2001 Standard Catalog of BASEBALL CARDS

10th Edition

Edited by

Bob Lemke

and the editors of Sports Collectors Digest

Special consultants

Chris Gallutia
Al Strumpf
Mark Macrae
Rob Lifson
Dwight Chapin
Larry Fritsch
John Spalding
Dick Goddard
Lee Temanson

Published by

krause publications

700 E. State Street • Iola, WI 54990-0001
Telephone: 715/445-2214

Please call or write for our free catalog.
Our toll-free number to place an order or obtain a free catalog is 800-258-0929
or please use our regular business telephone 715-445-2214
for editorial comment and further information.

Library of Congress Catalog Number: 88-80850
ISBN: 0-87341-936-7
Printed in the United States of America

ACKNOWLEDGMENTS

Dozens of individuals have been made countless valuable contributions which have been incorporated into the Standard Catalog of Baseball Cards. While all cannot be acknowledged, special appreciation is extended to the following principal contributors who have exhibited a special dedication by creating, revising or verifying listings and technical data, reviewing market valuations or loaning cards for photography.

Johnny Adams, Jr.
Ken Agona
Gary Agostino
Lisa Albano
Dan Albaugh
Will Allison
Mark Anker
Ellis Anmuth
Steve Applebaum
Rand Bailey
Bill Ballew
Gary Bartolett
Bob Bartosz
John Beisiegel
Karen Bell
Dr. Charles E. Belles
Dave Berman
Cathy Black
Mike Bodner
Bill Bossert
Bob Bostoff
Brian Boston
Mike Boyd
John Brigandi
Lou Brown
Dan Bruner
Greg Bussineau
Billy Caldwell
Len Caprisecca
Tony Carrafiell
Brian Cataquet
Lee Champion
Chriss Christiansen
Shane Cohen
Rich Cole
Charles Conlon
Eric Cooper
Bryan Couling
Bob Crabill
Clyde Cripe
Jim Cumpton
Robert Curtiss
James Davis
Tom Daniels
Ken Degnan
Dick DeCourcy
Dan DeKing
Mike Del Gado
Larry Dluhy
John Dorsey
Curtis Earl
Mark Elliott
Shirley Eross
Joe Esposito
Doak Ewing
David Festberg
Jay Finglass
Nick Flaviano
Rick Fleury
Jeff Fritsch
Gary Gagen
Richard Galasso
Tom Galic
Tony Galovich
Philip Garrou
Frank Giffune
Richard Gilkeson
Gerald J. Glasser
Philip Glazer
Keith David Goldfarb
Jack Goodman
Bill Goodwin
Howard Gordon
Mike Gordon
Bob Gray
Wayne Grove
Gerry Guenther
Don Guilbert
Tom Guilfoile
David, Joel & Walter Hall
Gary Hamilton
Tom Harbin
Don Harrison
Rich Hawksley
Herbert Hecht
Bill Henderson
Kathy Henry
Steve Hershkowitz
Gregg Hitesman
John Hoffmann
Dennis Hollenbeck
Jack Horkan
Jim Horne
Brent Horton
Ron Hosmer
Marvin Huck
Brad Hudecek
Bob Ivanjack
J.J. Teaparty
Robert Jacobsen
David Jenkins
Donn Jennings
Scott Jensen
Jim Johnston
Stewart Jones
Larry Jordan
Judy Kay
Allan Kaye
Michael Keedy
Mark Kemmerle
Rick Keplinger
John King
John Kitleson
Bob Koehler
David Kohler
Steve Lacasse
Lee Lasseigne
Mark K. Larson
William Lawrence
Scott Lawson
Richard Leech
Morley Leeking
Tom Leon
Don Lepore
Rod Lethbridge
Stuart Leviton
Howie Levy
Lew Lipset
Jeff Litteral
Chuck Lobenthal
Ken Magee
Paul Marchant
Bill Mastro
Ralph Maya
Jay McCracken
Dan McKee
Tony McLaughlin
Don McPherson
John Mehlin
Bill Mendel
Blake Meyer
Louis Middleton
Minnesota Sports Collectibles
Keith Mitchell
Joe Morano
Brian Morris
Mike Mosier
Mike Mowery
Peter Mudavin
Mark Murphy
Vincent Murray
David Musser
Frank Nagy
Steven Neimand
Joe Newman
Bill Nicolls
Chuck Nobriga
Mark Nochta
Wayne Nochta
Keith Olbermann
Joe Pasternack
Marty Perry
Tom Pfirrman
Dan Piepenbrok
Stan Pietruska
Paul Pollard
Harvey Poris
Pat Quinn
Ed Ransom
Fred Rapoport
Bob Richardson
Gavin Riley
Ron Ritzler
Tom Reid
Mike Rodell
Mike Rogers
Chris Ronan
Rocky Rosato
Alan Rosen
John Rumierz
Bob Rund
Jon Sands
Kevin Savage
Stephen Schauer
Allan Schoenberger
Dave Schwartz
Robert Scott
Corey Shanus
Max Silberman
Barry Sloate
Joe Smith
Mark Soltan
Kevin Spears
Gene Speranza
Nigel Spill
David Spivack
Don Steinbach
Dan Stickney
Larry Stone
Doug Stultz
Jim Suckow
Joe Szeremet
Erik Teller
K.J. Terplak
Dick Tinsley
Gary Tkac
Bud Tompkins
Scott Torrey
Dan Tripper
Rich Unruh
Jack Urban
Pete Waldman
Eric Waller
Gary Walter
Frank Ward
Dave Weber
Ken Weimer
Jeff T. Weis
Richard L. Weiss
Dale Weselowski
E.C. Wharton - Tigar
Charles Williamson
Frank Wozny
Bill Wright
Kit Young
Ted Zanidakis

2001 Standard Catalog of BASEBALL CARDS

HOW TO USE THIS CATALOG

This catalog has been uniquely designed to serve the needs of collectors and dealers at all levels from beginning to advanced. It provides a comprehensive guide to more than 125 years of baseball card issues, arranged so that even the most novice hobbyist can consult it with confidence and ease.

The following explanations summarize the general practices used in preparing this catalog's listings. However, because of specialized requirements which may vary from card set to card set, these must not be considered ironclad. Where these standards have been set aside, appropriate notations are usually incorporated.

ARRANGEMENT

The most important feature in identifying and pricing a baseball card is its set of origin. Therefore, the main body of this catalog, covering cards issued from 1869-date, has been alphabetically arranged within specific eras of issue according to the name by which the set is most popularly known to collectors, or by which it can be most easily identified by a person examining a card.

Previous editions of this catalog have relied heavily upon card set identification numbers that originated in the *American Card Catalog*. However, since that work was last updated more than 35 years ago its numbering system has become arcane and is of little use to the present generation of hobbyists. Where practical, sets which were listed in previous editions by their ACC designations have been reclassified alphabetically by a more readily identifiable signpost, such as manufacturer's name. Many of those sets continue to bear the ACC catalog number in the set heading and will be cross-referenced in the table of contents.

Among those card issuers who produced sets for more than a single year, their sets are then listed chronologically, from earliest to most recent, again within specific eras.

Within each set, the cards are listed by their designated card number, or in the absence of card numbers, alphabetically according to the last name of the player pictured. Listing numbers found in parentheses indicate the number does not appear on the card. Certain cards which fall outside the parameters of the normal card numbering for a specific set may be found at the beginning or end of the listings for that set.

Listings are generally arranged in two major sections — major league and minor league issues.

MAJOR LEAGUE ISSUES

The main body of the book details major league baseball card issues from 1869 through the first half of 2000, divided into two sections: Vintage (1869-1980) and Modern (1981-date). In general, prior to about 1990, this will include issues which picture one or more baseball players, usually contemporary with their playing days, printed on paper or cardboard in a variety of shapes and sizes and given away as a premium with the purchase of another product or service. After 1990 or so the definition is broadened to remove the restriction of the card as an ancillary product and to include those printed on plastic, wood, metal, etc.

Included within each era's listings are related collectibles featuring baseball players which do not fit under the definition previously given for baseball cards. These include many items on which players are depicted on materials other than paper or cardboard, such as pins, coins, silks, leathers, patches, felts, pennants, metallic ingots, statues, figurines, limited-edition artworks and others.

Also presented herein are foreign issues, one of the growth areas of the baseball card hobby in recent years. These encompass the various issues from countries outside of North America, particularly Latin America. Since the 1920s a variety of baseball cards, stamps and stickers have emanated from the Caribbean, South America and elsewhere chronicling the various winter baseball leagues which have flourished there, often stocked with former and future major league stars and, in the early years, providing the only contemporary cards of many U.S. and Latin Negro Leagues players.

Also incorporated into the listings are modern collectors' issues. There exists within the hobby a great body of cards known as "collectors issues" by virtue of their nature of having been produced solely for the hobby card market. These cards and sets are distinguished from "legitimate" issues in not having been created as a sales promotional item for another product or service — bubble gum, soda, snack cakes, dog food, cigarettes, gasoline, etc. This

BUYING

Baseball Cards

1948-1959

We are paying the highest prices in the history of sportscards for baseball Star and Common cards. What is a disappointment?...Sending your cards to PSA, thinking you will receive a 9 grade and receiving a 7. Not only is this discouraging, but it is a financial setback. We at Strike Zone can solve this problem for you and we will absorb this dilemma by purchasing your cards at PSA prices.

NEAR MINT TO MINT BUY PRICES

1948 Bowman Baseball

#1-36 Commons............$36
#1-36 Single Pr..............$52
#37-48 Commons...........$48
#3 Kiner........................$208
#4 Mize.........................$152
#5 Feller........................$312
#6 Berra........................$520
#8 Rizzuto......................$360
#18 Spahn....................$432
#36 Musial..................$1000
#38 Schoendienst.........$180

1948-49 Leaf Baseball

#1-168 Commons...........$56
#1-168 Singles Prints ...$300
#1 DiMaggio................$2880
#3 Ruth.......................$2800
#4 Musial....................$1240
#8 Paige......................$2720
#11 Rizzuto...................$300
#32 Spahn...................$380
#70 Wagner..................$416
#76 Williams...............$1200
#79 Robinson..............$1200
#83 Doerr.....................$208
#91 Kiner......................$240
#93 Feller....................$2000
#98 Newhouser.............$564
#106 Boudreau.............$128
#120 Kell.....................$632
#127 Slaughter............$560

1949 Bowman Baseball

#1-144 Commons...........$24
#145-240 Commons.......$60
#23 Doerr......................$65
#24 Musial...................$536
#27 Feller.....................$178
#29 Kiner.......................$88
#33 spahn....................$166
#36 Reese....................$192
#46 Roberts.................$208
#50 Robinson...............$813
#60 Berra.....................$306
#84 Campanella............$592
#98 Rizzuto..................$163
#98 Rizzuto..................$208
#100 Hodges................$244
#214 Ashburn...............$494
#224 Paige...................$975
#226 Snider...............$1008
#233 Doby...................$137

1950 Bowman Baseball

#1-72 Commons.............$59
#73-252 Commons.........$21
#1 Parnell....................$200
#6 Feller......................$400
#11 Rizzuto..................$360
#19 Spahn...................$280
#21 Reese....................$280
#22 Robinson.............$1160
#23 Newcombe............4208
#32 roberts..................$292
#33 Kiner.....................$160
#35 Slaughter..............$160
#46 Berra.....................$520
#62 Kluszewski............$116
#75 Campanella...........$440
#77 Snider...................$440
#84 Ashburn................$156
#98 Williams..............$1240
#217 Stengel...............$140
#252 DeMars...............$100

1951 Bowman Baseball

#1-252 Commons...........$21
#253-324 Commons.......$44
#1 Ford......................$1520
#2 Berra......................$520
#3 Roberts...................$128
#7 Hodges....................$112
#26 Rizzuto..................$204
#30 Feller.....................$160
#31 Campanella...........$340
#32 Snider...................$320
#80 Reese....................$196
#122 Garagiola.............$140
#134 Spahn..................$176
#165 Williams..............$972
#198 Irvin....................$168
#253 Mantle...............$9600
#305 Mays.................$3920

1952 Bowman Baseball

#1-216 Commons...........$20
#217-252 Commons.......$33
#1 Berra......................$800
#4 Roberts...................$120
#5 Minoso....................$176
#8 Reese......................$220
#33 McDougald..............$84
#43 Feller.....................$176
#44 Campanella...........$272
#101 Mantle...............$2720
#116 Snider.................$288
#158 Spahn..................$184
#196 Musial..................$656
#218 Mays.................$1460
#252 Crosetti................$180

1952 Topps Baseball

#1-80 Commons.............$84
#81-250 Commons.........$48
#251-310 Commons.......$76
#311-407 Commons.....$220
#1 Pafko.....................$6560
#11 Rizzuto..................$292
#20 Loes......................$280
#33 Spahn...................$512
#36 Hodges..................$248
#37 Snider...................$488
#48 Page.....................$656
#49 Sain......................$528
#59 Roberts..................$380
#65 Slaughter..............$260
#88 Feller....................$340
#191 Berra...................$740
#216 Ashburn...............$232
#246 Kell.....................$216
#261 Mays..................$3000
#277 Wynn...................$232
#312 Robinson............$1720
#314 Campanella........$2600
#315 Durocher.............$688
#333 Reese................$1800
#369 Groat...................$520
#372 McDougald..........$580
#392 Wilhelm...............$920
#400 Dickey...............$1120

1953 Bowman Color Baseball

#1-112 Commons...........$43
#113-160 Commons.......$95
#1 Williams..................$280
#9 Rizzuto...................$232
#10 Ashburn.................$228
#32 Musial...................$792
#33 Reese....................$960
#44 Bauer/Berra/Mantle $880
#46 Campanella...........$440
#59 Mantle.................$2880
#80 Kiner.....................$112
#81 Slaughter..............$140
#92 Hodges..................$304
#93 Rizzuto/Martin........$376
#97 Matthews...............$336
#99 Spahn...................$400
#114 Feller...................$800
#117 Snider...............$1040
#118 Martin..................$352
#212 Berra.................$1080
#153 Ford....................$880
#160 Abrams.................$500

1953 Topps Baseball

#1-165 Commons...........$36
#166-220 Commons.......$32
#221-280 Commons.....$104
#1 Robinson...............$1120
#27 Campanella...........$308
#37 Matthews...............$220
#54 Feller....................$172
#61 Wynn....................$160
#76 Reese....................$236
#82 Mantle.................$3920
#86 Martin...................4200
#104 Berra...................$416
#114 Rizzuto................$300
#147 Spahn.................$328
#207 Ford....................$264
#220 Paige...................$600
#228 Newhouser...........$180
#244 Mays.................$3840
#258 Gilliam.................$400
#263 Podres.................$480
#280 Bolling.................$720

1954 Bowman Baseball

#1-224 Commons...........$15
#1 Rizzuto....................$220
#15 Ashburn.................$220
#58 Reese....................$108
#65 Matnle.................$1140
#66 Williams..............$4600
#89 Mays.....................$560
#90 Campanella...........$204
#132 Feller..................$116
#161 Berra...................$224
#170 Snider.................$204
#177 Ford....................$132

1954 Topps Baseball

#1-50, 76-250 Commons $21
#51-75 Commons...........$39
#1 Williams..................$920
#17 Rizzuto..................$140
#20 Spahn...................$140
#30 Matthews...............$120
#32 Snider...................$288
#37 Ford.....................$176
#50 Berra.....................$320
#90 Mays.....................$688
#94 Banks..................$1080
#128 Aaron................$2080
#132 Lasorda...............$196
#201 Kaline..................$920
#250 Williams.............$1160

1955 Bowman Baseball

#1-224 Commons...........$12
#225-320 Commons.......$26
Umpire..........................$29
#1 Wilhelm...................$100
#22 Campanella...........$156
#23 Kaline...................$160
#37 Reese....................$104
#59 Ford.....................$112
#68 Howard....................$88
#134 Feller..................$104

1955 Topps Baseball

#168 Berra...................$184
#179 Aaron..................$336
#184 Mays...................$328
#202 Mantle.................$840
#1-150 Commons...........$16
#151-160 Commons.......$23
#161-210 Commons.......$36
#1 Rhodes....................$108
#2 Williams..................$580
#4 Kaline.....................$264
#28 Banks...................$252
#47 Aaron.....................$00
#50 Robinson...............$320
#123 Koufax.................$860
#124 Killebrew.............$312
#164 Clemente...........$2280
#187 Hodges................$180
#189 Rizzuto................$180
#194 Mays...................$600
#198 Berra...................$280
#210 Snider.................$600

1956 Topps Baseball

#1-100 Commons...........$15
#101-180, 261-349 Commons......................$20
#181-260 Commons.......$26
#1 Harridge..................$132
#5 Williams..................$420
#10 Spahn...................$112
#15 Banks...................$140
#30 Robinson...............$212
#31 Aaron....................$356
#33 Clemente...............$452
#79 Koufax..................$360
#101 Campanella..........$200
#110 Berra...................$160
#113 Rizzuto................$124
#130 Mays...................$500
#135 Mantle...............$1380
#166 Dodgers Team......$256
#240 Ford....................$176
#251 Yankees Team......$308
Checklist 1/3...............$320
Checklist 2/4...............$320

1957 Topps Baseball

#1-264, 353-407 Commons $16
#265-352 Commons.......$25
#1 Williams..................$620
#2 Berra......................$192
#10 Mays.....................$304
#18 Drysdale................$276
#20 Aaron....................$284
#35 Robinson...............$276
#55 Banks...................$176
#76 Clemente................$304
#95 Mantle.................$1280
#170 Snider.................$176
#210 Campanella..........$188
#212 Colavito...............$176
#286 Richardson...........$152
#302 Koufax.................$352
#324 Dodgers Team......$172
#328 Robinson..............$468
#400 Dodgers' Sluggers $300
#407 Yankee Power Hitters $640
Checklist 1/2...............$380
Checklist 2/3...............$580
Checklist 3/4.............$1080
Checklist 4/5.............$1280

1958 Topps Baseball

#1 Williams..................$540
#5 Mays.......................$228
#25 Drysdale..................$84
#30 Aaron....................$248
#30 Aaron YL................$460
#37 Maris....................$480
#52 Clemente................$280
#52 Clemente YL...........$492
#70 Kaline...................$120
#70 Kaline YL...............$272
#150 Mantle.................$920
#187 Koufax.................$220
#285 Robinson, F..........$116
#307 Robinson, B..........$136
#310 Banks..................$136
#370 Berra...................$124
#418 World Serires Batting Foes $212
#485 Ted Williams All-Star $132
#487 Mickey Mantle All-Star $168

1959 Topps Baseball

#10 Mantle...................$800
#40 Spahn.....................$80
#50 Mays.....................$176
#163 Koufax.................$180
#202 Maris..................$144
#380 Aaron..................$148
#514 Gibson.................$300
#550 Campanella..........$176
#561 Hank Aaron All-Star $136
#563 Willie Mays All-Star $124
#564 Mickey Mantle All-Star $304

Broadway Rick's STRIKE ZONE Gallery

Quality Autographs and Sports Memorabilia

Always Paying TOP DOLLAR For Autographs and Sports Memorabilia

American Express Cards · VISA · MasterCard

16008 NW 78th Avenue, Alachua, FL 32615
(904) 418-0385 • (800) 344-9103 • Fax (904) 418-0547
Visit us on the net at: www.strikezone.net Shipping & Handling Extra

Sports Collectors Digest · Krause Publications Customer Service Award 5 Year distinction, however, is no longer so easy to make since the early 1990s, when many baseball card issues by even the major national companies began to be sold without an accompanying product.

By their nature, and principally because the person issuing them was always free to print and distribute more of the same if they should ever attain any real value, collector issues were generally regarded by collectors as having little or no premium value. Since the leagues and players' unions began to enforce licensing restrictions in the early 1990s, the nature of collectors issues changed dramatically. The sets which were the work of an individual catering to the hobby market with an issue of relatively limited numbers and basic technology have given way to more sophisticated productions, often marketed to the general public, as well as the hobby.

More resources will be devoted to cataloging collector issues, particularly those from the hobby's early years, which have now become collectible in their own right. The distinction between "collectors" and "legitimate" cards may be barely perceptible but is noted whenever possible. Generally, those collectors' emissions share some or all of these characteristics: 1) Prior to around 1990 they were not licensed by the players depicted, their teams or leagues. 2) They were sold as complete sets rather than by pack or as singles. 3) The issue was marketed almost exclusively to the card collecting hobby audience through advertising in trade papers and public sporting press, and within the hobby's dealer network. 4) The cards were sold on a stand-alone basis, that is, not as a premium or adjunct to the sale of another product or service.

Persons with access to complete checklists of such cards are encouraged to correspond with the editor for possible inclusion in future editions.

MINOR LEAGUE ISSUES

Card sets in which all, or nearly all, of the players depicted are minor leaguers will be found in the second section of the catalog — minor league issues no distinction is made between baseball cards and memorabilia within the minor league section, which is itself divided into two segments based on the time and manner of issue.

MINOR LEAGUE ISSUES 1886-1969: Since the inception of the concept of using a baseball player's picture as a sales incentive minor league players were included, usually within the same issues as their major league brethren. This is particularly true of the 19th Century issues, in a time when the major leagues extended only in a triangle roughly from Boston to St. Louis to Washington, D.C., and there was not such a distinction between major and minor leagues. This section details those first issues as well as those of the next 80+ years.

Most such issues share the production values and method of distribution of their contemporary major league cards and are thus cataloged in much the same way, alphabetically by issuer/sponsor, chronologically within issuer. Because the majority of these cards were issued singly, rather than as sets, individual prices are shown for each card in this section.

MINOR LEAGUE SINGLES and TEAM SETS 1970-1999: Beginning about 1970 the preferred method of issue for minor league cards was in the form of team sets, usually sponsored by a local business and given away and/or sold by the team. Quite often dealers and manufacturers from within the baseball card industry contracted with several or several dozen teams to provide cards at minimal cost with the proviso that they be allowed to sell sets within the hobby.

Within this section of the catalog, listings are arranged chronologically by year of issue, then alphabetically by city. Because of vagaries in the computerized alphabetization program, some sets may not appear in strict alpha order, but will be found in the general vicinity.

Team-set cards within this section are priced only as complete sets because that is the manner in which they are almost exclusively bought and sold in the hobby market. Beginning in 1989, some of the major card manufacturers who were producing minor league team sets began to issue cards in wax-pack form; often similar in format to their team-set cards. Other companies who were not in the team-set market also began the issue of minor league singles. Because these wax-pack cards and their related inserts are usually sold as individuals, each card from those sets is prices.

Within each of these sections might be found a few sets depicting players who are not members of Organized Baseball's minor league system. Besides the independent professional leagues which have developed around the country in the mid-1990s, there are also listings for high school prospects' sets, draft picks, and the Cape Cod and Alaska summer college leagues which are generally considered to be steppingstones to pro ranks.

IDENTIFICATION

While most modern baseball cards are well identified on front, back, or both as to date and issue, such has not always been the case. In general, the back of the card is more useful in identifying the set of origin than the front. The issuer or sponsor's name will usually appear on the back since, after all, baseball cards were first produced as a promotional item to stimulate sales of other products. As often as not, that issuer's name is the name by which the set is known to collectors and under which it will be found listed in this catalog.

In some difficult cases, identifying a baseball card's general age, if not specific year of issue, can usually be accomplished by studying the biological or statistical information on the back of the card. The last year mentioned in either the biography or stats is usually the year which preceded the year of issue.

Over the years there have been many cards issued which bear no identification features at all with which to pinpoint the issuer. In such cases, they are cataloged by the names under which they are best known in the hobby. Many of the strip card issues of the 1920s, for example, remain listed under the "W" catalog number where they were listed in the *American Card Catalog*.

It is the ultimate goal, through the use of cross listings and more detailed indexes, to allow a person holding a card in his hand to find the catalog listing for that card with the greatest ease.

PHOTOGRAPHS

A photograph of the front and (prior to 1981) back of at least one representative card from virtually every set listed in this catalog has been incorporated into the listings to aid in identification. (Persons

who can provide sample cards for photography purposes for those sets which are missing photos in this volume are encouraged to contact the editor.)

Photographs have been printed in reduced size. The actual size of cards in each set is given in the introductory text preceding its listing, unless the card is the standard size (2.5" by 3.5").

DATING

The dating of baseball cards by year of issue on the front or back of the card itself is a relatively new phenomenon. In most cases, to accurately determine a date of issue for an unidentified card, it must be studied for clues. As mentioned, the biography, career summary or statistics on the back of the card are the best way to pinpoint a year of issue. In most cases, the year of issue will be the year after the last season mentioned on the card.

Luckily for today's collector, earlier generations have done much of the research in determining year of issue for those cards which bear no clues. The painstaking task of matching the players' listed and/or pictured team against their career records often allowed an issue date to be determined.

In some cases, particular card sets were issued over a period of more than one calendar year, but since they are collected together as a single set, their specific year of issue is not important. Such sets will be listed with their complete known range of issue years.

There remain some early issues for which an exact year of issue cannot be reliably pinpointed. In those cases a "best guess" date or one in the middle of the possible range has been used to identify the issue; such cases are usually noted in the introductory text.

NUMBERING

While many baseball card issues as far back as the 1880s have contained card numbers assigned by the issuer to facilitate the collecting of a complete set, the practice has by no means been universal. Even today, not every set bears card numbers.

Logically, those baseball cards which were numbered by their manufacturer are presented in that numerical order within the listings of this catalog whenever possible. In a few cases, complete player checklists were obtained from earlier published sources which did not note card numbers, and so numbers have been arbitrarily assigned. Many other unnumbered issues have been assigned catalog numbers to facilitate their universal identification within the hobby, especially when buying and selling by mail.

In all cases, numbers which have been assigned, or which otherwise do not appear on the card through error or by design, are shown in this catalog within parentheses. In virtually all cases, unless a more natural system suggested itself by the unique matter of a particular set, the assignment of numbers by the cataloging staff has been done by alphabetical arrangement of the players' last names or the card's principal title.

Significant collectible variations for any particular card are noted within the listings by the application of a suffix letter. In instances of variations, the suffix "a" is assigned to the variation which was created first, when it can be so identified.

NAMES

The identification of a player by full name on the front of his baseball card has been a common practice only since the 1920s. Prior to that, the player's last name and team were the usual information found on the card front.

As a general — though not universally applied — practice, the listings in this volume present the player's name exactly as it appears on the front of the card. If the player's full name only appears on the back, rather than on the front of the card, the listing may correspond to that designation.

A player's name checklisted in italic type indicates a rookie card.

In cases where only the player's last name is given on the card, the cataloging staff has included the first name by which he was most often known for ease of identification.

Cards which contain misspelled first or last names, or even wrong initials, will have included in their listings the incorrect information, with a correction accompanying in parentheses. This extends, also, to cases where the name on the card does not correspond to the player actually pictured.

In some cases, to facilitate efficient presentations, to maintain ease of use for the reader, or to allow for proper computer sorting of data, a player's name or card title may be listed other than as it appears on the card.

GRADING

It is necessary that some sort of grading standard be used so that buyer and seller (especially when dealing by mail) may reach an informed agreement on the value of a card.

Pre-1981 cards are generally priced in the three grades of preservation in which those cards are most commonly encountered in the daily buying and selling of the hobby marketplace. They are listed in grades of Near Mint (NR MT), Excellent (EX) and Very Good (VG), reflecting the basic fact that few cards were able to survive the 25, 50 or even 100 years in close semblance to the condition of their issue.

The pricing of cards in these three conditions will allow readers to accurately price cards which fall in intermediate grades, such as EX-MT, or VG-EX.

In general, although grades below Very Good are not generally priced, close approximations of low-grade card values may be figured on the following formula: Good condition cards are valued at about 50 percent of VG price, with Fair cards about 50 percent of Good.

Cards in Poor condition have no market value except in the cases of the rarest and most expensive cards. In such cases, value has to be negotiated individually.

More recent (1981-date) issues, which have been preserved in top condition in considerable number, are listed only in grade of Mint (MT), reflective of the fact that there exists in the current market little or no demand for cards of the recent past in lower grades.

As with older cards, values for low-grade cards from 1981-date may be generally figured by using a figure of 75% of the Mint price for Near Mint specimens, and 40% of the Mint price for Excellent cards.

For the benefit of the reader, we present herewith the grading guide which was originally formulated in 1981 by *Baseball Cards* magazine (now *SportsCards* magazine) and *Sports Collectors Digest*, and has been continually refined since that time.

CUBS

Negro League Baseball Stars
Negro League Baseball Stars
Josh Gibson

BASEBALL IMMORTALS
1926
BABE RUTH

These grading definitions have been used in the pricing of cards in this book, but they are by no means a universally-accepted grading standard.

The potential buyer of a baseball card should keep that in mind when encountering cards of nominally the same grade, but at a price which differs widely from that quoted in this book.

Ultimately, the collector himself must formulate his own personal grading standards in deciding whether cards available for purchase meet the needs of his own collection.

No collector is required to adhere to the grading standards presented herewith — nor to any other published grading standards.

Mint (MT): A perfect card. Well-centered, with parallel borders which appear equal to the naked eye. Four sharp, square corners. No creases, edge dents, surface scratches, paper flaws, loss of luster, yellowing or fading, regardless of age. No imperfectly printed card — out of register, badly cut or ink flawed — or card stained by contact with gum, wax or other substances can be considered truly Mint, even if new out of the pack. Generally, to be considered in Mint condition, a card's borders must exist in a ratio of 60/40 side to side and top to bottom.

Near Mint (NR MT): A nearly perfect card. At first glance, a Near Mint card appears perfect; upon closer examination, however, a minor flaw will be discovered. On well-centered cards, three of the four corners must be perfectly sharp; only one corner shows a minor imperfection upon close inspection. A slightly off-center card with one or more borders being noticeably unequal — but no worse than in a ratio of 70/30 S/S or T/B — would also fit this grade.

Excellent (EX): Corners are still fairly sharp with only moderate wear. Card borders may be off center as much as 80/20. No creases. May have very minor gum, wax or product stains, front or back. Surfaces may show slight loss of luster from rubbing across other cards.

Very Good (VG): Show obvious handling. Corners rounded and/or perhaps showing minor creases. Other minor creases may be visible. Surfaces may exhibit loss of luster, but all printing is intact. May show major gum, wax or other packaging stains. No major creases, tape marks or extraneous markings or writing. All four borders visible, though the ratio may be as poor as 95/5. Exhibits honest wear.

Good (G): A well-worn card, but exhibits no intentional damage or abuse. May have major or multiple creases. Corners rounded well beyond the border. A good card will generally sell for about 50% the value of a card in Very Good condition.

Fair (F or Fr.): Shows excessive wear, along with damage or abuse. Will show all the wear characteristics of a Good card, along with such damage as thumb tack holes in or near margins, evidence of having been taped or pasted, perhaps small tears around the edges, or creases so heavy as to break the cardboard. Backs may show minor added pen or pencil writing, or be missing small bits of paper. Still, basically a complete card. A Fair card will generally sell for 50% the value of a Good specimen.

Poor (P): A card that has been tortured to death. Corners or other areas may be torn off. Card may have been trimmed, show holes from a paper punch or have been used for BB gun practice. Front may have extraneous pen or pencil writing, or other defacement. Major portions of front or back design may be missing. Not a pretty sight.

In addition to these terms, collectors may encounter intermediate grades, such as VG-EX or EX-MT. These cards usually have characteristics of both the lower and higher grades, and are generally priced midway between those two values.

ROOKIE CARDS

While the status (and automatic premium value) which a player's rookie card used to carry has diminished in recent years, and though the hobby still has not reached a universal definition of a rookie card, many significant rookie cards are noted in this catalog's listings by the use of *italic* type. For purposes of this catalog, a player's rookie card is considered to be any card in a licensed set from a major manufacturer in the first year in which that player appears on a card.

VALUATIONS

Values quoted in this book represent the current retail market at the time of compilation (May, 2000). The quoted values are the result of a unique system of evaluation and verification created by the catalog's editors. Utilizing specialized computer analysis and drawing upon recommendations provided through their daily involvement in the publication of the hobby's leading sports collectors' periodicals as well as the input of consultants, dealers and collectors, each listing is, in the final analysis, the interpretation of that data by one or more of the editors.

It should be stressed, however, that this book is intended to serve only as an aid in evaluating cards; actual market conditions are constantly changing. This is especially true of the cards of current players, whose on-field performance during the course of a season can greatly affect the value of their cards — upwards or downwards.

Because of the extremely volatile nature of new card prices, especially high-end issues, we have chosen not to include the very latest releases such as most Series 2 products and premium-price brands from the major companies, feeling it is better to have no listings at all for those cards than to have inaccurate values in print.

Because this volume is intended to reflect the national market, users will find regional price variances caused by demand differences. Cards of Astros slugger Jeff Bagwell will, for instance, often sell at prices greater than quoted herein at shops and shows in the Houston area. Conversely, his cards may be acquired at a discount from these valuations when purchased on the East or West Coast.

Publication of this book is not intended as a solicitation to buy or sell the listed cards by the editors, publishers or contributors.

Again, the values here are retail prices — what a collector can expect to pay when buying a card from a dealer. The wholesale price, that which a collector can expect to receive from a dealer when selling cards, will be significantly lower.

Most dealers operate on a 100 percent mark-up, generally paying about 50 percent of a card's retail value for cards which they are purchasing for inventory. On some high-demand cards, dealers will pay up to 75 percent or even 100 percent or more of retail value, anticipating continued price increases. Conversely, for many low-

demand cards, such as common players' cards, dealers may pay as little as 10 percent or even less of retail with many base-brand cards of recent years having no resale value at all.

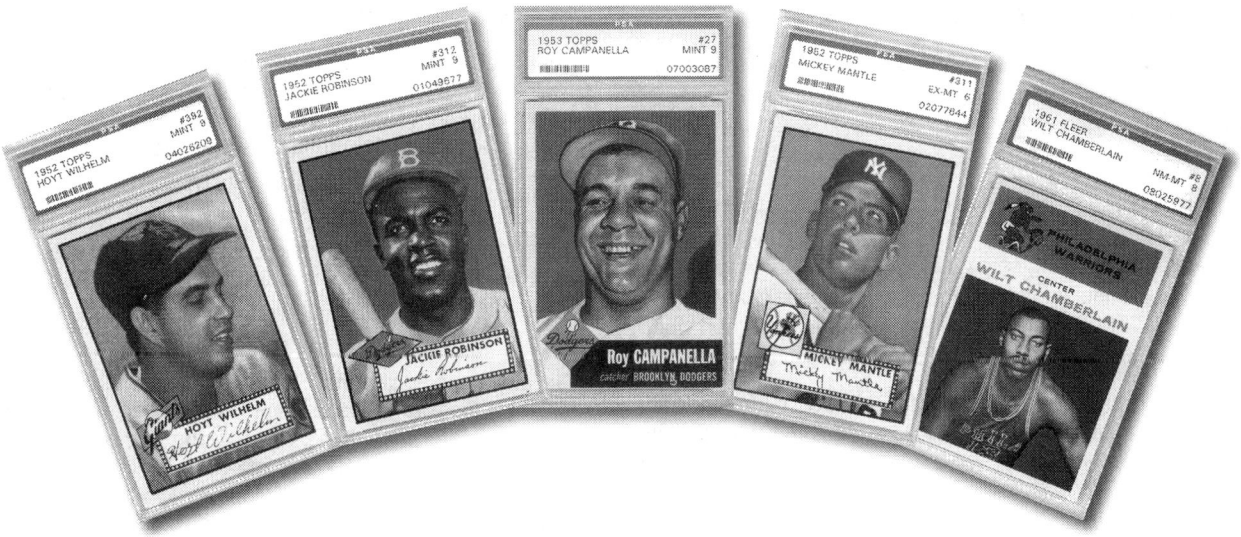

SETS

Collectors may note that the complete set prices for newer issues quoted in these listings are usually significantly lower than the total of the value of the individual cards which comprise the set. This reflects two factors in the baseball card market.

First, a seller is often willing to take a lower composite price for a complete set as a "volume discount" and to avoid carrying in inventory a large number of common player's or other lower-demand cards.

Second, to a degree, the value of common cards can be said to be inflated as a result of having a built-in overhead charge to justify the dealer's time in sorting cards, carrying them in stock and filling orders. This accounts for the fact that even brand new base-brand baseball cards, which cost the dealer around one cent each when bought in bulk, carry individual price tags of five cents or higher.

Some set prices shown, especially for old cards in top condition, are merely theoretical in that it is unlikely that a complete set exists in that condition. In general among older cards the range of conditions found in even the most painstakingly assembled complete set make the set values quoted useful only as a starting point for price negotiations.

ERRORS/VARIATIONS

It is often hard for the beginning collector to understand that an error on a baseball card, in and of itself, does not usually add premium value to that card. It is usually only when the correcting of an error in the subsequent printing creates a variation that premium value attaches to an error.

Minor errors, such as wrong stats or personal data, misspellings, inconsistencies, etc. — usually affecting the back of the card — are very common, especially in recent years. Unless a corrected variation was also printed, these errors are not noted in the listings of this book because they are not generally perceived by collectors to have premium value.

On the other hand, major effort has been expended to include the most complete listings ever for collectible variation cards. Many scarce and valuable variations are included in these listings because they are widely collected and often have significant premium value.

In the boom years of the early 1990s, some card companies produced their basic sets at more than one printing facility. This frequently resulted in numerous minor variations in photo cropping and back data presentation. Combined with a general decline in quality control from the mid-1980s through the early 1990s, which allowed unprecedented numbers of uncorrected error cards to be released, this caused a general softening of collector interest in errors and variations. Despite the fact most of these modern variations have no premium value, they are listed here as a matter of record.

COUNTERFEITS/REPRINTS

As the value of baseball cards has risen in the past 10-20 years, certain cards and sets have become too expensive for the average collector to obtain. This, along with changes in the technology of color printing, has given rise to increasing numbers of counterfeit and reprint cards.

While both terms describe essentially the same thing — a modern day copy which attempts to duplicate as closely as possible an original baseball card — there are differences which are important to the collector.

Generally, a counterfeit is made with the intention of deceiving somebody into believing it is genuine, and thus paying large amounts of money for it. The counterfeiter takes every pain to try to make his fakes look as authentic as possible.

A reprint, on the other hand, while it may have been made to look as close as possible to an original card, is made with the intention of allowing collectors to buy them as substitutes for cards they may never be otherwise able to afford. The big difference is that a reprint is generally marked as such, usually on the back of the card.

In other cases, like the Topps 1952 reprint set and 1953-54 Archives issues, the replicas are printed in a size markedly different from the originals. Collectors should be aware, however, that unscrupulous persons will sometimes cut off or otherwise obliterate the distinguishing word — "Reprint," "Copy," — or modern copyright date on the back of a reprint card in an attempt to pass it as genuine.

A collector's best defense against reprints and counterfeits is to acquire a knowledge of the look and feel of genuine baseball cards of various eras and issues.

UNLISTED CARDS

Persons encountering cards which are not listed in this reference should not immediately infer that they have something rare and/or valuable. With tens of thousands of baseball cards issued over the past century and thousands more being issued each year, this catalog's comprehensiveness will always remain relative. This is especially true in the area of modern cards and sets released regionally, and the vast universe of foreign and collectors' issues for which coverage has only recently begun. Readers who have cards or sets which are not covered in this edition are invited to correspond with the editor for purposes of adding to the compilation work now in progress. A photocopy of the card's front and back will assist in determining its status. Address: Bob Lemke, Standard Catalog of Baseball Cards, 700 E. State St., Iola, Wis. 54990. Contributors will be acknowledged in future editions.

NEW ISSUES

Because new baseball cards are being issued all the time, the cataloging, of them remains an on-going challenge. The editor will attempt to keep abreast of new issues so that they may be added to future editions of this book. Readers are invited to submit news of new issues, especially limited-edition or regionally issued cards, to the editor. Address: Bob Lemke, Standard Catalog of Baseball Cards, 700 E. State St., Iola, Wis. 54990.

VINTAGE MAJOR LEAGUE CARDS (1869-1980)

The vast majority of cards listed in this section were issued between 1869 and 1980 and feature major league players only. The term "card" is used rather loosely as in this context it is construed to include virtually any cardboard or paper product, of whatever size and/or shape, depicting baseball players and issued to stimulate the sales of another product or service.

In isolated cases, listings other than outlined here will be included in the vintage card section. For example, where a card sponsor's offerings began well prior to 1980, and continued for a few years into the early 1980s, all are grouped together in the section. Kellogg's is an example. For other, usually larger, card companies such as Topps or Fleer, the 1980 and earlier cards will be found in this section with the post-1980 cards in the modern card section which follows.

In all cases, selections for this section were made with an eye towards enhancing the book's utility to the user.

A

1976 A & P Brewers

The Aaron and Yount cards from this regional issue support the set price. The set was issued by the A & P grocery chain. Oversize - 5-7/8" x 9" - cards (actually printed on semi-gloss paper) were given out at the stores in 1976 in series of four with the purchase of select weekly grocery specials. Players are pictured in tight capless portraits. Each photo has a black facsimile autograph; backs are blank. The unnumbered cards are checklisted here in alphabetical order.

		NM	EX	VG
Complete Set (16):		35.00	17.50	10.50
Common Player:		.75	.40	.25
(1)	Henry Aaron	17.00	8.50	5.00
(2)	Pete Broberg	.75	.40	.25
(3)	Jim Colborn	.75	.40	.25
(4)	Mike Hegan	.75	.40	.25
(5)	Tim Johnson	.75	.40	.25
(6)	Von Joshua	.75	.40	.25
(7)	Sixto Lezcano	.75	.40	.25
(8)	Don Money	.75	.40	.25
(9)	Charlie Moore	.75	.40	.25
(10)	Darrell Porter	.75	.40	.25
(11)	George Scott	.75	.40	.25
(12)	Bill Sharp	.75	.40	.25
(13)	Jim Slaton	.75	.40	.25
(14)	Bill Travers	.75	.40	.25
(15)	Robin Yount	12.00	6.00	3.50
(16)	County Stadium	1.00	.50	.30

1976 A & P Royals

Identical in format to the Brewers' set issued around Milwaukee, these 5-7/8" x 9" photos picture players without their caps in posed portraits. The cards were given away four per week with the purchase of selected grocery item specials. Cards have a players' association logo in the upper-left corner, and a black facsimile autograph on front. Backs are blank. The unnumbered cards are checklisted here alphabetically.

		NM	EX	VG
Complete Set (16):		22.00	11.00	6.50
Common Player:		.75	.40	.25
(1)	Doug Bird	.75	.40	.25
(2)	George Brett	15.00	7.50	4.50
(3)	Steve Busby	.75	.40	.25
(4)	Al Cowens	.75	.40	.25
(5)	Al Fitzmorris	.75	.40	.25
(6)	Dennis Leonard	.75	.40	.25
(7)	Buck Martinez	.75	.40	.25
(8)	John Mayberry	.75	.40	.25
(9)	Hal McRae	1.00	.50	.30
(10)	Amos Otis	1.00	.50	.30
(11)	Fred Patek	.75	.40	.25
(12)	Tom Poquette	.75	.40	.25
(13)	Mel Rojas	.75	.40	.25
(14)	Tony Solaita	.75	.40	.25
(15)	Paul Splittorff	.75	.40	.25
(16)	Jim Wohlford	.75	.40	.25

1932 Abdulla Tobacco

Along with several other contemporary card issues from Germany, Babe Ruth is the lone representative from American baseball in this series of 200 cards. Cards are 1-11/16" x 2-1/2" and feature sepia-tone photos on front, with the celebrity's name and nation printed in the white border at bottom. Backs are in German and include a card number.

		NM	EX	VG
196	Babe Ruth	1200.	600.00	350.00

1970 Action Cartridge

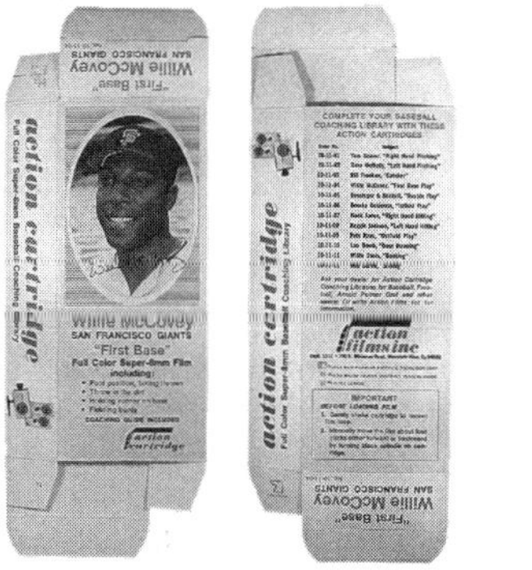

This set of boxes with baseball players' pictures on them was issued by Action Films Inc. of Mountain View, Calif., in 1970-71. The boxes, measuring 2-5/8" x 6" x 1" deep, contained 8mm film cartridges of various professional athletes demonstrating playing tips. The movie series included 12 baseball players. (Other sports represented were football, golf, tennis, hockey and skiing.) The movie cartridges are occasionally collected today, as are the boxes, which feature attractive, color player portraits. The photos appear inside an oval and include a facsimile autograph. The values listed are for complete boxes (without the movie cartridge).

		NM	EX	VG
Complete Set (12):		900.00	450.00	270.00
Common Player:		20.00	10.00	6.00
1	Tom Seaver	125.00	62.00	37.00
2	Dave McNally	20.00	10.00	6.00
3	Bill Freehan	20.00	10.00	6.00
4	Willie McCovey	90.00	45.00	27.00
5	Glenn Beckert, Don Kessinger	20.00	10.00	6.00
6	Brooks Robinson	110.00	55.00	33.00
7	Hank Aaron	190.00	95.00	57.00
8	Reggie Jackson	125.00	62.00	37.00
9	Pete Rose	175.00	87.00	52.00
10	Lou Brock	75.00	37.00	22.00
11	Willie Davis	20.00	10.00	6.00
12	Rod Carew	80.00	40.00	24.00

1913 A Fan For A Fan

These cardboard novelties were produced by the American Tobacco Co. About 7-1/4" in diameter, the bursting baseball and portrait are printed in color with a facsimile autograph. The handle is about 5" long. The back is blank. The known fans are listed here alphabetically; the checklist is likely incomplete.

		NM	EX	VG
Common Player:		1500.	750.00	450.00
(1)	Hal Chase	2200.	1100.	660.00
(2)	Larry Doyle	1500.	750.00	450.00
(3)	Christy Mathewson	2750.	1375.	825.00

1939 African Tobacco

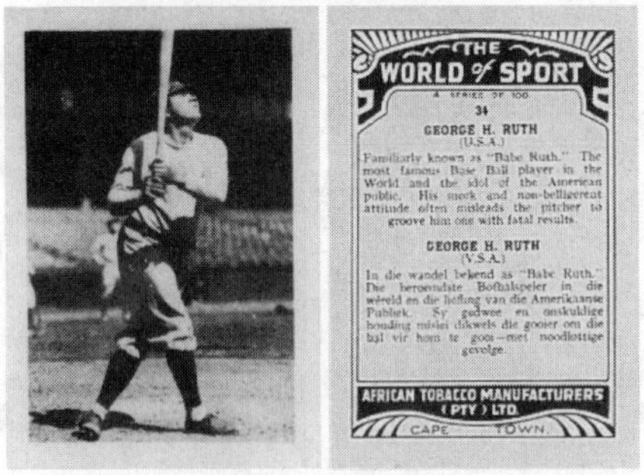

The unlikely venue of the "other" U.S.A. (Union of South Africa) is the provenance of this rare Babe Ruth card. The African Tobacco company issued a set of 100 cards in a series titled "The World of Sport". The cards were issued in both a large (2-1/4" x 3-1/4") and small (1-3/4" x 2-1/2") format. Fronts have a black-and-white photo of Ruth, with a white border all around. Backs are printed in both English and Afrikaner.

		NM	EX	VG
34	Babe Ruth (large)	600.00	300.00	180.00
34	Babe Ruth (small)	750.00	375.00	225.00

1936-52 Albertype Hall of Fame Plaque Postcards

(See 1936-63 Hall of Fame Black-and-White Plaque Postcards.)

1940s Antonio Alcalde Premium Pictures

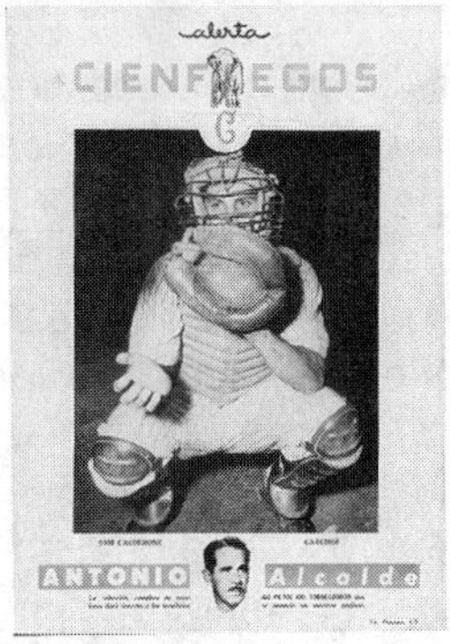

There are still gaps in the hobby's knowledge of this late-1940s/early-1950s Cuban issue. Evidently a premium used in a contest conducted by a newspaper or sports periodical, these pictures are printed on semi-gloss paper in an 8" x 11" format. Featured on front are black-and-white posed action or portrait photos. The team name and symbol are above and a portrait, presumably of Antonio, is at bottom. Pictures are highlighted by color graphics: blue for Almendares, green for Cienfuegos, red for Havana and orange for Marianao. Backs are blank, but are sometimes seen with a round rubber-stamped "Alerta" logo or red boxed "ANTONIO, ALCALDE". The unnumbered pictures are listed here alphabetically within team. The pictures include many American players and those who spent time in the major leagues.

		NM	EX	VG
Complete Set (70):		1125.	560.00	335.00
Common Player:		22.00	11.00	6.50
	ALMENDARES SCORPIONS			
(1)	Bill Antonello	26.00	13.00	7.75
(2)	Francisco Campos	26.00	13.00	7.75
(3)	Avelino Canizares	22.00	11.00	6.50
(4)	Yiqui De Souza	22.00	11.00	6.50
(5)	Rodolfo Fernandez	22.00	11.00	6.50
(6)	Andres Fleitas	22.00	11.00	6.50
(7)	Al Gionfriddo	37.00	18.50	11.00
(8)	Fermin Guerra	26.00	13.00	7.75
(9)	Bob Hooper	26.00	13.00	7.75
(10)	Vincente Lopez	22.00	11.00	6.50
(11)	Conrado Marrero	27.00	13.50	8.00
(12)	Agapito Mayor	22.00	11.00	6.50
(13)	Willy Miranda	37.00	18.50	11.00
(14)	Rene Monteagudo	26.00	13.00	7.75
(15)	Roberto Ortiz	26.00	13.00	7.75
(16)	Hector Rodriguez	26.00	13.00	7.75
(17)	Octavio Rubert	22.00	11.00	6.50
(18)	Rene Solis	22.00	11.00	6.50
	CIENFUEGOS ELEPHANTS			
(1)	Bob Addis	26.00	13.00	7.75
(2)	Sam Calderone	26.00	13.00	7.75
(3)	Jack Cassini	26.00	13.00	7.75
(4)	Alejandro Crespo	30.00	15.00	9.00
(5)	Paul (Al) Epperly	26.00	13.00	7.75
(6)	Thomas Fine	26.00	13.00	7.75
(7)	Pedro Formental (Formenthal)	22.00	11.00	6.50
(8)	Francisco Gallardo	22.00	11.00	6.50
(9)	Lloyd Gearhart	28.00	14.00	8.50
(10)	Leonardo Goicochea	22.00	11.00	6.50
(11)	Salvador Hernandez	26.00	13.00	7.75
(12)	Clarence (Buddy) Hicks	26.00	13.00	7.75
(13)	Max Manning	45.00	22.00	13.50
(14)	San (Ray) Noble	30.00	15.00	9.00
(15)	Regino Otero	26.00	13.00	7.75
(16)	Pedro Pages	22.00	11.00	6.50
(17)	Napoleon Reyes	30.00	15.00	9.00
(18)	Ernie Shore	27.00	13.50	8.00
(19)	Adrian Zabala	26.00	13.00	7.75
	HAVANA LIONS			
(1)	Ferrell Anderson	26.00	13.00	7.75
(2)	Wess Bailey	22.00	11.00	6.50
(3)	Vic Barnhart	28.00	14.00	8.50
(4)	Herberto Blanco	22.00	11.00	6.50
(5)	Emilio Cabrera	22.00	11.00	6.50
(6)	Pedro Formental (Formenthal)	22.00	11.00	6.50
(7)	Al Gerheauser	28.00	14.00	8.50
(8)	Miguel Angel Gonzalez	52.00	26.00	15.50
(9)	Chino Hidalgo	22.00	11.00	6.50
(10)	Jimmy Lenhart	22.00	11.00	6.50
(11)	Adolfo Luque	37.00	18.50	11.00
(12)	Max Manning	30.00	15.00	9.00
(13)	Julio Moreno	26.00	13.00	7.75
(14)	Lennox Pearson	26.00	13.00	7.75
(15)	Don Richmond	26.00	13.00	7.75
(16)	John Ford Smith	22.00	11.00	6.50
(17)	Don Thompson	26.00	13.00	7.75
(18)	Gilberto Torres	26.00	13.00	7.75
	MARIANAO TIGERS			
(1)	Mario Arencibia	22.00	11.00	6.50
(2)	Carlos Blanco	22.00	11.00	6.50
(3)	Chiquitin Cabbera	22.00	11.00	6.50
(4)	Sandalio Consuegra	30.00	15.00	9.00
(5)	Reinaldo Cordeiro	22.00	11.00	6.50
(6)	Talua (Ray) Dandridge	60.00	30.00	18.00
(7)	Mario Diaz	22.00	11.00	6.50
(8)	Claro Duany	30.00	15.00	9.00
(9)	Roberto Estalella	26.00	13.00	7.75
(10)	Chicuelo Garcia	22.00	11.00	6.50
(11)	Wesley Hamner	26.00	13.00	7.75
(12)	Rollie Hemsley	26.00	13.00	7.75
(13)	Amado Ibanez	22.00	11.00	6.50
(14)	Limonar (Rogelio) Martinez	26.00	13.00	7.75
(15)	Don Phillips	22.00	11.00	6.50
(16)	Bartholomew (Jim) Prendergast	26.00	13.00	7.75
(17)	John Trouppe	22.00	11.00	6.50

1970 Carl Aldana Orioles

Little is known about the distribution or origin of this 12-card regional set, which was available in 1970 in the Baltimore area. Measuring 3-1/4" x 2-1/8", the unnumbered cards picture members of the Baltimore Orioles and include two poses of Brooks Robinson. The cards feature line drawings of the players surrounded by a plain border. The player's last name appears below the portrait sketch. The set was named after Carl Aldana, who supplied the artwork for the cards.

		NM	EX	VG
Complete Set (12):		35.00	17.50	10.50
Common Player:		1.00	.50	.30
(1)	Mark Belanger	2.00	1.00	.60
(2)	Paul Blair	2.00	1.00	.60
(3)	Mike Cuellar	2.00	1.00	.60
(4)	Ellie Hendricks	1.00	.50	.30
(5)	Dave Johnson	2.00	1.00	.60
(6)	Dave McNally	2.00	1.00	.60
(7)	Jim Palmer	9.00	4.50	2.75
(8)	Boog Powell	4.00	2.00	1.25
(9)	Brooks Robinson (diving - face showing)	12.00	6.00	3.50
(10)	Brooks Robinson (diving - back showing)	12.00	6.00	3.50
(11)	Frank Robinson	12.00	6.00	3.50
(12)	Earl Weaver	3.00	2.25	1.25

1954 Alga Syrup Willie Mays Postcard

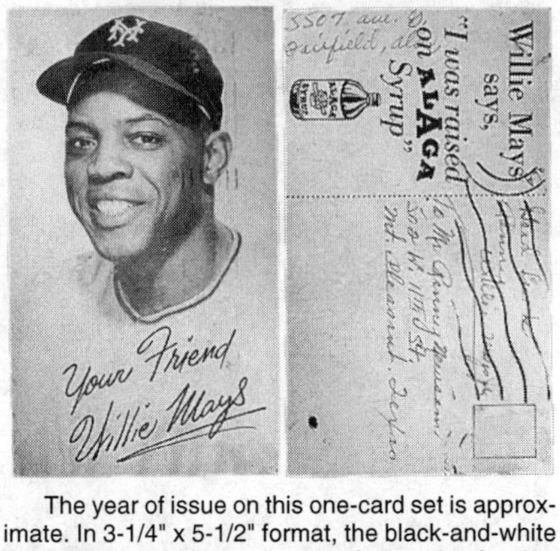

The year of issue on this one-card set is approximate. In 3-1/4" x 5-1/2" format, the black-and-white card has a borderless portrait on front with a facsimile autograph. Back has an ad for Alga Syrup, along with standard postcard elements.

		NM	EX	VG
(1)	Willie Mays	300.00	150.00	90.00

1904 Allegheny Card Co.

One of the rarest card issues of the early 20th Century is this baseball game set featuring only National League players. It is supposed that the sole known boxed set was produced as a prototype and never actually reached distribution. The issue contains 104 player cards and a "Ball Counter" card for each team. Cards are in playing-card format, about 2-1/2" x 3-1/2" with rounded corners. Backs are printed in red with baseball equipment pictured. Fronts are printed in blue with a circular player portrait at center. Team name is at top, with player's last name (occasionally with initials and occasionally misspelled) beneath. The unique boxed set was discovered in the late 1980s. It was sold at auction in 1991 for $26,400, and again in 1995 for $11,000, after which it was broken up for individual card sales. The checklist is presented here in alphabetical order.

		NM	EX	VG
Common Player:		400.00	200.00	120.00
(1)	Ed Abbaticchio	400.00	200.00	120.00
(2)	Harry Aubrey	400.00	200.00	120.00
(3)	Charlie Babb	400.00	200.00	120.00
(4)	George Barclay	400.00	200.00	120.00
(5)	Shad Barry	400.00	200.00	120.00
(6)	Bill Beagen ((Bergen))	400.00	200.00	120.00
(7)	Ginger Beaumont	400.00	200.00	120.00
(8)	Jake Beckley	550.00	275.00	165.00
(9)	Frank Bowerman	400.00	200.00	120.00
(10)	Dave Brain	400.00	200.00	120.00
(11)	Kitty Bransfield	400.00	200.00	120.00
(12)	Roger Bresnahan	550.00	275.00	165.00
(13)	Mordecai Brown	550.00	275.00	165.00
(14)	George Browne	400.00	200.00	120.00
(15)	Al Buckenberger	400.00	200.00	120.00
(16)	Jimmy Burke	400.00	200.00	120.00
(17)	Fred Carisch	400.00	200.00	120.00
(18)	Pat Carney	400.00	200.00	120.00
(19)	Doc Casey	400.00	200.00	120.00
(20)	Frank Chance	550.00	275.00	165.00
(21)	Fred Clarke	550.00	275.00	165.00
(22)	Dick Cooley	400.00	200.00	120.00
(23)	Bill Dahlen	400.00	200.00	120.00
(24)	Tom Daly	400.00	200.00	120.00
(25)	Charlie Dexter	400.00	200.00	120.00
(26)	Johnny Dobbs	400.00	200.00	120.00
(27)	Mike Donlin	400.00	200.00	120.00
(28)	Patsy Donovan	400.00	200.00	120.00
(29)	Red Dooin	400.00	200.00	120.00
(30)	Klondike Douglas (Douglass)	400.00	200.00	120.00
(31)	Jack Doyle	400.00	200.00	120.00
(32)	Bill Duggleby	400.00	200.00	120.00
(33)	Jack Dunn	450.00	225.00	135.00
(34)	Johnny Evers	550.00	275.00	165.00
(35)	John Farrel (Farrell)	400.00	200.00	120.00
(36)	Tim Flood	400.00	200.00	120.00
(37)	Chick Fraser	400.00	200.00	120.00
(38)	Ned Garver	400.00	200.00	120.00
(39)	Doc Gessler	400.00	200.00	120.00
(40)	Billy Gilbert	400.00	200.00	120.00
(41)	Kid Gleason	400.00	200.00	120.00
(42)	Ed Greminger (Gremminger)	400.00	200.00	120.00
(43)	Jim Hackett	400.00	200.00	120.00
(44)	Noodles Hahn	400.00	200.00	120.00
(45)	Ed. Hanlon	550.00	275.00	165.00
(46)	Jack Harper	400.00	200.00	120.00
(47)	Rudy Hulswitt	400.00	200.00	120.00
(48)	Fred Jacklitsch	400.00	200.00	120.00
(49)	Davy Jones	400.00	200.00	120.00
(50)	Oscar Jones	400.00	200.00	120.00
(51)	Bill Keister	400.00	200.00	120.00
(52)	Joe Kelley	550.00	275.00	165.00
(53)	Brickyard Kennedy	400.00	200.00	120.00
(54)	Johnny Kling	400.00	200.00	120.00
(55)	Otto Kruger (Krueger)	400.00	200.00	120.00
(56)	Tommy Leach	400.00	200.00	120.00
(57)	Sam Leever	400.00	200.00	120.00
(58)	Bobby Lowe	550.00	275.00	165.00
(59)	Carl Lundgren	400.00	200.00	120.00
(60)	Christy Mathewson	1500.	750.00	450.00
(61)	Tom McCreery	400.00	200.00	120.00
(62)	Chappie McFarland	400.00	200.00	120.00
(63)	Dan McGann	400.00	200.00	120.00
(64)	Iron Man McGinnity	550.00	275.00	165.00
(65)	John McGraw	550.00	275.00	165.00
(66)	Jock Menefee	400.00	200.00	120.00
(67)	Sam Mertes	400.00	200.00	120.00
(68)	Fred Mitchell	400.00	200.00	120.00
(69)	Pat Moran	400.00	200.00	120.00
(70)	Ed Murphy	400.00	200.00	120.00
(71)	Jack O'Neill	400.00	200.00	120.00
(72)	Mike O'Neill	400.00	200.00	120.00
(73)	Heinie Peitz	400.00	200.00	120.00
(74)	Ed Phelps	400.00	200.00	120.00
(75)	Deacon Phillippe	400.00	200.00	120.00
(76)	Togie Pittinger	400.00	200.00	120.00
(77)	Ed Poole	400.00	200.00	120.00
(78)	Tommy Raub	400.00	200.00	120.00
(79)	Bill Reidy	400.00	200.00	120.00
(80)	Claude Ritchie	400.00	200.00	120.00
(81)	Lew Ritter	400.00	200.00	120.00
(82)	Frank Roth	400.00	200.00	120.00
(83)	Jack Ryan	400.00	200.00	120.00
(84)	Jimmy Scheckard (Sheckard)	400.00	200.00	120.00
(85)	Jimmy Sebring	400.00	200.00	120.00
(86)	Frank Selee	550.00	275.00	165.00
(87)	Cy Seymour	400.00	200.00	120.00
(88)	Harry Smith	400.00	200.00	120.00
(89)	Homer Smoot	400.00	200.00	120.00
(90)	Tully Sparks	400.00	200.00	120.00
(91)	Joe Stanley	400.00	200.00	120.00
(92)	Harry Steinfeldt	400.00	200.00	120.00
(93)	Sammy Strang	400.00	200.00	120.00
(94)	Jack Suthoff (Sutthoff)	400.00	200.00	120.00
(95)	Jack Taylor	400.00	200.00	120.00
(96)	Luther Taylor	425.00	210.00	125.00
(97)	Roy Thomas	400.00	200.00	120.00
(98)	Joe Tinker	550.00	275.00	165.00
(99)	Fred Tinney (Tenney)	400.00	200.00	120.00
(100)	Honus Wagner	1750.	875.00	525.00
(101)	Jack Warner	400.00	200.00	120.00
(102)	Jake Weimer	400.00	200.00	120.00
(103)	Vic Willis	550.00	275.00	165.00
(104)	Harry Wolverton	400.00	200.00	120.00
(105)	Boston Ball Counter	75.00	37.00	22.00
(106)	Brooklyn Ball Counter	75.00	37.00	22.00
(107)	Chicago Ball Counter	75.00	37.00	22.00
(108)	Cincinnati Ball Counter	75.00	37.00	22.00
(109)	New York Ball Counter	75.00	37.00	22.00
(110)	Philadelphia Ball Counter	75.00	37.00	22.00
(111)	Pittsburgh Ball Counter	75.00	37.00	22.00
(112)	St. Louis Ball Counter	75.00	37.00	22.00

1887 Allen & Ginter World's Champions (N28)

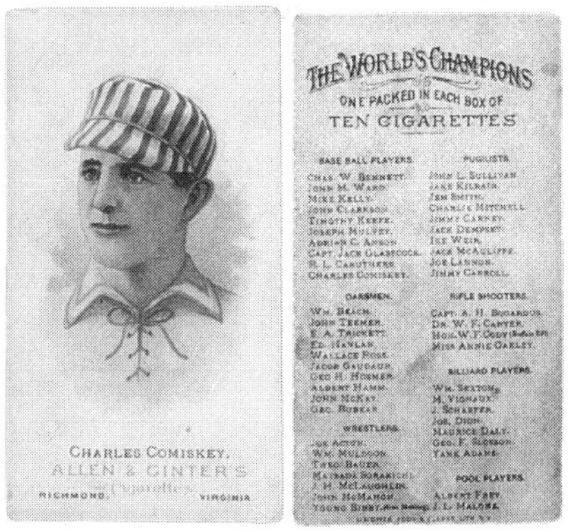

Generally considered the first of the tobacco card issues, this 50-card set was titled "The World Champions" and included 10 baseball players and 40 other sports personalities such as John L. Sullivan and Buffalo Bill Cody. The 1-1/2" x 2-3/4" cards were inserted in boxes of Allen & Ginter cigarettes. The card fronts are color lithographs on white card stock, and are considered among the most attractive cards ever produced. All card backs have a complete checklist for this unnumbered set, which includes six eventual Hall of Famers. Eight of the 10 players shown are from the National League and the other two from the American Association, then also considered a major league.

		NM	EX	VG
Complete Set (10):		11000.	5000.	3875.
Common Player:		500.00	225.00	175.00
Album:		4000.	2250.	1500.
(1)	Adrian C. Anson	2450.	1100.	850.00
(2)	Chas. W. Bennett	600.00	275.00	210.00
(3)	R.L. Caruthers	600.00	275.00	210.00
(4)	John Clarkson	1250.	560.00	435.00
(5)	Charles Comiskey	1750.	785.00	610.00
(6)	Capt. John Glasscock	600.00	275.00	210.00
(7)	Timothy Keefe	1500.	675.00	525.00
(8)	Mike Kelly	1750.	785.00	610.00
(9)	Joseph Mulvey	600.00	275.00	210.00
(10)	John M. Ward	1450.	650.00	500.00

1888 Allen & Ginter World's Champions (N29)

After their 1887 first series of tobacco cards proved a success, Allen & Ginter issued a second series of "World Champions" in 1888. Once again, 50 of these 1-1/2" x 2-3/4" color cards were produced, in virtually the same style as the year before. Only six baseball players are included in this set. The most obvious difference from the 1887 cards is the absence of the Allen & Ginter name on the card fronts. All six baseball players are from National League teams.

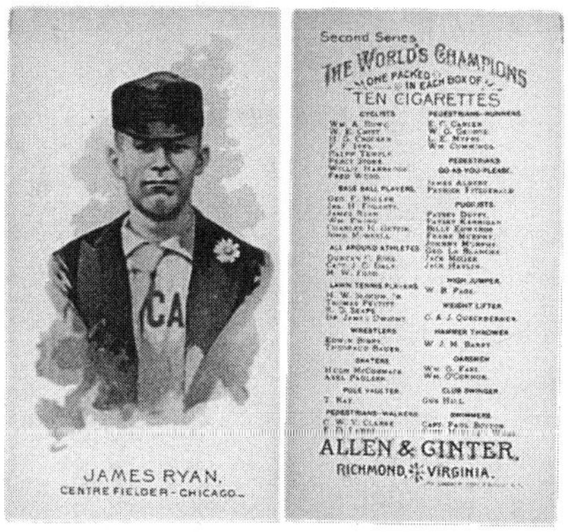

		NM	EX	VG
Complete Set (6):		6500.	2900.	2275.
Common Player:		950.00	425.00	330.00
Album:		2400.	1500.	900.00
(1)	Wm. Ewing	2800.	1260.	980.00
(2)	Jas. H. Fogarty (middle initial actually G.)	950.00	425.00	330.00
(3)	Charles H. Getzin (Getzien)	950.00	425.00	330.00
(4)	Geo. F. Miller	950.00	425.00	330.00
(5)	John Morrell (Morrill)	950.00	425.00	330.00
(6)	James Ryan	950.00	425.00	330.00

1888 Allen & Ginter World's Champions (N43)

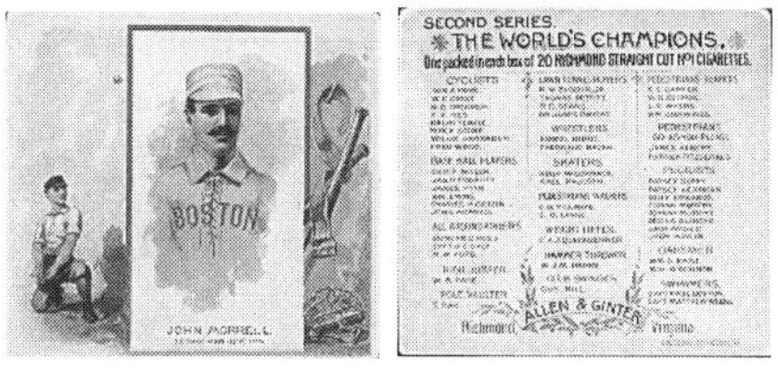

Presumably issued in a larger-than-standard cigarette package, the 50 cards designated N43 in the "American Card Catalog" are enhanced versions of the Allen & Ginter World's Champions (N29) series of 1888. As with the N29 set, six of the athletes in N43 are baseball players. The larger cards measure 3-1/4" x 2-7/8" compared to the 1-1/2" x 2-3/4" size of the N29s. The larger format allows for the use of baseball-related color lithography to the right and left of the central player portrait. Like the N29 cards, backs of the N43 A&Gs present the entire "Series Two" checklist along with advertising of the Richmond tobacco company. Only the baseball players are cataloged here.

		NM	EX	VG
Complete Set (6):		13500.	6100.	4725.
Common Player:		2200.	990.00	770.00
(1)	Wm. Ewing	4250.	1900.	1475.
(2)	Jas. H. Fogarty (middle initial actually G.)	2000.	900.00	700.00
(3)	Charles H. Getzin (Getzien)	2000.	900.00	700.00
(4)	Geo. F. Miller	2000.	900.00	700.00
(5)	John Morrell (Morrill)	2000.	900.00	700.00
(6)	James Ryan	2000.	900.00	700.00

1910 All Star Base-Ball

Issued circa 1910, this rare set was issued by candy maker J.H. Dockman & Son. The cards, measuring approximately 1-7/8" x 3-3/8", were printed on the front and back of boxes of candy sold as "All Star Base-Ball Package." There are two players on each box; one on front, the other on back. The cards consist of crude drawings that bear little resemblance to the player named below the drawing.

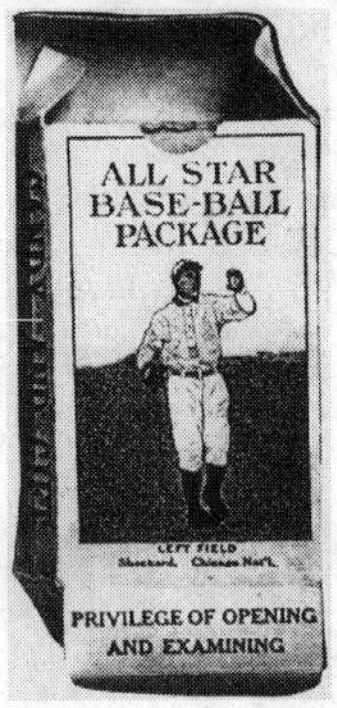

		NM	EX	VG
Complete Set (24):		9375.	4675.	2800.
Common Player:		325.00	155.00	90.00
(1)	Johnny Bates	325.00	155.00	90.00
(2)	Heinie Beckendorf	325.00	155.00	90.00
(3)	Joe Birmingham	325.00	155.00	90.00
(4)	Roger Bresnahan	500.00	250.00	150.00
(5)	Al Burch	325.00	155.00	90.00
(6)	Donie Bush	325.00	155.00	90.00
(7)	Frank Chance	500.00	250.00	150.00
(8)	Ty Cobb	1125.	560.00	335.00
(9)	Wid Conroy	325.00	155.00	90.00
(10)	Jack Coombs	325.00	155.00	90.00
(11)	George Gibson	325.00	155.00	90.00
(12)	Dick Hoblitzel	325.00	155.00	90.00
(13)	Johnny Kling	325.00	155.00	90.00
(14)	Frank LaPorte	325.00	155.00	90.00
(15)	Ed Lennox	325.00	155.00	90.00
(16)	Connie Mack	500.00	250.00	150.00
(17)	Christy Mathewson	750.00	375.00	225.00
(18)	Matty McIntyre	325.00	155.00	90.00
(19)	Al Schweitzer	325.00	155.00	90.00
(20)	Jimmy Sheckard	325.00	155.00	90.00
(21)	Bill Sweeney	325.00	155.00	90.00
(22)	Terry Turner	325.00	155.00	90.00
(23)	Hans Wagner	750.00	375.00	225.00
(24)	Harry Wolter	325.00	155.00	90.00

1950 All-Star Baseball "Pin-Ups"

This set of ten 7" diameter black-and-white player photos was issued in the form of a booklet, with the individual pictures perforated to be punched out. Each picture has a hole at the top for hanging. The front and back cover of the book are identical and picture Ted Williams, along with a list of the players inside. Backs of each player's picture have how-to tips for playing a specific position, hitting, base stealing, etc. Published by Garden City Publishing Co., Inc., the book carried a cover price of 50 cents. The unnumbered pictures are checklisted here alphabetically.

		NM	EX	VG
Complete Book:		1100.	550.00	325.00
Complete Set, Singles (10):		800.00	400.00	250.00
Common Player:		20.00	10.00	6.00
(1)	Joe DiMaggio	250.00	125.00	75.00
(2)	Jim Hegan	20.00	10.00	6.00
(3)	Gil Hodges	60.00	30.00	18.00
(4)	George Kell	30.00	15.00	9.00
(5)	Ralph Kiner	45.00	22.00	13.50
(6)	Stan Musial	125.00	62.00	37.00
(7)	Mel Parnell	20.00	10.00	6.00
(8)	Phil Rizzuto	75.00	37.00	22.00
(9)	Jackie Robinson	200.00	100.00	60.00
(10)	Ted Williams	200.00	100.00	60.00

1949 All Stars Photo Pack

This set of "American and National League All Stars" player pictures is comprised of 6-1/4" x 9" black-and-white photos bordered in white with a simulated signature printed on front. Backs are blank. The set came in a red, black and white paper envelope with several of the pictures shown on front and red stars for decoration. The unnumbered pictures are listed here alphabetically.

		NM	EX	VG
Complete Set (18):		300.00	150.00	80.00
Common Player:		10.00	5.00	3.00
(1)	Luke Appling	15.00	7.50	4.50
(2)	Lou Boudreau	15.00	7.50	4.50
(3)	Joe DiMaggio	50.00	25.00	15.00
(4)	Bobby Doerr	15.00	7.50	4.50
(5)	Bob Feller	20.00	10.00	6.00
(6)	Joe Gordon	10.00	5.00	3.00
(7)	Tommy Henrich	10.00	5.00	3.00
(8)	George Kell	15.00	7.50	4.50
(9)	Ralph Kiner	15.00	7.50	4.50
(10)	Bob Lemon	15.00	7.50	4.50
(11)	Marty Marion	10.00	5.00	3.00
(12)	Stan Musial	25.00	12.50	7.50
(13)	Don Newcombe	15.00	7.50	4.50
(14)	Phil Rizzuto	20.00	10.00	6.00
(15)	Jackie Robinson	35.00	17.50	10.50
(16)	Enos Slaughter	15.00	7.50	4.50
(17)	Vern Stephens	10.00	5.00	3.00
(18)	Ted Williams	35.00	17.50	10.50

1971 Allstate Insurance

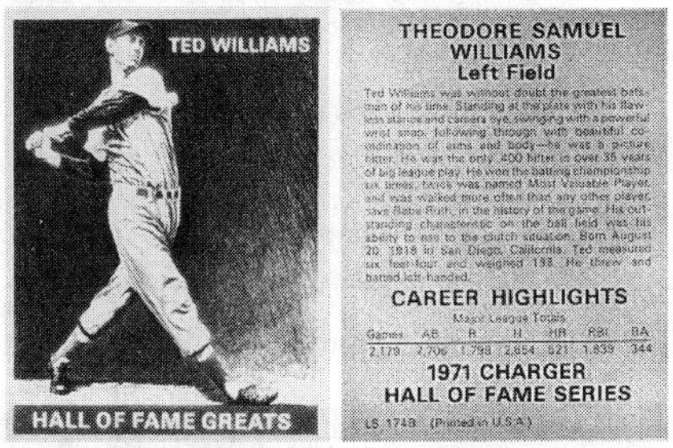

This 4-card series was distributed as part of an internal sales promotion for Allstate Insurance. Graphic artist Ray Lending, an Allstate employee, created the 2-1/2" x 3-1/4" cards in duo-tone black and green on white. Card fronts show the players in batting stance, with the player name in one of the upper corners and the "Hall of Fame Series" logo printed across the bottom of the card. The card backs carry the player's full name and position, followed by a brief career summary, biography, and Career Highlights chart listing major league totals. "1971 Charger" and "Hall of Fame Series" are printed at the bottom of the card back. 8,000 sets were distributed.

		NM	EX	VG
Complete Set (4):		80.00	40.00	24.00
Common Player:		20.00	10.00	6.00
(1)	Ty Cobb	20.00	10.00	6.00
(2)	Stan Musial	20.00	10.00	6.00
(3)	Babe Ruth	40.00	20.00	12.00
(4)	Ted Williams	20.00	10.00	6.00

1916 Altoona Tribune

This Pennsylvania daily newspaper was one of several regional advertisers to use this black-and-white, 1-5/8" x 3" 200-card set for promotional purposes. The Altoona issue shares the checklist and, by and large, the values of the 1916 Sporting News version of the set. Type card and superstar collectors may pay a premium for a Tribune version of a specific card.

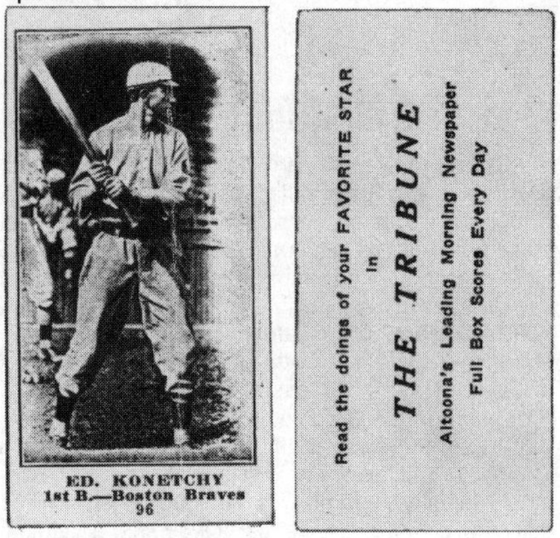

(See 1916 The Sporting News for checklist and price guide.)

1909-11 American Beauty Cigarettes

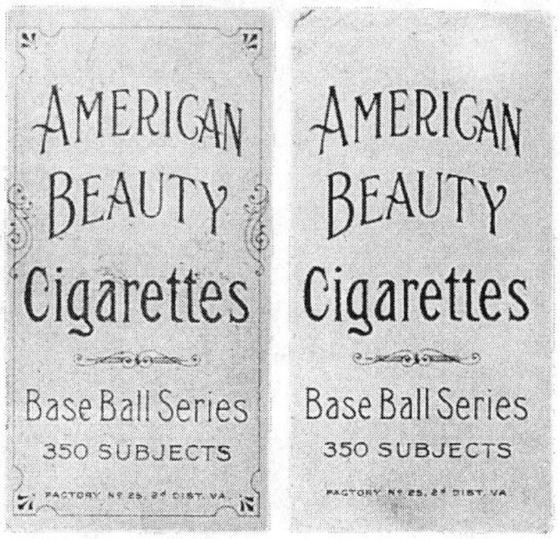

(See T205, T206. Premium: T205 - 2X, T206 - +75%.
Note: T206s with American Beauty backs may be somewhat narrower.)

1908 American Caramel (E91, Set A)

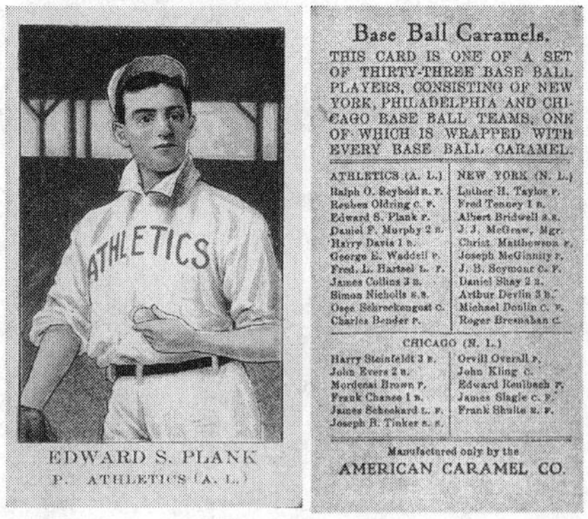

Issued by Philadelphia's American Caramel Company from 1908 through 1910, the E91 set of Base Ball Caramels is generally not popular with collectors because the color drawings show "generic" players, rather than actual major leaguers. In other words, the exact same drawing was used to depict two or three different players. For this reason, the set is sometimes referred to as "Fake Design". The player's name, position and team appear below the color drawing on the front of the card. The cards measure approximately 1-1/2" x 2-3/4" and were issued in three separate series. They can be differentiated by their backs, which checklist the cards. Set A backs list the Athletics in the upper left, the Giants in the upper right and the Cubs below. Set B backs list the Cubs and Athletics on top with the Giants below, and Set C backs list Pittsburg and Washington on top with Boston below. A line indicating the cards were "Manufactured Only by the American Caramel Co." appears at the bottom.

		NM	EX	VG
Complete Set (33):		4000.	1800.	1425.
Common Player:		75.00	34.00	22.00
(1)	Charles Bender	200.00	100.00	60.00
(2)	Roger Bresnahan	200.00	100.00	60.00
(3)	Albert Bridwell	75.00	34.00	22.00
(4)	Mordecai Brown	200.00	100.00	60.00
(5)	Frank Chance	200.00	100.00	60.00
(6)	James Collins	200.00	100.00	60.00
(7)	Harry Davis	75.00	37.00	22.00
(8)	Arthur Devlin	75.00	37.00	22.00
(9)	Michael Donlin	75.00	37.00	22.00
(10)	John Evers	200.00	100.00	60.00
(11)	Frederick L. Hartsel	75.00	37.00	22.00
(12)	John Kling	75.00	37.00	22.00
(13)	Christopher Matthewson (Mathewson)	400.00	200.00	120.00
(14)	Joseph McGinnity	200.00	100.00	60.00
(15)	John J McGraw	200.00	100.00	60.00
(16)	Daniel F Murphy	75.00	37.00	22.00
(17)	Simon Nicholls	75.00	37.00	22.00
(18)	Reuben Oldring	75.00	37.00	22.00
(19)	Orvill Overall (Orval)	75.00	37.00	22.00
(20)	Edward S. Plank	200.00	100.00	60.00
(21)	Edward Reulbach	75.00	37.00	22.00
(22)	James Scheckard (Sheckard)	75.00	37.00	22.00
(23)	Osee Schreckengost (Ossee)	75.00	37.00	22.00
(24)	Ralph O. Seybold	75.00	37.00	22.00
(25)	J. Bentley Seymour	75.00	37.00	22.00
(26)	Daniel Shay	75.00	37.00	22.00
(27)	Frank Shulte (Schulte)	75.00	37.00	22.00
(28)	James Slagle	75.00	37.00	22.00
(29)	Harry Steinfeldt	75.00	37.00	22.00
(30)	Luther H. Taylor	80.00	36.00	24.00
(31)	Fred Tenney	75.00	37.00	22.00
(32)	Joseph B. Tinker	200.00	100.00	60.00
(33)	George Edward Waddell	200.00	100.00	60.00

1909 American Caramel (E91, Set B)

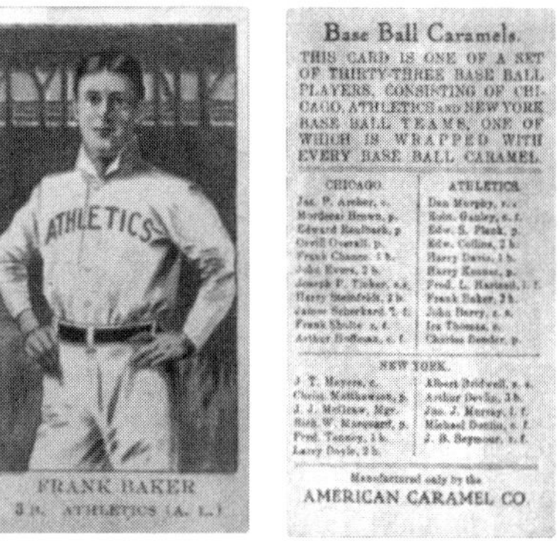

		NM	EX	VG
Complete Set (33):		3000.	1350.	900.00
Common Player:		75.00	34.00	22.00
(1)	James Archer	75.00	34.00	22.00
(2)	Frank Baker	200.00	90.00	60.00
(3)	John Barry	75.00	34.00	22.00
(4)	Charles Bender	200.00	90.00	60.00
(5)	Albert Bridwell	75.00	34.00	22.00
(6)	Mordecai Brown	200.00	90.00	60.00
(7)	Frank Chance	200.00	90.00	60.00
(8)	Edw. Collins	200.00	90.00	60.00
(9)	Harry Davis	75.00	34.00	22.00
(10)	Arthur Devlin	75.00	34.00	22.00
(11)	Michael Donlin	75.00	34.00	22.00
(12)	Larry Doyle	75.00	34.00	22.00
(13)	John Evers	200.00	90.00	60.00
(14)	Robt. Ganley	75.00	34.00	22.00
(15)	Frederick L. Hartsel	75.00	34.00	22.00
(16)	Arthur Hoffman (Hofman)	75.00	34.00	22.00
(17)	Harry Krause	75.00	34.00	22.00
(18)	Rich. W. Marquard	200.00	90.00	60.00
(19)	Christopher Matthewson (Mathewson)	400.00	180.00	120.00
(20)	John J. McGraw	200.00	90.00	60.00
(21)	J.T. Meyers	75.00	34.00	22.00
(22)	Dan Murphy	75.00	34.00	22.00
(23)	Jno. J. Murray	75.00	34.00	22.00
(24)	Orvill Overall (Orval)	75.00	34.00	22.00
(25)	Edward S. Plank	200.00	90.00	60.00
(26)	Edward Reulbach	75.00	34.00	22.00
(27)	James Scheckard (Sheckard)	75.00	34.00	22.00
(28)	J. Bentley Seymour	75.00	34.00	22.00
(29)	Harry Steinfeldt	75.00	34.00	22.00
(30)	Frank Shulte (Schulte)	75.00	34.00	22.00
(31)	Fred Tenney	75.00	34.00	22.00
(32)	Joseph B Tinker	200.00	90.00	60.00
(33)	Ira Thomas	75.00	34.00	22.00

1910 American Caramel (E91, Set C)

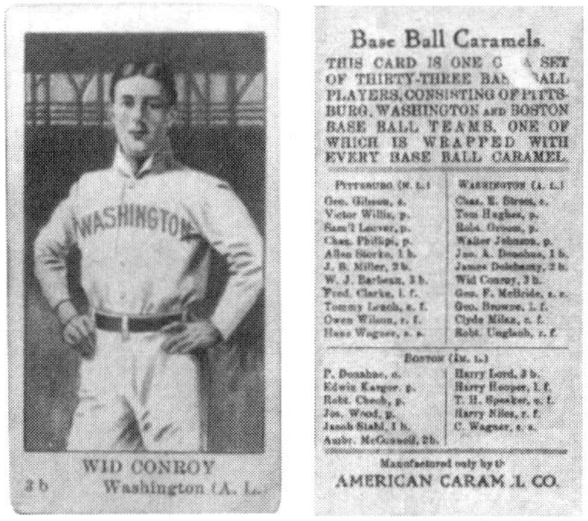

		NM	EX	VG
Complete Set (33):		3000.	1350.	900.00
Common Player:		65.00	32.00	19.50
(1)	W.J. Barbeau	75.00	34.00	22.00
(2)	Geo. Brown	75.00	34.00	22.00
(3)	Robt. Chech (Charles)	75.00	34.00	22.00
(4)	Fred Clarke	200.00	90.00	60.00
(5)	Wid Conroy	75.00	34.00	22.00
(6)	James Delehanty (Delahanty)	75.00	34.00	22.00
(7)	Jon A. Donohue (Donahue)	75.00	34.00	22.00
(8)	P. Donahue	75.00	34.00	22.00
(9)	Geo. Gibson	75.00	34.00	22.00
(10)	Robt. Groom	75.00	34.00	22.00
(11)	Harry Hooper	200.00	90.00	60.00
(12)	Tom Hughes	75.00	34.00	22.00
(13)	Walter Johnson	400.00	180.00	120.00
(14)	Edwin Karger	75.00	34.00	22.00
(15)	Tommy Leach	75.00	34.00	22.00
(16)	Sam'l Leever	75.00	34.00	22.00
(17)	Harry Lord	75.00	34.00	22.00
(18)	Geo. F. McBride	75.00	34.00	22.00
(19)	Ambr. McConnell	75.00	34.00	22.00
(20)	Clyde Milan	75.00	34.00	22.00
(21)	J.B. Miller	75.00	34.00	22.00
(22)	Harry Niles	75.00	34.00	22.00
(23)	Chas. Phillipi (Phillippe)	75.00	34.00	22.00
(24)	T.H. Speaker	300.00	135.00	90.00
(25)	Jacob Stahl	75.00	34.00	22.00
(26)	Chas. E. Street	75.00	34.00	22.00
(27)	Allen Storke	75.00	34.00	22.00
(28)	Robt. Unglaub	75.00	34.00	22.00
(29)	C. Wagner	75.00	34.00	22.00
(30)	Hans Wagner	500.00	225.00	150.00
(31)	Victor Willis	200.00	90.00	60.00
(32)	Owen Wilson	75.00	34.00	22.00
(33)	Jos. Wood	75.00	34.00	22.00

1909-11 American Caramel (E90-1)

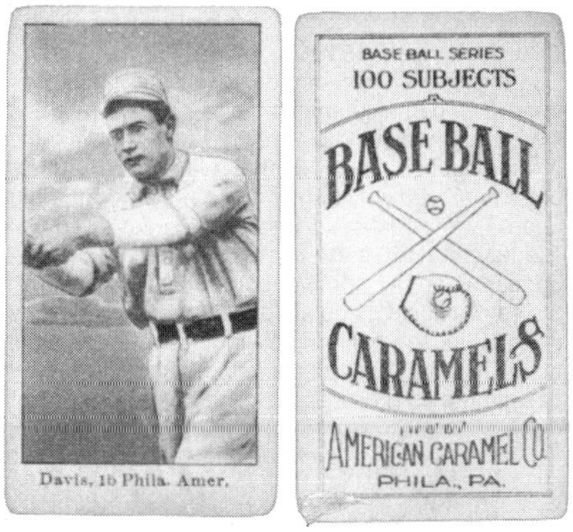

The E90-1 set was issued by the American Caramel Co. from 1909 through 1911, with the bulk of the set being produced in the first year. The cards, which measure 1-1/2" x 2-3/4" in size and were issued with sticks of caramel candy, are color reproductions of actual photographs. The card backs state that 100 subjects are included in the set though more actually do exist. There are several levels of scarcity in the set, those levels being mostly determined by the year the cards were issued. Mitchell (Cincinnati), Clarke (Pittsburg), Graham, and Sweeney (Boston) are the most difficult cards in the set to obtain. For the collector's convenience, the players' first names have been added in the checklist that follows. The complete set price includes all variations.

		NM	EX	VG
Complete Set (118):		50000.	25000.	15000.
Common Player:		120.00	55.00	35.00
(1)	Bill Bailey	120.00	55.00	35.00
(2)	Home Run Baker	400.00	185.00	115.00
(3)	Jack Barry	120.00	55.00	35.00
(4)	George Bell	120.00	55.00	35.00
(5)	Harry Bemis	200.00	92.00	58.00
(6)	Chief Bender	400.00	185.00	115.00
(7)	Bob Bescher	140.00	65.00	40.00
(8)	Cliff Blankenship	120.00	55.00	35.00
(9)	John Bliss	120.00	55.00	35.00
(10)	Bill Bradley	120.00	55.00	35.00
(11)	Kitty Bransfield ("P" on shirt)	120.00	55.00	35.00
(12)	Kitty Bransfield (no "P" on shirt)	140.00	65.00	40.00
(13)	Roger Bresnahan	350.00	160.00	100.00
(14)	Al Bridwell	120.00	55.00	35.00
(15)	Buster Brown (Boston)	120.00	55.00	35.00
(16)	Mordecai Brown (Chicago)	475.00	218.00	138.00
(17)	Donie Bush	120.00	55.00	35.00
(18)	John Butler	120.00	55.00	35.00
(19)	Howie Camnitz	120.00	55.00	35.00
(20)	Frank Chance	375.00	170.00	119.00
(21)	Hal Chase	140.00	65.00	40.00
(22a)	Fred Clarke (Philadelphia)	350.00	160.00	100.00
(22b)	Fred Clarke (Pittsburgh)	1125.	515.00	325.00
(23)	Wally Clement	140.00	65.00	40.00
(24)	Ty Cobb	3000.	1375.	850.00
(25)	Eddie Collins	375.00	170.00	119.00
(26)	Sam Crawford	360.00	165.00	105.00
(27)	Frank Corridon	120.00	55.00	35.00
(28)	Lou Criger	120.00	55.00	35.00
(29)	George Davis	300.00	138.00	87.00
(30)	Harry Davis	120.00	55.00	35.00
(31)	Ray Demmitt	290.00	135.00	85.00
(32)	Mike Donlin	120.00	55.00	35.00
(33)	Wild Bill Donovan	120.00	55.00	35.00
(34)	Red Dooin	120.00	55.00	35.00
(35)	Patsy Dougherty	160.00	75.00	45.00
(36)	Hugh Duffy	1400.	645.00	400.00
(37)	Jimmy Dygert	120.00	55.00	35.00
(38)	Rube Ellis	120.00	55.00	35.00
(39)	Clyde Engle	120.00	55.00	35.00
(40)	Art Fromme	350.00	160.00	100.00
(41)	George Gibson (back view)	425.00	195.00	125.00
(42)	George Gibson (front view)	120.00	55.00	35.00
(43)	Peaches Graham	1350.	620.00	390.00
(44)	Eddie Grant	120.00	55.00	35.00
(45)	Dolly Gray	120.00	55.00	35.00
(46)	Bob Groom	120.00	55.00	35.00
(47)	Charley Hall	120.00	55.00	35.00
(48)	Roy Hartzell (fielding)	120.00	55.00	35.00
(49)	Roy Hartzell (batting)	120.00	55.00	35.00
(50)	Heinie Heitmuller	120.00	55.00	35.00
(51)	Harry Howell (follow thru)	120.00	55.00	35.00
(52)	Harry Howell (windup)	125.00	57.00	36.00
(53)	Tex Irwin (Erwin)	120.00	55.00	35.00
(54)	Frank Isbell	120.00	55.00	35.00
(55)	Joe Jackson	9500.	4375.	2750.
(56)	Hughie Jennings	375.00	170.00	110.00
(57)	Buck Jordon (Jordan)	120.00	55.00	35.00
(58)	Addie Joss (portrait)	375.00	170.00	110.00
(59)	Addie Joss (pitching)	1500.	690.00	435.00
(60)	Ed Karger	1000.	460.00	290.00
(61a)	Willie Keeler (portrait, pink background)	400.00	185.00	115.00
(61b)	Willie Keeler (portrait, red background)	1125.	515.00	325.00
(62)	Willie Keeler (throwing)	1850.	850.00	535.00
(63)	John Knight	120.00	55.00	35.00
(64)	Harry Krause	120.00	55.00	35.00
(65)	Nap Lajoie	500.00	230.00	145.00
(66)	Tommy Leach (throwing)	120.00	55.00	35.00
(67)	Tommy Leach (batting)	120.00	55.00	35.00
(68)	Sam Leever	120.00	55.00	35.00
(69)	Hans Lobert	725.00	330.00	210.00
(70)	Harry Lumley	120.00	55.00	35.00
(71)	Rube Marquard	360.00	165.00	105.00
(72)	Christy Matthewson (Mathewson)	750.00	345.00	215.00
(73)	Stuffy McInnes (McInnis)	120.00	55.00	35.00
(74)	Harry McIntyre	120.00	55.00	35.00
(75)	Larry McLean	150.00	69.00	43.00
(76)	George McQuillan	120.00	55.00	35.00
(77)	Dots Miller	120.00	55.00	35.00
(78)	Fred Mitchell (New York)	120.00	55.00	35.00
(79)	Mike Mitchell (Cincinnati)	7500.	3450.	1750.
(80)	George Mullin	120.00	55.00	35.00
(81)	Rebel Oakes	120.00	55.00	35.00
(82)	Paddy O'Connor	120.00	55.00	35.00
(83)	Charley O'Leary	120.00	55.00	35.00
(84)	Orval Overall	600.00	275.00	175.00
(85)	Jim Pastorius	120.00	55.00	35.00
(86)	Ed Phelps	120.00	55.00	35.00
(87)	Eddie Plank	500.00	230.00	145.00
(88)	Lew Richie	120.00	55.00	35.00
(89)	Germany Schaefer	120.00	55.00	35.00
(90)	Biff Schlitzer	125.00	57.00	36.00
(91)	Johnny Seigle (Siegle)	160.00	75.00	45.00
(92)	Dave Shean	125.00	55.00	35.00
(93)	Jimmy Sheckard	125.00	55.00	35.00
(94)	Tris Speaker	1400.	645.00	400.00
(95)	Jake Stahl	1200.	550.00	350.00
(96)	Oscar Stanage	120.00	55.00	35.00

(97)	George Stone (no hands visible)	120.00	55.00	35.00
(98)	George Stone (left hand visible)	120.00	55.00	35.00
(99)	George Stovall	120.00	55.00	35.00
(100)	Ed Summers	120.00	55.00	35.00
(101)	Bill Sweeney (Boston)	1800.	825.00	525.00
(102)	Jeff Sweeney (New York)	120.00	55.00	35.00
(103)	Jesse Tannehill (Chicago A.L.)	120.00	55.00	35.00
(104)	Lee Tannehill (Chicago N.L.)	120.00	55.00	35.00
(105)	Fred Tenney	120.00	55.00	35.00
(106)	Ira Thomas (Philadelphia)	120.00	55.00	35.00
(107)	Roy Thomas (Boston)	120.00	55.00	35.00
(108)	Joe Tinker	375.00	170.00	110.00
(109)	Bob Unglaub	120.00	55.00	35.00
(110)	Jerry Upp	120.00	55.00	35.00
(111)	Honus Wagner (batting)	1250.	575.00	360.00
(112)	Honus Wagner (throwing)	1250.	575.00	360.00
(113)	Bobby Wallace	285.00	130.00	83.00
(114)	Ed Walsh	1200.	550.00	350.00
(115)	Vic Willis	300.00	138.00	87.00
(116)	Hooks Wiltse	160.00	75.00	45.00
(117)	Cy Young (Cleveland)	725.00	333.00	210.00
(118)	Cy Young (Boston)	585.00	270.00	170.00

1910 American Caramel Pirates (E90-2)

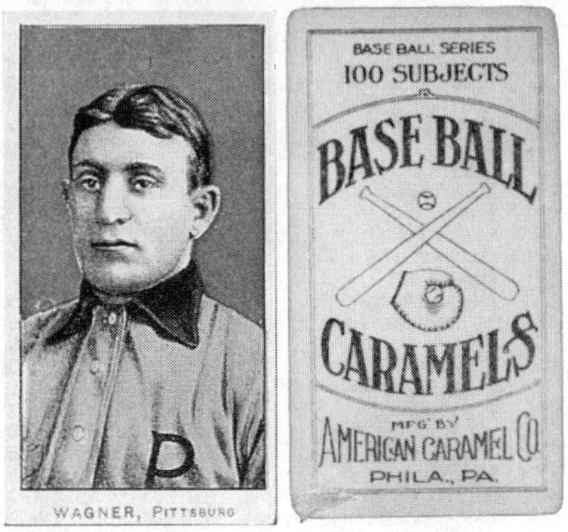

Closely related to the E90-1 American Caramel set, the E90-2 set consists of 11 cards featuring members of the 1909 champion Pittsburgh Pirates. The cards measure 1-1/2" x 2-3/4" and display a color lithograph on the front with a solid color background of either red, green, blue or pink. The player's name and "Pittsburg" appear in blue capital letters in the border beneath the portrait. The backs are identical to those in the E90-1 set, depicting a drawing of a ball, glove and crossed bats with the words "Base Ball Caramels" and a reference to "100 Subjects." The set includes Hall of Famers Honus Wagner and Fred Clarke.

		NM	EX	VG
Complete Set (11):		5625.	2575.	1625.
Common Player:		250.00	115.00	72.00
(1)	Babe Adams	250.00	115.00	72.00
(2)	Fred Clarke	500.00	230.00	145.00
(3)	George Gibson	250.00	115.00	72.00
(4)	Ham Hyatt	250.00	115.00	72.00
(5)	Tommy Leach	250.00	115.00	72.00
(6)	Sam Leever	250.00	115.00	72.00
(7)	Nick Maddox	250.00	115.00	72.00
(8)	Dots Miller	250.00	115.00	72.00
(9)	Deacon Phillippe	250.00	115.00	72.00
(10)	Honus Wagner	3250.	1500.	940.00
(11)	Owen Wilson	250.00	115.00	72.00

1910 American Caramel White Sox/Cubs (E90-3)

Similar in size (1-1/2" x 2-3/4") and style to the more popular E90-1 set, the E90-3 set was issued by the American Caramel Co. in 1910. The 20-card, color lithograph set includes 11 Chicago Cubs and nine White Sox. The fronts of the cards have a similar design to the E90-1 set, although different pictures were used. The backs can be differentiated by two major changes: The bottom of the card indicates the American Caramel Co. of "Chicago," rather than Philadelphia, and the top of the card contains the phrase "All The Star Players," rather than "100 Subjects."

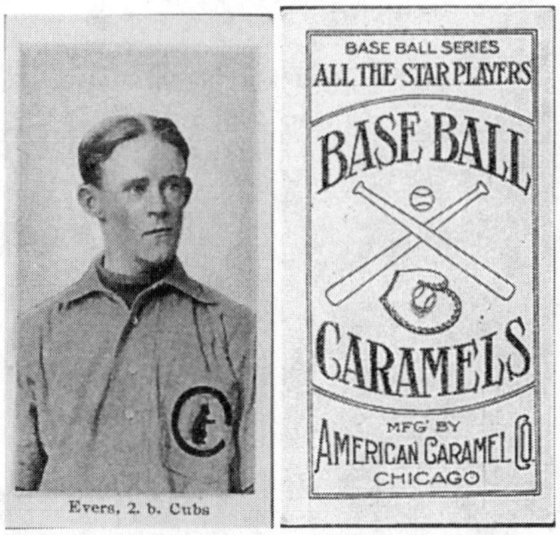

		NM	EX	VG
Complete Set (20):		4500.	2025.	1300.
Common Player:		200.00	92.00	58.00
(1)	Jimmy Archer	200.00	92.00	58.00
(2)	Lena Blackburne	200.00	92.00	58.00
(3)	Mordecai Brown	400.00	185.00	115.00
(4)	Frank Chance	400.00	185.00	115.00
(5)	King Cole	200.00	92.00	58.00
(6)	Patsy Dougherty	200.00	92.00	58.00
(7)	Johnny Evers	400.00	185.00	115.00
(8)	Chick Gandil	400.00	185.00	115.00
(9)	Ed Hahn	200.00	92.00	58.00
(10)	Solly Hofman	200.00	92.00	58.00
(11)	Orval Overall	200.00	92.00	58.00
(12)	Fred Payne	200.00	92.00	58.00
(13)	Billy Purtell	200.00	92.00	58.00
(14)	Wildfire Schulte	200.00	92.00	58.00
(15)	Jimmy Sheckard	200.00	92.00	58.00
(16)	Frank Smith	200.00	92.00	58.00
(17)	Harry Steinfeldt	200.00	92.00	58.00
(18a)	Joe Tinker (blue background)	400.00	185.00	115.00
(18b)	Joe Tinker (green background)	400.00	185.00	115.00
(19)	Ed Walsh	400.00	185.00	115.00
(20)	Rollie Zeider	200.00	92.00	58.00

1910 American Caramel Die-cuts (E125)

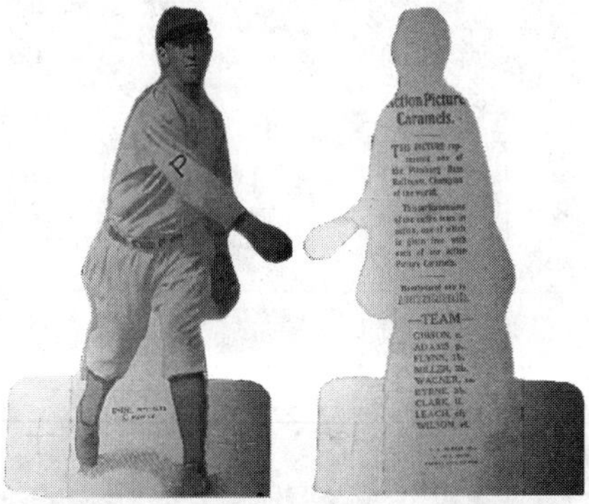

Issued circa 1910 by the American Caramel Co., this set of die-cut cards is so rare that it wasn't even known to exist until the late 1960s. Apparently inserted in boxes of caramels, these cards, which are die-cut figures of baseball players, vary in size but are all relatively large - some measuring 7" high and 4" wide. Players from the Athletics, Red Sox, Giants and Pirates are known with a team checklist appearing on the back. According to the checklists, the set would be complete at 41 cards (including two separate poses of Honus Wagner), but to date only about 20 different cards have been found. The set is designated as E125.

		NM	EX	VG
Common Player:		1200.	550.00	375.00
(1)	Babe Adams	1200.	550.00	375.00
(2)	Red Ames	1200.	550.00	375.00
(3)	Home Run Baker	1600.	725.00	480.00
(4)	Jack Barry	1200.	550.00	375.00
(5)	Chief Bender	1600.	725.00	480.00
(6)	Al Bridwell	1200.	550.00	375.00
(7)	Bobby Byrne (throwing)	1200.	550.00	375.00
(8)	Bill Carrigan	1200.	550.00	375.00
(9)	Ed Cicotte (throwing)	1500.	675.00	450.00
(10)	Fred Clark (Clarke)	1600.	725.00	480.00
(11)	Eddie Collins	1750.	785.00	525.00
(12)	Harry Davis (fielding)	1200.	550.00	375.00
(13)	Art Devlin	1200.	550.00	375.00
(14)	Josh Devore	1200.	550.00	375.00
(15)	Larry Doyle	1200.	550.00	375.00
(16)	John Flynn (running)	1200.	550.00	375.00
(17)	George Gibson (hands in glove)	1200.	550.00	375.00
(18)	Topsy Hartsell (Hartsel)	1200.	550.00	375.00
(19)	Harry Hooper (throwing)	1600.	725.00	480.00
(20)	Harry Krause	1200.	550.00	375.00
(21)	Tommy Leach	1200.	550.00	375.00
(22)	Harry Lord	1200.	550.00	375.00
(23)	Christy Mathewson	6500.	2925.	1950.
(24)	Amby McConnell	1200.	550.00	375.00
(25)	Fred Merkle	1200.	550.00	375.00
(26)	Dots Miller	1200.	550.00	375.00
(27)	Danny Murphy	1200.	550.00	375.00
(28)	Red Murray	1200.	550.00	375.00
(29)	Harry Niles	1200.	550.00	375.00
(30)	Rube Oldring	1200.	550.00	375.00
(31)	Eddie Plank	1750.	785.00	525.00
(32)	Cy Seymour	1200.	550.00	375.00
(33)	Tris Speaker (batting)	2400.	1080.	720.00
(34)	Tris Speaker (fielding)	2400.	1080.	720.00
(35)	Jake Stahl (fielding)	1200.	550.00	375.00
(36)	Ira Thomas	1200.	550.00	375.00
(37)	Heinie Wagner	1200.	550.00	375.00
(38)	Honus Wagner (batting)	7500.	3375.	2250.
(39)	Honus Wagner (throwing)	7500.	3375.	2250.
(40)	Art Wilson	1200.	550.00	375.00
(41)	Owen Wilson	1200.	550.00	375.00
(42)	Hooks Wiltse	1200.	550.00	375.00

1915 American Caramel (E106)

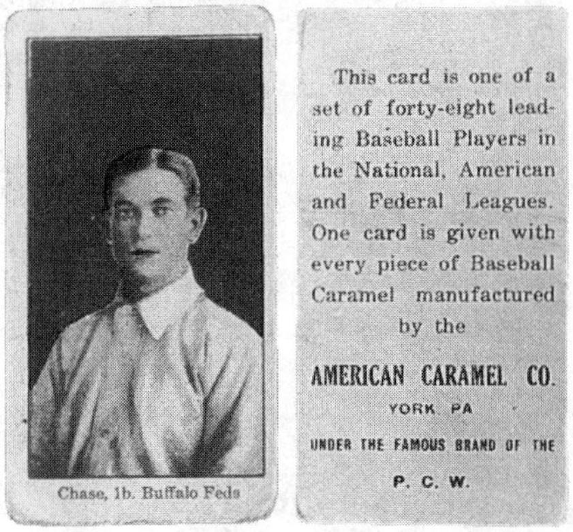

Chase, 1b. Buffalo Feds
This card is one of a set of forty-eight leading Baseball Players in the National, American and Federal Leagues. One card is given with every piece of Baseball Caramel manufactured by the
AMERICAN CARAMEL CO.
YORK PA
UNDER THE FAMOUS BRAND OF THE
P. C. W.

This 48-card set, designated E106 by the American Card Catalog, was produced by the American Caramel Co., of York, Pa., in 1915 and includes players from the National, American and Federal Leagues. Cards measure 1-1/2" x 2-3/4". The set is related to the E90-1 and E92 sets, from which the artwork is taken, but this issue has a glossy coating on front, which makes the cards very susceptible to cracking.

		NM	EX	VG
Complete Set (48):		25500.	11500.	9000.
Common Player:		200.00	90.00	58.00
(1)	Jack Barry	200.00	90.00	58.00
(2)	Chief Bender (white hat)	350.00	155.00	100.00
(3)	Chief Bender (striped hat)	350.00	155.00	100.00
(4)	Bob Bescher	200.00	90.00	58.00
(5)	Roger Bresnahan	350.00	155.00	100.00
(6)	Al Bridwell	200.00	90.00	58.00
(7)	Donie Bush	200.00	90.00	58.00
(8)	Hal Chase (portrait)	200.00	90.00	58.00
(9)	Hal Chase (catching)	200.00	90.00	58.00
(10)	Ty Cobb (w/bat, facing front)	4750.	2375.	1425.
(11)	Ty Cobb (batting, facing to side)	5500.	2475.	1595.
(12)	Eddie Collins	350.00	155.00	100.00
(13)	Sam Crawford	350.00	155.00	100.00
(14)	Ray Demmitt	200.00	90.00	58.00
(15)	Wild Bill Donovan	200.00	90.00	58.00
(16)	Red Dooin	200.00	90.00	58.00
(17)	Mickey Doolan	200.00	90.00	58.00
(18)	Larry Doyle	200.00	90.00	58.00
(19)	Clyde Engle	200.00	90.00	58.00
(20)	Johnny Evers	350.00	155.00	100.00
(21)	Art Fromme	200.00	90.00	58.00
(22)	George Gibson (catching, back view)	200.00	90.00	58.00
(23)	George Gibson (catching, front view)	200.00	90.00	58.00
(24)	Roy Hartzell	200.00	90.00	58.00
(25)	Fred Jacklitsch	200.00	90.00	58.00
(26)	Hugh Jennings	350.00	155.00	100.00
(27)	Otto Knabe	200.00	90.00	58.00
(28)	Nap Lajoie	400.00	180.00	115.00
(29)	Hans Lobert	200.00	90.00	58.00
(30)	Rube Marquard	350.00	155.00	100.00
(31)	Christy Matthewson (Mathewson)	900.00	400.00	260.00
(32)	John McGraw	350.00	155.00	100.00
(33)	George McQuillan	200.00	90.00	58.00
(34)	Dots Miller	200.00	90.00	58.00
(35)	Danny Murphy	200.00	90.00	58.00
(36)	Rebel Oakes	200.00	90.00	58.00
(37)	Eddie Plank	350.00	175.00	105.00
(38)	Germany Schaefer	200.00	90.00	58.00
(39)	Tris Speaker	500.00	225.00	145.00
(40)	Oscar Stanage	200.00	90.00	58.00

(41)	George Stovall	200.00	90.00	58.00
(42)	Jeff Sweeney	200.00	90.00	58.00
(43)	Joe Tinker (portrait)	350.00	155.00	100.00
(44)	Joe Tinker (batting)	350.00	155.00	100.00
(45)	Honus Wagner (batting)	2250.	1000.	650.00
(46)	Honus Wagner (throwing)	2250.	1000.	650.00
(47)	Hooks Wiltse	200.00	90.00	58.00
(48)	Heinie Zimmerman	200.00	90.00	58.00

1921 American Caramel Series of 80 (E121)

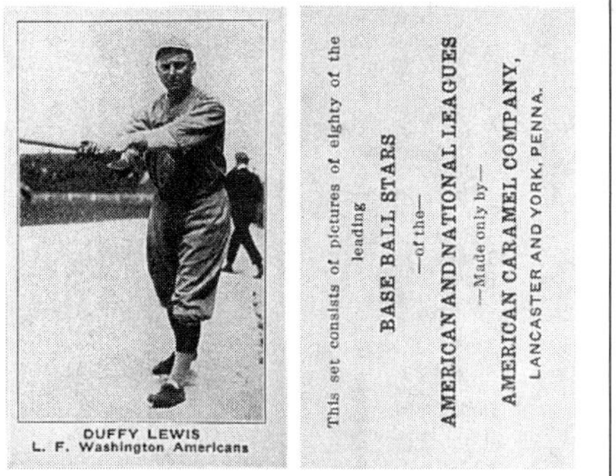
DUFFY LEWIS
L. F. Washington Americans
This set consists of pictures of eighty of the
leading
BASE BALL STARS
—of the—
AMERICAN AND NATIONAL LEAGUES
—Made only by—
AMERICAN CARAMEL COMPANY,
LANCASTER AND YORK, PENNA.

Issued circa 1921, the E121 Series of 80 is designated as such because of the card reverses which indicate the player pictured is just one of 80 baseball stars in the set. The figure of 80 supplied by the American Caramel Co. is incorrect as over 100 different pictures do exist. The unnumbered cards, which measure 2" x about 3-1/4", feature black and white photos. Two different backs exist for the Series of 80. The common back variation has the first line ending with the word "the," while the scarcer version ends with the word "eighty." The complete set price does not include the variations.

		NM	EX	VG
Complete Set (121):		9850.	4435.	3450.
Common Player:		40.00	18.00	11.50
(1)	G.C. Alexander (arms above head)	125.00	56.00	36.00
(2)	Grover Alexander	125.00	56.00	36.00
(3)	Jim Bagby	40.00	18.00	11.50
(4a)	J. Franklin Baker	125.00	56.00	36.00
(4b)	Frank Baker	125.00	56.00	36.00
(5)	Dave Bancroft (batting)	125.00	56.00	36.00
(6)	Dave Bancroft (leaping)	125.00	56.00	36.00
(7)	Ping Bodie	40.00	18.00	11.50
(8)	George Burns	40.00	18.00	11.50
(9)	Geo. J. Burns	40.00	18.00	11.50
(10)	Owen Bush	40.00	18.00	11.50
(11)	Max Carey (batting)	125.00	56.00	36.00
(12)	Max Carey (hands at hips)	125.00	56.00	36.00
(13)	Cecil Causey	40.00	18.00	11.50
(14)	Ty Cobb (throwing, looking front)	900.00	400.00	260.00
(15a)	Ty Cobb (throwing, looking right, Mgr. on front)	900.00	400.00	260.00
(15b)	Ty Cobb (throwing, looking right, Manager on front)	900.00	400.00	260.00
(16)	Eddie Collins	125.00	56.00	36.00
(17)	"Rip" Collins	40.00	18.00	11.50
(18)	Jake Daubert	40.00	18.00	11.50
(19)	George Dauss	40.00	18.00	11.50
(20)	Charles Deal (dark uniform)	40.00	18.00	11.50
(21)	Charles Deal (white uniform)	40.00	18.00	11.50
(22)	William Doak	40.00	18.00	11.50
(23)	Bill Donovan	40.00	18.00	11.50
(24)	"Phil" Douglas	40.00	18.00	11.50
(25a)	Johnny Evers (Manager)	125.00	56.00	36.00
(25b)	Johnny Evers (Mgr.)	125.00	56.00	36.00
(26)	Urban Faber (dark uniform)	125.00	56.00	36.00
(27)	Urban Faber (white uniform)	125.00	56.00	36.00
(28)	William Fewster (first name actually Wilson)	40.00	18.00	11.50
(29)	Eddie Foster	40.00	18.00	11.50
(30)	Frank Frisch	125.00	56.00	36.00
(31)	W.L. Gardner	40.00	18.00	11.50
(32a)	Alexander Gaston (no position on front)	40.00	18.00	11.50
(32b)	Alexander Gaston (position on front)	40.00	18.00	11.50
(33)	"Kid" Gleason	40.00	18.00	11.50
(34)	"Mike" Gonzalez	45.00	20.00	13.00
(35)	Hank Gowdy	40.00	18.00	11.50
(36)	John Graney	40.00	18.00	11.50
(37)	Tom Griffith	40.00	18.00	11.50
(38)	Heinie Groh	40.00	18.00	11.50
(39)	Harry Harper	40.00	18.00	11.50
(40)	Harry Heilman (Heilmann)	125.00	56.00	36.00
(41)	Walter Holke (portrait)	40.00	18.00	11.50
(42)	Walter Holke (throwing)	40.00	18.00	11.50
(43)	Charles Hollacher (Hollocher)	40.00	18.00	11.50
(44)	Harry Hooper	125.00	56.00	36.00
(45)	Rogers Hornsby	160.00	70.00	45.00
(46)	Waite Hoyt	125.00	56.00	36.00
(47)	Miller Huggins	125.00	56.00	36.00
(48)	Wm. C. Jacobson	40.00	18.00	11.50
(49)	Hugh Jennings	125.00	56.00	36.00
(50)	Walter Johnson (throwing)	325.00	145.00	95.00
(51)	Walter Johnson (hands at chest)	325.00	145.00	95.00
(52)	James Johnston	40.00	18.00	11.50
(53)	Joe Judge	40.00	18.00	11.50
(54)	George Kelly	125.00	56.00	36.00
(55)	Dick Kerr	40.00	18.00	11.50
(56)	P.J. Kilduff	40.00	18.00	11.50
(57a)	Bill Killifer (incorrect name)	40.00	18.00	11.50
(57b)	Bill Killefer (correct name)	40.00	18.00	11.50
(58)	John Lavan	40.00	18.00	11.50
(59)	"Nemo" Leibold	40.00	18.00	11.50
(60)	Duffy Lewis	40.00	18.00	11.50
(61)	Al. Mamaux	40.00	18.00	11.50
(62)	"Rabbit" Maranville	125.00	56.00	36.00
(63a)	Carl May (Mays)	75.00	34.00	22.00
(63b)	Carl Mays (correct name)	55.00	25.00	16.00
(64)	John McGraw	125.00	56.00	36.00
(65)	Jack McInnis	40.00	18.00	11.50
(66)	M.J. McNally	40.00	18.00	11.50
(67)	Emil Muesel (Photo actually Lou DeVormer)	45.00	20.00	13.00
(68)	R. Meusel	40.00	18.00	11.50
(69)	Clyde Milan	40.00	18.00	11.50
(70)	Elmer Miller	40.00	18.00	11.50
(71)	Otto Miller	40.00	18.00	11.50
(72)	Guy Morton	40.00	18.00	11.50
(73)	Eddie Murphy	40.00	18.00	11.50
(74)	"Hy" Myers	40.00	18.00	11.50
(75)	Arthur Nehf	40.00	18.00	11.50
(76)	Steve O'Neill	40.00	18.00	11.50
(77a)	Roger Peckinbaugh (incorrect name)	40.00	18.00	11.50
(77b)	Roger Peckinpaugh (correct name)	40.00	18.00	11.50
(78a)	Jeff Pfeffer (Brooklyn)	40.00	18.00	11.50
(78b)	Jeff Pfeffer (St. Louis)	40.00	18.00	11.50
(79)	Walter Pipp	40.00	18.00	11.50
(80)	Jack Quinn	40.00	18.00	11.50
(81)	John Rawlings	40.00	18.00	11.50
(82)	E.C. Rice	125.00	56.00	36.00
(83)	Eppa Rixey, Jr.	125.00	56.00	36.00
(84)	Robert Roth	40.00	18.00	11.50
(85a)	Ed. Roush (C.F.)	125.00	56.00	36.00
(85b)	Ed. Roush (L.F.)	125.00	56.00	36.00
(86a)	Babe Ruth	1875.	845.00	545.00
(86b)	"Babe" Ruth	1875.	845.00	545.00
(86c)	George Ruth	1875.	845.00	545.00
(87)	"Bill" Ryan	40.00	18.00	11.50
(88)	"Slim" Sallee (glove showing)	40.00	18.00	11.50
(89)	"Slim" Sallee (no glove showing)	40.00	18.00	11.50
(90)	Ray Schalk	125.00	56.00	36.00
(91)	Walter Schang	40.00	18.00	11.50
(92a)	Fred Schupp (name incorrect)	40.00	18.00	11.50
(92b)	Ferd Schupp (name correct)	40.00	18.00	11.50
(93)	Everett Scott	40.00	18.00	11.50
(94)	Hank Severeid	40.00	18.00	11.50
(95)	Robert Shawkey	40.00	18.00	11.50
(96a)	Pat Shea	40.00	18.00	11.50
(96b)	"Pat" Shea	40.00	18.00	11.50
(97)	George Sisler (batting)	125.00	56.00	36.00
(98)	George Sisler (throwing)	125.00	56.00	36.00
(99)	Earl Smith	40.00	18.00	11.50
(100)	Frank Snyder	40.00	18.00	11.50
(101a)	Tris Speaker (Mgr.)	175.00	80.00	50.00
(101b)	Tris Speaker (Manager - large projection)	175.00	80.00	50.00
(101c)	Tris Speaker (Manager - small projection)	175.00	80.00	50.00
(102)	Milton Stock	40.00	18.00	11.50
(103)	Amos Strunk	40.00	18.00	11.50
(104)	Zeb Terry	40.00	18.00	11.50
(105)	Chester Thomas	40.00	18.00	11.50
(106)	Fred Toney (trees in background)	40.00	18.00	11.50
(107)	Fred Toney (no trees in background)	40.00	18.00	11.50
(108)	George Tyler	40.00	18.00	11.50
(109)	Jim Vaughn (dark hat)	40.00	18.00	11.50
(110)	Jim Vaughn (white hat)	40.00	18.00	11.50
(111)	Bob Veach (glove in air)	40.00	18.00	11.50
(112)	Bob Veach (arms crossed)	40.00	18.00	11.50
(113)	Oscar Vitt	40.00	18.00	11.50
(114)	W. Wambsganss (photo actually Fred Coumbe)	40.00	18.00	11.50
(115)	Aaron Ward	40.00	18.00	11.50
(116)	Zach Wheat	125.00	56.00	36.00
(117)	George Whitted	40.00	18.00	11.50
(118)	Fred Williams	40.00	18.00	11.50
(119)	Ivy B. Wingo	40.00	18.00	11.50
(120)	Joe Wood	40.00	18.00	11.50
(121)	"Pep" Young	40.00	18.00	11.50

1922 American Caramel Series of 120 (E121)

Produced by American Caramel Co. circa 1922, the E121 Series of 120 is labeled as such by the company's claim that the set contained 120 subjects. Identical in design to the E121 Series of 80 set except for the card backs, the cards measure 2" x 3-1/2". Numerous variations are found in the set, most involving a change in the player's name, team or position. The complete set price does not include variations. To date, 118 different players are known.

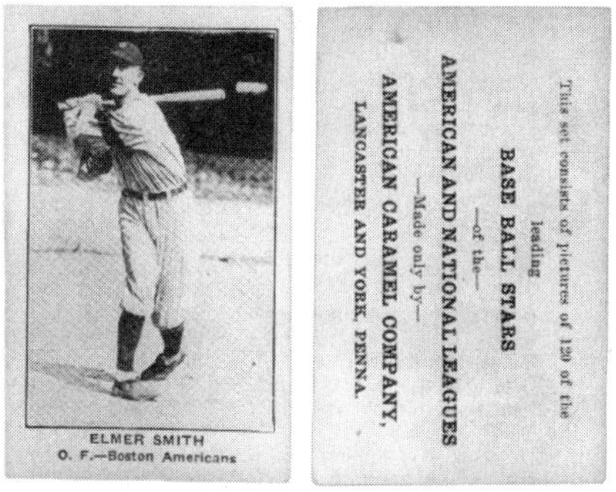
ELMER SMITH
O. F.—Boston Americans
This set consists of pictures of 120 of the
leading
BASE BALL STARS
—of the—
AMERICAN AND NATIONAL LEAGUES
—Made only by—
AMERICAN CARAMEL COMPANY,
LANCASTER AND YORK PENNA.

		NM	EX	VG
Complete Set (126):		13000.	5850.	4550.
Common Player:		40.00	18.00	11.50
(1)	Chas. "Babe" Adams	40.00	18.00	11.50
(2)	G.C. Alexander	150.00	67.00	43.00
(3)	Jim Bagby	40.00	18.00	11.50
(4)	Dave Bancroft	125.00	56.00	36.00
(5)	Turner Barber	40.00	18.00	11.50
(6a)	Carlson Bigbee (correct name Carson L. Bigbee)	40.00	18.00	11.50
(6b)	Carlson L. Bigbee	40.00	18.00	11.50
(6c)	Corson L. Bigbee	45.00	20.00	13.00
(6d)	L. Bigbee	40.00	18.00	11.50
(7)	"Bullet Joe" Bush	40.00	18.00	11.50
(8)	Max Carey	125.00	56.00	36.00
(9)	Cecil Causey	40.00	18.00	11.50
(10)	Ty Cobb (batting)	850.00	380.00	245.00
(11)	Ty Cobb (throwing)	850.00	380.00	245.00
(12)	Eddie Collins	125.00	56.00	36.00
(13)	A. Wilbur Cooper	40.00	18.00	11.50
(14)	Stanley Coveleskie (Coveleski)	125.00	56.00	36.00
(15)	Dave Danforth	40.00	18.00	11.50
(16)	Jake Daubert	40.00	18.00	11.50
(17)	George Dauss	40.00	18.00	11.50
(18)	Dixie Davis	40.00	18.00	11.50
(19)	Chas. A. Deal	40.00	18.00	11.50
(20)	Lou DeVormer	40.00	18.00	11.50
(21)	William Doak	40.00	18.00	11.50
(22)	Phil Douglas	40.00	18.00	11.50
(23)	Urban Faber	125.00	56.00	36.00
(24)	Bib Falk (Bibb)	40.00	18.00	11.50
(25)	Wm: Fewster (first name actually Wilson)	40.00	18.00	11.50
(26)	Max Flack	40.00	18.00	11.50
(27)	Ira Falgstead (Flagstead)	40.00	18.00	11.50
(28)	Frank Frisch	125.00	56.00	36.00
(29)	W.L. Gardner	40.00	18.00	11.50
(30)	Alexander Gaston	40.00	18.00	11.50
(31)	E.P. Gharrity	40.00	18.00	11.50
(32)	George Gibson	40.00	18.00	11.50
(33)	Chas. "Whitey" Glazner	40.00	18.00	11.50
(34)	"Kid" Gleason	40.00	18.00	11.50
(35)	Hank Gowdy	40.00	18.00	11.50
(36)	John Graney	40.00	18.00	11.50
(37)	Tom Griffith	40.00	18.00	11.50
(38)	Chas. Grimm	40.00	18.00	11.50
(39)	Heine Groh	40.00	18.00	11.50
(40)	Jess Haines	125.00	56.00	36.00
(41)	Harry Harper	40.00	18.00	11.50
(42a)	Harry Heilman (name incorrect)	165.00	75.00	48.00
(42b)	Harry Heilmann (name correct)	125.00	56.00	36.00
(43)	Clarence Hodge	40.00	18.00	11.50
(44)	Walter Holke (portrait)	40.00	18.00	11.50
(45)	Walter Holke (throwing)	40.00	18.00	11.50
(46)	Charles Hollocher	40.00	18.00	11.50
(47)	Harry Hooper	125.00	56.00	36.00
(48a)	Rogers Hornsby (2B.)	200.00	90.00	58.00
(48b)	Rogers Hornsby (O.F.)	200.00	90.00	58.00
(49)	Waite Hoyt	125.00	56.00	36.00
(50)	Miller Huggins	125.00	56.00	36.00
(51)	Walter Johnson	475.00	215.00	135.00
(52)	Joe Judge	40.00	18.00	11.50
(53)	George Kelly	125.00	56.00	36.00
(54)	Dick Kerr	40.00	18.00	11.50
(55)	P.J. Kilduff	40.00	18.00	11.50
(56)	Bill Killifer (Killefer) (batting)	40.00	18.00	11.50
(57)	Bill Killifer (Killefer) (throwing)	40.00	18.00	11.50
(58)	John Lavan	40.00	18.00	11.50
(59)	Walter Mails	40.00	18.00	11.50
(60)	"Rabbit" Maranville	125.00	56.00	36.00
(61)	Elwood Martin	40.00	18.00	11.50
(62)	Carl Mays	40.00	18.00	11.50
(63)	John J. McGraw	125.00	56.00	36.00
(64)	Jack McInnis	40.00	18.00	11.50
(65)	M.J. McNally	40.00	18.00	11.50
(66)	Emil Meusel (photo actually Lou DeVormer)	40.00	18.00	11.50
(67)	R. Meusel	40.00	18.00	11.50
(68)	Clyde Milan	40.00	18.00	11.50
(69)	Elmer Miller	40.00	18.00	11.50
(70)	Otto Miller	40.00	18.00	11.50
(71)	Johnny Mostil	40.00	18.00	11.50
(72)	Eddie Mulligan	40.00	18.00	11.50
(73a)	Hy Myers	40.00	18.00	11.50
(73b)	"Hy" Myers	40.00	18.00	11.50
(74)	Earl Neale	45.00	20.00	13.00
(75)	Arthur Nehf	40.00	18.00	11.50
(76)	Leslie Nunamaker	40.00	18.00	11.50
(77)	Joe Oeschger	40.00	18.00	11.50
(78)	Chas. O'Leary	40.00	18.00	11.50

(79)	Steve O'Neill	40.00	18.00	11.50
(80)	D.B. Pratt	40.00	18.00	11.50
(81a)	John Rawlings (2B.)	40.00	18.00	11.50
(81b)	John Rawlings (Utl.)	40.00	18.00	11.50
(82)	E.S. Rice (intials actually E.C.)	125.00	56.00	36.00
(83)	Eppa J. Rixey	125.00	56.00	36.00
(84)	Eppa Rixey, Jr.	125.00	56.00	36.00
(85)	Wilbert Robinson	125.00	56.00	36.00
(86)	Tom Rogers	40.00	18.00	11.50
(87a)	Ed Rounnel	40.00	18.00	11.50
(87b)	Ed. Rommel	40.00	18.00	11.50
(88)	Ed Roush	125.00	56.00	36.00
(89)	"Muddy" Ruel	40.00	18.00	11.50
(90)	Walter Ruether	40.00	18.00	11.50
(91a)	Babe Ruth (photo montage)	1895.	850.00	550.00
(91b)	"Babe" Ruth (photo montage)	2000.	900.00	580.00
(92a)	Babe Ruth (holding bird)	1800.	810.00	520.00
(92b)	"Babe" Ruth (holding bird)	1895.	850.00	550.00
(93)	"Babe" Ruth (holding ball)	1895.	850.00	550.00
(94)	Bill Ryan	40.00	18.00	11.50
(95)	Ray Schalk (catching)	125.00	56.00	36.00
(96)	Ray Schalk (batting)	125.00	56.00	36.00
(97)	Wally Schang	40.00	18.00	11.50
(98)	Ferd Schupp	40.00	18.00	11.50
(99)	Everett Scott	40.00	18.00	11.50
(100)	Joe Sewell	125.00	56.00	36.00
(101)	Robert Shawkey	40.00	18.00	11.50
(102)	Pat Shea	40.00	18.00	11.50
(103)	Earl Sheely	40.00	18.00	11.50
(104)	Urban Schocker	40.00	18.00	11.50
(105)	George Sisler (batting)	140.00	63.00	41.00
(106)	George Sisler (throwing)	125.00	56.00	36.00
(107)	Earl Smith	40.00	18.00	11.50
(108)	Elmer Smith	40.00	18.00	11.50
(109)	Frank Snyder	40.00	18.00	11.50
(110)	Bill Southworth	40.00	18.00	11.50
(111a)	Tris Speaker (large projection)	200.00	90.00	58.00
(111b)	Tris Speaker (small projection)	200.00	90.00	58.00
(112a)	Milton Stock	40.00	18.00	11.50
(112b)	Milton J. Stock	40.00	18.00	11.50
(113)	Amos Strunk	40.00	18.00	11.50
(114)	Zeb Terry	40.00	18.00	11.50
(115)	Fred Toney	40.00	18.00	11.50
(116)	George Topocer (Toporcer)	40.00	18.00	11.50
(117)	Bob Veach	40.00	18.00	11.50
(118)	Oscar Vitt	40.00	18.00	11.50
(119)	Curtis Walker	40.00	18.00	11.50
(120)	W. Wambsganss (photo actually Fred Coumbe)	40.00	18.00	11.50
(121)	Aaron Ward	40.00	18.00	11.50
(122)	Zach Wheat	125.00	56.00	36.00
(123a)	George Whitted (Pittsburgh)	40.00	18.00	11.50
(123b)	George Whitted (Brooklyn)	40.00	18.00	11.50
(124)	Fred Williams	40.00	18.00	11.50
(125)	Ivy B. Wingo	40.00	18.00	11.50
(126)	Ross Young (Youngs)	125.00	56.00	36.00

1922 American Caramel Series of 80 (E122)

Known as E122 in the American Card Catalog, this set is actually a parallel of the E121 American Caramel set. The cards are nearly identical to E121's "Series of 80," except the player's name, position and team are printed inside a gray rectangle at the bottom of the card, and the photos have a more coarse appearance. At 2" x 3-1/4," the E122s are slightly shorter than E121s.

		NM	EX	VG
Complete Set (80):		9000.	4000.	2500.
Common Player:		48.00	22.00	11.00
(1)	Grover Alexander	175.00	75.00	36.00
(2)	Jim Bagby	48.00	22.00	11.00
(3)	J. Franklin Baker	175.00	75.00	36.00
(4)	Dave Bancroft	175.00	75.00	36.00
(5)	Ping Bodie	48.00	22.00	11.00
(6)	George Burns	48.00	22.00	11.00
(7)	Geo. J. Burns	48.00	22.00	11.00
(8)	Owen Bush	48.00	22.00	11.00
(9)	Max Carey	175.00	75.00	36.00
(10)	Cecil Causey	48.00	22.00	11.00
(11)	Ty Cobb	1000.	500.00	300.00
(12)	Eddie Collins	175.00	75.00	36.00
(13)	Jake Daubert	48.00	22.00	11.00
(14)	George Dauss	48.00	22.00	11.00
(15)	Charles Deal	48.00	22.00	11.00
(16)	William Doak	48.00	22.00	11.00
(17)	Bill Donovan	48.00	22.00	11.00
(18)	Johnny Evers	175.00	75.00	36.00
(19)	Urban Faber	175.00	75.00	36.00
(20)	Eddie Foster	48.00	22.00	11.00
(21)	W.L. Gardner	48.00	22.00	11.00
(22)	"Kid" Gleason	48.00	22.00	11.00
(23)	Hank Gowdy	48.00	22.00	11.00
(24)	John Graney	48.00	22.00	11.00
(25)	Tom Griffith	48.00	22.00	11.00
(26)	Harry Heilman (Heilmann)	175.00	75.00	36.00
(27)	Walter Holke	48.00	22.00	11.00
(28)	Charles Hollacher (Hollocher)	48.00	22.00	11.00
(29)	Harry Hooper	175.00	75.00	36.00
(30)	Rogers Hornsby	200.00	90.00	45.00
(31)	Wm. C. Jacobson	48.00	22.00	11.00
(32)	Walter Johnson	625.00	312.00	187.00
(33)	James Johnston	48.00	22.00	11.00
(34)	Joe Judge	48.00	22.00	11.00
(35)	George Kelly	175.00	75.00	36.00
(36)	Dick Kerr	48.00	22.00	11.00
(37)	P.J. Kilduff	48.00	22.00	11.00
(38)	Bill Killefer	48.00	22.00	11.00
(39)	John Lavan	48.00	22.00	11.00
(40)	Duffy Lewis	48.00	22.00	11.00
(41)	Perry Lipe	48.00	22.00	11.00
(42)	Al. Mamaux	48.00	22.00	11.00
(43)	"Rabbit" Maranville	175.00	75.00	36.00
(44)	Carl May (Mays)	60.00	25.00	15.00
(45)	John McGraw	175.00	75.00	36.00
(46)	Jack McInnis	48.00	22.00	11.00
(47)	Clyde Milan	48.00	22.00	11.00
(48)	Otto Miller	48.00	22.00	11.00
(49)	Guy Morton	48.00	22.00	11.00
(50)	Eddie Murphy	48.00	22.00	11.00
(51)	"Hy" Myers	48.00	22.00	11.00
(52)	Steve O'Neill	48.00	22.00	11.00
(53)	Roger Peckinbaugh (Peckinpaugh)	48.00	22.00	11.00
(54)	Jeff Pfeffer	48.00	22.00	11.00
(55)	Walter Pipp	60.00	25.00	15.00
(56)	E.C. Rice	175.00	75.00	36.00
(57)	Eppa Rixey, Jr.	175.00	75.00	36.00
(58)	Babe Ruth	1600.	800.00	480.00
(59)	"Slim" Sallee	48.00	22.00	11.00
(60)	Ray Schalk	175.00	75.00	36.00
(61)	Walter Schang	48.00	22.00	11.00
(62a)	Fred Schupp (name incorrect)	48.00	22.00	11.00
(62b)	Ferd Schupp (name correct)	48.00	22.00	11.00
(63)	Everett Scott	48.00	22.00	11.00
(64)	Hank Severeid	48.00	22.00	11.00
(65)	George Sisler (batting)	175.00	75.00	36.00
(66)	George Sisler (throwing)	175.00	75.00	36.00
(67)	Tris Speaker	200.00	90.00	45.00
(68)	Milton Stock	48.00	22.00	11.00
(69)	Amos Strunk	48.00	22.00	11.00
(70)	Chester Thomas	48.00	22.00	11.00
(71)	George Tyler	48.00	22.00	11.00
(72)	Jim Vaughn	48.00	22.00	11.00
(73)	Bob Veach	48.00	22.00	11.00
(74)	Oscar Vitt	48.00	24.00	14.50
(75)	W. Wambsganss	55.00	27.00	16.50
(76)	Zach Wheat	175.00	75.00	36.00
(77)	Fred Williams	48.00	24.00	14.50
(78)	Ivy B. Wingo	48.00	22.00	11.00
(79)	Joe Wood	55.00	27.00	16.50
(80)	Pep Young	48.00	22.00	11.00

1922 American Caramel Series of 240 (E120)

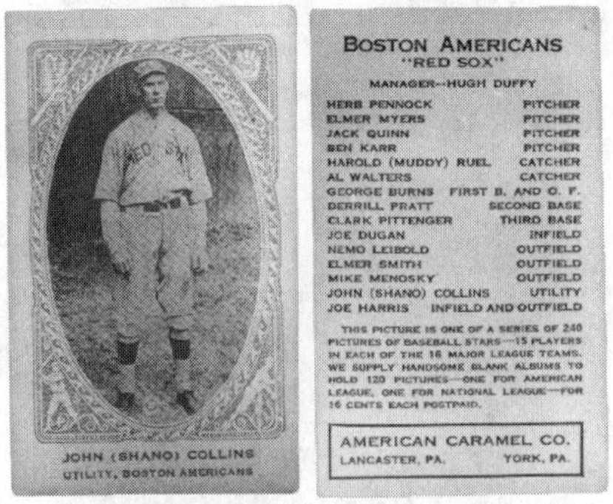

One of the most popular sets of the 1920s candy cards, the 1922 E120s were produced by the American Caramel Co. and distributed with sticks of caramel candy. The unnumbered cards measure 2" x 3-1/2". Cards depicting players from the American League are printed in brown ink on thin cream cardboard; National Leaguers are printed in green on blue-green stock. Backs carry team checklists. Many of the E120 photos were used in other sets of the era. A pair of 11-1/2" x 10-1/2" albums, holding 120 each and stamped American or National League were also issued.

		NM	EX	VG
Complete Set (240):		15000.	6750.	4350.
Common Player:		45.00	20.00	13.00
Album:		150.00	75.00	45.00
(1)	Charles (Babe) Adams	45.00	20.00	13.00
(2)	Eddie Ainsmith	45.00	20.00	13.00
(3)	Vic Aldridge	45.00	20.00	13.00
(4)	Grover C. Alexander	160.00	72.00	46.00
(5)	Jim Bagby	45.00	20.00	13.00
(6)	Frank (Home Run) Baker	160.00	72.00	46.00
(7)	Dave (Beauty) Bancroft	160.00	72.00	46.00
(8)	Walt Barbare	45.00	20.00	13.00
(9)	Turner Barber	45.00	20.00	13.00
(10)	Jess Barnes	45.00	20.00	13.00
(11)	Clyde Barnhart	45.00	20.00	13.00
(12)	John Bassler	45.00	20.00	13.00
(13)	Will Bayne	45.00	20.00	13.00
(14)	Walter (Huck) Betts	45.00	20.00	13.00
(15)	Carson Bigbee	45.00	20.00	13.00
(16)	Lu Blue	45.00	20.00	13.00
(17)	Norman Boeckel	45.00	20.00	13.00
(18)	Sammy Bohne	45.00	20.00	13.00
(19)	George Burns	45.00	20.00	13.00
(20)	George Burns	45.00	20.00	13.00
(21)	"Bullet Joe" Bush	45.00	20.00	13.00
(22)	Leon Cadore	45.00	20.00	13.00
(23)	Marty Callaghan	45.00	20.00	13.00
(24)	Frank Calloway (Callaway)	45.00	20.00	13.00
(25)	Max Carey	160.00	72.00	46.00
(26)	Jimmy Caveney	45.00	20.00	13.00
(27)	Virgil Cheeves	45.00	20.00	13.00
(28)	Vern Clemons	45.00	20.00	13.00
(29)	Ty Cob (Cobb)	1100.	495.00	320.00
(30)	Bert Cole	45.00	20.00	13.00
(31)	Eddie Collins	160.00	72.00	46.00
(32)	John (Shano) Collins	45.00	20.00	13.00
(33)	T.P. (Pat) Collins	45.00	20.00	13.00
(34)	Wilbur Cooper	45.00	20.00	13.00
(35)	Harry Courtney	45.00	20.00	13.00
(36)	Stanley Coveleskie (Coveleski)	160.00	72.00	46.00
(37)	Elmer Cox	45.00	20.00	13.00
(38)	Sam Crane	45.00	20.00	13.00
(39)	Walton Cruise	45.00	20.00	13.00
(40)	Bill Cunningham	45.00	20.00	13.00
(41)	George Cutshaw	45.00	20.00	13.00
(42)	Dave Danforth	45.00	20.00	13.00
(43)	Jake Daubert	45.00	20.00	13.00
(44)	George Dauss	45.00	20.00	13.00
(45)	Frank (Dixie) Davis	45.00	20.00	13.00
(46)	Hank DeBerry	45.00	20.00	13.00
(47)	Albert Devormer (Lou DeVormer)	45.00	20.00	13.00
(48)	Bill Doak	45.00	20.00	13.00
(49)	Pete Donohue	45.00	20.00	13.00
(50)	"Shufflin" Phil Douglas	45.00	20.00	13.00
(51)	Joe Dugan	45.00	20.00	13.00
(52)	Louis (Pat) Duncan	45.00	20.00	13.00
(53)	Jimmy Dykes	45.00	20.00	13.00
(54)	Howard Ehmke	45.00	20.00	13.00
(55)	Frank Ellerbe	45.00	20.00	13.00
(56)	Urban (Red) Faber	160.00	72.00	46.00
(57)	Bib Falk (Bibb)	45.00	20.00	13.00
(58)	Dana Fillingim	45.00	20.00	13.00
(59)	Max Flack	45.00	20.00	13.00
(60)	Ira Flagstead	45.00	20.00	13.00
(61)	Art Fletcher	45.00	20.00	13.00
(62)	Horace Ford	45.00	20.00	13.00
(63)	Jack Fournier	45.00	20.00	13.00
(64)	Frank Frisch	160.00	72.00	46.00
(65)	Ollie Fuhrman	45.00	20.00	13.00
(66)	Clarance Galloway	45.00	20.00	13.00
(67)	Larry Gardner	45.00	20.00	13.00
(68)	Walter Gerber	45.00	20.00	13.00
(69)	Ed Gharrity	45.00	20.00	13.00
(70)	John Gillespie	45.00	20.00	13.00
(71)	Chas. (Whitey) Glazner	45.00	20.00	13.00
(72)	Johnny Gooch	45.00	20.00	13.00
(73)	Leon Goslin	160.00	72.00	46.00
(74)	Hank Gowdy	45.00	20.00	13.00
(75)	John Graney	45.00	20.00	13.00
(76)	Tom Griffith	45.00	20.00	13.00
(77)	Burleigh Grimes	160.00	72.00	46.00
(78)	Oscar Ray Grimes	45.00	20.00	13.00
(79)	Charlie Grimm	45.00	20.00	13.00
(80)	Heinie Groh	45.00	20.00	13.00
(81)	Jesse Haines	160.00	72.00	46.00
(82)	Earl Hamilton	45.00	20.00	13.00
(83)	Gene (Bubbles) Hargrave	45.00	20.00	13.00
(84)	Bryan Harris (Harriss)	45.00	20.00	13.00
(85)	Joe Harris	45.00	20.00	13.00
(86)	Stanley Harris	160.00	72.00	46.00
(87)	Chas. (Dowdy) Hartnett	160.00	72.00	46.00
(88)	Bob Hasty	45.00	20.00	13.00
(89)	Joe Hauser	50.00	22.00	14.50
(90)	Clif Heathcote	45.00	20.00	13.00
(91)	Harry Heilmann	160.00	72.00	46.00
(92)	Walter (Butch) Henline	45.00	20.00	13.00
(93)	Clarence (Shovel) Hodge	45.00	20.00	13.00
(94)	Walter Holke	45.00	20.00	13.00
(95)	Charles Hollocher	45.00	20.00	13.00
(96)	Harry Hooper	160.00	72.00	46.00
(97)	Rogers Hornsby	200.00	90.00	58.00
(98)	Waite Hoyt	160.00	72.00	46.00
(99)	Wilbur Hubbell (Wilbert)	45.00	20.00	13.00
(100)	Bernard (Bud) Hungling	45.00	20.00	13.00
(101)	Will Jacobson	45.00	20.00	13.00
(102)	Charlie Jamieson	45.00	20.00	13.00
(103)	Ernie Johnson	45.00	20.00	13.00
(104)	Sylvester Johnson	45.00	20.00	13.00
(105)	Walter Johnson	500.00	225.00	145.00
(106)	Jimmy Johnston	45.00	20.00	13.00
(107)	W.R. (Doc) Johnston	45.00	20.00	13.00
(108)	"Deacon" Sam Jones	45.00	20.00	13.00

(109)	Bob Jones	45.00	20.00	13.00
(110)	Percy Jones	45.00	20.00	13.00
(111)	Joe Judge	45.00	20.00	13.00
(112)	Ben Karr	45.00	20.00	13.00
(113)	Johnny Kelleher	45.00	20.00	13.00
(114)	George Kelly	160.00	72.00	46.00
(115)	Lee King	45.00	20.00	13.00
(116)	Wm (Larry) Kopff (Kopf)	45.00	20.00	13.00
(117)	Marty Krug	45.00	20.00	13.00
(118)	Johnny Lavan	45.00	20.00	13.00
(119)	Nemo Leibold	45.00	20.00	13.00
(120)	Roy Leslie	45.00	20.00	13.00
(121)	George Leverette (Leverett)	45.00	20.00	13.00
(122)	Adolfo Luque	55.00	25.00	16.00
(123)	Walter Mails	45.00	20.00	13.00
(124)	Al Mamaux	45.00	20.00	13.00
(125)	"Rabbit" Maranville	160.00	72.00	46.00
(126)	Cliff Markle	45.00	20.00	13.00
(127)	Richard (Rube) Marquard	160.00	72.00	46.00
(128)	Carl Mays	65.00	29.00	19.00
(129)	Hervey McClellan (Harvey)	45.00	20.00	13.00
(130)	Austin McHenry	45.00	20.00	13.00
(131)	"Stuffy" McInnis	45.00	20.00	13.00
(132)	Martin McManus	45.00	20.00	13.00
(133)	Mike McNally	45.00	20.00	13.00
(134)	Hugh McQuillan	45.00	20.00	13.00
(135)	Lee Meadows	45.00	20.00	13.00
(136)	Mike Menosky	45.00	20.00	13.00
(137)	Bob (Dutch) Meusel	45.00	20.00	13.00
(138)	Emil (Irish) Meusel	45.00	20.00	13.00
(139)	Clyde Milan	45.00	20.00	13.00
(140)	Edmund (Bing) Miller	45.00	20.00	13.00
(141)	Elmer Miller	45.00	20.00	13.00
(142)	Lawrence (Hack) Miller	45.00	20.00	13.00
(143)	Clarence Mitchell	45.00	20.00	13.00
(144)	George Mogridge	45.00	20.00	13.00
(145)	Roy Moore	45.00	20.00	13.00
(146)	John L. Mokan	45.00	20.00	13.00
(147)	John Morrison	45.00	20.00	13.00
(148)	Johnny Mostil	45.00	20.00	13.00
(149)	Elmer Myers	45.00	20.00	13.00
(150)	Hy Myers	45.00	20.00	13.00
(151)	Roliene Naylor (Roleine)	45.00	20.00	13.00
(152)	Earl (Greasy) Neale	60.00	27.00	17.50
(153)	Art Nehf	45.00	20.00	13.00
(154)	Les Nunamaker	45.00	20.00	13.00
(155)	Joe Oeschger	45.00	20.00	13.00
(156)	Bob O'Farrell	45.00	20.00	13.00
(157)	Ivan Olson	45.00	20.00	13.00
(158)	George O'Neil	45.00	20.00	13.00
(159)	Steve O'Neill	45.00	20.00	13.00
(160)	Frank Parkinson	45.00	20.00	13.00
(161)	Roger Peckinpaugh	45.00	20.00	13.00
(162)	Herb Pennock	160.00	72.00	46.00
(163)	Ralph (Cy) Perkins	45.00	20.00	13.00
(164)	Will Pertica	45.00	20.00	13.00
(165)	Jack Peters	45.00	20.00	13.00
(166)	Tom Phillips	45.00	20.00	13.00
(167)	Val Picinich	45.00	20.00	13.00
(168)	Herman Pillette	45.00	20.00	13.00
(169)	Ralph Pinelli	45.00	20.00	13.00
(170)	Wallie Pipp	55.00	25.00	16.00
(171)	Clark Pittenger (Clarke)	45.00	20.00	13.00
(172)	Raymond Powell	45.00	20.00	13.00
(173)	Derrill Pratt	45.00	20.00	13.00
(174)	Jack Quinn	45.00	20.00	13.00
(175)	Joe (Goldie) Rapp	45.00	20.00	13.00
(176)	John Rawlings	45.00	20.00	13.00
(177)	Walter (Dutch) Reuther (Ruether)	45.00	20.00	13.00
(178)	Sam Rice	160.00	72.00	46.00
(179)	Emory Rigney	45.00	20.00	13.00
(180)	Jimmy Ring	45.00	20.00	13.00
(181)	Eppa Rixey	160.00	72.00	46.00
(182)	Charles Robertson	45.00	20.00	13.00
(183)	Ed Rommel	45.00	20.00	13.00
(184)	Eddie Roush	160.00	72.00	46.00
(185)	Harold (Muddy) Ruel (Herold)	45.00	20.00	13.00
(186)	Babe Ruth	2200.	990.00	635.00
(187)	Ray Schalk	160.00	72.00	46.00
(188)	Wallie Schang	45.00	20.00	13.00
(189)	Ray Schmandt	45.00	20.00	13.00
(190)	Walter Schmidt	45.00	20.00	13.00
(191)	Joe Schultz	45.00	20.00	13.00
(192)	Everett Scott	45.00	20.00	13.00
(193)	Henry Severeid	45.00	20.00	13.00
(194)	Joe Sewell	160.00	72.00	46.00
(195)	Howard Shanks	45.00	20.00	13.00
(196)	Bob Shawkey	45.00	20.00	13.00
(197)	Earl Sheely	45.00	20.00	13.00
(198)	Will Sherdel	45.00	20.00	13.00
(199)	Ralph Shinners	45.00	20.00	13.00
(200)	Urban Shocker	45.00	20.00	13.00
(201)	Charles (Chick) Shorten	45.00	20.00	13.00
(202)	George Sisler	160.00	72.00	46.00
(203)	Earl Smith	45.00	20.00	13.00
(204)	Earl Smith	45.00	20.00	13.00
(205)	Elmer Smith	45.00	20.00	13.00
(206)	Jack Smith	45.00	20.00	13.00
(207)	Sherrod Smith	45.00	20.00	13.00
(208)	Colonel Snover	45.00	20.00	13.00
(209)	Frank Snyder	45.00	20.00	13.00
(210)	Al Sothoron	45.00	20.00	13.00
(211)	Bill Southworth	45.00	20.00	13.00
(212)	Tris Speaker	200.00	90.00	58.00
(213)	Arnold Statz	45.00	20.00	13.00
(214)	Milton Stock	45.00	20.00	13.00
(215)	Amos Strunk	45.00	20.00	13.00
(216)	Jim Tierney	45.00	20.00	13.00
(217)	John Tobin	45.00	20.00	13.00
(218)	Fred Toney	45.00	20.00	13.00
(219)	George Toporcer	45.00	20.00	13.00
(220)	Harold (Pie) Traynor	160.00	72.00	46.00
(221)	George Uhle	45.00	20.00	13.00
(222)	Elam Vangilder	45.00	20.00	13.00
(223)	Bob Veach	45.00	20.00	13.00
(224)	Clarence (Tillie) Walker	45.00	20.00	13.00
(225)	Curtis Walker	45.00	20.00	13.00
(226)	Al Walters	45.00	20.00	13.00
(227)	Bill Wambsganss	45.00	20.00	13.00
(228)	Aaron Ward	45.00	20.00	13.00
(229)	John Watson	45.00	20.00	13.00
(230)	Frank Welch	45.00	20.00	13.00
(231)	Zach Wheat	160.00	72.00	46.00
(232)	Fred (Cy) Williams	45.00	20.00	13.00
(233)	Kenneth Williams	45.00	20.00	13.00
(234)	Ivy Wingo	45.00	20.00	13.00
(235)	Joe Wood	55.00	25.00	16.00
(236)	Lawrence Woodall	45.00	20.00	13.00
(237)	Russell Wrightstone	45.00	20.00	13.00
(238)	Everett Yaryan	45.00	20.00	13.00
(239)	Ross Young (Youngs)	160.00	72.00	46.00
(240)	J.T. Zachary	45.00	20.00	13.00

1927 American Caramel Series of 60 (E126)

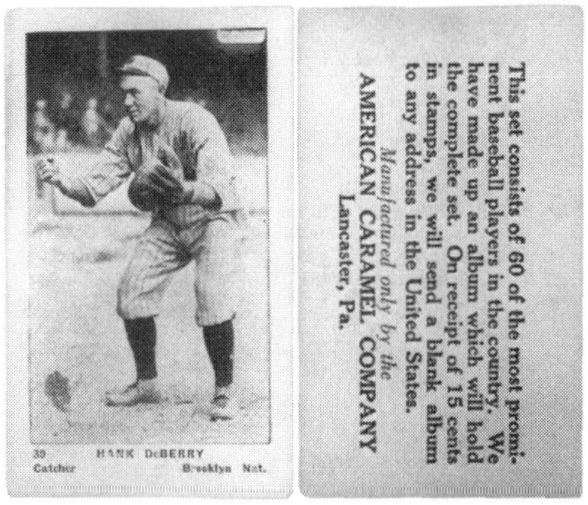

30 HANK DeBERRY
Catcher Brooklyn Nat.
This set consists of 60 of the most prominent baseball players in the country. We have made up an album which will hold the complete set. On receipt of 15 cents in stamps, we will send a blank album to any address in the United States.
Manufactured only by the
AMERICAN CARAMEL COMPANY
Lancaster, Pa.

Issued in 1927 by the American Caramel Co., of Lancaster, Pa., this obscure 60-card set was one of the last of the caramel card issues. Measuring 2" x 3-1/4", the cards differ from most sets of the period because they are numbered. The back of each card includes an offer for an album to house the set which includes players from all 16 major league teams. The set has the American Card Catalog designation E126.

		NM	EX	VG
Complete Set (60):		9250.	4100.	2200.
Common Player:		80.00	36.00	18.00
1	John Gooch	80.00	40.00	24.00
2	Clyde L. Barnhart	80.00	36.00	18.00
3	Joe Busch (Bush)	80.00	36.00	18.00
4	Lee Meadows	80.00	36.00	18.00
5	E.T. Cox	80.00	36.00	18.00
6	"Red" Faber	275.00	135.00	82.00
7	Aaron Ward	80.00	36.00	18.00
8	Ray Schalk	275.00	135.00	82.00
9	"Specks" Toporcer ("Specs")	80.00	36.00	18.00
10	Bill Southworth	80.00	36.00	18.00
11	Allen Sothoron	80.00	36.00	18.00
12	Will Sherdel	80.00	36.00	18.00
13	Grover Alexander	275.00	135.00	82.00
14	Jack Quinn	80.00	36.00	18.00
15	C. Galloway	80.00	36.00	18.00
16	"Eddie" Collins	275.00	135.00	82.00
17	"Ty" Cobb	1600.	725.00	375.00
18	Percy Jones	80.00	36.00	18.00
19	Chas. Grimm	80.00	36.00	18.00
20	"Bennie" Karr	80.00	36.00	18.00
21	Charlie Jamieson	80.00	36.00	18.00
22	Sherrod Smith	80.00	36.00	18.00
23	Virgil Cheeves	80.00	36.00	18.00
24	James Ring	80.00	36.00	18.00
25	"Muddy" Ruel	80.00	36.00	18.00
26	Joe Judge	80.00	36.00	18.00
27	Tris Speaker	350.00	175.00	105.00
28	Walter Johnson	550.00	275.00	165.00
29	E.C. "Sam" Rice	275.00	135.00	82.00
30	Hank DeBerry	80.00	36.00	18.00
31	Walter Henline	80.00	36.00	18.00
32	Max Carey	275.00	135.00	82.00
33	Arnold J. Statz	80.00	36.00	18.00
34	Emil Meusel	80.00	36.00	18.00
35	T.P. "Pat" Collins	80.00	36.00	18.00
36	Urban Shocker	80.00	36.00	18.00
37	Bob Shawkey	80.00	36.00	18.00
38	"Babe" Ruth	2900.	1300.	750.00
39	Bob Meusel	80.00	36.00	18.00
40	Alex Ferguson	80.00	36.00	18.00
41	"Stuffy" McInnis	80.00	36.00	18.00
42	"Cy" Williams	80.00	36.00	18.00
43	Russel Wrightstone (Russell)	80.00	36.00	18.00
44	John Tobin	80.00	36.00	18.00
45	Wm. C. Jacobson	80.00	36.00	18.00
46	Bryan "Slim" Harriss	80.00	36.00	18.00
47	Elam Vangilder	80.00	36.00	18.00
48	Ken Williams	80.00	36.00	18.00
49	Geo. R. Sisler	275.00	135.00	82.00
50	Ed Brown	80.00	36.00	18.00
51	Jack Smith	80.00	36.00	18.00
52	Dave Bancroft	275.00	135.00	82.00
53	Larry Woodall	80.00	36.00	18.00
54	Lu Blue	80.00	36.00	18.00
55	Johnny Bassler	80.00	36.00	18.00
56	"Jakie" May	80.00	36.00	18.00
57	Horace Ford	80.00	36.00	18.00
58	"Curt" Walker	80.00	36.00	18.00
59	"Artie" Nehf	80.00	36.00	18.00
60	Geo. Kelly	275.00	135.00	82.00

1908 American League Pub. Co. Postcards

Post Card

This set of black-and-white postcards was produced by the American League Publishing Co., Cleveland. The 3-1/2" x 5" cards have a large player posed-action photo against a white background and a smaller oval portrait photo in one of the top corners. A box at bottom contains some biographical data. The otherwise blank back has postcard indicia printed in black. The set carries an American Card Catalog designation of PC770. As might be expected, all but two of the players in the known checklist were contemporary members of the Cleveland ballclub.

		NM	EX	VG
Complete Set (16):		4500.	2250.	1350.
Common Player:		200.00	100.00	60.00
(1)	Harry Bay	200.00	100.00	60.00
(2)	Charles Berger	200.00	100.00	60.00
(3)	Joseph Birmingham	200.00	100.00	60.00
(4)	W. Bradley	200.00	100.00	60.00
(5)	Tyrus R. Cobb	1200.	600.00	360.00
(6)	Walter Clarkson	200.00	100.00	60.00
(7)	Elmer Flick	300.00	150.00	90.00
(8)	C.T. Hickman	200.00	100.00	60.00
(9)	William Hinchman	200.00	100.00	60.00
(10)	Addie Joss	350.00	175.00	105.00
(11)	Glen Liebhardt (Glenn)	200.00	100.00	60.00
(12)	Nap Lajoie	375.00	187.00	112.00
(13)	George Nill	200.00	100.00	60.00
(14)	George Perring	200.00	100.00	60.00
(16)	Honus Wagner	850.00	425.00	255.00

1950 American Nut & Chocolate Pennants (F150)

Although there is nothing on these small (1-7/8" x 4") felt pennants to identify the issuer, surviving ads show that the American Nut & Chocolate Co. of Boston sold them as a set of 22 for 50 cents. The pennants of American League players are printed in blue on white, while National Leaguers are printed in red on white. The pennants feature crude line-art drawings of the players at left, along with a facsimile autograph. A 10% variation in the size of the printing on the Elliott and Sain pennants has been noted, and may exist on others, as well. The checklist here is arranged alphabetically.

		NM	EX	VG
Complete Set (22):		400.00	200.00	120.00
Common Player:		15.00	7.50	4.50
(1)	Ewell Blackwell	15.00	7.50	4.50
(2)	Harry Brecheen	15.00	7.50	4.50
(3)	Phil Cavarretta	15.00	7.50	4.50
(4)	Bobby Doerr	20.00	10.00	6.00
(5)	Bob Elliott	15.00	7.50	4.50
(6)	Boo Ferriss	15.00	7.50	4.50
(7)	Joe Gordon	15.00	7.50	4.50
(8)	Tommy Holmes	15.00	7.50	4.50
(9)	Charles Keller	15.00	7.50	4.50

		NM	EX	VG
(10)	Ken Keltner	15.00	7.50	4.50
(11)	Ralph Kiner	24.00	12.00	7.25
(12)	Whitey Kurowski	15.00	7.50	4.50
(13)	Johnny Pesky	15.00	7.50	4.50
(14)	Pee Wee Reese	40.00	20.00	12.00
(15)	Phil Rizzuto	35.00	17.50	10.50
(16)	Johnny Sain	20.00	10.00	6.00
(17)	Enos Slaughter	20.00	10.00	6.00
(18)	Warren Spahn	25.00	12.50	7.50
(19)	Vern Stephens	15.00	7.50	4.50
(20)	Earl Torgeson	15.00	7.50	4.50
(21)	Dizzy Trout	15.00	7.50	4.50
(22)	Ted Williams	75.00	37.00	22.00

1968 American Oil Sweepstakes

Babe Ruth won fame as the greatest slugger in baseball history. He set many records including his 714 regular-season home runs which made him one of baseball's biggest attractions.
BABE RUTH
$1.00 ONE DOLLAR
Right side

One of several contemporary sweepstakes run by gas stations, this game called on players to match right- and left-side game pieces of the same athletic figure (or sporty auto) to win the stated cash prize or car. Naturally one side or the other was distributed in extremely limited quantities to avoid paying out too many prizes. Cards were given away in perforated pairs with a qualifying gasoline purchase. Uncut pairs carry a small premium over single cards. Data on which card halves were the rare part needed for redemption is incomplete and would have an effect on the collector value of surviving specimens. Individual game pieces measure 2-9/16" x 2-1/8" and are printed in color.

		NM	EX	VG
	Common Game Piece:	6.00	3.00	1.75
(1a)	Julius Boros (golfer, left side)	18.00	9.00	5.50
(1b)	Julius Boros (golfer, right side)	18.00	9.00	5.50
(2a)	Gay Brewer (golfer, left side)	18.00	9.00	5.50
(2b)	Gay Brewer (golfer, right side)	18.00	9.00	5.50
(3a)	Camaro (left side)	6.00	3.00	1.75
(3b)	Camaro (right side)	6.00	3.00	1.75
(4a)	Corvette (left side)	6.00	3.00	1.75
(4b)	Corvette (right side)	6.00	3.00	1.75
(5a)	Damascus (race horse, left side)	6.00	3.00	1.75
(5b)	Damascus (race horse, right side)	6.00	3.00	1.75
(6a)	Parnelli Jones (auto racer, left side)	15.00	7.50	4.50
(6b)	Parnelli Jones (auto racer, right side)	15.00	7.50	4.50
(7a)	Mickey Mantle (left side)	60.00	30.00	18.00
(7b)	Mickey Mantle (right side)	60.00	30.00	18.00
(8a)	Willie Mays (action, left side, $10)	36.00	18.00	11.00
(8b)	Willie Mays (portrait, right side, $10)	36.00	18.00	11.00
(9a)	Bob Richards (action, left side, 50 cents)	6.00	3.00	1.75
(9b)	Bob Richards (portrait, right side, 50 cents)	6.00	3.00	1.75
(10a)	Babe Ruth (action, left side, $1)	60.00	30.00	18.00
(10b)	Babe Ruth (portrait, right side, $1)	60.00	30.00	18.00
(11a)	Gale Sayers (action, left side, $5)	45.00	22.00	13.50
(11b)	Gale Sayers (portrait, right side, $5)	45.00	22.00	13.50
(12a)	Bart Starr (left side)	18.00	9.00	5.50
(12b)	Bart Starr (right side)	18.00	9.00	5.50

1962 American Tract Society

These full-color cards, which carry religious messages on the back, were issued in 1962 by the American Tract Society, an interdenominational, non-sectarian publisher of Christian literature in the United States since 1825. Known as "Tracards", the cards measure 2-3/4" x 3-1/2" and feature color photographs on the fronts. The set includes religious scenes along with photos of various celebrities and sports stars, including baseball players Felipe Alou, Bobby Richardson, Jerry Kindall and Al Worthington. (There are two poses each of Alou and Kindall.) The backs carry rather lengthy, first-person religious testimonials from the players. The cards are numbered on the back in the lower right corner.

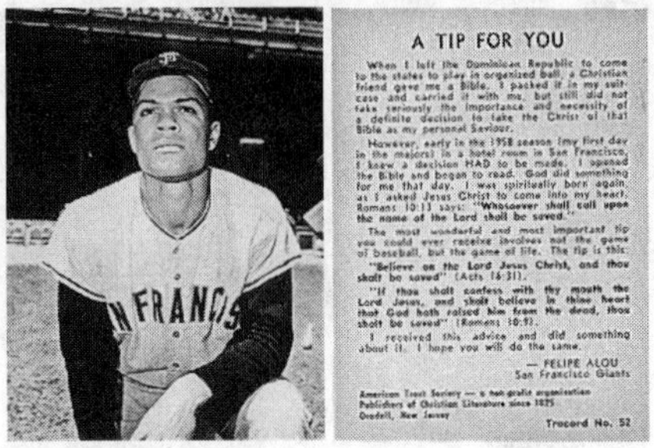
A TIP FOR YOU
— FELIPE ALOU
San Francisco Giants
Tracard No. 52

		NM	EX	VG
	Complete Set (6):	40.00	20.00	12.00
	Common Player:	8.00	4.00	2.50
43	Bobby Richardson	14.00	7.00	4.25
51a	Jerry Kindall (Cleveland)	8.00	4.00	2.50
51b	Jerry Kindall (Minnesota)	8.00	4.00	2.50
52a	Felipe Alou (kneeling on one knee)	12.00	6.00	3.50
52b	Felipe Alou (batting, full length)	12.00	6.00	3.50
66	Al Worthington	8.00	4.00	2.50

1973 John B. Anderson Former Greats

This set of postcard-sized black-and-white cards features the artwork of John B. Anderson, a New York collector. Each card includes a facsimile autograph on front; backs are blank. The unnumbered cards are checklisted here in alphabetical order.

		NM	EX	VG
	Complete Set (12):	30.00	15.00	9.00
	Common Player:	2.00	1.00	.60
(1)	Ty Cobb	3.00	1.50	.90
(2)	Mickey Cochrane	2.00	1.00	.60
(3)	Roberto Clemente	5.00	2.50	1.50
(4)	Lou Gehrig	5.00	2.50	1.50
(5)	Frank Frisch	2.00	1.00	.60
(6)	Gil Hodges	3.00	1.50	.90
(7)	Rogers Hornsby	2.00	1.00	.60
(8)	Connie Mack	2.00	1.00	.60
(9)	Christy Mathewson	2.50	1.25	.70
(10)	Jackie Robinson	5.00	2.50	1.50
(11)	Babe Ruth	5.00	2.50	1.50
(12)	Pie Traynor	2.00	1.00	.60

1977 John B. Anderson Aaron-Mays

This set of postcard size, black-and-white drawings is a collectors issue. Cards are blank-backed.

		NM	EX	VG
	Complete Set (4):	3.00	1.50	.90
	Common Card:	1.00	.50	.30
(1)	Hank Aaron (arm in air)	1.00	.50	.30
(2)	Hank Aaron (portrait)	1.00	.50	.30
(3)	Willie Mays (Giants)	1.00	.50	.30
(4)	Willie Mays (Mets)	1.00	.50	.30

1977 John B. Anderson New York Teams

Joe DiMaggio

Stars and local favorites of the three New York teams of the 1940s and 1950s are featured in this set of collectors cards. The 3-1/2" x 5-1/2" blank-back, black-and-white cards feature artwork by John B. Anderson. The unnumbered cards are checklisted here in alphabetical order.

		NM	EX	VG
	Complete Set (24):	45.00	22.50	13.50
	Common Player:	2.00	1.00	.60
(1)	Yogi Berra	3.00	1.50	.90
(2)	Ralph Branca	2.00	1.00	.60
(3)	Dolf Camilli	2.00	1.00	.60
(4)	Roy Campanella	3.00	1.50	.90
(5)	Jerry Coleman	2.00	1.00	.60
(6)	Frank Crosetti	2.00	1.00	.60
(7)	Bill Dickey	2.00	1.00	.60
(8)	Joe DiMaggio	8.00	4.00	2.50
(9)	Sid Gordon	2.00	1.00	.60
(10)	Babe Herman	2.00	1.00	.60
(11)	Carl Hubbell	2.00	1.00	.60
(12)	Billy Johnson	2.00	1.00	.60
(13)	Ernie Lombardi	2.00	1.00	.60
(14)	Willard Marshall	2.00	1.00	.60
(15)	Willie Mays	5.00	2.50	1.50
(16)	Joe McCarthy	2.00	1.00	.60
(17)	Joe Medwick	2.00	1.00	.60
(18)	Joe Moore	2.00	1.00	.60
(19)	Andy Pafko	2.00	1.00	.60
(20)	Jackie Robinson	5.00	2.50	1.50
(21)	Red Ruffing	2.00	1.00	.60
(22)	Bill Terry	2.00	1.00	.60
(23)	Hoyt Wilhelm	2.00	1.00	.60
(24)	Gene Woodling	2.00	1.00	.60

1971 Anonymous Collectors Issue

9
DON
Lang

In the absence of any indication of when produced or by whom, it is presumed this set of obscure players of the 1940s and 1950s was a collector's issue. The cards are blank-backed, about 2-1/8" x 2-3/4". Fronts have a bright red background with the player photo in blue. The player's last name and card number are in dark blue, his first name in white. For a few of the players, this is their only known baseball card. The set has been reportedly attributed to Carl Aldana circa 1971.

		NM	EX	VG
	Complete Set (16):	90.00	45.00	27.00
	Common Player:	8.00	4.00	2.50
1	Wally Hood	8.00	4.00	2.50
2	Jim Westlake	8.00	4.00	2.50
3	Stan McWilliams	8.00	4.00	2.50
4	Les Fleming	8.00	4.00	2.50
5	John Ritchey	8.00	4.00	2.50
6	Steve Nagy	8.00	4.00	2.50
7	Ken Gables	8.00	4.00	2.50
8	Maurice Fisher	8.00	4.00	2.50
9	Don Lang	8.00	4.00	2.50
10	Harry Malmburg (Malmberg)	8.00	4.00	2.50
11	Jack Conway	8.00	4.00	2.50
12	Don White	8.00	4.00	2.50
13	Dick Lajeskie	8.00	4.00	2.50
14	Walt Judnich	8.00	4.00	2.50
15	Joe Kirrene	8.00	4.00	2.50
16	Ed Sauer	8.00	4.00	2.50

1971 Arco

In 1971 players from four major league teams in the east were featured in a set of facsimile autographed color photos in a gas station giveaway program. Following the promotion, leftover pictures were sold directly to collectors in the pages of the existing hobby media. The photos share an 8" x 10" format, with virtually all of the players being pictured without caps. Red, white and blue stars flank the player name in the bottom border. Black-and-white backs have career summary and stats, personal data, team sponsor and union logos and an ad for frames for the pictures. The unnumbered photos are listed here alphabetically within team.

		NM	EX	VG
Complete Set (49):		150.00	75.00	45.00
Common Player:		3.00	1.50	.90
	Boston Red Sox team set:	45.00	22.00	13.50
(1)	Luis Aparicio	7.50	3.75	2.25
(2)	Ken Brett	3.00	1.50	.90
(3)	Billy Conigliaro	3.00	1.50	.90
(4)	Ray Culp	3.00	1.50	.90
(5)	Doug Griffin	3.00	1.50	.90
(6)	Bob Montgomery	3.00	1.50	.90
(7)	Gary Peters	3.00	1.50	.90
(8)	George Scott	4.00	2.00	1.25
(9)	Sonny Siebert	3.00	1.50	.90
(10)	Reggie Smith	4.50	2.25	1.25
(11)	Ken Tatum	3.00	1.50	.90
(12)	Carl Yastrzemski	10.00	5.00	3.00
	New York Yankees team set:	60.00	30.00	18.00
(1)	Jack Aker	5.00	2.50	1.50
(2)	Stan Bahnsen	5.00	2.50	1.50
(3)	Frank Baker	5.00	2.50	1.50
(4)	Danny Cater	5.00	2.50	1.50
(5)	Horace Clarke	5.00	2.50	1.50
(6)	John Ellis	5.00	2.50	1.50
(7)	Gene Michael	5.00	2.50	1.50
(8)	Thurman Munson	10.00	5.00	3.00
(9)	Bobby Murcer	6.00	3.00	1.75
(10)	Fritz Peterson	5.00	2.50	1.50
(11)	Mel Stottlemyre	6.00	3.00	1.75
(12)	Roy White	6.00	3.00	1.75
	Philadelphia Phillies team set:	45.00	22.00	13.50
(1)	Larry Bowa	4.00	2.00	1.25
(2)	Jim Bunning	9.00	4.50	2.75
(3)	Roger Freed	3.00	1.50	.90
(4)	Terry Harmon	3.00	1.50	.90
(5)	Larry Hisle	3.00	1.50	.90
(6)	Joe Hoerner	3.00	1.50	.90
(7)	Deron Johnson	3.00	1.50	.90
(8)	Tim McCarver	5.00	2.50	1.50
(9)	Don Money	3.00	1.50	.90
(10)	Dick Selma	3.00	1.50	.90
(11)	Chris Short	3.00	1.50	.90
(12)	Tony Taylor	3.00	1.50	.90
(13)	Rick Wise	3.00	1.50	.90
	Pittsburgh Pirates team set:	55.00	27.00	16.50
(1)	Gene Alley	3.00	1.50	.90
(2)	Steve Blass	3.00	1.50	.90
(3)	Roberto Clemente	35.00	17.50	10.50
(4)	Dave Giusti	3.00	1.50	.90
(5)	Richie Hebner	3.00	1.50	.90
(6)	Bill Mazeroski	9.00	4.50	2.75
(7)	Bob Moose	3.00	1.50	.90
(8)	Al Oliver	4.50	2.25	1.25
(9)	Bob Robertson	3.00	1.50	.90
(10)	Manny Sanguillen	3.00	1.50	.90
(11)	Willie Stargell	9.00	4.50	2.75
(12)	Luke Walker	3.00	1.50	.90

1980-81 Argus Publishing Reggie Jackson

Some of the cars from Reggie Jackson's collection of hot rods and vintage vehicles were featured on a series of promotional cards handed out at automotive conventions. Issued by the publisher of Hot Rodding and Super Chevy magazines, the standard-size color cars have photos of Jackson with his cars on front, along with magazine and other logos. Backs have information on Jackson's cars.

		MT	NM	EX
Complete Set (3):		30.00	22.00	12.00
(1)	1980 SEMA Show (Reggie Jackson) (1932 Ford highboy)	15.00	11.00	6.00
(2)	1981 SEMA (Reggie Jackson) (1932 Ford 5-window)	10.00	7.50	4.00
(3)	1981 Super Chevy Sunday (Reggie Jackson) (1955 Chev)	9.00	6.75	3.50

1955 Armour Coins

In 1955, Armour inserted a plastic "coin" in its packages of hot dogs. A raised profile of a ballplayer is on the front of each coin along with the player's name, position, birthplace and date, batting and throwing preference, and 1954 hitting or pitching record. The coins, which measure 1-1/2" in diameter and are unnumbered, came in a variety of colors, including the more common ones in aqua, dark blue, light green, orange, red and yellow. Scarcer colors are black, pale blue, lime green, very dark green, gold, pale orange, pink, silver, and tan. Scarce colors are double the value of the coins listed in the checklist that follows. Twenty-four different players are included in the set. Variations exist for Harvey Kuenn (letters in his name are condensed or spaced) and Mickey Mantle (name is spelled Mantle or incorrectly as Mantel). The complete set price includes the two variations.

		NM	EX	VG
Complete Set (26):		800.00	400.00	240.00
Common Player:		14.00	7.00	4.25
(1)	John "Johnny" Antonelli	14.00	7.00	4.25
(2)	Larry "Yogi" Berra	70.00	35.00	21.00
(3)	Delmar "Del" Crandall	14.00	7.00	4.25
(4)	Lawrence "Larry" Doby	35.00	17.50	10.50
(5)	James "Jim" Finigan	14.00	7.00	4.25
(6)	Edward "Whitey" Ford	70.00	35.00	21.00
(7)	James "Junior" Gilliam	22.00	11.00	6.50
(8)	Harvey "Kitten" Haddix	14.00	7.00	4.25
(9)	Ranson "Randy" Jackson (name actually Ransom)	14.00	7.00	4.25
(10)	Jack "Jackie" Jensen	22.00	11.00	6.50
(11)	Theodore "Ted" Kluszewski	24.00	12.00	7.25
(12a)	Harvey E. Kuenn (spaced letters in name)	30.00	15.00	9.00
(12b)	Harvey E. Kuenn (condensed letters in name)	48.00	24.00	14.50
(13a)	Charles "Mickey" Mantel (incorrect spelling)	175.00	87.00	52.00
(13b)	Charles "Mickey" Mantle (correct spelling)	360.00	180.00	108.00
(14)	Donald "Don" Mueller	14.00	7.00	4.25
(15)	Harold "Pee Wee" Reese	48.00	24.00	14.50
(16)	Allie P. Reynolds	20.00	10.00	6.00
(17)	Albert "Flip" Rosen	17.50	8.75	5.25
(18)	Curtis "Curt" Simmons	14.00	7.00	4.25
(19)	Edwin "Duke" Snider	70.00	35.00	21.00
(20)	Warren Spahn	48.00	24.00	14.50
(21)	Frank Thomas	18.00	9.00	5.50
(22)	Virgil "Fire" Trucks	14.00	7.00	4.25
(23)	Robert "Bob" Turley	22.00	11.00	6.50
(24)	James "Mickey" Vernon	14.00	7.00	4.25

1958 Armour S.F. Giants Tabs

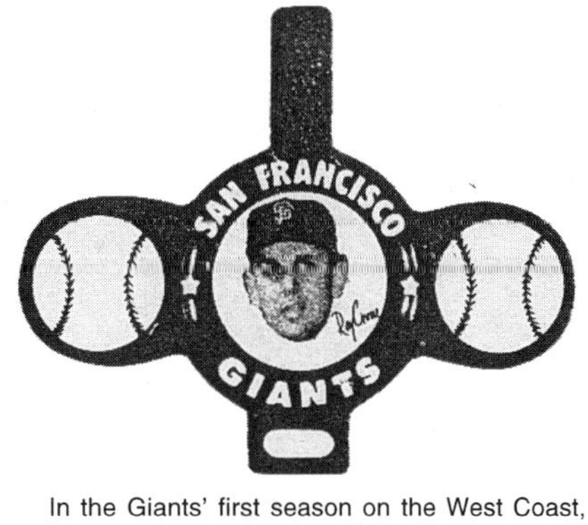

In the Giants' first season on the West Coast, packages of Armour hot dogs in the Bay Area could be found with a small (about 2" x 1-5/8") lithographed tin player "tab" enclosed. In team colors of black, white and orange the tabs have black-and-white portraits at center, around which is a round, square or diamond shaped device bearing the team name and other graphic touches. At the sides are wings with baseballs or caps printed thereon. A 1/2" tab is at top with a slotted panel at bottom. The tab of one piece could be inserted into the slot of another to create a chain of these pieces, or the top tab could be folded over a shirt pocket to wear the item as a badge. The unnumbered pieces are checklisted here alphabetically. NM values quoted are for unbent pieces only.

		NM	EX	VG
Complete Set (10):		550.00	275.00	165.00
Common Player:		45.00	22.50	13.50
(1)	Johnny Antonelli	45.00	22.50	13.50
(2)	Curt Barclay	45.00	22.50	13.50
(3)	Ray Crone	45.00	22.50	13.50
(4)	Whitey Lockman	45.00	22.50	13.50
(5)	Willie Mays	300.00	150.00	90.00
(6)	Don Mueller	45.00	22.50	13.50
(7)	Danny O'Connell	45.00	22.50	13.50
(8)	Hank Sauer	45.00	22.50	13.50
(9)	Daryl Spencer	45.00	22.50	13.50
(10)	Bobby Thomson	50.00	25.00	15.00

1959 Armour Bacon K.C. Athletics

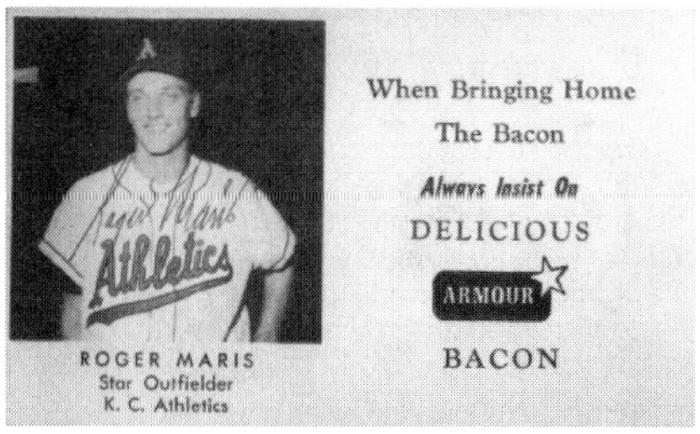

Not so much a baseball card set as a handful of related single-card issues used at player promotional appearances, a total of four cards are currently known of this issue. Measuring either 5-1/2" x 3-1/4" or 5-1/2" x 4", the horizontal-format cards are printed in black-and-white and are blank-backed. A posed player photo appears at left, with an ad for Armour bacon at right. Cards were given out at player appearances at local supermarkets. To date, all known specimens have been found autographed.

		NM	EX	VG
Complete Set (4):		900.00	450.00	275.00
Common Player:		75.00	37.00	22.00
(1)	Harry Chiti	75.00	37.00	22.00
(2)	Whitey Herzog	90.00	45.00	27.00
(3)	Roger Maris (photo to waist)	450.00	225.00	135.00
(4)	Roger Maris (hands on knees)	600.00	300.00	180.00

1959 Armour Coins

After a three-year layoff, Armour again inserted plastic baseball "coins" into its hot dog packages. The coins retained their 1-1/2" size but did not include as much detailed information as in 1955. Missing from the coins' backs is information such as birthplace and date, team, and batting and throwing preference. The fronts contain the player's name and, unlike 1955, only the team nickname is given. The set consists of 20 coins which come in a myriad of colors. Common colors are navy blue, royal blue, dark green, orange, red, and pale yellow. Scarce colors are pale blue, cream, grey-green, pale green, dark or light pink, pale red, tan, and translucent coins of any color with or without multi-colored flecks in the plastic mix. Scarce colors are double the value listed for coins in the checklist. In 1959, Armour had a write-in offer of 10 coins for $1. The same 10 players were part of the write-in offer, accounting for why half of the coins in the set are much more plentiful than the other.

		NM	EX	VG
Complete Set (20):		400.00	200.00	125.00
Common Player:		15.00	7.50	4.50
(1)	Hank Aaron	70.00	35.00	21.00
(2)	John Antonelli	15.00	7.50	4.50
(3)	Richie Ashburn	35.00	17.50	10.50
(4)	Ernie Banks	50.00	25.00	15.00
(5)	Don Blasingame	15.00	7.50	4.50
(6)	Bob Cerv	15.00	7.50	4.50
(7)	Del Crandall	15.00	7.50	4.50
(8)	Whitey Ford	50.00	25.00	15.00
(9)	Nellie Fox	35.00	17.50	10.50
(10)	Jackie Jensen	24.00	12.00	7.25
(11)	Harvey Kuenn	17.50	8.75	5.25
(12)	Frank Malzone	15.00	7.50	4.50
(13)	Johnny Podres	17.50	8.75	5.25
(14)	Frank Robinson	40.00	20.00	12.00
(15)	Roy Sievers	15.00	7.50	4.50
(16)	Bob Skinner	15.00	7.50	4.50
(17)	Frank Thomas	15.00	7.50	4.50
(18)	Gus Triandos	15.00	7.50	4.50
(19)	Bob Turley	24.00	12.00	7.25
(20)	Mickey Vernon	15.00	7.50	4.50

1960 Armour Coins

The 1960 Armour coin issue is identical in number and style to the 1959 set. The unnumbered coins, which measure 1-1/2" in diameter, once again came in a variety of colors. Common colors for 1960 are dark blue, light blue, dark green, light green, red-orange, dark red, and light yellow. Scarce colors are aqua, grey-blue, cream, tan, and dark yellow. Scarce colors are double the value of the coins in the checklist. The Bud Daley coin is very scarce, although it is not exactly known why. Theories for the scarcity center on broken printing molds, contract disputes, and that the coin was only inserted in a test product that quickly proved to be unsuccessful. As in 1959, a mail-in offer for 10 free coins was made available by Armour.

		NM	EX	VG
Complete Set (23):		950.00	475.00	275.00
Common Player:		10.00	5.00	3.00
(1a)	Hank Aaron (Braves)	40.00	20.00	12.00
(1b)	Hank Aaron (Milwaukee Braves)	65.00	32.00	19.50
(2)	Bob Allison	10.00	5.00	3.00
(3)	Ernie Banks	20.00	10.00	6.00
(4)	Ken Boyer	12.00	6.00	3.50
(5)	Rocky Colavito	13.00	6.50	4.00
(6)	Gene Conley	10.00	5.00	3.00
(7)	Del Crandall	10.00	5.00	3.00
(8)	Bud Daley	500.00	250.00	150.00
(9a)	Don Drysdale (L.A condensed)	20.00	10.00	6.00
(9b)	Don Drysdale (space between L. and A.)	24.00	12.00	7.25
(10)	Whitey Ford	20.00	10.00	6.00
(11)	Nellie Fox	20.00	10.00	6.00
(12)	Al Kaline	24.00	12.00	7.25
(13a)	Frank Malzone (Red Sox)	10.00	5.00	3.00
(13b)	Frank Malzone (Boston Red Sox)	21.00	10.50	6.25
(14)	Mickey Mantle	100.00	50.00	30.00
(15)	Ed Mathews	24.00	12.00	7.25
(16)	Willie Mays	48.00	24.00	14.50
(17)	Vada Pinson	10.00	5.00	3.00
(18)	Dick Stuart	10.00	5.00	3.00
(19)	Gus Triandos	10.00	5.00	3.00
(20)	Early Wynn	17.50	8.75	5.25

1953-63 Artvue Hall of Fame Plaque Postcards

(See 1963-98 Hall of Fame Yellow Plaque Postcards for checklist, value data.)

1967 Ashland Oil Grand Slam Baseball

These baseball player folders were issued in conjunction with a sweepstakes conducted at Ashland gas stations. The cards were originally issued in the form of a sealed tri-fold. When opened to 7-1/2" x 2", a black-and-white player photo is pictured at center. Back of the panel offers contest rules. The unnumbered panels are listed here in alphabetical order.

		NM	EX	VG
Complete Set (12):		150.00	75.00	45.00
Common Player:		8.00	4.00	2.50
(1)	Jim Bunning	12.00	6.00	3.50
(2)	Elston Howard	10.00	5.00	3.00
(3)	Al Kaline	20.00	10.00	6.00
(4)	Harmon Killebrew	12.00	6.00	3.50
(5)	Ed Kranepool	8.00	4.00	2.50
(6)	Jim Maloney (SP)	35.00	17.50	10.50
(7)	Bill Mazeroski	12.00	6.00	3.50
(8)	Frank Robinson	15.00	7.50	4.50
(9)	Ron Santo	12.00	6.00	3.50
(10)	Joe Torre	10.00	5.00	3.00
(11)	Leon Wagner	8.00	4.00	2.50
(12)	Pete Ward	8.00	4.00	2.50

1978 Atlanta Nobis Center

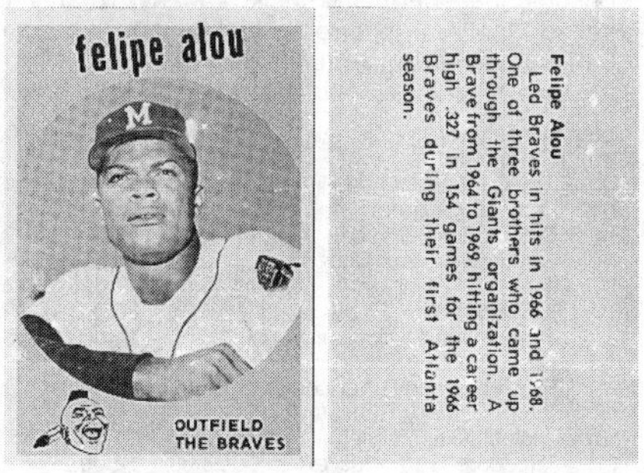

In conjunction with a May, 1978, card show to benefit the training/rehabilitation center supported by Hall of Fame linebacker Tommy Nobis, this collector's set was issued. Most of the players on the 2-1/2" x 3-1/2" cards are former stars of the Boston, Milwaukee or Atlanta Braves, though players from a few other teams and footballer Nobis are also included; several of the players appeared at the show as autograph guests. The cards are in the style of 1959 Topps, with black-and-white player photos in a circle at center and a light green background. The career summary on back is in black-and-white. The unnumbered cards are checklisted here in alphabetical order.

		NM	EX	VG
Complete Set (24):		20.00	10.00	6.00
Common Player:		1.00	.50	.30
(1)	Hank Aaron	4.00	2.00	1.25
(2)	Joe Adcock	1.00	.50	.30
(3)	Felipe Alou	1.25	.60	.40
(4)	Frank Bolling	1.00	.50	.30
(5)	Orlando Cepeda	1.25	.60	.40
(6)	Ty Cline	1.00	.50	.30
(7)	Tony Cloninger	1.00	.50	.30
(8)	Del Crandall	1.00	.50	.30
(9)	Fred Haney	1.00	.50	.30
(10)	Pat Jarvis	1.00	.50	.30
(11)	Ernie Johnson	1.00	.50	.30
(12)	Ken Johnson	1.00	.50	.30
(13)	Denny Lemaster	1.00	.50	.30
(14)	Eddie Mathews	1.25	.60	.40
(15)	Lee Maye	1.00	.50	.30
(16)	Denis Menke	1.00	.50	.30
(17)	Felix Millan	1.00	.50	.30
(18)	Johnny Mize	1.00	.50	.30
(19)	Tommy Nobis	1.00	.50	.30
(20)	Gene Oliver	1.00	.50	.30
(21)	Johnny Sain	1.00	.50	.30
(22)	Warren Spahn	1.25	.60	.40
(23)	Joe Torre	1.25	.60	.40
(24)	Bob Turley	1.00	.50	.30

1968 Atlantic Oil Play Ball Game Cards

Because some of the cards were redeemable either alone or in combination for cash awards, and thus were issued in lesser quantities, completion of this game issue was difficult from Day 1. Fifty different players are known in the issue, along with a number of variations. The majority of the cards can be found with card backs either explaining the game rules or picturing a pitcher throwing to a batter. The cards were issued in two-card panels, designed to be separated into a pair of 2-1/2" x 3-1/2" cards. For lack of an MLB license, the color player photos at center have the uniform logos removed. Printed at top is the face value of the particular card, while the player's name, team and league are printed in the bottom border. A large player number is printed in a white circle at bottom-right. American Leaguers' cards are bordered in red, while the National League cards have blue borders.

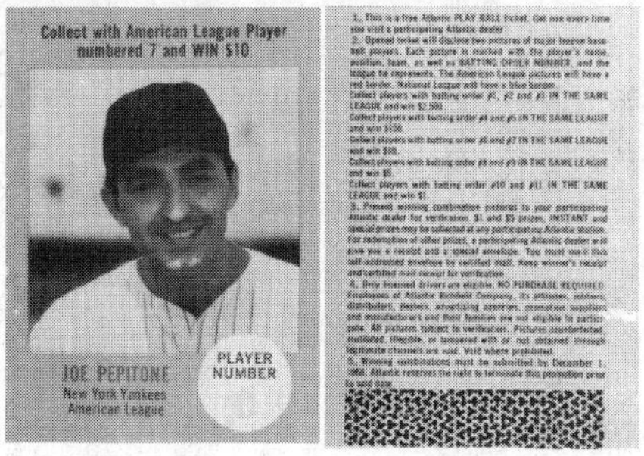

		NM	EX	VG
Complete Set (Non-winners) (40):		425.00	210.00	125.00
Common Player:		7.25	3.75	2.25
Instant Winner Card:		40.00	20.00	12.00
AMERICAN LEAGUE				
1a	Tony Oliva	7.25	3.75	2.25
1b	Brooks Robinson	22.00	11.00	6.50
1c	Pete Ward	7.25	3.75	2.25
2a	Max Alvis	7.25	3.75	2.25
2b	Campy Campaneris	7.25	3.75	2.25
2c	Jim Fregosi	7.25	3.75	2.25
2d	Al Kaline	30.00	15.00	9.00
2e	Tom Tresh	7.25	3.75	2.25
3	Bill Freehan ($2,500 winner)	400.00	200.00	120.00
4	Tommy Davis ($100 winner)	125.00	62.00	37.00
5a	Norm Cash	11.00	5.50	3.25
5b	Frank Robinson	22.00	11.00	6.50
5c	Carl Yastrzemski	30.00	15.00	9.00
6a	Joe Pepitone	9.50	4.75	2.75
6b	Boog Powell	15.00	7.50	4.50
6c	George Scott	7.25	3.75	2.25
6d	Fred Valentine	7.25	3.75	2.25
7	Tom McCraw ($10 winner)	100.00	50.00	30.00
8	Andy Etchebarren ($5 winner)	75.00	37.00	22.00
9a	Dean Chance	9.00	4.50	2.75
9b	Joel Horlen	7.25	3.75	2.25
9c	Jim Lonborg	9.00	4.50	2.75
9d	Sam McDowell	9.00	4.50	2.75
10	Earl Wilson ($1 winner)	50.00	25.00	15.00
11	Jose Santiago	7.25	3.75	2.25
NATIONAL LEAGUE				
1a	Bob Aspromonte	7.25	3.75	2.25
1b	Lou Brock	16.00	8.00	4.75
1c	Johnny Callison	7.25	3.75	2.25
1d	Pete Rose	30.00	15.00	9.00
1e	Maury Wills	9.50	4.75	2.75
2	Tommie Agee ($2,500 winner)	400.00	200.00	120.00
3a	Felipe Alou	10.00	5.00	3.00
3b	Jim Hart	7.25	3.75	2.25
3c	Vada Pinson	9.50	4.75	2.75
4a	Hank Aaron	35.00	17.50	10.50
4b	Orlando Cepeda	12.00	6.00	3.50
4c	Willie McCovey	18.00	9.00	5.50
4d	Ron Santo	12.00	6.00	3.50
5	Ernie Banks ($100 winner)	600.00	300.00	180.00
6	Ron Fairly ($10 winner)	100.00	50.00	30.00
7a	Roberto Clemente	75.00	37.00	22.00
7b	Roger Maris	24.00	12.00	7.25
7c a	Ron Swoboda (Collect w/ N.L. #6, win $10)	7.25	3.75	2.25
7c b	Ron Swoboda (Collect w/ N.L. #8, win $5)	60.00	30.00	18.00
8	Billy Williams ($5 winner)	125.00	62.00	37.00
9a	Jim Bunning	9.00	4.50	2.75
9b	Bob Gibson	22.00	11.00	6.50
9c	Jim Maloney	7.25	3.75	2.25
9d	Mike McCormick	7.25	3.75	2.25
10	Milt Pappas	7.25	3.75	2.25
11	Claude Osteen ($1 winner)	50.00	25.00	15.00

1969 Atlantic-Richfield Boston Red Sox

One of many larger-format (8" x 10") baseball premiums sponsored as gas station giveaways in the late 1960s and early 1970s was this set of Boston Red Sox player pictures by celebrity artist John Wheeldon sponsored by the Atlantic-Richfield Oil Co. Done in pastel colors, the pictures feature large portraits and smaller action pictures of the player against a bright background. A facsimile autograph is pencilled in beneath the pictures, and the player's name is printed in the white bottom border. Backs are printed in black-and-white and include biographical and career data, full major and minor league stats, a self-portrait and biography of the artist and the logos of the team, players' association and sponsor. The unnumbered pictures are checklisted here alphabetically.

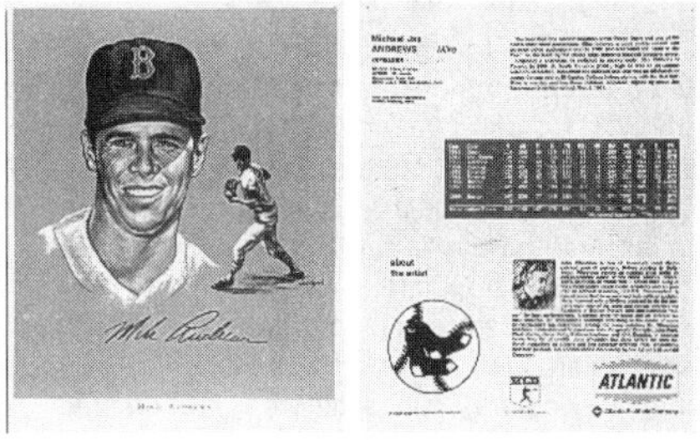

		NM	EX	VG
Complete Set (12):		75.00	37.00	22.00
Common Player:		6.00	3.00	1.75
(1)	Mike Andrews	6.00	3.00	1.75
(2)	Tony Conigliaro	9.00	4.50	2.75
(3)	Ray Culp	6.00	3.00	1.75
(4)	Russ Gibson	6.00	3.00	1.75
(5)	Dalton Jones	6.00	3.00	1.75
(6)	Jim Lonborg	7.50	3.75	2.25
(7)	Sparky Lyle	7.50	3.75	2.25
(8)	Syd O'Brien	6.00	3.00	1.75
(9)	George Scott	7.50	3.75	2.25
(10)	Reggie Smith	7.50	3.75	2.25
(11)	Rico Petrocelli	7.50	3.75	2.25
(12)	Carl Yastrzemski	24.00	12.00	7.25

1962 Auravision Records

Similar in design and format to the 16-record set which was issued in 1964, this test issue can be differentiated by the stats on the back. On the 1962 record, Mantle is shown in a right-handed batting pose, as compared to a follow-through on the 1964 record. Where Gentile and Colavito are shown in the uniform of K.C. A's on the 1964 records, they are shown as a Tiger (Colavito) and Oriole (Gentile) on the earlier version. The set is checklisted here alphabetically.

		NM	EX	VG
Complete Set (8):		650.00	350.00	200.00
Common Player:		45.00	22.00	13.50
(1)	Ernie Banks	75.00	37.00	22.00
(2)	Rocky Colavito	95.00	47.00	28.00
(3)	Whitey Ford	75.00	37.00	22.00
(4)	Jim Gentile	45.00	22.00	13.50
(5)	Mickey Mantle	145.00	72.00	43.00
(6)	Roger Maris	80.00	40.00	24.00
(7)	Willie Mays	100.00	50.00	30.00
(8)	Warren Spahn	75.00	37.00	22.00

1964 Auravision Records

Never a candidate for the Billboard "Hot 100," this series of baseball picture records has been popular with collectors due to the high-quality photos on front and back. On the grooved front side of the 6-3/4" x 6-3/4" plastic-laminated cardboard record is a color player photo with facsimile autograph, Sports Record trophy logo and 33-1/3 RPM notation. A color border surrounds the photo and is carried over to the unrecorded back side. There is another photo on back, along with a career summary and complete major and minor league stats and instructions for playing the record. In the bottom border is a copyright notice by Sports Champions Inc., and a notice that the Auravision Record is a product of Columbia Records. A hole at center of the record could be punched out for playing and the records featured a five-minute interview with the player by sportscaster Marty Glickman. Large quantities of the records made their way into the hobby as remainders. For early-1960s baseball items they remain reasonably priced today. The unnumbered records are checklisted here alphabetically. The Mays record is unaccountably much scarcer than the others.

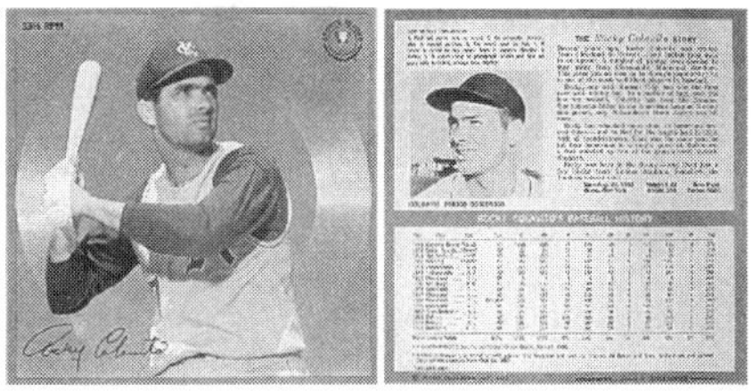

		NM	EX	VG
Complete Set (16):		300.00	150.00	90.00
Common Player:		5.50	2.75	1.75
(1)	Bob Allison	6.00	3.00	1.75
(2)	Ernie Banks	15.00	7.50	4.50
(3)	Ken Boyer	9.50	4.75	2.75
(4)	Rocky Colavito	11.00	5.50	3.25
(5)	Don Drysdale	15.00	7.50	4.50
(6)	Whitey Ford	15.00	7.50	4.50
(7)	Jim Gentile	6.00	3.00	1.75
(8)	Al Kaline	15.00	7.50	4.50
(9)	Sandy Koufax	25.00	12.50	7.50
(10)	Mickey Mantle	45.00	22.00	13.50
(11)	Roger Maris	22.00	11.00	6.50
(12)	Willie Mays	125.00	62.00	37.00
(13)	Bill Mazeroski	11.00	5.50	3.25
(14)	Frank Robinson	15.00	7.50	4.50
(15)	Warren Spahn	15.00	7.50	4.50
(16)	Pete Ward	6.00	3.00	1.75

B

1949 Baas Cheri-Cola

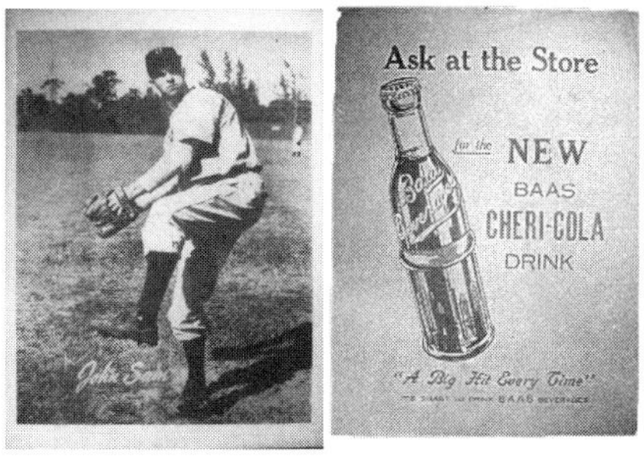

Only five of these premium issues have ever been cataloged so it's unknown how many comprise a set. The 7-5/8" x 9-1/2" pictures feature black-and-white player photos on front, with the player's name printed in white script. On back, printed in red, is an ad for Baas Cheri-Cola Drink. The unnumbered pictures are checklisted in alphabetical order.

		NM	EX	VG
Common Player:		110.00	55.00	33.00
(1)	Bobby Doerr	150.00	75.00	45.00
(2)	Bob Feller	225.00	110.00	67.00
(3)	Ken Keltner	110.00	55.00	33.00
(4)	John Sain	110.00	55.00	33.00
(5)	Ted Williams	450.00	225.00	135.00

1941 Ballantine Coasters

National League pitcher-catcher pairs are featured on this set of drink coasters issued by Ballentine Ale & Beer. The 4-1/2" diameter composition coasters are printed in black with orange, blue or red highlights. Fronts have line drawings of the batterymates and a few words about the previous or coming season. Backs have a Ballentine's ad. It is unknown whether there are more than these three coasters in the series.

		NM	EX	VG
Common Coaster:		30.00	15.00	9.00
(1)	Bob Klinger, Virgil Davis (Phillies)	30.00	15.00	9.00
(2)	Lon Warneke, Gus Mancuso (Cardinals)	30.00	15.00	9.00
(3)	Whit Wyatt, Mickey Owen (Dodgers)	30.00	15.00	9.00

1914 Baltimore News Terrapins

Players from both of Baltimore's professional baseball teams are included in this set of schedule cards from the local newspaper. That season fans could support the Orioles of the International League or the Terrapins of the Federal League. The newspaper's cards are 2-5/8" x 3-5/8", monochrome printed in either red or blue with a wide border. Players are pictured in full-length posed action photos with the backgrounds erased in favor of a few artificial shadows. The player name, position and league are shown on front. Backs have a schedule "AT HOME" and "ABROAD" of the appropriate team with an ad for the paper at top and a curious line at bottom which reads, "This Card is Given to", with space for a signature. The unnumbered cards are checklisted here in alphabetical order, though it is presumed the checklist is incomplete. Only the Federal Leaguers' cards are listed here; the Orioles will be found in the minor league section of this catalog.

		NM	EX	VG
Common Player:		1800.	900.00	550.00
(1)	Neal Ball	2100.	1050.	625.00
(2)	Mike Doolan	2250.	1125.	675.00
(3)	Fred Jacklitch (Jacklitsch)	1800.	900.00	550.00
(4)	Otto Knabe	1800.	900.00	550.00
(5)	Benny Meyers (Meyer)	1800.	900.00	550.00
(6)	Jack Quinn	1800.	900.00	550.00
(7)	Hack Simmons	1800.	900.00	550.00
(8)	Frank Smith	1800.	900.00	550.00
(9)	George Suggs	1800.	900.00	550.00
(10)	Harry (Swats) Swacina	1800.	900.00	550.00
(11)	Ducky Yount	1800.	900.00	550.00
(12)	Guy Zinn	1800.	900.00	550.00

1958 Baltimore Orioles team issue

These blank-backed, black-and-white cards are approximately postcard size at 3-1/4" x 5-1/2" and feature posed portraits of the players printed on semi-gloss cardboard. The unnumbered cards are checklisted here alphabetically.

		NM	EX	VG
Complete Set (16):		165.00	82.00	49.00
Common Player:		12.00	6.00	3.50
(1)	Bob Boyd	12.00	6.00	3.50
(2)	Harry Brecheen	12.00	6.00	3.50
(3)	Hal Brown	12.00	6.00	3.50
(4)	Jim Busby	12.00	6.00	3.50

(5)	Foster Castleman	12.00	6.00	3.50
(6)	Billy Gardner	12.00	6.00	3.50
(7)	Connie Johnson	12.00	6.00	3.50
(8)	Ken Lehman	12.00	6.00	3.50
(9)	Willie Miranda	12.00	6.00	3.50
(10)	Bob Nieman	12.00	6.00	3.50
(11)	Paul Richards	12.00	6.00	3.50
(12)	Brooks Robinson	36.00	18.00	11.00
(13)	Gus Triandos	12.00	6.00	3.50
(14)	Dick Williams	12.00	6.00	3.50
(15)	Gene Woodling	18.00	9.00	5.50
(16)	George Zuverink	12.00	6.00	3.50

1970 Baltimore Orioles Traffic Safety

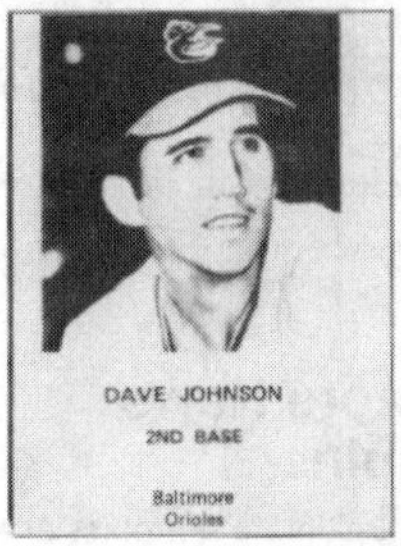

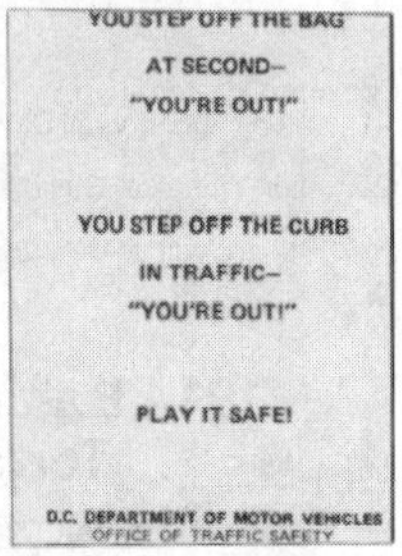

Similar in concept and design to the much more common Washington Senators safety issue of the same year, the Orioles cards are printed on yellow paper in 2-1/2" x 3-7/8" format. Fronts have player photo, name, team and position; backs have a safety message and notice of sponsorship by the D.C. Department of Motor Vehicles Office of Traffic Safety.

		NM	EX	VG
Complete Set (10):		125.00	62.50	37.50
Common Player:		10.00	5.00	3.00
(1)	Mark Bellanger (Belanger)	10.00	5.00	3.00
(2)	Paul Blair	10.00	5.00	3.00
(3)	Don Buford	10.00	5.00	3.00
(4)	Mike Cuellar (back in Spanish)	15.00	7.50	4.50
(5)	Dave Johnson	15.00	7.50	4.50
(6)	Dave McNally	10.00	5.00	3.00
(7)	Boog Powell	20.00	10.00	6.00
(8)	Merv Rettenmund	10.00	5.00	3.00
(9)	Brooks Robinson	35.00	17.50	10.50
(10)	Earl Weaver	15.00	7.50	4.50

1973-74 Baltimore Orioles team issue

Though approximately postcard-size, these color photocards are blank-backed. The 3-1/2" x 5-1/4" cards have player portait photos surrounded by a white border with the player's name at bottom. The presence of an orange and black knit collar on the jerseys differentiates this from earlier issues. The unnumbered cards are listed here alphabetically.

		NM	EX	VG
Complete Set (30):		75.00	37.00	22.00
Common Player:		3.00	1.50	.90
(1)	Doyle Alexander	3.00	1.50	.90
(2)	Frank Baker	3.00	1.50	.90
(3)	George Bamberger	3.00	1.50	.90
(4)	Don Baylor	3.50	1.75	1.00
(5)	Mark Belanger	3.00	1.50	.90
(6)	Paul Blair	3.00	1.50	.90
(7)	Larry Brown	3.00	1.50	.90
(8)	Al Bumbry	3.00	1.50	.90
(9)	Enos Cabell	3.00	1.50	.90
(10)	Richie Coggins	3.00	1.50	.90
(11)	Terry Crowley	3.00	1.50	.90
(12)	Mike Cuellar	3.00	1.50	.90
(13)	Tommy Davis	3.00	1.50	.90
(14)	Andy Etchebarren	3.00	1.50	.90
(15)	Jim Frey	3.00	1.50	.90
(16)	Bobby Grich	3.00	1.50	.90
(17)	Elrod Hendricks	3.00	1.50	.90
(18)	Bill Hunter	3.00	1.50	.90
(19)	Grant Jackson	3.00	1.50	.90
(20)	Dave McNally	3.00	1.50	.90
(21)	Jim Palmer	7.50	3.75	2.25
(22)	Orlando Pena	3.00	1.50	.90
(23)	John Powell	5.00	2.50	1.50
(24)	Merv Rettenmund	3.00	1.50	.90
(25)	Bob Reynolds	3.00	1.50	.90
(26)	Brooks Robinson	7.50	3.75	2.25
(27)	George Staller	3.00	1.50	.90
(28)	Eddie Watt	3.00	1.50	.90
(29)	Earl Weaver	5.00	2.50	1.50
(30)	Earl Williams	3.00	1.50	.90

1976 Baltimore Orioles team issue

Though an abbreviated issue of only 11 players in 1976, the O's team-issued photocards include three Hall of Famers and Reggie Jackson's only appearance on an Orioles' card. In standard post-card size, about 3-1/2" x 5-1/4", the cards are blank-backed. Fronts have a white border surrounding a color player portrait photo. The name is in black letters at bottom. All players in the 1976 issue are pictured in orange jerseys with script "Orioles" and black-and-white collar stripes. Caps have orange fronts with black body and bill. The unnumbered cards are listed here in alphabetical order.

		NM	EX	VG
Complete Set (11):		50.00	25.00	15.00
Common Player:		3.00	1.50	.90
(1)	Terry Crowley	3.00	1.50	.90
(2)	Mike Flanagan	4.50	2.25	1.25
(3)	Wayne Garland	3.00	1.50	.90
(4)	Tommy Harper	3.00	1.50	.90
(5)	Fred Holdsworth	3.00	1.50	.90
(6)	Bill Hunter	3.00	1.50	.90
(7)	Reggie Jackson	24.00	12.00	7.25
(8)	Dyar Miller	3.00	1.50	.90
(9)	Dave Pagan	3.00	1.50	.90
(10)	Jim Palmer	12.00	6.00	3.50
(11)	Brooks Robinson	12.00	6.00	3.50

1977 Baltimore Orioles team issue

The team-issued photocards for 1977 are very similar in format to the 1976 versions. Cards are again blank-backed and about postcard size (3-1/2" x 5-1/4"). Fronts have a white border around a posed color photo. The name is in black at bottom. Players who also appear on the cards of 1976 and 1978 can be differentiated in the 1977 issue by their uniforms. The 1977 cards show players in orange jerseys with script "Orioles" and black-and-white collar stripes. Caps are white on black with orange bills. The unnumbered cards are checklisted here in alphabetical order.

		NM	EX	VG
Complete Set (21):		75.00	37.50	22.00
Common Player:		3.00	1.50	.90
(1)	Mark Belanger	4.50	2.25	1.25
(2)	Al Bumbry	3.00	1.50	.90
(3)	Rich Dauer	3.00	1.50	.90
(4)	Doug DeCinces	3.00	1.50	.90
(5)	Rick Dempsey	3.00	1.50	.90
(6)	Kiko Garcia	3.00	1.50	.90
(7)	Ross Grimsley	3.00	1.50	.90
(8)	Larry Harlow	3.00	1.50	.90
(9)	Fred Holdsworth	3.00	1.50	.90
(10)	Bill Hunter	3.00	1.50	.90
(11)	Patrick Kelly	3.00	1.50	.90
(12)	Dennis Martinez	6.00	3.00	1.75
(13)	Tippy Martinez	3.00	1.50	.90
(14)	Scott McGregor	3.00	1.50	.90
(15)	Eddie Murray	15.00	7.50	4.50
(16a)	Brooks Robinson (dark background)	12.00	6.00	3.50
(16b)	Brooks Robinson (light background)	12.00	6.00	3.50
(17)	Tom Shopay	3.00	1.50	.90
(18)	Ken Singleton	4.50	2.25	1.25
(19)	Dave Skaggs	3.00	1.50	.90
(20)	Billy Smith	3.00	1.50	.90
(21)	Earl Weaver	6.00	3.00	1.75

1978 Baltimore Orioles team issue

Similar in format to previous years, the 1978 team-issued photocards retain the blank-back, 3-1/2" x 5-1/4" format. Player photos, mostly portraits on a blue background, are surrounded with a white border which carries the player name at bottom. The uniform of the day is a white jersey with black and orange color stripes, and white-on-black caps with orange bill. The corrected Kerrigan and Stephenson cards were late issues and are somewhat smaller than the others, with a different typography. The unnumbered cards are checklisted here in alphabetical order.

		NM	EX	VG
Complete Set (33):		100.00	50.00	30.00
Common Player:		3.00	1.50	.90
(1)	Mark Belanger	4.50	2.25	1.25
(2)	Nelson Briles	3.00	1.50	.90
(3)	Al Bumbry	3.00	1.50	.90
(4)	Terry Crowley	3.00	1.50	.90
(5)	Rich Dauer	3.00	1.50	.90
(6)	Doug DeCinces	3.00	1.50	.90
(7)	Rick Dempsey	3.00	1.50	.90
(8)	Mike Flanagan	4.50	2.25	1.25
(9)	Jim Frey	3.00	1.50	.90
(10)	Kiko Garcia	3.00	1.50	.90
(11)	Larry Harlow	3.00	1.50	.90
(12)	Ellie Hendricks	3.00	1.50	.90
(13)	Pat Kelly	3.00	1.50	.90
(14a)	Joe Kerrigan (photo actually Kevin Kennedy)	4.00	2.00	1.25
(14b)	Joe Kerrigan (correct photo)	6.00	3.00	1.75
(15)	Carlos Lopez	3.00	1.50	.90
(16)	Dennis Martinez	5.00	2.50	1.50
(17)	Tippy Martinez	3.00	1.50	.90
(18)	Lee May	3.00	1.50	.90
(19)	Scott McGregor	3.00	1.50	.90
(20)	Ray Miller	3.00	1.50	.90
(21)	Andres Mora	3.00	1.50	.90
(22)	Eddie Murray	12.00	6.00	3.50
(23)	Tony Muser	3.00	1.50	.90
(24)	Jim Palmer	12.00	6.00	3.50
(25)	Cal Ripken Sr.	3.00	1.50	.90
(26)	Frank Robinson	15.00	7.50	4.50
(27)	Gary Roenicke	3.00	1.50	.90
(28)	Ken Singleton	4.50	2.25	1.25
(29)	Dave Skaggs	3.00	1.50	.90
(30)	Billy Smith	3.00	1.50	.90
(31)	Don Stanhouse	3.00	1.50	.90
(32)	Earl Stephenson	5.00	2.50	1.50
(33)	Tim Stoddard	3.00	1.50	.90
(34)	Earl Weaver	6.00	3.00	1.80

1913 Tom Barker Game

Nearly identical in format to "The National Game" card set, this issue features a different back design of a red-and-white line art representation of a batter. Fronts of the round-cornered, 2-1/2" x 3-1/2" cards have a black-and-white player photo, or game action photo, along with two game scenarios used when playing the card game. There are nine action photos in the set. Player cards are checklisted here alphabetically. The set originally sold for 50 cents. Cards have been seen overprinted in the border with an advertisement for Fenway beer; they should command a premium or 25-50% or so.

		NM	EX	VG
Complete Set (54):		4500.	2250.	1350.
Common Player:		45.00	20.00	11.00
Action Photo Card:		22.00	10.00	5.50
Game Box:		125.00	71.00	43.00
(1)	Grover Alexander	95.00	43.00	24.00
(2)	Frank Baker	95.00	43.00	24.00
(3)	Chief Bender	95.00	43.00	24.00
(4)	Bob Bescher	45.00	20.00	11.00
(5)	Joe Birmingham	45.00	20.00	11.00
(6)	Roger Bresnahan	95.00	43.00	24.00
(7)	Nixey Callahan	45.00	20.00	11.00
(8)	Bill Carrigan	45.00	20.00	11.00
(9)	Frank Chance	95.00	43.00	24.00
(10)	Hal Chase	55.00	25.00	13.50
(11)	Fred Clarke	95.00	43.00	24.00
(12)	Ty Cobb	750.00	337.00	187.00
(13)	Sam Crawford	95.00	43.00	24.00
(14)	Jake Daubert	45.00	20.00	11.00
(15)	Red Dooin	45.00	20.00	11.00
(16)	Johnny Evers	95.00	43.00	24.00
(17)	Vean Gregg	45.00	20.00	11.00
(18)	Clark Griffith	95.00	43.00	24.00
(19)	Dick Hoblitzel	45.00	20.00	11.00
(20)	Miller Huggins	95.00	43.00	24.00
(21)	Joe Jackson	1100.	495.00	275.00
(22)	Hughie Jennings	95.00	43.00	24.00
(23)	Walter Johnson	225.00	101.00	56.00
(24)	Ed Konetchy	45.00	20.00	11.00
(25)	Nap Lajoie	95.00	43.00	24.00
(26)	Connie Mack	95.00	43.00	24.00
(27)	Rube Marquard	95.00	43.00	24.00
(28)	Christy Mathewson	225.00	101.00	56.00
(29)	John McGraw	95.00	43.00	24.00
(30)	Chief Meyers	45.00	20.00	11.00
(31)	Clyde Milan	45.00	20.00	11.00
(32)	Marty O'Toole	45.00	20.00	11.00
(33)	Nap Rucker	45.00	20.00	11.00
(34)	Tris Speaker	125.00	56.00	31.00
(35)	George Stallings	45.00	20.00	11.00
(36)	Bill Sweeney	45.00	20.00	11.00
(37)	Joe Tinker	95.00	43.00	24.00
(38)	Honus Wagner	250.00	112.00	62.00
(39)	Ed Walsh	95.00	43.00	24.00
(40)	Zach Wheat	95.00	43.00	24.00
(41)	Ivy Wingo	45.00	20.00	11.00
(42)	Joe Wood	45.00	20.00	11.00
(43)	Cy Young	150.00	67.00	37.00
(---)	Rules card	50.00	22.00	12.50
(---)	Score card	50.00	22.00	12.50
(1A)	Batter swinging, looking forward	15.00	6.75	3.75
(2A)	Batter swinging, looking back	15.00	6.75	3.75
(3A)	Runner sliding, fielder at bag	15.00	6.75	3.75
(4A)	Runner sliding, umpire behind	15.00	6.75	3.75
(5A)	Runner sliding, hugging base	15.00	6.75	3.75
(6A)	Sliding into home, umpire at left	15.00	6.75	3.75
(7A)	Sliding into home, umpire at right	15.00	6.75	3.75
(8A)	Play at home, runner standing	15.00	6.75	3.75
(9A)	Runner looking backwards	15.00	6.75	3.75

1974-80 Bob Bartosz Postcards

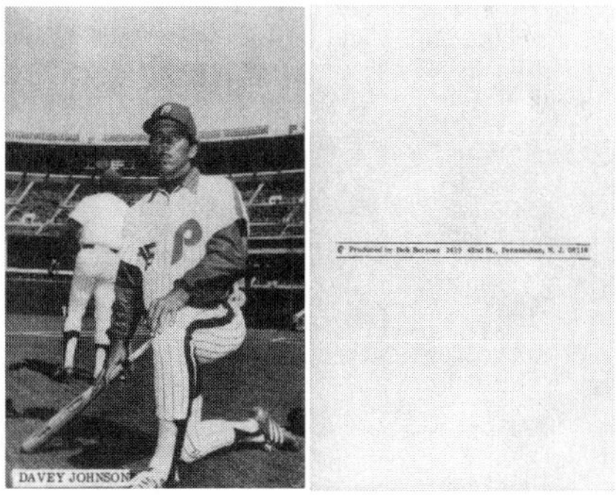

Through the last half of the 1970s, Bob Bartosz, who was a photographer covering the Phillies for a New Jersey daily newspaper, produced a series of player postcards. Most cards were produced at the request of the players for use in handling fan requests. Generally, no more than 500 cards of each player were ever produced. Most of the cards are in black-and-white with player name in a white stripe. Three cards were done in color. Size varies, but averages about 3-5/8" x 5-1/2". Back designs also vary, with most simply having Bartosz' credit line vertically at center. The unnumbered cards are checklisted here in alphabetical order.

		NM	EX	VG
Complete Set (32):				
Common Player:		2.00	1.00	.60
	Black-and-white postcards			
(1)	Hank Aaron (16th career grand slam)	5.00	2.50	1.50
(2)	Richie Ashburn (5th Delaware Valley Show)	2.00	1.00	.60
(3)	James Cool Papa Bell	2.00	1.00	.60
(4)	Bob Boone	2.50	1.25	.70
(5)	Jimmie Crutchfield	2.00	1.00	.60
(6)	Barry Foote	2.00	1.00	.60
(7)	Steve Garvey	2.50	1.25	.70
(8)	Tommy Hutton (Phillies)	2.00	1.00	.60
(9)	Tommy Hutton (Blue Jays)	2.00	1.00	.60
(10)	Dane Iorg	2.00	1.00	.60
(11)	Davey Johnson	2.00	1.00	.60
(12)	Jay Johnstone	2.00	1.00	.60
(13)	Dave Kingman (stadium background)	2.00	1.00	.60
(14)	Dave Kingman (black background)	2.00	1.00	.60
(15)	Greg Luzinski (both feet show)	2.00	1.00	.60
(16)	Greg Luzinski (only left foot shows)	2.00	1.00	.60
(17)	Jerry Martin (Phillies)	2.00	1.00	.60
(18)	Jerry Martin (Cubs)	2.00	1.00	.60
(19)	Tim McCarver	2.50	1.25	.70
(20)	John Montefusco	2.00	1.00	.60
(21)	Jerry Mumphrey	2.00	1.00	.60
(22)	Phil Niekro	2.50	1.25	.70
(23)	Robin Roberts (Hall of Fame induction)	2.00	1.00	.60
(24)	Robin Roberts (4th Delaware Valley Show)	2.00	1.00	.60
(25)	Steve Swisher	2.00	1.00	.60
(26)	Tony Taylor (uniform number visible)	2.00	1.00	.60
(27)	Tony Taylor (number is covered)	2.00	1.00	.60
(28)	Tom Underwood	2.00	1.00	.60
(29)	Billy Williams (N.L. umpire)	2.00	1.00	.60
(30)	1974 National League All-Stars Color postcards	2.50	1.25	.70
(1)	Greg Luzinski	5.00	2.50	1.50
(2)	Bill Madlock	5.00	2.50	1.50
(3)	Jason Thompson	4.00	2.00	1.25

1978 Bob Bartosz Baseball Postcards

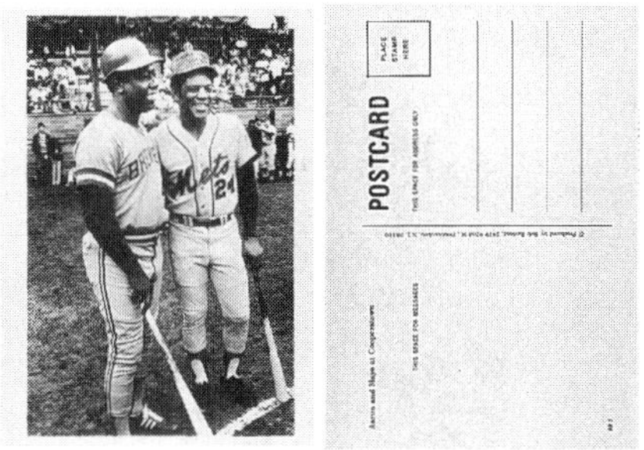

Newspaper photographer Bob Bartosz produced a book of postcards in 1978 combining player poses, action shots and stadium photos. Two dozen cards are printed in 4" x 5-1/2" black-and-white format and perforated on pages of four in the 8-1/2" x 11" book. Backs have standard postcard indicia and are numbered with a "BB" prefix and titled, all printing in black.

		NM	EX	VG
Complete Book (24):		20.00	10.00	6.00
Common Player:		1.00	.50	.30
1	25th anniversary of the 1950 Phillies (group photo at old-timers game)	1.00	.50	.30
2	Aaron and Mays at Cooperstown (Hank Aaron, Willie Mays)	2.50	1.25	.70
3	Willie Mays	5.00	2.50	1.50
4	Aaron signing autographs (Hank Aaron)	2.00	1.00	.60
5	Dizzy Dean (old-timers action sequence)	1.50	.70	.45
6	Jack Russell Stadium, Clearwater, Fla.	1.00	.50	.30
7	Paddy Livingston	1.00	.50	.30
8	Bob Feller (old-timers game)	1.50	.70	.45
9	Hall of Fame Game at Doubleday Field	1.00	.50	.30
10	Doubleday Field at Cooperstown, N.Y.	1.00	.50	.30
11	Three Rivers Stadium, Pittsburgh	1.00	.50	.30
12	Hall of Fame Game at Doubleday Field	1.00	.50	.30
13	Shibe Park from the air	1.00	.50	.30
14	Olympic Stadium, Montreal	1.00	.50	.30
15	A tree grows at home plate (Shibe Park - 1974)	1.00	.50	.30
16	The Bleachers, Wrigley Field	1.00	.50	.30
17	Another Home Run (Hank Aaron)	1.50	.70	.45
18	Home Run King (Hank Aaron)	1.50	.70	.45
19	Autograph Time - 1950 (Phillies signing balls)	1.00	.50	.30
20	The Champs (1976 Phillies)	1.00	.50	.30
21	Last Day - Shibe Park, 1977	1.00	.50	.30
22	Connie Mack Stadium, Philadelphia	1.00	.50	.30
23	Shibe Park	1.00	.50	.30
24	Shibe Park	1.00	.50	.30

1911 Baseball Bats

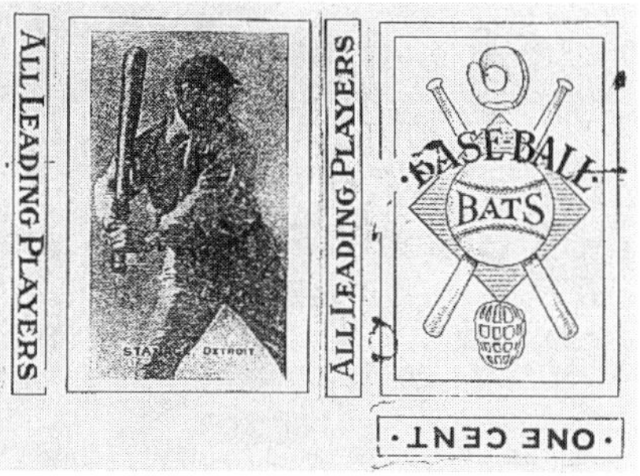

Issued circa 1911, cards in this rare 47-card issue were printed on the back panel of "Baseball Bats" penny candy. The cards themselves measure approximately 1-3/8" x 2-3/8" and feature a black-and-white player photo surrounded by an orange or white border. Player's name and team are printed in small, black capital letters near the bottom of the photo. Cards are blank-backed.

		NM	EX	VG
Complete Set (47):		13000.	4950.	2725.
Common Player:		200.00	75.00	42.00
(1)	Red Ames	200.00	75.00	42.00
(2)	Home Run Baker	350.00	135.00	75.00
(3)	Jack Barry	200.00	75.00	42.00
(4)	Ginger Beaumont	200.00	75.00	42.00
(5)	Chief Bender	350.00	135.00	75.00
(6)	Al Bridwell	200.00	75.00	42.00
(7)	Mordecai Brown	350.00	135.00	75.00
(8)	Bill Corrigan (Carrigan)	200.00	75.00	42.00
(9)	Frank Chance	350.00	135.00	75.00
(10)	Hal Chase	250.00	95.00	52.00
(11)	Ed Cicotte	300.00	114.00	63.00
(12)	Fred Clark (Clarke)	350.00	135.00	75.00
(13)	Ty Cobb	1600.	600.00	335.00
(14)	King Cole	200.00	75.00	42.00
(15)	Eddie Collins	350.00	135.00	75.00
(16)	Sam Crawford	350.00	135.00	75.00
(17)	Lou Criger	200.00	75.00	42.00
(18)	Harry Davis	200.00	75.00	42.00
(19)	Jim Delehanty	200.00	75.00	42.00
(20)	Art Devlin	200.00	75.00	42.00
(21)	Josh Devore	200.00	75.00	42.00
(22)	Wild Bill Donovan	200.00	75.00	42.00
(23)	Larry Doyle	200.00	75.00	42.00
(24)	Johnny Evers	350.00	135.00	75.00
(25)	John Flynn	200.00	75.00	42.00
(26)	George Gibson	200.00	75.00	42.00
(27)	Solly Hoffman (Hofman)	200.00	75.00	42.00
(28)	Walter Johnson	750.00	285.00	157.00
(29)	Johnny Kling	200.00	75.00	42.00
(30)	Nap Lajoie	350.00	135.00	75.00
(31)	Matty McIntyre	200.00	75.00	42.00
(32)	Fred Merkle	200.00	75.00	42.00
(33)	Tom Needham	200.00	75.00	42.00
(34)	Rube Oldring	200.00	75.00	42.00
(35)	Wildfire Schulte	200.00	75.00	42.00
(36)	Cy Seymour	200.00	75.00	42.00
(37)	Jimmy Sheckard	200.00	75.00	42.00
(38)	Tris Speaker	350.00	135.00	75.00
(39)	Oscar Stanage (batting - front view)	200.00	75.00	42.00
(40)	Oscar Stanage (batting - side view)	200.00	75.00	42.00
(41)	Ira Thomas	200.00	75.00	42.00
(42)	Joe Tinker	350.00	135.00	75.00
(43)	Heinie Wagner	200.00	75.00	42.00
(44)	Honus Wagner	500.00	190.00	105.00
(45)	Ed Walsh	350.00	135.00	75.00
(46)	Art Wilson	200.00	75.00	42.00
(47)	Owen Wilson	200.00	75.00	42.00

1979 Baseball Favorites "1953 Bowman"

This collectors' series was designed to represent an extension of the 64-card 1953 Bowman black-and-white card issue. This series uses the same design on its 2-1/2" x 3-3/4" format. Fronts have a black-and-white player photo with no extraneous graphics. Backs are printed in red and black and offer career highlights, stats and biographical data, written as if in 1953. Many of the players in this collectors' edition originally appeared in Bowman's 1953 color series. Issue price was about $7.

	NM	EX	VG
Complete Set (16):	18.00	9.00	5.50
Common Player:	.50	.25	.15
65 Monte Irvin	.50	.25	.15
66 Early Wynn	.50	.25	.15
67 Robin Roberts	.50	.25	.15
68 Stan Musial	2.00	1.00	.60
69 Ernie Banks	1.00	.50	.30
70 Willie Mays	3.00	1.50	.90
71 Yogi Berra	1.50	.70	.45
72 Mickey Mantle	6.00	3.00	1.75
73 Whitey Ford	.75	.40	.25
74 Bob Feller	.50	.25	.15
75 Ted Williams	3.00	1.50	.90
76 Satchel Paige	2.00	1.00	.60
77 Jackie Robinson	2.00	1.00	.60
78 Ed Mathews	.50	.25	.15
79 Warren Spahn	.50	.25	.15
80 Ralph Kiner	.50	.25	.15

1950 Baseball Player Charms

The date of issue for this novelty item is conjectural, based on known player selection. Packaged in plastic bubbles for sale in vending machines, these charms are found in several different shapes - rectangle, octagon, etc. - and colors of plastic. A black-and-white photo appears at center with a loop at top for hanging. Size also varies but is about 3/4" x 1-1/4". Players are not identified on the charm and there is no number. The checklist here is in alphabetical order, and likely not complete.

	NM	EX	VG
Common Player:	25.00	12.50	7.50
(1) Yogi Berra	50.00	25.00	15.00
(2) Ewell Blackwell	25.00	12.50	7.50
(3) Roy Campanella	50.00	25.00	15.00
(4) Joe DiMaggio	90.00	45.00	27.00
(5) Carl Erskine	25.00	12.50	7.50
(6) Bob Feller	25.00	12.50	7.50
(7) Carl Furillo	25.00	12.50	7.50
(8) Lou Gehrig	75.00	37.00	22.00
(9) Ralph Kiner	25.00	12.50	7.50
(10) Stan Musial	60.00	30.00	18.00
(11) Andy Pafko	25.00	12.50	7.50
(12) Pee Wee Reese	30.00	15.00	9.00
(13) Phil Rizzuto	30.00	15.00	9.00
(14) Jackie Robinson	75.00	37.00	22.00
(15) Babe Ruth	90.00	45.00	27.00
(16) Duke Snider	30.00	15.00	9.00
(17) Ted Williams	75.00	37.00	22.00

1952 Baseball Player Doubleheader Charms

These vending machine prizes were probably issued in the early 1950s, though pinning down a date via player selection is imprecise. About 7/8" in diameter, these novelties have black-and-white player photos on front and back, with the player's name in script beneath his portrait. A clear plastic dome covers the photos and is wrapped with a looped band for hanging. The unnumbered charms are listed here in alphabetical order.

	NM	EX	VG
Complete Set (29):	450.00	225.00	135.00
Common Player:	20.00	10.00	6.00
(1) Richie Ashburn, Phil Masi	25.00	12.50	7.50
(2) Hank Bauer, Johnny Pesky	20.00	10.00	6.00
(3) Yogi Berra, Duke Snider	35.00	17.50	10.50
(4) Ewell Blackwell, Jim Konstanty	20.00	10.00	6.00
(5) Roy Campanella, Bob Elliott	25.00	12.50	7.50
(6) Phil Cavarretta, Virgil Stallcup	20.00	10.00	6.00
(7) Sam Chapman, Larry Jansen	20.00	10.00	6.00
(8) Jerry Coleman, George Kell	20.00	10.00	6.00
(9) Billy Cox, Junior Thompson	20.00	10.00	6.00
(10) Walt Dropo, Myron McCormick	20.00	10.00	6.00
(11) Al Evans, Wes Westrum	20.00	10.00	6.00
(12) Walter Evers, Cliff Mapes	20.00	10.00	6.00
(13) Bob Feller, Phil Rizzuto	30.00	15.00	9.00
(14) Gordon Goldsberry, Stan Musial	25.00	12.50	7.50
(15) Clint Hartung, Don Kolloway	20.00	10.00	6.00
(16) Grady Hatton, Tommy Holmes	20.00	10.00	6.00
(17) Tommy Henrich, Ted Kluszewski	22.00	11.00	6.50
(18) Gene Hermanski, Hal Newhouser	20.00	10.00	6.00
(19) Art Houtteman, Jackie Robinson	30.00	15.00	9.00
(20) Sid Hudson, Andy Pafko	20.00	10.00	6.00
(21) Ed Kazak, Bob Lemon	20.00	10.00	6.00
(22) Ellis Kinder, Gus Zernial	20.00	10.00	6.00
(23) Ralph Kiner, Joe Page	20.00	10.00	6.00
(24) Ed Lopat, Paul Trout	20.00	10.00	6.00
(25) Don Newcombe, Vic Wertz	20.00	10.00	6.00
(26) Dave Philley, Aaron Robinson	20.00	10.00	6.00
(27) Vic Raschi, Enos Slaughter	20.00	10.00	6.00
(28) Pee Wee Reese, Gene Woodling	25.00	12.50	7.50
(29) George Tebbetts, Eddie Yost	20.00	10.00	6.00

1940 Baseball Player Pins

This was the first of two issues which share a nearly identical format. The 1-3/4" celluloid pin-back buttons feature a black-and-white player photo surrounded by a white border. The player's name is in black capital letters at bottom, and his team nickname in the same type size and style at top. These pins were originally sold at ballparks and other souvenir outlets. The checklist, arranged here in alphabetical order, is likely not complete.

	NM	EX	VG
Common Player:	40.00	20.00	10.00
(1) Dick Bartell	40.00	20.00	10.00
(2) Dolf Camilli	40.00	20.00	10.00
(3) Bill Dickey	65.00	32.00	19.50
(4) Joe DiMaggio	250.00	125.00	75.00
(5) Lou Gehrig	250.00	125.00	75.00
(6) Lefty Gomez	65.00	32.00	19.50
(7) Carl Hubbell	65.00	32.00	19.50
(8) Cliff Melton	40.00	20.00	10.00
(9) Pete Reiser	40.00	20.00	10.00
(10) Dixie Walker	40.00	20.00	10.00
(11) Whitlow Wyatt	40.00	20.00	10.00

1951 Baseball Player Pins

This was the second of two issues which share a nearly identical format. The 1-3/4" celluloid pin-back buttons feature a black-and-white player photo surrounded by a white border. The player's name is in black capital letters at bottom, and full team name in the same type size and style at top. These pins were originally sold at ballparks and other souvenir outlets. The checklist, arranged here in alphabetical order, is likely not complete. Note that the woeful Pittsburgh Pirates represent more than half the known players in this issue.

	NM	EX	VG
Common Player:	30.00	15.00	9.00
(1) Luke Easter	30.00	15.00	9.00
(2) Monte Irvin	40.00	20.00	12.00
(3) Ralph Kiner	40.00	20.00	12.00
(4) Willie Mays	150.00	75.00	45.00
(5) Clyde McCullouhg (McCullough)	30.00	15.00	9.00
(6) Billy Meyer	30.00	15.00	9.00
(7) Danny Murtaugh	30.00	15.00	9.00
(8) Saul Rogovin	30.00	15.00	9.00
(9) Stan Rojek	30.00	15.00	9.00
(10) Hank Thompson	30.00	15.00	9.00
(11) Bill Werle	30.00	15.00	9.00

1954-60 Baseball Player Pins

This series of baseball player pins is similar to contemporary issues in its 2-1/8" black-and-white celluloid format, but differs in that the player name appears at top, in all capital letters. Players known in the series indicate the buttons were issued over a period of several years, probably for sale in stadium concession stands and other souvenir outlets. The alphabetical checklist here is not believed to be complete.

	NM	EX	VG
Common Player:	20.00	10.00	6.00
(1) Luis Arroyo	20.00	10.00	6.00
(2) Hank Bauer	20.00	10.00	6.00
(3) Yogi Berra	45.00	22.00	13.50
(4) Johnny Blanchard	20.00	10.00	6.00
(5) Cletis Boyer	25.00	12.50	7.50
(6) Andy Carey	20.00	10.00	6.00
(7) Del Crandall	20.00	10.00	6.00
(8) Junior Gilliam	25.00	12.50	7.50
(9) Ruben Gomez	20.00	10.00	6.00
(10) Elston Howard	25.00	12.50	7.50
(11) Billy Loes	20.00	10.00	6.00
(12) Mickey Mantle	175.00	87.00	52.00
(13) Roger Maris	60.00	30.00	18.00
(14) Billy Martin	25.00	12.50	7.50
(15) Willie Mays	90.00	45.00	27.00
(16) Gil McDougald	20.00	10.00	6.00
(17) Irv Noren	20.00	10.00	6.00
(18) Johnny Podres	20.00	10.00	6.00
(19) Allie Reynolds	20.00	10.00	6.00
(20) Enos Slaughter	20.00	10.00	6.00
(21) Duke Snider	45.00	22.00	13.50
(22) Warren Spahn	40.00	20.00	12.00
(23) Gene Woodling	20.00	10.00	6.00

1910s Base Ball Stars Notebooks

Issued between 1911-15 (it's impossible to be more precise without a more complete checklist), this series of notebooks is one of several which carried the "Base Ball Stars" title. About 7-3/4" x 10-1/2", the cover of the notebook has a sepia posed action photo with player identification at bottom. Values shown are for complete notebooks; covers which have been removed have substantially less value.

		NM	EX	VG
(1)	Joe Jackson	2500.	1250.	750.00

1915+ Base Ball Stars Notebooks

The cover picture of Babe Ruth batting in a Red Sox uniform, plus the contents of the discovery specimen appear to date this notebook series from 1915-1920. The 6-3/4" x 8-1/2" tablets are similar in format to contemporary baseball player notebook series. Covers have only the player's name for identification and a "MADE IN U.S.A." notation at bottom. The black-and-white cover photo shows a large player figure on a ballpark action background photo.

	NM	EX	VG
Babe Ruth	600.00	300.00	180.00

1920s Base Ball Stars Notebooks

With only five players known, this series of notebooks can be dated no more precisely than 1920-26. The 6" x 9" tablets have a white background with a player photo printed in blue in a vaguely keyhole-shaped design. At top, also in blue, is "BASE BALL STARS" printed amid rayed stars and baseball equipment. It's likely other players may yet be reported. Values shown are for complete notebook; covers which have been removed are worth considerably less.

		NM	EX	VG
Common Notebook:		300.00	150.00	90.00
(1)	Grover Cleveland Alexander	200.00	100.00	60.00
(2)	Ty Cobb	400.00	200.00	120.00
(3)	Walter Johnson	300.00	150.00	90.00
(4)	Babe Ruth	600.00	300.00	180.00
(5)	Tris Speaker	250.00	125.00	75.00

1912 Base Ball Stars Series

This set of blank-backed, black-and-white 6" x 9" pictures features the contestants of the 1912 World Series - the Red Sox and Giants. It is possible these pictures were sold at the ballparks during the Series. The checklist here is probably incomplete. The unnumbered pictures have been listed alphabetically within team.

		NM	EX	VG
Common Player:		450.00	225.00	135.00
	BOSTON RED SOX			
(1)	Hugh Bedient	450.00	225.00	135.00
(2)	Joe Wood	480.00	240.00	145.00
	N.Y. GIANTS			
(1)	Rube Marquard	525.00	260.00	150.00
(2)	Christy Mathewson	1050.	525.00	315.00
(3)	Jeff Tesreau	450.00	225.00	135.00

1948 Baseball's Great Hall of Fame Exhibits

Titled "Baseball's Great Hall of Fame," this 32-player set features black and white player photos against a gray background. The photos are accented by Greek columns on either side with brief player information printed at the bottom. The blank-backed cards are unnumbered and are listed here alphabetically. The cards measure 3-3/8" x 5-3/8". Collectors should be aware that 23 of the cards in this set were reprinted on whiter stock in 1974.

		NM	EX	VG
Complete Set (33):		450.00	220.00	135.00
Common Player:		4.00	2.00	1.25
(1)	Grover Cleveland Alexander	4.00	2.00	1.25
(2)	Roger Bresnahan	4.00	2.00	1.25
(3)	Frank Chance	4.00	2.00	1.25
(4)	Jack Chesbro	4.00	2.00	1.25
(5)	Fred Clarke	4.00	2.00	1.25
(6)	Ty Cobb	50.00	25.00	15.00
(7)	Mickey Cochrane	4.00	2.00	1.25
(8)	Eddie Collins	4.00	2.00	1.25
(9)	Hugh Duffy	4.00	2.00	1.25
(10)	Johnny Evers	4.00	2.00	1.25
(11)	Frankie Frisch	4.00	2.00	1.25
(12)	Lou Gehrig	50.00	25.00	15.00
(13)	Clark Griffith	4.00	2.00	1.25
(14)	Robert "Lefty" Grove	4.00	2.00	1.25
(15)	Rogers Hornsby	5.00	2.50	1.50
(16)	Carl Hubbell	4.00	2.00	1.25
(17)	Hughie Jennings	4.00	2.00	1.25
(18)	Walter Johnson	10.00	5.00	3.00
(19)	Willie Keeler	4.00	2.00	1.25
(20)	Napolean Lajoie	5.00	2.50	1.50
(21)	Connie Mack	4.00	2.00	1.25
(22)	Christy Matthewson (Mathewson)	10.00	5.00	3.00
(23)	John J. McGraw	4.00	2.00	1.25
(24)	Eddie Plank	4.00	2.00	1.25
(25)	Babe Ruth (batting)	75.00	37.00	22.00
(26)	Babe Ruth (standing with bats)	200.00	100.00	60.00
(27)	George Sisler	4.00	2.00	1.25
(28)	Tris Speaker	5.00	2.50	1.50
(29)	Joe Tinker	4.00	2.00	1.25
(30)	Rube Waddell	4.00	2.00	1.25
(31)	Honus Wagner	12.00	6.00	3.50
(32)	Ed Walsh	4.00	2.00	1.25
(33)	Cy Young	5.00	2.50	1.50

1974 Baseball's Great Hall of Fame Exhibits

Two dozen of the cards from the 1948 issue were reprinted in 1974 by the original publisher, Exhibit Supply Co., Chicago. The 1974 reissues are in the same 3-3/8" x 5-3/8" format as the originals, and in the same design. They are blank-backed and printed on a thinner, slicker cardboard stock than the 1948 cards. The reprints can be found printed in black, blue or brown. The unnumbered cards are checklisted here alphabetically.

		NM	EX	VG
Complete Set (24):		9.00	4.50	2.75
Common Player:		.50	.25	.15
(1)	Grover Cleveland Alexander	.50	.25	.15
(2)	Roger Bresnahan	.50	.25	.15
(3)	Frank Chance	.50	.25	.15
(4)	Jack Chesbro	.50	.25	.15
(5)	Fred Clarke	.50	.25	.15
(6)	Ty Cobb	2.00	1.00	.60
(7)	Mickey Cochrane	.50	.25	.15
(8)	Eddie Collins	.50	.25	.15
(9)	Johnny Evers	.50	.25	.15
(10)	Frankie Frisch	.50	.25	.15
(11)	Clark Griffith	.50	.25	.15
(12)	Robert "Lefty" Grove	.50	.25	.15
(13)	Rogers Hornsby	.50	.25	.15
(14)	Hughie Jennings	.50	.25	.15
(15)	Walter Johnson	.65	.35	.20
(16)	Connie Mack	.50	.25	.15
(17)	Christy Mathewson	.65	.35	.20
(18)	John McGraw	.50	.25	.15
(19)	George Sisler	.50	.25	.15
(20)	Joe Tinker	.50	.25	.15
(21)	Rube Waddell	.50	.25	.15
(22)	Honus Wagner	.65	.35	.20
(23)	Ed Walsh	.50	.25	.15
(24)	Cy Young	.50	.25	.15

1977 Baseball's Great Hall of Fame Exhibits

A second set of "Baseball's Great Hall of Fame" exhibit cards was produced in 1977, most cards featuring more recent players than the 1948 issue. The cards were produced in the same 3-3/8" x 5-3/8" blank-back, black-and-white design as the 1948 cards, and are a genuine product of Exhibit Supply Co., Chicago. The new cards were printed on an extremely high grade of semi-gloss cardboard, in contrast to the earlier versions. Production was announced at 500,000 cards. The unnumbered cards are checklisted here alphabetically.

		NM	EX	VG
Complete Set (32):		95.00	47.00	28.00
Common Player:		2.00	1.00	.60
(1)	Luke Appling	2.00	1.00	.60
(2)	Ernie Banks	4.00	2.00	1.25
(3)	Yogi Berra	4.00	2.00	1.25
(4)	Roy Campanella	5.00	2.50	1.50
(5)	Roberto Clemente	12.00	6.00	3.50
(6)	Alvin Dark	2.00	1.00	.60
(7)	Joe DiMaggio	10.00	5.00	3.00
(8)	Whitey Ford	4.00	2.00	1.25
(9)	Bob Feller	3.00	1.50	.90
(10)	Jimmie Foxx	3.00	1.50	.90
(11)	Lou Gehrig	7.50	3.75	2.25
(12)	Charlie Gehringer	2.00	1.00	.60
(13)	Hank Greenberg	4.00	2.00	1.25
(14)	Gabby Hartnett	2.00	1.00	.60
(15)	Carl Hubbell	2.00	1.00	.60
(16)	Al Kaline	3.50	1.75	1.00
(17)	Mickey Mantle	15.00	7.50	4.50
(18)	Willie Mays	8.00	4.00	2.50
(19)	Johnny Mize	2.00	1.00	.60
(20)	Stan Musial	6.00	3.00	1.75
(21)	Mel Ott	2.00	1.00	.60
(22)	Satchel Paige	4.00	2.00	1.25
(23)	Robin Roberts	2.00	1.00	.60
(24)	Jackie Robinson	7.50	3.75	2.25
(25)	Babe Ruth	9.00	4.50	2.75
(26)	Duke Snider	3.00	1.50	.90
(27)	Warren Spahn	2.00	1.00	.60
(28)	Tris Speaker	2.00	1.00	.60
(29)	Honus Wagner	3.00	1.50	.90
(30)	Ted Williams	8.00	4.00	2.50
(31)	Rudy York	2.00	1.00	.60
(32)	Cy Young	3.00	1.50	.90

1934-36 Batter-Up

National Chicle's 192-card "Batter-Up" set was issued over a three-year period. The blank-backed cards are die-cut, enabling collectors of the era to fold the top of the card over so that it could stand upright on its own support. The cards can be found in black-and-white or a variety of color tints. Card numbers 1-80 measure 2-3/8" x 3-1/4" in size, while the high-numbered cards (#81-192) measure 2-3/8" x 3" (1/4" smaller in height). The high-numbered cards are significantly more difficult to find than the lower numbers. The set's ACC designation is R318.

		NM	EX	VG
Complete Set (192):		17500.	8500.	4650.
Common Player (1-80):		50.00	25.00	15.00
Common Player (81-192):		85.00	42.00	25.00
1	Wally Berger	100.00	35.00	22.00
2	Ed Brandt	50.00	25.00	15.00
3	Al Lopez	100.00	50.00	30.00
4	Dick Bartell	50.00	25.00	15.00
5	Carl Hubbell	125.00	62.00	37.00
6	Bill Terry	115.00	57.00	34.00
7	Pepper Martin	60.00	30.00	18.00
8	Jim Bottomley	100.00	50.00	30.00
9	Tommy Bridges	50.00	25.00	15.00
10	Rick Ferrell	100.00	50.00	30.00
11	Ray Benge	50.00	25.00	15.00
12	Wes Ferrell	50.00	25.00	15.00
13	Bill Cissell	50.00	25.00	15.00
14	Pie Traynor	100.00	50.00	30.00
15	Roy Mahaffey	50.00	25.00	15.00
16	Chick Hafey	100.00	50.00	30.00
17	Lloyd Waner	100.00	50.00	30.00
18	Jack Burns	50.00	25.00	15.00
19	Buddy Myer	50.00	25.00	15.00
20	Bob Johnson	50.00	25.00	15.00
21	Arky Vaughn (Vaughan)	100.00	50.00	30.00
22	Red Rolfe	50.00	25.00	15.00
23	Lefty Gomez	150.00	75.00	45.00
24	Earl Averill	100.00	50.00	30.00
25	Mickey Cochrane	100.00	50.00	30.00
26	Van Mungo	75.00	37.00	22.00
27	Mel Ott	125.00	62.00	37.00
28	Jimmie Foxx	200.00	100.00	60.00
29	Jimmy Dykes	50.00	25.00	15.00
30	Bill Dickey	150.00	75.00	45.00
31	Lefty Grove	200.00	100.00	60.00
32	Joe Cronin	100.00	50.00	30.00
33	Frankie Frisch	100.00	50.00	30.00
34	Al Simmons	100.00	50.00	30.00
35	Rogers Hornsby	175.00	87.00	52.00
36	Ted Lyons	100.00	50.00	30.00
37	Rabbit Maranville	100.00	50.00	30.00
38	Jimmie Wilson	50.00	25.00	15.00
39	Willie Kamm	50.00	25.00	15.00
40	Bill Hallahan	50.00	25.00	15.00
41	Gus Suhr	50.00	25.00	15.00
42	Charlie Gehringer	125.00	62.00	37.00
43	Joe Heving	50.00	25.00	15.00
44	Adam Comorosky	50.00	25.00	15.00
45	Tony Lazzeri	100.00	50.00	30.00
46	Sam Leslie	50.00	25.00	15.00
47	Bob Smith	50.00	25.00	15.00
48	Willis Hudlin	50.00	25.00	15.00
49	Carl Reynolds	50.00	25.00	15.00
50	Fred Schulte	50.00	25.00	15.00
51	Cookie Lavagetto	50.00	25.00	15.00
52	Hal Schumacher	50.00	25.00	15.00
53	Doc Cramer	50.00	25.00	15.00
54	Si Johnson	50.00	25.00	15.00
55	Ollie Bejma	50.00	25.00	15.00
56	Sammy Byrd	50.00	25.00	15.00
57	Hank Greenberg	200.00	100.00	60.00
58	Bill Knickerbocker	50.00	25.00	15.00
59	Billy Urbanski	50.00	25.00	15.00
60	Ed Morgan	50.00	25.00	15.00
61	Eric McNair	50.00	25.00	15.00
62	Ben Chapman	50.00	25.00	15.00
63	Roy Johnson	50.00	25.00	15.00
64	"Dizzy" Dean	400.00	200.00	120.00
65	Zeke Bonura	50.00	25.00	15.00
66	Firpo Marberry	50.00	25.00	15.00
67	Gus Mancuso	50.00	25.00	15.00
68	Joe Vosmik	50.00	25.00	15.00
69	Earl Grace	50.00	25.00	15.00
70	Tony Piet	50.00	25.00	15.00
71	Rollie Hemsley	50.00	25.00	15.00
72	Fred Fitzsimmons	50.00	25.00	15.00
73	Hack Wilson	175.00	87.00	52.00
74	Chick Fullis	50.00	25.00	15.00
75	Fred Frankhouse	50.00	25.00	15.00
76	Ethan Allen	50.00	25.00	15.00
77	Heinie Manush	100.00	50.00	30.00
78	Rip Collins	50.00	25.00	15.00
79	Tony Cuccinello	50.00	25.00	15.00
80	Joe Kuhel	50.00	25.00	15.00
81	Thomas Bridges	85.00	42.00	25.00
82	Clinton Brown	85.00	42.00	25.00
83	Albert Blanche	85.00	42.00	25.00
84	"Boze" Berger	85.00	42.00	25.00
85	Goose Goslin	200.00	100.00	60.00
86	Vernon Gomez	325.00	162.00	97.00
87	Joe Glen (Glenn)	85.00	42.00	25.00
88	Cy Blanton	85.00	42.00	25.00
89	Tom Carey	85.00	42.00	25.00
90	Ralph Birkhofer	85.00	42.00	25.00
91	Frank Gabler	85.00	42.00	25.00
92	Dick Coffman	85.00	42.00	25.00
93	Ollie Bejma	85.00	42.00	25.00
94	Leroy Earl Parmalee	85.00	42.00	25.00
95	Carl Reynolds	85.00	42.00	25.00
96	Ben Cantwell	85.00	42.00	25.00
97	Curtis Davis	85.00	42.00	25.00
98	Wallace Moses, Billy Webb	125.00	62.00	37.00
99	Ray Benge	85.00	42.00	25.00
100	"Pie" Traynor	200.00	100.00	60.00
101	Phil. Cavarretta	85.00	42.00	25.00
102	"Pep" Young	85.00	42.00	25.00
103	Willis Hudlin	85.00	42.00	25.00
104	Mickey Haslin	85.00	42.00	25.00
105	Oswald Bluege	85.00	42.00	25.00
106	Paul Andrews	85.00	42.00	25.00
107	Edward A. Brandt	85.00	42.00	25.00
108	Dan Taylor	85.00	42.00	25.00
109	Thornton T. Lee	85.00	42.00	25.00
110	Hal Schumacher	85.00	42.00	25.00
111	Minter Hayes, Ted Lyons	250.00	125.00	75.00
112	Odell Hale	85.00	42.00	25.00
113	Earl Averill	200.00	100.00	60.00
114	Italo Chelini	85.00	42.00	25.00
115	Ivy Andrews, Jim Bottomley	300.00	150.00	90.00
116	Bill Walker	85.00	42.00	25.00
117	Bill Dickey	325.00	162.00	97.00
118	Gerald Walker	85.00	42.00	25.00
119	Ted Lyons	200.00	100.00	60.00
120	Elden Auker (Eldon)	85.00	42.00	25.00
121	Wild Bill Hallahan	85.00	42.00	25.00
122	Freddy Lindstrom	200.00	100.00	60.00
123	Oral C. Hildebrand	85.00	42.00	25.00
124	Luke Appling	225.00	112.00	67.00
125	"Pepper" Martin	145.00	72.00	43.00
126	Rick Ferrell	200.00	100.00	60.00
127	Ival Goodman	85.00	42.00	25.00
128	Joe Kuhel	85.00	42.00	25.00
129	Ernest Lombardi	200.00	100.00	60.00
130	Charles Gehringer	300.00	150.00	90.00
131	Van L. Mungo	85.00	42.00	25.00
132	Larry French	85.00	42.00	25.00
133	"Buddy" Myer	85.00	42.00	25.00
134	Mel Harder	85.00	42.00	25.00
135	Augie Galan	85.00	42.00	25.00
136	"Gabby" Hartnett	200.00	100.00	60.00
137	Stan Hack	85.00	42.00	25.00
138	Billy Herman	200.00	100.00	60.00
139	Bill Jurges	85.00	42.00	25.00
140	Bill Lee	85.00	42.00	25.00
141	"Zeke" Bonura	85.00	42.00	25.00
142	Tony Piet	85.00	42.00	25.00
143	Paul Dean	150.00	75.00	45.00
144	Jimmy Foxx	325.00	162.00	97.00
145	Joe Medwick	200.00	100.00	60.00
146	Rip Collins	85.00	42.00	25.00
147	Melo Almada	110.00	55.00	33.00
148	Allan Cooke	85.00	42.00	25.00
149	Moe Berg	300.00	150.00	90.00
150	Adolph Camilli	85.00	42.00	25.00
151	Oscar Melillo	85.00	42.00	25.00
152	Bruce Campbell	85.00	42.00	25.00
153	Lefty Grove	300.00	150.00	90.00
154	John Murphy	85.00	42.00	25.00
155	Luke Sewell	85.00	42.00	25.00
156	Leo Durocher	200.00	100.00	60.00
157	Lloyd Waner	200.00	100.00	60.00
158	Guy Bush	85.00	42.00	25.00
159	Jimmy Dykes	85.00	42.00	25.00
160	Steve O'Neill	85.00	42.00	25.00
161	Gen. Crowder	85.00	42.00	25.00
162	Joe Cascarella	85.00	42.00	25.00
163	"Bud" Hafey	85.00	42.00	25.00
164	"Gilly" Campbell	85.00	42.00	25.00
165	Ray Hayworth	85.00	42.00	25.00
166	Frank Demaree	85.00	42.00	25.00
167	John Babich	85.00	42.00	25.00
168	Marvin Owen	85.00	42.00	25.00
169	Ralph Kress	85.00	42.00	25.00
170	"Mule" Haas	85.00	42.00	25.00
171	Frank Higgins	85.00	42.00	25.00
172	Walter Berger	85.00	42.00	25.00
173	Frank Frisch	200.00	100.00	60.00
174	Wess Ferrell (Wes)	85.00	42.00	25.00
175	Pete Fox	85.00	42.00	25.00
176	John Vergez	85.00	42.00	25.00
177	William Rogell	85.00	42.00	25.00
178	"Don" Brennan	85.00	42.00	25.00
179	James Bottomley	200.00	100.00	60.00
180	Travis Jackson	225.00	112.00	67.00
181	Robert Rolfe	85.00	42.00	25.00
182	Frank Crosetti	125.00	62.00	37.00
183	Joe Cronin	200.00	100.00	60.00
184	"Schoolboy" Rowe	125.00	62.00	37.00
185	"Chuck" Klein	200.00	100.00	60.00
186	Lon Warneke	85.00	42.00	25.00
187	Gus Suhr	85.00	42.00	25.00
188	Ben Chapman	125.00	62.00	37.00
189	Clint. Brown	125.00	62.00	37.00
190	Paul Derringer	125.00	62.00	37.00
191	John Burns	125.00	62.00	37.00
192	John Broaca	200.00	75.00	30.00

1959 Bazooka

The 1959 Bazooka set, consisting of 23 full-color, unnumbered cards, was printed on boxes of one-cent Topps bubble gum. The blank-backed cards measure 2-13/16" x 4-15/16", when properly cut. Nine cards were first issued, with 14 being added to the set later. The nine more plentiful cards are #'s 1, 5, 8, 9, 14, 15, 16, 17 and 22. Complete boxes would command double the price shown.

		NM	EX	VG
Complete Set (23):		8250.	4125.	2450.
Common Player:		115.00	57.00	34.00
(1a)	Hank Aaron (name in white)	650.00	325.00	195.00
(1b)	Hank Aaron (name in yellow)	650.00	325.00	195.00
(2)	Richie Ashburn (SP)	450.00	225.00	135.00
(3)	Ernie Banks (SP)	700.00	350.00	210.00
(4)	Ken Boyer (SP)	275.00	137.00	82.00
(5)	Orlando Cepeda	250.00	125.00	75.00
(6)	Bob Cerv (SP)	250.00	125.00	75.00
(7)	Rocky Colavito (SP)	500.00	250.00	150.00
(8)	Del Crandall	115.00	57.00	34.00
(9)	Jim Davenport	115.00	57.00	34.00
(10)	Don Drysdale (SP)	650.00	325.00	195.00
(11)	Nellie Fox (SP)	450.00	225.00	135.00
(12)	Jackie Jensen (SP)	275.00	137.00	82.00
(13)	Harvey Kuenn (SP)	275.00	137.00	82.00
(14)	Mickey Mantle	1500.	750.00	450.00
(15)	Willie Mays	545.00	272.00	163.00
(16)	Bill Mazeroski	200.00	100.00	60.00
(17)	Roy McMillan	115.00	57.00	34.00
(18)	Billy Pierce (SP)	250.00	125.00	75.00
(19)	Roy Sievers (SP)	250.00	125.00	75.00
(20)	Duke Snider (SP)	725.00	362.00	217.00
(21)	Gus Triandos (SP)	250.00	125.00	75.00
(22)	Bob Turley	175.00	87.00	52.00
(23)	Vic Wertz (SP)	250.00	125.00	75.00

1960 Bazooka

Three-card panels were printed on the bottoms of Bazooka bubble gum boxes in 1960. The blank-backed set is comprised of 36 cards with the card number located at the bottom of each full-color card. Individual cards measure 1-13/16" x 2-3/4"; the panels measure 2-3/4" x 5-1/2".

		NM	EX	VG
Complete Panel Set (12):		1800.	900.00	550.00
Complete Singles Set (36):		1300.	650.00	400.00
Common Player:		12.00	6.00	3.50
Panel 1		125.00	62.00	37.00
1	Ernie Banks	60.00	30.00	18.00
2	Bud Daley	12.00	6.00	3.50
3	Wally Moon	12.00	6.00	3.50
Panel 2		175.00	85.00	50.00
4	Hank Aaron	95.00	47.00	28.00
5	Milt Pappas	12.00	6.00	3.50
6	Dick Stuart	12.00	6.00	3.50
Panel 3		285.00	140.00	80.00
7	Bob Clemente	120.00	60.00	36.00
8	Yogi Berra	60.00	30.00	18.00
9	Ken Boyer	12.00	6.00	3.50
Panel 4		100.00	50.00	30.00
10	Orlando Cepeda	40.00	20.00	12.00
11	Gus Triandos	12.00	6.00	3.50
12	Frank Malzone	12.00	6.00	3.50
Panel 5		175.00	85.00	50.00
13	Willie Mays	95.00	47.00	28.00
14	Camilo Pascual	12.00	6.00	3.50
15	Bob Cerv	12.00	6.00	3.50
Panel 6		125.00	62.00	37.00
16	Vic Power	12.00	6.00	3.50
17	Larry Sherry	12.00	6.00	3.50
18	Al Kaline	60.00	30.00	18.00
Panel 7		150.00	75.00	45.00
19	Warren Spahn	48.00	24.00	14.50
20	Harmon Killebrew	36.00	18.00	11.00
21	Jackie Jensen	18.00	9.00	5.50
Panel 8		150.00	75.00	45.00
22	Luis Aparicio	30.00	15.00	9.00
23	Gil Hodges	36.00	18.00	11.00
24	Richie Ashburn	36.00	18.00	11.00
Panel 9		115.00	55.00	33.00
25	Nellie Fox	35.00	17.50	10.50
26	Robin Roberts	36.00	18.00	11.00
27	Joe Cunningham	12.00	6.00	3.50
Panel 10		170.00	85.00	50.00
28	Early Wynn	30.00	15.00	9.00
29	Frank Robinson	60.00	30.00	18.00
30	Rocky Colavito	24.00	12.00	7.25
Panel 11		450.00	225.00	135.00
31	Mickey Mantle	350.00	175.00	105.00
32	Glen Hobbie	12.00	6.00	3.50
33	Roy McMillan	12.00	6.00	3.50
Panel 12		55.00	27.50	16.50
34	Harvey Kuenn	12.00	6.00	3.50
35	Johnny Antonelli	12.00	6.00	3.50
36	Del Crandall	12.00	6.00	3.50

1961 Bazooka

Similar in design to the 1960 Bazooka set, the 1961 edition consists of 36 cards printed in panels of three on the bottom of Bazooka bubble gum boxes. The full-color cards, which measure 1-13/16" x 2-3/4" individually and 2-3/4" x 5-1/2" as panels, are numbered 1 through 36. The backs are blank.

		NM	EX	VG
Complete Panel Set (12):		1500.	750.00	450.00
Complete Singles Set (36):		935.00	465.00	280.00
Common Player:		10.00	5.00	3.00
Panel 1		475.00	240.00	140.00
1	Art Mahaffey	10.00	5.00	3.00
2	Mickey Mantle	300.00	150.00	90.00
3	Ron Santo	15.00	7.50	4.50
Panel 2		150.00	75.00	45.00
4	Bud Daley	10.00	5.00	3.00
5	Roger Maris	80.00	40.00	24.00
6	Eddie Yost	10.00	5.00	3.00
Panel 3		50.00	25.00	15.00
7	Minnie Minoso	15.00	7.50	4.50
8	Dick Groat	10.00	5.00	3.00
9	Frank Malzone	10.00	5.00	3.00
Panel 4		75.00	37.50	22.50
10	Dick Donovan	10.00	5.00	3.00
11	Ed Mathews	30.00	15.00	9.00
12	Jim Lemon	10.00	5.00	3.00
Panel 5		48.00	24.00	14.00
13	Chuck Estrada	10.00	5.00	3.00
14	Ken Boyer	10.00	5.00	3.00
15	Harvey Kuenn	10.00	5.00	3.00
Panel 6		68.00	34.00	20.00
16	Ernie Broglio	10.00	5.00	3.00
17	Rocky Colavito	20.00	10.00	6.00
18	Ted Kluszewski	16.00	8.00	4.75
Panel 7		200.00	100.00	60.00
19	Ernie Banks	75.00	37.00	22.00
20	Al Kaline	50.00	25.00	15.00
21	Ed Bailey	10.00	5.00	3.00
Panel 8		150.00	75.00	45.00
22	Jim Perry	10.00	5.00	3.00
23	Willie Mays	80.00	40.00	24.00
24	Bill Mazeroski	17.50	8.75	5.25
Panel 9		68.00	34.00	20.00
25	Gus Triandos	10.00	5.00	3.00
26	Don Drysdale	25.00	12.50	7.50
27	Frank Herrera	10.00	5.00	3.00
Panel 10		80.00	40.00	24.00
28	Earl Battey	10.00	5.00	3.00
29	Warren Spahn	35.00	17.50	10.50
30	Gene Woodling	10.00	5.00	3.00
Panel 11		80.00	40.00	24.00
31	Frank Robinson	35.00	17.50	10.50
32	Pete Runnels	10.00	5.00	3.00
33	Woodie Held	10.00	5.00	3.00
Panel 12		60.00	30.00	18.00
34	Norm Larker	10.00	5.00	3.00
35	Luis Aparicio	20.00	10.00	6.00
36	Bill Tuttle	10.00	5.00	3.00

1962 Bazooka

In 1962, Bazooka increased the size of its set to 45 full-color cards. The set is unnumbered and was printed in panels of three on the bottoms of bubble gum boxes. Individual cards measure 1-13/16" x 2-3/4" in size, with panels at 2-3/4" x 5-1/2". In the checklist that follows the cards have been numbered alphabetically, using the name of the player who appears on the left end of the panel. Panel #s 1, 11 and 15 were issued in much shorter supply and command a higher price.

		NM	EX	VG
Complete Panel Set (15):		5300.	2600.	1500.
Complete Singles Set (45):		3375.	1600.	1000.
Common Player:		11.00	5.50	3.25
Panel 1		1150.	580.00	348.00
(1)	Bob Allison	145.00	72.00	43.00
(2)	Ed Mathews	400.00	200.00	120.00
(3)	Vada Pinson	175.00	87.00	52.00
Panel 2		90.00	45.00	27.00
(4)	Earl Battey	11.00	5.50	3.25
(5)	Warren Spahn	35.00	17.50	10.50
(6)	Lee Thomas	11.00	5.50	3.25
Panel 3		100.00	50.00	30.00
(7)	Orlando Cepeda	35.00	17.50	10.50
(8)	Woodie Held	11.00	5.50	3.25
(9)	Bob Aspromonte	11.00	5.50	3.25
Panel 4		275.00	135.00	82.00
(10)	Dick Howser	11.00	5.50	3.25
(11)	Roberto Clemente	115.00	57.00	34.00
(12)	Al Kaline	50.00	25.00	15.00
Panel 5		175.00	85.00	50.00
(13)	Joey Jay	11.00	5.50	3.25
(14)	Roger Maris	85.00	42.00	25.00
(15)	Frank Howard	14.00	7.00	4.25
Panel 6		170.00	85.00	50.00
(16)	Sandy Koufax	85.00	42.00	25.00
(17)	Jim Gentile	11.00	5.50	3.25
(18)	Johnny Callison	11.00	5.50	3.25
Panel 7		55.00	27.50	16.50
(19)	Jim Landis	11.00	5.50	3.25
(20)	Ken Boyer	14.00	7.00	4.25
(21)	Chuck Schilling	11.00	5.50	3.25
Panel 8		400.00	200.00	120.00
(22)	Art Mahaffey	11.00	5.50	3.25
(23)	Mickey Mantle	300.00	150.00	90.00
(24)	Dick Stuart	11.00	5.50	3.25
Panel 9		120.00	60.00	35.00
(25)	Ken McBride	11.00	5.50	3.25
(26)	Frank Robinson	40.00	20.00	12.00
(27)	Gil Hodges	25.00	12.50	7.50
Panel 10		225.00	110.00	65.00
(28)	Milt Pappas	11.00	5.50	3.25
(29)	Hank Aaron	115.00	57.00	34.00
(30)	Luis Aparicio	24.00	12.00	7.25
Panel 11		1450.	725.00	435.00
(31)	Johnny Romano	175.00	87.00	52.00
(32)	Ernie Banks	575.00	287.00	172.00
(33)	Norm Siebern	175.00	87.00	52.00
Panel 12		80.00	40.00	24.00
(34)	Ron Santo	17.50	8.75	5.25
(35)	Norm Cash	17.50	8.75	5.25
(36)	Jim Piersall	14.50	7.25	4.25
Panel 13		220.00	110.00	66.00
(37)	Don Schwall	11.00	5.50	3.25
(38)	Willie Mays	115.00	57.00	34.00
(39)	Norm Larker	11.00	5.50	3.25
Panel 14		145.00	72.00	43.00
(40)	Bill White	11.00	5.50	3.25
(41)	Whitey Ford	55.00	27.00	16.50
(42)	Rocky Colavito	25.00	12.50	7.50
Panel 15		1100.	550.00	325.00
(43)	Don Zimmer	200.00	100.00	60.00
(44)	Harmon Killebrew	325.00	162.00	97.00
(45)	Gene Woodling	175.00	87.00	52.00

1963 Bazooka

The 1963 Bazooka issue reverted to a 12-panel, 36-card set, but saw a change in the size of the cards. Individual cards measure 1-9/16" x 2-1/2", while panels are 2-1/2" x 4-11/16". The card design was altered also, with the player's name, team and position situated in a white oval at the bottom of the card. The full-color, blank-backed set is numbered 1-36. Five Bazooka All-Time Greats cards were inserted in each box of bubble gum.

		NM	EX	VG
Complete Panel Set (12):		1500.	750.00	450.00
Complete Singles Set (36):		1000.	500.00	300.00
Common Player:		6.75	3.50	2.00
Panel 1		480.00	240.00	144.00
1	(Mickey Mantle) (batting righty)	290.00	145.00	87.00
2	Bob Rodgers	7.00	3.50	2.00
3	Ernie Banks	48.00	24.00	14.50
Panel 2		76.00	38.00	23.00
4	Norm Siebern	7.00	3.50	2.00
5	Warren Spahn (portrait)	29.00	14.50	8.75
6	Bill Mazeroski	14.50	7.25	4.25
Panel 3		172.00	86.00	52.00
7	Harmon Killebrew (batting)	30.00	15.00	9.00
8	Dick Farrell (portrait)	7.00	3.50	2.00
9	Hank Aaron (glove in front)	75.00	37.00	22.00
Panel 4		136.00	68.00	41.00
10	Dick Donovan	7.00	3.50	2.00
11	Jim Gentile (batting)	7.00	3.50	2.00
12	Willie Mays (bat in front)	75.00	37.00	22.00
Panel 5		136.00	68.00	41.00
13	Camilo Pascual (hands at waist)	7.00	3.50	2.00
14	Roberto Clemente (portrait)	75.00	37.00	22.00
15	Johnny Callison (wearing pinstripe uniform)	7.00	3.50	2.00
Panel 6		180.00	90.00	54.00
16	Carl Yastrzemski (kneeling)	72.00	36.00	22.00
17	Don Drysdale	40.00	20.00	12.00
18	Johnny Romano (portrait)	7.00	3.50	2.00
Panel 7		32.00	16.00	9.50
19	Al Jackson	7.00	3.50	2.00
20	Ralph Terry	7.00	3.50	2.00
21	Bill Monbouquette	7.00	3.50	2.00
Panel 8		150.00	75.00	45.00
22	Orlando Cepeda	30.00	15.00	9.00
23	Stan Musial	48.00	24.00	14.50
24	Floyd Robinson (no pinstripes on uniform)	7.00	3.50	2.00
Panel 9		44.00	22.00	13.00
25	Chuck Hinton (batting)	7.00	3.50	2.00
26	Bob Purkey	7.00	3.50	2.00
27	Ken Hubbs	14.50	7.25	4.25
Panel 10		72.00	36.00	22.00
28	Bill White	7.50	3.75	2.25
29	Ray Herbert	7.00	3.50	2.00
30	Brooks Robinson (glove in front)	32.00	16.00	9.50

		NM	EX	VG
Panel 11		110.00	55.00	33.00
31	Frank Robinson (batting, uniforn number doesn't show)	48.00	24.00	14.50
32	Lee Thomas	7.00	3.50	2.00
33	Rocky Colavito (Detroit)	17.50	8.75	5.25
Panel 12		72.00	36.00	22.00
34	Al Kaline (kneeling)	32.00	16.00	9.50
35	Art Mahaffey	7.00	3.50	2.00
36	Tommy Davis (batting follow-through)	7.50	3.75	2.25

1963 Bazooka All-Time Greats

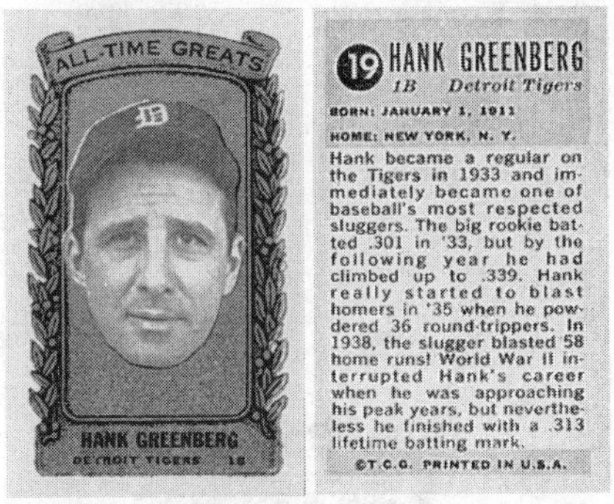

Consisting of 41 cards, the Bazooka All-Time Greats set was issued as inserts (5 per box) in boxes of Bazooka bubble gum. A black-and-white portrait photo of the player is placed inside a gold plaque within a white border. Card backs contain a brief biography of the player. The numbered cards measure 1-9/16" x 2-1/2" size. Cards can be found with silver fronts instead of gold; the silver are worth double the values listed.

		NM	EX	VG
Complete Set (41):		400.00	200.00	120.00
Common Player:		8.50	4.25	2.50
1	Joe Tinker	8.50	4.25	2.50
2	Harry Heilmann	8.50	4.25	2.50
3	Jack Chesbro	8.50	4.25	2.50
4	Christy Mathewson	15.00	7.50	4.50
5	Herb Pennock	8.50	4.25	2.50
6	Cy Young	13.00	6.50	4.00
7	Ed Walsh	8.50	4.25	2.50
8	Nap Lajoie	9.00	4.50	2.75
9	Eddie Plank	8.50	4.25	2.50
10	Honus Wagner	15.00	7.50	4.50
11	Chief Bender	8.50	4.25	2.50
12	Walter Johnson	15.00	7.50	4.50
13	Three-Fingered Brown	8.50	4.25	2.50
14	Rabbit Maranville	8.50	4.25	2.50
15	Lou Gehrig	55.00	27.00	16.50
16	Ban Johnson	8.50	4.25	2.50
17	Babe Ruth	80.00	40.00	24.00
18	Connie Mack	8.50	4.25	2.50
19	Hank Greenberg	11.00	5.50	3.25
20	John McGraw	8.50	4.25	2.50
21	Johnny Evers	8.50	4.25	2.50
22	Al Simmons	8.50	4.25	2.50
23	Jimmy Collins	8.50	4.25	2.50
24	Tris Speaker	9.00	4.50	2.75
25	Frank Chance	8.50	4.25	2.50
26	Fred Clarke	8.50	4.25	2.50
27	Wilbert Robinson	8.50	4.25	2.50
28	Dazzy Vance	8.50	4.25	2.50
29	Grover Alexander	10.00	5.00	3.00
30	Kenesaw Landis	8.50	4.25	2.50
31	Willie Keeler	8.50	4.25	2.50
32	Rogers Hornsby	10.00	5.00	3.00
33	Hugh Duffy	8.50	4.25	2.50
34	Mickey Cochrane	8.50	4.25	2.50
35	Ty Cobb	50.00	25.00	15.00
36	Mel Ott	8.50	4.25	2.50
37	Clark Griffith	8.50	4.25	2.50
38	Ted Lyons	8.50	4.25	2.50
39	Cap Anson	8.50	4.25	2.50
40	Bill Dickey	8.50	4.25	2.50
41	Eddie Collins	8.50	4.25	2.50

1964 Bazooka

The 1964 Bazooka set is identical in design and size to the previous year's effort. However, different photographs were used from year to year. The 1964 set consists of 36 full-color, blank-backed cards numbered 1 through 36. Individual cards measure 1-9/16" x 2-1/2"; three-card panels measure 2-1/2" x 4-11/16". Sheets of ten full-color baseball stamps were inserted in each box of bubble gum.

		NM	EX	VG
Complete Panel Set (12):		1000.	500.00	300.00
Complete Singles Set (36):		700.00	350.00	200.00
Common Player:		5.25	2.75	1.25
Panel 1		240.00	120.00	72.00
1	Mickey Mantle (portrait)	155.00	77.00	46.00
2	Dick Groat	7.50	3.75	2.25
3	Steve Barber	5.25	2.75	1.50
Panel 2		55.00	27.00	16.00
4	Ken McBride	5.25	2.75	1.50
5	Warren Spahn (head to waist shot)	26.00	13.00	7.75
6	Bob Friend	5.25	2.75	1.50
Panel 3		132.00	66.00	40.00
7	Harmon Killebrew (portrait)	24.00	12.00	7.25
8	Dick Farrell (hands above head)	5.25	2.75	1.50
9	Hank Aaron (glove to left)	60.00	30.00	18.00
Panel 4		100.00	50.00	30.00
10	Rich Rollins	5.25	2.75	1.50
11	Jim Gentile (portrait)	5.25	2.75	1.50
12	Willie Mays (looking to left)	60.00	30.00	18.00
Panel 5		100.00	50.00	30.00
13	Camilo Pascual (pitching follow-through)	5.25	2.75	1.50
14	Roberto Clemente (throwing)	60.00	30.00	18.00
15	Johnny Callison (batting, screen showing)	5.25	2.75	1.50
Panel 6		95.00	47.00	30.00
16	Carl Yastrzemski (batting)	40.00	20.00	12.00
17	Billy Williams (kneeling)	18.00	9.00	5.50
18	Johnny Romano (batting)	5.25	2.75	1.50
Panel 7		68.00	34.00	20.00
19	Jim Maloney	5.25	2.75	1.50
20	Norm Cash	12.00	6.00	3.50
21	Willie McCovey	28.00	14.00	8.50
Panel 8		24.00	12.00	7.25
22	Jim Fregosi (batting)	5.25	2.75	1.50
23	George Altman	5.25	2.75	1.50
24	Floyd Robinson (wearing pinstripe uniform)	5.25	2.75	1.50
Panel 9		24.00	12.00	7.25
25	Chuck Hinton (portrait)	5.25	2.75	1.50
26	Ron Hunt (batting)	6.50	3.25	2.00
27	Gary Peters (pitching)	5.25	2.75	1.50
Panel 10		68.00	34.00	20.00
28	Dick Ellsworth	5.25	2.75	1.50
29	Elston Howard (holding bat)	14.50	7.25	4.25
30	Brooks Robinson (kneeling with glove)	26.00	13.00	7.75
Panel 11		135.00	67.00	40.00
31	Frank Robinson (uniform number shows)	32.00	16.00	9.50
32	Sandy Koufax (glove in front)	48.00	24.00	14.50
33	Rocky Colavito (Kansas City)	12.00	6.00	3.50
Panel 12		60.00	30.00	18.00
34	Al Kaline (holding two bats)	24.00	12.00	7.25
35	Ken Boyer (head to waist shot)	8.00	4.00	2.50
36	Tommy Davis (batting)	8.00	4.00	2.50

1964 Bazooka Stamps

Occasionally mislabeled "Topps Stamps," the 1964 Bazooka stamps were produced by Topps, but found only in boxes of Bazooka bubble gum. Issued in sheets of ten, 100 color stamps make up the set. Each stamp measures 1" x 1-1/2" in size. While the stamps are not individually numbered, the sheets are numbered one through ten. The stamps are commonly found as complete sheets of ten and are priced in that fashion in the checklist that follows.

		NM	EX	VG
Complete Sheet Set (10x10):		600.00	300.00	180.00
Common Sheet:		25.00	12.50	7.50
Common Stamp:		3.00	1.50	.90
1	Max Alvis, Ed Charles, Dick Ellsworth, Jimmie Hall, Frank Malzone, Milt Pappas, Vada Pinson, Tony Taylor, Pete Ward, Bill White	25.00	12.50	7.50
2	Bob Aspromonte, Larry Jackson, Willie Mays, Al McBean, Bill Monbouquette, Bobby Richardson, Floyd Robinson, Frank Robinson, Norm Siebern, Don Zimmer	60.00	30.00	18.00
3	Ernie Banks, Roberto Clemente, Curt Flood, Jesse Gonder, Woody Held, Don Lock, Dave Nicholson, Joe Pepitone, Brooks Robinson, Carl Yastrzemski	90.00	45.00	27.00
4	Hank Aguirre, Jim Grant, Harmon Killebrew, Jim Maloney, Juan Marichal, Bill Mazeroski, Juan Pizarro, Boog Powell, Ed Roebuck, Ron Santo	60.00	30.00	18.00
5	Jim Bouton, Norm Cash, Orlando Cepeda, Tommy Harper, Chuck Hinton, Albie Pearson, Ron Perranoski, Dick Radatz, Johnny Romano, Carl Willey	35.00	17.50	10.50
6	Steve Barber, Jim Fregosi, Tony Gonzalez, Mickey Mantle, Jim O'Toole, Gary Peters, Rich Rollins, Warren Spahn, Dick Stuart, Joe Torre	125.00	62.00	37.00
7	Felipe Alou, George Altman, Ken Boyer, Rocky Colavito, Jim Davenport, Tommy Davis, Bill Freehan, Bob Friend, Ken Johnson, Billy Moran	30.00	15.00	9.00
8	Earl Battey, Ernie Broglio, Johnny Callison, Donn Clendenon, Don Drysdale, Jim Gentile, Elston Howard, Claude Osteen, Bill Williams, Hal Woodeshick	40.00	20.00	12.00
9	Hank Aaron, Jack Baldschun, Wayne Causey, Moe Drabowsky, Dick Groat, Frank Howard, Al Jackson, Jerry Lumpe, Ken McBride, Rusty Staub	50.00	25.00	15.00
10	Vic Davalillo, Dick Farrell, Ron Hunt, Al Kaline, Sandy Koufax, Eddie Mathews, Willie McCovey, Camilo Pascual, Lee Thomas	65.00	32.00	19.50

1965 Bazooka

The 1965 Bazooka set is identical to the 1963 and 1964 sets. Different players were added each year and different photographs were used for those players being included again. Individual cards cut from the boxes measure 1-9/16" x 2-1/2". Complete three-card panels measure 2-1/2" x 4-11/16". Thirty-six full-color, blank-backed, numbered cards comprise the set.

		NM	EX	VG
Complete Panel Set (12):		1000.	500.00	300.00
Complete Singles Set (36):		800.00	400.00	240.00
Common Player:		7.00	3.50	2.00
Panel 1		300.00	150.00	90.00
200.00 100.00 60.00				
1	Mickey Mantle (batting lefty)			
2	Larry Jackson	7.00	3.50	2.00
3	Chuck Hinton	7.00	3.50	2.00
Panel 2		34.00	17.00	10.00
4	Tony Oliva	10.00	5.00	3.00
5	Dean Chance	7.00	3.50	2.00
6	Jim O'Toole	7.00	3.50	2.00
Panel 3		110.00	55.00	35.00
7	Harmon Killebrew (bat on shoulder)	24.00	12.00	7.25
8	Pete Ward	7.00	3.50	2.00
9	Hank Aaron (batting)	48.00	24.00	14.50
Panel 4		95.00	47.00	29.00
10	Dick Radatz	7.00	3.50	2.00
11	Boog Powell	9.00	4.50	2.75

12	Willie Mays (looking down)	48.00	24.00	14.50
Panel 5		90.00	45.00	26.00
13	Bob Veale	7.00	3.50	2.00
14	Roberto Clemente (batting)	48.00	24.00	14.50
15	Johnny Callison (batting, no screen in background)	7.00	3.50	2.00
Panel 6		52.00	26.00	15.00
16	Joe Torre	10.00	5.00	3.00
17	Billy Williams (batting)	19.00	9.50	5.75
18	Bob Chance	7.00	3.50	2.00
Panel 7		40.00	20.00	12.00
19	Bob Aspromonte	7.00	3.50	2.00
20	Joe Christopher	7.00	3.50	2.00
21	Jim Bunning	17.50	8.75	5.25
Panel 8		75.00	37.00	22.00
22	Jim Fregosi (portrait)	7.50	3.75	2.25
23	Bob Gibson	24.00	12.00	7.25
24	Juan Marichal	19.00	9.50	5.75
Panel 9		30.00	15.00	9.00
25	Dave Wickersham	7.00	3.50	2.00
26	Ron Hunt (throwing)	7.50	3.75	2.25
27	Gary Peters (portrait)	7.00	3.50	2.00
Panel 10		72.00	36.00	22.00
28	Ron Santo	10.00	5.00	3.00
29	Elston Howard (with glove)	12.00	6.00	3.50
30	Brooks Robinson (portrait)	30.00	15.00	9.00
Panel 11		125.00	62.00	37.00
31	Frank Robinson (portrait)	30.00	15.00	9.00
32	Sandy Koufax (hands over head)	45.00	22.00	13.50
33	Rocky Colavito (Cleveland)	14.00	7.00	4.25
Panel 12		72.00	36.00	22.00
34	Al Kaline (portrait)	30.00	15.00	9.00
35	Ken Boyer (portrait)	10.00	5.00	3.00
36	Tommy Davis (fielding)	10.00	5.00	3.00

1966 Bazooka

The 1966 Bazooka set was increased to 48 cards. Printed in panels of three on the bottoms of boxes of bubble gum, the full-color cards are blank-backed and numbered. Individual cards measure 1-9/16" x 2-1/2", whereas panels measure 2-1/2" x 4-11/16".

		NM	EX	VG
Complete Panel Set (16):		1450.	725.00	425.00
Complete Singles Set (48):		1025.	500.00	300.00
Common Player:		6.00	3.00	1.75
Panel 1		105.00	50.00	30.00
1	Sandy Koufax	60.00	30.00	18.00
2	Willie Horton	6.00	3.00	1.75
3	Frank Howard	8.00	4.00	2.50
Panel 2		52.00	26.00	15.00
4	Richie Allen	9.50	4.75	2.75
5	Mel Stottlemyre	7.50	3.75	2.25
6	Tony Conigliaro	20.00	10.00	6.00
Panel 3		325.00	160.00	97.00
7	Mickey Mantle	240.00	120.00	72.00
8	Leon Wagner	6.00	3.00	1.75
9	Ed Kranepool	6.00	3.00	1.75
Panel 4		85.00	42.50	25.00
10	Juan Marichal	24.00	12.00	7.25
11	Harmon Killebrew	30.00	15.00	9.00
12	Johnny Callison	6.00	3.00	1.75
Panel 5		65.00	32.50	20.00
13	Roy McMillan	6.00	3.00	1.75
14	Willie McCovey	30.00	15.00	9.00
15	Rocky Colavito	12.00	6.00	3.50
Panel 6		110.00	55.00	32.50
16	Willie Mays	60.00	30.00	18.00
17	Sam McDowell	8.00	4.00	2.50
18	Vern Law	6.00	3.00	1.75
Panel 7		60.00	30.00	18.00
19	Jim Fregosi	6.00	3.00	1.75
20	Ron Fairly	6.00	3.00	1.75
21	Bob Gibson	30.00	15.00	9.00
Panel 8		90.00	45.00	27.00
22	Carl Yastrzemski	48.00	24.00	14.50
23	Bill White	8.00	4.00	2.50
24	Bob Aspromonte	6.00	3.00	1.75
Panel 9		100.00	50.00	30.00
25	Dean Chance (California)	6.00	3.00	1.75
26	Roberto Clemente	60.00	30.00	18.00
27	Tony Cloninger	6.00	3.00	1.75
Panel 10		100.00	50.00	30.00
28	Curt Blefary	6.00	3.00	1.75
29	Milt Pappas	6.00	3.00	1.75
30	Hank Aaron	60.00	30.00	18.00
Panel 11		95.00	47.00	28.00
31	Jim Bunning	22.00	11.00	6.50
32	Frank Robinson (portrait)	36.00	18.00	11.00
33	Bill Skowron	9.50	4.75	2.75
Panel 12		70.00	35.00	22.00
34	Brooks Robinson	36.00	18.00	11.00
35	Jim Wynn	6.00	3.00	1.75
36	Joe Torre	8.00	4.00	2.50
Panel 13		150.00	75.00	45.00
37	Jim Grant	6.00	3.00	1.75
38	Pete Rose	90.00	45.00	27.00
39	Ron Santo	12.00	6.00	3.50
Panel 14		72.00	36.00	22.00
40	Tom Tresh	9.50	4.75	2.75
41	Tony Oliva	12.00	6.00	3.50
42	Don Drysdale	30.00	15.00	9.00
Panel 15		28.00	14.00	8.50
43	Pete Richert	6.00	3.00	1.75
44	Bert Campaneris	8.00	4.00	2.50
45	Jim Maloney	6.00	3.00	1.75
Panel 16		95.00	47.00	28.00
46	Al Kaline	36.00	18.00	11.00
47	Eddie Fisher	6.00	3.00	1.75
48	Billy Williams	24.00	12.00	7.25

1967 Bazooka

The 1967 Bazooka set is identical in design to the sets of 1964-1966. Printed in panels of three on the bottoms of bubble gum boxes, the set is made up of 48 full-color, blank-backed, numbered cards. Individual cards measure 1-9/16" x 2-1/2"; complete panels measure 2-1/2" x 4-11/16".

		NM	EX	VG
Complete Panel Set (16):		1375.	675.00	400.00
Complete Singles Set (48):		950.00	475.00	275.00
Common Player:		6.00	3.00	1.75
Panel 1		30.00	15.00	9.00
1	Rick Reichardt	6.00	3.00	1.75
2	Tommy Agee	6.00	3.00	1.75
3	Frank Howard	8.00	4.00	2.50
Panel 2		50.00	25.00	15.00
4	Richie Allen	9.50	4.75	2.75
5	Mel Stottlemyre	6.00	3.00	1.75
6	Tony Conigliaro	20.00	10.00	6.00
Panel 3		350.00	175.00	105.00
7	Mickey Mantle	240.00	120.00	72.00
8	Leon Wagner	6.00	3.00	1.75
9	Gary Peters	6.00	3.00	1.75
Panel 4		85.00	42.50	25.00
10	Juan Marichal	24.00	12.00	7.25
11	Harmon Killebrew	30.00	15.00	9.00
12	Johnny Callison	6.00	3.00	1.75
Panel 5		80.00	40.00	24.00
13	Denny McLain	14.50	7.25	4.25
14	Willie McCovey	30.00	15.00	9.00
15	Rocky Colavito	12.00	6.00	3.50
Panel 6		95.00	47.50	29.00
16	Willie Mays	48.00	24.00	14.50
17	Sam McDowell	6.00	3.00	1.75
18	Jim Kaat	13.00	6.50	4.00
Panel 7		60.00	30.00	18.00
19	Jim Fregosi	6.00	3.00	1.75
20	Ron Fairly	6.00	3.00	1.75
21	Bob Gibson	30.00	15.00	9.00
Panel 8		80.00	40.00	24.00
22	Carl Yastrzemski	42.00	21.00	12.50
23	Bill White	8.00	4.00	2.50
24	Bob Aspromonte	6.00	3.00	1.75
Panel 9		85.00	42.50	25.00
25	Dean Chance (Minnesota)	6.00	3.00	1.75
26	Roberto Clemente	48.00	24.00	14.50
27	Tony Cloninger	6.00	3.00	1.75
Panel 10		85.00	42.50	25.00
28	Curt Blefary	6.00	3.00	1.75
29	Phil Regan	6.00	3.00	1.75
30	Hank Aaron	48.00	24.00	14.50
Panel 11		85.00	42.00	25.00
31	Jim Bunning	21.00	10.50	6.25
32	Frank Robinson (batting)	30.00	15.00	9.00
33	Ken Boyer	9.50	4.75	2.75
Panel 12		75.00	37.50	22.00
34	Brooks Robinson	36.00	18.00	11.00
35	Jim Wynn	6.00	3.00	1.75
36	Joe Torre	8.00	4.00	2.50
Panel 13		130.00	65.00	40.00
37	Tommy Davis	6.00	3.00	1.75
38	Pete Rose	72.00	36.00	22.00
39	Ron Santo	12.00	6.00	3.50
Panel 14		75.00	37.00	22.00
40	Tom Tresh	9.50	4.75	2.75
41	Tony Oliva	12.00	6.00	3.50
42	Don Drysdale	30.00	15.00	9.00
Panel 15		26.00	13.00	8.00
43	Pete Richert	6.00	3.00	1.75
44	Bert Campaneris	6.00	3.00	1.75
45	Jim Maloney	6.00	3.00	1.75
Panel 16		95.00	47.50	29.00
46	Al Kaline	36.00	18.00	11.00
47	Matty Alou	6.00	3.00	1.75
48	Billy Williams	24.00	12.00	7.25

1968 Bazooka

The design of the 1968 Bazooka set is radically different from previous years. The player cards are situated on the sides of the boxes with the box back containing "Tipps From The Topps." Four unnumbered player cards, measuring 1-1/4" x 3-1/8", are featured on each box. The box back includes a small player photo plus illustrated tips on various aspects of the game of baseball. Boxes are numbered 1-15 on the top panels. There are 56 different player cards in the set, with four of the cards (Agee, Drysdale, Rose, Santo) being used twice to round out the set of 15 boxes.

		NM	EX	VG
Complete Box Set (15):		2100.	1000.	625.00
Complete Singles Set (60):		1400.	700.00	425.00
Common Player:		6.00	3.00	1.75
1	Maury Wills (Bunting)	24.00	12.00	7.25
(1)	Clete Boyer	8.00	4.00	2.50
(2)	Paul Casanova	6.00	3.00	1.75
(3)	Al Kaline	36.00	18.00	11.00
(4)	Tom Seaver	85.00	42.00	25.00
Box 1		230.00	115.00	70.00
1	Maury Wills (bunting)	24.00	12.00	725.00
(1)	Clete Boyer	8.00	4.00	2.50
(2)	Paul Casanova	6.00	3.00	1.75
(3)	Al Kaline	40.00	20.00	12.00
(4)	Tom Seaver	80.00	40.00	24.00
Box 2		130.00	65.00	40.00
2	Carl Yastrzemski (Batting)	48.00	24.00	14.50
(5)	Matty Alou	6.00	3.00	1.75
(6)	Bill Freehan	6.00	3.00	1.75
(7)	Catfish Hunter	24.00	12.00	7.25
(8)	Jim Lefebvre	6.00	3.00	1.75
Box 3		110.00	55.00	33.00
3	Bert Campaneris (Stealing bases)	18.00	9.00	5.50
(9)	Bobby Knoop	6.00	3.00	1.75
(10)	Tim McCarver	14.50	7.25	4.25
(11)	Frank Robinson	30.00	15.00	9.00
(12)	Bob Veale	6.00	3.00	1.75
Box 4		95.00	47.50	28.00
4	Maury Wills (Sliding)	24.00	12.00	7.25
(13)	Joe Azcue	6.00	3.00	1.75
(14)	Tony Conigliaro	18.00	9.00	5.50
(15)	Ken Holtzman	6.00	3.00	1.75
(16)	Bill White	9.50	4.75	2.75
Box 5		155.00	77.00	47.00
5	Julian Javier (The Double Play)	18.00	9.00	5.50
(17)	Hank Aaron	48.00	24.00	14.50
(18)	Juan Marichal	24.00	12.00	7.25
(19)	Joe Pepitone	9.50	4.75	2.75
(20)	Rico Petrocelli	9.50	4.75	2.75
Box 6		200.00	100.00	60.00
6	Orlando Cepeda (Playing 1st Base)	35.00	17.50	10.50
(21)	Tommie Agee	6.00	3.00	1.75
(22a)	Don Drysdale (no period after "A" in team name)	30.00	15.00	9.00
(22b)	Don Drysdale (period after "A")	30.00	15.00	9.00
(23)	Pete Rose	60.00	30.00	18.00
(24)	Ron Santo	9.50	4.75	2.75
Box 7		110.00	55.00	33.00
7	Bill Mazeroski (Playing 2nd Base)	24.00	12.00	7.25
(25)	Jim Bunning	21.00	10.50	6.25
(26)	Frank Howard	8.00	4.00	2.50
(27)	John Roseboro	11.00	5.50	3.25
(28)	George Scott	11.00	5.50	3.25
Box 8		120.00	60.00	35.00
8	Brooks Robinson (Playing 3rd Base)	42.00	21.00	12.50
(29)	Tony Gonzalez	6.00	3.00	1.75
(30)	Willie Horton	6.00	3.00	1.75
(31)	Harmon Killebrew	30.00	15.00	9.00
(32)	Jim McGlothlin	6.00	3.00	1.75
Box 9		110.00	55.00	32.00
9	Jim Fregosi (Playing Shortstop)	18.00	9.00	5.50
(33)	Max Alvis	6.00	3.00	1.75
(34)	Bob Gibson	24.00	12.00	7.25
(35)	Tony Oliva	12.00	6.00	3.50

		NM	EX	VG
(36)	Vada Pinson	12.00	6.00	3.50
Box 10		90.00	45.00	27.00
10	Joe Torre (Catching)	22.00	11.00	6.50
(37)	Dean Chance	6.00	3.00	1.75
(38)	Tommy Davis	6.00	3.00	1.75
(39)	Ferguson Jenkins	24.00	12.00	7.25
(40)	Rick Monday	6.00	3.00	1.75
Box 11		325.00	165.00	99.00
11	Jim Lonborg (Pitching)	18.00	9.00	5.50
(41)	Curt Flood	9.00	4.50	2.75
(42)	Joel Horlen	6.00	3.00	1.75
(43)	Mickey Mantle	180.00	90.00	54.00
(44)	Jim Wynn	6.00	3.00	1.75
Box 12		140.00	70.00	45.00
12	Mike McCormick (Fielding the Pitcher's Position)	18.00	9.00	5.50
(45)	Roberto Clemente	48.00	24.00	14.50
(46)	Al Downing	6.00	3.00	1.75
(47)	Don Mincher	6.00	3.00	1.75
(48)	Tony Perez	24.00	12.00	7.25
Box 13		135.00	65.00	40.00
13	Frank Crosetti (Coaching)	18.00	9.00	5.50
(49)	Rod Carew	35.00	17.50	10.50
(50)	Willie McCovey	30.00	15.00	9.00
(51)	Ron Swoboda	6.00	3.00	1.75
(52)	Earl Wilson	6.00	3.00	1.75
Box 14		135.00	65.00	40.00
14	Willie Mays (Playing the Outfield)	42.00	21.00	12.50
(53)	Richie Allen	9.50	4.75	2.75
(54)	Gary Peters	6.00	3.00	1.75
(55)	Rusty Staub	12.00	6.00	3.50
(56)	Billy Williams	24.00	12.00	7.25
Box 15		200.00	100.00	60.00
15	Lou Brock (Base Running)	30.00	15.00	9.00
(57)	Tommie Agee	6.00	3.00	1.75
(58)	Don Drysdale	30.00	15.00	9.00
(59)	Pete Rose	60.00	30.00	18.00
(60)	Ron Santo	9.50	4.75	2.75

1969-70 Bazooka

Issued over a two-year span, the 1969-70 Bazooka set utilized the box bottom and sides. The bottom, entitled "Baseball Extra," features an historic event in baseball; the 3" x 6-1/4" panels are numbered 1-12. Two "All-Time Great" cards were located on each side of the box. These cards are not numbered and have no distinct borders; individual cards measure 1-1/4" x 3-1/8". The prices in the checklist that follows are for complete boxes only. Cards/panels cut from the boxes have a greatly reduced value - 25% of the complete box prices for all cut pieces.

		NM	EX	VG
Complete Set (12):		300.00	150.00	90.00
Common Box:		30.00	15.00	9.00
1	No-Hit Duel By Toney And Vaughn (Mordecai Brown, Ty Cobb, Willie Keeler, Eddie Plank)	28.00	14.00	8.50
2	Alexander Conquers Yanks (Rogers Hornsby, Ban Johnson, Walter Johnson, Al Simmons)	24.00	12.00	7.25
3	Yanks Lazzeri Sets A.L. Hit Record (Hugh Duffy, Lou Gehrig, Tris Speaker, Joe Tinker)	28.00	14.00	8.50
4	Home Run Almost Hit Out Of Stadium (Grover Alexander, Chief Bender, Christy Mathewson, Cy Young)	24.00	12.00	7.25
5	Four Consecutive Homers By Gehrig (Frank Chance, Mickey Cochrane, John McGraw, Babe Ruth)	42.00	21.00	12.50
6	No-Hit Game By Walter Johnson (Johnny Evers, Walter Johnson, John McGraw, Cy Young)	24.00	12.00	7.25
7	Twelve RBI's By Bottomley (Ty Cobb, Eddie Collins, Johnny Evers, Lou Gehrig)	36.00	18.00	11.00
8	Ty Ties Record (Mickey Cochrane, Eddie Collins, Mel Ott, Honus Wagner)	24.00	12.00	7.25
9	Babe Ruth Hits 3 HRs In Game (Cap Anson, Jack Chesbro, Al Simmons, Tris Speaker)	36.00	18.00	11.00
10	Calls Shot In Series Game (Nap Lajoie, Connie Mack, Rabbit Maranville, Ed Walsh)	36.00	18.00	11.00
11	Ruth's 60th HR Sets New Record (Frank Chance, Nap Lajoie, Mel Ott, Joe Tinker)	36.00	18.00	11.00
12	Double Shutout By Ed Reulbach (Rogers Hornsby, Rabbit Maranville, Christy Mathewson, Honus Wagner)	24.00	12.00	7.25

1971 Bazooka Numbered Set

The 1971 Bazooka numbered set is a proof set produced by the company after the unnumbered set was released. The set is comprised of 48 cards as opposed to the 36 cards which make up the unnumbered set. Issued in panels of three, the 12 cards not found in the unnumbered set are #1-3, 13-15, 34-36 and 43-45. All other cards are identical to those found in the unnumbered set. The cards, which measure 2" x 2-5/8", contain full-color photos and are blank-backed.

		NM	EX	VG
Complete Panel Set (16):		1025.	500.00	300.00
Complete Singles Set (48):		825.00	400.00	240.00
Common Player:		6.00	3.00	1.75
Panel 1		100.00	50.00	30.00
1	Tim McCarver	10.00	5.00	3.00
2	Frank Robinson	54.00	27.00	16.00
3	Bill Mazeroski	18.00	9.00	5.50
Panel 2		85.00	42.50	25.00
4	Willie McCovey	30.00	15.00	9.00
5	Carl Yastrzemski	32.00	16.00	9.50
6	Clyde Wright	6.00	3.00	1.75
Panel 3		44.00	22.00	13.00
7	Jim Merritt	6.00	3.00	1.75
8	Luis Aparicio	21.00	10.50	6.25
9	Bobby Murcer	8.50	4.25	2.50
Panel 4		27.00	13.50	8.25
10	Rico Petrocelli	6.00	3.00	1.75
11	Sam McDowell	6.00	3.00	1.75
12	Cito Gaston	8.00	4.00	2.50
Panel 5		72.00	36.00	22.00
13	Ferguson Jenkins	24.00	12.00	7.25
14	Al Kaline	30.00	15.00	9.00
15	Ken Harrelson	6.00	3.00	1.75
Panel 6		80.00	40.00	24.00
16	Tommie Agee	6.00	3.00	1.75
17	Harmon Killebrew	24.00	12.00	7.25
18	Reggie Jackson	36.00	18.00	11.00
Panel 7		48.00	24.00	14.50
19	Juan Marichal	24.00	12.00	7.25
20	Frank Howard	8.00	4.00	2.50
21	Bill Melton	6.00	3.00	1.75
Panel 8		145.00	72.00	43.00
22	Brooks Robinson	54.00	27.00	16.00
23	Hank Aaron	60.00	30.00	18.00
24	Larry Dierker	6.00	3.00	1.75
Panel 9		45.00	22.50	13.50
25	Jim Fregosi	6.00	3.00	1.75
26	Billy Williams	24.00	12.00	7.25
27	Dave McNally	6.00	3.00	1.75
Panel 10		50.00	25.00	15.00
28	Rico Carty	6.00	3.00	1.75
29	Johnny Bench	30.00	15.00	9.00
30	Tommy Harper	6.00	3.00	1.75
Panel 11		110.00	55.00	30.00
31	Bert Campaneris	6.00	3.00	1.75
32	Pete Rose	42.00	21.00	12.50
33	Orlando Cepeda	25.00	12.50	7.50
Panel 12		68.00	34.00	20.00
34	Maury Wills	10.00	5.00	3.00
35	Tom Seaver	35.00	17.50	10.50
36	Tony Oliva	10.00	5.00	3.00
Panel 13		90.00	45.00	27.00
37	Bill Freehan	6.00	3.00	1.75
38	Roberto Clemente	60.00	30.00	18.00
39	Claude Osteen	6.00	3.00	1.75
Panel 14		50.00	25.00	15.00
40	Rusty Staub	9.50	4.75	2.75
41	Bob Gibson	24.00	12.00	7.25
42	Amos Otis	7.50	3.75	2.25
Panel 15		45.00	22.50	13.50
43	Jim Wynn	6.00	3.00	1.75
44	Rich Allen	15.00	7.50	4.50
45	Tony Conigliaro	15.00	7.50	4.50
Panel 16		110.00	55.00	32.00
46	Randy Hundley	6.00	3.00	1.75
47	Willie Mays	60.00	30.00	18.00
48	Catfish Hunter	24.00	12.00	7.25

1971 Bazooka Unnumbered Set

This Bazooka set was issued in 1971, consisting of 36 full-color, blank-backed, unnumbered cards. Printed in panels of three on the bottoms of bubble gum boxes, individual cards measure 2" x 2-5/8"; complete panels measure 2-5/8" x 5-5/16". In the checklist that follows, the cards have been numbered by panel using the name of the player who appears on the left end of the panel.

		NM	EX	VG
Complete Panel Set (12):		425.00	210.00	125.00
Complete Singles Set (36):		340.00	170.00	100.00
Common Player:		3.00	1.50	.90
Panel 1		55.00	28.00	17.00
(1)	Tommie Agee	3.00	1.50	.90
(2)	Harmon Killebrew	14.50	7.25	4.25
(3)	Reggie Jackson	28.00	14.00	8.50
Panel 2		50.00	25.00	15.50
(4)	Bert Campaneris	3.00	1.50	.90
(5)	Pete Rose	24.00	12.00	7.25
(6)	Orlando Cepeda	12.50	6.25	3.75
Panel 3		36.00	18.00	11.00
(7)	Rico Carty	3.00	1.50	.90
(8)	Johnny Bench	24.00	12.00	7.25
(9)	Tommy Harper	3.00	1.50	.90
Panel 4		45.00	22.00	13.00
(10)	Bill Freehan	3.00	1.50	.90
(11)	Roberto Clemente	30.00	15.00	9.00
(12)	Claude Osteen	3.00	1.50	.90
Panel 5		24.00	12.00	7.25
(13)	Jim Fregosi	3.00	1.50	.90
(14)	Billy Williams	14.50	7.25	4.25
(15)	Dave McNally	3.00	1.50	.90
Panel 6		55.00	28.00	17.00
(16)	Randy Hundley	3.00	1.50	.90
(17)	Willie Mays	30.00	15.00	9.00
(18)	Catfish Hunter	13.00	6.50	4.00
Panel 7		28.00	14.00	8.50
(19)	Juan Marichal	14.50	7.25	4.25
(20)	Frank Howard	5.50	2.75	1.75
(21)	Bill Melton	3.00	1.50	.90
Panel 8		52.00	26.00	15.50
(22)	Willie McCovey	18.00	9.00	5.50
(23)	Carl Yastrzemski	21.00	10.50	6.25
(24)	Clyde Wright	3.00	1.50	.90
Panel 9		24.00	12.00	7.25
(25)	Jim Merritt	3.00	1.50	.90
(26)	Luis Aparicio	13.00	6.50	4.00
(27)	Bobby Murcer	4.50	2.25	1.25
Panel 10		12.00	6.00	3.50
(28)	Rico Petrocelli	3.00	1.50	.90
(29)	Sam McDowell	3.00	1.50	.90
(30)	Cito Gaston	3.00	1.50	.90
Panel 11		52.00	26.00	15.50
(31)	Brooks Robinson	19.00	9.50	5.75
(32)	Hank Aaron	30.00	15.00	9.00
(33)	Larry Dierker	3.00	1.50	.90
Panel 12		34.00	17.00	10.00
(34)	Rusty Staub	6.00	3.00	1.75
(35)	Bob Gibson	19.00	9.50	5.75
(36)	Amos Otis	4.00	2.00	1.25

1958 Bell Brand Dodgers

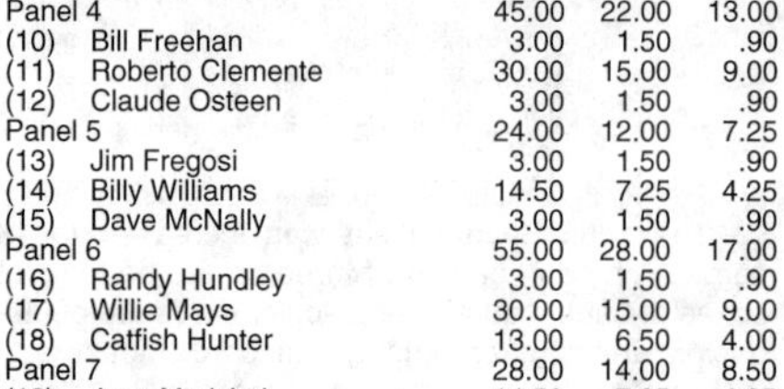

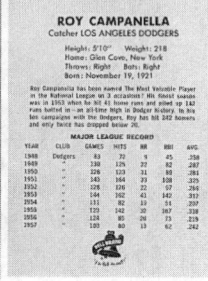

Celebrating the Dodgers first year of play in Los Angeles, Bell Brand inserted ten different unnumbered cards in their bags of potato chips and corn chips. The cards, which measure 3" x 4", have a sepia-colored photo inside a 1/4" green woodgrain border. The card backs feature statistical and biographical information and include the Bell Brand logo. Roy Campanella is included in the set despite a career-ending car wreck that prevented him from ever playing in Los Angeles.

		NM	EX	VG
Complete Set (10):		2000.	1000.	600.00
Common Player:		60.00	30.00	18.00
1	Roy Campanella	275.00	135.00	82.00
2	Gino Cimoli	185.00	92.00	55.00
3	Don Drysdale	150.00	75.00	45.00
4	Junior Gilliam	60.00	30.00	18.00
5	Gil Hodges	150.00	75.00	45.00
6	Sandy Koufax	400.00	200.00	120.00
7	Johnny Podres	185.00	92.00	55.00
8	Pee Wee Reese	200.00	100.00	60.00
9	Duke Snider	350.00	175.00	105.00
10	Don Zimmer	60.00	30.00	18.00

1960 Bell Brand Dodgers

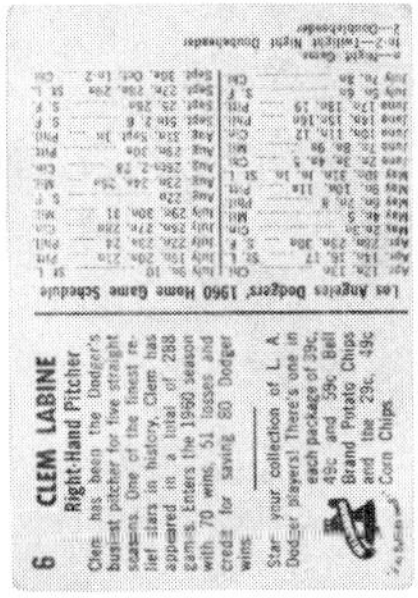

Bell Brand returned with a baseball card set in 1960 that was entirely different in style to their previous effort. The cards, which measure 2-1/2" x 3-1/2", feature beautiful, full-color photos. The backs carry a short player biography, the 1960 Dodgers home schedule, and the Bell Brand logo. Twenty different numbered cards were inserted in various size bags of potato chips and corn chips. Although sealed in cellophane, the cards were still subject to grease stains. Cards #'s 6, 12 and 18 are the scarcest in the set.

		NM	EX	VG
Complete Set (20):		1125.	560.00	330.00
Common Player:		35.00	17.50	10.50
1	Norm Larker	35.00	17.50	10.50
2	Duke Snider	150.00	75.00	45.00
3	Danny McDevitt	35.00	17.50	10.50
4	Jim Gilliam	40.00	20.00	12.00
5	Rip Repulski	35.00	17.50	10.50
6	Clem Labine	150.00	75.00	45.00
7	John Roseboro	35.00	17.50	10.50
8	Carl Furillo	55.00	27.00	16.50
9	Sandy Koufax	185.00	92.00	55.00
10	Joe Pignatano	35.00	17.50	10.50
11	Chuck Essegian	35.00	17.50	10.50
12	John Klippstein	120.00	60.00	36.00
13	Ed Roebuck	35.00	17.50	10.50
14	Don Demeter	35.00	17.50	10.50
15	Roger Craig	45.00	22.00	13.50
16	Stan Williams	35.00	17.50	10.50
17	Don Zimmer	45.00	22.00	13.50
18	Walter Alston	125.00	62.00	37.00
19	Johnny Podres	45.00	22.00	13.50
20	Maury Wills	55.00	27.00	16.50

1961 Bell Brand Dodgers

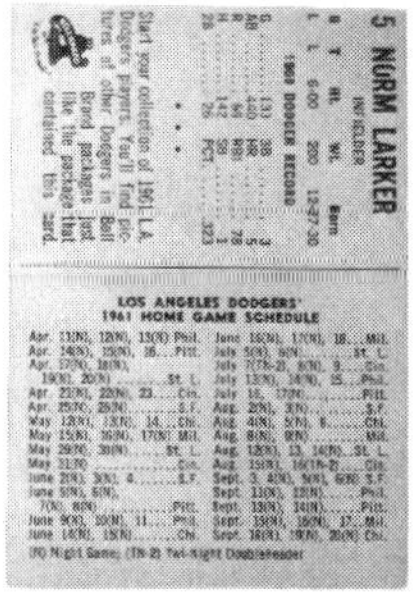

The 1961 Bell Brand set is identical in format to the previous year, although printed on thinner stock. Cards can be distinguished from the 1960 set by the 1961 schedule on the backs. The cards, which measure 2-7/16" x 3-1/2", are numbered by the player's uniform number. Twenty different cards were inserted into various size potato chip and corn chip packages, each card being sealed in a cellophane wrapper.

		NM	EX	VG
Complete Set (20):		800.00	400.00	240.00
Common Player:		27.00	13.50	8.00
3	Willie Davis	27.00	13.50	8.00
4	Duke Snider	100.00	50.00	30.00
5	Norm Larker	27.00	13.50	8.00
8	John Roseboro	27.00	13.50	8.00
9	Wally Moon	27.00	13.50	8.00
11	Bob Lillis	27.00	13.50	8.00
12	Tom Davis	27.00	13.50	8.00
14	Gil Hodges	75.00	37.00	22.00
16	Don Demeter	27.00	13.50	8.00
19	Jim Gilliam	30.00	15.00	9.00
22	John Podres	35.00	17.50	10.50
24	Walter Alston	60.00	30.00	18.00
30	Maury Wills	65.00	32.00	19.50
32	Sandy Koufax	180.00	90.00	54.00
34	Norm Sherry	27.00	13.50	8.00
37	Ed Roebuck	27.00	13.50	8.00
38	Roger Craig	30.00	15.00	9.00
40	Stan Williams	27.00	13.50	8.00
43	Charlie Neal	27.00	13.50	8.00
51	Larry Sherry	27.00	13.50	8.00

1962 Bell Brand Dodgers

The 1962 Bell Brand set is identical in style to the previous two years and cards can be distinguished by the 1962 Dodgers schedule on the back. Each card measures 2-7/16" x 3-1/2" and is numbered by the player's uniform number. Printed on glossy stock, the 1962 set was less susceptible to grease stains.

		NM	EX	VG
Complete Set (20):		550.00	275.00	160.00
Common Player:		20.00	10.00	6.00
3	Willie Davis	25.00	12.50	7.50
4	Duke Snider	100.00	50.00	30.00
6	Ron Fairly	20.00	10.00	6.00
8	John Roseboro	20.00	10.00	6.00
9	Wally Moon	20.00	10.00	6.00
12	Tom Davis	20.00	10.00	6.00
16	Ron Perranoski	20.00	10.00	6.00
19	Jim Gilliam	25.00	12.50	7.50
20	Daryl Spencer	20.00	10.00	6.00
22	John Podres	25.00	12.50	7.50
24	Walter Alston	45.00	22.00	13.50
25	Frank Howard	25.00	12.50	7.50
30	Maury Wills	40.00	20.00	12.00
32	Sandy Koufax	135.00	67.00	40.00
34	Norm Sherry	20.00	10.00	6.00
37	Ed Roebuck	20.00	10.00	6.00
40	Stan Williams	20.00	10.00	6.00
51	Larry Sherry	20.00	10.00	6.00
53	Don Drysdale	90.00	45.00	27.00
56	Lee Walls	20.00	10.00	6.00

1951 Berk Ross

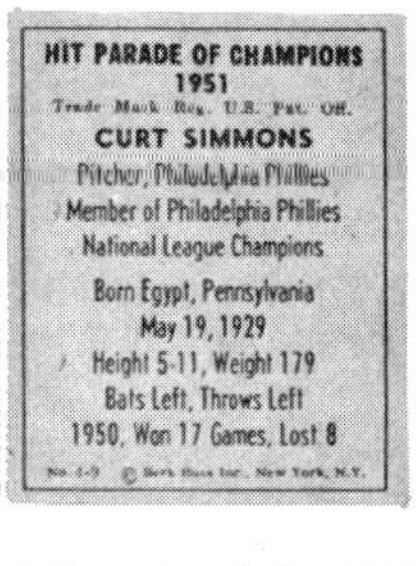

Entitled "Hit Parade of Champions," the 1951 Berk Ross set features 72 stars of various sports. The cards, which measure 2-1/16" x 2-1/2" and have tinted color photographs, were issued in boxes containing two-card panels. The issue is divided into four subsets with the first ten players of each series being baseball players. Only the baseball players are listed in the checklist that follows. Complete panels are valued 50 percent higher than the sum of the individual cards.

		NM	EX	VG
Complete Boxed Set (72):		1250.	625.00	375.00
Complete Baseball Set (40):		1000.	500.00	300.00
Common Player:		15.00	7.50	4.50
1-1	Al Rosen	15.00	7.50	4.50
1-2	Bob Lemon	25.00	12.50	7.50
1-3	Phil Rizzuto	60.00	30.00	18.00
1-4	Hank Bauer	17.50	8.75	5.25
1-5	Billy Johnson	15.00	7.50	4.50
1-6	Jerry Coleman	15.00	7.50	4.50
1-7	Johnny Mize	30.00	15.00	9.00
1-8	Dom DiMaggio	24.00	12.00	7.25
1-9	Richie Ashburn	35.00	17.50	10.50
1-10	Del Ennis	15.00	7.50	4.50
2-1	Stan Musial	250.00	125.00	75.00
2-2	Warren Spahn	30.00	15.00	9.00
2-3	Tommy Henrich	15.00	7.50	4.50
2-4	Larry "Yogi" Berra	150.00	75.00	45.00
2-5	Joe DiMaggio	400.00	200.00	120.00
2-6	Bobby Brown	15.00	7.50	4.50
2-7	Granville Hamner	15.00	7.50	4.50
2-8	Willie Jones	15.00	7.50	4.50
2-9	Stanley Lopata	15.00	7.50	4.50
2-10	Mike Goliat	15.00	7.50	4.50
3-1	Ralph Kiner	25.00	12.50	7.50
3-2	Billy Goodman	15.00	7.50	4.50
3-3	Allie Reynolds	17.50	8.75	5.25
3-4	Vic Raschi	17.50	8.75	5.25
3-5	Joe Page	15.00	7.50	4.50
3-6	Eddie Lopat	15.00	7.50	4.50
3-7	Andy Seminick	15.00	7.50	4.50
3-8	Dick Sisler	15.00	7.50	4.50
3-9	Eddie Waitkus	15.00	7.50	4.50
3-10	Ken Heintzelman	15.00	7.50	4.50
4-1	Gono Woodling	17.50	8.75	5.25
4-2	Cliff Mapes	15.00	7.50	4.50
4-3	Fred Sanford	15.00	7.50	4.50
4-4	Tommy Bryne	15.00	7.50	4.50
4-5	Eddie (Whitey) Ford	125.00	62.00	37.00
4-6	Jim Konstanty	15.00	7.50	4.50
4-7	Russ Meyer	15.00	7.50	4.50
4-8	Robin Roberts	25.00	12.50	7.50
4-9	Curt Simmons	15.00	7.50	4.50
4-10	Sam Jethroe	15.00	7.50	4.50

1952 Berk Ross

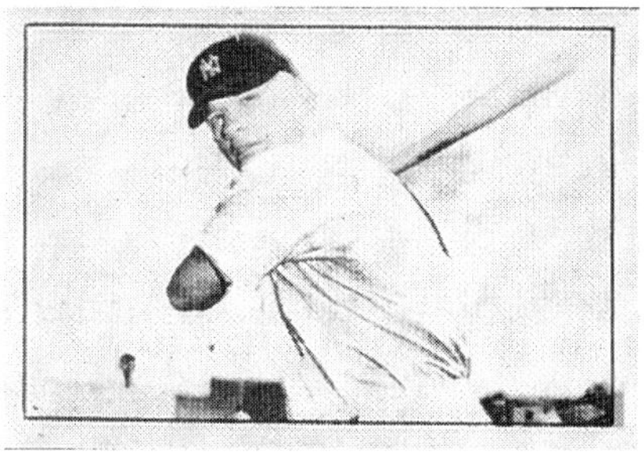
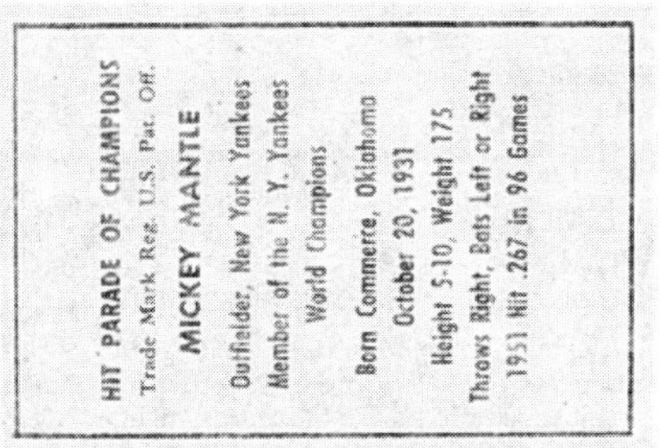

Although the card size is different (2" x 3"), the style of the fronts and backs of the 1952 Berk Ross set is similar to the previous year's effort. Seventy-two unnumbered cards make up the set. Rizzuto is included twice in the set and the Blackwell and Fox cards have transposed backs. The cards were issued individually rather than as two-card panels like in 1951.

		NM	EX	VG
Complete Set (72):		4250.	2100.	1250.
Common Player:		15.00	7.50	4.50
(1)	Richie Ashburn	32.00	16.00	9.50
(2)	Hank Bauer	17.50	8.75	5.25
(3)	Larry "Yogi" Berra	115.00	57.00	34.00
(4)	Ewell Blackwell (photo actually Nelson Fox)	40.00	20.00	12.00
(5)	Bobby Brown	15.00	7.50	4.50
(6)	Jim Busby	15.00	7.50	4.50

(7) Roy Campanella	125.00	62.00	37.00
(8) Chico Carrasquel	15.00	7.50	4.50
(9) Jerry Coleman	15.00	7.50	4.50
(10) Joe Collins	15.00	7.50	4.50
(11) Alvin Dark	15.00	7.50	4.50
(12) Dom DiMaggio	17.50	8.75	5.25
(13) Joe DiMaggio	650.00	325.00	195.00
(14) Larry Doby	25.00	12.50	7.50
(15) Bobby Doerr	25.00	12.50	7.50
(16) Bob Elliot (Elliott)	15.00	7.50	4.50
(17) Del Ennis	15.00	7.50	4.50
(18) Ferris Fain	15.00	7.50	4.50
(19) Bob Feller	65.00	32.00	19.50
(20) Nelson Fox (photo actually Ewell Blackwell)	18.00	9.00	5.50
(21) Ned Garver	15.00	7.50	4.50
(22) Clint Hartung	15.00	7.50	4.50
(23) Jim Hearn	15.00	7.50	4.50
(24) Gil Hodges	45.00	22.00	13.50
(25) Monte Irvin	25.00	12.50	7.50
(26) Larry Jansen	15.00	7.50	4.50
(27) George Kell	25.00	12.50	7.50
(28) Sheldon Jones	15.00	7.50	4.50
(29) Monte Kennedy	15.00	7.50	4.50
(30) Ralph Kiner	25.00	12.50	7.50
(31) Dave Koslo	15.00	7.50	4.50
(32) Bob Kuzava	15.00	7.50	4.50
(33) Bob Lemon	25.00	12.50	7.50
(34) Whitey Lockman	15.00	7.50	4.50
(35) Eddie Lopat	15.00	7.50	4.50
(36) Sal Maglie	15.00	7.50	4.50
(37) Mickey Mantle	1350.	675.00	405.00
(38) Billy Martin	35.00	17.50	10.50
(39) Willie Mays	400.00	200.00	120.00
(40) Gil McDougal (McDougald)	17.50	8.75	5.25
(41) Orestes Minoso	17.50	8.75	5.25
(42) Johnny Mize	30.00	15.00	9.00
(43) Tom Morgan	15.00	7.50	4.50
(44) Don Mueller	15.00	7.50	4.50
(45) Stan Musial	400.00	200.00	120.00
(46) Don Newcombe	20.00	10.00	6.00
(47) Ray Noble	15.00	7.50	4.50
(48) Joe Ostrowski	15.00	7.50	4.50
(49) Mel Parnell	15.00	7.50	4.50
(50) Vic Raschi	17.50	8.75	5.25
(51) Pee Wee Reese	50.00	25.00	15.00
(52) Allie Reynolds	17.50	8.75	5.25
(53) Bill Rigney	15.00	7.50	4.50
(54) Phil Rizzuto (bunting)	55.00	27.00	16.50
(55) Phil Rizzuto (swinging)	55.00	27.00	16.50
(56) Robin Roberts	25.00	12.50	7.50
(57) Eddie Robinson	15.00	7.50	4.50
(58) Jackie Robinson	400.00	200.00	120.00
(59) Elwin "Preacher" Roe	15.00	7.50	4.50
(60) Johnny Sain	17.50	8.75	5.25
(61) Albert "Red" Schoendienst	25.00	12.50	7.50
(62) Duke Snider	125.00	62.00	37.00
(63) George Spencer	15.00	7.50	4.50
(64) Eddie Stanky	15.00	7.50	4.50
(65) Henry Thompson	15.00	7.50	4.50
(66) Bobby Thomson	17.50	8.75	5.25
(67) Vic Wertz	15.00	7.50	4.50
(68) Waldon Westlake	15.00	7.50	4.50
(69) Wes Westrum	15.00	7.50	4.50
(70) Ted Williams	425.00	210.00	125.00
(71) Gene Woodling	17.50	8.75	5.25
(72) Gus Zernial	15.00	7.50	4.50

1956 Big League Stars Statues

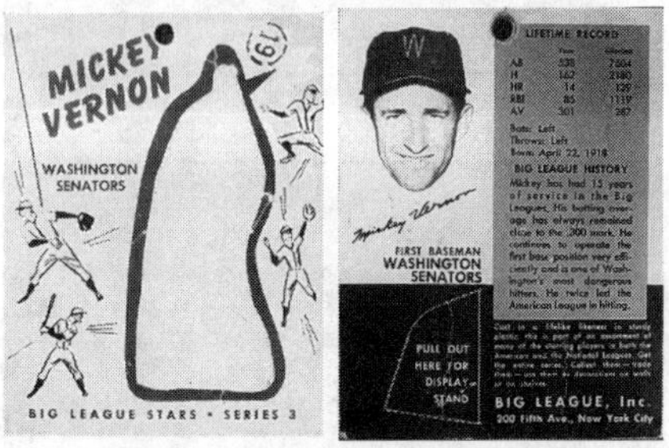

While the plastic statues in this set are virtually identical to the set issued in 1955 by Dairy Queen, the packaging of the Big League Stars statues on a card with all the usual elements of a baseball card makes them more collectible. The DQ versions of the statues are white, while the Big League versions are bronze colored. The statues measure about 3" tall and were sold in a 4" x 5" cardboard and plastic blister pack for about 19 cents. Complete league sets were also sold in a large package. The singles package features the player's name in a large banner near the top with his team printed below and line drawings of ballplayers in action around the statue. Backs have a player portrait photo with facsimile autograph, position, team, previous year and career stats and a career summary. A perforated tab at bottom can be pulled out to make a stand for the display. Most packages are found with the hole at top punched out to allow for hanging on a hook. Besides singles, larger packages of nine National or American league statues were also sold in a window-box. Values listed here are for complete statue/package combinations. Statues alone sell for $25-50 for non-Hall of Famers, up to $300 for Mantle. Packages without the statue should be priced about one-third the values quoted here. The set is checklisted alphabetically.

	NM	EX	VG
Complete Set (18):	2500.	1250.	750.00
Common Player:	60.00	30.00	18.00
(1) John Antonelli	60.00	30.00	18.00
(2) Bob Avila	60.00	30.00	18.00
(3) Yogi Berra	185.00	92.00	55.00
(4) Roy Campanella	200.00	100.00	60.00
(5) Larry Doby	90.00	45.00	27.00
(6) Del Ennis	60.00	30.00	18.00
(7) Jim Gilliam	65.00	32.00	19.50
(8) Gil Hodges	125.00	62.00	37.00
(9) Harvey Kuenn	60.00	30.00	18.00
(10) Bob Lemon	75.00	37.00	22.00
(11) Mickey Mantle	800.00	400.00	240.00
(12) Ed Mathews	125.00	62.00	37.00
(13) Minnie Minoso	65.00	32.00	19.50
(14) Stan Musial	250.00	125.00	75.00
(15) Pee Wee Reese	150.00	75.00	45.00
(16) Al Rosen	60.00	30.00	18.00
(17) Duke Snider	195.00	97.00	58.00
(18) Mickey Vernon	60.00	30.00	18.00

1978 Big T/Tastee Freeze discs

One player from each major league team was selected for inclusion in this discs set distributed by Big T family restaurants and Tastee Freeze stands in North Carolina, and possibly other parts of the country. The 3-3/8" diameter discs have a sepia-toned player portrait photo at center within a white diamond and surrounded by a brightly colored border with four colored stars at top. Licensed by the players' association through Michael Schecter Associates, the photos have had uniform logos removed. Backs are printed in red, white and blue and have the sponsor's logos and a line of 1977 stats, along with a card number.

	NM	EX	VG
Complete Set (26):	60.00	30.00	18.00
Common Player:	1.50	.75	.45
1 Buddy Bell	1.50	.75	.45
2 Jim Palmer	6.00	3.00	1.75
3 Steve Garvey	4.50	2.25	1.25
4 Jeff Burroughs	1.50	.75	.45
5 Greg Luzinski	1.50	.70	.45
6 Lou Brock	6.00	3.00	1.75
7 Thurman Munson	5.00	2.50	1.50
8 Rod Carew	6.00	3.00	1.75
9 George Brett	15.00	7.50	4.50
10 Tom Seaver	8.00	4.00	2.50
11 Willie Stargell	6.00	3.00	1.75
12 Jerry Koosman	2.00	1.00	.60
13 Bill North	1.50	.75	.45
14 Richie Zisk	1.50	.75	.45
15 Bill Madlock	1.50	.75	.45
16 Carl Yastrzemski	8.00	4.00	2.50
17 Dave Cash	1.50	.75	.45
18 Bob Watson	1.50	.75	.45
19 Dave Kingman	3.00	1.50	.90
20 Gene Tenace	1.50	.75	.45
21 Ralph Garr	1.50	.75	.45
22 Mark Fidrych	3.00	1.50	.90
23 Frank Tanana	1.50	.75	.45
24 Larry Hisle	1.50	.75	.45
25 Bruce Bochte	1.50	.75	.45
26 Bob Bailor	1.50	.75	.45

1955-60 Bill and Bob Braves Postcards

One of the most popular and scarce of the 1950s color postcard series is the run of Milwaukee Braves known as "Bill and Bobs". While some of the cards do carry a photo credit acknowledging the pair, and a few add a Bradenton, Fla., (spring training home of the Braves) address, little else is known about the issuer. The cards themselves appear to have been purchased by the players to honor photo and autograph requests. Several of the cards carry facsimile autographs pre-printed on the front. The cards feature crisp full-color photos on their borderless fronts. Postcard backs have a variety of printing including card numbers, photo credits, a Kodachrome logo and player name. Some cards are found with some of those elements, some with none. There is some question whether the Joe Torre card is actually a Bill and Bob product, because it is 1/16" narrower than the standard 3-1/2" x 5-1/2" format of the other cards, features the player with a Pepsi bottle in his hand and is rubber-stamped on back with a Pepsi bottler's address. The Torre card is usually collected along with the rest of the set.

	NM	EX	VG
Complete Set (20):	1850.	900.00	550.00
Common Player:	40.00	20.00	12.00
(1) Hank Aaron	500.00	250.00	150.00
(2) Joe Adcock (fielding)	75.00	37.00	22.00
(3) Joe Adcock (bat on shoulder)	60.00	30.00	18.00
(4) Joe Adcock (kneeling with two bats)	60.00	30.00	18.00
(5) Billy Bruton (kneeling)	75.00	37.00	22.00
(6) Billy Bruton (throwing)	100.00	50.00	30.00
(7) Bob Buhl	40.00	20.00	12.00
(8) Lou Burdette	40.00	20.00	12.00
(9) Gene Conley	40.00	20.00	12.00
(10) Wes Covington (kneeling with one bat)	60.00	30.00	18.00
(11) Wes Covington (kneeling with seven bats)	60.00	30.00	18.00
(12) Del Crandall (kneeling, one bat)	50.00	25.00	15.00
(13) Del Crandall (kneeling, two bats)	50.00	25.00	15.00
(14) Chuck Dressen	60.00	30.00	18.00
(15) Charlie Grimm	100.00	50.00	30.00
(16) Fred Haney	90.00	45.00	27.00
(17) Bob Keely	75.00	37.00	22.00
(18) Eddie Mathews	200.00	100.00	60.00
(19) Warren Spahn	200.00	100.00	60.00
(20) Frank Torre	100.00	50.00	30.00

1916 Block and Kuhl Co.

Best known for its use as a promotional medium for The Sporting News, this 200-card set can be found with ads on the back for several local and regional businesses. Among them is the Block and Kuhl department store, Peoria, Ill. While type card collectors and superstar collectors may pay a premium for individual cards with Block and Kuhl's advertising, prices will generally parallel the 1916 Sporting News values. Cards measure 1-5/8" x 3" and are printed in black-and-white.

(See 1916 Sporting News for checklist, price guide.)

1911 Blome's Chocolates

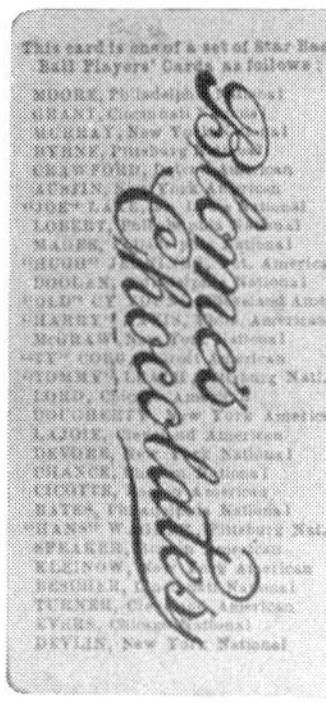

Advertising for Blome's Chocolates overprinted on the back of these cards is one of several brands produced by George Close Candy Co. Values are the same for cards with and without overprint.

(See 1911 George Close Candy Co. for checklist and price guide.)

1933 Blue Bird Babe Ruth

A small hoard of the (a) cards appeared in the market in early 1994 making available a card which had previously been virtually unknown. Printed in black-and-white on thin card stock, the piece measures 3-7/8" x 5-7/8". The photo on front was used in modified form on several other early-1930s issues. The back offers balls and gloves available for redemption with soft drink bottle caps and cash. The discovery of the (b) version came in 1999.

		NM	EX	VG
(1a)	Babe Ruth (batting follow-through, front view)	900.00	450.00	270.00
(1b)	Babe Ruth (batting follow-through, side view)	1500.	750.00	450.00

1930 Blue Ribbon Malt Chicago Cubs

These player pictures were originally printed as part of a 40" x 12" advertising piece by Blue Ribbon Malt. However, if cut from the piece, there is no identification of the issuer. Individual black-and-white pictures have facsimile autographs on front and measure 3-1/2" high by 1-7/16" to 3" wide. The backs are blank. The unnumbered pictures are checklisted here in alphabetical order, with names as they appear on the photos.

		NM	EX	VG
Complete Uncut Sheet:		900.00	450.00	275.00
Complete Set, Singles (28):		300.00	150.00	90.00
Common Player:		15.00	7.50	4.50
(1)	Clyde Beck	15.00	7.50	4.50
(2)	Lester Bell	15.00	7.50	4.50
(3)	Clarence Blair	15.00	7.50	4.50
(4)	Fred Blake	15.00	7.50	4.50
(5)	Jimmy Burke	15.00	7.50	4.50
(6)	Guy Bush	22.00	11.00	6.50
(7)	Hazen "Kiki" Cuyler	37.00	18.50	11.00
(8)	Woody English	15.00	7.50	4.50
(9)	Eddie Farrell	15.00	7.50	4.50
(10)	Charlie Grimm	22.00	11.00	6.50
(11)	Leo "Gabby" Hartnett	37.00	18.50	11.00
(12)	Clifton Heathcote	15.00	7.50	4.50
(13)	Rogers Hornsby	60.00	30.00	18.00
(14)	George L. Kelly	37.00	18.50	11.00
(15)	Pierce "Pat" Malone	15.00	7.50	4.50
(16)	Joe McCarthy	15.00	7.50	4.50
(17)	Lynn Nelson	15.00	7.50	4.50
(18)	Bob Osborn	15.00	7.50	4.50
(19)	Jesse Petty	15.00	7.50	4.50
(20)	Charlie Root	18.50	9.25	5.50
(21)	Ray Schalk	37.00	18.50	11.00
(22)	John Schulte	15.00	7.50	4.50
(23)	Al Shealy	15.00	7.50	4.50
(24)	Riggs Stephenson	22.00	11.00	6.50
(25)	Dan Taylor	15.00	7.50	4.50
(26)	Zack Taylor	15.00	7.50	4.50
(27)	Bud Teachout	15.00	7.50	4.50
(28)	Lewis "Hack" Wilson	52.00	26.00	15.50

1930 Blue Ribbon Malt Chicago White Sox

These player pictures were originally printed as part of a 40" x 12" advertising piece by Blue Ribbon Malt. However, if cut from the piece, there is no identification of the issuer. Individual black-and-white pictures have facsimile autographs on front and measure 3-1/2" high by 1-7/16" to 2-7/8" wide. The backs are blank. The unnumbered pictures are checklisted here in alphabetical order, with names as they appear on the photos.

		NM	EX	VG
Complete Uncut Sheet:		500.00	250.00	150.00
Complete Set (27):		200.00	100.00	60.00
Common Player:		10.00	5.00	3.00
(1)	"Chick" Autry	15.00	7.50	4.50
(2)	"Red" Barnes	10.00	5.00	3.00
(3)	Moe Berg	30.00	15.00	9.00
(4)	Garland Braxton	10.00	5.00	3.00
(5)	Donie Bush	10.00	5.00	3.00
(6)	Pat Caraway	10.00	5.00	3.00
(7)	Bill Cissell	10.00	5.00	3.00
(8)	"Bud" Clancy	10.00	5.00	3.00
(9)	Clyde Crouse	10.00	5.00	3.00
(10)	U.C. Faber	25.00	12.50	7.50
(11)	Bob Fothergill	10.00	5.00	3.00
(12)	Frank J. "Dutch" Henry	10.00	5.00	3.00
(13)	Smead Jolley	10.00	5.00	3.00
(14)	Bill "Willie" Kamm	10.00	5.00	3.00
(15)	Bernard "Mike" Kelly	10.00	5.00	3.00
(16)	Johnny Kerr	10.00	5.00	3.00
(17)	Ted Lyons	25.00	12.50	7.50
(18)	Harold McKain	10.00	5.00	3.00
(19)	"Jim" Moore	10.00	5.00	3.00
(20)	"Greg" Mulleavy	10.00	5.00	3.00
(21)	Carl N. Reynolds	10.00	5.00	3.00
(22)	Blondy Ryan	10.00	5.00	3.00
(23)	"Benny" Tate	10.00	5.00	3.00
(24)	Tommy Thomas	10.00	5.00	3.00
(25)	Ed Walsh, Jr.	10.00	5.00	3.00
(26)	Johnny Watwood	10.00	5.00	3.00
(27)	Bob Weiland	10.00	5.00	3.00

1931 Blue Ribbon Malt

Players of the Chicago Cubs and White Sox are featured in this series of 4-7/8" x 6-7/8" black-and-white photos. Each blank-backed photo is bordered in white with "Compliments of BLUE RIBBON MALT-America's Biggest Seller" printed in the bottom border and a facsimile autograph across the photo. It is likely players other than those listed here were also issued.

		NM	EX	VG
Common Player:		75.00	37.00	22.00
(1)	John Kerr	75.00	37.00	22.00
(2)	Bob Smith	75.00	37.00	22.00
(3)	Lewis "Hack" Wilson	125.00	62.00	37.00

1962 Bobbin' Head Doll Advertising Photos

This pair of color 5" x 7" photos depict the home run heroes of 1961 holding their Bobbin' Head dolls. The players are pictured in belt-to-cap photos wearing road uniforms and posed in a stadium setting. Backs are blank.

		NM	EX	VG
Complete Set (2):		500.00	250.00	150.00
(1)	Mickey Mantle	325.00	160.00	95.00
(2)	Roger Maris	175.00	85.00	50.00

1947 Bond Bread Jackie Robinson

(The listings formerly found under this heading will now be found under 1947 Homogonized Bond Bread Jackie

1912 Boston Garter

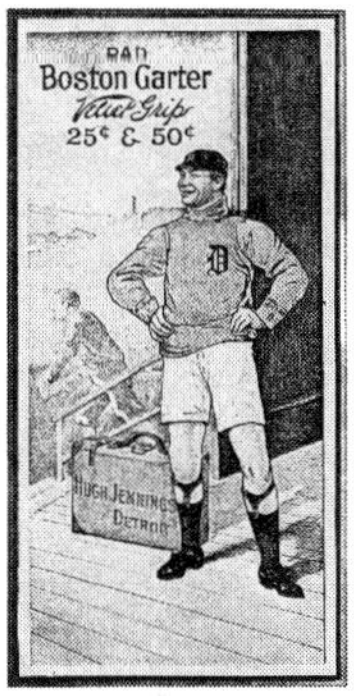

If it weren't for the checklist printed on the back of the few known specimens, the extent of this extremely rare issue would be unknown. Many of the cards mentioned on the back have yet to be seen. Issued by the George Frost Company of Boston, and packed one card per box of a dozen garters, the approximately 4" x 8-1/4" cards are printed in color lithography on the front, and black-and-white on the back. Fronts have a picture of the player standing near his locker or sitting in a chair, dressing in his uniform. The issuer's Boston-brand garter is prominently shown below the player's boxer shorts. A window in the background displays a cityscape or ballpark scene. There was a card issued for one player on each of the 16 major league teams of the day. Large-format (21-1/2" x 11-1/4") cardboard window display posters which reproduce pairs of the cards are sometimes seen in the hobby.

		NM	EX	VG
Complete Set (16):		75000.	37500.	22000.
Common Player:		4500.	2250.	1350.
(1)	Christy Mathewson	8000.	4000.	2400.
(2)	Nap Rucker	4500.	2250.	1350.
(3)	Frank Chance	5500.	2750.	1650.
(4)	Charles Dooin	4500.	2250.	1350.
(5)	Johnny Kling	4500.	2250.	1350.
(6)	Roger Bresnahan	5500.	2750.	1650.
(7)	Bob Bescher	4500.	2250.	1350.
(8)	Fred Clarke	5500.	2750.	1650.
(9)	Hal Chase	5000.	2500.	1500.
(10)	Hugh Jennings	5500.	2750.	1650.
(11)	Eddie Collins	5500.	2750.	1650.
(12)	Tris Speaker	6500.	3250.	1950.
(13)	Frank LaPorte	4500.	2250.	1350.
(14)	Larry Lajoie	6000.	3000.	1800.
(15)	Ed Walsh	5500.	2750.	1650.
(16)	Walter Johnson	8000.	4000.	2400.

1913 Boston Garter

The second of what are presumed to have been three annual issue by the George Frost Co., Boston, contains 12 cards. The colorful lithograph fronts have a player picture in front of a ballpark diagram. A large Boston-brand garter appears at the bottom. Baseballs with the Boston Garter name appear in each upper corner. Black-and-white backs have a checklist for the set, career statistics for the player pictured and details on the cards' availability. Retailers received one card per box of dozen garters and could write to the company to complete the set. The 4" x 8-1/4" cards were intended to be displayed in shop windows.

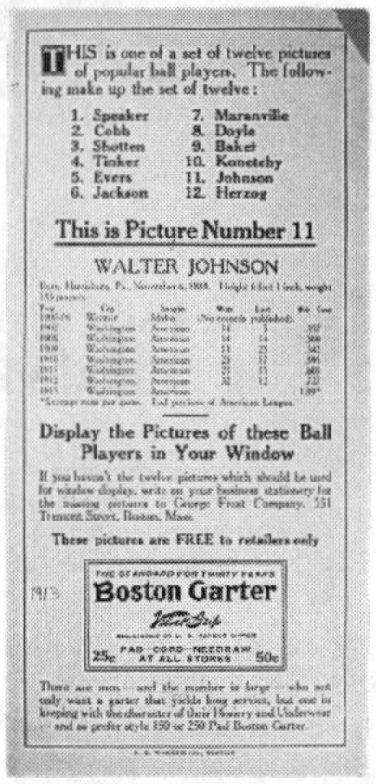

		NM	EX	VG
Complete Set (12):		80000.	40000.	25000.
Common Player:		4500.	2250.	1350.
1	Tris Speaker	7000.	3500.	2100.
2	Ty Cobb	13500.	6750.	4050.
3	Burt Shotten (Shotton)	4500.	2250.	1350.
4	Joe Tinker	6750.	3375.	2025.
5	Johnny Evers	6750.	3375.	2025.
6	Joe Jackson	15000.	7500.	4500.
7	Rabbit Maranville	6750.	3375.	2025.
8	Larry Doyle	4500.	2250.	1350.
9	Frank Baker	6750.	3375.	2025.
10	Ed Konetchy	4500.	2250.	1350.
11	Walter Johnson	11000.	5500.	3300.
12	Buck Herzog	4500.	2250.	1350.

1914 Boston Garter

The 1914 date attributed to this 10-card set may or may not be accurate. Since the company's other two known issues can be reliably dated and were produced using the color lithographic process, it is presumed that the use of photographs would have come. Fronts of the approximately 4" x 8" cards feature a green duo-tone photo of the player. His last name appears in white script at the bottom, along with a baseball with the Boston Garter name. Backs have a checklist of the set and information on how retail store owners can send for additional cards to supplement those which were packaged one per box of a dozen garters.

		NM	EX	VG
Complete Set (10):		30000.	15000.	9000.
Common Player:		2250.	1125.	675.00
1	Christy Mathewson	5600.	2800.	1680.
2	Red Murray	2250.	1125.	675.00
3	Eddie Collins	3350.	1675.	1005.
4	Hugh Jennings	3350.	1675.	1005.
5	Hal Chase	2500.	1250.	750.00
6	Bob Bescher	2250.	1125.	675.00
7	Red Dooin	2250.	1125.	675.00
8	Larry Lajoie	3750.	1875.	1125.
9	Tris Speaker	4000.	2000.	1200.
10	Heinie Zimmerman	2250.	1125.	675.00

1912 Boston Red Sox Tattoos

This set of tattoos is similar to a number of other issues of the era, most of which were made in Germany. This issue features members of the World Champion Boston Red Sox. Approximately 1-3/8" x 1-3/4", the tattoos are printed in mirror-image in bright colors. Images are crude line art with no resemblance to the actual players. Players are identified at bottom by at least a last name. A position is designated in the background of the picture. These items were issued on a perforated sheet. "Collins" may represent retired Red Sox Jimmy Collins or 1912 pitcher Ray Collins. The unnumbered tattoos are listed here alphabetically, though the listing may not be complete.

		NM	EX	VG
Complete Set (13):		475.00	235.00	140.00
Common Player:		35.00	17.50	10.50
(1)	Hugh Bedient	35.00	17.50	10.50
(2)	Hick Cady	35.00	17.50	10.50
(3)	Collins	35.00	17.50	10.50
(4)	Clyde Engle	35.00	17.50	10.50
(5)	Charley Hall	35.00	17.50	10.50
(6)	Martin Krug	35.00	17.50	10.50
(7)	Jerry McCarthy (mascot)	35.00	17.50	10.50
(8)	Les Nunamaker	35.00	17.50	10.50
(9)	Larry Pape	35.00	17.50	10.50
(10)	Tris Speaker	125.00	62.00	37.00
(11)	Jake Stahl	35.00	17.50	10.50
(12)	Heinie Wagner	35.00	17.50	10.50
(13)	Joe Wood	35.00	17.50	10.50

1946 Boston Red Sox Photo Pack

The American League champion Red Sox are featured in this team-issue photo pack. The player portraits are printed in black-and-white on heavy paper in 6" x 8-1/2" format. The photos have a white border and a facsimile autograph on front. Backs are blank. The unnumbered pictures are listed here in alphabetical order.

		NM	EX	VG
Complete Set (25):		125.00	62.00	37.00
Common Player:		3.00	1.50	.90
(1)	Ernie Andres	3.00	1.50	.90
(2)	Jim Bagby	3.00	1.50	.90
(3)	Mace Brown	3.00	1.50	.90
(4)	Joe Cronin	12.00	6.00	3.50
(5)	Leon Culbertston	3.00	1.50	.90
(6)	Mel Deutsch	3.00	1.50	.90
(7)	Dom DiMaggio	12.00	6.00	3.50
(8)	Joe Dobson	3.00	1.50	.90
(9)	Bobby Doerr	12.00	6.00	3.50
(10)	Boo Ferriss	3.00	1.50	.90
(11)	Mickey Harris	3.00	1.50	.90
(12)	Randy Heflin	3.00	1.50	.90
(13)	Tex Hughson	3.00	1.50	.90
(14)	Earl Johnson	3.00	1.50	.90
(15)	Ed McGah	3.00	1.50	.90
(16)	George Metkovich	3.00	1.50	.90
(17)	Roy Partee	3.00	1.50	.90
(18)	Eddie Pellagrini	3.00	1.50	.90
(19)	Johnny Pesky	4.50	2.25	1.25
(20)	Rip Russell	3.00	1.50	.90
(21)	Mike Ryba	3.00	1.50	.90
(22)	Charlie Wagner	3.00	1.50	.90
(23)	Hal Wagner	3.00	1.50	.90
(24)	Ted Williams	50.00	25.00	15.00
(25)	Rudy York	3.00	1.50	.90

1969 Boston Red Sox team issue

This team-issue photo pack features black-and-white portrait photos on a 4-1/4" x 7" blank-back format, similar to the team's 1971 issue. The player's name and team nickname are designated in the white border at top. The unnumbered cards are checklisted here in alphabetical order.

		NM	EX	VG
Complete Set (12):		60.00	30.00	15.00
Common Player:		4.00	2.00	1.25
(1)	Mike Andrews	4.00	2.00	1.25
(2)	Tony Conigliaro	9.00	4.50	2.75
(3)	Russ Gibson	4.00	2.00	1.25
(4)	Dalton Jones	4.00	2.00	1.25
(5)	Bill Landis	4.00	2.00	1.25
(6)	Jim Lonborg	5.00	2.50	1.50
(7)	Sparky Lyle	4.00	2.00	1.25
(8)	Rico Petrocelli	5.00	2.50	1.50
(9)	George Scott	5.00	2.50	1.50
(10)	Reggie Smith	4.00	2.00	1.25
(11)	Dick Williams	4.00	2.00	1.25
(12)	Carl Yastrzemski	15.00	7.50	4.50

1971 Boston Red Sox team issue

This enveloped, team-issue photo pack features black-and-white portrait photos on a 4-1/4" x 7" blank-back format, similar to the team's 1969 issue. The player's name and team nickname are printed in the wide white border at top. The unnumbered cards are checklisted here in alphabetical order.

		NM	EX	VG
Complete Set (12):		40.00	20.00	12.00
Common Player:		3.00	1.50	.90
(1)	Luis Aparicio	4.50	2.25	1.25
(2)	Billy Conigliaro	3.00	1.50	.90
(3)	Ray Culp	3.00	1.50	.90
(4)	Duane Josephson	3.00	1.50	.90
(5)	Jim Lonborg	4.50	2.25	1.25
(6)	Sparky Lyle	3.00	1.50	.90
(7)	Gary Peters	3.00	1.50	.90
(8)	Rico Petrocelli	4.50	2.25	1.25
(9)	George Scott	4.50	2.25	1.25
(10)	Sonny Siebert	3.00	1.50	.90
(11)	Reggie Smith	3.00	1.50	.90
(12)	Carl Yastrzemski	12.00	6.00	3.50

1975 Boston Red Sox Photo Pack

This is one of several team-issues from the Red Sox in the 1970s, sold at concession stands and souvenir outlets. This set features color photos in a 7" x 8" format with a white border all-around and the player name in capital letters in the bottom border. Backs are blank.

		NM	EX	VG
Complete Set (8):		17.50	8.75	5.25
Common Player:		2.00	1.00	.60
(1)	Rick Burleson	2.00	1.00	.60
(2)	Denny Doyle	2.00	1.00	.60
(3)	Dwight Evans	2.50	1.25	.70
(4)	Carlton Fisk	4.00	2.00	1.25
(5)	Fred Lynn	3.00	1.50	.90
(6)	Rico Petrocelli	2.50	1.25	.70
(7)	Jim Rice	4.00	2.00	1.25
(8)	Carl Yastrzemski	5.00	2.50	1.50

1978 Boston Red Sox of the 1950s

The date of actual issue, the name of the issuer and even the "official" title of this collectors' edition card set is currently unknown. The 2-1/2" x 3-1/2" cards are printed in black-and-white on front and backs. Fronts have the style of the 1953 Bowmans, with only a player photo and a white border. Backs are reminiscent of the 1955 Bowman, with player identification, career highlights, stats and a Red Sox trivia question.

		NM	EX	VG
Complete Set (64):		75.00	37.50	22.00
Common Player:		2.00	1.00	.60
1	Harry Agganis	6.00	3.00	1.75
2	Ken Aspromonte	2.00	1.00	.60
3	Bobby Avila	2.00	1.00	.60
4	Frank Baumann	2.00	1.00	.60
5	Lou Berberet	2.00	1.00	.60
6	Milt Bolling	2.00	1.00	.60
7	Lou Boudreau	3.00	1.50	.90
8	Ted Bowsfield	2.00	1.00	.60
9	Tom Brewer	2.00	1.00	.60
10	Don Buddin	2.00	1.00	.60
11	Jerry Casale	2.00	1.00	.60
12	Billy Consolo	2.00	1.00	.60
13	Pete Daley	2.00	1.00	.60
14	Ike Delock	2.00	1.00	.60
15	Dom DiMaggio	4.50	2.25	1.25
16	Bobby Doerr	3.00	1.50	.90
17	Walt Dropo	2.50	1.25	.70
18	Arnie Earley	2.00	1.00	.60
19	Hoot Evers	2.00	1.00	.60
20	Mike Fornieles	2.00	1.00	.60
21	Gary Geiger	2.00	1.00	.60
22	Don Gile	2.00	1.00	.60
23	Joe Ginsberg	2.00	1.00	.60
24	Billy Goodman	2.00	1.00	.60
25	Pumpsie Green	2.00	1.00	.60
26	Grady Hatton	2.00	1.00	.60
27	Billy Herman	2.50	1.25	.70
28	Jackie Jensen	2.50	1.25	.70
29	George Kell	3.00	1.50	.90
30	Marty Keough	2.00	1.00	.60
31	Leo Kiely	2.00	1.00	.60
32	Ellis Kinder	2.00	1.00	.60
33	Billy Klaus	2.00	1.00	.60
34	Don Lenhardt	2.00	1.00	.60
35	Ted Lepcio	2.00	1.00	.60
36	Frank Malzone	2.00	1.00	.60
37	Gene Mauch	2.00	1.00	.60
38	Maury McDermott	2.00	1.00	.60
39	Bill Monbouquette	2.00	1.00	.60
40	Chet Nichols	2.00	1.00	.60
41	Willard Nixon	2.00	1.00	.60
42	Jim Pagliaroni	2.00	1.00	.60
43	Mel Parnell	2.00	1.00	.60
44	Johnny Pesky	2.00	1.00	.60
45	Jimmy Piersall	2.50	1.25	.70
46	Bob Porterfield	2.00	1.00	.60
47	Pete Runnels	2.00	1.00	.60
48	Dave Sisler	2.00	1.00	.60
49	Riverboat Smith	2.00	1.00	.60
50	Gene Stephens	2.00	1.00	.60
51	Vern Stephens	2.00	1.00	.60
52	Chuck Stobbs	2.00	1.00	.60
53	Dean Stone	2.00	1.00	.60
54	Frank Sullivan	2.00	1.00	.60
55	Haywood Sullivan	2.00	1.00	.60
56	Birdie Tebbetts	2.00	1.00	.60
57	Mickey Vernon	2.00	1.00	.60
58	Vic Wertz	2.00	1.00	.60
59	Sammy White	2.00	1.00	.60
60	Ted Williams	12.00	6.00	3.50
61	Ted Wills	2.00	1.00	.60
62	Earl Wilson	2.00	1.00	.60
63	Al Zarilla	2.00	1.00	.60
64	Norm Zauchin	2.00	1.00	.60

1979 Boston Red Sox team issue

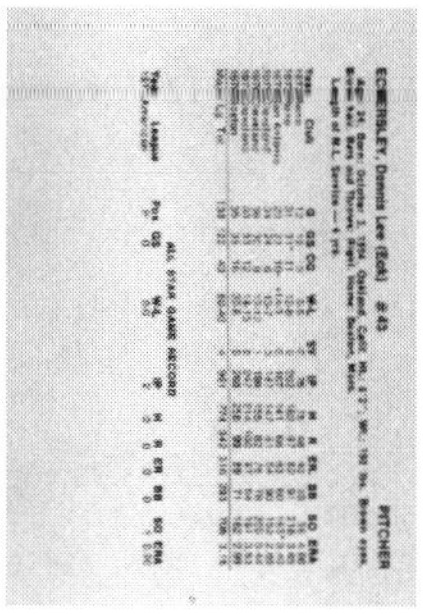

The origins of this Boston Red Sox card set are unclear. It may have been a team issue. The wide white bottom border beneath the black-and-white photo on the 2-1/2" x 3-1/2" cards may have been intended for autographing. Backs have player personal data and complete major and minor league stats. The checklist here, listed alphabetically, may not be complete.

		NM	EX	VG
Complete Set (23):		24.00	12.00	7.25
Common Player:		1.00	.50	.30
(1)	Gary Allenson	1.00	.50	.30
(2)	Jack Brohamer	1.00	.50	.30
(3)	Tom Burgmeier	1.00	.50	.30
(4)	Rick Burleson	1.00	.50	.30
(5)	Bill Campbell	1.00	.50	.30
(6)	Dick Drago	1.00	.50	.30
(7)	Dennis Eckersley	4.00	2.00	1.25
(8)	Dwight Evans	1.50	.70	.45
(9)	Carlton Fisk	4.00	2.00	1.25
(10)	Andy Hassler	1.00	.50	.30
(11)	Butch Hobson	1.00	.50	.30
(12)	Fred Lynn	2.00	1.00	.60
(13)	Bob Montgomery	1.00	.50	.30
(14)	Mike O'Berry	1.00	.50	.30
(15)	Jerry Remy	1.00	.50	.30
(16)	Steve Renko	1.00	.50	.30
(17)	Jim Rice	1.50	.70	.45
(18)	George Scott	1.00	.50	.30
(19)	Bob Stanley	1.00	.50	.30
(20)	Mike Torrez	1.00	.50	.30
(21)	Larry Wolfe	1.00	.50	.30
(22)	Jim Wright	1.00	.50	.30
(23)	Carl Yastrzemski	6.00	3.00	1.75

1916 Boston Store

One of several regional advertisers to use this 200-card set as a promotional medium was this Chicago department store chain. Checklist and pricing will be found elsewhere in these pages under the 1916 Collins-McCarthy listings. Collectors may pay a premium for individual cards to enhance a type card or superstar card collection. The American Card Catalog listed these 2" x 3-1/4" black-and-white cards as H801-8.

	NM	EX	VG
Common Player:	32.00	16.00	10.00
(See 1916 Collins-McCarthy.)			

1948 Bowman

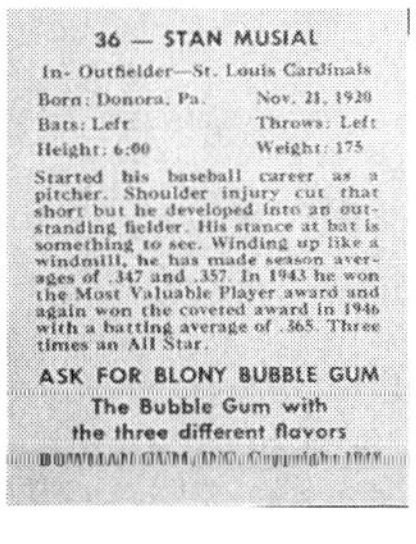

Bowman Gum Co.'s premiere set was produced in 1948, making it one of the first major issues of the post-war period. Forty-eight black-and-white cards comprise the set, with each card measuring 2-1/16" x 2-1/2" in size. The card backs, printed in black ink on grey stock, include the card number and the player's name, team, position, and a short biography. Twelve cards (marked with an "SP") were printed in short supply when they were removed from the 36-card printing sheet to make room for the set's high numbers (#37-48). These 24 cards command a higher price than the remaining cards in the set.

		NM	EX	VG
Complete Set (48):		3400.	1650.	950.00
Common Player (1-36):		20.00	10.00	6.50
Common Player (37-48):		32.00	16.00	9.50
1	*Bob Elliott*	80.00	24.00	15.00
2	*Ewell Blackwell*	34.00	17.00	10.00
3	*Ralph Kiner*	135.00	67.00	40.00
4	Johnny Mize	95.00	47.00	28.00
5	Bob Feller	220.00	110.00	66.00
6	*Yogi Berra*	425.00	212.00	127.00
7	Pete Reiser (SP)	50.00	25.00	15.00
8	Phil Rizzuto (SP)	250.00	125.00	75.00
9	Walker Cooper	20.00	10.00	6.50
10	Buddy Rosar	20.00	10.00	6.50
11	Johnny Lindell	25.00	12.50	7.50
12	*Johnny Sain*	50.00	25.00	15.00
13	*Willard Marshall* (SP)	32.00	16.00	9.50
14	*Allie Reynolds*	40.00	20.00	12.00
15	Eddie Joost	20.00	10.00	6.50
16	Jack Lohrke (SP)	32.00	16.00	9.50
17	Enos Slaughter	85.00	42.00	25.00
18	*Warren Spahn*	250.00	125.00	75.00
19	Tommy Henrich	35.00	17.50	10.50
20	Buddy Kerr (SP)	32.00	16.00	9.50
21	*Ferris Fain*	20.00	10.00	6.50
22	Floyd (Bill) Bevens (SP)	40.00	20.00	12.00
23	Larry Jansen	20.00	10.00	6.50
24	Emil (Dutch) Leonard (SP)	32.00	16.00	9.50
25	Barney McCoskey (McCosky)	20.00	10.00	6.50
26	Frank Shea (SP)	35.00	17.50	10.50
27	Sid Gordon	20.00	10.00	6.50
28	Emil Verban (SP)	32.00	16.00	9.50
29	*Joe Page* (SP)	50.00	25.00	15.00
30	*Whitey Lockman* (SP)	35.00	17.50	10.50
31	Bill McCahan	20.00	10.00	6.50
32	*Bill Rigney*	20.00	10.00	6.50
33	Billy Johnson	25.00	12.50	7.50
34	Sheldon Jones (SP)	32.00	16.00	9.50
35	Snuffy Stirnweiss	26.00	12.50	7.50
36	*Stan Musial*	775.00	385.00	230.00
37	Clint Hartung	32.00	16.00	9.50
38	*Red Schoendienst*	120.00	60.00	36.00
39	Augie Galan	32.00	16.00	9.50
40	*Marty Marion*	55.00	27.00	16.50
41	Rex Barney	32.00	16.00	9.50
42	Ray Poat	32.00	16.00	9.50
43	Bruce Edwards	32.00	16.00	9.50
44	Johnny Wyrostek	32.00	16.00	9.50
45	Hank Sauer	35.00	17.50	10.50
46	Herman Wehmeier	32.00	16.00	9.50
47	*Bobby Thomson*	75.00	37.00	22.00
48	Dave Koslo	70.00	20.00	9.00

1949 Bowman

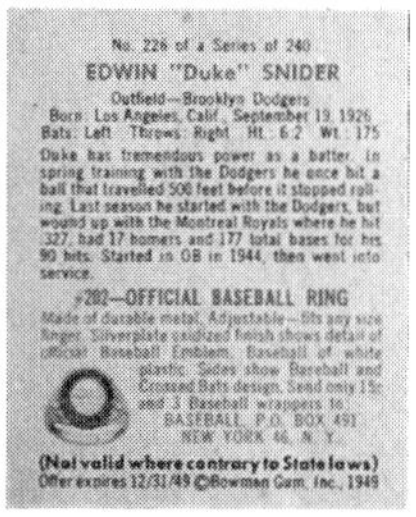

In 1949, Bowman increased the size of its issue to 240 numbered cards. The 2-1/16" x 2-1/2" cards are black-and-white photos overprinted with team uniform colors on a background of various solid pastel colors. Beginning with card #109 in the set, Bowman added the players' names on the card fronts. Twelve cards (#4, 78, 83, 85, 88, 98, 109, 124, 127, 132 and 143), which were produced in the first four series of printings, were reprinted in the seventh series with either a card front or back modification. These variations are noted in the checklist that follows. Card #1-3 and 5-73 can be found with either white or grey backs. The complete set value shown here does not include the higher priced variation cards.

		NM	EX	VG
Complete Set (240):		11000.	5500.	3250.
Common Player (1-144):		15.00	7.50	4.50
Common Player (145-240):		45.00	22.00	13.50
1	Vernon Bickford	125.00	25.00	8.00
2	"Whitey" Lockman	15.00	7.50	4.50
3	Bob Porterfield	15.00	7.50	4.50
4a	Jerry Priddy (no name on front)	15.00	7.50	4.50
4b	Jerry Priddy (name on front)	40.00	20.00	12.00
5	Hank Sauer	15.00	7.50	4.50
6	Phil Cavarretta	16.00	8.00	4.75
7	Joe Dobson	15.00	7.50	4.50
8	Murry Dickson	15.00	7.50	4.50
9	Ferris Fain	15.00	7.50	4.50
10	Ted Gray	15.00	7.50	4.50
11	Lou Boudreau	55.00	27.00	16.50

12	Cass Michaels	15.00	7.50	4.50
13	Bob Chesnes	15.00	7.50	4.50
14	*Curt Simmons*	30.00	15.00	9.00
15	*Ned Garver*	18.00	9.00	5.50
16	Al Kozar	15.00	7.50	4.50
17	Earl Torgeson	15.00	7.50	4.50
18	Bobby Thomson	27.50	13.50	8.25
19	*Bobby Brown*	35.00	17.50	10.50
20	Gene Hermanski	15.00	7.50	4.50
21	Frank Baumholtz	15.00	7.50	4.50
22	Harry "P-Nuts" Lowrey	15.00	7.50	4.50
23	Bobby Doerr	55.00	27.00	16.50
24	Stan Musial	500.00	250.00	150.00
25	Carl Scheib	15.00	7.50	4.50
26	George Kell	45.00	22.00	13.50
27	Bob Feller	165.00	82.00	49.00
28	Don Kolloway	15.00	7.50	4.50
29	Ralph Kiner	75.00	37.00	22.00
30	Andy Seminick	15.00	7.50	4.50
31	Dick Kokos	15.00	7.50	4.50
32	Eddie Yost	15.00	7.50	4.50
33	Warren Spahn	145.00	72.00	43.00
34	Dave Koslo	15.00	7.50	4.50
35	*Vic Raschi*	45.00	22.00	13.50
36	Pee Wee Reese	150.00	75.00	45.00
37	John Wyrostek	15.00	7.50	4.50
38	Emil Verban	15.00	7.50	4.50
39	Bill Goodman	15.00	7.50	4.50
40	"Red" Munger	15.00	7.50	4.50
41	Lou Brissie	15.00	7.50	4.50
42	"Hoot" Evers	15.00	7.50	4.50
43	Dale Mitchell	15.00	7.50	4.50
44	Dave Philley	15.00	7.50	4.50
45	Wally Westlake	15.00	7.50	4.50
46	*Robin Roberts*	200.00	100.00	60.00
47	Johnny Sain	32.00	16.00	9.50
48	Willard Marshall	15.00	7.50	4.50
49	Frank Shea	18.00	9.00	5.50
50	*Jackie Robinson*	800.00	400.00	240.00
51	Herman Wehmeier	15.00	7.50	4.50
52	Johnny Schmitz	15.00	7.50	4.50
53	Jack Kramer	15.00	7.50	4.50
54	Marty Marion	22.00	11.00	6.50
55	Eddie Joost	15.00	7.50	4.50
56	Pat Mullin	15.00	7.50	4.50
57	Gene Bearden	15.00	7.50	4.50
58	Bob Elliott	15.00	7.50	4.50
59	Jack Lohrke	15.00	7.50	4.50
60	Yogi Berra	265.00	130.00	80.00
61	Rex Barney	18.00	9.00	5.50
62	Grady Hatton	15.00	7.50	4.50
63	Andy Pafko	15.00	7.50	4.50
64	Dom DiMaggio	30.00	15.00	9.00
65	Enos Slaughter	55.00	27.00	16.50
66	Elmer Valo	15.00	7.50	4.50
67	Alvin Dark	18.00	9.00	5.50
68	Sheldon Jones	15.00	7.50	4.50
69	Tommy Henrich	24.00	12.00	7.25
70	*Carl Furillo*	75.00	37.50	22.50
71	Vern Stephens	15.00	7.50	4.50
72	Tommy Holmes	15.00	7.50	4.50
73	Billy Cox	18.00	9.00	5.50
74	Tom McBride	15.00	7.50	4.50
75	Eddie Mayo	15.00	7.50	4.50
76	Bill Nicholson	15.00	7.50	4.50
77	Ernie Bonham	15.00	7.50	4.50
78a	Sam Zoldak (no name on front)	15.00	7.50	4.50
78b	Sam Zoldak (name on front)	40.00	20.00	12.00
79	Ron Northey	15.00	7.50	4.50
80	Bill McCahan	15.00	7.50	4.50
81	Virgil "Red" Stallcup	15.00	7.50	4.50
82	Joe Page	24.00	12.00	7.25
83a	Bob Scheffing (no name on front)	15.00	7.50	4.50
83b	Bob Scheffing (name on front)	40.00	20.00	12.00
84	*Roy Campanella*	650.00	325.00	195.00
85a	Johnny Mize (no name on front)	80.00	40.00	24.00
85b	Johnny Mize (name on front)	120.00	60.00	36.00
86	Johnny Pesky	15.00	7.50	4.50
87	Randy Gumpert	15.00	7.50	4.50
88a	Bill Salkeld (no name on front)	15.00	7.50	4.50
88b	Bill Salkeld (name on front)	40.00	20.00	12.00
89	Mizell Platt	15.00	7.50	4.50
90	Gil Coan	15.00	7.50	4.50
91	Dick Wakefield	15.00	7.50	4.50
92	Willie Jones	15.00	7.50	4.50
93	Ed Stevens	15.00	7.50	4.50
94	*Mickey Vernon*	20.00	10.00	6.00
95	Howie Pollett	15.00	7.50	4.50
96	Taft Wright	15.00	7.50	4.50
97	Danny Litwhiler	15.00	7.50	4.50
98a	Phil Rizzuto (no name on front)	125.00	62.00	37.00
98b	Phil Rizzuto (name on front)	250.00	125.00	75.00
99	Frank Gustine	15.00	7.50	4.50
100	*Gil Hodges*	250.00	125.00	75.00
101	Sid Gordon	18.00	9.00	5.50
102	Stan Spence	15.00	7.50	4.50
103	Joe Tipton	15.00	7.50	4.50
104	*Ed Stanky*	30.00	15.00	9.00
105	Bill Kennedy	15.00	7.50	4.50
106	Jake Early	15.00	7.50	4.50
107	Eddie Lake	15.00	7.50	4.50
108	Ken Heintzelman	15.00	7.50	4.50
109a	Ed Fitz Gerald (script name on back)	15.00	7.50	4.50
109b	Ed Fitz Gerald (printed name on back)	40.00	20.00	12.00
110	*Early Wynn*	100.00	50.00	30.00
111	Red Schoendienst	70.00	35.00	21.00
112	Sam Chapman	15.00	7.50	4.50
113	Ray Lamanno	15.00	7.50	4.50
114	Allie Reynolds	30.00	15.00	9.00
115	Emil "Dutch" Leonard	15.00	7.50	4.50
116	Joe Hatten	15.00	7.50	4.50
117	Walker Cooper	15.00	7.50	4.50
118	Sam Mele	15.00	7.50	4.50
119	Floyd Baker	15.00	7.50	4.50
120	Cliff Fannin	15.00	7.50	4.50
121	Mark Christman	15.00	7.50	4.50
122	George Vico	15.00	7.50	4.50
123	Johnny Blatnick	15.00	7.50	4.50
124a	Danny Murtaugh (script name on back)	15.00	7.50	4.50
124b	Danny Murtaugh (printed name on back)	40.00	20.00	12.00
125	Ken Keltner	18.00	9.00	5.50
126a	Al Brazle (script name on back)	15.00	7.50	4.50
126b	Al Brazle (printed name on back)	40.00	20.00	12.00
127a	Henry Majeski (script name on back)	15.00	7.50	4.50
127b	Henry Majeski (printed name on back)	40.00	20.00	12.00
128	Johnny Vander Meer	24.00	12.00	7.25
129	Billy Johnson	18.00	9.00	5.50
130	Harry "The Hat" Walker	18.00	9.00	5.50
131	Paul Lehner	15.00	7.50	4.50
132a	Al Evans (script name on back)	15.00	7.50	4.50
132b	Al Evans (printed name on back)	40.00	20.00	12.00
133	Aaron Robinson	15.00	7.50	4.50
134	Hank Borowy	15.00	7.50	4.50
135	Stan Rojek	15.00	7.50	4.50
136	Hank Edwards	15.00	7.50	4.50
137	Ted Wilks	15.00	7.50	4.50
138	"Buddy" Rosar	15.00	7.50	4.50
139	Hank "Bow-Wow" Arft	15.00	7.50	4.50
140	Ray Scarborough	15.00	7.50	4.50
141	"Tony Lupien	15.00	7.50	4.50
142	Eddie Waitkus	15.00	7.50	4.50
143a	Bob Dillinger (script name on back)	15.00	7.50	4.50
143b	Bob Dillinger (printed name on back)	40.00	20.00	12.00
144	Mickey Haefner	15.00	7.50	4.50
145	"Blix" Donnelly	45.00	22.00	13.50
146	Mike McCormick	60.00	30.00	18.00
147	Elmer Singleton	45.00	22.00	13.50
148	Bob Swift	45.00	22.00	13.50
149	Roy Partee	55.00	27.00	16.50
150	Allie Clark	45.00	22.00	13.50
151	Mickey Harris	45.00	22.00	13.50
152	Clarence Maddern	45.00	22.00	13.50
153	Phil Masi	45.00	22.00	13.50
154	Clint Hartung	45.00	22.00	13.50
155	Mickey Guerra	45.00	22.00	13.50
156	Al Zarilla	45.00	22.00	13.50
157	Walt Masterson	45.00	22.00	13.50
158	Harry Brecheen	45.00	22.00	13.50
159	Glen Moulder	45.00	22.00	13.50
160	Jim Blackburn	45.00	22.00	13.50
161	"Jocko" Thompson	45.00	22.00	13.50
162	*Preacher Roe*	120.00	60.00	36.00
163	Clyde McCullough	45.00	22.00	13.50
164	*Vic Wertz*	60.00	30.00	18.00
165	"Snuffy" Stirnweiss	55.00	27.00	16.50
166	Mike Tresh	45.00	22.00	13.50
167	Boris "Babe" Martin	45.00	22.00	13.50
168	Doyle Lade	45.00	22.00	13.50
169	Jeff Heath	45.00	22.00	13.50
170	Bill Rigney	45.00	22.00	13.50
171	Dick Fowler	45.00	22.00	13.50
172	Eddie Pellagrini	45.00	22.00	13.50
173	Eddie Stewart	45.00	22.00	13.50
174	*Terry Moore*	75.00	37.00	22.00
175	Luke Appling	135.00	67.00	40.00
176	Ken Raffensberger	45.00	22.00	13.50
177	Stan Lopata	45.00	22.00	13.50
178	Tommy Brown	55.00	27.00	16.50
179	Hugh Casey	45.00	22.00	13.50
180	Connie Berry	45.00	22.00	13.50
181	Gus Niarhos	45.00	22.00	13.50
182	Hal Peck	45.00	22.00	13.50
183	Lou Stringer	45.00	22.00	13.50
184	Bob Chipman	45.00	22.00	13.50
185	Pete Reiser	85.00	42.00	25.00
186	"Buddy" Kerr	45.00	22.00	13.50
187	Phil Marchildon	45.00	22.00	13.50
188	Karl Drews	45.00	22.00	13.50
189	Earl Wooten	45.00	22.00	13.50
190	*Jim Hearn*	45.00	22.00	13.50
191	Joe Haynes	45.00	22.00	13.50
192	Harry Gumbert	45.00	22.00	13.50
193	Ken Trinkle	45.00	22.00	13.50
194	Ralph Branca	75.00	37.00	22.00
195	Eddie Bockman	45.00	22.00	13.50
196	Fred Hutchinson	45.00	22.00	13.50
197	Johnny Lindell	55.00	27.00	16.50
198	Steve Gromek	45.00	22.00	13.50
199	"Tex" Hughson	45.00	22.00	13.50
200	Jess Dobernic	45.00	22.00	13.50
201	Sibby Sisti	45.00	22.00	13.50
202	Larry Jansen	45.00	22.00	13.50
203	Barney McCosky	45.00	22.00	13.50
204	Bob Savage	45.00	22.00	13.50
205	Dick Sisler	45.00	22.00	13.50
206	Bruce Edwards	45.00	22.00	13.50
207	Johnny Hopp	45.00	22.00	13.50
208	"Dizzy" Trout	45.00	22.00	13.50
209	Charlie Keller	80.00	40.00	24.00
210	Joe Gordon	65.00	32.00	19.50
211	Dave "Boo" Ferris	45.00	22.00	13.50
212	Ralph Hamner	45.00	22.00	13.50
213	Charles "Red" Barrett	45.00	22.00	13.50
214	*Richie Ashburn*	550.00	275.00	165.00
215	Kirby Higbe	45.00	22.00	13.50
216	"Schoolboy" Rowe	55.00	27.00	16.50
217	Marino Pieretti	45.00	22.00	13.50
218	Dick Kryhoski	45.00	22.00	13.50
219	*Virgil "Fire" Trucks*	75.00	37.00	22.00
220	Johnny McCarthy	45.00	22.00	13.50
221	Bob Muncrief	45.00	22.00	13.50
222	Alex Kellner	45.00	22.00	13.50
223	Bob Hofman	45.00	22.00	13.50
224	*Satchel Paige*	950.00	475.00	285.00
225	*Gerry Coleman*	85.00	42.00	25.00
226	*Duke Snider*	850.00	425.00	255.00
227	Fritz Ostermueller	45.00	22.00	13.50
228	Jackie Mayo	45.00	22.00	13.50
229	*Ed Lopat*	120.00	60.00	36.00
230	Augie Galan	45.00	22.00	13.50
231	Earl Johnson	45.00	22.00	13.50
232	George McQuinn	45.00	22.00	13.50
233	*Larry Doby*	200.00	100.00	60.00
234	"Rip" Sewell	45.00	22.00	13.50
235	Jim Russell	45.00	22.00	13.50
236	Fred Sanford	55.00	27.00	16.50
237	Monte Kennedy	45.00	22.00	13.50
238	*Bob Lemon*	200.00	100.00	60.00
239	Frank McCormick	45.00	22.00	13.50
240	Norm "Babe" Young (Photo actually Bobby Young)	100.00	22.00	13.50

1950 Bowman

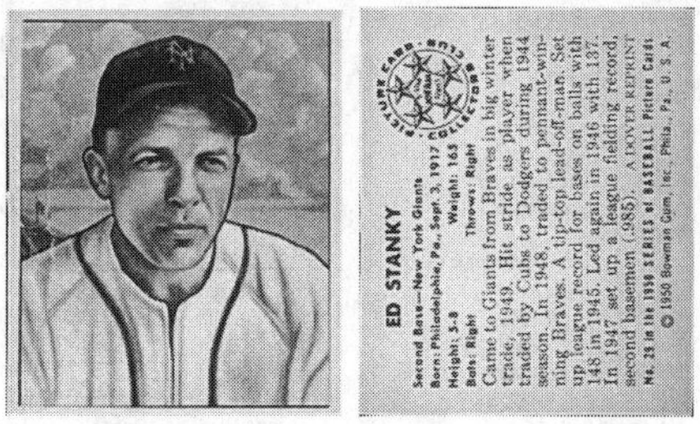

The quality of the 1950 Bowman issue showed a marked improvement over the company's previous efforts. The cards are beautiful color art reproductions of actual photographs and measure 2-1/16" x 2-1/2". Backs include the same type of information found in the previous year's issue but are designed in a horizontal format. Cards found in the first two series of the set (#1-72) are the scarcer of the issue. The backs of the final 72 cards in the set (#181-252) can be found with or without the copyright line at the bottom of the card, the "without" version being the less common.

		NM	EX	VG
Complete Set (252):		7000.	3500.	2100.
Common Player (1-72):		35.00	18.00	11.00
Common Player (73-252):		15.00	6.00	5.00
1	Mel Parnell	125.00	45.00	20.00
2	Vern Stephens	35.00	18.00	11.00
3	Dom DiMaggio	55.00	27.00	16.50
4	Gus Zernial	35.00	18.00	11.00
5	Bob Kuzava	35.00	18.00	11.00
6	Bob Feller	160.00	80.00	48.00
7	Jim Hegan	35.00	18.00	11.00
8	George Kell	65.00	32.00	19.50
9	Vic Wertz	35.00	18.00	11.00
10	Tommy Henrich	45.00	22.00	13.50
11	Phil Rizzuto	200.00	100.00	60.00
12	Joe Page	40.00	18.00	12.00
13	Ferris Fain	35.00	18.00	11.00
14	Alex Kellner	35.00	18.00	11.00
15	Al Kozar	35.00	18.00	11.00
16	*Roy Sievers*	50.00	25.00	11.00
17	Sid Hudson	35.00	18.00	11.00
18	Eddie Robinson	35.00	18.00	11.00
19	Warren Spahn	200.00	100.00	60.00
20	Bob Elliott	35.00	18.00	11.00
21	Pee Wee Reese	195.00	97.00	58.00
22	Jackie Robinson	625.00	300.00	185.00
23	*Don Newcombe*	115.00	57.00	34.00
24	Johnny Schmitz	35.00	18.00	11.00
25	Hank Sauer	35.00	18.00	11.00
26	Grady Hatton	35.00	18.00	11.00
27	Herman Wehmeier	35.00	18.00	11.00
28	Bobby Thomson	50.00	25.00	11.00
29	Ed Stanky	35.00	18.00	11.00
30	Eddie Waitkus	35.00	18.00	11.00
31	*Del Ennis*	50.00	25.00	11.00
32	Robin Roberts	135.00	67.00	40.00
33	Ralph Kiner	80.00	40.00	24.00
34	Murry Dickson	35.00	18.00	11.00
35	Enos Slaughter	90.00	45.00	27.00
36	Eddie Kazak	35.00	18.00	11.00
37	Luke Appling	70.00	35.00	21.00
38	Bill Wight	35.00	18.00	11.00
39	Larry Doby	125.00	62.00	37.00
40	Bob Lemon	70.00	35.00	21.00
41	"Hoot" Evers	35.00	18.00	11.00
42	Art Houtteman	35.00	18.00	11.00
43	Bobby Doerr	65.00	32.00	19.50
44	Joe Dobson	35.00	18.00	11.00
45	Al Zarilla	35.00	18.00	11.00
46	Yogi Berra	350.00	175.00	105.00
47	Jerry Coleman	45.00	22.00	13.50
48	Lou Brissie	35.00	18.00	11.00
49	Elmer Valo	35.00	18.00	11.00
50	Dick Kokos	35.00	18.00	11.00
51	Ned Garver	35.00	18.00	11.00
52	Sam Mele	35.00	18.00	11.00

53	Clyde Vollmer	35.00	18.00	11.00
54	Gil Coan	35.00	18.00	11.00
55	"Buddy" Kerr	35.00	18.00	11.00
56	*Del Crandell* (Crandall)	40.00	18.00	12.00
57	Vernon Bickford	35.00	18.00	11.00
58	Carl Furillo	55.00	27.00	16.50
59	Ralph Branca	40.00	18.00	12.00
60	Andy Pafko	35.00	18.00	11.00
61	Bob Rush	35.00	18.00	11.00
62	Ted Kluszewski	85.00	42.00	25.00
63	Ewell Blackwell	40.00	18.00	12.00
64	Alvin Dark	33.00	16.50	11.00
65	Dave Koslo	35.00	18.00	11.00
66	Larry Jansen	35.00	18.00	11.00
67	Willie Jones	35.00	18.00	11.00
68	Curt Simmons	35.00	18.00	11.00
69	Wally Westlake	35.00	18.00	11.00
70	Bob Chesnes	35.00	18.00	11.00
71	Red Schoendienst	65.00	32.00	19.50
72	Howie Pollet	35.00	18.00	11.00
73	Willard Marshall	15.00	6.00	5.00
74	*Johnny Antonelli*	32.00	16.00	9.50
75	Roy Campanella	275.00	135.00	82.00
76	Rex Barney	15.00	6.00	5.00
77	Duke Snider	235.00	117.00	70.00
78	Mickey Owen	15.00	6.00	5.00
79	Johnny Vander Meer	15.00	6.00	5.00
80	Howard Fox	15.00	6.00	5.00
81	Ron Northey	15.00	6.00	5.00
82	"Whitey" Lockman	15.00	6.00	5.00
83	Sheldon Jones	15.00	6.00	5.00
84	Richie Ashburn	100.00	50.00	30.00
85	Ken Heintzelman	15.00	6.00	5.00
86	Stan Rojek	15.00	6.00	5.00
87	Bill Werle	15.00	6.00	5.00
88	Marty Marion	18.00	9.00	5.50
89	George Munger	15.00	6.00	5.00
90	Harry Brecheen	15.00	6.00	5.00
91	Cass Michaels	15.00	6.00	5.00
92	Hank Majeski	15.00	6.00	5.00
93	Gene Bearden	15.00	6.00	5.00
94	Lou Boudreau	45.00	22.00	13.50
95	Aaron Robinson	15.00	6.00	5.00
96	Virgil "Fire" Trucks	15.00	6.00	5.00
97	Maurice McDermott	15.00	6.00	5.00
98	Ted Williams	700.00	375.00	175.00
99	Billy Goodman	15.00	6.00	5.00
100	Vic Raschi	22.00	11.00	6.50
101	Bobby Brown	18.00	9.00	5.50
102	Billy Johnson	15.00	6.00	5.00
103	Eddie Joost	15.00	6.00	5.00
104	Sam Chapman	15.00	6.00	5.00
105	Bob Dillinger	15.00	6.00	5.00
106	Cliff Fannin	15.00	6.00	5.00
107	Sam Dente	15.00	6.00	5.00
108	Ray Scarborough	15.00	6.00	5.00
109	Sid Gordon	15.00	6.00	5.00
110	Tommy Holmes	15.00	6.00	5.00
111	Walker Cooper	15.00	6.00	5.00
112	Gil Hodges	90.00	45.00	27.00
113	Gene Hermanski	15.00	6.00	5.00
114	*Wayne Terwilliger*	15.00	6.00	5.00
115	Roy Smalley	15.00	6.00	5.00
116	Virgil "Red" Stallcup	15.00	6.00	5.00
117	Bill Rigney	15.00	6.00	5.00
118	Clint Hartung	15.00	6.00	5.00
119	Dick Sisler	15.00	6.00	5.00
120	Jocko Thompson	15.00	6.00	5.00
121	Andy Seminick	15.00	6.00	5.00
122	Johnny Hopp	15.00	6.00	5.00
123	Dino Restelli	15.00	6.00	5.00
124	Clyde McCullough	15.00	6.00	5.00
125	Del Rice	15.00	6.00	5.00
126	Al Brazle	15.00	6.00	5.00
127	Dave Philley	15.00	6.00	5.00
128	Phil Masi	15.00	6.00	5.00
129	Joe Gordon	15.00	6.00	5.00
130	Dale Mitchell	15.00	6.00	5.00
131	Steve Gromek	15.00	6.00	5.00
132	Mickey Vernon	15.00	6.00	5.00
133	Don Kolloway	15.00	6.00	5.00
134	"Dizzy" Trout	15.00	6.00	5.00
135	Pat Mullin	15.00	6.00	5.00
136	"Buddy" Rosar	15.00	6.00	5.00
137	Johnny Pesky	15.00	6.00	5.00
138	Allie Reynolds	32.00	16.00	9.50
139	Johnny Mize	75.00	37.00	22.00
140	Pete Suder	15.00	6.00	5.00
141	Joe Coleman	15.00	6.00	5.00
142	*Sherman Lollar*	15.00	6.00	5.00
143	Eddie Stewart	15.00	6.00	5.00
144	Al Evans	15.00	6.00	5.00
145	Jack Graham	15.00	6.00	5.00
146	Floyd Baker	15.00	6.00	5.00
147	*Mike Garcia*	20.00	10.00	6.00
148	Early Wynn	55.00	27.00	16.50
149	Bob Swift	15.00	6.00	5.00
150	George Vico	15.00	6.00	5.00
151	Fred Hutchinson	15.00	6.00	5.00
152	Ellis Kinder	15.00	6.00	5.00
153	Walt Masterson	15.00	6.00	5.00
154	Gus Niarhos	15.00	6.00	5.00
155	Frank "Spec" Shea	15.00	6.00	5.00
156	Fred Sanford	15.00	6.00	5.00
157	Mike Guerra	15.00	6.00	5.00
158	Paul Lehner	15.00	6.00	5.00
159	Joe Tipton	15.00	6.00	5.00
160	Mickey Harris	15.00	6.00	5.00
161	Sherry Robertson	15.00	6.00	5.00
162	Eddie Yost	15.00	6.00	5.00
163	Earl Torgeson	15.00	6.00	5.00
164	Sibby Sisti	15.00	6.00	5.00
165	Bruce Edwards	15.00	6.00	5.00
166	Joe Hatten	15.00	6.00	5.00
167	Preacher Roe	19.00	9.50	5.75
168	Bob Scheffing	15.00	6.00	5.00
169	Hank Edwards	15.00	6.00	5.00
170	Emil Leonard	15.00	6.00	5.00
171	Harry Gumbert	15.00	6.00	5.00
172	Harry Lowrey	15.00	6.00	5.00
173	Lloyd Merriman	15.00	6.00	5.00
174	*Henry Thompson*	15.00	6.00	5.00
175	Monte Kennedy	15.00	6.00	5.00
176	"Blix" Donnelly	15.00	6.00	5.00
177	Hank Borowy	15.00	6.00	5.00
178	Eddy Fitz Gerald	15.00	6.00	5.00
179	Charles Diering	15.00	6.00	5.00
180	Harry "The Hat" Walker	15.00	6.00	5.00
181	Marino Pieretti	15.00	6.00	5.00
182	Sam Zoldak	15.00	6.00	5.00
183	Mickey Haefner	15.00	6.00	5.00
184	Randy Gumpert	15.00	6.00	5.00
185	Howie Judson	15.00	6.00	5.00
186	Ken Keltner	15.00	6.00	5.00
187	Lou Stringer	15.00	6.00	5.00
188	Earl Johnson	15.00	6.00	5.00
189	Owen Friend	15.00	6.00	5.00
190	Ken Wood	15.00	6.00	5.00
191	Dick Starr	15.00	6.00	5.00
192	Bob Chipman	15.00	6.00	5.00
193	Pete Reiser	18.00	9.00	5.50
194	Billy Cox	15.00	6.00	5.00
195	Phil Cavarretta	15.00	6.00	5.00
196	Doyle Lade	15.00	6.00	5.00
197	Johnny Wyrostek	15.00	6.00	5.00
198	Danny Litwhiler	15.00	6.00	5.00
199	Jack Kramer	15.00	6.00	5.00
200	Kirby Higbe	15.00	6.00	5.00
201	Pete Castiglione	15.00	6.00	5.00
202	Cliff Chambers	15.00	6.00	5.00
203	Danny Murtaugh	15.00	6.00	5.00
204	Granny Hamner	15.00	6.00	5.00
205	Mike Goliat	15.00	6.00	5.00
206	Stan Lopata	15.00	6.00	5.00
207	Max Lanier	15.00	6.00	5.00
208	Jim Hearn	15.00	6.00	5.00
209	Johnny Lindell	15.00	6.00	5.00
210	Ted Gray	15.00	6.00	5.00
211	Charlie Keller	15.00	6.00	5.00
212	Gerry Priddy	15.00	6.00	5.00
213	Carl Scheib	15.00	6.00	5.00
214	Dick Fowler	15.00	6.00	5.00
215	Ed Lopat	35.00	17.50	10.50
216	Bob Porterfield	15.00	6.00	5.00
217	Casey Stengel	100.00	50.00	30.00
218	Cliff Mapes	15.00	6.00	5.00
219	*Hank Bauer*	65.00	32.00	19.50
220	Leo Durocher	55.00	27.00	16.50
221	Don Mueller	15.00	6.00	5.00
222	Bobby Morgan	15.00	6.00	5.00
223	Jimmy Russell	15.00	6.00	5.00
224	Jack Banta	15.00	6.00	5.00
225	Eddie Sawyer	15.00	6.00	5.00
226	*Jim Konstanty*	28.00	14.00	8.50
227	Bob Miller	15.00	6.00	5.00
228	Bill Nicholson	15.00	6.00	5.00
229	Frank Frisch	37.00	18.50	11.00
230	Bill Serena	15.00	6.00	5.00
231	Preston Ward	15.00	6.00	5.00
232	*Al Rosen*	35.00	18.00	10.50
233	Allie Clark	15.00	6.00	5.00
234	*Bobby Shantz*	35.00	18.00	10.50
235	Harold Gilbert	15.00	6.00	5.00
236	Bob Cain	15.00	6.00	5.00
237	Bill Salkeld	15.00	6.00	5.00
238	Nippy Jones	15.00	6.00	5.00
239	Bill Howerton	15.00	6.00	5.00
240	Eddie Lake	15.00	6.00	5.00
241	Neil Berry	15.00	6.00	5.00
242	Dick Kryhoski	15.00	6.00	5.00
243	Johnny Groth	15.00	6.00	5.00
244	Dale Coogan	15.00	6.00	5.00
245	Al Papai	15.00	6.00	5.00
246	*Walt Dropo*	20.00	10.00	6.00
247	*Irv Noren*	22.00	11.00	6.50
248	*Sam Jethroe*	22.00	11.00	6.50
249	"Snuffy" Stirnweiss	15.00	6.00	5.00
250	Ray Coleman	15.00	6.00	5.00
251	Les Moss	15.00	6.00	5.00
252	Billy DeMars	45.00	10.00	6.00

1951 Bowman

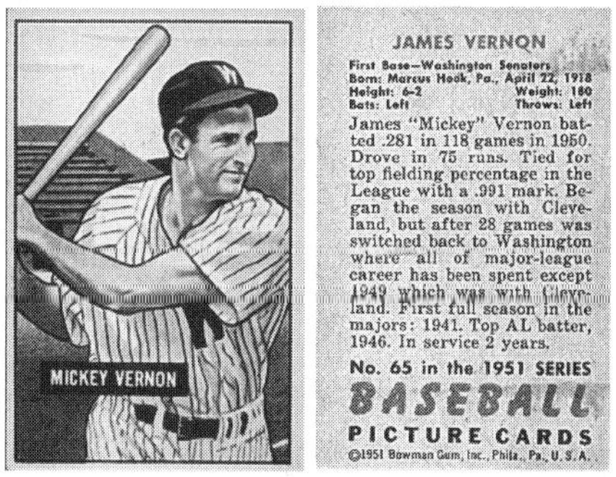

In 1951, Bowman increased the number of cards in its set for the third consecutive year when it issued 324 cards. The cards are, like 1950, color art reproductions of actual photographs but now measure 2-1/16" x 3-1/8" in size. The player's name is situated in a small, black box on the card front. Several of the card fronts are enlargements of the 1950 version. The high-numbered series of the set (#253-324), which includes the rookie cards of Mantle and Mays, are the scarcest of the issue.

		NM	EX	VG
Complete Set (324):		18000.	9000.	5000.
Common Player (1-36):		17.50	8.00	5.00
Common Player (37-252):		14.00	7.00	4.25
Common Player (253-324):		40.00	20.00	12.00
1	*Whitey Ford*	795.00	225.00	125.00
2	Yogi Berra	300.00	150.00	90.00
3	Robin Roberts	80.00	40.00	25.00
4	Del Ennis	17.50	8.00	5.00
5	Dale Mitchell	17.50	8.00	5.00
6	Don Newcombe	30.00	15.00	9.00
7	Gil Hodges	70.00	35.00	21.00
8	Paul Lehner	17.50	8.00	5.00
9	Sam Chapman	17.50	8.00	5.00
10	Red Schoendienst	55.00	27.00	16.50
11	"Red" Munger	17.50	8.00	5.00
12	Hank Majeski	17.50	8.00	5.00
13	Ed Stanky	17.50	8.00	5.00
14	Alvin Dark	20.00	10.00	6.00
15	Johnny Pesky	17.50	8.00	5.00
16	Maurice McDermott	17.50	8.00	5.00
17	Pete Castiglione	17.50	8.00	5.00
18	Gil Coan	17.50	8.00	5.00
19	Sid Gordon	17.50	8.00	5.00
20	Del Crandall	17.50	8.00	5.00
21	"Snuffy" Stirnweiss	17.50	8.00	5.00
22	Hank Sauer	17.50	8.00	5.00
23	"Hoot" Evers	17.50	8.00	5.00
24	Ewell Blackwell	22.00	11.00	6.50
25	Vic Raschi	29.00	14.50	8.75
26	Phil Rizzuto	115.00	57.00	34.00
27	Jim Konstanty	17.50	8.00	5.00
28	Eddie Waitkus	17.50	8.00	5.00
29	Allie Clark	17.50	8.00	5.00
30	Bob Feller	125.00	62.00	37.00
31	Roy Campanella	210.00	105.00	63.00
32	Duke Snider	210.00	105.00	63.00
33	Bob Hooper	17.50	8.00	5.00
34	Marty Marion	20.00	10.00	6.00
35	Al Zarilla	17.50	8.00	5.00
36	Joe Dobson	17.50	8.00	5.00
37	Whitey Lockman	14.00	7.00	4.25
38	Al Evans	14.00	7.00	4.25
39	Ray Scarborough	14.00	7.00	4.25
40	*Gus Bell*	27.50	13.50	8.25
41	Eddie Yost	14.00	7.00	4.25
42	Vern Bickford	14.00	7.00	4.25
43	Billy DeMars	14.00	7.00	4.25
44	Roy Smalley	14.00	7.00	4.25
45	Art Houtteman	14.00	7.00	4.25
46	George Kell	50.00	25.00	15.00
47	Grady Hatton	14.00	7.00	4.25
48	Ken Raffensberger	14.00	7.00	4.25
49	Jerry Coleman	17.50	8.00	5.00
50	Johnny Mize	48.00	24.00	14.50
51	Andy Seminick	14.00	7.00	4.25
52	Dick Sisler	14.00	7.00	4.25
53	Bob Lemon	45.00	22.00	13.50
54	*Ray Boone*	25.00	12.50	7.50
55	Gene Hermanski	14.00	7.00	4.25
56	Ralph Branca	24.00	12.00	7.25
57	Alex Kellner	14.00	7.00	4.25
58	Enos Slaughter	47.50	24.00	14.00
59	Randy Gumpert	14.00	7.00	4.25
60	"Chico" Carrasquel	14.00	7.00	4.25
61	Jim Hearn	14.00	7.00	4.25
62	Lou Boudreau	45.00	22.00	13.50
63	Bob Dillinger	14.00	7.00	4.25
64	Bill Werle	14.00	7.00	4.25
65	Mickey Vernon	14.00	7.00	4.25
66	Bob Elliott	14.00	7.00	4.25
67	Roy Sievers	14.00	7.00	4.25
68	Dick Kokos	14.00	7.00	4.25
69	Johnny Schmitz	14.00	7.00	4.25
70	Ron Northey	14.00	7.00	4.25
71	Jerry Priddy	14.00	7.00	4.25
72	Lloyd Merriman	14.00	7.00	4.25
73	Tommy Byrne	14.00	7.00	4.25
74	Billy Johnson	14.00	7.00	4.25
75	Russ Meyer	14.00	7.00	4.25
76	Stan Lopata	14.00	7.00	4.25
77	Mike Goliat	14.00	7.00	4.25
78	Early Wynn	45.00	22.00	13.50
79	Jim Hegan	14.00	7.00	4.25
80	Pee Wee Reese	125.00	62.00	37.00
81	Carl Furillo	28.00	14.00	8.50
82	Joe Tipton	14.00	7.00	4.25
83	Carl Scheib	14.00	7.00	4.25
84	Barney McCosky	14.00	7.00	4.25
85	Eddie Kazak	14.00	7.00	4.25
86	Harry Brecheen	14.00	7.00	4.25
87	Floyd Baker	14.00	7.00	4.25
88	Eddie Robinson	14.00	7.00	4.25
89	Henry Thompson	14.00	7.00	4.25
90	Dave Koslo	14.00	7.00	4.25
91	Clyde Vollmer	14.00	7.00	4.25
92	Vern Stephens	14.00	7.00	4.25
93	Danny O'Connell	14.00	7.00	4.25
94	Clyde McCullough	14.00	7.00	4.25
95	Sherry Robertson	14.00	7.00	4.25
96	Sandy Consuegra	14.00	7.00	4.25
97	Bob Kuzava	14.00	7.00	4.25
98	Willard Marshall	14.00	7.00	4.25
99	Earl Torgeson	14.00	7.00	4.25
100	Sherman Lollar	14.00	7.00	4.25
101	Owen Friend	14.00	7.00	4.25
102	Emil "Dutch" Leonard	14.00	7.00	4.25
103	Andy Pafko	14.00	7.00	4.25
104	Virgil "Fire" Trucks	14.00	7.00	4.25
105	Don Kolloway	14.00	7.00	4.25

106	Pat Mullin	14.00	7.00	4.25
107	Johnny Wyrostek	14.00	7.00	4.25
108	Virgil Stallcup	14.00	7.00	4.25
109	Allie Reynolds	29.00	14.50	8.75
110	Bobby Brown	17.50	8.75	5.25
111	Curt Simmons	14.00	7.00	4.25
112	Willie Jones	14.00	7.00	4.25
113	Bill "Swish" Nicholson	14.00	7.00	4.25
114	Sam Zoldak	14.00	7.00	4.25
115	Steve Gromek	14.00	7.00	4.25
116	Bruce Edwards	14.00	7.00	4.25
117	Eddie Miksis	14.00	7.00	4.25
118	Preacher Roe	22.00	11.00	6.50
119	Eddie Joost	14.00	7.00	4.25
120	Joe Coleman	14.00	7.00	4.25
121	Gerry Staley	14.00	7.00	4.25
122	*Joe Garagiola*	80.00	40.00	24.00
123	Howie Judson	14.00	7.00	4.25
124	Gus Niarhos	14.00	7.00	4.25
125	Bill Rigney	14.00	7.00	4.25
126	Bobby Thomson	29.00	14.50	8.75
127	*Sal Maglie*	35.00	17.50	10.50
128	Ellis Kinder	14.00	7.00	4.25
129	Matt Batts	14.00	7.00	4.25
130	Tom Saffell	14.00	7.00	4.25
131	Cliff Chambers	14.00	7.00	4.25
132	Cass Michaels	14.00	7.00	4.25
133	Sam Dente	14.00	7.00	4.25
134	Warren Spahn	125.00	62.00	37.00
135	Walker Cooper	14.00	7.00	4.25
136	Ray Coleman	14.00	7.00	4.25
137	Dick Starr	14.00	7.00	4.25
138	Phil Cavarretta	14.00	7.00	4.25
139	Doyle Lade	14.00	7.00	4.25
140	Eddie Lake	14.00	7.00	4.25
141	Fred Hutchinson	14.00	7.00	4.25
142	Aaron Robinson	14.00	7.00	4.25
143	Ted Kluszewski	40.00	20.00	12.00
144	Herman Wehmeier	14.00	7.00	4.25
145	Fred Sanford	14.00	7.00	4.25
146	Johnny Hopp	14.00	7.00	4.25
147	Ken Heintzelman	14.00	7.00	4.25
148	Granny Hamner	14.00	7.00	4.25
149	"Bubba" Church	14.00	7.00	4.25
150	Mike Garcia	17.50	8.00	5.00
151	Larry Doby	80.00	40.00	24.00
152	Cal Abrams	14.00	7.00	4.25
153	Rex Barney	14.00	7.00	4.25
154	Pete Suder	14.00	7.00	4.25
155	Lou Brissie	14.00	7.00	4.25
156	Del Rice	14.00	7.00	4.25
157	Al Brazle	14.00	7.00	4.25
158	Chuck Diering	14.00	7.00	4.25
159	Eddie Stewart	14.00	7.00	4.25
160	Phil Masi	14.00	7.00	4.25
161	Wes Westrum	14.00	7.00	4.25
162	Larry Jansen	14.00	7.00	4.25
163	Monte Kennedy	14.00	7.00	4.25
164	Bill Wight	14.00	7.00	4.25
165	Ted Williams	625.00	275.00	165.00
166	Stan Rojek	14.00	7.00	4.25
167	Murry Dickson	14.00	7.00	4.25
168	Sam Mele	14.00	7.00	4.25
169	Sid Hudson	14.00	7.00	4.25
170	Sibby Sisti	14.00	7.00	4.25
171	Buddy Kerr	14.00	7.00	4.25
172	Ned Garver	14.00	7.00	4.25
173	Hank Arft	14.00	7.00	4.25
174	Mickey Owen	14.00	7.00	4.25
175	Wayne Terwilliger	14.00	7.00	4.25
176	Vic Wertz	14.00	7.00	4.25
177	Charlie Keller	17.50	8.00	5.00
178	Ted Gray	14.00	7.00	4.25
179	Danny Litwhiler	14.00	7.00	4.25
180	Howie Fox	14.00	7.00	4.25
181	Casey Stengel	70.00	35.00	21.00
182	Tom Ferrick	14.00	7.00	4.25
183	Hank Bauer	25.00	12.50	7.50
184	Eddie Sawyer	14.00	7.00	4.25
185	Jimmy Bloodworth	14.00	7.00	4.25
186	Richie Ashburn	90.00	45.00	27.00
187	Al Rosen	17.50	8.00	5.00
188	*Roberto Avila*	17.50	8.00	5.00
189	Erv Palica	14.00	7.00	4.25
190	Joe Hatten	14.00	7.00	4.25
191	Billy Hitchcock	14.00	7.00	4.25
192	Hank Wyse	14.00	7.00	4.25
193	Ted Wilks	14.00	7.00	4.25
194	Harry "Peanuts" Lowrey	14.00	7.00	4.25
195	Paul Richards	18.00	9.00	5.50
196	*Bill Pierce*	32.00	16.00	9.50
197	Bob Cain	14.00	7.00	4.25
198	*Monte Irvin*	75.00	37.00	22.00
199	Sheldon Jones	14.00	7.00	4.25
200	Jack Kramer	14.00	7.00	4.25
201	Steve O'Neill	14.00	7.00	4.25
202	Mike Guerra	14.00	7.00	4.25
203	*Vernon Law*	24.00	12.00	7.25
204	Vic Lombardi	14.00	7.00	4.25
205	Mickey Grasso	14.00	7.00	4.25
206	Connie Marrero	14.00	7.00	4.25
207	Billy Southworth	14.00	7.00	4.25
208	"Blix" Donnelly	14.00	7.00	4.25
209	Ken Wood	14.00	7.00	4.25
210	Les Moss	14.00	7.00	4.25
211	Hal Jeffcoat	14.00	7.00	4.25
212	Bob Rush	14.00	7.00	4.25
213	Neil Berry	14.00	7.00	4.25
214	Bob Swift	14.00	7.00	4.25
215	Kent Peterson	14.00	7.00	4.25
216	Connie Ryan	14.00	7.00	4.25
217	Joe Page	19.00	9.50	5.75
218	Ed Lopat	25.00	12.50	7.50
219	*Gene Woodling*	40.00	20.00	12.00
220	Bob Miller	14.00	7.00	4.25
221	Dick Whitman	14.00	7.00	4.25
222	Thurman Tucker	14.00	7.00	4.25
223	Johnny Vander Meer	20.00	10.00	6.00
224	Billy Cox	17.50	8.00	5.00
225	*Dan Bankhead*	14.00	7.00	4.25
226	Jimmy Dykes	14.00	7.00	4.25
227	Bobby Shantz	17.50	8.00	5.00
228	*Cloyd Boyer*	14.00	7.00	4.25
229	Bill Howerton	14.00	7.00	4.25
230	Max Lanier	14.00	7.00	4.25
231	Luis Aloma	14.00	7.00	4.25
232	*Nellie Fox*	175.00	87.00	52.00
233	Leo Durocher	55.00	27.00	16.50
234	Clint Hartung	14.00	7.00	4.25
235	Jack Lohrke	14.00	7.00	4.25
236	"Buddy" Rosar	14.00	7.00	4.25
237	Billy Goodman	14.00	7.00	4.25
238	Pete Reiser	18.00	9.00	5.50
239	Bill MacDonald	14.00	7.00	4.25
240	Joe Haynes	14.00	7.00	4.25
241	Irv Noren	14.00	7.00	4.25
242	Sam Jethroe	14.00	7.00	5.50
243	Johnny Antonelli	14.00	7.00	4.25
244	Cliff Fannin	14.00	7.00	4.25
245	John Berardino	19.00	9.50	5.75
246	Bill Serena	14.00	7.00	4.25
247	Bob Ramazotti	14.00	7.00	4.25
248	*Johnny Klippstein*	14.00	7.00	4.25
249	Johnny Groth	14.00	7.00	4.25
250	Hank Borowy	14.00	7.00	4.25
251	Willard Ramsdell	14.00	7.00	4.25
252	"Dixie" Howell	14.00	7.00	4.25
253	*Mickey Mantle*	5500.	2750.	1900.
254	*Jackie Jensen*	90.00	45.00	27.00
255	Milo Candini	40.00	20.00	12.00
256	Ken Silvestri	40.00	20.00	12.00
257	Birdie Tebbetts	40.00	20.00	12.00
258	*Luke Easter*	45.00	22.00	13.50
259	Charlie Dressen	45.00	22.00	13.50
260	*Carl Erskine*	95.00	47.00	28.00
261	Wally Moses	40.00	20.00	12.00
262	Gus Zernial	40.00	20.00	12.00
263	Howie Pollet	40.00	20.00	12.00
264	Don Richmond	40.00	20.00	12.00
265	*Steve Bilko*	40.00	20.00	12.00
266	Harry Dorish	40.00	20.00	12.00
267	Ken Holcombe	40.00	20.00	12.00
268	Don Mueller	40.00	20.00	12.00
269	Ray Noble	40.00	20.00	12.00
270	Willard Nixon	40.00	20.00	12.00
271	Tommy Wright	40.00	20.00	12.00
272	Billy Meyer	40.00	20.00	12.00
273	Danny Murtaugh	40.00	20.00	12.00
274	George Metkovich	40.00	20.00	12.00
275	Bucky Harris	55.00	27.00	16.50
276	Frank Quinn	40.00	20.00	12.00
277	Roy Hartsfield	40.00	20.00	12.00
278	Norman Roy	40.00	20.00	12.00
279	Jim Delsing	40.00	20.00	12.00
280	Frank Overmire	40.00	20.00	12.00
281	Al Widmar	40.00	20.00	12.00
282	Frank Frisch	60.00	30.00	18.00
283	Walt Dubiel	40.00	20.00	12.00
284	Gene Bearden	40.00	20.00	12.00
285	Johnny Lipon	40.00	20.00	12.00
286	Bob Usher	40.00	20.00	12.00
287	Jim Blackburn	40.00	20.00	12.00
288	Bobby Adams	40.00	20.00	12.00
289	Cliff Mapes	40.00	20.00	12.00
290	Bill Dickey	90.00	45.00	27.00
291	Tommy Henrich	50.00	25.00	15.00
292	Eddie Pellagrini	40.00	20.00	12.00
293	Ken Johnson	40.00	20.00	12.00
294	Jocko Thompson	40.00	20.00	12.00
295	Al Lopez	65.00	32.00	19.50
296	Bob Kennedy	40.00	20.00	12.00
297	Dave Philley	40.00	20.00	12.00
298	Joe Astroth	40.00	20.00	12.00
299	Clyde King	40.00	20.00	12.00
300	Hal Rice	40.00	20.00	12.00
301	Tommy Glaviano	40.00	20.00	12.00
302	Jim Busby	40.00	20.00	12.00
303	Marv Rotblatt	40.00	20.00	12.00
304	Allen Gettel	40.00	20.00	12.00
305	*Willie Mays*	2500.	1100.	700.00
306	*Jim Piersall*	90.00	45.00	27.00
307	Walt Masterson	40.00	20.00	12.00
308	Ted Beard	40.00	20.00	12.00
309	Mel Queen	40.00	20.00	12.00
310	Erv Dusak	40.00	20.00	12.00
311	Mickey Harris	40.00	20.00	12.00
312	*Gene Mauch*	50.00	25.00	15.00
313	Ray Mueller	40.00	20.00	12.00
314	Johnny Sain	45.00	22.00	13.50
315	Zack Taylor	40.00	20.00	12.00
316	Duane Pillette	40.00	20.00	12.00
317	*Smoky Burgess*	70.00	35.00	21.00
318	Warren Hacker	40.00	20.00	12.00
319	Red Rolfe	40.00	20.00	12.00
320	Hal White	40.00	20.00	12.00
321	Earl Johnson	40.00	20.00	12.00
322	Luke Sewell	40.00	20.00	12.00
323	*Joe Adcock*	70.00	35.00	21.00
324	Johnny Pramesa	85.00	30.00	12.00

1952 Bowman

Bowman reverted back to a 252-card set in 1952, but retained the card size (2-1/16" x 3-1/8") employed the preceding year. The cards, which are color art reproductions of actual photographs, feature a facsimile autograph on the fronts.

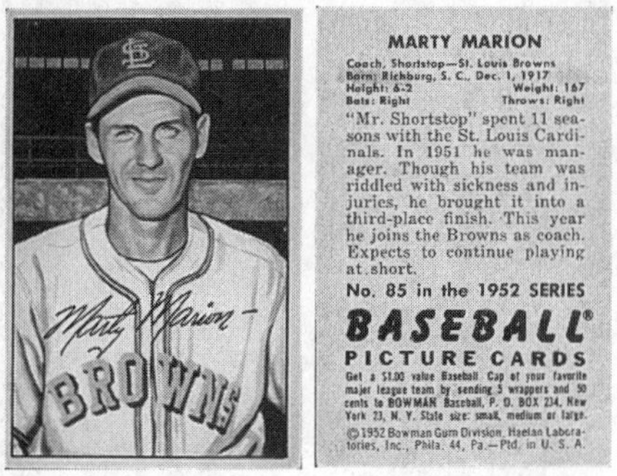

		NM	EX	VG
Complete Set (252):		9000.	4000.	2500.
Common Player (1-216):		12.00	6.00	3.50
Common Player (217-252):		32.00	16.00	9.00
1	Yogi Berra	550.00	200.00	80.00
2	Bobby Thomson	32.00	16.00	9.00
3	Fred Hutchinson	12.00	6.00	3.50
4	Robin Roberts	60.00	30.00	18.00
5	*Minnie Minoso*	115.00	57.00	34.00
6	Virgil "Red" Stallcup	12.00	6.00	3.50
7	Mike Garcia	12.00	6.00	3.50
8	Pee Wee Reese	95.00	47.00	28.00
9	Vern Stephens	12.00	6.00	3.50
10	Bob Hooper	12.00	6.00	3.50
11	Ralph Kiner	50.00	25.00	15.00
12	Max Surkont	12.00	6.00	3.50
13	Cliff Mapes	12.00	6.00	3.50
14	Cliff Chambers	12.00	6.00	3.50
15	Sam Mele	12.00	6.00	3.50
16	Omar Lown	12.00	6.00	3.50
17	Ed Lopat	25.00	12.50	7.50
18	Don Mueller	12.00	6.00	3.50
19	Bob Cain	12.00	6.00	3.50
20	Willie Jones	12.00	6.00	3.50
21	Nellie Fox	65.00	32.00	19.50
22	Willard Ramsdell	12.00	6.00	3.50
23	Bob Lemon	50.00	25.00	15.00
24	Carl Furillo	37.50	18.50	11.00
25	Maurice McDermott	12.00	6.00	3.50
26	Eddie Joost	12.00	6.00	3.50
27	Joe Garagiola	40.00	20.00	12.00
28	Roy Hartsfield	12.00	6.00	3.50
29	Ned Garver	12.00	6.00	3.50
30	Red Schoendienst	45.00	22.00	13.50
31	Eddie Yost	12.00	6.00	3.50
32	Eddie Miksis	12.00	6.00	3.50
33	*Gil McDougald*	60.00	30.00	18.00
34	Al Dark	16.00	8.00	4.75
35	Granny Hamner	12.00	6.00	3.50
36	Cass Michaels	12.00	6.00	3.50
37	Vic Raschi	21.00	10.50	6.25
38	Whitey Lockman	12.00	6.00	3.50
39	Vic Wertz	12.00	6.00	3.50
40	"Bubba" Church	12.00	6.00	3.50
41	"Chico" Carrasquel	12.00	6.00	3.50
42	Johnny Wyrostek	12.00	6.00	3.50
43	Bob Feller	100.00	50.00	30.00
44	Roy Campanella	200.00	100.00	60.00
45	Johnny Pesky	12.00	6.00	3.50
46	Carl Scheib	12.00	6.00	3.50
47	Pete Castiglione	12.00	6.00	3.50
48	Vernon Bickford	12.00	6.00	3.50
49	Jim Hearn	12.00	6.00	3.50
50	Gerry Staley	12.00	6.00	3.50
51	Gil Coan	12.00	6.00	3.50
52	Phil Rizzuto	130.00	65.00	39.00
53	Richie Ashburn	75.00	37.00	22.00
54	Billy Pierce	20.00	10.00	6.00
55	Ken Raffensberger	12.00	6.00	3.50
56	Clyde King	12.00	6.00	3.50
57	Clyde Vollmer	12.00	6.00	3.50
58	Hank Majeski	12.00	6.00	3.50
59	Murry Dickson	12.00	6.00	3.50
60	Sid Gordon	12.00	6.00	3.50
61	Tommy Byrne	12.00	6.00	3.50
62	Joe Presko	12.00	6.00	3.50
63	Irv Noren	12.00	6.00	3.50
64	Roy Smalley	12.00	6.00	3.50
65	Hank Bauer	19.00	9.50	5.75
66	Sal Maglie	18.00	9.00	5.50
67	Johnny Groth	12.00	6.00	3.50
68	Jim Busby	12.00	6.00	3.50
69	Joe Adcock	12.00	6.00	3.50
70	Carl Erskine	27.50	13.50	8.25
71	Vernon Law	12.00	6.00	3.50
72	Earl Torgeson	12.00	6.00	3.50
73	Jerry Coleman	12.00	6.00	3.50
74	Wes Westrum	12.00	6.00	3.50
75	George Kell	40.00	20.00	12.00
76	Del Ennis	12.00	6.00	3.50
77	Eddie Robinson	12.00	6.00	3.50
78	Lloyd Merriman	12.00	6.00	3.50
79	Lou Brissie	12.00	6.00	3.50
80	Gil Hodges	65.00	32.00	19.50
81	Billy Goodman	12.00	6.00	3.50
82	Gus Zernial	12.00	6.00	3.50
83	Howie Pollet	12.00	6.00	3.50
84	Sam Jethroe	12.00	6.00	3.50
85	Marty Marion	19.00	9.50	5.75
86	Cal Abrams	12.00	6.00	3.50
87	Mickey Vernon	12.00	6.00	3.50
88	Bruce Edwards	12.00	6.00	3.50
89	Billy Hitchcock	12.00	6.00	3.50
90	Larry Jansen	12.00	6.00	3.50

91	Don Kolloway	12.00	6.00	3.50
92	Eddie Waitkus	12.00	6.00	3.50
93	Paul Richards	12.00	6.00	3.50
94	Luke Sewell	12.00	6.00	3.50
95	Luke Easter	12.00	6.00	3.50
96	Ralph Branca	19.00	9.50	5.75
97	Willard Marshall	12.00	6.00	3.50
98	Jimmy Dykes	12.00	6.00	3.50
99	Clyde McCullough	12.00	6.00	3.50
100	Sibby Sisti	12.00	6.00	3.50
101	Mickey Mantle	2200.	1100.	400.00
102	Peanuts Lowrey	12.00	6.00	3.50
103	Joe Haynes	12.00	6.00	3.50
104	Hal Jeffcoat	12.00	6.00	3.50
105	Bobby Brown	16.00	8.00	4.75
106	Randy Gumpert	12.00	6.00	3.50
107	Del Rice	12.00	6.00	3.50
108	George Metkovich	12.00	6.00	3.50
109	Tom Morgan	12.00	6.00	3.50
110	Max Lanier	12.00	6.00	3.50
111	"Hoot" Evers	12.00	6.00	3.50
112	"Smoky" Burgess	18.00	9.00	5.50
113	Al Zarilla	12.00	6.00	3.50
114	Frank Hiller	12.00	6.00	3.50
115	Larry Doby	45.00	22.00	13.50
116	Duke Snider	210.00	105.00	63.00
117	Bill Wight	12.00	6.00	3.50
118	Ray Murray	12.00	6.00	3.50
119	Bill Howerton	12.00	6.00	3.50
120	Chet Nichols	12.00	6.00	3.50
121	Al Corwin	12.00	6.00	3.50
122	Billy Johnson	12.00	6.00	3.50
123	Sid Hudson	12.00	6.00	3.50
124	Birdie Tebbetts	12.00	6.00	3.50
125	Howie Fox	12.00	6.00	3.50
126	Phil Cavarretta	12.00	6.00	3.50
127	Dick Sisler	12.00	6.00	3.50
128	Don Newcombe	24.00	12.00	7.25
129	Gus Niarhos	12.00	6.00	3.50
130	Allie Clark	12.00	6.00	3.50
131	Bob Swift	12.00	6.00	3.50
132	Dave Cole	12.00	6.00	3.50
133	Dick Kryhoski	12.00	6.00	3.50
134	Al Brazle	12.00	6.00	3.50
135	Mickey Harris	12.00	6.00	3.50
136	Gene Hermanski	12.00	6.00	3.50
137	Stan Rojek	12.00	6.00	3.50
138	Ted Wilks	12.00	6.00	3.50
139	Jerry Priddy	12.00	6.00	3.50
140	Ray Scarborough	12.00	6.00	3.50
141	Hank Edwards	12.00	6.00	3.50
142	Early Wynn	50.00	25.00	15.00
143	Sandy Consuegra	12.00	6.00	3.50
144	Joe Hatten	12.00	6.00	3.50
145	Johnny Mize	45.00	22.00	13.50
146	Leo Durocher	35.00	17.50	10.50
147	Marlin Stuart	12.00	6.00	3.50
148	Ken Heintzelman	12.00	6.00	3.50
149	Howie Judson	12.00	6.00	3.50
150	Herman Wehmeier	12.00	6.00	3.50
151	Al Rosen	18.00	9.00	5.50
152	Billy Cox	12.00	6.00	3.50
153	Fred Hatfield	12.00	6.00	3.50
154	Ferris Fain	12.00	6.00	3.50
155	Billy Meyer	12.00	6.00	3.50
156	Warren Spahn	125.00	62.00	37.00
157	Jim Delsing	12.00	6.00	3.50
158	Bucky Harris	26.00	13.00	7.75
159	Dutch Leonard	12.00	6.00	3.50
160	Eddie Stanky	18.00	9.00	5.50
161	Jackie Jensen	24.00	12.00	7.25
162	Monte Irvin	42.00	21.00	12.50
163	Johnny Lipon	12.00	6.00	3.50
164	Connie Ryan	12.00	6.00	3.50
165	Saul Rogovin	12.00	6.00	3.50
166	Bobby Adams	12.00	6.00	3.50
167	Bob Avila	12.00	6.00	3.50
168	Preacher Roe	20.00	10.00	6.00
169	Walt Dropo	12.00	6.00	3.50
170	Joe Astroth	12.00	6.00	3.50
171	Mel Queen	12.00	6.00	3.50
172	Ebba St. Claire	12.00	6.00	3.50
173	Gene Bearden	12.00	6.00	3.50
174	Mickey Grasso	12.00	6.00	3.50
175	Ransom Jackson	12.00	6.00	3.50
176	Harry Brecheen	12.00	6.00	3.50
177	Gene Woodling	18.00	9.00	5.50
178	Dave Williams	12.00	6.00	3.50
179	Pete Suder	12.00	6.00	3.50
180	Eddie Fitz Gerald	12.00	6.00	3.50
181	Joe Collins	12.00	6.00	3.50
182	Dave Koslo	12.00	6.00	3.50
183	Pat Mullin	12.00	6.00	3.50
184	Curt Simmons	12.00	6.00	3.50
185	Eddie Stewart	12.00	6.00	3.50
186	Frank Smith	12.00	6.00	3.50
187	Jim Hegan	12.00	6.00	3.50
188	Charlie Dressen	12.00	6.00	3.50
189	Jim Piersall	20.00	10.00	6.00
190	Dick Fowler	12.00	6.00	3.50
191	*Bob Friend*	20.00	10.00	6.00
192	John Cusick	12.00	6.00	3.50
193	Bobby Young	12.00	6.00	3.50
194	Bob Porterfield	12.00	6.00	3.50
195	Frank Baumholtz	12.00	6.00	3.50
196	Stan Musial	500.00	240.00	130.00
197	*Charlie Silvera*	20.00	10.00	6.00
198	Chuck Diering	12.00	6.00	3.50
199	Ted Gray	12.00	6.00	3.50
200	Ken Silvestri	12.00	6.00	3.50
201	Ray Coleman	12.00	6.00	3.50
202	Harry Perkowski	12.00	6.00	3.50
203	Steve Gromek	12.00	6.00	3.50
204	Andy Pafko	12.00	6.00	3.50
205	Walt Masterson	12.00	6.00	3.50
206	Elmer Valo	12.00	6.00	3.50
207	George Strickland	12.00	6.00	3.50
208	Walker Cooper	12.00	6.00	3.50
209	Dick Littlefield	12.00	6.00	3.50
210	Archie Wilson	12.00	6.00	3.50
211	Paul Minner	12.00	6.00	3.50
212	Solly Hemus	12.00	6.00	3.50
213	Monte Kennedy	12.00	6.00	3.50
214	Ray Boone	12.00	6.00	3.50
215	Sheldon Jones	12.00	6.00	3.50
216	Matt Batts	12.00	6.00	3.50
217	Casey Stengel	120.00	60.00	36.00
218	Willie Mays	1100.	350.00	200.00
219	Neil Berry	32.00	16.00	9.00
220	Russ Meyer	32.00	16.00	9.00
221	Lou Kretlow	32.00	16.00	9.00
222	"Dixie" Howell	32.00	16.00	9.00
223	*Harry Simpson*	28.00	14.00	8.50
224	Johnny Schmitz	32.00	16.00	9.00
225	Del Wilber	32.00	16.00	9.00
226	Alex Kellner	32.00	16.00	9.00
227	Clyde Sukeforth	32.00	16.00	9.00
228	Bob Chipman	32.00	16.00	9.00
229	Hank Arft	32.00	16.00	9.00
230	Frank Shea	32.00	16.00	9.00
231	*Dee Fondy*	32.00	16.00	9.00
232	Enos Slaughter	80.00	40.00	24.00
233	Bob Kuzava	32.00	16.00	9.00
234	Fred Fitzsimmons	32.00	16.00	9.00
235	Steve Souchock	32.00	16.00	9.00
236	Tommy Brown	32.00	16.00	9.00
237	Sherman Lollar	32.00	16.00	9.00
238	*Roy McMillan*	32.00	16.00	9.00
239	Dale Mitchell	32.00	16.00	9.00
240	*Billy Loes*	42.00	21.00	12.50
241	Mel Parnell	32.00	16.00	9.00
242	Everett Kell	32.00	16.00	9.00
243	"Red" Munger	32.00	16.00	9.00
244	*Lew Burdette*	42.00	21.00	12.50
245	George Schmees	32.00	16.00	9.00
246	Jerry Snyder	32.00	16.00	9.00
247	John Pramesa	32.00	16.00	9.00
248	Bill Werle	32.00	16.00	9.00
249	Henry Thompson	32.00	16.00	9.00
250	Ike Delock	32.00	16.00	9.00
251	Jack Lohrke	32.00	16.00	9.00
252	Frank Crosetti	75.00	35.00	19.00

1952 Bowman Proofs

Coincident to Topps issue of its "Giant Size" baseball cards in 1952, Bowman began experimenting with up-sizing its card issues from the then-current 2-1/16" x 3-1/8". A group of proof cards was produced using 12 players from the '52 Bowman set. The proofs are 2-1/2" x 3-3/4", overall about 45% larger than the issued '52s. Each proof is found in two types, black-and-white and color. Both have blank-backs except for hand-written notes with the player's name, team and card number in the '52 set. Many of the proofs feature slight differences from the issued versions, such as uniform changes, elimination of background elements or picture cropping. The color proofs include a facsimile autograph. A small group of these proof cards entered the hobby early in the 1980s when a former Bowman executive disposed of his hobby card files. The proofs are numbered according to their number within the 1952 Bowman set.

		NM	EX	VG
Complete Set, B/W (13):		2300.	1150.	675.00
Common Player, B/W:		135.00	67.00	40.00
Complete Set, Color (13):		4400.	2200.	1350.
Common Player, Color:		300.00	150.00	80.00
1	Yogi Berra (b/w)	330.00	165.00	99.00
1	Yogi Berra (color)	725.00	362.00	217.00
2	Bobby Thomson (b/w)	210.00	105.00	63.00
2	Bobby Thomson (color)	450.00	225.00	135.00
3	Fred Hutchinson (b/w)	135.00	67.00	40.00
3	Fred Hutchinson (color)	225.00	110.00	65.00
4	Robin Roberts (b/w)	250.00	125.00	75.00
4	Robin Roberts (color)	550.00	275.00	165.00
10	Bob Hooper (b/w)	135.00	67.00	40.00
10	Bob Hooper (color)	225.00	110.00	65.00
11	Ralph Kiner (b/w)	250.00	125.00	75.00
11	Ralph Kiner (color)	550.00	275.00	165.00
12	Max Surkont (b/w)	135.00	67.00	40.00
12	Max Surkont (color)	225.00	110.00	65.00
13	Cliff Mapes (b/w)	135.00	67.00	40.00
13	Cliff Mapes (color)	225.00	110.00	65.00
14	Cliff Chambers (b/w)	135.00	67.00	40.00
14	Cliff Chambers (color)	225.00	110.00	65.00
34	Alvin Dark (b/w)	135.00	67.00	40.00
34	Alvin Dark (color)	225.00	110.00	65.00
39	William Wertz (b/w)	135.00	67.00	40.00
39	Vic Wertz (color)	225.00	110.00	65.00
142	Early Wynn (b/w)	250.00	125.00	75.00
142	Early Wynn (color)	550.00	275.00	165.00
176	Harry Brecheen (b/w)	135.00	67.00	40.00
176	Harry Brecheen (color)	225.00	110.00	65.00

1953 Bowman

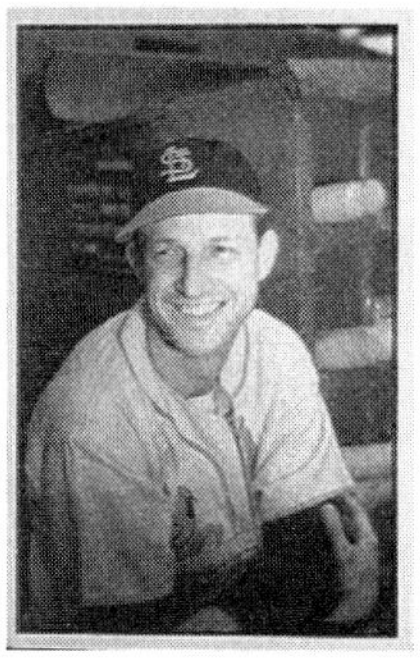

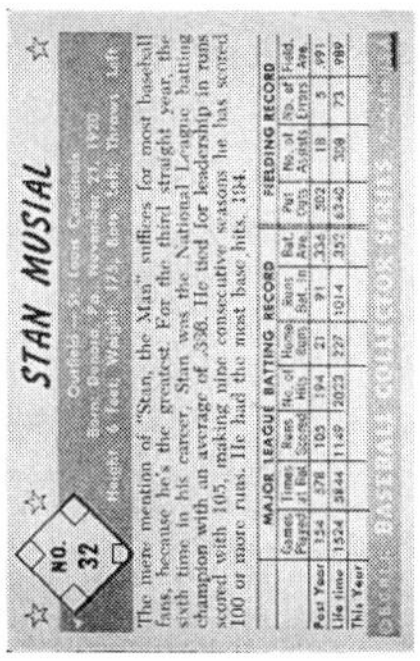

The first set of contemporary major league players featuring actual color photographs, the 160-card 1953 Bowman color set remains one of the most popular issues of the postwar era. The set is greatly appreciated for its uncluttered look; card fronts that contain no names, teams or facsimile autographs. Bowman increased the size of the cards to 2-1/2" x 3-3/4" to better compete with Topps' larger format. Bowman copied an idea from the 1952 Topps set and developed card backs that gave player career and previous-year statistics. The high-numbered cards (#113-160) are the scarcest of the set, with #113-128 being especially scarce.

		NM	EX	VG
Complete Set (160):		11000.	4750.	2650.
Common Player (1-112):		27.50	12.00	8.00
Common Player (113-128):		55.00	27.00	16.50
Common Player (129-160):		50.00	25.00	15.00
1	Davey Williams	85.00	40.00	17.00
2	Vic Wertz	27.50	12.00	8.00
3	Sam Jethroe	27.50	12.00	8.00
4	Art Houtteman	27.50	12.00	8.00
5	Sid Gordon	27.50	12.00	8.00
6	Joe Ginsberg	27.50	12.00	8.00
7	Harry Chiti	27.50	12.00	8.00
8	Al Rosen	36.00	18.00	11.00
9	Phil Rizzuto	170.00	85.00	50.00
10	Richie Ashburn	135.00	67.00	40.00
11	Bobby Shantz	30.00	15.00	9.00
12	Carl Erskine	40.00	20.00	12.00
13	Gus Zernial	27.50	12.00	8.00
14	Billy Loes	35.00	17.50	10.50
15	Jim Busby	27.50	12.00	8.00
16	Bob Friend	30.00	15.00	9.00
17	Gerry Staley	27.50	12.00	8.00
18	Nellie Fox	75.00	37.00	22.00
19	Al Dark	30.00	15.00	9.00
20	Don Lenhardt	27.50	12.00	8.00
21	Joe Garagiola	55.00	27.00	16.50
22	Bob Porterfield	27.50	12.00	8.00
23	Herman Wehmeier	27.50	12.00	8.00
24	Jackie Jensen	32.00	16.00	9.50
25	"Hoot" Evers	27.50	12.00	8.00
26	Roy McMillan	27.50	12.00	8.00
27	Vic Raschi	32.00	16.00	9.50
28	"Smoky" Burgess	29.00	14.50	8.75
29	Roberto Avila	30.00	15.00	9.00
30	Phil Cavarretta	27.50	12.00	8.00
31	Jimmy Dykes	27.50	12.00	8.00
32	Stan Musial	650.00	325.00	195.00
33	Pee Wee Reese	675.00	335.00	200.00
34	Gil Coan	27.50	12.00	8.00
35	Maury McDermott	27.50	12.00	8.00
36	Minnie Minoso	50.00	25.00	15.00
37	Jim Wilson	27.50	12.00	8.00
38	Harry Byrd	27.50	12.00	8.00
39	Paul Richards	27.50	12.00	8.00
40	Larry Doby	75.00	37.00	22.00
41	Sammy White	27.50	12.00	8.00
42	Tommy Brown	27.50	12.00	8.00
43	Mike Garcia	27.50	12.00	8.00
44	Hank Bauer, Yogi Berra, Mickey Mantle	550.00	275.00	165.00
45	Walt Dropo	27.50	12.00	8.00
46	Roy Campanella	275.00	135.00	80.00
47	Ned Garver	27.50	12.00	8.00
48	Hank Sauer	27.50	12.00	8.00
49	Eddie Stanky	27.50	12.00	8.00
50	Lou Kretlow	27.50	12.00	8.00
51	Monte Irvin	55.00	27.00	16.50
52	Marty Marion	40.00	20.00	12.00
53	Del Rice	27.50	12.00	8.00
54	"Chico" Carrasquel	27.50	12.00	8.00
55	Leo Durocher	55.00	27.00	16.50
56	Bob Cain	27.50	12.00	8.00
57	Lou Boudreau	50.00	25.00	15.00

58	Willard Marshall	27.50	12.00	8.00
59	Mickey Mantle	2400.	1025.	650.00
60	Granny Hamner	27.50	12.00	8.00
61	George Kell	55.00	27.00	16.50
62	Ted Kluszewski	55.00	27.00	16.50
63	Gil McDougald	55.00	27.00	16.50
64	Curt Simmons	27.50	12.00	8.00
65	Robin Roberts	125.00	62.00	37.00
66	Mel Parnell	27.50	12.00	8.00
67	Mel Clark	27.50	12.00	8.00
68	Allie Reynolds	50.00	25.00	15.00
69	Charlie Grimm	27.50	12.00	8.00
70	Clint Courtney	27.50	12.00	8.00
71	Paul Minner	27.50	12.00	8.00
72	Ted Gray	27.50	12.00	8.00
73	Billy Pierce	35.00	17.50	10.50
74	Don Mueller	27.50	12.00	8.00
75	Saul Rogovin	27.50	12.00	8.00
76	Jim Hearn	27.50	12.00	8.00
77	Mickey Grasso	27.50	12.00	8.00
78	Carl Furillo	35.00	17.50	10.50
79	Ray Boone	27.50	12.00	8.00
80	Ralph Kiner	90.00	45.00	27.00
81	Enos Slaughter	70.00	35.00	21.00
82	Joe Astroth	27.50	12.00	8.00
83	Jack Daniels	27.50	12.00	8.00
84	Hank Bauer	50.00	25.00	15.00
85	Solly Hemus	27.50	12.00	8.00
86	Harry Simpson	27.50	12.00	8.00
87	Harry Perkowski	27.50	12.00	8.00
88	Joe Dobson	27.50	12.00	8.00
89	Sandalio Consuegra	27.50	12.00	8.00
90	Joe Nuxhall	30.00	15.00	9.00
91	Steve Souchock	27.50	12.00	8.00
92	Gil Hodges	175.00	87.00	52.00
93	Billy Martin, Phil Rizzuto	275.00	125.00	75.00
94	Bob Addis	27.50	12.00	8.00
95	Wally Moses	27.50	12.00	8.00
96	Sal Maglie	30.00	15.00	9.00
97	Eddie Mathews	250.00	135.00	75.00
98	Hector Rodriquez	27.50	12.00	8.00
99	Warren Spahn	200.00	100.00	60.00
100	Bill Wight	27.50	12.00	8.00
101	Red Schoendienst	60.00	30.00	18.00
102	Jim Hegan	27.50	12.00	8.00
103	Del Ennis	27.50	12.00	8.00
104	Luke Easter	27.50	12.00	8.00
105	Eddie Joost	27.50	12.00	8.00
106	Ken Raffensberger	27.50	12.00	8.00
107	Alex Kellner	27.50	12.00	8.00
108	Bobby Adams	27.50	12.00	8.00
109	Ken Wood	27.50	12.00	8.00
110	Bob Rush	27.50	12.00	8.00
111	Jim Dyck	27.50	12.00	8.00
112	Toby Atwell	27.50	12.00	8.00
113	Karl Drews	55.00	27.00	16.50
114	Bob Feller	275.00	137.00	82.00
115	Cloyd Boyer	55.00	27.00	16.50
116	Eddie Yost	55.00	27.00	16.50
117	Duke Snider	450.00	225.00	145.00
118	Billy Martin	175.00	87.00	52.00
119	Dale Mitchell	55.00	27.00	16.50
120	Marlin Stuart	55.00	27.00	16.50
121	Yogi Berra	600.00	300.00	180.00
122	Bill Serena	55.00	27.00	16.50
123	Johnny Lipon	55.00	27.00	16.50
124	Charlie Dressen	65.00	32.00	19.50
125	Fred Hatfield	55.00	27.00	16.50
126	Al Corwin	55.00	27.00	16.50
127	Dick Kryhoski	55.00	27.00	16.50
128	"Whitey" Lockman	55.00	27.00	16.50
129	Russ Meyer	50.00	25.00	15.00
130	Cass Michaels	50.00	25.00	15.00
131	Connie Ryan	50.00	25.00	15.00
132	Fred Hutchinson	50.00	25.00	15.00
133	Willie Jones	50.00	25.00	15.00
134	Johnny Pesky	50.00	25.00	15.00
135	Bobby Morgan	50.00	25.00	15.00
136	Jim Bridewester	50.00	25.00	15.00
137	Sam Dente	50.00	25.00	15.00
138	"Bubba" Church	50.00	25.00	15.00
139	Pete Runnels	50.00	25.00	15.00
140	Alpha Brazle	50.00	25.00	15.00
141	Frank "Spec" Shea	50.00	25.00	15.00
142	Larry Miggins	50.00	25.00	15.00
143	Al Lopez	55.00	27.00	16.50
144	Warren Hacker	50.00	25.00	15.00
145	George Shuba	50.00	25.00	15.00
146	Early Wynn	110.00	55.00	33.00
147	Clem Koshorek	50.00	25.00	15.00
148	Billy Goodman	50.00	25.00	15.00
149	Al Corwin	50.00	25.00	15.00
150	Carl Scheib	50.00	25.00	15.00
151	Joe Adcock	50.00	25.00	15.00
152	Clyde Vollmer	50.00	25.00	15.00
153	Whitey Ford	425.00	212.00	127.00
154	Omar "Turk" Lown	50.00	25.00	15.00
155	Allie Clark	50.00	25.00	15.00
156	Max Surkont	50.00	25.00	15.00
157	Sherman Lollar	50.00	25.00	15.00
158	Howard Fox	50.00	25.00	15.00
159	Mickey Vernon (Photo actually Floyd Baker)	50.00	25.00	15.00
160	Cal Abrams	65.00	30.00	20.00

1953 Bowman Black & White

The 1953 Bowman black-and-white set is similar in all respects to the 1953 Bowman color cards, except that it lacks color. Purportedly, high costs in producing the color series forced Bowman to issue the set in black and white. Sixty-four cards, which measure 2-1/2" x 3-3/4", comprise the set.

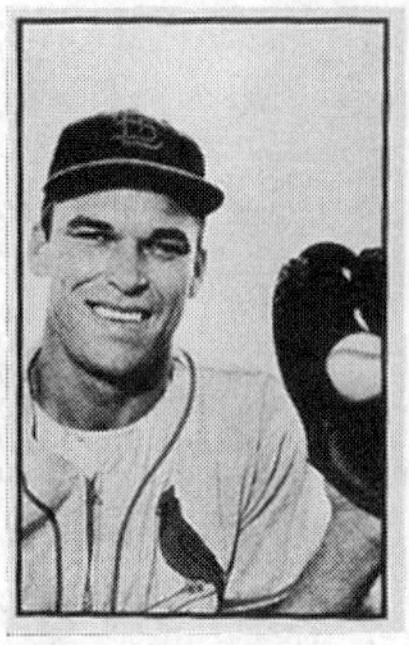

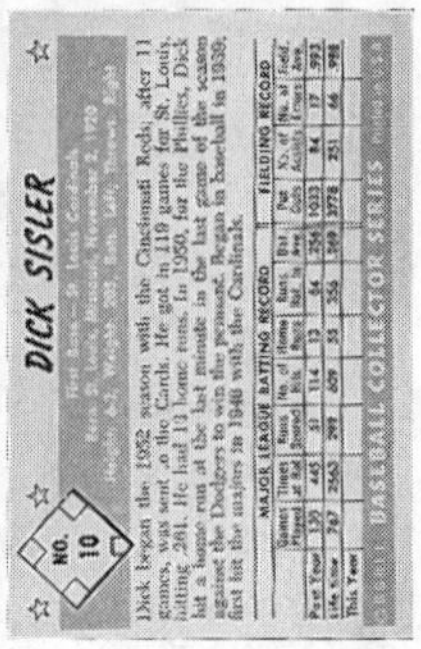

		NM	EX	VG
Complete Set (64):		2500.	1250.	750.00
Common Player:		35.00	20.00	14.00
1	Gus Bell	90.00	30.00	12.00
2	Willard Nixon	35.00	20.00	14.00
3	Bill Rigney	35.00	20.00	14.00
4	Pat Mullin	35.00	20.00	14.00
5	Dee Fondy	35.00	20.00	14.00
6	Ray Murray	35.00	20.00	14.00
7	Andy Seminick	35.00	20.00	14.00
8	Pete Suder	35.00	20.00	14.00
9	Walt Masterson	35.00	20.00	14.00
10	Dick Sisler	35.00	20.00	14.00
11	Dick Gernert	35.00	20.00	14.00
12	Randy Jackson	35.00	20.00	14.00
13	Joe Tipton	35.00	20.00	14.00
14	Bill Nicholson	35.00	20.00	14.00
15	Johnny Mize	115.00	57.00	34.00
16	Stu Miller	35.00	20.00	14.00
17	Virgil Trucks	35.00	20.00	14.00
18	Billy Hoeft	35.00	20.00	14.00
19	Paul LaPalme	35.00	20.00	14.00
20	Eddie Robinson	32.00	16.00	9.50
21	Clarence "Bud" Podbielan	35.00	20.00	14.00
22	Matt Batts	35.00	20.00	14.00
23	Wilmer Mizell	35.00	20.00	14.00
24	Del Wilber	35.00	20.00	14.00
25	Johnny Sain	48.00	24.00	14.50
26	Preacher Roe	40.00	20.00	12.00
27	Bob Lemon	110.00	55.00	33.00
28	Hoyt Wilhelm	135.00	67.00	40.00
29	Sid Hudson	35.00	20.00	14.00
30	Walker Cooper	35.00	20.00	14.00
31	Gene Woodling	40.00	20.00	12.00
32	Rocky Bridges	35.00	20.00	14.00
33	Bob Kuzava	35.00	20.00	14.00
34	Ebba St. Clair (St. Claire)	35.00	20.00	14.00
35	Johnny Wyrostek	35.00	20.00	14.00
36	Jim Piersall	50.00	25.00	15.00
37	Hal Jeffcoat	35.00	20.00	14.00
38	Dave Cole	35.00	20.00	14.00
39	Casey Stengel	300.00	150.00	90.00
40	Larry Jansen	35.00	20.00	14.00
41	Bob Ramazotti	35.00	20.00	14.00
42	Howie Judson	35.00	20.00	14.00
43	Hal Bevan	35.00	20.00	14.00
44	Jim Delsing	35.00	20.00	14.00
45	Irv Noren	35.00	20.00	14.00
46	Bucky Harris	42.00	21.00	12.50
47	Jack Lohrke	35.00	20.00	14.00
48	Steve Ridzik	35.00	20.00	14.00
49	Floyd Baker	35.00	20.00	14.00
50	Emil "Dutch" Leonard	35.00	20.00	14.00
51	Lew Burdette	32.00	16.00	9.50
52	Ralph Branca	40.00	20.00	12.00
53	Morris Martin	35.00	20.00	14.00
54	Bill Miller	35.00	20.00	14.00
55	Don Johnson	35.00	20.00	14.00
56	Roy Smalley	35.00	20.00	14.00
57	Andy Pafko	35.00	20.00	14.00
58	Jim Konstanty	35.00	20.00	14.00
59	Duane Pillette	35.00	20.00	14.00
60	Billy Cox	32.00	16.00	9.50
61	Tom Gorman	32.00	16.00	9.50
62	Keith Thomas	35.00	20.00	14.00
63	Steve Gromek	35.00	20.00	14.00
64	Andy Hansen	45.00	18.00	14.00

1954 Bowman

Bowman's 1954 set consists of 224 full-color cards that measure 2-1/2" x 3-3/4". It is believed that contractual problems caused the pulling of card #66 (Ted Williams) from the set, creating one of the most sought-after scarcities of the postwar era. The Williams card was replaced by Jim Piersall (who is also #210) in subsequent print runs. The set contains over 40 variations, most involving statistical errors on the card backs that were corrected. On most cards neither variation carries a premium value as both varieties appear to have been printed in equal amounts. The complete set price that follows does not include all variations or #66 Williams.

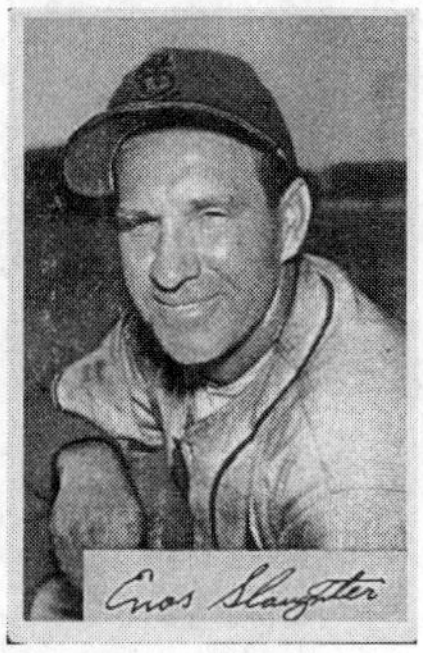

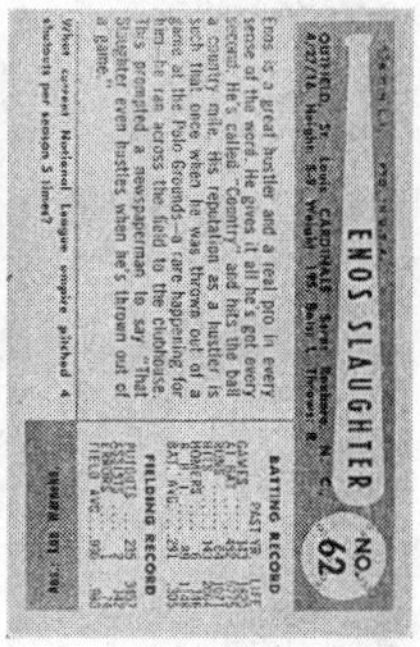

		NM	EX	VG
Complete Set (224):		4200.	2100.	1250.
Common Player (1-128):		8.00	4.00	2.50
Common Player (129-224):		10.00	5.00	3.00
1	Phil Rizzuto	120.00	45.00	25.00
2	Jack Jensen	16.00	8.00	4.75
3	Marion Fricano	8.00	4.00	2.50
4	Bob Hooper	8.00	4.00	2.50
5	Billy Hunter	8.00	4.00	2.50
6	Nellie Fox	28.00	14.00	8.50
7	Walter Dropo	8.00	4.00	2.50
8	Jim Busby	8.00	4.00	2.50
9	Dave Williams	8.00	4.00	2.50
10	Carl Erskine	12.50	6.25	3.75
11	Sid Gordon	8.00	4.00	2.50
12a	Roy McMillan (551/1290 At Bat)	8.00	4.00	2.50
12b	Roy McMillan (557/1296 At Bat)	8.00	4.00	2.50
13	Paul Minner	8.00	4.00	2.50
14	Gerald Staley	8.00	4.00	2.50
15	Richie Ashburn	60.00	30.00	18.00
16	Jim Wilson	8.00	4.00	2.50
17	Tom Gorman	8.00	4.00	2.50
18	"Hoot" Evers	8.00	4.00	2.50
19	Bobby Shantz	8.00	4.00	2.50
20	Artie Houtteman	8.00	4.00	2.50
21	Vic Wertz	8.00	4.00	2.50
22a	Sam Mele (213/1661 Putouts)	8.00	4.00	2.50
22b	Sam Mele (217/1665 Putouts)	8.00	4.00	2.50
23	*Harvey Kuenn*	30.00	15.00	9.00
24	Bob Porterfield	8.00	4.00	2.50
25a	Wes Westrum (1.000/.987 Field Avg.)	8.00	4.00	2.50
25b	Wes Westrum (.982/.986 Field Avg.)	8.00	4.00	2.50
26a	Billy Cox (1.000/.960 Field Avg.)	8.00	4.00	2.50
26b	Billy Cox (.972/.960 Field Avg.)	8.00	4.00	2.50
27	Dick Cole	8.00	4.00	2.50
28a	Jim Greengrass (Birthplace Addison, N.J.)	8.00	4.00	2.50
28b	Jim Greengrass (Birthplace Addison, N.Y.)	8.00	4.00	2.50
29	Johnny Klippstein	8.00	4.00	2.50
30	Del Rice	8.00	4.00	2.50
31	"Smoky" Burgess	8.00	4.00	2.50
32	Del Crandall	8.00	4.00	2.50
33a	Vic Raschi (no trade line)	16.00	8.00	4.75
33b	Vic Raschi (traded line)	30.00	15.00	9.00
34	Sammy White	8.00	4.00	2.50
35a	Eddie Joost (quiz answer is 8)	8.00	4.00	2.50
35b	Eddie Joost (quiz answer is 33)	8.00	4.00	2.50
36	George Strickland	8.00	4.00	2.50
37	Dick Kokos	8.00	4.00	2.50
38a	Minnie Minoso (.895/.961 Field Avg.)	24.00	12.00	7.25
38b	Minnie Minoso (.963/.963 Field Avg.)	24.00	12.00	7.25
39	Ned Garver	8.00	4.00	2.50
40	Gil Coan	8.00	4.00	2.50
41a	Alvin Dark (.986/.960 Field Avg.)	10.00	5.00	3.00
41b	Alvin Dark (.968/.960 Field Avg.)	10.00	5.00	3.00
42	Billy Loes	8.00	4.00	2.50
43a	Bob Friend (20 shutouts in quiz question)	8.00	4.00	2.50
43b	Bob Friend (16 shutouts in quiz question)	8.00	4.00	2.50
44	Harry Perkowski	8.00	4.00	2.50
45	Ralph Kiner	30.00	15.00	9.00
46	"Rip" Repulski	8.00	4.00	2.50
47a	Granny Hamner (.970/.953 Field Avg.)	8.00	4.00	2.50
47b	Granny Hamner (.953/.951 Field Avg.)	8.00	4.00	2.50
48	Jack Dittmer	8.00	4.00	2.50
49	Harry Byrd	8.00	4.00	2.50
50	George Kell	30.00	15.00	9.00
51	Alex Kellner	8.00	4.00	2.50
52	Joe Ginsberg	8.00	4.00	2.50
53a	Don Lenhardt (.969/.984 Field Avg.)	8.00	4.00	2.50
53b	Don Lenhardt (.966/.983 Field Avg.)	8.00	4.00	2.50
54	"Chico" Carrasquel	8.00	4.00	2.50
55	Jim Delsing	8.00	4.00	2.50
56	Maurice McDermott	8.00	4.00	2.50

57	Hoyt Wilhelm	27.50	13.50	8.25
58	Pee Wee Reese	65.00	32.00	19.50
59	Bob Schultz	8.00	4.00	2.50
60	Fred Baczewski	8.00	4.00	2.50
61a	Eddie Miksis (.954/.962 Field Avg.)	8.00	4.00	2.50
61b	Eddie Miksis (.954/.961 Field Avg.)	8.00	4.00	2.50
62	Enos Slaughter	40.00	20.00	12.00
63	Earl Torgeson	8.00	4.00	2.50
64	Eddie Mathews	52.50	26.00	15.50
65	Mickey Mantle	1000.	400.00	300.00
66a	Ted Williams	3500.	1450.	800.00
66b	Jimmy Piersall	70.00	35.00	21.00
67a	Carl Scheib (.306 Pct. with two lines under bio)	8.00	4.00	2.50
67b	Carl Scheib (.306 Pct. with one line under bio)	8.00	4.00	2.50
67c	Carl Scheib (.300 Pct.)	8.00	4.00	2.50
68	Bob Avila	8.00	4.00	2.50
69	Clinton Courtney	8.00	4.00	2.50
70	Willard Marshall	8.00	4.00	2.50
71	Ted Gray	8.00	4.00	2.50
72	Ed Yost	8.00	4.00	2.50
73	Don Mueller	8.00	4.00	2.50
74	Jim Gilliam	22.00	11.00	6.50
75	Max Surkont	8.00	4.00	2.50
76	Joe Nuxhall	8.00	4.00	2.50
77	Bob Rush	8.00	4.00	2.50
78	Sal Yvars	8.00	4.00	2.50
79	Curt Simmons	8.00	4.00	2.50
80a	Johnny Logan (106 Runs)	8.00	4.00	2.50
80b	Johnny Logan (100 Runs)	8.00	4.00	2.50
81a	Jerry Coleman (1.000/.975 Field Avg.)	8.00	4.00	2.50
81b	Jerry Coleman (.952/.975 Field Avg.)	8.00	4.00	2.50
82a	Bill Goodman (.965/.986 Field Avg.)	8.00	4.00	2.50
82b	Bill Goodman (.972/.985 Field Avg.)	8.00	4.00	2.50
83	Ray Murray	8.00	4.00	2.50
84	Larry Doby	30.00	15.00	9.00
85a	Jim Dyck (.926/.956 Field Avg.)	8.00	4.00	2.50
85b	Jim Dyck (.947/.960 Field Avg.)	8.00	4.00	2.50
86	Harry Dorish	8.00	4.00	2.50
87	Don Lund	8.00	4.00	2.50
88	Tommy Umphlett	8.00	4.00	2.50
89	Willie Mays	350.00	150.00	95.00
90	Roy Campanella	150.00	75.00	45.00
91	Cal Abrams	8.00	4.00	2.50
92	Ken Raffensberger	8.00	4.00	2.50
93a	Bill Serena (.983/.966 Field Avg.)	8.00	4.00	2.50
93b	Bill Serena (.977/.966 Field Avg.)	8.00	4.00	2.50
94a	Solly Hemus (476/1343 Assists)	8.00	4.00	2.50
94b	Solly Hemus (477/1343 Assists)	8.00	4.00	2.50
95	Robin Roberts	50.00	25.00	15.00
96	Joe Adcock	8.00	4.00	2.50
97	Gil McDougald	19.00	9.50	5.75
98	Ellis Kinder	8.00	4.00	2.50
99a	Peter Suder (.985/.974 Field Avg.)	8.00	4.00	2.50
99b	Peter Suder (.978/.974 Field Avg.)	8.00	4.00	2.50
100	Mike Garcia	8.00	4.00	2.50
101	*Don Larsen*	48.00	24.00	14.50
102	Bill Pierce	8.00	4.00	2.50
103a	Stephen Souchock (144/1192 Putouts)	8.00	4.00	2.50
103b	Stephen Souchock (147/1195 Putouts)	8.00	4.00	2.50
104	Frank Spec Shea	8.00	4.00	2.50
105a	Sal Maglie (quiz answer is 8)	14.00	7.00	4.25
105b	Sal Maglie (quiz answer is 1904)	14.00	7.00	4.25
106	Clem Labine	14.00	7.00	4.25
107	Paul LaPalme	8.00	4.00	2.50
108	Bobby Adams	8.00	4.00	2.50
109	Roy Smalley	8.00	4.00	2.50
110	Red Schoendienst	27.50	13.50	8.25
111	Murry Dickson	8.00	4.00	2.50
112	Andy Pafko	8.00	4.00	2.50
113	Allie Reynolds	17.50	8.75	5.00
114	Willard Nixon	8.00	4.00	2.50
115	Don Bollweg	8.00	4.00	2.50
116	Luke Easter	8.00	4.00	2.50
117	Dick Kryhoski	8.00	4.00	2.50
118	Bob Boyd	8.00	4.00	2.50
119	Fred Hatfield	8.00	4.00	2.50
120	Mel Hoderlein	8.00	4.00	2.50
121	Ray Katt	8.00	4.00	2.50
122	Carl Furillo	18.00	9.00	5.50
123	Toby Atwell	8.00	4.00	2.50
124a	Gus Bell (15/27 Errors)	8.00	4.00	2.50
124b	Gus Bell (11/26 Errors)	8.00	4.00	2.50
125	Warren Hacker	8.00	4.00	2.50
126	Cliff Chambers	8.00	4.00	2.50
127	Del Ennis	8.00	4.00	2.50
128	Ebba St. Claire	8.00	4.00	2.50
129	Hank Bauer	19.00	9.50	5.75
130	Milt Bolling	10.00	5.00	3.00
131	Joe Astroth	10.00	5.00	3.00
132	Bob Feller	75.00	37.00	22.00
133	Duane Pillette	10.00	5.00	3.00
134	Luis Aloma	10.00	5.00	3.00
135	Johnny Pesky	10.00	5.00	3.00
136	Clyde Vollmer	10.00	5.00	3.00
137	Al Corwin	10.00	5.00	3.00
138a	Gil Hodges (.993/.991 Field Avg.)	65.00	32.00	19.50
138b	Gil Hodges (.992/.991 Field Avg.)	65.00	32.00	19.50
139a	Preston Ward (.961/.992 Field Avg.)	10.00	5.00	3.00
139b	Preston Ward (.990/.992 Field Avg.)	10.00	5.00	3.00
140a	Saul Rogovin (7-12 Won/Lost with 2 Strikeouts)	10.00	5.00	3.00
140b	Saul Rogovin (7-12 Won/Lost with 62 Strikeouts)	10.00	5.00	3.00
140c	Saul Rogovin (8-12 Won/Lost)	10.00	5.00	3.00
141	Joe Garagiola	27.50	13.50	8.25
142	Al Brazle	10.00	5.00	3.00
143	Willie Jones	10.00	5.00	3.00
144	*Ernie Johnson*	16.00	8.00	4.75
145a	Billy Martin (.985/.983 Field Avg.)	45.00	22.00	13.50
145b	Billy Martin (.983/.982 Field Avg.)	45.00	22.50	13.50
146	Dick Gernert	10.00	5.00	3.00
147	Joe DeMaestri	10.00	5.00	3.00
148	Dale Mitchell	10.00	5.00	3.00
149	Bob Young	10.00	5.00	3.00
150	Cass Michaels	10.00	5.00	3.00
151	Pat Mullin	10.00	5.00	3.00
152	Mickey Vernon	10.00	5.00	3.00
153a	"Whitey" Lockman (100/331 Assists)	10.00	5.00	3.00
153b	"Whitey" Lockman (102/333 Assists)	10.00	5.00	3.00
154	Don Newcombe	24.00	12.00	7.25
155	*Frank Thomas*	15.00	7.50	4.50
156a	Rocky Bridges (320/467 Assists)	10.00	5.00	3.00
156b	Rocky Bridges (328/475 Assists)	10.00	5.00	3.00
157	Omar Lown	10.00	5.00	3.00
158	Stu Miller	10.00	5.00	3.00
159	John Lindell	10.00	5.00	3.00
160	Danny O'Connell	10.00	5.00	3.00
161	Yogi Berra	125.00	62.00	37.00
162	Ted Lepcio	10.00	5.00	3.00
163a	Dave Philley (152 Games, no traded line)	30.00	15.00	9.00
163b	Dave Philley (152 Games, traded line)	10.00	5.00	3.00
163c	Dave Philley (157 Games, traded line)	10.00	5.00	3.00
164	Early Wynn	45.00	22.00	13.50
165	Johnny Groth	10.00	5.00	3.00
166	Sandy Consuegra	10.00	5.00	3.00
167	Bill Hoeft	10.00	5.00	3.00
168	Edward Fitz Gerald	10.00	5.00	3.00
169	Larry Jansen	10.00	5.00	3.00
170	Duke Snider	150.00	75.00	45.00
171	Carlos Bernier	10.00	5.00	3.00
172	Andy Seminick	10.00	5.00	3.00
173	Dee Fondy	10.00	5.00	3.00
174a	Pete Castiglione (.966/.959 Field Avg.)	10.00	5.00	3.00
174b	Pete Castiglione (.970/.959 Field Avg.)	10.00	5.00	3.00
175	Mel Clark	10.00	5.00	3.00
176	Vernon Bickford	10.00	5.00	3.00
177	Whitey Ford	90.00	45.00	27.00
178	Del Wilber	10.00	5.00	3.00
179a	Morris Martin (44 ERA)	10.00	5.00	3.00
179b	Morris Martin (4.44 ERA)	10.00	5.00	3.00
180	Joe Tipton	10.00	5.00	3.00
181	Les Moss	10.00	5.00	3.00
182	Sherman Lollar	10.00	5.00	3.00
183	Matt Batts	10.00	5.00	3.00
184	Mickey Grasso	10.00	5.00	3.00
185a	*Daryl Spencer* (.941/.944 Field Avg.)	10.00	5.00	3.00
185b	*Daryl Spencer* (.933/.936 Field Avg.)	10.00	5.00	3.00
186	Russ Meyer	10.00	5.00	3.00
187	Vern Law	10.00	5.00	3.00
188	Frank Smith	10.00	5.00	3.00
189	Ransom Jackson	10.00	5.00	3.00
190	Joe Presko	10.00	5.00	3.00
191	Karl Drews	10.00	5.00	3.00
192	Lew Burdette	10.00	5.00	3.00
193	Eddie Robinson	10.00	5.00	3.00
194	Sid Hudson	10.00	5.00	3.00
195	Bob Cain	10.00	5.00	3.00
196	Bob Lemon	35.00	17.50	10.50
197	Lou Kretlow	10.00	5.00	3.00
198	Virgil Trucks	10.00	5.00	3.00
199	Steve Gromek	10.00	5.00	3.00
200	Connie Marrero	10.00	5.00	3.00
201	Bob Thomson	17.50	8.75	5.25
202	George Shuba	10.00	5.00	3.00
203	Vic Janowicz	15.00	7.50	4.50
204	Jack Collum	10.00	5.00	3.00
205	Hal Jeffcoat	10.00	5.00	3.00
206	Steve Bilko	10.00	5.00	3.00
207	Stan Lopata	10.00	5.00	3.00
208	Johnny Antonelli	10.00	5.00	3.00
209	Gene Woodling (photo reversed)	16.00	8.00	4.75
210	Jimmy Piersall	30.00	15.00	9.00
211	Jim Robertson	10.00	5.00	3.00
212a	Owen Friend (.964/.957 Field Avg.)	10.00	5.00	3.00
212b	Owen Friend (.967/.958 Field Avg.)	10.00	5.00	3.00
213	Dick Littlefield	10.00	5.00	3.00
214	Ferris Fain	10.00	5.00	3.00
215	Johnny Bucha	10.00	5.00	3.00
216a	Jerry Snyder (.988/.988 Field Avg.)	10.00	5.00	3.00
216b	Jerry Snyder (.968/.968 Field Avg.)	10.00	5.00	3.00
217a	Henry Thompson (.956/.951 Field Avg.)	10.00	5.00	3.00
217b	Henry Thompson (.958/.952 Field Avg.)	10.00	5.00	3.00
218	Preacher Roe	19.00	9.50	5.75
219	Hal Rice	10.00	5.00	3.00
220	Hobie Landrith	10.00	5.00	3.00
221	Frank Baumholtz	10.00	5.00	3.00
222	Memo Luna	10.00	5.00	3.00
223	Steve Ridzik	10.00	5.00	3.00
224	Billy Bruton	26.00	7.50	4.00

1955 Bowman

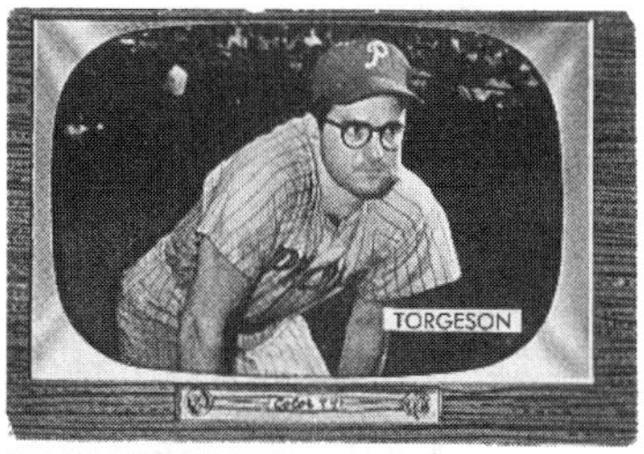

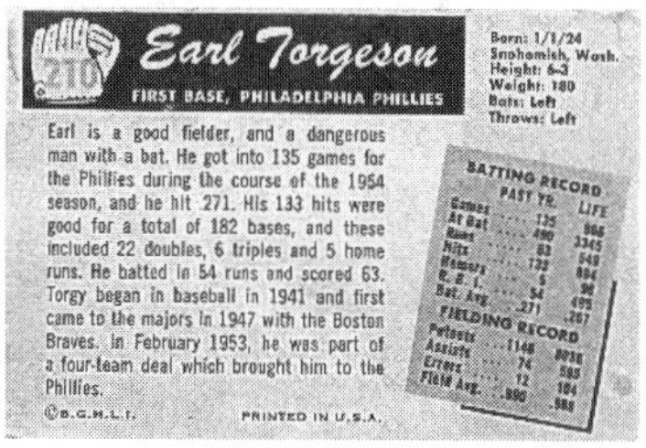

Bowman produced its final baseball card set as an independent card maker in 1955, a popular issue which has color player photographs placed inside a television set design. The set consists of 320 cards that measure 2-1/2" x 3-3/4" in size. High-numbered cards (#s 225-320) appear to have replaced certain low-numbered cards on the press sheets and are somewhat scarcer. The high series includes 31 umpire cards.

		NM	EX	VG
Complete Set (320):		4250.	2125.	1250.
Common Player (1-224):		8.00	4.00	2.50
Common Player (225-320):		16.00	8.00	4.75
1	Hoyt Wilhelm	100.00	30.00	17.50
2	Al Dark	8.00	4.00	2.50
3	Joe Coleman	8.00	4.00	2.50
4	Eddie Waitkus	8.00	4.00	2.50
5	Jim Robertson	8.00	4.00	2.50
6	Pete Suder	8.00	4.00	2.50
7	Gene Baker	8.00	4.00	2.50
8	Warren Hacker	8.00	4.00	2.50
9	Gil McDougald	18.00	9.00	5.50
10	Phil Rizzuto	65.00	32.00	19.50
11	Billy Bruton	8.00	4.00	2.50
12	Andy Pafko	8.00	4.00	2.50
13	Clyde Vollmer	8.00	4.00	2.50
14	Gus Keriazakos	8.00	4.00	2.50
15	*Frank Sullivan*	8.00	4.00	2.50
16	Jim Piersall	9.00	4.50	2.75
17	Del Ennis	8.00	4.00	2.50
18	Stan Lopata	8.00	4.00	2.50
19	Bobby Avila	9.00	4.50	2.75
20	Al Smith	8.00	4.00	2.50
21	Don Hoak	8.00	4.00	2.50
22	Roy Campanella	120.00	60.00	36.00
23	Al Kaline	145.00	72.00	43.00
24	Al Aber	8.00	4.00	2.50
25	Minnie Minoso	20.00	10.00	6.00
26	Virgil Trucks	8.00	4.00	2.50
27	Preston Ward	8.00	4.00	2.50
28	Dick Cole	8.00	4.00	2.50
29	Red Schoendienst	25.00	12.50	7.50
30	Bill Sarni	8.00	4.00	2.50
31	Johnny Temple	8.00	4.00	2.50
32	Wally Post	8.00	4.00	2.50
33	Nellie Fox	35.00	17.50	10.50
34	Clint Courtney	8.00	4.00	2.50
35	Bill Tuttle	8.00	4.00	2.50
36	Wayne Belardi	8.00	4.00	2.50
37	Pee Wee Reese	60.00	30.00	18.00
38	Early Wynn	24.00	12.00	7.25
39	Bob Darnell	8.00	4.00	2.50
40	Vic Wertz	8.00	4.00	2.50
41	Mel Clark	8.00	4.00	2.50
42	Bob Greenwood	8.00	4.00	2.50
43	Bob Buhl	8.00	4.00	2.50
44	Danny O'Connell	8.00	4.00	2.50
45	Tom Umphlett	8.00	4.00	2.50
46	Mickey Vernon	8.00	4.00	2.50
47	Sammy White	8.00	4.00	2.50
48a	Milt Bolling (Frank Bolling back)	8.00	4.00	2.50
48b	Milt Bolling (Milt Bolling back)	25.00	12.50	7.50
49	Jim Greengrass	8.00	4.00	2.50
50	Hobie Landrith	8.00	4.00	2.50
51	Elvin Tappe	8.00	4.00	2.50
52	Hal Rice	8.00	4.00	2.50
53	Alex Kellner	8.00	4.00	2.50
54	Don Bollweg	8.00	4.00	2.50
55	Cal Abrams	8.00	4.00	2.50
56	Billy Cox	8.00	4.00	2.50
57	Bob Friend	8.00	4.00	2.50

58	Frank Thomas	8.00	4.00	2.50
59	Whitey Ford	65.00	32.00	19.50
60	Enos Slaughter	30.00	15.00	9.00
61	Paul LaPalme	8.00	4.00	2.50
62	Royce Lint	8.00	4.00	2.50
63	Irv Noren	8.00	4.00	2.50
64	Curt Simmons	8.00	4.00	2.50
65	*Don Zimmer*	26.00	13.00	7.75
66	George Shuba	8.00	4.00	2.50
67	Don Larsen	20.00	10.00	6.00
68	*Elston Howard*	62.00	31.00	18.50
69	Bill Hunter	8.00	4.00	2.50
70	Lew Burdette	8.00	4.00	2.50
71	Dave Jolly	8.00	4.00	2.50
72	Chet Nichols	8.00	4.00	2.50
73	Eddie Yost	8.00	4.00	2.50
74	Jerry Snyder	8.00	4.00	2.50
75	Brooks Lawrence	8.00	4.00	2.50
76	Tom Poholsky	8.00	4.00	2.50
77	Jim McDonald	8.00	4.00	2.50
78	Gil Coan	8.00	4.00	2.50
79	Willie Miranda	8.00	4.00	2.50
80	Lou Limmer	8.00	4.00	2.50
81	Bob Morgan	8.00	4.00	2.50
82	Lee Walls	8.00	4.00	2.50
83	Max Surkont	8.00	4.00	2.50
84	George Freese	8.00	4.00	2.50
85	Cass Michaels	8.00	4.00	2.50
86	Ted Gray	8.00	4.00	2.50
87	Randy Jackson	8.00	4.00	2.50
88	Steve Bilko	8.00	4.00	2.50
89	Lou Boudreau	28.00	14.00	8.50
90	Art Ditmar	8.00	4.00	2.50
91	Dick Marlowe	8.00	4.00	2.50
92	George Zuverink	8.00	4.00	2.50
93	Andy Seminick	8.00	4.00	2.50
94	Hank Thompson	8.00	4.00	2.50
95	Sal Maglie	10.00	5.00	3.00
96	Ray Narleski	8.00	4.00	2.50
97	John Podres	22.00	11.00	6.50
98	Jim Gilliam	14.00	7.00	4.25
99	Jerry Coleman	8.00	4.00	2.50
100	Tom Morgan	8.00	4.00	2.50
101a	Don Johnson (Ernie Johnson (Braves) on front)	10.00	5.00	3.00
101b	Don Johnson (Don Johnson (Orioles) on front)	25.00	12.50	7.50
102	Bobby Thomson	12.00	6.00	3.50
103	Eddie Mathews	45.00	22.00	13.50
104	Bob Porterfield	8.00	4.00	2.50
105	Johnny Schmitz	8.00	4.00	2.50
106	Del Rice	8.00	4.00	2.50
107	Solly Hemus	8.00	4.00	2.50
108	Lou Kretlow	8.00	4.00	2.50
109	Vern Stephens	8.00	4.00	2.50
110	Bob Miller	8.00	4.00	2.50
111	Steve Ridzik	8.00	4.00	2.50
112	Granny Hamner	8.00	4.00	2.50
113	Bob Hall	8.00	4.00	2.50
114	Vic Janowicz	9.00	4.50	2.75
115	Roger Bowman	8.00	4.00	2.50
116	Sandy Consuegra	8.00	4.00	2.50
117	Johnny Groth	8.00	4.00	2.50
118	Bobby Adams	8.00	4.00	2.50
119	Joe Astroth	8.00	4.00	2.50
120	Ed Burtschy	8.00	4.00	2.50
121	Rufus Crawford	8.00	4.00	2.50
122	Al Corwin	8.00	4.00	2.50
123	Marv Grissom	8.00	4.00	2.50
124	Johnny Antonelli	8.00	4.00	2.50
125	Paul Giel	8.00	4.00	2.50
126	Billy Goodman	8.00	4.00	2.50
127	Hank Majeski	8.00	4.00	2.50
128	Mike Garcia	8.00	4.00	2.50
129	Hal Naragon	8.00	4.00	2.50
130	Richie Ashburn	30.00	15.00	9.00
131	Willard Marshall	8.00	4.00	2.50
132a	Harvey Kueen (misspelled last name)	11.00	5.50	3.25
132b	Harvey Kuenn (corrected)	35.00	17.50	10.50
133	Charles King	8.00	4.00	2.50
134	Bob Feller	65.00	32.00	19.50
135	Lloyd Merriman	8.00	4.00	2.50
136	Rocky Bridges	8.00	4.00	2.50
137	Bob Talbot	8.00	4.00	2.50
138	Davey Williams	8.00	4.00	2.50
139	Billy & Bobby Shantz	11.00	5.50	3.25
140	Bobby Shantz	9.00	4.50	2.75
141	Wes Westrum	8.00	4.00	2.50
142	Rudy Regalado	8.00	4.00	2.50
143	Don Newcombe	17.50	8.75	5.25
144	Art Houtteman	8.00	4.00	2.50
145	Bob Nieman	8.00	4.00	2.50
146	Don Liddle	8.00	4.00	2.50
147	Sam Mele	8.00	4.00	2.50
148	Bob Chakales	8.00	4.00	2.50
149	Cloyd Boyer	8.00	4.00	2.50
150	Bill Klaus	8.00	4.00	2.50
151	Jim Brideweser	8.00	4.00	2.50
152	Johnny Klippstein	8.00	4.00	2.50
153	Eddie Robinson	8.00	4.00	2.50
154	*Frank Lary*	8.00	4.00	2.50
155	Gerry Staley	8.00	4.00	2.50
156	Jim Hughes	8.00	4.00	2.50
157a	Ernie Johnson (Don Johnson (Orioles) picture on front)	10.00	5.00	3.00
157b	Ernie Johnson (Ernie Johnson (Braves) picture on front)	27.50	13.50	8.25
158	Gil Hodges	45.00	22.00	13.50
159	Harry Byrd	8.00	4.00	2.50
160	*Bill Skowron*	25.00	12.50	7.50
161	Matt Batts	8.00	4.00	2.50
162	Charlie Maxwell	8.00	4.00	2.50
163	Sid Gordon	8.00	4.00	2.50
164	Toby Atwell	8.00	4.00	2.50
165	Maurice McDermott	8.00	4.00	2.50
166	Jim Busby	8.00	4.00	2.50
167	Bob Grim	9.00	4.50	2.75
168	Yogi Berra	95.00	47.00	28.00
169	Carl Furillo	24.00	12.00	7.25
170	Carl Erskine	15.00	7.50	4.50
171	Robin Roberts	28.00	14.00	8.50
172	Willie Jones	8.00	4.00	2.50
173	"Chico" Carrasquel	8.00	4.00	2.50
174	Sherman Lollar	8.00	4.00	2.50
175	Wilmer Shantz	8.00	4.00	2.50
176	Joe DeMaestri	8.00	4.00	2.50
177	Willard Nixon	8.00	4.00	2.50
178	Tom Brewer	8.00	4.00	2.50
179	Hank Aaron	200.00	100.00	60.00
180	Johnny Logan	8.00	4.00	2.50
181	Eddie Miksis	8.00	4.00	2.50
182	Bob Rush	8.00	4.00	2.50
183	Ray Katt	8.00	4.00	2.50
184	Willie Mays	190.00	95.00	57.00
185	Vic Raschi	8.00	4.00	2.50
186	Alex Grammas	8.00	4.00	2.50
187	Fred Hatfield	8.00	4.00	2.50
188	Ned Garver	8.00	4.00	2.50
189	Jack Collum	8.00	4.00	2.50
190	Fred Baczewski	8.00	4.00	2.50
191	Bob Lemon	30.00	15.00	9.00
192	George Strickland	8.00	4.00	2.50
193	Howie Judson	8.00	4.00	2.50
194	Joe Nuxhall	8.00	4.00	2.50
195a	Erv Palica (no traded line)	9.00	4.50	2.75
195b	Erv Palica (traded line)	20.00	10.00	6.00
196	Russ Meyer	8.00	4.00	2.50
197	Ralph Kiner	30.00	15.00	9.00
198	Dave Pope	8.00	4.00	2.50
199	Vernon Law	8.00	4.00	2.50
200	Dick Littlefield	8.00	4.00	2.50
201	Allie Reynolds	12.50	6.25	3.75
202	Mickey Mantle	800.00	400.00	240.00
203	Steve Gromek	8.00	4.00	2.50
204a	Frank Bolling (Milt Bolling back)	10.00	5.00	3.00
204b	Frank Bolling (Frank Bolling back)	18.00	9.00	5.50
205	"Rip" Repulski	8.00	4.00	2.50
206	Ralph Beard	8.00	4.00	2.50
207	Frank Shea	8.00	4.00	2.50
208	Ed Fitz Gerald	8.00	4.00	2.50
209	"Smoky" Burgess	8.00	4.00	2.50
210	Earl Torgeson	8.00	4.00	2.50
211	John "Sonny" Dixon	8.00	4.00	2.50
212	Jack Dittmer	8.00	4.00	2.50
213	George Kell	30.00	15.00	9.00
214	Billy Pierce	8.00	4.00	2.50
215	Bob Kuzava	8.00	4.00	2.50
216	Preacher Roe	8.00	4.00	2.50
217	Del Crandall	8.00	4.00	2.50
218	Joe Adcock	8.00	4.00	2.50
219	"Whitey" Lockman	8.00	4.00	2.50
220	Jim Hearn	8.00	4.00	2.50
221	Hector "Skinny" Brown	8.00	4.00	2.50
222	Russ Kemmerer	8.00	4.00	2.50
223	Hal Jeffcoat	8.00	4.00	2.50
224	Dee Fondy	8.00	4.00	2.50
225	Paul Richards	16.00	8.00	4.75
226	W.F. McKinley (umpire)	25.00	12.50	7.50
227	Frank Baumholtz	16.00	8.00	4.75
228	John M. Phillips	16.00	8.00	4.75
229	Jim Brosnan	16.00	8.00	4.75
230	Al Brazle	16.00	8.00	4.75
231	Jim Konstanty	16.00	8.00	4.75
232	Birdie Tebbetts	16.00	8.00	4.75
233	Bill Serena	16.00	8.00	4.75
234	Dick Bartell	16.00	8.00	4.75
235	J.A. Paparella (umpire)	25.00	12.50	7.50
236	Murry Dickson	16.00	8.00	4.75
237	Johnny Wyrostek	16.00	8.00	4.75
238	Eddie Stanky	16.00	8.00	5.25
239	Edwin A. Rommel (umpire)	25.00	12.50	7.50
240	Billy Loes	16.00	8.00	4.75
241	John Pesky	16.00	8.00	4.75
242	Ernie Banks	300.00	150.00	90.00
243	Gus Bell	16.00	8.00	4.75
244	Duane Pillette	16.00	8.00	4.75
245	Bill Miller	16.00	8.00	4.75
246	Hank Bauer	24.00	12.00	7.25
247	Dutch Leonard	16.00	8.00	4.75
248	Harry Dorish	16.00	8.00	4.75
249	Billy Gardner	16.00	8.00	4.75
250	Larry Napp (umpire)	25.00	12.50	7.50
251	Stan Jok	16.00	8.00	4.75
252	Roy Smalley	16.00	8.00	4.75
253	Jim Wilson	16.00	8.00	4.75
254	Bennett Flowers	16.00	8.00	4.75
255	Pete Runnels	16.00	8.00	4.75
256	Owen Friend	16.00	8.00	4.75
257	Tom Alston	16.00	8.00	4.75
258	John W. Stevens (umpire)	25.00	12.50	7.50
259	*Don Mossi*	16.00	8.00	4.75
260	Edwin H. Hurley (umpire)	25.00	12.50	7.50
261	Walt Moryn	16.00	8.00	4.75
262	Jim Lemon	16.00	8.00	4.75
263	Eddie Joost	16.00	8.00	4.75
264	Bill Henry	16.00	8.00	4.75
265	Al Barlick (umpire)	65.00	32.00	19.50
266	Mike Fornieles	16.00	8.00	4.75
267	George Honochick (umpire)	60.00	30.00	18.00
268	Roy Lee Hawes	16.00	8.00	4.75
269	Joe Amalfitano	16.00	8.00	4.75
270	Chico Fernandez	16.00	8.00	4.75
271	Bob Hooper	16.00	8.00	4.75
272	John Flaherty (umpire)	25.00	12.50	7.50
273	"Bubba" Church	16.00	8.00	4.75
274	Jim Delsing	16.00	8.00	4.75
275	William T. Grieve (umpire)	25.00	12.50	7.50
276	Ike Delock	16.00	8.00	4.75
277	Ed Runge (umpire)	25.00	12.50	7.50
278	*Charles Neal*	20.00	10.00	6.00
279	Hank Soar (umpire)	25.00	12.50	7.50
280	Clyde McCullough	16.00	8.00	4.75
281	Charles Berry (umpire)	25.00	12.50	7.50
282	Phil Cavarretta	16.00	8.00	4.75
283	Nestor Chylak (umpire)	50.00	25.00	15.00
284	William A. Jackowski (umpire)	25.00	12.50	7.50
285	Walt Dropo	16.00	8.00	4.75
286	Frank Secory (umpire)	25.00	12.50	7.50
287	Ron Mrozinski	16.00	8.00	4.75
288	Dick Smith	16.00	8.00	4.75
289	Art Gore (umpire)	25.00	12.50	7.50
290	Hershell Freeman	16.00	8.00	4.75
291	Frank Dascoli (umpire)	25.00	12.50	7.50
292	Marv Blaylock	16.00	8.00	4.75
293	Thomas D. Gorman (umpire)	25.00	12.50	7.50
294	Wally Moses	16.00	8.00	4.75
295	Lee Ballanfant (umpire)	25.00	12.50	7.50
296	*Bill Virdon*	32.00	16.00	9.50
297	"Dusty" Boggess (umpire)	25.00	12.50	7.50
298	Charlie Grimm	16.00	8.00	4.75
299	Lonnie Warneke (umpire)	25.00	12.50	7.50
300	Tommy Byrne	16.00	8.00	4.75
301	William Engeln (umpire)	25.00	12.50	7.50
302	*Frank Malzone*	28.00	14.00	8.50
303	Jocko Conlan (umpire)	75.00	37.00	22.00
304	Harry Chiti	16.00	8.00	4.75
305	Frank Umont (umpire)	25.00	12.50	7.50
306	Bob Cerv	20.00	10.00	6.00
307	"Babe" Pinelli (umpire)	25.00	12.50	7.50
308	Al Lopez	42.00	21.00	12.50
309	Hal Dixon (umpire)	25.00	12.50	7.50
310	Ken Lehman	16.00	8.00	4.75
311	Larry Goetz (umpire)	25.00	12.50	7.50
312	Bill Wight	16.00	8.00	4.75
313	Augie Donatelli (umpire)	25.00	12.50	7.50
314	Dale Mitchell	16.00	8.00	4.75
315	Cal Hubbard (umpire)	65.00	32.00	19.50
316	Marion Fricano	16.00	8.00	4.75
317	Bill Summers (umpire)	25.00	12.50	7.50
318	Sid Hudson	16.00	8.00	4.75
319	Al Schroll	16.00	8.00	4.75
320	George Susce, Jr.	45.00	12.00	7.00

1963 George Brace All Time Chicago Cubs

The year of issue attributed here is only theoretical. The set consists of a window envelope which contains 18 5" x 7" black-and-white photos of former Cubs greats by famed Chicago baseball photographer George Brace. The blank-backed unnumbered pictures have player identification in the white border at bottom. They are checklisted here alphabetically.

		NM	EX	VG
Complete Set (18):		35.00	17.50	10.00
Common Player:		3.00	1.50	.90
(1)	Grover Cleveland Alexander	3.00	1.50	.90
(2)	Cap Anson	3.00	1.50	.90
(3)	Three Finger Brown	3.00	1.50	.90
(4)	Frank Chance	3.00	1.50	.90
(5)	Johnny Evers	3.00	1.50	.90
(6)	Charlie Grimm	3.00	1.50	.90
(7)	Stan Hack	3.00	1.50	.90
(8)	Gabby Hartnett	3.00	1.50	.90
(9)	Billy Herman	3.00	1.50	.90
(10)	Charlie Hollocher	3.00	1.50	.90
(11)	Billy Jurges	3.00	1.50	.90
(12)	Johnny Kling	3.00	1.50	.90
(13)	Joe McCarthy	3.00	1.50	.90
(14)	Ed Reulbach	3.00	1.50	.90
(15)	Albert Spalding	3.00	1.50	.90
(16)	Joe Tinker	3.00	1.50	.90
(17)	Hippo Vaughn	3.00	1.50	.90
(18)	Hack Wilson	3.00	1.50	.90

1974 Bramac 1933 National League All-Stars

This early collectors issue features black-and-white photos of the premiere N.L. All-Star team in their distinctive game uniforms. Cards are in a 2-1/2" x 3-1/4" format.

		NM	EX	VG
Complete Set (18):		24.00	12.00	7.50
Common Player:		2.00	1.00	.60
1	Paul Waner	2.00	1.00	.60

2	Woody English	2.00	1.00	.60
3	Dick Bartell	2.00	1.00	.60
4	Chuck Klein	2.00	1.00	.60
5	Tony Cuccinello	2.00	1.00	.60
6	Lefty O'Doul	2.00	1.00	.60
7	Gabby Hartnett	2.00	1.00	.60
8	Lon Warneke	2.00	1.00	.60
9	Wally Berger	2.00	1.00	.60
10	Chick Hafey	2.00	1.00	.60
11	Frank Frisch	2.00	1.00	.60
12	Carl Hubbell	2.00	1.00	.60
13	Bill Hallahan	2.00	1.00	.60
14	Hal Schumacher	2.00	1.00	.60
15	Pie Traynor	2.00	1.00	.60
16	Bill Terry	2.00	1.00	.60
17	Pepper Martin	2.00	1.00	.60
18	Jimmy Wilson	2.00	1.00	.60

1951 Bread for Energy Labels

(See 1951 Fischer's Bread for checklist and values.)

1953 Bread for Energy Labels

(See 1953 Northland Bread Labels for checklist and price guide.)

1909-11 H.H. Bregstone Browns/Cardinals Post Cards

Among the rarest of the early 20th Century baseball player postcards are those of the St. Louis Browns and Cardinals from H.H. Bregstone, also of St. Louis. The 3-1/2" x 5-1/2" cards feature sepia player photos that are borderless at top and sides. At bottom is a box with the player's name, team, position, league and the issuer's address. Backs are standard postcard format. The unnumbered cards are checklisted here alphabetically within team.

		NM	EX	VG
Complete Set, Browns (21):		5500.	2700.	1650.
Complete Set, Cardinals (22):		7800.	3750.	2300.
Common Player:		300.00	150.00	90.00
	ST. LOUIS BROWNS			
(1)	Bill Bailey	300.00	150.00	90.00
(2)	Lou Criger	300.00	150.00	90.00
(3)	Dode Criss	300.00	150.00	90.00
(4)	Bill Dineen	300.00	150.00	90.00
(5)	Hobe Ferris	300.00	150.00	90.00
(6)	Bill Graham	300.00	150.00	90.00
(7)	Art Griggs	300.00	150.00	90.00
(8)	Roy Hartzell	300.00	150.00	90.00
(9)	Danny Hoffman	300.00	150.00	90.00
(10)	Harry Howell	300.00	150.00	90.00
(11)	Tom Jones	300.00	150.00	90.00
(12)	Jimmy McAleer	300.00	150.00	90.00
(13)	Ham Patterson	300.00	150.00	90.00
(14)	Barney Pelty	300.00	150.00	90.00
(15)	Al Schweitzer	300.00	150.00	90.00
(16)	Wib Smith	300.00	150.00	90.00
(17)	Jim Stephens	300.00	150.00	90.00
(18)	George Stone	300.00	150.00	90.00
(19)	Rube Waddell	450.00	225.00	135.00
(20)	Bobby Wallace	450.00	225.00	135.00
(21)	Jimmy Williams	300.00	150.00	90.00
	ST. LOUIS CARDINALS			
(1)	Frank Betcher	300.00	150.00	90.00
(2)	Jack Bliss	300.00	150.00	90.00
(3)	Roger Bresnahan	450.00	225.00	135.00
(4)	Frank Corridon	300.00	150.00	90.00
(5)	Rube Ellis	300.00	150.00	90.00
(6)	Steve Evans	300.00	150.00	90.00
(7)	Rube Geyer	300.00	150.00	90.00
(8)	Bob Harmon	300.00	150.00	90.00
(9)	Tom Higgins	300.00	150.00	90.00
(10)	Art Hoelskoetter	300.00	150.00	90.00
(11)	Miller Huggins	450.00	225.00	135.00
(12)	Rudy Hulswitt	300.00	150.00	90.00
(13)	Adam Johnson	300.00	150.00	90.00
(14)	Ed Konetchy	300.00	150.00	90.00
(15)	Johnny Lush	300.00	150.00	90.00
(16)	Lee Magee	300.00	150.00	90.00
(17)	Rebel Oakes	300.00	150.00	90.00
(18)	Ed Phelps	300.00	150.00	90.00
(19)	Elmer Rieger	300.00	150.00	90.00
(20)	Charlie Rhodes	300.00	150.00	90.00
(21)	Slim Sallee	300.00	150.00	90.00
(22)	Vic Willis	450.00	225.00	135.00

1903 Breisch Williams Type I (E107)

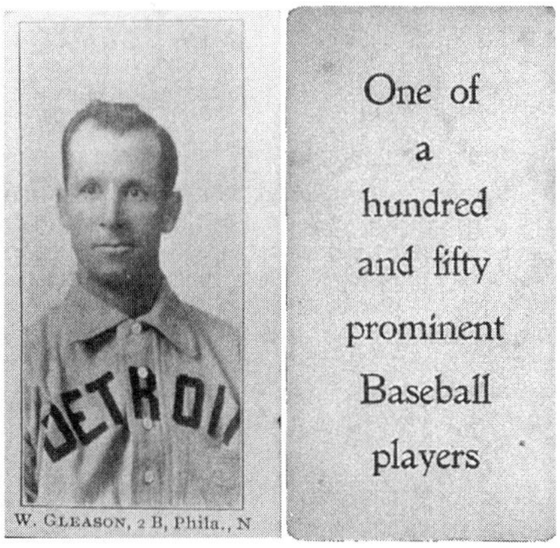

Identified by the American Card Catalog as E107, this circa 1903 set is significant because it was one of the first major baseball card sets since the days of the Old Judge issues in the 1880s. It established the pattern for most of the tobacco and candy cards that were to follow over the next two decades. Measuring approximately 1-3/8" x 2-5/8", cards feature black-and-white player photos with the name, position and team along the bottom. The back states simply "One of a hundred and fifty prominent Baseball players," although blank-backed varieties of this set are fairly common. Also found have been cards with a diagonal overprint stating "The Breisch-Williams Co." establishing the producer of the set. The Type I set consists of 147 different players although 11 additional variations can be found. The Type II cards are thicker than those in Type I and may have been cut from an advertising piece. The Keeler and Delehanty cards have captions different from those found in Type I. The 11 variations found in Type I are not included in the complete set price. Many of the photos were used in other sets, like T206 and M116 Sporting Life.

		NM	EX	VG
Complete Set (147):		70000.	35000.	21000.
Common Player:		425.00	210.00	125.00
(1a)	John Anderson (New York)	425.00	210.00	125.00
(1b)	John Anderson (St. Louis)	425.00	210.00	125.00
(2)	Jimmy Barret (Barrett)	425.00	210.00	125.00
(3)	Ginger Beaumont	425.00	210.00	125.00
(4)	Fred Beck	425.00	210.00	125.00
(5)	Jake Beckley	1100.	550.00	330.00
(6)	Harry Bemis	425.00	210.00	125.00
(7)	Chief Bender	1100.	550.00	330.00
(8)	Bill Bernhard	425.00	210.00	125.00
(9)	Harry Bey (Bay)	425.00	210.00	125.00
(10)	Bill Bradley	425.00	210.00	125.00
(11)	Fritz Buelow	425.00	210.00	125.00
(12)	Nixey Callahan	425.00	210.00	125.00
(13)	Scoops Carey	425.00	210.00	125.00
(14)	Charley Carr	425.00	210.00	125.00
(15)	Bill Carrick	425.00	210.00	125.00
(16)	Doc Casey	425.00	210.00	125.00
(17)	Frank Chance	1100.	550.00	330.00
(18)	Jack Chesbro	1100.	550.00	330.00
(19)	Boileryard Clark (Clarke)	425.00	210.00	125.00
(20)	Fred Clarke	1100.	550.00	330.00
(21)	Jimmy Collins	1100.	550.00	330.00
(22)	Duff Cooley	425.00	210.00	125.00
(23)	Tommy Corcoran	425.00	210.00	125.00
(24)	Bill Coughlan (Coughlin)	425.00	210.00	125.00
(25)	Lou Criger	425.00	210.00	125.00
(26)	Lave Cross	425.00	210.00	125.00
(27)	Monte Cross	425.00	210.00	125.00
(28)	Bill Dahlen	425.00	210.00	125.00
(29)	Tom Daly	425.00	210.00	125.00
(30)	George Davis	750.00	375.00	225.00
(31)	Harry Davis	425.00	210.00	125.00
(32)	Ed Delehanty (Delahanty)	1100.	550.00	330.00
(33)	Gene DeMont (DeMontreville)	425.00	210.00	125.00
(34a)	Pop Dillon (Detroit)	425.00	210.00	125.00
(34b)	Pop Dillon (Brooklyn)	425.00	210.00	125.00
(35)	Bill Dineen (Dinneen)	425.00	210.00	125.00
(36)	Red Donahue	425.00	210.00	125.00
(37)	Mike Donlin	425.00	210.00	125.00
(38)	Patsy Donovan	425.00	210.00	125.00
(39)	Patsy Dougherty	425.00	210.00	125.00
(40)	Klondike Douglass	425.00	210.00	125.00
(41a)	Jack Doyle (Brooklyn)	425.00	210.00	125.00
(41b)	Jack Doyle (Philadelphia)	425.00	210.00	125.00
(42)	Lew Drill	425.00	210.00	125.00
(43)	Jack Dunn	425.00	210.00	125.00
(44a)	Kid Elberfield (Elberfeld) (Detroit)	425.00	210.00	125.00
(44b)	Kid Elberfield (Elberfeld) (no team designation)	425.00	210.00	125.00
(45)	Duke Farrell	425.00	210.00	125.00
(46)	Hobe Ferris	425.00	210.00	125.00
(47)	Elmer Flick	1100.	550.00	330.00
(48)	Buck Freeman	425.00	210.00	125.00
(49)	Bill Freil (Friel)	425.00	210.00	125.00
(50)	Dave Fultz	425.00	210.00	125.00
(51)	Ned Garvin	425.00	210.00	125.00
(52)	Billy Gilbert	425.00	210.00	125.00
(53)	Harry Gleason	425.00	210.00	125.00
(54a)	Kid Gleason (New York)	425.00	210.00	125.00
(54b)	Kid Gleason (Philadelphia)	425.00	210.00	125.00
(55)	John Gochnauer (Gochnaur)	425.00	210.00	125.00
(56)	Danny Green	425.00	210.00	125.00
(57)	Noodles Hahn	425.00	210.00	125.00
(58)	Bill Hallman	425.00	210.00	125.00
(59)	Ned Hanlon	1100.	550.00	330.00
(60)	Dick Harley	425.00	210.00	125.00
(61)	Jack Harper	425.00	210.00	125.00
(62)	Topsy Hartsell (Hartsel)	425.00	210.00	125.00
(63)	Emmet Heidrick	425.00	210.00	125.00
(64)	Charlie Hemphill	425.00	210.00	125.00
(65)	Weldon Henley	425.00	210.00	125.00
(66)	Piano Legs Hickman	425.00	210.00	125.00
(67)	Harry Howell	425.00	210.00	125.00
(68)	Frank Isabel (Isbell)	425.00	210.00	125.00
(69)	Fred Jacklitzch (Jacklitsch)	425.00	210.00	125.00
(70)	Fielder Jones (Chicago)	425.00	210.00	125.00
(71)	Charlie Jones (Boston)	425.00	210.00	125.00
(72)	Addie Joss	1250.	625.00	375.00
(73)	Mike Kahoe	425.00	210.00	125.00
(74)	Wee Willie Keeler	1100.	550.00	330.00
(75)	Joe Kelley	1100.	550.00	330.00
(76)	Brickyard Kennedy	425.00	210.00	125.00
(77)	Frank Kitson	425.00	210.00	125.00
(78a)	Malachi Kittredge (Boston)	425.00	210.00	125.00
(78b)	Malachi Kittredge (Washington)	425.00	210.00	125.00
(79)	Candy LaChance	425.00	210.00	125.00
(80)	Nap Lajoie	1100.	550.00	330.00
(81)	Tommy Leach	425.00	210.00	125.00
(82a)	Watty Lee (Washington)	425.00	210.00	125.00
(82b)	Watty Lee (Pittsburg)	425.00	210.00	125.00
(83)	Sam Leever	425.00	210.00	125.00
(84)	Herman Long	425.00	210.00	125.00
(85a)	Billy Lush (Detroit)	425.00	210.00	125.00
(85b)	Billy Lush (Cleveland)	425.00	210.00	125.00
(86)	Christy Mathewson	3000.	1500.	900.00
(87)	Sport McAllister	425.00	210.00	125.00
(88)	Jack McCarthy	425.00	210.00	125.00
(89)	Barry McCormick	425.00	210.00	125.00
(90)	Ed McFarland (Chicago)	425.00	210.00	125.00
(91)	Herm McFarland (New York)	425.00	210.00	125.00
(92)	Joe McGinnity	1100.	550.00	330.00
(93)	John McGraw	1100.	550.00	330.00
(94)	Deacon McGuire	425.00	210.00	125.00
(95)	Jock Menefee	425.00	210.00	125.00
(96)	Sam Mertes	425.00	210.00	125.00
(97)	Roscoe Miller (picture actually George Mullin)	425.00	210.00	125.00
(98)	Fred Mitchell	425.00	210.00	125.00
(99)	Earl Moore	425.00	210.00	125.00
(100)	Danny Murphy	425.00	210.00	125.00
(101)	Jack O'Connor	425.00	210.00	125.00
(102)	Al Orth	425.00	210.00	125.00

		NM	EX	VG
(103)	Dick Padden	425.00	210.00	125.00
(104)	Freddy Parent	425.00	210.00	125.00
(105)	Roy Patterson	425.00	210.00	125.00
(106)	Heinie Peitz	425.00	210.00	125.00
(107)	Deacon Phillipi (Phillippe)	425.00	210.00	125.00
(108)	Wiley Piatt	425.00	210.00	125.00
(109)	Ollie Pickering	425.00	210.00	125.00
(110)	Eddie Plank	1100.	550.00	330.00
(111a)	Ed Poole (Cincinnati)	425.00	210.00	125.00
(111b)	Ed Poole (Brooklyn)	425.00	210.00	125.00
(112a)	Jack Powell (St. Louis)	425.00	210.00	125.00
(112b)	Jack Powell (New York)	425.00	210.00	125.00
(113)	Mike Powers	425.00	210.00	125.00
(114)	Claude Ritchie (Ritchey)	425.00	210.00	125.00
(115)	Jimmy Ryan	425.00	210.00	125.00
(116)	Ossee Schreckengost	425.00	210.00	125.00
(117)	Kip Selbach	425.00	210.00	125.00
(118)	Socks Seybold	425.00	210.00	125.00
(119)	Jimmy Sheckard	425.00	210.00	125.00
(120)	Ed Siever	425.00	210.00	125.00
(121)	Harry Smith	425.00	210.00	125.00
(122)	Tully Sparks	425.00	210.00	125.00
(123)	Jake Stahl	425.00	210.00	125.00
(124)	Harry Steinfeldt	425.00	210.00	125.00
(125)	Sammy Strang	425.00	210.00	125.00
(126)	Willie Sudhoff	425.00	210.00	125.00
(127)	Joe Sugden	425.00	210.00	125.00
(128)	Billy Sullivan	425.00	210.00	125.00
(129)	Jack Taylor	425.00	210.00	125.00
(130)	Fred Tenney	425.00	210.00	125.00
(131)	Ira Thomas	425.00	210.00	125.00
(132a)	Jack Thoney (Cleveland)	425.00	210.00	125.00
(132b)	Jack Thoney (New York)	425.00	210.00	125.00
(133)	Jack Townsend	425.00	210.00	125.00
(134)	George Van Haltren	425.00	210.00	125.00
(135)	Rube Waddell	1100.	550.00	330.00
(136)	Honus Wagner	3250.	1625.	975.00
(137)	Bobby Wallace	1100.	550.00	330.00
(138)	Jack Warner	425.00	210.00	125.00
(139)	Jimmy Wiggs	425.00	210.00	125.00
(140)	Jimmy Williams	425.00	210.00	125.00
(141)	Vic Willis	1100.	550.00	330.00
(142)	Snake Wiltse	425.00	210.00	125.00
(143)	George Winters (Winter)	425.00	210.00	125.00
(144)	Bob Wood	425.00	210.00	125.00
(145)	Joe Yeager	425.00	210.00	125.00
(146)	Cy Young	1500.	750.00	450.00
(147)	Chief Zimmer	425.00	210.00	125.00

1903 Breisch Williams Type II (E107)

		NM	EX	VG
Complete Set (6):		3450.	1725.	1025.
Common Player:		450.00	225.00	135.00
(1)	Ed Delehanty (Delahanty)	1000.	500.00	300.00
(2)	Jack Doyle	450.00	225.00	135.00
(3)	Wee Willie Keeler	1000.	500.00	300.00
(4)	Nap Lajoie	1100.	550.00	330.00
(5)	Tommy Leach	450.00	225.00	135.00
(6)	Socks Seybold	450.00	225.00	135.00
(7)	Fred Tenney	450.00	225.00	135.00

1909-10 C.A. Briggs Co. (E97)

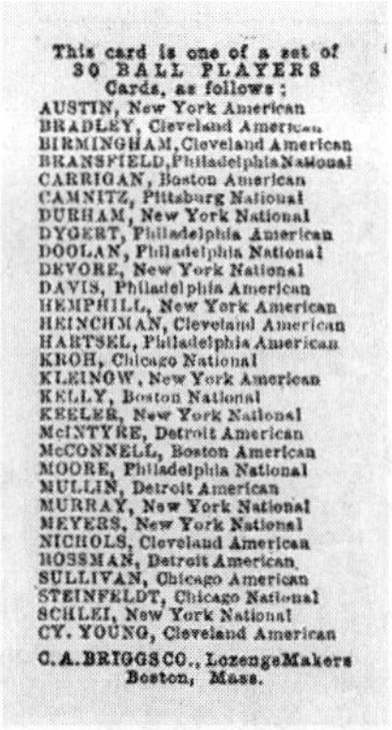

This card is one of a set of
30 BALL PLAYERS
Cards, as follows:
AUSTIN, New York American
BRADLEY, Cleveland American
BIRMINGHAM, Cleveland American
BRANSFIELD, Philadelphia National
CARRIGAN, Boston American
CAMNITZ, Pittsburg National
DURHAM, New York National
DYGERT, Philadelphia American
DOOLAN, Philadelphia National
DEVORE, New York National
DAVIS, Philadelphia American
HEMPHILL, New York American
HEINCHMAN, Cleveland American
HARTSEL, Philadelphia American
KROH, Chicago National
KLEINOW, New York American
KELLY, Boston National
KEELER, New York National
McINTYRE, Detroit American
McCONNELL, Boston American
MOORE, Philadelphia National
MULLIN, Detroit American
MURRAY, New York National
MEYERS, New York National
NICHOLS, Cleveland American
ROSSMAN, Detroit American
SULLIVAN, Chicago American
STEINFELDT, Chicago National
SCHLEI, New York National
CY. YOUNG, Cleveland American
C.A. BRIGGS CO., Lozenge Makers
Boston, Mass.

Measuring approximately 1-1/2" x 2-3/4", this set is nearly identical to several other candy issues of the same period. Designated as E97 in the American Card Catalog, the set was issued in 1909-1910 by "C.A. Briggs Co., Lozenge Makers of Boston, Mass." The front of the card shows a tinted player photo, with the player's last name, position and team printed below. Backs are printed in brown and checklist the 30 players in the set alphabetically. The C.A. Briggs Co. name appears at the bottom. Black-and-white examples of this set have also been found on a thin paper stock with blank backs and are believed to be "proof cards." Five variations are also found in the set. The more expensive variations are not included in the complete set price.

		NM	EX	VG
Complete Set (30):		8250.	4125.	2450.
Common Player:		200.00	100.00	60.00
(1)	Jimmy Austin	200.00	100.00	60.00
(2)	Joe Birmingham	200.00	100.00	60.00
(3)	Bill Bradley	200.00	100.00	60.00
(4)	Kitty Bransfield	200.00	100.00	60.00
(5)	Howie Camnitz	200.00	100.00	60.00
(6)	Bill Carrigan	200.00	100.00	60.00
(7)	Harry Davis	200.00	100.00	60.00
(8)	Josh Devore	200.00	100.00	60.00
(9a)	Mickey Dolan (Doolan)	200.00	100.00	60.00
(9b)	Mickey Doolan	200.00	100.00	60.00
(10)	Bull Durham	200.00	100.00	60.00
(11)	Jimmy Dygert	200.00	100.00	60.00
(12)	Topsy Hartsell (Hartsel)	200.00	100.00	60.00
(13)	Bill Heinchman (Hinchman)	200.00	100.00	60.00
(14)	Charlie Hemphill	200.00	100.00	60.00
(15)	Wee Willie Keeler	900.00	450.00	270.00
(16)	Joe Kelly (Kelley)	900.00	450.00	200.00
(17)	Red Kleinow	200.00	100.00	60.00
(18)	Rube Kroh	200.00	100.00	60.00
(19)	Matty McIntyre	200.00	100.00	60.00
(20)	Amby McConnell	200.00	100.00	60.00
(21)	Chief Meyers	200.00	100.00	60.00
(22)	Earl Moore	200.00	100.00	60.00
(23)	George Mullin	200.00	100.00	60.00
(24)	Red Murray	200.00	100.00	60.00
(25a)	Simon Nichols (Nicholls) (Philadelphia)	550.00	275.00	150.00
(25b)	Simon Nichols (Nicholls) (Cleveland)	200.00	100.00	60.00
(26)	Claude Rossman	200.00	100.00	60.00
(27)	Admiral Schlei	200.00	100.00	60.00
(28a)	Harry Steinfeld (name incorrect)	200.00	100.00	60.00
(28b)	Harry Steinfeldt (name correct)	550.00	275.00	150.00
(29a)	Dennis Sullivan (Chicago)	200.00	100.00	60.00
(29b)	Dennis Sullivan (Boston)	2500.	1250.	750.00
(30a)	Cy. Young (Cleveland)	1500.	750.00	450.00
(30b)	Cy. Young (Boston)	1500.	700.00	325.00

1933 C.A. Briggs Co. Babe Ruth

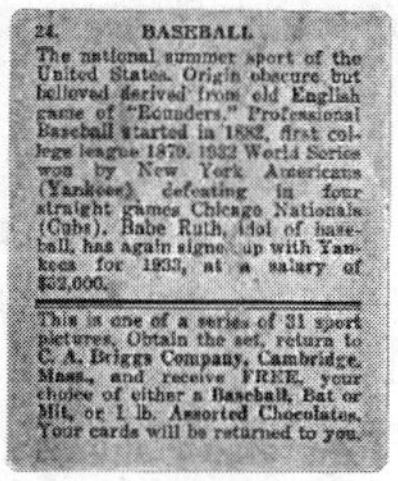

24. BASEBALL
The national summer sport of the United States. Origin obscure but believed derived from old English game of "Rounders." Professional Baseball started in 1882, first college league 1879. 1932 World Series won by New York Americans (Yankees) defeating in four straight games Chicago Nationals (Cubs). Babe Ruth, idol of baseball, has again signed up with Yankees for 1933, at a salary of $52,000.

This is one of a series of 31 sport pictures. Obtain the set, return to C. A. Briggs Company, Cambridge, Mass., and receive FREE, your choice of either a Baseball, Bat or Mit, or 1 lb. Assorted Chocolates. Your cards will be returned to you.

Stars in a variety of sports are featured in this series of candy issues. Card #24 has a drawing on front against a red background. The player bears more than a passing resemblance to Babe Ruth and on the back of the 2-3/8" x 2-7/8" card, along with a short history of baseball, Babe Ruth and his $52,000 contract for 1933 are mentioned. At bottom are details for redeeming a set of the 31 cards for baseball equipment or a pound of chocolates.

		NM	EX	VG
24	Baseball (Babe Ruth)	1000.	500.00	300.00

1953-54 Briggs Meats

The Briggs Meat set was issued over a two-year span (1953-54) and features 28 players from the Washington Senators and 12 from the New York teams. The set was issued in two-card panels on hot dog packages sold in the Washington, D.C. vicinity. The color cards, which are blank-backed and measure 2-1/4" x 3-1/2", are printed on waxed cardboard. Pictures of the New York players can also be found on cards in the 1954 Dan-Dee Potato Chips and 1953-1955 Stahl-Meyer Franks sets. There is a slight difference in style between the Senators cards and those of the New York players. The white panel beneath the photo of the Washington players includes a facsimile autograph plus a few biographical details about the player. The New York players' cards have only the player's name and facsimile signature in that panel. Several of the Senators cards command a premium for scarcity.

		NM	EX	VG
Complete Set (40):		11750.	5750.	3300.
Common Player:		200.00	100.00	60.00
(1)	Hank Bauer	250.00	125.00	75.00
(2)	James Busby	200.00	100.00	60.00
(3)	Tommy Byrne	250.00	125.00	75.00
(4)	Gil Coan	250.00	125.00	75.00
(5)	John Dixon	200.00	100.00	60.00
(6)	Carl Erskine	250.00	125.00	75.00
(7)	Edward Fitzgerald (Fitz Gerald)	200.00	100.00	60.00
(8)	Newton Grasso	250.00	125.00	75.00
(9)	Melvin Hoderlein	200.00	100.00	60.00
(10)	Gil Hodges	350.00	175.00	100.00
(11)	Monte Irvin	250.00	125.00	75.00
(12)	Jackie Jensen	250.00	125.00	75.00
(13)	Whitey Lockman	200.00	100.00	60.00
(14)	Mickey Mantle	3200.	1600.	960.00
(15)	Conrado Marrero	200.00	100.00	60.00
(16)	Walter Masterson	250.00	125.00	75.00
(17)	Carmen Mauro	250.00	125.00	75.00
(18)	Willie Mays	2000.	1000.	600.00
(19)	Mickey McDermott	200.00	100.00	60.00
(20)	Gil McDougald	250.00	125.00	75.00
(21)	Julio Moreno	250.00	125.00	75.00
(22)	Don Mueller	200.00	100.00	60.00
(23)	Don Newcombe	250.00	125.00	75.00
(24)	Robert Oldis	200.00	100.00	60.00
(25)	Erwin Porterfield	200.00	100.00	60.00
(26)	Phil Rizzuto	400.00	200.00	120.00
(27)	James Runnels	200.00	100.00	60.00
(28)	John Schmitz	200.00	100.00	60.00
(29)	Angel Scull	200.00	100.00	60.00
(30)	Frank Shea	200.00	100.00	60.00
(31)	Albert Sima	250.00	125.00	75.00
(32)	Duke Snider	800.00	400.00	240.00
(33)	Charles Stobbs	200.00	100.00	60.00
(34)	Willard Terwilliger	200.00	100.00	60.00
(35)	Joe Tipton	200.00	100.00	60.00
(36)	Thomas Umphlett	200.00	100.00	60.00
(37)	Gene Verble	250.00	125.00	75.00
(38)	James Vernon	200.00	100.00	60.00
(39)	Clyde Vollmer	200.00	100.00	60.00
(40)	Edward Yost	200.00	100.00	60.00

1909-12 Broad Leaf Cigarettes

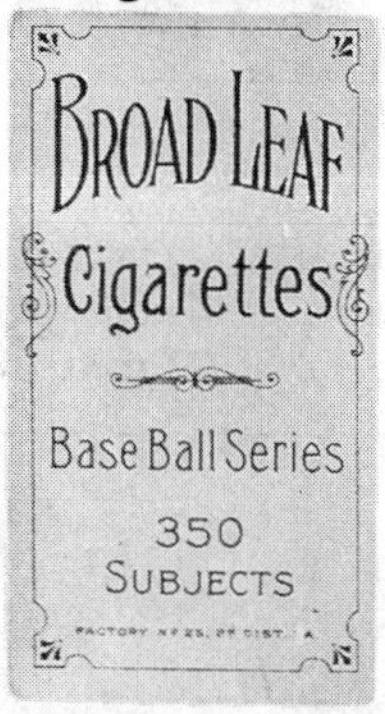

(See T205, T206, T207. Premium: 3X-4X)

1940 Brooklyn Dodgers Photo Pack

Rookie shortstop Pee Wee Reese appears in this team-issued set of black-and-white pictures. The 6" x 9" pictures have player portraits surrounded by a white border. A facsimile autograph appears on front. Backs are blank. The unnumbered pictures are checklisted here in alphabetical order. Players from this issue can be distinguished from later years' issues because the pictures have a stadium background and the players are wearing "Brooklyn" jerseys.

	NM	EX	VG
Complete Set (25):	150.00	75.00	45.00
Common Player:	8.00	4.00	2.50
(1) Dolf Camilli	8.00	4.00	2.50
(2) Tex Carleton	8.00	4.00	2.50
(3) Hugh Casey	8.00	4.00	2.50
(4) Pete Coscarart	8.00	4.00	2.50
(5) Curt Davis	8.00	4.00	2.50
(6) Leo Durocher	12.00	6.00	3.50
(7) Fred Fitzsimmons	8.00	4.00	2.50
(8) Herman Franks	8.00	4.00	2.50
(9) Joe Gallagher	8.00	4.00	2.50
(10) Charlie Gilbert	8.00	4.00	2.50
(11) Luke Hamlin	8.00	4.00	2.50
(12) Johnny Hudson	8.00	4.00	2.50
(13) Newt Kimball	8.00	4.00	2.50
(14) Cookie Lavagetto	8.00	4.00	2.50
(15) Gus Mancuso	8.00	4.00	2.50
(16) Joe Medwick	12.00	6.00	3.50
(17) Van Lingle Mungo	10.00	5.00	3.00
(18) Babe Phelps	8.00	4.00	2.50
(19) Tot Pressnell	8.00	4.00	2.50
(20) Pee Wee Reese	24.00	12.00	7.25
(21) Vito Tamulis	8.00	4.00	2.50
(22) Joe Vosmik	8.00	4.00	2.50
(23) Dixie Walker	8.00	4.00	2.50
(24) Jimmy Wasdell	8.00	4.00	2.50
(25) Whitlow Wyatt	8.00	4.00	2.50

1942 Brooklyn Dodgers Photo Pack

This set of 6" x 9" black-and-white team-issued pictures features player portrait photos in a studio setting. The pictures have a white border all around, and there is a facsimile autograph on front. Backs are blank. The unnumbered pictures are checklisted here alphabetically. Pictures from the 1942 and 1943 photo packs are indistinguishable except for player selection.

	NM	EX	VG
Complete Set (25):	150.00	75.00	45.00
Common Player:	8.00	4.00	2.50
(1) Johnny Allen	8.00	4.00	2.50
(2) Frenchy Bordagaray	8.00	4.00	2.50
(3) Dolf Camilli	8.00	4.00	2.50
(4) Hugh Casey	8.00	4.00	2.50
(5) Curt Davis	8.00	4.00	2.50
(6) Leo Durocher	12.00	6.00	3.50
(7) Larry French	8.00	4.00	2.50
(8) Augie Galan	8.00	4.00	2.50
(9) Ed Head	8.00	4.00	2.50
(10) Billy Herman	12.00	6.00	3.50
(11) Kirby Higbe	8.00	4.00	2.50
(12) Alex Kampouris	8.00	4.00	2.50
(13) Newt Kimball	8.00	4.00	2.50
(14) Joe Medwick	12.00	6.00	3.50
(15) Mickey Owen	8.00	4.00	2.50
(16) Pee Wee Reese	16.00	8.00	4.75
(17) Pete Reiser	10.00	5.00	3.00
(18) Lew Riggs	8.00	4.00	2.50
(19) Johnny Rizzo	8.00	4.00	2.50
(20) Schoolboy Rowe	10.00	5.00	3.00
(21) Billy Sullivan	8.00	4.00	2.50
(22) Arky Vaughan	12.00	6.00	3.50
(23) Dixie Walker	8.00	4.00	2.50
(24) Les Webber	8.00	4.00	2.50
(25) Whitlow Wyatt	8.00	4.00	2.50

1943 Brooklyn Dodgers Photo Pack

This set of 6" x 9" black-and-white team-issued pictures features player portrait photos in a studio setting. The pictures have a white border all around, and there is a facsimile autograph on front. Backs are blank. The unnumbered pictures are checklisted here alphabetically. Pictures from the 1942 and 1943 photo packs are indistinguishable except for player selection.

	NM	EX	VG
Complete Set (25):	150.00	75.00	45.00
Common Player:	8.00	4.00	2.50
(1) Johnny Allen	8.00	4.00	2.50
(2) Frenchy Bordagaray	8.00	4.00	2.50
(3) Bob Bragan	10.00	5.00	3.00
(4) Dolf Camilli	8.00	4.00	2.50
(5) Johnny Cooney	8.00	4.00	2.50
(6) John Corriden	8.00	4.00	2.50
(7) Curt Davis	8.00	4.00	2.50
(8) Leo Durocher	12.00	6.00	3.50
(9) Fred Fitzsimmons	8.00	4.00	2.50
(10) Augie Galan	8.00	4.00	2.50
(11) Al Glossop	8.00	4.00	2.50
(12) Ed Head	8.00	4.00	2.50
(13) Billy Herman	12.00	6.00	3.50
(14) Kirby Higbe	8.00	4.00	2.50
(15) Max Macon	8.00	4.00	2.50
(16) Joe Medwick	12.00	6.00	3.50
(17) Rube Melton	8.00	4.00	2.50
(18) Dee Moore	8.00	4.00	2.50
(19) Bobo Newsom	10.00	5.00	3.00
(20) Mickey Owen	8.00	4.00	2.50
(21) Arky Vaughan	12.00	6.00	3.50
(22) Dixie Walker	8.00	4.00	2.50
(23) Paul Waner	12.00	6.00	3.50
(24) Les Webber	8.00	4.00	2.50
(25) Whitlow Wyatt	8.00	4.00	2.50

1953-55 Brown & Bigelow

Some of baseball's biggest stars, either as they appeared in the mid-1950s or as spirit images, instruct All-American boys in the skills of baseball on this series of cards. Produced by the St. Paul firm of Brown & Bigelow, the 2-1/4" x 3-1/2", round-cornered cards can be found either as playing cards or with schedules printed on the back. The cards could be customized by local sponsors in a panel at the bottom of the artwork. The Medcalf artwork is also seen on contemporary wall and desk calendars and other printed items.

	NM	EX	VG
Individual Cards:	10.00	5.00	3.00
(1) Ty Cobb	15.00	7.50	4.50
(2) Lou Gehrig	22.00	11.00	6.50
(3) Connie Mack	10.00	5.00	3.00
(4) John McGraw	10.00	5.00	3.00
(5) Babe Ruth	30.00	15.00	9.00
(6) Honus Wagner	12.50	6.25	3.75

1911-14 Brunners Bread (D304)

(See 1911-1914 General Baking Co. for checklist and values.)

1910 Brush Detroit Tigers Postcards

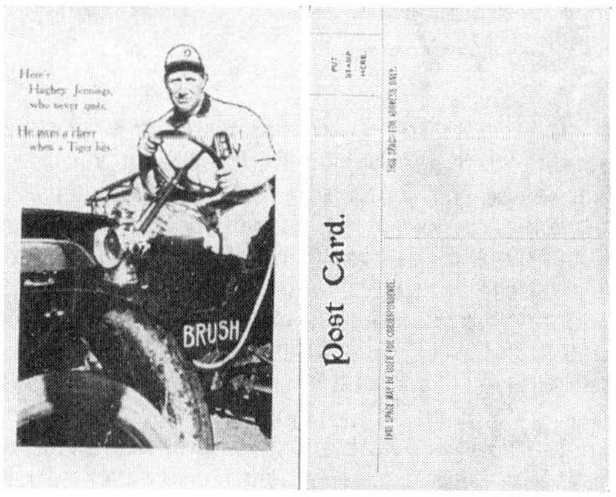

The makers of this short-lived (1907-11) automobile evidently engaged members of the hometown team to endorse their product. The 3-1/2" x 5-3/8" black-and-white postcards have a bordered photo on front showing a Tigers player (in uniform or suit) with the auto. A few lines of poetry about the player complete the design. Backs have typical postcard format. It is likely the checklist here is incomplete.

	NM	EX	VG
(1) Ty Cobb	2000.	1000.	600.00
(2) Hughie Jennings	750.00	375.00	225.00
(3) Matty McIntyre	350.00	175.00	100.00

1979 Bubble Yum Toronto Blue Jays

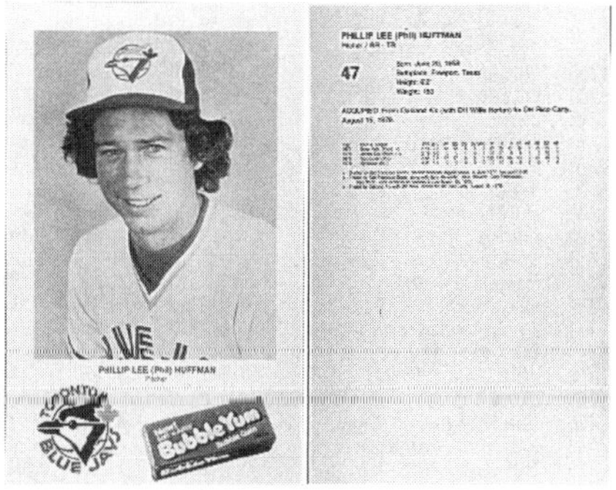

Members of the Toronto Blue Jays in the team's third season are featured in this set of 5-1/2" x 8-1/2" black-and-white player pictures. Fronts feature player portraits identified by their full name and position. In the wide bottom border are team and sponsor logos. Backs have player biographical data, major and minor league stats, acquisition information and career highlights. Cards are numbered by uniform number.

		NM	EX	VG
Complete Set (20):		80.00	40.00	24.00
Common Player:		4.00	2.00	1.25
1	Bob Bailor	5.00	2.50	1.50
4	Alfredo Griffin	5.00	2.50	1.50
7	Roy Hartsfield	4.00	2.00	1.25
9	Rick Cerone	6.00	3.00	1.75
10	John Mayberry	6.00	3.00	1.75
11	Luis Gomez	4.00	2.00	1.25
13	Roy Howell	4.00	2.00	1.25
18	Jim Clancy	6.00	3.00	1.75
19	Otto Velez	4.00	2.00	1.25
20	Al Woods	4.00	2.00	1.25
21	Rico Carty	5.00	2.50	1.50
22	Rick Bosetti	4.00	2.00	1.25
23	Dave Lemanczyk	4.00	2.00	1.25
24	Tom Underwood	4.00	2.00	1.25
31	Bobby Doerr	7.50	3.75	2.25
34	Jesse Jefferson	4.00	2.00	1.25
38	Balor Moore	4.00	2.00	1.25
44	Tom Buskey	4.00	2.00	1.25
46	Dave Freisleben	4.00	2.00	1.25
47	Phil Huffman	4.00	2.00	1.25

1976 Buckmans Discs

One of several regional sponsors of player disc sets in 1976 was Buckmans Ice Cream Village in Rochester, N.Y. The discs are 3-3/8" diameter with a black-and-white player portrait photo in the center of the baseball design. A line of red stars is above, while the left and right panels feature one of several bright colors. Produced by Michael Schecter Associates under license from the Major League Baseball Players Association, the player photos have had uniform and cap logos removed. Backs are printed in red and purple. The unnumbered checklist here is presented in alphabetical order.

		NM	EX	VG
Complete Set (70):		200.00	100.00	60.00
Common Player:		2.00	1.00	.60
(1)	Henry Aaron	24.00	12.00	7.25
(2)	Johnny Bench	15.00	7.50	4.50
(3)	Vida Blue	2.00	1.00	.60
(4)	Larry Bowa	2.00	1.00	.60
(5)	Lou Brock	9.00	4.50	2.75
(6)	Jeff Burroughs	2.00	1.00	.60
(7)	John Candelaria	2.00	1.00	.60
(8)	Jose Cardenal	2.00	1.00	.60
(9)	Rod Carew	9.00	4.50	2.75
(10)	Steve Carlton	9.00	4.50	2.75
(11)	Dave Cash	2.00	1.00	.60
(12)	Cesar Cedeno	2.00	1.00	.60
(13)	Ron Cey	2.00	1.00	.60
(14)	Carlton Fisk	9.00	4.50	2.75
(15)	Tito Fuentes	2.00	1.00	.60
(16)	Steve Garvey	9.00	4.50	2.75
(17)	Ken Griffey	2.00	1.00	.60
(18)	Don Gullett	2.00	1.00	.60
(19)	Willie Horton	2.00	1.00	.60
(20)	Al Hrabosky	2.00	1.00	.60
(21)	Catfish Hunter	9.00	4.50	2.75
(22)	Reggie Jackson	20.00	10.00	6.00
(23)	Randy Jones	2.00	1.00	.60
(24)	Jim Kaat	2.00	1.00	.60
(25)	Don Kessinger	2.00	1.00	.60
(26)	Dave Kingman	3.00	1.50	.90
(27)	Jerry Koosman	2.00	1.00	.60
(28)	Mickey Lolich	3.50	1.75	1.00
(29)	Greg Luzinski	2.00	1.00	.60
(30)	Fred Lynn	2.00	1.00	.60
(31)	Bill Madlock	2.00	1.00	.60
(32)	Carlos May	2.00	1.00	.60
(33)	John Mayberry	2.00	1.00	.60
(34)	Bake McBride	2.00	1.00	.60
(35)	Doc Medich	2.00	1.00	.60
(36)	Andy Messersmith	2.00	1.00	.60
(37)	Rick Monday	2.00	1.00	.60
(38)	John Montefusco	2.00	1.00	.60
(39)	Jerry Morales	2.00	1.00	.60
(40)	Joe Morgan	9.00	4.50	2.75
(41)	Thurman Munson	12.00	6.00	3.50
(42)	Bobby Murcer	2.00	1.00	.60
(43)	Al Oliver	2.00	1.00	.60
(44)	Jim Palmer	9.00	4.50	2.75
(45)	Dave Parker	2.00	1.00	.60
(46)	Tony Perez	9.00	4.50	2.75
(47)	Jerry Reuss	2.00	1.00	.60
(48)	Brooks Robinson	12.00	6.00	3.50
(49)	Frank Robinson	12.00	6.00	3.50
(50)	Steve Rogers	2.00	1.00	.60
(51)	Pete Rose	24.00	12.00	7.25
(52)	Nolan Ryan	48.00	24.00	14.50
(53)	Manny Sanguillen	2.00	1.00	.60
(54)	Mike Schmidt	18.00	9.00	5.50
(55)	Tom Seaver	10.00	5.00	3.00
(56)	Ted Simmons	2.00	1.00	.60
(57)	Reggie Smith	2.00	1.00	.60
(58)	Willie Stargell	9.00	4.50	2.75
(59)	Rusty Staub	2.50	1.25	.70
(60)	Rennie Stennett	2.00	1.00	.60
(61)	Don Sutton	9.00	4.50	2.75
(62)	Andy Thornton	2.00	1.00	.60
(63)	Luis Tiant	2.00	1.00	.60
(64)	Joe Torre	4.00	2.00	1.25
(65)	Mike Tyson	2.00	1.00	.60
(66)	Bob Watson	2.00	1.00	.60
(67)	Wilbur Wood	2.00	1.00	.60
(68)	Jimmy Wynn	2.00	1.00	.60
(69)	Carl Yastrzemski	10.00	5.00	3.00
(70)	Richie Zisk	2.00	1.00	.60

1932 Bulgaria Sport Tobacco

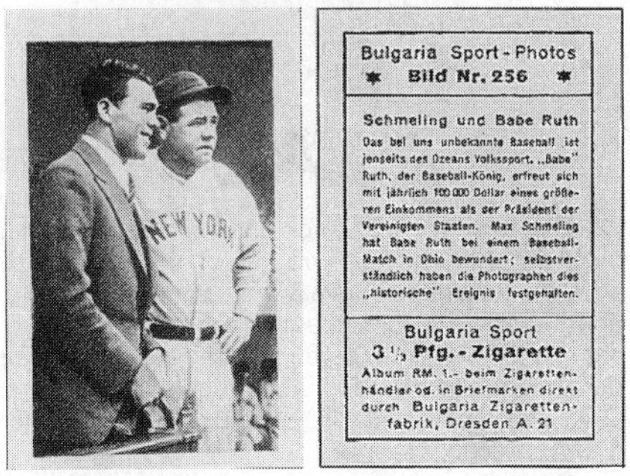

Despite the name of the sponsoring issuer, this set of cards is a product of Germany. Only a single major league ballplayer is pictured among the 272 cards in the set: Babe Ruth, who shares a card with boxing great Max Schmeling in a photo taken in the U.S. The black-and-white cards in the set measure 1-5/8" x 2-3/8" and have backs printed in German, including a card number.

		NM	EX	VG
256	Babe Ruth, Max Schmeling	500.00	250.00	150.00

1956 Burger Beer Cincinnati Reds

The first in a lengthy series of 8" x 10" black-and-white player photos from one of the Reds' broadcast sponsors, the '56 photos can be distinguished by the small line of type on the bottom of the otherwise blank black, "COURTESY OF BURGER - A FINER BEER YEAR AFTER YEAR". Players are identified on the lower front border in large capital letters.

		NM	EX	VG
Complete Set (12):		300.00	150.00	90.00
Common Player:		30.00	15.00	9.00
(1)	Ed Bailey	30.00	15.00	9.00
(2)	Gus Bell	30.00	15.00	9.00
(3)	Don Hoak	30.00	15.00	9.00
(4)	Waite Hoyt (broadcaster)	30.00	15.00	9.00
(5)	Hal Jeffcoat	30.00	15.00	9.00
(6)	Brooks Lawrence	30.00	15.00	9.00
(7a)	Roy McMillan (batting)	30.00	15.00	9.00
(7b)	Roy McMillan (fielding)	30.00	15.00	9.00
(8)	Jackie Moran (broadcaster)	30.00	15.00	9.00
(9)	Joe Nuxhall	30.00	15.00	9.00
(10)	Birdie Tebbetts	30.00	15.00	9.00
(11)	Johnny Temple	30.00	15.00	9.00

1959-64 Burger Beer Cincinnati Reds

The sponsor is not identified, nor the year of issue published on these 8-1/2" x 11" player photos. Uniform and cap styles can give some idea of when the photos were taken. Photos are black-and-white action poses surrounded by white borders with the player and team names at bottom. Backs are blank. The unnumbered photos are listed here in alphabetical order; this checklist may be incomplete.

		NM	EX	VG
Common Player:		12.00	6.00	3.50
(1)	Ed Bailey (portrait)	12.00	6.00	3.50
(2)	Gus Bell (fielding)	12.00	6.00	3.50
(3)	Gordy Coleman (batting)	12.00	6.00	3.50
(4)	John Edwards (portrait)	12.00	6.00	3.50
(5)	Gene Freese (fielding)	12.00	6.00	3.50
(6)	Waite Hoyt (portrait) (announcer)	12.00	6.00	3.50
(7)	Fred Hutchinson (portrait)	12.00	6.00	3.50
(8)	Joey Jay (pitching)	12.00	6.00	3.50
(9)	Eddie Kasko (fielding)	12.00	6.00	3.50
(10)	Gene Kelly (portrait) (announcer)	12.00	6.00	3.50
(11)	Jim Maloney (portrait)	12.00	6.00	3.50
(12)	Joe Nuxhall (pitching)	12.00	6.00	3.50
(13)	Jim O'Toole (windup)	12.00	6.00	3.50
(14)	Jim O'Toole (follow-through)	12.00	6.00	3.50
(15)	Don Pavletich (portrait)	12.00	6.00	3.50
(16)	Vada Pinson (batting)	15.00	7.50	4.50
(17)	Vada Pinson (catching fly ball)	15.00	7.50	4.50
(18)	Vada Pinson (hands on knees)	15.00	7.50	4.50
(19)	Wally Post (portrait)	12.00	6.00	3.50
(20)	Bob Purkey (pitching)	12.00	6.00	3.50
(21)	Bob Purkey (portrait)	12.00	6.00	3.50
(22)	Frank Robinson (fielding fly ball)	35.00	17.50	10.50
(23)	Frank Robinson (portrait)	35.00	17.50	10.50

1977 Burger Chef Funmeal Discs

The largest of the disc sets produced by Michael Schechter Associates is the 216-piece issue for the Burger Chef fast food restaurant chain. The discs were issued nine-per-team on a cardboard tray accompanying a 69-cent Funmeal for kids. The 2-3/8" discs could be punched out of the tray. They share the basic design of other MSA discs of the era. A black-and-white player photo is in the center of a baseball design. Because the discs were licensed only by the Players Association, the player photos have had cap logos airbrushed away. The left and right side panels are in one of several bright colors. Backs feature a Burger Chef cartoon character in color. The individual discs are unnumbered.

		NM	EX	VG
Complete Set, Trays (24):		300.00	150.00	90.00
Complete Set, Singles (216):		250.00	125.00	75.00
Common Player:		1.50	.70	.45
1A	Cincinnati Reds (full tray)	30.00	15.00	9.00
(1A1)	Johnny Bench	6.00	3.00	1.75
(1A2)	Dave Concepcion	1.50	.70	.45
(1A3)	Dan Driessen	1.50	.70	.45
(1A4)	George Foster	1.50	.70	.45
(1A5)	Cesar Geronimo	1.50	.70	.45
(1A6)	Ken Griffey	2.00	1.00	.60
(1A7)	Joe Morgan	4.50	2.25	1.25
(1A8)	Gary Nolan	1.50	.70	.45
(1A9)	Pete Rose	12.00	6.00	3.50
2A	St. Louis Cardinals (full tray)	18.00	9.00	5.50

(2A1)	Lou Brock	4.50	2.25	1.25
(2A2)	John Denny	1.50	.70	.45
(2A3)	Pete Falcone	1.50	.70	.45
(2A4)	Keith Hernandez	2.00	1.00	.60
(2A5)	Al Hrabosky	1.50	.70	.45
(2A6)	Bake McBride	1.50	.70	.45
(2A7)	Ken Reitz	1.50	.70	.45
(2A8)	Ted Simmons	1.50	.70	.45
(2A9)	Mike Tyson	1.50	.70	.45
3A	Detroit Tigers (full tray)	15.00	7.50	4.50
(3A1)	Mark Fidrych	2.50	1.25	.70
(3A2)	Bill Freehan	1.50	.70	.45
(3A3)	John Hiller	1.50	.70	.45
(3A4)	Willie Horton	1.50	.70	.45
(3A5)	Ron LeFlore	1.50	.70	.45
(3A6)	Ben Oglivie	1.50	.70	.45
(3A7)	Aurelio Rodriguez	1.50	.70	.45
(3A8)	Rusty Staub	2.00	1.00	.60
(3A9)	Jason Thompson	1.50	.70	.45
4A	Cleveland Indians (full tray)	15.00	7.50	4.50
(4A1)	Buddy Bell	1.50	.70	.45
(4A2)	Frank Duffy	1.50	.70	.45
(4A3)	Dennis Eckersley	3.00	1.50	.90
(4A4)	Ray Fosse	1.50	.70	.45
(4A5)	Wayne Garland	1.50	.70	.45
(4A6)	Duane Kuiper	1.50	.70	.45
(4A7)	Dave LaRoche	1.50	.70	.45
(4A8)	Rick Manning	1.50	.70	.45
(4A9)	Rick Waits	1.50	.70	.45
5A	Chicago White Sox (full tray)	15.00	7.50	4.50
(5A1)	Jack Brohamer	1.50	.70	.45
(5A2)	Bucky Dent	2.00	1.00	.60
(5A3)	Ralph Garr	1.50	.70	.45
(5A4)	Bart Johnson	1.50	.70	.45
(5A5)	Lamar Johnson	1.50	.70	.45
(5A6)	Chet Lemon	1.50	.70	.45
(5A7)	Jorge Orta	1.50	.70	.45
(5A8)	Jim Spencer	1.50	.70	.45
(5A9)	Richie Zisk	1.50	.70	.45
6A	Chicago Cubs (full tray)	15.00	7.50	4.50
(6A1)	Bill Bonham	1.50	.70	.45
(6A2)	Bill Buckner	2.00	1.00	.60
(6A3)	Ray Burris	1.50	.70	.45
(6A4)	Jose Cardenal	1.50	.70	.45
(6A5)	Bill Madlock	2.00	1.00	.60
(6A6)	Jerry Morales	1.50	.70	.45
(6A7)	Rick Reuschel	1.50	.70	.45
(6A8)	Manny Trillo	1.50	.70	.45
(6A9)	Joe Wallis	1.50	.70	.45
7A	Minnesota Twins (full tray)	18.00	9.00	5.50
(7A1)	Lyman Bostock	1.50	.70	.45
(7A2)	Rod Carew	6.00	3.00	1.75
(7A3)	Mike Cubbage	1.50	.70	.45
(7A4)	Dan Ford	1.50	.70	.45
(7A5)	Dave Goltz	1.50	.70	.45
(7A6)	Larry Hisle	1.50	.70	.45
(7A7)	Tom Johnson	1.50	.70	.45
(7A8)	Bobby Randall	1.50	.70	.45
(7A9)	Butch Wynegar	1.50	.70	.45
8A	Houston Astros (full tray)	15.00	7.50	4.50
(8A1)	Enos Cabell	1.50	.70	.45
(8A2)	Cesar Cedeno	1.50	.70	.45
(8A3)	Jose Cruz	1.50	.70	.45
(8A4)	Joe Ferguson	1.50	.70	.45
(8A5)	Ken Forsch	1.50	.70	.45
(8A6)	Roger Metzger	1.50	.70	.45
(8A7)	J.R. Richard	1.50	.70	.45
(8A8)	Leon Roberts	1.50	.70	.45
(8A9)	Bob Watson	1.50	.70	.45
1B	Baltimore Orioles (full tray)	27.00	13.50	8.00
(1B1)	Mark Belanger	1.50	.70	.45
(1B2)	Paul Blair	1.50	.70	.45
(1B3)	Al Bumbry	1.50	.70	.45
(1B4)	Doug DeCinces	1.50	.70	.45
(1B5)	Ross Grimsley	1.50	.70	.45
(1B6)	Lee May	1.50	.70	.45
(1B7)	Jim Palmer	6.00	3.00	1.75
(1B8)	Brooks Robinson	9.00	4.50	2.75
(1B9)	Ken Singleton	1.50	.70	.45
2B	Boston Red Sox (full tray)	27.00	13.50	8.00
(2B1)	Rick Burleson	1.50	.70	.45
(2B2)	Dwight Evans	2.00	1.00	.60
(2B3)	Carlton Fisk	4.50	2.25	1.25
(2B4)	Fergie Jenkins	4.50	2.25	1.25
(2B5)	Bill Lee	1.50	.70	.45
(2B6)	Fred Lynn	2.00	1.00	.60
(2B7)	Jim Rice	2.50	1.25	.70
(2B8)	Luis Tiant	2.00	1.00	.60
(2B9)	Carl Yastrzemski	7.50	3.75	2.25
3B	Kansas City Royals (full tray)	24.00	12.00	7.25
(3B1)	Doug Bird	1.50	.70	.45
(3B2)	George Brett	10.00	5.00	3.00
(3B3)	Dennis Leonard	1.50	.70	.45
(3B4)	John Mayberry	1.50	.70	.45
(3B5)	Hal McRae	2.00	1.00	.60
(3B6)	Amos Otis	1.50	.70	.45
(3B7)	Fred Patek	1.50	.70	.45
(3B8)	Tom Poquette	1.50	.70	.45
(3B9)	Paul Splittorff	1.50	.70	.45
4B	Milwaukee Brewers (full tray)	21.00	10.50	6.25
(4B1)	Jerry Augustine	1.50	.70	.45
(4B2)	Sal Bando	1.50	.70	.45
(4B3)	Von Joshua	1.50	.70	.45
(4B4)	Sixto Lezcano	1.50	.70	.45
(4B5)	Charlie Moore	1.50	.70	.45
(4B6)	Ed Rodriguez	1.50	.70	.45
(4B7)	Jim Slaton	1.50	.70	.45
(4B8)	Bill Travers	1.50	.70	.45
(4B9)	Robin Yount	9.00	4.50	2.75
5B	Texas Rangers (full tray)	18.00	9.00	5.50
(5B1)	Juan Beniquez	1.50	.70	.45
(5B2)	Bert Blyleven	2.00	1.00	.60
(5B3)	Bert Campaneris	2.00	1.00	.60
(5B4)	Tom Grieve	1.50	.70	.45
(5B5)	Mike Hargrove	2.00	1.00	.60
(5B6)	Toby Harrah	2.00	1.00	.60

(5B7)	Gaylord Perry	4.50	2.25	1.25
(5B8)	Lenny Randle	1.50	.70	.45
(5B9)	Jim Sundberg	1.50	.70	.45
6B	Atlanta Braves (full tray)	15.00	7.50	4.50
(6B1)	Jeff Burroughs	1.50	.70	.45
(6B2)	Darrel Chaney	1.50	.70	.45
(6B3)	Gary Matthews	1.50	.70	.45
(6B4)	Andy Messersmith	1.50	.70	.45
(6B5)	Willie Montanez	1.50	.70	.45
(6B6)	Phil Niekro	3.50	1.75	1.00
(6B7)	Tom Paciorek	1.50	.70	.45
(6B8)	Jerry Royster	1.50	.70	.45
(6B9)	Dick Ruthven	1.50	.70	.45
7B	Pittsburgh Pirates (full tray)	21.00	10.50	6.25
(7B1)	John Candelaria	1.50	.70	.45
(7B2)	Duffy Dyer	1.50	.70	.45
(7B3)	Al Oliver	2.00	1.00	.60
(7B4)	Dave Parker	2.00	1.00	.60
(7B5)	Jerry Reuss	1.50	.70	.45
(7B6)	Bill Robinson	1.50	.70	.45
(7B7)	Willie Stargell	6.00	3.00	1.75
(7B8)	Rennie Stennett	1.50	.70	.45
(7B9)	Frank Taveras	1.50	.70	.45
8B	New York Yankees (full tray)	30.00	15.00	9.00
(8B1)	Chris Chambliss	1.50	.70	.45
(8B2)	Don Gullett	1.50	.70	.45
(8B3)	Catfish Hunter	4.50	2.25	1.25
(8B4)	Reggie Jackson	9.00	4.50	2.75
(8B5)	Thurman Munson	7.50	3.75	2.25
(8B6)	Graig Nettles	1.50	.70	.45
(8B7)	Willie Randolph	1.50	.70	.45
(8B8)	Mickey Rivers	1.50	.70	.45
(8B9)	Roy White	1.50	.70	.45
1C	California Angels (full tray)	40.00	20.00	12.00
(1C1)	Bobby Bonds	2.00	1.00	.60
(1C2)	Dave Chalk	1.50	.70	.45
(1C3)	Bobby Grich	1.50	.70	.45
(1C4)	Paul Hartzell	1.50	.70	.45
(1C5)	Ron Jackson	1.50	.70	.45
(1C6)	Jerry Remy	1.50	.70	.45
(1C7)	Joe Rudi	1.50	.70	.45
(1C8)	Nolan Ryan	24.00	12.00	7.25
(1C9)	Frank Tanana	1.50	.70	.45
2C	Oakland A's (full tray)	15.00	7.50	4.50
(2C1)	Stan Bahnsen	1.50	.70	.45
(2C2)	Vida Blue	2.00	1.00	.60
(2C3)	Phil Garner	1.50	.70	.45
(2C4)	Paul Lindblad	1.50	.70	.45
(2C5)	Mike Norris	1.50	.70	.45
(2C6)	Bill North	1.50	.70	.45
(2C7)	Manny Sanguillen	1.50	.70	.45
(2C8)	Mike Torrez	1.50	.70	.45
(2C9)	Claudell Washington	1.50	.70	.45
3C	Los Angeles Dodgers (full tray)	18.00	9.00	5.50
(3C1)	Ron Cey	2.00	1.00	.60
(3C2)	Steve Garvey	3.00	1.50	.90
(3C3)	Davey Lopes	1.50	.70	.45
(3C4)	Rick Monday	1.50	.70	.45
(3C5)	Doug Rau	1.50	.70	.45
(3C6)	Rick Rhoden	1.50	.70	.45
(3C7)	Reggie Smith	2.00	1.00	.60
(3C8)	Don Sutton	4.00	2.00	1.25
(3C9)	Steve Yaeger	1.50	.70	.45
4C	Montreal Expos (full tray)	16.50	8.25	5.00
(4C1)	Gary Carter	3.00	1.50	.90
(4C2)	Dave Cash	1.50	.70	.45
(4C3)	Tim Foli	1.50	.70	.45
(4C4)	Barry Foote	1.50	.70	.45
(4C5)	Larry Parrish	1.50	.70	.45
(4C6)	Tony Perez	4.50	2.25	1.25
(4C7)	Steve Rogers	1.50	.70	.45
(4C8)	Del Unser	1.50	.70	.45
(4C9)	Ellis Valentine	1.50	.70	.45
5C	New York Mets (full tray)	24.00	12.00	7.25
(5C1)	Bud Harrelson	1.50	.70	.45
(5C2)	Dave Kingman	2.00	1.00	.60
(5C3)	Jerry Koosman	1.50	.70	.45
(5C4)	Ed Kranepool	2.00	1.00	.60
(5C5)	Skip Lockwood	1.50	.70	.45
(5C6)	Jon Matlack	1.50	.70	.45
(5C7)	Felix Millan	1.50	.70	.45
(5C8)	Tom Seaver	9.00	4.50	2.75
(5C9)	John Stearns	1.50	.70	.45
6C	Philadelphia Phillies (full tray)	27.00	13.50	8.00
(6C1)	Bob Boone	2.00	1.00	.60
(6C2)	Larry Bowa	1.50	.70	.45
(6C3)	Steve Carlton	6.00	3.00	1.75
(6C4)	Jay Johnstone	1.50	.70	.45
(6C5)	Jim Kaat	2.00	1.00	.60
(6C6)	Greg Luzinski	2.00	1.00	.60
(6C7)	Garry Maddox	1.50	.70	.45
(6C8)	Tug McGraw	2.00	1.00	.60
(6C9)	Mike Schmidt	9.00	4.50	2.75
7C	San Diego Padres (full tray)	18.00	9.00	5.50
(7C1)	Rollie Fingers	4.00	2.00	1.25
(7C2)	George Hendrick	1.50	.70	.45
(7C3)	Enzo Hernandez	1.50	.70	.45
(7C4)	Mike Ivie	1.50	.70	.45
(7C5)	Randy Jones	1.50	.70	.45
(7C6)	Butch Metzger	1.50	.70	.45
(7C7)	Dave Rader	1.50	.70	.45
(7C8)	Gene Tenace	1.50	.70	.45
(7C9)	Dave Winfield	4.50	2.25	1.25
8C	San Francisco Giants (full tray)	15.00	7.50	4.50
(8C1)	Jim Barr	1.50	.70	.45
(8C2)	Willie Crawford	1.50	.70	.45
(8C3)	Larry Herndon	1.50	.70	.45
(8C4)	Randy Moffitt	1.50	.70	.45
(8C5)	John Montefusco	1.50	.70	.45
(8C6)	Bobby Murcer	1.50	.70	.45
(8C7)	Marty Perez	1.50	.70	.45
(8C8)	Chris Speier	1.50	.70	.45
(8C9)	Gary Thomasson	1.50	.70	.45

1977 Burger King Yankees

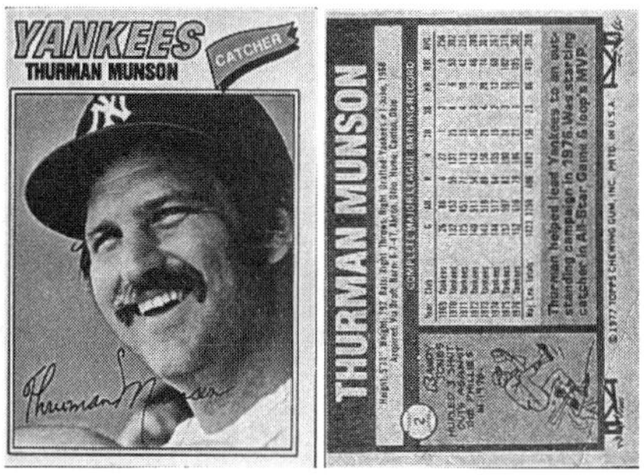

The first Topps-produced set for Burger King restaurants was issued in the New York area, featuring the A.L. Champion Yankees. Twenty-two players plus an unnumbered checklist were issued at the beginning of the promotion with card #23 (Lou Piniella) being added to the set later. The "New York Post" reported production of the first 22 player cards at about 170,000 of each. The Piniella card was issued in limited quantities. Cards are 2-1/2" x 3-1/2" and have fronts identical to the regular 1977 Topps set except for numbers 2, 6, 7, 13, 14, 15, 17, 20 and 21. These cards feature different poses or major picture-cropping variations. It should be noted that very minor cropping variations between the regular Topps sets and the Burger King issues exist throughout the years the sets were produced.

		NM	EX	VG
Complete Set (24):		20.00	10.00	6.00
Common Player:		.20	.10	.06
1	Yankees Team (Billy Martin)	.75	.40	.25
2	Thurman Munson	5.00	2.50	1.50
3	Fran Healy	.25	.13	.08
4	Catfish Hunter	1.50	.70	.45
5	Ed Figueroa	.25	.13	.08
6	Don Gullett	.25	.13	.08
7	Mike Torrez	.25	.13	.08
8	Ken Holtzman	.25	.13	.08
9	Dick Tidrow	.25	.13	.08
10	Sparky Lyle	.40	.20	.12
11	Ron Guidry	.45	.25	.14
12	Chris Chambliss	.25	.13	.08
13	Willie Randolph	.45	.25	.14
14	Bucky Dent	.45	.25	.14
15	Graig Nettles	.60	.30	.20
16	Fred Stanley	.25	.13	.08
17	Reggie Jackson	5.00	2.50	1.50
18	Mickey Rivers	.25	.13	.08
19	Roy White	.40	.20	.12
20	Jim Wynn	.40	.20	.12
21	Paul Blair	.25	.13	.08
22	Carlos May	.25	.13	.08
23	Lou Piniella	12.00	6.00	3.50
---	Checklist	.05	.03	.02

1977 Burger King Tigers

This series of color 8" x 10" player portraits was given away one per week at Detroit area Burger Kings. Backs are blank and there is no player identification on the front. The photos are checklisted here alphabetically.

		NM	EX	VG
Complete Set (4):		20.00	10.00	6.00
Common Player:		5.00	2.50	1.50
(1)	Mark Fidrych (holding glove)	7.50	3.75	2.25
(2)	Ron LeFlore (black guy w/bat)	5.00	2.50	1.50
(3)	Dave Rozema (winding up)	5.00	2.50	1.50
(4)	Mickey Stanley (white guy w/bat)	5.00	2.50	1.50

1978 Burger King Astros

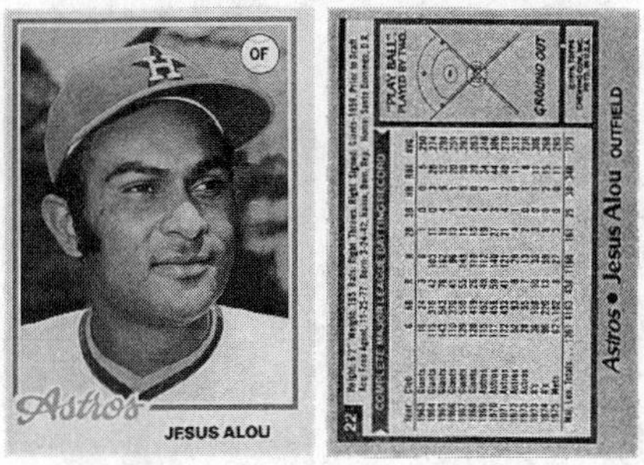

Burger King restaurants in the Houston area distributed a Topps-produced set showcasing the Astros. Cards are standard 2-1/2" x 3-1/2" and are numbered 1-22, plus an unnumbered checklist. Fronts are identical to the regular 1978 Topps set with the exception of card numbers 21, Dave Bergman, who appeared on a Rookie Outfielders card in the '78 Topps set; and 22, Jesus Alou, who did not have a card in the regular issue. Although not noted in the following checklist, it should be remembered that very minor picture-cropping variations between the regular Topps issues and the 1977-1980 Burger King sets do exist.

		NM	EX	VG
Complete Set (23):		7.00	3.50	2.00
Common Player:		.35	.20	.11
1	Bill Virdon	.50	.25	.15
2	Joe Ferguson	.35	.20	.11
3	Ed Herrmann	.35	.20	.11
4	J.R. Richard	.60	.30	.20
5	Joe Niekro	.60	.30	.20
6	Floyd Bannister	.35	.20	.11
7	Joaquin Andujar	.35	.20	.11
8	Ken Forsch	.35	.20	.11
9	Mark Lemongello	.35	.20	.11
10	Joe Sambito	.35	.20	.11
11	Gene Pentz	.35	.20	.11
12	Bob Watson	.40	.20	.12
13	Julio Gonzalez	.35	.20	.11
14	Enos Cabell	.35	.20	.11
15	Roger Metzger	.35	.20	.11
16	Art Howe	.40	.20	.12
17	Jose Cruz	.50	.25	.15
18	Cesar Cedeno	.50	.25	.15
19	Terry Puhl	.35	.20	.11
20	Wilbur Howard	.35	.20	.11
21	Dave Bergman	.35	.20	.11
22	Jesus Alou	.50	.25	.15
---	Checklist	.04	.02	.01

1978 Burger King Rangers

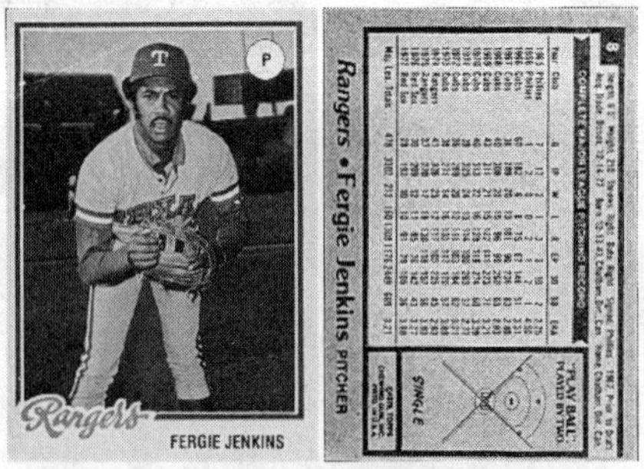

Issued by Burger King restaurants in the Dallas-Fort Worth area, this Topps-produced set features the Texas Rangers. Cards are standard 2-1/2" x 3-1/2" and identical in style to the regular 1978 Topps set with the following exceptions: #'s 5, 8, 10, 12, 17, 21 and 22. An unnumbered checklist card was included with the set.

		NM	EX	VG
Complete Set (23):		7.00	3.50	2.00
Common Player:		.35	.20	.11
1	Billy Hunter	.35	.20	.11
2	Jim Sundberg	.35	.20	.11
3	John Ellis	.35	.20	.11
4	Doyle Alexander	.35	.20	.11
5	Jon Matlack	.35	.20	.11
6	Dock Ellis	.35	.20	.11
7	George Medich	.35	.20	.11
8	Fergie Jenkins	2.50	1.25	.70
9	Len Barker	.35	.20	.11
10	Reggie Cleveland	.35	.20	.11
11	Mike Hargrove	.50	.25	.15
12	Bump Wills	.50	.25	.15
13	Toby Harrah	.50	.25	.15
14	Bert Campaneris	.50	.25	.15
15	Sandy Alomar	.50	.25	.15
16	Kurt Bevacqua	.35	.20	.11
17	Al Oliver	.75	.40	.25
18	Juan Beniquez	.35	.20	.11
19	Claudell Washington	.35	.20	.11
20	Richie Zisk	.35	.20	.11
21	John Lowenstein	.35	.20	.11
22	Bobby Thompson	.35	.20	.11
---	Checklist	.04	.02	.01

1978 Burger King Tigers

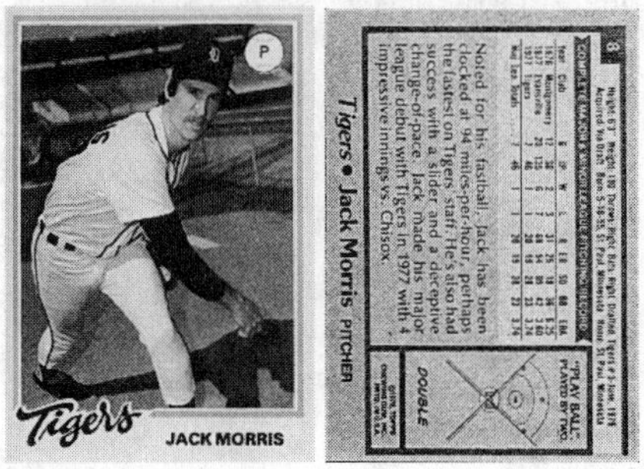

Rookie cards of Morris, Trammell and Whitaker make the Topps-produced 1978 Burger King Detroit Tigers issue the most popular of the BK sets. Twenty-two player cards and an unnumbered checklist make up the set which was issued in the Detroit area. Cards measure 2-1/2" x 3-1/2", and are identical to the regular 1978 Topps issue with the following exceptions: #'s 6, 7, 8, 13, 15 and 16. Numerous minor picture-cropping variations between the regular Topps issues and the Burger King sets appear from 1977-1980; these minor variations are not noted in the following checklist.

		NM	EX	VG
Complete Set (23):		30.00	15.00	9.00
Common Player:		.30	.15	.09
1	Ralph Houk	.40	.20	.12
2	Milt May	.30	.15	.09
3	John Wockenfuss	.30	.15	.09
4	Mark Fidrych	1.50	.70	.45
5	Dave Rozema	.30	.15	.09
6	Jack Billingham	.30	.15	.09
7	Jim Slaton	.30	.15	.09
8	Jack Morris	5.00	2.50	1.50
9	John Hiller	.30	.15	.09
10	Steve Foucault	.30	.15	.09
11	Milt Wilcox	.30	.15	.09
12	Jason Thompson	.30	.15	.09
13	Lou Whitaker	8.00	4.00	2.50
14	Aurelio Rodriguez	.30	.15	.09
15	Alan Trammell	15.00	7.50	4.50
16	Steve Dillard	.30	.15	.09
17	Phil Mankowski	.30	.15	.09
18	Steve Kemp	.30	.15	.09
19	Ron LeFlore	.40	.20	.12
20	Tim Corcoran	.30	.15	.09
21	Mickey Stanley	.30	.15	.09
22	Rusty Staub	.70	.35	.20
---	Checklist	.05	.03	.02

1978 Burger King Yankees

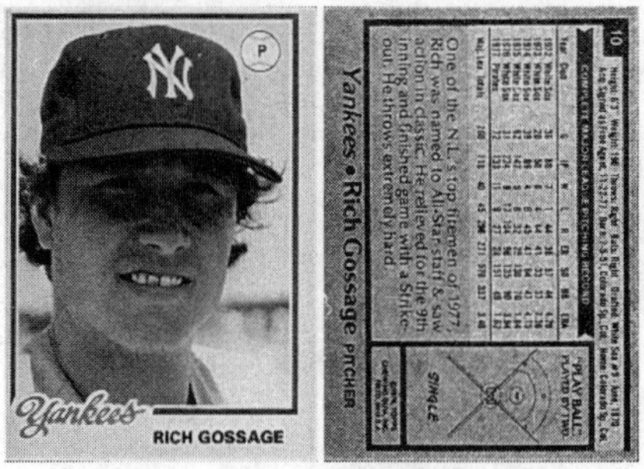

Produced by Topps for Burger King outlets in the New York area for the second year in a row, the 1978 Yankees set contains 22 cards plus an unnumbered checklist. The cards are numbered 1 through 22 and are the standard size of 2-1/2" x 3-1/2". The cards feature the same pictures found in the regular 1978 Topps set except for numbers 10, 11 and 16. Only those variations containing different poses or major picture-cropping differences are noted. Numerous minor picture-cropping variations, that are very insignificant in nature, exist between the regular Topps sets and the Burger King issues of 1977-1980.

		NM	EX	VG
Complete Set (23):		6.00	3.00	1.75
Common Player:		.25	.13	.08
1	Billy Martin	.70	.35	.20
2	Thurman Munson	2.50	1.25	.70
3	Cliff Johnson	.25	.13	.08
4	Ron Guidry	.35	.20	.11
5	Ed Figueroa	.25	.13	.08
6	Dick Tidrow	.25	.13	.08
7	Catfish Hunter	1.50	.70	.45
8	Don Gullett	.25	.13	.08
9	Sparky Lyle	.45	.25	.14
10	Rich Gossage	.60	.30	.20
11	Rawly Eastwick	.25	.13	.08
12	Chris Chambliss	.25	.13	.08
13	Willie Randolph	.45	.25	.14
14	Graig Nettles	.45	.25	.14
15	Bucky Dent	.45	.25	.14
16	Jim Spencer	.25	.13	.08
17	Fred Stanley	.25	.13	.08
18	Lou Piniella	.50	.25	.15
19	Roy White	.45	.25	.14
20	Mickey Rivers	.25	.13	.08
21	Reggie Jackson	3.00	1.50	.90
22	Paul Blair	.25	.13	.08
---	Checklist	.05	.03	.02

1979 Burger King Phillies

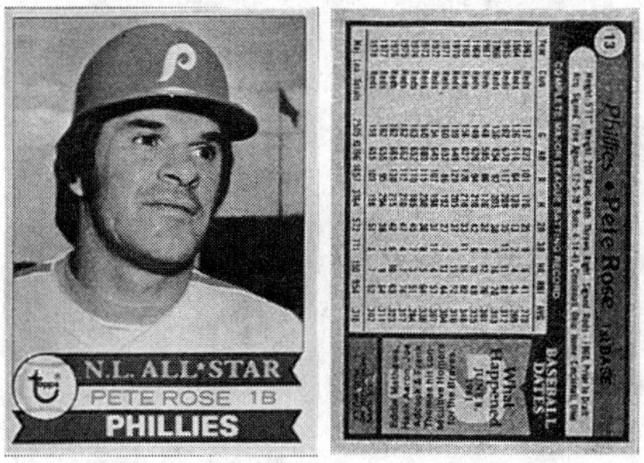

Twenty-two Phillies players are featured in the 1979 Burger King issue given out in the Philadelphia area. The Topps-produced set, measuring 2-1/2" x 3-1/2", also includes an unnumbered checklist. Cards are identical to the regular 1979 Topps set except #1, 11, 12, 13, 14, 17 and 22, which have different poses. Very minor picture-cropping variations between the regular Topps issues and the Burger King sets can be found throughout the four years the cards were produced, but only those variations featuring major changes are noted in the checklists.

		NM	EX	VG
Complete Set (23):		7.00	3.50	2.00
Common Player:		.15	.08	.05
1	Danny Ozark	.15	.08	.05
2	Bob Boone	.30	.15	.09
3	Tim McCarver	.35	.20	.11
4	Steve Carlton	2.00	1.00	.60
5	Larry Christenson	.15	.08	.05
6	Dick Ruthven	.15	.08	.05
7	Ron Reed	.15	.08	.05
8	Randy Lerch	.15	.08	.05
9	Warren Brusstar	.15	.08	.05
10	Tug McGraw	.25	.13	.08
11	Nino Espinosa	.15	.08	.05
12	Doug Bird	.15	.08	.05
13	Pete Rose	3.00	1.50	.90
14	Manny Trillo	.15	.08	.05
15	Larry Bowa	.25	.13	.08
16	Mike Schmidt	2.50	1.25	.70
17	Pete Mackanin	.15	.08	.05
18	Jose Cardenal	.15	.08	.05
19	Greg Luzinski	.35	.20	.11
20	Garry Maddox	.15	.08	.05
21	Bake McBride	.15	.08	.05
22	Greg Gross	.15	.08	.05
---	Checklist	.05	.03	.02

1979 Burger King Yankees

The New York Yankees were featured in a Topps-produced Burger King set for the third consecutive year in 1979. Once again, 22 numbered player cards and an unnumbered checklist made up the set. Cards measure 2-1/2" x 3-1/2", and are identical to the 1979 Topps regular set except for #4, 8, 9 and 22 which included new poses. Numerous minor picture cropping variations between the regular Topps issue and the Burger King sets of 1977-1980 exist.

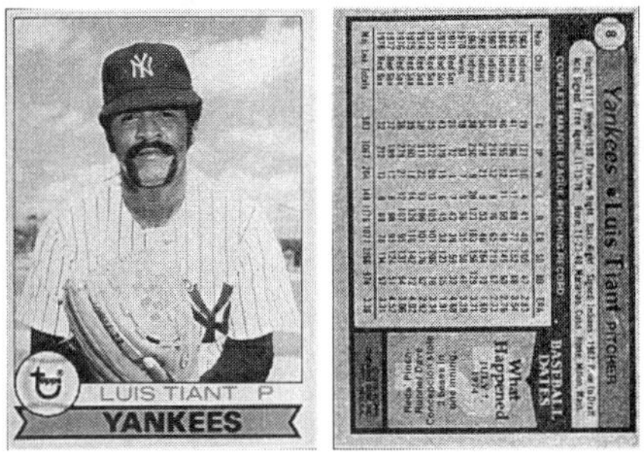

		NM	EX	VG
Complete Set (23):		6.00	4.50	2.50
Common Player:		.20	.10	.06
1	Yankees Team (Bob Lemon)	.30	.15	.09
2	Thurman Munson	1.50	.70	.45
3	Cliff Johnson	.20	.10	.06
4	Ron Guidry	.40	.20	.12
5	Jay Johnstone	.30	.15	.09
6	Catfish Hunter	.70	.35	.20
7	Jim Beattie	.20	.10	.06
8	Luis Tiant	.40	.20	.12
9	Tommy John	.60	.30	.20
10	Rich Gossage	.50	.25	.15
11	Ed Figueroa	.20	.10	.06
12	Chris Chambliss	.25	.13	.08
13	Willie Randolph	.30	.15	.09
14	Bucky Dent	.30	.15	.09
15	Graig Nettles	.30	.15	.09
16	Fred Stanley	.20	.10	.06
17	Jim Spencer	.20	.10	.06
18	Lou Piniella	.35	.20	.11
19	Roy White	.30	.15	.09
20	Mickey Rivers	.25	.13	.08
21	Reggie Jackson	2.00	1.00	.60
22	Juan Beniquez	.20	.10	.06
---	Checklist	.05	.03	.02

1980 Burger King Phillies

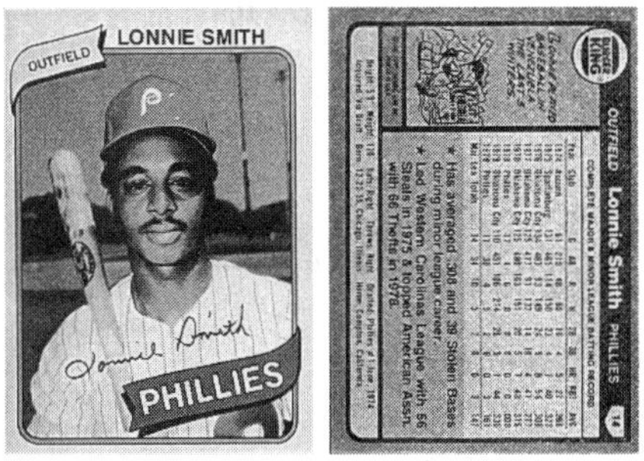

Philadelphia-area Burger King outlets issued a 23-card set featuring the Phillies for the second in a row in 1980. The Topps-produced set, measuring 2-1/2" x 3-1/2", contains 22 player cards and an unnumbered checklist. Fronts are identical in design to the regular 1980 Topps sets with the following exceptions: #1, 3, 8, 14 and 22 feature new poses. Very minor picture-cropping variations between the regular Topps issues and the Burger King sets exist in all years. Those minor differences are not noted in the checklists. The 1980 Burger King sets were the first to include the Burger King logo on the card backs.

		NM	EX	VG
Complete Set (23):		7.50	3.75	2.25
Common Player:		.10	.05	.03
1	Dallas Green	.40	.20	.12
2	Bob Boone	.40	.20	.12
3	Keith Moreland	.25	.13	.08
4	Pete Rose	2.25	1.25	.70
5	Manny Trillo	.10	.05	.03
6	Mike Schmidt	2.25	1.25	.70
7	Larry Bowa	.20	.10	.06
8	John Vukovich	.10	.05	.03
9	Bake McBride	.10	.05	.03
10	Garry Maddox	.10	.05	.03
11	Greg Luzinski	.25	.13	.08
12	Greg Gross	.10	.05	.03
13	Del Unser	.10	.05	.03
14	Lonnie Smith	.40	.20	.12
15	Steve Carlton	1.25	.60	.40
16	Larry Christenson	.10	.05	.03
17	Nino Espinosa	.10	.05	.03
18	Randy Lerch	.10	.05	.03
19	Dick Ruthven	.10	.05	.03
20	Tug McGraw	.15	.08	.05
21	Ron Reed	.10	.05	.03
22	Kevin Saucier	.10	.05	.03
---	Checklist	.05	.03	.02

1980 Burger King Pitch, Hit & Run

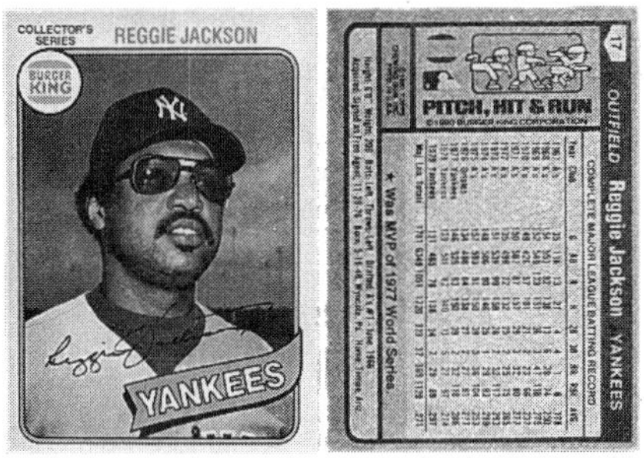

In 1980, Burger King issued, in conjunction with its "Pitch, Hit & Run" promotion, a Topps-produced set featuring pitchers (card #s 1-11), hitters (#s 12-22), and base stealers (#s 23-33). Fronts, which carry the Burger King logo, are identical in design to the regular 1980 Topps set except for numbers 1, 4, 5, 7, 9, 10, 16, 17, 18, 22, 23, 27, 28, 29 and 30, which feature different poses. Cards measure 2-1/2" x 3-1/2" in size. An unnumbered checklist was included with the set.

		NM	EX	VG
Complete Set (34):		9.00	4.50	2.75
Common Player:		.10	.05	.03
1	Vida Blue	.10	.05	.03
2	Steve Carlton	1.00	.50	.30
3	Rollie Fingers	.60	.30	.20
4	Ron Guidry	.15	.08	.05
5	Jerry Koosman	.10	.05	.03
6	Phil Niekro	.70	.35	.20
7	Jim Palmer	1.00	.50	.30
8	J.R. Richard	.10	.05	.03
9	Nolan Ryan	4.00	2.00	1.25
10	Tom Seaver	1.00	.50	.30
11	Bruce Sutter	.10	.05	.03
12	Don Baylor	.15	.08	.05
13	George Brett	2.00	1.00	.60
14	Rod Carew	1.00	.50	.30
15	George Foster	.10	.05	.03
16	Keith Hernandez	.10	.05	.03
17	Reggie Jackson	1.00	.50	.30
18	Fred Lynn	.15	.08	.05
19	Dave Parker	.15	.08	.05
20	Jim Rice	.20	.10	.06
21	Pete Rose	2.50	1.25	.70
22	Dave Winfield	.75	.40	.25
23	Bobby Bonds	.10	.05	.03
24	Enos Cabell	.10	.05	.03
25	Cesar Cedeno	.10	.05	.03
26	Julio Cruz	.10	.05	.03
27	Ron LeFlore	.10	.05	.03
28	Dave Lopes	.10	.05	.03
29	Omar Moreno	.10	.05	.03
30	Joe Morgan	.70	.35	.20
31	Bill North	.10	.05	.03
32	Frank Taveras	.10	.05	.03
33	Willie Wilson	.10	.05	.03
---	Checklist	.05	.03	.02

1916 Burgess-Nash Clothiers

Best known for its use as a promotional medium for The Sporting News, this 200-card set can be found with ads on the back for several local and regional businesses. Among them is Burgess-Nash clothiers, location unknown. While type card collectors and superstar collectors may pay a premium for individual cards with Burgess-Nash advertising, prices will generally parallel the 1916 Sporting News values. Cards measure 1-5/8" x 3" and are printed in black-and-white.

(See 1916 Sporting News for checklist, value information.)

1935 George Burke Detroit Tigers Photo Stamps

This team set of black-and-white, 1-1/16" x 1-1/4" photo stamps was produced by baseball photographer George Burke. The set was printed on two sheets of 12 players each. Each stamp has the player's name, position abbreviation and city in black or white typography. The blank-backed ungummed stamps of the 1935 World's Champs are checklisted here in alphabetical order.

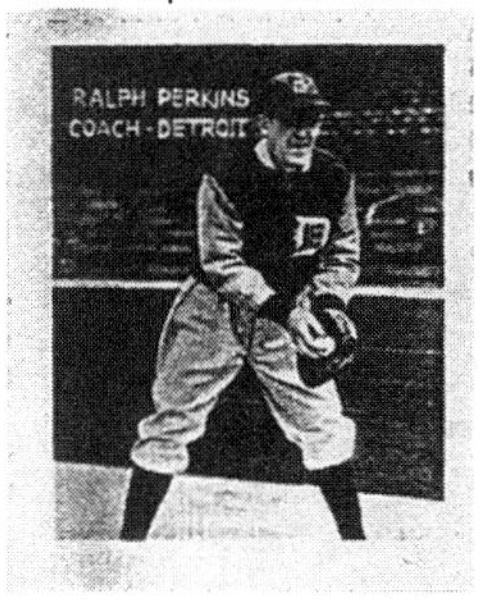

		NM	EX	VG
Complete Set (24):		275.00	135.00	82.50
Common Player:		8.00	4.00	2.50
(1)	Elden Auker	8.00	4.00	2.50
(2)	Del Baker	8.00	4.00	2.50
(3)	Tom Bridges	8.00	4.00	2.50
(4)	Herman Clifton	8.00	4.00	2.50
(5)	Mickey Cochrane	25.00	12.50	7.50
(6)	Alvin Crowder	8.00	4.00	2.50
(7)	Ervin Fox	8.00	4.00	2.50
(8)	Charles Gehringer	25.00	12.50	7.50
(9)	Leon Goslin	25.00	12.50	7.50
(10)	Henry Greenberg	40.00	20.00	12.00
(11)	Raymond Hayworth	8.00	4.00	2.50
(12)	Elon Hogsett	8.00	4.00	2.50
(13)	Roxie Lawson	8.00	4.00	2.50
(14)	Marvin Owen	8.00	4.00	2.50
(15)	Ralph Perkins	8.00	4.00	2.50
(16)	Frank Reiber	8.00	4.00	2.50
(17)	Wm. Rogell	8.00	4.00	2.50
(18)	Lynwood Rowe	12.00	6.00	3.50
(19)	Henry Schuble	8.00	4.00	2.50
(20)	Hugh Shelley	8.00	4.00	2.50
(21)	Victor Sorrell	8.00	4.00	2.50
(22)	Joseph Sullivan	8.00	4.00	2.50
(23)	Gerald Walker	8.00	4.00	2.50
(24)	Joyner White	8.00	4.00	2.50

1935-37 George Burke Postage Stamp Photos

These small (3/4" x 1") black-and-white stamps were produced by Chicago baseball portraitist George Burke for sale to individual players for use in answering fan mail. The stamps were not a big seller, though the checklist presented alphabetically here is surely incomplete. The unnumbered stamps, which are blank-backed, were not self-adhesive and were printed in sheets of at least six of the same player. Some of the photo-stamps have facsimile autographs, others do not.

		NM	EX	VG
Common Player:		8.00	4.00	2.50
(1)	Huck Betts	8.00	4.00	2.50
(2)	George Blaeholder	8.00	4.00	2.50
(3)	Jim Bottomley	25.00	12.50	7.50
(4)	Sam Byrd	8.00	4.00	2.50
(5)	Gilly Campbell	8.00	4.00	2.50
(6)	Hugh Casey	8.00	4.00	2.50
(7)	Kiki Cuyler	25.00	12.50	7.50
(8)	Bill Dietrich	8.00	4.00	2.50
(9)	Jim DeShong	8.00	4.00	2.50
(10)	Carl Doyle	8.00	4.00	2.50
(11)	Hank Erickson	8.00	4.00	2.50
(12)	Wes Ferrell	8.00	4.00	2.50
(13a)	Jimmie Foxx (facsimile autograph)	25.00	12.50	7.50
(13b)	Jimmie Foxx (no autograph)	25.00	12.50	7.50
(14)	Larry French	8.00	4.00	2.50
(15)	Benny Frey	8.00	4.00	2.50
(16)	Tony Freitas	8.00	4.00	2.50
(17)	Chick Hafey	25.00	12.50	7.50
(18)	Roy Henshaw	8.00	4.00	2.50
(19)	Leroy Herrmann	8.00	4.00	2.50
(20)	Al Hollingsworth	8.00	4.00	2.50
(21)	Bob Johnson	10.00	5.00	3.00
(22)	Douglas Johnson	8.00	4.00	2.50
(23)	Si Johnson	8.00	4.00	2.50
(24)	George L. Kelly	25.00	12.50	7.50

		NM	EX	VG
(25)	Bill Lee	8.00	4.00	2.50
(26)	Earle Mack	10.00	5.00	3.00
(27)	Roy Mahaffey	8.00	4.00	2.50
(28)	Johnny Marcum	8.00	4.00	2.50
(29)	Eric McNair	8.00	4.00	2.50
(30)	Skeeter Newsome	8.00	4.00	2.50
(31)	Billy Sullivan	8.00	4.00	2.50
(32)	Dan Taylor	8.00	4.00	2.50
(33)	Rube Walberg	8.00	4.00	2.50
(34)	"Rabbit" Warstler	8.00	4.00	2.50
(35)	Billy Webb	8.00	4.00	2.50

1933 Butter Cream (R306)

The 1933 Butter Cream set consists of unnumbered, black-and-white cards which measure 1-1/4" x 3-1/2". Backs feature a contest in which the collector was to estimate players' statistics by a specific date. Two different backs are known: 1) Estimate through Sept. 1 and no company address, and 2) Estimate through Oct. 1 with the Butter Cream address. The ACC designation for the set is R306.

		NM	EX	VG
Complete Set (30):		15000.	7500.	4500.
Common Player:		375.00	185.00	110.00
(1)	Earl Averill	600.00	300.00	180.00
(2)	Ed. Brandt	375.00	185.00	110.00
(3)	Guy T. Bush	375.00	185.00	110.00
(4)	Gordon Cochrane	600.00	300.00	180.00
(5)	Joe Cronin	600.00	300.00	180.00
(6)	George Earnshaw	375.00	185.00	110.00
(7)	Wesley Ferrell	375.00	185.00	110.00
(8)	"Jimmy" E. Foxx	750.00	375.00	225.00
(9)	Frank C. Frisch	600.00	300.00	180.00
(10)	Charles M. Gelbert	375.00	185.00	110.00
(11)	"Lefty" Robert M. Grove	675.00	335.00	200.00
(12)	Leo Charles Hartnett	600.00	300.00	180.00
(13)	"Babe" Herman	375.00	185.00	110.00
(14)	Charles Klein	600.00	300.00	180.00
(15)	Ray Kremer	375.00	185.00	110.00
(16)	Fred C. Linstrom (Lindstrom)	600.00	300.00	180.00
(17)	Ted A. Lyons	600.00	300.00	180.00
(18)	"Pepper" John L. Martin	450.00	225.00	135.00
(19)	Robert O'Farrell	375.00	185.00	110.00
(20)	Ed. A. Rommel	375.00	185.00	110.00
(21)	Charles Root	375.00	185.00	110.00
(22)	Harold "Muddy" Ruel (Herold)	375.00	185.00	110.00
(23)	Babe Ruth	4500.	2250.	1350.
(24)	"Al" Simmons	600.00	300.00	180.00
(25)	"Bill" Terry	600.00	300.00	180.00
(26)	George E. Uhle	375.00	185.00	110.00
(27)	Lloyd J. Waner	600.00	300.00	180.00
(28)	Paul G. Waner	600.00	300.00	180.00
(29)	Hack Wilson	600.00	300.00	180.00
(30)	Glen. Wright	375.00	185.00	110.00

1934 Butterfinger (R310)

Cards in this set were available as a premium with Butterfinger and other candy products. The unnumbered cards measure approximately 7-3/4" x 9-3/4" and can be found printed either on paper or heavy cardboard. The cardboard variety carry red advertising for Butterfinger and are valued about two to three times the paper version. The black-and-white cards feature a player photo with facsimile autograph. Similar cards in a 6-1/2" x 8-1/2" format are a companion Canadian issue.

		NM	EX	VG
Complete Set (65):		4100.	2050.	1225.
Common Player:		60.00	30.00	18.00
Cardboard Variety: 2-3x				
(1)	Earl Averill	115.00	57.00	34.00
(2)	Richard Bartell	60.00	30.00	18.00
(3)	Larry Benton	60.00	30.00	18.00
(4)	Walter Berger	60.00	30.00	18.00
(5)	Jim Bottomly (Bottomley)	115.00	57.00	34.00
(6)	Ralph Boyle	60.00	30.00	18.00
(7)	Tex Carleton	60.00	30.00	18.00
(8)	Owen T. Carroll	60.00	30.00	18.00
(9)	Ben Chapman	60.00	30.00	18.00
(10)	Gordon (Mickey) Cochrane	115.00	57.00	34.00
(11)	James Collins	60.00	30.00	18.00
(12)	Joe Cronin	115.00	57.00	34.00
(13)	Alvin Crowder	60.00	30.00	18.00
(14)	"Dizzy" Dean	235.00	115.00	70.00
(15)	Paul Derringer	60.00	30.00	18.00
(16)	William Dickey	145.00	72.00	43.00
(17)	Leo Durocher	115.00	57.00	34.00
(18)	George Earnshaw	60.00	30.00	18.00
(19)	Richard Ferrell	115.00	57.00	34.00
(20)	Lew Fonseca	60.00	30.00	18.00
(21a)	Jimmy Fox (name incorrect)	175.00	87.00	52.00
(21b)	Jimmy Foxx (name correct)	175.00	87.00	52.00
(22)	Benny Frey	60.00	30.00	18.00
(23)	Frankie Frisch	115.00	57.00	34.00
(24)	Lou Gehrig	700.00	350.00	210.00
(25)	Charles Gehringer	115.00	57.00	34.00
(26)	Vernon Gomez	115.00	57.00	34.00
(27)	Ray Grabowski	60.00	30.00	18.00
(28)	Robert (Lefty) Grove	115.00	57.00	34.00
(29)	George (Mule) Haas	60.00	30.00	18.00
(30)	"Chick" Hafey	115.00	57.00	34.00
(31)	Stanley Harris	115.00	57.00	34.00
(32)	J. Francis Hogan	60.00	30.00	18.00
(33)	Ed Holley	60.00	30.00	18.00
(34)	Rogers Hornsby	145.00	72.00	43.00
(35)	Waite Hoyt	115.00	57.00	34.00
(36)	Walter Johnson	200.00	100.00	60.00
(37)	Jim Jordan	60.00	30.00	18.00
(38)	Joe Kuhel	60.00	30.00	18.00
(39)	Hal Lee	60.00	30.00	18.00
(40)	Gus Mancuso	60.00	30.00	18.00
(41)	Henry Manush	115.00	57.00	34.00
(42)	Fred Marberry	60.00	30.00	18.00
(43)	Pepper Martin	90.00	45.00	27.00
(44)	Oscar Melillo	60.00	30.00	18.00
(45)	Johnny Moore	60.00	30.00	18.00
(46)	Joe Morrissey	60.00	30.00	18.00
(47)	Joe Mowrey	60.00	30.00	18.00
(48)	Bob O'Farrell	60.00	30.00	18.00
(49)	Melvin Ott	115.00	57.00	34.00
(50)	Monte Pearson	60.00	30.00	18.00
(51)	Carl Reynolds	60.00	30.00	18.00
(52)	Charles Ruffing	115.00	57.00	34.00
(53)	Babe Ruth	900.00	450.00	270.00
(54)	John "Blondy" Ryan	60.00	30.00	18.00
(55)	Al Simmons	115.00	57.00	34.00
(56)	Al Spohrer	60.00	30.00	18.00
(57)	Gus Suhr	60.00	30.00	18.00
(58)	Steve Swetonic	60.00	30.00	18.00
(59)	Dazzy Vance	115.00	57.00	34.00
(60)	Joe Vosmik	60.00	30.00	18.00
(61)	Lloyd Waner	115.00	57.00	34.00
(62)	Paul Waner	115.00	57.00	34.00
(63)	Sam West	60.00	30.00	18.00
(64)	Earl Whitehill	60.00	30.00	18.00
(65)	Jimmy Wilson	60.00	30.00	18.00

1934 Butterfinger - Canadian

Similar to the U.S. issue, though smaller in size at 6-1/2" x 8-1/2", these black-and-white paper cards include a number of players not found in the U.S. issue. Like the "regular" Butterfinger cards, each of the Canadian pieces includes a facsimile autograph on the front; backs are blank.

		NM	EX	VG
Complete Set (58):		5000.	2500.	1500.
Common Player:		50.00	25.00	15.00
(1)	Earl Averill	100.00	50.00	30.00
(2)	Larry Benton	50.00	25.00	15.00
(3)	Jim Bottomly (Bottomley)	100.00	50.00	30.00
(4)	Tom Bridges	50.00	25.00	15.00
(5)	Bob Brown	50.00	25.00	15.00
(6)	Owen T. Carroll	50.00	25.00	15.00
(7)	Gordon (Mickey) Cochrane	100.00	50.00	30.00
(8)	Roger Cramer	50.00	25.00	15.00
(9)	Joe Cronin	100.00	50.00	30.00
(10)	Alvin Crowder	50.00	25.00	15.00
(11)	"Dizzy" Dean	175.00	87.00	52.00
(12)	Edward Delker	50.00	25.00	15.00
(13)	William Dickey	125.00	62.00	37.00
(14)	Richard Ferrell	100.00	50.00	30.00
(15)	Lew Fonseca	50.00	25.00	15.00
(16a)	Jimmy Fox (name incorrect)	150.00	75.00	45.00
(16b)	Jimmy Foxx (name correct)	150.00	75.00	45.00
(17)	Chick Fullis	50.00	25.00	15.00
(18)	Lou Gehrig	600.00	300.00	180.00
(19)	Charles Gehringer	100.00	50.00	30.00
(20)	Vernon Gomez	100.00	50.00	30.00
(21)	Robert (Lefty) Grove	100.00	50.00	30.00
(22)	George (Mule) Haas	50.00	25.00	15.00
(23)	"Chick" Hafey	100.00	50.00	30.00
(24)	Stanley Harris	100.00	50.00	30.00
(25)	Frank Higgins	50.00	25.00	15.00
(26)	J. Francis Hogan	50.00	25.00	15.00
(27)	Ed Holley	50.00	25.00	15.00
(28)	Waite Hoyt	100.00	50.00	30.00
(29)	Jim Jordan	50.00	25.00	15.00
(30)	Hal Lee	50.00	25.00	15.00
(31)	Gus Mancuso	50.00	25.00	15.00
(32)	Oscar Melillo	50.00	25.00	15.00
(33)	Austin Moore	50.00	25.00	15.00
(34)	Randy Moore	50.00	25.00	15.00
(35)	Joe Morrissey	50.00	25.00	15.00
(36)	Joe Mowrey	50.00	25.00	15.00
(37)	Bobo Newsom	50.00	25.00	15.00
(38)	Ernie Orsatti	50.00	25.00	15.00
(39)	Carl Reynolds	50.00	25.00	15.00
(40)	Walter Roettger	50.00	25.00	15.00
(41)	Babe Ruth	800.00	400.00	240.00
(42)	John "Blondy" Ryan	50.00	25.00	15.00
(43)	John Salveson	50.00	25.00	15.00
(44)	Al Simmons	100.00	50.00	30.00
(45)	Al Smith	50.00	25.00	15.00
(46)	Harold Smith	50.00	25.00	15.00
(47)	Allyn Stout	50.00	25.00	15.00
(48)	Fresco Thompson	50.00	25.00	15.00
(49)	Art Veltman	50.00	25.00	15.00
(50)	Johnny Vergez	50.00	25.00	15.00
(51)	Gerald Walker	50.00	25.00	15.00
(52)	Paul Waner	100.00	50.00	30.00
(53)	Burgess Whitehead	50.00	25.00	15.00
(54)	Earl Whitehill	50.00	25.00	15.00
(55)	Robert Weiland	50.00	25.00	15.00
(56)	Jimmy Wilson	50.00	25.00	15.00
(57)	Bob Worthington			
(58)	Tom Zachary			

1911-14 Butter Krust Bread (D304)

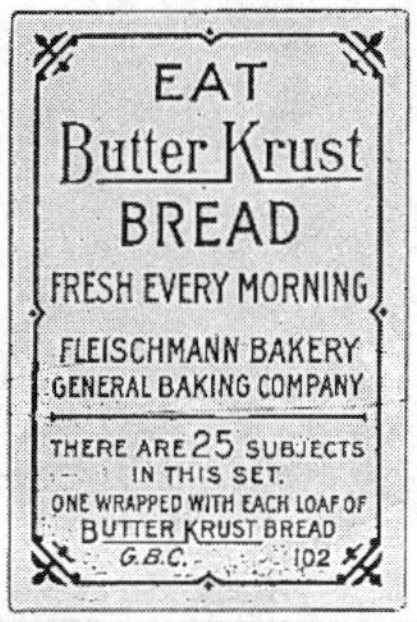

(See 1911-14 General Baking Co. for checklist and values.)

1914 B18 Blankets

These 5-1/4"-square flannels were issued in 1914 wrapped around several popular brands of tobacco. The flannels, whose American Card Catalog designation is B18, picked up the nickname blankets because many of them were sewn together to form bed covers or throws. Different color combinations on the flannels exist for all 10 teams included in the set. The complete set price includes only the lowest-priced variation for each of the 90 players.

		NM	EX	VG
Complete Set (90):		5000.	2500.	1500.
Common Player:		30.00	15.00	9.00
(1a)	Babe Adams (purple pennants)	60.00	30.00	18.00
(1b)	Babe Adams (red pennants)	70.00	35.00	21.00
(2a)	Sam Agnew (purple basepaths)	60.00	30.00	18.00
(2b)	Sam Agnew (red basepaths)	70.00	35.00	21.00
(3a)	Eddie Ainsmith (green pennants)	30.00	15.00	9.00
(3b)	Eddie Ainsmith (brown pennants)	30.00	15.00	9.00
(4a)	Jimmy Austin (purple basepaths)	60.00	30.00	18.00
(4b)	Jimmy Austin (red basepaths)	70.00	35.00	21.00
(5a)	Del Baker (white infield)	30.00	15.00	9.00
(5b)	Del Baker (brown infield)	115.00	57.00	34.00
(5c)	Del Baker (red infield)	1500.	750.00	450.00
(6a)	Johnny Bassler (purple pennants)	60.00	30.00	18.00
(6b)	Johnny Bassler (yellow pennants)	115.00	57.00	34.00
(7a)	Paddy Bauman (Baumann) (white infield)	30.00	15.00	9.00
(7b)	Paddy Bauman (Baumann) (brown infield)	115.00	57.00	34.00
(7c)	Paddy Bauman (Baumann) (red infield)	1500.	750.00	450.00
(8a)	Luke Boone (blue infield)	30.00	15.00	9.00
(8b)	Luke Boone (green infield)	30.00	15.00	9.00
(9a)	George Burns (brown basepaths)	30.00	15.00	9.00
(9b)	George Burns (green basepaths)	30.00	15.00	9.00
(10a)	Tioga George Burns (white infield)	30.00	15.00	9.00
(10b)	Tioga George Burns (brown infield)	115.00	57.00	34.00
(10c)	Tioga George Burns (red infield)	1500.	750.00	450.00
(11a)	Max Carey (purple pennants)	115.00	57.00	34.00
(11b)	Max Carey (red pennants)	130.00	65.00	39.00
(12a)	Marty Cavanaugh (Kavanagh) (white infield)	30.00	15.00	9.00
(12b)	Marty Cavanaugh (Kavanagh) (brown infield)	165.00	82.00	49.00
(12c)	Marty Cavanaugh (Kavanagh) (red infield)	1500.	750.00	450.00
(12d)	Marty Kavanaugh (Kavanagh)	30.00	15.00	9.00
(13a)	Frank Chance (green infield)	70.00	35.00	21.00
(13b)	Frank Chance (brown pennants, blue infield)	70.00	35.00	21.00
(13c)	Frank Chance (yellow pennants, blue infield)	350.00	175.00	105.00
(14a)	Ray Chapman (purple pennants)	70.00	35.00	21.00
(14b)	Ray Chapman (yellow pennants)	115.00	57.00	34.00
(15a)	Ty Cobb (white infield)	600.00	300.00	180.00
(15b)	Ty Cobb (brown infield)	700.00	350.00	210.00
(15c)	Ty Cobb (red infield)	4000.	2000.	1200.
(16a)	King Cole (blue infield)	30.00	15.00	9.00
(16b)	King Cole (green infield)	30.00	15.00	9.00
(17a)	Joe Connolly (white infield)	30.00	15.00	9.00
(17b)	Joe Connolly (brown infield)	115.00	57.00	34.00
(18a)	Harry Coveleski (white infield)	30.00	15.00	9.00
(18b)	Harry Coveleski (brown infield)	115.00	57.00	34.00
(18c)	Harry Coveleski (red infield)	1500.	750.00	450.00
(19a)	George Cutshaw (blue infield)	30.00	15.00	9.00
(19b)	George Cutshaw (green infield)	30.00	15.00	9.00
(20a)	Jake Daubert (blue infield)	35.00	17.50	10.50
(20b)	Jake Daubert (green infield)	35.00	17.50	10.50
(21a)	Ray Demmitt (white infield)	30.00	15.00	9.00
(21b)	Ray Demmitt (brown infield)	115.00	57.00	34.00
(21c)	Ray Demmitt (red infield)	1500.	750.00	450.00
(22a)	Bill Doak (purple pennants)	60.00	30.00	18.00
(22b)	Bill Doak (yellow pennants)	115.00	57.00	34.00
(23a)	Cozy Dolan (purple pennants)	60.00	30.00	18.00
(23b)	Cozy Dolan (yellow pennants)	115.00	57.00	34.00
(24a)	Larry Doyle (brown basepaths)	35.00	17.50	10.50
(24b)	Larry Doyle (green basepaths)	35.00	17.50	10.50
(25a)	Art Fletcher (brown basepaths)	30.00	15.00	9.00
(25b)	Art Fletcher (green basepaths)	30.00	15.00	9.00
(26a)	Eddie Foster (brown pennants)	30.00	15.00	9.00
(26b)	Eddie Foster (green pennants)	30.00	15.00	9.00
(27a)	Del Gainor (white infield)	30.00	15.00	9.00
(27b)	Del Gainor (brown infield)	115.00	57.00	34.00
(28a)	Chick Gandil (brown pennants)	55.00	27.00	16.50
(28b)	Chick Gandil (green pennants)	55.00	27.00	16.50
(29a)	George Gibson (purple pennants)	60.00	30.00	18.00
(29b)	George Gibson (red pennants)	70.00	35.00	21.00
(30a)	Hank Gowdy (white infield)	30.00	15.00	9.00
(30b)	Hank Gowdy (brown infield)	115.00	57.00	34.00
(30c)	Hank Gowdy (red infield)	1500.	750.00	450.00
(31a)	Jack Graney (purple pennants)	60.00	30.00	18.00
(31b)	Jack Graney (yellow pennants)	115.00	57.00	34.00
(32a)	Eddie Grant (brown basepaths)	30.00	15.00	9.00
(32b)	Eddie Grant (green basepaths)	30.00	15.00	9.00
(33a)	Tommy Griffith (white infield, green pennants)	30.00	15.00	9.00
(33b)	Tommy Griffith (white infield, red pennants)	1500.	750.00	450.00
(33c)	Tommy Griffith (brown infield)	115.00	57.00	34.00
(33d)	Tommy Griffith (red infield)	1500.	750.00	450.00
(34a)	Earl Hamilton (purple basepaths)	60.00	30.00	18.00
(34b)	Earl Hamilton (red basepaths)	70.00	35.00	21.00
(35a)	Roy Hartzell (blue infield)	30.00	15.00	9.00
(35b)	Roy Hartzell (green infield)	30.00	15.00	9.00
(36a)	Miller Huggins (purple pennants)	110.00	55.00	33.00
(36b)	Miller Huggin (yellow pennants)	190.00	95.00	57.00
(37a)	John Hummel (blue infield)	30.00	15.00	9.00
(37b)	John Hummel (green infield)	30.00	15.00	9.00
(38a)	Ham Hyatt (purple pennants)	60.00	30.00	18.00
(38b)	Ham Hyatt (red pennants)	70.00	35.00	21.00
(39a)	Shoeless Joe Jackson (purple pennants)	1000.	500.00	300.00
(39b)	Shoeless Joe Jackson (yellow pennants)	1250.	625.00	375.00
(40a)	Bill James (white infield)	30.00	15.00	9.00
(40b)	Bill James (brown infield)	115.00	57.00	34.00
(40c)	Bill James (red infield)	1500.	750.00	450.00
(41a)	Walter Johnson (brown pennants)	400.00	200.00	120.00
(41b)	Walter Johnson (green pennants)	400.00	200.00	120.00
(42a)	Ray Keating (blue infield)	30.00	15.00	9.00
(42b)	Ray Keating (green infield)	30.00	15.00	9.00
(43a)	Joe Kelley (Kelly) (purple pennants)	60.00	30.00	18.00
(43b)	Joe Kelley (Kelly) (red pennants)	70.00	35.00	21.00
(44a)	Ed Konetchy (purple pennants)	60.00	30.00	18.00
(44b)	Ed Konetchy (red pennants)	70.00	35.00	21.00
(45a)	Nemo Leibold (purple pennants)	60.00	30.00	18.00
(45b)	Nemo Leibold (yellow pennants)	115.00	57.00	34.00
(46a)	Fritz Maisel (blue infield)	30.00	15.00	9.00
(46b)	Fritz Maisel (green infield)	30.00	15.00	9.00
(47a)	Les Mann (white infield)	30.00	15.00	9.00
(47b)	Les Mann (brown infield)	115.00	57.00	34.00
(47c)	Les Mann (red infield)	1500.	750.00	450.00
(48a)	Rabbit Maranville (white infield)	70.00	35.00	21.00
(48b)	Rabbit Maranville (brown infield)	195.00	97.00	58.00
(48c)	Rabbit Maranville (red infield)	1750.	875.00	525.00
(49a)	Bill McAllister (McAllester) (purple basepaths)	60.00	30.00	18.00
(49b)	Bill McAllister (McAllester) (red basepaths)	70.00	35.00	21.00
(50a)	George McBride (brown pennants)	30.00	15.00	9.00
(50b)	George McBride (green pennants)	30.00	15.00	9.00
(51a)	Chief Meyers (brown basepaths)	30.00	15.00	9.00
(51b)	Chief Meyers (green basepaths)	30.00	15.00	9.00
(52a)	Clyde Milan (brown pennants)	30.00	15.00	9.00
(52b)	Clyde Milan (green pennants)	30.00	15.00	9.00
(53a)	Dots Miller (purple pennants)	60.00	30.00	18.00
(53b)	Dots Miller (yellow pennants)	115.00	57.00	34.00
(54a)	Otto Miller (blue infield)	30.00	15.00	9.00
(54b)	Otto Miller (green infield)	30.00	15.00	9.00
(55a)	Willie Mitchell (purple pennants)	60.00	30.00	18.00
(55b)	Willie Mitchell (yellow pennants)	115.00	57.00	34.00
(56a)	Danny Moeller (brown pennants)	30.00	15.00	9.00
(56b)	Danny Moeller (green pennants)	30.00	15.00	9.00
(57a)	Ray Morgan (brown pennants)	30.00	15.00	9.00
(57b)	Ray Morgan (green pennants)	30.00	15.00	9.00
(58a)	George Moriarty (white infield)	30.00	15.00	9.00
(58b)	George Moriarty (brown infield)	115.00	57.00	34.00
(58c)	George Moriarty (red infield)	1500.	750.00	450.00
(59a)	Mike Mowrey (purple pennants)	60.00	30.00	18.00
(59b)	Mike Mowrey (red pennants)	70.00	35.00	21.00
(60a)	Red Murray (brown basepaths)	30.00	15.00	9.00
(60b)	Red Murray (green basepaths)	30.00	15.00	9.00
(61a)	Ivy Olson (purple pennants)	60.00	30.00	18.00
(61b)	Ivy Olson (yellow pennants)	115.00	57.00	34.00
(62a)	Steve O'Neill (purple pennants)	60.00	30.00	18.00
(62b)	Steve O'Neill (red pennants)	115.00	57.00	34.00
(62c)	Steve O'Neill (yellow pennants)	115.00	57.00	34.00
(63a)	Marty O'Toole (purple pennants)	60.00	30.00	18.00
(63b)	Marty O'Toole (red pennants)	70.00	35.00	21.00
(64a)	Roger Peckinpaugh (blue infield)	35.00	17.50	10.50
(64b)	Roger Peckinpaugh (green infield)	35.00	17.50	10.50
(65a)	Hub Perdue (white infield)	30.00	15.00	9.00
(65b)	Hub Perdue (brown infield)	115.00	57.00	34.00
(65c)	Hub Purdue (red infield)	1500.	750.00	450.00
(66a)	Del Pratt (purple basepaths)	60.00	30.00	18.00
(66b)	Del Pratt (red basepaths)	70.00	35.00	21.00
(67a)	Hank Robinson (purple pennants)	60.00	30.00	18.00
(67b)	Hank Robinson (yellow pennants)	115.00	57.00	34.00
(68a)	Nap Rucker (blue infield)	30.00	15.00	9.00
(68b)	Nap Rucker (green infield)	30.00	15.00	9.00
(69a)	Slim Sallee (purple pennants)	60.00	30.00	18.00
(69b)	Slim Sallee (yellow pennants)	115.00	57.00	34.00
(70a)	Howard Shanks (brown pennants)	30.00	15.00	9.00
(70b)	Howard Shanks (green pennants)	30.00	15.00	9.00
(70c)	Howard Shanks (white infield)	30.00	15.00	9.00
(71a)	Burt Shotton (purple basepaths)	60.00	30.00	18.00
(71b)	Burt Shotton (red basepaths)	70.00	35.00	21.00
(72a)	Red Smith (blue infield)	30.00	15.00	9.00
(72b)	Red Smith (green infield)	30.00	15.00	9.00
(73a)	Fred Snodgrass (brown basepaths)	30.00	15.00	9.00
(73b)	Fred Snodgrass (green basepaths)	30.00	15.00	9.00
(74a)	Bill Steele (purple pennants)	60.00	30.00	18.00
74b	Bill Steele (yellow pennants)	115.00	57.00	34.00
(75a)	Casey Stengel (blue infield)	190.00	95.00	57.00
(75b)	Casey Stengel (green infield)	200.00	100.00	60.00
(76a)	Jeff Sweeney (blue infield)	30.00	15.00	9.00
(76b)	Jeff Sweeney (green infield)	30.00	15.00	9.00
(77a)	Jeff Tesreau (brown basepaths)	30.00	15.00	9.00
(77b)	Jeff Tesreau (green basepaths)	30.00	15.00	9.00
(78a)	Terry Turner (purple pennants)	60.00	30.00	18.00
(78b)	Terry Turner (yellow pennants)	115.00	57.00	34.00
(79a)	Lefty Tyler (white infield)	30.00	15.00	9.00
(79b)	Lefty Tyler (brown infield)	115.00	57.00	34.00
(79c)	Lefty Tyler (red infield)	1500.	750.00	450.00
(80a)	Jim Viox (purple pennants)	60.00	30.00	18.00
(80b)	Jim Viox (red pennants)	70.00	35.00	21.00
(81a)	Bull Wagner (blue infield)	30.00	15.00	9.00
(81b)	Bull Wagner (green infield)	30.00	15.00	9.00
(82a)	Bobby Wallace (purple basepaths)	115.00	57.00	34.00
(82b)	Bobby Wallace (red basepaths)	115.00	57.00	34.00
(83a)	Dee Walsh (purple basepaths)	60.00	30.00	18.00
(83b)	Dee Walsh (red basepaths)	70.00	35.00	21.00
(84a)	Jimmy Walsh (blue infield)	30.00	15.00	9.00
(84b)	Jimmy Walsh (green infield)	30.00	15.00	9.00
(85a)	Bert Whaling (white infield)	30.00	15.00	9.00
(85b)	Bert Whaling (brown infield)	115.00	57.00	34.00
(85c)	Bert Whaling (red infield)	1500.	750.00	450.00
(86a)	Zach Wheat (blue infield)	115.00	57.00	34.00
(86b)	Zach Wheat (green infield)	115.00	57.00	34.00
(87a)	Possum Whitted (purple pennants)	60.00	30.00	18.00
(87b)	Possum Whitted (yellow pennants)	115.00	57.00	34.00
(88a)	Gus Williams (purple basepaths)	60.00	30.00	18.00
(88b)	Gus Williams (red basepaths)	70.00	35.00	21.00
(89a)	Owen Wilson (purple pennants)	60.00	30.00	18.00
(89b)	Owen Wilson (yellow pennants)	115.00	57.00	34.00
(90a)	Hooks Wiltse (brown basepaths)	30.00	15.00	9.00
(90b)	Hooks Wiltse (green basepaths)	30.00	15.00	9.00

1916 BF2 Felt Pennants

Issued circa 1916, this unnumbered set consists of 97 felt pennants with a small black-and-white player photo glued to each. The triangular pennants measure approximately 8-1/4" long, while the photos are 1-3/4" x 1-1/4" and appear to be identical to photos used for The Sporting News issues of the same period. The pennants list the player's name and team. The pennants were given away as premiums with the purchase of 5-cent loaves of Ferguson Bakery bread in the Roxbury, Mass., area.

(See 1916 Ferguson Bakery Felt Pennants for checklist and values.)

1936-37 BF3 Felt Player/Team Pennants

The checklist for these series of felt pennants issued circa 1936-1937 is not complete, and new examples are still being reported. The pennants do not carry any manufacturer's name and their method of distribution is not certain, although it is believed they were issued as a premium with candy or gum. The pennants vary in size slightly but generally measure approximately 2-1/2" x 4-1/2" and were issued in various styles and colors. Most of the printing is white, although some pennants have been found with red or black printing, and the same pennant is often found in more than one color combination. The pennants feature both individual players and teams, including some minor league clubs. The pennants are grouped together under the American Card Catalog designation of BF3. Advanced collectors have categorized the pennants into 11 basic design types, depending on what elements are included on the pennant. The unnumbered felts are listed alphabetically within type.

	NM	EX	VG
Common Pennant:	25.00	12.50	7.50

1936-37 Type 1 - Player name and silhouette

		NM	EX	VG
Common Pennant:		35.00	17.50	10.50
(1)	Luke Appling (batting)	42.00	21.00	12.50
(2)	Wally Berger (fielding)	35.00	17.50	10.50
(3)	Zeke Bonura (fielding)	35.00	17.50	10.50
(4)	Dolph Camilli (fielding)	35.00	17.50	10.50
(5)	Ben Chapman (batting)	35.00	17.50	10.50
(6)	Mickey Cochrane (catching)	45.00	22.00	13.50
(7)	Rip Collins (batting)	35.00	17.50	10.50
(8)	Joe Cronin (batting)	42.00	21.00	12.50
(9)	Kiki Cuyler (running)	42.00	21.00	12.50
(10)	Dizzy Dean (pitching)	60.00	30.00	18.00
(11)	Frank Demaree (batting)	35.00	17.50	10.50
(12)	Paul Derringer (pitching)	35.00	17.50	10.50
(13)	Bill Dickey (catching)	45.00	22.00	13.50
(14)	Jimmy Dykes (fielding)	35.00	17.50	10.50
(15)	Bob Feller (pitching)	55.00	27.00	16.50
(16)	Wes Ferrell (batting)	35.00	17.50	10.50
(17)	Wes Ferrell (running)	35.00	17.50	10.50
(18)	Jimmy Foxx	50.00	25.00	15.00
(19)	Larry French (batting)	35.00	17.50	10.50
(20)	Frankie Frisch (running)	45.00	22.00	13.50
(21)	Lou Gehrig (fielding)	200.00	100.00	60.00
(22)	Lou Gehrig (throwing)	200.00	100.00	60.00
(23)	Charlie Gehringer (running)	45.00	22.00	13.50
(24)	Lefty Gomez (pitching)	42.00	21.00	12.50
(25)	Goose Goslin (batting)	42.00	21.00	12.50
(26)	Hank Greenberg (fielding)	55.00	27.00	16.50
(27)	Charlie Grimm (running)	35.00	17.50	10.50
(28)	Lefty Grove (pitching)	42.00	21.00	12.50
(29)	Gabby Hartnett (catching)	42.00	21.00	12.50
(30)	Rollie Hemsley (catching)	35.00	17.50	10.50
(31)	Billy Herman (fielding)	42.00	21.00	12.50
(32)	Frank Higgins (fielding)	35.00	17.50	10.50
(33)	Rogers Hornsby (batting)	47.50	24.00	14.00
(34)	Carl Hubbell (pitching)	45.00	22.00	13.50
(35)	Chuck Klein (throwing)	42.00	21.00	12.50
(36)	Tony Lazzeri (batting)	42.00	21.00	12.50
(37)	Hank Leiber (fielding)	35.00	17.50	10.50
(38)	Ernie Lombardi (catching)	42.00	21.00	12.50
(39)	Al Lopez (throwing)	42.00	21.00	12.50
(40)	Gus Mancuso (running)	35.00	17.50	10.50
(41)	Heinie Manush (batting)	42.00	21.00	12.50
(42)	Pepper Martin (batting)	40.00	20.00	12.00
(43)	Joe McCarthy (kneeling)	42.00	21.00	12.50
(44)	Wally Moses (running)	35.00	17.50	10.50
(45)	Van Mungo (standing)	35.00	17.50	10.50
(46)	Mel Ott (throwing)	45.00	22.00	13.50
(47)	Schoolboy Rowe (pitching)	35.00	17.50	10.50
(48)	Babe Ruth (batting)	300.00	150.00	90.00
(49)	George Selkirk (batting)	35.00	17.50	10.50
(50)	Luke Sewell (sliding)	35.00	17.50	10.50
(51)	Joe Stripp (batting)	35.00	17.50	10.50
(52)	Hal Trosky (fielding)	35.00	17.50	10.50
(53)	Floyd Vaughan (running, script name)	42.00	21.00	12.50
(54)	Floyd Vaughan (running, block name)	42.00	21.00	12.50
(55)	Joe Vosmik (running)	35.00	17.50	10.50
(56)	Paul Waner (batting)	42.00	21.00	12.50
(57)	Lon Warneke (pitching)	35.00	17.50	10.50
(58)	Jimmy Wilson (fielding)	35.00	17.50	10.50

1936-37 Type 2 - Player's name, team nickname, figure

		NM	EX	VG
Common Pennant:		35.00	17.50	10.50
(1)	Luke Appling (batting, block name)	42.00	21.00	12.50
(2)	Luke Appling (batting, script name)	42.00	21.00	12.50
(3)	Zeke Bonura (batting)	35.00	17.50	10.50
(4)	Dolph Camilli (batting)	35.00	17.50	10.50
(5)	Joe Cronin (throwing)	42.00	21.00	12.50
(6)	Dizzy Dean (batting)	60.00	30.00	18.00
(7)	Frank Demaree (batting)	35.00	17.50	10.50
(8)	Bob Feller (pitching)	55.00	27.00	16.50
(9)	Wes Ferrell (throwing)	35.00	17.50	10.50
(10)	Larry French (batting)	35.00	17.50	10.50
(11)	Frank Frisch (fielding)	45.00	22.00	13.50
(12)	Lou Gehrig (batting)	200.00	100.00	60.00
(13)	Lou Gehrig (fielding)	200.00	100.00	60.00
(14)	Hank Greenberg (throwing)	50.00	25.00	15.00
(15)	Charlie Grimm (fielding)	35.00	17.50	10.50
(16)	Charlie Grimm (throwing)	35.00	17.50	10.50
(17)	Lefty Grove (batting)	42.00	21.00	12.50
(18)	Lefty Grove (pitching)	42.00	21.00	12.50
(19)	Gabby Hartnett (batting)	42.00	21.00	12.50
(20)	Billy Herman (batting)	42.00	21.00	12.50
(21)	Tony Lazzeri (running)	42.00	21.00	12.50
(22)	Tony Lazzeri (throwing)	42.00	21.00	12.50
(23)	Hank Leiber (batting)	35.00	17.50	10.50
(24)	Ernie Lombardi (batting)	42.00	21.00	12.50
(25)	Pepper Martin (batting)	40.00	20.00	12.00
(26)	Joe Medwick (batting)	42.00	21.00	12.50
(27)	Van Lingle Mungo (batting)	35.00	17.50	10.50
(28)	Joe Stripp (batting)	35.00	17.50	10.50
(29)	Bill Terry (fielding)	42.00	21.00	12.50
(30)	Floyd Vaughan (batting)	42.00	21.00	12.50
(31)	Joe Vosmik (throwing)	35.00	17.50	10.50
(32)	Paul Waner (batting)	42.00	21.00	12.50
(33)	Lon Warneke (batting)	35.00	17.50	10.50
(34)	Lon Warneke (pitching)	35.00	17.50	10.50

1936-37 Type 3 - Player's name. Team nickname on ball

		NM	EX	VG
Common Pennant:		35.00	17.50	10.50
(1)	Wally Berger	35.00	17.50	10.50
(2)	Zeke Bonura	35.00	17.50	10.50
(3)	Dolph Camilli	35.00	17.50	10.50
(4)	Ben Chapman	35.00	17.50	10.50
(5)	Kiki Cuyler	42.00	21.00	12.50
(6)	Dizzy Dean	60.00	30.00	18.00
(7)	Frank Demaree	35.00	17.50	10.50
(8)	Bill Dickey	55.00	27.00	16.50
(9)	Joe DiMaggio (script name)	200.00	100.00	60.00
(10)	Bob Feller (script name)	55.00	27.00	16.50
(11)	Wes Ferrell	35.00	17.50	10.50
(12)	Jimmie Foxx	50.00	25.00	15.00
(13)	Larry French	35.00	17.50	10.50
(14)	Frank Frisch	45.00	22.00	13.50
(15)	Lou Gehrig (script name)	200.00	100.00	60.00
(16)	Charlie Gehringer	45.00	22.00	13.50
(17)	Lefty Gomez	42.00	21.00	12.50
(18)	Hank Greenberg	50.00	25.00	15.00
(19)	Lefty Grove	42.00	21.00	12.50
(20)	Gabby Hartnett	42.00	21.00	12.50
(21)	Billy Herman (script name)	42.00	21.00	12.50
(22)	Roger Hornsby (Rogers)	50.00	25.00	15.00
(23)	Carl Hubbell	45.00	22.00	13.50
(24)	Chuck Klein	42.00	21.00	12.50
(25)	Tony Lazzeri	42.00	21.00	12.50
(26)	Ernie Lombardi	42.00	21.00	12.50
(27)	Al Lopez	42.00	21.00	12.50
(28)	Johnny Marcum	35.00	17.50	10.50
(29)	Pepper Martin	40.00	20.00	12.00
(30)	Ducky Medwick	42.00	21.00	12.50
(31)	Van Mungo	35.00	17.50	10.50
(32)	Billy Myers	35.00	17.50	10.50
(33)	Mel Ott	45.00	22.00	13.50
(34)	Schoolboy Rowe	35.00	17.50	10.50
(35)	George Selkirk	35.00	17.50	10.50
(36)	Luke Sewell	35.00	17.50	10.50
(37)	Bill Terry	42.00	21.00	12.50
(38)	Pie Traynor	42.00	21.00	12.50
(39)	Hal Trosky	35.00	17.50	10.50
(40)	Floyd Vaughan	42.00	21.00	12.50
(41)	Lon Warneke	35.00	17.50	10.50
(42)	Earl Whitehill	35.00	17.50	10.50

1936-37 Type 4 - Team nickname and silhouette figure

		NM	EX	VG
Common Pennant:		25.00	12.50	7.50
(1)	Athletics (fielder)	25.00	12.50	7.50
(2)	Browns (catcher)	25.00	12.50	7.50
(3)	Cubs (batter)	25.00	12.50	7.50
(4)	Dodgers (batter)	25.00	12.50	7.50
(5)	Dodgers (fielder)	25.00	12.50	7.50
(6)	Giants (standing at base)	25.00	12.50	7.50
(7)	Giants (two players)	25.00	12.50	7.50
(8)	Phillies (pitcher)	25.00	12.50	7.50
(9)	Reds (batter)	25.00	12.50	7.50
(10)	Reds (pitcher)	25.00	12.50	7.50
(11)	White Sox (batter)	25.00	12.50	7.50
(12)	White Sox (catcher)	25.00	12.50	7.50
(13)	White Sox (pitcher)	25.00	12.50	7.50
(14)	Yankees (batter)	35.00	17.50	10.50
(15)	Yankees (fielder)	35.00	17.50	10.50

1936-37 Type 5 - Team nickname with emblem

		NM	EX	VG
Common Pennant:		25.00	12.50	7.50
(1)	Athletics (bat)	25.00	12.50	7.50
(2)	Athletics (elephant)	25.00	12.50	7.50
(3)	Bees (bee)	25.00	12.50	7.50
(4)	Browns (bat)	25.00	12.50	7.50
(5)	Cardinals (bat)	25.00	12.50	7.50
(6)	Cardinals (cardinal)	25.00	12.50	7.50
(7)	Cardinals (four birds flying)	25.00	12.50	7.50
(8)	Cubs (cub)	25.00	12.50	7.50
(9)	Cubs (cub's head)	25.00	12.50	7.50
(10)	Dodgers (ball)	25.00	12.50	7.50
(11)	Dodgers (ball, bat and glove)	25.00	12.50	7.50
(12)	Giants (crossed bats and ball)	25.00	12.50	7.50
(13)	Indians (Indians)	25.00	12.50	7.50
(14)	Indians (Indian Head)	25.00	12.50	7.50
(15)	Indians (Indian head with hat)	25.00	12.50	7.50
(16)	Phillies (Liberty Bell)	25.00	12.50	7.50
(17)	Pirates (skull and crossed bones)	25.00	12.50	7.50
(18)	Red Sox (ball)	25.00	12.50	7.50
(19)	Red Sox (bat)	25.00	12.50	7.50
(20)	Red Sox (ball and bat)	25.00	12.50	7.50
(21)	Senators (bat)	25.00	12.50	7.50
(22)	Senators (Capitol Dome)	25.00	12.50	7.50
(23)	Tigers (cap)	25.00	12.50	7.50
(24)	Tigers (tiger)	25.00	12.50	7.50

1936-37 Type 6 - Team nickname only

		NM	EX	VG
Common Pennant:		25.00	12.50	7.50
(1)	Cardinals	25.00	12.50	7.50
(2)	Cubs	25.00	12.50	7.50
(3)	Dodgers	25.00	12.50	7.50
(4)	Giants	25.00	12.50	7.50
(5)	Indians	25.00	12.50	7.50
(6)	Phillies (Phillies on spine)	25.00	12.50	7.50
(7)	Pirates	25.00	12.50	7.50
(8)	Pirates (Pirates on spine)	25.00	12.50	7.50
(9)	Yankees	35.00	17.50	10.50

1936-37 Type 7 - Player and team on two-tailed pennant

		NM	EX	VG
Common Pennant:		35.00	17.50	10.50
(1)	Luke Appling	42.00	21.00	12.50
(2)	Dolph Camilli	35.00	17.50	10.50
(3)	Joe DiMaggio	200.00	100.00	60.00
(4)	Lou Gehrig	200.00	100.00	60.00
(5)	Earl Grace	35.00	17.50	10.50
(6)	Rollie Hemsley	35.00	17.50	10.50
(7)	Carl Hubbell	45.00	22.00	13.50
(8)	Bob Johnson	35.00	17.50	10.50
(9)	Al Lopez	42.00	21.00	12.50
(10)	Joe Medwick	42.00	21.00	12.50
(11)	Frank Pytlak	35.00	17.50	10.50
(12)	Arky Vaughan	42.00	21.00	12.50
(13)	Paul Waner	42.00	21.00	12.50

1936-37 Type 8 - Player name, year and team on ball

		NM	EX	VG
Common Pennant:		35.00	17.50	10.50
(1)	Larry French	35.00	17.50	10.50

1936-37 Type 9 - Player's name, year on ball, team name

		NM	EX	VG
Common Pennant:		35.00	17.50	10.50
(1)	Zeke Bonura	35.00	17.50	10.50
(2)	Frenchy Bordagaray	35.00	17.50	10.50
(3)	Clint Brown	35.00	17.50	10.50
(4)	Clay Bryant	35.00	17.50	10.50
(5)	Guy Bush	35.00	17.50	10.50
(6)	Sugar Cain	35.00	17.50	10.50
(7)	Tex Carleton	35.00	17.50	10.50
(8a)	Phil Cavaretta (Cavarretta)	35.00	17.50	10.50
(8b)	Phil Cavarretta	35.00	17.50	10.50
(9)	Irving Cherry	35.00	17.50	10.50
(10)	Ripper Collins	35.00	17.50	10.50
(11)	Tony Cuccinello	35.00	17.50	10.50
(12)	Curt Davis	35.00	17.50	10.50
(13)	Dizzy Dean	60.00	30.00	18.00
(14)	Paul Dean	40.00	20.00	12.00
(15)	Frank Demaree	35.00	17.50	10.50
(16)	Bill Dietrich	35.00	17.50	10.50
(17)	Vince DiMaggio	40.00	20.00	12.00
(18)	Wes Flowers	35.00	17.50	10.50
(19)	Vic Frasier	35.00	17.50	10.50
(20)	Larry French	35.00	17.50	10.50
(21)	Linus Frey	35.00	17.50	10.50
(22)	Augie Galan	35.00	17.50	10.50
(23)	Charlie Grimm	35.00	17.50	10.50
(24)	Geo. Haas	35.00	17.50	10.50
(25)	Stan Hack	40.00	20.00	12.00
(26)	Gabby Hartnett	42.00	21.00	12.50
(27)	Billy Herman	42.00	21.00	12.50
(28)	Walter Highbee (Kirby Higbe)	35.00	17.50	10.50
(29)	Roy Johnson	35.00	17.50	10.50
(30)	Baxter Jordan	35.00	17.50	10.50
(31)	Billy Jurges	35.00	17.50	10.50
(32)	Vernon Kennedy	35.00	17.50	10.50
(33)	Mike Kreevich	35.00	17.50	10.50
(34)	Bill Lee	35.00	17.50	10.50
(35)	Thorn Lee	35.00	17.50	10.50
(36)	Al Lopez	42.00	21.00	12.50
(37)	Andy Lotshaw	35.00	17.50	10.50
(38)	Ted Lyons	42.00	21.00	12.50
(39)	Dan MacFayden	35.00	17.50	10.50
(40)	Henry Majeski	35.00	17.50	10.50
(41)	Pepper Martin	40.00	20.00	12.00
(42)	Stuart Martin	35.00	17.50	10.50
(43)	Joe Marty	35.00	17.50	10.50
(44)	Bill McKechnie	42.00	21.00	12.50
(45)	Joe Medwick	42.00	21.00	12.50
(46)	Steve Mesner	35.00	17.50	10.50
(47)	Hank Meyer	35.00	17.50	10.50
(48)	Johnny Mize	45.00	22.00	13.50
(49)	Gene Moore	35.00	17.50	10.50
(50)	Terry Moore	40.00	20.00	12.00
(51)	Brusie Ogrodowski	35.00	17.50	10.50
(52)	Tony Piet	35.00	17.50	10.50
(53)	Ray Radcliff	35.00	17.50	10.50
(54)	Bob Reis	35.00	17.50	10.50
(55)	Dunc Rigney	35.00	17.50	10.50
(56)	Les Rock	35.00	17.50	10.50
(57)	Chas. Root	35.00	17.50	10.50
(58)	Larry Rosenthal	35.00	17.50	10.50
(59)	Luke Sewell	35.00	17.50	10.50
(60)	Merv Shea	35.00	17.50	10.50
(61)	Tuck Stainback	35.00	17.50	10.50
(62)	Hank Steinbacher	35.00	17.50	10.50
(63)	Monty Stratton	40.00	20.00	12.00
(64)	Ken Sylvestri	35.00	17.50	10.50
(65)	Billie Urbanski	35.00	17.50	10.50
(66)	Fred Walker	35.00	17.50	10.50
(67)	Lon Warneke	35.00	17.50	10.50
(68)	Johnnie Whitehead	35.00	17.50	10.50

1936-37 Type 10 - Team nickname and year

		NM	EX	VG
Common Pennant:		25.00	12.50	7.50
(1)	Yankees (1936 Champions)	45.00	22.00	13.50

1936-37 Type 11 - Minor league and team

		NM	EX	VG
Common Pennant:		25.00	12.50	7.50
(1)	Bears - International	25.00	12.50	7.50
(2)	Blues - Amer. Assn.	25.00	12.50	7.50
(3)	Brewers - Amer. Assn.	25.00	12.50	7.50
(4)	Chicks - Southern	25.00	12.50	7.50
(5)	Colonels - Amer. Assn.	25.00	12.50	7.50
(6)	Giants - International	25.00	12.50	7.50
(7)	Maple Leafs - International	25.00	12.50	7.50
(8)	Millers - Amer. Assn.	25.00	12.50	7.50
(9)	Mud Hens - Amer. Assn.	25.00	12.50	7.50
(10)	Orioles - International	25.00	12.50	7.50
(11)	Red Birds - Amer. Assn.	25.00	12.50	7.50
(12)	Saints - Amer. Assn.	25.00	12.50	7.50
(13)	Smokies - Southern	25.00	12.50	7.50
(14)	Travelers - Southern	25.00	12.50	7.50

1937 BF104 Blankets

A throwback to the 1914 B18 blankets, little is known about these 3-1/2"-square felts. They were designated as BF104 in the American Card Catalog. The issuer and manner of distribution remain a mystery.

		NM	EX	VG
Common Player:		75.00	37.50	22.00
(1)	Moe Berg	250.00	125.00	75.00
(2)	Cy Blanton	75.00	37.50	22.00
(3)	Joe Cronin	125.00	62.00	37.00
(4)	Tony Cuccinello	75.00	37.50	22.00
(5)	Dizzy Dean	300.00	150.00	90.00
(6)	Jimmie Foxx	175.00	87.00	52.00
(7)	Woody Jensen	75.00	37.50	22.00
(8)	Harry Kelly (Kelley)	75.00	37.50	22.00
(9)	Thornton Lee	75.00	37.50	22.00
(10)	Stu Martin	75.00	37.50	22.00
(11)	Ray Mueller	75.00	37.50	22.00
(12)	L. Newsome	75.00	37.50	22.00
(13)	Monty Stratton	200.00	100.00	60.00
(14)	Jim Turner	75.00	37.50	22.00
(15)	Bill Werber	75.00	37.50	22.00
(16)	Rudy York	75.00	37.50	22.00

C

1966 California Angels Team-Issue Photos

This set of players and coaches photos was issued by the Angels, apparently for sale as a souvenir item. Nominally about 4" x 5", actual size varies considerably. Fronts are printed in black-and-white on glossy paper. Backs are blank. All pictures are chest-to-cap portrait photos. In the border at bottom are the player name, position, batting and throwing orientation and team name. The unnumbered photos are listed here in alphabetical order. A larger (7" x 5-1/2") postcard featuring a color artist's rendering of Anaheim Stadium was apparently sold with the photo set.

		NM	EX	VG
Complete Set (30):		125.00	62.00	37.00
Common Player:		5.00	2.50	1.50
(1)	Joe Adcock	7.50	3.75	2.25
(2)	George Brunet	5.00	2.50	1.50
(3)	Lew Burdette	5.00	2.50	1.50
(4)	Jose Cardenal	5.00	2.50	1.50
(5)	Dean Chance	6.50	3.25	2.00
(6)	Dick Egan	5.00	2.50	1.50
(7)	Jim Fregosi	5.00	2.50	1.50
(8)	Marv Grissom	5.00	2.50	1.50
(9)	Jack Hernandez	5.00	2.50	1.50
(10)	Eddie Kirkpatrick	5.00	2.50	1.50
(11)	Bobby Knoop	5.00	2.50	1.50
(12)	Bob Lee	5.00	2.50	1.50
(13)	Marcelino Lopez	5.00	2.50	1.50
(14)	Frank Malzone	5.00	2.50	1.50
(15)	Jim McGlothlin	5.00	2.50	1.50
(16)	Fred Newman	5.00	2.50	1.50
(17)	Jack Paepke	5.00	2.50	1.50
(18)	Salty Parker	5.00	2.50	1.50
(19)	Jimmy Piersall	7.50	3.75	2.25
(20)	Rick Reichardt	5.00	2.50	1.50
(21)	Del Rice	5.00	2.50	1.50
(22)	Bill Rigney	5.00	2.50	1.50
(23)	Bob Rodgers	5.00	2.50	1.50
(24)	Jack Sanford	5.00	2.50	1.50
(25)	Tom Satriano	5.00	2.50	1.50
(26)	Paul Schaal	5.00	2.50	1.50
(27)	Norm Siebern	5.00	2.50	1.50
(28)	Willie Smith	5.00	2.50	1.50
(29)	Ed Sukla	5.00	2.50	1.50
(30)	Jack Warner	5.00	2.50	1.50
---	Anaheim Stadium postcard	12.00	6.00	3.50

1972 California Angels Photocards

These black-and-white blank-back team-issued photocards are indentical in format to those issued in 1972. Some photos are even repeated. Measuring 3-1/4" x 4-3/4", the cards have a portrait photo surrounded by a white border. In the bottom border is the player name and position abbreviation. The unnumbered cards are checklisted here in alphabetical order.

		NM	EX	VG
Complete Set (30):		60.00	30.00	18.00
Common Player:		1.50	.75	.45
(1)	Lloyd Allen	1.50	.75	.45
(2)	Sandy Alomar	2.00	1.00	.60
(3)	Gene Autry (owner)	2.50	1.25	.70
(4)	Steve Barber	2.00	1.00	.60
(5)	Ken Berry	1.50	.75	.45
(6)	Leo Cardenas	1.50	.75	.45
(7)	Rick Clark	1.50	.75	.45
(8)	Eddie Fisher	1.50	.75	.45
(9)	Art Kusnyer	1.50	.75	.45
(10)	Winston Llenas	1.50	.75	.45
(11)	Peanuts Lowrey	1.50	.75	.45
(12)	Rudy May	1.50	.75	.45
(13)	Ken McMullen	1.50	.75	.45
(14)	Andy Messersmith	1.50	.75	.45
(15)	Tom Morgan	1.50	.75	.45
(16)	Bob Oliver	1.50	.75	.45
(17)	Vada Pinson	3.00	1.50	.90
(18)	Mel Queen	1.50	.75	.45
(19)	Jimmie Reese	2.00	1.00	.60
(20)	Del Rice	1.50	.75	.45
(21)	Mickey Rivers	2.00	1.00	.60
(22)	Don Rose	1.50	.75	.45
(23)	John Roseboro	1.50	.75	.45
(24)	Nolan Ryan	45.00	22.00	13.50
(25)	Jim Spencer	1.50	.75	.45
(26)	Lee Stanton	1.50	.75	.45
(27)	John Stephenson	1.50	.75	.45
(28)	Jeff Torborg	1.50	.75	.45
(29)	Bobby Winkles	1.50	.75	.45
(30)	Clyde Wright	1.50	.75	.45

1973 California Angels Photocards

These black-and-white blank-back photocards are a team issue. Measuring 3-1/4" x 4-3/4", the cards have a portrait photo surrounded by a white border. In the bottom border is the player name and position abbreviation. The unnumbered cards are checklisted here in alphabetical order.

		NM	EX	VG
Complete Set (40):		60.00	30.00	18.00
Common Player:		1.50	.75	.45
(1)	Lloyd Allen	1.50	.75	.45
(2)	Sandy Alomar	2.00	1.00	.60
(3)	Gene Autry (owner)	2.50	1.25	.70
(4)	Steve Barber	2.00	1.00	.60
(5)	Ken Berry	1.50	.75	.45
(6)	Harry Dalton	1.50	.75	.45
(7)	Jerry DaVanon	1.50	.75	.45
(8)	Don Drysdale (broadcaster)	4.50	2.25	1.25
(9)	Dick Enberg (broadcaster)	1.50	.75	.45
(10)	Mike Epstein	1.50	.75	.45
(11)	Alan Gallagher	1.50	.75	.45
(12)	Bill Grabarkewitz	1.50	.75	.45
(13)	Rich Hand	1.50	.75	.45
(14)	Art Kusnyer	1.50	.75	.45
(15)	Dick Lange	1.50	.75	.45
(16)	Winston Llenas	1.50	.75	.45
(17)	Rudy May	1.50	.75	.45
(18)	Tom McCraw	1.50	.75	.45
(19)	Rudy Meoli	1.50	.75	.45
(20)	Aurelio Monteagudo	1.50	.75	.45
(21)	Tom Morgan	1.50	.75	.45
(22)	Bob Oliver	1.50	.75	.45
(23)	Bill Parker	1.50	.75	.45
(24)	Salty Parker	1.50	.75	.45
(25)	Ron Perranoski	1.50	.75	.45
(26)	Vada Pinson	2.00	1.00	.60
(27)	Jimmie Reese	2.00	1.00	.60
(28)	Frank Robinson	6.00	3.00	1.75
(29)	John Roseboro	1.50	.75	.45
(30)	Nolan Ryan	45.00	22.00	13.50
(31)	Richie Scheinblum	1.50	.75	.45
(32)	Dave Sells	1.50	.75	.45
(33)	Bill Singer	1.50	.75	.45
(34)	Jim Spencer	1.50	.75	.45
(35)	Lee Stanton	1.50	.75	.45
(36)	John Stephenson	1.50	.75	.45
(37)	Jeff Torborg	1.50	.75	.45
(38)	Bob Valentine	2.00	1.00	.60
(39)	Bobby Winkles	1.50	.75	.45
(40)	Clyde Wright	1.50	.75	.45

1974 California Angels Photocards

These black-and-white, blank-back photocards are a team issue. Measuring 3-1/4" x 4-3/4", the cards have a portrait photo surrounded by a white border. In the bottom border is the player name and position abbreviation. Some photos were reused from previous years. The unnumbered cards are checklisted here in alphabetical order.

		NM	EX	VG
Complete Set (39):		60.00	30.00	18.00
Common Player:		1.50	.75	.45
(1)	Sandy Alomar	2.00	1.00	.60
(2)	Gene Autry (owner)	2.50	1.25	.70
(3)	Dave Chalk	1.50	.75	.45
(4)	Harry Dalton	1.50	.75	.45
(5)	John Doherty	1.50	.75	.45
(6)	Denny Doyle	1.50	.75	.45
(7)	Don Drysdale (broadcaster)	4.00	2.00	1.25
(8)	Tom Egan	1.50	.75	.45
(9)	Dick Enberg (broadcaster)	1.50	.75	.45
(10)	Eduardo Figueroa	1.50	.75	.45
(11)	Andy Hassler	1.50	.75	.45
(12)	Whitey Herzog	2.00	1.00	.60
(13)	Doug Howard	1.50	.75	.45
(14)	Joe Lahoud	1.50	.75	.45
(15)	Dick Lange	1.50	.75	.45
(16)	Winston Llenas	1.50	.75	.45
(17)	Skip Lockwood	1.50	.75	.45
(18)	Rudy May	1.50	.75	.45
(19)	Tom McCraw	1.50	.75	.45
(20)	Tom Morgan	1.50	.75	.45
(21)	Bob Oliver	1.50	.75	.45
(22)	Salty Parker	1.50	.75	.45
(23)	Jimmie Reese	2.00	1.00	.60
(24)	Mickey Rivers	2.00	1.00	.60
(25)	Frank Robinson	7.50	3.75	2.25
(26)	Ellie Rodriguez	1.50	.75	.45
(27)	John Roseboro	1.50	.75	.45
(28)	Nolan Ryan	45.00	22.00	13.50
(29)	Charlie Sands	1.50	.75	.45
(30)	Paul Schall	1.50	.75	.45
(31)	Dave Sells	1.50	.75	.45
(32)	Dick Selma	1.50	.75	.45
(33)	Bill Singer	1.50	.75	.45
(34)	Lee Stanton	1.50	.75	.45
(35)	Bill Stoneman	1.50	.75	.45
(36)	Frank Tanana	1.50	.75	.45
(37)	Bob Valentine	1.50	.75	.45
(38)	Dick Williams	1.50	.75	.45
(39)	Bobby Winkles	1.50	.75	.45

1975 California Angels Photocards

These black-and-white, blank-back photocards are a team issue. Measuring 3-1/4" x 5-1/2", the cards have a portrait photo surrounded by a white border. In the bottom border is the player name and position abbreviation. The unnumbered cards are checklisted here in alphabetical order.

		NM	EX	VG
Complete Set (44):		80.00	40.00	24.00
Common Player:		1.00	.50	.30
(1)	Jerry Adair	1.00	.50	.30
(2)	Bob Allietta	1.00	.50	.30
(3)	John Balaz	1.00	.50	.30
(4)	Steve Blateric	1.00	.50	.30
(5)	Bruce Bochte	1.00	.50	.30
(6)	Jim Brewer	1.00	.50	.30
(7)	Dave Chalk	1.00	.50	.30
(8)	Dave Collins	1.00	.50	.30
(9)	Chuck Dobson	1.00	.50	.30
(10)	John Doherty	1.00	.50	.30
(11)	Denny Doyle	1.00	.50	.30
(12)	Tom Egan	1.00	.50	.30
(13)	Ed Figueroa	1.00	.50	.30
(14)	Ike Hampton	1.00	.50	.30
(15)	Tommy Harper	1.00	.50	.30
(16)	Andy Hassler	1.00	.50	.30
(17)	Whitey Herzog	1.00	.50	.30
(18)	Chuck Hockenberry	1.00	.50	.30
(19)	Don Kirkwood	1.00	.50	.30
(20)	Joe Lahoud	1.00	.50	.30
(21)	Dick Lange	1.00	.50	.30
(22)	Winston Llenas	1.00	.50	.30
(23)	Rudy Meoli	1.00	.50	.30
(24)	Mike Miley	1.00	.50	.30
(25)	Billy Muffett	1.00	.50	.30
(26)	Morris Nettles	1.00	.50	.30
(27)	Orlando Pena	1.00	.50	.30
(28)	Orlando Ramirez	1.00	.50	.30
(29)	Jimmie Reese	2.50	1.25	.70
(30)	Jerry Remy	1.00	.50	.30
(31)	Grover Resinger	1.00	.50	.30
(32)	Mickey Rivers	1.50	.75	.45
(33)	Ellie Rodriguez	1.00	.50	.30
(34)	Nolan Ryan	40.00	20.00	12.00
(35)	Nolan Ryan (holding no-hit ball)	30.00	15.00	9.00
(36)	Mickey Scott	1.00	.50	.30
(37)	Bill Singer	1.00	.50	.30
(38)	Billy Smith	1.00	.50	.30
(39)	Lee Stanton	1.00	.50	.30
(40)	Bill Sudakis	1.00	.50	.30
(41)	Frank Tanana	1.00	.50	.30
(42)	Bobby Valentine	1.50	.70	.45
(43)	Dick Williams	1.00	.50	.30
(44)	Anaheim Stadium	1.50	.70	.45

1976 California Angels Photocards - b/w

These black-and-white blank-back photocards are a team issue. Measuring 3-1/4" x 5-1/2", the cards have a portrait photo surrounded by a white border. In the bottom border is the player name and position abbreviation. The unnumbered cards are checklisted here in alphabetical order.

		NM	EX	VG
Complete Set (39):		80.00	40.00	24.00
Common Player:		1.00	.50	.30
(1)	Orlando Alvarez	1.00	.50	.30
(2)	Bruce Bochte	1.50	.70	.45
(3)	Bobby Bonds	1.00	.50	.30
(4)	Jim Brewer	1.00	.50	.30
(5)	Dan Briggs	1.00	.50	.30
(6)	Dave Chalk	1.00	.50	.30
(7)	Bob Clear	1.00	.50	.30
(8)	Dave Collins	1.00	.50	.30
(9)	Paul Dade	1.00	.50	.30
(10)	Dick Drago	1.00	.50	.30
(11)	Andy Etchebarren	1.00	.50	.30
(12)	Adrian Garrett	1.00	.50	.30
(13)	Mario Guerrero	1.00	.50	.30
(14)	Ike Hampton	1.00	.50	.30
(15)	Paul Hartzell	1.00	.50	.30
(16)	Ed Herrmann	1.00	.50	.30
(17)	Vern Hoscheit	1.00	.50	.30
(18)	Terry Humphrey	1.00	.50	.30
(19)	Ron Jackson	1.00	.50	.30
(20)	Bob Jones	1.00	.50	.30
(21)	Bill Melton	1.00	.50	.30
(22)	Sid Monge	1.00	.50	.30
(23)	Billy Muffett	1.00	.50	.30
(24)	Mike Overy	1.00	.50	.30

		NM	EX	VG
(25)	Orlando Ramirez	1.00	.50	.30
(26)	Jimmie Reese	1.50	.70	.45
(27)	Jerry Remy (2B)	1.00	.50	.30
(28)	Jerry Remy (INF)	1.00	.50	.30
(29)	Grover Resinger	1.00	.50	.30
(30)	Gary Ross	1.00	.50	.30
(31)	Nolan Ryan (full color shows)	40.00	20.00	12.00
(32)	Nolan Ryan (collar cut off)	40.00	20.00	12.00
(33)	Mickey Scott	1.00	.50	.30
(34)	Norm Sherry	1.00	.50	.30
(35)	Lee Stanton	1.00	.50	.30
(36)	Frank Tanana	1.00	.50	.30
(37)	Rusty Torres	1.00	.50	.30
(38)	John Verhoeven	1.00	.50	.30
(39)	Dick Williams	1.00	.50	.30

1976 California Angels Photocards - color

Issued in conjunction with an album, these 8-1/2" x 8-1/2" square photocards have posed color action photos on front with a facsimile autograph. Backs are in black-and-white with a portrait photo, biographical information and stats. The unnumbered pictures are listed here alphabetically.

		NM	EX	VG
Complete Set (7):		65.00	32.00	19.50
Common Player:		6.00	3.00	1.75
(1)	Bobby Bonds	8.00	4.00	2.50
(2)	Dave Chalk	6.00	3.00	1.75
(3)	Bill Melton	6.00	3.00	1.75
(4)	Jerry Remy	6.00	3.00	1.75
(5)	Nolan Ryan	50.00	25.00	15.00
(6)	Leroy Stanton	6.00	3.00	1.75
(7)	Frank Tanana	6.00	3.00	1.75

1977 California Angels Photocards

These 3-1/4" x 5-1/2" black-and-white photocards feature portrait photos of the players surrounded by a white border. The player name and abbreviation for his position appear in the bottom border. Backs are blank. The unnumbered cards are checklisted here alphabetically.

		NM	EX	VG
Complete Set (49):		55.00	27.50	16.50
Common Player:		1.00	.50	.30
(1)	Willie Aikens	1.50	.70	.45
(2)	Mike Barlow	1.00	.50	.30
(3)	Don Baylor	2.00	1.00	.60
(4)	Bruce Bochte	1.00	.50	.30
(5)	Bobby Bonds	2.00	1.00	.60
(6)	Thad Bosley	1.00	.50	.30
(7)	Ken Brett	1.00	.50	.30
(8)	Dan Briggs	1.00	.50	.30
(9)	John Caneira	1.00	.50	.30
(10)	Dave Chalk	1.00	.50	.30
(11)	Bob Clear	1.00	.50	.30
(12)	Del Crandall	1.00	.50	.30
(13)	Mike Cuellar	1.50	.70	.45
(14)	Dick Drago	1.00	.50	.30
(15)	Dick Enberg (broadcaster)	1.00	.50	.30
(16)	Andy Etchebarren	1.00	.50	.30
(17)	Gil Flores	1.00	.50	.30
(18)	Dave Garcia	1.00	.50	.30
(19)	Dan Goodwin	1.00	.50	.30
(20)	Bobby Grich	2.00	1.00	.60
(21)	Marv Grissom	1.00	.50	.30
(22)	Mario Guerrero	1.00	.50	.30
(23)	Ike Hampton	1.00	.50	.30
(24)	Paul Hartzell	1.00	.50	.30
(25)	Terry Humphrey	1.00	.50	.30
(26)	Ron Jackson	1.00	.50	.30
(27)	Bob Jones	1.00	.50	.30
(28)	Don Kirkwood	1.00	.50	.30
(29)	Fred Kuhaulua	1.00	.50	.30
(30)	Ken Landreaux	1.00	.50	.30
(31)	Dave LaRoche	1.00	.50	.30
(32)	Carlos May	1.00	.50	.30
(33)	Billy Muffett	1.00	.50	.30
(34)	Rance Mulliniks	1.00	.50	.30
(35)	Dyar Miller	1.00	.50	.30
(36)	Gary Nolan	1.00	.50	.30
(37)	Jimmie Reese	1.50	.75	.45
(38)	Jerry Remy	1.00	.50	.30
(39)	Frank Robinson	4.00	2.00	1.25
(40)	Gary Ross	1.00	.50	.30
(41)	Joe Rudi	1.00	.50	.30
(42)	Nolan Ryan	24.00	12.00	7.25
(43)	Mickey Scott	1.00	.50	.30
(44)	Norm Sherry	1.00	.50	.30
(45)	Wayne Simpson	1.00	.50	.30
(46)	Tony Solaita	1.00	.50	.30
(47)	Frank Tanana	1.00	.50	.30
(48)	Rusty Torres	1.00	.50	.30
(49)	John Verhoeven	1.00	.50	.30

1950 Callahan Hall of Fame

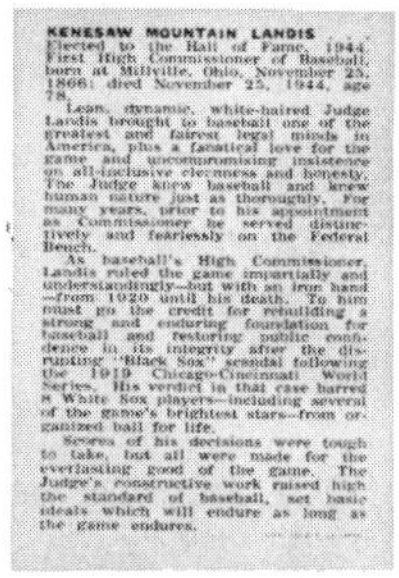
KENESAW MOUNTAIN LANDIS
Elected to the Hall of Fame, 1944. First High Commissioner of Baseball, born at Millville, Ohio, November 20, 1866; died November 25, 1944, age 78.

Lean, dynamic, white-haired Judge Landis brought to baseball one of the greatest and fairest legal minds in America, plus a fanatical love for the game and uncompromising insistence on all-inclusive cleanness and honesty. The Judge knew baseball and knew human nature just as thoroughly. For many years, prior to his appointment as Commissioner he served distinctively and fearlessly on the Federal Bench.

As baseball's High Commissioner, Landis ruled the game impartially and understandingly—but with an iron hand—from 1920 until his death. To him must go the credit for rebuilding a strong and enduring foundation for baseball and restoring public confidence in its integrity after the disrupting "Black Sox" scandal following the 1919 Chicago-Cincinnati World Series. His verdict in that case barred 8 White Sox players—including several of the game's brightest stars—from organized ball for life.

Severe of his decisions were tough to take, but all were made for the everlasting good of the game. The Judge's constructive work raised high the standard of baseball, set basic ideals which will endure as long as the game endures.

These cards, which feature drawings of Hall of Famers, were produced from 1950 through 1956 and sold by the Baseball Hall of Fame in Cooperstown. The cards measure 1-3/4" x 2-1/2" and include a detailed player biography on the back. When introduced in 1950 the set included all members of the Hall of Fame up to that time, and then new cards were added each year as more players were elected. Therefore, cards of players appearing in all previous editions are lesser in value than those players who appeared in just one or two years. When the set was discontinued in 1956 it consisted of 82 cards, which is now considered a complete set. The cards are not numbered and are listed here alphabetically.

		NM	EX	VG
Complete Set (82):		1100.	550.00	325.00
Common Player:		6.00	3.00	1.75
(1)	Grover Alexander	12.50	6.25	3.75
(2)	"Cap" Anson	10.00	5.00	3.00
(3)	J. Franklin "Home Run" Baker	20.00	10.00	6.00
(4)	Edward G. Barrow	15.00	7.50	4.50
(5a)	Charles "Chief" Bender (Bio ends ". . . immortal name for him.")	35.00	17.50	10.50
(5b)	Charles "Chief" Bender (Bio ends ". . . died in 1954.")	40.00	20.00	12.00
(6)	Roger Bresnahan	6.00	3.00	1.75
(7)	Dan Brouthers	6.00	3.00	1.75
(8)	Mordecai Brown	6.00	3.00	1.75
(9)	Morgan G. Bulkeley	6.00	3.00	1.75
(10)	Jesse Burkett	6.00	3.00	1.75
(11)	Alexander Cartwright	8.00	4.00	2.50
(12)	Henry Chadwick	6.00	3.00	1.75
(13)	Frank Chance	6.00	3.00	1.75
(14)	Albert B. Chandler	175.00	87.00	52.00
(15)	Jack Chesbro	6.00	3.00	1.75
(16)	Fred Clarke	6.00	3.00	1.75
(17)	Ty Cobb	80.00	40.00	24.00
(18a)	Mickey Cochran (name incorrect)	37.50	18.50	11.00
(18b)	Mickey Cochrane (name correct)	12.00	6.00	3.50
(19a)	Eddie Collins (Second paragraph of bio begins "Eddie had every . . . ")	10.00	5.00	3.00
(19b)	Eddie Collins (Second paragraph of bio begins "He was brilliant . . . ")	15.00	7.50	4.50
(20)	Jimmie Collins	6.00	3.00	1.75
(21)	Charles A. Comiskey	6.00	3.00	1.75
(22)	Tom Connolly	22.00	11.00	6.50
(23)	Candy Cummings	6.00	3.00	1.75
(24)	Dizzy Dean	60.00	30.00	18.00
(25)	Ed Delahanty	6.00	3.00	1.75
(26a)	Bill Dickey (first paragraph of bio ends ". . . He was right-handed all the way.")	40.00	20.00	12.00
(26b)	Bill Dickey (First paragraph of bio ends ". . . during his final year.")	40.00	20.00	12.00
(27)	Joe DiMaggio	200.00	100.00	60.00
(28)	Hugh Duffy	6.00	3.00	1.75
(29)	Johnny Evers	6.00	3.00	1.75
(30)	Buck Ewing	6.00	3.00	1.75
(31)	Jimmie Foxx	15.00	7.50	4.50
(32)	Frank Frisch	6.00	3.00	1.75
(33)	Lou Gehrig	125.00	62.00	37.00
(34a)	Charles Gehringer (white cap)	6.00	3.00	1.75
(34b)	Charlie Gehringer (dark cap)	12.00	6.00	3.50
(35)	Clark Griffith	6.00	3.00	1.75
(36)	Lefty Grove	11.00	5.50	3.25
(37)	Leo "Gabby" Hartnett	45.00	22.00	13.50
(38)	Harry Heilmann	12.50	6.25	3.75
(39)	Rogers Hornsby	12.00	6.00	3.50
(40)	Carl Hubbell	12.50	6.25	3.75
(41)	Hughey Jennings	6.00	3.00	1.75
(42)	Ban Johnson	6.00	3.00	1.75
(43)	Walter Johnson	15.00	7.50	4.50
(44)	Willie Keeler	10.00	5.00	3.00
(45)	Mike Kelly	20.00	10.00	6.00
(46)	Bill Klem	20.00	10.00	6.00
(47)	Napoleon Lajoie	12.00	6.00	3.50
(48)	Kenesaw M. Landis	6.00	3.00	1.75
(49)	Ted Lyons	40.00	20.00	12.00
(50)	Connie Mack	15.00	7.50	4.50
(51)	Walter Maranville	40.00	20.00	12.00
(52)	Christy Mathewson	15.00	7.50	4.50
(53)	Tommy McCarthy	6.00	3.00	1.75
(54)	Joe McGinnity	6.00	3.00	1.75
(55)	John McGraw	12.00	6.00	3.50
(56)	Charles Nichols	6.00	3.00	1.75
(57)	Jim O'Rourke	6.00	3.00	1.75
(58)	Mel Ott	12.50	6.25	3.75
(59)	Herb Pennock	6.00	3.00	1.75
(60)	Eddie Plank	6.00	3.00	1.75
(61)	Charles Radbourne	6.00	3.00	1.75
(62)	Wilbert Robinson	6.00	3.00	1.75
(63)	Babe Ruth	150.00	75.00	45.00
(64)	Ray "Cracker" Schalk	35.00	17.50	10.50
(65)	Al Simmons	20.00	10.00	6.00
(66a)	George Sisler (Bio ends "Sisler today is . . . ")	6.00	3.00	1.75
(66b)	George Sisler (Bio ends "Sisler was chosen as . . . ")	6.00	3.00	1.75
(67)	A. G. Spalding	6.00	3.00	1.75
(68)	Tris Speaker	12.00	6.00	3.50
(69)	Bill Terry	27.50	13.50	8.25
(70)	Joe Tinker	6.00	3.00	1.75
(71)	"Pie" Traynor	6.00	3.00	1.75
(72)	Clarence A. "Dazzy" Vance	15.00	7.50	4.50
(73)	Rube Waddell	6.00	3.00	1.75
(74)	Hans Wagner	55.00	27.00	16.50
(75)	Bobby Wallace	15.00	7.50	4.50
(76)	Ed Walsh	6.00	3.00	1.75
(77a)	Paul Waner (Complete black frame line around picture.)	10.00	5.00	3.00
(77b)	Paul Waner (Bottom missing on black frame line around picture.)	15.00	7.50	4.50
(78)	George Wright	6.00	3.00	1.75
(79)	Harry Wright	20.00	10.00	6.00
(80)	Cy Young	11.00	5.50	3.25
(---)	Museum Exterior View (No date at top of list on back)	15.00	7.50	4.50
(---)	Museum Exterior View (Date "1954" on top of list on back)	15.00	7.50	4.50
(---)	Museum Interior View (Back copy ends, ". . . to all baseball men.")	15.00	7.50	4.50
(---)	Museum Interior View (Back copy ends ". . . playing days are concluded.")	15.00	7.50	4.50

1898 Cameo Pepsin Gum Pins

The first large set of baseball player pins is this issue from Whitehead & Hoag, advertising Cameo Pepsin Gum. The 1-1/4" pins have a sepia player portrait photo at center, with name and team at top left and right. It is very difficult to find pins with clear pictures as they tend to darken or fade with time. Pins were issued with a paper inset in back advertising the gum, but are often found with the paper missing. It is likely that there will be future additions to this checklist. The unnumbered pins are presented here in alphabetical order.

		NM	EX	VG
Common Player:		600.00	300.00	180.00
(1)	John Anderson	600.00	300.00	180.00
(2)	Cap Anson	1300.	650.00	390.00
(3)	Jimmy Bannon	600.00	300.00	180.00
(4)	Marty Bergen	600.00	300.00	180.00
(5)	Beville (Indianapolis)	600.00	300.00	180.00
(6)	Louis Bierbauer	600.00	300.00	180.00
(7)	Frank Bowerman	600.00	300.00	180.00
(8)	Ted Breitenstein	600.00	300.00	180.00
(9)	Herbert Briggs	600.00	300.00	180.00
(10)	Richard Brown	600.00	300.00	180.00
(10.5)	Eddie Burk (Burke)	600.00	300.00	180.00
(11)	Jesse Burkett	900.00	450.00	270.00
(12)	William Clark (Clarke)	600.00	300.00	180.00
(13)	Jack Clements	600.00	300.00	180.00

		NM	EX	VG
(14)	Tommy Corcoran	600.00	300.00	180.00
(15)	Corkman (Indianapolis)	600.00	300.00	180.00
(16)	Lave Cross	600.00	300.00	180.00
(17)	Bill Dahlen	600.00	300.00	180.00
(18)	Bill Dammann	600.00	300.00	180.00
(19)	Dan Daub	600.00	300.00	180.00
(20)	George Decker	600.00	300.00	180.00
(21)	Cozy Dolan	600.00	300.00	180.00
(22)	Tim Donahue	600.00	300.00	180.00
(23)	Patsy Donovan	600.00	300.00	180.00
(24)	Hugh Duffy	900.00	450.00	270.00
(25)	Jack Dunn	670.00	335.00	200.00
(26)	Bones Ely	600.00	300.00	180.00
(27)	Buck Ewing	900.00	450.00	270.00
(28)	Fields (Buffalo)	600.00	300.00	180.00
(29)	Tim Flood	600.00	300.00	180.00
(30)	Foreman (Indianapolis)	600.00	300.00	180.00
(31)	Charlie Ganzel	600.00	300.00	180.00
(32a)	Jot Goar (Pittsburgh)	600.00	300.00	180.00
(32b)	Jot Goar (Indianapolis)	600.00	300.00	180.00
(33)	Gray (Indianapolis)	600.00	300.00	180.00
(34)	Mike Griffin	600.00	300.00	180.00
(35)	Billy Hamilton	900.00	450.00	270.00
(36)	Bill Hart	600.00	300.00	180.00
(37)	Charles Hastings	600.00	300.00	180.00
(38)	Pink Hawley	600.00	300.00	180.00
(39)	B. Hill (Cedar Rapids)	600.00	300.00	180.00
(40)	Bill Hoffer	600.00	300.00	180.00
(41)	Bug Holliday	600.00	300.00	180.00
(42)	Horton (Baltimore)	600.00	300.00	180.00
(43)	Dummy Hoy	670.00	335.00	200.00
(44)	Jim Hughey	600.00	300.00	180.00
(45)	Charlie Irwin	600.00	300.00	180.00
(46)	Hughie Jennings	900.00	450.00	270.00
(47)	Willie Keeler	900.00	450.00	270.00
(48)	Candy LaChance	600.00	300.00	180.00
(49)	Bill Lange	600.00	300.00	180.00
(50)	Herman Long	600.00	300.00	180.00
(51)	Bobby Lowe	600.00	300.00	180.00
(52)	Denny Lyons	600.00	300.00	180.00
(53)	Willard Mains	600.00	300.00	180.00
(54)	Barry McCormick	600.00	300.00	180.00
(55)	Chippy McGarr	600.00	300.00	180.00
(56)	John McGraw	950.00	475.00	285.00
(57)	Bid McPhee	650.00	325.00	195.00
(58)	Bill Merritt	600.00	300.00	180.00
(59)	Dusty Miller	600.00	300.00	180.00
(60)	Motz (Indianapolis)	600.00	300.00	180.00
(61)	Kid Nichols	900.00	450.00	270.00
(62)	Jack O'Connor	600.00	300.00	180.00
(63)	Heinie Peitz	600.00	300.00	180.00
(64)	Arlie Pond	600.00	300.00	180.00
(65)	Jack Powell	600.00	300.00	180.00
(66)	Bill Reidy	600.00	300.00	180.00
(67)	Heinie Reitz	600.00	300.00	180.00
(68)	Billy Rhines	600.00	300.00	180.00
(69)	Claude Richie (Ritchey)	600.00	300.00	180.00
(70)	Rowe (Buffalo)	600.00	300.00	180.00
(71)	John Ryan	600.00	300.00	180.00
(72)	Pop Schreiver (Schriver)	600.00	300.00	180.00
(73)	Bill Shindle	600.00	300.00	180.00
(74)	Broadway Aleck Smith	600.00	300.00	180.00
(75)	Elmer Smith	600.00	300.00	180.00
(76)	Germany Smith	600.00	300.00	180.00
(77)	Speer (Milwaukee)	600.00	300.00	180.00
(78)	Jake Stenzel	600.00	300.00	180.00
(79)	Joe Sugden	600.00	300.00	180.00
(80)	Jim Sullivan	600.00	300.00	180.00
(81)	Patsy Tebeau	600.00	300.00	180.00
(82)	Fred Tenney	600.00	300.00	180.00
(83)	Farmer Vaughn	600.00	300.00	180.00
(84)	Bobby Wallace	900.00	450.00	270.00
(85)	Watkins (Indianapolis)	600.00	300.00	180.00
(86)	Weaver (Milwaukee)	600.00	300.00	180.00
(87)	Wood (Indianapolis)	600.00	300.00	180.00
(88)	Cy Young	1100.	550.00	330.00
(89)	1897 Brooklyn team	370.00	185.00	110.00
(90)	1897 Buffalo team	370.00	185.00	110.00
(91)	1897 Indianapolis team	370.00	185.00	110.00
(92)	1897 Pittsburgh team	370.00	185.00	110.00
(93)	1897 Toronto team	600.00	300.00	180.00

1958 Roy Campanella Career Summary Card

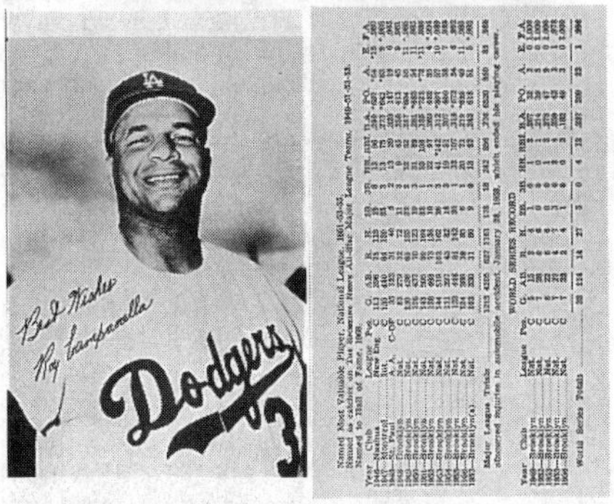

This card was probably produced to allow Campy to respond to fan mail following his career-ending auto wreck in 1957. The 3-1/8" x 5" card is printed in black-and-white on thin semi-gloss cardboard. Front has a portrait photo and facsimile autograph, with a white stripe at top and bottom. The back has a career statistical summary, apparently taken from a contemporary Baseball Register.

	NM	EX	VG
Roy Campanella	15.00	7.50	4.50

1974 Capital Publishing Co.

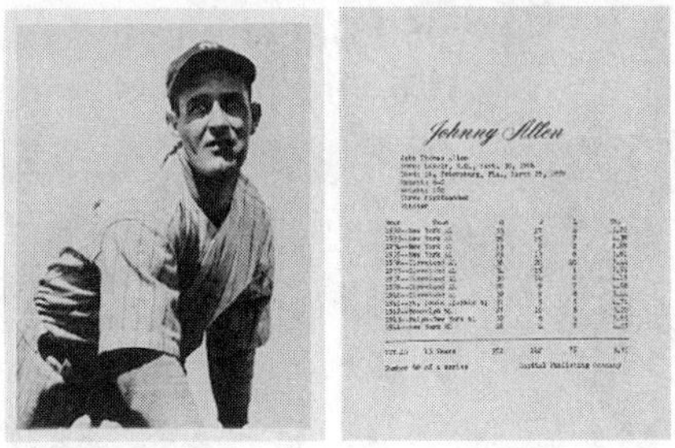

This ambitious collectors issue offered more than 100 cards of "old-timers" in an attractive 4-1/8" x 5-1/4" format. Card fronts have black-and-white photos with white borders all-around. Backs have player identification, biographical data and major league stats.

		NM	EX	VG
Copmplete Set (104):		50.00	25.00	15.00
Common Player:		.50	.25	.15
1	Babe Ruth	5.00	2.50	1.50
2	Lou Gehrig	4.00	2.00	1.25
3	Ty Cobb	3.00	1.50	.90
4	Jackie Robinson	4.00	2.00	1.25
5	Roger Connor	.50	.25	.15
6	Harry Heilmann	.50	.25	.15
7	Clark Griffith	.50	.25	.15
8	Ed Walsh	.50	.25	.15
9	Hugh Duffy	.50	.25	.15
10	Russ Christopher	.50	.25	.15
11	Snuffy Stirnweiss	.50	.25	.15
12	Willie Keeler	.50	.25	.15
13	Buck Ewing	.50	.25	.15
14	Tony Lazzeri	.50	.25	.15
15	King Kelly	.50	.25	.15
16	Jimmy McAleer	.50	.25	.15
17	Frank Chance	.50	.25	.15
18	Sam Zoldak	.50	.25	.15
19	Christy Mathewson	1.00	.50	.30
20	Eddie Collins	.50	.25	.15
21	Cap Anson	.50	.25	.15
22	Steve Evans	.50	.25	.15
23	Mordecai Brown	.50	.25	.15
24	Don Black	.50	.25	.15
25	Home Run Baker	.50	.25	.15
26	Jack Chesbro	.50	.25	.15
27	Gil Hodges	1.50	.70	.45
28	Dan Brouthers	.50	.25	.15
29	Don Hoak	.50	.25	.15
30	Herb Pennock	.50	.25	.15
31	Vern Stephens	.50	.25	.15
32	Cy Young	.75	.40	.25
33	Ed Cicotte	1.00	.50	.30
34	Sam Jones	.50	.25	.15
35	Ed Waitkus	.50	.25	.15
36	Roger Bresnahan	.50	.25	.15
37	Fred Merkle	.50	.25	.15
38	Ed Delehanty (Delahanty)	.50	.25	.15
39	Tris Speaker	.50	.25	.15
40	Fred Clarke	.50	.25	.15
41	Johnny Evers	.50	.25	.15
42	Mickey Cochrane	.50	.25	.15
43	Nap Lajoie	.50	.25	.15
44	Charles Comiskey	.50	.25	.15
45	Sam Crawford	.50	.25	.15
46	Ban Johnson	.50	.25	.15
47	Ray Schalk	.50	.25	.15
48	Pat Moran	.50	.25	.15
49	Walt Judnich	.50	.25	.15
50	Bill Killefer	.50	.25	.15
51	Jimmie Foxx	.50	.25	.15
52	Red Rolfe	.50	.25	.15
53	Howie Pollett	.50	.25	.15
54	Wally Pipp	.50	.25	.15
55	Chief Bender	.50	.25	.15
56	Connie Mack	.50	.25	.15
57	Bump Hadley	.50	.25	.15
58	Al Simmons	.50	.25	.15
59	Hughie Jennings	.50	.25	.15
60	Johnny Allen	.50	.25	.15
61	Fred Snodgrass	.50	.25	.15
62	Heinie Manush	.50	.25	.15
63	Dazzy Vance	.50	.25	.15
64	George Sisler	.50	.25	.15
65	Jim Bottomley	.50	.25	.15
66	Ray Chapman	.50	.25	.15
67	Hal Chase	.50	.25	.15
68	Jack Barry	.50	.25	.15
69	George Burns	.50	.25	.15
70	Jim Barrett	.50	.25	.15
71	Grover Alexander	.50	.25	.15
72	Elmer Flick	.50	.25	.15
73	Jake Flowers	.50	.25	.15
74	Al Orth	.50	.25	.15
75	Cliff Aberson	.50	.25	.15
76	Moe Berg	1.00	.50	.30
77	Bill Bradley	.50	.25	.15
78	Max Bishop	.50	.25	.15
79	Jimmy Austin	.50	.25	.15
80	Beals Becker	.50	.25	.15
81	Jack Clements	.50	.25	.15
82	Cy Blanton	.50	.25	.15
83	Garland Braxton	.50	.25	.15
84	Red Ames	.50	.25	.15
85	Hippo Vaughn	.50	.25	.15
86	Ray Caldwell	.50	.25	.15
87	Clint Brown	.50	.25	.15
88	Joe Jackson	4.00	2.00	1.25
89	Pete Appleton	.50	.25	.15
90	Ed Brandt	.50	.25	.15
91	Walter Johnson	.75	.40	.25
92	Dizzy Dean	.75	.40	.25
93	Nick Altrock	.50	.25	.15
94	Buck Weaver	1.00	.50	.30
95	George Blaeholder	.50	.25	.15
96	Jim Bagby	.50	.25	.15
97	Ted Blankenship	.50	.25	.15
98	Babe Adams	.50	.25	.15
99	Lefty Williams	1.00	.50	.30
100	Tommy Bridges	.50	.25	.15
101	Rube Benton	.50	.25	.15
102	Unknown	.50	.25	.15
103	Max Butcher	.50	.25	.15
104	Chick Gandil	1.00	.50	.30

1945-46 Caramelo Deportivo Cuban League

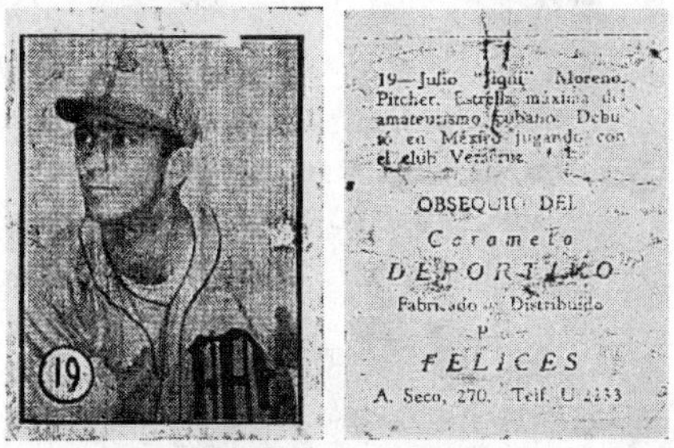

One of the better-known of Cuba's baseball card issues is the 100-card set issued by Caramelo Deportivo (Sporting Caramels) covering the 1945-46 Cuban winter league season. Printed in black-and-white on very thin 1-7/8" x 2-5/8" paper, the cards were intended to be pasted into an album issued for the purpose. Fronts have a card number, but no player identification; backs have the player's name, a few biographical and career details and an ad for the issuer, in as many as three different configurations. Many former and future Major Leaguers and stars of the U.S. Negro Leagues will be found on this checklist; sometimes providing the only cards issued contemporary with their playing careers.

		NM	EX	VG
Complete Set (100):		4275.	2100.	1250.
Common Player:		45.00	22.00	13.50
Album:		400.00	200.00	120.00
1	Caramelo Deportivo title card	15.00	7.50	4.50
2	Action scene	25.00	12.50	7.50
3	Amado Maestri (umpire)	45.00	22.00	13.50
4	Bernardino Rodriguez (umpire)	45.00	22.00	13.50
5	Quico Magrinat (umpire)	45.00	22.00	13.50
6	Cuco Conder (announcer)	45.00	22.00	13.50
7	Marianao team banner	20.00	10.00	6.00
8	Armando Marsans	60.00	30.00	18.00
9	Jose Fernandez	45.00	22.00	13.50
10	Jose Luis Colas	45.00	22.00	13.50
11	"Charlotio" Orta	45.00	22.00	13.50
12	Barney Serrell	55.00	27.00	16.50
13	Claro Duany	45.00	22.00	13.50
14	Antonio Castanos	45.00	22.00	13.50
15	Virgilio Arteaga	45.00	22.00	13.50
16	Gilberto Valdivia	45.00	22.00	13.50
17	Jugo Cabrera	45.00	22.00	13.50
18	Lazaro Salazar	45.00	22.00	13.50
19	Julio Moreno	50.00	25.00	15.00
20	Oliverio Ortiz	45.00	22.00	13.50
21	Lou Knerr	55.00	27.00	16.50
22	Francisco Campos	50.00	25.00	15.00
23	Red Adams	50.00	25.00	15.00
24	Sandalio Consuegra	50.00	25.00	15.00
25	Ray Dandridge	200.00	100.00	60.00
26	Booker McDaniels	75.00	37.00	22.00
27	Orestes Minoso	150.00	75.00	45.00
28	Daniel Parra	45.00	22.00	13.50
29	Roberto Estalella	50.00	25.00	15.00
30	Raymond Brown	60.00	30.00	18.00
31	Havana team banner	20.00	10.00	6.00
32	Miguel Gonzalez	65.00	32.00	19.50
33	Julio Rojo	45.00	22.00	13.50
34	Herberto Blanco	45.00	22.00	13.50
35	Pedro Formenthal	45.00	22.00	13.50
36	Rene Monteagudo	55.00	27.00	16.50
37	Carlos Blanco	45.00	22.00	13.50

38	Salvandor Hernandez	55.00	27.00	16.50
39	Rogelio Linares	45.00	22.00	13.50
40	Antionio Ordenana	55.00	27.00	16.50
41	Pedro Jiminez	45.00	22.00	13.50
42	Charley Kaiser	45.00	22.00	13.50
43	Manuel Garcia	45.00	22.00	13.50
44	Sagua Hernandez	45.00	22.00	13.50
45	Lou Klein	50.00	25.00	15.00
46	Manuel Hidalgo	45.00	22.00	13.50
47	Dick Sisler	55.00	27.00	16.50
48	Jim Rebel	45.00	22.00	13.50
49	Raul Navarro	45.00	22.00	13.50
50	Pedero Medina	45.00	22.00	13.50
51	Charlie McDuffie	65.00	32.00	19.50
52	Fred Martin	50.00	25.00	15.00
53	Julian Acosta	45.00	22.00	13.50
54	Cienfuegos team banner	20.00	10.00	6.00
55	Adolfo Luque	60.00	30.00	18.00
56	Jose Ramos	45.00	22.00	13.50
57	Conrado Perez	45.00	22.00	13.50
58	Antonio Rodriguez	45.00	22.00	13.50
59	Alejandro Crespo	45.00	22.00	13.50
60	Roland Gladu	50.00	25.00	15.00
61	Pedro Pages	45.00	22.00	13.50
62	Silvio Garcia	45.00	22.00	13.50
63	Carlos Colas	45.00	22.00	13.50
64	Salvatore Maglie	60.00	30.00	18.00
65	Martin Dihigo	200.00	100.00	60.00
66	Luis Tiant	50.00	25.00	15.00
67	Jim Roy	45.00	22.00	13.50
68	Ramon Roger	45.00	22.00	13.50
69	Adrian Zabala	55.00	27.00	16.50
70	Armando Gallart	45.00	22.00	13.50
71	Jose Zardon	55.00	27.00	16.50
72	Ray Berres	50.00	25.00	15.00
73	Napoleon Reyes (SP)	300.00	150.00	90.00
74	Jose Gomez	50.00	25.00	15.00
75	Loevigildo Xiques	45.00	22.00	13.50
76	Almendares team banner	20.00	10.00	6.00
77	Reinaldo Coreiro	45.00	22.00	13.50
78	Bartalo Portaundo	45.00	22.00	13.50
79	Jacinto Roque	45.00	22.00	13.50
80	Hector Arago	45.00	22.00	13.50
81	Gilberto Torres	55.00	27.00	16.50
82	Roberto Ortiz	55.00	27.00	16.50
83	Hector Rodriguez	50.00	25.00	15.00
84	Chifian Clark	45.00	22.00	13.50
85	Fermin Guerra	55.00	27.00	16.50
86	Jorge Comellas	55.00	27.00	16.50
87	Regino Otero	50.00	25.00	15.00
88	Tomas de la Cruz	55.00	27.00	16.50
89	Mario Diaz	45.00	22.00	13.50
90	Luis Aloma	50.00	25.00	15.00
91	Lloyd Davenport	55.00	27.00	16.50
92	Agapito Mayor	45.00	22.00	13.50
93	Ramon Bragana	45.00	22.00	13.50
94	Avelino Canizares	45.00	22.00	13.50
95	Santiago Ulrich	55.00	27.00	16.50
96	Beto Avila	95.00	47.00	28.00
97	Santos Amaro	45.00	22.00	13.50
98	Andres Fleitas	45.00	22.00	13.50
99	Limonar Martinez	55.00	27.00	16.50
100	Juan Montero	45.00	22.00	13.50

1946-47 Caramelo Deportivo Cuban League

Following its 100-card issue of the previous Cuban winter league season, this candy company issued a 185-card set for 1946-47. Besides more players, extra cards included banners, stadiums, managers, umpires and sportscasters. Printed on paper stock and intended to be pasted into an accompanying album, the cards measure about 1-7/8" x 2-1/2", though inconsistent cutting creates both over- and under-sized cards. Fronts have black-and-white player photos and a circle with a card number. Photos are often fuzzy or dark, indicative of their having been picked up from another source, such as a newspaper. Backs repeat the card number and have the player name at top, along with his Cuban League and, frequently, U.S. professional affiliation. Some 60 of the players in the set played in the segregated Negro Leagues of the era. A large ad for the candy and its sellers appear at bottom of the back. Because of the thin stock and placement in albums, these cards are usually found creased and/or with back damage.

		NM	EX	VG
Complete Set (185):		7000.	3500.	2100.
Common Player:		50.00	25.00	15.00
Album:		500.00	250.00	150.00
1	Introduction card	25.00	12.50	7.50
2	New El Cerro Stadium	25.00	12.50	7.50
3	Stadium La Tropical	25.00	12.50	7.50
4	Maestri, Bernardino and Magrinat (El Cerro umpires)	50.00	25.00	15.00
5	La Tropical umpires (Atan, Lopez, Vidal and Morales)	50.00	25.00	15.00
6	Cuco Conde (announcer)	25.00	12.50	7.50
7	Cienfuegos team banner	25.00	12.50	7.50
8	Martin Dihigo	200.00	100.00	60.00
9a	Napoleon Reyes	65.00	32.00	19.50
9b	Napoleon Reyes	65.00	32.00	19.50
10	Adrian Zabala	50.00	25.00	15.00
11	Roland Gladu	50.00	25.00	15.00
12	Alejandro Crespo	50.00	25.00	15.00
13	Alejandro Carrasquel	50.00	25.00	15.00
14	Napoleon Heredia	50.00	25.00	15.00
15	Andres Mesa	50.00	25.00	15.00
16	Pedro Pages	50.00	25.00	15.00
17	Danny Gardella	50.00	25.00	15.00
18	Conrado Perez	50.00	25.00	15.00
19	Myron Hayworth	50.00	25.00	15.00
20	Pedro Miro	50.00	25.00	15.00
21	Guillermo Vargas	50.00	25.00	15.00
22	Hoot Gibson	50.00	25.00	15.00
23	Rafael Noble	55.00	27.00	16.50
24	Ramon Roger	50.00	25.00	15.00
25	Luis Arango	50.00	25.00	15.00
26	Roy Zimmerman	50.00	25.00	15.00
27	Luis Tiant	80.00	40.00	24.00
28	Jean Roy	55.00	27.00	16.50
29	Stanislov Bread	50.00	25.00	15.00
30	Walter Nothe	50.00	25.00	15.00
31	Vinicio Garcia	50.00	25.00	15.00
32	Dan Manning	65.00	32.00	19.50
33	Habana Lions team banner	25.00	12.50	7.50
34	Miguel A. Gonzalez	75.00	37.00	22.00
35	Pedro Formental	50.00	25.00	15.00
36	Ray Navarro	50.00	25.00	15.00
37	Pedro Jiminez	50.00	25.00	15.00
38	Rene Montoagudo	50.00	25.00	15.00
39	Salvador Hernandez	50.00	25.00	15.00
40	Hugh Mc. Duffie	65.00	32.00	19.50
41	Herberto Blanco	50.00	25.00	15.00
42	Harry Kimbro	65.00	32.00	19.50
43	Lloyd Pearson	75.00	37.00	22.00
44	W. Bell	55.00	27.00	16.50
45	Carlos Blanco	50.00	25.00	15.00
46	Hank Thompson	70.00	35.00	21.00
47	Manuel Garcia	50.00	25.00	15.00
48	Alberto Hernandez	50.00	25.00	15.00
49	Tony Ordenana	50.00	25.00	15.00
50	Lazaro Medina	50.00	25.00	15.00
51	Fred Martin	50.00	25.00	15.00
52	Eddie Lamarque	50.00	25.00	15.00
53	Juan Montero	50.00	25.00	15.00
54	Lou Klein	50.00	25.00	15.00
55	Pablo Garcia	50.00	25.00	15.00
56	Julio Rojo	50.00	25.00	15.00
57	Almendares team banner	25.00	12.50	7.50
58	Adolfo Luque	75.00	37.00	22.00
59	Cheo Ramos	50.00	25.00	15.00
60	Avelino Canizares	50.00	25.00	15.00
61	George Hausmann	50.00	25.00	15.00
62	Homero Ariosa	50.00	25.00	15.00
63	Santos Amaro	50.00	25.00	15.00
64	Hank Robinson	60.00	30.00	18.00
65	Lazaro Salazar	50.00	25.00	15.00
66	Andres Fleitas	50.00	25.00	15.00
67	Hector Rodriguez	50.00	25.00	15.00
68	Jorge Comellas	50.00	25.00	15.00
69	Lloyd Davenport	55.00	27.00	16.50
70	Tomas de la Cruz	50.00	25.00	15.00
71a	Roberto Ortiz	50.00	25.00	15.00
71b	Roberto Ortiz	50.00	25.00	15.00
72	Jess Jessup	65.00	32.00	19.50
73	Agapito Mayor	50.00	25.00	15.00
74	William	50.00	25.00	15.00
75	Santiago Ullrich	50.00	25.00	15.00
76	Coty Leal	50.00	25.00	15.00
77	Max Lanier	55.00	27.00	16.50
78	Buck O'Neill	225.00	112.00	67.00
79	Mario Ariosa	50.00	25.00	15.00
80	Lefty Gaines	65.00	32.00	19.50
81	Marianao team banner	25.00	12.50	7.50
82	Armando Marsans	65.00	32.00	19.50
83	Antonio Castanos	50.00	25.00	15.00
84	Orestes Minoso	125.00	62.00	37.00
85	Murray Franklin	50.00	25.00	15.00
86	Roberto Estalella	50.00	25.00	15.00
87	A. Castro	50.00	25.00	15.00
88	Gilberto Valdivia	50.00	25.00	15.00
89	Baffeth	50.00	25.00	15.00
90	Oliverio Ortiz	50.00	25.00	15.00
91	Francisco Campos	50.00	25.00	15.00
92	Sandalio Consuegra	55.00	27.00	16.50
93	Lorenzo Cabrera	50.00	25.00	15.00
94	Roberto Avila	75.00	37.00	22.00
95	Chanquilon Diaz	50.00	25.00	15.00
96	Pedro Orta	50.00	25.00	15.00
97	Cochihuila Valenzuela	50.00	25.00	15.00
98	Ramon Carneado	50.00	25.00	15.00
99	Aristonico Correoso	50.00	25.00	15.00
100	Daniel Doy	50.00	25.00	15.00
101	Joe Lindsay	50.00	25.00	15.00
102	Habana Reds team banner	25.00	12.50	7.50
103	Gilberto Torres	50.00	25.00	15.00
104	Oscar Rodriguez	50.00	25.00	15.00
105	Isidoro Leon	50.00	25.00	15.00
106	Julio Moreno	50.00	25.00	15.00
107	Chulungo del Monte	50.00	25.00	15.00
108	Len Hooker	65.00	32.00	19.50
109	Antonio Napoles	50.00	25.00	15.00
110	Orlando Suarez	50.00	25.00	15.00
111	Guillermo Monje	50.00	25.00	15.00
112	Isasio Gonzalez	50.00	25.00	15.00
113	Regino Otero	50.00	25.00	15.00
114	Angel Fleitas	50.00	25.00	15.00
115	Jorge Torres	50.00	25.00	15.00
116	Claro Duany	50.00	25.00	15.00
117	Charles Perez	50.00	25.00	15.00
118	Francisco Quicutis	50.00	25.00	15.00
119	Lazaro Bernal	50.00	25.00	15.00
120	Tommy Warren	50.00	25.00	15.00
121	Clarence Iott	55.00	27.00	16.50
122	P. Newcomb (Don Newcombe)	150.00	75.00	45.00
123	Gilberto Castillo	50.00	25.00	15.00
124	Matanzas team banner	25.00	12.50	7.50
125	Silvio Garcia	50.00	25.00	15.00
126	Bartolo Portuondo	50.00	25.00	15.00
127	Pedro Arango	50.00	25.00	15.00
128	Yuyo Acosta	50.00	25.00	15.00
129	Jose Cendan	50.00	25.00	15.00
130	Eddie Chandler	50.00	25.00	15.00
131	Rogelio Martinez	50.00	25.00	15.00
132	Atares Garcia	50.00	25.00	15.00
133	Manuel Godinez	50.00	25.00	15.00
134	John Williams	55.00	27.00	16.50
135	Emilio Cabrera	50.00	25.00	15.00
136	Barney Serrell	55.00	27.00	16.50
137	Armando Gallart	50.00	25.00	15.00
138	Ruben Garcia	50.00	25.00	15.00
139	Loevigildo Xiques	50.00	25.00	15.00
140	Chifian Clark	50.00	25.00	15.00
141	Jacinto Roque	50.00	25.00	15.00
142	John Davis	65.00	32.00	19.50
143	Norman Wilson	50.00	25.00	15.00
144	Camaguey team banner	25.00	12.50	7.50
145	Antonio Rodriguez	50.00	25.00	15.00
146	Manuel Parrado	50.00	25.00	15.00
147	Leon Treadway	50.00	25.00	15.00
148	Amado Ibanez	50.00	25.00	15.00
149	Teodoro Oxamendi	50.00	25.00	15.00
150	Adolfo Cabrera	50.00	25.00	15.00
151	Oscar Garmendia	50.00	25.00	15.00
152	Hector Arago	50.00	25.00	15.00
153	Evelio Martinez	50.00	25.00	15.00
154	Raquel Antunez	50.00	25.00	15.00
155	Lino Donoso	50.00	25.00	15.00
156	Eliecer Alvarez	50.00	25.00	15.00
157	George Brown	50.00	25.00	15.00
158	Roberto Johnson	50.00	25.00	15.00
159	Rafael Franco	50.00	25.00	15.00
160	Miguel A. Carmona	50.00	25.00	15.00
161	Lilo Fano	50.00	25.00	15.00
162	Orestes Pereda	50.00	25.00	15.00
163	Pedro Diaz	50.00	25.00	15.00
164	Oriente team banner	25.00	12.50	7.50
165	Fermin Guerra	50.00	25.00	15.00
166	Jose M. Fernandez	50.00	25.00	15.00
167	Cando Lopez	50.00	25.00	15.00
168	Conrado Marrero	55.00	27.00	16.50
169	Oscar del Calvo	50.00	25.00	15.00
170	Booker McDaniels	55.00	27.00	16.50
171	Rafael Rivas	50.00	25.00	15.00
172	Daniel Parra	50.00	25.00	15.00
173	L. Holleman	50.00	25.00	15.00
174	Rogelio Valdes	50.00	25.00	15.00
175	Raymond Dandridge	200.00	100.00	60.00
176	Manuel Hidalgo	50.00	25.00	15.00
177	Miguel Lastra	50.00	25.00	15.00
178	Luis Minsal	50.00	25.00	15.00
179	Andres Vazquez	50.00	25.00	15.00
180	Jose A. Zardon	50.00	25.00	15.00
181	Jose Luis Colas	50.00	25.00	15.00
182	Rogelio Linares	50.00	25.00	15.00
183	Mario Diaz	50.00	25.00	15.00
184	R. Verdes	50.00	25.00	15.00
185	Indio Jiminez	50.00	25.00	15.00

1955 Carling Beer Cleveland Indians

Apparently the first of a line of premium photos which extended into the early 1960s. Measuring 8-1/2" x 12" and printed in black-and-white on semi-gloss thin card stock, these photocards are blank-backed. The 1955 Carling photos are identifiable from the 1956 issue, with which they share a "DBL" prefix to the card number in the lower-right corner, by the phrase "Great Champions" appearing just under the player photo.

		NM	EX	VG
Complete Set (11):		250.00	125.00	75.00
Common Player:		20.00	10.00	6.00
96A	Ralph Kiner	35.00	17.50	10.50
96Ba	Larry Doby	35.00	17.50	10.50
96Bb	Herb Score	25.00	12.50	7.50
96C	Al Rosen	25.00	12.50	7.50
96D	Mike Garcia	20.00	10.00	6.00
96E	Early Wynn	30.00	15.00	9.00
96F	Bob Feller	50.00	25.00	15.00
96G	Jim Hegan	20.00	10.00	6.00
96H	George Strickland	20.00	10.00	6.00
96K	Bob Lemon	30.00	15.00	9.00
96L	Art Houtteman	20.00	10.00	6.00

1956 Carling Beer Cleveland Indians

This set was sponsored by Carling Black Label Beer. The oversized (8-1/2" x 12") cards feature black-and-white posed photos with the player's name in a white strip and a Carling ad at the bottom of the card front. Backs are blank. Like the cards issued in 1955, the 1956 set carries a DBL 96 series indication in the lower-right corner and lists brewery locations as Cleveland, St. Louis and Belleville, Ill. Unlike the '55 photocards, however, the first line under the player photo on the 1956 issue is "Premium Quality". Cards numbered DBL 96I and DBL 96J are unknown.

		NM	EX	VG
Complete Set (10):		225.00	110.00	67.00
Common Player:		15.00	7.50	4.50
96A	Al Smith	15.00	7.50	4.50
96B	Herb Score	30.00	15.00	9.00
96C	Al Rosen	21.00	10.50	6.25
96D	Mike Garcia	15.00	7.50	4.50
96E	Early Wynn	30.00	15.00	9.00
96F	Bob Feller	60.00	30.00	18.00
96G	Jim Hegan	15.00	7.50	4.50
96H	George Strickland	15.00	7.50	4.50
96K	Bob Lemon	30.00	15.00	9.00
96L	Art Houtteman	15.00	7.50	4.50

1957 Carling Beer Cleveland Indians

The fact that Kerby Farrell managed the Indians only in 1957 pinpoints the year of issue for those Carling Beer photocards which carry a DBL 179 series number in the lower-right corner. Following the black-and-white, blank-backed 8-1/2" x 12" format of earlier issues, the 1957 Carlings list on the bottom line breweries at Cleveland; Frankenmuth, Mich.; Natick, Mass., and, Belleville, Ill. Cards numbered DBL 179I and DBL 179J are currently unknown.

		NM	EX	VG
Complete Set (10):		225.00	110.00	67.00
Common Player:		15.00	7.50	4.50
179A	Vic Wertz	15.00	7.50	4.50
179B	Early Wynn	27.00	13.50	8.00
179C	Herb Score	22.00	11.00	6.50
179D	Bob Lemon	27.00	13.50	8.00
179E	Ray Narleski	15.00	7.50	4.50
179F	Jim Hegan	15.00	7.50	4.50
179G	Bob Avila	22.00	11.00	6.50
179H	Al Smith	15.00	7.50	4.50
179K	Kerby Farrell	15.00	7.50	4.50
179L	Rocky Colavito	75.00	37.00	22.00

1958 Carling Beer Cleveland Indians

Identical in format to earlier issues, the 1958 premium photos can be distinguished by the card number printed in the lower-right corner. Cards in the 1958 series have numbers which begin with a DBL 2 or DBL 217 prefix.

		NM	EX	VG
Complete Set (10):		180.00	90.00	54.00
Common Player:		15.00	7.50	4.50
2	Vic Wertz	15.00	7.50	4.50
217	Minnie Minoso	27.00	13.50	8.00
217B	Gene Woodling	22.00	11.00	6.50
217C	Russ Nixon	15.00	7.50	4.50
217D	Bob Lemon	30.00	15.00	9.00
217E	Bobby Bragan	15.00	7.50	4.50
217F	Cal McLish	15.00	7.50	4.50
217G	Rocky Colavito	36.00	18.00	11.00
217H	Herb Score	27.00	13.50	8.00
217J	Chico Carrasquel	15.00	7.50	4.50

1959 Carling Beer Cleveland Indians

The appearance of Billy Martin among Carling photocards labeled with a DBL 266 prefix fixes the year of issue to 1959, the fiery second baseman's only year with the Tribe. Once again the 8-1/2" x 12" black-and-white, blank-backed cards follow the format of previous issues. Breweries listed on the bottom of the 1959 Carlings are Cleveland; Atlanta; Frankenmuth, Mich.; Natick, Mass.; Belleville, Ill., and Tacoma, Wash.

		NM	EX	VG
Complete Set (6):		150.00	75.00	45.00
Common Player:		15.00	7.50	4.50
266A	Vic Power	18.00	9.00	5.50
266B	Minnie Minoso	27.00	13.50	8.00
266C	Herb Score	27.00	13.50	8.00
266D	Rocky Colavito	36.00	18.00	11.00
266E	Jimmy Piersall	27.00	13.50	8.00
266F	Billy Martin	45.00	22.00	13.50

1961 Carling Beer Cleveland Indians

Totally different player selection and the use of an LB prefix to the number in the lower-right corner define the 1961 issue from Carling Beer. Otherwise the photocards share the same 8-1/2" x 12" black-and-white format with earlier issues. The blank-backed cards of the 1961 issue list only a single brewery, Cleveland, at the bottom of the ad portion of the issues. The checklist here is arranged alphabetically. Cards numbered LB 420I and LB420J are unknown.

		NM	EX	VG
Complete Set (10):		145.00	72.00	43.00
Common Player:		15.00	7.50	4.50
420A	Jimmy Piersall	24.00	12.00	7.25
420B	Willie Kirkland	15.00	7.50	4.50
420C	Johnny Antonelli	15.00	7.50	4.50
420D	John Romano	15.00	7.50	4.50
420E	Woodie Held	15.00	7.50	4.50
420F	Tito Francona	15.00	7.50	4.50
420G	Jim Perry	22.00	11.00	6.50
420H	Bubba Phillips	15.00	7.50	4.50
420K	John Temple	15.00	7.50	4.50
420L	Vic Power	15.00	7.50	4.50

1909-11 Carolina Brights

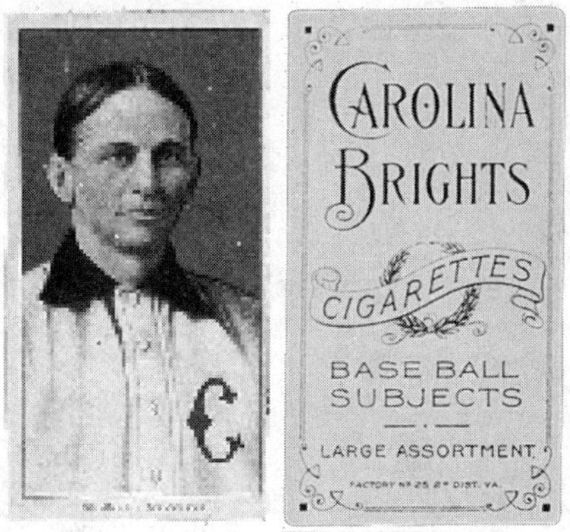

(See T206 for checklist. Premium for cards carrying Carolina Brights ad on back is 3X-4X.)

1976 Carousel Discs

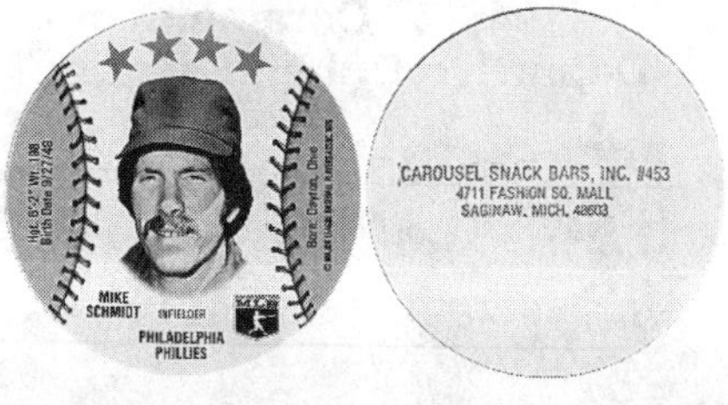

One of several regional sponsors of player disc sets in 1976 was the Michigan snack bar chain, Carousel. The sponsor's discs are unique in that they do not have pre-printed backs, but rather have a black rubber-stamp on the otherwise blank back. To date more than 20 such stamps have been seen, reportedly from New Jersey to Alaska. The discs are 3-3/8" diameter with a black-and-white player portrait photo in the center of the baseball design. A line of red stars is above, while the left and right panels feature one of several bright colors. Produced by Michael Schecter Associates under license from the Major League Baseball Players Association, the player photos have had uniform and cap logos removed. The unnumbered checklist here is presented in alphabetical order.

		NM	EX	VG
Complete Set (70):		175.00	87.00	52.00
Common Player:		2.00	1.00	.60
(1)	Henry Aaron	25.00	12.50	7.50
(2)	Johnny Bench	12.00	6.00	3.50
(3)	Vida Blue	2.00	1.00	.60
(4)	Larry Bowa	2.00	1.00	.60
(5)	Lou Brock	9.00	4.50	2.75
(6)	Jeff Burroughs	2.00	1.00	.60
(7)	John Candelaria	2.00	1.00	.60
(8)	Jose Cardenal	2.00	1.00	.60
(9)	Rod Carew	9.00	4.50	2.75
(10)	Steve Carlton	9.00	4.50	2.75

(11)	Dave Cash	2.00	1.00	.60
(12)	Cesar Cedeno	2.00	1.00	.60
(13)	Ron Cey	2.00	1.00	.60
(14)	Carlton Fisk	9.00	4.50	2.75
(15)	Tito Fuentes	2.00	1.00	.60
(16)	Steve Garvey	7.50	3.75	2.25
(17)	Ken Griffey	2.50	1.25	.70
(18)	Don Gullett	2.00	1.00	.60
(19)	Willie Horton	2.00	1.00	.60
(20)	Al Hrabosky	2.00	1.00	.60
(21)	Catfish Hunter	9.00	4.50	2.75
(22)	Reggie Jackson	15.00	7.50	4.50
(23)	Randy Jones	2.00	1.00	.60
(24)	Jim Kaat	2.00	1.00	.60
(25)	Don Kessinger	2.00	1.00	.60
(26)	Dave Kingman	3.00	1.50	.90
(27)	Jerry Koosman	2.00	1.00	.60
(28)	Mickey Lolich	3.00	1.50	.90
(29)	Greg Luzinski	2.00	1.00	.60
(30)	Fred Lynn	2.50	1.25	.70
(31)	Bill Madlock	2.00	1.00	.60
(32)	Carlos May	2.00	1.00	.60
(33)	John Mayberry	2.00	1.00	.60
(34)	Bake McBride	2.00	1.00	.60
(35)	Doc Medich	2.00	1.00	.60
(36)	Andy Messersmith	2.00	1.00	.60
(37)	Rick Monday	2.00	1.00	.60
(38)	John Montefusco	2.00	1.00	.60
(39)	Jerry Morales	2.00	1.00	.60
(40)	Joe Morgan	9.00	4.50	2.75
(41)	Thurman Munson	10.00	5.00	3.00
(42)	Bobby Murcer	2.00	1.00	.60
(43)	Al Oliver	2.00	1.00	.60
(44)	Jim Palmer	9.00	4.50	2.75
(45)	Dave Parker	2.00	1.00	.60
(46)	Tony Perez	9.00	4.50	2.75
(47)	Jerry Reuss	2.00	1.00	.60
(48)	Brooks Robinson	10.00	5.00	3.00
(49)	Frank Robinson	10.00	5.00	3.00
(50)	Steve Rogers	2.00	1.00	.60
(51)	Pete Rose	22.00	11.00	6.50
(52)	Nolan Ryan	48.00	24.00	14.50
(53)	Manny Sanguillen	2.00	1.00	.60
(54)	Mike Schmidt	15.00	7.50	4.50
(55)	Tom Seaver	10.00	5.00	3.00
(56)	Ted Simmons	2.00	1.00	.60
(57)	Reggie Smith	2.00	1.00	.60
(58)	Willie Stargell	9.00	4.50	2.75
(59)	Rusty Staub	2.50	1.25	.70
(60)	Rennie Stennett	2.00	1.00	.60
(61)	Don Sutton	9.00	4.50	2.75
(62)	Andy Thornton	2.00	1.00	.60
(63)	Luis Tiant	2.00	1.00	.60
(64)	Joe Torre	3.00	1.50	.90
(65)	Mike Tyson	2.00	1.00	.60
(66)	Bob Watson	2.00	1.00	.60
(67)	Wilbur Wood	2.00	1.00	.60
(68)	Jimmy Wynn	2.00	1.00	.60
(69)	Carl Yastrzemski	12.00	6.00	3.50
(70)	Richie Zisk	2.00	1.00	.60

1939 Centennial of Baseball Stamps

Part of the pagentry surrounding the 1939 centennial of the fabled beginnings of baseball was this set of player and history stamps and an accompanying 36-page album. The single stamps measure about 1-5/8" x 2-1/8" and are blank-backed. Stamps #1-13 deal with the game's history; most feature artwork by famed baseball artist and former major league pitcher Al Demaree. Stamps #14-25 feature photos of the game's greats in tombstone frames surrounded by colorful borders.

		NM	EX	VG
Complete Set, w/Album (25):		1225.	610.00	365.00
Common Player:		52.00	26.00	15.50
Common Historical:		24.00	12.00	7.25
Album:		87.00	43.00	26.00
1	Abner Doubleday	31.00	15.50	9.25
2	1849 Knickerbockers	31.00	15.50	9.25
3	Ball/bat Standards	24.00	12.00	7.25
4	1858 Brooklyn vs. New York Series	31.00	15.50	9.25
5	1859 Amherst vs. Williams Series	24.00	12.00	7.25
6	Curve Ball (Arthur Cummings)	31.00	15.50	9.25
7	First Admission Fee	24.00	12.00	7.25
8	First Professional Players	31.00	15.50	9.25
9	First No-Hitter (George Bradley)	31.00	15.50	9.25
10	Morgan G. Bulkeley	31.00	15.50	9.25
11	First World's Champions	24.00	12.00	7.25
12	Byron Bancroft (Ban) Johnson	31.00	15.50	9.25
13	First Night Game	24.00	12.00	7.25
14	Grover Cleveland Alexander	52.00	26.00	15.50
15	Tyrus Raymond Cobb	155.00	77.00	46.00
16	Eddie Collins	52.00	26.00	15.50
17	Wee Willie Keeler	52.00	26.00	15.50
18	Walter Perry Johnson	87.00	43.00	26.00
19	Napoleon (Larry) Lajoie	52.00	26.00	15.50
20	Christy Mathewson	70.00	35.00	21.00
21	George Herman (Babe) Ruth	280.00	140.00	84.00
22	George Sisler	52.00	26.00	15.50
23	Tristam E. (Tris) Speaker	52.00	26.00	15.50
24	Honus Wagner	70.00	35.00	21.00
25	Denton T. (Cy) Young	70.00	35.00	21.00

1930 Certified's Ice Cream Pins

Unless or until further players are seen in this series, the date of issue will have to remain uncertain. Apparently given away by Wrigley Field's ice cream concessionaire, these 1" diameter pin-backs feature player portraits and typography in sepia tones lithographed on a white background.

		NM	EX	VG
Complete Set (4):		900.00	450.00	275.00
Common Player:		150.00	75.00	45.00
(1)	Joe Bush	150.00	75.00	45.00
(2)	Kiki Cuyler	200.00	100.00	60.00
(3)	Rogers Hornsby	250.00	125.00	75.00
(4)	Riggs Stephenson	150.00	75.00	45.00
(5)	Hack Wilson	150.00	75.00	45.00

1964 Challenge the Yankees Game

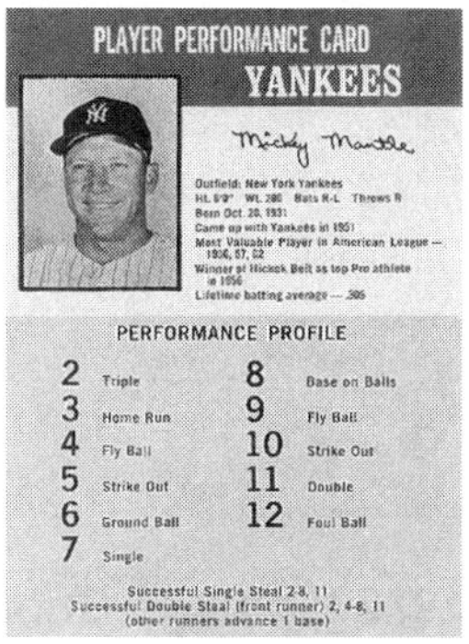

The 50 player cards in this set were part of a boxed dice baseball game produced by Hassenfeld Bros. of Pawtucket, R.I. Cards are approximately 4" x 5-1/2" and blank-backed, featuring a small black-and-white photo, a facsimile autograph and a few biographical details and stats. Player selection is virtually the same for the games issued in 1964 and 1965, and the only way to distinguish cards from each year is to study the stats. Cards are unnumbered and are checklisted below in alphabetical order.

		NM	EX	VG
Complete Boxed Set:		990.00	495.00	295.00
Complete Card Set (50):		650.00	320.00	195.00
Common Player:		3.50	1.75	1.00
(1)	Hank Aaron	80.00	40.00	24.00
(2)	Yogi Berra	50.00	25.00	15.00
(3)	Johnny Blanchard	7.00	3.50	2.00
(4)	Jim Bouton	12.00	6.00	3.50
(5)	Clete Boyer	11.00	5.50	3.25
(6)	Marshall Bridges	3.50	1.75	1.00
(7)	Harry Bright	3.50	1.75	1.00
(8)	Tom Cheney	3.50	1.75	1.00
(9)	Del Crandall	3.50	1.75	1.00
(10)	Al Downing	3.50	1.75	1.00
(11)	Whitey Ford	25.00	12.50	7.50
(12)	Tito Francona	3.50	1.75	1.00
(13)	Jake Gibbs	3.50	1.75	1.00
(14)	Pedro Gonzalez	3.50	1.75	1.00
(15)	Dick Groat	6.00	3.00	1.75
(16)	Steve Hamilton	3.50	1.75	1.00
(17)	Elston Howard	9.00	4.50	2.75
(18)	Al Kaline	35.00	17.50	10.50
(19)	Tony Kubek	12.00	6.00	3.50
(20)	Phil Linz	3.50	1.75	1.00
(21)	Hector Lopez	3.50	1.75	1.00
(22)	Art Mahaffey	3.50	1.75	1.00
(23)	Frank Malzone	3.50	1.75	1.00
(24)	Mickey Mantle	175.00	87.00	52.00
(25)	Juan Marichal	22.00	11.00	6.50
(26)	Roger Maris	70.00	35.00	21.00
(27)	Eddie Mathews	25.00	12.50	7.50
(28)	Bill Mazeroski	16.00	8.00	4.75
(29)	Ken McBride	3.50	1.75	1.00
(30)	Willie McCovey	22.00	11.00	6.50
(31)	Tom Metcalf	3.50	1.75	1.00
(32)	Jim O'Toole	3.50	1.75	1.00
(33)	Milt Pappas	3.50	1.75	1.00
(34)	Joe Pepitone	7.50	3.75	2.25
(35)	Ron Perranoski	3.50	1.75	1.00
(36)	Johnny Podres	9.00	4.50	2.75
(37)	Dick Radatz	3.50	1.75	1.00
(38)	Hal Reniff	3.50	1.75	1.00
(39)	Bobby Richardson	15.00	7.50	4.50
(40)	Rich Rollins	3.50	1.75	1.00
(41)	Ron Santo	7.50	3.75	2.25
(42)	Moose Skowron	12.00	6.00	3.50
(43)	Duke Snider	26.00	13.00	7.75
(44)	Bill Stafford	3.50	1.75	1.00
(45)	Ralph Terry	3.50	1.75	1.00
(46)	Tom Tresh	6.00	3.00	1.75
(47)	Pete Ward	3.50	1.75	1.00
(48)	Carl Warwick	3.50	1.75	1.00
(49)	Stan Williams	3.50	1.75	1.00
(50)	Carl Yastrzemski	60.00	30.00	18.00

1965 Challenge the Yankees Game

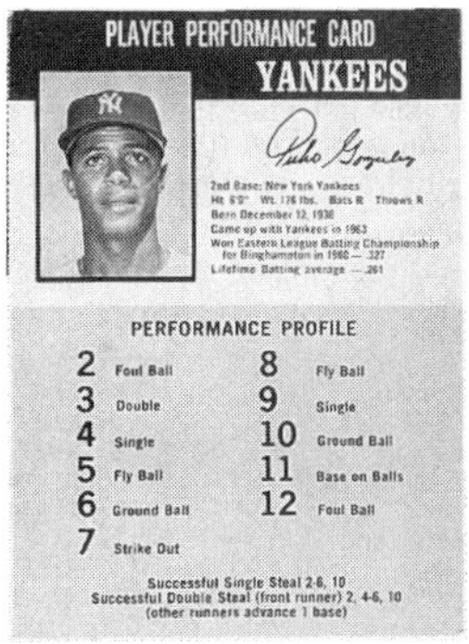

The player cards in this set were part of a boxed dice baseball game produced by Hassenfeld Bros. of Pawtucket, R.I. Cards are approximately 4" x 5-1/2" and blank-backed, featuring a small black-and-white photo, a facsimile autograph and a few biographical details and stats. Player selection is virtually the same for the games issued in 1964 and 1965, and the only way to distinguish cards from each year is to study the stats. Cards are unnumbered and are checklisted below in alphabetical order. The card of Yankee pitcher Rollie Sheldon was apparently withdrawn following his May 3 trade to Kansas City and is scarcer than the rest of the set.

		NM	EX	VG
Complete Boxed Set:		725.00	360.00	215.00
Complete Card Set (49):		450.00	225.00	135.00
Common Player:		3.50	1.75	1.00
(1)	Henry Aaron	55.00	27.00	16.50
(2)	Johnny Blanchard	3.50	1.75	1.00
(3)	Jim Bouton	6.00	3.00	1.75
(4)	Clete Boyer	3.50	1.75	1.00
(5)	Leon Carmel	3.50	1.75	1.00
(6)	Joe Christopher	3.50	1.75	1.00
(7)	Vic Davalillo	3.50	1.75	1.00
(8)	Al Downing	3.50	1.75	1.00
(9)	Whitey Ford	18.00	9.00	5.50
(10)	Bill Freehan	3.50	1.75	1.00
(11)	Jim Gentile	3.50	1.75	1.00
(12)	Jake Gibbs	3.50	1.75	1.00
(13)	Pedro Gonzalez	3.50	1.75	1.00
(14)	Dick Groat	4.00	2.00	1.25
(15)	Steve Hamilton	3.50	1.75	1.00
(16)	Elston Howard	7.00	3.50	2.00
(17)	Al Kaline	18.00	9.00	5.50
(18)	Tony Kubek	7.00	3.50	2.00
(19)	Phil Linz	3.50	1.75	1.00
(20)	Don Lock	3.50	1.75	1.00

(21)	Art Mahaffey	3.50	1.75	1.00
(22)	Frank Malzone	3.50	1.75	1.00
(23)	Mickey Mantle	120.00	60.00	36.00
(24)	Juan Marichal	18.00	9.00	5.50
(25)	Roger Maris	36.00	18.00	11.00
(26)	Eddie Mathews	18.00	9.00	5.50
(27)	Bill Mazeroski	9.00	4.50	2.75
(28)	Ken McBride	3.50	1.75	1.00
(29)	Tim McCarver	6.00	3.00	1.75
(30)	Willie McCovey	18.00	9.00	5.50
(31)	Tom Metcalf	3.50	1.75	1.00
(32)	Pete Mikkelsen	3.50	1.75	1.00
(33)	Jim O'Toole	3.50	1.75	1.00
(34)	Milt Pappas	3.50	1.75	1.00
(35)	Joe Pepitone	3.50	1.75	1.00
(36)	Ron Perranoski	3.50	1.75	1.00
(37)	Johnny Podres	6.00	3.00	1.75
(38)	Dick Radatz	3.50	1.75	1.00
(39)	Pedro Ramos	3.50	1.75	1.00
(40)	Hal Reniff	3.50	1.75	1.00
(41)	Bobby Richardson	8.00	4.00	2.50
(42)	Rich Rollins	3.50	1.75	1.00
(43)	Ron Santo	7.00	3.50	2.00
(44)	Rollie Sheldon (SP)	35.00	17.50	10.50
(45)	Bill Stafford	3.50	1.75	1.00
(46)	Mel Stottlemyre	3.50	1.75	1.00
(47)	Tom Tresh	3.50	1.75	1.00
(48)	Pete Ward	3.50	1.75	1.00
(49)	Carl Yaztrzemski	25.00	12.50	7.50

1961 Chemstrand Iron-On Patches

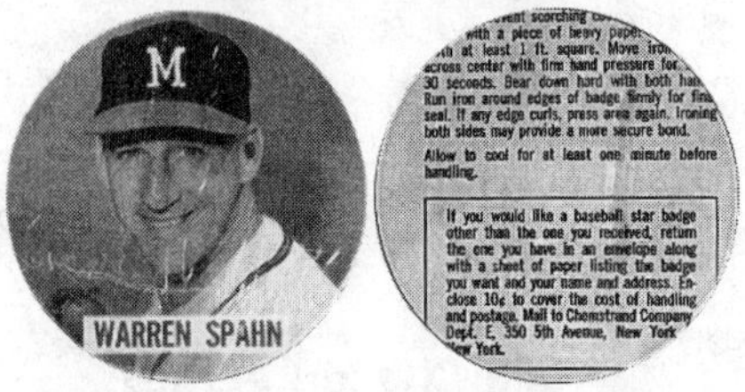

These colorful 2-1/2" diameter cloth patches were included with the purchase of a boy's sport shirt for a short period in 1961. The patches were issued in a cello package with instructions for ironing it onto the shirt. The package also offered the opportunity to trade the player patch for a different star.

		NM	EX	VG
Complete Set (9):		480.00	240.00	145.00
Common Player:		17.00	8.50	5.00
(1)	Ernie Banks	85.00	42.00	25.00
(2)	Yogi Berra	85.00	42.00	25.00
(3)	Nellie Fox	75.00	37.00	22.00
(4)	Dick Groat	28.00	14.00	8.50
(5)	Al Kaline	85.00	42.00	25.00
(6)	Harmon Killebrew	85.00	42.00	25.00
(7)	Frank Malzone	17.00	8.50	5.00
(8)	Willie Mays	140.00	70.00	42.00
(9)	Warren Spahn	85.00	42.00	25.00

1908 Chicago Cubs Postcards

The issuer of this postcard set is unknown. The only identification on the card is a dollar sign within a shield which apears near the center on back, along with standard postcard indicia. Fronts of the 3-7/16" x 5-3/8" cards have black-and-white player photos on a gray background. A plain strip at bottom has the player's name on a top line; his position and "CUBS" on a second line. The checklist presented here is probably not complete.

		NM	EX	VG
Common Player:		150.00	75.00	45.00
(1)	Mordecai Brown	350.00	175.00	100.00
(2)	Frank Chance	350.00	175.00	100.00
(3)	Johnny Evers	350.00	175.00	100.00
(4)	Solly Hoffman (Hofman)	150.00	75.00	45.00
(5)	Johnny Kling	150.00	75.00	45.00
(6)	Jake Pfeister (Pfiester)	150.00	75.00	45.00
(7)	Harry Steinfeldt	150.00	75.00	45.00
(8)	Joe Tinker	350.00	175.00	100.00

1931 Chicago Cubs Picture Pack

In the second-year of team-issued photo packs during the 1930s-1940s was this set of 1931 Cubs. The 6-1/8" x 9-1/2" sepia-toned pictures have facsimile autographs across the front and a white border around. Backs are blank. Like all the team's other photo packs, it is possible the specific make-up of the 30 pictures in each set changed as personnel came and went during the season. A number of non-playing team personnel are also in the set.

		NM	EX	VG
Complete Set (35):		450.00	225.00	135.00
Common Player:		15.00	7.50	4.50
(1)	Ed Baecht	12.50	6.25	3.75
(2)	Clyde Beck	12.50	6.25	3.75
(3)	Les Bell	12.50	6.25	3.75
(4)	Clarence Blair	12.50	6.25	3.75
(5)	John F. Blake	12.50	6.25	3.75
(6)	Guy Bush	15.00	7.50	4.50
(7)	Kiki Cuyler	35.00	17.50	10.50
(8)	Woody English	15.00	7.50	4.50
(9)	Earl Grace	12.50	6.25	3.75
(10)	Charlie Grimm	20.00	10.00	6.00
(11)	Gabby Hartnett	35.00	17.50	10.50
(12)	Rollie Hemsley	12.50	6.25	3.75
(13)	Rogers Hornsby	75.00	37.00	22.00
(14)	Bill Jurges	15.00	7.50	4.50
(15)	Pat Malone	12.50	6.25	3.75
(16)	Jakie May	12.50	6.25	3.75
(17)	John Moore	12.50	6.25	3.75
(18)	Charley O'Leary	12.50	6.25	3.75
(19)	Charlie Root	17.50	8.75	5.25
(20)	Ray Schalk	35.00	17.50	10.50
(21)	Bob Smith	12.50	6.25	3.75
(22)	Riggs Stephenson	20.00	10.00	6.00
(23)	Les Sweetland	12.50	6.25	3.75
(24)	Dan Taylor	12.50	6.25	3.75
(25)	Zack Taylor	12.50	6.25	3.75
(26)	Bud Teachout	12.50	6.25	3.75
(27)	Lon Warneke	12.50	6.25	3.75
(28)	Hack Wilson	50.00	25.00	15.00
	Non-Playing Personnel			
(29)	Margaret Donahue	12.50	6.25	3.75
(30)	Bob Lewis (traveling secretary)	12.50	6.25	3.75
(31)	Andy Lotshaw (trainer)	12.50	6.25	3.75
(32)	John Seys	12.50	6.25	3.75
(33)	William Veeck (President)	50.00	25.00	15.00
(34)	W.M. Walker (vp)	12.50	6.25	3.75
(35)	P.K. Wrigley	15.00	7.50	4.50
(36)	William Wrigley (owner)	17.50	8.75	5.25

1932 Chicago Cubs Picture Pack

This is one of many Cubs team issues of player pictures in the 1930s-1940s. The large format (6-1/8" x 9-1/4"), the set features action poses of the players in black-and-white on a black background. A bit of the ground at the players' feet is also included in the photo portion. A white facsimile autograph in the black background identifies the player. Backs are blank. The unnumbered pictures are checklisted here in alphabetical order. Some pictures of non-playing personnel were also issued.

		NM	EX	VG
Complete Set (35):		400.00	200.00	120.00
Common Player:		15.00	7.50	4.50
(1)	Guy Bush	15.00	7.50	4.50
(2)	Gilly Campbell	15.00	7.50	4.50
(3)	Red Corriden	15.00	7.50	4.50
(4)	Kiki Cuyler	30.00	15.00	9.00
(5)	Frank Demaree	15.00	7.50	4.50
(6)	Woody English	15.00	7.50	4.50
(7)	Burleigh Grimes	30.00	15.00	9.00
(8)	Charlie Grimm	20.00	10.00	6.00
(9)	Marv Gudat	15.00	7.50	4.50
(10)	Stan Hack	20.00	10.00	6.00
(11)	Gabby Hartnett	30.00	15.00	9.00
(12)	Rollie Hemsley	15.00	7.50	4.50
(13)	Billy Herman	30.00	15.00	9.00
(14)	LeRoy Herrmann	15.00	7.50	4.50
(15)	Billy Jurges	15.00	7.50	4.50
(16)	Mark Koenig	15.00	7.50	4.50
(17)	Pat Malone	15.00	7.50	4.50
(18)	Jake May	15.00	7.50	4.50
(19)	Johnny Moore	15.00	7.50	4.50
(20)	Charley O'Leary	15.00	7.50	4.50
(21)	Lance Richbourg	15.00	7.50	4.50
(22)	Charlie Root	20.00	10.00	6.00
(23)	Bob Smith	15.00	7.50	4.50
(24)	Riggs Stephenson	20.00	10.00	6.00
(25)	Harry Taylor	15.00	7.50	4.50
(26)	Zack Taylor	15.00	7.50	4.50
(27)	Bud Tinning	15.00	7.50	4.50
(28)	Lon Warneke	15.00	7.50	4.50
	Non-playing Personnel			
(29)	Marge Donahue	15.00	7.50	4.50
(30)	Bob Lewis (traveling secretary)	15.00	7.50	4.50
(31)	John Seys	15.00	7.50	4.50
(32)	Bill Veeck (president)	30.00	15.00	9.00
(33)	W.M. Walker	15.00	7.50	4.50
(34)	Phil Wrigley	15.00	7.50	4.50
(35)	William Wrigley	15.00	7.50	4.50

1936 Chicago Cubs Picture Pack

The use of a slightly narrower 6" x 9" format and the absence of white facsimile autographs helps differentiate this issue from the 1932 set. Both are printed on black paper. Backs are blank. The specific make-up of photo packs sold at Wrigley Field may have changed over the course of the season as players came and went. The unnumbered pictures are checklisted here in alphabetical order.

		NM	EX	VG
Complete Set (32):		240.00	120.00	72.00
Common Player:		9.00	4.50	2.75
(1)	Clay Bryant	9.00	4.50	2.75
(2)	Tex Carleton	9.00	4.50	2.75
(3)	Phil Cavarretta	12.00	6.00	3.50
(4)	John Corriden	9.00	4.50	2.75
(5)	Frank Demaree	9.00	4.50	2.75
(6)	Woody English	9.00	4.50	2.75
(7)	Larry French	9.00	4.50	2.75
(8)	Augie Galan	9.00	4.50	2.75
(9)	Johnny Gill	9.00	4.50	2.75
(10)	Charlie Grimm	12.00	6.00	3.50
(11)	Stan Hack	12.00	6.00	3.50
(12)	Gabby Hartnett	18.00	9.00	5.50
(13)	Roy Henshaw	9.00	4.50	2.75
(14)	Billy Herman	18.00	9.00	5.50
(15)	Roy Johnson	9.00	4.50	2.75
(16)	Bill Jurges	9.00	4.50	2.75
(17)	Chuck Klein	18.00	9.00	5.50
(18)	Fabian Kowalik	9.00	4.50	2.75
(19)	Bill Lee	9.00	4.50	2.75
(20)	Gene Lillard	9.00	4.50	2.75
(21)	Ken O'Dea	9.00	4.50	2.75
(22)	Charlie Root	12.00	6.00	3.50
(23)	Clyde Shoun	9.00	4.50	2.75
(24)	Walter Stephenson	9.00	4.50	2.75
(25)	Tuck Stainback	9.00	4.50	2.75
(26)	Lon Warneke	9.00	4.50	2.75
	Non-playing personnel			
(27)	Margaret Donahue	9.00	4.50	2.75
(28)	Bob Lewis (traveling secretary)	9.00	4.50	2.75
(29)	Andy Lotshaw (trainer)	9.00	4.50	2.75
(30)	John O. Seys	9.00	4.50	2.75
(31)	Charles Weber	9.00	4.50	2.75
(32)	Wrigley Field	18.00	9.00	5.50

1939 Chicago Cubs Picture Pack

The use of a textured paper stock for these 6-1/2" x 9" pictures helps identify the 1939 team issue.

The pictures once again feature sepia portrait photos with a white border. A facsimile autograph is at bottom. Backs are blank. The specific make-up of photo packs sold at Wrigley Field may have changed over the course of the season as players came and went. The unnumbered pictures are checklisted here in alphabetical order.

		NM	EX	VG
Complete Set (25):		225.00	115.00	65.00
Common Player:		9.00	4.50	2.75
(1)	Dick Bartell	9.00	4.50	2.75
(2)	Clay Bryant	9.00	4.50	2.75
(3)	Phil Cavarretta	12.00	6.00	3.50
(4)	John Corriden	9.00	4.50	2.75
(5)	Dizzy Dean	40.00	20.00	12.00
(6)	Larry French	9.00	4.50	2.75
(7)	Augie Galan	9.00	4.50	2.75
(8)	Bob Garbark	9.00	4.50	2.75
(9)	Jim Gleeson	9.00	4.50	2.75
(10)	Stan Hack	12.00	6.00	3.50
(11)	Gabby Hartnett	20.00	10.00	6.00
(12)	Billy Herman	20.00	10.00	6.00
(13)	Roy Johnson	9.00	4.50	2.75
(14)	Bill Lee	9.00	4.50	2.75
(15)	Hank Leiber	9.00	4.50	2.75
(16)	Gene Lillard	9.00	4.50	2.75
(17)	Gus Mancuso	9.00	4.50	2.75
(18)	Bobby Mattick	9.00	4.50	2.75
(19)	Vance Page	9.00	4.50	2.75
(20)	Claude Passeau	9.00	4.50	2.75
(21)	Carl Reynolds	9.00	4.50	2.75
(22)	Charlie Root	12.00	6.00	3.50
(23)	Glenn "Rip" Russell	9.00	4.50	2.75
(24)	Jack Russell	9.00	4.50	2.75
(25)	Earl Whitehill	9.00	4.50	2.75

1940 Chicago Cubs Picture Pack

The 1940 team-issue is identical in format to the 1939s: 6-1/2" x 9", printed on rough-surfaced paper stock with black-and-white portraits surrounded by a wide border and a facsimile autograph on front. Study of the uniforms, however, may help differentiate the issue from 1939, as the 1940 uniforms have no stripe on the shoulders. It is possible that 1939 pictures continued to be issued in the 1940 photo packs and that specific make-up of the packs changed with the team's roster. The blank-back pictures are unnumbered and checklisted here in alphabetical order.

		NM	EX	VG
Complete Set (9):		80.00	40.00	24.00
Common Player:		9.00	4.50	2.75
(1)	Dick Bartell	9.00	4.50	2.75
(2)	Clay Bryant	9.00	4.50	2.75
(3)	Phil Cavarretta	12.00	6.00	3.50
(4)	John Corriden	9.00	4.50	2.75
(5)	Larry French	9.00	4.50	2.75
(6)	Stan Hack	12.00	6.00	3.50
(7)	Gabby Hartnett	20.00	10.00	6.00
(8)	Roy Johnson	9.00	4.50	2.75
(9)	Bill Lee	9.00	4.50	2.75

1941 Chicago Cubs Picture Pack

A change of paper stock to a smooth finish helps differentiate the 1941 team-issue from previous years' offerings. Size remains at 6-1/2" x 9" with sepia player portraits surrounded by a white border and overprinted with a facsimile autograph. Backs are blank on these unnumbered photos. The pictures are listed here in alphabetical order.

		NM	EX	VG
Complete Set (25):		190.00	95.00	57.00
Common Player:		9.00	4.50	2.75
(1)	Phil Cavarretta	12.00	6.00	3.50
(2)	Dom Dallessandro	9.00	4.50	2.75
(3)	Paul Erickson	9.00	4.50	2.75
(4)	Larry French	9.00	4.50	2.75
(5)	Augie Galan	9.00	4.50	2.75
(6)	Greek George	9.00	4.50	2.75
(7)	Charlie Gilbert	9.00	4.50	2.75
(8)	Stan Hack	12.00	6.00	3.50
(9)	Johnny Hudson	9.00	4.50	2.75
(10)	Bill Lee	9.00	4.50	2.75
(11)	Hank Leiber	9.00	4.50	2.75
(12)	Clyde McCullough	9.00	4.50	2.75
(13)	Jake Mooty	9.00	4.50	2.75
(14)	Bill Myers	9.00	4.50	2.75
(15)	Bill Nicholson	9.00	4.50	2.75
(16)	Lou Novikoff	9.00	4.50	2.75
(17)	Vern Olsen	9.00	4.50	2.75
(18)	Vance Page	9.00	4.50	2.75
(19)	Claude Passeau	9.00	4.50	2.75
(20)	Tot Pressnell	9.00	4.50	2.75
(21)	Charlie Root	12.00	6.00	3.50
(22)	Bob Scheffing	9.00	4.50	2.75
(23)	Lou Stringer	9.00	4.50	2.75
(24)	Bob Sturgeon	9.00	4.50	2.75
(25)	Cubs Staff (Dizzy Dean, Charlie Grimm, Dick Spalding, Jimmie Wilson)	12.00	6.00	3.50

1942 Chicago Cubs Picture Pack

The relatively small number of photos in this team-issued set indicates it may have been issued as a supplement to update earlier photo packs with players who were new to the Cubs. In the same 6-1/2" x 9" format as previous issues, the 1942s are printed in sepia on a smooth-surfaced paper. A facsimile autograph graces the front and the portrait photo is surrounded by a border. Backs are blank and the pictures are not numbered. The checklist here is in alphabetical order.

		NM	EX	VG
Complete Set (22):		150.00	75.00	45.00
Common Player:		9.00	4.50	2.75
(1)	Hiram Bithorn	9.00	4.50	2.75
(2)	Phil Cavarretta	12.00	6.00	3.50
(3)	Dom Dallasandro	9.00	4.50	2.75
(4)	Paul Erickson	9.00	4.50	2.75
(5)	Bill Fleming	9.00	4.50	2.75
(6)	Charlie Gilbert	9.00	4.50	2.75
(7)	Stan Hack	15.00	7.50	4.50
(8)	Ed Hanyzewski	9.00	4.50	2.75
(9)	Chico Hernandez	9.00	4.50	2.75
(10)	Bill Lee	9.00	4.50	2.75
(11)	Harry Lowrey	9.00	4.50	2.75
(12)	Clyde McCullough	9.00	4.50	2.75
(13)	Lennie Merullo	9.00	4.50	2.75
(14)	Jake Mooty	9.00	4.50	2.75
(15)	Bill Nicholson	9.00	4.50	2.75
(16)	Lou Novikoff	9.00	4.50	2.75
(15)	Vern Olsen	9.00	4.50	2.75
(16)	Claude Passeau	9.00	4.50	2.75
(17)	Tot Pressnell	9.00	4.50	2.75
(18)	Glen "Rip" Russell	9.00	4.50	2.75
(19)	Bob Scheffing	9.00	4.50	2.75
(20)	Lou Stringer	9.00	4.50	2.75
(21)	Bob Sturgeon	9.00	4.50	2.75
(22)	Kiki Cuyler, Dick Spalding, Jimmie Wilson			

1943 Chicago Cubs Picture Pack

Lack of piping flanking the zipper on the uniforms helps differentiate these pictures from other early-1940s Cubs issues. Otherwise the format is identical: 6-1/2" x 9", black-and-white portrait photos with facsimile autograph and white borders. Backs are blank and the photos are not numbered. They are checklisted here alphabetically.

		NM	EX	VG
Complete Set (25):		215.00	105.00	65.00
Common Player:		9.00	4.50	2.75
(1)	Dick Barrett	9.00	4.50	2.75
(2)	Heinz Becker	9.00	4.50	2.75
(3)	Hiram Bithorn	9.00	4.50	2.75
(4)	Phil Cavarretta	12.00	6.00	3.50
(5)	Dom Dallasandro	9.00	4.50	2.75
(6)	Paul Derringer	9.00	4.50	2.75
(7)	Paul Erickson	9.00	4.50	2.75
(8)	Bill Fleming	9.00	4.50	2.75
(9)	Stan Hack	12.00	6.00	3.50
(10)	Ed Hanyzewski	9.00	4.50	2.75
(11)	Chico Hernandez	9.00	4.50	2.75
(12)	Bill Lee	9.00	4.50	2.75
(13)	Peanuts Lowrey	9.00	4.50	2.75
(14)	Stu Martin	9.00	4.50	2.75
(15)	Clyde McCullough	9.00	4.50	2.75
(16)	Len Merullo	9.00	4.50	2.75
(17)	Bill Nicholson	9.00	4.50	2.75
(18)	Lou Novikoff	9.00	4.50	2.75
(19)	Claude Passeau	9.00	4.50	2.75
(20)	Ray Prim	9.00	4.50	2.75
(21)	Eddie Stanky	12.00	6.00	3.50
(22)	Al Todd	9.00	4.50	2.75
(23)	Lon Warneke	9.00	4.50	2.75
(24)	Hank Wyse	9.00	4.50	2.75
(25)	Cubs Coaches (Kiki Cuyler, Dick Spalding, Jimmie Wilson)	9.00	4.50	2.75

1944 Chicago Cubs Picture Pack

A slight size reduction, to 6" x 8-1/2", helps identify the team's 1944 photo pack. The pictures feature black-and-white portrait photos with a white border. A facsimile autograph is at bottom. Backs are blank. The specific make-up of photo packs sold at Wrigley Field may have changed over the course of the season as players came and went. The unnumbered pictures are checklisted here in alphabetical order.

		NM	EX	VG
Complete Set (25):		215.00	105.00	64.00
Common Player:		9.00	4.50	2.75
(1)	Heinz Becker	9.00	4.50	2.75
(2)	John Burrows	9.00	4.50	2.75
(3)	Phil Cavarretta	12.00	6.00	3.50
(4)	Dom Dallassandro	9.00	4.50	2.75
(5)	Paul Derringer	9.00	4.50	2.75
(6)	Roy Easterwood	9.00	4.50	2.75
(7)	Paul Erickson	9.00	4.50	2.75
(8)	Bill Fleming	9.00	4.50	2.75
(9)	Jimmie Foxx	30.00	15.00	9.00
(10)	Ival Goodman	9.00	4.50	2.75
(11)	Ed Hanyzewski	9.00	4.50	2.75
(12)	Billy Holm	9.00	4.50	2.75
(13)	Don Johnson	9.00	4.50	2.75
(14)	Garth Mann	9.00	4.50	2.75
(15)	Len Merullo	9.00	4.50	2.75
(16)	John Miklos	9.00	4.50	2.75
(17)	Bill Nicholson	9.00	4.50	2.75
(18)	Lou Novikoff	9.00	4.50	2.75
(19)	Andy Pafko	12.00	6.00	3.50
(20)	Ed Sauer	9.00	4.50	2.75
(21)	Bill Schuster	9.00	4.50	2.75
(22)	Eddie Stanky	12.00	6.00	3.50
(23)	Hy Vandenberg	9.00	4.50	2.75
(24)	Hank Wyse	9.00	4.50	2.75
(25)	Tony York	9.00	4.50	2.75

1969 Chicago Cubs Picture Pack

This set of black-and-white player pictures was sold at souvenir stands in Wrigley Field. The pictures measure about 4-1/4" x 7" and feature portrait photo with a white border and facsimile autograph across the chest. Backs are blank. The pictures are unnumbered and arranged here in alphabetical order.

		NM	EX	VG
Complete Set (12):		24.00	12.00	7.25
Common Player:		1.50	.75	.45
(1)	Ted Abernathy	1.50	.75	.45
(2)	Ernie Banks	8.00	4.00	2.50
(3)	Glenn Beckert	2.50	1.25	.70
(4)	Leo Durocher	3.00	1.50	.90
(5)	Ken Holtzman	1.50	.75	.45
(6)	Randy Hundley	1.50	.70	.45
(7)	Ferguson Jenkins	3.00	1.50	.90
(8)	Don Kessinger	2.00	1.00	.60
(9)	Phil Regan	1.50	.75	.45
(10)	Ron Santo	3.00	1.50	.90
(11)	Al Spangler	1.50	.75	.45
(12)	Billy Williams	4.00	2.00	1.25

1972 Chicago Cubs Picture Pack

This set of black-and-white player pictures was sold in a white picture envelope at souvenir stands in Wrigley Field. The pictures measure about 4-1/4" x 7" and feature portrait photo with a white border and facsimile autograph across the chest. Backs are blank. The pictures are unnumbered and arranged here in alphabetical order.

		NM	EX	VG
Complete Set (12):		18.00	9.00	5.50
Common Player:		1.00	.50	.30
(1)	Ernie Banks	6.00	3.00	1.75
(2)	Glenn Beckert	2.00	1.00	.60
(3)	Billy Hands	1.00	.50	.30
(4)	Jim Hickman	1.00	.50	.30
(5)	Randy Hundley	1.00	.50	.30
(6)	Ferguson Jenkins	3.00	1.50	.90
(7)	Don Kessinger	2.00	1.00	.60
(8)	Rick Monday	1.00	.50	.30
(9)	Milt Pappas	1.00	.50	.30
(10)	Joe Pepitone	1.00	.50	.30
(11)	Ron Santo	2.00	1.00	.60
(12)	Billy Williams	3.00	1.50	.90

1922 Chicago Evening American Cubs/White Sox Pins

These 1-3/8" diameter pins were issued by the Chicago Evening American newspaper to promote its peach-colored sports section. Rather crude black-and-white line drawings of the players are at center, within an orange peach with the player's last name at bottom. Borders are either white or dark blue.

		NM	EX	VG
Complete Set (8):		750.00	375.00	225.00
Common Player:		75.00	37.00	22.00
(1)	Grover Alexander	200.00	100.00	60.00
(2)	Eddie Collins	200.00	100.00	60.00
(3)	Charlie Hollocher	75.00	37.00	22.00
(4)	Bill Killefer	75.00	37.00	22.00
(5)	Bob O'Farrell	75.00	37.00	22.00
(6)	Charlie Robertson	75.00	37.00	22.00
(7)	Ray Schalk	125.00	62.00	37.00
(8)	Jigger Statz	75.00	37.00	22.00

1930 Chicago Evening American Pins

Members of the Cubs and White Sox are featured on this series of pins issued by one of the local daily newspapers. Player portraits are featured in black-and-white on a white background on these 1-1/4" celluloid pins. Above the picture are the player's position, last name and team; below is the sponsor's name. The unnumbered pins are listed here in alphabetical order within team.

		NM	EX	VG
Complete Set (20):		750.00	375.00	225.00
Common Player:		45.00	22.50	13.50
	Chicago Cubs team set (11):	450.00	225.00	135.00
(1)	Les Bell	45.00	22.50	13.50
(2)	Guy Bush	45.00	22.50	13.50
(3)	Kiki Cuyler	60.00	30.00	18.00
(4)	Woody English	45.00	22.50	13.50
(5)	Charlie Grimm	45.00	22.50	13.50
(6)	Gabby Hartnett	60.00	30.00	18.00
(7)	Rogers Hornsby	90.00	45.00	27.00
(8)	Joe McCarthy	45.00	22.50	13.50
(9)	Charlie Root	45.00	22.50	13.50
(10)	Riggs Stephenson	45.00	22.50	13.50
(11)	Hack Wilson	60.00	30.00	18.00
	Chicago White So team set (9):	350.00	175.00	105.00
(1)	Moe Berg	60.00	30.00	18.00
(2)	Bill Cissel (Cissell)	45.00	22.50	13.50
(3)	Red Faber	60.00	30.00	18.00
(4)	Bill Hunnefield	45.00	22.50	13.50
(5)	Smead Jolley	45.00	22.50	13.50
(6)	Willie Kamm	45.00	22.50	13.50
(7)	Jimmy Moore	45.00	22.50	13.50
(8)	Carl Reynolds	45.00	22.50	13.50
(9)	Art Shires	45.00	22.50	13.50

1976 Chicagoland Collectors Association Chicago Greats

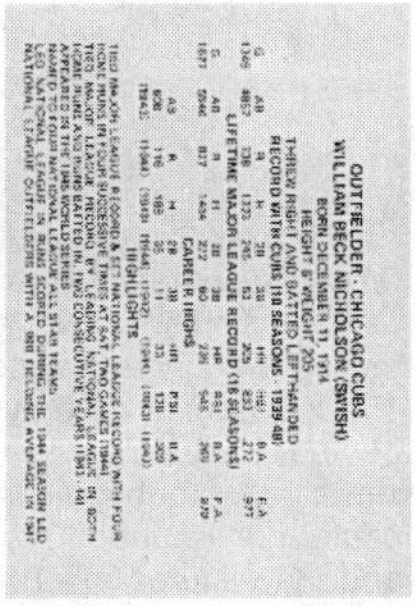

Former stars of the Cubs and White Sox are featured in this collectors issue produced in conjunction with an early sports card and memorabilia show in Chicago. The 2-1/2" x 3-1/2" cards feature black-and-white action photos at center of most cards, with a portrait photo inset at top. Graphics around the front are in red. Backs have detailed career summaries. A starting team, manager and president for each of the Chicago teams is represented in the issue. Complete sets were originally sold for about $2 with uncut sheets sold for $6.

		NM	EX	VG
Complete Set (25):		40.00	20.00	12.00
Common Player:		2.00	1.00	.60
(1)	Luke Appling	2.00	1.00	.60
(2)	Ernie Banks	3.50	1.75	1.00
(3)	Zeke Bonura	2.00	1.00	.60
(4)	Phil Cavarretta	2.00	1.00	.60
(5)	Jimmy Dykes	2.00	1.00	.60
(6)	Red Faber, Ted Lyons	2.00	1.00	.60
(7)	Nellie Fox	2.50	1.25	.70
(8)	Larry French	2.00	1.00	.60
(9)	Charlie Grimm	2.00	1.00	.60
(10)	Gabby Hartnett	2.00	1.00	.60
(11)	Billy Herman	2.00	1.00	.60
(12)	Mike Kreevich	2.00	1.00	.60
(13)	Sherman Lollar	2.00	1.00	.60
(14)	Al Lopez	2.00	1.00	.60
(15)	Minnie Minoso	2.50	1.25	.70
(16)	Wally Moses	2.00	1.00	.60
(17)	Bill Nicholson	2.00	1.00	.60
(18)	Claude Passeau	2.00	1.00	.60
(19)	Billy Pierce	2.00	1.00	.60
(20)	Ron Santo	2.00	1.00	.60
(21)	Hank Sauer	2.00	1.00	.60
(22)	Riggs Stephenson	2.00	1.00	.60
(23)	Bill Veeck	2.00	1.00	.60
(24)	P.K. Wrigley	2.00	1.00	.60
(25)	Checklist	2.00	1.00	.60

1915 Chicago Tribune Supplements

As the 1915 baseball season opened, the Chicago Sunday Tribune ran supplements in its April 4 and April 11 editions featuring pictures of Chicago players. The black-and-white pictures are 8" x 11". Saier is pictured in uniform, the others are in street clothes. Printed in the white border beneath each photo is "Supplement to The Chicago Sunday Tribune, April 4 (or) 11, 1915." Each picture bears a facsimile autograph of the player and is blank-backed.

		NM	EX	VG
Complete Set (4):		400.00	200.00	120.00
Common Player:		30.00	15.00	9.00
(1)	Roger Bresnahan (April 11)	100.00	50.00	30.00
(2)	Eddie Collins (April 11)	100.00	50.00	30.00
(3)	Vic Saier (April 11)	50.00	25.00	15.00
(4)	Joe Tinker (April 4)	150.00	75.00	45.00

1919 Chicago White Sox team issue

This set of the notorious Black Sox and their hapless teammates was produced by Davis Printing Works in Chicago and apparently sold as a complete boxed set by the team. Individual cards measure about 1-11/16" x 2-3/4". Fronts feature full-length black-and-white photos of the players on a white background with a whiter border. Player name and position is in black beneath the picture. Backs are blank. To date, only one set is known to exist. It sold at auction in 1991 for $45,100, and again in 1997 for $46,000. The unnumbered cards are checklisted here alphabetically.

		NM	EX	VG
Complete Set (25):		50000.	35000.	20000.
Common Player:		250.00	175.00	100.00
(1)	Joe Benz	250.00	175.00	100.00
(2)	Eddie Cicotte	4000.	2800.	1600.
(3)	Eddie Collins	1500.	1050.	600.00
(4)	Shano Collins	250.00	175.00	100.00
(5)	Charles Comiskey	2000.	1400.	800.00
(6)	Dave Danforth	250.00	175.00	100.00
(7)	Red Faber	1250.	875.00	500.00
(8)	Happy Felsch	2500.	1750.	1000.
(9)	Chick Gandil	4500.	3150.	1800.
(10)	Kid Gleason	250.00	175.00	100.00
(11)	Joe Jackson	22000.	15400.	8800.
(12)	Joe Jenkins	300.00	210.00	120.00
(13)	Ted Jourdan	300.00	210.00	120.00
(14)	Nemo Leibold	250.00	175.00	100.00
(15)	Byrd Lynn	250.00	175.00	100.00
(16)	Fred McMullin	1500.	1050.	600.00
(17)	Eddie Murphy	250.00	175.00	100.00
(18)	Swede Risberg	2000.	1400.	800.00
(19)	Pants Rowland	250.00	175.00	100.00
(20)	Reb Russell	250.00	175.00	100.00
(21)	Ray Schalk	1250.	875.00	500.00
(22)	James Scott	250.00	175.00	100.00
(23)	Buck Weaver	4000.	2800.	1600.
(24)	Lefty Williams	2000.	1400.	800.00
(25)	Mellie Wolfgang	250.00	175.00	100.00

1948 Chicago White Sox Photo Pack

The last-place White Sox of 1948 are immortalized in this team-issued set of player photos. Individual players are pictured in a 6-1/2" x 9" portrait photo with a thin white border around. A facsimile autograph also appears on front. Backs are blank. A team photo was also included in the set. The photo pack was sold in a large white envelope with a red and blue team logo. The unnumbered pictures are checklisted here in alphabetical order.

	NM	EX	VG
Complete Set (30):	180.00	90.00	54.00
Common Player:	7.50	3.75	2.25
(1) Luke Appling	18.00	9.00	5.50
(2) Floyd Baker	7.50	3.75	2.25
(3) Fred Bradley	7.50	3.75	2.25
(4) Earl Caldwell	7.50	3.75	2.25
(5) Red Faber	15.00	7.50	4.50
(6) Bob Gillespie	7.50	3.75	2.25
(7) Jim Goodwin	12.00	6.00	3.50
(8) Orval Grove	7.50	3.75	2.25
(9) Earl Harrist	7.50	3.75	2.25
(10) Joe Haynes	7.50	3.75	2.25
(11) Ralph Hodgin	7.50	3.75	2.25
(12) Howie Judson	7.50	3.75	2.25
(13) Bob Kennedy	7.50	3.75	2.25
(14) Don Kolloway	7.50	3.75	2.25
(15) Tony Lupien	7.50	3.75	2.25
(16) Ted Lyons	15.00	7.50	4.50
(17) Cass Michaels	7.50	3.75	2.25
(18) Bing Miller	7.50	3.75	2.25
(19) Buster Mills	7.50	3.75	2.25
(20) Glen Moulder	7.50	3.75	2.25
(21) Frank Papish	7.50	3.75	2.25
(22) Ike Pearson	7.50	3.75	2.25
(23) Dave Philley	7.50	3.75	2.25
(24) Aaron Robinson	7.50	3.75	2.25
(25) Mike Tresh	7.50	3.75	2.25
(26) Jack Wallaesa	7.50	3.75	2.25
(27) Ralph Weigel	7.50	3.75	2.25
(28) Bill Wight	7.50	3.75	2.25
(29) Taft Wright	7.50	3.75	2.25
(30) Team picture	18.00	9.00	5.50

1960-64 Chicago White Sox Ticket Stubs

From 1960-64 tickets to White Sox home games at Comiskey Park were issued bearing player photos. Along with the photos on the backs of the 1-5/16" x 2-5/8" ticket stubs are career information and facsimile autographs. Photos were generally re-used from year to year and color variations, depending on the type of ticket, are known. Players from each year are listed here alphabetically.

	NM	EX	VG
Complete Set (112):	450.00	225.00	135.00
Common Player:	6.00	3.00	1.75
60-1 Luis Aparicio	15.00	7.50	4.50
60-2 Earl Battey	6.00	3.00	1.75
60-3 Frank Baumann	6.00	3.00	1.75
60-4 Dick Donovan	6.00	3.00	1.75
60-5 Nelson Fox	15.00	7.50	4.50
60-6 Gene Freese	6.00	3.00	1.75
60-7 Ted Kluszewski	12.00	6.00	3.50
60-8 Jim Landis	6.00	3.00	1.75
60-9 Barry Latman	6.00	3.00	1.75
60-10 Sherm Lollar	6.00	3.00	1.75
60-11 Al Lopez	9.00	4.50	2.75
60-12 Turk Lown	6.00	3.00	1.75
60-13 Orestes Minoso	10.00	5.00	3.00
60-14 Bill Pierce	6.00	3.00	1.75
60-15 Jim Rivera	6.00	3.00	1.75
60-16 Bob Shaw	6.00	3.00	1.75
60-17 Roy Sievers	6.00	3.00	1.75
60-18 Al Smith	6.00	3.00	1.75
60-19 Gerry Staley	6.00	3.00	1.75
60-20 Early Wynn	9.00	4.50	2.75
61-1 Luis Aparicio	15.00	7.50	4.50
61-2 Frank Baumann	6.00	3.00	1.75
61-3 Camilo Carreon	6.00	3.00	1.75
61-4 Sam Esposito	6.00	3.00	1.75
61-5 Nelson Fox	15.00	7.50	4.50
61-6 Billy Goodman	6.00	3.00	1.75
61-7 Jim Landis	6.00	3.00	1.75
61-8 Sherman Lollar	6.00	3.00	1.75
61-9 Al Lopez	9.00	4.50	2.75
61-10 J.C. Martin	6.00	3.00	1.75
61-11 Cal McLish	6.00	3.00	1.75
61-12 Orestes Minoso	10.00	5.00	3.00
61-13 Bill Pierce	6.00	3.00	1.75
61-14 Juan Pizarro	6.00	3.00	1.75
61-15 Bob Roselli	6.00	3.00	1.75
61-16 Herb Score	7.50	3.75	2.25
61-17 Bob Shaw	6.00	3.00	1.75
61-18 Roy Sievers	6.00	3.00	1.75
61-19 Al Smith	6.00	3.00	1.75
61-20 Gerry Staley	6.00	3.00	1.75
61-21 Early Wynn	9.00	4.50	2.75
62-1 Luis Aparicio	15.00	7.50	4.50
62-2 Frank Baumann	6.00	3.00	1.75
62-3 John Buzhardt	6.00	3.00	1.75
62-4 Camilo Carreon	6.00	3.00	1.75
62-5 Joe Cunningham	6.00	3.00	1.75
62-6 Bob Farley	6.00	3.00	1.75
62-7 Eddie Fisher	6.00	3.00	1.75
62-8 Nelson Fox	15.00	7.50	4.50
62-9 Jim Landis	6.00	3.00	1.75
62-10 Sherm Lollar	6.00	3.00	1.75
62-11 Al Lopez	9.00	4.50	2.75
62-12 Turk Lown	6.00	3.00	1.75
62-13 J.C. Martin	6.00	3.00	1.75
62-14 Cal McLish	6.00	3.00	1.75
62-15 Gary Peters	6.00	3.00	1.75
62-16 Juan Pizarro	6.00	3.00	1.75
62-17 Floyd Robinson	6.00	3.00	1.75
62-18 Bob Roselli	6.00	3.00	1.75
62-19 Herb Score	7.50	3.75	2.25
62-20 Al Smith	6.00	3.00	1.75
62-21 Charles Smith	6.00	3.00	1.75
62-22 Early Wynn	9.00	4.50	2.75
63-1 Frank Baumann	6.00	3.00	1.75
63-2 John Buzhardt	6.00	3.00	1.75
63-3 Camilo Carreon	6.00	3.00	1.75
63-4 Joe Cunningham	6.00	3.00	1.75
63-5 Dave DeBusschere	8.00	4.00	2.50
63-6 Eddie Fisher	6.00	3.00	1.75
63-7 Nelson Fox	15.00	7.50	4.50
63-8 Ron Hansen	6.00	3.00	1.75
63-9 Ray Herbert	6.00	3.00	1.75
63-10 Mike Hershberger	6.00	3.00	1.75
63-11 Joe Horlen	6.00	3.00	1.75
63-12 Grover Jones	6.00	3.00	1.75
63-13 Mike Joyce	6.00	3.00	1.75
63-14 Frank Kreutzer	6.00	3.00	1.75
63-15 Jim Landis	6.00	3.00	1.75
63-16 Sherman Lollar	6.00	3.00	1.75
63-17 Al Lopez	9.00	4.50	2.75
63-18 J.C. Martin	6.00	3.00	1.75
63-19 Charlie Maxwell	6.00	3.00	1.75
63-20 Dave Nicholson	6.00	3.00	1.75
63-21 Juan Pizarro	6.00	3.00	1.75
63-22 Floyd Robinson	6.00	3.00	1.75
63-23 Charlie Smith	6.00	3.00	1.75
63-24 Pete Ward	6.00	3.00	1.75
63-25 Al Weis	6.00	3.00	1.75
63-26 Hoyt Wilhelm	9.00	4.50	2.75
63-27 Dom Zanni	6.00	3.00	1.75
64-1 Fritz Ackley	6.00	3.00	1.75
64-2 Frank Baumann	6.00	3.00	1.75
64-3 Don Buford	6.00	3.00	1.75
64-4 John Buzhardt	6.00	3.00	1.75
64-5 Camilo Carreon	6.00	3.00	1.75
64-6 Joe Cunningham	6.00	3.00	1.75
64-7 Dave DeBusschere	8.00	4.00	2.50
64-8 Eddie Fisher	6.00	3.00	1.75
64-9 Jim Golden	6.00	3.00	1.75
64-10 Ron Hansen	6.00	3.00	1.75
64-11 Ray Herbert	6.00	3.00	1.75
64-12 Mike Hershberger	6.00	3.00	1.75
64-13 Joe Horlen	6.00	3.00	1.75
64-14 Jim Landis	6.00	3.00	1.75
64-15 Al Lopez	9.00	4.50	2.75
64-16 J.C. Martin	6.00	3.00	1.75
64-17 Dave Nicholson	6.00	3.00	1.75
64-18 Gary Peters	6.00	3.00	1.75
64-19 Juan Pizarro	6.00	3.00	1.75
64-20 Floyd Robinson	6.00	3.00	1.75
64-21 Gene Stephens	6.00	3.00	1.75
64-22 Pete Ward	6.00	3.00	1.75
64-23 Hoyt Wilhelm	9.00	4.50	2.75

1977 Chilly Willee Discs

Virtually identical in format to the several locally sponsored disc sets of the previous year, these 3-3/8" diameter player discs were given away at participating frozen drink stands. Discs once again feature black-and-white player portrait photos in the center of a baseball design. The left and right panels are in one of several bright colors. Licensed by the players' association through Mike Schechter Associates, the player photos carry no uniform logos. Backs are printed in blue and red. The unnumbered discs are checklisted here alphabetically.

	NM	EX	VG
Complete Set (70):	125.00	62.00	37.00
Common Player:	1.00	.50	.30
(1) Sal Bando	1.00	.50	.30
(2) Buddy Bell	1.00	.50	.30
(3) Johnny Bench	8.00	4.00	2.50
(4) Larry Bowa	1.00	.50	.30
(5) Steve Braun	1.00	.50	.30
(6) George Brett	16.00	8.00	4.75
(7) Lou Brock	6.00	3.00	1.75
(8) Jeff Burroughs	1.00	.50	.30
(9) Bert Campaneris	1.00	.50	.30
(10) John Candelaria	1.00	.50	.30
(11) Jose Cardenal	1.00	.50	.30
(12) Rod Carew	6.50	3.25	2.00
(13) Steve Carlton	7.00	3.50	2.00
(14) Dave Cash	1.00	.50	.30
(15) Cesar Cedeno	1.00	.50	.30
(16) Ron Cey	1.00	.50	.30
(17) Dave Concepcion	1.00	.50	.30
(18) Dennis Eckersley	4.50	2.25	1.25
(19) Mark Fidrych	3.50	1.75	1.00
(20) Rollie Fingers	6.00	3.00	1.75
(21) Carlton Fisk	6.00	3.00	1.75
(22) George Foster	1.00	.50	.30
(23) Wayne Garland	1.00	.50	.30
(24) Ralph Garr	1.00	.50	.30
(25) Steve Garvey	4.00	2.00	1.25
(26) Cesar Geronimo	1.00	.50	.30
(27) Bobby Grich	1.00	.50	.30
(28) Ken Griffey Sr.	1.50	.70	.45
(29) Don Gullett	1.00	.50	.30
(30) Mike Hargrove	1.00	.50	.30
(31) Al Hrabosky	1.00	.50	.30
(32) Catfish Hunter	6.00	3.00	1.75
(33) Reggie Jackson	9.00	4.50	2.75
(34) Randy Jones	1.00	.50	.30
(35) Dave Kingman	2.00	1.00	.60
(36) Jerry Koosman	1.00	.50	.30
(37) Dave LaRoche	1.00	.50	.30
(38) Greg Luzinski	1.50	.70	.45
(39) Fred Lynn	1.50	.70	.45
(40) Bill Madlock	1.00	.50	.30
(41) Rick Manning	1.00	.50	.30
(42) Jon Matlock	1.00	.50	.30
(43) John Mayberry	1.00	.50	.30
(44) Hal McRae	1.00	.50	.30
(45) Andy Messersmith	1.00	.50	.30
(46) Rick Monday	1.00	.50	.30
(47) John Montefusco	1.00	.50	.30
(48) Joe Morgan	6.00	3.00	1.75
(49) Thurman Munson	6.50	3.25	2.00
(50) Bobby Murcer	1.00	.50	.30
(51) Bill North	1.00	.50	.30
(52) Jim Palmer	6.00	3.00	1.75
(53) Tony Perez	6.00	3.00	1.75
(54) Jerry Reuss	1.00	.50	.30
(55) Brooks Robinson	7.00	3.50	2.00
(56) Pete Rose	18.00	9.00	5.50
(57) Joe Rudi	1.00	.50	.30
(58) Nolan Ryan	24.00	12.00	7.25
(59) Manny Sanguillen	1.00	.50	.30
(60) Mike Schmidt	9.50	4.75	2.75
(61) Tom Seaver	7.00	3.50	2.00
(62) Bill Singer	1.00	.50	.30
(63) Willie Stargell	6.00	3.00	1.75
(64) Rusty Staub	1.50	.70	.45
(65) Luis Tiant	1.00	.50	.30
(66) Bob Watson	1.00	.50	.30
(67) Butch Wynegar	1.00	.50	.30
(68) Carl Yastrzemski	7.00	3.50	2.00
(69) Robin Yount	9.00	4.50	2.75
(70) Richie Zisk	1.00	.50	.30

1929 Churchman's Cigarettes

Though he is identified nowhere on this English cigarette card, the home run swing of Babe Ruth on the front is unmistakable. The last of a set of 25

"Sports & Games in Many Lands" series, the approximately 2-5/8" x 1-3/8" cards have color artwork on the front and black-and-white backs. The back of the baseball card provides a short history of "The great national sport of the U.S.A."

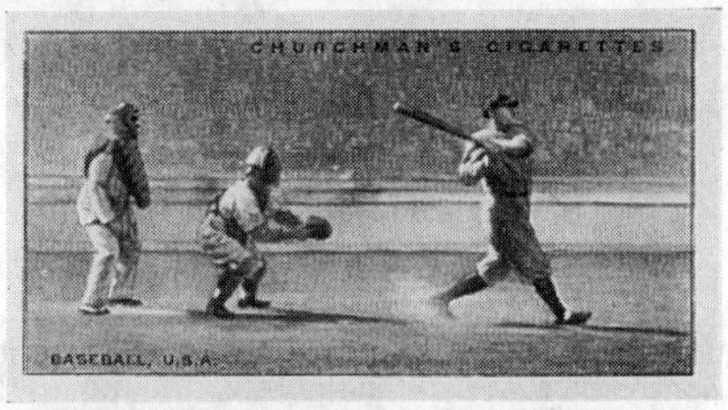

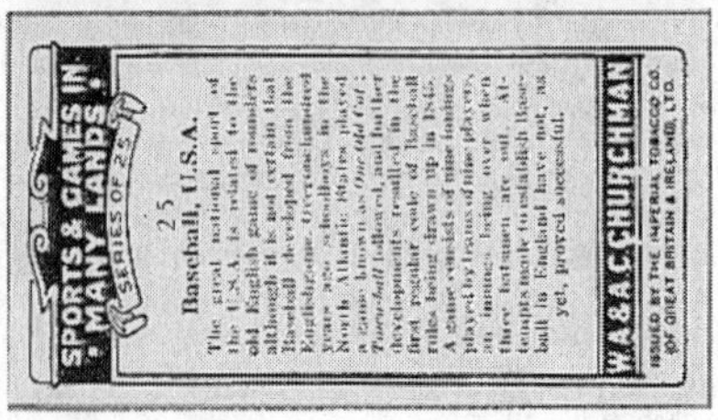

		NM	EX	VG
25	Baseball, U.S.A. (Babe Ruth)	375.00	187.00	112.00

1938 Cincinnati Post Reds

Over the course of several weeks during the summer of 1938, daily editions of the Cincinnati Post sports section carried a set of player portraits designed to be cut out and saved. The pieces measure 6" x 11" and feature a large photo with facsimile autograph, topped by a headline and carrying a short biography below. Everything is in black-and-white. The unnumbered series is checklisted here in alphabetical order.

		NM	EX	VG
Complete Set (25):		450.00	225.00	135.00
Common Player:		20.00	10.00	6.00
(1)	Wally Berger	30.00	15.00	9.00
(2)	Joe Cascarella	20.00	10.00	6.00
(3)	Harry Craft	20.00	10.00	6.00
(4)	Dusty Cooke	20.00	10.00	6.00
(5)	Peaches Davis	20.00	10.00	6.00
(6)	Paul Derringer	25.00	12.50	7.50
(7)	Linus (Junior) Frey	20.00	10.00	6.00
(8)	Lee Gamble	20.00	10.00	6.00
(9)	Ival Goodman	20.00	10.00	6.00
(10)	Hank Gowdy	20.00	10.00	6.00
(11)	Lee Grissom	20.00	10.00	6.00
(12)	Willard Hershberger	25.00	12.50	7.50
(13)	Don Lang	20.00	10.00	6.00
(14)	Ernie Lombardi	35.00	17.50	10.50
(15)	Buck McCormick	20.00	10.00	6.00
(16)	Bill McKechnie	35.00	17.50	10.50
(17)	Whitey Moore	20.00	10.00	6.00
(18)	Billy Myers	20.00	10.00	6.00
(19)	Clifford Richardson	20.00	10.00	6.00
(20)	Lewis Riggs	20.00	10.00	6.00
(21)	Edd Roush	35.00	17.50	10.50
(22)	Gene Schott	20.00	10.00	6.00
(23)	Johnny Vander Meer	30.00	15.00	9.00
(24)	Bucky Walter	20.00	10.00	6.00
(25)	James Weaver	20.00	10.00	6.00

1919-20 Cincinnati Reds Postcards

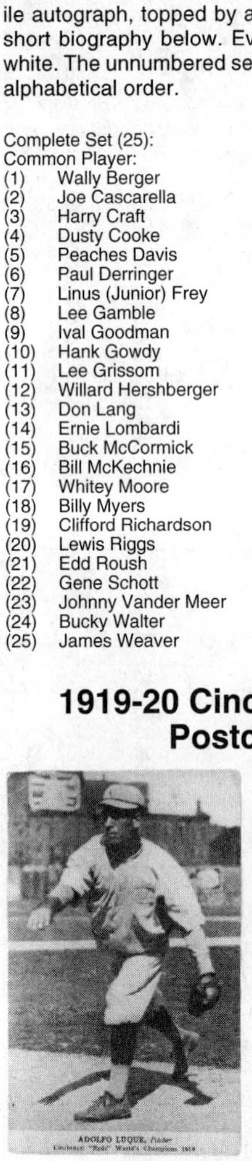
ADOLFO LUQUE, Pitcher
Cincinnati "Reds" World's Champions 1919

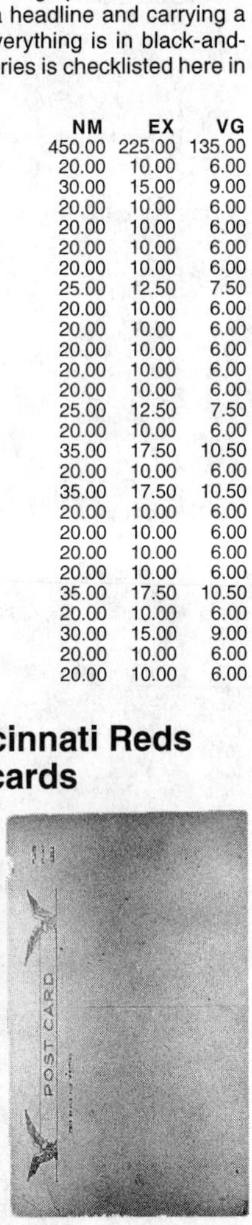

Two versions of each of the cards in this issue are known. Picturing members of the 1919 World Champions, the foils of the Black Sox scandal, these 3-1/2" x 5-1/2" cards have black-and-white player poses on front. In the white border at bottom (or occasionally, at top) are two lines of type. The top line has the player name and position. The second line can be found in two versions. One reads, "Cincinnati 'Reds' - Champions of National League 1919", the other, presumably a second printing following the World Series, reads, "Cincinnati 'Reds' World's Champions 1919". Backs are printed with standard postcard indicia. The unnumbered cards are checklisted here in alphabetical order.

		NM	EX	VG
Complete Set (24):		1500.	750.00	445.00
Common Player:		75.00	37.00	22.00
(1)	Nick Allen	75.00	37.00	22.00
(2)	Rube Bressler	75.00	37.00	22.00
(3)	Jake Daubert	75.00	37.00	22.00
(4)	Pat Duncan	75.00	37.00	22.00
(5)	Hod Eller	75.00	37.00	22.00
(6)	Ray Fisher	75.00	37.00	22.00
(7)	Eddie Gerner	75.00	37.00	22.00
(8)	Heinie Groh	75.00	37.00	22.00
(9)	Larry Kopf	75.00	37.00	22.00
(10)	Adolfo Luque	85.00	42.00	25.00
(11)	Sherwood Magee	75.00	37.00	22.00
(12)	Roy Mitchell	75.00	37.00	22.00
(13)	Pat Moran	75.00	37.00	22.00
(14)	Greasy Neale	85.00	42.00	25.00
(15)	Bill Rariden	75.00	37.00	22.00
(16)	Morris Rath	75.00	37.00	22.00
(17)	Walter Reuther	75.00	37.00	22.00
(18)	Jimmy Ring	75.00	37.00	22.00
(19)	Eddie Roush	100.00	50.00	30.00
(20)	Harry Sallee	75.00	37.00	22.00
(21)	Hank Schreiber	75.00	37.00	22.00
(22)	Charles See	75.00	37.00	22.00
(23)	Jimmy Smith	75.00	37.00	22.00
(24)	Ivy Wingo	75.00	37.00	22.00

1938 Cincinnati Reds team issue

This 32-card set is a challenge of particular interest to Cincinnati team collectors. The 2" x 3" cards were sold as a boxed set at the ballpark. Fronts feature a black-and-white photo of the player while backs have the player's name, position and a generally flattering description of the player's talents. The cards are not numbered. In the American Card Catalog, this issue was designated W711-1.

		NM	EX	VG
Complete Set (23):		325.00	160.00	97.00
Common Player:		10.00	5.00	3.00
(1)	Wally Berger ("... in a trade with the Giants in June.")	15.00	7.50	4.50
(2)	Joe Cascarella	15.00	7.50	4.50
(3)	Allen "Dusty" Cooke	15.00	7.50	4.50
(4)	Harry Craft	10.00	5.00	3.00
(5)	Ray "Peaches" Davis	10.00	5.00	3.00
(6)	Paul Derringer ("Won 22 games...this season.")	15.00	7.50	4.50
(7)	Linus Frey ("... only 25 now.")	15.00	7.50	4.50
(8)	Lee Gamble ("... Syracuse last year.")	15.00	7.50	4.50
(9)	Ival Goodman (no mention of 30 homers)	15.00	7.50	4.50
(10)	Harry "Hank" Gowdy	15.00	7.50	4.50
(11)	Lee Grissom (no mention of 1938)	15.00	7.50	4.50
(12)	Willard Hershberger	25.00	12.50	7.50
(13)	Ernie Lombardi (no mention of 1938 MVP)	30.00	15.00	9.00
(14)	Frank McCormick	15.00	7.50	4.50
(15)	Bill McKechnie ("Last year he led ...")	30.00	15.00	9.00
(16)	Lloyd "Whitey" Moore ("... last year with Syracuse.")	15.00	7.50	4.50
(17)	Billy Myers ("... in his fourth year.")	15.00	7.50	4.50
(18)	Lee Riggs ("... in his fourth season ...")	15.00	7.50	4.50
(19)	Eddie Roush	25.00	12.50	7.50
(20)	Gene Schott	15.00	7.50	4.50
(21)	Johnny Vander Meer (pitching pose)	20.00	10.00	6.00
(22)	Wm. "Bucky" Walter ("... won 14 games ...")	15.00	7.50	4.50
(23)	Jim Weaver	10.00	5.00	3.00

1939 Cincinnati Reds team issue

An updating by one season of the team-issued 1938 W711-1 set, most of the players and poses on the 2" x 3" cards remained the same. A close study of the career summary on the card's back is necessary to determine which year of issue is at hand.

		NM	EX	VG
Complete Set (27):		375.00	185.00	110.00
Common Player:		12.00	6.00	3.50
(1)	Wally Berger ("... in a trade with the Giants in June, 1938.")	30.00	15.00	9.00
(2)	Nino Bongiovanni	12.00	6.00	3.50
(3)	Stanley "Frenchy" Bordagaray	12.00	6.00	3.50
(4)	Harry Craft	12.00	6.00	3.50
(5)	Ray "Peaches" Davis	12.00	6.00	3.50
(6)	Paul Derringer ("Won 22 games ... last year.")	15.00	7.50	4.50
(7)	Linus Frey ("... only 26 now.")	12.00	6.00	3.50
(8)	Lee Gamble ("... Syracuse in 1937.")	12.00	6.00	3.50
(9)	Ival Goodman (mentions hitting 30 homers)	12.00	6.00	3.50
(10)	Harry "Hank" Gowdy	12.00	6.00	3.50
(11)	Lee Grissom (mentions 1938)	12.00	6.00	3.50
(12)	Willard Hershberger	24.00	12.00	7.25
(13)	Eddie Joost	12.00	6.00	3.50
(14)	Wes Livengood	12.00	6.00	3.50
(15)	Ernie Lombardi (mentions MVP of 1938)	50.00	25.00	15.00
(16)	Frank McCormick	12.00	6.00	3.50
(17)	Bill McKechnie ("In 1937 he led ...")	50.00	25.00	15.00
(18)	Lloyd "Whitey" Moore ("... in 1937 with Syracuse.")	12.00	6.00	3.50
(19)	Billy Myers ("... in his fifth year ...")	12.00	6.00	3.50
(20)	Lee Riggs ("... in his fifth season...")	12.00	6.00	3.50
(21)	Les Scarsella	12.00	6.00	3.50
(22)	Eugene "Junior" Thompson	12.00	6.00	3.50
(23)	Johnny Vander Meer (portrait)	20.00	10.00	6.00
(24)	Wm. "Bucky" Walters ("Won 15 games ...")	12.00	6.00	3.50
(25)	Jim Weaver	12.00	6.00	3.50
(26)	Bill Werber	12.00	6.00	3.50
(27)	Jimmy Wilson	12.00	6.00	3.50

1940 Cincinnati Reds team issue

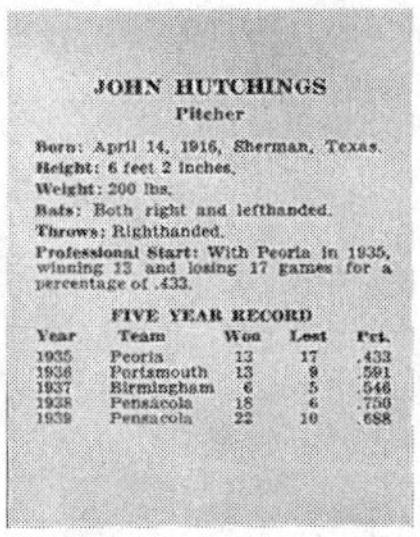
JOHN HUTCHINGS
Pitcher

Born: April 14, 1916, Sherman, Texas.
Height: 6 feet 2 inches.
Weight: 200 lbs.
Bats: Both right and lefthanded.
Throws: Righthanded.
Professional Start: With Peoria in 1935, winning 13 and losing 17 games for a percentage of .433.

FIVE YEAR RECORD

Year	Team	Won	Lost	Pct.
1935	Peoria	13	17	.433
1936	Portsmouth	13	9	.591
1937	Birmingham	6	5	.546
1938	Pensacola	18	6	.750
1939	Pensacola	22	10	.688

Another early Reds team issue, this set of black-and-white 2-1/8" x 2-5/8" cards is unnumbered and features player portrait photos on the front. Name, position, biographical information and five years' worth of stats are on the back. The Reds were World Champions in 1940 (defeating Detroit), and the set features several special World Series cards, making it one of the first to feature events as well as individuals. The set was listed in the American Card Catalog as W711-2.

		NM	EX	VG
Complete Set (35):		450.00	225.00	135.00
Common Player:		12.00	6.00	3.50
(1)	Morris Arnovich	12.00	6.00	3.50
(2)	William (Bill) Baker	12.00	6.00	3.50
(3)	Joseph Beggs	12.00	6.00	3.50
(4)	Harry Craft	12.00	6.00	3.50
(5)	Paul Derringer	20.00	10.00	6.00
(6)	Linus Frey	12.00	6.00	3.50
(7)	Ival Goodman	12.00	6.00	3.50
(8)	Harry (Hank) Gowdy	12.00	6.00	3.50
(9)	Witt Guise	12.00	6.00	3.50
(10)	Harry (Socko) Hartman	12.00	6.00	3.50
(11)	Willard Hershberger	20.00	10.00	6.00
(12)	John Hutchings	12.00	6.00	3.50
(13)	Edwin Joost	12.00	6.00	3.50
(14)	Ernie Lombardi	35.00	17.50	10.50
(15)	Frank McCormick	20.00	10.00	6.00
(16)	Myron McCormick	12.00	6.00	3.50
(17)	William Boyd McKechnie	30.00	15.00	9.00
(18)	Lloyd (Whitey) Moore	12.00	6.00	3.50
(19)	William (Bill) Myers	12.00	6.00	3.50
(20)	Lewis Riggs	12.00	6.00	3.50
(21)	Elmer Riddle	12.00	6.00	3.50
(22)	James A. Ripple	12.00	6.00	3.50
(23)	Milburn Shoffner	12.00	6.00	3.50
(24)	Eugene Thompson	12.00	6.00	3.50
(25)	James Turner	12.00	6.00	3.50
(26)	John Vander Meer	30.00	15.00	9.00
(27)	Wm. (Bucky) Walters	20.00	10.00	6.00
(28)	William (Bill) Werber	12.00	6.00	3.50
(29)	James Wilson	12.00	6.00	3.50
(30)	The Cincinnati Reds	12.00	6.00	3.50
(31)	The Cincinnati Reds World Champions	12.00	6.00	3.50
(32)	Tell the World About the Cincinnati Reds	12.00	6.00	3.50
(33)	Tell the World About the Cincinnati Reds Champions (Champions)	12.00	6.00	3.50
(34)	Results 1940 World's Series	15.00	7.50	4.50
(35)	Debt. of Gratitude to Wm. Koeh Co.	12.00	6.00	3.50

1957 Cincinnati Reds Postcards

The second in a long run of annual postcard issues, the 1957 cards are distinguished from the 1956 and 1958 cards by the appearance of players in dark caps in the portraits on front. On back, the card lacks the notice "This Space for Address" which appeared on the 1956 cards. The 3-1/2" x 5-3/4" cards have a black-and-white photo at top that is borderless at top and sides. At bottom is a 3/4" white strip for the application of an autograph. Backs are printed in black. The unnumbered cards are checklisted here in alphabetical order.

	NM	EX	VG
Complete Set (27):	200.00	100.00	60.00
Common Player:	9.00	4.50	2.75
(1) Tom Acker	9.00	4.50	2.75
(2) Ed Bailey	9.00	4.50	2.75
(3) Smoky Burgess	11.00	5.50	3.25
(4) George Crowe	9.00	4.50	2.75
(5) Bruce Edwards	9.00	4.50	2.75
(6) Tom Ferrick	9.00	4.50	2.75
(8) Hersh Freeman	9.00	4.50	2.75
(9) Don Gross	9.00	4.50	2.75
(10) Warren Hacker	9.00	4.50	2.75
(11) Bobby Henrich	9.00	4.50	2.75
(12) Don Hoak	11.00	5.50	3.25
(13) Hal Jeffcoat	9.00	4.50	2.75
(14) Johnny Klippstein	9.00	4.50	2.75
(15) Ted Kluszewski	18.00	9.00	5.50
(16) Brooks Lawrence	9.00	4.50	2.75
(17) Jerry Lynch	9.00	4.50	2.75
(18) Frank McCormick	9.00	4.50	2.75
(19) Roy McMillan	9.00	4.50	2.75
(20) Joe Nuxhall	9.00	4.50	2.75
(21) Wally Post	9.00	4.50	2.75
(22) Raul Sanchez	9.00	4.50	2.75
(23) Art Schult	9.00	4.50	2.75
(24) Birdie Tebbetts	9.00	4.50	2.75
(25) Johnny Temple	9.00	4.50	2.75
(26) Bob Thurman	9.00	4.50	2.75
(27) Pete Whisenant	9.00	4.50	2.75

1967 Cincinnati Reds Postcards

A lengthy run of team-issue black-and-white player portrait postcards began in 1967. The approximately 3-1/2" x 5-1/2" cards have white borders and standard postcard-style backs. The style of uniforms, color of team designation and facsimile autograph are useful in determining actual year of issue when the same players appeared from year to year. Only among 1969-70 cards is it sometimes necessary to compare poses. The '67 cards have players in pin-striped uniforms with the team name in red and facsimile signature in blue. Cards are not numbered and are checklisted here in alphabetical order.

	NM	EX	VG
Complete Set (35):	80.00	40.00	24.00
Common Player:	3.50	1.75	1.00
(1) Ted Abernathy	3.50	1.75	1.00
(2) Gerry Arrigo	3.50	1.75	1.00
(3) Jack Baldschun	3.50	1.75	1.00
(4) Johnny Bench	15.00	7.50	4.50
(5) Vern Benson	3.50	1.75	1.00
(6) Jimmy Bragan	3.50	1.75	1.00
(7) Dave Bristol	3.50	1.75	1.00
(8) Leo Cardenas	3.50	1.75	1.00
(9) Jim Coker	3.50	1.75	1.00
(10) Ted Davidson	3.50	1.75	1.00
(11) John Edwards	3.50	1.75	1.00
(12) Sam Ellis	3.50	1.75	1.00
(13) Ray Evans	3.50	1.75	1.00
(14) Mel Harder	3.50	1.75	1.00
(15) Tom Harper	5.00	2.50	1.50
(16) Tommy Helms	3.50	1.75	1.00
(17) Deron Johnson	3.50	1.75	1.00
(18) Bob Lee	3.50	1.75	1.00
(19) Jim Maloney	3.50	1.75	1.00
(20) Bill McCool	3.50	1.75	1.00
(21) Tom Murphy	3.50	1.75	1.00
(22) Gary Nolan	3.50	1.75	1.00
(23) Don Nottebart	3.50	1.75	1.00
(24) Milt Pappas	3.50	1.75	1.00
(25) Tony Perez	7.50	3.75	2.25
(26) Vada Pinson	6.00	3.00	1.75
(27) Mel Queen	3.50	1.75	1.00
(28) Floyd Robinson	3.50	1.75	1.00
(29) Pete Rose	15.00	7.50	4.50
(30) Chico Ruiz	3.50	1.75	1.00
(31) Art Shamsky	3.50	1.75	1.00
(32) Ray Shore	3.50	1.75	1.00
(33) Dick Simpson	3.50	1.75	1.00
(34) Whitey Wietelmann	3.50	1.75	1.00
(35) Jake Wood	3.50	1.75	1.00

1968 Cincinnati Reds Postcards

Similar in format to the 1967 and 1969 team-issue, the 1968 cards are distinguishable from the 1969s by the use of blue, rather than black, facsimile autographs. The '68s differ from the '67s in that the black-and-white portrait photos show the players in plain, rather than pin-striped, uniforms. Team designation is in red. The unnumbered cards are listed here alphabetically.

	NM	EX	VG
Complete Set (29):	55.00	27.50	16.50
Common Player:	3.00	1.50	.90
(1) Ted Abernathy	3.00	1.50	.90
(2) Gerry Arrigo	3.00	1.50	.90
(3) Johnny Bench	9.00	4.50	2.75
(4) Jimmy Bragan	3.00	1.50	.90
(5) Dave Bristol	3.00	1.50	.90
(6) Leo Cardenas	3.00	1.50	.90
(7) Clay Carroll	3.00	1.50	.90
(8) Tony Cloninger	3.00	1.50	.90
(9) George Culver	3.00	1.50	.90
(10) Tommy Helms	3.00	1.50	.90
(11) Alex Johnson	3.00	1.50	.90
(12) Mack Jones	3.00	1.50	.90
(13) Bill Kelso	3.00	1.50	.90
(14) Bob Lee	3.00	1.50	.90
(15) Jim Maloney	3.00	1.50	.90
(16) Lee May	3.00	1.50	.90
(17) Bill McCool	3.00	1.50	.90
(18) Gary Nolan	3.00	1.50	.90
(19) Don Pavletich	3.00	1.50	.90
(20) Tony Perez	6.00	3.00	1.75
(21) Vada Pinson	6.00	3.00	1.75
(22) Mel Queen	3.00	1.50	.90
(23) Jay Ritchie	3.00	1.50	.90
(24) Pete Rose	12.00	6.00	3.50
(25) Chico Ruiz	3.00	1.50	.90
(26) Jim Schaffer	3.00	1.50	.90
(27) Hal Smith	3.00	1.50	.90
(28) Fred Whitfield	3.00	1.50	.90
(29) Woody Woodward	3.00	1.50	.90

1969 Cincinnati Reds Postcards

The 1969 team-issued postcards are virtually identical in format to those of 1968 and 1970. They can be differentiated from the previous year's cards by the use of black, rather than blue facsimile autographs. The '69s, like the '70s, have team name in red and it is necessary to compare the black-and-white portrait photos to determine the year of issue. The unnumbered cards are checklisted here in alphabetical order.

	NM	EX	VG
Complete Set (28):	50.00	25.00	15.00
Common Player:	3.00	1.50	.90
(1) Gerry Arrigo	3.00	1.50	.90
(2) Jim Beauchamp	3.00	1.50	.90
(3) Johnny Bench (facing side)	7.50	3.75	2.25
(4) Vern Benson	3.00	1.50	.90
(5) Jimmy Bragan	3.00	1.50	.90
(6) Dave Bristol	3.00	1.50	.90
(7) Clay Carroll	3.00	1.50	.90
(8) Darrel Chaney (facing right)	3.00	1.50	.90
(9) Tony Cloninger	3.00	1.50	.90
(10) Pat Corrales (facing left)	3.00	1.50	.90
(11) George Culver	3.00	1.50	.90
(12) Jack Fisher	3.00	1.50	.90
(13) Wayne Granger (mouth open)	3.00	1.50	.90
(14) Harvey Haddix	4.00	2.00	1.25
(15) Tommy Helms (looking up)	3.00	1.50	.90
(16) Alex Johnson	3.00	1.50	.90
(17) Jim Maloney (facing left)	3.00	1.50	.90
(18) Lee May (looking right)	3.00	1.50	.90
(19) Jim Merritt	3.00	1.50	.90
(20) Tony Perez (looking up)	4.50	2.25	1.25
(21) Pete Rose (looking left)	12.00	6.00	3.50
(22) Chico Ruiz	3.00	1.50	.90
(23) Ted Savage	3.00	1.50	.90
(24) Hal Smith	3.00	1.50	.90
(25) Jim Stewart (facing left)	3.00	1.50	.90
(26) Bobby Tolan (no smile)	3.00	1.50	.90
(27) Fred Whitfield	3.00	1.50	.90
(28) Woody Woodward (no smile)	3.00	1.50	.90

1970 Cincinnati Reds Postcards

Like the previous year's team-issue, the 1970 series of postcards features black-and-white player portrait photos with the facsimile autograph in black and the team designation in red. Where possible, photo differences from the 1969 cards are noted in parentheses. The unnumbered cards are listed here alphabetically.

	NM	EX	VG
Complete Set (32):	45.00	22.50	13.50
Common Player:	2.00	1.00	.50
(1) George Anderson	4.50	2.25	1.25
(2) Johnny Bench (facing front)	6.00	3.00	1.75
(3) Bo Belinsky	3.00	1.50	.90
(4) Angel Bravo	2.00	1.00	.50
(5) Bernie Carbo	2.00	1.00	.50
(6) Clay Carroll (facing front)	2.00	1.00	.50
(7) Darrel Chaney (facing front)	2.00	1.00	.50
(8) Tony Cloninger (looking right)	2.00	1.00	.50
(9) Pat Corrales (looking right)	2.00	1.00	.50
(10) David Concepcion	3.00	1.50	.90
(11) Alex Grammas	2.00	1.00	.50
(12) Wayne Granger (mouth closed)	2.00	1.00	.50
(13) Don Gullett	2.00	1.00	.50
(14) Tommy Helms (facing front)	2.00	1.00	.50
(15) Ted Kluszewski	4.00	2.00	1.25
(16) Jim Maloney (facing right)	2.00	1.00	.50
(17) Lee May (facing front)	2.00	1.00	.50
(18) Jim Merritt	2.00	1.00	.50
(19) Jim McGlothlin	2.00	1.00	.50
(20) Hal McRae	3.50	1.75	1.00
(21) Gary Nolan	2.00	1.00	.50
(22) Tony Perez (facing front)	4.50	2.25	1.25
(23) George Scherger	2.00	1.00	.50
(24) Pete Rose (facing front)	10.00	5.00	3.00
(25) Larry Shepard	2.00	1.00	.50
(26) Wayne Simpson	2.00	1.00	.50
(27) Jim Stewart (facing right)	2.00	1.00	.50
(28) Bobby Tolan (smiling)	2.00	1.00	.50
(29) Ray Washburn	2.00	1.00	.50
(30) Woody Woodward (smiling)	2.00	1.00	.50

1971 Cincinnati Reds Postcards

This is the last year in which players were pictured in buttoned jerseys on the black-and-white team-issued cards. They can be differentiated from the previous year's issue by the team name appearing in black, rather than red. The unnumbered set is checklisted here in alphabetical order.

	NM	EX	VG
Complete Set (33):	40.00	20.00	12.00
Common Player:	2.00	1.00	1.50
(1) George Anderson	4.50	2.25	1.25
(2) Johnny Bench	6.00	3.00	1.75
(3) Buddy Bradford	2.00	1.00	1.50
(4) Bernie Carbo	2.00	1.00	1.50
(5) Clay Carroll	2.00	1.00	1.50
(6) Ty Cline	2.00	1.00	1.50
(7) Tony Cloninger	2.00	1.00	1.50
(8) David Concepcion	3.50	1.75	1.00
(9) Pat Corrales	2.00	1.00	1.50
(10) Al Ferrara	2.00	1.00	1.50
(11) George Foster	4.00	2.00	1.25
(12) Joe Gibbon	2.00	1.00	1.50
(13) Alex Grammas	2.00	1.00	1.50
(14) Wayne Granger	2.00	1.00	1.50
(15) Ross Grimsley	2.00	1.00	1.50
(16) Don Gullett	2.00	1.00	1.50
(17) Tommy Helms	2.00	1.00	1.50
(18) Ted Kluszewski	4.00	2.00	1.25
(19) Lee May	2.00	1.00	1.50
(20) Jim McGlothlin	2.00	1.00	1.50
(21) Hal McRae	3.50	1.75	1.00
(22) Jim Merritt	2.00	1.00	1.50
(23) Gary Nolan	2.00	1.00	1.50
(24) Tony Perez	4.00	2.00	1.25
(25) Pete Rose	10.00	5.00	3.00
(26) George Scherger	2.00	1.00	1.50
(27) Larry Shepard	2.00	1.00	1.50
(28) Wayne Simpson	2.00	1.00	1.50
(29) Willie Smith	2.00	1.00	1.50
(30) Jim Stewart	2.00	1.00	1.50
(31) Bobby Tolan	2.00	1.00	1.50
(32) Milt Wilcox	2.00	1.00	1.50
(33) Woody Woodward	2.00	1.00	1.50

1973 Cincinnati Reds Postcards

For the first time players in the annual team-issued postcard set are pictured in pull-over jerseys on these black-and-white postcards. The 1973 issue follows a one-year hiatus; no set was issued in 1972. The unnumbered cards are listed here alphabetically.

	NM	EX	VG
Complete Set (37):	45.00	22.00	13.50
Common Player:	2.00	1.00	.50
(1) George Anderson	3.50	1.75	1.00

(2)	Bob Barton	2.00	1.00	.50
(3)	Johnny Bench	6.00	3.00	1.75
(4)	Jack Billingham	2.00	1.00	.50
(5)	Pedro Borbon	2.00	1.00	.50
(6)	Clay Carroll	2.00	1.00	.50
(7)	Darrel Chaney	2.00	1.00	.50
(8)	David Concepcion	3.50	1.75	1.00
(9)	Ed Crosby	2.00	1.00	.50
(10)	Dan Driessen	2.00	1.00	.50
(11)	Phil Gagliano	2.00	1.00	.50
(12)	Cesar Geronimo	2.00	1.00	.50
(13)	Alex Grammas	2.00	1.00	.50
(14)	Ross Grimsley	2.00	1.00	.50
(15)	Don Gullett	2.00	1.00	.50
(16)	Joe Hague	2.00	1.00	.50
(17)	Tom Hall	2.00	1.00	.50
(18)	Hal King	2.00	1.00	.50
(19)	Ted Kluszewski	4.00	2.00	1.25
(20)	Andy Kosco	2.00	1.00	.50
(21)	Gene Locklear	2.00	1.00	.50
(22)	Jim McGlothlin	2.00	1.00	.50
(23)	Denis Menke	2.00	1.00	.50
(24)	Joe Morgan	5.00	2.50	1.50
(25)	Roger Nelson	2.00	1.00	.50
(26)	Gary Nolan	2.00	1.00	.50
(27)	Fred Norman	2.00	1.00	.50
(28)	Tony Perez	4.50	2.25	1.25
(29)	Bill Plummer	2.00	1.00	.50
(30)	Pete Rose	10.00	5.00	3.00
(31)	Richie Scheinblum	2.00	1.00	.50
(32)	George Scherger	2.00	1.00	.50
(33)	Larry Shepard	2.00	1.00	.50
(34)	Ed Sprague	2.00	1.00	.50
(35)	Larry Stahl	2.00	1.00	.50
(36)	Bobby Tolan	2.00	1.00	.50
(37)	Dave Tomlin	2.00	1.00	.50

1969 Citgo Coins

This 20-player set of small (about 1" in diameter) metal coins was issued by Citgo in 1969 to commemorate professional baseball's 100th anniversary. The brass-coated coins, susceptible to oxidation, display the player in a crude portrait with his name across the top. The backs honor the 100th anniversary of pro ball. The coins are unnumbered but are generally checklisted according to numbers that appear on a display card which was available from Citgo by mail.

		NM	EX	VG
Complete Set (20):		95.00	47.00	28.00
Common Player:		1.50	.70	.45
1	Denny McLain	3.00	1.50	.90
2	Dave McNally	1.50	.70	.45
3	Jim Lonborg	1.50	.70	.45
4	Harmon Killebrew	7.50	3.75	2.25
5	Mel Stottlemyre	1.50	.70	.45
6	Willie Horton	1.50	.70	.45
7	Jim Fregosi	2.25	1.25	.70
8	Rico Petrocelli	1.50	.70	.45
9	Stan Bahnsen	1.50	.70	.45
10	Frank Howard	3.00	1.50	.90
11	Joe Torre	3.00	1.50	.90
12	Jerry Koosman	1.50	.70	.45
13	Ron Santo	3.00	1.50	.90
14	Pete Rose	22.00	11.00	6.50
15	Rusty Staub	3.00	1.50	.90
16	Henry Aaron	25.00	12.50	7.50
17	Richie Allen	4.50	2.25	1.25
18	Ron Swoboda	1.50	.70	.45
19	Willie McCovey	7.50	3.75	2.25
20	Jim Bunning	6.00	3.00	1.75

1969 Citgo New York Mets

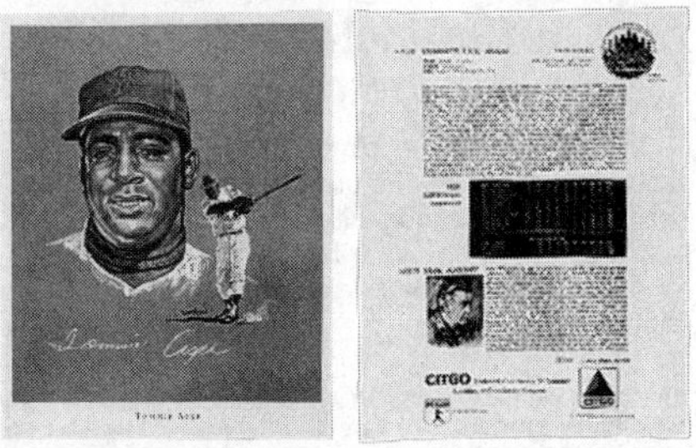

One of several regional issues in the Mets World Championship season of 1969, this set of player portraits was sponsored by Citgo, whose gas stations distributed the pictures with fuel purchases. Fronts feature large portraits and smaller action pictures of the player, done in pastels, set against a bright pastel background. The paintings are the work of noted celebrity artist John Wheeldon. Beneath the pictures is a facsimile autograph. The player's name is printed in the bottom border. Backs are printed in black-and-white and include biography and career details, full major and minor league stats and a self-portrait and biography of the artist. Logos of the Mets, the players' association and the sponsor complete the back design. The unnumbered player pictures are checklisted here in alphabetical order.

		NM	EX	VG
Complete Set (8):		100.00	50.00	30.00
Common Player:		10.00	5.00	3.00
(1)	Tommie Agee	12.00	6.00	3.50
(2)	Ken Boswell	10.00	5.00	3.00
(3)	Gary Gentry	10.00	5.00	3.00
(4)	Jerry Grote	10.00	5.00	3.00
(5)	Cleon Jones	10.00	5.00	3.00
(6)	Jerry Koosman	12.00	6.00	3.50
(7)	Ed Kranepool	10.00	5.00	3.00
(8)	Tom Seaver	35.00	17.50	10.50

1975 Clark & Sons Baseball Favorites

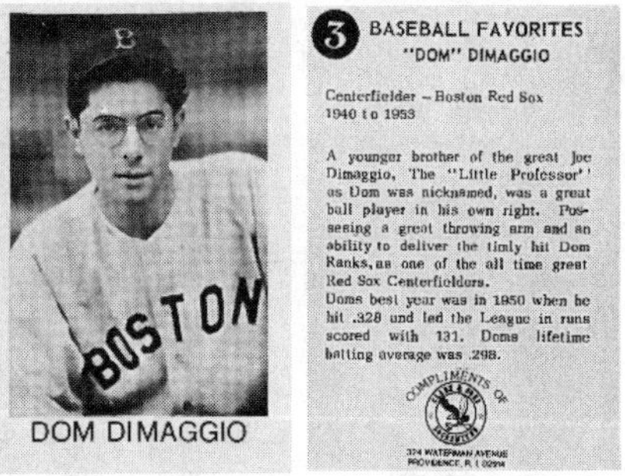

To commemorate the firm's 10 years in business and the Boston Red Sox first pennant since 1967, Clark & Sons Locksmiths of Rhode Island issued this set of Red Sox greats. Two versions were issued. The first has a "324 Waterman Avenue, Providence" address on back. A second printing corrected the errors to "324A Waterman Avenue, East Providence". Cards measure 2-1/2" x 3-5/8" and are printed in black-and-white.

		NM	EX	VG
Complete Set (4):		24.00	12.00	7.25
Common Player:		3.00	1.50	.90
1	Bobby Doerr	4.50	2.25	1.25
2	Ted Williams	15.00	7.50	4.50
3	Dom DiMaggio	4.50	2.25	1.25
4	Johnny Pesky	3.00	1.50	.90

1947 Cleveland Indians Picture Pack

The first of several annual issues of player photo packs, the 1947 version offered "autographed photos" of all players on the team's roster as of July 1. All players were presented in studio quality portraits in 6" x 8-1/2" format, lithographed on heavy paper with a facsimile autograph. A thin white border surrounds the photo. Backs are blank. The photos were sold in sets for 50 cents. The unnumbered pictures are checklisted here alphabetically.

		NM	EX	VG
Complete Set (25):		140.00	70.00	42.50
Common Player:		4.00	2.00	1.25
(1)	Don Black	6.00	3.00	1.75
(2)	Eddie Bockman	4.00	2.00	1.25
(3)	Lou Boudreau	12.00	6.00	3.50
(4)	Jack Conway	4.00	2.00	1.25
(5)	Larry Doby	25.00	12.50	7.50
(6)	Hank Edwards	4.00	2.00	1.25
(7)	"Red" Embree	4.00	2.00	1.25
(8)	Bob Feller	30.00	15.00	9.00
(9)	Les Fleming	4.00	2.00	1.25
(10)	Allen Gettel	4.00	2.00	1.25
(11)	Joe Gordon	4.00	2.00	1.25
(12)	Steve Gromek	4.00	2.00	1.25
(13)	Mel Harder	6.00	3.00	1.75
(14)	Jim Hegan	4.00	2.00	1.25
(15)	Ken Keltner	6.00	3.00	1.75
(16)	Ed Klieman	4.00	2.00	1.25
(17)	Bob Lemon	12.00	6.00	3.50
(18)	Al Lopez	12.00	6.00	3.50
(19)	George Metkovich	4.00	2.00	1.25
(20)	Dale Mitchell	6.00	3.00	1.75
(21)	Hal Peck	4.00	2.00	1.25
(22)	Eddie Robinson	4.00	2.00	1.25
(23)	Hank Ruszkowski	4.00	2.00	1.25
(24)	Pat Seerey	4.00	2.00	1.25
(25)	Bryan Stephens	4.00	2.00	1.25
(26)	Les Willis	4.00	2.00	1.25

1948 Cleveland Indians Picture Pack

For its second year of production as a souvenir sales item, the Indians picture pack utilized the basic format of the previous year: black-and-white photos with a white border and facsimile autograph. Backs were again blank. The 1948 set can be differentiated from the 1947 issue by its size; at 6-1/2" x 9", the '48s are larger by a half-inch horizontally and vertically. The unnumbered pictures are checklisted here in alphabetical order.

		NM	EX	VG
Complete Set (32):		200.00	100.00	60.00
Common Player:		4.00	2.00	1.25
(1)	Gene Bearden	4.00	2.00	1.25
(2)	Johnny Berardino	9.00	4.50	2.75
(3)	Don Black	5.00	2.50	1.50
(4)	Lou Boudreau	12.00	6.00	3.50
(5)	Russ Christopher	4.00	2.00	1.25
(6)	Allie Clark	4.00	2.00	1.25
(7)	Larry Doby	25.00	12.50	7.50
(8)	Hank Edwards	4.00	2.00	1.25
(9)	Bob Feller	30.00	15.00	9.00
(10)	Joe Gordon	4.00	2.00	1.25
(11)	Hank Greenberg (gm, in uniform)	16.00	8.00	4.75
(12)	Hank Greenberg (gm, in civies)	12.00	6.00	3.50
(13)	Steve Gromek	4.00	2.00	1.25
(14)	Mel Harder	4.00	2.00	1.25
(15)	Jim Hegan	4.00	2.00	1.25
(16)	Walt Judnich	4.00	2.00	1.25
(17)	Ken Keltner	5.00	2.50	1.50
(18)	Bob Kennedy	4.00	2.00	1.25
(19)	Ed Klieman	4.00	2.00	1.25
(20)	Bob Lemon	12.00	6.00	3.50
(21)	Al Lopez	12.00	6.00	3.50
(22)	Bill McKechnie	12.00	6.00	3.50
(23)	Dale Mitchell	4.00	2.00	1.25
(24)	Bob Muncrief	4.00	2.00	1.25
(25)	Satchel Paige	35.00	17.50	10.50
(26)	Hal Peck	4.00	2.00	1.25
(27)	Eddie Robinson	4.00	2.00	1.25
(28)	Muddy Ruel	4.00	2.00	1.25
(29)	Joe Tipton	4.00	2.00	1.25
(30)	Thurman Tucker	4.00	2.00	1.25
(31)	Bill Veeck (owner)	9.00	4.50	2.75
(32)	Sam Zoldak	4.00	2.00	1.25

1949 Cleveland Indians Picture Pack

Posed action photos are the focus of this team-issued picture pack. The black-and-white 6-1/2" x 9" photos feature white borders all around and a facsimile autograph on front. Backs are blank. The unnumbered pictures are checklisted here alphabetically.

		NM	EX	VG
Complete Set (31):		200.00	100.00	60.00
Common Player:		4.00	2.00	1.25
(1)	Bob Avila	6.00	3.00	1.75
(2)	Gene Bearden	4.00	2.00	1.25
(3)	Al Benton	4.00	2.00	1.25
(4)	John Berardino	12.00	6.00	3.50
(5)	Ray Boone	6.00	3.00	1.75
(6)	Lou Boudreau	16.00	8.00	4.75
(7)	Allie Clark	4.00	2.00	1.25
(8)	Larry Doby	17.50	8.75	5.25
(9)	Bob Feller	20.00	10.00	6.00
(10)	Mike Garcia	6.00	3.00	1.75
(11)	Joe Gordon	4.00	2.00	1.25
(12)	Hank Greenberg (gm)	12.00	6.00	3.50
(13)	Steve Gromek	4.00	2.00	1.25
(14)	Jim Hegan	4.00	2.00	1.25
(15)	Ken Keltner	4.00	2.00	1.25
(16)	Bob Kennedy	4.00	2.00	1.25
(17)	Bob Lemon	12.00	6.00	3.50
(18)	Dale Mitchell	4.00	2.00	1.25
(19)	Satchel Paige	40.00	20.00	12.00
(20)	Frank Papish	4.00	2.00	1.25
(21)	Hal Peck	4.00	2.00	1.25
(22)	Al Rosen	8.00	4.00	2.50
(23)	Mike Tresh	4.00	2.00	1.25
(24)	Thurman Tucker	4.00	2.00	1.25
(25)	Bill Veeck (owner)	12.00	6.00	3.50
(26)	Mickey Vernon	6.00	3.00	1.75
(27)	Early Wynn	12.00	6.00	3.50
(28)	Sam Zoldak	4.00	2.00	1.25
(29)	Indians coaches (Mel Harder, Steve O'Neill, Bill McKechnie, Muddy Ruel, George Susce)	4.00	2.00	1.25
(30)	Municipal Stadium	6.00	3.00	1.75

1950 Cleveland Indians Photoprints

Without further additions to this checklist, it is impossible to pinpoint the exact year of issue for these novelty cards. They are self-developing photoprints sold in a package which included a negative and a piece of photo-sensative paper which were used to make the 1-7/8" x 2" black-and-white blank-back pictures. Because existing negatives could be used to make many new prints, values for the prints themselves is low. Prices quoted here are for negative/print combinations.

		NM	EX	VG
Common Negative/Print:		125.00	62.50	37.50
(1)	Lou Boudreau	150.00	75.00	45.00
(2)	Allie Clark	125.00	62.50	37.50
(3)	Steve Gromek	125.00	62.50	37.50
(4)	Mickey Vernon	135.00	67.00	40.00

1950 Cleveland Indians Picture Pack

Similar in format to previous years' issues, these 6-1/2" x 9" black-and-white player poses have a white border and facsimile autograph on front. Backs are blank. The unnumbered photos are checklisted here alphabetically.

		NM	EX	VG
Complete Set (26):		150.00	75.00	45.00
Common Player:		4.00	2.00	1.20
(1)	Bobby Avila	5.00	2.50	1.50
(2)	Al Benton	4.00	2.00	1.20
(3)	Ray Boone	5.00	2.50	1.50
(4)	Lou Boudreau	12.00	6.00	3.50
(5)	Allie Clark	4.00	2.00	1.20
(6)	Larry Doby	17.50	8.75	5.25
(7)	Luke Easter	6.00	3.00	1.75
(8)	Bob Feller	20.00	10.00	6.00
(9)	Jess Flores	4.00	2.00	1.20
(10)	Mike Garcia	5.00	2.50	1.50
(11)	Joe Gordon	4.00	2.00	1.20
(12)	Hank Greenberg (gm)	12.00	6.00	3.50
(13)	Steve Gromek	4.00	2.00	1.20
(14)	Jim Hegan	4.00	2.00	1.20
(15)	Bob Kennedy	4.00	2.00	1.20
(16)	Bob Lemon	12.00	6.00	3.50
(17)	Dale Mitchell	4.00	2.00	1.20
(18)	Ray Murray	4.00	2.00	1.20
(19)	Chick Pieretti	4.00	2.00	1.20
(20)	Al Rosen	6.00	3.00	1.75
(21)	Dick Rozek	4.00	2.00	1.20
(22)	Ellis Ryan (owner)	4.00	2.00	1.20
(23)	Thurman Tucker	4.00	2.00	1.20
(24)	Early Wynn	12.00	6.00	3.50
(25)	Sam Zoldak	4.00	2.00	1.20
(26)	Cleveland Municipal Stadium	8.00	4.00	2.50

1955 Cleveland Indians Postcards

These team-issued black-and-white player postcards can be distinguished from earlier and later issues by the uniformity of the photos. All pictures are head-and-shoulder portraits against a white background. Players are wearing caps with Chief Wahoo inside a "C". Some cards are found with a notation on back, "Pub. by Ed Wood, Forestville, Calif." Cards were sent out to fans by the team and/or player and are usually found with an autograph on front.

		NM	EX	VG
Complete Set (29):		400.00	200.00	120.00
Common Player:		12.00	6.00	3.50
(1)	Bob Avila	15.00	7.50	4.50
(2)	Tony Cuccinello	12.00	6.00	3.50
(3)	Bud Daley	12.00	6.00	3.50
(4)	Sam Dente	12.00	6.00	3.50
(5)	Larry Doby	18.00	9.00	5.50
(6)	Bob Feller	30.00	15.00	9.00
(7)	Hank Foiles	12.00	6.00	3.50
(8)	Mike Garcia	12.00	6.00	3.50
(9)	Mel Harder	12.00	6.00	3.50
(10)	Jim Hegan	12.00	6.00	3.50
(11)	Art Houtteman	12.00	6.00	3.50
(12)	Ralph Kiner	20.00	10.00	6.00
(13)	Red Kress	12.00	6.00	3.50
(14)	Ken Kuhn	12.00	6.00	3.50
(15)	Bob Lemon	18.00	9.00	5.50
(16)	Bill Lobe	12.00	6.00	3.50
(17)	Dale Mitchell	12.00	6.00	3.50
(18)	Don Mossi	12.00	6.00	3.50
(19)	Hal Naragon	12.00	6.00	3.50
(20)	Ray Narleski	12.00	6.00	3.50
(21)	Dave Philley	12.00	6.00	3.50
(22)	Al Rosen	15.00	7.50	4.50
(23)	Herb Score	24.00	12.00	7.25
(24)	Al Smith	12.00	6.00	3.50
(25)	George Strickland	12.00	6.00	3.50
(26)	Vic Wertz	12.00	6.00	3.50
(27)	Wally Westlake	12.00	6.00	3.50
(28)	Bill Wright	12.00	6.00	3.50
(29)	Early Wynn	18.00	9.00	5.50

1963-69 Cleveland Indians Postcards

These black-and-white glossy postcards were issued by the team for player use in responding to fan mail. The example pictured here was autographed after issue. The 3-1/2" x 5-3/8" cards have no player identification on front or back. All of the player poses are in the team's sleeveless uniform which was used between 1963-69. It is otherwise impossible to differentiate year of issue. Multiple player listings in the checklist here indicate known pose variations. This list may be incomplete.

		NM	EX	VG
Common Player:		5.00	2.50	1.50
(1)	Ted Abernathy	5.00	2.50	1.50
(2)	Ted Abernathy	5.00	2.50	1.50
(3)	Joe Adcock	7.50	3.75	2.25
(4)	Joe Adcock	7.50	3.75	2.25
(5)	Joe Adcock	7.50	3.75	2.25
(6)	Bob Allen	5.00	2.50	1.50
(7)	Bob Allen	5.00	2.50	1.50
(8)	Max Alvis	5.00	2.50	1.50
(9)	Max Alvis	5.00	2.50	1.50
(10)	Max Alvis	5.00	2.50	1.50
(11)	Joe Azcue	5.00	2.50	1.50
(12)	Joe Azcue	5.00	2.50	1.50
(13)	Steve Bailey	5.00	2.50	1.50
(14)	Frank Baker	5.00	2.50	1.50
(15)	Gus Bell	6.00	3.00	1.75
(16)	Gus Bell	6.00	3.00	1.75
(17)	Buddy Booker	5.00	2.50	1.50
(18)	Larry Brown	5.00	2.50	1.50
(19)	Larry Brown	5.00	2.50	1.50
(20)	Larry Brown	5.00	2.50	1.50
(21)	Clay Bryant	5.00	2.50	1.50
(22)	Larry Burchart	5.00	2.50	1.50
(23)	Jose Cardenal	5.00	2.50	1.50
(24)	Jose Cardenal	5.00	2.50	1.50
(25)	Camilo Carreon	5.00	2.50	1.50
(26)	Bob Chance	5.00	2.50	1.50
(27)	Rocky Colavito	10.00	5.00	3.00
(28)	Rocky Colavito	10.00	5.00	3.00
(29)	Rocky Colavito	10.00	5.00	3.00
(30)	Rocky Colavito	10.00	5.00	3.00
(31)	Rocky Colavito	10.00	5.00	3.00
(32)	Ed Connolly	5.00	2.50	1.50
(33)	Del Crandall	5.00	2.50	1.50
(34)	George Culver	5.00	2.50	1.50
(35)	Alvin Dark	7.50	3.75	2.25
(36)	Alvin Dark	7.50	3.75	2.25
(37)	Vic Davalillo	5.00	2.50	1.50
(38)	Vic Davalillo	5.00	2.50	1.50
(39)	Vic Davalillo	5.00	2.50	1.50
(40)	Vic Davalillo	5.00	2.50	1.50
(41)	Bill Davis	5.00	2.50	1.50
(42)	Bill Davis	5.00	2.50	1.50
(43)	Don Demeter	5.00	2.50	1.50
(44)	Paul Dicken	5.00	2.50	1.50
(45)	Dick Donovan	5.00	2.50	1.50
(46)	Luke Easter	6.00	3.00	1.75
(47)	Dick Ellsworth	5.00	2.50	1.50
(48)	Eddie Fisher	5.00	2.50	1.50
(49)	Ray Fosse	5.00	2.50	1.50
(50)	Ray Fosse	5.00	2.50	1.50
(51)	Tito Francona	5.00	2.50	1.50
(52)	Vern Fuller	5.00	2.50	1.50
(53)	Vern Fuller	5.00	2.50	1.50
(54)	Vern Fuller	5.00	2.50	1.50
(55)	Jim Gentile	5.00	2.50	1.50
(56)	Gus Gil	5.00	2.50	1.50
(57)	Pedro Gonzalez	5.00	2.50	1.50
(58)	Mudcat Grant	5.00	2.50	1.50
(59)	Gene Green	5.00	2.50	1.50
(60)	Jimmie Hall	5.00	2.50	1.50
(61)	Jack Hamilton	5.00	2.50	1.50
(62)	Steve Hargan	5.00	2.50	1.50
(63)	Steve Hargan	5.00	2.50	1.50
(64)	Steve Hargan	5.00	2.50	1.50
(65)	Steve Hargan	5.00	2.50	1.50
(66)	Steve Hargan	5.00	2.50	1.50
(67)	Tommy Harper	5.00	2.50	1.50
(68)	Ken Harrelson	6.00	3.00	1.75
(69)	Billy Harris	5.00	2.50	1.50
(70)	Mike Hedlund	5.00	2.50	1.50
(71)	Jack Heidemann	5.00	2.50	1.50
(72)	Woodie Held	5.00	2.50	1.50
(73)	Solly Hemus	5.00	2.50	1.50
(74)	Chuck Hinton	5.00	2.50	1.50
(75)	Tony Horton	5.00	2.50	1.50

		NM	EX	VG
(76)	Dick Howser (ready to throw)	5.00	2.50	1.50
(77)	Dick Howser	5.00	2.50	1.50
(78)	Tommy John	7.50	3.75	2.25
(79)	Lou Johnson	5.00	2.50	1.50
(80)	Tom Kelley	5.00	2.50	1.50
(81)	Willie Kirkland	5.00	2.50	1.50
(82)	Lou Klimchock	5.00	2.50	1.50
(83)	Jack Kralick (looking for sign)	5.00	2.50	1.50
(84)	Jack Kralick	5.00	2.50	1.50
(85)	Gary Kroll	5.00	2.50	1.50
(86)	Hal Kurtz	5.00	2.50	1.50
(87)	Barry Latman	5.00	2.50	1.50
(88)	Jim Landis	5.00	2.50	1.50
(89)	Ron Law	5.00	2.50	1.50
(90)	Eddie Leon	5.00	2.50	1.50
(91)	Johnny Lipon	5.00	2.50	1.50
(92)	Al Luplow	5.00	2.50	1.50
(93)	Tony Martinez	5.00	2.50	1.50
(94)	Tony Martinez	5.00	2.50	1.50
(95)	Lee Maye	5.00	2.50	1.50
(96)	Sam McDowell	6.00	3.00	1.75
(97)	Sam McDowell	6.00	3.00	1.75
(98)	Sam McDowell	6.00	3.00	1.75
(99)	Sam McDowell	6.00	3.00	1.75
(100)	Don McMahon	5.00	2.50	1.50
(101)	Don McMahon	5.00	2.50	1.50
(102)	Billy Moran	5.00	2.50	1.50
(103)	Pat Mullin	5.00	2.50	1.50
(104)	Dave Nelson	5.00	2.50	1.50
(105)	Dave Nelson	5.00	2.50	1.50
(106)	Ron Nischwitz	5.00	2.50	1.50
(107)	John O'Donoghue	5.00	2.50	1.50
(108)	Reggie Otero	5.00	2.50	1.50
(109)	Mike Paul	5.00	2.50	1.50
(110)	Mike Paul	5.00	2.50	1.50
(111)	Orlando Pena	5.00	2.50	1.50
(112)	Cap Peterson	5.00	2.50	1.50
(113)	Horacio Pina	5.00	2.50	1.50
(114)	Juan Pizzaro	5.00	2.50	1.50
(115)	Dick Radatz	5.00	2.50	1.50
(116)	Pedro Ramos	5.00	2.50	1.50
(117)	Del Rice	5.00	2.50	1.50
(118)	Jim Rittwage	5.00	2.50	1.50
(119)	Billy Rohr	5.00	2.50	1.50
(120)	John Romano	5.00	2.50	1.50
(121)	John Romano	5.00	2.50	1.50
(122)	Vicente Romo	5.00	2.50	1.50
(123)	Phil Roof	5.00	2.50	1.50
(124)	Chico Salmon	5.00	2.50	1.50
(125)	Chico Salmon	5.00	2.50	1.50
(126)	John Sanford	5.00	2.50	1.50
(127)	Richie Scheinblum	5.00	2.50	1.50
(128)	Richie Scheinblum	5.00	2.50	1.50
(129)	Sonny Siebert	5.00	2.50	1.50
(130)	Sonny Siebert	5.00	2.50	1.50
(131)	Sonny Siebert	5.00	2.50	1.50
(132)	Sonny Siebert	5.00	2.50	1.50
(133)	Sonny Siebert	5.00	2.50	1.50
(134)	Duke Sims	5.00	2.50	1.50
(135)	Duke Sims	5.00	2.50	1.50
(136)	Duke Sims	5.00	2.50	1.50
(137)	Al Smith	5.00	2.50	1.50
(138)	Willie Smith	5.00	2.50	1.50
(139)	Russ Snyder	5.00	2.50	1.50
(140)	Lee Stange	5.00	2.50	1.50
(141)	George Strickland	5.00	2.50	1.50
(142)	George Strickland	5.00	2.50	1.50
(143)	Ken Suarez	5.00	2.50	1.50
(144)	Birdie Tebbetts	5.00	2.50	1.50
(145)	Birdie Tebbetts	5.00	2.50	1.50
(146)	Ralph Terry	5.00	2.50	1.50
(147)	Luis Tiant	7.50	3.75	2.25
(148)	Luis Tiant	7.50	3.75	2.25
(149)	Luis Tiant	7.50	3.75	2.25
(150)	Elmer Valo	5.00	2.50	1.50
(151)	Zoilo Versalles	5.00	2.50	1.50
(152)	Jose Vidal	5.00	2.50	1.50
(153)	Leon Wagner	7.50	3.75	2.25
(154)	Jerry Walker	5.00	2.50	1.50
(155)	Floyd Weaver	5.00	2.50	1.50
(156)	Fred Whitfield	5.00	2.50	1.50
(157)	Fred Whitfield	5.00	2.50	1.50
(158)	Stan Williams	5.00	2.50	1.50
(159)	Early Wynn	12.00	6.00	3.50

1969 Cleveland Indians Photo Pack

This set of color player photos features player poses taken at spring training. The blank-back pictures measure 6-1/4" x 8-3/4" and have a white border all around. The player name is printed in the bottom border. This checklist may not be complete and is arranged alphabetically.

		NM	EX	VG
Complete Set (10):		40.00	20.00	12.00
Common Player:		5.00	2.50	1.50
(1)	Larry Brown	5.00	2.50	1.50
(2)	Larry Burchart	5.00	2.50	1.50
(3)	Jose Cardenal	5.00	2.50	1.50
(4)	Ray Fosse	5.00	2.50	1.50
(5)	Ken "Hawk" Harrelson	7.50	3.75	2.25
(6)	Lee Maye	5.00	2.50	1.50
(7)	Sam McDowell	7.50	3.75	2.25
(8)	Richie Scheinblum	5.00	2.50	1.50
(9)	Zoilo Versalles	5.00	2.50	1.50
(10)	Stan Williams	5.00	2.50	1.50

1971 Cleveland Indians Photo Packs

These color player photos were issued in two six-picture sets. The 7" x 9" pictures have color poses bordered in white with the player name and team nickname printed at bottom. Backs are blank. Each set came in a cellophane bag with a paper checklist slip inside.

		NM	EX	VG
Complete Set (12):		10.00	5.00	3.00
Common Player:		1.00	.50	.30
(1)	Buddy Bradford	1.00	.50	.30
(2)	Alvin Dark	1.50	.70	.45
(3)	Steve Dunning	1.00	.50	.30
(4)	Ray Fosse	1.00	.50	.30
(5)	Steve Hargan	1.00	.50	.30
(6)	Ken Harrelson	1.00	.50	.30
(7)	Chuck Hinton	1.00	.50	.30
(8)	Ray Lamb	1.00	.50	.30
(9)	Sam McDowell	1.50	.70	.45
(10)	Vada Pinson	1.50	.70	.45
(11)	Ken Suarez	1.00	.50	.30
(12)	Ted Uhlaender	1.00	.50	.30

1973-74 Cleveland Indians Postcards - Type 1

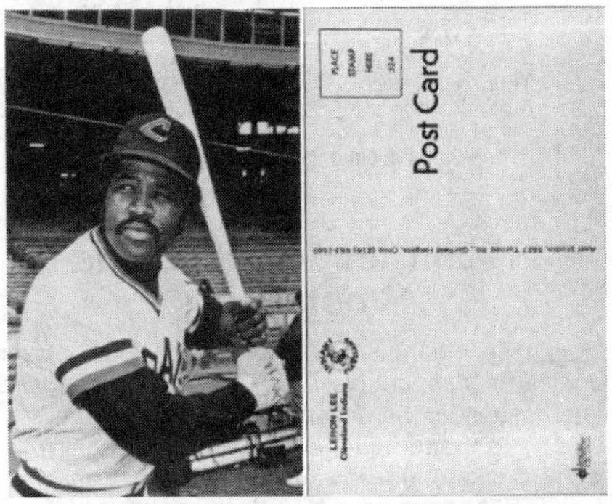

The first of several team-issued sets of color player postcards, Type 1s share the same basic format used in successive issues. The debut issue can be identified by the black-and-white back design, with a single vertical center line of the address and phone number for Axel Studios and, on most cards, a three-digit card number in the stamp box. Cards are numbered from 319-330 and 332-347; cards listed here after #347 have been arbitrarily assigned a number continuing the sequence. Fronts of the 3-7/16" x 5-7/16" cards are borderless poses with all players (except Fred Beene) wearing white uniforms. According to the player selection, cards continued to be issued into the 1974 season.

		NM	EX	VG
Complete Set (34):		90.00	45.00	27.00
Common Player:		4.00	2.00	1.25
319	Jim Perry	5.50	2.75	1.75
320	Fritz Peterson	4.00	2.00	1.25
321	Steve Kline	4.00	2.00	1.25
322	Fred Beene	4.00	2.00	1.25
323	Tom Buskey	4.00	2.00	1.25
324	Leron Lee	4.00	2.00	1.25
325	Clay Bryant	4.00	2.00	1.25
326	Larry Doby	9.00	4.50	2.75
327	Tony Pacheco	4.00	2.00	1.25
328	Ken Sanders	4.00	2.00	1.25
329	Bob Johnson	4.00	2.00	1.25
330	Ossie Blanco	4.00	2.00	1.25
332	Dwain Anderson	4.00	2.00	1.25
333	John Ellis	4.00	2.00	1.25
334	Charlie Spikes	4.00	2.00	1.25
335	Tom Hilgendorf	4.00	2.00	1.25
336	Frank Duffy	4.00	2.00	1.25
337	Milt Wilcox	4.00	2.00	1.25
338	Dick Bosman	4.00	2.00	1.25
339	Dave Duncan	4.00	2.00	1.25
340	Ken Aspromonte	4.00	2.00	1.25
341	Gaylord Perry	10.00	5.00	3.00
342	Rusty Torres	4.00	2.00	1.25
343	Jack Brohamer	4.00	2.00	1.25
344	Oscar Gamble	4.00	2.00	1.25
345	Buddy Bell	7.50	3.75	2.25
346	George Hendrick	5.50	2.75	1.75
347	John Lowenstein	4.00	2.00	1.25
(348)	Luis Alvardo	4.00	2.00	1.25
(349)	Steve Arlin	4.00	2.00	1.25
(350)	Alan Ashby	4.00	2.00	1.25
(351)	Ed Crosby	4.00	2.00	1.25
(352)	Bruce Ellingsen	4.00	2.00	1.25
(353)	Joe Lis	4.00	2.00	1.25

1973-74 Cleveland Indians Postcards - Type 2

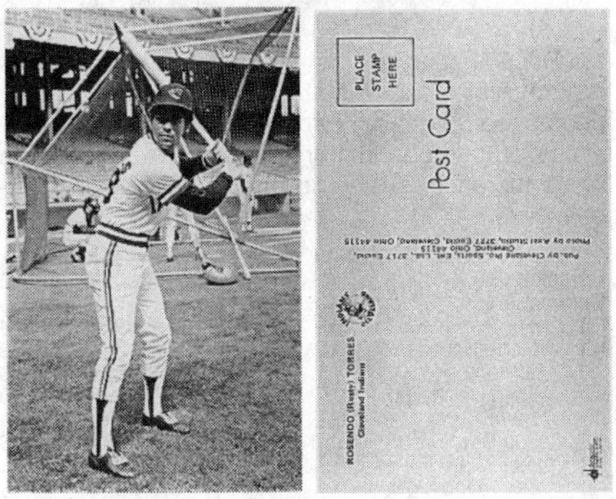

The Indians began a second series of color player postcards during the 1973 season. The 3-1/2" x 5-1/2" cards are similar in format to the Type 1 cards with borderless color poses on front and black-and-white backs. The Type 2 issue has no card number in the stamp box, however, and has three lines of type at center identifying the photographer and publisher. Players on Type 2 cards were active with the Indians in the 1973 and/or 1974 seasons.

		NM	EX	VG
Complete Set (31):		95.00	47.00	28.00
Common Player:		4.00	2.00	1.25
(1)	Ken Aspromonte	4.00	2.00	1.25
(2)	Buddy Bell	6.00	3.00	1.75
(3)	Dick Bosman	4.00	2.00	1.25
(4)	Jack Brohamer	4.00	2.00	1.25
(5a)	Leo Cardenas (Rusty Torres back)	4.00	2.00	1.25
(5b)	Leo Cardenas (correct back)	4.00	2.00	1.25
(6)	Chris Chambliss	4.00	2.00	1.25
(7)	Rocky Colavito	10.00	5.00	3.00
(8)	Frank Duffy	4.00	2.00	1.25
(9)	Dave Duncan	4.00	2.00	1.25
(10)	John Ellis	4.00	2.00	1.25
(11)	Ed Farmer	4.00	2.00	1.25
(12)	Oscar Gamble	4.00	2.00	1.25
(13)	George Hendrick	5.50	2.75	1.75
(14)	Tom Hilgendorf	4.00	2.00	1.25
(15)	Jerry Johnson	4.00	2.00	1.25
(16)	Ray Lamb	4.00	2.00	1.25
(17)	Ron Lolich	6.00	3.00	1.75
(18)	John Lowenstein	4.00	2.00	1.25
(19)	Joe Lutz	4.00	2.00	1.25
(20)	Steve Mingori	6.00	3.00	1.75
(21)	Gaylord Perry	10.00	5.00	3.00
(22)	Tom Ragland	4.00	2.00	1.25
(23)	Warren Spahn	10.00	5.00	3.00
(24)	Charlie Spikes	4.00	2.00	1.25
(25)	Brent Strom	4.00	2.00	1.25
(26)	Dick Tidrow	4.00	2.00	1.25
(27a)	Rusty Torres (Leo Cardenas back)	4.00	2.00	1.25
(27b)	Rusty Torres (correct back)	4.00	2.00	1.25
(28)	Milt Wilcox	4.00	2.00	1.25
(29)	Walt Williams	4.00	2.00	1.25

1975 Cleveland Indians Postcards

Players in red jerseys, white pants and blue caps distinguish this issue from earlier and later team issues. Fronts feature borderless posed action photos with no identification. Backs have player identification along with standard postcard indicia. Size is 3-1/2" x 5-1/2". The unnumbered cards are checklisted there alphabetically. The cards were printed by Calo, Crane Howard.

	NM	EX	VG
Complete Set (25):	65.00	32.00	19.50
Common Player:	3.00	1.50	.90
(1) Alan Ashby	3.00	1.50	.90
(2) Fred Beene	3.00	1.50	.90
(3) Buddy Bell	3.50	1.75	1.00
(4) Ken Berry	3.00	1.50	.90
(5) Dick Bosman	3.00	1.50	.90
(6) Jack Brohamer	3.00	1.50	.90
(7) Tom Buskey	3.00	1.50	.90
(8) Rico Carty	4.50	2.25	1.25
(9) Ed Crosby	3.00	1.50	.90
(10) Frank Duffy	3.00	1.50	.90
(11) John Ellis	3.00	1.50	.90
(12) Oscar Gamble	3.00	1.50	.90
(13) George Hendrick	3.00	1.50	.90
(14) Don Hood	3.00	1.50	.90
(15) Jim Kern	3.00	1.50	.90
(16) Dave LaRoche	3.00	1.50	.90
(17) Leron Lee	3.00	1.50	.90
(18) John Lowenstein	3.00	1.50	.90
(19) Gaylord Perry	7.50	3.75	2.25
(20) Jim Perry	3.50	1.75	1.00
(21) Fritz Peterson	3.00	1.50	.90
(22) Boog Powell	5.00	2.50	1.50
(23) Frank Robinson	6.00	3.00	1.75
(24) Charlie Spikes	3.00	1.50	.90
(25) Manager and coaches	3.00	1.50	.90

1976 Cleveland Indians Postcards

Axel Studios is credited on the postcard back for the production of this set. Along with player identification on back there is a stamp box which carries a card number, prefixed with a "P". Fronts are borderless color photos, either portraits or posed action shots, with the players almost all wearing blue jerseys and blue caps with red bills. Hood is pictured in a red shirt.

	NM	EX	VG
Complete Set (13):	45.00	22.00	13.00
Common Player:	3.00	1.50	.90
1548 Indian Coaches	3.00	1.50	.90
1549 Larvell Blanks	3.00	1.50	.90
1550 Dennis Eckersley	10.00	5.00	3.00
1551 Ray Fosse	3.00	1.50	.90
1552 Boog Powell	7.50	3.75	2.25
1553 Ron Pruitt	3.00	1.50	.90
1554 Rick Waits	3.00	1.50	.90
1555 Don Hood	3.00	1.50	.90
1556 Fritz Peterson	3.00	1.50	.90
1557 Dave LaRoche	3.00	1.50	.90
1558 Pat Dobson	3.00	1.50	.90
1559 Stan Thomas	3.00	1.50	.90
1560 Tom Buskey	3.00	1.50	.90

1977 Cleveland Indians Postcards - b/w

A separate series of black-and-white player postcards marked the final year of team-issued postcards by the Indians. Cards are in standard 3-1/2" x 5-1/2" format with a glossy photo on front. Backs have a printed "PHOTO POST CARD" notation at top-left, and "Kodak Paper" on the stamp box. The unnumbered cards are checklisted here alphabetically.

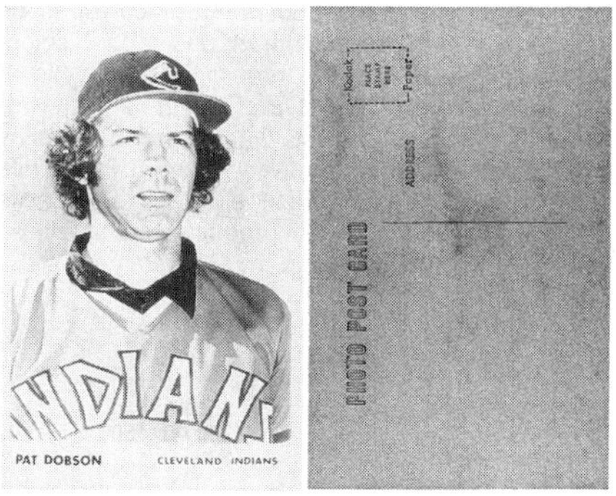

	NM	EX	VG
Complete Set (25):	40.00	20.00	12.00
Common Player:	1.50	.75	.45
(1) Jim Bibby	1.50	.75	.45
(2) Larvell Blanks	1.50	.75	.45
(3) Bruce Bochte	1.50	.75	.45
(4) Tom Buskey	1.50	.75	.45
(5) Rico Carty	2.00	1.00	.60
(6) Rocky Colavito	7.50	3.75	2.25
(7) Pat Dobson	1.50	.75	.45
(8) Frank Duffy	1.50	.75	.45
(9) Dennis Eckersley	6.00	3.00	1.75
(10) Al Fitzmorris	1.50	.75	.45
(11) Ray Fosse	1.50	.75	.45
(12) Fred Kendall	1.50	.75	.45
(13) Jim Kern	1.50	.75	.45
(14) Dave LaRoche	1.50	.75	.45
(15) John Lowenstein	1.50	.75	.45
(16) Rick Manning	1.50	.75	.45
(17) Bill Melton	1.50	.75	.45
(18) Sid Monge	1.50	.75	.45
(19) Jim Norris	1.50	.75	.45
(20) Joe Nossek	1.50	.75	.45
(21) Ron Pruitt	1.50	.75	.45
(22) Frank Robinson	4.00	2.00	1.25
(23) Andre Thornton	2.00	1.00	.60
(24) Jeff Torborg	1.50	.75	.45
(25) Rick Waits	1.50	.75	.45

1977 Cleveland Indians Postcards - color

The "K" for Kodachrome mark on back identifies the 1977 color team issued postcards as does the number centered at bottom on back. Player identification and a team logo also appear on back along with postcard indicia. Fronts are borderless color photos. Size is the standard 3-1/2" x 5-1/2".

	NM	EX	VG
Complete Set (7):	18.00	9.00	5.50
Common Player:	3.00	1.50	.90
144497 Eric Raich	3.00	1.50	.90
144498 Jackie Brown	3.00	1.50	.90
144499 Rick Manning	3.00	1.50	.90
144500 Jim Bibby	3.00	1.50	.90
144501 Roric Harrison	3.00	1.50	.90
144502 Dennis Eckersley	9.00	4.50	2.75
144503 Duane Kuiper	3.00	1.50	.90

1978 Cleveland Indians Photocards

From the late 1970s through the mid 1980s the Cleveland Indians issued through their souvenir outlets sets of player photo cards. In postcard size (3-1/2" x 5-1/2"), the cards share a basic format of framing black-and-white portrait photos in white borders with the name, team and, sometimes, position at bottom. Backs are blank. The unnumbered cards are checklisted here alphabetically.

	NM	EX	VG
Complete Set (36):	15.00	7.50	4.50
Common Player:	.50	.25	.15
(1) Gary Alexander	.50	.25	.15
(2) Buddy Bell	.75	.40	.25
(3) Larvell Blanks	.50	.25	.15
(4) Wayne Cage	.50	.25	.15
(5) Bernie Carbo	.50	.25	.15
(6) David Clyde	.50	.25	.15
(7) Rocky Colavito	4.00	2.00	1.25
(8) Ted Cox	.50	.25	.15
(9) Paul Dade	.50	.25	.15
(10) Bo Diaz	.50	.25	.15
(11) Dave Duncan	.50	.25	.15
(12) Al Fitzmorris	.50	.25	.15
(13) Dave Freisleben	.50	.25	.15
(14) Wayne Garland	.50	.25	.15
(15) Johnny Grubb	.50	.25	.15
(16) Harvey Haddix	.50	.25	.15
(17) Ron Hassey	.50	.25	.15
(18) Don Hood	.50	.25	.15
(19) Willie Horton	.50	.25	.15
(20) Jim Kern	.50	.25	.15
(21) Dennis Kinney	.50	.25	.15
(22) Duane Kuiper	.50	.25	.15
(23) Rick Manning	.50	.25	.15
(24) Sid Monge	.50	.25	.15
(25) Jim Norris	.50	.25	.15
(26) Joe Nossek	.50	.25	.15
(27) Mike Paxton	.50	.25	.15
(28) Ron Pruitt	.50	.25	.15
(29) Paul Reuschel	.50	.25	.15
(30) Horace Speed	.50	.25	.15
(31) Dan Spillner	.50	.25	.15
(32) Andre Thornton	.75	.40	.25
(33) Jeff Torborg	.50	.25	.15
(34) Tom Veryzer	.50	.25	.15
(35) Rick Waits	.50	.25	.15
(36) Rick Wise	.50	.25	.15

1979 Cleveland Indians Photocards

A simple format was once again used for the team's photo card set. The black-and-white, 3-1/2" x 5-1/2" cards have a player portrait at center, with his name and team in capital letters at bottom. Backs are blank. The cards were sold at team souvenir outlets. The unnumbered cards are checklisted here alphabetically.

	NM	EX	VG
Complete Set (36):	15.00	7.50	4.50
Common Player:	.50	.25	.15
(1) Gary Alexander	.50	.25	.15
(2) Dell Alston	.50	.25	.15
(3) Larry Anderson	.50	.25	.15
(4) Len Barker	.50	.25	.15
(5) Bobby Bonds	.75	.40	.25
(6) Wayne Cage	.50	.25	.15
(7) David Clyde	.50	.25	.15
(8) Victor Cruz	.50	.25	.15
(9) Ted Cox	.50	.25	.15
(10) Paul Dade	.50	.25	.15
(11) Bo Diaz	.50	.25	.15
(12) Dave Duncan	.50	.25	.15
(13) Dave Garcia	.50	.25	.15
(14) Wayne Garland	.50	.25	.15
(15) Mike Hargrove	.50	.25	.15
(16) Toby Harrah	.50	.25	.15
(17) Chuck Hartenstein	.50	.25	.15
(18) Don Hood	.50	.25	.15
(19) Cliff Johnson	.50	.25	.15
(20) Duane Kuiper	.50	.25	.15
(21) Rick Manning	.50	.25	.15
(22) Sid Monge	.50	.25	.15
(23) Jim Norris	.50	.25	.15
(24) Joe Nossek	.50	.25	.15
(25) Mike Paxton	.50	.25	.15
(26) Ron Pruitt	.50	.25	.15
(27) Paul Reuschel	.50	.25	.15
(28) Dave Rosello	.50	.25	.15
(29) Horace Speed	.50	.25	.15
(30) Dan Spillner	.50	.25	.15
(31) Andre Thornton	.75	.40	.25
(32) Jeff Torborg	.50	.25	.15
(33) Tom Veryzer	.50	.25	.15

(34)	Rick Waits	.50	.25	.15
(35)	Eric Wilkins	.50	.25	.15
(36)	Rick Wise	.50	.25	.15

1980 Cleveland Indians Photocards

In format similar to past and future issues, the Indians issued this set of player photo cards in 3-1/2" x 5-1/2" black-and-white, blank-back format. Player and team names are in capital letters in the white border at bottom. All photos are posed portraits, with players in dark caps with black "C", and white jerseys with triple stripes at the V-neck. The unnumbered cards are checklisted here in alphabetical order.

		NM	EX	VG
Complete Set (37):		14.00	10.50	5.50
Common Player:		.50	.25	.15
(1)	Gary Alexander	.50	.25	.15
(2)	Dell Alston	.50	.25	.15
(3)	Alan Bannister	.50	.25	.15
(4)	Len Barker	.50	.25	.15
(5)	Jack Brohamer	.50	.25	.15
(6)	Joe Charboneau	1.00	.50	.30
(7)	Victor Cruz	.50	.25	.15
(8)	John Denny	.50	.25	.15
(9)	Bo Diaz	.50	.25	.15
(10)	Miguel Dilone	.50	.25	.15
(11)	Dave Duncan	.50	.25	.15
(12)	Jerry Dybzinski	.50	.25	.15
(13)	Dave Garcia	.50	.25	.15
(14)	Wayne Garland	.50	.25	.15
(15)	Gary Gray	.50	.25	.15
(16)	Ross Grimsley	.50	.25	.15
(17)	Mike Hargrove	.65	.35	.20
(18)	Toby Harrah	.65	.35	.20
(19)	Ron Hassey	.50	.25	.15
(20)	Cliff Johnson	.50	.25	.15
(21)	Duane Kuiper	.50	.25	.15
(22)	Rick Manning	.50	.25	.15
(23)	Tom McCraw	.50	.25	.15
(24)	Sid Monge	.50	.25	.15
(25)	Andres Mora	.50	.25	.15
(26)	Joe Nossek	.50	.25	.15
(27)	Jorge Orta	.50	.25	.15
(28)	Bob Owchinko	.50	.25	.15
(29)	Ron Pruitt	.50	.25	.15
(30)	Dave Rosello	.50	.25	.15
(31)	Dennis Sommers	.50	.25	.15
(32)	Dan Spillner	.50	.25	.15
(33)	Mike Stanton	.50	.25	.15
(34)	Andre Thornton	.75	.40	.25
(35)	Tom Veryzer	.50	.25	.15
(36)	Rick Waits	.50	.25	.15
(37)	Sandy Wihtol	.50	.25	.15

1911 George Close Candy Co. (E94)

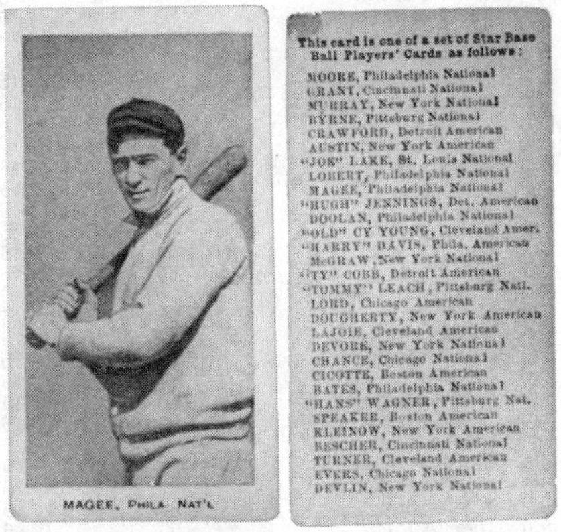

This 1911 issue is nearly identical to several contemporary candy and caramel sets. Issued by the George Close Candy Co. of Cambridge, Mass., many of the cards contain no indication of who issued them. The 1-1/2" x 2-3/4" cards feature tinted black-and-white player photos. Each card can be found with any of seven different background colors (blue, gold, green, olive, red, violet and yellow). Backs carry a set checklist. Eight different back variations are known to exist. One variation contains just the checklist without any advertising, while seven other variations include overprinted backs advertising various candy products manufactured by the George Close Company. The set carries the ACC designation E94.

		NM	EX	VG
Complete Set (30):		20000.	10000.	6000.
Common Player:		300.00	150.00	90.00
(1)	Jimmy Austin	300.00	150.00	90.00
(2)	Johnny Bates	300.00	150.00	90.00
(3)	Bob Bescher	300.00	150.00	90.00
(4)	Bobby Byrne	300.00	150.00	90.00
(5)	Frank Chance	700.00	350.00	210.00
(6)	Ed Cicotte	500.00	250.00	150.00
(7)	Ty Cobb	7200.	3600.	2150.
(8)	Sam Crawford	700.00	350.00	210.00
(9)	Harry Davis	300.00	150.00	90.00
(10)	Art Devlin	300.00	150.00	90.00
(11)	Josh Devore	300.00	150.00	90.00
(12)	Mickey Doolan	300.00	150.00	90.00
(13)	Patsy Dougherty	300.00	150.00	90.00
(14)	Johnny Evers	700.00	350.00	210.00
(15)	Eddie Grant	300.00	150.00	90.00
(16)	Hugh Jennings	700.00	350.00	210.00
(17)	Red Kleinow	300.00	150.00	90.00
(18)	Joe Lake	300.00	150.00	90.00
(19)	Nap Lajoie	800.00	400.00	240.00
(20)	Tommy Leach	300.00	150.00	90.00
(21)	Hans Lobert	300.00	150.00	90.00
(22)	Harry Lord	300.00	150.00	90.00
(23)	Sherry Magee	300.00	150.00	90.00
(24)	John McGraw	700.00	350.00	210.00
(25)	Earl Moore	300.00	150.00	90.00
(26)	Red Murray	300.00	150.00	90.00
(27)	Tris Speaker	1100.	550.00	330.00
(28)	Terry Turner	300.00	150.00	90.00
(29)	Honus Wagner	2400.	1200.	720.00
(30)	Cy Young	1500.	750.00	450.00

1961 Cloverleaf Dairy Minnesota Twins

These unnumbered cards pictures members of the debut Minnesota Twins team. Measuring approximately 3-3/4" x 7-3/4", the cards were actually side panels from Cloverleaf Milk cartons. Complete cartons are valued at about twice the prices listed. The card includes a black-and-white player photo with name, position, personal data and year-by-year statistics appearing below. Green graphics highlight the panels. Some pictures were reissued in 1962 but can be differentiated from the 1961 set by the stats at bottom.

		NM	EX	VG
Complete Set (17):		675.00	335.00	200.00
Common Player:		40.00	20.00	12.00
(1)	Earl Battey	40.00	20.00	12.00
(2)	Reno Bertoia	40.00	20.00	12.00
(3)	Billy Gardner	40.00	20.00	12.00
(4)	Paul Giel	40.00	20.00	12.00
(5)	Lenny Green	40.00	20.00	12.00
(6)	Jim Kaat	65.00	32.00	19.50
(7)	Jack Kralick	40.00	20.00	12.00
(8)	Don Lee	40.00	20.00	12.00
(9)	Jim Lemon	40.00	20.00	12.00
(10)	Billy Martin	80.00	40.00	24.00
(11)	Don Mincher	40.00	20.00	12.00
(12)	Camilo Pascual	50.00	25.00	15.00
(13)	Pedro Ramos	40.00	20.00	12.00
(14)	Chuck Stobbs	40.00	20.00	12.00
(15)	Bill Tuttle	40.00	20.00	12.00
(16)	Jose Valdivielso	40.00	20.00	12.00
(17)	Zoilo Versalles	50.00	25.00	15.00

1962 Cloverleaf Dairy Minnesota Twins

These unnumbered cards picture members of the Minnesota Twins. Measuring approximately 3-3/4" x 7-3/4", the cards were actually side panels from Cloverleaf Milk cartons. Complete cartons are valued at about twice the prices listed. The card includes a black-and-white player photo with name, position, personal data and year-by-year statistics appearing below. Green graphics highlight the panels. Some pictures were reissued in 1962 but can be differentiated from the 1961 set by the stats at bottom.

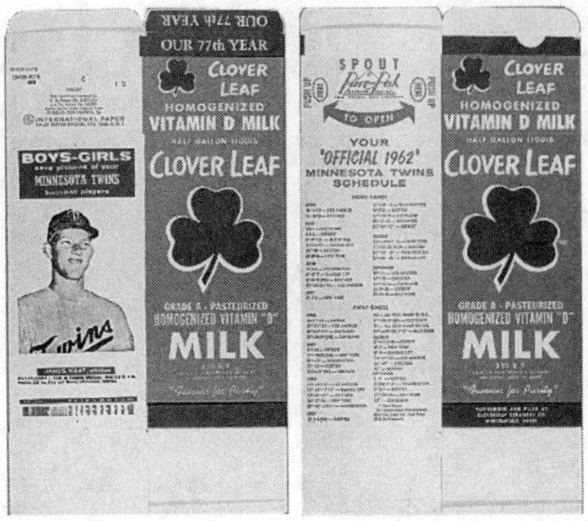

		NM	EX	VG
Complete Set (24):		835.00	415.00	250.00
Common Player:		40.00	20.00	12.00
(1)	Bernie Allen	40.00	20.00	12.00
(2)	George Banks	40.00	20.00	12.00
(3)	Earl Battey	40.00	20.00	12.00
(4)	Joe Bonikowski	40.00	20.00	12.00
(5)	John Goryl	40.00	20.00	12.00
(6)	Lenny Green	40.00	20.00	12.00
(7)	Jim Kaat	65.00	32.00	19.50
(8)	Jack Kralick	40.00	20.00	12.00
(9)	Jim Lemon	40.00	20.00	12.00
(10)	Georges Maranda	40.00	20.00	12.00
(11)	Orlando Martinez	40.00	20.00	12.00
(12)	Don Mincher	40.00	20.00	12.00
(13)	Ray Moore	40.00	20.00	12.00
(14)	Hal Naragon	40.00	20.00	12.00
(15)	Camilo Pascual	50.00	25.00	15.00
(16)	Vic Power	50.00	25.00	15.00
(17)	Rich Rollins	40.00	20.00	12.00
(18)	Theodore Sadowski	40.00	20.00	12.00
(19)	Albert Stange	40.00	20.00	12.00
(20)	Dick Stigman	40.00	20.00	12.00
(21)	Bill Tuttle	40.00	20.00	12.00
(22)	Zoilo Versalles	50.00	25.00	15.00
(23)	Gerald Zimmerman	40.00	20.00	12.00
(24)	Manager and Coaches (Floyd Baker, Edward Fitz Gerald, Gordon Maltzberger, Sam Mele, George Strickland)	40.00	20.00	12.00

1952 Coca-Cola Playing Tips Test Cards

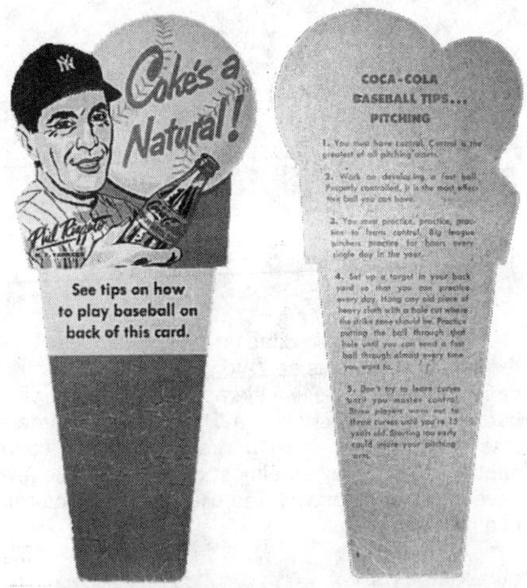

Apparently a regional issue to test the concept of baseball playing tips cards inserted into cartons of soda bottles, these test cards have a number of differences to the version which was more widely issued. The test cards are printed in black, red and yellow on the front, which features a drawing of the player with a bottle of Coke, along with his name in script and his team. Backs are printed in red on gray cardboard. The playing tips on back do not necessarily conform to the position of the player on front. Mays' card has a biography instead of playing tip. The cards are irregularly shaped, measuring about 3-1/2" at their widest point, and about 7-1/2" in length.

		NM	EX	VG
Complete Set (3):		6000.	3000.	1800.
(1)	Willie Mays	4000.	2000.	1200.
(2)	Phil Rizzuto	1000.	500.00	300.00
(3)	Phil Rizzuto	1000.	500.00	300.00

1952 Coca-Cola Playing Tips

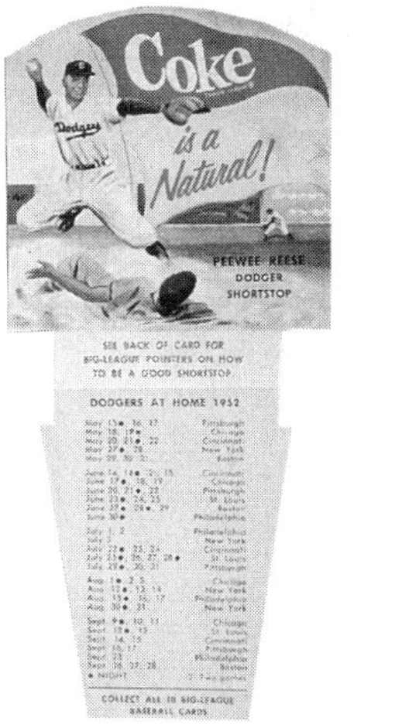

While it was more widely distributed than the three test cards, the 10-card set of playing tips cards is still scarce today. Apparently only issued in the metropolitan New York region, the cards include only players from the Yankees, Giants and Dodgers. Fronts feature paintings of players in action, though the artwork bears little actual resemblance to the players named. The phrase "Coke is a natural" is in the background on pennants, panels, etc. The player's name, team and position are included in the picture. In the portion of the card meant to be inserted into the soda-bottle carton, the home schedule of the player's team for 1952 is presented. Printed on back are tips for playing the position of the pictured player. Cards are irregularly shaped, measuring about 3-1/2" at their widest point, and 7-1/2" in length. The unnumbered cards are checklisted here in alphabetical order.

		NM	EX	VG
Complete Set (10):		4400.	2200.	1325.
Common Player:		315.00	155.00	94.00
(1)	Hank Bauer	550.00	275.00	165.00
(2)	Carl Furillo	715.00	355.00	215.00
(3)	Gil Hodges	935.00	465.00	280.00
(4)	Ed Lopat	385.00	190.00	115.00
(5)	Gil McDougald	495.00	245.00	150.00
(6)	Don Mueller	315.00	155.00	94.00
(7)	Pee Wee Reese	935.00	465.00	280.00
(8)	Bobby Thomson (3B)	495.00	245.00	150.00
(9)	Bobby Thomson (hitting)	495.00	245.00	150.00
(10)	Wes Westrum	315.00	155.00	94.00

1971 Coca-Cola Houston Astros

The constitution and distribution of these Coke premium pictures is unknown. Players are pictured in pastel drawings on the semi-gloss fronts of these 8" x 11" sheets. (The punch holes on the photographed card are not original.) A black facsimile autograph appears in the lower portion of the drawing and the player's name is printed in black in the white bottom border. Backs are printed in blue and red with a background photo of the Astrodome. Data on back includes biographical information, complete pro record and career summary. The unnumbered cards are checklisted here in alphabetical order; but this list is probably not complete.

		NM	EX	VG
Complete Set (12):		50.00	25.00	15.00
Common Player:		5.00	2.50	1.50
(1)	Jesus Alou	5.00	2.50	1.50
(2)	Wade Blasingame (SP)	9.00	4.50	2.75
(3)	Cesar Cedeno	7.50	3.75	2.25
(4)	Larry Dierker	7.50	3.75	2.25
(5)	John Edwards	5.00	2.50	1.50
(6)	Denis Menke	5.00	2.50	1.50
(7)	Roger Metzger	5.00	2.50	1.50
(8)	Joe Morgan	15.00	7.50	4.50
(9)	Doug Rader	5.00	2.50	1.50
(10)	Bob Watson	5.00	2.50	1.50
(11)	Don Wilson	5.00	2.50	1.50
(12)	Jim Wynn (SP)	12.00	6.00	3.50

1977 Coca-Cola Cleveland Indians Placemats

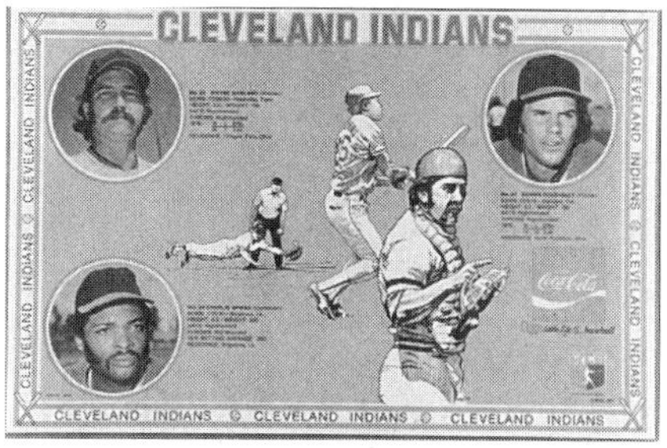

This series of plastic-laminated placemats features members of the 1977 Indians. Measuring 17" x 11", the mats' design combines player-action artwork with 3-1/2" round color portrait photos on a brightly colored background. Accompanying each player photo is personal data and 1976 stats. In the lower-right corner, are the logos of Coca-Cola and the Major League Baseball Player's Association. Like many other contemporary products licensed only by the players' union for Michael Schechter Associates, the photos and drawings on the placemats are devoid of uniform and cap logos. Backs have a simple weave pattern.

		NM	EX	VG
Complete Set (3):		18.00	9.00	5.50
(1)	Buddy Bell, John Grubb, Rick Manning	7.50	3.75	2.25
(2)	Dennis Eckersley, Wayne Garland, Charlie Spikes	10.00	5.00	3.00
(3)	Frank Duffy, Duane Kuiper, Jim Norris	6.00	3.00	1.75

1978 Coca-Cola/WPLO Atlanta Braves

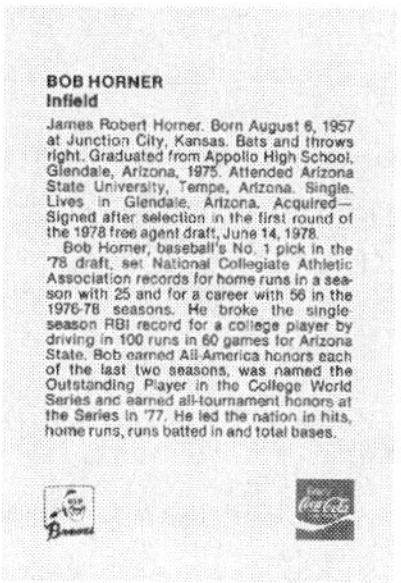

Co-sponsored by Coke and a local radio station, this set of Braves cards is rendered in blue-and-white line art portraits in a 3" x 4-1/4" format. A soda discount coupon was distributed with the set.

		NM	EX	VG
Complete Set (14):		16.00	8.00	4.75
Common Player:		1.50	.70	.45
(1)	Barry Bonnell	1.50	.70	.45
(2)	Jeff Burroughs	1.50	.70	.45
(3)	Rick Camp	1.50	.70	.45
(4)	Gene Garber	1.50	.70	.45
(5)	Rod Gilbreath	1.50	.70	.45
(6)	Bob Horner	2.25	1.25	.70
(7)	Glenn Hubbard	1.50	.70	.45
(8)	Gary Matthews	1.50	.70	.45
(9)	Larry McWilliams	1.50	.70	.45
(10)	Dale Murphy	4.00	2.00	1.25
(11)	Phil Niekro	4.00	2.00	1.25
(12)	Rowland Office	1.50	.70	.45
(13)	Biff Pocoroba	1.50	.70	.45
(14)	Jerry Royster	1.50	.70	.45

1909-11 Colgan's Chips Stars of the Diamond

This unusual set of 1-1/2"-diameter round cards was issued over a three-year period (1909-11) by the Colgan Gum Co., Louisville, Ky. The cards were inserted in five-cent tins of Colgan's Mint Chips and Violet Chips brands of gum. The borderless cards feature a black-and-white player portrait on the front along with the player's last name, team and league. On more than a dozen cards variations are known in the size of the photo and/or lettering on front. Since they cannot be identified without another card to compare with, they are noted here only with an asterisk. The card back identifies the set as "Stars of the Diamond" and carries advertising for Colgan's Gum. Over 230 different players were pictured over the three-year period, but because of team changes and other notable variations, more than 300 different cards exist. The complete set price does not include the more expensive variations. The issue was cataloged as E254 in the American Card Catalog.

		NM	EX	VG
Complete Set (237):		19000.	9500.	5500.
Common Player:		50.00	25.00	15.00
Round Tin Package:		80.00	40.00	24.00
(1)	Ed Abbaticchio	50.00	25.00	15.00
(2)	Fred Abbott	50.00	25.00	15.00
(3a)	Bill Abstein (Pittsburg)	50.00	25.00	15.00
(3b)	Bill Abstein (Jersey City)	50.00	25.00	15.00
(4)	Babe Adams	50.00	25.00	15.00
(5)	Doc Adkins	50.00	25.00	15.00
(6)	Joe Agler	50.00	25.00	15.00
(7a)	Dave Altizer (Cincinnati)	50.00	25.00	15.00
(7b)	Dave Altizer (Minneapolis)	50.00	25.00	15.00
(8)	Nick Altrock	50.00	25.00	15.00
(9)	Red Ames	50.00	25.00	15.00
(10)	Jimmy Archer	50.00	25.00	15.00
(11a)	Jimmy Austin (New York)	50.00	25.00	15.00
(11b)	Jimmy Austin (St. Louis)	50.00	25.00	15.00
(12a)	Charlie Babb (Memphis)	50.00	25.00	15.00
(12b)	Charlie Babb (Norfolk)	50.00	25.00	15.00
(13)	Baerwald	50.00	25.00	15.00
(14)	Bill Bailey	50.00	25.00	15.00
(15)	Home Run Baker (*)	150.00	75.00	45.00
(16)	Jack Barry (*)	50.00	25.00	15.00
(17a)	Bill Bartley (curved letters)	50.00	25.00	15.00
(17b)	Bill Bartley (horizontal letters)	50.00	25.00	15.00
(18a)	Johnny Bates (Cincinnati)	50.00	25.00	15.00
(18b)	Johnny Bates (Philadelphia, black letters)	50.00	25.00	15.00
(18c)	Johnny Bates (Philadelphia, white letters)	50.00	25.00	15.00
(19)	Dick Bayless	50.00	25.00	15.00
(20a)	Ginger Beaumont (Boston)	50.00	25.00	15.00
(20b)	Ginger Beaumont (Chicago)	50.00	25.00	15.00
(20c)	Ginger Beaumont (St. Paul)	50.00	25.00	15.00
(21)	Beals Becker	50.00	25.00	15.00
(22)	George Bell	50.00	25.00	15.00
(23a)	Harry Bemis (Cleveland)	50.00	25.00	15.00
(23b)	Harry Bemis (Columbus)	50.00	25.00	15.00
(24a)	Heinie Berger (Cleveland)	50.00	25.00	15.00
(24b)	Heinie Berger (Columbus)	50.00	25.00	15.00
(25)	Bob Bescher	50.00	25.00	15.00
(26)	Beumiller	50.00	25.00	15.00
(27)	Joe Birmingham	50.00	25.00	15.00
(28)	Kitty Bransfield	50.00	25.00	15.00
(29)	Roger Bresnahan	150.00	75.00	45.00
(30)	Al Bridwell	50.00	25.00	15.00
(31)	Lew Brockett	50.00	25.00	15.00
(32)	Al Burch (*)	50.00	25.00	15.00
(33a)	Burke (Ft. Wayne)	50.00	25.00	15.00
(33b)	Burke (Indianapolis)	50.00	25.00	15.00
(34)	Donie Bush	50.00	25.00	15.00
(35)	Bill Byers	50.00	25.00	15.00
(36)	Howie Cammitz (Camnitz)	50.00	25.00	15.00
(37a)	Charlie Carr (Indianapolis)	50.00	25.00	15.00
(37b)	Charlie Carr (Utica)	50.00	25.00	15.00
(38)	Frank Chance	165.00	82.00	49.00
(39)	Hal Chase	75.00	37.00	22.00
(40)	Bill Clancy (Clancey)	50.00	25.00	15.00
(41a)	Fred Clarke (Pittsburg)	150.00	75.00	45.00
(41b)	Fred Clarke (Pittsburgh)	150.00	75.00	45.00
(42)	Tommy Clarke (Cincinnati)	50.00	25.00	15.00
(43)	Bill Clymer	50.00	25.00	15.00
(44a)	Ty Cobb (*) (no team on uniform)	900.00	450.00	270.00
(44b)	Ty Cobb (team name on uniform))	1250.	625.00	375.00
(45)	Eddie Collins	150.00	75.00	45.00
(46)	Bunk Congalton	50.00	25.00	15.00
(47)	Wid Conroy	50.00	25.00	15.00
(48)	Ernie Courtney	50.00	25.00	15.00

(49a)	Harry Coveleski (Cincinnati)	50.00	25.00	15.00
(49b)	Harry Coveleski (Chattanooga)	50.00	25.00	15.00
(50)	Doc Crandall	50.00	25.00	15.00
(51)	Gavvy Cravath	50.00	25.00	15.00
(52)	Dode Criss	50.00	25.00	15.00
(53)	Bill Dahlen	50.00	25.00	15.00
(54a)	Jake Daubert (Memphis)	50.00	25.00	15.00
(54b)	Jake Daubert (Brooklyn)	50.00	25.00	15.00
(55)	Harry Davis (Philadelphia)	50.00	25.00	15.00
(56)	Davis (St. Paul)	50.00	25.00	15.00
(57)	Frank Delahanty	50.00	25.00	15.00
(58a)	Ray Demmett (Demmitt) (New York)	50.00	25.00	15.00
(58b)	Ray Demmett (Demmitt) (Montreal)	50.00	25.00	15.00
(58c)	Ray Demmett (Demmitt) (St. Louis)	50.00	25.00	15.00
(59)	Art Devlin	50.00	25.00	15.00
(60)	Wild Bill Donovan	50.00	25.00	15.00
(61)	Mickey Doolin (Doolan)	50.00	25.00	15.00
(62)	Patsy Dougherty	50.00	25.00	15.00
(63)	Tom Downey	50.00	25.00	15.00
(64)	Larry Doyle	50.00	25.00	15.00
(65)	Jack Dunn	50.00	25.00	15.00
(66)	Dick Eagan (Egan)	50.00	25.00	15.00
(67a)	Kid Elberfield (Elberfeld) (Washington)	50.00	25.00	15.00
(67b)	Kid Elberfield (Elberfeld) (New York)	50.00	25.00	15.00
(68)	Rube Ellis	50.00	25.00	15.00
(69a)	Clyde Engle (New York)	50.00	25.00	15.00
(69b)	Clyde Engle (Boston)	50.00	25.00	15.00
(70a)	Steve Evans (curved letters)	50.00	25.00	15.00
(70b)	Steve Evans (horizontal letters)	50.00	25.00	15.00
(71)	Johnny Evers	150.00	75.00	45.00
(72)	Cecil Ferguson	50.00	25.00	15.00
(73)	Hobe Ferris	50.00	25.00	15.00
(74)	Field (*)	50.00	25.00	15.00
(75)	Fitzgerald	50.00	25.00	15.00
(76a)	Patsy Flaherty (Kansas City)	50.00	25.00	15.00
(76b)	Patsy Flaherty (Atlanta)	50.00	25.00	15.00
(77)	Jack Flater	50.00	25.00	15.00
(78a)	Elmer Flick (Cleveland)	150.00	75.00	45.00
(78b)	Elmer Flick (Toledo)	150.00	75.00	45.00
(79a)	James Freck (Frick, Baltimore)	50.00	25.00	15.00
(79b)	James Freck (Frick, Toronto)	50.00	25.00	15.00
(80)	Jerry Freeman (photo actually Buck Freeman)	50.00	25.00	15.00
(81)	Art Fromme (*)	50.00	25.00	15.00
(82a)	Larry Gardner (Boston)	50.00	25.00	15.00
(82b)	Larry Gardner (New York)	50.00	25.00	15.00
(83)	Harry Gaspar	50.00	25.00	15.00
(84a)	Gus Getz (Boston)	50.00	25.00	15.00
(84b)	Gus Getz (Indianapolis)	50.00	25.00	15.00
(85)	George Gibson	50.00	25.00	15.00
(86a)	Moose Grimshaw (Toronto)	50.00	25.00	15.00
(86b)	Moose Grimshaw (Louisville)	50.00	25.00	15.00
(87)	Ed Hahn	50.00	25.00	15.00
(88)	John Halla (*)	50.00	25.00	15.00
(89)	Ed Hally (Holly)	50.00	25.00	15.00
(90)	Charlie Hanford	50.00	25.00	15.00
(91)	Topsy Hartsel	50.00	25.00	15.00
(92a)	Roy Hartzell (St. Louis)	50.00	25.00	15.00
(92b)	Roy Hartzell (New York)	50.00	25.00	15.00
(93)	Weldon Henley	50.00	25.00	15.00
(94)	Harry Hinchman	50.00	25.00	15.00
(95)	Solly Hofman	50.00	25.00	15.00
(96a)	Harry Hooper (Boston Na'l)	150.00	75.00	45.00
(96b)	Harry Hooper (Boston Am. L.)	150.00	75.00	45.00
(97)	Howard (*)	50.00	25.00	15.00
(98a)	Hughes (no name in uniform)	50.00	25.00	15.00
(98b)	Hughes (name and team name in uniform)	50.00	25.00	15.00
(99a)	Rudy Hulswitt (St. Louis, name incorrect)	50.00	25.00	15.00
(99b)	Rudy Hulswitt (St. Louis, name correct)	50.00	25.00	15.00
(99c)	Rudy Hulswitt (Chattanooga)	50.00	25.00	15.00
(100)	John Hummel	50.00	25.00	15.00
(101)	George Hunter	50.00	25.00	15.00
(102)	Shoeless Joe Jackson	3500.	1750.	1050.
(103)	Hugh Jennings	150.00	75.00	45.00
(104)	Davy Jones	50.00	25.00	15.00
(105)	Tom Jones	50.00	25.00	15.00
(106a)	Tim Jordon (Jordan, Brooklyn)	50.00	25.00	15.00
(106b)	Tim Jordon (Jordan, Atlanta)	50.00	25.00	15.00
(106c)	Tim Jordon (Jordan, Louisville)	50.00	25.00	15.00
(107)	Addie Joss	160.00	80.00	48.00
(108)	Al Kaiser	50.00	25.00	15.00
(109)	Wee Wille Keeler	150.00	75.00	45.00
(110)	Joe Kelly (Kelley)	155.00	77.00	46.00
(111)	Bill Killefer (*)	50.00	25.00	15.00
(112a)	Ed Killian (Detroit)	50.00	25.00	15.00
(112b)	Ed Killian (Toronto)	50.00	25.00	15.00
(113)	Johnny Kling	50.00	25.00	15.00
(114)	Otto Knabe	50.00	25.00	15.00
(115)	Jack Knight	50.00	25.00	15.00
(116)	Ed Konetchy	50.00	25.00	15.00
(117)	Rube Kroh	50.00	25.00	15.00
(118)	James Lafitte	50.00	25.00	15.00
(119)	Nap Lajoie	160.00	80.00	48.00
(120)	Lakoff	50.00	25.00	15.00
(121)	Frank Lange	50.00	25.00	15.00
(122a)	Frank LaPorte (St. Louis)	50.00	25.00	15.00
(122b)	Frank LaPorte (New York)	50.00	25.00	15.00
(123)	Tommy Leach	50.00	25.00	15.00
(124)	Jack Lelivelt	50.00	25.00	15.00
(125a)	Jack Lewis (Milwaukee)	50.00	25.00	15.00
(125b)	Jack Lewis (Indianapolis)	50.00	25.00	15.00
(126a)	Vive Lindaman (Boston)	50.00	25.00	15.00
(126b)	Vive Lindaman (Louisville)	50.00	25.00	15.00
(126c)	Vive Lindaman (Indianapolis)	50.00	25.00	15.00
(127)	Bris Lord	50.00	25.00	15.00
(128a)	Harry Lord (Boston)	50.00	25.00	15.00
(128b)	Harry Lord (Chicago)	50.00	25.00	15.00
(129a)	Bill Ludwig (Milwaukee)	50.00	25.00	15.00
(129b)	Bill Ludwig (St. Louis)	50.00	25.00	15.00
(130)	Madden	50.00	25.00	15.00
(131)	Nick Maddox	50.00	25.00	15.00
(132a)	Manser (Jersey City)	50.00	25.00	15.00
(132b)	Manser (Rochester)	50.00	25.00	15.00
(133)	Rube Marquard	150.00	75.00	45.00
(134)	Al Mattern	50.00	25.00	15.00
(135)	Bill Matthews	50.00	25.00	15.00
(136)	George McBride	50.00	25.00	15.00
(137)	McCarthy	50.00	25.00	15.00
(138)	McConnell	50.00	25.00	15.00
(139)	Moose McCormick	50.00	25.00	15.00
(140)	Dan McGann	50.00	25.00	15.00
(141)	Jim McGinley	50.00	25.00	15.00
(142)	Iron Man McGinnity	150.00	75.00	45.00
(143a)	Matty McIntyre (Detroit)	50.00	25.00	15.00
(143b)	Matty McIntyre (Chicago)	50.00	25.00	15.00
(144)	Larry McLean (*) (three photo size variations known)	50.00	25.00	15.00
(145)	Fred Merkle	50.00	25.00	15.00
(146a)	Merritt (Buffalo)	50.00	25.00	15.00
(146b)	Merritt (Jersey City)	50.00	25.00	15.00
(147a)	Meyer (Newark, name correct)	50.00	25.00	15.00
(147b)	Meyers (Newark, name incorrect)	50.00	25.00	15.00
(148)	Chief Meyers (New York)	50.00	25.00	15.00
(149)	Clyde Milan	50.00	25.00	15.00
(150)	Dots Miller	50.00	25.00	15.00
(151)	Mike Mitchell	50.00	25.00	15.00
(152)	Moran	50.00	25.00	15.00
(153a)	Bill Moriarty (Louisville)	50.00	25.00	15.00
(153b)	Bill Moriarty (Omaha)	50.00	25.00	15.00
(154)	George Moriarty	50.00	25.00	15.00
(155a)	George Mullen (name incorrect)	50.00	25.00	15.00
(155b)	George Mullin (name correct)	50.00	25.00	15.00
(156a)	Simmy Murch (Chattanooga)	50.00	25.00	15.00
(156b)	Simmy Murch (Indianapolis)	50.00	25.00	15.00
(157)	Danny Murphy	50.00	25.00	15.00
(158a)	Red Murray (New York, white letters)	50.00	25.00	15.00
(158b)	Red Murray (New York, black letters)	50.00	25.00	15.00
(158c)	Red Murray (St. Paul)	50.00	25.00	15.00
(159)	Billy Nattress (*)	50.00	25.00	15.00
(160a)	Red Nelson (St. Louis)	50.00	25.00	15.00
(160b)	Red Nelson (Toledo)	50.00	25.00	15.00
(161)	Rebel Oakes	50.00	25.00	15.00
(162)	Fred Odwell	50.00	25.00	15.00
(163)	O'Rourke	50.00	25.00	15.00
(164a)	Al Orth (New York)	50.00	25.00	15.00
(164b)	Al Orth (Indianapolis)	50.00	25.00	15.00
(165)	Fred Osborn	50.00	25.00	15.00
(166)	Orval Overall	50.00	25.00	15.00
(167)	Owens	50.00	25.00	15.00
(168)	Fred Parent	50.00	25.00	15.00
(169a)	Dode Paskert (Cincinnati)	50.00	25.00	15.00
(169b)	Dode Paskert (Philadelphia)	50.00	25.00	15.00
(170)	Heinie Peitz	50.00	25.00	15.00
(171)	Bob Peterson	50.00	25.00	15.00
(172)	Jake Pfeister	50.00	25.00	15.00
(173)	Deacon Phillipe (Phillippe)	50.00	25.00	15.00
(174a)	Ollie Pickering (Louisville)	50.00	25.00	15.00
(174b)	Ollie Pickering (Minneapolis)	50.00	25.00	15.00
(174c)	Ollie Pickering (Omaha)	50.00	25.00	15.00
(175a)	Billy Purtell (Chicago)	50.00	25.00	15.00
(175b)	Billy Purtell (Boston)	50.00	25.00	15.00
(176)	Bugs Raymond	50.00	25.00	15.00
(177)	Pat Regan (Ragan)	50.00	25.00	15.00
(178)	Barney Reilly	50.00	25.00	15.00
(179)	Duke Reilly (Reilley)	50.00	25.00	15.00
(180)	Ed Reulbach	50.00	25.00	15.00
(181)	Claude Ritchey	50.00	25.00	15.00
(182)	Lou Ritter	50.00	25.00	15.00
(183)	Robinson	50.00	25.00	15.00
(184)	Rock	50.00	25.00	15.00
(185a)	Jack Rowan (Cincinnati)	50.00	25.00	15.00
(185b)	Jack Rowan (Philadelphia)	50.00	25.00	15.00
(186)	Nap Rucker	50.00	25.00	15.00
(187a)	Dick Rudolph (New York)	50.00	25.00	15.00
(187b)	Dick Rudolph (Toronto)	50.00	25.00	15.00
(188)	Ryan	50.00	25.00	15.00
(189)	Slim Sallee	50.00	25.00	15.00
(190a)	Bill Schardt (Birmingham)	50.00	25.00	15.00
(190b)	Bill Schardt (Milwaukee)	50.00	25.00	15.00
(191)	Jimmy Scheckard (Sheckard)	50.00	25.00	15.00
(192a)	George Schirm (Birmingham)	50.00	25.00	15.00
(192b)	George Schirm (Buffalo)	50.00	25.00	15.00
(193)	Larry Schlafly	50.00	25.00	15.00
(194)	Wildfire Schulte	50.00	25.00	15.00
(195a)	James Seabaugh (looking to left, photo actually Julius Weisman)	50.00	25.00	15.00
(195b)	James Seabaugh (looking straight ahead, correct photo)	50.00	25.00	15.00
(196)	Selby (*)	50.00	25.00	15.00
(197a)	Cy Seymour (New York)	50.00	25.00	15.00
(197b)	Cy Seymour (Baltimore)	50.00	25.00	15.00
(198)	Hosea Siner	50.00	25.00	15.00
(199)	G. Smith	50.00	25.00	15.00
(200a)	Sid Smith (Atlanta)	50.00	25.00	15.00
(200b)	Sid Smith (Buffalo)	50.00	25.00	15.00
(201)	Fred Snodgrass	50.00	25.00	15.00
(202a)	Bob Spade (Cincinnati)	50.00	25.00	15.00
(202b)	Bob Spade (Newark)	50.00	25.00	15.00
(203a)	Tully Sparks (Philadelphia)	50.00	25.00	15.00
(203b)	Tully Sparks (Richmond)	50.00	25.00	15.00
(204a)	Tris Speaker (Boston Nat'l)	190.00	95.00	57.00
(204b)	Tris Speaker (Boston Am.)	190.00	95.00	57.00
(205)	Tubby Spencer	50.00	25.00	15.00
(206)	Jake Stahl	50.00	25.00	15.00
(207)	John Stansberry (Stansbury)	50.00	25.00	15.00
(208)	Harry Steinfeldt (*)	50.00	25.00	15.00
(209)	George Stone	50.00	25.00	15.00
(210)	George Stovall	50.00	25.00	15.00
(211)	Gabby Street	50.00	25.00	15.00
(212a)	Sullivan (Louisville)	50.00	25.00	15.00
(212b)	Sullivan (Omaha)	50.00	25.00	15.00
(213a)	Ed Summers (no white in uniform)	50.00	25.00	15.00
(213b)	Ed Summers (white in uniform)	50.00	25.00	15.00
(214)	Lee Tannehill	50.00	25.00	15.00
(215)	Taylor	50.00	25.00	15.00
(216)	Joe Tinker	150.00	75.00	45.00
(217)	John Titus	50.00	25.00	15.00
(218)	Terry Turner	50.00	25.00	15.00
(219a)	Bob Unglaub (Washington)	50.00	25.00	15.00
(219b)	Bob Unglaub (Lincoln)	50.00	25.00	15.00
(220a)	Rube Waddell (St. Louis)	150.00	75.00	45.00
(220b)	Rube Waddell (Minneapolis)	150.00	75.00	45.00
(220c)	Rube Waddell (Newark)	150.00	75.00	45.00
(221a)	Honus Wagner (Pittsburg, curved letters)	700.00	350.00	210.00
(221b)	Honus Wagner (Pittsburgh, curved letters) (*)	700.00	350.00	210.00
(221c)	Honus Wagner (Pittsburg, horizontal letters)	700.00	350.00	210.00
(222)	Walker	50.00	25.00	15.00
(223)	Waller	50.00	25.00	15.00
(224)	Clarence Wauner (Wanner)	50.00	25.00	15.00
(225)	Julius Weisman (name correct)	50.00	25.00	15.00
(226)	Jack White (Buffalo)	50.00	25.00	15.00
(227)	Kirby White (Boston)	50.00	25.00	15.00
(228)	Julius Wiesman (Weisman)	50.00	25.00	15.00
(229)	Ed Willett	50.00	25.00	15.00
(230a)	Otto Williams (Indianapolis)	50.00	25.00	15.00
(230b)	Otto Williams (Minneapolis)	50.00	25.00	15.00
(231)	Owen Wilson	50.00	25.00	15.00
(232)	Hooks Wiltse	50.00	25.00	15.00
(233a)	Orville Woodruff (Indianapolis)	50.00	25.00	15.00
(233b)	Orville Woodruff (Louisville)	50.00	25.00	15.00
(234)	Woods	50.00	25.00	15.00
(235)	Cy Young	375.00	187.00	112.00
(236)	Bill Zimmerman	50.00	25.00	15.00
(237)	Heinie Zimmerman	50.00	25.00	15.00

1912 Colgan's Chips Red Borders

This set, issued in 1912 by Colgan Gum Co., Louisville, Ky., is very similar to the 1909-11 Colgan's release. Measuring 1-1/2" in diameter, the black-and-white paper player photos were inserted in tins of Colgan's Mint and Violet Chips gum. They are differentiated from the earlier issues by their distinctive red borders and by the back of the cards, which advises collectors to "Send 25 Box Tops" for a photo of the "World's Pennant Winning Team." The issue is designated as the E270 Red Border set in the American Card Catalog.

		NM	EX	VG
Complete Set (182):		20000.	10000.	6000.
Common Player:		100.00	50.00	30.00
(1)	Ed Abbaticchio	100.00	45.00	27.00
(2)	Fred Abbott	100.00	45.00	27.00
(3)	Babe Adams	100.00	45.00	27.00
(4)	Doc Adkins	100.00	45.00	27.00
(5)	Red Ames	100.00	45.00	27.00
(6)	Charlie Babb	100.00	45.00	27.00
(7)	Bill Bailey	100.00	45.00	27.00
(8)	Home Run Baker	200.00	100.00	60.00
(9)	Jack Barry	100.00	45.00	27.00
(10)	Johnny Bates	100.00	45.00	27.00
(11)	Dick Bayless	100.00	45.00	27.00
(12)	Ginger Beaumont	100.00	45.00	27.00
(13)	Beals Becker	100.00	45.00	27.00
(14)	George Bell	100.00	45.00	27.00
(15)	Harry Bemis	100.00	45.00	27.00
(16)	Heinie Berger	100.00	45.00	27.00
(17)	Beumiller	100.00	45.00	27.00
(18)	Joe Birmingham	100.00	45.00	27.00
(19)	Kitty Bransfield	100.00	45.00	27.00
(20)	Roger Bresnahan	200.00	100.00	60.00
(21)	Lew Brockett	100.00	45.00	27.00
(22)	Al Burch	100.00	45.00	27.00
(23)	Donie Bush	100.00	45.00	27.00
(24)	Bill Byers	100.00	45.00	27.00
(25)	Howie Cammitz (Camnitz)	100.00	45.00	27.00
(26)	Charlie Carr	100.00	45.00	27.00
(27)	Frank Chance	200.00	100.00	60.00
(28)	Hal Chase	125.00	62.00	38.00
(29)	Fred Clarke (Pittsburg)	200.00	100.00	60.00
(30)	Tommy Clarke (Cincinnati)	100.00	45.00	27.00
(31)	Bill Clymer	100.00	45.00	27.00
(32)	Ty Cobb	1500.	750.00	450.00
(33)	Eddie Collins	200.00	100.00	60.00

(34)	Wid Conroy	100.00	45.00	27.00
(35)	Harry Coveleski	100.00	45.00	27.00
(36)	Gavvy Cravath	100.00	45.00	27.00
(37)	Dode Criss	100.00	45.00	27.00
(39)	Harry Davis (Philadelphia)	100.00	45.00	27.00
(40)	Davis (St. Paul)	100.00	45.00	27.00
(41)	Frank Delahanty	100.00	45.00	27.00
(42)	Ray Demmett (Demmitt)	100.00	45.00	27.00
(43)	Art Devlin	100.00	45.00	27.00
(44)	Wild Bill Donovan	100.00	45.00	27.00
(45)	Mickey Doolin (Doolan)	100.00	45.00	27.00
(46)	Patsy Dougherty	100.00	45.00	27.00
(47)	Tom Downey	100.00	45.00	27.00
(48)	Larry Doyle	100.00	45.00	27.00
(49)	Jack Dunn	100.00	45.00	27.00
(50)	Dick Eagan (Egan)	100.00	45.00	27.00
(51)	Kid Elberfield (Elberfeld)	100.00	45.00	27.00
(52)	Rube Ellis	100.00	45.00	27.00
(53)	Steve Evans	100.00	45.00	27.00
(54)	Johnny Evers	200.00	100.00	60.00
(55)	Cecil Ferguson	100.00	45.00	27.00
(56)	Hobe Ferris	100.00	45.00	27.00
(57)	Fisher	100.00	45.00	27.00
(58)	Fitzgerald	100.00	45.00	27.00
(59)	Elmer Flick	200.00	100.00	60.00
(60)	James Freck (Frick)	100.00	45.00	27.00
(61)	Art Fromme	100.00	45.00	27.00
(62)	Harry Gaspar	100.00	45.00	27.00
(63)	George Gibson	100.00	45.00	27.00
(64)	Moose Grimshaw	100.00	45.00	27.00
(65)	John Halla	100.00	45.00	27.00
(66)	Ed Hally (Holly)	100.00	45.00	27.00
(67)	Charlie Hanford	100.00	45.00	27.00
(68)	Topsy Hartsel	100.00	45.00	27.00
(69)	Roy Hartzell	100.00	45.00	27.00
(70)	Weldon Henley (two sizes photo variations noted)	100.00	45.00	27.00
(71)	Harry Hinchman	100.00	45.00	27.00
(72)	Solly Hofman	100.00	45.00	27.00
(73)	Harry Hooper	200.00	100.00	60.00
(74)	Howard	100.00	45.00	27.00
(75)	Hughes	100.00	45.00	27.00
(76)	Rudy Hulswitt	100.00	45.00	27.00
(77)	John Hummel	100.00	45.00	27.00
(78)	George Hunter	100.00	45.00	27.00
(79)	Hugh Jennings	200.00	100.00	60.00
(80)	Davy Jones	100.00	45.00	27.00
(81)	Tom Jones	100.00	45.00	27.00
(82)	Tim Jordon (Jordan)	100.00	45.00	27.00
(83)	Joe Kelly (Kelley)	200.00	100.00	60.00
(84)	Bill Killefer	100.00	45.00	27.00
(85)	Ed Killian	100.00	45.00	27.00
(86)	Otto Knabe	100.00	45.00	27.00
(87)	Jack Knight	100.00	45.00	27.00
(88)	Ed Konetchy	100.00	45.00	27.00
(89)	Rube Kroh	100.00	45.00	27.00
(90)	LaCrosse (photo actually Bill Schardt)	100.00	45.00	27.00
(91)	Frank LaPorte	100.00	45.00	27.00
(92)	Tommy Leach	100.00	45.00	27.00
(93)	Jack Lelivelt	100.00	45.00	27.00
(94)	Jack Lewis	100.00	45.00	27.00
(95)	Vive Lindaman	100.00	45.00	27.00
(96)	Bris Lord	100.00	45.00	27.00
(97)	Harry Lord	100.00	45.00	27.00
(98)	Bill Ludwig	100.00	45.00	27.00
(99)	Nick Maddox	100.00	45.00	27.00
(100)	Manser	100.00	50.00	30.00
(101)	Al Mattern	100.00	45.00	27.00
(102)	George McBride	100.00	45.00	27.00
(103)	McCarthy	100.00	45.00	27.00
(104)	McConnell	100.00	45.00	27.00
(105)	Moose McCormick	100.00	45.00	27.00
(106)	Dan McGann	100.00	45.00	27.00
(107)	Jim McGinley	100.00	45.00	27.00
(108)	Iron Man McGinnity	200.00	100.00	60.00
(109)	Matty McIntyre	100.00	45.00	27.00
(110)	Larry McLean	100.00	45.00	27.00
(111)	Fred Merkle	100.00	45.00	27.00
(112)	Merritt	100.00	45.00	27.00
(113)	Meyer (Newark)	100.00	45.00	27.00
(114)	Chief Meyers	100.00	45.00	27.00
(115)	Clyde Milan	100.00	45.00	27.00
(116)	Dots Miller	100.00	45.00	27.00
(117)	Mike Mitchell	100.00	45.00	27.00
(118)	Bill Moriarty (Omaha)	100.00	45.00	27.00
(119)	George Moriarty (Detroit)	100.00	45.00	27.00
(120)	George Mullen (Mullin)	100.00	45.00	27.00
(121)	Simmy Murch (Chattanooga)	100.00	45.00	27.00
(122)	Simmy Murch (Indianapolis)	100.00	45.00	27.00
(123)	Danny Murphy	100.00	45.00	27.00
(124)	Red Murray	100.00	45.00	27.00
(125)	Red Nelson	100.00	45.00	27.00
(126)	Rebel Oakes	100.00	45.00	27.00
(127)	Orval Overall	100.00	45.00	27.00
(128)	Owens	100.00	45.00	27.00
(129)	Fred Parent	100.00	45.00	27.00
(130)	Dode Paskert	100.00	45.00	27.00
(131)	Bob Peterson	100.00	45.00	27.00
(132)	Jake Pfeister (Pfiester)	100.00	45.00	27.00
(133)	Deacon Phillipe (Phillippe)	100.00	45.00	27.00
(134)	Ollie Pickering	100.00	45.00	27.00
(135)	Heinie Pietz (Peitz)	100.00	45.00	27.00
(136)	Bugs Raymond	100.00	45.00	27.00
(137)	Pat Regan (Ragan)	100.00	45.00	27.00
(138)	Ed Reulbach	100.00	45.00	27.00
(139)	Robinson	100.00	45.00	27.00
(140)	Rock	100.00	45.00	27.00
(141)	Jack Rowan	100.00	45.00	27.00
(142)	Nap Rucker	100.00	45.00	27.00
(143)	Dick Rudolph	100.00	45.00	27.00
(144)	Slim Sallee	100.00	45.00	27.00
(145)	Jimmy Scheckard (Sheckard)	100.00	45.00	27.00
(146)	George Schirm	100.00	45.00	27.00
(147)	Wildfire Schulte	100.00	45.00	27.00
(148)	James Seabaugh	100.00	45.00	27.00
(149)	Selby	100.00	45.00	27.00
(150)	Cy Seymour	100.00	45.00	27.00
(151)	Hosea Siner	100.00	45.00	27.00
(152)	Sid Smith	100.00	45.00	27.00
(153)	Fred Snodgrass	100.00	45.00	27.00
(154)	Bob Spade	100.00	45.00	27.00
(155)	Tully Sparks	100.00	45.00	27.00
(156)	Tris Speaker	350.00	175.00	105.00
(157)	Tubby Spencer	100.00	45.00	27.00
(158)	John Stausberry (Stansbury)	100.00	50.00	30.00
(159)	Harry Steinfeldt	100.00	50.00	30.00
(160)	George Stone	100.00	45.00	27.00
(161)	George Stovall	100.00	45.00	27.00
(162)	Gabby Street	100.00	45.00	27.00
(163)	Sullivan (Omaha)	100.00	45.00	27.00
(164)	John Sullivan (Louisville)	100.00	45.00	27.00
(165)	Ed Summers	100.00	45.00	27.00
(166)	Joe Tinker	200.00	100.00	60.00
(167)	John Titus	100.00	45.00	27.00
(168)	Terry Turner	100.00	45.00	27.00
(169)	Bob Unglaub	100.00	45.00	27.00
(170)	Rube Waddell	200.00	100.00	60.00
(171)	Walker	100.00	45.00	27.00
(172)	Waller	100.00	45.00	27.00
(173)	Kirby White (Boston)	100.00	50.00	30.00
(174)	Jack White (Buffalo)	100.00	45.00	27.00
(175)	Julius Wiesman (Weisman)	100.00	45.00	27.00
(176)	Otto Williams	100.00	45.00	27.00
(177)	Hooks Wiltse	100.00	45.00	27.00
(178)	Orville Woodruff	100.00	45.00	27.00
(179)	Woods	100.00	45.00	27.00
(180)	Cy Young	600.00	300.00	180.00
(181)	Bill Zimmerman	100.00	45.00	27.00
(182)	Heinie Zimmerman	100.00	45.00	27.00

1912 Colgan's Chips Tin Tops

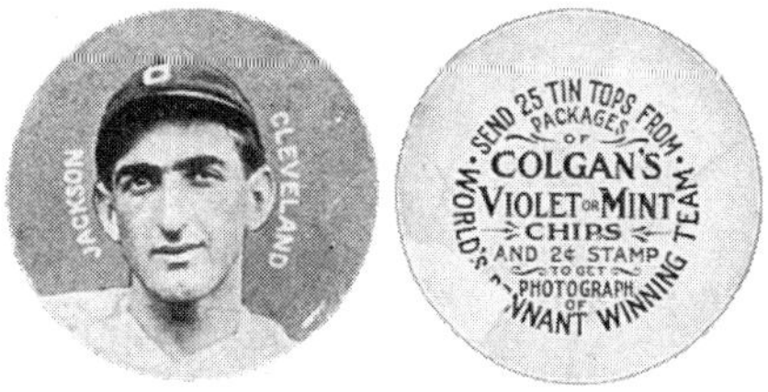

Except for the backs, these round, black-and-white paper cards (1-1/2" diameter) are identical to the 1909-11 Colgan's Chips issue, and were inserted in tin cannisters of Colgan's Mint Chips and Violet Chips. The front contains a player portrait photo along with the player's last name, team and league. The back advises collectors to "Send 25 Tin Tops" and a two-cent stamp to receive a photo of the "World's Pennant Winning Team." The set carries the designation E270 Tin Tops in the American Card Catalog.

		NM	EX	VG
Complete Set (214):		25000.	12500.	7500.
Common Player:		90.00	45.00	27.00
(1)	Ed Abbaticchio	90.00	45.00	27.00
(2)	Doc Adkins	90.00	45.00	27.00
(3)	Joe Agler	90.00	45.00	27.00
(4)	Eddie Ainsmith	90.00	45.00	27.00
(5)	Whitey Alperman	90.00	45.00	27.00
(6)	Red Ames (New York)	90.00	45.00	27.00
(7)	Red Ames (Cincinnati)	90.00	45.00	27.00
(8)	Tommy Atkins (Atlanta)	90.00	45.00	27.00
(9)	Tommy Atkins (Ft. Wayne)	90.00	45.00	27.00
(10)	Jake Atz (New Orleans)	90.00	45.00	27.00
(11)	Jake Atz (Providence)	90.00	45.00	27.00
(12)	Jimmy Austin	90.00	45.00	27.00
(13)	Home Run Baker	175.00	87.00	52.00
(14)	Johnny Bates	90.00	45.00	27.00
(15)	Beck (Buffalo)	90.00	45.00	27.00
(16)	Beebe	90.00	45.00	27.00
(17)	Harry Bemis	90.00	45.00	27.00
(18)	Bob Bescher	90.00	45.00	27.00
(19)	Beumiller (Louisville)	90.00	45.00	27.00
(20)	Joe Birmingham	90.00	45.00	27.00
(21)	Roger Bresnahan	175.00	87.00	52.00
(22)	Al Bridwell	90.00	45.00	27.00
(23)	George Brown (Browne)	90.00	45.00	27.00
(24)	Al Burch	90.00	45.00	27.00
(25)	Burns	90.00	45.00	27.00
(26)	Donie Bush	90.00	45.00	27.00
(27)	Bobby Byrne	90.00	45.00	27.00
(28)	Nixey Callahan	90.00	45.00	27.00
(29)	Howie Cammitz (Camnitz)	90.00	45.00	27.00
(30)	Billy Campbell	90.00	45.00	27.00
(31)	Charlie Carr	90.00	45.00	27.00
(32)	Jay Cashion	90.00	45.00	27.00
(33)	Frank Chance	175.00	87.00	52.00
(34)	Hal Chase	110.00	55.00	33.00
(35)	Ed Cicotte	125.00	62.00	37.00
(36)	Clarke (Indianapolis)	90.00	45.00	27.00
(37)	Fred Clarke (Pittsburg)	175.00	87.00	52.00
(38)	Tommy Clarke (Cincinnati)	90.00	45.00	27.00
(39)	Clemons	90.00	45.00	27.00
(40)	Bill Clymer	90.00	45.00	27.00
(41)	Ty Cobb	1200.	600.00	360.00
(42)	Eddie Collins	175.00	87.00	52.00
(43)	Bunk Congalton (Omaha)	90.00	45.00	27.00
(44)	Bunk Congalton (Toledo)	90.00	45.00	27.00
(45)	Cook	90.00	45.00	27.00
(46)	Jack Coombs	90.00	45.00	27.00
(47)	Corcoran	90.00	45.00	27.00
(48)	Gavvy Cravath	90.00	45.00	27.00
(49)	Sam Crawford	175.00	87.00	52.00
(50)	Bill Dahlen	90.00	45.00	27.00
(51)	Bert Daniels	90.00	45.00	27.00
(52)	Jake Daubert	90.00	45.00	27.00
(53)	Josh Devore (Cincinnati)	90.00	45.00	27.00
(54)	Josh Devore (New York)	90.00	45.00	27.00
(55)	Mike Donlin	90.00	45.00	27.00
(56)	Wild Bill Donovan	90.00	45.00	27.00
(57)	Red Dooin	90.00	45.00	27.00
(58)	Mickey Doolan	90.00	45.00	27.00
(59)	Larry Doyle	90.00	45.00	27.00
(60)	Delos Drake	90.00	45.00	27.00
(61)	Kid Elberfield (Elberfeld)	90.00	45.00	27.00
(62)	Roy Ellam	90.00	45.00	27.00
(63)	Elliott	90.00	45.00	27.00
(64)	Rube Ellis	90.00	45.00	27.00
(65)	Elwert	90.00	45.00	27.00
(66)	Clyde Engle	90.00	45.00	27.00
(67)	Jimmy Esmond	90.00	45.00	27.00
(68)	Steve Evans	90.00	45.00	27.00
(69)	Johnny Evers	175.00	87.00	52.00
(70)	Hobe Ferris	90.00	45.00	27.00
(71)	Russ Ford	90.00	45.00	27.00
(72)	Ed Foster	90.00	45.00	27.00
(73)	Friel	90.00	45.00	27.00
(74)	John Frill	90.00	45.00	27.00
(75)	Art Fromme	90.00	45.00	27.00
(76)	Gus Getz	90.00	45.00	27.00
(77)	George Gibson	90.00	45.00	27.00
(78)	Graham	90.00	45.00	27.00
(79)	Eddie Grant (Cincinnati)	90.00	45.00	27.00
(80)	Eddie Grant (New York)	90.00	45.00	27.00
(81)	Grief	90.00	45.00	27.00
(82)	Bob Groom	90.00	45.00	27.00
(83)	Charlie Hanford	90.00	45.00	27.00
(84)	Topsy Hartsel	90.00	45.00	27.00
(85)	Roy Hartzell	90.00	45.00	27.00
(86)	Harry Hinchman	90.00	45.00	27.00
(87)	Dick Hoblitzell	90.00	45.00	27.00
(88)	Happy Hogan (St. Louis)	90.00	45.00	27.00
(89)	Happy Hogan (San Francisco)	90.00	45.00	27.00
(90)	Harry Hooper	175.00	87.00	52.00
(91)	Miller Huggins	175.00	87.00	52.00
(92)	Hughes (Milwaukee)	90.00	45.00	27.00
(93)	Hughes (Rochester)	90.00	45.00	27.00
(94)	Rudy Hulswitt	90.00	45.00	27.00
(95)	John Hummel	90.00	45.00	27.00
(96)	George Hunter	90.00	45.00	27.00
(97)	Shoeless Joe Jackson	5500.	2750.	1650.
(98)	Jameson (Buffalo)	90.00	45.00	27.00
(99)	Hugh Jennings	175.00	87.00	52.00
(100)	Pete Johns	90.00	45.00	27.00
(101)	Walter Johnson	275.00	135.00	82.00
(102)	Davy Jones	90.00	45.00	27.00
(103)	Tim Jordan	90.00	45.00	27.00
(104)	Bob Keefe	90.00	45.00	27.00
(105)	Wee Willie Keeler	175.00	87.00	52.00
(106)	Joe Kelly (Kelley)	175.00	87.00	52.00
(107)	Ed Killian	90.00	45.00	27.00
(108)	Bill Killifer (Killefer)	90.00	45.00	27.00
(109)	Johnny Kling	90.00	45.00	27.00
(110)	Klipfer	90.00	45.00	27.00
(111)	Otto Knabe	90.00	45.00	27.00
(112)	Jack Knight	90.00	45.00	27.00
(113)	Ed Konetchy	90.00	45.00	27.00
(114)	Paul Krichell	90.00	45.00	27.00
(115)	James Lafitte	90.00	45.00	27.00
(116)	Nap Lajoie	200.00	100.00	60.00
(117)	Frank Lange	90.00	45.00	27.00
(118)	Lee	90.00	45.00	27.00
(119)	Jack Lewis	90.00	45.00	27.00
(120)	Harry Lord	90.00	45.00	27.00
(121)	Johnny Lush	90.00	45.00	27.00
(122)	Madden	90.00	45.00	27.00
(123)	Nick Maddox	90.00	45.00	27.00
(124)	Sherry Magee	90.00	45.00	27.00
(125)	Manser	90.00	45.00	27.00
(126)	Frank Manusch (Manush) (New Orleans)	90.00	45.00	27.00
(127)	Frank Manush (Toledo)	90.00	45.00	27.00
(128)	Rube Marquard	175.00	87.00	52.00
(129)	McAllister	90.00	45.00	27.00
(130)	George McBride	90.00	45.00	27.00
(131)	McCarthy (Newark)	90.00	45.00	27.00
(132)	McCarthy (Toledo)	90.00	45.00	27.00
(133)	McConnell	90.00	45.00	27.00
(134)	Moose McCormick	90.00	45.00	27.00
(135)	Larry McLean	90.00	45.00	27.00
(136)	Fred Merkle	90.00	45.00	27.00
(137)	Chief Meyers	90.00	45.00	27.00
(138)	Clyde Milan	90.00	45.00	27.00
(139)	Miller (Columbus)	90.00	45.00	27.00
(140)	Dots Miller (Pittsburg)	90.00	45.00	27.00
(141)	Clarence Mitchell	90.00	45.00	27.00
(142)	Mike Mitchell	90.00	45.00	27.00
(143)	Roy Mitchell	90.00	45.00	27.00
(144)	Carlton Molesworth	90.00	45.00	27.00
(145)	Herbie Moran	90.00	45.00	27.00
(146)	George Moriarty	90.00	45.00	27.00
(147)	George Mullen (Mullin)	90.00	45.00	27.00
(148)	Danny Murphy	90.00	45.00	27.00
(149)	Murray (Buffalo)	90.00	45.00	27.00
(150)	Jim Murray	90.00	45.00	27.00
(151)	Jake Northrop	90.00	45.00	27.00
(152)	Rebel Oakes	90.00	45.00	27.00
(153)	Rube Oldring	90.00	45.00	27.00
(154)	Steve O'Neil (O'Neill)	90.00	45.00	27.00
(155)	O'Rourke	90.00	45.00	27.00
(156)	Owens (Minneapolis)	90.00	45.00	27.00
(157)	Larry Pape	90.00	45.00	27.00
(158)	Fred Parent	90.00	45.00	27.00
(159)	Dode Paskert	90.00	45.00	27.00
(160)	Heinie Peitz	90.00	45.00	27.00
(161)	Perry	90.00	45.00	27.00

(162)	Billy Purtell	90.00	45.00	27.00
(163)	Bill Rariden	90.00	45.00	27.00
(164)	Morrie Rath	90.00	45.00	27.00
(165)	Bugs Raymond	90.00	45.00	27.00
(166)	Ed Reulbach	90.00	45.00	27.00
(167)	Nap Rucker	90.00	45.00	27.00
(168)	Dick Rudolph	90.00	45.00	27.00
(169)	Bud Ryan	90.00	45.00	27.00
(170)	Slim Sallee	90.00	45.00	27.00
(171)	Ray Schalk	90.00	45.00	27.00
(172)	Jimmy Scheckard (Sheckard)	90.00	45.00	27.00
(173)	Bob Shawkey	90.00	45.00	27.00
(174)	Skeeter Shelton	90.00	45.00	27.00
(175)	Burt Shotten (Shotton)	90.00	45.00	27.00
(176)	Smith (Montreal)	90.00	45.00	27.00
(177)	Sid Smith (Atlanta)	90.00	45.00	27.00
(178)	Sid Smith (Newark)	90.00	45.00	27.00
(179)	Fred Snodgrass	90.00	45.00	27.00
(180)	Tris Speaker	200.00	100.00	60.00
(181)	Jake Stahl	90.00	45.00	27.00
(182)	John Stansberry (Stansbury)	90.00	45.00	27.00
(183)	Amos Strunk	90.00	45.00	27.00
(184)	Sullivan	90.00	45.00	27.00
(185)	Harry Swacina	90.00	45.00	27.00
(186)	Bill Sweeney	90.00	45.00	27.00
(187)	Jeff Sweeney	90.00	45.00	27.00
(188)	Lee Tannehill	90.00	45.00	27.00
(189)	Taylor	90.00	45.00	27.00
(190)	Jim Thorpe	3000.	1500.	900.00
(191)	Joe Tinker	175.00	87.00	52.00
(192)	John Titus (Boston)	90.00	45.00	27.00
(193)	John Titus (Phiadelphia)	90.00	45.00	27.00
(194)	Terry Turner	90.00	45.00	27.00
(195)	Bob Unglaub	90.00	45.00	27.00
(196)	Viebahn	90.00	45.00	27.00
(197)	Rube Waddell	175.00	87.00	52.00
(198)	Honus Wagner	500.00	250.00	150.00
(199)	Bobby Wallace	175.00	87.00	52.00
(200)	Ed Walsh	175.00	87.00	52.00
(201)	Jack Warhop	90.00	45.00	27.00
(202)	Harry Welchouce (Welchonce)	90.00	45.00	27.00
(203)	Zach Wheat	175.00	87.00	52.00
(204)	Kirb. White	90.00	45.00	27.00
(205)	Kaiser Wilhelm	90.00	45.00	27.00
(206)	Ed Willett	90.00	45.00	27.00
(207)	Otto Williams	90.00	45.00	27.00
(208)	Owen Wilson	90.00	45.00	27.00
(209)	Hooks Wiltse	90.00	45.00	27.00
(210)	Joe Wood	90.00	45.00	27.00
(211)	Orville Woodruff	90.00	45.00	27.00
(212)	Joe Yeager	90.00	45.00	27.00
(213)	Bill Zimmerman	90.00	45.00	27.00
(214)	Heinie Zimmerman	90.00	45.00	27.00

1916 Collins-McCarthy (E135)

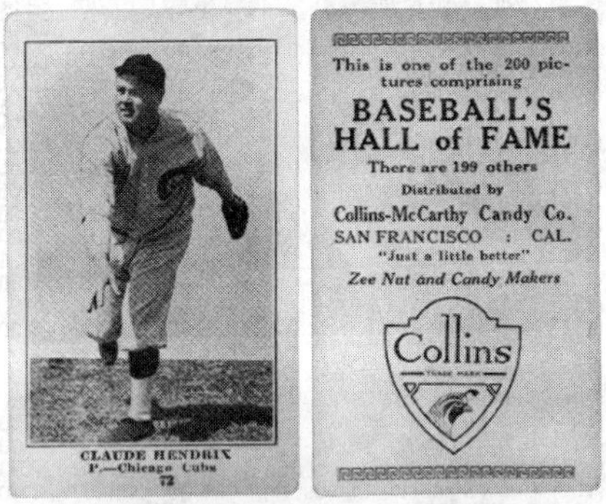

CLAUDE HENDRIX
P.—Chicago Cubs
72
This is one of the 200 pictures comprising
BASEBALL'S HALL of FAME
There are 199 others
Distributed by
Collins-McCarthy Candy Co.
SAN FRANCISCO : CAL.
"Just a little better"
Zee Nut and Candy Makers
Collins

Produced by the Collins-McCarthy Candy Co. of San Francisco, the 200-card, black-and-white set represents the company's only venture into issuing non-Pacific Coast League players. The cards, numbered alphabetically, measure 2" x 3-1/4" and are printed on thin stock. Though the set is entitled "Baseball's Hall of Fame," many nondescript players appear in the issue. The complete set price does not include the more expensive variations. The same cards can be found with the advertising of other regional issuers on back, or blank-backed.

		NM	EX	VG
Complete Set (200):		22500.	10000.	6000.
Common Player:		60.00	30.00	18.00
1	Sam Agnew	60.00	30.00	18.00
2	Grover Alexander	150.00	75.00	45.00
3	W.S. Alexander (W.E.)	60.00	30.00	18.00
4	Leon Ames	60.00	30.00	18.00
5	Fred Anderson	60.00	30.00	18.00
6	Ed Appleton	60.00	30.00	18.00
7	Jimmy Archer	60.00	30.00	18.00
8	Jimmy Austin	60.00	30.00	18.00
9	Jim Bagby	60.00	30.00	18.00
10	H.D. Baird	60.00	30.00	18.00
11	J. Franklin Baker	150.00	75.00	45.00
12	Dave Bancroft	150.00	75.00	45.00
13	Jack Barry	60.00	30.00	18.00
14	Joe Benz	60.00	30.00	18.00
15	Al Betzel	60.00	30.00	18.00
16	Ping Bodie	60.00	30.00	18.00
17	Joe Boehling	60.00	30.00	18.00
18	Eddie Burns	60.00	30.00	18.00
19	George Burns	60.00	30.00	18.00
20	Geo. J. Burns	60.00	30.00	18.00
21	Joe Bush	60.00	27.00	16.50
22	Owen Bush	60.00	30.00	18.00
23	Bobby Byrne	60.00	30.00	18.00
24	Forrest Cady	60.00	30.00	18.00
25	Max Carey	150.00	75.00	45.00
26	Ray Chapman	75.00	37.00	22.00
27	Larry Cheney	60.00	30.00	18.00
28	Eddie Cicotte	95.00	47.00	28.00
29	Tom Clarke	60.00	30.00	18.00
30	Ty Cobb	1900.	950.00	570.00
31	Eddie Collins	150.00	75.00	45.00
32	"Shauno" Collins (Shano)	60.00	30.00	18.00
33	Fred Coumbe	60.00	30.00	18.00
34	Harry Coveleskie (Coveleski)	60.00	30.00	18.00
35	Gavvy Cravath	60.00	30.00	18.00
36	Sam Crawford	150.00	75.00	45.00
37	Geo. Cutshaw	60.00	30.00	18.00
38	Jake Daubert	60.00	30.00	18.00
39	Geo. Dauss	60.00	30.00	18.00
40	Charles Deal	60.00	30.00	18.00
41	"Wheezer" Dell	60.00	30.00	18.00
42	William Doak	60.00	30.00	18.00
43	Bill Donovan	60.00	30.00	18.00
44	Larry Doyle	60.00	30.00	18.00
45	Johnny Evers	150.00	75.00	45.00
46	Urban Faber	150.00	75.00	45.00
47	"Hap" Felsch	75.00	37.00	22.00
48	Bill Fischer	60.00	30.00	18.00
49	Ray Fisher	60.00	30.00	18.00
50	Art Fletcher	60.00	30.00	18.00
51	Eddie Foster	60.00	30.00	18.00
52	Jacques Fournier	60.00	30.00	18.00
53	Del Gainer (Gainor)	60.00	30.00	18.00
54	Bert Gallia	60.00	30.00	18.00
55	"Chic" Gandil (Chick)	95.00	47.00	28.00
56	Larry Gardner	60.00	30.00	18.00
57	Joe Gedeon	60.00	30.00	18.00
58	Gus Getz	60.00	30.00	18.00
59	Frank Gilhooley	60.00	30.00	18.00
60	Wm. Gleason	60.00	30.00	18.00
61	M.A. Gonzales (Gonzalez)	70.00	35.00	21.00
62	Hank Gowdy	60.00	30.00	18.00
63	John Graney	60.00	30.00	18.00
64	Tom Griffith	60.00	30.00	18.00
65	Heinie Groh	60.00	27.00	16.50
66	Bob Groom	60.00	30.00	18.00
67	Louis Guisto	60.00	30.00	18.00
68	Earl Hamilton	60.00	30.00	18.00
69	Harry Harper	60.00	30.00	18.00
70	Grover Hartley	60.00	30.00	18.00
71	Harry Heilmann	150.00	75.00	45.00
72	Claude Hendrix	60.00	30.00	18.00
73	Olaf Henriksen	60.00	30.00	18.00
74	John Henry	60.00	30.00	18.00
75	"Buck" Herzog	60.00	30.00	18.00
76a	Hugh High (white stockings, photo actually Claude Williams)	150.00	75.00	45.00
76b	Hugh High (black stockings, correct photo)	75.00	37.00	22.00
77	Dick Hoblitzell	60.00	30.00	18.00
78	Walter Holke	60.00	30.00	18.00
79	Harry Hooper	150.00	75.00	45.00
80	Rogers Hornsby	200.00	100.00	60.00
81	Ivan Howard	60.00	30.00	18.00
82	Joe Jackson	4750.	2375.	1425.
83	Harold Janvrin	60.00	30.00	18.00
84	William James	60.00	30.00	18.00
85	C. Jamieson	60.00	30.00	18.00
86	Hugh Jennings	150.00	75.00	45.00
87	Walter Johnson	650.00	325.00	195.00
88	James Johnston	60.00	30.00	18.00
89	Fielder Jones	60.00	30.00	18.00
90a	Joe Judge (bat on right shoulder, photo actually Ray Morgan)	150.00	75.00	45.00
90b	Joe Judge (bat on left shoulder, correct photo)	75.00	37.00	22.00
91	Hans Lobert	60.00	30.00	18.00
92	Benny Kauff	60.00	30.00	18.00
93	Wm. Killefer Jr.	60.00	30.00	18.00
94	Ed. Konetchy	60.00	30.00	18.00
95	John Lavan	60.00	30.00	18.00
96	Jimmy Lavender	60.00	30.00	18.00
97	"Nemo" Leibold	60.00	30.00	18.00
98	H.B. Leonard	60.00	30.00	18.00
99	Duffy Lewis	60.00	27.00	16.50
100	Tom Long	60.00	30.00	18.00
101	Wm. Louden	60.00	30.00	18.00
102	Fred Luderus	60.00	30.00	18.00
103	Lee Magee	60.00	30.00	18.00
104	Sherwood Magee	60.00	30.00	18.00
105	Al Mamaux	60.00	30.00	18.00
106	Leslie Mann	60.00	30.00	18.00
107	"Rabbit" Maranville	150.00	75.00	45.00
108	Rube Marquard	150.00	75.00	45.00
109	Armando Marsans	65.00	32.00	19.50
110	J. Erskine Mayer	60.00	30.00	18.00
111	George McBride	60.00	30.00	18.00
112	Lew McCarty	60.00	30.00	18.00
113	John J. McGraw	150.00	75.00	45.00
114	Jack McInnis	60.00	30.00	18.00
115	Lee Meadows	60.00	30.00	18.00
116	Fred Merkle	60.00	27.00	16.50
117	"Chief" Meyers	60.00	30.00	18.00
118	Clyde Milan	60.00	30.00	18.00
119	Otto Miller	60.00	30.00	18.00
120	Clarence Mitchell	60.00	30.00	18.00
121a	Ray Morgan (bat on left shoulder, photo actually Joe Judge)	150.00	75.00	45.00
121b	Ray Morgan (bat on right shoulder, correct photo)	75.00	37.00	22.00
122	Guy Morton	60.00	30.00	18.00
123	"Mike" Mowrey	60.00	30.00	18.00
124	Elmer Myers	60.00	30.00	18.00
125	"Hy" Myers	60.00	30.00	18.00
126	A.E. Neale	70.00	35.00	21.00
127	Arthur Nehf	60.00	30.00	18.00
128	J.A. Niehoff	60.00	30.00	18.00
129	Steve O'Neill	60.00	30.00	18.00
130	"Dode" Paskert	60.00	30.00	18.00
131	Roger Peckinpaugh	60.00	27.00	16.50
132	"Pol" Perritt	60.00	30.00	18.00
133	"Jeff" Pfeffer	60.00	30.00	18.00
134	Walter Pipp	90.00	45.00	27.00
135	Derril Pratt (Derrill)	60.00	30.00	18.00
136	Bill Rariden	60.00	30.00	18.00
137	E.C. Rice	150.00	75.00	45.00
138	Wm. A. Ritter (Wm. H.)	60.00	30.00	18.00
139	Eppa Rixey	150.00	75.00	45.00
140	Davey Robertson	60.00	30.00	18.00
141	"Bob" Roth	60.00	30.00	18.00
142	Ed. Roush	150.00	75.00	45.00
143	Clarence Rowland	60.00	30.00	18.00
144	Dick Rudolph	60.00	30.00	18.00
145	William Rumler	60.00	30.00	18.00
146a	Reb Russell (pitching follow-thru, photo actually Mellie Wolfgang)	150.00	75.00	45.00
146b	Reb Russell (hands at side, correct photo)	75.00	37.00	22.00
147	"Babe" Ruth	4500.	2250.	1350.
148	Vic Saier	60.00	30.00	18.00
149	"Slim" Sallee	60.00	30.00	18.00
150	Ray Schalk	150.00	75.00	45.00
151	Walter Schang	60.00	30.00	18.00
152	Frank Schulte	60.00	30.00	18.00
153	Ferd Schupp	60.00	30.00	18.00
154	Everett Scott	60.00	30.00	18.00
155	Hank Severeid	60.00	30.00	18.00
156	Howard Shanks	60.00	30.00	18.00
157	Bob Shawkey	60.00	30.00	18.00
158	Jas. Sheckard	60.00	30.00	18.00
159	Ernie Shore	60.00	30.00	18.00
160	C.H. Shorten	60.00	30.00	18.00
161	Burt Shotton	60.00	30.00	18.00
162	Geo. Sisler	150.00	75.00	45.00
163	Elmer Smith	60.00	30.00	18.00
164	J. Carlisle Smith	60.00	30.00	18.00
165	Fred Snodgrass	60.00	30.00	18.00
166	Tris Speaker	200.00	100.00	60.00
167	Oscar Stanage	60.00	30.00	18.00
168	Charles Stengel	200.00	100.00	60.00
169	Milton Stock	60.00	30.00	18.00
170	Amos Strunk	60.00	30.00	18.00
171	"Zeb" Terry	60.00	30.00	18.00
172	"Jeff" Tesreau	60.00	30.00	18.00
173	Chester Thomas	60.00	30.00	18.00
174	Fred Toney	60.00	30.00	18.00
175	Terry Turner	60.00	30.00	18.00
176	George Tyler	60.00	30.00	18.00
177	Jim Vaughn	60.00	30.00	18.00
178	Bob Veach	60.00	30.00	18.00
179	Oscar Vitt	60.00	30.00	18.00
180	Hans Wagner	1200.	600.00	360.00
181	Clarence Walker	60.00	30.00	18.00
182	Jim Walsh	60.00	30.00	18.00
183	Al Walters	60.00	30.00	18.00
184	W. Wambsganss	60.00	27.00	16.50
185	Buck Weaver	95.00	47.00	28.00
186	Carl Weilman	60.00	30.00	18.00
187	Zack Wheat	150.00	75.00	45.00
188	Geo. Whitted	60.00	30.00	18.00
189	Joe Wilhoit	60.00	30.00	18.00
190a	Claude Williams (black stockings, photo actually Hugh High)	225.00	112.00	67.00
190b	Claude Williams (white stockings, correct photo)	80.00	40.00	24.00
191	Fred Williams	60.00	30.00	18.00
192	Art Wilson	60.00	30.00	18.00
193	Lawton Witt	60.00	30.00	18.00
194	Joe Wood	60.00	30.00	18.00
195	William Wortman	60.00	30.00	18.00
196	Steve Yerkes	60.00	30.00	18.00
197	Earl Yingling	60.00	30.00	18.00
198	"Pep" Young (photo actually Ralph Young)	60.00	30.00	18.00
199	Rollie Zeider	60.00	30.00	18.00
200	Henry Zimmerman	60.00	30.00	18.00

1910 Coupon Cigarettes Type 1 (T213)

Because they feature the same photos used in the contemporary T206 tobacco set, some collectors fail to recognize the T213 Coupon set as a separate issue. Actually, the Coupon Cigarette cards make up three distinct issues, produced from 1910 to 1919 and featuring a mix of players from the major leagues, the Federal League and the Southern League. While the fronts of the Coupon cards appear to be identical to the more popular T206 series, the backs clearly identify the cards as being a product of Coupon Cigarettes and allow the collector to easily differentiate between the three types. Type I cards, produced in 1910, carry a general advertisement for Coupon "Mild" Cigarettes, while the Type II cards, issued from 1914 to 1916, contain the words "20 for 5 cents." Type III cards, issued in 1919, advertise "16 for 10 cts." Distribution of the Coupon cards was limited to the Louisiana area, making the set very obscure and difficult to checklist. Numerous variations further complicate the situation. It is quite possible the checklists here are incomplete and additions will surface in the future. Type I cards are considered the rarest of the Coupon issues, and, because they were printed on a thinner stock, they are especially difficult to find in top condition. Although Type II cards are the most common, they were printed with a "glossy" coating, making them susceptible to cracking and creasing.

		NM	EX	VG
	Complete Set (68):	15750.	7100.	3450.
	Common Player:	150.00	67.00	33.00
(1)	Harry Bay	150.00	67.00	33.00
(2)	Beals Becker	150.00	67.00	33.00
(3)	Chief Bender	450.00	200.00	100.00
(4)	Bernhard	150.00	67.00	33.00
(5)	Ted Breitenstein	150.00	67.00	33.00
(6)	Bobby Byrne	150.00	67.00	33.00
(7)	Billy Campbell	150.00	67.00	33.00
(8)	Scoops Carey	450.00	200.00	100.00
(9)	Frank Chance	450.00	200.00	100.00
(10)	Chappy Charles	150.00	67.00	33.00
(11)	Hal Chase (portrait)	200.00	90.00	44.00
(12)	Hal Chase (throwing)	200.00	90.00	44.00
(13)	Ty Cobb	3000.	1500.	800.00
(14)	Bill Cranston	150.00	67.00	33.00
(15)	Birdie Cree	150.00	67.00	33.00
(16)	Wild Bill Donovan	150.00	67.00	33.00
(17)	Mickey Doolan	150.00	67.00	33.00
(18)	Jean Dubuc	150.00	67.00	33.00
(19)	Joe Dunn	150.00	67.00	33.00
(20)	Roy Ellam	150.00	67.00	33.00
(21)	Clyde Engle	150.00	67.00	33.00
(22)	Johnny Evers	450.00	200.00	100.00
(23)	Art Fletcher	150.00	67.00	33.00
(24)	Charlie Fritz	150.00	67.00	33.00
(25)	Ed Greminger	150.00	67.00	33.00
(26)	Bill Hart (Little Rock)	150.00	67.00	33.00
(27)	Jimmy Hart (Montgomery)	150.00	67.00	33.00
(28)	Topsy Hartsel	150.00	67.00	33.00
(29)	Gordon Hickman	150.00	67.00	33.00
(30)	Danny Hoffman	150.00	67.00	33.00
(31)	Harry Howell	150.00	67.00	33.00
(32)	Miller Huggins (hands at mouth)	450.00	200.00	100.00
(33)	Miller Huggins (portrait)	450.00	200.00	100.00
(34)	George Hunter	150.00	67.00	33.00
(35)	A.O. "Dutch" Jordan	150.00	67.00	33.00
(36)	Ed Killian	150.00	67.00	33.00
(37)	Otto Knabe	150.00	67.00	33.00
(38)	Frank LaPorte	150.00	67.00	33.00
(39)	Ed Lennox	150.00	67.00	33.00
(40)	Harry Lentz (Sentz)	150.00	67.00	33.00
(41)	Rube Marquard	450.00	200.00	100.00
(42)	Doc Marshall	150.00	67.00	33.00
(43)	Christy Mathewson	1250.	560.00	275.00
(44)	George McBride	150.00	67.00	33.00
(45)	Pryor McElveen	150.00	67.00	33.00
(46)	Matty McIntyre	150.00	67.00	33.00
(47)	Mike Mitchell	150.00	67.00	33.00
(48)	Carlton Molesworth	150.00	67.00	33.00
(49)	Mike Mowrey	150.00	67.00	33.00
(50)	Chief Myers (Meyers) (batting)	150.00	67.00	33.00
(51)	Chief Myers (Meyers) (fielding)	150.00	67.00	33.00
(52)	Dode Paskert	150.00	67.00	33.00
(53)	Hub Perdue	150.00	67.00	33.00
(54)	Arch Persons	150.00	67.00	33.00
(55)	Ed Reagan	150.00	67.00	33.00
(56)	Bob Rhoades (Rhoads)	150.00	67.00	33.00
(57)	Ike Rockenfeld	150.00	67.00	33.00
(58)	Claude Rossman	150.00	67.00	33.00
(59)	Boss Schmidt	150.00	67.00	33.00
(60)	Sid Smith	150.00	67.00	33.00
(61)	Charlie Starr	150.00	67.00	33.00
(62)	Gabby Street	150.00	67.00	33.00
(63)	Ed Summers	150.00	67.00	33.00
(64)	Jeff Sweeney	150.00	67.00	33.00
(65)	Ira Thomas	150.00	67.00	33.00
(66)	Woodie Thornton	150.00	67.00	33.00
(67)	Ed Willett	150.00	67.00	33.00
(68)	Owen Wilson	150.00	67.00	33.00

1914 Coupon Cigarettes Type 2 (T213)

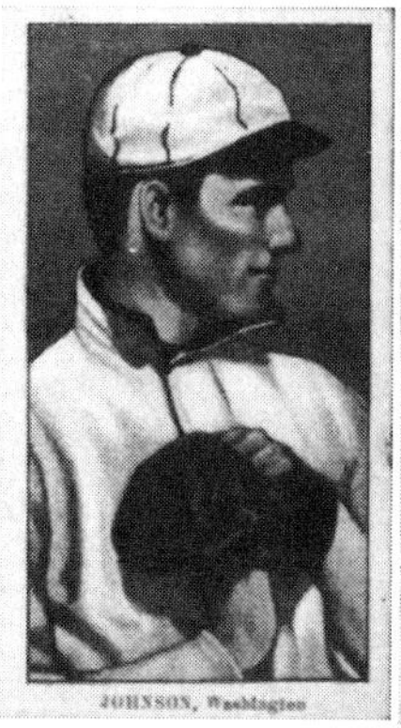

		NM	EX	VG
	Complete Set (188):	24000.	11000.	5300.
	Common Player:	100.00	45.00	22.00
(1)	Red Ames (Cincinnati)	100.00	45.00	22.00
(2)	Red Ames (St. Louis)	100.00	45.00	22.00
(3)	Home Run Baker (Phila. Amer.)	235.00	105.00	52.00
(4)	Home Run Baker (Philadelphia Amer.)	235.00	105.00	52.00
(5)	Home Run Baker (New York)	235.00	105.00	52.00
(6)	Cy Barger	100.00	45.00	22.00
(7)	Chief Bender (trees in background, Philadelphia Amer.)	235.00	105.00	52.00
(8)	Chief Bender (trees in background, Baltimore)	235.00	105.00	52.00
(9)	Chief Bender (trees in background, Philadelphia Nat.)	235.00	105.00	52.00
(10)	Chief Bender (no trees in background, Philadelphia Amer.)	235.00	105.00	52.00
(11)	Chief Bender (no trees in background, Baltimore)	235.00	105.00	52.00
(12)	Chief Bender (no trees in background, Philadelphia Na)	235.00	105.00	52.00
(13)	Bill Bradley	100.00	45.00	22.00
(14)	Roger Bresnahan (Chicago)	235.00	105.00	52.00
(15)	Roger Bresnahan (Toledo)	235.00	105.00	52.00
(16)	Al Bridwell (St. Louis)	100.00	45.00	22.00
(17)	Al Bridwell (Nashville)	100.00	45.00	22.00
(18)	Mordecai Brown (Chicago)	235.00	105.00	52.00
(19)	Mordecai Brown (St. Louis)	235.00	105.00	52.00
(20)	Bobby Byrne	100.00	45.00	22.00
(21)	Howie Camnitz (arm at side)	100.00	45.00	22.00
(22)	Howie Camnitz (Pittsburgh, hands above head)	100.00	45.00	22.00
(23)	Howie Camnitz (Savannah, hands above head)	100.00	45.00	22.00
(24)	Billy Campbell	100.00	45.00	22.00
(25)	Frank Chance (batting, New York)	235.00	105.00	52.00
(26)	Frank Chance (Los Angeles, batting)	235.00	105.00	52.00
(27)	Frank Chance (New York, portrait)	235.00	105.00	52.00
(28)	Frank Chance (Los Angeles, portrait)	235.00	105.00	52.00
(29)	Bill Chapelle (Brooklyn, "R" on shirt)	100.00	45.00	22.00
(30)	Larry Chapelle (Chappel) (Cleveland, no "R" on shirt, photo actually Bill Chapelle)	100.00	45.00	22.00
(31)	Hal Chase (Chicago, holding trophy)	125.00	55.00	27.00
(32)	Hal Chase (Buffalo, holding trophy)	125.00	55.00	27.00
(33)	Hal Chase (Chicago, portrait, blue background)	125.00	55.00	27.00
(34)	Hal Chase (Buffalo, portrait, blue background)	125.00	55.00	27.00
(35)	Hal Chase (Chicago, throwing)	125.00	55.00	27.00
(36)	Hal Chase (Buffalo, throwing)	125.00	55.00	27.00
(37)	Ty Cobb (portrait)	2500.	1125.	550.00
(38)	Ty Cobb (with bat off shoulder)	2500.	1125.	550.00
(39)	Eddie Collins (Philadelphia, "A" on shirt)	235.00	105.00	52.00
(40)	Eddie Collins (Chicago, "A" on shirt)	235.00	105.00	52.00
(41)	Eddie Collins (Chicago, no "A" on shirt)	235.00	105.00	52.00
(42)	Doc Crandall (St. Louis Fed.)	100.00	45.00	22.00
(43)	Doc Crandall (St. Louis Amer.)	100.00	45.00	22.00
(44)	Sam Crawford	235.00	105.00	52.00
(45)	Birdie Cree	100.00	45.00	22.00
(46)	Harry Davis (Phila. Amer.)	100.00	45.00	22.00
(47)	Harry Davis (Philadelphia Amer.)	100.00	45.00	22.00
(48)	Ray Demmitt (New York (A.L.) uniform)	100.00	45.00	22.00
(49)	Ray Demmitt (St. Louis (A.L.) uniform)	100.00	45.00	22.00
(50)	Josh Devore (Philadelphia)	100.00	45.00	22.00
(51)	Josh Devore (Chillicothe)	100.00	45.00	22.00
(52)	Mike Donlin (New York)	100.00	45.00	22.00
(53)	Mike Donlin (.300 batter 7 years)	100.00	45.00	22.00
(54)	Wild Bill Donovan	100.00	45.00	22.00
(55)	Mickey Doolan (Baltimore, batting)	100.00	45.00	22.00
(56)	Mickey Doolan (Chicago, batting)	100.00	45.00	22.00
(57)	Mickey Doolan (Baltimore, fielding)	100.00	45.00	22.00
(58)	Mickey Doolan (Chicago, fielding)	100.00	45.00	22.00
(59)	Tom Downey	100.00	45.00	22.00
(60)	Larry Doyle (batting)	100.00	45.00	22.00
(61)	Larry Doyle (portrait)	100.00	45.00	22.00
(62)	Jean Dubuc	100.00	45.00	22.00
(63)	Jack Dunn	100.00	45.00	22.00
(64)	Kid Elberfield (Elberfeld) (Brooklyn)	100.00	45.00	22.00
(65)	Kid Elberfield (Elberfeld) (Chatanooga)	100.00	45.00	22.00
(66)	Steve Evans	100.00	45.00	22.00
(67)	Johnny Evers	235.00	105.00	52.00
(68)	Russ Ford	100.00	45.00	22.00
(69)	Art Fromme	100.00	45.00	22.00
(70)	Chick Gandil (Washington)	175.00	75.00	38.00
(71)	Chick Gandil (Cleveland)	175.00	75.00	38.00
(72)	Rube Geyer	100.00	45.00	22.00
(73)	Clark Griffith	235.00	105.00	52.00
(74)	Bob Groom	100.00	45.00	22.00
(75)	Buck Herzog ("B" on shirt)	100.00	45.00	22.00
(76)	Buck Herzog (no "B" on shirt)	100.00	45.00	22.00
(77)	Dick Hoblitzell (Cincinnati)	100.00	45.00	22.00
(78)	Dick Hoblitzell (Boston Nat.)	100.00	45.00	22.00
(79)	Dick Hoblitzell (Boston Amer.)	100.00	45.00	22.00
(80)	Solly Hofman	100.00	45.00	22.00
(81)	Solly Hofmann (Hofman)	100.00	45.00	22.00
(82)	Miller Huggins (hands at mouth)	235.00	105.00	52.00
(83)	Miller Huggins (portrait)	235.00	105.00	52.00
(84)	John Hummel (Brooklyn Nat.)	100.00	45.00	22.00
(85)	John Hummel (Brooklyn)	100.00	45.00	22.00
(86)	Hughie Jennings (both hands showing)	235.00	105.00	52.00
(87)	Hughie Jennings (one hand showing)	235.00	105.00	52.00
(88)	Walter Johnson	1000.	450.00	220.00
(89)	Tim Jordan (Toronto)	100.00	45.00	22.00
(90)	Tim Jordan (Ft. Worth)	100.00	45.00	22.00
(91)	Joe Kelley (New York)	235.00	105.00	52.00
(92)	Joe Kelley (Toronto)	235.00	105.00	52.00
(93)	Otto Knabe	100.00	45.00	22.00
(94)	Ed Konetchy (Pittsburgh Nat.)	100.00	45.00	22.00
(95)	Ed Konetchy (Pittsburgh Fed.)	100.00	45.00	22.00
(96)	Ed Konetchy (Boston)	100.00	45.00	22.00
(97)	Harry Krause	100.00	45.00	22.00
(98)	Nap Lajoie (Phila. Amer.)	300.00	135.00	65.00
(99)	Nap Lajoie (Philadelphia Amer.)	300.00	135.00	65.00
(100)	Nap Lajoie (Cleveland)	300.00	135.00	65.00
(101)	Tommy Leach (Chicago)	100.00	45.00	22.00
(102)	Tommy Leach (Cincinnati)	100.00	45.00	22.00
(103)	Tommy Leach (Rochester)	100.00	45.00	22.00
(104)	Ed Lennox	100.00	45.00	22.00
(105)	Sherry Magee (Phila. Nat.)	100.00	45.00	22.00
(106)	Sherry Magee (Philadelphia Nat.)	100.00	45.00	22.00
(107)	Sherry Magee (Boston)	100.00	45.00	22.00
(108)	Rube Marquard (New York, pitching, "NY" on shirt)	235.00	105.00	52.00
(109)	Rube Marquard (Brooklyn, pitching, no "NY" on shirt)	235.00	105.00	52.00
(110)	Rube Marquard (New York, portrait, "NY" on shirt)	235.00	105.00	52.00
(111)	Rube Marquard (Brooklyn, portrait, no "NY" on shirt)	235.00	105.00	52.00
(112)	Christy Mathewson	1000.	450.00	220.00
(113)	John McGraw (glove at side)	235.00	105.00	52.00
(114)	John McGraw (portrait)	235.00	105.00	52.00
(115)	Larry McLean	100.00	45.00	22.00
(116)	George McQuillan (Pittsburgh)	100.00	45.00	22.00
(117)	George McQuillan (Phila. Nat.)	100.00	45.00	22.00
(118)	George McQuillan (Philadelphia Nat.)	100.00	45.00	22.00
(119)	Fred Merkle	100.00	45.00	22.00
(120)	Chief Meyers (New York, fielding)	100.00	45.00	22.00
(121)	Chief Meyers (Brooklyn, fielding)	100.00	45.00	22.00
(122)	Chief Meyers (New York, portrait)	100.00	45.00	22.00
(123)	Chief Meyers (Brooklyn, portrait)	100.00	45.00	22.00
(124)	Dots Miller	100.00	45.00	22.00
(125)	Mike Mitchell	100.00	45.00	22.00
(126)	Mike Mowrey (Pittsburgh Nat.)	100.00	45.00	22.00
(127)	Mike Mowrey (Pittsburgh Fed.)	100.00	45.00	22.00
(128)	Mike Mowrey (Brooklyn)	100.00	45.00	22.00
(129)	George Mullin (Indianapolis)	100.00	45.00	22.00
(130)	George Mullin (Newark)	100.00	45.00	22.00
(131)	Danny Murphy	100.00	45.00	22.00
(132)	Red Murray (New York)	100.00	45.00	22.00
(133)	Red Murray (Chicago)	100.00	45.00	22.00
(134)	Red Murray (Kansas City)	100.00	45.00	22.00
(135)	Tom Needham	100.00	45.00	22.00
(136)	Rebel Oakes	100.00	45.00	22.00
(137)	Rube Oldring (Phila. Amer.)	100.00	45.00	22.00
(138)	Rube Oldring (Philadelphia Amer.)	100.00	45.00	22.00
(139)	Dode Paskert (Phila. Nat.)	100.00	45.00	22.00
(140)	Dode Paskert (Philadelphia Nat.)	100.00	45.00	22.00

(141)	Billy Purtell	100.00	45.00	22.00
(142)	Jack Quinn (Baltimore)	100.00	45.00	22.00
(143)	Jack Quinn (Vernon)	100.00	45.00	22.00
(144)	Ed Reulbach (Brooklyn Nat.)	100.00	45.00	22.00
(145)	Ed Reulbach (Brooklyn Fed.)	100.00	45.00	22.00
(146)	Ed Reulbach (Pittsburgh)	100.00	45.00	22.00
(147)	Nap Rucker (Brooklyn)	100.00	45.00	22.00
(148)	Nap Rucker (Brooklyn Nat.)	100.00	45.00	22.00
(149)	Dick Rudolph	100.00	45.00	22.00
(150)	Germany Schaefer (Washington, "W" on shirt)	100.00	45.00	22.00
(151)	Germany Schaefer (K.C. Fed., "W" on shirt)	100.00	45.00	22.00
(152)	Germany Schaefer (New York, no "W" on shirt)	100.00	45.00	22.00
(153)	Admiral Schlei (batting)	100.00	45.00	22.00
(154)	Admiral Schlei (portrait)	100.00	45.00	22.00
(155)	Boss Schmidt	100.00	45.00	22.00
(156)	Wildfire Schulte	100.00	45.00	22.00
(157)	Frank Smith	100.00	45.00	22.00
(158)	Tris Speaker	300.00	140.00	65.00
(159)	George Stovall	100.00	45.00	22.00
(160)	Gabby Street (catching)	100.00	45.00	22.00
(161)	Gabby Street (portrait)	100.00	45.00	22.00
(162)	Ed Summers	100.00	45.00	22.00
(163)	Bill Sweeney (Boston)	100.00	45.00	22.00
(164)	Bill Sweeney (Chicago)	100.00	45.00	22.00
(165)	Jeff Sweeney (New York)	100.00	45.00	22.00
(166)	Jeff Sweeney (Richmond)	100.00	45.00	22.00
(167)	Ira Thomas (Phila. Amer.)	100.00	45.00	22.00
(168)	Ira Thomas (Philadelphia Amer.)	100.00	45.00	22.00
(169)	Joe Tinker (Chicago Fed., bat off shoulder)	235.00	105.00	52.00
(170)	Joe Tinker (Chicago Nat., bat off shoulder)	235.00	105.00	52.00
(171)	Joe Tinker (Chicago Fed., bat off shoulder)	235.00	105.00	52.00
(172)	Joe Tinker (Chicago Nat., bat off shoulder)	235.00	105.00	52.00
(173)	Heinie Wagner	100.00	45.00	22.00
(174)	Jack Warhop (New York, "NY" on shirt)	100.00	45.00	22.00
(175)	Jack Warhop (St. Louis, no "NY" on shirt)	100.00	45.00	22.00
(176)	Zach Wheat (Brooklyn)	235.00	105.00	52.00
(177)	Zach Wheat (Brooklyn Nat.)	235.00	105.00	52.00
(178)	Kaiser Wilhelm	100.00	45.00	22.00
(179)	Ed Willett (St. Louis)	100.00	45.00	22.00
(180)	Ed Willett (Memphis)	100.00	45.00	22.00
(181)	Owen Wilson	100.00	45.00	22.00
(182)	Hooks Wiltse (New York, pitching)	100.00	45.00	22.00
(183)	Hooks Wiltse (Brooklyn, pitching)	100.00	45.00	22.00
(184)	Hooks Wiltse (Jersey City, pitching)	100.00	45.00	22.00
(185)	Hooks Wiltse (New York, portrait)	100.00	45.00	22.00
(186)	Hooks Wiltse (Brooklyn, portrait)	100.00	45.00	22.00
(187)	Hooks Wiltse (Jersey City, portrait)	100.00	45.00	22.00
(188)	Heinie Zimmerman	100.00	45.00	22.00

1919 Coupon Cigarettes Type 3 (T213)

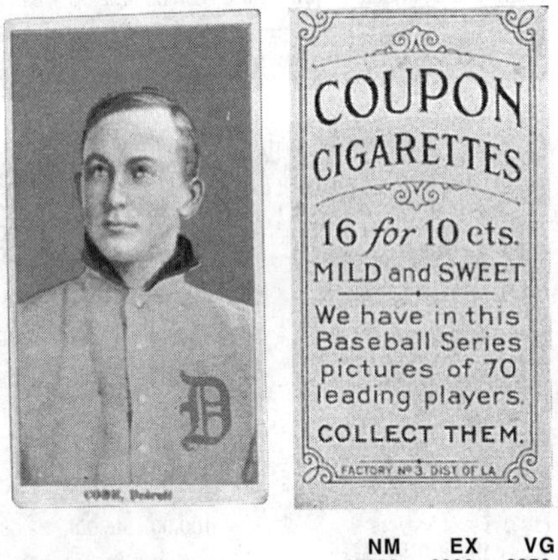

		NM	EX	VG
Complete Set (70):		15250.	6800.	3350.
Common Player:		130.00	58.00	29.00
(1)	Red Ames	130.00	58.00	29.00
(2)	Home Run Baker	300.00	135.00	66.00
(3)	Chief Bender (no trees in background)	300.00	135.00	66.00
(4)	Chief Bender (trees in background)	300.00	135.00	66.00
(5)	Roger Bresnahan	300.00	135.00	66.00
(6)	Al Bridwell	130.00	58.00	29.00
(7)	Miner Brown	300.00	135.00	66.00
(8)	Bobby Byrne	130.00	58.00	29.00
(9)	Frank Chance (batting)	300.00	135.00	66.00
(10)	Frank Chance (portrait)	300.00	135.00	66.00
(11)	Hal Chase (holding trophy)	150.00	67.00	33.00
(12)	Hal Chase (portrait)	150.00	67.00	33.00
(13)	Hal Chase (throwing)	150.00	67.00	33.00
(14)	Ty Cobb (batting)	2100.	945.00	465.00
(15)	Ty Cobb (portrait)	2100.	945.00	465.00
(16)	Eddie Collins	300.00	135.00	66.00
(17)	Sam Crawford	300.00	135.00	66.00
(18)	Harry Davis	130.00	58.00	29.00
(19)	Mike Donlin	130.00	58.00	29.00
(20)	Wild Bill Donovan	130.00	58.00	29.00
(21)	Mickey Doolan (batting)	130.00	58.00	29.00
(22)	Mickey Doolan (fielding)	130.00	58.00	29.00
(23)	Larry Doyle (batting)	130.00	58.00	29.00
(24)	Larry Doyle (portrait)	130.00	58.00	29.00
(25)	Jean Dubuc	130.00	58.00	29.00
(26)	Jack Dunn	130.00	58.00	29.00
(27)	Kid Elberfeld	130.00	58.00	29.00
(28)	Johnny Evers	300.00	135.00	66.00
(29)	Chick Gandil	150.00	67.00	33.00
(30)	Clark Griffith	300.00	135.00	66.00
(31)	Buck Herzog	130.00	58.00	29.00
(32)	Dick Hoblitzell	130.00	58.00	29.00
(33)	Miller Huggins (hands at mouth)	300.00	135.00	66.00
(34)	Miller Huggins (portrait)	300.00	135.00	66.00
(35)	John Hummel	130.00	58.00	29.00
(36)	Hughie Jennings (both hands showing)	300.00	135.00	66.00
(37)	Hughie Jennings (one hand showing)	300.00	135.00	66.00
(38)	Walter Johnson	750.00	335.00	165.00
(39)	Tim Jordan	130.00	58.00	29.00
(40)	Joe Kelley	300.00	135.00	66.00
(41)	Ed Konetchy	130.00	58.00	29.00
(42)	Larry Lajoie	300.00	135.00	66.00
(43)	Sherry Magee	130.00	58.00	29.00
(44)	Rube Marquard	300.00	135.00	66.00
(45)	Christy Mathewson	750.00	335.00	165.00
(47)	John McGraw (glove at side)	300.00	135.00	66.00
(48)	John McGraw (portrait)	300.00	135.00	66.00
(49)	George McQuillan	130.00	58.00	29.00
(50)	Fred Merkle	130.00	58.00	29.00
(51)	Dots Miller	130.00	58.00	29.00
(52)	Mike Mowrey	130.00	58.00	29.00
(53)	Chief Myers (Meyers) (Brooklyn)	130.00	58.00	29.00
(54)	Chief Myers (Meyers) (New Haven)	130.00	58.00	29.00
(55)	Dode Paskert	130.00	58.00	29.00
(56)	Jack Quinn	130.00	58.00	29.00
(57)	Ed Reulbach	130.00	58.00	29.00
(58)	Nap Rucker	130.00	58.00	29.00
(59)	Dick Rudolph	130.00	58.00	29.00
(60)	Herman Schaeffer (Schaefer)	130.00	58.00	29.00
(61)	Wildfire Schulte	130.00	58.00	29.00
(62)	Tris Speaker	350.00	155.00	75.00
(63)	Gabby Street (catching)	130.00	58.00	29.00
(64)	Gabby Street (portrait)	130.00	58.00	29.00
(65)	Jeff Sweeney	130.00	58.00	29.00
(66)	Ira Thomas	130.00	58.00	29.00
(67)	Joe Tinker	300.00	135.00	66.00
(68)	Zach Wheat	300.00	135.00	66.00
(69)	Geo. Wiltse	130.00	58.00	29.00
(70)	Heinie Zimmerman	130.00	58.00	29.00

1914 Cracker Jack

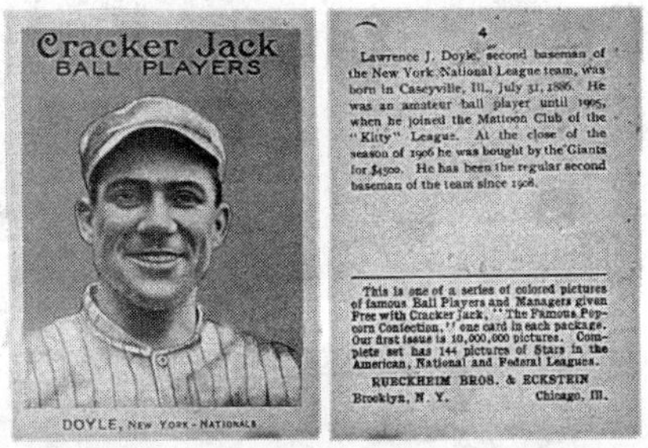

The 1914 Cracker Jack set, whose ACC designation is E145-1, is one of the most popular of the "E" card sets and features baseball stars from the American, National and Federal leagues. The 2-1/4" x 3" cards, are printed on thin stock and were inserted in boxes of Cracker Jack. The 1914 issue consists of 144 cards with tinted color photographs on a red background. Numbered backs feature a short biography plus an advertisement. The advertising on the low-numbered cards in the set indicates that 10 million cards were issued, while the high-numbered cards boast that 15 million were printed.

		NM	EX	VG
Complete Set (144):		65000.	26000.	13000.
Common Player:		200.00	80.00	40.00
1	Otto Knabe	750.00	250.00	130.00
2	Home Run Baker	900.00	360.00	180.00
3	Joe Tinker	600.00	240.00	120.00
4	Larry Doyle	200.00	80.00	40.00
5	Ward Miller	200.00	80.00	40.00
6	Eddie Plank	900.00	360.00	180.00
7	Eddie Collins	650.00	260.00	130.00
8	Rube Oldring	200.00	80.00	40.00
9	Artie Hoffman (Hofman)	200.00	80.00	40.00
10	Stuffy McInnis	200.00	80.00	40.00
11	George Stovall	200.00	80.00	40.00
12	Connie Mack	650.00	260.00	130.00
13	Art Wilson	200.00	80.00	40.00
14	Sam Crawford	400.00	160.00	80.00
15	Reb Russell	200.00	80.00	40.00
16	Howie Camnitz	200.00	80.00	40.00
17a	Roger Bresnahan (no number on back)	600.00	240.00	120.00
17b	Roger Bresnahan (number on back)	600.00	240.00	120.00
18	Johnny Evers	550.00	220.00	110.00
19	Chief Bender	600.00	240.00	120.00
20	Cy Falkenberg	200.00	80.00	40.00
21	Heinie Zimmerman	200.00	80.00	40.00
22	Smoky Joe Wood	200.00	80.00	40.00
23	Charles Comiskey	500.00	200.00	100.00
24	George Mullen (Mullin)	200.00	80.00	40.00
25	Mike Simon	200.00	80.00	40.00
26	Jim Scott	200.00	80.00	40.00
27	Bill Carrigan	200.00	80.00	40.00
28	Jack Barry	200.00	80.00	40.00
29	Vean Gregg	200.00	80.00	40.00
30	Ty Cobb	6000.	3000.	1350.
31	Heinie Wagner	200.00	80.00	40.00
32	Mordecai Brown	650.00	260.00	130.00
33	Amos Strunk	200.00	80.00	40.00
34	Ira Thomas	200.00	80.00	40.00
35	Harry Hooper	550.00	220.00	110.00
36	Ed Walsh	600.00	240.00	120.00
37	Grover C. Alexander	800.00	320.00	160.00
38	Red Dooin	200.00	80.00	40.00
39	Chick Gandil	325.00	130.00	65.00
40	Jimmy Austin	200.00	80.00	40.00
41	Tommy Leach	200.00	80.00	40.00
42	Al Bridwell	200.00	80.00	40.00
43	Rube Marquard	550.00	220.00	110.00
44	Jeff Tesreau	200.00	80.00	40.00
45	Fred Luderus	200.00	80.00	40.00
46	Bob Groom	200.00	80.00	40.00
47	Josh Devore	200.00	80.00	40.00
48	Harry Lord	450.00	180.00	90.00
49	Dots Miller	200.00	80.00	40.00
50	John Hummell (Hummel)	200.00	80.00	40.00
51	Nap Rucker	200.00	80.00	40.00
52	Zach Wheat	550.00	220.00	110.00
53	Otto Miller	200.00	80.00	40.00
54	Marty O'Toole	200.00	80.00	40.00
55	Dick Hoblitzel (Hoblitzell)	200.00	80.00	40.00
56	Clyde Milan	200.00	80.00	40.00
57	Walter Johnson	2400.	960.00	480.00
58	Wally Schang	200.00	80.00	40.00
59	Doc Gessler	200.00	80.00	40.00
60	Rollie Zeider	500.00	200.00	100.00
61	Ray Schalk	500.00	200.00	100.00
62	Jay Cashion	500.00	200.00	100.00
63	Babe Adams	200.00	80.00	40.00
64	Jimmy Archer	200.00	80.00	40.00
65	Tris Speaker	900.00	360.00	180.00
66	Nap Lajoie	950.00	380.00	190.00
67	Doc Crandall	200.00	80.00	40.00
68	Honus Wagner	3000.	1200.	600.00
69	John McGraw	650.00	260.00	130.00
70	Fred Clarke	450.00	180.00	90.00
71	Chief Meyers	200.00	80.00	40.00
72	Joe Boehling	200.00	80.00	40.00
73	Max Carey	400.00	160.00	80.00
74	Frank Owens	200.00	80.00	40.00
75	Miller Huggins	500.00	200.00	100.00
76	Claude Hendrix	200.00	80.00	40.00
77	Hughie Jennings	500.00	200.00	100.00
78	Fred Merkle	200.00	80.00	40.00
79	Ping Bodie	200.00	80.00	40.00
80	Ed Reulbach	200.00	80.00	40.00
81	Jim Delehanty (Delahanty)	200.00	80.00	40.00
82	Gavvy Cravath	200.00	80.00	40.00
83	Russ Ford	200.00	80.00	40.00
84	Elmer Knetzer	200.00	80.00	40.00
85	Buck Herzog	200.00	80.00	40.00
86	Burt Shotten	200.00	80.00	40.00
87	Hick Cady	200.00	80.00	40.00
88	Christy Mathewson	3000.	1200.	600.00
89	Larry Cheney	200.00	80.00	40.00
90	Frank Smith	200.00	80.00	40.00
91	Roger Peckinpaugh	200.00	80.00	40.00
92	Al Demaree	200.00	80.00	40.00
93	Del Pratt	600.00	240.00	120.00
94	Eddie Cicotte	275.00	110.00	55.00
95	Ray Keating	200.00	80.00	40.00
96	Beals Becker	200.00	80.00	40.00
97	Rube Benton	200.00	80.00	40.00
98	Frank Laporte (LaPorte)	200.00	80.00	40.00
99	Frank Chance	1600.	640.00	320.00
100	Tom Seaton	200.00	80.00	40.00
101	Wildfire Schulte	200.00	80.00	40.00
102	Ray Fisher	200.00	80.00	40.00
103	Shoeless Joe Jackson	15000.	6000.	3000.
104	Vic Saier	200.00	80.00	40.00
105	Jimmy Lavender	200.00	80.00	40.00
106	Joe Birmingham	200.00	80.00	40.00
107	Tom Downey	200.00	80.00	40.00
108	Sherry Magee	200.00	80.00	40.00
109	Fred Blanding	200.00	80.00	40.00
110	Bob Bescher	200.00	80.00	40.00
111	Nixey Callahan	600.00	240.00	120.00
112	Jeff Sweeney	200.00	80.00	40.00
113	George Suggs	200.00	80.00	40.00
114	George Moriarity (Moriarty)	200.00	80.00	40.00
115	Ad Brennan	200.00	80.00	40.00
116	Rollie Zeider	200.00	80.00	40.00
117	Ted Easterly	200.00	80.00	40.00
118	Ed Konetchy	200.00	80.00	40.00
119	George Perring	200.00	80.00	40.00
120	Mickey Doolan	200.00	80.00	40.00
121	Hub Perdue	200.00	80.00	40.00
122	Donie Bush	200.00	80.00	40.00
123	Slim Sallee	200.00	80.00	40.00
124	Earle Moore (Earl)	200.00	80.00	40.00
125	Bert Niehoff	200.00	80.00	40.00
126	Walter Blair	200.00	80.00	40.00
127	Butch Schmidt	200.00	80.00	40.00
128	Steve Evans	200.00	80.00	40.00
129	Ray Caldwell	200.00	80.00	40.00
130	Ivy Wingo	200.00	80.00	40.00
131	George Baumgardner	200.00	80.00	40.00

132	Les Nunamaker	200.00	80.00	40.00
133	Branch Rickey	600.00	240.00	120.00
134	Armando Marsans	250.00	100.00	50.00
135	Bill Killifer (Killefer)	200.00	80.00	40.00
136	Rabbit Maranville	600.00	240.00	120.00
137	Bill Rariden	200.00	80.00	40.00
138	Hank Gowdy	200.00	80.00	40.00
139	Rebel Oakes	200.00	80.00	40.00
140	Danny Murphy	200.00	80.00	40.00
141	Cy Barger	200.00	80.00	40.00
142	Gene Packard	200.00	80.00	40.00
143	Jake Daubert	200.00	80.00	40.00
144	Jimmy Walsh	500.00	200.00	100.00

1915 Cracker Jack

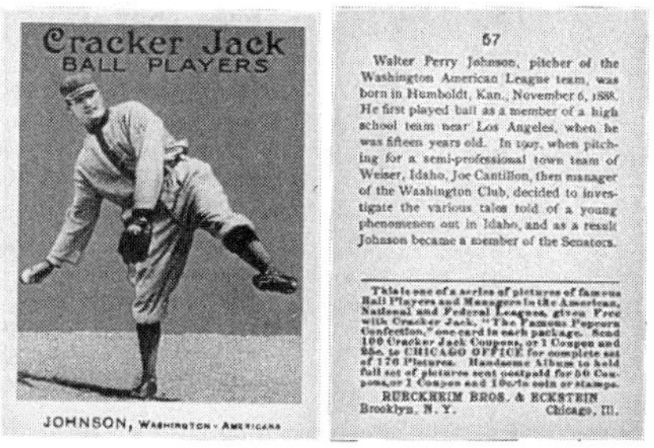

The 1915 Cracker Jack set (E145-2) is a reissue of the 1914 edition with some card additions and deletions, team designation changes, and new poses. A total of 176 cards comprise the set. Cards can be distinguished as either 1914 or 1915 by the advertising on the backs. The 1914 cards call the set complete at 144 pictures; the 1915 version notes 176 pictures. A complete set and an album were available from the company.

		NM	EX	VG
Complete Set (176):		40000.	16000.	8000.
Common Player (1-144):		160.00	65.00	35.00
Common Player (145-176):		240.00	95.00	50.00
Album:		750.00	375.00	225.00
1	Otto Knabe	500.00	200.00	100.00
2	Home Run Baker	650.00	260.00	130.00
3	Joe Tinker	575.00	230.00	115.00
4	Larry Doyle	160.00	64.00	32.00
5	Ward Miller	160.00	64.00	32.00
6	Eddie Plank	1000.	400.00	200.00
7	Eddie Collins	575.00	230.00	115.00
8	Rube Oldring	160.00	64.00	32.00
9	Artie Hoffman (Hofman)	160.00	64.00	32.00
10	Stuffy McInnis	160.00	64.00	32.00
11	George Stovall	160.00	64.00	32.00
12	Connie Mack	750.00	300.00	150.00
13	Art Wilson	160.00	64.00	32.00
14	Sam Crawford	450.00	180.00	90.00
15	Reb Russell	160.00	64.00	32.00
16	Howie Camnitz	160.00	64.00	32.00
17	Roger Bresnahan	525.00	210.00	105.00
18	Johnny Evers	600.00	240.00	120.00
19	Chief Bender	500.00	200.00	100.00
20	Cy Falkenberg	160.00	64.00	32.00
21	Heinie Zimmerman	160.00	64.00	32.00
22	Smoky Joe Wood	160.00	64.00	32.00
23	Charles Comiskey	800.00	320.00	160.00
24	George Mullen (Mullin)	160.00	64.00	32.00
25	Mike Simon	160.00	64.00	32.00
26	Jim Scott	160.00	64.00	32.00
27	Bill Carrigan	160.00	64.00	32.00
28	Jack Barry	160.00	64.00	32.00
29	Vean Gregg	160.00	64.00	32.00
30	Ty Cobb	6000.	2400.	1200.
31	Heinie Wagner	160.00	64.00	32.00
32	Mordecai Brown	500.00	200.00	100.00
33	Amos Strunk	160.00	64.00	32.00
34	Ira Thomas	160.00	64.00	32.00
35	Harry Hooper	500.00	200.00	100.00
36	Ed Walsh	500.00	200.00	100.00
37	Grover C. Alexander	800.00	320.00	160.00
38	Red Dooin	160.00	64.00	32.00
39	Chick Gandil	450.00	180.00	90.00
40	Jimmy Austin	160.00	64.00	32.00
41	Tommy Leach	160.00	64.00	32.00
42	Al Bridwell	160.00	64.00	32.00
43	Rube Marquard	525.00	210.00	105.00
44	Jeff Tesreau	160.00	64.00	32.00
45	Fred Luderus	160.00	64.00	32.00
46	Bob Groom	160.00	64.00	32.00
47	Josh Devore	160.00	64.00	32.00
48	Steve O'Neill	160.00	64.00	32.00
49	Dots Miller	160.00	64.00	32.00
50	John Hummell (Hummel)	160.00	64.00	32.00
51	Nap Rucker	160.00	64.00	32.00
52	Zach Wheat	500.00	200.00	100.00
53	Otto Miller	160.00	64.00	32.00
54	Marty O'Toole	160.00	64.00	32.00
55	Dick Hoblitzel (Hoblitzell)	160.00	64.00	32.00
56	Clyde Milan	160.00	64.00	32.00
57	Walter Johnson	1600.	650.00	325.00
58	Wally Schang	160.00	64.00	32.00
59	Doc Gessler	160.00	64.00	32.00
60	Oscar Dugey	160.00	64.00	32.00
61	Ray Schalk	600.00	240.00	120.00
62	Willie Mitchell	160.00	64.00	32.00
63	Babe Adams	160.00	64.00	32.00
64	Jimmy Archer	160.00	64.00	32.00
65	Tris Speaker	1150.	460.00	230.00
66	Nap Lajoie	1150.	460.00	230.00
67	Doc Crandall	160.00	64.00	32.00
68	Honus Wagner	2500.	1000.	500.00
69	John McGraw	600.00	240.00	120.00
70	Fred Clarke	450.00	180.00	90.00
71	Chief Meyers	160.00	64.00	32.00
72	Joe Boehling	160.00	64.00	32.00
73	Max Carey	450.00	180.00	90.00
74	Frank Owens	160.00	64.00	32.00
75	Miller Huggins	450.00	180.00	90.00
76	Claude Hendrix	160.00	64.00	32.00
77	Hughie Jennings	600.00	240.00	120.00
78	Fred Merkle	160.00	64.00	32.00
79	Ping Bodie	160.00	64.00	32.00
80	Ed Reulbach	160.00	64.00	32.00
81	Jim Delehanty (Delahanty)	160.00	64.00	32.00
82	Gavvy Cravath	160.00	64.00	32.00
83	Russ Ford	160.00	64.00	32.00
84	Elmer Knetzer	160.00	64.00	32.00
85	Buck Herzog	160.00	64.00	32.00
86	Burt Shotten	160.00	64.00	32.00
87	Hick Cady	160.00	64.00	32.00
88	Christy Mathewson	2500.	1000.	500.00
89	Larry Cheney	160.00	64.00	32.00
90	Frank Smith	160.00	64.00	32.00
91	Roger Peckinpaugh	160.00	64.00	32.00
92	Al Demaree	160.00	64.00	32.00
93	Del Pratt	160.00	64.00	32.00
94	Eddie Cicotte	450.00	180.00	90.00
95	Ray Keating	160.00	64.00	32.00
96	Beals Becker	160.00	64.00	32.00
97	Rube Benton	160.00	64.00	32.00
98	Frank Laporte (LaPorte)	160.00	64.00	32.00
99	Hal Chase	300.00	120.00	60.00
100	Tom Seaton	160.00	64.00	32.00
101	Wildfire Schulte	160.00	64.00	32.00
102	Ray Fisher	160.00	64.00	32.00
103	Shoeless Joe Jackson	12000.	4800.	2400.
104	Vic Saier	160.00	64.00	32.00
105	Jimmy Lavender	160.00	64.00	32.00
106	Joe Birmingham	160.00	64.00	32.00
107	Tom Downey	160.00	64.00	32.00
108	Sherry Magee	160.00	64.00	32.00
109	Fred Blanding	160.00	64.00	32.00
110	Bob Bescher	160.00	64.00	32.00
111	Herbie Moran	160.00	64.00	32.00
112	Jeff Sweeney	160.00	64.00	32.00
113	George Suggs	160.00	64.00	32.00
114	George Moriarity (Moriarty)	160.00	64.00	32.00
115	Ad Brennan	160.00	64.00	32.00
116	Rollie Zeider	160.00	64.00	32.00
117	Ted Easterly	160.00	64.00	32.00
118	Ed Konetchy	160.00	64.00	32.00
119	George Perring	160.00	64.00	32.00
120	Mickey Doolan	160.00	64.00	32.00
121	Hub Perdue	160.00	64.00	32.00
122	Donie Bush	160.00	64.00	32.00
123	Slim Sallee	160.00	64.00	32.00
124	Earle Moore (Earl)	160.00	64.00	32.00
125	Bert Niehoff	160.00	64.00	32.00
126	Walter Blair	160.00	64.00	32.00
127	Butch Schmidt	160.00	64.00	32.00
128	Steve Evans	160.00	64.00	32.00
129	Ray Caldwell	160.00	64.00	32.00
130	Ivy Wingo	160.00	64.00	32.00
131	George Baumgardner	160.00	64.00	32.00
132	Les Nunamaker	160.00	64.00	32.00
133	Branch Rickey	550.00	220.00	110.00
134	Armando Marsans	400.00	160.00	80.00
135	Bill Killifer (Killefer)	160.00	64.00	32.00
136	Rabbit Maranville	475.00	190.00	95.00
137	Bill Rariden	160.00	64.00	32.00
138	Hank Gowdy	160.00	64.00	32.00
139	Rebel Oakes	160.00	64.00	32.00
140	Danny Murphy	160.00	64.00	32.00
141	Cy Barger	160.00	64.00	32.00
142	Gene Packard	160.00	64.00	32.00
143	Jake Daubert	160.00	64.00	32.00
144	Jimmy Walsh	160.00	64.00	32.00
145	Ted Cather	240.00	95.00	50.00
146	Lefty Tyler	240.00	95.00	50.00
147	Lee Magee	240.00	95.00	50.00
148	Owen Wilson	240.00	95.00	50.00
149	Hal Janvrin	240.00	95.00	50.00
150	Doc Johnston	240.00	95.00	50.00
151	Possum Whitted	240.00	95.00	50.00
152	George McQuillen (McQuillan)	240.00	95.00	50.00
153	Bill James	240.00	95.00	50.00
154	Dick Rudolph	240.00	95.00	50.00
155	Joe Connolly	240.00	95.00	50.00
156	Jean Dubuc	240.00	95.00	50.00
157	George Kaiserling	240.00	95.00	50.00
158	Fritz Maisel	240.00	95.00	50.00
159	Heinie Groh	240.00	95.00	50.00
160	Benny Kauff	240.00	95.00	50.00
161	Edd Rousch (Roush)	450.00	180.00	90.00
162	George Stallings	240.00	95.00	50.00
163	Bert Whaling	240.00	95.00	50.00
164	Bob Shawkey	240.00	95.00	50.00
165	Eddie Murphy	240.00	95.00	50.00
166	Bullet Joe Bush	240.00	96.00	48.00
167	Clark Griffith	550.00	220.00	110.00
168	Vin Campbell	240.00	95.00	50.00
169	Ray Collins	240.00	95.00	50.00
170	Hans Lobert	240.00	95.00	50.00
171	Earl Hamilton	240.00	95.00	50.00
172	Erskine Mayer	240.00	96.00	48.00
173	Tilly Walker	240.00	95.00	50.00
174	Bobby Veach	240.00	95.00	50.00
175	Joe Benz	275.00	110.00	55.00
176	Hippo Vaughn	300.00	120.00	60.00

1976 Crane Potato Chips Discs

This unnumbered 70-card set of player discs was issued with Crane Potato Chips in 1976. The front of the discs are designed to look like a baseball with the player's black-and-white portrait in the center and vital data in side panels containing one of several bright colors. Discs measure 3-3/8" in diameter. This is the most common among several regionally issued sets sharing the same card fronts with different ads on back. The discs were produced by Michael Schechter Associates under license from the players' union. All uniform and cap logos have been deleted from the discs' photos. The unnumbered discs are checklisted here in alphabetical order. Several of the discs have team variations reflecting player moves. These are known only among the Crane discs and have not been verified in the issues of other advertisers.

		NM	EX	VG
Complete Set (70):		40.00	20.00	12.00
Common Player:		.50	.25	.15
(1)	Henry Aaron	4.50	2.25	1.25
(2)	Johnny Bench	2.50	1.25	.70
(3)	Vida Blue	.50	.25	.15
(4)	Larry Bowa	.50	.25	.15
(5)	Lou Brock	1.50	.70	.45
(6)	Jeff Burroughs	.50	.25	.15
(7)	John Candelaria	.50	.25	.15
(8)	Jose Cardenal	.50	.25	.15
(9)	Rod Carew	1.50	.70	.45
(10)	Steve Carlton	1.50	.70	.45
(11)	Dave Cash	.50	.25	.15
(12)	Cesar Cedeno	.50	.25	.15
(13)	Ron Cey	.50	.25	.15
(14)	Carlton Fisk	1.50	.70	.45
(15)	Tito Fuentes	.50	.25	.15
(16)	Steve Garvey	1.00	.50	.30
(17)	Ken Griffey	.50	.25	.15
(18)	Don Gullett	.50	.25	.15
(19)	Willie Horton	.50	.25	.15
(20)	Al Hrabosky	.50	.25	.15
(21)	Catfish Hunter	1.50	.70	.45
(22a)	Reggie Jackson (A's)	3.50	1.75	1.00
(22b)	Reggie Jackson (Orioles)	5.00	2.50	1.50
(23)	Randy Jones	.50	.25	.15
(24)	Jim Kaat	.50	.25	.15
(25)	Don Kessinger	.50	.25	.15
(26)	Dave Kingman	.75	.40	.25
(27)	Jerry Koosman	.50	.25	.15
(28)	Mickey Lolich	.60	.30	.20
(29)	Greg Luzinski	.50	.25	.15
(30)	Fred Lynn	.50	.25	.15
(31)	Bill Madlock	.50	.25	.15
(32a)	Carlos May (White Sox)	.50	.25	.15
(32b)	Carlos May (Yankees)	.50	.25	.15
(33)	John Mayberry	.50	.25	.15
(34)	Bake McBride	.50	.25	.15
(35)	Doc Medich	.50	.25	.15
(36a)	Andy Messersmith (Dodgers)	.50	.25	.15
(36b)	Andy Messersmith (Braves)	.50	.25	.15
(37)	Rick Monday	.50	.25	.15
(38)	John Montefusco	.50	.25	.15
(39)	Jerry Morales	.50	.25	.15
(40)	Joe Morgan	1.50	.70	.45
(41)	Thurman Munson	1.75	.90	.50
(42)	Bobby Murcer	.50	.25	.15
(43)	Al Oliver	.50	.25	.15
(44)	Jim Palmer	1.50	.70	.45
(45)	Dave Parker	.50	.25	.15
(46)	Tony Perez	1.50	.70	.45
(47)	Jerry Reuss	.50	.25	.15
(48)	Brooks Robinson	1.75	.90	.50
(49)	Frank Robinson	1.75	.90	.50
(50)	Steve Rogers	.50	.25	.15
(51)	Pete Rose	4.00	2.00	1.25
(52)	Nolan Ryan	8.00	4.00	2.50
(53)	Manny Sanguillen	.50	.25	.15
(54)	Mike Schmidt	3.00	1.50	.90
(55)	Tom Seaver	2.00	1.00	.60
(56)	Ted Simmons	.50	.25	.15
(57)	Reggie Smith	.50	.25	.15
(58)	Willie Stargell	1.50	.70	.45
(59)	Rusty Staub	.50	.25	.15
(60)	Rennie Stennett	.50	.25	.15
(61)	Don Sutton	1.50	.70	.45
(62a)	Andy Thornton (Cubs)	.50	.25	.15
(62b)	Andy Thornton (Expos)	.50	.25	.15
(63)	Luis Tiant	.50	.25	.15
(64)	Joe Torre	1.00	.50	.30
(65)	Mike Tyson	.50	.25	.15
(66)	Bob Watson	.50	.25	.15
(67)	Wilbur Wood	.50	.25	.15
(68)	Jimmy Wynn	.50	.25	.15
(69)	Carl Yastrzemski	2.00	1.00	.60
(70)	Richie Zisk	.50	.25	.15

1913 Cravats Felt Pennants

Little is known about this felt pennant issue, including the complete checklist. The name "Cravats" in the baseball above the player picture may represent the issuer, or describe the issue; the word "cravat" is an arcane term for a triangular piece of cloth. The pennants measure 4-1/8" across the top and are 9" long. Background colors are dark, with all printing in white. At center is a line art representation of the player, with his name horizontally beneath and his team nickname vertically at bottom. At top is a bat and ball logo with the "Cravats" name. Most specimens are seen with a metal ring reinforcing the hole punched at top center. The known checklist points to 1913 as the most probably year of issue.

		NM	EX	VG
Common Player:		100.00	50.00	30.00
(1)	Eddie Ainsmith	100.00	50.00	30.00
(2)	Hugh Bedient	100.00	50.00	30.00
(3)	Ray Caldwell	100.00	50.00	30.00
(4)	Jack Coombs	100.00	50.00	30.00
(5)	C.S. Dooin	100.00	50.00	30.00
(6)	Lawrence Doyle	100.00	50.00	30.00
(7)	Ed Konethy (Konetchy)	100.00	50.00	30.00
(8)	James Lavender	100.00	50.00	30.00
(9)	John J. McGraw	200.00	100.00	60.00
(10)	Stuffy McInnes (McInnis)	100.00	50.00	30.00
(11)	Christy Mathewson	400.00	200.00	120.00
(12)	J.T. (Chief) Meyer (Meyers)	100.00	50.00	30.00
(13)	Nap Rucker	100.00	50.00	30.00
(14)	Tris Speaker	200.00	100.00	60.00
(15)	Ed Sweeney	100.00	50.00	30.00
(16)	Jeff Tesreau	100.00	50.00	30.00
(17)	Ira Thomas	100.00	50.00	30.00
(18)	Joe Tinker	200.00	100.00	60.00
(19)	Ed Walsh	200.00	100.00	60.00

1909 Croft's Candy (E92)

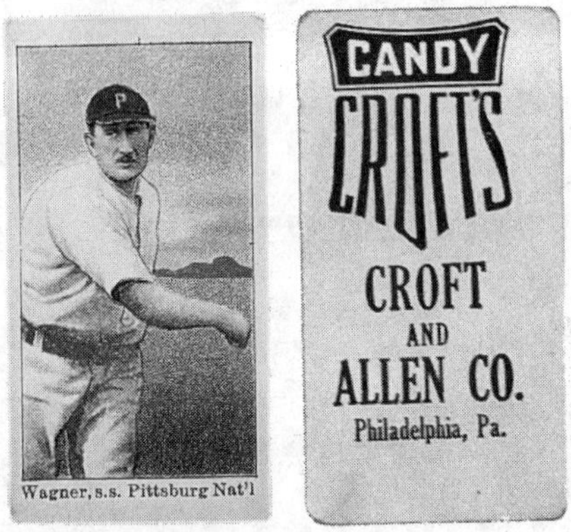

Because they share the format and pictures with several related issues (Croft's Cocoa, Dockman Gum, Nadja Caramels, etc.) this set shared the E92 designation in the American Card Catalog. It is more logical to present these sets as separate issues, based on the advertising which appears on back. Fronts of the 1-1/2" x 2-3/4" cards feature a color lithograph of the player. His last name, position and team are printed in black in the border below. Backs have a shield-shaped logo for Croft's Candy, a product of Croft & Allen Co., Philadelphia. Backs can be found printed in black or blue (scarcer). Cards are unnumbered and the checklist is presented here alphabetically.

		NM	EX	VG
Complete Set (50):		15500.	6200.	3000.
Common Player:		135.00	55.00	27.00
(1)	Jack Barry	300.00	120.00	60.00
(2)	Harry Bemis	135.00	54.00	27.00
(3)	Chief Bender (striped cap)	625.00	250.00	125.00
(4)	Chief Bender (white cap)	425.00	170.00	85.00
(5)	Bill Bergen	135.00	54.00	27.00
(6)	Bob Bescher	135.00	54.00	27.00
(7)	Al Bridwell	135.00	54.00	27.00
(8)	Doc Casey	135.00	54.00	27.00
(9)	Frank Chance	425.00	170.00	85.00
(10)	Hal Chase	175.00	70.00	35.00
(11)	Ty Cobb	4000.	1600.	800.00
(12)	Eddie Collins	600.00	240.00	120.00
(13)	Sam Crawford	350.00	140.00	70.00
(14)	Harry Davis	135.00	54.00	27.00
(15)	Art Devlin	135.00	54.00	27.00
(16)	Wild Bill Donovan	135.00	54.00	27.00
(17)	Red Dooin	275.00	110.00	55.00
(18)	Mickey Doolan	135.00	54.00	27.00
(19)	Patsy Dougherty	135.00	54.00	27.00
(20)	Larry Doyle (throwing)	135.00	54.00	27.00
(21)	Larry Doyle (with bat)	135.00	54.00	27.00
(22)	Johnny Evers	800.00	320.00	160.00
(23)	George Gibson	135.00	54.00	27.00
(24)	Topsy Hartsel	135.00	54.00	27.00
(25)	Fred Jacklitsch	300.00	120.00	60.00
(26)	Hugh Jennings	350.00	140.00	70.00
(27)	Red Kleinow	135.00	54.00	27.00
(28)	Otto Knabe	300.00	120.00	60.00
(29)	Jack Knight	300.00	120.00	60.00
(30)	Nap Lajoie	500.00	200.00	100.00
(31)	Hans Lobert	135.00	54.00	27.00
(32)	Sherry Magee	135.00	54.00	27.00
(33)	Christy Matthewson (Mathewson)	1100.	440.00	220.00
(34)	John McGraw	450.00	180.00	90.00
(35)	Larry McLean	135.00	54.00	27.00
(36)	Dots Miller (batting)	135.00	54.00	27.00
(37)	Dots Miller (fielding)	300.00	120.00	60.00
(38)	Danny Murphy	135.00	54.00	27.00
(39)	Bill O'Hara	135.00	54.00	27.00
(40)	Germany Schaefer	135.00	54.00	27.00
(41)	Admiral Schlei	135.00	54.00	27.00
(42)	Boss Schmidt	135.00	54.00	27.00
(43)	Johnny Seigle (Siegle)	135.00	54.00	27.00
(44)	Dave Shean	135.00	54.00	27.00
(45)	Boss Smith (Schmidt)	135.00	54.00	27.00
(46)	Joe Tinker	400.00	160.00	80.00
(47)	Honus Wagner (batting)	925.00	370.00	185.00
(48)	Honus Wagner (throwing)	925.00	370.00	185.00
(49)	Cy Young	750.00	300.00	150.00
(50)	Heinie Zimmerman	135.00	54.00	27.00

1909 Croft's Cocoa (E92)

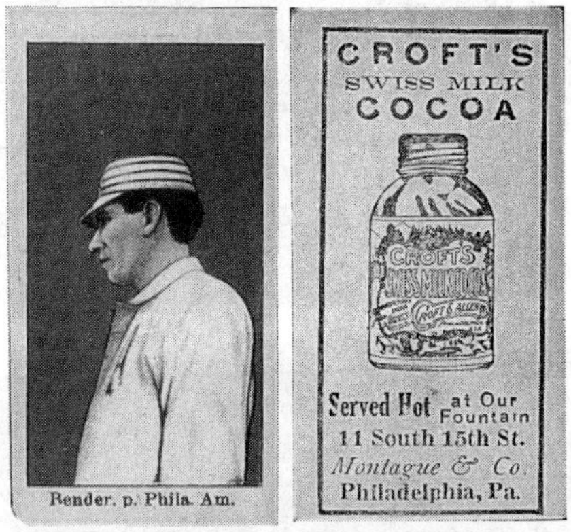

Like related issues once cataloged together as E92 (Croft's Candy, Dockman Gum, Nadja Caramels, etc.), these 1-1/2" x 2-3/4" cards feature a color player lithograph on front, which his name, position and team printed in the white border below. Backs have an ad for Crofts Swiss Milk Cocoa of Philadelphia. The checklist, presented here alphabetically, is identical to that of Croft's Candy.

		NM	EX	VG
Complete Set (50):		16000.	6400.	3100.
Common Player:		135.00	55.00	27.00
(1)	Jack Barry	350.00	175.00	105.00
(2)	Harry Bemis	135.00	55.00	27.00
(3)	Chief Bender (striped hat)	625.00	312.00	187.00
(4)	Chief Bender (white hat)	425.00	212.00	127.00
(5)	Bill Bergen	135.00	55.00	27.00
(6)	Bob Bescher	135.00	55.00	27.00
(7)	Al Bridwell	135.00	55.00	27.00
(8)	Doc Casey	135.00	55.00	27.00
(9)	Frank Chance	425.00	212.00	127.00
(10)	Hal Chase	175.00	87.00	52.00
(11)	Ty Cobb	4000.	2000.	1200.
(12)	Eddie Collins	600.00	300.00	180.00
(13)	Sam Crawford	350.00	175.00	105.00
(14)	Harry Davis	135.00	55.00	27.00
(15)	Art Devlin	135.00	55.00	27.00
(16)	Wild Bill Donovan	135.00	55.00	27.00
(17)	Red Dooin	300.00	150.00	90.00
(18)	Mickey Doolan	135.00	55.00	27.00
(19)	Patsy Dougherty	135.00	55.00	27.00
(20)	Larry Doyle (throwing)	135.00	55.00	27.00
(21)	Larry Doyle (with bat)	135.00	55.00	27.00
(22)	Johnny Evers	750.00	375.00	225.00
(23)	George Gibson	135.00	55.00	27.00
(24)	Topsy Hartsel	135.00	55.00	27.00
(25)	Fred Jacklitsch	300.00	150.00	90.00
(26)	Hugh Jennings	350.00	175.00	105.00
(27)	Red Kleinow	135.00	55.00	27.00
(28)	Otto Knabe	300.00	150.00	90.00
(29)	Jack Knight	300.00	150.00	90.00
(30)	Nap Lajoie	500.00	250.00	150.00
(31)	Hans Lobert	135.00	55.00	27.00
(32)	Sherry Magee	135.00	55.00	27.00
(33)	Christy Matthewson (Mathewson)	1100.	550.00	330.00
(34)	John McGraw	450.00	225.00	135.00
(35)	Larry McLean	135.00	55.00	27.00
(36)	Dots Miller (batting)	135.00	55.00	27.00
(37)	Dots Miller (fielding)	300.00	150.00	90.00
(38)	Danny Murphy	135.00	55.00	27.00
(39)	Bill O'Hara	135.00	55.00	27.00
(40)	Germany Schaefer	135.00	55.00	27.00
(41)	Admiral Schlei	135.00	55.00	27.00
(42)	Boss Schmidt	135.00	55.00	27.00
(43)	Johnny Seigle (Siegle)	135.00	55.00	27.00
(44)	Dave Shean	135.00	55.00	27.00
(45)	Boss Smith (Schmidt)	135.00	55.00	27.00
(46)	Joe Tinker	400.00	200.00	120.00
(47)	Honus Wagner (batting)	925.00	462.00	277.00
(48)	Honus Wagner (throwing)	925.00	462.00	277.00
(49)	Cy Young	750.00	375.00	225.00
(50)	Heinie Zimmerman	135.00	55.00	27.00

1977-78 Cubic Corp. Sports Decks playing cards

Playing cards featuring pencil drawings of stars in various sports were produced on a limited basis in the late 1970s by Cubic Corp. of San Diego. The cards are standard bridge size (2-1/4" x 3-1/2") with rounded corners and feature the artwork of Al Landsman along with a facsimile autograph within a colored frame. Each deck has the same athlete on the back and sold for $1.60. There is no indication of the manufacturer on individual cards, it is only found on the box. It is believed most of the decks were only produced in limited sample quantities. Similar cards were produced for Pepsi and are listed thereunder. Only the baseball players are checklisted here, in alphabetical order.

		NM	EX	VG
Complete Set, Boxed Decks (14):		500.00	250.00	150.00
Complete Set, One Card Each (14):		42.00	21.00	12.50
Common Boxed Deck:		15.00	7.50	4.50
Common Single Card:		.75	.40	.25
(1)	Johnny Bench (boxed deck)	30.00	15.00	9.00
(1)	Johnny Bench (single card)	1.50	.70	.45
(2)	Lou Gehrig (boxed deck)	75.00	37.00	22.00
(2)	Lou Gehrig (single card)	4.50	2.25	1.25
(3)	Catfish Hunter (boxed deck)	17.50	8.75	5.25
(3)	Catfish Hunter (single card)	1.50	.70	.45
(4)	Randy Jones (boxed deck)	15.00	7.50	4.50
(4)	Randy Jones (single card)	.75	.40	.25
(5)	Mickey Mantle (boxed deck)	125.00	62.00	37.00
(5)	Mickey Mantle (single card)	10.00	5.00	3.00
(6)	Butch Metzger (boxed deck)	15.00	7.50	4.50
(6)	Butch Metzger (single card)	.75	.40	.25
(7)	Joe Morgan (boxed deck)	17.50	8.75	5.25
(7)	Joe Morgan (single card)	1.50	.70	.45
(8)	Stan Musial (boxed deck)	62.00	31.00	18.50
(8)	Stan Musial (single card)	4.00	2.00	1.25
(9)	Jackie Robinson (boxed deck)	75.00	37.00	22.00
(9)	Jackie Robinson (single card)	4.50	2.25	1.25
(10)	Pete Rose (boxed deck)	50.00	25.00	15.00
(10)	Pete Rose (single card)	4.00	2.00	1.25
(11)	Babe Ruth (boxed deck)	100.00	50.00	30.00
(11)	Babe Ruth (single card)	6.00	3.00	1.75
(12)	Tom Seaver (boxed deck)	37.00	18.50	11.00
(12)	Tom Seaver (single card)	3.00	1.50	.90
(13)	Frank Tanana (boxed deck)	15.00	7.50	4.50
(13)	Frank Tanana (single card)	.75	.40	.25
(14)	Phillies logo/autographs (boxed deck)	10.00	5.00	3.00
(14)	Phillies logo/autographs (single card)	1.25	.60	.40

1911 Cullivan's Fireside Philadelphia A's

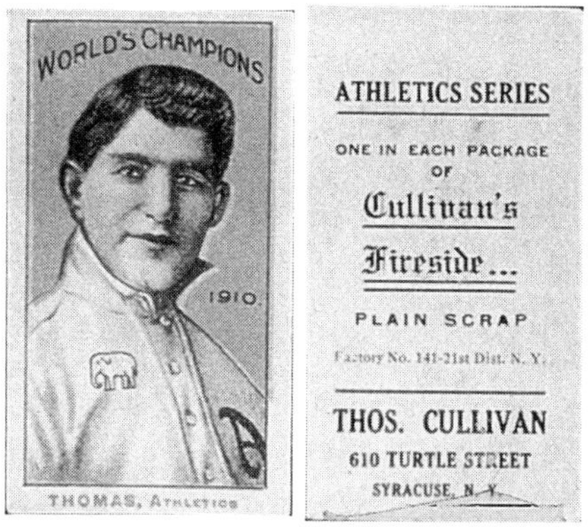

The 1911 T208 Firesides, an 18-card Philadelphia Athletics set issued by the Thomas Cullivan Tobacco Company of Syracuse, N.Y., is among the rarest of all 20th Century tobacco issues. Cullivan issued the set to commemorate the Athletics' 1910 Championship season, and, except for pitcher Jack Coombs, the checklist includes nearly all key members of the club, including manager Connie Mack. The cards are the standard cize for tobacco issues, about 1-1/2" x 2-5/8". The front of each card features a player portrait set against a colored background. The player's name and the word "Athletics" appear at the bottom, while "World's Champions 1910" is printed along the top. Backs advertise the set as the "Athletics Series" and advise that one card is included in each package of "Cullivan's Fireside Plain Scrap" tobacco. The same checklist was used for a similar Athletics set issued by Rochester Baking/Williams Baking (D359). Blank-backed versions are also known to exist.

		NM	EX	VG
Complete Set (18):		28000.	11250.	5600.
Common Player:		1250.	500.00	250.00
(1)	Home Run Baker	3000.	1200.	600.00
(2)	Jack Barry	1250.	500.00	250.00
(3)	Chief Bender	3000.	1200.	600.00
(4)	Eddie Collins	3000.	1200.	600.00
(5)	Harry Davis	1250.	500.00	250.00
(6)	Jimmy Dygert	1250.	500.00	250.00
(7)	Topsy Hartsel	1250.	500.00	250.00
(8)	Harry Krause	1250.	500.00	250.00
(9)	Jack Lapp	1250.	500.00	250.00
(10)	Paddy Livingstone (Livingston)	1250.	500.00	250.00
(11)	Bris Lord	1250.	500.00	250.00
(12)	Connie Mack	3000.	1200.	600.00
(13)	Cy Morgan	1250.	500.00	250.00
(14)	Danny Murphy	1250.	500.00	250.00
(15)	Rube Oldring	1250.	500.00	250.00
(16)	Eddie Plank	3000.	1200.	600.00
(17)	Amos Strunk	1250.	500.00	250.00
(18)	Ira Thomas	1250.	500.00	250.00

1964+ Curteichcolor Hall of Fame Plaque Postcards

(See Hall of Fame Yellow Plaque Postcards for checklist, price data.)

1909-12 Cycle Cigarettes

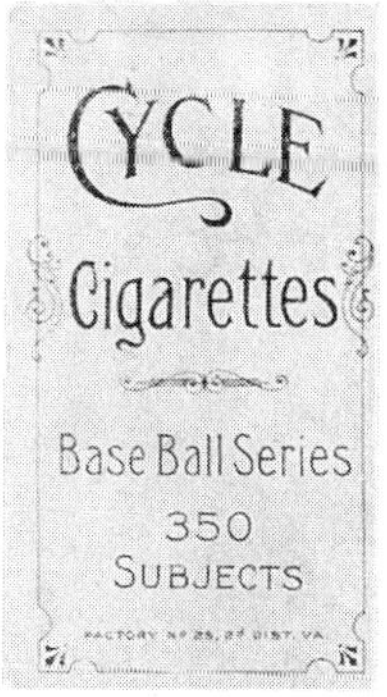

(See T205, T206, T207. Premium: T205 - 2X, T206/T207 - 1.75X.)

D

1977 Dad's Root Beer Cincinnati Reds Placemats

This series of plastic-laminated placemats features members of the 1977 Reds. Measuring 17" x 11", the mats' design combines player-action artwork with 3-1/2" round color portrait photos on a brightly colored background. Accompanying each player photo is personal data and 1976 stats. In the lower-right corner, are the logos of Dad's Root Beer and the Major League Baseball Player's Association. Like many other contemporary products licensed only by the players' union for Michael Schechter Associates, the photos and drawings on the placemats are devoid of uniform and cap logos. Backs have a simple weave pattern.

		NM	EX	VG
Complete Set (4):		32.00	16.00	9.50
Common Placemat:		6.00	3.00	1.75
(1)	Johnny Bench, Gary Nolan, Pat Zachry	12.00	6.00	3.50
(2)	Dave Concepcion, Dan Driessen, Joe Morgan	8.00	4.00	2.50
(3)	Rawly Eastwick, George Foster, Woodie Fryman	6.00	3.00	1.75
(4)	Cesar Geronimo, Ken Griffey, Pete Rose	16.00	8.00	4.75

1972 Daily Juice Co.

This one-card "set" was regionally issued to Roberto Clemente Fan Club members. Large numbers of the cards found their way into the hobby, including in uncut sheet form. The cards feature a full-color and black-and-white back. The card measures the standard 2-1/2" in width but is somewhat longer, at 3-3/4". This unnumbered card remains about the least expensive baseball card that was issued during Clemente's lifetime.

		NM	EX	VG
Complete Set:				
1	Roberto Clemente	17.50	8.75	5.25

1976 Dairy Isle Discs

One of several regional sponsors of player disc sets in 1976 was the upstate New York area chain, Dairy Isle. The discs are 3-3/8" diameter with a black-and-white player portrait photo in the center of the baseball design. A line of red stars is above, while the left and right panels feature one of several bright colors. Produced by Michael Schecter Associates under license from the Major League Baseball Players Association, the player photos have had uniform and cap logos removed. Backs are printed in red and purple. The unnumbered checklist here is presented in alphabetical order.

		NM	EX	VG
Complete Set (70):		90.00	45.00	27.00
Common Player:		1.00	.50	.30
(1)	Henry Aaron	10.00	5.00	3.00
(2)	Johnny Bench	6.00	3.00	1.75
(3)	Vida Blue	1.00	.50	.30
(4)	Larry Bowa	1.00	.50	.30
(5)	Lou Brock	3.50	1.75	1.00
(6)	Jeff Burroughs	1.00	.50	.30
(7)	John Candelaria	1.00	.50	.30
(8)	Jose Cardenal	1.00	.50	.30
(9)	Rod Carew	3.50	1.75	1.00
(10)	Steve Carlton	3.50	1.75	1.00
(11)	Dave Cash	1.00	.50	.30
(12)	Cesar Cedeno	1.00	.50	.30
(13)	Ron Cey	1.00	.50	.30
(14)	Carlton Fisk	3.50	1.75	1.00
(15)	Tito Fuentes	1.00	.50	.30
(16)	Steve Garvey	3.00	1.50	.90
(17)	Ken Griffey	1.25	.60	.40
(18)	Don Gullett	1.00	.50	.30
(19)	Willie Horton	1.00	.50	.30
(20)	Al Hrabosky	1.00	.50	.30
(21)	Catfish Hunter	3.50	1.75	1.00
(22)	Reggie Jackson	7.50	3.75	2.25
(23)	Randy Jones	1.00	.50	.30
(24)	Jim Kaat	2.00	1.00	.60
(25)	Don Kessinger	1.00	.50	.30
(26)	Dave Kingman	1.50	.70	.45
(27)	Jerry Koosman	1.00	.50	.30
(28)	Mickey Lolich	1.50	.70	.45
(29)	Greg Luzinski	1.00	.50	.30
(30)	Fred Lynn	1.00	.50	.30
(31)	Bill Madlock	1.00	.50	.30
(32)	Carlos May	1.00	.50	.30
(33)	John Mayberry	1.00	.50	.30
(34)	Bake McBride	1.00	.50	.30
(35)	Doc Medich	1.00	.50	.30
(36)	Andy Messersmith	1.00	.50	.30
(37)	Rick Monday	1.00	.50	.30
(38)	John Montefusco	1.00	.50	.30
(39)	Jerry Morales	1.00	.50	.30
(40)	Joe Morgan	3.50	1.75	1.00
(41)	Thurman Munson	4.50	2.25	1.25
(42)	Bobby Murcer	1.00	.50	.30
(43)	Al Oliver	1.00	.50	.30
(44)	Jim Palmer	3.50	1.75	1.00
(45)	Dave Parker	1.00	.50	.30
(46)	Tony Perez	3.50	1.75	1.00
(47)	Jerry Reuss	1.00	.50	.30
(48)	Brooks Robinson	4.50	2.25	1.25
(49)	Frank Robinson	4.50	2.25	1.25
(50)	Steve Rogers	1.00	.50	.30
(51)	Pete Rose	10.00	5.00	3.00
(52)	Nolan Ryan	20.00	10.00	6.00
(53)	Manny Sanguillen	1.00	.50	.30
(54)	Mike Schmidt	7.50	3.75	2.25
(55)	Tom Seaver	5.00	2.50	1.50
(56)	Ted Simmons	1.00	.50	.30
(57)	Reggie Smith	1.00	.50	.30
(58)	Willie Stargell	3.50	1.75	1.00
(59)	Rusty Staub	1.50	.70	.45
(60)	Rennie Stennett	1.00	.50	.30
(61)	Don Sutton	3.50	1.75	1.00
(62)	Andy Thornton	1.00	.50	.30
(63)	Luis Tiant	1.00	.50	.30
(64)	Joe Torre	2.50	1.25	.70
(65)	Mike Tyson	1.00	.50	.30
(66)	Bob Watson	1.00	.50	.30
(67)	Wilbur Wood	1.00	.50	.30
(68)	Jimmy Wynn	1.00	.50	.30
(69)	Carl Yastrzemski	5.00	2.50	1.50
(70)	Richie Zisk	1.00	.50	.30

1977 Dairy Isle Discs

Virtually identical in format to the 1976 issue (substituting red and blue for the back ad in 1977, instead of the previous year's red and purple), these 3-3/8" diameter player discs were given away at Dairy Isle outlets. Discs once again feature black-and-white player portrait photos in the center of a baseball design. The left and right panels are in one of several bright colors. Licensed by the players' association through Mike Schechter Associates, the player photos carry no uniform logos. The unnumbered discs are checklisted here alphabetically.

		NM	EX	VG
Complete Set (70):		110.00	55.00	33.00
Common Player:		1.00	.50	.30
(1)	Sal Bando	1.00	.50	.30
(2)	Buddy Bell	1.00	.50	.30
(3)	Johnny Bench	5.00	2.50	1.50
(4)	Larry Bowa	1.00	.50	.30
(5)	Steve Braun	1.00	.50	.30
(6)	George Brett	15.00	7.50	4.50
(7)	Lou Brock	4.50	2.25	1.25
(8)	Jeff Burroughs	1.00	.50	.30
(9)	Bert Campaneris	1.00	.50	.30
(10)	John Candelaria	1.00	.50	.30
(11)	Jose Cardenal	1.00	.50	.30
(12)	Rod Carew	4.50	2.25	1.25
(13)	Steve Carlton	4.50	2.25	1.25
(14)	Dave Cash	1.00	.50	.30
(15)	Cesar Cedeno	1.00	.50	.30
(16)	Ron Cey	1.00	.50	.30
(17)	Dave Concepcion	1.00	.50	.30
(18)	Dennis Eckersley	3.00	1.50	.90
(19)	Mark Fidrych	3.00	1.50	.90
(20)	Rollie Fingers	4.50	2.25	1.25
(21)	Carlton Fisk	4.50	2.25	1.25
(22)	George Foster	1.00	.50	.30
(23)	Wayne Garland	1.00	.50	.30
(24)	Ralph Garr	1.00	.50	.30
(25)	Steve Garvey	3.50	1.75	1.00
(26)	Cesar Geronimo	1.00	.50	.30
(27)	Bobby Grich	1.00	.50	.30
(28)	Ken Griffey Sr.	1.25	.60	.40
(29)	Don Gullett	1.00	.50	.30
(30)	Mike Hargrove	1.00	.50	.30
(31)	Willie Horton	1.00	.50	.30
(32)	Al Hrabosky	1.00	.50	.30
(33)	Reggie Jackson	7.50	3.75	2.25
(34)	Randy Jones	1.00	.50	.30
(35)	Dave Kingman	2.00	1.00	.60
(36)	Jerry Koosman	1.00	.50	.30
(37)	Dave LaRoche	1.00	.50	.30
(38)	Greg Luzinski	1.00	.50	.30
(39)	Fred Lynn	1.25	.60	.40
(40)	Bill Madlock	1.00	.50	.30
(41)	Rick Manning	1.00	.50	.30
(42)	Jon Matlock	1.00	.50	.30
(43)	John Mayberry	1.00	.50	.30
(44)	Hal McRae	1.00	.50	.30
(45)	Andy Messersmith	1.00	.50	.30
(46)	Rick Monday	1.00	.50	.30
(47)	John Montefusco	1.00	.50	.30
(48)	Joe Morgan	4.50	2.25	1.25
(49)	Thurman Munson	6.00	3.00	1.75
(50)	Bobby Murcer	1.00	.50	.30
(51)	Bill North	1.00	.50	.30
(52)	Jim Palmer	4.50	2.25	1.25
(53)	Tony Perez	4.50	2.25	1.25
(54)	Jerry Reuss	1.00	.50	.30
(55)	Pete Rose	15.00	7.50	4.50
(56)	Joe Rudi	1.00	.50	.30
(57)	Nolan Ryan	18.50	9.25	5.50
(58)	Manny Sanguillen	1.00	.50	.30
(59)	Mike Schmidt	9.00	4.50	2.75
(60)	Tom Seaver	6.00	3.00	1.75
(61)	Bill Singer	1.00	.50	.30
(62)	Willie Stargell	4.50	2.25	1.25
(63)	Rusty Staub	1.50	.70	.45
(64)	Luis Tiant	1.00	.50	.30
(65)	Mike Tyson	1.00	.50	.30
(66)	Bob Watson	1.00	.50	.30
(67)	Butch Wynegar	1.00	.50	.30
(68)	Carl Yastrzemski	9.00	4.50	2.75
(69)	Robin Yount	6.00	3.00	1.75
(70)	Richie Zisk	1.00	.50	.30

1974 Dairylea N.Y. Mets foldout

This unusual collectible was apparently sponsored as a stadium giveaway. When folded, the piece measures about 8" square. When unfolded, accordian style, it measures about 40" x 8". The foldout pictures nine members of the 1974 Mets, printed back-to-back. The pictures are color portrait photos set against solid pastel backgrounds with a facsimile autograph.

		NM	EX	VG
Complete Foldout:		22.00	11.00	6.50
(1)	Dairylea ad			
(2)	John Milner			
(3)	Harry Parker			
(4)	Don Hahn			
(5)	Jon Matlack			
(6)	Tom Seaver			
(7)	Bud Harrelson			
(8)	Ed Kranepool			
(9)	Rusty Staub			
(10)	Ray Sadecki			

1975 Dairylea N.Y. Mets foldout

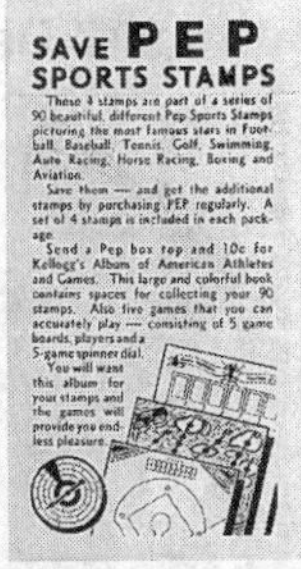

This unusual team set was a stadium giveaway. Packaged in a blue and orange envelope with a large team logo on front and sponsor's logo on back are a trio of foldouts. When unfolded, accordian style, each measures about 40" x 8" and pictures 10 members of the 1975 Mets, printed back-to-back. The pictures are color portrait photos set against solid pastel backgrounds with a facsimile autograph.

		NM	EX	VG
Complete Foldout:		30.00	15.00	9.00
	STRIP 1			
(1)	Jon Matlack			
(2)	Jesus Alou			
(3)	Wayne Garrett			
(4)	Del Unser			
(5)	Hank Webb			
(6)	Rusty Staub			
(7)	George Stone			
(8)	Jerry Grote			
(9)	Bob Gallagher			
(10)	Yogi Berra			
	STRIP 2			
(11)	Tom Seaver			
(12)	Felix Millan			
(13)	Dave Kingman			
(14)	Bob Apodaca			
(15)	Tom Hall			
(16)	Rick Baldwin			
(17)	John Milner			
(18)	Bud Harrelson			
(19)	Randy Tate			
(20)	Mike Phillips			
	STRIP 3			
(21)	Jerry Koosman			
(22)	Jack Heidemann			
(23)	Gene Clines			
(24)	Joe Torre			
(25)	Cleon Jones			
(26)	Harry Parker			
(27)	Ed Kranepool			
(28)	John Stearns			
(29)	Coaching staff			
(30)	Dairylea ad			

1976 Dairylea N.Y. Mets Photo Album

For the Bicentennial year, Dairylea switched the format of its stadium promotion to a bound "photo album." The 8" square album has a blue and orange tema logo on cover, with 13- and 50-star American flags. Inside are individual pages with player portraits. Each picture shows the player in home pinstripes but without a cap. There is a white border all around and a facsimile autograph. Backs are blank to allow the pictures to be removed and displayed. The unnumbered pictures are listed here in the order in which they appear in the album.

		NM	EX	VG
Complete Album:		17.50	8.75	5.25
(1)	Joe Frazier, Roy McMillan, Joe Pignatano, Rube Walker, Ed Yost			
(2)	Bob Apodaca			
(3)	Benny Ayala			
(4)	Bruce Boisclair			
(5)	Wayne Garrett			
(6)	Jerry Grote			
(7)	Tom Hall			
(8)	Bud Harrelson			
(9)	Dave Kingman			
(10)	Jerry Koosman			
(11)	Ed Kranepool			
(12)	Skip Lockwood			
(13)	Mickey Lolich			
(14)	Jon Matlack			
(15)	Felix Millan			
(16)	John Milner			
(17)	Mike Phillips			
(18)	Ken Sanders			
(19)	Tom Seaver			
(20)	Roy Staiger			
(21)	John Stearns			
(22)	Craig Swan			
(23)	Joe Torre			
(24)	Del Unser			
(25)	Mike Vail			
(26)	Hank Webb			

1956 Dairy Queen Stars Statues

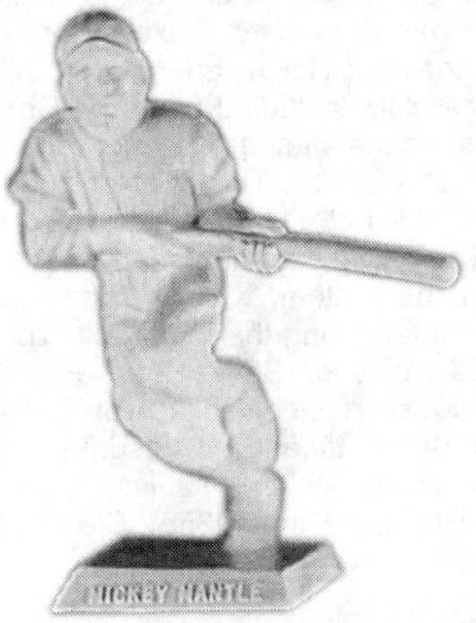

This set is identical in composition and manufacture to the carded figures sold as Big League Stars (see listing). The DQ versions of the statues are white, while the Big League versions are bronze colored. The statues measure about 3" tall and were evidently sold or given away with a purchase at the chain of ice cream shops.

		NM	EX	VG
Complete Set (18):		750.00	375.00	225.00
Common Player:		18.00	9.00	5.50
(1)	John Antonelli	18.00	9.00	5.50
(2)	Bob Avila	18.00	9.00	5.50
(3)	Yogi Berra	45.00	22.00	13.50
(4)	Roy Campanella	45.00	22.00	13.50
(5)	Larry Doby	30.00	15.00	9.00
(6)	Del Ennis	18.00	9.00	5.50
(7)	Jim Gilliam	18.00	9.00	5.50
(8)	Gil Hodges	35.00	17.50	10.50
(9)	Harvey Kuenn	18.00	9.00	5.50
(10)	Bob Lemon	25.00	12.50	7.50
(11)	Mickey Mantle	260.00	130.00	78.00
(12)	Ed Mathews	35.00	17.50	10.50
(13)	Minnie Minoso	18.00	9.00	5.50
(14)	Stan Musial	75.00	37.00	22.00
(15)	Pee Wee Reese	45.00	22.00	13.50
(16)	Al Rosen	18.00	9.00	5.50
(17)	Duke Snider	45.00	22.00	13.50
(18)	Mickey Vernon	18.00	9.00	5.50

1954 Dan-Dee Potato Chips

Issued in bags of potato chips, the cards in this 29-card set are commonly found with grease stains despite their waxed surface. The unnumbered cards, which measure 2-1/2" x 3-5/8", feature full-color photos. The card backs contain player statistical and biographical information. The set consists mostly of players from the Indians and Pirates. Photos of the Yankees players were also used for the Briggs Meats and Stahl-Meyer Franks sets. Cooper and Smith are the scarcest cards in the set.

		NM	EX	VG
Complete Set (29):		4475.	2225.	1345.
Common Player:		70.00	35.00	21.00
(1)	Bob Avila	70.00	35.00	21.00
(2)	Hank Bauer	75.00	37.00	22.00
(3)	Walker Cooper	375.00	187.00	112.00
(4)	Larry Doby	95.00	47.00	28.00
(5)	Luke Easter	70.00	35.00	21.00
(6)	Bob Feller	200.00	100.00	60.00
(7)	Bob Friend	70.00	35.00	21.00
(8)	Mike Garcia	70.00	35.00	21.00
(9)	Sid Gordon	70.00	35.00	21.00
(10)	Jim Hegan	70.00	35.00	21.00
(11)	Gil Hodges	150.00	75.00	45.00
(12)	Art Houtteman	70.00	35.00	21.00
(13)	Monte Irvin	95.00	47.00	28.00
(14)	Paul LaPalm (LaPalme)	70.00	35.00	21.00
(15)	Bob Lemon	95.00	47.00	28.00
(16)	Al Lopez	95.00	47.00	28.00
(17)	Mickey Mantle	1500.	750.00	450.00
(18)	Dale Mitchell	70.00	35.00	21.00
(19)	Phil Rizzuto	200.00	100.00	60.00
(20)	Curtis Roberts	70.00	35.00	21.00
(21)	Al Rosen	75.00	37.00	22.00
(22)	Red Schoendienst	95.00	47.00	28.00
(23)	Paul Smith	450.00	225.00	135.00
(24)	Duke Snider	245.00	122.00	73.00
(25)	George Strickland	70.00	35.00	21.00
(26)	Max Surkont	70.00	35.00	21.00
(27)	Frank Thomas	125.00	62.00	37.00
(28)	Wally Westlake	70.00	35.00	21.00
(29)	Early Wynn	95.00	47.00	28.00

1977 Tom Daniels Burleigh Grimes

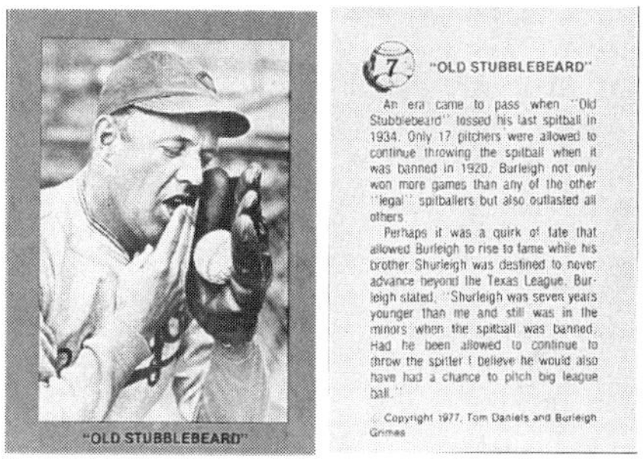

The career of Hall of Fame spitballer Burleigh Grimes is traced in this collectors issue. The 2-1/2" x 3-1/2" cards have black-and-white photos from Grimes' collection, bordered in bright blue. A card title is in black in the bottom border. Backs are printed in black and blue on white and have a description of the front photo. One card in each set is authentically autographed by Grimes. Price at issue was $3.50; uncut sheets were also available.

		NM	EX	VG
Complete Set (16):		8.00	4.00	2.50
Common Card:		.50	.25	.15
1	Dodger Manager 1937-38	.50	.25	.15
2	"Lord Burleigh"	.50	.25	.15
3	Last Spitballers	.50	.25	.15
4	Grimes, Hornsby, McGraw, Roush	.50	.25	.15
5	Winning Combination	.50	.25	.15
6	World Champion	.50	.25	.15
7	"Old Stubblebeard"	.50	.25	.15
8	Grimes Meets McCarthy	.50	.25	.15
9	Dodger Greats	.50	.25	.15
10	"The Babe"	1.00	.50	.30
11	Dodger Strategists	.50	.25	.15
12	Bender and Grimes	.50	.25	.15
13	Number '270'	.50	.25	.15
14	The Origin	.50	.25	.15
15	1964 HoF Inductees	.50	.25	.15
16	"Lord Burleigh" 1977	.50	.25	.15

1910 Darby Chocolates (E271)

The 1910 Darby Chocolates cards are among the rarest of all candy cards. The cards were printed on boxes of Darby's "Pennant" Chocolates, two players per box - one each on front and back. The cards feature black-and-white player action photos outlined with a thick dark shadow. The boxes are accented with orange or green graphics. Most of the 32 known examples of this set were not found until 1982, and there is speculation that the checklist is still not complete. Many of the known examples of this rare issue have been subjected to restoration. For such cards values must be adjusted downward.

		NM	EX	VG
Complete Set (32):		20000.	8000.	4000.
Common Player:		400.00	160.00	80.00
(1)	Jimmy Archer	400.00	160.00	80.00
(2)	Chief Bender	750.00	300.00	150.00
(3)	Bob Bescher	400.00	160.00	80.00
(4)	Roger Bresnahan	750.00	300.00	150.00
(5)	Al Bridwell	400.00	160.00	80.00
(6)	Mordicai Brown (Mordecai)	750.00	300.00	150.00
(7)	"Eddie" Cicotte	650.00	260.00	130.00
(8)	Fred Clark (Clarke)	750.00	300.00	150.00
(9)	Ty. Cobb	2750.	1100.	550.00
(10)	King Cole	400.00	160.00	80.00
(11)	E. Collins	800.00	325.00	160.00
(12)	Wid Conroy	400.00	160.00	80.00
(13)	"Sam" Crawford	750.00	300.00	150.00
(14)	Bill Dahlin (Dahlen)	400.00	160.00	80.00
(15)	Bill Donovan	400.00	160.00	80.00
(16)	"Pat" Dougherty	400.00	160.00	80.00
(17)	Kid Elberfeld	400.00	160.00	80.00
(18)	"Johnny" Evers	750.00	300.00	150.00
(19)	Charlie Herzog	400.00	160.00	80.00
(20)	Walter Johnson	1500.	600.00	300.00
(21)	Ed Konetchy	400.00	160.00	80.00
(22)	Tommy Leach	400.00	160.00	80.00
(23)	Fred Luderous (Luderus)	400.00	160.00	80.00
(24)	"Mike" Mowery (Mowrey)	400.00	160.00	80.00
(25)	Jack Powell	400.00	160.00	80.00
(26)	Slim Sallee	400.00	160.00	80.00
(27)	James Scheckard (Sheckard)	400.00	160.00	80.00
(28)	Walter Snodgrass	400.00	160.00	80.00
(29)	"Tris" Speaker	850.00	340.00	170.00
(30)	Charlie Suggs	400.00	160.00	80.00
(31)	Fred Tenney	400.00	160.00	80.00
(32)	"Hans" Wagner	1850.	750.00	375.00

1973 Dean's Photo Service San Diego Padres

A true rookie year issue for Dave Winfield is included in this set of 5-1/2" x 8-1/2" black-and-white, blank-backed player photos sponsored by Dean's Photo Service and given away by the team in five six-card series at various home games. Pictures have posed player portraits surrounded by a white border. Beneath are the name and position, with team and sponsor logos at bottom. The set is checklisted here alphabetically.

		NM	EX	VG
Complete Set (31):		80.00	40.00	24.00
Common Player:		3.00	1.50	.90
(1)	Steve Arlin	3.00	1.50	.90
(2)	Mike Caldwell	3.00	1.50	.90
(3)	Dave Campbell	3.00	1.50	.90
(4)	Nate Colbert	3.00	1.50	.90
(5)	Mike Corkins	3.00	1.50	.90
(6)	Pat Corrales	3.00	1.50	.90
(7)	Jim Davenport	3.00	1.50	.90
(8)	Dave Garcia	3.00	1.50	.90
(9)	Clarence Gaston	4.00	2.00	1.25
(10)	Bill Greif	3.00	1.50	.90
(11)	John Grubb	3.00	1.50	.90
(12)	Enzo Hernandez	3.00	1.50	.90
(13)	Randy Jones	3.00	1.50	.90
(14)	Fred Kendall	3.00	1.50	.90
(15)	Clay Kirby	3.00	1.50	.90
(16)	Leron Lee	3.00	1.50	.90
(17)	Dave Marshall	3.00	1.50	.90
(18)	Don Mason	3.00	1.50	.90
(19)	Jerry Morales	3.00	1.50	.90
(20)	Ivan Murrell	3.00	1.50	.90
(21)	Fred Norman	3.00	1.50	.90
(22)	Johnny Podres	4.00	2.00	1.25
(23)	Dave Roberts	3.00	1.50	.90
(24)	Vicente Romo	3.00	1.50	.90
(25)	Gary Ross	3.00	1.50	.90
(26)	Bob Skinner	3.00	1.50	.90
(27)	Derrel Thomas	3.00	1.50	.90
(28)	Rich Troedson	3.00	1.50	.90
(29)	Whitey Wietelmann	3.00	1.50	.90
(30)	Dave Winfield	24.00	12.00	7.25
(31)	Don Zimmer	4.50	2.25	1.25

1974 Dean's Photo Service San Diego Padres

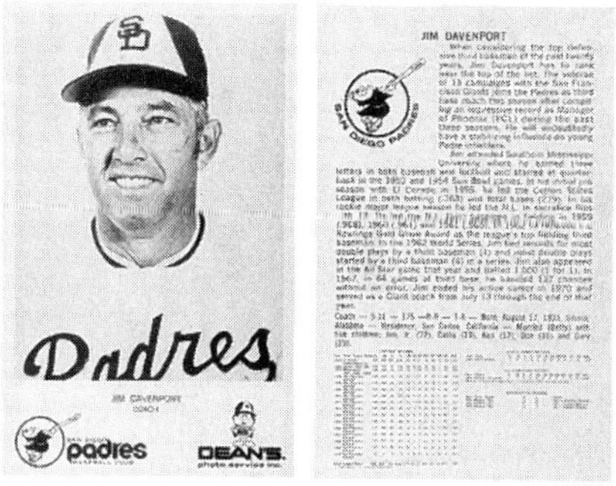

This issue shares the same basic format as the years which preceded it and succeeded it. Fronts of the 5-1/2" x 8-1/2" cards have a large player portrait or pose at top, with the player's name and position below. In the wide white border at bottom are the team and sponsor's logos. Backs, for the first time, have a lengthy career summary, personal data and full professional stats. All printing is in black-and-white. The unnumbered cards are checklisted here alphabetically.

		NM	EX	VG
Complete Set (30):		70.00	35.00	21.00
Common Player:		3.00	1.50	.90
(1)	Matty Alou	3.00	1.50	.90
(2)	Bob Barton	3.00	1.50	.90
(3)	Glenn Beckert	3.00	1.50	.90
(4)	Jack Bloomfield	3.00	1.50	.90
(5)	Nate Colbert	3.00	1.50	.90
(6)	Mike Corkins	3.00	1.50	.90
(7)	Jim Davenport	3.00	1.50	.90
(8)	Dave Freisleben	3.00	1.50	.90
(9)	Cito Gaston	4.50	2.25	1.25
(10)	Bill Greif	3.00	1.50	.90
(11)	Johnny Grubb	3.00	1.50	.90
(12)	Larry Hardy	3.00	1.50	.90
(13)	Enzo Hernandez	3.00	1.50	.90
(14)	Dave Hilton	3.00	1.50	.90
(15)	Randy Jones	3.00	1.50	.90
(16)	Fred Kendall	3.00	1.50	.90
(17)	Gene Locklear	3.00	1.50	.90
(18)	Willie McCovey	10.00	5.00	3.00
(19)	John McNamara	3.00	1.50	.90
(20)	Rich Morales	3.00	1.50	.90
(21)	Bill Posedel	3.00	1.50	.90
(22)	Dave Roberts	3.00	1.50	.90
(23)	Vicente Romo	3.00	1.50	.90
(24)	Dan Spillner	3.00	1.50	.90
(25)	Bob Tolan	3.00	1.50	.90
(26)	Derrel Thomas	3.00	1.50	.90
(27)	Rich Troedson	3.00	1.50	.90
(28)	Whitey Wietelmann	3.00	1.50	.90
(29)	Bernie Williams	3.00	1.50	.90
(30)	Dave Winfield	15.00	7.50	4.50

1975 Dean's Photo Service San Diego Padres

Player biographical data and stats continued on the backs of the cards in the 1975 series sponsored by Dean's. Once again the black-and-white pictures were in 5-1/2" x 8-1/2" format. Fronts have the player photo at top, with his name and position beneath. At bottom are the team and sponsor logos.

The Padres logo consists of a cartoon character robed monk in various baseball poses. The pictures were given away at autograph nights during the season. The unnumbered photos are checklisted here in alphabetical order.

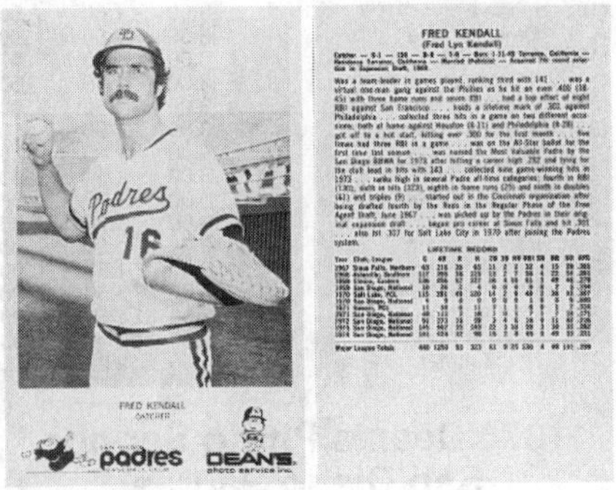

		NM	EX	VG
	Complete Set (30):	60.00	30.00	18.00
	Common Player:	2.00	1.00	.60
(1)	Jim Davenport	2.00	1.00	.60
(2)	Bob Davis	2.00	1.00	.60
(3)	Rich Folkers	2.00	1.00	.60
(4)	Alan Foster	2.00	1.00	.60
(5)	Dave Freisleben	2.00	1.00	.60
(6)	Danny Frisella	2.00	1.00	.60
(7)	Tito Fuentes	2.00	1.00	.60
(8)	Bill Greif	2.00	1.00	.60
(9)	Johnny Grubb	2.00	1.00	.60
(10)	Enzo Hernandez	2.00	1.00	.60
(11)	Randy Hundley (blank back)	2.00	1.00	.60
(12)	Mike Ivie	2.00	1.00	.60
(13)	Jerry Johnson	2.00	1.00	.60
(14)	Randy Jones	2.00	1.00	.60
(15)	Fred Kendall	2.00	1.00	.60
(16)	Ted Kubiak	2.00	1.00	.60
(17)	Gene Locklear	2.00	1.00	.60
(18)	Willie McCovey	8.00	4.00	2.50
(19)	Joe McIntosh	2.00	1.00	.60
(20)	John McNamara	2.00	1.00	.60
(21)	Tom Morgan	2.00	1.00	.60
(22)	Dick Sharon	2.00	1.00	.60
(23)	Dick Sisler	2.00	1.00	.60
(24)	Dan Spillner	2.00	1.00	.60
(25)	Brent Strom	2.00	1.00	.60
(26)	Bobby Tolan	2.00	1.00	.60
(27)	Dave Tomlin	2.00	1.00	.60
(28)	Hector Torres (blank back)	2.00	1.00	.60
(29)	Whitey Wietelmann	2.00	1.00	.60
(30)	Dave Winfield	12.00	6.00	3.50

1976 Dean's Photo Service San Diego Padres

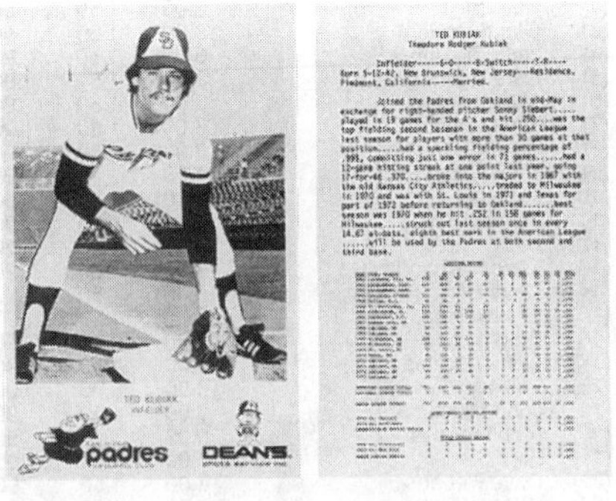

The last of four black-and-white team sets which were sponsored by Dean's was issued in 1976. The format was little different than previous years. Cards are 5-1/2" x 8-1/2" black-and-white. Fronts have a player portrait or pose surrounded by a white border. At bottom front are team and sponsor logos. Backs have personal data, a career summary and complete professional stats. The unnumbered cards are checklisted here in alphabetical order.

		NM	EX	VG
	Complete Set (30):	60.00	30.00	18.00
	Common Player:	2.00	1.00	.60
(1)	Joe Amalfitano	2.00	1.00	.60
(2)	Roger Craig	2.00	1.00	.60
(3)	Bob Davis	2.00	1.00	.60
(4)	Willie Davis	2.00	1.00	.60
(5)	Rich Folkers	2.00	1.00	.60
(6)	Alan Foster	2.00	1.00	.60
(7)	Dave Freisleben	2.00	1.00	.60
(8)	Tito Fuentes	2.00	1.00	.60
(9)	John Grubb	2.00	1.00	.60
(10)	Enzo Hernandez	2.00	1.00	.60
(11)	Mike Ivie	2.00	1.00	.60
(12)	Jerry Johnson	2.00	1.00	.60
(13)	Randy Jones	2.00	1.00	.60
(14)	Fred Kendall	2.00	1.00	.60
(15)	Ted Kubiak	2.00	1.00	.60
(16)	Willie McCovey	8.00	4.00	2.50
(17)	John McNamara	2.00	1.00	.60
(18)	Luis Melendez	2.00	1.00	.60
(19)	Butch Metzger	2.00	1.00	.60
(20)	Doug Rader	2.00	1.00	.60
(21)	Merv Rettenmund	2.00	1.00	.60
(22)	Ken Reynolds	2.00	1.00	.60
(23)	Dick Sisler	2.00	1.00	.60
(24)	Dan Spillner	2.00	1.00	.60
(25)	Brent Strom	2.00	1.00	.60
(26)	Dave Tomlin	2.00	1.00	.60
(27)	Hector Torres	2.00	1.00	.60
(28)	Jerry Turner	2.00	1.00	.60
(29)	Whitey Wietelmann	2.00	1.00	.60
(30)	Dave Winfield	12.00	6.00	3.50

1978 Dearborn Show

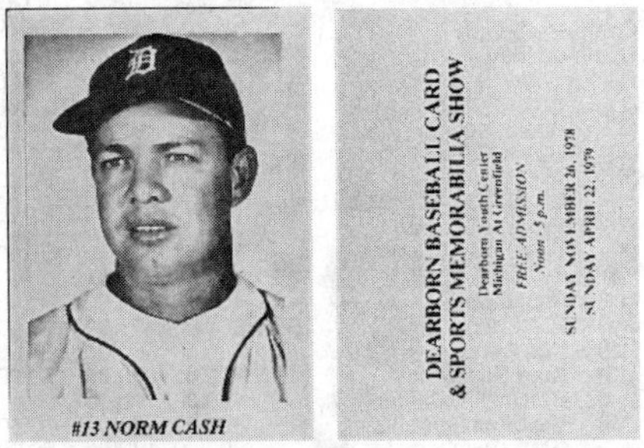

Former members of the Detroit Tigers, some of whom were scheduled to appear as autograph guests, are featured in this collectors issue produced in conjunction with the 1978 Dearborn Baseball Card & Sports Memorabilia Show. The 2-5/8" x 3-5/8" cards have black-and-white player photos on front with the player name and card number in the white border at bottom. Backs, also in black-and-white, advertise the fall, 1978, and spring, 1979 shows.

		NM	EX	VG
	Complete Set (18):	15.00	7.50	4.50
	Common Player:	.50	.25	.15
1	Rocky Colavito	2.00	1.00	.60
2	Ervin Fox	.50	.25	.15
3	Lynwood Rowe	.50	.25	.15
4	Gerald Walker	.50	.25	.15
5	Leon Goslin	.50	.25	.15
6	Harvey Kuenn	.75	.40	.25
7	Frank Howard	.50	.25	.15
8	Woodie Fryman	.50	.25	.15
9	Don Wert	.50	.25	.15
10	Jim Perry	.50	.25	.15
11	Mayo Smith	.50	.25	.15
12	Al Kaline	3.50	1.75	1.00
13	Norm Cash	1.50	.70	.45
14	Mickey Cochrane	1.00	.50	.30
15	Fred Marberry	.50	.25	.15
16	Bill Freehan	.75	.40	.25
17	Charlie Gehringer	1.00	.50	.30
18	Jim Northrup	.50	.25	.15

1971 Dell Today's Team Stamps

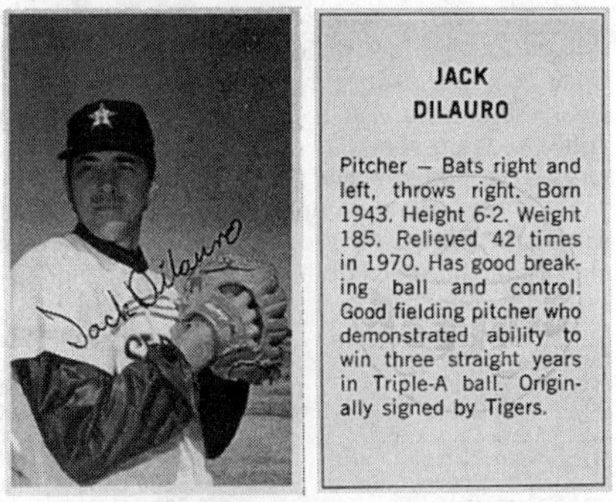
JACK
DILAURO
Pitcher – Bats right and left, throws right. Born 1943. Height 6-2. Weight 185. Relieved 42 times in 1970. Has good breaking ball and control. Good fielding pitcher who demonstrated ability to win three straight years in Triple-A ball. Originally signed by Tigers.

This issue was produced as a series of individual team (plus one All-Star) albums. The 8-1/2" x 10-7/8" booklets offer team and league histories and stats, photos of all-time team stars and two pages of 12 player stamps each. Each stamp is 1-7/8" x 2-15/16" and has a posed color photo and black facsimile autograph on front. Backs have the player name, biographical details and a few career highlights, along with an underprint of the team logo. The stamps are perforated for easy separation, though there are no spaces in the 12-page album for their housing once removed from the sheet. The team albums were sold individually as well as in divisional sets within each league. The checklist is arranged alphabetically by team within league; individual stamps are unnumbered.

		NM	EX	VG
	Complete Set, Albums (25):	360.00	180.00	108.00
	Complete Set, Stamps (600):	180.00	90.00	54.00
	Common Player:	.25	.13	.08
	Complete All-Star album:	30.00	15.00	9.00
(1)	Hank Aaron	8.00	4.00	2.50
(2)	Luis Aparicio	4.00	2.00	1.25
(3)	Ernie Banks	6.00	3.00	1.75
(4)	Johnny Bench	5.00	2.50	1.50
(5)	Rico Carty	.25	.13	.08
(6)	Roberto Clemente	10.00	5.00	3.00
(7)	Bob Gibson	4.00	2.00	1.25
(8)	Willie Horton	.25	.13	.08
(9)	Frank Howard	.75	.40	.25
(10)	Reggie Jackson	6.00	3.00	1.75
(11)	Fergie Jenkins	3.00	1.50	.90
(12)	Alex Johnson	.25	.13	.08
(13)	Al Kaline	4.00	2.00	1.25
(14)	Harmon Killebrew	4.00	2.00	1.25
(15)	Willie Mays	8.00	4.00	2.50
(16)	Sam McDowell	.50	.25	.15
(17)	Denny McLain	.75	.40	.25
(18)	Boog Powell	2.00	1.00	.60
(19)	Brooks Robinson	4.00	2.00	1.25
(20)	Frank Robinson	4.00	2.00	1.25
(21)	Pete Rose	8.00	4.00	2.50
(22)	Tom Seaver	4.00	2.00	1.25
(23)	Rusty Staub	.50	.25	.15
(24)	Carl Yastrzemski	4.00	2.00	1.25
	Complete Atlanta Braves album:	20.00	10.00	6.00
(1)	Hank Aaron	8.00	4.00	2.50
(2)	Tommie Aaron	.25	.13	.08
(3)	Hank Allen	.25	.13	.08
(4)	Clete Boyer	.50	.25	.15
(5)	Oscar Brown	.25	.13	.08
(6)	Rico Carty	.25	.13	.08
(7)	Orlando Cepeda	4.00	2.00	1.25
(8)	Bob Didier	.25	.13	.08
(9)	Ralph Garr	.25	.13	.08
(10)	Gil Garrido	.25	.13	.08
(11)	Ron Herbel	.25	.13	.08
(12)	Sonny Jackson	.25	.13	.08
(13)	Pat Jarvis	.25	.13	.08
(14)	Larry Jaster	.25	.13	.08
(15)	Hal King	.25	.13	.08
(16)	Mike Lum	.25	.13	.08
(17)	Felix Millan	.25	.13	.08
(18)	Jim Nash	.25	.13	.08
(19)	Phil Niekro	3.00	1.50	.90
(20)	Bob Priddy	.25	.13	.08
(21)	Ron Reed	.25	.13	.08
(22)	George Stone	.25	.13	.08
(23)	Cecil Upshaw	.25	.13	.08
(24)	Hoyt Wilhelm	3.00	1.50	.90
	Complete Chicago Cubs album:	20.00	10.00	6.00
(1)	Ernie Banks	6.00	3.00	1.75
(2)	Glenn Beckert	.25	.13	.08
(3)	Danny Breeden	.25	.13	.08
(4)	Johnny Callison	.25	.13	.08
(5)	Jim Colborn	.25	.13	.08
(6)	Joe Decker	.25	.13	.08
(7)	Bill Hands	.25	.13	.08
(8)	Jim Hickman	.25	.13	.08
(9)	Ken Holtzman	.25	.13	.08
(10)	Randy Hundley	.25	.13	.08
(11)	Fergie Jenkins	3.00	1.50	.90
(12)	Don Kessinger	.25	.13	.08
(13)	J.C. Martin	.25	.13	.08
(14)	Bob Miller	.25	.13	.08
(15)	Milt Pappas	.25	.13	.08
(16)	Joe Pepitone	.25	.13	.08
(17)	Juan Pizarro	.25	.13	.08
(18)	Paul Popovich	.25	.13	.08
(19)	Phil Regan	.25	.13	.08
(20)	Roberto Rodriguez	.25	.13	.08
(21)	Ken Rudolph	.25	.13	.08
(22)	Ron Santo	.75	.40	.25
(23)	Hector Torres	.25	.13	.08
(24)	Billy Williams	3.00	1.50	.90
	Complete Cincinnati Reds album:	25.00	12.50	7.50
(1)	Johnny Bench	5.00	2.50	1.50
(2)	Angel Bravo	.25	.13	.08
(3)	Bernie Carbo	.25	.13	.08
(4)	Clay Carroll	.25	.13	.08
(5)	Darrel Chaney	.25	.13	.08
(6)	Ty Cline	.25	.13	.08
(7)	Tony Cloninger	.25	.13	.08
(8)	Dave Concepcion	.25	.13	.08
(9)	Pat Corrales	.25	.13	.08
(10)	Greg Garrett	.25	.13	.08
(11)	Wayne Granger	.25	.13	.08
(12)	Don Gullett	.25	.13	.08
(13)	Tommy Helms	.25	.13	.08

(14)	Lee May	.25	.13	.08
(15)	Jim McGlothlin	.25	.13	.08
(16)	Hal McRae	.25	.13	.08
(17)	Jim Merritt	.25	.13	.08
(18)	Gary Nolan	.25	.13	.08
(19)	Tony Perez	4.00	2.00	1.25
(20)	Pete Rose	8.00	4.00	2.50
(21)	Wayne Simpson	.25	.13	.08
(22)	Jimmy Stewart	.25	.13	.08
(23)	Bobby Tolan	.25	.13	.08
(24)	Woody Woodward	.25	.13	.08
	Complete Houston Astros album:	15.00	7.50	4.50
(1)	Jesus Alou	.25	.13	.08
(2)	Jack Billingham	.25	.13	.08
(3)	Ron Cook	.25	.13	.08
(4)	George Culver	.25	.13	.08
(5)	Larry Dierker	.25	.13	.08
(6)	Jack DiLauro	.25	.13	.08
(7)	Johnny Edwards	.25	.13	.08
(8)	Fred Gladding	.25	.13	.08
(9)	Tom Griffin	.25	.13	.08
(10)	Skip Guinn	.25	.13	.08
(11)	Jack Hiatt	.25	.13	.08
(12)	Denny Lemaster	.25	.13	.08
(13)	Marty Martinez	.25	.13	.08
(14)	John Mayberry	.25	.13	.08
(15)	Denis Menke	.25	.13	.08
(16)	Norm Miller	.25	.13	.08
(17)	Joe Morgan	3.00	1.50	.90
(18)	Doug Rader	.25	.13	.08
(19)	Jim Ray	.25	.13	.08
(20)	Scipio Spinks	.25	.13	.08
(21)	Bob Watkins	.25	.13	.08
(22)	Bob Watson	.25	.13	.08
(23)	Don Wilson	.25	.13	.08
(24)	Jim Wynn	.25	.13	.08
	Complete Los Angeles Dodgers album:	20.00	10.00	6.00
(1)	Rich Allen	2.00	1.00	.60
(2)	Jim Brewer	.25	.13	.08
(3)	Bill Buckner	.25	.13	.08
(4)	Willie Crawford	.25	.13	.08
(5)	Willie Davis	.25	.13	.08
(6)	Al Downing	.25	.13	.08
(7)	Steve Garvey	6.00	3.00	1.75
(8)	Billy Grabarkewitz	.25	.13	.08
(9)	Tom Haller	.25	.13	.08
(10)	Jim Lefebvre	.25	.13	.08
(11)	Pete Mikkelsen	.25	.13	.08
(12)	Joe Moeller	.25	.13	.08
(13)	Manny Mota	.25	.13	.08
(14)	Claude Osteen	.25	.13	.08
(15)	Wes Parker	.25	.13	.08
(16)	Jose Pena	.25	.13	.08
(17)	Bill Russell	.25	.13	.08
(18)	Duke Sims	.25	.13	.08
(19)	Bill Singer	.25	.13	.08
(20)	Mike Strahler	.25	.13	.08
(21)	Bill Sudakis	.25	.13	.08
(22)	Don Sutton	3.00	1.50	.90
(23)	Jeff Torborg	.25	.13	.08
(24)	Maury Wills	.40	.20	.12
	Complete Montreal Expos album:	15.00	7.50	4.50
(1)	Bob Bailey	.25	.13	.08
(2)	John Bateman	.25	.13	.08
(3)	John Boccabella	.25	.13	.08
(4)	Ron Brand	.25	.13	.08
(5)	Boots Day	.25	.13	.08
(6)	Jim Fairey	.25	.13	.08
(7)	Ron Fairly	.25	.13	.08
(8)	Jim Gosger	.25	.13	.08
(9)	Don Hahn	.25	.13	.08
(10)	Ron Hunt	.25	.13	.08
(11)	Mack Jones	.25	.13	.08
(12)	Jose Laboy	.25	.13	.08
(13)	Mike Marshall	.25	.13	.08
(14)	Dan McGinn	.25	.13	.08
(15)	Carl Morton	.25	.13	.08
(16)	John O'Donoghue	.25	.13	.08
(17)	Adolfo Phillips	.25	.13	.08
(18)	Claude Raymond	.25	.13	.08
(19)	Steve Renko	.25	.13	.08
(20)	Marv Staehle	.25	.13	.08
(21)	Rusty Staub	.40	.20	.12
(22)	Bill Stoneman	.25	.13	.08
(23)	Gary Sutherland	.25	.13	.08
(24)	Bobby Wine	.25	.13	.08
	Complete New York Mets album:	35.00	17.50	10.50
(1)	Tommie Agee	.25	.13	.08
(2)	Bob Aspromonte	.25	.13	.08
(3)	Ken Boswell	.25	.13	.08
(4)	Dean Chance	.25	.13	.08
(5)	Donn Clendenon	.35	.20	.11
(6)	Duffy Dyer	.25	.13	.08
(7)	Dan Frisella	.25	.13	.08
(8)	Wayne Garrett	.25	.13	.08
(9)	Gary Gentry	.25	.13	.08
(10)	Jerry Grote	.25	.13	.08
(11)	Bud Harrelson	.40	.20	.12
(12)	Cleon Jones	.25	.13	.08
(13)	Jerry Koosman	.25	.13	.08
(14)	Ed Kranepool	.25	.13	.08
(15)	Dave Marshall	.25	.13	.08
(16)	Jim McAndrew	.25	.13	.08
(17)	Tug McGraw	.40	.20	.12
(18)	Nolan Ryan	30.00	15.00	9.00
(19)	Ray Sadecki	.25	.13	.08
(20)	Tom Seaver	5.00	2.50	1.50
(21)	Art Shamsky	.25	.13	.08
(22)	Ron Swoboda	.25	.13	.08
(23)	Ron Taylor	.25	.13	.08
(24)	Al Weis	.25	.13	.08
	Complete Philadelphia Phillies album:	15.00	7.50	4.50
(1)	Larry Bowa	.25	.13	.08

(2)	Johnny Briggs	.25	.13	.08
(3)	Bryon Browne	.25	.13	.08
(4)	Jim Bunning	4.00	2.00	1.25
(5)	Billy Champion	.25	.13	.08
(6)	Mike Compton	.25	.13	.08
(7)	Denny Doyle	.25	.13	.08
(8)	Roger Freed	.25	.13	.08
(9)	Woody Fryman	.25	.13	.08
(10)	Oscar Gamble	.25	.13	.08
(11)	Terry Harmon	.25	.13	.08
(12)	Larry Hisle	.25	.13	.08
(13)	Joe Hoerner	.25	.13	.08
(14)	Deron Johnson	.25	.13	.08
(15)	Barry Lersch	.25	.13	.08
(16)	Tim McCarver	1.50	.70	.45
(17)	Don Money	.25	.13	.08
(18)	Mike Ryan	.25	.13	.08
(19)	Dick Selma	.25	.13	.08
(20)	Chris Short	.25	.13	.08
(21)	Ron Stone	.25	.13	.08
(22)	Tony Taylor	.25	.13	.08
(23)	Rick Wise	.25	.13	.08
(24)	Billy Wilson	.25	.13	.08
	Complete Pittsburgh Pirates album:	25.00	12.50	7.50
(1)	Gene Alley	.25	.13	.08
(2)	Steve Blass	.25	.13	.08
(3)	Nelson Briles	.25	.13	.08
(4)	Jim Campanis	.25	.13	.08
(5)	Dave Cash	.25	.13	.08
(6)	Roberto Clemente	10.00	5.00	3.00
(7)	Vic Davalillo	.25	.13	.08
(8)	Dock Ellis	.25	.13	.08
(9)	Jim Grant	.25	.13	.08
(10)	Dave Giusti	.25	.13	.08
(11)	Richie Hebner	.25	.13	.08
(12)	Jackie Hernandez	.25	.13	.08
(13)	Johnny Jeter	.25	.13	.08
(14)	Lou Marone	.25	.13	.08
(15)	Jose Martinez	.25	.13	.08
(16)	Bill Mazeroski	3.50	1.75	1.00
(17)	Bob Moose	.25	.13	.08
(18)	Al Oliver	.40	.20	.12
(19)	Jose Pagan	.25	.13	.08
(20)	Bob Robertson	.25	.13	.08
(21)	Manny Sanguillen	.25	.13	.08
(22)	Willie Stargell	4.00	2.00	1.25
(23)	Bob Veale	.25	.13	.08
(24)	Luke Walker	.25	.13	.08
	Complete San Diego Padres album:	15.00	7.50	4.50
(1)	Jose Arcia	.25	.13	.08
(2)	Bob Barton	.25	.13	.08
(3)	Fred Beene	.25	.13	.08
(4)	Ollie Brown	.25	.13	.08
(5)	Dave Campbell	.25	.13	.08
(6)	Chris Cannizzaro	.25	.13	.08
(7)	Nate Colbert	.25	.13	.08
(8)	Mike Corkins	.25	.13	.08
(9)	Tommy Dean	.25	.13	.08
(10)	Al Ferrara	.25	.13	.08
(11)	Rod Gaspar	.25	.13	.08
(12)	Cito Gaston	.35	.20	.11
(13)	Enzo Hernandez	.25	.13	.08
(14)	Clay Kirby	.25	.13	.08
(15)	Don Mason	.25	.13	.08
(16)	Ivan Murrell	.25	.13	.08
(17)	Gerry Nyman	.25	.13	.08
(18)	Tom Phoebus	.25	.13	.08
(19)	Dave Roberts	.25	.13	.08
(20)	Gary Ross	.25	.13	.08
(21)	Al Santorini	.25	.13	.08
(22)	Al Severinsen	.25	.13	.08
(23)	Ron Slocum	.25	.13	.08
(24)	Ed Spiezio	.25	.13	.08
	Complete San Francisco Giants album:	20.00	10.00	6.00
(1)	Bobby Bonds	.50	.25	.15
(2)	Ron Bryant	.25	.13	.08
(3)	Don Carrithers	.25	.13	.08
(4)	John Cumberland	.25	.13	.08
(5)	Mike Davison	.25	.13	.08
(6)	Dick Dietz	.25	.13	.08
(7)	Tito Fuentes	.25	.13	.08
(8)	Russ Gibson	.25	.13	.08
(9)	Jim Ray Hart	.25	.13	.08
(10)	Bob Heise	.25	.13	.08
(11)	Ken Henderson	.25	.13	.08
(12)	Steve Huntz	.25	.13	.08
(13)	Frank Johnson	.25	.13	.08
(14)	Jerry Johnson	.25	.13	.08
(15)	Hal Lanier	.25	.13	.08
(16)	Juan Marichal	3.00	1.50	.90
(17)	Willie Mays	8.00	4.00	2.50
(18)	Willie McCovey	4.00	2.00	1.25
(19)	Don McMahon	.25	.13	.08
(20)	Jim Moyer	.25	.13	.08
(21)	Gaylord Perry	3.00	1.50	.90
(22)	Frank Reberger	.25	.13	.08
(23)	Rich Robertson	.25	.10	.08
(24)	Bernie Williams	.25	.13	.08
	Complete St. Louis Cardinals album:	15.00	7.50	4.50
(1)	Matty Alou	.25	.13	.08
(2)	Jim Beauchamp	.25	.13	.08
(3)	Frank Bertaina	.25	.13	.08
(4)	Lou Brock	4.00	2.00	1.25
(5)	George Brunet	.25	.13	.08
(6)	Jose Cardenal	.25	.13	.08
(7)	Steve Carlton	4.00	2.00	1.25
(8)	Moe Drabowsky	.25	.13	.08
(9)	Bob Gibson	4.00	2.00	1.25
(10)	Joe Hague	.25	.13	.08
(11)	Julian Javier	.25	.13	.08
(12)	Leron Lee	.25	.13	.08
(13)	Frank Linzy	.25	.13	.08
(14)	Dal Maxvill	.25	.13	.08
(15)	Jerry McNertney	.25	.13	.08

(16)	Fred Norman	.25	.13	.08
(17)	Milt Ramirez	.25	.13	.08
(18)	Dick Schofield	.25	.13	.08
(19)	Mike Shannon	.25	.13	.08
(20)	Ted Sizemore	.25	.13	.08
(21)	Bob Stinson	.25	.13	.08
(22)	Carl Taylor	.25	.13	.08
(23)	Joe Torre	2.00	1.00	.60
(24)	Mike Torrez	.25	.13	.08
	Complete Baltimore Orioles album:	25.00	12.50	7.50
(1)	Mark Belanger	.25	.13	.08
(2)	Paul Blair	.25	.13	.08
(3)	Don Buford	.25	.13	.08
(4)	Terry Crowley	.25	.13	.08
(5)	Mike Cuellar	.25	.13	.08
(6)	Clay Dalrymple	.25	.13	.08
(7)	Pat Dobson	.25	.13	.08
(8)	Andy Etchebarren	.25	.13	.08
(9)	Dick Hall	.25	.13	.08
(10)	Jim Hardin	.25	.13	.08
(11)	Elrod Hendricks	.25	.13	.08
(12)	Grant Jackson	.25	.13	.08
(13)	Dave Johnson	.25	.13	.08
(14)	Dave Leonhard	.25	.13	.08
(15)	Marcelino Lopez	.25	.13	.08
(16)	Dave McNally	.25	.13	.08
(17)	Curt Motton	.25	.13	.08
(18)	Jim Palmer	4.00	2.00	1.25
(19)	Boog Powell	2.00	1.00	.60
(20)	Merv Rettenmund	.25	.13	.08
(21)	Brooks Robinson	6.00	3.00	1.75
(22)	Frank Robinson	6.00	3.00	1.75
(23)	Pete Richert	.25	.13	.08
(24)	Chico Salmon	.25	.13	.08
	Complete Boston Red Sox album:	25.00	12.50	7.50
(1)	Luis Aparicio	4.00	2.00	1.25
(2)	Bobby Bolin	.25	.13	.08
(3)	Ken Brett	.25	.13	.08
(4)	Billy Conigliaro	.25	.13	.08
(5)	Ray Culp	.25	.13	.08
(6)	Mike Fiore	.25	.13	.08
(7)	John Kennedy	.25	.13	.08
(8)	Cal Koonce	.25	.13	.08
(9)	Joe Lahoud	.25	.13	.08
(10)	Bill Lee	.25	.13	.08
(11)	Jim Lonborg	.25	.13	.08
(12)	Sparky Lyle	.25	.13	.08
(13)	Mike Nagy	.25	.13	.08
(14)	Don Pavletich	.25	.13	.08
(15)	Gary Peters	.25	.13	.08
(16)	Rico Petrocelli	.40	.20	.12
(17)	Vicente Romo	.25	.13	.08
(18)	Tom Satriano	.25	.13	.08
(19)	George Scott	.25	.13	.08
(20)	Sonny Siebert	.25	.13	.08
(21)	Reggie Smith	.25	.13	.08
(22)	Jarvis Tatum	.25	.13	.08
(23)	Ken Tatum	.25	.13	.08
(24)	Carl Yastrzemski	4.00	2.00	1.25
	Complete California Angels album:	15.00	7.50	4.50
(1)	Sandy Alomar	.25	.13	.08
(2)	Joe Azcue	.25	.13	.08
(3)	Ken Berry	.25	.13	.08
(4)	Gene Brabender	.25	.13	.08
(5)	Billy Cowan	.25	.13	.08
(6)	Tony Conigliaro	.75	.40	.25
(7)	Eddie Fisher	.25	.13	.08
(8)	Jim Fregosi	.25	.13	.08
(9)	Tony Gonzales (Gonzalez)	.25	.13	.08
(10)	Alex Johnson	.25	.13	.08
(11)	Fred Lasher	.25	.13	.08
(12)	Jim Maloney	.25	.13	.08
(13)	Rudy May	.25	.13	.08
(14)	Ken McMullen	.25	.13	.08
(15)	Andy Messersmith	.25	.13	.08
(16)	Gerry Moses	.25	.13	.08
(17)	Syd O'Brien	.25	.13	.08
(18)	Mel Queen	.25	.13	.08
(19)	Roger Repoz	.25	.13	.08
(20)	Archie Reynolds	.25	.13	.08
(21)	Chico Ruiz	.25	.13	.08
(22)	Jim Spencer	.25	.13	.08
(23)	Clyde Wright	.25	.13	.08
(24)	Billy Wynne	.25	.13	.08
	Complete Chicago White Sox album:	15.00	7.50	4.50
	(Checklist not available)	.25	.13	.08
	Complete Cleveland Indians album:	15.00	7.50	4.50
(1)	Rick Austin	.25	.13	.08
(2)	Buddy Bradford	.25	.13	.08
(3)	Larry Brown	.25	.13	.08
(4)	Lou Camilli	.25	.13	.08
(5)	Vince Colbert	.25	.13	.08
(6)	Ray Fosse	.25	.13	.08
(7)	Alan Foster	.25	.13	.08
(8)	Roy Foster	.25	.13	.08
(9)	Rich Hand	.25	.13	.08
(10)	Steve Hargan	.25	.13	.08
(11)	Ken Harrelson	.25	.13	.08
(12)	Jack Heidemann	.25	.13	.08
(13)	Phil Hennigan	.25	.13	.08
(14)	Dennis Higgins	.25	.13	.08
(15)	Chuck Hinton	.25	.13	.08
(16)	Tony Horton	.25	.13	.08
(17)	Ray Lamb	.25	.13	.08
(18)	Eddie Leon	.25	.13	.08
(19)	Sam McDowell	.50	.25	.15
(20)	Graig Nettles	.50	.25	.15
(21)	Mike Paul	.25	.13	.08
(22)	Vada Pinson	.50	.25	.15
(23)	Ken Suarez	.25	.13	.08
(24)	Ted Uhlaender	.25	.13	.08
	Complete Detroit Tigers album:	17.50	8.75	5.25

(1)	Ed Brinkman	.25	.13	.08
(2)	Gates Brown	.25	.13	.08
(3)	Ike Brown	.25	.13	.08
(4)	Les Cain	.25	.13	.08
(5)	Norm Cash	.50	.25	.15
(6)	Joe Coleman	.25	.13	.08
(7)	Bill Freehan	.40	.20	.12
(8)	Cesar Gutierrez	.25	.13	.08
(9)	John Hiller	.25	.13	.08
(10)	Willie Horton	.40	.20	.12
(11)	Dalton Jones	.25	.13	.08
(12)	Al Kaline	4.00	2.00	1.25
(13)	Mike Kilkenny	.25	.13	.08
(14)	Mickey Lolich	.50	.25	.15
(15)	Dick McAuliffe	.25	.13	.08
(16)	Joe Niekro	.40	.20	.12
(17)	Jim Northrup	.25	.13	.08
(18)	Daryl Patterson	.25	.13	.08
(19)	Jimmie Price	.25	.13	.08
(20)	Bob Reed	.25	.13	.08
(21)	Aurelio Rodriguez	.25	.13	.08
(22)	Fred Scherman	.25	.13	.08
(23)	Mickey Stanley	.25	.13	.08
(24)	Tom Timmermann	.25	.13	.08
	Complete Kansas City Royals album:	15.00	7.50	4.50
(1)	Ted Abernathy	.25	.13	.08
(2)	Wally Bunker	.25	.13	.08
(3)	Tom Burgmeier	.25	.13	.08
(4)	Bill Butler	.25	.13	.08
(5)	Bruce Dal Canton	.25	.13	.08
(6)	Dick Drago	.25	.13	.08
(7)	Bobby Floyd	.25	.13	.08
(8)	Gail Hopkins	.25	.13	.08
(9)	Joe Keough	.25	.13	.08
(10)	Ed Kirkpatrick	.25	.13	.08
(11)	Tom Matchick	.25	.13	.08
(12)	Jerry May	.25	.13	.08
(13)	Aurelio Monteagudo	.25	.13	.08
(14)	Dave Morehead	.25	.13	.08
(15)	Bob Oliver	.25	.13	.08
(16)	Amos Otis	.40	.20	.12
(17)	Fred Patek	.25	.13	.08
(18)	Lou Piniella	.50	.25	.15
(19)	Cookie Rojas	.25	.13	.08
(20)	Jim Rooker	.25	.13	.08
(21)	Paul Schaal	.25	.13	.08
(22)	Rich Severson	.25	.13	.08
(23)	George Spriggs	.25	.13	.08
(24)	Carl Taylor	.25	.13	.08
	Complete Milwaukee Brewers album:	15.00	7.50	4.50
(1)	Dave Baldwin	.25	.13	.08
(2)	Dick Ellsworth	.25	.13	.08
(3)	John Gelnar	.25	.13	.08
(4)	Tommy Harper	.25	.13	.08
(5)	Mike Hegan	.25	.13	.08
(6)	Bob Humphreys	.25	.13	.08
(7)	Andy Kosco	.25	.13	.08
(8)	Lew Krausse	.25	.13	.08
(9)	Ted Kubiak	.25	.13	.08
(10)	Skip Lockwood	.25	.13	.08
(11)	Dave May	.25	.13	.08
(12)	Bob Meyer	.25	.13	.08
(13)	John Morris	.25	.13	.08
(14)	Marty Pattin	.25	.13	.08
(15)	Roberto Pena	.25	.13	.08
(16)	Eduardo Rodriguez	.25	.13	.08
(17)	Phil Roof	.25	.13	.08
(18)	Ken Sanders	.25	.13	.08
(19)	Ted Savage	.25	.13	.08
(20)	Russ Snyder	.25	.13	.08
(21)	Bob Tillman	.25	.13	.08
(22)	Bill Voss	.25	.13	.08
(23)	Danny Walton	.25	.13	.08
(24)	Floyd Wicker	.25	.13	.08
	Complete Minnesota Twins album:	15.00	7.50	4.50
(1)	Brant Alyea	.25	.13	.08
(2)	Bert Blyleven	.40	.20	.12
(3)	Dave Boswell	.25	.13	.08
(4)	Leo Cardenas	.25	.13	.08
(5)	Rod Carew	4.00	2.00	1.25
(6)	Tom Hall	.25	.13	.08
(7)	Jim Holt	.25	.13	.08
(8)	Jim Kaat	.50	.25	.15
(9)	Harmon Killebrew	4.00	2.00	1.25
(10)	Charlie Manuel	.25	.13	.08
(11)	George Mitterwald	.25	.13	.08
(12)	Tony Oliva	.50	.25	.15
(13)	Ron Perranoski	.25	.13	.08
(14)	Jim Perry	.25	.13	.08
(15)	Frank Quilici	.25	.13	.08
(16)	Rich Reese	.25	.13	.08
(17)	Rick Renick	.25	.13	.08
(18)	Danny Thompson	.25	.13	.08
(19)	Luis Tiant	.40	.20	.12
(20)	Tom Tischinski	.25	.13	.08
(21)	Cesar Tovar	.25	.13	.08
(22)	Stan Williams	.25	.13	.08
(23)	Dick Woodson	.25	.13	.08
(24)	Bill Zepp	.25	.13	.08
	Complete New York Yankees album:	24.00	12.00	7.25
(1)	Jack Aker	.25	.13	.08
(2)	Stan Bahnsen	.25	.13	.08
(3)	Curt Blefary	.25	.13	.08
(4)	Bill Burbach	.25	.13	.08
(5)	Danny Cater	.25	.13	.08
(6)	Horace Clarke	.25	.13	.08
(7)	John Ellis	.25	.13	.08
(8)	Jake Gibbs	.25	.13	.08
(9)	Ron Hansen	.25	.13	.08
(10)	Mike Kekich	.25	.13	.08
(11)	Jerry Kenney	.25	.13	.08
(12)	Ron Klimkowski	.25	.13	.08
(13)	Steve Kline	.25	.13	.08
(14)	Mike McCormick	.25	.13	.08
(15)	Lindy McDaniel	.25	.13	.08
(16)	Gene Michael	.25	.13	.08
(17)	Thurman Munson	8.00	4.00	2.50
(18)	Bobby Murcer	.50	.25	.15
(19)	Fritz Peterson	.25	.13	.08
(20)	Mel Stottlemyre	.25	.13	.08
(21)	Pete Ward	.25	.13	.08
(22)	Gary Waslewski	.25	.13	.08
(23)	Roy White	.35	.20	.11
(24)	Ron Woods	.25	.13	.08
	Complete Oakland A's album:	24.00	12.00	7.25
(1)	Felipe Alou	1.50	.70	.45
(2)	Sal Bando	.25	.13	.08
(3)	Vida Blue	.40	.20	.12
(4)	Bert Campaneris	.25	.13	.08
(5)	Ron Clark	.25	.13	.08
(6)	Chuck Dobson	.25	.13	.08
(7)	Dave Duncan	.25	.13	.08
(8)	Frank Fernandez	.25	.13	.08
(9)	Rollie Fingers	3.00	1.50	.90
(10)	Dick Green	.25	.13	.08
(11)	Steve Hovley	.25	.13	.08
(12)	Catfish Hunter	3.00	1.50	.90
(13)	Reggie Jackson	6.00	3.00	1.75
(14)	Marcel Lacheman	.25	.13	.08
(15)	Paul Lindblad	.25	.13	.08
(16)	Bob Locker	.25	.13	.08
(17)	Don Mincher	.25	.13	.08
(18)	Rick Monday	.25	.13	.08
(19)	John Odom	.25	.13	.08
(20)	Jim Roland	.25	.13	.08
(21)	Joe Rudi	.40	.20	.12
(22)	Diego Segui	.25	.13	.08
(23)	Bob Stickels	.25	.13	.08
(24)	Gene Tenace	.25	.13	.08
	Complete Washington Senators album:	15.00	7.50	4.50
(1)	Bernie Allen	.25	.13	.08
(2)	Dick Bosman	.25	.13	.08
(3)	Jackie Brown	.25	.13	.08
(4)	Paul Casanova	.25	.13	.08
(5)	Casey Cox	.25	.13	.08
(6)	Tim Cullen	.25	.13	.08
(7)	Mike Epstein	.25	.13	.08
(8)	Curt Flood	.50	.25	.15
(9)	Joe Foy	.25	.13	.08
(10)	Jim French	.25	.13	.08
(11)	Bill Gogolewski	.25	.13	.08
(12)	Tom Grieve	.25	.13	.08
(13)	Joe Grzenda	.25	.13	.08
(14)	Frank Howard	.50	.25	.15
(15)	Joe Janeski	.25	.13	.08
(16)	Darold Knowles	.25	.13	.08
(17)	Elliott Maddox	.25	.13	.08
(18)	Denny McLain	.50	.25	.15
(19)	Dave Nelson	.25	.13	.08
(20)	Horacio Pina	.25	.13	.08
(21)	Jim Shellenback	.25	.13	.08
(22)	Ed Stroud	.25	.13	.08
(23)	Del Unser	.25	.13	.08
(24)	Don Wert	.25	.13	.08

1980 Delacorte Press

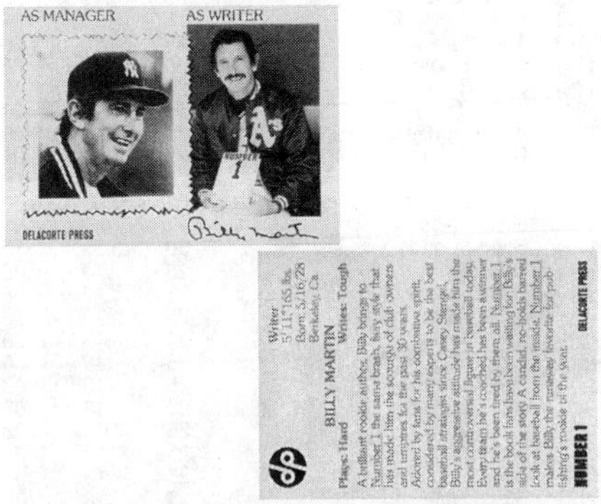

As a promotion for its book, "Number 1," written by Billy Martin, Delacorte Press issued this card picturing Martin somewhat in the style of a 1978 Topps manager card. The 3-1/2" x 2-1/2" card has a black-and-white photo of Martin as a Yankees manager, and a color photo as the A's manager. The front is bordered in red. Backs are printed in black, white and red with biographical details and promotional copy for the book.

		NM	EX	VG
1	Billy Martin	10.00	5.00	3.00

1933 DeLong

The DeLong company of Boston was among the first to sell baseball cards with gum, issuing a set of 24 cards in 1933, and making the company a pioneer in the field. DeLong cards measure 2" x 3" and feature black-and-white player photos on a color background. The photos show the players in various action poses and positions them in the middle of a miniature stadium setting so that they appear to be giants. Most of the cards are vertically designed, but a few are horizontal. Backs were by Austen Lake, editor of the Boston Transcript, and contain tips to help youngsters become better ballplayers. The ACC designation for this set is R333. The checklist below gives the players' names exactly as they appear on the fronts of the cards.

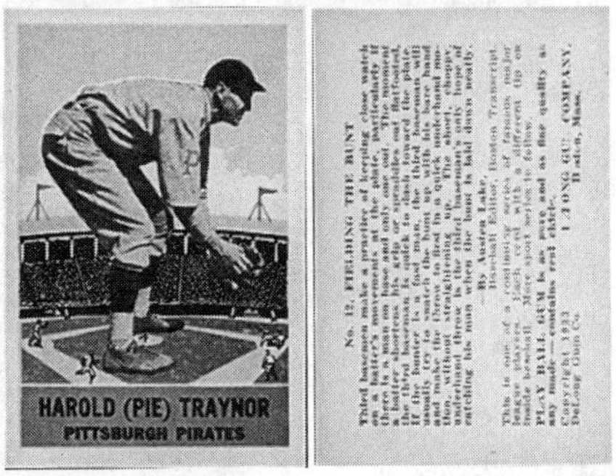

		NM	EX	VG
	Complete Set (24):	14000.	5500.	2750.
	Common Player:	325.00	130.00	65.00
1	"Marty" McManus	325.00	130.00	65.00
2	Al Simmons	500.00	200.00	100.00
3	Oscar Melillo	325.00	130.00	65.00
4	William (Bill) Terry	600.00	240.00	120.00
5	Charlie Gehringer	600.00	240.00	120.00
6	Gordon (Mickey) Cochrane	600.00	240.00	120.00
7	Lou Gehrig	5000.	2000.	1000.
8	Hazen S. (Kiki) Cuyler	400.00	160.00	80.00
9	Bill Urbanski	325.00	130.00	65.00
10	Frank J. (Lefty) O'Doul	350.00	140.00	70.00
11	Freddie Lindstrom	400.00	160.00	80.00
12	Harold (Pie) Traynor	400.00	160.00	80.00
13	"Rabbit" Maranville	400.00	200.00	120.00
14	Vernon "Lefty" Gomez	400.00	200.00	120.00
15	Riggs Stephenson	325.00	130.00	65.00
16	Lon Warneke	325.00	130.00	65.00
17	Pepper Martin	350.00	140.00	70.00
18	Jimmy Dykes	325.00	130.00	65.00
19	Chick Hafey	400.00	160.00	80.00
20	Joe Vosmik	325.00	130.00	65.00
21	Jimmy Foxx	800.00	325.00	160.00
22	Charles (Chuck) Klein	400.00	160.00	80.00
23	Robert (Lefty) Grove	450.00	180.00	90.00
24	"Goose" Goslin	400.00	160.00	80.00

1934 Al Demaree Die-cuts

Among the rarest 1930s gum cards are those issued by Dietz Gum Co., a Chicago confectioner, in packages of "Ball Players in Action Chewing Gum." The cards are so rare that the complete checklist may never be known. The set was cataloged as R304 in the American Card Catalog. The cards feature photographic portraits of players set upon cartoon bodies drawn by former major league pitcher Demaree. The photo and artwork are generally in black-and-white, while the players on some teams have blue or red uniform details printed on. The cards can be folded to create a stand-up figure, but did not have a background to be cut or torn away, as is common with most die-cut baseball cards. Unfolded, the cards measure 6-1/2" long and from 1-5/8" to 1-3/4" wide, depending on pose.

		NM	EX	VG
	Common Player:	250.00	125.00	75.00
3	Earle Combs	500.00	250.00	150.00
4	Babe Ruth	7500.	3750.	2250.

6	Tony Lazzeri	500.00	250.00	150.00
7	Frank Crosetti	350.00	175.00	105.00
9	Lou Gehrig	5000.	2500.	1500.
10	Lefty Gomez	500.00	250.00	150.00
11	Mule Haas	250.00	125.00	75.00
12	Evar Swenson	250.00	125.00	75.00
13	Marv Shea	250.00	125.00	75.00
14	Al Simmons (throwing)	500.00	250.00	150.00
15	Jack Hayes	250.00	125.00	75.00
16	Al Simmons (batting)	500.00	250.00	150.00
17	Jimmy Dykes	250.00	125.00	75.00
18	Luke Appling	500.00	250.00	150.00
19	Ted Lyons	500.00	250.00	150.00
20	Red Kress	250.00	125.00	75.00
21	Gee Walker	250.00	125.00	75.00
23	Mickey Cochrane (catching)	500.00	250.00	150.00
24	Mickey Cochrane (batting)	500.00	250.00	150.00
25	Pete Fox	250.00	125.00	75.00
26	Firpo Marberry	250.00	125.00	75.00
28	Mickey Owen	250.00	125.00	75.00
35	Joe Vosmik	250.00	125.00	75.00
41	Jack Burns	250.00	125.00	75.00
45	Ray Pepper	250.00	125.00	75.00
46	Bruce Campbell	250.00	125.00	75.00
48	Art Scharein	250.00	125.00	75.00
49	George Blaeholder	250.00	125.00	75.00
50	Rogers Hornsby	650.00	325.00	175.00
51	Eric McNair	250.00	150.00	75.00
54	Jimmie Foxx	600.00	300.00	180.00
56	Dib Williams	250.00	125.00	75.00
57	Lou Finney	250.00	125.00	75.00
61	Ossie Bluege	250.00	125.00	75.00
63	John Stone	250.00	150.00	75.00
64	Joe Cronin	500.00	250.00	150.00
66	Buddy Myer	250.00	125.00	75.00
67	Earl Whitehill	250.00	125.00	75.00
68	Fred Schulte	250.00	125.00	75.00
71	Ed Morgan	250.00	125.00	75.00
74	Carl Reynolds	250.00	125.00	75.00
76	Bill Cissell	250.00	125.00	75.00
77	Johnny Hodapp	250.00	125.00	75.00
78	Dusty Cooke	250.00	125.00	75.00
79	Lefty Grove	500.00	250.00	150.00
82	Gus Mancuso	250.00	125.00	75.00
83	Kiddo Davis	250.00	125.00	75.00
84	Blondy Ryan	250.00	125.00	75.00
86	Travis Jackson	500.00	250.00	150.00
89	Bill Terry	500.00	250.00	150.00
91	Tony Cuccinello	250.00	125.00	75.00
97	Danny Taylor	250.00	125.00	75.00
99	John Frederick	250.00	125.00	75.00
100	Sam Leslie	250.00	125.00	75.00
102	Mark Koenig	250.00	125.00	75.00
107	Syl Johnson	250.00	125.00	75.00
108	Jim Bottomley	500.00	250.00	150.00
111	Dick Bartell	250.00	125.00	75.00
112	Harvey Hendrick	250.00	125.00	75.00
115	Don Hurst	250.00	125.00	75.00
117	Prince Oana	250.00	125.00	75.00
121	Spud Davis	250.00	125.00	75.00
122	George Watkins	250.00	125.00	75.00
123	Frankie Frisch	500.00	250.00	150.00
124	Pepper Martin (batting)	300.00	150.00	90.00
125	Ripper Collins	250.00	125.00	75.00
126	Dizzy Dean	750.00	375.00	225.00
127	Pepper Martin (fielding)	300.00	150.00	90.00
128	Joe Medwick	500.00	250.00	150.00
129	Leo Durocher	500.00	250.00	150.00
130	Ernie Orsatti	250.00	125.00	75.00
132	Shanty Hogan	250.00	125.00	75.00
137	Wally Berger	250.00	125.00	75.00
140	Ben Cantwell	250.00	125.00	75.00
141	Gus Suhr	250.00	125.00	75.00
142	Earl Grace	250.00	125.00	75.00
146	Tommy Thevenow	250.00	150.00	75.00
151	Kiki Cuyler	500.00	250.00	150.00
152	Gabby Hartnett	500.00	250.00	150.00
154	Chuck Klein	500.00	250.00	150.00
156	Woody English	250.00	125.00	75.00
158	Billy Herman	500.00	250.00	150.00
160	Charlie Grimm	250.00	125.00	75.00
162	Bill Klem	750.00	375.00	225.00
167	George Hildebrand	250.00	125.00	75.00
	(All known specimens of cards below have had the tabs removed making it impossible to identify card number)			
----	Willie Kamm	250.00	125.00	75.00
----	Pinky Higgins	250.00	125.00	75.00
----	Bob Johnson	250.00	125.00	75.00
----	Roy Mahaffey	250.00	125.00	75.00

1932 Charles Denby Cigars Cubs

Actually a series of postcards, this Chicago Cubs set issued by the Charles Denby Company in 1932 is the last known tobacco issue produced before World War II. The cards are a standard postcard size (5-1/4" x 3-3/8") and feature a glossy black-and-white player photo with a facsimile autograph. In typical postcard style, the back of the card is divided in half, with a printed player profile on the left and room for the mailing address on the right. The back also includes an advertisement for Charles Denby Cigars, the mild five-cent cigar "for men who like to inhale". Only eight different subjects have been reported to date, but there is speculation that more probably exist.

		NM	EX	VG
Complete Set (8):		3500.	1400.	700.00
Common Player:		350.00	140.00	70.00
(1)	Hazen Cuyler	650.00	260.00	130.00
(2)	Elwood English	350.00	140.00	70.00
(3)	Charles J. Grimm	350.00	140.00	70.00
(4)	William Herman	650.00	260.00	130.00
(5)	Rogers Hornsby	700.00	280.00	140.00
(6)	William F. Jurges	350.00	140.00	70.00
(7)	Riggs Stephenson	350.00	140.00	70.00
(8)	Lonnie Warneke	350.00	140.00	70.00

1909 Derby Cigars N.Y. Giants

Although there is no advertising on these cards to indicate their origin, it is generally accepted that this set was issued by Derby Cigars, a product of American Tobacco Co. A dozen different subjects, all New York Giants, have been found. It is believed that the cards, which measure 1-3/4" x 2-3/4", were inserted in boxes of Derby "Little Cigars." The cards feature an oval black-and-white player portrait on a red background. The player's name and position are in a white strip at bottom.

		NM	EX	VG
Complete Set (12):		12000.	4900.	2450.
Common Player:		900.00	375.00	185.00
(1)	Josh Devore	900.00	375.00	185.00
(2)	Larry Doyle	900.00	375.00	185.00
(3)	Art Fletcher	900.00	375.00	185.00
(4)	Buck Herzog	900.00	375.00	185.00
(5)	Rube Marquard	1500.	600.00	300.00
(6)	Christy Mathewson	4000.	1600.	800.00
(7)	Fred Merkle	900.00	375.00	185.00
(8)	Chief Meyers	900.00	375.00	185.00
(9)	Red Murray	900.00	375.00	185.00
(10)	John McGraw	1550.	625.00	300.00
(11)	Fred Snodgrass	900.00	375.00	185.00
(12)	Hooks Wiltse	900.00	375.00	185.00

1977 Detroit Caesars discs

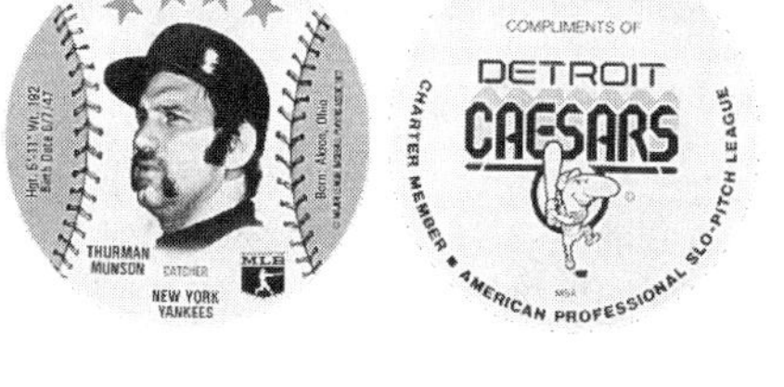

Virtually identical in format to the several locally sponsored disc sets of the previous year, these 3-3/8" diameter player discs were sponsored by a professional slow-pitch softball team. Discs once again feature black-and-white player portrait photos in the center of a baseball design. The left and right panels are in one of several bright colors. Licensed by the players' association through Mike Schechter Associates, the player photos carry no uniform logos. Backs are printed in green. The unnumbered discs are checklisted here alphabetically.

		NM	EX	VG
Complete Set (71):		300.00	150.00	90.00
Common Player:		3.00	1.50	.90
(1)	Sal Bando	3.00	1.50	.90
(2)	Buddy Bell	3.00	1.50	.90
(3)	Johnny Bench	15.00	7.50	4.50
(4)	Larry Bowa	3.00	1.50	.90
(5)	Steve Braun	3.00	1.50	.90
(6)	George Brett	35.00	17.50	10.50
(7)	Lou Brock	12.00	6.00	3.50
(8)	Jeff Burroughs	3.00	1.50	.90
(9)	Bert Campaneris	3.00	1.50	.90
(10)	John Candelaria	3.00	1.50	.90
(11)	Jose Cardenal	3.00	1.50	.90
(12)	Rod Carew	12.00	6.00	3.50
(13)	Steve Carlton	12.00	6.00	3.50
(14)	Dave Cash	3.00	1.50	.90
(15)	Cesar Cedeno	3.00	1.50	.90
(16)	Ron Cey	3.00	1.50	.90
(17)	Dave Concepcion	3.00	1.50	.90
(18)	Dennis Eckersley	9.00	4.50	2.75
(19)	Mark Fidrych	9.00	4.50	2.75
(20)	Rollie Fingers	12.00	6.00	3.50
(21)	Carlton Fisk	12.00	6.00	3.50
(22)	George Foster	3.00	1.50	.90
(23)	Wayne Garland	3.00	1.50	.90
(24)	Ralph Garr	3.00	1.50	.90
(25)	Steve Garvey	10.00	5.00	3.00
(26)	Cesar Geronimo	3.00	1.50	.90
(27)	Bobby Grich	3.00	1.50	.90
(28)	Ken Griffey Sr.	7.00	3.50	2.00
(29)	Don Gullett	3.00	1.50	.90
(30)	Mike Hargrove	3.00	1.50	.90
(31)	Willie Horton	3.00	1.50	.90
(32)	Al Hrabosky	3.00	1.50	.90
(33)	Catfish Hunter	12.00	6.00	3.50
(34)	Reggie Jackson	20.00	10.00	6.00
(35)	Randy Jones	3.00	1.50	.90
(36)	Dave Kingman	6.00	3.00	1.75
(37)	Jerry Koosman	3.00	1.50	.90
(38)	Dave LaRoche	3.00	1.50	.90
(39)	Greg Luzinski	3.00	1.50	.90
(40)	Fred Lynn	4.50	2.25	1.25
(41)	Bill Madlock	3.00	1.50	.90
(42)	Rick Manning	3.00	1.50	.90
(43)	Jon Matlock	3.00	1.50	.90
(44)	John Mayberry	3.00	1.50	.90
(45)	Hal McRae	3.00	1.50	.90
(46)	Andy Messersmith	3.00	1.50	.90
(47)	Rick Monday	3.00	1.50	.90
(48)	John Montefusco	3.00	1.50	.90
(49)	Joe Morgan	12.00	6.00	3.50
(50)	Thurman Munson	16.00	8.00	4.75
(51)	Bobby Murcer	3.00	1.50	.90
(52)	Bill North	3.00	1.50	.90
(53)	Jim Palmer	12.00	6.00	3.50
(54)	Tony Perez	12.00	6.00	3.50
(55)	Jerry Reuss	3.00	1.50	.90
(56)	Pete Rose	25.00	12.50	7.50
(57)	Joe Rudi	3.00	1.50	.90
(58)	Nolan Ryan	50.00	25.00	15.00
(59)	Manny Sanguillen	3.00	1.50	.90
(60)	Mike Schmidt	20.00	10.00	6.00
(61)	Tom Seaver	15.00	7.50	4.50
(62)	Bill Singer	3.00	1.50	.90
(63)	Willie Stargell	12.00	6.00	3.50
(64)	Rusty Staub	4.50	2.25	1.25
(65)	Luis Tiant	3.00	1.50	.90
(66)	Mike Tyson	3.00	1.50	.90
(67)	Bob Watson	3.00	1.50	.90
(68)	Butch Wynegar	3.00	1.50	.90
(69)	Carl Yastrzemski	15.00	7.50	4.50
(70)	Robin Yount	18.00	9.00	5.50
(71)	Richie Zisk	3.00	1.50	.90

1908 Detroit Free Press Tigers Postcards

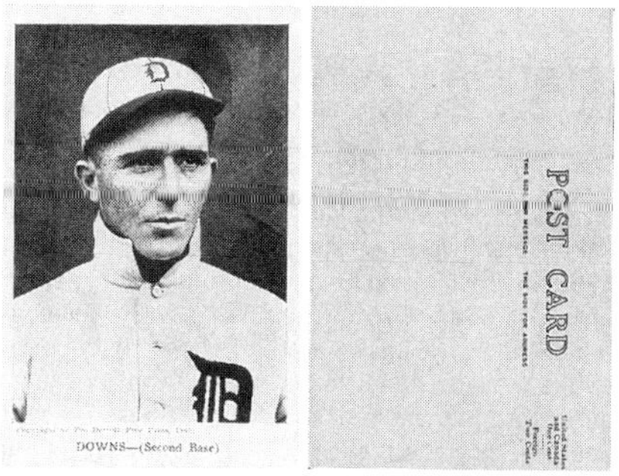

Most of the stars of the 1907-09 American League Champion Detroit Tigers are found in this set of postcards issued by a local newspaper and reportedly sold at the stadium for $1 a set. The cards are 3-1/2" x 5-1/4", printed in black-and-white. Fronts have a border around the photo with the line, "Copyright by the Detroit Free Press, 1908" beneath the photo. At bottom is the player's last name in capital letters with his position in parentheses. Backs have standard postcard indicia. The unnumbered cards are checklisted here alphabetically. It is possible this list is not complete.

		NM	EX	VG
Complete Set (11):		2750.	1350.	825.00
Common Player:		300.00	150.00	90.00
(1)	Ty Cobb	950.00	475.00	285.00
(2)	Sam Crawford	300.00	150.00	90.00
(3)	Wild Bill Donovan	300.00	150.00	90.00
(4)	Hughie Jennings	300.00	150.00	90.00
(5)	Ed Killian	300.00	150.00	90.00
(6)	Matty McIntyre	300.00	150.00	90.00
(7)	George Mullen (Mullin)	300.00	150.00	90.00
(8)	Charley O'Leary	300.00	150.00	90.00
(9)	Boss Schmidt	300.00	150.00	90.00
(10)	Ed Summer (Summers)	300.00	150.00	90.00
(11)	Ed Willett	300.00	150.00	90.00

1935 Detroit Free Press Tigers

Colorized photos with brightly colored backgrounds and borders are featured in this series of newspaper pictures featuring the World Champion Detroit Tigers. About 8" x 10-1/2", the pictures are blank-backed. It is unclear whether these pictures were included with newspaper purchases or were sold as sets. The unnumbered pictures are checklisted here in alphabetical order.

		NM	EX	VG
Complete Set (21):		500.00	250.00	150.00
Common Player:		20.00	10.00	6.00
(1)	Eldon Auker	20.00	10.00	6.00
(2)	Del Baker	20.00	10.00	6.00
(3)	Mickey Cochrane	35.00	17.50	10.50
(4)	Frank Doljack	20.00	10.00	6.00
(5)	Carl Fischer	20.00	10.00	6.00
(6)	Pete Fox	20.00	10.00	6.00
(7)	Charles Gehringer	50.00	25.00	15.00
(8)	Goose Goslin	50.00	25.00	15.00
(9)	Henry Greenberg	70.00	35.00	21.00
(10)	Luke Hamlin	20.00	10.00	6.00
(11)	Ray Hayworth	20.00	10.00	6.00
(12)	Elon Hogsett	20.00	10.00	6.00
(13)	Firpo Marberry	20.00	10.00	6.00
(14)	Marvin Owen	20.00	10.00	6.00
(15)	Cy Perkins	20.00	10.00	6.00
(16)	Billy Rogell	20.00	10.00	6.00
(17)	Schoolboy Rowe	25.00	12.50	7.50
(18)	Heinie Schuble	20.00	10.00	6.00
(19)	Vic Sorrell	20.00	10.00	6.00
(20)	Jerry Walker	20.00	10.00	6.00
(21)	Jo-Jo White	20.00	10.00	6.00

1968 Detroit Free Press Bubblegumless Tiger Cards

The World Champion Tigers are featured in this series of newspaper inserts published in August, 1968, by the "Detroit Magazine" rotogravure section of the Sunday "Detroit Free Press." The full-color fronts and the backs were printed on separate pages to allow them to be cut out and pasted on cardboard to make a baseball card. Backs are horizontally formatted and include a drawing of the player at left; biographical data and recent stats at right. Card elements measure 2-1/2" x 3-1/2". Values quoted are for front/back pairs. Unmatched fronts are priced at 45% of the prices shown; backs should be priced at 30%.

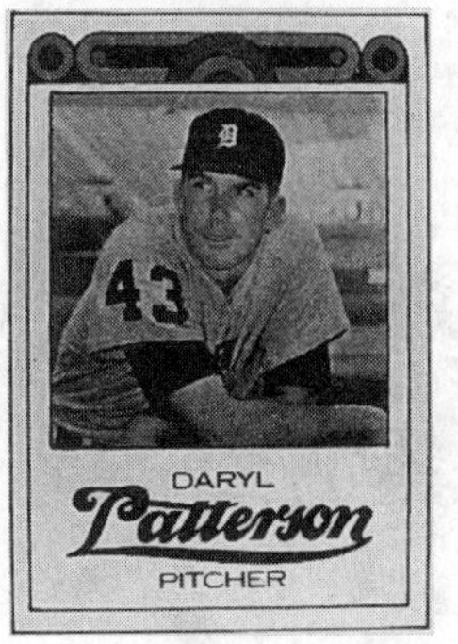

		NM	EX	VG
Complete Set, Uncut Pages:		200.00	100.00	60.00
Complete Set, Singles (28):		90.00	45.00	27.00
Common Player:		8.00	4.00	2.50
(1)	Gates Brown	8.00	4.00	2.50
(2)	Norm Cash	15.00	7.50	4.50
(3)	Tony Cuccinello	8.00	4.00	2.50
(4)	Pat Dobson	8.00	4.00	2.50
(5)	Bill Freehan	10.00	5.00	3.00
(6)	John Hiller	8.00	4.00	2.50
(7)	Willie Horton	8.00	4.00	2.50
(8)	Al Kaline	35.00	17.50	10.50
(9)	Fred Lasher	8.00	4.00	2.50
(10)	Mickey Lolich	15.00	7.50	4.50
(11)	Tom Matchick	8.00	4.00	2.50
(12)	Dick McAuliffe	8.00	4.00	2.50
(13)	Denny McLain	12.00	6.00	3.50
(14)	Don McMahon	8.00	4.00	2.50
(15)	Wally Moses	8.00	4.00	2.50
(16)	Jim Northrup	8.00	4.00	2.50
(17)	Ray Oyler	8.00	4.00	2.50
(18)	Daryl Patterson	8.00	4.00	2.50
(19)	Jim Price	8.00	4.00	2.50
(20)	Johnny Sain	10.00	5.00	3.00
(21)	Mayo Smith	8.00	4.00	2.50
(22)	Joe Sparma	8.00	4.00	2.50
(23)	Mickey Stanley	8.00	4.00	2.50
(24)	Dick Tracewski	8.00	4.00	2.50
(25)	Jon Warden	8.00	4.00	2.50
(26)	Don Wert	8.00	4.00	2.50
(27)	Earl Wilson	8.00	4.00	2.50
(28)	Jon Wyatt (John)	8.00	4.00	2.50

1978 Detroit Free Press Tigers

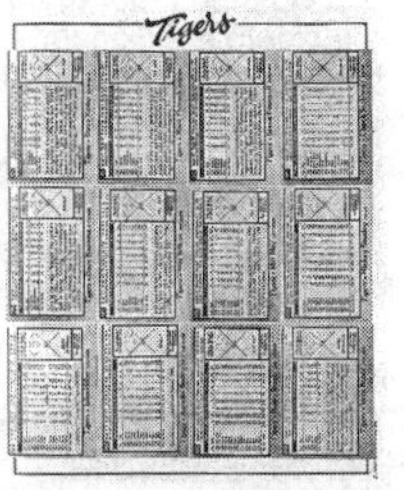

In its Sunday color magazine of April 16, 1978, the newspaper printed presumably authorized reproductions of all 1978 Topps cards which featured members of the Detroit Tigers. The magazine has a cover photo of Mark Fidrych. In the center-spread, reproduced in color, are pictures of the fronts of 20 Tigers cards. Two pages later the cards of three departed Tigers, five multi-player rookie cards and the team card are printed, also in full color. Three more pages have the backs of the cards, printed in black-and-white, rather than the orange-and-blue of genuine Topps cards. Instructions with the article invited readers to cut out the fronts and backs and paste them onto pieces of cardboard to make their own cards. Values shown are for complete front/back pairs.

		NM	EX	VG
Complete Magazine:		45.00	22.50	13.50
Complete Set, Singles (28):		30.00	15.00	9.00
Common Player:		2.00	1.00	.60
21	Steve Kemp	2.00	1.00	.60
45	Mark Fidrych	4.00	2.00	1.25
68	Steve Foucault	2.00	1.00	.60
94	Chuck Scrivener	2.00	1.00	.60
124	Dave Rozema	2.00	1.00	.60
151	Milt Wilcox	2.00	1.00	.60
176	Milt May	2.00	1.00	.60
232	Mickey Stanley	2.00	1.00	.60
258	John Hiller	2.00	1.00	.60
286	Ben Oglivie	2.00	1.00	.60
342	Aurelio Rodriguez	2.00	1.00	.60
370	Rusty Staub	4.00	2.00	1.25
385	Tito Fuentes	2.00	1.00	.60
404	Tigers team card (color checklist back)	4.00	2.00	1.25
456	Vern Ruhle	2.00	1.00	.60
480	Ron LeFlore	2.50	1.25	.70
515	Tim Corcoran	2.00	1.00	.60
536	Roric Harrison	2.00	1.00	.60
559	Phil Mankowski	2.00	1.00	.60
607	Fernando Arroyo	2.00	1.00	.60
633	Tom Veryzer	2.00	1.00	.60
660	Jason Thompson	2.00	1.00	.60
684	Ralph Houk	2.50	1.25	.70
701	Tom Hume, Larry Landreth, Steve McCatty, Bruce Taylor (Rookie Pitchers)	2.00	1.00	.60
703	Larry Andersen, Tim Jones, Mickey Mahler, Jack Morris (Rookie Pitchers)	5.00	2.50	1.50
704	Garth Iorg, Dave Oliver, Sam Perlozzo, Lou Whitaker (Rookie 2nd Basemen)	6.00	3.00	1.75
707	Mickey Klutts, Paul Molitor, Alan Trammell, U.L. Washington (Rookie Shortstops)	15.00	7.50	4.50
708	Bo Diaz, Dale Murphy, Lance Parrish, Ernie Whitt (Rookie Catchers)	7.50	3.75	2.25
723	Johnny Wockenfuss	2.00	1.00	.60

1907 Detroit Tigers Team Postcard

This black-and-white photographic postcard pictures the American League Champion Tigers of 1907, including a young Ty Cobb. The approximately 5-1/2" x 3-1/2" card has standard postcard markings on back and a credit line to H.M. Taylor.

	NM	EX	VG
Detroit Tigers team photo	250.00	125.00	75.00

1964 Detroit Tigers Milk Bottle Caps

These small (1-5/16" diameter) cardboard milk bottle caps feature line drawings of the 1964 Tigers. The caps are printed in dark blue and orange on front and blank on back. The unnumbered caps are checklisted here in alphabetical order. A wire staple is found in most caps. The caps were reportedly produced for Twin Pines Dairy for use on bottles of chocolate milk.

		NM	EX	VG
Complete Set (14):		375.00	187.00	112.00
Common Player:		22.00	11.00	6.50
(1)	Hank Aguirre	22.00	11.00	6.50
(2)	Billy Bruton	22.00	11.00	6.50
(3)	Norman Cash	40.00	20.00	12.00
(4)	Don Demeter	22.00	11.00	6.50
(5)	Chuck Dressen	22.00	11.00	6.50
(6)	Bill Freehan	30.00	15.00	9.00
(7)	Al Kaline	125.00	62.00	37.00
(8)	Frank Lary	22.00	11.00	6.50
(9)	Jerry Lumpe	22.00	11.00	6.50
(10)	Dick McAuliffe	22.00	11.00	6.50
(11)	Bubba Phillips	22.00	11.00	6.50
(12)	Ed Rakow	22.00	11.00	6.50

		NM	EX	VG
(13)	Phil Regan	22.00	11.00	6.50
(14)	Dave Wickersham	22.00	11.00	6.50

1969 Detroit Tigers team issue

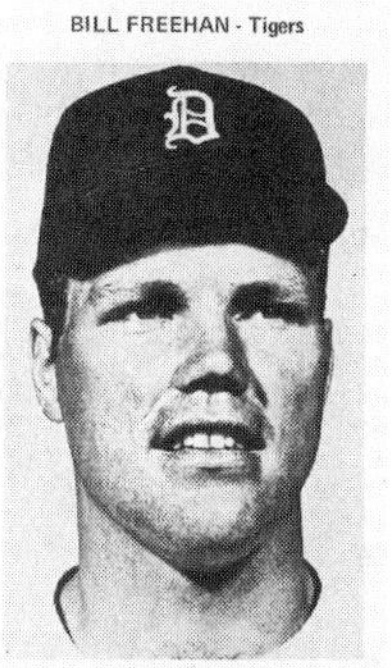

The top dozen players of the defending World Champion Tigers are featured in this team-issued picture set. In a 4-1/4" x 7" black-and-white, blank-back format, the pictures have portrait photos surrounded with a white border. The player's name is in the wide border at top. The unnumbered pictures are checklisted here in alphabetical order.

		NM	EX	VG
Complete Set (12):		35.00	17.50	10.50
Common Player:		3.00	1.50	.90
(1)	Norm Cash	4.50	2.25	1.25
(2)	Bill Freehan	3.00	1.50	.90
(3)	Willie Horton	3.00	1.50	.90
(4)	Al Kaline	12.00	6.00	3.50
(5)	Mike Kilkenny	3.00	1.50	.90
(6)	Mickey Lolich	4.50	2.25	1.25
(7)	Dick McAuliffe	3.00	1.50	.90
(8)	Denny McLain	4.50	2.25	1.25
(9)	Jim Northrup	3.00	1.50	.90
(10)	Mayo Smith	3.00	1.50	.90
(11)	Mickey Stanley	3.00	1.50	.90
(12)	Don Wert	3.00	1.50	.90

1978 Detroit Tigers Photocards

This set of photocards features borderless black-and-white photos on fronts, with player name in blue facsimile autograph. Backs are blank. Cards measure 3-1/4" x 5-1/4". The are checklisted here alphabetically.

		NM	EX	VG
Complete Set (30):		40.00	20.00	12.00
Common Player:		2.00	1.00	.60
(1)	Jack Billingham	2.00	1.00	.60
(2)	Gates Brown	2.00	1.00	.60
(3)	Jim Crawford	2.00	1.00	.60
(4)	Steve Dillard	2.00	1.00	.60
(5)	Mark Fidrych	4.00	2.00	1.25
(6)	Steve Foucault	2.00	1.00	.60
(7)	Fred Gladding	2.00	1.00	.60
(8)	Fred Hatfield	2.00	1.00	.60
(9)	Jim Hegan	2.00	1.00	.60
(10)	John Hiller	2.00	1.00	.60
(11)	Ralph Houk	2.50	1.25	.70
(12)	Steve Kemp	2.00	1.00	.60
(13)	Ron LeFlore	2.50	1.25	.70
(14)	Phil Mankowski	2.00	1.00	.60
(15)	Milt May	2.00	1.00	.60
(16)	Lance Parrish	2.50	1.25	.70
(17)	Aurelio Rodriguez	2.00	1.00	.60
(18)	Dave Rozema	2.00	1.00	.60
(19)	Jim Slaton	2.00	1.00	.60
(20)	Charlie Spikes	2.00	1.00	.60
(21)	Mickey Stanley	2.00	1.00	.60
(22)	Rusty Staub	2.50	1.25	.70
(23)	Bob Sykes	2.00	1.00	.60
(24)	Jason Thompson	2.00	1.00	.60
(25)	Dick Tracewski	2.00	1.00	.60
(26)	Alan Trammell	6.00	3.00	1.75
(27)	Mark Wagner	2.00	1.00	.60
(28)	Lou Whitaker	4.00	2.00	1.25
(29)	Milt Wilcox	2.00	1.00	.60
(30)	John B. Wockenfuss	2.00	1.00	.60

1966 Dexter Press California Angels

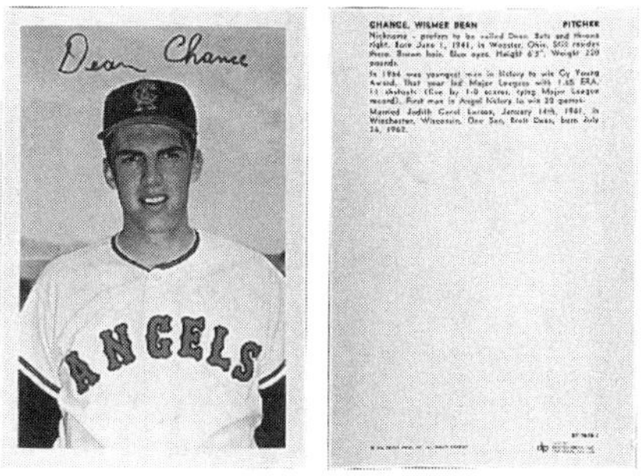

Less well-known than the New York firm's premium issues for Coca-Cola are Dexter Press' team issues. Sold for 50 cents in a cellophane bag with a colorful cardboard header the team issues are in the same basic design as the premium cards of 1967, but measure only 4" x 5-7/8". Though they were sold in sets of eight, more individual cards exist for the known teams, so it is evident there was some exchange of cards within the sets over the course of the sales period. Cards have color player poses with a black facsimile autograph at top and white border around. Backs are printed in blue with personal data and career highlights at top and copyright information at bottom. The cards are checklisted here alphabetically.

		NM	EX	VG
Complete Set (17):		100.00	50.00	30.00
Common Player:		8.00	4.00	2.50
(1)	Jose Cardenal	8.00	4.00	2.50
(2)	George Brunet	8.00	4.00	2.50
(3)	Dean Chance	10.00	5.00	3.00
(4)	Jim Fregosi	10.00	5.00	3.00
(5)	Ed Kirkpatrick	8.00	4.00	2.50
(6)	Bob Knoop	8.00	4.00	2.50
(7)	Bob Lee	8.00	4.00	2.50
(8)	Marcelino Lopez	8.00	4.00	2.50
(9)	Fred Newman	8.00	4.00	2.50
(10)	Albie Pearson	8.00	4.00	2.50
(11)	Jim Piersall	12.00	6.00	3.50
(12)	Rick Reichardt	8.00	4.00	2.50
(13)	Bob Rodgers	8.00	4.00	2.50
(14)	Paul Schaal	8.00	4.00	2.50
(15)	Norm Siebern	8.00	4.00	2.50
(16)	Willie Smith	8.00	4.00	2.50
(17)	Anaheim Stadium	8.00	4.00	2.50

1966 Dexter Press California Angels Booklet

This souvenir-stand bound booklet offered pictures of the 1966 California Angels in two different sizes. Each 8-1/8" x 3-1/2" page features a pair of identical color photo cards. A postcard-size (3-1/2" x 5-1/2") portrait has a facsimile autograph of the player at top, attached by perforations to a 2-1/4" x 3-1/2" card, which in turn is perforated into the bound end of the book. Booklets originally sold for 50 cents. The unnumbered cards are checklisted here in alphabetical order.

		NM	EX	VG
Complete Booket:		150.00	75.00	45.00
Complete Set, Large (10):		60.00	30.00	18.00
Complete Set, Small (10):		40.00	20.00	12.00
Common Player, Large:		8.00	4.00	2.40
Common Player, Small:		6.00	3.00	1.80
	Large Format (3-1/2" x 5-1/2")			
(1)	Jose Cardenal	8.00	4.00	2.50
(2)	Dean Chance	8.00	4.00	2.50
(3)	Jim Fregosi	8.00	4.00	2.50
(4)	Bob Knoop	8.00	4.00	2.50
(5)	Albie Pearson	8.00	4.00	2.50
(6)	Rick Reichardt	8.00	4.00	2.50
(7)	Bob Rodgers	8.00	4.00	2.50
(8)	Paul Schaal	8.00	4.00	2.50
(9)	Willie Smith	8.00	4.00	2.50
(10)	Anaheim Stadium	8.00	4.00	2.50
	Small Format (2-1/4" x 3-1/2")			
(1)	Jose Cardenal	6.00	3.00	1.80
(2)	Dean Chance	6.00	3.00	1.80
(3)	Jim Fregosi	6.00	3.00	1.80
(4)	Bob Knoop	6.00	3.00	1.80
(5)	Albie Pearson	6.00	3.00	1.80
(6)	Rick Reichardt	6.00	3.00	1.80
(7)	Bob Rodgers	6.00	3.00	1.80
(8)	Paul Schaal	6.00	3.00	1.80
(9)	Willie Smith	6.00	3.00	1.80
(10)	Anaheim Stadium	6.00	3.00	1.80

1966-67 Dexter Press N.Y. Yankees

Less commonly encountered than the later Dexter Press/Coca-Cola premium issues are the team-set photocards produced by the New York firm. Cards were sold in bagged sets with a colorful cardboard header. Virtually identical in design to the 5-1/2" x 7" premium cards of 1967, the team-set pictures measure 4" x 5-7/8" with a white border around, and a black facsimile autograph at the top of, color player poses. Backs are printed in blue with a few biographical details at top and copyright information at bottom. The unnumbered cards are checklisted here in alphabetical order.

		NM	EX	VG
Complete Set (10):		110.00	55.00	32.00
Common Player:		10.00	5.00	3.00
(1)	Jim Bouton	12.00	6.00	3.50
(2)	Al Downing	10.00	5.00	3.00
(3)	Whitey Ford	15.00	7.50	4.50
(4)	Steve Hamilton	10.00	5.00	3.00
(5)	Elston Howard	12.00	6.00	3.50
(6)	Mickey Mantle	50.00	25.00	15.00
(7)	Joe Pepitone	12.00	6.00	3.50
(8)	Bill Robinson	10.00	5.00	3.00
(9)	Tom Tresh	12.00	6.00	3.50
(10)	Steve Whitaker	10.00	5.00	3.00

1967 Dexter Press Premiums

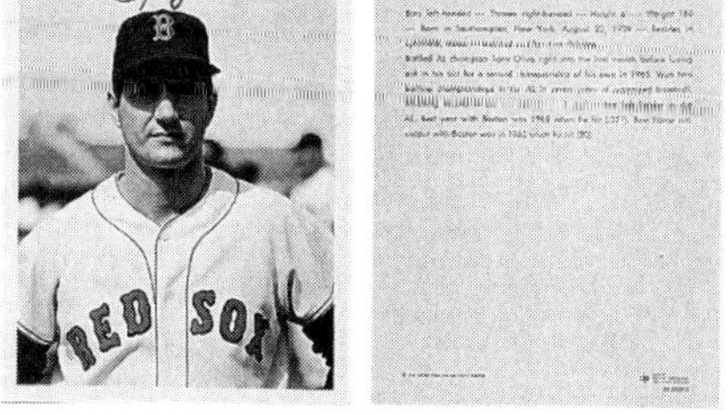

Among the most attractive baseball collectibles issued during the 1960s were the cards produced by Dexter Press and issued in team sets as a premium by Coca-Cola. Eighteen of the 20 Major League teams participated in the promotion (no California Angels or St. Louis Cardinals). The cards are in 5-1/2" x 7" glossy format. All of the color photos are waist-to-cap poses shot during spring training and all cards feature a black facsimile autograph at the top of the photo. The cards have a 1/4" white border around the picture. Backs are printed in blue on white and include a few biographical details and career highlights. The 12 players in the All-Star issue can be differentiated from the same players' cards in the team sets by the lengthier biographies on back. While each of the cards has a number printed on back in the lower-right, they are checklisted here alphabetically within team. Sixteen of the Dexter Press premiums were issued in a smaller, borderless sticker set in 1983; it is an unauthorized collector issue.

		NM	EX	VG
Complete Set (229):		750.00	375.00	225.00
Common Player:		4.00	2.00	1.25
All-Stars				
(1)	Jim Bunning	6.00	3.00	1.75
(2)	Roberto Clemente	8.00	4.00	2.50
(3)	Willie Davis	4.00	2.00	1.25
(4)	Al Kaline	6.00	3.00	1.75
(5)	Harmon Killebrew	6.00	3.00	1.75
(6)	Willie Mays	8.00	4.00	2.50
(7)	Joe Pepitone	4.00	2.00	1.25
(8)	Brooks Robinson	6.00	3.00	1.75
(9)	Frank Robinson	6.00	3.00	1.75
(10)	Ron Santo	4.00	2.00	1.25
(11)	Joe Torre	5.00	2.50	1.50
(12)	Carl Yastrzemski	6.00	3.00	1.75
Houston Astros				
(14)	Bob Aspromonte	4.00	2.00	1.25
(15)	John Bateman	4.00	2.00	1.25
(16)	Ron Davis	4.00	2.00	1.25
(17)	Larry Dierker	4.00	2.00	1.25
(18)	Dick Farrell	4.00	2.00	1.25
(19)	Dave Giusti	4.00	2.00	1.25
(20)	Chuck Harrison	4.00	2.00	1.25
(21)	Sonny Jackson	4.00	2.00	1.25
(22)	Jim Landis	4.00	2.00	1.25
(23)	Eddie Mathews	10.00	5.00	3.00
(24)	Joe Morgan	10.00	5.00	3.00
(25)	Rusty Staub	7.00	3.50	2.00
Kansas City Athletics				
(26)	Jack Aker	4.00	2.00	1.25
(27)	Campy Campaneris	5.00	2.50	1.50
(28)	Danny Cater	4.00	2.00	1.25
(29)	Ed Charles	4.00	2.00	1.25
(30)	Ossie Chavarria	4.00	2.00	1.25
(31)	Dick Green	4.00	2.00	1.25
(32)	Mike Hershberger	4.00	2.00	1.25
(33)	Lew Krausse	4.00	2.00	1.25
(34)	Jim Nash	4.00	2.00	1.25
(35)	Joe Nossek	4.00	2.00	1.25
(36)	Roger Repoz	4.00	2.00	1.25
(37)	Phil Roof	4.00	2.00	1.25
Atlanta Braves				
(38)	Hank Aaron	25.00	12.50	7.50
(39)	Felipe Alou	6.00	3.00	1.75
(40)	Wade Blasingame	4.00	2.00	1.25
(41)	Clete Boyer	4.00	2.00	1.25
(42)	Bob Bruce	4.00	2.00	1.25
(43)	Ty Cline	4.00	2.00	1.25
(44)	Tony Cloninger	4.00	2.00	1.25
(45)	Ken Johnson	4.00	2.00	1.25
(46)	Dennis Menke	4.00	2.00	1.25
(47)	Gene Oliver	4.00	2.00	1.25
(48)	Joe Torre	7.50	3.75	2.25
(49)	Woody Woodward	4.00	2.00	1.25
Chicago Cubs				
(50)	George Altman	4.00	2.00	1.25
(51)	Ernie Banks	18.00	9.00	5.50
(52)	Glen Beckert (Glenn)	4.00	2.00	1.25
(53)	John Boccabella	4.00	2.00	1.25
(54)	Ray Culp	4.00	2.00	1.25
(55)	Ken Holtzman	4.00	2.00	1.25
(56)	Randy Hundley	5.00	2.50	1.50
(57)	Cal Koonce	4.00	2.00	1.25
(58)	Adolfo Phillips	4.00	2.00	1.25
(59)	Ron Santo	7.50	3.75	2.25
(60)	Lee Thomas	4.00	2.00	1.25
(61)	Billy Williams	10.00	5.00	3.00
Los Angeles Dodgers				
(62)	Bob Bailey	4.00	2.00	1.25
(63)	Willie Davis	5.00	2.50	1.50
(64)	Ron Fairly	4.00	2.00	1.25
(65)	Ron Hunt	4.00	2.00	1.25
(66)	Lou Johnson	4.00	2.00	1.25
(67)	John Kennedy	4.00	2.00	1.25
(68)	Jim Lefebvre	5.00	2.50	1.50
(69)	Claude Osteen	4.00	2.00	1.25
(70)	Wes Parker	4.00	2.00	1.25
(71)	Ron Perranoski	4.00	2.00	1.25
(72)	Phil Regan	4.00	2.00	1.25
(73)	Don Sutton	7.50	3.75	2.25
San Francisco Giants				
(74)	Jesus Alou	4.00	2.00	1.25
(75)	Ollie Brown	4.00	2.00	1.25
(76)	Jim Davenport	4.00	2.00	1.25
(77)	Tito Fuentes	4.00	2.00	1.25
(78)	Tom Haller	4.00	2.00	1.25
(79)	Jim Hart	4.00	2.00	1.25
(80)	Hal Lanier	4.00	2.00	1.25
(81)	Willie Mays	25.00	12.50	7.50
(82)	Mike McCormick	4.00	2.00	1.25
(83)	Willie McCovey	12.00	6.00	3.50
(84)	Gaylord Perry	8.00	4.00	2.50
(85)	Norman Siebern	4.00	2.00	1.25
Cleveland Indians				
(86)	Max Alvis	4.00	2.00	1.25
(87)	Joe Azcue	4.00	2.00	1.25
(88)	Gary Bell	4.00	2.00	1.25
(89)	Larry Brown	4.00	2.00	1.25
(90)	Rocky Colavito	10.00	5.00	3.00
(91)	Vic Davalillo	4.00	2.00	1.25
(92)	Pedro Gonzalez	4.00	2.00	1.25
(93)	Chuck Hinton	4.00	2.00	1.25
(94)	Sam McDowell	5.00	2.50	1.50
(95)	Luis Tiant	5.00	2.50	1.50
(96)	Leon Wagner	4.00	2.00	1.25
(97)	Fred Whitfield	4.00	2.00	1.25
New York Mets				
(98)	Ed Bressoud	4.00	2.00	1.25
(99)	Ken Boyer	7.00	3.50	2.00
(100)	Tommy Davis	5.00	2.50	1.50
(101)	Jack Fisher	4.00	2.00	1.25
(102)	Jerry Grote	4.00	2.00	1.25
(103)	Jack Hamilton	4.00	2.00	1.25
(104)	Cleon Jones	5.00	2.50	1.50
(105)	Ed Kranepool	4.00	2.00	1.25
(106)	Johnny Lewis	4.00	2.00	1.25
(107)	Bob Shaw	4.00	2.00	1.25
(108)	John Stephenson	4.00	2.00	1.25
(109)	Ron Swoboda	4.00	2.00	1.25
Baltimore Orioles				
(110)	Luis Aparicio	10.00	5.00	3.00
(111)	Curt Blefary	4.00	2.00	1.25
(112)	Wally Bunker	4.00	2.00	1.25
(113)	Andy Etchebarren	4.00	2.00	1.25
(114)	Eddie Fisher	4.00	2.00	1.25
(115)	Dave Johnson	5.00	2.50	1.50
(116)	Dave McNally	4.00	2.00	1.25
(117)	Jim Palmer	10.00	5.00	3.00
(118)	John "Boog" Powell	8.00	4.00	2.50
(119)	Brooks Robinson	15.00	7.50	4.50
(120)	Frank Robinson	15.00	7.50	4.50
(121)	Russ Snyder	4.00	2.00	1.25
Philadelphia Phillies				
(122)	Rich Allen	7.50	3.75	2.25
(123)	John Briggs	4.00	2.00	1.25
(124)	Jim Bunning	6.00	3.00	1.75
(125)	Johnny Callison	4.00	2.00	1.25
(126)	Clay Dalrymple	4.00	2.00	1.25
(127)	Dick Groat	5.00	2.50	1.50
(128)	Larry Jackson	4.00	2.00	1.25
(129)	Don Lock	4.00	2.00	1.25
(130)	Cookie Rojas	4.00	2.00	1.25
(131)	Chris Short	4.00	2.00	1.25
(132)	Tony Taylor	4.00	2.00	1.25
(133)	Bill White	5.00	2.50	1.50
Pittsburgh Pirates				
(134)	Gene Alley	4.00	2.00	1.25
(135)	Matty Alou	4.00	2.00	1.25
(136)	Roberto Clemente	45.00	22.00	13.50
(137)	Donn Clendenon	4.00	2.00	1.25
(138)	Woodie Fryman	4.00	2.00	1.25
(139)	Vern Law	5.00	2.50	1.50
(140)	Bill Mazeroski	8.00	4.00	2.50
(141)	Manny Mota	4.00	2.00	1.25
(142)	Jim Pagliaroni	4.00	2.00	1.25
(143)	Wilver Stargell	12.00	6.00	3.50
(144)	Bob Veale	4.00	2.00	1.25
(145)	Maury Wills	6.00	3.00	1.75
Cincinnati Reds				
(146)	Leo Cardenas	4.00	2.00	1.25
(147)	Gordy Coleman	4.00	2.00	1.25
(148)	Johnny Edwards	4.00	2.00	1.25
(149)	Tommy Harper	5.00	2.50	1.50
(150)	Tommy Helms	4.00	2.00	1.25
(151)	Deron Johnson	4.00	2.00	1.25
(152)	Jim Maloney	4.00	2.00	1.25
(153)	Bill McCool	4.00	2.00	1.25
(154)	Milt Pappas	4.00	2.00	1.25
(155)	Vada Pinson	6.00	3.00	1.75
(156)	Pete Rose	20.00	10.00	6.00
(157)	Art Shamsky	4.00	2.00	1.25
Boston Red Sox				
(158)	Don Demeter	4.00	2.00	1.25
(159)	Bill Fischer	4.00	2.00	1.25
(160)	Joe Foy	4.00	2.00	1.25
(161)	Dalton Jones	4.00	2.00	1.25
(162)	Jim Lonborg	5.00	2.50	1.50
(163)	Rico Petrocelli	4.00	2.00	1.25
(164)	Jose Santiago	4.00	2.00	1.25
(165)	George Scott	4.00	2.00	1.25
(166)	George Smith	4.00	2.00	1.25
(167)	Jose Tartabull	4.00	2.00	1.25
(168)	Bob Tillman	4.00	2.00	1.25
(169)	Carl Yastrzemski	15.00	7.50	4.50
Washington Senators				
(170)	Bernie Allen	4.00	2.00	1.25
(171)	Ed Brinkman	4.00	2.00	1.25
(172)	Paul Casanova	4.00	2.00	1.25
(173)	Ken Harrelson	5.00	2.50	1.50
(174)	Frank Howard	6.00	3.00	1.75
(175)	Jim King	4.00	2.00	1.25
(176)	Ken McMullen	4.00	2.00	1.25
(177)	Dick Nen	4.00	2.00	1.25
(178)	Phil Ortega	4.00	2.00	1.25
(179)	Pete Richert	4.00	2.00	1.25
(180)	Bob Saverine	4.00	2.00	1.25
(181)	Fred Valentine	4.00	2.00	1.25
Detroit Tigers				
(182)	Norm Cash	6.00	3.00	1.75
(183)	Bill Freehan	4.00	2.00	1.25
(184)	Willie Horton	4.00	2.00	1.25
(185)	Al Kaline	12.00	6.00	3.50
(186)	Mickey Lolich	5.00	2.50	1.50
(187)	Jerry Lumpe	4.00	2.00	1.25
(188)	Dick McAuliffe	4.00	2.00	1.25
(189)	Johnny Podres	4.00	2.00	1.25
(190)	Joe Sparma	4.00	2.00	1.25
(191)	Dave Wickersham	4.00	2.00	1.25
(192)	Earl Wilson	4.00	2.00	1.25
(193)	Don Wert	4.00	2.00	1.25
Minnesota Twins				
(194)	Bob Allison	4.00	2.00	1.25
(195)	Earl Battey	4.00	2.00	1.25
(196)	Dave Boswell	4.00	2.00	1.25
(197)	Dean Chance	4.00	2.00	1.25
(198)	Mudcat Grant	4.00	2.00	1.25
(199)	Harmon Killebrew	12.00	6.00	3.50
(200)	Jim Merritt	4.00	2.00	1.25
(201)	Tony Oliva	8.00	4.00	2.50
(202)	Rich Rollins	4.00	2.00	1.25
(203)	Ted Uhlaender	4.00	2.00	1.25
(204)	Sandy Valdespino	4.00	2.00	1.25
(205)	Zoilo Versalles	4.00	2.00	1.25
Chicago White Sox				
(206)	Tommie Agee	4.00	2.00	1.25
(207)	Ken Berry	4.00	2.00	1.25
(208)	Don Buford	4.00	2.00	1.25
(209)	Ron Hansen	4.00	2.00	1.25
(210)	Joel Horlen	4.00	2.00	1.25
(211)	Tommy John	6.00	3.00	1.75
(212)	Bob Locker	4.00	2.00	1.25
(213)	Tommy McCraw	4.00	2.00	1.25
(214)	Jerry McNertney	4.00	2.00	1.25
(215)	Jim O'Toole	4.00	2.00	1.25
(216)	Bill "Moose" Skowron	7.00	3.50	2.00
(217)	Pete Ward	4.00	2.00	1.25
New York Yankees				
(218)	Jim Bouton	5.00	2.50	1.50
(219)	Horace Clarke	4.00	2.00	1.25
(220)	Al Downing	4.00	2.00	1.25
(221)	Steve Hamilton	4.00	2.00	1.25
(222)	Elston Howard	7.50	3.75	2.25
(223)	Mickey Mantle	50.00	25.00	15.00
(224)	Joe Pepitone	4.00	2.00	1.25
(225)	Fritz Peterson	4.00	2.00	1.25
(226)	Charley Smith	4.00	2.00	1.25
(227)	Mel Stottlemyre	5.00	2.50	1.50
(228)	Tom Tresh	6.00	3.00	1.75
(229)	Roy White	5.00	2.50	1.50

1968 Dexter Press Postcards

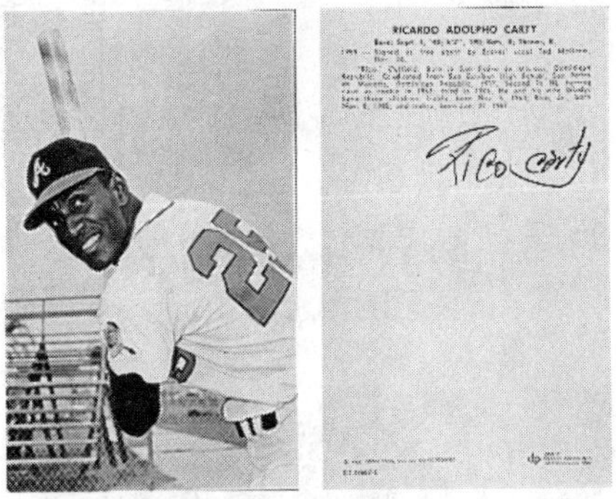

In its second year of printing premium cards for Coca-Cola, Dexter Press changed format and greatly reduced the number of participating teams and players. Only six teams were represented by 12-card sets, while an additional four teams had one or two players included. For 1968, Dexter Press produced its premiums in postcard (3-1/2" x 5-1/2") size. The cards featured borderless color player poses on front. Backs were printed in blue on white and included a facsimile autograph, biographical details and career highlights. Cards carry a Dexter Press serial number on back, but are checklisted here alphabetically within team.

		NM	EX	VG
Complete Set (77):		600.00	300.00	180.00
Common Player:		6.00	3.00	1.75
CALIFORNIA ANGELS				
(1)	Jim Fregosi	8.00	4.00	2.50
HOUSTON ASTROS				
(2)	Bob Aspromonte	6.00	3.00	1.75
(3)	John Bateman	6.00	3.00	1.75
(4)	Ron Brand	6.00	3.00	1.75
(5)	Mike Cuellar	6.00	3.00	1.75
(6)	Ron Davis	6.00	3.00	1.75
(7)	Dave Giusti	6.00	3.00	1.75
(8)	Julio Gotay	6.00	3.00	1.75
(9)	Denny Lemaster	6.00	3.00	1.75
(10)	Denis Menke	6.00	3.00	1.75
(11)	Joe Morgan	15.00	7.50	4.50
(12)	Rusty Staub	9.00	4.50	2.75
(13)	Jim Wynn	6.00	3.00	1.75
ATLANTA BRAVES				
(14)	Hank Aaron	30.00	15.00	9.00
(15)	Felipe Alou	9.00	4.50	2.75
(16)	Clete Boyer	6.00	3.00	1.75
(17)	Clay Carroll	6.00	3.00	1.75
(18)	Rico Carty	6.00	3.00	1.75
(19)	Tony Cloninger	6.00	3.00	1.75
(20)	Sonny Jackson	6.00	3.00	1.75
(21)	Ray Jarvis	6.00	3.00	1.75
(22)	Ken Johnson	6.00	3.00	1.75
(23)	Phil Niekro	11.00	5.50	3.25
(24)	Joe Torre	9.00	4.50	2.75

		NM	EX	VG
(25)	Woody Woodward	6.00	3.00	1.75
SAN FRANCISCO GIANTS				
(26)	Jesus Alou	6.00	3.00	1.75
(27)	Bob Bolin	6.00	3.00	1.75
(28)	Jim Davenport	6.00	3.00	1.75
(29)	Jim Hart	6.00	3.00	1.75
(30)	Jack Hiatt	6.00	3.00	1.75
(31)	Ron Hunt	6.00	3.00	1.75
(32)	Frank Linzy	6.00	3.00	1.75
(33)	Juan Marichal	15.00	7.50	4.50
(34)	Willie Mays	30.00	15.00	9.00
(35)	Mike McCormick	6.00	3.00	1.75
(36)	Gaylord Perry	12.00	6.00	3.50
(37)	Ray Sadecki	6.00	3.00	1.75
BALTIMORE ORIOLES				
(38)	Mark Belanger	6.00	3.00	1.75
(39)	Paul Blair	6.00	3.00	1.75
(40)	Curt Blefary	6.00	3.00	1.75
(41)	Don Buford	6.00	3.00	1.75
(42)	Moe Drabowsky	6.00	3.00	1.75
(43)	Andy Etchebarren	6.00	3.00	1.75
(44)	Dave Johnson	6.00	3.00	1.75
(45)	Dave McNally	6.00	3.00	1.75
(46)	Tom Phoebus	6.00	3.00	1.75
(47)	Boog Powell	8.00	4.00	2.50
(48)	Brooks Robinson	20.00	10.00	6.00
(49)	Frank Robinson	20.00	10.00	6.00
PHILADELPHIA PHILLIES				
(50)	Dick Allen	12.00	6.00	3.50
PITTSBURGH PIRATES				
(51)	Roberto Clemente	30.00	15.00	9.00
(52)	Bill Mazeroski	11.00	5.50	3.25
BOSTON RED SOX				
(53)	Jerry Adair	6.00	3.00	1.75
(54)	Mike Andrews	6.00	3.00	1.75
(55)	Gary Bell	6.00	3.00	1.75
(56)	Darrell Brandon	6.00	3.00	1.75
(57)	Dick Ellsworth	6.00	3.00	1.75
(58)	Joe Foy	6.00	3.00	1.75
(59)	Dalton Jones	6.00	3.00	1.75
(60)	Jim Lonborg	8.00	4.00	2.50
(61)	Dave Morehead	6.00	3.00	1.75
(62)	Rico Petrocelli	6.00	3.00	1.75
(63)	George Scott	6.00	3.00	1.75
(64)	John Wyatt	6.00	3.00	1.75
DETROIT TIGERS				
(65)	Bill Freehan	9.00	4.50	2.75
MINNESOTA TWINS				
(66)	Bob Allison	6.00	3.00	1.75
(67)	Dave Boswell	6.00	3.00	1.75
(68)	Rod Carew	20.00	10.00	6.00
(69)	Dean Chance	6.00	3.00	1.75
(70)	Jim Kaat	8.00	4.00	2.50
(71)	Harmon Killebrew	18.00	9.00	5.50
(72)	Russ Nixon	6.00	3.00	1.75
(73)	Tony Oliva	9.75	5.00	3.00
(74)	Rich Rollins	6.00	3.00	1.75
(75)	John Roseboro	6.00	3.00	1.75
(76)	Cesar Tovar	6.00	3.00	1.75
(77)	Ted Uhlaender	6.00	3.00	1.75

1979 Dexter Press Hall of Fame Plaque Postcards

(See Hall of Fame (Dexter Press) for checklist, value data.)

1977 DFF/LCF

(See listings under Larry Fritsch Cards)

1930s Diamond Dust Punchboard

Fifteen baseball stars of the 1930s, including Ruth, Gehrig, Foxx, etc., are pictured on this gambling device. The 5-3/4" x 8-7/8" x 9/16" board has 600 holes in which papers are rolled. For five cents a chance, gamblers could pick out a paper roll. If it had the number of one of the featured players, a $1 prize was awarded. Several different styles with a variety of featured players are known.

	NM	EX	VG
1930s Diamond Dust Punchboard (#33 is "Heine Manush")	300.00	150.00	90.00

1940s Diamond Dust Punchboard

Fifteen baseball stars of the 1940s, including DiMaggio, Feller, Greenberg, etc., are pictured on this gambling device. The 5-3/4" x 8-7/8" x 9/16" board has 600 holes in which papers are rolled. For five cents a chance, gamblers could pick out a paper roll. If it had the number of one of the featured players, a $1 prize was awarded. Several different styles with a variety of featured players are known.

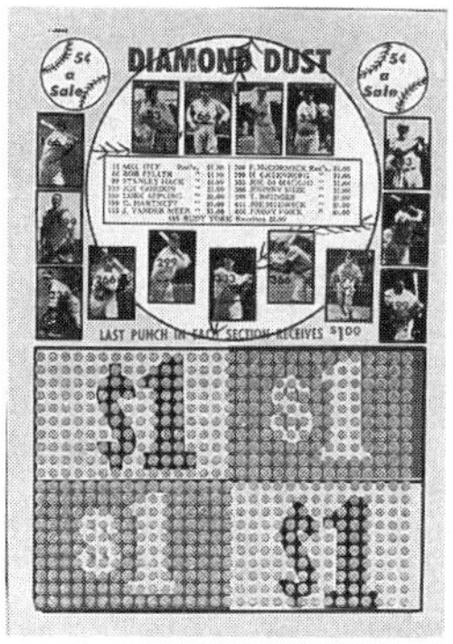

	NM	EX	VG
1940s Diamond Dust Punchboard	300.00	150.00	90.00

1940 Diamond Dust Punchboard Cards

These paper cards are the consolation prizes from a popular gambling device of the Depression era, the punchboard. For five cents a customer could choose one of 624 holes on the punchboard and push a wood or metal punch through the paper on front, driving out the back a 1" x about 1-3/4" picture of a baseball player. Fifteen of the players were $1 winners and were produced in much shorter supply than the others, any which were redeemed would probably have been destroyed. The pictures are printed on ribbed paper to assist in fitting them into the board. They are pictures taken from the photos on contemporary "Salutation" Exhibit cards, though without uniform logos. They are printed in bright colors with the player name in a color bar at bottom. Backs are blank. The unnumbered cards are listed here in alphabetical order, with an asterisk indicating winners. The punchboard itself is highly collectible, with colorful baseball graphics and player pictures and names. Earlier and later versions of Diamond Dust punchboards are also known, but have not been checklisted.

		NM	EX	VG
Complete Set (30):		850.00	425.00	250.00
Common Player:		15.00	7.50	4.50
Complete Unused Punchboard:		1200.	600.00	350.00
(1)	Luke Appling (*)	45.00	22.00	13.50
(2)	Earl Averill (*)	45.00	22.00	13.50
(3)	Adolf Camilli	15.00	7.50	4.50
(4)	Harland Clift (Harlond)	15.00	7.50	4.50
(5)	Joe Cronin (*) (unconfirmed)	45.00	22.00	13.50
(6)	Tony Cuccinello	15.00	7.50	4.50
(7)	Dizzy Dean	35.00	17.50	10.50
(8)	Bill Dickey (*)	50.00	25.00	15.00
(9)	Joe DiMaggio (*)	125.00	62.00	37.00
(10)	Bob Feller	30.00	15.00	9.00
(11)	Jimmie Foxx (*)	45.00	22.00	13.50
(12)	Charlie Gehringer (*)	45.00	22.00	13.50
(13)	Lefty Gomez	25.00	12.50	7.50
(14)	Hank Greenberg	30.00	15.00	9.00
(15)	Lefty Grove	25.00	12.50	7.50
(16)	Gabby Hartnett	15.00	7.50	4.50
(17)	Carl Hubbell	25.00	12.50	7.50
(18)	Bob Johnson	15.00	7.50	4.50
(19)	Chuck Klein	25.00	12.50	7.50
(20)	Bill Lee	15.00	7.50	4.50
(21)	Ernie Lombardi (*)	45.00	22.00	13.50
(22)	Frank McCormick (*)	25.00	12.50	7.50
(23)	Joe Medwick	25.00	12.50	7.50
(24)	Johnny Mize (*)	45.00	22.00	13.50
(25)	Buck Newson (Newsom)	15.00	7.50	4.50
(26)	Mel Ott (*)	45.00	22.00	13.50
(27)	Johnny Rizzo (*)	25.00	12.50	7.50
(28)	Red Ruffing (*) (unconfirmed)	45.00	22.00	13.50
(29)	Cecil Travis	15.00	7.50	4.50
(30)	Johnny Vander Meer	15.00	7.50	4.50
(31)	Arky Vaughan (*)	45.00	22.00	13.50
(32)	Lon Warneke	15.00	7.50	4.50
(33)	Rudy York (*) (unconfirmed)	25.00	12.50	7.50

1950 Diamond Dust Punchboard

A number of baseball stars circa 1950, including DiMaggio, Williams, Reese, etc., are pictured on this gambling device. The 7-1/4" x 10-3/4" x 9/16" board has 600 holes in which papers are rolled. For five cents a chance, gamblers could pick out a paper roll. If it had the number of one of the featured players, a $1 prize was awarded.

	NM	EX	VG
1950 New Diamond Dust Punchboard (#33 is Bob Feller)	250.00	125.00	75.00

1955 Diamond Dust Punchboard

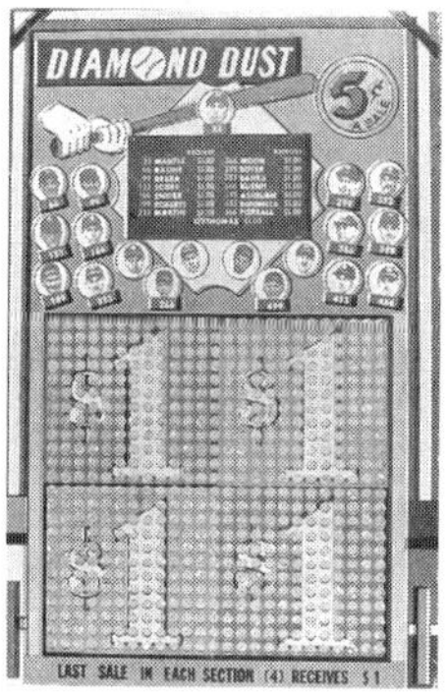

A number of baseball stars of the 1950s, including Mantle, Snider, Piersall, etc., are pictured on this gambling device. The 5-3/4" x 8-7/8" x 9/16" board has 600 holes in which papers are rolled. For five cents a chance, gamblers could pick out a paper roll. If it had the number of one of the featured players, a $1 prize was awarded.

	NM	EX	VG
1950s Diamond Dust Punchboard	250.00	125.00	75.00

1911 Diamond Gum Pins

The World's Champion Philadelphia A's are well represented and specially marked in this series of small 1" diameter pins. The sepia toned center portion of the pin has a player portrait photo with his last name, team and league in white at left and right. Around that is a metallic blue border with a white inscription; either "World's Champions" on the A's players, or "Free with Diamond Gum" on the other players.

		NM	EX	VG
Complete Set (28):		6000.	3000.	1800.
Common Player:		150.00	75.00	45.00
(1)	Babe Adams	150.00	75.00	45.00
(2)	Home Run Baker	350.00	175.00	105.00
(3)	Chief Bender	350.00	175.00	105.00
(4)	Mordecai Brown	350.00	175.00	105.00
(5)	Donie Bush	150.00	75.00	45.00
(6)	Bill Carrigan	150.00	75.00	45.00
(7)	Frank Chance	350.00	175.00	105.00

(8)	Hal Chase	200.00	100.00	60.00
(9)	Ty Cobb	950.00	475.00	285.00
(10)	Eddie Collins	350.00	175.00	105.00
(11)	George Davis	150.00	75.00	45.00
(12)	Red Dooin	150.00	75.00	45.00
(13)	Larry Doyle	150.00	75.00	45.00
(14)	Miller Huggins	350.00	175.00	105.00
(15)	Hughie Jennings	350.00	175.00	105.00
(16)	Nap Lajoie	350.00	175.00	105.00
(17)	Harry Lord	150.00	75.00	45.00
(18)	Christy Mathewson	550.00	275.00	165.00
(19)	Dots Miller	150.00	75.00	45.00
(20)	George Mullen (Mullin)	150.00	75.00	45.00
(21)	Danny Murphy	150.00	75.00	45.00
(22)	Orval Overall	150.00	75.00	45.00
(23)	Eddie Plank	350.00	175.00	105.00
(24)	Hack Simmons	150.00	75.00	45.00
(25)	Ira Thomas	150.00	75.00	45.00
(26)	Joe Tinker	350.00	175.00	105.00
(27)	Honus Wagner	550.00	275.00	165.00
(28)	Cy Young	400.00	200.00	120.00

1934 Diamond Matchbooks - silver border

During much of the Great Depression, the hobby of matchbook collecting swept the country. Generally selling at two for a penny, the matchbooks began to feature photos and artwork to attract buyers. In the late 1930s, several series of sports subjects were issued by Diamond Match Co., of New York City. The first issue was a set of 200 baseball players known to collectors as "silver border" for the color of the overall borders on front and back of the approximately 1-1/2" x 4-1/8" (open) matchbooks. Player portrait or posed photos are printed in sepia on front, and can be found framed in either red, green, blue or orange, theoretically creating an 800-piece color variation set. The player's name and team are printed on the "saddle" and there is a career summary on back, along with a design of glove, ball and bats. Matchbooks are commonly collected with the matches removed and the striker at back-bottom intact. Pieces without the striker are valued at 50% of these listed prices. Complete covers with matches bring a premium of 50-100%. The players are listed here alphabetically.

		NM	EX	VG
Complete Set (200):		2850.	1400.	850.00
Common Player:		15.00	7.50	4.50
(1)	Earl Adams	15.00	7.50	4.50
(2)	Ethan Allen	15.00	7.50	4.50
(3)	Eldon L. Auker	15.00	7.50	4.50
(4)	Delmar David Baker	15.00	7.50	4.50
(5)	Richard "Dick" Bartell	15.00	7.50	4.50
(6)	Walter Beck	15.00	7.50	4.50
(7)	Herman Bell	15.00	7.50	4.50
(8)	Ray Benge	15.00	7.50	4.50
(9)	Larry J. Benton	15.00	7.50	4.50
(10)	Louis W. Berger	15.00	7.50	4.50
(11)	Walter "Wally" Berger	15.00	7.50	4.50
(12)	Ray Berres	15.00	7.50	4.50
(13)	Charlie Berry	15.00	7.50	4.50
(14)	Walter M. "Huck" Betts	15.00	7.50	4.50
(15)	Ralph Birkofer	15.00	7.50	4.50
(16)	George F. Blaeholder	15.00	7.50	4.50
(17)	Jim Bottomley	30.00	15.00	9.00
(18)	Ralph Boyle	15.00	7.50	4.50
(19)	Ed Brandt	15.00	7.50	4.50
(20)	Don Brennan	15.00	7.50	4.50
(21)	Irving (Jack) Burns	15.00	7.50	4.50
(22)	Guy "Joe" Bush	20.00	10.00	6.00
(23)	Adolph Camilli	30.00	15.00	9.00
(24)	Ben Cantwell	15.00	7.50	4.50
(25)	Tex Carleton	15.00	7.50	4.50
(26)	Owen Carroll	15.00	7.50	4.50
(27)	Louis Chiozza	25.00	12.50	7.50
(28)	Watson Clark	15.00	7.50	4.50
(29)	James A. Collins	15.00	7.50	4.50
(30)	Phil Collins	15.00	7.50	4.50
(31)	Edward J. Connolly	15.00	7.50	4.50
(32)	Raymond F. Coombs	15.00	7.50	4.50
(33)	Roger Cramer	17.50	8.75	5.25
(34)	Clifford Crawford	15.00	7.50	4.50
(35)	Hugh M. Critz	15.00	7.50	4.50
(36)	Alvin Crowder	15.00	7.50	4.50
(37)	Tony Cuccinello	15.00	7.50	4.50
(38)	Hazen "Kiki" Cuyler	30.00	15.00	9.00
(39)	Virgil Davis	15.00	7.50	4.50
(40)	Jerome "Dizzy" Dean	45.00	22.00	13.50
(41)	Paul Dean	25.00	12.50	7.50
(42)	Edward Delker	15.00	7.50	4.50
(43)	Paul Derringer	15.00	7.50	4.50
(44)	Eugene DeSautel	15.00	7.50	4.50
(45)	William J. Dietrich	15.00	7.50	4.50
(46)	Frank F. Doljack	15.00	7.50	4.50
(47)	Edward F. Durham	15.00	7.50	4.50
(48)	Leo Durocher	25.00	12.50	7.50
(49)	Jim Elliott	15.00	7.50	4.50
(50)	Charles D. English	15.00	7.50	4.50
(51)	Elwood G. English	15.00	7.50	4.50
(52)	Richard Ferrell	25.00	12.50	7.50
(53)	Wesley Ferrell	15.00	7.50	4.50
(54)	Charles W. Fischer	15.00	7.50	4.50
(55)	Freddy Fitzsimmons	15.00	7.50	4.50
(56)	Lew Fonseca	15.00	7.50	4.50
(57)	Fred Frankhouse	15.00	7.50	4.50
(58)	John Frederick	15.00	7.50	4.50
(59)	Benny Frey (Reds)	15.00	7.50	4.50
(60)	Linus Frey (Dodgers)	17.50	8.75	5.25
(61)	Frankie Frisch	35.00	17.50	10.50
(62)	Chick Fullis	15.00	7.50	4.50
(63)	August Galan	15.00	7.50	4.50
(64)	Milton Galatzer	15.00	7.50	4.50
(65)	Dennis W. Galehouse	15.00	7.50	4.50
(66)	Milton Gaston	15.00	7.50	4.50
(67)	Chas. Gehringer	35.00	17.50	10.50
(68)	Edward P. Gharrity	15.00	7.50	4.50
(69)	George Gibson	15.00	7.50	4.50
(70)	Isidore Goldstein	15.00	7.50	4.50
(71)	"Hank" Gowdy	15.00	7.50	4.50
(72)	Earl Grace	15.00	7.50	4.50
(73)	Chas. Grimm (fielding)	15.00	7.50	4.50
(74)	Chas. Grimm (portrait)	15.00	7.50	4.50
(75)	Frank T. Grube	15.00	7.50	4.50
(76)	Richard Gyselman	15.00	7.50	4.50
(77)	Stanley C. Hack	20.00	10.00	6.00
(78)	Irving Hadley	15.00	7.50	4.50
(79)	Charles "Chick" Hafey	25.00	12.50	7.50
(80)	Harold A. Haid	15.00	7.50	4.50
(81)	Jesse Haines	30.00	15.00	9.00
(82)	Odell A. Hale	15.00	7.50	4.50
(83)	Bill Hallahan	15.00	7.50	4.50
(84)	Luke D. Hamlin	15.00	7.50	4.50
(85)	Roy Hansen	15.00	7.50	4.50
(86)	Melvin Harder	17.50	8.75	5.25
(87)	William M. Harris	15.00	7.50	4.50
(88)	Gabby Hartnett	30.00	15.00	9.00
(89)	Harvey Hendrick	15.00	7.50	4.50
(90)	Floyd "Babe" Herman	17.50	8.75	5.25
(91)	William Herman	30.00	15.00	9.00
(92)	J. Francis Hogan	15.00	7.50	4.50
(93)	Elon Hogsett	15.00	7.50	4.50
(94)	Waite Hoyt	30.00	15.00	9.00
(95)	Carl Hubbell	35.00	17.50	10.50
(96)	Silas K. Johnson	15.00	7.50	4.50
(97)	Sylvester Johnson	15.00	7.50	4.50
(98)	Roy M. Joiner	15.00	7.50	4.50
(99)	Baxter Jordan	15.00	7.50	4.50
(100)	Arndt Jorgens	15.00	7.50	4.50
(101)	William F. Jurges	15.00	7.50	4.50
(102)	Vernon Kennedy	15.00	7.50	4.50
(103)	John F. Kerr	15.00	7.50	4.50
(104)	Charles "Chuck" Klein	30.00	15.00	9.00
(105)	Theodore Kleinhans	15.00	7.50	4.50
(106)	Bill Klem (umpire)	30.00	15.00	9.00
(107)	Robert G. Kline	15.00	7.50	4.50
(108)	William Knickerbocker	15.00	7.50	4.50
(109)	Jack H. Knott	15.00	7.50	4.50
(110)	Mark Koenig	15.00	7.50	4.50
(111)	William Lawrence	15.00	7.50	4.50
(112)	Thornton S. Lee	15.00	7.50	4.50
(113)	Wm. C. "Bill" Lee	15.00	7.50	4.50
(114)	Emil Leonard	15.00	7.50	4.50
(115)	Ernest Lombardi	30.00	15.00	9.00
(116)	Alfonso Lopez	30.00	15.00	9.00
(117)	Red Lucas	15.00	7.50	4.50
(118)	Ted Lyons	30.00	15.00	9.00
(119)	Daniel MacFayden	17.50	8.75	5.25
(120)	Ed. Majeski	15.00	7.50	4.50
(121)	Leroy Mahaffey	15.00	7.50	4.50
(122)	Pat Malone	15.00	7.50	4.50
(123)	Leo Mangum	15.00	7.50	4.50
(124)	Rabbit Maranville	30.00	15.00	9.00
(125)	Charles K. Marrow	15.00	7.50	4.50
(126)	William McKechnie	30.00	15.00	9.00
(127)	Justin McLaughlin	15.00	7.50	4.50
(128)	Marty McManus	15.00	7.50	4.50
(129)	Eric McNair	15.00	7.50	4.50
(130)	Joe Medwick	30.00	15.00	9.00
(131)	Jim Mooney	15.00	7.50	4.50
(132)	Joe Moore	15.00	7.50	4.50
(133)	John Moore	15.00	7.50	4.50
(134)	Randy Moore	15.00	7.50	4.50
(135)	Joe Morrissey	15.00	7.50	4.50
(136)	Joseph Mowrey	15.00	7.50	4.50
(137)	Fred W. Muller	15.00	7.50	4.50
(138)	Van Mungo	17.50	8.75	5.25
(139)	Glenn Myatt	15.00	7.50	4.50
(140)	Lynn Nelson	15.00	7.50	4.50
(141)	Henry Oana	15.00	7.50	4.50
(142)	Lefty O'Doul	20.00	10.00	6.00
(143)	Robert O'Farrell	15.00	7.50	4.50
(144)	Ernest Orsatti	15.00	7.50	4.50
(145)	Fritz R. Ostermueller	15.00	7.50	4.50
(146)	Melvin Ott	35.00	17.50	10.50
(147)	Roy Parmelee	15.00	7.50	4.50
(148)	Ralph Perkins	15.00	7.50	4.50
(149)	Frank Pytlak	15.00	7.50	4.50
(150)	Ernest C. Quigley (umpire)	17.50	8.75	5.25
(151)	George Rensa	15.00	7.50	4.50
(152)	Harry Rice	15.00	7.50	4.50
(153)	Walter Roettger	15.00	7.50	4.50
(154)	William G. Rogell	15.00	7.50	4.50
(155)	Edwin A. Rommel	15.00	7.50	4.50
(156)	Charlie Root	15.00	7.50	4.50
(157)	John Rothrock	15.00	7.50	4.50
(158)	Jack Russell	15.00	7.50	4.50
(159)	Blondy Ryan	15.00	7.50	4.50
(160)	Alexander (Al) Schacht	20.00	10.00	6.00
(161)	Wesley Schultmerick	15.00	7.50	4.50
(162)	Truett B. Sewell	15.00	7.50	4.50
(163)	Gordon Slade	15.00	7.50	4.50
(164)	Bob Smith	15.00	7.50	4.50
(165)	Julius J. Solters	15.00	7.50	4.50
(166)	Glenn Spencer	15.00	7.50	4.50
(167)	Al Spohrer	15.00	7.50	4.50
(168)	George Stainback	15.00	7.50	4.50
(169)	Albert "Dolly" Stark (umpire)	20.00	10.00	6.00
(170)	Casey Stengel	35.00	17.50	10.50
(171)	Riggs Stephenson	17.50	8.75	5.25
(172)	Walter C. Stewart	15.00	7.50	4.50
(173)	Lin Storti	15.00	7.50	4.50
(174)	Allyn (Fish Hook) Stout	15.00	7.50	4.50
(175)	Joe Stripp	15.00	7.50	4.50
(176)	Gus Suhr	15.00	7.50	4.50
(177)	Billy Sullivan, Jr.	15.00	7.50	4.50
(178)	Benny Tate	15.00	7.50	4.50
(179)	Danny Taylor	15.00	7.50	4.50
(180)	Tommy Thevenow	15.00	7.50	4.50
(181)	Bud Tinning	15.00	7.50	4.50
(182)	Cecil Travis	15.00	7.50	4.50
(183)	Forest F. Twogood	15.00	7.50	4.50
(184)	Bill Urbanski	15.00	7.50	4.50
(185)	Dazzy Vance	30.00	15.00	9.00
(186)	Arthur Veltman	15.00	7.50	4.50
(187)	John L. Vergez	15.00	7.50	4.50
(188)	Gerald (Jerry) Walker	15.00	7.50	4.50
(189)	William H. Walker	15.00	7.50	4.50
(190)	Lloyd Waner	30.00	15.00	9.00
(191)	Paul Waner	30.00	15.00	9.00
(192)	Lon Warnecke	15.00	7.50	4.50
(193)	Harold B. Warstler	15.00	7.50	4.50
(194)	Bill Werber	15.00	7.50	4.50
(195)	Joyner White	15.00	7.50	4.50
(196)	Arthur Whitney	15.00	7.50	4.50
(197)	James Wilson	15.00	7.50	4.50
(198)	Lewis (Hack) Wilson	35.00	17.50	10.50
(199)	Ralph L. Winegarner	15.00	7.50	4.50
(200)	Thomas Zachary	15.00	7.50	4.50

1935 Diamond Matchbooks - black border

Only 24 players were issued in the 1935 Diamond Matchbook baseball series. Similar in design to the 1934 issue, these 1-1/2" x 4-1/8" matchbooks have sepia player portrait photos on front, framed in either red, green or blue. The overall borders of the cover are black. Backs of the 1935 issue feature a career summary overprinted on a silhouetted batting figure. The "saddle" has the player name and team superimposed on a baseball. These matchbooks are commonly collected with the matches removed and the striker at back-bottom intact. Pieces without the striker are valued at 50% of these listed prices. Complete covers with matches bring a premium of 50-100%. The players are listed here alphabetically.

		NM	EX	VG
Complete Set (24):		650.00	325.00	195.00
Common Player:		25.00	12.50	7.50
(1)	Ethan Allen (red)	25.00	12.50	7.50
(2)	Walter Berger (red)	25.00	12.50	7.50
(3)	Tommy Carey (blue)	25.00	12.50	7.50
(4)	Louis Chiozza (blue)	30.00	15.00	9.00
(5)	Jerome (Dizzy) Dean (green)	65.00	32.00	19.50
(6)	Frankie Frisch (red)	50.00	25.00	15.00
(7)	Charles Grimm (blue)	25.00	12.50	7.50
(8)	Charles Hafey (red)	40.00	20.00	12.00
(9)	J. Francis Hogan (red)	25.00	12.50	7.50
(10)	Carl Hubbell (green)	50.00	25.00	15.00
(11)	Charles Klein (green)	40.00	20.00	12.00
(12)	Ernest Lombardi (blue)	40.00	20.00	12.00
(13)	Alfonso Lopez (blue)	40.00	20.00	12.00
(14)	Rabbit Maranville (green)	40.00	20.00	12.00
(15)	Joe Moore (red)	25.00	12.50	7.50
(16)	Van Mungo (green)	25.00	12.50	7.50
(17)	Melvin (Mel) Ott (blue)	50.00	25.00	15.00
(18)	Gordon Slade (green)	25.00	12.50	7.50
(19)	Casey Stengel (green)	50.00	25.00	15.00
(20)	Tommy Thevenow (red)	25.00	12.50	7.50
(21)	Lloyd Waner (red)	40.00	20.00	12.00
(22)	Paul Waner (green)	50.00	25.00	15.00
(23)	Lon Warnecke (blue)	25.00	12.50	7.50
(24)	James Wilson (blue)	25.00	12.50	7.50

1935-36 Diamond Matchbooks

By the career summaries on back of these covers it is evident this series was issued over a two-year period. Measuring about 1-1/2" x 4-1/8", the fronts have posed player photos printed in sepia. Borders can be found in red, green or blue and it is believed that most, if not all, players, can be found in those three color varieties. Matchbooks in this series do not have the team name on back beneath the player name, as is the case on later series. Collectors generally prefer matchbooks to be complete with striker surface on bottom-back, though with matches removed. Values shown should be halved for covers without strikers. Complete with matches, covers will sell for a 50-100% premium over the values shown.

		NM	EX	VG
Complete Set (156):		1800.	900.00	550.00
Common Player:		12.50	6.25	3.75
(1)	Ethan Allen	12.50	6.25	3.75
(2)	Melo Almada	17.50	8.75	5.25
(3)	Eldon Auker	12.50	6.25	3.75
(4)	Dick Bartell	12.50	6.25	3.75
(5)	Aloysius Bejma	12.50	6.25	3.75
(6)	Ollie Bejma	12.50	6.25	3.75
(7)	Roy Chester Bell	12.50	6.25	3.75
(8)	Louis Berger	12.50	6.25	3.75
(9)	Walter Berger	12.50	6.25	3.75
(10)	Ralph Birkofer	12.50	6.25	3.75
(11)	Max Bishop	12.50	6.25	3.75
(12)	George Blaeholder	12.50	6.25	3.75
(13)	Henry (Zeke) Bonura	12.50	6.25	3.75
(14)	Jim Bottomley	20.00	10.00	6.00
(15)	Ed Brandt	12.50	6.25	3.75
(16)	Don Brennan	12.50	6.25	3.75
(17)	Lloyd Brown	12.50	6.25	3.75
(18)	Walter G. Brown	12.50	6.25	3.75
(19)	Claiborne Bryant	12.50	6.25	3.75
(20)	Jim Bucher	12.50	6.25	3.75
(21)	John Burnett	12.50	6.25	3.75
(22)	Irving Burns	12.50	6.25	3.75
(23)	Merritt Cain	12.50	6.25	3.75
(24)	Ben Cantwell	12.50	6.25	3.75
(25)	Tommy Carey	12.50	6.25	3.75
(26)	Tex Carleton	12.50	6.25	3.75
(27)	Joseph Cascarella	12.50	6.25	3.75
(28)	Thomas H. Casey	15.00	7.50	4.50
(29)	George Caster	12.50	6.25	3.75
(30)	Phil Cavarretta	15.00	7.50	4.50
(31)	Louis Chiozza	15.00	7.50	4.50
(32)	Edward Cihocki	12.50	6.25	3.75
(33)	Herman E. Clifton	12.50	6.25	3.75
(34)	Richard Coffman	12.50	6.25	3.75
(35)	Edward P. Coleman	12.50	6.25	3.75
(36)	James A. Collins	12.50	6.25	3.75
(37)	John Conlan	20.00	10.00	6.00
(38)	Roger Cramer	15.00	7.50	4.50
(39)	Hugh M. Critz	12.50	6.25	3.75
(40)	Alvin Crowder	12.50	6.25	3.75
(41)	Tony Cuccinello	12.50	6.25	3.75
(42)	Hazen "Kiki" Cuyler	20.00	10.00	6.00
(43)	Virgil Davis	12.50	6.25	3.75
(44)	Jerome "Dizzy" Dean	35.00	17.50	10.50
(45)	Paul Derringer	12.50	6.25	3.75
(46)	James DeShong	12.50	6.25	3.75
(47)	William Dietrich	12.50	6.25	3.75
(48)	Leo Durocher	20.00	10.00	6.00
(49)	George Earnshaw	12.50	6.25	3.75
(50)	Elwood English	12.50	6.25	3.75
(51)	Louis Finney	12.50	6.25	3.75
(52)	Charles Fischer	12.50	6.25	3.75
(53)	Freddy Fitzsimmons	12.50	6.25	3.75
(54)	Benny Frey	12.50	6.25	3.75
(55)	Linus B. Frey	12.50	6.25	3.75
(56)	Frankie Frisch	25.00	12.50	7.50
(57)	August Galan	12.50	6.25	3.75
(58)	Milton Galatzer	12.50	6.25	3.75
(59)	Dennis Galehouse	12.50	6.25	3.75
(60)	Debs Garms	12.50	6.25	3.75
(61)	Angelo J. Giuliani	12.50	6.25	3.75
(62)	Earl Grace	12.50	6.25	3.75
(63)	Charles Grimm	12.50	6.25	3.75
(64)	Frank Grube	12.50	6.25	3.75
(65)	Stanley Hack	15.00	7.50	4.50
(66)	Irving "Bump" Hadley	12.50	6.25	3.75
(67)	Odell Hale	12.50	6.25	3.75
(68)	Bill Hallahan	12.50	6.25	3.75
(69)	Roy Hansen	12.50	6.25	3.75
(70)	Melvin Harder	15.00	7.50	4.50
(71)	Charles Hartnett	20.00	10.00	6.00
(72)	"Gabby" Hartnett	20.00	10.00	6.00
(73)	Clyde Hatter	12.50	6.25	3.75
(74)	Raymond Hayworth	12.50	6.25	3.75
(75)	Raymond Hayworth (w/chest protector)	12.50	6.25	3.75
(76)	William Herman	20.00	10.00	6.00
(77)	Gordon Hinkle	12.50	6.25	3.75
(78)	George Hockette	12.50	6.25	3.75
(79)	James Holbrook	12.50	6.25	3.75
(80)	Alex Hooks	12.50	6.25	3.75
(81)	Waite Hoyt	20.00	10.00	6.00
(82)	Carl Hubbell	25.00	12.50	7.50
(83)	Roy M. Joiner	12.50	6.25	3.75
(84)	Sam Jones	12.50	6.25	3.75
(85)	Baxter Jordan	12.50	6.25	3.75
(86)	Arndt Jorgens	12.50	6.25	3.75
(87)	William F. Jurges	12.50	6.25	3.75
(88)	William Kamm	12.50	6.25	3.75
(89)	Vernon Kennedy	12.50	6.25	3.75
(90)	John Kerr	12.50	6.25	3.75
(91)	Charles Klein	25.00	12.50	7.50
(92)	Ted Kleinhans	12.50	6.25	3.75
(93)	Wm. Knickerbocker (thighs-up)	12.50	6.25	3.75
(94)	Wm. Knickerbocker (waist-up)	12.50	6.25	3.75
(95)	Jack Knott	12.50	6.25	3.75
(96)	Mark Koenig	12.50	6.25	3.75
(97)	Fabian L. Kowalik	12.50	6.25	3.75
(98)	Ralph Kress	12.50	6.25	3.75
(99)	Wm. C. "Bill" Lee	12.50	6.25	3.75
(100)	Louis Legett	12.50	6.25	3.75
(101)	Emil "Dutch" Leonard	12.50	6.25	3.75
(102)	Fred Lindstrom	20.00	10.00	6.00
(103)	Edward Linke (pole in background)	12.50	6.25	3.75
(104)	Edward Linke (no pole)	12.50	6.25	3.75
(105)	Ernest Lombardi	20.00	10.00	6.00
(106)	Al Lopez	20.00	10.00	6.00
(107)	John Marcum	12.50	6.25	3.75
(108)	William McKechnie	20.00	10.00	6.00
(109)	Eric McNair	12.50	6.25	3.75
(110)	Joe Medwick	20.00	10.00	6.00
(111)	Oscar Melillo	12.50	6.25	3.75
(112)	John Michaels	12.50	6.25	3.75
(113)	Joe Moore	12.50	6.25	3.75
(114)	John Moore	12.50	6.25	3.75
(115)	Wallace Moses	12.50	6.25	3.75
(116)	Joseph Milligan	12.50	6.25	3.75
(117)	Van Mungo	15.00	7.50	4.50
(118)	Glenn Myatt	12.50	6.25	3.75
(119)	James O'Dea	12.50	6.25	3.75
(120)	Ernest Orsatti	12.50	6.25	3.75
(121)	Fred Ostermueller	12.50	6.25	3.75
(122)	Melvin "Mel" Ott	25.00	12.50	7.50
(123)	LeRoy Parmelee	12.50	6.25	3.75
(124)	Monte Pearson	12.50	6.25	3.75
(125)	Raymond Pepper	12.50	6.25	3.75
(126)	Raymond Phelps	12.50	6.25	3.75
(127)	George Pipgras	12.50	6.25	3.75
(128)	Frank Pytlak	12.50	6.25	3.75
(129)	Gordon Rhodes	12.50	6.25	3.75
(130)	Charlie Root	12.50	6.25	3.75
(131)	John Rothrock	12.50	6.25	3.75
(132)	Herold "Muddy" Ruel	12.50	6.25	3.75
(133)	Jack Saltzgaver	12.50	6.25	3.75
(134)	Fred Schulte	12.50	6.25	3.75
(135)	George Selkirk	12.50	6.25	3.75
(136)	Mervyn Shea	12.50	6.25	3.75
(137)	Al Spohrer	12.50	6.25	3.75
(138)	George Stainback	12.50	6.25	3.75
(139)	Casey Stengel	25.00	12.50	7.50
(140)	Walter Stephenson	12.50	6.25	3.75
(141)	Lee Stine	12.50	6.25	3.75
(142)	John Stone	12.50	6.25	3.75
(143)	Gus Suhr	12.50	6.25	3.75
(144)	Tommy Thevenow	12.50	6.25	3.75
(145)	Fay Thomas	12.50	6.25	3.75
(146)	Leslie Tietje	12.50	6.25	3.75
(147)	Bill Urbanski	12.50	6.25	3.75
(148)	William H. Walker	12.50	6.25	3.75
(149)	Lloyd Waner	25.00	12.50	7.50
(150)	Paul Waner	25.00	12.50	7.50
(151)	Lon Warnecke	12.50	6.25	3.75
(152)	Harold Warstler	12.50	6.25	3.75
(153)	Bill Werber	12.50	6.25	3.75
(154)	Vernon Wiltshere	12.50	6.25	3.75
(155)	James Wilson	12.50	6.25	3.75
(156)	Ralph Winegarner	12.50	6.25	3.75

1936 Diamond Matchbooks - Chicago Cubs

This short series of baseball player matchbooks can each be found with borders of either red, green or blue. Except for Dean, all photos are portraits, printed in sepia or black-and-white. Dean and Paul Waner are the only subjects in the set who were not members of the Chicago Cubs. This series can be differentiated from Type 1 of Series 3 only by studying the career summary and stats on back. About 1-1/2" x 4-1/8", these matchbooks are commonly collected with the matches removed and the striker at back-bottom intact. Pieces without the striker are valued at 50% of these listed prices. Complete covers with matches bring a premium of 50-100%. The players are listed here alphabetically.

		NM	EX	VG
Complete Set (23):		300.00	150.00	90.00
Common Player:		10.00	5.00	3.00
10.00 5.00 3.00				
(1)	Claiborne Bryant			
(2)	Tex Carleton	10.00	5.00	3.00
(3)	Phil Cavarretta	12.00	6.00	3.50
(4)	James A. Collins	10.00	5.00	3.00
(5)	Curt Davis	10.00	5.00	3.00
(6)	Jerome "Dizzy" Dean	48.00	24.00	14.50
(7)	Frank Demaree	10.00	5.00	3.00
(8)	Larry French	10.00	5.00	3.00
(9)	Linus R. Frey	10.00	5.00	3.00
(10)	August Galan	10.00	5.00	3.00
(11)	Bob Garbark	10.00	5.00	3.00
(12)	Stanley Hack	15.00	7.50	4.50
(13)	Charles Hartnett	30.00	15.00	9.00
(14)	William Herman	30.00	15.00	9.00
(15)	William F. Jurges	10.00	5.00	3.00
(16)	William C. "Bill" Lee	10.00	5.00	3.00
(17)	Joe Marty	10.00	5.00	3.00
(18)	James K. O'Dea	10.00	5.00	3.00
(19)	LeRoy Parmelee	10.00	5.00	3.00
(20)	Charlie Root	12.00	6.00	3.50
(21)	Clyde Shoun	10.00	5.00	3.00
(22)	George Stainback	10.00	5.00	3.00
(23)	Paul Waner	40.00	20.00	12.00

1936 Diamond Matchbooks - team on back

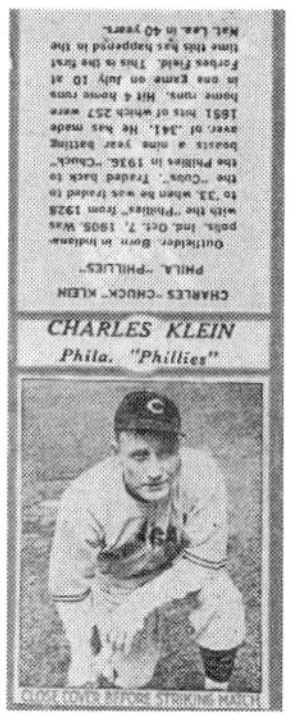

This is the smallest series of baseball player matchbooks, with only 12 subjects, each found with borders of red, green or blue. Player poses on front are printed in sepia or black-and-white. This series can be differentiated differentiated from contemporary series by the appearance of the player's team name on back, beneath his name. Backs have a career summary. About 1-1/2" x 4-1/8", these matchbooks are commonly collected with the matches removed and the striker at back bottom intact. Pieces without the striker are valued at 50% of these listed prices. Complete covers with matches bring a premium of 50-100%. The players are listed here alphabetically.

		NM	EX	VG
Complete Set (12):		350.00	175.00	100.00
Common Player:		20.00	10.00	6.00
(1)	Tommy Carey	20.00	10.00	6.00
(2)	Tony Cuccinello	20.00	10.00	6.00
(3)	Freddy Fitzsimmons	20.00	10.00	6.00
(4)	Frank Frisch	45.00	22.00	13.50
(5)	Charles Grimm	20.00	10.00	6.00
(6)	Carl Hubbell	45.00	22.00	13.50
(7)	Baxter Jordan	20.00	10.00	6.00
(8)	Chuck Klein	45.00	22.00	13.50
(9)	Al Lopez	35.00	17.50	10.50
(10)	Joe Medwick	35.00	17.50	10.50
(11)	Van Lingle Mungo	25.00	12.50	7.50
(12)	Mel Ott	45.00	22.00	13.50

1889 Diamond S Cigars Boston N.L.

(See 1889 Number 7 Cigars for checklist and value information.)

1934-36 Diamond Stars

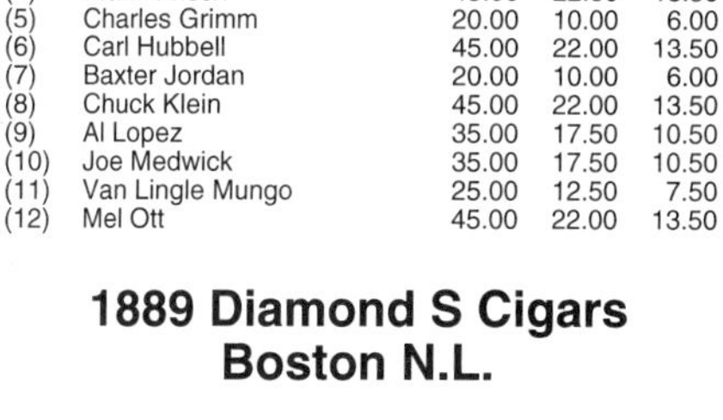

Issued from 1934-36, the Diamond Stars set (ACC designation R327) consists of 108 cards. Produced by National Chicle, the cards measure 2-3/8" x 2-7/8" and are color art reproductions of actual photographs. The year of issue can be determined by the player's statistics found on the reverse of the card. Backs also feature either a player biography or a playing tip. Some cards can be found with either green or blue printing on the backs. The complete set price does not include the higher priced variations.

		NM	EX	VG
Complete Set (108):		15000.	6000.	3500.
Common Player (1-31):		80.00	45.00	25.00
Common Player (32-72):		60.00	30.00	18.00
Common Player (73-84):		70.00	35.00	18.00
Common Player (85-96):		110.00	55.00	30.00
Common Player (97-108):		225.00	112.00	67.00
1a	"Lefty" Grove (1934 green back)	1250.	625.00	375.00
1b	"Lefty" Grove (1935 green back)	1150.	575.00	345.00
2a	Al Simmons (1934 green back)	180.00	90.00	55.00
2b	Al Simmons (1935 green back)	180.00	90.00	54.00
2c	Al Simmons (1936 blue back)	200.00	100.00	60.00
3a	"Rabbit" Maranville (1934 green back)	200.00	100.00	60.00
3b	"Rabbit" Maranville (1935 green back)	200.00	100.00	60.00
4a	"Buddy" Myer (1934 green back)	80.00	45.00	25.00
4b	"Buddy" Myer (1935 green back)	80.00	45.00	25.00
4c	"Buddy" Myer (1936 blue back)	80.00	45.00	25.00
5a	Tom Bridges (1934 green back)	80.00	45.00	25.00
5b	Tom Bridges (1935 green back)	80.00	45.00	25.00
5c	Tom Bridges (1936 blue back)	80.00	45.00	25.00
6a	Max Bishop (1934 green back)	80.00	45.00	25.00
6b	Max Bishop (1935 green back)	80.00	45.00	25.00
7a	Lew Fonseca (1934 green back)	80.00	45.00	25.00
7b	Lew Fonseca (1935 green back)	80.00	45.00	25.00
8a	Joe Vosmik (1934 green back)	80.00	45.00	25.00
8b	Joe Vosmik (1935 green back)	80.00	45.00	25.00
8c	Joe Vosmik (1936 blue back)	80.00	45.00	25.00
9a	"Mickey" Cochrane (1934 green back)	200.00	100.00	60.00
9b	"Mickey" Cochrane (1935 green back)	200.00	100.00	60.00
9c	"Mickey" Cochrane (1936 blue back)	200.00	100.00	60.00
10a	Roy Mahaffey (1934 green back)	80.00	45.00	25.00
10b	Roy Mahaffey (1935 green back)	80.00	45.00	25.00
10c	Roy Mahaffey (1936 blue back)	80.00	45.00	25.00
11a	Bill Dickey (1934 green back)	275.00	135.00	85.00
11b	Bill Dickey (1935 green back)	275.00	135.00	82.00
12a	"Dixie" Walker (1934 green back)	80.00	45.00	25.00
12b	"Dixie" Walker (1935 green back)	80.00	45.00	25.00
12c	"Dixie" Walker (1936 blue back)	80.00	45.00	25.00
13a	George Blaeholder (1934 green back)	80.00	45.00	25.00
13b	George Blaeholder (1935 green back)	80.00	45.00	25.00
14a	Bill Terry (1934 green back)	200.00	100.00	60.00
14b	Bill Terry (1935 green back)	200.00	100.00	60.00
15a	Dick Bartell (1934 green back)	80.00	45.00	25.00
15b	Dick Bartell (1935 green back)	80.00	45.00	25.00
16a	Lloyd Waner (1934 green back)	160.00	80.00	48.00
16b	Lloyd Waner (1935 green back)	160.00	80.00	48.00
16c	Lloyd Waner (1936 blue back)	180.00	90.00	54.00
17a	Frankie Frisch (1934 green back)	180.00	90.00	54.00
17b	Frankie Frisch (1935 green back)	180.00	90.00	54.00
18a	"Chick" Hafey (1934 green back)	200.00	100.00	60.00
18b	"Chick" Hafey (1935 green back)	200.00	100.00	60.00
19a	Van Mungo (1934 green back)	80.00	45.00	25.00
19b	Van Mungo (1935 green back)	80.00	45.00	25.00
20a	"Shanty" Hogan (1934 green back)	80.00	45.00	25.00
20b	"Shanty" Hogan (1935 green back)	80.00	45.00	25.00
21a	Johnny Vergez (1934 green back)	80.00	45.00	25.00
21b	Johnny Vergez (1935 green back)	80.00	45.00	25.00
22a	Jimmy Wilson (1934 green back)	80.00	45.00	25.00
22b	Jimmy Wilson (1935 green back)	80.00	45.00	25.00
22c	Jimmy Wilson (1936 blue back)	80.00	45.00	25.00
23a	Bill Hallahan (1934 green back)	80.00	45.00	25.00
23b	Bill Hallahan (1935 green back)	80.00	45.00	25.00
24a	"Sparky" Adams (1934 green back)	80.00	45.00	25.00
24b	"Sparky" Adams (1935 green back)	80.00	45.00	25.00
25	Walter Berger	80.00	45.00	25.00
26a	"Pepper" Martin (1935 green back)	110.00	55.00	30.00
26b	"Pepper" Martin (1936 blue back)	110.00	55.00	30.00
27	"Pie" Traynor	200.00	100.00	60.00
28	"Al" Lopez	200.00	100.00	60.00
29	Robert Rolfe	80.00	45.00	25.00
30a	"Heinie" Manush (1935 green back)	160.00	80.00	45.00
30b	"Heinie" Manush (1936 blue back)	160.00	80.00	45.00
31a	"Kiki" Cuyler (1935 green back)	160.00	80.00	45.00
31b	"Kiki" Cuyler (1936 blue back)	160.00	80.00	45.00
32	Sam Rice	160.00	80.00	45.00
33	"Schoolboy" Rowe	75.00	37.00	22.00
34	Stanley Hack	75.00	37.00	22.00
35	Earle Averill	165.00	82.00	49.00
36a	Earnie Lombardi	165.00	82.00	49.00
36b	Ernie Lombardi	160.00	80.00	48.00
37	"Billie" Urbanski	60.00	30.00	18.00
38	Ben Chapman	80.00	45.00	25.00
39	Carl Hubbell	220.00	110.00	66.00
40	"Blondy" Ryan	60.00	30.00	18.00
41	Harvey Hendrick	60.00	30.00	18.00
42	Jimmy Dykes	60.00	30.00	18.00
43	Ted Lyons	160.00	80.00	48.00
44	Rogers Hornsby	450.00	225.00	135.00
45	"Jo Jo" White	60.00	30.00	18.00
46	"Red" Lucas	60.00	30.00	18.00
47	Cliff Bolton	60.00	30.00	19.50
48	"Rick" Ferrell	160.00	80.00	48.00
49	"Buck" Jordan	60.00	30.00	18.00
50	"Mel" Ott	300.00	150.00	95.00
51	John Whitehead	60.00	30.00	18.00
52	George Stainback	60.00	30.00	18.00
53	Oscar Melillo	60.00	30.00	19.50
54a	"Hank" Greenburg (Greenberg)	350.00	175.00	105.00
54b	"Hank" Greenberg	250.00	125.00	75.00
55	Tony Cuccinello	60.00	30.00	18.00
56	"Gus" Suhr	60.00	30.00	18.00
57	Cy Blanton	60.00	30.00	18.00
58	Glenn Myatt	60.00	30.00	18.00
59	Jim Bottomley	160.00	80.00	48.00
60	Charley "Red" Ruffing	175.00	87.00	52.00
61	"Billie" Werber	60.00	30.00	18.00
62	Fred M. Frankhouse	60.00	30.00	18.00
63	"Stonewall" Jackson	175.00	87.00	52.00
64	Jimmie Foxx	400.00	200.00	120.00
65	"Zeke" Bonura	60.00	30.00	18.00
66	"Ducky" Medwick	175.00	87.00	52.00
67	Marvin Owen	60.00	30.00	18.00
68	"Sam" Leslie	60.00	30.00	18.00
69	Earl Grace	60.00	30.00	18.00
70	"Hal" Trosky	60.00	30.00	18.00
71	"Ossie" Bluege	60.00	30.00	18.00
72	"Tony" Piet	60.00	30.00	18.00
73a	"Fritz" Ostermueller (1935 green back)	70.00	35.00	18.00
73b	"Fritz" Ostermueller (1935 blue back)	70.00	35.00	18.00
73c	"Fritz" Ostermueller (1936 blue back)	70.00	35.00	18.00
74a	Tony Lazzeri (1935 green back)	200.00	100.00	60.00
74b	Tony Lazzeri (1935 blue back)	200.00	100.00	60.00
74c	Tony Lazzeri (1936 blue back)	200.00	100.00	60.00
75a	Irving Burns (1935 green back)	70.00	35.00	18.00
75b	Irving Burns (1935 blue back)	70.00	35.00	18.00
75c	Irving Burns (1936 blue back)	70.00	35.00	18.00
76a	Bill Rogell (1935 green back)	70.00	35.00	18.00
76b	Bill Rogell (1935 blue back)	70.00	35.00	18.00
76c	Bill Rogell (1936 blue back)	70.00	35.00	18.00
77a	Charlie Gehringer (1935 green back)	250.00	125.00	75.00
77b	Charlie Gehringer (1935 blue back)	250.00	125.00	75.00
77c	Charlie Gehringer (1936 blue back)	250.00	125.00	75.00
78a	Joe Kuhel (1935 green back)	70.00	35.00	18.00
78b	Joe Kuhel (1935 blue back)	70.00	35.00	18.00
78c	Joe Kuhel (1936 blue back)	70.00	35.00	18.00
79a	Willis Hudlin (1935 green back)	70.00	35.00	18.00
79b	Willis Hudlin (1935 blue back)	70.00	35.00	18.00
79c	Willis Hudlin (1936 blue back)	70.00	35.00	18.00
80a	Louis Chiozza (1935 green back)	70.00	35.00	18.00
80b	Louis Chiozza (1935 blue back)	70.00	35.00	18.00
80c	Louis Chiozza (1936 blue back)	70.00	35.00	18.00
81a	Bill DeLancey (1935 green back)	70.00	35.00	18.00
81b	Bill DeLancey (1935 blue back)	70.00	35.00	18.00
81c	Bill DeLancey (1936 blue back)	70.00	35.00	18.00
82a	John Babich (1935 green back)	70.00	35.00	18.00
82b	John Babich (1935 blue back)	70.00	35.00	18.00
82c	John Babich (1936 blue back)	70.00	35.00	18.00
83a	Paul Waner (1935 green back)	250.00	125.00	75.00
83b	Paul Waner (1935 blue back)	250.00	125.00	75.00
83c	Paul Waner (1936 blue back)	250.00	125.00	75.00
84a	Sam Byrd (1935 green back)	60.00	30.00	18.00
84b	Sam Byrd (1935 blue back)	60.00	30.00	18.00
84c	Sam Byrd (1936 blue back)	60.00	30.00	18.00
85	Julius Solters	110.00	55.00	30.00
86	Frank Crosetti	200.00	100.00	60.00
87	Steve O'Neil (O'Neill)	110.00	55.00	33.00
88	Geo. Selkirk	110.00	55.00	30.00
89	Joe Stripp	110.00	55.00	33.00
90	Ray Hayworth	110.00	55.00	33.00
91	Bucky Harris	175.00	87.00	52.00
92	Ethan Allen	110.00	55.00	33.00
93	Alvin Crowder	110.00	55.00	33.00
94	Wes Ferrell	110.00	55.00	30.00
95	Luke Appling	350.00	175.00	105.00
96	Lew Riggs	110.00	55.00	33.00
97	"Al" Lopez	500.00	250.00	150.00
98	"Schoolboy" Rowe	275.00	135.00	82.00
99	"Pie" Traynor	600.00	300.00	180.00
100	Earle Averill (Earl)	445.00	222.00	133.00
101	Dick Bartell	220.00	110.00	66.00
102	Van Mungo	300.00	150.00	90.00
103	Bill Dickey	850.00	425.00	255.00
104	Robert Rolfe	220.00	110.00	66.00
105	"Ernie" Lombardi	600.00	300.00	180.00
106	"Red" Lucas	225.00	112.00	67.00
107	Stanley Hack	225.00	112.00	67.00
108	Walter Berger	225.00	112.00	67.00

1924 Diaz Cigarettes

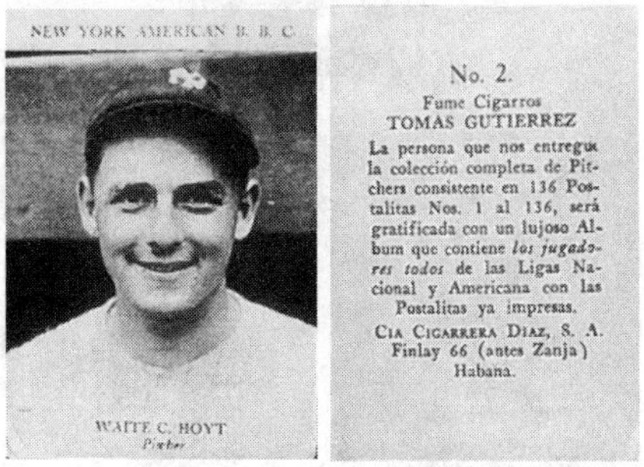

Because they were printed in Cuba and feature only pitchers, the 1924 Diaz Cigarette cards are among the rarest and most intriguing of all tobacco issues. Produced in Havana for the Diaz brand, the black-and-white cards measure 1-3/4" x 2-1/2" and were printed on a glossy-type stock. The player's name and position are listed at the bottom of the card, while his team and league appear at the top. According to the card backs, printed in Spanish, the set consists of 136 cards - all major league pitchers. But to date only the cards checklisted here have been discovered.

		NM	EX	VG
Common Player:		260.00	130.00	80.00
2	Waite C. Hoyt	400.00	200.00	120.00
12	Curtis Fullerton	260.00	130.00	80.00
14	George Walberg	260.00	130.00	80.00
40	A. Wilbur Cooper	260.00	130.00	80.00
51	Roy Meeker	260.00	130.00	80.00
58	Sam Gray	260.00	130.00	80.00
96	Philip B. Weinart	260.00	130.00	80.00
102	Howard	260.00	130.00	80.00
105	Hubert F. Pruett	260.00	130.00	80.00
121	Bert Cole	260.00	130.00	80.00
132	J. Martina	260.00	130.00	80.00
---	Victor Aldridge	260.00	130.00	80.00
---	Harry Baldwin	260.00	130.00	80.00
---	John M. Bentley (middle initial actually "N")	260.00	130.00	80.00
---	John C. Benton	260.00	130.00	80.00
---	Ted Blankenship	260.00	130.00	80.00
---	Dennis Burns	260.00	130.00	80.00
---	Leslie J. Bush (middle initial "A")	260.00	130.00	80.00
---	John W. Cooney	260.00	130.00	80.00
---	Mike Cvengros	260.00	130.00	80.00
---	Frank T. Davis	260.00	130.00	80.00
---	Arthur R. Decatur	260.00	130.00	80.00
---	Nicholas Dumovich	260.00	130.00	80.00
---	Burleigh A. Grimes	400.00	200.00	120.00
---	Jesse J. Haines	400.00	200.00	120.00
---	Earl Hamilton	260.00	130.00	80.00
---	Bryan Harris	260.00	130.00	80.00
---	Fred Heimach	260.00	130.00	80.00
---	Lester C. Howe	260.00	130.00	80.00
---	Walter H. Huntzinger	260.00	130.00	80.00
---	Claude Jonnard	260.00	130.00	80.00
---	Ray C. Kolp	260.00	130.00	80.00
---	Thomas F. Long	260.00	130.00	80.00
---	George K. Murray	260.00	130.00	80.00
---	Roline C. Naylor (Roleine)	260.00	130.00	80.00
---	Joseph Oeschger	260.00	130.00	80.00
---	Warren H. Ogden	260.00	130.00	80.00
---	Ernest P. Osborne (Earnest)	260.00	130.00	80.00
---	Wm. Piercy	260.00	130.00	80.00
---	Edwin A. Rommel	260.00	130.00	80.00
---	Chester Ross	260.00	130.00	80.00
---	Richard Rudolph	260.00	130.00	80.00
---	Walter H. Ruether	260.00	130.00	80.00
---	Charles Ruffing	400.00	200.00	120.00
---	Wilfred D. Ryan	260.00	130.00	80.00
---	Joseph B. Shaute	260.00	130.00	80.00
---	Allan S. Sothoron (Allen)	260.00	130.00	80.00
---	Arnold E. Stone	260.00	130.00	80.00
---	John D. Stuart	260.00	130.00	80.00
---	Hollis Thurston	260.00	130.00	80.00
---	Jesse F. Winters	260.00	130.00	80.00

1962 Dickson Orde & Co.

One of several English tobacco cards to include baseball among a series of world's sports, this card is of marginal interest to U.S. collectors because its color front pictures (from the back) a batter who could be Babe Ruth as part of a baseball scene on the front of the 2-5/8" x 1-3/8" card. The short description of baseball on the card's black-and-white back does mention Ruth. The "Sports of the Countries" series comprises 25 cards.

		NM	EX	VG
11	America (Babe Ruth)	125.00	62.00	37.00

1980 Did You Know . . . ?

This collectors' edition was produced by artist Mel (?) Anderson. The blank-backed 3-1/4" x 6-3/8" cards have black-and-white drawings of ballplayers and a "Did You Know" trivia fact. The unnumbered cards are checklisted here alphabetically.

		NM	EX	VG
Complete Set (30):		24.00	12.00	7.25
Common Player:		1.00	.50	.30
(1)	Richie Ashburn	2.00	1.00	.60
(2)	Hank Bauer	1.25	.60	.40
(3)	Ewell "The Whip" Blackwell	1.25	.60	.40
(4)	Johnny Callison	1.00	.50	.30
(5)	Roger "Doc" Cramer	1.00	.50	.30
(6)	Harry Danning	1.00	.50	.30
(7)	Ferris Fain	1.00	.50	.30
(8)	Ned Garver	1.00	.50	.30
(9)	Harvey Haddix	1.00	.50	.30
(10)	Clint Hartung	1.00	.50	.30
(11)	"Bobo" Holloman	1.00	.50	.30
(12)	Ron Hunt	1.00	.50	.30
(13)	Howard "Spud" Krist	1.00	.50	.30
(14)	Emil "Dutch" Leonard	1.00	.50	.30
(15)	Buddy Lewis	1.00	.50	.30
(16)	Jerry Lynch	1.00	.50	.30
(17)	Roy McMillan	1.00	.50	.30
(18)	Johnny Mize	1.50	.70	.45
(19)	Hugh Mulcahy	1.00	.50	.30
(20)	Hal Newhouser	1.00	.50	.30
(21)	Jim Perry	1.00	.50	.30
(22)	Phil Rizzuto	2.00	1.00	.60
(23)	Bobby Shantz	1.00	.50	.30
(24)	Roy Sievers	1.00	.50	.30
(25)	Nick Testa	1.50	.70	.45
(26)	Cecil Travis	1.00	.50	.30
(27)	Elmer "Valient" Valo	1.00	.50	.30
(28)	Bill Werber	1.00	.50	.30
(29)	Mickey Witek	1.00	.50	.30
(30)	Hal Woodeshick	1.00	.50	.30

1907 Dietsche Chicago Cubs Postcards

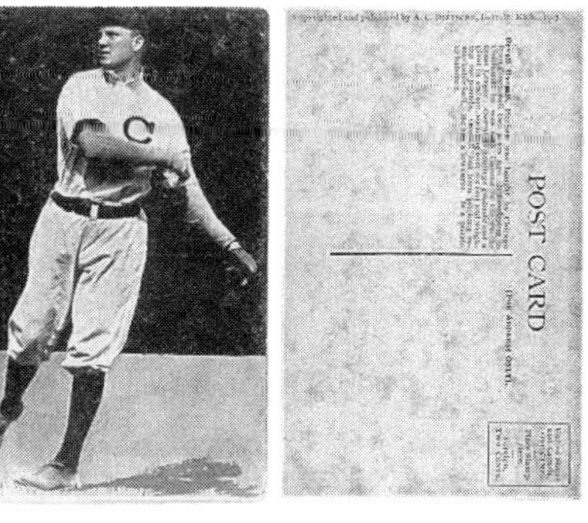

This series of early Cubs postcards was published by the same Detroit printer who issued Tigers postcard series from 1907-09. The Dietsche Cubs postcards are scarcer than the Tigers issues because they were only offered for sale in Detroit in conjunction with the 1907 World Series between the Tigers and Cubs, and few people bought the visiting team's cards. The 3-1/2" x 5-1/2" black-and-white cards have most of the photographic background blacked out on front. The player's last name may or may not appear on the front. Postcard style backs include a short career summary and a dated copyright line.

		NM	EX	VG
Complete Set (15):		2400.	1200.	725.00
Common Player:		165.00	82.00	49.00
(1)	Mordecai Brown	200.00	100.00	60.00
(2)	Frank L. Chance	250.00	125.00	75.00
(3)	John Evers	250.00	125.00	75.00
(4)	Arthur F. Hoffman (Hofman)	165.00	82.00	49.00
(5)	John Kling	165.00	82.00	49.00
(6)	Carl Lundgren	165.00	82.00	49.00
(7)	Patrick J. Moran	165.00	82.00	49.00
(8)	Orval Overall	165.00	82.00	49.00
(9)	John A. Pfeister	165.00	82.00	49.00
(10)	Edw. M. Ruelbach	165.00	82.00	49.00
(11)	Frank M. Schulte	165.00	82.00	49.00
(12)	James T. Sheckard	165.00	82.00	49.00
(13)	James Slagle	165.00	82.00	49.00
(14)	Harry Steinfeldt	165.00	82.00	49.00
(15)	Joseph B. Tinker	250.00	125.00	75.00

1907-09 Dietsche Detroit Tigers Postcards

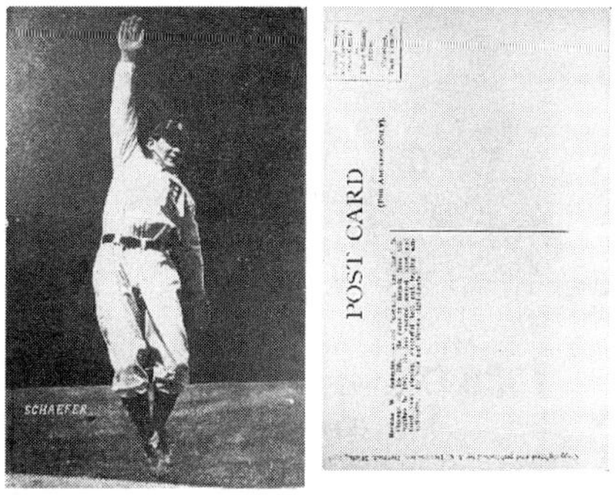

Three apparent annual issues (1907-09) of the home team by Detroit postcard publisher A.C. Dietsche, these 3-1/2" x 5-1/2" black-and-white postcards have most of the photographic background on front blackened out. The player's last name usually appears on the front. On back, along with the postcard legalities are a short player biography and a dated copyright line. The postcards were reportedly sold in sets for $.25.

		NM	EX	VG
Complete Set (35):		5500.	2700.	1650.
Common Player:		75.00	37.00	22.00
Series 1 - 1907				
(1a)	Tyrus R. Cobb (batting)	600.00	300.00	180.00
(1b)	Tyrus R. Cobb (fielding)	1100.	550.00	330.00
(2)	William Coughlin	75.00	37.00	22.00
(3)	Samuel S. Crawford	125.00	62.00	37.00
(4)	William E. Donovan	75.00	37.00	22.00
(5)	Jerome W. Downs	75.00	37.00	22.00
(6)	Hughie A. Jennings	125.00	62.00	37.00
(7)	David Jones	75.00	37.00	22.00
(8)	Edward H. Killian	75.00	37.00	22.00
(9)	George J. Mullin	75.00	37.00	22.00
(10)	Charles O'Leary	75.00	37.00	22.00
(11)	Fred T. Payne	75.00	37.00	22.00
(12)	Claude Rossman	75.00	37.00	22.00
(13)	Herman W. Schaefer	75.00	37.00	22.00
(14)	Schaefer & O'Leary (Germany Schaefer, Charles O'Leary)	90.00	45.00	27.00
(15)	Charles Schmidt	75.00	37.00	22.00
(16)	Edward Siever	75.00	37.00	22.00
Series 2 - 1908-1909				
(1)	Henry Beckendorf	90.00	45.00	27.00
(2)	Owen Bush	90.00	45.00	27.00
(3)	Tyrus R. Cobb	1250.	625.00	375.00
(4)	Sam Crawford	125.00	62.00	37.00
(5)	James Delahanty	90.00	45.00	27.00
(6)	William E. Donovan	90.00	45.00	27.00
(7)	Hughie A. Jennings	125.00	62.00	37.00
(8)	Tom Jones	90.00	45.00	27.00
(9)	Matthew McIntyre	90.00	45.00	27.00
(10)	George J. Moriarty	90.00	45.00	27.00
(11)	Germany Schaefer	90.00	45.00	27.00
(12)	Oscar Stanage	90.00	45.00	27.00
(13)	Oren Edgar Summers	90.00	45.00	27.00
(14)	Ira Thomas	90.00	45.00	27.00
(15)	Edgar Willett	90.00	45.00	27.00
(16)	George Winter	90.00	45.00	27.00
(17)	Ralph Works	90.00	45.00	27.00
(18)	Detroit Tigers Team	100.00	50.00	30.00

1972-83 Dimanche/Derniere Heure Photos

From 1972-74, and 1977-83, the Montreal magazine Dimanche / Derniere Heure (loosely translated, "Sunday / Latest Hour," issued color photos of Expos (and a few other) players. The 8-1/2" x 11" photos are printed on semi-gloss paper stock that is punched for a three-ring binder. Fronts have a large color photo with player data, stats and career highlights printed in black beneath - all in French. At left or top is usually the issue date in which the photo was included in the magazine. Backs are blank.

	NM	EX	VG
Common Player: (Stars are valued up to $50)	5.00	2.50	1.50

1972 Dimanche/Derniere Heure Expos

		NM	EX	VG
Complete Set (37):		155.00	78.00	47.00
Common Player:		5.00	2.50	1.50
(1)	Bill Stoneman (April 9)	5.00	2.50	1.50
(2)	John Boccabella (April 16)	5.00	2.50	1.50
(3)	Gene Mauch (April 23)	5.00	2.50	1.50
(4)	Ron Hunt (April 30)	5.00	2.50	1.50
(5)	Steve Renko (May 7)	5.00	2.50	1.50
(6)	Boots Day (May 14)	5.00	2.50	1.50
(7)	Bob Bailey (May 21)	5.00	2.50	1.50
(8)	Ernie McAnally (May 28)	5.00	2.50	1.50
(9)	Ken Singleton (June 4)	5.00	2.50	1.50
(10)	Ron Fairly (June 11)	5.00	2.50	1.50
(11)	Ron Woods (June 18)	5.00	2.50	1.50
(12)	Mike Jorgensen (June 25)	5.00	2.50	1.50
(13)	Bobby Wine (July 2)	5.00	2.50	1.50
(14)	Mike Torrez (July 9)	5.00	2.50	1.50
(15)	Terry Humphrey (July 16)	5.00	2.50	1.50
(16)	Jim Fairey (July 23)	5.00	2.50	1.50
(17)	Tim Foli (July 30)	5.00	2.50	1.50
(18)	Clyde Mashore (Aug. 6)	5.00	2.50	1.50
(19)	Tim McCarver (Aug. 13)	9.00	4.50	2.75
(20)	Hector Torres (Aug. 20)	5.00	2.50	1.50
(21)	Tom Walker (Aug. 27)	5.00	2.50	1.50
(22)	Cal McLish (Sept. 3)	5.00	2.50	1.50
(23)	Balor Moore (Sept. 10)	5.00	2.50	1.50
(24)	John Strohmayer (Sept. 17)	5.00	2.50	1.50
(25)	Larry Doby (Sept. 24)	12.00	6.00	3.50
(26)	Hal Breeden (Oct. 1)	5.00	2.50	1.50
(27)	Mike Marshall (Oct. 8)	5.00	2.50	1.50

1973 Dimanche/Derniere Heure National Leaguers

		NM	EX	VG
Complete Set (16):		375.00	185.00	110.00
Common Player:		12.00	6.00	3.50
(1)	Roberto Clemente (April 15)	50.00	25.00	15.00
(2)	Coco Laboy (April 22)	12.00	6.00	3.50
(3)	Rusty Staub (April 29)	16.00	8.00	4.75
(4)	Johnny Bench (May 6)	27.00	13.50	8.00
(5)	Ferguson Jenkins (May 13)	18.00	9.00	5.50

(6)	Bob Gibson (May 20)	22.00	11.00	6.50
(7)	Hank Aaron (May 27)	40.00	20.00	12.00
(8)	Willie Montanez (June 3)	12.00	6.00	3.50
(9)	Willie McCovey (June 10)	20.00	10.00	6.00
(10)	Willie Davis (June 17)	12.00	6.00	3.50
(11)	Steve Carlton (June 24)	22.00	11.00	6.50
(12)	Willie Stargell (July 1)	20.00	10.00	6.00
(13)	Dave Bristol (July 8)	12.00	6.00	3.50
(14)	Larry Bowa (July 15)	12.00	6.00	3.50
(15)	Pete Rose (July 22)	40.00	20.00	12.00
(16)	Pepe Frias (July 29)	12.00	6.00	3.50

1974 Dimanche/Derniere Heure Expos

		NM	EX	VG
Complete Set (10):		40.00	20.00	12.00
Common Player:		5.00	2.50	1.50
(1)	Dennis Blair	5.00	2.50	1.50
(2)	Don Carrithers	5.00	2.50	1.50
(3)	Jim Cox	5.00	2.50	1.50
(4)	Willie Davis	5.00	2.50	1.50
(5)	Don Demola	5.00	2.50	1.50
(6)	Barry Foote	5.00	2.50	1.50
(7)	Larry Lintz	5.00	2.50	1.50
(8)	John Montague	5.00	2.50	1.50
(9)	Steve Rogers	5.00	2.50	1.50
(10)	Chuck Taylor	5.00	2.50	1.50

1977 Dimanche/Derniere Heure Expos

		NM	EX	VG
Complete Set (26):		125.00	62.00	37.00
Common Player:		5.00	2.50	1.50
(1)	Steve Rogers (April 24)	5.00	2.50	1.50
(2)	Tim Foli (May 1)	5.00	2.50	1.50
(3)	Dick Williams (May 8)	5.00	2.50	1.50
(4)	Larry Parrish (May 15)	5.00	2.50	1.50
(5)	Jose Morales (May 22)	5.00	2.50	1.50
(6)	Don Stanhouse (May 29)	5.00	2.50	1.50
(7)	Gary Carter (June 5)	10.00	5.00	3.00
(8)	Ellis Valentine (June 12)	5.00	2.50	1.50
(9)	Dave Cash (June 19)	5.00	2.50	1.50
(10)	Jackie Brown (June 26)	5.00	2.50	1.50
(11)	Barry Foote (July 3)	5.00	2.50	1.50
(12)	Dan Warthen (July 10)	5.00	2.50	1.50
(13)	Tony Perez (July 17)	10.00	5.00	3.00
(14)	Wayne Garrett (July 24)	5.00	2.50	1.50
(15)	Bill Atkinson (July 31)	5.00	2.50	1.50
(16)	Joe Kerrigan (Aug. 7)	5.00	2.50	1.50
(17)	Mickey Vernon (Aug. 14)	5.00	2.50	1.50
(18)	Jeff Terpko (Aug. 21)	5.00	2.50	1.50
(19)	Andre Dawson (Aug. 28)	10.00	5.00	3.00
(20)	Del Unser (Sept. 4)	5.00	2.50	1.50
(21)	Stan Bahnsen (Sept. 11)	5.00	2.50	1.50
(22)	Warren Cromartie (Sept. 18)	5.00	2.50	1.50
(23)	Santo Alcala (Sept. 25)	5.00	2.50	1.50
(24)	Wayne Twitchell (Oct. 2)	5.00	2.50	1.50
(25)	Pepe Frias (Oct. 9)	5.00	2.50	1.50
(26)	Sam Mejias (Oct. 16)	5.00	2.50	1.50

1978 Dimanche/Derniere Heure Expos

		NM	EX	VG
Complete Set (13):		62.00	31.00	18.50
Common Player:		5.00	2.50	1.50
(1)	Ross Grimsley (May 7)	5.00	2.50	1.50
(2)	Chris Speier (May 14)	5.00	2.50	1.50
(3)	Norm Sherry (May 21)	5.00	2.50	1.50
(4)	Hal Dues (May 28)	5.00	2.50	1.50
(5)	Rudy May (June 4)	5.00	2.50	1.50
(6)	Stan Papi (June 11)	5.00	2.50	1.50
(7)	Darold Knowles (June 18)	5.00	2.50	1.50
(8)	Bob Reece (June 25)	5.00	2.50	1.50
(9)	Dan Schatzeder (July 2)	5.00	2.50	1.50
(10)	Jim Brewer (July 9)	5.00	2.50	1.50
(11)	Mike Garman (July 16)	5.00	2.50	1.50
(12)	Woodie Fryman (July 23)	5.00	2.50	1.50
(13)	Ed Hermann	5.00	2.50	1.50

1979 Dimanche/Derniere Heure Expos

		NM	EX	VG
Complete Set (8):		35.00	17.50	10.50
Common Player:		5.00	2.50	1.50
(1)	Bill Lee (May 6)	5.00	2.50	1.50
(2)	Elias Sosa (May 13)	5.00	2.50	1.50
(3)	Tommy Hutton (May 20)	5.00	2.50	1.50
(4)	Tony Solaita (May 27)	5.00	2.50	1.50
(5)	Rodney Scott (June 3)	5.00	2.50	1.50
(6)	Duffy Dyer (June 10)	5.00	2.50	1.50
(7)	Jim Mason (June 17)	5.00	2.50	1.50
(8)	Ken Macha (June 24)	5.00	2.50	1.50

1980 Dimanche/Derniere Heure Expos

		NM	EX	VG
Complete Set (23):		125.00	62.00	37.00
Common Player:		5.00	2.50	1.50
(1)	Steve Rogers (April 20)	5.00	2.50	1.50
(2)	Dick Williams (April 27)	5.00	2.50	1.50
(3)	Bill Lee (May 4)	5.00	2.50	1.50
(4)	Jerry White (May 11)	5.00	2.50	1.50
(5)	Scott Sanderson (May 18)	5.00	2.50	1.50
(6)	Ron LeFlore (May 25)	5.00	2.50	1.50
(7)	Elias Sosa (June 1)	5.00	2.50	1.50
(8)	Ellis Valentine (June 8)	5.00	2.50	1.50
(9)	Rodney Scott (June 22)	5.00	2.50	1.50
(10)	Woodie Fryman (June 29)	5.00	2.50	1.50
(11)	Chris Speier (July 6)	5.00	2.50	1.50
(12)	Warren Cromartie (July 13)	5.00	2.50	1.50
(13)	Stan Bahnsen (July 20)	5.00	2.50	1.50
(14)	Tommy Hutton (July 27)	5.00	2.50	1.50
(15)	Bill Almon (Aug. 3)	5.00	2.50	1.50
(16)	Fred Norman (Aug. 10)	5.00	2.50	1.50
(17)	Andre Dawson (Aug. 17)	10.00	5.00	3.00
(18)	John Tamargo (Aug. 24)	5.00	2.50	1.50
(19)	Larry Parrish (Aug. 31)	5.00	2.50	1.50
(20)	David Palmer (Sept. 7)	5.00	2.50	1.50
(21)	Tony Bernazard (Sept. 14)	5.00	2.50	1.50
(22)	Gary Carter (Sept. 21)	10.00	5.00	3.00
(23)	Ken Macha (Sept. 28)	5.00	2.50	1.50

1981 Dimanche/Derniere Heure Expos

		MT	NM	EX
Complete Set (9):		50.00	37.00	20.00
Common Player:		5.00	3.75	2.00
(1)	Tim Raines (May 17)	10.00	7.50	4.00
(2)	Willie Montanez (May 24)	5.00	3.75	2.00
(3)	Bill Gullickson (May 31)	5.00	3.75	2.00
(4)	Tim Wallach (June 7)	6.50	5.00	2.50
(5)	Charlie Lea (June 14)	5.00	3.75	2.00
(6)	Bobby Ramos (June 21)	5.00	3.75	2.00
(7)	Ray Burris (June 28)	5.00	3.75	2.00
(8)	Jerry Manuel (July 5)	5.00	3.75	2.00
(9)	Gary Carter (July 12)	10.00	7.50	4.00

1982 Dimanche/Derniere Heure Expos

		MT	NM	EX
Complete Set (14):		60.00	45.00	24.00
Common Player:		5.00	3.75	2.00
(1)	Jim Fanning (April 18)	5.00	3.75	2.00
(2)	Steve Rogers (April 25)	5.00	3.75	2.00
(3)	Frank Taveras (May 2)	5.00	3.75	2.00
(4)	Tim Blackwell (May 9)	5.00	3.75	2.00
(5)	Wallace Johnson (May 16)	5.00	3.75	2.00
(6)	Terry Francona (May 23)	5.00	3.75	2.00
(7)	Al Oliver (June 6)	7.50	5.75	3.00
(8)	John Milner (June 20)	5.00	3.75	2.00
(9)	Woodie Fryman, Jeff Reardon (June 27)	5.00	3.75	2.00
(10)	Tim Raines, Andre Dawson, Warren Cromartie (July 4)	9.00	6.75	3.50
(11)	Joel Youngblood (Aug. 22)	5.00	3.75	2.00
(12)	Dan Norman (Sept. 5)	5.00	3.75	2.00
(13)	Bryan Little (Sept. 12)	5.00	3.75	2.00
(14)	Doug Flynn (Sept. 26)	5.00	3.75	2.00

1983 Dimanche/Derniere Heure Expos

		MT	NM	EX
Complete Set (19):		100.00	70.00	40.00
Common Player:		5.00	3.75	2.00
(1)	Bill Virdon (June 5)	5.00	3.75	2.00
(2)	Tim Wallach (June 12)	5.00	3.75	2.00
(3)	Dan Schatzeder (June 19)	5.00	3.75	2.00
(4)	Andre Dawson (June 26)	10.00	7.50	4.00
(5)	Al Oliver (July 3)	7.50	5.75	3.00
(6)	Charlie Lea (July 10)	5.00	3.75	2.00
(7)	Tim Raines (July 17)	10.00	7.50	4.00
(8)	Gary Carter (July 24)	10.00	7.50	4.00
(9)	Ray Burris (July 31)	5.00	3.75	2.00
(10)	Steve Rogers (Aug. 7)	5.00	3.75	2.00
(11)	Jim Wohlford (Aug. 14)	5.00	3.75	2.00
(12)	Chris Speier (Aug. 21)	5.00	3.75	2.00
(13)	Bill Gullickson (Aug. 28)	5.00	3.75	2.00
(14)	Angel Salazar (Sept. 4)	5.00	3.75	2.00
(15)	Mike Stenhouse (Sept. 11)	5.00	3.75	2.00
(16)	Greg Bargar (Sept. 18)	5.00	3.75	2.00
(17)	Terry Crowley (Sept. 25)	5.00	3.75	2.00
(18)	Bob James (Oct. 2)	5.00	3.75	2.00
(19)	Gene Mauch (Oct. 9) (w/coaches)	5.00	3.75	2.00

1937 Dixie Lids

This unnumbered set of Dixie cup ice cream lids was issued in 1937 and consists of 24 different lids, although only six picture sports stars - four of whom are baseball stars. The lids are found in two different sizes, either 2-11/16" in diameter or 2-5/16" in diameter. The 1937 Dixie Lids were printed in black or dark red. The lids must have the small tab still intact to command top value.

	NM	EX	VG
Complete Set (4):	375.00	185.00	110.00
Common Player:	95.00	47.00	28.00
(1) Charles Gehringer	95.00	47.00	28.00
(2) Charles ("Gabby") Hartnett	95.00	47.00	28.00
(3) Carl Hubbell (mouth closed)	100.00	50.00	30.00
(4) Joe Medwick	95.00	47.00	28.00

1937 Dixie Lids Premiums

Issued as a premium offer in conjunction with the 1937 Dixie lids, this unnumbered set of color 8" x 10" pictures was printed on heavy paper and features the same subjects as the Dixie Lids set. The 1937 Dixie premiums have a distinctive dark green band along the left margin containing the player's name. The back has smaller photos of the player in action with a large star at the top and a player write-up.

	NM	EX	VG
Complete Set (4):	575.00	285.00	175.00
Common Player:	150.00	75.00	45.00
(1) Charles Gehringer	150.00	75.00	45.00
(2) Charles (Gabby) Hartnett	150.00	75.00	45.00
(3) Carl Hubbell	175.00	87.00	52.00
(4) Joe (Ducky) Medwick	150.00	75.00	45.00

1938 Dixie Lids

Similar to its set of the previous year, the 1938 Dixie Lids set is a 24-subject set that includes six sports stars - four of whom are baseball players. The lids are found in two sizes, either 2 11/16" in diameter or 2-5/16" in diameter. The 1938 Dixie lids are printed in blue ink. Dixie lids must have the small tab still intact to command top value.

	NM	EX	VG
Complete Set (4):	425.00	210.00	125.00
Common Player:	55.00	27.00	16.50
(1) Bob Feller	130.00	65.00	39.00
(2) Jimmie Foxx	130.00	65.00	39.00
(3) Carl Hubbell (mouth open)	130.00	65.00	39.00
(4) Wally Moses	55.00	27.00	16.50

1938 Dixie Lids Premiums

Issued in conjunction with the 1938 Dixie cup lids, this unnumbered set of 8" x 10" pictures contains the same subjects and is printed on surrounding the entire picture with the player's name to the left. The back contains smaller photos of the player in action with his name in script at the top and a short write-up.

	NM	EX	VG
Complete Set (4):	460.00	230.00	138.00
Common Player:	70.00	35.00	21.00
(1) Bob Feller	140.00	70.00	42.00
(2) Jimmy Foxx	140.00	70.00	42.00
(3) Carl Hubbell	140.00	70.00	42.00
(4) Wally Moses	70.00	35.00	21.00

1952 Dixie Lids

After a 14-year break, another Dixie lid set, featuring 24 baseball players, appeared in 1952. The unnumbered lids measure 2-11/16" in diameter and were printed with a blue tint. The Dixie lids of the 1950s can be distinguished from earlier issues because the bottom of the photo is squared off to accomodate the player's name. Dixie lids must contain the small tab to command top value.

	NM	EX	VG
Complete Set (24):	1750.	875.00	525.00
Common Player:	75.00	37.00	22.00
(1) Richie Ashburn	125.00	62.00	37.00
(2) Tommy Byrne	75.00	37.00	22.00
(3) Chico Carrasquel	75.00	37.00	22.00
(4) Pete Castiglione	75.00	37.00	22.00
(5) Walker Cooper	75.00	37.00	22.00
(6) Billy Cox	75.00	37.00	22.00
(7) Ferris Fain	75.00	37.00	22.00
(8) Bobby Feller	125.00	62.00	37.00
(9) Nelson Fox	125.00	62.00	37.00
(10) Monte Irvin	100.00	50.00	30.00
(11) Ralph Kiner	100.00	50.00	30.00
(12) Cass Michaels	75.00	37.00	22.00
(13) Don Mueller	75.00	37.00	22.00
(14) Mel Parnell	75.00	37.00	22.00
(15) Allie Reynolds	85.00	42.00	25.00
(16) Preacher Roe	75.00	37.00	22.00
(17) Connie Ryan	75.00	37.00	22.00
(18) Hank Sauer	75.00	37.00	22.00
(19) Al Schoendienst	100.00	50.00	30.00
(20) Andy Seminick	75.00	37.00	22.00
(21) Bobby Shantz	80.00	40.00	24.00
(22) Enos Slaughter	100.00	50.00	30.00
(23) Virgil Trucks	75.00	37.00	22.00
(24) Gene Woodling	75.00	37.00	22.00

1952 Dixie Lids Premiums

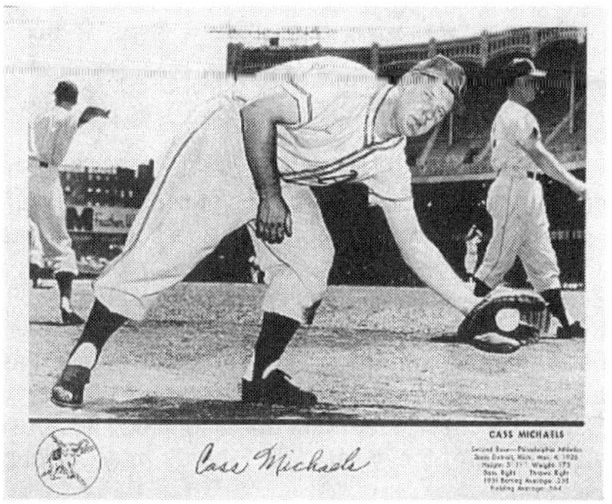

This unnumbered set of 24 player photos was issued as a premium in conjunction with the 1952 Dixie cup lids and features the same subjects. The player's team and facsimile autograph appear along the bottom of the 8" x 10" blank-backed photo, which was printed on heavy paper. The 1952 Dixie premiums show the player's 1951 season statistics in the lower right corner.

	NM	EX	VG
Complete Set (24):	800.00	400.00	240.00
Common Player:	40.00	20.00	12.00
(1) Richie Ashburn	100.00	50.00	30.00
(2) Tommy Byrne	40.00	20.00	12.00
(3) Chico Carrasquel	40.00	20.00	12.00
(4) Pete Castiglione	40.00	20.00	12.00
(5) Walker Cooper	40.00	20.00	12.00
(6) Billy Cox	40.00	20.00	12.00
(7) Ferris Fain	40.00	20.00	12.00
(8) Bob Feller	100.00	50.00	30.00
(9) Nelson Fox	90.00	45.00	27.00
(10) Monte Irvin	60.00	30.00	18.00
(11) Ralph Kiner	60.00	30.00	18.00
(12) Cass Michaels	40.00	20.00	12.00
(13) Don Mueller	40.00	20.00	12.00
(14) Mel Parnell	40.00	20.00	12.00
(15) Allie Reynolds	47.00	23.00	14.00
(16) Preacher Roe	40.00	20.00	12.00
(17) Connie Ryan	40.00	20.00	12.00
(18) Hank Sauer	40.00	20.00	12.00
(19) Al Schoendienst	60.00	30.00	18.00
(20) Andy Seminick	40.00	20.00	12.00
(21) Bobby Shantz	47.00	23.00	14.00
(22) Enos Slaughter	60.00	30.00	18.00
(23) Virgil Trucks	40.00	20.00	12.00
(24) Gene Woodling	47.00	23.00	14.00

1953 Dixie Lids

The 1953 Dixie Lids set again consists of 24 unnumbered players and is identical in design to the 1952 set. Each lid measures 2-11/16" in diameter and must include the small tab to command top value.

	NM	EX	VG
Complete Set (24):	1500.	750.00	450.00
Common Player:	35.00	17.50	10.50
(1) Richie Ashburn	75.00	37.00	22.00
(2) Chico Carrasquel	35.00	17.50	10.50
(3) Billy Cox	35.00	17.50	10.50
(4) Ferris Fain	35.00	17.50	10.50
(5) Nelson Fox	65.00	32.00	19.50
(6a) Sid Gordon (Boston)	70.00	35.00	21.00
(6b) Sid Gordon (Milwaukee)	35.00	17.50	10.50
(7) Warren Hacker	35.00	17.50	10.50
(8) Monte Irvin	55.00	27.00	16.50
(9) Jackie Jensen	40.00	20.00	12.00
(10a) Ralph Kiner (Pittsburgh)	100.00	50.00	30.00
(10b) Ralph Kiner (Chicago)	55.00	27.00	16.50
(11) Ted Kluszewski	50.00	25.00	15.00
(12) Bob Lemon	55.00	27.00	16.50
(13) Don Mueller	35.00	17.50	10.50
(14) Mel Parnell	35.00	17.50	10.50
(15) Jerry Priddy	35.00	17.50	10.50
(16) Allie Reynolds	40.00	20.00	12.00
(17) Preacher Roe	35.00	17.50	10.50
(18) Hank Sauer	35.00	17.50	10.50
(19) Al Schoendienst	55.00	27.00	16.50
(20) Bobby Shantz	40.00	20.00	12.00
(21) Enos Slaughter	55.00	27.00	16.50
(22a) Warren Spahn (Boston)	150.00	75.00	45.00
(22b) Warren Spahn (Milwaukee)	55.00	27.00	16.50
(23a) Virgil Trucks (Chicago)	75.00	37.00	22.00
(23b) Virgil Trucks (St. Louis)	35.00	17.50	10.50
(24) Gene Woodling	40.00	20.00	12.00

1953 Dixie Lids Premiums

This set of 24 8" x 10" photos was issued as a premium in conjunction with the 1953 Dixie Lids set and includes the same subjects. The player's team and facsimile autograph are at the bottom of the unnumbered, blank-backed photos. His 1952 season stats are shown in the lower right corner.

	NM	EX	VG
Complete Set (24):	750.00	350.00	210.00
Common Player:	30.00	15.00	9.00
(1) Richie Ashburn	75.00	37.00	22.00
(2) Chico Carrasquel	30.00	15.00	9.00
(3) Billy Cox	30.00	15.00	9.00
(4) Ferris Fain	30.00	15.00	9.00
(5) Nelson Fox	60.00	30.00	18.00
(6) Sid Gordon	30.00	15.00	9.00
(7) Warren Hacker	30.00	15.00	9.00
(8) Monte Irvin	50.00	25.00	15.00
(9) Jack Jensen	35.00	17.50	10.50
(10) Ralph Kiner	50.00	25.00	15.00
(11) Ted Kluszewski	45.00	22.00	13.50
(12) Bob Lemon	50.00	25.00	15.00
(13) Don Mueller	30.00	15.00	9.00
(14) Mel Parnell	30.00	15.00	9.00
(15) Jerry Priddy	30.00	15.00	9.00
(16) Allie Reynolds	35.00	17.50	10.50
(17) Preacher Roe	30.00	15.00	9.00
(18) Hank Sauer	30.00	15.00	9.00
(19) Al Schoendienst	50.00	25.00	15.00
(20) Bobby Shantz	35.00	17.50	10.50
(21) Enos Slaughter	50.00	25.00	15.00
(22) Warren Spahn	55.00	27.00	16.50
(23) Virgil Trucks	30.00	15.00	9.00
(24) Gene Woodling	35.00	17.50	10.50

1954 Dixie Lids

The 1954 Dixie Lids set consists of 18 players, and the lids are usually found with a gray tint. The lids usually measure 2-11/16" in diameter, although two other sizes also exist (2-1/4" in diameter and 3-3/16" in diameter), which are valued at about twice the prices listed. The 1954 Dixie Lids are similar to earlier issues, except they carry an offer for a "3-D Starviewer" around the outside edge. The small tabs must be attached to command top value. The lids are unnumbered.

	NM	EX	VG
Complete Set (18):	900.00	450.00	270.00
Common Player:	42.00	21.00	12.50
(1) Richie Ashburn	90.00	45.00	27.00
(2) Clint Courtney	42.00	21.00	12.50
(3) Sid Gordon	42.00	21.00	12.50
(4) Billy Hoeft	42.00	21.00	12.50
(5) Monte Irvin	65.00	32.00	19.50
(6) Jackie Jensen	45.00	22.00	13.50
(7) Ralph Kiner	65.00	32.00	19.50
(8) Ted Kluszewski	50.00	25.00	15.00
(9) Gil McDougald	50.00	25.00	15.00
(10) Minny Minoso	50.00	25.00	15.00
(11) Danny O'Connell	42.00	21.00	12.50
(12) Mel Parnell	42.00	21.00	12.50
(13) Preacher Roe	42.00	21.00	12.50
(14) Al Rosen	42.00	21.00	12.50
(15) Al Schoendienst	65.00	32.00	19.50
(16) Enos Slaughter	65.00	32.00	19.50
(17) Gene Woodling	50.00	25.00	15.00
(18) Gus Zernial	42.00	21.00	12.50

1938 Dizzy Dean's Service Station

The date of issue of this one-card set is only a guess. The 4" x 6" black-and-white card advertises Dean's Service Station in Florida.

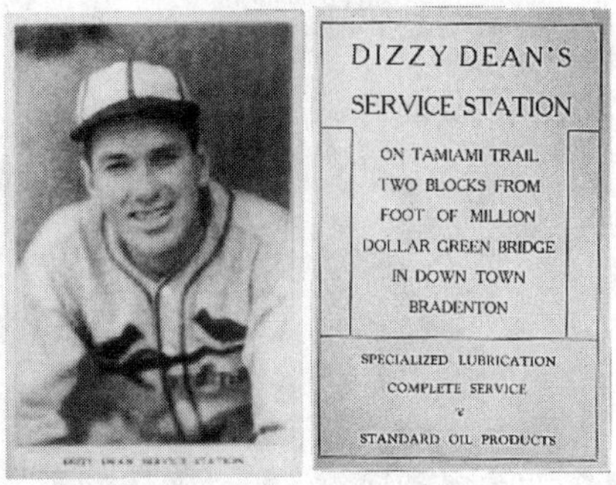

	NM	EX	VG
Dizzy Dean	250.00	125.00	75.00

1951 Joe DiMaggio Baseball Shoes

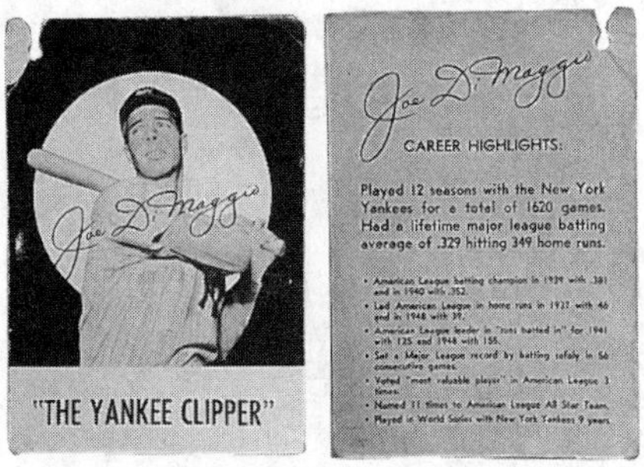

This 2-1/2" x 3-1/2" card was included with DiMaggio brand baseball shoes. A hole punch in the upper-left corner allowed the card to be attached to the shoe strings. Front has an action pose of DiMaggio printed in black-and-white on a dark green background. A facsimile autograph is at center. At bottom is printed: "THE YANKEE CLIPPER". The back has another facsimile signature and the player's career highlights through the 1950 season.

	NM	EX	VG
Joe DiMaggio	60.00	30.00	18.00

1909 Dockman & Sons Gum (E92)

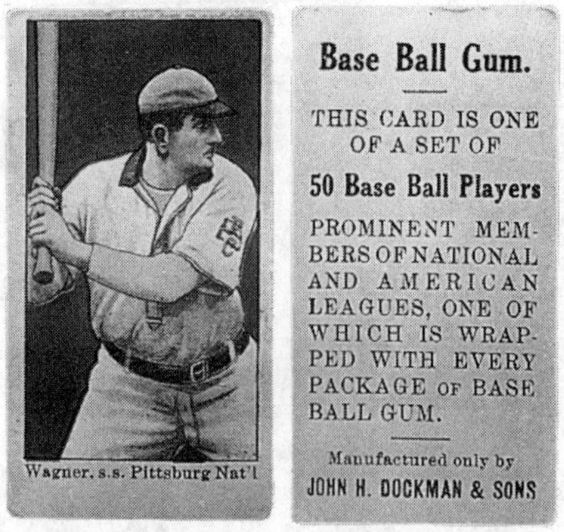

Once cataloged as a part of the E92 compendium, the John Dockman & Sons gum card issue differs from the Croft's Candy/Cocoa sets in that it has 10 fewer cards. Otherwise the format 1-1/2" x 2-3/4") and color litho player pictures are identical. Beneath the player picture on front is his last name, position and team. Backs, which describe the set as having 50 cards, have an ad for the gum company. Cards are checklisted here alphabetically. It is possible some of the "missing" 10 cards may yet surface.

	NM	EX	VG
Complete Set (40):	8500.	3550.	1750.
Common Player:	125.00	50.00	25.00
(1) Harry Bemis	125.00	50.00	25.00
(2) Chief Bender	350.00	140.00	70.00
(3) Bill Bergen	125.00	50.00	25.00
(4) Bob Bescher	125.00	50.00	25.00
(5) Al Bridwell	125.00	50.00	25.00
(6) Doc Casey	125.00	50.00	25.00
(7) Frank Chance	350.00	140.00	70.00
(8) Hal Chase	150.00	60.00	30.00
(9) Sam Crawford	350.00	140.00	70.00
(10) Harry Davis	125.00	50.00	25.00
(11) Art Devlin	125.00	50.00	25.00
(12) Wild Bill Donovan	125.00	50.00	25.00
(13) Mickey Doolan	125.00	50.00	25.00
(14) Patsy Dougherty	125.00	50.00	25.00
(15) Larry Doyle (throwing)	125.00	50.00	25.00
(16) Larry Doyle (with bat)	125.00	50.00	25.00
(17) George Gibson	125.00	50.00	25.00
(18) Topsy Hartsel	125.00	50.00	25.00
(19) Hugh Jennings	350.00	140.00	70.00
(20) Red Kleinow	125.00	50.00	25.00
(21) Nap Lajoie	350.00	140.00	70.00
(22) Hans Lobert	125.00	50.00	25.00
(23) Sherry Magee	125.00	50.00	25.00
(24) Christy Matthewson (Mathewson)	800.00	320.00	160.00
(25) John McGraw	350.00	140.00	70.00
(26) Larry McLean	125.00	50.00	25.00
(27) Dots Miller	125.00	50.00	25.00
(28) Danny Murphy	125.00	50.00	25.00
(29) Bill O'Hara	125.00	50.00	25.00
(30) Germany Schaefer	125.00	50.00	25.00
(31) Admiral Schlei	125.00	50.00	25.00
(32) Boss Schmidt	125.00	50.00	25.00
(33) Johnny Seigle	125.00	50.00	25.00
(34) Dave Shean	125.00	50.00	25.00
(35) Boss Smith (Schmidt)	125.00	50.00	25.00
(36) Joe Tinker	350.00	140.00	70.00
(37) Honus Wagner (batting)	1500.	600.00	300.00
(38) Honus Wagner (throwing)	1500.	600.00	300.00
(39) Cy Young	450.00	180.00	90.00
(40) Heinie Zimmerman	125.00	50.00	25.00

1888 Dog's Head Cabinets

(See Old Judge Cabinets)

1953-55 Dormand Postcards

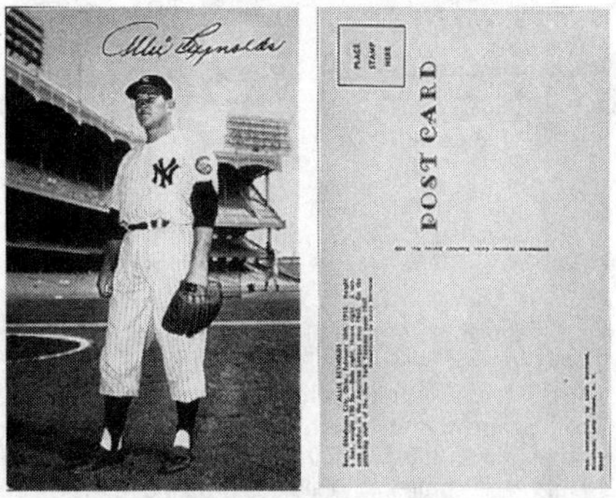

This mid-1950s issue features only selected players from the Yankees, Brooklyn Dodgers, White Sox and Philadelphia A's. Apparently produced on order by the players by Louis Dormand, a Long Island, N.Y., photographer, the cards were used to honor fan requests for photos and autographs. All cards have a facsimile autograph printed in front. Otherwise the fronts of these 3-1/2" x 5-1/2" postcards feature only sharp color photos with no border. Backs, printed in blue or green, feature a few player biographical and career details, one or two lines identifying the producer and usually product and series numbers. Most have a Kodachrome logo. Some cards do not have all of these elements and several are found blank-backed. The Gil Hodges card is considerably scarcer than the others in the set, with those of Jim Konstanty, Elston Howard, and Casey Stengel also seldom seen. Besides the standard-sized cards listed below, there are oversize versions of Rizzuto's and Mantle's cards. A variation of Johnny Sain's card shows his Arkansas Chevrolet dealership in a photo above the player's picture. Players are listed alphabetically here. The complete set price includes only the standard-size cards.

		NM	EX	VG
Complete Set (45):		2750.	1350.	825.00
Common Player:		25.00	12.50	7.50
(1a)	Hank Bauer (small autograph)	35.00	17.50	10.50
(1b)	Hank Bauer (large autograph)	35.00	17.50	10.50
(2)	Yogi Berra	70.00	35.00	21.00
(3)	Don Bollweg	25.00	12.50	7.50
(4)	Roy Campanella	150.00	75.00	45.00
(5)	Chico Carrasquel	25.00	12.50	7.50
(6)	Jerry Coleman	25.00	12.50	7.50
(7a)	Joe Collins (patch on sleeve, autograph at top)	60.00	30.00	18.00
(7b)	Joe Collins (patch on sleeve, autograph at bottom)	60.00	30.00	18.00
(8)	Joe Collins (no patch on sleeve)	40.00	20.00	12.00
(9)	Frank Crosetti	40.00	20.00	12.00
(10)	Carl Erskine	60.00	30.00	18.00
(11)	Whitey Ford	60.00	30.00	18.00
(12)	Carl Furillo	45.00	22.00	13.50
(13)	Tom Gorman	25.00	12.50	7.50
(14)	Gil Hodges	400.00	200.00	120.00
(15)	Ralph Houk	25.00	12.50	7.50
(16)	Elston Howard	150.00	75.00	45.00
(17)	Jim Konstanty	150.00	75.00	45.00
(18)	Ed Lopat	25.00	12.50	7.50
(19)	Mickey Mantle (bat on shoulder)	200.00	100.00	60.00
(20)	Mickey Mantle (batting stance, 3-1/2" x 5-1/2")	75.00	37.00	22.00
(21)	Mickey Mantle (bat on shoulder, 6" x 9")	850.00	425.00	255.00
(22)	Mickey Mantle (bat on shoulder, 9" x 12")	1150.	575.00	345.00
(23)	Billy Martin	35.00	17.50	10.50
(24)	Jim McDonald	25.00	12.50	7.50
(25a)	Gil McDougald (small autograph)	35.00	17.50	10.50
(25b)	Gil McDougald (large autograph)	30.00	15.00	9.00
(26)	Bill Miller	25.00	12.50	7.50
(27)	Willie Miranda	30.00	15.00	9.00
(28)	Johnny Mize	90.00	45.00	27.00
(29)	Irv Noren	35.00	17.50	10.50
(30)	Billy Pierce	35.00	17.50	10.50
(31)	Pee Wee Reese	70.00	35.00	21.00
(32)	Allie Reynolds	30.00	15.00	9.00
(33a)	Phil Rizzuto (autograph parallel to top)	45.00	22.00	13.50
(33b)	Phil Rizzuto (autograph angles downward, 3-1/2" x 5-1 /2")	45.00	22.00	13.50
(34)	Phil Rizzuto (autograph angles downward, 9" x 12")	110.00	55.00	33.00
(35)	Ed Robinson	40.00	20.00	12.00
(36)	Johnny Sain (beginning windup)	35.00	17.50	10.50
(37)	Johnny Sain (leg kick)	35.00	17.50	10.50
(38)	Johnny Sain (with auto dealership ad)	75.00	37.00	22.00
(39)	Ray Scarborough	35.00	17.50	10.50
(40a)	Bobby Shantz (autograph parallel to top)	40.00	20.00	12.00
(40b)	Bobby Shantz (autograph angles downward)	40.00	20.00	12.00
(41)	Charlie Silvera	30.00	15.00	9.00
(42)	Bill Skowron	45.00	22.00	13.50
(43)	Enos Slaughter	75.00	37.00	22.00
(44a)	Casey Stengel (autograph at top)	165.00	82.00	49.00
(44b)	Casey Stengel (autograph at bottom)	165.00	82.00	49.00
(45)	Gene Woodling	30.00	15.00	9.00

1941 Double Play

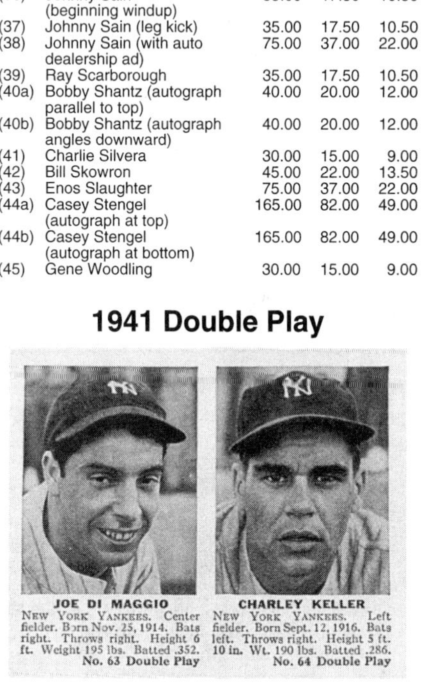
JOE DI MAGGIO
New York Yankees. Center fielder. Born Nov. 25, 1914. Bats right. Throws right. Height 6 ft. Weight 195 lbs. Batted .352.
No. 63 Double Play
CHARLEY KELLER
New York Yankees. Left fielder. Born Sept. 12, 1916. Bats left. Throws right. Height 5 ft. 10 in. Wt. 190 lbs. Batted .286.
No. 64 Double Play

Issued by Gum, Inc., this set includes 75 numbered cards (two consecutive numbers per card) featuring 150 players. The blank-backed cards measure 3-1/8" x 2-1/2" and feature black-and-white photos of the players, some in horizontal format, some in vertical. The last 50 cards in the series are scarcer than the early numbers. Cards which have been cut in half to form single cards have little collector value.

		NM	EX	VG
Complete Set (75):		6000.	3000.	1800.
Common Player:		40.00	20.00	12.00
1-2	Larry French, Vance Page	65.00	32.00	19.50
3-4	Billy Herman, Stanley Hack	75.00	37.00	22.00
5-6	Linus Frey, John Vander Meer	42.00	21.00	12.50
7-8	Paul Derringer, Bucky Walters	40.00	20.00	12.00
9-10	Frank McCormick, Bill Werber	40.00	20.00	12.00
11-12	Jimmy Ripple, Ernie Lombardi	60.00	30.00	18.00
13-14	Alex Kampouris, John Wyatt	40.00	20.00	12.00
15-16	Mickey Owen, Paul Waner	55.00	27.00	16.50
17-18	Cookie Lavagetto, Harold Reiser	45.00	22.00	13.50
19-20	Jimmy Wasdell, Dolph Camilli	42.00	21.00	12.50
21-22	Dixie Walker, Ducky Medwick	60.00	30.00	18.00
23-24	Harold Reese, Kirby Higbe	220.00	110.00	66.00
25-26	Harry Danning, Cliff Melton	40.00	20.00	12.00
27-28	Harry Gumbert, Burgess Whitehead	40.00	20.00	12.00
29-30	Joe Orengo, Joe Moore	40.00	20.00	12.00
31-32	Mel Ott, Babe Young	100.00	50.00	30.00
33-34	Lee Handley, Arky Vaughan	60.00	30.00	18.00
35-36	Bob Klinger, Stanley Brown	40.00	20.00	12.00
37-38	Terry Moore, Gus Mancuso	40.00	20.00	12.00
39-40	Johnny Mize, Enos Slaughter	95.00	47.00	28.00
41-42	John Cooney, Sibby Sisti	40.00	20.00	12.00
43-44	Max West, Carvel Rowell	40.00	20.00	12.00
45-46	Danny Litwhiler, Merrill May	40.00	20.00	12.00
47-48	Frank Hayes, Al Brancato	40.00	20.00	12.00
49-50	Bob Johnson, Bill Nagel	40.00	20.00	12.00
51-52	Buck Newsom, Hank Greenberg	95.00	47.00	28.00
53-54	Barney McCosky, Charley Gehringer	90.00	45.00	27.00
55-56	Pinky Higgins, Dick Bartell	40.00	20.00	12.00
57-58	Ted Williams, Jim Tabor	550.00	275.00	165.00
59-60	Joe Cronin, Jimmy Foxx	200.00	100.00	60.00
61-62	Lefty Gomez, Phil Rizzuto	275.00	137.00	82.00
63-64	Joe DiMaggio, Charley Keller	800.00	400.00	240.00
65-66	Red Rolfe, Bill Dickey	150.00	75.00	45.00
67-68	Joe Gordon, Red Ruffing	70.00	35.00	21.00
69-70	Mike Tresh, Luke Appling	55.00	27.00	16.50
71-72	Moose Solters, John Rigney	40.00	20.00	12.00
73-74	Buddy Meyer, Ben Chapman (Myer)	40.00	20.00	12.00
75-76	Cecil Travis, George Case	40.00	20.00	12.00
77-78	Joe Krakauskas, Bob Feller	175.00	87.00	52.00
79-80	Ken Keltner, Hal Trosky	40.00	20.00	12.00
81-82	Ted Williams, Joe Cronin	800.00	400.00	240.00
83-84	Joe Gordon, Charley Keller	50.00	25.00	15.00
85-86	Hank Greenberg, Red Ruffing	95.00	47.00	28.00
87-88	Hal Trosky, George Case	40.00	20.00	12.00
89-90	Mel Ott, Burgess Whitehead	90.00	45.00	27.00
91-92	Harry Danning, Harry Gumbert	40.00	20.00	12.00
93-94	Babe Young, Cliff Melton	40.00	20.00	12.00
95-96	Jimmy Ripple, Bucky Walters	40.00	20.00	12.00
97-98	Stanley Hack, Bob Klinger	40.00	20.00	12.00
99-100	Johnny Mize, Dan Litwhiler	55.00	27.00	16.50
101-102	Dom Dallessandro, Augie Galan	50.00	25.00	15.00
103-104	Bill Lee, Phil Cavarretta	55.00	27.00	16.50
105-106	Lefty Grove, Bobby Doerr	200.00	100.00	60.00
107-108	Frank Pytlak, Dom DiMaggio	65.00	32.00	19.50
109-110	Gerald Priddy, John Murphy	50.00	25.00	15.00
111-112	Tommy Henrich, Marius Russo	60.00	30.00	18.00
113-114	Frank Crossetti, John Sturm	55.00	27.00	16.50
115-116	Ival Goodman, Myron McCormick	50.00	25.00	15.00
117-118	Eddie Joost, Ernie Koy	50.00	25.00	15.00
119-120	Lloyd Waner, Hank Majeski	70.00	35.00	21.00
121-122	Buddy Hassett, Eugene Moore	50.00	25.00	15.00
123-124	Nick Etten, John Rizzo	50.00	25.00	15.00
125-126	Sam Chapman, Wally Moses	50.00	25.00	15.00
127-128	John Dabich, Richard Siebert	50.00	25.00	15.00
129-130	Nelson Potter, Benny McCoy	50.00	25.00	15.00
131-132	Clarence Campbell, Louis Boudreau	75.00	37.00	22.00
133-134	Rolly Hemsley, Mel Harder	55.00	27.00	16.50
135-136	Gerald Walker, Joe Heving	50.00	25.00	15.00
137-138	John Rucker, Ace Adams	50.00	25.00	15.00
139-140	Morris Arnovich, Carl Hubbell	120.00	60.00	36.00
141-142	Lew Riggs, Leo Durocher	85.00	42.00	25.00
143-144	Fred Fitzsimmons, Joe Vosmik	50.00	25.00	15.00
145-146	Frank Crespi, Jim Brown	50.00	25.00	15.00
147-148	Don Heffner, Harland Clift (Harlond)	50.00	25.00	15.00
149-150	Debs Garms, Elbie Fletcher	50.00	25.00	15.00

1976 Douglas Cool Papa Bell

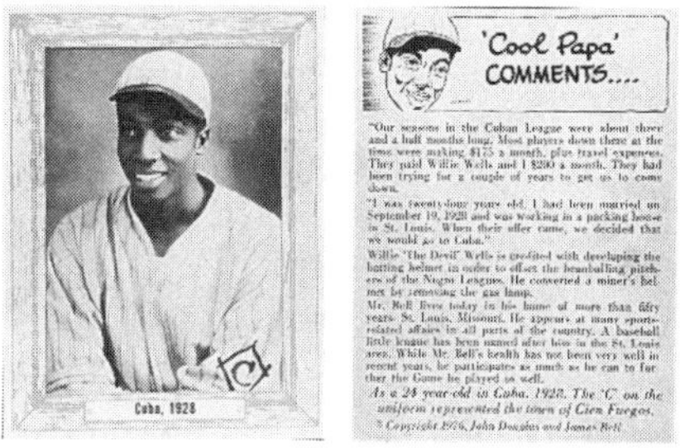

This collectors issue was produced following the 1974 induction of James "Cool Papa" Bell into the Hall of Fame. Collector John Douglas collaborated with Bell to produce the set chronicling Bell's career (1922-46) in the Negro and Latin American pro leagues. Fronts have vintage sepia-toned photos of Bell surrounded by a yellow, green or orange woodgrain, fame with a title plaque at bottom. Backs are in brown-and-white with a drawing of Bell at top and autobiographical material at center. A description of the photo and copyright data are at bottom. The unnumbered cards are checklisted here alphabetically by their title.

		NM	EX	VG
Complete Set (13):		12.00	6.00	3.50
Common Card:		1.00	.50	.30
(1)	Amazing Speed	1.00	.50	.30
(2)	Brock Sets SB Record	1.00	.50	.30
(3)	Cool Papa	1.00	.50	.30
(4)	Cuba, 1928	1.00	.50	.30
(5)	Great Fielder, Too	1.00	.50	.30
(6)	HOF, Cooperstown	1.00	.50	.30
(7)	HOF Favorite	1.00	.50	.30
(8)	Induction Day, 1974	1.00	.50	.30
(9)	Monarchs' Manager	1.00	.50	.30
(10)	On Deck in Cuba	1.00	.50	.30
(11)	The Mexican Leagues	1.00	.50	.30
(12)	Touring Havana	1.00	.50	.30
(13)	With Josh Gibson	1.00	.50	.30

1977 Douglas Johnny Mize

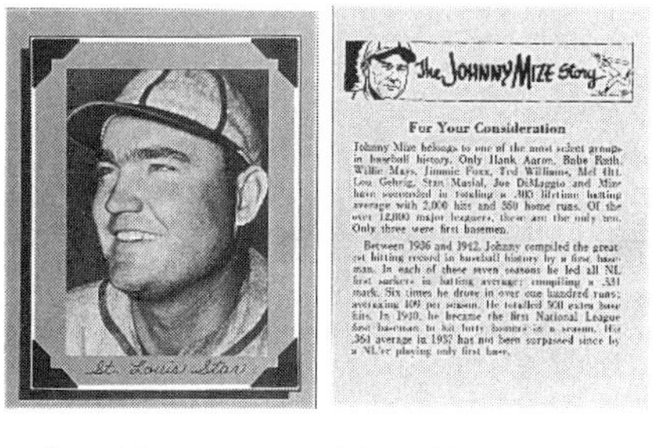

In an effort to promote Johnny Mize for induction to the Hall of Fame, John Douglas created this collectors issue. The Big Cat's career is traced on a series of 3-1/4" x 3-7/8" cards with black-and-white photos on a greenish-brown background. Black-and-white backs have a drawing of Mize at top with lengthy narrative below. The unnumbered cards are checklisted here by the title which appears on the front. Mize was selected for the Hall of Fame in 1981.

		NM	EX	VG
Complete Set (20):		12.00	6.00	3.50
Common Card:		.75	.40	.20
(1)	Blattner, Gordon, Lombardi, Mize, Marshall	.75	.40	.20
(2)	Call for Phillip Morris	.75	.40	.20
(3)	Cardinal Slugger	.75	.40	.20
(4)	Card's Big Stick	.75	.40	.20
(5)	Early Photo - 1913	.75	.40	.20
(6)	51 Homers, 1947	.75	.40	.20
(7)	Home Run, 1952 Series	.75	.40	.20
(8)	June 16, 1953	.75	.40	.20
(9)	Louisville Poster - 1947	.75	.40	.20
(10)	Mize, Happy Chandler, Bucky Harris	.75	.40	.20
(11)	Mize, Reynolds, Johnson	.75	.40	.20
(12)	N.L. Homer Champ 1948	.75	.40	.20
(13)	Series MVP - 1952	.75	.40	.20
(14)	St. Louis Star	.75	.40	.20
(15)	The Navy - 1943	.75	.40	.20
(16)	Vu-Master Slide	.75	.40	.20
(17)	With Enos Slaughter	.75	.40	.20
(18)	With Roy Rogers	.75	.40	.20
(19)	With Terry Moore	.75	.40	.20
(20)	Woodling, Raschi, Mize - 1952	.75	.40	.20

1978 Dover Publications Great Players Postcards

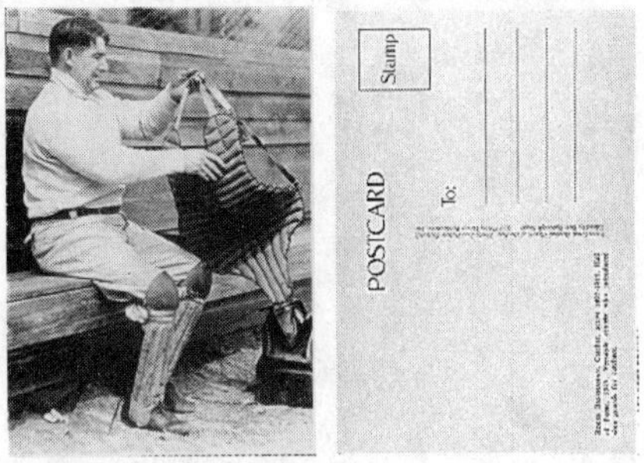

This set of 32 collectors' issue postcards was originally issued in the form of an 8" x 11" booklet from which individual cards could be separated. The 3-7/8" x 5-1/2" cards are perforated on two sides, depending on their placement on a four-card page. Fronts have borderless sepia photos. Black-and-white backs have standard postcard indicia, copyright data, player identification and a brief career summary. The unnumbered cards are checklisted here alphabetically.

		NM	EX	VG
Complete Set, Booklet:		6.00	3.00	1.75
Complete Set, Singles (32):		4.50	2.25	1.25
Common Player:		.25	.13	.08
(1)	Grover Cleveland Alexander	.25	.13	.08
(2)	Chief Bender	.25	.13	.08
(3)	Roger Bresnahan	.25	.13	.08
(4)	Bullet Joe Bush	.25	.13	.08
(5)	Frank Chance	.25	.13	.08
(6)	Ty Cobb	.60	.30	.20
(7)	Eddie Collins	.25	.13	.08
(8)	Stan Coveleski	.25	.13	.08
(9)	Sam Crawford	.25	.13	.08
(10)	Frankie Frisch	.25	.13	.08
(11)	Goose Goslin	.25	.13	.08
(12)	Harry Heilmann	.25	.13	.08
(13)	Rogers Hornsby	.35	.20	.11
(14)	Joe Jackson	2.00	1.00	.60
(15)	Hughie Jennings	.25	.13	.08
(16)	Walter Johnson	.50	.25	.15
(17)	Sad Sam Jones	.25	.13	.08
(18)	Rabbit Maranville	.25	.13	.08
(19)	Rube Marquard	.25	.13	.08
(20)	Christy Mathewson	.50	.25	.15
(21)	John McGraw	.25	.13	.08
(22)	Herb Pennock	.25	.13	.08
(23)	Eddie Plank	.25	.13	.08
(24)	Edd Roush	.25	.13	.08
(25)	Babe Ruth	2.00	1.00	.60
(26)	George Sisler	.25	.13	.08
(27)	Tris Speaker	.35	.20	.11
(28)	Casey Stengel	.25	.13	.08
(29)	Joe Tinker	.25	.13	.08
(30)	Pie Traynor	.25	.13	.08
(31)	Dazzy Vance	.25	.13	.08
(32)	Cy Young	.35	.20	.11

1925 Drake's

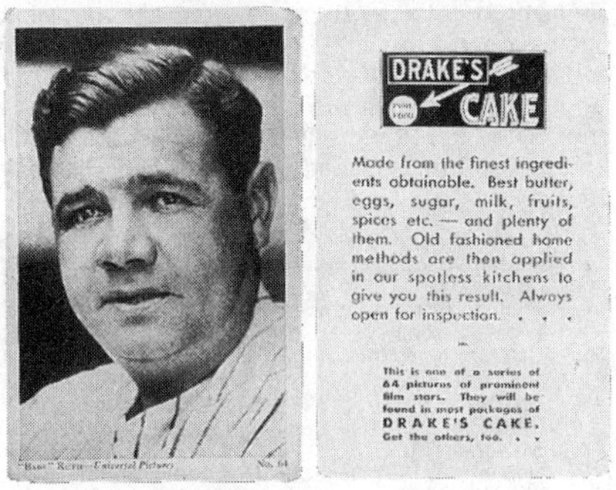

Among a series of 64 movie stars packaged with Drake's Cake in the mid-1920s was a card of Babe Ruth, who did some movie work for Universal Pictures at the time. The 2-7/16" x 4-3/16" black-and-white card has a portrait of Ruth on front, with his name, studio and card number in the bottom border. Backs have an ad for Drake's.

		NM	EX	VG
61	Babe Ruth	1350.	675.00	400.00

1950 Drake's

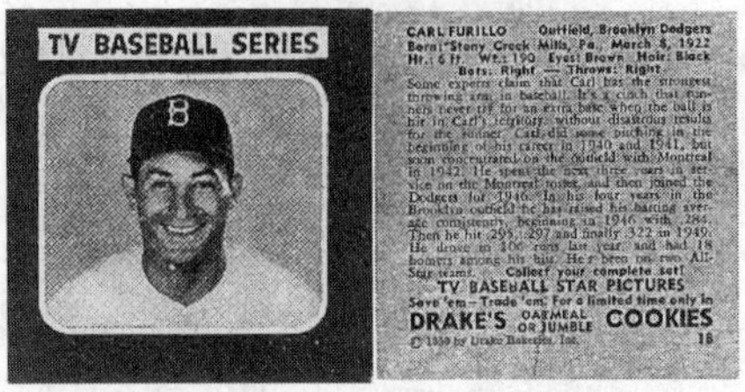

Entitled "TV Baseball Series," the 1950 Drake's Bakeries set pictures of 36 different players on a television screen format. The cards, 2-1/2" x 2-1/2", contain black-and-white photos surrounded by a black border. Backs carry a player biography plus an advertisement advising collectors to look for the cards in packages of Oatmeal or Jumble cookies.

		NM	EX	VG
Complete Set (36):		7225.	3600.	2175.
Common Player:		100.00	50.00	30.00
1	Elwin "Preacher" Roe	155.00	77.00	46.00
2	Clint Hartung	100.00	50.00	30.00
3	Earl Torgeson	100.00	50.00	30.00
4	Leland "Lou" Brissie	100.00	50.00	30.00
5	Edwin "Duke" Snider	750.00	375.00	225.00
6	Roy Campanella	750.00	375.00	225.00
7	Sheldon "Available" Jones	100.00	50.00	30.00
8	Carroll "Whitey" Lockman	100.00	50.00	30.00
9	Bobby Thomson	140.00	70.00	42.00
10	Dick Sisler	100.00	50.00	30.00
11	Gil Hodges	450.00	225.00	135.00
12	Eddie Waitkus	100.00	50.00	30.00
13	Bobby Doerr	300.00	150.00	90.00
14	Warren Spahn	425.00	210.00	125.00
15	John "Buddy" Kerr	100.00	50.00	30.00
16	Sid Gordon	100.00	50.00	30.00
17	Willard Marshall	100.00	50.00	30.00
18	Carl Furillo	155.00	77.00	46.00
19	Harold "Pee Wee" Reese	600.00	300.00	180.00
20	Alvin Dark	100.00	50.00	30.00
21	Del Ennis	100.00	50.00	30.00
22	Ed Stanky	100.00	50.00	30.00
23	Tommy "Old Reliable" Henrich	155.00	77.00	46.00
24	Larry "Yogi" Berra	750.00	375.00	225.00
25	Phil "Scooter" Rizzuto	600.00	300.00	180.00
26	Jerry Coleman	100.00	50.00	30.00
27	Joe Page	100.00	50.00	30.00
28	Allie Reynolds	155.00	77.00	46.00
29	Ray Scarborough	100.00	50.00	30.00
30	George "Birdie" Tebbetts	100.00	50.00	30.00
31	Maurice "Lefty" McDermott	100.00	50.00	30.00
32	Johnny Pesky	100.00	50.00	30.00
33	Dom "Little Professor" DiMaggio	200.00	100.00	60.00
34	Vern "Junior" Stephens	100.00	50.00	30.00
35	Bob Elliott	100.00	50.00	30.00
36	Enos "Country" Slaughter	425.00	210.00	125.00

1909-11 Drum Cigarettes

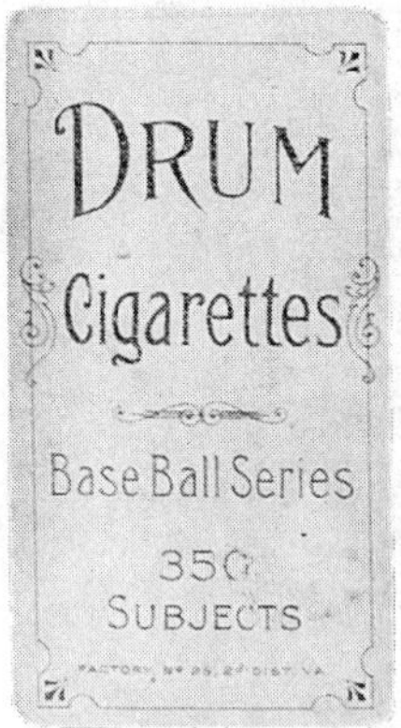

(See T205, T206. Premium: T205 - 15-25X, T206 - 8-10X.)

1888 Duke Talk of the Diamond (N135)

One of the more obscure 19th Century tobacco issues is a 25-card set issued by Honest Long Cut Tobacco in the late 1880's. Titled "Talk of the Diamond," the set features full-color cards measuring 4-1/8" x 2-1/2". Each card features a cartoon-like drawing illustrating a popular baseball term or expression. The left portion of the card pictures an unspecified player in a fielding position, and some of the artwork for that part of the set was borrowed from the more popular Buchner Gold Coin set (N284) issued about the same time. Because the "Talk of the Diamond" set does not feature individual players it has never really captured the attention of baseball card collectors. It does, however, hold interest as a novelty item of the period. It carries an N135 American Card Catalog designation.

		NM	EX	VG
Complete Set (25):		6575.	2625.	1325.
Common Card:		250.00	100.00	50.00
(1)	A Base Tender	250.00	100.00	50.00
(2)	A Big Hit	250.00	100.00	50.00
(3)	A Chronic Kicker	250.00	100.00	50.00
(4)	A Foul Balk	250.00	100.00	50.00
(5)	A Foul Catch	250.00	100.00	50.00
(6)	A Good Catch	250.00	100.00	50.00
(7)	A Good Throw	250.00	100.00	50.00
(8)	A Heavy Batter	250.00	100.00	50.00
(9)	A Home Run	250.00	100.00	50.00
(10)	A Hot Ball	250.00	100.00	50.00
(11)	A Low Ball	250.00	100.00	50.00
(12)	A Pitcher in the Box	250.00	100.00	50.00
(13)	A Regular Ball	250.00	100.00	50.00
(14)	A Rounder	250.00	100.00	50.00
(15)	A Short Stop	250.00	100.00	50.00
(16)	After the Ball	250.00	100.00	50.00
(17)	Going for Third Base	250.00	100.00	50.00
(18)	He Serves the Ball	250.00	100.00	50.00
(19)	Left Field	250.00	100.00	50.00
(20)	Left on Base	250.00	100.00	50.00
(21)	Lively Game	250.00	100.00	50.00
(22)	No Game	250.00	100.00	50.00
(23)	Out	250.00	100.00	50.00
(24)	Stealing a Base	250.00	100.00	50.00
(25)	Three out-All out	250.00	100.00	50.00

1972 Durochrome Chicago White Sox Decals

While they are technically stickers, rather than decals, this set of six White Sox was given away during the course of half a dozen "Decal Days" at Comiskey Park, as listed on the peel-off back. The stickers measure 3-9/16" x 4-9/16" and feature posed action photos of the players in their vintage red-trimmed uniforms. Fronts have a facsimile autograph and, in the bottom border, the team name. Backs are printed in green and have a few vital statistics, an ad by the manufacturer and an enigmatic row of numbers at the bottom. The unnumbered stickers are checklisted here in alphabetical order.

		NM	EX	VG
Complete Set (6):		48.00	24.00	14.50
Common Player:		6.00	3.00	1.75
(1)	Richard Allen	24.00	12.00	7.25
(2)	Ed Hermann	6.00	3.00	1.75
(3)	Bart Johnson	6.00	3.00	1.75
(4)	Carlos May	6.00	3.00	1.75
(5)	Bill Melton	6.00	3.00	1.75
(6)	Wilbur Wood	9.00	4.50	2.75

E

1914 E. & S. Publishing Co.

Only four players have been reported from this postcard issue. Front of the standard-size postcards has a large blue portrait of the player at center, with a number of cartoons around. The back is done in ornate typography with copyright line, stamp box, etc. Other players may yet be discovered.

		NM	EX	VG
(1)	Joe Benz	300.00	150.00	90.00
(2)	Ty Cobb	1500.	750.00	450.00
(3)	Joe Jackson	1600.	800.00	480.00
(4)	"Tex" Russell	300.00	150.00	90.00

1940s Eagle Hall of Fame

The date of this issue can only be approximated, probably in the late 1940s. The 9-1/4" x 11-1/4" cards have high-gloss sepia photos on thick cardboard. A wood-look frame and identification plaques are pictured around the central photo. Backs are blank. The pictures were issued by the Carnegie (Pa.) Aerie of the Eagles, Lodge #1134, according to the bottom "plaque" at top is "Eagle Hall of Fame." Presumably the four ballplayers and two boxers known were all members of that fraternal order. The unnumbered pieces are checklisted alphabetically.

		NM	EX	VG
Complete Set (6):		700.00	350.00	210.00
Common Player:		40.00	20.00	12.00
(1)	Bob Fitzsimmons (boxer)	40.00	20.00	12.00
(2)	Lefty Grove	150.00	75.00	45.00
(3)	Stan Musial	200.00	100.00	60.00
(4)	John Sullivan (boxer)	75.00	37.00	22.00
(5)	Honus Wagner	175.00	87.00	52.00
(6)	Cy Young	175.00	87.00	52.00

1979 Early Red Sox Favorites

This collectors' issue of unknown origin features players of the 1930s' Red Sox. Cards are printed in black-and-white in a 2-5/8" x 3-3/4" format. Front photos are bordered in white and have identification of the players overprinted in black. Backs have a few stats, highlights or an explanation of the photo on front. Many cards feature more than one player.

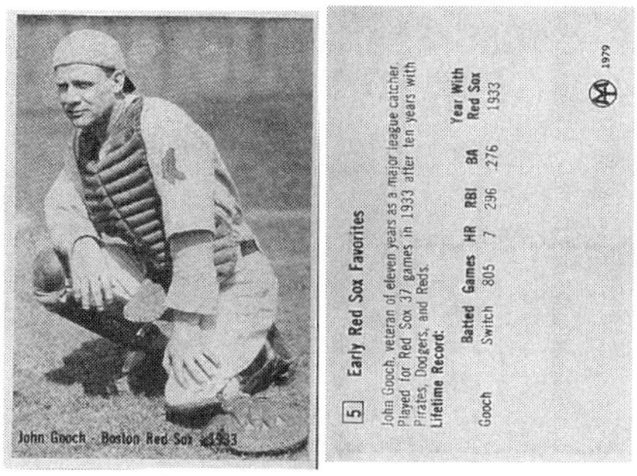

		NM	EX	VG
Complete Set (24):		45.00	22.50	13.50
Common Player:		2.00	1.00	.60
1	New Fenway Park	2.00	1.00	.60
2	Mrs. Tom Yawkey and Mrs. Eddie Collins	2.00	1.00	.60
3	Red Sox Outfielders - 1932 (Tom Oliver, Earl Webb, Jack Rothrock)	2.00	1.00	.60
4	Red Sox Ace Pitchers (John Marcum, Wes Ferrell, Lefty Grove, Fritz Ostermueller)	2.00	1.00	.60
5	John Gooch	2.00	1.00	.60
6	Red Sox Recruits at Sarasota, Fla. (Joe Cronin)	2.00	1.00	.60
7	Danny MacFayden	2.00	1.00	.60
8	Dale Alexander	2.00	1.00	.60
9	Robert (Fatsy) Fothergill	2.00	1.00	.60
10	Red Sox Sunday Morning Workout	2.00	1.00	.60
11	Jimmie Foxx (siging ball for Mrs, Yawkey)	2.50	1.25	.70
12	Lefty Grove (presented keys to new car)	2.50	1.25	.70
13	"Fireball" Lefty Grove	2.50	1.25	.70
14	Praciticng Base Stealing (Jack Rothrock, Urban Pickering)	2.00	1.00	.60
15	Tom Daly, Al Schacht, Herb Pennock	2.00	1.00	.60
16	Eddie Collins, Heinie Manush	2.50	1.25	.70
17	Tris Speaker	2.50	1.25	.70
18	Home Run Star (Jimmie Foxx)	2.50	1.25	.70
19	Smead Jolley	2.00	1.00	.60
20	Hal Trosky, Jimmie Foxx	2.00	1.00	.60
21	Herold "Muddy" Ruel, Wilcy "Fireman" Moore	2.00	1.00	.60
22	Bob Quinn, Shano Collins	2.00	1.00	.60
23	Tom Oliver	2.00	1.00	.60
24	Joe Cronin, Herb Pennock, Buetter	2.00	1.00	.60

1966 East Hills Pirates

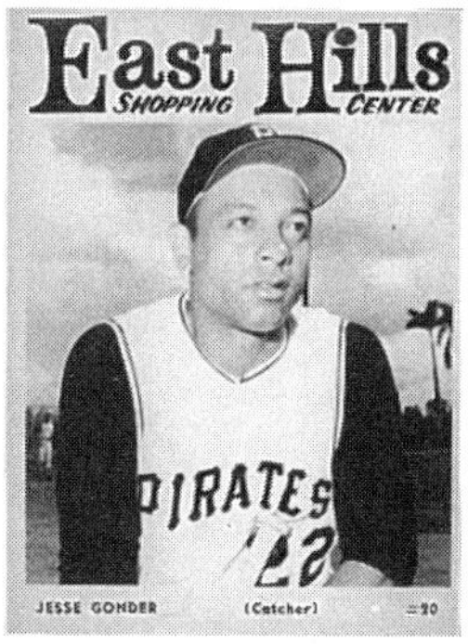

Stores in the East Hills Shopping Center, a large mall located in suburban Pittsburgh, distributed cards from this 25-card full-color set in 1966. The cards, which measure 3-1/4" x 4-1/4", are blank-backed and are numbered by the players' uniform numbers. The numbers appear in the lower right corners of the cards.

		NM	EX	VG
Complete Set (25):		115.00	57.00	33.00
Common Player:		5.00	2.50	1.50
3	Harry Walker	5.00	2.50	1.50
7	Bob Bailey	5.00	2.50	1.50
8	Willie Stargell	20.00	10.00	6.00
9	Bill Mazeroski	20.00	10.00	6.00
10	Jim Pagliaroni	5.00	2.50	1.50
11	Jose Pagan	5.00	2.50	1.50
12	Jerry May	5.00	2.50	1.50
14	Gene Alley	5.00	2.50	1.50
15	Manny Mota	5.50	2.75	1.75
16	Andy Rodgers	5.00	2.50	1.50
17	Donn Clendenon	5.00	2.50	1.50
18	Matty Alou	5.00	2.50	1.50
19	Pete Mikkelsen	5.00	2.50	1.50
20	Jesse Gonder	5.00	2.50	1.50
21	Roberto Clemente	50.00	25.00	15.00
22	Woody Fryman	5.00	2.50	1.50
24	Jerry Lynch	5.00	2.50	1.50
25	Tommie Sisk	5.00	2.50	1.50
26	Roy Face	6.50	3.25	2.00
28	Steve Blass	5.00	2.50	1.50
32	Vernon Law	6.50	3.25	2.00
34	Al McBean	5.00	2.50	1.50
39	Bob Veale	5.00	2.50	1.50
43	Don Cardwell	5.00	2.50	1.50
45	Gene Michael	5.00	2.50	1.50

1933 Eclipse Import

Issued in 1933, this set was sold in eight-card strips. Numbered from 401 through 424, the cards measure 2-7/16" x 2-7/8". The design features a crude colored drawing of the player on the front. The back of the card displays the card number at the top followed by the player's name, team and a brief write-up. Card numbers 403, 413, and 414 are missing and probably correspond to the three unnumbered cards in the set. The set carries an American Card Catalog designation of R337.

		NM	EX	VG
Complete Set (24):		2750.	1350.	825.00
Common Player:		70.00	35.00	21.00
401	Johnny Vergez	70.00	35.00	21.00
402	Babe Ruth	900.00	450.00	270.00
403	Not Issued			
404	George Pipgras	70.00	35.00	21.00
405	Bill Terry	120.00	60.00	36.00
406	George Connally	70.00	35.00	21.00
407	Watson Clark	70.00	35.00	21.00
408	"Lefty" Grove	120.00	60.00	36.00
409	Henry Johnson	70.00	35.00	21.00
410	Jimmy Dykes	70.00	35.00	21.00
411	Henry Hine Schuble	70.00	35.00	21.00
412	Bucky Harris	100.00	50.00	30.00
413	Not Issued			
414	Not Issued			
415	Al Simmons	100.00	50.00	30.00
416	Henry "Heinie" Manush	100.00	50.00	30.00
417	Glen Myatt (Glenn)	70.00	35.00	21.00
418	Babe Herman	80.00	40.00	24.00
419	Frank Frisch	120.00	60.00	36.00
420	Tony Lazzeri	100.00	50.00	30.00
421	Paul Waner	100.00	50.00	30.00
422	Jimmy Wilson	70.00	35.00	21.00
423	Charles Grimm	70.00	35.00	21.00
424	Dick Bartell	70.00	35.00	21.00
----	Jimmy Fox (Foxx)	150.00	75.00	45.00
----	Roy Johnson	70.00	35.00	21.00
----	Pie Traynor	100.00	50.00	30.00

1909-11 El Principe de Gales Cigarettes

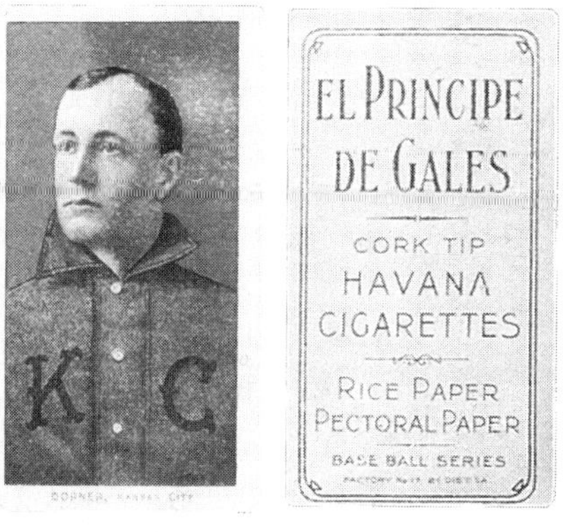

(See T206. Premium: +30%.)

1976 English's Chicken Baltimore Orioles Lids

It is uncertain whether the checklist presented here is complete. These 8-3/8" diameter fried chicken bucket lids are printed on heavy waxed cardboard in black-and-white. Cap logos have been airbrushed off. A few previous season's stats are printed to the left and right of the player photo.

		NM	EX	VG
Common Player:		4.00	2.00	1.20
(1)	Mike Cuellar	5.00	2.50	1.50
(2)	Ken Holtzman	4.00	2.00	1.20
(3)	Jim Palmer	12.00	6.00	3.50

1954 Esskay Hot Dogs Orioles

Measuring 2-1/4" x 3-1/2", the 1954 Esskay Hot Dogs set features the Baltimore Orioles. The unnumbered color cards were issued in panels of two on packages of hot dogs and are usually found with grease stains. The cards have waxed fronts with blank backs on a white stock. Complete boxes of Esskay Hot Dogs are scarce and command a price of 2-3 times greater than the single card values.

		NM	EX	VG
Complete Set (34):		4750.	2400.	1400.
Common Player:		150.00	75.00	45.00
(1)	Neil Berry	150.00	75.00	45.00
(2)	Michael Blyzka	150.00	75.00	45.00
(3)	Harry Brecheen	150.00	75.00	45.00
(4)	Gil Coan	150.00	75.00	45.00
(5)	Joe Coleman	150.00	75.00	45.00
(6)	Clinton Courtney	150.00	75.00	45.00
(7)	Charles E. Diering	150.00	75.00	45.00
(8)	Jimmie Dykes	150.00	75.00	45.00
(9)	Frank J. Fanovich	150.00	75.00	45.00
(10)	Howard Fox	150.00	75.00	45.00
(11)	Jim Fridley	150.00	75.00	45.00
(12)	Vinicio "Chico" Garcia	150.00	75.00	45.00
(13)	Jehosie Heard	350.00	175.00	105.00
(14)	Darrell Johnson	150.00	75.00	45.00
(15)	Bob Kennedy	150.00	75.00	45.00
(16)	Dick Kokos	150.00	75.00	45.00
(17)	Dave Koslo	150.00	75.00	45.00
(18)	Lou Kretlow	150.00	75.00	45.00
(19)	Richard D. Kryhoski	150.00	75.00	45.00
(20)	Don Larsen	250.00	125.00	75.00
(21)	Donald E. Lenhardt	150.00	75.00	45.00
(22)	Richard Littlefield	150.00	75.00	45.00
(23)	Sam Mele	150.00	75.00	45.00
(24)	Les Moss	150.00	75.00	45.00
(25)	Ray L. Murray	150.00	75.00	45.00
(26a)	"Bobo" Newsom (no stadium lights in background)	200.00	100.00	60.00
(26b)	"Bobo" Newson (stadium lights in background)	200.00	100.00	60.00
(27)	Tom Oliver	150.00	75.00	45.00
(28)	Duane Pillette	150.00	75.00	45.00
(29)	Francis M. Skaff	150.00	75.00	45.00
(30)	Marlin Stuart	150.00	75.00	45.00
(31)	Robert L. Turley	225.00	110.00	67.00
(32)	Eddie Waitkus	150.00	75.00	45.00
(33)	Vic Wertz	150.00	75.00	45.00
(34)	Robert G. Young	150.00	75.00	45.00

1955 Esskay Hot Dogs Orioles

For the second consecutive year, Esskay Meats placed baseball cards of Orioles players on their boxes of hot dogs. The unnumbered color cards measure 2-1/4" x 3-1/2" and can be distinguished from the previous year by their unwaxed fronts and blank gray backs. Many of the same photos from 1954 were used with only minor picture-cropping differences. For 1955, only one player card per box was printed. The space which was occupied by the second player card in 1954 carried a prize redemption coupon on 1955 boxes.

		NM	EX	VG
Complete Set (26):		3500.	1750.	1000.
Common Player:		150.00	75.00	45.00
(1)	Cal Abrams	150.00	75.00	45.00
(2)	Robert S. Alexander	150.00	75.00	45.00
(3)	Harry Byrd	150.00	75.00	45.00
(4)	Gil Coan	150.00	75.00	45.00
(5)	Joseph P. Coleman	150.00	75.00	45.00
(6)	William R. Cox	150.00	75.00	45.00
(7)	Charles E. Diering	150.00	75.00	45.00
(8)	Walter A. Evers	150.00	75.00	45.00
(9)	Don Johnson	150.00	75.00	45.00
(10)	Robert D. Kennedy	150.00	75.00	45.00
(11)	Lou Kretlow	150.00	75.00	45.00
(12)	Robert L. Kuzava	150.00	75.00	45.00
(13)	Fred Marsh	150.00	75.00	45.00
(14)	Charles Maxwell	150.00	75.00	45.00
(15)	Jimmie McDonald	150.00	75.00	45.00
(16)	Bill Miller	150.00	75.00	45.00
(17)	Willy Miranda	150.00	75.00	45.00
(18)	Raymond L. Moore	150.00	75.00	45.00
(19)	John Lester Moss	150.00	75.00	45.00
(20)	"Bobo" Newsom	150.00	75.00	45.00
(21)	Duane Pillette	150.00	75.00	45.00
(22)	Edward S. Waitkus	150.00	75.00	45.00
(23)	Harold W. Smith	150.00	75.00	45.00
(24)	Gus Triandos	150.00	75.00	45.00
(25)	Eugene R. Woodling	175.00	87.00	52.00
(26)	Robert G. Young	150.00	75.00	45.00

1977 Esso Hispanic Coins

Little is known of these coins, except that they were distributed in Puerto Rico. Even the sponsor, Esso Oil Co., is not mentioned anywhere on the pieces. Made of aluminum and 1-1/4" in diameter, coin fronts have a portrait of the player with his name above. Backs are in Spanish and have the player's position, team, height, weight, date and place of birth. The coins of Tony Perez and, to a lesser extent, Rod Carew are scarcer than the others. A person receiving a Perez coin was able to exchange it for a full tank of gas.

		NM	EX	VG
Complete Set (11):		160.00	80.00	48.00
Common Player:		6.00	3.00	1.75
(1)	Luis Aparicio	12.00	6.00	3.50
(2)	Rod Carew	36.00	18.00	11.00
(3)	Rico Carty	6.00	3.00	1.75
(4)	Cesar Cedeno	6.00	3.00	1.75
(5)	Orlando Cepeda	12.00	6.00	3.50
(6)	Mike Cuellar	6.00	3.00	1.75
(7)	Juan Marichal	12.00	6.00	3.50
(8)	Felix Millan	6.00	3.00	1.75
(9)	Tony Oliva	8.00	4.00	2.50
(10)	Tony Perez	70.00	35.00	21.00
(11)	Manny Sanguillen	6.00	3.00	1.75

1949 Eureka Sportstamps

The commissioner of baseball, president of the National League and 198 N.L. players are included in this issue. The stamps were issued on team sheets measuring 7-1/2" x 10", with individual stamps measuring 1-1/2" x 2". An album issued with the set provided short player biographies. The stamps feature colorized posed player action photos. At bottom is a yellow strip with the player's name, stamp number and copyright line. Stamps are numbered alphabetically within teams.

		NM	EX	VG
Complete Set (200):		1000.	500.00	300.00
Common Player:		5.50	2.75	1.75
Album w/mounted stamps:		300.00	150.00	90.00
1	Albert B. (Happy) Chandler	8.25	4.25	2.50
2	Ford Frick	6.75	3.50	2.00
3	Billy Southworth	5.50	2.75	1.75
4	Johnny Antonelli	5.50	2.75	1.75
5	Red Barrett	5.50	2.75	1.75
6	Clint Conaster	5.50	2.75	1.75
7	Alvin Dark	5.50	2.75	1.75
8	Bob Elliott	5.50	2.75	1.75
9	Glenn Elliott	5.50	2.75	1.75
10	Elbie Fletcher	5.50	2.75	1.75
11	Bob Hall	5.50	2.75	1.75
12	Jeff Heath	5.50	2.75	1.75
13	Bobby Hogue	5.50	2.75	1.75
14	Tommy Holmes	5.50	2.75	1.75
15	Al Lakeman	5.50	2.75	1.75
16	Phil Masi	5.50	2.75	1.75
17	Nelson Potter	5.50	2.75	1.75
18	Pete Reiser	9.00	4.50	2.75
19	Rick Rickert	5.50	2.75	1.75
20	Connie Ryan	5.50	2.75	1.75
21	Jim Russell	5.50	2.75	1.75
22	Johnny Sain	10.00	5.00	3.00
23	Bill Salkeld	5.50	2.75	1.75
24	Sibby Sisti	5.50	2.75	1.75
25	Warren Spahn	28.00	14.00	8.50
26	Eddie Stanky	5.50	2.75	1.75
27	Bill Voiselle	5.50	2.75	1.75
28	Bert Shotton	10.00	5.00	3.00
29	Jack Banta	10.00	5.00	3.00
30	Rex Barney	10.00	5.00	3.00
31	Ralph Branca	15.00	7.50	4.50
32	Tommy Brown	10.00	5.00	3.00
33	Roy Campanella	40.00	20.00	12.00
34	Billy Cox	10.00	5.00	3.00
35	Bruce Edwards	10.00	5.00	3.00
36	Carl Furillo	20.00	10.00	6.00
37	Joe Hatten	10.00	5.00	3.00
38	Gene Hermanski	10.00	5.00	3.00
39	Gil Hodges	22.00	11.00	6.50
40	Johnny Jorgensen	10.00	5.00	3.00
41	Lefty Martin	10.00	5.00	3.00
42	Mike McCormick	10.00	5.00	3.00
43	Eddie Miksis	10.00	5.00	3.00
44	Paul Minner	10.00	5.00	3.00
45	Sam Narron	10.00	5.00	3.00
46	Don Newcombe	20.00	10.00	6.00
47	Jake Pitler	10.00	5.00	3.00
48	Pee Wee Reese	35.00	17.50	10.50
49	Jackie Robinson	55.00	27.00	16.50
50	Duke Snider	45.00	22.00	13.50
51	Dick Whitman	10.00	5.00	3.00
52	Forrest Burgess	5.50	2.75	1.75
53	Phil Cavaretta	5.50	2.75	1.75
54	Bob Chipman	5.50	2.75	1.75
55	Walter Dubiel	5.50	2.75	1.75
56	Hank Edwards	5.50	2.75	1.75
57	Frankie Gustine	5.50	2.75	1.75
58	Hal Jeffcoat	5.50	2.75	1.75
59	Emil Kush	5.50	2.75	1.75
60	Doyle Lade	5.50	2.75	1.75
61	Dutch Leonard	5.50	2.75	1.75
62	Peanuts Lowrey	5.50	2.75	1.75
63	Gene Mauch	8.00	4.00	2.50
64	Cal McLish	5.50	2.75	1.75
65	Rube Novotney	5.50	2.75	1.75
66	Andy Pafko	5.50	2.75	1.75

67	Bob Ramozzotti	5.50	2.75	1.75
68	Herman Reich	5.50	2.75	1.75
69	Bob Rush	5.50	2.75	1.75
70	Johnny Schmitz	5.50	2.75	1.75
71	Bob Scheffing	5.50	2.75	1.75
72	Roy Smalley	5.50	2.75	1.75
73	Emil Verban	5.50	2.75	1.75
74	Al Walker	5.50	2.75	1.75
75	Harry Walker	5.50	2.75	1.75
76	Bucky Walters	5.50	2.75	1.75
77	Bob Adams	5.50	2.75	1.75
78	Ewell Blackwell	5.50	2.75	1.75
79	Jimmy Bloodworth	5.50	2.75	1.75
80	Walker Cooper	5.50	2.75	1.75
81	Tony Cuccinello	5.50	2.75	1.75
82	Jess Dobernic	5.50	2.75	1.75
83	Eddie Erautt	5.50	2.75	1.75
84	Frank Fanovich	5.50	2.75	1.75
85	Howie Fox	5.50	2.75	1.75
86	Grady Hatton	5.50	2.75	1.75
87	Homer Howell	5.50	2.75	1.75
88	Ted Kluszewski	20.00	10.00	6.00
89	Danny Litwhiler	5.50	2.75	1.75
90	Everett Lively	5.50	2.75	1.75
91	Lloyd Merriman	5.50	2.75	1.75
92	Phil Page	5.50	2.75	1.75
93	Kent Peterson	5.50	2.75	1.75
94	Ken Raffensberger	5.50	2.75	1.75
95	Luke Sewell	5.50	2.75	1.75
96	Virgil Stallcup	5.50	2.75	1.75
97	Johnny Vander Meer	10.00	5.00	3.00
98	Herman Wehmeier	5.50	2.75	1.75
99	Johnny Wyrostek	5.50	2.75	1.75
100	Benny Zientara	5.50	2.75	1.75
101	Leo Durocher	13.50	6.75	4.00
102	Hank Behrman	5.50	2.75	1.75
103	Augie Galan	5.50	2.75	1.75
104	Sid Gordon	5.50	2.75	1.75
105	Bert Haas	5.50	2.75	1.75
106	Andy Hansen	5.50	2.75	1.75
107	Clint Hartung	5.50	2.75	1.75
100	Kirby Higbe	5.50	2.75	1.75
109	George Hausman	5.50	2.75	1.75
110	Larry Jansen	5.50	2.75	1.75
111	Sheldon Jones	5.50	2.75	1.75
112	Monte Kennedy	5.50	2.75	1.75
113	Buddy Kerr	5.50	2.75	1.75
114	Dave Koslo	5.50	2.75	1.75
115	Joe Lafata	5.50	2.75	1.75
116	Whitey Lockman	5.50	2.75	1.75
117	Jack Lohrke	5.50	2.75	1.75
118	Willard Marshall	5.50	2.75	1.75
119	Bill Milne	5.50	2.75	1.75
120	Johnny Mize	15.00	7.50	4.50
121	Don Mueller	5.50	2.75	1.75
122	Ray Mueller	5.50	2.75	1.75
123	Bill Rigney	5.50	2.75	1.75
124	Bobby Thomson	8.00	4.00	2.50
125	Sam Webb	5.50	2.75	1.75
126	Wesley Westrum	5.50	2.75	1.75
127	Eddie Sawyer	5.50	2.75	1.75
128	Richie Ashburn	24.00	12.00	7.25
129	Benny Bengough	5.50	2.75	1.75
130	Charlie Bicknell	5.50	2.75	1.75
131	Buddy Blattner	5.50	2.75	1.75
132	Hank Borowy	5.50	2.75	1.75
133	Ralph Caballero	5.50	2.75	1.75
134	Blix Donnelly	5.50	2.75	1.75
135	Del Ennis	5.50	2.75	1.75
136	Granville Hamner	5.50	2.75	1.75
137	Ken Heintzelman	5.50	2.75	1.75
138	Stan Hollmig	5.50	2.75	1.75
139	Willie Jones	5.50	2.75	1.75
140	Jim Konstanty	5.50	2.75	1.75
141	Stan Lopata	5.50	2.75	1.75
142	Jackie Mayo	5.50	2.75	1.75
143	Bill Nicholson	5.50	2.75	1.75
144	Robin Roberts	22.00	11.00	6.50
145	Schoolboy Rowe	5.50	2.75	1.75
146	Andy Seminick	5.50	2.75	1.75
147	Ken Silvestri	5.50	2.75	1.75
148	Curt Simmons	5.50	2.75	1.75
149	Dick Sisler	5.50	2.75	1.75
150	Ken Trinkle	5.50	2.75	1.75
151	Eddie Waitkus	5.50	2.75	1.75
152	Bill Meyer	5.50	2.75	1.75
153	Monte Basgall	5.50	2.75	1.75
154	Eddie Bockman	5.50	2.75	1.75
155	Ernie Bonham	5.50	2.75	1.75
156	Hugh Casey	5.50	2.75	1.75
157	Pete Castiglione	5.50	2.75	1.75
158	Cliff Chambers	5.50	2.75	1.75
159	Murry Dickson	5.50	2.75	1.75
160	Ed Fitz Gerald	5.50	2.75	1.75
161	Les Fleming	5.50	2.75	1.75
162	Hal Gregg	5.50	2.75	1.75
163	Goldie Holt	5.50	2.75	1.75
164	Johnny Hopp	5.50	2.75	1.75
165	Ralph Kiner	22.00	11.00	6.50
166	Vic Lombardi	5.50	2.75	1.75
167	Clyde McCullough	5.50	2.75	1.75
168	Danny Murtaugh	5.50	2.75	1.75
169	Bill Posedel	5.50	2.75	1.75
170	Elmer Riddle	5.50	2.75	1.75
171	Stan Rojek	5.50	2.75	1.75
172	Rip Sewell	5.50	2.75	1.75
173	Eddie Stevens	5.50	2.75	1.75
174	Dixie Walker	5.50	2.75	1.75
175	Bill Werle	5.50	2.75	1.75
176	Wally Westlake	5.50	2.75	1.75
177	Eddie Dyer	5.50	2.75	1.75
178	Bill Baker	5.50	2.75	1.75
179	Al Brazle	5.50	2.75	1.75
180	Harry Brecheen	5.50	2.75	1.75
181	Chuck Diering	5.50	2.75	1.75
182	Joe Garagiola	13.50	6.75	4.00
183	Tom Galviano	5.50	2.75	1.75
184	Jim Hearn	5.50	2.75	1.75
185	Ken Johnson	5.50	2.75	1.75
186	Nippy Jones	5.50	2.75	1.75
187	Ed Kazak	5.50	2.75	1.75
188	Lou Klein	5.50	2.75	1.75
189	Marty Marion	5.50	2.75	1.75
190	George Munger	5.50	2.75	1.75
191	Stan Musial	40.00	20.00	12.00
192	Spike Nelson	5.50	2.75	1.75
193	Howie Pollet	5.50	2.75	1.75
194	Bill Reeder	5.50	2.75	1.75
195	Del Rice	5.50	2.75	1.75
196	Ed Sauer	5.50	2.75	1.75
197	Red Schoendienst	22.00	11.00	6.50
198	Enos Slaughter	22.00	11.00	6.50
199	Ted Wilks	5.50	2.75	1.75
200	Ray Yochim	5.50	2.75	1.75

1916 Everybody's

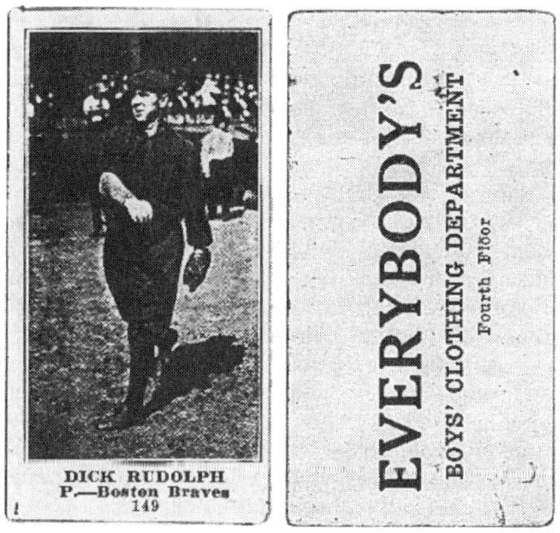

Where "Everybody's" department store was located is unknown, but in 1916 they chose to use baseball cards to promote their boy's wear department. The 2" x 3-1/2" black-and-white cards share the format and checklist with the much more common Sporting News version and many other regional advertisers. While Everybody's is one of the scarcest advertising backs to be found in this issue, the cards command only a small premium from type-card and superstar collectors.

(See 1916 Sporting News for checklist and price guide; Everybody's cards valued at 1.5X to 2X Sporting News Version.)

1921 Exhibits

The Exhibit Supply Company of Chicago issued the first in a long series of postcard-size (3-3/8" x 5-3/8") baseball cards in 1921. The Exhibit cards were commonly sold in "penny arcade" vending machines. The 1921 series consists of 64 cards and includes four players from each of the 16 major league teams. The cards feature black-and-white photos with the player's name printed in a fancy script. The player's position and team appear below the name in small, hand-lettered capital letters. American League is designated as "AM.L.," which can help differentiate the 1921 series from future years. Some of the cards contain white borders while others do not. All have blank backs. There are various spelling errors in the picture legends.

		NM	EX	VG
Complete Set (64):		4500.	2250.	1350.
Common Player:		40.00	20.00	12.00
(1)	Chas. B. Adams	40.00	20.00	12.00
(2)	Grover C. Alexander	100.00	50.00	30.00
(3)	David Bancroft	100.00	50.00	30.00
(4)	Geo. J. Burns	40.00	20.00	12.00
(5)	Owen Bush	40.00	20.00	12.00
(6)	Max J. Carey	100.00	50.00	30.00
(7)	Ty Cobb	565.00	282.00	169.00
(8)	Eddie T. Collins	100.00	50.00	30.00
(9)	John Collins	40.00	20.00	12.00
(10)	Stanley Coveleskie (Coveleski)	100.00	50.00	30.00
(11)	Walton E. Cruise	40.00	20.00	12.00
(12)	Jacob E. Daubert	40.00	20.00	12.00
(13)	George Dauss	40.00	20.00	12.00
(14)	Charles A. Deal	40.00	20.00	12.00
(15)	Joe A. Dugan	40.00	20.00	12.00
(16)	James Dykes	40.00	20.00	12.00
(17)	U.C. "Red" Faber	100.00	50.00	30.00
(18)	J.F. Fournier	40.00	20.00	12.00
(19)	Frank F. Frisch	100.00	50.00	30.00
(20)	W.L. Gardner	40.00	20.00	12.00
(21)	H.M. "Hank" Gowdy	40.00	20.00	12.00
(22)	Burleigh Grimes	100.00	50.00	30.00
(23)	Heinie Groh	40.00	20.00	12.00
(24)	Jesse Haines	100.00	50.00	30.00
(25)	Sam Harris (Stanley)	100.00	50.00	30.00
(26)	Walter L. Holke	40.00	20.00	12.00
(27)	Charles J. Hollicher (Hollocher)	40.00	20.00	12.00
(28)	Rogers Hornsby	125.00	62.00	37.00
(29)	James H. Johnson (Johnston)	40.00	20.00	12.00
(30)	Walter P. Johnson	350.00	175.00	105.00
(31)	Sam P. Jones	40.00	20.00	12.00
(32)	Geo. L. Kelly	100.00	50.00	30.00
(33)	Dick Kerr	40.00	20.00	12.00
(34)	William L. Killifer (Killefer)	40.00	20.00	12.00
(35)	Ed Konetchy	40.00	20.00	12.00
(36)	John "Doc" Lavan	40.00	20.00	12.00
(37)	Walter J. Maranville	100.00	50.00	30.00
(38)	Carl W. Mays	45.00	22.00	13.50
(39)	J. "Stuffy" McInnis	40.00	20.00	12.00
(40)	Rollie C. Naylor	40.00	20.00	12.00
(41)	A. Earl Neale (Earle)	50.00	25.00	15.00
(42)	Ivan M. Olsen	40.00	20.00	12.00
(43)	S.F. "Steve" O'Neil (O'Neill)	40.00	20.00	12.00
(44)	Robert (Roger) Peckinpaugh	40.00	20.00	12.00
(45)	Ralph "Cy" Perkins	40.00	20.00	12.00
(46)	Raymond R. Powell	40.00	20.00	12.00
(47)	Joe "Goldie" Rapp	40.00	20.00	12.00
(48)	Edgar S. Rice	100.00	50.00	30.00
(49)	Jimmy Ring	40.00	20.00	12.00
(50)	Geo. H. "Babe" Ruth	1000.	500.00	300.00
(51)	Ray W. Schalk	100.00	50.00	30.00
(52)	Wallie Schang	40.00	20.00	12.00
(53)	Everett Scott	40.00	20.00	12.00
(54)	H.S. Shanks (photo actually Wally Schang)	40.00	20.00	12.00
(55)	Urban Shocker	40.00	20.00	12.00
(56)	Geo. J. Sisler	100.00	50.00	30.00
(57)	Tris Speaker	200.00	100.00	60.00
(58)	John Tobin	40.00	20.00	12.00
(59)	Robt. Veach	40.00	20.00	12.00
(60)	Zack D. Wheat	100.00	50.00	30.00
(61)	Geo. B. Whitted	40.00	20.00	12.00
(62)	Cy Williams	40.00	20.00	12.00
(63)	Kenneth R. Williams	40.00	20.00	12.00
(64)	Ivy B. Wingo	40.00	20.00	12.00

1922 Exhibits

The Exhibit Supply Company continued the same 3-3/8" x 5-3/8" format in 1922 but doubled the number of cards in the series to 128, including eight players from each team. All but nine of the players who appeared in the 1921 series are pictured in the 1922 set, along with 74 new players. The cards again display black and white photos with blank backs. Some of the photos have white borders. The player's name appears in a plain script with the position and team below in small capital letters. American League is designated as "A.L." Again, there are several spelling errors and incorrect player identifications. In early printings the Earl Smith card actually pictured Brad Kocher. Only the 74 new additions are included in the checklist that follows.

		NM	EX	VG
Complete Set (74):		2750.	1350.	825.00
Common Player:		60.00	30.00	18.00
(1)	Jim Bagby	60.00	30.00	18.00
(2)	J. Frank Baker	80.00	40.00	24.00

(3)	Walter Barbare	60.00	30.00	18.00
(4)	Turner Barber	60.00	30.00	18.00
(5)	John Bassler	60.00	30.00	18.00
(6)	Carlson L. Bigbee (Carson)	60.00	30.00	18.00
(7)	Sam Bohne	60.00	30.00	18.00
(8)	Geo. Burns	60.00	30.00	18.00
(9)	George Burns	60.00	30.00	18.00
(10)	Jeo Bush (Joe)	50.00	25.00	15.00
(11)	Leon Cadore	60.00	30.00	18.00
(12)	Jim Caveney	60.00	30.00	18.00
(13)	Wilbur Cooper	60.00	30.00	18.00
(14)	George Cutshaw	60.00	30.00	18.00
(15)	Dave Danforth	60.00	30.00	18.00
(16)	Bill Doak	60.00	30.00	18.00
(17)	Joe Dugan	55.00	27.00	16.50
(18)	Pat Duncan	60.00	30.00	18.00
(19)	Howard Emke (Ehmke)	60.00	30.00	18.00
(20)	Wm. Evans (umpire)	80.00	40.00	24.00
(21)	Bib Falk (Bibb)	60.00	30.00	18.00
(22)	Dana Fillingin (Fillingim)	60.00	30.00	18.00
(23)	Ira Flagstead	60.00	30.00	18.00
(24)	Art Fletcher	60.00	30.00	18.00
(25)	Wally Gerber	60.00	30.00	18.00
(26)	Ray Grimes	60.00	30.00	18.00
(27)	Harry Heilman (Heilmann)	60.00	30.00	18.00
(28)	George Hildebrand (umpire)	80.00	40.00	24.00
(29)	Wibur Hubbell (Wilbert)	60.00	30.00	18.00
(30)	Bill Jacobson	60.00	30.00	18.00
(31)	E.R. Johnson	60.00	30.00	18.00
(32)	Joe Judge	60.00	30.00	18.00
(33)	Bill Klem (umpire)	80.00	40.00	24.00
(34)	Harry Liebold (Leibold)	60.00	30.00	18.00
(35)	Walter Mails	60.00	30.00	18.00
(36)	Geo. Maisel	60.00	30.00	18.00
(37)	Lee Meadows	60.00	30.00	18.00
(38)	Clyde Milam (Milan)	60.00	30.00	18.00
(39)	Ed (Bing) Miller	60.00	30.00	18.00
(40)	Hack Miller	60.00	30.00	18.00
(41)	George Moriarty (umpire)	60.00	30.00	18.00
(42)	Robert Muesel (Meusel)	55.00	27.00	16.50
(43)	Harry Myers	60.00	30.00	18.00
(44)	Arthur Nehf	60.00	30.00	18.00
(45)	Joe Oeschger	60.00	30.00	18.00
(46)	Geo. O'Neil	60.00	30.00	18.00
(47)	Roger Peckinpaugh	50.00	25.00	15.00
(48)	Val Picinich	60.00	30.00	18.00
(49)	Bill Piercy	60.00	30.00	18.00
(50)	Derrill Pratt	60.00	30.00	18.00
(51)	Jack Quinn	60.00	30.00	18.00
(52)	Walter Reuther (Ruether)	60.00	30.00	18.00
(53)	Charles Rigler (umpire)	60.00	30.00	18.00
(54)	Eppa Rixey	80.00	40.00	24.00
(55)	Chas. Robertson	60.00	30.00	18.00
(56)	Everett Scott	60.00	30.00	18.00
(57)	Earl Sheely	60.00	30.00	18.00
(58)	Earl Smith (portrait)	60.00	30.00	18.00
(59)	Earl Smith (standing) (photo actually Brad Kocher)	60.00	30.00	18.00
(60)	Elmer Smith	60.00	30.00	18.00
(61)	Jack Smith (photo actually Jimmy Smith)	60.00	30.00	18.00
(62)	Sherrod Smith	60.00	30.00	18.00
(63)	Frank Snyder	60.00	30.00	18.00
(64)	Allan Sothoron (Allen)	60.00	30.00	18.00
(65)	Arnold Statz	60.00	30.00	18.00
(66)	Milton Stock	60.00	30.00	18.00
(67)	James Tierney	60.00	30.00	18.00
(68)	George Toporcer	60.00	30.00	18.00
(69)	Clarence (Tilly) Walker	60.00	30.00	18.00
(70)	Curtis Walker	60.00	30.00	18.00
(71)	Aaron Ward	60.00	30.00	18.00
(72)	Joe Wood	50.00	25.00	15.00
(73)	Moses Yellowhorse	55.00	27.00	16.50
(74)	Ross Young (Youngs)	80.00	40.00	24.00

1922 Eastern Exhibit Supply Co.

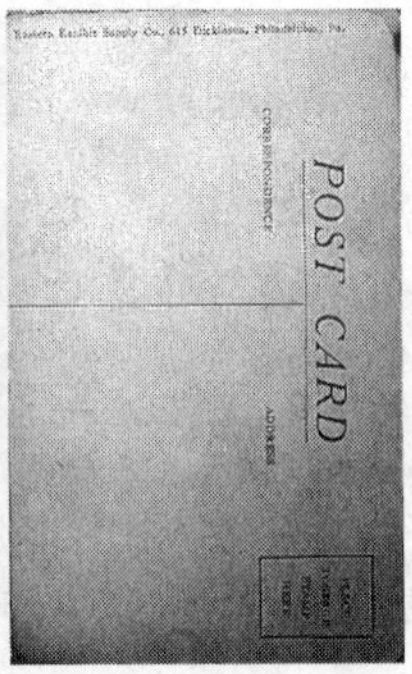

Postcard-style backs differentiate these cards from the more common Exhibit Supply Co., cards from Chicago. This 20-card series was produced by a Philadelphia company, although on some cards, the Eastern Exhibit copyright line on back can be found blacked out and that of the Chicago company printed beneath it. The black-and-white cards measure 3-3/8" x 5-5/8".

		NM	EX	VG
Complete Set (20):		2600.	1300.	800.00
Common Player:		45.00	22.00	13.50
(1)	Grover Alexander	100.00	50.00	30.00
(2)	Dave Bancroft	75.00	37.00	22.00
(3)	Jesse Barnes	45.00	22.00	13.50
(4)	Joe Bush	45.00	22.00	13.50
(5)	Ty Cobb	600.00	300.00	180.00
(6)	Eddie Collins	75.00	37.00	22.00
(7)	Urban Faber	75.00	37.00	22.00
(8)	Clarence Galloway	45.00	22.00	13.50
(9)	Heinie Groh	45.00	22.00	13.50
(10)	Harry Heilmann	75.00	37.00	22.00
(11)	Charlie Hollocher	45.00	22.00	13.50
(12)	Rogers Hornsby	100.00	50.00	30.00
(13)	Walter Johnson	250.00	125.00	75.00
(14)	Eddie Rommel	45.00	22.00	13.50
(15)	Babe Ruth	1200.	600.00	360.00
(16)	Ray Schalk	90.00	45.00	27.00
(17)	Wallie Schang	45.00	22.00	13.50
(18)	Tris Speaker	100.00	50.00	30.00
(19)	Zach Wheat	90.00	45.00	27.00
(20)	Kenneth Williams	45.00	22.00	13.50

1923-24 Exhibits

The Exhibit cards for 1923 and 1924 are generally collected as a single 128-card series. The format remained basically the same as the previous year, 3-3/8" x 5-3/8", with black-and-white photos (some surrounded by a white border) and blank backs. The player's name is again shown in a plain script with the position and team printed below in a small, square-block type style. Many of the same photos were used from previous years, although some are cropped differently, and some players have new team designations, background changes, team emblems removed, borders added or taken away, and other minor changes. Fifty-eight new cards are featured, including 38 players pictured for the first time in an Exhibit set. Only the 58 new cards are included in the checklist that follows.

		NM	EX	VG
Complete Set (58):		4250.	2100.	1250.
Common Player:		75.00	37.50	22.00
(1)	Clyde Barnhart	75.00	37.50	22.00
(2)	Ray Blades	75.00	37.50	22.00
(3)	James Bottomley	125.00	62.00	37.00
(4)	George Burns	75.00	37.50	22.00
(5)	Dan Clark	75.00	37.50	22.00
(6)	Bill Doak	75.00	37.50	22.00
(7)	Joe Dugan	75.00	37.50	22.00
(8)	Howard J. Ehmke	75.00	37.50	22.00
(9)	Ira Flagstead	75.00	37.50	22.00
(10)	J.F. Fournier	75.00	37.50	22.00
(11)	Howard Freigan (Freigau)	75.00	37.50	22.00
(12)	C.E. Galloway	75.00	37.50	22.00
(13)	Joe Genewich	75.00	37.50	22.00
(14)	Mike Gonzales (Gonzalez)	90.00	45.00	27.00
(15)	H.M. "Hank" Gowdy	75.00	37.50	22.00
(16)	Charles Grimm	75.00	37.50	22.00
(17)	Heinie Groh	75.00	37.50	22.00
(18)	Chas. L. Harnett (Hartnett)	125.00	62.00	37.00
(19)	George Harper	75.00	37.50	22.00
(20)	Slim Harris (Harriss)	75.00	37.50	22.00
(21)	Clifton Heathcote	75.00	37.50	22.00
(22)	Andy High	75.00	37.50	22.00
(23)	Walter L. Holke	75.00	37.50	22.00
(24)	Charles D. Jamieson	75.00	37.50	22.00
(25)	Willie Kamm	75.00	37.50	22.00
(26)	Tony Kaufmann	75.00	37.50	22.00
(27)	Dudley Lee	75.00	37.50	22.00
(28)	Harry Liebold (Leibold)	75.00	37.50	22.00
(29)	Aldofo Luque	75.00	37.50	22.00
(30)	W.C. (Wid) Matthews	75.00	37.50	22.00
(31)	John J. McGraw	125.00	62.00	37.00
(32)	J. "Stuffy" McInnis	75.00	37.50	22.00
(33)	Johnny Morrison	75.00	37.50	22.00
(34)	John A. Mostil	75.00	37.50	22.00
(35)	J.F. O'Neill (should be S.F.)	75.00	37.50	22.00
(36)	Ernest Padgett	75.00	37.50	22.00
(37)	Val Picinich	75.00	37.50	22.00
(38)	Bill Piercy	75.00	37.50	22.00
(39)	Herman Pillette	75.00	37.50	22.00
(40)	Wallie Pipp	90.00	45.00	27.00
(41)	Raymond R. Powell	75.00	37.50	22.00
(42)	Del. Pratt	75.00	37.50	22.00
(43)	E.E. Rigney	75.00	37.50	22.00
(44)	Eddie Rommel	75.00	37.50	22.00
(45)	Geo. H. "Babe" Ruth	775.00	387.00	232.00
(46)	Muddy Ruel	75.00	37.50	22.00
(47)	J.H. Sand	75.00	37.50	22.00
(48)	Henry Severeid	75.00	37.50	22.00
(49)	Joseph Sewell	125.00	62.00	37.00
(50)	Al. Simmons	125.00	62.00	37.00
(51)	R.E. Smith	75.00	37.50	22.00
(52)	Sherrod Smith	75.00	37.50	22.00
(53)	Casey Stengel	150.00	75.00	45.00
(54)	J.R. Stevenson (Stephenson)	75.00	37.50	22.00
(55)	James Tierney	75.00	37.50	22.00
(56)	Robt. Veach	75.00	37.50	22.00
(57)	L. Woodall	75.00	37.50	22.00
(58)	Russell G. Wrighstone	75.00	37.50	22.00

1925 Exhibits

The 1925 series of Exhibits contains 128 unnumbered cards, each measuring 3-3/8" x 5-3/8". The player's name (in all capital letters), position and team (along with a line reading "Made in U.S.A.) are printed in a small white box in a lower corner of the card. Most of the photos are vertical, however a few are horizontal. There are several misspellings in the set. Lou Gehrig's first baseball card appears in this issue. The cards are listed here in alphabetical order.

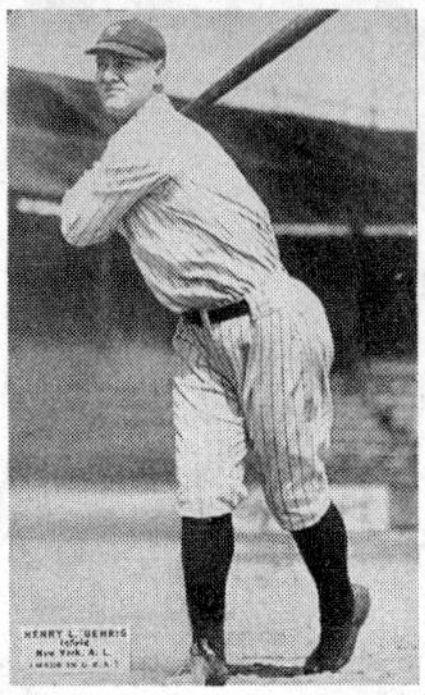

		NM	EX	VG
Complete Set (128):		10000.	5000.	3000.
Common Player:		60.00	30.00	18.00
(1)	Sparky Adams	60.00	30.00	18.00
(2)	Grover C. Alexander	90.00	45.00	27.00
(3)	David Bancroft	90.00	45.00	27.00
(4)	Jesse Barnes	60.00	30.00	18.00
(5)	John Bassler	60.00	30.00	18.00
(6)	Lester Bell	60.00	30.00	18.00
(7)	Lawrence Benton	60.00	30.00	18.00
(8)	Carson Bigbee	60.00	30.00	18.00
(9)	Max Bishop	60.00	30.00	18.00
(10)	Raymond Blates (Blades)	60.00	30.00	18.00
(11)	Oswald Bluege	60.00	30.00	18.00
(12)	James Bottomly (Bottomley)	90.00	45.00	27.00
(13)	Raymond Bressler	60.00	30.00	18.00
(14)	John Brooks	60.00	30.00	18.00
(15)	Maurice Burrus	60.00	30.00	18.00
(16)	Max Carey	90.00	45.00	27.00
(17)	Tyrus Cobb	750.00	375.00	225.00
(18)	Eddie Collins	90.00	45.00	27.00
(19)	Stanley Coveleski	90.00	45.00	27.00
(20)	Hugh M. Critz	60.00	30.00	18.00
(21)	Hazen Cuyler	90.00	45.00	27.00
(22)	George Dauss	60.00	30.00	18.00
(23)	I.M. Davis	60.00	30.00	18.00
(24)	John H. DeBerry	60.00	30.00	18.00
(25)	Art Decatur	60.00	30.00	18.00
(26)	Peter Donohue	60.00	30.00	18.00
(27)	Charles Dressen	60.00	30.00	18.00
(28)	James J. Dykes	60.00	30.00	18.00
(29)	Howard Ehmke	60.00	30.00	18.00
(30)	Bib Falk (Bibb)	60.00	30.00	18.00
(31)	Wilson Fewster	60.00	30.00	18.00
(32)	Max Flack	60.00	30.00	18.00
(33)	Ira Flagstead	60.00	30.00	18.00
(34)	Jacques F. Fournier	60.00	30.00	18.00
(35)	Howard Freigau	60.00	30.00	18.00
(36)	Frank Frisch	90.00	45.00	27.00
(37)	Henry L. Gehrig	3000.	1500.	900.00
(38)	Joseph Genewich	60.00	30.00	18.00
(39)	Walter Gerber	60.00	30.00	18.00
(40)	Frank Gibson	60.00	30.00	18.00
(41)	Leon Goslin	90.00	45.00	27.00
(42)	George Grantham	60.00	30.00	18.00
(43)	Samuel Gray	60.00	30.00	18.00
(44)	Burleigh A. Grimes	90.00	45.00	27.00
(45)	Charles Grimm	60.00	30.00	18.00
(46)	Heine Groh (Heinie)	60.00	30.00	18.00
(47)	Samuel Hale	60.00	30.00	18.00
(48)	George Harper	60.00	30.00	18.00
(49)	David Harris	60.00	30.00	18.00
(50)	Stanley Harris	90.00	45.00	27.00
(51)	Leo Hartnett	90.00	45.00	27.00
(52)	Nelson Hawks	60.00	30.00	18.00
(53)	Harry Heilmann	90.00	45.00	27.00
(54)	Walter Henline	60.00	30.00	18.00
(55)	Walter Holke	60.00	30.00	18.00
(56)	Harry Hooper	90.00	45.00	27.00
(57)	Rogers Hornsby	100.00	50.00	30.00
(58)	Wilbur Hubbell	60.00	30.00	18.00
(59)	Travis C. Jackson	90.00	45.00	27.00
(60)	William Jacobson	60.00	30.00	18.00
(61)	Charles Jamieson	60.00	30.00	18.00
(62)	James H. Johnson (Johnston)	60.00	30.00	18.00
(63)	Walter Johnson	185.00	92.00	55.00
(64)	Joseph Judge	60.00	30.00	18.00
(65)	Willie Kamm	60.00	30.00	18.00
(66)	Ray Kremer	60.00	30.00	18.00
(67)	Walter Lutzke	60.00	30.00	18.00
(68)	Walter Maranville	90.00	45.00	27.00
(69)	John ("Stuffy") McInnes (McInnis)	60.00	30.00	18.00
(70)	Martin McManus	60.00	30.00	18.00
(71)	Earl McNeely	60.00	30.00	18.00
(72)	Emil Meusel	60.00	30.00	18.00
(73)	Edmund (Bing) Miller	60.00	30.00	18.00
(74)	John Mokan	60.00	30.00	18.00
(75)	Clarence Mueller	60.00	30.00	18.00
(76)	Robert W. Muesel (Meusel)	75.00	37.00	22.00
(77)	Glenn Myatt	60.00	30.00	18.00
(78)	Arthur Nehf	60.00	30.00	18.00
(79)	George O'Neil	60.00	30.00	18.00
(80)	Frank O'Rourke	60.00	30.00	18.00
(81)	Ralph Perkins	60.00	30.00	18.00
(82)	Valentine Picinich	60.00	30.00	18.00
(83)	Walter C. Pipp	60.00	30.00	18.00

(84)	John Quinn	60.00	30.00	18.00
(85)	Emory Rigney	60.00	30.00	18.00
(86)	Eppa Rixey	90.00	45.00	27.00
(87)	Edwin Rommel	60.00	30.00	18.00
(88)	Ed (Edd) Roush	90.00	45.00	27.00
(89)	Harold Ruel (Herold)	60.00	30.00	18.00
(90)	Charles Ruffing	90.00	45.00	27.00
(91)	George H. "Babe" Ruth	1250.	625.00	375.00
(92)	John Sand	60.00	30.00	18.00
(93)	Henry Severid (Severeid)	60.00	30.00	18.00
(94)	Joseph Sewell	90.00	45.00	27.00
(95)	Ray Shalk (Schalk)	90.00	45.00	27.00
(96)	Walter H. Shang (Schang)	60.00	30.00	18.00
(97)	J.R. Shawkey	60.00	30.00	18.00
(98)	Earl Sheely	60.00	30.00	18.00
(99)	William Sherdell (Sherdel)	60.00	30.00	18.00
(100)	Urban J. Shocker	60.00	30.00	18.00
(101)	George Sissler (Sisler)	90.00	45.00	27.00
(102)	Earl Smith	60.00	30.00	18.00
(103)	Sherrod Smith	60.00	30.00	18.00
(104)	Frank Snyder	60.00	30.00	18.00
(105)	Wm. H. Southworth	60.00	30.00	18.00
(106)	Tristram Speaker	90.00	45.00	27.00
(107)	Milton J. Stock	60.00	30.00	18.00
(108)	Homer Summa	60.00	30.00	18.00
(109)	William Terry	90.00	45.00	27.00
(110)	Hollis Thurston	60.00	30.00	18.00
(111)	John Tobin	60.00	30.00	18.00
(112)	Philip Todt	60.00	30.00	18.00
(113)	George Torporcer (Toporcer)	60.00	30.00	18.00
(114)	Harold Traynor	90.00	45.00	27.00
(115)	A.C. "Dazzy" Vance	90.00	45.00	27.00
(116)	Robert Veach (photo actually Ernest Vache)	60.00	30.00	18.00
(117)	William Wambsganss	60.00	30.00	18.00
(118)	Aaron Ward	60.00	30.00	18.00
(119)	A.J. Weis	60.00	30.00	18.00
(120)	Frank Welch	60.00	30.00	18.00
(121)	Zack Wheat	90.00	45.00	27.00
(122)	Fred Williams	60.00	30.00	18.00
(123)	Kenneth Williams	60.00	30.00	18.00
(124)	Ernest Wingard	60.00	30.00	18.00
(125)	Ivy Wingo	60.00	30.00	18.00
(126)	Al Wings (Wingo)	60.00	30.00	18.00
(127)	Larry Woodall	60.00	30.00	18.00
(128)	Glen Wright (Glenn)	60.00	30.00	18.00

1926 Exhibits

The 1926 Exhibit cards are the same size (3-3/8" x 5-3/8") as previous Exhibit issues but are easily distinguished because of their blue-gray color. The set consists of 128 cards, 91 of which are identical to the photos in the 1925 series. The 37 new photos do not include the boxed caption used in 1925. There are several errors in the 1926 set: The photos of Hunnefield and Thomas are transposed; Bischoff's card identifies him as playing for Boston, N.L. (rather than A.L.) and the photo of Galloway is reversed. The cards are unnumbered and are listed here alphabetically.

		NM	EX	VG
Complete Set (128):		7750.	3750.	2200.
Common Player:		60.00	30.00	18.00
(1)	Sparky Adams	60.00	30.00	18.00
(2)	David Bancroft	90.00	45.00	27.00
(3)	John Bassler	60.00	30.00	18.00
(4)	Lester Bell	60.00	30.00	18.00
(5)	John M. Bentley	60.00	30.00	18.00
(6)	Lawrence Benton	60.00	30.00	18.00
(7)	Carson Bigbee	60.00	30.00	18.00
(8)	George Bischoff	60.00	30.00	18.00
(9)	Max Bishop	60.00	30.00	18.00
(10)	J. Fred Blake	60.00	30.00	18.00
(11)	Ted Blankenship	60.00	30.00	18.00
(12)	Raymond Blates (Blades)	60.00	30.00	18.00
(13)	Lucerne A. Blue (Luzerne)	60.00	30.00	18.00
(14)	Oswald Bluege	60.00	30.00	18.00
(15)	James Bottomly (Bottomley)	90.00	45.00	27.00
(16)	Raymond Bressler	60.00	30.00	18.00
(17)	Geo. H. Burns	60.00	30.00	18.00
(18)	Maurice Burrus	60.00	30.00	18.00
(19)	John Butler	60.00	30.00	18.00
(20)	Max Carey	90.00	45.00	27.00
(21)	Tyrus Cobb	750.00	375.00	225.00
(22)	Eddie Collins	90.00	45.00	27.00
(23)	Patrick T. Collins	60.00	30.00	18.00
(24)	Earl B. Combs (Earle)	90.00	45.00	27.00
(25)	James E. Cooney	60.00	30.00	18.00
(26)	Stanley Coveleski	90.00	45.00	27.00
(27)	Hugh M. Critz	60.00	30.00	18.00
(28)	Hazen Cuyler	90.00	45.00	27.00
(29)	George Dauss	60.00	30.00	18.00
(30)	Peter Donohue	60.00	30.00	18.00
(31)	Charles Dressen	60.00	30.00	18.00
(32)	James J. Dykes	60.00	30.00	18.00
(33)	Bib Falk (Bibb)	60.00	30.00	18.00
(34)	Edward S. Farrell	60.00	30.00	18.00
(35)	Wilson Fewster	60.00	30.00	18.00
(36)	Ira Flagstead	60.00	30.00	18.00
(37)	Howard Freigau	60.00	30.00	18.00
(38)	Bernard Friberg	60.00	30.00	18.00
(39)	Frank Frisch	90.00	45.00	27.00
(40)	Jacques F. Furnier (Fournier)	60.00	30.00	18.00
(41)	Joseph Galloway (Clarence)	60.00	30.00	18.00
(42)	Henry L. Gehrig	900.00	450.00	270.00
(43)	Charles Gehringer	90.00	45.00	27.00
(44)	Joseph Genewich	60.00	30.00	18.00
(45)	Walter Gerber	60.00	30.00	18.00
(46)	Leon Goslin	90.00	45.00	27.00
(47)	George Grantham	60.00	30.00	18.00
(48)	Burleigh A. Grimes	90.00	45.00	27.00
(49)	Charles Grimm	60.00	30.00	18.00
(50)	Fred Haney	60.00	30.00	18.00
(51)	Wm. Hargrave	60.00	30.00	18.00
(52)	George Harper	60.00	30.00	18.00
(53)	Stanley Harris	90.00	45.00	27.00
(54)	Leo Hartnett	90.00	45.00	27.00
(55)	Joseph Hauser	60.00	30.00	18.00
(56)	C.E. Heathcote	60.00	30.00	18.00
(57)	Harry Heilmann	90.00	45.00	27.00
(58)	Walter Henline	60.00	30.00	18.00
(59)	Ramon Herrera	60.00	30.00	18.00
(60)	Andrew A. High	60.00	30.00	18.00
(61)	Rogers Hornsby	100.00	50.00	30.00
(62)	Clarence Huber	60.00	30.00	18.00
(63)	Wm. Hunnefield (photo actually Tommy Thomas)	60.00	30.00	18.00
(64)	William Jacobson	60.00	30.00	18.00
(65)	Walter Johnson	175.00	87.00	52.00
(66)	Joseph Judge	60.00	30.00	18.00
(67)	Willie Kamm	60.00	30.00	18.00
(68)	Ray Kremer	60.00	30.00	18.00
(69)	Anthony Lazzeri	90.00	45.00	27.00
(70)	Frederick Lindstrom	90.00	45.00	27.00
(71)	Walter Lutzke	60.00	30.00	18.00
(72)	John Makan (Mokan)	60.00	30.00	18.00
(73)	Walter Maranville	90.00	45.00	27.00
(74)	Martin McManus	60.00	30.00	18.00
(75)	Earl McNeely	60.00	30.00	18.00
(76)	Hugh A. McQuillan	60.00	30.00	18.00
(77)	Douglas McWeeny	60.00	30.00	18.00
(78)	Oscar Melillo	60.00	30.00	18.00
(79)	Edmund (Bind) (Bing) Miller	60.00	30.00	18.00
(80)	Clarence Mueller	60.00	30.00	18.00
(81)	Robert W. Muesel (Meusel)	75.00	37.00	22.00
(82)	Joseph W. Munson	60.00	30.00	18.00
(83)	Emil Musel (Meusel)	60.00	30.00	18.00
(84)	Glenn Myatt	60.00	30.00	18.00
(85)	Bernie F. Neis	60.00	30.00	18.00
(86)	Robert O'Farrell	60.00	30.00	18.00
(87)	George O'Neil	60.00	30.00	18.00
(88)	Frank O'Rourke	60.00	30.00	18.00
(89)	Ralph Perkins	60.00	30.00	18.00
(90)	Walter C. Pipp	60.00	30.00	18.00
(91)	Emory Rigney	60.00	30.00	18.00
(92)	James J. Ring	60.00	30.00	18.00
(93)	Eppa Rixey	90.00	45.00	27.00
(94)	Edwin Rommel	60.00	30.00	18.00
(95)	Ed. Roush	90.00	45.00	27.00
(96)	Harold Ruel (Herold)	60.00	30.00	18.00
(97)	Charles Ruffing	90.00	45.00	27.00
(98)	Geo. H. "Babe" Ruth	1000.	500.00	300.00
(99)	John Sand	60.00	30.00	18.00
(100)	Joseph Sewell	90.00	45.00	27.00
(101)	Ray Shalk (Schalk)	90.00	45.00	27.00
(102)	J.R. Shawkey	60.00	30.00	18.00
(103)	Earl Sheely	60.00	30.00	18.00
(104)	William Sherdell (Sherdel)	60.00	30.00	18.00
(105)	Urban J. Shocker	60.00	30.00	18.00
(106)	George Sissler (Sisler)	90.00	45.00	27.00
(107)	Earl Smith	60.00	30.00	18.00
(108)	Sherrod Smith	60.00	30.00	18.00
(109)	Frank Snyder	60.00	30.00	18.00
(110)	Tristram Speaker	100.00	50.00	30.00
(111)	Fred Spurgeon	60.00	30.00	18.00
(112)	Homer Summa	60.00	30.00	18.00
(113)	Edward Taylor	60.00	30.00	18.00
(114)	J. Taylor	60.00	30.00	18.00
(115)	William Terry	90.00	45.00	27.00
(116)	Hollis Thurston	60.00	30.00	18.00
(117)	Philip Todt	60.00	30.00	18.00
(118)	George Torporcer (Toporcer)	60.00	30.00	18.00
(119)	Harold Traynor	90.00	45.00	27.00
(120)	Wm. Wambsganss	60.00	30.00	18.00
(121)	John Warner	60.00	30.00	18.00
(122)	Zach Wheat	90.00	45.00	27.00
(123)	Kenneth Williams	60.00	30.00	18.00
(124)	Ernest Wingard	60.00	30.00	18.00
(125)	Fred Wingfield	00.00	30.00	18.00
(126)	Ivy Wingo	60.00	30.00	18.00
(127)	Glen Wright (Glenn)	60.00	30.00	18.00
(128)	Russell Wrightstone	60.00	30.00	18.00

1927 Exhibits

The Exhibit Supply Company issued a set of 64 cards in 1927, each measuring 3-3/8" x 5-3/8". The set can be identified from earlier issues by its light green tint. The player's name and team appear in capital letters in one lower corner, while "Ex. Sup. Co., Chgo." and "Made in U.S.A." appear in the other. All 64 photos used in the 1927 set were borrowed from previous issues, but 13 players are listed with new teams. There are several misspellings and other labeling errors in the set. The unnumbered cards are listed here in alphabetical order.

		NM	EX	VG
Complete Set (64):		6500.	3250.	1950.
Common Player:		60.00	30.00	18.00
(1)	Sparky Adams	60.00	30.00	18.00
(2)	Grover C. Alexander	100.00	50.00	30.00
(3)	David Bancroft	90.00	45.00	27.00
(4)	John Bassler	60.00	30.00	18.00
(5)	John M. Bentley (middle initial actually N.)	60.00	30.00	18.00
(6)	Fred Blankenship (Ted)	60.00	30.00	18.00
(7)	James Bottomly (Bottomley)	90.00	45.00	27.00
(8)	Raymond Bressler	60.00	30.00	18.00
(9)	Geo. H. Burns	60.00	30.00	18.00
(10)	John Buttler (Butler)	60.00	30.00	18.00
(11)	Tyrus Cobb	950.00	475.00	285.00
(12)	Eddie Collins	90.00	45.00	27.00
(13)	Hazen Cuyler	90.00	45.00	27.00
(14)	George Daus (Dauss)	60.00	30.00	18.00
(15)	A.R. Decatur	60.00	30.00	18.00
(16)	Wilson Fewster	60.00	30.00	18.00
(17)	Ira Flagstead	60.00	30.00	18.00
(18)	Henry L. Gehrig	950.00	475.00	285.00
(19)	Charles Gehringer	90.00	45.00	27.00
(20)	Joseph Genewich	60.00	30.00	18.00
(21)	Leon Goslin	90.00	45.00	27.00
(22)	Burleigh A. Grimes	90.00	45.00	27.00
(23)	Charles Grimm	60.00	30.00	18.00
(24)	Fred Haney	60.00	30.00	18.00
(25)	Wm. Hargrave	60.00	30.00	18.00
(26)	George Harper	60.00	30.00	18.00
(27)	Leo Hartnett	90.00	45.00	27.00
(28)	Clifton Heathcote	60.00	30.00	18.00
(29)	Harry Heilman (Heillmann)	90.00	45.00	27.00
(30)	Walter Henline	60.00	30.00	18.00
(31)	Andrew High	60.00	30.00	18.00
(32)	Rogers Hornsby	150.00	75.00	45.00
(33)	Wm. Hunnefield (photo actually Tommy Thomas)	60.00	30.00	18.00
(34)	Walter Johnson	250.00	125.00	75.00
(35)	Willie Kamm	60.00	30.00	18.00
(36)	Ray Kremer	60.00	30.00	18.00
(37)	Anthony Lazzeri	90.00	45.00	27.00
(38)	Fredrick Lindstrom (Frederick)	90.00	45.00	27.00
(39)	Walter Lutzke	60.00	30.00	18.00
(40)	John "Stuffy" McInnes (McInnis)	60.00	30.00	18.00
(41)	John Mokan	60.00	30.00	18.00
(42)	Robert W. Muesel (Meusel)	60.00	30.00	18.00
(43)	Glenn Myatt	60.00	30.00	18.00
(44)	Bernie Neis	60.00	30.00	18.00
(45)	Robert O'Farrell	60.00	30.00	18.00
(46)	Walter C. Pipp	80.00	40.00	24.00
(47)	Eppa Rixey	90.00	45.00	27.00
(48)	Harold Ruel (Herold)	60.00	30.00	18.00
(49)	Geo. H. "Babe" Ruth	1200.	600.00	360.00
(50)	Ray Schalk	90.00	45.00	27.00
(51)	George Sissler (Sisler)	90.00	45.00	27.00
(52)	Earl Smith	60.00	30.00	18.00
(53)	Wm. H. Southworth	60.00	30.00	18.00
(54)	Tristam Speaker (Tristram)	150.00	75.00	45.00
(55)	J. Taylor	60.00	30.00	18.00
(56)	Philip Todt	60.00	30.00	18.00
(57)	Harold Traynor	90.00	45.00	27.00
(58)	William Wambsganns (Wambsganss)	60.00	30.00	18.00
(59)	Zach Wheat	90.00	45.00	27.00
(60)	Kenneth Williams	60.00	30.00	18.00
(61)	Ernest Wingard	60.00	30.00	18.00
(62)	Fred Wingfield	60.00	30.00	18.00
(63)	Ivy Wingo	60.00	30.00	18.00
(64)	Russell Wrightstone	60.00	30.00	18.00

1927-29 Postcard-back Exhibits

Probably issued in the Philadelphia area. these cards can be found with either plain or, more commonly, with a postcard-back which includes the legend: "Not to be used in Exhibit machines." The fronts are borderless photos which generally have the player's name, team and league designation printed thereon, though several variations in style have been noted. Cards can be found printed in any one of several different colors, and some or all players can be found in more than one color. Card size is about 3-3/8" x 5-3/8". The checklist below has been arranged alphabetically and is probably incomplete.

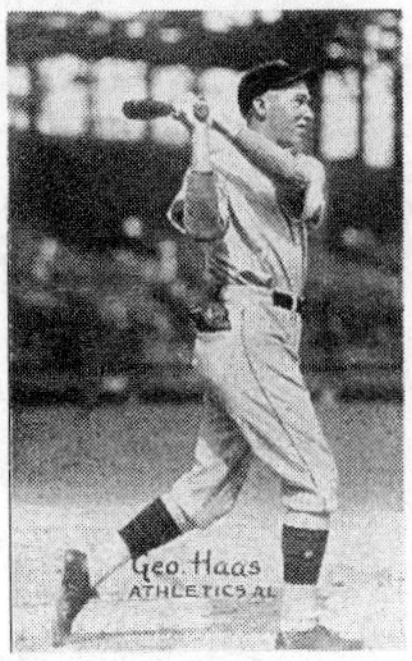

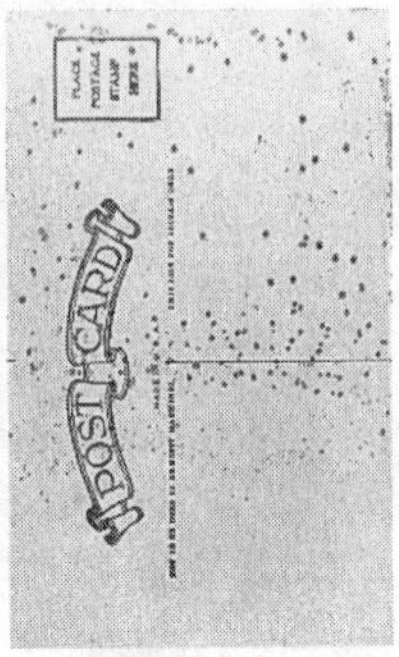

		NM	EX	VG
Complete Set (40):		5850.	2925.	1750.
Common Player:		50.00	25.00	15.00
(1)	Virgie Barnes	50.00	25.00	15.00
(2)	Jim Bottomley	100.00	50.00	30.00
(3)	Ty Cobb	800.00	400.00	240.00
(4)	Mickey Cochrane	100.00	50.00	30.00
(5)	Urban Faber	100.00	50.00	30.00
(6)	Jimmy Foxx (Jimmie)	125.00	62.00	37.00
(7)	Frank Frisch	100.00	50.00	30.00
(8)	Lou Gehrig	900.00	450.00	270.00
(9)	Lefty Grove	100.00	50.00	30.00
(10)	George Haas	50.00	25.00	15.00
(11)	Stanley Harris	100.00	50.00	30.00
(12)	Charlie Hartnett	100.00	50.00	30.00
(13)	Harry Heilmann	100.00	50.00	30.00
(14)	Rogers Hornsby	125.00	62.00	37.00
(15)	Walter Johnson	300.00	150.00	90.00
(16)	Joe Judge	50.00	25.00	15.00
(17)	Chuck Klein	100.00	50.00	30.00
(18)	Hugh McQuillan	50.00	25.00	15.00
(19)	Bob Meusel	65.00	32.00	19.50
(20)	Bing Miller	50.00	25.00	15.00
(21)	Lefty O'Doul	75.00	37.00	22.00
(22)	Roger Peckinpaugh	50.00	25.00	15.00
(23)	Ralph Pinelli	50.00	25.00	15.00
(24)	Walter Pipp	75.00	37.00	22.00
(25)	Jimmy Ring	50.00	25.00	15.00
(26)	Eppa Rixey	100.00	50.00	30.00
(27)	Ed Rouch (Edd Roush)	100.00	50.00	30.00
(28)	Babe Ruth (pose)	1000.	500.00	300.00
(29)	Babe Ruth (batting follow-through)	1000.	500.00	300.00
(30)	John Sand	50.00	25.00	15.00
(31)	Al Simmons	100.00	50.00	30.00
(32)	George Sisler	100.00	50.00	30.00
(33)	Tris Speaker	125.00	62.00	37.00
(34)	Pie Traynor	100.00	50.00	30.00
(35)	Phil Todt	50.00	25.00	15.00
(36)	Dazzy Vance	100.00	50.00	30.00
(37)	Rube Walberg	50.00	25.00	15.00
(38)	Paul Waner	100.00	50.00	30.00
(39)	Cy Williams	50.00	25.00	15.00
(40)	Hack Wilson	100.00	50.00	30.00

1928 Exhibits

The Exhibit Supply Company switched to a blue tint for the photos in its 64-card set in 1928. There are 36 new photos in the set, including 24 new players. Four players from the previous year are shown with new teams and 24 of the cards are identical to the 1927 series, except for the color of the card. Cards are found with either blank backs or postcard backs. The photos are captioned in the same style as the 1927 set. The set again includes some misspelling and incorrect labels. The cards are unnumbered and are listed here in alphabetical order.

		NM	EX	VG
Complete Set (64):		5525.	2750.	1650.
Common Player:		55.00	25.00	15.00
(1)	Grover C. Alexander	125.00	62.00	37.00
(2)	David Bancroft	100.00	50.00	30.00
(3)	Virgil Barnes	55.00	25.00	15.00
(4)	Francis R. Blades	55.00	25.00	15.00
(5)	L.A. Blue	55.00	25.00	15.00
(6)	Edward W. Brown	55.00	25.00	15.00
(7)	Max G. Carey	100.00	50.00	30.00
(8)	Chalmer W. Cissell	55.00	25.00	15.00
(9)	Gordon S. Cochrane	100.00	50.00	30.00
(10)	Pat Collins	55.00	25.00	15.00
(11)	Hugh M. Critz	55.00	25.00	15.00
(12)	Howard Ehmke	55.00	25.00	15.00
(13)	E. English	55.00	25.00	15.00
(14)	Bib Falk (Bibb)	55.00	25.00	15.00
(15)	Ira Flagstead	55.00	25.00	15.00
(16)	Robert Fothergill	55.00	25.00	15.00
(17)	Frank Frisch	100.00	50.00	30.00
(18)	Lou Gehrig	1000.	500.00	300.00
(19)	Leon Goslin	100.00	50.00	30.00
(20)	Eugene Hargrave	55.00	25.00	15.00
(21)	Charles R. Hargraves (Hargreaves)	55.00	25.00	15.00
(22)	Stanley Harris	100.00	50.00	30.00
(23)	Bryan "Slim" Harriss	55.00	25.00	15.00
(24)	Leo Hartnett	100.00	50.00	30.00
(25)	Joseph Hauser	55.00	25.00	15.00
(26)	Fred Hoffman (Hofmann)	55.00	25.00	15.00
(27)	J. Francis Hogan	55.00	25.00	15.00
(28)	Rogers Hornsby	125.00	62.00	37.00
(29)	Chas. Jamieson	55.00	25.00	15.00
(30)	Sam Jones	55.00	25.00	15.00
(31)	Ray Kremer	55.00	25.00	15.00
(32)	Fred Leach	55.00	25.00	15.00
(33)	Fredrick Lindstrom (Frederick)	100.00	50.00	30.00
(34)	Adolph Luque (Adolfo)	70.00	35.00	21.00
(35)	Theodore Lyons	100.00	50.00	30.00
(36)	Harry McCurdy	55.00	25.00	15.00
(37)	Glenn Myatt	55.00	25.00	15.00
(38)	John Ogden (photo actually Warren Ogden)	55.00	25.00	15.00
(39)	James Ring	55.00	25.00	15.00
(40)	A.C. Root (should be C.H.)	55.00	25.00	15.00
(41)	Edd. Roush	100.00	50.00	30.00
(42)	Harold Ruel (Herold)	55.00	25.00	15.00
(43)	Geo. H. "Babe" Ruth	1275.	635.00	380.00
(44)	Henry Sand	55.00	25.00	15.00
(45)	Fred Schulte	55.00	25.00	15.00
(46)	Joseph Sewell	100.00	50.00	30.00
(47)	Walter Shang (Schang)	55.00	25.00	15.00
(48)	Urban J. Shocker	55.00	25.00	15.00
(49)	Al. Simmons	100.00	50.00	30.00
(50)	Earl Smith	55.00	25.00	15.00
(51)	Robert Smith	55.00	25.00	15.00
(52)	Jack Tavener	55.00	25.00	15.00
(53)	J. Taylor	55.00	25.00	15.00
(54)	Philip Todt	55.00	25.00	15.00
(55)	Geo. Uhle	55.00	25.00	15.00
(56)	Arthur "Dazzy" Vance	100.00	50.00	30.00
(57)	Paul Waner	100.00	50.00	30.00
(58)	Earl G. Whitehill (middle intial actually O.)	55.00	25.00	15.00
(59)	Fred Williams	55.00	25.00	15.00
(60)	James Wilson	55.00	25.00	15.00
(61)	L.R. (Hack) Wilson	100.00	50.00	30.00
(62)	Lawrence Woodall	55.00	25.00	15.00
(63)	Glen Wright (Glenn)	55.00	25.00	15.00
(64)	William A. Zitzman (Zitzmann)	55.00	25.00	15.00

1929-30 Four-on-One Exhibits

Although the size of the card remained the same, the Exhibit Supply Company of Chicago began putting four player's pictures on each card in 1929 - a practice that would continue for the next decade. Known as "four-on-one" cards, the players are identified by name and team at the bottom of the photos, which are separated by borders. The 32 cards in the 1929-30 series have postcard backs and were printed in a wide range of color combinations including; black on orange, black on blue, brown on orange, blue on green, black on red, black on white, blue on white, black on yellow, brown on white, brown on yellow and red on yellow. Most of the backs are uncolored, however, cards with a black on red front have been seen with red backs, and cards with blue on yellow fronts have been seen with yellow backs. There are numerous spelling and caption errors in the set, and the player identified as Babe Herman is actually Jesse Petty.

		NM	EX	VG
Complete Set (32):		3000.	1500.	900.00
Common Card:		55.00	27.50	16.50
(1)	Earl J. Adams, R. Bartell, Earl Sheely, Harold Traynor	65.00	32.00	19.50
(2)	Dale Alexander, C. Gehringer, G.F. McManus (should be M.J.), H.F. Rice	65.00	32.00	19.50
(3)	Grover C. Alexander, James Bottomly (Bottomley), Frank Frisch, James Wilson	100.00	50.00	30.00
(4)	Martin G. Autrey (Autry), Alex Metzler, Carl Reynolds, Alphonse Thomas	55.00	27.50	16.50
(5)	Earl Averill, B.A. Falk, K. Holloway, L. Sewell	65.00	32.00	19.50
(6)	David Bancroft, Del L. Bisonette (Bissonette), John H. DeBerry, Floyd C. Herman (photo actually Jesse Petty)	65.00	32.00	19.50
(7)	C.E. Beck, Leo Hartnett, Rogers Hornsby, L.R. (Hack) Wilson	125.00	62.00	37.00
(8)	Ray Benge, Lester L. Sweetland, A.C. Whitney, Cy. Williams	55.00	27.50	16.50
(9)	Benny Bengough, Earl B. Coombs (Combs), Waite Hoyt, Anthony Lazzeri	70.00	35.00	21.00
(10)	L. Benton, Melvin Ott, Andrew Reese, William Terry	65.00	32.00	19.50
(11)	Max Bishop, James Dykes, Samuel Hale, Homer Summa	55.00	27.50	16.50
(12)	L.A. Blue, O. Melillo, F.O. Rourke (Frank O'Rourke), F. Schulte	55.00	27.50	16.50
(13)	Oswald Bluege, Leon Goslin, Joseph Judge, Harold Ruel (Herold)	65.00	32.00	19.50
(14)	Chalmer W. Cissell, John W. Clancy, Willie Kamm, John L. Kerr (Kerr's middle initial actually "F.")	55.00	27.50	16.50
(15)	Gordon S. Cochrane, Jimmy Foxx, Robert M. Grove, George Haas	145.00	72.00	43.00
(16)	Pat Collins, Joe Dugan, Edward Farrel (Farrell), George Sisler	65.00	32.00	19.50
(17)	H.M. Critz, G.L. Kelly, V.J. Picinich, W.C. Walker	65.00	32.00	19.50
(18)	Nick Cullop, D'Arcy Flowers, Harvey Hendrick, Arthur "Dazzy" Vance	65.00	32.00	19.50
(19)	Hazen Cuyler, E. English, C.J. Grimm, C.H. Root	65.00	32.00	19.50
(20)	Taylor Douthit, Chas. M. Gilbert (Gelbert), Chas. J. Hafey, Fred G. Haney	65.00	32.00	19.50
(21)	Leo Durocher, Henry L. Gehrig, Mark Koenig, Geo. H. "Babe" Ruth	1250.	625.00	375.00
(22)	L.A. Fonseca, Carl Lind, J. Sewell, J. Tavener	65.00	32.00	19.50
(23)	H.E. Ford, C.F. Lucas, C.A. Pittenger, E.V. Purdy	55.00	27.50	16.50
(24)	Bernard Friberg, Donald Hurst, Frank O'Doul, Fresco Thompson	55.00	27.50	16.50
(25)	S. Gray, R. Kress, H. Manush, W.H. Shang (Schang)	65.00	32.00	19.50
(26)	Charles R. Hargreaves, Ray Kremer, Lloyd Waner, Paul Waner	65.00	32.00	19.50
(27)	George Harper, Fred Maguire, Lance Richbourg, Robert Smith	55.00	27.50	16.50
(28)	Jack Hayes, Sam P. Jones, Chas. M. Myer, Sam Rice	65.00	32.00	19.50
(29)	Harry E. Heilman (Heilmann), C.N. Richardson, M.J. Shea, G.E. Uhle	65.00	32.00	19.50
(30)	J.A. Heving, R.R. Reeves (should be R.E.), J. Rothrock, C.H. Ruffing	65.00	32.00	19.50
(31)	J.F. Hogan, T.C. Jackson, Fred Lindstrom, J.D. Welsh	65.00	32.00	19.50
(32)	W.W. Regan, H. Rhyne, D. Taitt, P.J. Todt	55.00	27.50	16.50

1931-32 Four-on-One Exhibits

The 1931-1932 series issued by the Exhibit Company again consisted of 32 cards, each picturing four players. The series can be differentiated from the previous year by the coupon backs, which list various premiums available (including kazoos, toy pistols and other prizes). The cards again were printed in various color combinations, including; black on green, blue on green, black on orange, black on red, blue on white and black on yellow. There are numerous spelling and caption errors in the series. The Babe Herman/Jesse Petty error of the previous year was still not corrected, and the card of Rick Ferrell not only misspells his name ("Farrel"), but also pictures the wrong player (Edward Farrell).

		NM	EX	VG
Complete Set (32):		3000.	1500.	900.00
Common Card:		50.00	25.00	15.00
(1)	Earl J. Adams, James Bottomly (Bottomley), Frank Frisch, James Wilson	70.00	35.00	21.00
(2)	Dale Alexander, C. Gehringer, G.F. McManus (should be M.J.), G.E. Uhle	70.00	35.00	21.00
(3)	L.L. Appling (should be L.B.), Chalmer W. Cissell, Willie Kamm, Ted Lyons	70.00	35.00	21.00
(4)	Buzz Arlett, Ray Benge, Chuck Klein, A.C. Whitney	70.00	35.00	21.00
(5)	Earl Averill, B.A. Falk, L.A. Fonseca, L. Sewell	70.00	35.00	21.00
(6)	Richard Bartell, Bernard Friberg, Donald Hurst, Harry McCurdy	50.00	25.00	15.00
(7)	Walter Berger, Fred Maguire, Lance Richbourg, Earl Sheely	50.00	25.00	15.00
(8)	Chas. Berry, Robt. Reeves, R.R. Reeves (should be R.E.), J. Rothrock	50.00	25.00	15.00
(9)	Del L. Bisonette (Bissonette), Floyd C. Herman (photo - J. Petty, Jack Quinn, Glenn Wright	50.00	25.00	15.00
(10)	L.A. Blue, Smead Jolley, Carl Reynolds, Henry Tate	50.00	25.00	15.00
(11)	O. Bluege, Joe Judge, Chas. M. Myer, Sam Rice	70.00	35.00	21.00
(12)	John Boley, James Dykes, E.J. Miller, Al. Simmons	70.00	35.00	21.00
(13)	Gordon S. Chochrane, Jimmy Foxx, Robert M. Grove, George Haas	195.00	97.00	58.00
(14)	Adam Comorosky, Gus Suhr, T.J. Thevenow, Harold Traynor	70.00	35.00	21.00
(15)	Earl B. Coombs (Combs), W. Dickey, Anthony Lazzeri, H. Pennock	195.00	97.00	58.00
(16)	H.M. Critz, J.F. Hogan, T.C. Jackson, Fred Lindstrom	70.00	35.00	21.00
(17)	Joe Cronin, H. Manush, F. Marberry, Roy Spencer	70.00	35.00	21.00
(18)	Nick Cullop, Les Durocher (Leo), Harry Heilmann, W.C. Walker	70.00	35.00	21.00
(19)	Hazen Cuyler, E. English, C.J. Grimm, C.H. Root	70.00	35.00	21.00
(20)	Taylor Douthit, Chas. M. Gilbert (Gelbert), Chas. J. Hafey, Bill Hallahan	50.00	25.00	15.00
(21)	Richard Farrel (Ferrell), S. Gray, R. Kress, W. Stewart (photo actually Ed Farrell)	65.00	32.00	19.50
(22)	W. Ferrell, J. Goldman, Hunnefield, Ed Morgan	50.00	25.00	15.00
(23)	Fred Fitzsimmons, Robert O'Farrell, Melvin Ott, William Terry	70.00	35.00	21.00
(24)	D'Arcy Flowers, Frank O'Doul, Fresco Thompson, Arthur "Dazzy" Vance	70.00	35.00	21.00
(25)	H.E. Ford (should be H.H.), Gooch, C.F. Lucas, W. Roettger	50.00	25.00	15.00
(26)	E. Funk, W. Hoyt, Mark Koenig, Wallie Schang	70.00	35.00	21.00
(27)	Henry L. Gehrig, Lyn Lary, James Reese, Geo. H. "Babe" Ruth	1200.	600.00	360.00
(28)	George Grantham, Ray Kremer, Lloyd Waner, Paul Waner	70.00	35.00	21.00
(29)	Leon Goslin, O. Melillo, F.O. Rourke (Frank O'Rourke), F. Schulte	70.00	35.00	21.00
(30)	Leo Hartnett, Rogers Hornsby, J.R. Stevenson (Stephenson), L.R. (Hack) Wilson	115.00	57.00	34.00
(31)	D. MacFayden, H. Rhyne, Bill Sweeney, E.W. Webb	50.00	25.00	15.00
(32)	Walter Maranville, Randolph Moore, Alfred Spohrer, J.T. Zachary	70.00	35.00	21.00

1933 Four-on-One Exhibits

The 1933 series of four-on-one Exhibits consists of 16 cards with blank backs. Color combinations include: blue on green, black on orange, black on red, blue on white and black on yellow. Most have a plain, white back, although the black on yellow cards are also found with a yellow back. Most of the pictures used are reprinted from previous series, and there are some spelling and caption errors, including the Richard Ferrell/Edward Farrel mixup from the previous year. Al Lopez is shown as "Vincent" Lopez.

		NM	EX	VG
Complete Set (16):		1900.	950.00	550.00
Common Card:		50.00	25.00	15.00
(1)	Earl J. Adams, Frank Frisch, Chas. Gilbert (Gelbert), Bill Hallahan	70.00	35.00	21.00
(2)	Earl Averill, W. Ferrell, Ed Morgan, L. Sewell	70.00	35.00	21.00
(3)	Richard Bartell, Ray Benge, Donald Hurst, Chuck Klein	70.00	35.00	21.00
(4)	Walter Berger, Walter Maranville, Alfred Spohrer, J.T. Zachary	70.00	35.00	21.00
(5)	Charles Berry, L.A. Blue, Ted Lyons, Bob Seeds	70.00	35.00	21.00
(6)	Chas. Berry, D. MacFayden, H. Rhyne, E.W. Webb	50.00	25.00	15.00
(7)	Mickey Cochrane, Jimmy Foxx, Robert M. Grove, Al. Simmons	250.00	125.00	75.00
(8)	H.M. Critz, Fred Fitzsimmons, Fred Lindstrom, Robert O'Farrell	70.00	35.00	21.00
(9)	W. Dickey, Anthony Lazzeri, H. Pennock, George H. "Babe" Ruth	1000.	500.00	300.00
(10)	Taylor Douthit, George Grantham, Chas. J. Hafey, C.F. Lucas	70.00	35.00	21.00
(11)	E. English, C.J. Grimm, C.H. Root, J.R. Stevenson (Stephenson)	50.00	25.00	15.00
(12)	Richard Farrel (Ferrell), Leon Goslin, S. Gray, O. Melillo (photo actually Ed Farrell)	70.00	35.00	21.00
(13)	C. Gehringer, "Muddy" Ruel, Jonathan Stone (first name - John, G.E. Uhle	70.00	35.00	21.00
(14)	Joseph Judge, H. Manush, F. Marberry, Roy Spencer	70.00	35.00	21.00
(15)	Vincent Lopez (Al), Frank O'Doul, Arthur "Dazzy" Vance, Glenn Wright	70.00	35.00	21.00
(16)	Gus Suhr, Tom J. Thevenow, Lloyd Waner, Paul Waner	70.00	35.00	21.00

1934 Four-on-One Exhibits

This 16-card series issued by the Exhibit Co. in 1934 is again blank-backed and continues the four-on-one format. The 1934 series can be differentiated from previous years by the more subdued color combinations of the cards, which include lighter shades of blue, brown, green and violet - all printed on white card stock. Many new photos were also used in the 1934 series. Of the 64 players included, 25 appear for the first time and another 16 were given new poses. Spelling was improved, but Al Lopez is still identified as "Vincent."

		NM	EX	VG
Complete Set (16):		2150.	1075.	650.00
Common Card:		55.00	27.00	16.50
(1)	Luke Appling, George Earnshaw, Al Simmons, Evar Swanson	75.00	37.00	22.00
(2)	Earl Averill, W. Ferrell, Willie Kamm, Frank Pytlak	75.00	37.00	22.00
(3)	Richard Bartell, Donald Hurst, Wesley Schulmerich, Jimmy Wilson	55.00	27.00	16.50
(4)	Walter Berger, Ed Brandt, Frank Hogan, Bill Urbanski	55.00	27.00	16.50
(5)	Jim Bottomley, Chas. J. Hafey, Botchi Lombardi, Tony Piet	75.00	37.00	22.00
(6)	Irving Burns, Irving Hadley, Rollie Hemsley, O. Melillo	55.00	27.00	16.50
(7)	Bill Cissell, Rick Ferrell, Lefty Grove, Roy Johnson	75.00	37.00	22.00
(8)	Mickey Cochrane, C. Gehringer, Goose Goslin, Fred Marberry	115.00	57.00	34.00
(9)	George Cramer (Roger), Jimmy Foxx, Frank Higgins, Slug Mahaffey	115.00	57.00	34.00
(10)	Joe Cronin, Alvin Crowder, Joe Kuhel, H. Manush	75.00	37.00	22.00
(11)	W. Dickey, Lou Gehrig, Vernon Gomez, Geo. H. "Babe" Ruth	1600.	800.00	480.00
(12)	E. English, C.J. Grimm, Chas. Klein, Lon Warneke	75.00	37.00	22.00
(13)	Frank Frisch, Bill Hallahan, Pepper Martin, John Rothrock	75.00	37.00	22.00
(14)	Carl Hubbell, Mel Ott, Blondy Ryan, Bill Terry	115.00	57.00	34.00
(15)	Leonard Koenecke, Sam Leslie, Vincent Lopez (Al), Glenn Wright	50.00	25.00	15.00
(16)	T.J. Thevenow, Pie Traynor, Lloyd Waner, Paul Waner	105.00	52.00	31.00

1935 Four-on-One Exhibits

Continuing with the same four-on-one format, the Exhibit Supply Co. issued another 16-card series in 1935. All cards were printed in a slate-blue color with a plain, blank back. Seventeen of the players included in the 1935 series appear for the first time. While another 11 are shown with new poses. There are several spelling and caption errors. Babe Ruth appears in a regular Exhibit issue for the last time.

		NM	EX	VG
Complete Set (16):		2600.	1300.	775.00
Common Card:		40.00	20.00	12.00
(1)	Earl Averill, Mel Harder, Willie Kamm, Hal Trosky	60.00	30.00	18.00
(2)	Walter Berger, Ed Brandt, Frank Hogan, "Babe" Ruth	900.00	450.00	270.00
(3)	Henry Bonura, Jimmy Dykes, Ted Lyons, Al Simmons	60.00	30.00	18.00
(4)	Jimmy Bottomley, Paul Derringer, Chas. J. Hafey, Botchi Lombardi	85.00	42.00	25.00
(5)	Irving Burns, Rollie Hemsley, O. Melillo, L.N. Newson	40.00	20.00	12.00
(6)	Guy Bush, Pie Traynor, Floyd Vaughn (Vaughan), Paul Waner	85.00	42.00	25.00
(7)	Mickey Cochrane, C. Gehringer, Goose Goslin, Linwood Rowe (Lynwood)	85.00	42.00	25.00
(8)	Phil Collins, John "Blondy" Ryan, Geo. Watkins, Jimmy Wilson	40.00	20.00	12.00
(9)	George Cramer (Roger), Jimmy Foxx, Bob Johnson, Slug Mahaffey	85.00	42.00	25.00
(10)	Hughie Critz, Carl Hubbell, Mel Ott, Bill Terry	90.00	45.00	27.00
(11)	Joe Cronin, Rick Ferrell, Lefty Grove, Billy Werber	85.00	42.00	25.00
(12)	Tony Cuccinello, Vincent Lopez (Al), Van Mungo, Dan Taylor (photo actually George Puccinelli)	50.00	25.00	15.00
(13)	Jerome "Dizzy" Dean, Paul Dean, Frank Frisch, Pepper Martin	175.00	87.00	52.00
(14)	W. Dickey, Lou Gehrig, Vernon Gomez, Tony Lazzeri	900.00	450.00	270.00
(15)	C.J. Grimm, Gabby Hartnett, Chas. Klein, Lon Warneke	60.00	30.00	18.00
(16)	H. Manush, Buddy Meyer (Myer), Fred Schulte, Earl Whitehill	60.00	30.00	18.00

1936 Four-on-One Exhibits

The 1936 series of four-on-one cards again consisted of 16 cards in either green or slate blue with plain, blank backs. The series can be differentiated from the previous year's Exhibit cards by the line "PTD. IN U.S.A." at the bottom. Of the 64 players pictured, 16 appear for the first time and another nine are shown in new poses. The series is again marred by several spelling and caption errors.

		NM	EX	VG
	Complete Set (16):	1600.	800.00	475.00
	Common Card:	45.00	22.00	13.50
(1)	Paul Andrews, Harland Clift (Harlond), Rollie Hemsley, Sammy West	45.00	22.00	13.50
(2)	Luke Appling, Henry Bonura, Jimmy Dykes, Ted Lyons	55.00	27.00	16.50
(3)	Earl Averill, Mel Harder, Hal Trosky, Joe Vosmik	55.00	27.00	16.50
(4)	Walter Berger, Danny MacFayden, Bill Urbanski, Pinky Whitney	45.00	22.00	13.50
(5)	Charles Berry, Frank Higgins, Bob Johnson, Puccinelli	45.00	22.00	13.50
(6)	Ossie Bluege, Buddy Meyer (Myer), L.N. Newsom, Earl Whitehill	45.00	22.00	13.50
(7)	Stan. Bordagaray, Dutch Brandt, Fred Lindstrom, Van Mungo	55.00	27.00	16.50
(8)	Guy Bush, Pie Traynor, Floyd Vaughn (Vaughan), Paul Waner	75.00	37.00	22.00
(9)	Dolph Camilli, Curt Davis, Johnny Moore, Jimmy Wilson	45.00	22.00	13.50
(10)	Mickey Cochrane, C. Gehringer, Goose Goslin, Linwood Rowe (Lynwood)	75.00	37.00	22.00
(11)	Joe Cronin, Rick Ferrell, Jimmy Foxx, Lefty Grove	95.00	47.00	28.00
(12)	Jerome "Dizzy" Dean, Paul Dean, Frank Frisch, Joe "Ducky" Medwick	175.00	87.00	52.00
(13)	Paul Derringer, Babe Herman, Alex Kampouris, Botchi Lombardi	55.00	27.00	16.50
(14)	Augie Galan, Gabby Hartnett, Billy Herman, Lon Warneke	55.00	27.00	16.50
(15)	Lou Gehrig, Vernon Gomez, Tony Lazzeri, Red Ruffing	800.00	400.00	240.00
(16)	Carl Hubbell, Gus Mancuso, Mel Ott, Bill Terry	65.00	33.00	20.00

1937 Four-on-One Exhibits

The 1937 four-on-one Exhibit cards were printed in either green or bright blue. The backs are again blank. The 1937 cards are difficult to distinguish from the 1936 series, because both contain the "PTD. IN U.S.A." line along the bottom. Of the 64 photos, 47 are re-issues from previous series.

		NM	EX	VG
	Complete Set (16):	1775.	885.00	525.00
	Common Card:	45.00	22.00	13.50
(1)	Earl Averill, Bob Feller, Frank Pytlak, Hal Trosky	95.00	47.00	28.00
(2)	Luke Appling, Henry Bonura, Jimmy Dykes, Vernon Kennedy	60.00	30.00	18.00
(3)	Walter Berger, Alfonso Lopez, Danny MacFayden, Bill Urbanski	50.00	25.00	15.00
(4)	Cy Blanton, Gus Suhr, Floyd Vaughn (Vaughan), Paul Waner	60.00	30.00	18.00
(5)	Dolph Camilli, Johnny Moore, Wm. Walters, Pinky Whitney	45.00	22.00	13.50
(6)	Harland Clift (Harlond), Rollie Hemsley, Orval Hildebrand (Oral), Sammy West	45.00	22.00	13.50
(7)	Mickey Cochrane, C. Gehringer, Goose Goslin, Linwood Rowe (Lynwood)	80.00	40.00	24.00
(8)	Joe Cronin, Rick Ferrell, Jimmy Foxx, Lefty Grove	95.00	47.00	28.00
(9)	Jerome "Dizzy" Dean, Stuart Martin, Joe "Ducky" Medwick, Lon Warneke	140.00	70.00	42.00
(10)	Paul Derringer, Botchi Lombardi, Lew Riggs, Phil Weintraub	60.00	30.00	18.00
(11)	Joe DiMaggio, Lou Gehrig, Vernon Gomez, Tony Lazzeri	1000.	500.00	300.00
(12)	E. English, Johnny Moore, Van Mungo, Gordon Phelps	45.00	22.00	13.50
(13)	Augie Galan, Gabby Hartnett, Billy Herman, Bill Lee	60.00	30.00	18.00
(14)	Carl Hubbell, Sam Leslie, Gus. Mancuso, Mel Ott	60.00	30.00	18.00
(15)	Bob Johnson, Harry Kelly (Kelley), Wallace Moses, Billy Weber (Werber)	45.00	22.00	13.50
(16)	Joe Kuhel, Buddy Meyer (Myer), L.N. Newsom, Jonathan Stone (first name actually John)	45.00	22.00	13.50

1938 Four-on-One Exhibits

The Exhibit Co. used its four-on-one format for the final time in 1938, issuing another 16-card series. The cards feature brown printing on white stock with the line "MADE IN U.S.A." appearing along the bottom. The backs are blank. Twelve players appeared for the first time and three others are shown in new poses. Again, there are several spelling and caption mistakes.

		NM	EX	VG
	Complete Set (16):	1775.	875.00	525.00
	Common Card:	45.00	22.00	13.50
(1)	Luke Appling, Mike Kreevich, Ted Lyons, L. Sewell	60.00	30.00	18.00
(2)	Morris Arnovich, Chas. Klein, Wm. Walters, Pinky Whitney	60.00	30.00	18.00
(3)	Earl Averill, Bob Feller, Odell Hale, Hal Trosky	95.00	47.00	28.00
(4)	Beau Bell, Harland Clift (Harlond), L.N. Newsom, Sammy West	45.00	22.00	13.50
(5)	Cy Blanton, Gus Suhr, Floyd Vaughn (Vaughan), Paul Waner	60.00	30.00	18.00
(6)	Tom Bridges, C. Gehringer, Hank Greenberg, Rudy York	60.00	30.00	18.00
(7)	Dolph Camilli, Leo Durocher, Van Mungo, Gordon Phelps	50.00	25.00	15.00
(8)	Joe Cronin, Jimmy Foxx, Lefty Grove, Joe Vosmik	85.00	42.00	25.00
(9)	Tony Cuccinello, Vince DiMaggio, Roy Johnson, Danny MacFayden (photo actually George Puccinelli)	45.00	22.00	13.50
(10)	Jerome "Dizzy" Dean, Augie Galan, Gabby Hartnett, Billy Herman	125.00	62.00	37.00
(11)	Paul Derringer, Ival Goodman, Botchi Lombardi, Lew Riggs	60.00	30.00	18.00
(12)	W. Dickey, Joe DiMaggio, Lou Gehrig, Vernon Gomez	1000.	500.00	300.00
(13)	Rick Ferrell, W. Ferrell, Buddy Meyer (Myer), Jonathan Stone (first name actually John)	60.00	30.00	18.00
(14)	Carl Hubbell, Hank Leiber, Mel Ott, Jim Ripple	75.00	37.00	22.00
(15)	Bob Johnson, Harry Kelly (Kelley), Wallace Moses, Billy Weber (Werber)	45.00	22.00	13.50
(16)	Stuart Martin, Joe "Ducky" Medwick, Johnny Mize, Lon Warneke	60.00	30.00	18.00

1939-46 Salutation Exhibits

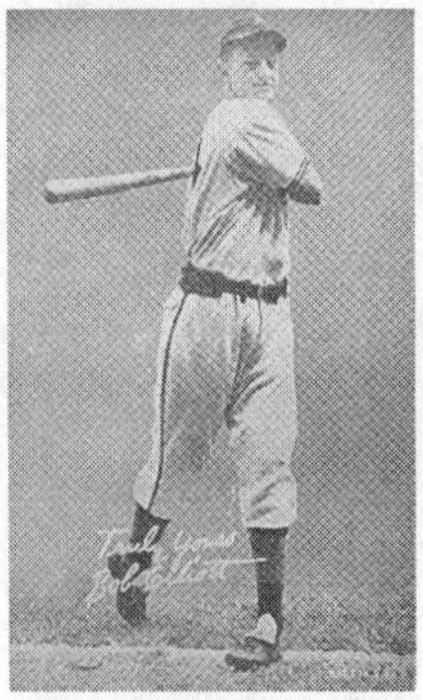

Referred to as "Exhibits" because they were issued by the Exhibit Supply Co. of Chicago, Ill., the bulk of this group was produced over an 8-year span, though production and sale of some players' cards continued into the range of the 1947-66 Exhibits. These cards are frequently called "Salutations" because of the personalized greeting found on the card. The black-and-white cards, which measure 3-3/8" x 5-3/8", are unnumbered and blank-backed. Most Exhibits were sold through vending machines for a penny. The complete set price includes all variations.

		NM	EX	VG
	Complete Set (83):	4500.	2200.	1350.
	Common Player:	8.00	4.00	2.50
(1)	Luke Appling ("Made In U.S.A." in left corner)	13.00	6.50	4.00
(2)	Luke Appling ("Made In U.S.A." in right corner)	7.50	3.75	2.25
(3)	Earl Averill	400.00	200.00	120.00
(4)	Charles "Red" Barrett	8.00	4.00	2.50
(5)	Henry "Hank" Borowy	8.00	4.00	2.50
(6)	Lou Boudreau	8.50	4.25	2.50
(7)	Adolf Camilli	27.00	13.50	8.00
(8)	Phil Cavarretta	8.00	4.00	2.50
(9)	Harland Clift (Harlond)	13.00	6.50	4.00
(10)	Tony Cuccinello	27.00	13.50	8.00
(11)	Dizzy Dean	85.00	42.00	25.00
(12)	Paul Derringer	8.00	4.00	2.50
(13)	Bill Dickey ("Made In U.S.A." in left corner)	27.00	13.50	8.00
(14)	Bill Dickey ("Made In U.S.A." in right corner)	27.00	13.50	8.00
(15)	Joe DiMaggio	100.00	50.00	30.00
(16)	Bob Elliott	8.00	4.00	2.50
(17)	Bob Feller (portrait)	100.00	50.00	30.00
(18)	Bob Feller (pitching)	32.00	16.00	9.50
(19)	Dave Ferriss	8.00	4.00	2.50
(20)	Jimmy Foxx	90.00	45.00	27.00
(21)	Lou Gehrig	900.00	450.00	270.00
(22)	Charlie Gehringer	135.00	67.00	40.00
(23)	Vernon Gomez	190.00	95.00	57.00
(24)	Joe Gordon (Cleveland)	27.00	13.50	8.00
(25)	Joe Gordon (New York)	8.00	4.00	2.50
(26)	Hank Greenberg (Truly yours)	21.00	10.50	6.25
(27)	Hank Greenberg (Very truly yours)	85.00	42.00	25.00
(28)	Robert Grove	55.00	27.00	16.50
(29)	Gabby Hartnett	275.00	137.00	82.00
(30)	Buddy Hassett	16.00	8.00	4.75
(31)	Jeff Heath (large projection)	27.00	13.50	8.00
(32)	Jeff Heath (small projection)	8.00	4.00	2.50
(33)	Kirby Higbe	16.00	8.00	4.75
(34)	Tommy Holmes (Yours truly)	8.00	4.00	2.50
(35)	Tommy Holmes (Sincerely yours)	130.00	65.00	39.00
(36)	Carl Hubbell	27.00	13.50	8.00
(37)	Bob Johnson	16.00	8.00	4.75
(38)	Charles Keller ("MADE IN U.S.A." left corner)	8.00	4.00	2.50
(39)	Charles Keller ("MADE IN U.S.A." right corner)	8.00	4.00	2.50
(40)	Ken Keltner	27.00	13.50	8.00
(41)	Chuck Klein	185.00	92.00	55.00
(42)	Mike Kreevich	85.00	42.00	25.00
(43)	Joe Kuhel	21.00	10.50	6.25
(44)	Bill Lee	21.00	10.50	6.25
(45)	Ernie Lombardi (Cordially)	210.00	105.00	63.00
(46)	Ernie Lombardi (Cordially yours)	8.50	4.25	2.50
(47)	Martin Marion ("Made in U.S.A." in left corner)	8.00	4.00	2.50
(48)	Martin Marion ("Made in U.S.A." in right corner)	8.00	4.00	2.50
(49)	Merrill May	21.00	10.50	6.25
(50)	Frank McCormick ("Made In U.S.A." in left corner)	21.00	10.50	6.25
(51)	Frank McCormick ("Made In U.S.A." in right corner)	8.00	4.00	2.50
(52)	George McQuinn ("Made In U.S.A." in left corner)	21.00	10.50	6.25
(53)	George McQuinn ("Made In U.S.A." in right corner)	8.00	4.00	2.50
(54)	Joe Medwick	32.00	16.00	9.50
(55)	Johnny Mize ("Made In U.S.A." in left corner)	27.00	13.50	8.00
(56)	Johnny Mize ("Made In U.S.A." in right corner)	16.00	8.00	4.75
(57)	Hugh Mulcahy	85.00	42.00	25.00
(58)	Hal Newhouser	8.00	4.00	2.50
(59)	Buck Newson (Newsom)	185.00	92.00	55.00
(60)	Louis (Buck) Newsom	8.00	4.00	2.50
(61)	Mel Ott ("Made In U.S.A." in left corner)	55.00	27.00	16.50
(62)	Mel Ott ("Made In U.S.A." in right corner)	27.00	13.50	8.00
(63)	Andy Pafko ("C" on cap)	8.00	4.00	2.50
(64)	Andy Pafko (plain cap)	8.00	4.00	2.50
(65)	Claude Passeau	8.00	4.00	2.50
(66)	Howard Pollet ("Made In U.S.A." in left corner)	12.00	6.00	3.50
(67)	Howard Pollet ("Made In U.S.A." in right corner)	8.00	4.00	2.50
(68)	Pete Reiser ("Made In U.S.A." in left corner)	85.00	42.00	25.00
(69)	Pete Reiser ("Made In U.S.A." in right corner)	8.00	4.00	2.50
(70)	Johnny Rizzo	95.00	47.00	28.00
(71)	Glenn Russell	95.00	47.00	28.00
(72)	George Stirnweiss	8.00	4.00	2.50
(73)	Cecil Travis	16.00	8.00	4.75
(74)	Paul Trout	8.00	4.00	2.50
(75)	Johnny Vander Meer	43.00	21.00	13.00
(76)	Arky Vaughn (Vaughan)	21.00	10.50	6.25
(77)	Fred "Dixie" Walker ("D" on cap)	8.00	4.00	2.50
(78)	Fred "Dixie" Walker ("D" blanked out)	60.00	30.00	18.00
(79)	"Bucky" Walters	8.00	4.00	2.50
(80)	Lon Warneke	8.00	4.00	2.50
(81)	Ted Williams (#9 shows)	450.00	225.00	135.00
(82)	Ted Williams (#9 not showing)	65.00	32.00	19.50
(83)	Rudy York	8.00	4.00	2.50

1947-66 Exhibits

Called "Exhibits" because they were produced by the Exhibit Supply Co. of Chicago, this group covers a span of 20 years. Each unnumbered, black-and-white card is printed on heavy cardboard measuring 3-3/8" x 5-3/8" and is blank-backed. The company issued new sets each year, with many players being repeated year after year. Other players appeared in only one or two years, thereby creating levels of scarcity. Many variations of the same basic pose are found in the group. The complete set values include all variations. Some pieces have been found printed on a semi-gloss paper stock, perhaps as proofs. Their value is 50% or less of the issued version.

		NM	EX	VG
Complete Set (336):		5250.	2600.	1500.
Common Player:		6.50	3.25	1.75
(1)	Hank Aaron	35.00	17.50	10.50
(2)	Joe Adcock (script signature)	6.50	3.25	1.75
(3)	Joe Adcock (plain signature)	7.75	4.00	2.25
(4)	Max Alvis	29.00	14.50	8.75
(5)	Johnny Antonelli (Braves)	6.50	3.25	1.75
(6)	Johnny Antonelli (Giants)	7.75	4.00	2.25
(7)	Luis Aparicio (portrait)	11.00	5.50	3.25
(8)	Luis Aparicio (batting)	29.00	14.50	8.75
(9)	Luke Appling	11.00	5.50	3.25
(10)	Ritchie Ashburn (Phillies, first name incorrect)	11.00	5.50	3.25
(11)	Richie Ashburn (Phillies, first name correct)	11.50	5.75	3.50
(12)	Richie Ashburn (Cubs)	15.50	7.75	4.75
(13)	Bob Aspromonte	6.50	3.25	1.75
(14)	Toby Atwell	6.50	3.25	1.75
(15)	Ed Bailey (with cap)	7.75	4.00	2.25
(16)	Ed Bailey (no cap)	6.50	3.25	1.75
(17)	Gene Baker	6.50	3.25	1.75
(18)	Ernie Banks (bat on shoulder, script signature)	30.00	15.00	9.00
(19)	Ernie Banks (bat on shoulder, plain signature)	18.00	9.00	5.50
(20)	Ernie Banks (portrait)	30.00	15.00	9.00
(21)	Steve Barber	6.50	3.25	1.75
(22)	Earl Battey	7.75	4.00	2.25
(23)	Matt Batts	6.50	3.25	1.75
(24)	Hank Bauer (N.Y. cap)	10.00	5.00	3.00
(25)	Hank Bauer (plain cap)	11.00	5.50	3.25
(26)	Frank Baumholtz	6.50	3.25	1.75
(27)	Gene Bearden	6.50	3.25	1.75
(28)	Joe Beggs	13.50	6.75	4.00
(29)	Larry "Yogi" Berra	32.00	16.00	9.50
(30)	Yogi Berra	23.00	11.50	7.00
(31)	Steve Bilko	7.75	4.00	2.25
(32)	Ewell Blackwell (pitching)	11.00	5.50	3.25
(33)	Ewell Blackwell (portrait)	6.50	3.25	1.75
(34)	Don Blasingame (St. Louis cap)	6.50	3.25	1.75
(35)	Don Blasingame (plain cap)	9.25	4.75	2.75
(36)	Ken Boyer	11.00	5.50	3.25
(37)	Ralph Branca	11.00	5.50	3.25
(38)	Jackie Brandt	50.00	25.00	15.00
(39)	Harry Brecheen	6.50	3.25	1.75
(40)	Tom Brewer	13.50	6.75	4.00
(41)	Lou Brissie	7.75	4.00	2.25
(42)	Bill Bruton	6.50	3.25	1.75
(43)	Lew Burdette (pitching, side view)	6.50	3.25	1.75
(44)	Lew Burdette (pitching, front view)	9.25	4.75	2.75
(45)	Johnny Callison	11.00	5.50	3.25
(46)	Roy Campanella	23.00	11.50	7.00
(47)	Chico Carrasquel (portrait)	16.00	8.00	4.75
(48)	Chico Carrasquel (leaping)	6.50	3.25	1.75
(49)	George Case	13.50	6.75	4.00
(50)	Hugh Casey	7.75	4.00	2.25
(51)	Norm Cash	11.00	5.50	3.25
(52)	Orlando Cepeda (portrait)	15.00	7.50	4.50
(53)	Orlando Cepeda (batting)	15.00	7.50	4.50
(54)	Bob Cerv (A's cap)	11.00	5.50	3.25
(55)	Bob Cerv (plain cap)	20.00	10.00	6.00
(56)	Dean Chance	6.50	3.25	1.75
(57)	Spud Chandler	13.50	6.75	4.00
(58)	Tom Cheney	6.50	3.25	1.75
(59)	Bubba Church	7.75	4.00	2.25
(60)	Roberto Clemente	50.00	25.00	15.00
(61)	Rocky Colavito (portrait)	35.00	17.50	10.50
(62)	Rocky Colavito (batting)	11.00	5.50	3.25
(63)	Choo Choo Coleman	15.50	7.75	4.75
(64)	Gordy Coleman	29.00	14.50	8.75
(65)	Jerry Coleman	7.75	4.00	2.25
(66)	Mort Cooper	13.50	6.75	4.00
(67)	Walker Cooper	6.50	3.25	1.75
(68)	Roger Craig	12.00	6.00	3.50
(69)	Delmar Crandall	6.50	3.25	1.75
(70)	Joe Cunningham (batting)	35.00	17.50	10.50
(71)	Joe Cunningham (portrait)	11.00	5.50	3.25
(72)	Guy Curtwright (Curtright)	7.75	4.00	2.25
(73)	Bud Daley	40.00	20.00	12.00
(74)	Alvin Dark (Braves)	11.00	5.50	3.25
(75)	Alvin Dark (Giants)	7.75	4.00	2.25
(76)	Alvin Dark (Cubs)	11.00	5.50	3.25
(77)	Murray Dickson (Murry)	7.75	4.00	2.25
(78)	Bob Dillinger	11.00	5.50	3.25
(79)	Dom DiMaggio	18.00	9.00	5.50
(80)	Joe Dobson	11.00	5.50	3.25
(81)	Larry Doby	15.00	7.50	4.50
(82)	Bobby Doerr	13.50	6.75	4.00
(83)	Dick Donovan (plain cap)	11.00	5.50	3.25
(84)	Dick Donovan (Sox cap)	6.50	3.25	1.75
(85)	Walter Dropo	6.50	3.25	1.75
(86)	Don Drysdale (glove at waist)	35.00	17.50	10.50
(87)	Don Drysdale (portrait)	35.00	17.50	10.50
(88)	Luke Easter	7.75	4.00	2.25
(89)	Bruce Edwards	7.75	4.00	2.25
(90)	Del Ennis	6.50	3.25	1.75
(91)	Al Evans	7.00	3.25	1.75
(92)	Walter Evers	6.50	3.25	1.75
(93)	Ferris Fain (fielding)	11.00	5.50	3.25
(94)	Ferris Fain (portrait)	6.50	3.25	1.75
(95)	Dick Farrell	6.50	3.25	1.75
(96)	Ed "Whitey" Ford	29.00	14.50	8.75
(97)	Whitey Ford (pitching)	17.50	8.75	5.25
(98)	Whitey Ford (portrait)	125.00	62.00	37.00
(99)	Dick Fowler	11.00	5.50	3.25
(100)	Nelson Fox	9.00	4.50	2.75
(101)	Tito Francona	6.50	3.25	1.75
(102)	Bob Friend	6.50	3.25	1.75
(103)	Carl Furillo	15.00	7.50	4.50
(104)	Augie Galan	11.00	5.50	3.25
(105)	Jim Gentile	6.50	3.25	1.75
(106)	Tony Gonzalez	6.50	3.25	1.75
(107)	Billy Goodman (leaping)	6.50	3.25	1.75
(108)	Billy Goodman (batting)	11.00	5.50	3.25
(109)	Ted Greengrass (Jim)	6.50	3.25	1.75
(110)	Dick Groat	11.00	5.50	3.25
(111)	Steve Gromek	6.50	3.25	1.75
(112)	Johnny Groth	6.50	3.25	1.75
(113)	Orval Grove	15.50	7.75	4.75
(114)	Frank Gustine (Pirates uniform)	7.75	4.00	2.25
(115)	Frank Gustine (plain uniform)	7.75	4.00	2.25
(116)	Berthold Haas	15.50	7.75	4.75
(117)	Grady Hatton	7.75	4.00	2.25
(118)	Jim Hegan	6.50	3.25	1.75
(119)	Tom Henrich	11.00	5.50	3.25
(120)	Ray Herbert	29.00	14.50	8.75
(121)	Gene Hermanski	7.00	3.25	1.75
(122)	Whitey Herzog	11.00	5.50	3.25
(123)	Kirby Higbe	15.50	7.75	4.75
(124)	Chuck Hinton	6.50	3.25	1.75
(125)	Don Hoak	15.50	7.75	4.75
(126)	Gil Hodges ("B" on cap)	14.50	7.25	4.25
(127)	Gil Hodges ("LA" on cap)	11.50	5.75	3.50
(128)	Johnny Hopp	13.50	6.75	4.00
(129)	Elston Howard	11.00	5.50	3.25
(130)	Frank Howard	11.00	5.50	3.25
(131)	Ken Hubbs	40.00	20.00	12.00
(132)	Tex Hughson	13.50	6.75	4.00
(133)	Fred Hutchinson	7.00	3.25	1.75
(134)	Monty Irvin (Monte)	11.00	5.50	3.25
(135)	Joey Jay	6.50	3.25	1.75
(136)	Jackie Jensen	35.00	17.50	10.50
(137)	Sam Jethroe	7.75	4.00	2.25
(138)	Bill Johnson	7.75	4.00	2.25
(139)	Walter Judnich	13.50	6.75	4.00
(140)	Al Kaline (kneeling)	35.00	17.50	10.50
(141)	Al Kaline (portrait)	35.00	17.50	10.50
(142)	George Kell	11.00	5.50	3.25
(143)	Charley Keller	7.00	3.25	1.75
(144)	Alex Kellner	6.50	3.25	1.75
(145)	Kenn (Ken) Keltner	7.75	4.00	2.25
(146)	Harmon Killebrew (batting)	35.00	17.50	10.50
(147)	Harmon Killebrew (throwing)	35.00	17.50	10.50
(148)	Harmon Killibrew (Killebrew) (portrait)	35.00	17.50	10.50
(149)	Ellis Kinder	6.50	3.25	1.75
(150)	Ralph Kiner	11.00	5.50	3.25
(151)	Billy Klaus	29.00	14.50	8.75
(152)	Ted Kluzewski (Kluszewski) (batting)	11.00	5.50	3.25
(153)	Ted Kluzewski (Kluszewski) (Pirates uniform)	11.00	5.50	3.25
(154)	Ted Kluzewski (Kluszewski) (plain uniform)	15.50	7.75	4.75
(155)	Don Kolloway	11.00	5.50	3.25
(156)	Jim Konstanty	7.75	4.00	2.25
(157)	Sandy Koufax	29.00	14.50	8.75
(158)	Ed Kranepool	55.00	27.00	16.50
(159)	Tony Kubek (light background)	11.00	5.50	3.25
(160)	Tony Kubek (dark background)	7.75	4.00	2.25
(161)	Harvey Kuenn ("D" on cap)	15.50	7.75	4.75
(162)	Harvey Kuenn (plain cap)	15.50	7.75	4.75
(163)	Harvey Kuenn ("SF" on cap)	11.00	5.50	3.25
(164)	Whitey Kurowski	7.00	3.25	1.75
(165)	Eddie Lake	7.75	4.00	2.25
(166)	Jim Landis	6.50	3.25	1.75
(167)	Don Larsen	11.00	5.50	3.25
(168)	Bob Lemon (glove not visible)	11.00	5.50	3.25
(169)	Bob Lemon (glove partially visible)	35.00	17.50	10.50
(170)	Buddy Lewis	13.50	6.75	4.00
(171)	Johnny Lindell	29.00	14.50	8.75
(172)	Phil Linz	29.00	14.50	8.75
(173)	Don Lock	29.00	14.50	8.75
(174)	Whitey Lockman	6.50	3.25	1.75
(175)	Johnny Logan	6.50	3.25	1.75
(176)	Dale Long ("P" on cap)	6.50	3.25	1.75
(177)	Dale Long ("C" on cap)	11.00	5.50	3.25
(178)	Ed Lopat	7.75	4.00	2.25
(179)	Harry Lowery (name misspelled)	7.75	4.00	2.25
(180)	Harry Lowrey (name correct)	7.75	4.00	2.25
(181)	Sal Maglie	6.50	3.25	1.75
(182)	Art Mahaffey	7.75	4.00	2.25
(183)	Hank Majeski	6.50	3.25	1.75
(184)	Frank Malzone	6.50	3.25	1.75
(185)	Mickey Mantle (batting, pinstriped uniform)	100.00	50.00	30.00
(186)	Mickey Mantle (batting, no pinstripes, first name outlined in white)	110.00	55.00	33.00
(187)	Mickey Mantle (batting, no pinstripes, first name not outlined in white)	70.00	35.00	21.00
(188)	Mickey Mantle (portrait)	500.00	250.00	150.00
(189)	Martin Marion	11.00	5.50	3.25
(190)	Roger Maris	29.00	14.50	8.75
(191)	Willard Marshall	8.00	4.00	2.50
(192)	Eddie Matthews (name incorrect)	15.50	7.75	4.75
(193)	Eddie Mathews (name correct)	15.50	7.75	4.75
(194)	Ed Mayo	8.00	4.00	2.50
(195)	Willie Mays (batting)	35.00	17.50	10.50
(196)	Willie Mays (portrait)	40.00	20.00	12.00
(197)	Bill Mazeroski (portrait)	12.00	6.00	3.50
(198)	Bill Mazeroski (batting)	18.00	9.00	5.50
(199)	Ken McBride	6.50	3.25	1.75
(200)	Barney McCaskey (McCosky)	15.50	7.75	4.75
(201)	Barney McCoskey (McCosky)	100.00	50.00	30.00
(202)	Lindy McDaniel	6.50	3.25	1.75
(203)	Gil McDougald	11.00	5.50	3.25
(204)	Albert Mele	15.50	7.75	4.75
(205)	Sam Mele	7.75	4.00	2.25
(206)	Orestes Minoso ("C" on cap)	12.50	6.25	3.75
(207)	Orestes Minoso (Sox on cap)	6.50	3.25	1.75
(208)	Dale Mitchell	6.50	3.25	1.75
(209)	Wally Moon	11.00	5.50	3.25
(210)	Don Mueller	8.00	4.00	2.50
(211)	Stan Musial (kneeling)	29.00	14.50	8.75
(212)	Stan Musial (batting)	40.00	20.00	12.00
(213)	Charley Neal	22.00	11.00	6.50
(214)	Don Newcombe (shaking hands)	11.00	5.50	3.25
(215)	Don Newcombe (Dodgers on jacket)	7.75	4.00	2.25
(216)	Don Newcombe (plain jacket)	7.75	4.00	2.25
(217)	Hal Newhouser	11.00	5.50	3.25
(218)	Ron Northey	13.50	6.75	4.00
(219)	Bill O'Dell	6.50	3.25	1.75
(220)	Joe Page	15.50	7.75	4.75
(221)	Satchel Paige	45.00	22.00	13.50
(222)	Milt Pappas	6.50	3.25	1.75
(223)	Camilo Pascual	6.50	3.25	1.75
(224)	Albie Pearson	29.00	14.50	8.75
(225)	Johnny Pesky	6.50	3.25	1.75
(226)	Gary Peters	29.00	14.50	8.75
(227)	Dave Philley	6.50	3.25	1.75
(228)	Billy Pierce	6.50	3.25	1.75
(229)	Jimmy Piersall	24.00	12.00	7.25
(230)	Vada Pinson	12.50	6.25	3.75
(231)	Bob Porterfield	6.50	3.25	1.75
(232)	John "Boog" Powell	50.00	25.00	15.00
(233)	Vic Raschi	7.00	3.25	1.75
(234)	Harold "Peewee" Reese (fielding, ball partially visible)	17.50	8.75	5.25
(235)	Harold "Peewee" Reese (fielding, ball not visible)	17.50	8.75	5.25
(236)	Del Rice	6.50	3.25	1.75
(237)	Bobby Richardson	60.00	30.00	18.00
(238)	Phil Rizzuto	18.00	9.00	5.50
(239)	Robin Roberts (script signature)	14.50	7.25	4.25
(240)	Robin Roberts (plain signature)	11.00	5.50	3.25
(241)	Brooks Robinson	35.00	17.50	10.50
(242)	Eddie Robinson	6.50	3.25	1.75
(243)	Floyd Robinson	29.00	14.50	8.75
(244)	Frankie Robinson	23.00	11.50	7.00
(245)	Jackie Robinson	35.00	17.50	10.50
(246)	Preacher Roe	11.00	5.50	3.25
(247)	Bob Rogers (Rodgers)	29.00	14.50	8.75
(248)	Richard Rollins	29.00	14.50	8.75
(249)	Pete Runnels	13.50	6.75	4.00
(250)	John Sain	7.75	4.00	2.25
(251)	Ron Santo	11.00	5.50	3.25
(252)	Henry Sauer	7.75	4.00	2.25
(253)	Carl Sawatski ("M" on cap)	6.50	3.25	1.75
(254)	Carl Sawatski ("P" on cap)	6.50	3.25	1.75
(255)	Carl Sawatski (plain cap)	17.50	8.75	5.25
(256)	Johnny Schmitz	7.75	4.00	2.25
(257)	Red Schoendeinst (Schoendienst) (fielding, name in white)	11.00	5.50	3.25
(258)	Red Schoendeinst (Schoendienst) (fielding, name in red-brown)	11.50	5.75	3.50
(259)	Red Schoendinst (Schoendienst) (batting)	11.00	5.50	3.25
(260)	Herb Score ("C" on cap)	7.75	4.00	2.25
(261)	Herb Score (plain cap)	15.50	7.75	4.75
(262)	Andy Seminick	6.50	3.25	1.75
(263)	Rip Sewell	11.00	5.50	3.25
(264)	Norm Siebern	6.50	3.25	1.75
(265)	Roy Sievers (batting)	7.75	4.00	2.25
(266)	Roy Sievers (portrait, "W" on cap, light background)	11.00	5.50	3.25
(267)	Roy Sievers (portrait, "W" on cap, dark background)	7.75	4.00	2.25

(268)	Roy Sievers (portrait, plain cap)	7.00	3.25	1.75
(269)	Curt Simmons	7.75	4.00	2.25
(270)	Dick Sisler	7.75	4.00	2.25
(271)	Bill Skowron	11.00	5.50	3.25
(272)	Bill "Moose" Skowron	60.00	30.00	18.00
(273)	Enos Slaughter	11.00	5.50	3.25
(274)	Duke Snider ("B" on cap)	17.50	8.75	5.25
(275)	Duke Snider ("LA" on cap)	20.00	10.00	6.00
(276)	Warren Spahn ("B" on cap)	11.50	5.75	3.50
(277)	Warren Spahn ("M" on cap)	16.00	8.00	4.75
(278)	Stanley Spence	15.50	7.75	4.75
(279)	Ed Stanky (plain uniform)	7.75	4.00	2.25
(280)	Ed Stanky (Giants uniform)	7.75	4.00	2.25
(281)	Vern Stephens (batting)	7.75	4.00	2.25
(282)	Vern Stephens (portrait)	7.75	4.00	2.25
(283)	Ed Stewart	7.75	4.00	2.25
(284)	Snuffy Stirnweiss	15.50	7.75	4.75
(285)	George "Birdie" Tebbetts	13.50	6.75	4.00
(286)	Frankie Thomas (photo actually Bob Skinner)	35.00	17.50	10.50
(287)	Frank Thomas (portrait)	16.00	8.00	4.75
(288)	Lee Thomas	6.50	3.25	1.75
(289)	Bobby Thomson	11.00	5.50	3.25
(290)	Earl Torgeson (Braves uniform)	6.50	3.25	1.75
(291)	Earl Torgeson (plain uniform)	7.75	4.00	2.25
(292)	Gus Triandos	11.00	5.50	3.25
(293)	Virgil Trucks	6.50	3.25	1.75
(294)	Johnny Vandermeer (VanderMeer)	15.00	7.50	4.50
(295)	Emil Verban	11.00	5.50	3.25
(296)	Mickey Vernon (throwing)	6.50	3.25	1.75
(297)	Mickey Vernon (batting)	6.50	3.25	1.75
(298)	Bill Voiselle	11.00	5.50	3.25
(299)	Leon Wagner	6.50	3.25	1.75
(300)	Eddie Waitkus (throwing, Chicago uniform)	11.00	5.50	3.25
(301)	Eddie Waitkus (throwing, plain uniform)	7.75	4.00	2.25
(302)	Eddie Waitkus (portrait)	15.00	7.50	4.50
(303)	Dick Wakefield	7.75	4.00	2.25
(304)	Harry Walker	11.00	5.50	3.25
(305)	Bucky Walters	7.00	3.25	1.75
(306)	Pete Ward	35.00	17.50	10.50
(307)	Herman Wehmeier	7.75	4.00	2.25
(308)	Vic Wertz (batting)	6.50	3.25	1.75
(309)	Vic Wertz (portrait)	6.50	3.25	1.75
(310)	Wally Westlake	7.75	4.00	2.25
(311)	Wes Westrum	15.50	7.75	4.75
(312)	Billy Williams	16.00	8.00	4.75
(313)	Maurice Wills	14.50	7.25	4.25
(314)	Gene Woodling (script signature)	6.50	3.25	1.75
(315)	Gene Woodling (plain signature)	11.00	5.50	3.25
(316)	Taffy Wright	7.75	4.00	2.25
(317)	Carl Yastrazemski (Yastrzemski)	195.00	97.00	58.00
(318)	Al Zarilla	7.75	4.00	2.25
(319)	Gus Zernial (script signature)	6.50	3.25	1.75
(320)	Gus Zernial (plain signature)	11.00	5.50	3.25
(321)	Braves Team - 1948	40.00	20.00	12.00
(322)	Dodgers Team - 1949	50.00	25.00	15.00
(323)	Dodgers Team - 1952	50.00	25.00	15.00
(324)	Dodgers Team - 1955	60.00	30.00	18.00
(325)	Dodgers Team - 1956	50.00	25.00	15.00
(326)	Giants Team - 1951	45.00	22.00	13.50
(327)	Giants Team - 1954	45.00	22.00	13.50
(328)	Indians Team - 1948	50.00	25.00	15.00
(329)	Indians Team - 1954	50.00	25.00	15.00
(330)	Phillies Team - 1950	50.00	25.00	15.00
(331)	Yankees Team - 1949	65.00	32.00	19.50
(332)	Yankees Team - 1950	65.00	32.00	19.50
(333)	Yankees Team - 1951	65.00	32.00	19.50
(334)	Yankees Team - 1952	65.00	32.00	19.50
(335)	Yankees Team - 1955	65.00	32.00	19.50
(336)	Yankees Team - 1956	65.00	32.00	19.50

1953 Canadian Exhibits

This Canadian-issued set consists of 64 cards and includes both major leaguers and players from the Montreal Royals of the International League. The cards are slightly smaller than the U.S. exhibit cards, measuring 3-1/4" x 5-1/4", and are numbered. The blank-backed cards were printed on gray stock. Card numbers 1-32 have a green or red tint, while card numbers 33-64 have a blue or reddish-brown tint.

		NM	EX	VG
Complete Set (64):		1100.	550.00	325.00
Common Player (1-32):		9.00	4.50	2.75
Common Player (33-64):		7.75	4.00	2.25
1	Preacher Roe	11.00	5.50	3.25
2	Luke Easter	9.00	4.50	2.75
3	Gene Bearden	9.00	4.50	2.75
4	Chico Carrasquel	9.00	4.50	2.75
5	Vic Raschi	11.00	5.50	3.25
6	Monty (Monte) Irvin	16.00	8.00	4.75
7	Henry Sauer	9.00	4.50	2.75
8	Ralph Branca	11.00	5.50	3.25
9	Ed Stanky	9.00	4.50	2.75
10	Sam Jethroe	9.00	4.50	2.75
11	Larry Doby	16.00	8.00	4.75
12	Hal Newhouser	16.00	8.00	4.75
13	Gil Hodges	25.00	12.50	7.50
14	Harry Brecheen	9.00	4.50	2.75
15	Ed Lopat	11.00	5.50	3.25
16	Don Newcombe	11.00	5.50	3.25
17	Bob Feller	30.00	15.00	9.00
18	Tommy Holmes	9.00	4.50	2.75
19	Jackie Robinson	150.00	75.00	45.00
20	Roy Campanella	100.00	50.00	30.00
21	Harold "Peewee" Reese	30.00	15.00	9.00
22	Ralph Kiner	20.00	10.00	6.00
23	Dom DiMaggio	11.00	5.50	3.25
24	Bobby Doerr	16.00	8.00	4.75
25	Phil Rizzuto	27.00	13.50	8.00
26	Bob Elliott	9.00	4.50	2.75
27	Tom Henrich	11.00	5.50	3.25
28	Joe DiMaggio	315.00	157.00	94.00
29	Harry Lowery (Lowrey)	9.00	4.50	2.75
30	Ted Williams	125.00	62.00	37.00
31	Bob Lemon	20.00	10.00	6.00
32	Warren Spahn	30.00	15.00	9.00
33	Don Hoak	11.00	5.50	3.25
34	Bob Alexander	9.00	4.50	2.75
35	John Simmons	9.00	4.50	2.75
36	Steve Lembo	9.00	4.50	2.75
37	Norman Larker	11.00	5.50	3.25
38	Bob Ludwick	9.00	4.50	2.75
39	Walter Moryn	11.00	5.50	3.25
40	Charlie Thompson	9.00	4.50	2.75
41	Ed Roebuck	11.00	5.50	3.25
42	Russell Rose	9.00	4.50	2.75
43	Edmundo (Sandy) Amoros	12.50	6.25	3.75
44	Bob Milliken	9.00	4.50	2.75
45	Art Fabbro	9.00	4.50	2.75
46	Spook Jacobs	9.00	4.50	2.75
47	Carmen Mauro	9.00	4.50	2.75
48	Walter Fiala	9.00	4.50	2.75
49	Rocky Nelson	9.00	4.50	2.75
50	Tom La Sorda (Lasorda)	50.00	25.00	15.00
51	Ronnie Lee	9.00	4.50	2.75
52	Hampton Coleman	9.00	4.50	2.75
53	Frank Marchio	9.00	4.50	2.75
54	William Sampson	9.00	4.50	2.75
55	Gil Mills	9.00	4.50	2.75
56	Al Ronning	9.00	4.50	2.75
57	Stan Musial	125.00	62.00	37.00
58	Walker Cooper	7.75	4.00	2.25
59	Mickey Vernon	7.75	4.00	2.25
60	Del Ennis	7.75	4.00	2.25
61	Walter Alston	25.00	12.50	7.50
62	Dick Sisler	7.75	4.00	2.25
63	Billy Goodman	7.75	4.00	2.25
64	Alex Kellner	7.75	4.00	2.25

1961 Exhibits - Wrigley Field

Distributed at Chicago's Wrigley Field circa 1961, this 24-card set features members of the Baseball Hall of Fame. The cards measure 3-3/8" x 5-3/8" and include the player's full name along the bottom. They were printed on gray stock and have a postcard back. The set is unnumbered.

		NM	EX	VG
Complete Set (24):		250.00	125.00	75.00
Common Player:		4.00	2.00	1.25
(1)	Grover Cleveland Alexander	6.00	3.00	1.75
(2)	Adrian Constantine Anson	6.00	3.00	1.75
(3)	John Franklin Baker	4.00	2.00	1.25
(4)	Roger Phillip Bresnahan	4.00	2.00	1.25
(5)	Mordecai Peter Brown	4.00	2.00	1.25
(6)	Frank Leroy Chance	5.00	2.50	1.50
(7)	Tyrus Raymond Cobb	50.00	25.00	15.00
(8)	Edward Trowbridge Collins	4.00	2.00	1.25
(9)	James J. Collins	4.00	2.00	1.25
(10)	John Joseph Evers	4.00	2.00	1.25
(11)	Henry Louis Gehrig	50.00	25.00	15.00
(12)	Clark C. Griffith	4.00	2.00	1.25
(13)	Walter Perry Johnson	10.00	5.00	3.00
(14)	Anthony Michael Lazzeri	4.00	2.00	1.25
(15)	James Walter Vincent Maranville	4.00	2.00	1.25
(16)	Christopher Mathewson	10.00	5.00	3.00
(17)	John Joseph McGraw	5.00	2.50	1.50
(18)	Melvin Thomas Ott	5.00	2.50	1.50
(19)	Herbert Jeffries Pennock	4.00	2.00	1.25
(20)	George Herman Ruth	70.00	35.00	21.00
(21)	Aloysius Harry Simmons	4.00	2.00	1.25
(22)	Tristram Speaker	12.00	6.00	3.50
(23)	Joseph B. Tinker	4.00	2.00	1.25
(24)	John Peter Wagner	10.00	5.00	3.00

1962 Statistic Back Exhibits

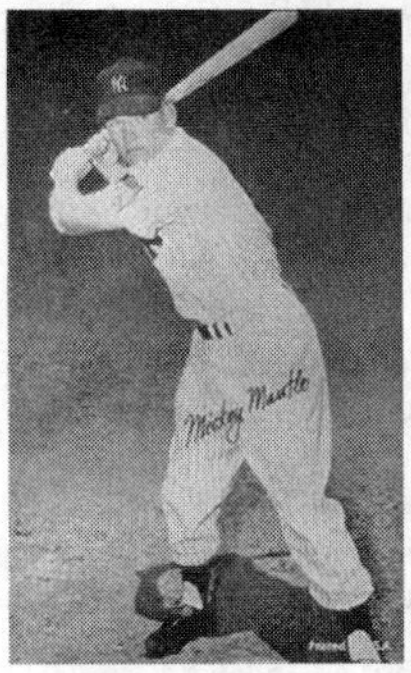

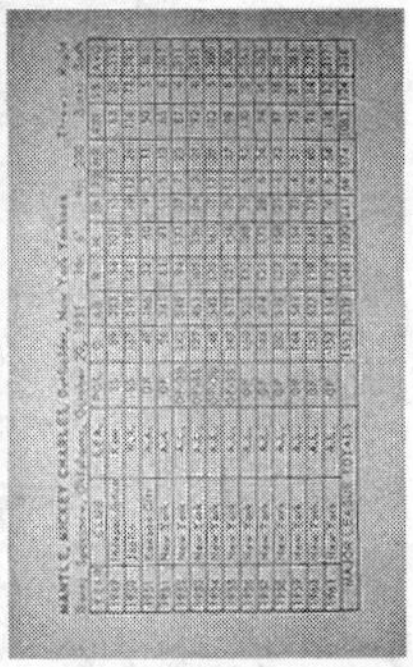

In 1962, the Exhibit Supply Co. added career statistics to the yearly set they produced. The black and white, unnumbered cards measure 3-3/8" x 5-3/8". The statistics found on the back are printed in black or red. The red backs are three times greater in value. The set is comprised of 32 cards.

		NM	EX	VG
Complete Set (32):		535.00	275.00	165.00
Common Player:		5.75	3.00	1.75
(1)	Hank Aaron	35.00	17.50	10.50
(2)	Luis Aparicio	15.00	7.50	4.50
(3)	Ernie Banks	24.00	12.00	7.25
(4)	Larry "Yogi" Berra	24.00	12.00	7.25
(5)	Ken Boyer	8.00	4.00	2.50
(6)	Lew Burdette	6.50	3.25	2.00
(7)	Norm Cash	6.50	3.25	2.00
(8)	Orlando Cepeda	9.50	4.75	2.75
(9)	Roberto Clemente	35.00	17.50	10.50
(10)	Rocky Colavito	15.00	7.50	4.50
(11)	Ed "Whitey" Ford	20.00	10.00	6.00
(12)	Nelson Fox	15.00	7.50	4.50
(13)	Tito Francona	5.75	3.00	1.75
(14)	Jim Gentile	5.75	3.00	1.75
(15)	Dick Groat	6.50	3.25	2.00
(16)	Don Hoak	6.50	3.25	2.00
(17)	Al Kaline	20.00	10.00	6.00
(18)	Harmon Killebrew	20.00	10.00	6.00
(19)	Sandy Koufax	35.00	17.50	10.50
(20)	Jim Landis	5.75	3.00	1.75
(21)	Art Mahaffey	5.75	3.00	1.75
(22)	Frank Malzone	5.75	3.00	1.75
(23)	Mickey Mantle	110.00	55.00	33.00
(24)	Roger Maris	20.00	10.00	6.00
(25)	Eddie Mathews	20.00	10.00	6.00
(26)	Willie Mays	35.00	17.50	10.50
(27)	Wally Moon	6.50	3.25	2.00
(28)	Stan Musial	35.00	17.50	10.50
(29)	Milt Pappas	5.75	3.00	1.75
(30)	Vada Pinson	7.50	3.75	2.25
(31)	Norm Siebern	5.75	3.00	1.75
(32)	Warren Spahn	20.00	10.00	6.00

1963 Statistic Back Exhibits

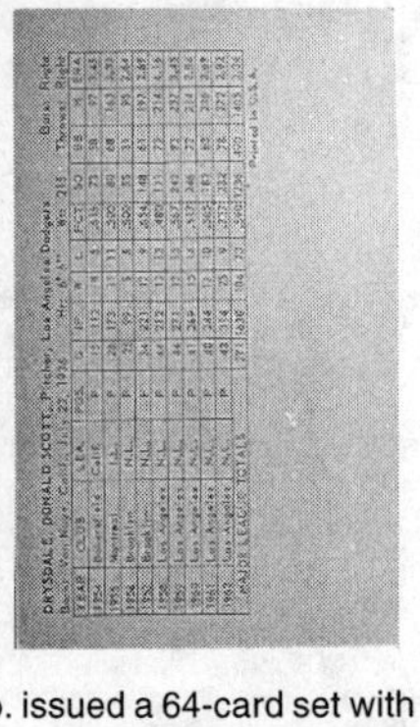

The Exhibit Supply Co. issued a 64-card set with career statistics on the backs of the cards in 1963. The unnumbered, black and white cards are printed on thick cardboard and measure 3-3/8" x 5-3/8" in size. The statistics on the back are usually found printed in black, though like the '62s, they have also been seen in red; a 3X premium should be attached to the red version.

	NM	EX	VG
Complete Set (64):	850.00	420.00	250.00
Common Player:	6.25	3.25	2.00
(1) Hank Aaron	40.00	20.00	12.00
(2) Luis Aparicio	18.50	9.25	5.50
(3) Bob Aspromonte	6.25	3.25	2.00
(4) Ernie Banks	25.00	12.50	7.50
(5) Steve Barber	6.25	3.25	2.00
(6) Earl Battey	6.25	3.25	2.00
(7) Larry "Yogi" Berra	30.00	15.00	9.00
(8) Ken Boyer	8.25	4.25	2.50
(9) Lew Burdette	7.00	3.50	2.00
(10) Johnny Callison	7.00	3.50	2.00
(11) Norm Cash	7.00	3.50	2.00
(12) Orlando Cepeda	12.50	6.25	3.75
(13) Dean Chance	6.25	3.25	2.00
(14) Tom Cheney	6.25	3.25	2.00
(15) Roberto Clemente	40.00	20.00	12.00
(16) Rocky Colavito	12.50	6.25	3.75
(17) Choo Choo Coleman	6.25	3.25	2.00
(18) Roger Craig	7.00	3.50	2.00
(19) Joe Cunningham	6.25	3.25	2.00
(20) Don Drysdale	18.50	9.25	5.50
(21) Dick Farrell	6.25	3.25	2.00
(22) Ed "Whitey" Ford	18.50	9.25	5.50
(23) Nelson Fox	15.00	7.50	4.50
(24) Tito Francona	6.25	3.25	2.00
(25) Jim Gentile	6.25	3.25	2.00
(26) Tony Gonzalez	6.25	3.25	2.00
(27) Dick Groat	7.00	3.50	2.00
(28) Ray Herbert	6.25	3.25	2.00
(29) Chuck Hinton	6.25	3.25	2.00
(30) Don Hoak	7.00	3.50	2.00
(31) Frank Howard	8.25	4.25	2.50
(32) Ken Hubbs	7.00	3.50	2.00
(33) Joey Jay	6.25	3.25	2.00
(34) Al Kaline	18.50	9.25	5.50
(35) Harmon Killebrew	18.50	9.25	5.50
(36) Sandy Koufax	30.00	15.00	9.00
(37) Harvey Kuenn	8.25	4.25	2.50
(38) Jim Landis	6.25	3.25	2.00
(39) Art Mahaffey	6.25	3.25	2.00
(40) Frank Malzone	6.25	3.25	2.00
(41) Mickey Mantle	120.00	60.00	36.00
(42) Roger Maris	18.50	9.25	5.50
(43) Eddie Mathews	18.50	9.25	5.50
(44) Willie Mays	40.00	20.00	12.00
(45) Bill Mazeroski	8.25	4.25	2.50
(46) Ken McBride	6.25	3.25	2.00
(47) Wally Moon	7.00	3.50	2.00
(48) Stan Musial	40.00	20.00	12.00
(49) Charlie Neal	6.25	3.25	2.00
(50) Bill O'Dell	6.25	3.25	2.00
(51) Milt Pappas	7.00	3.50	2.00
(52) Camilo Pascual	7.50	3.75	2.25
(53) Jimmy Piersall	8.25	4.25	2.50
(54) Vada Pinson	8.25	4.25	2.50
(55) Brooks Robinson	30.00	15.00	9.00
(56) Frankie Robinson	30.00	15.00	9.00
(57) Pete Runnels	7.00	3.50	2.00
(58) Ron Santo	8.25	4.25	2.50
(59) Norm Siebern	6.25	3.25	2.00
(60) Warren Spahn	25.00	12.50	7.50
(61) Lee Thomas	6.25	3.25	2.00
(62) Leon Wagner	6.25	3.25	2.00
(63) Billy Williams	18.50	9.25	5.50
(64) Maurice Wills	6.25	3.25	2.00

1980 Exhibits

Following the purchase of the "remains" of the Exhibit Supply Co., by a collector in the late 1970s, this set of Exhibits was issued in 1980. The set utilized photos from earlier issues in the same 3-3/8" x 5-3/8" size. Each card carries a notation in white at the bottom, "An Exhibit Card 1980", to distinguish them from the older version. Sets could be purchased printed in sepia, red or blue, at $4.50 per set. A total of 5,000 sets were reported printed. The unnumbered cards are checklisted here alphabetically.

	NM	EX	VG
Complete Set (32):	25.00	12.50	7.50
Common Player:	.50	.25	.15
(1) Johnny Antonelli	.50	.25	.15
(2) Richie Ashburn	.75	.40	.25
(3) Earl Averill	.50	.25	.15
(4) Ernie Banks	1.00	.50	.30
(5) Ewell Blackwell	.50	.25	.15
(6) Lou Brock	.50	.25	.15
(7) Dean Chance	.50	.25	.15
(8) Roger Craig	.50	.25	.15
(9) Lou Gehrig	4.00	2.00	1.25
(10) Gil Hodges	1.00	.50	.30
(11) Jack Jensen	.50	.25	.15
(12) Willie Keeler	.50	.25	.15
(13) George Kell	.50	.25	.15
(14) Alex Kellner	.50	.25	.15
(15) Harmon Killebrew	.75	.40	.25
(16) Dale Long	.50	.25	.15
(17) Sal Maglie	.50	.25	.15
(18) Roger Maris	2.00	1.00	.60
(19) Willie Mays	2.50	1.25	.70
(20) Minnie Minoso	.65	.35	.20
(21) Stan Musial	2.50	1.25	.70
(22) Billy Pierce	.50	.25	.15
(23) Jimmy Piersall	.60	.30	.20
(24) Eddie Plank	.50	.25	.15
(25) Pete Reiser	.50	.25	.15
(26) Brooks Robinson	.75	.40	.25
(27) Pete Runnels	.50	.25	.15
(28) Herb Score	.50	.25	.15
(29) Warren Spahn	.60	.30	.20
(30) Billy Williams	.50	.25	.15
(31) 1948 Boston Braves team	.50	.25	.15
(32) 1948 Cleveland Indians team	.50	.25	.15

1980 Hall of Fame Exhibits

Following the purchase of the "remains" of the Exhibit Supply Co., by a collector in the late 1970s, this set of Exhibits was issued in 1980. The set utilizies photos from earlier issues in the same 3-3/8" x 5-3/8" size. Each card has a notation in white at the bottom, "An Exhibit Card 1980 Hall Of Fame", to distinguish them from the older version. Sets could be purchased printed in sepia, red or blue for $5. The unnumbered cards are checklisted here alphabetically.

	NM	EX	VG
Complete Set (32):	30.00	15.00	9.00
Common Player:	.75	.35	.20
(1) Grover Cleveland Alexander	.75	.35	.20
(2) Lou Boudreau	.75	.35	.20
(3) Roger Bresnahan	.75	.35	.20
(4) Roy Campanella	1.25	.60	.40
(5) Frank Chance	.75	.35	.20
(6) Ty Cobb	2.50	1.25	.70
(7) Mickey Cochrane	.75	.35	.20
(8) Dizzy Dean	1.25	.60	.40
(9) Joe DiMaggio	4.00	2.00	1.25
(10) Bill Dickey	.75	.35	.20
(11) Johnny Evers	.75	.35	.20
(12) Jimmy Foxx	.75	.35	.20
(13) Vernon Gomez	.75	.35	.20
(14) Robert "Lefty" Grove	.75	.35	.20
(15) Hank Greenberg	1.25	.60	.40
(16) Rogers Hornsby	.75	.35	.20
(17) Carl Hubbell	.75	.35	.20
(18) Hughie Jennings	.75	.35	.20
(19) Walter Johnson	.75	.35	.20
(20) Napoleon Lajoie	.75	.35	.20
(21) Bob Lemon	.75	.35	.20
(22) Mickey Mantle	9.00	4.50	2.75
(23) Christy Mathewson	.75	.35	.20
(24) Mel Ott	.75	.35	.20
(25) Satchel Paige	1.25	.60	.40
(26) Jackie Robinson	2.50	1.25	.70
(27) Babe Ruth	7.50	3.75	2.25
(28) Tris Speaker	.75	.35	.20
(29) Joe Tinker	.75	.35	.20
(30) Honus Wagner	.75	.35	.20
(31) Ted Williams	3.00	1.50	.90
(32) Cy Young	.75	.35	.20

1909-11 E90-1, E90-2, E90-3 American Caramel

(See 1909-11 American Caramel Co. for checklists, values.)

1908-09 E91 American Caramel Co.

(See 1908-09 American Caramel Co. for checklists, values.)

1909 E92 Nadja Caramels

(See 1909 Nadja Caramels.)

1910 E93 Standard Caramel Co.

(See 1910 Standard Caramel Co. for checklist, values.)

1911 E94

(See 1911 George Close Candy Co. for checklist and value data.)

1909 E95 Philadelphia Caramel

(See 1909 Philadelphia Caramel for checklist, price guide.)

1910 E96 Philadelphia Caramel

(See 1910 Philadelphia Caramel for checklist, values.)

1910 E98 "Set of 30"

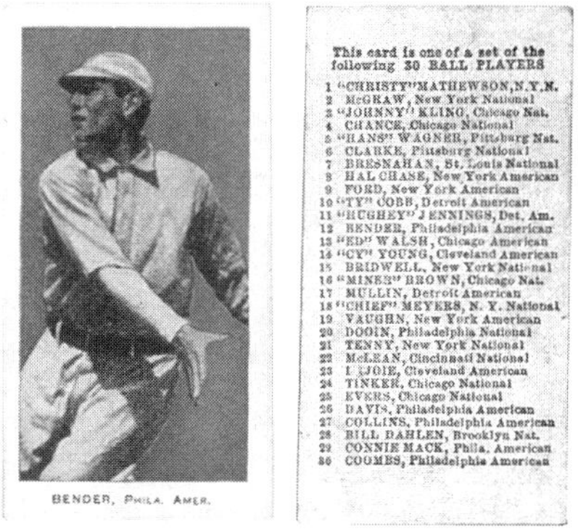

This card is one of a set of the following 30 BALL PLAYERS

1 "CHRISTY" MATHEWSON, N.Y.N.
2 McGRAW, New York National
3 "JOHNNY" KLING, Chicago Nat.
4 CHANCE, Chicago National
5 "HANS" WAGNER, Pittsburg Nat.
6 CLARKE, Pittsburg National
7 BRESNAHAN, St. Louis National
8 HAL CHASE, New York American
9 FORD, New York American
10 "TY" COBB, Detroit American
11 "HUGHEY" JENNINGS, Det. Am.
12 BENDER, Philadelphia American
13 "ED" WALSH, Chicago American
14 "CY" YOUNG, Cleveland American
15 BRIDWELL, New York National
16 "MINER" BROWN, Chicago Nat.
17 MULLIN, Detroit American
18 "CHIEF" MEYERS, N. Y. National
19 VAUGHN, New York American
20 DOOIN, Philadelphia National
21 TENNY, New York National
22 McLEAN, Cincinnati National
23 LAJOIE, Cleveland American
24 TINKER, Chicago National
25 EVERS, Chicago National
26 DAVIS, Philadelphia American
27 COLLINS, Philadelphia American
28 BILL DAHLEN, Brooklyn Nat.
29 CONNIE MACK, Phila. American
30 COOMBS, Philadelphia American

This set of 30 subjects was issued in 1910 and is closely related to several other early candy issues. that are nearly identical. The cards measure 1-1/2" x 2-3/4" and feature color lithograph player pictures. The backs, printed in brown, contain a checklist of the set but no advertising or other information indicating the manufacturer. The set was designated E98 by the "American Card Catalog." While the cards are unnumbered, they are listed here according to the numbers on the back checklist. Some or all of the cards may be found with different colored backgrounds.

	NM	EX	VG
Complete Set (30):	13500.	5000.	2500.
Common Player:	150.00	75.00	45.00
(1) Christy Matthewson (Mathewson)	900.00	360.00	180.00
(2) John McGraw	400.00	160.00	80.00
(3) Johnny Kling	150.00	75.00	45.00
(4) Frank Chance	400.00	160.00	80.00

(5)	Hans Wagner	1200.	480.00	240.00
(6)	Fred Clarke	400.00	160.00	80.00
(7)	Roger Bresnahan	400.00	160.00	80.00
(8)	Hal Chase	200.00	80.00	40.00
(9)	Russ Ford	150.00	75.00	45.00
(10)	Ty Cobb	3375.	1350.	675.00
(11)	Hughey Jennings	400.00	160.00	80.00
(12)	Chief Bender	400.00	160.00	80.00
(13)	Ed Walsh	400.00	160.00	80.00
(14)	Cy Young	600.00	240.00	120.00
(15)	Al Bridwell	150.00	75.00	45.00
(16)	Miner Brown	400.00	160.00	80.00
(17)	George Mullin	150.00	75.00	45.00
(18)	Chief Meyers	150.00	75.00	45.00
(19)	Hippo Vaughn	150.00	75.00	45.00
(20)	Red Dooin	150.00	75.00	45.00
(21)	Fred Tenny (Tenney)	150.00	75.00	45.00
(22)	Larry McLean	150.00	75.00	45.00
(23)	Nap Lajoie	400.00	160.00	80.00
(24)	Joe Tinker	400.00	160.00	80.00
(25)	Johnny Evers	400.00	160.00	80.00
(26)	Harry Davis	150.00	75.00	45.00
(27)	Eddie Collins	400.00	160.00	80.00
(28)	Bill Dahlen	150.00	75.00	45.00
(29)	Connie Mack	400.00	160.00	80.00
(30)	Jack Coombs	150.00	36.00	18.00

1909 E101 "Set of 50"

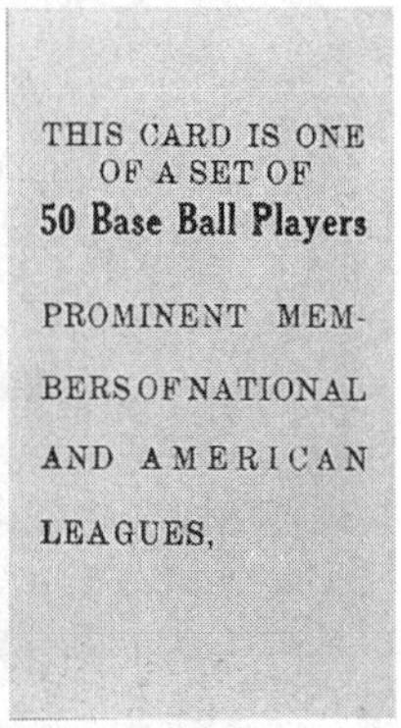

This 50-card set, issued in 1910, is closely related to the E92 set and is sometimes collected as part of that set. The fronts of the E101 cards are identical to the E92 set, but the back is an "anonymous" one, containing no advertising or any other information regarding the set's sponsor. The backs read simply "This card is one of a set of 50 Base Ball Players/Prominent Members of National and American Leagues."

		NM	EX	VG
Complete Set (50):		10000.	4000.	2000.
Common Player:		90.00	40.00	20.00
(1)	Jack Barry	90.00	40.00	20.00
(2)	Harry Bemis	90.00	40.00	20.00
(3)	Chief Bender (white hat)	350.00	140.00	70.00
(4)	Chief Bender (striped hat)	350.00	140.00	70.00
(5)	Bill Bergen	90.00	40.00	20.00
(6)	Bob Bescher	90.00	40.00	20.00
(7)	Al Bridwell	90.00	40.00	20.00
(8)	Doc Casey	90.00	40.00	20.00
(9)	Frank Chance	350.00	140.00	70.00
(10)	Hal Chase	200.00	80.00	40.00
(11)	Ty Cobb	2700.	1075.	540.00
(12)	Eddie Collins	350.00	140.00	70.00
(13)	Sam Crawford	350.00	140.00	70.00
(14)	Harry Davis	90.00	40.00	20.00
(15)	Art Devlin	90.00	40.00	20.00
(16)	Wild Bill Donovan	90.00	40.00	20.00
(17)	Red Dooin	90.00	40.00	20.00
(18)	Mickey Doolan	90.00	40.00	20.00
(19)	Patsy Dougherty	90.00	40.00	20.00
(20)	Larry Doyle (with bat)	90.00	40.00	20.00
(21)	Larry Doyle (throwing)	90.00	40.00	20.00
(22)	Johnny Evers	350.00	140.00	70.00
(23)	George Gibson	90.00	40.00	20.00
(24)	Topsy Hartsel	90.00	40.00	20.00
(25)	Fred Jacklitsch	90.00	40.00	20.00
(26)	Hugh Jennings	350.00	140.00	70.00
(27)	Red Kleinow	90.00	40.00	20.00
(28)	Otto Knabe	90.00	40.00	20.00
(29)	Jack Knight	90.00	40.00	20.00
(30)	Nap Lajoie	375.00	150.00	75.00
(31)	Hans Lobert	90.00	40.00	20.00
(32)	Sherry Magee	90.00	40.00	20.00
(33)	Christy Matthewson (Mathewson)	750.00	300.00	150.00
(34)	John McGraw	350.00	140.00	70.00
(35)	Larry McLean	90.00	40.00	20.00
(36)	Dots Miller (batting)	90.00	40.00	20.00
(37)	Dots Miller (fielding)	90.00	40.00	20.00
(38)	Danny Murphy	90.00	40.00	20.00
(39)	Bill O'Hara	90.00	40.00	20.00
(40)	Germany Schaefer	90.00	40.00	20.00
(41)	Admiral Schlei	90.00	40.00	20.00
(42)	Boss Schmidt	90.00	40.00	20.00
(43)	Johnny Seigle	90.00	40.00	20.00
(44)	Dave Shean	90.00	40.00	20.00
(45)	Boss Smith (Schmidt)	90.00	40.00	20.00
(46)	Joe Tinker	350.00	140.00	70.00
(47)	Honus Wagner (batting)	635.00	255.00	125.00
(48)	Honus Wagner (throwing)	635.00	255.00	125.00
(49)	Cy Young	450.00	180.00	90.00
(50)	Heinie Zimmerman	90.00	40.00	20.00

1908 E102 "Set of 25"

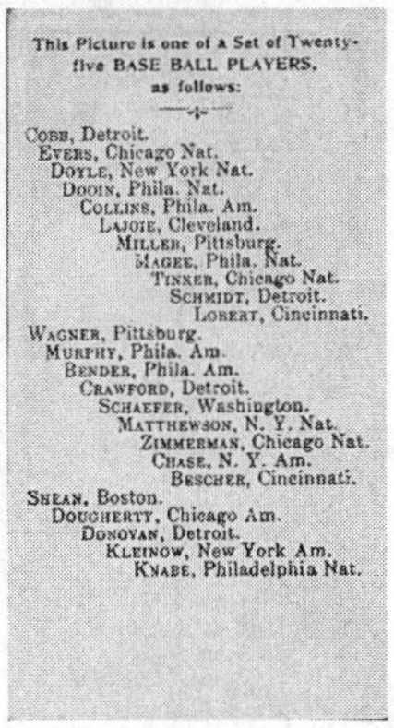

One of many similar early candy card sets, this set - designated as E102 in the American Card Catalog - was distributed around 1908. The producer of the set is unknown. Measuring approximately 1-1/2" x 2-3/4", the set is almost identical in design to the E101 set and other closely related issues. The set consists of 25 players, which are checklisted on the back of the card. Four of the players have been found in two variations, resulting in 29 different cards. Because there is no advertising on the cards, the set can best be identified by the words - "This Picture is one of a Set of Twenty-five Base Ball Players, as follows" - which appears at the top of the back of each card.

		NM	EX	VG
Complete Set (29):		9375.	3750.	1875.
Common Player:		120.00	50.00	25.00
(1)	Chief Bender	350.00	140.00	70.00
(2)	Bob Bescher	120.00	50.00	25.00
(3)	Hal Chase	200.00	80.00	40.00
(4)	Ty Cobb	4000.	1600.	800.00
(5)	Eddie Collins	350.00	140.00	70.00
(6)	Sam Crawford	350.00	140.00	70.00
(7)	Wild Bill Donovan	120.00	50.00	25.00
(8)	Red Dooin	120.00	50.00	25.00
(9)	Patsy Dougherty	120.00	50.00	25.00
(10)	Larry Doyle (batting)	120.00	50.00	25.00
(11)	Larry Doyle (throwing)	120.00	50.00	25.00
(12)	Johnny Evers	350.00	140.00	70.00
(13)	Red Kleinow	120.00	50.00	25.00
(14)	Otto Knabe	120.00	50.00	25.00
(15)	Nap Lajoie	400.00	160.00	80.00
(16)	Hans Lobert	120.00	50.00	25.00
(17)	Sherry Magee	120.00	50.00	25.00
(18)	Christy Matthewson (Mathewson)	900.00	360.00	180.00
(19)	Dots Miller (batting)	120.00	50.00	25.00
(20)	Dots Miller (fielding)	900.00	360.00	180.00
(21)	Danny Murphy	120.00	50.00	25.00
(22)	Germany Schaefer	120.00	50.00	25.00
(23)	Boss Schmidt	120.00	50.00	25.00
(24)	Dave Shean	120.00	50.00	25.00
(25)	Boss Smith (Schmidt)	120.00	50.00	25.00
(26)	Joe Tinker	350.00	140.00	70.00
(27)	Honus Wagner (batting)	850.00	340.00	170.00
(28)	Honus Wagner (fielding)	850.00	340.00	170.00
(29)	Heinie Zimmerman	120.00	50.00	25.00

1910 E104 Nadja Caramels

(See 1910 Nadja Caramels.)

1915 E106 American Caramel Co.

(See 1915 American Caramel Co.)

1922 E120 American Caramel Series of 240

(See 1922 American Caramel Series of 240.)

1921-22 E121 American Caramel Series of 80/120

(See 1921 American Caramel Series of 80, Series of 120.)

1922 E122 American Caramel Series of 80

(See 1922 American Caramel Series of 80 for checklist, values.)

1910 E125 American Caramel Die-Cuts

(See 1910 American Caramel Die-Cuts for checklist, values.)

1927 E126 American Caramel Series of 60

(See 1927 American Caramel Series of 60.)

1927 E210 (York Caramels)

(See York Caramels)

1910 E-UNC Candy

Little is known about these 1910-era cards except that they appear to have been cut from a candy box. Printed in blue or red duo-tone and blank-backed, the cards measure about 2-3/4" per side. A 1-3/8" x 2-1/2" central image has a player photo with a diamond design around. Player identification is in a white strip at bottom.

		NM	EX	VG
Common Player:				
(1)	Johnny Evers	300.00	150.00	90.00
(2)	"Christy" Mathewson	600.00	300.00	180.00
(3)	"Honus" Wagner	600.00	300.00	180.00

F

1961 F & M Bank Minnesota Twins Matchbook Covers

The star players on the inaugural Twins team are featured in this series of matchbook covers. The 1-1/2" x 4-7/16" matchbooks are printed in black, red and blue on white, and include a player portrait and team logo on front. The sponsoring bank's picture and logo are on back. Inside the front cover are a few details about the player. Values shown are for complete but empty covers, with the striker surface intact. Complete matchbooks with matches bring about 2X the values quoted.

	NM	EX	VG
Complete Set (10):	95.00	47.00	28.00
Common Player:	10.00	5.00	3.00
(1) Bob Allison	15.00	7.50	4.50
(2) Earl Battey	12.50	6.25	3.75
(3) Reno Bertoia	10.00	5.00	3.00
(4) Billy Gardner	10.00	5.00	3.00
(5) Lenny Green	10.00	5.00	3.00
(6) Harmon Killebrew	25.00	12.50	7.50
(7) Cookie Lavagetto	10.00	5.00	3.00
(8) Jim Lemon	15.00	7.50	4.50
(9) Camilo Pascual	15.00	7.50	4.50
(10) Pedro Ramos	10.00	5.00	3.00

1958-61 Falstaff Beer S.F. Giants team photos

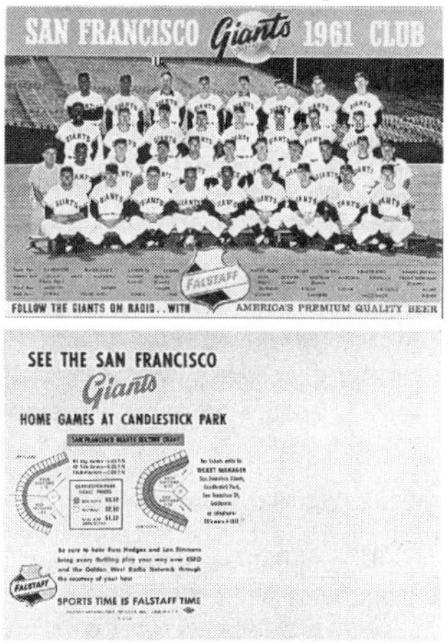

For the team's first four years on the West Coast, Falstaff beer sponsored this issue of color team photos. The 9" x 6-1/4" photos have team and year identification at top with players IDs and advertising message at bottom. Backs are printed in blue and orange on white with Falstaff ad and team promotional information.

	NM	EX	VG
Complete Set (4):	150.00	75.00	45.00
Common Photo:	40.00	20.00	12.00
(1) 1958 S.F. Giants	40.00	20.00	12.00
(2) 1959 S.F. Giants	40.00	20.00	12.00
(3) 1960 S.F. Giants	40.00	20.00	12.00
(4) 1961 S.F. Giants	40.00	20.00	12.00

1977 Family Fun Centers Padres

For 1977, Family Fun Centers, a chain of mini theme parks, took over sponsorship of the Padres annual issue of black-and-white player photos. The 5-1/2" x 8-1/2" photos have a large player pose at top-center, with his name and position below. In the bottom corners are team and sponsor logos. Backs have biographical data, complete stats and career highlights. Players are checklisted here alphabetically.

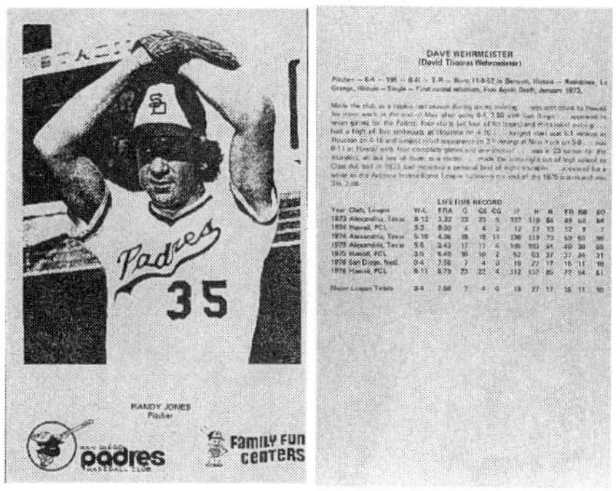

	NM	EX	VG
Complete Set (33):	60.00	30.00	18.00
Common Player:	2.00	1.00	.60
(1) Billy Almon	2.00	1.00	.60
(2) Joey Amalfitano	2.00	1.00	.60
(3) Tucker Ashford	2.00	1.00	.60
(4) Mike Champion	2.00	1.00	.60
(5) Roger Craig	2.00	1.00	.60
(6) Alvin Dark	2.00	1.00	.60
(7) Bob Davis	2.00	1.00	.60
(8) Rollie Fingers	6.00	3.00	1.75
(9) Dave Freisleben	2.00	1.00	.60
(10) Tom Griffin	2.00	1.00	.60
(11) George Hendrick	2.00	1.00	.60
(12) Mike Ivie	2.00	1.00	.60
(13) Randy Jones	2.00	1.00	.60
(14) John McNamara	2.00	1.00	.60
(15) Bob Owchinko	2.00	1.00	.60
(16) Merv Rettenmund	2.00	1.00	.60
(17) Gene Richards	2.00	1.00	.60
(18) Dave Roberts	2.00	1.00	.60
(19) Jackie Robinson	12.00	6.00	3.50
(20) Rick Sawyer	2.00	1.00	.60
(21) Pat Scanlon	2.00	1.00	.60
(22) Bob Shirley	2.00	1.00	.60
(23) Bob Skinner	2.00	1.00	.60
(24) Dan Spillner	2.00	1.00	.60
(25) Gary Sutherland	2.00	1.00	.60
(26) Gene Tenace	2.00	1.00	.60
(27) Dave Tomlin	2.00	1.00	.60
(28) Jerry Turner	2.00	1.00	.60
(29) Bobby Valentine	3.00	1.50	.90
(30) Dave Wehrmeister	2.00	1.00	.60
(31) Whitey Wietelmann	2.00	1.00	.60
(32) Don Williams	2.00	1.00	.60
(33) Dave Winfield	8.00	4.00	2.50

1978 Family Fun Centers Angels

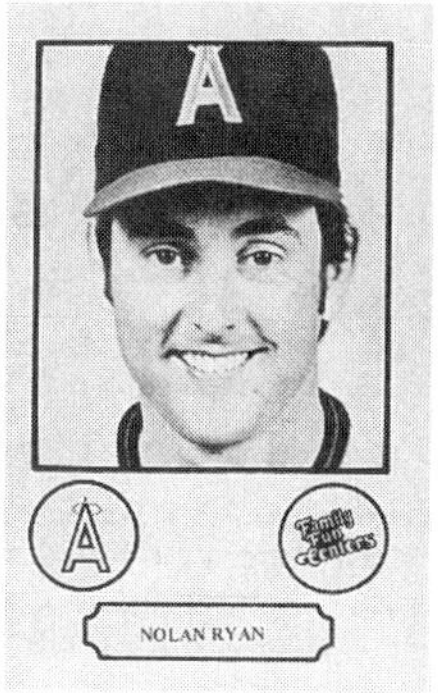

The players, manager and coaches of the '78 Angels are featured in this set of 3-1/2" x 5-1/2" sepia-tone cards. The unnumbered cards are checklisted here alphabetically.

	NM	EX	VG
Complete Set (38):	48.00	24.00	14.00
Common Player:	.50	.25	.15
(1) Don Aase	.50	.25	.15
(2) Mike Barlow	.50	.25	.15
(3) Don Baylor	.75	.40	.25
(4) Lyman Bostock	.60	.30	.20
(5) Ken Brett	.50	.25	.15
(6) Dave Chalk	.50	.25	.15
(7) Bob Clear	.50	.25	.15
(8) Brian Downing	.50	.25	.15
(9) Ron Fairly	.50	.25	.15
(10) Gil Flores	.50	.25	.15
(11) Dave Frost	.50	.25	.15
(12) Dave Garcia	.50	.25	.15
(13) Bobby Grich	.60	.30	.20
(14) Tom Griffin	.50	.25	.15
(15) Marv Grissom	.50	.25	.15
(16) Ike Hampton	.50	.25	.15
(17) Paul Hartzell	.50	.25	.15
(18) Terry Humphrey	.50	.25	.15
(19) Ron Jackson	.50	.25	.15
(20) Chris Knapp	.50	.25	.15
(21) Ken Landreaux	.50	.25	.15
(22) Carney Lansford	.50	.25	.15
(23) Dave LaRoche	.50	.25	.15
(24) John McNamara	.50	.25	.15
(25) Dyar Miller	.50	.25	.15
(26) Rick Miller	.50	.25	.15
(27) Balor Moore	.50	.25	.15
(28) Rance Mulliniks	.50	.25	.15
(29) Floyd Rayford	.50	.25	.15
(30) Jimmie Reese	.65	.35	.20
(31) Merv Rettenmund	.50	.25	.15
(32) Joe Rudi	.65	.35	.20
(33) Nolan Ryan	45.00	22.00	13.50
(34) Bob Skinner	.50	.25	.15
(35) Tony Solaita	.50	.25	.15
(36) Frank Tanana	.50	.25	.15
(37) Dickie Thon	.50	.25	.15
--- Header card	.50	.25	.15

1978 Family Fun Centers Padres

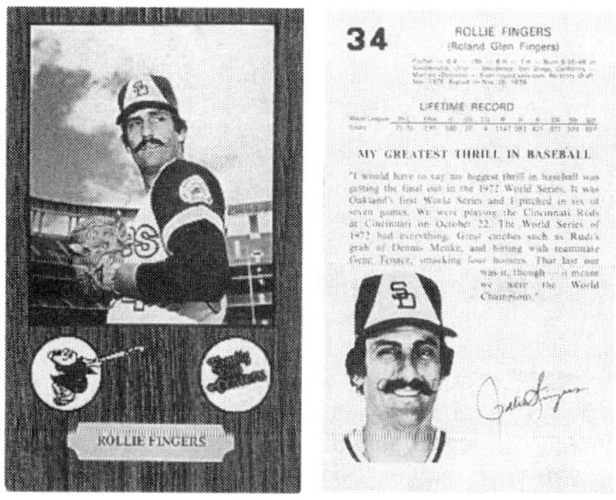

In conjunction with the Padres' hosting of the 1978 All-Star Game, Family Fun Centers issued this set of cards covering the players, coaches, announcers and even the owner. The 3-1/2" x 5-1/2" cards have a plaque look with a 3" x 3-1/4" posed color photo set on a wood background. The player's name is in a gold box at bottom, with the team and sponsor's logos in between. Backs are in black-and-white with a player portrait photo and facsimile autograph at bottom, a few biographical details and career stats at top and an essay in the middle titled, "My Greatest Thrill in Baseball". A uniform number appears at top-left. The set is checklisted here in alphabetical order.

	NM	EX	VG
Complete Set (39):	60.00	30.00	18.00
Common Player:	1.00	.50	.30
(1) Bill Almon	1.00	.50	.30
(2) Tucker Ashford	1.00	.50	.30
(3) Chuck Baker	1.00	.50	.30
(4) Dave Campbell (announcer)	1.00	.50	.30
(5) Mike Champion	1.00	.50	.30
(6) Jerry Coleman (announcer)	1.00	.50	.30
(7) Roger Craig	1.00	.50	.30
(8) John D'Acquisto	1.00	.50	.30
(9) Bob Davis	1.00	.50	.30
(10) Chuck Estrada	1.00	.50	.30
(11) Rollie Fingers	4.00	2.00	1.25
(12) Dave Freisleben	1.00	.50	.30
(13) Oscar Gamble	1.00	.50	.30
(14) Fernando Gonzalez	1.00	.50	.30
(15) Billy Herman	1.00	.50	.30
(16) Randy Jones	1.00	.50	.30
(17) Ray Kroc (owner)	1.00	.50	.30
(18) Mark Lee	1.00	.50	.30
(19) Mickey Lolich	2.50	1.25	.70
(20) Bob Owchinko	1.00	.50	.30
(21) Broderick Perkins	1.00	.50	.30
(22) Gaylord Perry	4.00	2.00	1.25
(23) Eric Rasmussen	1.00	.50	.30
(24) Don Reynolds	1.00	.50	.30
(25) Gene Richards	1.00	.50	.30
(26) Dave Roberts	1.00	.50	.30
(27) Phil Roof	1.00	.50	.30
(28) Bob Shirley	1.00	.50	.30
(29) Ozzie Smith	24.00	12.00	7.25
(30) Dan Spillner	1.00	.50	.30
(31) Rick Sweet	1.00	.50	.30
(32) Gene Tenace	1.00	.50	.30
(33) Derrel Thomas	1.00	.50	.30
(34) Jerry Turner	1.00	.50	.30
(35) Dave Wehrmeister	1.00	.50	.30
(36) Whitey Wietelmann	1.00	.50	.30
(37) Don Williams	1.00	.50	.30
(38) Dave Winfield	12.00	6.00	3.50
(39) All-Star Game	1.00	.50	.30

1979 Family Fun Centers Padres

Cards #25-30 have not been confirmed as issued.

		NM	EX	VG
Complete Set (30):		60.00	30.00	18.00
Common Player:		1.00	.50	.30
1	Roger Craig	1.00	.50	.30
2	John D'Acquisto	1.00	.50	.30
3	Ozzie Smith	16.00	8.00	4.75
4	KGB Chicken	1.00	.50	.30
5	Gene Richards	1.00	.50	.30
6	Jerry Turner	1.00	.50	.30
7	Bob Owchinko	1.00	.50	.30
8	Gene Tenace	1.00	.50	.30
9	Whitey Wietelmann	1.00	.50	.30
10	Bill Almon	1.00	.50	.30
11	Dave Winfield	9.00	4.50	2.75
12	Mike Hargrove	1.50	.70	.45
13	Fernando Gonzalez	1.00	.50	.30
14	Barry Evans	1.00	.50	.30
15	Steve Mura	1.00	.50	.30
16	Chuck Estrada	1.00	.50	.30
17	Bill Fahey	1.00	.50	.30
18	Gaylord Perry	6.00	3.00	1.75
19	Dan Briggs	1.00	.50	.30
20	Billy Herman	1.50	.70	.45
21	Mickey Lolich	2.50	1.25	.70
22	Broderick Perkins	1.00	.50	.30
23	Fred Kendall	1.00	.50	.30
24	Rollie Fingers	4.00	2.00	1.25
31	Bobby Tolan	1.00	.50	.30
32	Doug Rader	1.00	.50	.30
33	Dave Campbell	1.00	.50	.30
34	Jay Johnstone	1.00	.50	.30
35	Mark Lee	1.00	.50	.30
36	Bob Shirley	1.00	.50	.30

1980 Family Fun Centers Padres

Six Padres players or staff are featured on these 13" x 10" coupon sheets. At the right end of each glossy paper sheet is a group of coupons and advertising for the recreation centers, printed in black, yellow and green. At left are six photos. Each of the 3" x 5" photos has a color player pose. At either top or bottom, depending on placement on the sheet, is the player name in black, "FAMILY FUN CENTER" in green and a red building logo. Backs are blank and the sheets are not perforated. It is possible the checklist here is incomplete.

		NM	EX	VG
Complete Set (2):		16.00	8.00	4.75
Common Sheet:		4.00	2.00	1.25
(1)	Kurt Bevacqua, Dave Cash, Paul Dade, Rollie Fingers, Don Williams, Dave Winfield	12.00	6.00	3.50
(2)	Ed Brinkman, Dave Edwards, Jack Krol, Luis Salazar, Craig Stimac, John Urrea	4.00	2.00	1.25

1981 Family Fun Centers Padres

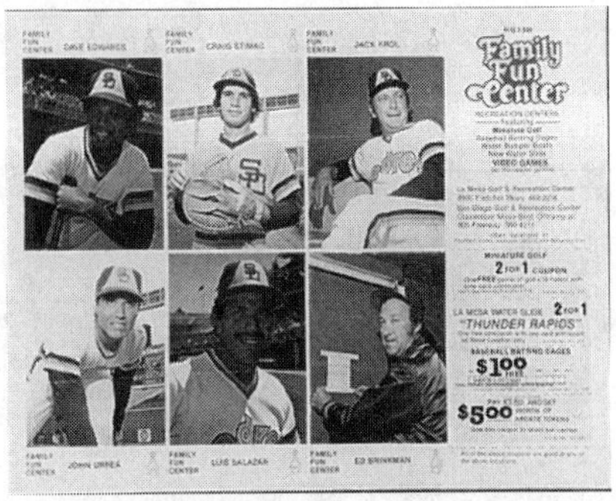

Six Padres players or staff are featured on these 13" x 10" coupon sheets. At the right end of each glossy paper sheet is a group of coupons and advertising for the recreation centers, printed in black, yellow and green. At left are six photos. Each of the 3" x 5" photos has a color player pose. At either top or bottom, depending on placement on the sheet, is the player name in black, "FAMILY FUN CENTER" in green and a red building logo. Backs are blank and the sheets are not perforated.

		MT	NM	EX
Complete Set (4):		110.00	75.00	40.00
Common Sheet:		10.00	7.50	4.00
(1)	Randy Bass, Frank Howard, Gary Lucas, Gene Richards, Ozzie Smith, Jerry Turner	75.00	56.00	30.00
(2)	Kurt Bevacqua, Dave Cash, Paul Dade, Rollie Fingers, Don Williams, Dave Winfield	55.00	41.00	22.00
(3)	Dan Boone, Chuck Estrada, Joe Lefebvre, Tim Lollar, Ed Stevens, Steve Swisher	10.00	7.50	4.00
(4)	Von Joshua, Fred Kendall, Dennis Kinney, Jerry Mumphrey, Steve Mura, Dick Phillips	10.00	7.50	4.00

1916 Famous and Barr Clothiers

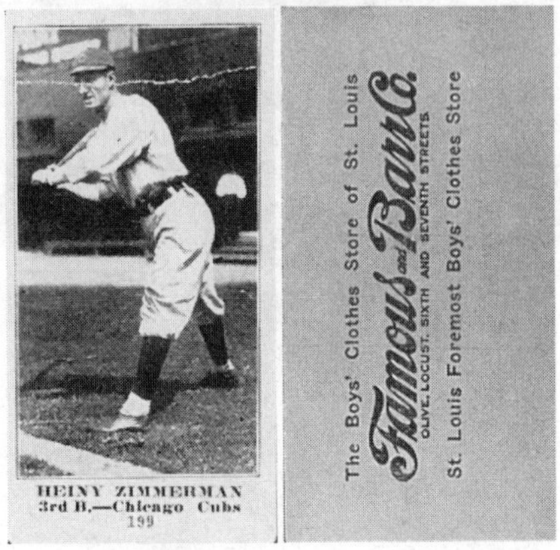

The advertisement for this St. Louis clothier is among the most commonly found on the backs of this 200-player set best known as the M101-4 Sporting News issue. Famous and Barr was one of many regional advertisers to use the cards for promotions. While type card or superstars collectors might pay a small premium for an example of the Famous and Barr back, prices will generally conform to those listed for 1916 Sporting News cards. Cards are printed in black-and-white and measure 1-5/8" x 3".

(See 1916 Sporting News for listings and values.)

1904 Fan Craze - American League

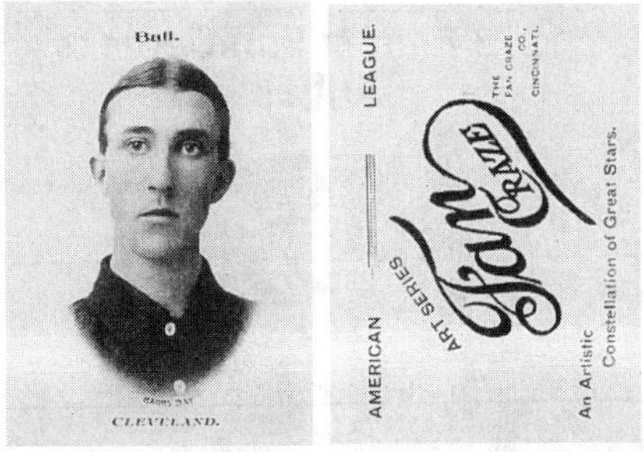

One of the earliest 20th Century baseball card sets, this 1904 issue from the Fan Craze Company of Cincinnati was designed as a deck of playing cards and was intended to be used as a baseball table game. Separate sets were issued for the National League, which are printed in red, and the American League, which are blue. Both sets feature sepia-toned, black and white player portraits inside an oval with the player's name and team below. The top of the card indicates one of many various baseball plays, such as "Single," "Out at First," "Strike," "Stolen Base," etc. The unnumbered cards measure 2-1/2" x 3-1/2" and are identified as "An Artistic Constellation of Great Stars."

		NM	EX	VG
Complete Set (51):		6000.	3000.	1800.
Complete Boxed Set:		7000.	3500.	2000.
Common Player:		80.00	40.00	24.00
(1)	Nick Altrock	80.00	40.00	24.00
(2)	Jim Barrett	80.00	40.00	24.00
(3)	Harry Bay	80.00	40.00	24.00
(4)	Albert Bender	230.00	115.00	69.00
(5)	Bill Bernhardt	80.00	40.00	24.00
(6)	W. Bradley	80.00	40.00	24.00
(7)	Jack Chesbro	265.00	132.00	79.00
(8)	Jimmy Collins	230.00	115.00	69.00
(9)	Sam Crawford	230.00	115.00	69.00
(10)	Lou Criger	80.00	40.00	24.00
(11)	Lave Cross	80.00	40.00	24.00
(12)	Monte Cross	80.00	40.00	24.00
(13)	Harry Davis	80.00	40.00	24.00
(14)	Bill Dinneen	80.00	40.00	24.00
(15)	Pat Donovan	80.00	40.00	24.00
(16)	"Pat" Dougherty	80.00	40.00	24.00
(17)	Norman Elberfield (Elberfeld)	80.00	40.00	24.00
(18)	Hoke Ferris (Hobe)	80.00	40.00	24.00
(19)	Elmer Flick	230.00	115.00	69.00
(20)	Buck Freeman	80.00	40.00	24.00
(21)	Fred Glade	80.00	40.00	24.00
(22)	Clark Griffith	230.00	115.00	69.00
(23)	Charley Hickman	80.00	40.00	24.00
(24)	Wm. Holmes	80.00	40.00	24.00
(25)	Harry Howell	80.00	40.00	24.00
(26)	Frank Isbel (Isbell)	80.00	40.00	24.00
(27)	Albert Jacobson	80.00	40.00	24.00
(28)	Ban Johnson	230.00	115.00	69.00
(29)	Fielder Jones	80.00	40.00	24.00
(30)	Adrian Joss	230.00	115.00	69.00
(31)	Billy Keeler	265.00	132.00	79.00
(32)	Napolean Lajoie	320.00	160.00	96.00
(33)	Connie Mack	480.00	240.00	144.00
(34)	Jimmy McAleer	80.00	40.00	24.00
(35)	Jim McGuire	80.00	40.00	24.00
(36)	Earl Moore	80.00	40.00	24.00
(37)	George Mullen (Mullin)	80.00	40.00	24.00
(38)	Billy Owen	80.00	40.00	24.00
(39)	Fred Parent	80.00	40.00	24.00
(40)	Case Patten	80.00	40.00	24.00
(41)	Ed Plank	230.00	115.00	69.00
(42)	Ossie Schreckengost	80.00	40.00	24.00
(43)	Jake Stahl	80.00	40.00	24.00
(44)	Fred Stone	80.00	40.00	24.00
(45)	Wm. Sudhoff	80.00	40.00	24.00
(46)	Roy Turner	80.00	40.00	24.00
(47)	G.E. Waddell	230.00	115.00	69.00
(48)	Bob Wallace	230.00	115.00	69.00
(49)	G. Harris White	80.00	40.00	24.00
(50)	Geo. Winters	80.00	40.00	24.00
(51)	Cy Young	600.00	300.00	180.00

1906 Fan Craze - National League

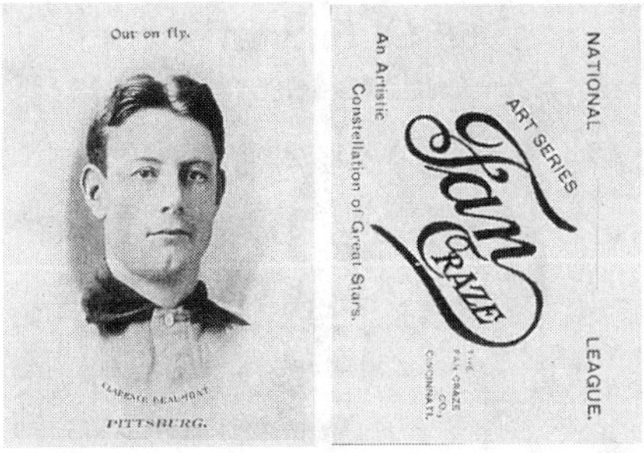

Identical in size and format to the American League set of two years previous, this set of unnumbered cards was issued by the Fan Craze Company of Cincinnati in 1906 and was designed like a deck of playing cards. The cards were intended to be used in playing a baseball table game. The National League cards are printed with red backs and sepia-toned player photos on front.

		NM	EX	VG
Complete Set (54):		4000.	2000.	1250.
Complete Boxed Set:		5000.	2500.	1500.
Common Player:		80.00	40.00	24.00
(1)	Leon Ames	80.00	40.00	24.00
(2)	Clarence Beaumont	80.00	40.00	24.00
(3)	Jake Beckley	250.00	125.00	75.00
(4)	Billy Bergen	80.00	40.00	24.00
(5)	Roger Bresnahan	250.00	125.00	75.00
(6)	George Brown (Browne)	80.00	40.00	24.00
(7)	Mordacai Brown	250.00	125.00	75.00
(8)	Jas. Casey	80.00	40.00	24.00
(9)	Frank Chance	250.00	125.00	75.00
(10)	Fred Clarke	250.00	125.00	75.00
(11)	Thos. Corcoran	80.00	40.00	24.00
(12)	Bill Dahlen	80.00	40.00	24.00
(13)	Mike Donlin	80.00	40.00	24.00
(14)	Charley Dooin	80.00	40.00	24.00
(15)	Mickey Doolin (Doolan)	80.00	40.00	24.00
(16)	Hugh Duffy	250.00	125.00	75.00
(17)	John E. Dunleavy	80.00	40.00	24.00
(18)	Bob Ewing	80.00	40.00	24.00
(19)	"Chick" Fraser	80.00	40.00	24.00
(20)	J. Edward Hanlon	250.00	125.00	75.00
(21)	G.E. Howard	80.00	40.00	24.00
(22)	Miller Huggins	250.00	125.00	75.00
(23)	Joseph Kelley	250.00	125.00	75.00
(24)	John Kling	80.00	40.00	24.00
(25)	Tommy Leach	80.00	40.00	24.00
(26)	Harry Lumley	80.00	40.00	24.00
(27)	Carl Lundgren	80.00	40.00	24.00
(28)	Bill Maloney	80.00	40.00	24.00
(29)	Dan McGann	80.00	40.00	24.00
(30)	Joe McGinnity	250.00	125.00	75.00
(31)	John J. McGraw	250.00	125.00	75.00
(32)	Harry McIntire (McIntyre)	80.00	40.00	24.00
(33)	Charley Nichols	80.00	40.00	24.00
(34)	Mike O'Neil (O'Neill)	80.00	40.00	24.00
(35)	Orville Overall (Orval)	80.00	40.00	24.00
(36)	Frank Pfeffer	80.00	40.00	24.00

		NM	EX	VG
(37)	Deacon Phillippe	80.00	40.00	24.00
(38)	Charley Pittinger	80.00	40.00	24.00
(39)	Harry C. Pulliam	80.00	40.00	24.00
(40)	Claude Ritchey	80.00	40.00	24.00
(41)	Ed Ruelbach (Reulbach)	80.00	40.00	24.00
(42)	J. Bentley Seymour	80.00	40.00	24.00
(43)	Jim Sheckard	80.00	40.00	24.00
(44)	Jack Taylor	80.00	40.00	24.00
(45)	Luther H. Taylor	100.00	50.00	30.00
(46)	Fred Tenny (Tenney)	80.00	40.00	24.00
(47)	Harry Theilman	80.00	40.00	24.00
(48)	Roy Thomas	80.00	40.00	24.00
(49)	Hans Wagner	750.00	375.00	225.00
(50)	Jake Weimer	80.00	40.00	24.00
(51)	Bob Wicker	80.00	40.00	24.00
(52)	Victor Willis	250.00	125.00	75.00
(53)	Lew Wiltsie	80.00	40.00	24.00
(54)	Irving Young	80.00	40.00	24.00

1920s Fan Favorites Notebooks

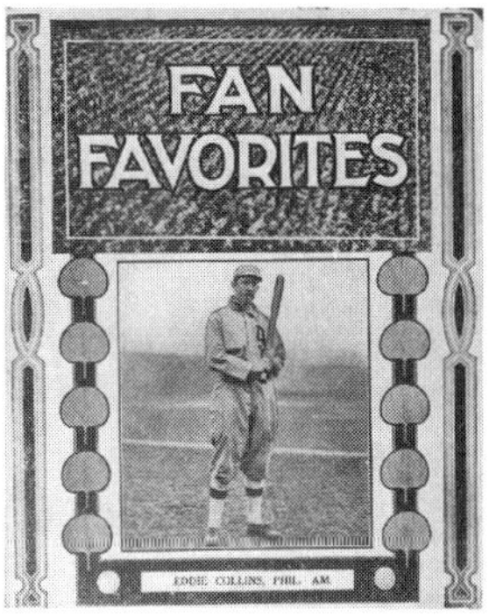

One of many contemporary notebooks to feature ballplayers on their covers, this series appears from the checklist to have been issued circa 1927-30. About 9" x 11", the notebooks have ornate backgrounds and borders on the cover with a black-and-white player photo at center. Values shown are for complete notebooks; covers which have been removed are valued substantially lower.

		NM	EX	VG
(1)	Mickey Cochrane	200.00	100.00	60.00
(2)	Eddie Collins	200.00	100.00	60.00
(3)	Babe Ruth	450.00	225.00	135.00
(4)	Hans Wagner	250.00	125.00	75.00

1922 Fans Cigarettes (T231)

More mystery surrounds this obscure set, issued in 1922 by Fans Cigarettes, than any other tobacco issue. In fact, the only evidence of its existence until 1992 was a photocopy of a single card of Pittsburgh Pirates outfielder Carson Bigbee. Even the owner of the card is unknown. Assuming the photocopy is actual size, the card measures approximately 2-1/2" x 1-1/2" and is believed to be sepia-toned. Adding to the mystery is the number "85" which appears in the lower right corner on the front of the card. apparently indicating there were at least that many cards in the set. In 1992 card "61" was reported. The back of Bigbee's card displays his batting averages for each season from 1918 through 1921 and includes the line: "I select C. Bigbee leading batter of all center fielders, packed with FANS cigarettes." The statement is followed by blanks for a person to fill in his name and address, as if the card were some sort of "ballot." Although they have not received much publicity, these are among the rarest baseball cards in the hobby. Their American Card Catalog designation is T231.

		NM	EX	VG
Complete Set:				
61	Frank Baker		7500.	4500.
85	Carson Bigbee		6000.	3500.

1939 Father & Son Shoes

This set features Phillies and A's players and was distributed in the Philadelphia area in 1939 by Father & Son Shoes stores. The unnumbered black and white cards measure 3" x 4". The player's name, position and team appear below the photo, along with the line "Compliments of Fathers & Son Shoes." The backs are blank. The checklist, arranged here alphabetically, may be incomplete.

		NM	EX	VG
Complete Set (17):		1200.	600.00	350.00
Common Player:		75.00	37.50	22.00
(1)	Morrie Arnovich	75.00	37.50	22.00
(2)	Earl Brucker	75.00	37.50	22.00
(3)	George Caster	75.00	37.50	22.00
(4)	Sam Chapman	75.00	37.50	22.00
(5)	Spud Davis	75.00	37.50	22.00
(6)	Joe Gantenbein	75.00	37.50	22.00
(7)	Bob Johnson	75.00	37.50	22.00
(8)	Chuck Klein	225.00	112.00	67.00
(9)	Herschel Martin	75.00	37.50	22.00
(10)	Merrill May	75.00	37.50	22.00
(11)	Wally Moses	75.00	37.50	22.00
(12)	Emmett Mueller	75.00	37.50	22.00
(13)	Hugh Mulcahy	75.00	37.50	22.00
(14)	Skeeter Newsome	75.00	37.50	22.00
(15)	Claude Passeau	75.00	37.50	22.00
(16)	George Scharien (Scharein)	75.00	37.50	22.00
(17)	Dick Siebert	75.00	37.50	22.00

1913 Fatima Team Cards (T200)

Issued by the Ligget & Myers Tobacco Co. in 1913 with Fatima brand cigarettes, the T200 set consists of eight National and eight American League team cards. The cards measure 2-5/8" x 4-3/4" and are glossy photographs on paper stock. Although it is unknown why, several of the cards are more difficult to obtain than others. The team cards feature 369 different players, managers and mascots. The card backs contain an offer for an enlarged copy (13" x 21") of a team card, minus the advertising on front, in exchange for 40 Fatima cigarette coupons. These large T200 premiums are very rare and have a value of 12-15 times greater than a common T200 card.

		NM	EX	VG
Complete Set (16):		12500.	6250.	3750.
(1)	Boston Nationals	700.00	350.00	275.00
(2)	Brooklyn Nationals	450.00	225.00	175.00
(3)	Chicago Nationals	450.00	225.00	175.00
(4)	Cincinnati Nationals	400.00	200.00	120.00
(5)	New York Nationals	800.00	500.00	325.00
(6)	Philadelphia Nationals	400.00	200.00	120.00
(7)	Pittsburgh Nationals	450.00	225.00	175.00
(8)	St. Louis Nationals	1000.	550.00	300.00
(9)	Boston Americans	500.00	300.00	185.00
(10)	Chicago Americans	650.00	400.00	195.00
(11)	Cleveland Americans	1000.	550.00	425.00
(12)	Detroit Americans	1100.	600.00	400.00
(13)	New York Americans	2100.	1000.	775.00
(14)	Philadelphia Americans	525.00	275.00	165.00
(15)	St. Louis Americans	2000.	1000.	600.00
(16)	Washington Americans	750.00	375.00	225.00

1913 Fatima Premiums

Among the rarest of the tobacco cards are the large-format (21" x 13") versions of the T200 Fatima team photos which could be obtained by redeeming 40 coupons from cigarette packs. The premium-size team photos are virtually identical to the smaller cards, except they do not carry the Fatima advertising on the front. Because of their large size, the premiums are seldom seen in top grade. The complete set price is quoted as a hypothetical proposition only; none is known.

		NM	EX	VG
Complete Set (16):		100000.	50000.	30000.
(1)	Boston Nationals	8000.	4000.	2400.
(2)	Brooklyn Nationals	7500.	3500.	2000.
(3)	Chicago Nationals	7500.	3500.	2000.
(4)	Cincinnati Nationals	7500.	3500.	2000.
(5)	New York Nationals	9000.	4500.	2700.
(6)	Philadelphia Nationals	7500.	3500.	2000.
(7)	Pittsburg Nationals	10000.	5000.	3000.
(8)	St. Louis Nationals	8000.	4000.	2400.
(9)	Boston Americans	7500.	3500.	2000.
(10)	Chicago Americans	8000.	4000.	2400.
(11)	Cleveland Americans	10000.	5000.	3000.
(12)	Detroit Americans	10000.	5000.	3000.
(13)	New York Americans	12500.	6250.	3750.
(14)	Philadelphia Americans	7500.	3500.	2000.
(15)	St. Louis Americans	9000.	4500.	2700.
(16)	Washington Americans	7500.	3500.	2000.

1914 Fatima (T222)

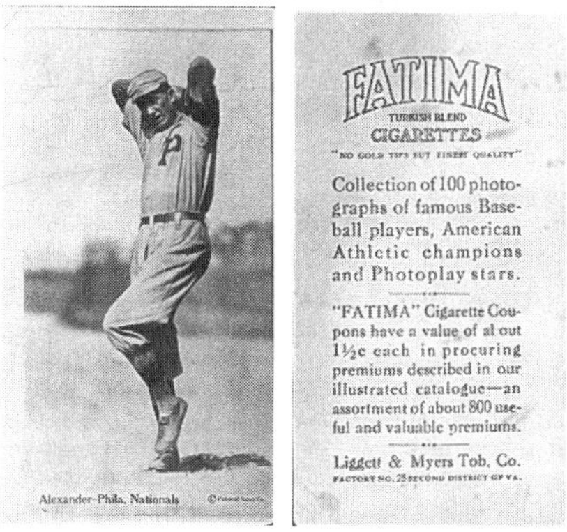

Unlike the typical 20th Century tobacco card issues, the T222 Fatima cards were glossy photographs on a thin paper stock and measure a larger 2-1/2" x 4-1/2". According to the back of the card, the set includes "100 photographs of famous Baseball Players, American Athletic Champions and Photoplay stars," but apparently not all were issued. The baseball portion of the set appears to be complete at 52, while only four other athletes and four "photoplay" stars have been found. The set, issued in 1913, includes players from 13 of the 16 major league teams (all except the Red Sox, White Sox and Pirates.) The set features a mix of star and lesser-known players.

		NM	EX	VG
Complete Set (52):		16250.	8125.	4875.
Common Player:		225.00	115.00	70.00
(1)	Grover Alexander	600.00	300.00	180.00
(2)	Jimmy Archer	225.00	115.00	70.00
(3)	Jimmy Austin	225.00	115.00	70.00
(4)	Jack Barry	225.00	115.00	70.00
(5)	George Baumgardner	225.00	115.00	70.00
(6)	Rube Benton	225.00	115.00	70.00
(7)	Roger Bresnahan	550.00	275.00	165.00
(8)	Boardwalk Brown	225.00	115.00	70.00
(9)	George Burns	225.00	115.00	70.00
(10)	Bullet Joe Bush	225.00	115.00	70.00
(11)	George Chalmers	225.00	115.00	70.00
(12)	Frank Chance	550.00	275.00	165.00
(13)	Al Demaree	225.00	115.00	70.00
(14)	Art Fletcher	225.00	115.00	70.00
(15)	Earl Hamilton	225.00	115.00	70.00
(16)	John Henry	225.00	115.00	70.00
(17)	Byron Houck	225.00	115.00	70.00
(18)	Miller Huggins	550.00	275.00	165.00
(19)	Hughie Jennings	550.00	275.00	165.00
(20)	Walter Johnson	1800.	900.00	540.00
(21)	Ray Keating	225.00	115.00	70.00
(22)	Jack Lapp	225.00	115.00	70.00
(23)	Tommy Leach	225.00	115.00	70.00
(24)	Nemo Leibold	225.00	115.00	70.00
(25)	Jack Lelivelt	225.00	115.00	70.00
(26)	Hans Lobert	225.00	115.00	70.00
(27)	Lee Magee	225.00	115.00	70.00
(28)	Sherry Magee	225.00	115.00	70.00
(29)	Fritz Maisel	225.00	115.00	70.00
(30)	Rube Marquard	600.00	300.00	180.00
(31)	George McBride	225.00	115.00	70.00
(32)	Stuffy McInnis	225.00	115.00	70.00
(33)	Stuffy McInnis	225.00	115.00	70.00
(34)	Ray Morgan	225.00	115.00	70.00
(35)	Eddie Murphy	225.00	115.00	70.00
(36)	Red Murray	225.00	115.00	70.00
(37)	Rube Oldring	225.00	115.00	70.00
(38)	Bill Orr	225.00	115.00	70.00
(39)	Hub Perdue	225.00	115.00	70.00
(40)	Art Phelan	225.00	115.00	70.00
(41)	Ed Reulbach	225.00	115.00	70.00
(42)	Vic Saier	225.00	115.00	70.00
(43)	Slim Sallee	225.00	115.00	70.00
(44)	Wally Schang	225.00	115.00	70.00
(45)	Wildfire Schulte	225.00	115.00	70.00
(46)	J.C. "Red" Smith	225.00	115.00	70.00
(47)	Amos Strunk	225.00	115.00	70.00
(48)	Bill Sweeney	225.00	115.00	70.00
(49)	Lefty Tyler	225.00	115.00	70.00
(50)	Ossie Vitt	225.00	115.00	70.00
(51)	Ivy Wingo	225.00	115.00	70.00
(52)	Heinie Zimmerman	225.00	115.00	70.00

1955 Felin's Franks

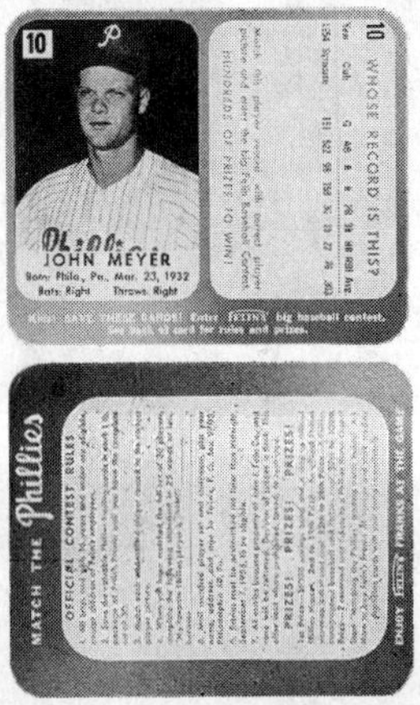

Because of the relatively few specimens in collectors hands, it is believed this hot dog issue was never actually released. The 4" x 3-5/8" round-cornered panels have a red border front and back with a color player photo on the left side of the front. At right-front are the 1954 stats of a player different than that pictured. Each half of the front shares a large black number. According to the card back, hot dog buyers were supposed to match the pictures and stats of 30 different players to have a chance to win prizes.

		NM	EX	VG
Common Player:		750.00	375.00	225.00
1	Mayo Smith	750.00	375.00	225.00
2	Unknown (probably coach Benny Bengough)			
3	Wally Moses	750.00	375.00	225.00
4	Whit Wyatt	750.00	375.00	225.00
5	(Maje McDonnell)	750.00	375.00	225.00
6	(Wiechec) (trainer)	450.00	225.00	135.00
7	Murry Dickson	750.00	375.00	225.00
8	Earl Torgeson	750.00	375.00	225.00
9	Bobby Morgan	750.00	375.00	225.00
10	John Meyer	750.00	375.00	225.00
11	Bob Miller	750.00	375.00	225.00
12	Jim Owens	750.00	375.00	225.00
13	(Steve Ridzik)	750.00	375.00	225.00
14	(Robin Roberts)	1250.	625.00	375.00
15	Unknown (probably Curt Simmons)			
16	(Herm Wehmeier)	750.00	375.00	225.00
17	(Smoky Burgess)	800.00	400.00	240.00
18	(Stan Lopata)	750.00	375.00	225.00
19	Gus Niarhos	750.00	375.00	225.00
20	Floyd Baker	750.00	375.00	225.00
21	Marv Blaylock	750.00	375.00	225.00
22	(Granny Hamner)	750.00	375.00	225.00
23	(Willie Jones)	750.00	375.00	225.00
24	Unknown	750.00	375.00	225.00
25	Unknown			
26	(Richie Ashburn)	1250.	625.00	375.00
27	Joe Lonnett	750.00	375.00	225.00
28	Mel Clark	750.00	375.00	225.00
29	Bob Greenwood	750.00	375.00	225.00
30	Unknown			

1913 Fenway Breweries/ Tom Barker Game

Presumably distributed as a promotion for its Fenway brand of beer, a specially labeled boxed set of the Tom Barker baseball game cards was issued. Apparently only the box itself and the card of Frank "Home Run" Baker can be found bearing the red advertising overprint.

	NM	EX	VG
Complete Set (54):	6000.	3000.	1800.
Frank Baker	200.00	100.00	60.00

1916 Ferguson Bakery Felt Pennants (BF2)

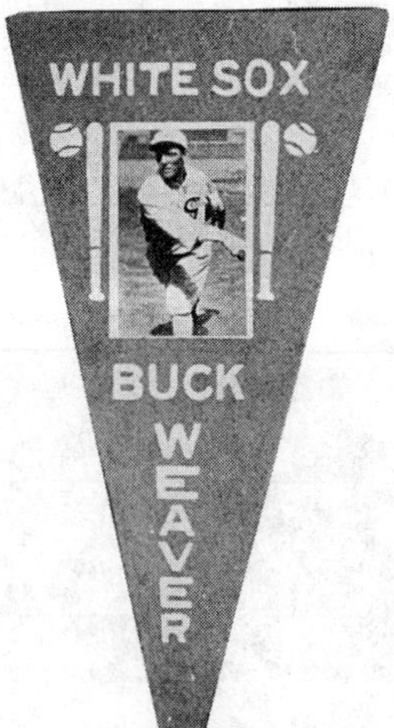

Issued circa 1916, this unnumbered set consists of 97 felt pennants with a small black-and-white player photo glued to each. The triangular pennants measure approximately 8-1/4" long, while the photos are 1-3/4" x 1-1/4" and appear to be identical to photos used for The Sporting News issues of the same period. The pennants list the player's name and team. The pennants were given away as premiums with the purchase of 5-cent loaves of Ferguson Bakery bread in the Roxbury, Mass., area.

		NM	EX	VG
Complete Set (97):		20000.	10000.	6000.
Common Player:		75.00	37.00	22.00
(1)	Grover Alexander	155.00	77.00	46.00
(2)	Jimmy Archer	75.00	37.00	22.00
(3)	Home Run Baker	95.00	47.00	28.00
(4)	Dave Bancroft	95.00	47.00	28.00
(5)	Jack Barry	75.00	37.00	22.00
(6)	Chief Bender	95.00	47.00	28.00
(7)	Joe Benz	75.00	37.00	22.00
(8)	Mordecai Brown	95.00	47.00	28.00
(9)	George J. Burns	75.00	37.00	22.00
(10)	Donie Bush	75.00	37.00	22.00
(11)	Hick Cady	75.00	37.00	22.00
(12)	Max Carey	95.00	47.00	28.00
(13)	Ray Chapman	90.00	45.00	27.00
(14)	Ty Cobb	750.00	375.00	225.00
(15)	Eddie Collins	95.00	47.00	28.00
(16)	Shano Collins	75.00	37.00	22.00
(17)	Commy Comiskey	95.00	47.00	28.00
(18)	Harry Coveleskie (Coveleski)	75.00	37.00	22.00
(19)	Gavvy Cravath	75.00	37.00	22.00
(20)	Sam Crawford	95.00	47.00	28.00
(21)	Jake Daubert	75.00	37.00	22.00
(22)	Josh Devore	75.00	37.00	22.00
(23)	Red Dooin	75.00	37.00	22.00
(24)	Larry Doyle	75.00	37.00	22.00
(25)	Jean Dubuc	75.00	37.00	22.00
(26)	Johnny Evers	95.00	47.00	28.00
(27)	Red Faber	95.00	47.00	28.00
(28)	Eddie Foster	75.00	37.00	22.00
(29)	Del Gainer (Gainor)	75.00	37.00	22.00
(30)	Chick Gandil	90.00	45.00	27.00
(31)	Joe Gedeon	75.00	37.00	22.00
(32)	Hank Gowdy	75.00	37.00	22.00
(33)	Earl Hamilton	75.00	37.00	22.00
(34)	Claude Hendrix	75.00	37.00	22.00
(35)	Buck Herzog	75.00	37.00	22.00
(36)	Harry Hooper	95.00	47.00	28.00
(37)	Miller Huggins	95.00	47.00	28.00
(38)	Shoeless Joe Jackson	1350.	675.00	405.00
(39)	Seattle Bill James	75.00	37.00	22.00
(40)	Hugh Jennings	95.00	47.00	28.00
(41)	Walter Johnson	400.00	200.00	120.00
(42)	Fielder Jones	75.00	37.00	22.00
(43)	Joe Judge	75.00	37.00	22.00
(44)	Benny Kauff	75.00	37.00	22.00
(45)	Bill Killefer	75.00	37.00	22.00
(46)	Nap Lajoie	95.00	47.00	28.00
(47)	Jack Lapp	75.00	37.00	22.00
(48)	Doc Lavan	75.00	37.00	22.00
(49)	Jimmy Lavender	75.00	37.00	22.00
(50)	Dutch Leonard	75.00	37.00	22.00
(51)	Duffy Lewis	75.00	37.00	22.00
(52)	Hans Lobert	75.00	37.00	22.00
(53)	Fred Luderus	75.00	37.00	22.00
(54)	Connie Mack	95.00	47.00	28.00
(55)	Sherry Magee	75.00	37.00	22.00
(56)	Al Mamaux	75.00	37.00	22.00
(57)	Rabbit Maranville	95.00	47.00	28.00
(58)	Rube Marquard	95.00	47.00	28.00
(59)	George McBride	75.00	37.00	22.00
(60)	John McGraw	95.00	47.00	28.00
(61)	Stuffy McInnes (McInnis)	75.00	37.00	22.00
(62)	Fred Merkle	75.00	37.00	22.00
(63)	Chief Meyers	75.00	37.00	22.00
(64)	Clyde Milan	75.00	37.00	22.00
(65)	Otto Miller	75.00	37.00	22.00
(66)	Pat Moran	75.00	37.00	22.00
(67)	Ray Morgan	75.00	37.00	22.00
(68)	Guy Morton	75.00	37.00	22.00
(69)	Eddie Murphy	75.00	37.00	22.00
(70)	Rube Oldring	75.00	37.00	22.00
(71)	Dode Paskert	75.00	37.00	22.00
(72)	Wally Pipp	65.00	32.00	19.50
(73)	Pants Rowland	75.00	37.00	22.00
(74)	Nap Rucker	75.00	37.00	22.00
(75)	Dick Rudolph	75.00	37.00	22.00
(76)	Reb Russell	75.00	37.00	22.00
(77)	Vic Saier	75.00	37.00	22.00
(78)	Slim Sallee	75.00	37.00	22.00
(79)	Ray Schalk	95.00	47.00	28.00
(80)	Wally Schang	75.00	37.00	22.00
(81)	Wildfire Schulte	75.00	37.00	22.00
(82)	Jim Scott	75.00	37.00	22.00
(83)	George Sisler	95.00	47.00	28.00
(84)	George Stallings	75.00	37.00	22.00
(85)	Oscar Stanage	75.00	37.00	22.00
(86)	Jeff Tesreau	75.00	37.00	22.00
(87)	Joe Tinker	95.00	47.00	28.00
(88)	Lefty Tyler	75.00	37.00	22.00
(89)	Hippo Vaughn	75.00	37.00	22.00
(90)	Bobby Veach	75.00	37.00	22.00
(91)	Honus Wagner	600.00	300.00	180.00
(92)	Ed Walsh	95.00	47.00	28.00
(93)	Buck Weaver	90.00	45.00	27.00
(94)	Ivy Wingo	75.00	37.00	22.00
(95)	Joe Wood	75.00	37.00	22.00
(96)	Ralph Young	75.00	37.00	22.00
(97)	Heinie Zimmerman	75.00	37.00	22.00

1916 Ferguson Bakery Photo Prize Pennants

As part of its baseball insert and premium program, the Roxbury, Mass., bakery issued this series of large (9" x 24") felt pennants bearing a black-and-white player photo (3" x 5"). The colorful pennants are decorated with baseball graphics and have player and team identification. The pennants were a premium for redeeming 50 tickets from 5-cent loaves of bread. Examples of the large-format pennants are so scarce only three players are checklisted thus far.

	NM	EX	VG
Common Player:	750.00	375.00	225.00
(1) Jack Barry	750.00	375.00	225.00
(2) Ty Cobb	5000.	2500.	1500.
(3) Miller Huggins	2000.	1000.	600.00
(4) John McGraw	2000.	1000.	600.00

1959 First Federal Savings Famous Senators Matchbooks

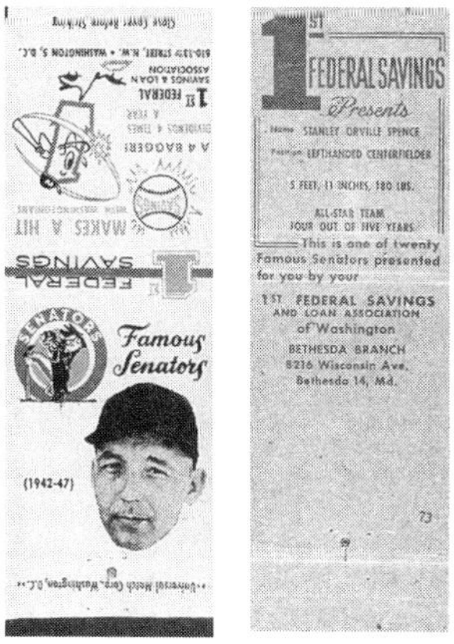

Star Senators of the 20th Century are featured in this series of matchbook covers. The 1-1/2" x 4-1/2" matchbooks include a black-and-white player portrait photo and team logo on front. The sponsoring bank's advertising is on back. Player identification and information are printed inside. Values shown are for complete but empty covers, with the striker surface intact. Complete matchbooks with matches bring about 2X the values quoted.

	NM	EX	VG
Complete Set (20):	325.00	160.00	95.00
Common Player:	15.00	7.50	4.50
(1) Nick Altrock	15.00	7.50	4.50
(2) Ossie Bluege	15.00	7.50	4.50
(3) Joe Cronin	20.00	10.00	6.00
(4) Alvin Crowder	15.00	7.50	4.50
(5) Goose Goslin	20.00	10.00	6.00
(6) Clark Griffith	20.00	10.00	6.00
(7) Bucky Harris	20.00	10.00	6.00
(8) Walter Johnson	45.00	22.00	13.50
(9) Joe Judge	15.00	7.50	4.50
(10) Harmon Killebrew	25.00	12.50	7.50
(11) Joe Kuhel	15.00	7.50	4.50
(12) Buddy Lewis	15.00	7.50	4.50
(13) Clyde Milan	15.00	7.50	4.50
(14) Buddy Myer	15.00	7.50	4.50
(15) Roger Peckinpaugh	15.00	7.50	4.50
(16) Sam Rice	20.00	10.00	6.00
(17) Roy Sievers	15.00	7.50	4.50
(18) Stanley Spence	15.00	7.50	4.50
(19) Mickey Vernon	15.00	7.50	4.50
(20) Samuel West	15.00	7.50	4.50

1953 First National Super Market Boston Red Sox

Four of the early 1950s Red Sox appear in this series issued by a Boston grocery chain. The cards may have been distributed in conjunction with players' in-store appearances. The cards measure 3-3/4" x 5" and are printed in black-and-white. A facsimile autograph appears on the front. Backs have the sponsor's advertising. The unnumbered cards are checklisted here alphabetically.

	NM	EX	VG
Complete Set (4):	300.00	150.00	90.00
Common Player:	75.00	37.00	22.00
(1) Billy Goodman	75.00	37.00	22.00
(2) Ellis Kinder	75.00	37.00	22.00
(3) Mel Parnell	75.00	37.00	22.00
(4) Sammy White	75.00	37.00	22.00

1951 Fischer's Bread Labels

This set of end labels from loaves of bread consists of 32 player photos, each measuring approximately 2-3/4" square. The labels include the player's name, team and position, along with a few words about him. The bakery's slogan "Bread For Energy" appears in a dark band along the bottom. The set, which is unnumbered, was distributed in the Northeast.

	NM	EX	VG
Complete Set (32):	7500.	3750.	2250.
Common Player:	250.00	125.00	75.00
(1) Vern Bickford	250.00	125.00	75.00
(2) Ralph Branca	275.00	135.00	82.00
(3) Harry Brecheen	250.00	125.00	75.00
(4) "Chico" Carrasquel	250.00	125.00	75.00
(5) Cliff Chambers	250.00	125.00	75.00
(6) "Hoot" Evers	250.00	125.00	75.00
(7) Ned Garver	250.00	125.00	75.00
(8) Billy Goodman	250.00	125.00	75.00
(9) Gil Hodges	375.00	185.00	110.00
(10) Larry Jansen	250.00	125.00	75.00
(11) Willie Jones	250.00	125.00	75.00
(12) Eddie Joost	250.00	125.00	75.00
(13) George Kell	350.00	175.00	105.00
(14) Alex Kellner	250.00	125.00	75.00
(15) Ted Kluszewski	325.00	160.00	97.00
(16) Jim Konstanty	250.00	125.00	75.00
(17) Bob Lemon	350.00	175.00	105.00
(18) Cass Michaels	250.00	125.00	75.00
(19) Johnny Mize	375.00	185.00	110.00
(20) Irv Noren	250.00	125.00	75.00
(21) Andy Pafko	250.00	125.00	75.00
(22) Joe Page	250.00	125.00	75.00
(23) Mel Parnell	250.00	125.00	75.00
(24) Johnny Sain	275.00	135.00	82.00
(25) "Red" Schoendienst	350.00	175.00	105.00
(26) Roy Sievers	250.00	125.00	75.00
(27) Roy Smalley	250.00	125.00	75.00
(28) Herman Wehmeier	250.00	125.00	75.00
(29) Bill Werle	250.00	125.00	75.00
(30) Wes Westrum	250.00	125.00	75.00
(31) Early Wynn	350.00	175.00	105.00
(32) Gus Zernial	250.00	125.00	75.00

1970 Flavor-est Milk Milwaukee Brewers

While purporting to be a dairy issue, this is actually a collectors' set produced by Illinois hobbyist Bob Solon. The cards picture members of the 1970 Brewers in their first year in Milwaukee. Posed action photos and portraits are printed in blue-and-white on a 2-3/8" x 4-1/4" format. The pictures are borderless at top and sides. At bottom in a white strip is the player name. Backs have a dairy ad. The unnumbered cards are checklisted here alphabetically. Ironically, this set was later reissued in a marked reprint.

	NM	EX	VG
Complete Set (24):	18.00	9.00	5.50
Common Player:	1.00	.50	.30
(1) Gene Brabender	1.00	.50	.30
(2) Dave Bristol	1.00	.50	.30
(3) Wayne Comer	1.00	.50	.30
(4) Cal Ermer	1.00	.50	.30
(5) Greg Goossen	1.00	.50	.30
(6) Tom Harper	1.25	.60	.40
(7) Mike Hegan	1.25	.60	.40
(8) Mike Hershberger	1.00	.50	.30
(9) Steve Hovley	1.00	.50	.30
(10) John Kennedy	1.00	.50	.30
(11) Lew Krausse	1.00	.50	.30
(12) Ted Kubiak	1.00	.50	.30
(13) Bob Locker	1.00	.50	.30
(14) Roy McMillan	1.00	.50	.30
(15) Jerry McNertney	1.00	.50	.30
(16) Bob Meyer	1.00	.50	.30
(17) John Morris	1.00	.50	.30
(18) John O'Donoghue	1.00	.50	.30
(19) Marty Pattin	1.00	.50	.30
(20) Rich Rollins	1.00	.50	.30
(21) Phil Roof	1.00	.50	.30
(22) Ted Savage	1.00	.50	.30
(23) Russ Snyder	1.00	.50	.30
(24) Dan Walton	1.50	.70	.45

1923 Fleer

While only a few specimens are known to date, from the print on the back it can be presumed that all 60 of the baseball players from the blank-back strip card set cataloged as W515 were also issued with Fleer advertising on the verso. Several cards are also known with boxers, indicating another 60 cards of non-baseball athletes and other famous people were also produced. The 1-5/8" x 2-3/8" cards feature crude color line art of the player on front, with a black-and-white ad on back. The cards pre-date by more than a decade Fleer's "Cops and Robbers" set of 1935, and are some 35 years in advance of Fleer's first modern baseball issue.

	NM	EX	VG
Complete Set (60):	7500.	3750.	2200.
Common Player:	100.00	50.00	30.00
1 Bill Cunningham	100.00	50.00	30.00
2 Al Mamaux	100.00	50.00	30.00
3 "Babe" Ruth	800.00	400.00	240.00
4 Dave Bancroft	200.00	100.00	60.00
5 Ed Rommel	100.00	50.00	30.00
6 "Babe" Adams	100.00	50.00	30.00
7 Clarence Walker	100.00	50.00	30.00
8 Waite Hoyt	200.00	100.00	60.00

9	Bob Shawkey	100.00	50.00	30.00
10	"Ty" Cobb	600.00	300.00	180.00
11	George Sisler	200.00	100.00	60.00
12	Jack Bentley	100.00	50.00	30.00
13	Jim O'Connell	100.00	50.00	30.00
14	Frank Frisch	200.00	100.00	60.00
15	Frank Baker	200.00	100.00	60.00
16	Burleigh Grimes	200.00	100.00	60.00
17	Wally Schang	100.00	50.00	30.00
18	Harry Heilman (Heilmann)	200.00	100.00	60.00
19	Aaron Ward	100.00	50.00	30.00
20	Carl Mays	115.00	57.00	34.00
21	The Meusel Bros. (Bob Meusel, Irish Meusel)	125.00	62.00	37.00
22	Arthur Nehf	100.00	50.00	30.00
23	Lee Meadows	100.00	50.00	30.00
24	"Casey" Stengel	200.00	100.00	60.00
25	Jack Scott	100.00	50.00	30.00
26	Kenneth Williams	100.00	50.00	30.00
27	Joe Bush	100.00	50.00	30.00
28	Tris Speaker	225.00	115.00	65.00
29	Ross Young (Youngs)	200.00	100.00	60.00
30	Joe Dugan	100.00	50.00	30.00
31	The Barnes Bros. (Jesse Barnes, Virgil Barnes)	100.00	50.00	30.00
32	George Kelly	200.00	100.00	60.00
33	Hugh McQuillen (McQuillan)	100.00	50.00	30.00
34	Hugh Jennings	200.00	100.00	60.00
35	Tom Griffith	100.00	50.00	30.00
36	Miller Huggins	200.00	100.00	60.00
37	"Whitey" Witt	100.00	50.00	30.00
38	Walter Johnson	250.00	125.00	75.00
39	"Wally" Pipp	115.00	57.00	34.00
40	"Dutch" Reuther	100.00	50.00	30.00
41	Jim Johnston	100.00	50.00	30.00
42	Willie Kamm	100.00	50.00	30.00
43	Sam Jones	100.00	50.00	30.00
44	Frank Snyder	100.00	50.00	30.00
45	John McGraw	200.00	100.00	60.00
46	Everett Scott	100.00	50.00	30.00
47	"Babe" Ruth	800.00	400.00	240.00
48	Urban Shocker	100.00	50.00	30.00
49	Grover Alexander	200.00	100.00	60.00
50	"Rabbit" Maranville	200.00	100.00	60.00
51	Ray Schalk	200.00	100.00	60.00
52	"Heinie" Groh	100.00	50.00	30.00
53	Wilbert Robinson	200.00	100.00	60.00
54	George Burns	100.00	50.00	30.00
55	Rogers Hornsby	200.00	100.00	60.00
56	Zack Wheat	200.00	100.00	60.00
57	Eddie Roush	200.00	100.00	60.00
58	Eddie Collins	200.00	100.00	60.00
59	Charlie Hollocher	100.00	50.00	30.00
60	Red Faber	200.00	100.00	60.00

1959 Fleer Ted Williams

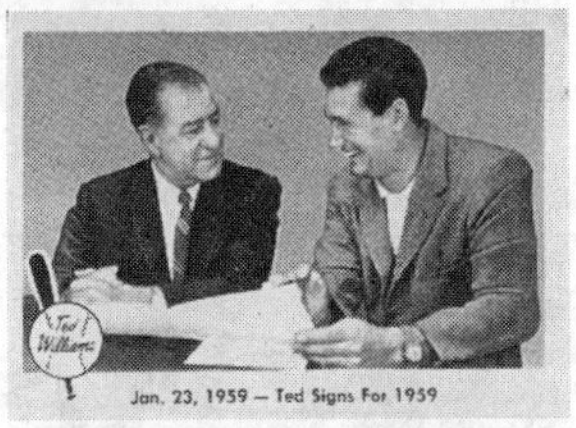

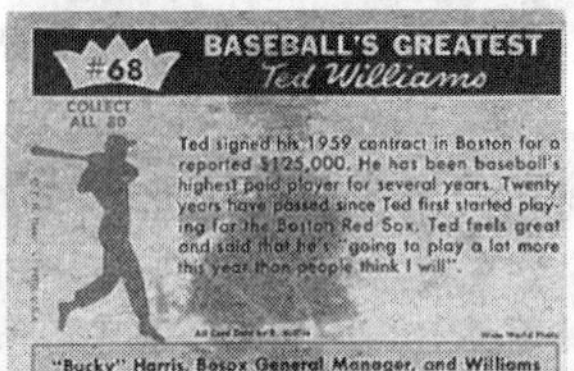

This 80-card 1959 Fleer set tells of the life of baseball great Ted Williams, from his childhood years up to 1958. The full-color cards measure 2-1/2" x 3-1/2" in size and make use of both horizontal and vertical formats. The card backs, all designed horizontally, contain a continuing biography of Williams. Card #68 was withdrawn from the set early in production and is scarce. Counterfeit cards of #68 have been produced and can be distinguished by a cross-hatch pattern which appears over the photo on the card fronts.

		NM	EX	VG
Complete Set (80):		1750.	875.00	525.00
Common Card:		11.00	5.50	3.25
1	The Early Years	45.00	15.00	9.00
2	Ted's Idol (Babe Ruth)	90.00	45.00	27.00
3	Practice Makes Perfect	11.00	5.50	3.25
4	1934 - Ted Learns The Fine Points	11.00	5.50	3.25
5	Ted's Fame Spreads - 1935-36	11.00	5.50	3.25
6	Ted Turns Professional	15.00	7.50	4.50
7	1936 - From Mound To Plate	11.00	5.50	3.25
8	1937 - First Full Season	15.00	7.50	4.50
9	1937 - First Step To The Majors (with Eddie Collins)	15.00	7.50	4.50
10	1938 - Gunning As A Pastime	11.00	5.50	3.25
11	1938 - First Spring Training (with Jimmie Foxx)	35.00	17.50	10.50
12	1939 - Burning Up The Minors	15.00	7.50	4.50
13	1939 - Ted Shows He Will Stay	11.00	5.50	3.25
14	Outstanding Rookie of 1939	11.00	5.50	3.25
15	1940 - Williams Licks Sophomore Jinx	11.00	5.50	3.25
16	1941 - Williams' Greatest Year	11.00	5.50	3.25
17	1941 - How Ted Hit .400	35.00	17.50	10.50
18	1941 - All-Star Hero	11.00	5.50	3.25
19	1942 - Ted Wins Triple Crown	11.00	5.50	3.25
20	1942 - On To Naval Training	11.00	5.50	3.25
21	1943 - Honors For Williams	11.00	5.50	3.25
22	1944 - Ted Solos	11.00	5.50	3.25
23	1944 - Williams Wins His Wings	11.00	5.50	3.25
24	1945 - Sharpshooter	11.00	5.50	3.25
25	1945 - Ted Is Discharged	11.00	5.50	3.25
26	1946 - Off To A Flying Start	11.00	5.50	3.25
27	July 9, 1946 - One Man Show	11.00	5.50	3.25
28	July 14, 1946 - The Williams Shift	11.00	5.50	3.25
29	July 21, 1946, Ted Hits For The Cycle	15.00	7.50	4.50
30	1946 - Beating The Williams Shift	11.00	5.50	3.25
31	Oct. 1946 - Sox Lose The Series	11.00	5.50	3.25
32	1946 - Most Valuable Player	11.00	5.50	3.25
33	1947 - Another Triple Crown For Ted	11.00	5.50	3.25
34	1947 - Ted Sets Runs-Scored Record	11.00	5.50	3.25
35	1948 - The Sox Miss The Pennant	11.00	5.50	3.25
36	1948 - Banner Year For Ted	11.00	5.50	3.25
37	1949 - Sox Miss Out Again	11.00	5.50	3.25
38	1949 - Power Rampage	11.00	5.50	3.25
39	1950 - Great Start (with Joe Cronin and Eddie Collins)	13.50	6.75	4.00
40	July 11, 1950 - Ted Crashes Into Wall	11.00	5.50	3.25
41	1950 - Ted Recovers	11.00	5.50	3.25
42	1951 - Williams Slowed By Injury	13.50	6.75	4.00
43	1951 - Leads Outfielders In Double Play	11.00	5.50	3.25
44	1952 - Back To The Marines	11.00	5.50	3.25
45	1952 - Farewell To Baseball?	11.00	5.50	3.25
46	1952 - Ready For Combat	11.00	5.50	3.25
47	1953 - Ted Crash Lands Jet	11.00	5.50	3.25
48	July 14, 1953 - Ted Returns	11.00	5.50	3.25
49	1953 - Smash Return	11.00	5.50	3.25
50	March 1954 - Spring Injury	11.00	5.50	3.25
51	May 16, 1954 - Ted Is Patched Up	11.00	5.50	3.25
52	1954 - Ted's Comeback	11.00	5.50	3.25
53	1954 - Ted's Comeback Is A Sucess	11.00	5.50	3.25
54	Dec. 1954, Fisherman Ted Hooks a Big On	11.00	5.50	3.25
55	1955 - Ted Decides Retirement Is "No Go (with Joe Cronin)	11.00	5.50	3.25
56	1955 - 2,000th Major League Hit	11.00	5.50	3.25
57	1956 - Ted Reaches 400th Homer	11.00	5.50	3.25
58	1957 - Williams Hits .388	11.00	5.50	3.25
59	1957 - Hot September For Ted	11.00	5.50	3.25
60	1957 - More Records For Ted	11.00	5.50	3.25
61	1957 - Outfielder Ted	11.00	5.50	3.25
62	1958 - 6th Batting Title For Ted	11.00	5.50	3.25
63	Ted's All-Star Record	40.00	20.00	12.00
64	1958 - Daughter And Famous Daddy	11.00	5.50	3.25
65	August 30, 1958	11.00	5.50	3.25
66	1958 - Powerhouse	11.00	5.50	3.25
67	Two Famous Fishermen (with Sam Snead)	35.00	17.50	10.50
68	Jan. 23, 1959 - Ted Signs For 1959	750.00	375.00	225.00
69	A Future Ted Williams?	11.00	5.50	3.25
70	Ted Williams & Jim Thorpe	35.00	17.50	10.50
71	Ted's Hitting Fundamentals #1	11.00	5.50	3.25
72	Ted's Hitting Fundamentals #2	11.00	5.50	3.25
73	Ted's Hitting Fundamentals #3	11.00	5.50	3.25
74	Here's How!	11.00	5.50	3.25
75	Williams' Value To Red Sox (with Babe Ruth, Eddie Collins)	50.00	25.00	15.00
76	Ted's Remarkable "On Base" Record	11.00	5.50	3.25
77	Ted Relaxes	11.00	5.50	3.25
78	Honors For Williams	11.00	5.50	3.25
79	Where Ted Stands	20.00	10.00	6.00
80	Ted's Goals For 1959	30.00	15.00	9.00

1960 Fleer Baseball Greats

The 1960 Fleer Baseball Greats set consists of 78 cards of the game's top players from the past, plus a card of Ted Williams, who was in his final major league season. The cards are standard size (2-1/2" x 3-1/2") and feature color photos inside blue, green, red or yellow borders. The card backs carry a short player biography plus career hitting or pitching statistics. Unissued cards with a Pepper Martin back (#80), but with another player pictured on the front are in existence, all have been cancelled with a slit cut out of the bottom.

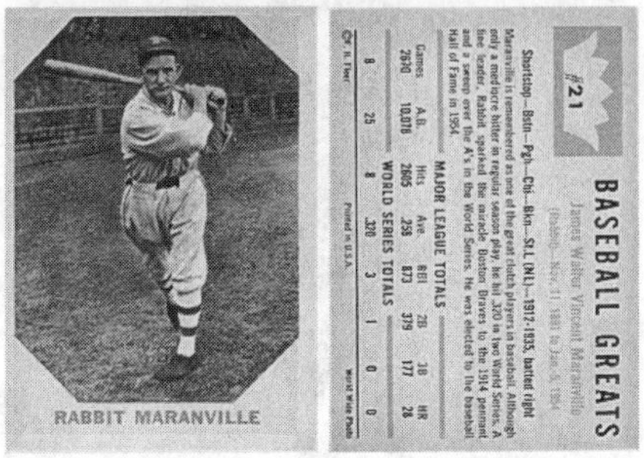

		NM	EX	VG
Complete Set (79):		450.00	225.00	135.00
Common Player:		4.00	2.00	1.25
1	Nap Lajoie	23.00	9.00	6.00
2	Christy Mathewson	15.00	7.50	4.50
3	Babe Ruth	75.00	37.00	22.00
4	Carl Hubbell	6.00	3.00	1.75
5	Grover Cleveland Alexander	8.00	4.00	2.50
6	Walter Johnson	11.00	5.50	3.25
7	Chief Bender	4.00	2.00	1.25
8	Roger Bresnahan	4.00	2.00	1.25
9	Mordecai Brown	4.00	2.00	1.25
10	Tris Speaker	6.00	3.00	1.75
11	Arky Vaughan	4.00	2.00	1.25
12	Zack Wheat	4.00	2.00	1.25
13	George Sisler	4.00	2.00	1.25
14	Connie Mack	4.00	2.00	1.25
15	Clark Griffith	4.00	2.00	1.25
16	Lou Boudreau	4.00	2.00	1.25
17	Ernie Lombardi	4.00	2.00	1.25
18	Heinie Manush	4.00	2.00	1.25
19	Marty Marion	4.00	2.00	1.25
20	Eddie Collins	4.00	2.00	1.25
21	Rabbit Maranville	4.00	2.00	1.25
22	Joe Medwick	4.00	2.00	1.25
23	Ed Barrow	4.00	2.00	1.25
24	Mickey Cochrane	4.00	2.00	1.25
25	Jimmy Collins	4.00	2.00	1.25
26	Bob Feller	15.00	7.50	4.50
27	Luke Appling	4.00	2.00	1.25
28	Lou Gehrig	85.00	42.00	25.00
29	Gabby Hartnett	4.00	2.00	1.25
30	Chuck Klein	4.00	2.00	1.25
31	Tony Lazzeri	4.00	2.00	1.25
32	Al Simmons	4.00	2.00	1.25
33	Wilbert Robinson	4.00	2.00	1.25
34	Sam Rice	4.00	2.00	1.25
35	Herb Pennock	4.00	2.00	1.25
36	Mel Ott	7.00	3.50	2.00
37	Lefty O'Doul	4.00	2.00	1.25
38	Johnny Mize	6.00	3.00	1.75
39	Bing Miller	4.00	2.00	1.25
40	Joe Tinker	4.00	2.00	1.25
41	Frank Baker	4.00	2.00	1.25
42	Ty Cobb	55.00	27.00	16.50
43	Paul Derringer	4.00	2.00	1.25
44	Cap Anson	4.00	2.00	1.25
45	Jim Bottomley	4.00	2.00	1.25
46	Eddie Plank	4.00	2.00	1.25
47	Cy Young	10.00	5.00	3.00
48	Hack Wilson	4.00	2.00	1.25
49	Ed Walsh	4.00	2.00	1.25
50	Frank Chance	4.00	2.00	1.25
51	Dazzy Vance	4.00	2.00	1.25
52	Bill Terry	4.00	2.00	1.25
53	Jimmy Foxx	8.00	4.00	2.50
54	Lefty Gomez	4.00	2.00	1.25
55	Branch Rickey	4.00	2.00	1.25
56	Ray Schalk	4.00	2.00	1.25
57	Johnny Evers	4.00	2.00	1.25
58	Charlie Gehringer	4.00	2.00	1.25
59	Burleigh Grimes	4.00	2.00	1.25
60	Lefty Grove	4.00	2.00	1.25
61	Rube Waddell	4.00	2.00	1.25
62	Honus Wagner	20.00	10.00	6.00
63	Red Ruffing	4.00	2.00	1.25
64	Judge Landis	4.00	2.00	1.25
65	Harry Heilmann	4.00	2.00	1.25
66	John McGraw	4.00	2.00	1.25
67	Hughie Jennings	4.00	2.00	1.25
68	Hal Newhouser	4.00	2.00	1.25
69	Waite Hoyt	4.00	2.00	1.25
70	Bobo Newsom	4.00	2.00	1.25
71	Earl Averill	4.00	2.00	1.25
72	Ted Williams	95.00	47.00	28.00
73	Warren Giles	4.00	2.00	1.25
74	Ford Frick	4.00	2.00	1.25
75	Ki Ki Cuyler	4.00	2.00	1.25
76	Paul Waner	4.00	2.00	1.25
77	Pie Traynor	4.00	2.00	1.25
78	Lloyd Waner	4.00	2.00	1.25
79	Ralph Kiner	8.00	4.00	2.50
80	Pepper Martin (Unissued, cancelled proof, Lefty Grove or Eddie Collins on front)	950.00	475.00	285.00

1960-62 Fleer Team Logo Decals

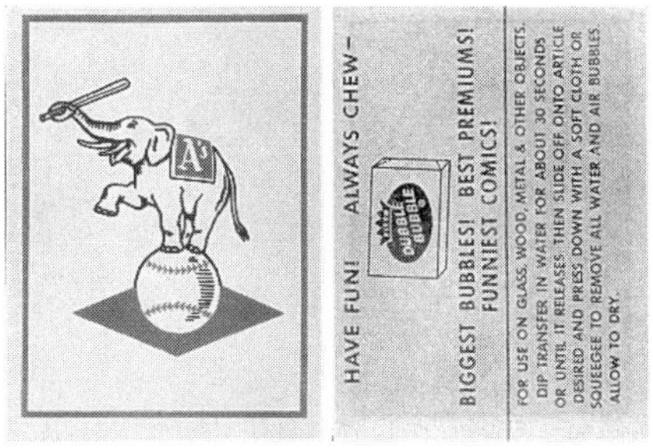

These colorful team logo decals were pack inserts in Fleer's 1960-62 baseball card issues. The decals measure 2-1/4" x 3". Those issued in 1960 have a blue background on front. The 1961-62 decals have a white background on front. Backs have advertising for Fleer bubblegum and instructions on applying the decals. The 1961 decals have back printing in blue; the 1962s are in red.

	NM	EX	VG
Complete Set, 1960 (16):	75.00	37.50	22.00
Complete Set, 1961 (18):	55.00	27.50	16.50
Complete Set, 1962 (20):	100.00	50.00	30.00
1960 team decal, blue background	7.00	3.50	2.00
1961 decal, white background, blue back	4.00	2.00	1.20
1962 decal, white background, red back	7.00	3.50	2.00

1961-62 Fleer Baseball Greats

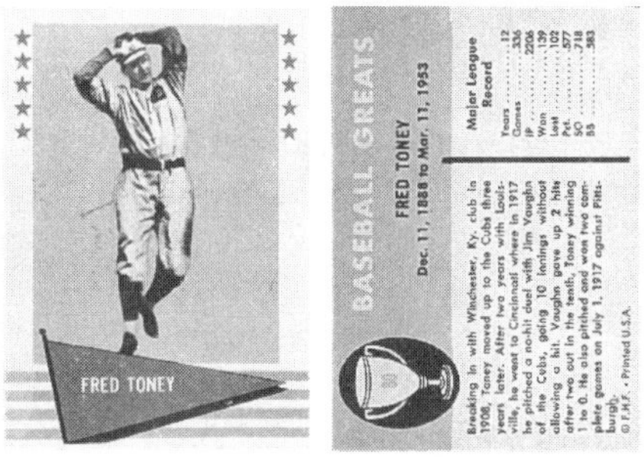

Over a two-year period, Fleer issued another set utilizing the Baseball Greats theme. The 154-card set was issued in two series and features a color player portrait against a color background. The player's name is located in a pennant set at the bottom of the card. The card backs feature orange and black on white stock and contain player biographical and statistical information. The cards measure 2-1/2" x 3-1/2" in size. The second series cards (#'s 89-154) were issued in 1962.

		NM	EX	VG
Complete Set (154):		800.00	400.00	240.00
Common Player (1-88):		3.00	1.50	.90
Common Player (89-154):		7.00	3.50	2.00
1	Checklist (Frank Baker, Ty Cobb, Zach Wheat)	45.00	16.00	8.00
2	G.C. Alexander	6.00	3.00	1.75
3	Nick Altrock	3.00	1.50	.90
4	Cap Anson	3.00	1.50	.90
5	Earl Averill	3.00	1.50	.90
6	Home Run Baker	3.00	1.50	.90
7	Dave Bancroft	3.00	1.50	.90
8	Chief Bender	3.00	1.50	.90
9	Jim Bottomley	3.00	1.50	.90
10	Roger Bresnahan	3.00	1.50	.90
11	Mordecai Brown	3.00	1.50	.90
12	Max Carey	3.00	1.50	.90
13	Jack Chesbro	3.00	1.50	.90
14	Ty Cobb	55.00	27.00	16.50
15	Mickey Cochrane	3.00	1.50	.90
16	Eddie Collins	3.00	1.50	.90
17	Earle Combs	3.00	1.50	.90
18	Charles Comiskey	3.00	1.50	.90
19	Ki Ki Cuyler	3.00	1.50	.90
20	Paul Derringer	3.00	1.50	.90
21	Howard Ehmke	3.00	1.50	.90
22	Billy Evans	3.00	1.50	.90
23	Johnny Evers	3.00	1.50	.90
24	Red Faber	3.00	1.50	.90
25	Bob Feller	11.00	5.50	3.25
26	Wes Ferrell	3.00	1.50	.90
27	Lew Fonseca	3.00	1.50	.90
28	Jimmy Foxx	7.50	3.75	2.25
29	Ford Frick	3.00	1.50	.90
30	Frankie Frisch	3.00	1.50	.90
31	Lou Gehrig	50.00	25.00	15.00
32	Charlie Gehringer	3.00	1.50	.90
33	Warren Giles	3.00	1.50	.90
34	Lefty Gomez	3.00	1.50	.90
35	Goose Goslin	3.00	1.50	.90
36	Clark Griffith	3.00	1.50	.90
37	Burleigh Grimes	3.00	1.50	.90
38	Lefty Grove	3.00	1.50	.90
39	Chick Hafey	3.00	1.50	.90
40	Jesse Haines	3.00	1.50	.90
41	Gabby Hartnett	3.00	1.50	.90
42	Harry Heilmann	3.00	1.50	.90
43	Rogers Hornsby	6.00	3.00	1.75
44	Waite Hoyt	3.00	1.50	.90
45	Carl Hubbell	3.00	1.50	.90
46	Miller Huggins	3.00	1.50	.90
47	Hughie Jennings	3.00	1.50	.90
48	Ban Johnson	3.00	1.50	.90
49	Walter Johnson	12.00	6.00	3.50
50	Ralph Kiner	6.00	3.00	1.75
51	Chuck Klein	3.00	1.50	.90
52	Johnny Kling	3.00	1.50	.90
53	Judge Landis	3.00	1.50	.90
54	Tony Lazzeri	3.00	1.50	.90
55	Ernie Lombardi	3.00	1.50	.90
56	Dolf Luque	4.50	2.25	1.25
57	Heinie Manush	3.00	1.50	.90
58	Marty Marion	3.00	1.50	.90
59	Christy Mathewson	15.00	7.50	4.50
60	John McGraw	3.00	1.50	.90
61	Joe Medwick	3.00	1.50	.90
62	Bing Miller	3.00	1.50	.90
63	Johnny Mize	3.00	1.50	.90
64	Johnny Mostil	3.00	1.50	.90
65	Art Nehf	3.00	1.50	.90
66	Hal Newhouser	3.00	1.50	.90
67	Bobo Newsom	3.00	1.50	.90
68	Mel Ott	3.00	1.50	.90
69	Allie Reynolds	3.00	1.50	.90
70	Sam Rice	3.00	1.50	.90
71	Eppa Rixey	3.00	1.50	.90
72	Edd Roush	3.00	1.50	.90
73	Schoolboy Rowe	3.00	1.50	.90
74	Red Ruffing	3.00	1.50	.90
75	Babe Ruth	100.00	60.00	30.00
76	Joe Sewell	3.00	1.50	.90
77	Al Simmons	3.00	1.50	.90
78	George Sisler	3.00	1.50	.90
79	Tris Speaker	5.00	2.50	1.50
80	Fred Toney	3.00	1.50	.90
81	Dazzy Vance	3.00	1.50	.90
82	Jim Vaughn	3.00	1.50	.90
83	Big Ed Walsh	3.00	1.50	.90
84	Lloyd Waner	3.00	1.50	.90
85	Paul Waner	3.00	1.50	.90
86	Zach Wheat	3.00	1.50	.90
87	Hack Wilson	3.00	1.50	.90
88	Jimmy Wilson	3.00	1.50	.90
89	Checklist (George Sisler, Pie Traynor)	50.00	25.00	15.00
90	Babe Adams	7.00	3.50	2.00
91	Dale Alexander	7.00	3.50	2.00
92	Jim Bagby	7.00	3.50	2.00
93	Ossie Bluege	7.00	3.50	2.00
94	Lou Boudreau	7.00	3.50	2.00
95	Tommy Bridges	7.00	3.50	2.00
96	Donnie Bush (Donie)	7.00	3.50	2.00
97	Dolph Camilli	7.00	3.50	2.00
98	Frank Chance	7.00	3.50	2.00
99	Jimmy Collins	7.00	3.50	2.00
100	Stanley Coveleskie (Coveleski)	7.00	3.50	2.00
101	Hughie Critz	7.00	3.50	2.00
102	General Crowder	7.00	3.50	2.00
103	Joe Dugan	7.00	3.50	2.00
104	Bibb Falk	7.00	3.50	2.00
105	Rick Ferrell	7.00	3.50	2.00
106	Art Fletcher	7.00	3.50	2.00
107	Dennis Galehouse	7.00	3.50	2.00
108	Chick Galloway	7.00	3.50	2.00
109	Mule Haas	7.00	3.50	2.00
110	Stan Hack	7.00	3.50	2.00
111	Bump Hadley	7.00	3.50	2.00
112	Billy Hamilton	7.00	3.50	2.00
113	Joe Hauser	7.00	3.50	2.00
114	Babe Herman	7.00	3.50	2.00
115	Travis Jackson	7.00	3.50	2.00
116	Eddie Joost	7.00	3.50	2.00
117	Addie Joss	7.00	3.50	2.00
118	Joe Judge	7.00	3.50	2.00
119	Joe Kuhel	7.00	3.50	2.00
120	Nap Lajoie	7.00	3.50	2.00
121	Dutch Leonard	7.00	3.50	2.00
122	Ted Lyons	7.00	3.50	2.00
123	Connie Mack	7.00	3.50	2.00
124	Rabbit Maranville	7.00	3.50	2.00
125	Fred Marberry	7.00	3.50	2.00
126	Iron Man McGinnity	7.00	3.50	2.00
127	Oscar Melillo	7.00	3.50	2.00
128	Ray Mueller	7.00	3.50	2.00
129	Kid Nichols	7.00	3.50	2.00
130	Lefty O'Doul	7.00	3.50	2.00
131	Bob O'Farrell	7.00	3.50	2.00
132	Roger Peckinpaugh	7.00	3.50	2.00
133	Herb Pennock	7.00	3.50	2.00
134	George Pipgras	7.00	3.50	2.00
135	Eddie Plank	7.00	3.50	2.00
136	Ray Schalk	7.00	3.50	2.00
137	Hal Schumacher	7.00	3.50	2.00
138	Luke Sewell	7.00	3.50	2.00
139	Bob Shawkey	7.00	3.50	2.00
140	Riggs Stephenson	7.00	3.50	2.00
141	Billy Sullivan	7.00	3.50	2.00
142	Bill Terry	7.00	3.50	2.00
143	Joe Tinker	7.00	3.50	2.00
144	Pie Traynor	7.00	3.50	2.00
145	George Uhle	7.00	3.50	2.00
146	Hal Troskey (Trosky)	7.00	3.50	2.00
147	Arky Vaughan	7.00	3.50	2.00
148	Johnny Vander Meer	7.00	3.50	2.00
149	Rube Waddell	7.00	3.50	2.00
150	Honus Wagner	45.00	22.00	13.50
151	Dixie Walker	7.00	3.50	2.00
152	Ted Williams	85.00	42.00	25.00
153	Cy Young	12.00	6.00	3.50
154	Ross Young (Youngs)	12.00	3.75	2.00

1961 Fleer World Champions Pennant Decals

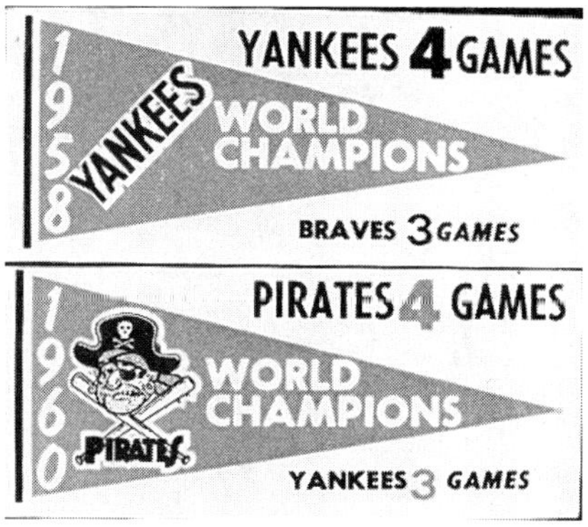

The winner of each World Series from 1913-1960 is honored in this pack insert. The 3" x 1-1/4" decals have a large red or blue pennant at center, with a team name or logo and the "WORLD CHAMPIONS" notation. The year of the Series win is at left on the pennant. The number of games won by each team is at top and bottom on right. Backs offer instructions for applying the decals.

		NM	EX	VG
Complete Set (xx):		225.00	110.00	65.00
Common Decal:		5.00	2.50	1.50
(1)	1913 - A's	5.00	2.50	1.50
(2)	1914 - Braves	5.00	2.50	1.50
(3)	1915 - Red Sox	5.00	2.50	1.50
(4)	1916 - Red Sox	5.00	2.50	1.50
(5)	1917 - White Sox	5.00	2.50	1.50
(6)	1918 - Red Sox	5.00	2.50	1.50
(7)	1919 - Reds	7.50	3.75	2.25
(8)	1920 - Indians	5.00	2.50	1.50
(9)	1921 - Giants	5.00	2.50	1.50
(10)	1922 - Giants	5.00	2.50	1.50
(11)	1923 - Yankees	6.00	3.00	1.75
(12)	1924 - Senators	5.00	2.50	1.50
(13)	1925 - Yankees	6.00	3.00	1.75
(14)	1926 - Cardinals	5.00	2.50	1.50
(15)	1927 - Yankees	6.00	3.00	1.75
(14)	1928 - Yankees	6.00	3.00	1.75
(15)	1929 - A's	5.00	2.50	1.50
(16)	1930 - A's	5.00	2.50	1.50
(17)	1931 - Cardinals	5.00	2.50	1.50
(18)	1932 - Yankees	6.00	3.00	1.75
(19)	1933 - Giants	5.00	2.50	1.50
(20)	1934 - Cardinals	5.00	2.50	1.50
(21)	1935 - Tigers	5.00	2.50	1.50
(22)	1936 - Yankees	6.00	3.00	1.75
(23)	1937 - Yankees	6.00	3.00	1.75
(24)	1938 - Yankees	6.00	3.00	1.75
(25)	1939 - Yankees	6.00	3.00	1.75
(26)	1940 - Reds	5.00	2.50	1.50
(27)	1941 - Yankees	6.00	3.00	1.75
(28)	1942 - Cardinals	5.00	2.50	1.50
(29)	1943 - Yankees	6.00	3.00	1.75
(30)	1944 - Cardinals	5.00	2.50	1.50
(31)	1945 - Tigers	5.00	2.50	1.50
(32)	1946 - Cardinals	5.00	2.50	1.50
(33)	1947 - Yankees	6.00	3.00	1.75
(34)	1948 - Indians	5.00	2.50	1.50
(35)	1949 - Yankees	6.00	3.00	1.75
(36)	1950 - Yankees	6.00	3.00	1.75
(37)	1951 - Yankees	6.00	3.00	1.75
(38)	1952 - Yankees	6.00	3.00	1.75
(41)	1953 - Yankees	6.00	3.00	1.75
(42)	1954 - Giants	5.00	2.50	1.50
(43)	1955 - Dodgers	7.50	3.75	2.25
(44)	1956 - Yankees	6.00	3.00	1.75
(45)	1957 - Braves	6.00	3.00	1.75
(46)	1958 - Yankees	6.00	3.00	1.75
(47)	1959 - Dodgers	7.50	3.75	2.25
(48)	1960 - Pirates	7.50	3.75	2.25

1963 Fleer

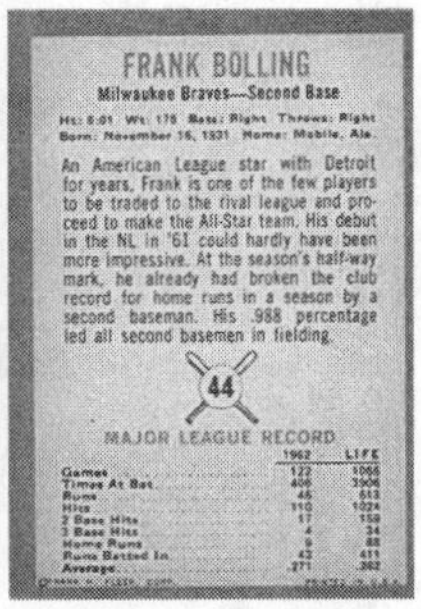

A lawsuit by Topps stopped Fleer's 1963 set at one series of 66 cards. Issued with a cookie rather than gum, the set features color photos of current players. The card backs include statistical information for 1962 and career plus a brief player biography. The cards, which measure 2-1/2" x 3-1/2", are numbered 1-66. An unnumbered checklist was issued with the set and is included in the complete set price in the checklist that follows. The checklist and #46 Adcock are scarce.

		NM	EX	VG
Complete Set (67):		1500.	750.00	450.00
Common Player:		11.00	5.50	3.25
1	Steve Barber	24.00	9.00	5.00
2	Ron Hansen	11.00	5.50	3.25
3	Milt Pappas	11.00	5.50	3.25
4	Brooks Robinson	80.00	40.00	24.00
5	Willie Mays	175.00	87.00	52.00
6	Lou Clinton	11.00	5.50	3.25
7	Bill Monbouquette	11.00	5.50	3.25
8	Carl Yastrzemski	75.00	37.00	22.00
9	Ray Herbert	11.00	5.50	3.25
10	Jim Landis	11.00	5.50	3.25
11	Dick Donovan	11.00	5.50	3.25
12	Tito Francona	11.00	5.50	3.25
13	Jerry Kindall	11.00	5.50	3.25
14	Frank Lary	11.00	5.50	3.25
15	Dick Howser	12.00	6.00	3.50
16	Jerry Lumpe	11.00	5.50	3.25
17	Norm Siebern	11.00	5.50	3.25
18	Don Lee	11.00	5.50	3.25
19	Albie Pearson	11.00	5.50	3.25
20	Bob Rodgers	11.00	5.50	3.25
21	Leon Wagner	11.00	5.50	3.25
22	Jim Kaat	19.00	9.50	5.75
23	Vic Power	11.00	5.50	3.25
24	Rich Rollins	11.00	5.50	3.25
25	Bobby Richardson	20.00	10.00	6.00
26	Ralph Terry	12.00	6.00	3.50
27	Tom Cheney	11.00	5.50	3.25
28	Chuck Cottier	11.00	5.50	3.25
29	Jimmy Piersall	15.00	7.50	4.50
30	Dave Stenhouse	11.00	5.50	3.25
31	Glen Hobbie	11.00	5.50	3.25
32	Ron Santo	24.00	12.00	7.25
33	Gene Freese	11.00	5.50	3.25
34	Vada Pinson	13.50	6.75	4.00
35	Bob Purkey	11.00	5.50	3.25
36	Joe Amalfitano	11.00	5.50	3.25
37	Bob Aspromonte	11.00	5.50	3.25
38	Dick Farrell	11.00	5.50	3.25
39	Al Spangler	11.00	5.50	3.25
40	Tommy Davis	13.50	6.75	4.00
41	Don Drysdale	55.00	27.00	16.50
42	Sandy Koufax	165.00	82.00	49.00
43	Maury Wills	95.00	47.00	28.00
44	Frank Bolling	11.00	5.50	3.25
45	Warren Spahn	55.00	27.00	16.50
46	Joe Adcock (SP)	160.00	80.00	48.00
47	Roger Craig	11.00	5.50	3.25
48	Al Jackson	11.00	5.50	3.25
49	Rod Kanehl	11.00	5.50	3.25
50	Ruben Amaro	11.00	5.50	3.25
51	John Callison	11.00	5.50	3.25
52	Clay Dalrymple	11.00	5.50	3.25
53	Don Demeter	11.00	5.50	3.25
54	Art Mahaffey	11.00	5.50	3.25
55	"Smoky" Burgess	11.00	5.50	3.25
56	Roberto Clemente	175.00	87.00	52.00
57	Elroy Face	11.00	5.50	3.25
58	Vernon Law	11.00	5.50	3.25
59	Bill Mazeroski	24.00	12.00	7.25
60	Ken Boyer	20.00	10.00	6.00
61	Bob Gibson	55.00	27.00	16.50
62	Gene Oliver	11.00	5.50	3.25
63	Bill White	13.50	6.75	4.00
64	Orlando Cepeda	21.00	10.50	6.25
65	Jimmy Davenport	11.00	5.50	3.25
66	Billy O'Dell	15.00	7.50	4.50
----	Checklist (SP)	500.00	200.00	100.00

1966 Fleer

This seldom-seen issue was produced in the years when Fleer was locked out of the "regular" baseball card market. Standard 2-1/2" x 3-1/2" format cards are designed for playing a baseball match game. Backs have a portion of a black-and-white photo of Dodger pitcher Don Drysdale, which can be assembled in jigsaw puzzle fashion. Fronts are printed in red, blue, yellow and black, and numbered F1-F66. Because single cards have little collector appeal, the value of a set is considerably higher than the sum of the parts.

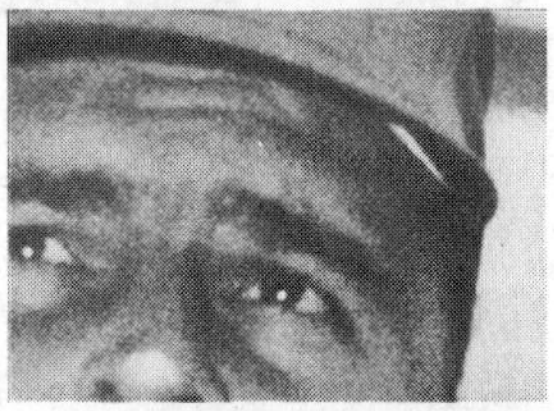

	NM	EX	VG
Complete Set (66):	375.00	185.00	110.00
Don Drysdale			

1968-69 Fleer Major League Baseball Patches

In 1968-69 Fleer sold its bubblegum in wax packs which also included four team logo/quiz cards and half a dozen cloth patches, all for a dime. The 2-9/16" x 4-1/16" cards are blank-back and have on front a color team logo at top and three baseball trivia questions at bottom. The cloth patches are about 2-1/2" x 3-5/16" and are die-cut to allow the team logos and nameplates to be removed from the paper backing and stuck on jackets, etc.

		NM	EX	VG
Complete Set Logo Cards (26):		12.00	6.00	3.50
Common Logo Card:		1.00	.50	.30
Complete Set Cloth Patches (27):		40.00	20.00	12.00
Common Cloth Patch:		2.00	1.00	.60
	LOGO/QUIZ CARDS			
(1)	Atlanta Braves	1.00	.50	.30
(2)	Baltimore Orioles	1.00	.50	.30
(3)	Boston Red Sox	1.00	.50	.30
(4)	California Angels	1.00	.50	.30
(5)	Chicago Cubs	1.00	.50	.30
(6)	Chicago White Sox	1.00	.50	.30
(7)	Cincinnati Reds	1.00	.50	.30
(8)	Cleveland Indians	1.00	.50	.30
(9)	Detroit Tigers	1.00	.50	.30
(10)	Houston Astros	1.00	.50	.30
(11)	Kansas City Royals	1.00	.50	.30
(12)	Los Angeles Dodgers	1.00	.50	.30
(13)	Minnesota Twins	1.00	.50	.30
(14)	Montreal Expos	1.50	.70	.45
(15)	New York Mets	2.00	1.00	.60
(16)	New York Yankees	2.50	1.25	.70
(17)	Oakland A's	1.50	.70	.45
(18)	Philadelphia Phillies	1.00	.50	.30
(19)	Pittsburgh Pirates	1.00	.50	.30
(20)	San Diego Padres	1.50	.70	.45
(21)	San Francisco Giants	1.00	.50	.30
(22)	Seattle Pilots	4.00	2.00	1.25
(23)	St. Louis Cardinals	1.00	.50	.30
(24)	Washington Senators	1.00	.50	.30
	TEAM LOGO CLOTH PATCHES			
(1)	Atlanta Braves	2.00	1.00	.60
(2)	Baltimore Orioles	2.00	1.00	.60
(3)	Boston Red Sox	2.00	1.00	.60
(4)	California Angels	2.00	1.00	.60
(5)	Chicago Cubs	2.00	1.00	.60
(6)	Chicago White Sox	2.00	1.00	.60
(7)	Cincinnati Reds	2.00	1.00	.60
(8)	Cleveland Indians	2.00	1.00	.60
(9)	Detroit Tigers	2.00	1.00	.60
(10)	Houston Astros	2.00	1.00	.60
(11)	Kansas City Royals	2.00	1.00	.60
(12)	Los Angeles Dodgers	2.00	1.00	.60
(13)	Minnesota Twins	2.00	1.00	.60
(14)	Montreal Expos	2.50	1.25	.70
(15)	New York Mets	2.50	1.25	.70
(16)	New York Yankees	3.00	1.50	.90
(17)	Oakland A's	2.50	1.25	.70
(18)	Philadelphia Phillies	2.00	1.00	.60
(19)	Pittsburgh Pirates	2.00	1.00	.60
(20)	San Diego Padres	2.50	1.25	.70
(21)	San Francisco Giants	2.00	1.00	.60
(22)	Seattle Pilots	4.00	2.00	1.25
(23)	St. Louis Cardinals	2.00	1.00	.60
(24)	Washington Senators	2.00	1.00	.60
(25)	Major League Baseball	2.00	1.00	.60

1970 Fleer World Series

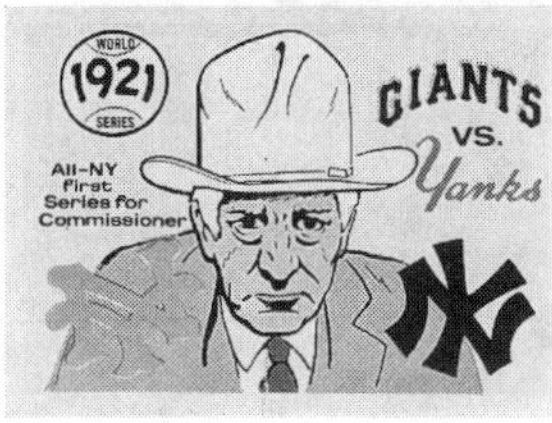

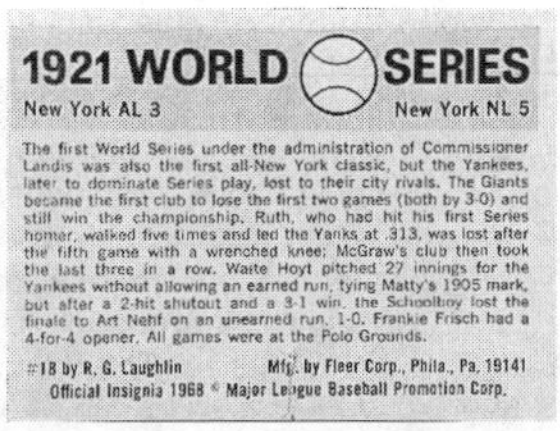

Utilizing the artwork done by Robert Laughlin a few years earlier for a privately marketed set, Fleer offered the first of two annual World Series highlights sets in 1970. Cards have color front with light blue backs. No card was issued for the 1904 World Series because no Series was played. Cards are checklisted in chronological order.

		NM	EX	VG
Complete Set (66):		325.00	160.00	97.00
Common Card:		3.00	1.50	.90
(1)	1903 Red Sox/Pirates	5.00	2.50	1.50
(2)	1905 Giants/A's (Christy Mathewson)	5.00	2.50	1.50
(3)	1906 White Sox/Cubs	3.00	1.50	.90
(4)	1907 Cubs/Tigers	3.00	1.50	.90
(5)	1908 Cubs/Tigers (Tinker/Evers/Chance)	6.00	3.00	1.75
(6)	1909 Pirates/Tigers (Honus Wagner/Ty Cobb)	15.00	7.50	4.50
(7)	1910 A's/Cubs (Chief Bender/Jack Coombs)	4.00	2.00	1.25
(8)	1911 A's/Giants (John McGraw)	4.00	2.00	1.25
(9)	1912 Red Sox/Giants	4.00	2.00	1.25
(10)	1913 A's/Giants	3.00	1.50	.90
(11)	1914 Braves/A's	4.00	2.00	1.25

(12)	1915 Red Sox/Phillies (Babe Ruth)	10.00	5.00	3.00
(13)	1916 Red Sox/Dodgers (Babe Ruth)	10.00	5.00	3.00
(14)	1917 White Sox/Giants	3.00	1.50	.90
(15)	1918 Red Sox/Cubs	3.00	1.50	.90
(16)	1919 Reds/White Sox	6.00	3.00	1.75
(17)	1920 Indians/Dodgers (Stan Coveleski)	4.00	2.00	1.25
(18)	1921 Giants/Yankees (Kenesaw Landis)	4.00	2.00	1.25
(19)	1922 Giants/Yankees (Heinie Groh)	4.00	2.00	1.25
(20)	1923 Yankees/Giants (Babe Ruth)	15.00	7.50	4.50
(21)	1924 Senators/Giants (John McGraw)	5.00	2.50	1.50
(22)	1925 Pirates/Senators (Walter Johnson)	6.00	3.00	1.75
(23)	1926 Cardinals/Yankees (Grover Cleveland Alexander/Tony Lazzeri)	6.00	3.00	1.75
(24)	1927 Yankees/Pirates	5.00	2.50	1.50
(25)	1928 Yankees/Cardinals (Babe Ruth/Lou Gehrig)	15.00	7.50	4.50
(26)	1929 A's/Cubs	3.00	1.50	.90
(27)	1930 A's/Cardinals	3.00	1.50	.90
(28)	1931 Cardinals/A's (Pepper Martin)	4.00	2.00	1.25
(29)	1932 Yankees/Cubs (Babe Ruth/Lou Gehrig)	15.00	7.50	4.50
(30)	1933 Giants/Senators (Mel Ott)	5.00	2.50	1.50
(31)	1934 Cardinals/Tigers	3.00	1.50	.90
(32)	1935 Tigers/Cubs (Charlie Gehringer/Tommy Bridges)	4.00	2.00	1.25
(33)	1936 Yankees/Giants	4.00	2.00	1.25
(34)	1937 Yankees/Giants (Carl Hubbell)	5.00	2.50	1.50
(35)	1938 Yankees/Cubs (Lou Gehrig)	8.00	4.00	2.50
(36)	1939 Yankees/Reds	3.00	1.50	.90
(37)	1940 Reds/Tigers	3.00	1.50	.90
(38)	1941 Yankees/Dodgers	4.00	2.00	1.25
(39)	1942 Cardinals/Yankees	3.00	1.50	.90
(40)	1943 Yankees/Cardinals	3.00	1.50	.90
(41)	1944 Cardinals/Browns	4.00	2.00	1.25
(42)	1945 Tigers/Cubs (Hank Greenberg)	5.00	2.50	1.50
(43)	1946 Cardinals/Red Sox (Enos Slaughter)	4.00	2.00	1.25
(44)	1947 Yankees/Dodgers (Al Gionfriddo)	4.00	2.00	1.25
(45)	1948 Indians/Braves	3.00	1.50	.90
(46)	1949 Yankees/Dodgers (Allie Reynolds/Preacher Roe)	4.00	2.00	1.25
(47)	1950 Yankees/Phillies	4.00	2.00	1.25
(48)	1951 Yankees/Giants	3.00	1.50	.90
(49)	1952 Yankees/Dodgers (Johnny Mize/Duke Snider)	5.00	2.50	1.50
(50)	1953 Yankees/Dodgers (Carl Erskine)	4.00	2.00	1.25
(51)	1954 Giants/Indians (Johnny Antonelli)	3.00	1.50	.90
(52)	1955 Dodgers/Yankees	4.00	2.00	1.25
(53)	1956 Yankees/Dodgers	4.00	2.00	1.25
(54)	1957 Braves/Yankees (Lew Burdette)	6.00	3.00	1.75
(55)	1958 Yankees/Braves (Bob Turley)	3.00	1.50	.90
(56)	1959 Dodgers/White Sox (Chuck Essegian)	4.00	2.00	1.25
(57)	1960 Pirates/Yankees	4.00	2.00	1.25
(58)	1961 Yankees/Reds (Whitey Ford)	4.00	2.00	1.25
(59)	1962 Yankees/Giants	3.00	1.50	.90
(60)	1963 Dodgers/Yankees (Bill Skowron)	3.00	1.50	.90
(61)	1964 Cardinals/Yankees (Bobby Richardson)	4.00	2.00	1.25
(62)	1965 Dodgers/Twins	4.00	2.00	1.25
(63)	1966 Orioles/Dodgers	3.00	1.50	.90
(64)	1967 Cardinals/Red Sox	3.00	1.50	.90
(65)	1968 Tigers/Cardinals	4.00	2.00	1.25
(66)	1969 Mets/Orioles	9.00	4.50	2.75

1971 Fleer World Series

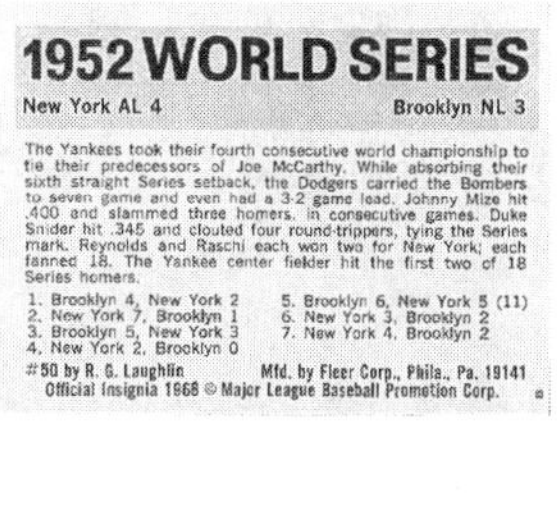
1952 WORLD SERIES

New York AL 4 Brooklyn NL 3

The Yankees took their fourth consecutive world championship to tie their predecessors of Joe McCarthy. While absorbing their sixth straight Series setback, the Dodgers carried the Bombers to seven game and even had a 3-2 game lead. Johnny Mize hit .400 and slammed three homers, in consecutive games. Duke Snider hit .345 and clouted four round-trippers, tying the Series mark. Reynolds and Raschi each won two for New York; each fanned 18. The Yankee center fielder hit the first two of 18 Series homers.

1. Brooklyn 4, New York 2
2. New York 7, Brooklyn 1
3. Brooklyn 5, New York 3
4. New York 2, Brooklyn 0
5. Brooklyn 6, New York 5 (11)
6. New York 3, Brooklyn 2
7. New York 4, Brooklyn 2

#50 by R. G. Laughlin Mfd. by Fleer Corp., Phila., Pa. 19141
Official Insignia 1968 © Major League Baseball Promotion Corp.

New artwork by Robert Laughlin is featured in the second of Fleer's World Series highlights sets. Fronts feature color art with backs printed in black. Cards are checklisted in chronological order.

		NM	EX	VG
Complete Set (68):		325.00	160.00	97.00
Common Card:		3.00	1.50	.90
(1)	1903 Red Sox/Pirates (Cy Young)	10.00	5.00	3.00
(2)	1904 No World Series (John McGraw)	8.00	4.00	2.50
(3)	1905 Giants/A's (Christy Mathewson/Chief Bender)	8.00	4.00	2.50
(4)	1906 White Sox/Cubs	3.00	1.50	.90
(5)	1907 Cubs/Tigers	3.00	1.50	.90
(6)	1908 Cubs/Tigers (Ty Cobb)	8.00	4.00	2.50
(7)	1909 Pirates/Tigers	4.00	2.00	1.25
(8)	1910 A's/Cubs (Eddie Collins)	4.00	2.00	1.25
(9)	1911 A's/Giants (Home Run Baker)	4.00	2.00	1.25
(10)	1912 Red Sox/Giants	3.00	1.50	.90
(11)	1913 A's/Giants (Christy Mathewson)	5.00	2.50	1.50
(12)	1914 Braves/A's	3.00	1.50	.90
(13)	1915 Red Sox/Phillies (Grover Cleveland Alexander)	5.00	2.50	1.50
(14)	1916 Red Sox/Dodgers (Jack Coombs)	3.00	1.50	.90
(15)	1917 White Sox/Giants (Red Faber)	4.00	2.00	1.25
(16)	1918 Red Sox/Cubs (Babe Ruth)	10.00	5.00	3.00
(17)	1919 Reds/White Sox	6.00	3.00	1.75
(18)	1920 Indians/Dodgers (Elmer Smith)	4.00	2.00	1.25
(19)	1921 Giants/Yankees (Waite Hoyt)	6.00	3.00	1.75
(20)	1922 Giants/Yankees (Art Nehf)	4.00	2.00	1.25
(21)	1923 Yankees/Giants (Herb Pennock)	4.00	2.00	1.25
(22)	1924 Senators/Giants (Walter Johnson)	6.00	3.00	1.75
(23)	1925 Pirates/Senators (Walter Johnson/Ki Ki Cuyler)	6.00	3.00	1.75
(24)	1926 Cardinals/Yankees (Rogers Hornsby)	6.00	3.00	1.75
(25)	1927 Yankees/Pirates	4.00	2.00	1.25
(26)	1928 Yankees/Cardinals (Lou Gehrig)	8.00	4.00	2.50
(27)	1929 A's/Cubs (Howard Ehmke)	3.00	1.50	.90
(28)	1930 A's/Cardinals (Jimmie Foxx)	5.00	2.50	1.50
(29)	1931 Cardinals/A's (Pepper Martin)	4.00	2.00	1.25
(30)	1932 Yankees/Cubs (Babe Ruth)	10.00	5.00	3.00
(31)	1933 Giants/Senators (Carl Hubbell)	5.00	2.50	1.50
(32)	1934 Cardinals/Tigers	3.00	1.50	.90
(33)	1935 Tigers/Cubs (Mickey Cochrane)	4.00	2.00	1.25
(34)	1936 Yankees/Giants (Red Rolfe)	4.00	2.00	1.25
(35)	1937 Yankees/Giants (Tony Lazzeri)	6.00	3.00	1.75
(36)	1938 Yankees/Cubs	5.00	2.50	1.50
(37)	1939 Yankees/Reds	5.00	2.50	1.50
(38)	1940 Reds/Tigers	3.00	1.50	.90
(39)	1941 Yankees/Dodgers (Charlie Keller)	4.00	2.00	1.25
(40)	1942 Cardinals/Yankees (Whitey Kurowski/Johnny Beazley)	3.00	1.50	.90
(41)	1943 Yankees/Cardinals (Spud Chandler)	3.00	1.50	.90
(42)	1944 Cardinals/Browns (Mort Cooper)	4.00	2.00	1.25
(43)	1945 Tigers/Cubs (Hank Greenberg)	5.00	2.50	1.50
(44)	1946 Cardinals/Red Sox (Enos Slaughter)	4.00	2.00	1.25
(45)	1947 Yankees/Dodgers (Johnny Lindell/Hugh Casey)	4.00	2.00	1.25
(46)	1948 Indians/Braves	3.00	1.50	.90
(47)	1949 Yankees/Dodgers (Preacher Roe)	3.00	1.50	.90
(48)	1950 Yankees/Phillies (Allie Reynolds)	4.00	2.00	1.25
(49)	1951 Yankees/Giants (Ed Lopat)	3.00	1.50	.90
(50)	1952 Yankees/Dodgers (Johnny Mize)	4.00	2.00	1.25
(51)	1953 Yankees/Dodgers	4.00	2.00	1.25
(52)	1954 Giants/Indians	3.00	1.50	.90
(53)	1955 Dodgers/Yankees (Duke Snider)	6.00	3.00	1.75
(54)	1956 Yankees/Dodgers	4.00	2.00	1.25
(55)	1957 Braves/Yankees	4.00	2.00	1.25
(56)	1958 Yankees/Braves (Hank Bauer)	4.00	2.00	1.25
(57)	1959 Dodgers/White Sox (Duke Snider)	5.00	2.50	1.50
(58)	1960 Pirates/Yankees (Bill Skowron/Bobby Richardson)	4.00	2.00	1.25
(59)	1961 Yankees/Reds (Whitey Ford)	4.00	2.00	1.25
(60)	1962 Yankees/Giants	3.00	1.50	.90
(61)	1963 Dodgers/Yankees	3.00	1.50	.90
(62)	1964 Cardinals/Yankees	4.00	2.00	1.25
(63)	1965 Dodgers/Twins	4.00	2.00	1.25
(64)	1966 Orioles/Dodgers	3.00	1.50	.90
(65)	1967 Cardinals/Red Sox	3.00	1.50	.90
(66)	1968 Tigers/Cardinals	4.00	2.00	1.25
(67)	1969 Mets/Orioles	9.00	4.50	2.75
(68)	1970 Orioles/Reds	8.00	4.00	2.50

1972 Fleer Famous Feats

BASEBALL'S FAMOUS FEATS

CHRISTY MATHEWSON

Christy Mathewson won 373 games with a .665 winning percentage. His manager, John McGraw, called him the greatest pitcher of all. Four times Matty won 30 or more, including 37 in 1908, the National League record. One of his greatest feats was pitching three shut-outs in the 1905 World Series, walking only one Athletic while fanning 18 and yielding but 14 hits in the three games. Matty had tough luck later on in Series play, but that performance has stood for all time. From 1903 through 1914, "Big Six" never won less than 22 in a season, and averaged 331 innings per year. He hurled 12 shutouts in 1908 and 83 in his career.

No. 3 of 40 CARDS by R. G. Laughlin ©1972 Fleer Corp., Phila., Pa. 19141

This 40-card set by sports artist R.G. Laughlin is oversized, 2-1/2" x 4". It features the pen and ink work of the artist, with several colors added to the front. The backs are printed in blue on white card stock. The Major League Baseball logo appears on the front of the card, one of the few Laughlin issues to do so. Selling price at issue was about $3.

		NM	EX	VG
Complete Set (40):		30.00	15.00	9.00
Common Player:		.60	.30	.20
1	Joe McGinnity	.70	.35	.20
2	Rogers Hornsby	1.50	.70	.45
3	Christy Mathewson	1.50	.70	.45
4	Dazzy Vance	.70	.35	.20
5	Lou Gehrig	2.50	1.25	.70
6	Jim Bottomley	.70	.35	.20
7	Johnny Evers	.70	.35	.20
8	Walter Johnson	1.50	.70	.45
9	Hack Wilson	.90	.45	.25
10	Wilbert Robinson	.70	.35	.20
11	Cy Young	1.25	.60	.40
12	Rudy York	.60	.30	.20
13	Grover C. Alexander	.90	.45	.25
14	Fred Toney, Hippo Vaughn	.60	.30	.20
15	Ty Cobb	2.50	1.25	.70
16	Jimmie Foxx	1.50	.70	.45
17	Hub Leonard	.60	.30	.20
18	Eddie Collins	.70	.35	.20
19	Joe Oeschger, Leon Cadore	.60	.30	.20
20	Babe Ruth	3.50	1.75	1.00
21	Honus Wagner	1.50	.70	.45
22	Red Rolfe	.60	.30	.20
23	Ed Walsh	.70	.35	.20
24	Paul Waner	.70	.35	.20
25	Mel Ott	1.25	.60	.40
26	Eddie Plank	.90	.45	.25
27	Sam Crawford	.70	.35	.20
28	Napoleon Lajoie	1.25	.60	.40
29	Ed Reulbach	.60	.30	.20
30	Pinky Higgins	.60	.30	.20
31	Bill Klem	.70	.35	.20
32	Tris Speaker	1.25	.60	.40
33	Hank Gowdy	.60	.30	.20
34	Lefty O'Doul	.60	.30	.20
35	Lloyd Waner	.70	.35	.20
36	Chuck Klein	.70	.35	.20
37	Deacon Phillippe	.60	.30	.20
38	Ed Delahanty	.70	.35	.20
39	Jack Chesbro	.70	.35	.20
40	Willie Keeler	.70	.35	.20

1973 Fleer Team Signs

Each of the major league teams was represented in this issue of thick oversize (7-3/4" x 11-1/2") team logo signs. The blank-back signs have rounded corners and a grommeted hole at top center for hanging. The unnumbered signs are checklisted here alphabetically.

		NM	EX	VG
Complete Set (24):		100.00	50.00	30.00
Common Team:		5.00	2.50	1.50
(1)	Atlanta Braves	5.00	2.50	1.50
(2)	Baltimore Orioles	5.00	2.50	1.50
(3)	Boston Red Sox	5.00	2.50	1.50
(4)	California Angels	5.00	2.50	1.50
(5)	Chicago Cubs	5.00	2.50	1.50
(6)	Chicago White Sox	5.00	2.50	1.50
(7)	Cincinnati Reds	7.00	3.50	2.00
(8)	Cleveland Indians	5.00	2.50	1.50
(9)	Detroit Tigers	5.00	2.50	1.50
(10)	Houston Astros	5.00	2.50	1.50
(11)	Kansas City Royals	5.00	2.50	1.50
(12)	Los Angeles Dodgers	5.00	2.50	1.50
(13)	Milwaukee Brewers	5.00	2.50	1.50
(14)	Minnesota Twins	5.00	2.50	1.50
(15)	Montreal Expos	5.00	2.50	1.50
(16)	New York Mets	7.00	3.50	2.00
(17)	New York Yankees	7.00	3.50	2.00
(18)	Oakland A's	7.00	3.50	2.00
(19)	Philadelphia Phillies	5.00	2.50	1.50
(20)	Pittsburgh Pirates	5.00	2.50	1.50
(21)	St. Louis Cardinals	5.00	2.50	1.50
(22)	San Francisco Giants	5.00	2.50	1.50
(23)	San Diego Padres	5.00	2.50	1.50
(24)	Texas Rangers	5.00	2.50	1.50

1973 Fleer Wildest Days and Plays

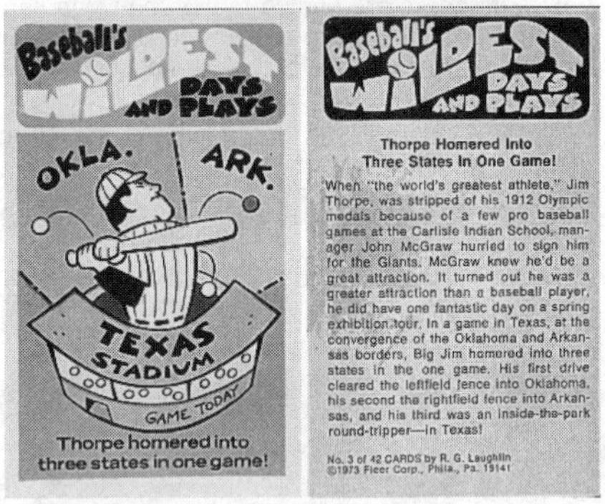

This 42-card set highlights unusual plays and happenings in baseball history, with the fronts featuring artwork by R.G. Laughlin. The cards are 2-1/2" x 4" and printed with color on the front and in red on the back. Original retail price was about $3.25.

		NM	EX	VG
Complete Set (42):		30.00	15.00	9.00
Common Player:		.75	.40	.25
1	Cubs and Phillies Score 49 Runs in Game	.75	.40	.25
2	Frank Chance Five HBP's in One Day	2.00	1.00	.60
3	Jim Thorpe Homered Into Three States	1.00	.50	.30
4	Eddie Gaedel Midget in Majors	1.00	.50	.30
5	Most Tied Game Ever	.75	.40	.25
6	Seven Errors in One Inning	.75	.40	.25
7	Four 20-Game Winners But No Pennant	.75	.40	.25
8	Dummy Hoy Umpire Signals Strikes	1.00	.50	.30
9	Fourteen Hits in One Inning	.75	.40	.25
10	Yankees Not Shut Out for Two Years	.75	.40	.25
11	Buck Weaver 17 Straight Fouls	1.00	.50	.30
12	George Sisler Greatest Thrill	.75	.40	.25
13	Wrong-Way Baserunner	.75	.40	.25
14	Kiki Cuyler Sits Out Series	.75	.40	.25
15	Grounder Climbed Wall	.75	.40	.25
16	Gabby Street Washington Monument	.75	.40	.25
17	Mel Ott Ejected Twice	1.00	.50	.30
18	Shortest Pitching Career	.75	.40	.25
19	Three Homers in One Inning	.75	.40	.25
20	Bill Byron Singing Umpire	.75	.40	.25
21	Fred Clarke Walking Steal of Home	.75	.40	.25
22	Christy Mathewson 373rd Win Discovered	1.00	.50	.30
23	Hitting Through the Unglaub Arc	.75	.40	.25
24	Jim O'Rourke Catching at 52	.75	.40	.25
25	Fired for Striking Out in Series	.75	.40	.25
26	Eleven Run Inning on One Hit	.75	.40	.25
27	58 Innings in 3 Days	.75	.40	.25
28	Homer on Warm-up Pitch	.75	.40	.25
29	Giants Win 26 Straight But Finish Fourth	.75	.40	.25
30	Player Who Stole First Base	.75	.40	.25
31	Ernie Shore Perfect Game in Relief	.75	.40	.25
32	Greatest Comeback	.75	.40	.25
33	All-Time Flash-in-the-Pan	.75	.40	.25
34	Pruett Fanned Ruth 19 Out of 31	1.00	.50	.30
35	Fixed Batting Race (Ty Cobb, Nap Lajoie)	1.00	.50	.30
36	Wild Pitch Rebound Play	.75	.40	.25
37	17 Straight Scoring Innings	.75	.40	.25
38	Wildest Opening Day	.75	.40	.25
39	Baseball's Strike One	.75	.40	.25
40	Opening Day No-Hitter That Didn't Count	.75	.40	.25
41	Jimmie Foxx 6 Straight Walks in One Game	1.00	.50	.30
42	Entire Team Hit and Scored in Inning	.75	.40	.25

1974 Fleer Baseball Firsts

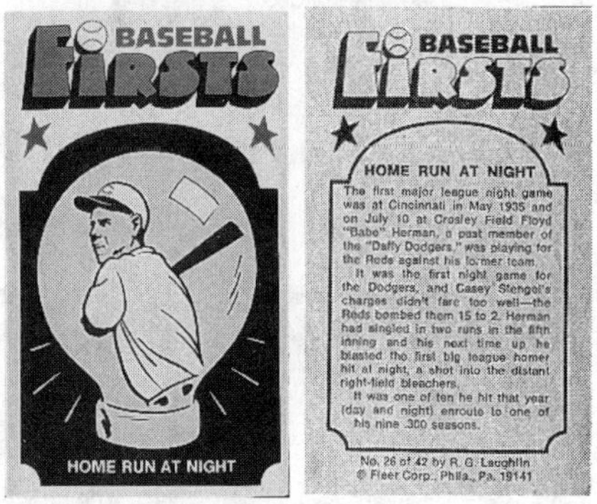

This 42-card set from Fleer is titled "Baseball Firsts" and features several historical moments in baseball, as captured through the artwork of sports artist R.G. Laughlin. The cards are 2-1/2" x 4" and are numbered on the back, which is gray card stock with black printing. The set is not licensed by Major League Baseball.

		NM	EX	VG
Complete Set (42):		12.00	6.00	3.50
Common Player:		.30	.15	.09
1	Slide	.30	.15	.09
2	Spring Training	.30	.15	.09
3	Bunt	.30	.15	.09
4	Catcher's Mask	.30	.15	.09
5	Four Straight Homers (Lou Gehrig)	2.00	1.00	.60
6	Radio Broadcast	.30	.15	.09
7	Numbered Uniforms	.30	.15	.09
8	Shin Guards	.30	.15	.09
9	Players Association	.30	.15	.09
10	Knuckleball	.30	.15	.09
11	Player With Glasses	.30	.15	.09
12	Baseball Cards	2.50	1.25	.70
13	Standardized Rules	.30	.15	.09
14	Grand Slam	.30	.15	.09
15	Player Fined	.30	.15	.09
16	Presidential Opener	.30	.15	.09
17	Player Transaction	.30	.15	.09
18	All-Star Game	.30	.15	.09
19	Scoreboard	.30	.15	.09
20	Cork-center Ball	.30	.15	.09
21	Scorekeeping	.30	.15	.09
22	Domed Stadium	.30	.15	.09
23	Batting Helmet	.30	.15	.09
24	Fatality	.60	.30	.20
25	Unassisted Triple Play	.30	.15	.09
26	Home Run at Night	.30	.15	.09
27	Black Major Leaguer	.60	.30	.20
28	Pinch Hitter	.30	.15	.09
29	Million Dollar World Series	.30	.15	.09
30	Tarpaulin	.30	.15	.09
31	Team Initials	.30	.15	.09
32	Pennant Playoff	.30	.15	.09
33	Glove	.30	.15	.09
34	Curve Ball	.30	.15	.09
35	Night Game	.30	.15	.09
36	Admission Charge	.30	.15	.09
37	Farm System	.30	.15	.09
38	Telecast	.30	.15	.09
39	Commissioner	.30	.15	.09
40	.400 Hitter	.30	.15	.09
41	World Series	.30	.15	.09
42	Player Into Service	.30	.15	.09

1975 Fleer Pioneers of Baseball

This 28-card set did not draw a great deal of interest in the hobby. The cards are slightly oversized (2-1/2" x 4") and feature sepia-toned photographs of old baseball players. The backs feature information about the player and the card number. A "Pioneers of Baseball" banner appears at the top of the card back. Each 10-cent pack included one card and one each cloth team pennant and patch, plus a stick of gum.

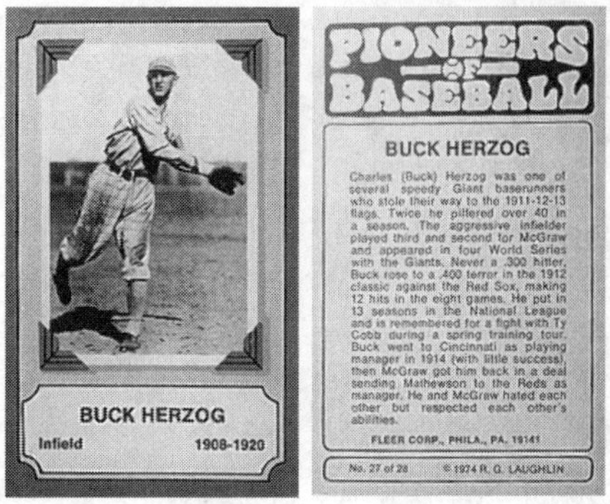

		NM	EX	VG
Complete Set (28):		16.00	8.00	4.75
Common Player:		.60	.30	.20
1	Cap Anson	.60	.30	.20
2	Harry Wright	.60	.30	.20
3	Buck Ewing	.60	.30	.20
4	A.G. Spalding	.60	.30	.20
5	Old Hoss Radbourn	.60	.30	.20
6	Dan Brouthers	.60	.30	.20
7	Roger Bresnahan	.60	.30	.20
8	Mike Kelly	.60	.30	.20
9	Ned Hanlon	.60	.30	.20
10	Ed Delahanty	.60	.30	.20
11	Pud Galvin	.60	.30	.20
12	Amos Rusie	.60	.30	.20
13	Tommy McCarthy	.60	.30	.20
14	Ty Cobb	1.25	.60	.40
15	John McGraw	.60	.30	.20
16	Home Run Baker	.60	.30	.20
17	Johnny Evers	.60	.30	.20
18	Nap Lajoie	.60	.30	.20
19	Cy Young	.60	.30	.20
20	Eddie Collins	.60	.30	.20
21	John Glasscock	.60	.30	.20
22	Hal Chase	.60	.30	.20
23	Mordecai Brown	.60	.30	.20
24	Jake Daubert	.60	.30	.20
25	Mike Donlin	.60	.30	.20
26	John Clarkson	.60	.30	.20
27	Buck Herzog	.60	.30	.20
28	Art Nehf	.60	.30	.20

1980 Fleer Baseball's Famous Feats

Yet another incarnation of Robert Laughlin's "Baseball's Famous Feats" cartoon artwork in this 22-card issue, in standard 2-1/2" x 3-1/2" format. The player art is backed with team logo and pennant stickers, creating a huge variety of possible front/back combinations. The cards are licensed by Major League Baseball and numbered on the front.

		NM	EX	VG
Complete Set (22):		12.00	6.00	3.50
Common Player:		.50	.25	.15
1	Grover Cleveland Alexander	.60	.30	.20
2	Jimmy Foxx	.60	.30	.20
3	Ty Cobb	1.25	.60	.40
4	Walter Johnson	.60	.30	.20
5	Hack Wilson	.50	.25	.15
6	Tris Speaker	.60	.30	.20
7	Hank Gowdy	.50	.25	.15
8	Bill Klem	.50	.25	.15
9	Ed Reulbach	.50	.25	.15
10	Fred Toney, Hippo Vaughn	.50	.25	.15
11	Joe Oeschger, Leon Cadore	.50	.25	.15
12	Lloyd Waner	.50	.25	.15
13	Eddie Plank	.50	.25	.15
14	Deacon Phillippe	.50	.25	.15
15	Ed Dalahanty (Delahanty)	.50	.25	.15
16	Eddie Collins	.50	.25	.15
17	Jack Chesbro	.50	.25	.15
18	Red Rolfe	.50	.25	.15
19	Cy Young	.60	.30	.20
20	Nap Lajoie	.50	.25	.15
21	Honus Wagner	.90	.45	.25
22	Ed Walsh	.50	.25	.15

1947 Fleetwood Slacks Jackie Robinson

The date of issue cited is conjectural. This card, about 5" x 8", depicts Jackie Robinson in a coat and tie in a black-and-white photo on front. In a strip at bottom is his name and an endorsement for Fleetwood Slacks. The back is blank. The card was probably used as an autograph vehicle for personal appearances by Robinson at clothing stores.

	NM	EX	VG
Jackie Robinson	450.00	225.00	135.00

1916 Fleischmann Bakery

These cards were issued by a New York City bakery, presumably given away with the purchase of bread or other goods. The blank-back cards are printed in black-and-white in a 2-3/4" x 5-3/8" format. Fronts have player photos with the name, team and position in two lines beneath. Most cards have an Underwood & Underwood copyright notice on the picture. At bottom is a coupon which could be redeemed for an album to house the cards. Prices shown here are for cards with the coupon. Cards without coupon are valued at about 35-50% of the values shown. Cards are checklisted here in alphabetical order. A nearly identical issue was produced contemporarily by Ferguson Bread. The two can be distinguished by the two-line identification on front of the Fleischmann cards, and one-line identification on Fergusons.

	NM	EX	VG
Complete Set (103):	20000.	10000.	6000.
Common Player:	200.00	100.00	60.00
(1) Babe Adams	200.00	100.00	60.00
(2) Grover Alexander	300.00	150.00	90.00
(3) Walt E. Alexander	200.00	100.00	60.00
(4) Frank Allen	200.00	100.00	60.00
(5) Fred Anderson	200.00	100.00	60.00
(6) Dave Bancroft	300.00	150.00	90.00
(7) Jack Barry	200.00	100.00	60.00
(8) Beals Becker	200.00	100.00	60.00
(9) Eddie Burns	200.00	100.00	60.00
(10) George J. Burns	200.00	100.00	60.00
(11) Bobby Byrne	200.00	100.00	60.00
(12) Ray Caldwell	200.00	100.00	60.00
(13) James Callahan	200.00	100.00	60.00
(14) William Carrigan	200.00	100.00	60.00
(15) Larry Cheney	200.00	100.00	60.00
(16) Tom Clarke	200.00	100.00	60.00
(17) Ty Cobb	2000.	1000.	600.00
(18) Ray W. Collins	200.00	100.00	60.00
(19) Jack Coombs	200.00	100.00	60.00
(20) A. Wilbur Cooper	200.00	100.00	60.00
(21) George Cutshaw	200.00	100.00	60.00
(22) Jake Daubert	200.00	100.00	60.00
(23) Wheezer Dell	200.00	100.00	60.00
(24) Bill Donovan	200.00	100.00	60.00
(25) Larry Doyle	200.00	100.00	60.00
(26) R.J. Egan	200.00	100.00	60.00
(27) Johnny Evers	300.00	150.00	90.00
(28) Ray Fisher	200.00	100.00	60.00
(29) Harry Gardner (Larry)	200.00	100.00	60.00
(30) Joe Gedeon	200.00	100.00	60.00
(31) Larry Gilbert	200.00	100.00	60.00
(32) Frank Gilhooley	200.00	100.00	60.00
(33) Hank Gowdy	200.00	100.00	60.00
(34) Sylvanus Gregg	200.00	100.00	60.00
(35) Tom Griffith	200.00	100.00	60.00
(36) Heinie Groh	200.00	100.00	60.00
(37) Bob Harmon	200.00	100.00	60.00
(38) Roy A. Hartzell	200.00	100.00	60.00
(39) Claude Hendrix	200.00	100.00	60.00
(40) Olaf Henriksen	200.00	100.00	60.00
(41) Buck Herzog	200.00	100.00	60.00
(42) Hugh High	200.00	100.00	60.00
(43) Dick Hoblitzell	200.00	100.00	60.00
(44) Herb Hunter	200.00	100.00	60.00
(45) Harold Janvrin	200.00	100.00	60.00
(46) Hugh Jennings	300.00	150.00	90.00
(47) John Johnston	200.00	100.00	60.00
(48) Erving Kantlehner	200.00	100.00	60.00
(49) Benny Kauff	200.00	100.00	60.00
(50) Ray Keating	200.00	100.00	60.00
(51) Wade Killefer	200.00	100.00	60.00
(52) Elmer Knetzer	200.00	100.00	60.00
(53) Bradley Kocher	200.00	100.00	60.00
(54) Ed Konetchy	200.00	100.00	60.00
(55) Fred Lauderous (Luderous)	200.00	100.00	60.00
(56) Dutch Leonard	200.00	100.00	60.00
(57) Duffy Lewis	200.00	100.00	60.00
(58) Slim Love	200.00	100.00	60.00
(59) Albert L. Mamaux	200.00	100.00	60.00
(60) Rabbit Maranville	300.00	150.00	90.00
(61) Rube Marquard	300.00	150.00	90.00
(62) Christy Mathewson	1350.	675.00	405.00
(63) Bill McKechnie	300.00	150.00	90.00
(64) Chief Meyer (Meyers)	200.00	100.00	60.00
(65) Otto Miller	200.00	100.00	60.00
(66) Fred Mollwitz	200.00	100.00	60.00
(67) Herbie Moran	200.00	100.00	60.00
(68) Mike Mowrey	200.00	100.00	60.00
(69) Dan Murphy	200.00	100.00	60.00
(70) Art Nehf	200.00	100.00	60.00
(71) Rube Oldring	200.00	100.00	60.00
(72) Oliver O'Mara	200.00	100.00	60.00
(73) Dode Paskert	200.00	100.00	60.00
(74) D.C. Pat Ragan	200.00	100.00	60.00
(75) William A. Rariden	200.00	100.00	60.00
(76) Davis Robertson	200.00	100.00	60.00
(77) Wm. Rodgers	200.00	100.00	60.00
(78) Edw. F. Rousch (Roush)	300.00	150.00	90.00
(79) Nap Rucker	200.00	100.00	60.00
(80) Dick Rudolph	200.00	100.00	60.00
(81) Wally Schang	200.00	100.00	60.00
(82) Rube Schauer	200.00	100.00	60.00
(83) Pete Schneider	200.00	100.00	60.00
(84) Ferd Schupp	200.00	100.00	60.00
(85) Ernie Shore	200.00	100.00	60.00
(86) Red Smith	200.00	100.00	60.00
(87) Fred Snodgrass	200.00	100.00	60.00
(88) Tris Speaker	350.00	175.00	105.00
(89) George Stallings	200.00	100.00	60.00
(90) Casey Stengel	600.00	300.00	180.00
(91) Sailor Stroud	200.00	100.00	60.00
(92) Amos Strunk	200.00	100.00	60.00
(93) Chas. (Jeff) Tesreau	200.00	100.00	60.00
(94) Charles Thomas	200.00	100.00	60.00
(95) Fred Toney	200.00	100.00	60.00
(96) Walt Tragesser	200.00	100.00	60.00
(97) Honus Wagner	1600.	800.00	480.00
(98) Carl Weilman	200.00	100.00	60.00
(99) Zack Wheat	300.00	150.00	90.00
(100) George Whitted	200.00	100.00	60.00
(101) Arthur Wilson	200.00	100.00	60.00
(102) Ivy Wingo	200.00	100.00	60.00
(103) Joe Wood	200.00	100.00	60.00

1961 Ford Pittsburgh Pirates Prints

The year after the team's dramatic World Series win over the Yankees, Pittsburgh area Ford dealers distributed a set of six player prints. The blank-back, 11-7/8 x 14-3/4" prints feature action drawings of the players by artist Robert Riger. Some of the prints are horizontal in format, some are vertical. A Ford Motor Company copyright line appears in the lower-left corner and a line at bottom center identifies the player in the form of a title for the picture.

The unnumbered prints are listed here in alphabetical order. The pictures were reprinted by an unauthorized party circa 1998.

	NM	EX	VG
Complete Set (6):	100.00	50.00	30.00
Common Player:			
(1) BOB FRIEND COMES IN WITH THE FAST ONE (Bob Friend)	5.00	2.50	1.50
(2) CLEMENTE LINES ONE OVER SECOND (Roberto Clemente)	75.00	37.50	22.00
(3) GROAT CUTS DOWN A BRAVE STEAL (Dick Groat)	5.00	2.50	1.50
(4) HOAK HANDLES A HOT SHOT AT THIRD (Don Hoak)	5.00	2.50	1.50
(5) MAZ GETS THE BIG HIT (Bill Mazeroski)	12.00	6.00	3.50
(6) THE LAW (Vern Law)	5.00	2.50	1.50

1962 Ford Detroit Tigers Postcards

Because baseball card collectors have to compete with auto memorabilia hobbyists for these scarce cards, they are among the most valuable postcard issues of the early 1960s. In standard 3-1/2" x 5-1/2" postcard format, the full-color cards feature photos taken on a golf course of players posed in front of various new Fords. White backs have a name, position and team, with a box for a stamp. Probably given out in conjunction with autograph appearances at car dealers (they are frequently found autographed), the set lacks some of the team's biggest stars (Al Kaline, Norm Cash), and includes coaches and even trainer Jack Homel. Probably because of lack of demand, the coaches' and trainer's cards are the scarcest to find today. The unnumbered cards are checklisted here alphabetically.

	NM	EX	VG
Complete Set (16):	950.00	475.00	275.00
Common Player:	60.00	30.00	18.00
(1) Hank Aguirre	60.00	30.00	18.00
(2) Steve Boros	80.00	40.00	24.00
(3) Dick Brown	60.00	30.00	18.00
(4) Phil Cavaretta	90.00	45.00	27.00
(5) Rocky Colavito	125.00	62.00	37.00
(6) Jim Bunning	110.00	55.00	33.00
(7) Terry Fox	60.00	30.00	18.00
(8) Purn Goldy	60.00	30.00	18.00
(9) Jack Homel	90.00	45.00	27.00
(10) Ron Kline	60.00	30.00	18.00
(11) Don Mossi	60.00	30.00	18.00
(12) George Myatt	80.00	40.00	24.00
(13) Ron Nischwitz	60.00	30.00	18.00
(14) Larry Osborne	60.00	30.00	18.00
(15) Mike Roarke	90.00	45.00	27.00
(16) Phil Regan	60.00	30.00	18.00

1938 Foto Fun

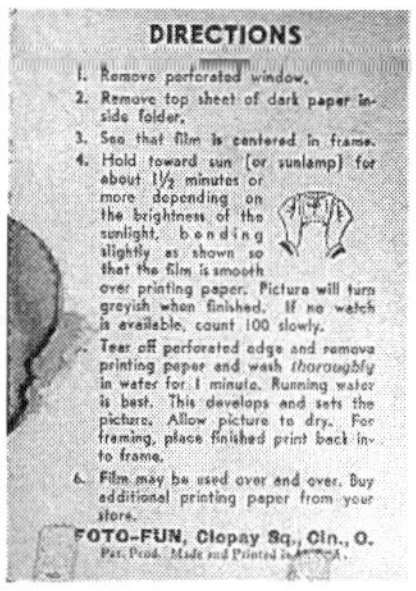

The first attempt at a self-developing player photocard (a technology which Topps would use in the 1940s-50s) used a black-and-white negative and a piece of photo paper to create a blue-tint photo which could be placed in a gold cardboard frame. The back of the 2-3/4" x 3-5/8" frame is printed in brown and gives instructions for developing the photo. The checklist of the the unnumbered cards, presented here alphabetically, may or may not be complete at 92.

		NM	EX	VG
Common Player:		50.00	25.00	15.00
(1)	Luke Appling	125.00	62.00	37.00
(2)	Morris Arnovich	50.00	25.00	15.00
(3)	Eldon Auker	50.00	25.00	15.00
(4)	Jim Bagby	50.00	25.00	15.00
(5)	Red Barrett	50.00	25.00	15.00
(6)	Roy Bell	50.00	25.00	15.00
(7)	Wally Berger	50.00	25.00	15.00
(8)	Oswald Bluege	50.00	25.00	15.00
(9)	Frenchy Bordagaray	50.00	25.00	15.00
(10)	Tom Bridges	50.00	25.00	15.00
(11)	Dolf Camilli	50.00	25.00	15.00
(12)	Ben Chapman	50.00	25.00	15.00
(13)	Harland Clift (Harlond)	50.00	25.00	15.00
(14)	Harry Craft	50.00	25.00	15.00
(15)	Roger Cramer	50.00	25.00	15.00
(16)	Joe Cronin	125.00	62.00	37.00
(17)	Tony Cuccinello	50.00	25.00	15.00
(18)	Kiki Cuyler	125.00	62.00	37.00
(19)	Ellsworth Dahlgren	50.00	25.00	15.00
(20)	Harry Danning	50.00	25.00	15.00
(21)	Frank Demaree	50.00	25.00	15.00
(22)	Gene Desautels	50.00	25.00	15.00
(23)	Jim Deshong	50.00	25.00	15.00
(24)	Bill Dickey	150.00	75.00	45.00
(25)	Lou Fette	50.00	25.00	15.00
(26)	Lou Finney	50.00	25.00	15.00
(27)	Larry French	50.00	25.00	15.00
(28)	Linus Frey	50.00	25.00	15.00
(29)	Debs Garms	50.00	25.00	15.00
(30)	Charles Gehringer	150.00	75.00	45.00
(31)	Lefty Gomez	150.00	75.00	45.00
(32)	Ival Goodman	50.00	25.00	15.00
(33)	Lee Grissom	50.00	25.00	15.00
(34)	Stan Hack	60.00	30.00	18.00
(35)	Irving Hadley	50.00	25.00	15.00
(36)	Rollie Hemsley	50.00	25.00	15.00
(37)	Tommy Henrich	50.00	25.00	15.00
(38)	Billy Herman	125.00	62.00	37.00
(39)	Willard Hershberger	50.00	25.00	15.00
(40)	Michael Higgins	50.00	25.00	15.00
(41)	Oral Hildebrand	50.00	25.00	15.00
(42)	Carl Hubbell	150.00	75.00	45.00
(43)	Willis Hudlin	50.00	25.00	15.00
(44)	Mike Kreevich	50.00	25.00	15.00
(45)	Ralph Kress	50.00	25.00	15.00
(46)	John Lanning	50.00	25.00	15.00
(47)	Lyn Lary	50.00	25.00	15.00
(48)	Cookie Lavagetto	50.00	25.00	15.00
(49)	Thornton Lee	50.00	25.00	15.00
(50)	Ernie Lombardi	125.00	62.00	37.00
(51)	Al Lopez	125.00	62.00	37.00
(52)	Ted Lyons	125.00	62.00	37.00
(53)	Danny MacFayden	50.00	25.00	15.00
(54)	Max Macon	50.00	25.00	15.00
(55)	Pepper Martin	65.00	32.00	19.50
(56)	Joe Marty	50.00	25.00	15.00
(57)	Frank McCormick	50.00	25.00	15.00
(58)	Bill McKechnie	125.00	62.00	37.00
(59)	Joe Medwick	125.00	62.00	37.00
(60)	Cliff Melton	50.00	25.00	15.00
(61)	Charley Meyer (Myer)	50.00	25.00	15.00
(62)	John Mize	150.00	75.00	45.00
(63)	Terry Moore	65.00	32.00	19.50
(64)	Whitey Moore	50.00	25.00	15.00
(65)	Emmett Mueller	50.00	25.00	15.00
(66)	Hugh Mulcahy	50.00	25.00	15.00
(67)	Van L. Mungo	50.00	25.00	15.00
(68)	Johnny Murphy	50.00	25.00	15.00
(69)	Lynn Nelson	50.00	25.00	15.00
(70)	Mel Ott	150.00	75.00	45.00
(71)	Monte Pearson	50.00	25.00	15.00
(72)	Bill Rogell	50.00	25.00	15.00
(73)	George Selkirk	50.00	25.00	15.00
(74)	Milt Shofner	50.00	25.00	15.00
(75)	Al Simmons	125.00	62.00	37.00
(76)	Clyde Shoun	50.00	25.00	15.00
(77)	Gus Suhr	50.00	25.00	15.00
(78)	Billy Sullivan	50.00	25.00	15.00
(79)	Cecil Travis	50.00	25.00	15.00
(80)	Pie Traynor	125.00	62.00	37.00
(81)	Hal Trosky	50.00	25.00	15.00
(82)	Jim Turner	50.00	25.00	15.00
(83)	Johnny Vander Meer	50.00	25.00	15.00
(84)	Oscar Vitt	50.00	25.00	15.00
(85)	Gerald Walker	50.00	25.00	15.00
(86)	Paul Waner	125.00	62.00	37.00
(87)	Rabbit Warstler	50.00	25.00	15.00
(88)	Bob Weiland	50.00	25.00	15.00
(89)	Burgess Whitehead	50.00	25.00	15.00
(90)	Earl Whitehill	50.00	25.00	15.00
(91)	Rudy York	50.00	25.00	15.00
(92)	Del Young	50.00	25.00	15.00

1887 Four Base Hits

Although the exact origin of this set is still in doubt, the Four Base Hits cards are among the rarest and most sought after of all 19th century tobacco issues. There is some speculation that the cards, measuring 2-1/4" x 3-7/8", were produced by Charles Gross & Co. because of their similarity to the Kalamazoo Bats issues, but there is also some evidence to support the theory that they were issued by August Beck & Co., producer of the Yum Yum set. The Four Base Hits cards feature sepia-toned photos with the player's name and position below the picture, and the words "Smoke Four Base Hits. Four For 10 Cents." along the bottom. The card labeled "Daily" is a double error. The name should have been spelled "Daly," but the card actually pictures Billy Sunday. Because new discoveries continue to surface for this issue, no complete-set value is listed.

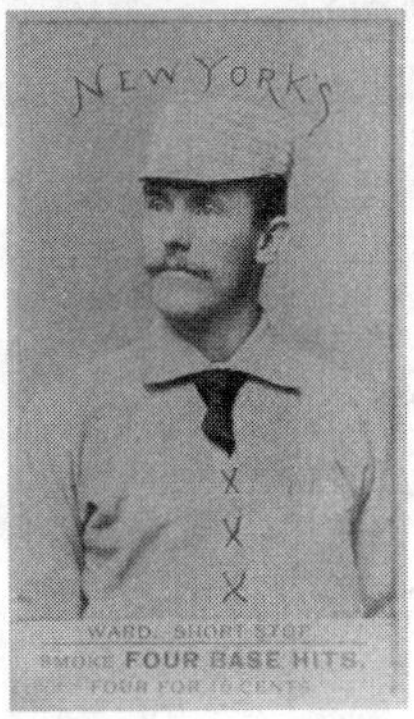

		NM	EX	VG
Common Player:		9000.	4500.	2700.
(1)	John Clarkson	15000.	7500.	4500.
(2)	Tido Daily (Daly)	9000.	4500.	2700.
(3)	Pat Deasley	9000.	4500.	2700.
(4)	Buck Ewing	15000.	7500.	4500.
(5)	Pete Gillespie	9000.	4500.	2700.
(6)	Frank Hankinson	9000.	4500.	2700.
(7)	King Kelly	25000.	12500.	7500.
(8)	Al Mays	9000.	4500.	2700.
(9)	Jim Mutrie	9000.	4500.	2700.
(10)	Chief Roseman	9000.	4500.	2700.
(11)	Marty Sullivan	9000.	4500.	2700.
(12)	Rip Van Haltren	9000.	4500.	2700.
(13)	Monte Ward	15000.	7500.	4500.
(14)	Mickey Welch	15000.	7500.	4500.

1980 Franchise Babe Ruth

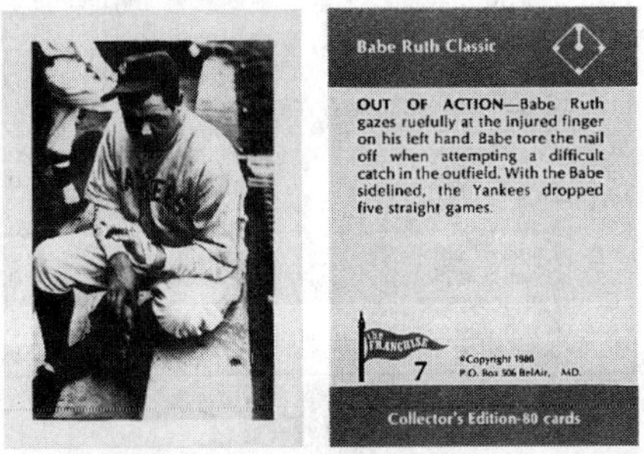

The first in a series of collectors issues relative to Maryland baseball, this 80-card set chronicles the life - on and off the field - of Babe Ruth. Fronts of the 2-1/2" x 3-1/2" cards have black-and-white photos surrounded by wide white borders. Backs are printed in red and black and include a caption and description of the front photo. At the time of issue, the set sold for about $8.

		NM	EX	VG
Complete Set (80):		65.00	32.00	19.50
Common Card:		1.00	.50	.30
1	Babe in Boston	1.00	.50	.30
2	Youthful Babe	1.00	.50	.30
3	Personal Touch	1.00	.50	.30
4	Takes A Cut	1.00	.50	.30
5	On Dotted Line	1.00	.50	.30
6	On Stage	1.00	.50	.30
7	Out of Action	1.00	.50	.30
8	All Smiles	1.00	.50	.30
9	Oriental Hero	1.00	.50	.30
10	Silent Babe	1.00	.50	.30
11	Old Times	1.00	.50	.30
12	Waiting his Turn	1.00	.50	.30
13	Speaking Out	1.00	.50	.30
14	Shadow Slugger	1.00	.50	.30
15	Youthful Ball Hawk	1.00	.50	.30
16	Speed On The Bases	1.00	.50	.30
17	Helping Hand	1.00	.50	.30
18	Babe in Disguise	1.00	.50	.30
19	Political Boss	1.00	.50	.30
20	Mail Clerk	1.00	.50	.30
21	Keeping Warm	1.00	.50	.30
22	Big Cut	1.00	.50	.30
23	Defense, Too	1.00	.50	.30
24	Playing Catch	1.00	.50	.30
25	Big Swing	1.00	.50	.30
26	Taking Aim	1.00	.50	.30
27	Double Trouble	1.00	.50	.30
28	Power Plus	1.00	.50	.30
29	Running Wild	1.00	.50	.30
30	Formidable Figure	1.00	.50	.30
31	Effort	1.00	.50	.30
32	Long Gone	1.00	.50	.30
33	Up the Shaft	1.00	.50	.30
34	Healthy Cut	1.00	.50	.30
35	Right Choice	1.00	.50	.30
36	At Rest	1.00	.50	.30
37	Count It	1.00	.50	.30
38	Bearded Babe	1.00	.50	.30
39	Solemn Babe	1.00	.50	.30
40	Good Cause	1.00	.50	.30
41	Powder Puff	1.00	.50	.30
42	He-Man Image	1.00	.50	.30
43	Shedding Pounds	1.00	.50	.30
44	Another Hit	1.00	.50	.30
45	An Ump, Too	1.00	.50	.30
46	Out of Action	1.00	.50	.30
47	New Start	1.00	.50	.30
48	Diet Food	1.00	.50	.30
49	Birthday Cake	1.00	.50	.30
50	Good Luck	1.00	.50	.30
51	Gourmet Chef	1.00	.50	.30
52	Long Gone	1.00	.50	.30
53	Getting Ready	1.00	.50	.30
54	Thanks, Pal	1.00	.50	.30
55	Called Shot	1.00	.50	.30
56	On the Farm	1.00	.50	.30
57	Itching to Play	1.00	.50	.30
58	Big Swing	1.00	.50	.30
59	Just Practice	1.00	.50	.30
60	On its Way	1.00	.50	.30
61	Easy Smile	1.00	.50	.30
62	In the Shade	1.00	.50	.30
63	Kingly Celebration	1.00	.50	.30
64	The Skipper	1.00	.50	.30
65	Sandy Swing	1.00	.50	.30
66	Deep Thought	1.00	.50	.30
67	Bundled Up	1.00	.50	.30
68	Stage Hand	1.00	.50	.30
69	Mechanic, Too	1.00	.50	.30
70	Serious Mood	1.00	.50	.30
71	Happy Face	1.00	.50	.30
72	Fashion Plate	1.00	.50	.30
73	Taking A Puff	1.00	.50	.30
74	Final Game as Yankee	1.00	.50	.30
75	New Team	1.00	.50	.30
76	Big Effort	1.00	.50	.30
77	Last Game	1.00	.50	.30
78	Solemn Look	1.00	.50	.30
79	End is Near	1.00	.50	.30
80	Farewell	1.00	.50	.30

1961 Franklin Milk

While it is not part of the contemporary Cloverleaf Dairy milk carton Minnesota Twins issues, this carton is often collected alongside the others. Printed in red and blue, the portion of the milk carton advertising Harmon Killebrew's radio show measures about 4" x 4-1/2".

		NM	EX	VG
(1)	Harmon Killebrew (complete carton)	300.00	150.00	90.00
(1)	Harmon Killebrew (cut panel)	90.00	45.00	27.00

1977 Franklin Mint American Hall of Fame

A single ballplayer was honored in this set of medallic art pieces depicting members of the American Hall of Fame. Issued in 32mm (about half-dollar size), the medals were struck in sterling silver and overlayed with 24K gold. Issue price was $15.75.

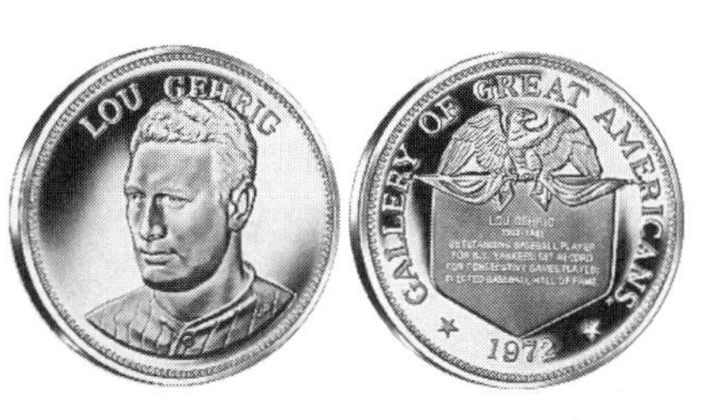

		NM	EX	VG
	1977- (?) American Hall of Fame			
---	Babe Ruth (32mm; 24K gold on sterling silver. Issued at $15.75)	45.00	22.00	13.50
	1968-74 American Negro Commemorative Society			
7	Jackie Robinson (Edition of 1,380. 39mm sterling silver. Issued at $9.)	50.00	25.00	15.00
14	Roberto Clemente (Edition of 900. 39mm sterling silver. Issued at $9.)	50.00	25.00	15.00
	1970-72 California History			
56	Giants and Dodgers Move to California (39mm proof sterling silver edition of 930; issued at $11.)	20.00	10.00	6.00
56	Giants and Dodgers Move to California (39mm proof bronze edition of 310; issued at $5.50)	15.00	7.50	4.50
	1971-77 Gallery of Great Americans			
	1971			
11	George "Babe" Ruth (39mm proof sterling silver. Edition of 8,757 issued at $8.75.)	40.00	20.00	12.00
11	George "Babe" Ruth (39mm bronze proof. Edition of 4,866 issued at $3.50.)	30.00	15.00	9.00
	1972			
11	Lou Gehrig (39mm proof sterling silver. Edition of 2,226 issued at $8.75.)	30.00	15.00	9.00
11	Lou Gehrig (39mm proof bronze. Edition of 1,338 issued at $3.50.)	25.00	12.50	7.50
	1973			
11	Connie Mack (39mm proof sterling silver. Edition of 1,514 issued at $9.50.)	25.00	12.50	7.50
11	Connie Mack (39mm proof bronze. Edition of 1,104 issued at $3.75.)	20.00	10.00	6.00
	1977- (?) Greatest Events in American Sports			
	(All medals 32mm proof sterling silver. Edition of 1,196 issued at $12.50.)			
3	Christy Mathewson	30.00	15.00	9.00
4	Cy Young	30.00	15.00	9.00
6	Rube Marquard	25.00	12.50	7.50
9	Boston Braves	20.00	10.00	6.00
10	Ty Cobb	40.00	20.00	12.00
11	Bill Wambsganss	20.00	10.00	6.00
18	Grover Cleveland Alexander	25.00	12.50	7.50
21	Walter Johnson	35.00	17.50	10.50
23	Babe Ruth (60 homers)	45.00	22.50	13.50
27	Babe Ruth (1932 World Series)	45.00	22.50	13.50
29	Lou Gehrig	40.00	20.00	12.00
36	Bob Feller	30.00	15.00	9.00
37	Lou Gehrig	40.00	20.00	12.00
40	Ted Williams	40.00	20.00	12.00
41	Cookie Lavagetto	20.00	10.00	6.00
46	Jackie Robinson	40.00	20.00	12.00
	(Unknown whether medals beyond #48 ever issued.)			
	1968-76 History of the U.S.			
129	Baseball Becomes Big League - 1904 (Cy Young) (45mm proof sterling silver. Edition of 10,000 issued at $9.75.)	30.00	15.00	9.00
129	Baseball Becomes Big League - 1904 (Cy Young) (45mm proof bronze. Edition of 24,836 issued at $3.)	25.00	12.50	7.50
129	Baseball Becomes Big League - 1904 (Cy Young) (13mm prooflike 24K gold. Edition of 63 issued in 1977 at $25.)	45.00	22.50	13.50
129	Baseball Becomes Big League - 1904 (Cy Young) (13mm prooflike sterling silver. Edition of 5,128 issued at	25.00	12.50	7.50
	1974- (?) Medallic Yearbook			
4	Hank Aaron ("Aaron Breaks Ruth's Home Run Record." 45mm proof sterling silver. Edition of 2,162 issued at	30.00	15.00	9.00
	Misc. Private Issues			
	1970 Three Rivers Stadium Dedication (39mm sterling silver; edition of 100)	40.00	20.00	12.00
	1970 Three Rivers Stadium Dedication (39mm gold on sterling silver; edition of 100)	30.00	15.00	9.00
	1970 Three Rivers Stadium Dedication (39mm bronze; edition of 738)	20.00	10.00	6.00
	1970 Three Rivers Stadium Dedication (39mm nickel-silver; edition of 769)	20.00	10.00	6.00
	1972 Jackie Robinson (39mm proof sterling silver; edition of 3,651 issued at $6.60)	40.00	20.00	12.00
	1972 Jackie Robinson (39mm proof bronze; edition of 1,104 issued at $3.)	30.00	15.00	7.50
	1964- (?) National Commemorative Society			
54	Babe Ruth (39mm proof sterling silver; edition of 5,249 issued $7.)	40.00	20.00	12.00
63	Baseball Centennial (39mm proof sterling silver; edition of 5,249 issued $7.)	15.00	7.50	4.50
148	Lou Gehrig (39mm proof sterling silver; edition of 5,249 issued $7.)	30.00	15.00	9.00
	1972 World Series- A's and Reds (39mm proof sterling silver; edition of 9,523 issued on postmarked cover at	25.00	12.50	7.50
	1968-71 Texas Under Six Flags			
50	Hemisfair & Astrodome (45mm proof sterling silver; edition of 777 issued at $11.)	15.00	7.50	4.50
50	Hemisfair & Astrodome (45mm proof bronze; edition of 337 issued at $4.50.)	12.00	6.00	3.50
	1977-85 20th Century's Greatest Events			
28	Babe Ruth (One-ounce gold on silver proof ingot; edition of 3,078.)	45.00	22.50	13.50

1963 French Bauer Reds Milk Caps

This regional set of cardboard milk bottle caps was issued in the Cincinnati area in 1963 and features 30 members of the Cincinnati Reds. The unnumbered, blank-backed discs are approximately 1-1/4" in diameter and feature rather crude drawings of the players with their names in script alongside the artwork and the words "Visit Beautiful Crosley Field/See The Reds in Action" along the outside. An album was issued to house the set.

		NM	EX	VG
Complete Set (30):		1650.	825.00	495.00
Common Player:		15.00	7.50	4.50
Album:		200.00	100.00	60.00
(1)	Don Blasingame	15.00	7.50	4.50
(2)	Leo Cardenas	15.00	7.50	4.50
(3)	Gordon Coleman	15.00	7.50	4.50
(4)	Wm. O. DeWitt	15.00	7.50	4.50
(5)	John Edwards	15.00	7.50	4.50
(6)	Jesse Gonder	15.00	7.50	4.50
(7)	Tommy Harper	15.00	7.50	4.50
(8)	Bill Henry	15.00	7.50	4.50
(9)	Fred Hutchinson	18.00	9.00	5.50
(10)	Joey Jay	15.00	7.50	4.50
(11)	Eddie Kasko	15.00	7.50	4.50
(12)	Marty Keough	15.00	7.50	4.50
(13)	Jim Maloney	20.00	10.00	6.00
(14)	Joe Nuxhall	20.00	10.00	6.00
(15)	Reggie Otero	15.00	7.50	4.50
(16)	Jim O'Toole	15.00	7.50	4.50
(17)	Jim Owens	15.00	7.50	4.50
(18)	Vada Pinson	50.00	25.00	15.00
(19)	Bob Purkey	15.00	7.50	4.50
(20)	Frank Robinson	200.00	100.00	60.00
(21)	Dr. Richard Rohde	15.00	7.50	4.50
(22)	Pete Rose	600.00	300.00	180.00
(23)	Ray Shore	15.00	7.50	4.50
(24)	Dick Sisler	15.00	7.50	4.50
(25)	Bob Skinner	15.00	7.50	4.50
(26)	John Tsitorius	15.00	7.50	4.50
(27)	Jim Turner	15.00	7.50	4.50
(28)	Ken Walters	15.00	7.50	4.50
(29)	Al Worthington	15.00	7.50	4.50
(30)	Dom Zanni	15.00	7.50	4.50

1946 Friedman's Dodger Aces Postcard

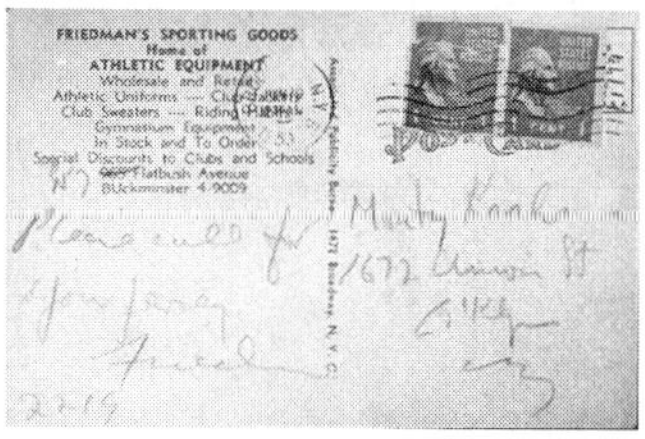

The date of issue is conjectural and could actually have been anytime in the 1940s until 1947, though the cards continued to be used at least into 1953 according to postally used examples. The 5-1/2" x 3-1/2" postcard has a linen finish on front and features color posed action photos of three Dodgers stars. Backs have information about the sporting goods store, a postage stamp box and a credit line to Associated Publicity Bureau.

	NM	EX	VG
Dodger Aces (Pete Reiser, Pewee Reese (Pee Wee), Dixie Walker)	35.00	17.50	10.50

1960-61 Fritos Ticket Folders

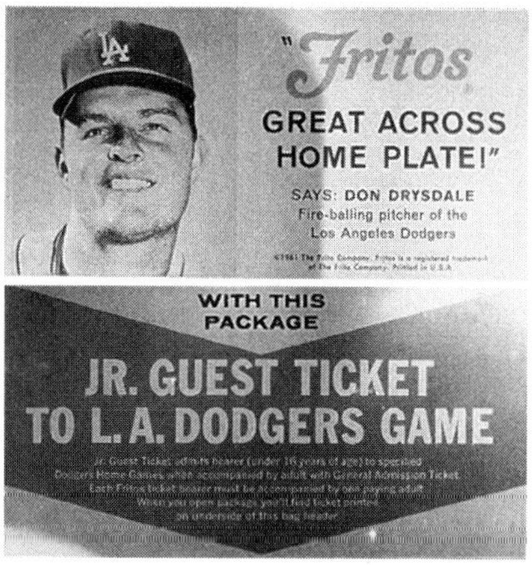

Only a few players are known in this issue of folders which includes a "Jr. Guest Ticket" to selected Dodgers games. About 5-5/8" x 3", the folder has a black-and-white player portrait on front and is highlighted in red and yellow. When opened, the folder has advertising for Fritos corn chips and a Dodgers home schedule. Others may exist.

		NM	EX	VG
Common Player:		60.00	30.00	18.00
(1)	Don Drysdale (1961)	100.00	50.00	30.00
(2)	Gil Hodges (1960)	150.00	75.00	45.00
(3)	Frank Howard (1961)	60.00	30.00	18.00
(4)	Wally Moon (1960)	60.00	30.00	18.00

1977 Fritsch One-Year Winners

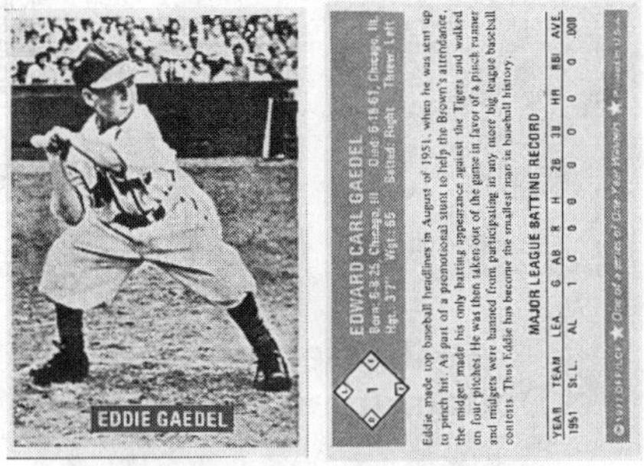

First printed in 1977, this collector's issue features players with brief, but often well-known, major league baseball careers. Because of the timing or duration of their playing days, few ever appeared on a major baseball card issue. The 2-1/2" x 3-1/2" cards have black-and-white photos on front, bordered in green, with the player name in white within a green strip at bottom. Backs are printed in black, red and white in similitude of the 1953 Bowman backs and contain personal data, stats and career highlights.

		NM	EX	VG
Complete Set (18):		5.00	3.75	2.00
Common Player:		.10	.08	.04
1	Eddie Gaedel	2.00	1.00	.60
2	Chuck Connors	1.00	.50	.30
3	Joe Brovia	.10	.08	.04
4	Ross Grimsley	.10	.08	.04
5	Bob Thorpe	.10	.08	.04
6	Pete Gray	2.00	1.00	.60
7	Cy Buker	.10	.08	.04
8	Ted Fritsch	.25	.13	.08
9	Ron Necciai	.25	.13	.08
10	Nino Escalera	.10	.08	.04
11	Bobo Holloman	.10	.08	.04
12	Tony Roig	.10	.08	.04
13	Paul Pettit	.10	.08	.04
14	Paul Schramka	.10	.08	.04
15	Hal Trosky	.10	.08	.04
16	Floyd Wooldridge	.10	.08	.04
17	Jim Westlake	.10	.08	.04
18	Leon Brinkopf	.10	.08	.04

1979 Fritsch One-Year Winners

Players with short major-league careers, few of whom appeared on contemporary baseball cards, are featured in the second collectors series of "One-Year Winners". The cards are numbered contiguously from the end of the 1977 issue and share a back format printed in red, white and black. Fronts of the 1979 issue have a white border and feature color player photos with a shadow box beneath carrying the name.

		NM	EX	VG
Complete Set (36):		10.00	5.00	3.00
Common Player:		.35	.20	.11
19	Daryl Robertson	.35	.20	.11
20	Gerry Schoen	.35	.20	.11
21	Jim Brenneman	.35	.20	.11
22	Pat House	.35	.20	.11
23	Ken Poulsen	.35	.20	.11
24	Arlo Brunsberg	.35	.20	.11
25	Jay Hankins	.35	.20	.11
26	Chuck Nieson	.35	.20	.11
27	Dick Joyce	.35	.20	.11
28	Jim Ellis	.35	.20	.11
29	John Duffie	.35	.20	.11
30	Vern Holtgrave	.35	.20	.11
31	Bill Bethea	.35	.20	.11
32	Joe Moock	.35	.20	.11
33	John Hoffman	.35	.20	.11
34	Jorge Rubio	.35	.20	.11
35	Fred Rath	.35	.20	.11
36	Jess Hickman	.35	.20	.11
37	Tom Fisher	.35	.20	.11
38	Dick Scott	.35	.20	.11
39	Jim Hibbs	.35	.20	.11
40	Paul Gilliford	.35	.20	.11
41	Bob Botz	.35	.20	.11
42	Jack Kubiszyn	.35	.20	.11
43	Rich Rusteck	.35	.20	.11
44	Roy Gleason	.35	.20	.11
45	Glenn Vaughn	.35	.20	.11
46	Bill Graham	.35	.20	.11
47	Dennis Musgraves	.35	.20	.11
48	Ron Henry	.35	.20	.11
49	Mike Jurewicz	.35	.20	.11
50	Pidge Browne	.35	.20	.11
51	Ron Keller	.35	.20	.11
52	Doug Gallagher	.35	.20	.11
53	Dave Thies	.35	.20	.11
54	Don Eaddy	.35	.20	.11

1928 Fro-joy

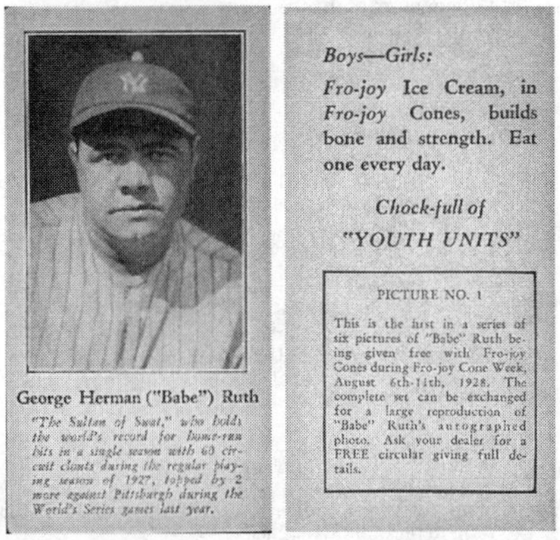

Capitalizing on the extreme popularity of Babe Ruth, these cards were given away with ice cream cones during the August 6-11, 1928 "Fro-joy Cone Week." The 2-1/16" x 4" cards have black-and-white photos on front with a title and a few sentences explaining the photo. Backs contain advertising for Fro-joy Ice Cream and Cones. Uncut sheets along with a large-format action photo of Ruth were available in a mail-in redemption offer. Virtually all uncut sheets offered in the market today, and all color Fro-joy cards are recent counterfeits.

		NM	EX	VG
Complete Set (6):		2400.	1200.	725.00
Common Card:		200.00	100.00	60.00
Uncut Sheet with Premium Photo:		6000.	3000.	1800.
1	George Herman ("Babe") Ruth	300.00	150.00	90.00
2	Look Out, Mr. Pitcher! (Babe Ruth)	250.00	125.00	75.00
3	"Babe" Ruth's Grip!	200.00	100.00	60.00
4	Ruth is a Crack Fielder	250.00	125.00	75.00
5	Bang! The Babe Lines One Out!	250.00	125.00	75.00
6	When the "Babe" Comes Home (Babe Ruth)	250.00	125.00	75.00

1928 Fro-joy Premium Photo

This 8-1/2" x 10" photo of Babe Ruth was given away when a complete set of individual Fro-joy Babe Ruth cards was sent in for redemption. It is extremely scarce in its own right and is vital for verification of the authenticity of uncut Fro-joy card sheets. The premium photo is printed in blue in the debossed center area of a cream-colored card. A facsimile autograph of Ruth adorns the image.

	NM	EX	VG
Babe Ruth	2500.	1250.	750.00

1976 Funky Facts

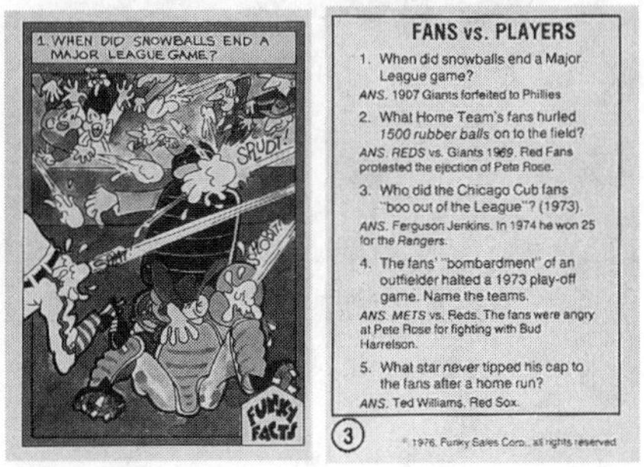

This set features color cartoons of famous and infamous baseball players and historical moments in the game. Cards are standard 2-1/2" x 3-1/2". Backs are black-and-white with several trivia questions.

		NM	EX	VG
Complete Set (40):		15.00	7.50	4.50
Common Card:		.50	.25	.15
1	Hit by Pitches	.50	.25	.15
2	Hypotism	.50	.25	.15
3	Fans vs. Players	.50	.25	.15
4	25-foot Pitches	.50	.25	.15
5	Language of Baseball	.50	.25	.15
6	Midget Pinch-hitter	.50	.25	.15
7	Names and Nicknames	.50	.25	.15
8	Find Hall of Famers	.50	.25	.15
9	"dem Bums"	.50	.25	.15
10	First Gloves	.50	.25	.15
11	Fan on Flagpole	.50	.25	.15
12	MVP in Both Leagues	.50	.25	.15
13	Bloomer Girl	.50	.25	.15
14	Wet Base Paths	.50	.25	.15
15	Pasquel's Raid	.50	.25	.15
16	$5,000 Fine	.50	.25	.15
17	Norm Cash	.50	.25	.15
18	Backwards Baserunning	.50	.25	.15
19	Hot Dogs	.50	.25	.15
20	Major League Brothers	.50	.25	.15
21	Shoe Polish	.50	.25	.15
22	NBA Superstar	.50	.25	.15
23	Acrobatic Hitter	.50	.25	.15
24	Three Dodgers on 3rd	.50	.25	.15
25	Smallest Attendance	.50	.25	.15
26	Evil Eye	.50	.25	.15
27	Outrunning Hans Lobert	.50	.25	.15
28	Wilbert Robinson	.50	.25	.15
29	Walking Batter	.50	.25	.15
30	World Series Snooze	.50	.25	.15
31	Most Steals	.50	.25	.15
32	Ott Loses HR Title	.50	.25	.15
33	Pitching Grips	.50	.25	.15
34	Bill Terry	.50	.25	.15
35	Hit Three Batters	.50	.25	.15
36	Three Hits in Inning	.50	.25	.15
37	Bandaged Yankees	.50	.25	.15
38	Ambidextrous Pitcher	.50	.25	.15
39	Nicknames	.50	.25	.15
(40)	International Baseball	.50	.25	.15

G

1888 G & B Chewing Gum (E223)

This set, issued with G&B Chewing Gum, is the first baseball card issued with candy or gum and the only 19th Century candy issue. The cards in the G&B set are small, measuring just 1" x 2-1/8". The cards are very similar in design to the August Beck Yum Yum issue (N403) and many of the photos appear to have been borrowed from that set. The player's name and position appear in thin capital letters below the photo, followed by either "National League" or "American League" (actually referring to the American Association). At the very bottom of the card, the manufacturer, "G&B N.Y." is indicated. (Some of the "National League" cards also include the words "Chewing Gum" after the league designation.) The set has been assigned the ACC number E223. Most of the action poses are line drawings rather than photographs.

		NM	EX	VG
Complete Set (68):		200000.	90000.	40000.
Common Player:		3000.	1200.	750.00
(1)	Cap Anson (portrait)	12000.	4800.	3000.
(2)	Fido Baldwin (bat at side)	3200.	1275.	800.00
(3)	Fido Baldwin (portrait)	4000.	1600.	1000.
(4)	Lady Baldwin (Detroit)	3200.	1275.	800.00
(5)	Stephen Brady (portrait)	4000.	1600.	1000.
(6)	Dan Brouthers	4000.	1600.	1000.
(7)	Bill Brown (portrait)	4000.	1600.	1000.
(8)	Bill Brown (line art)	3200.	1275.	800.00
(9)	Charles Buffington (Buffinton) (portrait)	4000.	1600.	1000.
(10)	Thomas Burns (portrait)	4000.	1600.	1000.
(11)	Bob Caruthers	3200.	1275.	800.00
(12)	John Clarkson (portrait)	6000.	2400.	1500.
(13)	John Coleman (portrait)	4000.	1600.	1000.
(14)	Commy Comiskey	6000.	2400.	1500.
(15)	Roger Connor (batting)	4000.	1600.	1000.
(16)	Roger Connor (portrait)	6000.	2400.	1500.
(17)	Con Daily (portrait)	4000.	1600.	1000.
(18)	Tom Deasley	4000.	1600.	1000.
(19)	Mike Dorgan (portrait)	4000.	1600.	1000.
(20)	Dude Esterbrook	4000.	1600.	1000.
(21)	Buck Ewing (batting)	4000.	1600.	1000.
(22)	Buck Ewing (portrait)	6000.	2400.	1500.
(23)	Charlie Ferguson	3200.	1275.	800.00
(24)	Silver Flint (portrait)	4000.	1600.	1000.
(25)	Charlie Getzein (Getzien)	3200.	1275.	800.00
(26)	Jack Glasscock (line art)	3200.	1275.	800.00
(27)	Will Gleason (line art)	3200.	1275.	800.00
(28)	Frank Hankinson (portrait)	4000.	1600.	1000.
(29)	Pete Hotaling	3200.	1275.	800.00
(30)	Spud Johnson	3200.	1275.	800.00
(31)	Tim Keefe (batting)	4000.	1600.	1000.
(32)	Tim Keefe (throwing)	4000.	1600.	1000.
(33)	Tim Keefe (portrait)	6500.	2600.	1625.
(34)	King Kelly (batting)	4000.	1600.	1000.
(35)	King Kelly (standing by urn)	6500.	2600.	1625.
(36)	Gus Krock (portrait)	4000.	1600.	1000.
(37)	Connie Mack	6000.	2400.	1500.
(38)	Doggie Miller	3200.	1275.	800.00
(39)	Honest John Morrill	3200.	1275.	800.00
(40)	James Mutrie	4000.	1600.	1000.
(41)	Little Nick Nicoll (Nicol)	4000.	1600.	1000.
(42)	Tip O'Neill	4000.	1600.	1000.
(43)	Orator Jim O'Rourke	6000.	2400.	1500.
(44)	Fred Pfeffer	3200.	1275.	800.00
(45)	Henry Porter	3200.	1275.	800.00
(46)	Danny Richardson (batting)	3200.	1275.	800.00
(47)	Danny Richardson (portrait)	4000.	1600.	1000.
(48)	Chief Roseman (portrait)	4000.	1600.	1000.
(49)	Jimmy Ryan (portrait)	4000.	1600.	1000.
(50)	Jimmy Ryan (throwing)	3200.	1275.	800.00
(51)	Pop Smith (portrait)	4000.	1600.	1000.
(52)	Little Bill Sowders (ball at chest)	3200.	1275.	800.00
(53)	Little Bill Sowders (throwing)	3200.	1275.	800.00
(54)	Marty Sullivan	4000.	1600.	1000.
(55)	Billy Sunday (fielding)	4000.	1600.	1000.
(56)	Billy Sunday (portrait)	6000.	2400.	1500.
(57)	Ezra Sutton	3200.	1275.	800.00
(58)	Silent Mike Tiernan (batting)	3200.	1275.	800.00
(59)	Silent Mike Tiernan (portrait)	4000.	1600.	1000.
(60)	Big Sam Thompson	4000.	1600.	1000.
(61)	Larry Twitchell	4000.	1600.	1000.
(62)	Rip Van Haltren	4000.	1600.	1000.
(63)	Monte Ward (portrait)	6000.	2400.	1500.
(64)	Smiling Mickey Welch (pitching)	4000.	1600.	1000.
(65)	Smiling Mickey Welch (portrait)	6000.	2400.	1500.
(66)	Curt Welsh (Welch)	4000.	1600.	1000.
(67)	Grasshopper Whitney	4000.	1600.	1000.
(68)	Pete Wood	3200.	1275.	800.00

1963 GAD Fun Cards

This cartoon-style set consists of 67 different baseball cards plus 17 cards concerning other sports. The 2-1/2" x 3-1/2" cards feature black, white and red illustrations on front. Backs are in green and have puzzles, riddles or checklists. Cards 1, 2, 4, 5 and 42 display a 1961 copyright but were apparently issued in 1963 with the rest of the set. Only the baseball related cards are checklisted here.

		NM	EX	VG
Complete Set (84):		80.00	40.00	24.00
Common Non-player:		1.00	.50	.30
Common Player:		1.25	.60	.40
1	Babe Ruth	6.00	3.00	1.75
2	40 Baseballs Lost	1.00	.50	.30
3	Baseball Slang - "Fireman"	1.00	.50	.30
4	Underhand Hurling	1.00	.50	.30
5	Lou Gehrig	4.00	2.00	1.25
6	Game Instructions	1.00	.50	.30
7	Consecutive HRs in Inning	1.00	.50	.30
8	Old Hoss Radbourne	1.50	.70	.45
9	Glen Gorbous	1.25	.60	.40
10	Joe Nuxhall	1.25	.60	.40
11	Ty Cobb	4.00	2.00	1.25
12	Baseball Slang - "Jake"	1.00	.50	.30
13	Pop Schriver	1.25	.60	.40
14	First Team to Fly	1.00	.50	.30
15	John Taylor	1.25	.60	.40
16	Longest Winning Streak	1.00	.50	.30
17	Most Runs Scored in Game	1.00	.50	.30
18	Baseball Slang - "Duster"	1.00	.50	.30
19	Baseball Scuffing Prohibited	1.00	.50	.30
20	Evar Swanson	1.25	.60	.40
21	Eight Pinch-hitters Used	1.00	.50	.30
22	Rogers Hornsby	2.00	1.00	.60
23	New York Highlanders	1.00	.50	.30
24	Baseball Slang - "Strawberry"	1.00	.50	.30
25	Lew Flick	1.25	.60	.40
26	Cy Young	2.00	1.00	.60
27	Jim Konstanti (Konstanty)	1.25	.60	.40
28	Carl Weilman	1.25	.60	.40
29	Warren Rosar	1.25	.60	.40
30	Baseball Slang - "Rabbit Ears"	1.00	.50	.30
31	Graham McNamee	1.25	.60	.40
32	Ty Cobb	4.00	2.00	1.25
33	Joe DiMaggio	5.00	2.50	1.50
34	Babe Ruth	5.00	2.50	1.50
35	Baseball Slang - "Chinese HR"	1.00	.50	.30
36	Ed Delahanty	1.50	.70	.45
37	Tiger Team on Strike	1.00	.50	.30
38	Bobo Holloman	1.25	.60	.40
39	Walter Johnson	2.00	1.00	.60
40	Sam Crawford	1.50	.70	.45
41	Ty Cobb	4.00	2.00	1.25
42	Baseball Slang - "Showboat"	1.00	.50	.30
43	Lou Gehrig	4.00	2.00	1.25
44	Yankee Stadium	1.00	.50	.30
45	Nick Altrock	1.25	.60	.40
46	M. Fleetwood Walker, W. Wilberforce Walker	1.75	.90	.50
47	Joseph Borden	1.25	.60	.40
48	Baseball Slang - "Around the Horn"	1.00	.50	.30
49	Hugh Duffy	1.50	.70	.45
50	Longest Game	1.00	.50	.30
51	Jim Scott	1.25	.60	.40
52	Babe Ruth	5.00	2.50	1.50
53	Most Runs in One Inning	1.00	.50	.30
54	Baseball Slang - "Jockey"	1.00	.50	.30
55	Umpires Worked Free	1.00	.50	.30
56	Bill Phillips	1.25	.60	.40
57	Eddie Collins	1.50	.70	.45
58	Milwaukee Nicknames	1.00	.50	.30
59	Bill Wambsganss	1.25	.60	.40
60	Baseball Slang - "Annie Oakley"	1.00	.50	.30
61	Robert Feller	2.00	1.00	.60
62	Wally Pipp	1.25	.60	.40
63	Shortest World Series	1.00	.50	.30
64	Chicago Invaders	1.00	.50	.30
65	Cleveland Nicknames	1.00	.50	.30
66	Baseball Slang - "Baltimore Chop"	1.00	.50	.30
67	Fourteen Pitchers Used in Game	1.00	.50	.30

1966 H.F. Gardner Postcards

Baseball players (and track legend Jesse Owens) who were born in Alabama are featured in this issue credited on some of the cards' backs to a Bessemer, Ala., firm, Scenic South Card Co. Fronts feature borderless color photos attributed to H.F. Gardner. The date given is somewhat arbitrary based on the mention of the Atlanta Braves on the back of a card. Cards are in standard 3-1/2" x 5-1/2" postcard size and format. A brief biography of the athletes appears on the back, along with the credits.

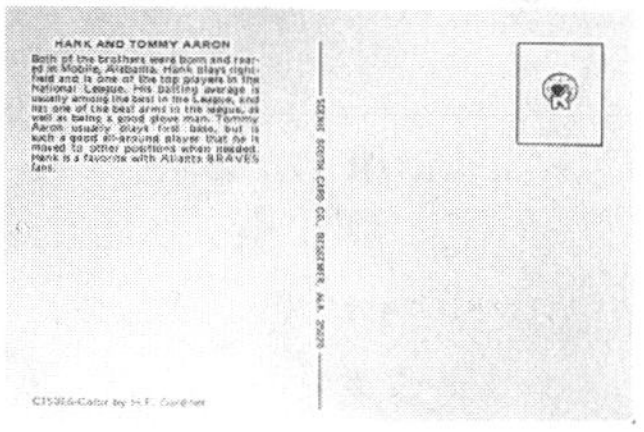

		NM	EX	VG
Complete Set (4):		180.00	90.00	54.00
Common Player:		18.00	9.00	5.50
(1)	Hank Aaron, Tommie Aaron	15.00	7.50	4.50
(2)	Bill Bruton	27.00	13.50	8.00
(3)	Lee Maye	18.00	9.00	5.50
(4)	Jesse Owens	36.00	18.00	11.00
(5)	Billy Williams	45.00	22.00	13.50

1922 Gassler's American Maid Bread

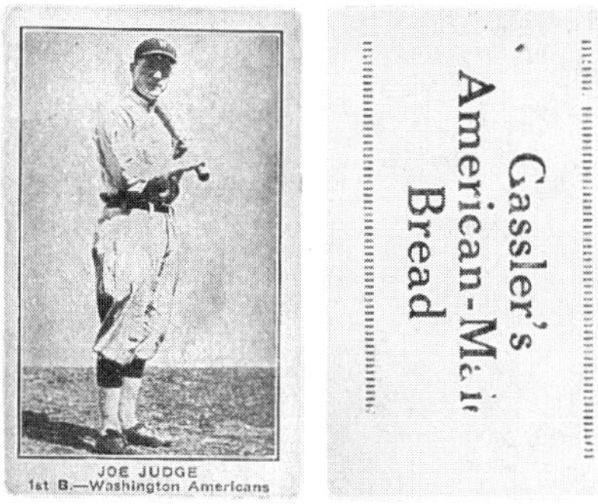

These 2" x 3-1/4" black-and-white cards are one of several versions of the W575-1 strip cards with custom-printed advertising on the backs. It is unknown whether each card in the W575-1 checklist can be found with the Gassler's back.

	NM	EX	VG
Common Player:	45.00	22.00	13.50

(See W575-1 for checklist. Gassler values 1.5X-2X W575-1.)

1962 Gehl's Ice Cream

Issued only in the Milwaukee area to promote sales of Gold-Mine brand ice cream, the six cards in this black-and-white set all feature Roger Maris, who the previous year had broken Babe Ruth's season home run record. The 4" x 5" cards are blank backed and each has a facsimile autograph on front reading "To My / Gold Mine Pal / Roger Maris". The cards are unnumbered; a descripiton of each is provided in the checklist.

		NM	EX	VG
Complete Set (6):		600.00	300.00	180.00
Common Card:		140.00	70.00	42.50
(1)	Roger Maris (bat on shoulder, close-up)	140.00	70.00	42.00
(2)	Roger Maris (bat on shoulder, photo to waist)	140.00	70.00	42.00
(3)	Roger Maris (batting stance)	140.00	70.00	42.00
(4)	Roger Maris ("Hitting My 61st," ballpark photo)	125.00	62.00	37.00
(5)	Roger Maris (holding bat in hands)	140.00	70.00	42.00
(6)	Roger Maris (portrait in warm-up jacket)	140.00	70.00	42.00

1911-14 General Baking Co. (D304)

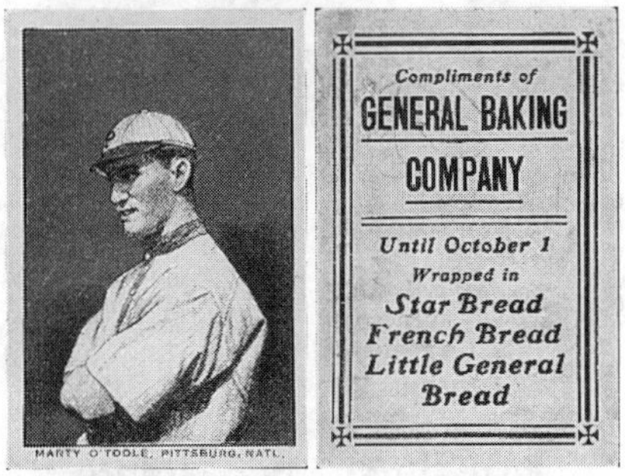

This issue by a bakery based in Buffalo, N.Y., is similar in design to contemporary tobacco and candy cards, but is larger in size, at 1-3/4" x 2-1/2". Fronts feature a color lithograph with the player's name and team below in capital letters. Some players who changed teams in 1913-14 are found with the team name obliterated at bottom by a black line. Four different back styles are known, listed here by the principal brand name: 1) Brunners, 2) Butter Krust, General Baking Co., 4) Weber Bakery. The complete set price does not include "no-team" variations.

		NM	EX	VG
Complete Set (25):		9500.	4750.	2800.
Common Player:		120.00	60.00	36.00
(1)	J. Frank Baker	300.00	150.00	90.00
(2)	Jack Barry	120.00	60.00	36.00
(3)	George Bell	120.00	60.00	36.00
(4)	Charles Bender	300.00	150.00	90.00
(5a)	Frank Chance (Chicago)	300.00	150.00	90.00
(5b)	Frank Chance (no team)	300.00	150.00	90.00
(6a)	Hal Chase (N.Y.)	150.00	75.00	45.00
(6b)	Hal Chase (no team)	150.00	75.00	45.00
(7)	Ty Cobb	2200.	1100.	660.00
(8)	Eddie Collins	300.00	150.00	90.00
(9a)	Otis Crandall (N.Y.)	120.00	60.00	36.00
(9b)	Otis Crandall (no team)	120.00	60.00	36.00
(10)	Sam Crawford	300.00	150.00	90.00
(11a)	John Evers (Chicago)	300.00	150.00	90.00
(11b)	John Evers (no team)	300.00	150.00	90.00
(12)	Arthur Fletcher	120.00	60.00	36.00
(13a)	Charles Herzog	120.00	60.00	36.00
(13b)	Charles Herzog (no team)	120.00	60.00	36.00
(14)	M. Kelly	120.00	60.00	36.00
(15)	Napoleon Lajoie	350.00	175.00	105.00
(16)	Rube Marquard	300.00	150.00	90.00
(17)	Christy Mathewson	900.00	450.00	270.00
(18)	Fred Merkle	120.00	60.00	36.00
(19)	"Chief" Meyers	120.00	60.00	36.00
(20)	Marty O'Toole	120.00	60.00	36.00
(21)	Nap. Rucker	120.00	60.00	36.00
(22)	Arthur Shafer	120.00	60.00	36.00
(23)	Fred Tenny (Tenney)	120.00	60.00	36.00
(24)	Honus Wagner	2400.	1200.	720.00
(25)	Cy Young	900.00	450.00	270.00

1914 General Baking Co. (D303)

Issued in 1914 by the General Baking Company, these unnumbered cards measure 1-1/2" x 2-3/4". The player pictures and format of the cards are identical to the E106 set, but the D303 cards are easily identified by the advertisement for General Baking on the back.

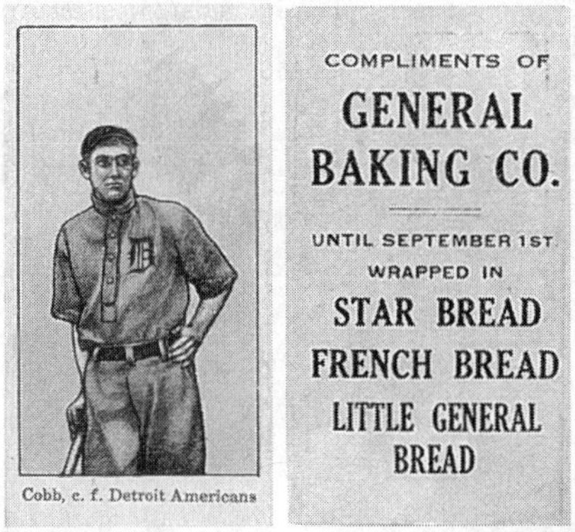

		NM	EX	VG
Complete Set (51):		17500.	8750.	5250.
Common Player:		200.00	100.00	60.00
(1)	Jack Barry	200.00	100.00	60.00
(2)	Chief Bender (blue background)	500.00	250.00	150.00
(3)	Chief Bender (green background)	500.00	250.00	150.00
(4)	Bob Bescher (New York)	200.00	100.00	60.00
(5)	Bob Bescher (St. Louis)	200.00	100.00	60.00
(6)	Roger Bresnahan	500.00	250.00	150.00
(7)	Al Bridwell	200.00	100.00	60.00
(8)	Donie Bush	200.00	100.00	60.00
(9)	Hal Chase (catching)	250.00	125.00	75.00
(10)	Hal Chase (portrait)	250.00	125.00	75.00
(11)	Ty Cobb (batting, front view)	2000.	1000.	600.00
(12)	Ty Cobb (batting, side view)	2000.	1000.	600.00
(13)	Eddie Collins	500.00	250.00	150.00
(14)	Sam Crawford	500.00	250.00	150.00
(15)	Ray Demmitt	200.00	100.00	60.00
(16)	Wild Bill Donovan	200.00	100.00	60.00
(17)	Red Dooin	200.00	100.00	60.00
(18)	Mickey Doolan	200.00	100.00	60.00
(19)	Larry Doyle	200.00	100.00	60.00
(20)	Clyde Engle	200.00	100.00	60.00
(21)	Johnny Evers	500.00	250.00	150.00
(22)	Art Fromme	200.00	100.00	60.00
(23)	George Gibson (catching, back view)	200.00	100.00	60.00
(24)	George Gibson (catching, front view)	200.00	100.00	60.00
(25)	Roy Hartzell	200.00	100.00	60.00
(26)	Fred Jacklitsch	200.00	100.00	60.00
(27)	Hugh Jennings	500.00	250.00	150.00
(28)	Otto Knabe	200.00	100.00	60.00
(29)	Nap Lajoie	600.00	300.00	180.00
(30)	Hans Lobert	200.00	100.00	60.00
(31)	Rube Marquard	500.00	250.00	150.00
(32)	Christy Mathewson	1200.	600.00	360.00
(33)	John McGraw	500.00	250.00	150.00
(34)	George McQuillan	200.00	100.00	60.00
(35)	Dots Miller	200.00	100.00	60.00
(36)	Danny Murphy	200.00	100.00	60.00
(37)	Rebel Oakes	200.00	100.00	60.00
(38)	Eddie Plank (no position on front)	500.00	250.00	150.00
(39)	Eddie Plank (position on front)	500.00	250.00	150.00
(40)	Germany Schaefer	200.00	100.00	60.00
(41)	Boss Smith (Schmidt)	200.00	100.00	60.00
(42)	Tris Speaker	600.00	300.00	180.00
(43)	Oscar Stanage	200.00	100.00	60.00
(44)	George Stovall	200.00	100.00	60.00
(45)	Jeff Sweeney	200.00	100.00	60.00
(46)	Joe Tinker (batting)	500.00	250.00	150.00
(47)	Joe Tinker (portrait)	500.00	250.00	150.00
(48)	Honus Wagner (batting)	1200.	600.00	360.00
(49)	Honus Wagner (throwing)	1200.	600.00	360.00
(50)	Hooks Wiltse	200.00	100.00	60.00
(51)	Heinie Zimmerman	200.00	100.00	60.00

1951 General Mills Premium Photos

The provenance on these 5" x 7" black-and-white player photos is shaky and the actual date of production is also unknown. The portraits on the blank-back pictures appear in most cases to be re-uses of team-issued images from photo packs and the like. Player names are in the bottom border in capital letters. Each picture has a small alpha-numeric identifier in the lower-right corner. The scope of the issue is unknown as at least one number from the sequence is missing. The letter shown in this checklist is preceded in each case by "A8491".

		NM	EX	VG
Common Player:		15.00	7.50	4.50
A	Stan Musial	35.00	17.50	10.50
C	Richie Ashburn	25.00	12.50	7.50
D	Bob Feller	25.00	12.50	7.50
E	Al Rosen	15.00	7.50	4.50
F	Yogi Berra	30.00	15.00	9.00
G	Mickey Mantle	150.00	75.00	45.00
J	Bob Lemon	20.00	10.00	6.00
K	Roy Campanella	30.00	15.00	9.00

1908 General Photo Co. St. Louis Browns Postcards

The extent of this postcard issue by a hometown printer is unknown. It is likely other single-player postcards were issued. Approximately 3-1/2" x 5-1/2", the cards are black-and-white with a credit line on bottom: "Photo by General Photo Co., 610 Granite Bldg., St. Louis". On the team photo card, players are identified below the group photo.

		NM	EX	VG
(1)	"Rube" Waddell	150.00	75.00	45.00
(2)	St. Louis Browns - 1908	200.00	100.00	60.00

1948 Gentle's Bread Boston Braves

These 3" x 9" waxed-paper end labels were found on loaves of Gentle's bread. Printed in blue and red, the labels depict action poses of the National League Champion '48 Braves. A facsimile autograph appears with the photo. Backs are blank. The unnumbered labels are checklisted here alphabetically.

		NM	EX	VG
Complete Set:		1500.	750.00	450.00
Common Player:		200.00	100.00	60.00
(1)	Alvin Dark	225.00	112.00	67.00
(2)	Bob Elliott	200.00	100.00	60.00
(3)	Tommy Heath	200.00	100.00	60.00
(4)	Tommy Holmes	200.00	100.00	60.00
(5)	Phil Masi	200.00	100.00	60.00

		NM	EX	VG
(6)	John Sain	225.00	112.00	67.00
(7)	Warren Spahn	300.00	150.00	90.00
(8)	Eddie Stanky	225.00	112.00	67.00
(9)	Earl Torgeson	200.00	100.00	60.00

1909-10 German Baseball Stamps

A marginal notation "Made in Germany" on one of the stamps in this series identifies its origins. Little else is known of them. The stamps measure about 1-3/8" to 1-1/2" by 1-3/4" to 1-7/8". They are printed in bright colors on a pink background with name and team in blue. Because of their European origins, there are many mistakes in player and team names. The crude pictures are not representative of the player named. Unnumbered stamps are listed here in alphabetical order.

		NM	EX	VG
Complete Sheet (35):		700.00	350.00	210.00
Common Player:		40.00	20.00	12.00
(1)	Ginger Beaumont	40.00	20.00	12.00
(2a)	Roger Bresnahan (light shirt)	65.00	32.00	19.50
(2b)	Roger Bresnahan (dark shirt)	65.00	32.00	19.50
(3)	Bill Carrigan	40.00	20.00	12.00
(4)	Hal Chase	45.00	22.00	13.50
(5)	Harry Davis	40.00	20.00	12.00
(6)	Larry Doyle	40.00	20.00	12.00
(7)	Kid Elberfield (Elberfeld)	40.00	20.00	12.00
(8)	Tim Jordan	40.00	20.00	12.00
(9)	Willie Keeler	65.00	32.00	19.50
(10)	Nap Lajoie	75.00	37.00	22.00
(11)	Tommy Leach	40.00	20.00	12.00
(12)	Christy Mathewson	175.00	87.00	52.00
(13)	Jack Rowan	40.00	20.00	12.00
(14)	Nap Rucker	40.00	20.00	12.00
(15)	Shannon (Boston)	40.00	20.00	12.00
(16)	Frank Smith	40.00	20.00	12.00
(17)	Jake Stahl	40.00	20.00	12.00
(18)	Fred Tenney	40.00	20.00	12.00
(19)	Cy Young	95.00	47.00	28.00
(20)	baseball	15.00	7.50	4.50
(21)	bat	15.00	7.50	4.50
(22)	body protector	15.00	7.50	4.50
(23)	catcher's mask	15.00	7.50	4.50
(24)	crossed bats	15.00	7.50	4.50
(25)	glove	15.00	7.50	4.50

1923 German Baseball Transfers

With crude artwork lifted from the W515 strip card set, this issue of baseball player (and boxers) transfers was produced in Germany. Approximately 1-3/16" x 1-1/2", the stamps are printed in red on a green background. All of the design, except for the "MADE IN GERMANY" notation in the white bottom margin, is in mirror-image, befitting their use as tattoos or transfers. Two of the baseball players are double-prints. The unnumbered stamps (baseball only) are checklisted here alphabetically.

		NM	EX	VG
Complete Set (13):		1100.	550.00	325.00
Common Player:		60.00	30.00	18.00
(1)	Grover Alexander	80.00	40.00	24.00
(2)	Dave Bancroft	75.00	37.00	22.00
(3)	George (J.) Burns	60.00	30.00	18.00
(4)	"Ty" Cobb	200.00	100.00	60.00
(5)	Red Faber (DP)	40.00	20.00	12.00
(6)	Arthur Nehf	60.00	30.00	18.00
(7)	"Babe" Ruth	400.00	200.00	120.00
(8)	Ray Schalk	75.00	37.00	22.00
(9)	Everett Scott	60.00	30.00	18.00
(10)	Bob Shawkey	60.00	30.00	18.00
(11)	Tris Speaker	80.00	40.00	24.00
(12)	"Casey" Stengel	80.00	40.00	24.00
(13)	Zack Wheat (DP)	60.00	30.00	18.00

1922 Lou Gertenrich

One of the most attractive advertising backs of the 1920s is found on this version of the 1922 issue which is most often found with American Caramel ads on back. Gertenrich had a three-game major league career between 1901-1903, supporting his advertising claim of "The Baseball Player Candy Manufacturer". Probably originating in Chicago, these cards are 2" x 3-1/2" black-and-white. The set shares the checklist with the American Caramel Co. (E121) set of 120. Because of the scarcity and appeal of this regional issue, the Gertenrich versions carry a substantial premium for type-card and superstar collectors.

(See 1922 American Caramel Series of 120 for checklist. Gertenrich cards valued at 2X to 3X American Caramels.)

1915-16 Gimbels

(See 1915, 1916 Sporting News for checklists and pricing.)

1953 Glendale Hot Dogs Tigers

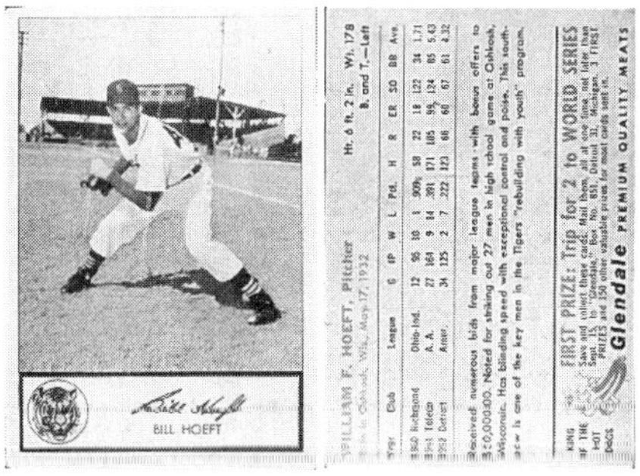

Glendale Meats issued these unnumbered, full-color cards (2-5/8" x 3-3/4") in packages of hot dogs Featuring only Detroit Tigers players, the card fronts contain a player picture with his name, a facsimile autograph, and the Tigers logo. Backs carry player statistical and biographical information plus an offer for a trip for two to the World Series. Collectors were advised to mail all the cards they had saved to Glendale Meats. The World Series trip plus 150 other prizes were to be given to the individuals sending in the most cards. As with most cards issued with food products, high-grade cards are tough to find because of the cards' susceptibilty to stains. The Houtteman card is extremely scarce.

		NM	EX	VG
Complete Set (28):		6600.	3300.	1900.
Common Player:		150.00	75.00	45.00
(1)	Matt Batts	150.00	75.00	45.00
(2)	Johnny Bucha	150.00	75.00	45.00
(3)	Frank Carswell	150.00	75.00	45.00
(4)	Jim Delsing	150.00	75.00	45.00
(5)	Walt Dropo	150.00	75.00	45.00
(6)	Hal Erickson	150.00	75.00	45.00
(7)	Paul Foytack	150.00	75.00	45.00
(8)	Owen Friend	175.00	87.00	52.00
(9)	Ned Garver	150.00	75.00	45.00
(10)	Joe Ginsberg	400.00	200.00	120.00
(11)	Ted Gray	150.00	75.00	45.00
(12)	Fred Hatfield	150.00	75.00	45.00
(13)	Ray Herbert	175.00	87.00	52.00
(14)	Bill Hitchcock	150.00	75.00	45.00
(15)	Bill Hoeft	325.00	162.00	97.00
(16)	Art Houtteman	2600.	1300.	780.00
(17)	Milt Jordan	225.00	112.00	67.00
(18)	Harvey Kuenn	375.00	187.00	112.00
(19)	Don Lund	150.00	75.00	45.00
(20)	Dave Madison	150.00	75.00	45.00
(21)	Dick Marlowe	150.00	75.00	45.00
(22)	Pat Mullin	150.00	75.00	45.00
(23)	Bob Neiman	150.00	75.00	45.00
(24)	Johnny Pesky	175.00	87.00	52.00
(25)	Jerry Priddy	150.00	75.00	45.00
(26)	Steve Souchock	150.00	75.00	45.00
(27)	Russ Sullivan	150.00	75.00	45.00
(28)	Bill Wight	225.00	112.00	67.00

1916 Globe Clothing Store

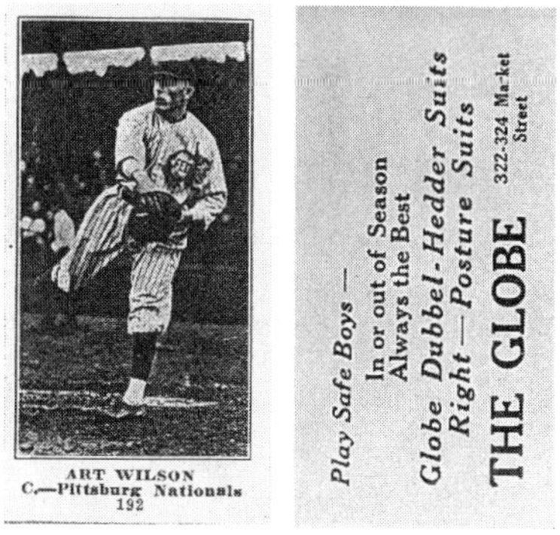

Best known for its use as a promotional medium for The Sporting News, this 200-card set can be found with ads on the back for several local and regional businesses. Among them is the Globe clothing store, location unknown. While type card collectors and superstar collectors may pay a premium for individual cards with the Globe store's advertising, prices will generally parallel the 1916 Sporting News values. This version carries an "American Card Catalog" designation of H801-9. Cards measure 1-5/8" x 3" and are printed in black-and-white.

(See 1916 Sporting News for checklist and individual card values.)

1969 Globe Imports Playing Cards

Largely ignored by collectors for more than 25 years, this issue has little to offer any but the most avid superstar collector. Printed in black-and-white on very thin white cardboard, with blank backs, the cards measure 1-5/8" x 2-1/4". Rather muddy player action photos are at center of each card, with the player's name reversed out of a black strip at the bottom. Single cards are never seen, but since the complete set is very inexpensive it should not deter the superstar collector from acquisition.

		NM	EX	VG
Complete Set (52):		16.00	8.00	4.75
Common Player:		.25	.13	.08
HEARTS				
J	Al Kaline	1.25	.60	.40
Q	Gene Alley	.25	.13	.08
K	Rusty Staub	.40	.20	.12
A	Willie Mays	2.00	1.00	.60
2	Chris Short	.25	.13	.08
3	Tony Conigliaro	.80	.40	.25
4	Bill Freehan	.40	.20	.12
5	Willie McCovey	1.00	.50	.30
6	Joel Horlen	.25	.13	.08
7	Ernie Banks	1.25	.60	.40
8	Jim Wynn	.25	.13	.08
9	Brooks Robinson	1.00	.50	.30
10	Orlando Cepeda	1.00	.50	.30
CLUBS				
J	Max Alvis	.25	.13	.08
Q	Ron Swoboda	.25	.13	.08
K	Johnny Callison	.25	.13	.08
A	Richie Allen	.80	.40	.25
2	Reggie Smith	.25	.13	.08
3	Jerry Koosman	.25	.13	.08
4	Tony Oliva	.40	.20	.12
5	Bud Harrelson	.25	.13	.08
6	Rick Reichardt	.25	.13	.08
7	Billy Williams	1.00	.50	.30
8	Pete Rose	2.00	1.00	.60
9	Jim Maloney	.25	.13	.08
10	Tim McCarver	.40	.20	.12
DIAMONDS				
J	Bob Aspromonte	.25	.13	.08
Q	Lou Brock	1.00	.50	.30
K	Jim Lonborg	.25	.13	.08
A	Bob Gibson	1.00	.50	.30
2	Paul Casanova	.25	.13	.08
3	Juan Marichal	1.00	.50	.30
4	Jim Fregosi	.25	.13	.08
5	Earl Wilson	.25	.13	.08
6	Tony Horton	.25	.13	.08
7	Harmon Killebrew	1.00	.50	.30
8	Tom Seaver	1.25	.60	.40
9	Curt Flood	.40	.20	.12
10	Frank Robinson	1.25	.60	.40
SPADES				
J	Ron Santo	.50	.25	.15
Q	Al Ferrara	.25	.13	.08
K	Clete Boyer	.25	.13	.08
A (a)	Ken Harrelson	.25	.13	.08
A (b)	Mickey Mantle	45.00	22.00	13.50
2	Denny McLain	.40	.20	.12
3	Rick Monday	.25	.13	.08
4	Richie Allen	.80	.40	.25
5	Mel Stottlemyre	.25	.13	.08
6	Tommy John	.40	.20	.12
7	Don Mincher	.25	.13	.08
8	Chico Cardenas	.25	.13	.08
9	Willie Davis	.25	.13	.08
10	Bert Campaneris	.25	.13	.08

1887 Gold Coin (Buchner) (N284)

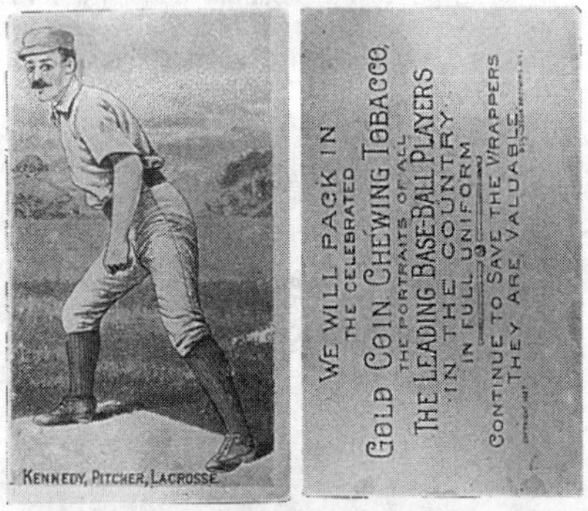
KENNEDY, PITCHER, LACROSSE
WE WILL PACK IN
THE CELEBRATED
GOLD COIN CHEWING TOBACCO
THE PORTRAITS OF ALL
THE LEADING BASE BALL PLAYERS
IN THE COUNTRY
IN FULL UNIFORM
CONTINUE TO SAVE THE WRAPPERS
THEY ARE VALUABLE

Issued circa 1887, the N284 issue was produced by D. Buchner & Company for its Gold Coin brand of chewing tobacco. Actually, the series was not comprised only of baseball players - actors, jockeys, firemen and policemen were also included. The cards, which measure 1-3/4" x 3", are color drawings. The set is not a popular one among collectors as the drawings do not in all cases represent the players designated on the cards. In most instances, players at a given position share the same drawing depicted on the card front. Three different card backs are found, all advising collectors to save the valuable chewing tobacco wrappers. Wrappers could be redeemed for various prizes.

		NM	EX	VG
Complete Set (143):		72500.	32750.	14550.
Common Player:		450.00	200.00	90.00
(1)	Ed Andrews (hands at neck)	450.00	200.00	90.00
(2)	Andrews (hands waist high)	545.00	245.00	110.00
(3)	Cap Anson (hands outstretched)	1225.	551.00	245.00
(4)	Cap Anson (left hand on hip)	2650.	1200.	530.00
(5)	Tug Arundel	450.00	200.00	90.00
(6)	Sam Barkley (Pittsburgh)	450.00	200.00	90.00
(7)	Sam Barkley (St. Louis)	635.00	285.00	125.00
(8)	Charley Bassett	450.00	200.00	90.00
(9)	Charlie Bastian	450.00	200.00	90.00
(10)	Ed Beecher	450.00	200.00	90.00
(11)	Charlie Bennett	450.00	200.00	90.00
(12)	Handsome Henry Boyle	545.00	245.00	110.00
(13)	Dan Brouthers (hands outstretched)	1100.	495.00	220.00
(14)	Dan Brouthers (with bat)	1275.	575.00	255.00
(15)	Tom Brown	450.00	200.00	90.00
(16)	Jack Burdock	450.00	200.00	90.00
(17)	Oyster Burns (Baltimore)	545.00	245.00	110.00
(18)	Tom Burns (Chicago)	450.00	200.00	90.00
(19)	Doc Bushong	635.00	285.00	125.00
(20)	John Cahill	545.00	245.00	110.00
(21)	Cliff Carroll (Washington)	450.00	200.00	90.00
(22)	Fred Carroll (Pittsburgh)	450.00	200.00	90.00
(23)	Parisian Bob Carruthers (Caruthers)	730.00	330.00	145.00
(24)	Dan Casey	635.00	285.00	125.00
(25)	John Clarkson (ball at chest)	1100.	495.00	220.00
(26)	John Clarkson (arm oustretched)	1275.	575.00	255.00
(27)	Jack Clements	450.00	200.00	90.00
(28)	John Coleman	450.00	200.00	90.00
(29)	Charles Comiskey	2275.	1025.	455.00
(30)	Roger Connor (hands outstretched)	1100.	495.00	220.00
(31)	Roger Connor (hands oustreteched, face level)	1275.	575.00	255.00
(32)	Corbett	545.00	245.00	110.00
(33)	Sam Craig (Crane)	545.00	245.00	110.00
(34)	Sam Crane	545.00	245.00	110.00
(35)	Crowley	545.00	245.00	110.00
(36)	Ed Cushmann (Cushman)	545.00	245.00	110.00
(37)	Ed Dailey (Daily)	450.00	200.00	90.00
(38)	Con Daley (Daily)	450.00	200.00	90.00
(39)	Pat Deasley	545.00	245.00	110.00
(40)	Jerry Denny (hands on knees)	450.00	200.00	90.00
(41)	Jerry Denny (hands on thighs)	545.00	245.00	110.00
(42)	Jim Donnelly	450.00	200.00	90.00
(43)	Jim Donohue (Donahue)	545.00	245.00	110.00
(44)	Mike Dorgan (right field)	450.00	200.00	90.00
(45)	Mike Dorgan (batter)	545.00	245.00	110.00
(46)	Sure Shot Dunlap	450.00	200.00	90.00
(47)	Dude Esterbrook	545.00	245.00	110.00
(48)	Buck Ewing (ready to tag)	1100.	495.00	220.00
(49)	Buck Ewing (hands at neck)	1275.	575.00	255.00
(50)	Sid Farrar	450.00	200.00	90.00
(51)	Jack Farrell (ready to tag)	450.00	200.00	90.00
(52)	Jack Farrell (hands at knees)	545.00	245.00	110.00
(53)	Charlie Ferguson	450.00	200.00	90.00
(54)	Silver Flint	450.00	200.00	90.00
(55)	Jim Fogerty (Fogarty)	450.00	200.00	90.00
(56)	Tom Forster	545.00	245.00	110.00
(57)	Dave Foutz	700.00	315.00	140.00
(58)	Chris Fulmer	545.00	245.00	110.00
(59)	Joe Gerhardt	545.00	245.00	110.00
(60)	Charlie Getzein (Getzien)	450.00	200.00	90.00
(61)	Pete Gillespie (left field)	450.00	200.00	90.00
(62)	Pete Gillespie (batter)	545.00	245.00	110.00
(63)	Barney Gilligan	450.00	200.00	90.00
(64)	Pebbly Jack Glasscock (fielding grounder)	545.00	245.00	110.00
(65)	Pebbly Jack Glasscock (hands on knees)	635.00	285.00	125.00
(66)	Will Gleason	635.00	285.00	125.00
(67)	Piano Legs Gore	450.00	200.00	90.00
(68)	Frank Hankinson	545.00	245.00	110.00
(69)	Ned Hanlon	1075.	485.00	215.00
(70)	Hart	545.00	245.00	110.00
(71)	Egyptian Healy	450.00	200.00	90.00
(72)	Paul Hines (centre field)	450.00	200.00	90.00
(73)	Paul Hines (batter)	545.00	245.00	110.00
(74)	Joe Hornung	450.00	200.00	90.00
(75)	Cutrate Irwin	450.00	200.00	90.00
(76)	Dick Johnston	450.00	200.00	90.00
(77)	Tim Keefe (right arm outstretched)	1100.	495.00	220.00
(78)	Tim Keefe (arm outstretched)	1275.	575.00	255.00
(79)	King Kelly (right field)	1275.	575.00	255.00
(80)	King Kelly (catcher)	1375.	620.00	275.00
(81)	Kennedy	545.00	245.00	110.00
(82)	Matt Kilroy	545.00	245.00	110.00
(83)	Arlie Latham	700.00	315.00	140.00
(84)	Jimmy Manning	450.00	200.00	90.00
(85)	Bill McClellan	545.00	245.00	110.00
(86)	Jim McCormick	545.00	245.00	110.00
(87)	Jack McGeachy	450.00	200.00	90.00
(88)	Jumbo McGinnis	635.00	285.00	125.00
(89)	George Meyers (Myers)	545.00	245.00	110.00
(90)	Doggie Miller	450.00	200.00	90.00
(91)	Honest John Morrill (hands outstretched)	450.00	200.00	90.00
(92)	Honest John Morrill (hands at neck)	545.00	245.00	110.00
(93)	Tom Morrissy (Morrissey)	545.00	245.00	110.00
(94)	Joe Mulvey (hands on knees)	450.00	200.00	90.00
(95)	Joe Mulvey (hands above head)	545.00	245.00	110.00
(96)	Al Myers	450.00	200.00	90.00
(97)	Candy Nelson	545.00	245.00	110.00
(98)	Little Nick Nichol	635.00	285.00	125.00
(99)	Billy O'Brien	450.00	200.00	90.00
(100)	Tip O'Neil (O'Neill)	700.00	315.00	140.00
(101)	Orator Jim O'Rourke (hands cupped)	1100.	495.00	220.00
(102)	Orator Jim O'Rourke (hands on thighs)	1275.	575.00	255.00
(103)	Dave Orr	545.00	245.00	110.00
(104)	Jimmy Peoples	450.00	200.00	90.00
(105)	Fred Pfeffer	450.00	200.00	90.00
(106)	Bill Phillips	450.00	200.00	90.00
(107)	Mark Polhemus	450.00	200.00	90.00
(108)	Henry Porter	450.00	200.00	90.00
(109)	Blondie Purcell	545.00	245.00	110.00
(110)	Old Hoss Radbourn (hands at chest)	1100.	495.00	220.00
(111)	Old Hoss Radbourn (hands above waist)	1275.	575.00	255.00
(112)	Danny Richardson (New York, hands at knees)	450.00	200.00	90.00
(113)	Danny Richardson (New York, foot on base)	545.00	245.00	110.00
(114)	Hardy Richardson (Detroit, hands at right shoulder)	450.00	200.00	90.00
(115)	Hardy Richardson (Detroit, hands above head)	545.00	245.00	110.00
(116)	Yank Robinson	635.00	285.00	125.00
(117)	George Rooks	545.00	245.00	110.00
(118)	Chief Rosemann (Roseman)	545.00	245.00	110.00
(119)	Jimmy Ryan	545.00	245.00	110.00
(120)	Emmett Seery (hands at right shoulder)	450.00	200.00	90.00
(121)	Emmett Seery (hands outstretched)	545.00	245.00	110.00
(122)	Otto Shomberg (Schomberg)	450.00	200.00	90.00
(123)	Pap Smith	450.00	200.00	90.00
(124)	Joe Strauss	545.00	245.00	110.00
(125)	Danny Sullivan	635.00	285.00	125.00
(126)	Marty Sullivan	450.00	200.00	90.00
(127)	Billy Sunday	635.00	285.00	125.00
(128)	Ezra Sutton	450.00	200.00	90.00
(129)	Big Sam Thompson (hand at belt)	1100.	495.00	220.00
(130)	Big Sam Thompson (hands chest high)	1275.	575.00	255.00
(131)	Chris Von Der Ahe	2275.	1025.	455.00
(132)	Monte Ward (fielding grounder)	1100.	495.00	220.00
(133)	Monte Ward (hands by knee)	1275.	575.00	255.00
(134)	Monte Ward (hands on knees)	1275.	575.00	255.00
(135)	Curt Welch	635.00	285.00	125.00
(136)	Deacon White	545.00	245.00	110.00
(137)	Art Whitney (Pittsburgh)	450.00	200.00	90.00
(138)	Grasshopper Whitney (Washington)	450.00	200.00	90.00
(139)	Ned Williamson (fielding grounder)	635.00	285.00	125.00
(140)	Ned Williamson (hands at chest)	700.00	315.00	140.00
(141)	Medoc Wise	450.00	200.00	90.00
(142)	Dandy Wood (hands at right shoulder)	450.00	200.00	90.00
(143)	Dandy Wood (stealing base)	545.00	245.00	110.00

1961 Golden Press

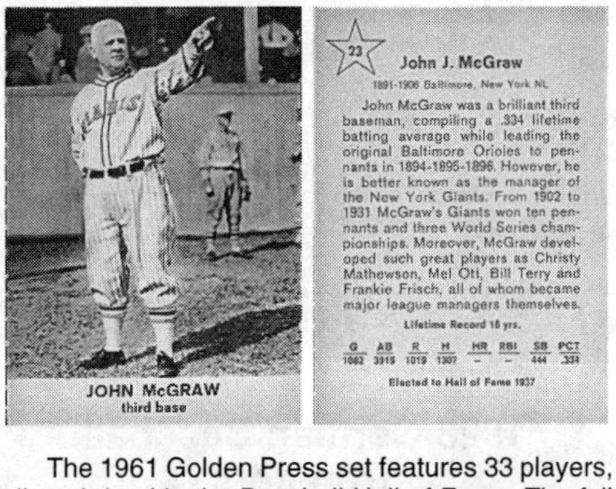
JOHN McGRAW
third base
John J. McGraw
Elected to Hall of Fame 1937

The 1961 Golden Press set features 33 players, all enshrined in the Baseball Hall of Fame. The full color cards measure 2-1/2" x 3-1/2" and came in a booklet with perforations so that they could be easily removed. Full books with the cards intact would command 50 percent over the set price in the checklist that follows. Card numbers 1-3 and 28-33 are slightly higher in price as they were located on the book's front and back covers, making them more susceptible to scuffing and wear.

		NM	EX	VG
Complete Set (33):		185.00	90.00	55.00
Complete Set in Book:		245.00	125.00	70.00
Common Player:		3.00	1.50	.90
1	Mel Ott	3.00	1.50	.90
2	Grover Cleveland Alexander	3.00	1.50	.90
3	Babe Ruth	30.00	15.00	9.00
4	Hank Greenberg	3.00	1.50	.90
5	Bill Terry	3.00	1.50	.90
6	Carl Hubbell	3.00	1.50	.90
7	Rogers Hornsby	4.00	2.00	1.25
8	Dizzy Dean	5.00	2.50	1.50
9	Joe DiMaggio	16.00	8.00	4.75
10	Charlie Gehringer	3.00	1.50	.90
11	Gabby Hartnett	3.00	1.50	.90
12	Mickey Cochrane	3.00	1.50	.90
13	George Sisler	3.00	1.50	.90
14	Joe Cronin	3.00	1.50	.90
15	Pie Traynor	3.00	1.50	.90
16	Lou Gehrig	20.00	10.00	6.00
17	Lefty Grove	3.00	1.50	.90
18	Chief Bender	3.00	1.50	.90
19	Frankie Frisch	3.00	1.50	.90
20	Al Simmons	3.00	1.50	.90

21	Home Run Baker	3.00	1.50	.90
22	Jimmy Foxx	4.00	2.00	1.25
23	John McGraw	3.00	1.50	.90
24	Christy Mathewson	6.00	3.00	1.75
25	Ty Cobb	20.00	10.00	6.00
26	Dazzy Vance	3.00	1.50	.90
27	Bill Dickey	3.00	1.50	.90
28	Eddie Collins	3.00	1.50	.90
29	Walter Johnson	6.00	3.00	1.75
30	Tris Speaker	4.00	2.00	1.25
31	Nap Lajoie	3.00	1.50	.90
32	Honus Wagner	6.00	3.00	1.75
33	Cy Young	6.00	3.00	1.75

1955 Golden Stamp Books

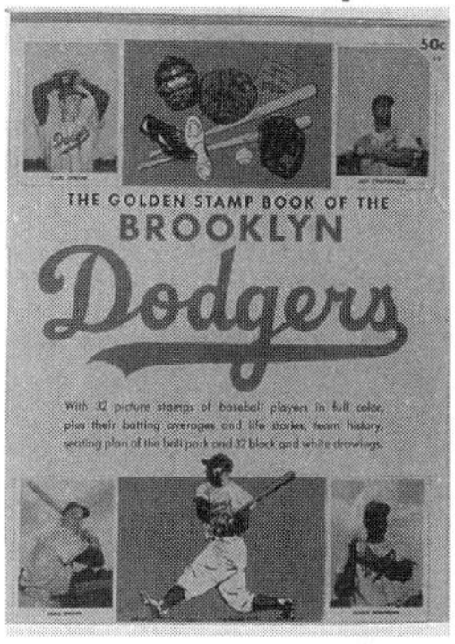

The 1954 World Series contestants, Cleveland and the Giants, along with the popular Dodgers and Braves are featured in this set of stamp books. The 32-page albums measure about 8-1/2" x 11" and include drawings and write-ups for each of the 32 players and managers featured. Other pages of the album include team histories, stats, etc. Sheets of 16 color stamps each are bound into the front and back of the album. Individual stamps measure about 2" x 2-5/8" and are unnumbered. Values shown are for complete albums with the stamps not pasted in; albums with stamps affixed to the pages are worth about 50%. The players for each team are listed in the order in which they appear in the album.

		NM	EX	VG
Complete Set (4):		350.00	175.00	100.00
Common Stamp:		2.00	1.00	.60
S-1	**NEW YORK GIANTS ALBUM**	100.00	50.00	30.00
(1)	1954 team photo	2.00	1.00	.60
(2)	Leo Durocher	4.00	2.00	1.25
(3)	Johnny Antonelli	2.00	1.00	.60
(4)	Sal Maglie	2.00	1.00	.60
(5)	Ruben Gomez	2.00	1.00	.60
(6)	Hoyt Wilhelm	4.00	2.00	1.25
(7)	Marv Grissom	2.00	1.00	.60
(8)	Jim Hearn	2.00	1.00	.60
(9)	Paul Giel	2.00	1.00	.60
(10)	Al Corwin	2.00	1.00	.60
(11)	George Spencer	2.00	1.00	.60
(12)	Don Liddle	2.00	1.00	.60
(13)	Windy McCall	2.00	1.00	.60
(14)	Al Worthington	2.00	1.00	.60
(15)	Wes Westrum	2.00	1.00	.60
(16)	Whitey Lockman	2.00	1.00	.60
(17)	Dave Williams	2.00	1.00	.60
(18)	Hank Thompson	3.00	1.50	.90
(19)	Alvin Dark	2.50	1.25	.70
(20)	Monte Irvin	5.00	2.50	1.50
(21)	Willie Mays	20.00	10.00	6.00
(22)	Don Mueller	2.00	1.00	.60
(23)	Dusty Rhodes	2.50	1.25	.70
(24)	Ray Katt	2.00	1.00	.60
(25)	Joe Amalfitano	2.00	1.00	.60
(26)	Bill Gardner	2.00	1.00	.60
(27)	Foster Castleman	2.00	1.00	.60
(28)	Bobby Hofman	2.00	1.00	.60
(29)	Bill Taylor	2.00	1.00	.60
(30)	Manager and coaches	2.00	1.00	.60
(31)	Bobby Weinstein (batboy)	2.00	1.00	.60
(32)	Polo Grounds	2.00	1.00	.60
S-2	**MILWAUKEE BRAVES ALBUM**	100.00	50.00	30.00
(1)	1954 team photo	2.00	1.00	.60
(2)	Charlie Grimm	2.00	1.00	.60
(3)	Warren Spahn	[illegible]	[illegible]	[illegible]
(4)	Lew Burdette	2.00	1.00	.60
(5)	Chet Nichols	2.00	1.00	.60
(6)	Gene Conley	2.00	1.00	.60
(7)	Bob Buhl	2.00	1.00	.60
(8)	Jim Wilson	2.00	1.00	.60
(9)	Dave Jolly	2.00	1.00	.60
(10)	Ernie Johnson	2.00	1.00	.60
(11)	Joey Jay	2.00	1.00	.60
(12)	Dave Koslo	2.00	1.00	.60
(13)	Charlie Gorin	2.00	1.00	.60
(14)	Ray Crone	2.00	1.00	.60
(15)	Del Crandall	2.50	1.25	.70
(16)	Joe Adcock	2.50	1.25	.70
(17)	Jack Dittmer	2.00	1.00	.60
(18)	Eddie Mathews	10.00	5.00	3.00
(19)	Johnny Logan	2.00	1.00	.60
(20)	Andy Pafko	2.00	1.00	.60
(21)	Bill Bruton	2.00	1.00	.60
(22)	Bobby Thomson	2.50	1.25	.70
(23)	Charlie White	2.00	1.00	.60
(24)	Danny O'Connell	2.00	1.00	.60
(25)	Hank Aaron	20.00	10.00	6.00
(26)	Jim Pendleton	2.00	1.00	.60
(27)	George Metkovich	2.00	1.00	.60
(28)	Mel Roach	2.00	1.00	.60
(29)	John Cooney	2.00	1.00	.60
(30)	Bucky Walters	2.00	1.00	.60
(31)	Charles Lacks (trainer)	2.00	1.00	.60
(32)	Milwaukee County Stadium	2.00	1.00	.60
S-3	**BROOKLYN DODGERS ALBUM**	150.00	75.00	45.00
(1)	Walter Alston	4.00	2.00	1.25
(2)	Don Newcombe	2.50	1.25	.70
(3)	Carl Erskine	2.00	1.00	.60
(4)	Johnny Podres	2.00	1.00	.60
(5)	Billy Loes	2.00	1.00	.60
(6)	Russ Meyer	2.00	1.00	.60
(7)	Jim Hughes	2.00	1.00	.60
(8)	Sandy Koufax	10.00	5.00	3.00
(9)	Joe Black	2.00	1.00	.60
(10)	Karl Spooner	2.00	1.00	.60
(11)	Clem Labine	2.00	1.00	.60
(12)	Roy Campanella	10.00	5.00	3.00
(13)	Gil Hodges	8.00	4.00	2.50
(14)	Jim Gilliam	2.50	1.25	.70
(15)	Jackie Robinson	25.00	12.50	7.50
(16)	Pee Wee Reese	10.00	5.00	3.00
(17)	Duke Snider	10.00	5.00	3.00
(18)	Carl Furillo	3.00	1.50	.90
(19)	Sandy Amoros	2.00	1.00	.60
(20)	Frank Kellert	2.00	1.00	.60
(21)	Don Zimmer	2.50	1.25	.70
(22)	Al Walker	2.00	1.00	.60
(23)	Tommy Lasorda	5.00	2.50	1.50
(24)	Ed Roebuck	2.00	1.00	.60
(25)	Don Hoak	2.00	1.00	.60
(26)	George Shuba	2.00	1.00	.60
(27)	Billy Herman	2.50	1.25	.70
(28)	Jake Pitlor	2.00	1.00	.60
(29)	Joe Becker	2.00	1.00	.60
(30)	Doc Wendler (trainer), Carl Furillo	2.00	1.00	.60
(31)	Charlie Di Giovanna (batboy)	2.00	1.00	.60
(32)	Ebbets Field	2.00	1.00	.60
S-4	**CLEVELAND INDIANS ALBUM**	2.00	1.00	.60
(1)	Al Lopez	2.00	1.00	.60
(2)	Bob Lemon	2.00	1.00	.60
(3)	Early Wynn	2.00	1.00	.60
(4)	Mike Garcia	2.00	1.00	.60
(5)	Bob Feller	2.00	1.00	.60
(6)	Art Houtteman	2.00	1.00	.60
(7)	Herb Score	2.00	1.00	.60
(8)	Don Mossi	2.00	1.00	.60
(9)	Ray Narleski	2.00	1.00	.60
(10)	Jim Hegan	2.00	1.00	.60
(11)	Vic Wertz	2.00	1.00	.60
(12)	Bobby Avila	2.00	1.00	.60
(13)	George Strickland	2.00	1.00	.60
(14)	Al Rosen	2.00	1.00	.60
(15)	Larry Doby	2.00	1.00	.60
(16)	Ralph Kiner	2.00	1.00	.60
(17)	Al Smith	2.00	1.00	.60
(18)	Wally Westlake	2.00	1.00	.60
(19)	Hal Naragon	2.00	1.00	.60
(20)	Hank Foiles	2.00	1.00	.60
(21)	Hank Majeski	2.00	1.00	.60
(22)	Bill Wight	2.00	1.00	.60
(23)	Sam Dente	2.00	1.00	.60
(24)	Dave Pope	2.00	1.00	.60
(25)	Dave Philley	2.00	1.00	.60
(26)	Dale Mitchell	2.00	1.00	.60
(27)	Hank Greenberg (gm)	2.00	1.00	.60
(28)	Mel Harder	2.00	1.00	.60
(29)	Ralph Kress	2.00	1.00	.60
(30)	Tony Cuccinello	2.00	1.00	.60
(31)	Bill Lobe	2.00	1.00	.60
(32)	Cleveland Municipal Stadium	2.00	1.00	.60

1934 Gold Medal Flour

This set of 12 unnumbered, blank-backed cards was issued by Gold Medal Flour to commemorate the 1934 World Series. The cards, which measure 3-1/4" x 5-3/8", feature members of the Detroit Tigers and the St. Louis Cardinals, who were participants in the '34 World Series.

		NM	EX	VG
Complete Set (12):		950.00	450.00	300.00
Common Player:		55.00	25.00	15.00
(1)	Tommy Bridges	55.00	25.00	15.00
(2)	Mickey Cochrane	100.00	50.00	30.00
(3)	Dizzy Dean	210.00	105.00	63.00
(4)	Paul Dean	75.00	37.00	22.00
(5)	Frank Frisch	100.00	50.00	30.00
(6)	"Goose" Goslin	100.00	50.00	30.00
(7)	Odell Hale	55.00	25.00	15.00
(8)	William Hallahan	55.00	25.00	15.00
(9)	Fred Marberry	55.00	25.00	15.00
(10)	Johnny "Pepper" Martin	70.00	35.00	21.00
(11)	Joe Medwick	100.00	50.00	30.00
(12)	William Rogell	55.00	25.00	15.00
(13)	"Jo Jo" White	55.00	25.00	15.00

1962 "Gold Mine Pal" Roger Maris

(See Gehl's Ice Cream.)

1888 Goodwin Champions (N162)

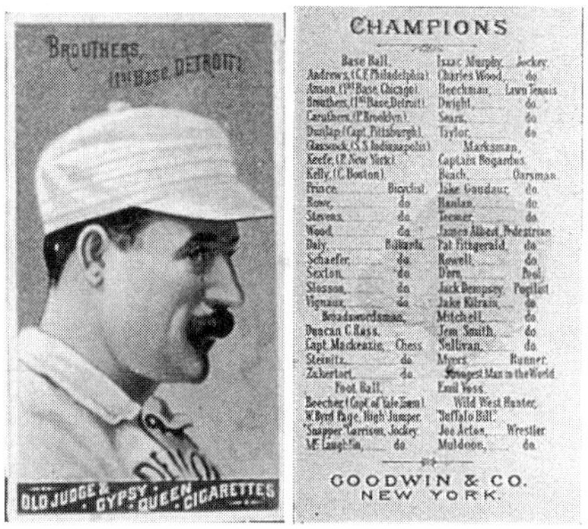

Issued in 1888 by New York's Goodwin & Co., the 50-card "Champions" set includes eight baseball players - seven from the National League and one from the American Association. The full-color cards, which measure 1-1/2" x 2-5/8", were inserted in packages of Old Judge and Gypsy Queen Cigarettes. A small ad for the cards lists all 50 subjects of the "Champions" set, which also included popular billiards players, bicyclists, marksmen, pugilists, runners, wrestlers, college football stars, weightlifters, and Wild West star Buffalo Bill Cody. Four of the eight baseball players in the set (Anson, Kelly, Keefe and Brouthers) are Hall of Famers. The cards feature very attractive player portraits, making the "Champions" set among the most beautiful of all the 19th Century tobacco inserts.

		NM	EX	VG
Complete Set (8):		13000.	5850.	2600.
Common Player:		650.00	290.00	130.00
Album:		[illegible]	[illegible]	[illegible]
(1)	Ed Andrews	650.00	290.00	130.00
(2)	Cap Anson	4500.	2025.	900.00
(3)	Dan Brouthers	2300.	1035.	460.00
(4)	Parisian Bob Caruthers	850.00	380.00	170.00
(5a)	Sure Shot Dunlap (Detroit)	650.00	290.00	130.00
(5b)	Sure Shot Dunlap (Pittsburgh)	1250.	625.00	375.00
(6)	Pebbly Jack Glasscock	900.00	400.00	180.00
(7)	Tim Keefe	2000.	900.00	400.00
(8)	King Kelly	3000.	1350.	600.00

1933 Goudey

Goudey Gum Co.'s first baseball card issue was a 239-card effort in 1933. The cards are color art reproductions of either portrait or action photos. The numbered cards measure 2-3/8" x 2-7/8" and carry a short player biography on the reverse. Card #106 (Napoleon Lajoie) is listed in the set though it was not actually issued until 1934. The card is very scarce and is unique in that it carries a 1934 design front and a 1933 back. The Lajoie card is not included in the complete set prices quoted here. The ACC designation for the set is R319.

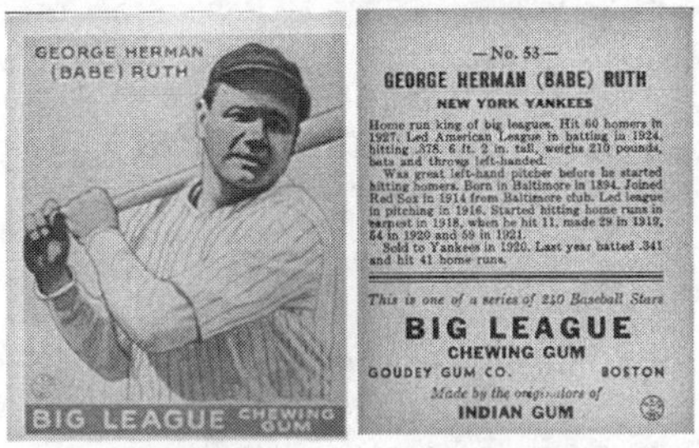

		NM	EX	VG
Complete Set (239):		48000.	19000.	9000.
Common Player (1-40):		150.00	35.00	20.00
Common Player (41-44):		80.00	30.00	15.00
Common Player (45-52):		110.00	40.00	22.00
Common Player (53-240):		80.00	30.00	15.00
1	Benny Bengough	5000.	750.00	200.00
2	Arthur (Dazzy) Vance	400.00	150.00	85.00
3	Hugh Critz	150.00	35.00	20.00
4	Henry "Heinie" Schuble	150.00	35.00	20.00
5	Floyd (Babe) Herman	250.00	75.00	45.00
6a	Jimmy Dykes (age is 26 in bio)	195.00	70.00	40.00
6b	Jimmy Dykes (age is 36 in bio)	195.00	70.00	40.00
7	Ted Lyons	400.00	150.00	55.00
8	Roy Johnson	150.00	35.00	20.00
9	Dave Harris	150.00	35.00	20.00
10	Glenn Myatt	150.00	35.00	20.00
11	Billy Rogell	150.00	35.00	20.00
12	George Pipgras	150.00	35.00	20.00
13	Lafayette Thompson	150.00	35.00	20.00
14	Henry Johnson	150.00	35.00	20.00
15	Victor Sorrell	150.00	35.00	20.00
16	George Blaeholder	150.00	35.00	20.00
17	Watson Clark	150.00	35.00	20.00
18	Herold (Muddy) Ruel	150.00	35.00	20.00
19	Bill Dickey	600.00	230.00	130.00
20	Bill Terry	425.00	160.00	80.00
21	Phil Collins	150.00	35.00	20.00
22	Harold (Pie) Traynor	450.00	170.00	75.00
23	Hazen (Ki-Ki) Cuyler	450.00	170.00	75.00
24	Horace Ford	150.00	35.00	20.00
25	Paul Waner	500.00	190.00	110.00
26	Chalmer Cissell	150.00	35.00	20.00
27	George Connally	150.00	35.00	20.00
28	Dick Bartell	150.00	35.00	20.00
29	Jimmy Foxx	800.00	305.00	175.00
30	Frank Hogan	150.00	35.00	20.00
31	Tony Lazzeri	450.00	170.00	75.00
32	John (Bud) Clancy	150.00	35.00	20.00
33	Ralph Kress	150.00	35.00	20.00
34	Bob O'Farrell	150.00	35.00	20.00
35	Al Simmons	475.00	180.00	90.00
36	Tommy Thevenow	150.00	35.00	20.00
37	Jimmy Wilson	150.00	35.00	20.00
38	Fred Brickell	150.00	35.00	20.00
39	Mark Koenig	150.00	35.00	20.00
40	Taylor Douthit	150.00	35.00	20.00
41	Gus Mancuso	80.00	30.00	15.00
42	Eddie Collins	350.00	90.00	50.00
43	Lew Fonseca	80.00	30.00	15.00
44	Jim Bottomley	275.00	105.00	55.00
45	Larry Benton	110.00	40.00	22.00
46	Ethan Allen	110.00	40.00	22.00
47	Henry "Heinie" Manush	325.00	120.00	65.00
48	Marty McManus	110.00	40.00	22.00
49	Frank Frisch	375.00	140.00	75.00
50	Ed Brandt	110.00	40.00	22.00
51	Charlie Grimm	110.00	40.00	22.00
52	Andy Cohen	110.00	40.00	22.00
53	George Herman (Babe) Ruth	6000.	2275.	1325.
54	Ray Kremer	80.00	30.00	15.00
55	Perce (Pat) Malone	80.00	30.00	15.00
56	Charlie Ruffing	290.00	110.00	55.00
57	Earl Clark	80.00	30.00	15.00
58	Frank (Lefty) O'Doul	160.00	60.00	30.00
59	Edmund (Bing) Miller	80.00	30.00	15.00
60	Waite Hoyt	250.00	95.00	40.00
61	Max Bishop	80.00	30.00	15.00
62	"Pepper" Martin	160.00	60.00	30.00
63	Joe Cronin	250.00	95.00	45.00
64	Burleigh Grimes	250.00	95.00	45.00
65	Milton Gaston	80.00	30.00	15.00
66	George Grantham	80.00	30.00	15.00
67	Guy Bush	80.00	30.00	15.00
68	Horace Lisenbee	80.00	30.00	15.00
69	Randy Moore	80.00	30.00	15.00
70	Floyd (Pete) Scott	80.00	30.00	15.00
71	Robert J. Burke	80.00	30.00	15.00
72	Owen Carroll	80.00	30.00	15.00
73	Jesse Haines	250.00	95.00	45.00
74	Eppa Rixey	250.00	95.00	45.00
75	Willie Kamm	80.00	30.00	15.00
76	Gordon (Mickey) Cochrane	375.00	125.00	60.00
77	Adam Comorosky	80.00	30.00	15.00
78	Jack Quinn	80.00	30.00	15.00
79	Urban (Red) Faber	250.00	95.00	45.00
80	Clyde Manion	80.00	30.00	15.00
81	Sam Jones	80.00	30.00	15.00
82	Dibrell Williams	80.00	30.00	15.00
83	Pete Jablonowski	80.00	30.00	15.00
84	Glenn Spencer	80.00	30.00	15.00
85	John Henry "Heinie" Sand	80.00	30.00	15.00
86	Phil Todt	80.00	30.00	15.00
87	Frank O'Rourke	80.00	30.00	15.00
88	Russell Rollings	80.00	30.00	15.00
89	Tris Speaker	525.00	200.00	115.00
90	Jess Petty	80.00	30.00	15.00
91	Tom Zachary	80.00	30.00	15.00
92	Lou Gehrig	4000.	1525.	880.00
93	John Welch	80.00	30.00	15.00
94	Bill Walker	80.00	30.00	15.00
95	Alvin Crowder	80.00	30.00	15.00
96	Willis Hudlin	80.00	30.00	15.00
97	Joe Morrissey	80.00	30.00	15.00
98	Walter Berger	80.00	30.00	15.00
99	Tony Cuccinello	80.00	30.00	15.00
100	George Uhle	80.00	30.00	15.00
101	Richard Coffman	80.00	30.00	15.00
102	Travis C. Jackson	250.00	95.00	45.00
103	Earl Combs (Earle)	250.00	95.00	45.00
104	Fred Marberry	80.00	30.00	15.00
105	Bernie Friberg	80.00	30.00	15.00
106	Napoleon (Larry) Lajoie	37500.	15000.	8500.
106p	Leo Durocher (unique proof card)			7500.
107	Henry (Heinie) Manush	250.00	95.00	45.00
108	Joe Kuhel	80.00	30.00	15.00
109	Joe Cronin	250.00	95.00	50.00
110	Leon (Goose) Goslin (portrait)	250.00	95.00	50.00
110p	Leon (Goose) Goslin (proof card, batting - same as #168 - name in two lines on front)	500.00	200.00	120.00
111	Monte Weaver	80.00	30.00	15.00
112	Fred Schulte	80.00	30.00	15.00
113	Oswald Bluege	80.00	30.00	15.00
114	Luke Sewell	80.00	30.00	15.00
115	Cliff Heathcote	80.00	30.00	15.00
116	Eddie Morgan	80.00	30.00	15.00
117	Walter (Rabbit) Maranville	250.00	95.00	50.00
118	Valentine J. (Val) Picinich	80.00	30.00	15.00
119	Rogers Hornsby	525.00	200.00	90.00
120	Carl Reynolds	80.00	30.00	15.00
121	Walter Stewart	80.00	30.00	15.00
122	Alvin Crowder	80.00	30.00	15.00
123	Jack Russell (orange background, white cap)	80.00	30.00	15.00
123p	Jack Russell (proof card, red background, dark cap - same as #167 - name in one line on front)	225.00	85.00	49.00
124	Earl Whitehill	80.00	30.00	15.00
125	Bill Terry	300.00	115.00	60.00
126	Joe Moore	80.00	30.00	15.00
127	Melvin Ott	525.00	200.00	100.00
128	Charles (Chuck) Klein	325.00	120.00	70.00
129	Harold Schumacher	80.00	30.00	15.00
130	Fred Fitzsimmons	80.00	30.00	15.00
131	Fred Frankhouse	80.00	30.00	15.00
132	Jim Elliott	80.00	30.00	15.00
133	Fred Lindstrom	225.00	85.00	40.00
134	Edgar (Sam) Rice	225.00	85.00	40.00
135	Elwood (Woody) English	80.00	30.00	15.00
136	Flint Rhem	80.00	30.00	15.00
137	Fred (Red) Lucas	80.00	30.00	15.00
138	Herb Pennock	225.00	85.00	40.00
139	Ben Cantwell	80.00	30.00	15.00
140	Irving (Bump) Hadley	80.00	30.00	15.00
141	Ray Benge	80.00	30.00	15.00
142	Paul Richards	100.00	40.00	20.00
143	Glenn Wright	80.00	30.00	15.00
144	George Herman (Babe) Ruth (double-print; replaced card #106 on press sheet)	5500.	2400.	1250.
145	George Walberg	80.00	30.00	15.00
146	Walter Stewart	80.00	30.00	15.00
147	Leo Durocher	225.00	85.00	40.00
148	Eddie Farrell	80.00	30.00	15.00
149	George Herman (Babe) Ruth	6000.	2500.	1350.
150	Ray Kolp	80.00	30.00	15.00
151	D'Arcy (Jake) Flowers	80.00	30.00	15.00
152	James (Zack) Taylor	80.00	30.00	15.00
153	Charles (Buddy) Myer	80.00	30.00	15.00
154	Jimmy Foxx	650.00	245.00	125.00
155	Joe Judge	80.00	30.00	15.00
156	Danny Macfayden (MacFayden)	80.00	30.00	15.00
157	Sam Byrd	80.00	30.00	15.00
158	Morris (Moe) Berg	400.00	150.00	90.00
159	Oswald Bluege	80.00	30.00	15.00
160	Lou Gehrig	5000.	1900.	1100.
161	Al Spohrer	80.00	30.00	15.00
162	Leo Mangum	80.00	30.00	15.00
163	Luke Sewell	80.00	30.00	15.00
164	Lloyd Waner	225.00	85.00	40.00
165	Joe Sewell	225.00	85.00	40.00
166	Sam West	80.00	30.00	15.00
167	Jack Russell (name on two lines, see also #123p)	80.00	30.00	15.00
168	Leon (Goose) Goslin (name on one line, see also #110p)	225.00	85.00	40.00
169	Al Thomas	80.00	30.00	15.00
170	Harry McCurdy	80.00	30.00	15.00
171	Charley Jamieson	80.00	30.00	15.00
172	Billy Hargrave	80.00	30.00	15.00
173	Roscoe Holm	80.00	30.00	15.00
174	Warren (Curley) Ogden	80.00	30.00	15.00
175	Dan Howley	80.00	30.00	15.00
176	John Ogden	80.00	30.00	15.00
177	Walter French	80.00	30.00	15.00
178	Jackie Warner	80.00	30.00	15.00
179	Fred Leach	80.00	30.00	15.00
180	Eddie Moore	80.00	30.00	15.00
181	George Herman (Babe) Ruth	6500.	2750.	1425.
182	Andy High	80.00	30.00	15.00
183	George Walberg	80.00	30.00	15.00
184	Charley Berry	80.00	30.00	15.00
185	Bob Smith	80.00	30.00	15.00
186	John Schulte	80.00	30.00	15.00
187	Henry (Heinie) Manush	225.00	85.00	40.00
188	Rogers Hornsby	550.00	210.00	120.00
189	Joe Cronin	250.00	95.00	50.00
190	Fred Schulte	80.00	30.00	15.00
191	Ben Chapman	80.00	30.00	15.00
192	Walter Brown	80.00	30.00	15.00
193	Lynford Lary	80.00	30.00	15.00
194	Earl Averill	225.00	85.00	40.00
195	Evar Swanson	80.00	30.00	15.00
196	Leroy Mahaffey	80.00	30.00	15.00
197	Richard (Rick) Ferrell	225.00	85.00	40.00
198	Irving (Jack) Burns	80.00	30.00	15.00
199	Tom Bridges	80.00	30.00	15.00
200	Bill Hallahan	80.00	30.00	15.00
201	Ernie Orsatti	80.00	30.00	15.00
202	Charles Leo (Gabby) Hartnett	225.00	85.00	40.00
203	Lonnie Warneke	80.00	30.00	15.00
204	Jackson Riggs Stephenson	90.00	35.00	20.00
205	Henry (Heinie) Meine	80.00	30.00	15.00
206	Gus Suhr	80.00	30.00	15.00
207	Melvin Ott	400.00	150.00	80.00
208	Byrne (Bernie) James	80.00	30.00	15.00
209	Adolfo Luque	150.00	55.00	30.00
210	Virgil Davis	80.00	30.00	15.00
211	Lewis (Hack) Wilson	400.00	150.00	85.00
212	Billy Urbanski	80.00	30.00	15.00
213	Earl Adams	80.00	30.00	15.00
214	John Kerr	80.00	30.00	15.00
215	Russell Van Atta	80.00	30.00	15.00
216	Vernon Gomez	350.00	135.00	70.00
217	Frank Crosetti	175.00	65.00	35.00
218	Wesley Ferrell	80.00	30.00	15.00
219	George (Mule) Haas	80.00	30.00	15.00
220	Robert (Lefty) Grove	675.00	255.00	130.00
221	Dale Alexander	80.00	30.00	15.00
222	Charley Gehringer	325.00	125.00	65.00
223	Jerome (Dizzy) Dean	900.00	340.00	185.00
224	Frank Demaree	80.00	30.00	15.00
225	Bill Jurges	80.00	30.00	15.00
226	Charley Root	80.00	30.00	15.00
227	Bill Herman	225.00	85.00	40.00
228	Tony Piet	80.00	30.00	15.00
229	Floyd Vaughan	225.00	85.00	40.00
230	Carl Hubbell	400.00	150.00	75.00
231	Joe Moore	80.00	30.00	15.00
232	Frank (Lefty) O'Doul	180.00	70.00	40.00
233	Johnny Vergez	80.00	30.00	15.00
234	Carl Hubbell	350.00	135.00	75.00
235	Fred Fitzsimmons	80.00	30.00	15.00
236	George Davis	80.00	30.00	15.00
237	Gus Mancuso	80.00	30.00	15.00
238	Hugh Critz	80.00	30.00	15.00
239	Leroy Parmelee	80.00	30.00	15.00
240	Harold Schumacher	275.00	90.00	30.00

1934 Goudey

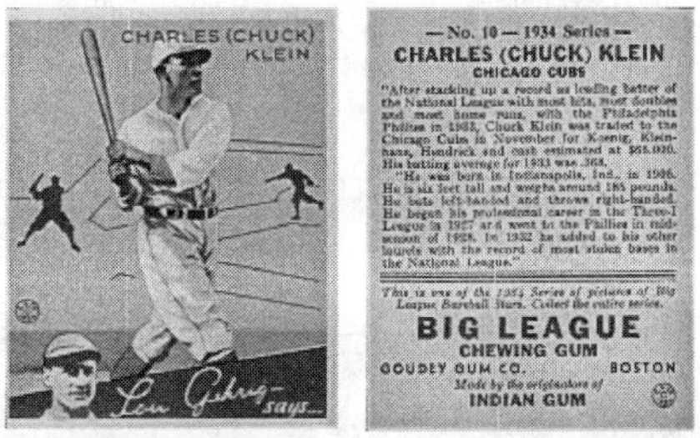

The 1934 Goudey set contains 96 cards (2-3/8" x 2-7/8") that feature color art reproductions of player photographs. Card fronts have two different designs; one featuring a small portrait photo of Lou Gehrig with the words "Lou Gehrig says..." inside a blue strip at the bottom, while the other design carries a red "Chuck Klein says..." strip and also has his photo. The card backs contain a short player biography that purports to have been written by Gehrig or Klein. The ACC designation for the set is R320. Albums, blue for A.L., pink for N.L., were given away to the person who bought the last penny pack in each box.

		NM	EX	VG
Complete Set (96):		18500.	7500.	4500.
Common Player (1-48):		65.00	30.00	15.00
Common Player (49-72):		100.00	40.00	20.00
Common Player (73-96):		225.00	100.00	60.00
Album:		200.00	100.00	60.00
1	Jimmy Foxx	1350.	600.00	185.00
2	Gordon (Mickey) Cochrane	250.00	125.00	60.00
3	Charlie Grimm	65.00	30.00	15.00
4	Elwood (Woody) English	65.00	30.00	15.00
5	Ed Brandt	65.00	30.00	15.00
6	Jerome (Dizzy) Dean	800.00	400.00	225.00
7	Leo Durocher	200.00	90.00	50.00
8	Tony Piet	65.00	30.00	15.00
9	Ben Chapman	65.00	30.00	15.00
10	Charles (Chuck) Klein	300.00	120.00	70.00
11	Paul Waner	200.00	100.00	50.00

12	Carl Hubbell	325.00	125.00	75.00
13	Frank Frisch	325.00	125.00	75.00
14	Willie Kamm	65.00	30.00	15.00
15	Alvin Crowder	65.00	30.00	15.00
16	Joe Kuhel	65.00	30.00	15.00
17	Hugh Critz	65.00	30.00	15.00
18	Henry (Heinie) Manush	225.00	110.00	45.00
19	Robert (Lefty) Grove	400.00	200.00	110.00
20	Frank Hogan	65.00	30.00	15.00
21	Bill Terry	250.00	125.00	60.00
22	Floyd Vaughan	200.00	100.00	45.00
23	Charley Gehringer	200.00	100.00	45.00
24	Ray Benge	65.00	30.00	15.00
25	Roger Cramer	65.00	30.00	15.00
26	Gerald Walker	65.00	30.00	15.00
27	Luke Appling	200.00	100.00	45.00
28	Ed. Coleman	65.00	30.00	15.00
29	Larry French	65.00	30.00	15.00
30	Julius Solters	65.00	30.00	15.00
31	Baxter Jordan	65.00	30.00	15.00
32	John (Blondy) Ryan	65.00	30.00	15.00
33	Frank (Don) Hurst	65.00	30.00	15.00
34	Charles (Chick) Hafey	200.00	100.00	45.00
35	Ernie Lombardi	200.00	100.00	45.00
36	Walter (Huck) Betts	65.00	30.00	15.00
37	Lou Gehrig	3750.	1875.	1000.
38	Oral Hildebrand	65.00	30.00	15.00
39	Fred Walker	65.00	30.00	15.00
40	John Stone	65.00	30.00	15.00
41	George Earnshaw	65.00	30.00	15.00
42	John Allen	65.00	30.00	15.00
43	Dick Porter	65.00	30.00	15.00
44	Tom Bridges	65.00	30.00	15.00
45	Oscar Melillo	65.00	30.00	15.00
46	Joe Stripp	65.00	30.00	15.00
47	John Frederick	65.00	30.00	15.00
48	James (Tex) Carleton	65.00	30.00	15.00
49	Sam Leslie	100.00	40.00	20.00
50	Walter Beck	100.00	40.00	20.00
51	Jim (Rip) Collins	100.00	40.00	20.00
52	Herman Bell	100.00	40.00	20.00
53	George Watkins	100.00	40.00	20.00
54	Wesley Schulmerich	100.00	40.00	20.00
55	Ed Holley	100.00	40.00	20.00
56	Mark Koenig	100.00	40.00	20.00
57	Bill Swift	100.00	40.00	20.00
58	Earl Grace	100.00	40.00	20.00
59	Joe Mowry	100.00	40.00	20.00
60	Lynn Nelson	100.00	40.00	20.00
61	Lou Gehrig	3000.	1500.	810.00
62	Henry Greenberg	600.00	300.00	150.00
63	Minter Hayes	100.00	40.00	20.00
64	Frank Grube	100.00	40.00	20.00
65	Cliff Bolton	100.00	40.00	20.00
66	Mel Harder	100.00	40.00	20.00
67	Bob Weiland	100.00	40.00	20.00
68	Bob Johnson	100.00	40.00	20.00
69	John Marcum	100.00	40.00	20.00
70	Ervin (Pete) Fox	100.00	40.00	20.00
71	Lyle Tinning	100.00	40.00	20.00
72	Arndt Jorgens	100.00	40.00	20.00
73	Ed Wells	225.00	100.00	60.00
74	Bob Boken	225.00	100.00	60.00
75	Bill Werber	225.00	100.00	60.00
76	Hal Trosky	225.00	100.00	60.00
77	Joe Vosmik	225.00	100.00	60.00
78	Frank (Pinkey) Higgins	225.00	100.00	60.00
79	Eddie Durham	225.00	100.00	60.00
80	Marty McManus	225.00	100.00	60.00
81	Bob Brown	225.00	100.00	60.00
82	Bill Hallahan	225.00	100.00	60.00
83	Jim Mooney	225.00	100.00	60.00
84	Paul Derringer	250.00	125.00	65.00
85	Adam Comorosky	225.00	100.00	60.00
86	Lloyd Johnson	225.00	100.00	60.00
87	George Darrow	225.00	100.00	60.00
88	Homer Peel	225.00	100.00	60.00
89	Linus Frey	225.00	100.00	60.00
90	Hazen (Ki-Ki) Cuyler	400.00	200.00	120.00
91	Dolph Camilli	225.00	100.00	60.00
92	Steve Larkin	225.00	100.00	60.00
93	Fred Ostermueller	225.00	100.00	60.00
94	Robert A. (Red) Rolfe	300.00	150.00	90.00
95	Myril Hoag	250.00	125.00	45.00
96	Jim DeShong	400.00	150.00	55.00

1934 Goudey Premiums (R309-1)

Consisting of just four unnumbered cards, this set of black-and-white photos was printed on heavy cardboard and issued as a premium by the Goudey Gum Co. in 1934. The cards measure 5-1/2" x 8-5/16" and are accented with a gold, picture frame border and an easel on the back.

		NM	EX	VG
Complete Set (4):		3500.	1700.	1020.
Common Card:		650.00	325.00	190.00
(1)	American League All-Stars of 1933	650.00	325.00	190.00
(2)	National League All-Stars	650.00	325.00	190.00
(3)	"Worlds Champions 1933" (New York Giants)	800.00	400.00	240.00
(4)	George Herman (Babe) Ruth	1450.	725.00	435.00

1935 Goudey 4-in-1

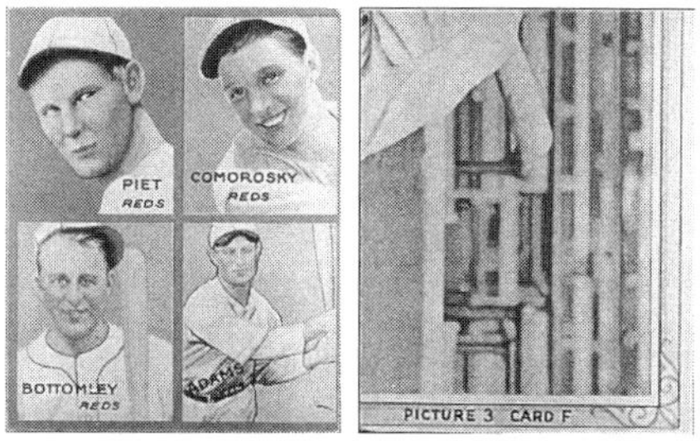

The 1935 Goudey set features color portraits of four players from the same team on each card. Thirty-six card fronts make up the set with numerous front/back combinations existing. The card backs form nine different puzzles: 1) Tigers Team, 2) Chuck Klein, 3) Frankie Frisch, 4) Mickey Cochrane, 5) Joe Cronin, 6) Jimmy Foxx, 7) Al Simmons, 8) Indians Team, and 9) Senators Team. The cards, which measure 2-3/8" x 2-7/8", have an ACC designation of R321.

		NM	EX	VG
Complete Set (36):		5100.	2000.	1000.
Common Card:		80.00	40.00	20.00
(1)	Sparky Adams, Jim Bottomley, Adam Comorosky, Tony Piet	100.00	50.00	30.00
(2)	Ethan Allen, Fred Brickell, Bubber Jonnard, Hack Wilson	100.00	50.00	30.00
(3)	Johnny Allen, Jimmie Deshong, Red Rolfe, Dixie Walker (DeShong)	80.00	40.00	20.00
(4)	Luke Appling, Jimmie Dykes, George Earnshaw, Luke Sewell	100.00	50.00	30.00
(5)	Earl Averill, Oral Hildebrand, Willie Kamm, Hal Trosky	200.00	100.00	60.00
(6)	Dick Bartell, Hughie Critz, Gus Mancuso, Mel Ott	125.00	62.00	37.00
(7)	Ray Benge, Fred Fitzsimmons, Mark Koenig, Tom Zachary	80.00	40.00	20.00
(8)	Larry Benton, Ben Cantwell, Flint Rhem, Al Spohrer	80.00	40.00	20.00
(9)	Charlie Berry, Bobby Burke, Red Kress, Dazzy Vance	100.00	50.00	30.00
(10)	Max Bishop, Bill Cissell, Joe Cronin, Carl Reynolds	125.00	62.00	37.00
(11)	George Blaeholder, Dick Coffman, Oscar Melillo, Sammy West	80.00	40.00	20.00
(12)	Cy Blanton, Babe Herman, Tom Padden, Gus Suhr	90.00	45.00	27.00
(13)	Zeke Bonura, Mule Haas, Jackie Hayes, Ted Lyons	100.00	50.00	30.00
(14)	Jim Bottomley, Adam Comorosky, Willis Hudlin, Glenn Myatt	100.00	50.00	30.00
(15)	Ed Brandt, Fred Frankhouse, Shanty Hogan, Gene Moore	100.00	50.00	30.00
(16)	Ed Brandt, Rabbit Maranville, Marty McManus, Babe Ruth	1600.	800.00	480.00
(17)	Tommy Bridges, Mickey Cochrane, Charlie Gehringer, Billy Rogell	165.00	80.00	50.00
(18)	Jack Burns, Frank Grube, Rollie Hemsley, Bob Weiland	80.00	40.00	20.00
(19)	Guy Bush, Waite Hoyt, Lloyd Waner, Paul Waner	195.00	95.00	55.00
(20)	Sammy Byrd, Danny MacFayden, Pepper Martin, Bob O'Farrell	80.00	40.00	20.00
(21)	Gilly Campbell, Ival Goodman, Alex Kampouris, Billy Meyers (Myers)	80.00	40.00	20.00
(22)	Tex Carleton, Dizzy Dean, Frankie Frisch, Ernie Orsatti	400.00	200.00	120.00
(23)	Watty Clark, Lonny Frey, Sam Leslie, Joe Stripp	80.00	40.00	20.00
(24)	Mickey Cochrane, Willie Kamm, Muddy Ruel, Al Simmons	135.00	67.00	40.00
(25)	Ed Coleman, Doc Cramer, Bob Johnson, Johnny Marcum	90.00	45.00	27.00
(26)	General Crowder, Goose Goslin, Firpo Marberry, Heinie Schuble	100.00	50.00	30.00
(27)	Kiki Cuyler, Woody English, Burleigh Grimes, Chuck Klein	200.00	100.00	60.00
(28)	Bill Dickey, Tony Lazzeri, Pat Malone, Red Ruffing	275.00	137.00	82.00
(29)	Rick Ferrell, Wes Ferrell, Fritz Ostermueller, Bill Werber	100.00	50.00	30.00
(30)	Pete Fox, Hank Greenberg, Schoolboy Rowe, Gee Walker	150.00	75.00	45.00
(31)	Jimmie Foxx, Pinky Higgins, Roy Mahaffey, Dib Williams	350.00	175.00	95.00
(32)	Bump Hadley, Lyn Lary, Heinie Manush, Monte Weaver	100.00	50.00	30.00
(33)	Mel Harder, Bill Knickerbocker, Lefty Stewart, Joe Vosmik	80.00	40.00	20.00
(34)	Travis Jackson, Gus Mancuso, Hal Schumacher, Bill Terry	165.00	82.00	49.00
(35)	Joe Kuhel, Buddy Meyer, John Stone, Earl Whitehill (Myer)	80.00	40.00	20.00
(36)	Red Lucas, Tommy Thevenow, Pie Traynor, Glenn Wright	100.00	50.00	30.00

1935 Goudey Premiums (R309-2)

The black-and-white photos in this set were issued as a premium by retailers in exchange for coupons from 10 Goudey wrappers in 1935. The pictures measure 5-1/2" x 9" (or a bit longer), and are printed on thin, glossy paper. The unnumbered set includes three team collages and players, whose names are written in script in the "wide pen" style.

		NM	EX	VG
Complete Set (16):		4875.	2425.	1450.
Common Player:		275.00	135.00	82.00
(1)	Elden Auker	275.00	135.00	82.00
(2)	Johnny Babich	275.00	135.00	82.00
(3)	Dick Bartell	275.00	135.00	82.00
(4)	Lester R. Bell	275.00	135.00	82.00
(5)	Wally Berger	275.00	135.00	82.00
(6)	Mickey Cochrane	500.00	250.00	150.00
(7)	Ervin Fox, Goose Goslin, Gerald Walker	325.00	160.00	97.00
(8)	Vernon Gomez	500.00	250.00	150.00
(9)	Hank Greenberg	500.00	250.00	150.00
(10)	Oscar Melillo	275.00	135.00	82.00
(11)	Mel Ott	500.00	250.00	150.00
(12)	Schoolboy Rowe	275.00	135.00	82.00
(13)	Vito Tamulis	275.00	135.00	82.00
(14)	Boston Red Sox	300.00	150.00	90.00
(15)	Cleveland Indians	300.00	150.00	90.00
(16)	Washington Senators	300.00	150.00	90.00

1936 Goudey

The 1936 Goudey set consists of black-and-white cards measuring 2-3/8" x 2-7/8". A facsimile autograph is positioned on the card fronts. Backs contain a brief player biography and were designed to be used to play a baseball game. Different game situations (out, single, double, etc.) are given on each card. Numerous front/back combinations exist in the set. The ACC designation for the set is R322.

		NM	EX	VG
Complete Set (25):		1500.	750.00	450.00
Common Player:		40.00	20.00	12.50
(1)	Walter Berger	55.00	25.00	15.00
(2)	Henry Bonura	40.00	20.00	12.50
(3)	Stan Bordagaray	40.00	20.00	12.50
(4)	Bill Brubaker	40.00	20.00	12.50
(5)	Dolf Camilli	40.00	20.00	12.50
(6)	Clydell Castleman	40.00	20.00	12.50
(7)	"Mickey" Cochrane	125.00	62.00	37.00
(8)	Joe Coscarart	40.00	20.00	12.50
(9)	Frank Crosetti	55.00	27.00	16.50
(10)	"Kiki" Cuyler	100.00	50.00	30.00
(11)	Paul Derringer	45.00	22.00	13.50
(12)	Jimmy Dykes	40.00	20.00	12.50
(13)	"Rick" Ferrell	80.00	40.00	24.00
(14)	"Lefty" Gomez	125.00	62.00	37.00
(15)	Hank Greenberg	195.00	97.00	58.00
(16)	"Bucky" Harris	100.00	50.00	30.00
(17)	"Rolly" Hemsley	40.00	20.00	12.50
(18)	Frank Higgins	40.00	20.00	12.50
(19)	Oral Hildebrand	40.00	20.00	12.50
(20)	"Chuck" Klein	100.00	50.00	30.00
(21)	"Pepper" Martin	55.00	27.00	16.50
(22)	"Buck" Newsom	40.00	20.00	12.50
(23)	Joe Vosmik	40.00	20.00	12.50
(24)	Paul Waner	125.00	62.00	37.00
(25)	Bill Werber	40.00	20.00	12.50

1936 Goudey "Wide Pen" Premiums (R314)

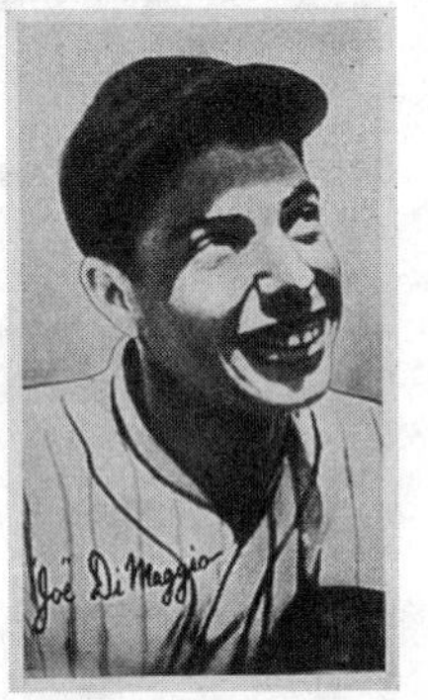

Issued in 1936 by the Goudey Gum Company in both the U.S. and Canada, these cards are known in the hobby as "Wide Pens" because of the distinctive, thick style of writing used for the black or white facsimile autographs. The black-and-white unnumbered cards measure 3-1/4" x 5-1/2" and are found in several different types. Some cards have borders, while others do not. Some cards are found with and/or without a "Litho USA" line along the bottom. Some cards in the set are found on a creamy paper stock (Canadian). The set includes both major and minor leaguers, the latter emphasizing the Canadian minor league teams in Montreal and Toronto. The cards were originally available as an in-store premium. Some players can be found in two or more poses. The set's American Card Catalog designation is R314. It is possible other poses or players may yet be reported.

		NM	EX	VG
Common Player:		36.00	15.00	9.00
(1)	Ethan Allen	36.00	15.00	9.25
(2)	Mel Almada	36.00	15.00	9.25
(3)	"Luke" Appling	55.00	23.00	14.50
(4)	Earl Averill	50.00	21.00	13.00
(5a)	Dick Bartell (portrait)	36.00	15.00	9.25
(5b)	Dick Bartell (sliding)	36.00	15.00	9.25
(6)	Buddy Bates	36.00	15.00	9.25
(7)	Walter Berger	36.00	15.00	9.25
(8)	Del Bissonnette	36.00	15.00	9.25
(9)	Geo Blaeholder	36.00	15.00	9.25
(10)	Lincoln Blakely	36.00	15.00	9.25
(11a)	Cy Blanton (portrait)	36.00	15.00	9.25
(11b)	"Cy" Blanton (pitching)	36.00	15.00	9.25
(12)	Cliff Bolton	36.00	15.00	9.25
(13a)	Henry Bonura (portrait)	36.00	15.00	9.25
(13b)	"Zeke" Bonura (batting)	36.00	15.00	9.25
(14)	Isaac J. Boone	36.00	15.00	9.25
(15)	Stan Bordagaray	36.00	15.00	9.25
(16a)	Tommy Bridges (portrait)	36.00	15.00	9.25
(16b)	Tom Bridges (pitching)	36.00	15.00	9.25
(17)	Bill Brubaker	36.00	15.00	9.25
(18)	John H. Burnett	36.00	15.00	9.25
(19)	Sam Byrd	36.00	15.00	9.25
(20)	Dolph Camilli	36.00	15.00	9.25
(21a)	Clydell Castleman (pitching)	36.00	15.00	9.25
(21b)	Clydell Castleman (portrait)	36.00	15.00	9.25
(22)	"Phil" Cavaretta (Cavarretta)	36.00	15.00	9.25
(23)	Leon Chagnon	36.00	15.00	9.25
(24)	Ben Chapman, Bill Werber	45.00	19.00	11.50
(25)	Herman Clifton	36.00	15.00	9.25
(26)	"Mickey" Cochrane	60.00	25.00	15.50
(27)	Earl Coombs (Earle Combs)	50.00	21.00	13.00
(28)	Joe Coscarart	36.00	15.00	9.25
(29)	Roger "Doc" Cramer	36.00	15.00	9.25
(30)	Joe Cronin	50.00	21.00	13.00
(31)	Frank Crosetti	36.00	15.00	9.25
(32)	Tony Cuccinello	36.00	15.00	9.25
(33)	"Kiki" Cuyler	50.00	21.00	13.00
(34)	Curt Davis	36.00	15.00	9.25
(35)	Virgil Davis	36.00	15.00	9.25
(36)	Paul Derringer	36.00	15.00	9.25
(37)	"Bill" Dickey	60.00	25.00	15.50
(38)	"Joe" DiMaggio	200.00	85.00	55.00
(39)	Joe DiMaggio, Joe McCarthy	250.00	105.00	65.00
(40)	"Bobby" Doeer (Doerr)	45.00	19.00	11.50
(41)	Gus Dugas	36.00	15.00	9.25
(42a)	Jimmy Dykes (kneeling)	36.00	15.00	9.25
(42b)	Jimmy Dykes (fielding)	36.00	15.00	9.25
(43)	Henry Erickson	36.00	15.00	9.25
(44)	"Bob" Feller	75.00	30.00	20.00
(45)	"Rick" Ferrell	50.00	21.00	13.00
(46)	"Wes" Ferrell	36.00	15.00	9.25
(47)	Rick Ferrell, Wes Ferrell	55.00	23.00	14.50
(48)	Lou Finney	36.00	15.00	9.25
(49)	"Elbie" Fletcher	36.00	15.00	9.25
(50a)	Pete Fox	36.00	15.00	9.25
(50b)	Erwin "Pete" Fox	36.00	15.00	9.25
(51)	"Jimmie" Foxx	55.00	23.00	14.50
(52)	Tony Freitas	36.00	15.00	9.25
(53)	Lonnie Frey	36.00	15.00	9.25
(54)	Frankie Frisch	50.00	21.00	13.00
(55)	Art Funk	36.00	15.00	9.25
(56a)	"Augie" Galan	36.00	15.00	9.25
(56b)	"Gus" Galan	36.00	15.00	9.25
(57)	Charles Gehringer	50.00	21.00	13.00
(58)	Charlie Gelbert	36.00	15.00	9.25
(59)	"Lefty" Gomez	50.00	21.00	13.00
(60)	"Goose" Goslin	50.00	21.00	13.00
(61)	Earl Grace	36.00	15.00	9.25
(62)	George Granger	36.00	15.00	9.25
(63)	Hank Greenberg	60.00	25.00	15.50
(64)	"Mule" Haas	36.00	15.00	9.25
(65)	Odell Hale	36.00	15.00	9.25
(66)	Bill Hallahan	36.00	15.00	9.25
(67a)	"Mel" Harder	36.00	15.00	9.25
(67b)	Mel Harder	36.00	15.00	9.25
(68)	"Bucky" Harris	50.00	21.00	13.00
(69)	"Gabby" Hartnett	50.00	21.00	13.00
(70)	Ray Hayworth	36.00	15.00	9.25
(71)	Tommy Heath	36.00	15.00	9.25
(72)	"Rolly" Hemsley	36.00	15.00	9.25
(73)	Phil Hensick	36.00	15.00	9.25
(74)	Babe Herman	36.00	15.00	9.25
(75)	LeRoy Herman	36.00	15.00	9.25
(76a)	Frank Higgins	36.00	15.00	9.25
(76b)	"Pinky" Higgins	36.00	15.00	9.25
(77a)	Oral Hildebrand (autograph across chest)	36.00	15.00	9.25
(77b)	Oral Hildebrand (autograph on left shoulder)	36.00	15.00	9.25
(78)	Myril Hoag	36.00	15.00	9.25
(79)	Alex Hooks	36.00	15.00	9.25
(80)	Waite Hoyt	50.00	21.00	13.00
(81)	Carl Hubbell	55.00	23.00	14.50
(82)	Willis Hudlin	36.00	15.00	9.25
(83)	Woody Jensen	36.00	15.00	9.25
(84)	Bob Johnson	36.00	15.00	9.25
(85)	Henry Johnson	36.00	15.00	9.25
(86)	"Buck" Jordan	36.00	15.00	9.25
(87)	Alex Kampouris	36.00	15.00	9.25
(88)	Hal King	36.00	15.00	9.25
(89)	"Chuck" Klein	50.00	21.00	13.00
(90)	Bill Knickerbocker	36.00	15.00	9.25
(91)	Joe Kuhel	36.00	15.00	9.25
(92)	Lyn Lary	36.00	15.00	9.25
(93)	Harry Lavagetto	36.00	15.00	9.25
(94)	Sam Leslie	36.00	15.00	9.25
(95a)	Freddie Lindstrom	50.00	21.00	13.00
(95b)	Fred Lindstrom	50.00	21.00	13.00
(96)	Ernie Lombardi	50.00	21.00	13.00
(97)	"Al" Lopez	50.00	21.00	13.00
(98)	Charles F. Lucas	36.00	15.00	9.25
(99)	Dan MacFayden	36.00	15.00	9.25
(100)	Heinie Manush	50.00	21.00	13.00
(101)	John Marcum	36.00	15.00	9.25
(102)	"Pepper" Martin	40.00	17.00	10.50
(103)	Eric McNair	36.00	15.00	9.25
(104)	"Ducky" Medwick	50.00	21.00	13.00
(105)	Edward S. Miller (Middle initial R.)	36.00	15.00	9.25
(106)	Gene Moore	36.00	15.00	9.25
(107)	Randy Moore	36.00	15.00	9.25
(108)	Terry Moore	36.00	15.00	9.25
(109)	Jake Mooty	36.00	15.00	9.25
(110)	Guy Moreau	36.00	15.00	9.25
(111)	Edward Moriarty	36.00	15.00	9.25
(112a)	"Wally" Moses (portrait)	36.00	15.00	9.25
(112b)	"Wally" Moses (batting)	36.00	15.00	9.25
(113)	George Murray	36.00	15.00	9.25
(114)	Glenn Myatt	36.00	15.00	9.25
(115)	"Buddy" Myer	36.00	15.00	9.25
(116)	Lauri Myllykangas	36.00	15.00	9.25
(117a)	Lou Newsom	36.00	15.00	9.25
(117b)	"Buck" Newsom	36.00	15.00	9.25
(118)	Francis J. Nicholas	36.00	15.00	9.25
(119)	Pat Nutticomb	36.00	15.00	9.25
(120)	Bill O'Brien	36.00	15.00	9.25
(121)	Thomas Oliver	36.00	15.00	9.25
(122)	Steve O'Neill	36.00	15.00	9.25
(123)	Steve O'Neill, Frank Pytlak	36.00	15.00	9.25
(124)	Fred Ostermueller	36.00	15.00	9.25
(125a)	Marvin Owen (portrait, top button shows)	36.00	15.00	9.25
(125b)	Marvin Owen (portrait, no button)	36.00	15.00	9.25
(126)	Tommy Padden	36.00	15.00	9.25
(127)	Andy Pattison	36.00	15.00	9.25
(128)	Ray Pepper	36.00	15.00	9.25
(129)	Tony Piet	36.00	15.00	9.25
(130)	Cup Polli	36.00	15.00	9.25
(131)	Harlan Pool	36.00	15.00	9.25
(132)	Walter Purcey	36.00	15.00	9.25
(133)	"Rabbit" Pytlak	36.00	15.00	9.25
(134)	"Rip" Radcliff	36.00	15.00	9.25
(135)	Bobby Reis	36.00	15.00	9.25
(136)	Bill Rhiel	36.00	15.00	9.25
(137)	"Lew" Riggs	36.00	15.00	9.25
(138)	Bill Rogell	36.00	15.00	9.25
(139)	"Red" Rolfe	36.00	15.00	9.25
(140a)	"Schoolboy" Rowe (portrait)	36.00	15.00	9.25
(140b)	"Schoolboy" Rowe (pitching)	36.00	15.00	9.25
(141)	Ben Sankey	36.00	15.00	9.25
(142)	Leslie Scarcella	36.00	15.00	9.25
(143)	Al Schacht	36.00	15.00	9.25
(144)	Bob Seeds	36.00	15.00	9.25
(145)	"Luke" Sewell	36.00	15.00	9.25
(146)	Frank Shaughnessy	36.00	15.00	9.25
(147)	Al Simmons	50.00	21.00	13.00
(148)	Harry Smythe	36.00	15.00	9.25
(149a)	Lem "Moose" Solters (border)	36.00	15.00	9.25
(149b)	Lem "Moose" Solters (no border)	36.00	15.00	9.25
(150)	John Stone	36.00	15.00	9.25
(151)	Gus Suhr	36.00	15.00	9.25
(152)	Joe Sullivan	36.00	15.00	9.25
(153)	Bill Swift	36.00	15.00	9.25
(154)	Vito Tamulis	36.00	15.00	9.25
(155)	Ben Tate	36.00	15.00	9.25
(156)	Dan Taylor	36.00	15.00	9.25
(157)	Fresco Thompson	36.00	15.00	9.25
(158)	Cecil Travis	36.00	15.00	9.25
(159a)	Hal Trosky (portrait)	36.00	15.00	9.25
(159b)	Hal Trosky (batting)	36.00	15.00	9.25
(159c)	"Hal" Trosky	36.00	15.00	9.25
(160)	"Bill" Urbanski	36.00	15.00	9.25
(161)	Russ Van Atta	36.00	15.00	9.25
(162)	"Arky" Vaughan	50.00	21.00	13.00
(163a)	Joe Vosmik (batting)	36.00	15.00	9.25
(163b)	Joe Vosmik (kneeling)	36.00	15.00	9.25
(164)	Gerald Walker	36.00	15.00	9.25
(165)	"Buck" Walter (Bucky)	36.00	15.00	9.25
(166)	Lloyd Waner	50.00	21.00	13.00
(167)	Paul Waner	50.00	21.00	13.00
(168)	"Lon" Warneke	36.00	15.00	9.25
(169)	"Rabbit" Warstler	36.00	15.00	9.25
(170)	Tom Webb	36.00	15.00	9.25
(171)	Bill Werber	36.00	15.00	9.25
(172)	"Jo Jo" White	36.00	15.00	9.25
(173)	Burgess Whitehead	36.00	15.00	9.25
(174a)	John Whitehead	36.00	15.00	9.25
(174b)	Johnnie Whitehead	36.00	15.00	9.25
(175)	Earl Whitehill	36.00	15.00	9.25
(176)	Charles Wilson	36.00	15.00	9.25
(177)	Francis Wistert	36.00	15.00	9.25
(178)	Whitlow Wyatt	36.00	15.00	9.25

1937 Goudey Thum Movies

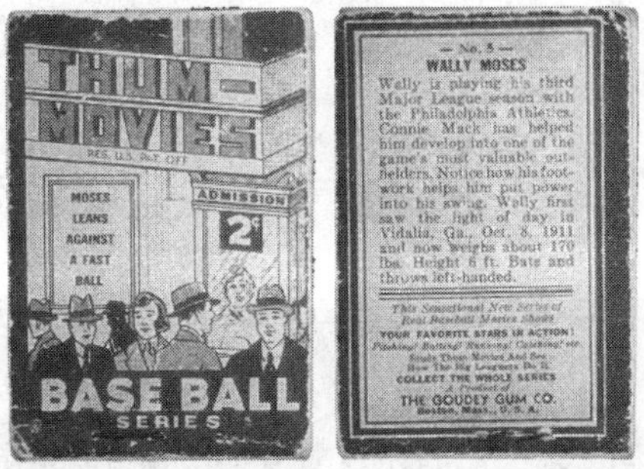

(Earlier editions of this catalog carried the Thum Movies issue date as 1934.) These 2" x 3" baseball novelty booklets create the illusion of baseball action in motion when the pages are rapidly flipped. The booklets are numbered on the top of the back page. Thum Movies were listed in the American Card Catalog as R342.

		NM	EX	VG
Complete Set (13):		1350.	650.00	400.00
Common Player:		55.00	27.00	16.50
1	John Irving Burns	55.00	27.00	16.50
2	Joe Vosmik	55.00	27.00	16.50
3	Mel Ott	140.00	70.00	42.00
4	Joe DiMaggio	450.00	225.00	135.00
5	Wally Moses	55.00	27.00	16.50
6	Van Lingle Mungo	55.00	27.00	16.50
7	Luke Appling	85.00	42.00	25.00
8	Bob Feller	140.00	70.00	42.00
9	Paul Derringer	55.00	27.00	16.50
10	Paul Waner	85.00	42.00	25.00
11	Joe Medwick	85.00	42.00	25.00
12	James Emory Foxx	140.00	70.00	42.00
13	Wally Berger	55.00	27.00	16.50

1938 Goudey

Sometimes referred to as the Goudey Heads-Up set, this issue begins numbering (#241) where the 1933 Goudey set left off. On the card fronts, a photo is used for the player's head with the body being a cartoon drawing. Twenty-four different players are pictured twice in the set. Cards #241-264 feature plain backgrounds on the fronts. Cards #265- 288 contain the same basic design and photo but include small drawings and comments within the background. Backs have player statistical and biographical information. The ACC designation for the issue is R323.

		NM	EX	VG
Complete Set (48):		16000.	7200.	4000.
Common Player (241-264):		125.00	60.00	30.00
Common Player (265-288):		145.00	70.00	40.00
241	Charlie Gehringer	400.00	180.00	100.00
242	Ervin Fox	125.00	60.00	30.00
243	Joe Kuhel	125.00	60.00	30.00
244	Frank DeMaree	125.00	60.00	30.00
245	Frank Pytlak	125.00	60.00	30.00
246	Ernie Lombardi	225.00	100.00	56.00
247	Joe Vosmik	125.00	60.00	30.00
248	Dick Bartell	125.00	60.00	30.00
249	Jimmy Foxx	500.00	225.00	110.00
250	Joe DiMaggio	4000.	1600.	750.00
251	Bump Hadley	125.00	60.00	30.00
252	Zeke Bonura	125.00	60.00	30.00
253	Hank Greenberg	525.00	230.00	130.00
254	Van Lingle Mungo	200.00	90.00	50.00
255	Julius Solters	125.00	60.00	30.00
256	Vernon Kennedy	125.00	60.00	30.00
257	Al Lopez	225.00	100.00	55.00
258	Bobby Doerr	300.00	135.00	75.00
259	Bill Werber	125.00	60.00	30.00
260	Rudy York	125.00	60.00	30.00
261	Rip Radcliff	125.00	60.00	30.00
262	Joe Ducky Medwick	300.00	135.00	75.00
263	Marvin Owen	125.00	60.00	30.00
264	Bob Feller	800.00	360.00	200.00
265	Charlie Gehringer	500.00	225.00	125.00
266	Ervin Fox	145.00	70.00	40.00
267	Joe Kuhel	145.00	70.00	40.00
268	Frank DeMaree	145.00	70.00	40.00
269	Frank Pytlak	145.00	70.00	40.00
270	Ernie Lombardi	260.00	117.00	65.00
271	Joe Vosmik	145.00	70.00	40.00
272	Dick Bartell	145.00	70.00	40.00
273	Jimmy Foxx	600.00	270.00	150.00
274	Joe DiMaggio	4250.	1750.	925.00
275	Bump Hadley	145.00	70.00	40.00
276	Zeke Bonura	145.00	70.00	40.00
277	Hank Greenberg	600.00	270.00	150.00
278	Van Lingle Mungo	145.00	70.00	40.00
279	Julius Solters	145.00	70.00	40.00
280	Vernon Kennedy	145.00	70.00	40.00
281	Al Lopez	250.00	112.00	62.00
282	Bobby Doerr	300.00	135.00	75.00
283	Bill Werber	145.00	70.00	40.00
284	Rudy York	145.00	70.00	40.00
285	Rip Radcliff	145.00	70.00	40.00
286	Joe Ducky Medwick	400.00	180.00	100.00
287	Marvin Owen	145.00	70.00	40.00
288	Bob Feller	900.00	400.00	225.00

1938 Goudey Big League Baseball Movies

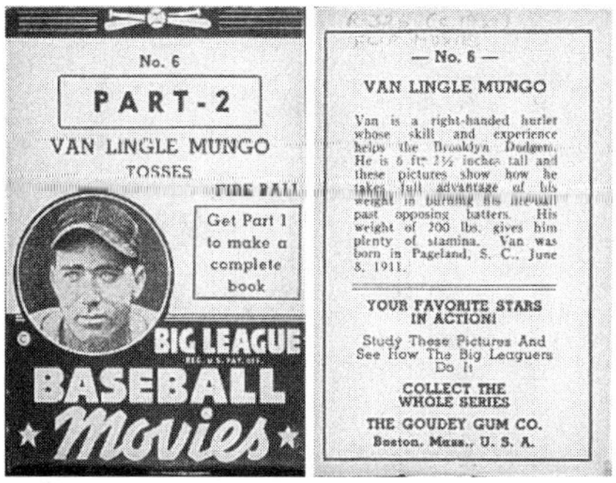

Probably issued in both 1937-38, according to the biographies on back, this set of "flip movies" was comprised of small (2" x 3") booklets whose pages produced a movie effect when flipped rapidly, similar to a penny arcade novelty popular at the time. There are 13 players in the set, each movie having two cleary labeled parts. The cover of the booklets identify the set as "Big League Baseball Movies." They carry the American Card Catalog designation R326.

		NM	EX	VG
Complete Set (26):		2900.	1400.	850.00
Common Player:		45.00	22.00	13.50
1a	John Irving Burns (Part 1)	45.00	22.00	13.50
1b	John Irving Burns (Part 2)	45.00	22.00	13.50
2a	Joe Vosmik (Part 1)	45.00	22.00	13.50
2b	Joe Vosmik (Part 2)	45.00	22.00	13.50
3a	Mel Ott (Part 1)	100.00	50.00	30.00
3b	Mel Ott (Part 2)	100.00	50.00	30.00
4a	Joe DiMaggio (Part 1, Joe DiMaggio cover photo)	750.00	375.00	225.00
4aa	Joe DiMaggio (Part 1, Vince DiMaggio cover photo)	350.00	175.00	105.00
4b	Joe DiMaggio (Part 2, Joe DiMaggio cover photo)	750.00	375.00	225.00
4ba	Joe DiMaggio (Part 2, Vince DiMaggio cover photo)	350.00	175.00	105.00
5a	Wally Moses (Part 1)	45.00	22.00	13.50
5b	Wally Moses (Part 2)	45.00	22.00	13.50
6a	Van Lingle Mungo (Part 1)	45.00	22.00	13.50
6b	Van Lingle Mungo (Part 2)	45.00	22.00	13.50
7a	Luke Appling (Part 1)	70.00	35.00	21.00
7b	Luke Appling (Part 2)	70.00	35.00	21.00
8a	Bob Feller (Part 1)	150.00	75.00	45.00
8b	Bob Feller (Part 2)	150.00	75.00	45.00
9a	Paul Derringer (Part 1)	45.00	22.00	13.50
9b	Paul Derringer (Part 2)	45.00	22.00	13.50
10a	Paul Waner (Part 1)	70.00	35.00	21.00
10b	Paul Waner (Part 2)	70.00	35.00	21.00
11a	Joe Medwick (Part 1)	70.00	35.00	21.00
11b	Joe Medwick (Part 2)	70.00	35.00	21.00
12a	James Emory Foxx (Part 1)	150.00	75.00	45.00
12b	James Emory Foxx (Part 2)	150.00	75.00	45.00
13a	Wally Berger (Part 1)	45.00	22.00	13.50
13b	Wally Berger (Part 2)	45.00	22.00	13.50

1939 Goudey Premiums (R303-A)

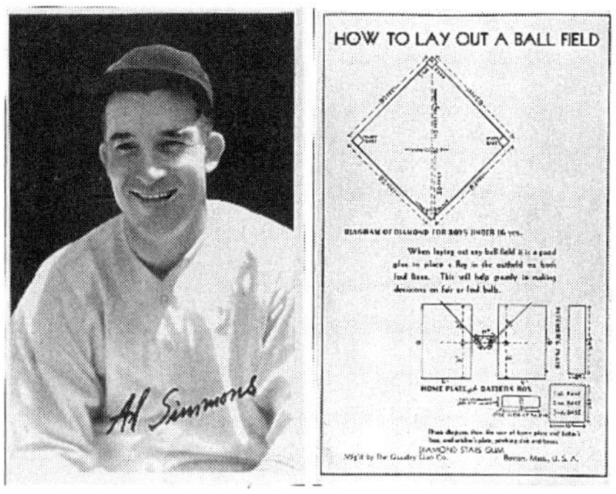

Although this unnumbered set of paper premiums has the name "Diamond Stars Gum" on the back, it is not related to National Chicle's Diamond Stars card sets. Rather, this 48-player set was a premium issued by the Goudey Gum Company. Each premium photo measures 4" x 6-3/16" and is printed in a brown-toned sepia. The front of the photo includes a facsimile autograph, while the back contains drawings that illustrate various baseball tips. These pictures are sometimes found with top and bottom border trimmed to a depth of 5-3/4" for distribution in Canada.

		NM	EX	VG
Complete Set (48):		6000.	2700.	1500.
Common Player:		75.00	34.00	18.50
(1)	Luke Appling	135.00	61.00	34.00
(2)	Earl Averill	135.00	61.00	34.00
(3)	Wally Berger	80.00	36.00	20.00
(4)	Darrell Blanton	75.00	34.00	18.50
(5)	Zeke Bonura	75.00	34.00	18.50
(6)	Mace Brown	75.00	34.00	18.50
(7)	George Case	75.00	34.00	18.50
(8)	Ben Chapman	80.00	36.00	20.00
(9)	Joe Cronin	135.00	61.00	34.00
(10)	Frank Crosetti	100.00	45.00	25.00
(11)	Paul Derringer	75.00	34.00	18.50
(12)	Bill Dickey	225.00	100.00	55.00
(13)	Joe DiMaggio	800.00	360.00	200.00
(14)	Bob Feller	235.00	105.00	60.00
(15)	Jimmy Foxx	235.00	105.00	60.00
(16)	Charles Gehringer	135.00	61.00	34.00
(17)	Lefty Gomez	135.00	61.00	34.00
(18)	Ival Goodman	75.00	34.00	18.50
(19)	Joe Gordon	75.00	34.00	18.50
(20)	Hank Greenberg	150.00	67.00	37.00
(21)	Buddy Hassett	75.00	34.00	18.50
(22)	Jeff Heath	75.00	34.00	18.50
(23)	Tom Henrich	75.00	34.00	18.50
(24)	Billy Herman	110.00	49.00	27.00
(25)	Frank Higgins	75.00	34.00	18.50
(26)	Fred Hutchinson	80.00	36.00	20.00
(27)	Bob Johnson	75.00	34.00	18.50
(28)	Ken Keltner	75.00	34.00	18.50
(29)	Mike Kreevich	75.00	34.00	18.50
(30)	Ernie Lombardi	135.00	61.00	34.00
(31)	Gus Mancuso	75.00	34.00	18.50
(32)	Eric McNair	75.00	34.00	18.50
(33)	Van Mungo	75.00	34.00	18.50
(34)	Buck Newsom	75.00	34.00	18.50
(35)	Mel Ott	135.00	61.00	34.00
(36)	Marvin Owen	75.00	34.00	18.50
(37)	Frank Pytlak	75.00	34.00	18.50
(38)	Woodrow Rich	75.00	34.00	18.50
(39)	Charley Root	75.00	34.00	18.50
(40)	Al Simmons	135.00	61.00	34.00
(41)	James Tabor	75.00	34.00	18.50
(42)	Cecil Travis	75.00	34.00	18.50
(43)	Hal Trosky	75.00	34.00	18.50
(44)	Arky Vaughan	135.00	61.00	34.00
(45)	Joe Vosmik	75.00	34.00	18.50
(46)	Lon Warneke	75.00	34.00	18.50
(47)	Ted Williams	1050.	475.00	265.00
(48)	Rudy York	75.00	34.00	18.50

1939 Goudey Premiums (R303-B)

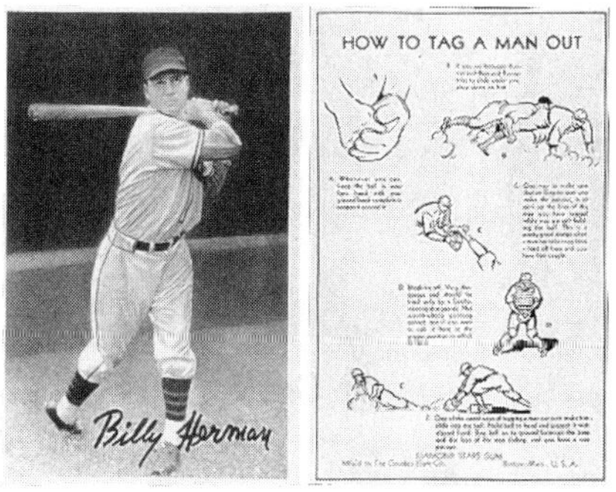

Although larger (4-3/4" x 7-1/4" to 7-3/8"), the photos in this 24-player set are identical to those in the R303-A issue of the same year, and the format of the set is unchanged. The set, designated as R303-B in the American Card Catalog, can be found in both black-and-white and sepia-toned, with backs printed in brown.

		NM	EX	VG
Complete Set (24):		2500.	1125.	625.00
Common Player:		60.00	27.00	15.00
(1)	Luke Appling	110.00	50.00	27.00
(2)	George Case	60.00	27.00	15.00
(3)	Ben Chapman	62.00	28.00	15.50
(4)	Joe Cronin	110.00	50.00	27.00
(5)	Bill Dickey	130.00	58.00	32.00
(6)	Joe DiMaggio	850.00	380.00	210.00
(7)	Bob Feller	175.00	80.00	44.00
(8)	Jimmy Foxx	175.00	80.00	44.00
(9)	Lefty Gomez	110.00	50.00	27.00
(10)	Ival Goodman	60.00	27.00	15.00
(11)	Joe Gordon	60.00	27.00	15.00
(12)	Hank Greenberg	125.00	56.00	31.00
(13)	Jeff Heath	60.00	27.00	15.00
(14)	Billy Herman	100.00	45.00	25.00
(15)	Frank Higgins	60.00	27.00	15.00
(16)	Ken Keltner	60.00	27.00	15.00
(17)	Mike Kreevich	60.00	27.00	15.00
(18)	Ernie Lombardi	100.00	45.00	25.00
(19)	Gus Mancuso	60.00	27.00	15.00
(20)	Mel Ott	110.00	50.00	27.00
(21)	Al Simmons	110.00	50.00	27.00
(22)	Arky Vaughan	110.00	50.00	27.00
(23)	Joe Vosmik	60.00	27.00	15.00
(24)	Rudy York	60.00	27.00	15.00

1941 Goudey

Goudey Gum Co.'s last set was issued in 1941. The 2-3/8" x 2-7/8" cards feature black-and-white photos set against blue, green, red or yellow backgrounds. The player's name, team and position plus the card number are situated in a box at the bottom of the card. The card backs are blank. The ACC designation for the set is R324.

		NM	EX	VG
Complete Set (33):		3200.	1250.	625.00
Common Player:		75.00	30.00	15.00
1	Hugh Mulcahy	125.00	50.00	25.00
2	Harlond Clift	75.00	30.00	15.00
3	Louis Chiozza	75.00	30.00	15.00
4	Warren (Buddy) Rosar	75.00	30.00	15.00
5	George McQuinn	75.00	30.00	15.00
6	Emerson Dickman	75.00	30.00	15.00
7	Wayne Ambler	75.00	30.00	15.00
8	Bob Muncrief	75.00	30.00	15.00
9	Bill Dietrich	75.00	30.00	15.00
10	Taft Wright	75.00	30.00	15.00
11	Don Heffner	75.00	30.00	15.00
12	Fritz Ostermueller	75.00	30.00	15.00
13	Frank Hayes	75.00	30.00	15.00
14	John (Jack) Kramer	75.00	30.00	15.00
15	Dario Lodigiani	75.00	30.00	15.00
16	George Case	75.00	30.00	15.00
17	Vito Tamulis	75.00	30.00	15.00
18	Whitlow Wyatt	75.00	30.00	15.00
19	Bill Posedel	75.00	30.00	15.00
20	Carl Hubbell	200.00	80.00	40.00
21	Harold Warstler	175.00	70.00	35.00
22	Joe Sullivan	275.00	110.00	55.00
23	Norman (Babe) Young	175.00	70.00	35.00
24	Stanley Andrews	275.00	110.00	55.00
25	Morris Arnovich	175.00	70.00	35.00
26	Elburt Fletcher	75.00	30.00	15.00
27	Bill Crouch	75.00	30.00	15.00
28	Al Todd	75.00	30.00	15.00
29	Debs Garms	75.00	30.00	15.00
30	Jim Tobin	75.00	30.00	15.00
31	Chester Ross	75.00	30.00	15.00
32	George Coffman	75.00	30.00	15.00
33	Mel Ott	300.00	120.00	60.00

1955 Robert Gould All Stars

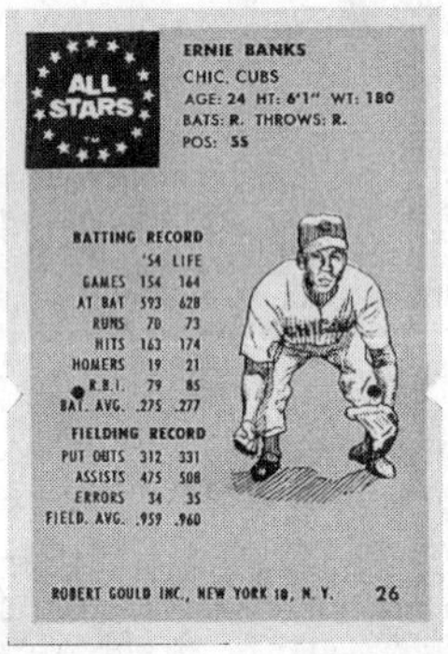

One of several issues of miniature plastic player statues issued in the mid-Fifties was the All-Stars series by Robert Gould Inc. of New York. The white plastic statues, which sold for about a quarter, came rubber-banded to a baseball card. The card measures 2-1/2" x 3-1/2" with a white border. A rather crude black-and-white line drawing of the player is set against a green background. There are a few biographical details and 1954 and lifetime stats. An "All Stars" logo is in an upper corner, while the card number is at lower-right. The cards are blank-backed. All cards have a pair of notches at the sides and two punch holes to hold the rubber band. Prices shown here are for the cards alone. Cards which retain the statues are valued from two to four times higher. A 2-5/8" x 3-5/8" album reproducing all 28 player cards was also issued.

		NM	EX	VG
Complete Set, Statues/Cards (28):		3000.	1500.	900.00
Complete Set, Cards (28):		1800.	900.00	540.00
Common Player:		60.00	30.00	18.00
Album:		250.00	125.00	75.00
1	Willie Mays	325.00	162.00	97.00
2	Gus Zernial	60.00	30.00	18.00
3	Red Schoendienst	95.00	47.00	28.00
4	Chico Carrasquel	60.00	30.00	18.00
5	Jim Hegan	60.00	30.00	18.00
6	Curt Simmons	60.00	30.00	18.00
7	Bob Porterfield	60.00	30.00	18.00
8	Jim Busby	60.00	30.00	18.00
9	Don Mueller	60.00	30.00	18.00
10	Ted Kluszewski	90.00	45.00	27.00
11	Ray Boone	60.00	30.00	18.00
12	Smoky Burgess	60.00	30.00	18.00
13	Bob Rush	60.00	30.00	18.00
14	Early Wynn	90.00	45.00	27.00
15	Bill Bruton	60.00	30.00	18.00
16	Gus Bell	60.00	30.00	18.00
17	Jim Finigan	60.00	30.00	18.00
18	Granny Hamner	60.00	30.00	18.00
19	Hank Thompson	60.00	30.00	18.00
20	Joe Coleman	60.00	30.00	18.00
21	Don Newcombe	65.00	32.00	19.50
22	Richie Ashburn	90.00	45.00	27.00
23	Bobby Thomson	65.00	32.00	19.50
24	Sid Gordon	60.00	30.00	18.00
25	Gerry Coleman	60.00	30.00	18.00
26	Ernie Banks	275.00	137.00	82.00
27	Billy Pierce	60.00	30.00	18.00
28	Mel Parnell	60.00	30.00	18.00

1978 Grand Slam

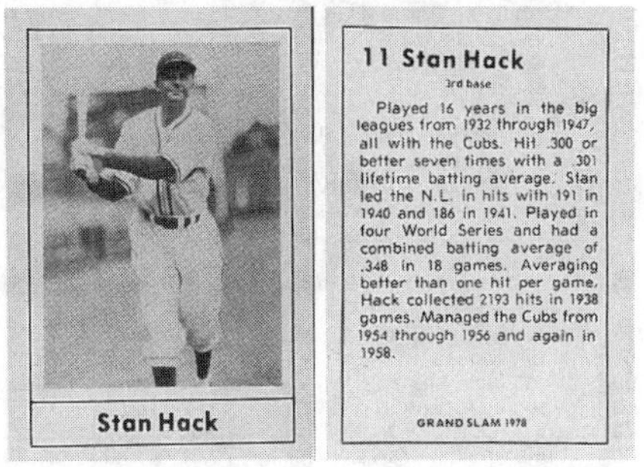

This collectors' edition card set was produced by Jack Wallin. The black-and-white 2-1/4" x 3-1/4" cards have player posed or action photos on front, with the name in the white border at bottom. Backs have a career summary.

		NM	EX	VG
Complete Set (200):		80.00	40.00	24.00
Common Player:		.50	.25	.15
1	Leo Durocher	.65	.35	.20
2	Bob Lemon	.55	.30	.15
3	Earl Averill	.50	.25	.15
4	Dale Alexander	.50	.25	.15
5	Hank Greenberg	1.50	.70	.45
6	Waite Hoyt	.50	.25	.15
7	Al Lopez	.50	.25	.15
8	Lloyd Waner	.50	.25	.15
9	Bob Feller	.65	.35	.20
10	Guy Bush	.50	.25	.15
11	Stan Hack	.50	.25	.15
12	Zeke Bonura	.50	.25	.15
13	Wally Moses	.50	.25	.15
14	Fred Fitzsimmons	.50	.25	.15
15	Johnny Vander Meer	.50	.25	.15
16	Riggs Stephenson	.50	.25	.15
17	Bucky Walters	.50	.25	.15
18	Charlie Grimm	.50	.25	.15
19	Phil Cavarretta	.50	.25	.15
20	Wally Berger	.50	.25	.15
21	Joe Sewell	.50	.25	.15
22	Edd Roush	.50	.25	.15
23	Johnny Mize	.55	.30	.15
24	Bill Dickey	.75	.40	.25
25	Lou Boudreau	.50	.25	.15
26	Bill Terry	.50	.25	.15
27	Willie Kamm	.50	.25	.15
28	Charlie Gehringer	.65	.35	.20
29	Stan Coveleski	.50	.25	.15
30	Larry French	.50	.25	.15
31	George Kelly	.50	.25	.15
32	Terry Moore	.50	.25	.15
33	Billy Herman	.50	.25	.15
34	Babe Herman	.50	.25	.15
35	Carl Hubbell	.50	.25	.15
36	Buck Leonard	.50	.25	.15
37	Gus Suhr	.50	.25	.15
38	Burleigh Grimes	.50	.25	.15
39	Al Fonseca	.50	.25	.15
40	Travis Jackson	.50	.25	.15
41	Enos Slaughter	.50	.25	.15
42	Fred Lindstrom	.50	.25	.15
43	Rick Ferrell	.50	.25	.15
44	Cookie Lavagetto	.50	.25	.15
45	Stan Musial	1.50	.70	.45
46	Hal Trosky	.50	.25	.15
47	Hal Newhouser	.50	.25	.15
48	Paul Dean	.60	.30	.20
49	George Halas	.85	.45	.25
50	Jocko Conlan	.50	.25	.15
51	Joe DiMaggio	4.00	2.00	1.25
52	Bobby Doerr	.50	.25	.15
53	Carl Reynolds	.50	.25	.15
54	Pete Reiser	.50	.25	.15
55	Frank McCormick	.50	.25	.15
56	Mel Harder	.50	.25	.15
57	George Uhle	.50	.25	.15
58	Doc Cramer	.50	.25	.15
59	Taylor Douthit	.50	.25	.15
60	Cecil Travis	.50	.25	.15
61	James Bell	.50	.25	.15
62	Charlie Keller	.50	.25	.15
63	Bill Hallahan	.50	.25	.15
64	Debs Garms	.50	.25	.15
65	Rube Marquard	.50	.25	.15
66	Rube Walberg	.50	.25	.15
67	Augie Galan	.50	.25	.15
68	George Pipgras	.50	.25	.15
69	Hal Schumacher	.50	.25	.15
70	Dolf Camilli	.50	.25	.15
71	Paul Richards	.50	.25	.15
72	Judy Johnson	.50	.25	.15
73	Frank Crosetti	.50	.25	.15
74	Harry Lowery	.50	.25	.15
75	Walter Alston	.50	.25	.15
76	Dutch Leonard	.50	.25	.15
77	Barney McCosky	.50	.25	.15
78	Joe Dobson	.50	.25	.15
79	George Kell	.50	.25	.15
80	Ted Lyons	.50	.25	.15
81	Johnny Pesky	.50	.25	.15
82	Hank Borowy	.50	.25	.15
83	Ewell Blackwell	.50	.25	.15
84	Pee Wee Reese	2.00	1.00	.60
85	Monte Irvin	.50	.25	.15
86	Joe Moore	.50	.25	.15
87	Joe Wood	.50	.25	.15
88	Babe Dahlgren	.50	.25	.15
89	Bibb Falk	.50	.25	.15
90	Ed Lopat	.50	.25	.15
91	Rip Sewell	.50	.25	.15
92	Marty Marion	.50	.25	.15
93	Taft Wright	.50	.25	.15
94	Allie Reynolds	.50	.25	.15
95	Harry Walker	.50	.25	.15
96	Tex Hughson	.50	.25	.15
97	George Selkirk	.50	.25	.15
98	Dom DiMaggio	1.00	.50	.30
99	Walker Cooper	.50	.25	.15
100	Phil Rizzuto	1.50	.70	.45
101	Robin Roberts	.50	.25	.15
102	Joe Adcock	.50	.25	.15
103	Hank Bauer	.50	.25	.15
104	Frank Baumholtz	.50	.25	.15
105	Ray Boone	.50	.25	.15
106	Smoky Burgess	.50	.25	.15
107	Walt Dropo	.50	.25	.15
108	Alvin Dark	.50	.25	.15
109	Carl Erskine	.50	.25	.15
110	Dick Donovan	.50	.25	.15
111	Dee Fondy	.50	.25	.15
112	Mike Garcia	.50	.25	.15
113	Bob Friend	.50	.25	.15
114	Ned Garver	.50	.25	.15
115	Billy Goodman	.50	.25	.15
116	Larry Jansen	.50	.25	.15
117	Jackie Jensen	.50	.25	.15
118	John Antonelli	.50	.25	.15
119	Ted Kluszewski	.75	.40	.25
120	Harvey Kuenn	.50	.25	.15
121	Clem Labine	.50	.25	.15
122	Red Schoendienst	.50	.25	.15
123	Don Larsen	.50	.25	.15
124	Vern Law	.50	.25	.15
125	Charlie Maxwell	.50	.25	.15
126	Wally Moon	.50	.25	.15
127	Bob Nieman	.50	.25	.15
128	Don Newcombe	.50	.25	.15
129	Wally Post	.50	.25	.15
130	Johnny Podres	.50	.25	.15
131	Vic Raschi	.50	.25	.15
132	Dusty Rhodes	.50	.25	.15
133	Jim Rivera	.50	.25	.15
134	Pete Runnels	.50	.25	.15
135	Hank Sauer	.50	.25	.15
136	Roy Sievers	.50	.25	.15
137	Bobby Shantz	.50	.25	.15
138	Curt Simmons	.50	.25	.15
139	Bob Skinner	.50	.25	.15
140	Bill Skowron	.75	.40	.25
141	Warren Spahn	.50	.25	.15
142	Gerry Staley	.50	.25	.15
143	Frank Thomas	.50	.25	.15
144	Bobby Thomson	.55	.30	.15
145	Bob Turley	.50	.25	.15
146	Vic Wertz	.50	.25	.15
147	Bill Virdon	.50	.25	.15
148	Gene Woodling	.50	.25	.15
149	Eddie Yost	.50	.25	.15
150	Sandy Koufax	3.00	1.50	.90
151	Lefty Gomez	.50	.25	.15
152	Al Rosen	.50	.25	.15
153	Vince DiMaggio	.55	.30	.15
154	Bill Nicholson	.50	.25	.15
155	Mark Koenig	.50	.25	.15
156	Max Lanier	.50	.25	.15
157	Ken Keltner	.50	.25	.15
158	Whit Wyatt	.50	.25	.15
159	Marv Owen	.50	.25	.15
160	Red Lucas	.50	.25	.15
161	Babe Phelps	.50	.25	.15
162	Pete Donohue	.50	.25	.15
163	Johnny Cooney	.50	.25	.15
164	Glenn Wright	.50	.25	.15
165	Willis Hudlin	.50	.25	.15
166	Tony Cuccinello	.50	.25	.15
167	Bill Bevens	.50	.25	.15
168	Dave Ferris	.50	.25	.15
169	Whitey Kurowski	.50	.25	.15
170	Buddy Hassett	.50	.25	.15
171	Ossie Bluege	.50	.25	.15
172	Hoot Evers	.50	.25	.15
173	Thornton Lee	.50	.25	.15
174	Virgil Davis	.50	.25	.15
175	Bob Shawkey	.50	.25	.15
176	Smead Jolley	.50	.25	.15
177	Andy High	.50	.25	.15
178	George McQuinn	.50	.25	.15
179	Mickey Vernon	.50	.25	.15
180	Birdie Tebbetts	.50	.25	.15
181	Jack Kramer	.50	.25	.15
182	Don Kolloway	.50	.25	.15
183	Claude Passeau	.50	.25	.15
184	Frank Shea	.50	.25	.15
185	Bob O'Farrell	.50	.25	.15
186	Bob Johnson	.50	.25	.15
187	Ival Goodman	.50	.25	.15
188	Mike Kreevich	.50	.25	.15
189	Joe Stripp	.50	.25	.15
190	Mickey Owen	.50	.25	.15
191	Hughie Critz	.50	.25	.15
192	Ethan Allen	.50	.25	.15

193	Billy Rogell	.50	.25	.15
194	Joe Kuhel	.50	.25	.15
195	Dale Mitchell	.50	.25	.15
196	Eldon Auker	.50	.25	.15
197	Johnny Beazley	.50	.25	.15
198	Spud Chandler	.50	.25	.15
199	Ralph Branca	.50	.25	.15
200	Joe Cronin	.50	.25	.15

1957-58 Graphics Arts Service Detroit Tigers Postcards

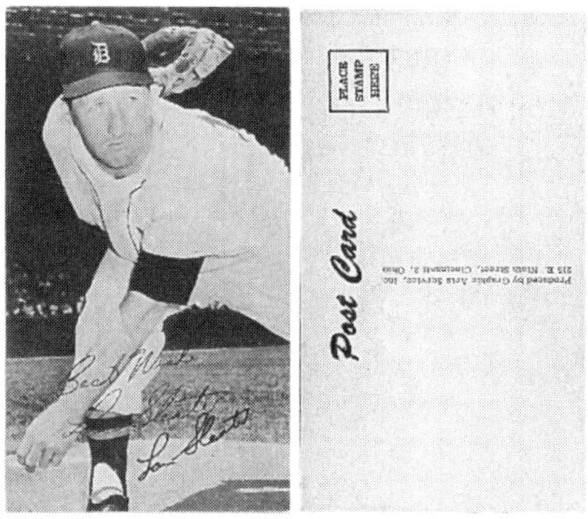

This series of Tigers postcards was issued over a two-year span by a Cincinnati printer. The 3-3/16" x 5-7/16" cards have black-and-white borderless player photos on front with a facsimile autograph. Backs have standard postcard indicia, including the producer's name and address.

		NM	EX	VG
Complete Set (22):		1300.	650.00	390.00
Common Player:		60.00	30.00	18.00
(1)	Al Aber	60.00	30.00	18.00
(2)	Hank Aguirre	60.00	30.00	18.00
(3)	Reno Bertoia (fielding)	60.00	30.00	18.00
(4)	Reno Bertoia (portrait)	60.00	30.00	18.00
(5)	Frank Bolling	60.00	30.00	18.00
(6)	Jim Bunning	120.00	60.00	36.00
(7)	Jack Dittmer	60.00	30.00	18.00
(8)	Paul Foytack	60.00	30.00	18.00
(9)	Jim Hegan	60.00	30.00	18.00
(10)	Tommy Henrich	80.00	40.00	24.00
(11)	Billy Hoeft	60.00	30.00	18.00
(12)	Frank House	60.00	30.00	18.00
(13)	Al Kaline	180.00	90.00	54.00
(14)	Harvey Kuenn	80.00	40.00	24.00
(15)	Don Lee	60.00	30.00	18.00
(16)	Billy Martin	90.00	45.00	27.00
(17)	Tom Morgan	60.00	30.00	18.00
(18)	J.W. Porter	60.00	30.00	18.00
(19)	Ron Samford	60.00	30.00	18.00
(20)	Bob Shaw	60.00	30.00	18.00
(21)	Lou Sleater	60.00	30.00	18.00
(22)	Tim Thompson	60.00	30.00	18.00

1975-76 Great Plains Greats

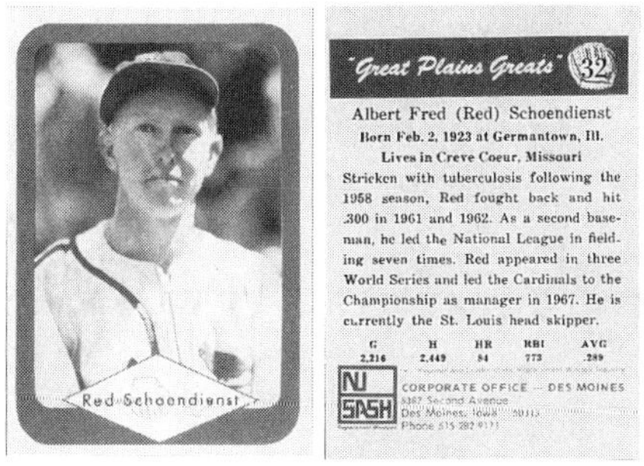

This collectors issue was issued in two series in conjunction with shows conducted by the Great Plains Sports Collectors Association. Cards are about 2-5/8" x 3-3/4". Fronts have black-and-white photos with heavy colored frames and white borders. Player name is overprinted on a diamond at bottom. Backs have a career summary and stats, and a sponsor's ad. The 1975 issue (#1-24) was sponsored by Sheraton Inns; the 1976 cards (#25-42) were sponsored by Nu-Sash Corp.

		NM	EX	VG
Complete Set (43):		22.00	11.00	6.50
Common Player:		.50	.25	.15
1	Bob Feller	.50	.25	.15
2	Carl Hubbell	.50	.25	.15
3	Jocko Conlan	.50	.25	.15
4	Hal Trosky	.50	.25	.15
5	Allie Reynolds	.50	.25	.15
6	Burleigh Grimes	.50	.25	.15
7	Jake Beckley	.50	.25	.15
8	Al Simmons	.50	.25	.15
9	Paul Waner	.50	.25	.15
10	Chief Bender	.50	.25	.15
11	Fred Clarke	.50	.25	.15
12	Jim Bottomley	.50	.25	.15
13	Dave Bancroft	.50	.25	.15
14	Bing Miller	.50	.25	.15
15	Walter Johnson	.75	.40	.25
16	Grover Alexander	.50	.25	.15
17	Bob Johnson	.50	.25	.15
18	Roger Maris	2.00	1.00	.60
19	Ken Keltner	.50	.25	.15
20	Red Faber	.50	.25	.15
21	"Cool Papa" Bell	.50	.25	.15
22	Yogi Berra	.65	.35	.20
23	Fred Lindstrom	.50	.25	.15
24	Ray Schalk	.50	.25	.15
---	Checklist	.50	.25	.15
25	Lloyd Waner	.50	.25	.15
26	Johnny Hopp	.50	.25	.15
27	Mel Harder	.50	.25	.15
28	Dutch Leonard	.50	.25	.15
29	Bob O'Farrell	.50	.25	.15
30	Cap Anson	.50	.25	.15
31	Dazzy Vance	.50	.25	.15
32	Red Schoendienst	.50	.25	.15
33	George Pipgras	.50	.25	.15
34	Harvey Kuenn	.50	.25	.15
35	Red Ruffing	.50	.25	.15
36	Roy Sievers	.50	.25	.15
37	Ken Boyer	.50	.25	.15
38	Al Smith	.50	.25	.15
39	Casey Stengel	.75	.40	.25
40	Bob Gibson	.50	.25	.15
41	Mickey Mantle	6.00	3.00	1.75
42	Denny McLain	.50	.25	.15

1916 Green-Joyce Clothiers

Best known for its use as a promotional medium for The Sporting News, this 200-card set can be found with ads on the back for several local and regional businesses. Among them is Green-Joyce Clothiers, location unknown. While type card collectors and superstar collectors may pay a premium for individual cards with Green-Joyce advertising, prices will generally parallel the 1916 Sporting News values. Cards measure 1-5/8" x 3" and are printed in black-and-white.

(See 1916 Sporting News for checklist, value information.)

1969 Greiner Tires Pittsburgh Pirates

One of the scarcer of the many Pirates regionals of the late 1960s is this eight-card issue. Printed on heavy paper in black-and-white, the 5-1/2" x 8-1/2" cards are blank-backed and unnumbered. They are checklisted here alphabetically. Some sources say the Matty Alou card is scarcer than the rest of the set.

		NM	EX	VG
Complete Set (8):		06.00	45.00	25.00
Common Player:		6.00	3.00	1.75
(1)	Gene Alley	6.00	3.00	1.75
(2)	Matty Alou	8.00	4.00	2.50
(3)	Steve Blass	6.00	3.00	1.75
(4)	Roberto Clemente	55.00	27.00	16.50
(5)	Jerry May	6.00	3.00	1.75
(6)	Bill Mazeroski	15.00	7.50	4.50
(7)	Larry Shepard	6.00	3.00	1.75
(8)	Willie Stargell	17.50	8.75	5.25

1974 Greyhound Heroes on the Base Paths

The first of three annual baseball card folders honoring the stolen base leaders and runners-up in each league, this 20" x 9" five-panel sheet features six 4" x 3" cards printed in black-and-white with sepia graphics. Backs are printed in black, brown and white. Besides the cards, the folder contains information about the bus company's award, as well as major league stolen base records and base-stealing tips. Besides individual cards of the 1974 winner and runner-up in each league, the folder has cards picturing all winners and runners-up since 1965.

		NM	EX	VG
Complete Set, Folder:		10.00	5.00	3.00
Complete Set, Singles:		8.00	4.00	2.50
Common Player:		1.00	.50	.30
(1)	Lou Brock	2.00	1.00	.60
(2)	Rod Carew	2.00	1.00	.60
(3)	Davey Lopes	1.00	.50	.30
(4)	Bill North	1.00	.50	.30
(5)	A.L. Winners/Runners-Up (Don Buford, Bert Campaneris, Rod Carew, Tommy Harper, Dave Nelson, Bill North, Amos Otis, Fred Patek)	1.00	.50	.30
(6)	N.L. Winners/Runners-Up (Lou Brock, Jose Cardenal, Sonny Jackson, Davey Lopes, Joe Morgan, Bobby Tolen, Maury Wills)	1.00	.50	.30

1975 Greyhound Heroes on the Base Paths

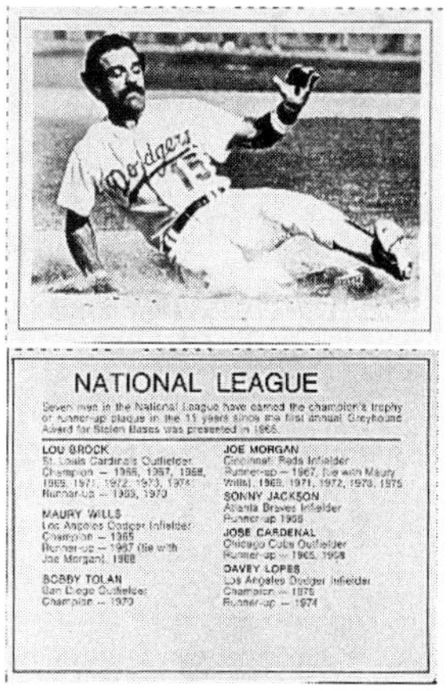

Six perforated 3-7/8" x 3" cards are featured on this folded five-panel 20" x 9" sheet honoring top base stealers in both leagues for the 1975 season. Four of the cards have each league's SB leader and runner-up in a black-and-white portrait photo with blue background. Backs are printed in black, blue and white and include major league stats. There are also two action photo cards with lists on the back of each year's winner and runner-up for the Greyhound Stolen Base Awards since 1965.

		NM	EX	VG
Complete Set, Folder:		10.00	5.00	3.00
Complete Set, Singles:		6.00	3.00	1.75
Common Player:		1.00	.50	.30
(1)	Davey Lopes	1.00	.50	.30
(2)	Davey Lopes (action)	1.00	.50	.30
(3)	Joe Morgan	2.00	1.00	.60
(4)	Bill North (action)	1.00	.50	.30
(5)	Mickey Rivers	1.00	.50	.30
(6)	Claudell Washington	1.00	.50	.30

1976 Greyhound Heroes on the Base Paths

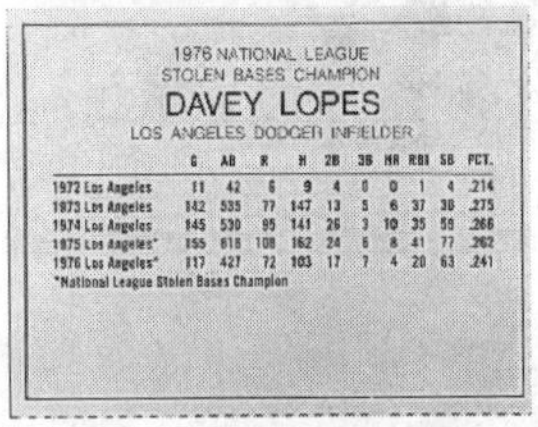

The last of three annual baseball card folders honoring the stolen base leaders and runners-up in each league, this 20" x 9" five-panel sheet features six 4" x 3" cards printed in black-and-white with sepia graphics. Backs are printed in black, brown and white. Besides the cards, the folder contains information about the bus company's award, as well as major league stolen base records and base-stealing tips. Besides individual cards of the 1974 winner and runner-up in each league, the folder has two action-photo cards listing all winners and runners-up since 1965.

		NM	EX	VG
Complete Set, Folder:		10.00	5.00	3.00
Complete Set, Singles:		6.00	3.00	1.75
Common Player:		1.00	.50	.30
(1)	Ronald Le Flore	1.00	.50	.30
(2)	Davey Lopes	1.00	.50	.30
(3)	Davey Lopes (action)	1.00	.50	.30
(4)	Joe Morgan	2.00	1.00	.60
(5)	(Bill North)	1.00	.50	.30
(6)	(Bill North) (action)	1.00	.50	.30

1907 Grignon Chicago Cubs Postcards

The eventual 1907 World Champion Cubs are featured in this set of novelty postcards. Fronts of the 3-1/2" x 5-1/2" horizontal cards have a green background with white border. The central figure on each is a teddy bear in a baseball pose. In an upper corner is a black-and-white circular portrait of one of the Cubs, with identification below. A line of infield chatter -- i.e., This is a Cinch -- completes the design. Backs have standard postcard markings and some have been seen with advertising for local businesses. The unnumbered cards are checklisted here alphabetically.

		NM	EX	VG
Complete Set (16):		1500.	750.00	450.00
Common Player:		260.00	130.00	75.00
(1)	Mordecai Brown	300.00	150.00	90.00
(2)	Frank Chance	375.00	185.00	110.00
(3)	John Evers	375.00	185.00	110.00
(4)	Arthur Hofman	260.00	130.00	75.00
(5)	John Kling	260.00	130.00	75.00
(6)	Carl Lundgren	260.00	130.00	75.00
(7)	Pat Moran	260.00	130.00	75.00
(8)	Orvie Overall	260.00	130.00	75.00
(9)	Jack Pfeister	260.00	130.00	75.00
(10)	Ed Reulbach	260.00	130.00	75.00
(11)	Frank Schulte	260.00	130.00	75.00
(12)	James Sheckard	260.00	130.00	75.00
(13)	James Slagle	260.00	130.00	75.00
(14)	Harry Steinfeldt	260.00	130.00	75.00
(15)	Jack Taylor	260.00	130.00	75.00
(16)	Joe Tinker	375.00	185.00	110.00

"1959-60" Gulf Oil Corporation

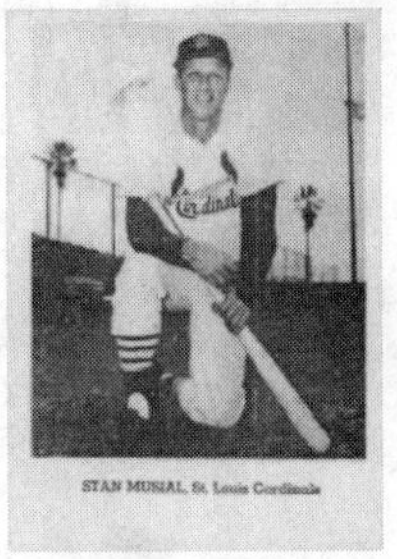

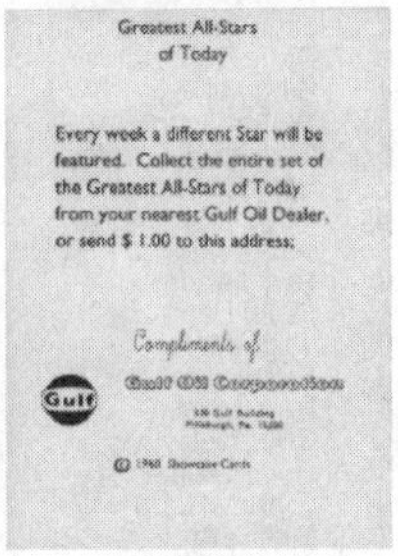

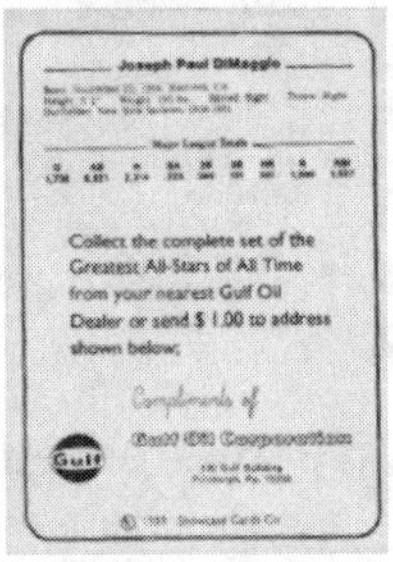

These fantasy/fraud cards were first reported in the hobby in 1999, though the copyright line on back purports to date them from 1959-1960. Two types of cards were produced, one series of eight featuring line-art portraits, the other featuring re-screened photos taken from team photo packs and similar sources. Cards are 2-1/2" x 3-1/2" printed in black-and-white. The unnumbered cards are checklisted here alphabetically within series. Because the cards were illegally produced in violation of player rights and team copyrights, no collector value is attributed.

Complete Set (16):

Artwork Series

(1) Ty Cobb
(2) Bill Dickey
(3) Joe DiMaggio
(4) Lou Gehrig
(5) Rogers Hornsby
(6) Walter Johnson
(7) Babe Ruth
(8) Pie Traynor

Photo Series

(1) Don Drysdale
(2) Bob Gibson
(3) Sandy Koufax
(4) Mickey Mantle
(5) Roger Maris
(6) Willie Mays
(7) Willie McCovey
(8) Stan Musial

1956 Gum Products Adventure

ADVENTURE

BOSTON'S GOLDEN GREEK - - - -

Harry Agganis, All-American football player, major leaguer, gentleman. Born in Lynn, Mass.; unanimous All-Scholastic football and baseball star for two years in high school; gained national honors as Boston University quarterback. Deadly passer, he held all BU passing records. Returned from Marines to win first base berth with Boston Red Sox in 1954; died unexpectedly following season.

CARD NO. 55 PRINTED IN U.S.A. GUM PRODUCTS, INC. 1956

This series of 100 cards depicts all manner of action and adventure scenes, including several sports subjects, one of which is a baseball player. The card depicts Boston U. quarterback and Boston Red Sox prospect Harry Agganis, who died unexpectedly in 1955. The 3-1/2" x 2-1/2" horizontal card has a central portrait artwork of Agganis as a Red Sox, surrounded by other scenes from his personal and sporting life. The black-and-white back has a short biography.

		NM	EX	VG
55	Harry Agganis (Boston's Golden Greek)	24.00	12.00	7.25

1948 Gunther Beer Washington Senators Postcards

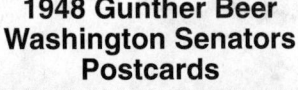

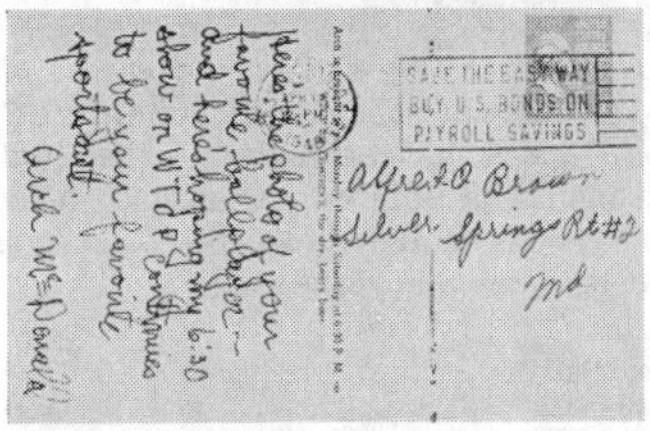

These postcards were apparently made available by writing to the radio voice of the Senators, Arch McDonald. A pre-printed message on the left side of the back urges the fan to keep listening to McDonald's program, sponsored by "Gunther's, the dry, beery beer." The black-and-white cards measure 3-1/2" x 5-1/2" and feature portrait photos of the Washington players. Most cards have two players side-by-side while manager Joe Kuhel has his own card. Player names are in heavy black letters across their chests. The cards are unnumbered and it is possible others will surface.

		NM	EX	VG
Complete Set (11):		950.00	450.00	275.00
Common Card:		100.00	50.00	30.00
(1)	Joe Kuhel	100.00	50.00	30.00
(2)	Gil Coan, Mickey Vernon	110.00	55.00	32.50
(3)	Al Evans, Scott Cary	100.00	50.00	30.00
(4)	Tom Ferrick, Harold Keller	100.00	50.00	30.00
(5)	Mickey Haefner, Forrest Thompson	100.00	50.00	30.00
(6)	Sid Hudson, Al Kozar	100.00	50.00	30.00
(7)	Walter Masterson, Rick Ferrell	125.00	62.00	37.00
(8)	Marino Pieretti, Leon Culberson	100.00	50.00	30.00
(9)	Sherrard Robertson, Eddie Lyons	100.00	50.00	30.00
(10)	Ray Scarborough, Kenneth McCreight	100.00	50.00	30.00
(11)	Early Wynn, Eddie Yost	125.00	62.00	37.00

1887 Gypsy Queen

The 1887 Gypsy Queen set is very closely related to the N172 Old Judge set and employs the same poses.The Gypsy Queens are easily identified by the advertising along the top. A line near the bottom lists the player's name, position and team, followed by an 1887 copyright line and words "Cigarettes" and "Goodwin & Co. N.Y." Although the checklist is still considered incomplete, 133 different poses have been discovered so far. Gypsy Queens were issued in two distinct sizes, the more common version measuring 1-1/2" x 2-1/2" (same as Old Judge) and a larger size measuring 2" x 3-1/2" which are considered extremely rare. The large Gypsy Queens are identical in format to the smaller size.

		NM	EX	VG
	Common Player:	900.00	550.00	325.00
(1)	J. (Tug) Arundel (Indianapolis, fielding)	900.00	550.00	325.00
(2)	Fido Baldwin	900.00	550.00	325.00
(3)	Sam Barkley (fielding)	900.00	550.00	325.00
(4)	Sam Barkley (tagging player)	900.00	550.00	325.00
(4.5)	Sam Barkley (throwing)	900.00	550.00	325.00
(5)	Handsome Boyle	900.00	550.00	325.00
(6)	Dan Brouthers (looking at ball)	1100.	660.00	385.00
(7)	Dan Brouthers (looking to right)	1100.	660.00	385.00
(8a)	California Brown (New York, throwing, large size)	4000.	2400.	1400.
(8b)	California Brown (New York, throwing, small size)	900.00	550.00	325.00
(9)	California Brown (New York, wearing mask)	900.00	550.00	325.00
(10)	Thomas Brown (Pittsburg, catching)	900.00	550.00	325.00
(11)	Thomas Brown (Pittsburg, with bat)	900.00	550.00	325.00
(12)	Black Jack Burdock	900.00	550.00	325.00
(13)	Watch Burnham	900.00	550.00	325.00
(14)	Doc Bushong	900.00	550.00	325.00
(15)	Patsy Cahill	900.00	550.00	325.00
(16)	Frederick Carroll	900.00	550.00	325.00
(17)	Parisian Bob Caruthers	900.00	550.00	325.00
(18)	Jack Clements (hands on knees)	900.00	550.00	325.00
(19)	Jack Clements (with bat)	900.00	550.00	325.00
(20)	John Coleman	900.00	550.00	325.00
(21)	Commy Comiskey	1000.	600.00	350.00
(22a)	Roger Connor (large size)	7500.	4500.	2625.
(22b)	Roger Connor (small size)	1000.	600.00	350.00
(23)	Dick Conway	900.00	550.00	325.00
(24)	Larry Corcoran	900.00	550.00	325.00
(25)	Samuel Crane (fielding)	900.00	550.00	325.00
(26)	Samuel Crane (with bat)	900.00	550.00	325.00
(27)	Edward Dailey	900.00	550.00	325.00
(28)	Abner Dalrymple	900.00	550.00	325.00
(29)	Dell Darling	900.00	550.00	325.00
(30)	Pat Dealey (bat at side)	900.00	550.00	325.00
(31)	Pat Dealey (bat on right shoulder)	900.00	550.00	325.00
(32)	Jerry Denny (catching)	900.00	550.00	325.00
(33)	Jerry Denny (with bat)	900.00	550.00	325.00
(34)	Jim Donnelly	900.00	550.00	325.00
(35)	Mike Dorgan	900.00	550.00	325.00
(36)	Buck Ewing (large size)	7500.	4500.	2625.
(37)	Buck Ewing (small size)	4000.	2400.	1400.
(38)	Jack Farrell (bat at side)	900.00	550.00	325.00
(39)	Jack Farrell (bat in air)	900.00	550.00	325.00
(40)	Jack Farrell (fielding)	900.00	550.00	325.00
(41)	Jack Farrell (hands on thighs)	900.00	550.00	325.00
(42)	Charlie Ferguson (hands at chest)	900.00	550.00	325.00
(43)	Charlie Ferguson (tagging player)	900.00	550.00	325.00
(44)	Charlie Ferguson (with bat)	900.00	550.00	325.00
(45)	Jocko Fields (catching)	900.00	550.00	325.00
(46)	Jocko Fields (throwing)	900.00	550.00	325.00
(47)	Dave Foutz	900.00	550.00	325.00
(48)	Honest John Gaffney	900.00	550.00	325.00
(49)	Pud Galvin (with bat)	1000.	600.00	350.00
(50)	Pud Galvin (without bat)	1000.	600.00	350.00
(51)	Emil Geiss (hands above waist)	900.00	550.00	325.00
(52)	Emil Geiss (right hand extended)	900.00	550.00	325.00
(53)	Barney Gilligan	900.00	550.00	325.00
(54)	Pebbly Jack Glasscock (hands on knees)	900.00	550.00	325.00
(55)	Pebbly Jack Glasscock (throwing)	900.00	550.00	325.00
(56)	Pebbly Jack Glasscock (with bat)	900.00	550.00	325.00
(57)	Will Gleason	900.00	550.00	325.00
(58)	Piano Legs Gore (fielding)	900.00	550.00	325.00
(59)	Piano Legs Gore (hand at head level)	900.00	550.00	325.00
(60)	Ed Greer	900.00	550.00	325.00
(61)	Tom Gunning (stooping to catch low ball on left)	900.00	550.00	325.00
(62)	Tom Gunning (bending, hands by right knee)	900.00	550.00	325.00
(63)	Ned Hanlon (catching)	1000.	600.00	350.00
(64)	Ned Hanlon (with bat)	1000.	600.00	350.00
(65)	Pa Harkins (hands above waist)	900.00	550.00	325.00
(66)	Pa Harkins (throwing)	900.00	550.00	325.00
(67)	Egyptian Healey (Healy)	900.00	550.00	325.00
(68)	Paul Hines	900.00	550.00	325.00
(69)	Joe Hornung	900.00	550.00	325.00
(70)	Nat Hudson	900.00	550.00	325.00
(71)	Cutrate Irwin	900.00	550.00	325.00
(72)	Dick Johnston (catching)	900.00	550.00	325.00
(73)	Dick Johnston (with bat)	900.00	550.00	325.00
(74a)	Tim Keefe (pitching, hands at chest, large size)	8500.	5100.	2975.
(74b)	Tim Keefe (pitching, hands at chest, small size)	1000.	600.00	350.00
(75)	Tim Keefe (pitching, hands above waist, facing fro nt)	1000.	600.00	350.00
(76)	Tim Keefe (right hand extended at head level)	1000.	600.00	350.00
(77)	Tim Keefe (with bat)	1000.	600.00	350.00
(78)	King Kelly (catching)	1200.	720.00	420.00
(79)	King Kelly (portrait)	1200.	720.00	420.00
(80a)	King Kelly (with bat, lg. size)	8500.	5100.	2975.
(80b)	King Kelly (with bat, sm. size)	1200.	720.00	420.00
(81)	Rudy Kemmler	900.00	550.00	325.00
(82)	Bill Krieg (catching)	900.00	550.00	325.00
(83)	Bill Krieg (with bat)	900.00	550.00	325.00
(84)	Arlie Latham	900.00	550.00	325.00
(85)	Mike Mattimore (hands above head)	900.00	550.00	325.00
(86)	Mike Mattimore (hands at neck)	900.00	550.00	325.00
(87)	Tommy McCarthy (catching)	1000.	600.00	350.00
(88)	Tommy McCarthy (with bat)	1000.	600.00	350.00
(89)	Bill McClellan	900.00	550.00	325.00
(90)	Jim McCormick	900.00	550.00	325.00
(91)	Jack McGeachy	900.00	550.00	325.00
(92)	Deacon McGuire	900.00	550.00	325.00
(93)	George Myers (Indianapolis, stooping)	900.00	550.00	325.00
(94)	George Myers (Indianapolis, with bat)	900.00	550.00	325.00
(95)	Al Myers (Washington)	900.00	550.00	325.00
(96)	Little Nick Nicol	900.00	550.00	325.00
(97)	Hank O'Day (ball in hand)	900.00	550.00	325.00
(98)	Hank O'Day (with bat)	900.00	550.00	325.00
(99)	Tip O'Neill	900.00	550.00	325.00
(100)	George Pinkney	900.00	550.00	325.00
(101)	Hardy Richardson (Detroit)	900.00	550.00	325.00
(102)	Danny Richardson (New York, large size)	4000.	2400.	1400.
(103)	Danny Richardson (New York, small size)	900.00	550.00	325.00
(104)	Yank Robinson	900.00	550.00	325.00
(105)	Jack Rowe	900.00	550.00	325.00
(106)	Emmett Seery (arms folded)	900.00	550.00	325.00
(107)	Emmett Seery (ball in hands)	900.00	550.00	325.00
(108)	Emmett Seery (catching)	900.00	550.00	325.00
(109)	George Shoch	900.00	550.00	325.00
(110)	Otto Shomberg (Schomberg)	900.00	550.00	325.00
(111)	Pap Smith	900.00	550.00	325.00
(112)	Cannonball Stemmyer (Stemmeyer) (pitching)	900.00	550.00	325.00
(113)	Cannonball Stemmyer (Stemmeyer) (with bat)	900.00	550.00	325.00
(114)	Ezra Sutton (with bat)	900.00	550.00	325.00
(115)	Ezra Sutton (throwing)	900.00	550.00	325.00
(116)	Big Sam Thompson (arms folded)	1000.	600.00	350.00
(117)	Big Sam Thompson (bat at side)	1000.	600.00	350.00
(118)	Big Sam Thompson (swinging at ball)	1000.	600.00	350.00
(119)	Silent Mike Tiernan (lg. size)	4000.	2400.	1400.
(120)	Stephen Toole	900.00	550.00	325.00
(121)	Larry Twitchell (hands by chest)	900.00	550.00	325.00
(122)	Larry Twitchell (right hand extended)	900.00	550.00	325.00
(123)	Chris Von Der Ahe	900.00	550.00	325.00
(124)	Monte Ward (large size)	7500.	4500.	2625.
(125)	Curt Welch	900.00	550.00	325.00
(126)	Art Whitney (Pittsburg, bending)	900.00	550.00	325.00
(127)	Art Whitney (Pittsburg, with bat)	900.00	550.00	325.00
(128)	Grasshopper Whitney (Washington)	900.00	550.00	325.00
(129)	Medoc Wise	900.00	550.00	325.00
(130)	George "Dandy" Wood	900.00	550.00	325.00

H

1953 H-O Instant Oatmeal Records

Baseball playing tips from several star New York players are featured in this set of box-top premium records. For 25 cents and two oatmeal box tops, a set of three of the four records could be ordered by mail. The records are 4-3/4" in diameter and have a color player portrait wuith facsimile autograph on the back side, while the grooved recording side has an action pose in single-color.

		NM	EX	VG
	Complete Set (4):	1500.	750.00	450.00
	Common Player:	250.00	125.00	75.00
(1)	Roy Campanella	500.00	250.00	150.00
(2)	"Whitey" Lockman	250.00	125.00	75.00
(3)	Allie Reynolds	350.00	175.00	105.00
(4)	Duke Snider	500.00	250.00	150.00

1922 Haffner's Big-Tayto-Loaf Bread

The bakery ad on the back is all that sets this issue apart from the blank-back W575-1 and several other versions with different sponsors named on back. The cards are 2" x 3-1/4" black-and-white. It is unknown whether each of the cards in the W575-1 checklist can be found in the Haffner's version.

	NM	EX	VG
Common Player:	45.00	22.00	13.50

(See W575-1 for checklist. Haffner's values 1.5X-2X W575-1.)

1951 Hage's Ice Cream Cleveland Indians

Similar in format to the Pacific Coast League cards produced by the dairy from 1949-51, these cards feature former members of the San Diego Padres, then a farm club of the Indians. Cards measure 2-5/8" x 3-1/8" and are printed in tones of sepia and green. Fronts have posed action photos similar to those found on contemporary Num Num and team photo pack pictures. A small white box on front has the player name and "CLEVELAND". There is a white border around the front photo. Backs are blank and unnumbered; the cards are presented here in alphabetical order.

		NM	EX	VG
	Complete Set (6):	250.00	125.00	75.00
	Common Player:	50.00	25.00	15.00
(1)	Ray Boone	50.00	25.00	15.00
(2)	Allie Clark	50.00	25.00	15.00
(3)	Jesse Flores	50.00	25.00	15.00
(4)	Al Olsen	50.00	25.00	15.00
(5)	Al Rosen	60.00	30.00	18.00
(6)	George Zuverink	50.00	25.00	15.00

1936-63 Hall of Fame Black-and-White Plaque Postcards

For nearly the first three decades of its existence, the Baseball Hall of Fame issued and made available for public sale postcards depicting the plaques of each inductee. While two different companies (Albertype, 1936-52, and Artvue, 1953-63) produced the cards, collectors generally do not distinguish between them The 3-1/2" x 5-1/2" cards' fronts have black-and-white photos of the plaques with a white border. Postcard-style backs have a bit of player data and identification of the specific producer. The unnumbered cards are checklisted here in alphabetical order.

		NM	EX	VG
Complete Set (98):		1000.	500.00	300.00
Common Player:		8.00	4.00	2.50
(1)	Grover Alexander	20.00	10.00	6.00
(2)	Cap Anson	25.00	12.50	7.50
(3)	Frank Baker	8.00	4.00	2.50
(4)	Ed Barrow	8.00	4.00	2.50
(5)	Chief Bender	8.00	4.00	2.50
(6)	Roger Bresnahan	8.00	4.00	2.50
(7)	Dan Brouthers	8.00	4.00	2.50
(8)	Mordecai Brown	15.00	7.50	4.50
(9)	Morgan Bulkeley	8.00	4.00	2.50
(10)	Jesse Burkett	8.00	4.00	2.50
(11)	Max Carey	8.00	4.00	2.50
(12)	Alexander Cartwright	8.00	4.00	2.50
(13)	Henry Chadwick	8.00	4.00	2.50
(14)	Frank Chance	20.00	10.00	6.00
(15)	Jack Chesbro	8.00	4.00	2.50
(16)	Fred Clarke	8.00	4.00	2.50
(17)	John Clarkson	8.00	4.00	2.50
(18)	Ty Cobb	50.00	25.00	15.00
(19)	Mickey Cochrane	20.00	10.00	6.00
(20)	Eddie Collins	20.00	10.00	6.00
(21)	Jimmy Collins	8.00	4.00	2.50
(22)	Charles Comiskey	8.00	4.00	2.50
(23)	Tom Connolly	8.00	4.00	2.50
(24)	Sam Crawford	8.00	4.00	2.50
(25)	Joe Cronin	8.00	4.00	2.50
(26)	Candy Cummings	8.00	4.00	2.50
(27)	Dizzy Dean	15.00	7.50	4.50
(28)	Ed Delahanty	8.00	4.00	2.50
(29)	Bill Dickey	8.00	4.00	2.50
(30)	Joe DiMaggio	50.00	25.00	15.00
(31)	Hugh Duffy	8.00	4.00	2.50
(32)	Johnny Evers	16.00	8.00	4.75
(33)	Buck Ewing	8.00	4.00	2.50
(34)	Bob Feller	15.00	7.50	4.50
(35)	Elmer Flick	8.00	4.00	2.50
(36)	Jimmie Foxx	25.00	12.50	7.50
(37)	Frank Frisch	15.00	7.50	4.50
(38)	Lou Gehrig	60.00	30.00	18.00
(39)	Charlie Gehringer	15.00	7.50	4.50
(40)	Hank Greenberg	15.00	7.50	4.50
(41)	Clark Griffith	8.00	4.00	2.50
(42)	Lefty Grove	20.00	10.00	6.00
(43)	Billy Hamilton	8.00	4.00	2.50
(44)	Gabby Hartnett	8.00	4.00	2.50
(45)	Harry Heilmann	8.00	4.00	2.50
(46)	Rogers Hornsby	20.00	10.00	6.00
(47)	Carl Hubbell	17.50	8.75	5.25
(48)	Hughie Jennings	8.00	4.00	2.50
(49)	Ban Johnson	8.00	4.00	2.50
(50)	Walter Johnson	40.00	20.00	12.00
(51)	Willie Keeler	8.00	4.00	2.50
(52)	Mike Kelly	8.00	4.00	2.50
(53)	Bill Klem	8.00	4.00	2.50
(54)	Nap Lajoie	15.00	7.50	4.50
(55)	Kenesaw M. Landis	8.00	4.00	2.50
(56)	Ted Lyons	8.00	4.00	2.50
(57)	Connie Mack	15.00	7.50	4.50
(58)	Rabbit Maranville	8.00	4.00	2.50
(59)	Christy Mathewson	40.00	20.00	12.00
(60)	Joe McCarthy	8.00	4.00	2.50
(61)	Tommy McCarthy	8.00	4.00	2.50
(62)	Iron Man McGinnity	8.00	4.00	2.50
(63)	John McGraw	15.00	7.50	4.50
(64)	Bill McKechnie	8.00	4.00	2.50
(65)	Kid Nichols	8.00	4.00	2.50
(66)	Jim O'Rourke	8.00	4.00	2.50
(67)	Mel Ott	15.00	7.50	4.50
(68)	Herb Pennock	12.00	6.00	3.50
(69)	Ed Plank	15.00	7.50	4.50
(70)	Charles Radbourn	8.00	4.00	2.50
(71)	Sam Rice	8.00	4.00	2.50
(72)	Eppa Rixey	8.00	4.00	2.50
(73)	Jackie Robinson	40.00	20.00	12.00
(74)	Wilbert Robinson	8.00	4.00	2.50
(75)	Edd Roush	8.00	4.00	2.50
(76)	Babe Ruth	75.00	37.00	22.00
(77)	Ray Schalk	8.00	4.00	2.50
(78)	Al Simmons	8.00	4.00	2.50
(79)	George Sisler	12.00	6.00	3.50
(80)	Albert Spalding	8.00	4.00	2.50
(81)	Tris Speaker	15.00	7.50	4.50
(82)	Bill Terry	8.00	4.00	2.50
(83)	Joe Tinker	20.00	10.00	6.00
(84)	Pie Traynor	8.00	4.00	2.50
(85)	Dazzy Vance	8.00	4.00	2.50
(86)	Rube Waddell	8.00	4.00	2.50
(87)	Honus Wagner	35.00	17.50	10.50
(88)	Bobby Wallace	8.00	4.00	2.50
(89)	Ed Walsh	8.00	4.00	2.50
(90)	Paul Waner	8.00	4.00	2.50
(91)	Zack Wheat	8.00	4.00	2.50
(92)	George Wright	8.00	4.00	2.50
(93)	Harry Wright	8.00	4.00	2.50
(94)	Cy Young	40.00	20.00	12.00
(95)	Abner Doubleday	8.00	4.00	2.50
(96)	Christy Mathewson (bust)	8.00	4.00	2.50
(97)	Hall of Fame Exterior	8.00	4.00	2.50
(98)	Hall of Fame Interior	8.00	4.00	2.50

1936-63 Hall of Fame B/W Plaque Postcards - Autographed

Collecting Hall of Fame plaque postcards autographed by inductees has long been popular in the hobby. Obviously completion of a set is impossible because many Hall of Famers have been inducted posthumously. Generally, the value of a genuinely autographed HoF plaque postcard is not so much dependent on star status of the player, but on the perception of how many such cards could have been autographed in his remaining lifetime. Players who died within months of their induction or who were un-cooperative with autograph requests have cards that are far more valuable than many players of greater renown. While the majority of the players checklisted here could have signed both Albertype and Artvue cards, some players are possible only on the later brand because their induction or death happened after 1962. Values quoted are for cards signed on the front. Cards signed on back can be worth 50% less.

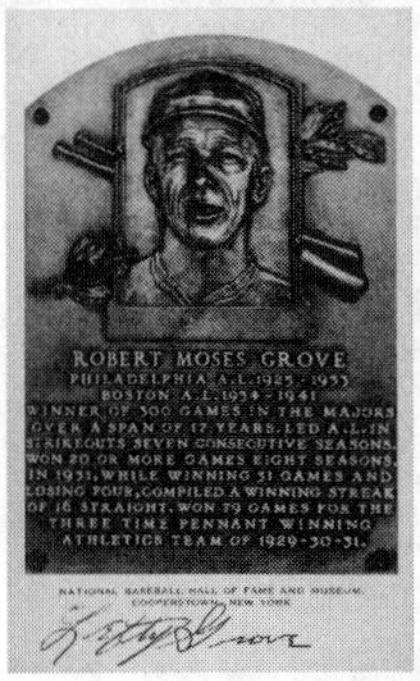

		NM	EX	VG
Complete Set (56) - value undetermined:				
Common Player:		30.00	27.00	22.00
(1)	Grover Alexander	600.00	540.00	450.00
(3)	Frank Baker	800.00	720.00	600.00
(4)	Ed Barrow	1500.	1350.	1125.
(5)	Chief Bender	400.00	360.00	300.00
(10)	Jesse Burkett	1100.	990.00	825.00
(11)	Max Carey	60.00	54.00	45.00
(16)	Fred Clarke	550.00	495.00	410.00
(18)	Ty Cobb	2000.	1800.	1500.
(19)	Mickey Cochrane	650.00	585.00	485.00
(20)	Eddie Collins	1200.	1080.	900.00
(23)	Tom Connolly	1750.	1575.	1300.
(24)	Sam Crawford	300.00	270.00	225.00
(25)	Joe Cronin	60.00	54.00	45.00
(26)	Dizzy Dean	130.00	117.00	97.00
(29)	Bill Dickey	45.00	40.00	34.00
(30)	Joe DiMaggio	145.00	130.00	109.00
(31)	Hugh Duffy	1500.	1350.	1125.
(32)	Johnny Evers	450.00	405.00	337.00
(34)	Bob Feller	25.00	22.00	18.50
(35)	Elmer Flick	400.00	360.00	300.00
(36)	Jimmie Foxx	775.00	697.00	581.00
(37)	Frank Frisch	250.00	225.00	187.00
(38)	Lou Gehrig	1500.	1350.	1125.
(39)	Charlie Gehringer	35.00	31.00	26.00
(40)	Hank Greenberg	80.00	72.00	60.00
(41)	Clark Griffith	550.00	495.00	412.00
(42)	Lefty Grove	85.00	76.00	64.00
(44)	Gabby Hartnett	250.00	225.00	187.00
(46)	Rogers Hornsby	550.00	495.00	412.00
(47)	Carl Hubbell (deduct 33% for post-stroke signature)	35.00	31.00	26.00
(50)	Walter Johnson	1200.	1080.	900.00
(54)	Nap Lajoie	1000.	900.00	750.00
(56)	Ted Lyons	40.00	36.00	30.00
(57)	Connie Mack	750.00	675.00	562.00
(60)	Joe McCarthy	85.00	76.00	64.00
(64)	Bill McKechnie	375.00	335.00	280.00
(65)	Kid Nichols	900.00	810.00	675.00
(67)	Mel Ott	650.00	585.00	487.00
(71)	Sam Rice	165.00	150.00	125.00
(72)	Eppa Rixey (possible but unlikely)			
(73)	Jackie Robinson	650.00	585.00	485.00
(74)	Wilbert Robinson	900.00	810.00	675.00
(75)	Edd Roush	40.00	36.00	30.00
(76)	Babe Ruth (value undetermined)			
(77)	Ray Schalk	450.00	405.00	335.00
(78)	Al Simmons	650.00	585.00	487.00
(79)	George Sisler	180.00	160.00	135.00
(81)	Tris Speaker	950.00	855.00	712.00
(82)	Bill Terry	40.00	36.00	30.00
(83)	Joe Tinker	450.00	405.00	337.00
(84)	Pie Traynor	400.00	360.00	300.00
(85)	Dazzy Vance	700.00	630.00	525.00
(87)	Honus Wagner	1600.	1440.	1200.
(88)	Bobby Wallace	1300.	1175.	975.00
(89)	Ed Walsh	425.00	382.00	319.00
(90)	Paul Waner	450.00	405.00	337.00
(91)	Zack Wheat	350.00	315.00	260.00
(94)	Cy Young	750.00	675.00	560.00

1973 Hall of Fame Picture Pack

This set of 5" x 6-3/4" black-and-white player photos pictures "Baseball's Greats Enshrined at Cooperstown, N.Y." Player career data is printed in the wide white border at bottom and there is a Hall of Fame logo at lower-left. The unnumbered pictures are listed here in alphabetical order.

		NM	EX	VG
Complete Set (20):		60.00	30.00	18.00
Common Player:		3.00	1.50	.90
(1)	Yogi Berra	4.50	2.25	1.25
(2)	Roy Campanella	4.50	2.25	1.25
(3)	Ty Cobb	5.00	2.50	1.50
(4)	Joe Cronin	3.00	1.50	.90
(5)	Dizzy Dean	4.50	2.25	1.25
(6)	Joe DiMaggio	12.00	6.00	3.50
(7)	Bob Feller	4.50	2.25	1.25
(8)	Lou Gehrig	7.50	3.75	2.25
(9)	Rogers Hornsby	3.00	1.50	.90
(10)	Sandy Koufax	6.00	3.00	1.75
(11)	Christy Mathewson	4.50	2.25	1.25
(12)	Stan Musial	4.50	2.25	1.25
(13)	Satchel Paige	4.50	2.25	1.25
(14)	Jackie Robinson	6.00	3.00	1.75
(15)	Babe Ruth	12.00	6.00	3.50
(16)	Warren Spahn	3.00	1.50	.90
(17)	Casey Stengel	4.50	2.25	1.25
(18)	Honus Wagner	4.50	2.25	1.25
(19)	Ted Williams	6.00	3.00	1.75
(20)	Cy Young	4.50	2.25	1.25

1979 Hall of Fame (Dexter Press) Plaque Postcards

This short-lived series, begun no later than 1979, features the Hall of Fame inductees' plaques on bright backgrounds of red, orange, blue and green. Because of the cards' color and finish, they are difficult to autograph.

		NM	EX	VG
Complete Set (53):		350.00	175.00	105.00
Common Player:		6.00	3.00	1.75
(1)	Grover Alexander	6.00	3.00	1.75
(2)	Lou Boudreau	6.00	3.00	1.75
(3)	Roy Campanella	12.00	6.00	3.50
(4)	Roberto Clemente	20.00	10.00	6.00
(5)	Ty Cobb	12.00	6.00	3.50
(6)	Stan Coveleski	6.00	3.00	1.75
(7)	Sam Crawford	6.00	3.00	1.75
(8)	Martin Dihigo	6.00	3.00	1.75
(9)	Joe DiMaggio	22.00	11.00	6.50
(10)	Billy Evans	6.00	3.00	1.75
(11)	Johnny Evers	6.00	3.00	1.75
(12)	Red Faber	6.00	3.00	1.75
(13)	Elmer Flick	6.00	3.00	1.75
(14)	Ford Frick	6.00	3.00	1.75
(15)	Frank Frisch	6.00	3.00	1.75
(16)	Pud Galvin	6.00	3.00	1.75
(17)	Lou Gehrig	20.00	10.00	6.00
(18)	Warren Giles	6.00	3.00	1.75
(19)	Will Harridge	6.00	3.00	1.75
(20)	Harry Heilmann	6.00	3.00	1.75
(21)	Harry Hooper	6.00	3.00	1.75
(22)	Waite Hoyt	6.00	3.00	1.75
(23)	Miller Huggins	6.00	3.00	1.75
(24)	Judy Johnson	6.00	3.00	1.75
(25)	Addie Joss	6.00	3.00	1.75
(26)	Tim Keefe	6.00	3.00	1.75
(27)	Willie Keeler	6.00	3.00	1.75
(28)	George Kelly	6.00	3.00	1.75
(29)	Sandy Koufax	12.00	6.00	3.50
(30)	Nap Lajoie	6.00	3.00	1.75
(31)	Pop Lloyd	6.00	3.00	1.75
(32)	Connie Mack	6.00	3.00	1.75
(33)	Larry MacPhail	6.00	3.00	1.75
(34)	Mickey Mantle	25.00	12.50	7.50
(35)	Heinie Manush	6.00	3.00	1.75
(36)	Eddie Mathews	6.00	3.00	1.75
(37)	Willie Mays	12.00	6.00	3.50
(38)	Ducky Medwick	6.00	3.00	1.75
(39)	Stan Musial	10.00	5.00	3.00
(40)	Herb Pennock	6.00	3.00	1.75
(41)	Edd Roush	6.00	3.00	1.75
(42)	Babe Ruth	25.00	12.50	7.50
(43)	Amos Rusie	6.00	3.00	1.75
(44)	Ray Schalk	6.00	3.00	1.75
(45)	Al Simmons	6.00	3.00	1.75
(46)	Albert Spalding	6.00	3.00	1.75
(47)	Joe Tinker	6.00	3.00	1.75
(48)	Pie Traynor	6.00	3.00	1.75
(49)	Dazzy Vance	6.00	3.00	1.75
(50)	Lloyd Waner	6.00	3.00	1.75
(51)	Ted Williams	20.00	10.00	6.00
(52)	Hack Wilson	6.00	3.00	1.75
(53)	Ross Youngs	6.00	3.00	1.75

1979 HoF (Dexter Press) Plaque Postcards - Autographed

		NM	EX	VG
Complete Set (15):		1100.	990.00	825.00
Common Player:		15.00	13.50	11.00
(2)	Lou Boudreau	12.00	11.00	9.00
(3)	Roy Campanella (value undetermined)			
(6)	Stan Coveleski	25.00	22.00	18.50
(9)	Joe DiMaggio	200.00	180.00	150.00
(22)	Waite Hoyt	27.50	25.00	21.00
(24)	Judy Johnson	25.00	22.00	18.50
(28)	George Kelly	27.50	25.00	21.00
(29)	Sandy Koufax	60.00	54.00	45.00
(34)	Mickey Mantle	300.00	270.00	225.00
(36)	Eddie Mathews	15.00	13.50	11.00
(37)	Willie Mays	40.00	36.00	30.00
(39)	Stan Musial	25.00	22.00	18.50
(41)	Edd Roush	25.00	22.00	18.50
(50)	Lloyd Waner	55.00	49.00	41.00
(51)	Ted Williams	250.00	225.00	187.00

1964-98 Hall of Fame Yellow Plaque Postcards

Since 1964 a number of related series of Hall of Fame Plaque Postcards have been produced by a pair of printers. The 3-1/2" x 5-1/2" postcards were first produced by Curteichcolor and, later, by Mike Roberts Color Productions. Like earlier HoF postcards, these series feature a color photo of an inductee's plaque on a yellow background. Black-and-white backs have a variety of player information, postcard indicia, copyright data and credit lines. Few hobbyists attmept to collect these by issuer, rather trying to assemble a complete set of each player regardless of who did the printing and when. Prior to 1977, single postcards sold for five cents at the HoF gift shop; in 1977 the price doubled to a dime, with complete sets (about 150) selling for $6. Today a complete set is available from the Hall of Fame for about $40.

1964-98 Hall of Fame Yellow Plaque Postcards - Autographed

This listing represents the Curteichcolor and Mike Roberts yellow Hall of Fame plaque postcards which are known to exist, or in a few cases are theoretically possible. Value of genuinely autographed HoF plaque postcards is not so much dependent on star status of the player, but on perception of how many such cards could exist given the time the player remained alive and in good health following his selection at Cooperstown. Players who died or were incapacitated shortly after induction may have more valuable autographed cards than currently living players of greater renown. Values quoted are for cards autographed on front; cards signed on the back can be worth 50% less.

	NM	EX	VG
	15.00	12.00	9.00
Hank Aaron	50.00	40.00	30.00
Walter Alston	160.00	130.00	96.00
Sparky Anderson	25.00	20.00	12.00
Luis Aparicio	20.00	16.00	12.00
Luke Appling	15.00	12.00	9.00
Richie Ashburn	40.00	32.00	24.00
Earl Averill	27.50	22.00	16.50
Dave Bancroft	900.00	720.00	540.00
Ernie Banks	32.50	26.00	19.50
Al Barlick	22.50	18.00	13.50
Cool Papa Bell	45.00	36.00	27.00
Johnny Bench	25.00	20.00	15.00
Yogi Berra	20.00	16.00	12.00
Lou Boudreau	10.00	8.00	6.00
George Brett	35.00	28.00	21.00
Lou Brock	15.00	12.00	9.00
Jim Bunning	35.00	28.00	21.00
Roy Campanella (value undetermined)			
Rod Carew	30.00	24.00	18.00
Max Carey	55.00	44.00	33.00
Steve Carlton	25.00	20.00	15.00
Orlando Cepeda	35.00	28.00	21.00
A.B. (Happy) Chandler	17.50	14.00	10.50
Earle Combs	95.00	75.00	57.00
Jocko Conlan	19.00	15.00	11.50
Stan Coveleski	25.00	20.00	15.00
"Stanislaus Kowalewski"	85.00	68.00	51.00
Sam Crawford	225.00	180.00	135.00
Joe Cronin	55.00	44.00	33.00
Ray Dandridge	20.00	16.00	12.00
Dizzy Dean	180.00	145.00	110.00
Bill Dickey	45.00	36.00	27.00
Joe DiMaggio	165.00	130.00	99.00
Larry Doby	27.50	22.00	16.50
Bobby Doerr	10.00	8.00	6.00
Don Drysdale	40.00	32.00	24.00
Red Faber	65.00	52.00	39.00
Bob Feller	10.00	8.00	6.00
Rick Ferrell	20.00	16.00	12.00
Rollie Fingers	17.50	14.00	10.50
Carlton Fisk	25.00	20.00	12.00
Elmer Flick	400.00	320.00	240.00
Whitey Ford	17.50	14.00	10.50
Jimmie Foxx	1600.	1280.	960.00
Ford Frick	150.00	120.00	90.00
Frank Frisch	225.00	180.00	135.00
Charlie Gehringer	22.50	18.00	13.50
Bob Gibson	15.00	12.00	9.00
Lefty Gomez	25.00	20.00	15.00
Goose Goslin (usually signed on back; value of such $500-1,000)	2000.	1600.	1200.
Hank Greenberg	70.00	56.00	42.00
Burleigh Grimes	40.00	32.00	24.00
Lefty Grove	150.00	120.00	90.00
Chick Hafey	450.00	360.00	270.00
Jesse Haines	100.00	80.00	60.00
Bucky Harris	160.00	130.00	96.00
Gabby Hartnett	300.00	240.00	180.00
Billy Herman	12.00	9.50	7.25
Harry Hooper	150.00	120.00	90.00
Waite Hoyt	35.00	28.00	21.00
Cal Hubbard	750.00	600.00	450.00
Carl Hubbell (pre-stroke)	20.00	16.00	12.00
Carl Hubbell (post-stroke)	15.00	12.00	9.00
Catfish Hunter	35.00	28.00	21.00
Monte Irvin	10.00	8.00	6.00
Reggie Jackson	45.00	36.00	27.00
Travis Jackson	35.00	28.00	21.00
Fergie Jenkins	10.00	8.00	6.00
Judy Johnson	25.00	20.00	15.00
Al Kaline	15.00	12.00	9.00
George Kell	10.00	8.00	6.00
George Kelly	40.00	32.00	24.00
Harmon Killebrew	20.00	16.00	12.00
Ralph Kiner	12.00	9.50	7.25
Sandy Koufax	45.00	36.00	27.00
Tommy Lasorda	30.00	24.00	18.00
Tony Lazzeri	25.00	20.00	15.00
Bob Lemon	10.00	8.00	6.00
Buck Leonard (post-stroke autographed cards worth 50%)	20.00	16.00	12.00
Freddie Lindstrom	47.50	38.00	28.00
Al Lopez	40.00	32.00	24.00
Ted Lyons	27.50	22.00	16.50
Mickey Mantle	180.00	145.00	110.00
Heinie Manush	300.00	240.00	180.00
Juan Marichal	35.00	28.00	21.00
Rube Marquard	40.00	32.00	24.00
Eddie Mathews	17.50	14.00	10.50
Willie Mays	45.00	36.00	27.00
Joe McCarthy	85.00	68.00	51.00
Willie McCovey	20.00	16.00	12.00
Bill McKechnie (possible, not likely)			
Lee McPhail	35.00	28.00	21.00
Ducky Medwick	165.00	130.00	99.00
Johnny Mize	20.00	16.00	12.00
Joe Morgan	25.00	20.00	15.00
Stan Musial	25.00	20.00	15.00
Hal Newhouser	20.00	16.00	12.00
Phil Niekro	25.00	20.00	15.00
Satchel Paige	140.00	110.00	84.00
Jim Palmer	25.00	20.00	15.00
Tony Perez	25.00	20.00	12.00
Gaylord Perry	10.00	8.00	6.00
Pee Wee Reese	40.00	32.00	24.00
Sam Rice	165.00	130.00	99.00
Phil Rizzuto	20.00	16.00	12.00
Robin Roberts	10.00	8.00	6.00
Brooks Robinson	15.00	12.00	9.00
Frank Robinson	20.00	16.00	12.00
Jackie Robinson	800.00	640.00	480.00
Edd Roush	25.00	20.00	15.00
Red Ruffing	70.00	56.00	42.00
Nolan Ryan	40.00	32.00	24.00
Ray Schalk	300.00	240.00	180.00
Mike Schmidt	45.00	36.00	27.00
Red Schoendienst	10.00	8.00	6.00
Tom Seaver	40.00	32.00	24.00
Joe Sewell	15.00	12.00	9.00
George Sisler	160.00	130.00	96.00
Enos Slaughter	10.00	8.00	6.00
Duke Snider	25.00	20.00	15.00
Warren Spahn	15.00	12.00	9.00
Willie Stargell	12.00	9.50	7.25
Casey Stengel	145.00	115.00	87.00
Don Sutton	25.00	18.50	10.00
Bill Terry	24.00	19.00	14.50
Pie Traynor	700.00	560.00	420.00
Lloyd Waner	30.00	24.00	18.00
Paul Waner (possible, not likely)			
Earl Weaver	30.00	24.00	18.00
George Weiss (possible, not likely)			
Zack Wheat	375.00	300.00	225.00
Hoyt Wilhelm	10.00	8.00	6.00
Billy Williams	15.00	12.00	9.00
Ted Williams	145.00	115.00	87.00
Early Wynn	22.50	18.00	13.50
Carl Yastrzemski	35.00	28.00	21.00
Robin Yount	35.00	28.00	21.00

1888 Joseph Hall Cabinets

These fourteen cabinet-size (6-1/2" x 4-1/2") cards feature team photos taken by Joseph Hall, a well-known photographer of the day. The cards, which are extremely rare, all have Hall's name beneath the photo and some include his Brooklyn address. The team is identified in large capital letters with the individual players identified in smaller type on both sides. Fourteen teams are known to date, but others may also exist, and Hall may have produced similar team cabinets in other years as well.

		NM	EX	VG
Common Team:		6000.	3000.	1800.
(1)	Athletic Ball Club, 1888	6000.	3000.	1800.
(2)	Baltimore Ball Club, 1888	9500.	4750.	2850.
(3)	Boston Ball Club, 1888	8500.	4250.	2550.
(4)	Brooklyn Ball Club, 1888	6500.	3250.	1950.
(5)	Chicago Ball Club, 1888	20000.	10000.	6000.
(6)	Cincinnati Ball Club, 1888	7500.	3750.	2250.
(7)	Cleveland Ball Club, 1888	8250.	4125.	2475.
(8)	Detroit Ball Club, 1888	9500.	4750.	2850.
(9)	Indianapolis Ball Club, 1888	7000.	3500.	2100.
(10)	Kansas City Ball Club, 1888	7500.	3750.	2250.
(11)	Louisville Ball Club, 1888	11500.	5750.	3450.
(12)	New York Ball Club, 1888 (wearing baseball uniforms)	9000.	4500.	2700.
(13)	New York Ball Club, 1888 (wearing tuxedos)	8500.	4250.	2550.
(14)	St. Louis Baseball Club, 1888	6250.	3125.	1875.
(15)	Washington Baseball Club, 1888	20000.	10000.	6000.

1928 Harrington's Ice Cream

Sharing the same format and checklist with several other (Tharp's, Yeungling's, Sweetman, etc.) contemporary ice cream sets this 60-card set includes all of the top stars of the day. Cards are printed in black and white on a 1-3/8" x 2-1/2" format. The player's name and a card number appear either in a strip within the frame of the photo, or printed in the border beneath the photo. Card backs have a redemption offer that includes an ice cream bar in exchange for a Babe Ruth card, or a gallon of ice cream for a complete set of 60.

		NM	EX	VG
Complete Set (60):		3500.	1750.	1000.
Common Player:		30.00	15.00	9.00
1	Burleigh Grimes	50.00	25.00	15.00
2	Walter Reuther	30.00	15.00	9.00
3	Joe Dugan	30.00	15.00	9.00
4	Red Faber	50.00	25.00	15.00
5	Gabby Hartnett	50.00	25.00	15.00
6	Babe Ruth	1100.	550.00	330.00
7	Bob Meusel	30.00	15.00	9.00
8	Herb Pennock	50.00	25.00	15.00
9	George Burns	30.00	15.00	9.00
10	Joe Sewell	50.00	25.00	15.00
11	George Uhle	30.00	15.00	9.00
12	Bob O'Farrell	30.00	15.00	9.00
13	Rogers Hornsby	65.00	32.00	19.50
14	"Pie" Traynor	50.00	25.00	15.00
15	Clarence Mitchell	30.00	15.00	9.00
16	Eppa Jepha Rixey	50.00	25.00	15.00
17	Carl Mays	30.00	15.00	9.00
18	Adolfo Luque	40.00	20.00	12.00
19	Dave Bancroft	50.00	25.00	15.00
20	George Kelly	50.00	25.00	15.00
21	Earl (Earle) Combs	50.00	25.00	15.00
22	Harry Heilmann	50.00	25.00	15.00
23	Ray W. Schalk	50.00	25.00	15.00
24	Johnny Mostil	30.00	15.00	9.00
25	Hack Wilson	50.00	25.00	15.00
26	Lou Gehrig	500.00	250.00	150.00
27	Ty Cobb	500.00	250.00	150.00
28	Tris Speaker	65.00	32.00	19.50
29	Tony Lazzeri	50.00	25.00	15.00
30	Waite Hoyt	50.00	25.00	15.00
31	Sherwood Smith	30.00	15.00	9.00
32	Max Carey	50.00	25.00	15.00
33	Eugene Hargrave	30.00	15.00	9.00
34	Miguel L. Gonzalez (Middle initial A.)	40.00	20.00	12.00
35	Joe Judge	30.00	15.00	9.00
36	E.C. (Sam) Rice	50.00	25.00	15.00
37	Earl Sheely	30.00	15.00	9.00
38	Sam Jones	30.00	15.00	9.00
39	Bib (Bibb) A. Falk	30.00	15.00	9.00
40	Willie Kamm	30.00	15.00	9.00
41	Stanley Harris	50.00	25.00	15.00
42	John J. McGraw	50.00	25.00	15.00
43	Artie Nehf	30.00	15.00	9.00
44	Grover Alexander	55.00	27.00	16.50
45	Paul Waner	50.00	25.00	15.00
46	William H. Terry	50.00	25.00	15.00
47	Glenn Wright	30.00	15.00	9.00
48	Earl Smith	30.00	15.00	9.00
49	Leon (Goose) Goslin	50.00	25.00	15.00
50	Frank Frisch	50.00	25.00	15.00
51	Joe Harris	30.00	15.00	9.00
52	Fred (Cy) Williams	30.00	15.00	9.00
53	Eddie Roush	50.00	25.00	15.00
54	George Sisler	50.00	25.00	15.00
55	Ed. Rommel	30.00	15.00	9.00
56	Rogers Peckinpaugh (Roger)	30.00	15.00	9.00
57	Stanley Coveleskie (Coveleski)	50.00	25.00	15.00
58	Lester Bell	30.00	15.00	9.00
59	L. Waner	50.00	25.00	15.00
60	John P. McInnis	30.00	15.00	9.00

1911-12 Hassan Cigarettes

(See T202, T205. Premium: T205 - +30%)

1952 Hawthorn-Mellody Chicago White Sox Pins

This issue was sponsored by a local dairy. The 1-3/8" diameter pins have sepia lithographs of the players with "Club of Champs" printed above. A non-pictorial membership button is also part of the set. The unnumbered pins are listed here in alphabetical order.

		NM	EX	VG
Complete Set (11):		325.00	160.00	98.00
Common Player:		30.00	15.00	9.00
(1)	Ray Coleman	30.00	15.00	9.00
(2)	Sam Dente	30.00	15.00	9.00
(3)	Joe Dobson	30.00	15.00	9.00
(4)	Nelson Fox	65.00	32.00	19.50
(5)	Sherman Lollar	40.00	20.00	12.00
(6)	Bill Pierce	40.00	20.00	12.00
(7)	Eddie Robinson	30.00	15.00	9.00
(8)	Hector Rodriguez	30.00	15.00	9.00
(9)	Eddie Stewart	30.00	15.00	9.00
(10)	Al Zarilla	30.00	15.00	9.00
(11)	Member's pin	15.00	7.50	4.50

1959 R.H. Hayes Postcards

Whether there are any other player postcards distributed by R.H. Hayes of Kansas is unknown. Produced for Hayes by Dexter Press, which issued cards for Coke in later years, the 3-1/2" x 5-1/2" postcard has a borderless color photo on front with a facsimile autograph at bottom. The postcard back has credit lines for Hayes and Dexter and a short biography of the player.

		NM	EX	VG
(1)	Hank Bauer	35.00	17.50	10.50

1909-10 Helmar Silks

(See S74)

1911 Helmar Stamps (T332)

In an interesting departure from the traditional tobacco cards of the period, Helmar Cigarettes in 1911 issued a series of small major league baseball player "stamps." The stamps, each measuring approximately 1-1/8" x 1-3/8", feature a black and white player portrait surrounded by a colorful, ornate frame. The stamps were originally issued in a 2" x 2-1/2" glassine envelope which advertised the Helmar brand and promoted "Philately - the Popular European Rage." To date, 181 different player stamps have been found. The set includes as many as 50 different frame designs are also known to exist. The Helmar stamp set has been assigned a T332 designation by the American Card Catalog.

		NM	EX	VG
Complete Set (180):		12000.	6000.	3500.
Common Player:		55.00	27.00	16.50
(1)	Babe Adams	55.00	27.00	16.50
(2)	Red Ames	55.00	27.00	16.50
(3)	Jimmy Archer	55.00	27.00	16.50
(4)	Jimmy Austin	55.00	27.00	16.50
(5)	Home Run Baker	150.00	75.00	45.00
(6)	Neal Ball	55.00	27.00	16.50
(7)	Cy Barger	55.00	27.00	16.50
(8)	Jack Barry	55.00	27.00	16.50
(9)	Johnny Bates	55.00	27.00	16.50
(10)	Fred Beck	55.00	27.00	16.50
(11)	Beals Becker	55.00	27.00	16.50
(12)	George Bell	55.00	27.00	16.50
(13)	Chief Bender	150.00	75.00	45.00
(14)	Bob Bescher	55.00	27.00	16.50
(15)	Joe Birmingham	55.00	27.00	16.50
(16)	John Bliss	55.00	27.00	16.50
(17)	Bruno Block	55.00	27.00	16.50
(18)	Ping Bodie	55.00	27.00	16.50
(19)	Roger Bresnahan	150.00	75.00	45.00
(20)	Al Bridwell	55.00	27.00	16.50
(21)	Lew Brockett	55.00	27.00	16.50
(22)	Mordecai Brown	150.00	75.00	45.00
(23)	Bill Burns	55.00	27.00	16.50
(24)	Donie Bush	55.00	27.00	16.50
(25)	Bobby Byrne	55.00	27.00	16.50
(26)	Nixey Callahan	55.00	27.00	16.50
(27)	Howie Camnitz	55.00	27.00	16.50
(28)	Max Carey	150.00	75.00	45.00
(29)	Bill Carrigan	55.00	27.00	16.50
(30)	Frank Chance	150.00	75.00	45.00
(31)	Hal Chase	75.00	37.00	22.00
(32)	Ed Cicotte	120.00	60.00	36.00
(33)	Fred Clarke	150.00	75.00	45.00
(34)	Tommy Clarke	55.00	27.00	16.50
(35)	Ty Cobb	1100.	550.00	330.00
(36)	King Cole	55.00	27.00	16.50
(37)	Eddie Collins (Philadelphia)	150.00	75.00	45.00
(38)	Shano Collins (Chicago)	55.00	27.00	16.50
(39)	Wid Conroy	55.00	27.00	16.50
(40)	Doc Crandall	55.00	27.00	16.50
(41)	Sam Crawford	150.00	75.00	45.00
(42)	Birdie Cree	55.00	27.00	16.50
(43)	Bill Dahlen	55.00	27.00	16.50
(44)	Jake Daubert	55.00	27.00	16.50
(45)	Harry Davis	55.00	27.00	16.50
(46)	Jim Delahanty	55.00	27.00	16.50
(47)	Art Devlin	55.00	27.00	16.50
(48)	Josh Devore	55.00	27.00	16.50
(49)	Mike Donlin	55.00	27.00	16.50
(50)	Wild Bill Donovan	55.00	27.00	16.50
(51)	Red Dooin	55.00	27.00	16.50
(52)	Mickey Doolan	55.00	27.00	16.50
(53)	Patsy Dougherty	55.00	27.00	16.50
(54)	Tom Downey	55.00	27.00	16.50
(55)	Larry Doyle	55.00	27.00	16.50
(56)	Louis Drucke	55.00	27.00	16.50
(57)	Clyde Engle	55.00	27.00	16.50
(58)	Tex Erwin	55.00	27.00	16.50
(59)	Steve Evans	55.00	27.00	16.50
(60)	Johnny Evers	150.00	75.00	45.00
(61)	Jack Ferry	55.00	27.00	16.50
(62)	Ray Fisher	55.00	27.00	16.50
(63)	Art Fletcher	55.00	27.00	16.50
(64)	Russ Ford	55.00	27.00	16.50
(65)	Art Fromme	55.00	27.00	16.50
(66)	Earl Gardner	55.00	27.00	16.50
(67)	Harry Gaspar	55.00	27.00	16.50
(68)	George Gibson	55.00	27.00	16.50
(69)	Roy Golden	55.00	27.00	16.50
(70)	Hank Gowdy	55.00	27.00	16.50
(71)	Peaches Graham	55.00	27.00	16.50
(72)	Eddie Grant	65.00	32.00	19.50
(73)	Dolly Gray	55.00	27.00	16.50
(74)	Clark Griffith	150.00	75.00	45.00
(75)	Bob Groom	55.00	27.00	16.50
(76)	Bob Harmon	55.00	27.00	16.50
(77)	Grover Hartley	55.00	27.00	16.50
(78)	Arnold Hauser	55.00	27.00	16.50
(79)	Buck Herzog	55.00	27.00	16.50
(80)	Dick Hoblitzell	55.00	27.00	16.50
(81)	Solly Hoffman (Hofman)	55.00	27.00	16.50
(82)	Miller Huggins	150.00	75.00	45.00
(83)	Long Tom Hughes	55.00	27.00	16.50
(84)	John Hummel	55.00	27.00	16.50
(85)	Hughie Jennings	150.00	75.00	45.00
(86)	Walter Johnson	400.00	200.00	120.00
(87)	Davy Jones	55.00	27.00	16.50
(88)	Johnny Kling	55.00	27.00	16.50
(89)	Otto Knabe	55.00	27.00	16.50
(90)	Jack Knight	55.00	27.00	16.50
(91)	Ed Konetchy	55.00	27.00	16.50
(92)	Harry Krause	55.00	27.00	16.50
(93)	Nap Lajoie	150.00	75.00	45.00
(94)	Joe Lake	55.00	27.00	16.50
(95)	Frank LaPorte	55.00	27.00	16.50
(96)	Tommy Leach	55.00	27.00	16.50
(97)	Lefty Leifield	55.00	27.00	16.50
(98)	Ed Lennox	55.00	27.00	16.50
(99)	Paddy Livingston	55.00	27.00	16.50
(100)	Hans Lobert	55.00	27.00	16.50
(101)	Harry Lord	55.00	27.00	16.50
(102)	Fred Luderas (Luderus)	55.00	27.00	16.50
(103)	Sherry Magee	55.00	27.00	16.50
(104)	Rube Marquard	150.00	75.00	45.00
(105)	Christy Mathewson	450.00	225.00	135.00
(106)	Al Mattern	55.00	27.00	16.50
(107)	George McBride	55.00	27.00	16.50
(108)	Amby McConnell	55.00	27.00	16.50
(109)	John McGraw	150.00	75.00	45.00
(110)	Harry McIntire (McIntyre)	55.00	27.00	16.50
(111)	Matty McIntyre	55.00	27.00	16.50
(112)	Larry McLean	55.00	27.00	16.50
(113)	Fred Merkle	55.00	27.00	16.50
(114)	Chief Meyers	55.00	27.00	16.50
(115)	Clyde Milan	55.00	27.00	16.50
(116)	Dots Miller	55.00	27.00	16.50
(117)	Mike Mitchell	55.00	27.00	16.50
(118)	Earl Moore	55.00	27.00	16.50
(119)	Pat Moran	55.00	27.00	16.50
(120)	George Moriarty	55.00	27.00	16.50
(121)	Mike Mowrey	55.00	27.00	16.50
(122)	George Mullin	55.00	27.00	16.50
(123)	Danny Murphy	55.00	27.00	16.50
(124)	Red Murray	55.00	27.00	16.50
(125)	Tom Needham	55.00	27.00	16.50
(126)	Rebel Oakes	55.00	27.00	16.50

(127)	Rube Oldring	55.00	27.00	16.50
(128)	Marty O'Toole	55.00	27.00	16.50
(129)	Fred Parent	55.00	27.00	16.50
(130)	Dode Paskert	55.00	27.00	16.50
(131)	Barney Pelty	55.00	27.00	16.50
(132)	Eddie Phelps	55.00	27.00	16.50
(133)	Jack Powell	55.00	27.00	16.50
(134)	Jack Quinn	55.00	27.00	16.50
(135)	Ed Reulbach	55.00	27.00	16.50
(136)	Lew Richie	55.00	27.00	16.50
(137)	Reggie Richter	55.00	27.00	16.50
(138)	Jack Rowan	55.00	27.00	16.50
(139)	Nap Rucker	55.00	27.00	16.50
(140)	Slim Sallee	55.00	27.00	16.50
(141)	Doc Scanlan	55.00	27.00	16.50
(142)	Germany Schaefer	55.00	27.00	16.50
(143)	Boss Schmidt	55.00	27.00	16.50
(144)	Wildfire Schulte	55.00	27.00	16.50
(145)	Jim Scott	55.00	27.00	16.50
(146)	Tillie Shafer	55.00	27.00	16.50
(147)	Dave Shean	55.00	27.00	16.50
(148)	Jimmy Sheckard	55.00	27.00	16.50
(149)	Mike Simon	55.00	27.00	16.50
(150)	Fred Snodgrass	55.00	27.00	16.50
(151)	Tris Speaker	200.00	100.00	60.00
(152)	Oscar Stanage	55.00	27.00	16.50
(153)	Bill Steele	55.00	27.00	16.50
(154)	Harry Stovall	55.00	27.00	16.50
(155)	Gabby Street	55.00	27.00	16.50
(156)	George Suggs	55.00	27.00	16.50
(157)	Billy Sullivan	55.00	27.00	16.50
(158)	Bill Sweeney	55.00	27.00	16.50
(159)	Jeff Sweeney	55.00	27.00	16.50
(160)	Lee Tannehill	55.00	27.00	16.50
(161)	Ira Thomas	55.00	27.00	16.50
(162)	Joe Tinker	150.00	75.00	45.00
(163)	John Titus	55.00	27.00	16.50
(164)	Fred Toney	55.00	27.00	16.50
(165)	Terry Turner	55.00	27.00	16.50
(166)	Hippo Vaughn	55.00	27.00	16.50
(167)	Heinie Wagner	55.00	27.00	16.50
(168)	Bobby Wallace	150.00	75.00	45.00
(169)	Ed Walsh	150.00	75.00	45.00
(170)	Jack Warhop	55.00	27.00	16.50
(171)	Zach Wheat	150.00	75.00	45.00
(172)	Doc White	55.00	27.00	16.50
(173)	Ed Willett	55.00	27.00	16.50
(174)	Art Wilson (New York)	55.00	27.00	16.50
(175)	Owen Wilson (Pittsburgh)	55.00	27.00	16.50
(176)	Hooks Wiltse	55.00	27.00	16.50
(177)	Harry Wolter	55.00	27.00	16.50
(178)	Harry Wolverton	55.00	27.00	16.50
(179)	Cy Young	600.00	300.00	180.00
(180)	Irv Young	55.00	27.00	16.50

1910 Hermes Ice Cream Pirates Pins

The World's Champion Pittsburgh Pirates are featured on this colorful set of 1-1/4" pins. Sepia player portraits at center have a yellow border aound with a blue banner at bottom and a skull and crossbones. The players are not identified on the buttons, making them difficult to collect.

		NM	EX	VG
Complete Set (12):		3000.	1500.	900.00
Common Player:		450.00	225.00	135.00
(1)	Bill Abstein	450.00	225.00	135.00
(2)	Red Adams	450.00	225.00	135.00
(3)	Bobby Byrne	450.00	225.00	135.00
(4)	Howie Camnitz	450.00	225.00	135.00
(5)	Fred Clarke	450.00	225.00	135.00
(6)	George Gibson	450.00	225.00	135.00
(7)	Tommy Leach	450.00	225.00	135.00
(8)	Sam Leever	450.00	225.00	135.00
(9)	Dots Miller	450.00	225.00	135.00
(10)	Mike Simon	450.00	225.00	135.00
(11)	Honus Wagner	600.00	300.00	180.00
(12)	Owen Wilson	450.00	225.00	135.00

1916 Herpolsheimer Co.

Advertising for a Michigan clothier is all that differentiates these cards from the more common Sporting News version and those of other regional advertisers. The cards are black-and-white, front and back, in 2" x 3-1/2" format. Though much scarcer than the Sporting News version, the Herpolsheimer cards command only a small premium from type-card and superstar collectors.

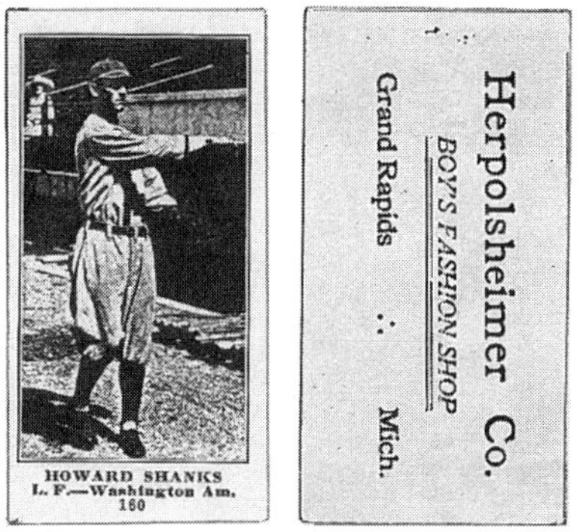

(See 1916 Sporting News for checklist and price guide.)

1888 S.F. Hess (N338-2)

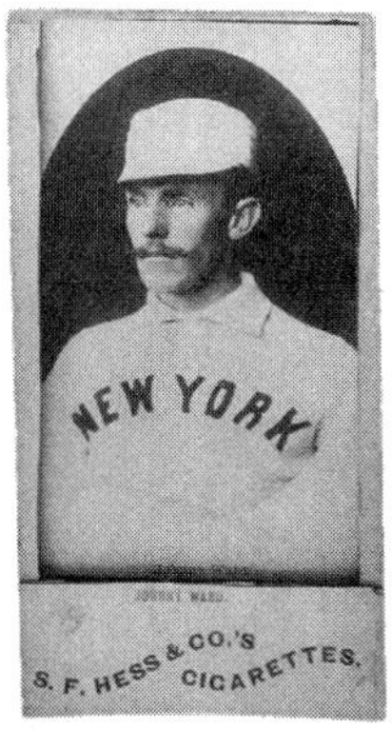

The most popular of the S.F. Hess & Co. issues, this 21-card set was issued in 1889 and pictures 16 players from the New York Giants, two New York Mets players, two from St. Louis and one from Detroit. The cards measure 2-3/4" x 1-1/2" and feature sepia-toned photographs, most of which are enclosed in ovals with a dark background. The player's name is printed in capital letters just beneath the photo, and the S.F. Hess & Co. logo appears at the bottom (without using the Creole Cigarette brand name).

		NM	EX	VG
Complete Set (23):		65000.	30000.	18000.
Common Player:		3200.	1600.	960.00
(1)	Bill Brown	3200.	1600.	960.00
(2)	Roger Conner (Connor)	4000.	2000.	1200.
(3)	Ed Crane	3200.	1600.	960.00
(4)	Buck Ewing	4000.	2000.	1200.
(5)	Elmer Foster	3200.	1600.	960.00
(6)	Wm. George	3200.	1600.	960.00
(7)	Joe Gerhardt	3200.	1600.	960.00
(8)	Chas. Getzein (Getzien)	3200.	1600.	960.00
(9)	Geo. Gore	3200.	1600.	960.00
(10)	Gil Hatfield	3200.	1600.	960.00
(11)	Tim Keefe	4000.	2000.	1200.
(12)	Arlie Latham	3200.	1600.	960.00
(13)	Pat Murphy	3200.	1600.	960.00
(14)	Jim Mutrie	3200.	1600.	960.00
(15)	Dave Orr	3200.	1600.	960.00
(16)	Danny Richardson	3200.	1600.	960.00
(17)	Mike Slattery	3200.	1600.	960.00
(18)	Silent Mike Tiernan	3200.	1600.	960.00
(19)	Lidell Titcomb	3200.	1600.	960.00
(20)	Johnny Ward	4000.	2000.	1200.
(21)	Curt Welch	3200.	1600.	960.00
(22)	Mickey Welch	4000.	2000.	1200.
(23)	Arthur Whitney	3200.	1600.	960.00

1909-11 Hindu Cigarettes

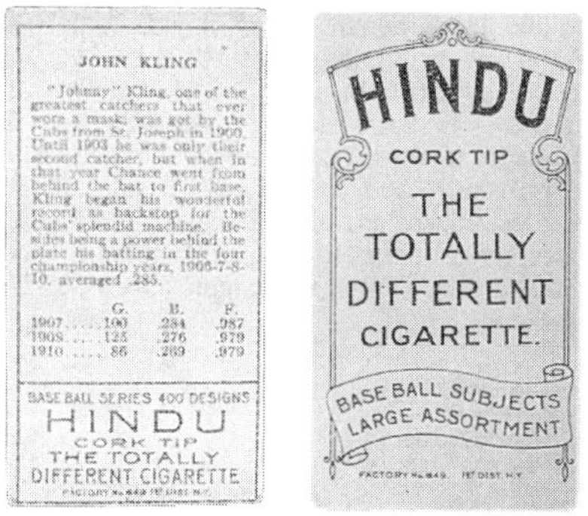

(See T205, T206. Premium: T205 - 3-4X, T206 - 1.25-2X)

1958 Hires Root Beer Test Set

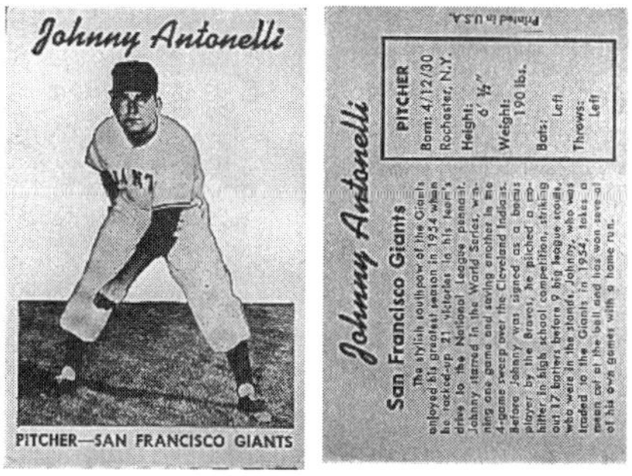

Among the scarcest of the regional issues of the late 1950s is the eight-card test issue which preceded the Hires Root Beer set of 66 cards. The test cards differ from the regular issue in that they have sepia-toned, rather than color pictures, which are set against plain yellow or orange backgrounds (much like the 1958 Topps), instead of viewed through a knothole. Like the regular Hires cards, the 2-5/16" x 3-1/2" cards were issued with an attached wedge-shaped tab of like size. The tab offered membership in Hires baseball fan club, and served to hold the card into the carton of bottled root beer with which it was given away. Values quoted here are for cards with tabs. Cards without tabs would be valued approximately 50 per cent lower.

		NM	EX	VG
Complete Set (8):		2700.	1300.	800.00
Common Player:		250.00	125.00	75.00
(1)	Johnny Antonelli	275.00	137.00	82.00
(2)	Jim Busby	250.00	125.00	75.00
(3)	Chico Fernandez	250.00	125.00	75.00
(4)	Bob Friend	250.00	125.00	75.00
(5)	Vern Law	275.00	137.00	82.00
(6)	Stan Lopata	250.00	125.00	75.00
(7)	Willie Mays	1000.	500.00	300.00
(8)	Al Pilarcik	250.00	125.00	75.00

1958 Hires Root Beer

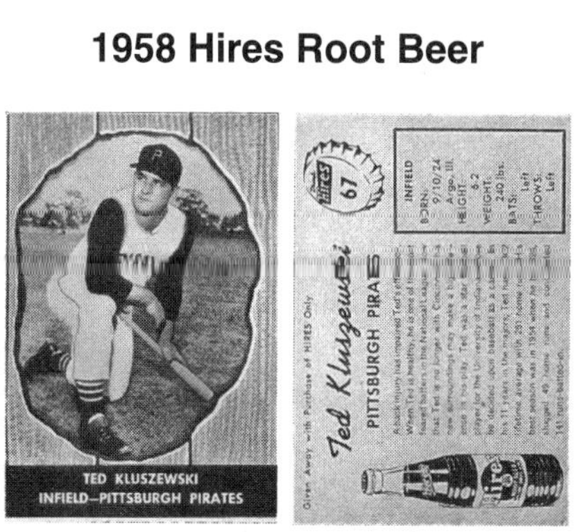

Like most baseball cards issued with a tab in the 1950s, the Hires cards are extremely scarce today in their original form. The basic card was attached to a wedge-shaped tab that served the dual purpose of offering a fan club membership and of holding the card into the cardboard carton of soda bottles with which it was distributed. Measurements of the card vary somewhat, from about 2-3/8" to 2-5/8" wide and 3-3/8" to 3-5/8" tall (without tab). The tab extends for another 3-1/2". Numbering of the Hires set begins at 10 and goes through 76, with card #69 never issued, making a set complete at 66 cards. Values given below are for cards with tabs. Cards without tabs would be valued approximately 50 percent lower.

		NM	EX	VG
Complete Set (66):		2975.	1485.	890.00
Common Player:		37.50	18.50	11.00
10	Richie Ashburn	135.00	67.00	40.00
11	Chico Carrasquel	37.50	18.50	11.00
12	Dave Philley	37.50	18.50	11.00
13	Don Newcombe	40.00	20.00	12.00
14	Wally Post	37.50	18.50	11.00
15	Rip Repulski	37.50	18.50	11.00
16	Chico Fernandez	37.50	18.50	11.00
17	Larry Doby	65.00	32.00	19.50
18	Hector Brown	37.50	18.50	11.00
19	Danny O'Connell	37.50	18.50	11.00
20	Granny Hamner	37.50	18.50	11.00
21	Dick Groat	37.50	18.50	11.00
22	Ray Narleski	37.50	18.50	11.00
23	Pee Wee Reese	100.00	50.00	30.00
24	Bob Friend	37.50	18.50	11.00
25	Willie Mays	260.00	130.00	78.00
26	Bob Nieman	37.50	18.50	11.00
27	Frank Thomas	37.50	18.50	11.00
28	Curt Simmons	37.50	18.50	11.00
29	Stan Lopata	37.50	18.50	11.00
30	Bob Skinner	37.50	18.50	11.00
31	Ron Kline	37.50	18.50	11.00
32	Willie Miranda	37.50	18.50	11.00
33	Bob Avila	37.50	18.50	11.00
34	Clem Labine	40.00	20.00	12.00
35	Ray Jablonski	37.50	18.50	11.00
36	Bill Mazeroski	50.00	25.00	15.00
37	Billy Gardner	37.50	18.50	11.00
38	Pete Runnels	37.50	18.50	11.00
39	Jack Sanford	37.50	18.50	11.00
40	Dave Sisler	37.50	18.50	11.00
41	Don Zimmer	40.00	20.00	12.00
42	Johnny Podres	40.00	20.00	12.00
43	Dick Farrell	37.50	18.50	11.00
44	Hank Aaron	260.00	130.00	78.00
45	Bill Virdon	37.50	18.50	11.00
46	Bobby Thomson	40.00	20.00	12.00
47	Willard Nixon	37.50	18.50	11.00
48	Billy Loes	37.50	18.50	11.00
49	Hank Sauer	37.50	18.50	11.00
50	Johnny Antonelli	37.50	18.50	11.00
51	Daryl Spencer	37.50	18.50	11.00
52	Ken Lehman	37.50	18.50	11.00
53	Sammy White	37.50	18.50	11.00
54	Charley Neal	37.50	18.50	11.00
55	Don Drysdale	90.00	45.00	27.00
56	Jack Jensen	37.50	18.50	11.00
57	Ray Katt	37.50	18.50	11.00
58	Franklin Sullivan	37.50	18.50	11.00
59	Roy Face	37.50	18.50	11.00
60	Willie Jones	37.50	18.50	11.00
61	Duke Snider (SP)	150.00	75.00	45.00
62	Whitey Lockman	37.50	18.50	11.00
63	Gino Cimoli	37.50	18.50	11.00
64	Marv Grissom	37.50	18.50	11.00
65	Gene Baker	37.50	18.50	11.00
66	George Zuverink	37.50	18.50	11.00
67	Ted Kluszewski	50.00	25.00	15.00
68	Jim Busby	37.50	18.50	11.00
69	Not issued			
70	Curt Barclay	37.50	18.50	11.00
71	Hank Foiles	37.50	18.50	11.00
72	Gene Stephens	37.50	18.50	11.00
73	Al Worthington	37.50	18.50	11.00
74	Al Walker	37.50	18.50	11.00
75	Bob Boyd	37.50	18.50	11.00
76	Al Pilarcik	37.50	18.50	11.00

1951-52 Hit Parade of Champions

(See 1951-52 Berk Ross)

1977 Holiday Inn Discs

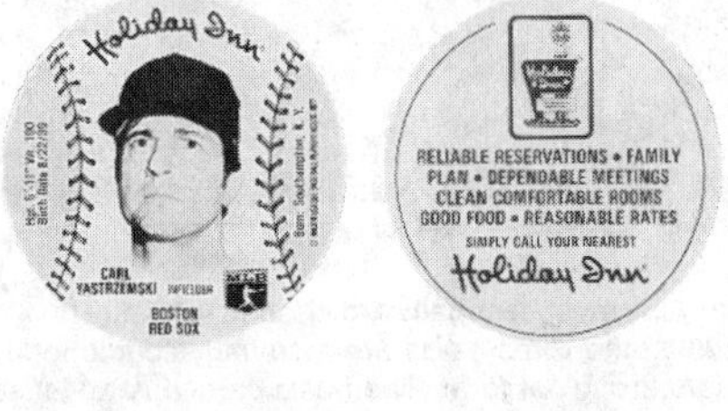

Virtually identical in format to the several locally sponsored disc sets of the previous year, these 3-3/8" diameter player discs were given away five at a time with the purchase of a children's dinner at some 72 participating Holiday Inns in the Midwest. Discs once again feature black-and-white player portrait photos in the center of a baseball design. The left and right panels are in one of several bright colors. Licensed by the players' association through Mike Schechter Associates, the player photos carry no uniform logos. Backs are printed in green. The unnumbered discs are checklisted here alphabetically.

		NM	EX	VG
Complete Set (70):		175.00	87.00	52.00
Common Player:		2.00	1.00	.60
(1)	Sal Bando	2.00	1.00	.60
(2)	Buddy Bell	2.00	1.00	.60
(3)	Johnny Bench	10.00	5.00	3.00
(4)	Larry Bowa	2.00	1.00	.60
(5)	Steve Braun	2.00	1.00	.60
(6)	George Brett	15.00	7.50	4.50
(7)	Lou Brock	7.50	3.75	2.25
(8)	Jeff Burroughs	2.00	1.00	.60
(9)	Bert Campaneris	2.00	1.00	.60
(10)	John Candelaria	2.00	1.00	.60
(11)	Jose Cardenal	2.00	1.00	.60
(12)	Rod Carew	8.00	4.00	2.50
(13)	Steve Carlton	8.00	4.00	2.50
(14)	Dave Cash	2.00	1.00	.60
(15)	Cesar Cedeno	2.00	1.00	.60
(16)	Ron Cey	2.00	1.00	.60
(17)	Dave Concepcion	2.00	1.00	.60
(18)	Dennis Eckersley	5.00	2.50	1.50
(19)	Mark Fidrych	6.00	3.00	1.75
(20)	Rollie Fingers	7.50	3.75	2.25
(21)	Carlton Fisk	8.00	4.00	2.50
(22)	George Foster	2.00	1.00	.60
(23)	Wayne Garland	2.00	1.00	.60
(24)	Ralph Garr	2.00	1.00	.60
(25)	Steve Garvey	6.00	3.00	1.75
(26)	Cesar Geronimo	2.00	1.00	.60
(27)	Bobby Grich	2.00	1.00	.60
(28)	Ken Griffey Sr.	3.00	1.50	.90
(29)	Don Gullett	2.00	1.00	.60
(30)	Mike Hargrove	2.00	1.00	.60
(31)	Willie Horton	2.00	1.00	.60
(32)	Al Hrabosky	2.00	1.00	.60
(33)	Reggie Jackson	11.00	5.50	3.25
(34)	Randy Jones	2.00	1.00	.60
(35a)	Dave Kingman (Mets)	3.00	1.50	.90
(35b)	Dave Kingman (Padres)	4.50	2.25	1.25
(36)	Jerry Koosman	2.00	1.00	.60
(37)	Dave LaRoche	2.00	1.00	.60
(38)	Greg Luzinski	2.00	1.00	.60
(39)	Fred Lynn	2.00	1.00	.60
(40)	Bill Madlock	2.00	1.00	.60
(41)	Rick Manning	2.00	1.00	.60
(42)	Jon Matlock	2.00	1.00	.60
(43)	John Mayberry	2.00	1.00	.60
(44)	Hal McRae	2.00	1.00	.60
(45)	Andy Messersmith	2.00	1.00	.60
(46)	Rick Monday	2.00	1.00	.60
(47)	John Montefusco	2.00	1.00	.60
(48)	Joe Morgan	7.50	3.75	2.25
(49)	Thurman Munson	8.00	4.00	2.50
(50)	Bobby Murcer	2.00	1.00	.60
(51)	Bill North	2.00	1.00	.60
(52)	Jim Palmer	7.50	3.75	2.25
(53)	Tony Perez	8.00	4.00	2.50
(54)	Jerry Reuss	2.00	1.00	.60
(55)	Pete Rose	24.00	12.00	7.25
(56)	Joe Rudi	2.00	1.00	.60
(57)	Nolan Ryan	30.00	15.00	9.00
(58)	Manny Sanguillen	2.00	1.00	.60
(59)	Mike Schmidt	12.00	6.00	3.50
(60)	Tom Seaver	10.00	5.00	3.00
(61)	Bill Singer	2.00	1.00	.60
(62)	Willie Stargell	7.50	3.75	2.25
(63)	Rusty Staub	3.00	1.50	.90
(64)	Luis Tiant	2.00	1.00	.60
(65)	Mike Tyson	2.00	1.00	.60
(66)	Bob Watson	2.00	1.00	.60
(67)	Butch Wynegar	2.00	1.00	.60
(68)	Carl Yastrzemski	10.00	5.00	3.00
(69)	Robin Yount	10.00	5.00	3.00
(70)	Richie Zisk	2.00	1.00	.60

1926 Holland World's Champions Washington Senators

The World's Champion Washington Senators were featured on a set issued in Winnipeg, Manitoba, of all places. The 1-1/2" x 3" cards have player portrait photos printed in blue on front. The black-printed back has a card number and details of a redemption offer of cards for ice cream. Like many such offers it appears as if card #16 was intentionally withheld or minimally distributed, making it very scarce today.

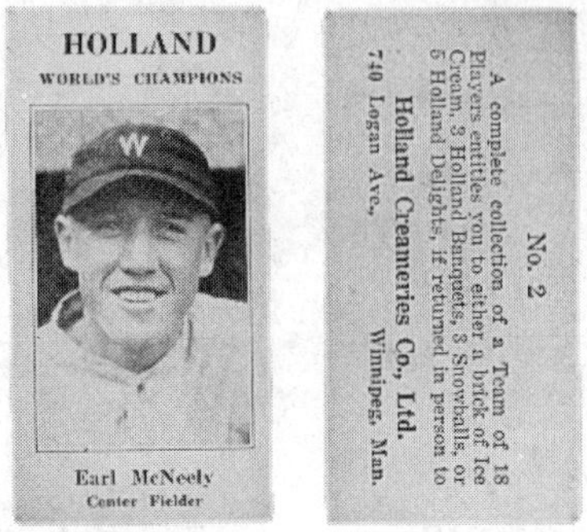

		NM	EX	VG
Complete Set, No #16 (17):		3800.	1900.	1140.
Common Player:		200.00	100.00	60.00
1	Ralph Miller	200.00	100.00	60.00
2	Earl McNeely	200.00	100.00	60.00
3	Allan Russell	200.00	100.00	60.00
4	Ernest Shirley	200.00	100.00	60.00
5	Sam Rice	300.00	150.00	90.00
6	Muddy Ruel	200.00	100.00	60.00
7	Ossie Bluege	200.00	100.00	60.00
8	Nemo Leibold	200.00	100.00	60.00
9	Paul Zahniser	200.00	100.00	60.00
10	Firpo Marberry	200.00	100.00	60.00
11	Warren Ogden	200.00	100.00	60.00
12	George Mogridge	200.00	100.00	60.00
13	Tom Zachary	200.00	100.00	60.00
14	Joe Judge	200.00	100.00	60.00
15	Goose Goslin	300.00	150.00	90.00
16	Roger Peckinpaugh	2500.	1250.	750.00
17	Bucky Harris	300.00	150.00	90.00
18	Walter Johnson	600.00	300.00	180.00

1921 Holsum Bread

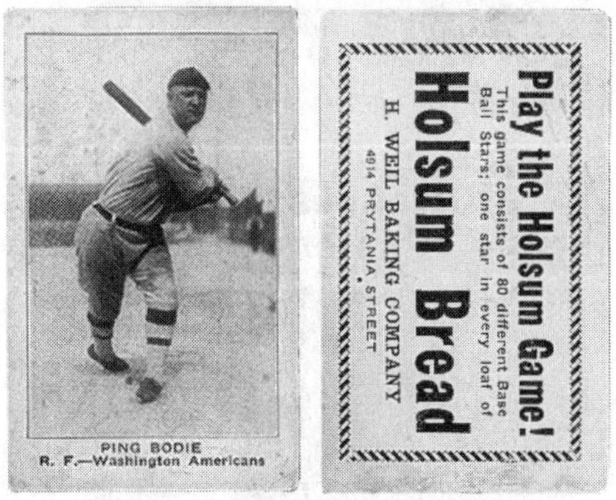

Issued by the Weil Baking Co., of New Orleans, which produced several sets in the 1910s, this issue is a variation of the 1921 American Caramel Series of 80 (E121), differing only in the advertising on the back. The 2-1/16" x 3-3/8" black-and-white cards are much scarcer than the candy company version, but do not bring too great a premium.

(See 1921 American Caramel Series of 80 for checklist; Holsum cards valued at 1.5X-2X.)

1959 Home Run Derby

This 20-card unnumbered set was produced by American Motors to publicize the Home Run Derby television program. The cards measure approximately 3-1/4" x 5-1/4" and feature black and white player photos on black-backed white stock. The player name and team are printed beneath the photo. This set was reprinted (and marked as such) in 1988 by Card Collectors' Company of New York. An advertising poster in sometimes seen which is essentially an uncut sheet of the cards with a promotional message at bottom.

		NM	EX	VG
Complete Set (20):		4500.	2250.	1350.
Common Player:		100.00	50.00	30.00
Advertising Poster:		2000.	1000.	600.00
(1)	Hank Aaron	465.00	232.00	139.00
(2)	Bob Allison	100.00	50.00	30.00
(3)	Ernie Banks	300.00	150.00	90.00
(4)	Ken Boyer	150.00	75.00	45.00
(5)	Bob Cerv	100.00	50.00	30.00
(6)	Rocky Colavito	235.00	117.00	70.00
(7)	Gil Hodges	250.00	125.00	75.00
(8)	Jackie Jensen	150.00	75.00	45.00
(9)	Al Kaline	300.00	150.00	90.00
(10)	Harmon Killebrew	290.00	145.00	87.00
(11)	Jim Lemon	100.00	50.00	30.00
(12)	Mickey Mantle	1200.	600.00	360.00
(13)	Ed Mathews	275.00	137.00	82.00
(14)	Willie Mays	465.00	232.00	139.00
(15)	Wally Post	100.00	50.00	30.00
(16)	Frank Robinson	275.00	137.00	82.00
(17)	Mark Scott (host)	150.00	75.00	45.00
(18)	Duke Snider	400.00	200.00	120.00
(19)	Dick Stuart	100.00	50.00	30.00
(20)	Gus Triandos	100.00	50.00	30.00

1947 Homogenized Bond Bread

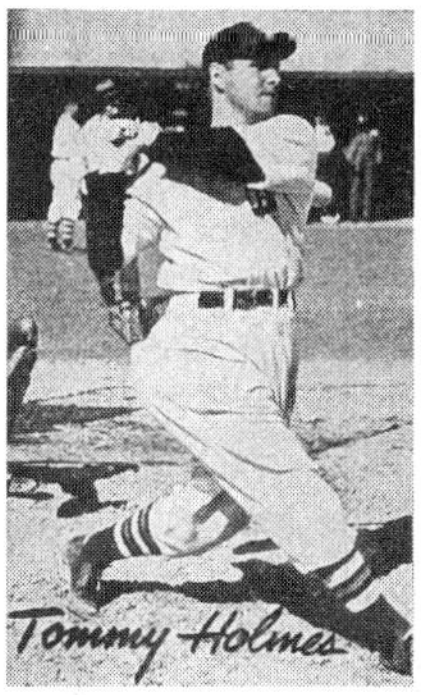

Issued by Homogenized Bond Bread in 1947, this set consists of 48 unnumbered black and white cards, each measuring 2-1/4" x 3-1/2". Of the 48 cards, 44 are baseball players; four picture boxers. The cards are usually found with rounded corners, although cards with square corners are also known to exist. The set contains both portrait and action photos, and features the player's facsimile autograph on front. In the 1980s a large quantity of half the cards in the set was uncovered in New York, creating a great disparity of supply between the 22 cards found in the hoard and the rest of the set. Current pricing reflects that fact. Scarcer cards are indicated in the checklist below with an "SP".

		NM	EX	VG
Complete Set (44):		1100.	550.00	325.00
Common Player:		6.00	3.00	1.75
(1)	Rex Barney (SP)	15.00	7.50	4.50
(2)	Yogi Berra (SP)	75.00	37.00	22.00
(3)	Ewell Blackwell	6.00	3.00	1.75
(4)	Lou Boudreau	9.00	4.50	2.75
(5)	Ralph Branca (SP)	15.00	7.50	4.50
(6)	Harry Brecheen	6.00	3.00	1.75
(7)	Dom DiMaggio (SP)	45.00	22.00	13.50
(8)	Joe DiMaggio (SP)	300.00	150.00	90.00
(9)	Bobbie Doerr (Bobby)	9.00	4.50	2.75
(10)	Bruce Edwards (SP)	15.00	7.50	4.50
(11)	Bob Elliott	6.00	3.00	1.75
(12)	Del Ennis	6.00	3.00	1.75
(13)	Bob Feller	13.50	6.75	4.00
(14)	Carl Furillo (SP)	35.00	17.50	10.50
(15)	Cid Gordon (Sid) (SP)	13.50	6.75	4.00
(16)	Joe Gordon	6.00	3.00	1.75
(17)	Joe Hatten (SP)	13.50	6.75	4.00
(18)	Gil Hodges (SP)	45.00	22.00	13.50
(19)	Tommy Holmes	6.00	3.00	1.75
(20)	Larry Janson (Jansen) (SP)	13.50	6.75	4.00
(21)	Sheldon Jones (SP)	13.50	6.75	4.00
(22)	Edwin Joost (SP)	13.50	6.75	4.00
(23)	Charlie Keller (SP)	17.50	8.75	5.25
(24)	Ken Keltner	6.00	3.00	1.75
(25)	Buddy Kerr (SP)	13.50	6.75	4.00
(26)	Ralph Kiner	11.00	5.50	3.25
(27)	John Lindell (SP)	13.50	6.75	4.00
(28)	Whitey Lockman (SP)	13.50	6.75	4.00
(29)	Willard Marshall (SP)	13.50	6.75	4.00
(30)	Johnny Mize	11.00	5.50	3.25
(31)	Stan Musial	70.00	35.00	21.00
(32)	Andy Pafko	6.00	3.00	1.75
(33)	Johnny Pesky	6.00	3.00	1.75
(34)	Pee Wee Reese (SP)	135.00	67.00	40.00
(35)	Phil Rizzuto	22.00	11.00	6.50
(36)	Aaron Robinson	6.00	3.00	1.75
(37)	Jackie Robinson	110.00	55.00	33.00
(38)	John Sain	7.00	3.50	2.00
(39)	Enos Slaughter	9.00	4.50	2.75
(40)	Vern Stephens	6.00	3.00	1.75
(41)	George Tebbetts (SP)	13.50	6.75	4.00
(42)	Bob Thomson (SP)	17.50	8.75	5.25
(43)	Johnny Vandermeer (VanderMeer) (SP)	18.00	9.00	5.50
(44)	Ted Williams	75.00	37.00	22.00

1947 Homogenized Bond Bread Jackie Robinson

The modern major leagues' first black player is featured in this set issued by Bond Bread in 1947. The cards, measuring 2-1/4" x 3-1/2", are black-and-white photos of Robinson in various action and portrait poses. The unnumbered cards bear three different backs advertising Bond Bread. Four cards use a horizontal format. Card #6 was issued in greater quantities and perhaps was a promotional card; its back is the only one containing a short biography of Robinson.

		NM	EX	VG
Complete Set (13):		6800.	3400.	2000.
Common Card:		400.00	200.00	120.00
(1)	(Jackie Robinson) (awaiting pitch)	595.00	300.00	175.00
(2)	(Jackie Robinson) (Batting followthrough, white shirtsleeves)	595.00	300.00	175.00
(3)	(Jackie Robinson) (Batting followthrough, no shirtsleeves)	595.00	300.00	175.00
(4)	(Jackie Robinson) (Leaping, scoreboard in background)	595.00	300.00	175.00
(5)	(Jackie Robinson) (Leaping, no scoreboard)	595.00	300.00	175.00
(6)	(Jackie Robinson) (Portrait, facsimile autograph)	400.00	200.00	120.00
(7)	(Jackie Robinson) (Portrait, holding glove in air)	595.00	300.00	175.00
(8)	(Jackie Robinson) (Running down baseline)	595.00	300.00	175.00
(9)	(Jackie Robinson) (Running to catch ball)	595.00	300.00	175.00
(10)	(Jackie Robinson) (Sliding)	595.00	300.00	175.00
(11)	(Jackie Robinson) (Stretching for throw, ball in glove)	595.00	300.00	175.00
(12)	(Jackie Robinson) (Stretching for throw, no ball visible)	595.00	300.00	175.00
(13)	(Jackie Robinson) (Throwing)	595.00	300.00	175.00

1893 Honest (Duke) Cabinets (N142)

These color cabinet cards, which measure 6" x 9-1/2", were produced by W.H. Duke between 1891 and 1893. The player name is centered at the bottom of the card front. The brand name "Honest" is located in the lower-left corner with the words "New York" in the lower-right corner. Three cyclists are also part of the set.

		NM	EX	VG
Complete Set (4):		40000.	20000.	12000.
Common Player:		10000.	5000.	3000.
(1)	G.S. Davis	10000.	5000.	3000.
(2)	E.J. Delahanty	12000.	6000.	3600.
(3)	W.M. Nash	10000.	5000.	3000.
(4)	W. Robinson	15000.	7500.	4500.

1911-12 Honest Long Cut Tobacco

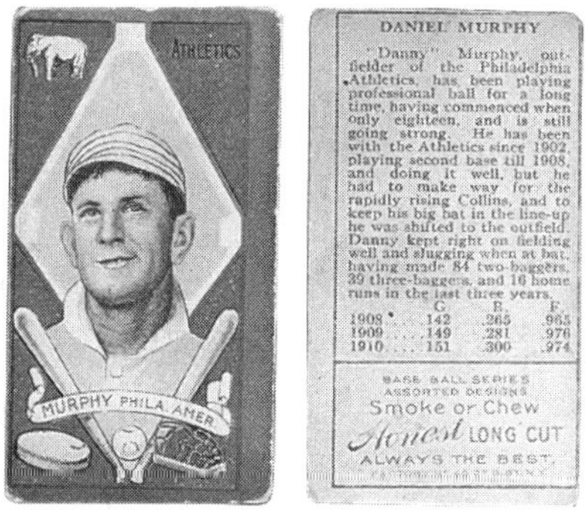

(See T207, T227 for checklists. Premium: T207 - +30%.)

1927 Honey Boy

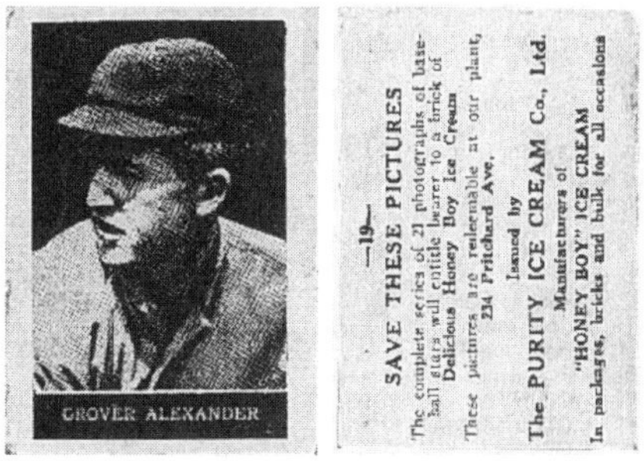

The date of issue for this rare Canadian issue is conjectural, as, apparently, are previously published checklists. What is known is that these black-and-white 1-5/8" x 2-3/8" cards were issued by an ice cream company and were redeemable as a set of 21 for a brick of "Delicious Honey Boy Ice Cream". Besides the major leaguers in the set, there are also cards of other players, perhaps local semi-pros.

		NM	EX	VG
Common (Major League) Player:		250.00	125.00	75.00
15	Harry Heilmann	350.00	175.00	105.00
16	Heinie Groh	250.00	125.00	75.00
18	Grover Alexander	350.00	175.00	105.00
19	Dave Bancroft	350.00	175.00	105.00
21	George Burns	250.00	125.00	75.00

1975 Hostess

The first of what would become five annual issues, the 1975 Hostess set consists of 50 three-card panels which formed the bottom of boxes of family-size snack cake products. Unlike many similar issues, the Hostess cards do not share common borders, so it was possible to cut them neatly and evenly from the box. Well-cut single cards measure 2-1/4" x 3-1/4", while a three-card panel measures 7-1/4" x 3-1/4". Because some of the panels were issued on packages of less popular snack cakes, they are somewhat scarcer today. Since the hobby was quite well-developed when the Hostess cards were first issued, there is no lack of complete panels. Even unused complete boxes are available today. Some of the photos in this issue also appear on Topps cards of the era.

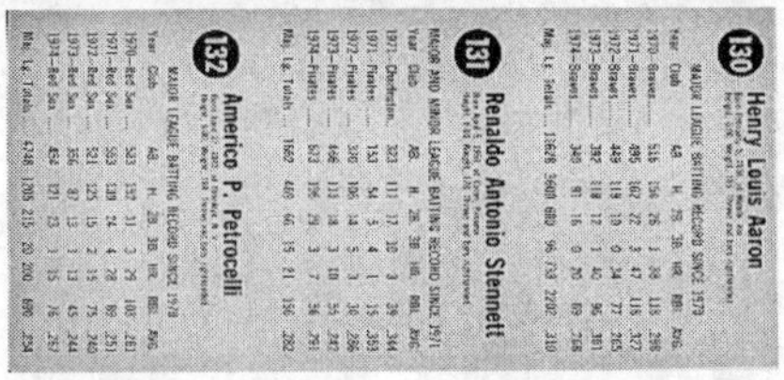

		NM	EX	VG
Complete Panel Set (50):		250.00	125.00	75.00
Complete Singles Set (150):		185.00	90.00	55.00
Common Panel:		3.50	1.75	1.00
Common Single Player:		.50	.25	.15
Panel 1		3.50	1.75	1.00
1	Bobby Tolan	.50	.25	.15
2	Cookie Rojas	.50	.25	.15
3	Darrell Evans	.65	.35	.20
Panel 2		7.50	3.75	2.25
4	Sal Bando	.50	.25	.15
5	Joe Morgan	2.00	1.00	.60
6	Mickey Lolich	.75	.40	.25
Panel 3		5.75	2.75	1.75
7	Don Sutton	1.50	.70	.45
8	Bill Melton	.50	.25	.15
9	Tim Foli	.50	.25	.15
Panel 4		5.75	2.75	1.75
10	Joe Lahoud	.50	.25	.15
11a	Bert Hooten (incorrect spelling)	1.50	.70	.45
11b	Burt Hooton (correct spelling)	1.50	.70	.45
12	Paul Blair	.50	.25	.15
Panel 5		3.50	1.75	1.00
13	Jim Barr	.50	.25	.15
14	Toby Harrah	.50	.25	.15
15	John Milner	.50	.25	.15
Panel 6		3.50	1.75	1.00
16	Ken Holtzman	.50	.25	.15
17	Cesar Cedeno	.50	.25	.15
18	Dwight Evans	.50	.25	.15
Panel 7		10.00	5.00	3.00
19	Willie McCovey	3.00	1.50	.90
20	Tony Oliva	.75	.40	.25
21	Manny Sanguillen	.50	.25	.15
Panel 8		10.00	5.00	3.00
22	Mickey Rivers	.50	.25	.15
23	Lou Brock	3.00	1.50	.90
24	Craig Nettles	.50	.25	.15
Panel 9		4.00	2.00	1.25
25	Jimmy Wynn	.50	.25	.15
26	George Scott	.50	.25	.15
27	Greg Luzinski	.50	.25	.15
Panel 10		21.00	10.50	6.25
28	Bert Campaneris	.50	.25	.15
29	Pete Rose	8.00	4.00	2.50
30	Buddy Bell	.50	.25	.15
Panel 11		3.50	1.75	1.00
31	Gary Matthews	.50	.25	.15
32	Fred Patek	.50	.25	.15
33	Mike Lum	.50	.25	.15
Panel 12		3.50	1.75	1.00
34	Ellie Rodriguez	.50	.25	.15
35	Milt May	.50	.25	.15
36	Willie Horton	.50	.25	.15
Panel 13		13.00	6.50	4.00
37	Dave Winfield	4.50	2.25	1.25
38	Tom Grieve	.50	.25	.15
39	Barry Foote	.50	.25	.15
Panel 14		3.50	1.75	1.00
40	Joe Rudi	.50	.25	.15
41	Bake McBride	.50	.25	.15
42	Mike Cuellar	.50	.25	.15
Panel 15		3.50	1.75	1.00
43	Garry Maddox	.50	.25	.15
44	Carlos May	.50	.25	.15
45	Bud Harrelson	.50	.25	.15
Panel 16		20.00	10.00	6.00
46	Dave Chalk	.50	.25	.15
47	Dave Concepcion	.50	.25	.15
48	Carl Yastrzemski	7.50	3.75	2.25
Panel 17		6.00	3.00	1.75
49	Steve Garvey	1.50	.70	.45
50	Amos Otis	.50	.25	.15
51	Rickey Reuschel	.50	.25	.15
Panel 18		7.00	3.50	2.00
52	Rollie Fingers	2.00	1.00	.60
53	Bob Watson	.50	.25	.15
54	John Ellis	.50	.25	.15
Panel 19		12.50	6.25	3.75
55	Bob Bailey	.50	.25	.15
56	Rod Carew	6.00	3.00	1.75
57	Richie Hebner	.50	.25	.15
Panel 20		26.00	13.00	7.75
58	Nolan Ryan	10.00	5.00	3.00
59	Reggie Smith	.50	.25	.15
60	Joe Coleman	.50	.25	.15
Panel 21		13.00	6.50	3.75
61	Ron Cey	.50	.25	.15
62	Darrell Porter	.50	.25	.15
63	Steve Carlton	6.00	3.00	1.75
Panel 22		3.50	1.75	1.00
64	Gene Tenace	.50	.25	.15
65	Jose Cardenal	.50	.25	.15
66	Bill Lee	.50	.25	.15
Panel 23		3.50	1.75	1.00
67	Dave Lopes	.50	.25	.15
68	Wilbur Wood	.50	.25	.15
69	Steve Renko	.50	.25	.15
Panel 24		4.00	2.00	1.25
70	Joe Torre	.85	.45	.25
71	Ted Sizemore	.50	.25	.15
72	Bobby Grich	.50	.25	.15
Panel 25		14.00	7.00	4.25
73	Chris Speier	.50	.25	.15
74	Bert Blyleven	.50	.25	.15
75	Tom Seaver	6.00	3.00	1.75
Panel 26		3.50	1.75	1.00
76	Nate Colbert	.50	.25	.15
77	Don Kessinger	.50	.25	.15
78	George Medich	.50	.25	.15
Panel 27		35.00	17.50	10.50
79	Andy Messersmith	.50	.25	.15
80	Robin Yount	15.00	7.50	4.50
81	Al Oliver	.60	.30	.20
Panel 28		22.00	11.00	6.50
82	Bill Singer	.50	.25	.15
83	Johnny Bench	7.50	3.75	2.25
84	Gaylord Perry	3.00	1.50	.90
Panel 29		4.00	2.00	1.25
85	Dave Kingman	.60	.30	.20
86	Ed Herrmann	.50	.25	.15
87	Ralph Garr	.50	.25	.15
Panel 30		22.00	11.00	6.50
88	Reggie Jackson	7.00	3.50	2.00
89a	Doug Radar (incorrect spelling)	2.00	1.00	.60
89b	Doug Rader (correct spelling)	2.00	1.00	.60
90	Elliott Maddox	.50	.25	.15
Panel 31		3.50	1.75	1.00
91	Bill Russell	.50	.25	.15
92	John Mayberry	.50	.25	.15
93	Dave Cash	.50	.25	.15
Panel 32		3.50	1.75	1.00
94	Jeff Burroughs	.50	.25	.15
95	Ted Simmons	.50	.25	.15
96	Joe Decker	.50	.25	.15
Panel 33		9.50	4.75	2.75
97	Bill Buckner	.60	.30	.20
98	Bobby Darwin	.50	.25	.15
99	Phil Niekro	2.00	1.00	.60
Panel 34		4.00	2.00	1.25
100	Mike Sundberg (Jim)	.50	.25	.15
101	Greg Gross	.50	.25	.15
102	Luis Tiant	.60	.30	.20
Panel 35		3.50	1.75	1.00
103	Glenn Beckert	.50	.25	.15
104	Hal McRae	.50	.25	.15
105	Mike Jorgensen	.50	.25	.15
Panel 36		3.50	1.75	1.00
106	Mike Hargrove	.50	.25	.15
107	Don Gullett	.50	.25	.15
108	Tito Fuentes	.50	.25	.15
Panel 37		4.00	2.00	1.25
109	John Grubb	.50	.25	.15
110	Jim Kaat	.90	.45	.25
111	Felix Millan	.50	.25	.15
Panel 38		3.50	1.75	1.00
112	Don Money	.50	.25	.15
113	Rick Monday	.50	.25	.15
114	Dick Bosman	.50	.25	.15
Panel 39		7.00	3.50	2.00
115	Roger Metzger	.50	.25	.15
116	Fergie Jenkins	2.00	1.00	.60
117	Dusty Baker	.50	.25	.15
Panel 40		11.00	5.50	3.25
118	Billy Champion	.50	.25	.15
119	Bob Gibson	4.00	2.00	1.25
120	Bill Freehan	.65	.35	.20
Panel 41		3.50	1.75	1.00
121	Cesar Geronimo	.50	.25	.15
122	Jorge Orta	.50	.25	.15
123	Cleon Jones	.50	.25	.15
Panel 42		12.00	6.00	3.50
124	Steve Busby	.50	.25	.15
125a	Bill Madlock (Pitcher)	2.00	1.00	.60
125b	Bill Madlock (Third Base)	2.00	1.00	.60
126	Jim Palmer	2.00	1.00	.60
Panel 43		6.00	3.00	1.75
127	Tony Perez	2.00	1.00	.60
128	Larry Hisle	.50	.25	.15
129	Rusty Staub	.60	.30	.20
Panel 44		25.00	12.50	7.50
130	Hank Aaron	11.00	5.50	3.25
131	Rennie Stennett	.50	.25	.15
132	Rico Petrocelli	.50	.25	.15
Panel 45		22.00	11.00	6.50
133	Mike Schmidt	7.00	3.50	2.00
134	Sparky Lyle	.50	.25	.15
135	Willie Stargell	2.50	1.25	.70
Panel 46		8.00	4.00	2.50
136	Ken Henderson	.50	.25	.15
137	Willie Montanez	.50	.25	.15
138	Thurman Munson	2.50	1.25	.70
Panel 47		3.50	1.75	1.00
139	Richie Zisk	.50	.25	.15
140	George Hendricks (Hendrick)	.50	.25	.15
141	Bobby Murcer	.50	.25	.15
Panel 48		14.00	7.00	4.25
142	Lee May	.50	.25	.15
143	Carlton Fisk	2.50	1.25	.70
144	Brooks Robinson	4.50	2.25	1.25
Panel 49		4.00	2.00	1.25
145	Bobby Bonds	.50	.25	.15
146	Gary Sutherland	.50	.25	.15
147	Oscar Gamble	.50	.25	.15
Panel 50		8.00	4.00	2.50
148	Catfish Hunter	2.50	1.25	.70
149	Tug McGraw	.50	.25	.15
150	Dave McNally	.50	.25	.15

1975 Hostess Twinkies

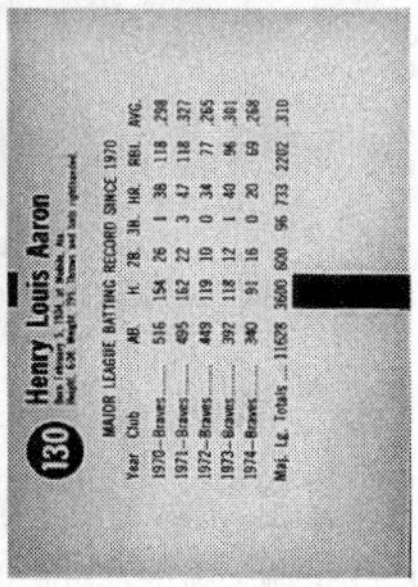

Believed to have been issued only in selected markets, and on a limited basis at that, the 1975 Hostess Twinkie set features 60 of the cards from the "regular" Hostess set of that year. The cards were issued one per pack with the popular snack cake. Cards #1-36 are a direct pick-up from the Hostess set, while the remaining 24 cards in the set were selected from the more popular names in the remainder of the Hostess issue - with an emphasis on West Coast players. Thus, after card #36, the '75 Twinkie cards are skip-numbered from 40-136. In identical 2-1/4" x 3-1/4" size, the Twinkie cards differ from the Hostess issue only in the presence of small black bars at top and bottom center of the back of the card.

		NM	EX	VG
Complete Set (60):		150.00	75.00	40.00
Common Player:		1.00	.50	.30
1	Bobby Tolan	1.00	.50	.30
2	Cookie Rojas	1.00	.50	.30
3	Darrell Evans	1.00	.50	.30
4	Sal Bando	1.00	.50	.30
5	Joe Morgan	5.00	2.50	1.50
6	Mickey Lolich	2.00	1.00	.60
7	Don Sutton	4.00	2.00	1.25
8	Bill Melton	1.00	.50	.30
9	Tim Foli	1.00	.50	.30
10	Joe Lahoud	1.00	.50	.30
11	Bert Hooten (Burt Hooton)	1.00	.50	.30
12	Paul Blair	1.00	.50	.30
13	Jim Barr	1.00	.50	.30
14	Toby Harrah	1.00	.50	.30
15	John Milner	1.00	.50	.30
16	Ken Holtzman	1.00	.50	.30
17	Cesar Cedeno	1.00	.50	.30
18	Dwight Evans	1.00	.50	.30
19	Willie McCovey	7.00	3.50	2.00
20	Tony Oliva	2.00	1.00	.60
21	Manny Sanguillen	1.00	.50	.30
22	Mickey Rivers	1.00	.50	.30
23	Lou Brock	5.00	2.50	1.50
24	Graig Nettles	1.50	.70	.45
25	Jim Wynn	1.00	.50	.30
26	George Scott	1.00	.50	.30
27	Greg Luzinski	1.00	.50	.30
28	Bert Campaneris	1.00	.50	.30
29	Pete Rose	20.00	10.00	6.00
30	Buddy Bell	1.00	.50	.30
31	Gary Matthews	1.00	.50	.30
32	Fred Patek	1.00	.50	.30
33	Mike Lum	1.00	.50	.30
34	Ellie Rodriguez	1.00	.50	.30
35	Milt May (photo actually Lee May)	1.00	.50	.30
36	Willie Horton	1.00	.50	.30
40	Joe Rudi	1.00	.50	.30
43	Garry Maddox	1.00	.50	.30
46	Dave Chalk	1.00	.50	.30
49	Steve Garvey	4.00	2.00	1.25
52	Rollie Fingers	4.00	2.00	1.25
58	Nolan Ryan	25.00	12.50	7.50
61	Ron Cey	1.00	.50	.30
64	Gene Tenace	1.00	.50	.30
65	Jose Cardenal	1.00	.50	.30
67	Dave Lopes	1.00	.50	.30
68	Wilbur Wood	1.00	.50	.30
73	Chris Speier	1.00	.50	.30
77	Don Kessinger	1.00	.50	.30
79	Andy Messersmith	1.00	.50	.30
80	Robin Yount	15.00	7.50	4.50
82	Bill Singer	1.00	.50	.30
103	Glenn Beckert	1.00	.50	.30
110	Jim Kaat	2.00	1.00	.60
112	Don Money	1.00	.50	.30
113	Rick Monday	1.00	.50	.30
122	Jorge Orta	1.00	.50	.30
125	Bill Madlock	1.00	.50	.30
130	Hank Aaron	15.00	7.50	4.50
136	Ken Henderson	1.00	.50	.30

1976 Hostess

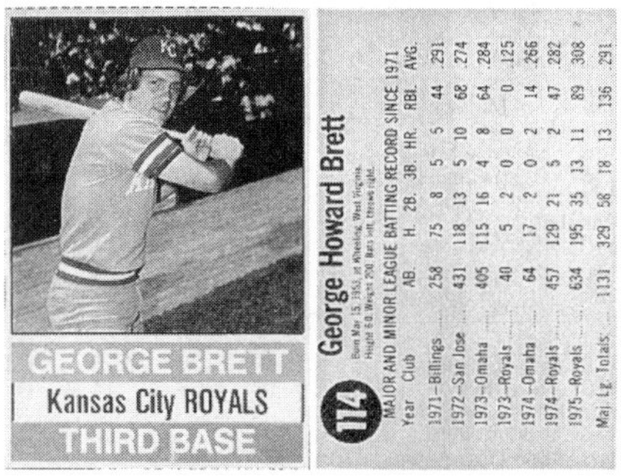

The second of five annual Hostess issues, the 1976 cards carried a "Bicentennial" color theme, with red, white and blue stripes at the bottom of the 2-1/4" x 3-1/4" cards. Like other Hostess issues, the cards were printed in panels of three as the bottom of family-size boxes of snack cake products. This leads to a degree of scarcity for some of the 150 cards in the set; those which were found on less-popular brands. A well-trimmed three-card panel measures 7-1/4" x 3-1/4" size. Some of the photos used in the 1976 Hostess set can also be found on Topps issues of the era.

		NM	EX	VG
Complete Panel Set (50):		250.00	125.00	75.00
Complete Single Set (150):		175.00	85.00	50.00
Common Panel:		3.50	1.75	1.00
Common Single Player:		.50	.25	.15
Panel 1		9.00	4.50	2.75
1	Fred Lynn	.60	.30	.20
2	Joe Morgan	2.00	1.00	.60
3	Phil Niekro	2.00	1.00	.60
Panel 2		6.00	3.00	1.75
4	Gaylord Perry	2.00	1.00	.60
5	Bob Watson	.50	.25	.15
6	Bill Freehan	.50	.25	.15
Panel 3		8.00	4.00	2.50
7	Lou Brock	3.00	1.50	.90
8	Al Fitzmorris	.50	.25	.15
9	Rennie Stennett	.50	.25	.15
Panel 4		12.50	6.25	3.75
10	Tony Oliva	.60	.30	.20
11	Robin Yount	5.00	2.50	1.50
12	Rick Manning	.50	.25	.15
Panel 5		3.50	1.75	1.00
13	Bobby Grich	.50	.25	.15
14	Terry Forster	.50	.25	.15
15	Dave Kingman	.60	.30	.20
Panel 6		9.00	4.50	2.75
16	Thurman Munson	3.00	1.50	.90
17	Rick Reuschel	.50	.25	.15
18	Bobby Bonds	.50	.25	.15
Panel 7		5.50	2.75	1.50
19	Steve Garvey	1.75	.90	.50
20	Vida Blue	.50	.25	.15
21	Dave Rader	.50	.25	.15
Panel 8		12.50	6.25	3.75
22	Johnny Bench	4.00	2.00	1.25
23	Luis Tiant	.50	.25	.15
24	Darrell Evans	.60	.30	.20
Panel 9		3.50	1.75	1.00
25	Larry Dierker	.50	.25	.15
26	Willie Horton	.50	.25	.15
27	John Ellis	.50	.25	.15
Panel 10		3.50	1.75	1.00
28	Al Cowens	.50	.25	.15
29	Jerry Reuss	.50	.25	.15
30	Reggie Smith	.50	.25	.15
Panel 11		14.50	7.25	4.25
31	Bobby Darwin	.50	.25	.15
32	Fritz Peterson	.50	.25	.15
33	Rod Carew	6.00	3.00	1.75
Panel 12		22.00	11.00	6.50
34	Carlos May	.50	.25	.15
35	Tom Seaver	5.00	2.50	1.50
36	Brooks Robinson	5.00	2.50	1.50
Panel 13		3.50	1.75	1.00
37	Jose Cardenal	.50	.25	.15
38	Ron Blomberg	.50	.25	.15
39	Lee Stanton	.50	.25	.15
Panel 14		3.50	1.75	1.00
40	Dave Cash	.50	.25	.15
41	John Montefusco	.50	.25	.15
42	Bob Tolan	.50	.25	.15
Panel 15		3.50	1.75	1.00
43	Carl Morton	.50	.25	.15
44	Rick Burleson	.50	.25	.15
45	Don Gullett	.50	.25	.15
Panel 16		3.50	1.75	1.00
46	Vern Ruhle	.50	.25	.15
47	Cesar Cedeno	.50	.25	.15
48	Toby Harrah	.50	.25	.15
Panel 17		8.00	4.00	2.50
49	Willie Stargell	3.00	1.50	.90
50	Al Hrabosky	.50	.25	.15
51	Amos Otis	.50	.25	.15
Panel 18		3.50	1.75	1.00
52	Bud Harrelson	.50	.25	.15
53	Jim Hughes	.50	.25	.15
54	George Scott	.50	.25	.15
Panel 19		10.00	5.00	3.00
55	Mike Vail	.50	.25	.15
56	Jim Palmer	3.50	1.75	1.00
57	Jorge Orta	.50	.25	.15
Panel 20		3.50	1.75	1.00
58	Chris Chambliss	.50	.25	.15
59	Dave Chalk	.50	.25	.15
60	Ray Burris	.50	.25	.15
Panel 21		6.00	3.00	1.75
61	Bert Campaneris	.50	.25	.15
62	Gary Carter	1.50	.70	.45
63a	Ron Cey	.50	.25	.15
63b	Ron Cey (negatives reversed, unissued proof)	35.00	17.50	10.50
Panel 22		27.50	13.50	8.25
64	Carlton Fisk	2.50	1.25	.70
65	Marty Perez	.50	.25	.15
66	Pete Rose	10.00	5.00	3.00
Panel 23		3.50	1.75	1.00
67	Roger Metzger	.50	.25	.15
68	Jim Sundberg	.50	.25	.15
69	Ron LeFlore	.50	.25	.15
Panel 24		3.50	1.75	1.00
70	Ted Sizemore	.50	.25	.15
71	Steve Busby	.50	.25	.15
72	Manny Sanguillen	.50	.25	.15
Panel 25		4.50	2.25	1.25
73	Larry Hisle	.50	.25	.15
74	Pete Broberg	.50	.25	.15
75	Boog Powell	1.00	.50	.30
Panel 26		5.00	2.50	1.50
76	Ken Singleton	.50	.25	.15
77	Rich Gossage	1.50	.70	.45
78	Jerry Grote	.50	.25	.15
Panel 27		25.00	12.50	7.50
79	Nolan Ryan	12.00	6.00	3.50
80	Rick Monday	.50	.25	.15
81	Graig Nettles	.50	.25	.15
Panel 28		22.00	11.00	6.50
82	Chris Speier	.50	.25	.15
83	Dave Winfield	4.00	2.00	1.25
84	Mike Schmidt	6.00	3.00	1.75
Panel 29		5.00	2.50	1.50
85	Buzz Capra	.50	.25	.15
86	Tony Perez	2.00	1.00	.60
87	Dwight Evans	.50	.25	.15
Panel 30		3.50	1.75	1.00
88	Mike Hargrove	.50	.25	.15
89	Joe Coleman	.50	.25	.15
90	Greg Gross	.50	.25	.15
Panel 31		3.50	1.75	1.00
91	John Mayberry	.50	.25	.15
92	John Candelaria	.50	.25	.15
93	Bake McBride	.50	.25	.15
Panel 32		17.50	8.75	5.25
94	Hank Aaron	9.00	4.50	2.75
95	Buddy Bell	.50	.25	.15
96	Steve Braun	.50	.25	.15
Panel 33		3.50	1.75	1.00
97	Jon Matlack	.50	.25	.15
98	Lee May	.50	.25	.15
99	Wilbur Wood	.50	.25	.15
Panel 34		3.50	1.75	1.00
100	Bill Madlock	.60	.30	.20
101	Frank Tanana	.50	.25	.15
102	Mickey Rivers	.50	.25	.15
Panel 35		6.00	3.00	1.75
103	Mike Ivie	.50	.25	.15
104	Rollie Fingers	2.00	1.00	.60
105	Dave Lopes	.50	.25	.15
Panel 36		3.50	1.75	1.00
106	George Foster	.65	.35	.20
107	Denny Doyle	.50	.25	.15
108	Earl Williams	.50	.25	.15
Panel 37		3.50	1.75	1.00
109	Tom Veryzer	.50	.25	.15
110	J.R. Richard	.50	.25	.15
111	Jeff Burroughs	.50	.25	.15
Panel 38		17.50	8.75	5.25
112	Al Oliver	.60	.30	.20
113	Ted Simmons	.50	.25	.15
114	George Brett	7.50	3.75	2.25
Panel 39		3.50	1.75	1.00
115	Frank Duffy	.50	.25	.15
116	Bert Blyleven	.50	.25	.15
117	Darrell Porter	.50	.25	.15
Panel 40		3.50	1.75	1.00
118	Don Baylor	.60	.30	.20
119	Bucky Dent	.50	.25	.15
120	Felix Millan	.50	.25	.15
Panel 41		3.50	1.75	1.00
121a	Mike Cuellar	.50	.25	.15
121b	Andy Messersmith (unissued proof)	25.00	12.50	7.50
122	Gene Tenace	.50	.25	.15
123	Bobby Murcer	.50	.25	.15
Panel 42		9.00	4.50	2.75
124	Willie McCovey	3.00	1.50	.90
125	Greg Luzinski	.50	.25	.15
126	Larry Parrish	.50	.25	.15
Panel 43		6.00	3.00	1.75
127	Jim Rice	2.00	1.00	.60
128	Dave Concepcion	.50	.25	.15
129	Jim Wynn	.50	.25	.15
Panel 44		3.50	1.75	1.00
130	Tom Grieve	.50	.25	.15
131	Mike Cosgrove	.50	.25	.15
132	Dan Meyer	.50	.25	.15
Panel 45		4.00	2.00	1.25
133	Dave Parker	1.00	.50	.30
134	Don Kessinger	.50	.25	.15
135	Hal McRae	.50	.25	.15
Panel 46		13.50	6.75	4.00
136	Don Money	.50	.25	.15
137	Dennis Eckersley	4.00	2.00	1.25
138a	Fergie Jenkins	2.00	1.00	.60
138b	Johnny Briggs (unissued proof)	25.00	12.50	7.50
Panel 47		6.00	3.00	1.75
139	Mike Torrez	.50	.25	.15
140	Jerry Morales	.50	.25	.15
141	Catfish Hunter	2.00	1.00	.60
Panel 48		3.50	1.75	1.00
142	Gary Matthews	.50	.25	.15
143	Randy Jones	.50	.25	.15
144	Mike Jorgensen	.50	.25	.15
Panel 49		15.00	7.50	4.50
145	Larry Bowa	.50	.25	.15
146	Reggie Jackson	6.00	3.00	1.75
147	Steve Yeager	.50	.25	.15
Panel 50		15.00	7.50	4.50
148	Dave May	.50	.25	.15
149	Carl Yastrzemski	6.00	3.00	1.75
150	Cesar Geronimo	.50	.25	.15

1976 Hostess Twinkies

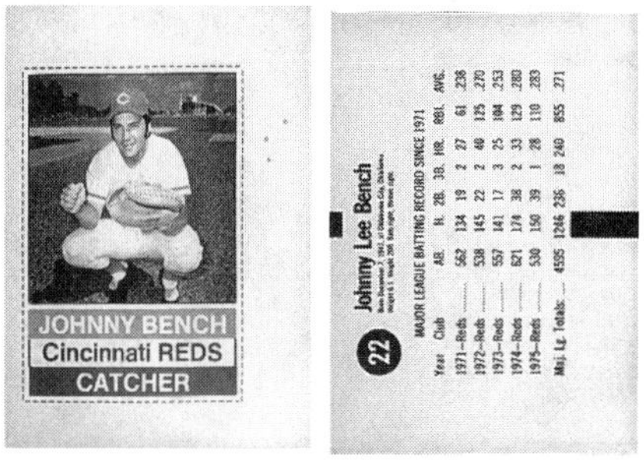

The 60 cards in this regionally-issued (test markets only) set closely parallel the first 60 cards in the numerical sequence of the "regular" 1976 Hostess issue. The singular difference is the appearance on the back of a black band toward the center of the card at top and bottom. Also unlike the three-card panels of the regular Hostess issue, the 2-1/4" x 3-1/4" Twinkie cards were issued singly, as the cardboard stiffener for the cellophane-wrapped snack cakes.

		NM	EX	VG
Complete Set (60):		100.00	50.00	30.00
Common Player:		1.00	.50	.30
1	Fred Lynn	1.50	.70	.45
2	Joe Morgan	5.00	2.50	1.50
3	Phil Niekro	5.00	2.50	1.50
4	Gaylord Perry	5.00	2.50	1.50
5	Bob Watson	1.00	.50	.30
6	Bill Freehan	1.25	.60	.40
7	Lou Brock	7.00	3.50	2.00
8	Al Fitzmorris	1.00	.50	.30
9	Rennie Stennett	1.00	.50	.30
10	Tony Oliva	1.50	.70	.45
11	Robin Yount	10.00	5.00	3.00
12	Rick Manning	1.00	.50	.30
13	Bobby Grich	1.00	.50	.30
14	Terry Forster	1.00	.50	.30
15	Dave Kingman	1.50	.70	.45
16	Thurman Munson	6.50	3.25	2.00
17	Rick Reuschel	1.00	.50	.30
18	Bobby Bonds	1.00	.50	.30
19	Steve Garvey	3.00	1.50	.90
20	Vida Blue	1.00	.50	.30
21	Dave Rader	1.00	.50	.30
22	Johnny Bench	8.00	4.00	2.50
23	Luis Tiant	1.00	.50	.30
24	Darrell Evans	1.25	.60	.40
25	Larry Dierker	1.00	.50	.30
26	Willie Horton	1.00	.50	.30
27	John Ellis	1.00	.50	.30
28	Al Cowens	1.00	.50	.30
29	Jerry Reuss	1.00	.50	.30
30	Reggie Smith	1.00	.50	.30
31	Bobby Darwin	1.00	.50	.30
32	Fritz Peterson	1.00	.50	.30
33	Rod Carew	8.00	4.00	2.50
34	Carlos May	1.00	.50	.30
35	Tom Seaver	8.00	4.00	2.50
36	Brooks Robinson	9.00	4.50	2.75
37	Jose Cardenal	1.00	.50	.30
38	Ron Blomberg	1.00	.50	.30
39	Lee Stanton	1.00	.50	.30
40	Dave Cash	1.00	.50	.30
41	John Montefusco	1.00	.50	.30
42	Bob Tolan	1.00	.50	.30
43	Carl Morton	1.00	.50	.30
44	Rick Burleson	1.00	.50	.30
45	Don Gullett	1.00	.50	.30
46	Vern Ruhle	1.00	.50	.30
47	Cesar Cedeno	1.00	.50	.30
48	Toby Harrah	1.00	.50	.30
49	Willie Stargell	6.00	3.00	1.75
50	Al Hrabosky	1.00	.50	.30
51	Amos Otis	1.00	.50	.30
52	Bud Harrelson	1.00	.50	.30
53	Jim Hughes	1.00	.50	.30
54	George Scott	1.00	.50	.30
55	Mike Vail	1.00	.50	.30
56	Jim Palmer	6.00	3.00	1.75
57	Jorge Orta	1.00	.50	.30
58	Chris Chambliss	1.00	.50	.30

59	Dave Chalk	1.00	.50	.30
60	Ray Burris	1.00	.50	.30

1976 Hostess Unissued Proofs

To help prevent a recurrance of the errors which plagued Hostess' debut set in 1975, the company prepared proof sheets of the cards before they were printed onto the bottoms of snack cake boxes. Probably to have ready substitutes in case problems were found, or a card had to be withdrawn at the last minute, there were seven players printed in proof version that were never issued on boxes. In addition, changes to cards #61, 121 and 138 were made between the proof stage and issued versions (they are detailed in the 1976 Hostess listings). The proofs share the format and 2-1/4" x 3-1/4" size of the issued cards.

		NM	EX	VG
Complete Set (9):		275.00	135.00	82.00
Common Player:		25.00	12.50	7.50
151	Fergie Jenkins (issued as #138)	45.00	22.00	13.50
152	Mike Cuellar (issued as #121)	30.00	15.00	9.00
153	Tom Murphy	25.00	12.50	7.50
154	Dusty Baker	35.00	17.50	10.50
155	Barry Foote	25.00	12.50	7.50
156	Steve Carlton	75.00	37.00	22.00
157	Richie Zisk	25.00	12.50	7.50
158	Ken Holtzman	25.00	12.50	7.50
159	Cliff Johnson	25.00	12.50	7.50

1977 Hostess

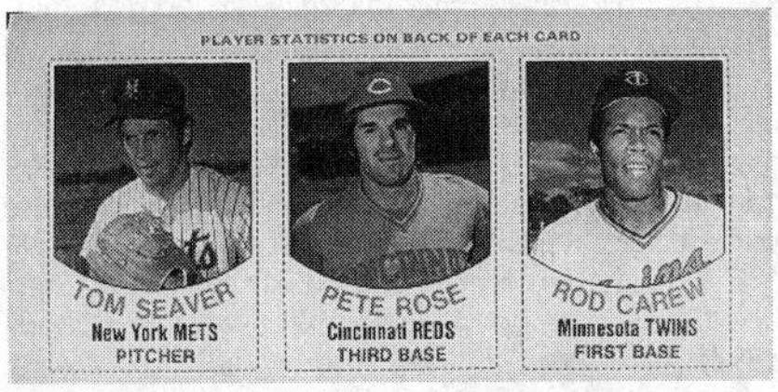

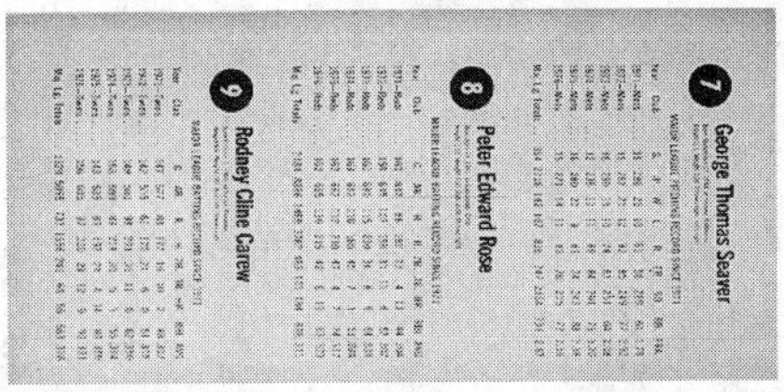

The third of five consecutive annual issues, the 1977 Hostess cards retained the same card size - 2-1/4" x 3-1/4", set size - 150 cards, and mode of issue - three cards on a 7-1/4" x 3-1/4" panel, as the previous two efforts. Because they were issued as the bottom panel of snack cake boxes, and because some brands of Hostess products were more popular than others, certain cards in the set are scarcer than others.

		NM	EX	VG
Complete Panel Set (50):		225.00	115.00	70.00
Complete Singles Set (150):		160.00	80.00	47.50
Common Panel:		3.50	1.75	1.00
Common Single Player:		.50	.25	.15
Panel 1		27.50	13.50	8.25
1	Jim Palmer	3.00	1.50	.90
2	Joe Morgan	3.00	1.50	.90
3a	Reggie Jackson	6.00	3.00	1.75
3b	Rod Carew (unissued proof)	60.00	30.00	18.00
Panel 2		30.00	15.00	9.00
4	Carl Yastrzemski	6.00	3.00	1.75
5	Thurman Munson	3.00	1.50	.90
6	Johnny Bench	6.00	3.00	1.75
Panel 3		34.00	17.00	10.00
7	Tom Seaver	3.00	1.50	.90
8	Pete Rose	8.00	4.00	2.50
9a	Rod Carew	4.00	2.00	1.25
9b	Reggie Jackson (unissued proof)	75.00	37.00	22.00
Panel 4		3.50	1.75	1.00
10	Luis Tiant	.50	.25	.15
11	Phil Garner	.50	.25	.15
12	Sixto Lezcano	.50	.25	.15
Panel 5		3.50	1.75	1.00
13	Mike Torrez	.50	.25	.15
14	Dave Lopes	.50	.25	.15
15	Doug DeCinces	.50	.25	.15
Panel 6		3.50	1.75	1.00
16	Jim Spencer	.50	.25	.15
17	Hal McRae	.50	.25	.15
18	Mike Hargrove	.50	.25	.15
Panel 7		3.50	1.75	1.00
19	Willie Montanez	.50	.25	.15
20	Roger Metzger	.50	.25	.15
21	Dwight Evans	.50	.25	.15
Panel 8		4.00	2.00	1.25
22	Steve Rogers	.50	.25	.15
23	Jim Rice	.75	.40	.25
24	Pete Falcone	.50	.25	.15
Panel 9		10.00	5.00	3.00
25	Greg Luzinski	.50	.25	.15
26	Randy Jones	.50	.25	.15
27	Willie Stargell	3.00	1.50	.90
Panel 10		3.50	1.75	1.00
28	John Hiller	.50	.25	.15
29	Bobby Murcer	.50	.25	.15
30	Rick Monday	.50	.25	.15
Panel 11		9.00	4.50	2.75
31	John Montefusco	.50	.25	.15
32	Lou Brock	3.00	1.50	.90
33	Bill North	.50	.25	.15
Panel 12		27.50	13.50	8.25
34	Robin Yount	5.00	2.50	1.50
35	Steve Garvey	2.00	1.00	.60
36	George Brett	6.00	3.00	1.75
Panel 13		3.50	1.75	1.00
37	Toby Harrah	.50	.25	.15
38	Jerry Royster	.50	.25	.15
39	Bob Watson	.50	.25	.15
Panel 14		7.50	3.75	2.25
40	George Foster	.75	.40	.25
41	Gary Carter	2.00	1.00	.60
42	John Denny	.50	.25	.15
Panel 15		25.00	12.50	7.50
43	Mike Schmidt	7.00	3.50	2.00
44	Dave Winfield	4.00	2.00	1.25
45	Al Oliver	.60	.30	.20
Panel 16		4.00	2.00	1.25
46	Mark Fidrych	.60	.30	.20
47	Larry Herndon	.50	.25	.15
48	Dave Goltz	.50	.25	.15
Panel 17		4.00	2.00	1.25
49	Jerry Morales	.50	.25	.15
50	Ron LeFlore	.50	.25	.15
51	Fred Lynn	.50	.25	.15
Panel 18		3.50	1.75	1.00
52	Vida Blue	.50	.25	.15
53	Rick Manning	.50	.25	.15
54	Bill Buckner	.60	.30	.20
Panel 19		3.50	1.75	1.00
55	Lee May	.50	.25	.15
56	John Mayberry	.50	.25	.15
57	Darrel Chaney	.50	.25	.15
Panel 20		4.00	2.00	1.25
58	Cesar Cedeno	.50	.25	.15
59	Ken Griffey	.60	.30	.20
60	Dave Kingman	.60	.30	.20
Panel 21		3.50	1.75	1.00
61	Ted Simmons	.50	.25	.15
62	Larry Bowa	.50	.25	.15
63	Frank Tanana	.50	.25	.15
Panel 22		3.50	1.75	1.00
64	Jason Thompson	.50	.25	.15
65	Ken Brett	.50	.25	.15
66	Roy Smalley	.50	.25	.15
Panel 23		3.50	1.75	1.00
67	Ray Burris	.50	.25	.15
68	Rick Burleson	.50	.25	.15
69	Buddy Bell	.50	.25	.15
Panel 24		5.50	2.75	1.50
70	Don Sutton	2.00	1.00	.60
71	Mark Belanger	.50	.25	.15
72	Dennis Leonard	.50	.25	.15
Panel 25		7.00	3.50	2.00
73	Gaylord Perry	2.00	1.00	.60
74	Dick Ruthven	.50	.25	.15
75	Jose Cruz	.50	.25	.15
Panel 26		3.50	1.75	1.00
76	Cesar Geronimo	.50	.25	.15
77	Jerry Koosman	.50	.25	.15
78	Garry Templeton	.50	.25	.15
Panel 27		28.00	14.00	8.50
79	Catfish Hunter	2.00	1.00	.60
80	John Candelaria	.50	.25	.15
81	Nolan Ryan	10.00	5.00	3.00
Panel 28		4.00	2.00	1.25
82	Rusty Staub	.60	.30	.20
83	Jim Barr	.50	.25	.15
84	Butch Wynegar	.50	.25	.15
Panel 29		3.50	1.75	1.00
85	Jose Cardenal	.50	.25	.15
86	Claudell Washington	.50	.25	.15
87	Bill Travers	.50	.25	.15
Panel 30		3.50	1.75	1.00
88	Rick Waits	.50	.25	.15
89	Ron Cey	.50	.25	.15
90	Al Bumbry	.50	.25	.15
Panel 31		3.50	1.75	1.00
91	Bucky Dent	.50	.25	.15
92	Amos Otis	.50	.25	.15
93	Tom Grieve	.50	.25	.15
Panel 32		3.50	1.75	1.00
94	Enos Cabell	.50	.25	.15
95	Dave Concepcion	.50	.25	.15
96	Felix Millan	.50	.25	.15
Panel 33		3.50	1.75	1.00
97	Bake McBride	.50	.25	.15
98	Chris Chambliss	.50	.25	.15
99	Butch Metzger	.50	.25	.15
Panel 34		3.50	1.75	1.00
100	Rennie Stennett	.50	.25	.15
101	Dave Roberts	.50	.25	.15
102	Lyman Bostock	.50	.25	.15
Panel 35		5.00	2.50	1.50
103	Rick Reuschel	.50	.25	.15
104	Carlton Fisk	2.50	1.25	.70
105	Jim Slaton	.50	.25	.15
Panel 36		5.00	2.50	1.50
106	Dennis Eckersley	1.50	.70	.45
107	Ken Singleton	.50	.25	.15
108	Ralph Garr	.50	.25	.15
Panel 37		5.00	2.50	1.50
109	Freddie Patek	.50	.25	.15
110	Jim Sundberg	.50	.25	.15
111	Phil Niekro	2.00	1.00	.60
Panel 38		4.00	2.00	1.25
112	J.R. Richard	.50	.25	.15
113	Gary Nolan	.50	.25	.15
114	Jon Matlack	.50	.25	.15
Panel 39		16.00	8.00	4.75
115	Keith Hernandez	.75	.40	.25
116	Graig Nettles	.60	.30	.20
117	Steve Carlton	5.00	2.50	1.50
Panel 40		6.00	3.00	1.75
118	Bill Madlock	.65	.35	.20
119	Jerry Reuss	.50	.25	.15
120	Aurelio Rodriguez	.50	.25	.15
Panel 41		3.50	1.75	1.00
121	Dan Ford	.50	.25	.15
122	Ray Fosse	.50	.25	.15
123	George Hendrick	.50	.25	.15
Panel 42		3.50	1.75	1.00
124	Alan Ashby	.50	.25	.15
125	Joe Lis	.50	.25	.15
126	Sal Bando	.50	.25	.15
Panel 43		4.00	2.00	1.25
127	Richie Zisk	.50	.25	.15
128	Rich Gossage	.60	.30	.20
129	Don Baylor	.60	.30	.20
Panel 44		3.50	1.75	1.00
130	Dave McKay	.50	.25	.15
131	Bob Grich	.50	.25	.15
132	Dave Pagan	.50	.25	.15
Panel 45		3.50	1.75	1.00
133	Dave Cash	.50	.25	.15
134	Steve Braun	.50	.25	.15
135	Dan Meyer	.50	.25	.15
Panel 46		4.50	2.25	1.25
136	Bill Stein	.50	.25	.15
137	Rollie Fingers	2.00	1.00	.60
138	Brian Downing	.50	.25	.15
Panel 47		3.50	1.75	1.00
139	Bill Singer	.50	.25	.15
140	Doyle Alexander	.50	.25	.15
141	Gene Tenace	.50	.25	.15
Panel 48		3.50	1.75	1.00
142	Gary Matthews	.50	.25	.15
143	Don Gullett	.50	.25	.15
144	Wayne Garland	.50	.25	.15
Panel 49		3.50	1.75	1.00
145	Pete Broberg	.50	.25	.15
146	Joe Rudi	.50	.25	.15
147	Glenn Abbott	.50	.25	.15
Panel 50		3.50	1.75	1.00
148	George Scott	.50	.25	.15
149	Bert Campaneris	.50	.25	.15
150	Andy Messersmith	.50	.25	.15

1977 Hostess Twinkies

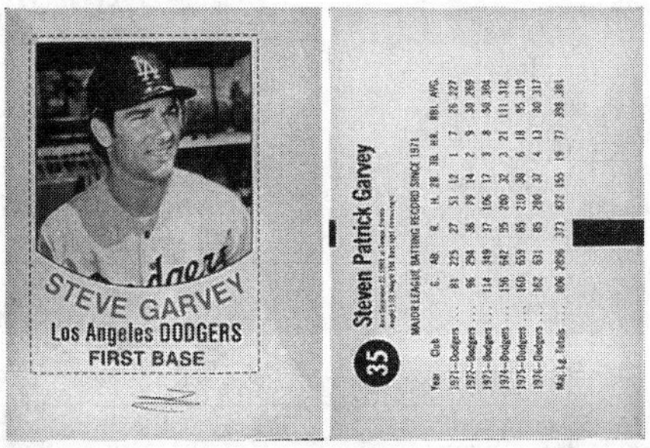

The 1977 Hostess Twinkie issue, at 150 different cards, is the largest of the single-panel Twinkie sets. It is also the most obscure. The cards, which measure 2-1/4" x 3-1/4", but are part of a larger panel, were found not only with Twinkies, but with Hostess Cupcakes as well. Cards #1-30 and 111-150 are Twinkies panels and #31-135 are Cupcakes panels. Complete Cupcakes panels are approximately 2-1/4" x 4-1/2" in size, while complete Twinkies panels measure 3-1/8" x 4-1/4". The photos used in the set are identical to those in the 1977 Hostess three-card panel set. The main difference is the appearance of a black band at the center of the card back.

		NM	EX	VG
Complete Set (150):		200.00	100.00	60.00
Common Player:		1.00	.50	.30
1	Jim Palmer	4.00	2.00	1.25
2	Joe Morgan	4.00	2.00	1.25
3	Reggie Jackson	10.00	5.00	3.00
4	Carl Yastrzemski	8.00	4.00	2.50
5	Thurman Munson	6.00	3.00	1.75
6	Johnny Bench	8.00	4.00	2.50
7	Tom Seaver	8.00	4.00	2.50
8	Pete Rose	15.00	7.50	4.50
9	Rod Carew	6.00	3.00	1.75
10	Luis Tiant	1.00	.50	.30
11	Phil Garner	1.00	.50	.30
12	Sixto Lezcano	1.00	.50	.30
13	Mike Torrez	1.00	.50	.30

14	Dave Lopes	1.00	.50	.30
15	Doug DeCinces	1.00	.50	.30
16	Jim Spencer	1.00	.50	.30
17	Hal McRae	1.00	.50	.30
18	Mike Hargrove	1.00	.50	.30
19	Willie Montanez	1.00	.50	.30
20	Roger Metzger	1.00	.50	.30
21	Dwight Evans	1.00	.50	.30
22	Steve Rogers	1.00	.50	.30
23	Jim Rice	2.50	1.25	.70
24	Pete Falcone	1.00	.50	.30
25	Greg Luzinski	1.00	.50	.30
26	Randy Jones	1.00	.50	.30
27	Willie Stargell	6.00	3.00	1.75
28	John Hiller	1.00	.50	.30
29	Bobby Murcer	1.00	.50	.30
30	Rick Monday	1.00	.50	.30
31	John Montefusco	1.00	.50	.30
32	Lou Brock	6.00	3.00	1.75
33	Bill North	1.00	.50	.30
34	Robin Yount	7.00	3.50	2.00
35	Steve Garvey	4.00	2.00	1.25
36	George Brett	9.00	4.50	2.75
37	Toby Harrah	1.00	.50	.30
38	Jerry Royster	1.00	.50	.30
39	Bob Watson	1.00	.50	.30
40	George Foster	1.00	.50	.30
41	Gary Carter	3.00	1.50	.90
42	John Denny	1.00	.50	.30
43	Mike Schmidt	9.00	4.50	2.75
44	Dave Winfield	6.00	3.00	1.75
45	Al Oliver	1.00	.50	.30
46	Mark Fidrych	1.50	.70	.45
47	Larry Herndon	1.00	.50	.30
48	Dave Goltz	1.00	.50	.30
49	Jerry Morales	1.00	.50	.30
50	Ron LeFlore	1.00	.50	.30
51	Fred Lynn	1.00	.50	.30
52	Vida Blue	1.00	.50	.30
53	Rick Manning	1.00	.50	.30
54	Bill Buckner	1.00	.50	.30
55	Lee May	1.00	.50	.30
56	John Mayberry	1.00	.50	.30
57	Darrel Chaney	1.00	.50	.30
58	Cesar Cedeno	1.00	.50	.30
59	Ken Griffey	1.25	.60	.40
60	Dave Kingman	1.50	.70	.45
61	Ted Simmons	1.00	.50	.30
62	Larry Bowa	1.00	.50	.30
63	Frank Tanana	1.00	.50	.30
64	Jason Thompson	1.00	.50	.30
65	Ken Brett	1.00	.50	.30
66	Roy Smalley	1.00	.50	.30
67	Ray Burris	1.00	.50	.30
68	Rick Burleson	1.00	.50	.30
69	Buddy Bell	1.00	.50	.30
70	Don Sutton	4.00	2.00	1.25
71	Mark Belanger	1.00	.50	.30
72	Dennis Leonard	1.00	.50	.30
73	Gaylord Perry	4.00	2.00	1.25
74	Dick Ruthven	1.00	.50	.30
75	Jose Cruz	1.00	.50	.30
76	Cesar Geronimo	1.00	.50	.30
77	Jerry Koosman	1.00	.50	.30
78	Garry Templeton	1.00	.50	.30
79	Catfish Hunter	4.00	2.00	1.25
80	John Candelaria	1.00	.50	.30
81	Nolan Ryan	25.00	12.50	7.50
82	Rusty Staub	1.50	.70	.45
83	Jim Barr	1.00	.50	.30
84	Butch Wynegar	1.00	.50	.30
85	Jose Cardenal	1.00	.50	.30
86	Claudell Washington	1.00	.50	.30
87	Bill Travers	1.00	.50	.30
88	Rick Waits	1.00	.50	.30
89	Ron Cey	1.00	.50	.30
90	Al Bumbry	1.00	.50	.30
91	Bucky Dent	1.00	.50	.30
92	Amos Otis	1.00	.50	.30
93	Tom Grieve	1.00	.50	.30
94	Enos Cabell	1.00	.50	.30
95	Dave Concepcion	1.00	.50	.30
96	Felix Millan	1.00	.50	.30
97	Bake McBride	1.00	.50	.30
98	Chris Chambliss	1.00	.50	.30
99	Butch Metzger	1.00	.50	.30
100	Rennie Stennett	1.00	.50	.30
101	Dave Roberts	1.00	.50	.30
102	Lyman Bostock	1.00	.50	.30
103	Rick Reuschel	1.00	.50	.30
104	Carlton Fisk	5.00	2.50	1.50
105	Jim Slaton	1.00	.50	.30
106	Dennis Eckersley	2.00	1.00	.60
107	Ken Singleton	1.00	.50	.30
108	Ralph Garr	1.00	.50	.30
109	Freddie Patek	1.00	.50	.30
110	Jim Sundberg	1.00	.50	.30
111	Phil Niekro	4.00	2.00	1.25
112	J.R. Richard	1.00	.50	.30
113	Gary Nolan	1.00	.50	.30
114	Jon Matlack	1.00	.50	.30
115	Keith Hernandez	1.00	.50	.30
116	Graig Nettles	1.00	.50	.30
117	Steve Carlton	6.00	3.00	1.75
118	Bill Madlock	1.00	.50	.30
119	Jerry Reuss	1.00	.50	.30
120	Aurelio Rodriguez	1.00	.50	.30
121	Dan Ford	1.00	.50	.30
122	Ray Fosse	1.00	.50	.30
123	George Hendrick	1.00	.50	.30
124	Alan Ashby	1.00	.50	.30
125	Joe Lis	1.00	.50	.30
126	Sal Bando	1.00	.50	.30
127	Richie Zisk	1.00	.50	.30
128	Rich Gossage	1.00	.50	.30
129	Don Baylor	1.50	.70	.45
130	Dave McKay	1.00	.50	.30
131	Bob Grich	1.00	.50	.30
132	Dave Pagan	1.00	.50	.30
133	Dave Cash	1.00	.50	.30
134	Steve Braun	1.00	.50	.30
135	Dan Meyer	1.00	.50	.30
136	Bill Stein	1.00	.50	.30
137	Rollie Fingers	4.00	2.00	1.25
138	Brian Downing	1.00	.50	.30
139	Bill Singer	1.00	.50	.30
140	Doyle Alexander	1.00	.50	.30
141	Gene Tenace	1.00	.50	.30
142	Gary Matthews	1.00	.50	.30
143	Don Gullett	1.00	.50	.30
144	Wayne Garland	1.00	.50	.30
145	Pete Broberg	1.00	.50	.30
146	Joe Rudi	1.00	.50	.30
147	Glenn Abbott	1.00	.50	.30
148	George Scott	1.00	.50	.30
149	Bert Campaneris	1.00	.50	.30
150	Andy Messersmith	1.00	.50	.30

1977 Hostess Unissued Proofs

The reason for the existence of these rare Hostess proofs is unknown, but there seems little doubt that they were never actually circulated; perhaps being held in reserve in case the cards actually printed on product boxes had to be replaced. The 10 cards were printed on a sheet in three-card panels, like the issued Hostess cards, plus a single of Briles. The proofs share the format of the issued cards, and the 2-1/4" x 3-1/4" size. Besides these "high number" proofs, there also exist numering-variation proofs of cards #3, 9, 65 and 119 (see 1977 Hostess listings).

		NM	EX	VG
Complete Set (10):		250.00	125.00	75.00
Common Single:		25.00	12.50	7.50
151	Ed Kranepool	35.00	17.50	10.50
152	Ross Grimsley	25.00	12.50	7.50
153	Ken Brett (#65 in regular-issue set)	25.00	12.50	7.50
154	Rowland Office	25.00	12.50	7.50
155	Rick Wise	25.00	12.50	7.50
156	Paul Splittorff	25.00	12.50	7.50
157	Jerry Augustine	25.00	12.50	7.50
158	Ken Forsch	25.00	12.50	7.50
159	Jerry Reuss	30.00	15.00	9.00
160	Nelson Briles	25.00	12.50	7.50

1978 Hostess

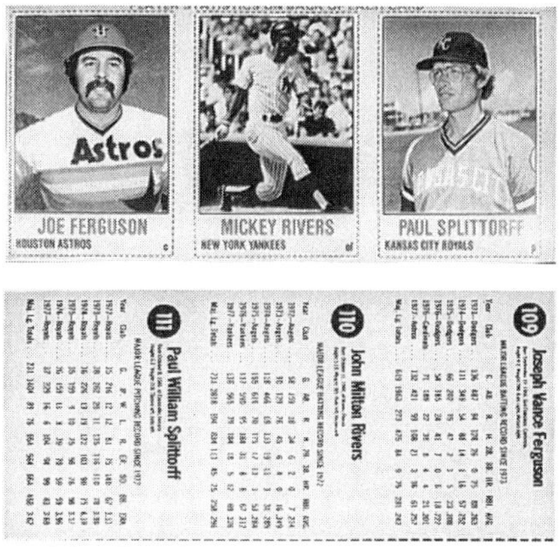

Other than the design on the front of the card, there was little different about the 1978 Hostess cards from the three years' issues which had preceded it, or the one which followed. The 2-1/4" x 3-1/4" cards were printed in panels of three (7-1/4" x 3-1/4") as the bottom of family-sized boxes of snake cakes. The 1978 set was again complete at 150 cards. Like other years of Hostess issues, there are scarcities within the 1978 set that are the result of those panels having been issued with less-popular brands of snack cakes.

		NM	EX	VG
Complete Panel Set (50):		250.00	125.00	75.00
Complete Singles Set (150):		165.00	82.00	48.00
Common Panel:		3.50	1.75	1.00
Common Single Player:		.50	.25	.15
Panel 1		3.50	1.75	1.00
1	Butch Hobson	.50	.25	.15
2	George Foster	.60	.30	.20
3	Bob Forsch	.50	.25	.15
Panel 2		7.00	3.50	2.00
4	Tony Perez	3.00	1.50	.90
5	Bruce Sutter	.50	.25	.15
6	Hal McRae	.60	.30	.20
Panel 3		6.00	3.00	1.75
7	Tommy John	1.00	.50	.30
8	Greg Luzinski	.50	.25	.15
9	Enos Cabell	.50	.25	.15
Panel 4		8.50	4.25	2.50
10	Doug DeCinces	.50	.25	.15
11	Willie Stargell	3.00	1.50	.90
12	Ed Halicki	.50	.25	.15
Panel 5		3.50	1.75	1.00
13	Larry Hisle	.50	.25	.15
14	Jim Slaton	.50	.25	.15
15	Buddy Bell	.50	.25	.15
Panel 6		3.50	1.75	1.00
16	Earl Williams	.50	.25	.15
17	Glenn Abbott	.50	.25	.15
18	Dan Ford	.50	.25	.15
Panel 7		3.50	1.75	1.00
19	Gary Mathews	.50	.25	.15
20	Eric Soderholm	.50	.25	.15
21	Bump Wills	.50	.25	.15
Panel 8		5.00	2.50	1.50
22	Keith Hernandez	.75	.40	.25
23	Dave Cash	.50	.25	.15
24	George Scott	.50	.25	.15
Panel 9		15.00	7.50	4.50
25	Ron Guidry	.60	.30	.20
26	Dave Kingman	.60	.30	.20
27	George Brett	6.00	3.00	1.75
Panel 10		3.50	1.75	1.00
28	Bob Watson	.50	.25	.15
29	Bob Boone	.60	.30	.20
30	Reggie Smith	.50	.25	.15
Panel 11		15.00	7.50	4.50
31	Eddie Murray	6.00	3.00	1.75
32	Gary Lavelle	.50	.25	.15
33	Rennie Stennett	.50	.25	.15
Panel 12		3.50	1.75	1.00
34	Duane Kuiper	.50	.25	.15
35	Sixto Lezcano	.50	.25	.15
36	Dave Rozema	.50	.25	.15
Panel 13		3.50	1.75	1.00
37	Butch Wynegar	.50	.25	.15
38	Mitchell Page	.50	.25	.15
39	Bill Stein	.50	.25	.15
Panel 14		3.50	1.75	1.00
40	Elliott Maddox	.50	.25	.15
41	Mike Hargrove	.50	.25	.15
42	Bobby Bonds	.50	.25	.15
Panel 15		18.00	9.00	5.50
43	Garry Templeton	.50	.25	.15
44	Johnny Bench	7.00	3.50	2.00
45	Jim Rice	2.00	1.00	.60
Panel 16		12.50	6.25	3.75
46	Bill Buckner	.60	.30	.20
47	Reggie Jackson	5.00	2.50	1.50
48	Freddie Patek	.50	.25	.15
Panel 17		10.00	5.00	3.00
49	Steve Carlton	4.00	2.00	1.25
50	Cesar Cedeno	.50	.25	.15
51	Steve Yeager	.50	.25	.15
Panel 18		3.50	1.75	1.00
52	Phil Garner	.50	.25	.15
53	Lee May	.50	.25	.15
54	Darrell Evans	.60	.30	.20
Panel 19		4.00	2.00	1.25
55	Steve Kemp	.50	.25	.15
56a	Dusty Baker	.50	.25	.15
56b	Andre Thornton (unissued proof)	12.00	6.00	3.50
57	Ray Fosse	.50	.25	.15
Panel 20		3.50	1.75	1.00
58	Manny Sanguillen	.50	.25	.15
59	Tom Johnson	.50	.25	.15
60	Lee Stanton	.50	.25	.15
Panel 21		12.00	6.00	3.50
61	Jeff Burroughs	.50	.25	.15
62	Bobby Grich	.50	.25	.15
63	Dave Winfield	5.00	2.50	1.50
Panel 22		3.50	1.75	1.00
64	Dan Driessen	.50	.25	.15
65	Ted Simmons	.50	.25	.15
66	Jerry Remy	.50	.25	.15
Panel 23		3.50	1.75	1.00
67	Al Cowens	.50	.25	.15
68	Sparky Lyle	.50	.25	.15
69	Manny Trillo	.50	.25	.15
Panel 24		6.00	3.00	1.75
70	Don Sutton	2.50	1.25	.70
71	Larry Bowa	.50	.25	.15
72	Jose Cruz	.50	.25	.15
Panel 25		8.50	4.25	2.50
73	Willie McCovey	3.00	1.50	.90
74	Bert Blyleven	.50	.25	.15
75	Ken Singleton	.50	.25	.15
Panel 26		4.00	2.00	1.25
76	Bill North	.50	.25	.15
77	Jason Thompson	.50	.25	.15
78	Dennis Eckersley	.75	.40	.25
Panel 27		3.50	1.75	1.00
79	Jim Sundberg	.50	.25	.15
80	Jerry Koosman	.50	.25	.15
81	Bruce Bochte	.50	.25	.15
Panel 28		23.00	11.50	7.00
82	George Hendrick	.50	.25	.15
83	Nolan Ryan	10.00	5.00	3.00
84	Roy Howell	.50	.25	.15
Panel 29		8.50	4.25	2.50
85	Butch Metzger	.50	.25	.15
86	George Medich	.50	.25	.15
87	Joe Morgan	3.00	1.50	.90
Panel 30		3.50	1.75	1.00
88	Dennis Leonard	.50	.25	.15
89	Willie Randolph	.50	.25	.15
90	Bobby Murcer	.50	.25	.15
Panel 31		3.50	1.75	1.00
91	Rick Manning	.50	.25	.15
92	J.R. Richard	.50	.25	.15
93	Ron Cey	.50	.25	.15
Panel 32		3.50	1.75	1.00
94	Sal Bando	.50	.25	.15
95	Ron LeFlore	.50	.25	.15
96	Dave Goltz	.50	.25	.15

Panel 33		3.50	1.75	1.00
97	Dan Meyer	.50	.25	.15
98	Chris Chambliss	.50	.25	.15
99	Biff Pocoroba	.50	.25	.15
Panel 34		3.50	1.75	1.00
100	Oscar Gamble	.50	.25	.15
101	Frank Tanana	.50	.25	.15
102	Lenny Randle	.50	.25	.15
Panel 35		3.50	1.75	1.00
103	Tommy Hutton	.50	.25	.15
104	John Candelaria	.50	.25	.15
105	Jorge Orta	.50	.25	.15
Panel 36		3.50	1.75	1.00
106	Ken Reitz	.50	.25	.15
107	Bill Campbell	.50	.25	.15
108	Dave Concepcion	.50	.25	.15
Panel 37		3.50	1.75	1.00
109	Joe Ferguson	.50	.25	.15
110	Mickey Rivers	.50	.25	.15
111	Paul Splittorff	.50	.25	.15
Panel 38		16.50	8.25	4.75
112	Davey Lopes	.50	.25	.15
113	Mike Schmidt	7.00	3.50	2.00
114	Joe Rudi	.50	.25	.15
Panel 39		8.50	4.25	2.50
115	Milt May	.50	.25	.15
116	Jim Palmer	3.00	1.50	.90
117	Bill Madlock	.50	.25	.15
Panel 40		3.50	1.75	1.00
118	Roy Smalley	.50	.25	.15
119	Cecil Cooper	.50	.25	.15
120	Rick Langford	.50	.25	.15
Panel 41		7.00	3.50	2.00
121	Ruppert Jones	.50	.25	.15
122	Phil Niekro	2.50	1.25	.70
123	Toby Harrah	.50	.25	.15
Panel 42		3.50	1.75	1.00
124	Chet Lemon	.50	.25	.15
125	Gene Tenace	.50	.25	.15
126	Steve Henderson	.50	.25	.15
Panel 43		24.00	12.00	7.25
127	Mike Torrez	.50	.25	.15
128	Pete Rose	10.00	5.00	3.00
129	John Denny	.50	.25	.15
Panel 44		3.50	1.75	1.00
130	Darrell Porter	.50	.25	.15
131	Rick Reuschel	.50	.25	.15
132	Graig Nettles	.50	.25	.15
Panel 45		4.75	2.25	1.25
133	Garry Maddox	.50	.25	.15
134	Mike Flanagan	.50	.25	.15
135	Dave Parker	1.00	.50	.30
Panel 46		18.00	9.00	5.50
136	Terry Whitfield	.50	.25	.15
137	Wayne Garland	.50	.25	.15
138	Robin Yount	6.50	3.25	2.00
Panel 47		16.00	8.00	4.75
139a	Gaylord Perry (San Diego)	2.50	1.25	.70
139b	Gaylord Perry (Texas Rangers, unissued proof)	20.00	10.00	6.00
140	Rod Carew	5.00	2.50	1.50
141	Wayne Gross	.50	.25	.15
Panel 48		6.25	3.25	1.75
142	Barry Bonnell	.50	.25	.15
143	Willie Montanez	.50	.25	.15
144	Rollie Fingers	2.00	1.00	.60
Panel 49		18.00	9.00	5.50
145	Bob Bailor	.50	.25	.15
146	Tom Seaver	5.00	2.50	1.50
147	Thurman Munson	2.50	1.25	.70
Panel 50		5.25	2.75	1.50
148	Lyman Bostock	.50	.25	.15
149	Gary Carter	1.50	.70	.45
150	Ron Blomberg	.50	.25	.15

1978 Hostess Unissued Proofs

Different versions of two of the issued cards (see 1978 Hostess #56, 139) plus 10 players who do not appear on the snack cake boxes constitute the proof set for '78 Hostess. The unissued proofs are identical in format to the cards actually issued and measure 2-1/4" x 3-1/4" at the dotted lines.

		NM	EX	VG
Complete Set (10):		240.00	120.00	72.50
Common Player:		25.00	12.50	7.50
151	Bill Robinson	25.00	12.50	7.50
152	Lou Piniella	35.00	17.50	10.50
153	Lamar Johnson	25.00	12.50	7.50
154	Mark Belanger	30.00	15.00	9.00
155	Ken Griffey	35.00	17.50	10.50
156	Ken Forsch	25.00	12.50	7.50
157	Ted Sizemore	25.00	12.50	7.50
158	Don Baylor	35.00	17.50	10.50
159	Dusty Baker	35.00	17.50	10.50
160	Al Oliver	35.00	17.50	10.50

1979 Hostess

The last of five consecutive annual issues, the 1979 Hostess set retained the 150-card set size, 2-1/4" x 3-1/4" single-card size and 7-1/4" x 3-1/4" three-card panel format from the previous years. The cards were printed as the bottom panel on family-size boxes of Hostess snack cakes. Some panels, which were printed on less-popular brands, are somewhat scarcer today than the rest of the set. Like all Hostess issues, because the hobby was in a well-developed state at the time of issue, the 1979s survive today in complete panels and complete unused boxes, for collectors who like original packaging.

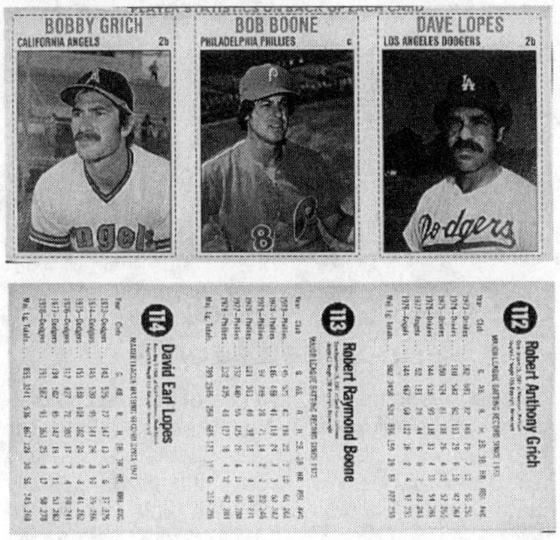

		NM	EX	VG
Complete Panel Set (50):		250.00	125.00	75.00
Complete Singles Set (150):		165.00	82.00	48.00
Common Panel:		3.50	1.75	1.00
Common Single Player:		.50	.25	.15
Panel 1		6.00	3.00	1.75
1	John Denny	.50	.25	.15
2a	Rod Carew (position "d-of", unissued proof)	15.00	7.50	4.50
2b	Jim Rice ("dh-of" corrected)	2.50	1.25	.70
3	Doug Bair	.50	.25	.15
Panel 2		3.50	1.75	1.00
4	Darrell Porter	.50	.25	.15
5	Ross Grimsley	.50	.25	.15
6	Bobby Murcer	.50	.25	.15
Panel 3		17.00	8.50	5.00
7	Lee Mazzilli	.50	.25	.15
8	Steve Garvey	2.00	1.00	.60
9	Mike Schmidt	6.00	3.00	1.75
Panel 4		8.50	4.25	2.50
10	Terry Whitfield	.50	.25	.15
11	Jim Palmer	3.00	1.50	.90
12	Omar Moreno	.50	.25	.15
Panel 5		3.50	1.75	1.00
13	Duane Kuiper	.50	.25	.15
14	Mike Caldwell	.50	.25	.15
15	Steve Kemp	.50	.25	.15
Panel 6		3.50	1.75	1.00
16	Dave Goltz	.50	.25	.15
17	Mitchell Page	.50	.25	.15
18	Bill Stein	.50	.25	.15
Panel 7		3.50	1.75	1.00
19	Gene Tenace	.50	.25	.15
20	Jeff Burroughs	.50	.25	.15
21	Francisco Barrios	.50	.25	.15
Panel 8		5.50	2.75	1.50
22	Mike Torrez	.50	.25	.15
23	Ken Reitz	.50	.25	.15
24	Gary Carter	1.50	.70	.45
Panel 9		7.50	3.75	2.25
25	Al Hrabosky	.50	.25	.15
26	Thurman Munson	2.50	1.25	.70
27	Bill Buckner	.50	.25	.15
Panel 10		6.50	3.25	1.75
28	Ron Cey	.60	.30	.20
29	J.R. Richard	.60	.30	.20
30	Greg Luzinski	.50	.25	.15
Panel 11		3.50	1.75	1.00
31	Ed Ott	.50	.25	.15
32	Denny Martinez	.75	.40	.25
33	Darrell Evans	.60	.30	.20
Panel 12		3.50	1.75	1.00
34	Ron LeFlore	.50	.25	.15
35	Rick Waits	.50	.25	.15
36	Cecil Cooper	.50	.25	.15
Panel 13		12.00	6.00	3.50
37	Leon Roberts	.50	.25	.15
38	Rod Carew	4.00	2.00	1.25
39	John Henry Johnson	.50	.25	.15
Panel 14		3.50	1.75	1.00
40	Chet Lemon	.50	.25	.15
41	Craig Swan	.50	.25	.15
42	Gary Matthews	.50	.25	.15
Panel 15		3.50	1.75	1.00
43	Lamar Johnson	.50	.25	.15
44	Ted Simmons	.50	.25	.15
45	Ken Griffey	.60	.30	.20
Panel 16		3.75	1.75	1.00
46	Freddie Patek	.50	.25	.15
47	Frank Tanana	.50	.25	.15
48	Rich Gossage	.60	.30	.20
Panel 17		3.50	1.75	1.00
49	Burt Hooton	.50	.25	.15
50	Ellis Valentine	.50	.25	.15
51	Ken Forsch	.50	.25	.15
Panel 18		4.50	2.25	1.25
52	Bob Knepper	.50	.25	.15
53	Dave Parker	1.00	.50	.30
54	Doug DeCinces	.50	.25	.15
Panel 19		14.00	7.00	4.25
55	Robin Yount	4.50	2.25	1.25
56	Rusty Staub	.60	.30	.20
57	Gary Alexander	.50	.25	.15
Panel 20		3.50	1.75	1.00
58	Julio Cruz	.50	.25	.15
59	Matt Keough	.50	.25	.15
60	Roy Smalley	.50	.25	.15
Panel 21		12.00	6.00	3.50
61	Joe Morgan	3.00	1.50	.90
62	Phil Niekro	2.50	1.25	.70
63	Don Baylor	.60	.30	.20
Panel 22		14.00	7.00	4.25
64	Dwight Evans	.50	.25	.15
65	Tom Seaver	5.00	2.50	1.50
66	George Hendrick	.50	.25	.15
Panel 23		16.00	8.00	4.75
67	Rick Reuschel	.50	.25	.15
68	George Brett	6.00	3.00	1.75
69	Lou Piniella	.75	.40	.25
Panel 24		9.50	4.75	3.00
70	Enos Cabell	.50	.25	.15
71	Steve Carlton	3.50	1.75	1.00
72	Reggie Smith	.50	.25	.15
Panel 25		3.50	1.75	1.00
73	Rick Dempsey	.50	.25	.15
74	Vida Blue	.50	.25	.15
75	Phil Garner	.50	.25	.15
Panel 26		3.50	1.75	1.00
76	Rick Manning	.50	.25	.15
77	Mark Fidrych	.60	.30	.20
78	Mario Guerrero	.50	.25	.15
Panel 27		3.50	1.75	1.00
79	Bob Stinson	.50	.25	.15
80	Al Oliver	.60	.30	.20
81	Doug Flynn	.50	.25	.15
Panel 28		6.00	3.00	1.75
82	John Mayberry	.50	.25	.15
83	Gaylord Perry	2.50	1.25	.70
84	Joe Rudi	.50	.25	.15
Panel 29		3.50	1.75	1.00
85	Dave Concepcion	.50	.25	.15
86	John Candelaria	.50	.25	.15
87	Pete Vuckovich	.50	.25	.15
Panel 30		3.50	1.75	1.00
88	Ivan DeJesus	.50	.25	.15
89	Ron Guidry	.60	.30	.20
90	Hal McRae	.50	.25	.15
Panel 31		5.00	2.50	1.50
91	Cesar Cedeno	.50	.25	.15
92	Don Sutton	2.00	1.00	.60
93	Andre Thornton	.50	.25	.15
Panel 32		3.50	1.75	1.00
94	Roger Erickson	.50	.25	.15
95	Larry Hisle	.50	.25	.15
96	Jason Thompson	.50	.25	.15
Panel 33		3.50	1.75	1.00
97	Jim Sundberg	.50	.25	.15
98	Bob Horner	.50	.25	.15
99	Ruppert Jones	.50	.25	.15
Panel 34		42.00	21.00	12.00
100	Willie Montanez	.50	.25	.15
101	Nolan Ryan	8.00	4.00	2.50
102	Ozzie Smith	12.00	6.00	3.50
Panel 35		8.50	4.25	2.50
103	Eric Soderholm	.50	.25	.15
104	Willie Stargell	3.00	1.50	.90
105a	Bob Bailor (photo reversed, unissued proof)	8.00	4.00	2.50
105b	Bob Bailor (photo corrected)	.50	.25	.15
Panel 36		10.00	5.00	3.00
106	Carlton Fisk	3.00	1.50	.90
107	George Foster	.60	.30	.20
108	Keith Hernandez	.65	.35	.20
Panel 37		3.50	1.75	1.00
109	Dennis Leonard	.50	.25	.15
110	Graig Nettles	.50	.25	.15
111	Jose Cruz	.50	.25	.15
Panel 38		3.50	1.75	1.00
112	Bobby Grich	.50	.25	.15
113	Bob Boone	.60	.30	.20
114	Dave Lopes	.50	.25	.15
Panel 39		12.00	6.00	3.50
115	Eddie Murray	4.00	2.00	1.25
116	Jack Clark	.50	.25	.15
117	Lou Whitaker	.75	.40	.25
Panel 40		13.00	6.50	4.00
118	Miguel Dilone	.50	.25	.15
119	Sal Bando	.50	.25	.15
120	Reggie Jackson	5.00	2.50	1.50
Panel 41		11.00	5.50	3.25
121	Dale Murphy	4.00	2.00	1.25
122	Jon Matlack	.50	.25	.15
123	Bruce Bochte	.50	.25	.15
Panel 42		11.00	5.50	3.25
124	John Stearns	.50	.25	.15
125	Dave Winfield	4.00	2.00	1.25
126	Jorge Orta	.50	.25	.15
Panel 43		16.00	8.00	4.75
127	Garry Templeton	.50	.25	.15
128	Johnny Bench	6.00	3.00	1.75
129	Butch Hobson	.50	.25	.15
Panel 44		3.50	1.75	1.00
130	Bruce Sutter	.50	.25	.15
131	Bucky Dent	.50	.25	.15
132	Amos Otis	.50	.25	.15
Panel 45		3.50	1.75	1.00
133	Bert Blyleven	.50	.25	.15
134	Larry Bowa	.50	.25	.15
135	Ken Singleton	.50	.25	.15
Panel 46		3.50	1.75	1.00
136	Sixto Lezcano	.50	.25	.15
137	Roy Howell	.50	.25	.15
138	Bill Madlock	.50	.25	.15
Panel 47		3.50	1.75	1.00
139	Dave Revering	.50	.25	.15
140	Richie Zisk	.50	.25	.15
141	Butch Wynegar	.50	.25	.15
Panel 48		22.00	11.00	6.50
142	Alan Ashby	.50	.25	.15
143	Sparky Lyle	.50	.25	.15
144	Pete Rose	10.00	5.00	3.00
Panel 49		4.50	2.25	1.25
145	Dennis Eckersley	.90	.45	.25

146	Dave Kingman	.60	.30	.20
147	Buddy Bell	.50	.25	.15
Panel 50		3.50	1.75	1.00
148	Mike Hargrove	.50	.25	.15
149	Jerry Koosman	.50	.25	.15
150	Toby Harrah	.50	.25	.15

1979 Hostess Unissued Proofs

Identical in format to the 150 cards which were issued on boxes of Hostess snack cakes, these cards were possibly prepared in the event trades of players in the issued set required quick replacement. The reason these cards were never released is unknown. Cards measure 2-1/4" x 3-1/4" at the dotted-line borders. While some of the proofs are numbered on back, others have no card number.

		NM	EX	VG
Complete Set (17):		550.00	275.00	165.00
Common Player:		25.00	12.50	7.50
151	Dusty Baker	35.00	17.50	10.50
152	Mark Belanger	30.00	15.00	9.00
154	Al Cowens	25.00	12.50	7.50
155	Dan Driessen	25.00	12.50	7.50
157	Steve Henderson	25.00	12.50	7.50
159	Tommy John	45.00	22.00	13.50
160	Garry Maddox	25.00	12.50	7.50
(161)	Willie McCovey	125.00	62.00	37.00
(162)	Scott McGregor	25.00	12.50	7.50
(163)	Bill Nahorodny	25.00	12.50	7.50
(164)	Terry Puhl	25.00	12.50	7.50
(165)	Willie Randolph	25.00	12.50	7.50
(166)	Jim Slaton	25.00	12.50	7.50
(167)	Paul Splittorff	25.00	12.50	7.50
(168)	Frank Taveras	25.00	12.50	7.50
(169)	Alan Trammell	60.00	30.00	18.00
(170)	Bump Wills	25.00	12.50	7.50

1971 House of Jazz

Controversy has dogged this card set since the first reports of its existence in the early 1970s. The legitimacy of the issue has been questioned though certain hobby journalists traced the cards to a record store which supposedly gave them away with music purchases, along with similar cards depicting musicians. The 2-3/8" x 3-1/2" cards are printed in black-and-white with round corners. Backs of some, but not all, cards have a blue-and-white address sticker for "HOUSE OF JAZZ, LTD." The unnumbered cards are checklisted here in alphabetical order.

		NM	EX	VG
Complete Set (35):		200.00	100.00	60.00
Common Player:		5.00	2.50	1.50
(1)	John Antonelli	5.00	2.50	1.50
(2)	Richie Ashburn	5.00	2.50	1.50
(3)	Ernie Banks	6.50	3.25	2.00
(4)	Hank Bauer	5.00	2.50	1.50
(5)	Joe DiMaggio	15.00	7.50	4.50
(6)	Bobby Doerr	5.00	2.50	1.50
(7)	Herman Franks	5.00	2.50	1.50
(8)	Lou Gehrig	10.00	5.00	3.00
(9)	Granny Hamner	5.00	2.50	1.50
(10)	Al Kaline	6.50	3.25	2.00
(11)	Harmon Killebrew	5.00	2.50	1.50
(12)	Jim Konstanty	5.00	2.50	1.50
(13)	Bob Lemon	5.00	2.50	1.50
(14)	Ed Lopat	5.00	2.50	1.50
(15)	Stan Lopata	5.00	2.50	1.50
(16)	Peanuts Lowrey	5.00	2.50	1.50
(17)	Mickey Mantle	45.00	22.00	13.50
(18)	Phil Marchildon	5.00	2.50	1.50
(19)	Walt Masterson	5.00	2.50	1.50
(20)	Ed Mathews	5.00	2.50	1.50
(21)	Willie Mays	10.00	5.00	3.00
(22)	Don Newcombe	5.00	2.50	1.50
(23)	Joe Nuxhall	5.00	2.50	1.50
(24)	Satchel Paige	7.50	3.75	2.25
(25)	Roy Partee	5.00	2.50	1.50
(26)	Jackie Robinson	7.50	3.75	2.25
(27)	Babe Ruth	20.00	10.00	6.00
(28)	Carl Scheib	5.00	2.50	1.50
(29)	Bobby Shantz	5.00	2.50	1.50
(30)	Burt Shotton	5.00	2.50	1.50
(31)	Duke Snider	6.50	3.25	2.00
(32)	Warren Spahn	5.00	2.50	1.50
(33)	Johnny Temple	5.00	2.50	1.50
(34)	Ted Williams	10.00	5.00	3.00
(35)	Early Wynn	5.00	2.50	1.50

1967 Houston Astros Team Issue

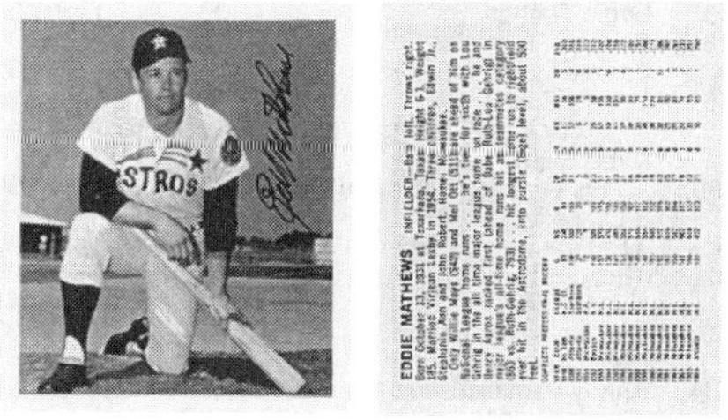

This set of 12 player cards was issued by the Houston Astros though the exact nature of the promotion is not known. Individual cards of 2-5/8" x 3-1/8" were printed on a perforated sheet about 9" x 10-1/2". Fronts have a posed color photo with a black facsimile autograph. Backs are printed in black on white with a yellow color block behind the player data and career notes. Full major and minor league stats are at bottom. The unnumbered cards are checklisted here in alphabetical order.

		NM	EX	VG
Complete Set, Sheet:		40.00	20.00	12.00
Complete Set, Singles (12):		35.00	17.50	10.00
Common Player:		4.00	2.00	1.25
(1)	Bob Aspromonte	4.00	2.00	1.25
(2)	John Bateman	4.00	2.00	1.25
(3)	Mike Cuellar	5.00	2.50	1.50
(4)	Larry Dierker	4.00	2.00	1.25
(5)	Dave Giusti	4.00	2.00	1.25
(6)	Grady Hatton	4.00	2.00	1.25
(7)	Bill Heath	4.00	2.00	1.25
(8)	Sonny Jackson	4.00	2.00	1.25
(9)	Ed Mathews	10.00	5.00	3.00
(10)	Joe Morgan	10.00	5.00	3.00
(11)	Rusty Staub	6.00	3.00	1.75
(12)	Jim Wynn	4.00	2.00	1.25

1962 Houston Colt .45s Booklets

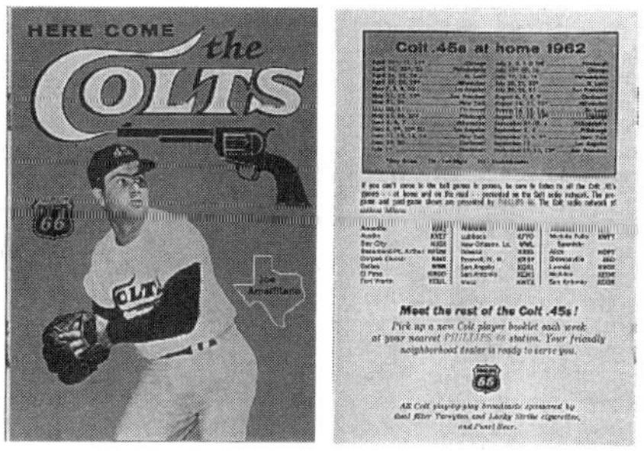

To introduce the members of the new Houston National League team Phillips 66 gasoline sponsored (along with the team's cigarette and beer broadcast sponsors) this set of 24 player profile booklets given away one per week during the season. Fronts of the 16-page 5-3/8" x 7-7/16" booklets feature a blue and white action photo of the player on a bright orange background. Black and white graphics complete the design. The player's name appears in a Texas map outline. Backs have the 1962 Houston Colt .45s home-game schedule and details of the team's statewide radio network. Inside the booklet are a complete biography, stats and both posed and action photos of the players, along with families, teammates, etc. Because of player trades during the season, and lessened demand for some of the non-player booklets, some of the series are quite scarce. Each of the booklets can be found with different sponsors logos on front.

		NM	EX	VG
Complete Set (24):		240.00	120.00	72.00
Common Booklet:		15.00	7.50	4.50
(1)	Joe Amalfitano	15.00	7.50	4.50
(2)	Bob Aspromonte	15.00	7.50	4.50
(3)	Bob Bruce	15.00	7.50	4.50
(4)	Jim Campbell	18.00	9.00	5.50
(5)	Harry Craft	15.00	7.50	4.50
(6)	Dick Farrell	15.00	7.50	4.50
(7)	Dave Giusti	15.00	7.50	4.50
(8)	Jim Golden	15.00	7.50	4.50
(9)	J.C. Hartman	18.00	9.00	5.50
(10)	Ken Johnson	15.00	7.50	4.50
(11)	Norm Larker	15.00	7.50	4.50
(12)	Bob Lillis	15.00	7.50	4.50
(13)	Don McMahon	15.00	7.50	4.50
(14)	Roman Mejias	15.00	7.50	4.50
(15)	Jim Pendleton	18.00	9.00	5.50
(16)	Paul Richards (GM)	15.00	7.50	4.50
(17)	Bobby Shantz	30.00	15.00	9.00
(18)	Hal Smith	15.00	7.50	4.50
(19)	Al Spangler	15.00	7.50	4.50
(20)	Jim Umbricht	15.00	7.50	4.50
(21)	Carl Warwick	15.00	7.50	4.50
(22)	Hal Woodeshick	15.00	7.50	4.50
(23)	Coaches (James Adair, Bobby Bragan, Cot Deal, Luman Harris)	25.00	12.50	7.50
(24)	Announcers (Rene Cardenas, Orlando Diego, Gene Elston, Al Helfer, Lowell Passe, Guy Savage)	19.00	9.50	5.75

1956 Howard Photo Service Postcards

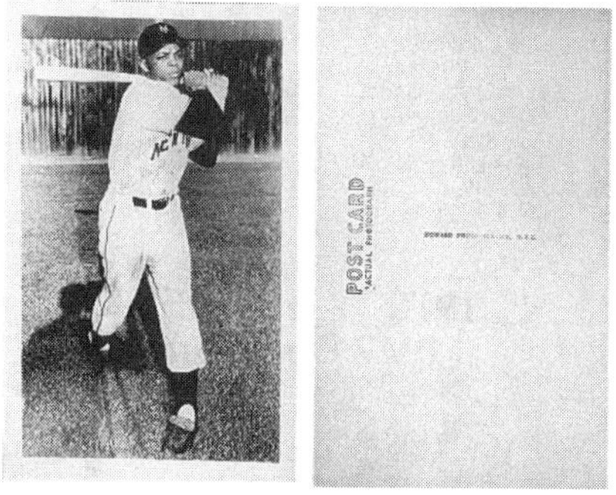

Little is known about these postcards. The year of issue is only a guess as it is unspecified on the cards and with only two players known, impossible to pinpoint. The 3-1/2" x 5-1/2" cards have a glossy black-and-white front photo. A rubber-stamp on the back attributes the card to "Howard Photo Service, N.Y.C." The specific photos of the two Turley cards is not known. It is possible other cards may yet be discovered.

		NM	EX	VG
Common Player:		15.00	7.50	4.50
(1)	Billy Hitchcock	15.00	7.50	4.50
(2)	Willie Mays	125.00	62.00	37.00
(3)	Bob Turley	15.00	7.50	4.50
(4)	Bob Turley	15.00	7.50	4.50

1976 HRT/RES 1942 Play Ball

This "phantom" continuation of the Play Ball series of 1939-41 was the creation of Ted Taylor and Bob Schmierer, whose initials appear in the copyright line on back. The 2-1/2" x 3-1/8" cards feature black-and-white photos on front and were printed on gray clay-content cardboard in a near replication of the stock found on the vintage Play Ball series. Backs were also done in style reminiscent of 1940s issues. Besides player data and career summaries, backs have a "1942 PLAY BALL - U.S.A." title line and either a "Buy War Bonds" or

"'Keep Baseball Going' - FDR" slogan above the 1976 copyright line. The pair produced a number of other original and reprint issues in the 1970s. All of the others carry advertisements for their "Philly" card shows.

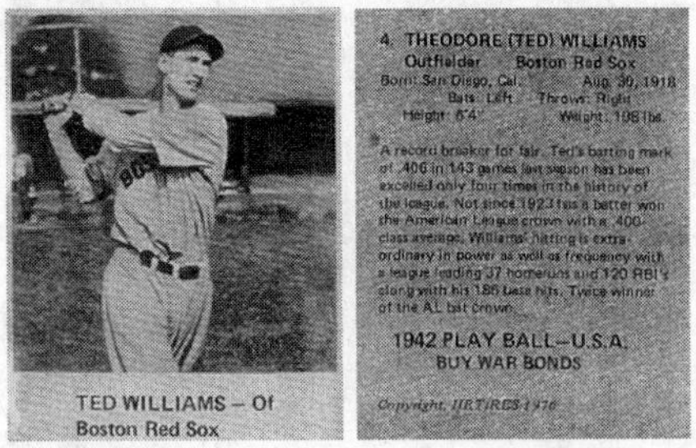

		NM	EX	VG
Complete Set (36):		30.00	15.00	9.00
Common Card:		.50	.25	.15
1	Lou Gehrig	4.00	2.00	1.25
2	Joe DiMaggio	4.00	2.00	1.25
3	Phil Rizzuto	1.50	.70	.45
4	Ted Williams	3.00	1.50	.90
5	Charles Wagner	.50	.25	.15
6	Thornton Lee	.50	.25	.15
7	Taft Wright	.50	.25	.15
8	Jeff Heath	.50	.25	.15
9	Roy Mack	.50	.25	.15
10	Pat Mullin	.50	.25	.15
11	Al Benton	.50	.25	.15
12	Bob Harris	.50	.25	.15
13	Roy Cullenbine	.50	.25	.15
14	Cecil Travis	.50	.25	.15
15	Buck Newsom	.50	.25	.15
16	Eddie Collins Jr.	.50	.25	.15
17	Dick Siebert	.50	.25	.15
18	Dee Miles	.50	.25	.15
19	Pete Reiser	.50	.25	.15
20	Dolph Camilli	.50	.25	.15
21	Curt Davis	.50	.25	.15
22	Spud Krist	.50	.25	.15
23	Frank Crespi	.50	.25	.15
24	Elmer Riddle	.50	.25	.15
25	Bucky Walters	.50	.25	.15
26	Vince DiMaggio	.75	.40	.25
27	Max Butcher	.50	.25	.15
28	Mel Ott	1.50	.70	.45
29	Bob Carpenter	.50	.25	.15
30	Claude Passeau	.50	.25	.15
31	Dom Dallessandro	.50	.25	.15
32	Casey Stengel	1.50	.70	.45
33	Alva Javery	.50	.25	.15
34	Hans Lobert	.50	.25	.15
35	Nick Etten	.50	.25	.15
36	John Podgajny	.50	.25	.15

1976-77 HRT/RES 1947 Bowman

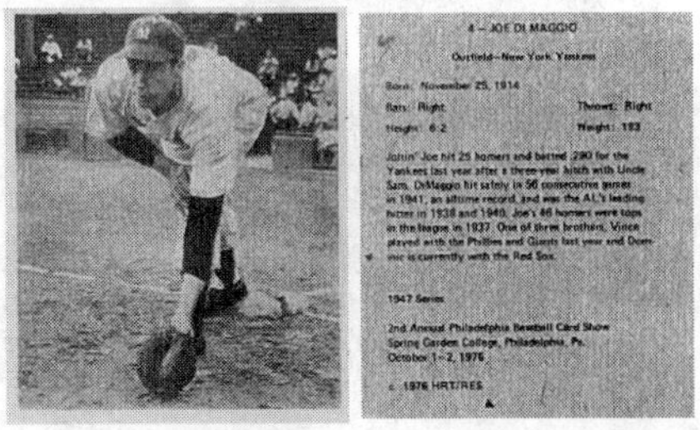

Advertised as "The Set That Never Was," this collectors issue from Ted Taylor and Bob Schmierer used a 2-1/8" x 2-1/2" black-and-white format and gray cardboard stock to replicate the feel of the first post-WWII baseball cards. The set was issued in three series with advertising on back promoting the second (1976) and third (1977) annual EPSCC "Philly" shows. Series one (#1-49) was issued in 1976; series two (#50-81) and three (#82-113) were 1977 issues.

		NM	EX	VG
Complete Set (113):		150.00	75.00	45.00
Common Player:		1.00	.50	.30
1	Bobby Doerr	1.00	.50	.30
2	Stan Musial	3.00	1.50	.90
3	Babe Ruth	8.00	4.00	2.50
4	Joe DiMaggio	6.00	3.00	1.75
5	Andy Pafko	1.00	.50	.30
6	Johnny Pesky	1.00	.50	.30
7	Gil Hodges	1.50	.70	.45
8	Tommy Holmes	1.00	.50	.30
9	Ralph Kiner	1.00	.50	.30
10	Yogi Berra	3.00	1.50	.90
11	Bob Feller	1.50	.70	.45
12	Joe Gordon	1.00	.50	.30
13	Eddie Joost	1.00	.50	.30
14	Del Ennis	1.00	.50	.30
15	Johnny Mize	1.00	.50	.30
16	Pee Wee Reese	1.25	.60	.40
17	Jackie Robinson	4.00	2.00	1.25
18	Enos Slaughter	1.00	.50	.30
19	Vern Stephens	1.00	.50	.30
20	Bobby Thomson	1.25	.60	.40
21	Ted Williams	6.00	3.00	1.75
22	Bob Elliott	1.00	.50	.30
23	Mickey Vernon	1.00	.50	.30
24	Ewell Blackwell	1.00	.50	.30
25	Lou Boudreau	1.00	.50	.30
26	Ralph Branca	1.00	.50	.30
27	Harry Breechen (Brecheen)	1.00	.50	.30
28	Dom DiMaggio	1.00	.50	.30
29	Bruce Edwards	1.00	.50	.30
30	Sam Chapman	1.00	.50	.30
31	George Kell	1.00	.50	.30
32	Jack Kramer	1.00	.50	.30
33	Hal Newhouser	1.00	.50	.30
34	Charlie Keller	1.00	.50	.30
35	Ken Keltner	1.00	.50	.30
36	Hank Greenberg	1.25	.60	.40
37	Howie Pollet	1.00	.50	.30
38	Luke Appling	1.00	.50	.30
39	Pete Suder	1.00	.50	.30
40	Johnny Sain	1.00	.50	.30
41	Phil Cavaretta (Cavarretta)	1.00	.50	.30
42	Johnny Vander Meer	1.00	.50	.30
43	Mel Ott	1.00	.50	.30
44	Walker Cooper	1.00	.50	.30
45	Birdie Tebbetts	1.00	.50	.30
46	George Stirnweiss	1.00	.50	.30
47	Connie Mack	1.00	.50	.30
48	Jimmie Foxx	1.00	.50	.30
49	Checklist (Joe DiMaggio, Babe Ruth)	1.50	.70	.45
(50)	Honus Wagner T206 card (First series)	1.00	.50	.30
51	(Ted Taylor) (First series)	1.00	.50	.30
52	(Bob Schmierer) (First series)	1.00	.50	.30
50	(Schoolboy Rowe) (Second series)	1.00	.50	.30
51	(Andy Seminick) (Second series)	1.00	.50	.30
52	Fred Walker (Second series)	1.00	.50	.30
53	Virgil Trucks	1.00	.50	.30
54	Dizzy Trout	1.00	.50	.30
55	Walter Evers	1.00	.50	.30
56	Thurman Tucker	1.00	.50	.30
57	Fritz Ostermueller	1.00	.50	.30
58	Augie Galan	1.00	.50	.30
59	Norman Young	1.00	.50	.30
60	Skeeter Newsome	1.00	.50	.30
61	Jack Lohrke	1.00	.50	.30
62	Rudy York	1.00	.50	.30
63	Tex Hughson	1.00	.50	.30
64	Sam Mele	1.00	.50	.30
65	Fred Hutchinson	1.00	.50	.30
66	Don Black	1.00	.50	.30
67	Les Fleming	1.00	.50	.30
68	George McQuinn	1.00	.50	.30
69	Mike McCormick	1.00	.50	.30
70	Mickey Witek	1.00	.50	.30
71	Blix Donnelly	1.00	.50	.30
72	Elbie Fletcher	1.00	.50	.30
73	Hal Gregg	1.00	.50	.30
74	Dick Whitman	1.00	.50	.30
75	Johnny Neun	1.00	.50	.30
76	Doyle Lade	1.00	.50	.30
77	Ron Northey	1.00	.50	.30
78	Walker Cooper	1.00	.50	.30
79	Warren Spahn	1.00	.50	.30
80	Happy Chandler	1.00	.50	.30
81	Checklist (Connie Mack, Roy Mack, Connie Mack III)	1.00	.50	.30
82	Earle Mack	1.00	.50	.30
83	Buddy Rosar	1.00	.50	.30
84	Walt Judnich	1.00	.50	.30
85	Bob Kennedy	1.00	.50	.30
86	Mike Tresh	1.00	.50	.30
87	Sid Hudson	1.00	.50	.30
88	Eugene Thompson	1.00	.50	.30
89	Bill Nicholson	1.00	.50	.30
90	Stan Hack	1.00	.50	.30
91	Terry Moore	1.00	.50	.30
92	Ted Lyons	1.00	.50	.30
93	Barney McCosky	1.00	.50	.30
94	Stan Spence	1.00	.50	.30
95	Larry Jansen	1.00	.50	.30
96	Whitey Kurowski	1.00	.50	.30
97	Honus Wagner	1.50	.70	.45
98	Billy Herman	1.00	.50	.30
99	Jim Tabor	1.00	.50	.30
100	Phil Marchildon	1.00	.50	.30
101	Dave Ferriss	1.00	.50	.30
102	Al Zarilla	1.00	.50	.30
103	Bob Dillinger	1.00	.50	.30
104	Bob Lemon	1.00	.50	.30
105	Jim Hegan	1.00	.50	.30
106	Johnny Lindell	1.00	.50	.30
107	Willard Marshall	1.00	.50	.30
108	Walt Masterson	1.00	.50	.30
109	Carl Scheib	1.00	.50	.30
110	Bobby Brown	1.00	.50	.30
111	Cy Block	1.00	.50	.30
112	Sid Gordon	1.00	.50	.30
113	Checklist (Ty Cobb, Babe Ruth, Tris Speaker)	1.50	.70	.45

1977 HRT/RES Philadelphia 'Favorites'

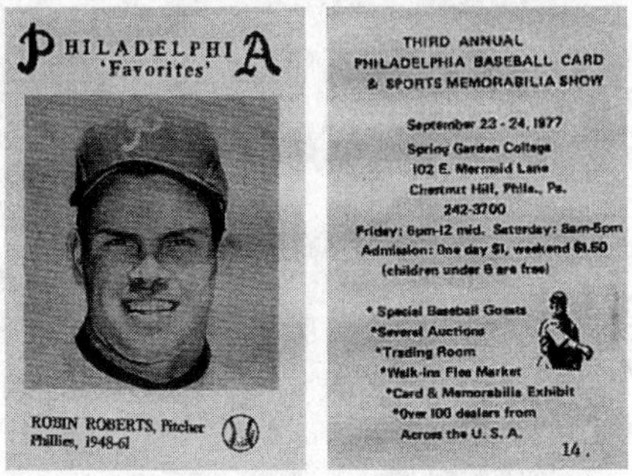

This collectors issue was produced by promoters Ted Taylor and Bob Schmierer to promote their third annual "Philly Show" in 1977. Printed in black-and-white on front and back, the 2-3/8" x 3-5/8" cards feature former Philadelphia A's and Phillies player photos on front, and an ad for the show on back. Cards were given away at area malls and sporting events to promote the show. Complete sets were originally sold for $2.75.

		NM	EX	VG
Complete Set (25):		12.00	6.00	3.50
Common Player:		.50	.25	.15
1	Connie Mack	.50	.25	.15
2	Larry Lajoie	.50	.25	.15
3	Eddie Collins	.50	.25	.15
4	Lefty Grove	.50	.25	.15
5	Al Simmons	.50	.25	.15
6	Jimmie Foxx	.50	.25	.15
7	Frank Baker	.50	.25	.15
8	Ferris Fain	.50	.25	.15
9	Jimmy Dykes	.50	.25	.15
10	Willie Jones	.50	.25	.15
11	Del Ennis	.50	.25	.15
12	Granny Hamner	.50	.25	.15
13	Andy Seminick	.50	.25	.15
14	Robin Roberts	.75	.40	.25
15	Ed Delahanty	.50	.25	.15
16	Gavvy Cravath	.50	.25	.15
17	Cy Williams	.50	.25	.15
18	Chuck Klein	.50	.25	.15
19	Rich Ashburn	.75	.40	.25
20	Bobby Shantz	.50	.25	.15
21	Gus Zernial	.50	.25	.15
22	Eddie Sawyer	.50	.25	.15
23	Grover Alexander	.50	.25	.15
24	Wally Moses	.50	.25	.15
25	Connie Mack Stadium	.50	.25	.15

1978 HRT/RES 1939 Father and Son Reprints

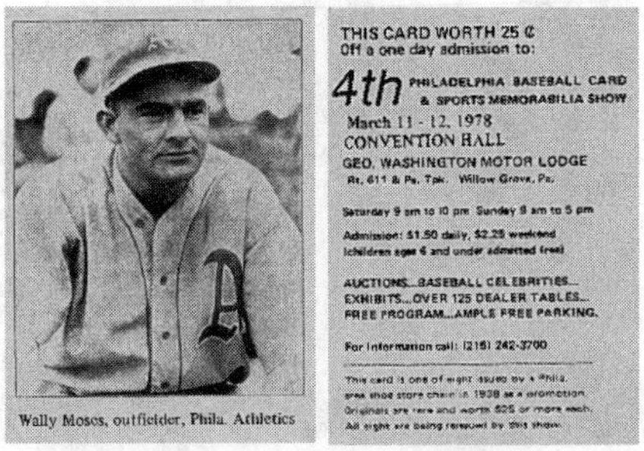

Reprints of scarce 1939 Father and Son Shoes stores cards of local ballplayers (minus the original advertising on front) were created by Ted Taylor and Bob Schmierer to promote their fourth "Philly Show" in March, 1978. The 3" x 4" cards have black-and-white player photos on front. Backs carry an ad for the show and information about the reprints.

		NM	EX	VG
Complete Set (8):		4.00	2.00	1.25
Common Player:		.50	.25	.15
(1)	Sam Chapman	.50	.25	.15
(2)	Chuck Klein	.75	.40	.25
(3)	Herschel Martin	.50	.25	.15
(4)	Wally Moses	.50	.25	.15
(5)	Hugh Mulcahy	.50	.25	.15
(6)	Skeeter Newsome	.50	.25	.15
(7)	George Scharien (Scharein)	.50	.25	.15
(8)	Dick Siebert	.50	.25	.15

1979 HRT/RES 1950 Phillies/A's "Doubleheaders"

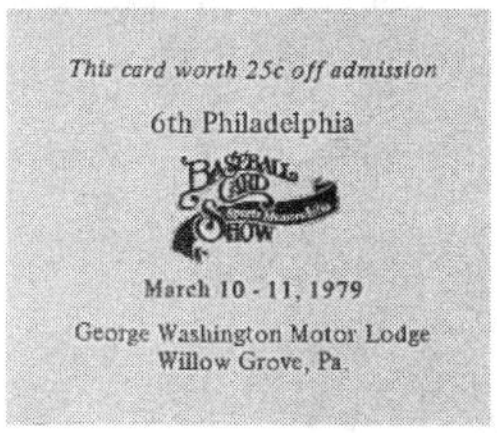

Though their names or initials do not appear on the cards, this collectors set was issued by Ted Taylor and Bob Schmierer to promote the March and September, 1979, "Philly Shows," the sixth and seventh in the show's history. Borrowing from the format of the 1941 "Doubleheaders" bubblegum card issue, these 2 1/2" x 2-1/8" cards depict members of the 1950 Phillies "Whiz Kids" and the 1950 A's, the last team managed by Connie Mack. Fronts are printed in blue and white, backs in maroon and white. The dual-player cards feature various ads on back, while the managers' cards have a team narrative. The unnumbered cards are checklisted here alphabetically within team, by the last name of the player on the left.

		NM	EX	VG
Complete Set (30):		24.00	12.00	7.25
Common Card:		.90	.45	.25
(1)	Joe Astroth, Dick Fowler	.90	.45	.25
(2)	Sam Chapman, Lou Brissie	.90	.45	.25
(3)	Bob Dillinger, Billy Hitchcock	.90	.45	.25
(4)	Ben Guintini, Joe Tipton	.90	.45	.25
(5)	Bob Hooper, Barney McCosky	.90	.45	.25
(6)	Eddie Joost, Kermit Wahl	.90	.45	.25
(7)	Ed Klieman, Mike Guerra	.90	.45	.25
(8)	Paul Lehner, Ferris Fain	.90	.45	.25
(9)	Connie Mack	.90	.45	.25
(10)	Earle Mack, Mickey Cochrane	.90	.45	.25
(11)	Wally Moses, Carl Scheib	.90	.45	.25
(12)	Pete Suder, Alex Kellner	.90	.45	.25
(13)	Elmer Valo, Bobby Shantz	.90	.45	.25
(14)	Bob Wellman, Joe Coleman	.90	.45	.25
(15)	Hank Wyse, Gene Markland	.90	.45	.25
(16)	Johnny Blatnik, Ed Wright	.90	.45	.25
(17)	Ralph Caballero, Bubba Church	.90	.45	.25
(18)	Milo Candini, Hank Borowy	.90	.45	.25
(19)	Blix Donnelly, Bill Nicholson	.90	.45	.25
(20)	Del Ennis, Ken Heintzelman	.90	.45	.25
(21)	Mike Goliat, Dick Whitman	.90	.45	.25
(22)	Granny Hamner, Rich Ashburn	2.25	1.25	.70
(23)	Willie Jones, Russ Meyer	.90	.45	.25
(24)	Jim Konstanty, Ken Silvestri	.90	.45	.25
(25)	Stan Lopata, Eddie Waitkus	.90	.45	.25
(26)	Ed Sanicki, Robin Roberts	1.75	.90	.50
(27)	Eddie Sawyer	.90	.45	.25
(28)	Andy Seminick, Ken Trinkle	.90	.45	.25
(29)	Dick Sisler, Stan Hollmig (DP)	.90	.45	.25
(30)	Jocko Thompson, Curt Simmons	.90	.45	.25

1907 Geo. W. Hull Chicago White Sox Postcards

Members of the World Champion White Sox are featured on this single-team issue. Horizontal in format, the black-and-white cards measure about 5-1/2" x 3-1/2". All of the cards share a basic design of a player action posed photo at right, with his name, position, and "White Sox, World's Champions" in a white box beneath. the main part of the card pictures a clothesline full of white socks, each of which has a small round portrait photo of one of the players - 15 in all. In a larger portrait at lower-left is team owner Charles Comiskey. In the white border at top, each card has a witty statement such as "String of World-Beaters" and "Not Worn By Ladies, But Admired By Them." In the bottom border is, "Copyright 1907, Geo. W. Hull". The unnumbered cards are listed here alphabetically. Because 15 players are pictured on the socks, it's possible one more card is yet to be reported.

		NM	EX	VG
Common Player:		300.00	150.00	90.00
(1)	Nick Altrock	300.00	150.00	90.00
(2)	George Davis	360.00	180.00	110.00
(3)	Jiggs Donahue	300.00	150.00	90.00
(4)	Pat Dougherty	300.00	150.00	90.00
(5)	Eddie Hahn	300.00	150.00	90.00
(6)	Frank Isbell	300.00	150.00	90.00
(7)	Fielder Jones	300.00	150.00	90.00
(8)	Ed McFarland	300.00	150.00	90.00
(9)	Frank Owens	300.00	150.00	90.00
(10)	Roy Patterson	300.00	150.00	90.00
(11)	Frank Smith	300.00	150.00	90.00
(12)	Lee Tannehill	300.00	150.00	90.00
(13)	Eddie Walsh	360.00	180.00	110.00
(14)	Doc White	300.00	150.00	90.00

1953 Hunter Wieners Cardinals

From the great era of the regionally issued hot dog cards in the mid-1950s, the 1953 Hunter wieners set of St. Louis Cardinals is certainly among the rarest today. Originally issued in two-card panels, the cards are most often found as 2-1/4" x 3-1/4" singles today when they can be found at all. The cards feature a light blue facsimile autograph printed over the stat box at the bottom. They are blank-backed.

		NM	EX	VG
Complete Set (26):		5600.	2800.	1675.
Common Player:		160.00	80.00	48.00
(1)	Steve Bilko	160.00	80.00	48.00
(2)	Cloyd Boyer	160.00	80.00	48.00
(3)	Al Brazle	160.00	80.00	48.00
(4)	Cliff Chambers	160.00	80.00	48.00
(5)	Michael Clark	160.00	80.00	48.00
(6)	Jack Crimian	160.00	80.00	48.00
(7)	Lester Fusselman	160.00	80.00	48.00
(8)	Harvey Haddix	175.00	87.00	52.00
(9)	Solly Hemus	160.00	80.00	48.00
(10)	Ray Jablonski	160.00	80.00	48.00
(11)	William Johnson	160.00	80.00	48.00
(12)	Harry Lowrey	160.00	80.00	48.00
(13)	Lawrence Miggins	160.00	80.00	48.00
(14)	Stuart Miller	160.00	80.00	48.00
(15)	Wilmer Mizell	160.00	80.00	48.00
(16)	Stanley Musial	1400.	700.00	420.00
(17)	Joseph Presko	160.00	80.00	48.00
(18)	Delbert Rice	160.00	80.00	48.00
(19)	Harold Rice	160.00	80.00	48.00
(20)	Willard Schmidt	160.00	80.00	48.00
(21)	Albert Schoendienst	350.00	175.00	105.00
(22)	Richard Sisler	160.00	80.00	48.00
(23)	Enos Slaughter	350.00	175.00	105.00
(24)	Gerald Staley	160.00	80.00	48.00
(25)	Edward Stanky	175.00	87.00	52.00
(26)	John Yuhas	160.00	80.00	48.00

1954 Hunter Wieners Cardinals

A nearly impossible set to complete today by virtue of the method of its issue, the 1954 Hunter hot dog set essentially features what would traditionally be the front and back of a normal baseball card on two different cards. The "front," containing a color photo of one of 30 St. Louis Cardinals has a box at bottom challenging the collector to name him and quote his stats. The "back" features cartoon Cardinals in action, and contains the answers. However, because both parts were printed on a single panel, and because most of the back (non-picture) panels were thrown away years ago, it is an impossible challenge to complete a '54 Hunter set today. There is no back printing on the 2-1/4" x 3-1/2" cards.

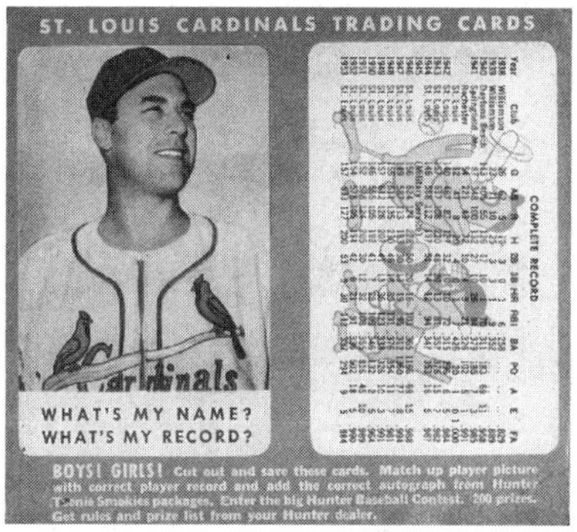

		NM	EX	VG
Complete Set (30):		6400.	3200.	1925.
Common Player:		160.00	80.00	48.00
(1)	Tom Alston	160.00	80.00	48.00
(2)	Steve Bilko	160.00	80.00	48.00
(3)	Al Brazle	160.00	80.00	48.00
(4)	Tom Burgess	160.00	80.00	48.00
(5)	Cot Deal	160.00	80.00	48.00
(6)	Alex Grammas	160.00	80.00	48.00
(7)	Harvey Haddix	175.00	87.00	52.00
(8)	Solly Hemus	160.00	80.00	48.00
(9)	Ray Jablonski	160.00	80.00	48.00
(10)	Royce Lint	160.00	80.00	48.00
(11)	Peanuts Lowrey	160.00	80.00	48.00
(12)	Memo Luna	160.00	80.00	48.00
(13)	Stu Miller	160.00	80.00	48.00
(14)	Stan Musial	1400.	700.00	420.00
(15)	Tom Poholsky	160.00	80.00	48.00
(16)	Bill Posedel	160.00	80.00	48.00
(17)	Joe Presko	100.00	00.00	48.00
(18)	Dick Rand	160.00	80.00	48.00
(19)	Vic Raschi	160.00	80.00	48.00
(20)	Rip Repulski	160.00	80.00	48.00
(21)	Del Rice	160.00	80.00	48.00
(22)	John Riddle	160.00	80.00	48.00
(23)	Mike Ryba	160.00	80.00	48.00
(24)	Red Schoendienst	350.00	175.00	105.00
(25)	Dick Schofield	260.00	130.00	78.00
(26)	Enos Slaughter	290.00	145.00	87.00
(27)	Gerry Staley	350.00	175.00	105.00
(28)	Ed Stanky	160.00	80.00	48.00
(29)	Ed Yuhas	160.00	80.00	48.00
(30)	Sal Yvars	160.00	80.00	48.00

1955 Hunter Wieners Cardinals

The 1955 team set of St. Louis Cardinals, included with packages of Hunter hot dogs, features the third format change in three years of issue. For 1955, the cards were printed in a tall, narrow 2" x 4-3/4" format, two to a panel. The cards featured both a posed action photo and a portrait photo, along with a facsimile autograph and brief biographical data on the front. There is no back printing, as the cards were part of the wrapping for packages of hot dogs.

		NM	EX	VG
Complete Set (30):		7125.	3550.	2125.
Common Player:		150.00	75.00	45.00
(1)	Thomas Edison Alston	150.00	75.00	45.00
(2)	Kenton Lloyd Boyer	450.00	225.00	135.00
(3)	Harry Lewis Elliott	150.00	75.00	45.00
(4)	John Edward Faszholz	150.00	75.00	45.00
(5)	Joseph Filmore Frazier	150.00	75.00	45.00
(6)	Alexander Pete Grammas	150.00	75.00	45.00
(7)	Harvey Haddix	165.00	82.00	49.00
(8)	Solly Joseph Hemus	150.00	75.00	45.00
(9)	Lawrence Curtis Jackson	150.00	75.00	45.00
(10)	Tony R. Jacobs	150.00	75.00	45.00
(11)	Gordon Bassett Jones	150.00	75.00	45.00

(12)	Paul Edmore LaPalme	150.00	75.00	45.00
(13)	Brooks Ulysses Lawrence	150.00	75.00	45.00
(14)	Wallace Wade Moon	225.00	110.00	67.00
(15)	Stanley Frank Musial	1800.	900.00	540.00
(16)	Thomas George Poholsky	150.00	75.00	45.00
(17)	William John Posedel	150.00	75.00	45.00
(18)	Victor Angelo John Raschi	150.00	75.00	45.00
(19)	Eldon John Repulski	150.00	75.00	45.00
(20)	Delbert Rice	150.00	75.00	45.00
(21)	John Ludy Riddle	150.00	75.00	45.00
(22)	William F. Sarni	150.00	75.00	45.00
(23)	Albert Fred Schoendienst	300.00	150.00	90.00
(24)	Richard John Schofield (actually John Richard)	150.00	75.00	45.00
(25)	Frank Thomas Smith	150.00	75.00	45.00
(26)	Edward R. Stanky	150.00	75.00	45.00
(27)	Bobby Gene Tiefenauer	150.00	75.00	45.00
(28)	William Charles Virdon	300.00	150.00	90.00
(29)	Frederick E. Walker	150.00	75.00	45.00
(30)	Floyd Lewis Woolridge	150.00	75.00	45.00

1980 Hunts Bread Cello Pack Header

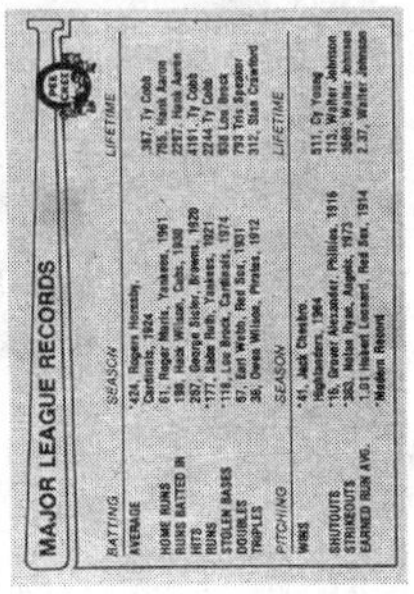

Hunts Bread of Canada used four-card cello packs of O-Pee-Chee baseball cards as a promotional premium. Besides the three regular-issue 1980 OPC cards in each pack, there was a header card with the sponsor's advertising in brown and yellow on front. On back of the header card is a list of some major league single-season or career records in various major statistical categories.

	NM	EX	VG
Hunts Bread/Major League Records	3.00	1.50	.90

I

1976 Icee Drinks Reds

Issued in 1976 in the Cincinnati area by Icee Drinks, this 12-card set of semi-circular cards features members of the Reds. The cards measure approximately 2" in diameter with the bottom of the disc squared off. The cards were originally issued as soft drink lids. Fronts have a portrait photo in black-and-white, with uniform logos removed. Backs are blank. The cards are unnumbered.

		NM	EX	VG
Complete Set (12):		90.00	45.00	27.00
Common Player:		3.00	1.50	.90
(1)	Johnny Bench	18.00	9.00	5.50
(2)	Dave Concepcion	4.50	2.25	1.25
(3)	Rawley Eastwick	3.00	1.50	.90
(4)	George Foster	4.50	2.25	1.25
(5)	Cesar Geronimo	3.00	1.50	.90
(6)	Ken Griffey	4.50	2.25	1.25
(7)	Don Gullett	3.00	1.50	.90
(8)	Will McEnaney	3.00	1.50	.90
(9)	Joe Morgan	11.00	5.50	3.25
(10)	Gary Nolan	3.00	1.50	.90
(11)	Tony Perez	6.00	3.00	1.75
(12)	Pete Rose	30.00	15.00	9.00

1963 I.D.L. Drug Store Pittsburgh Pirates

This set of 26 black-and-white cards was regionally distributed. The 4" x 5" semi-gloss cards are blank-backed and unnumbered. The checklist is arranged alphabetically. Johnny Logan's card is considered scarce and may have been pulled from distribution early.

		NM	EX	VG
Complete Set (26):		225.00	112.00	67.00
Common Player:		7.00	3.50	2.00
(1)	Bob Bailey	7.00	3.50	2.00
(2)	Forrest "Smokey" Burgess	7.00	3.50	2.00
(3)	Don Cardwell	7.00	3.50	2.00
(4)	Roberto Clemente	75.00	37.00	22.00
(5)	Donn Clendenon	10.00	5.00	3.00
(6)	Roy Face	7.00	3.50	2.00
(7)	Earl Francis	7.00	3.50	2.00
(8)	Bob Friend	7.00	3.50	2.00
(9)	Joe Gibbon	7.00	3.50	2.00
(10)	Julio Gotay	7.00	3.50	2.00
(11)	Harvey Haddix	10.00	5.00	3.00
(12)	Johnny Logan (SP)	25.00	12.50	7.50
(13)	Bill Mazeroski	25.00	12.50	7.50
(14)	Al McBean	7.00	3.50	2.00
(15)	Danny Murtaugh	7.00	3.50	2.00
(16)	Sam Narron	7.00	3.50	2.00
(17)	Ron Northey	7.00	3.50	2.00
(18)	Frank Oceak	7.00	3.50	2.00
(19)	Jim Pagliaroni	7.00	3.50	2.00
(20)	Ted Savage	7.00	3.50	2.00
(21)	Dick Schofield	7.00	3.50	2.00
(22)	Willie Stargell	30.00	15.00	9.00
(23)	Tom Sturdivant	7.00	3.50	2.00
(24)	Virgil "Fire" Trucks	7.00	3.50	2.00
(25)	Bob Veale	7.00	3.50	2.00
(26)	Bill Virdon	7.00	3.50	2.00

1921-23 IFS

(See 1921 W516 and 1923 W572)

1915 Indianapolis Brewing Co.

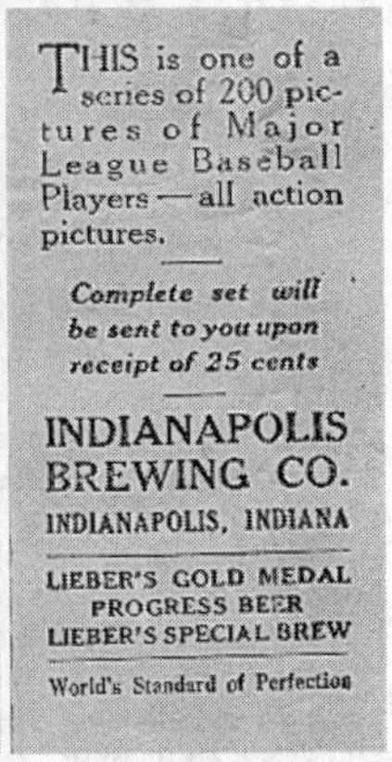

Best known for its use as a promotional medium for The Sporting News, this 200-card set can be found with ads on the back for several local and regional businesses. Among them is the Indianapolis Brewing Co. While type card collectors and superstar collectors may pay a premium for individual cards with Indianapolis brewing advertising, prices will generally parallel the 1915 Sporting News values. Cards measure 1-5/8" x 3" and are printed in black-and-white. The brewery originally advertised the set on its "Facts for Fans" booklet, at a cost of 25 cents.

(See 1916 Sporting News for checklist and value information)

1923 Curtis Ireland Candy (E123)

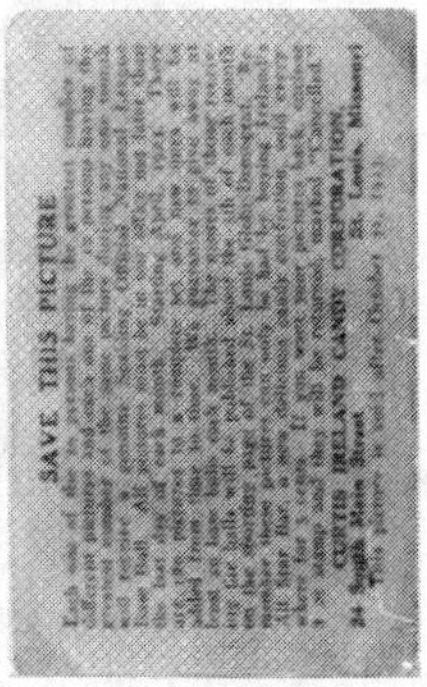

This set, identified in the ACC as E123, was issued in 1923 by the Curtis Ireland Candy Corporation of St. Louis and was distributed with Ireland's "All Star Bars." Except for the backs, the Ireland set is identical to the Willard Chocolate V100 set of the same year. Measuring 3-1/4" x 2-1/16", the cards feature sepia-toned photos with the player's name in script on the front. The backs advertise a contest which required the collector to mail in the cards in exchange for prizes, which probably explains their relative scarcity today.

		NM	EX	VG
Complete Set (180):		45000.	22000.	12000.
Common Player:		300.00	120.00	75.00
(1)	Chas. B Adams	300.00	120.00	75.00
(2)	Grover C. Alexander	650.00	260.00	160.00
(3)	J.P. Austin	300.00	120.00	75.00
(4)	J.C. Bagby	300.00	120.00	75.00
(5)	J. Franklin Baker	600.00	240.00	150.00
(6)	David J. Bancroft	600.00	240.00	150.00
(7)	Turner Barber	300.00	120.00	75.00
(8)	Jesse L. Barnes	300.00	120.00	75.00
(9)	J.C. Bassler	300.00	120.00	75.00
(10)	L.A. Blue	300.00	120.00	75.00
(11)	Norman D. Boeckel	300.00	120.00	75.00
(12)	F.L. Brazil (Brazill)	300.00	120.00	75.00
(13)	G.H. Burns	300.00	120.00	75.00
(14)	Geo. J. Burns	300.00	120.00	75.00
(15)	Leon Cadore	300.00	120.00	75.00
(16)	Max G. Carey	600.00	240.00	150.00
(17)	Harold G. Carlson	300.00	120.00	75.00
(18)	Lloyd R. Christenberry (Christenbury)	300.00	120.00	75.00
(19)	Vernon J. Clemons	300.00	120.00	75.00
(20)	T.R. Cobb	3600.	1450.	900.00
(21)	Bert Cole	300.00	120.00	75.00
(22)	John F. Collins	300.00	120.00	75.00
(23)	S. Coveleskie (Coveleski)	600.00	240.00	150.00
(24)	Walton E. Cruise	300.00	120.00	75.00
(25)	G.W. Cutshaw	300.00	120.00	75.00
(26)	Jacob E. Daubert	300.00	120.00	75.00
(27)	Geo. Dauss	300.00	120.00	75.00
(28)	F.T. Davis	300.00	120.00	75.00
(29)	Chas. A. Deal	300.00	120.00	75.00
(30)	William L. Doak	300.00	120.00	75.00
(31)	William E. Donovan	300.00	120.00	75.00
(32)	Hugh Duffy	600.00	240.00	150.00
(33)	J.A. Dugan	300.00	120.00	75.00
(34)	Louis B. Duncan	300.00	120.00	75.00
(35)	James Dykes	300.00	120.00	75.00
(36)	H.J. Ehmke	300.00	120.00	75.00
(37)	F.R. Ellerbe	300.00	120.00	75.00
(38)	E.G. Erickson	300.00	120.00	75.00
(39)	John J. Evers	600.00	240.00	150.00
(40)	U.C. Faber	600.00	240.00	150.00
(41)	B.A. Falk	300.00	120.00	75.00
(42)	Max Flack	300.00	120.00	75.00
(43)	Lee Fohl	300.00	120.00	75.00
(44)	Jacques F. Fournier	300.00	120.00	75.00
(45)	Frank F. Frisch	600.00	240.00	150.00
(46)	C.E. Galloway	300.00	120.00	75.00
(47)	W.C. Gardner	300.00	120.00	75.00
(48)	E.P. Gharrity	300.00	120.00	75.00
(49)	Geo. Gibson	300.00	120.00	75.00
(50)	Wm. Gleason	300.00	120.00	75.00
(51)	William Gleason	300.00	120.00	75.00
(52)	Henry M. Gowdy	300.00	120.00	75.00
(53)	I.M. Griffin	300.00	120.00	75.00
(54)	Clark Griffith	600.00	240.00	150.00

(55)	Burleigh A. Grimes	600.00	240.00	150.00
(56)	Charles J. Grimm	300.00	120.00	75.00
(57)	Jesse J. Haines	600.00	240.00	150.00
(58)	S.R. Harris	600.00	240.00	150.00
(59)	W.B. Harris	300.00	120.00	75.00
(60)	R.K. Hasty	300.00	120.00	75.00
(61)	H.E. Heilman (Heilmann)	600.00	240.00	150.00
(62)	Walter J. Henline	300.00	120.00	75.00
(63)	Walter L. Holke	300.00	120.00	75.00
(64)	Charles J. Hollocher	300.00	120.00	75.00
(65)	H.B. Hooper	600.00	240.00	150.00
(66)	Rogers Hornsby	650.00	260.00	160.00
(67)	W.C. Hoyt	600.00	240.00	150.00
(68)	Miller Huggins	600.00	240.00	150.00
(69)	W.C. Jacobsen (Jacobson)	300.00	120.00	75.00
(70)	C.D. Jamieson	300.00	120.00	75.00
(71)	Ernest Johnson	300.00	120.00	75.00
(72)	W.P. Johnson	1800.	720.00	450.00
(73)	James H. Johnston	300.00	120.00	75.00
(74)	R.W. Jones	300.00	120.00	75.00
(75)	Samuel Pond Jones	300.00	120.00	75.00
(76)	J.I. Judge	300.00	120.00	75.00
(77)	James W. Keenan	300.00	120.00	75.00
(78)	Geo. L. Kelly	600.00	240.00	150.00
(79)	Peter J. Kilduff	300.00	120.00	75.00
(80)	William Killefer	300.00	120.00	75.00
(81)	Lee King	300.00	120.00	75.00
(82)	Ray Kolp	300.00	120.00	75.00
(83)	John Lavan	300.00	120.00	75.00
(84)	H.L. Leibold	300.00	120.00	75.00
(85)	Connie Mack	600.00	240.00	150.00
(86)	J.W. Mails	300.00	120.00	75.00
(87)	Walter J. Maranville	600.00	240.00	150.00
(88)	Richard W. Marquard	600.00	240.00	150.00
(89)	C.W. Mays	325.00	130.00	81.00
(90)	Geo. F. McBride	300.00	120.00	75.00
(91)	H.M. McClellan	300.00	120.00	75.00
(92)	John J. McGraw	600.00	240.00	150.00
(93)	Austin B. McHenry	300.00	120.00	75.00
(94)	J. McInnis	300.00	120.00	75.00
(95)	Douglas McWeeney (MoWoony)	300.00	120.00	75.00
(96)	M. Menosky	300.00	120.00	75.00
(97)	Emil F. Meusel	300.00	120.00	75.00
(98)	R. Meusel	300.00	120.00	75.00
(99)	Henry W. Meyers	300.00	120.00	75.00
(100)	J.C. Milan	300.00	120.00	75.00
(101)	John K. Miljus	300.00	120.00	75.00
(102)	Edmund J. Miller	300.00	120.00	75.00
(103)	Elmer Miller	300.00	120.00	75.00
(104)	Otto L. Miller	300.00	120.00	75.00
(105)	Fred Mitchell	300.00	120.00	75.00
(106)	Geo. Mogridge	300.00	120.00	75.00
(107)	Patrick J. Moran	300.00	120.00	75.00
(108)	John D. Morrison	300.00	120.00	75.00
(109)	J.A. Mostil	300.00	120.00	75.00
(110)	Clarence F. Mueller	300.00	120.00	75.00
(111)	A. Earle Neale	325.00	130.00	81.00
(112)	Joseph Oeschger	300.00	120.00	75.00
(113)	Robert J. O'Farrell	300.00	120.00	75.00
(114)	J.C. Oldham	300.00	120.00	75.00
(115)	I.M. Olson	300.00	120.00	75.00
(116)	Geo. M. O'Neil	300.00	120.00	75.00
(117)	S.F. O'Neill	300.00	120.00	75.00
(118)	Frank J. Parkinson	300.00	120.00	75.00
(119)	Geo. H. Paskert	300.00	120.00	75.00
(120)	R.T. Peckinpaugh	300.00	120.00	75.00
(121)	H.J. Pennock	600.00	240.00	150.00
(122)	Ralph Perkins	300.00	120.00	75.00
(123)	Edw. J. Pfeffer	300.00	120.00	75.00
(124)	W.C. Pipp	325.00	130.00	81.00
(125)	Charles Elmer Ponder	300.00	120.00	75.00
(126)	Raymond R. Powell	300.00	120.00	75.00
(127)	D.B. Pratt	300.00	120.00	75.00
(128)	Joseph Rapp	300.00	120.00	75.00
(129)	John H. Rawlings	300.00	120.00	75.00
(130)	E.S. Rice (should be E.C.)	600.00	240.00	150.00
(131)	Branch Rickey	650.00	260.00	160.00
(132)	James J. Ring	300.00	120.00	75.00
(133)	Eppa J. Rixey	600.00	240.00	150.00
(134)	Davis A. Robertson	300.00	120.00	75.00
(135)	Edwin Rommel	300.00	120.00	75.00
(136)	Edd J. Roush	600.00	240.00	150.00
(137)	Harold Ruel (Herold)	300.00	120.00	75.00
(138)	Allen Russell	300.00	120.00	75.00
(139)	G.H. Ruth	4000.	1600.	1000.
(140)	Wilfred D. Ryan	300.00	120.00	75.00
(141)	Henry F. Sallee	300.00	120.00	75.00
(142)	W.H. Schang	300.00	120.00	75.00
(143)	Raymond H. Schmandt	300.00	120.00	75.00
(144)	Everett Scott	300.00	120.00	75.00
(145)	Henry Severeid	300.00	120.00	75.00
(146)	Jos. W. Sewell	600.00	240.00	150.00
(147)	Howard S. Shanks	300.00	120.00	75.00
(148)	E.H. Sheely	300.00	120.00	75.00
(149)	Ralph Shinners	300.00	120.00	75.00
(150)	U.J. Shocker	300.00	120.00	75.00
(151)	G.H. Sisler	600.00	240.00	150.00
(152)	Earl L. Smith	300.00	120.00	75.00
(153)	Earl S. Smith	300.00	120.00	75.00
(154)	Geo. A. Smith	300.00	120.00	75.00
(155)	J.W. Smith	300.00	120.00	75.00
(156)	Tris E. Speaker	650.00	260.00	160.00
(157)	Arnold Staatz	300.00	120.00	75.00
(158)	J.R. Stephenson	300.00	120.00	75.00
(159)	Milton J. Stock	300.00	120.00	75.00
(160)	John L. Sullivan	300.00	120.00	75.00
(161)	H.F. Tormahlen	300.00	120.00	75.00
(162)	Jas. A. Tierney	300.00	120.00	75.00
(163)	J.T. Tobin	300.00	120.00	75.00
(164)	Jas. L. Vaughn	300.00	120.00	75.00
(165)	R.H. Veach	300.00	120.00	75.00
(166)	C.W. Walker	300.00	120.00	75.00
(167)	A.L. Ward	300.00	120.00	75.00
(168)	Zack D. Wheat	600.00	240.00	150.00
(169)	George B. Whitted	300.00	120.00	75.00
(170)	Irvin K. Wilhelm	300.00	120.00	75.00
(171)	Roy H. Wilkinson	300.00	120.00	75.00
(172)	Fred C. Williams	300.00	120.00	75.00
(173)	K.R. Williams	300.00	120.00	75.00
(174)	Sam'l W. Wilson	300.00	120.00	75.00
(175)	Ivy B. Wingo	300.00	120.00	75.00
(176)	L.W. Witt	300.00	120.00	75.00
(177)	Joseph Wood	300.00	120.00	75.00
(178)	E. Yaryan	300.00	120.00	75.00
(179)	R.S. Young	300.00	120.00	75.00
(180)	Ross Young (Youngs)	600.00	240.00	150.00

1967 Irvindale Dairy Atlanta Braves

This quartet of Braves was printed in shades of deep red on the white background of a milk carton panel. Well-cut individual pieces measure 1-3/4" x 2-5/8" and are blank-backed.

		NM	EX	VG
Complete Set, Panel:		200.00	100.00	60.00
Complete Set, Singles:		150.00	75.00	45.00
Common Player:		40.00	20.00	12.00
(1)	Clete Boyer	40.00	20.00	12.00
(2)	Mack Jones	40.00	20.00	12.00
(3)	Denis Menke	40.00	20.00	12.00
(4)	Joe Torre	50.00	25.00	15.00

1976 Isaly's/Sweet William discs

One of several regional sponsors of player disc sets in 1976 was the Pittsburgh area dairy store chain, Isaly's, and Sweet William restaurants. The discs are 3-3/8" diameter with a black-and-white player portrait photo in the center of the baseball design. A line of red stars is above, while the left and right panels feature one of several bright colors. Produced by Michael Schecter Associates under license from the Major League Baseball Players Association, the player photos have had uniform and cap logos removed. Backs are printed in red and purple. The unnumbered checklist here is presented in alphabetical order.

		NM	EX	VG
Complete Set (70):		40.00	20.00	12.00
Common Player:		.40	.20	.12
(1)	Henry Aaron	5.00	2.50	1.50
(2)	Johnny Bench	2.75	1.50	.80
(3)	Vida Blue	.40	.20	.12
(4)	Larry Bowa	.40	.20	.12
(5)	Lou Brock	1.75	.90	.50
(6)	Jeff Burroughs	.40	.20	.12
(7)	John Candelaria	.40	.20	.12
(8)	Jose Cardenal	.40	.20	.12
(9)	Rod Carew	1.75	.90	.50
(10)	Steve Carlton	1.75	.90	.50
(11)	Dave Cash	.40	.20	.12
(12)	Cesar Cedeno	.40	.20	.12
(13)	Ron Cey	.40	.20	.12
(14)	Carlton Fisk	1.75	.90	.50
(15)	Tito Fuentes	.40	.20	.12
(16)	Steve Garvey	1.75	.90	.50
(17)	Ken Griffey	.40	.20	.12
(18)	Don Gullett	.40	.20	.12
(19)	Willie Horton	.40	.20	.12
(20)	Al Hrabosky	.40	.20	.12
(21)	Catfish Hunter	1.75	.90	.50
(22)	Reggie Jackson	3.50	1.75	1.00
(23)	Randy Jones	.40	.20	.12
(24)	Jim Kaat	.40	.20	.12
(25)	Don Kessinger	.40	.20	.12
(26)	Dave Kingman	.80	.40	.25
(27)	Jerry Koosman	.40	.20	.12
(28)	Mickey Lolich	.70	.35	.20
(29)	Greg Luzinski	.70	.35	.20
(30)	Fred Lynn	.50	.25	.15
(31)	Bill Madlock	.40	.20	.12
(32)	Carlos May	.40	.20	.12
(33)	John Mayberry	.40	.20	.12
(34)	Bake McBride	.40	.20	.12
(35)	Doc Medich	.40	.20	.12
(36)	Andy Messersmith	.40	.20	.12
(37)	Rick Monday	.40	.20	.12
(38)	John Montefusco	.40	.20	.12
(39)	Jerry Morales	.40	.20	.12
(40)	Joe Morgan	1.75	.90	.50
(41)	Thurman Munson	2.00	1.00	.60
(42)	Bobby Murcer	.40	.20	.12
(43)	Al Oliver	.40	.20	.12
(44)	Jim Palmer	1.75	.90	.50
(45)	Dave Parker	.50	.25	.15
(46)	Tony Perez	1.75	.90	.50
(47)	Jerry Reuss	.40	.20	.12
(48)	Brooks Robinson	2.00	1.00	.60
(49)	Frank Robinson	1.75	.90	.50
(50)	Steve Rogers	.40	.20	.12
(51)	Pete Rose	4.00	2.00	1.25
(52)	Nolan Ryan	12.00	6.00	3.50
(53)	Manny Sanguillen	.40	.20	.12
(54)	Mike Schmidt	3.00	1.50	.90
(55)	Tom Seaver	2.25	1.25	.70
(56)	Ted Simmons	.40	.20	.12
(57)	Reggie Smith	.40	.20	.12
(58)	Willie Stargell	1.75	.90	.50
(59)	Rusty Staub	.70	.35	.20
(60)	Rennie Stennett	.40	.20	.12
(61)	Don Sutton	1.75	.90	.50
(62)	Andy Thornton	.40	.20	.12
(63)	Luis Tiant	.40	.20	.12
(64)	Joe Torre	1.00	.50	.30
(65)	Mike Tyson	.40	.20	.12
(66)	Bob Watson	.40	.20	.12
(67)	Wilbur Wood	.40	.20	.12
(68)	Jimmy Wynn	.40	.20	.12
(69)	Carl Yastrzemski	2.25	1.25	.70
(70)	Richie Zisk	.40	.20	.12

1976 ISCA Hoosier Hot-Stove All-Stars

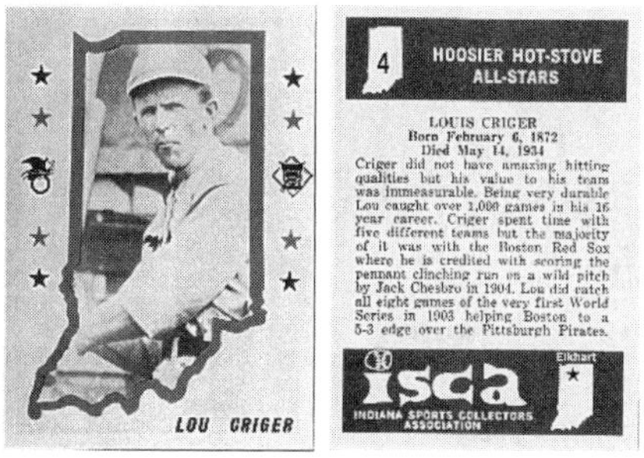

Famous native Hoosier ballplayers are featured in this collectors issue from the Indiana Sports Collectors Assn. The 2-5/8" x 3-5/8" cards have black-and-white player photos on front framed in the state's outline. Red and blue graphics on a white background complete the design. Backs are in black and blue on white and include a career summary. A star on the state map at bottom indicates where the player was born.

		NM	EX	VG
Complete Set (26):		35.00	17.50	10.50
Common Player:		2.00	1.00	.60
1	Edd Roush	2.00	1.00	.60
2	Sam Thompson	2.00	1.00	.60
3	Chuck Klein	2.00	1.00	.60
4	Lou Criger	2.00	1.00	.60
5	Amos Rusie	2.00	1.00	.60
6	Billy Herman	2.00	1.00	.60
7	George Dauss	2.00	1.00	.60
8	Tom Thevenow	2.00	1.00	.60
9	Mordecai Brown	2.00	1.00	.60
10	Freddie Fitzsimmons	2.00	1.00	.60
11	Art Nehf	2.00	1.00	.60
12	Carl Erskine	2.00	1.00	.60
13	Don Larsen	2.50	1.25	.70
14	Gil Hodges	2.50	1.25	.70
15	Pete Fox	2.00	1.00	.60
16	Butch Henline	2.00	1.00	.60
17	Doc Crandall	2.00	1.00	.60
18	Dizzy Trout	2.00	1.00	.60
19	Donie Bush	2.00	1.00	.60
20	Max Carey	2.00	1.00	.60
21	Eugene Hargrave, William Hargrave	2.00	1.00	.60

		NM	EX	VG
22	Sam Rice	2.00	1.00	.60
23	Babe Adams	2.00	1.00	.60
24	Cy Williams	2.00	1.00	.60
25	1913 Indianapolis Federal League Team	2.00	1.00	.60
26	Paul Frisz	2.00	1.00	.60

J

1910 J=K Candy

Originally printed on the front and back of candy boxes which advertised "100 Principal League Players," the actual extent of this series is currently unknown and the checklist presented here is almost certainly incomplete. The blank-back, black-and-white cards can be found in two sizes, 1-7/8" x 3-1/2" if printed on the box front, or 1-7/8" x 2-7/8" if printed on back. Player photos are framed with an ornate-cornered border. In a plaque at bottom, all in capital letters, are the player's name, position, team and league; the latter three designations are abbreviated.

	NM	EX	VG
Common Player:	250.00	125.00	75.00
(1) Eddie Collins	400.00	200.00	120.00
(2) Jim Delahanty	250.00	125.00	75.00
(3) Art Devlin	250.00	125.00	75.00
(4) Josh Devore	250.00	125.00	75.00
(5) Larry Doyle	250.00	125.00	75.00
(6) Larry Gardner	250.00	125.00	75.00
(7) George Gibson	250.00	125.00	75.00
(8) Charley Hall	250.00	125.00	75.00
(9) Buck Herzog	250.00	125.00	75.00
(10) Rube Marquard	400.00	200.00	120.00
(11) Christy Mathewson	900.00	450.00	270.00
(12) John McGraw	400.00	200.00	120.00
(13) Harry Niles	250.00	125.00	75.00
(14) Larry Pape	250.00	125.00	75.00
(15) Ed Reulbach	250.00	125.00	75.00
(16) Cy Seymour	250.00	125.00	75.00
(17) Jimmy Sheckard	250.00	125.00	75.00
(18) Hack Simmons	250.00	125.00	75.00
(19) Tris Speaker	465.00	230.00	140.00
(20) Jake Stahl	250.00	125.00	75.00
(21) Harry Steinfeldt	250.00	125.00	75.00
(22) Joe Tinker	250.00	125.00	75.00
(23) Owen Wilson	250.00	125.00	75.00

1969 Jack In The Box California Angels

This regional issue was distributed a few cards per week at the chain's fast food restaurants. Blank-back cards are printed in black-and-white on thin white stock in a 1-15/16" x 3-1/2" format. The checklist for the unnumbered cards is presented here alphabetically. A similar set depicting the 1971 Angels in horizontal format on tan paper is an unauthorized collectors issue with no connection to Jack In The Box or the team.

	NM	EX	VG
Complete Set (13):	40.00	20.00	12.00
Common Player:	3.00	1.50	.90
(1) Sandy Alomar	3.50	1.75	1.00
(2) Joe Azcue	3.00	1.50	.90
(3) Jim Fregosi	3.50	1.75	1.00
(4) Lou Johnson	3.00	1.50	.90
(5) Jay Johnstone	3.50	1.75	1.00
(6) Rudy May	3.00	1.50	.90
(7) Jim McGlothlin	3.00	1.50	.90
(8) Andy Messersmith	3.00	1.50	.90
(9) Tom Murphy	3.00	1.50	.90
(10) Rick Reichardt	3.00	1.50	.90
(11) Aurelio Rodriguez	3.00	1.50	.90
(12) Jim Spencer	3.00	1.50	.90
(13) Hoyt Wilhelm	15.00	7.50	4.50

1971 Jack In The Box California Angels

Unlike the legitimate issue of 1969, this is an unauthorized collectors issue with no official connection to either the team or the fast food restaurant chain. The cards are printed in horizontal format on 4" x 2-1/2" manila paper in black ink. Fronts have a player portrait photo at left. Stacked at right are the player's name, team, position and Jack in the Box logo. Backs are blank. The set is checklisted here in alphabetical order.

	NM	EX	VG
Complete Set (10):	24.00	12.00	7.25
Common Player:	1.50	.70	.45
(1) Sandy Alomar	2.25	1.25	.70
(2) Ken Berry	1.50	.70	.45
(3) Tony Conigliaro	15.00	7.50	4.50
(4) Jim Fregosi	1.50	.70	.45
(5) Alex Johnson	1.50	.70	.45
(6) Rudy May	1.50	.70	.45
(7) Andy Messersmith	1.50	.70	.45
(8) "Lefty" Phillips	1.50	.70	.45
(9) Jim Spencer	1.50	.70	.45
(10) Clyde Wright	1.50	.70	.45

1970 Jack in the Box Pittsburgh Pirates

Though this set is known within the hobby as the "Jack in the Box" Pirates, it bears no such advertising and has no actual connection to the restaurant chain; they are a collector's issue. The black-and-white cards measure 2" x 3-1/2" and are blank-backed. Beneath the photo on front is the player identification and a few stats from the 1969 season.

	NM	EX	VG
Complete Set (12):	30.00	15.00	9.00
Common Player:	1.50	.70	.45
(1) Gene Alley	1.50	.70	.45
(2) Dave Cash	1.50	.70	.45
(3) Dock Ellis	1.50	.70	.45
(4) Dave Giusti	1.50	.70	.45
(5) Jerry May	1.50	.70	.45
(6) Bill Mazeroski	6.00	3.00	1.75
(7) Al Oliver	3.00	1.50	.90
(8) Jose Pagan	1.50	.70	.45
(9) Fred Patek	1.50	.70	.45
(10) Bob Robertson	1.50	.70	.45
(11) Manny Sanguillen	3.00	1.50	.90
(12) Willie Stargell	9.00	4.50	2.75

1954 Bill Jacobellis N.Y. Giants

In the Giants' championship season, New York photographer Bill Jacobellis produced this set of player/team pictures, probably to be sold at the Polo Grounds souvenir stands. The black-and-white pictures are blank-backed and measure about 8-1/4" x 10-1/2", printed on semi-gloss paper. The player name is centered in bold type in the white bottom border; at right is "Bill Jacobellis Photo". The unnumbred pictures are listed here in alphabetical order.

	NM	EX	VG
Complete Set (8):	110.00	55.00	32.50
Common Player:	12.50	6.25	3.75
(1) John Antonelli	12.50	6.25	3.75
(2) Alvin Dark	12.50	6.25	3.75
(3) Ruben Gomez	12.50	6.25	3.75
(4) Whitey Lockman	12.50	6.25	3.75
(5) Willie Mays	60.00	30.00	18.00
(6) Don Mueller	12.50	6.25	3.75
(7) James (Dusty) Rhodes	12.50	6.25	3.75
(8) N.Y. Giants of 1954	20.00	10.00	6.00

1958 Jay Publishing 5x7 Photos Type 1

The name "Picture Packs" has been used to describe this massive series of 5" x 7" black-and-white player photos issued by Jay Publishing's Big League Books division over the eight-year period from 1958-1965. The company also produced yearbooks for various major league teams during that period; many of the photos used in the yearbooks also appear in the Picture Packs. Picture Packs were sold by teams, each set consisting of 12 player photos with name and team at the bottom. They were available by mail, at the ballparks and in stores. They were sold in either plain brown or white envelopes, or in clear plastic. Most were printed on a glossy, slick paper stock, although the quality of the paper may vary from team to team and year to year. The photos were issued anonymously, with no indication of the producer or year of issue, making it nearly impossible to checklist the sets completely. It is known that two different types were issued, based on the typeface used in the captions. Type I photos, issued from 1958 through 1961, were printed with a sans-serif style typeface, while Type II photos, issued from 1962 through 1965, used a serif typeface. Attempts to thoroughly checklist the Picture Packs began only recently. To date nearly 1,500 different poses have been found, but more may exist.

		NM	EX	VG
	Common Player:	3.00	1.50	.90
(1)	Henry Aaron (Outfielder)	15.00	7.50	4.50
(2)	Henry Aaron (batting)	15.00	7.50	4.50
(3)	Hank Aaron (portrait, pose to neck)	15.00	7.50	4.50
(4)	Joe Adcock (portrait, pose to waist)	3.00	1.50	.90
(5)	Joe Adcock (batting, pose to chest)	3.00	1.50	.90
(6)	Joseph Adcock (Infielder, portrait, pose to neck)	3.00	1.50	.90
(7)	Bob Allison (portrait, pose to neck)	3.00	1.50	.90
(8)	Bob Allison (batting, pose to chest)	3.00	1.50	.90
(9)	Bob Allison (batting, pose to chest, scored background)	3.00	1.50	.90
(10)	Felipe Alou (kneeling, pose to waist, arms crossed)	3.00	1.50	.90
(11)	Walter Alston (portrait, pose to neck)	3.00	1.50	.90
(12)	George Altman (portrait, pose to chest)	3.00	1.50	.90
(13)	Ruben Amaro (batting, pose to chest, dark background)	3.00	1.50	.90
(14)	Ruben Amaro (batting, pose to chest, light background)	3.00	1.50	.90
(15)	Bob Anderson (portrait, pose to chest)	3.00	1.50	.90
(16)	Bob Anderson (pitching)	3.00	1.50	.90
(17)	Harry Anderson (Phillies, portrait, pose to neck)	3.00	1.50	.90
(18)	Harry Anderson (Philadelphia Phillies, portrait, pose to chest)	3.00	1.50	.90
(19)	John Antonelli (Giants, pitching)	3.00	1.50	.90
(20)	John Antonelli (portrait, pose to neck)	3.00	1.50	.90
(21)	John Antonelli (Indians, pitching)	3.00	1.50	.90
(22)	Luis Aparicio (portrait, pose to chest)	4.50	2.25	1.25
(23)	Luis Aparicio (ready to throw)	4.50	2.25	1.25
(24)	Luis Aparicio (portrait, pose to neck)	4.50	2.25	1.25
(25)	Richie Ashburn (Phillies, portrait, pose to neck)	4.50	2.25	1.25
(26)	Richie Ashburn (Philadelphia Phillies, portrait, pose to waist)	4.50	2.25	1.25
(27)	Richie Asburn (Ashburn) (Cubs, portrait, pose to neck)	4.50	2.25	1.25
(28)	Richie Ashburn (Cubs, portrait, pose to waist)	4.50	2.25	1.25
(29)	Ken Aspromonte (portrait, pose to chest)	3.00	1.50	.90
(30)	Ed Bailey (portrait, pose to chest)	3.00	1.50	.90
(31)	Ed Bailey (batting, pose to waist)	3.00	1.50	.90
(32)	Ed Bailey (portrait, pose to neck, smile)	3.00	1.50	.90
(33)	Ed Bailey (portrait, pose to neck, no smile)	9.00	4.50	2.75
(34)	Ernie Banks (portrait, pose to neck)	9.00	4.50	2.75
(35)	Ernie Banks (portrait, pose to chest)	9.00	4.50	2.75
(36)	Curt Barclay (pitching, pitcher's follow through)	3.00	1.50	.90
(37)	Earl Battey (portrait, pose to neck)	3.00	1.50	.90
(38)	Earl Battey (catching, crouching)	3.00	1.50	.90
(39)	Hank Bauer (Yankees, portrait, pose to neck)	3.00	1.50	.90
(40)	Hank Bauer (Athletics, portrait, pose to neck)	3.00	1.50	.90
(41)	Hank Bauer (batting)	3.00	1.50	.90
(42)	Frank Baumann (portrait, pose to waist, glove)	3.00	1.50	.90
(43)	Jim Baumer (batting, pose to chest)	3.00	1.50	.90
(44)	Julio Becquer (portrait, pose to chest)	3.00	1.50	.90
(45)	Julio Becquer (kneeling, holding bat)	3.00	1.50	.90
(46)	Gus Bell (portrait, pose to neck)	3.00	1.50	.90
(47)	Gus Bell (hands on knees)	3.00	1.50	.90
(48)	Lou Berberet (portrait, pose to chest)	3.00	1.50	.90
(49)	Larry Berra (portrait, pose to neck)	10.50	5.25	3.25
(50)	Yogi Berra (batting, pose to waist)	10.50	5.25	3.25
(51)	Reno Bertoia (kneeling, holding bat)	3.00	1.50	.90
(52)	Reno Bertoia (fielding, Detroit uniform)	3.00	1.50	.90
(53)	Steve Bilko (portrait, pose to chest)	3.00	1.50	.90
(54)	Steve Bilko (portrait, pose to neck)	3.00	1.50	.90
(55)	Don Blasingame (bunting)	3.00	1.50	.90
(56)	Don Blasingame (fielding)	3.00	1.50	.90
(57)	Don Blasingame (portrait, pose to neck)	3.00	1.50	.90
(58)	Frank Bolling (Braves, portrait, pose to chest)	3.00	1.50	.90
(59)	Frank Bolling (Tigers, portrait, pose to chest)	3.00	1.50	.90
(60)	Steve Boros (portrait, pose to chest)	3.00	1.50	.90
(61)	Ed Bouchee (portrait, pose to waist, Philadelphia uniform)	3.00	1.50	.90
(62)	Ed Bouchee (portrait, pose to chest)	3.00	1.50	.90
(63)	Bob Bowman (portrait, pose to neck)	3.00	1.50	.90
(64)	Bob Boyd (portrait, pose to neck)	3.00	1.50	.90
(65)	Bob Boyd (Orioles, portrait, pose to chest)	3.00	1.50	.90
(66)	Bob Boyd (Athletics, portrait, pose to chest)	3.00	1.50	.90
(67)	Cletus Boyer (Cletis) (kneeling, holding bat)	3.00	1.50	.90
(68)	Ken Boyer (portrait, pose to neck)	3.00	1.50	.90
(69)	Ken Boyer (portrait, pose to chest)	3.00	1.50	.90
(70)	Jackie Brandt (Giants, portrait, pose to chest)	3.00	1.50	.90
(71)	Jackie Brandt (batting)	3.00	1.50	.90
(72)	Jackie Brandt (Orioles, portrait, pose to chest, dark background)	3.00	1.50	.90
(73)	Jackie Brandt (Orioles, portrait, pose to chest, light background)	3.00	1.50	.90
(74)	Marv Breeding (batting, pose to chest)	3.00	1.50	.90
(75)	Eddie Bressoud (fielding)	3.00	1.50	.90
(76)	Tom Brewer (portrait, pose to chest)	3.00	1.50	.90
(77)	Tom Brewer (portrait, pose to neck)	3.00	1.50	.90
(78)	Fritz Brickell (portrait, pose to chest)	3.00	1.50	.90
(79)	Rocky Bridges (portrait, pose to chest)	3.00	1.50	.90
(80)	Rocky Bridges (portrait, pose to neck)	3.00	1.50	.90
(81)	Harry Bright (portrait, pose to chest)	3.00	1.50	.90
(82)	Ernie Broglio (portrait, pose to chest)	3.00	1.50	.90
(83)	Jim Brosman (Brosnan) (portrait, pose to chest)	3.00	1.50	.90
(84)	Jim Brosnan (portrait, pose to neck)	3.00	1.50	.90
(85)	Dick Brown (catching, crouching)	3.00	1.50	.90
(86)	Bill Bruton (portrait, pose to chest)	3.00	1.50	.90
(87)	Billy Bruton (portrait, pose to waist)	3.00	1.50	.90
(88)	Billy Bruton (fielding, leaping)	3.00	1.50	.90
(89)	Don Buddin (portrait, pose to neck)	3.00	1.50	.90
(90)	Don Buddin (portrait, pose to chest)	3.00	1.50	.90
(91)	Don Buddin (fielding)	3.00	1.50	.90
(92)	Bob Buhl (portrait, pose to neck)	3.00	1.50	.90
(93)	Bob Buhl (pitching, pitcher's follow through)	3.00	1.50	.90
(94)	Jim Bunning (portrait, pose to chest)	4.00	2.00	1.25
(95)	Lewis Burdette (Pitcher, portrait, pose to neck)	3.00	1.50	.90
(96)	Lou Burdette (portrait, pose to chest)	3.00	1.50	.90
(97)	Lou Burdette (pitching)	3.00	1.50	.90
(98)	"Smokey" Burgess (portrait, pose to neck)	3.00	1.50	.90
(99)	Forrest "Smokey" Burgess (portrait, pose to chest)	3.00	1.50	.90
(100)	Smokey Burgess (sitting, 3 bats)	3.00	1.50	.90
(101)	Smokey Burgess (portrait, pose to chest)	3.00	1.50	.90
(102)	Jim Busby (portrait, pose to neck)	3.00	1.50	.90
(103)	John Callison (White Sox, portrait, pose to neck)	3.00	1.50	.90
(104)	John Callison (batting, pose to neck)	3.00	1.50	.90
(105)	John Callison (Phillies, batting, pose to chest, 2 bats)	3.00	1.50	.90
(106)	Roy Campanella (Catcher, portrait, pose to neck)	10.50	5.25	3.25
(107)	Andy Carey (portrait, pose to neck)	3.00	1.50	.90
(108)	Andy Carey (portrait, pose to waist)	3.00	1.50	.90
(109)	Chico Carrasquel (portrait, pose to chest)	3.00	1.50	.90
(110)	Jerry Casale (portrait, pose to chest)	3.00	1.50	.90
(111)	Jerry Casale (pitching)	3.00	1.50	.90
(112)	Norm Cash (portrait, pose to chest)	3.75	2.00	1.25
(113)	Orlando Cepeda (standing, 4 bats)	6.00	3.00	1.75
(114)	Bob Cerv (portrait, pose to chest)	3.00	1.50	.90
(115)	Bob Cerv (portrait, pose to neck)	3.00	1.50	.90
(116)	Bob Cerv (batting, pose to waist)	3.00	1.50	.90
(117)	Harry Chiti (catching, crouching)	3.00	1.50	.90
(118)	Gino Cimoli (outfielder, portrait, pose to neck)	3.00	1.50	.90
(119)	Gino Cimoli (portrait, pose to chest)	3.00	1.50	.90
(120)	Gino Cimoli (Cardinals, portrait, pose to neck)	3.00	1.50	.90
(121)	Roberto Clemente (portrait, pose to neck)	15.00	7.50	4.50
(122)	Roberto Clemente (batting, pose to chest)	15.00	7.50	4.50
(123)	Roberto Clemente (portrait, pose to chest)	15.00	7.50	4.50
(124)	Truman Clevenger (portrait, pose to chest)	3.00	1.50	.90
(125)	Truman Clevenger (pitching, pitcher's follow through)	3.00	1.50	.90
(126)	Jim Coker (catching, crouching)	3.00	1.50	.90
(127)	Rocco "Rocky" Colavito (batting)	4.50	2.25	1.25
(128)	Rocky Colavito (portrait, pose to chest, glove)	4.50	2.25	1.25
(129)	Rocky Colavito (hands on knees)	4.50	2.25	1.25
(130)	Gordon Coleman (batting, pose to chest)	3.00	1.50	.90
(131)	Billy Consolo (fielding)	3.00	1.50	.90
(132)	Chuck Cottier (throwing)	3.00	1.50	.90
(133)	Chuck Cottier (portrait, pose to chest, photo reversed)	3.00	1.50	.90
(134)	Clint Courtney (portrait, pose to neck, dark background)	3.00	1.50	.90
(135)	Clint Courtney (portrait, pose to neck, light background)	3.00	1.50	.90
(136)	John Covington (Outfield, batting, pose to neck)	3.00	1.50	.90
(137)	Wes Covington (batting)	3.00	1.50	.90
(138)	Wes Covington (kneeling, holding bat)	3.00	1.50	.90
(139)	Harry Craft (kneeling, pose to knees)	3.00	1.50	.90
(140)	Harry Craft (portrait, pose to neck)	3.00	1.50	.90
(141)	Roger Craig (portrait, pose to chest)	3.00	1.50	.90
(142)	Del Crandall (batting, pose to waist)	3.00	1.50	.90
(143)	Del Crandall (portrait, pose to neck)	3.00	1.50	.90
(144)	Delmar Crandall (Catcher, portrait, pose to neck)	3.00	1.50	.90
(145)	George Crowe (portrait, pose to neck)	3.00	1.50	.90
(146)	Joe Cunningham (portrait, pose to neck)	3.00	1.50	.90
(147)	Joe Cunningham (batting)	3.00	1.50	.90
(148)	Bud Daley (portrait, pose to chest)	3.00	1.50	.90
(149)	Bud Daley (pitching)	3.00	1.50	.90
(150)	Pete Daley (kneeling, pose to knees)	3.00	1.50	.90
(151)	Benny Daniels (portrait, pose to chest, hands over head)	3.00	1.50	.90
(152)	Al Dark (batting, pose to chest)	3.00	1.50	.90
(153)	Alvin Dark (Cardinals, portrait, pose to chest)	3.00	1.50	.90
(154)	Alvin Dark (Manager-Giants, portrait, pose to chest)	3.00	1.50	.90
(155)	Jim Davenport (throwing)	3.00	1.50	.90
(156)	Jim Davenport (fielding, glove out)	3.00	1.50	.90
(157)	Jim Davenport (fielding, low ball)	3.00	1.50	.90
(158)	Ike Delock (portrait, pose to chest, light background)	3.00	1.50	.90
(159)	Ivan Delock (portrait, pose to chest, dark background)	3.00	1.50	.90
(160)	Bobby Del Greco (portrait, pose to chest)	3.00	1.50	.90
(161)	Don Demeter (portrait, pose to waist)	3.00	1.50	.90
(162)	Joe DeMaestri (batting, pose to waist)	3.00	1.50	.90
(163)	Murray Dickson (Murry) (pitching, pitcher's follow through, pose to waist)	3.00	1.50	.90
(164)	Art Ditmar (pitching, pitcher's follow through, pose to knees)	3.00	1.50	.90
(165)	Dan Dobbek (portrait, pose to neck)	3.00	1.50	.90
(166)	Dan Dobbek (kneeling, holding bat)	3.00	1.50	.90
(167)	Dick Donovan (portrait, pose to neck)	3.00	1.50	.90
(168)	Dick Donovan (portrait, pose to chest)	3.00	1.50	.90
(169)	Dick Donovan (portrait, pose to chest, glove)	3.00	1.50	.90
(170)	Dutch Dotterer (batting, pose to waist)	3.00	1.50	.90
(171)	Moe Drabowski (Drabowsky) (portrait, pose to chest)	3.00	1.50	.90
(172)	Charlie Dressen (portrait, pose to chest)	3.00	1.50	.90
(173)	Don Drysdale (pitcher, portrait, pose to neck)	6.00	3.00	1.75
(174)	Don Drysdale (portrait, pose to neck)	6.00	3.00	1.75
(175)	Don Drysdale (portrait, pose to chest)	6.00	3.00	1.75

(176)	Jimmy Dykes (portrait, pose to chest)	3.00	1.50	.90
(177)	Bob Elliott (portrait, pose to neck)	3.00	1.50	.90
(178)	Dick Ellsworth (portrait, pose to waist, arms crossed)	3.00	1.50	.90
(179)	Don Elston (portrait, pose to neck)	3.00	1.50	.90
(180)	Del Ennis (portrait, pose to neck)	3.00	1.50	.90
(181)	Chuck Estrada (pitching, pose to knees)	3.00	1.50	.90
(182)	Roy Face (portrait, pose to chest)	3.00	1.50	.90
(183)	Roy Face (portrait, pose to neck)	3.00	1.50	.90
(184)	Dick Farrell (Phillies, portrait, pose to neck)	3.00	1.50	.90
(185)	Dick Farrell (Philadelphia Phillies, portrait, pose to neck, glove)	3.00	1.50	.90
(186)	Dick Farrell (portrait, pose to chest)	3.00	1.50	.90
(187)	Chico Fernandez (portrait, pose to neck)	3.00	1.50	.90
(188)	Chico Fernandez (portrait, pose to chest)	3.00	1.50	.90
(189)	Jack Fisher (portrait, pose to chest)	3.00	1.50	.90
(190)	Jack Fisher (pitching, pitcher's follow through)	3.00	1.50	.90
(191)	Ed FitzGerald (portrait, pose to neck)	3.00	1.50	.90
(192)	Curt Flood (portrait, pose to neck)	3.00	1.50	.90
(193)	Curt Flood (portrait, pose to waist)	3.00	1.50	.90
(194)	Hank Foiles (portrait, pose to neck)	3.00	1.50	.90
(195)	Hank Foiles (kneeling, holding bat)	3.00	1.50	.90
(196)	Whitey Ford (portrait, pose to neck)	7.50	3.75	2.25
(197)	Whitey Ford (portrait, pose to chest)	7.50	3.75	2.25
(198)	Nellie Fox (ready to throw)	6.00	3.00	1.75
(199)	Nelson Fox (portrait, pose to neck)	6.00	3.00	1.75
(200)	Nelson Fox (portrait, pose to waist, "S" visible)	6.00	3.00	1.75
(200.5)	Nelson Fox (portrait, pose to chest, top half of "S" visible)	6.00	3.00	1.75
(201)	Nelson Fox (portrait, pose to chest," Sox" visible)	4.50	2.25	1.25
(202)	Paul Foytack (portrait, pose to chest)	3.00	1.50	.90
(203)	Tito Francona (batting, pose to chest)	3.00	1.50	.90
(204)	Tito Francona (portrait, pose to neck)	3.00	1.50	.90
(205)	Gene Freese (portrait, pose to neck)	3.00	1.50	.90
(206)	Gene Freeze (portrait, pose to chest)	3.00	1.50	.90
(207)	Bob Friend (portrait, pose to neck)	3.00	1.50	.90
(208)	Bob Friend (pitching, pitcher's follow through)	3.00	1.50	.90
(209)	Bob Friend (portrait, pose to chest, "P" on helmet)	3.00	1.50	.90
(210)	Bob Friend (portrait, pose to neck, no "P" on cap)	3.00	1.50	.90
(211)	Carl Furillo (Outfielder, portrait, pose to neck)	4.50	2.25	1.25
(212)	Carl Furillo (portrait, pose to neck)	4.50	2.25	1.25
(213)	Billy Gardner (portrait, pose to neck)	3.00	1.50	.90
(214)	Billy Gardner (portrait, pose to chest)	3.00	1.50	.90
(215)	William (Billy) Gardner (portrait, pose to neck)	3.00	1.50	.90
(216)	Ned Garver (portrait, pose to chest)	3.00	1.50	.90
(217)	Ned Garver (pitching, pitcher's follow through)	3.00	1.50	.90
(218)	Ned Garver (pitching, hands over head)	3.00	1.50	.90
(219)	Gary Geiger (portrait, pose to chest)	3.00	1.50	.90
(220)	Jim Gentile (kneeling, holding bat)	3.00	1.50	.90
(221)	Jim Gentile (portrait, pose to chest)	3.00	1.50	.90
(222)	Dick Gernert (portrait, pose to neck)	3.00	1.50	.90
(223)	Dick Gernert (portrait, pose to chest)	3.00	1.50	.90
(224)	Paul Giel (portrait, pose to neck)	3.00	1.50	.90
(225)	Bob Giggie (pitching, pitcher's follow through)	3.00	1.50	.90
(226)	Junior Gilliam (portrait, pose to neck)	3.75	2.00	1.25
(227)	Junior Gilliam (portrait, pose to chest)	3.75	2.00	1.25
(228)	Reuben (Ruben) Gomez (portrait, pose to neck)	3.00	1.50	.90
(229)	Ruben Gomez (portrait, pose to chest)	3.00	1.50	.90
(230)	Bill Goodman (portrait, pose to neck)	3.00	1.50	.90
(231)	Bill Goodman (portrait, pose to chest)	3.00	1.50	.90
(232)	Joe Gordon (portrait, pose to chest)	3.00	1.50	.90
(233)	Alex Grammas (portrait, pose to neck)	3.00	1.50	.90
(234)	Jim Grant (pitching, pitcher's follow through, to knee)	3.00	1.50	.90
(235)	Jim Grant (pitching, pitcher's follow through, left leg visible)	3.00	1.50	.90
(236)	Dallas Green (portrait, pose to neck, hands over head)	3.00	1.50	.90
(237)	Gene Green (portrait, pose to neck)	3.00	1.50	.90
(238)	Jerry "Pumpsie" Green (portrait, pose to chest)	3.00	1.50	.90
(239)	Lenny Green (portraint, pose to neck)	3.00	1.50	.90
(240)	Lenny Green (portrait, pose to chest)	3.00	1.50	.90
(241)	Bob Grim (pitching, pitcher's follow through)	3.00	1.50	.90
(242)	Dick Groat (portrait, pose to neck)	3.00	1.50	.90
(243)	Dick Groat (portrait, pose to chest, light background)	3.00	1.50	.90
(244)	Dick Groat (portrait, pose to neck, dark background)	3.00	1.50	.90
(245)	Dick Groat (kneeling, holding bat)	3.00	1.50	.90
(246)	Harvey Haddix (portrait, pose to neck)	3.00	1.50	.90
(247)	Harvey Haddix (portrait, pose to chest)	3.00	1.50	.90
(248)	Granny Hammer (portrait, pose to neck)	3.00	1.50	.90
(249)	Harry Hanebrink (portrait, pose to waist, MILW uniform)	3.00	1.50	.90
(250)	Fred Haney (portrait, pose to neck)	3.00	1.50	.90
(251)	Ron Hansen (portrait, pose to chest)	3.00	1.50	.90
(252)	Ron Hansen (fielding)	3.00	1.50	.90
(253)	Bill Harrell (portrait, pose to chest)	3.00	1.50	.90
(254)	Jack Harshman (portrait, pose to chest)	3.00	1.50	.90
(255)	Robert Hazel (Hazle) (outfielder, portrait, pose to neck)	3.00	1.50	.90
(256)	Woody Held (batting, pose to waist)	3.00	1.50	.90
(257)	Woody Held (portrait, pose to neck)	3.00	1.50	.90
(258)	Solly Hemus (portrait, pose to chest)	3.00	1.50	.90
(259)	Ray Herbert (pitching, pitcher's follow through)	3.00	1.50	.90
(260)	Ray Herbert (portrait, pose to chest, "A" on cap)	3.00	1.50	.90
(261)	Ray Herbert (portrait, pose to neck, no "A" on cap)	3.00	1.50	.90
(262)	Frank Herrera (portrait, pose to neck, glove)	3.00	1.50	.90
(263)	Pancho Herrera (portrait, pose to waist, glove)	3.00	1.50	.90
(264)	Whitey Herzog (Orioles, portrait, pose to chest)	3.00	1.50	.90
(265)	Whitey Herzog (Athletics, portrait, pose to chest)	3.00	1.50	.90
(266)	Mike Higgins (portrait, pose to neck)	3.00	1.50	.90
(267)	Mike Higgins (portrait, pose to chest, one ear showin)	3.00	1.50	.90
(268)	Mike Higgins (portrait, pose to chest, two ears showing)	3.00	1.50	.90
(269)	Don Hoak (portrait, pose to neck)	3.00	1.50	.90
(270)	Don Hoak (portrait, pose to neck)	3.00	1.50	.90
(271)	Don Hoak (portrait, pose to waist)	3.00	1.50	.90
(272)	Glen Hobbie (portrait, pose to neck)	3.00	1.50	.90
(273)	Gil Hodges (first base, portrait, pose to neck)	6.00	3.00	1.75
(274)	Gil Hodges (portrait, pose to neck)	6.00	3.00	1.75
(275)	Jay Hook (portrait, pose to neck)	3.00	1.50	.90
(276)	Ralph Houk (portrait, pose to chest)	3.00	1.50	.90
(277)	Frank House (portrait, pose to neck)	3.00	1.50	.90
(278)	Elston Howard (portrait, pose to chest)	3.75	2.00	1.25
(278.5)	Elston Howard (portrait, pose to neck)	3.75	2.00	1.25
(279)	Elston Howard (batting, pose to chest)	3.75	2.00	1.25
(280)	Frank Howard (batting, pose to waist)	3.75	2.00	1.25
(281)	Fred Hutchinson (portrait, pose to neck)	3.00	1.50	.90
(282)	Fred Hutchinson (portrait, pose to chest)	3.00	1.50	.90
(283)	Dick Hyde (portrait, pose to chest)	3.00	1.50	.90
(284)	Dick Hyde (pitching, pitcher's follow through to, pose to thighs)	3.00	1.50	.90
(285)	Larry Jackson (portrait, pose to neck)	3.00	1.50	.90
(286)	Larry Jackson (portrait, pose to chest)	3.00	1.50	.90
(287)	Julian Javier (portrait, pose to chest)	3.00	1.50	.90
(288a)	Joey Jay (portrait, pose to chest)	3.00	1.50	.90
(288b)	Joey Jay (portrait, pose to neck)	3.00	1.50	.90
(289)	Joey Jay (pitching)	3.00	1.50	.90
(291)	Joey Jay (Reds, pitching, pitcher's follow throug)	3.00	1.50	.90
(292)	Hal Jeffcoat (portrait, portrait to neck)	3.00	1.50	.90
(293)	Jack Jensen (portrait, pose to neck)	3.00	1.50	.90
(294)	Jackie Jensen (portrait, pose to chest)	3.00	1.50	.90
(295)	Jackie Jensen (sitting, pose to knees)	3.00	1.50	.90
(296)	Bob Johnson (fielding)	3.00	1.50	.90
(297)	Connie Johnson (portrait, pose to neck)	3.00	1.50	.90
(298)	Sam Jones (portrait, pose to waist, trophy, St. Louis uniform)	3.00	1.50	.90
(299)	Sam Jones (pitching)	3.00	1.50	.90
(300)	Sam Jones (portrait, pose to neck)	3.00	1.50	.90
(301)	Willie Jones (batting, pose to chest)	3.00	1.50	.90
(302)	Bill Jurges (portrait, pose to waist)	3.00	1.50	.90
(303)	Al Kaline (portrait, pose to chest)	10.50	5.25	3.25
(304)	Al Kaline (kneeling, holding bat)	10.50	5.25	3.25
(305)	Eddie Kasco (Kasko) (batting, pose to chest)	3.00	1.50	.90
(306)	Eddie Kasko (portrait, pose to neck)	3.00	1.50	.90
(307)	Marty Keough (portrait, pose to chest)	3.00	1.50	.90
(308)	Harmon Killebrew (portrait, pose to chest)	7.50	3.75	2.25
(309)	Harmon Killebrew (kneeling, holding bat)	7.50	3.75	2.25
(310)	Harmon Killebrew (batting, pose to waist)	7.50	3.75	2.25
(311)	Jerry Kindall (portrait, pose to chest)	3.00	1.50	.90
(312)	Willie Kirkland (kneeling, five bats)	3.00	1.50	.90
(313)	Willie Kirkland (portrait, pose to chest)	3.00	1.50	.90
(314)	Willie Kirkland (batting)	3.00	1.50	.90
(315)	Willie Kirkland (portrait, pose to chest)	3.00	1.50	.90
(316)	Ronald Kline (portrait, pose to neck)	3.00	1.50	.90
(317)	Ronnie Kline (Pirates, portrait, pose to chest)	3.00	1.50	.90
(318)	Ronnie Kline (Cardinals, portrait, pose to chest)	3.00	1.50	.90
(319)	Ted Kluszewski (kneeling, holding bat)	4.50	2.25	1.25
(320)	Ted Kluszewski (batting, pose to chest)	4.50	2.25	1.25
(321)	Ted Kluzewski (Kluszewski) (portrait, pose to chest)	4.50	2.25	1.25
(322)	Steve Korcheck (batting, pose to chest)	3.00	1.50	.90
(323)	Jack Kralick (portrait, pose to neck)	3.00	1.50	.90
(324)	Tony Kubek (fielding)	3.75	2.00	1.25
(325)	Tony Kubek (portrait, pose to neck "NY" cap)	3.75	2.00	1.25
(326)	Tony Kubek (portrait, pose to neck, "NY" not visible on cap)	3.75	2.00	1.25
(327)	John Kucks (pitching)	3.00	1.50	.90
(328)	Johnny Kucks (portrait, pose to neck)	3.00	1.50	.90
(329)	Harvey Kuenn (Indians, portrait, pose to chest)	3.00	1.50	.90
(330)	Harvey Kuenn (Giants, portrait, pose to chest)	3.00	1.50	.90
(331)	Clem Labine (Pitcher, portrait, pose to neck)	3.00	1.50	.90
(332)	Clem Labine (portrait, pose to neck)	3.00	1.50	.90
(333)	Jim Landis (portrait, pose to chest)	3.00	1.50	.90
(334)	Jim Landis (batting)	3.00	1.50	.90
(335)	Hobie Landrith (catching, crouching)	3.00	1.50	.90
(336)	Norm Larker (portrait, pose to chest)	3.00	1.50	.90
(337)	Don Larsen (portrait, pose to neck)	3.00	1.50	.90
(338)	Don Larsen (pitching, pitcher's follow through)	3.00	1.50	.90
(339)	Frank Lary (portrait, pose to waist, arms crossed, one hand showing)	3.00	1.50	.90
(340)	Frank Lary (portrait, pose to waist, arms crossed, both hands showing)	3.00	1.50	.90
(341)	Barry Latman (portrait, pose to chest, W. SOX uniform)	3.00	1.50	.90
(342)	Cookie Lavagetto (portrait, pose to chest)	3.00	1.50	.90
(343)	Harry Lavagetto (portrait, pose to neck)	3.00	1.50	.90
(344)	Harry Lavagetto (portrait, pose to chest)	3.00	1.50	.90
(345)	Vern Law (portrait, pose to chest)	3.00	1.50	.90
(346)	Brooks Lawrence (portrait, pose to neck)	3.00	1.50	.90
(347)	Don Lee (portrait, pose to neck)	3.00	1.50	.90
(348)	Jim Lemon (portrait, pose to neck)	3.00	1.50	.90
(349)	Jim Lemon (kneeling, holding bat)	3.00	1.50	.90
(350)	Jim Lemon (portrait, pose to chest)	3.00	1.50	.90
(351)	Jim Lemon (batting, pose to chest)	3.00	1.50	.90

(352)	Bobbie Locke (pitching, pitcher's follow through)	3.00	1.50	.90
(353)	Carroll (Whitey) Lockman (portrait, pose to chest)	3.00	1.50	.90
(354)	Whitey Lockman (fielding)	3.00	1.50	.90
(355)	Billy Loes (portrait, pose to neck)	3.00	1.50	.90
(356)	John Logan (Infielder, portrait, pose to chest)	3.00	1.50	.90
(357)	Johnny Logan (batting, pose to waist)	3.00	1.50	.90
(358)	Sherman Lollar (portrait, pose to neck)	3.00	1.50	.90
(359)	Sherman Lollar (portrait, pose to chest)	3.00	1.50	.90
(360)	Sherman Lollar (kneeling, two bats)	3.00	1.50	.90
(361)	Dale Long (portrait, pose to neck)	3.00	1.50	.90
(362)	Stan Lopata (batting in cage)	3.00	1.50	.90
(363)	Stan Lopata (portrait, pose to chest)	3.00	1.50	.90
(364)	Stan Lopata (batting)	3.00	1.50	.90
(365)	Stan Lopata (portrait, pose to neck)	3.00	1.50	.90
(366)	Al Lopez (portrait, pose to chest, jacket)	4.50	2.25	1.25
(367)	Al Lopez (portrait, pose to chest, no jacket)	4.50	2.25	1.25
(368)	Hector Lopez (Athletics, batting, pose to waist)	3.00	1.50	.90
(369)	Hector Lopez (fielding)	3.00	1.50	.90
(370)	Hector Lopez (Yankees, batting)	3.00	1.50	.90
(371)	Jerry Lumpe (portrait, pose to neck)	3.00	1.50	.90
(372)	Jerry Lumpe (portrait, pose to chest)	3.00	1.50	.90
(373)	Jerry Lumpe (fielding)	3.00	1.50	.90
(374)	Jerry Lynch (portrait, pose to chest, one ear showing)	3.00	1.50	.90
(375)	Jerry Lynch (portrait, pose to chest, two ears showing)	3.00	1.50	.90
(376)	Art Mahaffey (portrait, pose to chest, glove)	3.00	1.50	.90
(377)	Bob Malkmus (portrait, pose to chest, glove)	3.00	1.50	.90
(378)	Frank Malzone (portrait, pose to neck)	3.00	1.50	.90
(379)	Frank Malzone (portrait, pose to chest, smile)	3.00	1.50	.90
(380)	Frank Malzone (portrait, pose to chest, no smile)	3.00	1.50	.90
(381)	Frank Malzone (batting, pose to thighs)	3.00	1.50	.90
(382)	Felix Mantilla (portrait, pose to neck)	3.00	1.50	.90
(383)	Felix Mantilla (fielding)	3.00	1.50	.90
(384)	Mickey Mantle (portrait, pose to neck)	22.00	11.00	6.50
(385)	Mickey Mantle (batting, pose to chest)	22.00	11.00	6.50
(386)	Juan Marichal (pitching, pose to waist, hands over head)	4.50	2.25	1.25
(387)	Roger Maris (batting, pose to chest)	7.50	3.75	2.25
(388)	Roger Maris (kneeling, holding bat)	7.50	3.75	2.25
(389)	Roger Maris (portrait, pose to neck)	7.50	3.75	2.25
(390)	Eddie Mathews (kneeling, holding bat, glove)	6.00	3.00	1.75
(391)	Eddie Mathews (kneeling, holding bat, no glove)	6.00	3.00	1.75
(392)	Edwin Mathews (Infielder, portrait, pose to chest)	6.00	3.00	1.75
(393)	Gene Mauch (portrait, pose to chest)	3.00	1.50	.90
(394)	Charlie Maxwell (portrait, pose to chest)	3.00	1.50	.90
(395)	Charlie Maxwell (kneeling, holding bat)	3.00	1.50	.90
(396)	Lee Maye (batting, pose to waist)	3.00	1.50	.90
(397)	Willie Mays (leaping)	15.00	7.50	4.50
(398)	Willie Mays (fielding)	15.00	7.50	4.50
(399)	Willie Mays (batting, pose to waist)	15.00	7.50	4.50
(400)	Willie Mays (batting)	15.00	7.50	4.50
(401)	Bill Mazeroski (Pirates, portrait, pose to neck)	6.00	3.00	1.75
(402)	Bill Mazeroski (Pittsburgh Pirates, portrait, pose to neck)	6.00	3.00	1.75
(403)	Bill Mazeroski (portrait, pose to chest)	6.00	3.00	1.75
(404)	Mike McCormick (pitching)	3.00	1.50	.90
(405)	Mike McCormick (pitching, pose to waist)	3.00	1.50	.90
(406)	Willie McCovey (kneeling, pose to waist, five bats)	6.00	3.00	1.75
(407)	Lindy McDaniel (portrait, pose to neck)	3.00	1.50	.90
(408)	Lindy McDaniel (portrait, pose to chest)	3.00	1.50	.90
(409)	Von McDaniel (portrait, pose to chest)	3.00	1.50	.90
(410)	Gil McDougald (portrait, pose to neck)	3.00	1.50	.90
(411)	Don McMahon (portrait, pose to waist)	3.00	1.50	.90
(412)	Don McMahon (pitching, pitcher's follow through)	3.00	1.50	.90
(413)	Donald McMahon (pitcher, portrait, pose to neck)	3.00	1.50	.90
(414)	Roy McMillan (portrait, pose to neck, glasses)	3.00	1.50	.90
(415)	Roy McMillan (portrait, pose to neck, no glasses)	3.00	1.50	.90
(416)	Roy McMillan (throwing, pose to knees)	3.00	1.50	.90
(417)	Roman Mejias (portrait, pose to neck)	3.00	1.50	.90
(418)	Stu Miller (portrait, pose to chest)	3.00	1.50	.90
(419)	Stu Miller (pitching, pitcher's follow through)	3.00	1.50	.90
(420)	Minnie Minoso (batting,)	3.00	1.50	.90
(421)	Orestes Minoso (portrait, pose to chest)	3.75	2.00	1.25
(422)	Willy Miranda (portrait, pose to neck)	3.00	1.50	.90
(423)	Wilmer Mizell (portrait, pose to neck)	3.00	1.50	.90
(424)	Bill Monbouquette (portrait, pose to chest)	3.00	1.50	.90
(425)	Wally Moon (Cardinals, portrait, pose to neck)	3.00	1.50	.90
(426)	Wally Moon (portrait, pose to waist)	3.00	1.50	.90
(427)	Wally Moon (Dodgers, portrait, pose to neck)	3.00	1.50	.90
(428)	Ray Moore (portrait, pose to neck)	3.00	1.50	.90
(429)	Seth Morehead (standing, pose to knees)	3.00	1.50	.90
(430)	Tom Morgan (portrait, pose to chest)	3.00	1.50	.90
(431)	Walt Moryn (portrait, pose to chest)	3.00	1.50	.90
(432)	Don Mossi (portrait, pose to chest)	3.00	1.50	.90
(433)	Billy Muffett (portrait, pose to chest)	3.00	1.50	.90
(434)	Danny Murtaugh (portrait, pose to neck)	3.00	1.50	.90
(435)	Danny Murtaugh (portrait, pose to chest, one ear showing)	3.00	1.50	.90
(436)	Danny Murtaugh (portrait, pose to chest, two ears showing)	3.00	1.50	.90
(437)	Stan Musial (portrait, pose to neck)	15.00	7.50	4.50
(438)	Stan Musial (portrait, pose to waist)	15.00	7.50	4.50
(439)	Ray Narleski (portrait, pose to chest)	3.00	1.50	.90
(440)	Charley Neal (Infielder, portrait, pose to neck)	3.00	1.50	.90
(441)	Charlie Neal (portrait, pose to neck)	3.00	1.50	.90
(442)	Charlie Neal (portrait, pose to chest)	3.00	1.50	.90
(443)	Don Newcombe (Pitcher, portrait, pose to neck)	3.00	1.50	.90
(444)	Don Newcombe (portrait, pose to neck)	3.00	1.50	.90
(445)	Don Newcombe (pitching, hands over head)	3.00	1.50	.90
(446)	Bob Nieman (Orioles, portrait, pose to neck)	3.00	1.50	.90
(447)	Bob Nieman (portrait, pose to chest)	3.00	1.50	.90
(448)	Bob Nieman (Cardinals, portrait, pose to neck)	3.00	1.50	.90
(449)	Russ Nixon (portrait, pose to chest)	3.00	1.50	.90
(450)	Russ Nixon (batting, pose to waist)	3.00	1.50	.90
(451)	Don Nottebart (portrait, pose to chest)	3.00	1.50	.90
(452)	Joe Nuxhall (pitching, pitcher's follow through)	3.00	1.50	.90
(453)	Joe Nuxhall (portrait, pose to neck)	3.00	1.50	.90
(454)	Danny O'Connell (portrait, pose to neck)	3.00	1.50	.90
(455)	Bill Odell (O'Dell) (portrait, pose to neck)	3.00	1.50	.90
(456)	Billy O'Dell (portrait, pose to chest)	3.00	1.50	.90
(457)	Claude Osteen (portrait, pose to waist, glove)	3.00	1.50	.90
(458)	Jim O'Toole (portrait, pose to neck)	3.00	1.50	.90
(459)	Jim O'Toole (portrait, pose to chest)	3.00	1.50	.90
(460)	Jim Owens (pitching, pitcher's follow through)	3.00	1.50	.90
(461)	Andrew Pafko (outfielder, portrait, pose to neck)	3.00	1.50	.90
(462)	Andy Pafko (batting, pose to waist)	3.00	1.50	.90
(463)	Jim Pagliaroni (catching, crouching)	3.00	1.50	.90
(464)	Milt Pappas (pitching, pitcher's follow through)	3.00	1.50	.90
(465)	Milt Pappas (portrait, pose to chest, dark background)	3.00	1.50	.90
(466)	Milt Pappas (portrait, pose to chest, light background)	3.00	1.50	.90
(467)	Camilo Pascual (portrait, pose to neck, light background)	3.00	1.50	.90
(468)	Camilo Pascual (pitching)	3.00	1.50	.90
(469)	Camilo Pascual (portrait, pose to neck, dark background)	3.00	1.50	.90
(470)	Camilo Pasqual (Pascual) (portrait, pose to neck)	3.00	1.50	.90
(471)	Albie Pearson (portrait, pose to chest)	3.00	1.50	.90
(472)	Albie Pearson (portrait, pose to neck, "W" on cap)	3.00	1.50	.90
(473)	Albie Pearson (portrait, pose to neck, "W" not visible on cap)	3.00	1.50	.90
(474)	Orlando Pena (batting, pose to waist)	3.00	1.50	.90
(474.5)	Orlando Pena (portrait, pose to neck)	3.00	1.50	.90
(475)	Bubba Phillips (hands on knees)	3.00	1.50	.90
(476)	Bubba Phillips (batting, pose to waist)	3.00	1.50	.90
(477)	Bubba Phillips (portrait, pose to chest)	3.00	1.50	.90
(478)	Bill Pierce (portrait, pose to neck)	3.00	1.50	.90
(479)	Billy Pierce (portrait, pose to chest)	3.00	1.50	.90
(480)	Billy Pierce (pitching, hands over head)	3.00	1.50	.90
(481)	Jim Piersall (portrait, pose to neck)	3.00	1.50	.90
(482)	Jim Piersall (batting, pose to chest)	3.00	1.50	.90
(483)	Jimmy Piersall (batting, pose to chest)	3.00	1.50	.90
(484)	Joe Pignatano (portrait, pose to chest)	3.00	1.50	.90
(485)	Al Pilarcik (portrait, pose to neck)	3.00	1.50	.90
(486)	Vada Pinson (portrait, pose to neck)	3.00	1.50	.90
(487)	Vada Pinson (batting, pose to waist)	3.00	1.50	.90
(488)	Juan Pizzarro (Pizarro) (pitching)	3.00	1.50	.90
(489)	Herb Plews (batting, pose to waist)	3.00	1.50	.90
(490)	Herb Plews (portrait, pose to neck)	3.00	1.50	.90
(491)	Johnny Podres (Pitcher, portrait, pose to neck)	3.00	1.50	.90
(492)	Johnny Podres (portrait, pose to neck)	3.00	1.50	.90
(493)	Johnny Podres (portrait, pose to chest)	3.00	1.50	.90
(494)	Arnie Portocarrero (portrait, pose to chest)	3.00	1.50	.90
(495)	Wally Post (portrait, pose to waist)	3.00	1.50	.90
(496)	Wally Post (batting, pose to waist)	3.00	1.50	.90
(497)	Vic Power (batting, pose to waist)	3.00	1.50	.90
(498)	Vic Power (batting, head shot)	3.00	1.50	.90
(499)	Vic Power (fielding, pose to knees)	3.00	1.50	.90
(500)	Bob Purkey (portrait, pose to neck)	3.00	1.50	.90
(501)	Pedro Ramos (portrait, pose to chest, hands over head)	3.00	1.50	.90
(502)	Pedro Ramos (Senators, portrait, pose to neck, dark background)	3.00	1.50	.90
(503)	Pedro Ramos (portrait, pose to neck, light background)	3.00	1.50	.90
(504)	Pedro Ramos (Twins, portrait, pose to neck)	3.00	1.50	.90
(505)	Pee Wee Reese (Infielder, portrait, pose to neck)	7.50	3.75	2.25
(506)	Rip Repulski (portrait, pose to neck)	3.00	1.50	.90
(507)	Rip Repulski (portrait, pose to neck)	3.00	1.50	.90
(508)	Paul Richards (portrait, pose to neck)	3.00	1.50	.90
(509)	Paul Richards (portrait, pose to chest, Orioles uniform)	3.00	1.50	.90
(510)	Paul Richards (portrait, pose to chest, Baltimore uniform)	3.00	1.50	.90
(511)	Bobby Richardson (batting,)	3.75	2.00	1.25
(512)	Bobby Richardson (fielding)	3.75	2.00	1.25
(513)	Bill Rigney (portrait, pose to chest)	3.00	1.50	.90
(514)	Jim Rivera (portrait, pose to neck)	3.00	1.50	.90
(515)	Mel Roach (throwing)	3.00	1.50	.90
(516)	Robin Roberts (portrait, pose to neck)	4.50	2.25	1.25
(517)	Robin Roberts (pitching, hands on knees)	4.50	2.25	1.25
(518)	Robin Roberts (portrait, pose to chest)	4.50	2.25	1.25
(519)	Brooks Robinson (portrait, pose to chest)	9.00	4.50	2.75
(520)	Brooks Robinson (fielding)	9.00	4.50	2.75
(521)	Frank Robinson (portrait, pose to neck)	7.50	3.75	2.25
(522)	Frank Robinson (portrait, pose to chest)	7.50	3.75	2.25
(523)	Frank Robinson (batting, pose to waist)	7.50	3.75	2.25
(524)	John Romano (portrait, pose to chest, W. Sox uniform)	3.00	1.50	.90
(525)	John Romano (portrait, pose to chest, Indians uniform)	3.00	1.50	.90
(526)	John Roseboro (portrait, pose to neck)	3.00	1.50	.90
(527)	John Roseboro (portrait, pose to chest)	3.00	1.50	.90
(528)	Pete Runnells (Runnels) (portrait, pose to neck)	3.00	1.50	.90
(529)	Pete Runnels (portrait, pose to chest)	3.00	1.50	.90
(530)	Pete Runnels (batting, pose to knees)	3.00	1.50	.90
(531)	Bob Rush (pitching)	3.00	1.50	.90

(532)	Ron Samford (kneeling, holding bat)	3.00	1.50	.90
(533)	Jack Sandford (Sanford) (portrait, pose to neck)	3.00	1.50	.90
(534)	Jack Sanford (pitching)	3.00	1.50	.90
(535)	Jack Sanford (pitching, pitcher's follow through)	3.00	1.50	.90
(536)	Ron Santo (portrait, pose to chest)	3.75	2.00	1.25
(537)	Hank Sauer (batting,)	3.00	1.50	.90
(538)	Hank Sauer (hands on knees)	3.00	1.50	.90
(539)	Eddie Sawyer (portrait, pose to chest)	3.00	1.50	.90
(540)	Bob Schmidt (catching, crouching)	3.00	1.50	.90
(541)	Bob Schmidt (catching, throwing mask)	3.00	1.50	.90
(542)	Bob Schmidt (portrait, pose to neck)	3.00	1.50	.90
(543)	Albert Schoendienst (infielder, batting, pose to neck)	4.50	2.25	1.25
(544)	Red Schoendienst (portrait, pose to neck)	4.50	2.25	1.25
(545)	Red Schoendienst (throwing)	4.50	2.25	1.25
(546)	Don Schwall (pitching, pitcher's follow through)	3.00	1.50	.90
(547)	Ray Semproch (portrait, pose to chest)	3.00	1.50	.90
(548)	Bobby Shantz (portrait, pose to neck)	3.00	1.50	.90
(549)	Bob Shaw (portrait, pose to neck)	3.00	1.50	.90
(550)	Bob Sheffing (portrait, pose to chest)	3.00	1.50	.90
(551)	Larry Sherry (portrait, pose to chest)	3.00	1.50	.90
(552)	Chuck Shilling (portrait, pose to chest)	3.00	1.50	.90
(553)	Norm Siebern (portrait, pose to chest)	3.00	1.50	.90
(554)	Norm Siebern (throwing)	3.00	1.50	.90
(555)	Roy Sievers (Senators, portrait, pose to neck)	3.00	1.50	.90
(556)	Roy Sievers (batting, pose to waist)	3.00	1.50	.90
(557)	Roy Sievers (White Sox, portrait, pose to neck)	3.00	1.50	.90
(558)	Roy Sievers (batting, pose to chest)	3.00	1.50	.90
(559)	Curt Simmons (portrait, pose to neck)	3.00	1.50	.90
(560)	Curt Simmons (portrait, pose to chest)	3.00	1.50	.90
(561)	Bob Skinner (Pirates, portrait, pose to neck)	3.00	1.50	.90
(562)	Bob Skinner (Pittsburgh Pirates, portrait, pose to neck)	3.00	1.50	.90
(563)	Bob Skinner (portrait, pose to thighs, five bats)	3.00	1.50	.90
(564)	Bob Skinner (batting, pose to chest)	3.00	1.50	.90
(565)	Bill Skowron (portrait, pose to neck)	3.75	2.00	1.25
(566)	Bill Skowron (batting, pose to waist)	3.75	2.00	1.25
(567)	Al Smith (portrait, pose to neck)	3.00	1.50	.90
(568)	Al Smith (portrait, pose to chest)	3.00	1.50	.90
(569)	Al Smith (kneeling, holding bat)	3.00	1.50	.90
(570)	Hal Smith (portrait, pose to neck)	3.00	1.50	.90
(571)	Hal Smith (catching, pose to waist)	3.00	1.50	.90
(572)	Hal Smith (batting)	3.00	1.50	.90
(573)	Hal Smith (batting, head shot)	3.00	1.50	.90
(574)	Mayo Smith (portrait, pose to neck)	3.00	1.50	.90
(575)	Duke Snider (Outfielder, portrait, pose to neck)	10.50	5.25	3.25
(576)	Duke Snider (portrait, pose to neck)	10.50	5.25	3.25
(577)	Duke Snider (portrait, pose to chest)	10.50	5.25	3.25
(578)	Russ Snyder (portrait, pose to chest)	3.00	1.50	.90
(579)	Warren Spahn (Pitcher, portrait, pose to neck)	6.00	3.00	1.75
(580)	Warren Spahn (portrait, pose to neck)	6.00	3.00	1.75
(581)	Warren Spahn (pitching)	6.00	3.00	1.75
(582)	Daryl Spencer (fielding)	3.00	1.50	.90
(583)	Daryl Spencer (throwing)	3.00	1.50	.90
(584)	Daryl Spencer (portrait, pose to neck)	3.00	1.50	.90
(585)	Daryl Spencer (portrait, pose to chest)	3.00	1.50	.90
(586)	Gerry Staley (fielding)	3.00	1.50	.90
(587)	Casey Stengel (portrait, pose to neck)	7.50	3.75	2.25
(588)	Gene Stephens (batting, pose to chest)	3.00	1.50	.90
(589)	Gene Stephens (portrait, pose to chest)	3.00	1.50	.90
(590)	R.C. Stevens (portrait, pose to chest)	3.00	1.50	.90
(591)	Chuck Stobbs (pitching, pitcher's follow through)	3.00	1.50	.90
(592)	George Strickland (kneeling, holding bat)	3.00	1.50	.90
(593)	Dick Stuart (portrait, pose to neck, no team designation)	3.00	1.50	.90
(594)	Dick Stuart (batting, pose to chest)	3.00	1.50	.90
(595)	Dick Stuart (kneeling, holding bat)	3.00	1.50	.90
(596)	Dick Stuart (portrait, pose to neck, Pirates)	3.00	1.50	.90
(597)	Tom Sturdivant (portrait, pose to neck)	3.00	1.50	.90
(598)	Tom Sturdivant (portrait, pose to chest)	3.00	1.50	.90
(599)	Frank Sullivan (portrait, pose to neck)	3.00	1.50	.90
(600)	Frank Sullivan (portrait, pose to chest)	3.00	1.50	.90
(601)	Haywood Sullivan (Red Sox, portrait, pose to chest)	3.00	1.50	.90
(602)	Haywood Sullivan (Athletics, portrait, pose to chest)	3.00	1.50	.90
(603)	Willie Tasby (batting, pose to chest)	3.00	1.50	.90
(604)	Willie Tasby (Orioles, portrait, pose to chest)	3.00	1.50	.90
(605)	Willie Tasby (Senators, portrait, pose to chest)	3.00	1.50	.90
(606)	Sam Taylor (portrait, pose to neck)	3.00	1.50	.90
(607)	Tony Taylor (portrait, pose to chest)	3.00	1.50	.90
(608)	Tony Taylor (batting, pose to chest)	3.00	1.50	.90
(609)	"Birdie" Tebbetts (portrait, pose to neck)	3.00	1.50	.90
(610)	John Temple (kneeling, holding bat)	3.00	1.50	.90
(611)	Johnny Temple (portrait, pose to neck)	3.00	1.50	.90
(612)	Johnny Temple (kneeling, holding bat)	3.00	1.50	.90
(613)	Ralph Terry (pitching, pitcher's follow through)	3.00	1.50	.90
(614)	Ralph Terry (pitching, pitcher's follow through, pose to knees)	3.00	1.50	.90
(615)	Moe Thacker (portrait, pose to chest)	3.00	1.50	.90
(616)	Frank J. Thomas (batting, pose to waist)	3.00	1.50	.90
(617)	Frank J. Thomas (batting, pose to chest)	3.00	1.50	.90
(618)	Frank J. Thomas (portrait, pose to neck)	3.00	1.50	.90
(619)	Bobby Thomson (batting, pose to waist, two bats)	3.00	1.50	.90
(620)	Fay Throneberry (Faye) (batting, pose to chest)	3.00	1.50	.90
(621)	Faye Throneberry (portrait, pose to chest)	3.00	1.50	.90
(622)	Marv Throneberry (throwing)	3.00	1.50	.90
(623)	Marv Throneberry (portrait, pose to chest)	3.00	1.50	.90
(624)	Dick Tomanek (pitching, pitcher's follow through)	3.00	1.50	.90
(625)	Frank Torre (portrait, pose to neck)	3.00	1.50	.90
(626)	Frank Torre (fielding)	3.00	1.50	.90
(627)	Gus Triandos (portrait, pose to neck)	3.00	1.50	.90
(628)	Gus Triandos (portrait, pose to chest)	3.00	1.50	.90
(629)	Gus Triandos (catching)	3.00	1.50	.90
(630)	Bob Trowbridge (portrait, pose to waist)	3.00	1.50	.90
(631)	Virgil Trucks (pitching, pitcher's follow through)	3.00	1.50	.90
(632)	Bob Turley (pitching, pitcher's follow through)	3.00	1.50	.90
(633)	Bob Turley (portrait, pose to neck, one ear showing)	3.00	1.50	.90
(634)	Bob Turley (portrait, pose to neck, two ears showing)	3.00	1.50	.90
(635)	Bill Tuttle (portrait, pose to neck, "A" on cap)	3.00	1.50	.90
(636)	Bill Tuttle (portrait, pose to neck, no "A" on cap)	3.00	1.50	.90
(637)	Bill Tuttle (batting, "KC" on cap)	3.00	1.50	.90
(638)	Bill Tuttle (batting, "A" on cap)	3.00	1.50	.90
(639)	Jack Urban (pitching, pitcher's follow through, pose to knees)	3.00	1.50	.90
(640)	Coot Veal (batting, pose to thighs)	3.00	1.50	.90
(641)	Mickey Vernon (portrait, pose to waist)	3.00	1.50	.90
(642)	Zoilo Versalles (portrait, pose to neck)	3.00	1.50	.90
(643)	Bill Virdon (portrait, pose to neck)	3.00	1.50	.90
(644)	Bill Virdon (kneeling, holding bat)	3.00	1.50	.90
(645)	Bill Virdon (batting, pose to chest)	3.00	1.50	.90
(646)	Jerry Walker (pitching, pitcher's follow through)	3.00	1.50	.90
(647)	Jerry Walker (portrait, pose to chest, tower background)	3.00	1.50	.90
(648)	Jerry Walker (portrait, pose to chest, no tower)	3.00	1.50	.90
(649)	Lee Walls (portrait, pose to neck)	3.00	1.50	.90
(650)	Ken Walters (portrait, pose to neck)	3.00	1.50	.90
(651)	Vic Wertz (portrait, pose to chest)	3.00	1.50	.90
(652)	Vic Wertz (batting, pose to chest)	3.00	1.50	.90
(653)	Bill White (portrait, pose to neck)	3.00	1.50	.90
(654)	Bill White (portrait, pose to chest)	3.00	1.50	.90
(655)	Sam White (portrait, pose to neck)	3.00	1.50	.90
(656)	Sammy White (portrait, pose to chest)	3.00	1.50	.90
(657)	Hoyt Wilhelm (portrait, pose to chest)	4.50	2.25	1.25
(658)	James (Hoyt) Wilhelm (portrait, pose to chest)	4.50	2.25	1.25
(659)	Carl Willey (portrait, pose to neck)	3.00	1.50	.90
(660)	Dick Williams (throwing)	3.00	1.50	.90
(661)	Stan Williams (portrait, pose to chest)	3.00	1.50	.90
(662)	Ted Williams (batting, pose to neck)	15.00	7.50	4.50
(663)	Ted Williams (batting, pose to chest)	15.00	7.50	4.50
(664)	Maury Wills (portrait, pose to waist)	3.75	2.00	1.25
(665)	Jim Wilson (portrait, pose to neck)	3.00	1.50	.90
(666)	Gene Woodling (portrait, pose to chest)	3.00	1.50	.90
(667)	Gene Woodling (portrait, pose to chest)	3.00	1.50	.90
(668)	Al Worthington (portrait, pose to neck)	3.00	1.50	.90
(669)	Early Wynn (portrait, pose to neck)	4.50	2.25	1.25
(670)	Early Wynn (portrait, pose to chest)	4.50	2.25	1.25
(671)	Early Wynn (fielding)	4.50	2.25	1.25
(672)	Carl Yastrzemski (portrait, pose to chest)	10.50	5.25	3.25
(673)	Ed Yost (kneeling, pose to waist)	3.00	1.50	.90
(674)	Ed Yost (portrait, pose to chest)	3.00	1.50	.90
(675)	Eddie Yost (portrait, pose to neck)	3.00	1.50	.90
(676)	Norm Zauchin (portrait, pose to neck)	3.00	1.50	.90
(677)	Don Zimmer (portrait, pose to neck)	3.00	1.50	.90
(678)	Don Zimmer (portrait, pose to chest)	3.00	1.50	.90
(679)	Jerry Zimmerman (portrait, pose to chest)	3.00	1.50	.90
(680)	George Zuverink (portrait, pose to neck)	3.00	1.50	.90
(681)	Marion Zipfel (fielding)	3.00	1.50	.90

1962 Jay Publishing 5x7 Photos Type 2

JOHN CALLISON, Philadelphia Phillies

		NM	EX	VG
	Common Player:	3.00	1.50	.90
(1)	Hank Aaron (batting, pose to chest)	20.00	10.00	6.00
(2)	Hank Aaron (batting)	20.00	10.00	6.00
(3)	Hank Aaron (kneeling, holding bat)	20.00	10.00	6.00
(4)	Tommy Aaron (fielding)	3.00	1.50	.90
(5)	Jerry Adair (batting, pose to chest,"B" on cap)	3.00	1.50	.90
(6)	Jerry Adair (batting, pose to chest, bird on cap)	3.00	1.50	.90
(7)	Joe Adcock (Braves, portrait, pose to waist)	5.00	2.50	1.50
(8)	Joe Adcock (batting, pose to chest)	5.00	2.50	1.50
(9)	Joe Adcock (Indians, portrait, pose to waist)	5.00	2.50	1.50
(9.5)	Joe Adcock (Angels, kneeling, portrait pose to waist)	5.00	2.50	1.50
(10)	Joe Adcock (batting, pose to neck)	5.00	2.50	1.50
(10.5)	Dave Adlesh (Houston, portrait, pose to waist)	3.00	1.50	.90
(11)	Hank Aguirre (pitching)	3.00	1.50	.90
(12)	Hank Aguirre (portrait, pose to waist, glove)	3.00	1.50	.90
(13)	Bernie Allen (batting, pose to waist)	3.00	1.50	.90
(14)	Bernie Allen (fielding)	3.00	1.50	.90
(15)	Bob Allison (batting, pose to chest, plain uniform)	4.00	2.00	1.25
(16)	Bob Allison (batting, pose to chest, towers in background)	4.00	2.00	1.25
(17)	Bob Allison (batting, pose to chest, wire background)	4.00	2.00	1.25

(18)	Bob Allison (kneeling, holding bat)	4.00	2.00	1.25
(19)	Felipe Alou (portrait, pose to neck)	4.00	2.00	1.25
(20)	Felipe Alou (batting, pose to thighs)	4.00	2.00	1.25
(21)	Jesus Alou (kneeling, pose to waist)	3.00	1.50	.90
(22)	Matty Alou (portrait, pose to chest)	4.00	2.00	1.25
(23)	Walt Alston (portrait, pose to neck)	3.50	1.75	1.00
(24)	Walt Alston (portrait, pose to chest, dark background)	3.50	1.75	1.00
(25)	Walt Alston (portrait, pose to chest, light background)	3.50	1.75	1.00
(26)	George Altman (portrait, pose to chest, dark background)	3.00	1.50	.90
(27)	George Altman (portrait, pose to chest, light background)	3.00	1.50	.90
(28)	Max Alvis (portrait, pose to chest)	3.00	1.50	.90
(29)	Max Alvis (batting, pose to chest)	3.00	1.50	.90
(30)	Joe Amalfitano (portrait, pose to chest)	3.00	1.50	.90
(31)	Ruben Amaro (batting, pose to chest)	3.00	1.50	.90
(32)	Bob Anderson (portrait, pose to chest)	3.00	1.50	.90
(33)	Luis Aparicio (fielding)	8.00	4.00	2.50
(34)	Luis Aparicio (batting, pose to chest,"B" on cap)	8.00	4.00	2.50
(35)	Luis Aparicio (batting, pose to chest, bird on cap)	8.00	4.00	2.50
(36)	Luis Aparicio (kneeling, pose to waist)	8.00	4.00	2.50
(37)	George Arrigo (Jerry) (portrait, pose to waist)	3.00	1.50	.90
(38)	Luis Arroyo (pitching, follow-through)	3.00	1.50	.90
(39)	Bob Aspromonte (portrait, pose to chest)	3.00	1.50	.90
(39.5)	Bob Aspromonte (Houston, portrait, pose to waist)	3.00	1.50	.90
(40)	Bob Aspromonte (batting, pose to chest)	3.00	1.50	.90
(41)	Earl Averill (batting, pose to chest)	3.00	1.50	.90
(42)	Joe Azcue (batting, pose to chest)	3.00	1.50	.90
(43)	Jim Archer (pitching, follow-through)	3.00	1.50	.90
(44)	Bob Bailey (batting, pose to chest)	3.00	1.50	.90
(45)	Bob Bailey (kneeling, holding bat)	3.00	1.50	.90
(46)	Ed Bailey (catching, lifting mask)	3.00	1.50	.90
(47)	Jack Baldschun (portrait, pose to chest)	3.00	1.50	.90
(48)	Jack Baldschun (portrait, pose to chest, hands over head)	3.00	1.50	.90
(49)	Ernie Banks (fielding)	12.00	6.00	3.50
(50)	Ernie Banks (portrait, pose to waist)	12.00	6.00	3.50
(51)	Ernie Banks (batting, pose to chest)	12.00	6.00	3.50
(52)	Steve Barber (pitching, pose to chest, hands over head)	3.00	1.50	.90
(53)	Steve Barber (portrait, pose to chest)	3.00	1.50	.90
(54)	Steve Barber (pitching, follow-through)	3.00	1.50	.90
(55)	Norm Bass (portrait, pose to chest)	3.00	1.50	.90
(56)	Norm Bass (portrait, pose to waist, glove)	3.00	1.50	.90
(56.5)	John Bateman (Houston, portrait, pose to waist)	3.00	1.50	.90
(57)	Earl Battey (batting, pose to chest)	3.00	1.50	.90
(58)	Earl Battey (catching, crouching)	3.00	1.50	.90
(59)	Hank Bauer (portrait, pose to chest)	3.00	1.50	.90
(60)	Frank Baumann (pitching, follow-through)	3.00	1.50	.90
(61)	Larry Bearnarth (pitching, follow-through)	3.00	1.50	.90
(62)	Bo Belinsky (portrait, pose to chest)	4.00	2.00	1.25
(63)	Gary Bell (portrait, pose to chest)	3.00	1.50	.90
(64)	Gary Bell (pitching)	3.00	1.50	.90
(65)	Gus Bell (portrait, pose to chest)	3.00	1.50	.90
(66)	Gus Bell (batting, pose to waist)	3.00	1.50	.90
(67)	Dennis Bennett (portrait, pose to chest)	3.00	1.50	.90
(68)	Yogi Berra (Manager, portrait, pose to chest)	14.00	7.00	4.25
(69)	Yogi Berra (portrait, pose to chest)	14.00	7.00	4.25
(70)	Yogi Berra (batting, pose to thighs)	14.00	7.00	4.25
(71)	Dick Bertell (portrait, pose to waist, home uniform)	3.00	1.50	.90
(72)	Dick Bertell (portrait, pose to chest, road uniform)	3.00	1.50	.90
(73)	Steve Bilko (batting, pose to chest)	3.00	1.50	.90
(74)	John Blanchard (batting, pose to chest)	4.00	2.00	1.25
(75)	Don Blasingame (portrait, pose to chest)	3.00	1.50	.90
(76)	Don Blasingame (batting, pose to chest)	3.00	1.50	.90
(77)	Wade Blasingame (pitching, follow-through)	3.00	1.50	.90
(78)	Frank Bolling (batting, pose to chest)	3.00	1.50	.90
(79)	Frank Bolling (fielding, throwing)	3.00	1.50	.90
(80)	Frank Bolling (kneeling, holding bat)	3.00	1.50	.90
(80.5)	Walt Bond (Houston, batting, pose to waist)	3.00	1.50	.90
(81)	Steve Boros (kneeling, holding bat)	3.00	1.50	.90
(82)	Jim Bouton (pitching, follow-through)	5.00	2.50	1.50
(83)	Sam Bowens (batting, pose to chest)	3.00	1.50	.90
(84)	Clete Boyer (fielding)	4.00	2.00	1.25
(85)	Clete Boyer (batting, pose to chest, bat tilted)	4.00	2.00	1.25
(86)	Cletis Boyer (batting, pose to chest, bat vertical)	4.00	2.00	1.25
(87)	Ken Boyer (portrait, pose to chest)	6.00	3.00	1.75
(88)	Ken Boyer (fielding)	6.00	3.00	1.75
(89)	Ken Boyer (kneeling, holding bat)	6.00	3.00	1.75
(90)	Bobbie Bragan (portrait, pose to waist, looks left)	3.00	1.50	.90
(90.5)	Bobby Bragan (portrait, kneeling, pose to thighs)	3.00	1.50	.90
(91)	Bobbie Bragan (portrait, pose to waist, looks right)	3.00	1.50	.90
(91.5)	Ron Brand (Houston, portrait, pose to waist)	3.00	1.50	.90
(92)	Jackie Brandt (kneeling, holding bat)	3.00	1.50	.90
(93)	Jackie Brandt (batting, pose to waist)	3.00	1.50	.90
(94)	Jackie Brandt (hands on knees)	3.00	1.50	.90
(95)	Marv Breeding (kneeling, holding bat)	3.00	1.50	.90
(96)	Ed Bressoud (portrait, pose to chest)	3.00	1.50	.90
(97)	Ed Bressoud (batting, pose to thighs)	3.00	1.50	.90
(98)	Ed Bressoud (kneeling, pose to knees, arms crossed)	3.00	1.50	.90
(99)	Ed Brinkman (portrait, pose to chest)	3.00	1.50	.90
(100)	Lou Brock (portrait, pose to chest, dark background)	10.00	5.00	3.00
(101)	Lou Brock (portrait, pose to waist, light background)	10.00	5.00	3.00
(102)	Ernie Broglio (pitching, follow-through)	3.00	1.50	.90
(103)	Ernie Broglio (pitching, pose to waist, one ear showing)	3.00	1.50	.90
(104)	Ernie Broglio (pitching, pose to waist, two ears showing)	3.00	1.50	.90
(105)	Ernie Broglio (portrait, pose to chest)	3.00	1.50	.90
(106)	Jim Brosnan (portrait, pose to chest, hands over head)	3.00	1.50	.90
(107)	Jim Brosnan (pitching, follow-through)	3.00	1.50	.90
(108)	Dick Brown (portrait, pose to waist, glove)	3.00	1.50	.90
(109)	Hector (Skinny) Brown (portrait, pose to chest)	3.00	1.50	.90
(110)	Larry Brown (portrait, pose to chest)	3.00	1.50	.90
(111)	Bob Bruce (pitching, pose to chest, hands over head)	3.00	1.50	.90
(112)	Bob Bruce (portrait, pose to chest)	3.00	1.50	.90
(113)	Mike Brumley (portrait, pose to chest)	3.00	1.50	.90
(114)	Bill Bruton (kneeling, holding bat)	3.00	1.50	.90
(115)	Bill Bryan (batting, pose to chest)	3.00	1.50	.90
(116)	Don Buddin (portrait, pose to chest)	3.00	1.50	.90
(117)	Bob Buhl (pitching)	3.00	1.50	.90
(118)	Bob Buhl (portrait, pose to waist, cage background)	3.00	1.50	.90
(119)	Bob Buhl (portrait, pose to neck, hook background)	3.00	1.50	.90
(120)	Bob Buhl (portrait, pose to chest, bleacher background)	3.00	1.50	.90
(121)	Wally Bunker (pitching, pose to waist)	3.00	1.50	.90
(122)	Jim Bunning (portrait, pose to chest)	4.00	2.00	1.25
(123)	Jim Bunning (pitching, follow-through)	4.00	2.00	1.25
(124)	Jim Bunning (kneeling, pose to knees, arms crossed)	4.00	2.00	1.25
(125)	Lew Burdette (pitching, photo reversed)	4.00	2.00	1.25
(126)	Lew Burdette (portrait, pose to thighs, glove)	4.00	2.00	1.25
(127)	Lou Burdette (pitching)	4.00	2.00	1.25
(128)	Lou Burdette (portrait, pose to chest)	4.00	2.00	1.25
(129)	Smokey Burgess (kneeling)	4.00	2.00	1.25
(130)	Pete Burnside (pitching)	3.00	1.50	.90
(131)	Larry Burright (portrait, pose to chest)	3.00	1.50	.90
(132)	Cecil Butler (pitching, follow-through)	3.00	1.50	.90
(133)	John Callison (batting, pose to chest)	4.00	2.00	1.25
(134)	John Callison (batting, pose to neck)	4.00	2.00	1.25
(135)	Chris Cannizzaro (batting, pose to chest)	3.00	1.50	.90
(136)	Leo Cardenas (fielding)	3.00	1.50	.90
(137)	Leo Cardenas (batting, pose to waist)	3.00	1.50	.90
(138)	Don Cardwell (portrait, pose to chest)	3.00	1.50	.90
(139)	Duke Carmel (portrait, pose to chest)	3.00	1.50	.90
(140)	Camilio Carreon (Camilo, batting, pose to chest)	3.00	1.50	.90
(141)	Camilio Carreon (Camilo, portrait, pose to chest)	3.00	1.50	.90
(142)	Norm Cash (batting, pose to chest)	4.00	2.00	1.25
(143)	Norm Cash (kneeling, holding bat)	4.00	2.00	1.25
(144)	Norm Cash (fielding)	4.00	2.00	1.25
(145)	Norm Cash (hands on knees)	4.00	2.00	1.25
(146)	Wayne Causey (kneeling, holding bat)	3.00	1.50	.90
(147)	Wayne Causey (portrait, pose to chest, stripe uniform)	3.00	1.50	.90
(148)	Wayne Causey (portrait, pose to chest, vest uniform)	3.00	1.50	.90
(148.5)	Wayne Causey (portrait, vest uniform, pose to waist)	3.00	1.50	.90
(149)	Orlando Cepeda (kneeling, pose to waist)	7.50	3.75	2.25
(150)	Orlando Cepeda (portrait, pose to chest, one ear showing)	7.50	3.75	2.25
(151)	Orlando Cepeda (portrait, pose to chest, two ears showing)	7.50	3.75	2.25
(152)	Orlando Cepeda (batting, pose to chest)	7.50	3.75	2.25
(153)	Elio Chacon (portrait, pose to waist)	3.00	1.50	.90
(154)	Dean Chance (pitching, follow-through, wrist over glove)	3.00	1.50	.90
(155)	Dean Chance (pitching, follow-through, hand over glove)	3.00	1.50	.90
(156)	Dean Chance (portrait, pose to chest)	3.00	1.50	.90
(157)	Ed Charles (batting, pose to chest, striped uniform)	3.00	1.50	.90
(158)	Ed Charles (batting, pose to chest, vest uniform)	3.00	1.50	.90
(159)	Tom Cheney (pitching, follow-through)	3.00	1.50	.90
(160)	Tom Cheney (portrait, pose to chest, hands over head, picture is Osteen)	3.00	1.50	.90
(161)	Frank Cipriani (batting, pose to waist)	3.00	1.50	.90
(162)	Galen Cisco (pitching, pose to knees)	3.00	1.50	.90
(163)	Roberto Clemente (batting, pose to chest, cap)	20.00	10.00	6.00
(164)	Roberto Clemente (batting, pose to chest, helmet)	20.00	10.00	6.00
(165)	Donn Clendenon (batting, pose to waist)	3.00	1.50	.90
(166)	Donn Clendenon (batting, pose to chest)	3.00	1.50	.90
(167)	Donn Clendenon (portrait, pose to chest)	3.00	1.50	.90
(168)	Lou Clinton (portrait, pose to chest)	3.00	1.50	.90
(169)	Lou Clinton (Red Sox, batting, pose to chest)	3.00	1.50	.90
(170)	Lou Clinton (Angels, batting, pose to chest)	3.00	1.50	.90
(171)	Tony Cloninger (pitching, hands over head)	3.00	1.50	.90
(172)	Tony Cloninger (portrait, pose to chest)	3.00	1.50	.90
(173)	Rocky Colavito (hands on knees)	8.00	4.00	2.50
(173.5)	Rocky Colavito (portrait, pose to waist)	8.00	4.00	2.50
(174)	Rocky Colavito (batting, pose to chest)	8.00	4.00	2.50
(175)	Choo Choo Coleman (portrait, pose to waist, glove)	3.00	1.50	.90
(176)	Gordy Coleman (batting, pose to chest)	3.00	1.50	.90
(177)	Gordy Coleman (fielding)	3.00	1.50	.90
(178)	Tony Conigliaro (portrait, pose to waist, glove)	4.00	2.00	1.25
(179)	Gene Conley (portrait, pose to chest)	3.00	1.50	.90
(180)	Jim Constable (pitching, follow-through)	3.00	1.50	.90
(181)	Chuck Cottier (kneeling, holding bat)	3.00	1.50	.90
(182)	Chuck Cottier (batting, pose to chest)	3.00	1.50	.90
(183)	Wes Covington (batting, pose to waist)	3.00	1.50	.90
(184)	Harry Craft (portrait, pose to chest, Colts uniform)	3.00	1.50	.90
(185)	Harry Craft (portrait, pose to chest, Houston uniform)	3.00	1.50	.90
(186)	Roger Craig (portrait, pose to waist)	4.00	2.00	1.25
(187)	Roger Craig (pitching, follow-through)	4.00	2.00	1.25
(188)	Del Crandall (portrait, pose to chest)	4.00	2.00	1.25
(189)	Del Crandall (kneeling, bats)	4.00	2.00	1.25
(190)	Del Crandall (catching, crouching)	4.00	2.00	1.25
(191)	Del Crandall (catching, crouching, throwing)	4.00	2.00	1.25

(192)	Del Crandall (kneeling, pose to waist)	4.00	2.00	1.25
(193)	Joe Cunningham (portrait, pose to chest)	3.00	1.50	.90
(194)	Joe Cunningham (batting, pose to chest)	3.00	1.50	.90
(195)	Jack Curtis (portrait, pose to chest)	3.00	1.50	.90
(196)	Bill Dailey (pitching, pose to chest, hands over head)	3.00	1.50	.90
(197)	Bud Daley (portrait, pose to chest, glove)	3.00	1.50	.90
(198)	Clay Dalrymple (batting, pose to chest)	3.00	1.50	.90
(199)	Clay Dalrymple (portrait, pose to chest)	3.00	1.50	.90
(200)	Bennie Daniels (pitching, follow-through)	3.00	1.50	.90
(201)	Bennie Daniels (portrait, pose to waist, glove)	3.00	1.50	.90
(202)	Alvin Dark (kneeling, pose to waist)	4.00	2.00	1.25
(203)	Alvin Dark (portriat, pose to chest)	4.00	2.00	1.25
(204)	Alvin Dark (sitting)	4.00	2.00	1.25
(205)	Jose Davalillo (Vic) (portrait, pose to waist)	3.00	1.50	.90
(206)	Jose Davalillo (Vic) (batting, pose to neck)	3.00	1.50	.90
(207)	Jose Davalillo (Vic) (batting, pose to chest)	3.00	1.50	.90
(208)	Jim Davenport (fielding)	3.00	1.50	.90
(209)	Jim Davenport (fielding, over bag)	3.00	1.50	.90
(210)	Jim Davenport (portrait, pose to chest, San Francisco uniform)	3.00	1.50	.90
(211)	Jim Davenport (portrait, pose to chest, Giants uniform)	3.00	1.50	.90
(212)	Tom Davis (batting, pose to waist)	4.00	2.00	1.25
(213)	Tom Davis (portrait, pose to chest)	4.00	2.00	1.25
(213.5)	Tom Davis (ready to field, hands on knees)	4.00	2.00	1.25
(214)	Willie Davis (batting, pose to chest)	4.00	2.00	1.25
(214.5)	Willie Davis (batting, pose to waist)	4.00	2.00	1.25
(215)	Willie Davis (hands on knees)	4.00	2.00	1.25
(216)	Mike de la Hoz (portrait, pose to waist, arms crossed)	3.00	1.50	.90
(217)	Charlie Dees (portrait, pose to chest)	3.00	1.50	.90
(218)	Ike Delock (sitting, pose to knees)	3.00	1.50	.90
(219)	Don Demeter (portrait, pose to chest)	3.00	1.50	.90
(220)	Don Demeter (batting, pose to chest)	3.00	1.50	.90
(221)	Dick Donovan (portrait, pose to chest)	3.00	1.50	.90
(222)	Dick Donovan (pitching, follow-through, pose to knees)	3.00	1.50	.90
(223)	Dick Donovan (crouching)	3.00	1.50	.90
(224)	Al Downing (portrait, pose to chest)	4.00	2.00	1.25
(225)	Al Downing (pitching, follow-through)	4.00	2.00	1.25
(226)	Moe Drabowski (Drabowsky) (portrait, pose to chest)	3.00	1.50	.90
(227)	Chuck Dressen (kneeling, pose to knees)	3.00	1.50	.90
(228)	Chuck Dressen (portrait, pose to chest)	3.00	1.50	.90
(229)	Don Drysdale (portrait, pose to chest, two ears showing)	5.00	2.50	1.50
(230)	Don Drysdale (portrait, pose to chest, one ear showing)	5.00	2.50	1.50
(230.5)	Don Drysdale (portrait, pose to waist, one ear showing)	5.00	2.50	1.50
(231)	Ryne Duran (Duren) (pitching, follow-through)	4.00	2.00	1.25
(232)	Doc Edwards (kneeling, holding bat)	3.00	1.50	.90
(233)	Sammy Ellis (portrait, pose to chest)	3.00	1.50	.90
(234)	Dick Ellsworth (portrait, pose to chest, Cubs uniform)	3.00	1.50	.90
(235)	Dick Ellsworth (portrait, pose to waist, Chicago)	3.00	1.50	.90
(236)	Don Elston (portrait, pose to waist, arms crossed)	3.00	1.50	.90
(237)	Sam Esposito (portrait, pose to chest)	3.00	1.50	.90
(238)	Chuck Estrada (pitching, follow-through)	3.00	1.50	.90
(239)	Chuck Estrada (pitching, pose to knees)	3.00	1.50	.90
(240)	Roy Face (portrait, pose to chest, pole background)	4.00	2.00	1.25
(241)	Roy Face (portrait, pose to chest, no pole)	4.00	2.00	1.25
(242)	Ron Fairley (Fairly) (batting, pose to chest, tower in background)	3.00	1.50	.90
(243)	Ron Fairly (portrait, pose to chest, #6 visible)	3.00	1.50	.90
(244)	Ron Fairly (batting, pose to chest, no tower)	3.00	1.50	.90
(245)	Ron Fairly (portrait, pose to waist)	3.00	1.50	.90
(246)	Dick Farrell (portrait, pose to chest, Colts uniform)	3.00	1.50	.90
(247)	Dick Farrell (portrait, pose to chest, Houston uniform)	3.00	1.50	.90
(248)	Dick Farrell (portrait, pose to chest, glove)	3.00	1.50	.90
(249)	Bill Faul (portrait, pose to chest)	3.00	1.50	.90
(250)	Chico Fernandez (batting, pose to chest)	3.00	1.50	.90
(251)	Hank Fischer (pitching, follow-through)	3.00	1.50	.90
(252)	Bill Fisher (Fischer) (pitching, follow-through)	3.00	1.50	.90
(253)	Jack Fisher (kneeling, pose to waist, arms crossed)	3.00	1.50	.90
(254)	Curt Flood (portrait, pose to chest)	5.00	2.50	1.50
(255)	Curt Flood (hands on knees, background shows two men on left and one on right)	5.00	2.50	1.50
(256)	Curt Flood (hands on knees, background shows two men on left and none on right)	5.00	2.50	1.50
(257)	Curt Flood (hands on knees, background shows one man on left and none on right)	5.00	2.50	1.50
(258)	Whitey Ford (portrait, pose to chest)	10.00	5.00	3.00
(259)	Whitey Ford (pitching, pose to knees)	10.00	5.00	3.00
(260)	Whitey Ford (kneeling, pose to waist, arms crossed)	10.00	5.00	3.00
(261)	Nellie Fox (portrait, pose to chest)	6.00	3.00	1.75
(261.1)	Nellie Fox (Houston, portrait, pose to waist)	6.00	3.00	1.75
(262)	Nellie Fox (portrait, pose to neck)	6.00	3.00	1.75
(263)	Nellie Fox (fielding)	6.00	3.00	1.75
(264)	Paul Foytack (pitching, hands over head)	3.00	1.50	.90
(265)	Tito Francona (batting, pose to waist)	3.00	1.50	.90
(266)	Tito Francona (hands on knees)	3.00	1.50	.90
(267)	Herman Franks (portrait, pose to chest)	3.00	1.50	.90
(268)	Bill Freehan (kneeling, holding bat)	4.00	2.00	1.25
(269)	Bill Freehan (portrait, pose to waist, arms crossed)	4.00	2.00	1.25
(270)	Jim Fregosi (portrait, pose to chest)	4.00	2.00	1.25
(271)	Jim Fregosi (batting, pose to chest)	4.00	2.00	1.25
(272)	Bob Friend (pitching, follow-through)	4.00	2.00	1.25
(273)	Bob Friend (portrait, pose to chest)	4.00	2.00	1.25
(274)	Frank Funk (pitching, follow-through)	3.00	1.50	.90
(275)	Gary Geiger (portrait, pose to chest)	3.00	1.50	.90
(276)	Gary Geiger (batting, pose to waist)	3.00	1.50	.90
(277)	Jim Gentile (kneeling, holding bat)	3.00	1.50	.90
(278)	Jim Gentile (batting, pose to chest)	3.00	1.50	.90
(279)	Jim Gentile (batting, pose to waist)	3.00	1.50	.90
(280)	Jim Gentile (kneeling, pose to waist, arms crossed)	3.00	1.50	.90
(281)	Bob Gibson (portrait, pose to chest)	5.00	2.50	1.50
(282)	Bob Gibson (pitching, follow-through)	5.00	2.50	1.50
(283)	Bob Gibson (pitching, pose to knees)	5.00	2.50	1.50
(284)	Jim Gilliam (portrait, pose to chest, clouds)	5.00	2.50	1.50
(285)	Jim Gilliam (portrait, pose to chest, no clouds)	5.00	2.50	1.50
(286)	Jim Gilliam (batting, pose to waist)	6.00	3.00	1.75
(287)	Jess Gonder (batting, pose to chest)	5.00	2.50	1.50
(288)	Jesse Gonder (portrait, pose to chest)	3.00	1.50	.90
(289)	Tony Gonzalez (hands on knees)	3.00	1.50	.90
(290)	Jim Grant (portrait, pose to thighs, glove)	3.00	1.50	.90
(291)	Jim Grant (pitching, follow-through, fuzzy background)	3.00	1.50	.90
(292)	Jim Grant (pitching, follow-through, stands in background)	3.00	1.50	.90
(293)	Eli Grba (pitching, follow-through)	3.00	1.50	.90
(294)	Dallas Green (pitching, pose to chest, hands over head)	3.00	1.50	.90
(295)	Dallas Green (pitching, follow-through)	3.00	1.50	.90
(296)	Dick Green (batting, pose to waist)	3.00	1.50	.90
(297)	Lenny Green (kneeling, holding bat)	3.00	1.50	.90
(298)	Dick Groat (kneeling, holding bat)	5.00	2.50	1.50
(299)	Dick Groat (kneeling, holding bat)	5.00	2.50	1.50
(300)	Dick Groat (batting, pose to waist)	5.00	2.50	1.50
(300.5)	Jerry Grote (Houston, portrait, pose to waist)	3.00	1.50	.90
(301)	Harvey Haddox (Haddix) (pitching, follow-through)	4.00	2.00	1.25
(302)	Jimmie Hall (portrait, pose to chest)	3.00	1.50	.90
(303)	Tom Haller (catching, crouching)	3.00	1.50	.90
(304)	Tom Haller (catching, throwing)	3.00	1.50	.90
(305)	Tom Haller (portrait, pose to chest, Giants uniform)	3.00	1.50	.90
(306)	Tom Haller (portrait, pose to chest, San Francisco uniform)	3.00	1.50	.90
(307)	Ken Hamlin (portrait, pose to chest)	3.00	1.50	.90
(308)	Ron Hansen (batting, pose to waist)	3.00	1.50	.90
(309)	Ron Hansen (fielding)	3.00	1.50	.90
(310)	Ron Hansen (kneeling, holding bat)	3.00	1.50	.90
(311)	Carroll Hardy (batting)	3.00	1.50	.90
(312)	Tim Harkness (fielding)	3.00	1.50	.90
(313)	Tommy Harper (hands on knees)	3.00	1.50	.90
(314)	Ken Harrelson (batting, pose to chest)	4.00	2.00	1.25
(315)	Ken Harrelson (portrait, pose to chest)	4.00	2.00	1.25
(315.5)	Lum Harris (Houston, portrait, pose to waist)	3.00	1.50	.90
(316)	Woody Held (batting, pose to waist)	3.00	1.50	.90
(317)	Woody Held (portrait, pose to chest)	3.00	1.50	.90
(318)	Bob Hendley (portrait, pose to chest)	3.00	1.50	.90
(319)	Bob Hendley (pitching, follow-through)	3.00	1.50	.90
(320)	Ron Henry (batting, pose to chest)	3.00	1.50	.90
(321)	Ray Herbert (pitching, follow-through)	3.00	1.50	.90
(322)	Ron Herbert (pitching)	3.00	1.50	.90
(323)	Billy Herman (portrait, pose to chest)	6.00	3.00	1.75
(324)	Mike Hershberger (kneeling, holding bat)	3.00	1.50	.90
(325)	Mike Hershberger (portrait, pose to chest, arms crossed)	3.00	1.50	.90
(326)	Whitey Herzog (portrait, pose to chest)	5.00	2.50	1.50
(327)	Jim Hickman (batting, pose to chest)	3.00	1.50	.90
(328)	Jim Hickman (kneeling, pose to knees)	3.00	1.50	.90
(329)	Mike Higgins (portrait, pose to chest)	3.00	1.50	.90
(330)	Chuck Hiller (batting, pose to chest)	3.00	1.50	.90
(331)	Chuck Hiller (portrait, pose to chest, Giants uniform)	3.00	1.50	.90
(332)	Chuck Hiller (portrait, pose to chest, San Francisco uniform)	3.00	1.50	.90
(333)	Chuck Hinton (batting, pose to chest)	3.00	1.50	.90
(334)	Chuck Hinton (portrait, pose to chest)	3.00	1.50	.90
(335)	Chuck Hinton (portrait, pose to waist)	3.00	1.50	.90
(336)	Billy Hitchcock (portrait, pose to chest)	3.00	1.50	.90
(337)	Don Hoak (kneeling, holding bat)	3.00	1.50	.90
(338)	Don Hoak (batting, pose to chest)	3.00	1.50	.90
(339)	Glen Hobbie (portrait, pose to chest)	3.00	1.50	.90
(340)	Gil Hodges (portrait, pose to chest, dark background)	6.00	3.00	1.75
(341)	Gil Hodges (portrait, pose to chest, light background)	6.00	3.00	1.75
(342)	Gil Hodges (portrait, pose to waist)	5.50	2.75	1.75
(343)	Gil Hodges (batting, pose to chest)	5.50	2.75	1.75
(344)	Jay Hook (portrait, pose to waist)	3.00	1.50	.90
(345)	Jay Hook (pitching, pose to knees)	3.00	1.50	.90
(346)	Joel Horlen (pitching, pose to chest, hands over head)	3.00	1.50	.90
(347)	Ralph Houk (portrait, pose to chest, Mgr. on front)	4.00	2.00	1.25
(348)	Ralph Houk (portrait, pose to chest, Manager on front)	4.00	2.00	1.25
(349)	Elston Howard (batting, pose to waist)	6.00	3.00	1.75
(350)	Elston Howard (kneeling, holding bat, pose to knees)	6.00	3.00	1.75
(351)	Elston Howard (catching, crouching)	6.00	3.00	1.75
(352)	Frank Howard (batting, pose to thighs)	6.00	3.00	1.75
(353)	Frank Howard (kneeling, holding bat to thigh)	6.00	3.00	1.75
(354)	Frank Howard (kneeling, holding bat, tower background)	6.00	3.00	1.75
(355)	Frank Howard (portrait, pose to chest)	6.00	3.00	1.75
(356)	Dick Howser (portrait, pose to chest)	4.00	2.00	1.25
(357)	Ken Hubbs (portrait, pose to chest)	4.00	2.00	1.25
(358)	Ken Hunt (portrait, pose to chest)	3.00	1.50	.90
(359)	Ken Hunt (batting, pose to chest)	3.00	1.50	.90
(360)	Ron Hunt (batting, pose to waist)	3.00	1.50	.90
(361)	Ron Hunt (fielding)	3.00	1.50	.90

(362) Fred Hutchinson (portrait, pose to chest)	3.00	1.50	.90
(363) Al Jackson (portrait, pose to chest)	3.00	1.50	.90
(364) Al Jackson (pitching, follow-through)	3.00	1.50	.90
(365) Larry Jackson (portrait, pose to waist, tank in background)	3.00	1.50	.90
(366) Larry Jackson (Cardinals, portrait, pose to chest, mouth closed)	3.00	1.50	.90
(367) Larry Jackson (Cubs, portrait, pose to neck, mouth open)	3.00	1.50	.90
(368) Larry Jackson (portrait, pose to neck)	3.00	1.50	.90
(368.5) Sonny Jackson (Houston, batting, pose to waist)	3.00	1.50	.90
(369) Charlie James (fielding)	3.00	1.50	.90
(370) Julian Javier (batting, pose to waist)	3.00	1.50	.90
(371) Julian Javier (portrait, pose to chest)	3.00	1.50	.90
(372) Joey Jay (portrait, pose to chest)	3.00	1.50	.90
(373) Joey Jay (pitching, follow-through)	3.00	1.50	.90
(374) Manny Jiminez (Jimenez) (portrait, pose to chest)	3.00	1.50	.90
(375) Manny Jiminez (Jimenez) (kneeling, holding bat)	3.00	1.50	.90
(376) Manny Jiminez (Jimenez) (batting, pose to waist)	3.00	1.50	.90
(377) Bob Johnson (batting, pose to waist)	3.00	1.50	.90
(378) Ken Johnson (portrait, pose to chest)	3.00	1.50	.90
(379) Mack Jones (batting)	3.00	1.50	.90
(380) Mack Jones (batting, pose to chest)	3.00	1.50	.90
(381) Jim Kaat (pitching, follow-through)	6.00	3.00	1.75
(382) Jim Kaat (portrait, pose to waist, glove)	6.00	3.00	1.75
(383) Al Kaline (portrait, pose to chest)	12.00	6.00	3.50
(384) Al Kaline (hands on knees)	12.00	6.00	3.50
(385) Al Kaline (batting, pose to chest)	12.00	6.00	3.50
(385.5) Al Kaline (batting, pose to waist)	12.00	6.00	3.50
(386) Rod Kanehl (batting, pose to chest, bat straight up)	3.00	1.50	.90
(387) Rod Kanehl (batting, pose to chest, bat angled)	3.00	1.50	.90
(388) Eddie Kasko (batting, pose to chest)	3.00	1.50	.90
(388.5) Eddie Kasco (Kasko) (Houston, batting, pose to waist)	3.00	1.50	.90
(389) John Keane (portrait, pose to waist)	3.00	1.50	.90
(390) John Keane (standing)	3.00	1.50	.90
(391) Johnny Keane (portrait, pose to waist)	3.00	1.50	.90
(392) Russ Kemmerer (pitching, pose to knees)	3.00	1.50	.90
(393) Bob Kennedy (portrait, pose to chest)	3.00	1.50	.90
(394) Bob Kennedy (kneeling, holding bat)	3.00	1.50	.90
(395) John Kennedy (batting, pose to waist)	3.00	1.50	.90
(396) Marty Keough (batting, pose to chest)	3.00	1.50	.90
(397) Marty Keough (hands on knees)	3.00	1.50	.90
(398) Harmon Killebrew (batting, pose to chest)	6.50	3.25	2.00
(399) Harmon Killebrew (portrait, pose to chest)	6.50	3.25	2.00
(399.5) Harmon Killebrew (Twins, holding bats on dugout steps)	6.50	3.25	2.00
(400) Jim King (batting, pose to chest)	3.00	1.50	.90
(401) Jim King (portrait, pose to chest)	3.00	1.50	.90
(402) Willie Kirkland (Indians, batting, pose to waist)	3.00	1.50	.90
(403) Willie Kirkland (Orioles, batting, pose to waist)	3.00	1.50	.90
(404) Ron Kline (pitching, follow-through)	3.00	1.50	.90
(405) Ted Kluszewski (batting, pose to chest)	8.00	4.00	2.50
(406) Bob Knoop (portrait, pose to chest)	3.00	1.50	.90
(407) Sandy Koufax (portrait, pose to waist, arms crossed)	15.00	7.50	4.50
(408) Sandy Koufax (portrait, pose to chest, smiling)	15.00	7.50	4.50
(409) Sandy Koufax (portrait, pose to chest, palm trees in background)	15.00	7.50	4.50
(410) Jack Kralick (pitching, follow-through)	3.00	1.50	.90
(411) Jim Kralick (portrait, pose to chest)	3.00	1.50	.90
(412) John Kralick (pitching, follow-through)	3.00	1.50	.90
(413) Ed Kranepool (batting, pose to chest)	3.00	1.50	.90
(414) Tony Kubek (fielding)	6.00	3.00	1.75
(415) Tony Kubek (batting)	6.00	3.00	1.75
(416) Harvey Kuenn (portrait, pose to chest, Giants uniform)	4.00	2.00	1.25
(417) Harvey Kuenn (portrait, pose to chest, San Francisco uniform)	4.00	2.00	1.25
(418) Marty Kutyna (pitching, follow-through)	3.00	1.50	.90
(419) Jim Landis (batting)	3.00	1.50	.90
(420) Jim Landis (kneeling, holding bat)	3.00	1.50	.90
(421) Jim Landis (kneeling, pose to knees, arms crossed)	3.00	1.50	.90
(422) Jim Landis (hands on knees)	3.00	1.50	.90
(423) Hobie Landrith (batting)	3.00	1.50	.90
(424) Don Landrum (fielding)	3.00	1.50	.90
(425) Norm Larker (portrait, pose to chest)	3.00	1.50	.90
(426) Norm Larker (fielding)	3.00	1.50	.90
(427) Frank Lary (pitching, follow-through)	3.00	1.50	.90
(428) Barry Latman (portrait)	3.00	1.50	.90
(429) Barry Latman (pitching)	3.00	1.50	.90
(430) Charlie Lau (batting)	3.00	1.50	.90
(431) Vern Law (portrait)	4.00	2.00	1.25
(432) Vernon Law (pitching)	4.00	2.00	1.25
(433) Don Lee (pitching)	3.00	1.50	.90
(434) Don Lee (portrait)	3.00	1.50	.90
(435) Denny Lemaster (pitching, follow-through)	3.00	1.50	.90
(436) Denny Lemaster (pitching, pose to knees)	3.00	1.50	.90
(437) Jim Lemon (batting)	3.00	1.50	.90
(438) Don Leppert (batting)	3.00	1.50	.90
(439) Bob Lillis (batting)	3.00	1.50	.90
(439.5) Bob Lillis (Houston, portrait, pose to waist)	3.00	1.50	.90
(440) Don Lock (portrait, pose to chest, light background)	3.00	1.50	.90
(441) Don Lock (portrait, pose to chest, dark background, Senators in block letters)	3.00	1.50	.90
(442) Don Lock (portrait, pose to waist, dark background, Senators in script)	3.00	1.50	.90
(443) Sherman Lollar (kneeling)	3.00	1.50	.90
(444) Sherman Lollar (portrait)	3.00	1.50	.90
(445) Ed Lopat (portrait)	4.00	2.00	1.25
(446) Al Lopez (portrait)	6.00	3.00	1.75
(447) Al Lopez (portrait, pose to chest, jacket has top of "S" visible)	6.00	3.00	1.75
(448) Al Lopez (portrait, pose to chest, jacket has "S" and part of "O" visible)	6.00	3.00	1.75
(448.5) Al Lopez (portrait, pose to waist)	6.00	3.00	1.75
(449) Jerry Lumpe (batting, pose to waist)	3.00	1.50	.90
(450) Jerry Lumpe (kneeling, pose to thighs)	3.00	1.50	.90
(451) Jerry Lumpe (batting, pose to chest)	3.00	1.50	.90
(452) Jerry Lynch (portrait, pose to chest)	3.00	1.50	.90
(453) Art Mahaffey (portrait)	3.00	1.50	.90
(454) Art Mahaffey (pitching)	3.00	1.50	.90
(455) Roman Majias (portrait)	3.00	1.50	.90
(456) Jim Maloney (pitching)	3.00	1.50	.90
(457) Frank Malzone (batting, pose to chest, one ear showing)	3.00	1.50	.90
(458) Frank Malzone (batting, pose to chest, two ears showing)	3.00	1.50	.90
(459) Frank Malzone (portrait)	3.00	1.50	.90
(460) Felix Mantilla (portrait, pose to neck, one ear showing)	3.00	1.50	.90
(461) Felix Mantilla (portrait, pose to chest, two ears showing)	3.00	1.50	.90
(462) Felix Mantilla (portrait, pose to waist)	3.00	1.50	.90
(463) Mickey Mantle (portrait)	30.00	15.00	9.00
(464) Mickey Mantle (batting, pose to chest, one ear showing)	30.00	15.00	9.00
(465) Mickey Mantle (batting, pose to chest, two ears showing)	30.00	15.00	9.00
(466) Juan Marichal (portrait, pose to waist, hands over head)	5.00	2.50	1.50
(467) Juan Marichal (pitching)	5.00	2.50	1.50
(468) Juan Marichal (portrait, pose to chest)	5.00	2.50	1.50
(469) Roger Maris (kneeling)	16.00	8.00	4.75
(470) Roger Maris (batting, pose to chest, one ear showing)	16.00	8.00	4.75
(471) Roger Maris (batting, pose to chest, two ears showing)	3.00	1.50	.90
(472) J.C. Martin (batting, pose to waist)	3.00	1.50	.90
(473) Joe Martin (batting, pose to waist)	3.00	1.50	.90
(474) Eddie Mathews (batting)	6.50	3.25	2.00
(475) Eddie Mathews (batting, pose to waist)	6.50	3.25	2.00
(476) Eddie Mathews (kneeling)	6.50	3.25	2.00
(476.5) Eddie Mathews (portrait, kneeling, leaning on bat)	6.50	3.25	2.00
(477) Gene Mauch (portrait, pose to knees, one ear showing)	4.00	2.00	1.25
(478) Gene Mauch (portrait, pose to knees, two ears showing)	4.00	2.00	1.25
(479) Gene Mauch (portrait, pose to chest)	4.00	2.00	1.25
(480) Dal Maxvill (fielding)	3.00	1.50	.90
(481) Charley Maxwell (batting)	3.00	1.50	.90
(482) Lee Maye (portrait, pose to chest, holding bat)	3.00	1.50	.90
(483) Lee Maye (portrait, pose to chest, no bat)	3.00	1.50	.90
(484) Lee Maye (fielding)	3.00	1.50	.90
(485) Willie Mays (portrait, pose to neck)	20.00	10.00	6.00
(486) Willie Mays (portrait, pose to chest)	20.00	10.00	6.00
(487) Willie Mays (kneeling)	20.00	10.00	6.00
(488) Willie Mays (hat, pose to waist)	20.00	10.00	6.00
(489) Bill Mazeroski (portrait)	5.00	2.50	1.50
(490) Bill Mazeroski (batting)	5.00	2.50	1.50
(491) Bill Mazeroski (fielding)	5.00	2.50	1.50
(492) Ken McBride (portrait)	3.00	1.50	.90
(493) Ken McBride (pitching)	3.00	1.50	.90
(494) Tim McCarver (portrait)	5.00	2.50	1.50
(495) Tim McCarver (catching)	5.00	2.50	1.50
(496) Joe McClain (pitching)	3.00	1.50	.90
(497) Mike McCormick (pitching)	3.00	1.50	.90
(498) Willie McCovey (portrait)	6.50	3.25	2.00
(499) Willie McCovey (batting)	6.50	3.25	2.00
(500) Willie McCovey (kneeling)	6.50	3.25	2.00
(501) Tom McCraw (batting)	3.00	1.50	.90
(502) Lindy McDaniel (portrait, pose to chest, Chicago uniform)	3.00	1.50	.90
(503) Lindy McDaniel (portrait, pose to chest, Cubs uniform)	3.00	1.50	.90
(504) Lindy McDaniel (Cardinals, portrait, pose to chest)	3.00	1.50	.90
(505) Sam McDowell (portrait, pose to chest)	4.00	2.00	1.25
(506) Mel McGaha (portrait, pose to waist, holding bat)	3.00	1.50	.90
(507) Mel McGaha (portrait, pose to chest)	3.00	1.50	.90
(508) Roy McMillan (fielding)	3.00	1.50	.90
(509) Roy McMillan (batting)	3.00	1.50	.90
(510) Roy McMillan (portrait)	3.00	1.50	.90
(511) Ken McMullen (portrait)	3.00	1.50	.90
(512) Sam Mele (portrait)	3.00	1.50	.90
(513) Dennis Menke (Denis) (throwing)	3.00	1.50	.90
(514) Dennis Menke (Denis) (portrait, pose to neck)	3.00	1.50	.90
(515) Bob Miller (portrait)	3.00	1.50	.90
(516) Stu Miller (pitching)	3.00	1.50	.90
(517) Minnie Minoso (batting)	5.00	2.50	1.50
(518) Bill Monbouquette (pitching, follow-through)	3.00	1.50	.90
(519) Bill Monbouquette (kneeling, pose to knees)	3.00	1.50	.90
(520) William Monbouquette (kneeling, pose to knees)	3.00	1.50	.90
(521) Wally Moon (batting)	3.00	1.50	.90
(522) Wally Moon (portrait)	3.00	1.50	.90
(523) Billy Moran (batting)	3.00	1.50	.90
(524) Tom Morgan (portrait)	3.00	1.50	.90
(525) Don Mossi (portrait)	3.00	1.50	.90
(526) Manny Mota (portrait)	4.00	2.00	1.25
(527) Danny Murtaugh (portrait)	3.00	1.50	.90
(528) Stan Musial (fielding)	20.00	10.00	6.00
(529) Stan Musial (kneeling)	20.00	10.00	6.00
(530) Don McMahon (pitching)	3.00	1.50	.90
(531) Buster Narum (portrait)	3.00	1.50	.90
(532) Charlie Neal (batting)	3.00	1.50	.90
(533) Fred Newman (portrait)	3.00	1.50	.90
(534) Dave Nicholson (kneeling, pose to waist, holding bat)	3.00	1.50	.90
(535) Dave Nicholson (hands on knees)	3.00	1.50	.90
(536) Phil Niekro (pitching)	4.50	2.25	1.25
(536.5) Phil Niekro (Nierko) (pitching, follow-through, stands in background)	4.50	2.25	1.25
(537) Bob Nieman (hands on knees)	3.00	1.50	.90
(538) Russ Nixon (batting)	3.00	1.50	.90
(539) Joe Nuxhall (portrait)	4.00	2.00	1.25
(540) Danny O'Connell (batting)	3.00	1.50	.90
(541) Billy O'Dell (portrait)	3.00	1.50	.90
(542) Billy O'Dell (Giants, pitching, pitcher's follow)	3.00	1.50	.90
(543) Billy O'Dell (pitching)	3.00	1.50	.90
(544) Billy O'Dell (Braves, pitching, follow-through)	3.00	1.50	.90
(545) Jim O'Toole (portrait)	3.00	1.50	.90
(546) Jim O'Toole (pitching)	3.00	1.50	.90
(547) Tony Oliva (batting)	8.00	4.00	2.50
(548) Gene Oliver (batting)	3.00	1.50	.90
(549) Nate Oliver (batting)	3.00	1.50	.90
(550) John Orsino (batting, pose to waist, one ear showing)	3.00	1.50	.90
(551) John Orsino (batting, pose to waist, two ears showing)	3.00	1.50	.90
(552) John Orsino (kneeling, pose to waist)	3.00	1.50	.90
(553) Phil Ortega (portrait)	3.00	1.50	.90
(554) Dan Osinski (portrait, pose to neck)	3.00	1.50	.90
(555) Dan Osinski (portrait, pose to chest)	3.00	1.50	.90
(556) Claude Osteen (portrait, pose to waist, glove)	3.00	1.50	.90
(557) Claude Osteen (portrait, pose to chest)	3.00	1.50	.90
(558) Claude Osteen (pitching, pose to knees) (photo actually Tom Cheney)	3.00	1.50	.90
(559) Jose Pagan (portrait, pose to chest, Giants uniform)	3.00	1.50	.90
(560) Jose Pagan (portrait, pose to chest, San Francisco uniform)	3.00	1.50	.90
(561) Jose Pagan (portrait, pose to waist)	3.00	1.50	.90
(562) Jose Pagan (fielding)	3.00	1.50	.90
(563) James Pagliaroni (portrait, pose to chest)	3.00	1.50	.90
(564) Jim Pagliaroni (portrait, pose to waist)	3.00	1.50	.90
(565) Milt Pappas (pitching, pose to chest, hands over head)	4.00	2.00	1.25
(566) Milt Pappas (pitching, follow-through, stands empty)	4.00	2.00	1.25

(567)	Milt Pappas (pitching, follow-through, people in stands)	4.00	2.00	1.25
(568)	Camilo Pascual (pitching, follow-through)	4.00	2.00	1.25
(569)	Camilo Pascual (pitching, pose to knees, glove at knee)	4.00	2.00	1.25
(570)	Camilo Pascual (pitching, pose to waist, glove in front)	4.00	2.00	1.25
(571)	Don Pavletich (batting)	3.00	1.50	.90
(572)	Albie Pearson (hands on knees)	3.00	1.50	.90
(573)	Albie Pearson (kneeling, holding bat)	3.00	1.50	.90
(574)	Jim Pendleton (batting)	3.00	1.50	.90
(575)	Joe Pepitone (portrait)	5.00	2.50	1.50
(576)	Joe Pepitone (batting)	5.00	2.50	1.50
(577)	Gaylord Perry (kneeling, pose to waist, holding bat)	4.50	2.25	1.25
(578)	Johnny Pesky (portrait, pose to chest)	3.00	1.50	.90
(579)	Johnny Pesky (portrait, pose to waist, arms crossed)	3.00	1.50	.90
(580)	Gary Peters (kneeling)	3.00	1.50	.90
(581)	Gary Peters (pitching)	3.00	1.50	.90
(582)	Bubba Phillips (kneeling)	3.00	1.50	.90
(583)	Bubba Phillips (hands on knees)	3.00	1.50	.90
(584)	Ron Piche (portrait)	3.00	1.50	.90
(585)	Billy Pierce (pitching)	4.00	2.00	1.25
(586)	Billy Pierce (portrait)	4.00	2.00	1.25
(587)	Jim Piersall (hands on knees)	5.00	2.50	1.50
(588)	Vada Pinson (batting, pose to waist, tower in background)	5.00	2.50	1.50
(589)	Vada Pinson (batting, pose to chest, stands in background)	3.00	1.50	.90
(590)	Juan Pizzaro (pitching, pose to waist)	3.00	1.50	.90
(591)	Juan Pizzaro (pitching, follow-through)	3.00	1.50	.90
(592)	John Podres (portrait)	5.00	2.50	1.50
(593)	John Podres (pitching)	5.00	2.50	1.50
(594)	Leo Posada (batting)	3.00	1.50	.90
(595)	Wally Post (batting)	3.00	1.50	.90
(596)	Boog Powell (portrait)	6.00	3.00	1.75
(597)	Boog Powell (batting)	6.00	3.00	1.75
(598)	Vic Power (batting, pose to chest)	3.00	1.50	.90
(599)	Vic Power (kneeling, holding bat)	3.00	1.50	.90
(600)	Vic Power (batting, pose to waist)	3.00	1.50	.90
(601)	Bob Purkey (pitching)	3.00	1.50	.90
(602)	Bob Purkey (kneeling)	3.00	1.50	.90
(603)	Mel Queen (batting, pose to waist)	3.00	1.50	.90
(604)	Dick Radatz (portrait, pose to neck)	3.00	1.50	.90
(605)	Dick Radatz (portrait, pose to chest, two players in background)	3.00	1.50	.90
(606)	Dick Radatz (portrait, pose to chest, sky in background)	3.00	1.50	.90
(607)	Ed Rakow (portrait, pose to chest)	3.00	1.50	.90
(608)	Ed Rakow (kneeling, pose to knees, arms crossed)	3.00	1.50	.90
(609)	Ed Rakow (portrait, pose to chest)	3.00	1.50	.90
(610)	Pedro Ramos (standing)	3.00	1.50	.90
(611)	Merritt Ranew (batting)	3.00	1.50	.90
(612)	Claude Raymond (pitching)	3.00	1.50	.90
(613)	Phil Regan (portrait)	3.00	1.50	.90
(614)	Phil Regan (pitching)	3.00	1.50	.90
(615)	Ken Retzer (batting)	3.00	1.50	.90
(616)	Ken Retzer (kneeling)	3.00	1.50	.90
(617)	Paul Richards (portrait)	3.00	1.50	.90
(618)	Bobby Richardson (fielding)	6.00	3.00	1.75
(619)	Robby Richardson (portrait)	6.00	3.00	1.75
(620)	Pete Richert (portrait)	3.00	1.50	.90
(621)	Bill Rigney (portrait, pose to chest, one ear showing)	3.00	1.50	.90
(622)	Bill Rigney (portrait, pose to chest, two ears showing)	3.00	1.50	.90
(623)	Mike Roarke (catching)	3.00	1.50	.90
(624)	Robin Roberts (pitching)	5.00	2.50	1.50
(625)	Robin Roberts (kneeling)	5.00	2.50	1.50
(626)	Brooks Robinson (batting, pose to chest)	12.00	6.00	3.50
(627)	Brooks Robinson (kneeling, pose to waist, "B" on cap)	12.00	6.00	3.50
(628)	Brooks Robinson (kneeling, holding bat, bird on cap)	12.00	6.00	3.50
(629)	Earl Robinson (hands on knees)	3.00	1.50	.90
(630)	Floyd Robinson (kneeling, holding bat)	3.00	1.50	.90
(631)	Floyd Robinson (batting, pose to chest, mouth open)	3.00	1.50	.90
(632)	Floyd Robinson (batting, pose to chest, mouth closed)	3.00	1.50	.90
(633)	Frank Robinson (batting, pose to thigh)	6.50	3.25	2.00
(634)	Frank Robinson (kneeling, holding bat)	6.50	3.25	2.00
(635)	Andre Rodgers (portrait, pose to chest, Chicago uniform)	3.00	1.50	.90
(636)	Andre Rodgers (portrait, pose to waist, Cubs uniform)	3.00	1.50	.90
(637)	Bob Rodgers (portrait)	4.00	2.00	1.25
(638)	Bob Rodgers (batting)	4.00	2.00	1.25
(639)	Ed Roebuck (pitching, pose to chest, hands over head)	3.00	1.50	.90
(640)	Rich Rollins (fielding)	3.00	1.50	.90
(641)	Rich Rollins (batting)	3.00	1.50	.90
(642)	John Romano (batting, pose to waist)	3.00	1.50	.90
(643)	John Romano (batting, pose to chest)	3.00	1.50	.90
(644)	Pete Rose (portrait)	20.00	10.00	6.00
(645)	Pete Rose (kneeling)	20.00	10.00	6.00
(646)	John Roseboro (portrait)	3.00	1.50	.90
(647)	John Roseboro (catching)	3.00	1.50	.90
(648)	Don Rudolph (pitching, pose to knees, glove on knee)	3.00	1.50	.90
(649)	Don Rudolph (pitching, follow-through, picture is Stenhouse)	3.00	1.50	.90
(650)	Pete Runnels (portrait, pose to chest)	3.00	1.50	.90
(651)	Pete Runnels (portrait, pose to chest)	3.00	1.50	.90
(652)	Pete Runnels (portrait, pose to neck)	3.00	1.50	.90
(653)	Ray Sadecki (pitching, follow-through, glasses)	3.00	1.50	.90
(654)	Ray Sadecki (pitching, follow-through, no glasses)	3.00	1.50	.90
(655)	Bob Sadowski (portrait, pose to neck)	3.00	1.50	.90
(656)	Amado Samuel (fielding, horizontal)	3.00	1.50	.90
(657)	Jack Sanford (pitching)	3.00	1.50	.90
(658)	Jack Sanford (pitching, follow-through)	3.00	1.50	.90
(659)	Jack Sanford (pitching, pose to chest)	3.00	1.50	.90
(660)	Ron Santo (portrait, pose to chest, teeth apart)	5.00	2.50	1.50
(661)	Ron Santo (portrait, pose to chest, teeth together)	5.00	2.50	1.50
(662)	Ron Santo (portrait, pose to waist, tank in background)	5.00	2.50	1.50
(663)	Ron Santo (kneeling, holding bat)	3.00	1.50	.90
(664)	Bob Scheffing (portrait, pose to chest)	3.00	1.50	.90
(665)	Bob Sheffing (Scheffing) (portrait, pose to chest)	3.00	1.50	.90
(666)	Charles Schilling (portrait, pose to chest)	3.00	1.50	.90
(667)	Chuck Schilling (batting, pose to waist)	3.00	1.50	.90
(668)	Chuck Schilling (batting, pose to chest)	3.00	1.50	.90
(669)	Bob Schmidt (batting, pose to chest)	3.00	1.50	.90
(670)	Red Schoendienst (portrait, pose to knees)	3.50	1.75	1.00
(671)	Dick Schofield (batting, stands in background)	3.00	1.50	.90
(672)	Dick Schofield (batting, screen in background)	3.00	1.50	.90
(673)	Barney Schultz (portrait, pose to waist, arms crossed)	3.00	1.50	.90
(674)	Don Schwall (portrait, pose to chest)	3.00	1.50	.90
(675)	Diego Segui (portrait, pose to chest)	3.00	1.50	.90
(676)	Mike Shannon (batting, pose to waist)	3.00	1.50	.90
(677)	Bob Shaw (portrait, pose to chest)	3.00	1.50	.90
(678)	Bob Shaw (pitching, follow-through)	3.00	1.50	.90
(679)	Larry Sherry (portrait, pose to chest)	3.00	1.50	.90
(680)	Chris Short (portrait, pose to chest)	3.00	1.50	.90
(681)	Chris Short (pitching, follow-through)	3.00	1.50	.90
(682)	Norm Siebern (batting, pose to waist)	3.00	1.50	.90
(683)	Norm Siebern (portrait, pose to chest)	3.00	1.50	.90
(684)	Norm Siebern (batting, pose to chest)	3.00	1.50	.90
(685)	Roy Sievers (kneeling, holding bat)	4.00	2.00	1.25
(686)	Roy Sievers (portrait, pose to chest)	4.00	2.00	1.25
(687)	Roy Sievers (batting, pose to chest)	4.00	2.00	1.25
(688)	Curt Simmons (portrait, pose to chest)	4.00	2.00	1.25
(689)	Curt Simmons (portrait, pose to chest, glove)	4.00	2.00	1.25
(690)	Dick Sisler (portrait, pose to chest)	3.00	1.50	.90
(691)	Bob Skinner (batting, pose to waist)	3.00	1.50	.90
(692)	Bill Skowron (Yankees, kneeling, holding bat)	6.00	3.00	1.75
(693)	Bill Skowron (White Sox, kneeling, holding bat)	3.00	1.50	.90
(694)	Ed Sadowski (batting, pose to waist)	3.00	1.50	.90
(695)	Al Smith (White Sox, kneeling, holding bat)	3.00	1.50	.90
(696)	Al Smith (Indians, kneeling, holding bat)	3.00	1.50	.90
(697)	Hal Smith (portrait, pose to chest)	3.00	1.50	.90
(698)	Hal Smith (batting, pose to chest)	3.00	1.50	.90
(699)	Duke Snider (batting, pose to waist)	14.00	7.00	4.25
(700)	Duke Snider (batting)	14.00	7.00	4.25
(701)	Duke Snider (portrait, pose to chest)	14.00	7.00	4.25
(702)	Russ Snyder (portrait, pose to chest)	3.00	1.50	.90
(703)	Warren Spahn (pitching)	6.00	3.00	1.75
(704)	Warren Spahn (pitching, follow-through)	6.00	3.00	1.75
(705)	Warren Spahn (kneeling, pose to knees, glove)	6.00	3.00	1.75
(706)	Al Spangler (portrait, pose to chest)	3.00	1.50	.90
(707)	Al Spangler (batting, pose to chest)	3.00	1.50	.90
(708)	Tracy Stallard (portrait, pose to waist, arms crossed)	3.00	1.50	.90
(709)	Willie Stargell (portrait, pose to waist)	6.00	3.00	1.75
(710)	Willie Stargell (hands on knees)	6.00	3.00	1.75
(711)	Casey Stengel (portrait, pose to chest)	10.00	5.00	3.00
(712)	Dave Stenhouse (pitching, follow-through) (picture is actually Don Rudolph)	3.00	1.50	.90
(713)	Jim Stewart (batting, pose to waist)	3.00	1.50	.90
(714)	Dick Stigman (pitching, follow-through, arm down)	3.00	1.50	.90
(715)	Dick Stigman (pitching, follow-through, arm bent)	3.00	1.50	.90
(716)	Mel Stottlemeyer (Stottlemyre) (portrait, pose to waist)	5.00	2.50	1.50
(717)	Dick Stuart (portrait, pose to chest)	3.00	1.50	.90
(718)	Dick Stuart (batting, pose to neck)	3.00	1.50	.90
(719)	Dick Stuart (Pirates, batting, pose to chest)	3.00	1.50	.90
(720)	Dick Stuart (batting, pose to waist)	3.00	1.50	.90
(721)	Dick Stuart (Red Sox, batting, pose to chest)	3.00	1.50	.90
(722)	Frank Sullivan (portrait, pose to chest, glove)	3.00	1.50	.90
(723)	Hay Sullivan (portrait, pose to waist, arms crossed)	3.00	1.50	.90
(724)	Haywood Sullivan (batting, pose to chest)	3.00	1.50	.90
(725)	Rusty Staub (portrait, pose to chest)	5.00	2.50	1.50
(726)	Wes Stock (pitching, follow-through)	3.00	1.50	.90
(727)	Wes Stock (kneeling, pose to waist, arms crossed)	3.00	1.50	.90
(728)	Fred Talbot (portrait, pose to chest, arms crossed)	3.00	1.50	.90
(729)	Jose Tartabull (portrait, pose to waist, arms crossed)	3.00	1.50	.90
(730)	Jose Tartabull (batting, pose to chest)	3.00	1.50	.90
(731)	Willie Tasby (batting, pose to waist)	3.00	1.50	.90
(732)	Sam Taylor (portrait, pose to chest, stripe uniform)	3.00	1.50	.90
(733)	Sam Taylor (portrait, pose to chest, plain uniform)	3.00	1.50	.90
(734)	Tony Taylor (batting, pose to chest, one ear)	3.00	1.50	.90
(735)	Tony Taylor (batting, pose to chest, two ears)	3.00	1.50	.90
(736)	Birdie Tebbets (portrait, pose to neck)	3.00	1.50	.90
(737)	Birdie Tebbetts (arms crossed on knees)	3.00	1.50	.90
(738)	George "Birdie" Tebbetts (portrait, pose to chest)	3.00	1.50	.90
(738.5)	Manager Birdie Tebbetts (portrait, pose to chest)	3.00	1.50	.90
(739)	Johnny Temple (portrait, pose to chest)	3.00	1.50	.90
(740)	Ralph Terry (pitching, follow-through)	4.00	2.00	1.25
(741)	Ralph Terry (portrait, pose to neck)	3.00	1.50	.90
(742)	Frank J. Thomas (portrait, pose to chest)	3.00	1.50	.90
(743)	Frank J. Thomas (batting, pose to chest)	3.00	1.50	.90
(744)	George Thomas (portrait, pose to chest)	3.00	1.50	.90
(745)	Lee Thomas (portrait, pose to chest)	3.00	1.50	.90
(746)	Lee Thomas (batting, pose to chest, two ears)	3.00	1.50	.90
(747)	Lee Thomas (batting, pose to waist, one ear showing)	3.00	1.50	.90
(748)	Marv Throneberry (portrait, pose to chest)	4.00	2.00	1.25
(749)	Luis Tiant (portrait, pose to neck)	6.00	3.00	1.75
(750)	Bob Tillman (batting, pose to chest, one ear showing)	3.00	1.50	.90
(751)	Bob Tillman (batting, pose to chest, two ears showing)	3.00	1.50	.90
(752)	Joe Torre (batting)	6.00	3.00	1.75
(753)	Joe Torre (portrait, pose to chest, no "M" seen on cap)	6.00	3.00	1.75
(754)	Joe Torre (portrait, pose to chest, sky in background)	6.00	3.00	1.75
(755)	Joe Torre (portrait, pose to chest, stands in background)	6.00	3.00	1.75
(756)	Dick Tracewksi (portrait, pose to chest)	3.00	1.50	.90
(757)	Tom Tresh (fielding)	4.00	2.00	1.25
(758)	Tom Tresh (portrait, pose to chest)	4.00	2.00	1.25
(759)	Tom Tresh (batting, pose to waist)	4.00	2.00	1.25
(760)	Gus Triandos (catching, crouching)	3.00	1.50	.90

(761)	Gus Triandos (batting, pose to waist)	3.00	1.50	.90
(762)	Gus Triandos (kneeling, holding bat)	3.00	1.50	.90
(763)	Bob Uecker (catching, crouching)	6.00	3.00	1.75
(764)	Jose Valdivielso (batting, pose to waist)	3.00	1.50	.90
(765)	Bob Veale (portrait, pose to chest)	3.00	1.50	.90
(766)	Mickey Vernon (standing)	4.00	2.00	1.25
(767)	Zoilo Versalles (batting, pose to chest)	3.00	1.50	.90
(768)	Zoilo Versalles (fielding, left leg extended)	3.00	1.50	.90
(769)	Zoilo Versalles (fielding, legs spaced evenly)	3.00	1.50	.90
(770)	Dave Vineyard (portrait, pose to chest)	3.00	1.50	.90
(771)	Bill Virdon (batting, pose to waist, screen in background)	4.00	2.00	1.25
(772)	Bill Virdon (batting, pose to chest, dark background)	4.00	2.00	1.25
(773)	Leon Wagner (hands on knees)	3.00	1.50	.90
(774)	Leon Wagner (portrait, pose to waist)	3.00	1.50	.90
(775)	Harry Walker (portrait, pose to chest, arms crossed)	3.00	1.50	.90
(776)	Jerry Walker (portrait, pose to waist, glove)	3.00	1.50	.90
(777)	Jerry Walker (pitching)	3.00	1.50	.90
(778)	Ken Walter (batting, pose to chest)	3.00	1.50	.90
(779)	Pete Ward (fielding)	3.00	1.50	.90
(780)	Pete Ward (kneeling, holding bat)	3.00	1.50	.90
(781)	Carl Warwick (batting, pose to chest)	3.00	1.50	.90
(782)	Carl Warwick (batting, pose to chest)	3.00	1.50	.90
(783)	Bill White (portrait, pose to chest)	4.00	2.00	1.25
(784)	Bill White (batting, pose to chest)	4.00	2.00	1.25
(784.5)	Mike White (Houston, portrait, pose to waist)	3.00	1.50	.90
(784.6)	Hoyt Wilhelm (pitching, looking in for sign)	6.00	3.00	1.75
(785)	Carl Willey (pitching)	3.00	1.50	.90
(786)	Carlton Willey (pitching, pose to chest, hands over head)	3.00	1.50	.90
(787)	Billy Williams (portrait, pose to waist, fence background)	5.00	2.50	1.50
(788)	Billy Williams (portrait, pose to waist, arms crossed)	5.00	2.50	1.50
(789)	Billy Williams (portrait, pose to chest, dark background)	5.00	2.50	1.50
(790)	Hoyt Williams (Wilhelm) (pitching)	8.00	4.00	2.50
(791)	Stan Williams (portrait, pose to chest)	3.00	1.50	.90
(792)	Maury Wills (portrait, pose to chest)	6.00	3.00	1.75
(793)	Maury Wills (batting, pose to waist)	6.00	3.00	1.75
(794)	Maury Wills (batting, pose to waist, photo reversed)	6.00	3.00	1.75
(795)	Earl Wilson (portrait, pose to waist)	3.00	1.50	.90
(796)	Bob Wine (fielding)	3.00	1.50	.90
(797)	Bob Wine (portrait, pose to chest)	3.00	1.50	.90
(798)	Jake Wood (batting, pose to chest)	3.00	1.50	.90
(799)	Jake Wood (fielding)	3.00	1.50	.90
(800)	Hal Woodeshick (portrait, pose to chest)	3.00	1.50	.90
(801)	Gene Woodling (batting, pose to waist)	4.00	2.00	1.25
(802)	Early Wynn (pitching)	5.00	2.50	1.50
(803)	Jim Wynn (portrait, pose to chest)	3.00	1.50	.90
(804)	Carl Yastrzemski (batting)	20.00	10.00	6.00
(805)	Carl Yastrzemski (portrait, pose to chest, Red Sox uniform)	20.00	10.00	6.00
(806)	Carl Yastrzemski (portrait, pose to chest, Boston uniform)	20.00	10.00	6.00
(807)	Carl Yastrzemski (batting, pose to waist, one ear showing)	20.00	10.00	6.00
(808)	Carl Yastrzemski (batting, pose to waist, two ears showing)	20.00	10.00	6.00
(809)	Eddie Yost (batting, pose to chest)	3.00	1.50	.90
(810)	Don Zimmer (batting, pose to chest)	4.00	2.00	1.25
(811)	Marion Zipfel (fielding)	3.00	1.50	.90

1962 Jell-O

Virtually identical in content to the 1962 Post cereal cards, the '62 Jell-O set of 197 was only issued in the Midwest. Players and card numbers are identical in the two sets, except Brooks Robinson (#29), Ted Kluszewski (#82) and Smoky Burgess (#176) were not issued in the Jell-O version. The Jell-O cards are easy to distinguish from the Post of that year by the absence of the red oval Post logo and red or blue border around the stat box. Cards which have been neatly trimmed from the box which they were printed will measure 3-1/2" x 2-1/2".

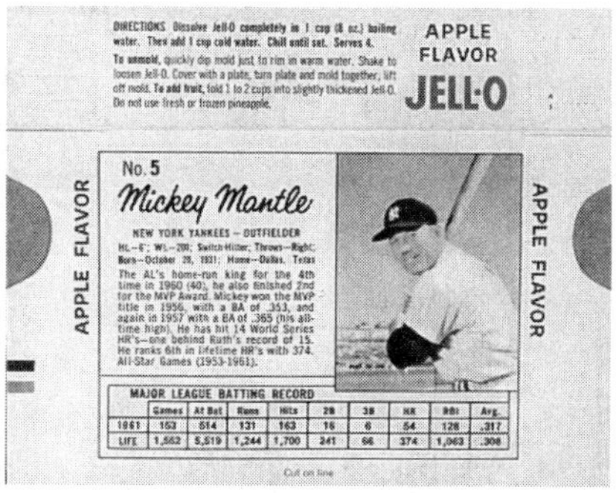

		NM	EX	VG
Complete Set (200):		4500.	2250.	1350.
Common Player:		5.00	2.50	1.50
1	Bill Skowron	20.00	10.00	6.00
2	Bobby Richardson	20.00	10.00	6.00
3	Cletis Boyer	10.00	5.00	3.00
4	Tony Kubek	15.00	7.50	4.50
5	Mickey Mantle	300.00	150.00	90.00
6	Roger Maris	125.00	62.00	37.00
7	Yogi Berra	60.00	30.00	18.00
8	Elston Howard	15.00	7.50	4.50
9	Whitey Ford	40.00	20.00	12.00
10	Ralph Terry	10.00	5.00	3.00
11	John Blanchard	6.00	3.00	1.75
12	Luis Arroyo	6.00	3.00	1.75
13	Bill Stafford	20.00	10.00	6.00
14	Norm Cash	10.00	5.00	3.00
15	Jake Wood	5.00	2.50	1.50
16	Steve Boros	5.00	2.50	1.50
17	Chico Fernandez	5.00	2.50	1.50
18	Billy Bruton	5.00	2.50	1.50
19	Ken Aspromonte	5.00	2.50	1.50
20	Al Kaline	40.00	20.00	12.00
21	Dick Brown	5.00	2.50	1.50
22	Frank Lary	6.00	3.00	1.75
23	Don Mossi	6.00	3.00	1.75
24	Phil Regan	5.00	2.50	1.50
25	Charley Maxwell	5.00	2.50	1.50
26	Jim Bunning	18.00	9.00	5.50
27	Jim Gentile	6.00	3.00	1.75
28	Marv Breeding	5.00	2.50	1.50
29	Not issued			
30	Ron Hansen	5.00	2.50	1.50
31	Jackie Brandt	20.00	10.00	6.00
32	Dick Williams	6.00	3.00	1.75
33	Gus Triandos	6.00	3.00	1.75
34	Milt Pappas	6.00	3.00	1.75
35	Hoyt Wilhelm	20.00	10.00	6.00
36	Chuck Estrada	5.00	2.50	1.50
37	Vic Power	5.00	2.50	1.50
38	Johnny Temple	5.00	2.50	1.50
39	Bubba Phillips	20.00	10.00	6.00
40	Tito Francona	6.00	3.00	1.75
41	Willie Kirkland	5.00	2.50	1.50
42	John Romano	5.00	2.50	1.50
43	Jim Perry	10.00	5.00	3.00
44	Woodie Held	5.00	2.50	1.50
45	Chuck Essegian	5.00	2.50	1.50
46	Roy Sievers	6.00	3.00	1.75
47	Nellie Fox	16.00	8.00	4.75
48	Al Smith	5.00	2.50	1.50
49	Luis Aparicio	20.00	10.00	6.00
50	Jim Landis	5.00	2.50	1.50
51	Minnie Minoso	10.00	5.00	3.00
52	Andy Carey	20.00	10.00	6.00
53	Sherman Lollar	6.00	3.00	1.75
54	Bill Pierce	6.00	3.00	1.75
55	Early Wynn	20.00	10.00	6.00
56	Chuck Schilling	20.00	10.00	6.00
57	Pete Runnels	6.00	3.00	1.75
58	Frank Malzone	6.00	3.00	1.75
59	Don Buddin	10.00	5.00	3.00
60	Gary Geiger	5.00	2.50	1.50
61	Carl Yastrzemski	175.00	87.00	52.00
62	Jackie Jensen	20.00	10.00	6.00
63	Jim Pagliaroni	20.00	10.00	6.00
64	Don Schwall	5.00	2.50	1.50
65	Dale Long	6.00	3.00	1.75
66	Chuck Cottier	10.00	5.00	3.00
67	Billy Klaus	20.00	10.00	6.00
68	Coot Veal	5.00	2.50	1.50
69	Marty Keough	40.00	20.00	12.00
70	Willie Tasby	40.00	20.00	12.00
71	Gene Woodling	6.00	3.00	1.75
72	Gene Green	40.00	20.00	12.00
73	Dick Donovan	10.00	5.00	3.00
74	Steve Bilko	10.00	5.00	3.00
75	Rocky Bridges	20.00	10.00	6.00
76	Eddie Yost	10.00	5.00	3.00
77	Leon Wagner	10.00	5.00	3.00
78	Albie Pearson	10.00	5.00	3.00
79	Ken Hunt	10.00	5.00	3.00
80	Earl Averill	40.00	20.00	12.00
81	Ryne Duren	10.00	5.00	3.00
82	Not issued			
83	Bob Allison	6.00	3.00	1.75
84	Billy Martin	15.00	7.50	4.50
85	Harmon Killebrew	40.00	20.00	12.00
86	Zoilo Versalles	6.00	3.00	1.75
87	Lennie Green	20.00	10.00	6.00
88	Bill Tuttle	5.00	2.50	1.50
89	Jim Lemon	6.00	3.00	1.75
90	Earl Battey	20.00	10.00	6.00
91	Camilo Pascual	6.00	3.00	1.75
92	Norm Siebern	10.00	5.00	3.00
93	Jerry Lumpe	10.00	5.00	3.00
94	Dick Howser	10.00	5.00	3.00
95	Gene Stephens	40.00	20.00	12.00
96	Leo Posada	10.00	5.00	3.00
97	Joe Pignatano	10.00	5.00	3.00
98	Jim Archer	10.00	5.00	3.00
99	Haywood Sullivan	20.00	10.00	6.00
100	Art Ditmar	10.00	5.00	3.00
101	Gil Hodges	40.00	20.00	12.00
102	Charlie Neal	10.00	5.00	3.00
103	Daryl Spencer	10.00	5.00	3.00
104	Maury Wills	20.00	10.00	6.00
105	Tommy Davis	10.00	5.00	3.00
106	Willie Davis	10.00	5.00	3.00
107	John Roseboro	40.00	20.00	12.00
108	John Podres	12.00	6.00	3.50
109	Sandy Koufax	80.00	40.00	24.00
110	Don Drysdale	50.00	25.00	15.00
111	Larry Sherry	20.00	10.00	6.00
112	Jim Gilliam	20.00	10.00	6.00
113	Norm Larker	40.00	20.00	12.00
114	Duke Snider	70.00	35.00	21.00
115	Stan Williams	20.00	10.00	6.00
116	Gordon Coleman	70.00	35.00	21.00
117	Don Blasingame	20.00	10.00	6.00
118	Gene Freese	40.00	20.00	12.00
119	Ed Kasko	40.00	20.00	12.00
120	Gus Bell	20.00	10.00	6.00
121	Vada Pinson	10.00	5.00	3.00
122	Frank Robinson	40.00	20.00	12.00
123	Bob Purkey	10.00	5.00	3.00
124	Joey Jay	10.00	5.00	3.00
125	Jim Brosnan	10.00	5.00	3.00
126	Jim O'Toole	10.00	5.00	3.00
127	Jerry Lynch	10.00	5.00	3.00
128	Wally Post	10.00	5.00	3.00
129	Ken Hunt	10.00	5.00	3.00
130	Jerry Zimmerman	10.00	5.00	3.00
131	Willie McCovey	40.00	20.00	12.00
132	Jose Pagan	20.00	10.00	6.00
133	Felipe Alou	10.00	5.00	3.00
134	Jim Davenport	10.00	5.00	3.00
135	Harvey Kuenn	10.00	5.00	3.00
136	Orlando Cepeda	18.00	9.00	5.50
137	Ed Bailey	10.00	5.00	3.00
138	Sam Jones	10.00	5.00	3.00
139	Mike McCormick	10.00	5.00	3.00
140	Juan Marichal	40.00	20.00	12.00
141	Jack Sanford	10.00	5.00	3.00
142	Willie Mays	150.00	75.00	45.00
143	Stu Miller	70.00	35.00	21.00
144	Joe Amalfitano	10.00	5.00	3.00
145	Joe Adcock	10.00	5.00	3.00
146	Frank Bolling	5.00	2.50	1.50
147	Ed Mathews	40.00	20.00	12.00
148	Roy McMillan	6.00	3.00	1.75
149	Hank Aaron	150.00	75.00	45.00
150	Gino Cimoli	20.00	10.00	6.00
151	Frank J. Thomas	6.00	3.00	1.75
152	Joe Torre	10.00	5.00	3.00
153	Lou Burdette	6.00	3.00	1.75
154	Bob Buhl	6.00	3.00	1.75
155	Carlton Willey	5.00	2.50	1.50
156	Lee Maye	18.00	9.00	5.50
157	Al Spangler	40.00	20.00	12.00
158	Bill White	40.00	20.00	12.00
159	Ken Boyer	15.00	7.50	4.50
160	Joe Cunningham	10.00	5.00	3.00
161	Carl Warwick	10.00	5.00	3.00
162	Carl Sawatski	5.00	2.50	1.50
163	Lindy McDaniel	5.00	2.50	1.50
164	Ernie Broglio	10.00	5.00	3.00
165	Larry Jackson	5.00	2.50	1.50
166	Curt Flood	15.00	7.50	4.50
167	Curt Simmons	40.00	20.00	12.00
168	Alex Grammas	20.00	10.00	6.00
169	Dick Stuart	6.00	3.00	1.75
170	Bill Mazeroski	20.00	10.00	6.00
171	Don Hoak	10.00	5.00	3.00
172	Dick Groat	10.00	5.00	3.00
173	Roberto Clemente	150.00	75.00	45.00
174	Bob Skinner	20.00	10.00	6.00
175	Bill Virdon	40.00	20.00	12.00
176	Not issued			
177	Elroy Face	10.00	5.00	3.00
178	Bob Friend	6.00	3.00	1.75
179	Vernon Law	20.00	10.00	6.00
180	Harvey Haddix	40.00	20.00	12.00
181	Hal Smith	20.00	10.00	6.00
182	Ed Bouchee	20.00	10.00	6.00
183	Don Zimmer	8.00	4.00	2.50
184	Ron Santo	10.00	5.00	3.00
185	Andre Rodgers	5.00	2.50	1.50
186	Richie Ashburn	15.00	7.50	4.50
187	George Altman	5.00	2.50	1.50
188	Ernie Banks	40.00	20.00	12.00
189	Sam Taylor	5.00	2.50	1.50
190	Don Elston	5.00	2.50	1.50
191	Jerry Kindall	20.00	10.00	6.00
192	Pancho Herrera	5.00	2.50	1.50
193	Tony Taylor	5.00	2.50	1.50
194	Ruben Amaro	20.00	10.00	6.00
195	Don Demeter	5.00	2.50	1.50
196	Bobby Gene Smith	5.00	2.50	1.50
197	Clay Dalrymple	5.00	2.50	1.50
198	Robin Roberts	25.00	12.50	7.50
199	Art Mahaffey	5.00	2.50	1.50
200	John Buzhardt	5.00	2.50	1.50

1963 Jell-O

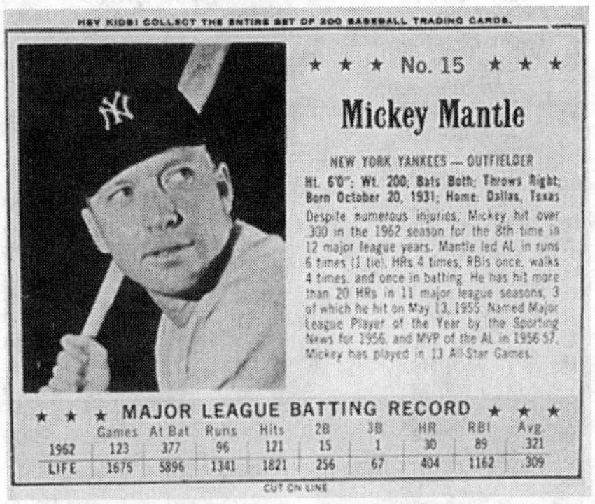
HEY KIDS! COLLECT THE ENTIRE SET OF 200 BASEBALL TRADING CARDS.
★ ★ ★ No. 15 ★ ★ ★
Mickey Mantle
NEW YORK YANKEES — OUTFIELDER
Ht. 6'0"; Wt. 200; Bats Both; Throws Right; Born October 20, 1931; Home: Dallas, Texas
Despite numerous injuries, Mickey hit over .300 in the 1962 season for the 8th time in 12 major league years. Mantle led AL in runs 6 times (1 tie), HRs 4 times, RBIs once, walks 4 times, and once in batting. He has hit more than 20 HRs in 11 major league seasons, 3 of which he hit on May 13, 1955. Named Major League Player of the Year by the Sporting News for 1956, and MVP of the AL in 1956-57. Mickey has played in 13 All-Star Games.
★ ★ ★ MAJOR LEAGUE BATTING RECORD ★ ★ ★
Games At Bat Runs Hits 2B 3B HR RBI Avg.
1962 123 377 96 121 15 1 30 89 .321
LIFE 1675 5896 1341 1821 256 67 404 1162 .309
CUT ON LINE

Like the other Post and Jell-O issues of the era, the '63 Jell-O set includes many scarce cards; primarily those which were printed as the backs of less popular brands and sizes of the gelatin dessert. Slightly smaller than the virtually identical Post cereal cards of the same year, the 200 cards in the Jell-O issue measure 3-3/8" x 2-1/2". The easiest way to distinguish 1963 Jell-O cards from Post cards is by the red line that separates the 1962 stats from the lifetime stats. On Post cards, the line extends almost all the way to the side borders, on the Jell-O cards, the line begins and ends much closer to the stats.

		NM	EX	VG
Complete Set (200):		3000.	1500.	900.00
Common Player:		3.00	1.50	.90
1	Vic Power	3.00	1.50	.90
2	Bernie Allen	20.00	10.00	6.00
3	Zoilo Versalles	20.00	10.00	6.00
4	Rich Rollins	3.00	1.50	.90
5	Harmon Killebrew	8.00	4.00	2.50
6	Lenny Green	20.00	10.00	6.00
7	Bob Allison	3.00	1.50	.90
8	Earl Battey	15.00	7.50	4.50
9	Camilo Pascual	3.00	1.50	.90
10	Jim Kaat	35.00	17.50	10.50
11	Jack Kralick	3.00	1.50	.90
12	Bill Skowron	20.00	10.00	6.00
13	Bobby Richardson	5.00	2.50	1.50
14	Cletis Boyer	3.00	1.50	.90
15	Mickey Mantle	200.00	100.00	60.00
16	Roger Maris	20.00	10.00	6.00
17	Yogi Berra	20.00	10.00	6.00
18	Elston Howard	20.00	10.00	6.00
19	Whitey Ford	10.00	5.00	3.00
20	Ralph Terry	3.00	1.50	.90
21	John Blanchard	15.00	7.50	4.50
22	Bill Stafford	20.00	10.00	6.00
23	Tom Tresh	3.00	1.50	.90
24	Steve Bilko	3.00	1.50	.90
25	Bill Moran	3.00	1.50	.90
26	Joe Koppe	3.00	1.50	.90
27	Felix Torres	3.00	1.50	.90
28	Leon Wagner	3.00	1.50	.90
29	Albie Pearson	3.00	1.50	.90
30	Lee Thomas	3.00	1.50	.90
31	Bob Rodgers	20.00	10.00	6.00
32	Dean Chance	3.00	1.50	.90
33	Ken McBride	20.00	10.00	6.00
34	George Thomas	20.00	10.00	6.00
35	Joe Cunningham	20.00	10.00	6.00
36	Nelson Fox	6.00	3.00	1.75
37	Luis Aparicio	6.00	3.00	1.75
38	Al Smith	3.00	1.50	.90
39	Floyd Robinson	3.00	1.50	.90
40	Jim Landis	3.00	1.50	.90
41	Charlie Maxwell	3.00	1.50	.90
42	Sherman Lollar	3.00	1.50	.90
43	Early Wynn	6.00	3.00	1.75
44	Juan Pizarro	20.00	10.00	6.00
45	Ray Herbert	20.00	10.00	6.00
46	Norm Cash	3.50	1.75	1.00
47	Steve Boros	20.00	10.00	6.00
48	Dick McAuliffe	3.00	1.50	.90
49	Bill Bruton	3.00	1.50	.90
50	Rocky Colavito	5.00	2.50	1.50
51	Al Kaline	12.00	6.00	3.50
52	Dick Brown	20.00	10.00	6.00
53	Jim Bunning	7.50	3.75	2.25
54	Hank Aguirre	3.00	1.50	.90
55	Frank Lary	20.00	10.00	6.00
56	Don Mossi	20.00	10.00	6.00
57	Jim Gentile	3.00	1.50	.90
58	Jackie Brandt	3.00	1.50	.90
59	Brooks Robinson	15.00	7.50	4.50
60	Ron Hansen	3.00	1.50	.90
61	Jerry Adair	55.00	27.00	16.50
62	John Powell	3.50	1.75	1.00
63	Russ Snyder	20.00	10.00	6.00
64	Steve Barber	3.00	1.50	.90
65	Milt Pappas	20.00	10.00	6.00
66	Robin Roberts	6.00	3.00	1.75
67	Tito Francona	3.00	1.50	.90
68	Jerry Kindall	20.00	10.00	6.00
69	Woodie Held	3.00	1.50	.90
70	Bubba Phillips	3.00	1.50	.90
71	Chuck Essegian	3.00	1.50	.90
72	Willie Kirkland	20.00	10.00	6.00
73	Al Luplow	3.00	1.50	.90
74	Ty Cline	20.00	10.00	6.00
75	Dick Donovan	3.00	1.50	.90
76	John Romano	3.00	1.50	.90
77	Pete Runnels	3.00	1.50	.90
78	Ed Bressoud	20.00	10.00	6.00
79	Frank Malzone	3.00	1.50	.90
80	Carl Yastrzemski	75.00	37.00	22.00
81	Gary Geiger	3.00	1.50	.90
82	Lou Clinton	20.00	10.00	6.00
83	Earl Wilson	3.00	1.50	.90
84	Bill Monbouquette	3.00	1.50	.90
85	Norm Siebern	3.00	1.50	.90
86	Jerry Lumpe	3.00	1.50	.90
87	Manny Jimenez	3.00	1.50	.90
88	Gino Cimoli	3.00	1.50	.90
89	Ed Charles	55.00	27.00	16.50
90	Ed Rakow	3.00	1.50	.90
91	Bob Del Greco	20.00	10.00	6.00
92	Haywood Sullivan	20.00	10.00	6.00
93	Chuck Hinton	3.00	1.50	.90
94	Ken Retzer	20.00	10.00	6.00
95	Harry Bright	20.00	10.00	6.00
96	Bob Johnson	3.00	1.50	.90
97	Dave Stenhouse	20.00	10.00	6.00
98	Chuck Cottier	3.00	1.50	.90
99	Tom Cheney	3.00	1.50	.90
100	Claude Osteen	20.00	10.00	6.00
101	Orlando Cepeda	7.50	3.75	2.25
102	Charley Hiller	20.00	10.00	6.00
103	Jose Pagan	20.00	10.00	6.00
104	Jim Davenport	3.00	1.50	.90
105	Harvey Kuenn	3.50	1.75	1.00
106	Willie Mays	75.00	37.00	22.00
107	Felipe Alou	3.00	1.50	.90
108	Tom Haller	3.00	1.50	.90
109	Juan Marichal	6.00	3.00	1.75
110	Jack Sanford	3.00	1.50	.90
111	Bill O'Dell	3.00	1.50	.90
112	Willie McCovey	90.00	45.00	27.00
113	Lee Walls	20.00	10.00	6.00
114	Jim Gilliam	20.00	10.00	6.00
115	Maury Wills	5.00	2.50	1.50
116	Ron Fairly	3.00	1.50	.90
117	Tommy Davis	3.00	1.50	.90
118	Duke Snider	9.00	4.50	2.75
119	Willie Davis	3.00	1.50	.90
120	John Roseboro	3.00	1.50	.90
121	Sandy Koufax	20.00	10.00	6.00
122	Stan Williams	20.00	10.00	6.00
123	Don Drysdale	9.00	4.50	2.75
124	Daryl Spencer	3.00	1.50	.90
125	Gordy Coleman	3.00	1.50	.90
126	Don Blasingame	20.00	10.00	6.00
127	Leo Cardenas	3.00	1.50	.90
128	Eddie Kasko	20.00	10.00	6.00
129	Jerry Lynch	3.00	1.50	.90
130	Vada Pinson	4.00	2.00	1.25
131	Frank Robinson	9.00	4.50	2.75
132	John Edwards	20.00	10.00	6.00
133	Joey Jay	3.00	1.50	.90
134	Bob Purkey	3.00	1.50	.90
135	Marty Keough	55.00	27.00	16.50
136	Jim O'Toole	20.00	10.00	6.00
137	Dick Stuart	3.00	1.50	.90
138	Bill Mazeroski	5.00	2.50	1.50
139	Dick Groat	3.00	1.50	.90
140	Don Hoak	3.00	1.50	.90
141	Bob Skinner	3.00	1.50	.90
142	Bill Virdon	3.00	1.50	.90
143	Roberto Clemente	90.00	45.00	27.00
144	Smoky Burgess	3.00	1.50	.90
145	Bob Friend	3.00	1.50	.90
146	Al McBean	20.00	10.00	6.00
147	ElRoy Face	3.00	1.50	.90
148	Joe Adcock	3.50	1.75	1.00
149	Frank Bolling	3.00	1.50	.90
150	Roy McMillan	3.00	1.50	.90
151	Eddie Mathews	8.00	4.00	2.50
152	Hank Aaron	75.00	37.00	22.00
153	Del Crandall	20.00	10.00	6.00
154	Bob Shaw	3.00	1.50	.90
155	Lew Burdette	3.50	1.75	1.00
156	Joe Torre	20.00	10.00	6.00
157	Tony Cloninger	35.00	17.50	10.50
158	Bill White	4.00	2.00	1.25
159	Julian Javier	20.00	10.00	6.00
160	Ken Boyer	4.00	2.00	1.25
161	Julio Gotay	20.00	10.00	6.00
162	Curt Flood	3.00	1.50	.90
163	Charlie James	35.00	17.50	10.50
164	Gene Oliver	20.00	10.00	6.00
165	Ernie Broglio	3.00	1.50	.90
166	Bob Gibson	75.00	37.00	22.00
167	Lindy McDaniel	20.00	10.00	6.00
168	Ray Washburn	3.00	1.50	.90
169	Ernie Banks	12.00	6.00	3.50
170	Ron Santo	4.00	2.00	1.25
171	George Altman	3.00	1.50	.90
172	Billy Williams	75.00	37.00	22.00
173	Andre Rodgers	20.00	10.00	6.00
174	Ken Hubbs	4.00	2.00	1.25
175	Don Landrum	20.00	10.00	6.00
176	Dick Bertell	20.00	10.00	6.00
177	Roy Sievers	3.00	1.50	.90
178	Tony Taylor	20.00	10.00	6.00
179	John Callison	3.00	1.50	.90
180	Don Demeter	3.00	1.50	.90
181	Tony Gonzalez	20.00	10.00	6.00
182	Wes Covington	20.00	10.00	6.00
183	Art Mahaffey	3.00	1.50	.90
184	Clay Dalrymple	3.00	1.50	.90
185	Al Spangler	3.00	1.50	.90
186	Roman Mejias	3.00	1.50	.90
187	Bob Aspromonte	50.00	25.00	15.00
188	Norm Larker	3.00	1.50	.90
189	Johnny Temple	3.00	1.50	.90
190	Carl Warwick	20.00	10.00	6.00
191	Bob Lillis	20.00	10.00	6.00
192	Dick Farrell	50.00	25.00	15.00
193	Gil Hodges	8.00	4.00	2.50
194	Marv Throneberry	3.00	1.50	.90
195	Charlie Neal	20.00	10.00	6.00
196	Frank J. Thomas	3.00	1.50	.90
197	Richie Ashburn	5.00	2.50	1.50
198	Felix Mantilla	20.00	10.00	6.00
199	Rod Kanehl	20.00	10.00	6.00
200	Roger Craig	20.00	10.00	6.00

1973 Jewel Food Baseball Photos

Jewel Food Stores, a midwestern grocery chain, issued three team sets of large-format baseball player photos in 1973. The 5-7/8" x 9" blank-back photos are full color and feature a facsimile autograph. Photos were sold in groups of four or five per week at five or ten cents per picture. There are 24 Milwaukee Brewers in the issue, and 16 each Chicago Cubs and Chicago White Sox. The unnumbered cards are alphabetized by team in the checklist below.

		NM	EX	VG
CHICAGO CUBS				
Complete Set (16):		40.00	20.00	12.00
Common Player:		2.00	1.00	.60
(1)	Jack Aker	2.00	1.00	.60
(2)	Glenn Beckert	3.00	1.50	.90
(3)	Jose Cardenal	2.00	1.00	.60
(4)	Carmen Fanzone	2.00	1.00	.60
(5)	Burt Hooton	2.00	1.00	.60
(6)	Fergie Jenkins	7.50	3.75	2.25
(7)	Don Kessinger	3.00	1.50	.90
(8)	Jim Hickman	2.00	1.00	.60
(9)	Randy Hundley	3.00	1.50	.90
(10)	Bob Locker	2.00	1.00	.60
(11)	Rick Monday	2.00	1.00	.60
(12)	Milt Pappas	2.00	1.00	.60
(13)	Rick Reuschel	2.00	1.00	.60
(14)	Ken Rudolph	2.00	1.00	.60
(15)	Ron Santo	7.50	3.75	2.25
(16)	Billy Williams	9.00	4.50	2.75
CHICAGO WHITE SOX				
Complete Set (16):		30.00	15.00	9.00
Common Player:		2.00	1.00	.60
(17)	Dick Allen	5.00	2.50	1.50
(18)	Mike Andrews	2.00	1.00	.60
(19)	Stan Bahnsen	2.00	1.00	.60
(20)	Eddie Fisher	2.00	1.00	.60
(21)	Terry Forster	2.00	1.00	.60
(22)	Ken Henderson	2.00	1.00	.60
(23)	Ed Hermann	2.00	1.00	.60
(24)	John Jeter	2.00	1.00	.60
(25)	Pat Kelly	2.00	1.00	.60
(26)	Eddie Leon	2.00	1.00	.60
(27)	Carlos May	2.00	1.00	.60
(28)	Bill Melton	2.00	1.00	.60
(29)	Tony Muser	2.00	1.00	.60
(30)	Jorge Orta	2.00	1.00	.60
(31)	Rick Reichardt	2.00	1.00	.60
(32)	Wilbur Wood	2.00	1.00	.60
MILWAUKEE BREWERS				
Complete Set (25):		35.00	22.50	13.50
Common Player:		2.00	1.00	.60
(33)	Jerry Bell	2.00	1.00	.60
(34)	John Briggs	2.00	1.00	.60
(35)	Ollie Brown	2.00	1.00	.60
(36)	Billy Champion	2.00	1.00	.60
(37)	Jim Colborn	2.00	1.00	.60
(38)	Bob Coluccio	2.00	1.00	.60
(39)	John Felske	2.00	1.00	.60
(40)	Pedro Garcia	2.00	1.00	.60
(41)	Rob Gardner	2.00	1.00	.60
(42)	Bob Heise	2.00	1.00	.60
(43)	Tim Johnson	2.00	1.00	.60
(44)	Joe Lahoud	2.00	1.00	.60
(45)	Frank Linzy	2.00	1.00	.60
(46)	Skip Lockwood	2.00	1.00	.60
(47)	Dave May	2.00	1.00	.60
(48)	Bob Mitchell	2.00	1.00	.60
(49)	Don Money	3.00	1.50	.90
(50)	Bill Parsons	2.00	1.00	.60
(51)	Darrell Porter	2.00	1.00	.60
(52)	Eduardo Rodriguez	2.00	1.00	.60
(53)	Ellie Rodriguez	2.00	1.00	.60
(54)	George Scott	4.00	2.00	1.20
(55)	Chris Short	2.00	1.00	.60

(56)	Jim Slaton	2.00	1.00	.60
(57)	John Vukovich	2.00	1.00	.60

1977 Jewel Food Chicago Cubs/White Sox

Once again in 1977 Jewel grocery stores in the Chicago area offered photos of local players with specific product purchases over a four-week period. The 5-7/8" x 9" color photos are printed on heavy paper. Fronts have player poses, a facsimile signature and the MLB Players Association logo in the upper-left corner. Backs are blank. The pictures are not numbered and are checklisted here alphabetically within each team. It was reported 12,000 of each picture were produced.

		NM	EX	VG
Complete Set, Cubs (16):		8.00	4.00	2.50
Complete Set, White Sox (16):		8.00	4.00	2.50
Common Player:		.50	.40	.20
	CHICAGO CUBS			
(1)	Larry Biittner	.50	.25	.15
(2)	Bill Bonham	.50	.25	.15
(3)	Bill Buckner	.75	.40	.25
(4)	Ray Burris	.50	.25	.15
(5)	Jose Cardenal	.50	.25	.15
(6)	Gene Clines	.50	.25	.15
(7)	Ivan DeJesus	.50	.25	.15
(8)	Willie Hernandez	.50	.25	.15
(9)	Mike Krukow	.50	.25	.15
(10)	George Mitterwald	.50	.25	.15
(11)	Jerry Morales	.50	.25	.15
(12)	Bobby Murcer	.75	.40	.25
(13)	Steve Ontiveros	.50	.25	.15
(14)	Rick Reuschel	.50	.25	.15
(15)	Bruce Sutter	.60	.30	.20
(16)	Manny Trillo	.50	.25	.15
	CHICAGO WHITE SOX			
(1)	Alan Bannister	.50	.25	.15
(2)	Francisco Barrios	.50	.25	.15
(3)	Jim Essian	.50	.25	.15
(4)	Oscar Gamble	.50	.25	.15
(5)	Ralph Garr	.50	.25	.15
(6)	Lamar Johnson	.50	.25	.15
(7)	Chris Knapp	.50	.25	.15
(8)	Ken Kravec	.50	.25	.15
(9)	Lerrin LaGrow	.50	.25	.15
(10)	Chet Lemon	.50	.25	.15
(11)	Jorge Orta	.50	.25	.15
(12)	Eric Soderholm	.50	.25	.15
(13)	Jim Spencer	.50	.25	.15
(14)	Steve Stone	.75	.40	.25
(15)	Wilbur Wood	.50	.25	.15
(16)	Richie Zisk	.50	.25	.15

1948 Jimmy Fund Ted Williams Tag

The year of issue is speculative. This 2-1/4" square hang tag was, according to the wording thereon, appears to have been given away for contributions to the childhood cancer charity which was supported by Williams and the Red Sox for several decades. The tag is printed in blue on white and has a hole on top through which a string was attached. The back has a drawing of "The Jimmy Bldg."

	NM	EX	VG
Ted Williams	25.00	12.50	7.50

1949 Jimmy Fund Boston Braves Die-cuts

The reigning National League champions undertook the support of the Jimmy Fund, a Boston charity for children's cancer research, with a set of die-cut counter cards accompanying contributions boxes. Between about 6" and 8" at the base, and up to a foot tall, these heavy cardboard pieces feature sepia-toned player action photos in front of a large baseball on which is written, "THANK YOU! in behalf of 'JIMMY', with a facsimile signature below. Backs have a fold-out easel to stand the card up, and a notation that following the fund drive, the card should be given to the largest contributor at that location.

		NM	EX	VG
Complete Set (20):		3950.	1900.	1100.
Common Player:		225.00	112.00	65.00
(1)	Johnny Antonelli	225.00	112.00	65.00
(2)	Red Barrett	225.00	112.00	65.00
(3)	Vern Bickford	225.00	112.00	65.00
(4)	Clint Conatser	225.00	112.00	65.00
(5)	Al Dark	225.00	112.00	65.00
(6)	Bob Elliott	225.00	112.00	65.00
(7)	Glenn Elliott	225.00	112.00	65.00
(8)	Bobby Hogue	225.00	112.00	65.00
(9)	Tommy Holmes	225.00	112.00	65.00
(10)	Pete Reiser	225.00	112.00	65.00
(11)	Marv Rickert	225.00	112.00	65.00
(12)	Jim Russell	225.00	112.00	65.00
(13)	Connie Ryan	225.00	112.00	65.00
(14)	Johnny Sain	250.00	125.00	75.00
(15)	Bill Salkeld	225.00	112.00	65.00
(16)	Sibby Sisti	225.00	112.00	65.00
(17)	Warren Spahn	300.00	150.00	90.00
(18)	Don Thompson	225.00	112.00	65.00
(19)	Earl Torgeson	225.00	112.00	65.00
(20)	Bill Voiselle	225.00	112.00	65.00

1978 JJH Reading Remembers

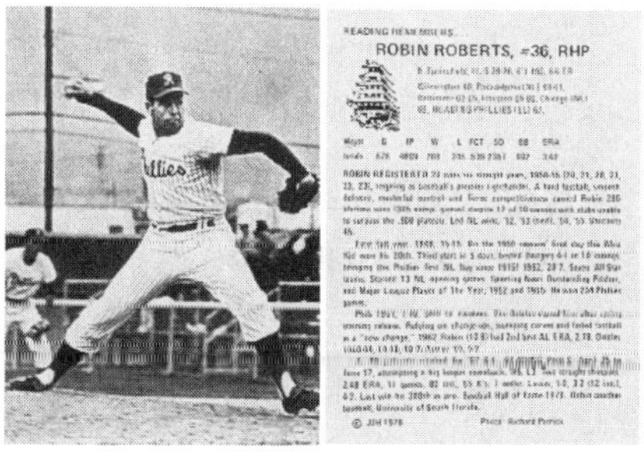

This collectors' issue was created to honor baseball players (and a few others) who were born, lived in or played in Berks County, Pa., particularly in Reading. The cards are 3" x 4" featuring borderless sepia photos on front. Most of the photos picture players in big league uniforms. Backs are in black-and-white and have career stats and summaries. A number of major leaguers who did not have cards contemporary with their careers are found in this set. Cards are numbered by uniform number.

		NM	EX	VG
Complete Set (23):		12.00	6.00	3.50
Common Player:		.50	.25	.15
1	Whitey Kurowski	.50	.25	.15
6	Carl Furillo	1.00	.50	.30
9	Roger Maris	6.00	3.00	1.75
12	Stan Wetzel	.50	.25	.15
17	Doug Clemens	.50	.25	.15
18	Randy Gumpert	.50	.25	.15
18	Ty Stofflet (softball)	.50	.25	.15
21	George Eyrich	.50	.25	.15
23	Vic Wertz	.50	.25	.15
24	Lenny Moore (football)	.50	.25	.15
25	Dick Gernert	.50	.25	.15
27	Herb Score	.50	.25	.15
27	Charlie Wagner	.50	.25	.15
28	Carl Mathias	.50	.25	.15
32	Jesse Levan	.50	.25	.15
34	Betz Klopp	.50	.25	.15
36	Robin Roberts	3.00	1.50	.90
39	Bob Katz	.50	.25	.15
39	Harry Schaeffer	.50	.25	.15
40	Tommy Brown (baseball/football)	.75	.40	.25
46	Dom Dallessandro	.50	.25	.15
---	Lauer's Park	.50	.25	.15
---	John Updike (author)	.50	.25	.15

1973 Johnny Pro Orioles

This regional set of large (4-1/2" x 7-1/4,") die-cut cards was issued by Johnny Pro Enterprises Inc. of Baltimore and features only Orioles. The cards were designed to be punched out and folded to make baseball player figures that can stand up. The full-color die-cut figures appear against a green background. The cards are numbered according to the player's uniform number, which appears in a white box along with his name and position. The backs are blank. Three players (Robinson, Grich, and Palmer) appear in two poses each, and cards of Orlando Pena were not die-cut. Values listed are for complete cards not punched out. Cards originally sold for 15Û apiece.

		NM	EX	VG
Complete Set (28):		145.00	60.00	30.00
Common Player:		3.00	1.50	.90
1	Al Bumbry	3.00	1.50	.90
2	Rich Coggins	3.00	1.50	.90
3a	Bobby Grich (batting)	5.00	2.50	1.50
3b	Bobby Grich (fielding)	5.00	2.50	1.50
4	Earl Weaver	6.00	3.00	1.75
5a	Brooks Robinson (batting)	20.00	10.00	6.00
5b	Brooks Robinson (fielding)	20.00	10.00	6.00
6	Paul Blair	4.00	2.00	1.25
7	Mark Belanger	4.00	2.00	1.25
8	Andy Etchebarren	3.00	1.50	.90
10	Elrod Hendricks	3.00	1.50	.90
11	Terry Crowley	3.00	1.50	.90
12	Tommy Davis	4.00	2.00	1.25
13	Doyle Alexander	3.00	1.50	.90
14	Merv Rettenmund	3.00	1.50	.90
15	Frank Baker	3.00	1.50	.90
19	Dave McNally	4.00	2.00	1.25
21	Larry Brown	3.00	1.50	.90
22a	Jim Palmer (follow-thru)	20.00	10.00	6.00
22b	Jim Palmer (wind up)	20.00	10.00	6.00
23	Grant Jackson	3.00	1.50	.90
25	Don Baylor	6.00	3.00	1.75
26	Boog Powell	7.00	3.50	2.00
27	Orlando Pena	8.00	4.00	2.50
32	Earl Williams	3.00	1.50	.90
34	Bob Reynolds	3.00	1.50	.90
35	Mike Cuellar	5.00	2.50	1.50
39	Eddie Watt	3.00	1.50	.90

1974 Johnny Pro Phillies

Although slightly smaller (3-3/4" x 7-1/8") and featuring members of the Phillies, this set is very similar to the 1973 Johnny Pro Orioles set. The full-color die-cut player figures are set against a white background. Again, the set is numbered according to the player's uniform number. The values listed are for complete cards.

		NM	EX	VG
Complete Set (12):		125.00	65.00	40.00
Common Player:		3.00	1.50	.90
8	Bob Boone	6.00	3.00	1.75
10	Larry Bowa	4.00	2.00	1.25
16	Dave Cash	3.00	1.50	.90
19	Greg Luzinski	6.00	3.00	1.75
20	Mike Schmidt	90.00	45.00	27.00
22	Mike Anderson	3.00	1.50	.90
24	Bill Robinson	3.00	1.50	.90
25	Del Unser	3.00	1.50	.90
27	Willie Montanez	3.00	1.50	.90
32	Steve Carlton	25.00	12.50	7.50
37	Ron Schueler	3.00	1.50	.90
41	Jim Lonborg	3.00	1.50	.90

1953 Johnston Cookies Braves

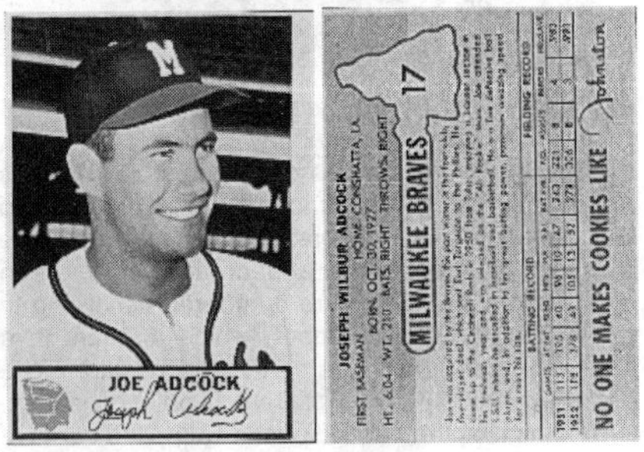

The first and most common of three annual issues, the '53 Johnstons were inserted into boxes of cookies on a regional basis. Complete sets were also available via a mail-in offer from the company, whose factory sits in the shadow of Milwaukee County Stadium. While at first glance appearing to be color photos, the pictures on the 25 cards in the set are actually well-done colorizations of black-and-white photos. Cards measure 2-9/16" x 3-5/8". Write-ups on the backs were "borrowed" from the Braves' 1953 yearbook.

		NM	EX	VG
Complete Set (25):		500.00	250.00	150.00
Common Player:		15.00	7.50	4.50
1	Charlie Grimm	15.00	7.50	4.50
2	John Antonelli	15.00	7.50	4.50
3	Vern Bickford	15.00	7.50	4.50
4	Bob Buhl	15.00	7.50	4.50
5	Lew Burdette	15.00	7.50	4.50
6	Dave Cole	15.00	7.50	4.50
7	Ernie Johnson	15.00	7.50	4.50
8	Dave Jolly	15.00	7.50	4.50
9	Don Liddle	15.00	7.50	4.50
10	Warren Spahn	60.00	30.00	18.00
11	Max Surkont	15.00	7.50	4.50
12	Jim Wilson	15.00	7.50	4.50
13	Sibby Sisti	15.00	7.50	4.50
14	Walker Cooper	15.00	7.50	4.50
15	Del Crandall	15.00	7.50	4.50
16	Ebba St. Claire	15.00	7.50	4.50
17	Joe Adcock	15.00	7.50	4.50
18	George Crowe	15.00	7.50	4.50
19	Jack Dittmer	15.00	7.50	4.50
20	Johnny Logan	15.00	7.50	4.50
21	Ed Mathews	60.00	30.00	18.00
22	Bill Bruton	15.00	7.50	4.50
23	Sid Gordon	15.00	7.50	4.50
24	Andy Pafko	15.00	7.50	4.50
25	Jim Pendleton	15.00	7.50	4.50

1954 Johnston Cookies Braves

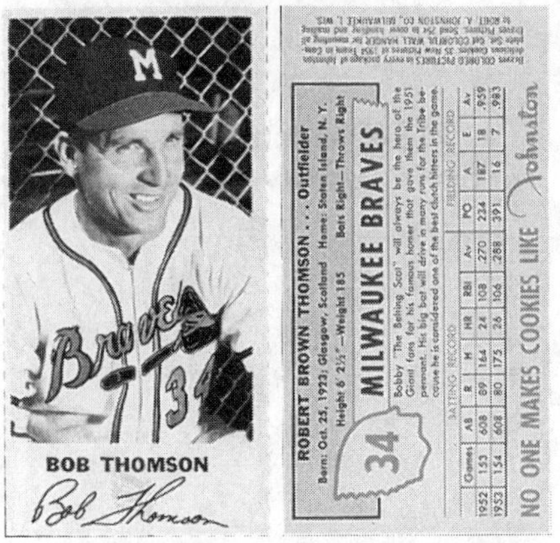

In its second of three annual issues, Johnston's increased the number of cards in its 1954 Braves issue to 35, and switched to an unusual size, a narrow format, 2" x 3-7/8". Besides the players and manager, the '54 set also includes unnumbered cards of the team trainer and equipment manager. Other cards are numbered by uniform number. After his early-season injury (which gave Hank Aaron a chance to play regularly), Bobby Thomson's card was withdrawn, accounting for its scarcity and high value. A cardboard wall-hanging display into which cards could be inserted was available as a premium offer.

		NM	EX	VG
Complete Set (35):		1350.	675.00	400.00
Common Player:		15.00	7.50	4.50
1	Del Crandall	15.00	7.50	4.50
3	Jim Pendleton	15.00	7.50	4.50
4	Danny O'Connell	15.00	7.50	4.50
5	Henry Aaron	450.00	225.00	135.00
6	Jack Dittmer	15.00	7.50	4.50
9	Joe Adcock	15.00	7.50	4.50
10	Robert Buhl	15.00	7.50	4.50
11	Phillip Paine (Phillips)	15.00	7.50	4.50
12	Ben Johnson	15.00	7.50	4.50
13	Sibby Sisti	15.00	7.50	4.50
15	Charles Gorin	15.00	7.50	4.50
16	Chet Nichols	15.00	7.50	4.50
17	Dave Jolly	15.00	7.50	4.50
19	Jim Wilson	15.00	7.50	4.50
20	Ray Crone	15.00	7.50	4.50
21	Warren Spahn	95.00	47.00	28.00
22	Gene Conley	15.00	7.50	4.50
23	Johnny Logan	15.00	7.50	4.50
24	Charlie White	15.00	7.50	4.50
27	George Metkovich	15.00	7.50	4.50
28	John Cooney	15.00	7.50	4.50
29	Paul Burris	15.00	7.50	4.50
31	Wm. Walters	15.00	7.50	4.50
32	Ernest T. Johnson	15.00	7.50	4.50
33	Lew Burdette	15.00	7.50	4.50
34	Bob Thomson	260.00	130.00	78.00
35	Robert Keely	15.00	7.50	4.50
38	Billy Bruton	15.00	7.50	4.50
40	Charles Grimm	15.00	7.50	4.50
41	Ed Mathews	95.00	47.00	28.00
42	Sam Calderone	15.00	7.50	4.50
47	Joey Jay	15.00	7.50	4.50
48	Andy Pafko	15.00	7.50	4.50
---	Dr. Charles Lacks (asst. trainer)	15.00	7.50	4.50
---	Joseph F. Taylor (asst. trainer)	15.00	7.50	4.50

1955 Johnston Cookies Braves

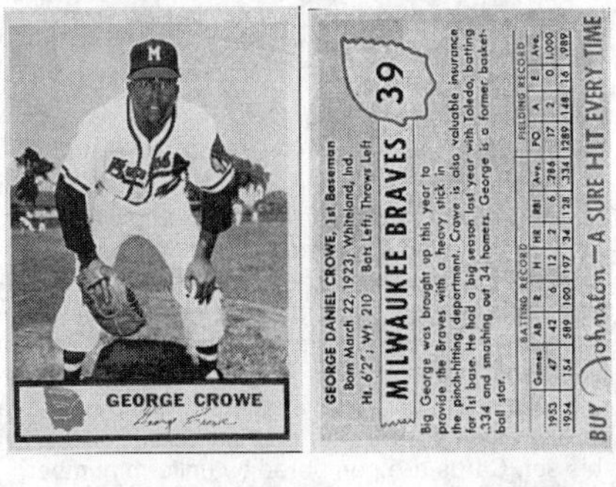

A third change in size and format was undertaken in the final year of Braves sets produced by Johnston's. The 35 cards in the 1955 set were issued in six fold-out panels of six cards each (Andy Pafko was double-printed). As in 1954, cards are numbered by uniform number, except those of the team equipment manager, trainer and road secretary (former Boston star Duffy Lewis). Single cards measure 2-7/8" x 4". Besides including panels in boxes of cookies, the '55 Johnstons could be ordered for 5¢ per panel by mail. The scarcest of the Johnston's issues, the 1955 set can be found today still in complete panels, or as single cards.

		NM	EX	VG
Complete Folder Set:		1600.	800.00	475.00
Complete Singles Set (35):		750.00	375.00	225.00
Common Player:		20.00	10.00	6.00
Common Folder:		125.00	62.00	37.00
1	Del Crandall	20.00	10.00	6.00
3	Jim Pendleton	20.00	10.00	6.00
4	Danny O'Connell	20.00	10.00	6.00
6	Jack Dittmer	20.00	10.00	6.00
9	Joe Adcock	20.00	10.00	6.00
10	Bob Buhl	20.00	10.00	6.00
11	Phil Paine	20.00	10.00	6.00
12	Ray Crone	20.00	10.00	6.00
15	Charlie Gorin	20.00	10.00	6.00
16	Dave Jolly	20.00	10.00	6.00
17	Chet Nichols	20.00	10.00	6.00
18	Chuck Tanner	20.00	10.00	6.00
19	Jim Wilson	20.00	10.00	6.00
20	Dave Koslo	20.00	10.00	6.00
21	Warren Spahn	80.00	40.00	24.00
22	Gene Conley	20.00	10.00	6.00
23	John Logan	20.00	10.00	6.00
24	Charlie White	20.00	10.00	6.00
28	Johnny Cooney	20.00	10.00	6.00
30	Roy Smalley	20.00	10.00	6.00
31	Bucky Walters	20.00	10.00	6.00
32	Ernie Johnson	20.00	10.00	6.00
33	Lew Burdette	20.00	10.00	6.00
34	Bobby Thomson	25.00	12.50	7.50
35	Bob Keely	20.00	10.00	6.00
38	Billy Bruton	20.00	10.00	6.00
39	George Crowe	20.00	10.00	6.00
40	Charlie Grimm	20.00	10.00	6.00
41	Eddie Mathews	80.00	40.00	24.00
44	Hank Aaron	400.00	200.00	120.00
47	Joe Jay	20.00	10.00	6.00
48	Andy Pakfo	20.00	10.00	6.00
----	Dr. Charles K. Lacks	20.00	10.00	6.00
---	Duffy Lewis	20.00	10.00	6.00
---	Joe Taylor	20.00	10.00	6.00
Series 1 Folder	Hank Aaron, Lew Burdette, Del Crandall, Charlie Gorin, Bob Keely, Danny O'Connell	550.00	275.00	165.00
Series 2 Folder	Joe Adcock, Joe Jay, Dr. Charles K. Lacks, Chet Nichols, Andy Pafko, Charlie White	175.00	85.00	50.00
Series 3 Folder	Gene Conley, George Crowe, Jim Pendleton, Roy Smalley, Warren Spahn, Joe Taylor	225.00	110.00	65.00
Series 4 Folder	Billy Bruton, John Cooney, Dave Jolly, Dave Koslo, Johnny Logan, Andy Pafko	175.00	85.00	50.00
Series 5 Folder	Ray Crone, Ernie Johnson, Duffy Lewis, Eddie Mathews, Phil Paine, Chuck Tanner	250.00	125.00	75.00
Series 6 Folder	Bob Buhl, Jack Dittmer, Charlie Grimm, Bobby Thomson, Bucky Walters, Jim Wilson	175.00	85.00	50.00

1933 Josetti Tobacco

This is one of several early 1930s German cigarette cards to picture Babe Ruth. In this case he is pictured on the 1-5/8" x 2-3/8" black-and-white card with American comedic actor Harold Lloyd. The card is part of a numbered set of 256 celebrity cards. Backs are printed in German. The card can be found with Ruth's first name printed as George or as Babe.

		NM	EX	VG
151a	George Ruth, Harold Lloyd	500.00	250.00	150.00
151b	Babe Ruth, Harold Lloyd	500.00	250.00	150.00

1910 Ju-Ju Drums (E286)

Issued in 1910 with Ju-Ju Drum Candy, this extremely rare set of circular baseball cards is very similar in design to the more common Colgan's Chips cards. About the size of a silver dollar (1-7/16" in diameter) the cards display a player photo on the front with the player's name and team printed below in a semi-circle design. The backs carry advertising for Ju Ju Drums. The checklist contains 45 different players to date, but the issue - known as E286 in the American Card Catalog - is so rare that others are likely to exist.

		NM	EX	VG
Complete Set (45):		25600.	10250.	6150.
Common Player:		400.00	160.00	95.00
(1)	Eddie Ainsmith	400.00	160.00	95.00
(2)	Jimmy Austin	400.00	160.00	95.00
(3)	Chief Bender	600.00	240.00	145.00
(4)	Bob Bescher	400.00	160.00	95.00
(5)	Bruno Bloch (Block)	400.00	160.00	95.00
(6)	Frank Burke	400.00	160.00	95.00
(7)	Donie Bush	400.00	160.00	95.00
(8)	Frank Chance	600.00	240.00	145.00
(9)	Harry Cheek	400.00	160.00	95.00
(10)	Ed Cicotte	500.00	200.00	120.00
(11)	Ty Cobb	4000.	1600.	960.00
(12)	King Cole	400.00	160.00	95.00
(13)	Jack Coombs	400.00	160.00	95.00
(14)	Bill Dahlen	400.00	160.00	95.00
(15)	Bert Daniels	400.00	160.00	95.00
(16)	Harry Davis	400.00	160.00	95.00
(17)	Larry Doyle	400.00	160.00	95.00
(18)	Rube Ellis	400.00	160.00	95.00
(19)	Cecil Ferguson	400.00	160.00	95.00
(20)	Russ Ford	400.00	160.00	95.00
(21)	Bob Harnion (Harmon)	400.00	160.00	95.00
(22)	Ham Hyatt	400.00	160.00	95.00
(23)	Red Kellifer (Killifer)	400.00	160.00	95.00
(24)	Art Kruger (Krueger)	400.00	160.00	95.00
(25)	Tommy Leach	400.00	160.00	95.00
(26)	Harry Lumley	400.00	160.00	95.00
(27)	Christy Mathewson	1200.	480.00	290.00
(28)	John McGraw	600.00	240.00	145.00
(29)	Deacon McGuire	400.00	160.00	95.00
(30)	Chief Meyers	400.00	160.00	95.00
(31)	Otto Miller	400.00	160.00	95.00
(32)	Charlie Mullen	400.00	160.00	95.00
(33)	Tom Needham	400.00	160.00	95.00
(34)	Rube Oldring	400.00	160.00	95.00
(35)	Barney Pelty	400.00	160.00	95.00
(36)	Ed Reulbach	400.00	160.00	95.00
(37)	Jack Rowan	400.00	160.00	95.00
(38)	Dave Shean	400.00	160.00	95.00
(39)	Tris Speaker	750.00	300.00	180.00
(40)	Ed Sweeney	400.00	160.00	95.00
(41)	Honus Wagner	1200.	480.00	290.00
(42)	Jimmy Walsh	400.00	160.00	95.00
(43)	Kirby White	400.00	160.00	95.00
(44)	Ralph Works	400.00	160.00	95.00
(45)	Elmer Zacher	400.00	160.00	95.00

1893 Just So Tobacco

This set, issued by the Just So tobacco brand in 1893, is so rare that only a dozen or so examples are known, although more undoubtedly exist. The set features only members of the Cleveland club, known then as the "Spiders." Measuring 2-1/2" x 3-7/8", these sepia-colored cards were printed on heavy paper. The player appears in a portrait photo with his name beneath and an ad for Just So Tobacco along the bottom. The existence of this set wasn't even established until the 1960s, and for 15 years only two subjects were known. In 1981 and 1989 several more cards were discovered. To date only one or two copies of the known cards have turned up in collectors' hands, making it among the rarest of all baseball card issues.

		NM	EX	VG
Common Player:		2500.	1000.	600.00
(1)	F.W. Boyd	2500.	1000.	600.00
(2)	Burkette (Jesse Burkett)	3000.	1200.	720.00
(3)	C.L. Childs ("Cupid")	2500.	1000.	600.00
(4)	John Clarkson	3500.	1400.	840.00
(5)	J.O. Connor (John O'Connor)	2500.	1000.	600.00
(6)	G. Cuppy	2500.	1000.	600.00
(7)	G.W. Davies	2500.	1000.	600.00
(8)	C.M. Hastings	2500.	1000.	600.00
(9)	E.J. McKean	2500.	1000.	600.00
(10)	CAPt Tebeau ("Patsy")	2500.	1000.	600.00
(11)	J.K. Virtue	2500.	1000.	600.00
(12)	T.C. Williams	2500.	1000.	600.00
(13)	D.T. Young (Cy)	4500.	1800.	1080.
(14)	C.L. Zimmer ("Chief")	2500.	1000.	600.00

K

1980 K-Mart Cello Pack Header Card

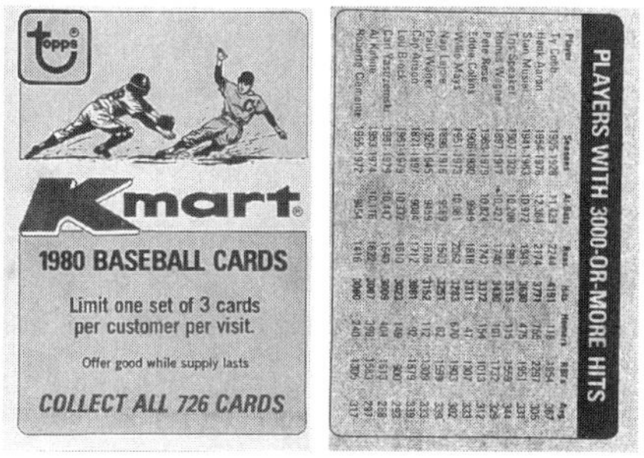

Squirt was one of several businesses in 1980 which used four-card cello packs of Topps baseball cards as a promotional premium. Besides the three regular-issue 1980 cards in each pack, there was a header card with the sponsor's advertising in full color on front. On back of the header card is a chart of major league lifetime .300 hitters.

	NM	EX	VG
K-Mart/3,000+ hits	2.00	1.00	.60

1950s Kabaya Caramel Babe Ruth

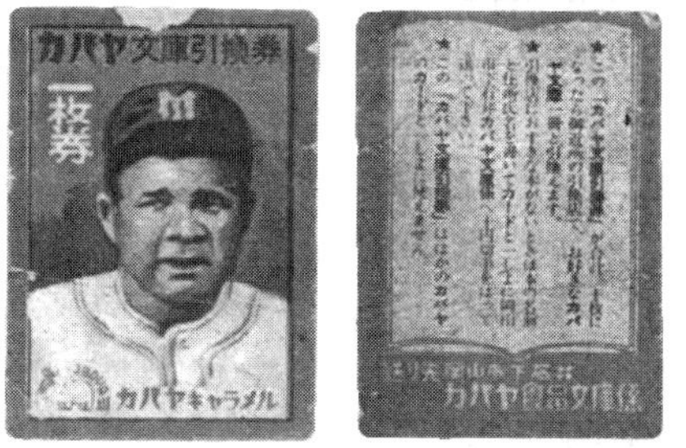

This card was part of a series produced by an Okayama, Japan candy company. The card measures about 1-1/2" x 2-1/8" with color artwork of Ruth on front. On back is Japanese script within the design of an open book.

	NM	EX	VG
Babe Ruth	1200.	600.00	350.00

1955 Kahn's Wieners Reds

The first of what would become 15 successive years of baseball card issues by the Kahn's meat company of Cincinnati is also the rarest. The set consists of six Cincinnati Redlegs player cards, 3-1/4" x 4". Printed in black and white, with blank backs, the '55 Kahn's cards were distributed at a one-day promotional event at a Cincinnati amusement park, where the featured players were on hand to sign autographs. Like the other Kahn's issues through 1963, the '55 cards have a 1/2" white panel containing an advertising message below the player photo. These cards are sometimes found with this portion cut off, greatly reducing the value of the card.

		NM	EX	VG
Complete Set (6):		3250.	1600.	975.00
Common Player:		450.00	225.00	135.00
(1)	Gus Bell	750.00	375.00	225.00
(2)	Ted Kluszewski	800.00	400.00	240.00
(3)	Roy McMillan	450.00	225.00	135.00
(4)	Joe Nuxhall	450.00	225.00	135.00
(5)	Wally Post	450.00	225.00	135.00
(6)	Johnny Temple	450.00	225.00	135.00

1956 Kahn's Wieners Reds

In 1956, Kahn's expanded its baseball card program to include 15 Redlegs players, and began issuing the cards one per pack in packages of hot dogs. Because the cards were packaged in direct contact with the meat, they are often found today in stained condition. In 3-1/4" x 4" format, black and white with blank backs, the '56 Kahn's cards can be distinguished from later issues by the presence of full stadium photographic backgrounds behind the player photos. Like all Kahn's issues, the 1956 set is unnumbered; the checklists are arranged alphabetically for convenience. The set features the first-ever baseball card of Hall of Famer Frank Robinson.

		NM	EX	VG
Complete Set (15):		1800.	900.00	550.00
Common Player:		95.00	47.00	28.00
(1)	Ed Bailey	95.00	47.00	28.00
(2)	Gus Bell	100.00	50.00	30.00

(3)	Joe Black	125.00	62.00	37.00
(4)	"Smokey" Burgess	125.00	62.00	37.00
(5)	Art Fowler	95.00	47.00	28.00
(6)	Hershell Freeman	95.00	47.00	28.00
(7)	Ray Jablonski	95.00	47.00	28.00
(8)	John Klippstein	95.00	47.00	28.00
(9)	Ted Kluszewski	225.00	112.00	67.00
(10)	Brooks Lawrence	95.00	47.00	28.00
(11)	Roy McMillan	95.00	47.00	28.00
(12)	Joe Nuxhall	95.00	47.00	28.00
(13)	Wally Post	95.00	47.00	28.00
(14)	Frank Robinson	425.00	212.00	127.00
(15)	Johnny Temple	95.00	47.00	28.00

1957 Kahn's Wieners

In its third season of baseball card issue, Kahn's kept the basic 3-1/4" x 4" format, with black-and-white photos and blank backs. The issue was expanded to 28 players, all Pirates or Reds. The last of the blank-backed Kahn's sets until 1966, the 1957 Reds players can be distinguished from the 1956 issue by the general lack of background photo detail, in favor of a neutral light gray background. The Dick Groat card appears with two name variations, a facsimile autograph, "Richard Groat," and a printed "Dick Groat." Both Groat varieties are included in the complete set price.

		NM	EX	VG
Complete Set (29):		4000.	2000.	1200.
Common Player:		95.00	45.00	25.00
(1)	Tom Acker	95.00	45.00	25.00
(2)	Ed Bailey	95.00	45.00	25.00
(3)	Gus Bell	125.00	62.00	37.00
(4)	Smokey Burgess	125.00	62.00	37.00
(5)	Roberto Clemente	950.00	475.00	285.00
(6)	George Crowe	95.00	45.00	25.00
(7)	Elroy Face	125.00	62.00	37.00
(8)	Hershell Freeman	95.00	45.00	25.00
(9)	Robert Friend	95.00	45.00	25.00
(10a)	Dick Groat	250.00	125.00	75.00
(10b)	Richard Groat	250.00	125.00	75.00
(11)	Don Gross	95.00	45.00	25.00
(12)	Warren Hacker	95.00	45.00	25.00
(13)	Don Hoak	110.00	55.00	33.00
(14)	Hal Jeffcoat	95.00	45.00	25.00
(15)	Ron Kline	95.00	45.00	25.00
(16)	John Klippstein	95.00	45.00	25.00
(17)	Ted Kluszewski	200.00	100.00	60.00
(18)	Brooks Lawrence	95.00	45.00	25.00
(19)	Dale Long	95.00	45.00	25.00
(20)	Bill Mazeroski	200.00	100.00	60.00
(21)	Roy McMillan	95.00	45.00	25.00
(22)	Joe Nuxhall	95.00	45.00	25.00
(23)	Wally Post	95.00	45.00	25.00
(24)	Frank Robinson	375.00	175.00	105.00
(25)	Johnny Temple	95.00	45.00	25.00
(26)	Frank Thomas	95.00	45.00	25.00
(27)	Bob Thurman	95.00	45.00	25.00
(28)	Lee Walls	95.00	45.00	25.00

1958 Kahn's Wieners

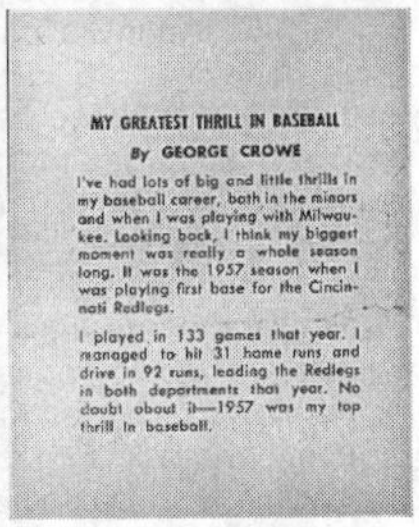
MY GREATEST THRILL IN BASEBALL

By GEORGE CROWE

I've had lots of big and little thrills in my baseball career, both in the minors and when I was playing with Milwaukee. Looking back, I think my biggest moment was really a whole season long. It was the 1957 season when I was playing first base for the Cincinnati Redlegs.

I played in 133 games that year. I managed to hit 31 home runs and drive in 92 runs, leading the Redlegs in both departments that year. No doubt about it—1957 was my top thrill in baseball.

Long-time Cincinnati favorite Wally Post became the only Philadelphia Phillies ballplayer to appear in the 15-year run of Kahn's issues when he was traded in 1958, but included as part of the otherwise exclusively Pirates-Reds set. Like previous years, the '58 Kahn's were 3-1/4" x 4", with black and white player photos. Unlike previous years, however, the cards had printing on the back, a story by the pictured player, titled "My Greatest Thrill in Baseball." Quite similar to the 1959 issue, the '58 Kahn's can be distinguished by the fact that the top line of the advertising panel at bottom has the word "Wieners" in 1958, but not in 1959.

		NM	EX	VG
Complete Set (29):		3500.	1750.	1050.
Common Player:		70.00	35.00	21.00
(1)	Ed Bailey	70.00	35.00	21.00
(2)	Gene Baker	70.00	35.00	21.00
(3)	Gus Bell	80.00	40.00	24.00
(4)	Smokey Burgess	80.00	40.00	24.00
(5)	Roberto Clemente	575.00	287.00	172.00
(6)	George Crowe	70.00	35.00	21.00
(7)	Elroy Face	75.00	37.00	22.00
(8)	Henry Foiles	70.00	35.00	21.00
(9)	Dee Fondy	70.00	35.00	21.00
(10)	Robert Friend	80.00	40.00	24.00
(11)	Richard Groat	90.00	45.00	27.00
(12)	Harvey Haddix	80.00	40.00	24.00
(13)	Don Hoak	80.00	40.00	24.00
(14)	Hal Jeffcoat	80.00	40.00	24.00
(15)	Ronald L. Kline	80.00	40.00	24.00
(16)	Ted Kluszewski	150.00	75.00	45.00
(17)	Vernon Law	80.00	40.00	24.00
(18)	Brooks Lawrence	70.00	35.00	21.00
(19)	Bill Mazeroski	150.00	75.00	45.00
(20)	Roy McMillan	70.00	35.00	21.00
(21)	Joe Nuxhall	80.00	40.00	24.00
(22)	Wally Post	300.00	150.00	90.00
(23)	John Powers	70.00	35.00	21.00
(24)	Robert T. Purkey	70.00	35.00	21.00
(25)	Charles Rabe	300.00	150.00	90.00
(26)	Frank Robinson	350.00	175.00	105.00
(27)	Robert Skinner	70.00	35.00	21.00
(28)	Johnny Temple	70.00	35.00	21.00
(29)	Frank Thomas	300.00	150.00	90.00

1959 Kahn's Wieners

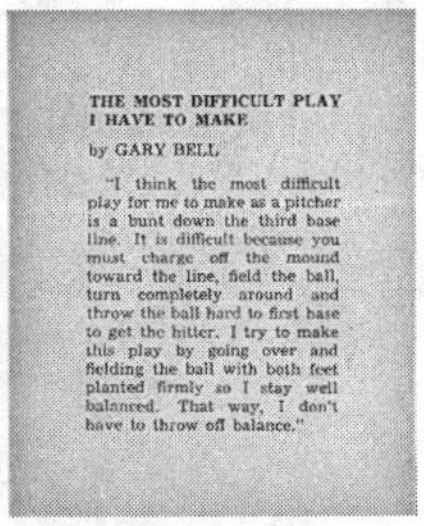
THE MOST DIFFICULT PLAY I HAVE TO MAKE

by GARY BELL

"I think the most difficult play for me to make as a pitcher is a bunt down the third base line. It is difficult because you must charge off the mound toward the line, field the ball, turn completely around and throw the ball hard to first base to get the hitter. I try to make this play by going over and fielding the ball with both feet planted firmly so I stay well balanced. That way, I don't have to throw off balance."

A third team was added to the Kahn's lineup in 1959, the Cleveland Indians joining the Pirates and Reds, bringing the number of cards in the set to 38. Again printed in black and white in the 3-1/4" x 4" size, the 1959 Kahn's cards can be differentiated from the previous issue by the lack of the word "Wieners" on the top line of the advertising panel at bottom. Backs again featured a story written by the pictured player, titled "The Toughest Play I Had to Make," "My Most Difficult Moment in Baseball," or "The Toughest Batters I Have to Face."

		NM	EX	VG
Complete Set (38):		5100.	2550.	1500.
Common Player:		70.00	35.00	21.00
(1)	Ed Bailey	70.00	35.00	21.00
(2)	Gary Bell	70.00	35.00	21.00
(3)	Gus Bell	70.00	35.00	21.00
(4)	Richard Brodowski	495.00	247.00	148.00
(5)	Forrest Burgess	70.00	35.00	21.00
(6)	Roberto Clemente	600.00	300.00	180.00
(7)	Rocky Colavito	125.00	62.00	37.00
(8)	ElRoy Face	75.00	37.00	22.00
(9)	Robert Friend	75.00	37.00	22.00
(10)	Joe Gordon	75.00	37.00	22.00
(11)	Jim Grant	70.00	35.00	21.00
(12)	Richard M. Groat	80.00	40.00	24.00
(13)	Harvey Haddix	445.00	222.00	133.00
(14)	Woodie Held	445.00	222.00	133.00
(15)	Don Hoak	75.00	37.00	22.00
(16)	Ronald Kline	70.00	35.00	21.00
(17)	Ted Kluszewski	125.00	62.00	37.00
(18)	Vernon Law	70.00	35.00	21.00
(19)	Jerry Lynch	70.00	35.00	21.00
(20)	Billy Martin	115.00	57.00	34.00
(21)	Bill Mazeroski	125.00	62.00	37.00
(22)	Cal McLish	445.00	222.00	133.00
(23)	Roy McMillan	70.00	35.00	21.00
(24)	Minnie Minoso	80.00	40.00	24.00
(25)	Russell Nixon	70.00	35.00	21.00
(26)	Joe Nuxhall	70.00	35.00	21.00
(27)	Jim Perry	75.00	37.00	22.00
(28)	Vada Pinson	80.00	40.00	24.00
(29)	Vic Power	70.00	35.00	21.00
(30)	Robert Purkey	70.00	35.00	21.00
(31)	Frank Robinson	235.00	117.00	70.00
(32)	Herb Score	70.00	35.00	21.00
(33)	Robert Skinner	70.00	35.00	21.00
(34)	George Strickland	70.00	35.00	21.00
(35)	Richard L. Stuart	70.00	35.00	21.00
(36)	John Temple	70.00	35.00	21.00
(37)	Frank Thomas	75.00	37.00	22.00
(38)	George A. Witt	70.00	35.00	21.00

1960 Kahn's Wieners

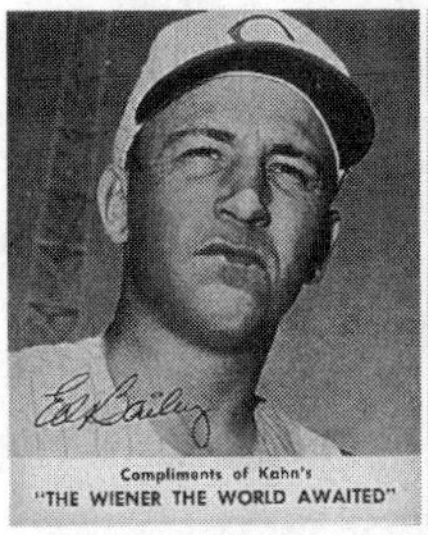

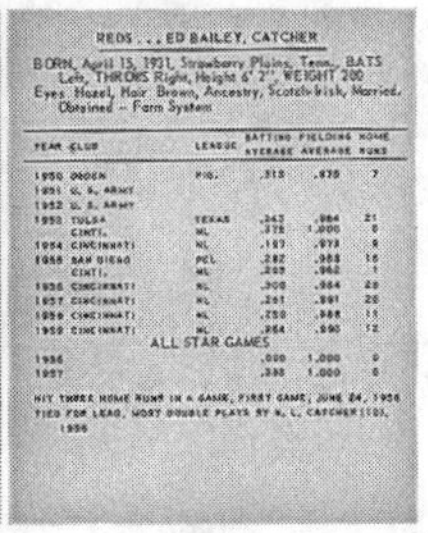

Three more teams joined the Kahn's roster in 1960, the Chicago Cubs, Chicago White Sox and St. Louis Cardinals. A total of 42 different players are represented in the set. Again 3-1/4" x 4" with black and white photos, the 1960 Kahn's cards featured for the first time player stats and personal data on the back, except Harvey Kuenn, which was issued with blank back, probably because of the lateness of his trade to the Indians.

		NM	EX	VG
Complete Set (42):		2500.	1250.	750.00
Common Player:		40.00	20.00	12.00
(1)	Ed Bailey	40.00	20.00	12.00
(2)	Gary Bell	40.00	20.00	12.00
(3)	Gus Bell	45.00	22.00	13.50
(4)	Forrest Burgess	45.00	22.00	13.50
(5)	Gino N. Cimoli	40.00	20.00	12.00
(6)	Roberto Clemente	400.00	200.00	120.00
(7)	ElRoy Face	45.00	22.00	13.50
(8)	Tito Francona	45.00	22.00	13.50
(9)	Robert Friend	45.00	22.00	13.50
(10)	Jim Grant	40.00	20.00	12.00
(11)	Richard Groat	50.00	25.00	15.00
(12)	Harvey Haddix	45.00	22.00	13.50
(13)	Woodie Held	40.00	20.00	12.00
(14)	Bill Henry	40.00	20.00	12.00
(15)	Don Hoak	45.00	22.00	13.50
(16)	Jay Hook	40.00	20.00	12.00
(17)	Eddie Kasko	40.00	20.00	12.00
(18)	Ronnie Kline	50.00	25.00	15.00
(19)	Ted Kluszewski	100.00	50.00	30.00
(20)	Harvey Kuenn	200.00	100.00	60.00
(21)	Vernon S. Law	45.00	22.00	13.50
(22)	Brooks Lawrence	40.00	20.00	12.00
(23)	Jerry Lynch	40.00	20.00	12.00
(24)	Billy Martin	90.00	45.00	27.00
(25)	Bill Mazeroski	100.00	50.00	30.00
(26)	Cal McLish	40.00	20.00	12.00
(27)	Roy McMillan	40.00	20.00	12.00
(28)	Don Newcombe	45.00	22.00	13.50
(29)	Russ Nixon	40.00	20.00	12.00
(30)	Joe Nuxhall	45.00	22.00	13.50
(31)	James J. O'Toole	40.00	20.00	12.00
(32)	Jim Perry	45.00	22.00	13.50
(33)	Vada Pinson	50.00	25.00	15.00
(34)	Vic Power	40.00	20.00	12.00
(35)	Robert T. Purkey	40.00	20.00	12.00
(36)	Frank Robinson	200.00	100.00	60.00
(37)	Herb Score	45.00	22.00	13.50
(38)	Robert R. Skinner	40.00	20.00	12.00
(39)	Richard L. Stuart	45.00	22.00	13.50
(40)	John Temple	40.00	20.00	12.00
(41)	Frank Thomas	50.00	25.00	15.00
(42)	Lee Walls	45.00	22.00	13.50

1961 Kahn's Wieners

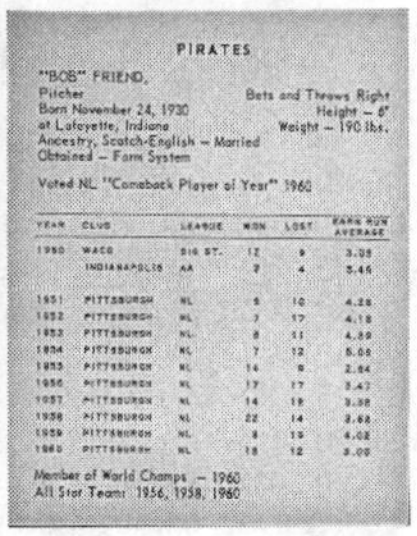

After a single season, the Chicago and St. Louis teams dropped out of the Kahn's program, but the 1961 set was larger than ever, at 43 cards. The same basic format - 3-1/4" x 4" size, black-and-white photos and statistical information on the back - was retained. For the first time in '61, the meat company made complete sets of the Kahn's cards available to collectors via a mail-in offer. This makes the 1961 and later Kahn's cards considerably easier to obtain than the earlier issues.

		NM	EX	VG
Complete Set (43):		1150.	600.00	350.00
Common Player:		18.00	9.00	5.50
(1)	John A. Antonelli	20.00	10.00	6.00
(2)	Ed Bailey	18.00	9.00	5.50
(3)	Gary Bell	18.00	9.00	5.50
(4)	Gus Bell	20.00	10.00	6.00
(5)	James P. Brosnan	18.00	9.00	5.50
(6)	Forrest Burgess	20.00	10.00	6.00
(7)	Gino Cimoli	18.00	9.00	5.50
(8)	Roberto Clemente	400.00	200.00	120.00
(9)	Gordon Coleman	18.00	9.00	5.50
(10)	Jimmie Dykes	18.00	9.00	5.50
(11)	ElRoy Face	22.00	11.00	6.50
(12)	Tito Francona	18.00	9.00	5.50
(13)	Gene L. Freese	18.00	9.00	5.50
(14)	Robert Friend	20.00	10.00	6.00
(15)	Jim Grant	18.00	9.00	5.50
(16)	Richard M. Groat	25.00	12.50	7.50
(17)	Harvey Haddix	20.00	10.00	6.00
(18)	Woodie Held	18.00	9.00	5.50
(19)	Don Hoak	20.00	10.00	6.00
(20)	Jay Hook	18.00	9.00	5.50
(21)	Joe Jay	18.00	9.00	5.50
(22)	Eddie Kasko	18.00	9.00	5.50
(23)	Willie Kirkland	18.00	9.00	5.50
(24)	Vernon S. Law	22.00	11.00	6.50
(25)	Jerry Lynch	18.00	9.00	5.50
(26)	Jim Maloney	22.00	11.00	6.50
(27)	Bill Mazeroski	40.00	20.00	12.00
(28)	Wilmer D. Mizell	18.00	9.00	5.50
(29)	Glenn R. Nelson	18.00	9.00	5.50
(30)	James J. O'Toole	18.00	9.00	5.50
(31)	Jim Perry	20.00	10.00	6.00
(32)	John M. Phillips	18.00	9.00	5.50
(33)	Vada E. Pinson Jr.	25.00	12.50	7.50
(34)	Wally Post	18.00	9.00	5.50
(35)	Vic Power	18.00	9.00	5.50
(36)	Robert T. Purkey	18.00	9.00	5.50
(37)	Frank Robinson	120.00	60.00	36.00
(38)	John A. Romano Jr.	18.00	9.00	5.50
(39)	Dick Schofield	18.00	9.00	5.50
(40)	Robert Skinner	18.00	9.00	5.50
(41)	Hal Smith	18.00	9.00	5.50
(42)	Richard Stuart	20.00	10.00	6.00
(43)	John E. Temple	18.00	9.00	5.50

1962 Kahn's Wieners

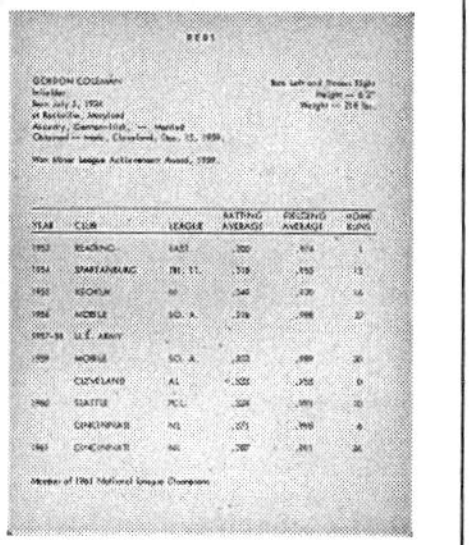

Besides the familiar Reds, Pirates and Indians players in the 1962 Kahn's set, a fourth team was added, the Minnesota Twins, though the overall size of the set was decreased from the previous year, to 38 players in 1962. The cards retained the 3-1/4" x 4" black-and-white format of previous years. The '62 Kahn's set is awash in variations. Besides the photo and front design variations on the Bell, Purkey and Power cards, each Cleveland player can be found with two back variations, listing the team either as "Cleveland" or "Cleveland Indians." The complete set values listed below include all variations.

		NM	EX	VG
Complete Set (51):		2100.	1050.	625.00
Common Player:		13.50	6.75	4.00
(1a)	Gary Bell (fat man in background)	135.00	67.00	40.00
(1b)	Gary Bell (no fat man)	34.00	17.00	10.00
(2)	James P. Brosnan	13.50	6.75	4.00
(3)	Forrest Burgess	18.00	9.00	5.50
(4)	Leonardo Cardenas	13.50	6.75	4.00
(5)	Roberto Clemente	175.00	87.00	52.00
(6a)	Ty Cline (Cleveland Indians back)	65.00	32.00	19.50
(6b)	Ty Cline (Cleveland back)	25.00	12.50	7.50
(7)	Gordon Coleman	13.50	6.75	4.00
(8)	Dick Donovan	25.00	12.50	7.50
(9)	John Edwards	13.50	6.75	4.00
(10a)	Tito Francona (Cleveland Indians back)	65.00	32.00	19.50
(10b)	Tito Francona (Cleveland back)	25.00	12.50	7.50
(11)	Gene Freese	13.50	6.75	4.00
(12)	Robert B. Friend	18.00	9.00	5.50
(13)	Joe Gibbon	75.00	37.00	22.00
(14a)	Jim Grant (Cleveland Indians back)	65.00	32.00	19.50
(14b)	Jim Grant (Cleveland back)	25.00	12.50	7.50
(15)	Richard M. Groat	25.00	12.50	7.50
(16)	Harvey Haddix	18.00	9.00	5.50
(17a)	Woodie Held (Cleveland Indians back)	75.00	37.00	22.00
(17b)	Woodie Held (Cleveland back)	25.00	12.50	7.50
(18)	Bill Henry	13.50	6.75	4.00
(19)	Don Hoak	18.00	9.00	5.50
(20)	Ken Hunt	13.50	6.75	4.00
(21)	Joseph R. Jay	13.50	6.75	4.00
(22)	Eddie Kasko	13.50	6.75	4.00
(23a)	Willie Kirkland (Cleveland Indians back)	65.00	32.00	19.50
(23b)	Willie Kirkland (Cleveland back)	25.00	12.50	7.50
(24a)	Barry Latman (Cleveland Indians back)	65.00	32.00	19.50
(24b)	Barry Latman (Cleveland back)	25.00	12.50	7.50
(25)	Jerry Lynch	13.50	6.75	4.00
(26)	Jim Maloney	18.00	9.00	5.50
(27)	Bill Mazeroski	25.00	12.50	7.50
(28)	Jim O'Toole	13.50	6.75	4.00
(29a)	Jim Perry (Cleveland Indians back)	75.00	37.00	22.00
(29b)	Jim Perry (Cleveland back)	25.00	12.50	7.50
(30a)	John M. Phillips (Cleveland Indians back)	65.00	32.00	19.50
(30b)	John M. Phillips (Cleveland back)	25.00	12.50	7.50
(31)	Vada E. Pinson	25.00	12.50	7.50
(32)	Wally Post	13.50	6.75	4.00
(33a)	Vic Power (Cleveland Indians back)	65.00	32.00	19.50
(33b)	Vic Power (Cleveland back)	25.00	12.50	7.50
(33c)	Vic Power (Minnesota Twins back)	135.00	67.00	40.00
(34a)	Robert T. Purkey (no autograph)	135.00	67.00	40.00
(34b)	Robert T. Purkey (with autograph)	34.00	17.00	10.00
(35)	Frank Robinson	75.00	37.00	22.00
(36a)	John Romano (Cleveland Indians back)	65.00	32.00	19.50
(36b)	John Romano (Cleveland back)	25.00	12.50	7.50
(37)	Dick Stuart	18.00	9.00	5.50
(38)	Bill Virdon	18.00	9.00	5.50

1963 Kahn's Wieners

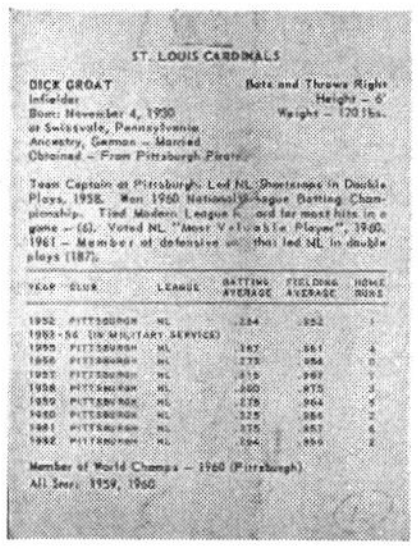

In 1963, for the first time since Kahn's began issuing baseball cards in 1955, the design underwent a significant change, white borders were added to the top and sides of player photo. Also, the card size was changed to 3-3/16" x 4-1/4". Statistical and personal data continued to be printed on the card backs. Joining traditional Reds, Pirates and Indians personnel in the 30-card 1963 set were a handful of New York Yankees and Dick Groat, in his new identity as a St. Louis Cardinal.

		NM	EX	VG
Complete Set (30):		800.00	400.00	240.00
Common Player:		15.00	7.50	4.50
(1)	Robert Bailey	15.00	7.50	4.50
(2)	Don Blasingame	15.00	7.50	4.50
(3)	Clete Boyer	25.00	12.50	7.50
(4)	Forrest Burgess	20.00	10.00	6.00
(5)	Leonardo Cardenas	15.00	7.50	4.50
(6)	Roberto Clemente	180.00	90.00	54.00
(7)	Don Clendennon (Donn Clendenon)	15.00	7.50	4.50
(8)	Gordon Coleman	15.00	7.50	4.50
(9)	John A. Edwards	15.00	7.50	4.50
(10)	Gene Freese	15.00	7.50	4.50
(11)	Robert B. Friend	20.00	10.00	6.00
(12)	Joe Gibbon	15.00	7.50	4.50
(13)	Dick Groat	25.00	12.50	7.50
(14)	Harvey Haddix	20.00	10.00	6.00
(15)	Elston Howard	30.00	15.00	9.00
(16)	Joey Jay	15.00	7.50	4.50
(17)	Eddie Kasko	15.00	7.50	4.50
(18)	Tony Kubek	30.00	15.00	9.00
(19)	Jerry Lynch	15.00	7.50	4.50
(20)	Jim Maloney	20.00	10.00	6.00
(21)	Bill Mazeroski	40.00	20.00	12.00
(22)	Joe Nuxhall	20.00	10.00	6.00
(23)	Jim O'Toole	15.00	7.50	4.50
(24)	Vada E. Pinson	24.00	12.00	7.25
(25)	Robert T. Purkey	15.00	7.50	4.50
(26)	Bob Richardson	30.00	15.00	9.00
(27)	Frank Robinson	80.00	40.00	24.00
(28)	Bill Stafford	20.00	10.00	6.00
(29)	Ralph W. Terry	24.00	12.00	7.25
(30)	Bill Virdon	22.00	11.00	6.50

1964 Kahn's Wieners

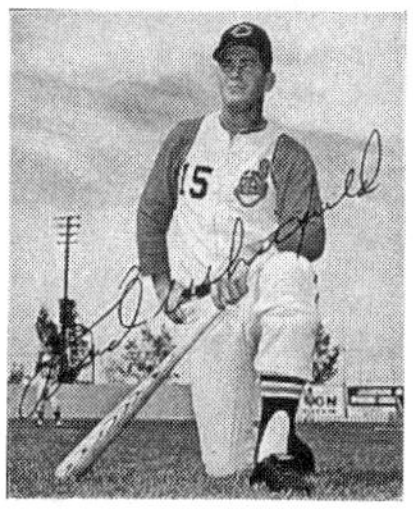

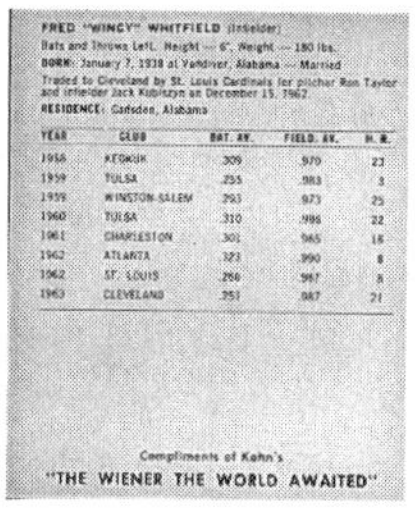

After nearly a decade of virtually identical card issues, the 1964 Kahn's issue was an abrupt change. In a new size, 3" x 3-1/2", the nearly square cards featured a borderless color photo. The only other design element on the front of the card was a facsimile autograph. The advertising slogan which had traditionally appeared on the front of the card was moved to the back, where it joined the player's stats and personal data. The teams in the 1964 issue once again reverted to the Reds, Pirates and Indians, for a total of 31 cards.

		NM	EX	VG
Complete Set (31):		900.00	450.00	270.00
Common Player:		10.00	5.00	3.00
(1)	Max Alvis	10.00	5.00	3.00
(2)	Bob Bailey	10.00	5.00	3.00
(3)	Leonardo Cardenas	10.00	5.00	3.00
(4)	Roberto Clemente	150.00	75.00	45.00
(5)	Donn A. Clendenon	10.00	5.00	3.00
(6)	Victor Davalillo	10.00	5.00	3.00
(7)	Dick Donovan	10.00	5.00	3.00
(8)	John A. Edwards	10.00	5.00	3.00
(9)	Robert Friend	12.00	6.00	3.50
(10)	Jim Grant	10.00	5.00	3.00
(11)	Tommy Harper	10.00	5.00	3.00
(12)	Woodie Held	10.00	5.00	3.00
(13)	Joey Jay	10.00	5.00	3.00
(14)	Jack Kralick	10.00	5.00	3.00
(15)	Jerry Lynch	10.00	5.00	3.00
(16)	Jim Maloney	14.00	7.00	4.25
(17)	Bill Mazeroski	35.00	17.50	10.50
(18)	Alvin McBean	10.00	5.00	3.00
(19)	Joe Nuxhall	14.00	7.00	4.25
(20)	Jim Pagliaroni	10.00	5.00	3.00
(21)	Vada E. Pinson Jr.	20.00	10.00	6.00
(22)	Robert T. Purkey	10.00	5.00	3.00
(23)	Pedro Ramos	10.00	5.00	3.00
(24)	Frank Robinson	80.00	40.00	24.00
(25)	John Romano	10.00	5.00	3.00
(26)	Pete Rose	350.00	175.00	105.00
(27)	John Tsitouris	10.00	5.00	3.00
(28)	Robert A. Veale Jr.	10.00	5.00	3.00
(29)	Bill Virdon	14.00	7.00	4.25
(30)	Leon Wagner	10.00	5.00	3.00
(31)	Fred Whitfield	10.00	5.00	3.00

1965 Kahn's Wieners

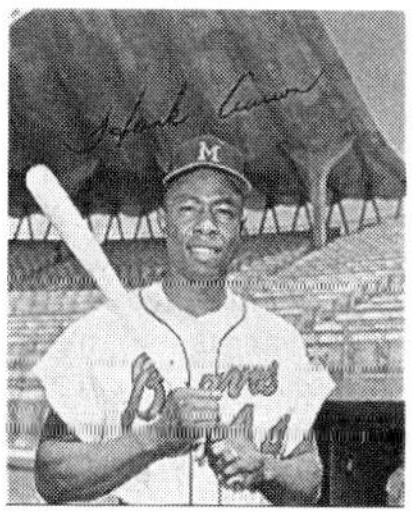

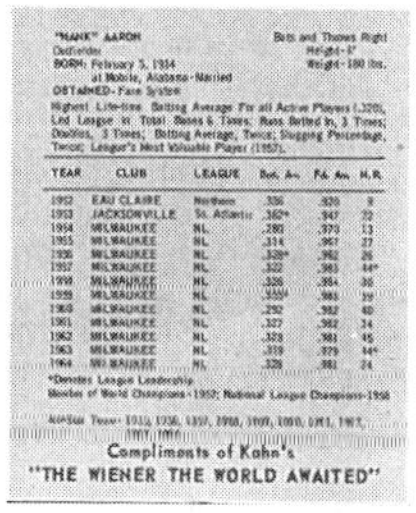

There was little change for the Kahn's issue in 1965 beyond the addition of Milwaukee Braves players to the Reds, Pirates and Indians traditionally included in the set. At 45 players, the 1965 issue was the largest of the Kahn's sets. Once again in 3" x 3-1/2" size, the 1965s retained the borderless color photo design of the previous season. A look at the stats on the back will confirm the year of issue, however, since the last year of statistics is the year prior to the card's issue.

		NM	EX	VG
Complete Set (45):		1100.	550.00	325.00
Common Player:		13.00	6.50	4.00
(1)	Hank Aaron	160.00	80.00	48.00
(2)	Max Alvis	13.00	6.50	4.00
(3)	Jose Azcue	13.00	6.50	4.00
(4)	Bob Bailey	13.00	6.50	4.00
(5)	Frank Bolling	13.00	6.50	4.00
(6)	Leonardo Cardenas	13.00	6.50	4.00
(7)	Rico Ricardo Carty	16.50	8.25	5.00
(8)	Donn A. Clendenon	13.00	6.50	4.00
(9)	Tony Cloninger	13.00	6.50	4.00
(10)	Gordon Coleman	13.00	6.50	4.00
(11)	Victor Davalillo	13.00	6.50	4.00
(12)	John A. Edwards	13.00	6.50	4.00
(13)	Sam Ellis	13.00	6.50	4.00
(14)	Robert Friend	16.50	8.25	5.00
(15)	Tommy Harper	13.00	6.50	4.00
(16)	Chuck Hinton	13.00	6.50	4.00
(17)	Dick Howser	16.50	8.25	5.00
(18)	Joey Jay	13.00	6.50	4.00
(19)	Deron Johnson	13.00	6.50	4.00
(20)	Jack Kralick	13.00	6.50	4.00
(21)	Denny Lemaster	13.00	6.50	4.00
(22)	Jerry Lynch	13.00	6.50	4.00
(23)	Jim Maloney	16.50	8.25	5.00
(24)	Lee Maye	13.00	6.50	4.00
(25)	Bill Mazeroski	35.00	17.50	10.50
(26)	Alvin McBean	13.00	6.50	4.00
(27)	Bill McCool	13.00	6.50	4.00
(28)	Sam McDowell	16.50	8.25	5.00
(29)	Donald McMahon	13.00	6.50	4.00
(30)	Denis Menke	13.00	6.50	4.00
(31)	Joe Nuxhall	16.50	8.25	5.00
(32)	Gene Oliver	13.00	6.50	4.00
(33)	Jim O'Toole	13.00	6.50	4.00
(34)	Jim Pagliaroni	13.00	6.50	4.00
(35)	Vada E. Pinson Jr.	24.00	12.00	7.25
(36)	Frank Robinson	120.00	60.00	36.00
(37)	Pete Rose	250.00	125.00	75.00
(38)	Willie Stargell	120.00	60.00	36.00
(39)	Ralph W. Terry	13.00	6.50	4.00
(40)	Luis Tiant	22.00	11.00	6.50
(41)	Joe Torre	27.50	13.50	8.25
(42)	John Tsitouris	13.00	6.50	4.00
(43)	Robert A. Veale Jr.	13.00	6.50	4.00
(44)	Bill Virdon	16.50	8.25	5.00
(45)	Leon Wagner	13.00	6.50	4.00

1966 Kahn's Wieners

The fourth new format in five years greeted collectors with the introduction of Kahn's 1966 issue. The design consists of a color photo bordered by white and yellow vertical stripes. The player's name is printed above the photo, and a facsimile autograph appears across the photo. As printed, the cards were 2-13/16" x 4" in size. However, the top portion consists of a 2-13/16" x 1-3/8" advertising panel with a red rose logo and the word "Kahn's," separated from the player portion of the card by a black dotted line. Naturally, many of the cards are found today with the top portion cut off. Values listed here are for cards with the top portion intact; cards without the ad portion are valued at 50% or less. Players from the Cincinnati Reds, Pittsburgh Pirates, Cleveland Indians and Atlanta Braves were included in the set. Since the cards are blank-backed, collectors must learn to differentiate player poses to determine year of issue for some cards.

		NM	EX	VG
Complete Set (32):		1200.	600.00	350.00
Common Player:		20.00	10.00	6.00
(1)	Henry Aaron	200.00	100.00	60.00
(2)	Felipe Alou	30.00	15.00	9.00
(3)	Max Alvis	20.00	10.00	6.00
(4)	Robert Bailey	20.00	10.00	6.00
(5)	Wade Blasingame	20.00	10.00	6.00
(6)	Frank Bolling	20.00	10.00	6.00
(7)	Leo Cardenas	20.00	10.00	6.00
(8)	Roberto Clemente	250.00	125.00	75.00
(9)	Tony Cloninger	20.00	10.00	6.00
(10)	Vic Davalillo	20.00	10.00	6.00
(11)	John Edwards	20.00	10.00	6.00
(12)	Sam Ellis	20.00	10.00	6.00
(13)	Pedro Gonzalez	20.00	10.00	6.00
(14)	Tommy Harper	20.00	10.00	6.00
(15)	Deron Johnson	20.00	10.00	6.00
(16)	Mack Jones	20.00	10.00	6.00
(17)	Denny Lemaster	20.00	10.00	6.00
(18)	Jim Maloney	24.00	12.00	7.25
(19)	Bill Mazeroski	45.00	22.00	13.50
(20)	Bill McCool	20.00	10.00	6.00
(21)	Sam McDowell	24.00	12.00	7.25
(22)	Denis Menke	20.00	10.00	6.00
(23)	Joe Nuxhall	24.00	12.00	7.25
(24)	Jim Pagliaroni	20.00	10.00	6.00
(25)	Milt Pappas	24.00	12.00	7.25
(26)	Vada Pinson	35.00	17.50	10.50
(27)	Pete Rose	275.00	137.00	82.00
(28)	Sonny Siebert	20.00	10.00	6.00
(29)	Willie Stargell	80.00	40.00	24.00
(30)	Joe Torre	30.00	15.00	9.00
(31)	Bob Veale	20.00	10.00	6.00
(32)	Fred Whitfield	20.00	10.00	6.00

1967 Kahn's Wieners

Retaining the 1966 format, the '67 Kahn's set was expanded to 41 players by adding several New York Mets to the previous season's lineup of Reds, Pirates, Indians and Braves. Making this set especially challenging for collectors is the fact that some cards are found in a smaller size and/or with different colored stripes bordering the color player photo. On the majority of cards, the size remained 2-13/16" x 4" (with ad at top; 2-13/16" x 2-5/8" without ad at top). However, because of packing in different products, some cards can be found in 2-13/16" x 3-1/4" size (with ad; 2-13/16" x 2-1/8" without ad). The border stripe variations are listed below. Values quoted are for cards with the top ad panel intact; values drop by 50% or more for cards without the ad portion. All variation cards are included in the valuations given for the complete set.

		NM	EX	VG
Complete Set (51):		1200.	600.00	350.00
Common Player:		15.00	7.50	4.50
(1a)	Henry Aaron (large size)	150.00	75.00	45.00
(1b)	Henry Aaron (small size)	150.00	75.00	45.00
(2)	Gene Alley	15.00	7.50	4.50
(3)	Felipe Alou	24.00	12.00	7.25
(4a)	Matty Alou (yellow & white striped border)	20.00	10.00	6.00
(4b)	Matty Alou (red & white striped border)	24.00	12.00	7.25
(5)	Max Alvis	15.00	7.50	4.50
(6a)	Ken Boyer (yellow & white striped border)	25.00	12.50	7.50
(6b)	Ken Boyer (red, white & green striped border)	30.00	15.00	9.00
(7)	Leo Cardenas	15.00	7.50	4.50
(8)	Rico Carty	18.00	9.00	5.50
(9)	Tony Cloninger	15.00	7.50	4.50
(10)	Tommy Davis	18.00	9.00	5.50
(11)	John Edwards	15.00	7.50	4.50
(12a)	Sam Ellis (large size)	15.00	7.50	4.50
(12b)	Sam Ellis (small size)	28.00	14.00	8.50
(13)	Jack Fisher	15.00	7.50	4.50
(14)	Steve Hargan	15.00	7.50	4.50
(15)	Tom Harper	15.00	7.50	4.50
(16a)	Tom Helms (large size)	15.00	7.50	4.50
(16b)	Tom Helms (small size)	30.00	15.00	9.00
(17)	Deron Johnson	15.00	7.50	4.50
(18)	Ken Johnson	15.00	7.50	4.50
(19)	Cleon Jones	15.00	7.50	4.50
(20a)	Ed Kranepool (yellow & white striped border)	15.00	7.50	4.50
(20b)	Ed Kranepool (red & white striped border)	25.00	12.50	7.50
(21a)	James Maloney (yellow & white striped border)	20.00	10.00	6.00
(21b)	James Maloney (red & white striped border)	24.00	12.00	7.25
(22)	Lee May	18.00	9.00	5.50
(23a)	Wm. Mazeroski (large size)	35.00	17.50	10.50
(23b)	Wm. Mazeroski (small size)	35.00	17.50	10.50
(24)	Wm. McCool	15.00	7.50	4.50
(25)	Sam McDowell	18.00	9.00	5.50
(26)	Dennis Menke (Denis)	15.00	7.50	4.50
(27)	Jim Pagliaroni	15.00	7.50	4.50
(28)	Don Pavletich	15.00	7.50	4.50
(29)	Tony Perez	35.00	17.50	10.50
(30)	Vada Pinson	26.00	13.00	7.75
(31)	Dennis Ribant	15.00	7.50	4.50
(32)	Pete Rose	175.00	87.00	52.00
(33)	Art Shamsky	15.00	7.50	4.50
(34)	Bob Shaw	15.00	7.50	4.50
(35)	Sonny Siebert	15.00	7.50	4.50
(36)	Wm. Stargell (first name actually Wilver)	60.00	30.00	18.00
(37a)	Joe Torre (large size)	24.00	12.00	7.25
(37b)	Joe Torre (small size)	30.00	15.00	9.00
(38)	Bob Veale	15.00	7.50	4.50
(39)	Leon Wagner	15.00	7.50	4.50
(40a)	Fred Whitfield (large size)	15.00	7.50	4.50
(40b)	Fred Whitfield (small size)	15.00	7.50	4.50
(41)	Woody Woodward	15.00	7.50	4.50

1968 Kahn's Wieners

The number of card size and stripe color variations increased with the 1968 Kahn's issue, though the basic card format was retained: 2-13/16" x 4" size (with ad panel at top; 2-13/16" x 2-5/8" with ad panel cut off), color photo bordered by yellow and white vertical stripes. In addition to the basic issue, a number of the cards appear in a smaller, 2-13/16" x 3-1/4", size, while some of them, and others, appear with variations in the color of border stripes. One card, Maloney, can be found with a top portion advertising Blue Mountain brand meats, as well as Kahn's. The 1968 set features the largest number of teams represented in any Kahn's issue: Braves, Cubs, White Sox, Reds, Indians, Tigers, Mets and Pirates. Values quoted are for cards with intact ad panel at top; cards without the ad are worth 50% or less. Complete set prices include all variations.

		NM	EX	VG
Complete Set (56):		1400.	700.00	420.00
Common Player:		17.00	8.50	5.00
(1a)	Hank Aaron (large size)	140.00	70.00	42.00
(1b)	Hank Aaron (small size)	170.00	85.00	51.00
(2)	Tommy Agee	17.00	8.50	5.00
(3a)	Gene Alley (large size)	17.00	8.50	5.00
(3b)	Gene Alley (small size)	28.00	14.00	8.50
(4)	Felipe Alou	21.00	10.50	6.25
(5a)	Matty Alou (yellow striped border)	23.00	11.50	7.00
(5b)	Matty Alou (red striped border)	28.00	14.00	8.50
(6a)	Max Alvis (large size)	17.00	8.50	5.00
(6b)	Max Alvis (small size)	28.00	14.00	8.50
(7)	Gerry Arrigo	17.00	8.50	5.00
(8)	John Bench	375.00	187.00	112.00
(9a)	Clete Boyer (large size)	17.00	8.50	5.00
(9b)	Clete Boyer (small size)	28.00	14.00	8.50
(10)	Larry Brown	17.00	8.50	5.00
(11a)	Leo Cardenas (large size)	17.00	8.50	5.00
(11b)	Leo Cardenas (small size)	28.00	14.00	8.50
(12a)	Bill Freehan (large size)	28.00	14.00	8.50
(12b)	Bill Freehan (small size)	33.00	16.50	10.00
(13)	Steve Hargan	17.00	8.50	5.00
(14)	Joel Horlen	17.00	8.50	5.00
(15)	Tony Horton	21.00	10.50	6.25
(16)	Willie Horton	21.00	10.50	6.25
(17)	Ferguson Jenkins	38.00	19.00	11.50
(18)	Deron Johnson	17.00	8.50	5.00
(19)	Mack Jones	17.00	8.50	5.00
(20)	Bob Lee	17.00	8.50	5.00
(21a)	Jim Maloney (large size, rose logo)	21.00	10.50	6.25
(21b)	Jim Maloney (large size, blue mountain logo)	38.00	19.00	11.50
(21c)	Jim Maloney (small size, yellow & white striped border)	28.00	14.00	8.50
(21d)	Jim Maloney (small size, yellow, white & green strip ed border)	28.00	14.00	8.50
(22a)	Lee May (large size)	23.00	11.50	7.00
(22b)	Lee May (small size)	28.00	14.00	8.50
(23a)	Wm. Mazeroski (large size)	35.00	17.50	10.50
(23b)	Wm. Mazeroski (small size)	38.00	19.00	11.50
(24)	Dick McAuliffe	17.00	8.50	5.00
(25)	Bill McCool	17.00	8.50	5.00
(26a)	Sam McDowell (yellow striped border)	23.00	11.50	7.00

		NM	EX	VG
(26b)	Sam McDowell (red striped border)	28.00	14.00	8.50
(27a)	Tony Perez (yellow striped border)	42.00	21.00	12.50
(27b)	Tony Perez (red striped border)	47.00	23.00	14.00
(28)	Gary Peters	17.00	8.50	5.00
(29a)	Vada Pinson (large size)	28.00	14.00	8.50
(29b)	Vada Pinson (small size)	33.00	16.50	10.00
(30)	Chico Ruiz	17.00	8.50	5.00
(31a)	Ron Santo (yellow striped border)	28.00	14.00	8.50
(31b)	Ron Santo (red striped border)	33.00	16.50	10.00
(32)	Art Shamsky	17.00	8.50	5.00
(33)	Luis Tiant	28.00	14.00	8.50
(34a)	Joe Torre (large size)	28.00	14.00	8.50
(34b)	Joe Torre (small size)	35.00	17.50	10.50
(35a)	Bob Veale (large size)	17.00	8.50	5.00
(35b)	Bob Veale (small size)	28.00	14.00	8.50
(36)	Leon Wagner	17.00	8.50	5.00
(37)	Billy Williams	55.00	27.00	16.50
(38)	Earl Wilson	17.00	8.50	5.00

1969 Kahn's Wieners

In its 15th consecutive year of baseball card issue, Kahn's continued the basic format adopted in 1966. The basic 22 players' cards were printed in 2-13/16" x 4" size (with ad panel at top; 2-13/16" x 2-5/8" without panel) and are blank-backed. Teams represented in the set are the Braves, Cubs, White Sox, Reds, Cardinals, Indians and Pirates. Cards feature a color photo and facsimile autograph bordered by yellow and white vertical stripes. At top is an ad panel consisting of the Kahn's red rose logo. However, because some cards were produced for inclusion in packages other than the standard hot dogs, a number of variations in card size and stripe color were created, as noted in the listings below. The smaller size cards, 2-13/16" x 3-1/4" with ad, 2-13/16" x 2-1/8" without ad, were created by more closely cropping the player photo at top and bottom. Values quoted are for cards with the top logo panel intact; deduct a minimum 50% for cards without the ad panel. Complete set values include all variations.

		NM	EX	VG
Complete Set (29):		1025.	510.00	300.00
Common Player:		19.00	9.50	5.75
(1a)	Hank Aaron (large size)	160.00	80.00	48.00
(1b)	Hank Aaron (small size)	190.00	95.00	57.00
(2)	Matty Alou	24.00	12.00	7.25
(3)	Max Alvis	19.00	9.50	5.75
(4)	Gerry Arrigo	19.00	9.50	5.75
(5)	Steve Blass	19.00	9.50	5.75
(6)	Clay Carroll	19.00	9.50	5.75
(7)	Tony Cloninger	19.00	9.50	5.75
(8)	George Culver	19.00	9.50	5.75
(9)	Joel Horlen	19.00	9.50	5.75
(10)	Tony Horton	24.00	12.00	7.25
(11)	Alex Johnson	19.00	9.50	5.75
(12a)	Jim Maloney (large size)	25.00	12.50	7.50
(12b)	Jim Maloney (small size)	30.00	15.00	9.00
(13a)	Lee May (yellow striped border)	25.00	12.50	7.50
(13b)	Lee May (red striped border)	30.00	15.00	9.00
(14a)	Bill Mazeroski (yellow striped border)	45.00	22.00	13.50
(14b)	Bill Mazeroski (red striped border)	50.00	25.00	15.00
(15a)	Sam McDowell (yellow striped border)	25.00	12.50	7.50
(15b)	Sam McDowell (red striped border)	30.00	15.00	9.00
(16a)	Tony Perez (large size)	45.00	22.00	13.50
(16b)	Tony Perez (small size)	50.00	25.00	15.00
(17)	Gary Peters	19.00	9.50	5.75
(18a)	Ron Santo (yellow striped border)	30.00	15.00	9.00
(18b)	Ron Santo (red striped border)	35.00	17.50	10.50
(19)	Luis Tiant	30.00	15.00	9.00
(20)	Joe Torre	30.00	15.00	9.00
(21)	Bob Veale	19.00	9.50	5.75
(22)	Billy Williams	65.00	32.00	19.50

1970s Kahn's Kielbasa Singles Carl Yastrzemski

The exact year or years of this label's issue are not known. The 4-7/8" x 3-1/8" cardboard package insert has a color portrait photo of baseball's most famous Polish player endorsing the polish sausage product.

	NM	EX	VG
Carl Yastrzemski	15.00	7.50	4.50

1887 Kalamazoo Bats (N690)

This set, issued circa 1887 by Charles Gross & Co. Philadelphia, is one of the most difficult of all 19th Century tobacco issues. The cards measure a rather large 2-1/4" x 4" and feature a sepia-toned photograph on heavy cardboard. The player's name and team appear inside a white strip at the bottom of the photo, while a small ad for Kalamazoo Bats cigarettes is printed at the very bottom of the card. Some cards carry an 1887 copyright line, but there are indications that some of the cards date from 1886 or 1888. The unnumbered set pictures players from four teams - two from New York (Giants and Mets) and two from Philadelphia (Athletics and Phillies). A few of the cards picture more than one player, and some cards have been found with an ad on the back offering various prizes in exchange for saving the cards. The set has been assigned the American Card Catalog number N690. Because of the rarity of Kalamazoo Bats, and the uncertainty as to completeness of this checklist, no complete set value is given.

		NM	EX	VG
Common Player:		2750.	1000.	600.00
(1)	Ed Andrews	2750.	1000.	600.00
(2)	Charles Bastian, Lyons	3500.	1250.	770.00
(3)	Louis Bierbauer	2750.	1000.	600.00
(4)	Louis Bierbauer, Gallagher	3500	1250.	770.00
(5)	Buffington (Buffinton)	2750.	1000.	600.00
(6)	Daniel Casey	2750.	1000.	600.00
(7)	Jack Clements	2750.	1000.	600.00
(8)	Roger Connor	8500.	3050.	1875.
(9)	Larry Corcoran	3500.	1250.	770.00
(10)	Ed Cushman	3500.	1250.	770.00
(11)	Pat Deasley	3500.	1250.	770.00
(12)	Jim Devlin	2750.	1000.	600.00
(13)	Jim Donahue	3500.	1250.	770.00
(14)	Mike Dorgan	3500.	1250.	770.00
(15)	Dude Esterbrooke (Esterbrook)	3500.	1250.	770.00
(16)	Buck Ewing	8500.	3050.	1875.
(17)	Sid Farrar	2750.	1000.	600.00
(18)	Charlie Ferguson	2750.	1000.	600.00
(19)	Jim Fogarty	2750.	1000.	600.00
(20)	Fogarty, Deacon McGuire	3500.	1250.	770.00
(21)	Elmer Foster	3500.	1250.	770.00
(22)	Whitey Gibson	2750.	1000.	600.00
(23)	Pete Gillespie	2750.	1000.	600.00
(24)	Tom Gunning	2750.	1000.	600.00
(25)	Cutrate Irwin	2750.	1000.	600.00
(26)	Irwin, Smiling Al Maul	3500.	1250.	770.00
(27)	Tim Keefe	8500.	3050.	1875.
(28)	Ted Larkin	2750.	1000.	600.00
(29)	Ted Larkins, Jocko Milligan (Larkin)	3500.	1250.	770.00
(30)	Jack Lynch	3500.	1250.	770.00
(31)	Denny Lyons	2750.	1000.	600.00
(32)	Denny Lyons, Taylor	2750.	1000.	600.00
(33)	Fred Mann	2750.	1000.	600.00
(34)	Fred Mann, Uncle Robbie Robinson	8500.	3050.	1875.
(35)	Charlie Mason	2750.	1000.	600.00
(36)	Bobby Mathews	2750.	1000.	600.00
(37)	Smiling Al Maul	2750.	1000.	600.00
(38)	Al Mays	3500.	1250.	770.00
(39)	Jim McGan (McGarr)	2750.	1000.	600.00
(40)	Deacon McGuire (catching)	2750.	1000.	600.00
(41)	Deacon McGuire (throwing)	2750.	1000.	600.00
(42)	Tom McLaughlin	2750.	1000.	600.00
(43)	Jocko Milligan, Harry Stowe (Stovey)	3500.	1250.	770.00
(44)	Joseph Mulvey	2750.	1000.	600.00
(45)	Candy Nelson	3500.	1250.	770.00
(46)	Orator Jim O'Rourke	8500.	3050.	1875.
(47)	Dave Orr	3500.	1250.	770.00
(48)	Tom Poorman	2750.	1000.	600.00
(49)	Danny Richardson	3500.	1250.	770.00
(50)	Uncle Robbie Robinson	8500.	3050.	1875.
(51)	Chief Roseman	3500.	1250.	770.00
(52)	Harry Stowe (Stovey) (hands on hips)	3500.	1250.	770.00
(53)	Harry Stowe (Stovey) (hands outstretched)	3500.	1250.	770.00
(54)	Sleepy Townsend	2750.	1000.	600.00
(55)	Jocko Milligan, Sleepy Townsend	3500.	1250.	770.00
(56)	Monte Ward	8500.	3050.	1875.
(57)	Gus Weyhing	2750.	1000.	600.00
(58)	George "Dandy" Wood	2750.	1000.	600.00
(59)	Harry Wright	8500.	3050.	1875.

1887 Kalamazoo Bats Cabinets (N690)

This extremely rare issue of cabinet cards was issued as a premium by Charles Gross & Co. of Philadelphia, makers of the Kalamazoo Bats brand of cigarettes. Two distinct types have been found, both measuring 4-1/4" x 6-1/2". One variety displays the photo on a black mount with the words "Smoke Kalamazoo Bats" embossed in gold to the left. The other contains no advertising, although there is an oval embossment on the card, along with the words "Chas. Gross & Co." and an 1887 copyright line. These cards also have a distinctive pink color on the back of the cardboard mount. Because of the rarity of Kalamazoo Bats cabinets, and uncertainty as to completeness of this checklist, no complete set value is quoted.

		NM	EX	VG
Common Player:		2500.	900.00	550.00
Common Team:		10000.	5000.	3000.
(1)	Ed Andrews	2500.	900.00	550.00
(2)	Charles Bastian, Daniel Casey, Taylor	2500.	900.00	550.00
(3)	Charles Bastian, Denny Lyons	2500.	900.00	550.00
(4)	Louis Bierbauer, Gallagher	2500.	900.00	550.00
(5)	Charles Buffington (Buffinton)	2500.	900.00	550.00
(6)	Daniel Casey	2500.	900.00	550.00
(7)	Jack Clements	2500.	900.00	550.00
(8)	Jim Devlin	2500.	900.00	550.00
(9)	Sid Farrar	2500.	900.00	550.00
(10)	Charlie Ferguson	2500.	900.00	550.00
(11)	Jim Fogarty	2500.	900.00	550.00
(12)	Whitey Gibson	2500.	900.00	550.00
(13)	Tom Gunning	2500.	900.00	550.00
(14)	Cutrate Irwin	2500.	900.00	550.00
(15)	Cutrate Irwin, Smiling Al Maul	2500.	900.00	550.00
(16)	Ted Larkins (Larkin), Jocko Milligan	2500.	900.00	550.00
(17)	Denny Lyons	2500.	900.00	550.00
(18)	Denny Lyons, Taylor	2500.	900.00	550.00
(19)	Fred Mann	2500.	900.00	550.00
(20)	Bobby Mathews	2500.	900.00	550.00
(21)	Smiling Al Maul	2500.	900.00	550.00
(22)	Chippy McCan (McGarr)	2500.	900.00	550.00
(23)	Deacon McGuire	2500.	900.00	550.00
(24)	Jocko Milligan, Harry Stowe (Stovey)	2500.	900.00	550.00
(25)	Joseph Mulvey	2500.	900.00	550.00

(26)	Tim Poorman	2500.	900.00	550.00
(27)	Ed Seward	2500.	900.00	550.00
(28)	Harry Stowe (Stovey)	2500.	900.00	550.00
(29)	Sleepy Townsend	2500.	900.00	550.00
(30)	George "Dandy" Wood	2500.	900.00	550.00
(31)	Athletic Club	10000.	3600.	2200.
(32)	Boston B.B.C.	20000.	7200.	4400.
(33)	Philadelphia B.B.C.	10000.	3600.	2200.
(34)	Pittsburg B.B.C.	10000.	3600.	2200.

1887 Kalamazoo Bats Team Cards (N690-1)

The team photos in this set were issued by Charles Gross & Co. of Philadelphia as a promotion for its Kalamazoo Bats brand of cigarettes. The cards, which are similar in design to the related N690 series, are extremely rare. They feature a team photo with the caption in a white box at the bottom of the photo and an ad for Kalamazoo Bats to the left.

		NM	EX	VG
Complete Set (6):		62500.	21000.	13125.
Common Team:		12000.	4500.	2775.
(1)	Athletic Club	12000.	4500.	2775.
(2)	Baltimore B.B.C.	12000.	4500.	2775.
(3)	Boston B.B.C.	15000.	5400.	3300.
(4)	Detroit B.B.C.	16000.	5750.	3525.
(5)	Philadelphia B.B.C.	12000.	4500.	2775.
(6)	Pittsburg B.B.C.	12000.	4500.	2775.

1958-61 Kansas City Athletics team issue

Issued over a period of six years these black-and-white photo cards share an identical format. The cards are 3-1/4" x 5-1/2" with borderless poses and facsimile autographs on front. Backs are blank. The unnumbered cards are checklisted here in alphabetical order.

		NM	EX	VG
Complete Set (37):		250.00	125.00	75.00
Common Player:		6.00	3.00	1.75
(1)	Jim Archer	6.00	3.00	1.75
(2)	Mike Baxes	6.00	3.00	1.75
(3)	Zeke Bella	6.00	3.00	1.75
(4)	Lou Boudreau	12.00	6.00	3.50
(5)	Cletis Boyer	9.00	4.50	2.75
(6)	Bob Cerv	6.00	3.00	1.75
(7)	Harry Chiti	6.00	3.00	1.75
(8)	Bud Daley	6.00	3.00	1.75
(9)	Joe DeMaestri	6.00	3.00	1.75
(10)	Art Ditmar	6.00	3.00	1.75
(11)	Jim Ewell (trainer)	6.00	3.00	1.75
(12)	Jim Finigan	6.00	3.00	1.75
(13)	Ned Garver	7.50	3.75	2.25
(14)	Tom Gorman (cap-to-knees)	6.00	3.00	1.75
(15)	Tom Gorman (pitching)	6.00	3.00	1.75
(16)	Bob Grim	6.00	3.00	1.75
(17)	Kent Hadley	6.00	3.00	1.75
(18)	Ray Herbert	6.00	3.00	1.75
(19)	Troy Herriage	6.00	3.00	1.75
(20)	Whitey Herzog	9.00	4.50	2.75
(21)	Frank House	6.00	3.00	1.75
(22)	Alex Kellner	6.00	3.00	1.75
(23)	Lou Kretlow	6.00	3.00	1.75
(24)	Hec Lopez	6.00	3.00	1.75
(25)	Roger Maris	45.00	22.00	13.50
(26)	Rance Pless	6.00	3.00	1.75
(27)	Vic Power	9.00	4.50	2.75
(28)	Bobby Shantz	10.00	5.00	3.00
(29)	Enos Slaughter	12.00	6.00	3.50
(30)	Hal Smith	6.00	3.00	1.75
(31)	Wayne Terwilliger	6.00	3.00	1.75
(32)	Charles Thompson	6.00	3.00	1.75
(33)	Dick Tomanek	6.00	3.00	1.75
(34)	Bill Tuttle	6.00	3.00	1.75
(35)	Jack Urban	6.00	3.00	1.75
(36)	Preston Ward	6.00	3.00	1.75
(37)	Dick Williams	7.50	3.75	2.25

1969 Kansas City Royals Photocards

These team-issued photocards are printed in black-and-white in a 4-1/4" x 7" blank-back format. Posed photos are bordered in white with player identification at top. The unnumbered pictures are checklisted here in alphabetical order.

		NM	EX	VG
Complete Set (12):		12.00	6.00	3.50
Common Player:		1.00	.50	.30
(1)	Jerry Adair	1.00	.50	.30
(2)	Jimmy Campanis	1.00	.50	.30
(3)	Moe Drabowsky	1.50	.70	.45
(4)	Mike Fiore	1.00	.50	.30
(5)	Joe Foy	1.00	.50	.30
(6)	Joe Gordon	1.00	.50	.30
(7)	Pat Kelly	1.00	.50	.30
(8)	Joe Keough	1.00	.50	.30
(9)	Roger Nelson	1.00	.50	.30
(10)	Bob Oliver	1.00	.50	.30
(11)	Juan Rios	1.00	.50	.30
(12)	Dave Wickersham	1.00	.50	.30

1974 Kansas City Royals Photocards

Off and on through the 1970s, the Royals issued series of player photocards in a blank-backed, black-and-white 3-1/4" x 5" format. The design didn't always change from year to year and unless a complete set is at hand, distinguishing the year of issue can be impossible. The 1974 cards are 3-1/2" x 5-1/2" with a portrait photo that is borderless at top and sides and has a facsimile autograph. In the bottom margin is the player name, team and position in three lines of bold sans-serif type. The unnumbered cards are checklisted here in alphabetical order.

		NM	EX	VG
Complete Set (29):		3.00	1.50	.90
Common Player:		75.00	37.50	22.00
(1)	Kurt Bevacqua	3.00	1.50	.90
(2)	Doug Bird	3.00	1.50	.90
(3)	George Brett	30.00	15.00	9.00
(4)	Nellie Briles	3.00	1.50	.90
(5)	Steve Busby	3.00	1.50	.90
(6)	Orlando Cepeda	9.00	4.50	2.75
(7)	Galen Cisco	3.00	1.50	.90
(8)	Al Cowens	3.00	1.50	.90
(9)	Bruce Dal Canton	3.00	1.50	.90
(10)	Harry Dunlop	3.00	1.50	.90
(11)	Al Fitzmorris	3.00	1.50	.90
(12)	Fran Healy	3.00	1.50	.90
(13)	Joe Hoerner	3.00	1.50	.90
(14)	Charley Lau	3.00	1.50	.90
(15)	Buck Martinez	3.00	1.50	.90
(16)	John Mayberry	3.00	1.50	.90
(17)	Lindy McDaniel	3.00	1.50	.90
(18)	Jack McKeon	3.00	1.50	.90
(19)	Hal McRae	4.50	2.25	1.25
(20)	Steve Mingori	3.00	1.50	.90
(21)	Amos Otis	4.50	2.25	1.25
(22)	Fred Patek	4.50	2.25	1.25
(23)	Marty Pattin	3.00	1.50	.90
(24)	Vada Pinson	4.50	2.25	1.25
(25)	Cookie Rojas	3.00	1.50	.90
(26)	Tony Solaita	3.00	1.50	.90
(27)	Paul Splittorff	3.00	1.50	.90
(28)	Frank White	4.50	2.25	1.25
(29)	Jim Wohlford	3.00	1.50	.90

1978 Kansas City Royals Photocards

Off and on through the 1970s, the Royals issued series of player photocards in a blank-backed, black-and-white 3-1/4" x 5" format. The design didn't always change from year to year and unless a complete set is at hand, distinguishing the year of issue can be impossible. The 1978 cards have a portrait photo surrounded with white borders. The bottom margin is extra wide and has the player name, team and position in a single line of sans-serif type. The unnumbered cards are checklisted here in alphabetical order.

		NM	EX	VG
Complete Set (27):		50.00	25.00	15.00
Common Player:		2.50	1.25	.75
(1)	Doug Bird	2.50	1.25	.75
(2)	Steve Braun	2.50	1.25	.75
(3)	George Brett	8.00	4.00	2.50
(4)	Al Cowens	2.50	1.25	.75
(5)	Rich Gale	2.50	1.25	.75
(6)	Larry Gura	2.50	1.25	.75
(7)	Whitey Herzog	3.00	1.50	.90
(8)	Al Hrabosky	3.00	1.50	.90
(9)	Clint Hurdle	2.50	1.25	.75
(10)	Pete LaCock	2.50	1.25	.75
(11)	Dennis Leonard	2.50	1.25	.75
(12)	John Mayberry	2.50	1.25	.75
(13)	Hal McRae	3.00	1.50	.90
(14)	Steve Mingori	2.50	1.25	.75
(15)	Dave Nelson	2.50	1.25	.75
(16)	Amos Otis	3.00	1.50	.90
(17)	Fred Patek	3.00	1.50	.90
(18)	Marty Pattin	2.50	1.25	.75
(19)	Tom Poquette	2.50	1.25	.75
(20)	Darrell Porter	2.50	1.25	.75
(21)	Paul Splittorff	2.50	1.25	.75
(22)	Jerry Terrell	2.50	1.25	.75
(23)	U.L. Washington	2.50	1.25	.75
(24)	John Wathan	2.50	1.25	.75
(25)	Frank White	4.00	2.00	1.25
(26)	Willie Wilson	5.00	2.50	1.50
(27)	Joe Zdeb	2.50	1.25	.75

1979 Kansas City Royals Photocards

This series of team-issued photocards features color photos in a 4-1/4" x 5-1/2" format. Fronts have a thin white border; backs are blank. The only identification on the card is a facsimile signature printed in blue. The unnumbered pictures are listed here alphabetically.

		NM	EX	VG
Complete Set (28):		30.00	15.00	9.00
Common Player:		1.00	.50	.30
(1)	Steve Braun	1.00	.50	.30
(2)	Steve Boros, Galen Cisco	1.00	.50	.30
(3)	George Brett	6.00	3.00	1.75
(4)	Steve Busby	1.00	.50	.30
(5)	Al Cowens	1.00	.50	.30
(6)	Rich Gale	1.00	.50	.30

(7)	Larry Gura	1.00	.50	.30
(8)	Whitey Herzog	1.50	.70	.45
(9)	Chuck Hiller, John Sullivan	1.00	.50	.30
(10)	Al Hrabosky	1.00	.50	.30
(11)	Clint Hurdle	1.00	.50	.30
(12)	Pete LaCock	1.00	.50	.30
(13)	Dennis Leonard	1.00	.50	.30
(14)	Hal McRae	1.50	.70	.45
(15)	Steve Mingori	1.00	.50	.30
(16)	Amos Otis	1.50	.70	.45
(17)	Fred Patek	1.50	.70	.45
(18)	Marty Pattin	1.00	.50	.30
(19)	Darrell Porter	1.00	.50	.30
(20)	Jamie Quirk	1.00	.50	.30
(21)	Ed Rodriguez	1.00	.50	.30
(22)	Paul Splittorff	1.00	.50	.30
(23)	Jerry Terrell	1.00	.50	.30
(24)	U.L. Washington	1.00	.50	.30
(25)	John Wathan	1.00	.50	.30
(26)	Frank White	1.50	.70	.45
(27)	Willie Wilson	2.50	1.25	.70
(28)	Joe Zdeb	1.00	.50	.30

1929 Kashin Publications (R316)

This set of 101 unnumbered cards was issued in 25-card boxed series, with cards measuring 3-1/2" x 4-1/2". The cards feature black-and-white photos with the player's name printed in script near the bottom of the photo. Team and league are designated at bottom in printed letters. The backs of the cards are blank. Four of the cards (Hadley, Haines, Siebold and Todt) are considered to be scarcer than the rest of the set.

		NM	EX	VG
Complete Set (101):		7000.	3500.	2100.
Common Player:		60.00	30.00	18.00
(1)	Dale Alexander	60.00	30.00	18.00
(2)	Ethan N. Allen	60.00	30.00	18.00
(3)	Larry Benton	60.00	30.00	18.00
(4)	Moe Berg	160.00	80.00	48.00
(5)	Max Bishop	60.00	30.00	18.00
(6)	Del Bissonette	60.00	30.00	18.00
(7)	Lucerne A. Blue	60.00	30.00	18.00
(8)	James Bottomley	95.00	47.00	28.00
(9)	Guy T. Bush	60.00	30.00	18.00
(10)	Harold G. Carlson	60.00	30.00	18.00
(11)	Owen Carroll	60.00	30.00	18.00
(12)	Chalmers W. Cissell (Chalmer)	60.00	30.00	18.00
(13)	Earl Combs	95.00	47.00	28.00
(14)	Hugh M. Critz	60.00	30.00	18.00
(15)	H.J. DeBerry	60.00	30.00	18.00
(16)	Pete Donohue	60.00	30.00	18.00
(17)	Taylor Douthit	60.00	30.00	18.00
(18)	Chas. W. Dressen	60.00	30.00	18.00
(19)	Jimmy Dykes	60.00	30.00	18.00
(20)	Howard Ehmke	60.00	30.00	18.00
(21)	Elwood English	60.00	30.00	18.00
(22)	Urban Faber	95.00	47.00	28.00
(23)	Fred Fitzsimmons	60.00	30.00	18.00
(24)	Lewis A. Fonseca	60.00	30.00	18.00
(25)	Horace H. Ford	60.00	30.00	18.00
(26)	Jimmy Foxx	120.00	60.00	36.00
(27)	Frank Frisch	100.00	50.00	30.00
(28)	Lou Gehrig	500.00	250.00	150.00
(29)	Charles Gehringer	95.00	47.00	28.00
(30)	Leon Goslin	95.00	47.00	28.00
(31)	George Grantham	60.00	30.00	18.00
(32)	Burleigh Grimes	95.00	47.00	28.00
(33)	Robert Grove	100.00	50.00	30.00
(34)	Bump Hadley	150.00	75.00	45.00
(35)	Charlie Hafey	95.00	47.00	28.00
(36)	Jesse J. Haines	250.00	125.00	75.00
(37)	Harvey Hendrick	60.00	30.00	18.00
(38)	Floyd C. Herman	60.00	30.00	18.00
(39)	Andy High	60.00	30.00	18.00
(40)	Urban J. Hodapp	60.00	30.00	18.00
(41)	Frank Hogan	60.00	30.00	18.00
(42)	Rogers Hornsby	110.00	55.00	33.00
(43)	Waite Hoyt	95.00	47.00	28.00
(44)	Willis Hudlin	60.00	30.00	18.00
(45)	Frank O. Hurst	60.00	30.00	18.00
(46)	Charlie Jamieson	60.00	30.00	18.00
(47)	Roy C. Johnson	60.00	30.00	18.00
(48)	Percy Jones	60.00	30.00	18.00
(49)	Sam Jones	60.00	30.00	18.00
(50)	Joseph Judge	60.00	30.00	18.00
(51)	Willie Kamm	60.00	30.00	18.00
(52)	Charles Klein	95.00	47.00	28.00
(53)	Mark Koenig	60.00	30.00	18.00
(54)	Ralph Kress	60.00	30.00	18.00
(55)	Fred M. Leach	60.00	30.00	18.00
(56)	Fred Lindstrom	95.00	47.00	28.00
(57)	Ad Liska	60.00	30.00	18.00
(58)	Fred Lucas (Red)	60.00	30.00	18.00
(59)	Fred Maguire	60.00	30.00	18.00
(60)	Perce L. Malone	60.00	30.00	18.00
(61)	Harry Manush (Henry)	95.00	47.00	28.00
(62)	Walter Maranville	95.00	47.00	28.00
(63)	Douglas McWeeney (McWeeny)	60.00	30.00	18.00
(64)	Oscar Melillo	60.00	30.00	18.00
(65)	Ed "Bing" Miller	60.00	30.00	18.00
(66)	Frank O'Doul	65.00	32.00	19.50
(67)	Melvin Ott	100.00	50.00	30.00
(68)	Herbert Pennock	95.00	47.00	28.00
(69)	William W. Regan	60.00	30.00	18.00
(70)	Harry F. Rice	60.00	30.00	18.00
(71)	Sam Rice	95.00	47.00	28.00
(72)	Lance Richbourgh (Richbourg)	60.00	30.00	18.00
(73)	Eddie Rommel	60.00	30.00	18.00
(74)	Chas. H. Root	60.00	30.00	18.00
(75)	Edd Roush	95.00	47.00	28.00
(76)	Harold Ruel (Herold)	60.00	30.00	18.00
(77)	Charles Ruffing	95.00	47.00	28.00
(78)	Jack Russell	60.00	30.00	18.00
(79)	Babe Ruth	500.00	250.00	150.00
(80)	Fred Schulte	60.00	30.00	18.00
(81)	Harry Seibold	150.00	75.00	45.00
(82)	Joe Sewell	95.00	47.00	28.00
(83)	Luke Sewell	60.00	30.00	18.00
(84)	Art Shires	60.00	30.00	18.00
(85)	Al Simmons	95.00	47.00	28.00
(86)	Bob Smith	60.00	30.00	18.00
(87)	Riggs Stephenson	60.00	30.00	18.00
(88)	Wm. H. Terry	95.00	47.00	28.00
(89)	Alphonse Thomas	60.00	30.00	18.00
(90)	Lafayette F. Thompson	60.00	30.00	18.00
(91)	Phil Todt	150.00	75.00	45.00
(92)	Harold J. Traynor	95.00	47.00	28.00
(93)	Dazzy Vance	95.00	47.00	28.00
(94)	Lloyd Waner	95.00	47.00	28.00
(95)	Paul Waner	95.00	47.00	28.00
(96)	Jimmy Welsh	60.00	30.00	18.00
(97)	Earl Whitehill	60.00	30.00	18.00
(98)	A.C. Whitney	60.00	30.00	18.00
(99)	Claude Willoughby	60.00	30.00	18.00
(100)	Hack Wilson	95.00	47.00	28.00
(101)	Tom Zachary	60.00	30.00	18.00

1964 KDKA Pittsburgh Pirates Portraits

Issued prior to the radio/TV stations' much more common color player cards of 1968, this seldom-seen regional issue presents the 1964 Pittsburgh Pirates in a set of 28 large-format (8" x 11-7/8") schedule cards. The cards are printed in sepia tones on blank-backed cardboard. Fronts present a player pose and a '64 Pirates schedule. A redemption offer states that a pair of Bucs' tickets will be given in exchange for a complete set of the portraits, and the pictures will be returned, presumably cancelled in some fashion. The unnumbered cards are checklisted here alphabetically. While the cards advertise the Pirates' broadcasting partners, they were actually issued by Sweet Clean laundry as stiffeners for men's shirts that had been washed. The laundry's name is not mentioned anywhere on the cards.

		NM	EX	VG
Complete Set (28):		1200.	600.00	350.00
Common Player:		30.00	15.00	9.00
(1)	Gene Alley	30.00	15.00	9.00
(2)	Bob Bailey	30.00	15.00	9.00
(3)	Frank Bork	30.00	15.00	9.00
(4)	Smokey Burgess	30.00	15.00	9.00
(5)	Tom Butters	30.00	15.00	9.00
(6)	Don Cardwell	30.00	15.00	9.00
(7)	Roberto Clemente	350.00	175.00	105.00
(8)	Donn Clendenon	30.00	15.00	9.00
(9)	Elroy Face	30.00	15.00	9.00
(10)	Gene Freese	30.00	15.00	9.00
(11)	Bob Friend	30.00	15.00	9.00
(12)	Joe Gibbon	30.00	15.00	9.00
(13)	Julio Gotay	30.00	15.00	9.00
(14)	Rex Johnston	30.00	15.00	9.00
(15)	Vernon Law	30.00	15.00	9.00
(16)	Jerry Lynch	30.00	15.00	9.00
(17)	Bill Mazeroski	65.00	32.00	19.50
(18)	Al McBean	30.00	15.00	9.00
(19)	Orlando McFarlane	30.00	15.00	9.00
(20)	Manny Mota	30.00	15.00	9.00
(21)	Danny Murtaugh	30.00	15.00	9.00
(22)	Jim Pagliaroni	30.00	15.00	9.00
(23)	Dick Schofield	30.00	15.00	9.00
(24)	Don Schwall	30.00	15.00	9.00
(25)	Tommie Sisk	30.00	15.00	9.00
(26)	Willie Stargell	65.00	32.00	19.50
(27)	Bob Veale	30.00	15.00	9.00
(28)	Bill Virdon	35.00	17.50	10.50

1968 KDKA Pittsburgh Pirates

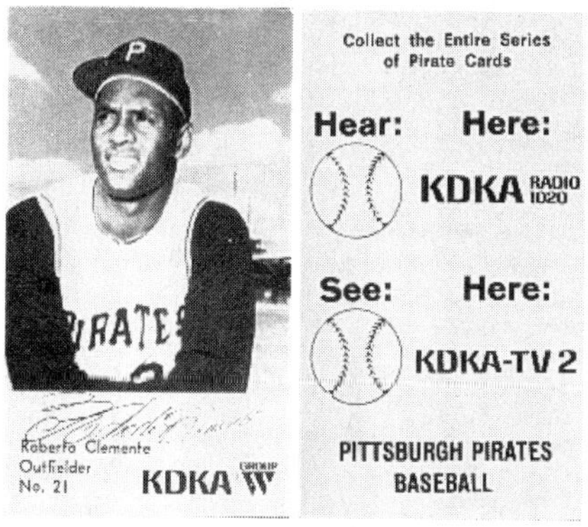

The most common of the many Pirates regional issues of the late 1960s, this 23-card set was sponsored by the Pirates' TV and radio flagship stations, KDKA in Pittsburgh. Cards measure 2-1/2" x 4" and feature at top front a color posed photo of the player, with no top or side borders. In the white panel beneath the photo are a facsimile autograph, the player's name, position and uniform number and the broadcasters' logo. Backs are printed in black on white and feature advertising for the radio and TV station. The checklist is presented here by uniform number.

		NM	EX	VG
Complete Set (23):		200.00	100.00	60.00
Common Player:		6.00	3.00	1.75
7	Larry Shepard	6.00	3.00	1.75
8	Willie Stargell	24.00	12.00	7.25
9	Bill Mazeroski	22.00	11.00	6.50
10	Gary Kolb	6.00	3.00	1.75
11	Jose Pagan	6.00	3.00	1.75
12	Gerry May (Jerry)	6.00	3.00	1.75
14	Jim Bunning	12.00	6.00	3.50
15	Manny Mota	7.50	3.75	2.25
17	Donn Clendenon	6.00	3.00	1.75
18	Matty Alou	6.00	3.00	1.75
21	Roberto Clemente	50.00	25.00	15.00
22	Gene Alley	6.00	3.00	1.75
25	Tommy Sisk	6.00	3.00	1.75
26	Roy Face	6.00	3.00	1.75
27	Ron Kline	6.00	3.00	1.75
28	Steve Blass	6.00	3.00	1.75
29	Juan Pizarro	6.00	3.00	1.75
30	Maury Wills	8.00	4.00	2.50
34	Al McBean	6.00	3.00	1.75
35	Manny Sanguillen	6.00	3.00	1.75
38	Bob Moose	6.00	3.00	1.75
39	Bob Veale	6.00	3.00	1.75
41	Dave Wickersham	6.00	3.00	1.75

1937 Kellogg's Pep Sports Stamps

Kellogg's packaged a four-stamp panel of "Sports Stamps" in boxes of Pep cereal. While 24 panels comprise a complete set, six of the stamps were double-printed, creating a set of 90. Backs of the stamp panels gave details for ordering an album and game boards for playing with the stamps. The color-tinted stamps measure 1-1/8" x 2-3/4" individually, and 2-1/4" x 4-1/4" as a panel. Besides the ballplayers checklisted here, the Kellogg's/Pep stamps included football, tennis and golf players, swimmers, boxers, aviators and race horses. Baseball player stamps are listed here according to the number of the four-stamp panel on which they appeared. Prices for complete panels would be considerably higher, factoring in the other stamps on the sheet.

		NM	EX	VG
Complete Set (18):		675.00	335.00	200.00
Common Player:		35.00	17.50	10.00
1	Joe Medwick	45.00	22.00	13.50
3	Leo Durocher	45.00	22.00	13.50
5	Gabby Hartnett	45.00	22.00	13.50
6	Billy Herman	45.00	22.00	13.50
7	Luke Appling	45.00	22.00	13.50
8	Floyd Vaughan	45.00	22.00	13.50
9	Paul Waner	45.00	22.00	13.50
11	Bill Terry	45.00	22.00	13.50
12	George Selkirk	35.00	17.50	10.00
13	Walter Johnson	90.00	45.00	27.00
15	Lew Fonseca	35.00	17.50	10.00
16	Richard Ferrell	45.00	22.00	13.50
17	Johnny Evers	45.00	22.00	13.50
18	Sam West	35.00	17.50	10.00
19	Charles Myer	35.00	17.50	10.00
20	Tris Speaker (double print, also on Panel 23)	50.00	25.00	15.00
21	Joe Tinker	45.00	22.00	13.50
22	Mordecai Brown	45.00	22.00	13.50
23	Tris Speaker (double-print, also on Panel 20)	50.00	25.00	15.00

1948 Kellogg's Pep Celebrities

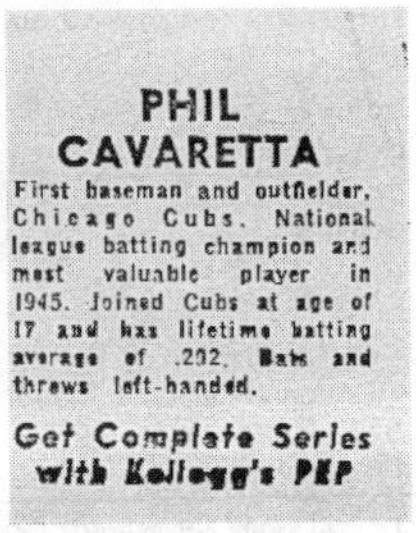

PHIL
CAVARETTA
First baseman and outfielder, Chicago Cubs. National league batting champion and most valuable player in 1945. Joined Cubs at age of 17 and has lifetime batting average of .292. Bats and throws left-handed.
Get Complete Series with Kellogg's PEP

Five baseball players are included among the 18 athletes in this set of 1-3/8" x 1-5/8" cards. Fronts have player photos bordered in white. Backs have player name at top, a short career summary and a Kellogg's ad. The baseball players from the unnumbered set are listed here alphabetically.

		NM	EX	VG
Complete Set (5):		150.00	75.00	45.00
Common Player:		35.00	17.50	10.50
(1)	Phil Cavarretta	35.00	17.50	10.50
(2)	Orval Grove	35.00	17.50	10.50
(3)	Mike Tresh	35.00	17.50	10.50
(4)	Paul "Dizzy" Trout	35.00	17.50	10.50
(5)	Dick Wakefield	35.00	17.50	10.50

1970 Kellogg's

For 14 years in the 1970s and early 1980s, the Kellogg's cereal company provided Topps with virtually the only meaningful national competition in the baseball card market. Kellogg's kicked off its baseball card program in 1970 with a 75-player set of simulated 3-D cards. Single cards were available in selected brands of the company's cereal, while a mail-in program offered complete sets. The 3-D effect was achieved by the sandwiching of a clear color player photo between a purposely blurred stadium background scene and a layer of ribbed plastic. The relatively narrow dimension of the card, 2-1/4" x 3-1/2" and the nature of the plastic overlay seem to conspire to cause the cards to curl, often cracking the plastic layer, if not stored properly. Cards with major cracks in the plastic can be considered in Fair condition, at best.

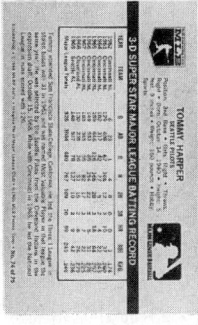

		NM	EX	VG
Complete Set (75):		300.00	150.00	90.00
Common Player:		2.00	1.00	.60
1	Ed Kranepool	2.00	1.00	.60
2	Pete Rose	15.00	7.50	4.50
3	Cleon Jones	2.00	1.00	.60
4	Willie McCovey	8.00	4.00	2.50
5	Mel Stottlemyre	3.00	1.50	.90
6	Frank Howard	3.00	1.50	.90
7	Tom Seaver	10.00	5.00	3.00
8	Don Sutton	6.00	3.00	1.75
9	Jim Wynn	2.00	1.00	.60
10	Jim Maloney	2.00	1.00	.60
11	Tommie Agee	2.00	1.00	.60
12	Willie Mays	17.50	8.75	5.25
13	Juan Marichal	7.50	3.75	2.25
14	Dave McNally	2.00	1.00	.60
15	Frank Robinson	10.00	5.00	3.00
16	Carlos May	2.00	1.00	.60
17	Bill Singer	2.00	1.00	.60
18	Rick Reichardt	2.00	1.00	.60
19	Boog Powell	3.00	1.50	.90
20	Gaylord Perry	7.50	3.75	2.25
21	Brooks Robinson	10.00	5.00	3.00
22	Luis Aparicio	8.00	4.00	2.50
23	Joel Horlen	2.00	1.00	.60
24	Mike Epstein	2.00	1.00	.60
25	Tom Haller	2.00	1.00	.60
26	Willie Crawford	2.00	1.00	.60
27	Roberto Clemente	18.00	9.00	5.50
28	Matty Alou	2.00	1.00	.60
29	Willie Stargell	7.50	3.75	2.25
30	Tim Cullen	2.00	1.00	.60
31	Randy Hundley	2.00	1.00	.60
32	Reggie Jackson	12.50	6.25	3.75
33	Rich Allen	5.00	2.50	1.50
34	Tim McCarver	2.50	1.25	.70
35	Ray Culp	2.00	1.00	.60
36	Jim Fregosi	2.00	1.00	.60
37	Billy Williams	8.00	4.00	2.50
38	Johnny Odom	2.00	1.00	.60
39	Bert Campaneris	2.00	1.00	.60
40	Ernie Banks	10.00	5.00	3.00
41	Chris Short	2.00	1.00	.60
42	Ron Santo	3.00	1.50	.90
43	Glenn Beckert	2.00	1.00	.60
44	Lou Brock	7.50	3.75	2.25
45	Larry Hisle	2.00	1.00	.60
46	Reggie Smith	2.00	1.00	.60
47	Rod Carew	7.50	3.75	2.25
48	Curt Flood	2.00	1.00	.60
49	Jim Lonborg	2.00	1.00	.60
50	Sam McDowell	2.00	1.00	.60
51	Sal Bando	2.00	1.00	.60
52	Al Kaline	10.00	5.00	3.00
53	Gary Nolan	2.00	1.00	.60
54	Rico Petrocelli	2.00	1.00	.60
55	Ollie Brown	2.00	1.00	.60
56	Luis Tiant	2.00	1.00	.60
57	Bill Freehan	2.00	1.00	.60
58	Johnny Bench	10.00	5.00	3.00
59	Joe Pepitone	2.00	1.00	.60
60	Bobby Murcer	2.00	1.00	.60
61	Harmon Killebrew	7.50	3.75	2.25
62	Don Wilson	2.00	1.00	.60
63	Tony Oliva	2.50	1.25	.70
64	Jim Perry	2.00	1.00	.60
65	Mickey Lolich	2.50	1.25	.70
66	Coco Laboy	2.00	1.00	.60
67	Dean Chance	2.00	1.00	.60
68	Ken Harrelson	2.00	1.00	.60
69	Willie Horton	2.00	1.00	.60
70	Wally Bunker	2.00	1.00	.60
71a	Bob Gibson (1959 IP blank)	9.00	4.50	2.75
71b	Bob Gibson (1959 IP 76)	9.00	4.50	2.75
72	Joe Morgan	7.50	3.75	2.25
73	Denny McLain	2.50	1.25	.70
74	Tommy Harper	2.00	1.00	.60
75	Don Mincher	2.00	1.00	.60

1971 Kellogg's

The scarcest and most valuable of the Kellogg's editions, the 75-card 1971 set was the only one not offered by the company on a mail-in basis. The only way to complete it was to buy ... and buy and buy ... boxes of cereal. Kellogg's again used the simulated 3-D effect in the cards' design, with the same result being many of the 2-1/4" x 3-1/2" cards are found today with cracks resulting from the cards' curling. A number of scarcer back variations are checklisted below. In addition, all 75 cards can be found with and without the 1970 date before the "Xograph" copyright line on the back; though there is no difference in value.

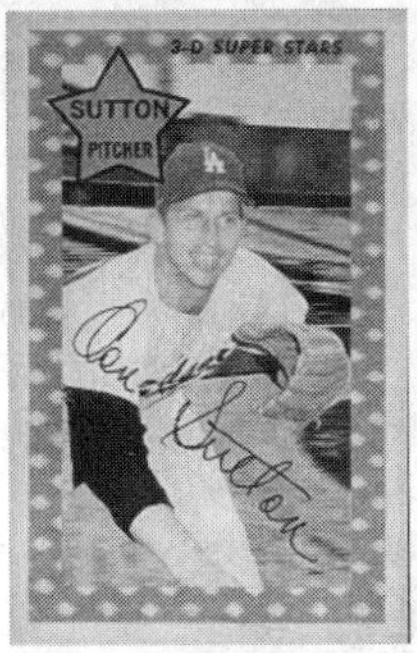

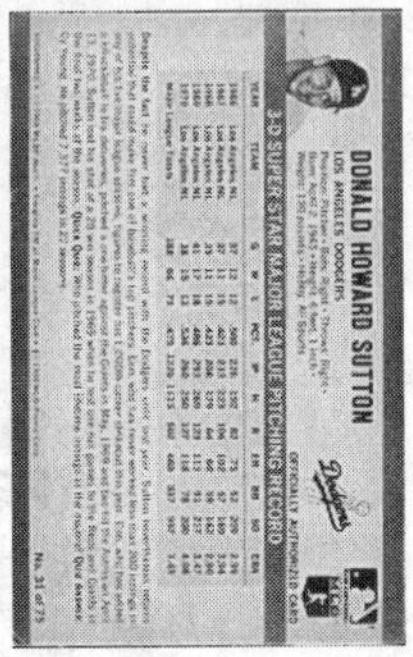

		NM	EX	VG
Complete Set (75):		800.00	400.00	240.00
Common Player:		9.00	4.50	2.75
1a	Wayne Simpson (SO 120)	9.00	4.50	2.75
1b	Wayne Simpson (SO 119)	13.50	6.75	4.00
2	Tom Seaver	25.00	12.50	7.50
3a	Jim Perry (IP 2238)	9.00	4.50	2.75
3b	Jim Perry (IP 2239)	13.50	6.75	4.00
4a	Bob Robertson (RBI 94)	9.00	4.50	2.75
4b	Bob Robertson (RBI 95)	13.50	6.75	4.00
5	Roberto Clemente	40.00	20.00	12.00
6a	Gaylord Perry (IP 2014)	20.00	10.00	6.00
6b	Gaylord Perry (IP 2015)	25.00	12.50	7.50
7a	Felipe Alou (1970 Oakland NL)	13.50	6.75	4.00
7b	Felipe Alou (1970 Oakland AL)	15.00	7.50	4.50
8	Denis Menke	9.00	4.50	2.75
9a	Don Kessinger (Hits 849)	9.00	4.50	2.75
9b	Don Kessinger (Hits 850)	13.50	6.75	4.00
10	Willie Mays	35.00	17.50	10.50
11	Jim Hickman	9.00	4.50	2.75
12	Tony Oliva	12.50	6.25	3.75
13	Manny Sanguillen	9.00	4.50	2.75
14a	Frank Howard (1968 Washington NL)	20.00	10.00	6.00
14b	Frank Howard (1968 Washington AL)	13.50	6.75	4.00
15	Frank Robinson	25.00	12.50	7.50
16	Willie Davis	9.00	4.50	2.75
17	Lou Brock	22.00	11.00	6.50
18	Cesar Tovar	9.00	4.50	2.75
19	Luis Aparicio	20.00	10.00	6.00
20	Boog Powell	12.50	6.25	3.75
21a	Dick Selma (SO 584)	9.00	4.50	2.75
21b	Dick Selma (SO 587)	13.50	6.75	4.00
22	Danny Walton	9.00	4.50	2.75
23	Carl Morton	9.00	4.50	2.75
24a	Sonny Siebert (SO 1054)	9.00	4.50	2.75
24b	Sonny Siebert (SO 1055)	13.50	6.75	4.00
25	Jim Merritt	9.00	4.50	2.75
26a	Jose Cardenal (Hits 828)	9.00	4.50	2.75
26b	Jose Cardenal (Hits 829)	13.50	6.75	4.00
27	Don Mincher	9.00	4.50	2.75
28a	Clyde Wright (California state logo)	9.00	4.50	2.75
28b	Clyde Wright (Angels crest logo)	13.50	6.75	4.00
29	Les Cain	9.00	4.50	2.75
30	Danny Cater	9.00	4.50	2.75
31	Don Sutton	20.00	10.00	6.00
32	Chuck Dobson	9.00	4.50	2.75
33	Willie McCovey	24.00	12.00	7.25
34	Mike Epstein	9.00	4.50	2.75
35a	Paul Blair (Runs 386)	9.00	4.50	2.75
35b	Paul Blair (Runs 385)	13.50	6.75	4.00
36a	Gary Nolan (SO 577)	9.00	4.50	2.75
36b	Gary Nolan (SO 581)	13.50	6.75	4.00
37	Sam McDowell	9.00	4.50	2.75
38	Amos Otis	9.00	4.50	2.75
39a	Ray Fosse (RBI 69)	9.00	4.50	2.75
39b	Ray Fosse (RBI 70)	13.50	6.75	4.00
40	Mel Stottlemyre	9.00	4.50	2.75
41	Cito Gaston	9.00	4.50	2.75
42	Dick Dietz	9.00	4.50	2.75
43	Roy White	9.00	4.50	2.75
44	Al Kaline	25.00	12.50	7.50
45	Carlos May	9.00	4.50	2.75
46a	Tommie Agee (RBI 313)	9.00	4.50	2.75
46b	Tommie Agee (RBI 314)	13.50	6.75	4.00
47	Tommy Harper	9.00	4.50	2.75
48	Larry Dierker	9.00	4.50	2.75
49	Mike Cuellar	9.00	4.50	2.75
50	Ernie Banks	25.00	12.50	7.50
51	Bob Gibson	24.00	12.00	7.25
52	Reggie Smith	9.00	4.50	2.75
53a	Matty Alou (RBI 273)	9.00	4.50	2.75
53b	Matty Alou (RBI 274)	13.50	6.75	4.00
54a	Alex Johnson (California state logo)	9.00	4.50	2.75
54b	Alex Johnson (Angels crest logo)	13.50	6.75	4.00
55	Harmon Killebrew	24.00	12.00	7.25
56	Billy Grabarkewitz	9.00	4.50	2.75

57	Rich Allen	15.00	7.50	4.50
58	Tony Perez	22.00	11.00	6.50
59a	Dave McNally (SO 1065)	9.00	4.50	2.75
59b	Dave McNally (SO 1067)	13.50	6.75	4.00
60a	Jim Palmer (SO 564)	20.00	10.00	6.00
60b	Jim Palmer (SO 567)	25.00	12.50	7.50
61	Billy Williams	22.00	11.00	6.50
62	Joe Torre	18.00	9.00	5.50
63a	Jim Northrup (AB 2773)	9.00	4.50	2.75
63b	Jim Northrup (AB 2772)	13.50	6.75	4.00
64a	Jim Fregosi (Calif. state logo - Hits 1326)	9.00	4.50	2.75
64b	Jim Fregosi (Calif. state logo - Hits 1327)	13.50	6.75	4.00
64c	Jim Fregosi (Angels crest logo)	13.50	6.75	4.00
65	Pete Rose	45.00	22.00	13.50
66a	Bud Harrelson (RBI 112)	9.00	4.50	2.75
66b	Bud Harrelson (RBI 113)	13.50	6.75	4.00
67	Tony Taylor	9.00	4.50	2.75
68	Willie Stargell	22.00	11.00	6.50
69	Tony Horton	9.00	4.50	2.75
70a	Claude Osteen (no number)	18.00	9.00	5.50
70b	Claude Osteen (#70 on back)	9.00	4.50	2.75
71	Glenn Beckert	9.00	4.50	2.75
72	Nate Colbert	9.00	4.50	2.75
73a	Rick Monday (AB 1705)	9.00	4.50	2.75
73b	Rick Monday (AB 1704)	13.50	6.75	4.00
74a	Tommy John (BB 444)	13.50	6.75	4.00
74b	Tommy John (BB 443)	18.00	9.00	5.50
75	Chris Short	9.00	4.50	2.75

1972 Kellogg's

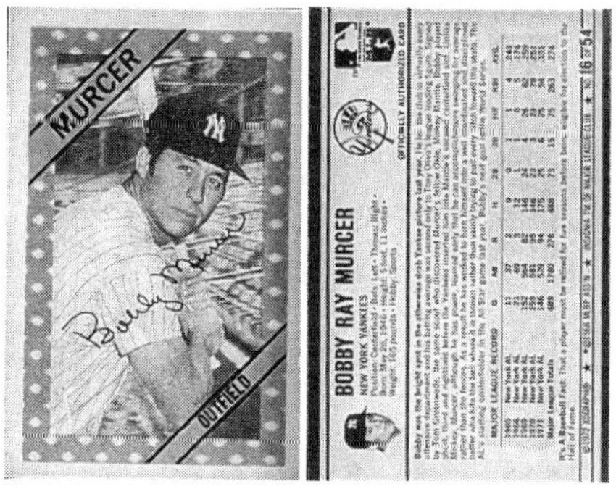

For 1972, Kellogg's reduced both the number of cards in its set and the dimensions of each card, moving to a 2-1/8" x 3-1/4" size and fixing the set at 54 cards. Once again, the cards were produced to simulate a 3-D effect (see description for 1970 Kellogg's). The set was available via a mail-in offer. The checklist includes variations which resulted from the correction of erroneous statistics on the backs of some cards. The complete set values quoted do not include the scarcer variations.

		NM	EX	VG
Complete Set (54):		75.00	37.50	22.00
Common Player:		.75	.40	.25
1a	Tom Seaver (1970 ERA 2.85)	12.00	6.00	3.50
1b	Tom Seaver (1970 ERA 2.81)	7.00	3.50	2.00
2	Amos Otis	.75	.40	.25
3a	Willie Davis (Runs 842)	1.25	.60	.40
3b	Willie Davis (Runs 841)	.90	.45	.25
4	Wilbur Wood	.75	.40	.25
5	Bill Parsons	.75	.40	.25
6	Pete Rose	20.00	10.00	6.00
7a	Willie McCovey (HR 360)	5.50	2.75	1.75
7b	Willie McCovey (HR 370)	3.75	2.00	1.25
8	Fergie Jenkins	3.25	1.75	1.00
9a	Vida Blue (ERA 2.35)	1.50	.70	.45
9b	Vida Blue (ERA 2.31)	1.00	.50	.30
10	Joe Torre	2.50	1.25	.70
11	Merv Rettenmund	.75	.40	.25
12	Bill Melton	.75	.40	.25
13a	Jim Palmer (Games 170)	5.25	2.75	1.50
13b	Jim Palmer (Games 168)	3.25	1.75	1.00
14	Doug Rader	.75	.40	.25
15a	Dave Roberts (...Seaver, the NL leader...)	1.25	.60	.40
15b	Dave Roberts (...Seaver, the league leader...)	.75	.10	.25
16	Bobby Murcer	.75	.40	.25
17	Wes Parker	.75	.40	.25
18a	Joe Coleman (BB 394)	1.25	.60	.40
18b	Joe Coleman (BB 393)	.75	.40	.25
19	Manny Sanguillen	.75	.40	.25
20	Reggie Jackson	8.00	4.00	2.50
21	Ralph Garr	.75	.40	.25
22	Jim "Catfish" Hunter	3.25	1.75	1.00
23	Rick Wise	.75	.40	.25
24	Glenn Beckert	.75	.40	.25
25	Tony Oliva	1.00	.50	.30
26a	Bob Gibson (SO 2577)	5.25	2.75	1.50
26b	Bob Gibson (SO 2578)	3.25	1.75	1.00
27a	Mike Cuellar (1971 ERA 3.80)	1.25	.60	.40
27b	Mike Cuellar (1971 ERA 3.08)	.90	.45	.25
28	Chris Speier	.75	.40	.25
29a	Dave McNally (ERA 3.18)	1.25	.60	.40
29b	Dave McNally (ERA 3.15)	.90	.45	.25
30	Chico Cardenas	.75	.40	.25
31a	Bill Freehan (AVG. .263)	1.25	.60	.40
31b	Bill Freehan (AVG. .262)	.90	.45	.25
32a	Bud Harrelson (Hits 634)	1.25	.60	.40
32b	Bud Harrelson (Hits 624)	.75	.40	.25
33a	Sam McDowell (...less than 200 innings...)	1.25	.60	.40
33b	Sam McDowell (...less than 225 innings...)	.90	.45	.25
34a	Claude Osteen (1971 ERA 3.25)	1.25	.60	.40
34b	Claude Osteen (1971 ERA 3.51)	.75	.40	.25
35	Reggie Smith	.75	.40	.25
36	Sonny Siebert	.75	.40	.25
37	Lee May	.75	.40	.25
38	Mickey Lolich	1.00	.50	.30
39a	Cookie Rojas (2B 149)	1.25	.60	.40
39b	Cookie Rojas (2B 150)	.75	.40	.25
40	Dick Drago	.75	.40	.25
41	Nate Colbert	.75	.40	.25
42	Andy Messersmith	.75	.40	.25
43a	Dave Johnson (AVG. .262)	1.50	.70	.45
43b	Dave Johnson (AVG. .264)	1.00	.50	.30
44	Steve Blass	.75	.40	.25
45	Bob Robertson	.75	.40	.25
46a	Billy Williams (...missed only one last season...)	5.00	2.50	1.50
46b	Billy Williams (phrase omitted)	3.00	1.50	.90
47	Juan Marichal	3.00	1.50	.90
48	Lou Brock	3.00	1.50	.90
49	Roberto Clemente	12.50	6.25	3.75
50	Mel Stottlemyre	.75	.40	.25
51	Don Wilson	.75	.40	.25
52a	Sal Bando (RBI 355)	1.25	.60	.40
52b	Sal Bando (RBI 356)	.75	.40	.25
53a	Willie Stargell (2B 197)	6.00	3.00	1.75
53b	Willie Stargell (2B 196)	3.50	1.75	1.00
54a	Willie Mays (RBI 1855)	15.00	7.50	4.50
54b	Willie Mays (RBI 1856)	12.00	0.00	0.50

1972 Kellogg's All-Time Baseball Greats

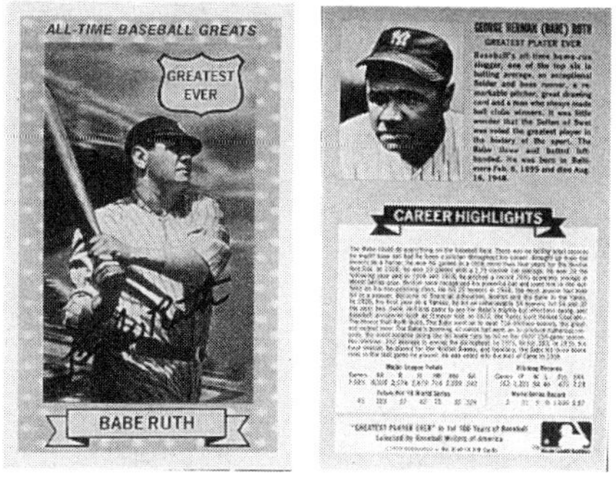

Kellogg's issued a second baseball card set in 1972, inserted into packages of breakfast rolls. The 2-1/4" x 3-1/2" cards also featured a simulated 3-D effect, but the 15 players in the set were "All-Time Baseball Greats", rather than current players. The set is virtually identical to a Rold Gold pretzel issue of 1970; the only difference being the 1972 copyright date on the back of the Kellogg's cards, while the pretzel issue bears a 1970 date. The pretzel cards are considerably scarcer than the Kellogg's.

		NM	EX	VG
Complete Set (15):		30.00	15.00	9.00
Common Player:		1.50	.70	.45
1	Walter Johnson	2.00	1.00	.60
2	Rogers Hornsby	1.50	.70	.45
3	John McGraw	1.50	.70	.45
4	Mickey Cochrane	1.50	.70	.45
5	George Sisler	1.50	.70	.45
6	Babe Ruth (portrait photo on back)	9.00	4.50	2.75
7	Robert "Lefty" Grove	1.50	.70	.45
8	Harold "Pie" Traynor	1.50	.70	.45
9	Honus Wagner	4.00	2.00	1.25
10	Eddie Collins	1.50	.70	.45
11	Tris Speaker	1.50	.70	.45
12	Cy Young	2.00	1.00	.60
13	Lou Gehrig	6.00	3.00	1.75
14	Babe Ruth (action photo on back)	9.00	4.50	2.75
15	Ty Cobb	6.00	3.00	1.75

1973 Kellogg's

The lone exception to Kellogg's long run of simulated 3-D effect cards came in 1973, when the cereal company's 54-card set was produced by "normal" printing methods. In 2-1/4" x 3-1/2" size, the design was otherwise quite compatible with the issues which preceded and succeeded it. Because it was available via a mail-in offer ($1.25 and two Raisin Bran boxtops), it is not as scarce as the earlier Kellogg's issues.

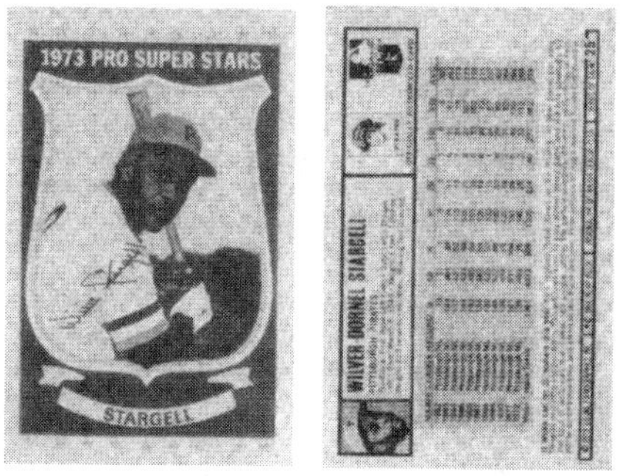

		NM	EX	VG
Complete Set (54):		90.00	45.00	27.00
Common Player:		.75	.40	.20
1	Amos Otis	.75	.40	.20
2	Ellie Rodriguez	.75	.40	.20
3	Mickey Lolich	1.50	.70	.45
4	Tony Oliva	1.50	.70	.45
5	Don Sutton	3.50	1.75	1.00
6	Pete Rose	12.50	6.25	3.75
7	Steve Carlton	5.00	2.50	1.50
8	Bobby Bonds	1.00	.50	.30
9	Wilbur Wood	.75	.40	.20
10	Billy Williams	3.50	1.75	1.00
11	Steve Blass	.75	.40	.20
12	Jon Matlack	.75	.40	.20
13	Cesar Cedeno	.75	.40	.20
14	Bob Gibson	4.00	2.00	1.25
15	Sparky Lyle	.75	.40	.20
16	Nolan Ryan	18.00	9.00	5.50
17	Jim Palmer	3.50	1.75	1.00
18	Ray Fosse	.75	.40	.20
19	Bobby Murcer	.75	.40	.20
20	Jim "Catfish" Hunter	3.50	1.75	1.00
21	Tug McGraw	.75	.40	.25
22	Reggie Jackson	7.50	3.75	2.25
23	Bill Stoneman	.75	.40	.20
24	Lou Piniella	.75	.40	.20
25	Willie Stargell	3.50	1.75	1.00
26	Dick Allen	3.00	1.50	.90
27	Carlton Fisk	3.50	1.75	1.00
28	Fergie Jenkins	3.50	1.75	1.00
29	Phil Niekro	3.50	1.75	1.00
30	Gary Nolan	.75	.40	.20
31	Joe Torre	2.00	1.00	.60
32	Bobby Tolan	.75	.40	.20
33	Nate Colbert	.75	.40	.20
34	Joe Morgan	3.50	1.75	1.00
35	Bert Blyleven	.75	.40	.20
36	Joe Rudi	.75	.40	.20
37	Ralph Garr	.75	.40	.20
38	Gaylord Perry	3.50	1.75	1.00
39	Bobby Grich	.75	.40	.20
40	Lou Brock	3.50	1.75	1.00
41	Pete Broberg	.75	.40	.20
42	Manny Sanguillen	.75	.40	.20
43	Willie Davis	.75	.40	.20
44	Dave Kingman	1.00	.50	.30
45	Carlos May	.75	.40	.20
46	Tom Seaver	5.00	2.50	1.50
47	Mike Cuellar	.75	.40	.20
48	Joe Coleman	.75	.40	.20
49	Claude Osteen	.75	.40	.20
50	Steve Kline	.75	.40	.20
51	Rod Carew	5.00	2.50	1.50
52	Al Kaline	5.00	2.50	1.50
53	Larry Dierker	.75	.40	.20
54	Ron Santo	1.50	.70	.45

1974 Kellogg's

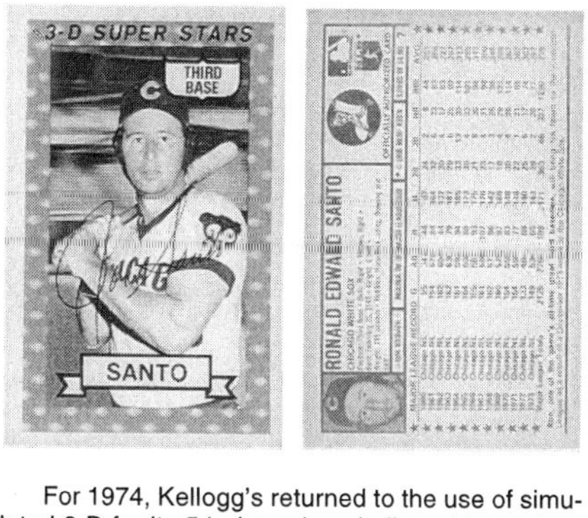

For 1974, Kellogg's returned to the use of simulated 3-D for its 54-player baseball card issue (see 1970 Kellogg's listing for description). In 2-1/8" x 3-1/4" size, the cards were available as a complete set via a mail-in offer. The complete set price listed here does not include the more expensive variations.

		NM	EX	VG
Complete Set (54):		50.00	25.00	15.00
Common Player:		.60	.30	.20
1	Bob Gibson	4.50	2.25	1.25
2	Rick Monday	.60	.30	.20
3	Joe Coleman	.60	.30	.20
4	Bert Campaneris	.60	.30	.20
5	Carlton Fisk	4.00	2.00	1.25
6	Jim Palmer	4.00	2.00	1.25
7a	Ron Santo (Chicago Cubs)	2.00	1.00	.60
7b	Ron Santo (Chicago White Sox)	.90	.45	.25
8	Nolan Ryan	15.00	7.50	4.50
9	Greg Luzinski	.60	.30	.20
10a	Buddy Bell (Runs 134)	2.00	1.00	.60
10b	Buddy Bell (Runs 135)	.90	.45	.25
11	Bob Watson	.60	.30	.20
12	Bill Singer	.60	.30	.20
13	Dave May	.60	.30	.20
14	Jim Brewer	.60	.30	.20
15	Manny Sanguillen	.60	.30	.20
16	Jeff Burroughs	.60	.30	.20
17	Amos Otis	.60	.30	.20
18	Ed Goodson	.60	.30	.20
19	Nate Colbert	.60	.30	.20
20	Reggie Jackson	5.00	2.50	1.50
21	Ted Simmons	.60	.30	.20
22	Bobby Murcer	.60	.30	.20
23	Willie Horton	.60	.30	.20
24	Orlando Cepeda	4.00	2.00	1.25
25	Ron Hunt	.60	.30	.20
26	Wayne Twitchell	.60	.30	.20
27	Ron Fairly	.60	.30	.20
28	Johnny Bench	4.50	2.25	1.25
29	John Mayberry	.60	.30	.20
30	Rod Carew	4.00	2.00	1.25
31	Ken Holtzman	.60	.30	.20
32	Billy Williams	4.00	2.00	1.25
33	Dick Allen	2.50	1.25	.70
34a	Wilbur Wood (SO 959)	1.50	.70	.45
34b	Wilbur Wood (SO 960)	.70	.35	.20
35	Danny Thompson	.60	.30	.20
36	Joe Morgan	4.00	2.00	1.25
37	Willie Stargell	4.00	2.00	1.25
38	Pete Rose	10.00	5.00	3.00
39	Bobby Bonds	.70	.35	.20
40	Chris Speier	.60	.30	.20
41	Sparky Lyle	.60	.30	.20
42	Cookie Rojas	.60	.30	.20
43	Tommy Davis	.60	.30	.20
44	Jim "Catfish" Hunter	4.00	2.00	1.25
45	Willie Davis	.60	.30	.20
46	Bert Blyleven	.60	.30	.20
47	Pat Kelly	.60	.30	.20
48	Ken Singleton	.60	.30	.20
49	Manny Mota	.60	.30	.20
50	Dave Johnson	.60	.30	.20
51	Sal Bando	.60	.30	.20
52	Tom Seaver	4.50	2.25	1.25
53	Felix Millan	.60	.30	.20
54	Ron Blomberg	.60	.30	.20

1975 Kellogg's

While the card size remained the same at 2-1/8" x 3-1/4", the size of the 1975 Kellogg's "3-D" set was increased by three, to 57 cards. Despite the fact cards could be obtained by a mail-in offer, as well as in cereal boxes, the '75 Kellogg's are noticeably scarcer than the company's other issues, with the exception of the 1971 set. Also helping to raise the value of the cards is the presence of an unusually large number of current and future Hall of Famers.

		NM	EX	VG
Complete Set (57):		150.00	75.00	45.00
Common Player:		2.00	1.00	.60
1	Roy White	2.00	1.00	.60
2	Ross Grimsley	2.00	1.00	.60
3	Reggie Smith	2.00	1.00	.60
4a	Bob Grich ("...1973 work..." in last line)	4.00	2.00	1.25
4b	Bob Grich (no "...1973 work...")	2.50	1.25	.70
5	Greg Gross	2.00	1.00	.60
6	Bob Watson	2.00	1.00	.60
7	Johnny Bench	12.00	6.00	3.50
8	Jeff Burroughs	2.00	1.00	.60
9	Elliott Maddox	2.00	1.00	.60
10	Jon Matlack	2.00	1.00	.60
11	Pete Rose	22.00	11.00	6.50
12	Leroy Stanton	2.00	1.00	.60
13	Bake McBride	2.00	1.00	.60
14	Jorge Orta	2.00	1.00	.60
15	Al Oliver	2.50	1.25	.70
16	John Briggs	2.00	1.00	.60
17	Steve Garvey	6.00	3.00	1.75
18	Brooks Robinson	12.00	6.00	3.50
19	John Hiller	2.00	1.00	.60
20	Lynn McGlothen	2.00	1.00	.60
21	Cleon Jones	2.00	1.00	.60
22	Fergie Jenkins	7.50	3.75	2.25
23	Bill North	2.00	1.00	.60
24	Steve Busby	2.00	1.00	.60
25	Richie Zisk	2.00	1.00	.60
26	Nolan Ryan	25.00	12.50	7.50
27	Joe Morgan	7.50	3.75	2.25
28	Joe Rudi	2.00	1.00	.60
29	Jose Cardenal	2.00	1.00	.60
30	Andy Messersmith	2.00	1.00	.60
31	Willie Montanez	2.00	1.00	.60
32	Bill Buckner	2.00	1.00	.60
33	Rod Carew	9.00	4.50	2.75
34	Lou Piniella	2.00	1.00	.60
35	Ralph Garr	2.00	1.00	.60
36	Mike Marshall	2.00	1.00	.60
37	Garry Maddox	2.00	1.00	.60
38	Dwight Evans	2.00	1.00	.60
39	Lou Brock	7.50	3.75	2.25
40	Ken Singleton	2.00	1.00	.60
41	Steve Braun	2.00	1.00	.60
42	Dick Allen	4.00	2.00	1.25
43	Johnny Grubb	2.00	1.00	.60
44a	Jim Hunter (Oakland)	11.00	5.50	3.25
44b	Jim Hunter (New York)	8.00	4.00	2.50
45	Gaylord Perry	7.50	3.75	2.25
46	George Hendrick	2.00	1.00	.60
47	Sparky Lyle	2.00	1.00	.60
48	Dave Cash	2.00	1.00	.60
49	Luis Tiant	2.50	1.25	.70
50	Cesar Geronimo	2.00	1.00	.60
51	Carl Yastrzemski	15.00	7.50	4.50
52	Ken Brett	2.00	1.00	.60
53	Hal McRae	2.00	1.00	.60
54	Reggie Jackson	15.00	7.50	4.50
55	Rollie Fingers	6.00	3.00	1.75
56	Mike Schmidt	18.00	9.00	5.50
57	Richie Hebner	2.00	1.00	.60

1976 Kellogg's

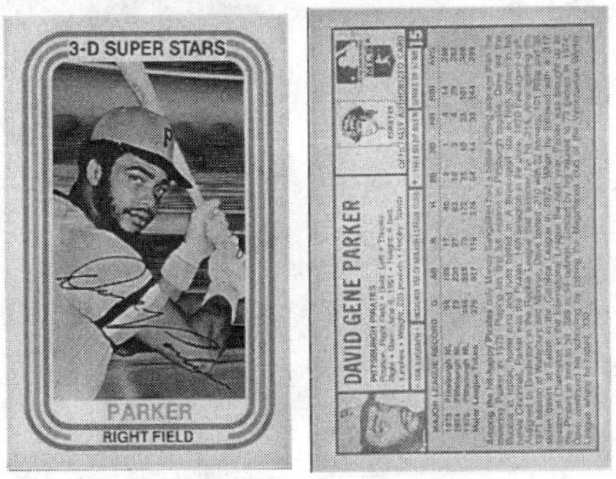

A sizeable list of corrected errors and other variation cards dots the checklist for the 57-card 1976 Kellogg's 3-D set. Again containing 57 cards, the first three cards in the set are found far less often than cards #4-57, indicating they were short-printed in relation to the rest of the set. The complete set values quoted below do not include the scarcer variation cards. Card size remained at 2-1/8" x 3-1/4". Cards #1-3 were short-printed.

		NM	EX	VG
Complete Set (57):		60.00	30.00	18.00
Common Player:		1.25	.60	.40
1	Steve Hargan	7.50	3.75	2.25
2	Claudell Washington	7.50	3.75	2.25
3	Don Gullett	7.50	3.75	2.25
4	Randy Jones	1.25	.60	.40
5	Jim "Catfish" Hunter	4.50	2.25	1.25
6a	Clay Carroll (Cincinnati)	2.25	1.25	.70
6b	Clay Carroll (Chicago)	1.25	.60	.40
7	Joe Rudi	1.25	.60	.40
8	Reggie Jackson	6.00	3.00	1.75
9	Felix Millan	1.25	.60	.40
10	Jim Rice	1.50	.70	.45
11	Bert Blyleven	1.25	.60	.40
12	Ken Singleton	1.25	.60	.40
13	Don Sutton	3.50	1.75	1.00
14	Joe Morgan	4.50	2.25	1.25
15	Dave Parker	2.00	1.00	.60
16	Dave Cash	1.25	.60	.40
17	Ron LeFlore	1.25	.60	.40
18	Greg Luzinski	1.25	.60	.40
19	Dennis Eckersley	3.00	1.50	.90
20	Bill Madlock	1.25	.60	.40
21	George Scott	1.25	.60	.40
22	Willie Stargell	4.50	2.25	1.25
23	Al Hrabosky	1.25	.60	.40
24	Carl Yastrzemski	8.00	4.00	2.50
25	Jim Kaat	2.50	1.25	.70
26	Marty Perez	1.25	.60	.40
27	Bob Watson	1.25	.60	.40
28	Eric Soderholm	1.25	.60	.40
29	Bill Lee	1.25	.60	.40
30a	Frank Tanana (1975 ERA 2.63)	2.00	1.00	.60
30b	Frank Tanana (1975 ERA 2.62)	1.25	.60	.40
31	Fred Lynn	1.50	.70	.45
32a	Tom Seaver (1967 PCT. 552)	7.50	3.75	2.25
32b	Tom Seaver (1967 Pct. .552)	6.00	3.00	1.75
33	Steve Busby	1.25	.60	.40
34	Gary Carter	2.25	1.25	.70
35	Rick Wise	1.25	.60	.40
36	Johnny Bench	6.00	3.00	1.75
37	Jim Palmer	4.50	2.25	1.25
38	Bobby Murcer	1.25	.60	.40
39	Von Joshua	1.25	.60	.40
40	Lou Brock	4.50	2.25	1.25
41a	Mickey Rivers (last line begins "In three...")	2.00	1.00	.60
41b	Mickey Rivers (last line begins "The Yankees...")	1.25	.60	.40
42	Manny Sanguillen	1.25	.60	.40
43	Jerry Reuss	1.25	.60	.40
44	Ken Griffey	1.25	.60	.40
45a	Jorge Orta (AB 1616)	1.75	.90	.50
45b	Jorge Orta (AB 1615)	1.25	.60	.40
46	John Mayberry	1.25	.60	.40
47a	Vida Blue (2nd line reads "...pitched more innings ...")	2.25	1.25	.70
47b	Vida Blue (2nd line reads "...struck out more...")	1.25	.60	.40
48	Rod Carew	5.00	2.50	1.50
49a	Jon Matlack (1975 ER 87)	1.75	.90	.50
49b	Jon Matlack (1975 ER 86)	1.25	.60	.40
50	Boog Powell	2.25	1.25	.70
51a	Mike Hargrove (AB 935)	1.75	.90	.50
51b	Mike Hargrove (AB 934)	1.25	.60	.40
52a	Paul Lindblad (1975 ERA 2.72)	1.75	.90	.50
52b	Paul Lindblad (1975 ERA 2.73)	1.25	.60	.40
53	Thurman Munson	5.00	2.50	1.50
54	Steve Garvey	2.50	1.25	.70
55	Pete Rose	10.00	5.00	3.00
56a	Greg Gross (Games 302)	1.75	.90	.50
56b	Greg Gross (Games 334)	1.25	.60	.40
57	Ted Simmons	1.25	.60	.40

1977 Kellogg's

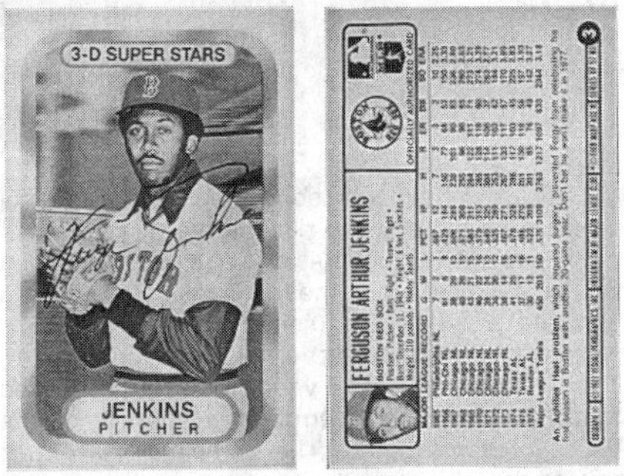

Other than another innovative card design to complement the simulated 3-D effect, there was little change in the 1977 Kellogg's issue. Set size remained at 57 cards, the set remained in the 2-1/8" x 3-1/4" format, and the cards were available either individually in boxes of cereal, or as a complete set via a mail-in box top offer. The 1977 set is the last in which Kellogg's used a player portrait photo on the back of the card.

		NM	EX	VG
Complete Set (57):		45.00	22.00	13.00
Common Player:		.50	.25	.15
1	George Foster	.50	.25	.15
2	Bert Campaneris	.50	.25	.15
3	Fergie Jenkins	2.00	1.00	.60
4	Dock Ellis	.50	.25	.15
5	John Montefusco	.50	.25	.15
6	George Brett	12.00	6.00	3.50
7	John Candelaria	.50	.25	.15
8	Fred Norman	.50	.25	.15
9	Bill Travers	.50	.25	.15
10	Hal McRae	.50	.25	.15
11	Doug Rau	.50	.25	.15
12	Greg Luzinski	.50	.25	.15
13	Ralph Garr	.50	.25	.15
14	Steve Garvey	1.50	.70	.45
15	Rick Manning	.50	.25	.15
16a	Lyman Bostock (Back photo is N.Y. Yankee Dock Ellis)	6.00	3.00	1.75
16b	Lyman Bostock (correct back photo)	.50	.25	.15
17	Randy Jones	.50	.25	.15
18a	Ron Cey (58 homers in first sentence)	1.00	.50	.30
18b	Ron Cey (48 homers in first sentence)	.60	.30	.20
19	Dave Parker	1.00	.50	.30
20	Pete Rose	10.00	5.00	3.00
21a	Wayne Garland (last line begins "Prior to...")	.90	.45	.25
21b	Wayne Garland (last line begins "There he...")	.50	.25	.15
22	Bill North	.50	.25	.15

23	Thurman Munson	5.00	2.50	1.50
24	Tom Poquette	.50	.25	.15
25	Ron LeFlore	.50	.25	.15
26	Mark Fidrych	.75	.40	.25
27	Sixto Lezcano	.50	.25	.15
28	Dave Winfield	4.00	2.00	1.25
29	Jerry Koosman	.50	.25	.15
30	Mike Hargrove	.50	.25	.15
31	Willie Montanez	.50	.25	.15
32	Don Stanhouse	.50	.25	.15
33	Jay Johnstone	.50	.25	.15
34	Bake McBride	.50	.25	.15
35	Dave Kingman	.75	.40	.25
36	Freddie Patek	.50	.25	.15
37	Garry Maddox	.50	.25	.15
38a	Ken Reitz (last line begins "The previous...")	.90	.45	.25
38b	Ken Reitz (last line begins "In late...")	.50	.25	.15
39	Bobby Grich	.50	.25	.15
40	Cesar Geronimo	.50	.25	.15
41	Jim Lonborg	.50	.25	.15
42	Ed Figueroa	.50	.25	.15
43	Bill Madlock	.50	.25	.15
44	Jerry Remy	.50	.25	.15
45	Frank Tanana	.50	.25	.15
46	Al Oliver	.75	.40	.25
47	Charlie Hough	.50	.25	.15
48	Lou Piniella	.50	.25	.15
49	Ken Griffey	.50	.25	.15
50	Jose Cruz	.50	.25	.15
51	Rollie Fingers	2.00	1.00	.60
52	Chris Chambliss	.50	.25	.15
53	Rod Carew	4.00	2.00	1.25
54	Andy Messersmith	.50	.25	.15
55	Mickey Rivers	.50	.25	.15
56	Butch Wynegar	.50	.25	.15
57	Steve Carlton	3.00	1.50	.90

1978 Kellogg's

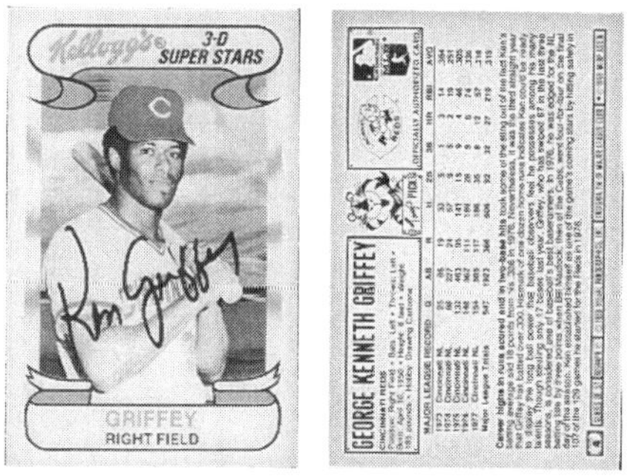

Besides the substitution of a Tony the Tiger drawing for a player portrait photo on the back of the card, the 1978 Kellogg's set offered no major changes from the previous few years issues. Cards were once again in the 2-1/8" x 3-1/4" format, with 57 cards comprising a complete set. Single cards were available in selected brands of the company's cereal, while complete sets could be obtained by a mail-in offer.

		NM	EX	VG
Complete Set (57):		40.00	20.00	12.00
Common Player:		.50	.25	.15
1	Steve Carlton	3.00	1.50	.90
2	Bucky Dent	.50	.25	.15
3	Mike Schmidt	6.00	3.00	1.75
4	Ken Griffey	.50	.25	.15
5	Al Cowens	.50	.25	.15
6	George Brett	8.00	4.00	2.50
7	Lou Brock	3.00	1.50	.90
8	Rich Gossage	.60	.30	.20
9	Tom Johnson	.50	.25	.15
10	George Foster	.50	.25	.15
11	Dave Winfield	3.00	1.50	.90
12	Dan Meyer	.50	.25	.15
13	Chris Chambliss	.50	.25	.15
14	Paul Dade	.50	.25	.15
15	Jeff Burroughs	.50	.25	.15
16	Jose Cruz	.50	.25	.15
17	Mickey Rivers	.50	.25	.15
18	John Candelaria	.50	.25	.15
19	Ellis Valentine	.50	.25	.15
20	Hal McRae	.50	.25	.15
21	Dave Rozema	.50	.25	.15
22	Lenny Randle	.50	.25	.15
23	Willie McCovey	3.00	1.50	.90
24	Ron Cey	.50	.25	.15
25	Eddie Murray	12.50	6.25	3.75
26	Larry Bowa	.50	.25	.15
27	Tom Seaver	3.50	1.75	1.00
28	Garry Maddox	.50	.25	.15
29	Rod Carew	3.00	1.50	.90
30	Thurman Munson	3.50	1.75	1.00
31	Garry Templeton	.50	.25	.15
32	Eric Soderholm	.50	.25	.15
33	Greg Luzinski	.50	.25	.15
34	Reggie Smith	.50	.25	.15
35	Dave Goltz	.50	.25	.15
36	Tommy John	.60	.30	.20
37	Ralph Garr	.50	.25	.15
38	Alan Bannister	.50	.25	.15
39	Bob Bailor	.50	.25	.15
40	Reggie Jackson	3.50	1.75	1.00
41	Cecil Cooper	.50	.25	.15
42	Burt Hooton	.50	.25	.15
43	Sparky Lyle	.50	.25	.15
44	Steve Ontiveros	.50	.25	.15
45	Rick Reuschel	.50	.25	.15
46	Lyman Bostock	.50	.25	.15
47	Mitchell Page	.50	.25	.15
48	Bruce Sutter	.50	.25	.15
49	Jim Rice	.75	.40	.25
50	Bob Forsch	.50	.25	.15
51	Nolan Ryan	12.50	6.25	3.75
52	Dave Parker	.75	.40	.25
53	Bert Blyleven	.50	.25	.15
54	Frank Tanana	.50	.25	.15
55	Ken Singleton	.50	.25	.15
56	Mike Hargrove	.50	.25	.15
57	Don Sutton	3.00	1.50	.90

1979 Kellogg's

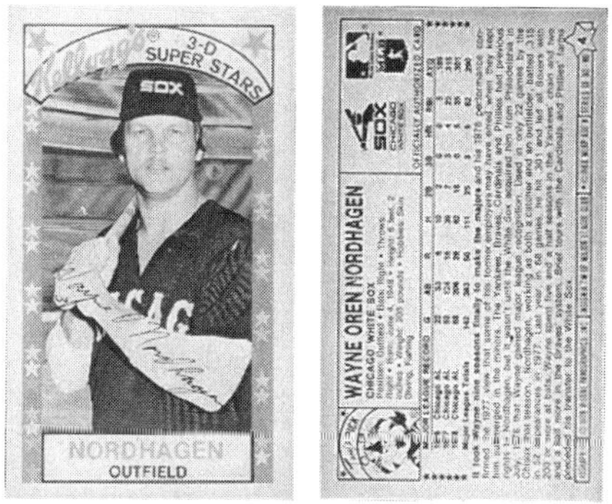

For its 1979 3-D issue, Kellogg's increased the size of the set to 60 cards, but reduced the width of the cards to 1-15/16". Depth stayed the same as in previous years, 3-1/4". The narrower card format seems to have compounded the problem of curling and subsequent cracking of the ribbed plastic surface which helps give the card a 3-D effect. Cards with major cracks can be graded no higher than VG. The complete set price in the checklist that follows does not include the scarcer variations. Numerous minor variations featuring copyright and trademark logos can be found in the set.

		NM	EX	VG
Complete Set (60):		25.00	12.50	7.50
Common Player:		.50	.25	.15
1	Bruce Sutter	.50	.25	.15
2	Ted Simmons	.50	.25	.15
3	Ross Grimsley	.50	.25	.15
4	Wayne Nordhagen	.50	.25	.15
5a	Jim Palmer (PCT. .649)	2.00	1.00	.60
5b	Jim Palmer (PCT. .650)	1.25	.60	.40
6	John Henry Johnson	.50	.25	.15
7	Jason Thompson	.50	.25	.15
8	Pat Zachry	.50	.25	.15
9	Dennis Eckersley	1.00	.50	.30
10a	Paul Splittorff (IP 1665)	.50	.25	.15
10b	Paul Splittorff (IP 1666)	.50	.25	.15
11a	Ron Guidry (Hits 397)	.90	.45	.25
11b	Ron Guidry (Hits 396)	.50	.25	.15
12	Jeff Burroughs	.50	.25	.15
13	Rod Carew	2.50	1.25	.70
14a	Buddy Bell (no trade line in bio)	1.00	.50	.30
14b	Buddy Bell (trade line in bio)	.50	.25	.15
15	Jim Rice	.65	.35	.20
16	Garry Maddox	.50	.25	.15
17	Willie McCovey	2.50	1.25	.70
18	Steve Carlton	2.50	1.25	.70
19a	J. R. Richard (stats begin with 1972)	.50	.25	.15
19b	J. R. Richard (stats begin with 1971)	.50	.25	.15
20	Paul Molitor	2.50	1.25	.70
21a	Dave Parker (AVG. .281)	1.50	.70	.45
21b	Dave Parker (AVG. .318)	.90	.45	.25
22a	Pete Rose (1978 3B 3)	5.00	2.50	1.50
22b	Pete Rose (1978 3B 33)	4.00	2.00	1.25
23a	Vida Blue (Runs 819)	.80	.40	.25
23b	Vida Blue (Runs 818)	.50	.25	.15
24	Richie Zisk	.50	.25	.15
25a	Darrell Porter (2B 101)	.70	.35	.20
25b	Darrell Porter (2B 111)	.50	.25	.15
26a	Dan Driessen (Games 642)	.70	.35	.20
26b	Dan Driessen (Games 742)	.50	.25	.15
27a	Geoff Zahn (1978 Minnesota)	.50	.25	.15
27b	Geoff Zahn (1978 Minnesota)	.50	.25	.15
28	Phil Niekro	3.00	1.50	.90
29	Tom Seaver	2.50	1.25	.70
30	Fred Lynn	.75	.40	.25
31	Bill Bonham	.50	.25	.15
32	George Foster	.50	.25	.15
33a	Terry Puhl (last line of bio begins "Terry...")	.50	.25	.15
33b	Terry Puhl (last line of bio begins "His...")	.50	.25	.15
34a	John Candelaria (age is 24)	.80	.40	.25
34b	John Candelaria (age is 25)	.50	.25	.15
35	Bob Knepper	.50	.25	.15
36	Freddie Patek	.50	.25	.15
37	Chris Chambliss	.50	.25	.15
38a	Bob Forsch (1977 Games 86)	.70	.35	.20
38b	Bob Forsch (1977 Games 35)	.50	.25	.15
39a	Ken Griffey (1978 AB 674)	.80	.40	.25
39b	Ken Griffey (1978 AB 614)	.50	.25	.15
40	Jack Clark	.50	.25	.15
41a	Dwight Evans (1978 Hits 13)	1.25	.60	.40
41b	Dwight Evans (1978 Hits 123)	.80	.40	.25
42	Lee Mazzilli	.50	.25	.15
43	Mario Guerrero	.50	.25	.15
44	Larry Bowa	.50	.25	.15
45a	Carl Yastrzemski (Games 9930)	5.50	2.75	1.75
45b	Carl Yastrzemski (Games 9929)	3.50	1.75	1.00
46a	Reggie Jackson (1978 Games 162)	4.00	2.00	1.25
46b	Reggie Jackson (1978 Games 139)	2.50	1.25	.70
47	Rick Reuschel	.50	.25	.15
48a	Mike Flanagan (1976 SO 57)	.80	.40	.25
48b	Mike Flanagan (1976 SO 56)	.50	.25	.15
49a	Gaylord Perry (1973 Hits 325)	1.75	.90	.50
49b	Gaylord Perry (1973 Hits 315)	1.00	.50	.30
50	George Brett	5.00	2.50	1.50
51a	Craig Reynolds (last line of bio begins "He spent...")	.50	.25	.15
51b	Craig Reynolds (last line of bio begins "In those...")	.50	.25	.15
52	Davey Lopes	.50	.25	.15
53a	Bill Almon (2B 31)	.50	.25	.15
53b	Bill Almon (2B 41)	.50	.25	.15
54	Roy Howell	.50	.25	.15
55	Frank Tanana	.50	.25	.15
56a	Doug Rau (1978 PCT. .577)	.50	.25	.15
56b	Doug Rau (1978 PCT. .625)	.50	.25	.15
57a	Rick Monday (1976 Runs 197)	.80	.40	.25
57b	Rick Monday (1976 Runs 107)	.50	.25	.15
58	Jon Matlack	.50	.25	.15
59a	Ron Jackson (last line of bio begins "His best...")	.50	.25	.15
59b	Ron Jackson (last line of bio begins "The Twins...")	.50	.25	.15
60	Jim Sundberg	.50	.25	.15

1980 Kellogg's

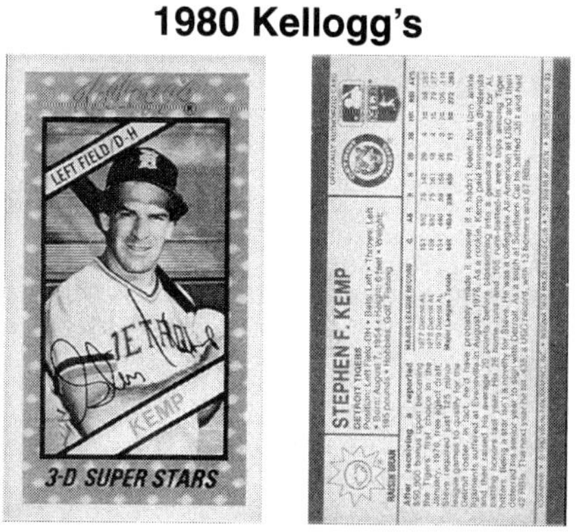

The 1980 cereal company issue featured the narrowest format of any Kellogg's card, 1-7/8" x 3-1/4". For the second straight year, set size remained at 60 cards, available either singly in boxes of cereal, or as complete sets by a mail-in offer.

		NM	EX	VG
Complete Set (60):		22.00	11.00	6.50
Common Player:		.50	.25	.15
1	Ross Grimsley	.50	.25	.15
2	Mike Schmidt	4.00	2.00	1.25
3	Mike Flanagan	.50	.25	.15
4	Ron Guidry	.50	.25	.15
5	Bert Blyleven	.50	.25	.15
6	Dave Kingman	.75	.40	.25
7	Jeff Newman	.50	.25	.15
8	Steve Rogers	.50	.25	.15
9	George Brett	5.00	2.50	1.50
10	Bruce Sutter	.50	.25	.15
11	Gorman Thomas	.50	.25	.15
12	Darrell Porter	.50	.25	.15
13	Roy Smalley	.50	.25	.15
14	Steve Carlton	2.00	1.00	.60
15	Jim Palmer	2.00	1.00	.60
16	Bob Bailor	.50	.25	.15
17	Jason Thompson	.50	.25	.15
18	Graig Nettles	.50	.25	.15
19	Ron Cey	.50	.25	.15
20	Nolan Ryan	10.00	5.00	3.00
21	Ellis Valentine	.50	.25	.15
22	Larry Hisle	.50	.25	.15
23	Dave Parker	.75	.40	.25
24	Eddie Murray	3.00	1.50	.90
25	Willie Stargell	2.50	1.25	.70
26	Reggie Jackson	3.00	1.50	.90
27	Carl Yastrzemski	3.00	1.50	.90
28	Andre Thornton	.50	.25	.15
29	Davey Lopes	.50	.25	.15
30	Ken Singleton	.50	.25	.15
31	Steve Garvey	1.00	.50	.30
32	Dave Winfield	2.50	1.25	.70

33	Steve Kemp	.50	.25	.15
34	Claudell Washington	.50	.25	.15
35	Pete Rose	7.50	3.75	2.25
36	Cesar Cedeno	.50	.25	.15
37	John Stearns	.50	.25	.15
38	Lee Mazzilli	.50	.25	.15
39	Larry Bowa	.50	.25	.15
40	Fred Lynn	.50	.25	.15
41	Carlton Fisk	2.00	1.00	.60
42	Vida Blue	.50	.25	.15
43	Keith Hernandez	.50	.25	.15
44	Jim Rice	.75	.40	.25
45	Ted Simmons	.50	.25	.15
46	Chet Lemon	.50	.25	.15
47	Fergie Jenkins	2.00	1.00	.60
48	Gary Matthews	.50	.25	.15
49	Tom Seaver	3.00	1.50	.90
50	George Foster	.50	.25	.15
51	Phil Niekro	2.00	1.00	.60
52	Johnny Bench	3.00	1.50	.90
53	Buddy Bell	.50	.25	.15
54	Lance Parrish	.50	.25	.15
55	Joaquin Andujar	.50	.25	.15
56	Don Baylor	.60	.30	.20
57	Jack Clark	.50	.25	.15
58	J.R. Richard	.50	.25	.15
59	Bruce Bochte	.50	.25	.15
60	Rod Carew	3.00	1.50	.90

1981 Kellogg's

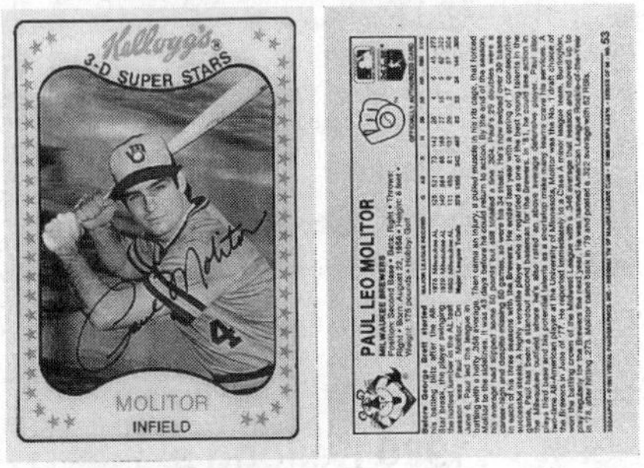

"Bigger" is the word to best describe Kellogg's 1981 card set. Not only were the cards themselves larger than ever before at 2-1/2" x 3-1/2", but the size of the set was increased to 66, the largest since the 75-card issues of 1970-71. The '81 Kellogg's set was available only as complete sets by mail. It is thought that the wider format of the 1981s may help prevent the problems of curling and cracking from which other years of Kellogg's issues suffer.

		MT	NM	EX
	Complete Set (66):	12.50	9.50	5.00
	Common Player:	.25	.20	.10
1	George Foster	.25	.20	.10
2	Jim Palmer	1.00	.70	.40
3	Reggie Jackson	2.50	2.00	1.00
4	Al Oliver	.25	.20	.10
5	Mike Schmidt	2.50	2.00	1.00
6	Nolan Ryan	6.00	4.50	2.50
7	Bucky Dent	.25	.20	.10
8	George Brett	2.50	2.00	1.00
9	Jim Rice	.50	.40	.20
10	Steve Garvey	.50	.40	.20
11	Willie Stargell	1.00	.70	.40
12	Phil Niekro	.75	.60	.30
13	Dave Parker	.30	.25	.12
14	Cesar Cedeno	.25	.20	.10
15	Don Baylor	.35	.25	.14
16	J.R. Richard	.25	.20	.10
17	Tony Perez	1.00	.70	.40
18	Eddie Murray	1.00	.70	.40
19	Chet Lemon	.25	.20	.10
20	Ben Oglivie	.25	.20	.10
21	Dave Winfield	1.00	.70	.40
22	Joe Morgan	1.00	.70	.40
23	Vida Blue	.25	.20	.10
24	Willie Wilson	.25	.20	.10
25	Steve Henderson	.25	.20	.10
26	Rod Carew	1.00	.70	.40
27	Garry Templeton	.25	.20	.10
28	Dave Concepcion	.25	.20	.10
29	Davey Lopes	.25	.20	.10
30	Ken Landreaux	.25	.20	.10
31	Keith Hernandez	.25	.20	.10
32	Cecil Cooper	.25	.20	.10
33	Rickey Henderson	2.00	1.50	.80
34	Frank White	.25	.20	.10
35	George Hendrick	.25	.20	.10
36	Reggie Smith	.25	.20	.10
37	Tug McGraw	.25	.20	.10
38	Tom Seaver	1.50	1.25	.60
39	Ken Singleton	.25	.20	.10
40	Fred Lynn	.25	.20	.10
41	Rich "Goose" Gossage	.25	.20	.10
42	Terry Puhl	.25	.20	.10
43	Larry Bowa	.25	.20	.10
44	Phil Garner	.25	.20	.10
45	Ron Guidry	.25	.20	.10
46	Lee Mazzilli	.25	.20	.10
47	Dave Kingman	.25	.20	.10
48	Carl Yastrzemski	2.00	1.50	.80
49	Rick Burleson	.25	.20	.10
50	Steve Carlton	1.00	.70	.40
51	Alan Trammell	.50	.40	.20
52	Tommy John	.25	.20	.10
53	Paul Molitor	1.00	.70	.40
54	Joe Charboneau	.50	.40	.20
55	Rick Langford	.25	.20	.10
56	Bruce Sutter	.25	.20	.10
57	Robin Yount	1.00	.70	.40
58	Steve Stone	.25	.20	.10
59	Larry Gura	.25	.20	.10
60	Mike Flanagan	.25	.20	.10
61	Bob Horner	.25	.20	.10
62	Bruce Bochte	.25	.20	.10
63	Pete Rose	4.00	3.00	1.50
64	Buddy Bell	.25	.20	.10
65	Johnny Bench	2.00	1.50	.80
66	Mike Hargrove	.25	.20	.10

1982 Kellogg's

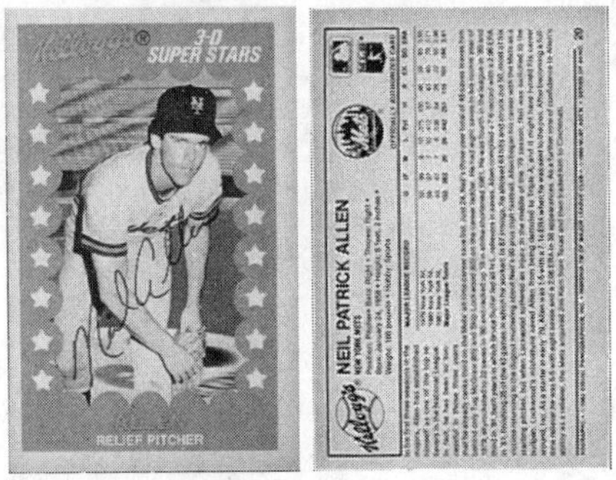

For the second straight year in 1982, Kellogg's cards were not inserted into cereal boxes, but had to be obtained by sending cash and box tops to the company for complete sets. The '82 cards were downsized both in number of cards in the set - 64 - and in physical dimensions, 2-1/8" x 3-1/4".

		MT	NM	EX
	Complete Set (64):	15.00	11.00	6.00
	Common Player:	.25	.20	.10
1	Richie Zisk	.25	.20	.10
2	Bill Buckner	.25	.20	.10
3	George Brett	3.00	2.25	1.25
4	Rickey Henderson	1.00	.70	.40
5	Jack Morris	.25	.20	.10
6	Ozzie Smith	2.00	1.50	.80
7	Rollie Fingers	1.00	.70	.40
8	Tom Seaver	2.00	1.50	.80
9	Fernando Valenzuela	.25	.20	.10
10	Hubie Brooks	.25	.20	.10
11	Nolan Ryan	6.00	4.50	2.50
12	Dave Winfield	1.00	.70	.40
13	Bob Horner	.25	.20	.10
14	Reggie Jackson	1.50	1.25	.60
15	Burt Hooton	.25	.20	.10
16	Mike Schmidt	3.00	2.25	1.25
17	Bruce Sutter	.25	.20	.10
18	Pete Rose	4.00	3.00	1.50
19	Dave Kingman	.25	.20	.10
20	Neil Allen	.25	.20	.10
21	Don Sutton	.75	.60	.30
22	Dave Concepcion	.25	.20	.10
23	Keith Hernandez	.25	.20	.10
24	Gary Carter	.50	.40	.20
25	Carlton Fisk	1.00	.70	.40
26	Ron Guidry	.25	.20	.10
27	Steve Carlton	1.00	.70	.40
28	Robin Yount	1.00	.70	.40
29	John Castino	.25	.20	.10
30	Johnny Bench	2.00	1.50	.80
31	Bob Knepper	.25	.20	.10
32	Rich "Goose" Gossage	.25	.20	.10
33	Buddy Bell	.25	.20	.10
34	Art Howe	.25	.20	.10
35	Tony Armas	.25	.20	.10
36	Phil Niekro	1.00	.70	.40
37	Len Barker	.25	.20	.10
38	Bobby Grich	.25	.20	.10
39	Steve Kemp	.25	.20	.10
40	Kirk Gibson	.25	.20	.10
41	Carney Lansford	.25	.20	.10
42	Jim Palmer	1.00	.70	.40
43	Carl Yastrzemski	1.50	1.25	.60
44	Rick Burleson	.25	.20	.10
45	Dwight Evans	.25	.20	.10
46	Ron Cey	.25	.20	.10
47	Steve Garvey	.60	.45	.25
48	Dave Parker	.30	.25	.12
49	Mike Easler	.25	.20	.10
50	Dusty Baker	.25	.20	.10
51	Rod Carew	1.00	.70	.40
52	Chris Chambliss	.25	.20	.10
53	Tim Raines	.60	.45	.25
54	Chet Lemon	.25	.20	.10
55	Bill Madlock	.25	.20	.10
56	George Foster	.25	.20	.10
57	Dwayne Murphy	.25	.20	.10
58	Ken Singleton	.25	.20	.10
59	Mike Norris	.25	.20	.10
60	Cecil Cooper	.25	.20	.10
61	Al Oliver	.25	.20	.10
62	Willie Wilson	.25	.20	.10
63	Vida Blue	.25	.20	.10
64	Eddie Murray	1.00	.70	.40

1983 Kellogg's

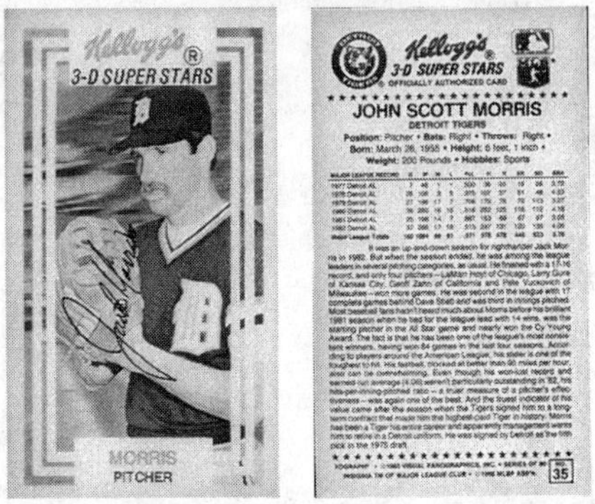

In its 14th consecutive year of baseball card issue, Kellogg's returned to the policy of inserting single cards into cereal boxes, as well as offering complete sets by a mail-in box top redemption offer. The 3-D cards themselves returned to a narrow 1-7/8" x 3-1/4" format, while the set size was reduced to 60 cards.

		MT	NM	EX
	Complete Set (60):	12.50	9.50	5.00
	Common Player:	.25	.20	.10
1	Rod Carew	1.50	1.25	.60
2	Rollie Fingers	1.00	.70	.40
3	Reggie Jackson	1.50	1.25	.60
4	George Brett	2.00	1.50	.80
5	Hal McRae	.25	.20	.10
6	Pete Rose	3.00	2.25	1.25
7	Fernando Valenzuela	.25	.20	.10
8	Rickey Henderson	1.00	.70	.40
9	Carl Yastrzemski	1.50	1.25	.60
10	Rich "Goose" Gossage	.25	.20	.10
11	Eddie Murray	1.00	.70	.40
12	Buddy Bell	.25	.20	.10
13	Jim Rice	.50	.40	.20
14	Robin Yount	1.00	.70	.40
15	Dave Winfield	1.00	.70	.40
16	Harold Baines	.25	.20	.10
17	Garry Templeton	.25	.20	.10
18	Bill Madlock	.25	.20	.10
19	Pete Vuckovich	.25	.20	.10
20	Pedro Guerrero	.25	.20	.10
21	Ozzie Smith	1.00	.70	.40
22	George Foster	.25	.20	.10
23	Willie Wilson	.25	.20	.10
24	Johnny Ray	.25	.20	.10
25	George Hendrick	.25	.20	.10
26	Andre Thornton	.25	.20	.10
27	Leon Durham	.25	.20	.10
28	Cecil Cooper	.25	.20	.10
29	Don Baylor	.35	.25	.14
30	Lonnie Smith	.25	.20	.10
31	Nolan Ryan	5.00	3.75	2.00
32	Dan Quiesenberry (Quisenberry)	.25	.20	.10
33	Len Barker	.25	.20	.10
34	Neil Allen	.25	.20	.10
35	Jack Morris	.25	.20	.10
36	Dave Stieb	.25	.20	.10
37	Bruce Sutter	.25	.20	.10
38	Jim Sundberg	.25	.20	.10
39	Jim Palmer	1.00	.70	.40
40	Lance Parrish	.25	.20	.10
41	Floyd Bannister	.25	.20	.10
42	Larry Gura	.25	.20	.10
43	Britt Burns	.25	.20	.10
44	Toby Harrah	.25	.20	.10
45	Steve Carlton	1.00	.70	.40
46	Greg Minton	.25	.20	.10
47	Gorman Thomas	.25	.20	.10
48	Jack Clark	.25	.20	.10
49	Keith Hernandez	.25	.20	.10
50	Greg Luzinski	.25	.20	.10
51	Fred Lynn	.25	.20	.10
52	Dale Murphy	.75	.60	.30
53	Kent Hrbek	.30	.25	.12
54	Bob Horner	.25	.20	.10
55	Gary Carter	.30	.25	.12
56	Carlton Fisk	1.00	.70	.40
57	Dave Concepcion	.25	.20	.10
58	Mike Schmidt	2.00	1.50	.80
59	Bill Buckner	.25	.20	.10
60	Bobby Grich	.25	.20	.10

1969 Kelly's Potato Chips Pins

Consisting of 20 pins, each measuring approximately 1-3/16" in diameter, this set was issued by Kelly's Potato Chips in 1969 and has a heavy emphasis on St. Louis Cardinals. The pin has a black and white player photo in the center surrounded by either a red border (for A.L. players) or a blue border (for N.L. players) that displays the player's team and name at the top and bottom. "Kelly's" appears to the left while the word "Zip!" is printed to the right. The pins are unnumbered.

		NM	EX	VG
Complete Set (20):		125.00	62.00	37.00
Common Player:		1.50	.70	.45
(1)	Luis Aparicio	6.00	3.00	1.75
(2)	Ernie Banks	12.00	6.00	3.50
(3)	Glenn Beckert	1.50	.70	.45
(4)	Lou Brock	8.00	4.00	2.50
(5)	Curt Flood	2.00	1.00	.60
(6)	Bob Gibson	8.00	4.00	2.50
(7)	Joel Horlen	1.50	.70	.45
(8)	Al Kaline	12.00	6.00	3.50
(9)	Don Kessinger	1.50	.70	.45
(10)	Mickey Lolich	2.50	1.25	.70
(11)	Juan Marichal	8.00	4.00	2.50
(12)	Willie Mays	20.00	10.00	6.00
(13)	Tim McCarver	2.50	1.25	.70
(14)	Denny McLain	2.50	1.25	.70
(15)	Pete Rose	22.00	11.00	6.50
(16)	Ron Santo	2.50	1.25	.70
(17)	Joe Torre	3.00	1.50	.90
(18)	Pete Ward	1.50	.70	.45
(19)	Billy Williams	6.00	3.00	1.75
(20)	Carl Yastrzemski	12.00	6.00	3.50

1961 Key Chain Inserts

The maker of these postage-stamp size (1-1/8" x 1-1/2") black-and-white, blank-back cards is unknown. From the inclusion of numerous journeyman Pirates players in the set, it probably has a Pittsburgh origin. Possibly intended for sale at stadium souvenir counters, they were made to be inserted into clear plastic key chain novelties, and have a semi-gloss front surface. Unnumbered, they are checklisted here alphabetically.

		NM	EX	VG
Complete Set (69):		250.00	125.00	75.00
Common Player:		2.00	1.00	.60
(1)	Hank Aaron	12.00	6.00	3.50
(2)	Bob Allison	2.00	1.00	.60
(3)	George Altman	2.00	1.00	.60
(4)	Luis Aparicio	4.00	2.00	1.25
(5)	Richie Ashburn	6.00	3.00	1.75
(6)	Ernie Banks	7.50	3.75	2.25
(7)	Earl Battey	2.00	1.00	.60
(8)	Hank Bauer	2.00	1.00	.60
(9)	Gus Bell	2.00	1.00	.60
(10)	Yogi Berra	7.50	3.75	2.25
(11)	Ken Boyer	3.00	1.50	.90
(12)	Lew Burdette	2.00	1.00	.60
(13)	Smoky Burgess	2.00	1.00	.60
(14)	Orlando Cepeda	4.00	2.00	1.25
(15)	Gino Cimoli	2.00	1.00	.60
(16)	Roberto Clemente	16.00	8.00	4.75
(17)	Del Crandall	2.00	1.00	.60
(18)	Dizzy Dean	6.00	3.00	1.75
(19)	Don Drysdale	4.00	2.00	1.25
(20)	Sam Esposito	2.00	1.00	.60
(21)	Roy Face	2.00	1.00	.60
(22)	Nelson Fox	4.00	2.00	1.25
(23)	Bob Friend	2.00	1.00	.60
(24)	Lou Gehrig	9.00	4.50	2.75
(25)	Joe Gibbon	2.00	1.00	.60
(26)	Jim Gilliam	2.00	1.00	.60
(27)	Fred Green	2.00	1.00	.60
(28)	Pumpsie Green	2.00	1.00	.60
(29)	Dick Groat	2.00	1.00	.60
(30)	Harvey Haddix	2.00	1.00	.60
(31)	Don Hoak	2.00	1.00	.60
(32)	Glen Hobbie	2.00	1.00	.60
(33)	Frank Howard	2.00	1.00	.60
(34)	Jackie Jensen	2.00	1.00	.60
(35)	Sam Jones	2.00	1.00	.60
(36)	Al Kaline	6.00	3.00	1.75
(37)	Harmon Killebrew	4.00	2.00	1.25
(38)	Harvey Kuenn	2.00	1.00	.60
(39)	Norm Larker	2.00	1.00	.60
(40)	Vernon Law	2.00	1.00	.60
(41)	Mickey Mantle	24.00	12.00	7.25
(42)	Roger Maris	10.00	5.00	3.00
(43)	Eddie Mathews	4.00	2.00	1.25
(44)	Willie Mays	8.00	4.00	2.50
(45)	Bill Mazeroski	3.50	1.75	1.00
(46)	Willie McCovey	4.00	2.00	1.25
(47)	Lindy McDaniel	2.00	1.00	.60
(48)	Roy McMillan	2.00	1.00	.60
(49)	Minnie Minoso	2.00	1.00	.60
(50)	Danny Murtaugh	2.00	1.00	.60
(51)	Stan Musial	8.00	4.00	2.50
(52)	Rocky Nelson	2.00	1.00	.60
(53)	Bob Oldis	2.00	1.00	.60
(54)	Vada Pinson	2.00	1.00	.60
(55)	Vic Power	2.00	1.00	.60
(56)	Robin Roberts	4.00	2.00	1.25
(57)	Pete Runnels	2.00	1.00	.60
(58)	Babe Ruth	12.00	6.00	3.50
(59)	Ron Santo	3.00	1.50	.90
(60)	Dick Schofield	2.00	1.00	.60
(61)	Bob Skinner	2.00	1.00	.60
(62)	Hal Smith	2.00	1.00	.60
(63)	Duke Snider	6.00	3.00	1.75
(64)	Warren Spahn	4.00	2.00	1.25
(65)	Dick Stuart	2.00	1.00	.60
(66)	Willie Tasby	2.00	1.00	.60
(67)	Tony Taylor	2.00	1.00	.60
(68)	Bill Virdon	2.00	1.00	.60
(69)	Ted Williams	12.00	6.00	3.50

1887 W.S. Kimball Champions (N184)

Similar to sets issued by Allen & Ginter and Goodwin, the Kimball tobacco company of Rochester, N.Y., issued its own 50-card set of "Champions of Games and Sport" in 1888, and included four baseball players among the "billiardists, girl riders, tight-rope walkers" and other popular celebrities featured in the series. Measuring 1-1/2" x 2-3/4", the color lithographs were inserted in packages of Kimball Cigarettes. The artwork on the card features a posed portrait, which occupies the top three-fourths, and a drawing of the player in action at the bottom. The back of the card contains an ad for Kimball Cigarettes along with a list of the various sports and activities depicted in the set. James O'Neill, whose name is misspelled on the card, is the best known of the four baseball players. His .435 batting average in 1887 is the highest ever recorded. The Kimball promotion also included an album to house the card set.

		NM	EX	VG
Complete Set (4):		4500.	1800.	1350.
Common Player:		1100.	440.00	330.00
Album:		3500.	1750.	1000.
(1)	E.A. Burch	1100.	440.00	330.00
(2)	Dell Darling	1100.	440.00	330.00
(3)	Hardie Henderson	1100.	440.00	330.00
(4)	James O'Neil (O'Neill)	1350.	540.00	405.00

1921 Koester Bread N.Y. Giants/Yankees

The 1921 World Series was the first of many for the N.Y. Yankees, and it was the first "subway series," as their opponents were the Giants. This special card issue, essentially a blank-backed version of the American Caramel Series of 120 (E121), featured the players, managers and coaches of each team. The 2" x about 3-1/4" cards feature black-and-white photos on front. They were distributed in October, 1921, by E.H. Koester, a New York bakery. The unnumbered cards are checklisted here alphabetically within team. Several of the players in this issue do not appear in the contemporary American Caramel sets. A rarely seen album was issued to house the cards. New evidence indicates a previously checklisted card of Ping Bodie does not exist and that theirs was a card issued of Bill Piercy.

		NM	EX	VG
Complete Set (52):		8000.	3600.	2000.
Common Player:		90.00	40.00	22.00
Album:		800.00	350.00	200.00
	N.Y. Giants Team Set:	3200.	1440.	800.00
(1)	Dave Bancroft	200.00	90.00	50.00
(2)	Jesse Barnes	90.00	40.00	22.00
(3)	Howard Berry	90.00	40.00	22.00
(4)	"Ed." Brown	90.00	40.00	22.00
(5)	Jesse Burkett	250.00	112.00	62.00
(6)	Geo. J. Burns	90.00	40.00	22.00
(7)	Cecil Causey	90.00	40.00	22.00
(8)	"Bill" Cunningham	90.00	40.00	22.00
(9)	"Phil" Douglas	90.00	40.00	22.00
(10)	Frank Frisch	250.00	112.00	62.00
(11)	Alexander Gaston	90.00	40.00	22.00
(12)	"Mike" Gonzalez	150.00	67.00	37.00
(13)	Hugh Jennings	200.00	90.00	50.00
(14)	George Kelly	200.00	90.00	50.00
(15)	John McGraw	200.00	90.00	50.00
(16)	Emil Meusel	90.00	40.00	22.00
(17)	Arthur Nehf	90.00	40.00	22.00
(18)	John Rawlings	90.00	40.00	22.00
(19)	"Bill" Ryan	90.00	40.00	22.00
(20)	"Slim" Sallee	90.00	40.00	22.00
(21)	"Pat" Shea	90.00	40.00	22.00
(22)	Earl Smith	90.00	40.00	22.00
(23)	Frank Snyder	90.00	40.00	22.00
(24)	Chas. Stengel	250.00	112.00	62.00
(25)	Fred Toney	90.00	40.00	22.00
(26)	Ross Young (Youngs)	200.00	90.00	50.00
	N.Y. Yankees Team Set:	4800.	2150.	1200.
(1)	Frank Baker	200.00	90.00	50.00
(2)	"Rip" Collins	90.00	40.00	22.00
(3)	Lou De Vormer	90.00	40.00	22.00
(4)	Alex Ferguson	90.00	40.00	22.00
(5)	William Fewster	90.00	40.00	22.00
(6)	Harry Harper	90.00	40.00	22.00
(7)	"Chicken" Hawks	100.00	45.00	25.00
(8)	Fred Hoffmann (Hofmann)	100.00	45.00	25.00
(9)	Waite Hoyt	200.00	90.00	50.00
(10)	Miller Huggins	200.00	90.00	50.00
(11)	Carl Mays	115.00	52.00	29.00
(12)	M.J. McNally	90.00	40.00	22.00
(13)	R. Meusel	90.00	40.00	22.00
(14)	Elmer Miller	90.00	40.00	22.00
(15)	John Mitchell	90.00	40.00	22.00
(16)	Chas. O'Leary	90.00	40.00	22.00
(17)	Roger Peckinpaugh	90.00	40.00	22.00
(18)	William Piercy	90.00	40.00	22.00
(19)	Walter Pipp	90.00	40.00	22.00
(20)	Jack Quinn	90.00	40.00	22.00
(21)	Tom Rogers	90.00	40.00	22.00
(22)	Robert Roth	90.00	40.00	22.00
(23)	George Ruth	2200.	990.00	550.00
(24)	Walter Schang	90.00	40.00	22.00
(25)	Robert Shawkey	90.00	40.00	22.00
(26)	Aaron Ward	90.00	40.00	22.00

Suffix letters after a card number indicate a variation card.

1914 Kotton Cigarettes

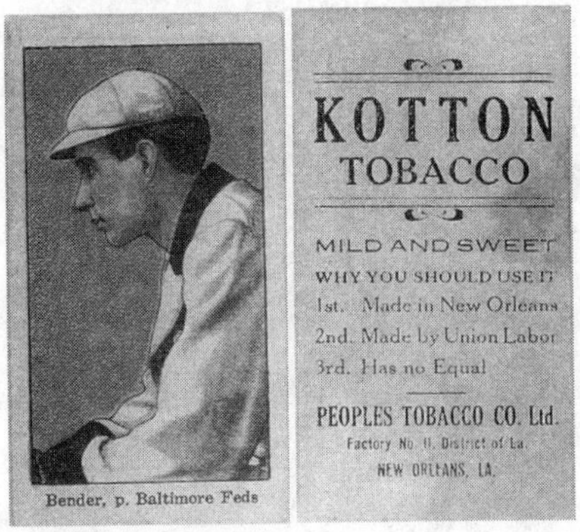

(See 1914 T216 Peoples Tobacco for checklist)

1969 Krewe of Grela Mel Ott Medal

Louisiana native and Hall of Famer Mel Ott is honored on this medallion struck for throwing to the crowds in the Mardi Gras tradition. Front of the 1-9/16" diameter aluminum piece depicts Ott at bat and bears the date 1969. Back has the name and logo of the sponsoring krewe.

	NM	EX	VG
Mel Ott	15.00	7.50	4.50

1976 Kroger Cincinnati Reds

These 5-7/8" x 9" color photos were grocery store giveaways. Blank-backed and unnumbered, they are checklisted here alphabetically. Because the photos were licensed only by the players' union, and not Major League Baseball, photos do not show uniform logos.

		NM	EX	VG
Complete Set (16):		32.00	16.00	9.75
Common Player:		1.00	.50	.30
(1)	Ed Armbrister	1.00	.50	.30
(2)	Bob Bailey	1.00	.50	.30
(3)	Johnny Bench	8.00	4.00	2.50
(4)	Jack Billingham	1.00	.50	.30
(5)	Dave Concepcion	1.50	.70	.45
(6)	Dan Driessen	1.00	.50	.30
(7)	Rawly Eastwick	1.00	.50	.30
(8)	George Foster	2.00	1.00	.60
(9)	Cesar Geronimo	1.00	.50	.30
(10)	Ken Griffey	1.50	.70	.45
(11)	Don Gullett	1.00	.50	.30
(12)	Joe Morgan	7.00	3.50	2.00
(13)	Gary Nolan	1.00	.50	.30
(14)	Fred Norman	1.00	.50	.30
(15)	Tony Perez	3.50	1.75	1.00
(16)	Pete Rose	12.00	6.00	3.50

1926 Kut Outs Giants/Yankees die-cuts

These black-and-white die-cut cards were sold as complete sets for 10 cents per team. The size varies with the pose depicted, but the cards are generally about 2" wide and 4-1/2" tall. The player's name is printed at the bottom of his photo. The unnumbered cards are checklisted here in alphabetical order by team. The issue is very similar to the Middy Bread Cardinals/Browns cards of 1927.

		NM	EX	VG
Complete Set (20):		8425.	3375.	1675.
Common Player:		250.00	100.00	50.00
	N.Y. Giants team set:	2675.	1075.	535.00
(1)	Ed Farrell	250.00	100.00	50.00
(2)	Frank Frisch	350.00	140.00	70.00
(3)	George Kelly	300.00	120.00	60.00
(4)	Freddie Lindstrom	300.00	120.00	60.00
(5)	John McGraw	300.00	120.00	60.00
(6)	Emil Meusel	250.00	100.00	50.00
(7)	John Scott	250.00	100.00	50.00
(8)	Frank Snyder	250.00	100.00	50.00
(9)	Billy Southworth	250.00	100.00	50.00
(10)	Ross Youngs	300.00	120.00	60.00
	N.Y. Yankees team set:	5600.	2250.	1125.
(11)	Pat Collins	250.00	100.00	50.00
(12)	Earle Combs	300.00	120.00	60.00
(13)	Joe Dugan	250.00	100.00	50.00
(14)	Lou Gehrig	1500.	600.00	300.00
(15)	Miller Huggins	300.00	120.00	60.00
(16)	Mark Koenig	250.00	100.00	50.00
(17)	Tony Lazzeri	300.00	120.00	60.00
(18)	Bob Meusel	250.00	100.00	50.00
(19)	Herb Pennock	300.00	120.00	60.00
(20)	Babe Ruth	2250.	900.00	450.00

L

1958-60 L.A. Dodgers Premium Pictures

Apparently issued over a period of years from 1958 through at least 1960, these black-and-white, 8-1/2" x 11" premium pictures were sold as a set through Dodgers souvenir outlets, though the make-up of a set changed with the comings and goings of players. The blank-backed pictures feature on front a pencil portrait of the player, with his name printed towards the bottom. The signature of sports artist Nicholas Volpe also appears on front. The unnumbered pictures are checklisted here alphabetically.

		NM	EX	VG
Complete Set (16):		500.00	250.00	150.00
Common Player:		20.00	10.00	6.00
(1)	Walter Alston	25.00	12.50	7.50
(2)	Roy Campanella	90.00	45.00	27.00
(3)	Gino Cimoli	20.00	10.00	6.00
(4)	Don Drysdale	40.00	20.00	12.00
(5)	Carl Erskine	20.00	10.00	6.00
(6)	Carl Furillo	25.00	12.50	7.50
(7)	Jim Gilliam	25.00	12.50	7.50
(8)	Gil Hodges	35.00	17.50	10.50
(9)	Clem Labine	20.00	10.00	6.00
(10)	Wally Moon	20.00	10.00	6.00
(11)	Don Newcombe	20.00	10.00	6.00
(12)	Johnny Podres	20.00	10.00	6.00
(13)	Pee Wee Reese	40.00	20.00	12.00
(14)	Rip Repulski	20.00	10.00	6.00
(15)	Vin Scully, Jerry Doggett (announcers)	20.00	10.00	6.00
(16)	Duke Snider	50.00	25.00	15.00

1959 L.A. Dodgers Postcards

In the team's second year in California, the Dodgers began production of an on-going set of color player postcards. Cards were usually sold in 10-card packs in stadium souvenir stands. The makeup of the packs sold varied as players came and went and cards were issued or withdrawn. When supplies of any player's cards were exhausted, he would be included in the current printing. Various photographers and printers were responsible for the issue over the years, but all utilized a similar format of 3-1/2" x 5-1/2" glossy borderless fronts and postcard style backs. The initial effort in 1959 has no player identification on the front. Backs are printed in brown, including player ID, copyright date and credits to Mirro Krome and Crocker Co. Cards are numbered as shown here, but with an "LA-D-" prefix.

		NM	EX	VG
Complete Set (12):		260.00	130.00	78.00
Common Player:		22.00	11.00	6.50
901	Duke Snider	35.00	17.50	10.50
902	Gil Hodges	30.00	15.00	9.00
903	Johnny Podres	22.00	11.00	6.50
904	Carl Furillo	22.00	11.00	6.50
905	Don Drysdale	35.00	17.50	10.50
906	Sandy Koufax	50.00	25.00	15.00
907	Jim Gilliam	22.00	11.00	6.50
908	Don Zimmer	22.00	11.00	6.50
909	Charlie Neal	22.00	11.00	6.50
910	Norm Larker (photo actually Joe Pignatano)	22.00	11.00	6.50
911	Clem Labine (photo actually Stan Williams)	22.00	11.00	6.50
912	John Roseboro	22.00	11.00	6.50

1960 L.A. Dodgers Postcards

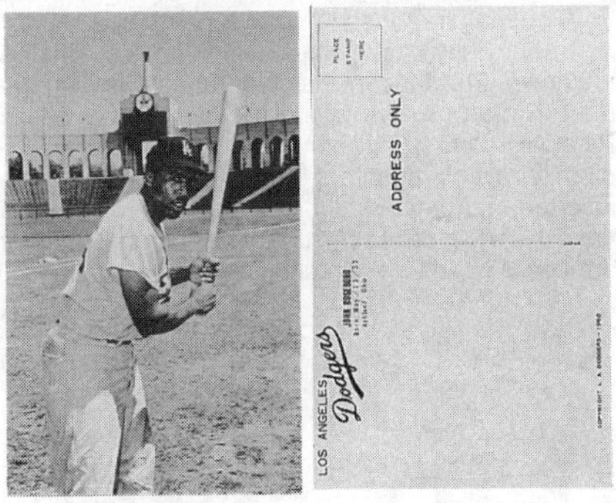

Like many baseball souvenirs, this set of team-issued postcards was "Made in Japan". The 3-1/2" x 5-1/2" cards share the basic format of the 1959 premiere issue with borderless color poses on front and postcard-style back. Backs are printed in blue with player ID and copyright date, but the cards are unnumbered. They are checklisted here alphabetically. The Carl Furillo card is scarce because it was withdrawn when he retired after playing only eight games in 1960.

		NM	EX	VG
Complete Set (12):		225.00	110.00	65.00
Common Player:		12.00	6.00	3.50
(1)	Walt Alston	15.00	7.50	4.50
(2)	Roger Craig	12.00	6.00	3.50
(3)	Don Drysdale	20.00	10.00	6.00
(4)	Carl Furillo	75.00	37.00	22.00
(5)	Gil Hodges	15.00	7.50	4.50
(6)	Sandy Koufax	25.00	12.50	7.50
(7)	Wally Moon	12.00	6.00	3.50
(8)	Charlie Neal	12.00	6.00	3.50
(9)	Johnny Podres	12.00	6.00	3.50
(10)	John Roseboro	12.00	6.00	3.50
(11)	Larry Sherry	12.00	6.00	3.50
(12)	Duke Snider	15.00	7.50	4.50

1962-65 L.A. Dodgers Postcards

The new Dodger Stadium was the backdrop for player photos on the 1962-65 postcard issues. The same 10 players' cards were issued each year with the same photos. Beginning in 1962, the borderless fronts began to carry a white facsimile autograph. Backs credit Plastichrome as printer and Mitock and Sons as distributer. The specific year of issue can be determined by the backs, as follows: 1962-3 - printed in red and black with drawing of stadium; 1964 - all-black back printing, no stadium picture; 1965 - card number moved inside stamp box. A few special cards issued over this time span are also checklisted here. The cards all carry the "P" prefix.

	NM	EX	VG
Complete Set (10):	65.00	32.00	19.50
Common Player:	6.00	3.00	1.75
50315 Willie Davis	6.00	3.00	1.75
50316 Larry Sherry	6.00	3.00	1.75
50317 Ron Perranoski	6.00	3.00	1.75
50318 Sandy Koufax	15.00	7.50	4.50
50319 Frank Howard	8.00	4.00	2.50
50320 Tommy Davis	8.00	4.00	2.50
50321 Don Drysdale	12.00	6.00	3.50
50322 John Roseboro	6.00	3.00	1.75
50323 Ron Fairly	6.00	3.00	1.75
50324 Maury Wills	8.00	4.00	2.50
SPECIAL CARDS			
49774 Vin Scully, Jerry Doggett (announcers) (1962-3))	6.00	3.00	1.75
49780 1962 Dodgers Team Photo	9.00	4.50	2.75
53767 Stadium photo with player insets (1962-63)	7.50	3.75	2.25
62008 Baseball Greats (Dean Chance, Don Drysdale, Sandy Koufax, Willie Mays) (1962-63)	9.00	4.50	2.75
55773 1963 Dodgers Team Photo	9.00	4.50	2.75

1963 L.A. Dodgers Motion Pins

The year of issue quoted here is speculative. It is also not known whether the two players listed comprise the entire issue. These 2-1/2" diameter pins feature player portraits on a seamed blue background resembling a baseball. When the angle of view is changed, the player's name and team logo and the starbursts pop in and out of sight.

	NM	EX	VG
Don Drysdale	15.00	7.50	4.50
Sandy Koufax	25.00	12.50	7.50

1963 L.A. Dodgers Pin-Ups

Borrowing on the concept of the 1938 Goudey Heads-up cards, this set was sold, probably at the stadium souvenir stands, in a white envelope labeled "Los Angeles Dodgers Pin-Ups." The cards feature large full-color head-and-cap photos set atop cartoon ballplayers' bodies. Cards are printed on 7-1/4" x 8-1/2" semi-gloss cardboard with blank backs. The player's name appears in black on the front, along with the instructions, "Push out character carefully. Take scissors and trim white around player's head." Each figure was die-cut to allow its easy removal from the background.

		NM	EX	VG
Complete Set (10):		75.00	37.00	22.00
Common Player:		6.00	3.00	1.75
(1)	Tommy Davis	7.00	3.50	2.00
(2)	Willie Davis	7.00	3.50	2.00
(3)	Don Drysdale	11.00	5.50	3.25
(4)	Ron Fairly	6.00	3.00	1.75
(5)	Frank Howard	7.50	3.75	2.25
(6)	Sandy Koufax	26.00	13.00	7.75
(7)	Joe Moeller	6.00	3.00	1.75
(8)	Ron Perranoski	6.00	3.00	1.75
(9)	John Roseboro	6.00	3.00	1.75
(10)	Maury Wills	7.50	3.75	2.25

1966 L.A. Dodgers Postcards

Similar in style to earlier team-issued postcards, these color, glossy cards have borderless posed photos on front with a facsimile autograph in white. Backs are printed in black with credits to "Plastichrome" as printer and Mitock and Sons as distributor. Player identification appears in the upper-left corner. Card numbers as shown appear in the stamp box at upper-right with the letter "P" prefix.

	NM	EX	VG
Complete Set (9):	45.00	22.50	13.50
Common Player:	4.00	2.00	1.25
67392 Sandy Koufax	12.00	6.00	3.50
69766 Wes Parker	4.00	2.00	1.25
69767 Jeff Torborg	4.00	2.00	1.25
69768 Jim Lefebvre	4.00	2.00	1.25
69769 Lou Johnson	4.00	2.00	1.25
69770 Don Sutton	10.00	5.00	3.00
69771 Claude Osteen	4.00	2.00	1.25
69885 Vin Scully (announcer)	4.00	2.00	1.25
69950 1966 Dodgers team photo	6.00	3.00	1.75
70455 1966 Dodgers team photo (5-1/2" x 7")	6.00	3.00	1.75

1967 L.A. Dodgers Postcards

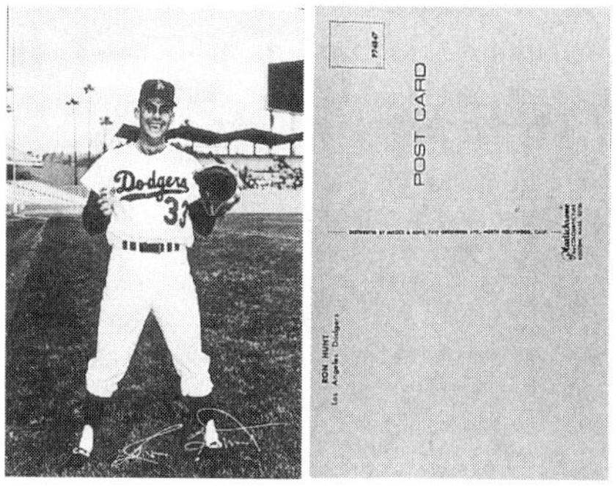

Only four new Dodgers postcards were issued in 1967, in the same format and by the same suppliers as indicated on the 1966 cards. Player identification in the upper-left corner is in visibly smaller type size than the previous year. They are numbered with the "P" prefix.

	NM	EX	VG
Complete Set (4):	15.00	7.50	4.50
Common Player:	4.00	2.00	1.25
70454 Vin Scully, Jerry Doggett (announcers)	4.00	2.00	1.25
74846 Gene Michael	4.00	2.00	1.25
74847 Ron Hunt	4.00	2.00	1.25
70455 1967 Dodgers team photo (6" x 4")	5.00	2.50	1.50

1967-77 L.A. Dodgers 8x10 Photocards

Contemporary with its on-going issue of player postcards in the 1960-70s, the souvenir stands at Dodger Stadium also carried a line of 8" x 10" color player photos. Generally sold in packs of five for a dollar, the players changed as the team's roster changed, with new faces being added and traded or retired players being dropped. The many Dodgers who enjoyed long careers in L.A. in that era often appeared on two or more different photocards; as supplies of old cards were exhausted, new ones were made. The style of all cards is identical. Color posed or game-action photos are centered on front, with a white border all around. Backs are blank. The only player identification is a facsimile autograph on front in either black or white. Minor cropping differences are not listed here.

		NM	EX	VG
Complete Set (109):		325.00	160.00	95.00
Common Player:		4.00	2.00	1.25
(1)	Richie Allen (kneeling, waist-up)	7.50	3.75	2.25
(2)	Rick Auerbach (horizontal, batting)	4.00	2.00	1.25
(3)	Rick Auerbach (vertical, batting)	4.00	2.00	1.25
(4)	Bob Bailey (full-body pose)	4.00	2.00	1.25
(5)	Dusty Baker (posed, bat on shoulder)	6.00	3.00	1.75

(6)	Bill Buckner (posed in batting stance)	6.00	3.00	1.75
(7)	Bill Buckner (horizontal, game-action, batting)	6.00	3.00	1.75
(8)	Ron Cey (game-action, batting, spring training)	5.00	2.50	1.50
(9)	Ron Cey (game-action, batting, Dodger Stadium)	5.00	2.50	1.50
(10)	Ron Cey (game-action, batting, knees-up, red, white and blue wrist band)	5.00	2.50	1.50
(11)	Willie Crawford (full-length batting pose)	4.00	2.00	1.25
(12)	Willie Crawford (game-action, batting follow-through)	4.00	2.00	1.25
(13)	Henry Cruz (pose, glove at waist)	4.00	2.00	1.25
(14)	Tommy Davis (pose, catching fly ball, hands over head)	6.00	3.00	1.75
(15)	Willie Davis (posed, full-body, fielding, black autograph)	4.00	2.00	1.25
(16)	Willie Davis (posed, full-body, fielding, horizontal white autograph)	4.00	2.00	1.25
(17)	Willie Davis (posed, full-body, fielding, white autograph at angle)	4.00	2.00	1.25
(18)	Al Downing (horizontal, pitching, autograph level with base)	4.00	2.00	1.25
(19)	Al Downing (horizontal, pitching, autograph below base)	4.00	2.00	1.25
(20)	Don Drysdale (pose, glove at waist, L.A. Colisuem)	9.00	4.50	2.75
(21)	Don Drysdale (pose, pitching follow-through)	9.00	4.50	2.75
(22)	Don Drysdale (pose, pitching, hands over head)	9.00	4.50	2.75
(23)	Ron Fairly (pose, full-length batting)	4.00	2.00	1.25
(24)	Joe Ferguson (game-action batting)	4.00	2.00	1.25
(25)	Joe Ferguson (horizontal, game-action batting)	4.00	2.00	1.25
(26)	Al Ferrera (pose, full-length batting)	4.00	2.00	1.25
(27)	Alan Foster (pitching pose, followthrough)	4.00	2.00	1.25
(28)	Terry Forster (pitching pose, chest-up)	4.00	2.00	1.25
(29)	Len Gabrielson (pose, full-length batting follow-through)	4.00	2.00	1.25
(30)	Steve Garvey (horizontal, game-action batting)	8.00	4.00	2.50
(31)	Steve Garvey (game-action, batting)	8.00	4.00	2.50
(32)	Steve Garvey (game-action, fielding)	8.00	4.00	2.50
(33)	Bill Grabarkewitz (pose, full-length, fielding, autograph over left foot)	4.00	2.00	1.25
(34)	Billy Grabarkewitz (same pose as above, autograph below left foot)	4.00	2.00	1.25
(35)	Jim "Mudcat" Grant (pose, full-body, standing on mound)	4.00	2.00	1.25
(36)	John Hale (game-action, batting)	4.00	2.00	1.25
(37)	Tom Haller (game-action, batting)	4.00	2.00	1.25
(38)	Jim Hickman (pose, full-body, throwing)	4.00	2.00	1.25
(39)	Burt Hooton (pose, belt-up, on mound)	4.00	2.00	1.25
(40)	Charlie Hough (pose, pitching follow-through)	5.00	2.50	1.50
(41)	Frank Howard (pose, batting, knees-up)	5.00	2.50	1.50
(42)	Frank Howard (pose, full-body, batting)	5.00	2.50	1.50
(43)	Ron Hunt (pose, full-body, fielding)	4.00	2.00	1.25
(44)	Tommy John (game-action, pitching wind-up)	5.00	2.50	1.50
(45)	Tommy John (game-action, pitching release)	5.00	2.50	1.50
(46)	Tommy John (pose, pitching, belt-up)	5.00	2.50	1.50
(47)	Lou Johnson (pose, full-length, batting)	4.00	2.00	1.25
(48)	Von Joshua (horizontal, pose, shoulders-up)	4.00	2.00	1.25
(49)	Sandy Koufax (full-body pitching pose, printed name)	12.00	6.00	3.50
(50)	Sandy Koufax (pose, pitching follow-through, facsimile signature)	12.00	6.00	3.50
(51)	Lee Lacy (game-action, batting)	4.00	2.00	1.25
(52)	Norm Larker (pose, knees-up, batting)	4.00	2.00	1.25
(53)	Tommy Lasorda (waist-up pose, arm on bat)	8.00	4.00	2.50
(54)	Jim Lefebvre (full-length pose)	4.00	2.00	1.25
(55)	Davey Lopes (game-action, batting, knees-up)	4.00	2.00	1.25
(56)	Davey Lopes (game-action, full-length, batting, view from center field)	4.00	2.00	1.25
(57)	Davey Lopes (game-action, batting, knees-up)	4.00	2.00	1.25
(58)	Mike Marshall (game-action, pitching, side view)	4.00	2.00	1.25
(59)	Mike Marshall (game-action, pitching follow-through, NOB visible)	4.00	2.00	1.25
(60)	Mike Marshall (horizontal, game-action, pitching)	4.00	2.00	1.25
(61)	Andy Messersmith (full-body, pitching, in bullpen)	4.00	2.00	1.25
(62)	Gene Michael (full-length pose)	4.00	2.00	1.25
(63)	Bob Miller (pose, full-length)	4.00	2.00	1.25
(64)	Rick Monday (game-action, batting follow-through)	4.00	2.00	1.25
(65)	Wally Moon (pose, knees-up, batting)	5.00	2.50	1.50
(66)	Manny Mota (game-action, batting follow-through)	4.00	2.00	1.25
(67)	Manny Mota (pose, full-length, batting)	4.00	2.00	1.25
(68)	Manny Mota (horizontal, game-action, batting)	4.00	2.00	1.25
(69)	Johnny Oates (pose, batting follow-through)	4.00	2.00	1.25
(70)	Claude Osteen (pose, full-body, pitching)	4.00	2.00	1.25
(71)	Tom Paciorek (pose, batting, waist-up)	4.00	2.00	1.25
(72)	Wes Parker (pose, full-body, lunging at ball)	4.00	2.00	1.25
(73)	Wes Parker (pose, full-body, kneeling w/ bat)	4.00	2.00	1.25
(74)	Paul Popovich (pose, full-body, batting)	4.00	2.00	1.25
(75)	Doug Rau (game-action, full-body, pitching delivery)	4.00	2.00	1.25
(76)	Doug Rau (game-action, full-body, pitching, scoreboard in background)	4.00	2.00	1.25
(77)	Doug Rau (game-action, full-body, pitching, hands above head)	4.00	2.00	1.25
(78)	Phil Regan (pose, full-length, on mound)	4.00	2.00	1.25
(79)	Rick Rhoden (game-action, full-body, pitching)	4.00	2.00	1.25
(80)	Frank Robinson (game-action, full-length, at bat)	9.00	4.50	2.75
(81)	Ed Roebuck (pitching pose, knees-up, heads over head)	4.00	2.00	1.25
(82)	John Roseboro (pose, full-body, catching)	4.00	2.00	1.25
(83)	Bill Russell (game-action, full-length, ready to throw)	5.00	2.50	1.50
(84)	Bill Russell (fielding pose)	5.00	2.50	1.50
(85)	Bill Russell (game-action, batting)	5.00	2.50	1.50
(86)	Duke Sims (kneeling pose)	4.00	2.00	1.25
(87)	Bill Singer (full-body pose)	4.00	2.00	1.25
(88)	Ted Sizemore (full-body pose, leaning on bat)	4.00	2.00	1.25
(89)	Ted Sizemore (full-body fielding pose)	4.00	2.00	1.25
(90)	Reggie Smith (game-action, batting)	5.00	2.50	1.50
(91)	Bill Sudakis (game-action, batting)	4.00	2.00	1.25
(92)	Bill Sudakis (fielding pose)	4.00	2.00	1.25
(93)	Don Sutton (game-action, full-body, pitching)	6.00	3.00	1.75
(94)	Don Sutton (horizontal, game-action, pitching)	6.00	3.00	1.75
(95)	Don Sutton (pitching pose, wind-up)	6.00	3.00	1.75
(96)	Don Sutton (pitching pose, follow-through)	6.00	3.00	1.75
(97)	Jeff Torborg (pose, in catcher's gear)	4.00	2.00	1.25
(98)	Bobby Valentine (shoulders-up pose)	4.00	2.00	1.25
(99)	Zoilo Versalles (pose, full-length, batting)	4.00	2.00	1.25
(100)	Maury Wills (kneeling pose)	6.00	3.00	1.75
(101)	Maury Wills (batting pose, waist-up)	6.00	3.00	1.75
(102)	Maury Wills (batting pose, knees-up, left-handed)	6.00	3.00	1.75
(103)	Maury Wills (game-action, sliding into base)	6.00	3.00	1.75
(104)	Jim Wynn (game-action, batting)	4.00	2.00	1.25
(105)	Jim Wynn (game-action, sliding)	4.00	2.00	1.25
(106)	Steve Yeager (game-action, batting follow-through)	4.00	2.00	1.25
(107)	Steve Yeager (game-action, batting swing)	4.00	2.00	1.25
(108)	Steve Yeager (horizontal, game-action, batting)	4.00	2.00	1.25
(109)	Geoff Zahn (game-action, pitching wind-up)	4.00	2.00	1.25

1968 L.A. Dodgers Postcards

The Dodgers team-issued postcards for 1968 retained the same format used in the prior two years; borderless color poses on front with a white facsimile autograph. All photos for the issue were taken at spring training in Florida with the players wearing road gray uniforms. Postcard style backs are similar to earlier issues. Cards are numbered with the "P" prefix.

	NM	EX	VG
Complete Set (6):	20.00	10.00	6.00
Common Player:	4.00	2.00	1.25
77501 Jim Grant	4.00	2.00	1.25
77502 Zoilo Versalles	4.00	2.00	1.25
77503 Bill Singer	4.00	2.00	1.25
77504 Tom Haller	4.00	2.00	1.25
77505 Alan Foster	4.00	2.00	1.25
77506 Al Ferrara	4.00	2.00	1.25

1969 L.A. Dodgers Postcards

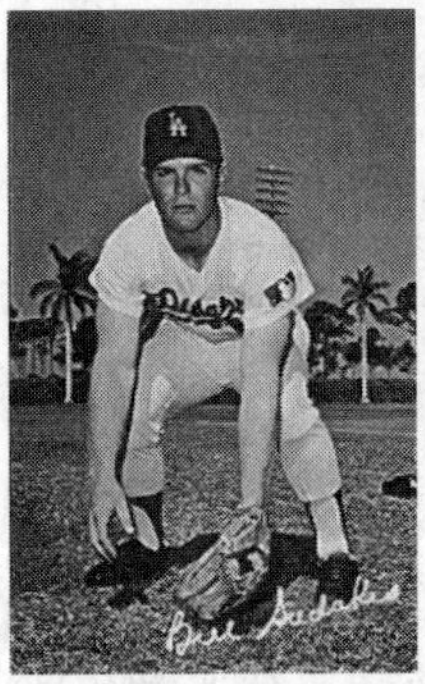

Except for the card of Bill Russell, spring training in Vero Beach was again the backdrop for the photos in the Dodgers on-going postcard issue in 1969. This time the players are posed in their home white uniforms, many displaying the 100th anniversary of professionall baseball patch. Cards are numbered with the "P" prefix.

	NM	EX	VG
Complete Set (6):	25.00	12.50	7.50
Common Player:	4.00	2.00	1.25
86213 Bill Sudakis	4.00	2.00	1.25
86214 Ted Sizemore	4.00	2.00	1.25
86215 Bil Grabarkewitz	4.00	2.00	1.25
86216 Willie Crawford	4.00	2.00	1.25
86497 Bill Russell	6.00	3.00	1.75
86707 Walt Alston	9.00	4.50	2.75

1970 L.A. Dodgers Team Postcard

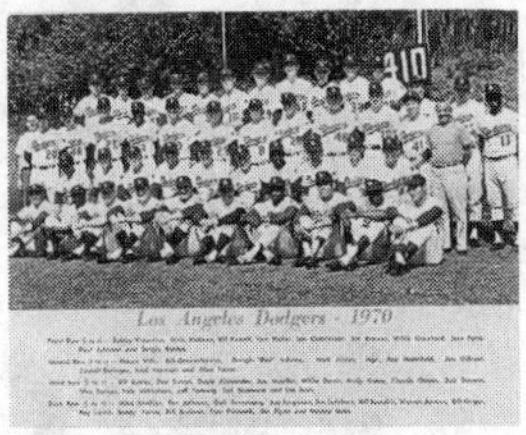

It does not appear that the Dodgers issued any new postcards in 1970 for individual players, but a team-photo postcard was issued. The 7" x 5-1/2"

card has a color team photo and players identification on front. On the postcard-style back are credits for the photo and distributor. Within the stamp box is the card number.

	NM	EX	VG
P88530 Dodgers team photo	4.00	2.00	1.25

1971 L.A. Dodgers Postcards

After issuing no new player cards in 1970, the Dodgers updated their on-going team issue with five new players in 1971. The set also marked a change of printers to Dexter Press. Format remained basically the same with borderless color poses on front including a facsimile autograph. Postcard style backs are printed in blue with card numbers carrying a "C" suffix in the stamp box at upper-right and player identification in the upper-left corner.

	NM	EX	VG
Complete Set (5):	12.50	6.25	3.75
Common Player:	2.00	1.00	.60
74802 Steve Garvey	5.00	2.50	1.50
74803 Duke Sims	2.00	1.00	.60
74804 Bob Valentine	2.00	1.00	.60
74805 Rich Allen	3.75	2.00	1.25
74806 Jim Brewer	2.00	1.00	.60

1972 L.A. Dodgers Postcards

Dexter Press added another half-dozen cards to the team's on-going series for 1972. Both front and back formats are identical to the 1971 cards. Cards are numbered with a "C" suffix.

	NM	EX	VG
Complete Set (6):	13.50	6.75	4.00
Common Player:	2.00	1.00	.60
86153 Tommy John	3.00	1.50	.90
86154 Frank Robinson	5.00	2.50	1.50
86155 Al Downing	2.00	1.00	.60
86156 Bill Buckner	3.00	1.50	.90
86157 Hoyt Wilhelm	4.00	2.00	1.25
86158 Pete Richert	2.00	1.00	.60

1973 L.A. Dodgers Postcards

Kolor View Press took over production of the Dodgers postcards for 1973. The fronts remained unchanged while the backs returned to black printing. All cards, except that of the announcers, share the number KV5251. They are listed here in alphabetical order.

		NM	EX	VG
Complete Set (17):		30.00	15.00	9.00
Common Player:		2.00	1.00	.60
(1)	Bill Buckner	3.00	1.50	.90
(2)	Ron Cey	3.75	2.00	1.25
(3)	Willie Davis	2.50	1.25	.70
(4)	Joe Ferguson	2.00	1.00	.60
(5)	Tommy John	2.50	1.25	.70
(6)	Lee Lacy	2.00	1.00	.60
(7)	Tommy Lasorda	4.00	2.00	1.25
(8)	Davey Lopes	2.00	1.00	.60
(9)	Andy Messersmith	2.00	1.00	.60
(10)	Manny Mota	2.00	1.00	.60
(11)	Claude Osteen	2.00	1.00	.60
(12)	Tom Paciorek	2.00	1.00	.60
(13)	Bill Russell	2.50	1.25	.70
(14)	Don Sutton	3.75	2.00	1.25
(15)	Steve Yeager	2.00	1.00	.60
(16)	Vin Scully, Jerry Doggett (announcers)	2.00	1.00	.60
(17)	Dodgers team jet (Kayo 2)	3.75	2.00	1.25

1974 L.A. Dodgers Postcards

Six additional players were printed in Kolor View postcards for 1974. Format remained virtually unchanged though individual card numbers returned to the back. They all have the "KV" prefix.

		NM	EX	VG
Complete Set (7):		13.50	6.75	4.00
Common Player:		2.00	1.00	.60
6412	Mike Marshall	2.00	1.00	.60
6413	Charlie Hough	2.00	1.00	.60
6514	Jim Wynn	2.00	1.00	.60
6515	Doug Rau	2.00	1.00	.60
6427	Steve Garvey	3.75	2.00	1.25
6428	Willie Crawford	2.00	1.00	.60
6432	Dodgers team photo (7" x 5-1/2")	2.00	1.00	.60

1975 L.A. Dodgers Postcards

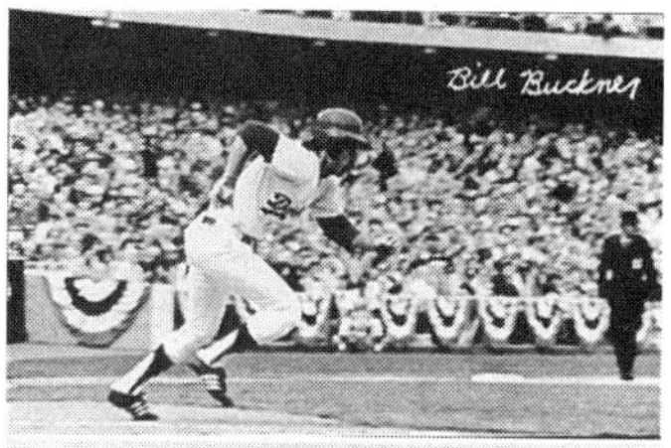

Other than the disappearance of credit lines on the postcard style backs, the 1975 continuation of the Dodgers' player postcard series conforms to the design of previous years. The KV7813- prefix on most of the cards indicates this was another production of Kolor View Press.

		NM	EX	VG
Complete Set (17):		25.00	12.50	7.50
Common Player:		2.00	1.00	.60
1	Bill Buckner	2.50	1.25	.70
2	Jim Wynn	2.00	1.00	.60
3	Henry Cruz	2.00	1.00	.60
4	Rick Auerbach	2.00	1.00	.60
5	Bill Russell	2.50	1.25	.70
6	Tom Paciorek	2.00	1.00	.60
7	Steve Yeager	2.00	1.00	.60
8	Don Sutton	3.75	2.00	1.25
9	Mike Marshall	2.00	1.00	.60
10	Ron Cey	2.00	1.00	.60
11	Rick Rhoden	2.00	1.00	.60
12	Joe Ferguson	2.00	1.00	.60
15	Davey Lopes	2.00	1.00	.60
31	Doug Rau	2.00	1.00	.60
57	Willie Crawford	2.00	1.00	.60
6427	Steve Garvey (MVP mention on back)	3.75	2.00	1.25
----	Vin Scully, Jerry Doggett (announcers)	2.00	1.00	.60

1976 L.A. Dodgers Postcards

Card numbers preceeded by the prefix KV8861 within the stamp box identify these cards as a 1976 issue. Otherwise the format is virtually identical to the previous year. Fronts of the 3-1/2" x 5-1/2" cards have borderless color action photos with the player's facsimile signature in white. Postcard-style backs are printed in black with no identification of publisher, printer or distributor.

		NM	EX	VG
Complete Set (11):		16.00	8.00	4.75
Common Player:		2.00	1.00	.60
1	Walter Alston	4.00	2.00	1.25
2	Ron Cey	3.00	1.50	.90
3	Tommy John	2.50	1.25	.70
4a	Davey Lopes ("p" beneath right foot)	2.00	1.00	.60
4b	Davey Lopes ("L" beneath right foot)	2.00	1.00	.60
5	Charlie Hough	2.00	1.00	.60
6	Steve Garvey	4.00	2.00	1.25
7	Mike Marshall	2.00	1.00	.60
8	Joe Ferguson	2.00	1.00	.60
9	Dusty Baker	2.50	1.25	.70
10	Burt Hooton	2.00	1.00	.60

1977 L.A. Dodgers Postcards

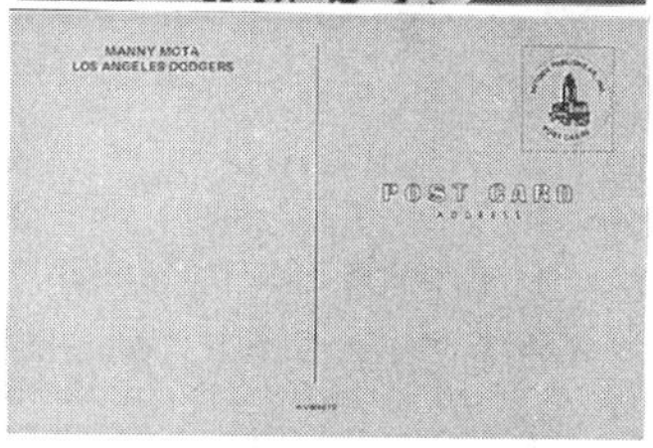

The newly issued cards for 1977 can be differentiated from those of the previous years by the appearance of a Mitock Publishers logo within the stamp box and individual card numbers in the range of KVB9869-KVB9876. Otherwise the 3-1/2" x 5-1/2" cards share the basic format of previous years, with borderless color photos on front overprinted with a white facsimile autograph. Postcard-style backs are printed in black.

	NM	EX	VG
Complete Set (8):	16.00	8.00	4.75
Common Player:	2.00	1.00	.60
9869a Reggie Smith	2.00	1.00	.60
9869b Reggie Smith (blank back)	2.00	1.00	.60
9870 Manny Mota	2.00	1.00	.60
9871 Rick Monday	2.00	1.00	.60
9872a Johnny Oates	2.00	1.00	.60
9872b Johnny Oates (blank back)	2.00	1.00	.60
9873a Ron Cey	2.50	1.25	.70
9873b Ron Cey (blank back)	2.00	1.00	.60
9874 Doug Rau	2.00	1.00	.60
9875 Steve Garvey	4.00	2.00	1.25
9876a Tommy Lasorda	4.00	2.00	1.25
9876b Tommy Lasorda (blank back)	4.00	2.00	1.25

1978 L.A. Dodgers Postcards

Only a single addition to the team's line-up of color player postcards is known from 1978, Terry Forster, who had signed as a free agent after 1977. Format of the 3-1/2" x 5-1/2" card is similar to previous years' efforts with a borderless photo on front and white facsimile signature. Black postcard-style back has a Mitock Publishers logo in the stamp box and four dotted lines for addressing.

	NM	EX	VG
B10975 Terry Forster	2.00	1.00	.60

1979 L.A. Dodgers

Presumed to be a collectors' issue due to lack of sponsors' or licensors' logos, this set features the top players of the '79 Dodgers. Fronts of the 2-1/2" x 3-3/8" cards are borderless color photos. Backs are printed in blue and white with career highlights and personal data. Cards are checklisted here in alphabetical order.

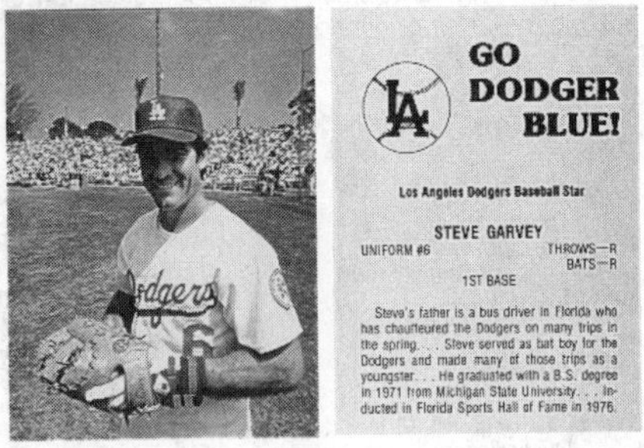

		NM	EX	VG
Complete Set (15):		18.00	9.00	5.50
Common Player:		1.00	.50	.30
(1)	Dusty Baker	1.50	.70	.45
(2)	Ron Cey	1.00	.50	.30
(3)	Terry Forster	1.00	.50	.30
(4)	Steve Garvey	2.50	1.25	.70
(5)	Burt Hooton	1.00	.50	.30
(6)	Charlie Hough	1.00	.50	.30
(7)	Tommy Lasorda	2.00	1.00	.60
(8)	Dave Lopes	1.00	.50	.30
(9)	Rick Monday	1.00	.50	.30
(10)	Manny Mota	1.00	.50	.30
(11)	Doug Rau	1.00	.50	.30
(12)	Bill Russell	1.00	.50	.30
(13)	Reggie Smith	1.50	.70	.45
(14)	Don Sutton	2.00	1.00	.60
(15)	Steve Yeager	1.00	.50	.30

1979 L.A. Dodgers Postcards

Continuing a successful format from previous seasons, the team's 1979 color player postcards were again printed by Kolor View as evidenced by the KVB prefix to the card number on back. Fronts of the 3-1/2" x 5-1/2" cards have borderless color photos with white facsimile autographs. Backs have the Mitock Publishers logo within the stamp box. Unlike the 1978 issue, there are no lines on back for addressing. Each of the card numbers in the checklist here is preceded by a prefix of "KVB11". The Rauthzan card is scarce because it was withdrawn only a month into the season when he was traded.

		NM	EX	VG
Complete Set (9):		32.00	16.00	9.50
Common Player:		2.00	1.00	.60
99-2	Sandy Koufax	7.50	3.75	2.25
055-4	Derrel Thomas	2.00	1.00	.60
955-1	Bob Welch	2.00	1.00	.60
955-2	Lance Rautzhan	15.00	7.50	4.50
955-3	Joe Ferguson	2.00	1.00	.60
955-5	Andy Messersmith	2.00	1.00	.60
955-6	Gary Thomasson	2.00	1.00	.60
956-2	Terry Forster	2.00	1.00	.60
956-3	Charlie Hough	2.00	1.00	.60

1980 L.A. Dodgers Police

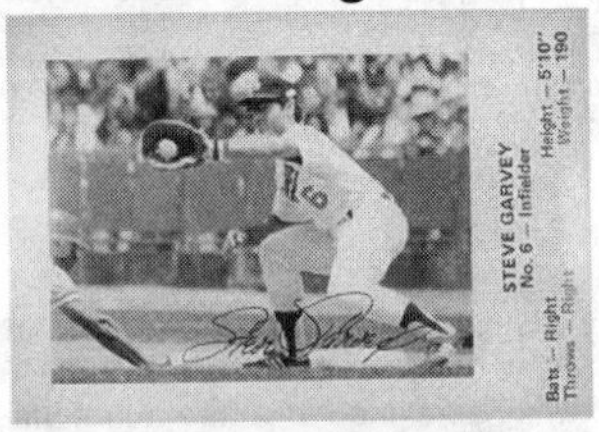

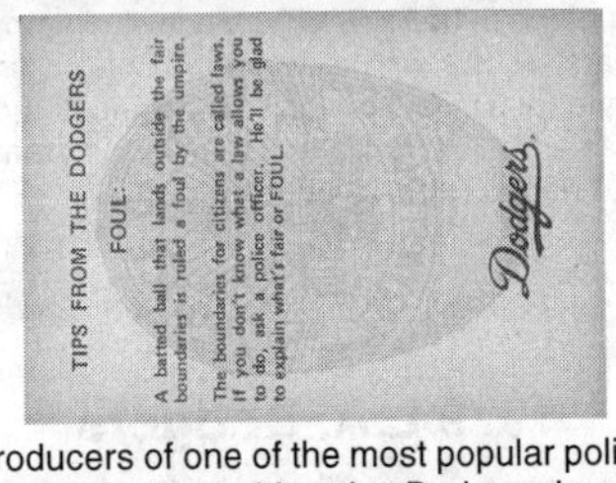

Producers of one of the most popular police and safety sets in the hobby, the Dodgers began this successful promotion in 1980. The 2-13/16" x 4-1/8" cards feature full-color photos on front, along with brief personal statistics. Backs include "Tips from the Dodgers" along with the team and LAPD logos. Cards are numbered by player uniform number, with an unnumbered team card also included in the set.

		NM	EX	VG
Complete Set (30):		15.00	7.50	4.50
Common Player:		.80	.40	.25
5	Johnny Oates	.80	.40	.25
6	Steve Garvey	3.00	1.50	.90
7	Steve Yeager	.80	.40	.25
8	Reggie Smith	1.00	.50	.30
9	Gary Thomasson	.80	.40	.25
10	Ron Cey	1.00	.50	.30
12	Dusty Baker	.90	.45	.25
13	Joe Ferguson	.80	.40	.25
15	Davey Lopes	1.00	.50	.30
16	Rick Monday	.80	.40	.25
18	Bill Russell	.90	.45	.25
20	Don Sutton	3.00	1.50	.90
21	Jay Johnstone	.80	.40	.25
23	Teddy Martinez	.80	.40	.25
27	Joe Beckwith	.80	.40	.25
28	Pedro Guerrero	.80	.40	.25
29	Don Stanhouse	.80	.40	.25
30	Derrel Thomas	.80	.40	.25
31	Doug Rau	.80	.40	.25
34	Ken Brett	.80	.40	.25
35	Bob Welch	.80	.40	.25
37	Robert Castillo	.80	.40	.25
38	Dave Goltz	.80	.40	.25
41	Jerry Reuss	.80	.40	.25
43	Rick Sutcliffe	1.00	.50	.30
44	Mickey Hatcher	.80	.40	.25
46	Burt Hooton	.80	.40	.25
49	Charlie Hough	.80	.40	.25
51	Terry Forster	.80	.40	.25
---	Team photo	.80	.40	.25

1980 L.A. Dodgers Postcards

Though the 1980 team-issued color player postcards share a basic format - 3-1/2" x 5-1/2", glossy color borderless photo and facsimile autograph on front - as those of previous years they can identified on the backs by the removal of the Mitock logo from the stamp box, leaving only USA there. All cards have a prefix of KVB129, except Baker, which has a KVB130 prefix.

		NM	EX	VG
Complete Set (10):		20.00	10.00	6.00
Common Player:		2.00	1.00	.60
953-1	Derrel Thomas	2.00	1.00	.60
953-2	Jerry Reuss	2.00	1.00	.60
953-3	Dave Goltz	2.00	1.00	.60
953-4	Rudy Law	2.00	1.00	.60
953-5	Jay Johnstone	2.50	1.25	.70
953-6	Rick Sutcliffe	3.00	1.50	.90
953-7	Don Stanhouse	2.00	1.00	.60
956-1	Don Sutton	3.75	2.00	1.25
956-2	Terry Forster	2.00	1.00	.60
066	Dusty Baker	2.50	1.25	.70

1960 Lake To Lake Dairy Braves

This 28-card set of unnumbered 2-1/2" x 3-1/4" cards offers a special challenge for the condition-conscious collector. Originally issued by being stapled to milk cartons, the cards were redeemable for prizes ranging from pen and pencil sets to Braves tickets. When sent in for redemption, the cards had a hole punched in the corner. Naturally, collectors most desire cards without the staple or punch holes. Cards are printed in blue ink on front, red ink on back. Because he was traded in May, and his card withdrawn, the Ray Boone card is scarce; the Billy Bruton card is unaccountably scarcer still.

		NM	EX	VG
Complete Set (28):		2175.	1075.	650.00
Common Player:		25.00	12.50	7.50
(1)	Henry Aaron	495.00	245.00	150.00
(2)	Joe Adcock	25.00	12.50	7.50
(3)	Ray Boone	225.00	110.00	67.00
(4)	Bill Bruton	495.00	245.00	150.00
(5)	Bob Buhl	25.00	12.50	7.50
(6)	Lou Burdette	25.00	12.50	7.50
(7)	Chuck Cottier	25.00	12.50	7.50
(8)	Wes Covington	25.00	12.50	7.50
(9)	Del Crandall	25.00	12.50	7.50
(10)	Charlie Dressen	25.00	12.50	7.50
(11)	Bob Giggie	25.00	12.50	7.50
(12)	Joey Jay	25.00	12.50	7.50
(13)	Johnny Logan	25.00	12.50	7.50
(14)	Felix Mantilla	25.00	12.50	7.50
(15)	Lee Maye	25.00	12.50	7.50
(16)	Don McMahon	25.00	12.50	7.50
(17)	George Myatt	25.00	12.50	7.50
(18)	Andy Pafko	25.00	12.50	7.50
(19)	Juan Pizarro	25.00	12.50	7.50
(20)	Mel Roach	25.00	12.50	7.50
(21)	Bob Rush	25.00	12.50	7.50
(22)	Bob Scheffing	25.00	12.50	7.50
(23)	Red Schoendienst	55.00	27.00	16.50
(24)	Warren Spahn	110.00	55.00	33.00
(25)	Al Spangler	25.00	12.50	7.50
(26)	Frank Torre	25.00	12.50	7.50
(27)	Carl Willey	25.00	12.50	7.50
(28)	Whitlow Wyatt	25.00	12.50	7.50

1913 Napoleon Lajoie Game Card

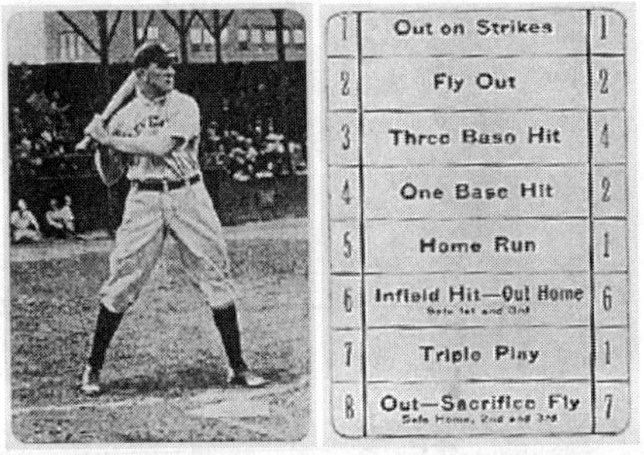

Although individual cards are not marked, these cards were produced as part of a Parker Brothers baseball board game called "The National American Baseball Game." Each of the approximately 2-3/8" x 3-1/4", round-cornered cards has a borderless photo on front picturing the Hall of Famer at bat. Backs have a chart of various baseball plays used in the game. Cards can be found with the Lajoie photo tinted either blue or red, the latter being somewhat scarcer.

	NM	EX	VG
Napoleon Lajoie	35.00	17.50	10.50

1970 La Pizza Royale Expos

This colorful collectors issue features only Montreal Expos. Each of the 2-1/2" x 5" cards can be found printed in red, yellow, blue or green duotones. "La Pizza Royale" is printed in white above the player photo. Below the photo is the player's name and, in French, his position. Backs are blank and the cards are unnumbered. The checklist is presented here alphabetically. The La Pizza Royale cards are a fantasy issue produced by a collector for sale within the hobby.

	NM	EX	VG
Complete Set (14):	25.00	18.50	10.00
Common Player:	2.00	1.00	.60
(1) Bob Bailey	2.00	1.00	.60
(2) John Boccabella	2.00	1.00	.60
(3) Ron Fairly	3.00	1.50	.90
(4) Jim Gosger	2.00	1.00	.60
(5) Coco Laboy	2.00	1.00	.60
(6) Gene Mauch	3.00	1.50	.90
(7) Rich Nye	2.00	1.00	.60
(8) John O'Donoghue	2.00	1.00	.60
(9) Adolfo Phillips	2.00	1.00	.60
(10) Howie Reed	2.00	1.00	.60
(11) Marv Staehle	2.00	1.00	.60
(12) Rusty Staub	4.50	2.25	1.25
(13) Gary Sutherland	2.00	1.00	.60
(14) Bobby Wine	3.00	1.50	.90

1967 Laughlin World Series

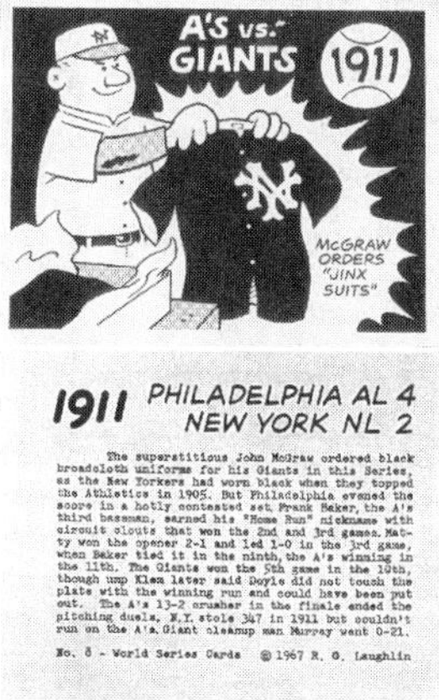

Apparently a prototype set for subsequent offerings by the sports artist R.G. Laughlin that were produced by Fleer, this set of 64 cards was printed in black and white with the cartoon line drawings for which Laughlin was noted. The cards are an odd size, 2-3/4" x 3-1/2", like so many of the Laughlin/Fleer issues of the period. The texts on the back are printed in red and offer details of the World Series from that year.

	NM	EX	VG
Complete Set (64):	200.00	100.00	60.00
Common Card:	2.00	1.00	.60
1 1903 Red Sox/Pirates	2.00	1.00	.60
2 1905 Giants/A's (Christy Mathewson)	4.50	2.25	1.25
3 1906 White Sox/Cubs	2.00	1.00	.60
4 1907 Cubs/Tigers	2.00	1.00	.60
5 1908 Cubs/Tigers (Joe Tinker, Evers, Frank Chance)	6.00	3.00	1.75
6 1909 Pirates/Tigers (Honus Wagner, Ty Cobb)	7.00	3.50	2.00
7 1910 A's/Cubs	2.00	1.00	.60
8 1911 A's/Giants (John McGraw)	4.50	2.25	1.25
9 1912 Red Sox/Giants	2.00	1.00	.60
10 1913 A's/Giants	2.00	1.00	.60
11 1914 Braves/A's	2.00	1.00	.60
12 1915 Red Sox/Phillies (Babe Ruth)	9.00	4.50	2.75
13 1916 White Sox/Dodgers (Babe Ruth)	9.00	4.50	2.75
14 1917 White Sox/Giants	2.00	1.00	.60
15 1918 Red Sox/Cubs	2.00	1.00	.60
16 1919 Reds/White Sox	6.00	3.00	1.75
17 1920 Indians/Dodgers (Bill Wambsganss)	2.00	1.00	.60
18 1921 Giants/Yankees (Waite Hoyt)	3.00	1.50	.90
19 1922 Giants/Yankees (Frank Frisch, Heinie Groh)	3.00	1.50	.90
20 1923 Yankees/Giants (Babe Ruth)	9.00	4.50	2.75
21 1924 Senators/Giants (Walter Johnson)	2.00	1.00	.60
22 1925 Pirates/Senators (Walter Johnson)	5.00	2.50	1.50
23 1926 Cardinals/Yankees (Grover Alexander, Anthony Lazzeri)	4.50	2.25	1.25
24 1927 Yankees/Pirates	2.00	1.00	.60
25 1928 Yankees/Cardinals (Babe Ruth, Lou Gehrig)	9.00	4.50	2.75
26 1929 A's/Cubs	2.00	1.00	.60
27 1930 A's/Cardinals	2.00	1.00	.60
28 1931 Cardinals/A's (Pepper Martin)	3.50	1.75	1.00
29 1932 Yankees/Cubs (Babe Ruth)	9.00	4.50	2.75
30 1933 Giants/Senators (Mel Ott)	4.50	2.25	1.25
31 1934 Cardinals/Tigers (Dizzy Dean, Paul Dean)	6.00	3.00	1.75
32 1935 Tigers/Cubs	2.00	1.00	.60
33 1936 Yankees/Giants	2.00	1.00	.60
34 1937 Yankees/Giants (Carl Hubbell)	4.50	2.25	1.25
35 1938 Yankees/Cubs	2.00	1.00	.60
36 1939 Yankees/Reds (Joe DiMaggio)	7.00	3.50	2.00
37 1940 Reds/Tigers	2.00	1.00	.60
38 1941 Yankees/Dodgers (Mickey Owen)	3.00	1.50	.90
39 1942 Cardinals/Yankees	2.00	1.00	.60
40 1943 Yankees/Cardinals (Joe McCarthy)	3.00	1.50	.90
41 1944 Cardinals/Browns	2.00	1.00	.60
42 1945 Tigers/Cubs (Hank Greenberg)	4.50	2.25	1.25
43 1946 Cardinals/Red Sox (Enos Slaughter)	4.50	2.25	1.25
44 1947 Yankees/Dodgers (Al Gionfriddo)	2.00	1.00	.60
45 1948 Indians/Braves (Bob Feller)	4.50	2.25	1.25
46 1949 Yankees/Dodgers (Allie Reynolds, Preacher Roe)	3.50	1.75	1.00
47 1950 Yankees/Phillies	2.00	1.00	.60
48 1951 Yankees/Giants	2.00	1.00	.60
49 1952 Yankees/Dodgers (Johnny Mize, Duke Snider)	4.50	2.25	1.25
50 1953 Yankees/Dodgers (Casey Stengel)	4.50	2.25	1.25
51 1954 Giants/Indians (Dusty Rhodes)	2.00	1.00	.60
52 1955 Dodgers/Yankees (Johnny Podres)	3.50	1.75	1.00
53 1956 Yankees/Dodgers (Don Larsen)	3.50	1.75	1.00
54 1957 Braves/Yankees (Lew Burdette)	2.00	1.00	.60
55 1958 Yankees/Braves (Hank Bauer)	2.00	1.00	.60
56 1959 Dodgers/White Sox (Larry Sherry)	2.00	1.00	.60
57 1960 Pirates/Yankees	3.50	1.75	1.00
58 1961 Yankees/Reds (Whitey Ford)	4.50	2.25	1.25
59 1962 Yankees/Giants	2.00	1.00	.60
60 1963 Dodgers/Yankees (Sandy Koufax)	4.50	2.25	1.25
61 1964 Cardinals/Yankees (Mickey Mantle)	9.00	4.50	2.75
62 1965 Dodgers/Twins (Sandy Koufax)	2.00	1.00	.60
63 1966 Orioles/Dodgers	2.00	1.00	.60
64 1967 Cardinals/Red Sox (Bob Gibson)	4.50	2.25	1.25

1972 Laughlin Great Feats

George Sisler made 257 hits in 1920

Sports artist R.G. Laughlin created this set of 50 numbered cards and one unnumbered title card highlighting top performances by stars over the years. The cards depict the player in pen and ink, with one variation of the set adding flesh tones to the players. One variation of the set has red borders, the other (with the flesh tones) blue. The cards are blank backed and numbered on the front with a brief caption. Sets originally sold for about $3.

	NM	EX	VG
Complete Set (51):	60.00	30.00	18.00
Common Player:	1.00	.50	.30
1 Joe DiMaggio	8.00	4.00	2.50
2 Walter Johnson	3.00	1.50	.90
3 Rudy York	1.00	.50	.30
4 Sandy Koufax	4.00	2.00	1.25
5 George Sisler	1.00	.50	.30
6 Iron Man McGinnity	1.00	.50	.30
7 Johnny VanderMeer	1.00	.50	.30
8 Lou Gehrig	6.00	3.00	1.75
9 Max Carey	1.00	.50	.30
10 Ed Delahanty	1.00	.50	.30
11 Pinky Higgins	1.00	.50	.30
12 Jack Chesbro	1.00	.50	.30
13 Jim Bottomley	1.00	.50	.30
14 Rube Marquard	1.00	.50	.30
15 Rogers Hornsby	1.00	.50	.30
16 Lefty Grove	1.00	.50	.30
17 Johnny Mize	1.00	.50	.30
18 Lefty Gomez	1.00	.50	.30
19 Jimmie Fox	1.00	.50	.30
20 Casey Stengel	1.50	.70	.45
21 Dazzy Vance	1.00	.50	.30
22 Jerry Lynch	1.00	.50	.30
23 Hughie Jennings	1.00	.50	.30
24 Stan Musial	4.00	2.00	1.25
25 Christy Mathewson	3.00	1.50	.90
26 Elroy Face	1.00	.50	.30
27 Hack Wilson	1.00	.50	.30
28 Smoky Burgess	1.00	.50	.30
29 Cy Young	1.50	.70	.45
30 Wilbert Robinson	1.00	.50	.30
31 Wee Willie Keeler	1.00	.50	.30
32 Babe Ruth	10.00	5.00	3.00
33 Mickey Mantle	10.00	5.00	3.00
34 Hub Leonard	1.00	.50	.30
35 Ty Cobb	4.00	2.00	1.25
36 Carl Hubbell	1.00	.50	.30
37 Joe Oeschger, Leon Cadore	1.00	.50	.30
38 Don Drysdale	1.50	.70	.45
39 Fred Toney, Hippo Vaughn	1.00	.50	.30
40 Joe Sewell	1.00	.50	.30
41 Grover Cleveland Alexander	1.00	.50	.30
42 Joe Adcock	1.00	.50	.30
43 Eddie Collins	1.00	.50	.30
44 Bob Feller	1.50	.70	.45
45 Don Larsen	1.50	.70	.45
46 Dave Philley	1.00	.50	.30
47 Bill Fischer	1.00	.50	.30
48 Dale Long	1.00	.50	.30
49 Bill Wambsganss	1.00	.50	.30
50 Roger Maris	4.00	2.00	1.25
--- Title card	1.00	.50	.30

1973 Laughlin Super Stand-Ups

A dozen Hall of Famers are featured in this collectors' issue of stand-up figures. Printed in color on heavy cardboard, each is die-cut around the player action picture with typical measurements being 7" x 11". The stand-ups are much scarcer than most of the artist's other baseball issues. They are listed here alphabetically. The stand-ups originally retailed for $3.50 apiece.

	NM	EX	VG
Complete Set (12):	850.00	425.00	250.00
Common Player:	30.00	15.00	9.00
(1) Hank Aaron	50.00	25.00	15.00
(2) Roberto Clemente	75.00	37.00	22.00
(3) Joe DiMaggio	125.00	62.00	37.00
(4) Lou Gehrig	150.00	75.00	45.00
(5) Gil Hodges	45.00	22.00	13.50
(6) Sandy Koufax	50.00	25.00	15.00
(7) Mickey Mantle	200.00	100.00	60.00
(8) Willie Mays	50.00	25.00	15.00
(9) Stan Musial	50.00	25.00	15.00
(10) Babe Ruth	175.00	87.00	52.00
(11) Tom Seaver	30.00	15.00	9.00
(12) Ted Williams	60.00	30.00	18.00

1974 Laughlin All-Star Games

With pen and ink drawings by R.G. Laughlin on the fronts, this set (40 cards) features one card from each year of the game from 1933 to 1973. The 2-3/4" x 3-3/8" cards show a player in black ink in front of a light blue background with a glossy finish, with red printing for the title of the set and the year. The backs are printed in blue, with the year of the All-Star Game serving as the card number. Issue price was $3.50.

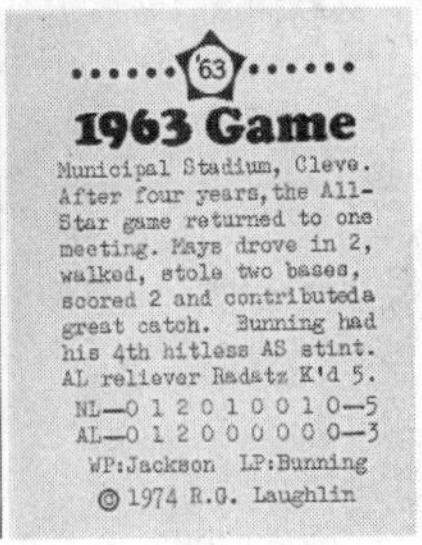

		NM	EX	VG
Complete Set (40):		27.00	13.50	8.00
Common Player:		.50	.25	.15
33	Babe's Homer (Babe Ruth)	5.00	2.50	1.50
34a	Hub Fans Five (Carl Hubbell) (uniform #11)	.70	.35	.20
34b	Hub Fans Five (Carl Hubbell) (uniform #14)	.70	.35	.20
35	Foxx Smashes HR (Jimmie Foxx)	.70	.35	.20
36	Ol' Diz Fogs 'Em (Dizzy Dean)	.70	.35	.20
37	Four Hits for Ducky (Ducky Medwick)	.50	.25	.15
38	No-Hit Vandy (John VanderMeer)	.50	.25	.15
39	DiMaggio Homers (Joe DiMaggio)	3.50	1.75	1.00
40	West's 3-Run Shot (Max West)	.50	.25	.15
41	Vaughan Busts Two (Arky Vaughan)	.50	.25	.15
42	York's 2-Run Smash (Rudy York)	.50	.25	.15
43	Doerr's 3-Run Blast (Bobby Doerr)	.50	.25	.15
44	Cavarretta Reaches (Phil Cavarretta)	.50	.25	.15
46	Field Day for Ted (Ted Williams)	3.00	1.50	.90
47	Big Cat Plants One (Johnny Mize)	.50	.25	.15
48	Raschi Pitches (Vic Raschi)	.50	.25	.15
49	Jackie Scores (Jackie Robinson)	3.00	1.50	.90
50	Schoendienst Breaks (Red Schoendienst)	.50	.25	.15
51	Kiner Homers (Ralph Kiner)	.50	.25	.15
52	Sauer's Shot (Hank Sauer)	.50	.25	.15
53	Slaughter Hustles (Enos Slaughter)	.50	.25	.15
54	Rosen Hits (Al Rosen)	.50	.25	.15
55	Stan the Man's HR (Stan Musial)	2.00	1.00	.60
56	Boyer Super (Ken Boyer)	.50	.25	.15
57	Kaline's Hits (Al Kaline)	.70	.35	.20
58	Nellie Gets Two (Nellie Fox)	.50	.25	.15
59	Robbie Perfect (Frank Robinson)	.70	.35	.20
60	Willie 3-for-4 (Willie Mays)	2.00	1.00	.60
61	Bunning Hitless (Jim Bunning)	.50	.25	.15
62	Roberto Perfect (Roberto Clemente)	3.00	1.50	.90
63	Monster Strikeouts (Dick Radatz)	.50	.25	.15
64	Callison's Homer (Johnny Callison)	.50	.25	.15
65	Stargell's Big Day (Willie Stargell)	.50	.25	.15
66	Brooks Gets Triple (Brooks Robinson)	.70	.35	.20
67	Fergie Fans Six (Fergie Jenkins)	.50	.25	.15
68	Tom Terrific (Tom Seaver)	1.00	.50	.30
69	Stretch Belts Two (Willie McCovey)	.50	.25	.15
70	Yaz' Four Hits (Carl Yastrzemski)	.70	.35	.20
71	Reggie Unloads (Reggie Jackson)	1.00	.50	.30
72	Henry Hammers (Hank Aaron)	2.00	1.00	.60
73	Bonds Perfect (Bobby Bonds)	.50	.25	.15

1974 Laughlin Old-Time Black Stars

This set of slightly oversized cards (2-5/8" x 3-1/2") features drawings by R.G. Laughlin. The artwork is printed in brown and a light tan; backs are printed in brown on white stock. The set features many of the greatest players from the Negro Leagues. The cards carry no copyright date and no mention of the prolific Laughlin, but the simple line drawings are obviously his work, and a subsequent issue four years later by Laughlin removes any doubt. Original retail price at time of issue was about $3.25.

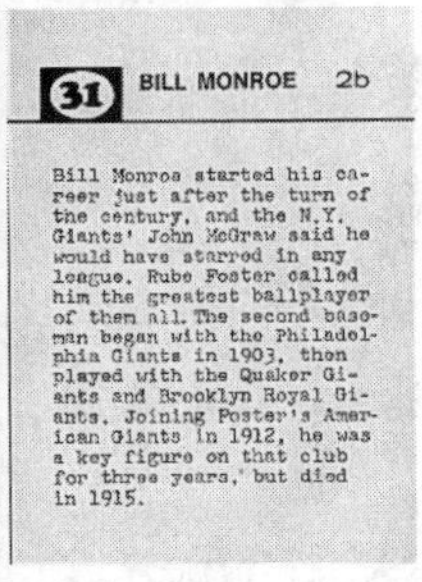

		NM	EX	VG
Complete Set (36):		50.00	25.00	15.00
Common Player:		1.50	.70	.45
1	Smokey Joe Williams	5.00	2.50	1.50
2	Rap Dixon	1.50	.70	.45
3	Oliver Marcelle	1.50	.70	.45
4	Bingo DeMoss	3.00	1.50	.90
5	Willie Foster	2.00	1.00	.60
6	John Beckwith	1.50	.70	.45
7	Floyd (Jelly) Gardner	1.50	.70	.45
8	Josh Gibson	7.00	3.50	2.00
9	Jose Mendez	1.50	.70	.45
10	Pete Hill	1.50	.70	.45
11	Buck Leonard	4.00	2.00	1.25
12	Jud Wilson	1.50	.70	.45
13	Willie Wells	4.00	2.00	1.25
14	Jimmie Lyons	1.50	.70	.45
15	Satchel Paige	8.00	4.00	2.50
16	Louis Santop	1.50	.70	.45
17	Frank Grant	1.50	.70	.45
18	Christobel Torrienti	1.50	.70	.45
19	Bullet Rogan	3.00	1.50	.90
20	Dave Malarcher	2.00	1.00	.60
21	Spot Poles	1.50	.70	.45
22	Home Run Johnson	2.00	1.00	.60
23	Charlie Grant	3.00	1.50	.90
24	Cool Papa Bell	4.00	2.00	1.25
25	Cannonball Dick Redding	1.50	.70	.45
26	Ray Dandridge	4.00	2.00	1.25
27	Biz Mackey	3.00	1.50	.90
28	Fats Jenkins	1.50	.70	.45
29	Martin Dihigo	3.00	1.50	.90
30	Mule Suttles	1.50	.70	.45
31	Bill Monroe	1.50	.70	.45
32	Dan McClellan	1.50	.70	.45
33	Pop Lloyd	2.50	1.25	.70
34	Oscar Charleston	4.00	2.00	1.25
35	Andrew (Rube) Foster	4.00	2.00	1.25
36	William (Judy) Johnson	4.00	2.00	1.25

1974 Laughlin Sportslang

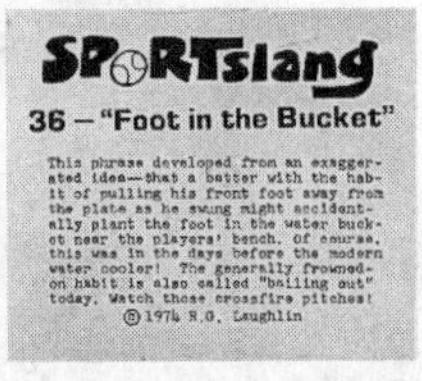

Featuring the cartoon artwork of R.G. Laughlin, this 41-card set features 40 cards (plus one unnumbered title card) detailing the history and derivation of slang terms from several sports. The cards are 2-3/4" x 3-1/4", with red and blue printing on the front and red on the back. The cards are numbered on the back.

		NM	EX	VG
Complete Set (41):		8.00	4.00	2.50
Common Card:		.25	.13	.08
1	Bull Pen	.25	.13	.08
2	Charley Horse	.25	.13	.08
3	Derby	.25	.13	.08
4	Anchor Man	.25	.13	.08
5	Mascot	.25	.13	.08
6	Annie Oakley	.25	.13	.08
7	Taxi Squad	.25	.13	.08
8	Dukes	.25	.13	.08
9	Rookie	.25	.13	.08
10	Jinx	.25	.13	.08
11	Dark Horse	.25	.13	.08
12	Hat Trick	.25	.13	.08
13	Bell Wether	.25	.13	.08
14	Love	.25	.13	.08
15	Red Dog	.25	.13	.08
16	Barnstorm	.25	.13	.08
17	Bull's Eye	.25	.13	.08
18	Rabbit Punch	.25	.13	.08
19	The Upper Hand	.25	.13	.08
20	Handi Cap	.25	.13	.08
21	Marathon	.25	.13	.08
22	Southpaw	.25	.13	.08
23	Boner	.25	.13	.08
24	Gridiron	.25	.13	.08
25	Fan	.25	.13	.08
26	Moxie	.25	.13	.08
27	Birdie	.25	.13	.08
28	Sulky	.25	.13	.08
29	Dribble	.25	.13	.08
30	Donnybrook	.25	.13	.08
31	The Real McCoy	.25	.13	.08
32	Even Stephen	.25	.13	.08
33	Chinese Homer	.25	.13	.08
34	English	.25	.13	.08
35	Garrison Finish	.25	.13	.08
36	Foot in the Bucket	.25	.13	.08
37	Steeple Chase	.25	.13	.08
38	Long Shot	.25	.13	.08
39	Nip and Tuck	.25	.13	.08
40	Battery	.25	.13	.08
----	Header card	.25	.13	.08

1975 Laughlin Batty Baseball

This 25-card set depicts one humorous nickname for each of 24 Major League teams, plus one unnumbered title card. The cards are approximately standard size at 2-1/2" x 3-1/2", with simple black and white cartoon drawings on the front with orange back-grounds. The backs are blank and the cards are numbered on front.

		NM	EX	VG
Complete Set (25):		40.00	20.00	12.00
Common Card:		2.00	1.00	.60
1	Oakland Daze	2.00	1.00	.60
2	Boston Wet Sox	2.00	1.00	.60
3	Cincinnati Dreads	2.00	1.00	.60
4	Chicago Wide Sox	2.00	1.00	.60
5	Milwaukee Boozers	2.00	1.00	.60
6	Philadlephia Fillies	2.00	1.00	.60
7	Cleveland Engines	2.00	1.00	.60
8	New York Mitts	2.00	1.00	.60
9	Texas Ranchers	2.00	1.00	.60
10	San Francisco Gents	2.00	1.00	.60
11	Houston Disastros	2.00	1.00	.60
12	Chicago Clubs	2.00	1.00	.60
13	Minnesota Wins	2.00	1.00	.60
14	St. Louis Gardeners	2.00	1.00	.60
15	New York Yankers	2.00	1.00	.60
16	California Angles	2.00	1.00	.60
17	Pittsburgh Irates	2.00	1.00	.60
18	Los Angeles Smoggers	2.00	1.00	.60
19	Baltimore Oreos	2.00	1.00	.60
20	Montreal Expose	2.00	1.00	.60
21	San Diego Parties	2.00	1.00	.60
22	Detroit Taggers	2.00	1.00	.60
23	Kansas City Broils	2.00	1.00	.60
24	Atlanta Briefs	2.00	1.00	.60
----	Header card	2.00	1.00	.60

Vintage cards in Good condition are valued at about 50% of the Very Good value shown here. Fair cards are valued at 25% or less of VG.
The ratio of Excellent and Very Good prices to Near Mint can vary depending on relative collectibility for each grade in a specific set. Current listings reflect such adjustments.

1976 Laughlin Diamond Jubilee

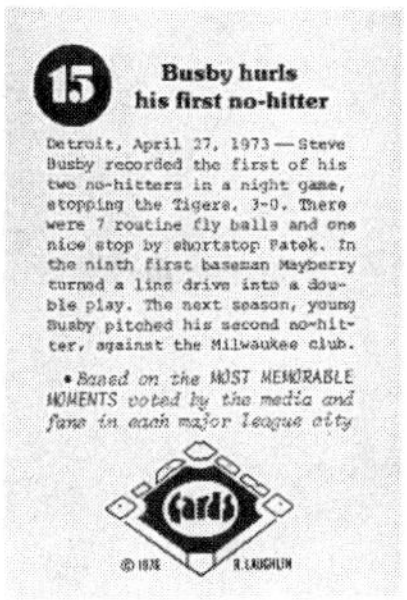

This set of 32 oversized cards (2-3/4" x 4") features Laughlin's drawings of baseball stars highlighting specific events or records. The fronts are printed in black and blue over a red background; the backs are numbered and printed in blue with information about the specific event. Sets originally sold for $3.50.

		NM	EX	VG
Complete Set (32):		90.00	45.00	27.00
Common Player:		1.25	.60	.40
1	Nolan Ryan	20.00	10.00	6.00
2	Ernie Banks	4.00	2.00	1.25
3	Mickey Lolich	1.25	.60	.40
4	Sandy Koufax	6.00	3.00	1.75
5	Frank Robinson	2.00	1.00	.60
6	Bill Mazeroski	2.00	1.00	.60
7	Catfish Hunter	1.25	.60	.40
8	Hank Aaron	6.00	3.00	1.75
9	Carl Yastrzemski	2.00	1.00	.60
10	Jim Bunning	1.25	.60	.40
11	Brooks Robinson	2.00	1.00	.60
12	John VanderMeer	1.25	.60	.40
13	Harmon Killebrew	1.50	.70	.45
14	Lou Brock	1.50	.70	.45
15	Steve Busby	1.25	.60	.40
16	Nate Colbert	1.25	.60	.40
17	Don Larsen	2.00	1.00	.60
18	Willie Mays	6.00	3.00	1.75
19	David Clyde	1.25	.60	.40
20	Mack Jones	1.25	.60	.40
21	Mike Hegan	1.25	.60	.40
22	Jerry Koosman	1.25	.60	.40
23	Early Wynn	1.50	.70	.45
24	Nellie Fox	2.00	1.00	.60
25	Joe DiMaggio	12.50	6.25	3.75
26	Jackie Robinson	8.00	4.00	2.50
27	Ted Williams	8.00	4.00	2.50
28	Lou Gehrig	8.00	4.00	2.50
29	Bobby Thomson	2.00	1.00	.60
30	Roger Maris	5.00	2.50	1.50
31	Harvey Haddix	1.25	.60	.40
32	Babe Ruth	15.00	7.50	4.50

1976 Laughlin Indianapolis Clowns

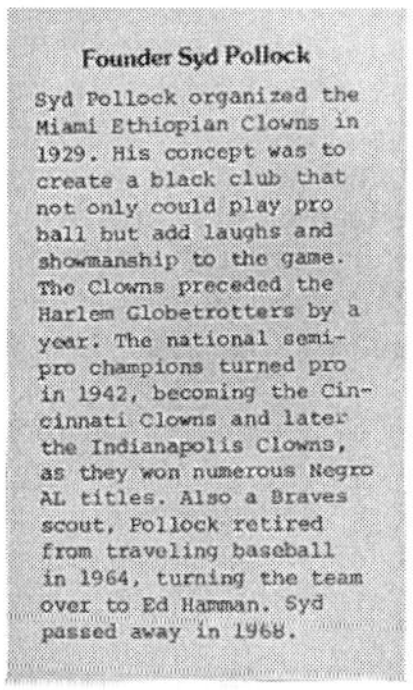

In a departure from the style of most Laughlin issues, this 42-card set does not use his artwork, but rather black and white photos framed by a light blue border. The cards are oversized at 2-5/8" x 4-1/4", with red printing on front and back. The cards are numbered on the front.

		NM	EX	VG
Complete Set (42):		40.00	20.00	12.00
Common Player:		.75	.40	.25
1	Ed Hamman (Ed the Clown)	1.25	.60	.40
2	Dero Austin	.75	.40	.25
3	James Williams (Natureboy)	.75	.40	.25
4	Sam Brison (Birmingham)	.75	.40	.25
5	Richard King (King Tut)	.75	.40	.25
6	Syd Pollock (Founder)	.75	.40	.25
7	Nataniel (Lefty) Small	.75	.40	.25
8	Grant Greene (Double Duty)	.75	.40	.25
9	Nancy Miller (Lady Umpire)	.75	.40	.25
10	Billy Vaughn	.75	.40	.25
11	Sam Brison (Putout for Sam)	.75	.40	.25
12	Ed Hamman	.75	.40	.25
13	Dero Austin (Home Delivery)	.75	.40	.25
14	Steve (Nub) Anderson	.75	.40	.25
15	Joe Cherry	.75	.40	.25
16	Reece (Goose) Tatum	4.00	2.00	1.25
17	James Williams (Natureboy)	.75	.40	.25
18	Byron Purnell	.75	.40	.25
19	Bat Boy	.75	.40	.25
20	Spec BeBop	.75	.40	.25
21	Satchel Paige	7.00	3.50	2.00
22	Prince Jo Henry	.75	.40	.25
23	Ed Hamman, Syd Pollock	.75	.40	.25
24	Paul Casanova	1.00	.50	.30
25	Steve (Nub) Anderson (Nub Singles)	.75	.40	.25
26	Comiskey Park	.75	.40	.25
27	Toni Stone (Second basewoman)	2.00	1.00	.60
28	Dero Austin (Small target)	.75	.40	.25
29	Calling Dr. Kildare (Sam Brison, Natureboy Williams)	.75	.40	.25
30	Oscar Charleston	2.50	1.25	.70
31	Richard King (King Tut)	.75	.40	.25
32	Ed and Prospects (Ed Hamman, Joe Cherry, Hal King)	.75	.40	.25
33	Team bus	.75	.40	.25
34	Hank Aaron	7.50	3.75	2.25
35	The Greta Yogi	2.00	1.00	.60
36	W.H. (Chauff) Wilson	.75	.40	.25
37	Doin' Their Thing (Sam Brison, Sonny Jackson)	.75	.40	.25
38	Billy Vaughn (The hard way)	.75	.40	.25
39	James Williams (18 the easy way)	.75	.40	.25
40	Casey & Ed (Ed Hamman, Casey Stengel)	1.50	.70	.45
---	Header card	.75	.40	.25
---	Baseball Laff Book	.75	.40	.25

1978 Laughlin Long Ago Black Stars

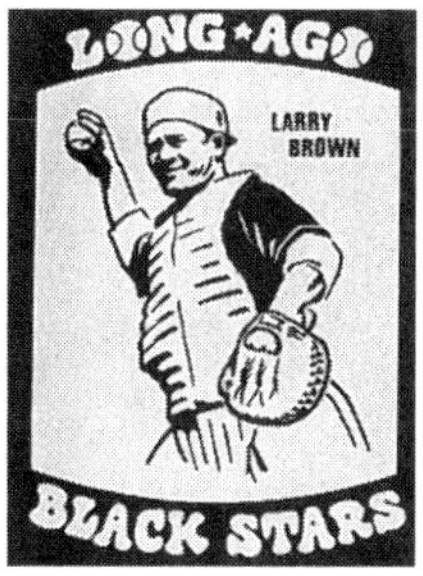

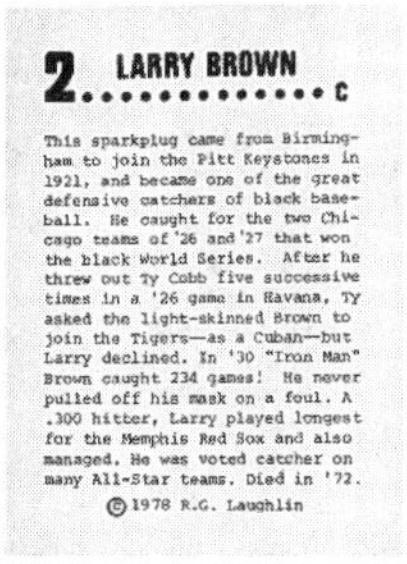

In what appears very much like a second series save for slight title alteration, sports artist R.G. Laughlin produced this 36-card set in a format very similar to his 1974 issue highlighting Negro League stars. This set is printed in dark and light green on a non-glossy front, with printing on the back in black. Most of the more widely known Negro League stars appeared in the 1974 issue.

		NM	EX	VG
Complete Set (36):		30.00	15.00	9.00
Common Player:		.75	.40	.25
1	Ted Trent	.75	.40	.25
2	Larry Brown	.75	.40	.25
3	Newt Allen	1.50	.70	.45
4	Norman Stearns	2.00	1.00	.60
5	Leon Day	3.00	1.50	.90
6	Dick Lundy	.75	.40	.25
7	Bruce Petway	.75	.40	.25
8	Bill Drake	.75	.40	.25
9	Chaney White	.75	.40	.25
10	Webster McDonald	1.25	.60	.40
11	Tommy Butts	.75	.40	.25
12	Ben Taylor	.75	.40	.25
13	James (Joe) Greene	.75	.40	.25
14	Dick Seay	.75	.40	.25
15	Sammy Hughes	.75	.40	.25
16	Ted Page	1.50	.70	.45
17	Willie Cornelius	.75	.40	.25
18	Pat Patterson	.75	.40	.25
19	Frank Wickware	.75	.40	.25
20	Albert Haywood	.75	.40	.25
21	Bill Holland	.75	.40	.25
22	Sol White	1.25	.60	.40
23	Chet Brewer	1.50	.70	.45
24	Crush Holloway	.75	.40	.25
25	George Johnson	.75	.40	.25
26	George Scales	.75	.40	.25
27	Dave Brown	.75	.40	.25
28	John Donaldson	.75	.40	.25
29	William Johnson	1.50	.70	.45
30	Bill Yancey	1.50	.70	.45
31	Sam Bankhead	2.00	1.00	.60
32	Leroy Matlock	.75	.40	.25
33	Quincy Troupe	1.25	.60	.40
34	Hilton Smith	.75	.40	.25
35	Jim Crutchfield	1.50	.70	.45
36	Ted Radcliffe	2.00	1.00	.60

1980 Laughlin Famous Feats

A set of 40 cards, this Famous Feats set by sports artist R.G. Laughlin carries a subtitle as the Second Series, apparently a reference to a 1972 issue of the same name by Laughlin that was produced by Fleer. Unlike many of the odd sized Laughlin issues, this one is the standard 2-1/2" x 3-1/2", with full color used with the artist's pen and ink drawings on the front. The cards are numbered on the front and the backs are blank.

		NM	EX	VG
Complete Set (40):		30.00	15.00	9.00
Common Player:		.90	.45	.25
1	Honus Wagner	3.00	1.50	.90
2	Herb Pennock	.90	.45	.25
3	Al Simmons	.90	.45	.25
4	Hack Wilson	.90	.45	.25
5	Dizzy Dean	2.00	1.00	.60
6	Chuck Klein	.90	.45	.25
7	Nellie Fox	1.50	.70	.45
8	Lefty Grove	.90	.45	.25
9	George Sisler	.90	.45	.25
10	Lou Gehrig	4.00	2.00	1.25
11	Rube Waddell	.90	.45	.25
12	Max Carey	.90	.45	.25
13	Thurman Munson	2.00	1.00	.60
14	Mel Ott	.90	.45	.25
15	Doc White	.90	.45	.25
16	Babe Ruth	7.50	3.75	2.25
17	Schoolboy Rowe	.90	.45	.25
18	Jackie Robinson	5.00	2.50	1.50
19	Joe Medwick	.90	.45	.25
20	Casey Stengel	2.00	1.00	.60
21	Roberto Clemente	7.50	3.75	2.25
22	Christy Mathewson	2.00	1.00	.60
23	Jimmie Foxx	1.50	.70	.45
24	Joe Jackson	7.50	3.75	2.25
25	Walter Johnson	2.00	1.00	.60
26	Tony Lazzeri	.90	.45	.25
27	Hugh Casey	.90	.45	.25
28	Ty Cobb	4.00	2.00	1.25
29	Stuffy McInnis	.90	.45	.25
30	Cy Young	1.50	.70	.45
31	Lefty O'Doul	.90	.45	.25
32	Eddie Collins	.90	.45	.25
33	Joe McCarty	.90	.45	.25
34	Ed Walsh	.90	.45	.25
35	George Burns	.90	.45	.25
36	Walt Dropo	.90	.45	.25
37	Connie Mack	.90	.45	.25
38	Babe Adams	.90	.45	.25
39	Rogers Hornsby	1.25	.60	.40
40	Grover C. Alexander	1.25	.60	.40

1980 Laughlin 300/400/500

This unusual set features a combination of the line drawings of R.G. Laughlin and a photo head shot of the player depicted. The cards are actually square, 3-1/4" x 3-1/4", with a background in color depicting a baseball diamond. The set is based on 300 wins, batting .400 or better and 500 homers, with a total of 30 cards in the blank backed set. The cards are numbered on the front.

		NM	EX	VG
Complete Set (30):		16.00	8.00	4.75
Common Player:		.50	.25	.15
1	Header card	.50	.25	.15
2	Babe Ruth	4.00	2.00	1.25
3	Walter Johnson	1.00	.50	.30
4	Ty Cobb	1.50	.70	.45
5	Christy Mathewson	1.00	.50	.30
6	Ted Williams	1.50	.70	.45
7	Bill Terry	.75	.40	.25
8	Grover C. Alexander	.75	.40	.25
9	Napoleon Lajoie	.75	.40	.25
10	Willie Mays	1.50	.70	.45
11	Cy Young	.75	.40	.25
12	Mel Ott	.50	.25	.15
13	Joe Jackson	3.00	1.50	.90
14	Harmon Killebrew	.75	.40	.25
15	Warren Spahn	.75	.40	.25
16	Hank Aaron	2.00	1.00	.60
17	Rogers Hornsby	.75	.40	.25
18	Mickey Mantle	4.00	2.00	1.25
19	Lefty Grove	.75	.40	.25
20	Ted Williams	2.00	1.00	.60
21	Jimmie Fox	.75	.40	.25
22	Eddie Plank	.50	.25	.15
23	Frank Robinson	.75	.40	.25
24	George Sisler	.50	.25	.15
25	Eddie Mathews	.75	.40	.25
26	Early Wynn	.50	.25	.15
27	Ernie Banks	1.00	.50	.30
28	Harry Heilmann	.50	.25	.15
29	Lou Gehrig	3.00	1.50	.90
30	Willie McCovey	.75	.40	.25

1948-49 Leaf

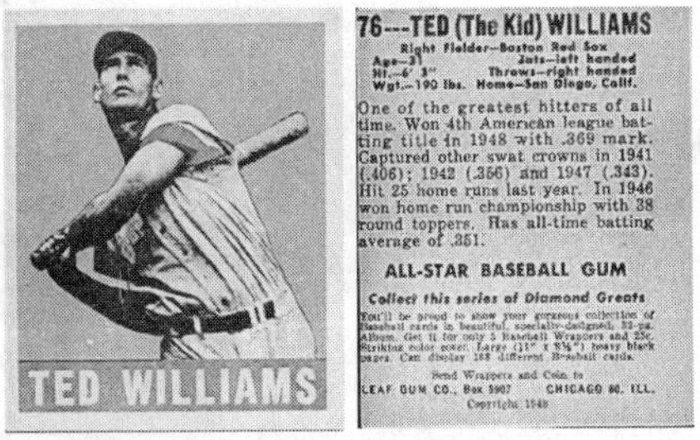

The first color baseball cards of the post-World War II era were the 98-card, 2-3/8" x 2-7/8", set produced by Chicago's Leaf Gum Company in 1948-1949. The color was crude, probably helping to make the set less popular than the Bowman issues of the same era. One of the toughest post-war sets to complete, exactly half of the Leaf issue - 49 of the cards - are significantly harder to find than the other 49. Probably intended to confound bubble gum buyers of the day, the set is skip-numbered between 1-168. Card backs contain offers of felt pennants, an album for the cards or 5-1/2" x 7-1/2" premium photos of Hall of Famers.

		NM	EX	VG
Complete Set (98):		24000.	12000.	7250.
Common Player:		25.00	12.50	7.50
Common Short-print:		200.00	100.00	60.00
1	Joe DiMaggio	2100.	900.00	550.00
3	Babe Ruth	2000.	1000.	550.00
4	*Stan Musial*	700.00	350.00	210.00
5	*Virgil Trucks* (SP)	275.00	137.00	82.00
8	*Satchel Paige* (SP)	2400.	1200.	720.00
10	Paul Trout	25.00	12.50	7.50
11	*Phil Rizzuto*	225.00	112.00	67.00
13	Casimer Michaels (SP)	200.00	100.00	60.00
14	Billy Johnson	30.00	15.00	9.00
17	Frank Overmire	25.00	12.50	7.50
19	John Wyrostek (SP)	200.00	100.00	60.00
20	*Hank Sauer* (SP)	250.00	125.00	75.00
22	Al Evans	25.00	12.50	7.50
26	Sam Chapman	25.00	12.50	7.50
27	Mickey Harris	25.00	12.50	7.50
28	*Jim Hegan*	30.00	15.00	9.00
29	*Elmer Valo*	30.00	15.00	9.00
30	*Bill Goodman* (SP)	200.00	100.00	60.00
31	Lou Brissie	25.00	12.50	7.50
32	*Warren Spahn*	260.00	130.00	78.00
33	Harry Lowrey (SP)	200.00	100.00	60.00
36	Al Zarilla (SP)	200.00	100.00	60.00
38	*Ted Kluszewski*	140.00	70.00	42.00
39	*Ewell Blackwell*	45.00	22.00	13.50
42	Kent Peterson	25.00	12.50	7.50
43	Eddie Stevens (SP)	200.00	100.00	60.00
45	Ken Keltner (SP)	200.00	100.00	60.00
46	Johnny Mize	100.00	50.00	30.00
47	George Vico	25.00	12.50	7.50
48	Johnny Schmitz (SP)	200.00	100.00	60.00
49	*Del Ennis*	35.00	17.50	10.50
50	Dick Wakefield	25.00	12.50	7.50
51	*Alvin Dark* (SP)	275.00	137.00	82.00
53	John Vandermeer (Vander Meer)	50.00	25.00	15.00
54	Bobby Adams (SP)	200.00	100.00	60.00
55	Tommy Henrich (SP)	300.00	150.00	90.00
56	*Larry Jensen*	30.00	15.00	9.00
57	Bob McCall	25.00	12.50	7.50
59	Luke Appling	90.00	45.00	27.00
61	Jake Early	25.00	12.50	7.50
62	Eddie Joost (SP)	200.00	100.00	60.00
63	Barney McCosky (SP)	200.00	100.00	60.00
65	Bob Elliot (Elliott)	25.00	12.50	7.50
66	Orval Grove (SP)	200.00	100.00	60.00
68	Ed Miller (SP)	200.00	100.00	60.00
70	Honus Wagner	265.00	130.00	80.00
72	Hank Edwards	25.00	12.50	7.50
73	Pat Seerey	25.00	12.50	7.50
75	Dom DiMaggio (SP)	450.00	225.00	135.00
76	Ted Williams	750.00	375.00	225.00
77	Roy Smalley	25.00	12.50	7.50
78	Walter Evers (SP)	200.00	100.00	60.00
79	*Jackie Robinson*	750.00	400.00	250.00
81	George Kurowski (SP)	200.00	100.00	60.00
82	Johnny Lindell	25.00	12.50	7.50
83	Bobby Doerr	100.00	50.00	30.00
84	Sid Hudson	25.00	12.50	7.50
85	*Dave Philley* (SP)	250.00	125.00	75.00
86	Ralph Weigel	25.00	12.50	7.50
88	Frank Gustine (SP)	200.00	100.00	60.00
91	*Ralph Kiner*	175.00	87.00	52.00
93	Bob Feller (SP)	1250.	625.00	375.00
95	George Stirnweiss	25.00	12.50	7.50
97	*Martin Marion*	55.00	27.00	16.50
98	*Hal Newhouser* (SP)	550.00	275.00	165.00
102a	Gene Hermansk (incorrect spelling)	2100.	1050.	630.00
102b	Gene Hermanski (correct spelling)	25.00	12.50	7.50
104	Edward Stewart (SP)	200.00	100.00	60.00
106	Lou Boudreau	95.00	47.00	28.00
108	Matthew Batts (SP)	200.00	100.00	60.00
111	Gerald Priddy	25.00	12.50	7.50
113	Emil Leonard (SP)	200.00	100.00	60.00
117	Joe Gordon	25.00	12.50	7.50
120	*George Kell* (SP)	500.00	250.00	150.00
121	*John Pesky* (SP)	300.00	150.00	90.00
123	Clifford Fannin (SP)	200.00	100.00	60.00
125	*Andy Pafko*	35.00	17.50	10.50
127	Enos Slaughter (SP)	725.00	362.00	217.00
128	Warren Rosar	25.00	12.50	7.50
129	Kirby Higbe (SP)	200.00	100.00	60.00
131	Sid Gordon (SP)	200.00	100.00	60.00
133	Tommy Holmes (SP)	275.00	137.00	82.00
136a	Cliff Aberson (full sleeve)	25.00	12.50	7.50
136b	Cliff Aberson (short sleeve)	300.00	150.00	90.00
137	Harry Walker (SP)	200.00	100.00	60.00
138	*Larry Doby* (SP)	525.00	262.00	157.00
139	Johnny Hopp	25.00	12.50	7.50
142	*Danny Murtaugh* (SP)	275.00	137.00	82.00
143	Dick Sisler (SP)	200.00	100.00	60.00
144	Bob Dillinger (SP)	200.00	100.00	60.00
146	Harold Reiser (SP)	450.00	225.00	135.00
149	Henry Majeski (SP)	200.00	100.00	60.00
153	Floyd Baker (SP)	200.00	100.00	60.00
158	*Harry Brecheen* (SP)	275.00	137.00	82.00
159	Mizell Platt	25.00	12.50	7.50
160	Bob Scheffing (SP)	250.00	125.00	75.00
161	*Vernon Stephens* (SP)	275.00	137.00	82.00
163	*Freddy Hutchinson* (SP)	275.00	137.00	82.00
165	*Dale Mitchell* (SP)	275.00	137.00	82.00
168	Phil Cavaretta (SP)	300.00	150.00	90.00

1948-49 Leaf Premiums

These blank-back, sepia photos were available with the purchase of 1948 Leaf baseball cards. Measuring 5-5/8" x 7-1/4", the pictures have a facsimile autograph and a black box labeled "BASEBALL'S IMMORTALS" at bottom containing a short biography. The unnumbered pictures are checklisted alphabetically.

		NM	EX	VG
Complete Set (9):		2400.	1200.	725.00
Common Player:		200.00	100.00	60.00
(1)	Grover Alexander	250.00	125.00	75.00
(2)	Mickey Cochrane	200.00	100.00	60.00
(3)	Lou Gehrig	500.00	250.00	150.00
(4)	Walter Johnson	250.00	125.00	75.00
(5)	Christy Mathewson	275.00	135.00	82.00
(6)	John McGraw	200.00	100.00	60.00
(7)	Babe Ruth	600.00	300.00	180.00
(8)	Babe Ruth	600.00	300.00	180.00
(9)	Ed Walsh	200.00	100.00	60.00

1960 Leaf Pre-production

Evidently produced prior to final approval for the design of the 1960 Leaf set, these cards all feature much larger player photos than the issued versions. Generally the issued cards have cap-to-waist photos while the pre-production cards have cap-to-chin shots. Backs of the pre-production cards are virtually identical to the regular cards. The pre-production cards were never publically issued and show evidence of having been hand-cut.

		NM	EX	VG
Complete Set (8):		12500.	6250.	3750.
Common Player:		1500.	750.00	450.00
1	Luis Aparicio	2200.	1100.	660.00
12	Ken Boyer	2000.	1000.	600.00
17	Walt Moryn	1500.	750.00	450.00
23	Joey Jay	1500.	750.00	450.00
35	Jim Coates	1500.	750.00	450.00
58	Hal Smith	1500.	750.00	450.00
61	Vic Rehm	1500.	750.00	450.00
72	Dick Donovan	1500.	750.00	450.00

1960 Leaf

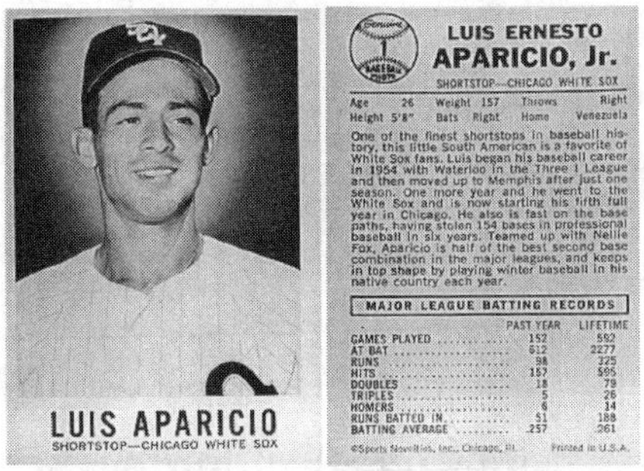

While known to the hobby as "Leaf" cards, this set of 144 carries the copyright of Sports Novelties Inc., Chicago. The 2-1/2" x 3-1/2" cards feature black-and-white player portrait photos, with plain background. Cards were sold in nickel wax packs with a marble, rather than a piece of bubble gum. The second half of the set, #73-144, are quite scarce. Card #25, Jim Grant, is found in two versions, with his own picture (black cap) and with a photo of Brooks Lawrence (white cap). Three back variations of Hal Smith card #58 are also known. Complete set prices do not include variations. In the late 1990s, a large group of high-number wax packs - in excess of 4,000 cards - was added to the surviving supply.

		NM	EX	VG
Complete Set (144):		1250.	650.00	400.00
Common Player (1-72):		4.00	2.00	1.25
Common Player (73-144):		15.00	7.50	4.50
1	Luis Aparicio	30.00	15.00	9.00
2	Woody Held	4.00	2.00	1.25
3	Frank Lary	4.00	2.00	1.25
4	Camilo Pascual	4.00	2.00	1.25
5	Frank Herrera	4.00	2.00	1.25
6	Felipe Alou	12.00	6.00	3.50
7	Bennie Daniels	4.00	2.00	1.25
8	Roger Craig	5.00	2.50	1.50
9	Eddie Kasko	4.00	2.00	1.25
10	Bob Grim	4.00	2.00	1.25
11	Jim Busby	4.00	2.00	1.25
12	Ken Boyer	11.00	5.50	3.25
13	Bob Boyd	4.00	2.00	1.25
14	Sam Jones	4.00	2.00	1.25
15	Larry Jackson	4.00	2.00	1.25

16	Roy Face	4.00	2.00	1.25
17	Walt Moryn	4.00	2.00	1.25
18	Jim Gilliam	5.00	2.50	1.50
19	Don Newcombe	5.00	2.50	1.50
20	Glen Hobbie	4.00	2.00	1.25
21	Pedro Ramos	4.00	2.00	1.25
22	Ryne Duren	4.50	2.25	1.25
23	Joe Jay	4.00	2.00	1.25
24	Lou Berberet	4.00	2.00	1.25
25a	Jim Grant (white cap, photo actually Brooks Lawrence)	20.00	10.00	6.00
25b	Jim Grant (dark cap, correct photo)	30.00	15.00	9.00
26	Tom Borland	4.00	2.00	1.25
27	Brooks Robinson	50.00	25.00	15.00
28	Jerry Adair	4.00	2.00	1.25
29	Ron Jackson	4.00	2.00	1.25
30	George Strickland	4.00	2.00	1.25
31	Rocky Bridges	4.00	2.00	1.25
32	Bill Tuttle	4.00	2.00	1.25
33	Ken Hunt	4.00	2.00	1.25
34	Hal Griggs	4.00	2.00	1.25
35	Jim Coates	4.00	2.00	1.25
36	Brooks Lawrence	4.00	2.00	1.25
37	Duke Snider	50.00	25.00	15.00
38	Al Spangler	4.00	2.00	1.25
39	Jim Owens	4.00	2.00	1.25
40	Bill Virdon	4.00	2.00	1.25
41	Ernie Broglio	4.00	2.00	1.25
42	Andre Rodgers	4.00	2.00	1.25
43	Julio Becquer	4.00	2.00	1.25
44	Tony Taylor	4.00	2.00	1.25
45	Jerry Lynch	4.00	2.00	1.25
46	Clete Boyer	4.00	2.00	1.25
47	Jerry Lumpe	4.00	2.00	1.25
48	Charlie Maxwell	4.00	2.00	1.25
49	Jim Perry	4.00	2.00	1.25
50	Danny McDevitt	4.00	2.00	1.25
51	Juan Pizarro	4.00	2.00	1.25
52	*Dallas Green*	12.00	6.00	3.50
53	Bob Friend	4.00	2.00	1.25
54	Jack Sanford	4.00	2.00	1.25
55	Jim Rivera	4.00	2.00	1.25
56	Ted Wills	4.00	2.00	1.25
57	Milt Pappas	4.00	2.00	1.25
58a	Hal Smith (team & position on back)	4.00	2.00	1.25
58b	Hal Smith (team blackened out on back)	65.00	32.00	19.50
58c	Hal Smith (team missing on back)	65.00	32.00	19.50
59	Bob Avila	4.00	2.00	1.25
60	Clem Labine	5.00	2.50	1.50
61	Vic Rehm	4.00	2.00	1.25
62	John Gabler	4.00	2.00	1.25
63	John Tsitouris	4.00	2.00	1.25
64	Dave Sisler	4.00	2.00	1.25
65	Vic Power	4.00	2.00	1.25
66	Earl Battey	4.00	2.00	1.25
67	Bob Purkey	4.00	2.00	1.25
68	Moe Drabowsky	4.00	2.00	1.25
69	Hoyt Wilhelm	21.00	10.50	6.25
70	Humberto Robinson	4.00	2.00	1.25
71	Whitey Herzog	8.00	4.00	2.50
72	Dick Donovan	4.00	2.00	1.25
73	Gordon Jones	15.00	7.50	4.50
74	Joe Hicks	15.00	7.50	4.50
75	*Ray Culp*	15.00	7.50	4.50
76	Dick Drott	15.00	7.50	4.50
77	Bob Duliba	15.00	7.50	4.50
78	Art Ditmar	15.00	7.50	4.50
79	Steve Korcheck	15.00	7.50	4.50
80	Henry Mason	15.00	7.50	4.50
81	Harry Simpson	15.00	7.50	4.50
82	Gene Green	15.00	7.50	4.50
83	Bob Shaw	15.00	7.50	4.50
84	Howard Reed	15.00	7.50	4.50
85	Dick Stigman	15.00	7.50	4.50
86	Rip Repulski	15.00	7.50	4.50
87	Seth Morehead	15.00	7.50	4.50
88	Camilo Carreon	15.00	7.50	4.50
89	John Blanchard	18.00	9.00	5.50
90	Billy Hoeft	15.00	7.50	4.50
91	Fred Hopke	15.00	7.50	4.50
92	Joe Martin	15.00	7.50	4.50
93	Wally Shannon	15.00	7.50	4.50
94	Baseball's Two Hal Smiths	25.00	12.50	7.50
95	Al Schroll	15.00	7.50	4.50
96	John Kucks	15.00	7.50	4.50
97	Tom Morgan	15.00	7.50	4.50
98	Willie Jones	15.00	7.50	4.50
99	Marshall Renfroe	15.00	7.50	4.50
100	Willie Tasby	15.00	7.50	4.50
101	Irv Noren	15.00	7.50	4.50
102	Russ Snyder	15.00	7.50	4.50
103	Bob Turley	18.00	9.00	5.50
104	Jim Woods	15.00	7.50	4.50
105	Ronnie Kline	15.00	7.50	4.50
106	Steve Bilko	15.00	7.50	4.50
107	Elmer Valo	15.00	7.50	4.50
108	Tom McAvoy	15.00	7.50	4.50
109	Stan Williams	15.00	7.50	4.50
110	Earl Averill	15.00	7.50	4.50
111	Lee Walls	15.00	7.50	4.50
112	Paul Richards	15.00	7.50	4.50
113	Ed Sadowski	15.00	7.50	4.50
114	Stover McIlwain	15.00	7.50	4.50
115	Chuck Tanner (photo actually Ken Kuhn)	20.00	10.00	6.00
116	Lou Klimchock	15.00	7.50	4.50
117	Neil Chrisley	15.00	7.50	4.50
118	Johnny Callison	18.00	9.00	5.50
119	Hal Smith	15.00	7.50	4.50
120	Carl Sawatski	15.00	7.50	4.50
121	Frank Leja	15.00	7.50	4.50
122	Earl Torgeson	15.00	7.50	4.50
123	Art Schult	15.00	7.50	4.50
124	Jim Brosnan	15.00	7.50	4.50
125	Sparky Anderson	80.00	40.00	24.00
126	Joe Pignatano	15.00	7.50	4.50
127	Rocky Nelson	15.00	7.50	4.50
128	Orlando Cepeda	65.00	32.00	19.50
129	Daryl Spencer	15.00	7.50	4.50
130	Ralph Lumenti	15.00	7.50	4.50
131	Sam Taylor	15.00	7.50	4.50
132	Harry Brecheen	15.00	7.50	4.50
133	Johnny Groth	15.00	7.50	4.50
134	Wayne Terwilliger	15.00	7.50	4.50
135	Kent Hadley	15.00	7.50	4.50
136	Faye Throneberry	15.00	7.50	4.50
137	Jack Meyer	15.00	7.50	4.50
138	*Chuck Cottier*	15.00	7.50	4.50
139	Joe DeMaestri	15.00	7.50	4.50
140	Gene Freese	15.00	7.50	4.50
141	Curt Flood	35.00	17.50	10.50
142	Gino Cimoli	15.00	7.50	4.50
143	Clay Dalrymple	15.00	7.50	4.50
144	Jim Bunning	80.00	40.00	24.00

1950 Leather Key Tags

Little information about the issue of these homely little (1-1/2" square) souvenirs is known. Player selection suggests an issue date between 1947-1952. Each tag has a rather crude player picture in red, white, blue and black arranged in a diamond shape on the natural brown leather background. A facsimile autograph also appears on front. Backs are blank.

		NM	EX	VG
Complete Set (7):		250.00	125.00	75.00
Common Player:		25.00	12.50	7.50
(1)	Joe DiMaggio	75.00	37.00	22.00
(2)	Bob Feller	45.00	22.00	13.50
(3)	Sid Luckman (football)	25.00	12.50	7.50
(4)	John Mize	25.00	12.50	7.50
(5)	Stan Musial	45.00	22.00	13.50
(6)	Jackie Robinson	65.00	32.00	19.50
(7)	Ted Williams	25.00	12.50	7.50

1923 Lections

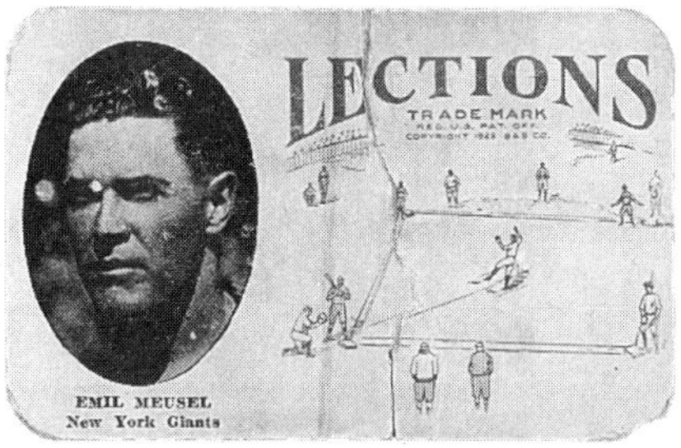

This series of cards was virtually unknown in the hobby until 1997 when 28 cards turned up in Albany, N.Y. The cards measure about 4" x 2-1/2" with rounded corners and are printed on very thick cardboard. At left front is an oval black-and-white player photo with name and team below. At right is green or orange art of a baseball game with the issuer's logo and trademark information. It is likely the checklist here is incomplete. It is unknown with what, if any, product these cards were issued. A candy premium seems the most likely source. Most of the cards seen so far are in grades from Fair-Good, though a few are known in Ex-Mt.

		NM	EX	VG
Common Player:		1200.	600.00	350.00
(1)	Howard Ehmke	750.00	375.00	225.00
(2)	Frank Frisch	2250.	1125.	675.00
(3)	Roger (Rogers) Hornsby	2250.	1125.	675.00
(4)	Charles Jamieson	750.00	375.00	225.00
(5)	"Bob" Meusel	900.00	450.00	270.00
(6)	Emil Meusel	750.00	375.00	225.00
(7)	"Babe" Ruth	3500.	1750.	1050.
(8)	Charles Schmidt	750.00	375.00	225.00
(9)	"Bob" Shawkey	750.00	375.00	225.00

1975 Lee's Sweets

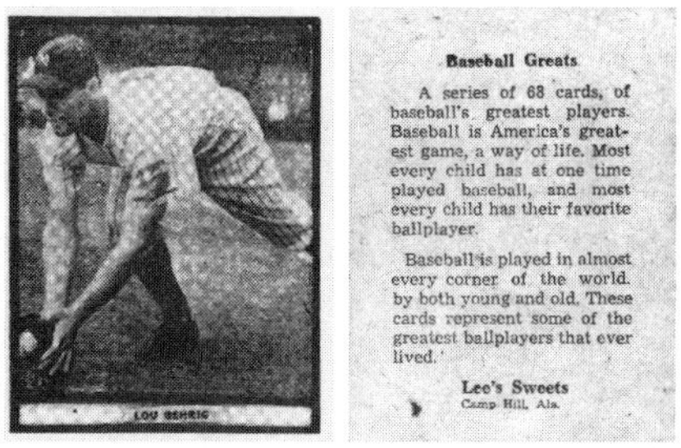

Purporting to be an issue of 68 cards of "Baseball Greats," this collector's issue first appeared about 1975. Only four players are currently known. Fronts of the 2-1/2" x 3-3/16" cards have crudely printed black-and-white player photos. Backs describe the series and give the Lee's Sweets address as Camp Hill, Ala.

		NM	EX	VG
Complete Set (4):		8.00	4.00	2.50
Common Player:		2.00	1.00	.60
(1)	Ty Cobb	2.00	1.00	.60
(2)	Joe DiMaggio	2.00	1.00	.60
(3)	Lou Gehrig	2.00	1.00	.60
(4)	Babe Ruth	4.00	2.00	1.25

1909-11 Lenox Cigarettes

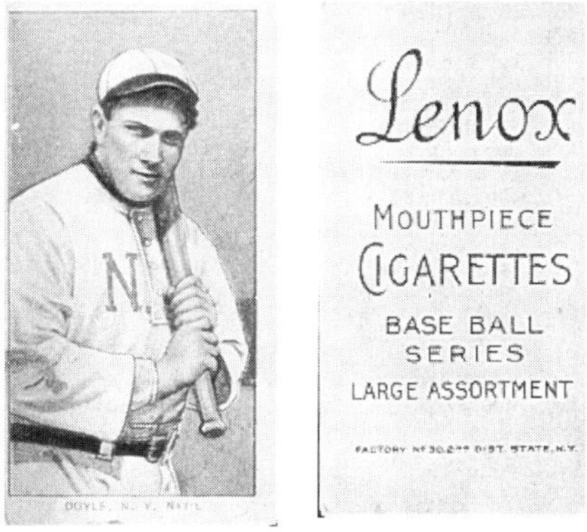

(See T206. Premium: 3-5X.)

1976 Linnett Portraits

This series of pencil-portrait prints was done by sports artist Charles Linnett of Walpole, Mass., and includes baseball, football, hockey, NBA and Harlem Globetrotters players (only baseball listed here). The black-and-white prints are on 8-1/2" x 11" textured paper, featuring a facsimile autograph of the player. Because the portraits are licensed only by the players' association, the players are pictured capless with no uniform logos visible. Backs are blank. The portraits originally sold for 50 cents apiece by mail.

		NM	EX	VG
Complete Baseball Set (175):		265.00	132.00	80.00
Common Player:		1.00	.50	.30
(1)	Hank Aaron	12.00	6.00	3.50
(2)	Dick Allen	3.00	1.50	.90
(3)	Matty Alou	1.00	.50	.30
(4)	Mike Anderson	1.00	.50	.30
(5)	Luis Aparicio	4.00	2.00	1.25
(6)	Sal Bando	1.00	.50	.30
(7)	Mark Belanger	1.50	.70	.45
(8)	Buddy Bell	1.00	.50	.30
(9)	Johnny Bench	6.00	3.00	1.75
(10)	Jim Bibby	1.00	.50	.30
(11)	Paul Blair	1.00	.50	.30
(12)	Bert Blyleven	2.50	1.25	.70
(13)	Ron Blomberg	1.00	.50	.30
(14)	Bob Bolin	1.00	.50	.30
(15)	Bill Bonham	1.00	.50	.30
(16)	Pedro Borbon	1.00	.50	.30
(17)	Bob Boone	1.50	.70	.45
(18)	Larry Bowa	1.00	.50	.30
(19)	Steve Braun	1.00	.50	.30
(20)	Ken Brett	1.00	.50	.30
(21)	John Briggs	1.00	.50	.30
(22)	Lou Brock	4.00	2.00	1.25
(23)	Jack Brohamer	1.00	.50	.30
(24)	Steve Brye	1.00	.50	.30
(25)	Bill Buckner	1.50	.70	.45
(26)	Jeff Burroughs	1.00	.50	.30
(27)	Steve Busby	1.00	.50	.30
(28)	Bert Campaneris	1.00	.50	.30
(29)	Bernie Carbo	1.00	.50	.30
(30)	Jose Cardenal	1.00	.50	.30
(31)	Steve Carlton	4.00	2.00	1.25
(32)	Rod Carew	4.00	2.00	1.25
(33)	Dave Cash	1.00	.50	.30
(34)	Norm Cash	1.50	.70	.45
(35)	Danny Cater	1.00	.50	.30
(36)	Cesar Cedeno	1.00	.50	.30
(37)	Orlando Cepeda	3.00	1.50	.90
(38)	Ron Cey	1.50	.70	.45
(39)	Chris Chambliss	1.00	.50	.30
(40)	David Clyde	1.00	.50	.30
(41)	Rich Coggins	1.00	.50	.30
(42)	Jim Colborn	1.00	.50	.30
(43)	Dave Concepcion	1.50	.70	.45
(44)	Willie Crawford	1.00	.50	.30
(45)	John Curtis	1.00	.50	.30
(46)	Bobby Darwin	1.00	.50	.30
(47)	Dan Driessen	1.00	.50	.30
(48)	Duffy Dyer	1.00	.50	.30
(49)	John Ellis	1.00	.50	.30
(50)	Darrell Evans	1.50	.70	.45
(51)	Dwight Evans	1.50	.70	.45
(52)	Joe Ferguson	1.00	.50	.30
(53)	Rollie Fingers	4.00	2.00	1.25
(54)	Carlton Fisk	3.00	1.50	.90
(55)	Bill Freehan	1.50	.70	.45
(56)	Jim Fregosi	1.50	.70	.45
(57)	Oscar Gamble	1.00	.50	.30
(58)	Pedro Garcia	1.00	.50	.30
(59)	Ralph Garr	1.00	.50	.30
(60)	Wayne Garrett	1.00	.50	.30
(61)	Steve Garvey	2.50	1.25	.70
(62)	Cesar Geronimo	1.00	.50	.30
(63)	Bob Gibson	4.00	2.00	1.25
(64)	Dave Giusti	1.00	.50	.30
(65)	Bobby Grich	1.50	.70	.45
(66)	Doug Griffin	1.00	.50	.30
(67)	Mario Guerrero	1.00	.50	.30
(68)	Don Gullett	1.00	.50	.30
(69)	Tommy Harper	1.00	.50	.30
(70)	Toby Harrah	1.50	.70	.45
(71)	Bud Harrelson	1.50	.70	.45
(72)	Vic Harris	1.00	.50	.30
(73)	Richie Hebner	1.00	.50	.30
(74)	George Hendrick	1.00	.50	.30
(75)	Ed Hermann	1.00	.50	.30
(76)	John Hiller	1.00	.50	.30
(77)	Willie Horton	1.00	.50	.30
(78)	Jim Hunter	4.00	2.00	1.25
(79)	Tommy Hutton	1.00	.50	.30
(80)	Reggie Jackson	6.00	3.00	1.75
(81)	Fergie Jenkins	4.00	2.00	1.25
(82)	Dave Johnson	1.00	.50	.30
(83)	Cleon Jones	1.00	.50	.30
(84)	Al Kaline	6.00	3.00	1.75
(85)	John Kennedy	1.00	.50	.30
(86)	Steve Kline	1.00	.50	.30
(87)	Jerry Koosman	1.50	.70	.45
(88)	Bill Lee	1.00	.50	.30
(89)	Eddie Leon	1.00	.50	.30
(90)	Bob Locker	1.00	.50	.30
(91)	Mickey Lolich	2.00	1.00	.60
(92)	Jim Lonborg	1.50	.70	.45
(93)	Davey Lopes	1.50	.70	.45
(94)	Mike Lum	1.00	.50	.30
(95)	Greg Luzinski	2.00	1.00	.60
(96)	Sparky Lyle	1.50	.70	.45
(97)	Teddy Martinez	1.00	.50	.30
(98)	Jon Matlack	1.00	.50	.30
(99)	Dave May	1.00	.50	.30
(100)	John Mayberry	1.00	.50	.30
(101)	Willie Mays	12.00	6.00	3.50
(102)	Jim McAndrew	1.00	.50	.30
(103)	Dick McAuliffe	1.00	.50	.30
(104)	Sam McDowell	1.50	.70	.45
(105)	Lynn McGlothen	1.00	.50	.30
(106)	Tug McGraw	1.50	.70	.45
(107)	Hal McRae	2.00	1.00	.60
(108)	Bill Melton	1.00	.50	.30
(109)	Andy Messersmith	1.00	.50	.30
(110)	Gene Michael	1.00	.50	.30
(111)	Felix Millan	1.00	.50	.30
(112)	Rick Miller	1.00	.50	.30
(113)	John Milner	1.00	.50	.30
(114)	Rick Monday	1.00	.50	.30
(115)	Don Money	1.00	.50	.30
(116)	Bob Montgomery	1.00	.50	.30
(117)	Joe Morgan	4.00	2.00	1.25
(118)	Carl Morton	1.00	.50	.30
(119)	Thurman Munson	4.00	2.00	1.25
(120)	Bobby Murcer	1.00	.50	.30
(121)	Graig Nettles	1.50	.70	.45
(122)	Jim Northrup	1.00	.50	.30
(123)	Ben Oglivie	1.00	.50	.30
(124)	Al Oliver	1.50	.70	.45
(125)	Bob Oliver	1.00	.50	.30
(126)	Jorge Orta	1.00	.50	.30
(127)	Amos Otis	1.00	.50	.30
(128)	Jim Palmer	4.00	2.00	1.25
(129)	Harry Parker	1.00	.50	.30
(130)	Fred Patek	1.00	.50	.30
(131)	Marty Pattin	1.00	.50	.30
(132)	Tony Perez	2.50	1.25	.70
(133)	Gaylord Perry	4.00	2.00	1.25
(134)	Jim Perry	1.00	.50	.30
(135)	Rico Petrocelli	1.00	.50	.30
(136)	Rick Reichardt	1.00	.50	.30
(137)	Ken Reitz	1.00	.50	.30
(138)	Jerry Reuss	1.00	.50	.30
(139)	Bill Robinson	1.00	.50	.30
(140)	Brooks Robinson	6.00	3.00	1.75
(141)	Frank Robinson	6.00	3.00	1.75
(142)	Cookie Rojas	1.00	.50	.30
(143)	Pete Rose	9.00	4.50	2.75
(144)	Bill Russell	1.00	.50	.30
(145)	Nolan Ryan	15.00	7.50	4.50
(146)	Manny Sanguillen	1.00	.50	.30
(147)	George Scott	1.00	.50	.30
(148)	Mike Schmidt	7.50	3.75	2.25
(149)	Tom Seaver	7.50	3.75	2.25
(150)	Sonny Siebert	1.00	.50	.30
(151)	Ted Simmons	1.00	.50	.30
(152)	Bill Singer	1.00	.50	.30
(153)	Reggie Smith	1.50	.70	.45
(154)	Chris Speier	1.00	.50	.30
(155)	Charlie Spikes	1.00	.50	.30
(156)	Paul Splittorff	1.00	.50	.30
(157)	Mickey Stanley	1.00	.50	.30
(158)	Lee Stanton	1.00	.50	.30
(159)	Willie Stargell	4.00	2.00	1.25
(160)	Rusty Staub	2.00	1.00	.60
(161)	Rennie Stennett	1.00	.50	.30
(162)	Steve Stone	1.50	.70	.45
(163)	Mel Stottlemyre	1.00	.50	.30
(164)	Don Sutton	3.00	1.50	.90
(165)	George Theodore	1.00	.50	.30
(166)	Danny Thompson	1.00	.50	.30
(167)	Luis Tiant	2.50	1.25	.70
(168)	Joe Torre	2.50	1.25	.70
(169)	Bobby Valentine	1.00	.50	.30
(170)	Bob Veale	1.00	.50	.30
(171)	Billy Williams	4.00	2.00	1.25
(172)	Wilbur Wood	1.00	.50	.30
(173)	Jim Wynn	1.00	.50	.30
(174)	Carl Yastrzemski	6.00	3.00	1.75
(175)	Richie Zisk	1.00	.50	.30

1976 Linnett Superstars

This frequently encountered set of 36 cards has enjoyed little collector interest since its issue in 1976. Officially known as "Pee-Wee Superstars," the cards measure 4" x 5-5/8". Player portraits by artist Charles Linnett are rendered in black-and-white pencil and set against a pale yellow background. Players are shown without caps or uniforms (most appear to be wearing white T-shirts). According to the logos at top the set was fully licensed by both the players' association and Major League Baseball, and team logos do appear in the lower-left corner. A facsimile autograph in red or purple appears on each card. Front borders are bright purple, red, green, dark brown or white. Card backs feature either a photo of an antique auto or a drawing of a historic sailing ship. Each of the 12 different back designs appears on one card from each team set. The Linnetts were sold in panels of six perforated cards. An offer on the back of each card makes 8" x 10" premium portraits of each player available for 95 cents. The premium pictures have about the same value as the cards. Inexplicably, the cards are numbered from 90-125. Only the World's Champion Cincinnati Reds, A.L. Champion Boston Red Sox and N.L. runner-up Dodgers are represented in the issue.

		NM	EX	VG
Complete Panel Set (6):		26.00	13.00	7.75
Complete Singles Set (36):		21.00	10.50	6.25
Common Player:		.90	.45	.25
Panel 1		11.50	5.75	3.50
90	Don Gullett	.90	.45	.25
91	Johnny Bench	3.50	1.75	1.00
92	Tony Perez	1.50	.70	.45
93	Mike Lum	.90	.45	.25
94	Ken Griffey	1.00	.50	.30
95	George Foster	1.00	.50	.30
Panel 2		14.00	7.00	4.25
96	Joe Morgan	3.00	1.50	.90
97	Pete Rose	5.00	2.50	1.50
98	Dave Concepcion	1.00	.50	.30
99	Cesar Geronimo	.90	.45	.25
100	Dan Driessen	.90	.45	.25
101	Pedro Borbon	.90	.45	.25
Panel 3		12.00	6.00	3.50
102	Carl Yastrzemski	3.50	1.75	1.00
103	Fred Lynn	1.50	.70	.45
104	Dwight Evans	1.00	.50	.30
105	Ferguson Jenkins	1.75	.90	.50
106	Rico Petrocelli	.90	.45	.25
107	Denny Doyle	.90	.45	.25
Panel 4		8.75	4.50	2.75
108	Luis Tiant	1.00	.50	.30
109	Carlton Fisk	1.75	.90	.50
110	Rick Burleson	.90	.45	.25
111	Bill Lee	.90	.45	.25
112	Rick Wise	.90	.45	.25
113	Jim Rice	1.25	.60	.40
Panel 5		8.75	4.50	2.75
114	Davey Lopes	1.00	.50	.30
115	Steve Garvey	1.75	.90	.50
116	Bill Russell	1.00	.50	.30
117	Ron Cey	1.00	.50	.30
118	Steve Yaeger	.90	.45	.25
119	Doug Rau	.90	.45	.25
Panel 6		8.25	4.25	2.50
120	Don Sutton	2.00	1.00	.60
121	Joe Ferguson	.90	.45	.25
122	Mike Marshall	.90	.45	.25
123	Bill Buckner	1.00	.50	.30
124	Rick Rhoden	.90	.45	.25
125	Ted Sizemore	.90	.45	.25

1923 Little Wonder Picture Series

(See W515-2)

1887 Lone Jack St. Louis Browns (N370)

The 1886 Lone Jack set is among the rarest of all 19th Century tobacco issues. Issued by the Lone Jack Cigarette Co. of Lynchburg, Va., the set consists of 13 subjects, all members of the champion St. Louis Browns. Photos for the set are enlarged versions of those used in the more popular N172

Old Judge series. Cards in the set measure 2-1/2" x 1-1/2" and carry an ad for Lone Jack Cigarettes along the bottom of the front. The set features the Browns' starting lineup for 1886 along with their two top pitchers, backup catcher and owner, Chris Von Der Ahe.

		NM	EX	VG
Complete Set (13):		70000.	28000.	17500.
Common Player:		5000.	2000.	1250.
(1)	Doc Bushong	5000.	2000.	1250.
(2)	Parisian Bob Caruthers	5000.	2000.	1250.
(3)	Charles Commiskey (Comiskey)	17500.	7000.	4375.
(4)	Dave Foutz	5000.	2000.	1250.
(5)	Will Gleason	5000.	2000.	1250.
(6)	Nat Hudson	5000.	2000.	1250.
(7)	Rudy Kimler (Kemmler)	5000.	2000.	1250.
(8)	Arlie Latham	5000.	2000.	1250.
(9)	Little Nick Nicol	5000.	2000.	1250.
(10)	Tip O'Neil (O'Neill)	5000.	2000.	1250.
(11)	Yank Robinson	5000.	2000.	1250.
(12)	Chris Von Der Ahe	9000.	3600.	2250.
(13)	Curt Welsh (Welch)	5000.	2000.	1250.

1886 Lorillard Team Card

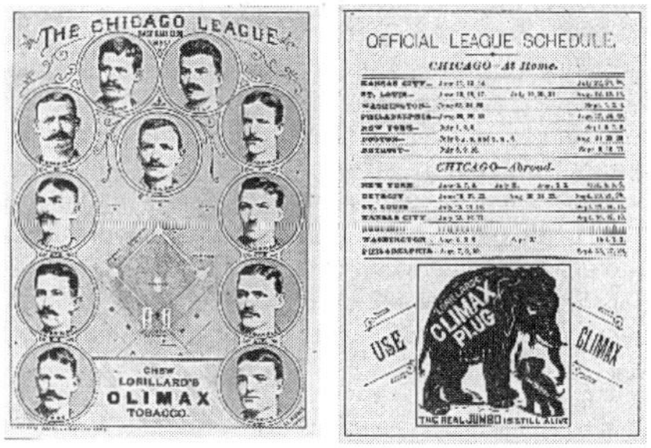

Issued in 1886 by Lorillard Tobacco Co., these 4" x 5-1/2" cards were issued for the Chicago, Detroit and New York baseball clubs. Each card carries the team's schedule (starting with June) on one side and features 11 player portraits enclosed in circles on the other. Each side has advertising for one of Lorillard's tobacco brands - Climax, Rebecca, etc.

		NM	EX	VG
Complete Set (4):		22000.	11000.	6550.
Common Team:		4375.	2175.	1300.
(1)	Chicago League Base Ball Club	5675.	2825.	1700.
(2)	Detroit League Base Ball Club	6500.	3250.	1950.
(3)	New York League Base Ball Club	7875.	3925.	2350.
(4)	Philadelphia League Base Ball Club	4375.	2175.	1300.

1949 Lummis Peanut Butter Phillies

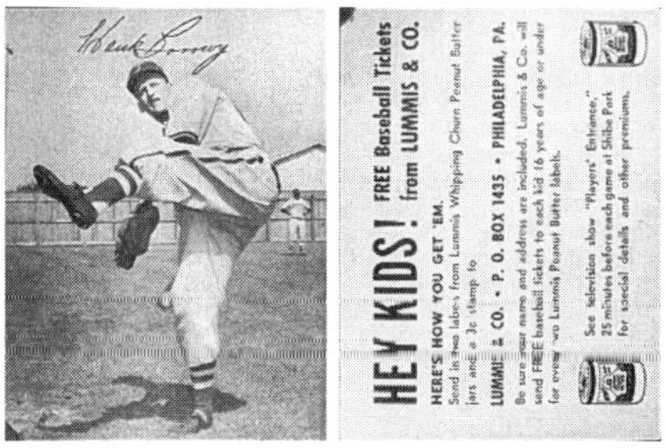

This 12-card regional set featuring the Phillies was issued in the Philadelphia area by Lummis Peanut Butter in 1949. The cards measure 3-1/4" x 4-1/4" and are unnumbered. The fronts feature an action photo with a facsimile autograph, while the backs advertise a game ticket promotion by Lummis Peanut Butter. The same photos and checklist were also used for a regional sticker card set issued by Sealtest Dairy the same year.

		NM	EX	VG
Complete Set (12):		850.00	425.00	255.00
Common Player:		60.00	30.00	18.00
(1)	Rich Ashburn	225.00	112.00	67.00
(2)	Hank Borowy	60.00	30.00	18.00
(3)	Del Ennis	90.00	45.00	27.00
(4)	Granny Hamner	60.00	30.00	18.00
(5)	Puddinhead Jones	60.00	30.00	18.00
(6)	Russ Meyer	60.00	30.00	18.00
(7)	Bill Nicholson	60.00	30.00	18.00
(8)	Robin Roberts	200.00	100.00	60.00
(9)	"Schoolboy" Rowe	90.00	45.00	27.00
(10)	Andy Seminick	60.00	30.00	18.00
(11)	Curt Simmons	90.00	45.00	27.00
(12)	Eddie Waitkus	60.00	30.00	18.00

1910 Luxello Cigars A's/Phillies Pins

Players from the two Philadelphia teams are pictured in this series of 7/8" black-and-white pins. The player's last name, team and position are printed below the photo; the Luxello Cigar name at top. On left and right are a horseshoe with monogram inside.

		NM	EX	VG
Complete Set (21):		4575.	2275.	1375.
Common Player:		250.00	125.00	75.00
	Philadelphia Athletics			
(1)	Franklin Baker	350.00	175.00	105.00
(2)	Jack Barry	250.00	125.00	75.00
(3)	Eddie Collins	350.00	175.00	105.00
(4)	John W. Coombs	250.00	125.00	75.00
(5)	Harry Davis	250.00	125.00	75.00
(6)	James Dygert	250.00	125.00	75.00
(7)	Heinie Heitmuller	250.00	125.00	75.00
(8)	Harry Krause	250.00	125.00	75.00
(9)	Paddy Livingston	250.00	125.00	75.00
(10)	Danny Murphy	250.00	125.00	75.00
(11)	Ed Plank	350.00	175.00	105.00
	Philadelphia Phillies			
(12)	John W. Bates	250.00	125.00	75.00
(13)	Chas. S. Dooin	250.00	125.00	75.00
(14)	Mike Doolan	250.00	125.00	75.00
(15)	Eddie Grant	250.00	125.00	75.00
(16)	Otto Knabe	250.00	125.00	75.00
(17)	Geo. McQuillan	250.00	125.00	75.00
(18)	Earl Moore	250.00	125.00	75.00
(19)	Lew Moren	250.00	125.00	75.00
(20)	Tully Sparks	250.00	125.00	75.00
(21)	John Titus	250.00	125.00	75.00

1912 L1 Leathers

One of the more unusual baseball collectibles of the tobacco era, the L1 "Leathers" were issued by Helmar Tobacco Co. in 1912 as a premium with its "Turkish Trophies" brand of cigarettes. The set featured 25 of the top baseball players and shared a checklist with the closely-related S81 "Silks," which were another part of the same promotion. The "Leathers," advertised as being 10" x 12", featured drawings of baseball players on horsehide-shaped pieces of leather. The drawings were based on the pictures used for the popular T3 Turkey Red series issued a year earlier. Twenty of the 25 players in the "Leathers" set are from the T3 set. Five pitchers (Rube Marquard, Rube Benton, Marty O'Toole, Grover Alexander and Russ Ford) not pictured in T3 were added to the "Leathers" set, and the Frank Baker error was corrected. According to the promotion, each "Leather" was available in exchange for 50 Helmar coupons. In addition to the 25 baseball stars, the "Leathers" set also included more than 100 other subjects, including female athletes and bathing beauties, famous generals, Indian chiefs, actresses, national flags, college mascots and others.

		NM	EX	VG
Complete Set (25):		68500.	34000.	20000.
Common Player:		1700.	850.00	500.00
86	Rube Marquard	3200.	1600.	960.00
87	Marty O'Toole	2000.	1000.	600.00
88	Rube Benton	2000.	1000.	600.00
89	Grover Alexander	4000.	2000.	1200.
90	Russ Ford	2000.	1000.	600.00
91	John McGraw	3200.	1600.	960.00
92	Nap Rucker	2000.	1000.	600.00
93	Mike Mitchell	2000.	1000.	600.00
94	Chief Bender	3200.	1600.	960.00
95	Home Run Baker	3200.	1600.	960.00
96	Nap Lajoie	4000.	2000.	1200.
97	Joe Tinker	3200.	1600.	960.00
98	Sherry Magee	2000.	1000.	600.00
99	Howie Camnitz	2000.	1000.	600.00
100	Eddie Collins	3200.	1600.	960.00
101	Red Dooin	2000.	1000.	600.00
102	Ty Cobb	11000.	5500.	3300.
103	Hugh Jennings	3200.	1600.	960.00
104	Roger Bresnahan	3200.	1600.	960.00
105	Jake Stahl	2000.	1000.	600.00
100	Tris Speaker	3500.	1750.	1050.
107	Ed Walsh	3200.	1600.	960.00
108	Christy Mathewson	5500.	2750.	1650.
109	Johnny Evers	3200.	1600.	960.00
110	Walter Johnson	5500.	2750.	1650.

M

1950s-70s MacGregor Advisory Staff Photos

Advisory staff photos were a promotional item which debuted in the early 1950s, flourished in the 1960s and died in the early 1970s. Generally 8" x 10" (sometimes a little larger), these black-and-white (a few later were color) glossy photos picture players who had contracted with a major baseball equipment company to endorse and use their product. Usually the product - most often a glove - was prominently displayed in the photo. The pictures were often displayed in the windows of sporting goods stores or the walls of sports departments and were sometimes made available to customers. Because the companies tended to stick with players over the years, some photos were reissued, sometimes with and sometimes without a change of team, pose or typography. All MacGregor staff photos of the era are checklisted here in alphabetical order. Team designation and pose description is given for each known picture. The photos are checklisted here in alphabetical order. It is unlikely this list is complete. Several arrangements of typography in the bottom border are seen and some photos have a facsimile autograph.

		NM	EX	VG
Common Player:		12.00	6.00	3.50
(1)	Richie Ashburn (Cubs, full-length, hands on knees)	25.00	12.50	7.50
(2)	Gus Bell (Reds, kneeling)	12.00	6.00	3.50
(3)	Ed Bouchee (Phillies, upper body)	12.00	6.00	3.50
(4)	Ed Brinkman (Senators, upper body)	12.00	6.00	3.50
(5)	Roberto Clemente (full-length)	125.00	62.00	37.00
(6)	Del Crandall (Braves, catching crouch in gear, large)	12.00	6.00	3.50
(7)	Del Crandall (Braves, catching crouch in gear, small)	12.00	6.00	3.50
(8)	Del Crandall (Bravces, catching crouch, no gear)	12.00	6.00	3.50
(9)	Del Crandall (Braves, kneeling, glove on knee)	12.00	6.00	3.50
(10)	Al Downing (Yankees, upper body)	12.00	6.00	3.50
(11)	Ron Hansen (White Sox, fielding)	12.00	6.00	3.50
(12)	Tommy Helms (Reds, full-length)	12.00	6.00	3.50
(13)	Randy Hundley (Cubs, upper body)	12.50	6.25	3.75
(14)	Jack Jensen (Red Sox, upper body)	15.00	7.50	4.50
(15)	Jack Jensen (Red Sox, full-length, hands on knees)	15.00	7.50	4.50
(16)	Ralph Kiner (Pirates, full-length)	25.00	12.50	7.50
(17)	Ted Kluszewski (Reds, fielding)	22.00	11.00	6.50
(18)	Johnny Kucks (Yankees, pitching)	13.50	6.75	4.00
(19)	Willie Mays (Giants, full-length)	95.00	47.00	28.00
(20)	Bill Mazeroski (Pirates, batting)	24.00	12.00	7.25
(21)	Mike McCormick (Giants, pitching follow-through)	12.00	6.00	3.50
(22)	Gil McDougald (Yankees, throwing)	15.00	7.50	4.50
(23)	Gil McDougald (Yankees, upper-body portrait)	15.00	7.50	4.50
(24)	Tony Oliva (Twins, batting)	15.00	7.50	4.50
(25)	Tony Oliva (Twins, upper body)	15.00	7.50	4.50
(26)	Claude Osteen (Dodgers, pitching)	12.00	6.00	3.50
(27)	Claude Osteen (Dodgers, portrait)	12.00	6.00	3.50
(28)	Juan Pizzaro (White Sox, pitching follow-through)	12.00	6.00	3.50
(29)	Robin Roberts (Phillies, portrait)	24.00	12.00	7.25
(30)	Robin Roberts (Phillies, pitching follow-through)	24.00	12.00	7.25
(31)	Frank Robinson (Orioles, portrait)	24.00	12.00	7.25
(32)	Pete Rose (Reds, kneeling)	35.00	17.50	10.50
(33)	Al Schoendienst (Cardinals, kneeling)	24.00	12.00	7.25
(34)	Warren Spahn (Boston Braves, pitching follow-through)	24.00	12.00	7.25
(35)	Don Sutton (Dodgers, color, ready to pitch)	24.00	12.00	7.25
(36)	Frank Torre (Braves, ready to throw)	12.00	6.00	3.50

1960 MacGregor

The MacGregor Sporting Goods Company was one of the pioneers in celebrity marketing, creating an advisory staff in 1960 to promote its products. The 25-card set features black-and-white photography of several stars and lesser lights, and even a couple of managers. The cards are 3-3/4" x 5" with a thin white border and the words "MacGregor Baseball Advisory Staff of Champions" on the bottom panel. The cards are not numbered and are blank-backed, and include a facsimile autograph in white on the front photo. The checklist is arranged here alphabetically.

		NM	EX	VG
Complete Set (25):		800.00	400.00	240.00
Common Player:		15.00	7.50	4.50
1	Hank Aaron	200.00	100.00	60.00
2	Richie Ashburn	40.00	20.00	12.00
3	Gus Bell	15.00	7.50	4.50
4	Lou Berberet	15.00	7.50	4.50
5	Jerry Casale	15.00	7.50	4.50
6	Del Crandall	15.00	7.50	4.50
7	Art Ditmar	15.00	7.50	4.50
8	Gene Freese	15.00	7.50	4.50
9	James Gilliam	20.00	10.00	6.00
10	Ted Kluszewski	30.00	15.00	9.00
11	Jim Landis	15.00	7.50	4.50
12	Al Lopez	20.00	10.00	6.00
13	Willie Mays	200.00	100.00	60.00
14	Bill Mazeroski	35.00	17.50	10.50
15	Mike McCormick	15.00	7.50	4.50
16	Gil McDougald	20.00	10.00	6.00
17	Russ Nixon	15.00	7.50	4.50
18	Bill Rigney	15.00	7.50	4.50
19	Robin Roberts	30.00	16.50	9.00
20	Frank Robinson	50.00	25.00	15.00
21	John Roseboro	15.00	7.50	4.50
22	Red Schoendienst	30.00	15.00	9.00
23	Bill Skowron	20.00	10.00	6.00
24	Daryl Spencer	15.00	7.50	4.50
25	Johnny Temple	15.00	7.50	4.50

1965 MacGregor

The 1965 MacGregor set is similar to earlier issues, with only a slight change in dimension to 3-1/2" x 5" and reduced in size to only 10 players. The cards are blank-backed and unnumbered and have a glossy finish. They are checklisted here alphabetically.

		NM	EX	VG
Complete Set (10):		345.00	170.00	100.00
Common Player:		10.00	5.00	3.00
(1)	Roberto Clemente	150.00	75.00	45.00
(2)	Al Downing	10.00	5.00	3.00
(3)	Johnny Edwards	10.00	5.00	3.00
(4)	Ron Hansen	10.00	5.00	3.00
(5)	Deron Johnson	10.00	5.00	3.00
(6)	Willie Mays	135.00	67.00	40.00
(7)	Tony Oliva	15.00	7.50	4.50
(8)	Claude Osteen	10.00	5.00	3.00
(9)	Bobby Richardson	15.00	7.50	4.50
(10)	Zoilo Versalles	10.00	5.00	3.00

1951 Connie Mack Book

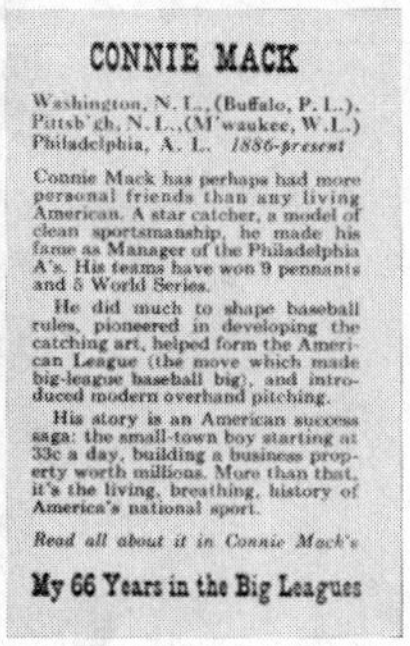
CONNIE MACK

Washington, N. L., (Buffalo, P. L.), Pittsb'gh, N. L., (M'waukee, W. L.) Philadelphia, A. L. *1886-present*

Connie Mack has perhaps had more personal friends than any living American. A star catcher, a model of clean sportsmanship, he made his fame as Manager of the Philadelphia A's. His teams have won 9 pennants and 5 World Series.

He did much to shape baseball rules, pioneered in developing the catching art, helped form the American League (the move which made big-league baseball big), and introduced modern overhand pitching.

His story is an American success saga: the small-town boy starting at 33c a day, building a business property worth millions. More than that, it's the living, breathing, history of America's national sport.

Read all about it in Connie Mack's

My 66 Years in the Big Leagues

In conjunction with the publication of Connie Mack's book "My 66 Years in the Big Leagues," a folder of cards titled, "Four Mighty Heroes" was also issued. The folder contained a quartet of black-and-white player cards. Fronts feature a player photo against a white background. Backs have a bit of player career data and an ad for Mack's book. Cards measure 2-1/4" x 3-1/2".

		NM	EX	VG
Complete Set (4):		900.00	450.00	270.00
Common Player:		180.00	90.00	54.00
(1)	Connie Mack	180.00	90.00	54.00
(2)	Christy Mathewson	250.00	125.00	75.00
(3)	Babe Ruth	550.00	275.00	165.00
(4)	Rube Waddell	180.00	90.00	54.00

1923 Walter Mails Card Game

This set of playing cards features 56 subjects. Card backs are printed in either red or blue, featuring player and umpire figures in each corner. At center is the picture of a pitcher with the name of the game's creator beneath. Walter Mails was a major league pitcher between 1915-26. Fronts feature a black-and-white player photo with a facsimile autograph. Printed beneath are the player's name, position and team. At bottom is the designation of a play used in the card game. Both major and minor league players are included in the set. Cards are round-cornered and measure 2-5/16" x 3-1/2". The unnumbered cards are checklisted here alphabetically.

		NM	EX	VG
Complete Set (56):		4500.	1800.	1125.
Common Player, Major Leaguer:		90.00	36.00	22.00
Common Player, Minor Leaguer:		72.00	29.00	18.00
Rules Card:		36.00	14.50	9.00
(1)	Russell "Buzz" Arlett	72.00	29.00	18.00
(2)	J.C. "Jim" Bagby	72.00	29.00	18.00
(3)	Dave "Beauty" Bancroft	180.00	72.00	45.00
(4)	Johnny Basseler (Bassler)	90.00	36.00	22.00
(5)	Jack Bentley	90.00	36.00	22.00
(6)	J.C. "Rube" Benton	90.00	36.00	22.00
(7)	Geo. Burns	90.00	36.00	22.00
(8)	"Bullet Joe" Bush	75.00	30.00	18.50
(9)	Harold P. Chavezo	72.00	29.00	18.00
(10)	Hugh Critz	72.00	29.00	18.00
(11)	"Jake" E. Daubert	90.00	36.00	22.00
(12)	Wheezer Dell	72.00	29.00	18.00
(13)	Joe Dugan	90.00	36.00	22.00
(14)	Pat Duncan	90.00	36.00	22.00
(15)	Howard J. Ehmke	90.00	36.00	22.00
(16)	Lewis Fonseca	90.00	36.00	22.00
(17)	Ray French	90.00	36.00	22.00
(18)	Ed Gharity (Gharrity)	90.00	36.00	22.00
(19)	Heinie Groh	90.00	36.00	22.00
(20)	George N. Groves	72.00	29.00	18.00
(21)	E.F. "Red" Hargrave	90.00	36.00	22.00
(22)	Elmer Jacobs	90.00	36.00	22.00
(23)	Walter Johnson	450.00	180.00	110.00
(24)	WM. "Duke" Kenworthy	72.00	29.00	18.00
(25)	Harry Krause	72.00	29.00	18.00
(26)	Ray Kremer	90.00	36.00	22.00
(27)	Walter Mails	80.00	32.00	20.00
(28)	Walter "Rabbitt" Maranville	180.00	72.00	45.00
(29)	John "Stuffy" McInnis	90.00	36.00	22.00
(30)	Marty McManus	90.00	36.00	22.00
(31)	Bob Meusel	110.00	44.00	27.00
(32)	Hack Miller	90.00	36.00	22.00
(33)	Pat J. Moran	90.00	36.00	22.00
(34)	Guy Morton	90.00	36.00	22.00
(35)	Johnny Mostil	90.00	36.00	22.00
(36)	Rod Murphy	72.00	29.00	18.00
(37)	Jimmy O'Connell	90.00	36.00	22.00
(38)	Steve O'Neil	90.00	36.00	22.00
(39)	Joe Oeschger	90.00	36.00	22.00
(40)	Roger Peckinpaugh	90.00	36.00	22.00
(41)	Ralph "Babe" Pinelli	90.00	36.00	22.00
(42)	Wally Pipp	110.00	44.00	27.00
(43)	Elmer Ponder	72.00	29.00	18.00
(44)	Sam Rice	180.00	72.00	45.00
(45)	Edwin Rommell (Rommel)	110.00	44.00	27.00
(46)	Walter Schmidt	90.00	36.00	22.00
(47)	Wilford Shupes	72.00	29.00	18.00
(48)	Joe Sewell	180.00	72.00	45.00
(49)	Pat Shea	72.00	29.00	18.00
(50)	W. "Paddy" Siglin	72.00	29.00	18.00
(51)	Geo. H. Sisler	180.00	72.00	45.00
(52)	William "Bill" Skiff	72.00	29.00	18.00
(53)	J. Smith	90.00	36.00	22.00
(54)	Harry "Suds" Sutherland	72.00	29.00	18.00
(55)	James A. Tierney	90.00	36.00	22.00
(56)	Geo. Uhle	90.00	36.00	22.00

1921-30 Major League Ball Die-cuts

These die-cut black-and-white, blank-back player cards were issued over the period 1921-30 for use with a board game called, "Major League Ball - The Indoor Baseball Game Supreme," from The National Game Makers of Washington, D.C. Measuring about 2-1/2" to 2-3/4" tall x 1" to 1-1/4" wide, the cards were originally printed on a sheet of 14 from which they were punched out to play the game. The cards were issued in team sets with on-field roster changes reflected in the player cards over the years. Individual cards are generic, liberally sharing the same poses and portraits with identification possible only by changes to the uniform and the player ID printed in the box below the figure. That player data changed from year to year and the only way to determine exact year of issue is when the player card is found with a complete team set, often in a small pre-printed manila envelope. It is unknown whether all teams were issued in all years so the checklist for this issue will continue to grow as new data is reported. According to information found with the game, stickers could be purchased each year to update the game's figures with new player identification. Beginning in at least 1925 player cards were numbered at bottom, but since that information is lacking for most of these team set lists, most teams are arranged alphabetically.

		NM	EX	VG
	Common Player:	30.00	15.00	9.00
	1921 Red Sox team set:	250.00	125.00	75.00
(1)	(Joe Bush)	30.00	15.00	9.00
(2)	(J. Collins) (Shano)	30.00	15.00	9.00
(3)	(Eddie Foster)	30.00	15.00	9.00
(4)	(Sam Jones)	30.00	15.00	9.00
(5)	(Nemo Leibold)	30.00	15.00	9.00
(6)	(Stuffy McInnis)	30.00	15.00	9.00
(7)	(Elmer Meyers) (Myers)	30.00	15.00	9.00
(8)	(Herb Pennock)	50.00	25.00	15.00
(9)	(Pinky Pittinger) (Pettenger)	30.00	15.00	9.00
(10)	(Del Pratt)	30.00	15.00	9.00
(11)	(Muddy Ruel)	30.00	15.00	9.00
(12)	(Everett Scott)	30.00	15.00	9.00
(13)	(Hank Thormahlan) (Thormahlen)	30.00	15.00	9.00
(14)	(Roxy Walters)	30.00	15.00	9.00
	1921 Chicago White Sox team set:	250.00	125.00	75.00
(1)	(Eddie Collins)	60.00	30.00	18.00
(2)	(Red Faber)	50.00	25.00	15.00
(3)	(Bibb Falk)	30.00	15.00	9.00
(4)	(Harry Hooper)	50.00	25.00	15.00
(5)	(Ernie Johnson)	30.00	15.00	9.00
(6)	(Dicky Kerr)	30.00	15.00	9.00
(7)	(Eddie Mulligan)	30.00	15.00	9.00
(8)	(John Russell)	30.00	15.00	9.00
(9)	(Ray Schalk)	50.00	25.00	15.00
(10)	(Earl Sheely)	30.00	15.00	9.00
(11)	(Amos Strunk)	30.00	15.00	9.00
(12)	(Roy Wilkinson)	30.00	15.00	9.00
(13)	(Everett Yaryan)	30.00	15.00	9.00
(--)	Unknown pitcher	30.00	15.00	9.00
	1921 Cleveland Indians team set:	250.00	125.00	75.00
(--)	(Doc Johnston)	30.00	15.00	9.00
(--)	(Les Nunamaker)	30.00	15.00	9.00
(--)	(Steve O'Neil) (O'Neill)	30.00	15.00	9.00
(--)	(Allen Sothoron)	30.00	15.00	9.00
(--)	(George Uhle)	30.00	15.00	9.00
	1921 Tigers team set:	300.00	150.00	90.00
(1)	Johnny Bassler	30.00	15.00	9.00
(2)	Lu Blue	30.00	15.00	9.00
(3)	Ty Cobb	100.00	50.00	30.00
(4)	George Dauss	30.00	15.00	9.00
(5)	Howard Ehmke	30.00	15.00	9.00
(6)	Harry Heilmann	50.00	25.00	15.00
(7)	Bob Jones	30.00	15.00	9.00
(8)	Dutch Leonard	30.00	15.00	9.00
(9)	Jim Middleton	30.00	15.00	9.00
(10)	Red Oldham	30.00	15.00	9.00
(11)	Joe Sargent	30.00	15.00	9.00
(12)	Bobby Veach	30.00	15.00	9.00
(13)	Larry Woodall	30.00	15.00	9.00
(14)	Ralph Young	30.00	15.00	9.00
	1921 St. Louis Browns team set:	250.00	125.00	75.00
(1)	(Bill Bayne)	30.00	15.00	9.00
(2)	(Pat Collins)	30.00	15.00	9.00
(3)	(Dixie Davis)	30.00	15.00	9.00
(4)	(Frank Ellerby) (Ellerbee)	30.00	15.00	9.00
(5)	(Wally Gerber)	30.00	15.00	9.00
(6)	(Baby Doll Jacobson)	30.00	15.00	9.00
(7)	(Ray Kolp)	30.00	15.00	9.00
(8)	(Marty McManus)	30.00	15.00	9.00
(9)	(Urban Schocker) (Shocker)	30.00	15.00	9.00
(10)	(Hank Severeid)	30.00	15.00	9.00
(11)	(George Sisler)	50.00	25.00	15.00
(12)	(Jack Tobin)	30.00	15.00	9.00
(13)	(Elam Vangilder)	30.00	15.00	9.00
(14)	(Ken Williams)	30.00	15.00	9.00
	1921 Washington Senators team set:	300.00	150.00	90.00
(1)	(Jose Acosta)	40.00	20.00	12.00
(2)	(Eric Erickson)	30.00	15.00	9.00
(3)	(Patsy Gharrity)	30.00	15.00	9.00
(4)	(Goose Goslin)	50.00	25.00	15.00
(5)	(S. Harris)	50.00	25.00	15.00
(6)	(Walter Johnson)	80.00	40.00	24.00
(7)	(Joe Judge)	30.00	15.00	9.00
(8)	(Clyde Milan)	30.00	15.00	9.00
(9)	(George Mogridge)	30.00	15.00	9.00
(10)	(Frank O'Rourke)	30.00	15.00	9.00
(11)	(Val Picinich)	30.00	15.00	9.00
(12)	(Sam Rice)	50.00	25.00	15.00
(13)	(Howard Shanks)	30.00	15.00	9.00
(14)	(Tom Zachary)	30.00	15.00	9.00
	1923-24 Giants team set:	250.00	125.00	75.00
(1)	Virgil Barnes	30.00	15.00	9.00
(2)	Jack Bentley	30.00	15.00	9.00
(3)	Frankie Frisch	50.00	25.00	15.00
(4)	Hank Gowdy	30.00	15.00	9.00
(5)	Heinie Groh	30.00	15.00	9.00
(6)	Travis Jackson	50.00	25.00	15.00
(7)	George Kelly	50.00	25.00	15.00
(8)	Hugh McQuillan	30.00	15.00	9.00
(9)	Irish Meusel	30.00	15.00	9.00
(10)	Art Nehf	30.00	15.00	9.00
(11)	Rosy Ryan	30.00	15.00	9.00
(12)	Frank Snyder	30.00	15.00	9.00
(13)	L. (Hack) Wilson	60.00	30.00	18.00
(14)	Ross Young (Youngs)	50.00	25.00	15.00
	1924 Philadelhpia A's team set:	250.00	125.00	75.00
(1)	Max Bishop	30.00	15.00	9.00
(2)	Frank Bruggy	30.00	15.00	9.00
(3)	Chick Galloway	30.00	15.00	9.00
(4)	Bob Hasty	30.00	15.00	9.00
(5)	Joe Hauser	40.00	20.00	12.00
(6)	Fred Heimach	30.00	15.00	9.00
(7)	Bill Lamar	30.00	15.00	9.00
(8)	Roy Meeker	30.00	15.00	9.00
(9)	Bing Miller	30.00	15.00	9.00
(10)	Cy Perkins	30.00	15.00	9.00
(11)	Harry Riconda	30.00	15.00	9.00
(12)	Eddie Rommel	30.00	15.00	9.00
(13)	Al Simmons	50.00	25.00	15.00
(14)	Frank Welch	30.00	15.00	9.00
	1924 Boston Braves team set:	250.00	125.00	75.00
(1)	(Dave Bancroft)	50.00	25.00	15.00
(2)	(Jesse Barnes)	30.00	15.00	9.00
(3)	(Larry Benton)	30.00	15.00	9.00
(4)	(Johnny Cooney)	30.00	15.00	9.00
(5)	(Bill Cunningham)	30.00	15.00	9.00
(6)	(Gus Felix)	30.00	15.00	9.00
(7)	(Joe Genewich)	30.00	15.00	9.00
(8)	(Rube Marquard)	50.00	25.00	15.00
(9)	(Stuffy McInnis)	30.00	15.00	9.00
(10)	(Mickey O'Neill) (O'Neil)	30.00	15.00	9.00
(11)	(Ernie Padgett)	30.00	15.00	9.00
(12)	(Bob Smith)	30.00	15.00	9.00
(13)	(Casey Stengel)	65.00	32.00	19.50
(14)	(Cotton Tierney)	30.00	15.00	9.00
	1924 St. Louis Browns team set:	250.00	125.00	75.00
(1)	Pat Collins	30.00	15.00	9.00
(2)	Dave Danforth	30.00	15.00	9.00
(3)	Dixie Davis	30.00	15.00	9.00
(4)	Wally Gerber	30.00	15.00	9.00
(5)	William Jacobson	30.00	15.00	9.00
(6)	Ray Kolp	30.00	15.00	9.00
(7)	Marty McManus	30.00	15.00	9.00
(8)	Gene Robertson	30.00	15.00	9.00
(9)	Hank Severeid	30.00	15.00	9.00
(10)	Urban Shocker	50.00	25.00	15.00
(11)	George Sisler	50.00	25.00	15.00
(12)	Jack Tobin	30.00	15.00	9.00
(13)	Ken Williams	30.00	15.00	9.00
(14)	Ernie Wingard	30.00	15.00	9.00
	1924 St. Louis Cardinals team set:	250.00	125.00	75.00
(1)	Jim Bottomly (Bottomley)	50.00	25.00	15.00
(2)	Jimmy Cooney	30.00	15.00	9.00
(3)	Eddie Dyer	30.00	15.00	9.00
(4)	Max Flack	30.00	15.00	9.00
(5)	Howard Freigau	30.00	15.00	9.00
(6)	Mike Gonzales (Gonzalez)	40.00	20.00	12.00
(7)	Jesse Haines	50.00	25.00	15.00
(8)	Rogers Hornsby	75.00	37.00	22.00
(9)	Heinie Mueller	30.00	15.00	9.00
(10)	Charlie Neibergalls (Niebergall)	30.00	15.00	9.00
(11)	Jeff Pfeffer	30.00	15.00	9.00
(12)	Bill Sherdell (Sherdel)	30.00	15.00	9.00
(13)	Jack Smith	30.00	15.00	9.00
(14)	Allen Sothoron	30.00	15.00	9.00
	1924 Chicago Cubs team set:	250.00	125.00	75.00
(1)	(Grover Alexander)	60.00	30.00	18.00
(2)	(Bernie Friberg)	30.00	15.00	9.00
(3)	(George Grantham)	30.00	15.00	9.00
(4)	(Ray Grimes)	30.00	15.00	9.00
(5)	(Gabby Hartnett)	50.00	25.00	15.00
(6)	(Cliff Heathcote)	30.00	15.00	9.00
(7)	(Charlie Hollocher)	30.00	15.00	9.00
(8)	(Elmer Jacobs)	30.00	15.00	9.00
(9)	(Tony Kaufman (Kaufmann))	30.00	15.00	9.00
(10)	(Vic Keen)	30.00	15.00	9.00
(11)	(Hack Miller)	30.00	15.00	9.00
(12)	(Bob O'Farrell)	30.00	15.00	9.00
(13)	(Jigger Statz)	30.00	15.00	9.00
(14)	(Rip Wheeler)	30.00	15.00	9.00
	1924 Cleveland Indians team set:	250.00	125.00	75.00
(1)	George Burns	30.00	15.00	9.00
(2)	Stan Coveleskie (Coveleski)	50.00	25.00	15.00
(3)	Charlie Jamieson	30.00	15.00	9.00
(4)	Rube Lutzke	30.00	15.00	9.00
(5)	Dewey Metevier (Metivier)	30.00	15.00	9.00
(6)	Pat McNulty	30.00	15.00	9.00
(7)	Glenn Myatt	30.00	15.00	9.00
(8)	Joe Sewell	50.00	25.00	15.00
(9)	Luke Sewell	30.00	15.00	9.00
(10)	Joe Shaute	30.00	15.00	9.00
(11)	Sherry Smith	30.00	15.00	9.00
(12)	Tris Speaker	75.00	37.00	22.00
(13)	Riggs Stephenson	30.00	15.00	9.00
(14)	George Uhle	30.00	15.00	9.00
	1924 Pittsburgh Pirates team set:	250.00	125.00	75.00
(1)	Clyde Barnhart	30.00	15.00	9.00
(2)	Carson Bigbee	30.00	15.00	9.00
(3)	Max Carey	50.00	25.00	15.00
(4)	Wilbur Cooper	30.00	15.00	9.00
(5)	Johnny Gooch	30.00	15.00	9.00
(6)	Charlie Grimm	30.00	15.00	9.00
(7)	Ray Kremer	30.00	15.00	9.00
(8)	Rabbit Maranville	50.00	25.00	15.00
(9)	Lee Meadows	30.00	15.00	9.00
(10)	Johnny Morrison	30.00	15.00	9.00
(11)	Walter Schmidt	30.00	15.00	9.00
(12)	Pie Traynor	50.00	25.00	15.00
(13)	Glenn Wright	30.00	15.00	9.00
(14)	Emil Yde	30.00	15.00	9.00
	1924 Philadelphia Phillies team set:	200.00	100.00	60.00
(1)	Hal Carlson	30.00	15.00	9.00
(2)	Hod Ford	30.00	15.00	9.00
(3)	Whitey Glazner	30.00	15.00	9.00
(4)	George Harper	30.00	15.00	9.00
(5)	Butch Henline	30.00	15.00	9.00
(6)	Walter Holke	30.00	15.00	9.00
(7)	Bill Hubbell	30.00	15.00	9.00
(8)	Clarence Mitchell	30.00	15.00	9.00
(9)	Jimmy Ring	30.00	15.00	9.00
(10)	Heinie Sand	30.00	15.00	9.00
(11)	Joe Schultz	30.00	15.00	9.00
(12)	Cy Williams	30.00	15.00	9.00
(13)	Jimmie Wilson	30.00	15.00	9.00
(14)	Russell Wrightstone	30.00	15.00	9.00
	1924 Cincinnati Reds team set:	250.00	125.00	75.00
(1)	Rube Benton	30.00	15.00	9.00
(2)	George Burns	30.00	15.00	9.00
(3)	Jimmy Caveney	30.00	15.00	9.00
(4)	Hughie Critz	30.00	15.00	9.00
(5)	Jake Daubert	30.00	15.00	9.00
(6)	Pete Donohue	30.00	15.00	9.00
(7)	Pat Duncan	30.00	15.00	9.00
(8)	Bubbles Hargrave	30.00	15.00	9.00
(9)	Dolf Luque	40.00	20.00	12.00
(10)	Carl Mays	35.00	17.50	10.50
(11)	"Babe" Pinelli	30.00	15.00	9.00
(12)	Eppa Rixey	50.00	25.00	15.00
(13)	Edd Rousch (Roush)	50.00	25.00	15.00
(14)	Ivy Wingo	30.00	15.00	9.00
	1924 Boston Red Sox team set:	250.00	125.00	75.00
(1)	(Ike Boone)	30.00	15.00	9.00
(2)	(Danny Clarke) (Clark)	30.00	15.00	9.00
(3)	(Howard Ehmke)	30.00	15.00	9.00
(4)	(Alex Ferguson)	30.00	15.00	9.00
(5)	(Ira Flagstead)	30.00	15.00	9.00
(6)	(Oscar Fuhr)	30.00	15.00	9.00
(7)	(Joe Harris)	30.00	15.00	9.00
(8)	(Dud Lee)	30.00	15.00	9.00
(9)	(Steve O'Neill)	30.00	15.00	9.00
(10)	(Val Picinich)	30.00	15.00	9.00
(11)	(Bill Piercy)	30.00	15.00	9.00
(12)	(Jack Quinn)	30.00	15.00	9.00
(13)	(Bobby Veach)	30.00	15.00	9.00
(14)	(Bill Wamsganss) (Wambsganss)	30.00	15.00	9.00
	1924 Brooklyn Robins team set:	250.00	125.00	75.00
(1)	Hank DeBerry	30.00	15.00	9.00
(2)	Art Decatur	30.00	15.00	9.00
(3)	Rube Erhardt (Ehrhardt)	30.00	15.00	9.00
(4)	Jack Fournier	30.00	15.00	9.00
(5)	Tommy Griffith	30.00	15.00	9.00
(6)	Burleigh Grimes	50.00	25.00	15.00
(7)	Dutch Henry	30.00	15.00	9.00
(8)	Andy High	30.00	15.00	9.00
(9)	Jimmy Johnson (Johnston)	30.00	15.00	9.00
(10)	Dutch Ruether	30.00	15.00	9.00
(11)	Milt Stock	30.00	15.00	9.00
(12)	Zack Taylor	30.00	15.00	9.00
(13)	Dazzy Vance	50.00	25.00	15.00
(14)	Zack Wheat	50.00	25.00	15.00
	1924 Washington Senators team set:	250.00	125.00	75.00
(1)	Ossie Bluege	30.00	15.00	9.00
(2)	Goose Goslin	50.00	25.00	15.00
(3)	S. Harris	50.00	25.00	15.00
(4)	Walter Johnson	80.00	40.00	24.00
(5)	Joe Judge	30.00	15.00	9.00
(6)	Firpo Marberry	30.00	15.00	9.00
(7)	George Mogridge	30.00	15.00	9.00
(8)	Curly Ogden	30.00	15.00	9.00
(9)	Roger Peckinpaugh	30.00	15.00	9.00
(10)	Muddy Ruel	30.00	15.00	9.00
(11)	Bennie Tate	30.00	15.00	9.00
(12)	Tom Zachary	30.00	15.00	9.00

(--)	Unknown position player	30.00	15.00	9.00
(--)	Unknown position player	30.00	15.00	9.00
	1924 Detroit Tigers team set:	300.00	150.00	90.00
(1)	Johnny Bassler	30.00	15.00	9.00
(2)	Lu Blue	30.00	15.00	9.00
(3)	Les Burke	30.00	15.00	9.00
(4)	Ty Cobb	100.00	50.00	30.00
(5)	Bert Cole	30.00	15.00	9.00
(6)	George Dauss	30.00	15.00	9.00
(7)	Harry Heilmann	50.00	25.00	15.00
(8)	Bob Jones	30.00	15.00	9.00
(9)	Heinie Manush	50.00	25.00	15.00
(10)	Herman Pillette	30.00	15.00	9.00
(11)	Emory Rigney	30.00	15.00	9.00
(12)	Lil Stoner	30.00	15.00	9.00
(13)	Earl Whitehill	30.00	15.00	9.00
(14)	Larry Woodall	30.00	15.00	9.00
	1924 Chicago White Sox team set:	275.00	137.00	82.00
(1)	Maurice Archdeacon	30.00	15.00	9.00
(2)	Bill Barrett	30.00	15.00	9.00
(3)	Eddie Collins	50.00	25.00	15.00
(4)	George Connally	30.00	15.00	9.00
(5)	Buck Crouse	30.00	15.00	9.00
(6)	Mike Cvengros	30.00	15.00	9.00
(7)	Red Faber	50.00	25.00	15.00
(8)	Bibb Falk	30.00	15.00	9.00
(9)	Harry Hooper	50.00	25.00	15.00
(10)	Willie Kamm	30.00	15.00	9.00
(11)	Ted Lyons	50.00	25.00	15.00
(12)	Ray Schalk	50.00	25.00	15.00
(13)	Earl Sheely	30.00	15.00	9.00
(14)	Sloppy Thurston	30.00	15.00	9.00
	1924 New York Yankees team set:	400.00	200.00	120.00
(1)	Joe Bush	30.00	15.00	9.00
(2)	Joe Dugan	30.00	15.00	9.00
(3)	Fred Hofmann	30.00	15.00	9.00
(4)	Waite Hoyt	50.00	25.00	15.00
(5)	Sam Jones	30.00	15.00	9.00
(6)	Bob Meusel	30.00	15.00	9.00
(7)	Herb Pennock	50.00	25.00	15.00
(8)	Wally Pipp	35.00	17.50	10.50
(9)	Babe Ruth	200.00	100.00	60.00
(10)	Wally Schang	30.00	15.00	9.00
(11)	Everett Scott	30.00	15.00	9.00
(12)	Bob Shawkey	30.00	15.00	9.00
(13)	Aaron Ward	30.00	15.00	9.00
(14)	Whitey Witt	30.00	15.00	9.00
	1925 New York Giants team set:	400.00	200.00	120.00
1	(Jack Scott)	30.00	15.00	9.00
2	(Virgil Barnes)	30.00	15.00	9.00
3	(Jack Bentley)	30.00	15.00	9.00
4	(Hugh McQuillan)	30.00	15.00	9.00
5	(Art Nehf)	30.00	15.00	9.00
6	(Hank Gowdy)	30.00	15.00	9.00
7	(Frank Snyder)	30.00	15.00	9.00
8	(Frank Frisch)	50.00	25.00	15.00
9	(Irish Meusel)	30.00	15.00	9.00
10	(Bill Terry)	50.00	25.00	15.00
11	(George Kelly)	50.00	25.00	15.00
12	(L. (Hack) Wilson)	50.00	25.00	15.00
13	(Travis Jackson)	50.00	25.00	15.00
14	(Ross Young (Youngs))	50.00	25.00	15.00
	1925 Philadelphia Phillies team set:	250.00	125.00	75.00
1	(Hal Carlson)	30.00	15.00	9.00
2	(Jack Knight)	30.00	15.00	9.00
3	(Johnny Couch)	30.00	15.00	9.00
4	(Jimmy Ring)	30.00	15.00	9.00
5	(Clarence Mitchell)	30.00	15.00	9.00
6	(Butch Henline)	30.00	15.00	9.00
7	(Jimmie Wilson)	30.00	15.00	9.00
8	(Barney Friberg)	30.00	15.00	9.00
9	(Russell Wrightstone)	30.00	15.00	9.00
10	(Chicken Hawks)	30.00	15.00	9.00
11	(Lew Fonseca)	30.00	15.00	9.00
12	(George Harper)	30.00	15.00	9.00
13	(Heinie Sand)	30.00	15.00	9.00
14	(Geo. J. Burns)	30.00	15.00	9.00
	1925 Brooklyn Robins			
(--)	(Lloyd Brown)	30.00	15.00	9.00
(--)	(Hod Ford)	30.00	15.00	9.00
	1925 Washington Senators team set	350.00	175.00	100.00
(1)	(Ossie Bluege)	30.00	15.00	9.00
(2)	(Stan Coveleski)	50.00	25.00	15.00
(3)	(Goose Goslin)	50.00	25.00	15.00
(4)	(Bucky Harris)	50.00	25.00	15.00
(5)	(Walter Johnson)	90.00	45.00	27.00
(6)	(Joe Judge)	30.00	15.00	9.00
(7)	(Firpo Marberry)	30.00	15.00	9.00
(8)	(Earl McNeely)	30.00	15.00	9.00
(9)	(Roger Peckinpaugh)	30.00	15.00	9.00
(10)	(Sam Rice)	50.00	25.00	15.00
(11)	(Muddy Ruel)	30.00	15.00	9.00
(12)	(Dutch Ruether)	30.00	15.00	9.00
(13)	(Hank Severeid)	30.00	15.00	9.00
(14)	(Tom Zachary)	30.00	15.00	9.00
	1926 Philadelphia A's team set:	250.00	125.00	75.00
(1)	Max Bishop	30.00	15.00	9.00
(2)	Mickey Cochrane	50.00	25.00	15.00
(3)	Jimmy Dykes	30.00	15.00	9.00
(4)	Howard Ehmke	30.00	15.00	9.00
(5)	Walt French	30.00	15.00	9.00
(6)	Chick Galloway	30.00	15.00	9.00
(7)	Sam Gray	30.00	15.00	9.00
(8)	Lefty Grove	50.00	25.00	15.00
(9)	Joe Hauser	30.00	15.00	9.00
(10)	Bill Lamar	30.00	15.00	9.00
(11)	Cy Perkins	30.00	15.00	9.00
(12)	Eddie Rommel	30.00	15.00	9.00
(13)	Al Simmons	50.00	25.00	15.00
(14)	Rube Walberg	30.00	15.00	9.00
	1926 Boston Braves team set:	250.00	125.00	75.00
(1)	Dave Bancroft	50.00	25.00	15.00
(2)	Larry Benton	30.00	15.00	9.00
(3)	Eddie Brown	30.00	15.00	9.00
(4)	Dick Burrus	30.00	15.00	9.00
(5)	Johnny Cooney	30.00	15.00	9.00
(6)	Dick Gautreau	30.00	15.00	9.00
(7)	Joe Genewich	30.00	15.00	9.00
(8)	Frank Gibson	30.00	15.00	9.00
(9)	Andy High	30.00	15.00	9.00
(10)	George Mogridge	30.00	15.00	9.00
(11)	Bob Smith	30.00	15.00	9.00
(12)	Zack Taylor	30.00	15.00	9.00
(13)	Jimmy Welsh	30.00	15.00	9.00
(14)	Frank Wilson	30.00	15.00	9.00
	1926 St. Louis Browns team set:	250.00	125.00	75.00
(1)	Dixie Davis	30.00	15.00	9.00
(2)	Cedric Durst	30.00	15.00	9.00
(3)	Milt Gaston	30.00	15.00	9.00
(4)	Wally Gerber	30.00	15.00	9.00
(5)	Joe Giard	30.00	15.00	9.00
(6)	Pinky Hargrave	30.00	15.00	9.00
(7)	Marty McManus	30.00	15.00	9.00
(8)	Oscar Melillo	30.00	15.00	9.00
(9)	Bing Miller	30.00	15.00	9.00
(10)	Harry Rice	30.00	15.00	9.00
(11)	Wally Schang	30.00	15.00	9.00
(12)	George Sisler	50.00	25.00	15.00
(13)	Elam Vangilder	30.00	15.00	9.00
(14)	Tom Zachary	30.00	15.00	9.00
	1926 St. Louis Cardinals team set:	300.00	150.00	90.00
(1)	Grover Alexander	60.00	30.00	18.00
(2)	Les Bell	30.00	15.00	9.00
(3)	Ray Blades	30.00	15.00	9.00
(4)	Jim Bottomley	50.00	25.00	15.00
(5)	Taylor Douthit	30.00	15.00	9.00
(6)	Jesse Haines	50.00	25.00	15.00
(7)	Rogers Hornsby	65.00	32.00	19.50
(8)	Vic Keen	30.00	15.00	9.00
(9)	Bob O'Farrell	30.00	15.00	9.00
(10)	Flint Rhem	30.00	15.00	9.00
(11)	Bill Sherdel	30.00	15.00	9.00
(12)	Billy Southworth	30.00	15.00	9.00
(13)	Tommy Thevenow	30.00	15.00	9.00
(14)	Bill Warwick	30.00	15.00	9.00
	1926 Chicago Cubs team set:	250.00	125.00	75.00
(1)	Sparky Adams	30.00	15.00	9.00
(2)	Sheriff Blake	30.00	15.00	9.00
(3)	Guy Bush	30.00	15.00	9.00
(4)	Jim Cooney	30.00	15.00	9.00
(5)	Howard Freigau	30.00	15.00	9.00
(6)	Mike Gonzalez	40.00	20.00	12.00
(7)	Charlie Grimm	30.00	15.00	9.00
(8)	Gabby Hartnett	50.00	25.00	15.00
(9)	Cliff Heathcote	30.00	15.00	9.00
(10)	Percy Jones	30.00	15.00	9.00
(11)	Tony Kaufmann	30.00	15.00	9.00
(12)	Charlie Root	30.00	15.00	9.00
(13)	Riggs Stephenson	30.00	15.00	9.00
(14)	Hack Wilson	50.00	25.00	15.00
	1926 New York Giants team set:	300.00	150.00	90.00
(1)	Virgil Barnes	30.00	15.00	9.00
(2)	Chick Davies	30.00	15.00	9.00
(3)	Freddie Fitzsimmons	30.00	15.00	9.00
(4)	Paul Florence	30.00	15.00	9.00
(5)	Frankie Frisch	50.00	25.00	15.00
(6)	Kent Greenfield	30.00	15.00	9.00
(7)	Travis Jackson	50.00	25.00	15.00
(8)	George Kelly	50.00	25.00	15.00
(9)	Freddie Lindstrom	50.00	25.00	15.00
(10)	Irish Meusel	30.00	15.00	9.00
(11)	Heinie Mueller	30.00	15.00	9.00
(12)	Jimmy Ring	30.00	15.00	9.00
(13)	Frank Snyder	30.00	15.00	9.00
(14)	Ross Young (Youngs)	50.00	25.00	15.00
	1926 Cleveland Indians team set:	250.00	125.00	75.00
(1)	George Burns	30.00	15.00	9.00
(2)	Charlie Jamieson	30.00	15.00	9.00
(3)	Ben Kerr (Karr)	30.00	15.00	9.00
(4)	Emil Levsen	30.00	15.00	9.00
(5)	Rube Lutzke	30.00	15.00	9.00
(6)	Glenn Myatt	30.00	15.00	9.00
(7)	Joe Sewell	50.00	25.00	15.00
(8)	Luke Sewell	30.00	15.00	9.00
(9)	Joe Shaute	30.00	15.00	9.00
(10)	Sherry Smith	30.00	15.00	9.00
(11)	Tris Speaker	60.00	30.00	18.00
(12)	Fred Spurgeon	30.00	15.00	9.00
(13)	Homer Summa	30.00	15.00	9.00
(14)	George Uhle	30.00	15.00	9.00
	1926 Pittsburgh Pirates team set:	250.00	125.00	75.00
(1)	Vic Aldridge	30.00	15.00	9.00
(2)	Max Carey	50.00	25.00	15.00
(3)	Kiki Cuyler	50.00	25.00	15.00
(4)	Johnny Gooch	30.00	15.00	9.00
(5)	George Grantham	30.00	15.00	9.00
(6)	Ray Kremer	30.00	15.00	9.00
(7)	Lee Meadows	30.00	15.00	9.00
(8)	Johnny Morrison	30.00	15.00	9.00
(9)	Hal Rhyne	30.00	15.00	9.00
(10)	Earl Smith	30.00	15.00	9.00
(11)	Pie Traynor	50.00	25.00	15.00
(12)	Paul Waner	50.00	25.00	15.00
(13)	Glenn Wright	30.00	15.00	9.00
(14)	Emil Yde	30.00	15.00	9.00
	1926 Philadelphia Phillies team set:	250.00	125.00	75.00
(1)	Hal Carlson	30.00	15.00	9.00
(2)	Wayland Dean	30.00	15.00	9.00
(3)	Bennie Friberg	30.00	15.00	9.00
(4)	Ray Grimes	30.00	15.00	9.00
(5)	George Harper	30.00	15.00	9.00
(6)	Butch Henline	30.00	15.00	9.00
(7)	Clarence Huber	30.00	15.00	9.00
(8)	Jack Knight	30.00	15.00	9.00
(9)	Fred Leach	30.00	15.00	9.00
(10)	John McKan (Mokan)	30.00	15.00	9.00
(11)	Clarence Mitchell	30.00	15.00	9.00
(12)	Heinie Sand	30.00	15.00	9.00
(13)	Claude Willoughby	30.00	15.00	9.00
(14)	Jimmie Wilson	30.00	15.00	9.00
	1926 Cincinnati Reds team set:	250.00	125.00	75.00
(1)	Rube Bressler	30.00	15.00	9.00
(2)	Hughie Critz	30.00	15.00	9.00
(3)	Pete Donohue	30.00	15.00	9.00
(4)	Chuck Dressen	30.00	15.00	9.00
(5)	Frank Emmer	30.00	15.00	9.00
(6)	Bubbles Hargrave	30.00	15.00	9.00
(7)	Dolf Luque	40.00	20.00	12.00
(8)	Jakie May	30.00	15.00	9.00
(9)	Carl Mays	35.00	17.50	10.50
(10)	Val Picinich	30.00	15.00	9.00
(11)	Wally Pipp	35.00	17.50	10.50
(12)	Edd Rousch (Roush)	50.00	25.00	15.00
(13)	Eppa Rixey	50.00	25.00	15.00
(14)	Curt Walker	30.00	15.00	9.00
	1926 Boston Red Sox team set:	250.00	125.00	75.00
(1)	George Bischoff	30.00	15.00	9.00
(2)	Ira Flagstead	30.00	15.00	9.00
(3)	Alex Gaston	30.00	15.00	9.00
(4)	Fred Haney	30.00	15.00	9.00
(5)	B. Harris (Harriss)	30.00	15.00	9.00
(6)	Fred Heimach	30.00	15.00	9.00
(7)	Baby Doll Jacobsen (Jacobson)	30.00	15.00	9.00
(8)	Bill Regan	30.00	15.00	9.00
(9)	Emory Rigney	30.00	15.00	9.00
(10)	Red Ruffing	50.00	25.00	15.00
(11)	Wally Shaner	30.00	15.00	9.00
(12)	Phil Todt	30.00	15.00	9.00
(13)	Ted Wingfield	30.00	15.00	9.00
(14)	Hal Wiltse	30.00	15.00	9.00
	1926 Brooklyn Robins team set:	250.00	125.00	75.00
(1)	Jesse Barnes	30.00	15.00	9.00
(2)	Jimmy Butler	30.00	15.00	9.00
(3)	Dick Cox	30.00	15.00	9.00
(4)	Hank DeBerry	30.00	15.00	9.00
(5)	Chick Fewster	30.00	15.00	9.00
(6)	Burleigh Grimes	50.00	25.00	15.00
(7)	Babe Herman	30.00	15.00	9.00
(8)	Rabbit Maranville	50.00	25.00	15.00
(9)	Bob McGraw	30.00	15.00	9.00
(10)	Mickey O'Neil	30.00	15.00	9.00
(11)	Jesse Petty	30.00	15.00	9.00
(12)	Dazzy Vance	50.00	25.00	15.00
(13)	Zack Wheat	50.00	25.00	15.00
(14)	Whitey Witt	30.00	15.00	9.00
	1926 Washington Senators team set:	300.00	150.00	90.00
(1)	Ossie Bluege	30.00	15.00	9.00
(2)	Stan Coveleskie (Coveleski)	50.00	25.00	15.00
(3)	Goose Goslin	50.00	25.00	15.00
(4)	S. Harris	50.00	25.00	15.00
(5)	Walter Johnson	80.00	40.00	24.00
(6)	Joe Judge	30.00	15.00	9.00
(7)	Firpo Marberry	30.00	15.00	9.00
(8)	Emilio Palmero	30.00	15.00	9.00
(9)	Roger Peckinpaugh	30.00	15.00	9.00
(10)	Dutch Ruether	30.00	15.00	9.00
(11)	Sam Rice	50.00	25.00	15.00
(12)	Muddy Ruel	30.00	15.00	9.00
(13)	Hank Severeid	30.00	15.00	9.00
(14)	Dan Taylor	30.00	15.00	9.00
	1926 Detroit Tigers team set:	300.00	150.00	90.00
(1)	Johnny Bassler	30.00	15.00	9.00
(2)	Lu Blue	30.00	15.00	9.00
(3)	Ty Cobb	100.00	50.00	30.00
(4)	George Dauss	30.00	15.00	9.00
(5)	Harry Heilmann	50.00	25.00	15.00
(6)	Ken Holloway	30.00	15.00	9.00
(7)	Frank O'Rourke	30.00	15.00	9.00
(8)	Lil Stoner	30.00	15.00	9.00
(9)	Jack Tavener	30.00	15.00	9.00
(10)	Jack Warner	30.00	15.00	9.00
(11)	Ed Wells	30.00	15.00	9.00
(12)	Earl Whitehill	30.00	15.00	9.00
(13)	Al Wingo	30.00	15.00	9.00
(14)	Larry Woodall	30.00	15.00	9.00
	1926 Chicago White Sox team set:	250.00	125.00	75.00
(1)	Bill Barret (Barrett)	30.00	15.00	9.00
(2)	Ted Blankenship	30.00	15.00	9.00
(3)	Eddie Collins	50.00	25.00	15.00
(4)	Buck Crouse	30.00	15.00	9.00
(5)	Ike Davis	30.00	15.00	9.00
(6)	Jim Joe Edwards	30.00	15.00	9.00
(7)	Red Faber	50.00	25.00	15.00
(8)	Bibb Falk	30.00	15.00	9.00
(9)	Willie Kamm	30.00	15.00	9.00
(10)	Ted Lyons	50.00	25.00	15.00
(11)	Johnny Mostil	30.00	15.00	9.00
(12)	Ray Schalk	50.00	25.00	15.00
(13)	Earl Sheely	30.00	15.00	9.00
(14)	A. Thomas	30.00	15.00	9.00
	1926 New York Yankees team set:	450.00	225.00	135.00
(1)	Benny Bengough	30.00	15.00	9.00
(2)	Pat Collins	30.00	15.00	9.00
(3)	Earle Combs	50.00	25.00	15.00
(4)	Joe Dugan	30.00	15.00	9.00
(5)	Lou Gehrig	100.00	50.00	30.00
(6)	Waite Hoyt	50.00	25.00	15.00
(7)	Sam Jones	30.00	15.00	9.00
(8)	Mark Koenig	30.00	15.00	9.00
(9)	Tony Lazzeri	50.00	25.00	15.00
(10)	Bob Meusel	30.00	15.00	9.00
(11)	Herb Pennock	50.00	25.00	15.00
(12)	Babe Ruth	200.00	100.00	60.00
(13)	Urban Schocker (Shocker)	30.00	15.00	9.00

(14)	Myles Thomas	30.00	15.00	9.00
	1927 Philadelphia Phillies team set:	250.00	125.00	75.00
(1)	(Alex Ferguson)	30.00	15.00	9.00
(2)	(Barney Friberg)	30.00	15.00	9.00
(3)	(Bubber Jonnard)	30.00	15.00	9.00
(4)	(Tony Kaufmann)	30.00	15.00	9.00
(5)	(Fred Leach)	30.00	15.00	9.00
(6)	(Clarence Mitchell)	30.00	15.00	9.00
(7)	(Hub Pruett)	30.00	15.00	9.00
(8)	(Heinie Sand)	30.00	15.00	9.00
(9)	(Jack Scott)	30.00	15.00	9.00
(10)	(Dick Spaulding) (Spalding)	30.00	15.00	9.00
(11)	(Fresco Thompson)	30.00	15.00	9.00
(12)	(Cy Williams)	30.00	15.00	9.00
(13)	(Jimmie Wilson)	30.00	15.00	9.00
(14)	(Russell Wrightstone)	30.00	15.00	9.00
	1929 Philadelphia A's team set:	300.00	150.00	90.00
(1)	Max Bishop	30.00	15.00	9.00
(2)	Joe Boley	30.00	15.00	9.00
(3)	Mickey Cochrane	50.00	25.00	15.00
(4)	George Earnshaw	30.00	15.00	9.00
(5)	Jimmie Foxx	60.00	30.00	18.00
(6)	Lefty Grove	50.00	25.00	15.00
(7)	Mule Haas	30.00	15.00	9.00
(8)	Sammy Hale	30.00	15.00	9.00
(9)	E. Miller	30.00	15.00	9.00
(10)	Cy Perkins	30.00	15.00	9.00
(11)	Al Simmons	50.00	25.00	15.00
(12)	Jack Quinn	30.00	15.00	9.00
(13)	Rube Walberg	30.00	15.00	9.00
(14)	Unknown pitcher	30.00	15.00	9.00
	1929 New York Giants team set:	300.00	150.00	90.00
1	Joe Genewich	30.00	15.00	9.00
2	Bill Walker	30.00	15.00	9.00
3	Freddie Fitzsimmons	30.00	15.00	9.00
4	Larry Benton	30.00	15.00	9.00
5	Carl Hubbell	50.00	25.00	15.00
6	Bob O'Farrell	30.00	15.00	9.00
7	Shanty Hogan	30.00	15.00	9.00
8	Freddie Lindstrom	50.00	25.00	15.00
9	Fred Leach	30.00	15.00	9.00
10	Bill Terry	50.00	25.00	15.00
11	Andy Cohen	30.00	15.00	9.00
12	Edd Roush	50.00	25.00	15.00
13	Travis Jackson	50.00	25.00	15.00
14	Mel Ott	50.00	25.00	15.00
	1929 Pittsburgh Pirates team set:	250.00	125.00	75.00
(1)	Dick Bartell	30.00	15.00	9.00
(2)	Adam Comorosky	30.00	15.00	9.00
(3)	Larry French	30.00	15.00	9.00
(4)	George Grantham	30.00	15.00	9.00
(5)	Burleigh Grimes	50.00	25.00	15.00
(6)	Charlie Hargreaves	30.00	15.00	9.00
(7)	Rollie Hemsley	30.00	15.00	9.00
(8)	Carmen Hill	30.00	15.00	9.00
(9)	Ray Kremer	30.00	15.00	9.00
(10)	Barney Pelty	30.00	15.00	9.00
(11)	Earl Sheely	30.00	15.00	9.00
(12)	Pie Traynor	50.00	25.00	15.00
(13)	L. Waner	50.00	25.00	15.00
(14)	P. Waner	50.00	25.00	15.00
	1929 Cincinnati Reds team set:	250.00	125.00	75.00
(1)	Ethan Allen	30.00	15.00	9.00
(2)	Hughie Critz	30.00	15.00	9.00
(3)	Pete Donohue	30.00	15.00	9.00
(4)	Chuck Dressen	30.00	15.00	9.00
(5)	Hod Ford	30.00	15.00	9.00
(6)	Johnny Gooch	30.00	15.00	9.00
(7)	George Kelly	50.00	25.00	15.00
(8)	Red Lucas	30.00	15.00	9.00
(9)	Dolf Luque	30.00	15.00	9.00
(10)	Jakie May	30.00	15.00	9.00
(11)	Eppa Rixey	50.00	25.00	15.00
(12)	Clyde Sukeforth	30.00	15.00	9.00
(13)	Evar Swanson	30.00	15.00	9.00
(14)	Curt Walker	30.00	15.00	9.00
	1929 Boston Red Sox team set:	250.00	125.00	75.00
(1)	Bill Barrett	30.00	15.00	9.00
(2)	Charlie Berry	30.00	15.00	9.00
(3)	M. Gaston	30.00	15.00	9.00
(4)	John Heving	30.00	15.00	9.00
(5)	Danny MacFayden	30.00	15.00	9.00
(6)	Ed Morris	30.00	15.00	9.00
(7)	Bill Narlesky (Narleski)	30.00	15.00	9.00
(8)	Bobby Reeves	30.00	15.00	9.00
(9)	Hal Rhyne	30.00	15.00	9.00
(10)	Red Ruffing	50.00	25.00	15.00
(11)	Jack Russell	30.00	15.00	9.00
(12)	Russ Scarritt	30.00	15.00	9.00
(13)	Phil Todt	30.00	15.00	9.00
(14)	Ken Williams	30.00	15.00	9.00
	1929 Washington Senators team set:	250.00	125.00	75.00
(1)	Ossie Bluege	30.00	15.00	9.00
(2)	Garland Braxton	30.00	15.00	9.00
(3)	Joe Cronin	50.00	25.00	15.00
(4)	Goose Goslin	50.00	25.00	15.00
(5)	Bump Hadley	30.00	15.00	9.00
(6)	Sam Jones	30.00	15.00	9.00
(7)	Joe Judge	30.00	15.00	9.00
(8)	Ad Liska	30.00	15.00	9.00
(9)	Firpo Marberry	30.00	15.00	9.00
(10)	Buddy Myer	30.00	15.00	9.00
(11)	Sam Rice	50.00	25.00	15.00
(12)	Muddy Ruel	30.00	15.00	9.00
(13)	Benny Tate	30.00	15.00	9.00
(14)	Sammy West	30.00	15.00	9.00
	1929 Detroit Tigers			
(1)	Emil Yde	30.00	15.00	9.00
	1929 New York Yankees			
(1)	Lou Gehrig	200.00	100.00	60.00
(2)	Johnny Grabowski	30.00	15.00	9.00
(3)	Fred Heimach	30.00	15.00	9.00
(4)	Waite Hoyt	50.00	25.00	15.00
(5)	Hank Johnson	30.00	15.00	9.00
(6)	Tony Lazzeri	50.00	25.00	15.00
(7)	Bob Meusel	30.00	15.00	9.00
(8)	Herb Pennock	50.00	25.00	15.00
(9)	George Pipgras	30.00	15.00	9.00
(10)	Gene Robertson	30.00	15.00	9.00
	1930 Cincinnati Reds			
(--)	Leo Durocher	50.00	25.00	15.00
	1930 Brooklyn Robins			
(--)	Al Lopez	50.00	25.00	15.00

1969 Major League Baseball Photostamps

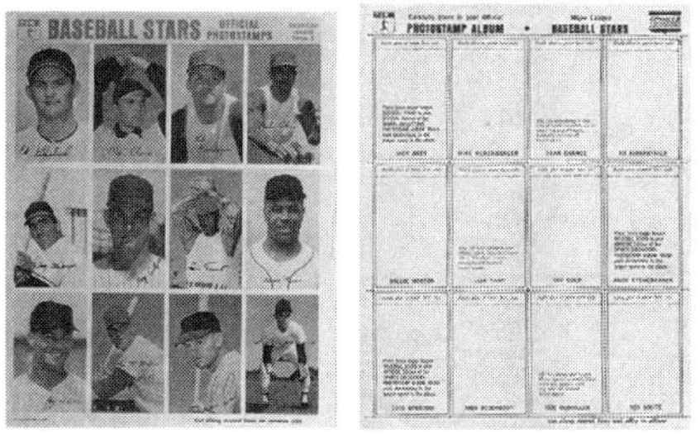

This set of 216 player stamps, sponsored by the Major League Baseball Players Association (not authorized by MLB, thus the lack of team uniform insignia) was issued in professional baseball's centennial year of 1969 and was sold in 18 different uncut sheets, with 12 stamps on each sheet. Each individual stamp measured 2" x 3-1/4". There were nine sheets picturing National League players and nine picturing American Leaguers. The full-color stamps displayed facsimilie autographs on the fronts. The backs carried instructions to moisten the stamps and place them in a special album that was also available. Many sheets of these stamps were uncovered by a dealer in the early 1980s and they were available at inexpensive prices.

		NM	EX	VG
Complete Sheet Set (18):		60.00	30.00	18.00
Complete Singles Set (216):		45.00	22.00	13.50
Common Sheet:		1.75	.90	.50
Common Player:		.25	.13	.08
Sheet A.L. 1		3.75	2.00	1.25
(1)	Don Buford	.25	.13	.08
(2)	Mike Andrews	.25	.13	.08
(3)	Max Alvis	.25	.13	.08
(4)	Bill Freehan	.40	.20	.12
(5)	Horace Clarke	.25	.13	.08
(6)	Bernie Allen	.25	.13	.08
(7)	Jim Fregosi	.35	.20	.11
(8)	Joe Horlen	.25	.13	.08
(9)	Jerry Adair	.25	.13	.08
(10)	Harmon Killebrew	1.50	.70	.45
(11)	Johnny Odom	.25	.13	.08
(12)	Steve Barber	.25	.13	.08
Sheet A.L. 2		2.50	1.25	.70
(13)	Tom Harper	.25	.13	.08
(14)	Boog Powell	.50	.25	.15
(15)	Jose Santiago	.25	.13	.08
(16)	Sonny Siebert	.25	.13	.08
(17)	Mickey Lolich	.50	.25	.15
(18)	Tom Tresh	.50	.25	.15
(19)	Camilo Pascual	.25	.13	.08
(20)	Bob Rodgers	.25	.13	.08
(21)	Pete Ward	.25	.13	.08
(22)	Dave Morehead	.25	.13	.08
(23)	John Roseboro	.25	.13	.08
(24)	Bert Campaneris	.35	.20	.11
Sheet A.L. 3		3.75	2.00	1.25
(25)	Danny Cater	.25	.13	.08
(26)	Rich Rollins	.25	.13	.08
(27)	Brooks Robinson	1.50	.70	.45
(28)	Rico Petrocelli	.25	.13	.08
(29)	Larry Brown	.25	.13	.08
(30)	Norm Cash	.40	.20	.12
(31)	Jake Gibbs	.25	.13	.08
(32)	Mike Epstein	.25	.13	.08
(33)	George Brunet	.25	.13	.08
(34)	Tom McCraw	.25	.13	.08
(35)	Steve Whitaker	.25	.13	.08
(36)	Bob Allison	.25	.13	.08
Sheet A.L. 4		2.50	1.25	.70
(37)	Jim Kaat	.40	.20	.12
(38)	Sal Bando	.25	.13	.08
(39)	Ray Oyler	.25	.13	.08
(40)	Dave McNally	.25	.13	.08
(41)	George Scott	.25	.13	.08
(42)	Joe Azcue	.25	.13	.08
(43)	Jim Northrup	.25	.13	.08
(44)	Fritz Peterson	.25	.13	.08
(45)	Paul Casanova	.25	.13	.08
(46)	Roger Repoz	.25	.13	.08
(47)	Tommy John	.40	.20	.12
(48)	Moe Drabowsky	.25	.13	.08
Sheet A.L. 5		2.50	1.25	.70
(49)	Ed Kirkpatrick	.25	.13	.08
(50)	Dean Chance	.25	.13	.08
(51)	Mike Hershberger	.25	.13	.08
(52)	Jack Aker	.25	.13	.08
(53)	Andy Etchebarren	.25	.13	.08
(54)	Ray Culp	.25	.13	.08
(55)	Luis Tiant	.35	.20	.11
(56)	Willie Horton	.25	.13	.08
(57)	Roy White	.25	.13	.08
(58)	Ken McMullen	.25	.13	.08
(59)	Rick Reichardt	.25	.13	.08
(60)	Luis Aparicio	1.50	.70	.45
Sheet A.L. 6		2.50	1.25	.70
(61)	Ken Berry	.25	.13	.08
(62)	Wally Bunker	.25	.13	.08
(63)	Tony Oliva	.45	.25	.14
(64)	Rick Monday	.25	.13	.08
(65)	Chico Salmon	.25	.13	.08
(66)	Paul Blair	.25	.13	.08
(67)	Jim Lonborg	.25	.13	.08
(68)	Zoilo Versalles	.25	.13	.08
(69)	Denny McLain	.50	.25	.15
(70)	Mel Stottlemyre	.25	.13	.08
(71)	Joe Coleman	.25	.13	.08
(72)	Bob Knoop	.25	.13	.08
Sheet A.L. 7		2.50	1.25	.70
(73)	Chuck Hinton	.25	.13	.08
(74)	Duane Josephson	.25	.13	.08
(75)	Roger Nelson	.25	.13	.08
(76)	Ted Uhlaender	.25	.13	.08
(77)	John Donaldson	.25	.13	.08
(78)	Tommy Davis	.25	.13	.08
(79)	Frank Robinson	1.50	.70	.45
(80)	Dick Ellsworth	.25	.13	.08
(81)	Sam McDowell	.35	.20	.11
(82)	Dick McAuliffe	.25	.13	.08
(83)	Bill Robinson	.25	.13	.08
(84)	Frank Howard	.35	.20	.11
Sheet A.L. 8		5.00	2.50	1.50
(85)	Ed Brinkman	.25	.13	.08
(86)	Vic Davalillo	.25	.13	.08
(87)	Gary Peters	.25	.13	.08
(88)	Joe Foy	.25	.13	.08
(89)	Rod Carew	1.50	.70	.45
(90)	Jim "Catfish" Hunter	1.00	.50	.30
(91)	Gary Bell	.25	.13	.08
(92)	Dave Johnson	.25	.13	.08
(93)	Ken Harrelson	.25	.13	.08
(94)	Tony Horton	.25	.13	.08
(95)	Al Kaline	1.50	.70	.45
(96)	Steve Hamilton	.25	.13	.08
Sheet A.L. 9		2.50	1.25	.70
(97)	Joseph Pepitone	.35	.20	.11
(98)	Ed Stroud	.25	.13	.08
(99)	Jim McGlothlin	.25	.13	.08
(100)	Wilbur Wood	.25	.13	.08
(101)	Paul Schaal	.25	.13	.08
(102)	Cesar Tovar	.25	.13	.08
(103)	Jim Nash	.25	.13	.08
(104)	Don Mincher	.25	.13	.08
(105)	Thomas Phoebus	.25	.13	.08
(106)	Reggie Smith	.30	.15	.09
(107)	Jose Cardenal	.25	.13	.08
(108)	Mickey Stanley	.25	.13	.08
Sheet N.L. 1		5.00	2.50	1.50
(109)	Billy Williams	1.00	.50	.30
(110)	Mack Jones	.25	.13	.08
(111)	Tom Seaver	1.50	.70	.45
(112)	Rich Allen	.75	.40	.25
(113)	Bob Veale	.25	.13	.08
(114)	Curt Flood	.40	.20	.12
(115)	Pat Jarvis	.25	.13	.08
(116)	Jim Merritt	.25	.13	.08
(117)	Joe Morgan	1.00	.50	.30
(118)	Tom Haller	.25	.13	.08
(119)	Larry Stahl	.25	.13	.08
(120)	Willie McCovey	1.25	.60	.40
Sheet N.L. 2		6.25	3.25	2.00
(121)	Ron Hunt	.25	.13	.08
(122)	Ernie Banks	1.50	.70	.45
(123)	Jim Fairey	.25	.13	.08
(124)	Tommy Agee	.25	.13	.08
(125)	Cookie Rojas	.25	.13	.08
(126)	Mateo Alou	.25	.13	.08
(127)	Mike Shannon	.25	.13	.08
(128)	Milt Pappas	.25	.13	.08
(129)	Johnny Bench	1.50	.70	.45
(130)	Larry Dierker	.25	.13	.08
(131)	Willie Davis	.25	.13	.08
(132)	Tony Gonzalez	.25	.13	.08
Sheet N.L. 3		3.75	2.00	1.25
(133)	Dick Selma	.25	.13	.08
(134)	Jim Ray Hart	.25	.13	.08
(135)	Phil Regan	.25	.13	.08
(136)	Manny Mota	.25	.13	.08
(137)	Cleon Jones	.25	.13	.08
(138)	Rick Wise	.25	.13	.08
(139)	Willie Stargell	1.25	.60	.40
(140)	Robert Gibson	1.25	.60	.40
(141)	Rico Carty	.25	.13	.08
(142)	Gary Nolan	.25	.13	.08
(143)	Doug Rader	.25	.13	.08
(144)	Wes Parker	.25	.13	.08
Sheet N.L. 4		2.50	1.25	.70
(145)	Bill Singer	.25	.13	.08
(146)	Bill McCool	.25	.13	.08
(147)	Juan Marichal	1.00	.50	.30
(148)	Randy Hundley	.25	.13	.08
(149)	"Mudcat" Grant	.25	.13	.08
(150)	Ed Kranepool	.25	.13	.08
(151)	Tony Taylor	.25	.13	.08
(152)	Gene Alley	.25	.13	.08
(153)	Dal Maxvill	.25	.13	.08
(154)	Felipe Alou	.30	.15	.09
(155)	Jim Maloney	.25	.13	.08
(156)	Jesus Alou	.25	.13	.08
Sheet N.L. 5		8.00	4.00	2.50
(157)	Curt Blefary	.25	.13	.08
(158)	Ron Fairly	.25	.13	.08
(159)	Dick Kelley	.25	.13	.08

(160) Frank Linzy	.25	.13	.08
(161) Fergie Jenkins	1.00	.50	.30
(162) Maury Wills	.45	.25	.14
(163) Jerry Grote	.25	.13	.08
(164) Chris Short	.25	.13	.08
(165) Jim Bunning	1.00	.50	.30
(166) Nelson Briles	.25	.13	.08
(167) Orlando Cepeda	1.00	.50	.30
(168) Pete Rose	4.00	2.00	1.25
Sheet N.L. 6	3.00	1.50	.90
(169) Tony Cloninger	.25	.13	.08
(170) Jim Wynn	.25	.13	.08
(171) Jim Lefebvre	.25	.13	.08
(172) Ron Davis	.25	.13	.08
(173) Mike McCormick	.25	.13	.08
(174) Ron Santo	.40	.20	.12
(175) Ty Cline	.25	.13	.08
(176) Jerry Koosman	.25	.13	.08
(177) Mike Ryan	.25	.13	.08
(178) Jerry May	.25	.13	.08
(179) Tim McCarver	.30	.15	.09
(180) Phil Niekro	1.00	.50	.30
Sheet N.L. 7	15.00	7.50	4.50
(181) Hank Aaron	2.50	1.25	.70
(182) Tommy Helms	.25	.13	.08
(183) Denis Menke	.25	.13	.08
(184) Don Sutton	1.00	.50	.30
(185) Al Ferrera	.25	.13	.08
(186) Willie Mays	2.50	1.25	.70
(187) Bill Hands	.25	.13	.08
(188) Rusty Staub	.35	.20	.11
(189) Bud Harrelson	.25	.13	.08
(190) Johnny Callison	.25	.13	.08
(191) Roberto Clemente	4.00	2.00	1.25
(192) Julian Javier	.25	.13	.08
Sheet N.L. 8	2.50	1.25	.70
(193) Joe Torre	.65	.35	.20
(194) Bob Aspromonte	.25	.13	.08
(195) Lee May	.25	.13	.08
(196) Don Wilson	.25	.13	.08
(197) Claude Osteen	.25	.13	.08
(198) Ed Spiezio	.25	.13	.08
(199) Hal Lanier	.25	.13	.08
(200) Glenn Beckert	.25	.13	.08
(201) Bob Bailey	.25	.13	.08
(202) Ron Swoboda	.25	.13	.08
(203) John Briggs	.25	.13	.08
(204) Bill Mazeroski	.75	.40	.25
Sheet N.L. 9	3.75	2.00	1.25
(205) Tommie Sisk	.25	.13	.08
(206) Lou Brock	1.25	.60	.40
(207) Felix Millan	.25	.13	.08
(208) Tony Perez	1.00	.50	.30
(209) John Edwards	.25	.13	.08
(210) Len Gabrielson	.25	.13	.08
(211) Ollie Brown	.25	.13	.08
(212) Gaylord Perry	1.00	.50	.30
(213) Don Kessinger	.25	.13	.08
(214) John Bateman	.25	.13	.08
(215) Ed Charles	.25	.13	.08
(216) Woodie Fryman	.25	.13	.08

1969 Major League Baseball Players Ass'n Pins

Issued by the Major League Baseball Players Association in 1969, this unnumbered set consists of 60 pins - 30 players from the N.L. and 30 from the A.L. Each pin measures approximately 7/8" in diameter and features a black-and-white player photo. A.L. players are surrounded by a red border, while N.L. players are framed in blue. The player's name and team appear at the top and bottom. Also along the bottom is a line reading "1969 MLBPA MFG. R.R. Winona, MINN."

	NM	EX	VG
Complete Set (60):	325.00	160.00	98.00
Common Player:	2.50	1.25	.70
(1) Hank Aaron	30.00	15.00	9.00
(2) Richie Allen	6.00	3.00	1.75
(3) Felipe Alou	3.00	1.50	.90
(4) Max Alvis	2.50	1.25	.70
(5) Luis Aparicio	8.00	4.00	2.50
(6) Ernie Banks	16.00	8.00	4.75
(7) Johnny Bench	16.00	8.00	4.75
(8) Lou Brock	8.00	4.00	2.50
(9) George Brunet	2.50	1.25	.70
(10) Johnny Callison	3.00	1.50	.90
(11) Rod Carew	14.00	7.00	4.25
(12) Orlando Cepeda	8.00	4.00	2.50
(13) Dean Chance	2.50	1.25	.70
(14) Roberto Clemente	30.00	15.00	9.00
(15) Willie Davis	3.00	1.50	.90
(16) Don Drysdale	14.00	7.00	4.25
(17) Ron Fairly	3.00	1.50	.90
(18) Curt Flood	5.00	2.50	1.50
(19) Bill Freehan	3.00	1.50	.90
(20) Jim Fregosi	3.00	1.50	.90
(21) Bob Gibson	14.00	7.00	4.25
(22) Ken Harrelson	2.50	1.25	.70
(23) Bud Harrelson	2.50	1.25	.70
(24) Jim Ray Hart	2.50	1.25	.70
(25) Tommy Helms	2.50	1.25	.70
(26) Joe Horlen	2.50	1.25	.70
(27) Willie Horton	3.00	1.50	.90
(28) Frank Howard	3.00	1.50	.90
(29) Tony Horton	3.00	1.50	.90
(30) Al Kaline	16.00	8.00	4.75
(31) Don Kessinger	3.00	1.50	.90
(32) Harmon Killebrew	16.00	8.00	4.75
(33) Jerry Koosman	3.00	1.50	.90
(34) Mickey Lolich	3.00	1.50	.90
(35) Jim Lonborg	3.00	1.50	.90
(36) Jim Maloney	2.50	1.25	.70
(37) Juan Marichal	14.00	7.00	4.25
(38) Willie Mays	30.00	15.00	9.00
(39) Tim McCarver	4.00	2.00	1.25
(40) Willie McCovey	14.00	7.00	4.25
(41) Sam McDowell	3.00	1.50	.90
(42) Denny McLain	4.00	2.00	1.25
(43) Rick Monday	3.00	1.50	.90
(44) Tony Oliva	4.00	2.00	1.25
(45) Joe Pepitone	3.00	1.50	.90
(46) Boog Powell	5.00	2.50	1.50
(47) Rick Reichardt	2.50	1.25	.70
(48) Pete Richert	2.50	1.25	.70
(49) Brooks Robinson	16.00	8.00	4.75
(50) Frank Robinson	16.00	8.00	4.75
(51) Pete Rose	30.00	15.00	9.00
(52) Ron Santo	4.00	2.00	1.25
(53) Mel Stottlemyre	3.00	1.50	.90
(54) Ron Swoboda	2.50	1.25	.70
(55) Luis Tiant	3.00	1.50	.90
(56) Joe Torre	5.00	2.50	1.50
(57) Pete Ward	2.50	1.25	.70
(58) Billy Williams	10.00	5.00	3.00
(59) Jim Wynn	2.50	1.25	.70
(60) Carl Yastrzemski	25.00	12.50	7.50

1970 Major League Baseball Photostamps

For a second year, ballplayer "stamps" were sold in conjunction with team albums. Approximately 1-7/8" x 3", the pieces are printed on glossy paper in full color with a white border and facsimile autograph. Backs, which are not gummed, have gluing instructions and the players name at bottom. The 1970 issue can be differentiated from the 1969 issue in that backs do not carry a notation at bottom about using the "Official" collectors album. The unnumbered stamps are checklisted here alphabetically within team.

	NM	EX	VG
Complete Set (288):	175.00	85.00	50.00
Common Player:	.50	.25	.15
ATLANTA BRAVES			
(1) Hank Aaron	8.00	4.00	2.50
(2) Bob Aspromonte	.50	.25	.15
(3) Rico Carty	.60	.30	.20
(4) Orlando Cepeda	3.00	1.50	.90
(5) Bob Didier	.50	.25	.15
(6) Tony Gonzalez	.50	.25	.15
(7) Pat Jarvis	.50	.25	.15
(8) Felix Millan	.50	.25	.15
(9) Jim Nash	.50	.25	.15
(10) Phil Niekro	2.00	1.00	.60
(11) Milt Pappas	.50	.25	.15
(12) Ron Reed	.50	.25	.15
BALTIMORE ORIOLES			
(1) Mark Belanger	.50	.25	.15
(2) Paul Blair	.50	.25	.15
(3) Don Buford	.50	.25	.15
(4) Mike Cuellar	.60	.30	.20
(5) Andy Etchebarren	.50	.25	.15
(6) Dave Johnson	.60	.30	.20
(7) Dave McNally	.50	.25	.15
(8) Tom Phoebus	.50	.25	.15
(9) Boog Powell	1.00	.50	.30
(10) Brooks Robinson	3.50	1.75	1.00
(11) Frank Robinson	3.50	1.75	1.00
(12) Chico Salmon	.50	.25	.15
BOSTON RED SOX			
(1) Mike Andrews	.50	.25	.15
(2) Ray Culp	.50	.25	.15
(3) Jim Lonborg	.60	.30	.20
(4) Sparky Lyle	.60	.30	.20
(5) Gary Peters	.50	.25	.15
(6) Rico Petrocelli	.60	.30	.20
(7) Vicente Romo	.50	.25	.15
(8) Tom Satriano	.50	.25	.15
(9) George Scott	.50	.25	.15
(10) Sonny Seibert	.50	.25	.15
(11) Reggie Smith	.60	.30	.20
(12) Carl Yastrzemski	3.50	1.75	1.00
CALIFORNIA ANGELS			
(1) Sandy Alomar	.50	.25	.15
(2) Jose Azcue	.50	.25	.15
(3) Tom Egan	.50	.25	.15
(4) Jim Fregosi	.50	.25	.15
(5) Alex Johnson	.50	.25	.15
(6) Jay Johnstone	.50	.25	.15
(7) Rudy May	.50	.25	.15
(8) Andy Messersmith	.50	.25	.15
(9) Rick Reichardt	.50	.25	.15
(10) Roger Repoz	.50	.25	.15
(11) Aurelio Rodriguez	.50	.25	.15
(12) Ken Tatum	.50	.25	.15
CHICAGO CUBS			
(1) Ernie Banks	4.00	2.00	1.25
(2) Glenn Beckert	.50	.25	.15
(3) Johnny Callison	.50	.25	.15
(4) Bill Hands	.50	.25	.15
(5) Randy Hundley	.60	.30	.20
(6) Ken Holtzman	.50	.25	.15
(7) Fergie Jenkins	2.00	1.00	.60
(8) Don Kessinger	.60	.30	.20
(9) Phil Regan	.50	.25	.15
(10) Ron Santo	1.00	.50	.30
(11) Dick Selma	.50	.25	.15
(12) Billy Williams	2.50	1.25	.70
CHICAGO WHITE SOX			
(1) Luis Aparicio	2.50	1.25	.70
(2) Ken Berry	.50	.25	.15
(3) Buddy Bradford	.50	.25	.15
(4) Ron Hansen	.50	.25	.15
(5) Joel Horlen	.50	.25	.15
(6) Tommy John	.75	.40	.25
(7) Duane Josephson	.50	.25	.15
(8) Bobby Knoop	.50	.25	.15
(9) Tom McCraw	.50	.25	.15
(10) Bill Melton	.50	.25	.15
(11) Walt Williams	.50	.25	.15
(12) Wilbur Wood	.50	.25	.15
CINCINNATI REDS			
(1) Johnny Bench	5.00	2.50	1.50
(2) Tony Cloninger	.50	.25	.15
(3) Wayne Granger	.50	.25	.15
(4) Tommy Helms	.50	.25	.15
(5) Jim Maloney	.50	.25	.15
(6) Lee May	.50	.25	.15
(7) Jim McGlothlin	.50	.25	.15
(8) Jim Merritt	.50	.25	.15
(9) Gary Nolan	.50	.25	.15
(10) Tony Perez	2.00	1.00	.60
(11) Pete Rose	8.00	4.00	2.50
(12) Bobby Tolan	.50	.25	.15
CLEVELAND INDIANS			
(1) Max Alvis	.50	.25	.15
(2) Larry Brown	.50	.25	.15
(3) Dean Chance	.60	.30	.20
(4) Dick Ellsworth	.50	.25	.15
(5) Vern Fuller	.50	.25	.15
(6) Ken Harrelson	.50	.25	.15
(7) Chuck Hinton	.50	.25	.15
(8) Tony Horton	.50	.25	.15
(9) Sam McDowell	.60	.30	.20
(10) Vada Pinson	.60	.30	.20
(11) Duke Sims	.50	.25	.15
(12) Ted Uhlaender	.50	.25	.15
DETROIT TIGERS			
(1) Norm Cash	.60	.30	.20
(2) Bill Freehan	.60	.30	.20
(3) Willie Horton	.50	.25	.15
(4) Al Kaline	4.00	2.00	1.25
(5) Mike Kilkenny	.50	.25	.15
(6) Mickey Lolich	.60	.30	.20
(7) Dick McAuliffe	.50	.25	.15
(8) Denny McLain	.75	.40	.25
(9) Jim Northrup	.50	.25	.15
(10) Mickey Stanley	.50	.25	.15
(11) Tom Tresh	.50	.25	.15
(12) Earl Wilson	.50	.25	.15
HOUSTON ASTROS			
(1) Jesus Alou	.50	.25	.15
(2) Tommy Davis	.60	.30	.20
(3) Larry Dierker	.50	.25	.15
(4) Johnny Edwards	.50	.25	.15
(5) Fred Gladding	.50	.25	.15
(6) Denver Lemaster	.50	.25	.15
(7) Denis Menke	.50	.25	.15
(8) Joe Morgan	2.00	1.00	.60
(9) Joe Pepitone	.60	.30	.20
(10) Doug Rader	.50	.25	.15
(11) Don Wilson	.50	.25	.15
(12) Jim Wynn	.60	.30	.20
KANSAS CITY ROYALS			
(1) Jerry Adair	.50	.25	.15
(2) Wally Bunker	.50	.25	.15
(3) Bill Butler	.50	.25	.15
(4) Moe Drabowsky	.50	.25	.15
(5) Jackie Hernandez	.50	.25	.15

(6)	Pat Kelly	.50	.25	.15
(7)	Ed Kirkpatrick	.50	.25	.15
(8)	Dave Morehead	.50	.25	.15
(9)	Roger Nelson	.50	.25	.15
(10)	Bob Oliver	.50	.25	.15
(11)	Lou Piniella	.60	.30	.20
(12)	Paul Schaal	.50	.25	.15
	LOS ANGELES DODGERS			
(1)	Willie Davis	.60	.30	.20
(2)	Len Gabrielson	.50	.25	.15
(3)	Tom Haller	.50	.25	.15
(4)	Jim Lefebvre	.50	.25	.15
(5)	Manny Mota	.60	.30	.20
(6)	Claude Osteen	.50	.25	.15
(7)	Wes Parker	.50	.25	.15
(8)	Bill Russell	.60	.30	.20
(9)	Bill Singer	.50	.25	.15
(10)	Ted Sizemore	.50	.25	.15
(11)	Don Sutton	2.50	1.25	.70
(12)	Maury Wills	.75	.40	.25
	MINNESOTA TWINS			
(1)	Bob Allison	.50	.25	.15
(2)	Dave Boswell	.50	.25	.15
(3)	Leo Cardenas	.50	.25	.15
(4)	Rod Carew	3.00	1.50	.90
(5)	Jim Kaat	1.00	.50	.30
(6)	Harmon Killebrew	3.00	1.50	.90
(7)	Tony Oliva	1.00	.50	.30
(8)	Jim Perry	.60	.30	.20
(9)	Ron Perranoski	.50	.25	.15
(10)	Rich Reese	.50	.25	.15
(11)	Luis Tiant	.60	.30	.20
(12)	Cesar Tovar	.50	.25	.15
	MONTREAL EXPOS			
(1)	John Bateman	.50	.25	.15
(2)	Bob Bailey	.50	.25	.15
(3)	Ron Brand	.50	.25	.15
(4)	Ty Cline	.50	.25	.15
(5)	Ron Fairly	.50	.25	.15
(6)	Mack Jones	.50	.25	.15
(7)	Jose Laboy	.50	.25	.15
(8)	Claude Raymond	.50	.25	.15
(9)	Joe Sparma	.50	.25	.15
(10)	Rusty Staub	.75	.40	.25
(11)	Bill Stoneman	.50	.25	.15
(12)	Bobby Wine	.50	.25	.15
	NEW YORK METS			
(1)	Tommie Agee	.60	.30	.20
(2)	Donn Clendenon	.60	.30	.20
(3)	Joe Foy	.50	.25	.15
(4)	Jerry Grote	.50	.25	.15
(5)	Bud Harrelson	.60	.30	.20
(6)	Cleon Jones	.60	.30	.20
(7)	Jerry Koosman	.60	.30	.20
(8)	Ed Kranepool	.60	.30	.20
(9)	Nolan Ryan	21.00	10.50	6.25
(10)	Tom Seaver	3.50	1.75	1.00
(11)	Ron Swoboda	.50	.25	.15
(12)	Al Weis	.50	.25	.15
	NEW YORK YANKEES			
(1)	Jack Aker	.50	.25	.15
(2)	Curt Blefary	.50	.25	.15
(3)	Danny Cater	.50	.25	.15
(4)	Horace Clarke	.50	.25	.15
(5)	Jake Gibbs	.50	.25	.15
(6)	Steve Hamilton	.50	.25	.15
(7)	Bobby Murcer	.60	.30	.20
(8)	Fritz Peterson	.50	.25	.15
(9)	Bill Robinson	.50	.25	.15
(10)	Mel Stottlemyre	.60	.30	.20
(11)	Pete Ward	.50	.25	.15
(12)	Roy White	.60	.30	.20
	OAKLAND A's			
(1)	Felipe Alou	.60	.30	.20
(2)	Sal Bando	.50	.25	.15
(3)	Bert Campaneris	.75	.40	.25
(4)	Chuck Dobson	.50	.25	.15
(5)	Tito Francona	.50	.25	.15
(6)	Dick Green	.50	.25	.15
(7)	Catfish Hunter	2.00	1.00	.60
(8)	Reggie Jackson	7.50	3.75	2.25
(9)	Don Mincher	.50	.25	.15
(10)	Rick Monday	.60	.30	.20
(11)	John Odom	.60	.30	.20
(12)	Ray Oyler	.50	.25	.15
	PHILADELPHIA PHILLIES			
(1)	Johnny Briggs	.50	.25	.15
(2)	Jim Bunning	2.00	1.00	.60
(3)	Curt Flood	.75	.40	.25
(4)	Woodie Fryman	.50	.25	.15
(5)	Larry Hisle	.50	.25	.15
(6)	Joe Hoerner	.50	.25	.15
(7)	Grant Jackson	.50	.25	.15
(8)	Tim McCarver	.75	.40	.25
(9)	Mike Ryan	.50	.25	.15
(10)	Chris Short	.50	.25	.15
(11)	Tony Taylor	.50	.25	.15
(12)	Rick Wise	.50	.25	.15
	PITTSBURGH PIRATES			
(1)	(Gene Alley)	.50	.25	.15
(2)	Matty Alou	.50	.25	.15
(3)	Roberto Clemente	21.00	10.50	6.25
(4)	Ron Davis	.50	.25	.15
(5)	Richie Hebner	.50	.25	.15
(6)	Jerry May	.50	.25	.15
(7)	Bill Mazeroski	2.50	1.25	.70
(8)	Bob Moose	.50	.25	.15
(9)	Al Oliver	.75	.40	.25
(10)	Manny Sanguillen	.50	.25	.15
(11)	Willie Stargell	2.50	1.25	.70
(12)	Bob Veale	.50	.25	.15
	SAN DIEGO PADRES			
(1)	Ollie Brown	.50	.25	.15
(2)	Dave Campbell	.50	.25	.15
(3)	Nate Colbert	.50	.25	.15
(4)	Pat Dobson	.50	.25	.15
(5)	Al Ferrera	.50	.25	.15
(6)	Dick Kelley	.50	.25	.15
(7)	Clay Kirby	.50	.25	.15
(8)	Bill McCool	.50	.25	.15
(9)	Frank Reberger	.50	.25	.15
(10)	Tommie Sisk	.50	.25	.15
(11)	Ed Spiezio	.50	.25	.15
(12)	Larry Stahl	.50	.25	.15
	SAN FRANCISCO GIANTS			
(1)	Bobby Bonds	.60	.30	.20
(2)	Jim Davenport	.50	.25	.15
(3)	Dick Dietz	.50	.25	.15
(4)	Jim Ray Hart	.50	.25	.15
(5)	Ron Hunt	.50	.25	.15
(6)	Hal Lanier	.50	.25	.15
(7)	Frank Linzy	.50	.25	.15
(8)	Juan Marichal	2.50	1.25	.70
(9)	Willie Mays	8.00	4.00	2.50
(10)	Mike McCormick	.50	.25	.15
(11)	Willie McCovey	3.50	1.75	1.00
(12)	Gaylord Perry	2.00	1.00	.60
	SEATTLE PILOTS			
(1)	Steve Barber	.50	.25	.15
(2)	Bobby Bolin	.50	.25	.15
(3)	George Brunet	.50	.25	.15
(4)	Wayne Comer	.50	.25	.15
(5)	John Donaldson	.50	.25	.15
(6)	Tommy Harper	.70	.35	.20
(7)	Mike Hegan	.60	.30	.20
(8)	Mike Hershberger	.50	.25	.15
(9)	Steve Hovley	.50	.25	.15
(10)	Bob Locker	.50	.25	.15
(11)	Gerry McNertney	.50	.25	.15
(12)	Rich Rollins	.50	.25	.15
	ST. LOUIS CARDINALS			
(1)	Richie Allen	1.50	.70	.45
(2)	Nelson Briles	.50	.25	.15
(3)	Lou Brock	3.00	1.50	.90
(4)	Jose Cardenal	.50	.25	.15
(5)	Steve Carlton	3.50	1.75	1.00
(6)	Vic Davalillo	.50	.25	.15
(7)	Bob Gibson	3.00	1.50	.90
(8)	Julian Javier	.50	.25	.15
(9)	Dal Maxvill	.50	.25	.15
(10)	Cookie Rojas	.50	.25	.15
(11)	Mike Shannon	.50	.25	.15
(12)	Joe Torre	2.00	1.00	.60
	WASHINGTON SENATORS			
(1)	Bernie Allen	.50	.25	.15
(2)	Dick Bosman	.50	.25	.15
(3)	Ed Brinkman	.50	.25	.15
(4)	Paul Casanova	.50	.25	.15
(5)	Joe Coleman	.50	.25	.15
(6)	Mike Epstein	.75	.40	.25
(7)	Frank Howard	.60	.30	.20
(8)	Ken McMullen	.50	.25	.15
(9)	John Roseboro	.50	.25	.15
(10)	Ed Stroud	.50	.25	.15
(11)	Del Unser	.50	.25	.15
(12)	Zoilo Versalles	.50	.25	.15

1961 Manny's Baseball Land 8x10s

In 1961, Manny's Baseball Land issued 18 10-piece 8" x 10" printed black-and-white photo packs, arranged by team. Manny's was a next-door neighbor of Yankee Stadium and the nation's largest purveyor of baseball souvenirs. These photo sets were sold for $1.50 per team. The blank-back photos were printed on semi-gloss paper. Portraits or posed action photos were surrounded by a white border which contains the player's name in all caps at bottom. The unnumbered pictures are checklisted here alphabetically by and within team.

		NM	EX	VG
	Complete Set (180):	600.00	300.00	175.00
	Common Player:	3.00	1.50	.90
	BALTIMORE ORIOLES			
(1)	Jackie Brandt	3.00	1.50	.90
(2)	Marv Breeding	3.00	1.50	.90
(3)	Chuck Estrada	3.00	1.50	.90
(4)	Jack Fisher	3.00	1.50	.90
(5)	Jim Gentile	3.00	1.50	.90
(6)	Ron Hansen	3.00	1.50	.90
(7)	Milt Pappas	3.00	1.50	.90
(8)	Brooks Robinson	10.00	5.00	3.00
(9)	Gus Triandos	3.00	1.50	.90
(10)	Jerry Walker	3.00	1.50	.90
	BOSTON RED SOX			
(11)	Tom Brewer	3.00	1.50	.90
(12)	Don Buddin	3.00	1.50	.90
(13)	Gene Conley	3.00	1.50	.90
(14)	Mike Fornieles	3.00	1.50	.90
(15)	Gary Geiger	3.00	1.50	.90
(16)	Pumpsie Green	3.00	1.50	.90
(17)	Jackie Jensen	5.00	2.50	1.50
(18)	Frank Malzone	3.00	1.50	.90
(19)	Pete Runnels	3.00	1.50	.90
(20)	Vic Wertz	3.00	1.50	.90
	CHICAGO CUBS			
(21)	George Altman	3.00	1.50	.90
(22)	Bob Anderson	3.00	1.50	.90
(23)	Richie Ashburn	10.00	5.00	3.00
(24)	Ernie Banks	10.00	5.00	3.00
(25)	Don Cardwell	3.00	1.50	.90
(26)	Moe Drabowsky	3.00	1.50	.90
(27)	Don Elston	3.00	1.50	.90
(28)	Jerry Kindall	3.00	1.50	.90
(29)	Ron Santo	5.00	2.50	1.50
(30)	Bob Will	3.00	1.50	.90
	CHICAGO WHITE SOX			
(31)	Luis Aparicio	9.00	4.50	2.75
(32)	Frank Baumann	3.00	1.50	.90
(33)	Sam Esposito	3.00	1.50	.90
(34)	Nellie Fox	9.00	4.50	2.75
(35)	Jim Landis	3.00	1.50	.90
(36)	Sherman Lollar	3.00	1.50	.90
(37)	Minnie Minoso	6.00	3.00	1.75
(38)	Billy Pierce	4.00	2.00	1.25
(39)	Bob Shaw	3.00	1.50	.90
(40)	Early Wynn	9.00	4.50	2.75
	CINCINNATI REDLEGS			
(41)	Ed Bailey	3.00	1.50	.90
(42)	Gus Bell	3.00	1.50	.90
(43)	Gordon Coleman	3.00	1.50	.90
(44)	Bill Henry	3.00	1.50	.90
(45)	Jerry Lynch	3.00	1.50	.90
(46)	Claude Osteen	3.00	1.50	.90
(47)	Vada Pinson	4.00	2.00	1.25
(48)	Wally Post	3.00	1.50	.90
(49)	Bob Purkey	3.00	1.50	.90
(50)	Frank Robinson	10.00	5.00	3.00
	CLEVELAND INDIANS			
(51)	Mike de la Hoz	3.00	1.50	.90
(52)	Tito Francona	3.00	1.50	.90
(53)	Woody Held	3.00	1.50	.90
(54)	Barry Latman	3.00	1.50	.90
(55)	Jim Perry	4.00	2.00	1.25
(56)	Bubba Phillips	3.00	1.50	.90
(57)	Jim Piersall	4.00	2.00	1.25
(58)	Vic Power	3.00	1.50	.90
(59)	John Romano	3.00	1.50	.90
(60)	Johnny Temple	3.00	1.50	.90
	DETROIT TIGERS			
(61)	Hank Aguirre	3.00	1.50	.90
(62)	Billy Bruton	3.00	1.50	.90
(63)	Jim Bunning	8.00	4.00	2.50
(64)	Norm Cash	7.50	3.75	2.25
(65)	Rocky Colavito	8.00	4.00	2.50
(66)	Chico Fernandez	3.00	1.50	.90
(67)	Paul Foytack	3.00	1.50	.90
(68)	Al Kaline	10.00	5.00	3.00
(69)	Frank Lary	3.00	1.50	.90
(70)	Don Mossi	3.00	1.50	.90
	KANSAS CITY ATHLETICS			
(71)	Hank Bauer	4.00	2.00	1.25
(72)	Andy Carey	3.00	1.50	.90
(73)	Leo "Bud" Daley	3.00	1.50	.90
(74)	Ray Herbert	3.00	1.50	.90
(75)	John Kucks	3.00	1.50	.90
(76)	Jerry Lumpe	3.00	1.50	.90
(77)	Norm Siebern	3.00	1.50	.90
(78)	Haywood Sullivan	3.00	1.50	.90
(79)	Marv Throneberry	4.00	2.00	1.25
(80)	Dick Williams	3.00	1.50	.90
	LOS ANGELES ANGELS			
(81)	Ken Aspromonte	3.00	1.50	.90
(82)	Steve Bilko	3.00	1.50	.90
(83)	Bob Cerv	3.00	1.50	.90
(84)	Ned Garver	3.00	1.50	.90
(85)	Ken Hunt	3.00	1.50	.90
(86)	Ted Kluszewski	7.50	3.75	2.25
(87)	Jim McAnany	3.00	1.50	.90
(88)	Duke Maas	3.00	1.50	.90
(89)	Albie Pearson	3.00	1.50	.90
(90)	Eddie Yost	3.00	1.50	.90
	LOS ANGELES DODGERS			
(91)	Don Drysdale	10.00	5.00	3.00
(92)	Jim Gilliam	4.00	2.00	1.25
(93)	Frank Howard	4.00	2.00	1.25
(94)	Sandy Koufax	15.00	7.50	4.50
(95)	Norm Larker	3.00	1.50	.90
(96)	Wally Moon	4.00	2.00	1.25
(97)	Charles Neal	3.00	1.50	.90
(98)	Johnny Podres	4.00	2.00	1.25
(99)	Larry Sherry	3.00	1.50	.90
(100)	Maury Wills	4.00	2.00	1.25
	MILWAUKEE BRAVES			
(101)	Hank Aaron	15.00	7.50	4.50
(102)	Joe Adcock	3.00	1.50	.90
(103)	Frank Bolling	3.00	1.50	.90
(104)	Bob Buhl	3.00	1.50	.90
(105)	Lew Burdette	3.00	1.50	.90
(106)	Del Crandall	3.00	1.50	.90
(107)	Ed Mathews	10.00	5.00	3.00
(108)	Roy McMillan	3.00	1.50	.90
(109)	Warren Spahn	10.00	5.00	3.00
(110)	Al Spangler	3.00	1.50	.90
	MINNESOTA TWINS			
(111)	Bob Allison	3.00	1.50	.90
(112)	Earl Battey	3.00	1.50	.90
(113)	Reno Bertola (Bertoia)	3.00	1.50	.90
(114)	Billy Consolo	3.00	1.50	.90
(115)	Billy Gardner	3.00	1.50	.90
(116)	Harmon Killebrew	10.00	5.00	3.00
(117)	Jim Lemon	3.00	1.50	.90
(118)	Camilo Pascual	3.00	1.50	.90
(119)	Pedro Ramos	3.00	1.50	.90

		NM	EX	VG
(120)	Chuck Stobbs	3.00	1.50	.90
	NEW YORK YANKEES			
(121)	Larry "Yogi" Berra	10.00	5.00	3.00
(122)	John Blanchard	3.00	1.50	.90
(123)	Ed "Whitey" Ford	10.00	5.00	3.00
(124)	Elston Howard	4.00	2.00	1.25
(125)	Tony Kubek	4.00	2.00	1.25
(126)	Mickey Mantle	20.00	10.00	6.00
(127)	Roger Maris	12.50	6.25	3.75
(128)	Bobby Richardson	4.00	2.00	1.25
(129)	Bill Skowron	4.00	2.00	1.25
(130)	Bob Turley	3.00	1.50	.90
	PHILADELPHIA PHILLIES			
(131)	John Callison	3.00	1.50	.90
(132)	Dick Farrell	3.00	1.50	.90
(133)	Pancho Herrera	3.00	1.50	.90
(134)	Joe Koppe	3.00	1.50	.90
(135)	Art Mahaffey	3.00	1.50	.90
(136)	Gene Mauch	3.00	1.50	.90
(137)	Jim Owens	3.00	1.50	.90
(138)	Robin Roberts	10.00	5.00	3.00
(139)	Frank Sullivan	3.00	1.50	.90
(140)	Tony Taylor	3.00	1.50	.90
	PITTSBURGH PIRATES			
(141)	Roberto Clemente	17.50	8.75	5.25
(142)	Roy Face	3.00	1.50	.90
(143)	Bob Friend	3.00	1.50	.90
(144)	Dick Groat	3.00	1.50	.90
(145)	Harvey Haddix	3.00	1.50	.90
(146)	Don Hoak	3.00	1.50	.90
(147)	Vern Law	3.00	1.50	.90
(148)	Bill Mazeroski	8.00	4.00	2.50
(149)	Wilmer Mizell	3.00	1.50	.90
(150)	Bill Virdon	3.00	1.50	.90
	SAN FRANCISCO GIANTS			
(151)	Felipe Alou	4.00	2.00	1.25
(152)	Orlando Cepeda	9.00	4.50	2.75
(153)	Sam Jones	3.00	1.50	.90
(154)	Harvey Kuenn	4.00	2.00	1.25
(155)	Willie Mays	15.00	7.50	4.50
(156)	Mike McCormick	3.00	1.50	.90
(157)	Willie McCovey	9.00	4.50	2.75
(158)	Stu Miller	3.00	1.50	.90
(159)	Billy O'Dell	3.00	1.50	.90
(160)	Jack Sanford	3.00	1.50	.90
	ST. LOUIS CARDINALS			
(161)	Ernie Broglio	3.00	1.50	.90
(162)	Ken Boyer	4.00	2.00	1.25
(163)	Joe Cunningham	3.00	1.50	.90
(164)	Alex Grammas	3.00	1.50	.90
(165)	Larry Jackson	3.00	1.50	.90
(166)	Julian Javier	3.00	1.50	.90
(167)	Lindy McDaniel	3.00	1.50	.90
(168)	Stan Musial	12.50	6.25	3.75
(169)	Hal Smith	3.00	1.50	.90
(170)	Daryl Spencer	3.00	1.50	.90
	WASHINGTON SENATORS			
(171)	Pete Daley	3.00	1.50	.90
(172)	Dick Donovan	3.00	1.50	.90
(173)	Bob Johnson	3.00	1.50	.90
(174)	Marty Keough	3.00	1.50	.90
(175)	Billy Klaus	3.00	1.50	.90
(176)	Dale Long	3.00	1.50	.90
(177)	Carl Mathias	3.00	1.50	.90
(178)	Willie Tasby	3.00	1.50	.90
(179)	Mickey Vernon	3.00	1.50	.90
(180)	Gene Woodling	4.00	2.00	1.25

1923 Maple Crispette

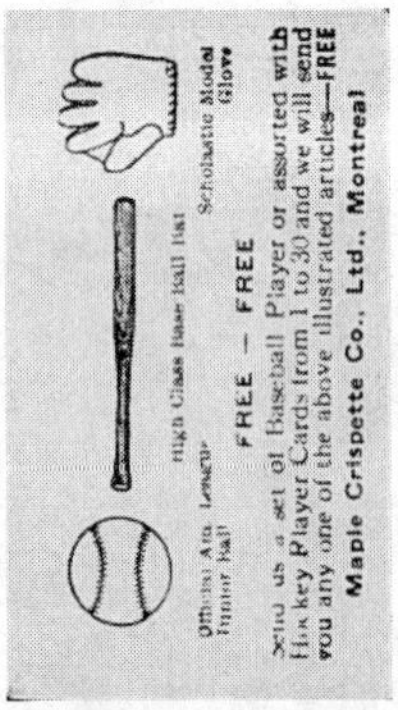

Issued by a Montreal candy company, these small (1-3/8" x 2-1/4") black-and-white cards were redeemable for baseball equipment, accounting for their scarcity today. Card #15, Stengel, was only discovered in 1992 and was obviously short-printed by the issuer to avoid giving away many bats, balls and gloves. Only a single specimen of the Stengel card is currently known; it is not included in the complete set prices.

		NM	EX	VG
Complete Set, no Stengel (29):		9375.	3750.	2350.
Common Player:		130.00	50.00	30.00
1	Jesse Barnes	130.00	50.00	30.00
2	Harold Traynor	350.00	140.00	85.00
3	Ray Schalk	350.00	140.00	85.00
4	Eddie Collins	350.00	140.00	85.00
5	Lee Fohl	130.00	50.00	30.00
6	Howard Summa	130.00	50.00	30.00
7	Waite Hoyt	350.00	140.00	85.00
8	Babe Ruth	2625.	1050.	650.00
9	Cozy Dolan	130.00	50.00	30.00
10	Johnny Bassler	130.00	50.00	30.00
11	George Dauss	130.00	50.00	30.00
12	Joe Sewell	350.00	140.00	85.00
13	Syl Johnson	130.00	50.00	30.00
14a	Wingo	130.00	50.00	30.00
14b	Ivy Wingo	130.00	50.00	30.00
15	Casey Stengel	12000.	4800.	3000.
16	Arnold Statz	130.00	50.00	30.00
17	Emil Meusel	130.00	50.00	30.00
18	Bill Jacobson	130.00	50.00	30.00
19	Jim Bottomley	350.00	140.00	85.00
20	Sam Bohne	130.00	50.00	30.00
21	Bucky Harris	350.00	140.00	85.00
22	Ty Cobb	1800.	725.00	450.00
23	Roger Peckinpaugh	130.00	50.00	30.00
24	Muddy Ruel	130.00	50.00	30.00
25	Bill McKechnie	350.00	140.00	85.00
26	Riggs Stephenson	130.00	50.00	30.00
27	Herb Pennock	350.00	140.00	85.00
28	Edd Roush	350.00	140.00	85.00
29	Bill Wambsganss	130.00	50.00	30.00
30	Walter Johnson	1125.	450.00	280.00

1955 Mascot Dog Food

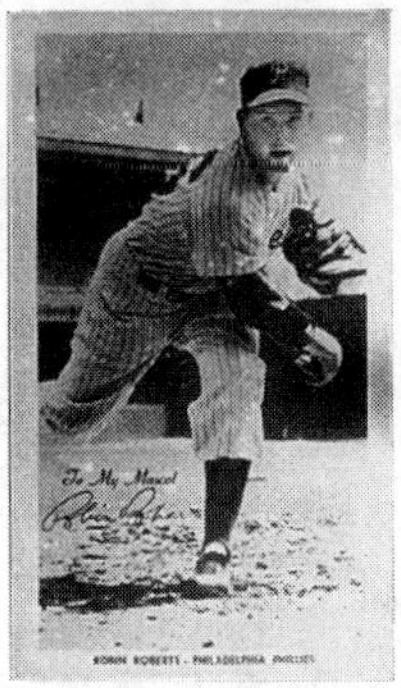

The date of issue shown is approximate. It is likely other players' cards exist, since the back mentions eight stars printed on the label, presumably of the dog food can. In black-and-white, the 3-1/2" x 5-1/2" card has on front a glossy action pose with a facsimile autograph personalized, "To My Mascot" and the player name and position printed in black in the bottom border. The back has an ad for a fan club offering an autographed 8x10, membership card and pin and set of eight postcards for a quarter and a label.

		NM	EX	VG
(1)	Robin Roberts	150.00	75.00	45.00

1971 Mattel Instant Replay Records

These 2-3/8" diameter plastic records were produced in conjunction with a hand-held, battery-operated record player. Paper inserts featured illustrations of players in baseball, football and basketball, as well as various racing vehicles and airplanes. The audio recounts career highlights of the depicted player. Additional records were sold in sets of four.

		NM	EX	VG
Complete Set (11):		200.00	100.00	60.00
Common Player:		10.00	5.00	3.00
(1)	Hank Aaron	25.00	12.50	7.50
(2)	Ernie Banks	20.00	10.00	6.00
(3)	Al Kaline	20.00	10.00	6.00
(4)	Sandy Koufax	30.00	15.00	9.00
(5)	Roger Maris	40.00	20.00	12.00
(6)	Willie Mays (plays one side only; came with record player purchase)	25.00	12.50	7.50
(7)	Willie McCovey	20.00	10.00	6.00
(8)	Tony Oliva	10.00	5.00	3.00
(9)	Frank Robinson	20.00	10.00	6.00
(10)	Tom Seaver	25.00	12.50	7.50
(11)	Willie Stargell	20.00	10.00	6.00

1895 Mayo's Cut Plug (N300)

These 1-5/8" x 2-7/8" cards were issued by the Mayo Tobacco Works of Richmond, Va. There are 48 cards in the set, with 40 different players pictured. Twenty-eight of the players are pictured in uniform and 12 are shown in street clothes. Eight players appear both ways. Eight of the uniformed players also appear in two variations, creating the 48-card total. Card fronts are black-and-white or sepia portraits on black cardboard, with a Mayo's Cut Plug ad at the bottom of each card. Cards are blank-backed and unnumbered.

		NM	EX	VG
Complete Set (48):		58500.	29250.	17550.
Common Player:		825.00	410.00	245.00
(1)	Charlie Abbey	825.00	410.00	245.00
(2)	Cap Anson	3000.	1500.	900.00
(3)	Jimmy Bannon	825.00	410.00	245.00
(4a)	Dan Brouthers (Baltimore on shirt)	2100.	1050.	630.00
(4b)	Dan Brouthers (Louisville on shirt)	2400.	1200.	720.00
(5)	Ed Cartwright	825.00	410.00	245.00
(6)	John Clarkson	2100.	1050.	630.00
(7)	Tommy Corcoran	825.00	410.00	245.00
(8)	Lave Cross	825.00	410.00	245.00
(9)	Bill Dahlen	825.00	410.00	245.00
(10)	Tom Daly	825.00	410.00	245.00
(11)	Ed Delehanty (Delahanty)	2400.	1200.	720.00
(12)	Hugh Duffy	2100.	1050.	630.00
(13a)	Buck Ewing (Cleveland on shirt)	2100.	1050.	630.00
(13b)	Buck Ewing (Cincinnati on shirt)	2400.	1200.	720.00
(14)	Dave Foutz	825.00	410.00	245.00
(15)	Charlie Ganzel	825.00	410.00	245.00
(16a)	Jack Glasscock (Pittsburg on shirt)	825.00	410.00	245.00
(16b)	Jack Glasscock (Louisville on shirt)	900.00	450.00	270.00
(17)	Mike Griffin	825.00	410.00	245.00
(18a)	George Haddock (no team on shirt)	900.00	450.00	270.00
(18b)	George Haddock (Philadelphia on shirt)	825.00	410.00	245.00
(19)	Bill Hallman	825.00	410.00	245.00
(20)	Billy Hamilton	2100.	1050.	630.00
(21)	Bill Joyce	825.00	410.00	245.00
(22)	Brickyard Kennedy	825.00	410.00	245.00
(23a)	Tom Kinslow (no team on shirt)	900.00	450.00	270.00
(23b)	Tom Kinslow (Pittsburg on shirt)	825.00	410.00	245.00
(24)	Arlie Latham	825.00	410.00	245.00
(25)	Herman Long	825.00	410.00	245.00
(26)	Tom Lovett	825.00	410.00	245.00
(27)	Bobby Lowe	825.00	410.00	245.00
(28)	Tommy McCarthy	1350.	675.00	405.00
(29)	Yale Murphy	825.00	410.00	245.00
(30)	Billy Nash	825.00	410.00	245.00
(31)	Kid Nichols	2400.	1200.	720.00
(32a)	Fred Pfeffer (2nd Base)	825.00	410.00	245.00
(32b)	Fred Pfeffer (Retired)	900.00	450.00	270.00
(33)	Wilbert Robinson	1875.	935.00	560.00
(34a)	Amos Russie (incorrect spelling)	1875.	935.00	560.00
(34b)	Amos Rusie (correct)	1650.	825.00	495.00
(35)	Jimmy Ryan	825.00	410.00	245.00
(36)	Bill Shindle	825.00	410.00	245.00
(37)	Germany Smith	825.00	410.00	245.00
(38)	Otis Stocksdale (Stockdale)	825.00	410.00	245.00
(39)	Tommy Tucker	825.00	410.00	245.00
(40a)	Monte Ward (2nd Base)	1875.	935.00	560.00
(40b)	Monte Ward (Retired)	2400.	1200.	720.00

1896 Mayo's Die-Cut Game Cards (N301)

Mayo Tobacco Works of Richmond, Va., issued an innovative, if not very popular, series of die-cut baseball player figures in 1896. These tiny (1-1/2" long by just 3/16" wide) cardboard figures were inserted in packages of Mayo's Cut Plug Tobacco and were designed to be used as part of a baseball board game. A "grandstand, base and teetotum" were available free by mail to complete the game pieces. Twenty-eight different die-cut figures were available, representing 26 unspecified New York and Boston players along with two umpires. The players are shown in various action poses - either running, batting, pitching or fielding. The backs carry an ad for Mayo's Tobacco. The players shown do not relate to any actual members of the New York or Boston clubs, diminishing the popularity of this issue, which has an American Card Catalog designation of N301.

		NM	EX	VG
Complete Set (28):		1400.	490.00	275.00
Common Player:		50.00	17.50	10.00
(1a)	Pitcher (Boston)	50.00	17.50	10.00
(1b)	Pitcher (New York)	50.00	17.50	10.00
(2a)	1st Baseman (Boston)	50.00	17.50	10.00
(2b)	1st Baseman (New York)	50.00	17.50	10.00
(3a)	2nd Baseman (Boston)	50.00	17.50	10.00
(3b)	2nd Baseman (New York)	50.00	17.50	10.00
(4a)	3rd Baseman (Boston)	50.00	17.50	10.00
(4b)	3rd Baseman (New York)	50.00	17.50	10.00
(5a)	Right Fielder (Boston)	50.00	17.50	10.00
(5b)	Right Fielder (New York)	50.00	17.50	10.00
(6a)	Center Fielder (Boston)	50.00	17.50	10.00
(6b)	Center Fielder (New York)	50.00	17.50	10.00
(7a)	Left Fielder (Boston)	50.00	17.50	10.00
(7b)	Left Fielder (New York)	50.00	17.50	10.00
(8a)	Short Stop (Boston)	50.00	17.50	10.00
(8b)	Short Stop (New York)	50.00	17.50	10.00
(9a)	Catcher (Boston)	50.00	17.50	10.00
(9b)	Catcher (New York)	50.00	17.50	10.00
(10a)	Batman (Boston)	50.00	17.50	10.00
(10b)	Batman (New York)	50.00	17.50	10.00
(11a)	Runner (Boston, standing upright)	50.00	17.50	10.00
(11b)	Runner (New York, standing upright)	50.00	17.50	10.00
(12a)	Runner (Boston, bent slightly forward)	50.00	17.50	10.00
(12b)	Runner (New York, bent slightly forward)	50.00	17.50	10.00
(13a)	Runner (Boston, bent well forward)	50.00	17.50	10.00
(13b)	Runner (New York, bent well forward)	50.00	17.50	10.00
(14)	Umpire (facing front)	50.00	17.50	10.00
(15)	Field Umpire (rear view)	50.00	17.50	10.00

1900 Mayo's Baseball Comics (T203)

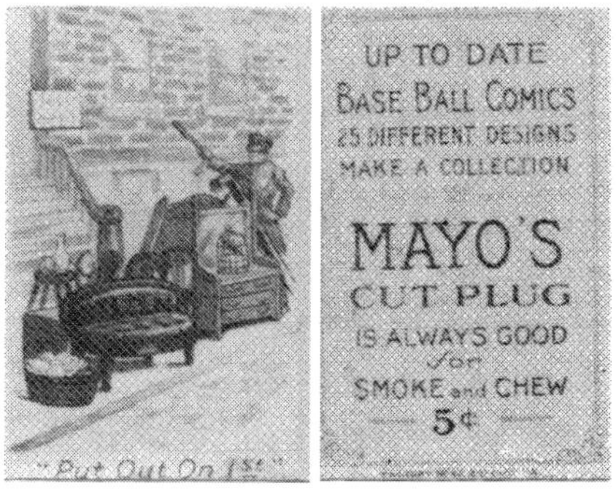

As their name implies, the T203 Baseball Comics feature cartoon-like drawings that illustrate various baseball phrases and terminology. Issued with Winner Cut Plug and Mayo Cut Plug tobacco products, the complete set consists of 25 different comics, each measuring approximately 2-1/16" x 3-1/8". Because they do not picture individual players, these cards have never attracted much of a following among serious baseball card collectors. They do, however, hold some interest as a novelty item of the period.

		NM	EX	VG
Complete Set (25):		850.00	300.00	175.00
Common Player:		35.00	12.50	7.50
(1)	"A Crack Outfielder"	35.00	12.50	7.50
(2)	"A Fancy Twirler"	35.00	12.50	7.50
(3)	"A Fine Slide"	35.00	12.50	7.50
(4)	"A Fowl Bawl"	35.00	12.50	7.50
(5)	"A Great Game"	35.00	12.50	7.50
(6)	"A Home Run"	35.00	12.50	7.50
(7)	"An All Star Battery"	35.00	12.50	7.50
(8)	"A Short Stop"	35.00	12.50	7.50
(9)	"A Star Catcher"	35.00	12.50	7.50
(10)	"A White Wash"	35.00	12.50	7.50
(11)	"A Tie Game"	35.00	12.50	7.50
(12)	"A Two Bagger"	35.00	12.50	7.50
(13)	"A Wild Pitch"	35.00	12.50	7.50
(14)	"Caught Napping"	35.00	12.50	7.50
(15)	"On To The Curves"	35.00	12.50	7.50
(16)	"Out"	35.00	12.50	7.50
(17)	"Put Out On 1st"	35.00	12.50	7.50
(18)	"Right Over The Plate"	35.00	12.50	7.50
(19)	"Rooting For The Home Team"	35.00	12.50	7.50
(20)	"Stealing A Base"	35.00	12.50	7.50
(21)	"Stealing Home"	35.00	12.50	7.50
(22)	"Strike One"	35.00	12.50	7.50
(23)	"The Bleacher"	35.00	12.50	7.50
(24)	"The Naps"	35.00	12.50	7.50
(25)	"The Red Sox"	35.00	12.50	7.50

1970 McDonald's Brewers

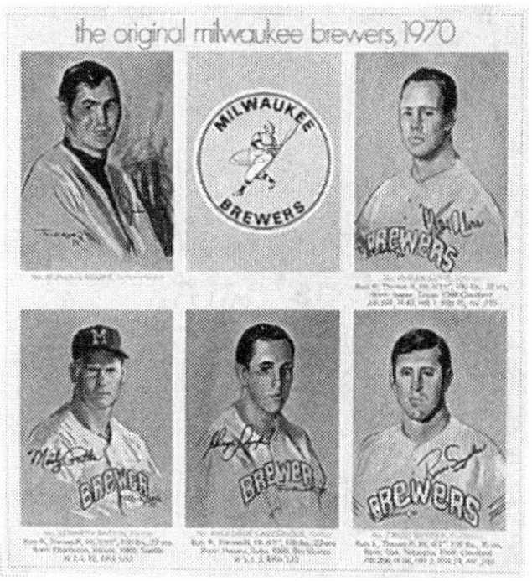

McDonald's welcomed the Brewers to Milwaukee in 1970 by issuing a set of six baseball card panels. Five of the panels picture five players and a team logo, while the sixth panel contains six players, resulting in 31 different players. The panels measure 9" x 9-1/2" and feature full-color paintings of the players. Each sheet displays the heading, "the original milwaukee brewers, 1970". The cards are numbered by uniform number and the backs are blank. Although distributed by McDonald's, their name does not appear on the cards.

		NM	EX	VG
Complete Sheet Set (6):		12.00	6.00	3.50
Complete Singles Set (32):		8.00	4.00	2.50
Common Player:		.25	.13	.08
1	Ted Kubiak	.25	.13	.08
2	Ted Savage	.25	.13	.08
4	Dave Bristol	.25	.13	.08
5	Phil Roof	.25	.13	.08
6	Mike Hershberger	.25	.13	.08
7	Russ Snyder	.25	.13	.08
8	Mike Hegan	.25	.13	.08
9	Rich Rollins	.25	.13	.08
10	Max Alvis	.25	.13	.08
11	John Kennedy	.25	.13	.08
12	Dan Walton	.25	.13	.08
15	Jerry McNertney	.25	.13	.08
18	Wes Stock	.25	.13	.08
20	Wayne Comer	.25	.13	.08
21	Tommy Harper	.30	.15	.09
23	Bob Locker	.25	.13	.08
24	Lew Krausse	.25	.13	.08
25	John Gelnar	.25	.13	.08
26	Roy McMillan	.25	.13	.08
27	Cal Ermer	.25	.13	.08
28	Sandy Valdespino	.25	.13	.08
30	Jackie Moore	.25	.13	.08
32	Gene Brabender	.25	.13	.08
33	Marty Pattin	.25	.13	.08
34	Greg Goossen	.25	.13	.08
35	John Morris	.25	.13	.08
36	Steve Hovley	.25	.13	.08
38	Bob Meyer	.25	.13	.08
39	Bob Bolin	.25	.13	.08
43	John O'Donoghue	.25	.13	.08
49	George Lauzerique	.25	.13	.08
---	Logo Card	.25	.13	.08

1974 McDonald's Gene Michael

Though there is no advertising or logo on this one-card "set," this black-and-white card of "The Stick" in his last year as a Yankee was distributed by Staten Island McDonalds restaurants. The card measures 2-5/8" x 4-3/8" and is blank-backed.

	NM	EX	VG
Gene "The Stick" Michael	15.00	7.50	4.50

1974 McDonald's Padres Discs

Envisioned as part of a line of sports promotional sets, this concept died following the test with San Diego area McDonalds. At the July 30, 1974, game, Padres fans were given a hinged plastic baseball containing five Padres player photo discs plus a disc with the team's schedule and a Ronald McDonald disc which listed the dates on which the remaining eight player cards would be distributed at area McDonalds. Only 60,000 of the "starter set" discs were made, while 180,000 of each of the other player discs were printed. The 2-3/8" diameter discs feature a color photo on front and player stats on back. The promotion was the work of Photo Sports, Inc., of Los Angeles.

		NM	EX	VG
Complete Set (15):		60.00	30.00	18.00
Common Player:		1.50	.70	.45
(1)	Matty Alou	2.00	1.00	.60
(2)	Glenn Beckert	6.00	3.00	1.75
(3)	Nate Colbert	1.50	.70	.45
(4)	Bill Grief	1.50	.70	.45
(5)	John Grubb	1.50	.70	.45
(6)	Enzo Hernandez	6.00	3.00	1.75
(7)	Randy Jones	6.00	3.00	1.75
(8)	Fred Kendall	6.00	3.00	1.75
(9)	Willie McCovey	9.00	4.50	2.75
(10)	John McNamara	6.00	3.00	1.75
(11)	Dave Roberts	1.50	.70	.45
(12)	Bobby Tolan	1.50	.70	.45
(13)	Dave Winfield	30.00	15.00	9.00
(14)	Padres home game schedule	4.00	2.00	1.25
(15)	Ronald McDonald	6.00	3.00	1.75

1970s-80s Doug McWilliams Postcards

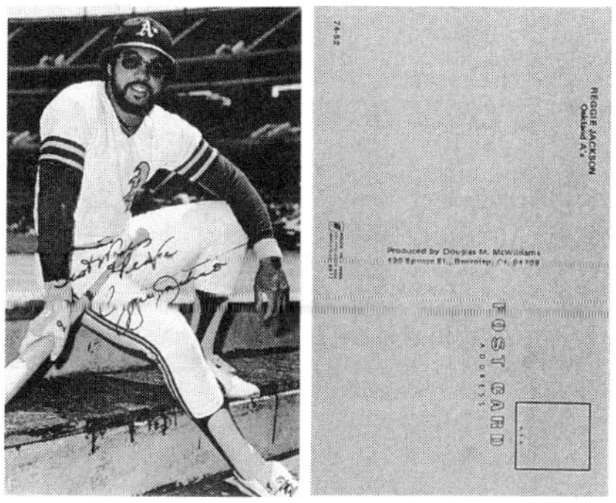

For more than two decades, California photographer Doug McWilliams (who also worked for Topps for 23 years) produced a series of black-and-white and color postcards for individual use by ballplayers, mostly members of the Oakland A's. Almost uniformly, the 3-1/2" x 5-1/2" cards have no graphics on front (a few have facsimile autographs), just a player pose or portrait. Backs have standard postcard markings, player identification, and McWilliams' credit lines. Backs carry a two-digit year of issue prefix to the card number. Postcards are printed in black-and-white unless noted.

	NM	EX	VG
Common Player: (See individual years for checklists and values)	1.00	.50	.30

1970 Doug McWilliams Collectors' Issue Postcards

This set of black-and-white player postcards was produced by S.F. area photographer Doug McWilliams as a custom order for an Eastern collector. Fewer than 50 sets were reportedly produced. The 3-1/2" x 5-1/2" cards have glossy photographic fronts and standard postcard backs with player identification. The unnumbered cards are checklisted here in alphabetical order.

		NM	EX	VG
Complete Set (22):		400.00	200.00	125.00
Common Player:		20.00	10.00	6.00
(1)	Jerry Adair	20.00	10.00	6.00
(2)	Brant Alyea	20.00	10.00	6.00
(3)	Brant Alyea	20.00	10.00	6.00
(4)	Dwain Anderson	20.00	10.00	6.00
(5)	Curt Blefary	20.00	10.00	6.00
(6)	Bill Daniels	20.00	10.00	6.00
(7)	Mike Epstein	22.50	11.00	6.75
(8)	Adrian Garrett	20.00	10.00	6.00
(9)	Frank Fernandez	20.00	10.00	6.00
(10)	Mike Hegan	20.00	10.00	6.00
(11)	George Hendrick	20.00	10.00	6.00
(12)	Reggie Jackson	125.00	62.00	37.00
(13)	Reggie Jackson	125.00	62.00	37.00
(14)	Ron Klimkowski	20.00	10.00	6.00
(15)	Darold Knowles	20.00	10.00	6.00
(16)	Jerry Lumpe	20.00	10.00	6.00
(17)	Angel Mangual	20.00	10.00	6.00
(18)	Denny McLain	30.00	15.00	9.00
(19)	Denny McLain	30.00	15.00	9.00
(20)	Irv Noren	20.00	10.00	6.00
(21)	Ramon Webster	20.00	10.00	6.00
(22)	Dick Williams	20.00	10.00	6.00

1970 Doug McWilliams Oakland A's Postcards

This set of 3-1/2" x 5-1/2" player postcards was produced by San Francisco photographer Doug McWilliams for sale by Sports Cards for Collectors, a forerunner of TCMA. Each card can be found either with or without borders on front, the latter having a slightly enlarged image. Player identification is on back. The unnumbered cards are checklisted here alphabetically. Fewer than 50 sets were reported produced.

		NM	EX	VG
Complete Set (42):		400.00	200.00	125.00
Common Player:		15.00	7.50	4.50
(1)	Felipe Alou	20.00	10.00	6.00
(2)	Sal Bando	20.00	10.00	6.00
(3)	Vida Blue	25.00	12.50	7.50
(4)	Bobby Brooks	15.00	7.50	4.50
(5)	Bert Campaneris	25.00	12.50	7.50
(6)	"Babe" Dahlgren	15.00	7.50	4.50
(7)	Tommy Davis	17.50	8.75	5.25
(8)	Chuck Dobson	15.00	7.50	4.50
(9)	John Donaldson	15.00	7.50	4.50
(10)	Al Downing	15.00	7.50	4.50
(11)	Jim Driscoll	15.00	7.50	4.50
(12)	Dave Duncan	15.00	7.50	4.50
(13)	Frank Fernandez	15.00	7.50	4.50
(14)	Rollie Fingers	45.00	22.00	13.50
(15)	Tito Francona	15.00	7.50	4.50
(16)	Jim Grant	20.00	10.00	6.00
(17)	Dick Green	15.00	7.50	4.50
(18)	Larry Haney	15.00	7.50	4.50
(19)	Bobby Hofman	15.00	7.50	4.50
(20)	Steve Hovley	15.00	7.50	4.50
(21)	Jim Hunter	45.00	22.00	13.50
(22)	Reggie Jackson	125.00	62.00	37.00
(23)	Dave Johnson	15.00	7.50	4.50
(24)	Marcel Lacheman	15.00	7.50	4.50
(25)	Tony LaRussa	40.00	20.00	12.00
(26)	Paul Lindblad	15.00	7.50	4.50
(27)	Bob Locker	15.00	7.50	4.50
(28)	John McNamara	15.00	7.50	4.50
(29)	Don Mincher	15.00	7.50	4.50
(30)	Rick Monday	15.00	7.50	4.50
(31)	"Blue Moon" Odom	17.50	8.75	5.25
(32)	Darrell Osteen	15.00	7.50	4.50
(33)	Ray Oyler	15.00	7.50	4.50
(34)	Roberto Pena	15.00	7.50	4.50
(35)	Bill Posedel	15.00	7.50	4.50
(36)	Roberto Rodriguez	15.00	7.50	4.50
(37)	Jim Roland	15.00	7.50	4.50
(38)	Joe Rudi	20.00	10.00	6.00
(39)	Diego Segui	15.00	7.50	4.50
(40)	Jose Tartabull	15.00	7.50	4.50
(41)	Gene Tenace	15.00	7.50	4.50
(42)	Dooley Womack	15.00	7.50	4.50

1970 Doug McWilliams Postcards

		NM	EX	VG
1	Jim Roland	1.00	.50	.30
2a	Mudcat Grant, Mudcat Grant	1.50	.75	.45
2b	Mudcat Grant	1.50	.75	.45
3	Reggie Jackson (color - only 50 produced)	150.00	75.00	45.00
4	Darrell Osteen	1.00	.50	.30
5a	Tom Hafey (first printing)	1.00	.50	.30
5b	Tom Hafey (second printing)	1.00	.50	.30
6	Chick Hafey	1.50	.75	.45

1971 Doug McWilliams Postcards

		NM	EX	VG
7	Larry Brown	1.00	.50	.30
8a	Vida Blue (color - first printing - KV3321)	2.00	1.00	.60
8b	Vida Blue (color - second printing - KV3509)	2.00	1.00	.60
8c	Vida Blue (color - third printing - KV4403)	2.00	1.00	.60
9	Dave Duncan	1.00	.50	.30
10	George Hendrick (color)	3.00	1.50	.90
11	Mudcat Grant	1.00	.50	.30
12	Mudcat Grant	1.00	.50	.30

1972 Doug McWilliams Postcards

		NM	EX	VG
13	John Odom (color)	2.00	1.00	.60
14	Reggie Jackson (color)	7.50	3.75	2.25
15	Sal Bando (color)	2.00	1.00	.60
16	Dan Cater	1.00	.50	.30
17	Bob Locker	1.00	.50	.30
18a	Joe Rudi (equal edges to player)	1.00	.50	.30
18b	Joe Rudi (bat close at bottom)	1.00	.50	.30
18c	Joe Rudi (hand close to edge)	1.00	.50	.30
19	Larry Brown	1.00	.50	.30
20a	Dick Green (first printing - glossy)	1.00	.50	.30
20b	Dick Green (second printing - glossy, more contrast)	1.00	.50	.30
20c	Dick Green (third printing - matte)	1.00	.50	.30
21	Vida Blue (color)	2.00	1.00	.60
22a	Joe Horlen (first printing - bright)	1.00	.50	.30
22b	Joe Horlen (second printing - dark)	1.00	.50	.30
23	Gene Tenace (color)	2.00	1.00	.60
24a	Ted Kubiak (glossy)	1.00	.50	.30
24b	Ted Kubiak (matte)	1.00	.50	.30
A	Emeryville Ball Park	1.00	.50	.30
B	Oakland Coliseum	1.00	.50	.30

1973 Doug McWilliams Postcards

		NM	EX	VG
25	Rene Lachemann	1.00	.50	.30
26	Tom Greive	1.00	.50	.30
27	John Odom (color)	2.00	1.00	.60
28a	Rollie Fingers (first printing)	3.00	1.50	.90
28b	Rollie Fingers (second printing - thinner stock)	3.00	1.50	.90
29	Jim Hunter (color)	3.00	1.50	.90
30	Ray Fosse (color)	2.00	1.00	.60
31	Charley Pride (color)	6.00	3.00	1.75
32	Charley Pride (color)	6.00	3.00	1.75
33	Bill North	1.00	.50	.30
34	Damasco Blanco	1.00	.50	.30
35	Paul Lindblad	1.00	.50	.30
36	Rollie Fingers (color)	3.00	1.50	.90
37	Horacio Pina	1.00	.50	.30
38	Bert Campaneris (color)	2.50	1.25	.70
39	Jim Holt (color)	2.00	1.00	.60
40	Sal Bando (color)	2.00	1.00	.60
41	Joe Rudi (color)	2.00	1.00	.60
42	Dick Williams (color)	2.00	1.00	.60
43	Jesus Alou	1.00	.50	.30
44	Joe Niekro	1.25	.60	.40
45	Johnny Oates	1.00	.50	.30

1974 Doug McWilliams Postcards

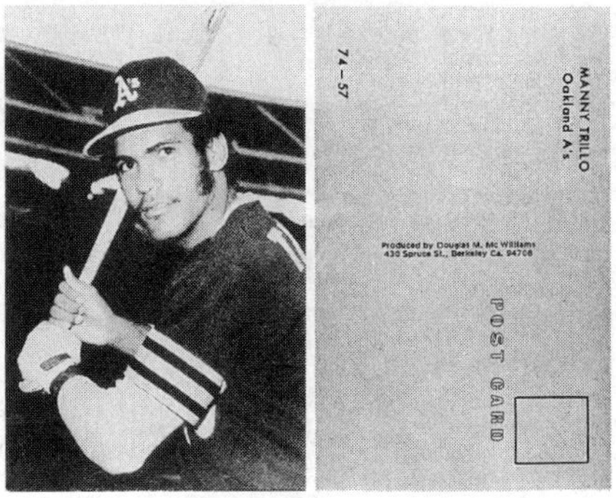

		NM	EX	VG
46a	Ray Fosse (color - first printing - w/signature)	2.00	1.00	.60
46b	Ray Fosse (color - second printing - no signature)	2.00	1.00	.60
46c	Ray Fosse (color - third printing - no sig., very green grass)	2.00	1.00	.60
47	Jesus Alou	1.00	.50	.30
48	John Summers	1.00	.50	.30
49	Dal Maxvill	1.00	.50	.30
50	Joe Rudi (color)	2.00	1.00	.60
51	Sal Bando (color)	2.00	1.00	.60
52	Reggie Jackson (color)	7.50	3.75	2.25
53	Ted Kubiak (color)	2.00	1.00	.60
54	Dave Hamilton	1.00	.50	.30
55	Gene Tenace (color)	2.00	1.00	.60
56a	Bob Locker (first printing - back foot near edge)	1.00	.50	.30
56b	Bob Locker (second printing - foot 3/4" from edge)	1.00	.50	.30
57	Manny Trillo	1.00	.50	.30

1975 Doug McWilliams Postcards

		NM	EX	VG
58a	Dan Godby (first printing)	1.00	.50	.30
58b	Dan Godby (second printing - blank back)	1.00	.50	.30
58c	Dan Godby (third printing - flat contrast)	1.00	.50	.30
59	Bob Locker	1.00	.50	.30
60	Rollie Fingers (color)	3.00	1.50	.90
61	Glenn Abbott	1.00	.50	.30
62	Jim Todd	1.00	.50	.30
63	Phil Garner	1.00	.50	.30
64	Paul Lindblad	1.00	.50	.30
65	Bill North (color)	2.00	1.00	.60
66	Dick Sisler	1.00	.50	.30
67	Angel Mangual	1.00	.50	.30
68	Claudell Washington	1.00	.50	.30

1976 Doug McWilliams Postcards

		NM	EX	VG
69	Oakland Coliseum (color)	2.00	1.00	.60
70	Sal Bando (color)	2.00	1.00	.60
71	Mike Torrez (color)	2.00	1.00	.60
72	Joe Lonnett	1.00	.50	.30
73	Chuck Tanner	1.00	.50	.30

74	Tommy Sandt	1.00	.50	.30
75	Dick Bosman (color)	2.00	1.00	.60
76	Bert Campaneris (color)	2.00	1.00	.60
77	Ken Brett	2.00	1.00	.60
78	Jim Todd (color)	2.00	1.00	.60
79	Jeff Newman	1.00	.50	.30
80	John McCall	1.00	.50	.30

1977 Doug McWilliams Postcards

		NM	EX	VG
81	Don Baylor (color)	3.00	1.50	.90
82	Lee Stange	1.00	.50	.30
83	Rob Picciolo	1.00	.50	.30
84	Jack Mc Keon (color)	2.00	1.00	.60
85	Rollie Fingers (color)	3.00	1.50	.90
86	Manny Sanguillen	1.00	.50	.30
87	Tony Armas	1.00	.50	.30
88	Jim Tyrone	1.00	.50	.30
89	Wayne Gross	1.00	.50	.30
90	Rick Langford	1.00	.50	.30
91	Rich Gossage	1.00	.50	.30
92	Phil Garner (color)	2.00	1.00	.60
93	Del Alston	1.00	.50	.30
94	Bert Blyleven (color)	2.50	1.25	.70
95	Willie McCovey (color)	3.00	1.50	.90
96	Ken Brett (color)	2.00	1.00	.60
97	Doyle Alexander (color)	2.00	1.00	.60

1978 Doug McWilliams Postcards

		NM	EX	VG
98	Rene Lacheman	1.00	.50	.30
99	Del Alston	1.00	.50	.30
100	Lee Stange (color)	2.00	1.00	.60
101	Taylor Duncan	1.00	.50	.30
102	Matt Keough	1.00	.50	.30
103	Bruce Robinson	1.00	.50	.30
104	Sal Bando (color)	2.00	1.00	.60

1979 Doug McWilliams Postcards

		NM	EX	VG
105	Alan Wirth	1.00	.50	.30
106	Mike Edwards	1.00	.50	.30
107	Craig Minetto	1.00	.50	.30
108	Mike Morgan	1.00	.50	.30
109	Brian Kingman	1.00	.50	.30

1980 Doug McWilliams Postcards

		NM	EX	VG
110	Jim Essian	1.00	.50	.30
111a	Willie McCovey (color - first printing - no signature)	3.00	1.50	.90
111b	Willie McCovey (color - second printing - w/signature, stamp at top)	3.00	1.50	.90
111c	Willie McCovey (color - third printing - w/sig., stamp at bottom)	3.00	1.50	.90
112a	Willie McCovey (color - first printing - no signature)	3.00	1.50	.90
112b	Willie McCovey (color - second printing - w/signature)	3.00	1.50	.90

1936 H.A. Meade St. Louis Cardinals Postcard

The St. Louis Cardinals are pictured in insect-size portrait photos on this color linen-finish post-card. Back of the approximately 5-1/2" x 3-1/2" card has standard postcard markings.

	NM	EX	VG
St. Louis Cardinals team composite	200.00	100.00	60.00

1964 Meadowgold Dairy

Four of the mid-Sixties' biggest stars appear as a panel on this milk carton issue. The four-player portion measures about 3-3/4" x 4-1/4" and is printed in shades of blue on the white background. Individual cards measure about 1-1/8" x 2-1/16" and are, of course blank backed. In 1998, a complete milk carton was sold at auction for $2,475.

	NM	EX	VG
Complete Set, Panel:	700.00	350.00	200.00
Complete Set, Singles (4):	450.00	225.00	125.00
Common Player:	40.00	20.00	12.00
(1) Sandy Koufax	85.00	42.00	25.00
(2) Mickey Mantle	260.00	130.00	78.00
(3) Willie Mays	80.00	40.00	24.00
(4) Bill Mazeroski	60.00	30.00	18.00

1911 Mecca Cigarettes

(See 1911 T201 Double Folders)

1910 Mello-Mint (E105)

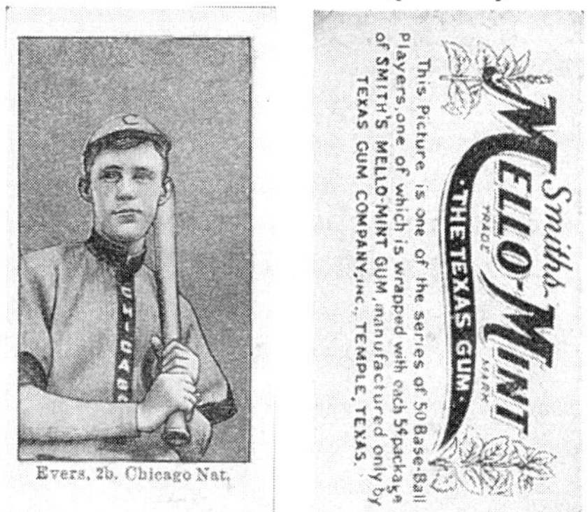

Issued circa 1910 by Smith's Mello-Mint, "The Texas Gum", this set of 50 cards shares the same checklist and artwork as the better known E101 set. The Mello-Mint cards, however, are slightly smaller, measuring approximately 1-3/8" x 2-5/8", and were printed on thin paper, making them difficult to find in top condition. Also contributing to condition problems is the fact that many cards were folded vertically to fit the packaging. The backs contain an advertisement for Mello-Mint Gum. The set carries an ACC designation of E105.

	NM	EX	VG
Complete Set (50):	27500.	11000.	7000.
Common Player:	400.00	160.00	100.00
(1) Jack Barry	400.00	160.00	100.00
(2) Harry Bemis	400.00	160.00	100.00
(3) Chief Bender (white hat)	660.00	265.00	165.00
(4) Chief Bender (striped hat)	660.00	265.00	165.00
(5) Bill Bergen	400.00	160.00	100.00
(6) Bob Bescher	400.00	160.00	100.00
(7) Al Bridwell	400.00	160.00	100.00
(8) Doc Casey	400.00	160.00	100.00
(9) Frank Chance	660.00	265.00	165.00
(10) Hal Chase	515.00	205.00	130.00
(11) Ty Cobb	2700.	1075.	675.00
(12) Eddie Collins	660.00	265.00	165.00
(13) Sam Crawford	660.00	265.00	165.00
(14) Harry Davis	400.00	160.00	100.00
(15) Art Devlin	400.00	160.00	100.00
(16) Wild Bill Donovan	400.00	160.00	100.00
(17) Red Dooin	400.00	160.00	100.00
(18) Mickey Doolan	400.00	160.00	100.00
(19) Patsy Dougherty	400.00	160.00	100.00
(20) Larry Doyle (with bat)	400.00	160.00	100.00
(21) Larry Doyle (throwing)	400.00	160.00	100.00
(22) Johnny Evers	660.00	265.00	165.00
(23) George Gibson	400.00	160.00	100.00
(24) Topsy Hartsel	400.00	160.00	100.00
(25) Fred Jacklitsch	400.00	160.00	100.00
(26) Hugh Jennings	660.00	265.00	165.00
(27) Red Kleinow	400.00	160.00	100.00
(28) Otto Knabe	400.00	160.00	100.00
(29) Jack Knight	400.00	160.00	100.00
(30) Nap Lajoie	745.00	300.00	185.00
(31) Hans Lobert	400.00	160.00	100.00
(32) Sherry Magee	400.00	160.00	100.00
(33) Christy Matthewson (Mathewson)	1600.	640.00	400.00
(34) John McGraw	660.00	265.00	165.00
(35) Larry McLean	400.00	160.00	100.00
(36) Dots Miller (batting)	400.00	160.00	100.00
(37) Dots Miller (fielding)	400.00	160.00	100.00
(38) Danny Murphy	400.00	160.00	100.00
(39) Bill O'Hara	400.00	160.00	100.00
(40) Germany Schaefer	400.00	160.00	100.00
(41) Admiral Schlei	400.00	160.00	100.00
(42) Boss Schmidt	400.00	160.00	100.00
(43) Johnny Seigle	400.00	160.00	100.00
(44) Dave Shean	400.00	160.00	100.00
(45) Boss Smith (Schmidt)	400.00	160.00	100.00
(46) Joe Tinker	660.00	265.00	165.00
(47) Honus Wagner (batting)	1850.	740.00	460.00
(48) Honus Wagner (throwing)	1850.	740.00	460.00
(49) Cy Young	745.00	300.00	185.00
(50) Heinie Zimmerman	400.00	160.00	100.00

1953-54 Marshall Merrell Milwaukee Braves Portfolio

One of several portfolios of Milwaukee Braves artwork produced during the team's first few years, this issue of 8" x 10" black-and-white lithographs was sold at County Stadium for 25 cents apiece. The player checklist here is believed to be complete, but it is possible other poses may yet be reported. The cards are blank-backed and unnumbered; the checklist here has been arranged alphabetically.

	NM	EX	VG
Complete Set (25):	750.00	375.00	225.00
Common Player:	25.00	12.50	7.50
(1) Henry Aaron	200.00	100.00	60.00
(2) Joe Adcock	25.00	12.50	7.50
(3) Johnny Antonelli	25.00	12.50	7.50
(4) Billy Bruton	25.00	12.50	7.50
(5) Bob Buhl	25.00	12.50	7.50
(6) Lou Burdette (follow-through)	25.00	12.50	7.50
(7) Lew Burdette (wind-up)	25.00	12.50	7.50
(8) Gene Conley	25.00	12.50	7.50
(9) Del Crandall	25.00	12.50	7.50
(10) Jack Dittmer	25.00	12.50	7.50
(11) Sid Gordon (batting)	25.00	12.50	7.50
(12) Sid Gordon (standing)	25.00	12.50	7.50
(13) Charlie Grimm (tomahawk on jersey)	25.00	12.50	7.50
(14) Charlie Grimm (no tomahawk)	25.00	12.50	7.50
(15) Don Liddle	25.00	12.50	7.50
(16) Johnny Logan	25.00	12.50	7.50
(17) Ed Mathews (batting)	75.00	37.00	22.00
(18) Ed Mathews (standing)	75.00	37.00	22.00
(19) Danny O'Connell	25.00	12.50	7.50
(20) Andy Pafko	25.00	12.50	7.50
(21) Jim Pendleton	25.00	12.50	7.50
(22) Warren Spahn	70.00	35.00	21.00
(23) Max Surkont	25.00	12.50	7.50
(24) Bobby Thomson	45.00	22.00	13.50
(25) Jim Wilson	25.00	12.50	7.50

Vintage cards in Good condition are valued at about 50% of the Very Good value shown here. Fair cards are valued at 25% or less of VG.
The ratio of Excellent and Very Good prices to Near Mint can vary depending on relative collectibility for each grade in a specific set. Current listings reflect such adjustments.

1938-39 Metropolitan Clothing Cincinnati Reds postcards

(See 1937-39 Orcajo Cincinnati Reds postcards for checklist, values.)

1968 Metropolitan Museum of Art Burdick Collection

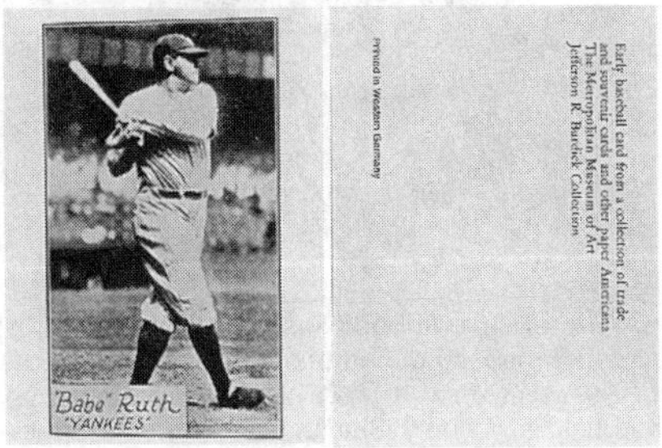

The date of issue is approximate for this set promoting New York's Metropolitan Museum of Art as the repository for the Jefferson Burdick collection, once the world's premier accumulation of trading cards. Burdick, author of the once-standard "American Card Catalog" donated his collection to the Met. The 2-3/4" x 3-5/8" black-and-white glossy card fronts reproduce 1928 R315 cards of major leaguers and earlier Zeenuts cards of minor leaguers. Backs have a few words about the museum and a "Printed in Western Germany" line. The unnumbered cards are checklisted here in alphabetical order.

		NM	EX	VG
Complete Set (8):		90.00	45.00	27.00
Common Player:		9.00	4.50	2.75
(1)	Max Bishop	9.00	4.50	2.75
(2)	Lou Gehrig	37.00	18.50	11.00
(3)	Carl Hubbell	15.00	7.50	4.50
(4)	Art Kores	9.00	4.50	2.75
(5)	Bill Leard	9.00	4.50	2.75
(6)	Babe Ruth	45.00	22.00	13.50
(7)	Dazzy Vance	9.00	4.50	2.75
(8)	Elmer Zacher	9.00	4.50	2.75

1931 Metropolitan Studio St. Louis Cardinals

Members of the St. Louis Cardinals are featured in this 30-card set. The cards were printed on heavy paper and feature sepia-toned photos. The player's name appears along the bottom white border below the photo. The cards measure 6-1/4" x 9-1/2" and are not numbered. Most cards feature the logo of Metropolitan Studio in a bottom corner, while others have "Sid Whiting St. Louis MO", and a few have no sponsor's credit.

		NM	EX	VG
Complete Set (30):		1600.	725.00	400.00
Common Player:		40.00	18.00	10.00
(1)	Earl "Sparky" Adams	40.00	18.00	10.00
(2)	Ray Bladco	40.00	18.00	10.00
(3)	James Bottomley	85.00	38.00	21.00
(4)	Sam Breadon	40.00	18.00	10.00
(5)	James "Rip" Collins	45.00	20.00	11.00
(6)	Dizzy Dean	200.00	90.00	50.00
(7)	Paul Derringer	45.00	20.00	11.00
(8)	Jake Flowers	40.00	18.00	10.00
(9)	Frank Frisch	95.00	43.00	24.00
(10)	Charles Gelbert	40.00	18.00	10.00
(11)	Miguel Gonzales (Gonzalez)	75.00	34.00	18.50
(12)	Burleigh Grimes	85.00	38.00	21.00
(13)	Charles "Chick" Hafey	85.00	38.00	21.00
(14)	William Hallahan	40.00	18.00	10.00
(15)	Jesse Haines	85.00	38.00	21.00
(16)	Andrew High	40.00	18.00	10.00
(17)	Sylvester Johnson	40.00	18.00	10.00
(18)	Tony Kaufmann	40.00	18.00	10.00
(19)	James Lindsey	40.00	18.00	10.00
(20)	Gus Mancuso	40.00	18.00	10.00
(21)	John Leonard "Pepper" Martin	65.00	29.00	16.00
(22)	Ernest Orsatti	40.00	18.00	10.00
(23)	Charles Flint Rhem	40.00	18.00	10.00
(24)	Branch Rickey	100.00	45.00	25.00
(25)	Walter Roettger	40.00	18.00	10.00
(26)	Allyn Stout	40.00	18.00	10.00
(27)	"Gabby" Street	40.00	18.00	10.00
(28)	Clyde Wares	40.00	18.00	10.00
(29)	George Watkins	40.00	18.00	10.00
(30)	James Wilson	40.00	18.00	10.00

1975 Michael Schechter Associates Test Discs

Prior to rolling out it's 70-disc set in 1976, Michael Schecter Associates issued this sample set of discs the previous year. Slightly larger, at 3-9/16" diameter, than the '76 issues, the '75 sample discs share a similar format. Fronts have a black-and-white player photo from which uniform logos details have been removed due to lack of licensing by Major League Baseball. Backs are blank. The Seaver and Bench discs are considerably scarcer than the other four players in the set.

		NM	EX	VG
Complete Set (6):		250.00	125.00	75.00
Common Player:		7.50	3.75	2.25
(1)	Hank Aaron	25.00	12.50	7.50
(2)	Johnny Bench	85.00	42.00	25.00
(3)	Catfish Hunter	12.50	6.25	3.75
(4)	Fred Lynn	12.50	6.25	3.75
(5)	Pete Rose	25.00	12.50	7.50
(6)	Tom Seaver	150.00	75.00	45.00

Suffix letters after a card number indicate a variation card.

1976 Michael Schechter Associates Discs

Following its test issue of 1975, Michael Schechter Associates ran out its baseball player disc issues on a large scale in 1976. While most were sold with specific sponsor advertising on back, they were also made available with blank backs. The discs are 3-3/8" diameter with a black-and-white player portrait photo in the center of the baseball design. A line of red stars is above, while the left and right panels feature one of several bright colors. Produced by MSA under license from the Major League Players Association, the player photos have had uniform and cap logos removed. The unnumbered checklist here is presented in alphabetical order.

		NM	EX	VG
Complete Set (70):		90.00	67.00	36.00
Common Player:		.50	.40	.20
(1)	Henry Aaron	12.00	6.00	3.50
(2)	Johnny Bench	7.50	3.75	2.25
(3)	Vida Blue	.50	.40	.20
(4)	Larry Bowa	.50	.40	.20
(5)	Lou Brock	4.50	2.25	1.25
(6)	Jeff Burroughs	.50	.40	.20
(7)	John Candelaria	.50	.40	.20
(8)	Jose Cardenal	.50	.40	.20
(9)	Rod Carew	4.50	2.25	1.25
(10)	Steve Carlton	4.50	2.25	1.25
(11)	Dave Cash	.50	.40	.20
(12)	Cesar Cedeno	.50	.40	.20
(13)	Ron Cey	.50	.40	.20
(14)	Carlton Fisk	4.50	2.25	1.25
(15)	Tito Fuentes	.50	.40	.20
(16)	Steve Garvey	3.50	1.75	1.00
(17)	Ken Griffey	.50	.40	.20
(18)	Don Gullett	.50	.40	.20
(19)	Willie Horton	.50	.40	.20
(20)	Al Hrabosky	.50	.40	.20
(21)	Catfish Hunter	4.50	2.25	1.25
(22)	Reggie Jackson	10.00	5.00	3.00
(23)	Randy Jones	.50	.40	.20
(24)	Jim Kaat	.50	.40	.20
(25)	Don Kessinger	.50	.40	.20
(26)	Dave Kingman	1.50	.70	.45
(27)	Jerry Koosman	.50	.40	.20
(28)	Mickey Lolich	1.00	.50	.30
(29)	Greg Luzinski	1.00	.50	.30
(30)	Fred Lynn	1.00	.50	.30
(31)	Bill Madlock	.50	.40	.20
(32)	Carlos May	.50	.40	.20
(33)	John Mayberry	.50	.40	.20
(34)	Bake McBride	.50	.40	.20
(35)	Doc Medich	.50	.40	.20
(36)	Andy Messersmith	.50	.40	.20
(37)	Rick Monday	.50	.40	.20
(38)	John Montefusco	.50	.40	.20
(39)	Jerry Morales	.50	.40	.20
(40)	Joe Morgan	4.50	2.25	1.25
(41)	Thurman Munson	6.00	3.00	1.75
(42)	Bobby Murcer	.50	.40	.20
(43)	Al Oliver	.50	.40	.20
(44)	Jim Palmer	4.50	2.25	1.25
(45)	Dave Parker	1.00	.50	.30
(46)	Tony Perez	4.50	2.25	1.25
(47)	Jerry Reuss	.50	.40	.20
(48)	Brooks Robinson	6.00	3.00	1.75
(49)	Frank Robinson	6.00	3.00	1.75
(50)	Steve Rogers	.50	.40	.20
(51)	Pete Rose	12.00	6.00	3.50
(52)	Nolan Ryan	24.00	12.00	7.25
(53)	Manny Sanguillen	.50	.40	.20
(54)	Mike Schmidt	9.00	4.50	2.75
(55)	Tom Seaver	6.00	3.00	1.75
(56)	Ted Simmons	.50	.40	.20
(57)	Reggie Smith	.50	.40	.20
(58)	Willie Stargell	4.50	2.25	1.25
(59)	Rusty Staub	1.00	.50	.30
(60)	Rennie Stennett	.50	.40	.20
(61)	Don Sutton	4.50	2.25	1.25
(62)	Andy Thornton	.50	.40	.20
(63)	Luis Tiant	.50	.40	.20
(64)	Joe Torre	.50	.40	.20
(65)	Mike Tyson	.50	.40	.20
(66)	Bob Watson	.50	.40	.20
(67)	Wilbur Wood	.50	.40	.20
(68)	Jimmy Wynn	.50	.40	.20
(69)	Carl Yastrzemski	6.00	3.00	1.75
(70)	Richie Zisk	.50	.40	.20

1977 Michael Schechter Associates Cup Lids

One of MSA's early baseball novelty issues was a set of drink-cup lids. The 3-1/2" diameter pieces are made of pressed and waxed cardboard. They are 3/16" thick and have a 3/8" die-cut hole for inserting a straw. Design is similar to other MSA issues of the era, with a black-and-white player portrait photo at center of a simulated baseball design. Personal data is printed in colored panels at left and right, and there is a row of colored stars above the photo. Player caps do not show team insignia because the issue was licensed only by the players' union, and not the owners. The unnumbered lids are checklisted here in alphabetical order.

		NM	EX	VG
Complete Set (48):		650.00	325.00	195.00
Common Player:		10.00	5.00	3.00
(1)	Sal Bando	10.00	5.00	3.00
(2)	Johnny Bench	40.00	20.00	12.00
(3)	Larry Bowa	10.00	5.00	3.00
(4)	Steve Braun	10.00	5.00	3.00
(5)	George Brett	40.00	20.00	12.00
(6)	Lou Brock	20.00	10.00	6.00
(7)	Bert Campaneris	10.00	5.00	3.00
(8)	Bill Campbell	10.00	5.00	3.00
(9)	Jose Cardenal	10.00	5.00	3.00
(10)	Rod Carew	25.00	12.50	7.50
(11)	Dave Cash	10.00	5.00	3.00
(12)	Cesar Cedeno	10.00	5.00	3.00
(13)	Chris Chambliss	10.00	5.00	3.00
(14)	Dave Concepcion	10.00	5.00	3.00
(15)	Mark Fidrych	10.00	5.00	3.00
(16)	Rollie Fingers	15.00	7.50	4.50
(17)	George Foster	10.00	5.00	3.00
(18)	Wayne Garland	10.00	5.00	3.00
(19)	Steve Garvey	15.00	7.50	4.50
(20)	Cesar Geronimo	10.00	5.00	3.00
(21)	Bobby Grich	10.00	5.00	3.00
(22)	Don Gullett	10.00	5.00	3.00
(23)	Mike Hargrove	10.00	5.00	3.00
(24)	Catfish Hunter	15.00	7.50	4.50
(25)	Randy Jones	10.00	5.00	3.00
(26)	Dave Kingman	12.50	6.25	3.75
(27)	Dave LaRoche	10.00	5.00	3.00
(28)	Greg Luzinski	10.00	5.00	3.00
(29)	Fred Lynn	10.00	5.00	3.00
(30)	Jon Matlack	10.00	5.00	3.00
(31)	Bake McBride	10.00	5.00	3.00
(32)	Joe Morgan	15.00	7.50	4.50
(33)	Phil Niekro	15.00	7.50	4.50
(34)	Jim Palmer	15.00	7.50	4.50
(35)	Dave Parker	12.50	6.25	3.75
(36)	Fred Patek	10.00	5.00	3.00
(37)	Mickey Rivers	10.00	5.00	3.00
(38)	Brooks Robinson	25.00	12.50	7.50
(39)	Pete Rose	40.00	20.00	12.00
(40)	Nolan Ryan	80.00	40.00	24.00
(41)	Mike Schmidt	40.00	20.00	12.00
(42)	Bill Singer	10.00	5.00	3.00
(43)	Chris Speier	10.00	5.00	3.00
(44)	Willie Stargell	20.00	10.00	6.00
(45)	Luis Tiant	12.50	6.25	3.75
(46)	Butch Wynegar	10.00	5.00	3.00
(47)	Robin Yount	30.00	15.00	9.00
(48)	Richie Zisk	10.00	5.00	3.00

1977 Mike Schechter Associates Customized Sports Discs

Virtually identical in format to the several locally sponsored disc sets of the previous year, these 3-3/8" diameter player discs once again feature black-and-white player portrait photos in the center of a baseball design. The left and right panels are in one of several bright colors. Licensed by the players' association the photos carry no uniform logos. Backs of the discs are printed in dark blue and carry an ad from MSA for "Customized Sports Discs" and novelties for which Schechter held the licenses. The unnumbered discs are checklisted here alphabetically.

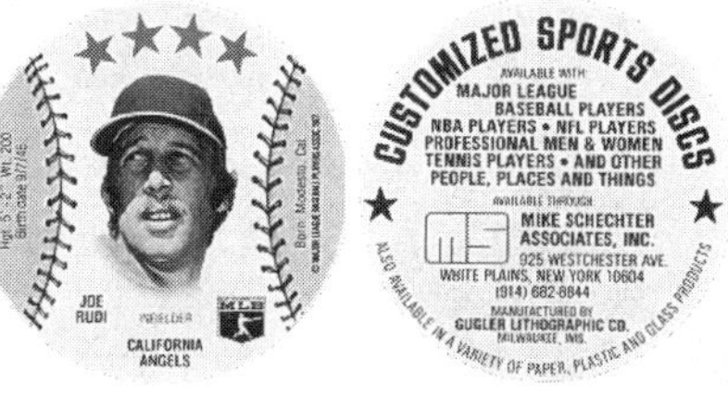

		NM	EX	VG
Complete Set (70):		525.00	260.00	155.00
Common Player:		6.00	3.00	1.75
(1)	Sal Bando	6.00	3.00	1.75
(2)	Buddy Bell	6.00	3.00	1.75
(3)	Johnny Bench	30.00	15.00	9.00
(4)	Larry Bowa	6.00	3.00	1.75
(5)	Steve Braun	6.00	3.00	1.75
(6)	George Brett	60.00	30.00	18.00
(7)	Lou Brock	22.00	11.00	6.50
(8)	Jeff Burroughs	6.00	3.00	1.75
(9)	Bert Campaneris	6.00	3.00	1.75
(10)	John Candelaria	6.00	3.00	1.75
(11)	Jose Cardenal	6.00	3.00	1.75
(12)	Rod Carew	24.00	12.00	7.25
(13)	Steve Carlton	24.00	12.00	7.25
(14)	Dave Cash	6.00	3.00	1.75
(15)	Cesar Cedeno	6.00	3.00	1.75
(16)	Ron Cey	6.00	3.00	1.75
(17)	Dave Concepcion	6.00	3.00	1.75
(18)	Dennis Eckersley	18.00	9.00	5.50
(19)	Mark Fidrych	18.00	9.00	5.50
(20)	Rollie Fingers	22.00	11.00	6.50
(21)	Carlton Fisk	24.00	12.00	7.25
(22)	George Foster	6.00	3.00	1.75
(23)	Wayne Garland	6.00	3.00	1.75
(24)	Ralph Garr	6.00	3.00	1.75
(25)	Steve Garvey	20.00	10.00	6.00
(26)	Cesar Geronimo	6.00	3.00	1.75
(27)	Bobby Grich	6.00	3.00	1.75
(28)	Ken Griffey Sr.	10.00	5.00	3.00
(29)	Don Gullett	6.00	3.00	1.75
(30)	Mike Hargrove	6.00	3.00	1.75
(31)	Willie Horton	6.00	3.00	1.75
(32)	Al Hrabosky	6.00	3.00	1.75
(33)	Reggie Jackson	35.00	17.50	10.50
(34)	Randy Jones	6.00	3.00	1.75
(35)	Dave Kingman	12.00	6.00	3.50
(36)	Jerry Koosman	6.00	3.00	1.75
(37)	Dave LaRoche	6.00	3.00	1.75
(38)	Greg Luzinski	6.00	3.00	1.75
(39)	Fred Lynn	7.50	3.75	2.25
(40)	Bill Madlock	6.00	3.00	1.75
(41)	Rick Manning	6.00	3.00	1.75
(42)	Jon Matlock	6.00	3.00	1.75
(43)	John Mayberry	6.00	3.00	1.75
(44)	Hal McRae	6.00	3.00	1.75
(45)	Andy Messersmith	6.00	3.00	1.75
(46)	Rick Monday	6.00	3.00	1.75
(47)	John Montefusco	6.00	3.00	1.75
(48)	Joe Morgan	22.00	11.00	6.50
(49)	Thurman Munson	24.00	12.00	7.25
(50)	Bobby Murcer	6.00	3.00	1.75
(51)	Bill North	6.00	3.00	1.75
(52)	Jim Palmer	22.00	11.00	6.50
(53)	Tony Perez	22.00	11.00	6.50
(54)	Jerry Reuss	6.00	3.00	1.75
(55)	Pete Rose	60.00	30.00	18.00
(56)	Joe Rudi	6.00	3.00	1.75
(57)	Nolan Ryan	90.00	45.00	27.00
(58)	Manny Sanguillen	6.00	3.00	1.75
(59)	Mike Schmidt	35.00	17.50	10.50
(60)	Tom Seaver	30.00	15.00	9.00
(61)	Bill Singer	6.00	3.00	1.75
(62)	Willie Stargell	24.00	12.00	7.25
(63)	Rusty Staub	9.00	4.50	2.75
(64)	Luis Tiant	6.00	3.00	1.75
(65)	Mike Tyson	6.00	3.00	1.75
(66)	Bob Watson	6.00	3.00	1.75
(67)	Butch Wynegar	6.00	3.00	1.75
(68)	Carl Yastrzemski	27.00	13.50	8.00
(69)	Robin Yount	24.00	12.00	7.25
(70)	Richie Zisk	6.00	3.00	1.75

1979 Michigan Sports Collectors

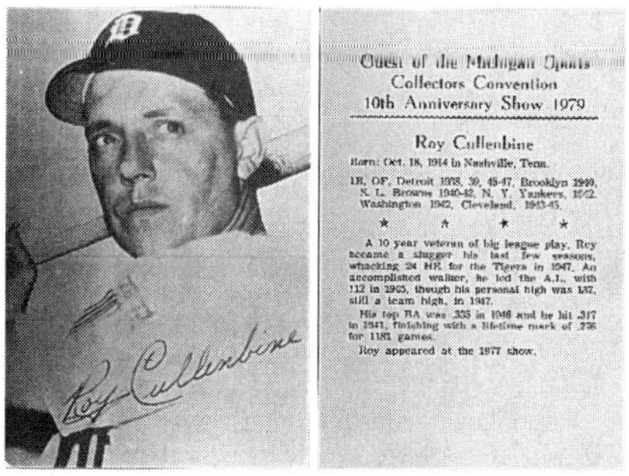

Former Detroit Tigers, along with several baseball writers and announcers, including some who were appearing as autograph guests were featured in this collectors set issued in conjunction with the 1979 Troy, Mich. show. Cards are 3-1/2" x 5-1/16" black-and-white. Backs have personal data and a career summary of the pictured player, along with mention of the show. The unnumbered cards are checklisted here alphabetically.

		NM	EX	VG
Complete Set (20):		16.00	8.00	4.75
Common Player:		.50	.25	.15
(1)	Gates Brown	.50	.25	.15
(2)	Norm Cash	.85	.45	.25
(3)	Al Cicotte	.50	.25	.15
(4)	Roy Cullenbine	.50	.25	.15
(5)	Gene Desautels	.50	.25	.15
(6)	Hoot Evers	.50	.25	.15
(7)	Joe Falls	.50	.25	.15
(8)	Joe Ginsberg	.50	.25	.15
(9)	Ernie Harwell	.50	.25	.15
(10)	Ray Herbert	.50	.25	.15
(11)	John Hiller	.50	.25	.15
(12)	Billy Hoeft	.50	.25	.15
(13)	Ralph Houk	.50	.25	.15
(14)	Cliff Kachline	.50	.25	.15
(15)	George Kell	1.00	.50	.30
(16)	Ron LeFlore	.50	.25	.15
(17)	Barney McCosky	.50	.25	.15
(18)	Jim Northrup	.50	.25	.15
(19)	Dick Radatz	.50	.25	.15
(20)	Tom Timmermann	.50	.25	.15

1940 Michigan Sportservice Detroit Tigers

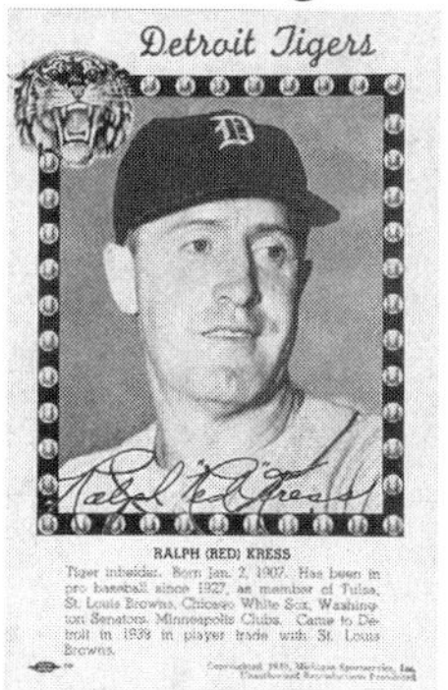

Apparently a team issue sent to persons who wrote the team or players for photos, these blank-back cards measure 4-1/8" x 6-1/4" and are printed in black-and-white. A facsimile autograph is printed over the central portrait, which is surrounded by a border of baseballs. A few career notes are printed under the photo. At bottom-left is a union printing label. At bottom-right is printed, "Copyrighted 1939, Michigan Sportservice, Inc. Unauthorized Reproduction Prohibited". The unnumbered cards are checklisted here alphabetically.

		NM	EX	VG
Complete Set (21):		5400.	2700.	1650.
Common Player:		300.00	150.00	90.00
(1)	Earl Averill	350.00	175.00	105.00
(2)	Dick Bartell	300.00	150.00	90.00
(3)	Roy "Beau" Bell	300.00	150.00	90.00
(4)	Al Benton	300.00	150.00	90.00
(5)	Tommy Bridges	300.00	150.00	90.00
(6)	Frank Croucher	300.00	150.00	90.00
(7)	Pete Fox	300.00	150.00	90.00
(8)	Charlie Gehringer	400.00	200.00	120.00
(9)	Hank Greenberg	550.00	275.00	165.00
(10)	John Gorsica	300.00	150.00	90.00
(11)	Pinky Higgins	300.00	150.00	90.00
(12)	Fred Hutchinson	300.00	150.00	90.00
(13)	Ralph "Red" Kress	300.00	150.00	90.00
(14)	Barney McCosky	300.00	150.00	90.00
(15)	Archie R. McKain	300.00	150.00	90.00
(16)	Hal Newhouser	350.00	175.00	105.00
(17)	Louis "Buck" Newsom	300.00	150.00	90.00
(18)	Schoolboy Rowe	300.00	150.00	90.00
(19)	Birdie Tebbetts	300.00	150.00	90.00
(20)	Dizzy Trout	300.00	150.00	90.00
(21)	Rudy York	300.00	150.00	90.00

1975 Mid-Atlantic Sports Collectors Assn.

This "Baseball Royalty" collectors set was issued in conjunction with the 1975 convention of the Mid-Atlantic Sports Collectors Association in Pikesville, Md. The blank-backed, 2-1/2" x 4-3/4" cards are printed in red and blue on white with player photos in blue. Each of the players in the set has a name or nickname pertaining to royalty. The unnumbered cards are checklisted here in alphabetical order.

		NM	EX	VG
Complete Set (8):		7.00	3.50	2.00
Common Player:		.50	.25	.15
(1)	Paul (Duke) Derringer	.50	.25	.15
(2)	Elroy (Baron of the Bullpen) Face	.50	.25	.15
(3)	Rogers (Rajah) Hornsby	.75	.40	.25
(4)	(King) Carl Hubbell	.75	.40	.25
(5)	Charley (King Kong) Keller	.50	.25	.15
(6)	Babe (Sultan of Swat) Ruth	3.00	1.50	.90
(7)	(Prince) Hal Schumacher	.50	.25	.15
(8)	Edwin (Duke) Snider	1.00	.50	.30

1927 Middy Bread Browns/Cardinals Die-Cuts

The emphasis is on St. Louis Cardinals and St. Louis Browns players in this set, although a handful of Yankees and a few Giants are salted throughout the checklist. The black-and-white, blank-backed cards are known only in die-cut form, and vary in size according to the player pose, with a typical card measuring 2-1/4" x 4" or so. The checklist, arranged here alphabetically, currently consists of just over 50 cards, but may be subject to future additions. Similar to the previous year's issue of Kut Outs Yankees and Giants die-cut cards, this issue features black-and-white player photos with the backgrounds cut away and the player and team name printed at the bottom of the photo. Unlike the earlier New York issue, however, these cards carry an advertisement at bottom for Midday Bread, and were presumably issued in the St. Louis area, though the exact method of their distribution is unknown. Depending on the exact pose, cards measure about 2" wide by 4" tall and are blank-backed and unnumbered. The issue includes 22 cards each of the Browns and Cardinals. As with all die-cut cards, various appendages and bat ends were easily torn off and cards with such defects suffer severe loss of value.

		NM	EX	VG
Complete Set (44):		5500.	2200.	1100.
Common Player:		100.00	50.00	30.00
St. Louis Browns				
(1)	Spencer Adams	150.00	60.00	30.00
(2)	Win Ballou	150.00	60.00	30.00
(3)	Walter Beck	150.00	60.00	30.00
(4)	Herschel Bennett	150.00	60.00	30.00
(5)	Stewart Bolen	150.00	60.00	30.00
(6)	Leo Dixon	150.00	60.00	30.00
(7)	Chester Falk	150.00	60.00	30.00
(8)	Milton Gaston	150.00	60.00	30.00
(9)	Walter Gerber	150.00	60.00	30.00
(10)	Sam Jones	150.00	60.00	30.00
(11)	Oscar Melillo	150.00	60.00	30.00
(12)	Bing Miller	150.00	60.00	30.00
(13)	Otis Miller	150.00	60.00	30.00
(14)	Billie Mullen	150.00	60.00	30.00
(15)	Ernie Nevers	300.00	120.00	60.00
(16)	Steve O'Neill	150.00	60.00	30.00
(17)	Harry Rice	150.00	60.00	30.00
(18)	George Sisler	250.00	100.00	50.00
(19)	Walter Stewart	150.00	60.00	30.00
(20)	Elam VanGilder	150.00	60.00	30.00
(21)	Ken Williams	150.00	60.00	30.00
(22)	Ernie Wingard	150.00	60.00	30.00
St. Louis Cardinals				
(1)	Grover Alexander	300.00	120.00	60.00
(2)	Herman Bell	150.00	60.00	30.00
(3)	Lester Bell	150.00	60.00	30.00
(4)	Ray Blades	150.00	60.00	30.00
(5)	Jim Bottomley	250.00	100.00	50.00
(6)	Danny Clark	150.00	60.00	30.00
(7)	Taylor Douthit	150.00	60.00	30.00
(8)	Frank Frisch	250.00	100.00	50.00
(9)	Chick Hafey	225.00	90.00	45.00
(10)	Jesse Haines	150.00	60.00	30.00
(11)	Vic Keen	150.00	60.00	30.00
(12)	Carlise Littlejohn	150.00	60.00	30.00
(13)	Bob McGraw	150.00	60.00	30.00
(14)	Bob O'Farrell	150.00	60.00	30.00
(15)	Art Reinhardt	150.00	60.00	30.00
(16)	Jimmy Ring	150.00	60.00	30.00
(17)	Walter Roettger	150.00	60.00	30.00
(18)	Robert Schang	150.00	60.00	30.00
(19)	Willie Sherdel	150.00	60.00	30.00
(20)	Billy Southworth	150.00	60.00	30.00
(21)	Tommy Thevenow	150.00	60.00	30.00
(22)	George Toporcer	150.00	60.00	30.00

1976 Midwest Sports Collectors Convention

This collectors issue was produced in conjunction with the 7th annual convention of the Midwest Sports Collectors in Troy, Mich. Former members of the Detroit Tigers, with an emphasis on the 1930s, are featured on the black-and-white, 2-3/8" x 2-7/8" cards. Players are depicted in portrait and action drawings, with personal data and career highlights added in either written or comic form. Backs advertise the show. The unnumbered cards are checklisted here in alphabetical order.

		NM	EX	VG
Complete Set (23):		12.00	6.00	3.50
Common Player:		.50	.25	.15
(1)	Eldon Auker	.50	.25	.15
(2)	Tommy Bridges	.50	.25	.15
(3)	Flea Clifton	.50	.25	.15
(4)	Mickey Cochrane	.75	.40	.25
(5)	General Crowder	.50	.25	.15
(6)	Frank Doljack	.50	.25	.15
(7)	Carl Fischer	.50	.25	.15
(8)	Pete Fox	.50	.25	.15
(9)	Charlie Gehringer	.75	.40	.25
(10)	Goose Goslin	.75	.40	.25
(11)	Hank Greenberg	1.50	.70	.45
(12)	Luke Hamlin	.50	.25	.15
(13)	Ray Hayworth	.50	.25	.15
(14)	Chief Hogsett	.50	.25	.15
(15)	Firpo Marberry	.50	.25	.15
(16)	Marvin Owen	.50	.25	.15
(17)	Cy Perkins	.50	.25	.15
(18)	Bill Rogell	.50	.25	.15
(19)	Schoolboy Rowe	.50	.25	.15
(20)	Heinie Schuble	.50	.25	.15
(21)	Vic Sorrell	.50	.25	.15
(22)	Gee Walker	.50	.25	.15
(23)	Jo Jo White	.50	.25	.15

1980 Midwest Sports Collectors Convention

Reprints of a number of the player postcards of J.D. McCarthy were produced in conjunction with the 1980 Detroit show. The blank-backed, black-and-white postcards are 3-1/4" x 5-1/2" and all feature former Detroit Tigers. The unnumbered cards are checklisted here alphabetically.

		NM	EX	VG
Complete Set (11):		4.50	2.25	1.25
Common Player:		.25	.13	.08
(1)	Bob Anderson	.25	.13	.08
(2)	Babe Birrer	.25	.13	.08
(3)	Frank Bolling	.25	.13	.08
(4)	Jim Bunning	.75	.40	.25
(5)	Al Cicotte	.25	.13	.08
(6)	Paul Foytack	.25	.13	.08
(7)	Joe Ginsberg	.25	.13	.08
(8)	Steve Gromek	.25	.13	.08
(9)	Art Houtteman	.25	.13	.08
(10)	Al Kaline	1.50	.70	.45
(11)	Harvey Kuenn	.45	.25	.14

1964+ Mike Roberts Color HoF Plaque Postcards

(See Hall of Fame Yellow Plaque Postcards for checklist, price data.)

1971 Milk Duds

These cards were issued on the backs of five-cent packages of Milk Duds candy. Most collectors prefer complete boxes, rather than cut-out cards, which measure approximately 1-13/16" x 2-5/8" when trimmed tightly. Values quoted below are for complete boxes. Cut cards will bring 50-75% of the quoted values. The set includes 37 National League and 32 American League players. Card numbers appear on the box flap, with each number from 1 through 24 being shared by three different players. A suffix (a, b and c) has been added for the collector's convenience. Harmon Killebrew, Brooks Robinson and Pete Rose were double-printed.

		NM	EX	VG
Complete Set, Boxes:		1000.	500.00	300.00
Complete Set, Singles (72):		800.00	400.00	240.00
Common Player:		9.00	4.50	2.75
1a	Frank Howard	9.00	4.50	2.75
1b	Fritz Peterson	9.00	4.50	2.75
1c	Pete Rose	70.00	35.00	21.00
2a	Johnny Bench	35.00	17.50	10.50
2b	Rico Carty	9.00	4.50	2.75
2c	Pete Rose	70.00	35.00	21.00
3a	Ken Holtzman	9.00	4.50	2.75
3b	Willie Mays	50.00	25.00	15.00
3c	Cesar Tovar	9.00	4.50	2.75
4a	Willie Davis	9.00	4.50	2.75
4b	Harmon Killebrew	17.50	8.75	5.25
4c	Felix Millan	9.00	4.50	2.75
5a	Billy Grabarkewitz	9.00	4.50	2.75
5b	Andy Messersmith	9.00	4.50	2.75
5c	Thurman Munson	30.00	15.00	9.00
6a	Luis Aparicio	17.50	8.75	5.25

6b	Lou Brock	17.50	8.75	5.25
6c	Bill Melton	9.00	4.50	2.75
7a	Ray Culp	9.00	4.50	2.75
7b	Willie McCovey	17.50	8.75	5.25
7c	Luke Walker	9.00	4.50	2.75
8a	Roberto Clemente	75.00	37.00	22.00
8b	Jim Merritt	9.00	4.50	2.75
8c	Claud Osteen (Claude)	9.00	4.50	2.75
9a	Stan Bahnsen	9.00	4.50	2.75
9b	Sam McDowell	9.00	4.50	2.75
9c	Billy Williams	17.50	8.75	5.25
10a	Jim Hickman	9.00	4.50	2.75
10b	Dave McNally	9.00	4.50	2.75
10c	Tony Perez	12.00	6.00	3.50
11a	Hank Aaron	50.00	25.00	15.00
11b	Glen Beckert (Glenn)	9.00	4.50	2.75
11c	Ray Fosse	9.00	4.50	2.75
12a	Alex Johnson	9.00	4.50	2.75
12b	Gaylord Perry	15.00	7.50	4.50
12c	Wayne Simpson	9.00	4.50	2.75
13a	Dave Johnson	9.00	4.50	2.75
13b	George Scott	9.00	4.50	2.75
13c	Tom Seaver	25.00	12.50	7.50
14a	Bill Freehan	9.00	4.50	2.75
14b	Bud Harrelson	9.00	4.50	2.75
14c	Manny Sanguillen	9.00	4.50	2.75
15a	Bob Gibson	17.50	8.75	5.25
15b	Rusty Staub	9.00	4.50	2.75
15c	Roy White	9.00	4.50	2.75
16a	Jim Fregosi	9.00	4.50	2.75
16b	Catfish Hunter	15.00	7.50	4.50
16c	Mel Stottlemyer (Stottlemyre)	9.00	4.50	2.75
17a	Tommy Harper	9.00	4.50	2.75
17b	Frank Robinson	25.00	12.50	7.50
17c	Reggie Smith	9.00	4.50	2.75
18a	Orlando Cepeda	12.00	6.00	3.50
18b	Rico Petrocelli	9.00	4.50	2.75
18c	Brooks Robinson	25.00	12.50	7.50
19a	Tony Oliva	9.00	4.50	2.75
19b	Milt Pappas	9.00	4.50	2.75
19c	Bobby Tolan	9.00	4.50	2.75
20a	Ernie Banks	25.00	12.50	7.50
20b	Don Kessinger	9.00	4.50	2.75
20c	Joe Torre	12.00	6.00	3.50
21a	Fergie Jenkins	15.00	7.50	4.50
21b	Jim Palmer	17.50	8.75	5.25
21c	Ron Santo	12.50	6.25	3.75
22a	Randy Hundley	9.00	4.50	2.75
22b	Dennis Menke (Denis)	9.00	4.50	2.75
22c	Boog Powell	10.00	5.00	3.00
23a	Dick Dietz	9.00	4.50	2.75
23b	Tommy John	9.00	4.50	2.75
23c	Brooks Robinson	25.00	12.50	7.50
24a	Danny Cater	9.00	4.50	2.75
24b	Harmon Killebrew	17.50	8.75	5.25
24c	Jim Perry	9.00	4.50	2.75

1933 George C. Miller

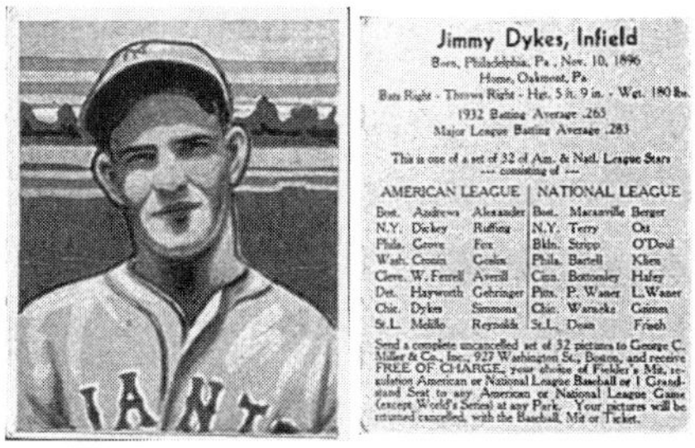

George C. Miller & Co. of Boston, Mass., issued a 32-card set in 1933. The set, which received limited distribution, consists of 16 National League and 16 American League players. The cards are color art reproductions of actual photographs and measure 2-3/8" x 2-7/8". Two distinct variations can be found for each card in the set. Two different typefaces were used, one being much smaller than the other. The most substantial difference is "R" and "L" being used for the "Bats/Throws" information on one version, while the other spells out "Right" and "Left." Collectors were advised on the card backs to collect all 32 cards and return them for prizes. (Ivy Andrews' card was short-printed to avoid giving out too many prizes.) The cards, with a cancellation at the bottom, were returned to the collector with the prize. Two forms of cancellation were used; one involved the complete trimming of the bottom one-quarter of the card, the other a series of diamond-shaped punch holes. Cancelled cards have a significantly decreased value.

		NM	EX	VG
Complete Set (32):		16000.	7200.	4000.
Common Player:		400.00	180.00	100.00
(1)	Dale Alexander	400.00	180.00	100.00
(2)	"Ivy" Paul Andrews	2600.	1175.	650.00
(3)	Earl Averill	575.00	250.00	145.00
(4)	Dick Bartell	400.00	180.00	100.00
(5)	Walter Berger	400.00	180.00	100.00
(6)	Jim Bottomley	575.00	250.00	145.00
(7)	Joe Cronin	600.00	275.00	150.00
(8)	Jerome "Dizzy" Dean	1200.	550.00	300.00
(9)	William Dickey	650.00	290.00	160.00
(10)	Jimmy Dykes	400.00	180.00	100.00
(11)	Wesley Ferrell	400.00	180.00	100.00
(12)	Jimmy Foxx	700.00	315.00	175.00
(13)	Frank Frisch	575.00	250.00	145.00
(14)	Charlie Gehringer	600.00	275.00	150.00
(15)	Leon "Goose" Goslin	575.00	250.00	145.00
(16)	Charlie Grimm	400.00	180.00	100.00
(17)	Bob "Lefty" Grove	600.00	275.00	150.00
(18)	Charles "Chick" Hafey	575.00	250.00	145.00
(19)	Ray Hayworth	400.00	180.00	100.00
(20)	Charles "Chuck" Klein	575.00	250.00	145.00
(21)	Walter "Rabbit" Maranville	575.00	250.00	145.00
(22)	Oscar Melillo	400.00	180.00	100.00
(23)	Frank "Lefty" O'Doul	425.00	190.00	105.00
(24)	Melvin Ott	650.00	290.00	160.00
(25)	Carl Reynolds	400.00	180.00	100.00
(26)	Charles Ruffing	575.00	250.00	145.00
(27)	Al Simmons	575.00	250.00	145.00
(28)	Joe Stripp	400.00	180.00	100.00
(29)	Bill Terry	575.00	250.00	145.00
(30)	Lloyd Waner	575.00	250.00	145.00
(31)	Paul Waner	575.00	250.00	145.00
(32)	Lonnie Warneke	400.00	180.00	100.00

1969 Milton Bradley

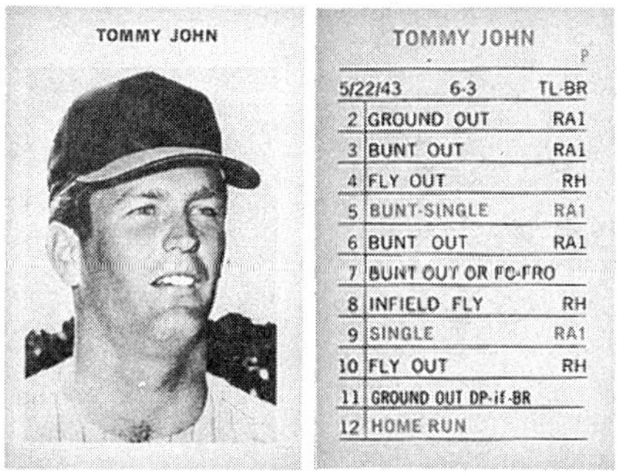

The first of three sets issued by Milton Bradley over a four-year period, these cards were part of a baseball board game. The unnumbered cards measure 2" x 3" and have a white border surrounding the black-and-white player photo. The player's name appears above the photo in upper case letters. There are no team designations and the photos are airbrushed to eliminate team logos. Backs display biographical data along the top followed by a list of various game situations used in playing the board game. The cards have square corners. Because the 1969 and 1972 game cards are virtually identical in format it will help in differentiating the two to know that on back if there is a numeral "1" in a line of red type, it will not have a base on a 1969 card, but will have a base if the card is a 1972.

		NM	EX	VG
Complete Boxed Set:		400.00	200.00	120.00
Complete Set (296):		250.00	125.00	75.00
Common Player:		.50	.25	.15
(1)	Hank Aaron	30.00	15.00	9.00
(2)	Ted Abernathy	.50	.25	.15
(3)	Jerry Adair	.50	.25	.15
(4)	Tommy Agee	.50	.25	.15
(5)	Bernie Allen	.50	.25	.15
(6)	Hank Allen	.50	.25	.15
(7)	Richie Allen	2.50	1.25	.70
(8)	Gene Alley	.50	.25	.15
(9)	Bob Allison	.50	.25	.15
(10)	Felipe Alou	1.00	.50	.30
(11)	Jesus Alou	.50	.25	.15
(12)	Matty Alou	.50	.25	.15
(13)	Max Alvis	.50	.25	.15
(14)	Mike Andrews	.50	.25	.15
(15)	Luis Aparicio	7.50	3.75	2.25
(16)	Jose Arcia	.50	.25	.15
(17)	Bob Aspromonte	.50	.25	.15
(18)	Joe Azcue	.50	.25	.15
(19)	Ernie Banks	18.00	9.00	5.50
(20)	Steve Barber	.50	.25	.15
(21)	John Bateman	.50	.25	.15
(22)	Glen Beckert (Glenn)	.50	.25	.15
(23)	Gary Bell	.50	.25	.15
(24)	John Bench	20.00	10.00	6.00
(25)	Ken Berry	.50	.25	.15
(26)	Frank Bertaina	.50	.25	.15
(27)	Paul Blair	.50	.25	.15
(28)	Wade Blasingame	.50	.25	.15
(29)	Curt Blefary	.50	.25	.15
(30)	John Boccabella	.50	.25	.15
(31)	Bobby Lee Bonds	1.00	.50	.30
(32)	Sam Bowens	.50	.25	.15
(33)	Ken Boyer	1.00	.50	.30
(34)	Charles Bradford	.50	.25	.15
(35)	Darrell Brandon	.50	.25	.15
(36)	Jim Brewer	.50	.25	.15
(37)	John Briggs	.50	.25	.15
(38)	Nelson Briles	.50	.25	.15
(39)	Ed Brinkman	.50	.25	.15
(40)	Lou Brock	12.50	6.25	3.75
(41)	Gates Brown	.50	.25	.15
(42)	Larry Brown	.50	.25	.15
(43)	George Brunet	.50	.25	.15
(44)	Jerry Buchek	.50	.25	.15
(45)	Don Buford	.50	.25	.15
(46)	Jim Bunning	7.50	3.75	2.25
(47)	Johnny Callison	.50	.25	.15
(48)	Campy Campaneris	.50	.25	.15
(49)	Jose Cardenal	.50	.25	.15
(50)	Leo Cardenas	.50	.25	.15
(51)	Don Cardwell	.50	.25	.15
(52)	Rod Carew	12.50	6.25	3.75
(53)	Paul Casanova	.50	.25	.15
(54)	Norm Cash	1.50	.70	.45
(55)	Danny Cater	.50	.25	.15
(56)	Orlando Cepeda	9.00	4.50	2.75
(57)	Dean Chance	.50	.25	.15
(58)	Ed Charles	.50	.25	.15
(59)	Horace Clarke	.50	.25	.15
(60)	Roberto Clemente	45.00	22.00	13.50
(61)	Donn Clendenon	.50	.25	.15
(62)	Ty Cline	.50	.25	.15
(63)	Nate Colbert	.50	.25	.15
(64)	Joe Coleman	.50	.25	.15
(65)	Bob Cox	.50	.25	.15
(66)	Mike Cuellar	.50	.25	.15
(67)	Ray Culp	.50	.25	.15
(68)	Clay Dalrymple	.50	.25	.15
(69)	Vic Davalillo	.50	.25	.15
(70)	Jim Davenport	.50	.25	.15
(71)	Ron Davis	.50	.25	.15
(72)	Tommy Davis	.50	.25	.15
(73)	Willie Davis	.50	.25	.15
(74)	Chuck Dobson	.50	.25	.15
(75)	John Donaldson	.50	.25	.15
(76)	Al Downing	.50	.25	.15
(77)	Moe Drabowsky	.50	.25	.15
(78)	Dick Ellsworth	.50	.25	.15
(79)	Mike Epstein	.50	.25	.15
(80)	Andy Etchebarren	.50	.25	.15
(81)	Ron Fairly	.50	.25	.15
(82)	Dick Farrell	.50	.25	.15
(83)	Curt Flood	1.00	.50	.30
(84)	Joe Foy	.50	.25	.15
(85)	Tito Francona	.50	.25	.15
(86)	Bill Freehan	.75	.40	.25
(87)	Jim Fregosi	.50	.25	.15
(88)	Woodie Fryman	.50	.25	.15
(89)	Len Gabrielson	.50	.25	.15
(90)	Cito Gaston	.50	.25	.15
(91)	Jake Gibbs	.50	.25	.15
(92)	Russ Gibson	.50	.25	.15
(93)	Dave Giusti	.50	.25	.15
(94)	Tony Gonzalez	.50	.25	.15
(95)	Jim Gosger	.50	.25	.15
(96)	Julio Gotay	.50	.25	.15
(97)	Dick Green	.50	.25	.15
(98)	Jerry Grote	.50	.25	.15
(99)	Jimmie Hall	.50	.25	.15
(100)	Tom Haller	.50	.25	.15
(101)	Steve Hamilton	.50	.25	.15
(102)	Ron Hansen	.50	.25	.15
(103)	Jim Hardin	.50	.25	.15
(104)	Tommy Harper	.50	.25	.15
(105)	Bud Harrelson	.50	.25	.15
(106)	Ken Harrelson	.50	.25	.15
(107)	Jim Hart	.50	.25	.15
(108)	Woodie Held	.50	.25	.15
(109)	Tommy Helms	.50	.25	.15
(110)	Elrod Hendricks	.50	.25	.15
(111)	Mike Hershberger	.50	.25	.15
(112)	Jack Hiatt	.50	.25	.15
(113)	Jim Hickman	.50	.25	.15
(114)	John Hiller	.50	.25	.15
(115)	Chuck Hinton	.50	.25	.15
(116)	Ken Holtzman	.50	.25	.15
(117)	Joel Horlen	.50	.25	.15
(118)	Tony Horton	.50	.25	.15
(119)	Willie Horton	.50	.25	.15
(120)	Frank Howard	1.00	.50	.30
(121)	Dick Howser	.50	.25	.15
(122)	Randy Hundley	.50	.25	.15
(123)	Ron Hunt	.50	.25	.15
(124)	Catfish Hunter	7.50	3.75	2.25
(125)	Al Jackson	.50	.25	.15
(126)	Larry Jackson	.50	.25	.15
(127)	Reggie Jackson	35.00	17.50	10.50
(128)	Sonny Jackson	.50	.25	.15
(129)	Pat Jarvis	.50	.25	.15
(130)	Julian Javier	.50	.25	.15
(131)	Ferguson Jenkins	7.50	3.75	2.25
(132)	Manny Jimenez	.50	.25	.15
(133)	Tommy John	2.00	1.00	.60
(134)	Bob Johnson	.50	.25	.15
(135)	Dave Johnson	.50	.25	.15
(136)	Deron Johnson	.50	.25	.15
(137)	Lou Johnson	.50	.25	.15
(138)	Jay Johnstone	.50	.25	.15
(139)	Cleon Jones	.50	.25	.15
(140)	Dalton Jones	.50	.25	.15
(141)	Duane Josephson	.50	.25	.15
(142)	Jim Kaat	1.50	.70	.45
(143)	Al Kaline	15.00	7.50	4.50
(144)	Don Kessinger	.50	.25	.15
(145)	Harmon Killebrew	12.50	6.25	3.75
(146)	Harold King	.50	.25	.15
(147)	Ed Kirkpatrick	.50	.25	.15
(148)	Fred Klages	.50	.25	.15
(149)	Ron Kline	.50	.25	.15
(150)	Bobby Knoop	.50	.25	.15
(151)	Gary Kolb	.50	.25	.15
(152)	Andy Kosco	.50	.25	.15
(153)	Ed Kranepool	.50	.25	.15
(154)	Lew Krausse	.50	.25	.15
(155)	Harold Lanier	.50	.25	.15
(156)	Jim Lefebvre	.50	.25	.15
(157)	Denny Lemaster	.50	.25	.15
(158)	Dave Leonhard	.50	.25	.15

(159) Don Lock	.50	.25	.15
(160) Mickey Lolich	1.50	.70	.45
(161) Jim Lonborg	.75	.40	.25
(162) Mike Lum	.50	.25	.15
(163) Al Lyle	.50	.25	.15
(164) Jim Maloney	.50	.25	.15
(165) Juan Marichal	8.00	4.00	2.50
(166) J.C. Martin	.50	.25	.15
(167) Marty Martinez	.50	.25	.15
(168) Tom Matchick	.50	.25	.15
(169) Ed Mathews	12.50	6.25	3.75
(170) Dal Maxvill	.50	.25	.15
(171) Jerry May	.50	.25	.15
(172) Lee May	.50	.25	.15
(173) Lee Maye	.50	.25	.15
(174) Willie Mays	30.00	15.00	9.00
(175) Bill Mazeroski	5.00	2.50	1.50
(176) Richard McAuliffe	.50	.25	.15
(177) Al McBean	.50	.25	.15
(178) Tim McCarver	.75	.40	.25
(179) Bill McCool	.50	.25	.15
(180) Mike McCormick	.50	.25	.15
(181) Willie McCovey	12.50	6.25	3.75
(182) Tom McCraw	.50	.25	.15
(183) Lindy McDaniel	.50	.25	.15
(184) Sam McDowell	.75	.40	.25
(185) Orlando McFarlane	.50	.25	.15
(186) Jim McGlothlin	.50	.25	.15
(187) Denny McLain	1.25	.60	.40
(188) Ken McMullen	.50	.25	.15
(189) Dave McNally	.50	.25	.15
(190) Gerry McNertney	.50	.25	.15
(191) Dennis Menke (Denis)	.50	.25	.15
(192) Felix Millan	.50	.25	.15
(193) Don Mincher	.50	.25	.15
(194) Rick Monday	.50	.25	.15
(195) Joe Morgan	7.50	3.75	2.25
(196) Bubba Morton	.50	.25	.15
(197) Manny Mota	.50	.25	.15
(198) Jim Nash	.50	.25	.15
(199) Dave Nelson	.50	.25	.15
(200) Dick Nen	.50	.25	.15
(201) Phil Niekro	7.50	3.75	2.25
(202) Jim Northrup	.50	.25	.15
(203) Richard Nye	.50	.25	.15
(204) Johnny Odom	.50	.25	.15
(205) Tony Oliva	2.00	1.00	.60
(206) Gene Oliver	.50	.25	.15
(207) Phil Ortega	.50	.25	.15
(208) Claude Osteen	.50	.25	.15
(209) Ray Oyler	.50	.25	.15
(210) Jose Pagan	.50	.25	.15
(211) Jim Pagliaroni	.50	.25	.15
(212) Milt Pappas	.50	.25	.15
(213) Wes Parker	.50	.25	.15
(214) Camilo Pascual	.50	.25	.15
(215) Don Pavletich	.50	.25	.15
(216) Joe Pepitone	.50	.25	.15
(217) Tony Perez	8.00	4.00	2.50
(218) Gaylord Perry	7.50	3.75	2.25
(219) Jim Perry	.50	.25	.15
(220) Gary Peters	.50	.25	.15
(221) Rico Petrocelli	.50	.25	.15
(222) Adolfo Phillips	.50	.25	.15
(223) Tom Phoebus	.50	.25	.15
(224) Vada Pinson	2.00	1.00	.60
(225) Boog Powell	2.25	1.25	.70
(226) Frank Quilici	.50	.25	.15
(227) Doug Rader	.50	.25	.15
(228) Rich Reese	.50	.25	.15
(229) Phil Regan	.50	.25	.15
(230) Rick Reichardt	.50	.25	.15
(231) Rick Renick	.50	.25	.15
(232) Roger Repoz	.50	.25	.15
(233) Dave Ricketts	.50	.25	.15
(234) Bill Robinson	.50	.25	.15
(235) Brooks Robinson	15.00	7.50	4.50
(236) Frank Robinson	12.50	6.25	3.75
(237) Bob Rodgers	.50	.25	.15
(238) Cookie Rojas	.50	.25	.15
(239) Rich Rollins	.50	.25	.15
(240) Phil Roof	.50	.25	.15
(241) Pete Rose	30.00	15.00	9.00
(242) John Roseboro	.50	.25	.15
(243) Chico Ruiz	.50	.25	.15
(244) Ray Sadecki	.50	.25	.15
(245) Chico Salmon	.50	.25	.15
(246) Jose Santiago	.50	.25	.15
(247) Ron Santo	2.50	1.25	.70
(248) Tom Satriano	.50	.25	.15
(249) Paul Schaal	.50	.25	.15
(250) Tom Seaver	12.50	6.25	3.75
(251) Art Shamsky	.50	.25	.15
(252) Mike Shannon	.50	.25	.15
(253) Chris Short	.50	.25	.15
(254) Dick Simpson	.50	.25	.15
(255) Duke Sims	.50	.25	.15
(256) Reggie Smith	.50	.25	.15
(257) Willie Smith	.50	.25	.15
(258) Russ Snyder	.50	.25	.15
(259) Al Spangler	.50	.25	.15
(260) Larry Stahl	.50	.25	.15
(261) Lee Stange	.50	.25	.15
(262) Mickey Stanley	.50	.25	.15
(263) Willie Stargell	10.00	5.00	3.00
(264) Rusty Staub	1.00	.50	.30
(265) Mel Stottlemyre	.50	.25	.15
(266) Ed Stroud	.50	.25	.15
(267) Don Sutton	7.50	3.75	2.25
(268) Ron Swoboda	.50	.25	.15
(269) Jose Tartabull	.50	.25	.15
(270) Tony Taylor	.50	.25	.15
(271) Luis Tiant	1.00	.50	.30
(272) Bob Tillman	.50	.25	.15
(273) Bobby Tolan	.50	.25	.15
(274) Jeff Torborg	.50	.25	.15
(275) Joe Torre	1.50	.70	.45
(276) Cesar Tovar	.50	.25	.15
(277) Dick Tracewski	.50	.25	.15
(278) Tom Tresh	.75	.40	.25
(279) Ted Uhlaender	.50	.25	.15
(280) Del Unser	.50	.25	.15
(281) Hilario Valdespino	.50	.25	.15
(282) Fred Valentine	.50	.25	.15
(283) Bob Veale	.50	.25	.15
(284) Zoilo Versalles	.50	.25	.15
(285) Pete Ward	.50	.25	.15
(286) Al Weis	.50	.25	.15
(287) Don Wert	.50	.25	.15
(288) Bill White	.50	.25	.15
(289) Roy White	.50	.25	.15
(290) Fred Whitfield	.50	.25	.15
(291) Hoyt Wilhelm	7.50	3.75	2.25
(292) Billy Williams	11.00	5.50	3.25
(293) Maury Wills	.75	.40	.25
(294) Earl Wilson	.50	.25	.15
(295) Wilbur Wood	.50	.25	.15
(296) Jerry Zimmerman	.50	.25	.15

1970 Milton Bradley

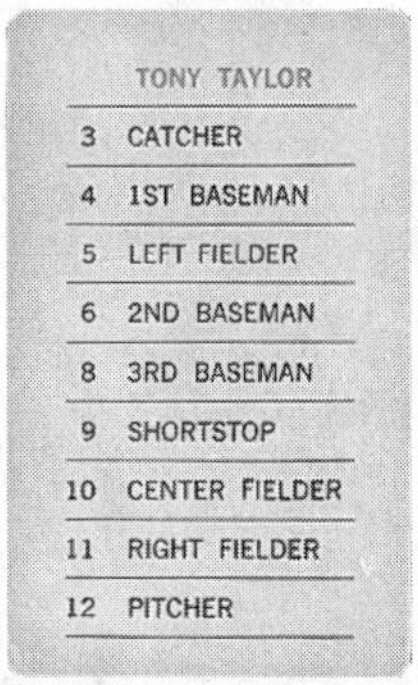

TONY TAYLOR
3 CATCHER
4 1ST BASEMAN
5 LEFT FIELDER
6 2ND BASEMAN
8 3RD BASEMAN
9 SHORTSTOP
10 CENTER FIELDER
11 RIGHT FIELDER
12 PITCHER

Except for the slightly larger (2-3/8" x 3-1/2") size, the format of the 1970 Milton Bradley set is similar to the 1969 Milton Bradley issue. Again designed for use with a baseball board game, the unnumbered black-and-white cards have rounded corners and wide white borders. The player's name appears in capital letters beneath the photo with his position, birthdate, height and batting and throwing preference on a line below. The back of the card shows the player's name along the top followed by a list of possible game situations used in playing the board game. There are no team designations on the cards and all team insignias have been airbrushed from the photos.

	NM	EX	VG
Complete Boxed Set:	300.00	150.00	90.00
Complete Card Set (28):	240.00	120.00	70.00
Common Player:	2.50	1.25	.70
(1) Hank Aaron	33.00	16.50	10.00
(2) Ernie Banks	21.00	10.50	6.25
(3) Lou Brock	14.50	7.25	4.25
(4) Rod Carew	17.00	8.50	5.00
(5) Roberto Clemente	35.00	17.50	10.50
(6) Tommy Davis	2.50	1.25	.70
(7) Bill Freehan	2.50	1.25	.70
(8) Jim Fregosi	2.50	1.25	.70
(9) Tom Haller	2.50	1.25	.70
(10) Frank Howard	2.50	1.25	.70
(11) Reggie Jackson	24.00	12.00	7.25
(12) Harmon Killebrew	17.00	8.50	5.00
(13) Mickey S. Lolich	3.50	1.75	1.00
(14) Juan Marichal	12.00	6.00	3.50
(15) Willie Mays	33.00	16.50	10.00
(16) Willie McCovey	14.50	7.25	4.25
(17) Sam McDowell	2.50	1.25	.70
(18) Dennis Menke (Denis)	2.50	1.25	.70
(19) Don Mincher	2.50	1.25	.70
(20) Phil Niekro	12.00	6.00	3.50
(21) Rico Petrocelli	2.50	1.25	.70
(22) Boog Powell	3.50	1.75	1.00
(23) Frank Robinson	17.00	8.50	5.00
(24) Pete Rose	33.00	16.50	10.00
(25) Ron Santo	4.25	2.25	1.25
(26) Tom Seaver	21.00	10.50	6.25
(27) Mel Stottlemyre	2.50	1.25	.70
(28) Tony Taylor	2.50	1.25	.70

1972 Milton Bradley

The 1972 Milton Bradley set was again designed for use with a baseball table game. The 1972 cards are similar to the 1969 and 1970 issues. The unnumbered black-and-white cards measure 2" x 3" and display the player's name along the top of the card. Again, all team insignias have been eliminated by airbrushing, and there are no team designations indicated. Backs carry the player's name and personal data followed by a list of possible game situations used in playing the game. To differentiate a 1972 card from a 1969, look on back for a line of red type which contains the numeral "1". If the digit has a base, the card is a '72; if there is no base to the red "1", it is a 1969.

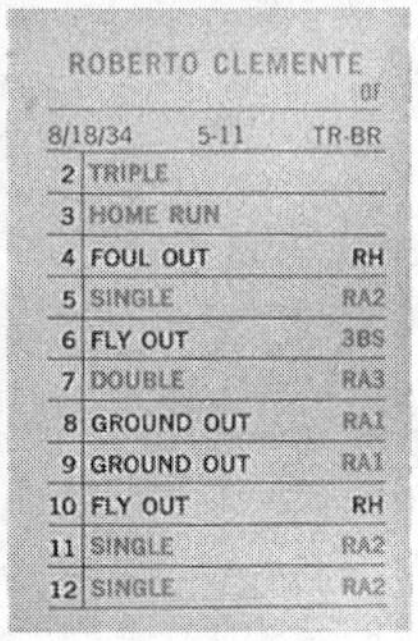

	NM	EX	VG
Complete Boxed Set:	450.00	225.00	135.00
Complete Card Set (378):	400.00	200.00	120.00
Common Player:	.50	.25	.15
(1) Hank Aaron	24.00	12.00	7.25
(2) Tommie Aaron	.50	.25	.15
(3) Ted Abernathy	.50	.25	.15
(4) Jerry Adair	.50	.25	.15
(5) Tommy Agee	.50	.25	.15
(6) Bernie Allen	.50	.25	.15
(7) Hank Allen	.50	.25	.15
(8) Richie Allen	.90	.45	.25
(9) Gene Alley	.50	.25	.15
(10) Bob Allison	.50	.25	.15
(11) Sandy Alomar	.50	.25	.15
(12) Felipe Alou	.75	.40	.25
(13) Jesus Alou	.50	.25	.15
(14) Matty Alou	.50	.25	.15
(15) Max Alvis	.50	.25	.15
(16) Brant Alyea	.50	.25	.15
(17) Mike Andrews	.50	.25	.15
(18) Luis Aparicio	7.50	3.75	2.25
(19) Jose Arcia	.50	.25	.15
(20) Gerald Arrigo	.50	.25	.15
(21) Bob Aspromonte	.50	.25	.15
(22) Joe Azcue	.50	.25	.15
(23) Robert Bailey	.50	.25	.15
(24) Sal Bando	.50	.25	.15
(25) Ernie Banks	15.00	7.50	4.50
(26) Steve Barber	.50	.25	.15
(27) Robert Barton	.50	.25	.15
(28) John Bateman	.50	.25	.15
(29) Glen Beckert (Glenn)	.50	.25	.15
(30) John Bench	15.00	7.50	4.50
(31) Ken Berry	.50	.25	.15
(32) Frank Bertaina	.50	.25	.15
(33) Paul Blair	.50	.25	.15
(34) Stephen Blass	.50	.25	.15
(35) Curt Blefary	.50	.25	.15
(36) Bobby Bolin	.50	.25	.15
(37) Bobby Lee Bonds	1.00	.50	.30
(38) Donald Bosch	.50	.25	.15
(39) Richard Bosman	.50	.25	.15
(40) Dave Boswell	.50	.25	.15
(41) Kenneth Boswell	.50	.25	.15
(42) Cletis Boyer	.50	.25	.15
(43) Ken Boyer	1.25	.60	.40
(44) Charles Bradford	.50	.25	.15
(45) Ronald Brand	.50	.25	.15
(46) Ken Brett	.50	.25	.15
(47) Jim Brewer	.50	.25	.15
(48) John Briggs	.50	.25	.15
(49) Nelson Briles	.50	.25	.15
(50) Ed Brinkman	.50	.25	.15
(51) James Britton	.50	.25	.15
(52) Lou Brock	9.00	4.50	2.75
(53) Gates Brown	.50	.25	.15
(54) Larry Brown	.50	.25	.15
(55) Ollie Brown	.50	.25	.15
(56) George Brunet	.50	.25	.15
(57) Don Buford	.50	.25	.15
(58) Wallace Bunker	.50	.25	.15
(59) Jim Bunning	6.00	3.00	1.75
(60) William Butler	.50	.25	.15
(61) Johnny Callison	.50	.25	.15
(62) Campy Campaneris	.50	.25	.15
(63) Jose Cardenal	.50	.25	.15
(64) Leo Cardenas	.50	.25	.15
(65) Don Cardwell	.50	.25	.15
(66) Rod Carew	10.00	5.00	3.00
(67) Cisco Carlos	.50	.25	.15
(68) Steve Carlton	10.00	5.00	3.00
(69) Clay Carroll	.50	.25	.15
(70) Paul Casanova	.50	.25	.15
(71) Norm Cash	1.25	.60	.40
(72) Danny Cater	.50	.25	.15
(73) Orlando Cepeda	9.00	4.50	2.75
(74) Dean Chance	.50	.25	.15
(75) Horace Clarke	.50	.25	.15
(76) Roberto Clemente	27.50	13.50	8.25
(77) Donn Clendenon	.50	.25	.15
(78) Ty Cline	.50	.25	.15
(79) Nate Colbert	.50	.25	.15
(80) Joe Coleman	.50	.25	.15
(81) William Conigliaro	.75	.40	.25
(82) Casey Cox	.50	.25	.15
(83) Mike Cuellar	.50	.25	.15
(84) Ray Culp	.50	.25	.15
(85) George Culver	.50	.25	.15
(86) Vic Davalillo	.50	.25	.15
(87) Jim Davenport	.50	.25	.15

(88)	Tommy Davis	.50	.25	.15
(89)	Willie Davis	.50	.25	.15
(90)	Larry Dierker	.50	.25	.15
(91)	Richard Dietz	.50	.25	.15
(92)	Chuck Dobson	.50	.25	.15
(93)	Pat Dobson	.50	.25	.15
(94)	John Donaldson	.50	.25	.15
(95)	Al Downing	.50	.25	.15
(96)	Moe Drabowsky	.50	.25	.15
(97)	John Edwards	.50	.25	.15
(98)	Thomas Egan	.50	.25	.15
(99)	Dick Ellsworth	.50	.25	.15
(100)	Mike Epstein	.50	.25	.15
(101)	Andy Etchebarren	.50	.25	.15
(102)	Ron Fairly	.50	.25	.15
(103)	Frank Fernandez	.50	.25	.15
(104)	Alfred Ferrara	.50	.25	.15
(105)	Michael Fiore	.50	.25	.15
(106)	Curt Flood	1.00	.50	.30
(107)	Vern Fuller	.50	.25	.15
(108)	Joe Foy	.50	.25	.15
(109)	Tito Francona	.50	.25	.15
(110)	Bill Freehan	.50	.25	.15
(111)	Jim Fregosi	.50	.25	.15
(112)	Woodie Fryman	.50	.25	.15
(113)	Len Gabrielson	.50	.25	.15
(114)	Philip Gagliano	.50	.25	.15
(115)	Cito Gaston	.50	.25	.15
(116)	Jake Gibbs	.50	.25	.15
(117)	Russ Gibson	.50	.25	.15
(118)	Dave Giusti	.50	.25	.15
(119)	Fred Gladding	.50	.25	.15
(120)	Tony Gonzalez	.50	.25	.15
(121)	Jim Gosger	.50	.25	.15
(122)	James Grant	.50	.25	.15
(123)	Thomas Griffin	.50	.25	.15
(124)	Dick Green	.50	.25	.15
(125)	Jerry Grote	.50	.25	.15
(126)	Tom Hall	.50	.25	.15
(127)	Tom Haller	.50	.25	.15
(128)	Steve Hamilton	.50	.25	.15
(129)	William Hands	.50	.25	.15
(130)	James Hannan	.50	.25	.15
(131)	Ron Hansen	.50	.25	.15
(132)	Jim Hardin	.50	.25	.15
(133)	Steve Hargan	.50	.25	.15
(134)	Tommy Harper	.50	.25	.15
(135)	Bud Harrelson	.50	.25	.15
(136)	Ken Harrelson	.50	.25	.15
(137)	Jim Hart	.50	.25	.15
(138)	Rich Hebner	.50	.25	.15
(139)	Michael Hedlund	.50	.25	.15
(140)	Tommy Helms	.50	.25	.15
(141)	Elrod Hendricks	.50	.25	.15
(142)	Ronald Herbel	.50	.25	.15
(143)	Jack Hernandez	.50	.25	.15
(144)	Mike Hershberger	.50	.25	.15
(145)	Jack Hiatt	.50	.25	.15
(146)	Jim Hickman	.50	.25	.15
(147)	Dennis Higgins	.50	.25	.15
(148)	John Hiller	.50	.25	.15
(149)	Chuck Hinton	.50	.25	.15
(150)	Larry Hisle	.50	.25	.15
(151)	Ken Holtzman	.50	.25	.15
(152)	Joel Horlen	.50	.25	.15
(153)	Tony Horton	.50	.25	.15
(154)	Willie Horton	.50	.25	.15
(155)	Frank Howard	.75	.40	.25
(156)	Robert Humphreys	.50	.25	.15
(157)	Randy Hundley	.50	.25	.15
(158)	Ron Hunt	.50	.25	.15
(159)	Catfish Hunter	6.00	3.00	1.75
(160)	Grant Jackson	.50	.25	.15
(161)	Reggie Jackson	15.00	7.50	4.50
(162)	Sonny Jackson	.50	.25	.15
(163)	Pat Jarvis	.50	.25	.15
(164)	Larry Jaster	.50	.25	.15
(165)	Julian Javier	.50	.25	.15
(166)	Ferguson Jenkins	6.00	3.00	1.75
(167)	Tommy John	2.00	1.00	.60
(168)	Alexander Johnson	.50	.25	.15
(169)	Bob Johnson	.50	.25	.15
(170)	Dave Johnson	.50	.25	.15
(171)	Deron Johnson	.50	.25	.15
(172)	Jay Johnstone	.50	.25	.15
(173)	Cleon Jones	.50	.25	.15
(174)	Dalton Jones	.50	.25	.15
(175)	Mack Jones	.50	.25	.15
(176)	Richard Joseph	.50	.25	.15
(177)	Duane Josephson	.50	.25	.15
(178)	Jim Kaat	2.50	1.25	.70
(179)	Al Kaline	12.00	6.00	3.50
(180)	Richard Kelley	.50	.25	.15
(181)	Harold Kelly	.50	.25	.15
(182)	Gerald Kenney	.50	.25	.15
(183)	Don Kessinger	.50	.25	.15
(184)	Harmon Killebrew	10.00	5.00	3.00
(185)	Ed Kirkpatrick	.50	.25	.15
(186)	Bobby Knoop	.50	.25	.15
(187)	Calvin Koonce	.50	.25	.15
(188)	Jerry Koosman	.50	.25	.15
(189)	Andy Kosco	.50	.25	.15
(190)	Ed Kranepool	.50	.25	.15
(191)	Ted Kubiak	.50	.25	.15
(192)	Jose Laboy	.50	.25	.15
(193)	Joseph Lahoud	.50	.25	.15
(194)	William Landis	.50	.25	.15
(195)	Harold Lanier	.50	.25	.15
(196)	Fred Lasher	.50	.25	.15
(197)	John Lazar	.50	.25	.15
(198)	Jim Lefebvre	.50	.25	.15
(199)	Denny Lemaster	.50	.25	.15
(200)	Dave Leonhard	.50	.25	.15
(201)	Frank Linzy	.50	.25	.15
(202)	Mickey Lolich	1.25	.60	.40
(203)	Jim Lonborg	.50	.25	.15
(204)	Mike Lum	.50	.25	.15
(205)	Al Lyle	.50	.25	.15
(206)	Jim Maloney	.50	.25	.15
(207)	Juan Marichal	9.00	4.50	2.75
(208)	David Marshall	.50	.25	.15
(209)	J.C. Martin	.50	.25	.15
(210)	Marty Martinez	.50	.25	.15
(211)	Tom Matchick	.50	.25	.15
(212)	Dal Maxvill	.50	.25	.15
(213)	Carlos May	.50	.25	.15
(214)	Jerry May	.50	.25	.15
(215)	Lee May	.50	.25	.15
(216)	Lee Maye	.50	.25	.15
(217)	Willie Mays	24.00	12.00	7.25
(218)	Bill Mazeroski	4.00	2.00	1.25
(219)	Richard McAuliffe	.50	.25	.15
(220)	Al McBean	.50	.25	.15
(221)	Tim McCarver	.60	.30	.20
(222)	Bill McCool	.50	.25	.15
(223)	Mike McCormick	.50	.25	.15
(224)	Willie McCovey	10.00	5.00	3.00
(225)	Tom McCraw	.50	.25	.15
(226)	Lindy McDaniel	.50	.25	.15
(227)	Sam McDowell	.50	.25	.15
(228)	Leon McFadden	.50	.25	.15
(229)	Daniel McGinn	.50	.25	.15
(230)	Jim McGlothlin	.50	.25	.15
(231)	Fred McGraw	.50	.25	.15
(232)	Denny McLain	1.00	.50	.30
(233)	Ken McMullen	.50	.25	.15
(234)	Dave McNally	.50	.25	.15
(235)	Gerry McNertney	.50	.25	.15
(236)	William Melton	.50	.25	.15
(237)	Dennis Menke (Denis)	.50	.25	.15
(238)	John Messersmith	.50	.25	.15
(239)	Felix Millan	.50	.25	.15
(240)	Norman Miller	.50	.25	.15
(241)	Don Mincher	.50	.25	.15
(242)	Rick Monday	.50	.25	.15
(243)	Donald Money	.50	.25	.15
(244)	Barry Moore	.50	.25	.15
(245)	Bob Moose	.50	.25	.15
(246)	David Morehead	.50	.25	.15
(247)	Joe Morgan	9.00	4.50	2.75
(248)	Curt Motton	.50	.25	.15
(249)	Manny Mota	.50	.25	.15
(250)	Bob Murcer	.50	.25	.15
(251)	Thomas Murphy	.50	.25	.15
(252)	Ivan Murrell	.50	.25	.15
(253)	Jim Nash	.50	.25	.15
(254)	Joe Niekro	1.50	.70	.45
(255)	Phil Niekro	6.00	3.00	1.75
(256)	Gary Nolan	.50	.25	.15
(257)	Jim Northrup	.50	.25	.15
(258)	Richard Nye	.50	.25	.15
(259)	Johnny Odom	.50	.25	.15
(260)	John O'Donaghue	.50	.25	.15
(261)	Tony Oliva	1.00	.50	.30
(262)	Al Oliver	1.00	.50	.30
(263)	Robert Oliver	.50	.25	.15
(264)	Claude Osteen	.50	.25	.15
(265)	Ray Oyler	.50	.25	.15
(266)	Jose Pagan	.50	.25	.15
(267)	Jim Palmer	9.00	4.50	2.75
(268)	Milt Pappas	.50	.25	.15
(269)	Wes Parker	.50	.25	.15
(270)	Fred Patek	.50	.25	.15
(271)	Mike Paul	.50	.25	.15
(272)	Joe Pepitone	.50	.25	.15
(273)	Tony Perez	7.50	3.75	2.25
(274)	Gaylord Perry	6.00	3.00	1.75
(275)	Jim Perry	.50	.25	.15
(276)	Gary Peters	.50	.25	.15
(277)	Rico Petrocelli	.50	.25	.15
(278)	Tom Phoebus	.50	.25	.15
(279)	Lou Piniella	1.00	.50	.30
(280)	Vada Pinson	1.50	.70	.45
(281)	Boog Powell	2.00	1.00	.60
(282)	Jim Price	.50	.25	.15
(283)	Frank Quilici	.50	.25	.15
(284)	Doug Rader	.50	.25	.15
(285)	Ron Reed	.50	.25	.15
(286)	Rich Reese	.50	.25	.15
(287)	Phil Regan	.50	.25	.15
(288)	Rick Reichardt	.50	.25	.15
(289)	Rick Renick	.50	.25	.15
(290)	Roger Repoz	.50	.25	.15
(291)	Mervin Rettenmund	.50	.25	.15
(292)	Dave Ricketts	.50	.25	.15
(293)	Juan Rios	.50	.25	.15
(294)	Bill Robinson	.50	.25	.15
(295)	Brooks Robinson	12.00	6.00	3.50
(296)	Frank Robinson	12.00	6.00	3.50
(297)	Aurelio Rodriguez	.50	.25	.15
(298)	Ellie Rodriguez	.50	.25	.15
(299)	Cookie Rojas	.50	.25	.15
(300)	Rich Rollins	.50	.25	.15
(301)	Vicente Romo	.50	.25	.15
(302)	Phil Roof	.50	.25	.15
(303)	Pete Rose	24.00	12.00	7.25
(304)	John Roseboro	.50	.25	.15
(305)	Chico Ruiz	.50	.25	.15
(306)	Mike Ryan	.50	.25	.15
(307)	Ray Sadecki	.50	.25	.15
(308)	Chico Salmon	.50	.25	.15
(309)	Manuel Sanguillen	.50	.25	.15
(310)	Ron Santo	2.50	1.25	.70
(311)	Tom Satriano	.50	.25	.15
(312)	Theodore Savage	.50	.25	.15
(313)	Paul Schaal	.50	.25	.15
(314)	Dick Schofield	.50	.25	.15
(315)	George Scott	.50	.25	.15
(316)	Tom Seaver	10.00	5.00	3.00
(317)	Art Shamsky	.50	.25	.15
(318)	Mike Shannon	.50	.25	.15
(319)	Chris Short	.50	.25	.15
(320)	Sonny Siebert	.50	.25	.15
(321)	Duke Sims	.50	.25	.15
(322)	William Singer	.50	.25	.15
(323)	Reggie Smith	.50	.25	.15
(324)	Willie Smith	.50	.25	.15
(325)	Russ Snyder	.50	.25	.15
(326)	Al Spangler	.50	.25	.15
(327)	James Spencer	.50	.25	.15
(328)	Ed Spiezio	.50	.25	.15
(329)	Larry Stahl	.50	.25	.15
(330)	Lee Stange	.50	.25	.15
(331)	Mickey Stanley	.50	.25	.15
(332)	Willie Stargell	9.00	4.50	2.75
(333)	Rusty Staub	2.00	1.00	.60
(334)	James Stewart	.50	.25	.15
(335)	George Stone	.50	.25	.15
(336)	William Stoneman	.50	.25	.15
(337)	Mel Stottlemyre	.50	.25	.15
(338)	Ed Stroud	.50	.25	.15
(339)	Ken Suarez	.50	.25	.15
(340)	Gary Sutherland	.50	.25	.15
(341)	Don Sutton	6.00	3.00	1.75
(342)	Ron Swoboda	.50	.25	.15
(343)	Fred Talbot	.50	.25	.15
(344)	Jose Tartabull	.50	.25	.15
(345)	Kenneth Tatum	.50	.25	.15
(346)	Tony Taylor	.50	.25	.15
(347)	Luis Tiant	.75	.40	.25
(348)	Bob Tillman	.50	.25	.15
(349)	Bobby Tolan	.50	.25	.15
(350)	Jeff Torborg	.50	.25	.15
(351)	Joe Torre	1.50	.70	.45
(352)	Cesar Tovar	.50	.25	.15
(353)	Tom Tresh	.75	.40	.25
(354)	Ted Uhlaender	.50	.25	.15
(355)	Del Unser	.50	.25	.15
(356)	Bob Veale	.50	.25	.15
(357)	Zoilo Versalles	.50	.25	.15
(358)	Luke Walker	.50	.25	.15
(359)	Pete Ward	.50	.25	.15
(360)	Eddie Watt	.50	.25	.15
(361)	Ramon Webster	.50	.25	.15
(362)	Al Weis	.50	.25	.15
(363)	Don Wert	.50	.25	.15
(364)	Bill White	.50	.25	.15
(365)	Roy White	.50	.25	.15
(366)	Hoyt Wilhelm	6.00	3.00	1.75
(367)	Billy Williams	9.00	4.50	2.75
(368)	Walter Williams	.50	.25	.15
(369)	Maury Wills	.90	.45	.25
(370)	Don Wilson	.50	.25	.15
(371)	Earl Wilson	.50	.25	.15
(372)	Robert Wine	.50	.25	.15
(373)	Richard Wise	.50	.25	.15
(374)	Wilbur Wood	.50	.25	.15
(375)	William Woodward	.50	.25	.15
(376)	Clyde Wright	.50	.25	.15
(377)	James Wynn	.50	.25	.15
(378)	Jerry Zimmerman	.50	.25	.15

1970 Milwaukee Brewers picture pack

This was a souvenir-stand set of player pictures. The 4-1/4" x 7" pictures are black-and-white portraits or poses. The player's name and "Brewers" is printed in the top border. Backs are blank. The set was sold in a window envelope with a checklist on front. The pictures are unnumbered.

		NM	EX	VG
Complete Set (12):		35.00	17.50	10.50
Common Player:		3.00	1.50	.90
(1)	Max Alvis	3.00	1.50	.90
(2)	Dave Bristol	3.00	1.50	.90
(3)	Tommy Harper	4.50	2.25	1.25
(4)	Mike Hegan	4.50	2.25	1.25
(5)	Mike Hershberger	3.00	1.50	.90
(6)	Lew Krausse	0.00	1.50	.00
(7)	Ted Kubiak	3.00	1.50	.90
(8)	Dave May	3.00	1.50	.90
(9)	Jerry McNertney	3.00	1.50	.90
(10)	Phil Roof	3.00	1.50	.90
(11)	Ted Savage	3.00	1.50	.90
(12)	Danny Walton	3.75	2.00	1.25

1970 Milwaukee Brewers team issue

One of the first souvenir items issued by the Brewers upon their move from Seattle was this set of 8" x 10" player photo cards. The cards have semi-gloss fronts on which are printed black-and-white portrait photos. In the white border at bottom an unfinished Brewers logo is at center, with the player name at left and position at right, in capital letters. Backs are blank. The unnumbered cards are listed here alphabetically. The set was sold in a large envelope with artwork printed in blue of a player at bat.

		NM	EX	VG
Complete Set (24):		75.00	37.50	22.00
Common Player:		4.00	2.00	1.25
(1)	Max Alvis	4.00	2.00	1.25
(2)	Bob Bolin	4.00	2.00	1.25
(3)	Gene Brabender	4.00	2.00	1.25
(4)	Dave Bristol	4.00	2.00	1.25
(5)	Wayne Comer	4.00	2.00	1.25
(6)	John Gelnar	4.00	2.00	1.25
(7)	Greg Goossen	4.00	2.00	1.25
(8)	Mike Hegan	6.00	3.00	1.75
(9)	Mike Hershberger	4.00	2.00	1.25
(10)	Steve Hovley	4.00	2.00	1.25
(11)	John Kennedy	4.00	2.00	1.25
(12)	Lew Krausse	4.00	2.00	1.25
(13)	Ted Kubiak	4.00	2.00	1.25
(14)	George Lauzerique	4.00	2.00	1.25
(15)	Bob Locker	4.00	2.00	1.25
(16)	Jerry McNertney	4.00	2.00	1.25
(17)	Bob Meyer	4.00	2.00	1.25
(18)	Johnnie Morris	4.00	2.00	1.25
(19)	John O'Donoghue	4.00	2.00	1.25
(20)	Marty Pattin	4.00	2.00	1.25
(21)	Rich Rollins	4.00	2.00	1.25
(22)	Phil Roof	4.00	2.00	1.25
(23)	Ted Savage	4.00	2.00	1.25
(24)	Russ Snyder	4.00	2.00	1.25

1971 Milwaukee Brewers picture pack

This was a souvenir stand set of player pictures. The 4-1/4" x 7" pictures are black-and-white portraits or poses. The player's name and "Brewers" is printed in the top border. Backs are blank. The set was sold in a window envelope with a checklist on front. The pictures are unnumbered.

		NM	EX	VG
Complete Set (12):		35.00	17.50	10.50
Common Player:		3.00	1.50	.90
(1)	Dave Bristol	3.00	1.50	.90
(2)	Tommy Harper	4.50	2.25	1.25
(3)	Lew Krausse	3.00	1.50	.90
(4)	Ted Kubiak	3.00	1.50	.90
(5)	Dave May	3.00	1.50	.90
(6)	Bill Parsons	3.00	1.50	.90
(7)	Marty Pattin	3.00	1.50	.90
(8)	Roberto Pena	3.00	1.50	.90
(9)	Ellie Rodriguez	3.00	1.50	.90
(10)	Phil Roof	3.00	1.50	.90
(11)	Ken Sanders	3.00	1.50	.90
(12)	Bill Voss	3.00	1.50	.90

1972 Milwaukee Brewers picture pack

This was a souvenir-stand set of player pictures. The 4-1/4" x 7" pictures are black-and-white portraits or poses. The player name and "Brewers" is printed in the bottom border. Backs are blank. The set was sold in a window envelope with a checklist on front. The pictures are unnumbered.

		NM	EX	VG
Complete Set (12):		24.00	12.00	7.50
Common Player:		2.00	1.00	.60
(1)	Rick Auerbach	2.00	1.00	.60
(2)	Ken Brett	2.00	1.00	.60
(3)	John Briggs	2.00	1.00	.60
(4)	Del Crandall	2.50	1.25	.70
(5)	Joe Lahoud	2.00	1.00	.60
(6)	Jim Lonborg	2.50	1.25	.70
(7)	Dave May	2.00	1.00	.60
(8)	Bill Parsons	2.00	1.00	.60
(9)	Ellie Rodriguez	2.00	1.00	.60
(10)	Ken Sanders	2.00	1.00	.60
(11)	George Scott	3.00	1.50	.90
(12)	Ron Theobald	2.00	1.00	.60

1975 Milwaukee Brewers photo pack

This stadium souvenir photo pack offers six color portraits, each about 7" x 9" with blank back. The unnumbered pictures are listed here in alphabetical order.

		NM	EX	VG
Complete Set (6):		40.00	20.00	12.00
Common Player:		3.00	1.50	.90
(1)	Bob Coluccio	3.00	1.50	.90
(2)	Pedro Garcia	3.00	1.50	.90
(3)	Dave May	3.00	1.50	.90
(4)	Darrell Porter	3.00	1.50	.90
(5)	George Scott	4.50	2.25	1.25
(6)	Robin Yount	30.00	15.00	9.00

1976 Milwaukee Brewer team-issue 5x7s

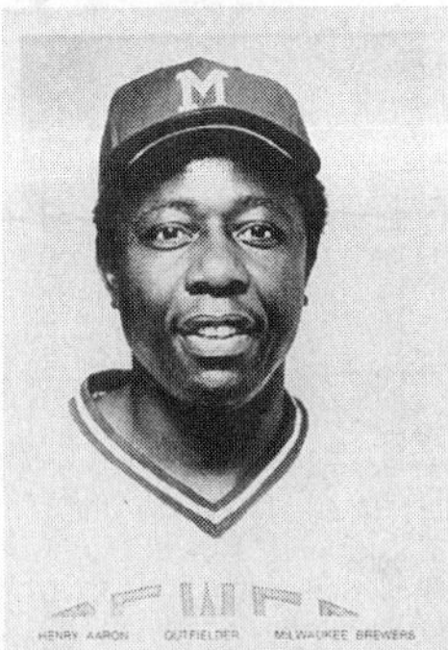

Issued by the team for media distribution and for players' use in answering fan requests, this series of 5" x 7" black-and-white, blank-back photos features chest-to-cap portraits. All pictures have the player name, position and team printed in the bottom border. The unnumbered pictures are checklisted here in alphabetical order, but the list may not be complete.

		NM	EX	VG
Complete Set (21):		80.00	40.00	24.00
Common Player:		3.00	1.50	.90
(1)	Hank Aaron	15.00	7.50	4.50
(2)	Kurt Bevacqua	3.00	1.50	.90
(3)	Jimmy Bragan	3.00	1.50	.90
(4)	Pete Broberg	3.00	1.50	.90
(5)	Bill Champion	3.00	1.50	.90
(6)	Jim Colborn	3.00	1.50	.90
(7)	Bob Darwin	3.00	1.50	.90
(8)	Pedro Garcia	3.00	1.50	.90
(9)	Alex Grammas	3.00	1.50	.90
(10)	Tim Johnson	3.00	1.50	.90
(11)	Mike Hegan	4.50	2.25	1.25
(12)	Harvey Kuenn	4.50	2.25	1.25
(13)	Cal McLish	3.00	1.50	.90
(14)	Tom Murphy	3.00	1.50	.90
(15)	Darrell Porter	3.00	1.50	.90
(16)	Ed Rodriguez	3.00	1.50	.90
(17)	George Scott	6.00	3.00	1.75
(18)	Bill Sharp	3.00	1.50	.90
(19)	Hal Smith	3.00	1.50	.90
(20)	Dan Thomas	4.50	2.25	1.25
(21)	Robin Yount	9.00	4.50	2.75

1977 Milwaukee Brewers team issue

Twenty-five Milwaukee Brewers players, coaches and manager are included in this team-issued picture pack. Printed in black-and-white on heavy paper, the pictures are 4" x 6" and feature tight portrait photos on front. Backs are blank. The unnumbered pictures are checklisted here alphabetically.

		NM	EX	VG
Complete Set (25):		30.00	15.00	9.00
Common Player:		1.00	.50	.30
(1)	Jerry Augustine	1.00	.50	.30
(2)	Sal Bando	1.25	.60	.40
(3)	Gary Beare	1.00	.50	.30
(4)	Steve Brye	1.00	.50	.30
(5)	Bill Castro	1.00	.50	.30
(6)	Cecil Cooper	2.00	1.00	.60
(7)	Barry Cort	1.00	.50	.30
(8)	Alex Grammas	1.00	.50	.30
(9)	Bryan Haas	1.00	.50	.30
(10)	Larry Haney	1.00	.50	.30
(11)	Mike Hegan	1.00	.50	.30
(12)	Frank Howard	1.25	.60	.40
(13)	Tim Johnson	1.00	.50	.30
(14)	Von Joshua	1.00	.50	.30
(15)	Sixto Lezcano	1.00	.50	.30
(16)	Bob McClure	1.00	.50	.30
(17)	Ken McMullen	1.00	.50	.30
(18)	Don Money	1.00	.50	.30
(19)	Charlie Moore	1.00	.50	.30
(20)	Jamie Quirk	1.00	.50	.30
(21)	Ed Rodriguez	1.00	.50	.30
(22)	Jim Slaton	1.00	.50	.30
(23)	Bill Travers	1.00	.50	.30
(24)	Jim Wohlford	1.00	.50	.30
(25)	Robin Yount	8.00	4.00	2.50

1980-81 Milwaukee Brewers team issue 5x7s

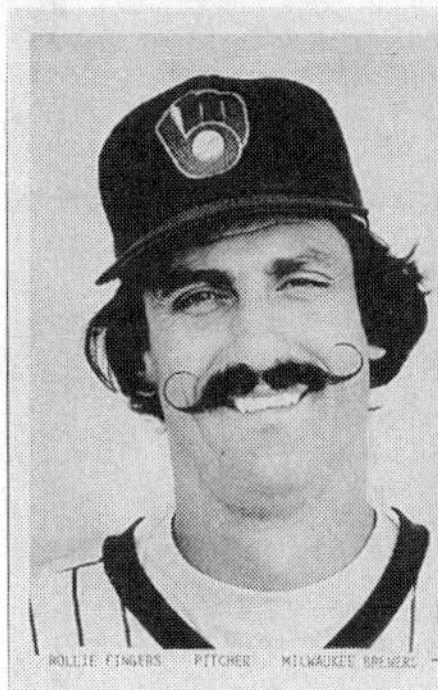

Issued by the team for media distribution and for players' use in answering fan requests, this series of 5" x 7" black-and-white, blank-back photos was produced over a two-season span. All pictures are portraits, either from chest- or neck-to-cap. All pictures have the player name, position and team at bottom. On most, this information is on a strip at the bottom of the photo, rather than in the bottom border. The unnumbered pictures are checklisted here in alphabetical order.

	NM	EX	VG
Complete Set (32):	45.00	22.00	13.50
Common Player:	1.00	.50	.30
(1) Jerry Augustine	1.00	.50	.30
(2) George Bamberger	1.00	.50	.30
(3) Sal Bando	1.00	.50	.30
(4) Mark Brouhard	1.00	.50	.30
(5) Mike Caldwell	1.00	.50	.30
(6) Reggie Cleveland	1.00	.50	.30
(7) Cecil Cooper	1.50	.70	.45
(8) Jamie Easterly	1.00	.50	.30
(9) Marshall Edwards	1.00	.50	.30
(10) Rollie Fingers	4.00	2.00	1.25
(11) Jim Gantner	1.00	.50	.30
(12) Larry Haney	1.00	.50	.30
(13) Ron Hansen	1.00	.50	.30
(14) Larry Hisle	1.25	.60	.40
(15) Roy Howell	1.00	.50	.30
(16) Rickey Keeton	1.00	.50	.30
(17) Harvey Kuenn	1.50	.70	.45
(18) Randy Lerch	1.00	.50	.30
(19) Bob McClure	1.00	.50	.30
(20) Cal McLish	1.00	.50	.30
(21) Paul Molitor	7.50	3.75	2.25
(22) Don Money	1.25	.60	.40
(23) Charlie Moore	1.00	.50	.30
(24) Ben Oglivie	1.25	.60	.40
(25) Bob (Buck) Rodgers	1.00	.50	.30
(26) Ed Romero	1.00	.50	.30
(27) Ted Simmons	1.25	.60	.40
(28) Jim Slaton	1.00	.50	.30
(29) Gorman Thomas	1.00	.50	.30
(30) Harry Warner	1.00	.50	.30
(31) Ned Yost	1.00	.50	.30
(32) Robin Yount	7.50	3.75	2.25

1912 Miner's Extra Series of Champions

(See 1912 T227 Series of Champions for checklist, price guide)

1970 Minnesota Twins team issue

These black-and-white team-issued player photos are printed on semi-gloss paper in a 7" x 8-3/4" format. Fronts have player poses with a white border. Player and team identification are in the bottom border. Backs are blank. The unnumbered pictures are checklisted here alphabetically.

	NM	EX	VG
Complete Set (12):	75.00	37.50	22.00
Common Player:	7.50	3.75	2.25
(1) Bert Blyleven	9.00	4.50	2.75
(2) Steve Braun	7.50	3.75	2.25
(3) Steve Brye	7.50	3.75	2.25
(4) Rod Carew	15.00	7.50	4.50
(5) Bob Darwin	7.50	3.75	2.25
(6) Larry Hisle	7.50	3.75	2.25
(7) Jim Holt	7.50	3.75	2.25
(8) Harmon Killebrew	12.00	6.00	3.50
(9) Tony Oliva	9.00	4.50	2.75
(10) Frank Quillici	7.50	3.75	2.25
(11) Jerry Terrell	7.50	3.75	2.25
(12) Danny Thompson	7.50	3.75	2.25

1977-78 Minnesota Twins team issue

Produced by collector Barry Fritz, and sold by the team through its normal concession outlets, this set consists of two 25-card series. Cards 1-25 were issued in 1977; cards 26-50 in 1978. Measuring 2-1/2" x 3-3/4", card fronts feature quality color player poses with no other graphics. Backs are in black-and-white and have all player data, stats with the Twins and overall major league numbers, plus career highlights. Besides being sold as individual cards, the sets were also offered in uncut sheet form.

	NM	EX	VG
Complete Set (50):	40.00	20.00	12.00
Common Player:	1.00	.50	.30
1 Bob Allison	1.00	.50	.30
2 Earl Battey	1.00	.50	.30
3 Dave Boswell	1.00	.50	.30
4 Dean Chance	1.25	.60	.40
5 Jim Grant	1.25	.60	.40
6 Calvin Griffith	1.25	.60	.40
7 Jimmie Hall	1.00	.50	.30
8 Harmon Killebrew	6.00	3.00	1.75
9 Jim Lemon	1.00	.50	.30
10 Billy Martin	3.00	1.50	.90
11 Gene Mauch	1.00	.50	.30
12 Sam Mele	1.00	.50	.30
13 Metropolitan Stadium	1.50	.70	.45
14 Don Mincher	1.00	.50	.30
15 Tony Oliva	3.00	1.50	.90
16 Camilo Pascual	1.00	.50	.30
17 Jim Perry	1.25	.60	.40
18 Frank Quilici	1.00	.50	.30
19 Rich Reese	1.00	.50	.30
20 Bill Rigney	1.00	.50	.30
21 Cesar Tovar	1.00	.50	.30
22 Zoilo Versalles	1.00	.50	.30
23 Al Worthington	1.00	.50	.30
24 Jerry Zimmerman	1.00	.50	.30
25 Checklist / Souvenir List	1.00	.50	.30
26 Bernie Allen	1.00	.50	.30
27 Leo Cardenas	1.00	.50	.30
28 Ray Corbin	1.00	.50	.30
29 Joe Decker	1.00	.50	.30
30 Johnny Goryl	1.00	.50	.30
31 Tom Hall	1.00	.50	.30
32 Bill Hands	1.00	.50	.30
33 Jim Holt	1.00	.50	.30
34 Randy Hundley	1.00	.50	.30
35 Jerry Kindall	1.00	.50	.30
36 Johnny Klippstein	1.00	.50	.30
37 Jack Kralick	1.00	.50	.30
38 Jim Merritt	1.00	.50	.30
39 Joe Nossek	1.00	.50	.30
40 Ron Perranoski	1.00	.50	.30
41 Bill Pleis	1.00	.50	.30
42 Rick Renick	1.00	.50	.30
43 Jim Roland	1.00	.50	.30
44 Lee Stange	1.00	.50	.30
45 Dick Stigman	1.00	.50	.30
46 Danny Thompson	1.00	.50	.30
47 Ted Uhlaender	1.00	.50	.30
48 Sandy Valdespino	1.00	.50	.30
49 Dick Woodson	1.00	.50	.30
50 Checklist #26-50	1.00	.50	.30

1980 Minnesota Twins Postcards

One of the scarcest in a long line of Twins team issues, this postcard set features the photos of Barry Fritz, whose initials appear on the back. Card fronts feature borderless color photos, with or without black facsimile autographs overprinted (cards without autographs are worth twice the values quoted here). Backs of the 3-1/2" x 5-1/2" cards have a ghost-image team logo at left, above which is the player name and a few biographical details. The unnumbered cards are checklisted here alphabetically.

	NM	EX	VG
Complete Set (33):	60.00	30.00	18.00
Common Player:	2.25	1.25	.70
(1) Glenn Adams	2.25	1.25	.70
(2) Sal Butera	2.25	1.25	.70
(3) John Castino	2.25	1.25	.70
(4) Doug Corbett	2.25	1.25	.70
(5) Mike Cubbage	2.25	1.25	.70
(6) Dave Edwards	2.25	1.25	.70
(7) Roger Erickson	2.25	1.25	.70
(8) Terry Felton	2.25	1.25	.70
(9) Danny Goodwin	2.25	1.25	.70
(10) John Goryl	2.25	1.25	.70
(11) Darrell Jackson	2.25	1.25	.70
(12) Ron Jackson	2.25	1.25	.70
(13) Harmon Killebrew	12.00	6.00	3.50
(14) Jerry Koosman	3.00	1.50	.90
(15) Karl Kuehl	2.25	1.25	.70
(16) Ken Landreaux	2.25	1.25	.70
(17) Pete Mackanin	2.25	1.25	.70
(18) Mike Marshall	2.25	1.25	.70
(19) Gene Mauch	2.25	1.25	.70
(20) Jose Morales	2.25	1.25	.70
(21) Willie Norwood	2.25	1.25	.70
(22) Camilo Pascual	2.25	1.25	.70
(23) Hosken Powell	2.25	1.25	.70
(24) Bobby Randall	2.25	1.25	.70
(25) Pete Redfern	2.25	1.25	.70
(26) Bombo Rivera	2.25	1.25	.70
(27) Roy Smalley	2.25	1.25	.70
(28) Rick Sofield	2.25	1.25	.70
(29) John Verhoeven	2.25	1.25	.70
(30) Rob Wilfong	2.25	1.25	.70
(31) Buth Wynegar	2.25	1.25	.70
(32) Geoff Zahn	2.25	1.25	.70
(33) Jerry Zimmerman	2.25	1.25	.70

1914 Mino Cigarettes

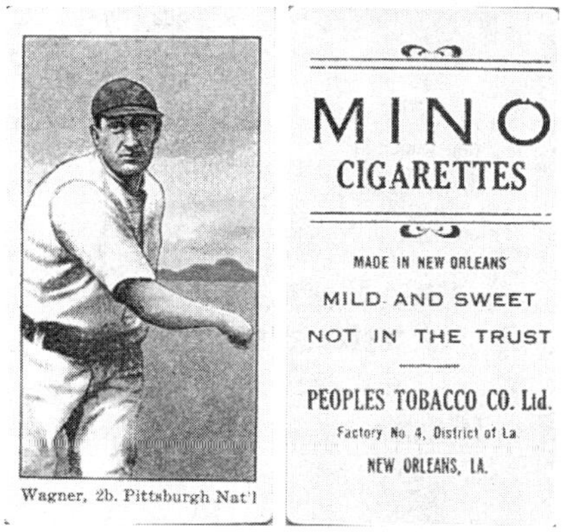

(See 1914 T216 Peoples Tobacco for checklist; Mino values are 1.5X-2X)

1911 Monarch Typewriter Philadelphia A's

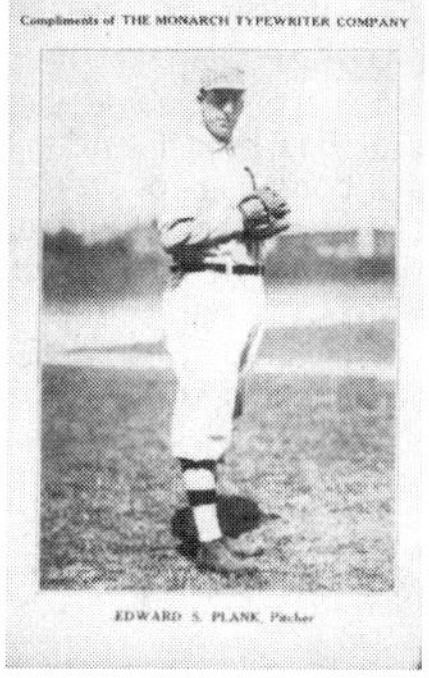

These black-and-white postcards (about 3-1/2" x 5") depict the World Champion 1910 Philadelphia A's. Fronts have posed player photos with a black pinstripe and white borders. The player's name and position are printed in the bottom border. "Compliments of THE MONARCH TYPEWRITER COMPANY" appears in the top border. Backs are rather standard postcard fare, but include data about the World Series between 1903-1910. The alphabetized checklist here may be incomplete.

	NM	EX	VG
Common Player:	250.00	125.00	75.00
(1) Jack Barry	175.00	87.00	52.00
(2) Chief Bender	250.00	125.00	75.00
(3) Eddie Collins	250.00	125.00	75.00
(4) Rube Oldring	175.00	87.00	52.00
(5) Eddie Plank	250.00	125.00	75.00
(6) Ira Thomas	175.00	87.00	52.00

Near Mint-Mint and Mint examples of vintage cards carry a significant premium over the Near Mint values quoted here. This premium reflects availability of the highest-grade cards as well as demand for a particular card or set in top grade. Premiums of 2X to 3X are not uncommon and many are even higher.

1969 Montreal Expos Postcards - b/w

Evidently a continuation of the color postcard series of 1969, these cards are numbered on the back but carry no issuer identification. They are in the same style as the color cards, featuring black-and-white borderless portrait photos on front and a facsimile autograph. Player identification is also provided on back. The black-and-white cards are generally regarded as scarcer than the colored.

		NM	EX	VG
Complete Set (15):		95.00	47.00	28.00
Common Player:		7.50	3.75	2.25
17	Howie Reed	7.50	3.75	2.25
18	Steve Renko	7.50	3.75	2.25
19	Jerry Robertson	7.50	3.75	2.25
20	Gary Waslewski	7.50	3.75	2.25
21	Kevin Collins	7.50	3.75	2.25
22	Ron Fairly	7.50	3.75	2.25
23	Jose Herrera	7.50	3.75	2.25
24	Ty Cline	7.50	3.75	2.25
25	Adolfo Phillips	7.50	3.75	2.25
26	Floyd Wicker	7.50	3.75	2.25
27	Gene Mauch	7.50	3.75	2.25
28	Harry Lee (Peanuts) Lowrey	7.50	3.75	2.25
29	Calvin (Cal) McLish	7.50	3.75	2.25
30	Robert (Bob) Oldis	7.50	3.75	2.25
31	Gerald (Jerry) Zimmerman	7.50	3.75	2.25

1969 Montreal Expos Postcards - color

This is the first of many team-issued color player postcard sets for the Expos. Fronts of the 3-1/2" x 5-1/2" cards have borderless photos with a facsimile autograph. Backs have a card number in the upper-left corner, with player name, position and team at top-left. A stamp box is at upper-right. The center is divided by this credit line: "Distributed by S.N.S./5000 Victoria, Montreal / Tel. 381-1264".

		NM	EX	VG
Complete Set (16):		75.00	37.00	22.00
Common Player:		5.00	2.50	1.50
1	Elroy Face	7.00	3.50	2.00
2	Don Shaw	5.00	2.50	1.50
3	Dan McGinn	5.00	2.50	1.50
4	Bill Stoneman	5.00	2.50	1.50
5	Mike Wegener	5.00	2.50	1.50
6	Bob Bailey	5.00	2.50	1.50
7	Gary Sutherland	5.00	2.50	1.50
8	Jose (Coco) Laboy	5.00	2.50	1.50
9	Bobby Wine	5.00	2.50	1.50
10	Mack Jones	5.00	2.50	1.50
11	Rusty Staub	7.00	3.50	2.00
12	Don Bosch	5.00	2.50	1.50
13	Larry Jaster	5.00	2.50	1.50
14	John Bateman	5.00	2.50	1.50
15	John Boccabella	5.00	2.50	1.50
16	Ron Brand	5.00	2.50	1.50

1970 Montreal Expos Player Pins

Produced by "Best in Sports" for sale in the Montreal area for 35¢ apiece, these 1-3/4" diameter pinbacks feature action poses of the players set against a white background. The player's name at top is in black.

		NM	EX	VG
Complete Set (16):		150.00	75.00	45.00
Common Player:		15.00	7.50	4.50
(1)	John Bateman	15.00	7.50	4.50
(2)	Ron Brand	15.00	7.50	4.50
(3)	Ron Fairly	15.00	7.50	4.50
(4)	Mack Jones	15.00	7.50	4.50
(5)	Coco Laboy	15.00	7.50	4.50
(6)	Gene Mauch	15.00	7.50	4.50
(7)	Dan McGinn	15.00	7.50	4.50
(8)	Adolfo Phillips	15.00	7.50	4.50
(9)	Claude Raymond	15.00	7.50	4.50
(10)	Steve Renko	15.00	7.50	4.50
(11)	Marv Staehle	15.00	7.50	4.50
(12)	Rusty Staub	20.00	10.00	6.00
(13)	Bill Stoneman	15.00	7.50	4.50
(14)	Gary Sutherland	15.00	7.50	4.50
(15)	Bobby Wine	15.00	7.50	4.50
(16)	Expos team logo	5.00	2.50	1.50

1972-76 Montreal Expos Matchbook Covers

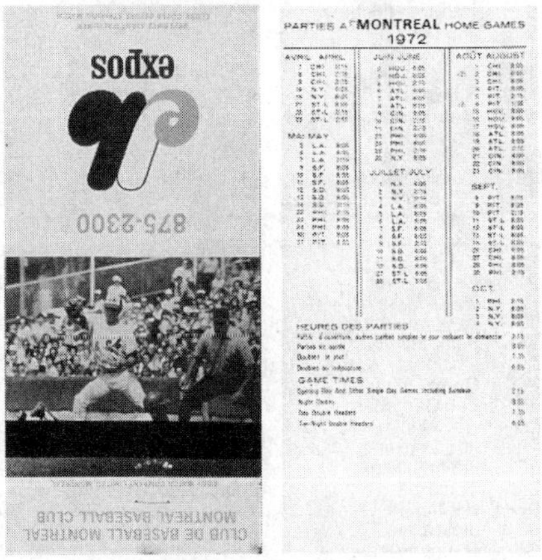

In 1972, 1973 and 1976, the Eddy Match Co., Montreal, issued a series of seven matchbook covers featuring action photos. Fronts have a red, white and blue team logo on a white background. Backs have a bluetone action photo with the match-striking surface across the lower portion. The player in the photo is not identified on the matchbook. Inside of the 2-1/8" x 4-3/8" cover, printed in blue, is the team home schedule for that season. The unnumbered matchbook covers are checklisted here alphabetically by year. Values shown are for empty matchbooks; full matchbooks would be valued at 2-3X.

		NM	EX	VG
Complete Set (21):		40.00	20.00	12.00
Common Player:		2.00	1.00	.60
	1972			
(1)	Boots Day	2.00	1.00	.60
(2)	Ron Fairly	2.00	1.00	.60
(3)	Ron Hunt	2.00	1.00	.60
(4)	Steve Renko	2.00	1.00	.60
(5)	Rusty Staub	3.00	1.50	.90
(6)	Bobby Wine	2.00	1.00	.60
(7)	Hunt's 50th HBP (Scoreboard)	2.00	1.00	.60
	1973			
(1)	Tim Foli	2.00	1.00	.60
(2)	Ron Hunt	2.00	1.00	.60
(3)	Mike Jorgensen	2.00	1.00	.60
(4)	Gene Mauch	2.00	1.00	.60
(5)	Balor Moore	2.00	1.00	.60
(6)	Ken Singleton	2.00	1.00	.60
(7)	Bill Stoneman	2.00	1.00	.60
	1976			
(1)	Barry Foote	2.00	1.00	.60
(2)	Mike Jorgensen	2.00	1.00	.60
(3)	Pete Mackanin	2.00	1.00	.60
(4)	Dale Murray	2.00	1.00	.60
(5)	Larry Parrish	2.00	1.00	.60
(6)	Steve Rogers	2.00	1.00	.60
(7)	Dan Warthen	2.00	1.00	.60

1916 Morehouse Baking Co.

While this 200-card set is most often found with the advertising of "The Sporting News" newspaper on the back, a number of scarce regional advertisers also can be found. This Massachusetts baker inserted the cards into bread loaves and offered a redemption program.

	NM	EX	VG
Complete Set (200):	22000.	11000.	6500.
Common Player:	55.00	27.00	16.50

(See 1916 Sporting News for checklist and price guide.)

1907 Morgan Stationery "Red Belt" Postcards

Only one player is individually identified in this series of postcards. The 3-1/2" x 5-1/2" cards have colorized player and group posed photos on front with a title printed in white in the lower-left corner. All photos were taken at the Reds ballpark, then known as the Palace of Fans, and include pictures of Reds and Pirates of the National League, and Toledo of the minors. Many of the players have bright red belts, thus the set's nickname. Postcard backs have a credit line: "The Morgan Stationery Co., Cincinnati, O., Publishers". The unnumbered cards are checklisted here alphabetically by title.

		NM	EX	VG
Complete Set (11):		2250.	1125.	675.00
Common Card:		225.00	110.00	67.00
(1)	After A High One	225.00	110.00	67.00
(2)	A Home Run	225.00	110.00	67.00
(3)	Hit & Run	225.00	110.00	67.00
(4)	In Consultation	225.00	110.00	67.00
(5)	It's All in the Game - "Noise"	225.00	110.00	67.00
(6)	Huggins Second Baseman Par Excellence (Miller Huggins)	450.00	225.00	135.00
(7)	Opening of the Season 1907	225.00	110.00	67.00
(8)	Out to the Long Green	225.00	110.00	67.00
(9)	Practice Makes Perfect	225.00	110.00	67.00
(10)	Safe	225.00	110.00	67.00
(11)	Use Two If Necessary	270.00	135.00	81.00

1959 Morrell Meats Dodgers

This popular set of Los Angeles Dodgers player cards was the first issue of a three-year run for the Southern California meat company. The 12 cards in this 2-1/2" x 3-1/2" set are unnumbered and feature fullframe, unbordered color photos. Card backs feature a company ad and list only the player's name, birthdate and birthplace. Two interesting errors exist in the set, as the cards for Clem Labine and Norm Larker show photos of Stan Williams and Joe Pignatano, respectively. Dodger greats Sandy Koufax and Duke Snider are key cards in the set.

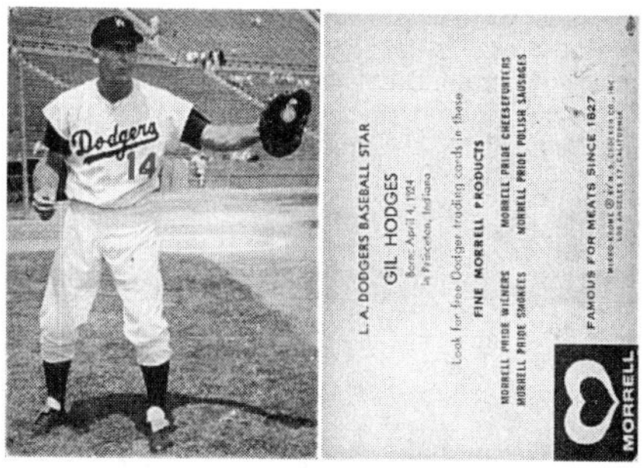

	NM	EX	VG
Complete Set (12):	950.00	475.00	280.00
Common Player:	40.00	20.00	12.00
(1) Don Drysdale	120.00	60.00	36.00
(2) Carl Furillo	60.00	30.00	18.00
(3) Jim Gilliam	50.00	25.00	15.00
(4) Gil Hodges	100.00	50.00	30.00
(5) Sandy Koufax	250.00	125.00	75.00
(6) Clem Labine (photo actually Stan Williams)	40.00	20.00	12.00
(7) Norm Larker (photo actually Joe Pignatano)	40.00	20.00	12.00
(8) Charlie Neal	40.00	20.00	12.00
(9) Johnny Podres	45.00	22.00	13.50
(10) John Roseboro	40.00	20.00	12.00
(11) Duke Snider	180.00	90.00	54.00
(12) Don Zimmer	60.00	30.00	18.00

1960 Morrell Meats Dodgers

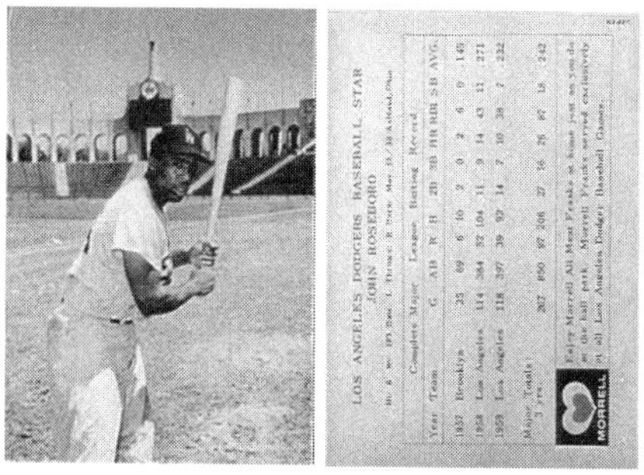

This 12-card set is the same 2-1/2" x 3-1/2" size as the 1959 set, and again features unbordered color card fronts. Five of the players included are new to the Morrell's sets. Card backs in 1960 list player statistics and brief personal data on each player. Cards for Gil Hodges, Carl Furillo and Duke Snider are apparently more scarce than others in the set. The 1960 set is again unnumbered.

	NM	EX	VG
Complete Set (12):	800.00	400.00	240.00
Common Player:	16.00	8.00	4.75
(1) Walt Alston	24.00	12.00	7.25
(2) Roger Craig	20.00	10.00	6.00
(3) Don Drysdale	48.00	24.00	14.50
(4) Carl Furillo	95.00	47.00	28.00
(5) Gil Hodges	140.00	70.00	42.00
(6) Sandy Koufax	250.00	125.00	75.00
(7) Wally Moon	16.00	8.00	4.75
(8) Charlie Neal	16.00	8.00	4.75
(9) Johnny Podres	20.00	10.00	6.00
(10) John Roseboro	16.00	8.00	4.75
(11) Larry Sherry	16.00	8.00	4.75
(12) Duke Snider	200.00	100.00	60.00

1961 Morrell Meats Dodgers

The Morrell set shrunk to just six cards in 1961, with a format almost identical to the 1960 cards. Card fronts are again full-color, unbordered photos, with player statistics on the backs. The unnumbered cards measure a slightly smaller 2-1/4" x 3-1/4", and comparison of statistical information can also distinguish the cards from the 1960 version. Top cards in the set are Don Drysdale and Sandy Koufax, who are also the only two players to appear in all three years of the Morrell Meats sets.

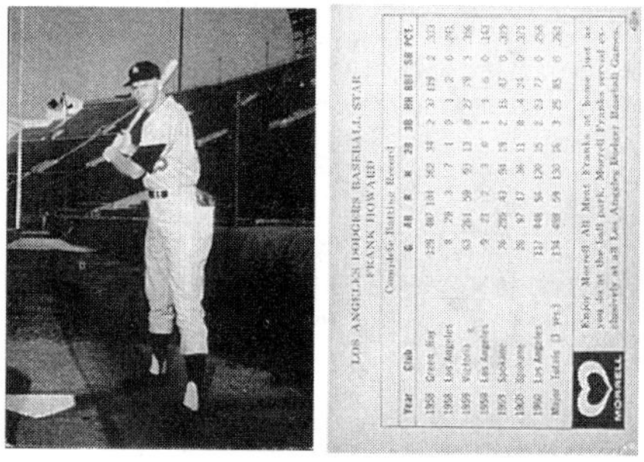

	NM	EX	VG
Complete Set (6):	200.00	100.00	60.00
Common Player:	15.00	7.50	4.50
(1) Tommy Davis	18.00	9.00	5.50
(2) Don Drysdale	55.00	27.00	16.50
(3) Frank Howard	18.00	9.00	5.50
(4) Sandy Koufax	90.00	45.00	27.00
(5) Norm Larker	15.00	7.50	4.50
(6) Maury Wills	20.00	10.00	6.00

1910 Morton's Buster Brown Bread Tigers Pins

Dating of these two issues is arbitrary, since there is no indication on the pins of vintage. Both sets feature members of the Detroit Tigers, American League champions of 1907-09. The Buster Brown Bread pins measure 1-1/4" in diameter and have a small black-and-white player portrait photo surrounded by a yellow border. Artwork to the left depicts Buster Brown with a tiger holding a blue banner with the Morton's name. The player photos carry no identification, which may make the checklist presented here somewhat tentative.

	NM	EX	VG
Complete Set (15):	4000.	2000.	1200.
Common Player:	250.00	125.00	75.00
(1) Jimmy Archer	250.00	125.00	75.00
(2) Heinie Beckendorf	250.00	125.00	75.00
(3) Donie Bush	250.00	125.00	75.00
(4) Ty Cobb	1200.	600.00	360.00
(5) Sam Crawford	400.00	200.00	120.00
(6) Wild Bill Donovan	250.00	125.00	75.00
(7) Hughie Jennings	400.00	200.00	120.00
(8) Tom Jones	250.00	125.00	75.00
(9) Red Killefer	250.00	125.00	75.00
(10) George Moriarty	250.00	125.00	75.00
(11) George Mullin	250.00	125.00	75.00
(12) Claude Rossman	250.00	125.00	75.00
(13) "Germany" Schaefer	250.00	125.00	75.00
(14) Ed Summers	250.00	125.00	75.00
(15) Ed Willett	250.00	125.00	75.00

1910 Morton's Pennant Winner Bread Tigers Pins

The American League champion Detroit Tigers (1907-1909) are featured on this set of pins advertising -- appropriately -- Pennant Winner Bread. The 1-1/4" pins have black-and-white player photos surrounded by a yellow border. A Detroit banner with tiger head superimposed is at bottom. The players are not identified anywhere on the pins, which may make this checklist somewhat arbitrary.

	NM	EX	VG
Complete Set (16):	4800.	2400.	1400.
Common Player:	250.00	125.00	75.00
(1) Jimmy Archer	250.00	125.00	75.00
(2) Heinie Beckendorf	250.00	125.00	75.00
(3) Donie Bush	250.00	125.00	75.00
(4) Ty Cobb	1200.	600.00	360.00
(5) Sam Crawford	400.00	200.00	120.00
(6) Wild Bill Donovan	250.00	125.00	75.00
(7) Hughie Jennings	400.00	200.00	120.00
(8) Davy Jones	250.00	125.00	75.00
(9) Matty McIntyre	250.00	125.00	75.00
(10) George Moriarty	250.00	125.00	75.00
(11) George Mullin	250.00	125.00	75.00
(12) Claude Rossman	250.00	125.00	75.00
(13) Herman Schaeffer (Schaefer)	250.00	125.00	75.00
(14) Charles Schmidt	250.00	125.00	75.00
(15) Ed Summers	250.00	125.00	75.00
(16) Ed Willett	250.00	125.00	75.00

1919 Mother's Bread

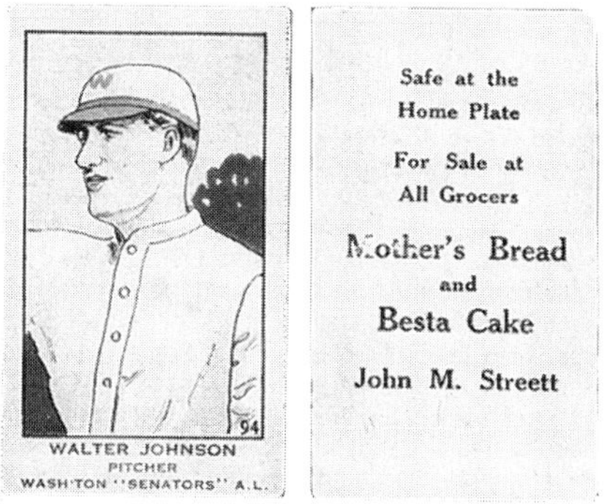

Essentially a version of the W514 strip cards with an advertisement on the back, the Mother's Bread cards are much scarcer than the blank-backs with which they share a checklist. The cards are 1-1/2" x 2-1/2" with color drawings of the players on front, along with name, position, team, league and card number.

(See 1919 W514 for checklist; cards valued at 2.5X-3X W514 version.)

1976 Motorola

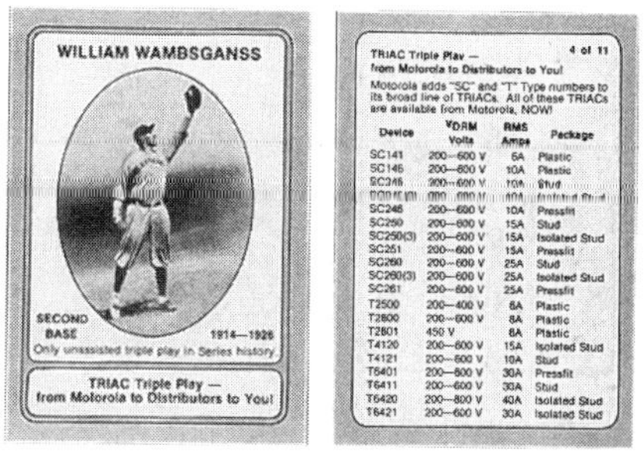

This set of (mostly) Hall of Famers was issued in conjunction with the annual convention of Motorola electronics dealers. Cards were issued singly in a wax wrapper with a piece of bubblegum. Sepia player photos are featured in an oval at center.

Player identification and a career highlight are in the white frame around the photo. A sales message appears in a white box at bottom. Overall borders are rust colored. Backs have information about various Motorola products.

		NM	EX	VG
Complete Set (11):		40.00	20.00	12.00
Common Player:		3.00	1.50	.90
1	Honus Wagner	4.50	2.25	1.25
2	Nap Lajoie	3.00	1.50	.90
3	Ty Cobb	9.00	4.50	2.75
4	William Wambsganss	3.00	1.50	.90
5	Three Finger Brown	3.00	1.50	.90
6	Ray Schalk	3.00	1.50	.90
7	Frank Frisch	3.00	1.50	.90
8	Pud Galvin	3.00	1.50	.90
9	Babe Ruth	18.00	9.00	5.50
10	Grover Cleveland Alexander	3.00	1.50	.90
11	Frank L. Chance	3.00	1.50	.90

1943 M.P. & Co. (R302-1)

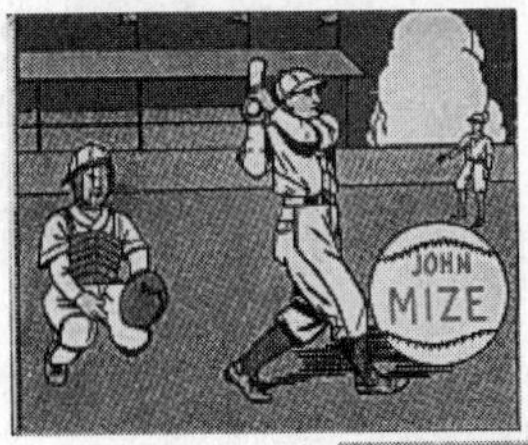

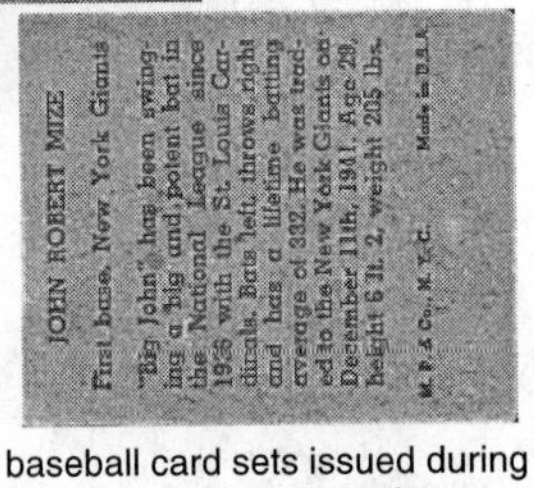

One of the few baseball card sets issued during World War II, this set of unnumbered cards, measuring approximately 2-5/8" x 2-1/4" was produced in two major types and at least five subtypes. The cards feature crude color drawings that have little resemblance to the player named. They were originally produced in strips and sold inexpensively in candy stores. The backs contain brief player write-ups. One major type has the player's full name, team and position on back. The second type has only the player's first and last name and position on back; no team. Variations in ink color and wording of the biographies on back are also seen. M.P. & Co., stands for Michael Pressner and Co., a New York City novelty and carnival supply firm.

		NM	EX	VG
Complete Set (24):		950.00	450.00	250.00
Common Player:		40.00	14.00	6.00
(1)	Ernie Bonham	40.00	14.00	6.00
(2)	Lou Boudreau	50.00	17.50	7.50
(3)	Dolph Camilli	40.00	14.00	6.00
(4)	Mort Cooper	40.00	14.00	6.00
(5)	Walker Cooper	40.00	14.00	6.00
(6)	Joe Cronin	50.00	17.50	7.50
(7)	Hank Danning	40.00	14.00	6.00
(8)	Bill Dickey	60.00	21.00	9.00
(9)	Joe DiMaggio	350.00	150.00	65.00
(10)	Bobby Feller	50.00	17.50	7.50
(11)	Jimmy Foxx	60.00	21.00	9.00
(12)	Hank Greenberg	75.00	26.00	11.00
(13)	Stan Hack	40.00	14.00	6.00
(14)	Tom Henrich	40.00	14.00	6.00
(15)	Carl Hubbell	50.00	17.50	7.50
(16)	Joe Medwick	50.00	17.50	7.50
(17)	John Mize	50.00	17.50	7.50
(18)	Lou Novikoff	40.00	14.00	6.00
(19)	Mel Ott	50.00	17.50	7.50
(20)	Pee Wee Reese	60.00	21.00	9.00
(21)	Pete Reiser	40.00	14.00	6.00
(22)	Charlie Ruffing	50.00	17.50	7.50
(23)	Johnny Vander Meer	40.00	14.00	6.00
(24)	Ted Williams	200.00	75.00	35.00

1948-49 M.P. & Co. Photoprints

One of several 1930s-1940s kits for do-it-yourself production of photos, this issue was produced in New York City by the novelty firm M.P. & Co. A complete outfit consists of a film negative and a piece of light-sensitive paper for producing the photo. The negative and resulting print measure about 2" x 2-1/4". The issue includes 13 subjects, mostly non-sport, but including Babe Ruth. Values shown are for negative/print pairs; individual pieces would be pro-rated, with the negative the most valuable component.

	NM	EX	VG
Babe Ruth	350.00	175.00	100.00

1949 M.P. & Co. (R302-2)

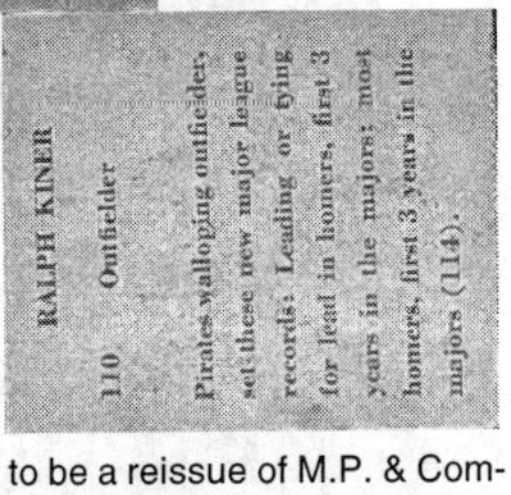

This set appears to be a reissue of M.P. & Company's 1943 cards with several different players (although reusing the same pictures as the '43s). The cards, which measure about 2-11/16" x 2-1/4", feature crude drawings of generic baseball players which have little resemblance to the player named. Most backs include card number and player information. The numbering sequence begins with card 100. Numbers 104, 118, and 120 are unknown, while three of the cards are unnumbered. The set is assigned the American Card Catalog number R302-2.

		NM	EX	VG
Complete Set (25):		950.00	450.00	250.00
Common Player:		40.00	14.00	6.00
100	Lou Boudreau	50.00	17.50	7.50
101	Ted Williams	200.00	75.00	35.00
102	Buddy Kerr	40.00	14.00	6.00
103	Bobby Feller	60.00	21.00	9.00
104	Unknown			
105	Joe DiMaggio	350.00	150.00	65.00
106	Pee Wee Reese	60.00	21.00	9.00
107	Ferris Fain	40.00	14.00	6.00
108	Andy Pafko	40.00	14.00	6.00
109	Del Ennis	40.00	14.00	6.00
110	Ralph Kiner	50.00	17.50	7.50
111	Nippy Jones	40.00	14.00	6.00
112	Del Rice	40.00	14.00	6.00
113	Hank Sauer	40.00	14.00	6.00
114	Gil Coan	40.00	14.00	6.00
115	Eddie Joost	40.00	14.00	6.00
116	Alvin Dark	40.00	14.00	6.00
117	Larry Berra	60.00	21.00	9.00
118	Unknown			
119	Bob Lemon	50.00	17.50	7.50
120	Unknown			
121	Johnny Pesky	40.00	14.00	6.00
122	Johnny Sain	40.00	14.00	6.00
123	Hoot Evers	40.00	14.00	6.00
124	Larry Doby	50.00	17.50	7.50
----	Jimmy Foxx	60.00	21.00	9.00
----	Tom Henrich	40.00	14.00	6.00
----	Al Kozar	40.00	14.00	6.00

1980 Mrs. Butterworth's Cello Pack Header

Mrs. Butterworth's was one of several businesses in 1980 which used four-card cello packs of Topps (or, in Canada, O-Pee-Chee) baseball cards as a promotional premium. Besides the three regular-issue 1980 cards in each pack, there was a header card with the sponsor's advertising in brown and red on front. On back of the header card is a list of players holding single-season or career records in various major statistical categories.

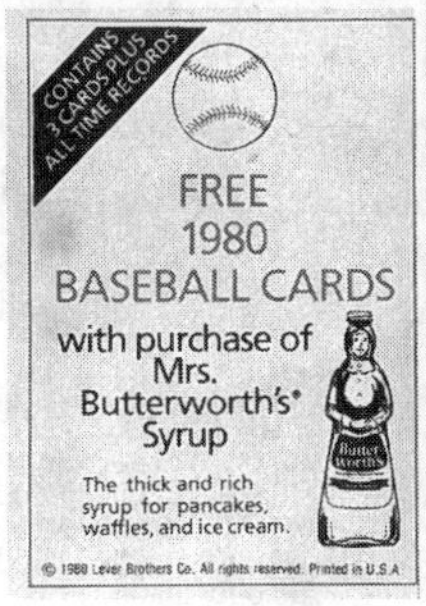

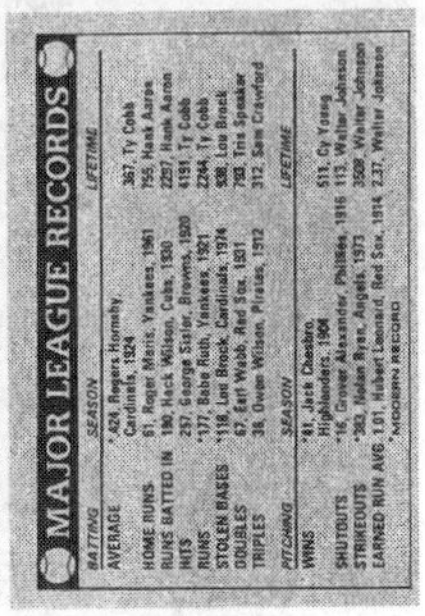

	NM	EX	VG
Mrs. Butterworth's/Major League Records	2.00	1.00	.60

1977 Mrs. Carter's Bread Sports Illustrated Covers

This two-sport card set was issued by Mrs. Carter's Bread. Fronts of the 3-1/2" x 4-3/4" cards reproduce SI covers in full color, surrounded by a white border. Backs have a special offer for SI subscriptions, and are printed in black and blue on white. Despite the higher card numbers, it does not appear any more than five were ever issued.

		NM	EX	VG
Complete Set (5):		20.00	10.00	6.00
Common Card:		3.00	1.50	.90
(1)	George Brett	15.00	7.50	4.50
(2)	George Foster	3.00	1.50	.90
(3)	Bump Wills	3.00	1.50	.90
(4)	Oakland Wins a Big One (football)	3.00	1.50	.90
(5)	Michigan is No. 1 (football)	5.00	2.50	1.50

1921 Mrs. Sherlock's Bread Pins

The date of issue for these pins is uncertain. The 7/8" diameter pins feature black-and-white player photos with a red border. The player's last name and team are printed beneath the photo;

above is "Mrs. Sherlock's Home Made Bread". The set is one of several sponsored by the Toledo bakery.

		NM	EX	VG
Complete Set (10):		3500.	1600.	975.00
Common Player:		200.00	100.00	60.00
(1)	Grover Alexander	300.00	150.00	90.00
(2)	Ty Cobb	800.00	400.00	240.00
(3)	Rogers Hornsby	300.00	150.00	90.00
(4)	Walter Johnson	300.00	150.00	90.00
(5)	Rabbit Maranville	300.00	150.00	90.00
(6)	Pat Moran	100.00	50.00	30.00
(7)	"Babe" Ruth	900.00	450.00	270.00
(8)	George Sisler	350.00	175.00	105.00
(9)	Tris Speaker	350.00	175.00	105.00
(10)	Honus Wagner	500.00	250.00	150.00

1975-96 MSA

(See listings under Michael Schechter Associates)

N

1969 Nabisco Team Flakes

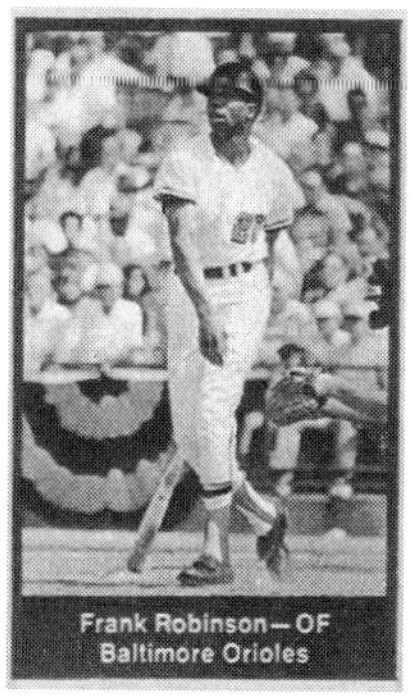

This set of cards is seen in two different sizes: 1-15/16" x 3" and 1-3/4" x 2-15/16". This is explained by the varying widths of the card borders on the backs of Nabisco cereal packages. Cards are action color photos bordered in yellow. Twenty-four of the top players in the game are included in the set, which was issued in three series of eight cards each. No team insignias are visible on any of the cards. Packages described the cards as "Mini Posters."

		NM	EX	VG
Complete Set (24):		300.00	150.00	90.00
Common Player:		3.25	1.75	1.00
(1)	Hank Aaron	50.00	25.00	15.00
(2)	Richie Allen	10.00	5.00	3.00
(3)	Lou Brock	24.00	12.00	7.25
(4)	Paul Casanova	3.00	1.50	.90
(5)	Roberto Clemente	60.00	30.00	18.00
(6)	Al Ferrara	3.00	1.50	.90
(7)	Bill Freehan	4.00	2.00	1.25
(8)	Jim Fregosi	4.00	2.00	1.25
(9)	Bob Gibson	24.00	12.00	7.25
(10)	Tony Horton	4.00	2.00	1.25
(11)	Tommy John	7.00	3.50	2.00
(12)	Al Kaline	32.00	16.00	9.50
(13)	Jim Lonborg	4.00	2.00	1.25
(14)	Juan Marichal	20.00	10.00	6.00
(15)	Willie Mays	50.00	25.00	15.00
(16)	Rick Monday	3.00	1.50	.90
(17)	Tony Oliva	4.00	2.00	1.25
(18)	Brooks Robinson	32.00	16.00	9.50
(19)	Frank Robinson	32.00	16.00	9.50
(20)	Pete Rose	50.00	25.00	15.00
(21)	Ron Santo	6.50	3.25	2.00
(22)	Tom Seaver	35.00	17.50	10.50
(23)	Rusty Staub	4.00	2.00	1.25
(24)	Mel Stottlemyre	3.50	1.75	1.00

1909 Nadja Caramels (E92)

One of several 1909-10 issues produced for Nadja Caramels, this set can be distinguished by the players in the checklist (alphabetized here) and the type beneath the color player lithograph. In this set, the player's last name is in upper- and lower-case letters, and his position is given, along with the team. Backs of these 1-1/2" x 2-3/4" cards are identical to later Nadja issues, featuring an ad for the candy brand. Cataloged (along with the cards of Croft's Candy/Cocoa and Dockman Gum) as E92 in the "American Card Catalog," the Nadja set checklist differs from those issues in that it is larger and contains a group of St. Louis players not found in the other sets.

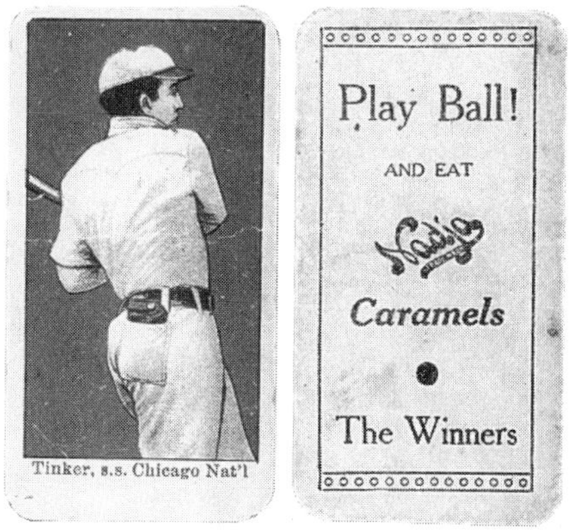

		NM	EX	VG
Complete Set (62):		13000.	6150.	4200.
Common Player:		135.00	65.00	40.00
(1)	Bill Bailey	135.00	65.00	40.00
(2)	Jack Barry	135.00	65.00	40.00
(3)	Harry Bemis	135.00	65.00	40.00
(4)	Chief Bender (striped cap)	300.00	135.00	90.00
(5)	Chief Bender (white cap)	300.00	135.00	90.00
(6)	Bill Bergen	135.00	65.00	40.00
(7)	Bob Bescher	135.00	65.00	40.00
(8)	Roger Bresnahan	300.00	135.00	90.00
(9)	Al Bridwell	135.00	65.00	40.00
(10)	Doc Casey	135.00	65.00	40.00
(11)	Frank Chance	300.00	135.00	90.00
(12)	Hal Chase	150.00	67.00	45.00
(13)	Ty Cobb	3500.	1575.	1050.
(14)	Eddie Collins	300.00	135.00	90.00
(15)	Sam Crawford	300.00	135.00	90.00
(16)	Harry Davis	135.00	65.00	40.00
(17)	Art Devlin	135.00	65.00	40.00
(18)	Bill Donovan	135.00	65.00	40.00
(19)	Red Dooin	135.00	65.00	40.00
(20)	Mickey Doolan	135.00	65.00	40.00
(21)	Patsy Dougherty	135.00	65.00	40.00
(22)	Larry Doyle (throwing)	135.00	65.00	40.00
(23)	Larry Doyle (with bat)	135.00	65.00	40.00
(24)	Rube Ellis	135.00	65.00	40.00
(25)	Johnny Evers	300.00	135.00	90.00
(26)	George Gibson	135.00	65.00	40.00
(27)	Topsy Hartsel	135.00	65.00	40.00
(28)	Roy Hartzell (batting)	135.00	65.00	40.00
(29)	Roy Hartzell (fielding)	135.00	65.00	40.00
(30)	Harry Howell (ready to pitch)	135.00	65.00	40.00
(31)	Harry Howell (follow-through)	135.00	65.00	40.00
(32)	Fred Jacklitsch	135.00	65.00	40.00
(33)	Hugh Jennings	300.00	135.00	90.00
(34)	Red Kleinow	135.00	65.00	40.00
(35)	Otto Knabe	135.00	65.00	40.00
(36)	Jack Knight	135.00	65.00	40.00
(37)	Nap Lajoie	300.00	135.00	90.00
(38)	Hans Lobert	135.00	65.00	40.00
(39)	Sherry Magee	135.00	65.00	40.00
(40)	Christy Matthewson (Mathewson)	500.00	225.00	150.00
(41)	John McGraw	300.00	135.00	90.00
(42)	Larry McLean	135.00	65.00	40.00
(43)	Dots Miller (batting)	135.00	65.00	40.00
(44)	Dots Miller (fielding)	135.00	65.00	40.00
(45)	Danny Murphy	135.00	65.00	40.00
(46)	Rebel Oakes	135.00	65.00	40.00
(47)	Bill O'Hara	135.00	65.00	40.00
(48)	Eddie Phelps	135.00	65.00	40.00
(49)	Germany Schaefer	135.00	65.00	40.00
(50)	Admiral Schlei	135.00	65.00	40.00
(51)	Boss Schmidt	135.00	65.00	40.00
(52)	Johnny Seigle (Siegle)	135.00	65.00	40.00
(53)	Dave Shean	135.00	65.00	40.00
(54)	Boss Smith (Schmidt)	135.00	65.00	40.00
(55)	George Stone (blue background)	135.00	65.00	40.00
(56)	George Stone (green background)	135.00	65.00	40.00
(57)	Joe Tinker	300.00	135.00	90.00
(58)	Honus Wagner (batting)	500.00	225.00	150.00
(59)	Honus Wagner (throwing)	500.00	225.00	150.00
(60)	Bobby Wallace	300.00	135.00	90.00
(61)	Cy Young	450.00	200.00	135.00
(62)	Heinie Zimmerman	135.00	65.00	40.00

1910 Nadja Carmels (E104-III)

It should be assumed that the 30 cards in this issue can each be found with or without a Nadja ad on back; the latter being somewhat scarcer and carrying a premium of 10 to 20 percent over the values quoted. These 1-1/2" x 2-3/4" cards can be distinguished from the 1909 issue by the line of type beneath the player portrait. On the 1910 cards, the player's last name is in all blue capital letters and there is no position designation given.

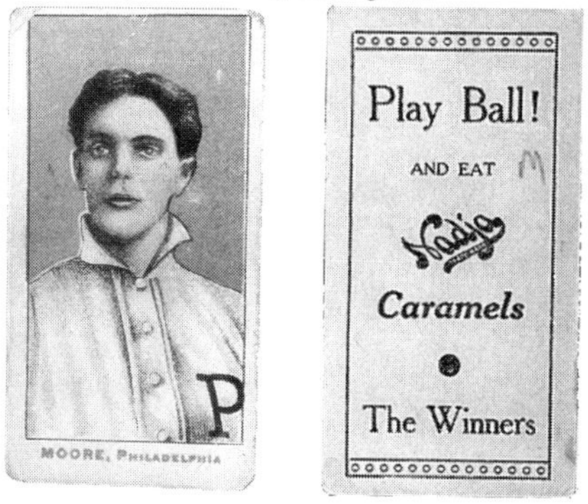

		NM	EX	VG
Complete Set (30):		6000.	2700.	1800.
Common Player:		200.00	90.00	60.00
(1)	Bill Abstein	200.00	90.00	60.00
(2)	Red Ames	200.00	90.00	60.00
(3)	Johnny Bates	200.00	90.00	60.00
(4)	Kitty Bransfield	200.00	90.00	60.00
(5)	Al Bridwell	200.00	90.00	60.00
(6)	Doc Crandall	200.00	90.00	60.00
(7)	Sam Crawford	400.00	180.00	120.00
(8)	Jim Delehanty (Delahanty)	200.00	90.00	60.00
(9)	Larry Doyle	200.00	90.00	60.00
(10)	Eddie Grant	200.00	90.00	60.00
(11)	Fred Jacklitsch	200.00	90.00	60.00
(12)	Hugh Jennings	400.00	180.00	120.00
(13)	Davy Jones	200.00	90.00	60.00
(14)	Tom Jones	200.00	90.00	60.00
(15)	Otto Knabe	200.00	90.00	60.00
(16)	John McGraw	400.00	180.00	120.00
(17)	Matty McIntyre	200.00	90.00	60.00
(18)	Earl Moore	200.00	90.00	60.00
(19)	Pat Moren (Moran)	200.00	90.00	60.00
(20)	George Moriarity	200.00	90.00	60.00
(21)	George Mullin	200.00	90.00	60.00
(22)	Red Murray	200.00	90.00	60.00
(23)	Simon Nicholls	200.00	90.00	60.00
(24)	Charley O'Leary	200.00	90.00	60.00
(25)	Admiral Schlei	200.00	90.00	60.00
(26)	Cy Seymore (Seymour)	200.00	90.00	60.00
(27)	Tully Sparks	200.00	90.00	60.00
(28)	Ed Summers	200.00	90.00	60.00
(29)	Ed Willetts (Willett)	200.00	90.00	60.00
(30)	Vic Willis	300.00	135.00	90.00

1910 Nadja Philadelphia Athletics (E104-I)

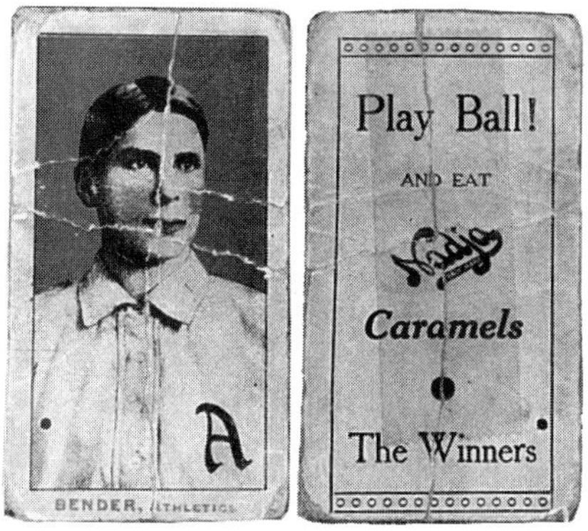

While there are 18 Philadelphia Athletics players in this set, it should be assumed that each can be found in three different variations. Each of the 1-1/2" x 2-3/4" cards can be found with a plain portrait lithograph on front, with either a blank back or a back containing a Nadja ad. Each player can also be found with a black overprint on front, comprised of a white elephant figure on the uniform and the notation "World's Champions 1910" above. The overprinted cards are known only with blank backs, and are somewhat scarcer than the plain cards of either type. Nadja-back cards should be value about the same as the overprinted type.

		NM	EX	VG
Complete Set (18):		3250.	1600.	950.00
Common Player:		135.00	61.00	40.00
(1a)	Home Run Baker (no "World's Champions" at top)	300.00	135.00	90.00
(1b)	Home Run Baker ("World's Champions" at top)	400.00	180.00	120.00

(2a)	Jack Barry (no "World's Champions" at top)	135.00	61.00	40.00
(2b)	Jack Barry ("World's Champions" at top)	150.00	67.00	45.00
(3a)	Chief Bender (no "World's Champions" at top)	300.00	135.00	90.00
(3b)	Chief Bender ("World's Champions" at top)	400.00	180.00	120.00
(4a)	Eddie Collins (no "World's Champions" at top)	300.00	135.00	90.00
(4b)	Eddie Collins ("World's Champions" at top)	400.00	180.00	120.00
(5a)	Harry Davis (no "World's Champions" at top)	135.00	61.00	40.00
(5b)	Harry Davis ("World's Champions" at top)	150.00	67.00	45.00
(6a)	Jimmy Dygert (no "World's Champions" at top)	135.00	61.00	40.00
(6b)	Jimmy Dygert ("World's Champions" at top)	150.00	67.00	45.00
(7a)	Topsy Hartsel (no "World's Champions" at top)	135.00	61.00	40.00
(7b)	Topsy Hartel ("World's Champions" at top)	150.00	67.00	45.00
(8a)	Harry Krause (no "World's Champions" at top)	135.00	61.00	40.00
(8b)	Harry Krause ("World's Champions" at top)	150.00	67.00	45.00
(9a)	Jack Lapp (no "World's Champions" at top)	135.00	61.00	40.00
(9b)	Jack Lapp ("World's Champions" at top)	150.00	67.00	45.00
(10a)	Paddy Livingstone (Livingston) (no "World's Champions" at top)	135.00	61.00	40.00
(10b)	Paddy Livingstone (Livingston) ("World's Champions" at top)	150.00	67.00	45.00
(11a)	Bris Lord (no "World's Champions" at top)	135.00	61.00	40.00
(11b)	Bris Lord ("World's Champions" at top)	150.00	67.00	45.00
(12a)	Connie Mack (no "World's Champions" at top)	350.00	157.00	105.00
(12b)	Connie Mack ("World's Champions" at top)	450.00	202.00	135.00
(13a)	Cy Morgan (no "World's Champions" at top)	135.00	61.00	40.00
(13b)	Cy Morgan ("World's Champions" at top)	150.00	67.00	45.00
(14a)	Danny Murphy (no "World's Champions" at top)	135.00	61.00	40.00
(14b)	Danny Murphy ("World's Champions" at top)	150.00	67.00	45.00
(15a)	Rube Oldring (no "World's Champions" at top)	135.00	61.00	40.00
(15b)	Rube Oldring ("World's Champions" at top)	150.00	67.00	45.00
(16a)	Eddie Plank (no "World's Champions" at top)	300.00	135.00	90.00
(16b)	Eddie Plank ("World's Champions" at top)	400.00	180.00	120.00
(17a)	Amos Strunk (no "World's Champions" at top)	135.00	61.00	40.00
(17b)	Amos Strunk ("World's Champions" at top)	150.00	67.00	45.00
(18a)	Ira Thomas (no "World's Champions" at top)	135.00	61.00	40.00
(18b)	Ira Thomas ("World's Champions" at top)	150.00	67.00	45.00

1910 Nadja Pittsburgh Pirates (E104-II)

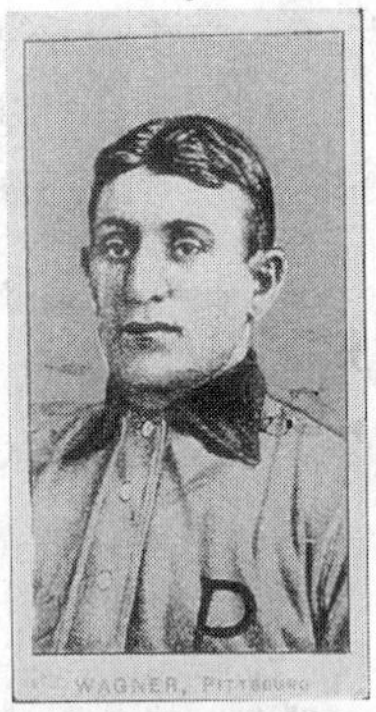
WAGNER, PITTSBURG

Similar to the contemporary American Caramel issue, this set of 1-1/2" x 2-3/4" cards features portrait color lithographs of the 1909 World's champion Pittsburgh (spelled "Pittsburg" on the cards) Pirates. Each card can be presumed to have been issued with both blank back and with a back bearing a Nadja ad. The Nadja-backed cards are scarcer but command little or no premium.

		NM	EX	VG
Complete Set (11):		3200.	1500.	900.00
Common Player:		135.00	61.00	40.00
(1)	Babe Adams	135.00	61.00	40.00
(2)	Fred Clarke	300.00	135.00	90.00
(3)	George Gibson	135.00	61.00	40.00
(4)	Ham Hyatt	135.00	61.00	40.00
(5)	Tommy Leach	135.00	61.00	40.00
(6)	Sam Leever	135.00	61.00	40.00
(7)	Nick Maddox	135.00	61.00	40.00
(8)	Dots Miller	135.00	61.00	40.00
(9)	Deacon Phillippe	135.00	61.00	40.00
(10)	Honus Wagner	2000.	900.00	600.00
(11)	Owen Wilson	135.00	61.00	40.00

1912 Napoleon Little Cigars

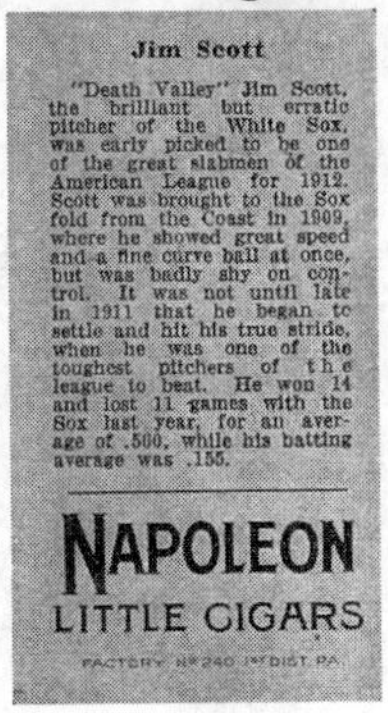
Jim Scott
"Death Valley" Jim Scott, the brilliant but erratic pitcher of the White Sox, was early picked to be one of the great slabmen of the American League for 1912. Scott was brought to the Sox fold from the Coast in 1909, where he showed great speed and a fine curve ball at once, but was badly shy on control. It was not until late in 1911 that he began to settle and hit his true stride, when he was one of the toughest pitchers of the league to beat. He won 14 and lost 11 games with the Sox last year, for an average of .560, while his batting average was .155.
NAPOLEON
LITTLE CIGARS

(See T207 for checklist, values.)

1963 Nassau County Boy Scouts

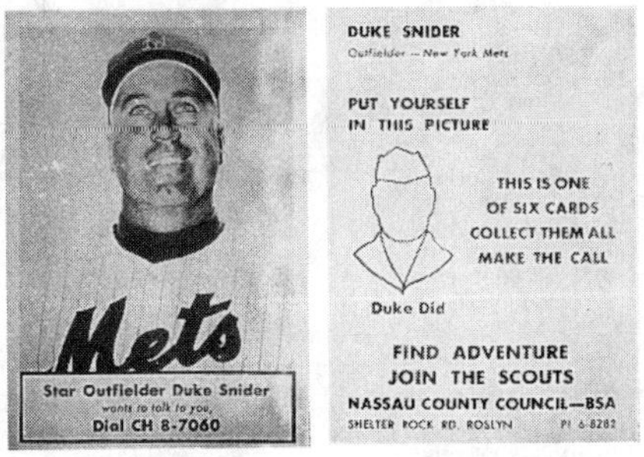
Mets
Star Outfielder Duke Snider
wants to talk to you,
Dial CH 8-7060
DUKE SNIDER
Outfielder — New York Mets
PUT YOURSELF
IN THIS PICTURE
THIS IS ONE
OF SIX CARDS
COLLECT THEM ALL
MAKE THE CALL
Duke Did
FIND ADVENTURE
JOIN THE SCOUTS
NASSAU COUNTY COUNCIL—BSA
SHELTER ROCK RD. ROSLYN

According to the text on the back, six cards were issued in this set. The other subjects are unknown, and may not feature any additional baseball players. The standard-size cards are printed in blue-and-white, both front and back, including a duo-tone photo of Snider in his only season with the Mets.

		NM	EX	VG
(1)	Duke Snider	150.00	75.00	45.00

1921-23 National Caramel (E220)

LARRY GARDNER
3rd.B. Cleveland
This set consists of pictures of 120 of the leading
BASE BALL STARS
—of the—
AMERICAN AND NATIONAL LEAGUES
—Made only by—
NATIONAL CARAMEL COMPANY
LANCASTER, PENNA.

Issued circa 1921 to 1923, this 120-card set is sometimes confused with contemporary American Caramel issues, but is easy to identify because of the words "Made only by National Caramel Company" on the back. It is the only baseball card set issued by that Lancaster, PA., confectioner. Cards measure 2" x 3-1/4" and feature black-and-white photos with the player's name, position and team at the bottom. In addition to the line indicating the manufacturer, the backs read "This set consists of pictures of 120 of the leading Base Ball Stars of the American and National Leagues". There are 115 different players included in the set, with five players shown on two cards each. About half of the photos in the set are identical to those used in various American Caramel sets, leading to some confusion regarding the three sets.

		NM	EX	VG
Complete Set (121):		9400.	4225.	2825.
Common Player:		50.00	22.00	15.00
(1)	Charles "Babe" Adams	50.00	22.00	15.00
(2)	G.C. Alexander	165.00	74.00	49.00
(3)	James Austin	50.00	22.00	15.00
(4)	Jim Bagbyk (Bagby)	50.00	22.00	15.00
(5)	Franklin "Home Run Baker"	150.00	67.00	45.00
(6)	Dave Bancroft	125.00	56.00	37.00
(7)	Turner Barber	50.00	22.00	15.00
(8)	George Burns (Cincinnati)	50.00	22.00	15.00
(9)	George Burns (Cleveland)	50.00	22.00	15.00
(10)	Joe Bush	50.00	22.00	15.00
(11)	Leon Cadore	50.00	22.00	15.00
(12)	Max Carey	125.00	56.00	37.00
(13)	Ty Cobb	800.00	360.00	240.00
(14)	Eddie Collins	150.00	67.00	45.00
(15)	John Collins	50.00	22.00	15.00
(16)	Wilbur Cooper	50.00	22.00	15.00
(17)	S. Coveleskie (Coveleski)	125.00	56.00	37.00
(18)	Walton Cruise	50.00	22.00	15.00
(19)	Wm. Cunningham	50.00	22.00	15.00
(20)	George Cutshaw	50.00	22.00	15.00
(21)	Jake Daubert	50.00	22.00	15.00
(22)	Chas. A. Deal	50.00	22.00	15.00
(23)	Bill Doak	50.00	22.00	15.00
(24)	Joe Dugan	50.00	22.00	15.00
(25)	Jimmy Dykes (batting)	50.00	22.00	15.00
(26)	Jimmy Dykes (fielding)	50.00	22.00	15.00
(27)	"Red" Faber	125.00	56.00	37.00
(28)	"Chick" Fewster	50.00	22.00	15.00
(29)	Wilson Fewster	50.00	22.00	15.00
(30)	Ira Flagstead	50.00	22.00	15.00
(31)	Arthur Fletcher	50.00	22.00	15.00
(32)	Frank Frisch	150.00	67.00	45.00
(33)	Larry Gardner	50.00	22.00	15.00
(34)	Walter Gerber	50.00	22.00	15.00
(35)	Charles Glazner	50.00	22.00	15.00
(36)	Hank Gowdy	50.00	22.00	15.00
(37)	J.C. Graney (should be J.G.)	50.00	22.00	15.00
(38)	Tommy Griffith	50.00	22.00	15.00
(39)	Charles Grimm	50.00	22.00	15.00
(40)	Heinie Groh	50.00	22.00	15.00
(41)	Byron Harris	50.00	22.00	15.00
(42)	Sam Harris (Stanley or Bucky)	125.00	56.00	37.00
(43)	Harry Heilman (Heilmann)	125.00	56.00	37.00
(44)	Claude Hendrix	50.00	22.00	15.00
(45)	Walter Henline	50.00	22.00	15.00
(46)	Chas. Hollocher	50.00	22.00	15.00
(47)	Harry Hooper	125.00	56.00	37.00
(48)	Rogers Hornsby	150.00	67.00	45.00
(49)	Waite Hoyt	125.00	56.00	37.00
(50)	Wilbert Hubbell	50.00	22.00	15.00
(51)	Wm. Jacobson	50.00	22.00	15.00
(52)	Walter Johnson	400.00	180.00	120.00
(53)	Jimmy Johnston	50.00	22.00	15.00
(54)	Joe Judge	50.00	22.00	15.00
(55)	Geo. "Bingo" Kelly	125.00	56.00	37.00
(56)	Dick Kerr	50.00	22.00	15.00
(57)	Pete Kilduff (bending)	50.00	22.00	15.00
(58)	Pete Kilduff (leaping)	50.00	22.00	15.00
(59)	Larry Kopf	50.00	22.00	15.00
(60)	H.B. Leonard	50.00	22.00	15.00
(61)	Harry Liebold (Leibold)	50.00	22.00	15.00
(62)	Walter "Buster" Mails ("Duster")	50.00	22.00	15.00
(63)	Walter "Rabbit" Maranville	125.00	56.00	37.00
(64)	Carl Mays	50.00	22.00	15.00
(65)	Lee Meadows	50.00	22.00	15.00
(66)	Bob Meusel	50.00	22.00	15.00
(67)	Emil Meusel	50.00	22.00	15.00
(68)	J.C. Milan	50.00	22.00	15.00
(69)	Earl Neale	50.00	22.00	15.00
(70)	Albert Nehf (Arthur)	50.00	22.00	15.00
(71)	Robert Nehf (Arthur)	50.00	22.00	15.00
(72)	Bernie Neis	50.00	22.00	15.00
(73)	Joe Oeschger	50.00	22.00	15.00
(74)	Robert O'Farrell	50.00	22.00	15.00
(75)	Ivan Olson	50.00	22.00	15.00
(76)	Steve O'Neill	50.00	22.00	15.00
(77)	Geo. Paskert	50.00	22.00	15.00
(78)	Roger Peckinpaugh	50.00	22.00	15.00
(79)	Herb Pennock	125.00	56.00	37.00
(80)	Ralph "Cy" Perkins	50.00	22.00	15.00
(81)	Scott Perry (photo actually Ed Rommel)	50.00	22.00	15.00
(82)	Jeff Pfeffer	50.00	22.00	15.00
(83)	V.J. Picinich	50.00	22.00	15.00
(84)	Walter Pipp	60.00	27.00	18.00
(85)	Derrill Pratt	50.00	22.00	15.00
(86)	Goldie Rapp	50.00	22.00	15.00
(87)	Edgar Rice	125.00	56.00	37.00
(88)	Jimmy Ring	50.00	22.00	15.00
(89)	Eddie Rousch (Roush)	125.00	56.00	37.00
(90)	Babe Ruth	2500.	1125.	750.00
(91)	Raymond Schmandt	50.00	22.00	15.00
(92)	Everett Scott	50.00	22.00	15.00
(93)	Joe Sewell	125.00	56.00	37.00
(94)	Wally Shang (Schang)	50.00	22.00	15.00
(95)	Maurice Shannon	50.00	22.00	15.00
(96)	Bob Shawkey	50.00	22.00	15.00
(97)	Urban Shocker	50.00	22.00	15.00
(98)	George Sisler	125.00	56.00	37.00
(99)	Earl Smith	50.00	22.00	15.00
(100)	John Smith	50.00	22.00	15.00
(101)	Sherrod Smith	50.00	22.00	15.00
(102)	Frank Snyder (crouching)	50.00	22.00	15.00

(103) Frank Snyder (standing)	50.00	22.00	15.00
(104) Tris Speaker	150.00	67.00	45.00
(105) Vernon Spencer	50.00	22.00	15.00
(106) Chas. "Casey" Stengle (Stengel)	175.00	79.00	52.00
(107) Milton Stock (batting)	50.00	22.00	15.00
(108) Milton Stock (fielding)	50.00	22.00	15.00
(109) James Vaughn	50.00	22.00	15.00
(110) Robert Veach	50.00	22.00	15.00
(111) Wm. Wambsgauss (Wambsganss)	50.00	22.00	15.00
(112) Aaron Ward	50.00	22.00	15.00
(113) Zach Wheat	125.00	56.00	37.00
(114) George Whitted (batting)	50.00	22.00	15.00
(115) George Whitted (fielding)	50.00	22.00	15.00
(116) Fred C. Williams	50.00	22.00	15.00
(117) Arthur Wilson	50.00	22.00	15.00
(118) Ivy Wingo	50.00	22.00	15.00
(119) Lawton Witt	50.00	22.00	15.00
(120) "Pep" Young (photo actually Ralph Young)	50.00	22.00	15.00
(121) Ross Young (Youngs)	125.00	56.00	37.00

1936 National Chicle Co. "Fine Pens" (R313)

Issued in 1936 by the National Chicle Company, this set consists of 120 cards, measuring 3-1/4" x 5-3/8". The black-and-white cards are blank-backed and unnumbered. Although issued by National Chicle, the name of the company does not appear on the cards. The set includes individual player portraits with facsimile autographs, multi-player cards and action photos. The cards, known in the hobby as "Fine Pen" because of the thin style of writing used for the facsimile autographs, were originally available as an in-store premium.

	NM	EX	VG
Complete Set (120):	3850.	1750.	1150.
Common Player:	30.00	13.50	7.50
(1) Melo Almada	35.00	15.50	8.75
(2) Nick Altrock, Al Schacht	30.00	13.50	7.50
(3) Paul Andrews	30.00	13.50	7.50
(4) Elden Auker (Eldon)	30.00	13.50	7.50
(5) Earl Averill	48.00	22.00	12.00
(6) John Babich, James Bucher	30.00	13.50	7.50
(7) Jim Becher (Bucher)	30.00	13.50	7.50
(8) Moe Berg	250.00	112.00	62.00
(9) Walter Berger	30.00	13.50	7.50
(10) Charles Berry	30.00	13.50	7.50
(11) Ralph Birkhofer (Birkofer)	30.00	13.50	7.50
(12) Cy Blanton	30.00	13.50	7.50
(13) O. Bluege	30.00	13.50	7.50
(14) Cliff Bolton	30.00	13.50	7.50
(15) Zeke Bonura	30.00	13.50	7.50
(16) Stan Bordagaray, George Earnshaw	30.00	13.50	7.50
(17) Jim Bottomley, Charley Gelbert	35.00	15.50	8.75
(18) Thos. Bridges	30.00	13.50	7.50
(19) Sam Byrd	30.00	13.50	7.50
(20) Dolph Camilli	30.00	13.50	7.50
(21) Dolph Camilli, Billy Jurges	30.00	13.50	7.50
(22) Bruce Campbell	30.00	13.50	7.50
(23) Walter "Kit" Carson	30.00	13.50	7.50
(24) Ben Chapman	30.00	13.50	7.50
(25) Harlond Clift, Luke Sewell	30.00	13.50	7.50
(26) Mickey Cochrane, Jimmy Fox (Foxx), Al Simmons	60.00	27.00	15.00
(27) "Rip" Collins	30.00	13.50	7.50
(28) Joe Cronin	48.00	22.00	12.00
(29) Frank Crossetti (Crosetti)	30.00	13.50	7.50
(30) Frank Crosetti, Jimmy Dykes	30.00	13.50	7.50
(31) Kiki Cuyler, Gabby Hartnett	48.00	22.00	12.00
(32) Paul Derringer	30.00	13.50	7.50
(33) Bill Dickey, Hank Greenberg	60.00	27.00	15.00
(34) Bill Dietrich	30.00	13.50	7.50
(35) Joe DiMaggio, Hank Erickson	525.00	235.00	130.00
(36) Carl Doyle	30.00	13.50	7.50
(37) Charles Dressen, Bill Myers	30.00	13.50	7.50
(38) Jimmie Dykes	30.00	13.50	7.50
(39) Rick Ferrell, Wess Ferrell (Wes)	48.00	22.00	12.00
(40) Pete Fox	30.00	13.50	7.50
(41) Frankie Frisch	48.00	22.00	12.00
(42) Milton Galatzer	30.00	13.50	7.50
(43) Chas. Gehringer	48.00	22.00	12.00
(44) Charley Gelbert	30.00	13.50	7.50
(45) Joe Glenn	30.00	13.50	7.50
(46) Jose Gomez	30.00	13.50	7.50
(47) Lefty Gomez, Red Ruffing	48.00	22.00	12.00
(48) Vernon Gomez	48.00	22.00	12.00
(49) Leon Goslin	48.00	22.00	12.00
(50) Hank Gowdy	30.00	13.50	7.50
(51) "Hank" Greenberg	55.00	25.00	13.50
(52) "Lefty" Grove	48.00	22.00	12.00
(53) Stan Hack	30.00	13.50	7.50
(54) Odell Hale	30.00	13.50	7.50
(55) Wild Bill Hallahan	30.00	13.50	7.50
(56) Mel Harder	30.00	13.50	7.50
(57) Stanley Bucky Harriss (Harris)	48.00	22.00	12.00
(58) Gabby Hartnett, Rip Radcliff	35.00	15.50	8.75
(59) Gabby Hartnett, L. Waner	35.00	15.50	8.75
(60) Gabby Hartnett, Lon Warnecke (Warneke)	30.00	13.50	7.50
(61) Buddy Hassett	30.00	13.50	7.50
(62) Babe Herman	30.00	13.50	7.50
(63) Frank Higgins	30.00	13.50	7.50
(64) Oral C. Hildebrand	30.00	13.50	7.50
(65) Myril Hoag	30.00	13.50	7.50
(66) Rogers Hornsby	60.00	27.00	15.00
(67) Waite Hoyt	48.00	22.00	12.00
(68) Willis G. Hudlin	30.00	13.50	7.50
(69) "Woody" Jensen	30.00	13.50	7.50
(70) Woody Jenson (Jensen)	30.00	13.50	7.50
(71) William Knickerbocker	30.00	13.50	7.50
(72) Joseph Kuhel	30.00	13.50	7.50
(73) Cookie Lavagetto	30.00	13.50	7.50
(74) Thornton Lee	30.00	13.50	7.50
(75) Ernie Lombardi	48.00	22.00	12.00
(76) Red Lucas	30.00	13.50	7.50
(77) Connie Mack, John McGraw	55.00	25.00	13.50
(78) Pepper Martin	30.00	13.50	7.50
(79) George McQuinn	30.00	13.50	7.50
(80) George McQuinn, Lee Stine	30.00	13.50	7.50
(81) Joe Medwick	48.00	22.00	12.00
(82) Oscar Melillo	30.00	13.50	7.50
(83) "Buddy" Meyer (Myer)	30.00	13.50	7.50
(84) Randy Moore	30.00	13.50	7.50
(85) T. Moore, Jimmie Wilson	30.00	13.50	7.50
(86) Wallace Moses	30.00	13.50	7.50
(87) V. Mungo	30.00	13.50	7.50
(88) Lamar Newsom (Newsome)	30.00	13.50	7.50
(89) Lewis "Buck" Newsom (Louis)	30.00	13.50	7.50
(90) Steve O'Neill	30.00	13.50	7.50
(91) Tommie Padden	30.00	13.50	7.50
(92) E. Babe Philips (Phelps)	30.00	13.50	7.50
(93) Bill Rogel (Rogell)	30.00	13.50	7.50
(94) Lynn "Schoolboy" Rowe	30.00	13.50	7.50
(95) Luke Sewell	30.00	13.50	7.50
(96) Al Simmons	48.00	22.00	12.00
(97) Casey Stengel	55.00	25.00	13.50
(98) Bill Swift	30.00	13.50	7.50
(99) Cecil Travis	30.00	13.50	7.50
(100) "Pie" Traynor	48.00	22.00	12.00
(101) William Urbansky (Urbanski)	30.00	13.50	7.50
(102) Arky Vaughn (Vaughan)	48.00	22.00	12.00
(103) Joe Vosmik	30.00	13.50	7.50
(104) Honus Wagner	95.00	43.00	24.00
(105) Rube Walberg	30.00	13.50	7.50
(106) Bill Walker	30.00	13.50	7.50
(107) Gerald Walker	30.00	13.50	7.50
(108) L. Waner, P. Waner, Big Jim Weaver	48.00	22.00	12.00
(109) George Washington	30.00	13.50	7.50
(110) Bill Werber	30.00	13.50	7.50
(111) Sam West	30.00	13.50	7.50
(112) Pinkey Whitney	30.00	13.50	7.50
(113) Vernon Wiltshere (Wilshere)	30.00	13.50	7.50
(114) "Pep" Young	30.00	13.50	7.50
(115) Chicago White Sox 1936	30.00	13.50	7.50
(116) Fence Busters	30.00	13.50	7.50
(117) Talking It Over (Leo Durocher)	30.00	13.50	7.50
(118) There She Goes! Chicago City Series	30.00	13.50	7.50
(119) Ump Says No - Cleveland vs. Detroit	30.00	13.50	7.50
(120) World Series 1935 (Phil Cavarretta, Goose Goslin, Lon Warneke)	30.00	13.50	7.50

1936 National Chicle Rabbit Maranville 'How To'

Issued by National Chicle in 1936, this 20-card set was a paper issue distributed with Batter-Up Gum. Unfolded, each paper measured 3-5/8" x 6". The numbered set featured a series of baseball tips from Rabbit Maranville and are illustrated with line drawings. American Card Catalog designation was R344.

	NM	EX	VG
Complete Set (20):	600.00	300.00	180.00
Common Card:	35.00	17.50	10.00
1 How to Pitch the Out Shoot	35.00	17.50	10.00
2 How to Throw the In Shoot	35.00	17.50	10.00
3 How to Pitch the Drop	35.00	17.50	10.00
4 How to Pitch the Floater	35.00	17.50	10.00
5 How to Run Bases	35.00	17.50	10.00
6 How to Slide	35.00	17.50	10.00
7 How to Catch Flies	35.00	17.50	10.00
8 How to Field Grounders	35.00	17.50	10.00
9 How to Tag A Man Out	35.00	17.50	10.00
10 How to Cover A Base	35.00	17.50	10.00
11 How to Bat	35.00	17.50	10.00
12 How to Steal Bases	35.00	17.50	10.00
13 How to Bunt	35.00	17.50	10.00
14 How to Coach Base Runner	35.00	17.50	10.00
15 How to Catch Behind the Bat	35.00	17.50	10.00
16 How to Throw to Bases	35.00	17.50	10.00
17 How to Signal	35.00	17.50	10.00
18 How to Umpire Balls and Strikes	35.00	17.50	10.00
19 How to Umpire Bases	35.00	17.50	10.00
20 How to Lay Out a Ball Field	35.00	17.50	10.00

1898-99 National Copper Plate Co. Portraits

Besides supplying The Sporting News with the player portrait supplements issued during 1899-1900, this Grand Rapids, Mich., firm also sold nearly identical pieces in portfolios of 50 in a hard-cover, string-bound book. Approximately 10" x 13", the pictures feature the players at the turn of the century in formal portrait poses; some are in uniform, some in civilian clothes. The pictures are vignetted on a white background with the player's full name, team and year of issue printed at bottom. At lower-left is National Copper Plate's credit line. Backs have player biographies in elaborate scrollwork frames.

	NM	EX	VG
Complete Set (50):	23000.	11500.	6900.
Common Player:	500.00	250.00	150.00
(1) M.F. Amole (M.G. "Doc")	550.00	275.00	165.00
(2) A.C. Anson	1200.	600.00	360.00
(3) Robert Becker	550.00	275.00	165.00
(4) Martin Bergen	500.00	250.00	150.00
(5) James A. Collins	900.00	450.00	270.00
(6) Joe Corbett	550.00	275.00	165.00
(7) Louis Criger	500.00	250.00	150.00
(8) Lave Cross	500.00	250.00	150.00
(9) Montford Cross	500.00	250.00	150.00
(10) Eugene DeMontreville	500.00	250.00	150.00
(11) Charles Dexter	500.00	250.00	150.00
(12) P.J. Donovan	500.00	250.00	150.00
(13) Thomas Dowd	550.00	275.00	165.00
(14) John J. Doyle	500.00	250.00	150.00
(15) Hugh Duffy	900.00	450.00	270.00
(16) Frank Dwyer	500.00	250.00	150.00
(17) Fred Ely ("Bones")	500.00	250.00	150.00
(18) A.F. Esterquest	550.00	275.00	165.00
(19) Wm. Ewing	900.00	450.00	270.00
(20) Elmer Flick	900.00	450.00	270.00
(21) Daniel Friend	550.00	275.00	165.00
(22) George F. Gilpatrick (Gillpatrick)	550.00	275.00	165.00
(23) J.M. Goar	500.00	250.00	150.00
(24) Michael Griffin	500.00	250.00	150.00
(25) Clark C. Griffith	900.00	450.00	270.00
(26) William Hill	500.00	250.00	150.00
(27) Dummy Hoy	600.00	300.00	180.00
(28) James Hughes	500.00	250.00	150.00
(29) William Joyce	500.00	250.00	150.00
(30) William Keeler	900.00	450.00	270.00
(31) Joseph J. Kelley	900.00	450.00	270.00
(32) William Kennedy	500.00	250.00	150.00
(33) William Lange	500.00	250.00	150.00
(34) John J. McGraw	900.00	450.00	270.00
(35) W.B. Mercer (George B. "Win")	550.00	275.00	165.00
(36) Charles A. Nichols	900.00	450.00	270.00
(37) Jerry Nops	500.00	250.00	150.00
(38) John O'Connor	500.00	250.00	150.00
(39) Richard Padden	500.00	250.00	150.00
(40) Wilbert Robinson	900.00	450.00	270.00
(41) William Shindle	500.00	250.00	150.00
(42) Charles Stahl	500.00	250.00	150.00
(43) E.F. Stein	550.00	275.00	165.00
(44) S.L. Thompson	900.00	450.00	270.00
(45) John Wagner	1200.	600.00	360.00
(46) R.J. Wallace	900.00	450.00	270.00
(47) Victor Willis	900.00	450.00	270.00
(48) Parke Wilson	500.00	250.00	150.00
(49) George Yeager	550.00	275.00	165.00
(50) C.L. Zimmer	500.00	250.00	150.00

1913 National Game

The patent date on the ornate red-and-white backs identify this as a 1913 issue. Fronts of the 2-1/2" x 3-1/2" cards have a black-and-white photo and a pair of baseball play scenarios used to play the card game. Corners are rounded. The set contains 43 identified player cards, a group of nine action photos in which the players are not identified and two header cards. Recent research indicates earlier checklists which included cards of Chief Meyers and Zach Wheat are in error. The unnumbered cards are checklisted in alphabetical order. This set carries the ACC designation of WG5.

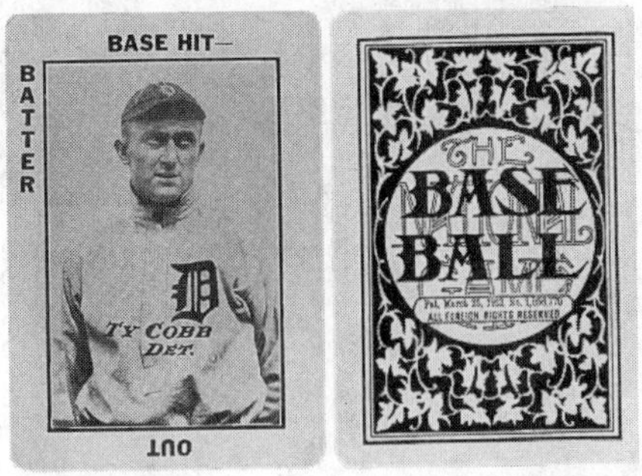

		NM	EX	VG
Complete Set (54):		4000.	1625.	1000.
Common Player:		50.00	20.00	12.50
Action Photo Card:		18.50	7.50	4.75
(1)	Grover Alexander	94.00	38.00	23.00
(2)	Frank Baker	87.00	35.00	22.00
(3)	Chief Bender	87.00	35.00	22.00
(4)	Bob Bescher	50.00	20.00	12.50
(5)	Joe Birmingham	50.00	20.00	12.50
(6)	Roger Bresnahan	87.00	35.00	22.00
(7)	Nixey Callahan	50.00	20.00	12.50
(8)	Frank Chance	87.00	35.00	22.00
(9)	Hal Chase	56.00	22.00	14.00
(10)	Fred Clarke	87.00	35.00	22.00
(11)	Ty Cobb	745.00	300.00	185.00
(12)	Sam Crawford	87.00	35.00	22.00
(13)	Bill Dahlen	50.00	20.00	12.50
(14)	Jake Daubert	50.00	20.00	12.50
(15)	Red Dooin	50.00	20.00	12.50
(16)	Johnny Evers	87.00	35.00	22.00
(17)	Vean Gregg	50.00	20.00	12.50
(18)	Clark Griffith	87.00	35.00	22.00
(19)	Dick Hoblitzel	50.00	20.00	12.50
(20)	Miller Huggins	87.00	35.00	22.00
(21)	Joe Jackson	1400.	560.00	350.00
(22)	Hughie Jennings	87.00	35.00	22.00
(23)	Walter Johnson	155.00	62.00	39.00
(24)	Ed Konetchy	50.00	20.00	12.50
(25)	Nap Lajoie	87.00	35.00	22.00
(26)	Connie Mack	87.00	35.00	22.00
(27)	Rube Marquard	87.00	35.00	22.00
(28)	Christy Mathewson	155.00	62.00	39.00
(29)	John McGraw	87.00	35.00	22.00
(30)	Larry McLean	50.00	20.00	12.50
(31)	Clyde Milan	50.00	20.00	12.50
(32)	Marty O'Toole	50.00	20.00	12.50
(33)	Nap Rucker	50.00	20.00	12.50
(34)	Tris Speaker	100.00	40.00	25.00
(35)	Jake Stahl	50.00	20.00	12.50
(36)	George Stallings	50.00	20.00	12.50
(37)	George Stovall	50.00	20.00	12.50
(38)	Bill Sweeney	50.00	20.00	12.50
(39)	Joe Tinker	87.00	35.00	22.00
(40)	Honus Wagner	385.00	155.00	96.00
(41)	Ed Walsh	87.00	35.00	22.00
(42)	Joe Wood	50.00	20.00	12.50
(43)	Cy Young	135.00	54.00	34.00
(---)	Rules card	50.00	20.00	12.50
(---)	Score card	50.00	20.00	12.50
(1A)	Batter swinging, looking forward	18.50	7.50	4.75
(2A)	Batter swinging, looking back	18.50	7.50	4.75
(3A)	Runner sliding, fielder at bag	18.50	7.50	4.75
(4A)	Runner sliding, umpire behind	18.50	7.50	4.75
(5A)	Runner sliding, hugging base	18.50	7.50	4.75
(6A)	Sliding play at plate, umpire at left	18.50	7.50	4.75
(7A)	Sliding play at plate, umpire at right	18.50	7.50	4.75
(8A)	Play at plate, runner standing	18.50	7.50	4.75
(9A)	Runner looking backwards	18.50	7.50	4.75

1952 National Tea Labels

Another set of bread end-labels, this checklist now comprises 44 players, although there is speculation that others remain to be cataloged. The unnumbered labels measure approximately 2-3/4" x 2-11/16" and are sometimes referred to as "Red Borders" because of their wide, red margins. The player's name and team are printed alongside his photo, and the slogan "Eat More Bread for Health" also appears on some labels.

		NM	EX	VG
Complete Set (44):		5000.	2500.	1500.
Common Player:		125.00	62.00	37.00
(1)	Gene Bearden	125.00	62.00	37.00
(2)	Yogi Berra	325.00	160.00	97.00
(3)	Lou Brissie	125.00	62.00	37.00
(4)	Sam Chapman	125.00	62.00	37.00
(5)	Chuck Diering	125.00	62.00	37.00
(6)	Dom DiMaggio	150.00	75.00	45.00
(7)	Bruce Edwards	125.00	62.00	37.00
(8)	Del Ennis	125.00	62.00	37.00
(9)	Ferris Fain	125.00	62.00	37.00
(10)	Bob Feller	225.00	110.00	67.00
(11)	Howie Fox	125.00	62.00	37.00
(12)	Sid Gordon	125.00	62.00	37.00
(13)	John Groth	125.00	62.00	37.00
(14)	Granny Hamner	125.00	62.00	37.00
(15)	Jim Hegan	125.00	62.00	37.00
(16)	Sheldon Jones	125.00	62.00	37.00
(17)	Howie Judson	125.00	62.00	37.00
(18)	Sherman Lollar	125.00	62.00	37.00
(19)	Clarence Marshall	125.00	62.00	37.00
(20)	Don Mueller	125.00	62.00	37.00
(21)	Danny Murtaugh	125.00	62.00	37.00
(22)	Dave Philley	125.00	62.00	37.00
(23)	Jerry Priddy	125.00	62.00	37.00
(24)	Bill Rigney	125.00	62.00	37.00
(25)	Robin Roberts	200.00	100.00	60.00
(26)	Eddie Robinson	125.00	62.00	37.00
(27)	Preacher Roe	135.00	67.00	40.00
(28)	Stan Rojek	125.00	62.00	37.00
(29)	Al Rosen	135.00	67.00	40.00
(30)	Bob Rush	125.00	62.00	37.00
(31)	Hank Sauer	125.00	62.00	37.00
(32)	Johnny Schmitz	125.00	62.00	37.00
(33)	Enos Slaughter	200.00	100.00	60.00
(34)	Duke Snider	325.00	160.00	97.00
(35)	Warren Spahn	225.00	110.00	67.00
(36)	Gerry Staley	125.00	62.00	37.00
(37)	Virgil Stallcup	125.00	62.00	37.00
(38)	George Stirnweiss	125.00	62.00	37.00
(39)	Earl Torgeson	125.00	62.00	37.00
(40)	Dizzy Trout	125.00	62.00	37.00
(41)	Mickey Vernon	125.00	62.00	37.00
(42)	Wally Westlake	125.00	62.00	37.00
(43)	Johnny Wyrostek	125.00	62.00	37.00
(44)	Eddie Yost	125.00	62.00	37.00

1922 Neilson's Chocolate (V61)

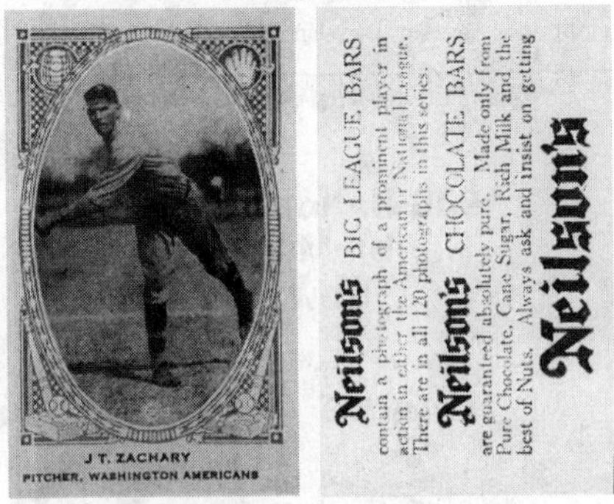

This set is closely related to the popular 1922 American Caramels (E120). The 120-card set was issued in Canada by Neilson's Chocolate Bars and carries the American Card Catalog designation V61. The front of the black-and-white cards is very similar to the E120 set, while the backs contain an ad for Neilson's Chocolates. Two types of cards exist. Type I is printed on heavy paper (similar to E120), has a card number in the lower-left corner and features Old English typography of the sponsor's name on back. Type II is printed on cardboard, has no card numbers and has no Old English typography on back. The Type II unnumbered cardboard version carries a 50 percent premium over the values shown here.

		NM	EX	VG
Complete Set (120):		13000.	5200.	2600.
Common Player:		80.00	32.00	16.00
1	George Burns	80.00	32.00	16.00
2	John Tobin	80.00	32.00	16.00
3	J.T. Zachary	80.00	32.00	16.00
4	"Bullet" Joe Bush	80.00	32.00	16.00
5	Lu Blue	80.00	32.00	16.00
6	Clarence (Tillie) Walker	80.00	32.00	16.00
7	Carl Mays	90.00	36.00	18.00
8	Leon Goslin	150.00	60.00	30.00
9	Ed Rommel	80.00	32.00	16.00
10	Charles Robertson	80.00	32.00	16.00
11	Ralph (Cy) Perkins	80.00	32.00	16.00
12	Joe Sewell	150.00	60.00	30.00
13	Harry Hooper	150.00	60.00	30.00
14	Urban (Red) Faber	150.00	60.00	30.00
15	Bib Falk ((Bibb))	80.00	32.00	16.00
16	George Uhle	80.00	32.00	16.00
17	Emory Rigney	80.00	32.00	16.00
18	George Dauss	80.00	32.00	16.00
19	Herman Pillette	80.00	32.00	16.00
20	Wallie Schang	80.00	32.00	16.00
21	Lawrence Woodall	80.00	32.00	16.00
22	Steve O'Neill	80.00	32.00	16.00
23	Edmund (Bing) Miller	80.00	32.00	16.00
24	Sylvester Johnson	80.00	32.00	16.00
25	Henry Severeid	80.00	32.00	16.00
26	Dave Danforth	80.00	32.00	16.00
27	Harry Heilmann	150.00	60.00	30.00
28	Bert Cole	80.00	32.00	16.00
29	Eddie Collins	150.00	60.00	30.00
30	Ty Cobb	2000.	800.00	400.00
31	Bill Wambsganss	80.00	32.00	16.00
32	George Sisler	150.00	60.00	30.00
33	Bob Veach	80.00	32.00	16.00
34	Earl Sheely	80.00	32.00	16.00
35	T.P. (Pat) Collins	80.00	32.00	16.00
36	Frank (Dixie) Davis	80.00	32.00	16.00
37	Babe Ruth	3000.	1200.	600.00
38	Bryan Harris	80.00	32.00	16.00
39	Bob Shawkey	80.00	32.00	16.00
40	Urban Shocker	80.00	32.00	16.00
41	Martin McManus	80.00	32.00	16.00
42	Clark Pittenger	80.00	32.00	16.00
43	"Deacon" Sam Jones	80.00	32.00	16.00
44	Waite Hoyt	150.00	60.00	30.00
45	Johnny Mostil	80.00	32.00	16.00
46	Mike Menosky	80.00	32.00	16.00
47	Walter Johnson	750.00	300.00	150.00
48	Wallie Pipp (Wally)	90.00	36.00	18.00
49	Walter Gerber	80.00	32.00	16.00
50	Ed Gharrity	80.00	32.00	16.00
51	Frank Ellerbe	80.00	32.00	16.00
52	Kenneth Williams	80.00	32.00	16.00
53	Joe Hauser	80.00	32.00	16.00
54	Carson Bigbee	80.00	32.00	16.00
55	Emil (Irish) Meusel	80.00	32.00	16.00
56	Milton Stock	80.00	32.00	16.00
57	Wilbur Cooper	80.00	32.00	16.00
58	Tom Griffith	80.00	32.00	16.00
59	Walter (Butch) Henline	80.00	32.00	16.00
60	Gene (Bubbles) Hargrave	80.00	32.00	16.00
61	Russell Wrightstone	80.00	32.00	16.00
62	Frank Frisch	150.00	60.00	30.00
63	Frank Parkinson	80.00	32.00	16.00
64	Walter (Dutch) Reuther	80.00	32.00	16.00
65	Bill Doak	80.00	32.00	16.00
66	Marty Callaghan	80.00	32.00	16.00
67	Sammy Bohne	80.00	32.00	16.00
68	Earl Hamilton	80.00	32.00	16.00
69	Grover C. Alexander	150.00	60.00	30.00
70	George Burns	80.00	32.00	16.00
71	Max Carey	150.00	60.00	30.00
72	Adolfo Luque	95.00	38.00	19.00
73	Dave (Beauty) Bancroft	150.00	60.00	30.00
74	Vic Aldridge	80.00	32.00	16.00
75	Jack Smith	80.00	32.00	16.00
76	Bob O'Farrell	80.00	32.00	16.00
77	Pete Donohue	80.00	32.00	16.00
78	Ralph Pinelli	80.00	32.00	16.00
79	Eddie Roush	150.00	60.00	30.00
80	Norman Boeckel	80.00	32.00	16.00
81	Rogers Hornsby	250.00	100.00	50.00
82	George Toporcer	80.00	32.00	16.00
83	Ivy Wingo	80.00	32.00	16.00
84	Virgil Cheeves	80.00	32.00	16.00
85	Vern Clemons	80.00	32.00	16.00
86	Lawrence (Hack) Miller	80.00	32.00	16.00
87	Johnny Kelleher	80.00	32.00	16.00
88	Heinie Groh	80.00	32.00	16.00
89	Burleigh Grimes	150.00	60.00	30.00
90	"Rabbit" Maranville	150.00	60.00	30.00
91	Charles (Babe) Adams	80.00	32.00	16.00
92	Lee King	80.00	32.00	16.00
93	Art Nehf	80.00	32.00	16.00
94	Frank Snyder	80.00	32.00	16.00
95	Raymond Powell	80.00	32.00	16.00
96	Wilbur Hubbell	80.00	32.00	16.00
97	Leon Cadore	80.00	32.00	16.00
98	Joe Oeschger	80.00	32.00	16.00
99	Jake Daubert	80.00	32.00	16.00
100	Will Sherdel	80.00	32.00	16.00
101	Hank DeBerry	80.00	32.00	16.00
102	Johnny Lavan	80.00	32.00	16.00
103	Jesse Haines	150.00	60.00	30.00
104	Joe (Goldie) Rapp	80.00	32.00	16.00
105	Oscar Ray Grimes	80.00	32.00	16.00
106	Ross Young (Youngs)	150.00	60.00	30.00
107	Art Fletcher	80.00	32.00	16.00
108	Clyde Barnhart	80.00	32.00	16.00
109	Louis (Pat) Duncan	80.00	32.00	16.00
110	Charlie Hollocher	80.00	32.00	16.00

111	Horace Ford	80.00	32.00	16.00
112	Bill Cunningham	80.00	32.00	16.00
113	Walter Schmidt	80.00	32.00	16.00
114	Joe Schultz	80.00	32.00	16.00
115	John Morrison	80.00	32.00	16.00
116	Jimmy Caveney	80.00	32.00	16.00
117	Zach Wheat	150.00	60.00	30.00
118	Fred (Cy) Williams	80.00	32.00	16.00
119	George Kelly	150.00	60.00	30.00
120	Jimmy Ring	80.00	32.00	16.00

1923 "Neilson's Chocolates"

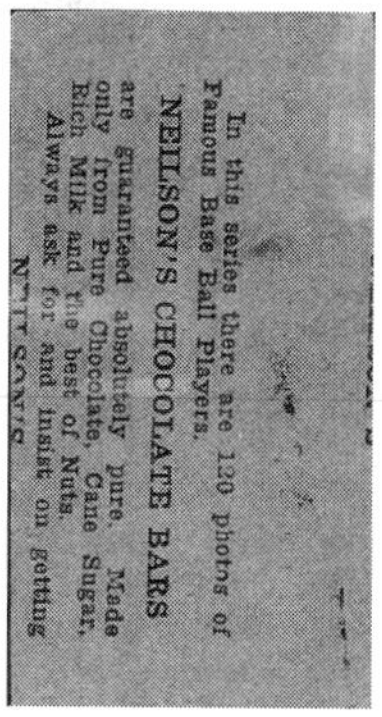

This issue, purporting to come from the Canadian candy maker which had produced a 1922 set, was first reported in 1996. The cards appear to be genuine W572 strip cards which have had a Neilson's ad overprinted on the back many years later in an apparent effort to defraud collectors. These altered W572s would have to be significantly downgraded to adjust for the defacing. It can be expected that any card which appears in W572 can be found with the Neilson's back, but the "discovery" was contained to 47 different players.

(See W572 for checklist)

1976-81 New England Sports Collectors

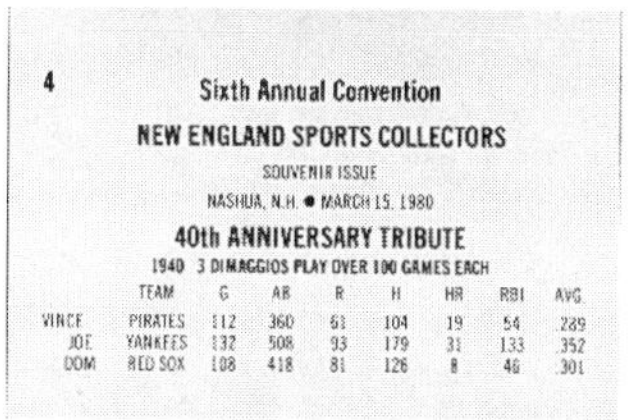

From the period 1976-81, the New England Sports Collectors club issued a series of postcard-size (3-1/2" x 5-1/4") black-and-white cards promoting their annual shows in Nashua, N.H. No card was issued in 1978.

		NM	EX	VG
Complete Set (5):		30.00	15.00	9.00
Common Player:		6.00	3.00	1.75
1	Joe DiMaggio (1976)	8.00	4.00	2.50
2	Jackie Robinson (1977)	6.00	3.00	1.75
3	Ted Williams (1979)	7.00	3.50	2.00
4	Vince DiMaggio, Joe DiMaggio, Dom DiMaggio (1980)	6.00	3.00	1.75
5	Mickey Mantle (1981)	9.00	4.50	2.75

1895 Newsboy Cabinets (N566)

Issued in the 1890s by the National Tobacco Works, this massive cabinet card set was distributed as a premium with the Newsboy tobacco brand. Although the set contained over 500 popular actresses, athletes, politicians and other celebrities of the day, only about a dozen cards of baseball players have been found. The cards measure 4-1/4" x 6-1/2" and feature sepia-toned photographs mounted on a backing that usually has "Newsboy New York" printed at bottom. Each portrait photograph is numbered and a few are numbered and a few are round. The ballplayers in the set are mostly members of the 1894 New York Giants with a couple of Brooklyn players. There are two known poses of John Ward. At least one card is known with advertising on the back for Keystone cigars.

		NM	EX	VG
Complete (Baseball) Set (14):		25000.	11000.	6000.
Common Player:		1500.	675.00	375.00
174	W.H. Murphy	1500.	675.00	375.00
175	Amos Rusie	5000.	2250.	1250.
176	Michael Tiernan	1500.	675.00	375.00
177	E.D. Burke	1500.	675.00	375.00
178	J.J. Doyle	1500.	675.00	375.00
179	W.B. Fuller	1500.	675.00	375.00
180	Geo. Van Haltren	1500.	675.00	375.00
181	Dave Foutz	1500.	675.00	375.00
182	Jouett Meekin	1500.	675.00	375.00
183	Michael Griffin	1500.	675.00	375.00
201	W.H. (Dad) Clark (Clarke)	1500.	675.00	375.00
202	Parke Wilson	1500.	675.00	375.00
586	John M. Ward (portrait, arms folded)	4500.	2025.	1125.
587	John M. Ward (standing, with bat)	3500.	1575.	875.00

1886 New York Baseball Club

This rare 19th Century baseball issue can be classified under the general category of "trade" cards, a popular advertising vehicle of the period. The cards measure 3" x 4-3/4" and feature blue line drawing portraits of members of the "New York Base Ball Club," which is printed along the top. As was common with this type of trade card, the bottom was left blank to accomodate various messages. The known examples of this set carry ads for local tobacco merchants and other businesses. The portraits are all based on the photographs used in the 1886 Old Judge set. The cards, which have been assigned an ACC designation of H812, are printed on thin paper rather than cardboard.

		NM	EX	VG
Complete Set (8):		27000.	12000.	6500.
Common Player:		3000.	1500.	900.00
(1)	T. Dealsey	3000.	1350.	600.00
(2)	M. Dorgan	3000.	1350.	600.00
(3)	T. Esterbrook	3000.	1350.	600.00
(4)	W. Ewing	5000.	2250.	1000.
(5)	J. Gerhardt	3000.	1350.	600.00
(6)	J. O'Rourke	5000.	2250.	1000.
(7)	D. Richardson	3000.	1350.	600.00
(8)	M. Welch	5000.	2250.	1000.

1953 Northland Bread Labels

This bread end-label set consists of 32 players - two from each major league team. The unnumbered black-and-white labels measure approximately 2-11/16" square and include the slogan "Bread for Energy" along the top. An album to house the labels was also part of the promotion.

		NM	EX	VG
Complete Set (32):		3650.	1825.	1100.
Common Player:		125.00	60.00	35.00
(1)	Cal Abrams	125.00	62.00	37.00
(2)	Richie Ashburn	200.00	100.00	60.00
(3)	Gus Bell	125.00	62.00	37.00
(4)	Jim Busby	125.00	62.00	37.00
(5)	Clint Courtney	125.00	62.00	37.00
(6)	Billy Cox	125.00	62.00	37.00
(7)	Jim Dyck	125.00	62.00	37.00
(8)	Nellie Fox	180.00	90.00	54.00
(9)	Sid Gordon	125.00	62.00	37.00
(10)	Warren Hacker	125.00	62.00	37.00
(11)	Jim Hearn	125.00	62.00	37.00
(12)	Fred Hutchinson	125.00	62.00	37.00
(13)	Monte Irvin	180.00	90.00	54.00
(14)	Jackie Jensen	150.00	75.00	45.00
(15)	Ted Kluszewski	170.00	85.00	51.00
(16)	Bob Lemon	180.00	90.00	54.00
(17)	Maury McDermott	125.00	62.00	37.00
(18)	Minny Minoso	170.00	85.00	51.00
(19)	Johnny Mize	180.00	90.00	54.00
(20)	Mel Parnell	125.00	62.00	37.00
(21)	Howie Pollet	125.00	62.00	37.00
(22)	Jerry Priddy	125.00	62.00	37.00
(23)	Allie Reynolds	150.00	75.00	45.00
(24)	Preacher Roe	150.00	75.00	45.00
(25)	Al Rosen	150.00	75.00	45.00
(26)	Connie Ryan	125.00	62.00	37.00
(27)	Hank Sauer	125.00	62.00	37.00
(28)	Red Schoendienst	180.00	90.00	54.00
(29)	Bobby Shantz	150.00	75.00	45.00
(30)	Enos Slaughter	180.00	90.00	54.00
(31)	Warren Spahn	100.00	90.00	54.00
(32)	Gus Zernial	125.00	62.00	37.00

1978 North Shore Dodge Cecil Cooper

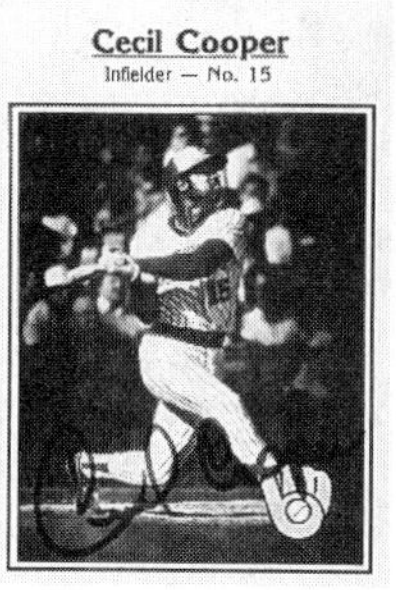

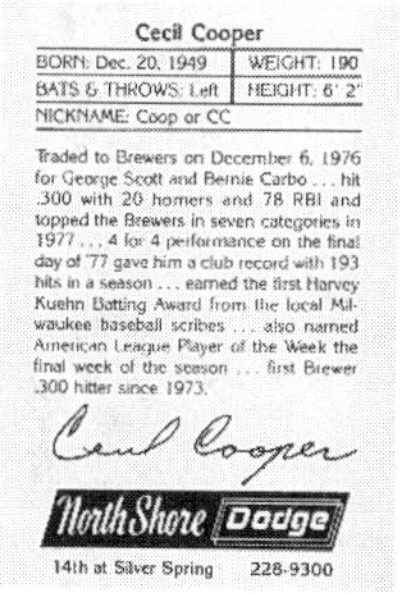

As part of his work as promotional spokesman for a local auto dealership, popular Brewers first baseman Cecil Cooper appears on a one-card set which was given to fans and collectors during public appearances. The card is printed in black-and-white in standard 2-1/2" x 3-1/2" size and is often found with a genuine autograph on the front.

	NM	EX	VG
Cecil Cooper	6.00	3.00	1.75
Cecil Cooper (autographed)	15.00	7.50	4.50

1980 Nostalgic Enterprises 1903 N.Y. Highlanders

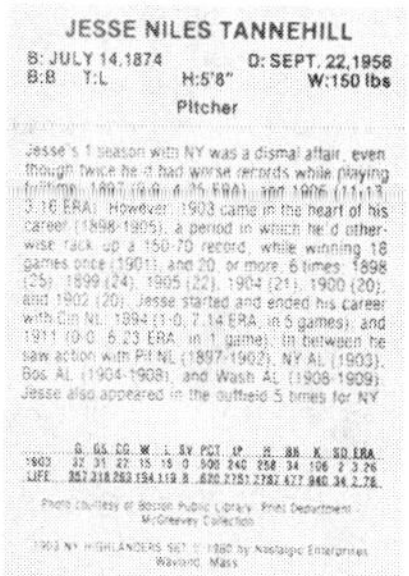

New York City's first team in the American League, the 1903 Highlanders, are featured in this collectors' issue. Fronts of the 2-1/2" x 3-1/2" cards have black-and-white portrait photos with ornate graphics, highlighted in yellow, and a white border. Backs have season and lifetime stats, player data and an extensive career summary. The unnumbered cards are checklisted here in alphabetical order. Sets originally sold for about $2.50.

		NM	EX	VG
Complete Set (17):		35.00	17.50	10.50
Common Player:		2.00	1.00	.60
(1)	Monte Beville	2.50	1.25	.70
(2)	Jack Chesbro	2.00	1.00	.60
(3)	Wid Conroy	2.00	1.00	.60
(4)	Lefty Davis	2.00	1.00	.60
(5)	John Deering	2.50	1.25	.70
(6)	Kid Elberfeld	2.00	1.00	.60
(7)	Dave Fultz	2.00	1.00	.60
(8)	John Ganzel	2.00	1.00	.60
(9)	Clark Griffith	2.00	1.00	.60
(10)	Harry Howell	2.00	1.00	.60
(11)	Willie Keeler	2.00	1.00	.60
(12)	Herm McFarland	2.00	1.00	.60
(13)	Jack O'Connor	2.00	1.00	.60
(14)	Jesse Tannehill	2.00	1.00	.60
(15)	Jimmy Williams	2.00	1.00	.60
(16)	Jack Zalusky	2.50	1.25	.70
(17)	Header card/checklist	2.00	1.00	.60

1910 Notebook Covers - color

These colorful notebook covers are one of several issues in many sizes and styles which were found on children's notebooks after the turn of the century. This series of eight measures 5" x 7-1/4" (about the size of the popular Turkey Red cabinets of the era) and feature color player pictures within a red frame. The player's last name is on front of the blank-backed picture. Values shown are for covers alone; covers still attached to original notebooks would command a premium of at least 2-3X.

		NM	EX	VG
Complete Set (8):		2500.	1250.	750.00
Common Player:		175.00	87.00	52.00
(1)	Roger Bresnahan	175.00	87.00	52.00
(2)	Ty Cobb	1250.	625.00	375.00
(3)	Eddie Collins	175.00	87.00	52.00
(4)	Johnny Evers	175.00	87.00	52.00
(5)	Clark Griffith	175.00	87.00	52.00
(6)	Nap Lajoie	175.00	87.00	52.00
(7)	Christy Mathewson	300.00	150.00	90.00
(8)	Honus Wagner	300.00	150.00	90.00

1914 Notebook Covers - Series of 12

These sepia-tone notebook covers are one of several issues in many sizes and styles which were found on children's notebooks after the turn of the century. This series of 12 measures 8" x 11". Covers have large central photos of the day's star with an action photo at bottom. Either two or four other players from the series are featured in the corners of the blank-back piece. Values shown are for covers alone; covers still attached to original notebooks would command a premium of at least 1.5X-2X. The unnumbered covers are listed here in alphabetical order, with the corner player photos identified in parentheses.

		NM	EX	VG
Complete Set (12):		3500.	1750.	1050.
Common Player:		95.00	47.00	28.00
(1)	Frank Baker (Milan, Mathewson)	125.00	62.00	37.00
(2)	Ty Cobb (Milan, Mathewson, Herzog, Johnson)	1200.	600.00	360.00
(3)	Eddie Collins (Schang, Johnson, Milan, McInnis)	125.00	62.00	37.00
(4)	Vean Gregg (Wood, Jackson, Collins, Johnson)	95.00	47.00	28.00
(5)	Charlie Herzog (McInnis, Collins, Schang, Cobb)	95.00	47.00	28.00
(6)	Joe Jackson (Milan, Wood, Herzog, Gregg)	2000.	1000.	600.00
(7)	Walter Johnson (Beker, Herzog, Mathewson, Jackson)	200.00	100.00	60.00
(8)	Christy Matthewson (Mathewson) (Baker, Jackson, McInnis, Gregg)	200.00	100.00	60.00
(9)	"Stuffy" McInnis (Cobb, Gregg)	95.00	47.00	28.00
(10)	Clyde Milan (Wood, Cobb, Gregg, Collins)	95.00	47.00	28.00
(11)	"Li Hung" (Wally) Schang (Jackson, Johnson)	95.00	47.00	28.00
(12)	Smokey (Smoky) Joe Wood (Collins, Herzog)	95.00	47.00	28.00

1907-09 Novelty Cutlery Postcards

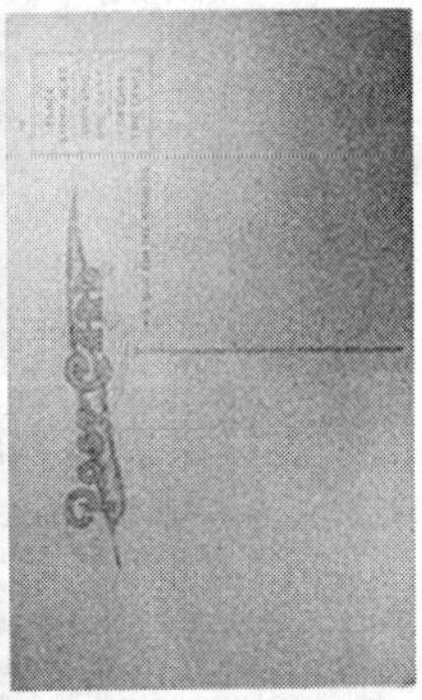

An ornately bordered black-and-white or sepia portrait or action pose of the day's great players identifies these postcards from a Canton, Ohio, knife company. Cards measure the standard 3-1/2" x 5-1/2" size with postcard indicia on the back. The sponsor is identified in a tiny line of type beneath the lower-right corner of the player photo.

		NM	EX	VG
Complete Set (26):		11000.	4350.	2175.
Common Player:		340.00	135.00	68.00
(1)	Roger Bresnahan	550.00	220.00	110.00
(2)	Al Bridwell	340.00	135.00	68.00
(3)	Three Finger Brown	550.00	220.00	110.00
(4)	Frank Chance	550.00	220.00	110.00
(5)	Hal Chase	375.00	150.00	75.00
(6)	Ty Cobb	1500.	600.00	300.00
(7)	Eddie Collins	550.00	220.00	110.00
(8)	Sam Crawford	550.00	220.00	110.00
(9)	Art Devlin	340.00	135.00	68.00
(10)	Red Dooin	340.00	135.00	68.00
(11)	Elmer Flick	550.00	220.00	110.00
(12)	Sam Frock	340.00	135.00	68.00
(13)	George Gibson	340.00	135.00	68.00
(14)	Solly Hofman	340.00	135.00	68.00
(15)	Walter Johnston (Johnson)	750.00	300.00	150.00
(16)	Nap Lajoie	550.00	220.00	110.00
(17)	Bris Lord	340.00	135.00	68.00
(18)	Christy Mathewson	750.00	300.00	150.00
(19)	Orval Overall	340.00	135.00	68.00
(20)	Eddie Plank	550.00	220.00	110.00
(21)	Tris Speaker	550.00	220.00	110.00
(22)	Gabby Street	340.00	135.00	68.00
(23)	Honus Wagner	1025.	410.00	205.00
(24)	Ed Walsh	550.00	220.00	110.00
(25)	Ty Cobb, Honus Wagner	1500.	600.00	300.00
(26)	Johnny Evers, Germany Schaefer	500.00	200.00	100.00

1960 Nu-Card Baseball Hi-Lites

These large, 3-1/4" x 5-3/8" cards are printed in a mock newspaper format, with a headline, picture and story describing one of baseball's greatest events. There are 72 events featured in the set, which is printed in red and black. Each card is numbered in the upper left corner. The card backs offer a quiz question and answer. Certain cards in the set can be found with the fronts printed entirely in black. These cards may command a slight premium.

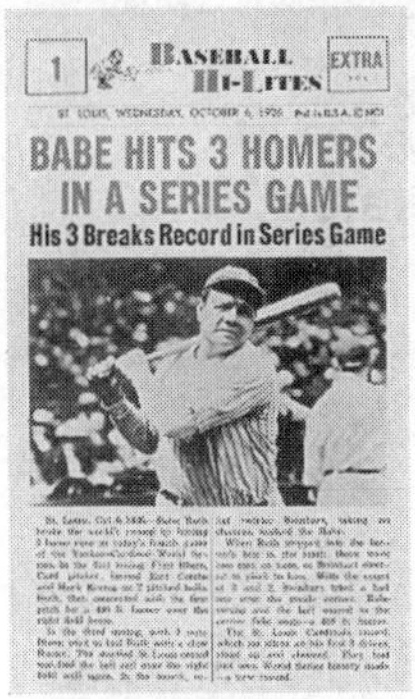

		NM	EX	VG
Complete Set (72):		400.00	200.00	120.00
Common Player:		4.00	2.00	1.25
1	Babe Hits 3 Homers In A Series Game	32.00	16.00	9.50
2	Podres Pitching Wins Series	6.00	3.00	1.75
3	Bevans Pitches No Hitter, Almost	4.00	2.00	1.25
4	Box Score Devised By Reporter	4.00	2.00	1.25
5	VanderMeer Pitches 2 No Hitters	4.00	2.00	1.25
6	Indians Take Bums	4.00	2.00	1.25
7	DiMag Comes Thru	16.00	8.00	4.75
8	Mathewson Pitches 3 W.S. Shutouts	6.00	3.00	1.75
9	Haddix Pitches 12 Perfect Innings	4.00	2.00	1.25
10	Thomson's Homer Sinks Dodgers	6.00	3.00	1.75
11	Hubbell Strikes Out 5 A.L. Stars	4.00	2.00	1.25
12	Pickoff Ends Series (Marty Marion)	4.00	2.00	1.25
13	Cards Take Series From Yanks (Grover Cleveland Alexander)	4.00	2.00	1.25
14	Dizzy And Daffy Win Series	6.00	3.00	1.75
15	Owen Drops 3rd Strike	4.00	2.00	1.25
16	Ruth Calls His Shot	32.00	16.00	9.50
17	Merkle Pulls Boner	4.00	2.00	1.25
18	Larsen Hurls Perfect World Series Game	7.25	3.75	2.25
19	Bean Ball Ends Career of Mickey Cochrane	4.00	2.00	1.25
20	Banks Belts 47 Homers, Earns MVP Honors	4.00	2.00	1.25
21	Stan Musial Hits 5 Homers In 1 Day	4.75	2.50	1.50
22	Mickey Mantle Hits Longest Homer	35.00	17.50	10.50
23	Sievers Captures Home Run Title	4.00	2.00	1.25
24	Gehrig Consecutive Game Record Ends	20.00	10.00	6.00
25	Red Schoendienst Key Player In Victory	4.00	2.00	1.25
26	Midget Pinch-Hits For St. Louis Browns (Eddie Gaedel)	6.00	3.00	1.75
27	Willie Mays Makes Greatest Catch	9.50	4.75	2.75
28	Homer By Berra Puts Yanks In 1st Place	4.00	2.00	1.25
29	Campy National League's MVP	4.00	2.00	1.25
30	Bob Turley Hurls Yanks To Championship	4.00	2.00	1.25
31	Dodgers Take Series From Sox In Six	4.00	2.00	1.25
32	Furillo Hero As Dodgers Beat Chicago	4.00	2.00	1.25
33	Adcock Gets Four Homers And A Double	4.00	2.00	1.25
34	Dickey Chosen All Star Catcher	4.00	2.00	1.25
35	Burdette Beats Yanks In 3 Series Games	4.00	2.00	1.25
36	Umpires Clear White Sox Bench	4.00	2.00	1.25
37	Reese Honored As Greatest Dodger S.S.	4.00	2.00	1.25
38	Joe DiMaggio Hits In 56 Straight Games	28.00	14.00	8.50
39	Ted Williams Hits .406 For Season	20.00	10.00	6.00
40	Johnson Pitches 56 Scoreless Innings	4.00	2.00	1.25
41	Hodges Hits 4 Home Runs In Nite Game	4.00	2.00	1.25
42	Greenberg Returns To Tigers From Army	7.25	3.75	2.25
43	Ty Cobb Named Best Player Of All Time	16.00	8.00	4.75
44	Robin Roberts Wins 28 Games	4.00	2.00	1.25
45	Rizzuto's 2 Runs Save 1st Place	4.00	2.00	1.25

		NM	EX	VG
46	Tigers Beat Out Senators For Pennant (Hal Newhouser)	4.00	2.00	1.25
47	Babe Ruth Hits 60th Home Run	32.00	16.00	9.50
48	Cy Young Honored	4.00	2.00	1.25
49	Killebrew Starts Spring Training	4.00	2.00	1.25
50	Mantle Hits Longest Homer At Stadium	35.00	17.50	10.50
51	Braves Take Pennant (Hank Aaron)	4.00	2.00	1.25
52	Ted Williams Hero Of All Star Game	16.00	8.00	4.75
53	Robinson Saves Dodgers For Playoffs (Jackie Robinson)	7.25	3.75	2.25
54	Snodgrass Muffs A Fly Ball	4.00	2.00	1.25
55	Snider Belts 2 Homers	4.00	2.00	1.25
56	New York Giants Win 26 Straight Games (Christy Mathewson)	4.00	2.00	1.25
57	Ted Kluszewski Stars In 1st Game Win	4.00	2.00	1.25
58	Ott Walks 5 Times In A Single Game (Mel Ott)	4.00	2.00	1.25
59	Harvey Kuenn Takes Batting Title	4.00	2.00	1.25
60	Bob Feller Hurls 3rd No-Hitter Of Caree	4.00	2.00	1.25
61	Yanks Champs Again! (Casey Stengel)	4.00	2.00	1.25
62	Aaron's Bat Beats Yankees In Series	7.25	3.75	2.25
63	Warren Spahn Beats Yanks in World Serie	4.00	2.00	1.25
64	Ump's Wrong Call Helps Dodgers	4.00	2.00	1.25
65	Kaline Hits 3 Homers, 2 In Same Inning	4.00	2.00	1.25
66	Bob Allison Named A.L. Rookie of Year	4.00	2.00	1.25
67	McCovey Blasts Way Into Giant Lineup	4.00	2.00	1.25
68	Colavito Hits Four Homers In One Game	7.25	3.75	2.25
69	Erskine Sets Strike Out Record In W.S.	4.00	2.00	1.25
70	Sal Maglie Pitches No-Hit Game	4.00	2.00	1.25
71	Early Wynn Victory Crushes Yanks	4.00	2.00	1.25
72	Nellie Fox American League's M.V.P.	4.00	2.00	1.25

1961 Nu-Card Baseball Scoops

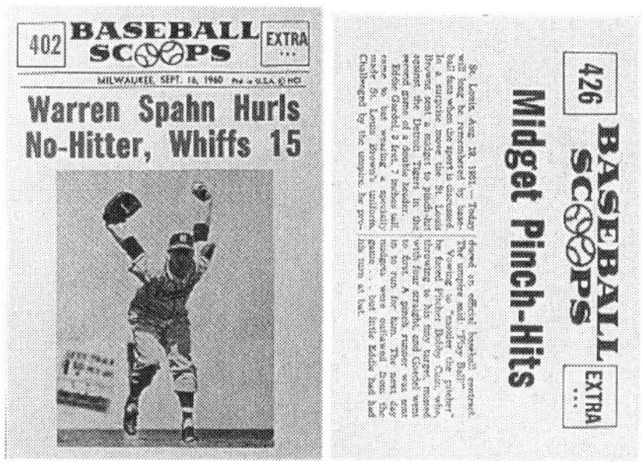

Very similar in style to their set of the year before, the Nu-Card Baseball Scoops were issued in a smaller 2-1/2" x 3-1/2" size, but still featured the mock newspaper card front. This 80-card set is numbered from 401 to 480, with numbers shown on both the card front and back. These cards, which commemorate great moments in individual players' careers, included only the headline and black and white photo on the fronts, with the descriptive story on the card backs. Cards are again printed in red and black. It appears the set may have been counterfeited, though when is not known. These cards can be determined by examining the card photo for unusual blurring and fuzziness.

		NM	EX	VG
	Complete Set (80):	375.00	185.00	110.00
	Common Player:	2.00	1.50	.80
401	Gentile Powers Birds Into 1st	2.00	1.50	.80
402	Warren Spahn Hurls No-Hitter, Whiffs 15	4.00	2.00	1.25
403	Mazeroski's Homer Wins Series For Bucs	15.00	7.50	4.50
404	Willie Mays' 3 Triples Paces Giants	9.00	4.50	2.75
405	Woodie Held Slugs 2 Homers, 6 RBIs	2.00	1.50	.80
406	Vern Law Winner Of Cy Young Award	2.00	1.50	.80
407	Runnels Makes 9 Hits in Twin-Bill	2.00	1.50	.80
408	Braves' Lew Burdette Wins No-Hitter	2.00	1.50	.80
409	Dick Stuart Hits 3 Homers, Single	2.00	1.50	.80
410	Don Cardwell Of Cubs Pitches No-Hit Game	2.00	1.50	.80
411	Camilo Pascual Strikes Out 15 Bosox	2.00	1.50	.80
412	Eddie Mathews Blasts 300th Big League HR	2.00	1.50	.80
413	Groat, NL Bat King, Named Loop's MVP	2.00	1.50	.80
414	AL Votes To Expand To 10 Teams (Gene Autry)	2.00	1.50	.80
415	Bobby Richardson Sets Series Mark	2.00	1.50	.80
416	Maris Nips Mantle For AL MVP Award	10.00	5.00	3.00
417	Merkle Pulls Boner	2.00	1.50	.80
418	Larsen Hurls Perfect World Series Game	5.00	2.50	1.50
419	Bean Ball Ends Career Of Mickey Cochrane	2.00	1.50	.80
420	Banks Belts 47 Homers, Earns MVP Award	2.00	1.50	.80
421	Stan Musial Hits 5 Homers In 1 Day	4.00	2.00	1.25
422	Mickey Mantle Hits Longest Homer	25.00	12.50	7.50
423	Sievers Captures Home Run Title	2.00	1.50	.80
424	Gehrig Consecutive Game Record Ends	20.00	10.00	6.00
425	Red Schoendienst Key Player In Victory	2.00	1.50	.80
426	Midget Pinch-Hits For St. Louis Browns (Eddie Gaedel)	4.00	2.00	1.25
427	Willie Mays Makes Greatest Catch	12.00	6.00	3.50
428	Robinson Saves Dodgers For Playoffs	7.50	3.75	2.25
429	Campy Most Valuable Player	2.00	1.00	.60
430	Turley Hurls Yanks To Championship	2.00	1.50	.80
431	Dodgers Take Series From Sox In Six (Larry Sherry)	2.00	1.50	.80
432	Furillo Hero In 3rd World Series Game	2.00	1.50	.80
433	Adcock Gets Four Homers, Double	2.00	1.50	.80
434	Dickey Chosen All Star Catcher	2.00	1.50	.80
435	Burdette Beats Yanks In 3 Series Games	2.00	1.50	.80
436	Umpires Clear White Sox Bench	2.00	1.50	.80
437	Reese Honored As Greatest Dodgers S.S.	2.00	1.50	.80
438	Joe DiMaggio Hits In 56 Straight Games	20.00	10.00	6.00
439	Ted Williams Hits .406 For Season	15.00	7.50	4.50
440	Johnson Pitches 56 Scoreless Innings	2.00	1.50	.80
441	Hodges Hits 4 Home Runs In Nite Game	2.00	1.50	.80
442	Greenberg Returns To Tigers From Army	4.00	2.00	1.25
443	Ty Cobb Named Best Player Of All Time	15.00	7.50	4.50
444	Robin Roberts Wins 28 Games	2.00	1.50	.80
445	Rizzuto's 2 Runs Save 1st Place	2.00	1.50	.80
446	Tigers Beat Out Senators For Pennant (Hal Newhouser)	2.00	1.50	.80
447	Babe Ruth Hits 60th Home Run	25.00	12.50	7.50
448	Cy Young Honored	2.00	1.00	.60
449	Killebrew Starts Spring Training	2.00	1.50	.80
450	Mantle Hits Longest Homer At Stadium	25.00	12.50	7.50
451	Braves Take Pennant	2.00	1.50	.80
452	Ted Williams Hero Of All Star Game	15.00	7.50	4.50
453	Homer By Berra Puts Yanks In 1st Place	2.00	1.50	.80
454	Snodgrass Muffs A Fly Ball	2.00	1.50	.80
455	Babe Hits 3 Homers In A Series Game	25.00	12.50	7.50
456	New York Wins 26 Straight Games	2.00	1.50	.80
457	Ted Kluszewski Stars In 1st Series Win	2.00	1.50	.80
458	Ott Walks 5 Times In A Single Game	2.00	1.50	.80
459	Harvey Kuenn Takes Batting Title	2.00	1.50	.80
460	Bob Feller Hurls 3rd No-Hitter Of Career	2.00	1.50	.80
461	Yanks Champs Again! (Casey Stengel)	2.00	1.50	.80
462	Aaron's Bat Beats Yankees In Series	9.00	4.50	2.75
463	Warren Spahn Beats Yanks In World Serie	2.00	1.50	.80
464	Ump's Wrong Call Helps Dodgers	2.00	1.50	.80
465	Kaline Hits 3 Homers, 2 In Same Inning	2.00	1.50	.80
466	Bob Allison Named A.L. Rookie Of Year	2.00	1.50	.80
467	DiMag Comes Thru	20.00	10.00	6.00
468	Colavito Hits Four Homers In One Game	3.00	1.50	.90
469	Erskine Sets Strike Out Record In W.S.	2.00	1.50	.80
470	Sal Maglie Pitches No-Hit Game	2.00	1.50	.80
471	Early Wynn Victory Crushes Yanks	2.00	1.50	.80
472	Nellie Fox American League's MVP	2.00	1.50	.80
473	Pickoff Ends Series (Marty Marion)	2.00	1.50	.80
474	Podres Pitching Wins Series	3.00	1.50	.90
475	Owen Drops 3rd Strike	2.00	1.50	.80
476	Dizzy And Daffy Win Series	4.00	2.00	1.25
477	Mathewson Pitches 3 W.S. Shutouts	2.00	1.50	.80
478	Haddix Pitches 12 Perfect Innings	2.00	1.50	.80
479	Hubbell Strike Out 5 A.L. Stars	2.00	1.00	.60
480	Homer Sinks Dodgers (Bobby Thomson)	5.00	2.50	1.50

1889 Number 7 Cigars

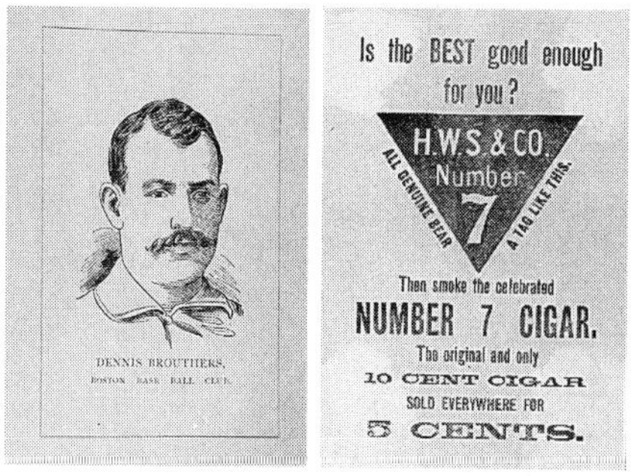

At least three versions of this set picturing Boston Beaneaters (N.L.) players were issued in 1889. Number 7 and Diamond S brand cigars are the most commonly encountered advertising printed on the cards' backs. Cards with "C.S. White & Co." at top front are also known. The cards measure approximately 3-1/8" x 4-1/2" and feature black-and-white portrait drawings of the players with their name printed below in capital letters along with the team name. Backs carry ads for either Number 7 Cigars, a product of H.W.S. & Co., or Diamond S Cigars, advertised as the "Best 10 cent Cigar in America."

		NM	EX	VG
	Complete Set (15):	12000.	4800.	2400.
	Common Player:	1000.	400.00	200.00
(1)	C.W. Bennett	1000.	400.00	200.00
(2)	Dennis Brouthers	1450.	580.00	290.00
(3)	T.T. Brown	1000.	400.00	200.00
(4)	John G. Clarkson	1450.	580.00	290.00
(5)	C.W. Ganzel	1000.	400.00	200.00
(6)	James A. Hart	1000.	400.00	200.00
(7)	R.F. Johnston	1000.	400.00	200.00
(8)	M.J. Kelly	1650.	660.00	330.00
(9)	M.J. Madden	1000.	400.00	200.00
(10)	Wm. Nash	1000.	400.00	200.00
(11)	Jos. Quinn	1000.	400.00	200.00
(12)	Chas. Radbourn	1450.	580.00	290.00
(13)	J.B. Ray (should be I.B.)	1000.	400.00	200.00
(14)	Hardie Richardson	1000.	400.00	200.00
(15)	Wm. Sowders	1000.	400.00	200.00

1950 Num Num Cleveland Indians

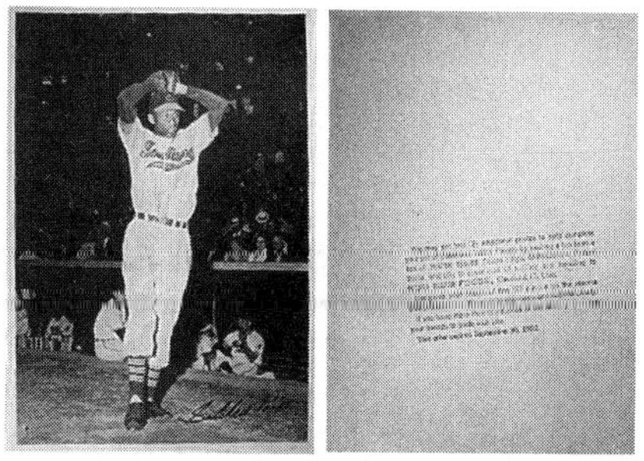

The 6-1/2" x 9" photopack pictures sold at Municipal Stadium did double duty in 1950 when they were also used as a premium for Num Num snack foods. A rubber-stamped notice on the back of the black-and-white photos offered two pictures for 10 cents and a box top, while encouraging trading. The pictures generally feature posed action shots with a facsimile autograph and white border. Backs are blank except for the rubber stamping. The unnumbered cards are checklisted here alphabetically.

		NM	EX	VG
Complete Set (34):		1600.	725.00	400.00
Common Player:		35.00	15.50	8.75
(1)	Bob Avila	35.00	15.50	8.75
(2)	Gene Bearden	35.00	15.50	8.75
(3)	Al Benton	35.00	15.50	8.75
(4)	John Berardino	50.00	22.00	12.50
(5)	Ray Boone	35.00	15.50	8.75
(6)	Lou Boudreau	65.00	29.00	16.00
(7)	Allie Clark	35.00	15.50	8.75
(8)	Larry Doby	65.00	29.00	16.00
(9)	Luke Easter	35.00	15.50	8.75
(10)	Bob Feller	125.00	56.00	31.00
(11)	Jess Flores	35.00	15.50	8.75
(12)	Mike Garcia	35.00	15.50	8.75
(13)	Joe Gordon	35.00	15.50	8.75
(14)	Hank Greenberg	90.00	40.00	22.00
(15)	Steve Gromek	35.00	15.50	8.75
(16)	Jim Hegan	35.00	15.50	8.75
(17)	Ken Keltner	35.00	15.50	8.75
(18)	Bob Kennedy	150.00	67.00	37.00
(19)	Bob Lemon	65.00	29.00	16.00
(20)	Dale Mitchell	35.00	15.50	8.75
(21)	Ray Murray	35.00	15.50	8.75
(22)	Satchell Paige	200.00	90.00	50.00
(23)	Frank Papish	35.00	15.50	8.75
(24)	Hal Peck	35.00	15.50	8.75
(25)	Chick Pieretti	35.00	15.50	8.75
(26)	Al Rosen	35.00	15.50	8.75
(27)	Dick Rozek	35.00	15.50	8.75
(28)	Mike Tresh	35.00	15.50	8.75
(29)	Thurman Tucker	35.00	15.50	8.75
(30)	Bill Veeck	65.00	29.00	16.00
(31)	Mickey Vernon	35.00	15.50	8.75
(32)	Early Wynn	65.00	29.00	16.00
(33)	Sam Zoldak	35.00	15.50	8.75
(34)	Coaches (George Susce, Herold Ruel, Bill McKechnie, Steve O'Neill, Mel Harder)	35.00	15.50	8.75

1952 Num Num Cleveland Indians

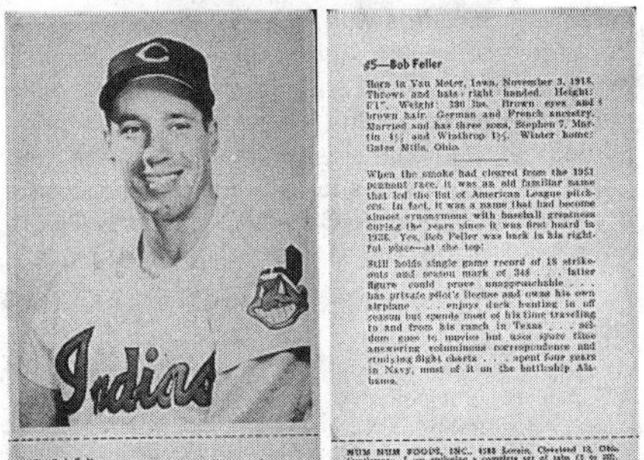

Distributed with packages of Num Num potato chips, pretzels and other snack foods, this black-and-white set, like the 1950 issue, was also issued in a slightly different format directly by the team. The Num Num cards have a 1" tab at the bottom which could be redeemed, when a complete set was collected, for an autographed baseball. The team-issued version of the cards was printed without the tabs. Also like the 1950 Num Nums, Bob Kennedy's card is unaccountably scarce in the 1952 set. The '52 cards measure 3-1/2" x 5-1/2" including the tab, which has the card number on front, along with redemption details. Backs, also printed in black-and-white, repeat the card number in the upper-left corner. There is significant player biographical information and some 1951 season highlights. Cards with no tabs are worth about 1/3 less than the values quoted.

		NM	EX	VG
Complete Set (20):		2175.	875.00	435.00
Common Player:		75.00	30.00	15.00
1	Lou Brissie	75.00	30.00	15.00
2	Jim Hegan	75.00	30.00	15.00
3	Birdie Tebbetts	75.00	30.00	15.00
4	Bob Lemon	150.00	60.00	30.00
5	Bob Feller	300.00	120.00	60.00
6	Early Wynn	150.00	60.00	30.00
7	Mike Garcia	75.00	30.00	15.00
8	Steve Gromek	75.00	30.00	15.00
9	Bob Chakales	75.00	30.00	15.00
10	Al Rosen	75.00	30.00	15.00
11	Dick Rozek	75.00	30.00	15.00
12	Luke Easter	75.00	30.00	15.00
13	Ray Boone	75.00	30.00	15.00
14	Bobby Avila	75.00	30.00	15.00
15	Dale Mitchell	75.00	30.00	15.00
16	Bob Kennedy	500.00	200.00	100.00
17	Harry Simpson	75.00	30.00	15.00
18	Larry Doby	125.00	50.00	25.00
19	Sam Jones	75.00	30.00	15.00
20	Al Lopez	135.00	54.00	27.00

1969 N.Y. Boy Scouts

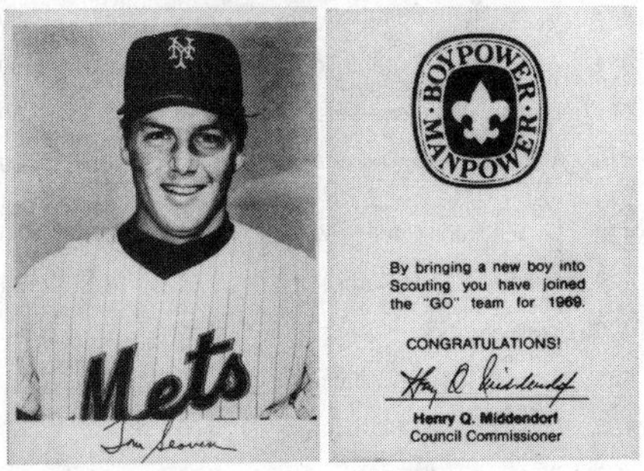

Cards featuring N.Y. Mets and Yankees players were used as a recruitment incentive in 1969. Cards are 2-1/2" x 3-1/2" and printed in black-and-white on thin cardboard. It is unknown, but likely, that players other than those checklisted here were also issued.

		NM	EX	VG
Common Player:		60.00	30.00	18.00
(1)	Tommy Agee	75.00	37.00	22.00
(2)	Bud Harrelson	75.00	37.00	22.00
(3)	Cleon Jones	75.00	37.00	22.00
(4)	Bobby Murcer	75.00	37.00	22.00
(5)	Art Shamsky	60.00	30.00	18.00
(6)	Tom Seaver	450.00	225.00	135.00
(7)	Mel Stottlemyre	75.00	37.00	22.00
(8)	Ron Swoboda	75.00	37.00	22.00

1949 N.Y. Giants Photo Pack

This set of player photos was sold at Polo Grounds souvenir stands. Pictures have player portraits in a 6-1/2" x 9" format. The black-and-white photos are blank-backed and have facsimile autographs printed near the bottom on front. A white border surrounds the front. The unnumbered photos are checklisted here in alphabetical order.

		NM	EX	VG
Complete Set (25):		200.00	100.00	60.00
Common Player:		5.00	2.50	1.50
(1)	Hank Behrman	5.00	2.50	1.50
(2)	Walker Cooper	5.00	2.50	1.50
(3)	Leo Durocher	9.00	4.50	2.75
(4)	Fred Fitzsimmons	5.00	2.50	1.50
(5)	Frank Frisch	12.00	6.00	3.50
(6)	Augie Galan	5.00	2.50	1.50
(7)	Sid Gordon	7.50	3.75	2.25
(8)	Bert Haas	5.00	2.50	1.50
(9)	Andy Hansen	5.00	2.50	1.50
(10)	Clint Hartung	5.00	2.50	1.50
(11)	Bob Hofman	5.00	2.50	1.50
(12)	Larry Jansen	5.00	2.50	1.50
(13)	Sheldon Jones	5.00	2.50	1.50
(14)	Monte Kennedy	5.00	2.50	1.50
(15)	Buddy Kerr	5.00	2.50	1.50
(16)	Dave Koslo	5.00	2.50	1.50
(17)	Mickey Livingston	5.00	2.50	1.50
(18)	Whitey Lockman	5.00	2.50	1.50
(19)	Willard Marshall	5.00	2.50	1.50
(20)	Johnny Mize	12.00	6.00	3.50
(21)	Don Mueller	5.00	2.50	1.50
(22)	Ray Poat	5.00	2.50	1.50
(23)	Bobby Rhawn	5.00	2.50	1.50
(24)	Bill Rigney	5.00	2.50	1.50
(25)	Bobby Thomson	10.00	5.00	3.00

1954 N.Y. Journal-American

Issued during the Golden Age of baseball in New York City, this 59-card set features only players from the three New York teams of the day - the Giants, Yankees and Dodgers. The 2" x 4" cards were issued at newsstands with the purchase of the now-extinct newspaper. Card fronts have promotional copy and a contest serial number in addition to the player's name and photo. Cards are black-and-white and unnumbered. Many of the game's top stars are included, such as Mickey Mantle, Willie Mays, Gil Hodges, Duke Snider, Jackie Robinson and Yogi Berra. Card backs feature team schedules. It has been theorized that a 60th Dodgers card should exist. Don Hoak and Bob Milliken have been suggested as the missing card, but the existence of either card has never been confirmed.

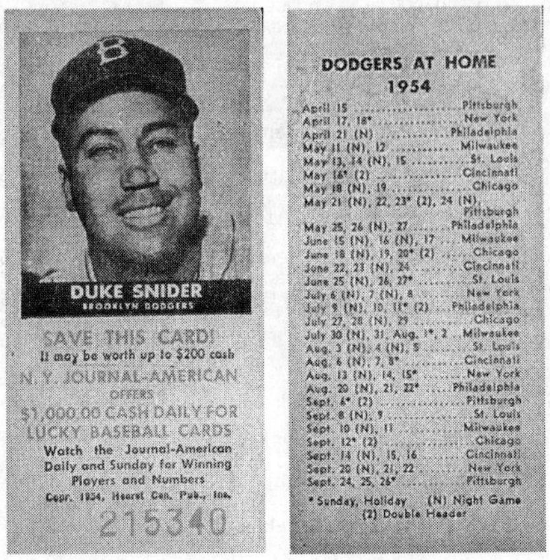

		NM	EX	VG
Complete Set (59):		3250.	1600.	975.00
Common Player:		24.00	12.00	7.25
(1)	Johnny Antonelli	24.00	12.00	7.25
(2)	Hank Bauer	32.00	16.00	9.50
(3)	Yogi Berra	200.00	100.00	60.00
(4)	Joe Black	24.00	12.00	7.25
(5)	Harry Byrd	24.00	12.00	7.25
(6)	Roy Campanella	200.00	100.00	60.00
(7)	Andy Carey	24.00	12.00	7.25
(8)	Jerry Coleman	24.00	12.00	7.25
(9)	Joe Collins	24.00	12.00	7.25
(10)	Billy Cox	24.00	12.00	7.25
(11)	Al Dark	24.00	12.00	7.25
(12)	Carl Erskine	32.00	16.00	9.50
(13)	Whitey Ford	75.00	37.00	22.00
(14)	Carl Furillo	40.00	20.00	12.00
(15)	Junior Gilliam	40.00	20.00	12.00
(16)	Ruben Gomez	24.00	12.00	7.25
(17)	Marv Grissom	24.00	12.00	7.25
(18)	Jim Hearn	24.00	12.00	7.25
(19)	Gil Hodges	75.00	37.00	22.00
(20)	Bobby Hofman	24.00	12.00	7.25
(21)	Jim Hughes	24.00	12.00	7.25
(22)	Monte Irvin	50.00	25.00	15.00
(23)	Larry Jansen	24.00	12.00	7.25
(24)	Ray Katt	24.00	12.00	7.25
(25)	Steve Kraly	24.00	12.00	7.25
(26)	Bob Kuzava	24.00	12.00	7.25
(27)	Clem Labine	24.00	12.00	7.25
(28)	Frank Leja	24.00	12.00	7.25
(29)	Don Liddle	24.00	12.00	7.25
(30)	Whitey Lockman	24.00	12.00	7.25
(31)	Billy Loes	24.00	12.00	7.25
(32)	Eddie Lopat	24.00	12.00	7.25
(33)	Sal Maglie	24.00	12.00	7.25
(34)	Mickey Mantle	500.00	250.00	150.00
(35)	Willie Mays	300.00	150.00	90.00
(36)	Gil McDougald	40.00	20.00	12.00
(37)	Russ Meyer	24.00	12.00	7.25
(38)	Bill Miller	24.00	12.00	7.25
(39)	Tom Morgan	24.00	12.00	7.25
(40)	Don Mueller	24.00	12.00	7.25
(41)	Don Newcombe	40.00	20.00	12.00
(42)	Irv Noren	24.00	12.00	7.25
(43)	Erv Palica	24.00	12.00	7.25
(44)	Pee Wee Reese	120.00	60.00	36.00
(45)	Allie Reynolds	40.00	20.00	12.00
(46)	Dusty Rhodes	24.00	12.00	7.25
(47)	Phil Rizzuto	120.00	60.00	36.00
(48)	Ed Robinson	24.00	12.00	7.25
(49)	Jackie Robinson	350.00	175.00	105.00
(50)	Preacher Roe	32.00	16.00	9.50
(51)	George Shuba	24.00	12.00	7.25
(52)	Duke Snider	250.00	125.00	75.00
(53)	Hank Thompson	24.00	12.00	7.25
(54)	Wes Westrum	24.00	12.00	7.25
(55)	Hoyt Wilhelm	50.00	25.00	15.00
(56)	Davey Williams	24.00	12.00	7.25
(57)	Dick Williams	24.00	12.00	7.25
(58)	Gene Woodling	24.00	12.00	7.25
(59)	Al Worthington	24.00	12.00	7.25

1969 N.Y. News Mets Portfolio of Stars

To commemorate the N.Y. Mets miracle season of 1969, one of the city's daily newspapers, The News, issued a portfolio of player portraits done by editorial cartoonist Bruce Stark. The 9" x 12" pencil drawings are printed on heavy textured paper and were sold as a set in a folder labeled, "The 1969 Mets / A Portfolio of Stars". The black-and-white drawings are on a white background. A facsimile player autograph is printed at lower left. At lower right is the signature of the artist, Stark, along with the paper's logo and a union label. The blank-backed, unnumbered pieces are checklisted here alphabetically.

		NM	EX	VG
	Complete Set (20):	485.00	240.00	145.00
	Common Player:	15.00	7.50	4.50
(1)	Tommie Agee	15.00	7.50	4.50
(2)	Ken Boswell	15.00	7.50	4.50
(3)	Don Cardwell	15.00	7.50	4.50
(4)	Donn Clendenon	20.00	10.00	6.00
(5)	Wayne Garrett	15.00	7.50	4.50
(6)	Gary Gentry	15.00	7.50	4.50
(7)	Jerry Grote	15.00	7.50	4.50
(8)	Bud Harrelson	18.00	9.00	5.50
(9)	Gil Hodges	45.00	22.00	13.50
(10)	Cleon Jones	15.00	7.50	4.50
(11)	Jerry Koosman	15.00	7.50	4.50
(12)	Ed Kranepool	15.00	7.50	4.50
(13)	Jim McAndrew	15.00	7.50	4.50
(14)	Tug McGraw	18.00	9.00	5.50
(15)	Nolan Ryan	225.00	110.00	67.00
(16)	Tom Seaver	75.00	37.00	22.00
(17)	Art Shamsky	15.00	7.50	4.50
(18)	Ron Swoboda	15.00	7.50	4.50
(19)	Ron Taylor	15.00	7.50	4.50
(20)	Al Weis	15.00	7.50	4.50

1944 N.Y. Yankees Stamps

One of the few paper collectibles issued during World War II, this set includes several players who do not appear on any other contemporary baseball card issue. The 1-3/4" x 2-3/8" stamps were issued on a single sheet with an album marking the Yankees 1943 World Series win. Stamps are in full color with the player's name in white on a red strip at bottom. The unnumbered stamps are checklisted here alphabetically.

		NM	EX	VG
	Complete Set (30):	250.00	125.00	75.00
	Common Player:	12.00	6.00	3.50
	Album:	50.00	25.00	15.00
(1)	Ernie Bonham	12.00	6.00	3.50
(2)	Hank Borowy	12.00	6.00	3.50
(3)	Marvin Breuer	12.00	6.00	3.50
(4)	Tommy Byrne	12.00	6.00	3.50
(5)	Spud Chandler	15.00	7.50	4.50
(6)	Earl Combs (Earle)	25.00	12.50	7.50
(7)	Frank Crosetti	20.00	10.00	6.00
(8)	Bill Dickey	35.00	17.50	10.50
(9)	Atley Donald	12.00	6.00	3.50
(10)	Nick Etten	12.00	6.00	3.50
(11)	Art Fletcher	12.00	6.00	3.50
(12)	Joe Gordon	15.00	7.50	4.50
(13)	Oscar Grimes	12.00	6.00	3.50
(14)	Rollie Hemsley	12.00	6.00	3.50
(15)	Bill Johnson	12.00	6.00	3.50
(16)	Charlie Keller	15.00	7.50	4.50
(17)	John Lindell	15.00	7.50	4.50
(18)	Joe McCarthy	25.00	12.50	7.50
(19)	Bud Metheny	12.00	6.00	3.50
(20)	Johnny Murphy	12.00	6.00	3.50
(21)	Pat O'Daugherty	12.00	6.00	3.50
(22)	Marius Russo	12.00	6.00	3.50
(23)	John Schulte	12.00	6.00	3.50
(24)	Ken Sears	12.00	6.00	3.50
(25)	Tuck Stainback	12.00	6.00	3.50
(26)	George Stirnweiss	12.00	6.00	3.50
(27)	Jim Turner	12.00	6.00	3.50
(28)	Roy Weatherly	12.00	6.00	3.50
(29)	Charley Wensloff	12.00	6.00	3.50
(30)	Bill Zuber	12.00	6.00	3.50

1947-50 N.Y. Yankees Picture Pack

These team-issued sets offered fans at the souvenir stand more than two dozen pictures of the players and staff. The 6-1/2" x 9" pictures are in black-and-white with a white border and a facsimile autograph. Backs are blank. Players repeated over the years were represented by the same picture. The unnumbered pictures are listed in alphabetical order by year of issue.

		NM	EX	VG
	Common Player:	8.00	4.00	2.50
	Complete 1947 Set (25):	300.00	150.00	90.00
(1)	Yogi Berra	40.00	20.00	12.00
(2)	Bill Bevens	8.00	4.00	2.50
(3)	Bobby Brown	8.00	4.00	2.50
(4)	Spud Chandler	8.00	4.00	2.50
(5)	Frank Colman	8.00	4.00	2.50
(6)	John Corriden	8.00	4.00	2.50
(7)	Frank Crosetti	10.00	5.00	3.00
(8)	Joe DiMaggio	80.00	40.00	24.00
(9)	Chuck Dressen	8.00	4.00	2.50
(10)	Randy Gumpert	8.00	4.00	2.50
(11)	Bucky Harris	10.00	5.00	3.00
(12)	Tommy Henrich	8.00	4.00	2.50
(13)	Ralph Houk	10.00	5.00	3.00
(14)	Don Johnson	8.00	4.00	2.50
(15)	Bill Johnson	8.00	4.00	2.50
(16)	Charlie Keller	10.00	5.00	3.00
(17)	John Lindell	8.00	4.00	2.50
(18)	George McQuinn	8.00	4.00	2.50
(19)	Joe Page	8.00	4.00	2.50
(20)	Allie Reynolds	10.00	5.00	3.00
(21)	Phil Rizzuto	27.00	13.50	8.00
(22)	Aaron Robinson	8.00	4.00	2.50
(23)	Frank Shea	8.00	4.00	2.50
(24)	Ken Silvestri	8.00	4.00	2.50
(26)	George Stirnweiss	8.00	4.00	2.50
	Complete 1948 Set (25):	300.00	150.00	90.00
(1)	Yogi Berra	40.00	20.00	12.00
(2)	Bobby Brown	8.00	4.00	2.50
(3)	Red Corriden	8.00	4.00	2.50
(4)	Frank Crosetti	10.00	5.00	3.00
(5)	Joe DiMaggio	80.00	40.00	24.00
(6)	Chuck Dressen	8.00	4.00	2.50
(7)	Karl Drews	8.00	4.00	2.50
(8)	Red Embree	8.00	4.00	2.50
(9)	Randy Gumpert	8.00	4.00	2.50
(10)	Bucky Harris	10.00	5.00	3.00
(11)	Tommy Henrich	8.00	4.00	2.50
(12)	Frank Hiller	8.00	4.00	2.50
(13)	Bill Johnson	8.00	4.00	2.50
(14)	Charlie Keller	10.00	5.00	3.00
(15)	Eddie Lopat	10.00	5.00	3.00
(16)	John Lindell	8.00	4.00	2.50
(17)	Cliff Mapes	8.00	4.00	2.50
(18)	Gus Niarhos	8.00	4.00	2.50
(19)	George McQuinn	8.00	4.00	2.50
(20)	Joe Page	8.00	4.00	2.50
(21)	Vic Raschi	10.00	5.00	3.00
(22)	Allie Reynolds	10.00	5.00	3.00
(23)	Phil Rizzuto	27.00	13.50	8.00
(24)	Frank Shea	8.00	4.00	2.50
(25)	Snuffy Stirnweiss	8.00	4.00	2.50
	Complete 1949 Set (25):	330.00	165.00	99.00
(1)	Mel Allen	16.00	8.00	4.75
(2)	Larry Berra	40.00	20.00	12.00
(3)	Bobby Brown	8.00	4.00	2.50
(4)	Tommy Byrne	8.00	4.00	2.50
(5)	Jerry Coleman	8.00	4.00	2.50
(6)	Frank Crosetti	10.00	5.00	3.00
(7)	Bill Dickey	20.00	10.00	6.00
(8)	Joe DiMaggio	80.00	40.00	24.00
(9)	Tommy Henrich	8.00	4.00	2.50
(10)	Bill Johnson	8.00	4.00	2.50
(11)	Charlie Keller	10.00	5.00	3.00
(12)	John Lindell	8.00	4.00	2.50
(13)	Ed Lopat	10.00	5.00	3.00
(14)	Gus Niarhos	8.00	4.00	2.50
(15)	Joe Page	8.00	4.00	2.50
(16)	Bob Porterfield	8.00	4.00	2.50
(17)	Vic Raschi	8.00	4.00	2.50
(18)	Allie Reynolds	10.00	5.00	3.00
(19)	Phil Rizzuto	27.00	13.50	8.00
(20)	Fred Sanford	8.00	4.00	2.50
(21)	Frank Shea	8.00	4.00	2.50
(22)	Casey Stengel	33.00	16.50	10.00
(23)	George Stirnweiss	8.00	4.00	2.50
(24)	Jim Turner	8.00	4.00	2.50
(25)	Gene Woodling	10.00	5.00	3.00
	Complete 1950 Set (25):	330.00	165.00	99.00
(1)	Mel Allen	16.00	8.00	4.75
(2)	Hank Bauer	12.00	6.00	3.50
(3)	Larry Berra	40.00	20.00	12.00
(4)	Bobby Brown	8.00	4.00	2.50
(5)	Tommy Byrne	8.00	4.00	2.50
(6)	Jerry Coleman	8.00	4.00	2.50
(7)	Frank Crosetti	10.00	5.00	3.00
(8)	Bill Dickey	20.00	10.00	6.00
(9)	Joe DiMaggio	80.00	40.00	24.00
(10)	Tommy Henrich	8.00	4.00	2.50
(11)	Jack Jensen	13.50	6.75	4.00
(12)	Bill Johnson	8.00	4.00	2.50
(13)	Ed Lopat	10.00	5.00	3.00
(14)	Cliff Mapes	8.00	4.00	2.50
(15)	Joe Page	8.00	4.00	2.50
(16)	Bob Porterfield	8.00	4.00	2.50
(17)	Vic Raschi	10.00	5.00	3.00
(18)	Allie Reynolds	10.00	5.00	3.00
(19)	Phil Rizzuto	27.00	13.50	8.00
(20)	Fred Sanford	8.00	4.00	2.50
(21)	Charlie Silvera	10.00	5.00	3.00
(22)	Casey Stengel	33.00	16.50	10.00
(23)	George Stirnweiss	8.00	4.00	2.50
(24)	Jim Turner	8.00	4.00	2.50
(25)	Gene Woodling	10.00	5.00	3.00

1956 N.Y. Yankees Photo Pack

This set was issued, probably for sale at Yankee Stadium souvenir stands, in 1956, though some of the photos date as far back as 1951, and a few appear to have been taken during the 1955 World Series at Ebbets Field. Printed in black-and-white on semi-gloss paper, the pictures measure about 6" x 8-7/8". There is a 1/4" white border around the photo and a white strip at the bottom of each photo with the player's name. Backs are blank. The pictures are checklisted here in alphabetical order, but the list may not be complete. Some of the photos are familiar from their use on baseball cards, including the 1951 Bowman Mantle.

		NM	EX	VG
	Complete Set (22):	200.00	100.00	60.00
	Common Player:	8.00	4.00	2.50
(1)	Hank Bauer	10.00	5.00	3.00
(2)	Larry "Yogi" Berra	20.00	10.00	6.00
(3)	Tommy Byrne	8.00	4.00	2.50
(4)	Andy Carey	8.00	4.00	2.50
(5)	Bob Cerv	8.00	4.00	2.50
(6)	Gerry Coleman	8.00	4.00	2.50
(7)	Joe Collins	8.00	4.00	2.50
(8)	Ed "Whitey" Ford	20.00	10.00	6.00
(9)	Bob Grim	8.00	4.00	2.50
(10)	Elston Howard	10.00	5.00	3.00
(11)	Johnny Kucks	8.00	4.00	2.50
(12)	Don Larsen	12.00	6.00	3.50
(13)	Jerry Lumpe	8.00	4.00	2.50
(14)	Mickey Mantle	60.00	30.00	18.00
(15)	Billy Martin	13.50	6.75	4.00
(16)	Mickey McDermott	8.00	4.00	2.50
(17)	Gil McDougald	10.00	5.00	3.00
(18)	Tom Morgan	8.00	4.00	2.50
(19)	Irv Noren	8.00	4.00	2.50
(20)	Charlie Silvera	8.00	4.00	2.50
(21)	Bill Skowron	10.00	5.00	3.00
(22)	Bob Turley	10.00	5.00	3.00

1970 N.Y. Yankees Clinic Schedule Postcards

This series of postcards was issued in conjunction with a series of baseball clinics which the Yankees put on for youngsters prior to selected home games. Fronts of the 3-1/2 x 5-1/2" glossy color cards have player portraits with a facsimile autograph in a white panel at bottom. Backs have player identification and career highlights, a schedule of the clinic days and credit line for Howard Photo Service. White and Murcer cards are scarce because of rainouts on their scheduled clinic appaearance days. Cards are checklisted here in alphabetical order.

		NM	EX	VG
Complete Set (13):		115.00	55.00	35.00
Common Player:		3.00	1.50	.90
(1)	Stan Bahnsen	3.00	1.50	.90
(2)	Curt Blefary	3.00	1.50	.90
(3)	Danny Cater	3.00	1.50	.90
(4)	Horace Clarke	3.00	1.50	.90
(5)	Joe DiMaggio, Mickey Mantle	30.00	15.00	9.00
(6)	John Ellis	3.00	1.50	.90
(7)	Jerry Kenney	3.00	1.50	.90
(8)	Gene Michael	3.00	1.50	.90
(9)	Thurman Munson	15.00	7.50	4.50
(10)	Bobby Murcer	12.50	6.25	3.75
(11)	Fritz Peterson	3.00	1.50	.90
(12)	Mel Stottlemyre	4.50	2.25	1.25
(13)	Roy White	35.00	17.50	10.50

1971 N.Y. Yankess Clinic Schedule Postcards

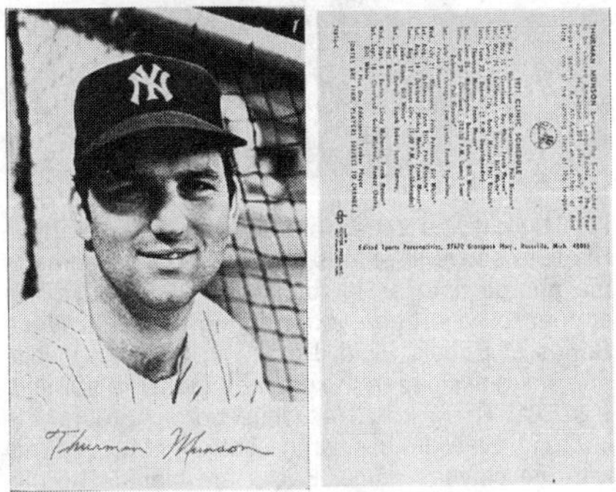

This series of postcards was issued in conjunction with a series of baseball clinics which the Yankees put on for youngsters prior to selected home games. Fronts of the 3-1/2 x 5-1/2" glossy color cards have player portraits with a facsimile autograph in a white panel at bottom. Backs are printed in blue , have player identification and career highlights and a schedule of the clinic days. Cards are checklisted here in alphabetical order.

		NM	EX	VG
Complete Set (16):		75.00	37.50	22.00
Common Player:		3.00	1.50	.90
(1)	Felipe Alou, Jim Lyttle	3.00	1.50	.90
(2)	Stan Bahnsen	3.00	1.50	.90
(3)	Frank Baker, Jerry Kenney	3.00	1.50	.90
(4)	Curt Blefary	3.00	1.50	.90
(5)	Danny Cater	3.00	1.50	.90
(6)	Horace Clarke, Gene Michael	3.00	1.50	.90
(7)	John Ellis	3.00	1.50	.90
(8)	Jake Gibbs	3.00	1.50	.90
(9)	Ralph Houk	4.50	2.25	1.25
(10)	Mickey Mantle	35.00	17.50	10.50
(11)	Lindy McDaniel	3.00	1.50	.90
(12)	Thurman Munson	12.00	6.00	3.50
(13)	Bobby Murcer	3.00	1.50	.90
(14)	Fritz Peterson	3.00	1.50	.90
(15)	Mel Stottlemyre	3.00	1.50	.90
(16)	Roy White	3.00	1.50	.90

1972 N.Y. Yankees Schedule Cards

The origins and distribution of these cards is unclear. They may have been a collector issue. The 2-1/4" x 3-1/2" cards are printed in blue and sepia. Fronts have player photos with a facsimile autograph in the white border at bottom, between a pair of team insignia. Backs have the team schedule. The unnumbered cards are listed here alphabetically.

		NM	EX	VG
Complete Set (8):		300.00	150.00	75.00
Common Player:		20.00	10.00	6.00
(1)	Felipe Alou	35.00	17.50	10.50
(2)	Ron Blomberg	20.00	10.00	6.00
(3)	Thurman Munson	150.00	75.00	45.00
(4)	Bobby Murcer	25.00	12.50	7.50
(5)	Mel Stottlemyre	20.00	10.00	6.00
(6)	Ron Swoboda	20.00	10.00	6.00
(7)	Roy White	25.00	12.50	7.50
(8)	Frank Messer, Phil Rizzuto, Bill White (announcers)	25.00	12.50	7.50

1979 N.Y. Yankees Photo Album

This stadium giveaway was sponsored by Dellwood, whose logo appears on the outside back cover of the approximately 8"-square album. The cover is printed in red, white and blue on a pin-striped background. Inside the album are color portrait photos of the players, manager and coaches. Except for group pages of coaches and bench-warmers, each of the 26 blank-back pages has a single player picture with a white border and (usually) a facsimile autograph. The individual pictures could be removed for display. The picture of Thurman Munson is framed in black and indicates the years of his birth and death. The pictures are arranged alphabetically and checklisted here in that fashion.

		NM	EX	VG
Complete Album:		15.00	7.50	4.50
Common Player:		1.00	.50	.30
(1)	Billy Martin	2.00	1.00	.60
(2)	Yogi Berra, Mike Ferraro, Art Fowler, Jim Hegan, Charley Lau	1.00	.50	.30
(3)	Jim Beattie	1.00	.50	.30
(4)	Juan Beniquez	1.00	.50	.30
(5)	Bobby Brown	1.00	.50	.30
(6)	Chris Chambliss	1.00	.50	.30
(7)	Ron Davis	1.00	.50	.30
(8)	Bucky Dent	1.50	.70	.45
(9)	Ed Figueroa	1.00	.50	.30
(10)	Rich Gossage	1.25	.60	.40
(11)	Ron Guidry	1.50	.70	.45
(12)	Don Hood	1.00	.50	.30
(13)	Jim Catfish Hunter	1.50	.70	.45
(14)	Reggie Jackson	6.00	3.00	1.75
(15)	Tommy John	1.50	.70	.45
(16)	Jim Kaat	1.50	.70	.45
(17)	Thurman Munson	6.00	3.00	1.75
(18)	Bobby Murcer	1.50	.70	.45
(19)	Jerry Narron	1.00	.50	.30
(20)	Graig Nettles	1.25	.60	.40
(21)	Lou Piniella	1.50	.70	.45
(22)	Willie Randolph	1.25	.60	.40
(23)	Jim Spencer	1.00	.50	.30
(24)	Luis Tiant	1.00	.50	.30
(25)	Roy White	1.25	.60	.40
(26)	Ray Burris, Kenny Clay, Brian Doyle, Don Gullett	1.00	.50	.30

O

1937 O-Pee-Chee

Kind of a combination of 1934 Goudeys and 1934-36 Batter Ups, the '37 OPC "Baseball Stars" set features black-and-white action photos against a stylized ballpark. About halfway up the 2-5/8" x 2-15/16" cards, the background was die-cut to allow it to be folded back to create a stand-up card. Backs are printed in English and French. The 40 cards in "Series A" are all American Leaguers, leading to speculation that a Series B of National League players was to have been issued at a later date. The set carries the American Card Catalog designation of V300.

		NM	EX	VG
Complete Set (40):		13000.	6500.	4000.
Common Player:		150.00	75.00	45.00
101	John Lewis	150.00	75.00	45.00
102	"Jack" Hayes	150.00	75.00	45.00
103	Earl Averill	375.00	187.00	112.00
104	Harland Clift (Harlond)	150.00	75.00	45.00
105	"Beau" Bell	150.00	75.00	45.00
106	Jimmy Foxx (Jimmie)	800.00	400.00	240.00
107	Hank Greenberg	1100.	550.00	330.00
108	George Selkirk	150.00	75.00	45.00
109	Wally Moses	150.00	75.00	45.00
110	"Gerry" Walker	150.00	75.00	45.00
111	"Goose" Goslin	375.00	187.00	112.00
112	Charlie Gehringer	500.00	250.00	150.00
113	Hal Trosky	150.00	75.00	45.00
114	"Buddy" Myer	150.00	75.00	45.00
115	Luke Appling	375.00	187.00	112.00
116	"Zeke" Bonura	150.00	75.00	45.00
117	Tony Lazzeri	375.00	187.00	112.00
118	Joe DiMaggio	4500.	2250.	1350.
119	Bill Dickey	650.00	325.00	195.00
120	Bob Feller	1100.	550.00	330.00
121	Harry Kelley	150.00	75.00	45.00
122	Johnny Allen	150.00	75.00	45.00
123	Bob Johnson	165.00	82.00	49.00
124	Joe Cronin	375.00	187.00	112.00
125	"Rip" Radcliff	150.00	75.00	45.00
126	Cecil Travis	150.00	75.00	45.00
127	Joe Kuhel	150.00	75.00	45.00
128	Odell Hale	150.00	75.00	45.00
129	Sam West	150.00	75.00	45.00
130	Ben Chapman	150.00	75.00	45.00
131	Monte Pearson	150.00	75.00	45.00
132	"Rick" Ferrell	375.00	187.00	112.00
133	Tommy Bridges	150.00	75.00	45.00
134	"Schoolboy" Rowe	165.00	82.00	49.00
135	Vernon Kennedy	150.00	75.00	45.00
136	"Red" Ruffing	375.00	187.00	112.00
137	"Lefty" Grove	600.00	300.00	180.00
138	Wes Farrell	150.00	75.00	45.00
139	"Buck" Newsom	150.00	75.00	45.00
140	Rogers Hornsby	700.00	350.00	210.00

1965 O-Pee-Chee

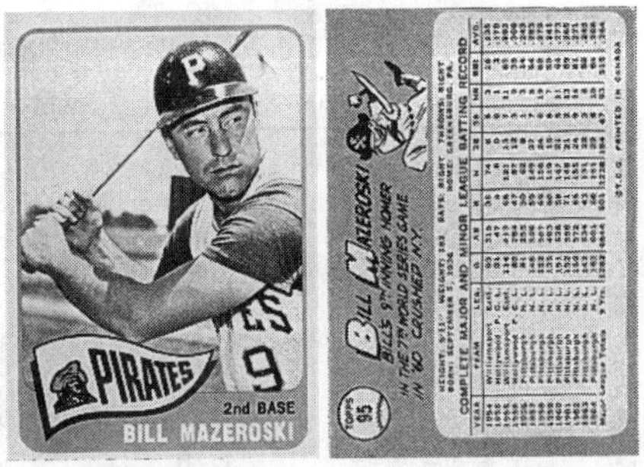

Identical in design to the 1965 Topps set, the Canadian-issued 1965 O-Pee-Chee set was printed on gray stock and consists of 283 cards, each measuring the standard 2-1/2" x 3-1/2". The words "Printed in Canada" appear along the bottom of the back of the cards.

		NM	EX	VG
Complete Set (283):		2400.	1200.	725.00
Common Player (1-196):		3.00	1.50	.90
Common Player (197-283):		7.00	3.50	2.00
1	A.L. Batting Leaders (Elston Howard, Tony Oliva, Brooks Robinson)	23.00	11.50	7.00
2	N.L. Batting Leaders (Hank Aaron, Rico Carty, Bob Clemente)	24.00	12.00	7.25
3	A.L. Home Run Leaders (Harmon Killebrew, Mickey Mantle, Boog Powell)	50.00	25.00	15.00
4	N.L. Home Run Leaders (Johnny Callison, Jim Ray Hart, Willie Mays, Billy Williams)	12.00	6.00	3.50

5	A.L. RBI Leaders (Harmon Killebrew, Mickey Mantle, Brooks Robinson, Dick Stuart)	50.00	25.00	15.00
6	N.L. RBI Leaders (Ken Boyer, Willie Mays, Ron Santo)	9.00	4.50	2.75
7	A.L. ERA Leaders (Dean Chance, Joel Horlen)	3.00	1.50	.90
8	N.L. ERA Leaders (Don Drysdale, Sandy Koufax)	24.00	12.00	7.25
9	A.L. Pitching Leaders (Wally Bunker, Dean Chance, Gary Peters, Juan Pizarro, Dave Wickersham)	3.00	1.50	.90
10	N.L. Pitching Leaders (Larry Jackson, Juan Marichal, Ray Sadecki)	3.00	1.50	.90
11	A.L. Strikeout Leaders (Dean Chance, Al Downing, Camilo Pascual)	3.00	1.50	.90
12	N.L. Strikeout Leaders (Don Drysdale, Bob Gibson, Bob Veale)	3.00	1.50	.90
13	Pedro Ramos	3.00	1.50	.90
14	Len Gabrielson	3.00	1.50	.90
15	Robin Roberts	20.00	10.00	6.00
16	Astros Rookies (Sonny Jackson, Joe Morgan)	125.00	62.00	37.00
17	Johnny Romano	3.00	1.50	.90
18	Bill McCool	3.00	1.50	.90
19	Gates Brown	3.00	1.50	.90
20	Jim Bunning	22.00	11.00	6.50
21	Don Blasingame	3.00	1.50	.90
22	Charlie Smith	3.00	1.50	.90
23	Bob Tiefenauer	3.00	1.50	.90
24	Twins Team	6.00	3.00	1.75
25	Al McBean	3.00	1.50	.90
26	Bobby Knoop	3.00	1.50	.90
27	Dick Bertell	3.00	1.50	.90
28	Barney Schultz	3.00	1.50	.90
29	Felix Mantilla	3.00	1.50	.90
30	Jim Bouton	4.50	2.25	1.25
31	Mike White	3.00	1.50	.90
32	Herman Franks	3.00	1.50	.90
33	Jackie Brandt	3.00	1.50	.90
34	Cal Koonce	3.00	1.50	.90
35	Ed Charles	3.00	1.50	.90
36	Bobby Wine	3.00	1.50	.90
37	Fred Gladding	3.00	1.50	.90
38	Jim King	3.00	1.50	.90
39	Gerry Arrigo	3.00	1.50	.90
40	Frank Howard	3.50	1.75	1.00
41	White Sox Rookies (Bruce Howard, Marv Staehle)	3.00	1.50	.90
42	Earl Wilson	3.00	1.50	.90
43	Mike Shannon	3.00	1.50	.90
44	Wade Blasingame	3.00	1.50	.90
45	Roy McMillan	3.00	1.50	.90
46	Bob Lee	3.00	1.50	.90
47	Tommy Harper	3.00	1.50	.90
48	Claude Raymond	3.00	1.50	.90
49	Orioles Rookies (Curt Blefary, John Miller)	3.00	1.50	.90
50	Juan Marichal	24.00	12.00	7.25
51	Billy Bryan	3.00	1.50	.90
52	Ed Roebuck	3.00	1.50	.90
53	Dick McAuliffe	3.00	1.50	.90
54	Joe Gibbon	3.00	1.50	.90
55	Tony Conigliaro	18.00	9.00	5.50
56	Ron Kline	3.00	1.50	.90
57	Cards Team	3.00	1.50	.90
58	Fred Talbot	3.00	1.50	.90
59	Nate Oliver	3.00	1.50	.90
60	Jim O'Toole	3.00	1.50	.90
61	Chris Cannizzaro	3.00	1.50	.90
62	Jim Katt (Kaat)	6.00	3.00	1.75
63	Ty Cline	3.00	1.50	.90
64	Lou Burdette	3.00	1.50	.90
65	Tony Kubek	3.25	1.75	1.00
66	(Bill Rigney)	3.00	1.50	.90
67	Harvey Haddix	3.00	1.50	.90
68	Del Crandall	3.00	1.50	.90
69	Bill Virdon	3.00	1.50	.90
70	Bill Skowron	3.00	1.50	.90
71	John O'Donoghue	3.00	1.50	.90
72	Tony Gonzalez	3.00	1.50	.90
73	Dennis Ribant	3.00	1.50	.90
74	Red Sox Rookies (Rico Petrocelli, Jerry Stephenson)	7.00	3.50	2.00
75	Deron Johnson	3.00	1.50	.90
76	Sam McDowell	3.00	1.50	.90
77	Doug Camilli	3.00	1.50	.90
78	Dal Maxvill	3.00	1.50	.90
79	Checklist 1	12.00	6.00	3.50
80	Turk Farrell	3.00	1.50	.90
81	Don Buford	3.00	1.50	.90
82	Brave Rookies (Santos Alomar, John Braun)	3.00	1.50	.90
83	George Thomas	3.00	1.50	.90
84	Ron Herbel	3.00	1.50	.90
85	Willie Smith	3.00	1.50	.90
86	Les Narum	3.00	1.50	.90
87	Nelson Mathews	3.00	1.50	.90
88	Jack Lamabe	3.00	1.50	.90
89	Mike Hershberger	3.00	1.50	.90
90	Rich Rollins	3.00	1.50	.90
91	Cubs Team	3.00	1.50	.90
92	Dick Howser	3.00	1.50	.90
93	Jack Fisher	3.00	1.50	.90
94	Charlie Lau	3.00	1.50	.90
95	Bill Mazeroski	12.00	6.00	3.50
96	Sonny Siebert	3.00	1.50	.90
97	Pedro Gonzalez	3.00	1.50	.90
98	Bob Miller	3.00	1.50	.90
99	Gil Hodges	18.00	9.00	5.50
100	Ken Boyer	6.00	3.00	1.75
101	Fred Newman	3.00	1.50	.90
102	Steve Boros	3.00	1.50	.90
103	Harvey Kuenn	3.00	1.50	.90
104	Checklist 2	12.00	6.00	3.50
105	Chico Salmon	3.00	1.50	.90
106	Gene Oliver	3.00	1.50	.90
107	Phillies Rookies (Pat Corrales, Costen Shockley)	3.00	1.50	.90
108	Don Mincher	3.00	1.50	.90
109	Walt Bond	3.00	1.50	.90
110	Ron Santo	3.25	1.75	1.00
111	Lee Thomas	3.00	1.50	.90
112	Derrell Griffith	3.00	1.50	.90
113	Steve Barber	3.00	1.50	.90
114	Jim Hickman	3.00	1.50	.90
115	Bobby Richardson	3.50	1.75	1.00
116	Cardinals Rookies (Dave Dowling, Bob Tolan)	3.00	1.50	.90
117	Wes Stock	3.00	1.50	.90
118	Hal Lanier	3.00	1.50	.90
119	John Kennedy	3.00	1.50	.90
120	Frank Robinson	35.00	17.50	10.50
121	Gene Alley	3.00	1.50	.90
122	Bill Pleis	3.00	1.50	.90
123	Frank Thomas	3.00	1.50	.90
124	Tom Satriano	3.00	1.50	.90
125	Juan Pizarro	3.00	1.50	.90
126	Dodgers Team	3.25	1.75	1.00
127	Frank Lary	3.00	1.50	.90
128	Vic Davalillo	3.00	1.50	.90
129	Bennie Daniels	3.00	1.50	.90
130	Al Kaline	35.00	17.50	10.50
131	Johnny Keane	3.00	1.50	.90
132	World Series Game 1 (Cards Take Opener)	3.00	1.50	.90
133	World Series Game 2 (Stottlemyre Wins)	3.00	1.50	.90
134	World Series Game 3 (Mantle's Clutch HR)	125.00	62.00	37.00
135	World Series Game 4 (Boyer's Grand Slam)	4.00	2.00	1.25
136	World Series Game 5 (10th Inning Triumph)	3.00	1.50	.90
137	World Series Game 6 (Bouton Wins Again)	3.00	1.50	.90
138	World Series Game 7 (Gibson Wins Finale)	14.00	7.00	4.25
139	World Series Summary (The Cards Celebrate)	3.00	1.50	.90
140	Dean Chance	3.00	1.50	.90
141	Charlie James	3.00	1.50	.90
142	Bill Monbouquette	3.00	1.50	.90
143	Pirates Rookies (John Gelnar, Jerry May)	3.00	1.50	.90
144	Ed Kranepool	3.00	1.50	.90
145	Luis Tiant	16.00	8.00	4.75
146	Ron Hansen	3.00	1.50	.90
147	Dennis Bennett	3.00	1.50	.90
148	Willie Kirkland	3.00	1.50	.90
149	Wayne Schurr	3.00	1.50	.90
150	Brooks Robinson	35.00	17.50	10.50
151	Athletics Team	3.00	1.50	.90
152	Phil Ortega	3.00	1.50	.90
153	Norm Cash	3.50	1.75	1.00
154	Bob Humphreys	3.00	1.50	.90
155	Roger Maris	75.00	37.00	22.00
156	Bob Sadowski	3.00	1.50	.90
157	Zoilo Versalles	3.00	1.50	.90
158	Dick Sisler	3.00	1.50	.90
159	Jim Duffalo	3.00	1.50	.90
160	Bob Clemente	175.00	87.00	52.00
161	Frank Baumann	3.00	1.50	.90
162	Russ Nixon	3.00	1.50	.90
163	John Briggs	3.00	1.50	.90
164	Al Spangler	3.00	1.50	.90
165	Dick Ellsworth	3.00	1.50	.90
166	Indians Rookies (Tommie Agee, George Culver)	3.00	1.50	.90
167	Bill Wakefield	3.00	1.50	.90
168	Dick Green	3.00	1.50	.90
169	Dave Vineyard	3.00	1.50	.90
170	Hank Aaron	120.00	60.00	36.00
171	Jim Roland	3.00	1.50	.90
172	Jim Piersall	3.25	1.75	1.00
173	Tigers Team	3.00	1.50	.90
174	Joe Jay	3.00	1.50	.90
175	Bob Aspromonte	3.00	1.50	.90
176	Willie McCovey	30.00	15.00	9.00
177	Pete Mikkelsen	3.00	1.50	.90
178	Dalton Jones	3.00	1.50	.90
179	Hal Woodeshick	3.00	1.50	.90
180	Bob Allison	3.00	1.50	.90
181	Senators Rookies (Don Loun, Joe McCabe)	3.00	1.50	.90
182	Mike de la Hoz	3.00	1.50	.90
183	Dave Nicholson	3.00	1.50	.90
184	John Boozer	3.00	1.50	.90
185	Max Alvis	3.00	1.50	.90
186	Billy Cowan	3.00	1.50	.90
187	Casey Stengel	24.00	12.00	7.25
188	Sam Bowens	3.00	1.50	.90
189	Checklist 3	12.00	6.00	3.50
190	Bill White	3.00	1.50	.90
191	Phil Regan	3.00	1.50	.90
192	Jim Coker	3.00	1.50	.90
193	Gaylord Perry	24.00	12.00	7.25
194	Rookie Stars (Bill Kelso, Rick Reichardt)	3.00	1.50	.90
195	Bob Veale	3.00	1.50	.90
196	Ron Fairly	3.00	1.50	.90
197	Diego Segui	7.00	3.50	2.00
198	Smoky Burgess	7.00	3.50	2.00
199	Bob Heffner	7.00	3.50	2.00
200	Joe Torre	12.00	6.00	3.50
201	Twins Rookies (Cesar Tovar, Sandy Valdespino)	7.00	3.50	2.00
202	Leo Burke	7.00	3.50	2.00
203	Dallas Green	7.00	3.50	2.00
204	Russ Snyder	7.00	3.50	2.00
205	Warren Spahn	45.00	22.00	13.50
206	Willie Horton	7.00	3.50	2.00
207	Pete Rose	200.00	100.00	60.00
208	Tommy John	15.00	7.50	4.50
209	Pirates Team	7.00	3.50	2.00
210	Jim Fregosi	7.00	3.50	2.00
211	Steve Ridzik	7.00	3.50	2.00
212	Ron Brand	7.00	3.50	2.00
213	Jim Davenport	7.00	3.50	2.00
214	Bob Purkey	7.00	3.50	2.00
215	Pete Ward	7.00	3.50	2.00
216	Al Worthington	7.00	3.50	2.00
217	Walt Alston	20.00	10.00	6.00
218	Dick Schofield	7.00	3.50	2.00
219	Bob Meyer	7.00	3.50	2.00
220	Billy Williams	35.00	17.50	10.50
221	John Tsitouris	7.00	3.50	2.00
222	Bob Tillman	7.00	3.50	2.00
223	Dan Osinski	7.00	3.50	2.00
224	Bob Chance	7.00	3.50	2.00
225	Bo Belinsky	7.00	3.50	2.00
226	Yankees Rookies (Jake Gibbs, Elvio Jimenez)	7.00	3.50	2.00
227	Bobby Klaus	7.00	3.50	2.00
228	Jack Sanford	7.00	3.50	2.00
229	Lou Clinton	7.00	3.50	2.00
230	Ray Sadecki	7.00	3.50	2.00
231	Jerry Adair	7.00	3.50	2.00
232	Steve Blass	7.00	3.50	2.00
233	Don Zimmer	7.00	3.50	2.00
234	White Sox Team	7.00	3.50	2.00
235	Chuck Hinton	7.00	3.50	2.00
236	Dennis McLain	20.00	10.00	6.00
237	Bernie Allen	7.00	3.50	2.00
238	Joe Moeller	7.00	3.50	2.00
239	Doc Edwards	7.00	3.50	2.00
240	Bob Bruce	7.00	3.50	2.00
241	Mack Jones	7.00	3.50	2.00
242	George Brunet	7.00	3.50	2.00
243	Reds Rookies (Ted Davidson, Tommy Helms)	7.00	3.50	2.00
244	Lindy McDaniel	7.00	3.50	2.00
245	Joe Pepitone	7.00	3.50	2.00
246	Tom Butters	7.00	3.50	2.00
247	Wally Moon	7.00	3.50	2.00
248	Gus Triandos	7.00	3.50	2.00
249	Dave McNally	7.00	3.50	2.00
250	Willie Mays	135.00	67.00	40.00
251	Billy Herman	9.00	4.50	2.75
252	Pete Richert	7.00	3.50	2.00
253	Danny Cater	7.00	3.50	2.00
254	Roland Sheldon	7.00	3.50	2.00
255	Camilo Pascual	7.00	3.50	2.00
256	Tito Francona	7.00	3.50	2.00
257	Jim Wynn	7.00	3.50	2.00
258	Larry Bearnarth	7.00	3.50	2.00
259	Tigers Rookies (Jim Northrup, Ray Oyler)	7.00	3.50	2.00
260	Don Drysdale	45.00	22.00	13.50
261	Duke Carmel	7.00	3.50	2.00
262	Bud Daley	7.00	3.50	2.00
263	Marty Keough	7.00	3.50	2.00
264	Bob Buhl	7.00	3.50	2.00
265	Jim Pagliaroni	7.00	3.50	2.00
266	Bert Campaneris	9.00	4.50	2.75
267	Senators Team	7.00	3.50	2.00
268	Ken McBride	7.00	3.50	2.00
269	Frank Bolling	7.00	3.50	2.00
270	Milt Pappas	7.00	3.50	2.00
271	Don Wert	7.00	3.50	2.00
272	Chuck Schilling	7.00	3.50	2.00
273	Checklist 4	15.00	7.50	4.50
274	Lum Harris	7.00	3.50	2.00
275	Dick Groat	7.00	3.50	2.00
276	Hoyt Wilhelm	20.00	10.00	6.00
277	Johnny Lewis	7.00	3.50	2.00
278	Ken Retzer	7.00	3.50	2.00
279	Dick Tracewski	7.00	3.50	2.00
280	Dick Stuart	7.00	3.50	2.00
281	Bill Stafford	7.00	3.50	2.00
282	Giants Rookies (Dick Estelle, Masanori Murakami)	20.00	10.00	6.00
283	Fred Whitfield	7.00	3.50	2.00

1966 O-Pee-Chee

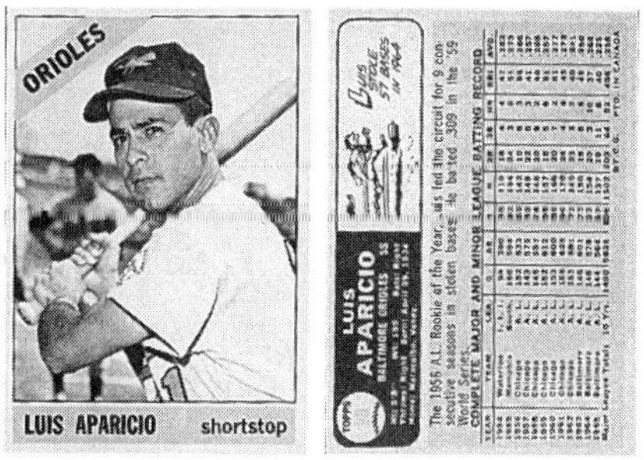

Utilizing the same design as the 1966 Topps set, the 1966 O-Pee-Chee set consists of 196 cards, measuring 2-1/2" x 3-1/2". The words "Ptd. in Canada" appear along the bottom on the back of the cards.

		NM	EX	VG
	Complete Set (196):	1600.	800.00	475.00
	Common Player (1-109):	3.00	1.50	.90
	Common Player (110-196):	3.50	1.75	1.00
1	Willie Mays	200.00	100.00	60.00
2	Ted Abernathy	3.00	1.50	.90
3	Sam Mele	3.00	1.50	.90
4	Ray Culp	3.00	1.50	.90
5	Jim Fregosi	3.00	1.50	.90
6	Chuck Schilling	3.00	1.50	.90
7	Tracy Stallard	3.00	1.50	.90
8	Floyd Robinson	3.00	1.50	.90
9	Clete Boyer	3.00	1.50	.90
10	Tony Cloninger	3.00	1.50	.90
11	Senators Rookies (Brant Alyea, Pete Craig)	3.00	1.50	.90
12	John Tsitouris	3.00	1.50	.90
13	Lou Johnson	3.00	1.50	.90
14	Norm Siebern	3.00	1.50	.90
15	Vern Law	3.00	1.50	.90
16	Larry Brown	3.00	1.50	.90
17	Johnny Stephenson	3.00	1.50	.90
18	Roland Sheldon	3.00	1.50	.90
19	Giants Team	3.00	1.50	.90
20	Willie Horton	3.00	1.50	.90
21	Don Nottebart	3.00	1.50	.90
22	Joe Nossek	3.00	1.50	.90
23	Jack Sanford	3.00	1.50	.90
24	Don Kessinger	3.50	1.75	1.00
25	Pete Ward	3.00	1.50	.90
26	Ray Sadecki	3.00	1.50	.90
27	Orioles Rookies (Andy Etchebarren, Darold Knowles)	3.00	1.50	.90
28	Phil Niekro	15.00	7.50	4.50
29	Mike Brumley	3.00	1.50	.90
30	Pete Rose	65.00	32.00	19.50
31	Jack Cullen	3.00	1.50	.90
32	Adolfo Phillips	3.00	1.50	.90
33	Jim Pagliaroni	3.00	1.50	.90
34	Checklist 1	8.00	4.00	2.50
35	Ron Swoboda	3.00	1.50	.90
36	Jim Hunter	21.00	10.50	6.25
37	Billy Herman	4.00	2.00	1.25
38	Ron Nischwitz	3.00	1.50	.90
39	Ken Henderson	3.00	1.50	.90
40	Jim Grant	3.00	1.50	.90
41	Don LeJohn	3.00	1.50	.90
42	Aubrey Gatewood	3.00	1.50	.90
43	Don Landrum	3.00	1.50	.90
44	Indians Rookies (Bill Davis, Tom Kelley)	3.00	1.50	.90
45	Jim Gentile	3.00	1.50	.90
46	Howie Koplitz	3.00	1.50	.90
47	J.C. Martin	3.00	1.50	.90
48	Paul Blair	3.00	1.50	.90
49	Woody Woodward	3.00	1.50	.90
50	Mickey Mantle	325.00	162.00	97.00
51	Gordon Richardson	3.00	1.50	.90
52	Power Plus (Johnny Callison, Wes Covington)	3.00	1.50	.90
53	Bob Duliba	3.00	1.50	.90
54	Jose Pagan	3.00	1.50	.90
55	Ken Harrelson	3.00	1.50	.90
56	Sandy Valdespino	3.00	1.50	.90
57	Jim Lefebvre	3.00	1.50	.90
58	Dave Wickersham	3.00	1.50	.90
59	Reds Team	3.00	1.50	.90
60	Curt Flood	3.00	1.50	.90
61	Bob Bolin	3.00	1.50	.90
62	Merritt Ranew	3.00	1.50	.90
63	Jim Stewart	3.00	1.50	.90
64	Bob Bruce	3.00	1.50	.90
65	Leon Wagner	3.00	1.50	.90
66	Al Weis	3.00	1.50	.90
67	Mets Rookies (Cleon Jones, Dick Selma)	3.00	1.50	.90
68	Hal Reniff	3.00	1.50	.90
69	Ken Hamlin	3.00	1.50	.90
70	Carl Yastrzemski	40.00	20.00	12.00
71	Frank Carpin	3.00	1.50	.90
72	Tony Perez	16.00	8.00	4.75
73	Jerry Zimmerman	3.00	1.50	.90
74	Don Mossi	3.00	1.50	.90
75	Tommy Davis	3.00	1.50	.90
76	Red Schoendienst	7.50	3.75	2.25
77	Johnny Orsino	3.00	1.50	.90
78	Frank Linzy	3.00	1.50	.90
79	Joe Pepitone	3.00	1.50	.90
80	Richie Allen	7.50	3.75	2.25
81	Ray Oyler	3.00	1.50	.90
82	Bob Hendley	3.00	1.50	.90
83	Albie Pearson	3.00	1.50	.90
84	Braves Rookies (Jim Beauchamp, Dick Kelley)	3.00	1.50	.90
85	Eddie Fisher	3.00	1.50	.90
86	John Bateman	3.00	1.50	.90
87	Dan Napoleon	3.00	1.50	.90
88	Fred Whitfield	3.00	1.50	.90
89	Ted Davidson	3.00	1.50	.90
90	Luis Aparicio	15.00	7.50	4.50
91	Bob Uecker	15.00	7.50	4.50
92	Yankees Team	5.00	2.50	1.50
93	Jim Lonborg	3.00	1.50	.90
94	Matty Alou	3.00	1.50	.90
95	Pete Richert	3.00	1.50	.90
96	Felipe Alou	3.50	1.75	1.00
97	Jim Merritt	3.00	1.50	.90
98	Don Demeter	3.00	1.50	.90
99	Buc Belters (Donn Clendenon, Willie Stargell)	3.50	1.75	1.00
100	Sandy Koufax	150.00	75.00	45.00
101	Checklist 2	8.00	4.00	2.50
102	Ed Kirkpatrick	3.00	1.50	.90
103	Dick Groat	3.00	1.50	.90
104	Alex Johnson	3.00	1.50	.90
105	Milt Pappas	3.00	1.50	.90
106	Rusty Staub	3.50	1.75	1.00
107	Athletics Rookies (Larry Stahl, Ron Tompkins)	3.00	1.50	.90
108	Bobby Klaus	3.00	1.50	.90
109	Ralph Terry	3.00	1.50	.90
110	Ernie Banks	25.00	12.50	7.50
111	Gary Peters	3.50	1.75	1.00
112	Manny Mota	3.50	1.75	1.00
113	Hank Aguirre	3.50	1.75	1.00
114	Jim Gosger	3.50	1.75	1.00
115	Bill Henry	3.50	1.75	1.00
116	Walt Alston	7.50	3.75	2.25
117	Jake Gibbs	3.50	1.75	1.00
118	Mike McCormick	3.50	1.75	1.00
119	Art Shamsky	3.50	1.75	1.00
120	Harmon Killebrew	24.00	12.00	7.25
121	Ray Herbert	3.50	1.75	1.00
122	Joe Gaines	3.50	1.75	1.00
123	Pirates Rookies (Frank Bork, Jerry May)	3.50	1.75	1.00
124	Tug McGraw	3.50	1.75	1.00
125	Lou Brock	21.00	10.50	6.25
126	Jim Palmer	150.00	75.00	45.00
127	Ken Berry	3.50	1.75	1.00
128	Jim Landis	3.50	1.75	1.00
129	Jack Kralick	3.50	1.75	1.00
130	Joe Torre	6.00	3.00	1.75
131	Angels Team	3.50	1.75	1.00
132	Orlando Cepeda	18.00	9.00	5.50
133	Don McMahon	3.50	1.75	1.00
134	Wes Parker	3.50	1.75	1.00
135	Dave Morehead	3.50	1.75	1.00
136	Woody Held	3.50	1.75	1.00
137	Pat Corrales	3.50	1.75	1.00
138	Roger Repoz	3.50	1.75	1.00
139	Cubs Rookies (Byron Browne, Don Young)	3.50	1.75	1.00
140	Jim Maloney	3.50	1.75	1.00
141	Tom McCraw	3.50	1.75	1.00
142	Don Dennis	3.50	1.75	1.00
143	Jose Tartabull	3.50	1.75	1.00
144	Don Schwall	3.50	1.75	1.00
145	Bill Freehan	3.50	1.75	1.00
146	George Altman	3.50	1.75	1.00
147	Lum Harris	3.50	1.75	1.00
148	Bob Johnson	3.50	1.75	1.00
149	Dick Nen	3.50	1.75	1.00
150	Rocky Colavito	12.00	6.00	3.50
151	Gary Wagner	3.50	1.75	1.00
152	Frank Malzone	3.50	1.75	1.00
153	Rico Carty	3.50	1.75	1.00
154	Chuck Hiller	3.50	1.75	1.00
155	Marcelino Lopez	3.50	1.75	1.00
156	Double Play Combo (Hal Lanier, Dick Schofield)	3.50	1.75	1.00
157	Rene Lachemann	3.50	1.75	1.00
158	Jim Brewer	3.50	1.75	1.00
159	Chico Ruiz	3.50	1.75	1.00
160	Whitey Ford	30.00	15.00	9.00
161	Jerry Lumpe	3.50	1.75	1.00
162	Lee Maye	3.50	1.75	1.00
163	Tito Francona	3.50	1.75	1.00
164	White Sox Rookies (Tommie Agee, Marv Staehle)	3.50	1.75	1.00
165	Don Lock	3.50	1.75	1.00
166	Chris Krug	3.50	1.75	1.00
167	Boog Powell	4.00	2.00	1.25
168	Dan Osinski	3.50	1.75	1.00
169	Duke Sims	3.50	1.75	1.00
170	Cookie Rojas	3.50	1.75	1.00
171	Nick Willhite	3.50	1.75	1.00
172	Mets Team	4.00	2.00	1.25
173	Al Spangler	3.50	1.75	1.00
174	Ron Taylor	3.50	1.75	1.00
175	Bert Campaneris	3.50	1.75	1.00
176	Jim Davenport	3.50	1.75	1.00
177	Hector Lopez	3.50	1.75	1.00
178	Bob Tillman	3.50	1.75	1.00
179	Cards Rookies (Dennis Aust, Bob Tolan)	3.50	1.75	1.00
180	Vada Pinson	3.50	1.75	1.00
181	Al Worthington	3.50	1.75	1.00
182	Jerry Lynch	3.50	1.75	1.00
183	Checklist 3	9.00	4.50	2.75
184	Denis Menke	3.50	1.75	1.00
185	Bob Buhl	3.50	1.75	1.00
186	Ruben Amaro	3.50	1.75	1.00
187	Chuck Dressen	3.50	1.75	1.00
188	Al Luplow	3.50	1.75	1.00
189	John Roseboro	3.50	1.75	1.00
190	Jimmie Hall	3.50	1.75	1.00
191	Darrell Sutherland	3.50	1.75	1.00
192	Vic Power	3.50	1.75	1.00
193	Dave McNally	3.50	1.75	1.00
194	Senators Team	3.50	1.75	1.00
195	Joe Morgan	18.00	9.00	5.50
196	Don Pavletich	3.50	1.75	1.00

1967 O-Pee-Chee

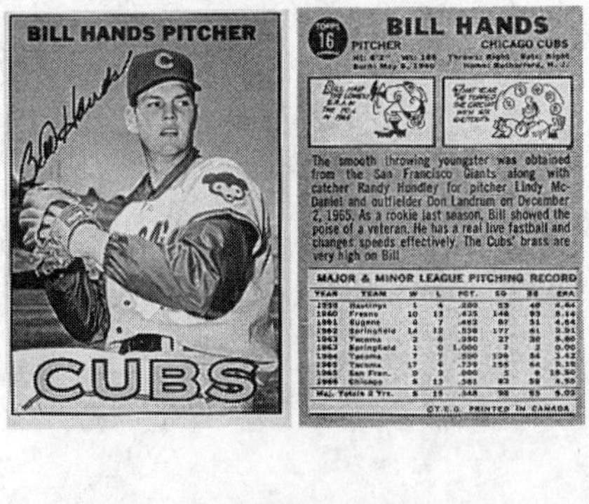

Cards in the 196-card Canadian set are nearly identical in design to the 1967 Topps set, except the words "Printed in Canada" are found on the back in the lower right corner. Cards measure 2-1/2" x 3-1/2".

		NM	EX	VG
	Complete Set (196):	1350.	675.00	400.00
	Common Player (1-109):	2.50	1.25	.70
	Common Player (110-196):	3.00	1.50	.90
1	The Champs (Hank Bauer, Brooks Robinson, Frank Robinson)	30.00	15.00	9.00
2	Jack Hamilton	2.50	1.25	.70
3	Duke Sims	2.50	1.25	.70
4	Hal Lanier	2.50	1.25	.70
5	Whitey Ford	25.00	12.50	7.50
6	Dick Simpson	2.50	1.25	.70
7	Don McMahon	2.50	1.25	.70
8	Chuck Harrison	2.50	1.25	.70
9	Ron Hansen	2.50	1.25	.70
10	Matty Alou	2.50	1.25	.70
11	Barry Moore	2.50	1.25	.70
12	Dodgers Rookies (Jim Campanis, Bill Singer)	2.50	1.25	.70
13	Joe Sparma	2.50	1.25	.70
14	Phil Linz	2.50	1.25	.70
15	Earl Battey	2.50	1.25	.70
16	Bill Hands	2.50	1.25	.70
17	Jim Gosger	2.50	1.25	.70
18	Gene Oliver	2.50	1.25	.70
19	Jim McGlothlin	2.50	1.25	.70
20	Orlando Cepeda	8.00	4.00	2.50
21	Dave Bristol	2.50	1.25	.70
22	Gene Brabender	2.50	1.25	.70
23	Larry Elliot	2.50	1.25	.70
24	Bob Allen	2.50	1.25	.70
25	Elston Howard	3.00	1.50	.90
26	Bob Priddy	2.50	1.25	.70
27	Bob Saverine	2.50	1.25	.70
28	Barry Latman	2.50	1.25	.70
29	Tom McCraw	2.50	1.25	.70
30	Al Kaline	25.00	12.50	7.50
31	Jim Brewer	2.50	1.25	.70
32	Bob Bailey	2.50	1.25	.70
33	Athletic Rookies (Sal Bando, Randy Schwartz)	3.00	1.50	.90
34	Pete Cimino	2.50	1.25	.70
35	Rico Carty	2.50	1.25	.70
36	Bob Tillman	2.50	1.25	.70
37	Rick Wise	2.50	1.25	.70
38	Bob Johnson	2.50	1.25	.70
39	Curt Simmons	2.50	1.25	.70
40	Rick Reichardt	2.50	1.25	.70
41	Joe Hoerner	2.50	1.25	.70
42	Mets Team	7.00	3.50	2.00
43	Chico Salmon	2.50	1.25	.70
44	Joe Nuxhall	2.50	1.25	.70
45	Roger Maris	75.00	37.00	22.00
46	Lindy McDaniel	2.50	1.25	.70
47	Ken McMullen	2.50	1.25	.70
48	Bill Freehan	2.50	1.25	.70
49	Roy Face	2.50	1.25	.70
50	Tony Oliva	2.50	1.25	.70
51	Astros Rookies (Dave Adlesh, Wes Bales)	2.50	1.25	.70
52	Dennis Higgins	2.50	1.25	.70
53	Clay Dalrymple	2.50	1.25	.70
54	Dick Green	2.50	1.25	.70
55	Don Drysdale	25.00	12.50	7.50
56	Jose Tartabull	2.50	1.25	.70
57	Pat Jarvis	2.50	1.25	.70
58	Paul Schaal	2.50	1.25	.70
59	Ralph Terry	2.50	1.25	.70
60	Luis Aparicio	8.50	4.25	2.50
61	Gordy Coleman	2.50	1.25	.70
62	Checklist 1 (Frank Robinson)	8.00	4.00	2.50
63	Cards' Clubbers (Lou Brock, Curt Flood)	7.00	3.50	2.00
64	Fred Valentine	2.50	1.25	.70
65	Tom Haller	2.50	1.25	.70
66	Manny Mota	2.50	1.25	.70
67	Ken Berry	2.50	1.25	.70
68	Bob Buhl	2.50	1.25	.70
69	Vic Davalillo	2.50	1.25	.70
70	Ron Santo	3.50	1.75	1.00
71	Camilo Pascual	2.50	1.25	.70
72	Tigers Rookies (George Korince, John Matchick)	2.50	1.25	.70
73	Rusty Staub	3.00	1.50	.90
74	Wes Stock	2.50	1.25	.70
75	George Scott	2.50	1.25	.70
76	Jim Barbieri	2.50	1.25	.70
77	Dooley Womack	2.50	1.25	.70
78	Pat Corrales	2.50	1.25	.70
79	Bubba Morton	2.50	1.25	.70
80	Jim Maloney	2.50	1.25	.70
81	Eddie Stanky	2.50	1.25	.70
82	Steve Barber	2.50	1.25	.70
83	Ollie Brown	2.50	1.25	.70
84	Tommie Sisk	2.50	1.25	.70
85	Johnny Callison	2.50	1.25	.70
86	Mike McCormick	2.50	1.25	.70
87	George Altman	2.50	1.25	.70
88	Mickey Lolich	2.50	1.25	.70
89	Felix Millan	2.50	1.25	.70
90	Jim Nash	2.50	1.25	.70
91	Johnny Lewis	2.50	1.25	.70
92	Ray Washburn	2.50	1.25	.70
93	Yankees Rookies (Stan Bahnsen, Bobby Murcer)	4.00	2.00	1.25
94	Ron Fairly	2.50	1.25	.70
95	Sonny Siebert	2.50	1.25	.70
96	Art Shamsky	2.50	1.25	.70
97	Mike Cuellar	2.50	1.25	.70
98	Rich Rollins	2.50	1.25	.70
99	Lee Stange	2.50	1.25	.70
100	Frank Robinson	24.00	12.00	7.25

101	Ken Johnson	2.50	1.25	.70
102	Phillies Team	2.50	1.25	.70
103	Checklist 2 (Mickey Mantle)	17.50	8.75	5.25
104	Minnie Rojas	2.50	1.25	.70
105	Ken Boyer	2.50	1.25	.70
106	Randy Hundley	2.50	1.25	.70
107	Joel Horlen	2.50	1.25	.70
108	Alex Johnson	2.50	1.25	.70
109	Tribe Thumpers (Rocky Colavito, Leon Wagner)	6.00	3.00	1.75
110	Jack Aker	3.00	1.50	.90
111	John Kennedy	3.00	1.50	.90
112	Dave Wickersham	3.00	1.50	.90
113	Dave Nicholson	3.00	1.50	.90
114	Jack Balschun	3.00	1.50	.90
115	Paul Casanova	3.00	1.50	.90
116	Herman Franks	3.00	1.50	.90
117	Darrell Brandon	3.00	1.50	.90
118	Bernie Allen	3.00	1.50	.90
119	Wade Blasingame	3.00	1.50	.90
120	Floyd Robinson	3.00	1.50	.90
121	Ed Bressoud	3.00	1.50	.90
122	George Brunet	3.00	1.50	.90
123	Pirates Rookies (Jim Price, Luke Walker)	3.00	1.50	.90
124	Jim Stewart	3.00	1.50	.90
125	Moe Drabowsky	3.00	1.50	.90
126	Tony Taylor	3.00	1.50	.90
127	John O'Donoghue	3.00	1.50	.90
128	Ed Spiezio	3.00	1.50	.90
129	Phil Roof	3.00	1.50	.90
130	Phil Regan	3.00	1.50	.90
131	Yankees Team	12.00	6.00	3.50
132	Ozzie Virgil	3.00	1.50	.90
133	Ron Kline	3.00	1.50	.90
134	Gates Brown	3.00	1.50	.90
135	Deron Johnson	3.00	1.50	.90
136	Carroll Sembera	3.00	1.50	.90
137	Twins Rookies (Ron Clark, Jim Ollum)	3.00	1.50	.90
138	Dick Kelley	3.00	1.50	.90
139	Dalton Jones	3.00	1.50	.90
140	Willie Stargell	25.00	12.50	7.50
141	John Miller	3.00	1.50	.90
142	Jackie Brandt	3.00	1.50	.90
143	Sox Sockers (Don Buford, Pete Ward)	3.00	1.50	.90
144	Bill Hepler	3.00	1.50	.90
145	Larry Brown	3.00	1.50	.90
146	Steve Carlton	45.00	22.00	13.50
147	Tom Egan	3.00	1.50	.90
148	Adolfo Phillips	3.00	1.50	.90
149	Joe Moeller	3.00	1.50	.90
150	Mickey Mantle	325.00	162.00	97.00
151	World Series Game 1 (Moe Mows Down 11)	3.00	1.50	.90
152	World Series Game 2 (Palmer Blanks Dodgers)	6.00	3.00	1.75
153	World Series Game 3 (Blair's Homer Defeats L.A.)	3.00	1.50	.90
154	World Series Game 4 (Orioles Win 4th Straight)	3.00	1.50	.90
155	World Series Summary (The Winners Celebrate)	3.00	1.50	.90
156	Ron Herbel	3.00	1.50	.90
157	Danny Cater	3.00	1.50	.90
158	Jimmy Coker	3.00	1.50	.90
159	Bruce Howard	3.00	1.50	.90
160	Willie Davis	3.00	1.50	.90
161	Dick Williams	3.00	1.50	.90
162	Billy O'Dell	3.00	1.50	.90
163	Vic Roznovsky	3.00	1.50	.90
164	Dwight Siebler	3.00	1.50	.90
165	Cleon Jones	3.00	1.50	.90
166	Ed Mathews	25.00	12.50	7.50
167	Senators Rookies (Joe Coleman, Tim Cullen)	3.00	1.50	.90
168	Ray Culp	3.00	1.50	.90
169	Horace Clarke	3.00	1.50	.90
170	Dick McAuliffe	3.00	1.50	.90
171	Calvin Koonce	3.00	1.50	.90
172	Bill Heath	3.00	1.50	.90
173	Cards Team	3.00	1.50	.90
174	Dick Radatz	3.00	1.50	.90
175	Bobby Knoop	3.00	1.50	.90
176	Sammy Ellis	3.00	1.50	.90
177	Tito Fuentes	3.00	1.50	.90
178	John Buzhardt	3.00	1.50	.90
179	Braves Rookies (Cecil Upshaw, Charles Vaughan)	3.00	1.50	.90
180	Curt Blefary	3.00	1.50	.90
181	Terry Fox	3.00	1.50	.90
182	Ed Charles	3.00	1.50	.90
183	Jim Pagliaroni	3.00	1.50	.90
184	George Thomas	3.00	1.50	.90
185	Ken Holtzman	3.00	1.50	.90
186	Mets Maulers (Ed Kranepool, Ron Swoboda)	3.00	1.50	.90
187	Pedro Ramos	3.00	1.50	.90
188	Ken Harrelson	3.00	1.50	.90
189	Chuck Hinton	3.00	1.50	.90
190	Turk Farrell	3.00	1.50	.90
191	Checklist 3 (Willie Mays)	12.50	6.25	3.75
192	Fred Gladding	3.00	1.50	.90
193	Jose Cardenal	3.00	1.50	.90
194	Bob Allison	3.00	1.50	.90
195	Al Jackson	3.00	1.50	.90
196	Johnny Romano	3.00	1.50	.90

1967-68 O-Pee-Chee Posters

The 5" x 7" "All Star Pin-ups" were inserts to 1968 OPC wax packs, but are virtually identical to the Topps version issued in 1967. The OPC posters have a small "Ptd. in Canada" line at bottom. They feature a full color picture with the player's name, position and team in a circle in the lower-right corner on front. The numbered set consists of 32 players (generally big names). Even so, they are rather inexpensive. Because the large paper pin-ups had to be folded several times to fit into the wax packs, they are almost never found in technical Mint or NM condition.

		NM	EX	VG
Complete Set (32):		250.00	125.00	75.00
Common Player:		3.00	1.50	.90
1	Boog Powell	4.00	2.00	1.25
2	Bert Campaneris	3.00	1.50	.90
3	Brooks Robinson	18.00	9.00	5.50
4	Tommie Agee	3.00	1.50	.90
5	Carl Yastrzemski	18.00	9.00	5.50
6	Mickey Mantle	60.00	30.00	18.00
7	Frank Howard	4.00	2.00	1.25
8	Sam McDowell	3.00	1.50	.90
9	Orlando Cepeda	12.00	6.00	3.50
10	Chico Cardenas	3.00	1.50	.90
11	Roberto Clemente	36.00	18.00	11.00
12	Willie Mays	30.00	15.00	9.00
13	Cleon Jones	3.00	1.50	.90
14	John Callison	3.00	1.50	.90
15	Hank Aaron	30.00	15.00	9.00
16	Don Drysdale	15.00	7.50	4.50
17	Bobby Knoop	3.00	1.50	.90
18	Tony Oliva	4.00	2.00	1.25
19	Frank Robinson	15.00	7.50	4.50
20	Denny McLain	4.00	2.00	1.25
21	Al Kaline	15.00	7.50	4.50
22	Joe Pepitone	3.00	1.50	.90
23	Harmon Killebrew	12.00	6.00	3.50
24	Leon Wagner	3.00	1.50	.90
25	Joe Morgan	12.00	6.00	3.50
26	Ron Santo	5.00	2.50	1.50
27	Joe Torre	6.00	3.00	1.75
28	Juan Marichal	12.00	6.00	3.50
29	Matty Alou	3.00	1.50	.90
30	Felipe Alou	5.00	2.50	1.50
31	Ron Hunt	3.00	1.50	.90
32	Willie McCovey	12.00	6.00	3.50

1968 O-Pee-Chee

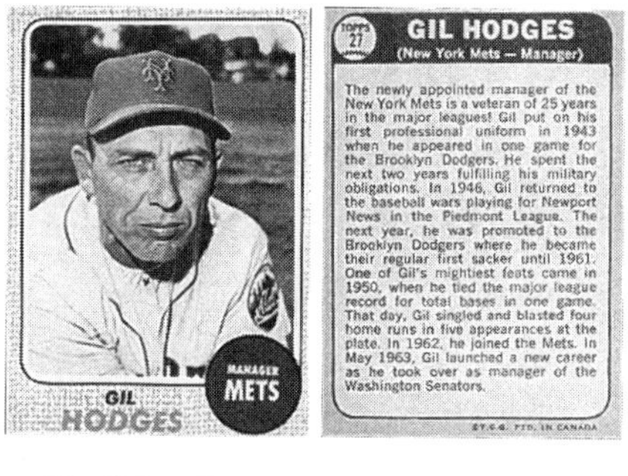

The O-Pee-Chee set for 1968 again consists of 196 cards, in the standard 2-1/2" x 3-1/2". The design is identical to the 1968 Topps set, except the color of the backs is slightly different and the words "Ptd. in Canada" appear in the lower-right corner of the back.

		NM	EX	VG
Complete Set (196):		2500.	1250.	750.00
Common Player:		2.50	1.25	.70
1	N.L. Batting Leaders (Matty Alou, Bob Clemente, Tony Gonzales) (Gonzalez)	45.00	22.00	13.50
2	A.L. Batting Leaders (Al Kaline, Frank Robinson, Carl Yastrzemski)	15.00	7.50	4.50
3	N.L. RBI Leaders (Hank Aaron, Orlando Cepeda, Bob Clemente)	30.00	15.00	9.00
4	A.L. RBI Leaders (Harmon Killebrew, Frank Robinson, Carl Yastrzemski)	17.50	8.75	5.25
5	N.L. Home Run Leaders (Hank Aaron, Willie McCovey, Ron Santo, Jim Wynn)	12.50	6.25	3.75
6	N.L. Home Run Leaders (Frank Howard, Harmon Killebrew, Carl Yastrzemski)	11.50	5.75	3.50
7	N.L. ERA Leaders (Jim Bunning, Phil Niekro, Chris Short)	4.00	2.00	1.25
8	A.L. ERA Leaders (Joe Horlen, Gary Peters, Sonny Siebert)	2.50	1.25	.70
9	N.L. Pitching Leaders (Jim Bunning, Ferguson Jenkins, Mike McCormick, Claude Osteen)	4.00	2.00	1.25
10	A.L. Pitching Leaders (Dean Chance, Jim Lonborg, Earl Wilson)	2.50	1.25	.70
11	N.L. Strikeout Leaders (Jim Bunning, Ferguson Jenkins, Gaylord Perry)	5.00	2.50	1.50
12	A.L. Strikeout Leaders (Dean Chance, Jim Lonborg, Sam McDowell)	2.50	1.25	.70
13	Chuck Hartenstein	2.50	1.25	.70
14	Jerry McNertney	2.50	1.25	.70
15	Ron Hunt	2.50	1.25	.70
16	Indians Rookies (Lou Piniella, Richie Scheinblum)	3.50	1.75	1.00
17	Dick Hall	2.50	1.25	.70
18	Mike Hershberger	2.50	1.25	.70
19	Juan Pizarro	2.50	1.25	.70
20	Brooks Robinson	32.00	16.00	9.50
21	Ron Davis	2.50	1.25	.70
22	Pat Dobson	2.50	1.25	.70
23	Chico Cardenas	2.50	1.25	.70
24	Bobby Locke	2.50	1.25	.70
25	Julian Javier	2.50	1.25	.70
26	Darrell Brandon	2.50	1.25	.70
27	Gil Hodges	15.00	7.50	4.50
28	Ted Uhlaender	2.50	1.25	.70
29	Joe Verbanic	2.50	1.25	.70
30	Joe Torre	5.00	2.50	1.50
31	Ed Stroud	2.50	1.25	.70
32	Joe Gibbon	2.50	1.25	.70
33	Pete Ward	2.50	1.25	.70
34	Al Ferrara	2.50	1.25	.70
35	Steve Hargan	2.50	1.25	.70
36	Pirates Rookies (Bob Moose, Bob Robertson)	2.50	1.25	.70
37	Billy Williams	16.00	8.00	4.75
38	Tony Pierce	2.50	1.25	.70
39	Cookie Rojas	2.50	1.25	.70
40	Denny McLain	12.50	6.25	3.75
41	Julio Gotay	2.50	1.25	.70
42	Larry Haney	2.50	1.25	.70
43	Gary Bell	2.50	1.25	.70
44	Frank Kostro	2.50	1.25	.70
45	Tom Seaver	165.00	82.00	49.00
46	Dave Ricketts	2.50	1.25	.70
47	Ralph Houk	2.50	1.25	.70
48	Ted Davidson	2.50	1.25	.70
49	Ed Brinkman	2.50	1.25	.70
50	Willie Mays	115.00	57.00	34.00
51	Bob Locker	2.50	1.25	.70
52	Hawk Taylor	2.50	1.25	.70
53	Gene Alley	2.50	1.25	.70
54	Stan Williams	2.50	1.25	.70
55	Felipe Alou	4.50	2.25	1.25
56	Orioles Rookies (Dave Leonhard, Dave May)	2.50	1.25	.70
57	Dan Schneider	2.50	1.25	.70
58	Ed Mathews	20.00	10.00	6.00
59	Don Lock	2.50	1.25	.70
60	Ken Holtzman	2.50	1.25	.70
61	Reggie Smith	2.50	1.25	.70
62	Chuck Dobson	2.50	1.25	.70
63	Dick Kenworthy	2.50	1.25	.70
64	Jim Merritt	2.50	1.25	.70
65	John Roseboro	2.50	1.25	.70
66	Casey Cox	2.50	1.25	.70
67	Checklist 1 (Jim Kaat)	2.50	1.25	.70
68	Ron Willis	2.50	1.25	.70
69	Tom Tresh	2.50	1.25	.70
70	Bob Veale	2.50	1.25	.70
71	Vern Fuller	2.50	1.25	.70
72	Tommy John	2.50	1.25	.70
73	Jim Hart	2.50	1.25	.70
74	Milt Pappas	2.50	1.25	.70
75	Don Mincher	2.50	1.25	.70
76	Braves Rookies (Jim Britton, Ron Reed)	2.50	1.25	.70
77	Don Wilson	2.50	1.25	.70
78	Jim Northrup	2.50	1.25	.70
79	Ted Kubiak	2.50	1.25	.70
80	Rod Carew	75.00	37.00	22.00
81	Larry Jackson	2.50	1.25	.70
82	Sam Bowens	2.50	1.25	.70
83	John Stephenson	2.50	1.25	.70
84	Bob Tolan	2.50	1.25	.70
85	Gaylord Perry	18.00	9.00	5.50
86	Willie Stargell	20.00	10.00	6.00
87	Dick Williams	2.50	1.25	.70
88	Phil Regan	2.50	1.25	.70
89	Jake Gibbs	2.50	1.25	.70
90	Vada Pinson	2.50	1.25	.70
91	Jim Ollom	2.50	1.25	.70
92	Ed Kranepool	2.50	1.25	.70
93	Tony Cloninger	2.50	1.25	.70
94	Lee Maye	2.50	1.25	.70
95	Bob Aspromonte	2.50	1.25	.70
96	Senators Rookies (Frank Coggins, Dick Nold)	2.50	1.25	.70
97	Tom Phoebus	2.50	1.25	.70
98	Gary Sutherland	2.50	1.25	.70
99	Rocky Colavito	12.00	6.00	3.50
100	Bob Gibson	25.00	12.50	7.50
101	Glenn Beckert	2.50	1.25	.70
102	Jose Cardenal	2.50	1.25	.70
103	Don Sutton	18.00	9.00	5.50
104	Dick Dietz	2.50	1.25	.70
105	Al Downing	2.50	1.25	.70
106	Dalton Jones	2.50	1.25	.70
107	Checklist 2 (Juan Marichal)	2.75	1.50	.80
108	Don Pavletich	2.50	1.25	.70
109	Bert Campaneris	2.50	1.25	.70
110	Hank Aaron	95.00	47.00	28.00
111	Rich Reese	2.50	1.25	.70
112	Woody Fryman	2.50	1.25	.70
113	Tigers Rookies (Tom Matchick, Daryl Patterson)	2.50	1.25	.70
114	Ron Swoboda	2.50	1.25	.70
115	Sam McDowell	2.50	1.25	.70
116	Ken McMullen	2.50	1.25	.70
117	Larry Jaster	2.50	1.25	.70
118	Mark Belanger	2.50	1.25	.70

119	Ted Savage	2.50	1.25	.70
120	Mel Stottlemyre	2.50	1.25	.70
121	Jimmie Hall	2.50	1.25	.70
122	Gene Mauch	2.50	1.25	.70
123	Jose Santiago	2.50	1.25	.70
124	Nate Oliver	2.50	1.25	.70
125	Joe Horlen	2.50	1.25	.70
126	Bob Etheridge	2.50	1.25	.70
127	Paul Lindblad	2.50	1.25	.70
128	Astros Rookies (Tom Dukes, Alonzo Harris)	2.50	1.25	.70
129	Mickey Stanley	2.50	1.25	.70
130	Tony Perez	18.00	9.00	5.50
131	Frank Bertaina	2.50	1.25	.70
132	Bud Harrelson	2.50	1.25	.70
133	Fred Whitfield	2.50	1.25	.70
134	Pat Jarvis	2.50	1.25	.70
135	Paul Blair	2.50	1.25	.70
136	Randy Hundley	2.50	1.25	.70
137	Twins Team	2.50	1.25	.70
138	Ruben Amaro	2.50	1.25	.70
139	Chris Short	2.50	1.25	.70
140	Tony Conigliaro	9.00	4.50	2.75
141	Dal Maxvill	2.50	1.25	.70
142	White Sox Rookies (Buddy Bradford, Bill Voss)	2.50	1.25	.70
143	Pete Cimino	2.50	1.25	.70
144	Joe Morgan	19.00	9.50	5.75
145	Don Drysdale	27.50	13.50	8.25
146	Sal Bando	2.50	1.25	.70
147	Frank Linzy	2.50	1.25	.70
148	Dave Bristol	2.50	1.25	.70
149	Bob Saverine	2.50	1.25	.70
150	Bob Clemente	175.00	87.00	52.00
151	World Series Game 1 (Brock Socks 4-Hits)	6.00	3.00	1.75
152	World Series Game 2 (Yaz Smashes Two Homers)	10.00	5.00	3.00
153	World Series Game 3 (Briles Cools Off Boston)	2.50	1.25	.70
154	World Series Game 4 (Gibson Hurls Shutout)	8.00	4.00	2.50
155	World Series Game 5 (Lonborg Wins Again)	2.50	1.25	.70
156	World Series Game 6 (Petrocelli Socks Two Homers)	3.00	1.50	.90
157	World Series Game 7 (St. Louis Wins It)	2.50	1.25	.70
158	World Series Summary (The Cardinals Celebrate)	2.50	1.25	.70
159	Don Kessinger	2.50	1.25	.70
160	Earl Wilson	2.50	1.25	.70
161	Norm Miller	2.50	1.25	.70
162	Cards Rookies (Hal Gilson, Mike Torrez)	2.50	1.25	.70
163	Gene Brabender	2.50	1.25	.70
164	Ramon Webster	2.50	1.25	.70
165	Tony Oliva	3.00	1.50	.90
166	Claude Raymond	2.50	1.25	.70
167	Elston Howard	3.00	1.50	.90
168	Dodgers Team	2.50	1.25	.70
169	Bob Bolin	2.50	1.25	.70
170	Jim Fregosi	2.50	1.25	.70
171	Don Nottebart	2.50	1.25	.70
172	Walt Williams	2.50	1.25	.70
173	John Boozer	2.50	1.25	.70
174	Bob Tillman	2.50	1.25	.70
175	Maury Wills	3.00	1.50	.90
176	Bob Allen	2.50	1.25	.70
177	Mets Rookies (Jerry Koosman, Nolan Ryan)	1500.	750.00	450.00
178	Don Wert	2.50	1.25	.70
179	Bill Stoneman	2.50	1.25	.70
180	Curt Flood	2.50	1.25	.70
181	Jerry Zimmerman	2.50	1.25	.70
182	Dave Gusti	2.50	1.25	.70
183	Bob Kennedy	2.50	1.25	.70
184	Lou Johnson	2.50	1.25	.70
185	Tom Haller	2.50	1.25	.70
186	Eddie Watt	2.50	1.25	.70
187	Sonny Jackson	2.50	1.25	.70
188	Cap Peterson	2.50	1.25	.70
189	Bill Landis	2.50	1.25	.70
190	Bill White	2.50	1.25	.70
191	Dan Frisella	2.50	1.25	.70
192	Checklist 3 (Carl Yastrzemski)	4.00	2.00	1.25
193	Jack Hamilton	2.50	1.25	.70
194	Don Buford	2.50	1.25	.70
195	Joe Pepitone	2.50	1.25	.70
196	Gary Nolan	2.50	1.25	.70

1969 O-Pee-Chee

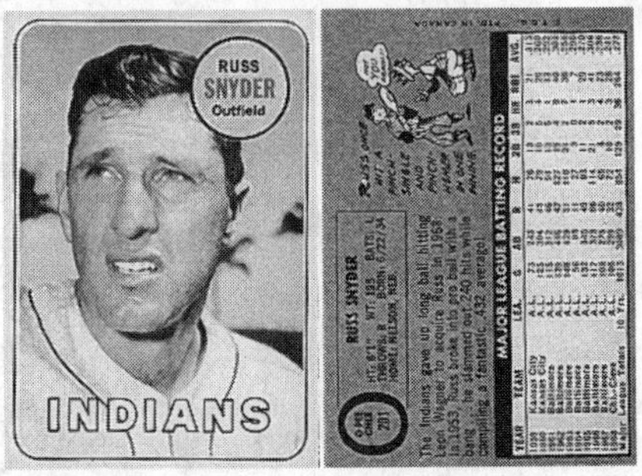

O-Pee-Chee increased the number of cards in its 1969 set to 218, maintaining the standard 2-1/2" x 3-1/2" size. The card design is identical to the 1969 Topps set, except for the appearance of an OPC logo on back, a slightly different color on the back and the words "Ptd. in Canada," which appear along the bottom.

		NM	EX	VG
	Complete Set (218):	850.00	425.00	250.00
	Common Player:	2.50	1.25	.75
1	A.L. Batting Leaders (Danny Cater, Tony Oliva, Carl Yastrzemski)	15.00	7.50	4.50
2	N.L. Batting Leaders (Felipe Alou, Matty Alou, Pete Rose)	10.00	5.00	3.00
3	A.L. RBI Leaders (Ken Harrelson, Frank Howard, Jim Northrup)	2.50	1.25	.70
4	N.L. RBI Leaders (Willie McCovey, Ron Santo, Billy Williams)	7.50	3.75	2.25
5	A.L. Home Run Leaders (Ken Harrelson, Willie Horton, Frank Howard)	2.50	1.25	.70
6	N.L. Home Run Leaders (Richie Allen, Ernie Banks, Willie McCovey)	8.50	4.25	2.50
7	A.L. ERA Leaders (Sam McDowell, Dave McNally, Luis Tiant)	2.50	1.25	.70
8	N.L. ERA Leaders (Bobby Bolin, Bob Gibson, Bob Veale)	2.50	1.25	.70
9	A.L. Pitching Leaders (Denny McLain, Dave McNally, Mel Stottlemyre, Luis Tiant)	2.50	1.25	.70
10	N.L. Pitching Leaders (Bob Gibson, Fergie Jenkins, Juan Marichal)	8.50	4.25	2.50
11	A.L. Strikeout Leaders (Sam McDowell, Denny McLain, Luis Tiant)	2.50	1.25	.70
12	N.L. Strikeout Leaders (Bob Gibson, Fergie Jenkins, Bill Singer)	2.50	1.25	.70
13	Mickey Stanley	2.50	1.25	.70
14	Al McBean	2.50	1.25	.70
15	Boog Powell	3.00	1.50	.90
16	Giants Rookies (Cesar Gutierrez, Rich Robertson)	2.50	1.25	.70
17	Mike Marshall	2.50	1.25	.70
18	Dick Schofield	2.50	1.25	.70
19	Ken Suarez	2.50	1.25	.70
20	Ernie Banks	20.00	10.00	6.00
21	Jose Santiago	2.50	1.25	.70
22	Jesus Alou	3.50	1.75	1.00
23	Lew Krausse	2.50	1.25	.70
24	Walt Alston	6.00	3.00	1.75
25	Roy White	2.50	1.25	.70
26	Clay Carroll	2.50	1.25	.70
27	Bernie Allen	2.50	1.25	.70
28	Mike Ryan	2.50	1.25	.70
29	Dave Morehead	2.50	1.25	.70
30	Bob Allison	2.50	1.25	.70
31	Mets Rookies (Gary Gentry, Amos Otis)	3.50	1.75	1.00
32	Sammy Ellis	2.50	1.25	.70
33	Wayne Causey	2.50	1.25	.70
34	Gary Peters	2.50	1.25	.70
35	Joe Morgan	12.00	6.00	3.50
36	Luke Walker	2.50	1.25	.70
37	Curt Motton	2.50	1.25	.70
38	Zoilo Versalles	2.50	1.25	.70
39	Dick Hughes	2.50	1.25	.70
40	Mayo Smith	2.50	1.25	.70
41	Bob Barton	2.50	1.25	.70
42	Tommy Harper	2.50	1.25	.70
43	Joe Niekro	2.50	1.25	.70
44	Danny Cater	2.50	1.25	.70
45	Maury Wills	4.00	2.00	1.25
46	Fritz Peterson	2.50	1.25	.70
47	Paul Popovich	2.50	1.25	.70
48	Brant Alyea	2.50	1.25	.70
49	Royals Rookies (Steve Jones, Eliseo Rodriguez)	2.50	1.25	.70
50	Bob Clemente	120.00	60.00	36.00
51	Woody Fryman	2.50	1.25	.70
52	Mike Andrews	2.50	1.25	.70
53	Sonny Jackson	2.50	1.25	.70
54	Cisco Carlos	2.50	1.25	.70
55	Jerry Grote	2.50	1.25	.70
56	Rich Reese	2.50	1.25	.70
57	Checklist 1 (Denny McLain)	3.00	1.50	.90
58	Fred Gladding	2.50	1.25	.70
59	Jay Johnstone	2.50	1.25	.70
60	Nelson Briles	2.50	1.25	.70
61	Jimmie Hall	2.50	1.25	.70
62	Chico Salmon	2.50	1.25	.70
63	Jim Hickman	2.50	1.25	.70
64	Bill Monbouquette	2.50	1.25	.70
65	Willie Davis	2.50	1.25	.70
66	Orioles Rookies (Mike Adamson, Merv Rettenmund)	2.50	1.25	.70
67	Bill Stoneman	3.00	1.50	.90
68	Dave Duncan	2.50	1.25	.70
69	Steve Hamilton	2.50	1.25	.70
70	Tommy Helms	2.50	1.25	.70
71	Steve Whitaker	2.50	1.25	.70
72	Ron Taylor	2.50	1.25	.70
73	Johnny Briggs	2.50	1.25	.70
74	Preston Gomez	2.50	1.25	.70
75	Luis Aparicio	12.00	6.00	3.50
76	Norm Miller	2.50	1.25	.70
77	Ron Perranoski	2.50	1.25	.70
78	Tom Satriano	2.50	1.25	.70
79	Milt Pappas	2.50	1.25	.70
80	Norm Cash	2.50	1.25	.70
81	Mel Queen	2.50	1.25	.70
82	Pirates Rookies (Rich Hebner, Al Oliver)	15.00	7.50	4.50
83	Mike Ferraro	2.50	1.25	.70
84	Bob Humphreys	2.50	1.25	.70
85	Lou Brock	18.00	9.00	5.50
86	Pete Richert	2.50	1.25	.70
87	Horace Clarke	2.50	1.25	.70
88	Rich Nye	2.50	1.25	.70
89	Russ Gibson	2.50	1.25	.70
90	Jerry Koosman	3.00	1.50	.90
91	Al Dark	2.50	1.25	.70
92	Jack Billingham	3.00	1.50	.90
93	Joe Foy	2.50	1.25	.70
94	Hank Aguirre	2.50	1.25	.70
95	Johnny Bench	90.00	45.00	27.00
96	Denver Lemaster	2.50	1.25	.70
97	Buddy Bradford	2.50	1.25	.70
98	Dave Giusti	2.50	1.25	.70
99	Twins Rookies (Danny Morris, Graig Nettles)	18.00	9.00	5.50
100	Hank Aaron	75.00	37.00	22.00
101	Daryl Patterson	2.50	1.25	.70
102	Jim Davenport	2.50	1.25	.70
103	Roger Repoz	2.50	1.25	.70
104	Steve Blass	2.50	1.25	.70
105	Rick Monday	2.50	1.25	.70
106	Jim Hannan	2.50	1.25	.70
107	Checklist 2 (Bob Gibson)	4.00	2.00	1.25
108	Tony Taylor	2.50	1.25	.70
109	Jim Lonborg	2.50	1.25	.70
110	Mike Shannon	2.50	1.25	.70
111	Johnny Morris	2.50	1.25	.70
112	J.C. Martin	2.50	1.25	.70
113	Dave May	2.50	1.25	.70
114	Yankees Rookies (Alan Closter, John Cumberland)	2.50	1.25	.70
115	Bill Hands	2.50	1.25	.70
116	Chuck Harrison	2.50	1.25	.70
117	Jim Fairey	3.00	1.50	.90
118	Stan Williams	2.50	1.25	.70
119	Doug Rader	2.50	1.25	.70
120	Pete Rose	60.00	30.00	18.00
121	Joe Grzenda	2.50	1.25	.70
122	Ron Fairly	2.50	1.25	.70
123	Wilbur Wood	2.50	1.25	.70
124	Hank Bauer	2.50	1.25	.70
125	Ray Sadecki	2.50	1.25	.70
126	Dick Tracewski	2.50	1.25	.70
127	Kevin Collins	2.50	1.25	.70
128	Tommie Aaron	2.50	1.25	.70
129	Bill McCool	2.50	1.25	.70
130	Carl Yastrzemski	32.00	16.00	9.50
131	Chris Cannizzaro	2.50	1.25	.70
132	Dave Baldwin	2.50	1.25	.70
133	Johnny Callison	2.50	1.25	.70
134	Jim Weaver	2.50	1.25	.70
135	Tommy Davis	2.50	1.25	.70
136	Cards Rookies (Steve Huntz, Mike Torrez)	2.50	1.25	.70
137	Wally Bunker	2.50	1.25	.70
138	John Bateman	3.00	1.50	.90
139	Andy Kosco	2.50	1.25	.70
140	Jim Lefebvre	2.50	1.25	.70
141	Bill Dillman	2.50	1.25	.70
142	Woody Woodward	2.50	1.25	.70
143	Joe Nossek	2.50	1.25	.70
144	Bob Hendley	2.50	1.25	.70
145	Max Alvis	2.50	1.25	.70
146	Jim Perry	2.50	1.25	.70
147	Leo Durocher	4.00	2.00	1.25
148	Lee Stange	2.50	1.25	.70
149	Ollie Brown	2.50	1.25	.70
150	Denny McLain	2.50	1.25	.70
151	Clay Dalrymple	2.50	1.25	.70
152	Tommie Sisk	2.50	1.25	.70
153	Ed Brinkman	2.50	1.25	.70
154	Jim Britton	2.50	1.25	.70
155	Pete Ward	2.50	1.25	.70
156	Astros Rookies (Hal Gilson, Leon McFadden)	2.50	1.25	.70
157	Bob Rodgers	2.50	1.25	.70
158	Joe Gibbon	2.50	1.25	.70
159	Jerry Adair	2.50	1.25	.70
160	Vada Pinson	2.50	1.25	.70
161	John Purdin	2.50	1.25	.70
162	World Series Game 1 (Gibson Fans 17; Sets New Record)	8.50	4.25	2.50
163	World Series Game 2 (Tiger Homers Deck The Cards)	2.50	1.25	.70
164	World Series Game 3 (McCarver's Homer Puts St. Louis Ahead)	6.00	3.00	1.75
165	World Series Game 4 (Brock's Lead-Off Homer Starts Cards' Ro mp)	6.00	3.00	1.75
166	World Series Game 5 (Kaline's Key Hit Sparks Tiger Rally)	9.00	4.50	2.75
167	World Series Game 6 (Tiger 10-Run Inning Ties Mark)	2.50	1.25	.70
168	World Series Game 7 (Lolich Series Hero, Outduels Gibson)	6.00	3.00	1.75
169	World Series Summary (Tigers Celebrate Their Victory)	2.50	1.25	.70
170	Frank Howard	2.75	1.50	.80
171	Glenn Beckert	2.50	1.25	.70
172	Jerry Stephenson	2.50	1.25	.70
173	White Sox Rookies (Bob Christian, Gerry Nyman)	2.50	1.25	.70
174	Grant Jackson	2.50	1.25	.70
175	Jim Bunning	12.00	6.00	3.50
176	Joe Azcue	2.50	1.25	.70

177	Ron Reed	2.50	1.25	.70
178	Ray Oyler	2.50	1.25	.70
179	Don Pavletich	2.50	1.25	.70
180	Willie Horton	2.50	1.25	.70
181	Mel Nelson	2.50	1.25	.70
182	Bill Rigney	2.50	1.25	.70
183	Don Shaw	3.00	1.50	.90
184	Roberto Pena	2.50	1.25	.70
185	Tom Phoebus	2.50	1.25	.70
186	John Edwards	2.50	1.25	.70
187	Leon Wagner	2.50	1.25	.70
188	Rick Wise	2.50	1.25	.70
189	Red Sox Rookies (Joe Lahoud, John Thibdeau)	2.50	1.25	.70
190	Willie Mays	75.00	37.00	22.00
191	Lindy McDaniel	2.50	1.25	.70
192	Jose Pagan	2.50	1.25	.70
193	Don Cardwell	2.50	1.25	.70
194	Ted Uhlaender	2.50	1.25	.70
195	John Odom	2.50	1.25	.70
196	Lum Harris	2.50	1.25	.70
197	Dick Selma	2.50	1.25	.70
198	Willie Smith	2.50	1.25	.70
199	Jim French	2.50	1.25	.70
200	Bob Gibson	18.00	9.00	5.50
201	Russ Snyder	2.50	1.25	.70
202	Don Wilson	2.50	1.25	.70
203	Dave Johnson	2.50	1.25	.70
204	Jack Hiatt	2.50	1.25	.70
205	Rick Reichardt	2.50	1.25	.70
206	Phillies Rookies (Larry Hisle, Barry Lersch)	2.50	1.25	.70
207	Roy Face	2.50	1.25	.70
208	Donn Clendenon	2.75	1.50	.80
209	Larry Haney	2.50	1.25	.70
210	Felix Millan	2.50	1.25	.70
211	Galen Cisco	2.50	1.25	.70
212	Tom Tresh	2.50	1.25	.70
213	Gerry Arrigo	2.50	1.25	.70
214	Checklist 3	2.50	1.25	.70
215	Rico Petrocelli	3.00	1.50	.90
216	Don Sutton	12.00	6.00	3.50
217	John Donaldson	2.50	1.25	.70
218	John Roseboro	2.50	1.25	.70

1969 O-Pee-Chee Deckle

Very similar in design to the Topps Deckle Edge set of the same year, the 1969 O-Pee-Chee set consists of 24 unnumbered black-and-white cards. The Canadian-issued version measures 2-1/8" x 3-1/8", slightly smaller than the Topps set, but features the same "deckle cut" borders. The OPC set is blank-backed and has the facsimile autographs in black ink, rather than blue.

		NM	EX	VG
Complete Set (24):		360.00	180.00	100.00
Common Player:		5.00	2.50	1.50
(1)	Rich Allen	7.50	3.75	2.25
(2)	Luis Aparicio	12.00	6.00	3.50
(3)	Rodney Carew	16.00	8.00	4.75
(4)	Roberto Clemente	90.00	45.00	27.00
(5)	Curt Flood	5.00	2.50	1.50
(6)	Bill Freehan	5.00	2.50	1.50
(7)	Robert Gibson	14.00	7.00	4.25
(8)	Ken Harrelson	5.00	2.50	1.50
(9)	Tommy Helms	5.00	2.50	1.50
(10)	Tom Haller	5.00	2.50	1.50
(11)	Willie Horton	5.00	2.50	1.50
(12)	Frank Howard	5.00	2.50	1.50
(13)	Willie McCovey	16.00	8.00	4.75
(14)	Denny McLain	6.00	3.00	1.75
(15)	Juan Marichal	14.00	7.00	4.25
(16)	Willie Mays	65.00	32.00	19.50
(17)	John "Boog" Powell	6.50	3.25	2.00
(18)	Brooks Robinson	30.00	15.00	9.00
(19)	Ronald Santo	6.50	3.25	2.00
(20)	Rusty Staub	6.50	3.25	2.00
(21)	Mel Stottlemyre	5.00	2.50	1.50
(22)	Luis Tiant	5.00	2.50	1.50
(23)	Maurie Wills	5.00	2.50	1.50
(24)	Carl Yastrzemski	30.00	15.00	9.00

1970 O-Pee-Chee

The 1970 O-Pee-Chee set, identical in design to the 1970 Topps set, expanded to 546 cards, measuring 2-1/2" x 3-1/2". The Canadian-issued O-Pee-Chee set is easy to distinguish because the backs are printed in both French and English and include the words "Printed in Canada."

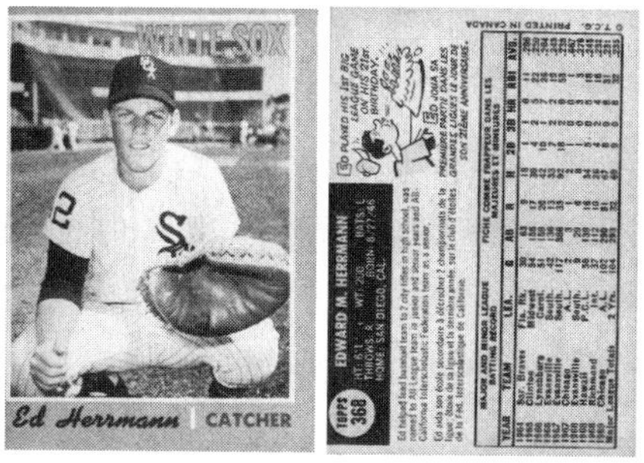

		NM	EX	VG
Complete Set (546):		1800.	900.00	550.00
Common Player (1-263):		1.50	.70	.45
Common Player (264-459):		2.00	1.00	.60
Common Player (460-546):		2.50	1.25	.70
1	World Champions (Mets Team)	15.00	7.50	4.50
2	Diego Segui	1.50	.70	.45
3	Darrel Chaney	1.50	.70	.45
4	Tom Egan	1.50	.70	.45
5	Wes Parker	1.50	.70	.45
6	Grant Jackson	1.50	.70	.45
7	Indians Rookies (Gary Boyd, Russ Nagelson)	1.50	.70	.45
8	Jose Martinez	1.50	.70	.45
9	Checklist 1	1.50	.70	.45
10	Carl Yastrzemski	21.00	10.50	6.25
11	Nate Colbert	1.50	.70	.45
12	John Hiller	1.50	.70	.45
13	Jack Hiatt	1.50	.70	.45
14	Hank Allen	1.50	.70	.45
15	Larry Dierker	1.50	.70	.45
16	Charlie Metro	1.50	.70	.45
17	Hoyt Wilhelm	6.00	3.00	1.75
18	Carlos May	1.50	.70	.45
19	John Boccabella	2.50	1.25	.70
20	Dave McNally	1.50	.70	.45
21	Athletics Rookies (Vida Blue, Gene Tenace)	4.00	2.00	1.25
22	Ray Washburn	1.50	.70	.45
23	Bill Robinson	1.50	.70	.45
24	Dick Selma	1.50	.70	.45
25	Cesar Tovar	1.50	.70	.45
26	Tug McGraw	1.50	.70	.45
27	Chuck Hinton	1.50	.70	.45
28	Billy Wilson	1.50	.70	.45
29	Sandy Alomar	1.50	.70	.45
30	Matty Alou	1.50	.70	.45
31	Marty Pattin	1.50	.70	.45
32	Harry Walker	1.50	.70	.45
33	Don Wert	1.50	.70	.45
34	Willie Crawford	1.50	.70	.45
35	Joe Horlen	1.50	.70	.45
36	Red Rookies (Danny Breeden, Bernie Carbo)	1.50	.70	.45
37	Dick Drago	1.50	.70	.45
38	Mack Jones	2.50	1.25	.70
39	Mike Nagy	1.50	.70	.45
40	Rich Allen	2.50	1.25	.70
41	George Lauzerique	1.50	.70	.45
42	Tito Fuentes	1.50	.70	.45
43	Jack Aker	1.50	.70	.45
44	Roberto Pena	1.50	.70	.45
45	Dave Johnson	1.50	.70	.45
46	Ken Rudolph	1.50	.70	.45
47	Bob Miller	1.50	.70	.45
48	Gil Garrido	1.50	.70	.45
49	Tim Cullen	1.50	.70	.45
50	Tommie Agee	1.50	.70	.45
51	Bob Christian	1.50	.70	.45
52	Bruce Dal Canton	1.50	.70	.45
53	John Kennedy	1.50	.70	.45
54	Jeff Torborg	1.50	.70	.45
55	John Odom	1.50	.70	.45
56	Phillies Rookies (Joe Lis, Scott Reid)	1.50	.70	.45
57	Pat Kelly	1.50	.70	.45
58	Dave Marshall	1.50	.70	.45
59	Dick Ellsworth	1.50	.70	.45
60	Jim Wynn	1.50	.70	.45
61	N.L. Batting Leaders (Bob Clemente, Cleon Jones, Pete Rose)	8.50	4.25	2.50
62	A.L. Batting Leaders (Rod Carew, Tony Oliva, Reggie Smith)	2.00	1.00	.60
63	N.L. RBI Leaders (Willie McCovey, Tony Perez, Ron Santo)	2.00	1.00	.60
64	A.L. RBI Leaders (Reggie Jackson, Harmon Killebrew, Boog Powell)	2.50	1.25	.70
65	N.L. Home Run Leaders (Hank Aaron, Lee May, Willie McCovey)	2.50	1.25	.70
66	A.L. Home Run Leaders (Frank Howard, Reggie Jackson, Harmon Killebrew)	2.50	1.25	.70
67	N.L. ERA Leaders (Steve Carlton, Bob Gibson, Juan Marichal)	7.50	3.75	2.25
68	A.L. ERA Leaders (Dick Bosman, Mike Cuellar, Jim Palmer)	1.50	.70	.45
69	N.L. Pitching Leaders (Fergie Jenkins, Juan Marichal, Phil Niekro, Tom Seaver)	9.00	4.50	2.75
70	A.L. Pitching Leaders (Dave Boswell, Mike Cuellar, Dennis McLain, Dave McNally, Jim Perry, Mel	1.50	.70	.45
71	N.L. Strikeout Leaders (Bob Gibson, Fergie Jenkins, Bill Singer)	2.00	1.00	.60
72	A.L. Strikeout Leaders (Mickey Lolich, Sam McDowell, Andy Messersmith)	1.50	.70	.45
73	Wayne Granger	1.50	.70	.45
74	Angels Rookies (Greg Washburn, Wally Wolf)	1.50	.70	.45
75	Jim Kaat	1.50	.70	.45
76	Carl Taylor	1.50	.70	.45
77	Frank Linzy	1.50	.70	.45
78	Joe Lahoud	1.50	.70	.45
79	Clay Kirby	1.50	.70	.45
80	Don Kessinger	1.50	.70	.45
81	Dave May	1.50	.70	.45
82	Frank Fernandez	1.50	.70	.45
83	Don Cardwell	1.50	.70	.45
84	Paul Casanova	1.50	.70	.45
85	Max Alvis	1.50	.70	.45
86	Lum Harris	1.50	.70	.45
87	Steve Renko	2.50	1.25	.70
88	Pilots Rookies (Dick Baney, Miguel Fuentes)	2.00	1.00	.60
89	Juan Rios	1.50	.70	.45
90	Tim McCarver	1.50	.70	.45
91	Rich Morales	1.50	.70	.45
92	George Culver	1.50	.70	.45
93	Rick Renick	1.50	.70	.45
94	Fred Patek	1.50	.70	.45
95	Earl Wilson	1.50	.70	.45
96	Cards Rookies (Leron Lee, Jerry Reuss)	1.50	.70	.45
97	Joe Moeller	1.50	.70	.45
98	Gates Brown	1.50	.70	.45
99	Bobby Pfeil	1.50	.70	.45
100	Mel Stottlemyre	1.50	.70	.45
101	Bobby Floyd	1.50	.70	.45
102	Joe Rudi	1.50	.70	.45
103	Frank Reberger	1.50	.70	.45
104	Gerry Moses	1.50	.70	.45
105	Tony Gonzalez	1.50	.70	.45
106	Darold Knowles	1.50	.70	.45
107	Bobby Etheridge	1.50	.70	.45
108	Tom Burgmeier	1.50	.70	.45
109	Expos Rookies (Garry Jestadt, Carl Morton)	5.00	2.50	1.50
110	Bob Moose	1.50	.70	.45
111	Mike Hegan	1.50	.70	.45
112	Dave Nelson	1.50	.70	.45
113	Jim Ray	1.50	.70	.45
114	Gene Michael	1.50	.70	.45
115	Alex Johnson	1.50	.70	.45
116	Sparky Lyle	1.50	.70	.45
117	Don Young	1.50	.70	.45
118	George Mitterwald	1.50	.70	.45
119	Chuck Taylor	1.50	.70	.45
120	Sal Bando	1.50	.70	.45
121	Orioles Rookies (Fred Beene, Terry Crowley)	1.50	.70	.45
122	George Stone	1.50	.70	.45
123	Don Gutteridge	1.50	.70	.45
124	Larry Jaster	2.50	1.25	.70
125	Deron Johnson	1.50	.70	.45
126	Marty Martinez	1.50	.70	.45
127	Joe Coleman	1.50	.70	.45
128	Checklist 2	1.50	.70	.45
129	Jimmie Price	1.50	.70	.45
130	Ollie Brown	1.50	.70	.45
131	Dodgers Rookies (Ray Lamb, Bob Stinson)	1.50	.70	.45
132	Jim McGlothlin	1.50	.70	.45
133	Clay Carroll	1.50	.70	.45
134	Danny Walton	1.50	.70	.45
135	Dick Dietz	1.50	.70	.45
136	Steve Hargan	1.50	.70	.45
137	Art Shamsky	1.50	.70	.45
138	Joe Foy	1.50	.70	.45
139	Rich Nye	1.50	.70	.45
140	Reggie Jackson	65.00	32.00	19.50
141	Pirates Rookies (Dave Cash, Johnny Jeter)	1.50	.70	.45
142	Fritz Peterson	1.50	.70	.45
143	Phil Gagliano	1.50	.70	.45
144	Ray Culp	1.50	.70	.45
145	Rico Carty	1.50	.70	.45
146	Danny Murphy	1.50	.70	.45
147	Angel Hermoso	2.50	1.25	.70
148	Earl Weaver	2.00	1.00	.60
149	Billy Champion	1.50	.70	.45
150	Harmon Killebrew	10.00	5.00	3.00
151	Dave Roberts	1.50	.70	.45
152	Ike Brown	1.50	.70	.45
153	Gary Gentry	1.50	.70	.45
154	Senators Rookies (Jan Dukes, Jim Miles)	1.50	.70	.45
155	Denis Menke	1.50	.70	.45
156	Eddie Fisher	1.50	.70	.45
157	Manny Mota	1.50	.70	.45
158	Jerry McNertney	1.50	.70	.45
159	Tommy Helms	1.50	.70	.45
160	Phil Niekro	5.00	2.50	1.50
161	Richie Scheinblum	1.50	.70	.45
162	Jerry Johnson	1.50	.70	.45
163	Syd O'Brien	1.50	.70	.45
164	Ty Cline	2.50	1.25	.70
165	Ed Kirkpatrick	1.50	.70	.45

166	Al Oliver	2.50	1.25	.70
167	Bill Burbach	1.50	.70	.45
168	Dave Watkins	1.50	.70	.45
169	Tom Hall	1.50	.70	.45
170	Billy Williams	8.50	4.25	2.50
171	Jim Nash	1.50	.70	.45
172	Braves Rookies (Ralph Garr, Garry Hill)	2.00	1.00	.60
173	Jim Hicks	1.50	.70	.45
174	Ted Sizemore	1.50	.70	.45
175	Dick Bosman	1.50	.70	.45
176	Jim Hart	1.50	.70	.45
177	Jim Northrup	1.50	.70	.45
178	Denny Lemaster	1.50	.70	.45
179	Ivan Murrell	1.50	.70	.45
180	Tommy John	2.00	1.00	.60
181	Sparky Anderson	1.50	.70	.45
182	Dick Hall	1.50	.70	.45
183	Jerry Grote	1.50	.70	.45
184	Ray Fosse	1.50	.70	.45
185	Don Mincher	1.50	.70	.45
186	Rick Joseph	1.50	.70	.45
187	Mike Hedlund	1.50	.70	.45
188	Manny Sanguillen	1.50	.70	.45
189	Yankees Rookies (Dave McDonald, Thurman Munson)	90.00	45.00	27.00
190	Joe Torre	1.50	.70	.45
191	Vicente Romo	1.50	.70	.45
192	Jim Qualls	1.50	.70	.45
193	Mike Wegener	2.50	1.25	.70
194	Chuck Manuel	1.50	.70	.45
195	N.L. Playoff Game 1 (Seaver Wins Opener!)	18.00	9.00	5.50
196	N.L. Playoff Game 2 (Mets Show Muscle!)	1.50	.70	.45
197	N.L. Playoff Game 3 (Ryan Saves The Day!)	60.00	30.00	18.00
198	N.L. Playoff Summary (We're Number One!)	12.00	6.00	3.50
199	A.L. Playoff Game 1 (Orioles Win A Squeaker!)	1.50	.70	.45
200	A.L. Playoff Game 2 (Powell Scores Winning Run!)	2.50	1.25	.70
201	A.L. Playoff Game 3 (Birds Wrap It Up!)	1.50	.70	.45
202	A.L. Playoffs Summary (Sweep Twins In Three!)	1.50	.70	.45
203	Rudy May	1.50	.70	.45
204	Len Gabrielson	1.50	.70	.45
205	Bert Campaneris	1.50	.70	.45
206	Clete Boyer	1.50	.70	.45
207	Tigers Rookies (Norman McRae, Bob Reed)	1.50	.70	.45
208	Fred Gladding	1.50	.70	.45
209	Ken Suarez	1.50	.70	.45
210	Juan Marichal	7.50	3.75	2.25
211	Ted Williams	25.00	12.50	7.50
212	Al Santorini	1.50	.70	.45
213	Andy Etchebarren	1.50	.70	.45
214	Ken Boswell	1.50	.70	.45
215	Reggie Smith	1.50	.70	.45
216	Chuck Hartenstein	1.50	.70	.45
217	Ron Hansen	1.50	.70	.45
218	Ron Stone	1.50	.70	.45
219	Jerry Kenney	1.50	.70	.45
220	Steve Carlton	21.00	10.50	6.25
221	Ron Brand	2.50	1.25	.70
222	Jim Rooker	1.50	.70	.45
223	Nate Oliver	1.50	.70	.45
224	Steve Barber	1.50	.70	.45
225	Lee May	1.50	.70	.45
226	Ron Perranoski	1.50	.70	.45
227	Astros Rookies (John Mayberry, Bob Watkins)	1.50	.70	.45
228	Aurelio Rodriguez	1.50	.70	.45
229	Rich Robertson	1.50	.70	.45
230	Brooks Robinson	18.00	9.00	5.50
231	Luis Tiant	1.50	.70	.45
232	Bob Didier	1.50	.70	.45
233	Lew Krausse	1.50	.70	.45
234	Tommy Dean	1.50	.70	.45
235	Mike Epstein	1.50	.70	.45
236	Bob Veale	1.50	.70	.45
237	Russ Gibson	1.50	.70	.45
238	Jose Laboy	3.00	1.50	.90
239	Ken Berry	1.50	.70	.45
240	Fergie Jenkins	15.00	7.50	4.50
241	Royals Rookies (Al Fitzmorris, Scott Northey)	1.50	.70	.45
242	Walter Alston	3.00	1.50	.90
243	Joe Sparma	2.50	1.25	.70
244	Checklist 3	1.50	.70	.45
245	Leo Cardenas	1.50	.70	.45
246	Jim McAndrew	1.50	.70	.45
247	Lou Klimchock	1.50	.70	.45
248	Jesus Alou	1.50	.70	.45
249	Bob Locker	1.50	.70	.45
250	Willie McCovey	12.50	6.25	3.75
251	Dick Schofield	1.50	.70	.45
252	Lowell Palmer	1.50	.70	.45
253	Ron Woods	1.50	.70	.45
254	Camilo Pascual	1.50	.70	.45
255	Jim Spencer	1.50	.70	.45
256	Vic Davalillo	1.50	.70	.45
257	Dennis Higgins	1.50	.70	.45
258	Paul Popovich	1.50	.70	.45
259	Tommie Reynolds	1.50	.70	.45
260	Claude Osteen	1.50	.70	.45
261	Curt Motton	1.50	.70	.45
262	Padres Rookies (Jerry Morales, Jim Williams)	1.50	.70	.45
263	Duane Josephson	1.50	.70	.45
264	Rich Hebner	2.00	1.00	.60
265	Randy Hundley	2.00	1.00	.60
266	Wally Bunker	2.00	1.00	.60
267	Twins Rookies (Herman Hill, Paul Ratliff)	2.00	1.00	.60
268	Claude Raymond	2.00	1.00	.60
269	Cesar Gutierrez	2.00	1.00	.60
270	Chris Short	2.00	1.00	.60
271	Greg Goossen	2.00	1.00	.60
272	Hector Torres	2.00	1.00	.60
273	Ralph Houk	2.00	1.00	.60
274	Gerry Arrigo	2.00	1.00	.60
275	Duke Sims	2.00	1.00	.60
276	Ron Hunt	2.00	1.00	.60
277	Paul Doyle	2.00	1.00	.60
278	Tommie Aaron	2.00	1.00	.60
279	Bill Lee	2.00	1.00	.60
280	Donn Clendenon	2.00	1.00	.60
281	Casey Cox	2.00	1.00	.60
282	Steve Huntz	2.00	1.00	.60
283	Angel Bravo	2.00	1.00	.60
284	Jack Baldschun	2.00	1.00	.60
285	Paul Blair	2.00	1.00	.60
286	Dodgers Rookies (Bill Buckner, Jack Jenkins)	9.00	4.50	2.75
287	Fred Talbot	2.00	1.00	.60
288	Larry Hisle	2.00	1.00	.60
289	Gene Brabender	2.00	1.00	.60
290	Rod Carew	22.00	11.00	6.50
291	Leo Durocher	3.00	1.50	.90
292	Eddie Leon	2.00	1.00	.60
293	Bob Bailey	2.50	1.25	.70
294	Jose Azcue	2.00	1.00	.60
295	Cecil Upshaw	2.00	1.00	.60
296	Woody Woodward	2.00	1.00	.60
297	Curt Blefary	2.00	1.00	.60
298	Ken Henderson	2.00	1.00	.60
299	Buddy Bradford	2.00	1.00	.60
300	Tom Seaver	40.00	20.00	12.00
301	Chico Salmon	2.00	1.00	.60
302	Jeff James	2.00	1.00	.60
303	Brant Alyea	2.00	1.00	.60
304	Bill Russell	2.00	1.00	.60
305	World Series Game 1 (Buford Belts Leadoff Homer!)	2.00	1.00	.60
306	World Series Game 2 (Clendenon's Homer Breaks Ice!)	2.00	1.00	.60
307	World Series Game 3 (Agee's Catch Saves The Day!)	2.00	1.00	.60
308	World Series Game 4 (Martin's Bunt Ends Deadlock!)	2.00	1.00	.60
309	World Series Game 5 (Koosman Shuts The Door!)	2.00	1.00	.60
310	World Series Summary (Mets Whoop It Up!)	2.00	1.00	.60
311	Dick Green	2.00	1.00	.60
312	Mike Torrez	2.00	1.00	.60
313	Mayo Smith	2.00	1.00	.60
314	Bill McCool	2.00	1.00	.60
315	Luis Aparicio	11.00	5.50	3.25
316	Skip Guinn	2.00	1.00	.60
317	Red Sox Rookies (Luis Alvarado, Billy Conigliaro)	2.00	1.00	.60
318	Willie Smith	2.00	1.00	.60
319	Clayton Dalrymple	2.00	1.00	.60
320	Jim Maloney	2.00	1.00	.60
321	Lou Piniella	2.00	1.00	.60
322	Luke Walker	2.00	1.00	.60
323	Wayne Comer	2.00	1.00	.60
324	Tony Taylor	2.00	1.00	.60
325	Dave Boswell	2.00	1.00	.60
326	Bill Voss	2.00	1.00	.60
327	Hal King	2.00	1.00	.60
328	George Brunet	2.00	1.00	.60
329	Chris Cannizzaro	2.00	1.00	.60
330	Lou Brock	11.00	5.50	3.25
331	Chuck Dobson	2.00	1.00	.60
332	Bobby Wine	3.50	1.75	1.00
333	Bobby Murcer	2.00	1.00	.60
334	Phil Regan	2.00	1.00	.60
335	Bill Freehan	2.00	1.00	.60
336	Del Unser	2.00	1.00	.60
337	Mike McCormick	2.00	1.00	.60
338	Paul Schaal	2.00	1.00	.60
339	Johnny Edwards	2.00	1.00	.60
340	Tony Conigliaro	4.50	2.25	1.25
341	Bill Sudakis	2.00	1.00	.60
342	Wilbur Wood	2.00	1.00	.60
343	Checklist 4	2.50	1.25	.70
344	Marcelino Lopez	2.00	1.00	.60
345	Al Ferrara	2.00	1.00	.60
346	Red Schoendienst	4.00	2.00	1.25
347	Russ Snyder	2.00	1.00	.60
348	Mets Rookies (Jesse Hudson, Mike Jorgensen)	2.00	1.00	.60
349	Steve Hamilton	2.00	1.00	.60
350	Roberto Clemente	95.00	47.00	28.00
351	Tom Murphy	2.00	1.00	.60
352	Bob Barton	2.00	1.00	.60
353	Stan Williams	2.00	1.00	.60
354	Amos Otis	2.00	1.00	.60
355	Doug Rader	2.00	1.00	.60
356	Fred Lasher	2.00	1.00	.60
357	Bob Burda	2.00	1.00	.60
358	Pedro Borbon	2.00	1.00	.60
359	Phil Roof	2.00	1.00	.60
360	Curt Flood	2.00	1.00	.60
361	Ray Jarvis	2.00	1.00	.60
362	Joe Hague	2.00	1.00	.60
363	Tom Shopay	2.00	1.00	.60
364	Dan McGinn	3.00	1.50	.90
365	Zoilo Versalles	2.00	1.00	.60
366	Barry Moore	2.00	1.00	.60
367	Mike Lum	2.00	1.00	.60
368	Ed Herrmann	2.00	1.00	.60
369	Alan Foster	2.00	1.00	.60
370	Tommy Harper	2.00	1.00	.60
371	Rod Gaspar	2.00	1.00	.60
372	Dave Giusti	2.00	1.00	.60
373	Roy White	2.00	1.00	.60
374	Tommie Sisk	2.00	1.00	.60
375	Johnny Callison	2.00	1.00	.60
376	Lefty Phillips	2.00	1.00	.60
377	Bill Butler	2.00	1.00	.60
378	Jim Davenport	2.00	1.00	.60
379	Tom Tischinski	2.00	1.00	.60
380	Tony Perez	7.50	3.75	2.25
381	Athletics Rookies (Bobby Brooks, Mike Olivo)	2.00	1.00	.60
382	Jack DiLauro	2.00	1.00	.60
383	Mickey Stanley	2.00	1.00	.60
384	Gary Neibauer	2.00	1.00	.60
385	George Scott	2.00	1.00	.60
386	Bill Dillman	2.00	1.00	.60
387	Orioles Team	2.00	1.00	.60
388	Byron Browne	2.00	1.00	.60
389	Jim Shellenback	2.00	1.00	.60
390	Willie Davis	2.00	1.00	.60
391	Larry Brown	2.00	1.00	.60
392	Walt Hriniak	2.00	1.00	.60
393	John Gelnar	2.00	1.00	.60
394	Gil Hodges	7.50	3.75	2.25
395	Walt Williams	2.00	1.00	.60
396	Steve Blass	2.00	1.00	.60
397	Roger Repoz	2.00	1.00	.60
398	Bill Stoneman	3.50	1.75	1.00
399	Yankees Team	2.50	1.25	.70
400	Denny McLain	3.00	1.50	.90
401	Giants Rookies (John Harrell, Bernie Williams)	2.00	1.00	.60
402	Ellie Rodriguez	2.00	1.00	.60
403	Jim Bunning	10.00	5.00	3.00
404	Rich Reese	2.00	1.00	.60
405	Bill Hands	2.00	1.00	.60
406	Mike Andrews	2.00	1.00	.60
407	Bob Watson	2.00	1.00	.60
408	Paul Lindblad	2.00	1.00	.60
409	Bob Tolan	2.00	1.00	.60
410	Boog Powell	2.50	1.25	.70
411	Dodgers Team	2.00	1.00	.60
412	Larry Burchart	2.00	1.00	.60
413	Sonny Jackson	2.00	1.00	.60
414	Paul Edmondson	2.00	1.00	.60
415	Julian Javier	2.00	1.00	.60
416	Joe Verbanic	2.00	1.00	.60
417	John Bateman	2.00	1.00	.60
418	John Donaldson	2.00	1.00	.60
419	Ron Taylor	2.00	1.00	.60
420	Ken McMullen	2.00	1.00	.60
421	Pat Dobson	2.00	1.00	.60
422	Royals Team	2.00	1.00	.60
423	Jerry May	2.00	1.00	.60
424	Mike Kilkenny	2.00	1.00	.60
425	Bobby Bonds	10.00	5.00	3.00
426	Bill Rigney	2.00	1.00	.60
427	Fred Norman	2.00	1.00	.60
428	Don Buford	2.00	1.00	.60
429	Cubs Rookies (Randy Bobb, Jim Cosman)	2.00	1.00	.60
430	Andy Messersmith	2.00	1.00	.60
431	Ron Swoboda	2.00	1.00	.60
432	Checklist 5	2.00	1.00	.60
433	Ron Bryant	2.00	1.00	.60
434	Felipe Alou	4.00	2.00	1.25
435	Nelson Briles	2.00	1.00	.60
436	Phillies Team	2.00	1.00	.60
437	Danny Cater	2.00	1.00	.60
438	Pat Jarvis	2.00	1.00	.60
439	Lee Maye	2.00	1.00	.60
440	Bill Mazeroski	4.00	2.00	1.25
441	John O'Donoghue	2.00	1.00	.60
442	Gene Mauch	3.50	1.75	1.00
443	Al Jackson	2.00	1.00	.60
444	White Sox Rookies (Billy Farmer, John Matias)	2.00	1.00	.60
445	Vada Pinson	2.00	1.00	.60
446	Billy Grabarkewitz	2.00	1.00	.60
447	Lee Stange	2.00	1.00	.60
448	Astros Team	2.00	1.00	.60
449	Jim Palmer	21.00	10.50	6.25
450	Willie McCovey AS	2.50	1.25	.70
451	Boog Powell AS	2.00	1.00	.60
452	Felix Millan AS	2.00	1.00	.60
453	Rod Carew AS	5.00	2.50	1.50
454	Ron Santo AS	2.50	1.25	.70
455	Brooks Robinson AS	9.00	4.50	2.75
456	Don Kessinger AS	2.00	1.00	.60
457	Rico Petrocelli AS	2.00	1.00	.60
458	Pete Rose AS	12.00	6.00	3.50
459	Reggie Jackson AS	9.00	4.50	2.75
460	Matty Alou AS	2.50	1.25	.70
461	Carl Yastrzemski AS	7.00	3.50	2.00
462	Hank Aaron AS	15.00	7.50	4.50
463	Frank Robinson AS	7.00	3.50	2.00
464	Johnny Bench AS	10.00	5.00	3.00
465	Bill Freehan (All-Star)	2.50	1.25	.70
466	Juan Marichal AS	3.00	1.50	.90
467	Denny McLain AS	3.00	1.50	.90
468	Jerry Koosman AS	2.50	1.25	.70
469	Sam McDowell AS	2.50	1.25	.70
470	Willie Stargell	11.00	5.50	3.25
471	Chris Zachary	2.50	1.25	.70
472	Braves Team	2.50	1.25	.70
473	Don Bryant	2.50	1.25	.70
474	Dick Kelley	2.50	1.25	.70
475	Dick McAuliffe	2.50	1.25	.70
476	Don Shaw	3.00	1.50	.90
477	Orioles Rookies (Roger Freed, Al Severinsen)	2.50	1.25	.70
478	Bob Heise	2.50	1.25	.70
479	Dick Woodson	2.50	1.25	.70
480	Glenn Beckert	2.50	1.25	.70
481	Jose Tartabull	2.50	1.25	.70
482	Tom Hilgendorf	2.50	1.25	.70
483	Gail Hopkins	2.50	1.25	.70
484	Gary Nolan	2.50	1.25	.70
485	Jay Johnstone	2.50	1.25	.70
486	Terry Harmon	2.50	1.25	.70
487	Cisco Carlos	2.50	1.25	.70

488	J.C. Martin	2.50	1.25	.70
489	Eddie Kasko	2.50	1.25	.70
490	Bill Singer	2.50	1.25	.70
491	Graig Nettles	4.50	2.25	1.25
492	Astros Rookies (Keith Lampard, Scipio Spinks)	2.50	1.25	.70
493	Lindy McDaniel	2.50	1.25	.70
494	Larry Stahl	2.50	1.25	.70
495	Dave Morehead	2.50	1.25	.70
496	Steve Whitaker	2.50	1.25	.70
497	Eddie Watt	2.50	1.25	.70
498	Al Weis	2.50	1.25	.70
499	Skip Lockwood	2.50	1.25	.70
500	Hank Aaron	75.00	37.00	22.00
501	White Sox Team	2.50	1.25	.70
502	Rollie Fingers	16.00	8.00	4.75
503	Dal Maxvill	2.50	1.25	.70
504	Don Pavletich	2.50	1.25	.70
505	Ken Holtzman	2.50	1.25	.70
506	Ed Stroud	2.50	1.25	.70
507	Pat Corrales	2.50	1.25	.70
508	Joe Niekro	2.50	1.25	.70
509	Expos Team	6.00	3.00	1.75
510	Tony Oliva	2.50	1.25	.70
511	Joe Hoerner	2.50	1.25	.70
512	Billy Harris	2.50	1.25	.70
513	Preston Gomez	2.50	1.25	.70
514	Steve Hovley	2.50	1.25	.70
515	Don Wilson	2.50	1.25	.70
516	Yankees Rookies (John Ellis, Jim Lyttle)	2.50	1.25	.70
517	Joe Gibbon	2.50	1.25	.70
518	Bill Melton	2.50	1.25	.70
519	Don McMahon	2.50	1.25	.70
520	Willie Horton	2.50	1.25	.70
521	Cal Koonce	2.50	1.25	.70
522	Angels Team	2.50	1.25	.70
523	Jose Pena	2.50	1.25	.70
524	Alvin Dark	2.50	1.25	.70
525	Jerry Adair	2.50	1.25	.70
526	Ron Herbel	2.50	1.25	.70
527	Don Bosch	4.00	2.00	1.25
528	Elrod Hendricks	2.50	1.25	.70
529	Bob Aspromonte	2.50	1.25	.70
530	Bob Gibson	18.00	9.00	5.50
531	Ron Clark	2.50	1.25	.70
532	Danny Murtaugh	2.50	1.25	.70
533	Buzz Stephen	2.50	1.25	.70
534	Twins Team	2.50	1.25	.70
535	Andy Kosco	2.50	1.25	.70
536	Mike Kekich	2.50	1.25	.70
537	Joe Morgan	12.00	6.00	3.50
538	Bob Humphreys	2.50	1.25	.70
539	Phillies Rookies (Larry Bowa, Dennis Doyle)	4.50	2.25	1.25
540	Gary Peters	2.50	1.25	.70
541	Bill Heath	2.50	1.25	.70
542	Checklist 6	2.50	1.25	.70
543	Clyde Wright	2.50	1.25	.70
544	Reds Team	2.50	1.25	.70
545	Ken Harrelson	2.50	1.25	.70
546	Ron Reed	2.50	1.25	.70

1971 O-Pee-Chee

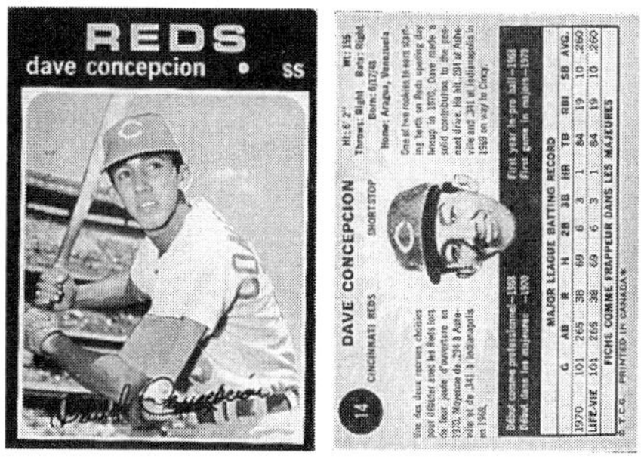

For 1971 O-Pee-Chee increased the number of cards in its set to 752, the same as the 1971 Topps set, which shares the same black-bordered design. The backs of the OPC are printed in yellow, rather than green, in a slightly different format and (except card numbers 524-752) are printed in both French and English. The words "Printed in Canada" appear on the back. Fourteen of the OPC cards have different photos from their corresponding Topps cards or list the player with a different team. The cards measure the standard 2-1/2" x 3-1/2".

		NM	EX	VG
	Complete Set (752):	2900.	1400.	850.00
	Common Player (1-393):	2.00	1.00	.60
	Common Player (394-523):	2.50	1.25	.70
	Common Player (524-643):	4.00	2.00	1.25
	Common Player (644-752):	6.00	3.00	1.75
1	World Champions (Orioles Team)	15.00	7.50	4.50
2	Dock Ellis	2.00	1.00	.60
3	Dick McAuliffe	2.00	1.00	.60
4	Vic Davalillo	2.00	1.00	.60
5	Thurman Munson	35.00	17.50	10.50
6	Ed Spiezio	2.00	1.00	.60
7	Jim Holt	2.00	1.00	.60
8	Mike McQueen	2.00	1.00	.60
9	George Scott	2.00	1.00	.60
10	Claude Osteen	2.00	1.00	.60
11	Elliott Maddox	2.00	1.00	.60
12	Johnny Callison	2.00	1.00	.60
13	White Sox Rookies (Charlie Brinkman, Dick Moloney)	2.00	1.00	.60
14	Dave Concepcion	18.00	9.00	5.50
15	Andy Messersmith	2.00	1.00	.60
16	Ken Singleton	2.00	1.00	.60
17	Billy Sorrell	2.00	1.00	.60
18	Norm Miller	2.00	1.00	.60
19	Skip Pitlock	2.00	1.00	.60
20	Reggie Jackson	55.00	27.00	16.50
21	Dan McGinn	3.00	1.50	.90
22	Phil Roof	2.00	1.00	.60
23	Oscar Gamble	2.00	1.00	.60
24	Rich Hand	2.00	1.00	.60
25	Clarence Gaston	3.50	1.75	1.00
26	Bert Blyleven	22.00	11.00	6.50
27	Pirates Rookies (Fred Cambria, Gene Clines)	2.00	1.00	.60
28	Ron Klimkowski	2.00	1.00	.60
29	Don Buford	2.00	1.00	.60
30	Phil Niekro	6.00	3.00	1.75
31	John Bateman	3.50	1.75	1.00
32	Jerry DaVanon	2.00	1.00	.60
33	Del Unser	2.00	1.00	.60
34	Sandy Vance	2.00	1.00	.60
35	Lou Piniella	2.00	1.00	.60
36	Dean Chance	2.00	1.00	.60
37	Rich McKinney	2.00	1.00	.60
38	Jim Colborn	2.00	1.00	.60
39	Tigers Rookies (Gene Lamont, Lerrin LaGrow)	2.00	1.00	.60
40	Lee May	2.00	1.00	.60
41	Rick Austin	2.00	1.00	.60
42	Boots Day	3.50	1.75	1.00
43	Steve Kealey	2.00	1.00	.60
44	Johnny Edwards	2.00	1.00	.60
45	Jim Hunter	9.00	4.50	2.75
46	Dave Campbell	2.00	1.00	.60
47	Johnny Jeter	2.00	1.00	.60
48	Dave Baldwin	2.00	1.00	.60
49	Don Money	2.00	1.00	.60
50	Willie McCovey	11.00	5.50	3.25
51	Steve Kline	2.00	1.00	.60
52	Braves Rookies (Oscar Brown, Earl Williams)	2.00	1.00	.60
53	Paul Blair	2.00	1.00	.60
54	Checklist 1	2.00	1.00	.60
55	Steve Carlton	24.00	12.00	7.25
56	Duane Josephson	2.00	1.00	.60
57	Von Joshua	2.00	1.00	.60
58	Bill Lee	2.00	1.00	.60
59	Gene Mauch	3.50	1.75	1.00
60	Dick Bosman	2.00	1.00	.60
61	A.L. Batting Leaders (Alex Johnson, Tony Oliva, Carl Yastrzemski)	2.00	1.00	.60
62	N.L. Batting Leaders (Rico Carty, Manny Sanguillen, Joe Torre)	2.00	1.00	.60
63	A.L. RBI Leaders (Tony Conigliaro, Frank Howard, Boog Powell)	2.00	1.00	.60
64	N.L. RBI Leaders (Johnny Bench, Tony Perez, Billy Williams)	2.50	1.25	.70
65	A.L. HR Leaders (Frank Howard, Harmon Killebrew, Carl Yastrzemski)	2.50	1.25	.70
66	N.L. HR Leaders (Johnny Bench, Tony Perez, Billy Williams)	2.50	1.25	.70
67	A.L. ERA Leaders (Jim Palmer, Diego Segui, Clyde Wright)	2.00	1.00	.60
68	N.L. ERA Leader (Tom Seaver, Wayne Simpson, Luke Walker)	2.00	1.00	.60
69	A.L. Pitching Leaders (Mike Cuellar, Dave McNally, Jim Perry)	2.00	1.00	.60
70	N.L. Pitching Leaders (Bob Gibson, Fergie Jenkins, Gaylord Perry)	2.00	1.00	.60
71	A.L. Strikeout Leaders (Bob Johnson, Mickey Lolich, Sam McDowell)	2.00	1.00	.60
72	N.L. Strikeout Leaders (Bob Gibson, Fergie Jenkins, Tom Seaver)	6.00	3.00	1.75
73	George Brunet	2.00	1.00	.60
74	Twins Rookies (Pete Hamm, Jim Nettles)	2.00	1.00	.60
75	Gary Nolan	2.00	1.00	.60
76	Ted Savage	2.00	1.00	.60
77	Mike Compton	2.00	1.00	.60
78	Jim Spencer	2.00	1.00	.60
79	Wade Blasingame	2.00	1.00	.60
80	Bill Melton	2.00	1.00	.60
81	Felix Millan	2.00	1.00	.60
82	Casey Cox	2.00	1.00	.60
83	Met Rookies (Randy Bobb, Tim Foli)	2.00	1.00	.60
84	Marcel Lachemann	2.00	1.00	.60
85	Billy Grabarkewitz	2.00	1.00	.60
86	Mike Kilkenny	2.00	1.00	.60
87	Jack Heidemann	2.00	1.00	.60
88	Hal King	2.00	1.00	.60
89	Ken Brett	2.00	1.00	.60
90	Joe Pepitone	2.00	1.00	.60
91	Bob Lemon	3.00	1.50	.90
92	Fred Wenz	2.00	1.00	.60
93	Senators Rookies (Norm McRae, Denny Riddleberger)	2.00	1.00	.60
94	Don Hahn	3.00	1.50	.90
95	Luis Tiant	2.00	1.00	.60
96	Joe Hague	2.00	1.00	.60
97	Floyd Wicker	2.00	1.00	.60
98	Joe Decker	2.00	1.00	.60
99	Mark Belanger	2.00	1.00	.60
100	Pete Rose	60.00	30.00	18.00
101	Les Cain	2.00	1.00	.60
102	Astros Rookies (Ken Forsch, Larry Howard)	2.00	1.00	.60
103	Rich Severson	2.00	1.00	.60
104	Dan Frisella	2.00	1.00	.60
105	Tony Conigliaro	3.50	1.75	1.00
106	Tom Dukes	2.00	1.00	.60
107	Roy Foster	2.00	1.00	.60
108	John Cumberland	2.00	1.00	.60
109	Steve Hovley	2.00	1.00	.60
110	Bill Mazeroski	3.50	1.75	1.00
111	Yankees Rookies (Loyd Colson, Bobby Mitchell)	2.00	1.00	.60
112	Manny Mota	2.00	1.00	.60
113	Jerry Crider	2.00	1.00	.60
114	Billy Conigliaro	2.00	1.00	.60
115	Donn Clendenon	2.00	1.00	.60
116	Ken Sanders	2.00	1.00	.60
117	Ted Simmons	9.00	4.50	2.75
118	Cookie Rojas	2.00	1.00	.60
119	Frank Lucchesi	2.00	1.00	.60
120	Willie Horton	2.00	1.00	.60
121	Cubs Rookies (Jim Dunegan, Roe Skidmore)	2.00	1.00	.60
122	Eddie Watt	2.00	1.00	.60
123	Checklist 2	2.00	1.00	.60
124	Don Gullett	2.00	1.00	.60
125	Ray Fosse	2.00	1.00	.60
126	Danny Coombs	2.00	1.00	.60
127	Danny Thompson	2.00	1.00	.60
128	Frank Johnson	2.00	1.00	.60
129	Aurelio Monteagudo	2.00	1.00	.60
130	Denis Menke	2.00	1.00	.60
131	Curt Blefary	2.00	1.00	.60
132	Jose Laboy	3.00	1.50	.90
133	Mickey Lolich	2.00	1.00	.60
134	Jose Arcia	2.00	1.00	.60
135	Rick Monday	2.00	1.00	.60
136	Duffy Dyer	2.00	1.00	.60
137	Marcelino Lopez	2.00	1.00	.60
138	Phillies Rookies (Joe Lis, Willie Montanez)	2.00	1.00	.60
139	Paul Casanova	2.00	1.00	.60
140	Gaylord Perry	9.00	4.50	2.75
141	Frank Quilici	2.00	1.00	.60
142	Mack Jones	3.00	1.50	.90
143	Steve Blass	2.00	1.00	.60
144	Jackie Hernandez	2.00	1.00	.60
145	Bill Singer	2.00	1.00	.60
146	Ralph Houk	2.00	1.00	.60
147	Bob Priddy	2.00	1.00	.60
148	John Mayberry	2.00	1.00	.60
149	Mike Hershberger	2.00	1.00	.60
150	Sam McDowell	2.00	1.00	.60
151	Tommy Davis	2.00	1.00	.60
152	Angels Rookies (Lloyd Allen, Winston Llenas)	2.00	1.00	.60
153	Gary Ross	2.00	1.00	.60
154	Cesar Gutierrez	2.00	1.00	.60
155	Ken Henderson	2.00	1.00	.60
156	Bart Johnson	2.00	1.00	.60
157	Bob Bailey	3.00	1.50	.90
158	Jerry Reuss	2.00	1.00	.60
159	Jarvis Tatum	2.00	1.00	.60
160	Tom Seaver	42.00	21.00	12.50
161	Ron Hunt	3.00	1.50	.90
162	Jack Billingham	2.00	1.00	.60
163	Buck Martinez	2.00	1.00	.60
164	Reds Rookies (Frank Duffy, Milt Wilcox)	2.00	1.00	.60
165	Cesar Tovar	2.00	1.00	.60
166	Joe Hoerner	2.00	1.00	.60
167	Tom Grieve	2.00	1.00	.60
168	Bruce Dal Canton	2.00	1.00	.60
169	Ed Herrmann	2.00	1.00	.60
170	Mike Cuellar	2.00	1.00	.60
171	Bobby Wine	3.50	1.75	1.00
172	Duke Sims	2.00	1.00	.60
173	Gil Garrido	2.00	1.00	.60
174	Dave LaRoche	2.00	1.00	.60
175	Jim Hickman	2.00	1.00	.60
176	Red Sox Rookies (Doug Griffin, Bob Montgomery)	2.00	1.00	.60
177	Hal McRae	2.00	1.00	.60
178	Dave Duncan	2.00	1.00	.60
179	Mike Corkins	2.00	1.00	.60
180	Al Kaline	25.00	12.50	7.50
181	Hal Lanier	2.00	1.00	.60
182	Al Downing	2.00	1.00	.60
183	Gil Hodges	4.00	2.00	1.25
184	Stan Bahnsen	2.00	1.00	.60
185	Julian Javier	2.00	1.00	.60
186	Bob Spence	2.00	1.00	.60
187	Ted Abernathy	2.00	1.00	.60
188	Dodgers Rookies (Mike Strahler, Bob Valentine)	2.00	1.00	.60
189	George Mitterwald	2.00	1.00	.60
190	Bob Tolan	2.00	1.00	.60
191	Mike Andrews	2.00	1.00	.60
192	Billy Wilson	2.00	1.00	.60
193	Bob Grich	2.00	1.00	.60
194	Mike Lum	2.00	1.00	.60
195	A.L. Playoff Game 1 (Powell Muscles Twins!)	2.00	1.00	.60
196	A.L. Playoff Game 2 (McNally Makes It Two Straight!)	2.00	1.00	.60
197	A.L. Playoff Game 3 (Palmer Mows 'Em Down!)	3.00	1.50	.90
198	A.L. Playoffs Summary (A Team Effort!)	2.00	1.00	.60
199	N.L. Playoff Game 1 (Cline Pinch-Triple Decides It!)	2.00	1.00	.60

200	N.L. Playoff Game 2 (Tolan Scores For Third Time!)	2.00	1.00	.60
201	N.L. Playoff Game 3 (Cline Scores Winning Run!)	2.00	1.00	.60
202	Claude Raymond	2.00	1.00	.60
203	Larry Gura	2.00	1.00	.60
204	Brewers Rookies (George Kopacz, Bernie Smith)	2.00	1.00	.60
205	Gerry Moses	2.00	1.00	.60
206	Checklist 3	2.00	1.00	.60
207	Alan Foster	2.00	1.00	.60
208	Billy Martin	2.50	1.25	.70
209	Steve Renko	3.00	1.50	.90
210	Rod Carew	35.00	17.50	10.50
211	Phil Hennigan	2.00	1.00	.60
212	Rich Hebner	2.00	1.00	.60
213	Frank Baker	2.00	1.00	.60
214	Al Ferrara	2.00	1.00	.60
215	Diego Segui	2.00	1.00	.60
216	Cardinals Rookies (Reggie Cleveland, Luis Melendez)	2.00	1.00	.60
217	Ed Stroud	2.00	1.00	.60
218	Tony Cloninger	2.00	1.00	.60
219	Elrod Hendricks	2.00	1.00	.60
220	Ron Santo	2.50	1.25	.70
221	Dave Morehead	2.00	1.00	.60
222	Bob Watson	2.00	1.00	.60
223	Cecil Upshaw	2.00	1.00	.60
224	Alan Gallagher	2.00	1.00	.60
225	Gary Peters	2.00	1.00	.60
226	Bill Russell	2.00	1.00	.60
227	Floyd Weaver	2.00	1.00	.60
228	Wayne Garrett	2.00	1.00	.60
229	Jim Hannan	2.00	1.00	.60
230	Willie Stargell	11.00	5.50	3.25
231	Indians Rookies (Vince Colbert, John Lowenstein)	2.00	1.00	.60
232	John Strohmayer	3.00	1.50	.90
233	Larry Bowa	2.00	1.00	.60
234	Jim Lyttle	2.00	1.00	.60
235	Nate Colbert	2.00	1.00	.60
236	Bob Humphreys	2.00	1.00	.60
237	Cesar Cedeno	2.00	1.00	.60
238	Chuck Dobson	2.00	1.00	.60
239	Red Schoendienst	3.00	1.50	.90
240	Clyde Wright	2.00	1.00	.60
241	Dave Nelson	2.00	1.00	.60
242	Jim Ray	2.00	1.00	.60
243	Carlos May	2.00	1.00	.60
244	Bob Tillman	2.00	1.00	.60
245	Jim Kaat	2.50	1.25	.70
246	Tony Taylor	2.00	1.00	.60
247	Royals Rookies (Jerry Cram, Paul Splittorff)	2.00	1.00	.60
248	Hoyt Wilhelm	3.50	1.75	1.00
249	Chico Salmon	2.00	1.00	.60
250	Johnny Bench	35.00	17.50	10.50
251	Frank Reberger	2.00	1.00	.60
252	Eddie Leon	2.00	1.00	.60
253	Bill Sudakis	2.00	1.00	.60
254	Cal Koonce	2.00	1.00	.60
255	Bob Robertson	2.00	1.00	.60
256	Tony Gonzalez	2.00	1.00	.60
257	Nelson Briles	2.00	1.00	.60
258	Dick Green	2.00	1.00	.60
259	Dave Marshall	2.00	1.00	.60
260	Tommy Harper	2.00	1.00	.60
261	Darold Knowles	2.00	1.00	.60
262	Padres Rookies (Dave Robinson, Jim Williams)	2.00	1.00	.60
263	John Ellis	2.00	1.00	.60
264	Joe Morgan	9.00	4.50	2.75
265	Jim Northrup	2.00	1.00	.60
266	Bill Stoneman	3.00	1.50	.90
267	Rich Morales	2.00	1.00	.60
268	Phillies Team	2.00	1.00	.60
269	Gail Hopkins	2.00	1.00	.60
270	Rico Carty	2.00	1.00	.60
271	Bill Zepp	2.00	1.00	.60
272	Tommy Helms	2.00	1.00	.60
273	Pete Richert	2.00	1.00	.60
274	Ron Slocum	2.00	1.00	.60
275	Vada Pinson	2.00	1.00	.60
276	Giants Rookies (Mike Davison, George Foster)	4.00	2.00	1.25
277	Gary Waslewski	2.00	1.00	.60
278	Jerry Grote	2.00	1.00	.60
279	Lefty Phillips	2.00	1.00	.60
280	Fergie Jenkins	25.00	12.50	7.50
281	Danny Walton	2.00	1.00	.60
282	Jose Pagan	2.00	1.00	.60
283	Dick Such	2.00	1.00	.60
284	Jim Gosger	3.00	1.50	.90
285	Sal Bando	2.00	1.00	.60
286	Jerry McNertney	2.00	1.00	.60
287	Mike Fiore	2.00	1.00	.60
288	Joe Moeller	2.00	1.00	.60
289	Rusty Staub	4.00	2.00	1.25
290	Tony Oliva	2.00	1.00	.60
291	George Culver	2.00	1.00	.60
292	Jay Johnstone	2.00	1.00	.60
293	Pat Corrales	2.00	1.00	.60
294	Steve Dunning	2.00	1.00	.60
295	Bobby Bonds	2.00	1.00	.60
296	Tom Timmermann	2.00	1.00	.60
297	Johnny Briggs	2.00	1.00	.60
298	Jim Nelson	2.00	1.00	.60
299	Ed Kirkpatrick	2.00	1.00	.60
300	Brooks Robinson	24.00	12.00	7.25
301	Earl Wilson	2.00	1.00	.60
302	Phil Gagliano	2.00	1.00	.60
303	Lindy McDaniel	2.00	1.00	.60
304	Ron Brand	3.00	1.50	.90
305	Reggie Smith	2.00	1.00	.60
306	Jim Nash	2.00	1.00	.60
307	Don Wert	2.00	1.00	.60
308	Cards Team	2.00	1.00	.60
309	Dick Ellsworth	2.00	1.00	.60

310	Tommie Agee	2.00	1.00	.60
311	Lee Stange	2.00	1.00	.60
312	Harry Walker	2.00	1.00	.60
313	Tom Hall	2.00	1.00	.60
314	Jeff Torborg	2.00	1.00	.60
315	Ron Fairly	3.50	1.75	1.00
316	Fred Scherman	2.00	1.00	.60
317	Athletics Rookies (Jim Driscoll, Angel Mangual)	2.00	1.00	.60
318	Rudy May	2.00	1.00	.60
319	Ty Cline	2.00	1.00	.60
320	Dave McNally	2.00	1.00	.60
321	Tom Matchick	2.00	1.00	.60
322	Jim Beauchamp	2.00	1.00	.60
323	Billy Champion	2.00	1.00	.60
324	Graig Nettles	2.00	1.00	.60
325	Juan Marichal	8.00	4.00	2.50
326	Richie Scheinblum	2.00	1.00	.60
327	World Series Game 1 (Powell Homers To Opposite Field!)	2.50	1.25	.70
328	World Series Game 2 (Buford Goes 2-For 4!)	2.00	1.00	.60
329	World Series Game 3 (F. Robinson Shows Muscle!)	3.00	1.50	.90
330	World Series Game 4 (Reds Stay Alive!)	2.00	1.00	.60
331	World Series Game 5 (B. Robinson Commits Robbery!)	3.00	1.50	.90
332	World Series Summary (Clinching Performance!)	2.00	1.00	.60
333	Clay Kirby	2.00	1.00	.60
334	Roberto Pena	2.00	1.00	.60
335	Jerry Koosman	2.00	1.00	.60
336	Tigers Team	2.00	1.00	.60
337	Jesus Alou	2.00	1.00	.60
338	Gene Tenace	2.00	1.00	.60
339	Wayne Simpson	2.00	1.00	.60
340	Rico Petrocelli	2.00	1.00	.60
341	Steve Garvey	55.00	27.00	16.50
342	Frank Tepedino	2.00	1.00	.60
343	Pirates Rookies (Ed Acosta, Milt May)	2.00	1.00	.60
344	Ellie Rodriguez	2.00	1.00	.60
345	Joe Horlen	2.00	1.00	.60
346	Lum Harris	2.00	1.00	.60
347	Ted Uhlaender	2.00	1.00	.60
348	Fred Norman	2.00	1.00	.60
349	Rich Reese	2.00	1.00	.60
350	Billy Williams	7.00	3.50	2.00
351	Jim Shellenback	2.00	1.00	.60
352	Denny Doyle	2.00	1.00	.60
353	Carl Taylor	2.00	1.00	.60
354	Don McMahon	2.00	1.00	.60
355	Bud Harrelson	2.00	1.00	.60
356	Bob Locker	2.00	1.00	.60
357	Reds Team	2.00	1.00	.60
358	Danny Cater	2.00	1.00	.60
359	Ron Reed	2.00	1.00	.60
360	Jim Fregosi	2.00	1.00	.60
361	Don Sutton	6.50	3.25	2.00
362	Orioles Rookies (Mike Adamson, Roger Freed)	2.00	1.00	.60
363	Mike Nagy	2.00	1.00	.60
364	Tommy Dean	2.00	1.00	.60
365	Bob Johnson	2.00	1.00	.60
366	Ron Stone	2.00	1.00	.60
367	Dalton Jones	2.00	1.00	.60
368	Bob Veale	2.00	1.00	.60
369	Checklist 4	2.00	1.00	.60
370	Joe Torre	4.00	2.00	1.25
371	Jack Hiatt	2.00	1.00	.60
372	Lew Krausse	2.00	1.00	.60
373	Tom McCraw	2.00	1.00	.60
374	Clete Boyer	2.00	1.00	.60
375	Steve Hargan	2.00	1.00	.60
376	Expos Rookies (Clyde Mashore, Ernie McAnally)	4.00	2.00	1.25
377	Greg Garrett	2.00	1.00	.60
378	Tito Fuentes	2.00	1.00	.60
379	Wayne Granger	2.00	1.00	.60
380	Ted Williams	10.00	5.00	3.00
381	Fred Gladding	2.00	1.00	.60
382	Jake Gibbs	2.00	1.00	.60
383	Rod Gaspar	2.00	1.00	.60
384	Rollie Fingers	9.00	4.50	2.75
385	Maury Wills	2.00	1.00	.60
386	Red Sox Team	2.00	1.00	.60
387	Ron Herbel	2.00	1.00	.60
388	Al Oliver	2.00	1.00	.60
389	Ed Brinkman	2.00	1.00	.60
390	Glenn Beckert	2.00	1.00	.60
391	Twins Rookies (Steve Brye, Cotton Nash)	2.00	1.00	.60
392	Grant Jackson	2.00	1.00	.60
393	Merv Rettenmund	2.00	1.00	.60
394	Clay Carroll	2.50	1.25	.70
395	Roy White	2.50	1.25	.70
396	Dick Schofield	2.50	1.25	.70
397	Alvin Dark	2.50	1.25	.70
398	Howie Reed	4.00	2.00	1.25
399	Jim French	2.50	1.25	.70
400	Hank Aaron	65.00	32.00	19.50
401	Tom Murphy	2.50	1.25	.70
402	Dodgers Team	2.50	1.25	.70
403	Joe Coleman	2.50	1.25	.70
404	Astros Rookies (Buddy Harris, Roger Metzger)	2.50	1.25	.70
405	Leo Cardenas	2.50	1.25	.70
406	Ray Sadecki	2.50	1.25	.70
407	Joe Rudi	2.50	1.25	.70
408	Rafael Robles	2.50	1.25	.70
409	Don Pavletich	2.50	1.25	.70
410	Ken Holtzman	2.50	1.25	.70
411	George Spriggs	2.50	1.25	.70
412	Jerry Johnson	2.50	1.25	.70
413	Pat Kelly	2.50	1.25	.70
414	Woodie Fryman	2.50	1.25	.70
415	Mike Hegan	2.50	1.25	.70

416	Gene Alley	2.50	1.25	.70
417	Dick Hall	2.50	1.25	.70
418	Adolfo Phillips	4.00	2.00	1.25
419	Ron Hansen	2.50	1.25	.70
420	Jim Merritt	2.50	1.25	.70
421	John Stephenson	2.50	1.25	.70
422	Frank Bertaina	2.50	1.25	.70
423	Tigers Rookies (Tim Marting, Dennis Saunders)	2.50	1.25	.70
424	Roberto Rodriguez	2.50	1.25	.70
425	Doug Rader	2.50	1.25	.70
426	Chris Cannizzaro	2.50	1.25	.70
427	Bernie Allen	2.50	1.25	.70
428	Jim McAndrew	2.50	1.25	.70
429	Chuck Hinton	2.50	1.25	.70
430	Wes Parker	2.50	1.25	.70
431	Tom Burgmeier	2.50	1.25	.70
432	Bob Didier	2.50	1.25	.70
433	Skip Lockwood	2.50	1.25	.70
434	Gary Sutherland	4.00	2.00	1.25
435	Jose Cardenal	2.50	1.25	.70
436	Wilbur Wood	2.50	1.25	.70
437	Danny Murtaugh	2.50	1.25	.70
438	Mike McCormick	2.50	1.25	.70
439	Phillie Rookies (Greg Luzinski, Scott Reid)	4.50	2.25	1.25
440	Bert Campaneris	2.50	1.25	.70
441	Milt Pappas	2.50	1.25	.70
442	Angels Team	2.50	1.25	.70
443	Rich Robertson	2.50	1.25	.70
444	Jimmie Price	2.50	1.25	.70
445	Art Shamsky	2.50	1.25	.70
446	Bobby Bolin	2.50	1.25	.70
447	Cesar Geronimo	2.50	1.25	.70
448	Dave Roberts	2.50	1.25	.70
449	Brant Alyea	2.50	1.25	.70
450	Bob Gibson	18.00	9.00	5.50
451	Joe Keough	2.50	1.25	.70
452	John Boccabella	4.00	2.00	1.25
453	Terry Crowley	2.50	1.25	.70
454	Mike Paul	2.50	1.25	.70
455	Don Kessinger	2.50	1.25	.70
456	Bob Meyer	2.50	1.25	.70
457	Willie Smith	2.50	1.25	.70
458	White Sox Rookies (Dave Lemonds, Ron Lolich)	2.50	1.25	.70
459	Jim LeFebvre	2.50	1.25	.70
460	Fritz Peterson	2.50	1.25	.70
461	Jim Hart	2.50	1.25	.70
462	Senators Team	2.50	1.25	.70
463	Tom Kelley	2.50	1.25	.70
464	Aurelio Rodriguez	2.50	1.25	.70
465	Tim McCarver	3.00	1.50	.90
466	Ken Berry	2.50	1.25	.70
467	Al Santorini	2.50	1.25	.70
468	Frank Fernandez	2.50	1.25	.70
469	Bob Aspromonte	2.50	1.25	.70
470	Bob Oliver	2.50	1.25	.70
471	Tom Griffin	2.50	1.25	.70
472	Ken Rudolph	2.50	1.25	.70
473	Gary Wagner	2.50	1.25	.70
474	Jim Fairey	4.00	2.00	1.25
475	Ron Perranoski	2.50	1.25	.70
476	Dal Maxvill	2.50	1.25	.70
477	Earl Weaver	5.00	2.50	1.50
478	Bernie Carbo	2.50	1.25	.70
479	Dennis Higgins	2.50	1.25	.70
480	Manny Sanguillen	2.50	1.25	.70
481	Daryl Patterson	2.50	1.25	.70
482	Padres Team	2.50	1.25	.70
483	Gene Michael	2.50	1.25	.70
484	Don Wilson	2.50	1.25	.70
485	Ken McMullen	2.50	1.25	.70
486	Steve Huntz	2.50	1.25	.70
487	Paul Schaal	2.50	1.25	.70
488	Jerry Stephenson	2.50	1.25	.70
489	Luis Alvarado	2.50	1.25	.70
490	Deron Johnson	2.50	1.25	.70
491	Jim Hardin	2.50	1.25	.70
492	Ken Boswell	2.50	1.25	.70
493	Dave May	2.50	1.25	.70
494	Braves Rookies (Ralph Garr, Rick Kester)	2.50	1.25	.70
495	Felipe Alou	6.00	3.00	1.75
496	Woody Woodward	2.50	1.25	.70
497	Horacio Pina	2.50	1.25	.70
498	John Kennedy	2.50	1.25	.70
499	Checklist 5	2.50	1.25	.70
500	Jim Perry	2.50	1.25	.70
501	Andy Etchebarren	2.50	1.25	.70
502	Cubs Team	2.50	1.25	.70
503	Gates Brown	2.50	1.25	.70
504	Ken Wright	2.50	1.25	.70
505	Ollie Brown	2.50	1.25	.70
506	Bobby Knoop	2.50	1.25	.70
507	George Stone	2.50	1.25	.70
508	Roger Repoz	2.50	1.25	.70
509	Jim Grant	2.50	1.25	.70
510	Ken Harrelson	2.50	1.25	.70
511	Chris Short	2.50	1.25	.70
512	Red Sox Rookies (Mike Garman, Dick Mills)	2.50	1.25	.70
513	Nolan Ryan	315.00	157.00	94.00
514	Ron Woods	2.50	1.25	.70
515	Carl Morton	4.50	2.25	1.25
516	Ted Kubiak	2.50	1.25	.70
517	Charlie Fox	2.50	1.25	.70
518	Joe Grzenda	2.50	1.25	.70
519	Willie Crawford	2.50	1.25	.70
520	Tommy John	2.50	1.25	.70
521	Leron Lee	2.50	1.25	.70
522	Twins Team	2.50	1.25	.70
523	John Odom	2.50	1.25	.70
524	Mickey Stanley	4.00	2.00	1.25
525	Ernie Banks	50.00	25.00	15.00
526	Ray Jarvis	4.00	2.00	1.25
527	Cleon Jones	4.00	2.00	1.25
528	Wally Bunker	4.00	2.00	1.25

529	N.L. Rookies (Bill Buckner, Enzo Hernandez, Marty Perez)	4.00	2.00	1.25
530	Carl Yastrzemski	50.00	25.00	15.00
531	Mike Torrez	4.00	2.00	1.25
532	Bill Rigney	4.00	2.00	1.25
533	Mike Ryan	4.00	2.00	1.25
534	Luke Walker	4.00	2.00	1.25
535	Curt Flood	4.00	2.00	1.25
536	Claude Raymond	6.00	3.00	1.75
537	Tom Egan	4.00	2.00	1.25
538	Angel Bravo	4.00	2.00	1.25
539	Larry Brown	4.00	2.00	1.25
540	Larry Dierker	4.00	2.00	1.25
541	Bob Burda	4.00	2.00	1.25
542	Bob Miller	4.00	2.00	1.25
543	Yankees Team	4.00	2.00	1.25
544	Vida Blue	4.00	2.00	1.25
545	Dick Dietz	4.00	2.00	1.25
546	John Matias	4.00	2.00	1.25
547	Pat Dobson	4.00	2.00	1.25
548	Don Mason	4.00	2.00	1.25
549	Jim Brewer	4.00	2.00	1.25
550	Harmon Killebrew	30.00	15.00	9.00
551	Frank Linzy	4.00	2.00	1.25
552	Buddy Bradford	4.00	2.00	1.25
553	Kevin Collins	4.00	2.00	1.25
554	Lowell Palmer	4.00	2.00	1.25
555	Walt Williams	4.00	2.00	1.25
556	Jim McGlothlin	4.00	2.00	1.25
557	Tom Satriano	4.00	2.00	1.25
558	Hector Torres	4.00	2.00	1.25
559	A.L. Rookies (Terry Cox, Bill Gogolewski, Gary Jones)	4.00	2.00	1.25
560	Rusty Staub	9.00	4.50	2.75
561	Syd O'Brien	4.00	2.00	1.25
562	Dave Giusti	4.00	2.00	1.25
563	Giants Team	4.00	2.00	1.25
564	Al Fitzmorris	4.00	2.00	1.25
565	Jim Wynn	4.00	2.00	1.25
566	Tim Cullen	4.00	2.00	1.25
567	Walt Alston	6.00	3.00	1.75
568	Sal Campisi	4.00	2.00	1.25
569	Ivan Murrell	4.00	2.00	1.25
570	Jim Palmer	40.00	20.00	12.00
571	Ted Sizemore	4.00	2.00	1.25
572	Jerry Kenney	4.00	2.00	1.25
573	Ed Kranepool	4.00	2.00	1.25
574	Jim Bunning	24.00	12.00	7.25
575	Bill Freehan	4.00	2.00	1.25
576	Cubs Rookies (Brock Davis, Adrian Garrett, Garry Jestadt)	4.00	2.00	1.25
577	Jim Lonborg	4.00	2.00	1.25
578	Eddie Kasko	4.00	2.00	1.25
579	Marty Pattin	4.00	2.00	1.25
580	Tony Perez	9.00	4.50	2.75
581	Roger Nelson	4.00	2.00	1.25
582	Dave Cash	4.00	2.00	1.25
583	Ron Cook	4.00	2.00	1.25
584	Indians Team	4.00	2.00	1.25
585	Willie Davis	4.00	2.00	1.25
586	Dick Woodson	4.00	2.00	1.25
587	Sonny Jackson	4.00	2.00	1.25
588	Tom Bradley	4.00	2.00	1.25
589	Bob Barton	4.00	2.00	1.25
590	Alex Johnson	4.00	2.00	1.25
591	Jackie Brown	4.00	2.00	1.25
592	Randy Hundley	4.00	2.00	1.25
593	Jack Aker	4.00	2.00	1.25
594	Cards Rookies (Bob Chlupsa, Al Hrabosky, Bob Stinson)	4.00	2.00	1.25
595	Dave Johnson	4.00	2.00	1.25
596	Mike Jorgensen	4.00	2.00	1.25
597	Ken Suarez	4.00	2.00	1.25
598	Rick Wise	4.00	2.00	1.25
599	Norm Cash	4.00	2.00	1.25
600	Willie Mays	135.00	67.00	40.00
601	Ken Tatum	4.00	2.00	1.25
602	Marty Martinez	4.00	2.00	1.25
603	Pirates Team	4.00	2.00	1.25
604	John Gelnar	4.00	2.00	1.25
605	Orlando Cepeda	22.00	11.00	6.50
606	Chuck Taylor	4.00	2.00	1.25
607	Paul Ratliff	4.00	2.00	1.25
608	Mike Wegener	6.00	3.00	1.75
609	Leo Durocher	6.00	3.00	1.75
610	Amos Otis	4.00	2.00	1.25
611	Tom Phoebus	4.00	2.00	1.25
612	Indians Rookies (Lou Camilli, Ted Ford, Steve Mingori)	4.00	2.00	1.25
613	Pedro Borbon	4.00	2.00	1.25
614	Billy Cowan	4.00	2.00	1.25
615	Mel Stottlemyre	4.00	2.00	1.25
616	Larry Hisle	4.00	2.00	1.25
617	Clay Dalrymple	4.00	2.00	1.25
618	Tug McGraw	4.00	2.00	1.25
619	Checklist 6	4.00	2.00	1.25
620	Frank Howard	4.00	2.00	1.25
621	Ron Bryant	4.00	2.00	1.25
622	Joe LaHoud	4.00	2.00	1.25
623	Pat Jarvis	4.00	2.00	1.25
624	Athletics Team	4.00	2.00	1.25
625	Lou Brock	32.00	16.00	9.50
626	Freddie Patek	4.00	2.00	1.25
627	Steve Hamilton	4.00	2.00	1.25
628	John Bateman	6.00	3.00	1.75
629	John Hiller	4.00	2.00	1.25
630	Roberto Clemente	150.00	75.00	45.00
631	Eddie Fisher	4.00	2.00	1.25
632	Darrel Chaney	4.00	2.00	1.25
633	A.L. Rookies (Bobby Brooks, Pete Koegel, Scott Northey)	4.00	2.00	1.25
634	Phil Regan	4.00	2.00	1.25
635	Bob Murcer	4.00	2.00	1.25
636	Denny Lemaster	4.00	2.00	1.25
637	Dave Bristol	4.00	2.00	1.25
638	Stan Williams	4.00	2.00	1.25
639	Tom Haller	4.00	2.00	1.25
640	Frank Robinson	50.00	25.00	15.00
641	Mets Team	12.00	6.00	3.50
642	Jim Roland	4.00	2.00	1.25
643	Rick Reichardt	4.00	2.00	1.25
644	Jim Stewart (SP)	12.00	6.00	3.50
645	Jim Maloney (SP)	12.00	6.00	3.50
646	Bobby Floyd (SP)	12.00	6.00	3.50
647	Juan Pizarro	6.00	3.00	1.75
648	Mets Rookies (Rich Folkers, Ted Martinez, Jon Matlack) (SP)	12.00	6.00	3.50
649	Sparky Lyle (SP)	12.00	6.00	3.50
650	Rich Allen	24.00	12.00	7.25
651	Jerry Robertson (SP)	12.00	6.00	3.50
652	Braves Team	7.00	3.75	2.25
653	Russ Snyder (SP)	12.00	6.00	3.50
654	Don Shaw (SP)	12.00	6.00	3.50
655	Mike Epstein (SP)	12.00	6.00	3.50
656	Gerry Nyman (SP)	12.00	6.00	3.50
657	Jose Azcue	6.00	3.00	1.75
658	Paul Lindblad (SP)	12.00	6.00	3.50
659	Byron Browne (SP)	12.00	6.00	3.50
660	Ray Culp	6.00	3.00	1.75
661	Chuck Tanner (SP)	12.00	6.00	3.50
662	Mike Hedlund (SP)	12.00	6.00	3.50
663	Marv Staehle	6.00	3.00	1.75
664	Major League Rookies (Archie Reynolds, Bob Reynolds, Ken Reynolds) (SP)	15.00	7.50	4.50
665	Ron Swoboda (SP)	15.00	7.50	4.50
666	Gene Brabender (SP)	12.00	6.00	3.50
667	Pete Ward	6.00	3.00	1.75
668	Gary Neibauer	6.00	3.00	1.75
669	Ike Brown (SP)	12.00	6.00	3.50
670	Bill Hands	6.00	3.00	1.75
671	Bill Voss (SP)	12.00	6.00	3.50
672	Ed Crosby (SP)	12.00	6.00	3.50
673	Gerry Janeski (SP)	12.00	6.00	3.50
674	Expos Team	12.00	6.00	3.50
675	Dave Boswell	6.00	3.00	1.75
676	Tommie Reynolds	6.00	3.00	1.75
677	Jack DiLauro (SP)	12.00	0.00	0.50
678	George Thomas	6.00	3.00	1.75
679	Don O'Riley	6.00	3.00	1.75
680	Don Mincher (SP)	12.00	6.00	3.50
681	Bill Butler	6.00	3.00	1.75
682	Terry Harmon	6.00	3.00	1.75
683	Bill Burbach (SP)	12.00	6.00	3.50
684	Curt Motton	6.00	3.00	1.75
685	Moe Drabowsky	6.00	3.00	1.75
686	Chico Ruiz (SP)	12.00	6.00	3.50
687	Ron Taylor (SP)	12.00	6.00	3.50
688	Sparky Anderson	24.00	12.00	7.25
689	Frank Baker	6.00	3.00	1.75
690	Bob Moose	6.00	3.00	1.75
691	Bob Heise	6.00	3.00	1.75
692	A.L. Rookies (Hal Haydel, Rogelio Moret, Wayne Twitchell) (SP)	12.00	6.00	3.50
693	Jose Pena (SP)	12.00	6.00	3.50
694	Rick Renick (SP)	12.00	6.00	3.50
695	Joe Niekro	6.00	3.00	1.75
696	Jerry Morales	6.00	3.00	1.75
697	Rickey Clark (SP)	12.00	6.00	3.50
698	Brewers Team	9.00	4.50	2.75
699	Jim Britton	9.00	4.50	2.75
700	Boog Powell	21.00	10.50	6.25
701	Bob Garibaldi	6.00	3.00	1.75
702	Milt Ramirez	6.00	3.00	1.75
703	Mike Kekich	6.00	3.00	1.75
704	J.C. Martin (SP)	12.00	6.00	3.50
705	Dick Selma (SP)	12.00	6.00	3.50
706	Joe Foy (SP)	12.00	6.00	3.50
707	Fred Lasher	6.00	3.00	1.75
708	Russ Nagelson (SP)	12.00	6.00	3.50
709	Major League Rookies (Dusty Baker, Don Baylor, Tom Paciorek)	75.00	37.00	22.00
710	Sonny Siebert	6.00	3.00	1.75
711	Larry Stahl (SP)	12.00	6.00	3.50
712	Jose Martinez	6.00	3.00	1.75
713	Mike Marshall (SP)	16.00	8.00	4.75
714	Dick Williams (SP)	12.00	6.00	3.50
715	Horace Clarke (SP)	12.00	6.00	3.50
716	Dave Leonhard	6.00	3.00	1.75
717	Tommie Aaron (SP)	12.00	6.00	3.50
718	Billy Wynne	6.00	3.00	1.75
719	Jerry May (SP)	12.00	6.00	3.50
720	Matty Alou	6.00	3.00	1.75
721	John Morris	6.00	3.00	1.75
722	Astros Team	12.00	6.00	3.50
723	Vicente Romo (SP)	12.00	6.00	3.50
724	Tom Tischinski (SP)	12.00	6.00	3.50
725	Gary Gentry (SP)	12.00	6.00	3.50
726	Paul Popovich	6.00	3.00	1.75
727	Ray Lamb (SP)	12.00	6.00	3.50
728	N.L. Rookies (Keith Lampard, Wayne Redmond, Bernie Williams)	6.00	3.00	1.75
729	Dick Billings	6.00	3.00	1.75
730	Jim Rooker	6.00	3.00	1.75
731	Jim Qualls (SP)	12.00	6.00	3.50
732	Bob Reed	6.00	3.00	1.75
733	Lee Maye (SP)	12.00	6.00	3.50
734	Rob Gardner (SP)	12.00	6.00	3.50
735	Mike Shannon (SP)	12.00	6.00	3.50
736	Mel Queen (SP)	12.00	6.00	3.50
737	Preston Gomez (SP)	12.00	6.00	3.50
738	Russ Gibson (SP)	12.00	6.00	3.50
739	Barry Lersch (SP)	12.00	6.00	3.50
740	Luis Aparicio	30.00	15.00	9.00
741	Skip Guinn	6.00	3.00	1.75
742	Royals Team	6.00	3.00	1.75
743	John O'Donoghue (SP)	15.00	7.50	4.50
744	Chuck Manuel (SP)	12.00	6.00	3.50
745	Sandy Alomar (SP)	12.00	6.00	3.50
746	Andy Kosco	6.00	3.00	1.75
747	N.L. Rookies (Balor Moore, Al Severinsen, Scipio Spinks)	15.00	7.50	4.50
748	John Purdin (SP)	12.00	6.00	3.50
749	Ken Szotkiewicz	6.00	3.00	1.75
750	Denny McLain (SP)	12.00	6.00	3.50
751	Al Weis (SP)	12.00	6.00	3.50
752	Dick Drago	6.00	3.00	1.75

1972 O-Pee-Chee

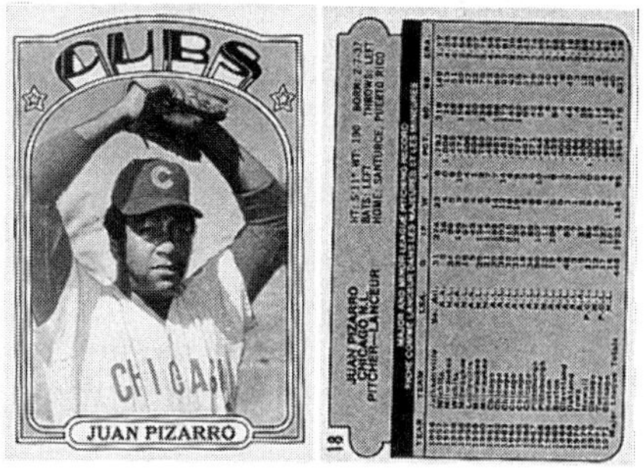

Identical in design to the Topps cards of the same year, the Canadian-issued 1972 O-Pee-Chee set numbers 525 cards, measuring 2-1/2" x 3-1/2". The backs state "Printed in Canada" and are written in both French and English. Unlike the 1972 Topps set, the O-Pee-Chee card of Gil Hodges notes the Mets' manager's death.

		NM	EX	VG
	Complete Set (525):	1400.	700.00	425.00
	Common Player (1-132):	.75	.40	.25
	Common Player (133-263):	1.00	.50	.30
	Common Player (264-394):	1.50	.75	.40
	Common Player (395-525):	2.00	1.00	.60
1	World Champions (Pirates Team)	9.00	4.50	2.75
2	Ray Culp	.75	.40	.25
3	Bob Tolan	.75	.40	.25
4	Checklist 1	1.50	.70	.45
5	John Bateman	1.50	.70	.45
6	Fred Scherman	.75	.40	.25
7	Enzo Hernandez	.75	.40	.25
8	Ron Swoboda	.75	.40	.25
9	Stan Williams	.75	.40	.25
10	Amos Otis	.75	.40	.25
11	Bobby Valentine	.75	.40	.25
12	Jose Cardenal	.75	.40	.25
13	Joe Grzenda	.75	.40	.25
14	Phillies Rookies (Mike Anderson, Pete Koegel, Wayne Twitchell)	.75	.40	.25
15	Walt Williams	.75	.40	.25
16	Mike Jorgensen	.75	.40	.25
17	Dave Duncan	.75	.40	.25
18	Juan Pizarro	.75	.40	.25
19	Billy Cowan	.75	.40	.25
20	Don Wilson	.75	.40	.25
21	Braves Team	.75	.40	.25
22	Rob Gardner	.75	.40	.25
23	Ted Kubiak	.75	.40	.25
24	Ted Ford	.75	.40	.25
25	Bill Singer	.75	.40	.25
26	Andy Etchebarren	.75	.40	.25
27	Bob Johnson	.75	.40	.25
28	Twins Rookies (Steve Brye, Bob Gebhard, Hal Haydel)	.75	.40	.25
29	Bill Bonham	.75	.40	.25
30	Rico Petrocelli	.75	.40	.25
31	Cleon Jones	.75	.40	.25
32	Cleon Jones (In Action)	.75	.40	.25
33	Billy Martin	1.50	.70	.45
34	Billy Martin (IA)	.75	.40	.25
35	Jerry Johnson	.75	.40	.25
36	Jerry Johnson (IA)	.75	.40	.25
37	Carl Yastrzemski	15.00	7.50	4.50
38	Carl Yastrzemski (IA)	7.50	3.75	2.25
39	Bob Barton	.75	.40	.25
40	Bob Barton (IA)	.75	.40	.25
41	Tommy Davis	.75	.40	.25
42	Tommy Davis (IA)	.75	.40	.25
43	Rick Wise	.75	.40	.25
44	Rick Wise (IA)	.75	.40	.25
45	Glenn Beckert	.75	.40	.25
46	Glenn Beckert (IA)	.75	.40	.25
47	John Ellis	.75	.40	.25
48	John Ellis (IA)	.75	.40	.25
49	Willie Mays	32.00	16.00	9.50
50	Willie Mays (IA)	15.00	7.50	4.50
51	Harmon Killebrew	7.50	3.75	2.25
52	Harmon Killebrew (IA)	3.00	1.50	.90
53	Bud Harrelson	.75	.40	.25
54	Bud Harrelson (IA)	.75	.40	.25
55	Clyde Wright	.75	.40	.25
56	Rich Chiles	.75	.40	.25
57	Bob Oliver	.75	.40	.25
58	Ernie McAnally	1.50	.70	.45
59	Fred Stanley	.75	.40	.25
60	Manny Sanguillen	.75	.40	.25
61	Cubs Rookies (Gene Hiser, Burt Hooton, Earl Stephenson)	.75	.40	.25
62	Angel Mangual	.75	.40	.25
63	Duke Sims	.75	.40	.25

64	Pete Broberg	.75	.40	.25
65	Cesar Cedeno	.75	.40	.25
66	Ray Corbin	.75	.40	.25
67	Red Schoendienst	2.00	1.00	.60
68	Jim York	.75	.40	.25
69	Roger Freed	.75	.40	.25
70	Mike Cuellar	.75	.40	.25
71	Angels Team	.75	.40	.25
72	Bruce Kison	.75	.40	.25
73	Steve Huntz	.75	.40	.25
74	Cecil Upshaw	.75	.40	.25
75	Bert Campaneris	.75	.40	.25
76	Don Carrithers	.75	.40	.25
77	Ron Theobald	.75	.40	.25
78	Steve Arlin	.75	.40	.25
79	Red Sox Rookies (Cecil Cooper, Carlton Fisk Mike Garman)	95.00	47.00	28.00
80	Tony Perez	4.00	2.00	1.25
81	Mike Hedlund	.75	.40	.25
82	Ron Woods	1.50	.70	.45
83	Dalton Jones	.75	.40	.25
84	Vince Colbert	.75	.40	.25
85	N.L. Batting Leaders (Glenn Beckert, Ralph Garr, Joe Torre)	.75	.40	.25
86	A.L. Batting Leaders (Bobby Murcer, Tony Oliva, Merv Rettenmund)	.75	.40	.25
87	N.L. RBI Leaders (Hank Aaron, Willie Stargell, Joe Torre)	1.50	.70	.45
88	A.L. RBI Leaders (Harmon Killebrew, Frank Robinson, Reggie Smith)	1.50	.70	.45
89	N.L. Home Run Leaders (Hank Aaron, Lee May, Willie Stargell)	1.50	.70	.45
90	A.L. Home Run Leaders (Norm Cash, Reggie Jackson, Bill Melton)	1.00	.50	.30
91	N.L. ERA Leaders (Dave Roberts, Tom Seaver, Don Wilson) (photo actually Danny Coombs)	1.00	.50	.30
92	A.L ERA Leaders (Vida Blue, Jim Palmer, Wilbur Wood)	1.00	.50	.30
93	N.L. Pitching Leaders (Steve Carlton, Al Downing, Fergie Jenkins, Tom Seaver)	5.00	2.50	1.50
94	A.L. Pitching Leaders (Vida Blue, Mickey Lolich, Wilbur Wood)	.75	.40	.25
95	N.L. Strikeout Leaders (Fergie Jenkins, Tom Seaver, Bill Stoneman)	1.50	.70	.45
96	A.L. Strikeout Leaders (Vida Blue, Joe Coleman, Mickey Lolich)	.75	.40	.25
97	Tom Kelley	.75	.40	.25
98	Chuck Tanner	.75	.40	.25
99	Ross Grimsley	.75	.40	.25
100	Frank Robinson	6.75	3.50	2.00
101	Astros Rookies (Ray Busse, Bill Greif, J.R. Richard)	1.00	.50	.30
102	Lloyd Allen	.75	.40	.25
103	Checklist 2	1.50	.70	.45
104	Toby Harrah	.75	.40	.25
105	Gary Gentry	.75	.40	.25
106	Brewers Team	.75	.40	.25
107	Jose Cruz	1.00	.50	.30
108	Gary Waslewski	.75	.40	.25
109	Jerry May	.75	.40	.25
110	Ron Hunt	1.50	.70	.45
111	Jim Grant	.75	.40	.25
112	Greg Luzinski	.75	.40	.25
113	Rogelio Moret	.75	.40	.25
114	Bill Buckner	.75	.40	.25
115	Jim Fregosi	.75	.40	.25
116	Ed Farmer	.75	.40	.25
117	Cleo James	.75	.40	.25
118	Skip Lockwood	.75	.40	.25
119	Marty Perez	.75	.40	.25
120	Bill Freehan	.75	.40	.25
121	Ed Sprague	.75	.40	.25
122	Larry Biittner	.75	.40	.25
123	Ed Acosta	.75	.40	.25
124	Yankees Rookies (Alan Closter, Roger Hambright, Rusty Torres)	.75	.40	.25
125	Dave Cash	.75	.40	.25
126	Bart Johnson	.75	.40	.25
127	Duffy Dyer	.75	.40	.25
128	Eddie Watt	.75	.40	.25
129	Charlie Fox	.75	.40	.25
130	Bob Gibson	7.50	3.75	2.25
131	Jim Nettles	.75	.40	.25
132	Joe Morgan	6.25	3.25	2.00
133	Joe Keough	1.00	.50	.30
134	Carl Morton	2.00	1.00	.60
135	Vada Pinson	1.00	.50	.30
136	Darrel Chaney	1.00	.50	.30
137	Dick Williams	1.00	.50	.30
138	Mike Kekich	1.00	.50	.30
139	Tim McCarver	1.00	.50	.30
140	Pat Dobson	1.00	.50	.30
141	Mets Rookies (Buzz Capra, Jon Matlack, Leroy Stanton)	1.00	.50	.30
142	Chris Chambliss	1.00	.50	.30
143	Garry Jestadt	1.00	.50	.30
144	Marty Pattin	1.00	.50	.30
145	Don Kessinger	1.00	.50	.30
146	Steve Kealey	1.00	.50	.30
147	Dave Kingman	4.00	2.00	1.25
148	Dick Billings	1.00	.50	.30
149	Gary Neibauer	1.00	.50	.30
150	Norm Cash	1.00	.50	.30
151	Jim Brewer	1.00	.50	.30
152	Gene Clines	1.00	.50	.30
153	Rick Auerbach	1.00	.50	.30
154	Ted Simmons	1.00	.50	.30
155	Larry Dierker	1.00	.50	.30
156	Twins Team	1.00	.50	.30
157	Don Gullett	1.00	.50	.30
158	Jerry Kenney	1.00	.50	.30
159	John Boccabella	2.00	1.00	.60
160	Andy Messersmith	1.00	.50	.30
161	Brock Davis	1.00	.50	.30
162	Brewers Rookies (Jerry Bell, Darrell Porter, Bob Reynolds) (Porter and Bell photos transposed)	1.00	.50	.30
163	Tug McGraw	1.00	.50	.30
164	Tug McGraw (IA)	1.00	.50	.30
165	Chris Speier	1.00	.50	.30
166	Chris Speier (IA)	1.00	.50	.30
167	Deron Johnson	1.00	.50	.30
168	Deron Johnson (IA)	1.00	.50	.30
169	Vida Blue	1.00	.50	.30
170	Vida Blue (IA)	1.00	.50	.30
171	Darrell Evans	1.00	.50	.30
172	Darrell Evans (IA)	1.00	.50	.30
173	Clay Kirby	1.00	.50	.30
174	Clay Kirby (IA)	1.00	.50	.30
175	Tom Haller	1.00	.50	.30
176	Tom Haller (IA)	1.00	.50	.30
177	Paul Schaal	1.00	.50	.30
178	Paul Schaal (IA)	1.00	.50	.30
179	Dock Ellis	1.00	.50	.30
180	Dock Ellis (IA)	1.00	.50	.30
181	Ed Kranepool	1.00	.50	.30
182	Ed Kranepool (IA)	1.00	.50	.30
183	Bill Melton	1.00	.50	.30
184	Bill Melton (IA)	1.00	.50	.30
185	Ron Bryant	1.00	.50	.30
186	Ron Bryant (IA)	1.00	.50	.30
187	Gates Brown	1.00	.50	.30
188	Frank Lucchesi	1.00	.50	.30
189	Gene Tenace	1.00	.50	.30
190	Dave Giusti	1.00	.50	.30
191	Jeff Burroughs	1.00	.50	.30
192	Cubs Team	1.00	.50	.30
193	Kurt Bevacqua	1.00	.50	.30
194	Fred Norman	1.00	.50	.30
195	Orlando Cepeda	6.00	3.00	1.75
196	Mel Queen	1.00	.50	.30
197	Johnny Briggs	1.00	.50	.30
198	Dodgers Rookies (Charlie Hough, Bob O'Brien, Mike Strahler)	6.00	3.00	1.75
199	Mike Fiore	1.00	.50	.30
200	Lou Brock	7.50	3.75	2.25
201	Phil Roof	1.00	.50	.30
202	Scipio Spinks	1.00	.50	.30
203	Ron Blomberg	1.00	.50	.30
204	Tommy Helms	1.00	.50	.30
205	Dick Drago	1.00	.50	.30
206	Dal Maxvill	1.00	.50	.30
207	Tom Egan	1.00	.50	.30
208	Milt Pappas	1.00	.50	.30
209	Joe Rudi	1.00	.50	.30
210	Denny McLain	1.50	.70	.45
211	Gary Sutherland	2.00	1.00	.60
212	Grant Jackson	1.00	.50	.30
213	Angels Rookies (Art Kusnyer, Billy Parker, Tom Silverio)	1.00	.50	.30
214	Mike McQueen	1.00	.50	.30
215	Alex Johnson	1.00	.50	.30
216	Joe Niekro	1.00	.50	.30
217	Roger Metzger	1.00	.50	.30
218	Eddie Kasko	1.00	.50	.30
219	Rennie Stennett	1.00	.50	.30
220	Jim Perry	1.00	.40	.30
221	N.L. Playoffs	1.00	.50	.30
222	A.L. Playoffs	1.00	.50	.30
223	World Series Game 1	1.00	.50	.30
224	World Series Game 2	1.00	.50	.30
225	World Series Game 3	1.00	.50	.30
226	World Series Game 4 (Roberto Clemente)	5.00	2.50	1.50
227	World Series Game 5	1.00	.50	.30
228	World Series Game 6	1.00	.50	.30
229	World Series Game 7	1.00	.50	.30
230	World Series Summary	1.00	.50	.30
231	Casey Cox	1.00	.50	.30
232	Giants Rookies (Chris Arnold, Jim Barr, Dave Rader)	1.00	.50	.30
233	Jay Johnstone	1.00	.50	.30
234	Ron Taylor	2.00	1.00	.60
235	Merv Rettenmund	1.00	.50	.30
236	Jim McGlothlin	1.00	.50	.30
237	Yankees Team	1.00	.50	.30
238	Leron Lee	1.00	.50	.30
239	Tom Timmermann	1.00	.50	.30
240	Rich Allen	2.00	1.00	.60
241	Rollie Fingers	8.00	4.00	2.50
242	Don Mincher	1.00	.50	.30
243	Frank Linzy	1.00	.50	.30
244	Steve Braun	1.00	.50	.30
245	Tommie Agee	1.00	.50	.30
246	Tom Burgmeier	1.00	.50	.30
247	Milt May	1.00	.50	.30
248	Tom Bradley	1.00	.50	.30
249	Harry Walker	1.00	.50	.30
250	Boog Powell	2.00	1.00	.60
251	Checklist 3	1.50	.70	.45
252	Ken Reynolds	1.00	.50	.30
253	Sandy Alomar	1.00	.50	.30
254	Boots Day	2.00	1.00	.60
255	Jim Lonborg	1.50	.70	.45
256	George Foster	1.50	.70	.45
257	Tigers Rookies (Jim Foor, Tim Hosley, Paul Jata)	1.00	.50	.30
258	Randy Hundley	1.00	.50	.30
259	Sparky Lyle	1.00	.50	.30
260	Ralph Garr	1.00	.50	.30
261	Steve Mingori	1.00	.50	.30
262	Padres Team	1.00	.50	.30
263	Felipe Alou	4.50	2.25	1.25
264	Tommy John	1.50	.70	.45
265	Wes Parker	1.50	.70	.45
266	Bobby Bolin	1.50	.70	.45
267	Dave Concepcion	1.50	.70	.45
268	A's Rookies (Dwain Anderson, Chris Floethe)	1.50	.70	.45
269	Don Hahn	1.50	.70	.45
270	Jim Palmer	12.00	6.00	3.50
271	Ken Rudolph	1.50	.70	.45
272	Mickey Rivers	1.50	.70	.45
273	Bobby Floyd	1.50	.70	.45
274	Al Severinsen	1.50	.70	.45
275	Cesar Tovar	1.50	.70	.45
276	Gene Mauch	2.50	1.25	.70
277	Elliot Maddox	1.50	.70	.45
278	Dennis Higgins	1.50	.70	.45
279	Larry Brown	1.50	.70	.45
280	Willie McCovey	8.00	4.00	2.50
281	Bill Parsons	1.50	.70	.45
282	Astros Team	1.50	.70	.45
283	Darrell Brandon	1.50	.70	.45
284	Ike Brown	1.50	.70	.45
285	Gaylord Perry	7.00	3.50	2.00
286	Gene Alley	1.50	.70	.45
287	Jim Hardin	1.50	.70	.45
288	Johnny Jeter	1.50	.70	.45
289	Syd O'Brien	1.50	.70	.45
290	Sonny Siebert	1.50	.70	.45
291	Hal McRae	1.50	.70	.45
292	Hal McRae (IA)	1.50	.70	.45
293	Danny Frisella	1.50	.70	.45
294	Dan Frisella (IA)	1.50	.70	.45
295	Dick Dietz	1.50	.70	.45
296	Dick Dietz (IA)	1.50	.70	.45
297	Claude Osteen	1.50	.70	.45
298	Claude Osteen (IA)	1.50	.70	.45
299	Hank Aaron	38.00	19.00	11.50
300	Hank Aaron (IA)	18.00	9.00	5.50
301	George Mitterwald	1.50	.70	.45
302	George Mitterwald (IA)	1.50	.70	.45
303	Joe Pepitone	1.50	.70	.45
304	Joe Pepitone (IA)	1.50	.70	.45
305	Ken Boswell	1.50	.70	.45
306	Ken Boswell (IA)	1.50	.70	.45
307	Steve Renko	1.50	.70	.45
308	Steve Renko (IA)	1.50	.70	.45
309	Roberto Clemente	50.00	25.00	15.00
310	Roberto Clemente (IA)	21.00	10.50	6.25
311	Clay Carroll	1.50	.70	.45
312	Clay Carroll (IA)	1.50	.70	.45
313	Luis Aparicio	6.00	3.00	1.75
314	Luis Aparicio (IA)	3.00	1.50	.90
315	Paul Splittorff	1.50	.70	.45
316	Cardinals Rookies (Jim Bibby, Santiago Guzman, Jorge Roque)	1.50	.70	.45
317	Rich Hand	1.50	.70	.45
318	Sonny Jackson	1.50	.70	.45
319	Aurelio Rodriguez	1.50	.70	.45
320	Steve Blass	1.50	.70	.45
321	Joe Lahoud	1.50	.70	.45
322	Jose Pena	1.50	.70	.45
323	Earl Weaver	1.50	.70	.45
324	Mike Ryan	1.50	.70	.45
325	Mel Stottlemyre	1.50	.70	.45
326	Pat Kelly	1.50	.70	.45
327	Steve Stone	1.50	.70	.45
328	Red Sox Team	1.50	.70	.45
329	Roy Foster	1.50	.70	.45
330	Jim Hunter	6.00	3.00	1.75
331	Stan Swanson	2.50	1.25	.70
332	Buck Martinez	1.50	.70	.45
333	Steve Barber	1.50	.70	.45
334	Rangers Rookies (Bill Fahey, Jim Mason, Tom Ragland)	1.50	.70	.45
335	Bill Hands	1.50	.70	.45
336	Marty Martinez	1.50	.70	.45
337	Mike Kilkenny	1.50	.70	.45
338	Bob Grich	1.50	.70	.45
339	Ron Cook	1.50	.70	.45
340	Roy White	1.50	.70	.45
341	Boyhood Photo (Joe Torre)	1.50	.70	.45
342	Boyhood Photo (Wilbur Wood)	1.50	.70	.45
343	Boyhood Photo (Willie Stargell)	1.50	.70	.45
344	Boyhood Photo (Dave McNally)	1.50	.70	.45
345	Boyhood Photo (Rick Wise)	1.50	.70	.45
346	Boyhood Photo (Jim Fregosi)	1.50	.70	.45
347	Boyhood Photo (Tom Seaver)	5.00	2.50	1.50
348	Boyhood Photo (Sal Bando)	1.50	.70	.45
349	Al Fitzmorris	1.50	.70	.45
350	Frank Howard	1.50	.70	.45
351	Braves Rookies (Jimmy Britton, Tom House, Rick Kester)	1.50	.70	.45
352	Dave LaRoche	1.50	.70	.45
353	Art Shamsky	1.50	.70	.45
354	Tom Murphy	1.50	.70	.45
355	Bob Watson	1.50	.70	.45
356	Gerry Moses	1.50	.70	.45
357	Woodie Fryman	1.50	.70	.45
358	Sparky Anderson	1.50	.70	.45
359	Don Pavletich	1.50	.70	.45
360	Dave Roberts	1.50	.70	.45
361	Mike Andrews	1.50	.70	.45
362	Mets Team	1.50	.70	.45
363	Ron Klimkowski	1.50	.70	.45
364	Johnny Callison	1.50	.70	.45
365	Dick Bosman	1.50	.70	.45
366	Jimmy Rosario	1.50	.70	.45
367	Ron Perranoski	1.50	.70	.45
368	Danny Thompson	1.50	.70	.45

369	Jim LeFebvre	1.50	.70	.45
370	Don Buford	1.50	.70	.45
371	Denny LeMaster	2.50	1.25	.70
372	Royals Rookie (Lance Clemons, Monty Montgomery)	1.50	.70	.45
373	John Mayberry	1.50	.70	.45
374	Jack Heidemann	1.50	.70	.45
375	Reggie Cleveland	1.50	.70	.45
376	Andy Kosco	1.50	.70	.45
377	Terry Harmon	1.50	.70	.45
378	Checklist 4	1.50	.70	.45
379	Ken Berry	1.50	.70	.45
380	Earl Williams	1.50	.70	.45
381	White Sox Team	1.50	.70	.45
382	Joe Gibbon	1.50	.70	.45
383	Brant Alyea	1.50	.70	.45
384	Dave Campbell	1.50	.70	.45
385	Mickey Stanley	1.50	.70	.45
386	Jim Colborn	1.50	.70	.45
387	Horace Clarke	1.50	.70	.45
388	Charlie Williams	1.50	.70	.45
389	Bill Rigney	1.50	.70	.45
390	Willie Davis	1.50	.70	.45
391	Ken Sanders	1.50	.70	.45
392	Pirates Rookies (Fred Cambria, Richie Zisk)	1.50	.70	.45
393	Curt Motton	1.50	.70	.45
394	Ken Forsch	1.50	.70	.45
395	Matty Alou	2.00	1.00	.60
396	Paul Lindblad	2.00	1.00	.60
397	Phillies Team	2.00	1.00	.60
398	Larry Hisle	2.00	1.00	.60
399	Milt Wilcox	2.00	1.00	.60
400	Tony Oliva	2.00	1.00	.60
401	Jim Nash	2.00	1.00	.60
402	Bobby Heise	2.00	1.00	.60
403	John Cumberland	2.00	1.00	.60
404	Jeff Torborg	2.00	1.00	.60
405	Ron Fairly	3.00	1.50	.90
406	George Hendrick	2.00	1.00	.60
407	Chuck Taylor	2.00	1.00	.60
408	Jim Northrup	2.00	1.00	.60
409	Frank Baker	2.00	1.00	.60
410	Fergie Jenkins	9.00	4.50	2.75
411	Bob Montgomery	2.00	1.00	.60
412	Dick Kelley	2.00	1.00	.60
413	White Sox Rookies (Don Eddy, Dave Lemonds)	2.00	1.00	.60
414	Bob Miller	2.00	1.00	.60
415	Cookie Rojas	2.00	1.00	.60
416	Johnny Edwards	2.00	1.00	.60
417	Tom Hall	2.00	1.00	.60
418	Tom Shopay	2.00	1.00	.60
419	Jim Spencer	2.00	1.00	.60
420	Steve Carlton	25.00	12.50	7.50
421	Ellie Rodriguez	2.00	1.00	.60
422	Ray Lamb	2.00	1.00	.60
423	Oscar Gamble	2.00	1.00	.60
424	Bill Gogolewski	2.00	1.00	.60
425	Ken Singleton	2.00	1.00	.60
426	Ken Singleton (IA)	2.00	1.00	.60
427	Tito Fuentes	2.00	1.00	.60
428	Tito Fuentes (IA)	2.00	1.00	.60
429	Bob Robertson	2.00	1.00	.60
430	Bob Robertson (IA)	2.00	1.00	.60
431	Clarence Gaston	3.50	1.75	1.00
432	Clarence Gaston (IA)	2.00	1.00	.60
433	Johnny Bench	32.00	16.00	9.50
434	Johnny Bench (IA)	16.00	8.00	4.75
435	Reggie Jackson	32.00	16.00	9.50
436	Reggie Jackson (IA)	17.00	8.50	5.00
437	Maury Wills	2.50	1.25	.70
438	Maury Wills (IA)	2.00	1.00	.60
439	Billy Williams	6.00	3.00	1.75
440	Billy Williams (IA)	3.00	1.50	.90
441	Thurman Munson	25.00	12.50	7.50
442	Thurman Munson (IA)	12.00	6.00	3.50
443	Ken Henderson	2.00	1.00	.60
444	Ken Henderson (IA)	2.00	1.00	.60
445	Tom Seaver	25.00	12.50	7.50
446	Tom Seaver (IA)	17.00	8.50	5.00
447	Willie Stargell	8.00	4.00	2.50
448	Willie Stargell (IA)	4.00	2.00	1.25
449	Bob Lemon	2.00	1.00	.60
450	Mickey Lolich	2.00	1.00	.60
451	Tony LaRussa	2.00	1.00	.60
452	Ed Herrmann	2.00	1.00	.60
453	Barry Lersch	2.00	1.00	.60
454	A's Team	2.00	1.00	.60
455	Tommy Harper	2.00	1.00	.60
456	Mark Belanger	2.00	1.00	.60
457	Padres Rookies (Darcy Fast, Mike Ivie, Derrel Thomas)	2.00	1.00	.60
458	Aurelio Monteagudo	2.00	1.00	.60
459	Rick Renick	2.00	1.00	.60
460	Al Downing	2.00	1.00	.60
461	Tim Cullen	2.00	1.00	.60
462	Rickey Clark	2.00	1.00	.60
463	Bernie Carbo	2.00	1.00	.60
464	Jim Roland	2.00	1.00	.60
465	Gil Hodges	5.00	2.50	1.50
466	Norm Miller	2.00	1.00	.60
467	Steve Kline	2.00	1.00	.60
468	Richie Scheinblum	2.00	1.00	.60
469	Ron Herbel	2.00	1.00	.60
470	Ray Fosse	2.00	1.00	.60
471	Luke Walker	2.00	1.00	.60
472	Phil Gagliano	2.00	1.00	.60
473	Dan McGinn	3.00	1.50	.90
474	Orioles Rookies (Don Baylor, Roric Harrison, Johnny Oates)	11.00	5.50	3.25
475	Gary Nolan	2.00	1.00	.60
476	Lee Richard	2.00	1.00	.60
477	Tom Phoebus	2.00	1.00	.60
478	Checklist 5	2.00	1.00	.60
479	Don Shaw	2.00	1.00	.60
480	Lee May	2.00	1.00	.60
481	Billy Conigliaro	2.00	1.00	.60
482	Joe Hoerner	2.00	1.00	.60
483	Ken Suarez	2.00	1.00	.60
484	Lum Harris	2.00	1.00	.60
485	Phil Regan	2.00	1.00	.60
486	John Lowenstein	2.00	1.00	.60
487	Tigers Team	2.00	1.00	.60
488	Mike Nagy	2.00	1.00	.60
489	Expos Rookies (Terry Humphrey, Keith Lampard)	4.00	2.00	1.25
490	Dave McNally	2.00	1.00	.60
491	Boyhood Photos (Lou Piniella)	2.00	1.00	.60
492	Boyhood Photos (Mel Stottlemyre)	2.00	1.00	.60
493	Boyhood Photos (Bob Bailey)	3.00	1.50	.90
494	Boyhood Photos (Willie Horton)	2.00	1.00	.60
495	Boyhood Photos (Bill Melton)	2.00	1.00	.60
496	Boyhood Photos (Bud Harrelson)	2.00	1.00	.60
497	Boyhood Photos (Jim Perry)	2.00	1.00	.60
498	Boyhood Photos (Brooks Robinson)	2.25	1.25	.70
499	Vicente Romo	2.00	1.00	.60
500	Joe Torre	4.00	2.00	1.25
501	Pete Hamm	2.00	1.00	.60
502	Jackie Hernandez	2.00	1.00	.60
503	Gary Peters	2.00	1.00	.60
504	Ed Spiezio	2.00	1.00	.60
505	Mike Marshall	3.50	1.75	1.00
506	Indians Rookies (Terry Ley, Jim Moyer, Dick Tidrow)	2.00	1.00	.60
507	Fred Gladding	2.00	1.00	.60
508	Ellie Hendricks	2.00	1.00	.60
509	Don McMahon	2.00	1.00	.60
510	Ted Williams	9.00	4.50	2.75
511	Tony Taylor	2.00	1.00	.60
512	Paul Popovich	2.00	1.00	.60
513	Lindy McDaniel	2.00	1.00	.60
514	Ted Sizemore	2.00	1.00	.60
515	Bert Blyleven	3.50	1.75	1.00
516	Oscar Brown	2.00	1.00	.60
517	Ken Brett	2.00	1.00	.60
518	Wayne Garrett	2.00	1.00	.60
519	Ted Abernathy	2.00	1.00	.60
520	Larry Bowa	2.00	1.00	.60
521	Alan Foster	2.00	1.00	.60
522	Dodgers Team	2.00	1.00	.60
523	Chuck Dobson	2.00	1.00	.60
524	Reds Rookies (Ed Armbrister, Mel Behney)	2.00	1.00	.60
525	Carlos May	2.00	1.00	.60

1973 O-Pee-Chee

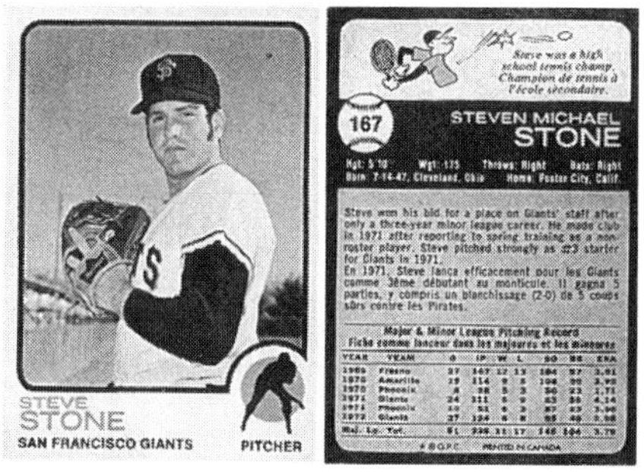

The 1973 Canadian-issued O-Pee-Chee set numbers 660 cards and is identical in design to the 1973 Topps set. The backs of the OPC cards are written in both French and English and contain the line "Printed in Canada" along the bottom. The cards measure 2-1/2" x 3-1/2". Unlike the '73 Topps set, which was issued in series of increasing scarcity throughout the summer, the '73 OPC cards were issued in a single series, with cards #529-660 being scarcer than the lower numbers.

		NM	EX	VG
Complete Set (660):		1100.	550.00	325.00
Common Player (1-528):		1.25	.60	.40
Common Player (529-660):		2.50	1.25	.70
1	All Time Home Run Leaders (Hank Aaron, Willie Mays, Babe Ruth)	35.00	17.50	10.50
2	Rich Hebner	1.25	.60	.40
3	Jim Lonborg	1.25	.60	.40
4	John Milner	1.25	.60	.40
5	Ed Brinkman	1.25	.60	.40
6	Mac Scarce	1.25	.60	.40
7	Rangers Team	1.25	.60	.40
8	Tom Hall	1.25	.60	.40
9	Johnny Oates	1.25	.60	.40
10	Don Sutton	4.00	2.00	1.25
11	Chris Chambliss	1.25	.60	.40
12	Padres Mgr./Coaches (Dave Garcia, Johnny Podres, Bob Skinner, Whitey Wietelmann, Don Zimmer)	1.25	.60	.40
13	George Hendrick	1.25	.60	.40
14	Sonny Siebert	1.25	.60	.40
15	Ralph Garr	1.25	.60	.40
16	Steve Braun	1.25	.60	.40
17	Fred Gladding	1.25	.60	.40
18	Leroy Stanton	1.25	.60	.40
19	Tim Foli	2.00	1.00	.60
20	Stan Bahnsen	1.25	.60	.40
21	Randy Hundley	1.25	.60	.40
22	Ted Abernathy	1.25	.60	.40
23	Dave Kingman	1.25	.60	.40
24	Al Santorini	1.25	.60	.40
25	Roy White	1.25	.60	.40
26	Pirates Team	1.25	.60	.40
27	Bill Gogolewski	1.25	.60	.40
28	Hal McRae	1.25	.60	.40
29	Tony Taylor	1.25	.60	.40
30	Tug McGraw	1.25	.60	.40
31	Buddy Bell	2.50	1.25	.70
32	Fred Norman	1.25	.60	.40
33	Jim Breazeale	1.25	.60	.40
34	Pat Dobson	1.25	.60	.40
35	Willie Davis	1.25	.60	.40
36	Steve Barber	1.25	.60	.40
37	Bill Robinson	1.25	.60	.40
38	Mike Epstein	1.25	.60	.40
39	Dave Roberts	1.25	.60	.40
40	Reggie Smith	1.25	.60	.40
41	Tom Walker	2.00	1.00	.60
42	Mike Andrews	1.25	.60	.40
43	Randy Moffitt	1.25	.60	.40
44	Rick Monday	1.25	.60	.40
45	Ellie Rodriguez	1.25	.60	.40
46	Lindy McDaniel	1.25	.60	.40
47	Luis Melendez	1.25	.60	.40
48	Paul Splittorff	1.25	.60	.40
49	Twins Mgr./Coaches (Vern Morgan, Frank Quilici, Bob Rodgers, Ralph Rowe, Al Worthington)	1.25	.60	.40
50	Roberto Clemente	65.00	32.00	19.50
51	Chuck Seelbach	1.25	.60	.40
52	Denis Menke	1.25	.60	.40
53	Steve Dunning	1.25	.60	.40
54	Checklist 1	1.25	.60	.40
55	Jon Matlack	1.25	.60	.40
56	Merv Rettenmund	1.25	.60	.40
57	Derrel Thomas	1.25	.60	.40
58	Mike Paul	1.25	.60	.40
59	Steve Yeager	1.25	.60	.40
60	Ken Holtzman	1.25	.60	.40
61	Batting Leaders (Rod Carew, Billy Williams)	1.25	.60	.40
62	Home Run Leaders (Dick Allen, Johnny Bench)	1.25	.60	.40
63	Runs Batted In Leaders (Dick Allen, Johnny Bench)	1.25	.60	.40
64	Stolen Base Leaders (Lou Brock, Bert Campaneris)	1.25	.60	.40
65	Earned Run Average Leaders (Steve Carlton, Luis Tiant)	1.25	.60	.40
66	Victory Leaders (Steve Carlton, Gaylord Perry, Wilbur Wood)	1.25	.60	.40
67	Strikeout Leaders (Steve Carlton, Nolan Ryan)	30.00	15.00	9.00
68	Leading Firemen (Clay Carroll, Sparky Lyle)	1.25	.60	.40
69	Phil Gagliano	1.25	.60	.40
70	Milt Pappas	1.25	.60	.40
71	Johnny Briggs	1.25	.60	.40
72	Ron Reed	1.25	.60	.40
73	Ed Herrmann	1.25	.60	.40
74	Billy Champion	1.25	.60	.40
75	Vada Pinson	1.25	.60	.40
76	Doug Rader	1.25	.60	.40
77	Mike Torrez	2.50	1.25	.70
78	Richie Scheinblum	1.25	.60	.40
79	Jim Willoughby	1.25	.60	.40
80	Tony Oliva	1.25	.60	.40
81	Cubs Mgr./Coaches (Hank Aguirre, Ernie Banks, Larry Jansen, Whitey Lockman, Pete Reiser)	1.50	.70	.45
82	Fritz Peterson	1.25	.60	.40
83	Leron Lee	1.25	.60	.40
84	Rollie Fingers	6.00	3.00	1.75
85	Ted Simmons	1.25	.60	.40
86	Tom McCraw	1.25	.60	.40
87	Ken Boswell	1.25	.60	.40
88	Mickey Stanley	1.25	.60	.40
89	Jack Billingham	1.25	.60	.40
90	Brooks Robinson	9.50	4.75	2.75
91	Dodgers Team	1.25	.60	.40
92	Jerry Bell	1.25	.60	.40
93	Jesus Alou	1.25	.60	.40
94	Dick Billings	1.25	.60	.40
95	Steve Blass	1.25	.60	.40
96	Doug Griffin	1.25	.60	.40
97	Willie Montanez	1.25	.60	.40
98	Dick Woodson	1.25	.60	.40
99	Carl Taylor	1.25	.60	.40
100	Hank Aaron	45.00	22.00	13.50
101	Ken Henderson	1.25	.60	.40
102	Rudy May	1.25	.60	.40
103	Celerino Sanchez	1.25	.60	.40
104	Reggie Cleveland	1.25	.60	.40
105	Carlos May	1.25	.60	.40
106	Terry Humphrey	2.00	1.00	.60
107	Phil Hennigan	1.25	.60	.40
108	Bill Russell	1.25	.60	.40
109	Doyle Alexander	1.25	.60	.40
110	Bob Watson	1.25	.60	.40
111	Dave Nelson	1.25	.60	.40
112	Gary Ross	1.25	.60	.40
113	Jerry Grote	1.25	.60	.40
114	Lynn McGlothen	1.25	.60	.40

115	Ron Santo	1.50	.70	.45
116	Yankees Mgr./Coache (Jim Hegan, Ralph Houk, Elston Howard, Dick Howser, Jim Turner)	1.25	.60	.40
117	Ramon Hernandez	1.25	.60	.40
118	John Mayberry	1.25	.60	.40
119	Larry Bowa	1.25	.60	.40
120	Joe Coleman	1.25	.60	.40
121	Dave Rader	1.25	.60	.40
122	Jim Strickland	1.25	.60	.40
123	Sandy Alomar	1.25	.60	.40
124	Jim Hardin	1.25	.60	.40
125	Ron Fairly	2.00	1.00	.60
126	Jim Brewer	1.25	.60	.40
127	Brewers Team	1.25	.60	.40
128	Ted Sizemore	1.25	.60	.40
129	Terry Forster	1.25	.60	.40
130	Pete Rose	35.00	17.50	10.50
131	Red Sox Mgr./Coaches (Doug Camilli, Eddie Kasko, Don Lenhardt, Eddie Popowski, Lee Stange)	1.25	.60	.40
132	Matty Alou	1.25	.60	.40
133	Dave Roberts	1.25	.60	.40
134	Milt Wilcox	1.25	.60	.40
135	Lee May	1.25	.60	.40
136	Orioles Mgr./Coaches (George Bamberger, Jim Frey, Billy Hunter, George Staller, Earl Weaver)	1.25	.60	.40
137	Jim Beauchamp	1.25	.60	.40
138	Horacio Pina	1.25	.60	.40
139	Carmen Fanzone	1.25	.60	.40
140	Lou Piniella	1.25	.60	.40
141	Bruce Kison	1.25	.60	.40
142	Thurman Munson	11.00	5.50	3.25
143	John Curtis	1.25	.60	.40
144	Marty Perez	1.25	.60	.40
145	Bobby Bonds	1.25	.60	.40
146	Woodie Fryman	1.25	.60	.40
147	Mike Anderson	1.25	.60	.40
148	Dave Goltz	1.25	.60	.40
149	Ron Hunt	2.00	1.00	.60
150	Wilbur Wood	1.25	.60	.40
151	Wes Parker	1.25	.60	.40
152	Dave May	1.25	.60	.40
153	Al Hrabosky	1.25	.60	.40
154	Jeff Torborg	1.25	.60	.40
155	Sal Bando	1.25	.60	.40
156	Cesar Geronimo	1.25	.60	.40
157	Denny Riddleberger	1.25	.60	.40
158	Astros Team	1.25	.60	.40
159	Clarence Gaston	2.50	1.25	.70
160	Jim Palmer	11.00	5.50	3.25
161	Ted Martinez	1.25	.60	.40
162	Pete Broberg	1.25	.60	.40
163	Vic Davalillo	1.25	.60	.40
164	Monty Montgomery	1.25	.60	.40
165	Luis Aparicio	5.00	2.50	1.50
166	Terry Harmon	1.25	.60	.40
167	Steve Stone	1.25	.60	.40
168	Jim Northrup	1.25	.60	.40
169	Ron Schueler	1.25	.60	.40
170	Harmon Killebrew	7.00	3.50	2.00
171	Bernie Carbo	1.25	.60	.40
172	Steve Kline	1.25	.60	.40
173	Hal Breeden	2.00	1.00	.60
174	Rich Gossage	12.00	6.00	3.50
175	Frank Robinson	9.00	4.50	2.75
176	Chuck Taylor	1.25	.60	.40
177	Bill Plummer	1.25	.60	.40
178	Don Rose	1.25	.60	.40
179	A's Mgr./Coaches (Jerry Adair, Vern Hoscheit, Irv Noren, Wes Stock, Dick Williams)	1.25	.60	.40
180	Fergie Jenkins	8.00	4.00	2.50
181	Jack Brohamer	1.25	.60	.40
182	Mike Caldwell	1.25	.60	.40
183	Don Buford	1.25	.60	.40
184	Jerry Koosman	1.25	.60	.40
185	Jim Wynn	1.25	.60	.40
186	Bill Fahey	1.25	.60	.40
187	Luke Walker	1.25	.60	.40
188	Cookie Rojas	1.25	.60	.40
189	Greg Luzinski	1.25	.60	.40
190	Bob Gibson	7.00	3.50	2.00
191	Tigers Team	1.25	.60	.40
192	Pat Jarvis	1.25	.60	.40
193	Carlton Fisk	30.00	15.00	9.00
194	Jorge Orta	1.25	.60	.40
195	Clay Carroll	1.25	.60	.40
196	Ken McMullen	1.25	.60	.40
197	Ed Goodson	1.25	.60	.40
198	Horace Clarke	1.25	.60	.40
199	Bert Blyleven	1.50	.70	.45
200	Billy Williams	6.00	3.00	1.75
201	A.L. Playoffs (Hendrick Scores Winning Run)	1.25	.60	.40
202	N.L. Playoffs (Foster's Run Decides It)	1.25	.60	.40
203	World Series Game 1 (Tenace The Menace)	1.25	.60	.40
204	World Series Game 2 (A's Make It Two Straight)	1.25	.60	.40
205	World Series Game 3 (Reds Win Squeeker)	1.25	.60	.40
206	World Series Game 4 (Tenace Singles In Ninth)	1.25	.60	.40
207	World Series Game 5 (Odom Out At Plate)	1.25	.60	.40
208	World Series Game 6 (Reds' Slugging Ties Series)	1.25	.60	.40
209	World Series Game 7 (Campy Starts Winning Rally)	1.25	.60	.40
210	World Series Summary (World Champions)	1.25	.60	.40
211	Balor Moore	2.00	1.00	.60
212	Joe Lahoud	1.25	.60	.40
213	Steve Garvey	6.00	3.00	1.75
214	Dave Hamilton	1.25	.60	.40
215	Dusty Baker	1.25	.60	.40
216	Toby Harrah	1.25	.60	.40
217	Don Wilson	1.25	.60	.40
218	Aurelio Rodriguez	1.25	.60	.40
219	Cardinals Team	1.25	.60	.40
220	Nolan Ryan	125.00	62.00	37.00
221	Fred Kendall	1.25	.60	.40
222	Rob Gardner	1.25	.60	.40
223	Bud Harrelson	1.25	.60	.40
224	Bill Lee	1.25	.60	.40
225	Al Oliver	1.25	.60	.40
226	Ray Fosse	1.25	.60	.40
227	Wayne Twitchell	1.25	.60	.40
228	Bobby Darwin	1.25	.60	.40
229	Roric Harrison	1.25	.60	.40
230	Joe Morgan	6.00	3.00	1.75
231	Bill Parsons	1.25	.60	.40
232	Ken Singleton	2.50	1.25	.70
233	Ed Kirkpatrick	1.25	.60	.40
234	Bill North	1.25	.60	.40
235	Jim Hunter	5.00	2.50	1.50
236	Tito Fuentes	1.25	.60	.40
237	Braves Mgr./Coaches (Lew Burdette, Jim Busby, Roy Hartsfield, Eddie Mathews, Ken Silvestri)	1.50	.70	.45
238	Tony Muser	1.25	.60	.40
239	Pete Richert	1.25	.60	.40
240	Bobby Murcer	1.25	.60	.40
241	Dwain Anderson	1.25	.60	.40
242	George Culver	1.25	.60	.40
243	Angels Team	1.25	.60	.40
244	Ed Acosta	1.25	.60	.40
245	Carl Yastrzemski	15.00	7.50	4.50
246	Ken Sanders	1.25	.60	.40
247	Del Unser	1.25	.60	.40
248	Jerry Johnson	1.25	.60	.40
249	Larry Biittner	1.25	.60	.40
250	Manny Sanguillen	1.25	.60	.40
251	Roger Nelson	1.25	.60	.40
252	Giants Mgr./Coaches (Joe Amalfitano, Charlie Fox, Andy Gilbert, Don McMahon, John McNamara)	1.25	.60	.40
253	Mark Belanger	1.25	.60	.40
254	Bill Stoneman	2.00	1.00	.60
255	Reggie Jackson	20.00	10.00	6.00
256	Chris Zachary	1.25	.60	.40
257	Mets Mgr./Coaches (Yogi Berra, Roy McMillan, Joe Pignatano, Rube Walker, Eddie Yost)	1.50	.70	.45
258	Tommy John	1.25	.60	.40
259	Jim Holt	1.25	.60	.40
260	Gary Nolan	1.25	.60	.40
261	Pat Kelly	1.25	.60	.40
262	Jack Aker	1.25	.60	.40
263	George Scott	1.25	.60	.40
264	Checklist 2	1.25	.60	.40
265	Gene Michael	1.25	.60	.40
266	Mike Lum	1.25	.60	.40
267	Lloyd Allen	1.25	.60	.40
268	Jerry Morales	1.25	.60	.40
269	Tim McCarver	1.50	.70	.45
270	Luis Tiant	1.25	.60	.40
271	Tom Hutton	1.25	.60	.40
272	Ed Farmer	1.25	.60	.40
273	Chris Speier	1.25	.60	.40
274	Darold Knowles	1.25	.60	.40
275	Tony Perez	1.50	.70	.45
276	Joe Lovitto	1.25	.60	.40
277	Bob Miller	1.25	.60	.40
278	Orioles Team	1.25	.60	.40
279	Mike Strahler	1.25	.60	.40
280	Al Kaline	8.00	4.00	2.50
281	Mike Jorgensen	2.00	1.00	.60
282	Steve Hovley	1.25	.60	.40
283	Ray Sadecki	1.25	.60	.40
284	Glenn Borgmann	1.25	.60	.40
285	Don Kessinger	1.25	.60	.40
286	Frank Linzy	1.25	.60	.40
287	Eddie Leon	1.25	.60	.40
288	Gary Gentry	1.25	.60	.40
289	Bob Oliver	1.25	.60	.40
290	Cesar Cedeno	1.25	.60	.40
291	Rogelio Moret	1.25	.60	.40
292	Jose Cruz	1.25	.60	.40
293	Bernie Allen	1.25	.60	.40
294	Steve Arlin	1.25	.60	.40
295	Bert Campaneris	1.25	.60	.40
296	Reds Mgr./Coaches (Sparky Anderson, Alex Grammas, Ted Kluszewski, George Scherger, Larry Shepard)	1.25	.60	.40
297	Walt Williams	1.25	.60	.40
298	Ron Bryant	1.25	.60	.40
299	Ted Ford	1.25	.60	.40
300	Steve Carlton	15.00	7.50	4.50
301	Billy Grabarkewitz	1.25	.60	.40
302	Terry Crowley	1.25	.60	.40
303	Nelson Briles	1.25	.60	.40
304	Duke Sims	1.25	.60	.40
305	Willie Mays	45.00	22.00	13.50
306	Tom Burgmeier	1.25	.60	.40
307	Boots Day	1.25	.60	.40
308	Skip Lockwood	1.25	.60	.40
309	Paul Popovich	1.25	.60	.40
310	Dick Allen	2.50	1.25	.70
311	Joe Decker	1.25	.60	.40
312	Oscar Brown	1.25	.60	.40
313	Jim Ray	1.25	.60	.40
314	Ron Swoboda	1.25	.60	.40
315	John Odom	1.25	.60	.40
316	Padres Team	1.25	.60	.40
317	Danny Cater	1.25	.60	.40
318	Jim McGlothlin	1.25	.60	.40
319	Jim Spencer	1.25	.60	.40
320	Lou Brock	7.50	3.75	2.25
321	Rich Hinton	1.25	.60	.40
322	Garry Maddox	1.25	.60	.40
323	Tigers Mgr./Coaches (Art Fowler, Billy Martin, Charlie Silvera, Dick Tracewski)	1.25	.60	.40
324	Al Downing	1.25	.60	.40
325	Boog Powell	1.50	.70	.45
326	Darrell Brandon	1.25	.60	.40
327	John Lowenstein	1.25	.60	.40
328	Bill Bonham	1.25	.60	.40
329	Ed Kranepool	1.25	.60	.40
330	Rod Carew	9.00	4.50	2.75
331	Carl Morton	2.00	1.00	.60
332	John Felske	1.25	.60	.40
333	Gene Clines	1.25	.60	.40
334	Freddie Patek	1.25	.60	.40
335	Bob Tolan	1.25	.60	.40
336	Tom Bradley	1.25	.60	.40
337	Dave Duncan	1.25	.60	.40
338	Checklist 3	1.25	.60	.40
339	Dick Tidrow	1.25	.60	.40
340	Nate Colbert	1.25	.60	.40
341	Boyhood Photo (Jim Palmer)	1.25	.60	.40
342	Boyhood Photo (Sam McDowell)	1.25	.60	.40
343	Boyhood Photo (Bobby Murcer)	1.25	.60	.40
344	Boyhood Photo (Jim Hunter)	1.25	.60	.40
345	Boyhood Photo (Chris Speier)	1.25	.60	.40
346	Boyhood Photo (Gaylord Perry)	1.25	.60	.40
347	Royals Team	1.25	.60	.40
348	Rennie Stennett	1.25	.60	.40
349	Dick McAuliffe	1.25	.60	.40
350	Tom Seaver	20.00	10.00	6.00
351	Jimmy Stewart	1.25	.60	.40
352	Don Stanhouse	1.25	.60	.40
353	Steve Brye	1.25	.60	.40
354	Billy Parker	1.25	.60	.40
355	Mike Marshall	1.25	.60	.40
356	White Sox Mgr./Coaches (Joe Lonnett, Jim Mahoney, Al Monchak, Johnny Sain, Chuck Tanner)	1.25	.60	.40
357	Ross Grimsley	1.25	.60	.40
358	Jim Nettles	1.25	.60	.40
359	Cecil Upshaw	1.25	.60	.40
360	Joe Rudi (photo actually Gene Tenace)	1.25	.60	.40
361	Fran Healy	1.25	.60	.40
362	Eddie Watt	1.25	.60	.40
363	Jackie Hernandez	1.25	.60	.40
364	Rick Wise	1.25	.60	.40
365	Rico Petrocelli	1.25	.60	.40
366	Brock Davis	1.25	.60	.40
367	Burt Hooton	1.25	.60	.40
368	Bill Buckner	1.25	.60	.40
369	Lerrin LaGrow	1.25	.60	.40
370	Willie Stargell	6.00	3.00	1.75
371	Mike Kekich	1.25	.60	.40
372	Oscar Gamble	1.25	.60	.40
373	Clyde Wright	1.25	.60	.40
374	Darrell Evans	1.25	.60	.40
375	Larry Dierker	1.25	.60	.40
376	Frank Duffy	1.25	.60	.40
377	Expos Mgr./Coaches (Dave Bristol, Larry Doby, Gene Mauch, Cal McLish, Jerry Zimmerman)	2.50	1.25	.70
378	Lenny Randle	1.25	.60	.40
379	Cy Acosta	1.25	.60	.40
380	Johnny Bench	19.00	9.50	5.75
381	Vicente Romo	1.25	.60	.40
382	Mike Hegan	1.25	.60	.40
383	Diego Segui	1.25	.60	.40
384	Don Baylor	1.50	.70	.45
385	Jim Perry	1.25	.60	.40
386	Don Money	1.25	.60	.40
387	Jim Barr	1.25	.60	.40
388	Ben Oglivie	1.25	.60	.40
389	Mets Team	1.25	.60	.40
390	Mickey Lolich	1.25	.60	.40
391	Lee Lacy	1.25	.60	.40
392	Dick Drago	1.25	.60	.40
393	Jose Cardenal	1.25	.60	.40
394	Sparky Lyle	1.25	.60	.40
395	Roger Metzger	1.25	.60	.40
396	Grant Jackson	1.25	.60	.40
397	Dave Cash	1.25	.60	.40
398	Rich Hand	1.25	.60	.40
399	George Foster	1.25	.60	.40
400	Gaylord Perry	6.00	3.00	1.75
401	Clyde Mashore	2.50	1.25	.70
402	Jack Hiatt	1.25	.60	.40
403	Sonny Jackson	1.25	.60	.40
404	Chuck Brinkman	1.25	.60	.40
405	Cesar Tovar	1.25	.60	.40
406	Paul Lindblad	1.25	.60	.40
407	Felix Millan	1.25	.60	.40
408	Jim Colborn	1.25	.60	.40
409	Ivan Murrell	1.25	.60	.40
410	Willie McCovey	7.00	3.50	2.00
411	Ray Corbin	1.25	.60	.40
412	Manny Mota	1.25	.60	.40
413	Tom Timmermann	1.25	.60	.40
414	Ken Rudolph	1.25	.60	.40
415	Marty Pattin	1.25	.60	.40
416	Paul Schaal	1.25	.60	.40
417	Scipio Spinks	1.25	.60	.40
418	Bobby Grich	1.25	.60	.40
419	Casey Cox	1.25	.60	.40
420	Tommie Agee	1.25	.60	.40

421	Angels Mgr./Coaches (Tom Morgan, Salty Parker, Jimmie Reese, John Roseboro, Bobby Winkles)	1.25	.60	.40
422	Bob Robertson	1.25	.60	.40
423	Johnny Jeter	1.25	.60	.40
424	Denny Doyle	1.25	.60	.40
425	Alex Johnson	1.25	.60	.40
426	Dave Laroche	1.25	.60	.40
427	Rick Auerbach	1.25	.60	.40
428	Wayne Simpson	1.25	.60	.40
429	Jim Fairey	2.50	1.25	.70
430	Vida Blue	1.25	.60	.40
431	Gerry Moses	1.25	.60	.40
432	Dan Frisella	1.25	.60	.40
433	Willie Horton	1.25	.60	.40
434	Giants Team	1.25	.60	.40
435	Rico Carty	1.25	.60	.40
436	Jim McAndrew	1.25	.60	.40
437	John Kennedy	1.25	.60	.40
438	Enzo Hernandez	1.25	.60	.40
439	Eddie Fisher	1.25	.60	.40
440	Glenn Beckert	1.25	.60	.40
441	Gail Hopkins	1.25	.60	.40
442	Dick Dietz	1.25	.60	.40
443	Danny Thompson	1.25	.60	.40
444	Ken Brett	1.25	.60	.40
445	Ken Berry	1.25	.60	.40
446	Jerry Reuss	1.25	.60	.40
447	Joe Hague	1.25	.60	.40
448	John Hiller	1.25	.60	.40
449	Indians Mgr./Coaches (Ken Aspromonte, Rocky Colavito, Joe Lutz, Warren Spahn)	1.50	.70	.45
450	Joe Torre	2.50	1.25	.70
451	John Vukovich	1.25	.60	.40
452	Paul Casanova	1.25	.60	.40
453	Checklist 4	1.25	.60	.40
454	Tom Haller	1.25	.60	.40
455	Bill Melton	1.25	.60	.40
456	Dick Green	1.25	.60	.40
457	John Strohmayer	2.50	1.25	.70
458	Jim Mason	1.25	.60	.40
459	Jimmy Howarth	1.25	.60	.40
460	Bill Freehan	1.25	.60	.40
461	Mike Corkins	1.25	.60	.40
462	Ron Blomberg	1.25	.60	.40
463	Ken Tatum	1.25	.60	.40
464	Cubs Team	1.25	.60	.40
465	Dave Giusti	1.25	.60	.40
466	Jose Arcia	1.25	.60	.40
467	Mike Ryan	1.25	.60	.40
468	Tom Griffin	1.25	.60	.40
469	Dan Monzon	1.25	.60	.40
470	Mike Cuellar	1.25	.60	.40
471	Hit Leader (Ty Cobb)	7.50	3.75	2.25
472	Grand Slam Leader (Lou Gehrig)	10.00	5.00	3.00
473	Total Bases Leader (Hank Aaron)	7.50	3.75	2.25
474	R.B.I. Leader (Babe Ruth)	15.00	7.50	4.50
475	Batting Leader (Ty Cobb)	7.00	3.50	2.00
476	Shutout Leader (Walter Johnson)	2.50	1.25	.70
477	Victory Leader (Cy Young)	1.25	.60	.40
478	Strikeout Leader (Walter Johnson)	2.50	1.25	.70
479	Hal Lanier	1.25	.60	.40
480	Juan Marichal	5.00	2.50	1.50
481	White Sox Team	1.25	.60	.40
482	Rick Reuschel	1.50	.70	.45
483	Dal Maxvill	1.25	.60	.40
484	Ernie McAnally	2.50	1.25	.70
485	Norm Cash	1.25	.60	.40
486	Phillies Mgr./Coaches (Carroll Beringer, Billy DeMars, Danny Ozark, Ray Rippelmeyer, Bobby Wine)	1.25	.60	.40
487	Bruce Dal Canton	1.25	.60	.40
488	Dave Campbell	1.25	.60	.40
489	Jeff Burroughs	1.25	.60	.40
490	Claude Osteen	1.25	.60	.40
491	Bob Montgomery	1.25	.60	.40
492	Pedro Borbon	1.25	.60	.40
493	Duffy Dyer	1.25	.60	.40
494	Rich Morales	1.25	.60	.40
495	Tommy Helms	1.25	.60	.40
496	Ray Lamb	1.25	.60	.40
497	Cardinals Mgr./Coaches (Vern Benson, George Kissell, Red Schoendienst, Barney Schultz)	1.50	.70	.45
498	Graig Nettles	1.50	.70	.45
499	Bob Moose	1.25	.60	.40
500	A's Team	1.25	.60	.40
501	Larry Gura	1.25	.60	.40
502	Bobby Valentine	1.25	.60	.40
503	Phil Niekro	6.00	3.00	1.75
504	Earl Williams	1.25	.60	.40
505	Bob Bailey	2.50	1.25	.70
506	Bart Johnson	1.25	.60	.40
507	Darrel Chaney	1.25	.60	.40
508	Gates Brown	1.25	.60	.40
509	Jim Nash	1.25	.60	.40
510	Amos Otis	1.25	.60	.40
511	Sam McDowell	1.25	.60	.40
512	Dalton Jones	1.25	.60	.40
513	Dave Marshall	1.25	.60	.40
514	Jerry Kenney	1.25	.60	.40
515	Andy Messersmith	1.25	.60	.40
516	Danny Walton	1.25	.60	.40
517	Pirates Mgr./Coaches (Don Leppert, Bill Mazeroski, Dave Ricketts, Bill Virdon, Mel Wright)	1.25	.60	.40
518	Bob Veale	1.25	.60	.40
519	John Edwards	1.25	.60	.40
520	Mel Stottlemyre	1.25	.60	.40

521	Braves Team	1.25	.60	.40
522	Leo Cardenas	1.25	.60	.40
523	Wayne Granger	1.25	.60	.40
524	Gene Tenace	1.25	.60	.40
525	Jim Fregosi	1.25	.60	.40
526	Ollie Brown	1.25	.60	.40
527	Dan McGinn	1.25	.60	.40
528	Paul Blair	1.25	.60	.40
529	Milt May	2.50	1.25	.70
530	Jim Kaat	3.00	1.50	.90
531	Ron Woods	5.00	2.50	1.50
532	Steve Mingori	2.50	1.25	.70
533	Larry Stahl	2.50	1.25	.70
534	Dave Lemonds	2.50	1.25	.70
535	John Callison	2.50	1.25	.70
536	Phillies Team	2.50	1.25	.70
537	Bill Slayback	2.50	1.25	.70
538	Jim Hart	2.50	1.25	.70
539	Tom Murphy	2.50	1.25	.70
540	Cleon Jones	2.50	1.25	.70
541	Bob Bolin	2.50	1.25	.70
542	Pat Corrales	2.50	1.25	.70
543	Alan Foster	2.50	1.25	.70
544	Von Joshua	2.50	1.25	.70
545	Orlando Cepeda	15.00	7.50	4.50
546	Jim York	2.50	1.25	.70
547	Bobby Heise	2.50	1.25	.70
548	Don Durham	2.50	1.25	.70
549	Rangers Mgr./Coaches (Chuck Estrada, Whitey Herzog, Chuck Hiller, Jackie Moore)	2.50	1.25	.70
550	Dave Johnson	2.50	1.25	.70
551	Mike Kilkenny	2.50	1.25	.70
552	J.C. Martin	2.50	1.25	.70
553	Mickey Scott	2.50	1.25	.70
554	Dave Concepcion	2.50	1.25	.70
555	Bill Hands	2.50	1.25	.70
556	Yankees Team	2.50	1.25	.70
557	Bernie Williams	2.50	1.25	.70
558	Jerry May	2.50	1.25	.70
559	Barry Lersch	2.50	1.25	.70
560	Frank Howard	3.00	1.50	.90
561	Jim Geddes	2.50	1.25	.70
562	Wayne Garrett	2.50	1.25	.70
563	Larry Haney	2.50	1.25	.70
564	Mike Thompson	2.50	1.25	.70
565	Jim Hickman	2.50	1.25	.70
566	Lew Krausse	2.50	1.25	.70
567	Bob Fenwick	2.50	1.25	.70
568	Ray Newman	2.50	1.25	.70
569	Dodgers Mgr./Coaches (Red Adams, Walt Alston, Monty Basgall, Jim Gilliam, Tom Lasorda)	5.00	2.50	1.50
570	Bill Singer	2.50	1.25	.70
571	Rusty Torres	2.50	1.25	.70
572	Gary Sutherland	2.50	1.25	.70
573	Fred Beene	2.50	1.25	.70
574	Bob Didier	2.50	1.25	.70
575	Dock Ellis	2.50	1.25	.70
576	Expos Team	6.00	3.00	1.75
577	Eric Soderholm	2.50	1.25	.70
578	Ken Wright	2.50	1.25	.70
579	Tom Grieve	2.50	1.25	.70
580	Joe Pepitone	2.50	1.25	.70
581	Steve Kealey	2.50	1.25	.70
582	Darrell Porter	2.50	1.25	.70
583	Bill Grief	2.50	1.25	.70
584	Chris Arnold	2.50	1.25	.70
585	Joe Niekro	2.50	1.25	.70
586	Bill Sudakis	2.50	1.25	.70
587	Rich McKinney	2.50	1.25	.70
588	Checklist 5	5.00	2.50	1.50
589	Ken Forsch	2.50	1.25	.70
590	Deron Johnson	2.50	1.25	.70
591	Mike Hedlund	2.50	1.25	.70
592	John Boccabella	5.00	2.50	1.50
593	Royals Mgr./Coaches (Galen Cisco, Harry Dunlop, Charlie Lau, Jack McKeon)	2.50	1.25	.70
594	Vic Harris	2.50	1.25	.70
595	Don Gullett	2.50	1.25	.70
596	Red Sox Team	2.50	1.25	.70
597	Mickey Rivers	2.50	1.25	.70
598	Phil Roof	2.50	1.25	.70
599	Ed Crosby	2.50	1.25	.70
600	Dave McNally	2.50	1.25	.70
601	Rookie Catchers (George Pena, Sergio Robles, Rick Stelmaszek)	2.50	1.25	.70
602	Rookie Pitchers (Mel Behney, Ralph Garcia, Doug Rau)	2.50	1.25	.70
603	Rookie Third Basemen (Terry Hughes, Bill McNulty, Ken Reitz)	2.50	1.25	.70
604	Rookie Pitchers (Jesse Jefferson, Dennis O'Toole, Bob Strampe)	2.50	1.25	.70
605	Rookie First Basemen (Pat Bourque, Enos Cabell, Gonzalo Marquez)	2.50	1.25	.70
606	Rookie Outfielders (Gary Matthews, Tom Paciorek, Jorge Roque)	5.00	2.50	1.50
607	Rookie Shortstops (Ray Busse, Pepe Frias, Mario Guerrero)	5.00	2.50	1.50
608	Rookie Pitchers (Steve Busby, Dick Colpaert, George Medich)	2.50	1.25	.70
609	Rookie Second Basemen (Larvell Blanks, Pedro Garcia, Dave Lopes)	2.50	1.25	.70
610	Rookie Pitchers (Jimmy Freeman, Charlie Hough, Hank Webb)	2.50	1.25	.70

611	Rookie Outfielders (Rich Coggins, Jim Wohlford, Richie Zisk)	2.50	1.25	.70
612	Rookie Pitchers (Steve Lawson, Bob Reynolds, Brent Strom)	2.50	1.25	.70
613	Rookie Catchers (Bob Boone, Mike Ivie, Skip Jutze)	35.00	17.50	10.50
614	Rookie Outfielders (Alonza Bumbry, Dwight Evans, Charlie Spikes)	30.00	15.00	9.00
615	Rookie Third Basemen (Ron Cey, John Hilton, Mike Schmidt)	375.00	185.00	110.00
616	Rookie Pitchers (Norm Angelini, Steve Blateric, Mike Garman)	2.50	1.25	.70
617	Rich Chiles	2.50	1.25	.70
618	Andy Etchebarren	2.50	1.25	.70
619	Billy Wilson	2.50	1.25	.70
620	Tommy Harper	2.50	1.25	.70
621	Joe Ferguson	2.50	1.25	.70
622	Larry Hisle	2.50	1.25	.70
623	Steve Renko	5.00	2.50	1.50
624	Astros Mgr./Coaches (Leo Durocher, Preston Gomez, Grady Hatton, Hub Kittle, Jim Owens)	2.50	1.25	.70
625	Angel Mangual	2.50	1.25	.70
626	Bob Barton	2.50	1.25	.70
627	Luis Alvarado	2.50	1.25	.70
628	Jim Slaton	2.50	1.25	.70
629	Indians Team	2.50	1.25	.70
630	Denny McLain	4.00	2.00	1.25
631	Tom Matchick	2.50	1.25	.70
632	Dick Selma	2.50	1.25	.70
633	Ike Brown	2.50	1.25	.70
634	Alan Closter	2.50	1.25	.70
635	Gene Alley	2.50	1.25	.70
636	Rick Clark	2.50	1.25	.70
637	Norm Miller	2.50	1.25	.70
638	Ken Reynolds	2.50	1.25	.70
639	Willie Crawford	2.50	1.25	.70
640	Dick Bosman	2.50	1.25	.70
641	Reds Team	2.50	1.25	.70
642	Jose LaBoy	5.00	2.50	1.50
643	Al Fitzmorris	2.50	1.25	.70
644	Jack Heidemann	2.50	1.25	.70
645	Bob Locker	2.50	1.25	.70
646	Brewers Mgr./Coaches (Del Crandall, Harvey Kuenn, Joe Nossek, Bob Shaw, Jim Walton)	2.50	1.25	.70
647	George Stone	2.50	1.25	.70
648	Tom Egan	2.50	1.25	.70
649	Rich Folkers	2.50	1.25	.70
650	Felipe Alou	7.50	3.75	2.25
651	Don Carrithers	2.50	1.25	.70
652	Ted Kubiak	2.50	1.25	.70
653	Joe Hoerner	2.50	1.25	.70
654	Twins Team	2.50	1.25	.70
655	Clay Kirby	2.50	1.25	.70
656	John Ellis	2.50	1.25	.70
657	Bob Johnson	2.50	1.25	.70
658	Elliott Maddox	2.50	1.25	.70
659	Jose Pagan	2.50	1.25	.70
660	Fred Scherman	2.50	1.25	.70

1973 O-Pee-Chee Team Checklists

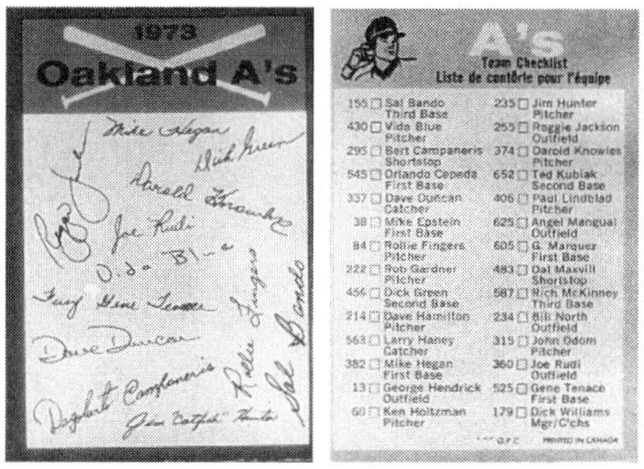

Similar to the 1973 Topps team checklist cards, this set was produced in Canada. The set consists of 24 unnumbered cards (2-1/2" x 3-1/2") with blue borders. The card fronts contain facsimile autographs of players from the same team. The backs contain team checklists of players found in the 1973 O-Pee-Chee regular issue set. The card backs contain the French translation for Team Checklist plus a copyright line "O.P.C. Printed in Canada."

		NM	EX	VG
Complete Set (24):		45.00	22.00	13.50
Common Card:		2.00	1.00	.60
(1)	Atlanta Braves	2.00	1.00	.60
(2)	Baltimore Orioles	2.00	1.00	.60
(3)	Boston Red Sox	2.00	1.00	.60
(4)	California Angels	2.00	1.00	.60
(5)	Chicago Cubs	2.00	1.00	.60
(6)	Chicago White Sox	2.00	1.00	.60
(7)	Cincinnati Reds	2.50	1.25	.70

(8)	Cleveland Indians	2.00	1.00	.60
(9)	Detroit Tigers	3.50	1.75	1.00
(10)	Houston Astros	2.00	1.00	.60
(11)	Kansas City Royals	2.00	1.00	.60
(12)	Los Angeles Dodgers	2.00	1.00	.60
(13)	Milwaukee Brewers	2.00	1.00	.60
(14)	Minnesota Twins	2.00	1.00	.60
(15)	Montreal Expos	4.00	2.00	1.25
(16)	New York Mets	2.50	1.25	.70
(17)	New York Yankees	2.00	1.00	.60
(18)	Oakland A's	3.00	1.50	.90
(19)	Philadelphia Phillies	2.00	1.00	.60
(20)	Pittsburgh Pirates	2.00	1.00	.60
(21)	St. Louis Cardinals	2.00	1.00	.60
(22)	San Diego Padres	2.00	1.00	.60
(23)	San Francisco Giants	2.00	1.00	.60
(24)	Texas Rangers	2.00	1.00	.60

1974 O-Pee-Chee

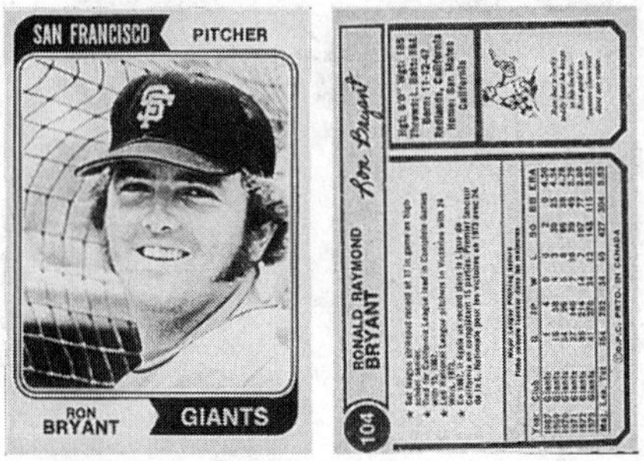

Again numbering 660 cards, the 1974 O-Pee-Chee set borrows its design from the Topps set of the same year. The cards measure the standard 2-1/2" x 3-1/2" and the backs are printed in both French and English and state "Printed in Canada." Ten of the cards in the O-Pee-Chee set have fronts that differ from their corresponding Topps cards, including most of the Hank Aaron "specials" that lead off the set. And, because the O-Pee-Chee cards were printed later than the corresponding Topps cards, there are no "Washington, Nat'l. League" variations in the O-Pee-Chee set.

		NM	EX	VG
Complete Set (660):		900.00	450.00	275.00
Common Player:		.75	.40	.25
1	Hank Aaron	40.00	20.00	12.00
2	Aaron Special 1954-57	8.00	4.00	2.50
3	Aaron Special 1958-59	8.00	4.00	2.50
4	Aaron Special 1960-61	8.00	4.00	2.50
5	Aaron Special 1962-63	8.00	4.00	2.50
6	Aaron Special 1964-65	8.00	4.00	2.50
7	Aaron Special 1966-67	8.00	4.00	2.50
8	Aaron Special 1968-69	8.00	4.00	2.50
9	Aaron Special 1970-73	8.00	4.00	2.50
10	Johnny Bench	19.00	9.50	5.75
11	Jim Bibby	.75	.40	.25
12	Dave May	.75	.40	.25
13	Tom Hilgendorf	.75	.40	.25
14	Paul Popovich	.75	.40	.25
15	Joe Torre	2.50	1.25	.70
16	Orioles Team	.75	.40	.25
17	Doug Bird	.75	.40	.25
18	Gary Thomasson	.75	.40	.25
19	Gerry Moses	.75	.40	.25
20	Nolan Ryan	175.00	87.00	52.00
21	Bob Gallagher	.75	.40	.25
22	Cy Acosta	.75	.40	.25
23	Craig Robinson	.75	.40	.25
24	John Hiller	.75	.40	.25
25	Ken Singleton	2.00	1.00	.60
26	Bill Campbell	.75	.40	.25
27	George Scott	.75	.40	.25
28	Manny Sanguillen	.75	.40	.25
29	Phil Niekro	5.00	2.50	1.50
30	Bobby Bonds	1.00	.50	.30
31	Astros Mgr./Coaches (Roger Craig, Preston Gomez, Grady Hatton, Hub Kittle, Bob Lillis)	.75	.40	.25
32	John Grubb	.75	.40	.25
33	Don Newhauser	.75	.40	.25
34	Andy Kosco	.75	.40	.25
35	Gaylord Perry	5.00	2.50	1.50
36	Cardinals Team	.75	.40	.25
37	Dave Sells	.75	.40	.25
38	Don Kessinger	.75	.40	.25
39	Ken Suarez	.75	.40	.25
40	Jim Palmer	9.00	4.50	2.75
41	Bobby Floyd	.75	.40	.25
42	Claude Osteen	.75	.40	.25
43	Jim Wynn	.75	.40	.25
44	Mel Stottlemyre	.75	.40	.25
45	Dave Johnson	.75	.40	.25
46	Pat Kelly	.75	.40	.25
47	Dick Ruthven	.75	.40	.25
48	Dick Sharon	.75	.40	.25
49	Steve Renko	1.50	.70	.45
50	Rod Carew	9.00	4.50	2.75
51	Bob Heise	.75	.40	.25
52	Al Oliver	1.00	.50	.30
53	Fred Kendall	.75	.40	.25
54	Elias Sosa	.75	.40	.25
55	Frank Robinson	8.00	4.00	2.50
56	Mets Team	1.00	.50	.30
57	Darold Knowles	.75	.40	.25
58	Charlie Spikes	.75	.40	.25
59	Ross Grimsley	.75	.40	.25
60	Lou Brock	7.00	3.50	2.00
61	Luis Aparicio	6.00	3.00	1.75
62	Bob Locker	.75	.40	.25
63	Bill Sudakis	.75	.40	.25
64	Doug Rau	.75	.40	.25
65	Amos Otis	.75	.40	.25
66	Sparky Lyle	.75	.40	.25
67	Tommy Helms	.75	.40	.25
68	Grant Jackson	.75	.40	.25
69	Del Unser	.75	.40	.25
70	Dick Allen	1.50	.70	.45
71	Danny Frisella	.75	.40	.25
72	Aurelio Rodriguez	.75	.40	.25
73	Mike Marshall	2.00	1.00	.60
74	Twins Team	.75	.40	.25
75	Jim Colborn	.75	.40	.25
76	Mickey Rivers	.75	.40	.25
77	Rich Troedson	.75	.40	.25
78	Giants Mgr./Coaches (Joe Amalfitano, Charlie Fox, Andy Gilbert, Don McMahon, John McNamara)	.75	.40	.25
79	Gene Tenace	.75	.40	.25
80	Tom Seaver	15.00	7.50	4.50
81	Frank Duffy	.75	.40	.25
82	Dave Giusti	.75	.40	.25
83	Orlando Cepeda	8.00	4.00	2.50
84	Rick Wise	.75	.40	.25
85	Joe Morgan	7.00	3.50	2.00
86	Joe Ferguson	.75	.40	.25
87	Fergie Jenkins	9.00	4.50	2.75
88	Freddie Patek	.75	.40	.25
89	Jackie Brown	.75	.40	.25
90	Bobby Murcer	.75	.40	.25
91	Ken Forsch	.75	.40	.25
92	Paul Blair	.75	.40	.25
93	Rod Gilbreath	.75	.40	.25
94	Tigers Team	.75	.40	.25
95	Steve Carlton	11.00	5.50	3.25
96	Jerry Hairston	.75	.40	.25
97	Bob Bailey	1.50	.70	.45
98	Bert Blyleven	1.00	.50	.30
99	George Theodore	1.00	.50	.30
100	Willie Stargell	7.00	3.50	2.00
101	Bobby Valentine	.75	.40	.25
102	Bill Greif	.75	.40	.25
103	Sal Bando	.75	.40	.25
104	Ron Bryant	.75	.40	.25
105	Carlton Fisk	12.00	6.00	3.50
106	Harry Parker	.75	.40	.25
107	Alex Johnson	.75	.40	.25
108	Al Hrabosky	.75	.40	.25
109	Bob Grich	.75	.40	.25
110	Billy Williams	7.00	3.50	2.00
111	Clay Carroll	.75	.40	.25
112	Dave Lopes	.75	.40	.25
113	Dick Drago	.75	.40	.25
114	Angels Team	.75	.40	.25
115	Willie Horton	.75	.40	.25
116	Jerry Reuss	.75	.40	.25
117	Ron Blomberg	.75	.40	.25
118	Bill Lee	.75	.40	.25
119	Phillies Mgr./Coaches (Carroll Beringer, Billy DeMars, Danny Ozark, Ray Ripplemeyer, Bobby Wine)	.75	.40	.25
120	Wilbur Wood	.75	.40	.25
121	Larry Lintz	1.50	.70	.45
122	Jim Holt	.75	.40	.25
123	Nelson Briles	.75	.40	.25
124	Bob Coluccio	.75	.40	.25
125	Nate Colbert	.75	.40	.25
126	Checklist 1	1.00	.50	.30
127	Tom Paciorek	.75	.40	.25
128	John Ellis	.75	.40	.25
129	Chris Speier	.75	.40	.25
130	Reggie Jackson	30.00	15.00	9.00
131	Bob Boone	1.00	.50	.30
132	Felix Millan	.75	.40	.25
133	David Clyde	.75	.40	.25
134	Denis Menke	.75	.40	.25
135	Roy White	.75	.40	.25
136	Rick Reuschel	.75	.40	.25
137	Al Bumbry	.75	.40	.25
138	Ed Brinkman	.75	.40	.25
139	Aurelio Monteagudo	.75	.40	.25
140	Darrell Evans	.75	.40	.25
141	Pat Bourque	.75	.40	.25
142	Pedro Garcia	.75	.40	.25
143	Dick Woodson	.75	.40	.25
144	Dodgers Mgr./Coaches (Red Adams, Walter Alston, Monty Basgall, Jim Gilliam, Tom Lasorda)	1.50	.70	.45
145	Dock Ellis	.75	.40	.25
146	Ron Fairly	1.50	.70	.45
147	Bart Johnson	.75	.40	.25
148	Dave Hilton	.75	.40	.25
149	Mac Scarce	.75	.40	.25
150	John Mayberry	.75	.40	.25
151	Diego Segui	.75	.40	.25
152	Oscar Gamble	.75	.40	.25
153	Jon Matlack	.75	.40	.25
154	Astros Team	.75	.40	.25
155	Bert Campaneris	.75	.40	.25
156	Randy Moffitt	.75	.40	.25
157	Vic Harris	.75	.40	.25
158	Jack Billingham	.75	.40	.25
159	Jim Ray Hart	.75	.40	.25
160	Brooks Robinson	9.00	4.50	2.75
161	Ray Burris	.75	.40	.25
162	Bill Freehan	.75	.40	.25
163	Ken Berry	.75	.40	.25
164	Tom House	.75	.40	.25
165	Willie Davis	.75	.40	.25
166	Mickey Lolich	1.50	.70	.45
167	Luis Tiant	.75	.40	.25
168	Danny Thompson	.75	.40	.25
169	Steve Rogers	2.50	1.25	.70
170	Bill Melton	.75	.40	.25
171	Eduardo Rodriguez	.75	.40	.25
172	Gene Clines	.75	.40	.25
173	Randy Jones	.75	.40	.25
174	Bill Robinson	.75	.40	.25
175	Reggie Cleveland	.75	.40	.25
176	John Lowenstein	.75	.40	.25
177	Dave Roberts	.75	.40	.25
178	Garry Maddox	.75	.40	.25
179	Mets Mgr./Coaches (Yogi Berra, Roy McMillan, Joe Pignatano, Rube Walker, Eddie Yost)	1.00	.50	.30
180	Ken Holtzman	.75	.40	.25
181	Cesar Geronimo	.75	.40	.25
182	Lindy McDaniel	.75	.40	.25
183	Johnny Oates	.75	.40	.25
184	Rangers Team	.75	.40	.25
185	Jose Cardenal	.75	.40	.25
186	Fred Scherman	.75	.40	.25
187	Don Baylor	.75	.40	.25
188	Rudy Meoli	.75	.40	.25
189	Jim Brewer	.75	.40	.25
190	Tony Oliva	.75	.40	.25
191	Al Fitzmorris	.75	.40	.25
192	Mario Guerrero	.75	.40	.25
193	Tom Walker	1.50	.70	.45
194	Darrell Porter	.75	.40	.25
195	Carlos May	.75	.40	.25
196	Jim Hunter	6.00	3.00	1.75
197	Vicente Romo	.75	.40	.25
198	Dave Cash	.75	.40	.25
199	Mike Kekich	.75	.40	.25
200	Cesar Cedeno	.75	.40	.25
201	Batting Leaders (Rod Carew, Pete Rose)	6.00	3.00	1.75
202	1963 - MVPs (Ken Boyer, Reggie Jackson, Willie Stargell)	6.00	3.00	1.75
203	Runs Batted In (Reggie Jackson, Willie Stargell)	6.00	3.00	1.75
204	Stolen Base Leaders (Lou Brock, Tommy Harper)	1.00	.50	.30
205	Victory Leaders (Ron Bryant, Wilbur Wood)	.75	.40	.25
206	Earned Run Average Leaders (Jim Palmer, Tom Seaver)	6.00	3.00	1.75
207	Strikeout Leaders (Nolan Ryan, Tom Seaver)	25.00	12.50	7.50
208	Leading Firemen (John Hiller, Mike Marshall)	1.25	.60	.40
209	Ted Sizemore	.75	.40	.25
210	Bill Singer	.75	.40	.25
211	Cubs Team	.75	.40	.25
212	Rollie Fingers	6.00	3.00	1.75
213	Dave Rader	.75	.40	.25
214	Billy Grabarkewitz	.75	.40	.25
215	Al Kaline	9.00	4.50	2.75
216	Ray Sadecki	.75	.40	.25
217	Tim Foli	2.00	1.00	.60
218	Johnny Briggs	.75	.40	.25
219	Doug Griffin	.75	.40	.25
220	Don Sutton	6.00	3.00	1.75
221	White Sox Mgr./Coaches (Joe Lonnett, Jim Mahoney, Alex Monchak, Johnny Sain, Chuck Tanner)	.75	.40	.25
222	Ramon Hernandez	.75	.40	.25
223	Jeff Burroughs	.75	.40	.25
224	Roger Metzger	.75	.40	.25
225	Paul Splittorff	.75	.40	.25
226	Padres Team	.75	.40	.25
227	Mike Lum	.75	.40	.25
228	Ted Kubiak	.75	.40	.25
229	Fritz Peterson	.75	.40	.25
230	Tony Perez	4.00	2.00	1.25
231	Dick Tidrow	.75	.40	.25
232	Steve Brye	.75	.40	.25
233	Jim Barr	.75	.40	.25
234	John Milner	.75	.40	.25
235	Dave McNally	.75	.40	.25
236	Cardinals Mgr./Coaches (Vern Benson, George Kissell, Johnny Lewis, Red Schoendienst, Barney	1.00	.50	.30
237	Ken Brett	.75	.40	.25
238	Fran Healy	.75	.40	.25
239	Bill Russell	.75	.40	.25
240	Joe Coleman	.75	.40	.25
241	Glenn Beckert	.75	.40	.25
242	Bill Gogolewski	.75	.40	.25
243	Bob Oliver	.75	.40	.25
244	Carl Morton	.75	.40	.25
245	Cleon Jones	.75	.40	.25
246	A's Team	.75	.40	.25
247	Rick Miller	.75	.40	.25
248	Tom Hall	.75	.40	.25
249	George Mitterwald	.75	.40	.25
250	Willie McCovey	8.00	4.00	2.50
251	Graig Nettles	1.25	.60	.40
252	Dave Parker	12.00	6.00	3.50
253	John Boccabella	1.50	.70	.45
254	Stan Bahnsen	.75	.40	.25
255	Larry Bowa	.75	.40	.25
256	Tom Griffin	.75	.40	.25
257	Buddy Bell	.75	.40	.25
258	Jerry Morales	.75	.40	.25
259	Bob Reynolds	.75	.40	.25
260	Ted Simmons	.75	.40	.25
261	Jerry Bell	.75	.40	.25

262	Ed Kirkpatrick	.75	.40	.25
263	Checklist 2	1.00	.50	.30
264	Joe Rudi	.75	.40	.25
265	Tug McGraw	.75	.40	.25
266	Jim Northrup	.75	.40	.25
267	Andy Messersmith	.75	.40	.25
268	Tom Grieve	.75	.40	.25
269	Bob Johnson	.75	.40	.25
270	Ron Santo	1.00	.50	.30
271	Bill Hands	.75	.40	.25
272	Paul Casanova	.75	.40	.25
273	Checklist 3	1.00	.50	.30
274	Fred Beene	.75	.40	.25
275	Ron Hunt	1.50	.70	.45
276	Angels Mgr./Coaches (Tom Morgan, Salty Parker, Jimmie Reese, John Roseboro, Bobby Winkles)	.75	.40	.25
277	Gary Nolan	.75	.40	.25
278	Cookie Rojas	.75	.40	.25
279	Jim Crawford	.75	.40	.25
280	Carl Yastrzemski	11.00	5.50	3.25
281	Giants Team	.75	.40	.25
282	Doyle Alexander	.75	.40	.25
283	Mike Schmidt	90.00	45.00	27.00
284	Dave Duncan	.75	.40	.25
285	Reggie Smith	.75	.40	.25
286	Tony Muser	.75	.40	.25
287	Clay Kirby	.75	.40	.25
288	Gorman Thomas	.75	.40	.25
289	Rick Auerbach	.75	.40	.25
290	Vida Blue	.75	.40	.25
291	Don Hahn	.75	.40	.25
292	Chuck Seelbach	.75	.40	.25
293	Milt May	.75	.40	.25
294	Steve Foucault	.75	.40	.25
295	Rick Monday	.75	.40	.25
296	Ray Corbin	.75	.40	.25
297	Hal Breeden	1.50	.70	.45
298	Roric Harrison	.75	.40	.25
299	Gene Michael	.75	.40	.25
300	Pete Rose	15.00	7.50	4.50
301	Bob Montgomery	.75	.40	.25
302	Rudy May	.75	.40	.25
303	George Hendrick	.75	.40	.25
304	Don Wilson	.75	.40	.25
305	Tito Fuentes	.75	.40	.25
306	Orioles Mgr./Coaches (George Bamberger, Jim Frey, Billy Hunter, George Staller, Earl Weaver)	.75	.40	.25
307	Luis Melendez	.75	.40	.25
308	Bruce Dal Canton	.75	.40	.25
309	Dave Roberts	.75	.40	.25
310	Terry Forster	.75	.40	.25
311	Jerry Grote	.75	.40	.25
312	Deron Johnson	.75	.40	.25
313	Barry Lersch	.75	.40	.25
314	Brewers Team	.75	.40	.25
315	Ron Cey	.75	.40	.25
316	Jim Perry	.75	.40	.25
317	Richie Zisk	.75	.40	.25
318	Jim Merritt	.75	.40	.25
319	Randy Hundley	.75	.40	.25
320	Dusty Baker	.75	.40	.25
321	Steve Braun	.75	.40	.25
322	Ernie McAnally	1.50	.70	.45
323	Richie Scheinblum	.75	.40	.25
324	Steve Kline	.75	.40	.25
325	Tommy Harper	.75	.40	.25
326	Reds Mgr./Coaches (Sparky Anderson, Alex Grammas, Ted Kluszewski, George Scherger, Larry Shepard)	1.00	.50	.30
327	Tom Timmermann	.75	.40	.25
328	Skip Jutze	.75	.40	.25
329	Mark Belanger	.75	.40	.25
330	Juan Marichal	6.00	3.00	1.75
331	All-Star Catchers (Johnny Bench, Carlton Fisk)	3.50	1.75	1.00
332	All-Star First Basemen (Hank Aaron, Dick Allen)	3.50	1.75	1.00
333	All-Star Second Basemen (Rod Carew, Joe Morgan)	3.50	1.75	1.00
334	All-Star Third Baseman (Brooks Robinson, Ron Santo)	3.00	1.50	.90
335	All-Star Shortstops (Bert Campaneris, Chris Speier)	.75	.40	.25
336	All-Star Left Fielders (Bobby Murcer, Pete Rose)	2.00	1.00	.60
337	All-Star Center Fielders (Cesar Cedeno, Amos Otis)	.75	.40	.25
338	All-Star Right Fielders (Reggie Jackson, Billy Williams)	3.50	1.75	1.00
339	All-Star Pitchers (Jim Hunter, Rick Wise)	.75	.40	.25
340	Thurman Munson	11.00	5.50	3.25
341	Dan Driessen	.75	.40	.25
342	Jim Lonborg	1.00	.50	.30
343	Royals Team	.75	.40	.25
344	Mike Caldwell	.75	.40	.25
345	Bill North	.75	.40	.25
346	Ron Reed	.75	.40	.25
347	Sandy Alomar	.75	.40	.25
348	Pete Richert	.75	.40	.25
349	John Vukovich	.75	.40	.25
350	Bob Gibson	7.00	3.50	2.00
351	Dwight Evans	2.00	1.00	.60
352	Bill Stoneman	1.50	.70	.45
353	Rich Coggins	.75	.40	.25
354	Cubs Mgr./Coaches (Hank Aguirre, Whitey Lockman, Jim Marshall, J.C. Martin, Al Spangler)	.75	.40	.25
355	Dave Nelson	.75	.40	.25
356	Jerry Koosman	.75	.40	.25
357	Buddy Bradford	.75	.40	.25
358	Dal Maxvill	.75	.40	.25
359	Brent Strom	.75	.40	.25
360	Greg Luzinski	.75	.40	.25
361	Don Carrithers	.75	.40	.25
362	Hal King	.75	.40	.25
363	Yankees Team	1.00	.50	.30
364	Clarence Gaston	2.50	1.25	.70
365	Steve Busby	.75	.40	.25
366	Larry Hisle	.75	.40	.25
367	Norm Cash	.75	.40	.25
368	Manny Mota	.75	.40	.25
369	Paul Lindblad	.75	.40	.25
370	Bob Watson	.75	.40	.25
371	Jim Slaton	.75	.40	.25
372	Ken Reitz	.75	.40	.25
373	John Curtis	.75	.40	.25
374	Marty Perez	.75	.40	.25
375	Earl Williams	.75	.40	.25
376	Jorge Orta	.75	.40	.25
377	Ron Woods	1.50	.70	.45
378	Burt Hooton	.75	.40	.25
379	Rangers Mgr./Coaches (Art Fowler, Frank Lucchesi, Billy Martin, Jackie Moore, Charlie Silvera)	.75	.40	.25
380	Bud Harrelson	.75	.40	.25
381	Charlie Sands	.75	.40	.25
382	Bob Moose	.75	.40	.25
383	Phillies Team	.75	.40	.25
384	Chris Chambliss	.75	.40	.25
385	Don Gullett	.75	.40	.25
386	Gary Matthews	.75	.40	.25
387	Rich Morales	.75	.40	.25
388	Phil Roof	.75	.40	.25
389	Gates Brown	.75	.40	.25
390	Lou Piniella	1.00	.50	.30
391	Billy Champion	.75	.40	.25
392	Dick Green	.75	.40	.25
393	Orlando Pena	.75	.40	.25
394	Ken Henderson	.75	.40	.25
395	Doug Rader	.75	.40	.25
396	Tommy Davis	.75	.40	.25
397	George Stone	.75	.40	.25
398	Duke Sims	.75	.40	.25
399	Mike Paul	.75	.40	.25
400	Harmon Killebrew	7.00	3.50	2.00
401	Elliot Maddox	.75	.40	.25
402	Jim Rooker	.75	.40	.25
403	Red Sox Mgr./Coaches (Don Bryant, Darrell Johnson, Eddie Popowski, Lee Stange, Don Zimmer)	.75	.40	.25
404	Jim Howarth	.75	.40	.25
405	Ellie Rodriguez	.75	.40	.25
406	Steve Arlin	.75	.40	.25
407	Jim Wohlford	.75	.40	.25
408	Charlie Hough	.75	.40	.25
409	Ike Brown	.75	.40	.25
410	Pedro Borbon	.75	.40	.25
411	Frank Baker	.75	.40	.25
412	Chuck Taylor	1.50	.70	.45
413	Don Money	.75	.40	.25
414	Checklist 4	1.00	.50	.30
415	Gary Gentry	.75	.40	.25
416	White Sox Team	.75	.40	.25
417	Rich Folkers	.75	.40	.25
418	Walt Williams	.75	.40	.25
419	Wayne Twitchell	.75	.40	.25
420	Ray Fosse	.75	.40	.25
421	Dan Fife	.75	.40	.25
422	Gonzalo Marquez	.75	.40	.25
423	Fred Stanley	.75	.40	.25
424	Jim Beauchamp	.75	.40	.25
425	Pete Broberg	.75	.40	.25
426	Rennie Stennett	.75	.40	.25
427	Bobby Bolin	.75	.40	.25
428	Gary Sutherland	.75	.40	.25
429	Dick Lange	.75	.40	.25
430	Matty Alou	.75	.40	.25
431	Gene Garber	.75	.40	.25
432	Chris Arnold	.75	.40	.25
433	Lerrin LaGrow	.75	.40	.25
434	Ken McMullen	.75	.40	.25
435	Dave Concepcion	.75	.40	.25
436	Don Hood	.75	.40	.25
437	Jim Lyttle	1.50	.70	.45
438	Ed Herrmann	.75	.40	.25
439	Norm Miller	.75	.40	.25
440	Jim Kaat	1.00	.50	.30
441	Tom Ragland	.75	.40	.25
442	Alan Foster	.75	.40	.25
443	Tom Hutton	.75	.40	.25
444	Vic Davalillo	.75	.40	.25
445	George Medich	.75	.40	.25
446	Len Randle	.75	.40	.25
447	Twins Mgr./Coaches (Vern Morgan, Frank Quilici, Bob Rodgers, Ralph Rowe)	.75	.40	.25
448	Ron Hodges	.75	.40	.25
449	Tom McCraw	.75	.40	.25
450	Rich Hebner	.75	.40	.25
451	Tommy John	1.25	.60	.40
452	Gene Hiser	.75	.40	.25
453	Balor Moore	1.50	.70	.45
454	Kurt Bevacqua	.75	.40	.25
455	Tom Bradley	.75	.40	.25
456	Dave Winfield	90.00	45.00	27.00
457	Chuck Goggin	.75	.40	.25
458	Jim Ray	.75	.40	.25
459	Reds Team	.75	.40	.25
460	Boog Powell	1.00	.50	.30
461	John Odom	.75	.40	.25
462	Luis Alvarado	.75	.40	.25
463	Pat Dobson	.75	.40	.25
464	Jose Cruz	.75	.40	.25
465	Dick Bosman	.75	.40	.25
466	Dick Billings	.75	.40	.25
467	Winston Llenas	.75	.40	.25
468	Pepe Frias	1.50	.70	.45
469	Joe Decker	.75	.40	.25
470	A.L. Playoffs (Reggie Jackson)	3.50	1.75	1.00
471	N.L. Playoffs	.75	.40	.25
472	World Series Game 1	.75	.40	.25
473	World Series Game 2 (Willie Mays)	5.00	2.50	1.50
474	World Series Game 3	.75	.40	.25
475	World Series Game 4	.75	.40	.25
476	World Series Game 5	.75	.40	.25
477	World Series Game 6 (Reggie Jackson)	4.50	2.25	1.25
478	World Series Game 7	.75	.40	.25
479	World Series Summary	.75	.40	.25
480	Willie Crawford	.75	.40	.25
481	Jerry Terrell	.75	.40	.25
482	Bob Didier	.75	.40	.25
483	Braves Team	.75	.40	.25
484	Carmen Fanzone	.75	.40	.25
485	Felipe Alou	4.00	2.00	1.25
486	Steve Stone	.75	.40	.25
487	Ted Martinez	.75	.40	.25
488	Andy Etchebarren	.75	.40	.25
489	Pirates Mgr./Coaches (Don Leppert, Bill Mazeroski, Danny Murtaugh, Don Osborn, Bob Skinner)	.75	.40	.25
490	Vada Pinson	.75	.40	.25
491	Roger Nelson	.75	.40	.25
492	Mike Rogodzinski	.75	.40	.25
493	Joe Hoerner	.75	.40	.25
494	Ed Goodson	.75	.40	.25
495	Dick McAuliffe	.75	.40	.25
496	Tom Murphy	.75	.40	.25
497	Bobby Mitchell	.75	.40	.25
498	Pat Corrales	.75	.40	.25
499	Rusty Torres	.75	.40	.25
500	Lee May	.75	.40	.25
501	Eddie Leon	.75	.40	.25
502	Dave LaRoche	.75	.40	.25
503	Eric Soderholm	.75	.40	.25
504	Joe Niekro	.75	.40	.25
505	Bill Buckner	.75	.40	.25
506	Ed Farmer	.75	.40	.25
507	Larry Stahl	.75	.40	.25
508	Expos Team	2.50	1.25	.70
509	Jesse Jefferson	.75	.40	.25
510	Wayne Garrett	.75	.40	.25
511	Toby Harrah	.75	.40	.25
512	Joe Lahoud	.75	.40	.25
513	Jim Campanis	.75	.40	.25
514	Paul Schaal	.75	.40	.25
515	Willie Montanez	.75	.40	.25
516	Horacio Pina	.75	.40	.25
517	Mike Hegan	.75	.40	.25
518	Derrel Thomas	.75	.40	.25
519	Bill Sharp	.75	.40	.25
520	Tim McCarver	.75	.40	.25
521	Indians Mgr./Coaches (Ken Aspromonte, Clay Bryant, Tony Pacheco)	.75	.40	.25
522	J.R. Richard	.75	.40	.25
523	Cecil Cooper	.75	.40	.25
524	Bill Plummer	.75	.40	.25
525	Clyde Wright	.75	.40	.25
526	Frank Tepedino	.75	.40	.25
527	Bobby Darwin	.75	.40	.25
528	Bill Bonham	.75	.40	.25
529	Horace Clarke	.75	.40	.25
530	Mickey Stanley	.75	.40	.25
531	Expos Mgr./Coaches (Dave Bristol, Larry Doby, Gene Mauch, Cal McLish, Jerry Zimmerman)	2.50	1.25	.70
532	Skip Lockwood	.75	.40	.25
533	Mike Phillips	.75	.40	.25
534	Eddie Watt	.75	.40	.25
535	Bob Tolan	.75	.40	.25
536	Duffy Dyer	.75	.40	.25
537	Steve Mingori	.75	.40	.25
538	Cesar Tovar	.75	.40	.25
539	Lloyd Allen	.75	.40	.25
540	Bob Robertson	.75	.40	.25
541	Indians Team	.75	.40	.25
542	Rich Gossage	1.00	.50	.30
543	Danny Cater	.75	.40	.25
544	Ron Schueler	.75	.40	.25
545	Billy Conigliaro	.75	.40	.25
546	Mike Corkins	.75	.40	.25
547	Glenn Borgmann	.75	.40	.25
548	Sonny Siebert	.75	.40	.25
549	Mike Jorgensen	1.50	.70	.45
550	Sam McDowell	.75	.40	.25
551	Von Joshua	.75	.40	.25
552	Denny Doyle	.75	.40	.25
553	Jim Willoughby	.75	.40	.25
554	Tim Johnson	.75	.40	.25
555	Woodie Fryman	.75	.40	.25
556	Dave Campbell	.75	.40	.25
557	Jim McGlothlin	.75	.40	.25
558	Bill Fahey	.75	.40	.25
559	Darrel Chaney	.75	.40	.25
560	Mike Cuellar	.75	.40	.25
561	Ed Kranepool	.75	.40	.25
562	Jack Aker	.75	.40	.25
563	Hal McRae	.75	.40	.25
564	Mike Ryan	.75	.40	.25
565	Milt Wilcox	.75	.40	.25
566	Jackie Hernandez	.75	.40	.25
567	Red Sox Team	.75	.40	.25
568	Mike Torrez	2.00	1.00	.60
569	Rick Dempsey	.75	.40	.25
570	Ralph Garr	.75	.40	.25
571	Rich Hand	.75	.40	.25
572	Enzo Hernandez	.75	.40	.25
573	Mike Adams	.75	.40	.25

574	Bill Parsons	.75	.40	.25
575	Steve Garvey	6.00	3.00	1.75
576	Scipio Spinks	.75	.40	.25
577	Mike Sadek	.75	.40	.25
578	Ralph Houk	.75	.40	.25
579	Cecil Upshaw	.75	.40	.25
580	Jim Spencer	.75	.40	.25
581	Fred Norman	.75	.40	.25
582	Bucky Dent	.75	.40	.25
583	Marty Pattin	.75	.40	.25
584	Ken Rudolph	.75	.40	.25
585	Merv Rettenmund	.75	.40	.25
586	Jack Brohamer	.75	.40	.25
587	Larry Christenson	.75	.40	.25
588	Hal Lanier	.75	.40	.25
589	Boots Day	1.50	.70	.45
590	Rogelio Moret	.75	.40	.25
591	Sonny Jackson	.75	.40	.25
592	Ed Bane	.75	.40	.25
593	Steve Yeager	.75	.40	.25
594	Lee Stanton	.75	.40	.25
595	Steve Blass	.75	.40	.25
596	Rookie Pitchers (Wayne Garland, Fred Holdsworth, Mark Littell, Dick Pole)	.75	.40	.25
597	Rookie Shortstops (Dave Chalk, John Gamble, Pete MacKanin, Manny Trillo)	.75	.40	.25
598	Rookie Outfielders (Dave Augustine, Ken Griffey, Steve Ontiveros, Jim Tyrone)	15.00	7.50	4.50
599	Rookie Pitchers (Ron Diorio, Dave Freisleben, Frank Riccelli, Greg Shanahan)	.75	.40	.25
600	Rookie Infielders (Ron Cash, Jim Cox, Bill Madlock, Reggie Sanders)	4.00	2.00	1.25
601	Rookie Outfielders (Ed Armbrister, Rich Bladt, Brian Downing, Bake McBride)	5.50	2.75	1.75
602	Rookie Pitchers (Glenn Abbott, Rick Henninger, Craig Swan, Dan Vossler)	.75	.40	.25
603	Rookie Catchers (Barry Foote, Tom Lundstedt, Charlie Moore, Sergio Robles)	1.50	.70	.45
604	Rookie Infielders (Terry Hughes, John Knox, Andy Thornton, Frank White)	5.50	2.75	1.75
605	Rookie Pitchers (Vic Albury, Ken Frailing, Kevin Kobel, Frank Tanana)	6.00	3.00	1.75
606	Rookie Outfielders (Jim Fuller, Wilbur Howard, Tommy Smith, Otto Velez)	.75	.40	.25
607	Rookie Shortstops (Leo Foster, Tom Heintzelman, Dave Rosello, Frank Taveras)	.75	.40	.25
608	Rookie Pitchers (Bob Apodaco, Dick Baney, John D'Acquisto, Mike Wallace)	.75	.40	.25
609	Rico Petrocelli	.75	.40	.25
610	Dave Kingman	1.00	.50	.30
611	Rick Stelmaszek	.75	.40	.25
612	Luke Walker	.75	.40	.25
613	Dan Monzon	.75	.40	.25
614	Adrian Devine	.75	.40	.25
615	Rookie Pitchers (Johnny Jeter, Tom Underwood)	.75	.40	.25
616	Larry Gura	.75	.40	.25
617	Ted Ford	.75	.40	.25
618	Jim Mason	.75	.40	.25
619	Mike Anderson	.75	.40	.25
620	Al Downing	.75	.40	.25
621	Bernie Carbo	.75	.40	.25
622	Phil Gagliano	.75	.40	.25
623	Celerino Sanchez	.75	.40	.25
624	Bob Miller	.75	.40	.25
625	Ollie Brown	.75	.40	.25
626	Pirates Team	.75	.40	.25
627	Carl Taylor	.75	.40	.25
628	Ivan Murrell	.75	.40	.25
629	Rusty Staub	1.50	.70	.45
630	Tommie Agee	.75	.40	.25
631	Steve Barber	.75	.40	.25
632	George Culver	.75	.40	.25
633	Dave Hamilton	.75	.40	.25
634	Braves Mgr./Coaches (Jim Busby, Eddie Mathews, Connie Ryan, Ken Silvestri, Herm Starrette)	1.00	.50	.30
635	John Edwards	.75	.40	.25
636	Dave Goltz	.75	.40	.25
637	Checklist 5	1.00	.50	.30
638	Ken Sanders	.75	.40	.25
639	Joe Lovitto	.75	.40	.25
640	Milt Pappas	.75	.40	.25
641	Chuck Brinkman	.75	.40	.25
642	Terry Harmon	.75	.40	.25
643	Dodgers Team	.75	.40	.25
644	Wayne Granger	.75	.40	.25
645	Ken Boswell	.75	.40	.25
646	George Foster	.75	.40	.25
647	Juan Beniquez	.75	.40	.25
648	Terry Crowley	.75	.40	.25
649	Fernando Gonzalez	.75	.40	.25
650	Mike Epstein	.75	.40	.25
651	Leron Lee	.75	.40	.25
652	Gail Hopkins	.75	.40	.25
653	Bob Stinson	1.50	.70	.45
654	Jesus Alou	.75	.40	.25
655	Mike Tyson	.75	.40	.25
656	Adrian Garrett	.75	.40	.25
657	Jim Shellenback	.75	.40	.25
658	Lee Lacy	.75	.40	.25
659	Joe Lis	.75	.40	.25
660	Larry Dierker	.75	.40	.25

1974 O-Pee-Chee Team Checklists

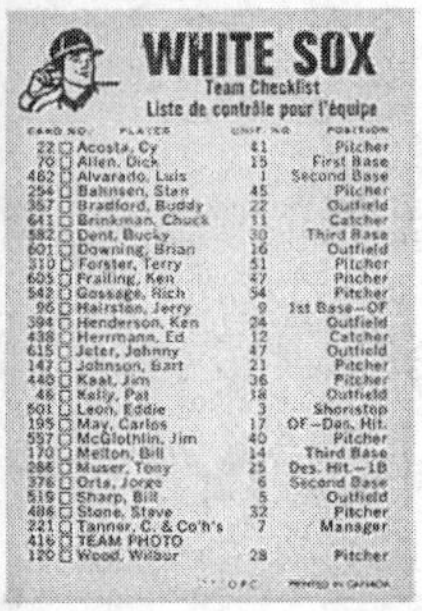

The 1974 O-Pee-Chee Team Checklists set is nearly identical to its Topps counterpart of the same year. Twenty-four unnumbered cards that measure 2-1/2" x 3-1/2" make up the set. The card fronts contain facsimile autographs while the backs carry a team checklist of players found in the regular issue O-Pee-Chee set of 1974. The cards have red borders and can be differentiated from the U.S. version by the "O.P.C. Printed in Canada" line on the back.

		NM	EX	VG
Complete Set (24):		30.00	15.00	9.00
Common Checklist:		1.50	.70	.40
(1)	Atlanta Braves	1.50	.70	.45
(2)	Baltimore Orioles	1.50	.70	.45
(3)	Boston Red Sox	1.50	.70	.45
(4)	California Angels	1.50	.70	.45
(5)	Chicago Cubs	1.50	.70	.45
(6)	Chicago White Sox	1.50	.70	.45
(7)	Cincinnati Reds	1.50	.70	.45
(8)	Cleveland Indians	1.50	.70	.45
(9)	Detroit Tigers	1.50	.70	.45
(10)	Houston Astros	1.50	.70	.45
(11)	Kansas City Royals	1.50	.70	.45
(12)	Los Angeles Dodgers	1.50	.70	.45
(13)	Milwaukee Brewers	1.50	.70	.45
(14)	Minnesota Twins	1.50	.70	.45
(15)	Montreal Expos	3.00	1.50	.90
(16)	New York Mets	1.50	.70	.45
(17)	New York Yankees	1.50	.70	.45
(18)	Oakland A's	1.50	.70	.45
(19)	Philadelphia Phillies	1.50	.70	.45
(20)	Pittsburgh Pirates	1.50	.70	.45
(21)	St. Louis Cardinals	1.50	.70	.45
(22)	San Diego Padres	1.50	.70	.45
(23)	San Francisco Giants	1.50	.70	.45
(24)	Texas Rangers	1.50	.70	.45

1975 O-Pee-Chee

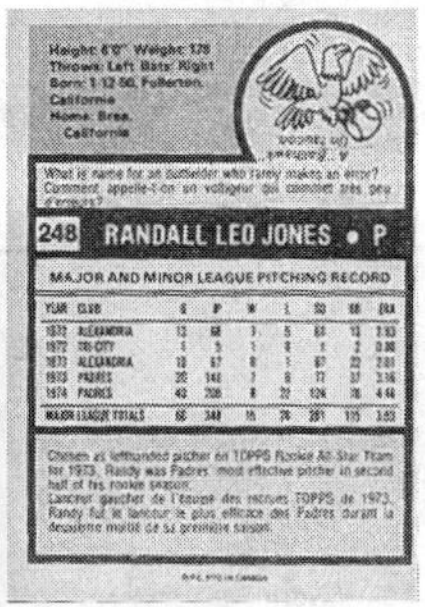

The 1975 O-Pee-Chee set was again complete at 660 cards, each measuring 2-1/2" x 3-1/2", and using the same design as the 1975 Topps set. The backs of the O-Pee-Chee cards are written in both French and English and state that the cards were printed in Canada.

		NM	EX	VG
Complete Set (660):		850.00	425.00	250.00
Common Player:		.55	.30	.15
1	'74 Highlights (Hank Aaron)	30.00	15.00	9.00
2	'74 Highlights (Lou Brock)	1.25	.60	.40
3	'74 Highlights (Bob Gibson)	1.25	.60	.40
4	'74 Highlights (Al Kaline)	4.50	2.25	1.25
5	'74 Highlights (Nolan Ryan)	35.00	17.50	10.50
6	'74 Highlights (Mike Marshall)	.55	.30	.15
7	'74 Highlights (Dick Bosman, Steve Busby, Nolan Ryan)	9.00	4.50	2.75
8	Rogelio Moret	.55	.30	.15
9	Frank Tepedino	.55	.30	.15
10	Willie Davis	1.50	.70	.45
11	Bill Melton	.55	.30	.15
12	David Clyde	.55	.30	.15
13	Gene Locklear	.55	.30	.15
14	Milt Wilcox	.55	.30	.15
15	Jose Cardenal	.55	.30	.15
16	Frank Tanana	.55	.30	.15
17	Dave Concepcion	.55	.30	.15
18	Tigers Team (Ralph Houk)	.75	.40	.25
19	Jerry Koosman	.55	.30	.15
20	Thurman Munson	7.00	3.50	2.00
21	Rollie Fingers	4.00	2.00	1.25
22	Dave Cash	.55	.30	.15
23	Bill Russell	.55	.30	.15
24	Al Fitzmorris	.55	.30	.15
25	Lee May	.55	.30	.15
26	Dave McNally	.55	.30	.15
27	Ken Reitz	.55	.30	.15
28	Tom Murphy	.55	.30	.15
29	Dave Parker	3.00	1.50	.90
30	Bert Blyleven	.75	.40	.25
31	Dave Rader	.55	.30	.15
32	Reggie Cleveland	.55	.30	.15
33	Dusty Baker	.65	.35	.20
34	Steve Renko	1.00	.50	.30
35	Ron Santo	.75	.40	.25
36	Joe Lovitto	.55	.30	.15
37	Dave Freisleben	.55	.30	.15
38	Buddy Bell	.75	.40	.25
39	Andy Thornton	.60	.30	.20
40	Bill Singer	.55	.30	.15
41	Cesar Geronimo	.55	.30	.15
42	Joe Coleman	.55	.30	.15
43	Cleon Jones	.55	.30	.15
44	Pat Dobson	.55	.30	.15
45	Joe Rudi	.55	.30	.15
46	Phillies Team (Danny Ozark)	.55	.30	.15
47	Tommy John	1.00	.50	.30
48	Freddie Patek	.55	.30	.15
49	Larry Dierker	.55	.30	.15
50	Brooks Robinson	8.00	4.00	2.50
51	Bob Forsch	.75	.40	.25
52	Darrell Porter	.55	.30	.15
53	Dave Giusti	.55	.30	.15
54	Eric Soderholm	.55	.30	.15
55	Bobby Bonds	.55	.30	.15
56	Rick Wise	.55	.30	.15
57	Dave Johnson	.55	.30	.15
58	Chuck Taylor	1.00	.50	.30
59	Ken Henderson	.55	.30	.15
60	Fergie Jenkins	6.00	3.00	1.75
61	Dave Winfield	25.00	12.50	7.50
62	Fritz Peterson	.55	.30	.15
63	Steve Swisher	.55	.30	.15
64	Dave Chalk	.55	.30	.15
65	Don Gullett	.55	.30	.15
66	Willie Horton	.55	.30	.15
67	Tug McGraw	.55	.30	.15
68	Ron Blomberg	.55	.30	.15
69	John Odom	.55	.30	.15
70	Mike Schmidt	60.00	30.00	18.00
71	Charlie Hough	.55	.30	.15
72	Royals Team (Jack McKeon)	.55	.30	.15
73	J.R. Richard	.55	.30	.15
74	Mark Belanger	.55	.30	.15
75	Ted Simmons	.55	.30	.15
76	Ed Sprague	.55	.30	.15
77	Richie Zisk	.55	.30	.15
78	Ray Corbin	.55	.30	.15
79	Gary Matthews	.55	.30	.15
80	Carlton Fisk	6.00	3.00	1.75
81	Ron Reed	.55	.30	.15
82	Pat Kelly	.55	.30	.15
83	Jim Merritt	.55	.30	.15
84	Enzo Hernandez	.55	.30	.15
85	Bill Bonham	.55	.30	.15
86	Joe Lis	.55	.30	.15
87	George Foster	.65	.35	.20
88	Tom Egan	.55	.30	.15
89	Jim Ray	.55	.30	.15
90	Rusty Staub	1.00	.50	.30
91	Dick Green	.55	.30	.15
92	Cecil Upshaw	.55	.30	.15
93	Dave Lopes	.55	.30	.15
94	Jim Lonborg	.55	.30	.15
95	John Mayberry	.55	.30	.15
96	Mike Cosgrove	.55	.30	.15
97	Earl Williams	.55	.30	.15
98	Rich Folkers	.55	.30	.15
99	Mike Hegan	.55	.30	.15
100	Willie Stargell	6.00	3.00	1.75
101	Expos Team (Gene Mauch)	1.50	.70	.45
102	Joe Decker	.55	.30	.15
103	Rick Miller	.55	.30	.15
104	Bill Madlock	.75	.40	.25
105	Buzz Capra	.55	.30	.15
106	Mike Hargrove	.55	.30	.15
107	Jim Barr	.55	.30	.15
108	Tom Hall	.55	.30	.15
109	George Hendrick	.55	.30	.15
110	Wilbur Wood	.55	.30	.15
111	Wayne Garrett	.55	.30	.15
112	Larry Hardy	.55	.30	.15
113	Elliott Maddox	.55	.30	.15
114	Dick Lange	.55	.30	.15
115	Joe Ferguson	.55	.30	.15
116	Lerrin LaGrow	.55	.30	.15
117	Orioles Team (Earl Weaver)	.75	.40	.25
118	Mike Anderson	.55	.30	.15
119	Tommy Helms	.55	.30	.15
120	Steve Busby (photo actually Fran Healy)	.55	.30	.15
121	Bill North	.55	.30	.15
122	Al Hrabosky	.55	.30	.15
123	Johnny Briggs	.55	.30	.15
124	Jerry Reuss	.55	.30	.15
125	Ken Singleton	1.50	.70	.45
126	Checklist 1-132	1.00	.50	.30
127	Glenn Borgmann	.55	.30	.15
128	Bill Lee	.55	.30	.15
129	Rick Monday	.55	.30	.15
130	Phil Niekro	4.00	2.00	1.25
131	Toby Harrah	.55	.30	.15
132	Randy Moffitt	.55	.30	.15

133	Dan Driessen	.55	.30	.15
134	Ron Hodges	.55	.30	.15
135	Charlie Spikes	.55	.30	.15
136	Jim Mason	.55	.30	.15
137	Terry Forster	.55	.30	.15
138	Del Unser	.55	.30	.15
139	Horacio Pina	.55	.30	.15
140	Steve Garvey	4.00	2.00	1.25
141	Mickey Stanley	.55	.30	.15
142	Bob Reynolds	.55	.30	.15
143	Cliff Johnson	.55	.30	.15
144	Jim Wohlford	.55	.30	.15
145	Ken Holtzman	.55	.30	.15
146	Padres Team (John McNamara)	.55	.30	.15
147	Pedro Garcia	.55	.30	.15
148	Jim Rooker	.55	.30	.15
149	Tim Foli	1.00	.50	.30
150	Bob Gibson	7.00	3.50	2.00
151	Steve Brye	.55	.30	.15
152	Mario Guerrero	.55	.30	.15
153	Rick Reuschel	.55	.30	.15
154	Mike Lum	.55	.30	.15
155	Jim Bibby	.55	.30	.15
156	Dave Kingman	1.00	.50	.30
157	Pedro Borbon	.55	.30	.15
158	Jerry Grote	.55	.30	.15
159	Steve Arlin	.55	.30	.15
160	Graig Nettles	.75	.40	.25
161	Stan Bahnsen	.55	.30	.15
162	Willie Montanez	.55	.30	.15
163	Jim Brewer	.55	.30	.15
164	Mickey Rivers	.55	.30	.15
165	Doug Rader	.55	.30	.15
166	Woodie Fryman	.55	.30	.15
167	Rich Coggins	.55	.30	.15
168	Bill Greif	.55	.30	.15
169	Cookie Rojas	.55	.30	.15
170	Bert Campaneris	.55	.30	.15
171	Ed Kirkpatrick	.55	.30	.15
172	Red Sox Team (Darrell Johnson)	.55	.30	.15
173	Steve Rogers	1.25	.60	.40
174	Bake McBride	.55	.30	.15
175	Don Money	.55	.30	.15
176	Burt Hooton	.55	.30	.15
177	Vic Correll	.55	.30	.15
178	Cesar Tovar	.55	.30	.15
179	Tom Bradley	.55	.30	.15
180	Joe Morgan	7.00	3.50	2.00
181	Fred Beene	.55	.30	.15
182	Don Hahn	.55	.30	.15
183	Mel Stottlemyre	.55	.30	.15
184	Jorge Orta	.55	.30	.15
185	Steve Carlton	7.00	3.50	2.00
186	Willie Crawford	.55	.30	.15
187	Denny Doyle	.55	.30	.15
188	Tom Griffin	.55	.30	.15
189	1951 - MVPs (Larry (Yogi) Berra, Roy Campanella)	3.00	1.50	.90
190	1952 - MVPs (Hank Sauer, Bobby Shantz)	.55	.30	.15
191	1953 - MVPs (Roy Campanella, Al Rosen)	.75	.40	.25
192	1954 - MVPs (Yogi Berra, Willie Mays)	5.00	2.50	1.50
193	1955 - MVPs (Yogi Berra, Roy Campanella)	3.00	1.50	.90
194	1956 - MVPs (Mickey Mantle, Don Newcombe)	7.50	3.75	2.25
195	1957 - MVPs (Hank Aaron, Mickey Mantle)	15.00	7.50	4.50
196	1958 - MVPs (Ernie Banks, Jackie Jensen)	3.00	1.50	.90
197	1959 - MVPs (Ernie Banks, Nellie Fox)	3.25	1.75	1.00
198	1960 - MVPs (Dick Groat, Roger Maris)	3.00	1.50	.90
199	1961 - MVPs (Roger Maris, Frank Robinson)	3.50	1.75	1.00
200	1962- MVPs (Mickey Mantle, Maury Wills)	7.50	3.75	2.25
201	1963 - MVPs (Elston Howard, Sandy Koufax)	3.50	1.75	1.00
202	1964 - MVPs (Ken Boyer, Brooks Robinson)	2.00	1.00	.60
203	1965 - MVPs (Willie Mays, Zoilo Versalles)	5.00	2.50	1.50
204	1966 - MVPs (Bob Clemente, Frank Robinson)	4.00	2.00	1.25
205	1967 - MVPs (Orlando Cepeda, Carl Yastrzemski)	3.50	1.75	1.00
206	1968 - MVPs (Bob Gibson, Denny McLain)	2.00	1.00	.60
207	1969 - MVPs (Harmon Killebrew, Willie McCovey)	2.00	1.00	.60
208	1970 - MVPs (Johnny Bench, Boog Powell)	3.00	1.50	.90
209	1971 - MVPs (Vida Blue, Joe Torre)	.55	.30	.15
210	1972 - MVPs (Rich Allen, Johnny Bench)	3.00	1.50	.90
211	1973 - MVPs (Reggie Jackson, Pete Rose)	6.00	3.00	1.75
212	1974 - MVPs (Jeff Burroughs, Steve Garvey)	.65	.35	.20
213	Oscar Gamble	.55	.30	.15
214	Harry Parker	.55	.30	.15
215	Bobby Valentine	.55	.30	.15
216	Giants Team (Wes Westrum)	.55	.30	.15
217	Lou Piniella	.65	.35	.20
218	Jerry Johnson	.55	.30	.15
219	Ed Herrmann	.55	.30	.15
220	Don Sutton	4.00	2.00	1.25
221	Aurelio Rodriquez (Rodriguez)	.55	.30	.15
222	Dan Spillner	.55	.30	.15
223	Robin Yount	150.00	75.00	45.00
224	Ramon Hernandez	.55	.30	.15
225	Bob Grich	.55	.30	.15
226	Bill Campbell	.55	.30	.15
227	Bob Watson	.55	.30	.15
228	George Brett	175.00	87.00	52.00
229	Barry Foote	1.00	.50	.30
230	Jim Hunter	4.00	2.00	1.25
231	Mike Tyson	.55	.30	.15
232	Diego Segui	.55	.30	.15
233	Billy Grabarkewitz	.55	.30	.15
234	Tom Grieve	.55	.30	.15
235	Jack Billingham	.55	.30	.15
236	Angels Team (Dick Williams)	.55	.30	.15
237	Carl Morton	.55	.30	.15
238	Dave Duncan	.55	.30	.15
239	George Stone	.55	.30	.15
240	Garry Maddox	.55	.30	.15
241	Dick Tidrow	.55	.30	.15
242	Jay Johnstone	.55	.30	.15
243	Jim Kaat	.75	.40	.25
244	Bill Buckner	.55	.30	.15
245	Mickey Lolich	.55	.30	.15
246	Cardinals Team (Red Schoendienst)	.60	.30	.20
247	Enos Cabell	.55	.30	.15
248	Randy Jones	.55	.30	.15
249	Danny Thompson	.55	.30	.15
250	Ken Brett	.55	.30	.15
251	Fran Healy	.55	.30	.15
252	Fred Scherman	.55	.30	.15
253	(Jesus Alou)	.55	.30	.15
254	Mike Torrez	1.50	.70	.45
255	Dwight Evans	1.00	.50	.30
256	Billy Champion	.55	.30	.15
257	Checklist 133-264	1.00	.50	.30
258	Dave LaRoche	.55	.30	.15
259	Len Randle	.55	.30	.15
260	Johnny Bench	10.00	5.00	3.00
261	Andy Hassler	.55	.30	.15
262	Rowland Office	.55	.30	.15
263	Jim Perry	.55	.30	.15
264	John Milner	.55	.30	.15
265	Ron Bryant	.55	.30	.15
266	Sandy Alomar	.55	.30	.15
267	Dick Ruthven	.55	.30	.15
268	Hal McRae	.55	.30	.15
269	Doug Rau	.55	.30	.15
270	Ron Fairly	1.00	.50	.30
271	Jerry Moses	.55	.30	.15
272	Lynn McGlothen	.55	.30	.15
273	Steve Braun	.55	.30	.15
274	Vicente Romo	.55	.30	.15
275	Paul Blair	.55	.30	.15
276	White Sox Team (Chuck Tanner)	.55	.30	.15
277	Frank Taveras	.55	.30	.15
278	Paul Lindblad	.55	.30	.15
279	Milt May	.55	.30	.15
280	Carl Yastrzemski	10.00	5.00	3.00
281	Jim Slaton	.55	.30	.15
282	Jerry Morales	.55	.30	.15
283	Steve Foucault	.55	.30	.15
284	Ken Griffey	2.00	1.00	.60
285	Ellie Rodriguez	.55	.30	.15
286	Mike Jorgensen	1.00	.50	.30
287	Roric Harrison	.55	.30	.15
288	Bruce Ellingsen	.55	.30	.15
289	Ken Rudolph	.55	.30	.15
290	Jon Matlack	.55	.30	.15
291	Bill Sudakis	.55	.30	.15
292	Ron Schueler	.55	.30	.15
293	Dick Sharon	.55	.30	.15
294	Geoff Zahn	.55	.30	.15
295	Vada Pinson	.55	.30	.15
296	Alan Foster	.55	.30	.15
297	Craig Kusick	.55	.30	.15
298	Johnny Grubb	.55	.30	.15
299	Bucky Dent	.55	.30	.15
300	Reggie Jackson	15.00	7.50	4.50
301	Dave Roberts	.55	.30	.15
302	Rick Burleson	.55	.30	.15
303	Grant Jackson	.55	.30	.15
304	Pirates Team (Danny Murtaugh)	.55	.30	.15
305	Jim Colborn	.55	.30	.15
306	Batting Leaders (Rod Carew, Ralph Garr)	.75	.40	.25
307	Home Run Leaders (Dick Allen, Mike Schmidt)	4.00	2.00	1.25
308	Runs Batted In (Johnny Bench, Jeff Burroughs)	1.50	.70	.45
309	Stolen Base Leaders (Lou Brock, Bill North)	.75	.40	.25
310	Victory Leaders (Jim Hunter, Fergie Jenkins, Andy Messersmith, Phil Niekro)	1.00	.50	.30
311	Earned Run Average Leaders (Buzz Capra, Jim Hunter)	.55	.30	.15
312	Strikeout Leaders (Steve Carlton, Nolan Ryan)	25.00	12.50	7.50
313	Leading Firemen (Terry Forster, Mike Marshall)	1.00	.50	.30
314	Buck Martinez	.55	.30	.15
315	Don Kessinger	.55	.30	.15
316	Jackie Brown	.55	.30	.15
317	Joe Lahoud	.55	.30	.15
318	Ernie McAnally	1.00	.50	.30
319	Johnny Oates	.55	.30	.15
320	Pete Rose	35.00	17.50	10.50
321	Rudy May	.55	.30	.15
322	Ed Goodson	.55	.30	.15
323	Fred Holdsworth	.55	.30	.15
324	Ed Kranepool	.55	.30	.15
325	Tony Oliva	.75	.40	.25
326	Wayne Twitchell	.55	.30	.15
327	Jerry Hairston	.55	.30	.15
328	Sonny Siebert	.55	.30	.15
329	Ted Kubiak	.55	.30	.15
330	Mike Marshall	.55	.30	.15
331	Indians Team (Frank Robinson)	.60	.30	.20
332	Fred Kendall	.55	.30	.15
333	Dick Drago	.55	.30	.15
334	Greg Gross	.55	.30	.15
335	Jim Palmer	7.00	3.50	2.00
336	Rennie Stennett	.55	.30	.15
337	Kevin Kobel	.55	.30	.15
338	Rick Stelmaszek	.55	.30	.15
339	Jim Fregosi	.55	.30	.15
340	Paul Splittorff	.55	.30	.15
341	Hal Breeden	1.00	.50	.30
342	Leroy Stanton	.55	.30	.15
343	Danny Frisella	.55	.30	.15
344	Ben Oglivie	.55	.30	.15
345	Clay Carroll	.55	.30	.15
346	Bobby Darwin	.55	.30	.15
347	Mike Caldwell	.55	.30	.15
348	Tony Muser	.55	.30	.15
349	Ray Sadecki	.55	.30	.15
350	Bobby Murcer	.55	.30	.15
351	Bob Boone	.55	.30	.15
352	Darold Knowles	.55	.30	.15
353	Luis Melendez	.55	.30	.15
354	Dick Bosman	.55	.30	.15
355	Chris Cannizzaro	.55	.30	.15
356	Rico Petrocelli	.55	.30	.15
357	Ken Forsch	.55	.30	.15
358	Al Bumbry	.55	.30	.15
359	Paul Popovich	.55	.30	.15
360	George Scott	.55	.30	.15
361	Dodgers Team (Walter Alston)	.75	.40	.25
362	Steve Hargan	.55	.30	.15
363	Carmen Fanzone	.55	.30	.15
364	Doug Bird	.55	.30	.15
365	Bob Bailey	1.00	.50	.30
366	Ken Sanders	.55	.30	.15
367	Craig Robinson	.55	.30	.15
368	Vic Albury	.55	.30	.15
369	Merv Rettenmund	.55	.30	.15
370	Tom Seaver	15.00	7.50	4.50
371	Gates Brown	.55	.30	.15
372	John D'Acquisto	.55	.30	.15
373	Bill Sharp	.55	.30	.15
374	Eddie Watt	.55	.30	.15
375	Roy White	.55	.30	.15
376	Steve Yeager	.55	.30	.15
377	Tom Hilgendorf	.55	.30	.15
378	Derrel Thomas	.55	.30	.15
379	Bernie Carbo	.55	.30	.15
380	Sal Bando	.55	.30	.15
381	John Curtis	.55	.30	.15
382	Don Baylor	.75	.40	.25
383	Jim York	.55	.30	.15
384	Brewers Team (Del Crandall)	.55	.30	.15
385	Dock Ellis	.55	.30	.15
386	Checklist 265-396	1.00	.50	.30
387	Jim Spencer	.55	.30	.15
388	Steve Stone	.55	.30	.15
389	Tony Solaita	.55	.30	.15
390	Ron Cey	.55	.30	.15
391	Don DeMola	1.00	.50	.30
392	Bruce Bochte	.55	.30	.15
393	Gary Gentry	.55	.30	.15
394	Larvell Blanks	.55	.30	.15
395	Bud Harrelson	.55	.30	.15
396	Fred Norman	.55	.30	.15
397	Bill Freehan	.55	.30	.15
398	Elias Sosa	.55	.30	.15
399	Terry Harmon	.55	.30	.15
400	Dick Allen	.75	.40	.25
401	Mike Wallace	.55	.30	.15
402	Bob Tolan	.55	.30	.15
403	Tom Buskey	.55	.30	.15
404	Ted Sizemore	.55	.30	.15
405	John Montague	1.00	.50	.30
406	Bob Gallagher	.55	.30	.15
407	Herb Washington	.55	.30	.15
408	Clyde Wright	.55	.30	.15
409	Bob Robertson	.55	.30	.15
410	Mike Cueller (Cuellar)	.55	.30	.15
411	George Mitterwald	.55	.30	.15
412	Bill Hands	.55	.30	.15
413	Marty Pattin	.55	.30	.15
414	Manny Mota	.55	.30	.15
415	John Hiller	.55	.30	.15
416	Larry Lintz	1.00	.50	.30
417	Skip Lockwood	.55	.30	.15
418	Leo Foster	.55	.30	.15
419	Dave Goltz	.55	.30	.15
420	Larry Bowa	.55	.30	.15
421	Mets Team (Yogi Berra)	.75	.40	.25
422	Brian Downing	.55	.30	.15
423	Clay Kirby	.55	.30	.15
424	John Lowenstein	.55	.30	.15
425	Tito Fuentes	.55	.30	.15
426	George Medich	.55	.30	.15
427	Clarence Gaston	1.50	.70	.45
428	Dave Hamilton	.55	.30	.15
429	Jim Dwyer	.55	.30	.15
430	Luis Tiant	.55	.30	.15
431	Rod Gilbreath	.55	.30	.15
432	Ken Berry	.55	.30	.15
433	Larry Demery	.55	.30	.15
434	Bob Locker	.55	.30	.15
435	Dave Nelson	.55	.30	.15
436	Ken Frailing	.55	.30	.15
437	Al Cowens	.55	.30	.15
438	Don Carrithers	1.00	.50	.30
439	Ed Brinkman	.55	.30	.15
440	Andy Messersmith	.55	.30	.15
441	Bobby Heise	.55	.30	.15
442	Maximino Leon	.55	.30	.15
443	Twins Team (Frank Quillici)	.55	.30	.15
444	Gene Garber	.55	.30	.15

445	Felix Millan	.55	.30	.15
446	Bart Johnson	.55	.30	.15
447	Terry Crowley	.55	.30	.15
448	Frank Duffy	.55	.30	.15
449	Charlie Williams	.55	.30	.15
450	Willie McCovey	7.00	3.50	2.00
451	Rick Dempsey	.55	.30	.15
452	Angel Mangual	.55	.30	.15
453	Claude Osteen	.55	.30	.15
454	Doug Griffin	.55	.30	.15
455	Don Wilson	.55	.30	.15
456	Bob Coluccio	.55	.30	.15
457	Mario Mendoza	.55	.30	.15
458	Ross Grimsley	.55	.30	.15
459	A.L. Championships	.75	.40	.25
460	N.L. Championships	.75	.40	.25
461	World Series Game 1 (Reggie Jackson)	3.50	1.75	1.00
462	World Series Game 2	.75	.40	.25
463	World Series Game 3 (Rollie Fingers)	1.00	.50	.30
464	World Series Game 4	.75	.40	.25
465	World Series Game 5	.75	.40	.25
466	World Series Summary	.75	.40	.25
467	Ed Halicki	.55	.30	.15
468	Bobby Mitchell	.55	.30	.15
469	Tom Dettore	.55	.30	.15
470	Jeff Burroughs	.55	.30	.15
471	Bob Stinson	1.00	.50	.30
472	Bruce Dal Canton	.55	.30	.15
473	Ken McMullen	.55	.30	.15
474	Luke Walker	.55	.30	.15
475	Darrell Evans	.55	.30	.15
476	Ed Figueroa	.55	.30	.15
477	Tom Hutton	.55	.30	.15
478	Tom Burgmeier	.55	.30	.15
479	Ken Boswell	.55	.30	.15
480	Carlos May	.55	.30	.15
481	Will McEnaney	.55	.30	.15
482	Tom McCraw	.55	.30	.15
483	Steve Ontiveros	.55	.30	.15
484	Glenn Beckert	.55	.30	.15
485	Sparky Lyle	.55	.30	.15
486	Ray Fosse	.55	.30	.15
487	Astros Team (Preston Gomez)	.55	.30	.15
488	Bill Travers	.55	.30	.15
489	Cecil Cooper	.55	.30	.15
490	Reggie Smith	.55	.30	.15
491	Doyle Alexander	.55	.30	.15
492	Rich Hebner	.55	.30	.15
493	Don Stanhouse	.55	.30	.15
494	Pete LaCock	.55	.30	.15
495	Nelson Briles	.55	.30	.15
496	Pepe Frias	1.00	.50	.30
497	Jim Nettles	.55	.30	.15
498	Al Downing	.55	.30	.15
499	Marty Perez	.55	.30	.15
500	Nolan Ryan	90.00	45.00	27.00
501	Bill Robinson	.55	.30	.15
502	Pat Bourque	.55	.30	.15
503	Fred Stanley	.55	.30	.15
504	Buddy Bradford	.55	.30	.15
505	Chris Speier	.55	.30	.15
506	Leron Lee	.55	.30	.15
507	Tom Carroll	.55	.30	.15
508	Bob Hansen	.55	.30	.15
509	Dave Hilton	.55	.30	.15
510	Vida Blue	.55	.30	.15
511	Rangers Team (Billy Martin)	.60	.30	.20
512	Larry Milbourne	.55	.30	.15
513	Dick Pole	.55	.30	.15
514	Jose Cruz	.55	.30	.15
515	Manny Sanguillen	.55	.30	.15
516	Don Hood	.55	.30	.15
517	Checklist 397-528	1.00	.50	.30
518	Leo Cardenas	.55	.30	.15
519	Jim Todd	.55	.30	.15
520	Amos Otis	.55	.30	.15
521	Dennis Blair	1.00	.50	.30
522	Gary Sutherland	.55	.30	.15
523	Tom Paciorek	.55	.30	.15
524	John Doherty	.55	.30	.15
525	Tom House	.55	.30	.15
526	Larry Hisle	.55	.30	.15
527	Mac Scarce	.55	.30	.15
528	Eddie Leon	.55	.30	.15
529	Gary Thomasson	.55	.30	.15
530	Gaylord Perry	4.00	2.00	1.25
531	Reds Team (Sparky Anderson)	.75	.40	.25
532	Gorman Thomas	.55	.30	.15
533	Rudy Meoli	.55	.30	.15
534	Alex Johnson	.55	.30	.15
535	Gene Tenace	.55	.30	.15
536	Bob Moose	.55	.30	.15
537	Tommy Harper	.55	.30	.15
538	Duffy Dyer	.55	.30	.15
539	Jesse Jefferson	.55	.30	.15
540	Lou Brock	7.00	3.50	2.00
541	Roger Metzger	.55	.30	.15
542	Pete Broberg	.55	.30	.15
543	Larry Biittner	1.00	.50	.30
544	Steve Mingori	.55	.30	.15
545	Billy Williams	6.00	3.00	1.75
546	John Knox	.55	.30	.15
547	Von Joshua	.55	.30	.15
548	Charlie Sands	.55	.30	.15
549	Bill Butler	.55	.30	.15
550	Ralph Garr	.55	.30	.15
551	Larry Christenson	.55	.30	.15
552	Jack Brohamer	.55	.30	.15
553	John Boccabella	.55	.30	.15
554	Rich Gossage	.75	.40	.25
555	Al Oliver	.75	.40	.25
556	Tim Johnson	.55	.30	.15
557	Larry Gura	.55	.30	.15
558	Dave Roberts	.55	.30	.15
559	Bob Montgomery	.55	.30	.15
560	Tony Perez	4.00	2.00	1.25
561	A's Team (Alvin Dark)	.55	.30	.15
562	Gary Nolan	.55	.30	.15
563	Wilbur Howard	.55	.30	.15
564	Tommy Davis	.55	.30	.15
565	Joe Torre	1.25	.60	.40
566	Ray Burris	.55	.30	.15
567	Jim Sundberg	.55	.30	.15
568	Dale Murray	1.00	.50	.30
569	Frank White	.55	.30	.15
570	Jim Wynn	.55	.30	.15
571	Dave Lemanczyk	.55	.30	.15
572	Roger Nelson	.55	.30	.15
573	Orlando Pena	.55	.30	.15
574	Tony Taylor	.55	.30	.15
575	Gene Clines	.55	.30	.15
576	Phil Roof	.55	.30	.15
577	John Morris	.55	.30	.15
578	Dave Tomlin	.55	.30	.15
579	Skip Pitlock	.55	.30	.15
580	Frank Robinson	6.00	3.00	1.75
581	Darrel Chaney	.55	.30	.15
582	Eduardo Rodriguez	.55	.30	.15
583	Andy Etchebarren	.55	.30	.15
584	Mike Garman	.55	.30	.15
585	Chris Chambliss	.55	.30	.15
586	Tim McCarver	.55	.30	.15
587	Chris Ward	.55	.30	.15
588	Rick Auerbach	.55	.30	.15
589	Braves Team (Clyde King)	.55	.30	.15
590	Cesar Cedeno	.55	.30	.15
591	Glenn Abbott	.55	.30	.15
592	Balor Moore	1.00	.50	.30
593	Gene Lamont	.55	.30	.15
594	Jim Fuller	.55	.30	.15
595	Joe Niekro	.55	.30	.15
596	Ollie Brown	.55	.30	.15
597	Winston Llenas	.55	.30	.15
598	Bruce Kison	.55	.30	.15
599	Nate Colbert	.55	.30	.15
600	Rod Carew	7.00	3.50	2.00
601	Juan Beniquez	.55	.30	.15
602	John Vukovich	.55	.30	.15
603	Lew Kruasse	.55	.30	.15
604	Oscar Zamora	.55	.30	.15
605	John Ellis	.55	.30	.15
606	Bruce Miller	.55	.30	.15
607	Jim Holt	.55	.30	.15
608	Gene Michael	.55	.30	.15
609	Ellie Hendricks	.55	.30	.15
610	Ron Hunt	.55	.30	.15
611	Yankees Team (Bill Virdon)	.75	.40	.25
612	Terry Hughes	.55	.30	.15
613	Bill Parsons	.55	.30	.15
614	Rookie Pitchers (Jack Kecek, Dyar Miller, Vern Ruhle, Paul Siebert)	.55	.30	.15
615	Rookie Pitchers (Pat Darcy, Dennis Leonard, Tom Underwood, Hank Webb)	.55	.30	.15
616	Rookie Outfielders (Dave Augustine, Pepe Mangual, Jim Rice, John Scott)	12.00	6.00	3.50
617	Rookie Infielders (Mike Cubbage, Doug DeCinces, Reggie Sanders, Manny Trillo)	1.00	.50	.30
618	Rookie Pitchers (Jamie Easterly, Tom Johnson, Scott McGregor, Rick Rhoden)	2.00	1.00	.60
619	Rookie Outfielders (Benny Ayala, Nyls Nyman, Tommy Smith, Jerry Turner)	.55	.30	.15
620	Catchers-Outfielders (Gary Carter, Marc Hill, Danny Meyer, Leon Roberts)	45.00	22.00	13.50
621	Rookie Pitchers (John Denny, Rawly Eastwick, Jim Kern, Juan Veintidos)	.55	.30	.15
622	Rookie Outfielders (Ed Armbrister, Fred Lynn, Tom Poquette, Terry Whitfield)	12.00	6.00	3.50
623	Rookie Infielders (Phil Garner, Keith Hernandez, Bob Sheldon, Tom Veryzer)	12.00	6.00	3.50
624	Rookie Pitchers (Doug Knoieczny, Gary Lavelle, Jim Otten, Eddie Solomon)	.55	.30	.15
625	Boog Powell	.60	.30	.20
626	Larry Haney	.55	.30	.15
627	Tom Walker	1.00	.50	.30
628	Ron LeFlore	.60	.30	.20
629	Joe Hoerner	.55	.30	.15
630	Greg Luzinski	.55	.30	.15
631	Lee Lacy	.55	.30	.15
632	Morris Nettles	.55	.30	.15
633	Paul Casanova	.55	.30	.15
634	Cy Acosta	.55	.30	.15
635	Chuck Dobson	.55	.30	.15
636	Charlie Moore	.55	.30	.15
637	Ted Martinez	.55	.30	.15
638	Cubs Team (Jim Marshall)	.55	.30	.15
639	Steve Kline	.55	.30	.15
640	Harmon Killebrew	7.00	3.50	2.00
641	Jim Northrup	.55	.30	.15
642	Mike Phillips	.55	.30	.15
643	Brent Strom	.55	.30	.15
644	Bill Fahey	.55	.30	.15
645	Danny Cater	.55	.30	.15
646	Checklist 529-660	1.00	.50	.30
647	Claudell Washington	.55	.30	.15
648	Dave Pagan	.55	.30	.15
649	Jack Heidemann	.55	.30	.15
650	Dave May	.55	.30	.15
651	John Morlan	.55	.30	.15
652	Lindy McDaniel	.55	.30	.15
653	Lee Richards	.55	.30	.15
654	Jerry Terrell	.55	.30	.15
655	Rico Carty	.55	.30	.15
656	Bill Plummer	.55	.30	.15
657	Bob Oliver	.55	.30	.15
658	Vic Harris	.55	.30	.15
659	Bob Apodaca	.55	.30	.15
660	Hank Aaron	40.00	20.00	12.00

1976 O-Pee-Chee

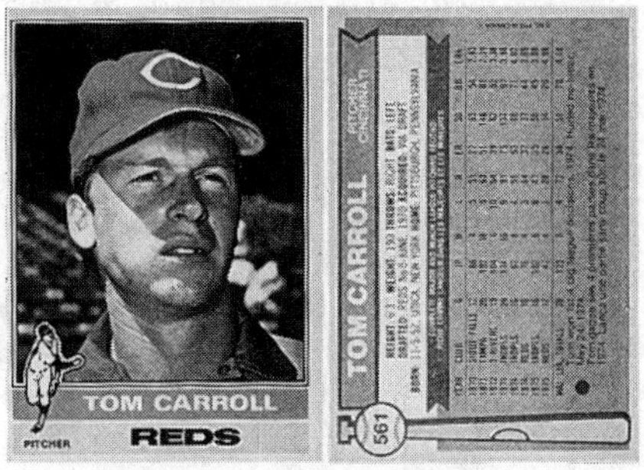

Identical in design to the 1976 Topps set, the Canadian-issued 1976 O-Pee-Chee set contains 660 cards, each 2-1/2" x 3-1/2". The backs are printed in both French and English and state "Ptd. in Canada."

		NM	EX	VG
Complete Set (660):		425.00	210.00	125.00
Common Player:		.25	.13	.08
1	'75 Record Breaker (Hank Aaron)	13.00	6.50	4.00
2	'75 Record Breaker (Bobby Bonds)	.40	.13	.12
3	'75 Record Breaker (Mickey Lolich)	.25	.13	.08
4	'75 Record Breaker (Dave Lopes)	.25	.13	.08
5	'75 Record Breaker (Tom Seaver)	3.50	1.75	1.00
6	'75 Record Breaker (Rennie Stennett)	.25	.13	.08
7	Jim Umbarger	.25	.13	.08
8	Tito Fuentes	.25	.13	.08
9	Paul Lindblad	.25	.13	.08
10	Lou Brock	6.00	3.00	1.75
11	Jim Hughes	.25	.13	.08
12	Richie Zisk	.25	.13	.08
13	Johnny Wockenfuss	.25	.13	.08
14	Gene Garber	.25	.13	.08
15	George Scott	.25	.13	.08
16	Bob Apodaca	.25	.13	.08
17	Yankees Team (Billy Martin)	.55	.30	.15
18	Dale Murray	.75	.40	.25
19	George Brett	50.00	25.00	15.00
20	Bob Watson	.25	.13	.08
21	Dave LaRoche	.25	.13	.08
22	Bill Russell	.25	.13	.08
23	Brian Downing	.25	.13	.08
24	Cesar Geronimo	.25	.13	.08
25	Mike Torrez	.25	.13	.08
26	Andy Thornton	.25	.13	.08
27	Ed Figueroa	.25	.13	.08
28	Dusty Baker	.25	.13	.08
29	Rick Burleson	.25	.13	.08
30	John Montefusco	.25	.13	.08
31	Len Randle	.25	.13	.08
32	Danny Frisella	.25	.13	.08
33	Bill North	.25	.13	.08
34	Mike Garman	.25	.13	.08
35	Tony Oliva	.50	.25	.15
36	Frank Taveras	.25	.13	.08
37	John Hiller	.25	.13	.08
38	Garry Maddox	.25	.13	.08
39	Pete Broberg	.25	.13	.08
40	Dave Kingman	.75	.40	.25
41	Tippy Martinez	.25	.13	.08
42	Barry Foote	.75	.40	.25
43	Paul Splittorff	.25	.13	.08
44	Doug Rader	.25	.13	.08
45	Boog Powell	.40	.13	.12
46	Dodgers Team (Walter Alston)	.85	.45	.25
47	Jesse Jefferson	.25	.13	.08
48	Dave Concepcion	.25	.13	.08
49	Dave Duncan	.25	.13	.08
50	Fred Lynn	1.50	.70	.45
51	Ray Burris	.25	.13	.08
52	Dave Chalk	.25	.13	.08
53	Mike Beard	.25	.13	.08
54	Dave Rader	.25	.13	.08
55	Gaylord Perry	4.00	2.00	1.25
56	Bob Tolan	.25	.13	.08
57	Phil Garner	.25	.13	.08
58	Ron Reed	.25	.13	.08
59	Larry Hisle	.25	.13	.08
60	Jerry Reuss	.25	.13	.08
61	Ron LeFlore	.25	.13	.08
62	Johnny Oates	.25	.13	.08
63	Bobby Darwin	.25	.13	.08
64	Jerry Koosman	.25	.13	.08
65	Chris Chambliss	.25	.13	.08

66	Father and Son (Buddy Bell, Gus Bell)	.40	.13	.12
67	Father and Son (Bob Boone, Ray Boone)	.45	.25	.14
68	Father and Son (Joe Coleman, Joe Coleman, Jr.)	.25	.13	.08
69	Father and Son (Jim Hegan, Mike Hegan)	.25	.13	.08
70	Father and Son (Roy Smalley, III, Roy Smalley, Jr.)	.25	.13	.08
71	Steve Rogers	1.00	.50	.30
72	Hal McRae	.25	.13	.08
73	Orioles Team (Earl Weaver)	.75	.40	.25
74	Oscar Gamble	.25	.13	.08
75	Larry Dierker	.25	.13	.08
76	Willie Crawford	.25	.13	.08
77	Pedro Borbon	.25	.13	.08
78	Cecil Cooper	.25	.13	.08
79	Jerry Morales	.25	.13	.08
80	Jim Kaat	.55	.30	.15
81	Darrell Evans	.25	.13	.08
82	Von Joshua	.25	.13	.08
83	Jim Spencer	.25	.13	.08
84	Brent Strom	.25	.13	.08
85	Mickey Rivers	.25	.13	.08
86	Mike Tyson	.25	.13	.08
87	Tom Burgmeier	.25	.13	.08
88	Duffy Dyer	.25	.13	.08
89	Vern Ruhle	.25	.13	.08
90	Sal Bando	.25	.13	.08
91	Tom Hutton	.25	.13	.08
92	Eduardo Rodriguez	.25	.13	.08
93	Mike Phillips	.25	.13	.08
94	Jim Dwyer	.75	.40	.25
95	Brooks Robinson	6.50	3.25	2.00
96	Doug Bird	.25	.13	.08
97	Wilbur Howard	.25	.13	.08
98	Dennis Eckersley	25.00	12.50	7.50
99	Lee Lacy	.25	.13	.08
100	Jim Hunter	4.00	2.00	1.25
101	Pete LaCock	.25	.13	.08
102	Jim Willoughby	.25	.13	.08
103	Biff Pocoroba	.25	.13	.08
104	Reds Team (Sparky Anderson)	.75	.40	.25
105	Gary Lavelle	.25	.13	.08
106	Tom Grieve	.25	.13	.08
107	Dave Roberts	.25	.13	.08
108	Don Kirkwood	.25	.13	.08
109	Larry Lintz	.25	.13	.08
110	Carlos May	.25	.13	.08
111	Danny Thompson	.25	.13	.08
112	Kent Tekulve	.25	.13	.08
113	Gary Sutherland	.25	.13	.08
114	Jay Johnstone	.25	.13	.08
115	Ken Holtzman	.25	.13	.08
116	Charlie Moore	.25	.13	.08
117	Mike Jorgensen	.75	.40	.25
118	Red Sox Team (Darrell Johnson)	.25	.13	.08
119	Checklist 1-132	1.00	.50	.30
120	Rusty Staub	1.00	.50	.30
121	Tony Solaita	.25	.13	.08
122	Mike Cosgrove	.25	.13	.08
123	Walt Williams	.25	.13	.08
124	Doug Rau	.25	.13	.08
125	Don Baylor	.40	.20	.12
126	Tom Dettore	.25	.13	.08
127	Larvell Blanks	.25	.13	.08
128	Ken Griffey	.25	.13	.08
129	Andy Etchebarren	.25	.13	.08
130	Luis Tiant	.25	.13	.08
131	Bill Stein	.25	.13	.08
132	Don Hood	.25	.13	.08
133	Gary Matthews	.25	.13	.08
134	Mike Ivie	.25	.13	.08
135	Bake McBride	.25	.13	.08
136	Dave Goltz	.25	.13	.08
137	Bill Robinson	.25	.13	.08
138	Lerrin LaGrow	.25	.13	.08
139	Gorman Thomas	.25	.13	.08
140	Vida Blue	.45	.25	.14
141	Larry Parrish	2.00	1.00	.60
142	Dick Drago	.25	.13	.08
143	Jerry Grote	.25	.13	.08
144	Al Fitzmorris	.25	.13	.08
145	Larry Bowa	.25	.13	.08
146	George Medich	.25	.13	.08
147	Astros Team (Bill Virdon)	.25	.13	.08
148	Stan Thomas	.25	.13	.08
149	Tommy Davis	.25	.13	.08
150	Steve Garvey	3.00	1.50	.90
151	Bill Bonham	.25	.13	.08
152	Leroy Stanton	.25	.13	.08
153	Buzz Capra	.25	.13	.08
154	Bucky Dent	.25	.13	.08
155	Jack Billingham	.25	.13	.08
156	Rico Carty	.25	.13	.08
157	Mike Caldwell	.25	.13	.08
158	Ken Reitz	.25	.13	.08
159	Jerry Terrell	.25	.13	.08
160	Dave Winfield	15.00	7.50	4.50
161	Bruce Kison	.25	.13	.08
162	Jack Pierce	.25	.13	.08
163	Jim Slaton	.25	.13	.08
164	Pepe Mangual	.75	.40	.25
165	Gene Tenace	.25	.13	.08
166	Skip Lockwood	.25	.13	.08
167	Freddie Patek	.25	.13	.08
168	Tom Hilgendorf	.25	.13	.08
169	Graig Nettles	.25	.13	.08
170	Rick Wise	.25	.13	.08
171	Greg Gross	.25	.13	.08
172	Rangers Team (Frank Lucchesi)	.25	.13	.08
173	Steve Swisher	.25	.13	.08

174	Charlie Hough	.25	.13	.08
175	Ken Singleton	.25	.13	.08
176	Dick Lange	.25	.13	.08
177	Marty Perez	.25	.13	.08
178	Tom Buskey	.25	.13	.08
179	George Foster	.25	.13	.08
180	Rich Gossage	.65	.35	.20
181	Willie Montanez	.25	.13	.08
182	Harry Rasmussen	.25	.13	.08
183	Steve Braun	.25	.13	.08
184	Bill Greif	.25	.13	.08
185	Dave Parker	2.00	1.00	.60
186	Tom Walker	.25	.13	.08
187	Pedro Garcia	.25	.13	.08
188	Fred Scherman	.75	.40	.25
189	Claudell Washington	.25	.13	.08
190	Jon Matlack	.25	.13	.08
191	N.L. Batting Leaders (Bill Madlock, Manny Sanguillen, Ted Simmons)	.50	.25	.15
192	A.L. Batting Leaders (Rod Carew, Fred Lynn, Thurman Munson)	2.00	1.00	.60
193	N.L. Home Run Leaders (Dave Kingman, Greg Luzinski, Mike Schmidt)	2.00	1.00	.60
194	A.L. Home Run Leaders (Reggie Jackson, John Mayberry, George Scott)	2.00	1.00	.60
195	N.L. Runs Batted In Ldrs. (Johnny Bench, Greg Luzinski, Tony Perez)	2.00	1.00	.60
196	A.L. Runs Batted In Ldrs. (Fred Lynn, John Mayberry, George Scott)	.50	.25	.15
197	N.L. Stolen Base Leaders (Lou Brock, Dave Lopes, Joe Morgan)	2.00	1.00	.60
198	A.L. Stolen Base Leaders (Amos Otis, Mickey Rivers, Claudell Washington)	.40	.13	.12
199	N.L. Victory Leaders (Randy Jones, Andy Messersmith, Tom Seaver)	2.00	1.00	.60
200	A.L. Victory Leaders (Vida Blue, Jim Hunter, Jim Palmer)	2.00	1.00	.60
201	N.L. Earned Run Average Ldrs. (Randy Jones, Andy Messersmith, Tom Seaver)	2.00	1.00	.60
202	A.L. Earned Run Average Ldrs. (Dennis Eckersley, Jim Hunter, Jim Palmer)	4.00	2.00	1.25
203	N.L. Strikeout Leaders (Andy Messersmith, John Montefusco, Tom Seaver)	2.00	1.00	.60
204	A.L. Strikeout Leaders (Bert Blyleven, Gaylord Perry, Frank Tanana)	.50	.25	.15
205	Major League Leading Firemen (Rich Gossage, Al Hrabosky)	.40	.13	.12
206	Manny Trillo	.25	.13	.08
207	Andy Hassler	.25	.13	.08
208	Mike Lum	.25	.13	.08
209	Alan Ashby	.25	.13	.08
210	Lee May	.25	.13	.08
211	Clay Carroll	.25	.13	.08
212	Pat Kelly	.25	.13	.08
213	Dave Heaverlo	.25	.13	.08
214	Eric Soderholm	.25	.13	.08
215	Reggie Smith	.25	.13	.08
216	Expos Team (Karl Kuehl)	1.00	.50	.30
217	Dave Freisleben	.25	.13	.08
218	John Knox	.25	.13	.08
219	Tom Murphy	.25	.13	.08
220	Manny Sanguillen	.25	.13	.08
221	Jim Todd	.25	.13	.08
222	Wayne Garrett	.25	.13	.08
223	Ollie Brown	.25	.13	.08
224	Jim York	.25	.13	.08
225	Roy White	.25	.13	.08
226	Jim Sundberg	.25	.13	.08
227	Oscar Zamora	.25	.13	.08
228	John Hale	.25	.13	.08
229	Jerry Remy	.25	.13	.08
230	Carl Yastrzemski	6.50	3.25	2.00
231	Tom House	.25	.13	.08
232	Frank Duffy	.25	.13	.08
233	Grant Jackson	.25	.13	.08
234	Mike Sadek	.25	.13	.08
235	Bert Blyleven	.25	.13	.08
236	Royals Team (Whitey Herzog)	.25	.13	.08
237	Dave Hamilton	.25	.13	.08
238	Larry Biittner	.75	.40	.25
239	John Curtis	.25	.13	.08
240	Pete Rose	20.00	10.00	6.00
241	Hector Torres	.25	.13	.08
242	Dan Meyer	.25	.13	.08
243	Jim Rooker	.25	.13	.08
244	Bill Sharp	.25	.13	.08
245	Felix Millan	.25	.13	.08
246	Cesar Tovar	.25	.13	.08
247	Terry Harmon	.25	.13	.08
248	Dick Tidrow	.25	.13	.08
249	Cliff Johnson	.25	.13	.08
250	Fergie Jenkins	6.00	3.00	1.75
251	Rick Monday	.25	.13	.08
252	Tim Nordbrook	.25	.13	.08
253	Bill Buckner	.25	.13	.08
254	Rudy Meoli	.25	.13	.08
255	Fritz Peterson	.25	.13	.08
256	Rowland Office	.25	.13	.08
257	Ross Grimsley	.25	.13	.08
258	Nyls Nyman	.25	.13	.08

259	Darrel Chaney	.25	.13	.08
260	Steve Busby	.25	.13	.08
261	Gary Thomasson	.25	.13	.08
262	Checklist 133-264	1.00	.50	.30
263	Lyman Bostock	.75	.40	.25
264	Steve Renko	.75	.40	.25
265	Willie Davis	.25	.13	.08
266	Alan Foster	.25	.13	.08
267	Aurelio Rodriguez	.25	.13	.08
268	Del Unser	.25	.13	.08
269	Rick Austin	.25	.13	.08
270	Willie Stargell	5.00	2.50	1.50
271	Jim Lonborg	.25	.13	.08
272	Rick Dempsey	.25	.13	.08
273	Joe Niekro	.25	.13	.08
274	Tommy Harper	.25	.13	.08
275	Rick Manning	.25	.13	.08
276	Mickey Scott	.25	.13	.08
277	Cubs Team (Jim Marshall)	.25	.13	.08
278	Bernie Carbo	.25	.13	.08
279	Roy Howell	.25	.13	.08
280	Burt Hooton	.25	.13	.08
281	Dave May	.25	.13	.08
282	Dan Osborn	.25	.13	.08
283	Merv Rettenmund	.25	.13	.08
284	Steve Ontiveros	.25	.13	.08
285	Mike Cuellar	.25	.13	.08
286	Jim Wohlford	.25	.13	.08
287	Pete Mackanin	.75	.40	.25
288	Bill Campbell	.25	.13	.08
289	Enzo Hernandez	.25	.13	.08
290	Ted Simmons	.25	.13	.08
291	Ken Sanders	.25	.13	.08
292	Leon Roberts	.25	.13	.08
293	Bill Castro	.25	.13	.08
294	Ed Kirkpatrick	.25	.13	.08
295	Dave Cash	.25	.13	.08
296	Pat Dobson	.25	.13	.08
297	Roger Metzger	.25	.13	.08
298	Dick Bosman	.25	.13	.08
299	Champ Summers	.25	.13	.08
300	Johnny Bench	7.00	3.50	2.00
301	Jackie Brown	.25	.13	.08
302	Rick Miller	.25	.13	.08
303	Steve Foucault	.25	.13	.08
304	Angels Team (Dick Williams)	.25	.13	.08
305	Andy Messersmith	.25	.13	.08
306	Rod Gilbreath	.25	.13	.08
307	Al Bumbry	.25	.13	.08
308	Jim Barr	.25	.13	.08
309	Bill Melton	.25	.13	.08
310	Randy Jones	.25	.13	.08
311	Cookie Rojas	.25	.13	.08
312	Don Carrithers	.75	.40	.25
313	Dan Ford	.25	.13	.08
314	Ed Kranepool	.25	.13	.08
315	Al Hrabosky	.25	.13	.08
316	Robin Yount	30.00	15.00	9.00
317	John Candelaria	1.75	.90	.50
318	Bob Boone	.25	.13	.08
319	Larry Gura	.25	.13	.08
320	Willie Horton	.25	.13	.08
321	Jose Cruz	.25	.13	.08
322	Glenn Abbott	.25	.13	.08
323	Rob Sperring	.25	.13	.08
324	Jim Bibby	.25	.13	.08
325	Tony Perez	4.00	2.00	1.25
326	Dick Pole	.25	.13	.08
327	Dave Moates	.25	.13	.08
328	Carl Morton	.25	.13	.08
329	Joe Ferguson	.25	.13	.08
330	Nolan Ryan	75.00	37.00	22.00
331	Padres Team (John McNamara)	.25	.13	.08
332	Charlie Williams	.25	.13	.08
333	Bob Coluccio	.25	.13	.08
334	Dennis Leonard	.25	.13	.08
335	Bob Grich	.25	.13	.08
336	Vic Albury	.25	.13	.08
337	Bud Harrelson	.25	.13	.08
338	Bob Bailey	.25	.13	.08
339	John Denny	.25	.13	.08
340	Jim Rice	1.00	.50	.30
341	(Lou Gehrig) (All-Time All-Stars)	7.00	3.50	2.00
342	(Rogers Hornsby) (All-Time All-Stars)	1.50	.70	.45
343	(Pie Traynor) (All-Time All-Stars)	.25	.13	.08
344	(Honus Wagner) (All-Time All-Stars)	4.50	2.25	1.25
345	(Babe Ruth) (All-Time All-Stars)	7.50	3.75	2.25
346	(Ty Cobb) (All-Time All-Stars)	7.00	3.50	2.00
347	(Ted Williams) (All-Time All-Stars)	8.00	4.00	2.50
348	(Mickey Cochrane) (All-Time All-Stars)	.25	.13	.08
349	(Walter Johnson) (All-Time All-Stars)	2.00	1.00	.60
350	(Lefty Grove) (All-Time All-Stars)	.65	.35	.20
351	Randy Hundley	.25	.13	.08
352	Dave Giusti	.25	.13	.08
353	Sixto Lezcano	.25	.13	.08
354	Ron Blomberg	.25	.13	.08
355	Steve Carlton	6.00	3.00	1.75
356	Ted Martinez	.25	.13	.08
357	Ken Forsch	.25	.13	.08
358	Buddy Bell	.25	.13	.08
359	Rick Reuschel	.25	.13	.08
360	Jeff Burroughs	.25	.13	.08
361	Tigers Team (Ralph Houk)	.25	.13	.08
362	Will McEnaney	.25	.13	.08
363	Dave Collins	.25	.13	.08

364	Elias Sosa	.25	.13	.08
365	Carlton Fisk	5.00	2.50	1.50
366	Bobby Valentine	.25	.13	.08
367	Bruce Miller	.25	.13	.08
368	Wilbur Wood	.25	.13	.08
369	Frank White	.25	.13	.08
370	Ron Cey	.25	.13	.08
371	Ellie Hendricks	.25	.13	.08
372	Rick Baldwin	.25	.13	.08
373	Johnny Briggs	.25	.13	.08
374	Dan Warthen	.75	.40	.25
375	Ron Fairly	.25	.13	.08
376	Rich Hebner	.25	.13	.08
377	Mike Hegan	.25	.13	.08
378	Steve Stone	.25	.13	.08
379	Ken Boswell	.25	.13	.08
380	Bobby Bonds	.25	.13	.08
381	Denny Doyle	.25	.13	.08
382	Matt Alexander	.25	.13	.08
383	John Ellis	.25	.13	.08
384	Phillies Team (Danny Ozark)	.25	.13	.08
385	Mickey Lolich	.25	.13	.08
386	Ed Goodson	.25	.13	.08
387	Mike Miley	.25	.13	.08
388	Stan Perzanowski	.25	.13	.08
389	Glenn Adams	.25	.13	.08
390	Don Gullett	.25	.13	.08
391	Jerry Hairston	.25	.13	.08
392	Checklist 265-396	1.00	.50	.30
393	Paul Mitchell	.25	.13	.08
394	Fran Healy	.25	.13	.08
395	Jim Wynn	.25	.13	.08
396	Bill Lee	.25	.13	.08
397	Tim Foli	.75	.40	.25
398	Dave Tomlin	.25	.13	.08
399	Luis Melendez	.25	.13	.08
400	Rod Carew	6.50	3.25	2.00
401	Ken Brett	.25	.13	.08
402	Don Money	.25	.13	.08
403	Geoff Zahn	.25	.13	.08
404	Enos Cabell	.25	.13	.08
405	Rollie Fingers	4.00	2.00	1.25
406	Ed Herrmann	.25	.13	.08
407	Tom Underwood	.25	.13	.08
408	Charlie Spikes	.25	.13	.08
409	Dave Lemanczyk	.25	.13	.08
410	Ralph Garr	.25	.13	.08
411	Bill Singer	.25	.13	.08
412	Toby Harrah	.25	.13	.08
413	Pete Varney	.25	.13	.08
414	Wayne Garland	.25	.13	.08
415	Vada Pinson	.25	.13	.08
416	Tommy John	.50	.25	.15
417	Gene Clines	.25	.13	.08
418	Jose Morales	.75	.40	.25
419	Reggie Cleveland	.25	.13	.08
420	Joe Morgan	6.00	3.00	1.75
421	A's Team	.25	.13	.08
422	Johnny Grubb	.25	.13	.08
423	Ed Halicki	.25	.13	.08
424	Phil Roof	.25	.13	.08
425	Rennie Stennett	.25	.13	.08
426	Bob Forsch	.25	.13	.08
427	Kurt Bevacqua	.25	.13	.08
428	Jim Crawford	.25	.13	.08
429	Fred Stanley	.25	.13	.08
430	Jose Cardenal	.25	.13	.08
431	Dick Ruthven	.25	.13	.08
432	Tom Veryzer	.25	.13	.08
433	Rick Waits	.25	.13	.08
434	Morris Nettles	.25	.13	.08
435	Phil Niekro	5.00	2.50	1.50
436	Bill Fahey	.25	.13	.08
437	Terry Forster	.25	.13	.08
438	Doug DeCinces	.25	.13	.08
439	Rick Rhoden	.25	.13	.08
440	John Mayberry	.25	.13	.08
441	Gary Carter	8.00	4.00	2.50
442	Hank Webb	.25	.13	.08
443	Giants Team	.25	.13	.08
444	Gary Nolan	.25	.13	.08
445	Rico Petrocelli	.25	.13	.08
446	Larry Haney	.25	.13	.08
447	Gene Locklear	.25	.13	.08
448	Tom Johnson	.25	.13	.08
449	Bob Robertson	.25	.13	.08
450	Jim Palmer	6.00	3.00	1.75
451	Buddy Bradford	.25	.13	.08
452	Tom Hausman	.25	.13	.08
453	Lou Piniella	.25	.13	.08
454	Tom Griffin	.25	.13	.08
455	Dick Allen	.50	.25	.15
456	Joe Coleman	.25	.13	.08
457	Ed Crosby	.25	.13	.08
458	Earl Williams	.25	.13	.08
459	Jim Brewer	.25	.13	.08
460	Cesar Cedeno	.25	.13	.08
461	NL and AL Championships	.75	.40	.25
462	1975 World Series	.75	.40	.25
463	Steve Hargan	.25	.13	.08
464	Ken Henderson	.25	.13	.08
465	Mike Marshall	.25	.13	.08
466	Bob Stinson	.25	.13	.08
467	Woodie Fryman	1.00	.50	.30
468	Jesus Alou	.25	.13	.08
469	Rawly Eastwick	.25	.13	.08
470	Bobby Murcer	.25	.13	.08
471	Jim Burton	.25	.13	.08
472	Bob Davis	.25	.13	.08
473	Paul Blair	.25	.13	.08
474	Ray Corbin	.25	.13	.08
475	Joe Rudi	.25	.13	.08
476	Bob Moose	.25	.13	.08
477	Indians Team (Frank Robinson)	.60	.30	.20
478	Lynn McGlothen	.25	.13	.08
479	Bobby Mitchell	.25	.13	.08
480	Mike Schmidt	15.00	7.50	4.50
481	Rudy May	.25	.13	.08
482	Tim Hosley	.25	.13	.08
483	Mickey Stanley	.25	.13	.08
484	Eric Raich	.25	.13	.08
485	Mike Hargrove	.25	.13	.08
486	Bruce Dal Canton	.25	.13	.08
487	Leron Lee	.25	.13	.08
488	Claude Osteen	.25	.13	.08
489	Skip Jutze	.25	.13	.08
490	Frank Tanana	.25	.13	.08
491	Terry Crowley	.25	.13	.08
492	Marty Pattin	.25	.13	.08
493	Derrel Thomas	.25	.13	.08
494	Craig Swan	.25	.13	.08
495	Nate Colbert	1.00	.50	.30
496	Juan Beniquez	.25	.13	.08
497	Joe McIntosh	.25	.13	.08
498	Glenn Borgmann	.25	.13	.08
499	Mario Guerrero	.25	.13	.08
500	Reggie Jackson	10.00	5.00	3.00
501	Billy Champion	.25	.13	.08
502	Tim McCarver	.25	.13	.08
503	Elliott Maddox	.25	.13	.08
504	Pirates Team (Danny Murtaugh)	.25	.13	.08
505	Mark Belanger	.25	.13	.08
506	George Mitterwald	.25	.13	.08
507	Ray Bare	.25	.13	.08
508	Duane Kuiper	.25	.13	.08
509	Bill Hands	.25	.13	.08
510	Amos Otis	.25	.13	.08
511	Jamie Easterley	.25	.13	.08
512	Ellie Rodriguez	.25	.13	.08
513	Bart Johnson	.25	.13	.08
514	Dan Driessen	.25	.13	.08
515	Steve Yeager	.25	.13	.08
516	Wayne Granger	.25	.13	.08
517	John Milner	.25	.13	.08
518	Doug Flynn	.25	.13	.08
519	Steve Brye	.25	.13	.08
520	Willie McCovey	6.00	3.00	1.75
521	Jim Colborn	.25	.13	.08
522	Ted Sizemore	.25	.13	.08
523	Bob Montgomery	.25	.13	.08
524	Pete Falcone	.25	.13	.08
525	Billy Williams	4.00	2.00	1.25
526	Checklist 397-528	1.00	.50	.30
527	Mike Anderson	.25	.13	.08
528	Dock Ellis	.25	.13	.08
529	Deron Johnson	.25	.13	.08
530	Don Sutton	4.00	2.00	1.25
531	Mets Team (Joe Frazier)	.25	.13	.08
532	Milt May	.25	.13	.08
533	Lee Richard	.25	.13	.08
534	Stan Bahnsen	.25	.13	.08
535	Dave Nelson	.25	.13	.08
536	Mike Thompson	.25	.13	.08
537	Tony Muser	.25	.13	.08
538	Pat Darcy	.25	.13	.08
539	John Balaz	.25	.13	.08
540	Bill Freehan	.25	.13	.08
541	Steve Mingori	.25	.13	.08
542	Keith Hernandez	.75	.40	.25
543	Wayne Twitchell	.25	.13	.08
544	Pepe Frias	.75	.40	.25
545	Sparky Lyle	.25	.13	.08
546	Dave Rosello	.25	.13	.08
547	Roric Harrison	.25	.13	.08
548	Manny Mota	.25	.13	.08
549	Randy Tate	.25	.13	.08
550	Hank Aaron	25.00	12.50	7.50
551	Jerry DaVanon	.25	.13	.08
552	Terry Humphrey	.25	.13	.08
553	Randy Moffitt	.25	.13	.08
554	Ray Fosse	.25	.13	.08
555	Dyar Miller	.25	.13	.08
556	Twins Team (Gene Mauch)	.25	.13	.08
557	Dan Spillner	.25	.13	.08
558	Clarence Gaston	.25	.13	.08
559	Clyde Wright	.25	.13	.08
560	Jorge Orta	.25	.13	.08
561	Tom Carroll	.25	.13	.08
562	Adrian Garrett	.25	.13	.08
563	Larry Demery	.25	.13	.08
564	Bubble Gum Blowing Champ (Kurt Bevacqua)	.25	.13	.08
565	Tug McGraw	.25	.13	.08
566	Ken McMullen	.25	.13	.08
567	George Stone	.25	.13	.08
568	Rob Andrews	.25	.13	.08
569	Nelson Briles	.25	.13	.08
570	George Hendrick	.25	.13	.08
571	Don DeMola	.75	.40	.25
572	Rich Coggins	.25	.13	.08
573	Bill Travers	.25	.13	.08
574	Don Kessinger	.25	.13	.08
575	Dwight Evans	.65	.35	.20
576	Maximino Leon	.25	.13	.08
577	Marc Hill	.25	.13	.08
578	Ted Kubiak	.25	.13	.08
579	Clay Kirby	.25	.13	.08
580	Bert Campaneris	.25	.13	.08
581	Cardinals Team (Red Schoendienst)	.60	.30	.20
582	Mike Kekich	.25	.13	.08
583	Tommy Helms	.25	.13	.08
584	Stan Wall	.25	.13	.08
585	Joe Torre	.25	.13	.08
586	Ron Schueler	.25	.13	.08
587	Leo Cardenas	.25	.13	.08
588	Kevin Kobel	.25	.13	.08
589	Rookie Pitchers (Santo Alcala, Mike Flanagan, Joe Pactwa, Pablo Torrealba)	1.25	.60	.40
590	Rookie Outfielders (Henry Cruz, Chet Lemon, Ellis Valentine, Terry Whitfield)	1.50	.70	.45
591	Rookie Pitchers (Steve Grilli, Craig Mitchell, Jose Sosa, George Throop)	.25	.13	.08
592	Rookie Infielders (Dave McKay, Willie Randolph, Jerry Royster, Roy Staiger)	4.50	2.25	1.25
593	Rookie Pitchers (Larry Anderson, Ken Crosby, Mark Littell, Butch Metzger)	.25	.13	.08
594	Rookie Catchers & Outfielders (Andy Merchant, Ed Ott, Royle Stillman, Jerry White)	1.00	.50	.30
595	Rookie Pitchers (Steve Barr, Art DeFilippis, Randy Lerch, Sid Monge)	.25	.13	.08
596	Rookie Infielders (Lamar Johnson, Johnnie LeMaster, Jerry Manuel, Craig Reynolds)	.25	.13	.08
597	Rookie Pitchers (Don Aase, Jack Kucek, Frank LaCorte, Mike Pazik)	.25	.13	.08
598	Rookie Outfielders (Hector Cruz, Jamie Quirk, Jerry Turner, Joe Wallis)	.25	.13	.08
599	Rookie Pitchers (Rob Dressler, Ron Guidry, Bob McClure, Pat Zachry)	6.00	3.00	1.75
600	Tom Seaver	7.00	3.50	2.00
601	Ken Rudolph	.25	.13	.08
602	Doug Konieczny	.25	.13	.08
603	Jim Holt	.25	.13	.08
604	Joe Lovitto	.25	.13	.08
605	Al Downing	.25	.13	.08
606	Brewers Team (Alex Grammas)	.25	.13	.08
607	Rich Hinton	.25	.13	.08
608	Vic Correll	.25	.13	.08
609	Fred Norman	.25	.13	.08
610	Greg Luzinski	.25	.13	.08
611	Rich Folkers	.25	.13	.08
612	Joe Lahoud	.25	.13	.08
613	Tim Johnson	.25	.13	.08
614	Fernando Arroyo	.25	.13	.08
615	Mike Cubbage	.25	.13	.08
616	Buck Martinez	.25	.13	.08
617	Darold Knowles	.25	.13	.08
618	Jack Brohamer	.25	.13	.08
619	Bill Butler	.25	.13	.08
620	Al Oliver	.25	.13	.08
621	Tom Hall	.25	.13	.08
622	Rick Auerbach	.25	.13	.08
623	Bob Allietta	.25	.13	.08
624	Tony Taylor	.25	.13	.08
625	J.R. Richard	.25	.13	.08
626	Bob Sheldon	.25	.13	.08
627	Bill Plummer	.25	.13	.08
628	John D'Acquisto	.25	.13	.08
629	Sandy Alomar	.25	.13	.08
630	Chris Speier	.25	.13	.08
631	Braves Team (Dave Bristol)	.25	.13	.08
632	Rogelio Moret	.25	.13	.08
633	John Stearns	.25	.13	.08
634	Larry Christenson	.25	.13	.08
635	Jim Fregosi	.25	.13	.08
636	Joe Decker	.25	.13	.08
637	Bruce Bochte	.25	.13	.08
638	Doyle Alexander	.25	.13	.08
639	Fred Kendall	.25	.13	.08
640	Bill Madlock	.25	.13	.08
641	Tom Paciorek	.25	.13	.08
642	Dennis Blair	.75	.40	.25
643	Checklist 529-660	1.00	.50	.30
644	Tom Bradley	.25	.13	.08
645	Darrell Porter	.25	.13	.08
646	John Lowenstein	.25	.13	.08
647	Ramon Hernandez	.25	.13	.08
648	Al Cowens	.25	.13	.08
649	Dave Roberts	.25	.13	.08
650	Thurman Munson	7.00	3.50	2.00
651	John Odom	.25	.13	.08
652	Ed Armbrister	.25	.13	.08
653	Mike Norris	.25	.13	.08
654	Doug Griffin	.25	.13	.08
655	Mike Vail	.25	.13	.08
656	White Sox Team (Chuck Tanner)	.25	.13	.08
657	Roy Smalley	.25	.13	.08
658	Jerry Johnson	.25	.13	.08
659	Ben Oglivie	.25	.13	.08
660	Dave Lopes	.25	.13	.08

Vintage cards in Good condition are valued at about 50% of the Very Good value shown here. Fair cards are valued at 25% or less of VG.
The ratio of Excellent and Very Good prices to Near Mint can vary depending on relative collectibility for each grade in a specific set. Current listings reflect such adjustments.

1977 O-Pee-Chee

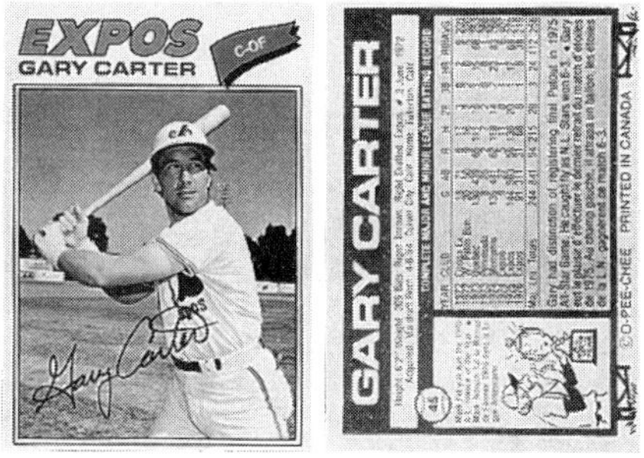

The 1977 O-Pee-Chee set represents a change in philosophy for the Canadian company. The design of the set is still identical to the Topps set of the same year, but the number of cards was reduced to 264 with more emphasis on players from the two Canadian teams. The backs are printed in both French and English and state "O-Pee-Chee Printed in Canada." About 1/3 of the photos in the OPC set differ from the corresponding Topps cards either with entirely different photos, airbrushed uniform changes, the removal of All-Star and Rookie Team designations, or significant photo cropping variations. Cards measure the standard 2-1/2" x 3-1/2".

		NM	EX	VG
Complete Set (264):		200.00	100.00	60.00
Common Player:		.25	.13	.08
1	Batting Leaders (George Brett, Bill Madlock)	4.50	2.25	1.25
2	Home Run Leaders (Graig Nettles, Mike Schmidt)	3.00	1.50	.90
3	Runs Batted In Leaders (George Foster, Lee May)	.40	.20	.12
4	Stolen Base Leaders (Dave Lopes, Bill North)	.25	.13	.08
5	Victory Leaders (Randy Jones, Jim Palmer)	1.50	.70	.45
6	Strikeout Leaders (Nolan Ryan, Tom Seaver)	18.00	9.00	5.50
7	Earned Run Avg. Leaders (John Denny, Mark Fidrych)	.25	.13	.08
8	Leading Firemen (Bill Campbell, Rawly Eastwick)	.25	.13	.08
9	Mike Jorgensen	.25	.13	.08
10	Jim Hunter	2.00	1.00	.60
11	Ken Griffey	.25	.13	.08
12	Bill Campbell	.25	.13	.08
13	Otto Velez	.25	.13	.08
14	Milt May	.25	.13	.08
15	Dennis Eckersley	7.00	3.50	2.00
16	John Mayberry	.25	.13	.08
17	Larry Bowa	.25	.13	.08
18	Don Carrithers	.25	.13	.08
19	Ken Singleton	.25	.13	.08
20	Bill Stein	.25	.13	.08
21	Ken Brett	.25	.13	.08
22	Gary Woods	.25	.13	.08
23	Steve Swisher	.25	.13	.08
24	Don Sutton	2.00	1.00	.60
25	Willie Stargell	3.00	1.50	.90
26	Jerry Koosman	.25	.13	.08
27	Del Unser	.25	.13	.08
28	Bob Grich	.25	.13	.08
29	Jim Slaton	.25	.13	.08
30	Thurman Munson	5.00	2.50	1.50
31	Dan Driessen	.25	.13	.08
32	Tom Bruno (not in Topps)	.25	.13	.08
33	Larry Hisle	.25	.13	.08
34	Phil Garner	.25	.13	.08
35	Mike Hargrove	.25	.13	.08
36	Jackie Brown	.25	.13	.08
37	Carl Yastrzemski	6.00	3.00	1.75
38	Dave Roberts	.25	.13	.08
39	Ray Fosse	.25	.13	.08
40	Dave McKay	.25	.13	.08
41	Paul Splittorff	.25	.13	.08
42	Garry Maddox	.25	.13	.08
43	Phil Niekro	4.00	2.00	1.25
44	Roger Metzger	.25	.13	.08
45	Gary Carter	6.00	3.00	1.75
46	Jim Spencer	.25	.13	.08
47	Ross Grimsley	.25	.13	.08
48	Bob Bailor	.25	.13	.08
49	Chris Chambliss	.25	.13	.08
50	Will McEnaney	.25	.13	.08
51	Lou Brock	4.00	2.00	1.25
52	Rollie Fingers	3.50	1.75	1.00
53	Chris Speier	.25	.13	.08
54	Bombo Rivera	.25	.13	.08
55	Pete Broberg	.25	.13	.08
56	Bill Madlock	.25	.13	.08
57	Rick Rhoden	.25	.13	.08
58	Blue Jay Coaches (Don Leppert, Bob Miller, Jackie Moore, Harry Warner)	.50	.25	.15
59	John Candelaria	.25	.13	.08
60	Ed Kranepool	.25	.13	.08
61	Dave LaRoche	.25	.13	.08
62	Jim Rice	1.00	.50	.30
63	Don Stanhouse	.25	.13	.08
64	Jason Thompson	.25	.13	.08
65	Nolan Ryan	60.00	30.00	18.00
66	Tom Poquette	.25	.13	.08
67	Leon Hooten	.25	.13	.08
68	Bob Boone	.25	.13	.08
69	Mickey Rivers	.25	.13	.08
70	Gary Nolan	.25	.13	.08
71	Sixto Lezcano	.25	.13	.08
72	Larry Parrish	.25	.13	.08
73	Dave Goltz	.25	.13	.08
74	Bert Campaneris	.25	.13	.08
75	Vida Blue	.25	.13	.08
76	Rick Cerone	.25	.13	.08
77	Ralph Garr	.25	.13	.08
78	Ken Forsch	.25	.13	.08
79	Willie Montanez	.25	.13	.08
80	Jim Palmer	6.00	3.00	1.75
81	Jerry White	.25	.13	.08
82	Gene Tenace	.25	.13	.08
83	Bobby Murcer	.25	.13	.08
84	Garry Templeton	.25	.13	.08
85	Bill Singer	.25	.13	.08
86	Buddy Bell	.25	.13	.08
87	Luis Tiant	.25	.13	.08
88	Rusty Staub	.25	.13	.08
89	Sparky Lyle	.25	.13	.08
90	Jose Morales	.25	.13	.08
91	Dennis Leonard	.25	.13	.08
92	Tommy Smith	.25	.13	.08
93	Steve Carlton	6.00	3.00	1.75
94	John Scott	.25	.13	.08
95	Bill Bonham	.25	.13	.08
96	Dave Lopes	.25	.13	.08
97	Jerry Reuss	.25	.13	.08
98	Dave Kingman	.50	.25	.15
99	Dan Warthen	.25	.13	.08
100	Johnny Bench	9.50	4.75	2.75
101	Bert Blyleven	.25	.13	.08
102	Cecil Cooper	.25	.13	.08
103	Mike Willis	.25	.13	.08
104	Dan Ford	.25	.13	.08
105	Frank Tanana	.25	.13	.08
106	Bill North	.25	.13	.08
107	Joe Ferguson	.25	.13	.08
108	Dick Williams	.25	.13	.08
109	John Denny	.25	.13	.08
110	Willie Randolph	.25	.13	.08
111	Reggie Cleveland	.25	.13	.08
112	Doug Howard	.25	.13	.08
113	Randy Jones	.25	.13	.08
114	Rico Carty	.25	.13	.08
115	Mark Fidrych	3.00	1.50	.90
116	Darrell Porter	.25	.13	.08
117	Wayne Garrett	.25	.13	.08
118	Greg Luzinski	.25	.13	.08
119	Jim Barr	.25	.13	.08
120	George Foster	.25	.13	.08
121	Phil Roof	.25	.13	.08
122	Bucky Dent	.25	.13	.08
123	Steve Braun	.25	.13	.08
124	Checklist 1-132	1.00	.50	.30
125	Lee May	.25	.13	.08
126	Woodie Fryman	.25	.13	.08
127	Jose Cardenal	.25	.13	.08
128	Doug Rau	.25	.13	.08
129	Rennie Stennett	.25	.13	.08
130	Pete Vuckovich	.25	.13	.08
131	Cesar Cedeno	.25	.13	.08
132	Jon Matlack	.25	.13	.08
133	Don Baylor	.35	.20	.11
134	Darrel Chaney	.25	.13	.08
135	Tony Perez	4.00	2.00	1.25
136	Aurelio Rodriguez	.25	.13	.08
137	Carlton Fisk	4.00	2.00	1.25
138	Wayne Garland	.25	.13	.08
139	Dave Hilton	.25	.13	.08
140	Rawly Eastwick	.25	.13	.08
141	Amos Otis	.25	.13	.08
142	Tug McGraw	.25	.13	.08
143	Rod Carew	6.00	3.00	1.75
144	Mike Torrez	.25	.13	.08
145	Sal Bando	.25	.13	.08
146	Dock Ellis	.25	.13	.08
147	Jose Cruz	.25	.13	.08
148	Alan Ashby	.25	.13	.08
149	Gaylord Perry	3.00	1.50	.90
150	Keith Hernandez	.50	.25	.15
151	Dave Pagan	.25	.13	.08
152	Richie Zisk	.25	.13	.08
153	Steve Rogers	.25	.13	.08
154	Mark Belanger	.25	.13	.08
155	Andy Messersmith	.25	.13	.08
156	Dave Winfield	12.00	6.00	3.50
157	Chuck Hartenstein	.25	.13	.08
158	Manny Trillo	.25	.13	.08
159	Steve Yeager	.25	.13	.08
160	Cesar Geronimo	.25	.13	.08
161	Jim Rooker	.25	.13	.08
162	Tim Foli	.25	.13	.08
163	Fred Lynn	.60	.30	.20
164	Ed Figueroa	.25	.13	.08
165	Johnny Grubb	.25	.13	.08
166	Pedro Garcia	.25	.13	.08
167	Ron LeFlore	.25	.13	.08
168	Rich Hebner	.25	.13	.08
169	Larry Herndon	.25	.13	.08
170	George Brett	25.00	12.50	7.50
171	Joe Kerrigan	.25	.13	.08
172	Bud Harrelson	.25	.13	.08
173	Bobby Bonds	.25	.13	.08
174	Bill Travers	.25	.13	.08
175	John Lowenstein	.25	.13	.08
176	Butch Wynegar	.25	.13	.08
177	Pete Falcone	.25	.13	.08
178	Claudell Washington	.25	.13	.08
179	Checklist 133-264	1.00	.50	.30
180	Dave Cash	.25	.13	.08
181	Fred Norman	.25	.13	.08
182	Roy White	.25	.13	.08
183	Marty Perez	.25	.13	.08
184	Jesse Jefferson	.25	.13	.08
185	Jim Sundberg	.25	.13	.08
186	Dan Meyer	.25	.13	.08
187	Fergie Jenkins	4.00	2.00	1.25
188	Tom Veryzer	.25	.13	.08
189	Dennis Blair	.25	.13	.08
190	Rick Manning	.25	.13	.08
191	Doug Bird	.25	.13	.08
192	Al Bumbry	.25	.13	.08
193	Dave Roberts	.25	.13	.08
194	Larry Christenson	.25	.13	.08
195	Chet Lemon	.25	.13	.08
196	Ted Simmons	.25	.13	.08
197	Ray Burris	.25	.13	.08
198	Expos Coaches (Jim Brewer, Billy Gardner, Mickey Vernon, Ozzie Virgil)	.25	.13	.08
199	Ron Cey	.25	.13	.08
200	Reggie Jackson	10.00	5.00	3.00
201	Pat Zachry	.25	.13	.08
202	Doug Ault	.25	.13	.08
203	Al Oliver	.25	.13	.08
204	Robin Yount	20.00	10.00	6.00
205	Tom Seaver	8.00	4.00	2.50
206	Joe Rudi	.25	.13	.08
207	Barry Foote	.25	.13	.08
208	Toby Harrah	.25	.13	.08
209	Jeff Burroughs	.25	.13	.08
210	George Scott	.25	.13	.08
211	Jim Mason	.25	.13	.08
212	Vern Ruhle	.25	.13	.08
213	Fred Kendall	.25	.13	.08
214	Rick Reuschel	.25	.13	.08
215	Hal McRae	.25	.13	.08
216	Chip Lang	.25	.13	.08
217	Graig Nettles	.35	.20	.11
218	George Hendrick	.25	.13	.08
219	Glenn Abbott	.25	.13	.08
220	Joe Morgan	5.00	2.50	1.50
221	Sam Ewing	.25	.13	.08
222	George Medich	.25	.13	.08
223	Reggie Smith	.25	.13	.08
224	Dave Hamilton	.25	.13	.08
225	Pepe Frias	.25	.13	.08
226	Jay Johnstone	.25	.13	.08
227	J.R. Richard	.25	.13	.08
228	Doug DeCinces	.25	.13	.08
229	Dave Lemanczyk	.25	.13	.08
230	Rick Monday	.25	.13	.08
231	Manny Sanguillen	.25	.13	.08
232	John Montefusco	.25	.13	.08
233	Duane Kuiper	.25	.13	.08
234	Ellis Valentine	.25	.13	.08
235	Dick Tidrow	.25	.13	.08
236	Ben Oglivie	.25	.13	.08
237	Rick Burleson	.25	.13	.08
238	Roy Hartsfield	.25	.13	.08
239	Lyman Bostock	.25	.13	.08
240	Pete Rose	12.00	6.00	3.50
241	Mike Ivie	.25	.13	.08
242	Dave Parker	1.00	.50	.30
243	Bill Greif	.25	.13	.08
244	Freddie Patek	.25	.13	.08
245	Mike Schmidt	20.00	10.00	6.00
246	Brian Downing	.25	.13	.08
247	Steve Hargan	.25	.13	.08
248	Dave Collins	.25	.13	.08
249	Felix Millan	.25	.13	.08
250	Don Gullett	.25	.13	.08
251	Jerry Royster	.25	.13	.08
252	Earl Williams	.25	.13	.08
253	Frank Duffy	.25	.13	.08
254	Tippy Martinez	.25	.13	.08
255	Steve Garvey	4.00	2.00	1.25
256	Alvis Woods	.25	.13	.08
257	John Hiller	.25	.13	.08
258	Dave Concepcion	.25	.13	.08
259	Dwight Evans	.25	.13	.08
260	Pete MacKanin	.25	.13	.08
261	(George Brett) (Record Breaker)	9.00	4.50	2.75
262	(Minnie Minoso) (Record Breaker)	.25	.13	.08
263	(Jose Morales) (Record Breaker)	.25	.13	.08
264	(Nolan Ryan) (Record Breaker)	19.00	9.50	5.75

1978 O-Pee-Chee

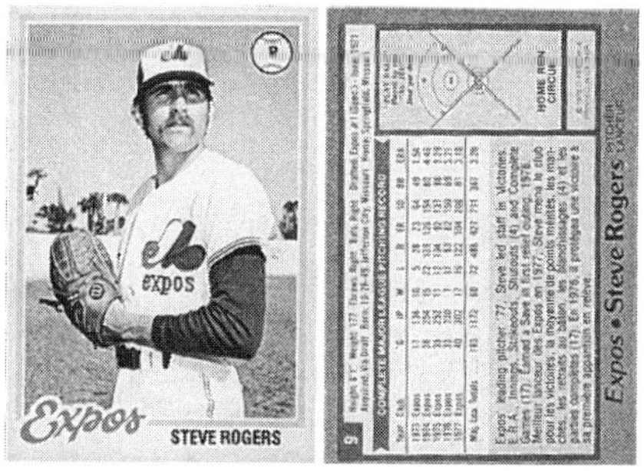

The 1978 O-Pee-Chee set was further reduced to 242 cards and again had heavy representation from the two Canadian teams. The cards measure the standard 2-1/2" x 3-1/2" and the backs are printed in both French and English. The cards use the same design as the 1978 Topps set. Some of the cards contain an extra line on the front indicating a team change.

		NM	EX	VG
	Complete Set (242):	150.00	75.00	45.00
	Common Player:	.30	.15	.09
1	Batting Leaders (Rod Carew, Dave Parker)	.75	.40	.25
2	Home Run Leaders (George Foster, Jim Rice)	.30	.15	.09
3	Runs Batted In Leaders (George Foster, Larry Hisle)	.30	.15	.09
4	Stolen Base Leaders (Freddie Patek, Frank Taveras)	.30	.15	.09
5	Victory Leaders (Steve Carlton, Dave Goltz, Dennis Leonard, Jim Palmer)	.50	.25	.15
6	Strikeout Leaders (Phil Niekro, Nolan Ryan)	4.00	2.00	1.25
7	Earned Run Avg. Ldrs. (John Candelaria, Frank Tanana)	.30	.15	.09
8	Leading Firemen (Bill Campbell, Rollie Fingers)	.50	.25	.15
9	Steve Rogers	.30	.15	.09
10	Graig Nettles	.30	.15	.09
11	Doug Capilla	.30	.15	.09
12	George Scott	.30	.15	.09
13	Gary Woods	.30	.15	.09
14	Tom Veryzer	.30	.15	.09
15	Wayne Garland	.30	.15	.09
16	Amos Otis	.30	.15	.09
17	Larry Christenson	.30	.15	.09
18	Dave Cash	.30	.15	.09
19	Jim Barr	.30	.15	.09
20	Ruppert Jones	.30	.15	.09
21	Eric Soderholm	.30	.15	.09
22	Jesse Jefferson	.30	.15	.09
23	Jerry Morales	.30	.15	.09
24	Doug Rau	.30	.15	.09
25	Rennie Stennett	.30	.15	.09
26	Lee Mazzilli	.30	.15	.09
27	Dick Williams	.30	.15	.09
28	Joe Rudi	.30	.15	.09
29	Robin Yount	16.00	8.00	4.75
30	Don Gullett	.30	.15	.09
31	Roy Howell	.30	.15	.09
32	Cesar Geronimo	.30	.15	.09
33	Rick Langford	.30	.15	.09
34	Dan Ford	.30	.15	.09
35	Gene Tenace	.30	.15	.09
36	Santo Alcala	.30	.15	.09
37	Rick Burleson	.30	.15	.09
38	Dave Rozema	.30	.15	.09
39	Duane Kulper	.30	.15	.09
40	Ron Fairly	.30	.15	.09
41	Dennis Leonard	.30	.15	.09
42	Greg Luzinski	.30	.15	.09
43	Willie Montanez	.30	.15	.09
44	Enos Cabell	.30	.15	.09
45	Ellis Valentine	.30	.15	.09
46	Steve Stone	.30	.15	.09
47	Lee May	.30	.15	.09
48	Roy White	.30	.15	.09
49	Jerry Garvin	.30	.15	.09
50	Johnny Bench	5.00	2.50	1.50
51	Garry Templeton	.30	.15	.09
52	Doyle Alexander	.30	.15	.09
53	Steve Henderson	.30	.15	.09
54	Stan Bahnsen	.30	.15	.09
55	Dan Meyer	.30	.15	.09
56	Rick Reuschel	.30	.15	.09
57	Reggie Smith	.30	.15	.09
58	Blue Jays Team	.60	.30	.20
59	John Montefusco	.30	.15	.09
60	Dave Parker	.75	.40	.25
61	Jim Bibby	.30	.15	.09
62	Fred Lynn	.75	.40	.25
63	Jose Morales	.30	.15	.09
64	Aurelio Rodriguez	.30	.15	.09
65	Frank Tanana	.30	.15	.09
66	Darrell Porter	.30	.15	.09
67	Otto Velez	.30	.15	.09
68	Larry Bowa	.30	.15	.09
69	Jim Hunter	1.50	.70	.45
70	George Foster	.30	.15	.09
71	Cecil Cooper	.30	.15	.09
72	Gary Alexander	.30	.15	.09
73	Paul Thormodsgard	.30	.15	.09
74	Toby Harrah	.30	.15	.09
75	Mitchell Page	.30	.15	.09
76	Alan Ashby	.30	.15	.09
77	Jorge Orta	.30	.15	.09
78	Dave Winfield	9.00	4.50	2.75
79	Andy Messersmith	.30	.15	.09
80	Ken Singleton	.30	.15	.09
81	Will McEnaney	.30	.15	.09
82	Lou Piniella	.30	.15	.09
83	Bob Forsch	.30	.15	.09
84	Dan Driessen	.30	.15	.09
85	Dave Lemanczyk	.30	.15	.09
86	Paul Dade	.30	.15	.09
87	Bill Campbell	.30	.15	.09
88	Ron LeFlore	.30	.15	.09
89	Bill Madlock	.30	.15	.09
90	Tony Perez	.30	.15	.09
91	Freddie Patek	.30	.15	.09
92	Glenn Abbott	.30	.15	.09
93	Garry Maddox	.30	.15	.09
94	Steve Staggs	.30	.15	.09
95	Bobby Murcer	.30	.15	.09
96	Don Sutton	1.00	.50	.30
97	Al Oliver	.30	.15	.09
98	Jon Matlack	.30	.15	.09
99	Sam Mejias	.30	.15	.09
100	Pete Rose	12.00	6.00	3.50
101	Randy Jones	.30	.15	.09
102	Sixto Lezcano	.30	.15	.09
103	Jim Clancy	.30	.15	.09
104	Butch Wynegar	.30	.15	.09
105	Nolan Ryan	50.00	25.00	15.00
106	Wayne Gross	.30	.15	.09
107	Bob Watson	.30	.15	.09
108	Joe Kerrigan	.30	.15	.09
109	Keith Hernandez	.60	.30	.20
110	Reggie Jackson	7.50	3.75	2.25
111	Denny Doyle	.30	.15	.09
112	Sam Ewing	.30	.15	.09
113	Bert Blyleven	.30	.15	.09
114	Andre Thornton	.30	.15	.09
115	Milt May	.30	.15	.09
116	Jim Colborn	.30	.15	.09
117	Warren Cromartie	.30	.15	.09
118	Ted Sizemore	.30	.15	.09
119	Checklist 1-121	.75	.40	.25
120	Tom Seaver	6.00	3.00	1.75
121	Luis Gomez	.30	.15	.09
122	Jim Spencer	.30	.15	.09
123	Leroy Stanton	.30	.15	.09
124	Luis Tiant	.30	.15	.09
125	Mark Belanger	.30	.15	.09
126	Jackie Brown	.30	.15	.09
127	Bill Buckner	.30	.15	.09
128	Bill Robinson	.30	.15	.09
129	Rick Cerone	.30	.15	.09
130	Ron Cey	.30	.15	.09
131	Jose Cruz	.30	.15	.09
132	Len Randle	.30	.15	.09
133	Bob Grich	.30	.15	.09
134	Jeff Burroughs	.30	.15	.09
135	Gary Carter	4.50	2.25	1.25
136	Milt Wilcox	.30	.15	.09
137	Carl Yastrzemski	4.25	2.25	1.25
138	Dennis Eckersley	4.00	2.00	1.25
139	Tim Nordbrook	.30	.15	.09
140	Ken Griffey	.30	.15	.09
141	Bob Boone	.30	.15	.09
142	Dave Goltz	.30	.15	.09
143	Al Cowens	.30	.15	.09
144	Bill Atkinson	.30	.15	.09
145	Chris Chambliss	.30	.15	.09
146	Jim Slaton	.30	.15	.09
147	Bill Stein	.30	.15	.09
148	Bob Bailor	.30	.15	.09
149	J.R. Richard	.30	.15	.09
150	Ted Simmons	.30	.15	.09
151	Rick Manning	.30	.15	.09
152	Lerrin LaGrow	.30	.15	.09
153	Larry Parrish	.30	.15	.09
154	Eddie Murray	90.00	45.00	27.00
155	Phil Niekro	4.00	2.00	1.25
156	Bake McBride	.30	.15	.09
157	Pete Vuckovich	.30	.15	.09
158	Ivan DeJesus	.30	.15	.09
159	Rick Rhoden	.30	.15	.09
160	Joe Morgan	3.50	1.75	1.00
161	Ed Ott	.30	.15	.09
162	Don Stanhouse	.30	.15	.09
163	Jim Rice	.75	.40	.25
164	Bucky Dent	.30	.15	.09
165	Jim Kern	.30	.15	.09
166	Doug Rader	.30	.15	.09
167	Steve Kemp	.30	.15	.09
168	John Mayberry	.30	.15	.09
169	Tim Foli	.30	.15	.09
170	Steve Carlton	5.00	2.50	1.50
171	Pepe Frias	.30	.15	.09
172	Pat Zachry	.30	.15	.09
173	Don Baylor	.30	.15	.09
174	Sal Bando	.30	.15	.09
175	Alvis Woods	.30	.15	.09
176	Mike Hargrove	.30	.15	.09
177	Vida Blue	.30	.15	.09
178	George Hendrick	.30	.15	.09
179	Jim Palmer	4.00	2.00	1.25
180	Andre Dawson	19.00	9.50	5.75
181	Paul Moskau	.30	.15	.09
182	Mickey Rivers	.30	.15	.09
183	Checklist 122-242	.75	.40	.25
184	Jerry Johnson	.30	.15	.09
185	Willie McCovey	1.75	.90	.50
186	Enrique Romo	.30	.15	.09
187	Butch Hobson	.30	.15	.09
188	Rusty Staub	.50	.25	.15
189	Wayne Twitchell	.30	.15	.09
190	Steve Garvey	1.50	.70	.45
191	Rick Waits	.30	.15	.09
192	Doug DeCinces	.30	.15	.09
193	Tom Murphy	.30	.15	.09
194	Rich Hebner	.30	.15	.09
195	Ralph Garr	.30	.15	.09
196	Bruce Sutter	.30	.15	.09
197	Tom Poquette	.30	.15	.09
198	Wayne Garrett	.30	.15	.09
199	Pedro Borbon	.30	.15	.09
200	Thurman Munson	4.25	2.25	1.25
201	Rollie Fingers	2.50	1.25	.70
202	Doug Ault	.30	.15	.09
203	Phil Garner	.30	.15	.09
204	Lou Brock	3.50	1.75	1.00
205	Ed Kranepool	.30	.15	.09
206	Bobby Bonds	.30	.15	.09
207	Expos Team	.30	.15	.09
208	Bump Wills	.30	.15	.09
209	Gary Matthews	.30	.15	.09
210	Carlton Fisk	5.00	2.50	1.50
211	Jeff Byrd	.30	.15	.09
212	Jason Thompson	.30	.15	.09
213	Larvell Blanks	.30	.15	.09
214	Sparky Lyle	.30	.15	.09
215	George Brett	22.00	11.00	6.50
216	Del Unser	.30	.15	.09
217	Manny Trillo	.30	.15	.09
218	Roy Hartsfield	.30	.15	.09
219	Carlos Lopez	.30	.15	.09
220	Dave Concepcion	.30	.15	.09
221	John Candelaria	.30	.15	.09
222	Dave Lopes	.30	.15	.09
223	Tim Blackwell	.30	.15	.09
224	Chet Lemon	.30	.15	.09
225	Mike Schmidt	15.00	7.50	4.50
226	Cesar Cedeno	.30	.15	.09
227	Mike Willis	.30	.15	.09
228	Willie Randolph	.30	.15	.09
229	Doug Bair	.30	.15	.09
230	Rod Carew	5.00	2.50	1.50
231	Mike Flanagan	.30	.15	.09
232	Chris Speier	.30	.15	.09
233	Don Aase	.30	.15	.09
234	Buddy Bell	.30	.15	.09
235	Mark Fidrych	.35	.20	.11
236	(Lou Brock) (Record Breaker)	1.25	.60	.40
237	(Sparky Lyle) (Record Breaker)	.30	.15	.09
238	(Willie McCovey) (Record Breaker)	.60	.30	.20
239	(Brooks Robinson) (Record Breaker)	1.00	.50	.30
240	(Pete Rose) (Record Breaker)	3.25	1.75	1.00
241	(Nolan Ryan) (Record Breaker)	15.00	7.50	4.50
242	(Reggie Jackson) (Record Breaker)	6.00	3.00	1.75

1979 O-Pee-Chee

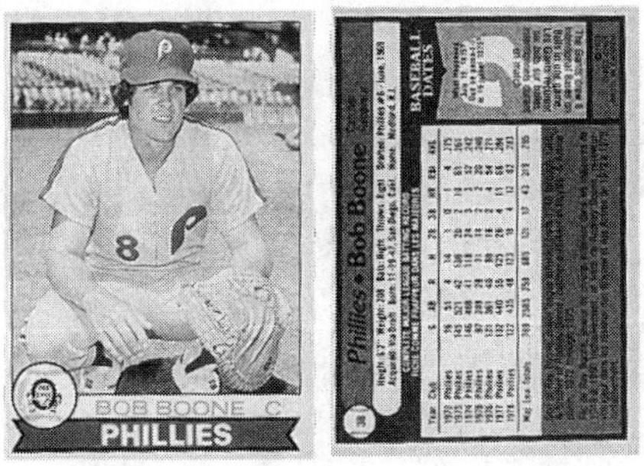

The 1979 O-Pee-Chee cards are nearly identical in design to the Topps set of the same year, but display the O-Pee-Chee logo inside the baseball in the lower-left corner of the front. The number of cards in the set was increased to 374, each measuring 2-1/2" x 3-1/2".

		NM	EX	VG
	Complete Set (374):	125.00	60.00	40.00
	Common Player:	.25	.13	.08
1	Lee May	.25	.13	.08
2	Dick Drago	.25	.13	.08
3	Paul Dade	.25	.13	.08
4	Ross Grimsley	.25	.13	.08
5	Joe Morgan	3.00	1.50	.90
6	Kevin Kobel	.25	.13	.08
7	Terry Forster	.25	.13	.08
8	Paul Molitor	35.00	17.50	10.50
9	Steve Carlton	4.25	2.25	1.25
10	Dave Goltz	.25	.13	.08
11	Dave Winfield	8.00	4.00	2.50
12	Dave Rozema	.25	.13	.08
13	Ed Figueroa	.25	.13	.08
14	Alan Ashby	.25	.13	.08
15	Dale Murphy	5.00	2.50	1.50
16	Dennis Eckersley	3.00	1.50	.90
17	Ron Blomberg	.25	.13	.08
18	Wayne Twitchell	.25	.13	.08
19	Al Hrabosky	.25	.13	.08
20	Fred Norman	.25	.13	.08
21	Steve Garvey	1.00	.50	.30
22	Willie Stargell	2.50	1.25	.70
23	John Hale	.25	.13	.08
24	Mickey Rivers	.25	.13	.08
25	Jack Brohamer	.25	.13	.08
26	Tom Underwood	.25	.13	.08
27	Mark Belanger	.25	.13	.08
28	Elliott Maddox	.25	.13	.08
29	John Candelaria	.25	.13	.08
30	Shane Rawley	.25	.13	.08
31	Steve Yeager	.25	.13	.08
32	Warren Cromartie	.25	.13	.08
33	Jason Thompson	.25	.13	.08
34	Roger Erickson	.25	.13	.08
35	Gary Matthews	.25	.13	.08
36	Pete Falcone	.25	.13	.08
37	Dick Tidrow	.25	.13	.08
38	Bob Boone	.25	.13	.08
39	Jim Bibby	.25	.13	.08
40	Len Barker	.25	.13	.08
41	Robin Yount	15.00	7.50	4.50
42	Sam Mejias	.25	.13	.08

43	Ray Burris	.25	.13	.08
44	Tom Seaver	3.25	1.75	1.00
45	Roy Howell	.25	.13	.08
46	Jim Todd	.25	.13	.08
47	Frank Duffy	.25	.13	.08
48	Joel Youngblood	.25	.13	.08
49	Vida Blue	.25	.13	.08
50	Cliff Johnson	.25	.13	.08
51	Nolan Ryan	45.00	22.00	13.50
52	Ozzie Smith	90.00	45.00	27.00
53	Jim Sundberg	.25	.13	.08
54	Mike Paxton	.25	.13	.08
55	Lou Whitaker	4.00	2.00	1.25
56	Dan Schatzeder	.25	.13	.08
57	Rick Burleson	.25	.13	.08
58	Doug Bair	.25	.13	.08
59	Ted Martinez	.25	.13	.08
60	Bob Watson	.25	.13	.08
61	Jim Clancy	.25	.13	.08
62	Rowland Office	.25	.13	.08
63	Bobby Murcer	.25	.13	.08
64	Don Gullett	.25	.13	.08
65	Tom Paciorek	.25	.13	.08
66	Rick Rhoden	.25	.13	.08
67	Duane Kuiper	.25	.13	.08
68	Bruce Boisclair	.25	.13	.08
69	Manny Sarmiento	.25	.13	.08
70	Wayne Cage	.25	.13	.08
71	John Hiller	.25	.13	.08
72	Rick Cerone	.25	.13	.08
73	Dwight Evans	.25	.13	.08
74	Buddy Solomon	.25	.13	.08
75	Roy White	.25	.13	.08
76	Mike Flanagan	.25	.13	.08
77	Tom Johnson	.25	.13	.08
78	Glenn Burke	.25	.13	.08
79	Frank Taveras	.25	.13	.08
80	Don Sutton	1.25	.60	.40
81	Leon Roberts	.25	.13	.08
82	George Hendrick	.25	.13	.08
83	Aurelio Rodriguez	.25	.13	.08
84	Ron Reed	.25	.13	.08
85	Alvis Woods	.25	.13	.08
86	Jim Beattie	.25	.13	.08
87	Larry Hisle	.25	.13	.08
88	Mike Garman	.25	.13	.08
89	Tim Johnson	.25	.13	.08
90	Paul Splittorff	.25	.13	.08
91	Darrel Chaney	.25	.13	.08
92	Mike Torrez	.25	.13	.08
93	Eric Soderholm	.25	.13	.08
94	Ron Cey	.25	.13	.08
95	Randy Jones	.25	.13	.08
96	Bill Madlock	.25	.13	.08
97	Steve Kemp	.25	.13	.08
98	Bob Apodaca	.25	.13	.08
99	Johnny Grubb	.25	.13	.08
100	Larry Milbourne	.25	.13	.08
101	Johnny Bench	2.75	1.50	.80
102	Dave Lemanczyk	.25	.13	.08
103	Reggie Cleveland	.25	.13	.08
104	Larry Bowa	.25	.13	.08
105	Denny Martinez	3.00	1.50	.90
106	Bill Travers	.25	.13	.08
107	Willie McCovey	2.50	1.25	.70
108	Wilbur Wood	.25	.13	.08
109	Dennis Leonard	.25	.13	.08
110	Roy Smalley	.25	.13	.08
111	Cesar Geronimo	.25	.13	.08
112	Jesse Jefferson	.25	.13	.08
113	Dave Revering	.25	.13	.08
114	Rich Gossage	.60	.30	.20
115	Steve Stone	.25	.13	.08
116	Doug Flynn	.25	.13	.08
117	Bob Forsch	.25	.13	.08
118	Paul Mitchell	.25	.13	.08
119	Toby Harrah	.25	.13	.08
120	Steve Rogers	.25	.13	.08
121	Checklist 1-125	.25	.13	.08
122	Balor Moore	.25	.13	.08
123	Rick Reuschel	.25	.13	.08
124	Jeff Burroughs	.25	.13	.08
125	Willie Randolph	.25	.13	.08
126	Bob Stinson	.25	.13	.08
127	Rick Wise	.25	.13	.08
128	Luis Gomez	.25	.13	.08
129	Tommy John	.25	.13	.08
130	Richie Zisk	.25	.13	.08
131	Mario Guerrero	.25	.13	.08
132	Oscar Gamble	.25	.13	.08
133	Don Money	.25	.13	.08
134	Joe Rudi	.25	.13	.08
135	Woodie Fryman	.25	.13	.08
136	Butch Hobson	.25	.13	.08
137	Jim Colborn	.25	.13	.08
138	Tom Grieve	.25	.13	.08
139	Andy Messersmith	.25	.13	.08
140	Andre Thornton	.25	.13	.08
141	Kevin Kravec	.25	.13	.08
142	Bobby Bonds	.25	.13	.08
143	Jose Cruz	.25	.13	.08
144	Dave Lopes	.25	.13	.08
145	Jerry Garvin	.25	.13	.08
146	Pepe Frias	.25	.13	.08
147	Mitchell Page	.25	.13	.08
148	Ted Sizemore	.25	.13	.08
149	Rich Gale	.25	.13	.08
150	Steve Ontiveros	.25	.13	.08
151	Rod Carew	3.50	1.75	1.00
152	Lary Sorensen	.25	.13	.08
153	Willie Montanez	.25	.13	.08
154	Floyd Bannister	.25	.13	.08
155	Bert Blyleven	.30	.15	.09
156	Ralph Garr	.25	.13	.08
157	Thurman Munson	3.00	1.50	.90
158	Bob Robertson	.25	.13	.08
159	Jon Matlack	.25	.13	.08
160	Carl Yastrzemski	3.50	1.75	1.00
161	Gaylord Perry	2.00	1.00	.60
162	Mike Tyson	.25	.13	.08
163	Cecil Cooper	.25	.13	.08
164	Pedro Borbon	.25	.13	.08
165	Art Howe	.25	.13	.08
166	Joe Coleman	.25	.13	.08
167	George Brett	20.00	10.00	6.00
168	Gary Alexander	.25	.13	.08
169	Chet Lemon	.25	.13	.08
170	Craig Swan	.25	.13	.08
171	Chris Chambliss	.25	.13	.08
172	John Montague	.25	.13	.08
173	Ron Jackson	.25	.13	.08
174	Jim Palmer	3.75	2.00	1.25
175	Willie Upshaw	.75	.40	.25
176	Tug McGraw	.25	.13	.08
177	Bill Buckner	.25	.13	.08
178	Doug Rau	.25	.13	.08
179	Andre Dawson	10.00	5.00	3.00
180	Jim Wright	.25	.13	.08
181	Garry Templeton	.25	.13	.08
182	Bill Bonham	.25	.13	.08
183	Lee Mazzilli	.25	.13	.08
184	Alan Trammell	9.00	4.50	2.75
185	Amos Otis	.25	.13	.08
186	Tom Dixon	.25	.13	.08
187	Mike Cubbage	.25	.13	.08
188	Sparky Lyle	.25	.13	.08
189	Juan Bernhardt	.25	.13	.08
190	Bump Wills	.25	.13	.08
191	Dave Kingman	.30	.15	.09
192	Lamar Johnson	.25	.13	.08
193	Lance Rautzhan	.25	.13	.08
194	Ed Herrmann	.25	.13	.08
195	Bill Campbell	.25	.13	.08
196	Gorman Thomas	.25	.13	.08
197	Paul Moskau	.25	.13	.08
198	Dale Murray	.25	.13	.08
199	John Mayberry	.25	.13	.08
200	Phil Garner	.25	.13	.08
201	Dan Ford	.25	.13	.08
202	Gary Thomasson	.25	.13	.08
203	Rollie Fingers	2.00	1.00	.60
204	Al Oliver	.25	.13	.08
205	Doug Ault	.25	.13	.08
206	Scott McGregor	.25	.13	.08
207	Dave Cash	.25	.13	.08
208	Bill Plummer	.25	.13	.08
209	Ivan DeJesus	.25	.13	.08
210	Jim Rice	.80	.40	.25
211	Ray Knight	.25	.13	.08
212	Paul Hartzell	.25	.13	.08
213	Tim Foli	.25	.13	.08
214	Butch Wynegar	.25	.13	.08
215	Darrell Evans	.25	.13	.08
216	Ken Griffey	.25	.13	.08
217	Doug DeCinces	.25	.13	.08
218	Ruppert Jones	.25	.13	.08
219	Bob Montgomery	.25	.13	.08
220	Rick Manning	.25	.13	.08
221	Chris Speier	.25	.13	.08
222	Bobby Valentine	.25	.13	.08
223	Dave Parker	.65	.35	.20
224	Larry Biittner	.25	.13	.08
225	Ken Clay	.25	.13	.08
226	Gene Tenace	.25	.13	.08
227	Frank White	.25	.13	.08
228	Rusty Staub	.35	.20	.11
229	Lee Lacy	.25	.13	.08
230	Doyle Alexander	.25	.13	.08
231	Bruce Bochte	.25	.13	.08
232	Steve Henderson	.25	.13	.08
233	Jim Lonborg	.25	.13	.08
234	Dave Concepcion	.25	.13	.08
235	Jerry Morales	.25	.13	.08
236	Len Randle	.25	.13	.08
237	Bill Lee	.25	.13	.08
238	Bruce Sutter	.25	.13	.08
239	Jim Essian	.25	.13	.08
240	Graig Nettles	.25	.13	.08
241	Otto Velez	.25	.13	.08
242	Checklist 126-250	.25	.13	.08
243	Reggie Smith	.25	.13	.08
244	Stan Bahnsen	.25	.13	.08
245	Garry Maddox	.25	.13	.08
246	Joaquin Andujar	.25	.13	.08
247	Dan Driessen	.25	.13	.08
248	Bob Grich	.25	.13	.08
249	Fred Lynn	.60	.30	.20
250	Skip Lockwood	.25	.13	.08
251	Craig Reynolds	.25	.13	.08
252	Willie Horton	.25	.13	.08
253	Rick Waits	.25	.13	.08
254	Bucky Dent	.25	.13	.08
255	Bob Knepper	.25	.13	.08
256	Miguel Dilone	.25	.13	.08
257	Bob Owchinko	.25	.13	.08
258	Al Cowens	.25	.13	.08
259	Bob Bailor	.25	.13	.08
260	Larry Christenson	.25	.13	.08
261	Tony Perez	3.00	1.50	.90
262	Blue Jays Team	.25	.13	.08
263	Glenn Abbott	.25	.13	.08
264	Ron Guidry	.75	.40	.25
265	Ed Kranepool	.25	.13	.08
266	Charlie Hough	.25	.13	.08
267	Ted Simmons	.25	.13	.08
268	Jack Clark	.75	.40	.25
269	Enos Cabell	.25	.13	.08
270	Gary Carter	3.75	2.00	1.25
271	Sam Ewing	.25	.13	.08
272	Tom Burgmeier	.25	.13	.08
273	Freddie Patek	.25	.13	.08
274	Frank Tanana	.25	.13	.08
275	Leroy Stanton	.25	.13	.08
276	Ken Forsch	.25	.13	.08
277	Ellis Valentine	.25	.13	.08
278	Greg Luzinski	.25	.13	.08
279	Rick Bosetti	.25	.13	.08
280	John Stearns	.25	.13	.08
281	Enrique Romo	.25	.13	.08
282	Bob Bailey	.25	.13	.08
283	Sal Bando	.25	.13	.08
284	Matt Keough	.25	.13	.08
285	Biff Pocoroba	.25	.13	.08
286	Mike Lum	.25	.13	.08
287	Jay Johnstone	.25	.13	.08
288	John Montefusco	.25	.13	.08
289	Ed Ott	.25	.13	.08
290	Dusty Baker	.25	.13	.08
291	Rico Carty	.25	.13	.08
292	Nino Espinosa	.25	.13	.08
293	Rich Hebner	.25	.13	.08
294	Cesar Cedeno	.25	.13	.08
295	Darrell Porter	.25	.13	.08
296	Rod Gilbreath	.25	.13	.08
297	Jim Kern	.25	.13	.08
298	Claudell Washington	.25	.13	.08
299	Luis Tiant	.25	.13	.08
300	Mike Parrott	.25	.13	.08
301	Pete Broberg	.25	.13	.08
302	Greg Gross	.25	.13	.08
303	Darold Knowles	.25	.13	.08
304	Paul Blair	.25	.13	.08
305	Julio Cruz	.25	.13	.08
306	Hal McRae	.25	.13	.08
307	Ken Reitz	.25	.13	.08
308	Tom Murphy	.25	.13	.08
309	Terry Whitfield	.25	.13	.08
310	J.R. Richard	.25	.13	.08
311	Mike Hargrove	.25	.13	.08
312	Rick Dempsey	.25	.13	.08
313	Phil Niekro	3.50	1.75	1.00
314	Bob Stanley	.25	.13	.08
315	Jim Spencer	.25	.13	.08
316	George Foster	.25	.13	.08
317	Dave LaRoche	.25	.13	.08
318	Rudy May	.25	.13	.08
319	Jeff Newman	.25	.13	.08
320	Rick Monday	.25	.13	.08
321	Omar Moreno	.25	.13	.08
322	Dave McKay	.25	.13	.08
323	Mike Schmidt	8.50	4.25	2.50
324	Ken Singleton	.25	.13	.08
325	Jerry Remy	.25	.13	.08
326	Bert Campaneris	.25	.13	.08
327	Pat Zachry	.25	.13	.08
328	Larry Herndon	.25	.13	.08
329	Mark Fidrych	.25	.13	.08
330	Del Unser	.25	.13	.08
331	Gene Garber	.25	.13	.08
332	Bake McBride	.25	.13	.08
333	Jorge Orta	.25	.13	.08
334	Don Kirkwood	.25	.13	.08
335	Don Baylor	.25	.13	.08
336	Bill Robinson	.25	.13	.08
337	Manny Trillo	.25	.13	.08
338	Eddie Murray	25.00	12.50	7.50
339	Tom Hausman	.25	.13	.08
340	George Scott	.25	.13	.08
341	Rick Sweet	.25	.13	.08
342	Lou Piniella	.25	.13	.08
343	Pete Rose	10.00	5.00	3.00
344	Stan Papi	.25	.13	.08
345	Jerry Koosman	.25	.13	.08
346	Hosken Powell	.25	.13	.08
347	George Medich	.25	.13	.08
348	Ron LeFlore	.25	.13	.08
349	Expos Team	.75	.40	.25
350	Lou Brock	3.00	1.50	.90
351	Bill North	.25	.13	.08
352	Jim Hunter	2.00	1.00	.60
353	Checklist 251-374	.25	.13	.08
354	Ed Halicki	.25	.13	.08
355	Tom Hutton	.25	.13	.08
356	Mike Caldwell	.25	.13	.08
357	Larry Parrish	.25	.13	.08
358	Geoff Zahn	.25	.13	.08
359	Derrel Thomas	.25	.13	.08
360	Carlton Fisk	3.00	1.50	.90
361	John Henry Johnson	.25	.13	.08
362	Dave Chalk	.25	.13	.08
363	Dan Meyer	.25	.13	.08
364	Sixto Lezcano	.25	.13	.08
365	Rennie Stennett	.25	.13	.08
366	Mike Willis	.25	.13	.08
367	Buddy Bell	.25	.13	.08
368	Mickey Stanley	.25	.13	.08
369	Dave Rader	.25	.13	.08
370	Burt Hooton	.25	.13	.08
371	Keith Hernandez	.25	.13	.08
372	Bill Stein	.25	.13	.08
373	Hal Dues	.25	.13	.08
374	Reggie Jackson	2.50	1.25	.70

1980 O-Pee-Chee

The 1980 Canadian-issued O-Pee-Chee set was again complete at 374 cards, which measure 2-1/2" x 3-1/2" and share the same design as the 1980 Topps set. The OPC cards are printed on a white stock, rather than the traditional gray stock used by Topps, and their backs are written in both French and English. Some of the cards include an extra line on the front indicating a new team designation.

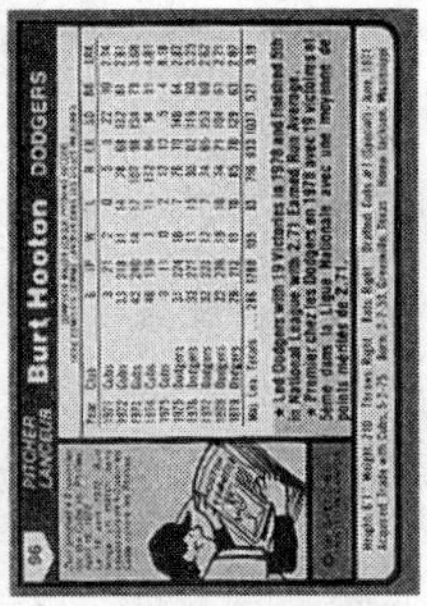

#	Player	NM	EX	VG
Complete Set (374):		125.00	62.00	37.00
Common Player:		.20	.10	.06
1	Craig Swan	.20	.10	.06
2	Denny Martinez	.20	.10	.06
3	Dave Cash	.20	.10	.06
4	Bruce Sutter	.20	.10	.06
5	Ron Jackson	.20	.10	.06
6	Balor Moore	.20	.10	.06
7	Dan Ford	.20	.10	.06
8	Pat Putnam	.20	.10	.06
9	Derrel Thomas	.20	.10	.06
10	Jim Slaton	.20	.10	.06
11	Lee Mazzilli	.20	.10	.06
12	Del Unser	.20	.10	.06
13	Mark Wagner	.20	.10	.06
14	Vida Blue	.20	.10	.06
15	Jay Johnstone	.20	.10	.06
16	Julio Cruz	.20	.10	.06
17	Tony Scott	.20	.10	.06
18	Jeff Newman	.20	.10	.06
19	Luis Tiant	.20	.10	.06
20	Carlton Fisk	1.00	.50	.30
21	Dave Palmer	.20	.10	.06
22	Bombo Rivera	.20	.10	.06
23	Bill Fahey	.20	.10	.06
24	Frank White	.20	.10	.06
25	Rico Carty	.20	.10	.06
26	Bill Bonham	.20	.10	.06
27	Rick Miller	.20	.10	.06
28	J.R. Richard	.20	.10	.06
29	Joe Ferguson	.20	.10	.06
30	Bill Madlock	.20	.10	.06
31	Pete Vuckovich	.20	.10	.06
32	Doug Flynn	.20	.10	.06
33	Bucky Dent	.20	.10	.06
34	Mike Ivie	.20	.10	.06
35	Bob Stanley	.20	.10	.06
36	Al Bumbry	.20	.10	.06
37	Gary Carter	2.50	1.25	.70
38	John Milner	.20	.10	.06
39	Sid Monge	.20	.10	.06
40	Bill Russell	.20	.10	.06
41	John Stearns	.20	.10	.06
42	Dave Stieb	2.00	1.00	.60
43	Ruppert Jones	.20	.10	.06
44	Bob Owchinko	.20	.10	.06
45	Ron LeFlore	.20	.10	.06
46	Ted Sizemore	.20	.10	.06
47	Ted Simmons	.20	.10	.06
48	Pepe Frias	.20	.10	.06
49	Ken Landreaux	.20	.10	.06
50	Manny Trillo	.20	.10	.06
51	Rick Dempsey	.20	.10	.06
52	Cecil Cooper	.20	.10	.06
53	Bill Lee	.20	.10	.06
54	Victor Cruz	.20	.10	.06
55	Johnny Bench	4.00	2.00	1.25
56	Rich Dauer	.20	.10	.06
57	Frank Tanana	.20	.10	.06
58	Francisco Barrios	.20	.10	.06
59	Bob Horner	.90	.45	.25
60	Fred Lynn	.30	.15	.09
61	Bob Knepper	.20	.10	.06
62	Sparky Lyle	.20	.10	.06
63	Larry Cox	.20	.10	.06
64	Dock Ellis	.20	.10	.06
65	Phil Garner	.20	.10	.06
66	Greg Luzinski	.20	.10	.06
67	Checklist 1-125	.40	.20	.12
68	Dave Lemanczyk	.20	.10	.06
69	Tony Perez	2.00	1.00	.60
70	Gary Thomasson	.20	.10	.06
71	Craig Reynolds	.20	.10	.06
72	Amos Otis	.20	.10	.06
73	Biff Pocoroba	.20	.10	.06
74	Matt Keough	.20	.10	.06
75	Bill Buckner	.20	.10	.06
76	John Castino	.20	.10	.06
77	Rich Gossage	.50	.25	.15
78	Gary Alexander	.20	.10	.06
79	Phil Huffman	.20	.10	.06
80	Bruce Bochte	.20	.10	.06
81	Darrell Evans	.20	.10	.06
82	Terry Puhl	.20	.10	.06
83	Jason Thompson	.20	.10	.06
84	Lary Sorenson	.20	.10	.06
85	Jerry Remy	.20	.10	.06
86	Tony Brizzolara	.20	.10	.06
87	Willie Wilson	.20	.10	.06
88	Eddie Murray	12.00	6.00	3.50
89	Larry Christenson	.20	.10	.06
90	Bob Randall	.20	.10	.06
91	Greg Pryor	.20	.10	.06
92	Glenn Abbott	.20	.10	.06
93	Jack Clark	.20	.10	.06
94	Rick Waits	.20	.10	.06
95	Luis Gomez	.20	.10	.06
96	Burt Hooton	.20	.10	.06
97	John Henry Johnson	.20	.10	.06
98	Ray Knight	.20	.10	.06
99	Rick Reuschel	.20	.10	.06
100	Champ Summers	.20	.10	.06
101	Ron Davis	.20	.10	.06
102	Warren Cromartie	.20	.10	.06
103	Ken Reitz	.20	.10	.06
104	Hal McRae	.20	.10	.06
105	Alan Ashby	.20	.10	.06
106	Kevin Kobel	.20	.10	.06
107	Buddy Bell	.20	.10	.06
108	Dave Goltz	.20	.10	.06
109	John Montefusco	.20	.10	.06
110	Lance Parrish	1.25	.60	.40
111	Mike LaCoss	.20	.10	.06
112	Jim Rice	.20	.10	.06
113	Steve Carlton	4.00	2.00	1.25
114	Sixto Lezcano	.20	.10	.06
115	Ed Halicki	.20	.10	.06
116	Jose Morales	.20	.10	.06
117	Dave Concepcion	.20	.10	.06
118	Joe Cannon	.20	.10	.06
119	Willie Montanez	.20	.10	.06
120	Lou Piniella	.20	.10	.06
121	Bill Stein	.20	.10	.06
122	Dave Winfield	3.50	1.75	1.00
123	Alan Trammell	2.00	1.00	.60
124	Andre Dawson	9.00	4.50	2.75
125	Marc Hill	.20	.10	.06
126	Don Aase	.20	.10	.06
127	Dave Kingman	.40	.20	.12
128	Checklist 126-250	.40	.20	.12
129	Dennis Lamp	.20	.10	.06
130	Phil Niekro	2.00	1.00	.60
131	Tim Foli	.20	.10	.06
132	Jim Clancy	.20	.10	.06
133	Bill Atkinson	.20	.10	.06
134	Paul Dade	.20	.10	.06
135	Dusty Baker	.20	.10	.06
136	Al Oliver	.20	.10	.06
137	Dave Chalk	.20	.10	.06
138	Bill Robinson	.20	.10	.06
139	Robin Yount	12.00	6.00	3.50
140	Dan Schatzeder	.20	.10	.06
141	Mike Schmidt	4.25	2.25	1.25
142	Ralph Garr	.20	.10	.06
143	Dale Murphy	3.50	1.75	1.00
144	Jerry Koosman	.20	.10	.06
145	Tom Veryzer	.20	.10	.06
146	Rick Bosetti	.20	.10	.06
147	Jim Spencer	.20	.10	.06
148	Gaylord Perry	1.25	.60	.40
149	Paul Blair	.20	.10	.06
150	Don Baylor	.20	.10	.06
151	Dave Rozema	.20	.10	.06
152	Steve Garvey	.90	.45	.25
153	Elias Sosa	.20	.10	.06
154	Larry Gura	.20	.10	.06
155	Tim Johnson	.20	.10	.06
156	Steve Henderson	.20	.10	.06
157	Ron Guidry	.50	.25	.15
158	Mike Edwards	.20	.10	.06
159	Butch Wynegar	.20	.10	.06
160	Randy Jones	.20	.10	.06
161	Denny Walling	.20	.10	.06
162	Mike Hargrove	.20	.10	.06
163	Dave Parker	.75	.40	.25
164	Roger Metzger	.20	.10	.06
165	Johnny Grubb	.20	.10	.06
166	Steve Kemp	.20	.10	.06
167	Bob Lacey	.20	.10	.06
168	Chris Speier	.20	.10	.06
169	Dennis Eckersley	1.50	.70	.45
170	Keith Hernandez	.20	.10	.06
171	Claudell Washington	.20	.10	.06
172	Tom Underwood	.20	.10	.06
173	Dan Driessen	.20	.10	.06
174	Al Cowens	.20	.10	.06
175	Rich Hebner	.20	.10	.06
176	Willie McCovey	2.00	1.00	.60
177	Carney Lansford	.20	.10	.06
178	Ken Singleton	.20	.10	.06
179	Jim Essian	.20	.10	.06
180	Mike Vail	.20	.10	.06
181	Randy Lerch	.20	.10	.06
182	Larry Parrish	.20	.10	.06
183	Checklist 251-374	.40	.20	.12
184	George Hendrick	.20	.10	.06
185	Bob Davis	.20	.10	.06
186	Gary Matthews	.20	.10	.06
187	Lou Whitaker	.75	.40	.25
188	Darrell Porter	.20	.10	.06
189	Wayne Gross	.20	.10	.06
190	Bobby Murcer	.20	.10	.06
191	Willie Aikens	.20	.10	.06
192	Jim Kern	.20	.10	.06
193	Cesar Cedeno	.20	.10	.06
194	Joel Youngblood	.20	.10	.06
195	Ross Grimsley	.20	.10	.06
196	Jerry Mumphrey	.20	.10	.06
197	Kevin Bell	.20	.10	.06
198	Garry Maddox	.20	.10	.06
199	Dave Freisleben	.20	.10	.06
200	Ed Ott	.20	.10	.06
201	Enos Cabell	.20	.10	.06
202	Pete LaCock	.20	.10	.06
203	Fergie Jenkins	2.00	1.00	.60
204	Milt Wilcox	.20	.10	.06
205	Ozzie Smith	18.00	9.00	5.50
206	Ellis Valentine	.20	.10	.06
207	Dan Meyer	.20	.10	.06
208	Barry Foote	.20	.10	.06
209	George Foster	.20	.10	.06
210	Dwight Evans	.20	.10	.06
211	Paul Molitor	18.00	9.00	5.50
212	Tony Solaita	.20	.10	.06
213	Bill North	.20	.10	.06
214	Paul Splittorff	.20	.10	.06
215	Bobby Bonds	.20	.10	.06
216	Butch Hobson	.20	.10	.06
217	Mark Belanger	.20	.10	.06
218	Grant Jackson	.20	.10	.06
219	Tom Hutton	.20	.10	.06
220	Pat Zachry	.20	.10	.06
221	Duane Kuiper	.20	.10	.06
222	Larry Hisle	.20	.10	.06
223	Mike Krukow	.20	.10	.06
224	Johnnie LeMaster	.20	.10	.06
225	Billy Almon	.20	.10	.06
226	Joe Niekro	.20	.10	.06
227	Dave Revering	.20	.10	.06
228	Don Sutton	1.00	.50	.30
229	John Hiller	.20	.10	.06
230	Alvis Woods	.20	.10	.06
231	Mark Fidrych	.20	.10	.06
232	Duffy Dyer	.20	.10	.06
233	Nino Espinosa	.20	.10	.06
234	Doug Bair	.20	.10	.06
235	George Brett	16.00	8.00	4.75
236	Mike Torrez	.20	.10	.06
237	Frank Taveras	.20	.10	.06
238	Bert Blyleven	.20	.10	.06
239	Willie Randolph	.20	.10	.06
240	Mike Sadek	.20	.10	.06
241	Jerry Royster	.20	.10	.06
242	John Denny	.20	.10	.06
243	Rick Monday	.20	.10	.06
244	Jesse Jefferson	.20	.10	.06
245	Aurelio Rodriguez	.20	.10	.06
246	Bob Boone	.20	.10	.06
247	Cesar Geronimo	.20	.10	.06
248	Bob Shirley	.20	.10	.06
249	Expos Team	.35	.20	.11
250	Bob Watson	.20	.10	.06
251	Mickey Rivers	.20	.10	.06
252	Mike Tyson	.20	.10	.06
253	Wayne Nordhagen	.20	.10	.06
254	Roy Howell	.20	.10	.06
255	Lee May	.20	.10	.06
256	Jerry Martin	.20	.10	.06
257	Bake McBride	.20	.10	.06
258	Silvio Martinez	.20	.10	.06
259	Jim Mason	.20	.10	.06
260	Tom Seaver	3.50	1.75	1.00
261	Rick Wortham	.20	.10	.06
262	Mike Cubbage	.20	.10	.06
263	Gene Garber	.20	.10	.06
264	Bert Campaneris	.20	.10	.06
265	Tom Buskey	.20	.10	.06
266	Leon Roberts	.20	.10	.06
267	Ron Cey	.20	.10	.06
268	Steve Ontiveros	.20	.10	.06
269	Mike Caldwell	.20	.10	.06
270	Nelson Norman	.20	.10	.06
271	Steve Rogers	.20	.10	.06
272	Jim Morrison	.20	.10	.06
273	Clint Hurdle	.20	.10	.06
274	Dale Murray	.20	.10	.06
275	Jim Barr	.20	.10	.06
276	Jim Sundberg	.20	.10	.06
277	Willie Horton	.20	.10	.06
278	Andre Thornton	.20	.10	.06
279	Bob Forsch	.20	.10	.06
280	Joe Strain	.20	.10	.06
281	Rudy May	.20	.10	.06
282	Pete Rose	12.00	6.00	3.50
283	Jeff Burroughs	.20	.10	.06
284	Rick Langford	.20	.10	.06
285	Ken Griffey	.20	.10	.06
286	Bill Nahorodny	.20	.10	.06
287	Art Howe	.20	.10	.06
288	Ed Figueroa	.20	.10	.06
289	Joe Rudi	.20	.10	.06
290	Alfredo Griffin	.20	.10	.06
291	Dave Lopes	.20	.10	.06
292	Rick Manning	.20	.10	.06
293	Dennis Leonard	.20	.10	.06
294	Bud Harrelson	.20	.10	.06
295	Skip Lockwood	.20	.10	.06
296	Roy Smalley	.20	.10	.06
297	Kent Tekulve	.20	.10	.06
298	Scot Thompson	.20	.10	.06
299	Ken Kravec	.20	.10	.06
300	Blue Jays Team	.35	.20	.11
301	Scott Sanderson	.20	.10	.06
302	Charlie Moore	.20	.10	.06
303	Nolan Ryan	45.00	22.00	13.50
304	Bob Bailor	.20	.10	.06
305	Bob Stinson	.20	.10	.06
306	Al Hrabosky	.20	.10	.06
307	Mitchell Page	.20	.10	.06
308	Garry Templeton	.20	.10	.06
309	Chet Lemon	.20	.10	.06
310	Jim Palmer	3.00	1.50	.90
311	Rick Cerone	.20	.10	.06
312	Jon Matlack	.20	.10	.06
313	Don Money	.20	.10	.06
314	Reggie Jackson	5.00	2.50	1.50
315	Brian Downing	.20	.10	.06
316	Woodie Fryman	.20	.10	.06
317	Alan Bannister	.20	.10	.06
318	Ron Reed	.20	.10	.06
319	Willie Stargell	2.00	1.00	.60
320	Jerry Garvin	.20	.10	.06
321	Cliff Johnson	.20	.10	.06
322	Doug DeCinces	.20	.10	.06
323	Gene Richards	.20	.10	.06
324	Joaquin Andujar	.20	.10	.06
325	Richie Zisk	.20	.10	.06
326	Bob Grich	.20	.10	.06
327	Gorman Thomas	.20	.10	.06

328	Chris Chambliss	.20	.10	.06
329	Blue Jays Future Stars (Butch Edge, Pat Kelly, Ted Wilborn)	.30	.15	.09
330	Larry Bowa	.20	.10	.06
331	Barry Bonnell	.20	.10	.06
332	John Candelaria	.20	.10	.06
333	Toby Harrah	.20	.10	.06
334	Larry Biittner	.20	.10	.06
335	Mike Flanagan	.20	.10	.06
336	Ed Kranepool	.20	.10	.06
337	Ken Forsch	.20	.10	.06
338	John Mayberry	.20	.10	.06
339	Rick Burleson	.20	.10	.06
340	Milt May	.20	.10	.06
341	Roy White	.20	.10	.06
342	Joe Morgan	3.00	1.50	.90
343	Rollie Fingers	1.50	.70	.45
344	Mario Mendoza	.20	.10	.06
345	Stan Bahnsen	.20	.10	.06
346	Tug McGraw	.20	.10	.06
347	Rusty Staub	.25	.13	.08
348	Tommy John	.50	.25	.15
349	Ivan DeJesus	.20	.10	.06
350	Reggie Smith	.20	.10	.06
351	Expos Future Stars (Tony Bernazard, Randy Miller, John Tamargo)	.45	.25	.14
352	Floyd Bannister	.20	.10	.06
353	Rod Carew	3.00	1.50	.90
354	Otto Velez	.20	.10	.06
355	Gene Tenace	.20	.10	.06
356	Freddie Patek	.20	.10	.06
357	Elliott Maddox	.20	.10	.06
358	Pat Underwood	.20	.10	.06
359	Graig Nettles	.20	.10	.06
360	Rodney Scott	.20	.10	.06
361	Terry Whitfield	.20	.10	.06
362	Fred Norman	.20	.10	.06
363	Sal Bando	.20	.10	.06
364	Greg Gross	.20	.10	.06
365	Carl Yastrzemski	2.50	1.25	.70
366	Paul Hartzell	.20	.10	.06
367	Jose Cruz	.20	.10	.06
368	Shane Rawley	.20	.10	.06
369	Jerry White	.20	.10	.06
370	Rick Wise	.20	.10	.06
371	Steve Yeager	.20	.10	.06
372	Omar Moreno	.20	.10	.06
373	Bump Wills	.20	.10	.06
374	Craig Kusick	.20	.10	.06

1969 Oakland A's (Andersen)

Though they are sometimes identified as an issue of Jack in the Box restaurants, there is no identifier of that nature on these cards. In fact, they are a collectors' fantasy issue sold only within the hobby by Boston photographer Mike Andersen. The blank-back black-and-white cards measure 2-1/8" x 3-5/8". Beneath the portrait photo on front is the player's name, position and uniform number. The team name is in gothic script at bottom. Cards are checklisted here by uniform number.

		NM	EX	VG
Complete Set (21):		60.00	30.00	18.00
Common Player:		2.00	1.00	.60
1	Dick Green	2.00	1.00	.60
2	Danny Cater	2.00	1.00	.60
3	Mike Hershberger	2.00	1.00	.60
5	Joe DiMaggio (coach)	30.00	15.00	9.00
6	Sal Bando	2.00	1.00	.60
7	Rick Monday	2.00	1.00	.60
9a	Bert Campaneris	4.00	2.00	1.25
9b	Reggie Jackson	20.00	10.00	6.00
13	Blue Moon Odom	4.00	2.00	1.25
17	Jim Pagliaroni	2.00	1.00	.60
19	Bert Campaneris	2.00	1.00	.60
20	Lew Krausse	2.00	1.00	.60
24	Joe Nossek	2.00	1.00	.60
25	Paul Lindblad	2.00	1.00	.60
27	Catfish Hunter	6.00	3.00	1.75
29	Chuck Dobson	2.00	1.00	.60
30	Jim Nash	2.00	1.00	.60
31	Ramon Webster	2.00	1.00	.60
35	Tom Reynolds	2.00	1.00	.60
42	Hank Bauer	4.00	2.00	1.25

1969 Oakland A's (Broder)

A second issue of black-and-white collector cards featuring the 1969 A's was produced by West Coast collector/dealer Ed Broder. In larger (2-3/4" x 4") format the Broder issue is considerably scarcer than that produced by Mike Andersen. Availability of the Broders was advertised at 100 sets. The blank-back Broder cards have the player name in the wide white border beneath the photo. At bottom the city name is in gothic script with the A's logo on a baseball flying out of a stadium. The unnumbered cards are checklisted here alphabetically.

		NM	EX	VG
Complete Set (14):		65.00	32.00	19.50
Common Player:		2.00	1.00	.60
(1)	Sal Bando	2.00	1.00	.60
(2)	Hank Bauer	2.00	1.00	.60
(3)	Bert Campaneris	3.00	1.50	.90
(4)	Dan Cater	2.00	1.00	.60
(5)	Joe DiMaggio	25.00	12.50	7.50
(6)	Chuck Dobson	2.00	1.00	.60
(7)	Dick Green	2.00	1.00	.60
(8)	Mike Hershberger	2.00	1.00	.60
(9)	Jim Hunter	8.00	4.00	2.50
(10)	Reggie Jackson	15.00	7.50	4.50
(11)	Bob Johnson	2.00	1.00	.60
(12)	Rick Monday	2.00	1.00	.60
(13)	Johnny Moon Odom	2.00	1.00	.60
(14)	Phil Roof	2.00	1.00	.60

1969 Oakland A's Picture Pack

These blank-backed, black-and-white player portraits were sold in a picture pack. Photos measure approximately 4-5/8" x 7". The unnumbered pictures are checklisted here alphabetically.

		NM	EX	VG
Complete Set (12):		70.00	35.00	21.00
Common Player:		4.00	2.00	1.25
(1)	Sal Bando	4.00	2.00	1.25
(2)	Bert Campaneris	6.00	3.00	1.75
(3)	Danny Cater	4.00	2.00	1.25
(4)	Chuck Dobson	4.00	2.00	1.25
(5)	Dick Green	4.00	2.00	1.25
(6)	Mike Hershberger	4.00	2.00	1.25
(7)	Jim Hunter	16.00	8.00	4.75
(8)	Reggie Jackson	36.00	18.00	11.00
(9)	Lew Krausse	4.00	2.00	1.25
(10)	Rick Monday	6.00	3.00	1.75
(11)	Jim Nash	4.00	2.00	1.25
(12)	John Odom	6.00	3.00	1.75

1970 Oakland A's (Andersen)

Boston baseball photographer Mike Andersen produced a second collectors' issue of Oakland A's cards in 1970. Nearly identical in format to his 1969 issue, the '70 team set measures 2-1/4" x 3-5/8" with black-and-white player poses at center. Uniform number, name and team are in the bottom border. Backs are blank. Cards are checklisted here by uniform number.

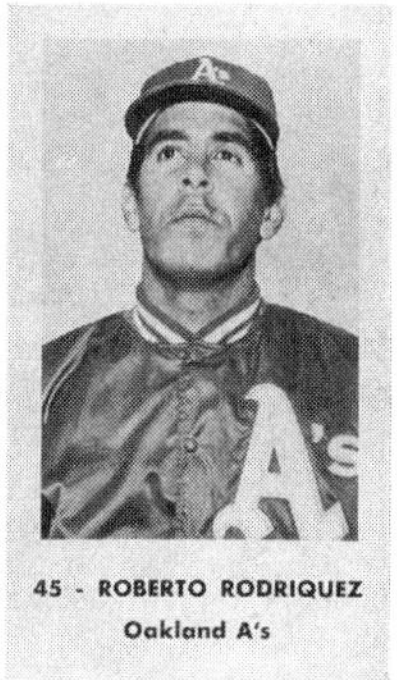

		NM	EX	VG
Complete Set (24):		32.00	16.00	9.50
Common Player:		1.50	.75	.45
1	Dick Green	1.50	.75	.45
6	Sal Bando	1.50	.75	.45
7	Rick Monday	1.50	.75	.45
8	Felipe Alou	2.50	1.25	.70
9	Reggie Jackson	12.50	6.25	3.75
10	Dave Duncan	1.50	.75	.45
11	John McNamera (McNamara)	1.50	.75	.45
12	Larry Haney	1.50	.75	.45
13	Blue Moon Odom	2.00	1.00	.60
17	Roberto Pena	1.50	.75	.45
19	Bert Campaneris	2.00	1.00	.60
24	Diego Segui	1.50	.75	.45
25	Paul Lindblad	1.50	.75	.45
27	Catfish Hunter	4.00	2.00	1.25
28	Mudcat Grant	1.50	.75	.45
29	Chuck Dobson	1.50	.75	.45
30	Don Mincher	1.50	.75	.45
31	Jose Tartabull	1.50	.75	.45
33	Jim Roland	1.50	.75	.45
34	Rollie Fingers	4.00	2.00	1.25
36	Tito Francona	1.50	.75	.45
38	Al Downing	1.50	.75	.45
39	Frank Fernandez	1.50	.75	.45
45	Roberto Rodriguez	1.50	.75	.45

1974 Oh Henry! Henry Aaron Premium Photo

This 8" x 10" black-and-white photo was prepared as a premium for Oh Henry! candy. It features a full-length pose of Aaron and has a facsimile inscribed autographed on front.

	NM	EX	VG
Henry Aaron	15.00	7.50	4.50

1949 Old Gold Jackie Robinson

The stated date of issue is approximate. This postcard-size advertising piece pictures Jackie Robinson and a pack of Old Gold cigarettes on its black-and-white front. In the wide white border at bottom is an endorsement from the player, along with his facsimile autograph. Back has a short biography and career summary.

	NM	EX	VG
Jackie Robinson	300.00	150.00	90.00

1886 Old Judge New York Giants (N167)

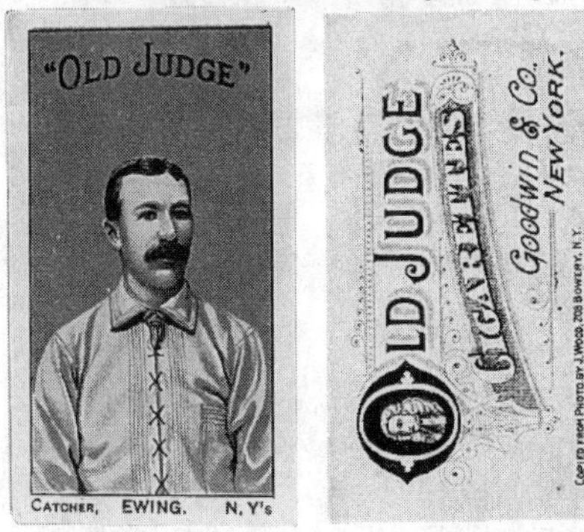

Produced in 1886, the rare N167 Old Judge tobacco cards were the first to be issued by New York's Goodwin & Co., the parent firm of Old Judge Cigarettes. The 1-1/2" x 2-1/2" sepia-toned cards were printed on thin paper and featured only members of the New York National League club. Twelve subjects are known to exist, five of whom are Hall of Famers. The front of each card lists the player's name, position and team and has the words "Old Judge" at the top. The backs contain another ad for the Old Judge brand and also include a line noting that the player poses were "copied from by J. Wood, 208, N.Y."

		NM	EX	VG
Complete Set (12):		80000.	35000.	17500.
Common Player:		4500.	2025.	1125.
(1)	Roger Connor	9000.	4500.	2700.
(2)	Larry Corcoran	4500.	2025.	1125.
(3)	Mike Dorgan	4500.	2025.	1125.
(4)	Dude Esterbrook	4500.	2025.	1125.
(5)	Buck Ewing	9000.	4500.	2700.
(6)	Joe Gerhardt	4500.	2025.	1125.
(7)	Pete Gillespie	4500.	2025.	1125.
(8)	Tim Keefe	9000.	4500.	2700.
(9)	Orator Jim O'Rourke	9000.	4500.	2700.
(10)	Danny Richardson	4500.	2025.	1125.
(11)	Monte Ward	9000.	4500.	2700.
(12)	Mickey Welsh (Welch)	9000.	4500.	2700.

1887 Old Judge (N172)

This is one of the most fascinating of all card sets, as the number of cards issued will probably never be finally determined. These cards were issued by the Goodwin & Co. tobacco firm in their Old Judge and, to a lesser extent, Gypsy Queen cigarettes. Players from more than 40 major and minor league teams are pictured on the approximately 1-7/16" x 2-1/2" cards, with some 518 different players known to exist. Up to 17 different pose and team variations exist for some players, and the cards were issued both with and without dates on the card fronts, numbered and unnumbered, and with both handwritten and machine-printed names. Known variations number in the thousands. The cards themselves are sepia-toned photographs pasted onto thick cardboard. They are blank-backed. The N172 listings are based on the recordings in The Cartophilic Society's (of Great Britian) World Index, Part IV, compiled by E.C. Wharton-Tigar with the help of many collectors, especially Donald J. McPherson of California and Lew Lipset of New York. Because of the vastness of the N172 issue, no complete set price is given.

		NM	EX	VG
Common Player:		260.00	115.00	65.00
Browns Champions:		290.00	130.00	72.00
Dotted Ties:		375.00	170.00	94.00
1	Gus Albert (Alberts)	260.00	115.00	65.00
2	Alcott	260.00	115.00	65.00
3	Alexander	260.00	115.00	65.00
4	Myron Allen (Kansas City - fielding, 32)	260.00	115.00	65.00
5	Bob Allen (Pittsburgh, Philadelphia)	260.00	115.00	65.00
6	Uncle Bill Alvord	260.00	115.00	65.00
7	Varney Anderson	260.00	115.00	65.00
8	Wally Andrews (Omaha)	260.00	115.00	65.00
9	Ed Andrews (Philadelphia)	260.00	115.00	65.00
9-6	Ed Andrews, Buster Hoover	320.00	145.00	80.00
10	Bill Annis	260.00	115.00	65.00
11	Cap Anson	3700.	1675.	925.00
12	Old Hoss Ardner	260.00	115.00	65.00
13	Tug Arundel	260.00	115.00	65.00
14	Jersey Bakley (Bakely)	260.00	115.00	65.00
15	Fido Baldwin (Chicago, Columbus)	260.00	115.00	65.00
16	Kid Baldwin (Cincinnati)	260.00	115.00	65.00
17	Lady Baldwin (Detroit, Cincinnati)	260.00	115.00	65.00
18	James Banning	260.00	115.00	65.00
19	Samuel Barkley	260.00	115.00	65.00
20	John Barnes	260.00	115.00	65.00
21	Bald Billy Barnie	260.00	115.00	65.00
22	Charles Bassett	260.00	115.00	65.00
23	Charles Bastian	260.00	115.00	65.00
23-6	Charles Bastian, Schriver	320.00	145.00	80.00
24	Ed Beatin	260.00	115.00	65.00
25	Jake Beckley	2025.	910.00	505.00
26	Stephen Behel (dotted tie)	435.00	195.00	110.00
27	Charles Bennett	260.00	115.00	65.00
28	Louis Bierbauer	260.00	115.00	65.00
28-5	Louis Bierbauer, Gamble	320.00	145.00	80.00
29	Bill Bishop	260.00	115.00	65.00
30	Bill Blair	260.00	115.00	65.00
31	Ned Bligh	260.00	115.00	65.00
32	Bogart	260.00	115.00	65.00
33	Boyce	260.00	115.00	65.00
34	Boyd	260.00	115.00	65.00
35	Honest John Boyle (St. Louis, Chicago)	260.00	115.00	65.00
36	Handsome Boyle (Indianapolis, New York)	260.00	115.00	65.00
37	Nick Bradley (Kansas City, Worcester)	260.00	115.00	65.00
38	Grin Bradley (Sioux City)	260.00	115.00	65.00
39	Stephen Brady (dotted tie)	435.00	195.00	110.00
40	Breckenridge	435.00	195.00	110.00
41	Timothy Brosnam	260.00	115.00	65.00
42	Cal Broughton	260.00	115.00	65.00
43	Dan Brouthers	1050.	470.00	260.00
44	Thomas Brown (Pittsburgh, Boston)	260.00	115.00	65.00
45	California Brown (New York)	260.00	115.00	65.00
46	Pete Browning	320.00	145.00	80.00
47	Charles Brynan	260.00	115.00	65.00
48	Al Buckenberger	320.00	145.00	80.00
49	Dick Buckley	260.00	115.00	65.00
50	Charles Buffinton	260.00	115.00	65.00
51	Ernest Burch	260.00	115.00	65.00
52	Bill Burdick	260.00	115.00	65.00
53	Black Jack Burdock	260.00	115.00	65.00
54	Robert Burks (Burk)	260.00	115.00	65.00
55	Watch Burnham	320.00	145.00	80.00
56	James Burns (Kansas City, Omaha)	260.00	115.00	65.00
57	No World Index listing	260.00	115.00	65.00
58	Oyster Burns (Baltimore, Brooklyn)	260.00	115.00	65.00
59	Thomas Burns (Chicago)	260.00	115.00	65.00
60	Doc Bushong (Brooklyn)	260.00	115.00	65.00
60-1	Doc Bushong (Brown's Champions)	340.00	155.00	85.00
61	Patsy Cahill	260.00	115.00	65.00
62	Count Campau	260.00	115.00	65.00
63	Jimmy Canavan	260.00	115.00	65.00
64	Bart Cantz	260.00	115.00	65.00
65	Handsome Jack Carney	260.00	115.00	65.00
66	Hick Carpenter	260.00	115.00	65.00
67	Cliff Carroll (Washington)	260.00	115.00	65.00
68	Scrappy Carroll (St. Paul, Chicago)	260.00	115.00	65.00
69	Fred Carroll (Pittsburgh)	260.00	115.00	65.00
70	Jumbo Cartwright	260.00	115.00	65.00
71	Parisian Bob Caruthers (Brooklyn)	260.00	115.00	65.00
71-1	Parisian Bob Caruthers (Brown's Champions)	405.00	180.00	100.00
72	Dan Casey	260.00	115.00	65.00
73	Icebox Chamberlain	260.00	115.00	65.00
74	Cupid Childs	260.00	115.00	65.00
75	Spider Clark (Washington)	260.00	115.00	65.00
76	Bob Clark (Brooklyn)	260.00	115.00	65.00
76-6	Bob Clark, Mickey Hughes	320.00	145.00	80.00
77	Dad Clarke (also spelled Clark)	260.00	115.00	65.00
78	John Clarkson	1400.	630.00	350.00
79	Jack Clements	260.00	115.00	65.00
80	Elmer Cleveland	260.00	115.00	65.00
81	Monk Cline	260.00	115.00	65.00
82	Cody	260.00	115.00	65.00
83	John Coleman	260.00	115.00	65.00
84	Bill Collins (NY, Newark)	260.00	115.00	65.00
85	Hub Collins (Louisville, Brooklyn)	260.00	115.00	65.00
86	Commy Comiskey (St. Louis, Chicago)	1750.	785.00	435.00
86-1	Commy Comiskey (Brown's Champions)	1850.	830.00	460.00
87	Pete Connell	260.00	115.00	65.00
88	Roger Connor	1100.	495.00	275.00
89	Dick Conway (Boston, Worcester)	260.00	115.00	65.00
90	Pete Conway (Detroit, Pittsburgh, Indianapolis)	260.00	115.00	65.00
91	Jim Conway (Kansas City)	260.00	115.00	65.00
92	Paul Cook	260.00	115.00	65.00
93	Jimmy Cooney	520.00	235.00	130.00
94	Larry Corcoran	260.00	115.00	65.00
95	Pop Corkhill	260.00	115.00	65.00
96	Cannonball Crane (NY)	260.00	115.00	65.00
97	Samuel Crane (Washington)	260.00	115.00	65.00
98	Jack Crogan (Croghan)	260.00	115.00	65.00
99	John Crooks	260.00	115.00	65.00
100	Lave Cross	260.00	115.00	65.00
101	N.C. Crossley	260.00	115.00	65.00
102	Joe Crotty (Sioux City)	260.00	115.00	65.00
102-1	Joe Crotty (dotted tie)	435.00	195.00	110.00
103	Billy Crowell	260.00	115.00	65.00
104	Jim Cudworth	260.00	115.00	65.00
105	Bert Cunningham	260.00	115.00	65.00
106	Tacks Curtis	260.00	115.00	65.00
107	Ed Cushman (dotted tie)	435.00	195.00	110.00
107-2	Ed Cushman (Toledo)	320.00	145.00	80.00
108	Tony Cusick	260.00	115.00	65.00
109	Dailey (Oakland)	405.00	180.00	100.00
110	Edward Dailey (Daily) (Philadelphia, Washington, Columbus)	260.00	115.00	65.00
111	Bill Daley (Boston)	260.00	115.00	65.00
112	Con Daley (Daily) (Boston, Indianapolis)	260.00	115.00	65.00
113	Abner Dalrymple	260.00	115.00	65.00
114	Tido Daly (Chicago, Washington)	260.00	115.00	65.00
115	Sun Daly (Minneapolis)	260.00	115.00	65.00
116	Law Daniels	260.00	115.00	65.00
117	Dell Darling	260.00	115.00	65.00
118	William Darnbrough	260.00	115.00	65.00
118-1	Davin	405.00	180.00	100.00
119	Jumbo Davis	260.00	115.00	65.00
120	Pat Dealey	260.00	115.00	65.00
121	Tom Deasley	260.00	115.00	65.00
122	Harry Decker	260.00	115.00	65.00
123	Ed Delahanty	1750.	785.00	435.00
124	Jerry Denny	260.00	115.00	65.00
125	Jim Devlin	260.00	115.00	65.00
126	Tom Dolan	260.00	115.00	65.00
127	Jack Donahue (San Fran)	405.00	180.00	100.00
128	Jim Donahue (Kansas City)	260.00	115.00	65.00
128-1	Jim Donohue (Donahue) (dotted tie)	600.00	270.00	150.00
129	Jim Donnelly	260.00	115.00	65.00
130	Dooley	435.00	195.00	110.00
131	Doran	260.00	115.00	65.00
132	Mike Dorgan	260.00	115.00	65.00
133	Doyle	435.00	195.00	110.00
134	Home Run Duffe (Duffee)	260.00	115.00	65.00
135	Hugh Duffy	930.00	420.00	230.00
136	Dan Dugdale	260.00	115.00	65.00
137	Duck Duke	260.00	115.00	65.00
138	Sure Shot Dunlap	260.00	115.00	65.00
139	Dunn	260.00	115.00	65.00
140	Jesse Duryea	260.00	115.00	65.00
141	Frank Dwyer	260.00	115.00	65.00
142	Billy Earle	260.00	115.00	65.00
143	Buck Ebright	260.00	115.00	65.00
144	Red Ehret	260.00	115.00	65.00
145	R. Emmerke	260.00	115.00	65.00
146	Dude Esterbrook	260.00	115.00	65.00
147	Henry Esterday	260.00	115.00	65.00
148	Long John Ewing (Louisville)	260.00	115.00	65.00
149	Buck Ewing (New York)	985.00	445.00	245.00
149-11	Willie Breslin - mascot, Buck Ewing	810.00	365.00	200.00
150	Jay Faatz	260.00	115.00	65.00
151	Bill Fagan	260.00	115.00	65.00
152	Bill Farmer	260.00	115.00	65.00
153	Sid Farrar	260.00	115.00	65.00
154	Jack Farrell (Washington, Baltimore)	260.00	115.00	65.00
155	Duke Farrell (Chicago)	260.00	115.00	65.00
156	Frank Fennelly	260.00	115.00	65.00
157	Charlie Ferguson	260.00	115.00	65.00
158	Alex Ferson	260.00	115.00	65.00
159	Wallace Fessenden (umpire)	1400.	630.00	350.00
160	Jocko Fields	260.00	115.00	65.00
161	Fischer	260.00	115.00	65.00
162	Thomas Flanigan (Flanagan)	260.00	115.00	65.00
163	Silver Flint	260.00	115.00	65.00
164	Thomas Flood	260.00	115.00	65.00

164-1	Jocko Flynn	390.00	175.00	97.00
165	Jim Fogarty	260.00	115.00	65.00
166	Frank Foreman	260.00	115.00	65.00
167	Tom Forster (Hartford)	320.00	145.00	80.00
167-2	Tom Forster (dotted tie, incorrect name (F.W. Foster) on front)	435.00	195.00	110.00
168	Elmer Foster (New York, Minneapolis)	260.00	115.00	65.00
168-1	Elmer Foster (dotted tie)	435.00	195.00	110.00
169	No listing in World Index	260.00	115.00	65.00
170	Dave Foutz (Brooklyn)	260.00	115.00	65.00
170-1	Dave Foutz (Brown's Champions)	340.00	155.00	85.00
171	Julie Freeman	260.00	115.00	65.00
172	Will Fry	260.00	115.00	65.00
172-1	Fudger	405.00	180.00	100.00
173	William Fuller (Milwaukee)	260.00	115.00	65.00
174	Shorty Fuller (St. Louis)	260.00	115.00	65.00
175	Chris Fulmer	260.00	115.00	65.00
175-6	Chris Fulmer, Foghorn Tucker	320.00	145.00	80.00
176	Honest John Gaffney	260.00	115.00	65.00
177	Pud Galvin	1750.	785.00	435.00
178	Bob Gamble	260.00	115.00	65.00
179	Charlie Ganzel	260.00	115.00	65.00
180	Gid Gardner	260.00	115.00	65.00
180-5	Gid Gardner, Miah Murray	320.00	145.00	80.00
181	Hank Gastreich	260.00	115.00	65.00
182	Emil Geiss	260.00	115.00	65.00
183	Frenchy Genins	260.00	115.00	65.00
184	Bill George	260.00	115.00	65.00
185	Joe Gerhardt	260.00	115.00	65.00
186	Charlie Getzein (Getzien)	260.00	115.00	65.00
187	Bobby Gilks	260.00	115.00	65.00
188	Pete Gillespie	260.00	115.00	65.00
189	Barney Gilligan	260.00	115.00	65.00
190	Frank Gilmore	260.00	115.00	65.00
191	Pebbly Jack Glasscock	260.00	115.00	65.00
192	Kid Gleason (Philadelphia)	260.00	115.00	65.00
193	Will Gleason (Athletics)	260.00	115.00	65.00
193-1	Will Gleason (Brown's Champions)	340.00	155.00	85.00
194	Mouse Glenn	260.00	115.00	65.00
195	Mike Goodfellow	260.00	115.00	65.00
196	Piano Legs Gore	260.00	115.00	65.00
197	Frank Graves	260.00	115.00	65.00
198	Bill Greenwood	260.00	115.00	65.00
199	Ed Greer	260.00	115.00	65.00
200	Mike Griffin	260.00	115.00	65.00
201	Clark Griffith	1150.	515.00	285.00
202	Henry Gruber	260.00	115.00	65.00
203	Ad Gumbert	260.00	115.00	65.00
204	Tom Gunning	260.00	115.00	65.00
205	Joe Gunson	260.00	115.00	65.00
206	Gentleman George Haddock	260.00	115.00	65.00
207	Bill Hafner (Hoffner)	260.00	115.00	65.00
208	Willie Hahm (mascot) (mascot)	260.00	115.00	65.00
209	Bill Hallman	260.00	115.00	65.00
210	Sliding Billy Hamilton	1150.	515.00	285.00
211	Frank Hankinson (dotted tie)	340.00	155.00	85.00
212	Ned Hanlon	1400.	630.00	350.00
213	William Hanrahan	260.00	115.00	65.00
213-1	Hapeman	435.00	195.00	110.00
214	Pa Harkins	260.00	115.00	65.00
215	Bill Hart	260.00	115.00	65.00
216	Bill Hasamdear	260.00	115.00	65.00
217	Gill Hatfield	260.00	115.00	65.00
218	Egyptian Healey (Healy)	260.00	115.00	65.00
219	Healy	260.00	115.00	65.00
220	Guy Hecker	260.00	115.00	65.00
221	Tony Hellman	260.00	115.00	65.00
222	Hardie Henderson	260.00	115.00	65.00
222-10	Ed Greer, Henderson	640.00	290.00	160.00
223	Moxie Hengle	260.00	115.00	65.00
224	John Henry	260.00	115.00	65.00
225	Ed Herr	260.00	115.00	65.00
226	Hunkey Hines (St. Louis Whites)	260.00	115.00	65.00
227	Paul Hines (Washington, Indianapolis)	260.00	115.00	65.00
228	Texas Wonder Hoffman	260.00	115.00	65.00
229	Eddie Hogan	260.00	115.00	65.00
230	Bill Holbert	260.00	115.00	65.00
230-1	Bill Holbert (dotted tie)	435.00	195.00	110.00
231	Bug Holliday	260.00	115.00	65.00
232	Charles Hoover (Chicago, Kansas City)	260.00	115.00	65.00
233	Buster Hoover (Philadelphia)	260.00	115.00	65.00
234	Jack Horner	260.00	115.00	65.00
234-3	Jack Horner, E.H. Warner	320.00	145.00	80.00
235	Joe Hornung	260.00	115.00	65.00
236	Pete Hotaling	260.00	115.00	65.00
237	Bill Howes (Hawes)	260.00	115.00	65.00
238	Dummy Hoy	435.00	195.00	110.00
239	Nat Hudson (St. Louis)	260.00	115.00	65.00
239-1	Nat Hudson (Brown's Champions)	340.00	155.00	85.00
240	Mickey Hughes	260.00	115.00	65.00
241	Hungler	260.00	115.00	65.00
242	Wild Bill Hutchinson	260.00	115.00	65.00
243	John Irwin (Washington)	260.00	115.00	65.00
244	Cutrate Irwin (Philadelphia)	260.00	115.00	65.00
245	A.C. Jantzen	260.00	115.00	65.00
246	Frederick Jevne	260.00	115.00	65.00
247	Spud Johnson	260.00	115.00	65.00
248	Dick Johnston	260.00	115.00	65.00
249	Jordan	260.00	115.00	65.00
250	Heinie Kappell (Kappel)	260.00	115.00	65.00
251	Tim Keefe (New York)	1400.	630.00	350.00
251-8	Keefe, Danny Richardson	1450.	650.00	360.00
252	George Keefe (Washington)	260.00	115.00	65.00
253	Jim Keenan	260.00	115.00	65.00
254	King Kelly (Boston)	1750.	785.00	435.00
255	John Kelly (Louisville)	260.00	115.00	65.00
255-3	Honest John Kelly (umpire)	260.00	115.00	65.00
255-4	Kelly, Jim Powell	320.00	145.00	80.00

256	No listing in World Index	260.00	115.00	65.00
257	Charles Kelly (Philadelphia)	260.00	115.00	65.00
258	Rudy Kemmler (St. Paul)	260.00	115.00	65.00
258-1	Rudy Kemler (Kemmler) (Brown's Champions)	340.00	155.00	85.00
259	Theodore Kennedy	260.00	115.00	65.00
260	J.J. Kenyon	260.00	115.00	65.00
261	John Kerins	260.00	115.00	65.00
262	Matt Kilroy	260.00	115.00	65.00
263	Silver King	520.00	235.00	130.00
264	August Kloff (Klopf)	260.00	115.00	65.00
265	William Klusman	260.00	115.00	65.00
266	Philip Knell	260.00	115.00	65.00
267	Fred Knouff	260.00	115.00	65.00
268	Charles Kremmeyer (Krehmeyer)	435.00	195.00	110.00
269	Bill Krieg	260.00	115.00	65.00
269-10	August Kloff, Bill Krieg	320.00	145.00	80.00
270	Gus Krock	260.00	115.00	65.00
271	Willie Kuehne	260.00	115.00	65.00
272	Fred Lange	260.00	115.00	65.00
273	Ted Larkin	260.00	115.00	65.00
274	Arlie Latham (St. Louis)	260.00	115.00	65.00
274-1	Arlie Latham (Brown's Champions)	320.00	145.00	80.00
275	Chuck Lauer (Laver)	260.00	115.00	65.00
276	John Leighton	260.00	115.00	65.00
276-5	Levy	435.00	195.00	110.00
277	Tom Loftus	320.00	145.00	80.00
278	Germany Long (Kansas City, Chicago Maroons)	260.00	115.00	65.00
279	Danny Long (Oakland)	405.00	180.00	100.00
280	Tom Lovett	260.00	115.00	65.00
281	Bobby Lowe	320.00	145.00	80.00
282	Jack Lynch	260.00	115.00	65.00
282-1	Jack Lynch (dotted tie)	435.00	195.00	110.00
283	Denny Lyons (Athletics)	260.00	115.00	65.00
284	Harry Lyons (St. Louis)	260.00	115.00	65.00
285	Connie Mack (Washington)	2425.	1100.	605.00
286	Reddie Mack (Louisville, Baltimore)	260.00	115.00	65.00
287	Little Mac Macullar	260.00	115.00	65.00
288	Kid Madden	260.00	115.00	65.00
289	Danny Mahoney	260.00	115.00	65.00
290	Grasshopper Maines (Mains)	260.00	115.00	65.00
291	Fred Mann	260.00	115.00	65.00
292	Jimmy Manning	260.00	115.00	65.00
293	Lefty Marr	260.00	115.00	65.00
294	Willie Breslin (N.Y. mascot)	695.00	315.00	175.00
295	Leech Maskrey	260.00	115.00	65.00
296	Bobby Mathews	260.00	115.00	65.00
297	Mike Mattimore	260.00	115.00	65.00
298	Smiling Al Maul	260.00	115.00	65.00
299	Al Mays (Columbus)	260.00	115.00	65.00
299-1	Al Mays (dotted tie)	435.00	195.00	110.00
300	Jimmy McAleer	260.00	115.00	65.00
301	Tommy McCarthy (Philadelphia, St. Louis)	870.00	390.00	215.00
302	John McCarthy (McCarty) (Kansas City)	260.00	115.00	65.00
303	Jim McCauley	260.00	115.00	65.00
304	Bill McClellan	260.00	115.00	65.00
305	Jerry McCormack (McCormick)	260.00	115.00	65.00
306	Jim McCormick	260.00	115.00	65.00
307	McCreachery (photo actually Deacon White)	260.00	115.00	65.00
308	McCullum (McCallum)	260.00	115.00	65.00
308-1	Jim McDonald	435.00	195.00	110.00
309	Chippy McGarr	260.00	115.00	65.00
310	Jack McGeachy	260.00	115.00	65.00
311	John McGlone	260.00	115.00	65.00
312	Deacon McGuire	260.00	115.00	65.00
313	Bill McGunnigle	320.00	145.00	80.00
314	Ed McKean	260.00	115.00	65.00
315	Alex McKinnon	260.00	115.00	65.00
316	Tom McLaughlin (dotted tie)	435.00	195.00	110.00
317	Bid McPhee	435.00	195.00	110.00
318	James McQuaid (Denver)	260.00	115.00	65.00
319	John McQuaid (umpire)	320.00	145.00	80.00
320	Jim McTamany	260.00	115.00	65.00
321	George McVey	260.00	115.00	65.00
321-1	Steady Pete Meegan	435.00	195.00	110.00
322	John Messitt	260.00	115.00	65.00
323	Doggie Miller (Pittsburgh)	260.00	115.00	65.00
324	Joseph Miller (Omaha, Minneapolis)	260.00	115.00	65.00
325	Jocko Milligan	260.00	115.00	65.00
326	E.L. Mills	260.00	115.00	65.00
327	Daniel Minnehan (Minahan)	260.00	115.00	65.00
328	Sam Moffet	260.00	115.00	65.00
329	Honest John Morrill	260.00	115.00	65.00
330	Ed Morris	260.00	115.00	65.00
331	Count Mullane	260.00	115.00	65.00
332	Joseph Mulvey	260.00	115.00	65.00
333	P.L. Murphy (St. Paul)	260.00	115.00	65.00
334	Pat Murphy (New York)	260.00	115.00	65.00
335	Miah Murray	260.00	115.00	65.00
336	Truthful Jim Mutrie	305.00	135.00	76.00
337	George Myers (Indianapolis)	260.00	115.00	65.00
338	Al Myers (Washington, Philadelphia)	260.00	115.00	65.00
339	Tom Nagle	260.00	115.00	65.00
340	Billy Nash	260.00	115.00	65.00
341	Candy Nelson (dotted tie)	435.00	195.00	110.00
342	Kid Nichols (Omaha)	2100.	945.00	525.00
343	Samuel Nichols (Nichol) (Pittsburgh)	260.00	115.00	65.00
344	J.W. Nicholson (Chicago Maroons)	260.00	115.00	65.00
345	Parson Nicholson (St. Louis, Cleveland)	260.00	115.00	65.00
346	Little Nick Nicol (Cincinnati)	260.00	115.00	65.00
346-1	Little Nick Nicoll (Nicol) (Brown's Champions)	340.00	155.00	85.00
346-8	Little Nick Nicol, Big John Reilly	320.00	145.00	80.00
347	Frederick Nyce	260.00	115.00	65.00

348	Doc Oberlander	260.00	115.00	65.00
349	Jack O'Brien (Brooklyn, Baltimore)	260.00	115.00	65.00
350	Billy O'Brien (Washington)	260.00	115.00	65.00
351	Darby O'Brien (Brooklyn)	260.00	115.00	65.00
352	John O'Brien (Cleveland)	260.00	115.00	65.00
353	P.J. O'Connell	260.00	115.00	65.00
354	Rowdy Jack O'Connor	260.00	115.00	65.00
355	Hank O'Day	260.00	115.00	65.00
356	Tip O'Neil (O'Neill) (St. Louis)	260.00	115.00	65.00
356-6	Tip O'Neil (O'Neill) (Brown's Champions)	340.00	155.00	85.00
357	Tip O'Neill (photo actually Deacon White, St. Louis)	260.00	115.00	65.00
357-1	O'Neill (Oakland)	405.00	180.00	100.00
358	Orator Jim O'Rourke (New York)	985.00	445.00	245.00
359	Tom O'Rourke (Boston)	260.00	115.00	65.00
360	Dave Orr	260.00	115.00	65.00
360-1	Dave Orr (dotted tie)	435.00	195.00	110.00
361	Charles Parsons	260.00	115.00	65.00
362	Owen Patton	260.00	115.00	65.00
363	Jimmy Peeples (Peoples)	260.00	115.00	65.00
363-3	Hardie Henderson, Jimmy Peeples	320.00	145.00	80.00
364	Hip Perrier	435.00	195.00	110.00
365	Patrick Pettee	260.00	115.00	65.00
365-5	Bobby Lowe, Patrick Pettee	320.00	145.00	80.00
366	Fred Pfeffer	260.00	115.00	65.00
367	Dick Phelan	260.00	115.00	65.00
368	Bill Phillips	260.00	115.00	65.00
369	Jack Pickett	260.00	115.00	65.00
370	George Pinkney	260.00	115.00	65.00
371	Tom Poorman	260.00	115.00	65.00
372	Henry Porter	260.00	115.00	65.00
373	Jim Powell	260.00	115.00	65.00
373-1	Thomas Powers	435.00	195.00	110.00
374	Blondie Purcell	260.00	115.00	65.00
375	Tom Quinn (Baltimore)	260.00	115.00	65.00
376	Joe Quinn (Boston, Des Moines)	260.00	115.00	65.00
377	Old Hoss Radbourn	3500.	1575.	875.00
378	Shorty Radford	260.00	115.00	65.00
379	Toad Ramsey	260.00	115.00	65.00
380	Rehse	260.00	115.00	65.00
381	Long John Reilly (Cincinnati)	260.00	115.00	65.00
382	Princeton Charlie Reilly (St. Paul)	260.00	115.00	65.00
383	Charlie Reynolds	260.00	115.00	65.00
384	Hardy Richardson (Detroit, Boston)	260.00	115.00	65.00
385	Danny Richardson (NY)	260.00	115.00	65.00
386	Charles Ripslager (dotted tie)	435.00	195.00	110.00
387	John Roach	260.00	115.00	65.00
388	Uncle Robbie Robinson (Athletics)	1050.	470.00	260.00
389	M.C. Robinson (Minneapolis)	260.00	115.00	65.00
390	Yank Robinson (St. Louis)	260.00	115.00	65.00
390-6	Yank Robinson (Brown's Champions)	340.00	155.00	85.00
391	George Rooks	260.00	115.00	65.00
392	Chief Roseman (dotted tie)	435.00	195.00	110.00
393	Dave Rowe (Kansas City)	260.00	115.00	65.00
394	Jack Rowe (Detroit)	260.00	115.00	65.00
395	Amos Rusie (Indianapolis)	2000.	900.00	500.00
396	Jimmy Ryan	260.00	115.00	65.00
397	Doc Sage	260.00	115.00	65.00
397-4	Doc Sage, Bill Van Dyke	320.00	145.00	80.00
398	Ben Sanders	260.00	115.00	65.00
399	Frank Scheibeck	260.00	115.00	65.00
400	Al Schellhase (Schellhasse)	260.00	115.00	65.00
401	William Schenkel	260.00	115.00	65.00
402	Schildknecht	260.00	115.00	65.00
403	Gus Schmelz	260.00	115.00	65.00
404	Jumbo Schoeneck	260.00	115.00	65.00
405	Pop Schriver	260.00	115.00	65.00
406	Emmett Seery	260.00	115.00	65.00
407	Billy Serad	260.00	115.00	65.00
408	Ed Seward	260.00	115.00	65.00
409	Orator Shafer (Shaffer) (Des Moines)	260.00	115.00	65.00
410	Taylor Shafer (Shaffer) (St. Paul)	260.00	115.00	65.00
411	Daniel Shannon	260.00	115.00	65.00
412	William Sharsig	260.00	115.00	65.00
413	Samuel Shaw (Baltimore, Newark)	260.00	115.00	65.00
414	John Shaw (Minneapolis)	260.00	115.00	65.00
415	Bill Shindle	260.00	115.00	65.00
416	George Shoch	260.00	115.00	65.00
417	Otto Shomberg (Schomberg)	260.00	115.00	65.00
418	Lev Shreve	260.00	115.00	65.00
419	Ed Silch	260.00	115.00	65.00
420	Mike Slattery	260.00	115.00	65.00
421	Skyrocket Smith (Louisville)	260.00	115.00	65.00
422	Phenomenal Smith (Baltimore, Athletics)	520.00	235.00	130.00
423	Elmer Smith (Cincinnati)	260.00	115.00	65.00
424	Sam Smith (Des Moines)	260.00	115.00	65.00
425	Germany Smith (Brooklyn)	260.00	115.00	65.00
426	Pap Smith (Pittsburgh, Boston)	260.00	115.00	65.00
427	Nick Smith (St. Joseph)	260.00	115.00	65.00
428	P.T. Somers	260.00	115.00	65.00
429	Joe Sommer	260.00	115.00	65.00
430	Pete Sommers	260.00	115.00	65.00
431	Little Bill Sowders (Boston)	260.00	115.00	65.00
432	John Sowders (St. Paul, Kansas City)	260.00	115.00	65.00
433	Charlie Sprague	260.00	115.00	65.00
434	Ed Sproat	260.00	115.00	65.00
435	Harry Staley	260.00	115.00	65.00
436	Dan Stearns	260.00	115.00	65.00
437	Cannonball Stemmyer (Stemmeyer)	260.00	115.00	65.00
438	B.F. Stephens	260.00	115.00	65.00
439	John Sterling	260.00	115.00	65.00
439-1	Stockwell	435.00	195.00	110.00

440	Harry Stovey	320.00	145.00	80.00
441	Scott Stratton	260.00	115.00	65.00
442	Joe Straus (Strauss)	260.00	115.00	65.00
443	Cub Stricker	260.00	115.00	65.00
444	Marty Sullivan (Chicago, Indianapolis)	260.00	115.00	65.00
445	Mike Sullivan (Athletics)	260.00	115.00	65.00
446	Billy Sunday	1000.	450.00	250.00
447	Sy Sutcliffe	260.00	115.00	65.00
448	Ezra Sutton	260.00	115.00	65.00
449	Ed Swartwood	260.00	115.00	65.00
450	Park Swartzel	260.00	115.00	65.00
451	Pete Sweeney	260.00	115.00	65.00
451-1	Louis Sylvester	435.00	195.00	110.00
452	Pop Tate	260.00	115.00	65.00
453	Patsy Tebeau	260.00	115.00	65.00
454	John Tener	260.00	115.00	65.00
455	Adonis Terry	260.00	115.00	65.00
456	Big Sam Thompson	620.00	280.00	155.00
457	Silent Mike Tiernan	260.00	115.00	65.00
458	Cannonball Titcomb	260.00	115.00	65.00
459	Buster Tomney	260.00	115.00	65.00
460	Stephen Toole	810.00	365.00	200.00
461	Sleepy Townsend	260.00	115.00	65.00
462	Bill Traffley	260.00	115.00	65.00
463	George Treadway	260.00	115.00	65.00
464	Sam Trott	260.00	115.00	65.00
464-6	Oyster Burns, Sam Trott	320.00	145.00	80.00
465	Foghorn Tucker	260.00	115.00	65.00
466	A.M. Tuckerman	260.00	115.00	65.00
467	George Turner	260.00	115.00	65.00
468	Larry Twitchell	260.00	115.00	65.00
469	Jim Tyng	260.00	115.00	65.00
470	Bill Van Dyke	260.00	115.00	65.00
471	Rip Van Haltren	260.00	115.00	65.00
472	Farmer Vaughn	260.00	115.00	65.00
472-1	Veach	435.00	195.00	110.00
473	Lee Viau	260.00	115.00	65.00
474	Bill Vinton	260.00	115.00	65.00
475	Joe Visner	260.00	115.00	65.00
476	Christian Von Der Ahe (Brown's Champions)	435.00	195.00	110.00
477	Reddy Walsh	260.00	115.00	65.00
478	Monte Ward	1050.	470.00	260.00
479	E.H. Warner	260.00	115.00	65.00
480	Bill Watkins	260.00	115.00	65.00
481	Farmer Weaver	260.00	115.00	65.00
482	Count Weber	260.00	115.00	65.00
483	Stump Weidman	260.00	115.00	65.00
484	Wild Bill Weidner (Widner)	260.00	115.00	65.00
485	Curt Welch (Athletics)	260.00	115.00	65.00
485-1	Curt Welch (Brown's Champions)	340.00	155.00	85.00
485-7	Will Gleason, Curt Welch	320.00	145.00	80.00
486	Smiling Mickey Welch (New York)	985.00	445.00	245.00
487	Jake Wells (Kansas City)	260.00	115.00	65.00
488	Frank Wells (Milwaukee)	260.00	115.00	65.00
489	Joe Werrick	260.00	115.00	65.00
490	Buck West	260.00	115.00	65.00
491	A.C. "Cannonball" Weyhing	260.00	115.00	65.00
492	John Weyhing	260.00	115.00	65.00
493	Bobby Wheelock	260.00	115.00	65.00
494	Pat Whitacre (Whitaker)	260.00	115.00	65.00
495	Pat Whitaker	260.00	115.00	65.00
496	Deacon White (Detroit, Pittsburgh)	260.00	115.00	65.00
497	Bill White (Louisville)	260.00	115.00	65.00
498	Grasshopper Whitney (Washington, Indianapolis)	260.00	115.00	65.00
499	Art Whitney (Pittsburgh, New York)	260.00	115.00	65.00
500	G. Whitney (St. Joseph)	260.00	115.00	65.00
501	James Williams	260.00	115.00	65.00
502	Ned Williamson	640.00	290.00	160.00
502-7	Willie Hahm (mascot), Ned Williamson	405.00	180.00	100.00
503	C.H. Willis	260.00	115.00	65.00
504	Watt Wilmot	260.00	115.00	65.00
505	George Winkleman (Winkelman)	260.00	115.00	65.00
506	Medoc Wise	260.00	115.00	65.00
507	Chicken Wolf	260.00	115.00	65.00
508	George "Dandy" Wood (L.F.)	260.00	115.00	65.00
509	Pete Wood (P.)	260.00	115.00	65.00
510	Harry Wright	1800.	810.00	450.00
511	Chief Zimmer	260.00	115.00	65.00
512	Frank Zinn	260.00	115.00	65.00

1888 Old Judge Cabinets (N173)

These cabinet cards were issued by Goodwin & Co. in 1888-89 as a premium available by exchanging coupons found in Old Judge or Dogs Head brand cigarettes. The cabinet cards consist of 3-3/4" x 5-3/4" photographs affixed to a cardboard backing that measures approximately 4-1/4" x 6-1/2". The mounting is usually a yellow color, but backings have also been found in shades of red, blue or black. An ad for Old Judge Cigarettes appears along the bottom of the cabinet. (Cabinets obtained by exchanging coupons from Dogs Head cigarettes include an ad for both Old Judge and Dogs Head, and are considered scarcer, valued at 2-3x the same player on an Old Judge cabinet.) According to an advertising sheet, cabinets were available of "every prominent player in the National League, Western League and American Association." There will likely be additions to this checklist. The poses on the cabinet photos are enlarged versions of the popular N172 Old Judge cards.

		NM	EX	VG
	Common Player:	900.00	405.00	225.00
	Common Player, black or colored mount:	1650.	740.00	410.00
(1)	Bob Allen	900.00	405.00	225.00
(2)	Varney Anderson	900.00	405.00	225.00
(3)	Ed Andrews (both hands at shoulder level)	900.00	405.00	225.00
(4)	Ed Andrews (one hand above head)	900.00	405.00	225.00
(5)	Ed Andrews, Buster Hoover	1300.	585.00	325.00
(6)	Cap Anson (portrait)	10500.	4725.	2625.
(7)	Fido Baldwin (Chicago, pitching)	900.00	405.00	225.00
(8)	Fido Baldwin (Chicago, with bat)	900.00	405.00	225.00
(9)	Kid Baldwin (Detroit)	900.00	405.00	225.00
(10)	John Barnes	900.00	405.00	225.00
(11)	Bald Billy Barnie	1200.	540.00	300.00
(12)	Charles Bassett	900.00	405.00	225.00
(13)	Charles Bastian (Chicago)	900.00	405.00	225.00
(14)	Charles Bastian (Philly)	900.00	405.00	225.00
(15)	Bastian, Pop Schriver	1300.	585.00	325.00
(16)	Ed Beatin	900.00	405.00	225.00
(17)	Charles Bennett	900.00	405.00	225.00
(18)	Louis Bierbauer	900.00	405.00	225.00
(19)	Ned Bligh	900.00	405.00	225.00
(20)	Bogart	900.00	405.00	225.00
(21)	Handsome Boyle (Indy)	900.00	405.00	225.00
(22)	Honest John Boyle (St. Louis, bat at side)	900.00	405.00	225.00
(23)	Honest John Boyle (St. Louis, bat in air)	900.00	405.00	225.00
(24)	Grin Bradley	900.00	405.00	225.00
(25)	Dan Brouthers (fielding)	2400.	1075.	600.00
(26)	Dan Brouthers (batting)	2400.	1075.	600.00
(27)	California Brown (Boston, catching)	900.00	405.00	225.00
(28)	California Brown (Boston, with bat)	900.00	405.00	225.00
(29)	Thomas Brown (New York, throwing)	900.00	405.00	225.00
(30)	Thomas Brown (New York, with bat)	900.00	405.00	225.00
(31)	Pete Browning (batting)	1000.	450.00	250.00
(32)	Charles Brynan (Chicago)	900.00	405.00	225.00
(33)	Charles Brynan (Des Moines)	900.00	405.00	225.00
(34)	Al Buckenberger	900.00	405.00	225.00
(35)	Dick Buckley	900.00	405.00	225.00
(36)	Charles Buffinton (hands chest high)	900.00	405.00	225.00
(37)	Charles Buffinton (right hand above head)	900.00	405.00	225.00
(38)	Black Jack Burdock	900.00	405.00	225.00
(39)	James Burns (Kansas City)	900.00	405.00	225.00
(40)	Oyster Burns (Brooklyn)	900.00	405.00	225.00
(41)	Thomas Burns (Chicago, bat at side)	900.00	405.00	225.00
(42)	Thomas Burns (Chicago, bat in air)	900.00	405.00	225.00
(43)	Thomas Burns (catching)	900.00	405.00	225.00
(44)	Doc Bushong (fielding)	900.00	405.00	225.00
(45)	Doc Bushong (throwing)	900.00	405.00	225.00
(46)	Hick Carpenter	900.00	405.00	225.00
(47)	Fred Carroll	900.00	405.00	225.00
(48)	Jumbo Cartwright	900.00	405.00	225.00
(50)	Parisian Bob Caruthers (holding ball)	900.00	405.00	225.00
(51)	Parisian Bob Caruthers (with bat)	900.00	405.00	225.00
(52)	Daniel Casey	900.00	405.00	225.00
(53)	Icebox Chamberlain (boths hands at chest level)	900.00	405.00	225.00
(54)	Icebox Chamberlain (St. Louis, right hand extended w/ball)	900.00	405.00	225.00
(55)	Chamberlain (with bat)	900.00	405.00	225.00
(56)	Cupid Childs	900.00	405.00	225.00
(57)	Clark (Brooklyn, catching)	900.00	405.00	225.00
(58)	Bob Clark (Brooklyn, right hand shoulder high)	900.00	405.00	225.00
(59)	Bob Clark, Mickey Hughes	900.00	405.00	225.00
(60)	Dad Clark (Clarke) (Chicago)	900.00	405.00	225.00
(61)	Spider Clark (Washington)	900.00	405.00	225.00
(62)	John Clarkson (pitching, arm at thigh level)	3000.	1350.	750.00
(63)	John Clarkson (with bat)	3000.	1350.	750.00
(64)	Jack Clements (hands on knees)	900.00	405.00	225.00
(65)	Jack Clements (hands outstreched at neck level)	900.00	405.00	225.00
(66)	Jack Clements (with bat)	900.00	405.00	225.00
(67)	Elmer Cleveland (New York)	900.00	405.00	225.00
(68)	Monk Cline	900.00	405.00	225.00
(69)	John Coleman (holding ball)	900.00	405.00	225.00
(70)	John Coleman (with bat)	900.00	405.00	225.00
(71)	Hub Collins	900.00	405.00	225.00
(72)	Commy Comiskey (arms folded)	4800.	2150.	1200.
(73)	Commy Comiskey (fielding)	4800.	2150.	1200.
(74)	Roger Connor (catching)	2000.	900.00	500.00
(75)	Roger Connor (hands on knees)	2000.	900.00	500.00
(76)	Roger Connor (with bat)	2000.	900.00	500.00
(77)	Jim Conway (Kansas City) (pitching)	900.00	405.00	225.00
(78)	Pete Conway (Detroit)	900.00	405.00	225.00
(79)	Paul Cook (tagging baserunner)	900.00	405.00	225.00
(80)	Paul Cook (wearing mask)	900.00	405.00	225.00
(81)	Pop Corkhill	900.00	405.00	225.00
(82)	Samuel Crane	900.00	405.00	225.00
(83)	Lave Cross	900.00	405.00	225.00
(84)	Bert Cunningham (both arms waist level)	900.00	405.00	225.00
(85)	Edward Daily	900.00	405.00	225.00
(86)	Bill Daley (Boston)	900.00	405.00	225.00
(87)	Con Daley (Daily) (Indianapolis)	900.00	405.00	225.00
(88)	Abner Dalrymple	900.00	405.00	225.00
(89)	Sun Daly (Minneapolis)	900.00	405.00	225.00
(90)	Tido Daly (Washington)	900.00	405.00	225.00
(91)	Tido Daly (Chicago)	900.00	405.00	225.00
(92)	Dell Darling	900.00	405.00	225.00
(93)	William Darnbrough	900.00	405.00	225.00
(94)	Big Ed Delehanty (bat at right shoulder)	3475.	1575.	870.00
(95)	Big Ed Delehanty (bat horizontal)	3475.	1575.	870.00
(96)	Jerry Denny	900.00	405.00	225.00
(97)	Jim Devlin (pitching)	900.00	405.00	225.00
(98)	Jim Devlin (sliding)	900.00	405.00	225.00
(99)	Jim Donnelly	900.00	405.00	225.00
(100)	Home Run Duffe (Duffee) (bending)	900.00	405.00	225.00
(101)	Home Run Duffe (Duffee) (catching, standing upright)	900.00	405.00	225.00
(102)	Home Run Duffe (Duffee) (with bat)	900.00	405.00	225.00
(103)	Hugh Duffy (catching)	3000.	1350.	750.00
(104)	Hugh Duffy (fielding)	3000.	1350.	750.00
(105)	Hugh Duffy (with bat)	3000.	1350.	750.00
(106)	Duck Duke	900.00	405.00	225.00
(107)	Sure Shot Dunlap (arms at side)	900.00	405.00	225.00
(108)	Sure Shot Dunlap (holding ball aloft)	900.00	405.00	225.00
(109)	Jesse Duryea	900.00	405.00	225.00
(110)	Frank Dwyer (bat at side)	900.00	405.00	225.00
(111)	Frank Dwyer (bat in air)	900.00	405.00	225.00
(112)	Frank Dwyer (ball in hands)	900.00	405.00	225.00
(113)	Frank Dwyer (hands cupped at chest)	900.00	405.00	225.00
(114)	Billy Earle	900.00	405.00	225.00
(115)	Red Ehret (Louisville, batting)	900.00	405.00	225.00
(116)	Dude Esterbrook	900.00	405.00	225.00
(117)	Buck Ewing (New York, bat at side)	3000.	1350.	750.00
(118)	Buck Ewing (New York, bat in air)	3000.	1350.	750.00
(119)	Buck Ewing (New York, hands at head level)	3000.	1350.	750.00
(120)	Buck Ewing (New York, hands on knees)	3000.	1350.	750.00
(121)	Willie Breslin - mascot, Buck Ewing	3500.	1575.	875.00
(122)	Long John Ewing (Louisville)	900.00	405.00	225.00
(123)	Jay Faatz	900.00	405.00	225.00
(124)	Bill Farmer	900.00	405.00	225.00
(125)	Sid Farrar (hands outstreched at head level)	900.00	405.00	225.00
(126)	Sid Farrar (stooping)	900.00	405.00	225.00
(127)	Duke Farrell (fielding)	900.00	405.00	225.00
(128)	Duke Farrell (hands on knees)	900.00	405.00	225.00
(129)	Frank Fennelly	900.00	405.00	225.00
(130)	Charlie Ferguson	900.00	405.00	225.00
(131)	Alex Ferson	900.00	405.00	225.00
(132)	Jocko Fields	900.00	405.00	225.00
(133)	Silver Flint (with bat)	900.00	405.00	225.00
(134)	Silver Flint (with mask)	900.00	405.00	225.00
(135)	Jim Fogarty (catching, hands at neck level)	900.00	405.00	225.00
(136)	Jim Fogarty (running to left)	900.00	405.00	225.00
(137)	Jim Fogarty (sliding)	900.00	405.00	225.00
(138)	Jim Fogarty (with bat)	900.00	405.00	225.00
(139)	Elmer Foster (Minneapolis)	900.00	405.00	225.00
(140)	Elmer Foster (New York)	900.00	405.00	225.00
(141)	Dave Foutz	900.00	405.00	225.00
(142)	Shorty Fuller (St. Louis, catching)	900.00	405.00	225.00
(143)	Shorty Fuller (hands on knees)	900.00	405.00	225.00
(144)	Shorty Fuller (swinging bat)	900.00	405.00	225.00
(145)	Chris Fulmer, Foghorn Tucker	1900.	855.00	475.00
(146)	Pud Galvin	1050.	470.00	260.00
(147)	Charlie Ganzel (catching, hands at shoulder level)	900.00	405.00	225.00
(148)	Charlie Ganzel (catching, hands at thigh level)	900.00	405.00	225.00
(150)	Charlie Ganzel (with bat)	900.00	405.00	225.00
(151)	Gid Gardner	900.00	405.00	225.00
(152)	Hank Gastreich	900.00	405.00	225.00
(153)	Frenchy Genins (bat in air, looking at camera)	900.00	405.00	225.00
(154)	Frenchy Genins (swinging at ball)	900.00	405.00	225.00
(155)	Bill George	900.00	405.00	225.00

(156)	Charlie Getzein (Getzien)	900.00	405.00	225.00
(157)	Bobby Gilks	900.00	405.00	225.00
(158)	Barney Gilligan	900.00	405.00	225.00
(159)	Frank Gilmore	900.00	405.00	225.00
(160)	Pebbly Jack Glasscock (hands on knees)	900.00	405.00	225.00
(161)	Pebbly Jack Glasscock (throwing)	900.00	405.00	225.00
(162)	Kid Gleason (Philadelphia, fielding)	900.00	405.00	225.00
(163)	Kid Gleason (Philadelphia, pitching)	900.00	405.00	225.00
(164)	Will Gleason (Louisville)	900.00	405.00	225.00
(165)	Mouse Glenn	900.00	405.00	225.00
(166)	Piano Legs Gore (fielding)	900.00	405.00	225.00
(167)	Piano Legs Gore (with bat)	900.00	405.00	225.00
(168)	Henry Gruber	900.00	405.00	225.00
(169)	Ad Gumbert (right hand at eye level)	900.00	405.00	225.00
(170)	Ad Gumbert (right hand at waist level)	900.00	405.00	225.00
(171)	Tom Gunning	900.00	405.00	225.00
(172)	Joe Gunson	900.00	405.00	225.00
(173)	Bill Hallman	900.00	405.00	225.00
(174)	Billy Hamilton (fielding grounder)	2000.	900.00	500.00
(175)	Billy Hamilton (with bat)	2000.	900.00	500.00
(176)	Ned Hanlon	2000.	900.00	500.00
(177)	William Hanrahan	900.00	405.00	225.00
(178)	Gill Hatfield (bat at waist)	900.00	405.00	225.00
(179)	Hatfield (bat over shoulder)	900.00	405.00	225.00
(180)	Gill Hatfield (catching)	900.00	405.00	225.00
(181)	Egyptian Healey (Healy)	900.00	405.00	225.00
(182)	Hardie Henderson	900.00	405.00	225.00
(183)	Moxie Hengle	900.00	405.00	225.00
(184)	John Henry	900.00	405.00	225.00
(185)	Hunkey Hines (St. Louis)	900.00	405.00	225.00
(186)	Paul Hines	900.00	405.00	225.00
(187)	Texas Wonder Hoffman	900.00	405.00	225.00
(188)	Bug Holliday	900.00	405.00	225.00
(189)	Buster Hoover (Philadelphia)	900.00	405.00	225.00
(190)	Charles Hoover (Chicago)	900.00	405.00	225.00
(191)	Charles Hoover (Kansas City)	900.00	405.00	225.00
(192)	Joe Hornung	900.00	405.00	225.00
(193)	Dummy Hoy	900.00	405.00	225.00
(194)	Nat Hudson	900.00	405.00	225.00
(195)	Mickey Hughes (holding ball at chest)	900.00	405.00	225.00
(196)	Mickey Hughes (holding ball at side)	900.00	405.00	225.00
(197)	Mickey Hughes (right hand extended)	900.00	405.00	225.00
(198)	Wild Bill Hutchinson (ball in hand, right heel hidden)	900.00	405.00	225.00
(200)	Wild Bill Hutchinson (ball in hand, right heel visible)	900.00	405.00	225.00
(201)	Bill Hutchinson (with bat)	900.00	405.00	225.00
(202)	Cutrate Irwin (Philadelphia, catching)	900.00	405.00	225.00
(203)	Cutrate Irwin (Philadelphia, throwing)	900.00	405.00	225.00
(204)	John Irwin (Washington)	900.00	405.00	225.00
(205)	A.C. Jantzen	900.00	405.00	225.00
(206)	Spud Johnson	900.00	405.00	225.00
(207)	Johnston (hands on hip)	900.00	405.00	225.00
(208)	Dick Johnston (with bat)	900.00	405.00	225.00
(209)	Tim Keefe (Dogs Head)	3675.	1650.	920.00
(210)	Tim Keefe (batting)	2000.	900.00	500.00
(211)	Tim Keefe (hands at chest)	2000.	900.00	500.00
(212)	Tim Keefe (pitching, right hand at head level)	2000.	900.00	500.00
(213)	Tim Keefe (pitching, right hand at waist level)	2000.	900.00	500.00
(214)	Charles Kelly (Philadelphia)	900.00	405.00	225.00
(215)	Mike Kelly ("Kelly, Boston.", bat at 45-degree angle)	6000.	2700.	1500.
(215.5)	Mike Kelly ("Mike Kelly, C, Boston.", bat at 45-degree angle)	6000.	2700.	1500.
(216)	Rudy Kemmler	900.00	405.00	225.00
(217)	John Kerins	900.00	405.00	225.00
(218)	C.C. "Silver" King (hands at chest level; initials actually C.F.)	900.00	405.00	225.00
(219)	Silver King (hands at chin)	900.00	405.00	225.00
(220)	William Klusman	900.00	405.00	225.00
(221)	Gus Krock (right hand extended)	900.00	405.00	225.00
(222)	Gus Krock (with bat)	900.00	405.00	225.00
(223)	Willie Kuehne	900.00	405.00	225.00
(224)	Ted Larkin	900.00	405.00	225.00
(225)	Chuck Lauer (Laver)	900.00	405.00	225.00
(226)	Arlie Latham (throwing)	900.00	405.00	225.00
(227)	Arlie Latham (with bat)	900.00	405.00	225.00
(228)	Germany Long	900.00	405.00	225.00
(229)	Tom Lovett (right hand extended)	900.00	405.00	225.00
(230)	Tom Lovett (with bat)	900.00	405.00	225.00
(231)	Denny Lyons (left hand above head)	900.00	405.00	225.00
(232)	Denny Lyons (with bat)	900.00	405.00	225.00
(233)	Harry Lyons (St. Louis, at first base)	900.00	405.00	225.00
(234)	Connie Mack	10000.	4500.	2500.
(235)	Little Mac Macullar	900.00	405.00	225.00
(236)	Kid Madden (ball in left hand at eye level)	900.00	405.00	225.00
(237)	Kid Madden (ball in hand above head)	900.00	405.00	225.00
(238)	Kid Madden (ball in hands at neck level)	900.00	405.00	225.00
(239)	Jimmy Manning (fielding)	900.00	405.00	225.00
(240)	Jimmy Manning (with bat)	900.00	405.00	225.00
(241)	Lefty Marr	900.00	405.00	225.00
(242)	Leech Maskrey	900.00	405.00	225.00
(243)	Mike Mattimore	900.00	405.00	225.00
(244)	Smiling Al Maul	900.00	405.00	225.00
(245)	Al Mays	900.00	405.00	225.00
(246)	Jimmy McAleer	900.00	405.00	225.00
(247)	Tommy McCarthy (pitching, hand at head level)	2850.	1275.	710.00
(248)	Tommy McCarthy (with bat)	2850.	1275.	710.00
(250)	Deacon McGuire	900.00	405.00	225.00
(251)	Bill McGunnigle	900.00	405.00	225.00
(252)	Ed McKean (hands above head)	900.00	405.00	225.00
(253)	Ed McKean (with bat)	900.00	405.00	225.00
(254)	James McQuaid	900.00	405.00	225.00
(255)	Doggie Miller (Pittsburgh, ball in hands)	900.00	405.00	225.00
(256)	Joseph Miller (Minneapolis, hands outstretched)	900.00	405.00	225.00
(257)	Joseph Miller (Minneapolis, with bat)	900.00	405.00	225.00
(258)	Jocko Milligan (bat at side)	900.00	405.00	225.00
(259)	Jocko Milligan (bat in air)	900.00	405.00	225.00
(260)	Jocko Milligan (stooping)	900.00	405.00	225.00
(261)	Jocko Milligan (throwing)	900.00	405.00	225.00
(262)	Daniel Minnehan (Minahan)	900.00	405.00	225.00
(263)	Sam Moffet	900.00	405.00	225.00
(264)	Honest John Morrill	900.00	405.00	225.00
(265)	Joseph Mulvey (catching)	900.00	405.00	225.00
(266)	Joseph Mulvey (with bat)	900.00	405.00	225.00
(267)	Pat Murphy	900.00	405.00	225.00
(268)	Miah Murray	900.00	405.00	225.00
(269)	Truthful Jim Mutrie (standing)	900.00	405.00	225.00
(270)	Al Myers (Washington)	900.00	405.00	225.00
(271)	George Myers (Indianapolis)	900.00	405.00	225.00
(272)	Tom Nagle	900.00	405.00	225.00
(273)	Billy Nash (hands on knees)	900.00	405.00	225.00
(274)	Billy Nash (throwing)	900.00	405.00	225.00
(275)	Kid Nichols	3900.	1750.	975.00
(276)	Little Nick Nicol, Big John Reilly	1300.	585.00	325.00
(277)	Darby O'Brien (Brooklyn)	900.00	405.00	225.00
(278)	John O'Brien (Cleveland)	900.00	405.00	225.00
(279)	Rowdy Jack O'Connor	900.00	405.00	225.00
(280)	Hank O'Day	900.00	405.00	225.00
(281)	Tip O'Neill (bat held horizontally)	900.00	405.00	225.00
(282)	O'Neill (bat over shoulder)	900.00	405.00	225.00
(283)	Tip O'Neill (fielding)	900.00	405.00	225.00
(284)	J.E. (Tip) O'Neill (throwing)	1125.	505.00	280.00
(285)	Orator Jim O'Rourke (New York, pitching, hand at head level)	2000.	900.00	500.00
(286)	Orator Jim O'Rourke (New York, with bat)	2000.	900.00	500.00
(287)	Tom O'Rourke (Boston)	900.00	405.00	225.00
(288)	Dave Orr	900.00	405.00	225.00
(289)	Fred Pfeffer (right hand at neck level)	900.00	405.00	225.00
(290)	Fred Pfeffer (with bat)	900.00	405.00	225.00
(291)	Dick Phelan	900.00	405.00	225.00
(292)	Jack Pickett (right hand at head level)	900.00	405.00	225.00
(293)	Jack Pickett (stooping)	900.00	405.00	225.00
(294)	Jack Pickett (with bat)	900.00	405.00	225.00
(295)	George Pinkney (bat in air, nearly vertical)	900.00	405.00	225.00
(296)	George Pinkney (bat over right shoulder)	900.00	405.00	225.00
(297)	Jim Powell	900.00	405.00	225.00
(298)	Blondie Purcell	900.00	405.00	225.00
(300)	Joe Quinn (ball in hands)	900.00	405.00	225.00
(301)	Joe Quinn (ready to run)	900.00	405.00	225.00
(302)	Old Hoss Radbourn (hands on hips with bat)	2000.	900.00	500.00
(303)	Toad Ramsey	900.00	405.00	225.00
(304)	Princeton Charlie Reilly (St. Paul)	900.00	405.00	225.00
(305)	Long John Reilly (Cincinnati)	900.00	405.00	225.00
(306)	Danny Richardson (New York, arms at side)	900.00	405.00	225.00
(307)	Danny Richardson (New York, right hand at head level)	900.00	405.00	225.00
(308)	Hardy Richardson (Boston, hands at head level)	900.00	405.00	225.00
(309)	Hardy Richardson (Boston or Detroit, with bat)	975.00	440.00	245.00
(310)	Uncle Robbie Robinson (Athletics, catching)	3150.	1425.	785.00
(311)	Uncle Robbie Robinson (Athletics, with bat)	3150.	1425.	785.00
(312)	W.H. (Yank) Robinson (St. Louis, fielding)	975.00	440.00	245.00
(313)	Yank Robinson (St. Louis, with bat)	975.00	440.00	245.00
(314)	Dave Rowe (Kansas City)	900.00	405.00	225.00
(315)	Jack Rowe (Detroit)	900.00	405.00	225.00
(316)	Jimmy Ryan (fielding)	900.00	405.00	225.00
(317)	Jimmy Ryan (with bat)	900.00	405.00	225.00
(318)	Ben Sanders (hands at neck level)	900.00	405.00	225.00
(319)	Ben Sanders (right hand at head level)	900.00	405.00	225.00
(320)	Frank Scheibeck	900.00	405.00	225.00
(321)	Gus Schmelz	900.00	405.00	225.00
(322)	Jumbo Schoeneck	900.00	405.00	225.00
(323)	Pop Schriver (hands at ankle level)	900.00	405.00	225.00
(324)	Pop Schriver (hands cupped at chest level)	900.00	405.00	225.00
(325)	Emmett Seery	900.00	405.00	225.00
(326)	Ed Seward	900.00	405.00	225.00
(327)	Daniel Shannon	900.00	405.00	225.00
(328)	William Sharsig	900.00	405.00	225.00
(329)	George Shoch	900.00	405.00	225.00
(330)	Otto Shomberg (Schomberg)	900.00	405.00	225.00
(331)	Lev Shreve	900.00	405.00	225.00
(332)	Mike Slattery (fielding)	900.00	405.00	225.00
(333)	Germany Smith (Brooklyn, hands on knees)	900.00	405.00	225.00
(334)	Germany Smith (Brooklyn, right hand at head level)	900.00	405.00	225.00
(335)	Germany Smith (Brooklyn, with bat)	900.00	405.00	225.00
(336)	Pap Smith (Pittsburg, hands on knees)	900.00	405.00	225.00
(337)	Pap Smith (Pittsburg or Boston, with bat)	900.00	405.00	225.00
(338)	Pete Sommers	900.00	405.00	225.00
(339)	Little Bill Sowders	900.00	405.00	225.00
(340)	Charlie Sprague	900.00	405.00	225.00
(341)	Harry Staley	900.00	405.00	225.00
(342)	Dan Stearns	900.00	405.00	225.00
(343)	Stovey (hands on knees)	900.00	405.00	225.00
(344)	Harry Stovey (with bat)	900.00	405.00	225.00
(345)	C. (Scott) Stratton (Louisville)	900.00	405.00	225.00
(346)	Joe Straus (Strauss)	900.00	405.00	225.00
(347)	Cub Stricker	900.00	405.00	225.00
(348)	Marty Sullivan (Indianapolis)	900.00	405.00	225.00
(350)	Marty Sullivan (Chicago)	900.00	405.00	225.00
(351)	Billy Sunday (bending to left)	3000.	1350.	750.00
(352)	Billy Sunday (with bat)	3000.	1350.	750.00
(353)	Ezra Sutton (hands at shoulder level)	900.00	405.00	225.00
(354)	Ezra Sutton (with bat)	900.00	405.00	225.00
(355)	Park Swartzel	900.00	405.00	225.00
(356)	Pop Tate	900.00	405.00	225.00
(357)	Patsy Tebeau	900.00	405.00	225.00
(358)	John Tener	900.00	405.00	225.00
(359)	Adonis Terry (arms extended)	900.00	405.00	225.00
(360)	Adonis Terry (with bat)	900.00	405.00	225.00
(361)	Big Sam Thompson (Detroit)	2000.	900.00	500.00
(362)	Big Sam Thompson (Philadelphia)	2000.	900.00	500.00
(363)	Silent Mike Tiernan (throwing, hand at head level)	900.00	405.00	225.00
(364)	Cannonball Titcomb	900.00	405.00	225.00
(365)	Phil Tomney (fielding, hands over head)	900.00	405.00	225.00
(366)	Sleepy Townsend (hands at head level)	900.00	405.00	225.00
(367)	Sleepy Townsend (with bat)	900.00	405.00	225.00
(368)	Bill Traffley	900.00	405.00	225.00
(369)	Foghorn Tucker	900.00	405.00	225.00
(370)	George Turner	900.00	405.00	225.00
(371)	Larry Twitchell	900.00	405.00	225.00
(372)	Jim Tyng	900.00	405.00	225.00
(373)	Rip Van Haltren (hands above waist)	900.00	405.00	225.00
(374)	Rip Van Haltren (right hand at right thigh)	900.00	405.00	225.00
(375)	Rip Van Haltren (with bat)	900.00	405.00	225.00
(376)	Farmer Vaughn	900.00	405.00	225.00
(377)	Joe Visner (arms at side)	900.00	405.00	225.00
(378)	Joe Visner (with bat)	900.00	405.00	225.00
(379)	Monte Ward (hands on hips)	4125.	1850.	1025.
(380)	J. (Monte) Ward (sliding, horizontal)	3375.	1525.	845.00
(381)	Monte Ward (throwing)	3225.	1450.	805.00
(382)	Bill Watkins	900.00	405.00	225.00
(383)	Farmer Weaver	900.00	405.00	225.00
(384)	Stump Weidman	900.00	405.00	225.00
(385)	Wild Bill Weidner	900.00	405.00	225.00
(386)	Curt Welch (Athletics)	900.00	405.00	225.00
(387)	Will Gleason, Curt Welch	1900.	855.00	475.00
(388)	Mickey Welsh (New York) (pitching hand shoulder high, name incorrect))	1950.	875.00	485.00
(389)	Mickey Welch (New York) (pitching hand shoulder high, name correct))	1950.	875.00	485.00
(390)	A.C. "Cannonball" Weyhing	900.00	405.00	225.00
(391)	John Weyhing	900.00	405.00	225.00
(392)	Deacon White (hands above head)	900.00	405.00	225.00
(393)	Deacon White (looking down at ball)	900.00	405.00	225.00
(394)	Art Whitney (Pittsburg)	900.00	405.00	225.00
(395)	Art Whitney (New York)	900.00	405.00	225.00
(396)	Grasshopper Whitney (Washington)	900.00	405.00	225.00
(397)	Grasshopper Whitney (St. Joseph)	900.00	405.00	225.00
(398)	Ned Williamson (arms folded)	900.00	405.00	225.00
(399)	Ned Williamson (fielding)	900.00	405.00	225.00
(400)	Ned Williamson (with bat)	900.00	405.00	225.00
(401)	Watt Wilmot	900.00	405.00	225.00
(402)	Medoc Wise	900.00	405.00	225.00
(403)	Chicken Wolf	900.00	405.00	225.00
(404)	George "Dandy" Wood (L.F., both hands at neck level)	900.00	405.00	225.00
(405)	George "Dandy" Wood (L.F., right hand at head level)	900.00	405.00	225.00
(406)	Pete Wood (P., with bat)	900.00	405.00	225.00
(407)	Harry Wright (portrait)	7500.	3375.	1875.

1965 Old London Coins

These 1-1/2" diameter metal coins were included in Old London snack food packages. The 40 coins in this set feature two players from each of the major leagues' 20 teams, except St. Louis (3) and the New York Mets (1). Coin fronts have color photos and player names, while the silver-colored coin backs give brief biographies of each player. An Old London logo is also displayed on each coin back. Space Magic Ltd. produced the coins. This is the same company which produced similar sets for Topps in 1964 and 1971.

		NM	EX	VG
Complete Set (40):		500.00	250.00	150.00
Common Player:		3.50	1.75	1.00
(1)	Henry Aaron	45.00	22.00	13.50
(2)	Richie Allen	6.00	3.00	1.75
(3)	Bob Allison	3.50	1.75	1.00
(4)	Ernie Banks	20.00	10.00	6.00
(5)	Ken Boyer	5.00	2.50	1.50
(6)	Jim Bunning	15.00	7.50	4.50
(7)	Orlando Cepeda	10.00	5.00	3.00
(8)	Dean Chance	3.50	1.75	1.00
(9)	Rocky Colavito	9.00	4.50	2.75
(10)	Vic Davalillo	3.50	1.75	1.00
(11)	Tommy Davis	3.50	1.75	1.00
(12)	Ron Fairly	3.50	1.75	1.00
(13)	Dick Farrell	3.50	1.75	1.00
(14)	Jim Fregosi	3.50	1.75	1.00
(15)	Bob Friend	3.50	1.75	1.00
(16)	Dick Groat	3.50	1.75	1.00
(17)	Ron Hunt	3.50	1.75	1.00
(18)	Chuck Hinton	3.50	1.75	1.00
(19)	Ken Johnson	3.50	1.75	1.00
(20)	Al Kaline	20.00	10.00	6.00
(21)	Harmon Killebrew	20.00	10.00	6.00
(22)	Don Lock	3.50	1.75	1.00
(23)	Mickey Mantle	150.00	75.00	45.00
(24)	Roger Maris	30.00	15.00	9.00
(25)	Willie Mays	45.00	22.00	13.50
(26)	Bill Mazeroski	10.00	5.00	3.00
(27)	Gary Peters	3.50	1.75	1.00
(28)	Vada Pinson	4.00	2.00	1.25
(29)	Boog Powell	4.50	2.25	1.25
(30)	Dick Radatz	3.50	1.75	1.00
(31)	Brooks Robinson	20.00	10.00	6.00
(32)	Frank Robinson	20.00	10.00	6.00
(33)	Tracy Stallard	3.50	1.75	1.00
(34)	Joe Torre	5.00	2.50	1.50
(35)	Leon Wagner	3.50	1.75	1.00
(36)	Pete Ward	3.50	1.75	1.00
(37)	Dave Wickersham	3.50	1.75	1.00
(38)	Billy Williams	16.00	8.00	4.75
(39)	John Wyatt	3.50	1.75	1.00
(40)	Carl Yastrzemski	25.00	12.50	7.50

1909-11 Old Mill Cigarettes

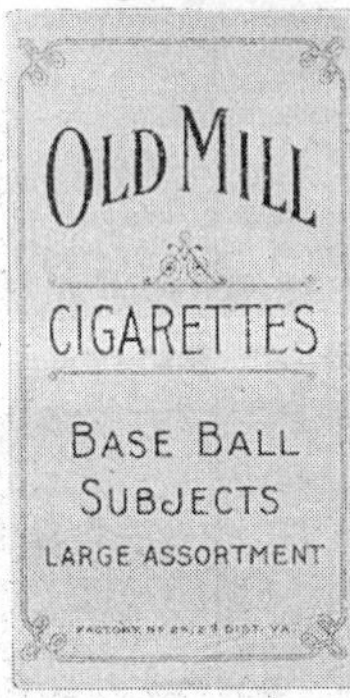

(See S74, T3, T206. Premium: T206 - +30%)

1951 Olmes Studio Postcards

This line of Philadelphia player postcards (all but one from the A's) was produced by a local photographer, probably for player use in satisfying fans' autograph requests. The 3-1/2" x 5-1/2" cards have a glossy black-and-white player photo on front, with his name, team and position printed in black in the bottom border. Backs have only standard postcard indicia and the Olmes credit line. Other players may remain to be checklisted. The unnumbered cards are listed here alphabetically. Two poses of Ferris Fain are reported, but not specified.

		NM	EX	VG
Complete Set (9):		665.00	335.00	200.00
Common Player:		65.00	32.00	20.00
(1)	Sam Chapman	65.00	32.00	20.00
(2)	Ferris Fain (batting)	65.00	32.00	20.00
(3)	Ferris Fain	65.00	32.00	20.00
(4)	Dick Fowler	65.00	32.00	20.00
(5)	Bob Hooper	65.00	32.00	20.00
(6)	Barney McCosky	65.00	32.00	20.00
(7)	Robin Roberts	265.00	135.00	79.00
(8)	Carl Scheib	65.00	32.00	20.00
(9)	Joe Tipton	65.00	32.00	20.00

1979 Open Pantry/ Lake to Lake MACC

To benefit Milwaukee Athletes Against Childhood Cancer (MACC) the Open Pantry convenience stores in Wisconsin teamed with Lake to Lake Dairy to produce this card set. Red, white and black fronts of the 5" x 6" cards have a player photo, facsimile autograph and team logo. Backs are printed in red with a message from the player about the MACC fund and a note that the sponsors are donating 10 cents per gallon of milk sold to MACC. Besides members of the Milwaukee Brewers, the set features Green Bay Packers football players and Milwaukee Bucks basketball players. The unnumbered cards are checklisted here alphabetically.

		NM	EX	VG
Complete Set (12):		20.00	10.00	6.00
Common Player:		2.00	1.00	.60
(1)	Jerry Augustine	2.00	1.00	.60
(2)	Sal Bando	2.00	1.00	.60
(3)	Kent Benson (Bucks)	2.00	1.00	.60
(4)	Junior Bridgeman (Bucks)	2.00	1.00	.60
(5)	Quinn Buckner (Bucks)	2.00	1.00	.60
(6)	Cecil Cooper	3.00	1.50	.90
(7)	Larry Hisle	2.00	1.00	.60
(8)	Marques Johnson (Bucks)	2.00	1.00	.60
(9)	Rich McGeorge (Packers)	2.00	1.00	.60
(10)	John McGlocklin (Bucks)	2.00	1.00	.60
(11)	Lary Sorensen	2.00	1.00	.60
(12)	Steve Wagner (Packers)	2.00	1.00	.60

1910 "Orange Borders"

Known in the hobby as "Orange Borders", these 1-1/2" x 2-7/16" cards were issued in 1910 and were printed on candy boxes that displayed the words "American Sports and Candy and Jewelry." The end flaps indicate the producers as the "Geo. Davis Co., Inc." and the "P.R. Warren Co., Warrenville Lowell, Mass." According to the box, the complete set includes "144 leading ballplayers," but to date just over two dozen different subjects are known. When found today, these black and white photos are often surrounded by orange borders which, in reality, were part of the candy box. Similar in format to the "Baseball Bats" cards, Orange Borders have player names which are hand-lettered, rather than typeset.

		NM	EX	VG
Common Player:		210.00	85.00	40.00
(1)	Bill Bergen	210.00	85.00	40.00
(2)	Bill Bradley	210.00	85.00	40.00
(3)	Bill Carrigan	210.00	85.00	40.00
(4)	Hal Chase	250.00	100.00	50.00
(5)	Fred Clark (Clarke)	315.00	125.00	60.00
(6)	Ty Cobb	1250.	500.00	250.00
(7)	Sam Crawford	315.00	125.00	63.00
(8)	Lou Criger	210.00	85.00	40.00
(9)	Art Devlin	210.00	85.00	40.00
(10)	Mickey Doolan	210.00	85.00	40.00
(11)	George Gibson	210.00	85.00	40.00
(12)	Addie Joss	350.00	140.00	70.00
(13)	Nap Lajoie	315.00	125.00	63.00
(14)	Frank LaPorte	210.00	85.00	40.00
(15)	Harry Lord	210.00	85.00	40.00
(16)	Christy Mathewson	625.00	250.00	125.00
(17)	Amby McConnell	210.00	85.00	40.00
(18)	John McGraw	315.00	125.00	63.00
(19)	Dots Miller	210.00	85.00	40.00
(20)	George Mullin	210.00	85.00	40.00
(21)	Eddie Plank	315.00	125.00	63.00
(22)	Tris Speaker	350.00	140.00	70.00
(23)	Jake Stahl	210.00	85.00	40.00
(24)	Honus Wagner (batting)	625.00	250.00	125.00
(25)	Honus Wagner (portrait)	625.00	250.00	125.00
(26)	Jack Warhop	210.00	85.00	40.00
(27)	American League Champions, 1909 (Detroit)	210.00	85.00	40.00
(28)	National League Champions, 1909 (Pittsburgh)	210.00	85.00	40.00

1976 Orbaker's discs

One of several regional sponsors of player disc sets in 1976 was the Orbaker's restaurant chain. The discs are 3-3/8" diameter with a black-and-white player portrait photo in the center of the baseball design. A line of red stars is above, while the left and right panels feature one of several bright colors. Produced by Michael Schecter Associates under license from the Major League Baseball Players Association, the player photos have had uniform and cap logos removed. Backs are printed in red and purple. The unnumbered checklist here is presented in alphabetical order.

		NM	EX	VG
Complete Set (70):		80.00	40.00	24.00
Common Player:		.90	.45	.25
(1)	Henry Aaron	9.00	4.50	2.75
(2)	Johnny Bench	5.00	2.50	1.50
(3)	Vida Blue	.90	.45	.25
(4)	Larry Bowa	.90	.45	.25
(5)	Lou Brock	3.00	1.50	.90
(6)	Jeff Burroughs	.90	.45	.25
(7)	John Candelaria	.90	.45	.25
(8)	Jose Cardenal	.90	.45	.25
(9)	Rod Carew	3.00	1.50	.90
(10)	Steve Carlton	3.00	1.50	.90
(11)	Dave Cash	.90	.45	.25
(12)	Cesar Cedeno	.90	.45	.25
(13)	Ron Cey	.90	.45	.25
(14)	Carlton Fisk	3.00	1.50	.90
(15)	Tito Fuentes	.90	.45	.25
(16)	Steve Garvey	3.00	1.50	.90
(17)	Ken Griffey	.90	.45	.25
(18)	Don Gullett	.90	.45	.25
(19)	Willie Horton	.90	.45	.25
(20)	Al Hrabosky	.90	.45	.25
(21)	Catfish Hunter	3.00	1.50	.90
(22)	Reggie Jackson	6.00	3.00	1.75
(23)	Randy Jones	.90	.45	.25
(24)	Jim Kaat	.90	.45	.25
(25)	Don Kessinger	.90	.45	.25
(26)	Dave Kingman	1.50	.70	.45
(27)	Jerry Koosman	.90	.45	.25
(28)	Mickey Lolich	1.25	.60	.40
(29)	Greg Luzinski	.90	.45	.25
(30)	Fred Lynn	.90	.45	.25
(31)	Bill Madlock	.90	.45	.25
(32)	Carlos May	.90	.45	.25
(33)	John Mayberry	.90	.45	.25
(34)	Bake McBride	.90	.45	.25
(35)	Doc Medich	.90	.45	.25
(36)	Andy Messersmith	.90	.45	.25
(37)	Rick Monday	.90	.45	.25
(38)	John Montefusco	.90	.45	.25
(39)	Jerry Morales	.90	.45	.25
(40)	Joe Morgan	3.00	1.50	.90
(41)	Thurman Munson	3.50	1.75	1.00
(42)	Bobby Murcer	.90	.45	.25
(43)	Al Oliver	.90	.45	.25
(44)	Jim Palmer	3.00	1.50	.90
(45)	Dave Parker	.90	.45	.25
(46)	Tony Perez	3.00	1.50	.90
(47)	Jerry Reuss	.90	.45	.25
(48)	Brooks Robinson	4.00	2.00	1.25
(49)	Frank Robinson	4.00	2.00	1.25
(50)	Steve Rogers	.90	.45	.25
(51)	Pete Rose	9.00	4.50	2.75
(52)	Nolan Ryan	16.00	8.00	4.75
(53)	Manny Sanguillen	.90	.45	.25
(54)	Mike Schmidt	6.00	3.00	1.75

(55)	Tom Seaver	4.00	2.00	1.25
(56)	Ted Simmons	.90	.45	.25
(57)	Reggie Smith	.90	.45	.25
(58)	Willie Stargell	3.00	1.50	.90
(59)	Rusty Staub	1.00	.50	.30
(60)	Rennie Stennett	.90	.45	.25
(61)	Don Sutton	3.00	1.50	.90
(62)	Andy Thornton	.90	.45	.25
(63)	Luis Tiant	.90	.45	.25
(64)	Joe Torre	.90	.45	.25
(65)	Mike Tyson	.90	.45	.25
(66)	Bob Watson	.90	.45	.25
(67)	Wilbur Wood	.90	.45	.25
(68)	Jimmy Wynn	.90	.45	.25
(69)	Carl Yastrzemski	4.00	2.00	1.25
(70)	Richie Zisk	.90	.45	.25

1932 Orbit Gum Pins - Numbered

Issued circa 1932, this skip-numbered set of small (13/16" diameter) pins was produced by Orbit Gum and carries the American Card Catalog designation of PR2. A player lithograph is set against a green background with the player's name and team printed on a strip of yellow below. The pin number is at the very bottom; pins after #40 are skip-numbered.

		NM	EX	VG
Complete Set (54):		1800.	900.00	525.00
Common Player:		25.00	12.50	7.50
1	Ivy Andrews	25.00	12.50	7.50
2	Carl Reynolds	25.00	12.50	7.50
3	Riggs Stephenson	27.50	13.50	8.25
4	Lon Warneke	25.00	12.50	7.50
5	Frank Grube	25.00	12.50	7.50
6	Kiki Cuyler	45.00	22.00	13.50
7	Marty McManus	25.00	12.50	7.50
8	Lefty Clark	25.00	12.50	7.50
9	George Blaeholder	25.00	12.50	7.50
10	Willie Kamm	25.00	12.50	7.50
11	Jimmy Dykes	25.00	12.50	7.50
12	Earl Averill	45.00	22.00	13.50
13	Pat Malone	25.00	12.50	7.50
14	Dizzy Dean	150.00	75.00	45.00
15	Dick Bartell	25.00	12.50	7.50
16	Guy Bush	25.00	12.50	7.50
17	Bud Tinning	25.00	12.50	7.50
18	Jimmy Foxx	75.00	37.00	22.00
19	Mule Haas	25.00	12.50	7.50
20	Lew Fonseca	25.00	12.50	7.50
21	Pepper Martin	35.00	17.50	10.50
22	Phil Collins	25.00	12.50	7.50
23	Bill Cissell	25.00	12.50	7.50
24	Bump Hadley	25.00	12.50	7.50
25	Smead Jolley	25.00	12.50	7.50
26	Burleigh Grimes	45.00	22.00	13.50
27	Dale Alexander	25.00	12.50	7.50
28	Mickey Cochrane	50.00	25.00	15.00
29	Mel Harder	25.00	12.50	7.50
30	Mark Koenig	25.00	12.50	7.50
31a	Lefty O'Doul (Dodgers)	40.00	20.00	12.00
31b	Lefty O'Doul (Giants)	75.00	37.00	22.00
32a	Woody English (with bat)	25.00	12.50	7.50
32b	Woody English (without bat)	65.00	32.00	19.50
33a	Billy Jurges (with bat)	25.00	12.50	7.50
33b	Billy Jurges (without bat)	65.00	32.00	19.50
34	Bruce Campbell	25.00	12.50	7.50
35	Joe Vosmik	25.00	12.50	7.50
36	Dick Porter	25.00	12.50	7.50
37	Charlie Grimm	25.00	12.50	7.50
38	George Earnshaw	25.00	12.50	7.50
39	Al Simmons	45.00	22.00	13.50
40	Red Lucas	25.00	12.50	7.50
51	Wally Berger	25.00	12.50	7.50
52	Jim Levey	25.00	12.50	7.50
55	Jim Levey	25.00	12.50	7.50
58	Ernie Lombardi	45.00	22.00	13.50
64	Jack Burns	25.00	12.50	7.50
67	Billy Herman	45.00	22.00	13.50
72	Bill Hallahan	25.00	12.50	7.50
92	Don Brennan	25.00	12.50	7.50
96	Sam Byrd	25.00	12.50	7.50
99	Ben Chapman	25.00	12.50	7.50
103	John Allen	25.00	12.50	7.50
107	Tony Lazzeri	45.00	22.00	13.50
111	Earl Combs (Earle)	45.00	22.00	13.50
116	Joe Sewell	45.00	22.00	13.50
120	Vernon Gomez	50.00	25.00	15.00

1932 Orbit Gum Pins - Unnumbered

This set, issued by Orbit Gum circa 1932, has the American Card Catalog designation PR3. The pins are identical to the PR2 set, except they are unnumbered.

		NM	EX	VG
Complete Set (60):		2650.	1350.	825.00
Common Player:		35.00	17.50	10.50
(1)	Dale Alexander	35.00	17.50	10.50
(2)	Ivy Andrews	35.00	17.50	10.50
(3)	Earl Averill	60.00	30.00	18.00
(4)	Dick Bartell	35.00	17.50	10.50
(5)	Wally Berger	35.00	17.50	10.50
(6)	George Blaeholder	35.00	17.50	10.50
(7)	Jack Burns	35.00	17.50	10.50
(8)	Guy Bush	35.00	17.50	10.50
(9)	Bruce Campbell	35.00	17.50	10.50
(10)	Bill Cissell	35.00	17.50	10.50
(11)	Lefty Clark	35.00	17.50	10.50
(12)	Mickey Cochrane	60.00	30.00	18.00
(13)	Phil Collins	35.00	17.50	10.50
(14)	Kiki Cuyler	60.00	30.00	18.00
(15)	Dizzy Dean	175.00	87.00	52.00
(16)	Jimmy Dykes	35.00	17.50	10.50
(17)	George Earnshaw	35.00	17.50	10.50
(18)	Woody English	35.00	17.50	10.50
(19)	Lew Fonseca	35.00	17.50	10.50
(20)	Jimmy Foxx	95.00	47.00	28.00
(21)	Burleigh Grimes	60.00	30.00	18.00
(22)	Charlie Grimm	35.00	17.50	10.50
(23)	Lefty Grove	60.00	30.00	18.00
(24)	Frank Grube	35.00	17.50	10.50
(25)	Mule Haas	35.00	17.50	10.50
(26)	Bump Hadley	35.00	17.50	10.50
(27)	Chick Hafey	60.00	30.00	18.00
(28)	Jesse Haines	60.00	30.00	18.00
(29)	Bill Hallahan	35.00	17.50	10.50
(30)	Mel Harder	35.00	17.50	10.50
(31)	Gabby Hartnett	60.00	30.00	18.00
(32)	Babe Herman	45.00	22.00	13.50
(33)	Billy Herman	60.00	30.00	18.00
(34)	Rogers Hornsby	75.00	37.00	22.00
(35)	Roy Johnson	35.00	17.50	10.50
(36)	Smead Jolley	35.00	17.50	10.50
(37)	Billy Jurges	35.00	17.50	10.50
(38)	Willie Kamm	35.00	17.50	10.50
(39)	Mark Koenig	35.00	17.50	10.50
(40)	Jim Levey	35.00	17.50	10.50
(41)	Ernie Lombardi	60.00	30.00	18.00
(42)	Red Lucas	35.00	17.50	10.50
(43)	Ted Lyons	60.00	30.00	18.00
(44)	Connie Mack	60.00	30.00	18.00
(45)	Pat Malone	35.00	17.50	10.50
(46)	Pepper Martin	45.00	22.00	13.50
(47)	Marty McManus	35.00	17.50	10.50
(48)	Lefty O'Doul	45.00	22.00	13.50
(49)	Dick Porter	35.00	17.50	10.50
(50)	Carl Reynolds	35.00	17.50	10.50
(51)	Charlie Root	35.00	17.50	10.50
(52)	Bob Seeds	35.00	17.50	10.50
(53)	Al Simmons	60.00	30.00	18.00
(54)	Riggs Stephenson	35.00	17.50	10.50
(55)	Bud Tinning	35.00	17.50	10.50
(56)	Joe Vosmik	35.00	17.50	10.50
(57)	Rube Walberg	35.00	17.50	10.50
(58)	Paul Waner	60.00	30.00	18.00
(59)	Lon Warneke	35.00	17.50	10.50
(60)	Pinky Whitney	35.00	17.50	10.50

1937-39 Orcajo Cincinnati Reds postcards

Orcajo, a Dayton, Ohio, photo firm, issued a series of Reds player postcards (plus, inexplicably, Joe DiMaggio) from 1937-39. Besides those found with just the issuer's imprint on the back, some or all of the players' cards can be found with the advertising on front of the Val Decker Packing Co., a meat dealer, Metropolitan Clothing Co., and an inset photo of WHIO radio announcer Si Burick (the latter are the 1937 cards and have no Orcajo imprint on back, utilizing different photos than the 1938-39 cards). The 3-1/2" x 5-1/2" cards have glossy black-and-white player poses on front with the player's name overprinted. Backs have standard postcard indicia. A number of spelling errors and several variations exist. The unnumbered cards are checklisted here alphabetically; those with ads for the meat company, men's store or radio station are appropriately noted.

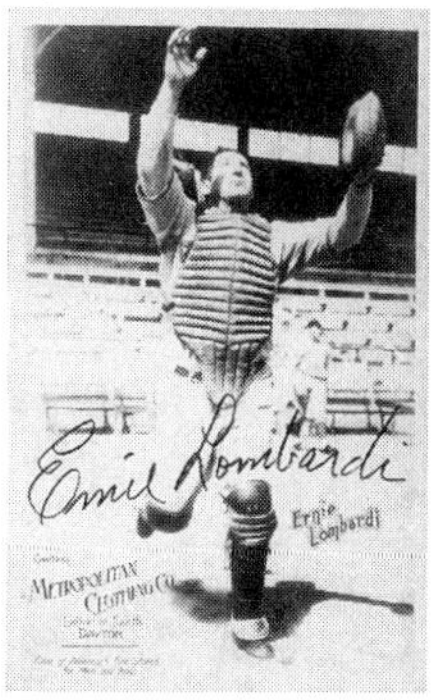

		NM	EX	VG
Complete Set (37):		3200.	1600.	950.00
Common Player:		85.00	40.00	24.00
(1)	Wally Berger	85.00	36.00	20.00
(2)	Bongiovanni (first name Nino)	85.00	36.00	20.00
(3)	Frenchy Bordagaray	85.00	36.00	20.00
(4)	Joe Cascarella, Gene Schott (Val Decker only)	85.00	36.00	20.00
(5)	Allan Cooke (Allen) (Val Decker only)	85.00	36.00	20.00
(6)	Harry Craft (also Val Decker)	85.00	36.00	20.00
(7)	Kiki Cuyler (WHIO only)	135.00	61.00	34.00
(8)	Ray Davis	85.00	36.00	20.00
(9)	Virgil Davis (Val Decker only)	85.00	36.00	20.00
(10)	Paul Derringer (also Val Decker)	85.00	36.00	20.00
(11)	Joe DiMaggio	700.00	315.00	175.00
(12)	Linus Frey (also Val Decker)	85.00	36.00	20.00
(13)	Lee Gamble	85.00	36.00	20.00
(14)	Ivan Goodman (Ival) (also Val Decker)	85.00	36.00	20.00
(15)	Hank Gowdy	85.00	36.00	20.00
(16)	Lee Grissom	85.00	36.00	20.00
(17a)	Willard Hershberger (Hershberger, name in white) (also Val Decker)	85.00	36.00	20.00
(17b)	Willard Hershberger (name in black)	85.00	36.00	20.00
(18a)	Al Hollingsworth	85.00	36.00	20.00
(18b)	Al Hollingsworth (WHIO)	85.00	36.00	20.00
(18c)	Al Hollingsworth (Val Decker)	85.00	36.00	20.00
(19)	Hank Johnson	85.00	36.00	20.00
(20)	Edwin Joost	85.00	36.00	20.00
(21a)	Ernie Lombardi (plain letters) (also Val Decker, Metro)	135.00	61.00	34.00
(21b)	Ernie Lombardi (fancy letters) (also Val Decker, Metro)	135.00	61.00	34.00
(22)	Frank McCormick (also Val Decker, Metro)	85.00	36.00	20.00
(23)	Bill McKecknie (McKechnie)	125.00	56.00	31.00
(24)	Billy Meyers (Myers) (also Val Decker)	85.00	36.00	20.00
(25a)	Whitey Moore (photo actually Bucky Walters)	85.00	36.00	20.00
(25b)	Whitey Moore (correct photo)	85.00	36.00	20.00
(26)	Lew Riggs	85.00	36.00	20.00
(27)	Edd Roush (Val Decker only)	125.00	56.00	31.00
(28a)	Leo Scarsella (Les)	135.00	61.00	34.00
(28b)	Les Scarsella (WHIO)	85.00	36.00	20.00
(29)	Gene Schott (WHIO)	85.00	36.00	20.00
(30)	Milburn Shoffner	85.00	36.00	20.00
(31)	Junior Thompson	85.00	36.00	20.00
(32a)	Johnny Vander Meer (throwing) (also Metro, Val Decker)	150.00	67.00	37.00
(32b)	Johnny Vander Meer (fielding) (also Metro)	150.00	67.00	37.00
(33)	Bucky Walters	85.00	36.00	20.00
(34)	Bill Werber	85.00	36.00	20.00
(35)	Dick West	85.00	36.00	20.00
(36)	Jimmie Wilson	85.00	36.00	20.00
(37)	Cincinnati Reds composite team card	85.00	36.00	20.00

1963 Otto Milk

The attributed issue date of this commemorative milk carton is approximate. A 4" x 8" panel on the front of the milk carton has a picture and history of Honus Wagner printed in red and blue. Wagner is the only ballplayer in the milk carton series honoring Western Pennsylvania celebrities.

		NM	EX	VG
(1)	Honus Wagner (complete carton)	135.00	65.00	40.00
(1)	Honus Wagner (cut panel)	45.00	22.00	13.50

1938 Our National Game Pins

This unnumbered 30-pin set issued circa 1938 carries the American Card Catalog designation of PM8. The pins, which measure 7/8" in diameter, have a bendable "tab" rather than a pin back. The player photo is printed in blue-and-white. The player's name and team are printed at bottom. The pins were originally sold on a square of cardboard decorated with stars and stripes and imprinted "OUR NATIONAL GAME" above the pin, and "A BASEBALL HERO" below. A large number of the pins, complete with their cardboard backing, were found in a hoard in Oklahoma in the early 1990s.

		NM	EX	VG
Complete Set (30):		600.00	300.00	180.00
Common Player:		11.00	5.50	3.25
(1)	Wally Berger	11.00	5.50	3.25
(2)	Lou Chiozza	11.00	5.50	3.25
(3)	Joe Cronin	25.00	12.50	7.50
(4)	Frank Crosetti	15.00	7.50	4.50
(5)	Jerome (Dizzy) Dean	45.00	22.00	13.50
(6)	Frank DeMaree (Demaree)	11.00	5.50	3.25
(7)	Joe DiMaggio	130.00	65.00	39.00
(8)	Bob Feller	35.00	17.50	10.50
(9)	Jimmy Foxx (Jimmie)	35.00	17.50	10.50
(10)	Lou Gehrig	130.00	65.00	39.00
(11)	Charles Gehringer	25.00	12.50	7.50
(12)	Lefty Gomez	25.00	12.50	7.50
(13)	Hank Greenberg	30.00	15.00	9.00
(14)	Irving (Bump) Hadley	11.00	5.50	3.25
(15)	Leo Hartnett	25.00	12.50	7.50
(16)	Carl Hubbell	25.00	12.50	7.50
(17)	John (Buddy) Lewis	11.00	5.50	3.25
(18)	Gus Mancuso	11.00	5.50	3.25
(19)	Joe McCarthy	25.00	12.50	7.50
(20)	Joe Medwick	25.00	12.50	7.50
(21)	Joe Moore	11.00	5.50	3.25
(22)	Mel Ott	25.00	12.50	7.50
(23)	Jake Powell	11.00	5.50	3.25
(24)	Jimmy Ripple	11.00	5.50	3.25
(25)	Red Ruffing	25.00	12.50	7.50
(26)	Hal Schumacher	11.00	5.50	3.25
(27)	George Selkirk	11.00	5.50	3.25
(28)	"Al" Simmons	25.00	12.50	7.50
(29)	Bill Terry	25.00	12.50	7.50
(30)	Harold Trosky	11.00	5.50	3.25

1936 Overland Candy Co. (R301)

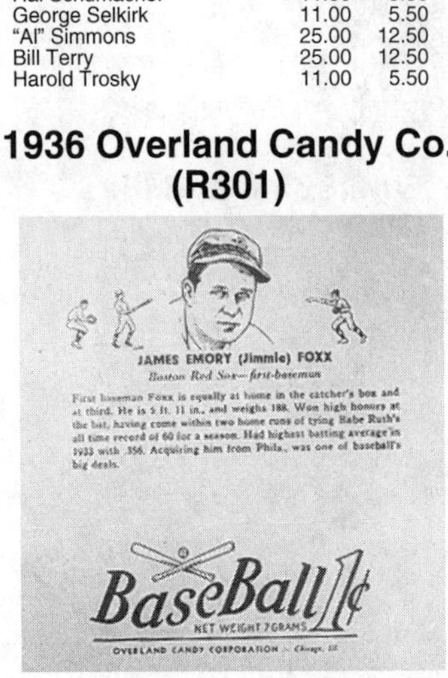

Used as wrappers for a piece of penny candy, these 5" x 5-1/4" waxed papers are usually found with resultant folds and creases, though unfolded examples are known. Printed in dark blue, the top of the wrapper features a line drawing portrait of the player, his formal name and nickname, team, position and career summary. The unnumbered wrappers are checklisted here alphabetically.

		NM	EX	VG
Complete Set (54):		15500.	7000.	3100.
Common Player:		275.00	125.00	55.00
(1)	Melo (Mel) Almada	350.00	155.00	70.00
(2)	Lucius B. (Luke) Appling	475.00	215.00	95.00
(3)	Howard Earl Averill	475.00	215.00	95.00
(4)	Walter Antone (Wally) Berger	275.00	125.00	55.00
(5)	Henry John (Zeke) Bonura	275.00	125.00	55.00
(6)	Philip Joseph (Phil) Cavarretta	300.00	150.00	60.00
(7)	William Ben (Chappy) Chapman	275.00	125.00	55.00
(8)	Harland Clift (first name Harlond)	275.00	125.00	25.00
(9a)	John Walter (Johnny) Cooney (Bees)	275.00	125.00	55.00
(9b)	John Walter (Johnny) Cooney (Dodgers)	275.00	125.00	55.00
(10)	Harry Danning	275.00	125.00	55.00
(11)	William N. (Bill) Dickey (middle initial is N)	500.00	225.00	100.00
(12a)	William J. (Bill) Dietrich (Athletics)	275.00	125.00	55.00
(12b)	William J. (Bill) Dietrich (White Sox)	275.00	125.00	55.00
(13)	Joseph (Deadpan Joe) DiMaggio	1600.	725.00	320.00
(14)	Wesley Cheek Ferrell	275.00	125.00	55.00
(15)	James Emory (Jimmie) Foxx	600.00	275.00	120.00
(16)	Henry Louis (Lou) Gehrig	1500.	675.00	300.00
(17)	Charles Leonard (Charley) Gehringer	475.00	215.00	95.00
(18)	Jose Luis (Chile) Gomez	275.00	125.00	55.00
(19)	Vernon (Lefty) Gomez	475.00	215.00	95.00
(20)	Joe Gordon	275.00	125.00	55.00
(21)	Henry (Hank) Greenberg	600.00	275.00	120.00
(22)	Robert Moses (Lefty) Grove	475.00	215.00	95.00
(23)	George W. (Mule) Haas	275.00	125.00	55.00
(24)	Ralston Burdett (Rollie) Hemsley	275.00	125.00	55.00
(25)	Michael Francis (Pinky) Higgins (middle name Franklin)	275.00	125.00	55.00
(26)	Oral Clyde (Hildy) Hildebrand	275.00	125.00	55.00
(27)	Robert Lee (Cherokee) Johnson	275.00	125.00	55.00
(28)	Baxter Byerly (Buck) Jordan	275.00	125.00	55.00
(29)	Ken Keltner	275.00	125.00	55.00
(30)	Fabian Kowalik	275.00	125.00	55.00
(31)	Harry A. Lavagetto	275.00	125.00	55.00
(32)	Anthony Michael (Poosh 'em Up) Lazzeri	475.00	215.00	95.00
(33)	Samuel A. Leslie	275.00	125.00	55.00
(34)	Dan (Slug) Lithwhiler (last name Litwhiler)	275.00	125.00	55.00
(35)	Theodore A. (Ted) Lyons	475.00	215.00	95.00
(36)	George McQuinn	275.00	125.00	55.00
(37)	John Robert (Skippy) Mize	475.00	215.00	95.00
(38)	Charles Solomon (Buddy) Myer	275.00	125.00	55.00
(39)	Louis Norman (Buck) Newsom	275.00	125.00	55.00
(40)	Frank A. (Pity) Pytlak	275.00	125.00	55.00
(41)	Raymond Allen (Rip) Radcliff	275.00	125.00	55.00
(42)	Peter (Pete) Reiser (Correct name Harold Patrick)	275.00	125.00	55.00
(43)	Carl Nettles (Sheeps) Reynolds	275.00	125.00	55.00
(44)	Robert Abial (Red) Rolfe	275.00	125.00	55.00
(45)	Lynwood Thomas (Schoolboy) Rowe	275.00	125.00	55.00
(46)	Aloysius Harry (Al) Simmons	475.00	215.00	95.00
(47)	Cecil Howard Travis (middle name is Howell)	275.00	125.00	55.00
(48)	Harold Arthus (Hal) Trosky	275.00	125.00	55.00
(49)	Joseph Franklin (Joe) Vosmik	275.00	125.00	55.00
(50)	Harold Burton (Rabbit) Warstler	275.00	125.00	55.00
(51)	William M. (Bill) Werber	275.00	125.00	55.00
(52)	Max West	275.00	125.00	55.00
(53)	Samuel F. (Sam) West	275.00	125.00	55.00
(54)	Whitlow (Whit) Wyatt	275.00	125.00	55.00

1921 Oxford Confectionery (E253)

Issued in 1921 by Oxford Confectionery of Oxford, Pa., this 20-card set was printed on thin paper and distributed with caramels. Each card measures 1-5/8" x 2-3/4" and features a black-and-white player photo with the player's name and team printed in a white band along the bottom. The back carries a checklist of the players in the set, 14 of whom are now in the Hall of Fame. The set is designated as E253 in the ACC.

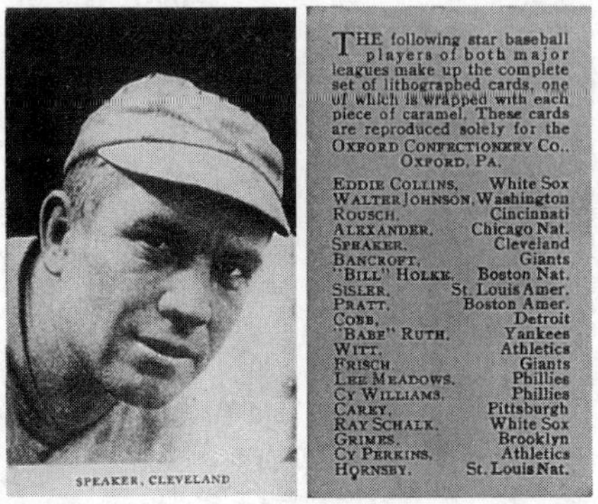

		NM	EX	VG
Complete Set (20):		6250.	2800.	1250.
Common Player:		80.00	36.00	16.00
(1)	Grover Alexander	150.00	67.00	30.00
(2)	Dave Bancroft	150.00	65.00	30.00
(3)	Max Carey	150.00	65.00	30.00
(4)	Ty Cobb	1500.	675.00	300.00
(5)	Eddie Collins	150.00	65.00	30.00
(6)	Frankie Frisch	150.00	65.00	30.00
(7)	Burleigh Grimes	150.00	65.00	30.00
(8)	"Bill" Holke (Walter)	80.00	36.00	16.00
(9)	Rogers Hornsby	175.00	79.00	35.00
(10)	Walter Johnson	600.00	270.00	120.00
(11)	Lee Meadows	80.00	36.00	16.00
(12)	Cy Perkins	80.00	36.00	16.00
(13)	Derrill Pratt	80.00	36.00	16.00
(14)	Ed Rousch (Roush)	150.00	65.00	30.00
(15)	"Babe" Ruth	2000.	900.00	400.00
(16)	Ray Schalk	150.00	65.00	30.00
(17)	George Sisler	150.00	65.00	30.00
(18)	Tris Speaker	175.00	79.00	35.00
(19)	Cy Williams	80.00	36.00	16.00
(20)	Whitey Witt	80.00	36.00	16.00

P

1958 Packard-Bell

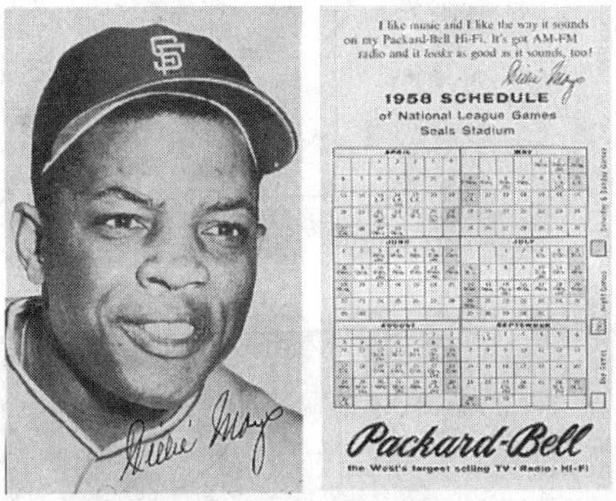

Issued by the "world's largest seller of TVs, radios and hi-fis", this set was distributed in California and features members of the newly arrived Los Angeles Dodgers and San Francisco Giants. The 3-1/2" x 5-1/2" black-and-white cards are unnumbered, checklisted here alphabetically.

		NM	EX	VG
Complete Set (7):		435.00	215.00	130.00
Common Player:		25.00	12.50	7.50
(1)	Walter Alston	35.00	17.50	10.50
(2)	John A. Antonelli	25.00	12.50	7.50
(3)	Jim Gilliam	35.00	17.50	10.50
(4)	Gil Hodges	90.00	45.00	27.00
(5)	Willie Mays	250.00	125.00	75.00
(6)	Bill Rigney	25.00	12.50	7.50
(7)	Hank Sauer	25.00	12.50	7.50

1978 Papa Gino's Discs

This promotion was largely confined to the Boston area, as 25 of the 40 players represented are Red Sox, the other 15 are all from American League teams. The 3-3/8" discs were given away with the purchase of soft drinks at the restaurant chain. Fronts have player portraits at center with name in the dark blue border at top and team below. Photos have the uniform logos airbrushed away because the discs were licensed only by the players' union, not MLB. Backs retain the color scheme with player data, previous season's stats, uniform and card numbers, sponsor's ad, etc.

	NM	EX	VG
Complete Set (40):	150.00	75.00	45.00
Common Player:	4.00	2.00	1.25
1 Allen Ripley	4.00	2.00	1.25
2 Jerry Remy	4.00	2.00	1.25
3 Jack Brohamer	4.00	2.00	1.25
4 Butch Hobson	4.00	2.00	1.25
5 Dennis Eckersley	5.00	2.50	1.50
6 Sam Bowen	4.00	2.00	1.25
7 Rick Burleson	4.00	2.00	1.25
8 Carl Yastrzemski	12.00	6.00	3.50
9 Bill Lee	4.00	2.00	1.25
10 Bob Montgomery	4.00	2.00	1.25
11 Dick Drago	4.00	2.00	1.25
12 Bob Stanley	4.00	2.00	1.25
13 Fred Kendall	4.00	2.00	1.25
14 Jim Rice	7.50	3.75	2.25
15 George Scott	4.00	2.00	1.25
16 Tom Burgmeier	4.00	2.00	1.25
17 Frank Duffy	4.00	2.00	1.25
18 Jim Wright	4.00	2.00	1.25
19 Fred Lynn	4.00	2.00	1.25
20 Bob Bailey	4.00	2.00	1.25
21 Mike Torrez	4.00	2.00	1.25
22 Bill Campbell	4.00	2.00	1.25
23 Luis Tiant	4.00	2.00	1.25
24 Dwight Evans	5.00	2.50	1.50
25 Carlton Fisk	9.00	4.50	2.75
26 Reggie Jackson	12.00	6.00	3.50
27 Thurman Munson	10.00	5.00	3.00
28 Ron Guidry	4.00	2.00	1.25
29 Bruce Bochte	4.00	2.00	1.25
30 Richie Zisk	4.00	2.00	1.25
31 Jim Palmer	12.00	6.00	3.50
32 Mark Fidrych	6.00	3.00	1.75
33 Frank Tanana	4.00	2.00	1.25
34 Buddy Bell	4.00	2.00	1.25
35 Rod Carew	12.00	6.00	3.50
36 George Brett	20.00	10.00	6.00
37 Ralph Garr	4.00	2.00	1.25
38 Larry Hisle	4.00	2.00	1.25
39 Mitchell Page	4.00	2.00	1.25
40 John Mayberry	4.00	2.00	1.25

1976 Bob Parker More Baseball Cartoons

This collectors' issue showcased the pen and ink artwork of Ohio cartoonist Bob Parker on cards featuring current and former ballplayers from the great to the obscure. Cards are in 3-1/2" x 5" format with black-and-white fronts and blank backs.

	NM	EX	VG
Complete Set (24):	20.00	10.00	6.00
Common Card:	.50	.25	.15
1 Hank Aaron, Babe Ruth (All-Time HR Specialists)	2.00	1.00	.60
2 Ernie Banks	1.00	.50	.30
3 Rod Carew	.50	.25	.15
4 Joe DiMaggio	4.00	2.00	1.25
5 Doug Flynn	.50	.25	.15
6 Mike Garcia	.50	.25	.15
7 Steve Garvey, Greg Luzinski (All-Stars)	.50	.25	.15
8 Lou Gehrig	4.00	2.00	1.25
9 Chuck Klein, Hack Wilson (Hall of Famers?)	.50	.25	.15
10 Don Larsen	.50	.25	.15
11 Fred Lynn	.50	.25	.15
12 Roy Majtyka	.50	.25	.15
13 Pepper Martin	.50	.25	.15
14 Christy Mathewson	.75	.40	.25
15 Cal McVey	.50	.25	.15
16 Tony Perez	.50	.25	.15
17 Lou Gehrig, Babe Ruth (Great Moments)	4.00	2.00	1.25
18 Everett Scott	.50	.25	.15
19 Bobby Thomson	.50	.25	.15
20 Ted Williams (1939)	2.00	1.00	.60
21 Ted Williams (Great Moments)	2.00	1.00	.60
22 Bill Madlock	.50	.25	.15
23 Henry Chadwick, Buck Ewing, Albert Spalding, Honus Wagner (Hall of Famers)	.50	.25	.15
--- Checklist	.50	.25	.15

1974 Bob Parker 2nd Best

Star players who came in second, often to lesser-known players, in various statistical categories between 1899-1955 are featured in this collectors issue from Bob Parker. The blank-backed, black-and-white cards measure an unusual 3" x 8" and feature the story of the 1-2 finish in cartoon form. The unnumbered cards are listed here in chronological order.

	NM	EX	VG
Complete Set (25):	14.00	7.00	4.25
Common Player:	.50	.25	.15
(1) Jesse Burkett, Ed Delahanty (1899)	.50	.25	.15
(2) Hans Wagner, Cy Seymour (1905)	.75	.40	.25
(3) Gavvy Cravath, Jake Daubert (1913)	.50	.25	.15
(4) Joe Jackson, Ty Cobb (1913)	2.50	1.25	.70
(5) Eddie Collins, Ty Cobb (1914)	1.00	.50	.30
(6) Babe Ruth, Heinie Manush (1926)	2.00	1.00	.60
(7) Chick Hafey, Jim Bottomley, Hack Wilson (1928)	.50	.25	.15
(8) Paul Waner, Rogers Hornsby (1928)	.50	.25	.15
(9) Babe Herman, Lefty O'Doul (1929)	.50	.25	.15
(10) Al Simmons, Lew Fonseca (1929)	.50	.25	.15
(11) Lou Gehrig, Babe Ruth (1930)	2.50	1.25	.70
(12) Babe Herman, Bill Terry (1930)	.50	.25	.15
(13) Chuck Klein, Hack Wilson (1930)	.50	.25	.15
(14) Jim Bottomley, Bill Terry, Chick Hafey (1931)	.50	.25	.15
(15) Jimmy (Jimmie) Foxx, Dale Alexander (1932)	.50	.25	.15
(16) Spud Davis, Chuck Klein (1933)	.50	.25	.15
(17) Heinie Manush, Jimmy (Jimmie) Foxx (1933)	.50	.25	.15
(18) Mel Ott, Wally Berger (1935)	.50	.25	.15
(19) Joe Vosmik, Buddy Myer (1935)	.50	.25	.15
(20) Blimp Phelps, Paul Waner (1936)	.50	.25	.15
(21) Bobby Doerr, Lou Boudreau (1944)	.50	.25	.15
(22) Stan Musial, Dixie Walker (1944)	.75	.40	.25
(23) George Kell, Billy Goodman (1950)	.50	.25	.15
(24) Al Rosen, Mickey Vernon (1953)	.50	.25	.15
(25) Vic Power, Al Kaline (1955)	.50	.25	.15

1977 Bob Parker Hall of Fame

This is one of many collectors issues produced in the mid to late 1970s by midwestern sports artist Bob Parker. The 3-3/8" x 5-1/2" cards are printed in sepia on tan cardboard; they are blank-backed. Fronts have a portrait drawing of the player, with career highlights in cartoon form.

	NM	EX	VG
Complete Set (54):	40.00	20.00	12.00
Common Player:	.50	.25	.15
1 Grover Alexander	.50	.25	.15
2 Cap Anson	.50	.25	.15
3 Luke Appling	.50	.25	.15
4 Ernie Banks	.75	.40	.25
5 Chief Bender	.50	.25	.15
6 Jim Bottomley	.50	.25	.15
7 Dan Brouthers	.50	.25	.15
8 Morgan Bulkeley	.50	.25	.15
9 Roy Campanella	1.50	.70	.45
10 Alexander Cartwright	.50	.25	.15
11 Henry Chadwick	.50	.25	.15
12 John Clarkson	.50	.25	.15
13 Ty Cobb	2.00	1.00	.60
14 Eddie Collins	.50	.25	.15
16 Charles Comiskey	.50	.25	.15
17 Sam Crawford	.50	.25	.15
18 Dizzy Dean	.65	.35	.20
19 Joe DiMaggio	3.00	1.50	.90
20 Buck Ewing	.50	.25	.15
21 Bob Feller	.65	.35	.20
22 Lou Gehrig	3.00	1.50	.90
23 Goose Goslin	.50	.25	.15
24 Burleigh Grimes	.50	.25	.15
25 Chick Hafey	.50	.25	.15
26 Rogers Hornsby	.50	.25	.15
27 Carl Hubbell	.50	.25	.15
28 Miller Huggins	.50	.25	.15
29 Tim Keefe	.50	.25	.15
30 Mike Kelly	.50	.25	.15
31 Nap Lajoie	.50	.25	.15
32 Freddie Lindstrom	.50	.25	.15
33 Connie Mack	.50	.25	.15
34 Mickey Mantle	7.50	3.75	2.25
35 Heinie Manush	.50	.25	.15
36 Joe McGinnity	.50	.25	.15
37 John McGraw	.50	.25	.15
38 Ed Plank	.50	.25	.15
39 Eppa Rixey	.50	.25	.15
40 Jackie Robinson	3.00	1.50	.90
41 Edd Roush	.50	.25	.15
42 Babe Ruth	6.00	3.00	1.75
43 Al Simmons	.50	.25	.15
44 Al Spalding	.50	.25	.15
45 Tris Speaker	.50	.25	.15
46 Casey Stengel	.50	.25	.15
47 Bill Terry	.50	.25	.15
48 Rube Waddell	.50	.25	.15
49 Honus Wagner	.75	.40	.25
50 Paul Waner	.50	.25	.15
51 John Montgomery Ward	.50	.25	.15
52 Ted Williams	2.00	1.00	.60
53 George Wright	.50	.25	.15
54 Harry Wright	.50	.25	.15

1977 Bob Parker Cincinnati Reds

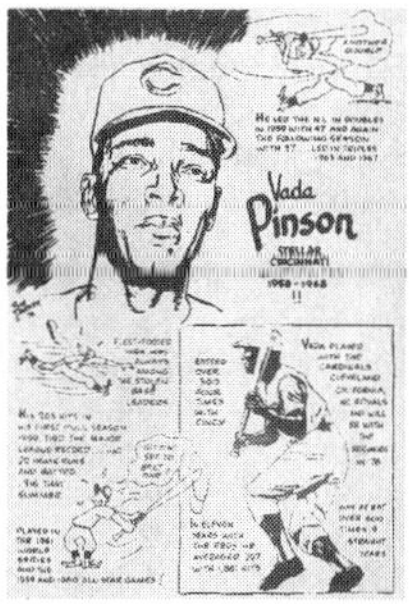

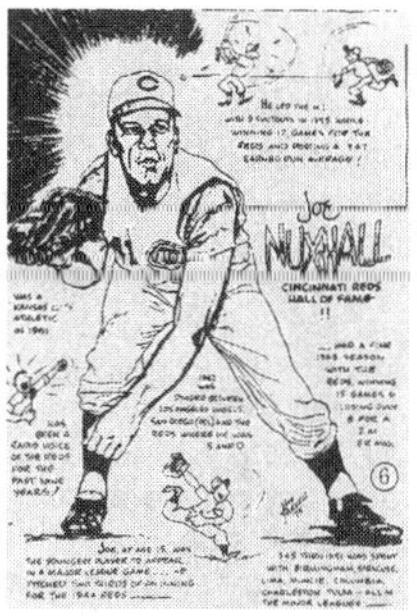

In the late 1970s, Ohio cartoonist Bob Parker drew a series of Reds feature cartoons for the weekly "Reds Alert." Later, he assembled two groups of those cartoons into collectors' issue card sets. The cards are black-and-white with blank backs. Fronts have portraits and/or action main drawings, usually with some cartoon figures included to draw attention to the player's career highlights. Size is 3-1/2" x 5". The unnumbered series is listed in alphabetical order.

		NM	EX	VG
Complete Set (47):		35.00	17.50	10.50
Common Player:		.75	.40	.25
	UNNUMBERED SERIES (23):	15.00	7.50	4.50
(1)	Sparky Anderson	1.00	.50	.30
(2)	Wally Berger	.75	.40	.25
(3)	Pedro Borbon	.75	.40	.25
(4)	Rube Bressler	.75	.40	.25
(5)	Gordy Coleman	.75	.40	.25
(6)	Dave Concepcion	.75	.40	.25
(7)	Harry Craft	.75	.40	.25
(8)	Hugh Critz	.75	.40	.25
(9)	Dan Driessen	.75	.40	.25
(10)	Pat Duncan	.75	.40	.25
(11)	Lonnie Frey	.75	.40	.25
(12)	Ival Goodman	.75	.40	.25
(13)	Heinie Groh	.75	.40	.25
(14)	Noodles Hahn	.75	.40	.25
(15)	Mike Lum	.75	.40	.25
(16)	Bill McKechnie	.75	.40	.25
(17)	Pat Moran	.75	.40	.25
(18)	Billy Myers	.75	.40	.25
(19)	Gary Nolan	.75	.40	.25
(20)	Fred Norman	.75	.40	.25
(21)	Jim O'Toole	.75	.40	.25
(22)	Vada Pinson	1.00	.50	.30
(23)	Bucky Walters	.75	.40	.25
	NUMBERED SERIES (24):	22.00	11.00	6.50
1	Ted Kluszewski	1.50	.70	.45
2	Johnny Bench	2.50	1.25	.70
3	Jim Maloney	.75	.40	.25
4	Bubbles Hargrave	.75	.40	.25
5	Don Gullett	.75	.40	.25
6	Joe Nuxhall	1.00	.50	.30
7	Edd Roush	.75	.40	.25
8	Wally Post	.75	.40	.25
9	George Wright	.75	.40	.25
10	George Foster	.75	.40	.25
11	Pete Rose	4.00	2.00	1.25
12	Red Lucas	.75	.40	.25
13	Joe Morgan	1.00	.50	.30
14	Eppa Rixey	.75	.40	.25
15	Bill Werber	.75	.40	.25
16	Frank Robinson	1.50	.70	.45
17	Dolf Luque	1.00	.50	.30
18	Paul Derringer	.75	.40	.25
19	Frank McCormick	.75	.40	.25
20	Ken Griffey	.75	.40	.25
21	Jack Billingham	.75	.40	.25
22	Larry Kopf	.75	.40	.25
23	Ernie Lombardi	.75	.40	.25
24	Johnny Vander Meer	.75	.40	.25

1968-70 Partridge Meats Reds

The extent of the checklist for this scarce regional issue is unknown. The cards were produced in conjunction with Reds' autograph appearances at Kroger food stores in the Cincinnati area. Players' service with the Reds indicates this set was issued over a period of several years. Similar cards are known for other Cincinnati pro sports teams. The 1968 cards measure 4" x 5" and feature a black-and-white player photo set against a borderless white background. The player's name and team and the word "Likes" are printed in black, the ad for the issuing meat company at bottom is printed in red. Cards have a blank back. The 1969-70 cards are in the same format but in 3-3/4" x 5-1/2" format. The unnumbered cards are checklisted here in alphabetical order.

		NM	EX	VG
Common Player:		30.00	15.00	9.00
(1)	Ted Abernathy	30.00	15.00	9.00
(2)	John Bench	150.00	75.00	45.00
(3)	Jimmy Bragan	30.00	15.00	9.00
(4)	Dave Bristol	30.00	15.00	9.00
(5)	Tommy Helms	30.00	15.00	9.00
(6)	Gary Nolan	30.00	15.00	9.00
(7)	Milt Pappas	30.00	15.00	9.00
(8)	Don Pavletich	30.00	15.00	9.00
(9)	Mel Queen	30.00	15.00	9.00
(10)	Pete Rose	175.00	87.00	52.00
(11)	Jim Stewart	30.00	15.00	9.00

1972 Partridge Meats Reds

Similar in format to the meat company's 1968-70 issue, these later cards are in a slightly different size - 3-3/4" x 5-1/2". The ad on the '72 cards reads "Photo courtesy of Partridge Meats." The extent of the issue is as yet unknown. All known players are listed below.

		NM	EX	VG
Common Player:		25.00	12.50	7.50
(1)	Don Gullett	25.00	12.50	7.50
(2)	Lee May	25.00	12.50	7.50
(3)	Denis Menke	25.00	12.50	7.50
(4)	Jim Merritt	25.00	12.50	7.50
(5)	Gary Nolan	25.00	12.50	7.50
(6)	Tony Perez	60.00	30.00	18.00
(7)	Bob Tolan	25.00	12.50	7.50

1922 Wm. Paterson

Believed to have been a Canadian candy premium, this 50-card set of 2" x 3-1/4" cards features black-and-white portrait or posed action photos with wide white borders. Beneath the photo is a card number, player name, team, and in two lines, "Wm. Paterson, Limited / Brantford, Canada". Backs are blank.

		NM	EX	VG
Complete Set (50):		10000.	5000.	3000.
Common Player:		125.00	60.00	40.00
1	Eddie Roush	200.00	100.00	60.00
2	Rube Marquard	200.00	100.00	60.00
3	Del Gainor	125.00	60.00	40.00
4	George Sisler	200.00	100.00	60.00
5	Joe Bush	125.00	60.00	40.00
6	Joe Oeschger	125.00	60.00	40.00
7	Willie Kamm	125.00	60.00	40.00
8	John Watson	125.00	60.00	40.00
9	Dolf Luque	150.00	75.00	45.00
10	Miller Huggins	200.00	100.00	60.00
11	Wally Schang	125.00	60.00	40.00
12	Bob Shawkey	125.00	60.00	40.00
13	Tris Speaker	250.00	125.00	75.00
14	Hugh McQuillan	125.00	60.00	40.00
15	"Long George" Kelly	200.00	100.00	60.00
16	Ray Schalk	200.00	100.00	60.00
17	Sam Jones	125.00	60.00	40.00
18	Grover Alexander	225.00	110.00	67.00
19	Bob Meusel	125.00	60.00	40.00
20	"Irish" Emil Meusel	125.00	60.00	40.00
21	Rogers Hornsby	250.00	125.00	75.00
22	Harry Heilmann	200.00	100.00	60.00
23	Heinie Groh	125.00	60.00	40.00
24	Frank Frisch	200.00	100.00	60.00
25	Babe Ruth	2000.	1000.	600.00
26	Jack Bentley	125.00	60.00	40.00
27	Everett Scott	125.00	60.00	40.00
28	Max Carey	200.00	100.00	60.00
29	Chick Fewster	125.00	60.00	40.00
30	Cy Williams	125.00	60.00	40.00
31	Burleigh Grimes	200.00	100.00	60.00
32	Waite Hoyt	200.00	100.00	60.00
33	Frank Snyder	125.00	60.00	40.00
34	Clyde Milan	125.00	60.00	40.00
35	Eddie Collins	200.00	100.00	60.00
36	Travis Jackson	200.00	100.00	60.00
37	Ken Williams	125.00	60.00	40.00
38	Dave Bancroft	200.00	100.00	60.00
39	Mike McNally	125.00	60.00	40.00
40	John McGraw	200.00	100.00	60.00
41	Art Nehf	125.00	60.00	40.00
42	"Rabbit" Maranville	200.00	100.00	60.00
43	Charlie Grimm	125.00	60.00	40.00
44	Joe Judge	125.00	60.00	40.00
45	Wally Pipp	125.00	60.00	40.00
46	Ty Cobb	1250.	625.00	375.00
47	Walter Johnson	750.00	375.00	225.00
48	Jake Daubert	125.00	60.00	40.00
49	Zack Wheat	200.00	100.00	60.00
50	Herb Pennock	200.00	100.00	60.00

1921 Pathe Freres Phonograph Co.

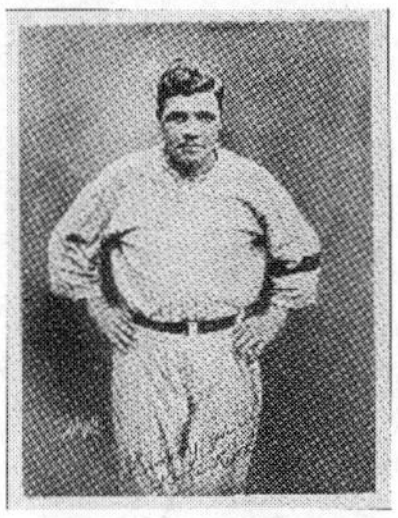

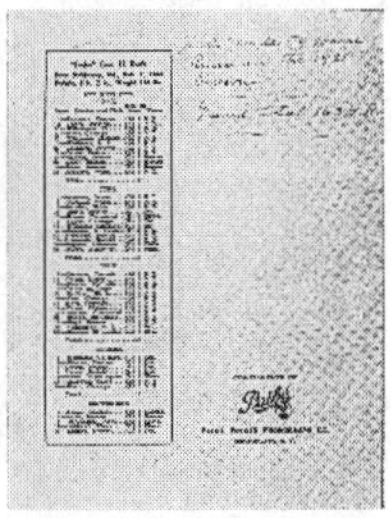

One of the rarest early-1920s Babe Ruth items is this premium photo issued by Pathe Freres Phonograph Co. of Brooklyn. Ruth is pictured bareheaded in a pinstriped uniform on the front of this approximately 7" x 9" card, printed in green and gray tones with a white border. A photo credit to White Studios of New York is given on the front and there is a facsimile autograph at bottom front. The black-and-white back has a listing of Ruth's 1920 homers in a box at left, and a Pathe ad at bottom-right.

	NM	EX	VG
Babe Ruth	2000.	1000.	600.00

1910 PC796 Sepia Postcards

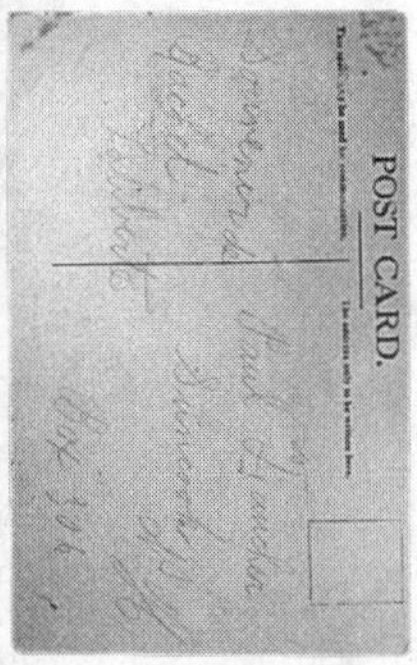

The manufacturer of these sepia-toned 3-1/2" x 5-1/2" postcards is unknown, but most of the photos utilized are familiar from other card issues of the era. Fronts have the player name at bottom in fancy capital letters. Backs have a standard divided postcard indicia. The set was given the PC796 designation in the "American Card Catalog." The unnumbered cards are checklisted here alphabetically.

		NM	EX	VG
Complete Set (25):		7000.	3150.	1750.
Common Player:		150.00	60.00	30.00
(1)	Roger Bresnahan	300.00	120.00	60.00
(2)	Al Bridwell	150.00	60.00	30.00

(3)	Mordecai Brown	300.00	120.00	60.00
(4)	Frank Chance	300.00	120.00	60.00
(5)	Hal Chase	200.00	80.00	40.00
(6)	Ty Cobb	1000.	400.00	200.00
(7)	Ty Cobb, Honus Wagner	825.00	330.00	165.00
(8)	Eddie Collins	300.00	120.00	60.00
(9)	Sam Crawford	300.00	120.00	60.00
(10)	Art Devlin	150.00	60.00	30.00
(11)	Red Dooin	150.00	60.00	30.00
(12)	Johnny Evers, Germany Schaefer	200.00	80.00	40.00
(13)	Sam Frock	150.00	60.00	30.00
(14)	George Gibson	150.00	60.00	30.00
(15)	Artie Hoffman (Hofman)	150.00	60.00	30.00
(16)	Walter Johnson	600.00	240.00	120.00
(17)	Nap Lajoie	300.00	120.00	60.00
(18)	Harry Lord	150.00	60.00	30.00
(19)	Christy Mathewson	750.00	300.00	150.00
(20)	Orval Overall	150.00	60.00	30.00
(21)	Eddie Plank	300.00	120.00	60.00
(22)	Tris Speaker	400.00	160.00	80.00
(23)	Gabby Street	150.00	60.00	30.00
(24)	Honus Wagner	750.00	300.00	150.00
(25)	Ed Walsh	300.00	120.00	60.00

1869 Peck & Snyder Cincinnati Red Stockings

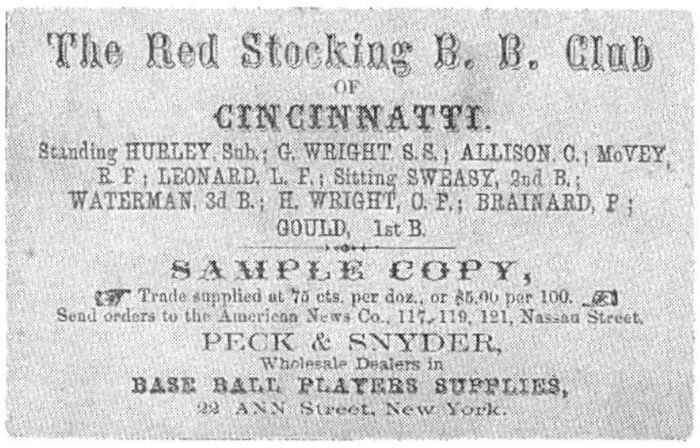
The Red Stocking B. B. Club
OF
CINCINNATTI.
Standing HURLEY, Sub.; G. WRIGHT S. S.; ALLISON, C.; McVEY, R. F.; LEONARD, L. F.; Sitting SWEASY, 2nd B.; WATERMAN, 3d B.; H. WRIGHT, C. F.; BRAINARD, P.; GOULD, 1st B.
SAMPLE COPY,
Trade supplied at 75 cts. per doz., or $5.00 per 100.
Send orders to the American News Co., 117, 119, 121, Nassau Street.
PECK & SNYDER,
Wholesale Dealers in
BASE BALL PLAYERS SUPPLIES,
22 ANN Street, New York.

Many consider this to be the first true baseball card in that it was produced in large quantities (relative to the cabinets and carte de visites of the era) and offered to firms wishing to place their advertising on the back. The 3-15/16" x 2-3/8" card features a sepia team photo on front of baseball's first real professional team, including Hall of Famers George and Harry Wright. The Peck & Snyder ad back is the most commonly found, but others are known, including a back which lists only the team's line-up.

	NM	EX	VG
Cincinnati Red Stocking team photo	22000.	11000.	6600.

1963 Pepsi-Cola Colt .45's

This issue was distributed regionally in Texas in bottled six-packs of Pepsi. The cards were issued on 2-3/8" x 9-1/8" panels, which were fit in between the bottles in each carton. Values quoted in the checklist below are for complete panels. A standard 2-3/8" x 3-3/4" card was printed on each panel, which also included promos for Pepsi and the Colt .45's, as well as a team schedule. Card fronts are black-and-white posed action photos with blue and red trim. Player name and position and Pepsi logo are also included. Card backs offer player statistics and career highlights. The John Bateman card, which was apparently never distributed publicly, is among the rarest collectible baseball cards of the 1960s. The complete set price does not include the Bateman card. The unnumbered cards are checklisted here alphabetically.

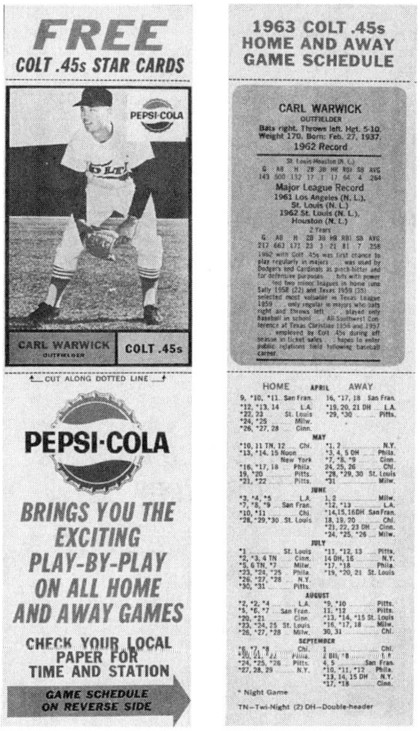

		NM	EX	VG
Complete Set (16):		2200.	1100.	650.00
Common Player:		12.50	6.25	3.75
(1)	Bob Aspromonte	12.50	6.25	3.75
(2)	John Bateman	1250.	625.00	375.00
(3)	Bob Bruce	12.50	6.25	3.75
(4)	Jim Campbell	12.50	6.25	3.75
(5)	Dick Farrell	12.50	6.25	3.75
(6)	Ernie Fazio	12.50	6.25	3.75
(7)	Carroll Hardy	12.50	6.25	3.75
(8)	J.C. Hartman	12.50	6.25	3.75
(9)	Ken Johnson	12.50	6.25	3.75
(10)	Bob Lillis	12.50	6.25	3.75
(11)	Don McMahon	12.50	6.25	3.75
(12)	Pete Runnels	20.00	10.00	6.00
(13)	Al Spangler	12.50	6.25	3.75
(14)	Rusty Staub	25.00	12.50	7.50
(15)	Johnny Temple	12.50	6.25	3.75
(16)	Carl Warwick	100.00	50.00	30.00

1977 Pepsi-Cola Baseball Stars

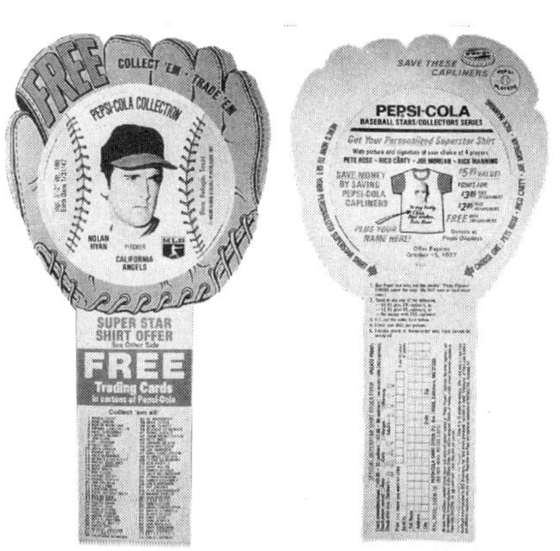

An Ohio regional promotion (the checklist is extra heavy with Indians and Reds players), large numbers of these cards found their way into hobby dealers' hands. Designed to be inserted into cartons of soda, the cards have a 3-3/8" diameter central disc attached with perforations to a baseball glove design. A tab beneath the glove contains the checklist (the card discs themselves are unnumbered) and a coupon on back for ordering a player t-shirt, the offer for which is made on the back of the player disc. The players' association logo appears on front, but the producer, Mike Schechter Associates, did not seek licensing by Major League Baseball, with the result that uniform logos have been removed from the black-and-white player photos. Prices shown are for complete glove/disc/tab cards. Values for unattached player discs would be no more than one-half of those shown. The discs of Reggie Jackson and Mike Schmidt can be found with either orange, green, purple or light blue side panels; the other player discs are known in only one color each.

		NM	EX	VG
Complete Set (72):		100.00	50.00	30.00
Common Player:		.75	.40	.25
1	Robin Yount	7.50	3.75	2.25
2	Rod Carew	3.75	2.00	1.25
3	Butch Wynegar	.75	.40	.25
4	Manny Sanguillen	.75	.40	.25
5	Mike Hargrove	.75	.40	.25
6	Larvel (Larvell) Blanks	.75	.40	.25
7	Jim Kern	.75	.40	.25
8	Pat Dobson	.75	.40	.25
9	Rico Carty	.75	.40	.25
10	John Grubb	.75	.40	.25
11	Buddy Bell	.75	.40	.25
12	Rick Manning	.75	.40	.25
13	Dennis Eckersley	2.00	1.00	.60
14	Wayne Garland	.75	.40	.25
15	Dave LaRoche	.75	.40	.25
16	Rick Waits	.75	.40	.25
17	Ray Fosse	.75	.40	.25
18	Frank Duffy	.75	.40	.25
19	Duane Kuiper	.75	.40	.25
20	Jim Palmer	3.75	2.00	1.25
21	Fred Lynn	1.00	.50	.30
22	Carlton Fisk	3.75	2.00	1.25
23	Carl Yastrzemski	5.00	2.50	1.50
24	Nolan Ryan	12.50	6.25	3.75
25	Bobby Grich	.75	.40	.25
26	Ralph Garr	.75	.40	.25
27	Richie Zisk	.75	.40	.25
28	Ron LeFlore	.75	.40	.25
29	Rusty Staub	1.25	.60	.40
30	Mark Fidrych	1.25	.60	.40
31	Willie Horton	.75	.40	.25
32	George Brett	9.00	4.50	2.75
33	Amos Otis	.75	.40	.25
34	Reggie Jackson	6.00	3.00	1.75
35	Don Gullett	.75	.40	.25
36	Thurman Munson	2.50	1.25	.70
37	Al Hrabosky	.75	.40	.25
38	Mike Tyson	.75	.40	.25
39	Gene Tenace	.75	.40	.25
40	George Hendrick	.75	.40	.25
41	Chris Speier	.75	.40	.25
42	John Montefusco	.75	.40	.25
43	Pete Rose	10.00	5.00	3.00
44	Johnny Bench	7.00	3.50	2.00
45	Dan Driessen	.75	.40	.25
46	Joe Morgan	3.75	2.00	1.25
47	Dave Concepcion	.75	.40	.25
48	George Foster	.90	.45	.25
49	Cesar Geronimo	.75	.40	.25
50	Ken Griffey	.90	.45	.25
51	Gary Nolan	.75	.40	.25
52	Santo Alcala	.75	.40	.25
53	Jack Billingham	.75	.40	.25
54	Pedro Borbon	.75	.40	.25
55	Rawly Eastwick	.75	.40	.25
56	Fred Norman	.75	.40	.25
57	Pat Zachary (Zachry)	.75	.40	.25
58	Jeff Burroughs	.75	.40	.25
59	Manny Trillo	.75	.40	.25
60	Bob Watson	.75	.40	.25
61	Steve Garvey	1.25	.60	.40
62	Don Sutton	3.75	2.00	1.25
63	John Candelaria	.75	.40	.25
64	Willie Stargell	3.75	2.00	1.25
65	Jerry Reuss	.75	.40	.25
66	Dave Cash	.75	.40	.25
67	Tom Seaver	3.75	2.00	1.25
68	Jon Matlock	.75	.40	.25
69	Dave Kingman	.90	.45	.25
70	Mike Schmidt	9.00	4.50	2.75
71	Jay Johnstone	.75	.40	.25
72	Greg Luzinski	.75	.40	.25

1977 Pepsi Cincinnati Reds playing cards

Similar to a multi-sport series produced by Cubic Corp. (see also), these playing card sets feature on back the pencil drawings of Al Landsman. Each boxed deck featured one Reds star player within a red border. Also on each card back is a facsimile autograph and Pepsi logo. Cards are standard bridge size (2-1/4" x 3-1/2") with rounded corners. Decks were available by sending in 250 16-oz. Pepsi cap liners or a combination of cash and cap liners.

		NM	EX	VG
Complete Set, Boxed Decks:		60.00	30.00	18.00
Complete Set, One Card Each:		15.00	7.50	4.50
Common Boxed Deck:		20.00	10.00	6.00
Common Single Card:		5.00	2.50	1.50
(1)	Johnny Bench (boxed deck)	25.00	12.50	7.50
(1)	Johnny Bench (single card)	7.50	3.75	2.25
(2)	Joe Morgan (boxed deck)	20.00	10.00	6.00
(2)	Joe Morgan (single card)	5.00	2.50	1.50
(3)	Pete Rose (boxed deck)	30.00	15.00	9.00
(3)	Pete Rose (single card)	10.00	5.00	3.00

1978 Pepsi-Cola Superstars

In its second year of producing carton-stuffer baseball cards, Cincinnati area Pepsi bottlers issued a 40-card set featuring 25 Reds players and 15 other major league stars. The entire carton insert measured 2-1/8" x 9-1/2". Besides the baseball card at top, there is a checklist and mail-in offer for playing cards featuring Johnny Bench, Joe Morgan and Pete Rose. The card element at the top measured 2-1/8" x 2-1/2". A player portrait, with uniform logos airbrushed off, is featured in black-and-white in a white star on a red background. The Major League Baseball Player's Association logo appears in dark blue in the upper-left. Printed in black below are the player's name, team, position, birthdate and place and a few 1977 stats. On back, printed in red, white and blue, is part of the offer for the playing cards. Large quantities of this set found their way into hobby hands and they remain common today.

		NM	EX	VG
Complete Set (40):		60.00	30.00	18.00
Common Player:		.50	.25	.15
(1)	Sparky Anderson	2.00	1.00	.60
(2)	Rick Auerbach	.50	.25	.15
(3)	Doug Bair	.50	.25	.15
(4)	Buddy Bell	.50	.25	.15
(5)	Johnny Bench	4.00	2.00	1.25
(6)	Bill Bonham	.50	.25	.15
(7)	Pedro Borbon	.50	.25	.15
(8)	Larry Bowa	.50	.25	.15
(9)	George Brett	6.00	3.00	1.75
(10)	Jeff Burroughs	.50	.25	.15
(11)	Rod Carew	2.00	1.00	.60
(12)	Dave Collins	.50	.25	.15
(13)	Dave Concepcion	.50	.25	.15
(14)	Dan Driessen	.50	.25	.15
(15)	George Foster	.50	.25	.15
(16)	Steve Garvey	1.00	.50	.30
(17)	Cesar Geronimo	.50	.25	.15
(18)	Ken Griffey	.75	.40	.25
(19)	Ken Henderson	.50	.25	.15
(20)	Tom Hume	.50	.25	.15
(21)	Reggie Jackson	4.00	2.00	1.25
(22)	Junior Kennedy	.50	.25	.15
(23)	Dave Kingman	.60	.30	.20
(24)	Ray Knight	.50	.25	.15
(25)	Jerry Koosman	.50	.25	.15
(26)	Mike Lum	.50	.25	.15
(27)	Bill Madlock	.50	.25	.15
(28)	Joe Morgan	2.00	1.00	.60
(29)	Paul Moskau	.50	.25	.15
(30)	Fred Norman	.50	.25	.15
(31)	Jim Palmer	2.00	1.00	.60
(32)	Pete Rose	7.50	3.75	2.25
(33)	Nolan Ryan	12.00	6.00	3.50
(34)	Manny Sarmiento	.50	.25	.15
(35)	Tom Seaver	2.50	1.25	.70
(36)	Ted Simmons	.50	.25	.15
(37)	Dave Tomlin	.50	.25	.15
(38)	Don Werner	.50	.25	.15
(39)	Carl Yastrzemski	4.00	2.00	1.25
(40)	Richie Zisk	.50	.25	.15

1980 Pepsi-Cola All-Stars Prototypes

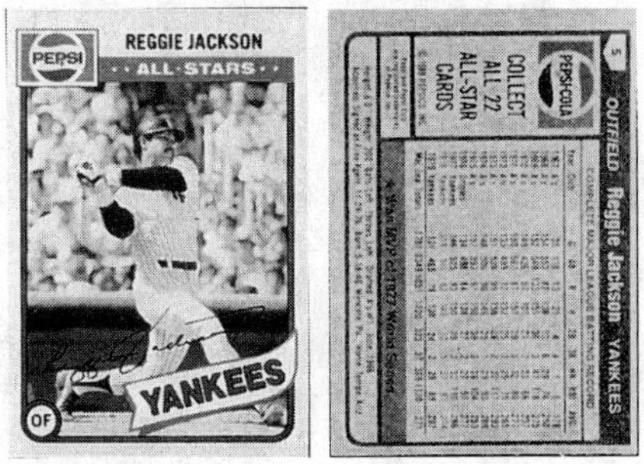

These prototype cards were prepared by Topps and Mike Schechter Associates for a proposed Pepsi promotion. Three sets of the cards were given to Pepsi officials for consideration but only two were returned when the deal fell through. The third sheet was cut up and sold into the hobby. The Pepsi cards share the format of Topps' regular 1980 issue, although Pepsi logos have been added on front and back, name and banner colors changed on front and a position circle added. The release of the two archived sets in some sort of charitable sale remains a possibility, which would probably have a negative effect on the values of these currently unique specimens.

		NM	EX	VG
Common Player:		600.00	300.00	180.00
1	Rod Carew	2200.	1100.	660.00
2	Paul Molitor	2200.	1100.	660.00
3	George Brett	3000.	1500.	900.00
4	Robin Yount	2500.	1250.	750.00
5	Reggie Jackson	2750.	1375.	825.00
6	Fred Lynn	1200.	600.00	360.00
7	Ken Landreaux	600.00	300.00	180.00
8	Jim Sundberg	600.00	300.00	180.00
9	Ron Guidry (one known, other two cut from sheets and destroyed; negatives reversed)	2400.	1200.	720.00
10	Jim Palmer	2500.	1250.	750.00
11	Goose Gossage	850.00	425.00	255.00
12	Keith Hernandez	650.00	325.00	195.00
13	Dave Lopes	600.00	300.00	180.00
14	Mike Schmidt	3500.	1750.	1050.
15	Garry Templeton	600.00	300.00	180.00
16	Dave Parker	750.00	375.00	225.00
17	George Foster	750.00	375.00	225.00
18	Dave Winfield	2750.	1375.	825.00
19	Ted Simmons	600.00	300.00	180.00
20	Steve Carlton	2200.	1100.	660.00
21	J.R. Richard	750.00	375.00	225.00
22	Bruce Sutter	600.00	300.00	180.00

1961 Peters Meats Twins

This set, featuring the first-year 1961 Minnesota Twins, is in a large, 4-5/8" x 3-1/2", format. Cards are on thick cardboard and heavily waxed, as they were used as partial packaging for the company's meat products. Card fronts feature full-color photos, team and Peters logos, and biographical information. The cards are blank-backed. Prices shown are for cards without the surrounding packaging. Uncut cards are worth 1.5X to 2X the prices shown.

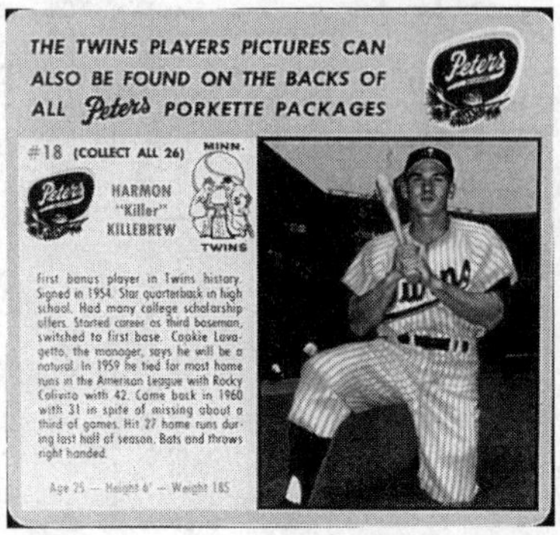

		NM	EX	VG
Complete Set (26):		750.00	375.00	225.00
Common Player:		24.00	12.00	7.25
1	Zoilo Versalles	32.00	16.00	9.50
2	Eddie Lopat	30.00	15.00	9.00
3	Pedro Ramos	25.00	12.50	7.50
4	Charles "Chuck" Stobbs	25.00	12.50	7.50
5	Don Mincher	25.00	12.50	7.50
6	Jack Kralick	25.00	12.50	7.50
7	Jim Kaat	60.00	30.00	18.00
8	Hal Naragon	25.00	12.50	7.50
9	Don Lee	25.00	12.50	7.50
10	Harry "Cookie" Lavagetto	25.00	12.50	7.50
11	Tom "Pete" Whisenant	25.00	12.50	7.50
12	Elmer Valo	25.00	12.50	7.50
13	Ray Moore	25.00	12.50	7.50
14	Billy Gardner	25.00	12.50	7.50
15	Lenny Green	25.00	12.50	7.50
16	Sam Mele	25.00	12.50	7.50
17	Jim Lemon	25.00	12.50	7.50
18	Harmon "Killer" Killebrew	225.00	112.00	67.00
19	Paul Giel	25.00	12.50	7.50
20	Reno Bertoia	25.00	12.50	7.50
21	Clyde McCullough	25.00	12.50	7.50
22	Earl Battey	32.00	16.00	9.50
23	Camilo Pascual	32.00	16.00	9.50
24	Dan Dobbek	25.00	12.50	7.50
25	Joe "Valvy" Valdivielso	25.00	12.50	7.50
26	Billy Consolo	25.00	12.50	7.50

1938-53 Philadelphia A's team-issue photos

For a decade and a half the Philadelphia A's issued souvenir sets of black-and-white player photos. All are in a 7" x 10" format but the size of picture, the use of posed action and portrait photos and the type style of the name printed in the bottom border differ among the years. In many cases, pictures were re-issued year after year making it impossible 50 years later to reconstruct the composition of any particular year's issue. The unnumbered pictures are checklisted here alphabetically. Multiple player listings are the result of known pose variations.

		NM	EX	VG
Common Player:		6.00	3.00	1.75
(1)	Joe Astroth	6.00	3.00	1.75
(2)	Loren Babe	6.00	3.00	1.75
(3)	Johnny Babich	6.00	3.00	1.75
(4)	Bill Beckman	6.00	3.00	1.75
(5)	Joe Berry	6.00	3.00	1.75
(6)	Herman Besse	6.00	3.00	1.75
(7)	Hal Bevan	6.00	3.00	1.75
(8)	Henry Biasatti	6.00	3.00	1.75
(9)	Don Black	6.00	3.00	1.75
(10)	Lena Blackburne	6.00	3.00	1.75
(11)	Buddy Blair	6.00	3.00	1.75
(12)	Don Bollweg	6.00	3.00	1.75
(13)	Al Brancato	6.00	3.00	1.75
(14)	Lou Brissie	6.00	3.00	1.75
(15)	Earle Brucker	6.00	3.00	1.75
(16)	Earle Brucker	6.00	3.00	1.75
(17)	Earle Brucker	6.00	3.00	1.75
(18)	William Burgo	7.50	3.75	2.25
(19)	Joe Burns	6.00	3.00	1.75

(20)	Ed Burtschy	6.00	3.00	1.75
(21)	Harry Byrd	6.00	3.00	1.75
(22)	Fred Caligiuri	9.00	4.50	2.75
(23)	George Caster	6.00	3.00	1.75
(24)	Jim Castiglia	6.00	3.00	1.75
(25)	Sam Chapman	6.00	3.00	1.75
(26)	Sam Chapman	6.00	3.00	1.75
(27)	Sam Chapman	6.00	3.00	1.75
(28)	Russ Christopher	6.00	3.00	1.75
(29)	Joe Coleman	6.00	3.00	1.75
(30)	Eddie Collins Jr.	7.50	3.75	2.25
(31)	Lawrence Davis	6.00	3.00	1.75
(32)	Tom Davis	6.00	3.00	1.75
(33)	Chubby Dean	6.00	3.00	1.75
(34)	Joe DeMaestri	6.00	3.00	1.75
(35)	Russ Derry	6.00	3.00	1.75
(36)	Art Ditmar	6.00	3.00	1.75
(37)	Jimmy Dykes	6.00	3.00	1.75
(38)	Bob Estalella	6.00	3.00	1.75
(39)	Nick Etten	6.00	3.00	1.75
(40)	Ferris Fain	9.00	4.50	2.75
(41)	Tom Ferrick	6.00	3.00	1.75
(42)	Jim Finigan	6.00	3.00	1.75
(43)	Lewis Flick	6.00	3.00	1.75
(44)	Jesse Flores	6.00	3.00	1.75
(45)	Richard Fowler	6.00	3.00	1.75
(46)	Nelson Fox	15.00	7.50	4.50
(47)	Marion Fricano	6.00	3.00	1.75
(48)	Joe Gantenbein	6.00	3.00	1.75
(49)	Mike Guerra	6.00	3.00	1.75
(50)	Irv Hadley	6.00	3.00	1.75
(51)	Irv Hall	6.00	3.00	1.75
(52)	Luke Hamlin	6.00	3.00	1.75
(53)	Gene Handley	6.00	3.00	1.75
(54)	Bob Harris	6.00	3.00	1.75
(55)	Charlie Harris	6.00	3.00	1.75
(56)	Luman Harris	6.00	3.00	1.75
(57)	Luman Harris	6.00	3.00	1.75
(58)	Frank Hayes	6.00	3.00	1.75
(59)	Bob Johnson	7.50	3.75	2.25
(60)	Bob Johnson	7.50	3.75	2.25
(61)	Eddie Joost	6.00	3.00	1.75
(62)	David Keefe	6.00	3.00	1.75
(63)	George Kell	10.00	5.00	3.00
(64)	Everett Kell	7.50	3.75	2.25
(65)	Alex Kellner	6.00	3.00	1.75
(66)	Alex Kellner	6.00	3.00	1.75
(67)	Lou Klein	6.00	3.00	1.75
(68)	Bill Knickerbocker	6.00	3.00	1.75
(69)	Jack Knott	6.00	3.00	1.75
(70)	Mike Kreevich	6.00	3.00	1.75
(71)	John Kucab	6.00	3.00	1.75
(72)	Paul Lehner	6.00	3.00	1.75
(73)	Bill Lillard	6.00	3.00	1.75
(74)	Lou Limmer	6.00	3.00	1.75
(75)	Lou Limmer	6.00	3.00	1.75
(76)	Dario Lodigiani	6.00	3.00	1.75
(77)	Connie Mack	10.00	5.00	3.00
(78)	Connie Mack	10.00	5.00	3.00
(79)	Connie Mack	10.00	5.00	3.00
(80)	Connie Mack	10.00	5.00	3.00
(81)	Earle Mack	7.50	3.75	2.25
(82)	Earle Mack	7.50	3.75	2.25
(83)	Felix Mackiewicz	6.00	3.00	1.75
(84)	Hank Majeski	6.00	3.00	1.75
(85)	Hank Majeski	6.00	3.00	1.75
(86)	Phil Marchildon	6.00	3.00	1.75
(87)	Phil Marchildon	6.00	3.00	1.75
(88)	Phil Marchildon	6.00	3.00	1.75
(89)	Morris Martin	6.00	3.00	1.75
(90)	Barney McCosky	6.00	3.00	1.75
(91)	Bennie McCoy	6.00	3.00	1.75
(92)	Les McCrabb	6.00	3.00	1.75
(93)	Bill McGhee	9.00	4.50	2.75
(94)	George McQuinn	6.00	3.00	1.75
(95)	Charlie Metro	6.00	3.00	1.75
(96)	Cass Michaels	6.00	3.00	1.75
(97)	Dee Miles	6.00	3.00	1.75
(98)	Wally Moses	6.00	3.00	1.75
(99)	Wally Moses	6.00	3.00	1.75
(100)	Ray Murray	6.00	3.00	1.75
(101)	Bill Nagel	6.00	3.00	1.75
(102)	Bobo Newsom	6.00	3.00	1.75
(103)	Skeeter Newsome	6.00	3.00	1.75
(104)	Hal Peck	6.00	3.00	1.75
(105)	Dave Philley	6.00	3.00	1.75
(106)	Cotton Pippen	6.00	3.00	1.75
(107)	Arnie Portocarrero	6.00	3.00	1.75
(108)	Nelson Potter	6.00	3.00	1.75
(109)	Vic Power	6.00	3.00	1.75
(110)	Jim Pruett	6.00	3.00	1.75
(111)	Bill Renna	6.00	3.00	1.75
(112)	Al Robertson	6.00	3.00	1.75
(113)	Ed Robinson	6.00	3.00	1.75
(114)	Buddy Rosar	6.00	3.00	1.75
(115)	Buddy Rosar	6.00	3.00	1.75
(116)	Al Rubeling	6.00	3.00	1.75
(117)	Joseph Rullo	9.00	4.50	2.75
(118)	Carl Scheib	6.00	3.00	1.75
(119)	Bill Shantz	7.50	3.75	2.25
(120)	Bob Shantz	9.00	4.50	2.75
(121)	Newman Shirley	6.00	3.00	1.75
(122)	Dick Siebert	6.00	3.00	1.75
(123)	Dick Siebert	6.00	3.00	1.75
(124)	Al Simmons	12.00	6.00	3.50
(125)	Al Simmons	12.00	6.00	3.50
(126)	Tuck Stainback	6.00	3.00	1.75
(127)	Pete Suder	6.00	3.00	1.75
(128)	Pete Suder	6.00	3.00	1.75
(129)	Bob Swift	6.00	3.00	1.75
(130)	Keith Thomas	6.00	3.00	1.75
(131)	Eric Tipton	6.00	3.00	1.75
(132)	Bob Trice	6.00	3.00	1.75
(133)	Elmer Valo	6.00	3.00	1.75
(134)	Elmer Valo	6.00	3.00	1.75
(135)	Ozzie Van Brabant	9.00	4.50	2.75
(136)	Porter Vaughan	6.00	3.00	1.75
(137)	Harold Wagner	6.00	3.00	1.75
(138)	Harold Wagner	6.00	3.00	1.75
(139)	Jack Wallaesa	6.00	3.00	1.75
(140)	Johnny Welaj	6.00	3.00	1.75
(141)	Don White	6.00	3.00	1.75
(142)	Jo Jo White	6.00	3.00	1.75
(143)	Roger Wolff	6.00	3.00	1.75
(144)	Tom Wright	6.00	3.00	1.75
(145)	Gus Zernial	9.00	4.50	2.75
(146)	1938 A's team	15.00	7.50	4.50
(147)	1939 A's team	15.00	7.50	4.50
(148)	1940 A's team	15.00	7.50	4.50
(149)	1941 A's team	15.00	7.50	4.50
(150)	1942 A's team	15.00	7.50	4.50
(151)	1943 A's team	15.00	7.50	4.50
(152)	1944 A's team	15.00	7.50	4.50
(153)	1945 A's team	15.00	7.50	4.50
(154)	1946 A's team	12.00	6.00	3.50
(155)	1949 A's team	12.00	6.00	3.50
(156)	Shibe Park	15.00	7.50	4.50

1952 Philadelphia A's/ Phillies Player Pins

Only players on the Philadelphia A's and Phillies are found in this series of player pin-backs. The 1-3/4" diameter celluloid pins have black-and-white player portraits on front. The player name is printed in block letters across his shoulders, while the team name is printed in script across the chest. It is possible other player pins may exist. The unnumbered pieces are checklisted here in alphabetical order.

		NM	EX	VG
	Common Player:	40.00	20.00	12.00
	Philadelphia Athletics			
(1)	Bobby Shantz	45.00	22.00	13.50
(2)	Gus Zernial	45.00	22.00	13.50
	Philadelphia Phillies			
(1)	Richie Ashburn	60.00	30.00	18.00
(2)	Del Ennis	40.00	20.00	12.00
(3)	Granny Hamner	40.00	20.00	12.00
(4)	Willie Jones	40.00	20.00	12.00
(5)	Jim Konstanty	40.00	20.00	12.00
(6)	Robin Roberts	75.00	37.00	22.00
(7)	Andy Seminick	40.00	20.00	12.00
(8)	Curt Simmons	40.00	20.00	12.00
(9)	Eddie Waitkus	40.00	20.00	12.00

1949-50 Philadelphia Bulletin Pin-Ups

This series of 8" x 10" black-and-white portraits of A's and Phillies players, coaches and managers was issued in the Sunday rotogravure section of the Bulletin, in series of five or six per week. Each picture has a facsimile autgraph on front. The unnumbered pictures are checklisted here in alphabetical order, and may be incomplete.

		NM	EX	VG
	Complete Set (63):	300.00	150.00	90.00
	Common Player:	6.00	3.00	1.75
(1)	Rich Ashburn	15.00	7.50	4.50
(2)	Joe Astroth	6.00	3.00	1.75
(3)	Bennie Bengough	6.00	3.00	1.75
(4)	Henry Biasetti	6.00	3.00	1.75
(5)	Charles Bicknell	6.00	3.00	1.75
(6)	Bud Blattner	6.00	3.00	1.75
(7)	Hank Borowy	6.00	3.00	1.75
(8)	Leland (Lou) Brissie	6.00	3.00	1.75
(9)	Earle Brucker	6.00	3.00	1.75
(10)	Ralph Caballero	6.00	3.00	1.75
(11)	Sam Chapman	6.00	3.00	1.75
(12)	Emory Church	6.00	3.00	1.75
(13)	Joe Coleman	6.00	3.00	1.75
(14)	Dusty Cooke	6.00	3.00	1.75
(15)	Thomas O. Davis	6.00	3.00	1.75
(16)	Sylvester (Blix) Donnolly	6.00	3.00	1.75
(17)	Jimmy Dykes	6.00	3.00	1.75
(18)	Del Ennis	7.50	3.75	2.25
(19)	Ferris Fain	7.50	3.75	2.25
(20)	Dick Fowler	6.00	3.00	1.75
(21)	Nellie Fox	15.00	7.50	4.50
(22)	Mike Goliat	6.00	3.00	1.75
(23)	Mike Guerra	6.00	3.00	1.75
(24)	Granville Hamner	6.00	3.00	1.75
(25)	Charley Harris	6.00	3.00	1.75
(26)	Ken Heintzelman	6.00	3.00	1.75
(27)	Stan Hollmig	6.00	3.00	1.75
(28)	Ken Johnson	6.00	3.00	1.75
(29)	Willie Jones	6.00	3.00	1.75
(30)	Eddie Joost	6.00	3.00	1.75
(31)	Alex Kellner	6.00	3.00	1.75
(32)	Jim Konstanty	6.00	3.00	1.75
(33)	Stan Lopata	6.00	3.00	1.75
(34)	Connie Mack	15.00	7.50	4.50
(35)	Earle Mack	6.00	3.00	1.75
(36)	Hank Majeski	6.00	3.00	1.75
(37)	Phil Marchildon	6.00	3.00	1.75
(38)	Jackie Mayo	6.00	3.00	1.75
(39)	Bill McCahan	6.00	3.00	1.75
(40)	Barney McCosky	6.00	3.00	1.75
(41)	Russ Meyer	6.00	3.00	1.75
(42)	Bob Miller	6.00	3.00	1.75
(43)	Eddie Miller	6.00	3.00	1.75
(44)	Wally Moses	6.00	3.00	1.75
(45)	Bill Nicholson	6.00	3.00	1.75
(46)	Cy Perkins	6.00	3.00	1.75
(47)	Robin Roberts	15.00	7.50	4.50
(48)	Buddy Rosar	6.00	3.00	1.75
(49)	Schoolboy Rowe	7.50	3.75	2.25
(50)	Eddie Sawyer	6.00	3.00	1.75
(51)	Carl Scheib	6.00	3.00	1.75
(52)	Andy Seminick	6.00	3.00	1.75
(53)	Bobby Shantz	7.50	3.75	2.25
(54)	Ken Silvestri	6.00	3.00	1.75
(55)	Al Simmons	15.00	7.50	4.50
(56)	Curtis T. Simmons	9.00	4.50	2.75
(57)	Dick Sisler	6.00	3.00	1.75
(58)	Pete Suder	6.00	3.00	1.75
(59)	Ken Trinkle	6.00	3.00	1.75
(60)	Elmer Valo	6.00	3.00	1.75
(61)	Eddie Waitkus	6.00	3.00	1.75
(62)	Don White	6.00	3.00	1.75
(63)	Taft Wright	6.00	3.00	1.75

1950 Philadelphia Bulletin 1950 Phillies Panorama

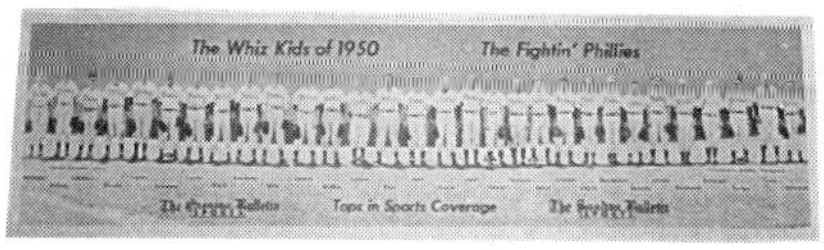

Characterized as "The Whiz Kids of 1950" and "The Fightin' Phillies," the members of the team are pictured on this 36" x 10" black-and-white panoramic insert from the Philadelphia Bulletin newspaper. Thirty members of the team and staff are pictured and identified.

	NM	EX	VG
1950 Philadelphia Phillies	200.00	100.00	60.00

1964 Philadelphia Bulletin Phillies Album

Color artwork by Jim Ponter is featured in this series of newspaper inserts. Portrait and action figures are combined on a blank-backed 8" x 10" format, along with a facsimile autograph. The unnumbered pictures are checklisted here alphabetically, two varieties of Jim Bunning's picture have been reported.

		NM	EX	VG
Complete Set (28):		225.00	110.00	65.00
Common Player:		8.00	4.00	2.50
(1)	Richie Allen	25.00	12.50	7.50
(2)	Ruben Amaro	8.00	4.00	2.50
(3)	Jack Baldschun	8.00	4.00	2.50
(4)	Dennis Bennett	8.00	4.00	2.50
(5)	John Boozer	8.00	4.00	2.50
(6)	Johnny Briggs	8.00	4.00	2.50
(7)	Jim Bunning	25.00	12.50	7.50
(8)	Jim Bunning	25.00	12.50	7.50
(9)	Johnny Callison	10.00	5.00	3.00
(10)	Danny Cater	8.00	4.00	2.50
(11)	Wes Covington	8.00	4.00	2.50
(12)	Ray Culp	8.00	4.00	2.50
(13)	Clay Dalrymple	8.00	4.00	2.50
(14)	Tony Gonzalez	8.00	4.00	2.50
(15)	John Herrnstein	8.00	4.00	2.50
(16)	Alex Johnson	8.00	4.00	2.50
(17)	Art Mahaffey	8.00	4.00	2.50
(18)	Gene Mauch	8.00	4.00	2.50
(19)	Vic Power	8.00	4.00	2.50
(20)	Ed Roebuck	8.00	4.00	2.50
(21)	Cookie Rojas	8.00	4.00	2.50
(22)	Bobby Shantz	8.00	4.00	2.50
(23)	Tony Taylor	8.00	4.00	2.50
(24)	Frank Thomas	8.00	4.00	2.50
(25)	Gus Triandos	8.00	4.00	2.50
(26)	Bobby Wine	8.00	4.00	2.50
(27)	Rick Wise	8.00	4.00	2.50

1909 Philadelphia Caramel (E95)

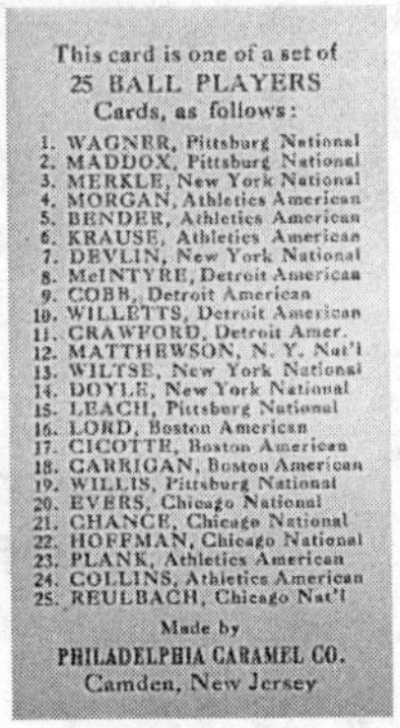

Similar in style to the many other early candy and caramel cards, the set designated as E95 by the American Card Catalog is a 25-card issue produced by the Philadelphia Caramel Co. (actually of Camden, N.J.) in 1909. The cards measure approximately 2-5/8" x 1-1/2" and contain a full-color player drawing. The back, which differentiates the set from other similar issues, checklists the 25 players in black ink and displays the Philadelphia Caramel Co. name at the bottom.

		NM	EX	VG
Complete Set (25):		10000.	5000.	3000.
Common Player:		125.00	62.00	37.00
(1)	Chief Bender	350.00	175.00	105.00
(2)	Bill Carrigan	125.00	62.00	37.00
(3)	Frank Chance	350.00	175.00	105.00
(4)	Ed Cicotte	235.00	115.00	70.00
(5)	Ty Cobb	2500.	1250.	750.00
(6)	Eddie Collins	350.00	175.00	105.00
(7)	Sam Crawford	350.00	175.00	105.00
(8)	Art Devlin	125.00	62.00	37.00
(9)	Larry Doyle	125.00	62.00	37.00
(10)	Johnny Evers	350.00	175.00	105.00
(11)	Solly Hoffman (Hofman)	125.00	62.00	37.00
(12)	Harry Krause	125.00	62.00	37.00
(13)	Tommy Leach	125.00	62.00	37.00
(14)	Harry Lord	125.00	62.00	37.00
(15)	Nick Maddox	125.00	62.00	37.00
(16)	Christy Matthewson (Mathewson)	1000.	500.00	300.00
(17)	Matty McIntyre	125.00	62.00	37.00
(18)	Fred Merkle	125.00	62.00	37.00
(19)	Cy Morgan	125.00	62.00	37.00
(20)	Eddie Plank	350.00	175.00	105.00
(21)	Ed Reulbach	125.00	62.00	37.00
(22)	Honus Wagner	1250.	625.00	375.00
(23)	Ed Willetts (Willett)	125.00	62.00	37.00
(24)	Vic Willis	125.00	62.00	37.00
(25)	Hooks Wiltse	125.00	62.00	37.00

1910 Philadelphia Caramel (E96)

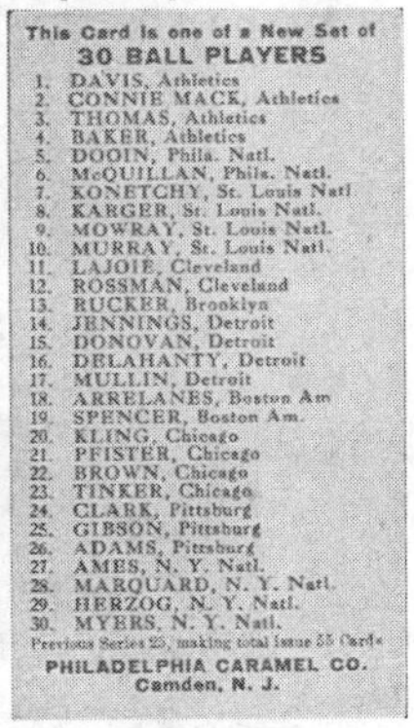

This set of 30 subjects, known by the ACC designation E96, was issued in 1910 by the Philadelphia Caramel Co. as a continuation of the E95 set of the previous year. The front design remained the same, but the two issues can be identified by the backs. The backs of the E96 cards are printed in red and carry a checklist of 30 players. There is also a line at the bottom advising "Previous series 25, making total issue 55 cards." Just below that appears "Philadelphia Caramel Co./Camden, N.J."

		NM	EX	VG
Complete Set (30):		5750.	2300.	1150.
Common Player:		140.00	56.00	28.00
(1)	Babe Adams	140.00	56.00	28.00
(2)	Red Ames	140.00	56.00	28.00
(3)	Frank Arrelanes (Arellanes)	140.00	56.00	28.00
(4)	Home Run Baker	400.00	160.00	80.00
(5)	Mordecai Brown	400.00	160.00	80.00
(6)	Fred Clark (Clarke)	400.00	160.00	80.00
(7)	Harry Davis	140.00	56.00	28.00
(8)	Wild Bill Donovan	140.00	56.00	28.00
(9)	Jim Delehanty	140.00	56.00	28.00
(10)	Red Dooin	140.00	56.00	28.00
(11)	George Gibson	140.00	56.00	28.00
(12)	Buck Herzog	140.00	56.00	28.00
(13)	Hugh Jennings	400.00	160.00	80.00
(14)	Ed Karger	140.00	56.00	28.00
(15)	Johnny Kling	140.00	56.00	28.00
(16)	Ed Konetchy	140.00	56.00	28.00
(17)	Nap Lajoie	425.00	170.00	85.00
(18)	Connie Mack	400.00	160.00	80.00
(19)	Rube Marquard	400.00	160.00	80.00
(20)	George McQuillan	140.00	56.00	28.00
(21)	Chief Meyers	140.00	56.00	28.00
(22)	Mike Mowrey	140.00	56.00	28.00
(23)	George Mullin	140.00	56.00	28.00
(24)	Red Murray	140.00	56.00	28.00
(25)	Jack Pfeister (Pfiester)	140.00	56.00	28.00
(26)	Nap Rucker	140.00	56.00	28.00
(27)	Claude Rossman	140.00	56.00	28.00
(28)	Tubby Spencer	140.00	56.00	28.00
(29)	Ira Thomas	140.00	56.00	28.00
(30)	Joe Tinker	400.00	160.00	80.00

1950 Philadelphia Inquirer Fightin' Phillies

As the Whiz Kids battled to a National League pennant the "Philadelphia Inquirer" instituted a set of cut-out baseball cards in the Sunday rotogravure editions during September. The 4-7/8" x 6-7/8" cards have colored portrait photos surrounded with a white border. A facsimile autograph is printed across the chest. In the bottom border are the player's formal name, position, career summary and the line, "Inquirer Fightin' Phillies Album". Backs have whatever articles or ads were on the next page. The unnumbered cards are printed here in alphabetical order.

		NM	EX	VG
Complete Set (24):		350.00	175.00	105.00
Common Player:		15.00	7.50	4.50
(1)	Richie Ashburn	35.00	17.50	10.50
(2)	James Henry Bloodworth	15.00	7.50	4.50
(3)	Ralph Joseph Caballero	15.00	7.50	4.50
(4)	Milo Candini	15.00	7.50	4.50
(5)	Emory Church	15.00	7.50	4.50
(6)	Sylvester Urban Donnelly	15.00	7.50	4.50
(7)	Delmer Ennis	15.00	7.50	4.50
(8)	Mike Mitchel Goliat (Mitchell)	15.00	7.50	4.50
(9)	Granville Wilbur Hamner	15.00	7.50	4.50
(10)	Kenneth Alphonse Heintzelman	15.00	7.50	4.50
(11)	Stanley Ernst Hollmig	15.00	7.50	4.50
(12)	Kenneth W. Johnson	15.00	7.50	4.50
(13)	Willie Edward Jones	15.00	7.50	4.50
(14)	Stanley Edward Lopata	15.00	7.50	4.50
(15)	Russell Charles Meyer	15.00	7.50	4.50
(16)	Robert Miller	15.00	7.50	4.50
(17)	William Beck Nicholson	15.00	7.50	4.50
(18)	Robin Evan Roberts	35.00	17.50	10.50
(19)	Andrew Wasal Seminick	15.00	7.50	4.50
(20)	Kenneth Joseph Silvestri	15.00	7.50	4.50
(21)	Curtis Thomas Simmons	15.00	7.50	4.50
(22)	Richard Alan Sisler	15.00	7.50	4.50
(23)	Edward Stephen Waitkus	15.00	7.50	4.50
(24)	Dick Whitman	15.00	7.50	4.50

1958-60 Philadelphia Phillies team issue

Thus far 18 different cards have been discovered in this format; it is likely the checklist here is not yet complete. Like many teams, the Phillies issued these cards to players and staff to honor fan requests for photos and autographs. The cards are 3-1/4" x 5-1/2" and have black-and-white portrait photos with white borders. Backs are blank. The unnumbered cards are listed here alphabetically.

		NM	EX	VG
Common Player:		6.00	3.00	1.75
(1)	Harry Anderson	6.00	3.00	1.75
(2)	Richie Ashburn	12.00	6.00	3.50
(3)	Ed Bouchee	6.00	3.00	1.75
(4)	Johnny Callison	8.00	4.00	2.50
(5)	Jim Coker	6.00	3.00	1.75
(6)	Clay Dalrymple	6.00	3.00	1.75
(7)	Tony Gonzalez	6.00	3.00	1.75
(8)	Granny Hamner	6.00	3.00	1.75
(9)	Willie Jones	6.00	3.00	1.75
(10)	Stan Lopata	6.00	3.00	1.75
(11)	Art Mahaffey	6.00	3.00	1.75
(12)	Gene Mauch	6.00	3.00	1.75
(13)	Wally Post	6.00	3.00	1.75
(14)	Robin Roberts	12.00	6.00	3.50
(15)	Eddie Sawyer	6.00	3.00	1.75

		NM	EX	VG
(16)	Ray Semproch	6.00	3.00	1.75
(17)	Chris Short	6.00	3.00	1.75
(18)	Curt Simmons	8.00	4.00	2.50

1964 Philadelphia Phillies Player Pins

Only four players are checklisted in this series, but it is expected more will be added in the future. These pinbacks are 2-3/16" in diameter and have black-and-white player portraits on front, on a white background. The player's name is printed at bottom in block letters.

		NM	EX	VG
Common Player:		20.00	10.00	6.00
(1)	Dick Allen	30.00	15.00	9.00
(2)	Jim Bunning	30.00	15.00	9.00
(3)	Chris Short	20.00	10.00	6.00
(4)	Roy Sievers	20.00	10.00	6.00

1967 Philadelphia Phillies Safe Driving

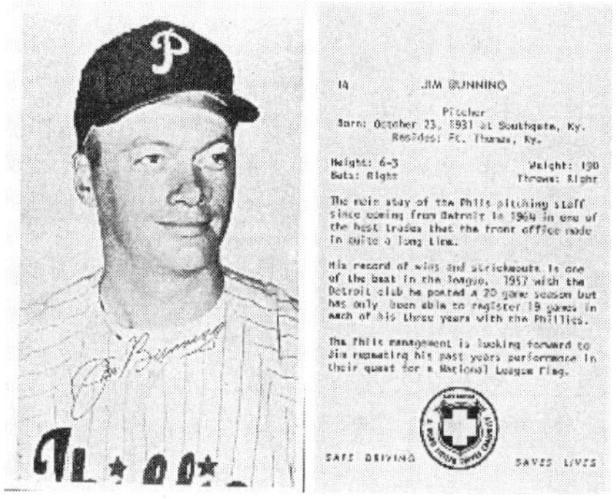

The honor of producing the only safety set of the 1960s goes to the Phillies for this traffic safety set. Measuring 2-3/4" x 4-1/2", the cards have a black-and-white front featuring the standard publicity photo of the player, with a facsimile autograph superimposed. Backs are printed in blue and include a few career and biographical details, along with the player's uniform number, by which the set is checklisted here. At bottom is a circle and shield design with the safety message.

		NM	EX	VG
Complete Set (13):		95.00	47.00	28.00
Common Player:		8.00	4.00	2.50
4	Gene Mauch	8.00	4.00	2.50
6	Johnny Callison	10.00	5.00	3.00
10	Bill White	10.00	5.00	3.00
11	Clay Dalrymple	8.00	4.00	2.50
12	Johnny Briggs	8.00	4.00	2.50
14	Jim Bunning	20.00	10.00	6.00
15	Dick Allen	18.00	9.00	5.50
16	Cookie Rojas	8.00	4.00	2.50
24	Dick Groat	10.00	5.00	3.00
25	Tony Gonzalez	8.00	4.00	2.50
37	Dick Ellsworth	8.00	4.00	2.50
41	Chris Short	8.00	4.00	2.50
46	Larry Jackson	8.00	4.00	2.50

1975 Philadelphia Phillies Photocards

These 3-1/4" x 5-1/2" blank-back, black-and-white cards, probably team issued, feature player portrait photos with only the player name in the white border at bottom. Fronts have a semi-gloss finish. It is likely the checklist, presented here alphabetically, is incomplete.

		NM	EX	VG
Common Player:		3.00	1.50	.90
(1)	Tom Hilgendorf	3.00	1.50	.90
(2)	Terry Harmon	3.00	1.50	.90
(3)	Joe Hoerner	3.00	1.50	.90
(4)	Tommy Hutton	3.00	1.50	.90
(5)	Jim Lonborg	4.00	2.00	1.25
(6)	John Oates	3.00	1.50	.90

1961 Phillies Cigar Mickey Mantle

This 5" x 7" blank-back color photo card of Mickey Mantle was part of a redemption program for Phillies cigars. For $3.39 and 20 cigar bands, a person could receive a Mickey Mantle model baseball glove and this "autographed" (facsimile) photo.

	NM	EX	VG
Mickey Mantle	125.00	62.50	37.50

1949-59 Photo-Film Fotos Pirates Postcards

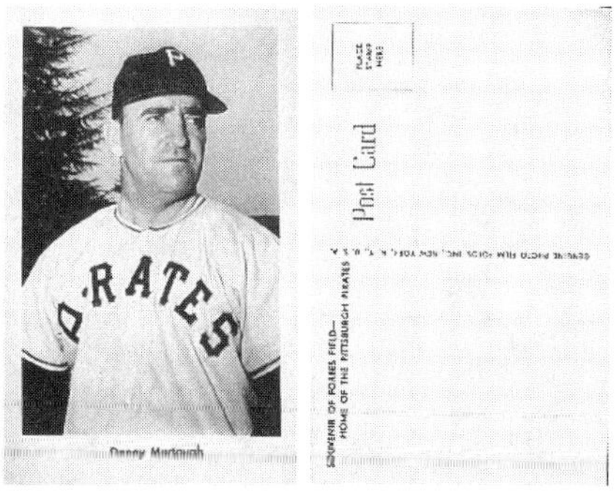

This series of black-and-white postcards was issued over a period which seems to have spanned 1949 through the 1950s. In standard 3-1/2" x 5-1/2" size, the cards have minor variations in the size and styles of type used for the player name in the bottom border on front and for the typography on the backs. Some cards are seen with pre-printed autographs on front. Most cards have printing on the back which includes versions of "Genuine Photo-Film Fotos, Inc., New York, N.Y., U.S.A." and "Souvenir of Forbes Field Home of the Pittsburgh Pirates." The checklist here, arranged alphabetically, indicates by the use of "a, b, c" and "d" suffixes different known poses for that particular player. Future additions to the checklist are likely, therefore no complete set price is given.

		NM	EX	VG
Common Player:		15.00	7.50	4.50
(1)	Gair Allie	15.00	7.50	4.50
(2)	Toby Atwell	15.00	7.50	4.50
(3)	Tony Bartirome	15.00	7.50	4.50
(4)	Ron Blackburn	15.00	7.50	4.50
(5)	Don Carlsen	15.00	7.50	4.50
(6a)	Pete Castiglione	15.00	7.50	4.50
(6b)	Pete Castiglione	15.00	7.50	4.50
(7)	Cliff Chambers	15.00	7.50	4.50
(8)	Dick Cole	15.00	7.50	4.50
(9)	Dale Coogan	15.00	7.50	4.50
(10)	Bobby Del Greco	15.00	7.50	4.50
(11a)	Roy Face	20.00	10.00	6.00
(11b)	Roy Face	20.00	10.00	6.00
(11c)	Roy Face	20.00	10.00	6.00
(12)	Hank Foiles	15.00	7.50	4.50
(13)	Gene Freese	15.00	7.50	4.50
(14a)	Bob Friend	17.00	8.50	5.00
(14b)	Bob Friend	17.00	8.50	5.00
(14c)	Bob Friend	17.00	8.50	5.00
(15)	Dick Groat	20.00	10.00	6.00
(16)	Fred Haney	15.00	7.50	4.50
(17)	Johnny Hopp	15.00	7.50	4.50
(18)	Ralph Kiner	50.00	25.00	15.00
(19a)	Ron Kline	15.00	7.50	4.50
(19b)	Ron Kline	15.00	7.50	4.50
(20)	Clem Koshorek	15.00	7.50	4.50
(21a)	Vern Law	17.00	8.50	5.00
(21b)	Vern Law	17.00	8.50	5.00
(21c)	Vern Law	17.00	8.50	5.00
(21d)	Vern Law	17.00	8.50	5.00
(22a)	Dale Long	15.00	7.50	4.50
(22b)	Dale Long	15.00	7.50	4.50
(23a)	Jerry Lynch	15.00	7.50	4.50
(23b)	Jerry Lynch	15.00	7.50	4.50
(24)	Bill MacDonald	15.00	7.50	4.50
(25a)	Bill Mazeroski	30.00	15.00	9.00
(25b)	Bill Mazeroski	30.00	15.00	9.00
(26)	Danny Murtaugh	15.00	7.50	4.50
(27)	Johnny O'Brien	15.00	7.50	4.50
(28)	Bob Oldis	15.00	7.50	4.50
(29)	Laurin Pepper	15.00	7.50	4.50
(30)	Hardy Peterson	15.00	7.50	4.50
(31)	Jack Phillips	15.00	7.50	4.50
(32)	Buddy Pritchard	15.00	7.50	4.50
(33)	Bob Purkey	15.00	7.50	4.50
(34)	Dino Restelli	15.00	7.50	4.50
(35)	Rip Sewell	15.00	7.50	4.50
(36)	Bob Smith	15.00	7.50	4.50
(37)	Red Swanson	15.00	7.50	4.50
(38a)	Frank Thomas	17.00	8.50	5.00
(38b)	Frank Thomas	17.00	8.50	5.00
(38c)	Frank Thomas	17.00	8.50	5.00
(39)	Bill Virdon	17.00	8.50	5.00
(40a)	Lee Walls	15.00	7.50	4.50
(40b)	Lee Walls	15.00	7.50	4.50
(41)	Junior Walsh	15.00	7.50	4.50
(42)	Pete Ward	15.00	7.50	4.50
(43)	Fred Waters	15.00	7.50	4.50
(44)	Bill Werle	15.00	7.50	4.50
(45)	Wally Westlake	15.00	7.50	4.50

1972 Photo Sports Co. L.A. Dodgers

This is the first known issue of a sports novelty marketed by Photo Sports Co., Los Angeles. The company is best known to collectors for its 1974 McDonald's promotional "Foto Balls" with player discs. The Dodgers set is similar in concept with a hinged plastic baseball which opens to reveal player discs. A "keyhole" punched at the bottom of the discs keeps them in place within the ball. The Dodgers never rolled out the project and surviving sets are extremely rare. Discs are 2-5/8" diameter with borderless color photos on front. Backs have player stats and the team logo. The unnumbered discs are checklisted here in alphabetical order.

		NM	EX	VG
Complete Set (ball and discs):		300.00	150.00	90.00
Common Player:		16.00	8.00	4.75
(1)	Red Adams	16.00	8.00	4.75

		NM	EX	VG
(2)	Walt Alston	35.00	17.50	10.50
(3)	Willie Crawford	16.00	8.00	4.75
(4)	Willie Davis	24.00	12.00	7.25
(5)	Al Downing	16.00	8.00	4.75
(6)	Jim Gilliam	24.00	12.00	7.25
(7)	Bill Grabarkewitz	16.00	8.00	4.75
(8)	Jim Lefebvre	16.00	8.00	4.75
(9)	Pete Mikkelsen	16.00	8.00	4.75
(10)	Manny Mota	18.00	9.00	5.50
(11)	Claude Osteen	16.00	8.00	4.75
(12)	Wes Parker	16.00	8.00	4.75
(13)	Duke Sims	16.00	8.00	4.75
(14)	Bill Singer	16.00	8.00	4.75
(15)	Bill Sudakis	16.00	8.00	4.75
(16)	Don Sutton	30.00	15.00	9.00
(17)	Bob Valentine	18.00	9.00	5.50
(18)	Maury Wills	22.00	11.00	6.50

1970 Pictures of Champions Baltimore Orioles

Issued in 1970 in the Baltimore area, this 16-card set pictures members of the Baltimore Orioles. The 2-1/8" x 2-3/4" cards feature black and white player photos on orange card stock. The method of distribution is unknown.

		NM	EX	VG
Complete Set (16):		60.00	30.00	18.00
Common Player:		1.00	.50	.30
4	Earl Weaver	6.00	3.00	1.75
5	Brooks Robinson	20.00	10.00	6.00
7	Mark Belanger	1.50	.70	.45
8	Andy Etchebarren	1.00	.50	.30
9	Don Buford	1.00	.50	.30
10	Ellie Hendricks	1.00	.50	.30
12	Dave May	1.00	.50	.30
15	Dave Johnson	2.00	1.00	.60
16	Dave McNally	1.50	.70	.45
20	Frank Robinson	16.00	8.00	4.75
22	Jim Palmer	14.00	7.00	4.25
24	Pete Richert	1.00	.50	.30
29	Dick Hall	1.00	.50	.30
35	Mike Cuellar	1.50	.70	.45
39	Eddie Watt	1.00	.50	.30
40	Dave Leonhard	1.00	.50	.30

1914 Piedmont Art Stamps (T330-2)

This series of "Piedmont Art Stamps" looks like a fragile version of the more popular T205 Gold Border tobacco cards of 1911, employing the same basic design on front. The Piedmont stamps measure 1-1/2" x 2-5/8". Though the backs of the stamps advertise "100 designs," 110 different players are known. And, because four of the players are pictured in two separate poses, there are actually 114 different stamps known, with new discoveries still being made. All but three of the subjects in the Piedmont set were taken from the T205 set; the exceptions being Joe Wood, Walt Blair and Bill Killifer. Because of their fragile composition, and since they are stamps that were frequently stuck to album pages, examples of Piedmont Art Stamps in Near Mint or better condition are very scarce. The back of the stamps offered a "handsome" album in exchange for 25 Piedmont coupons. The set has an American Card Catalog designation of T330-2.

		NM	EX	VG
Complete Set (114):		16000.	6400.	3200.
Common Player:		150.00	60.00	30.00
(1)	Leon K. Ames	150.00	60.00	30.00
(2)	Jimmy Archer	150.00	60.00	30.00
(3)	Jimmy Austin	150.00	60.00	30.00
(4)	Home Run Baker	250.00	100.00	50.00
(5)	Cy Barger	150.00	60.00	30.00
(6)	Jack Barry	150.00	60.00	30.00
(7)	Johnny Bates	150.00	60.00	30.00
(8)	Beals Becker	150.00	60.00	30.00
(9)	Chief Bender	250.00	100.00	50.00
(10)	Bob Bescher	150.00	60.00	30.00
(11)	Joe Birmingham	150.00	60.00	30.00
(12)	Walt Blair	150.00	60.00	30.00
(13)	Roger Bresnahan	250.00	100.00	50.00
(14)	Al Bridwell	150.00	60.00	30.00
(15)	Mordecai Brown	250.00	100.00	50.00
(16)	Bobby Byrne	150.00	60.00	30.00
(17)	Howie Camnitz	150.00	60.00	30.00
(18)	Bill Carrigan	150.00	60.00	30.00
(19)	Frank Chance	250.00	100.00	50.00
(20)	Hal Chase ("Chase" on front)	165.00	66.00	33.00
(21)	Hal Chase ("Hal Chase" on front)	165.00	66.00	33.00
(22)	Ed Cicotte	185.00	74.00	37.00
(23)	Fred Clarke	250.00	100.00	50.00
(24)	Ty Cobb	1200.	480.00	240.00
(25)	Eddie Collins (mouth closed)	250.00	100.00	50.00
(26)	Eddie Collins (mouth open)	250.00	100.00	50.00
(27)	Otis "Doc" Crandall	150.00	60.00	30.00
(28)	Bill Dahlen	150.00	60.00	30.00
(29)	Jake Daubert	150.00	60.00	30.00
(30)	Jim Delahanty	150.00	60.00	30.00
(31)	Josh Devore	150.00	60.00	30.00
(32)	Red Dooin	150.00	60.00	30.00
(33)	Mickey Doolan	150.00	60.00	30.00
(34)	Tom Downey	150.00	60.00	30.00
(35)	Larry Doyle	150.00	60.00	30.00
(36)	Dick Egan	150.00	60.00	30.00
(37)	Kid Elberfield (Elberfeld)	150.00	60.00	30.00
(38)	Clyde Engle	150.00	60.00	30.00
(39)	Louis Evans	150.00	60.00	30.00
(40)	Johnny Evers	250.00	100.00	50.00
(41)	Ray Fisher	150.00	60.00	30.00
(42)	Art Fletcher	150.00	60.00	30.00
(43)	Russ Ford (dark cap)	150.00	60.00	30.00
(44)	Russ Ford (white cap)	150.00	60.00	30.00
(45)	Art Fromme	150.00	60.00	30.00
(46)	George Gibson	150.00	60.00	30.00
(47)	William Goode (Wilbur Good)	150.00	60.00	30.00
(48)	Clark Griifith	250.00	100.00	50.00
(49)	Bob Groom	150.00	60.00	30.00
(50)	Bob Harmon	150.00	60.00	30.00
(51)	Arnold Hauser	150.00	60.00	30.00
(52)	Buck Herzog	150.00	60.00	30.00
(53)	Dick Hoblitzell	150.00	60.00	30.00
(54)	Miller Huggins	250.00	100.00	50.00
(55)	John Hummel	150.00	60.00	30.00
(56)	Hughie Jennings	250.00	100.00	50.00
(57)	Walter Johnson	750.00	300.00	150.00
(58)	Davy Jones	150.00	60.00	30.00
(59)	Bill Killifer (Killefer)	150.00	60.00	30.00
(60)	Jack Knight	150.00	60.00	30.00
(61)	Ed Konetchy	150.00	60.00	30.00
(62)	Frank LaPorte	150.00	60.00	30.00
(63)	Thomas Leach	150.00	60.00	30.00
(64)	Edgar Lennox	150.00	60.00	30.00
(65)	Hans Lobert	150.00	60.00	30.00
(66)	Harry Lord	150.00	60.00	30.00
(67)	Sherry Magee	150.00	60.00	30.00
(68)	Rube Marquard	250.00	100.00	50.00
(69)	Christy Mathewson	750.00	300.00	150.00
(70)	George McBride	150.00	60.00	30.00
(71)	J.J. McGraw	250.00	100.00	50.00
(72)	Larry McLean	150.00	60.00	30.00
(73)	Fred Merkle	150.00	60.00	30.00
(74)	Chief Meyers	150.00	60.00	30.00
(75)	Clyde Milan	150.00	60.00	30.00
(76)	Dots Miller	150.00	60.00	30.00
(77)	Mike Mitchell	150.00	60.00	30.00
(78)	Pat Moran	150.00	60.00	30.00
(79)	George Moriarity (Moriarty)	150.00	60.00	30.00
(80)	George Mullin	150.00	60.00	30.00
(81)	Danny Murphy	150.00	60.00	30.00
(82)	Jack "Red" Murray	150.00	60.00	30.00
(83)	Tom Needham	150.00	60.00	30.00
(84)	Rebel Oakes	150.00	60.00	30.00
(85)	Rube Oldring	150.00	60.00	30.00
(86)	Fred Parent	150.00	60.00	30.00
(87)	Dode Paskert	150.00	60.00	30.00
(88)	Jack Quinn	150.00	60.00	30.00
(89)	Ed Reulbach	150.00	60.00	30.00
(90)	Lewis Ritchie	150.00	60.00	30.00
(91)	Jack Rowan	150.00	60.00	30.00
(92)	Nap Rucker	150.00	60.00	30.00
(93)	Germany Schaefer	150.00	60.00	30.00
(94)	Wildfire Schulte	150.00	60.00	30.00
(95)	Jim Scott	150.00	60.00	30.00
(96)	Fred Snodgrass	150.00	60.00	30.00
(97)	Tris Speaker	300.00	120.00	60.00
(98)	Oscar Stamage (Stanage)	150.00	60.00	30.00
(99)	George Suggs	150.00	60.00	30.00
(100)	Jeff Sweeney	150.00	60.00	30.00
(101)	Ira Thomas	150.00	60.00	30.00
(102)	Joe Tinker	250.00	100.00	50.00
(103)	Terry Turner	150.00	60.00	30.00
(104)	Hippo Vaughn	150.00	60.00	30.00
(105)	Heinie Wagner	150.00	60.00	30.00
(106)	Bobby Wallace (no cap)	250.00	100.00	50.00
(107)	Bobby Wallace (with cap)	250.00	100.00	50.00
(108)	Ed Walsh	250.00	100.00	50.00
(109)	Zach Wheat	250.00	100.00	50.00
(110)	Irwin "Kaiser" Wilhelm	150.00	60.00	30.00
(111)	Ed Willett	150.00	60.00	30.00
(112)	Owen Wilson	150.00	60.00	30.00
(113)	Hooks Wiltse	150.00	60.00	30.00
(114)	Joe Wood	150.00	60.00	30.00

1909-11 Piedmont Cigarettes

(See T205, T206)

1911 Pinkerton Cabinets

(See T5)

1912 Pirate Cigarettes (T215)

This set can be considerd a British version of the Red Cross set. Distributed by Pirate brand cigarettes of Bristol and London, England, the fronts of the cards are identical to the Type I Red Cross cards, but the green backs carry advertising for Pirate Cigarettes. It is believed that the Pirate cards were printed for distribution to U.S. servicemen in the South Seas. They are very rare in both England and the United States.

		NM	EX	VG
Common Player:		1250.	625.00	375.00
(1)	Red Ames	1250.	625.00	375.00
(2)	Home Run Baker	3125.	1550.	935.00
(3)	Neal Ball	1250.	625.00	375.00
(4)	Chief Bender	3125.	1550.	935.00
(5)	Al Bridwell	1250.	625.00	375.00
(6)	Bobby Byrne	1250.	625.00	375.00
(7)	Howie Camnitz	1250.	625.00	375.00
(8)	Frank Chance	3325.	1650.	995.00
(9)	Hal Chase	1575.	785.00	470.00
(10)	Eddie Collins	3325.	1650.	995.00
(11)	Doc Crandall	1250.	625.00	375.00
(12)	Sam Crawford	3125.	1550.	935.00
(13)	Birdie Cree	1250.	625.00	375.00
(14)	Harry Davis	1250.	625.00	375.00
(15)	Josh Devore	1250.	625.00	375.00
(16)	Mike Donlin	1250.	625.00	375.00
(17)	Mickey Doolan (batting)	1250.	625.00	375.00
(18)	Mickey Doolan (fielding)	1250.	625.00	375.00
(19)	Patsy Dougherty	1250.	625.00	375.00
(20)	Larry Doyle (batting)	1250.	625.00	375.00
(21)	Larry Doyle (portrait)	1250.	625.00	375.00
(22)	Jean Dubuc	1250.	625.00	375.00
(23)	Kid Elberfeld	1250.	625.00	375.00
(24)	Steve Evans	1250.	625.00	375.00
(25)	Johnny Evers	3125.	1550.	935.00
(26)	Russ Ford	1250.	625.00	375.00
(27)	Art Fromme	1250.	625.00	375.00
(28)	Clark Griffith	3125.	1550.	935.00

(29)	Bob Groom	1250.	625.00	375.00
(30)	Topsy Hartsel	1250.	625.00	375.00
(31)	Buck Herzog	1250.	625.00	375.00
(32)	Dick Hoblitzell	1250.	625.00	375.00
(33)	Solly Hofman	1250.	625.00	375.00
(34)	Del Howard	1250.	625.00	375.00
(35)	Miller Huggins (hands at mouth)	3125.	1550.	935.00
(36)	Miller Huggins (portrait)	3125.	1550.	935.00
(37)	John Hummel	1250.	625.00	375.00
(38)	Hughie Jennings (both hands showing)	3125.	1550.	935.00
(39)	Hughie Jennings (one hand showing)	3125.	1550.	935.00
(40)	Walter Johnson	6250.	3125.	1875.
(41)	Joe Kelley	3125.	1550.	935.00
(42)	Ed Konetchy	1250.	625.00	375.00
(43)	Harry Krause	1250.	625.00	375.00
(44)	Nap Lajoie	3325.	1650.	995.00
(45)	Joe Lake	1250.	625.00	375.00
(46)	Lefty Leifield	1250.	625.00	375.00
(47)	Harry Lord	1250.	625.00	375.00
(48)	Sherry Magee	1250.	625.00	375.00
(49)	Rube Marquard (pitching)	3125.	1550.	935.00
(50)	Rube Marquard (portrait)	3125.	1550.	935.00
(51)	Joe McGinnity	3125.	1550.	935.00
(52)	John McGraw (glove at side)	3125.	1550.	935.00
(53)	John McGraw (portrait)	3125.	1550.	935.00
(54)	Harry McIntyre (Chicago)	1250.	625.00	375.00
(55)	Harry McIntyre (Brooklyn & Chicago)	1250.	625.00	375.00
(56)	Larry McLean	1250.	625.00	375.00
(57)	Fred Merkle	1250.	625.00	375.00
(58)	Chief Meyers	1250.	625.00	375.00
(59)	Mike Mitchell	1250.	625.00	375.00
(60)	Mike Mowrey	1250.	625.00	375.00
(61)	George Mullin	1250.	625.00	375.00
(62)	Danny Murphy	1250.	625.00	375.00
(63)	Red Murray	1250.	625.00	375.00
(64)	Rebel Oakes	1250.	625.00	375.00
(65)	Rube Oldring	1250.	625.00	375.00
(66)	Charley O'Leary	1250.	625.00	375.00
(67)	Dode Paskert	1250.	625.00	375.00
(68)	Barney Pelty	1250.	625.00	375.00
(69)	Billy Purtell	1250.	625.00	375.00
(70)	Jack Quinn	1250.	625.00	375.00
(71)	Ed Reulbach	1250.	625.00	375.00
(72)	Nap Rucker	1250.	625.00	375.00
(73)	Germany Schaefer	1250.	625.00	375.00
(74)	Wildfire Schulte	1250.	625.00	375.00
(75)	Jimmy Sheckard	1250.	625.00	375.00
(76)	Frank Smith	1250.	625.00	375.00
(77)	Tris Speaker	3750.	1875.	1125.
(78)	Jake Stahl	1250.	625.00	375.00
(79)	Harry Steinfeldt	1250.	625.00	375.00
(80)	Gabby Street	1250.	625.00	375.00
(81)	Ed Summers	1250.	625.00	375.00
(82)	Jeff Sweeney	1250.	625.00	375.00
(83)	Lee Tannehill	1250.	625.00	375.00
(84)	Ira Thomas	1250.	625.00	375.00
(85)	Joe Tinker	3125.	1550.	935.00
(86)	Heinie Wagner	1250.	625.00	375.00
(87)	Jack Warhop	1250.	625.00	375.00
(88)	Zack Wheat	3125.	1550.	935.00
(89)	Ed Willetts (Willett)	1250.	625.00	375.00
(90)	Owen Wilson	1250.	625.00	375.00
(91)	Hooks Wiltse (pitching)	1250.	625.00	375.00
(92)	Hooks Wiltse (portrait)	1250.	625.00	375.00

1949-59 Pittsburgh Pirates Postcards

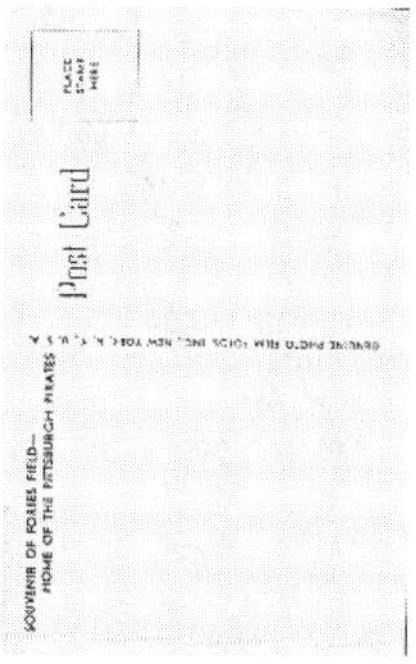

(See Photo-Film Fotos Pirates Postcards)

1950 Pittsburgh Pirates Photo Pack

The player photos in this picture pack which was sold at Forbes Field measure 6-1/2" x 9" and are printed in black-and-white on heavy, blank-backed paper. A facsimile "autograph" is printed on front of each picture, though all were written in the same hand. Several of the photos from this set were the basis for the color paintings found on 1951 Bowman cards. The unnumbered pictures are checklisted here alphabetically.

		NM	EX	VG
Complete Set (26):		175.00	85.00	50.00
Common Player:		8.00	4.00	2.50
(1)	Ted Beard	8.00	4.00	2.50
(2)	Gus Bell	12.00	6.00	3.50
(3)	Pete Castiglione	8.00	4.00	2.50
(4)	Cliff Chambers	8.00	4.00	2.50
(5)	Dale Coogan	8.00	4.00	2.50
(6)	Murry Dickson	8.00	4.00	2.50
(7)	Bob Dillinger	8.00	4.00	2.50
(8)	Froilan Fernandez	8.00	4.00	2.50
(9)	Johnny Hopp	8.00	4.00	2.50
(10)	Ralph Kiner	18.00	9.00	5.50
(11)	Vernon Law	12.00	6.00	3.50
(12)	Vic Lombardi	8.00	4.00	2.50
(13)	Bill MacDonald	8.00	4.00	2.50
(14)	Clyde McCullough	8.00	4.00	2.50
(15)	Bill Meyer	8.00	4.00	2.50
(16)	Ray Mueller	8.00	4.00	2.50
(17)	Danny Murtaugh	8.00	4.00	2.50
(18)	Jack Phillips	8.00	4.00	2.50
(19)	Mel Queen	8.00	4.00	2.50
(20)	Stan Rojek	8.00	4.00	2.50
(21)	Henry Schenz	8.00	4.00	2.50
(22)	George Strickland	8.00	4.00	2.50
(23)	Earl Turner	8.00	4.00	2.50
(24)	Jim Walsh	8.00	4.00	2.50
(25)	Bill Werle	8.00	4.00	2.50
(26)	Wally Westlake	8.00	4.00	2.50

1960 Pittsburgh Pirates Bat/Fan

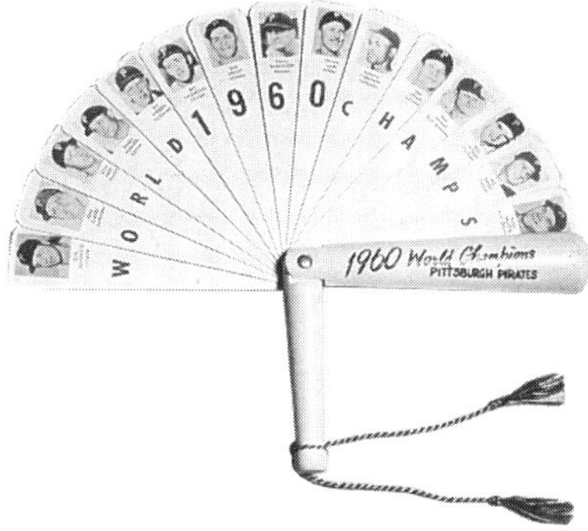

This unusual souvenir honors the World Champion Pirates. The piece takes the form of an 11" celluloid baseball bat, inscribed "1960 World Champions / Pittsburgh Pirates. The bat can be "broken" at center to reveal a set of 15 "blades" which can be folded out to create a fan. Each of the fans has a black-and-white portrait at top, with the player's name and position printed beneath the photo. The souvenir borrowed the design of a similar Pirates player fan issued in the first decade of the 1950s.

		NM	EX	VG
Complete Bat/Fan:		415.00	210.00	130.00
W	Dick Schofield			
O	Gino Cimoli			
R	Roy Face			
L	Smokey Burgess			
D	Bill Virdon			
1	Bill Mazeroski			
9	Dick Groat			
6	Danny Murtaugh			
0	Vern Law			
C	Roberto Clemente			
H	Don Hoak			
A	Dick Stuart			
M	Bob Skinner			
P	Hal Smith			
S	Rocky Nelson			

1967 Pittsburgh Pirates Autograph Cards

A souvenir stand item introduced by the Pirates in 1967 was a series of color player cards bearing facsimile autographs. The 3-1/4" x 4-1/4" cards identify the player with a line of type beneath the photo giving name, position and uniform number. Backs are blank. The cards are checklisted here in alphabetical order.

		NM	EX	VG
Complete Set (24):		100.00	50.00	30.00
Common Player:		4.00	2.00	1.25
	SERIES A			
(1)	(Gene Alley)	4.00	2.00	1.25
(2)	(Steve Blass)	4.00	2.00	1.25
(3)	(Roberto Clemente)	40.00	20.00	12.00
(4)	(Donn Clendenon)	5.00	2.50	1.50
(5)	(Roy Face)	5.00	2.50	1.50
(6)	Jesse Gonder	4.00	2.00	1.25
(7)	Jerry May	4.00	2.00	1.25
(8)	Manny Mota	5.00	2.50	1.50
(9)	Jose Pagan	4.00	2.00	1.25
(10)	Dennis Ribant	4.00	2.00	1.25
(11)	Tommie Sisk	4.00	2.00	1.25
(12)	Bob Veale	4.00	2.00	1.25
	SERIES B			
(13)	Matty Alou	4.00	2.00	1.25
(14)	Woody Fryman	4.00	2.00	1.25
(15)	Vernon Law	5.00	2.50	1.50
(16)	Bill Mazeroski	15.00	7.50	4.50
(17)	Al McBean	4.00	2.00	1.25
(18)	Pete Mikkelsen	4.00	2.00	1.25
(19)	Jim Pagliaroni	4.00	2.00	1.25
(20)	Juan Pizarro	4.00	2.00	1.25
(21)	Andy Rodgers	4.00	2.00	1.25
(22)	Willie Stargell	15.00	7.50	4.50
(23)	Harry Walker	4.00	2.00	1.25
(24)	Maury Wills	6.50	3.25	2.00

1968 Pittsburgh Pirates Autograph Cards

These team-issued autograph cards were sold in packages at Forbes Field. The 3-1/4" x 4-1/4" cards feature a color player photo and facsimile autograph. They are blank-backed. Cards were issued in Series A and Series B, with header cards in each series providing a checklist. Cards are listed here by series according to the uniform number found on the card.

		NM	EX	VG
Complete Set (26):		45.00	22.00	13.50
Common Player:		2.00	1.00	.60
	SERIES A			
7	Larry Shepard	2.00	1.00	.60
11	Jose Pagan	2.00	1.00	.60
12	Jerry May	2.00	1.00	.60
14	Jim Bunning	7.50	3.75	2.25
15	Manny Mota	2.00	1.00	.60
17	Donn Clendenon	3.00	1.50	.90
21	Roberto Clemente	15.00	7.50	4.50
22	Gene Alley	2.00	1.00	.60
25	Tommie Sisk	2.00	1.00	.60

26	Roy Face	2.00	1.00	.60
28	Steve Blass	2.00	1.00	.60
39	Bob Veale	2.00	1.00	.60
--	Checklist card, Series A	2.00	1.00	.60
	SERIES B			
8	Willie Stargell	8.00	4.00	2.50
9	Bill Mazeroski	8.00	4.00	2.50
10	Gary Kolb	2.00	1.00	.60
18	Matty Alou	2.50	1.25	.70
27	Ronnie Kline	2.00	1.00	.60
29	Juan Pizzaro	2.00	1.00	.60
30	Maury Wills	4.00	2.00	1.25
34	Al McBean	2.00	1.00	.60
35	Manny Sanguillen	2.00	1.00	.60
38	Bob Moose	2.00	1.00	.60
40	Dave Wickersham	2.00	1.00	.60
--	Jim Shellenback	2.00	1.00	.60
--	Checklist card, Series B	2.00	1.00	.60

1969 Pittsburgh Pirates Autograph Cards

Sold in Series A with a blue header card/checklist and Series B with a pink header card/checklist, these team-issued autograph cards were available at Forbes Field. Identical in format to the previous year's issue, the 3-1/4" x 4-1/4" cards are blank-backed and feature a color player photo on front with a facsimile autograph in the wide white bottom border. Cards are checklisted here by series and uniform number (found on card fronts) within series.

		NM	EX	VG
	Complete Set:	45.00	22.50	13.50
	Common Player:	2.00	1.00	.60
	Series A			
2	Fred Patek	2.00	1.00	.60
4	Larry Shepard	2.00	1.00	.60
8	Willie Stargell	6.00	3.00	1.75
9	Bill Mazeroski	8.00	4.00	2.50
10	Gary Kolb	2.00	1.00	.60
23	Luke Walker	2.00	1.00	.60
28	Steve Blass	2.00	1.00	.60
29	Al Oliver	4.00	2.00	1.25
35	Manny Sanguillen	2.50	1.25	.70
38	Bob Moose	2.00	1.00	.60
39	Bob Veale	2.00	1.00	.60
42	Chuck Hartenstein	2.00	1.00	.60
Series B				
7	Bill Virdon	2.50	1.25	.70
11	Jose Pagan	2.00	1.00	.60
12	Jerry May	2.00	1.00	.60
14	Jim Bunning	7.50	3.75	2.25
18	Matty Alou	2.50	1.25	.70
20	Richie Hebner	3.00	1.50	.90
21	Roberto Clemente	15.00	7.50	4.50
22	Gene Alley	2.00	1.00	.60
32	Vernon Law	2.50	1.25	.70
36	Carl Taylor	2.00	1.00	.60
40	Dock Ellis	2.50	1.25	.70
43	Bruce Dal Canton	2.00	1.00	.60

1969 Pittsburgh Pirates Photo Album

This 8-1/8" x 10-3/4" color 20-page album features posed portraits of 14 Pirates. Most of the photos are the same pictures seen on the 1968 KDKA Pirates card set. The pictures are back-to-back in the stapled album. Besides the player pictures, the book has ads for the sponsor, Foodland, and a 1969 Pirates' schedule. A panoramic picture of Forbes Field is on the front and back covers.

		NM	EX	VG
	Complete Album:	35.00	17.50	10.00
2	Fred Patek			
8	Willie Stargell			
9	Bill Mazeroski			
12	Jerry May			
14	Jim Bunning			
18	Matty Alou			
20	Richie Hebner			
21	Roberto Clemente			
22	Gene Alley			
28	Steve Blass			
29	Al Oliver			
37	Dock Ellis			
38	Bob Moose			
39	Bob Veale			

1970 Pittsburgh Pirates Autograph Cards

Retaining the 3-1/4" x 4-1/4" format from previous years, these team-issued autograph cards can be distinguished from the 1968-69 issues by the Three Rivers Stadium photo background on each card. The Pirates moved from Forbes Field in June, 1970. The set is checklisted here by uniform number without regard to Series A and B.

		NM	EX	VG
	Complete Set (25):	55.00	27.50	16.50
	Common Player:	2.00	1.00	.60
2	Fred Patek	2.00	1.00	.60
5	Dave Ricketts	2.00	1.00	.60
8	Willie Stargell	8.00	4.00	2.50
9	Bill Mazeroski	8.00	4.00	2.50
10	Richie Hebner	2.50	1.25	.70
11	Jose Pagan	2.00	1.00	.60
12	Jerry May	2.00	1.00	.60
16	Al Oliver	4.00	2.00	1.25
17	Dock Ellis	2.00	1.00	.60
18	Matty Alou	2.00	1.00	.60
19	Joe Gibbon	2.00	1.00	.60
21	Roberto Clemente	20.00	10.00	6.00
22	Gene Alley	2.00	1.00	.60
22	Orlando Pena	2.00	1.00	.60
23	Luke Walker	2.00	1.00	.60
25	John Jeter	2.00	1.00	.60
25	Bob Robertson	2.00	1.00	.60
30	Dave Cash	2.00	1.00	.60
31	Dave Giusti	2.00	1.00	.60
35	Manny Sanguillen	2.50	1.25	.70
36	Dick Calpaert (Colpaert)	2.00	1.00	.60
38	Bob Moose	2.00	1.00	.60
39	Bob Veale	2.00	1.00	.60
40	Danny Murtaugh	2.00	1.00	.60
50	Jim Nelson	2.00	1.00	.60

1971 Pittsburgh Pirates Action Photos

A successor to the team-issued autograph cards of 1968-70, this set of souvenir photos was produced in a 4" x 5-1/2" black-and-white format on semi-gloss paper. The player's name, position, and uniform number were printed on front. Backs are blank. Some cards have the player's name printed in the white bottom border, some have it within the photo. The set was issued in two series. The checklist is presented here alphabetically within series.

		NM	EX	VG
	Complete Set (24):	45.00	22.00	13.50
	Common Player:	2.00	1.00	.60
	SERIES 1			
(1)	Gene Alley	2.00	1.00	.60
(2)	Nellie Briles	2.00	1.00	.60
(3)	Dave Cash	2.00	1.00	.60
(4)	Roberto Clemente	15.00	7.50	4.50
(5)	Dock Ellis	2.00	1.00	.60
(6)	Mudcat Grant	3.00	1.50	.90
(7)	Bob Johnson	2.00	1.00	.60
(8)	Milt May	2.00	1.00	.60
(9)	Jose Pagan	2.00	1.00	.60
(10)	Manny Sanguillen	3.00	1.50	.90
(11)	Bob Veale	2.00	1.00	.60
(12)	Luke Walker	2.00	1.00	.60
	SERIES 2			
(13)	Steve Blass	2.00	1.00	.60
(14)	Gene Clines	2.00	1.00	.60
(15)	Vic Davalillo	2.00	1.00	.60
(16)	Dave Giusti	2.00	1.00	.60
(17)	Richie Hebner	3.00	1.50	.90
(18)	Jackie Hernandez	2.00	1.00	.60
(19)	Bill Mazeroski	8.00	4.00	2.50
(20)	Bob Moose	2.00	1.00	.60
(21)	Al Oliver	4.00	2.00	1.25
(22)	Bob Robertson	2.00	1.00	.60
(23)	Charlie Sands	2.00	1.00	.60
(24)	Willie Stargell	8.00	4.00	2.50

1971 Pittsburgh Pirates Autograph Cards

The final year of team-issued Pirates autograph cards are distinguished by the appearance of mustard-yellow caps on the players' portraits. Otherwise the blank-back 3-1/4" x 4-1/2" photocards are identical in format to those of earlier seasons. Players are checklisted here alphabetically within series.

		NM	EX	VG
	Complete Set (20):	45.00	22.50	13.50
	Common Player:	2.00	1.00	.60
	Series A			
(1)	Gene Alley	2.00	1.00	.60
(2)	Nelson Briles	2.00	1.00	.60
(3)	Dave Cash	2.00	1.00	.60
(4)	Dock Ellis	2.00	1.00	.60
(5)	Mudcat Grant	2.50	1.25	.70
(6)	Bill Mazeroski	8.00	4.00	2.50
(7)	Jim Nelson	2.00	1.00	.60
(8)	Al Oliver	4.00	2.00	1.25
(9)	Manny Sanguillen	2.50	1.25	.70
(10)	Luke Walker	2.00	1.00	.60
	Series B			
(11)	Steve Blass	2.00	1.00	.60
(12)	Bob Clemente	15.00	7.50	4.50
(13)	Dave Giusti	2.00	1.00	.60
(14)	Richie Hebner	2.50	1.25	.70
(15)	Bob Johnson	2.00	1.00	.60
(16)	Bob Moose	2.00	1.00	.60
(17)	Jose Pagan	2.00	1.00	.60
(18)	Bob Robertson	2.00	1.00	.60
(19)	Willie Stargell	8.00	4.00	2.50
(20)	Bob Veale	2.00	1.00	.60

1971-72 Pittsburgh Pirates team issue

Given the checklist printed on the envelope in which these player pictures were sold, it is impossible to pinpoint the year of issue. Pictures are in black-and-back and feature close-up player poses with the name and team in the white border at top. Backs are blank. The unnumbered pictures are checklisted here alphabetically.

		NM	EX	VG
Complete Set (12):		27.50	13.50	8.25
Common Player:		3.00	1.50	.90
(1)	Gene Alley	3.00	1.50	.90
(2)	Roberto Clemente	15.00	7.50	4.50
(3)	Vic Davalillo	3.00	1.50	.90
(4)	Dock Ellis	3.00	1.50	.90
(5)	Dave Giusti	3.00	1.50	.90
(6)	Richie Hebner	3.00	1.50	.90
(7)	Bob Johnson	3.00	1.50	.90
(8)	Bill Mazeroski	8.00	4.00	2.50
(9)	Bob Moose	3.00	1.50	.90
(10)	Jose Pagan	3.00	1.50	.90
(11)	Willie Stargell	8.00	4.00	2.50
(12)	Bob Veale	3.00	1.50	.90

1973 Pittsburgh Post-Gazette Pirates

This set of Pirates pictures was printed on newspaper stock one per day in the sports section of the daily paper. The black-bordered black-and-white photos are 5-1/4" x 9-1/4". At top is "'73 Pirate Album" and a short career summary. At bottom are 1972 and career stats. The first six pictures are unnumbered, the others are numbered alphabetically.

		NM	EX	VG
Complete Set (25):		125.00	60.00	35.00
Common Player:		6.00	3.00	1.75
	Gene Alley	6.00	3.00	1.75
	Steve Blass	6.00	3.00	1.75
	Nellie Briles	6.00	3.00	1.75
	Dave Cash	6.00	3.00	1.75
	Roberto Clemente	40.00	20.00	12.00
	Gene Clines	6.00	3.00	1.75
6	Vic Davalillo	6.00	3.00	1.75
7	Dock Ellis	6.00	3.00	1.75
8	Dave Giusti	6.00	3.00	1.75
9	Richie Hebner	6.00	3.00	1.75
10	Jackie Hernandez	6.00	3.00	1.75
11	Ramon Hernandez	6.00	3.00	1.75
12	Bob Johnson	6.00	3.00	1.75
13	Bruce Kison	6.00	3.00	1.75
14	Milt May	6.00	3.00	1.75
15	Bob Miller	6.00	3.00	1.75
16	Bob Moose	6.00	3.00	1.75
17	Al Oliver	7.50	3.75	2.25
18	Bob Robertson	6.00	3.00	1.75
19	Charlie Sands	6.00	3.00	1.75
20	Manny Sanguillen	6.00	3.00	1.75
21	Willie Stargell	12.00	6.00	3.50
22	Rennie Stennett	6.00	3.00	1.75
23	Luke Walker	6.00	3.00	1.75
24	Bill Virdon	7.50	3.75	2.25

1972 Pittsburgh Press "Buc-A-Day" Pirates

Through the month of March, 1972, the daily Pittsburgh Press carried a "Buc-A-Day" feature highlighting members of the team. The feature was intended to be cut out of the paper and saved. Individual pieces measure 3-3/8" wide and vary in length from 9-1/4" to 11-1/16" depending on the length of the biographical information provided. Each player is pictured in a black-and-white photo in street clothes. Some are pictured with golf clubs, fishing poles, with their children, etc. Because of the nature of their distribution and their fragile nature, complete sets are very scarce.

		NM	EX	VG
Complete Set (25):		600.00	300.00	180.00
Common Player:		15.00	7.50	4.50
1	Willie Stargell	60.00	30.00	18.00
2	Steve Blass	15.00	7.50	4.50
3	Al Oliver	20.00	10.00	6.00
4	Bob Moose	15.00	7.50	4.50
5	Dave Cash	15.00	7.50	4.50
6	Bill Mazeroski	50.00	25.00	15.00
7	Bob Johnson	15.00	7.50	4.50
8	Nellie Briles	15.00	7.50	4.50
9	Manny Sanguillen	20.00	10.00	6.00
10	Vic Davalillo	15.00	7.50	4.50
11	Dave Giusti	15.00	7.50	4.50
12	Luke Walker	15.00	7.50	4.50
13	Gene Clines	15.00	7.50	4.50
14	Milt May	15.00	7.50	4.50
15	Bob Robertson	15.00	7.50	4.50
16	Roberto Clemente	100.00	50.00	30.00
17	Gene Alley	15.00	7.50	4.50
18	Bruce Kison	15.00	7.50	4.50
19	Jose Pagan	15.00	7.50	4.50
20	Dock Ellis	15.00	7.50	4.50
21	Richie Hebner	15.00	7.50	4.50
22	Bob Miller	15.00	7.50	4.50
23	Jackie Hernandez	15.00	7.50	4.50
24	Rennie Stennett	15.00	7.50	4.50
25	Bob Veale	15.00	7.50	4.50

1939 Play Ball Samples

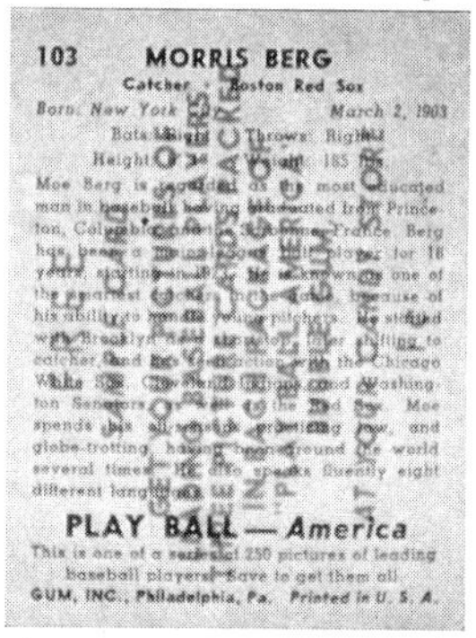

Each of the first 115 cards in the 1939 Play Ball set can be found with red overprinting on the back indicating sample card status. The overprint reads: FREE / SAMPLE CARD / GET YOUR PICTURES OF / LEADING BASEBALL PLAYERS. / THREE PICTURE CARDS PACKED / IN EACH PACKAGE OF / "PLAY BALL AMERICA" / BUBBLE GUM. / AT YOUR CANDY STORE / 1c". Collectors will pay a small premium for a type card of a common player. Sample cards of most star players sell for about double the price of the regular-issue cards, while DiMaggio and Williams samples sell for about the same price as their regular-issue cards.

		NM	EX	VG
Common Player:		25.00	11.00	8.00
26	Joe DiMaggio	2200.	1000.	725.00
92	Ted Williams	2000.	900.00	650.00

1939 Play Ball

With the issue of this card set by Gum Inc., a new era of baseball cards was born. Although the cards are black-and-white, the photos on the fronts are of better quality than previously seen, and the 2-1/2" x 3-1/8" size was larger than virtually all of the tobacco and caramel cards of the early 20th Century. Card backs feature full player names, "Joseph Paul DiMaggio" instead of "Joe DiMaggio" and extensive biographies. Regardless of the name on back, players are listed here by their most commonly used name. Similarly, minor corrections of names, biographical data, dates or stats are not noted. There are 161 cards in the set; card #126 was never issued. The complete set price does not include all back variations found in the low-numbered series. Most of the cards between #2-115 can be found with the player name on back either in all capital letters, or in both upper- and lower-case letters. No premium currently attaches to either version.

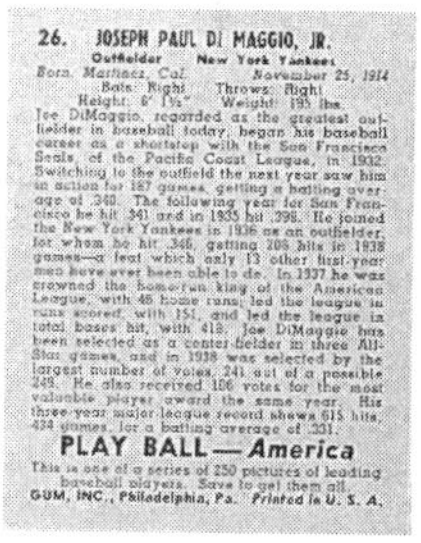

		NM	EX	VG
Complete Set (161):		9000.	4000.	2150.
Common Player (1-115):		18.00	9.00	6.00
Common Player (116-162):		95.00	50.00	30.00
1	Jake Powell	185.00	75.00	50.00
2	Lee Grissom	18.00	9.00	6.00
3	Red Ruffing	115.00	55.00	38.00
4	Eldon Auker	18.00	9.00	6.00
5	Luke Sewell	18.00	9.00	6.00
6	Leo Durocher	115.00	57.00	34.00
7	Bobby Doerr	95.00	47.00	28.00
8	Cotton Pippen	18.00	9.00	6.00
9	Jim Tobin	18.00	9.00	6.00
10	Jimmie DeShong	18.00	9.00	6.00
11	Johnny Rizzo	18.00	9.00	6.00
12	Hersh Martin	18.00	9.00	6.00
13	Luke Hamlin	18.00	9.00	6.00
14	Jim Tabor	18.00	9.00	6.00
15	Paul Derringer	22.00	11.00	6.50
16	Johnny Peacock	18.00	9.00	6.00
17	Emerson Dickman	18.00	9.00	6.00
18	Harry Danning	18.00	9.00	6.00
19	Paul Dean	40.00	20.00	12.00
20	Joe Heving	18.00	9.00	6.00
21	Dutch Leonard	18.00	9.00	6.00
22	Bucky Walters	18.00	9.00	6.00
23	Burgess Whitehead	18.00	9.00	6.00
24	Dick Coffman	18.00	9.00	6.00
25	George Selkirk	18.00	9.00	6.00
26	Joe DiMaggio	2000.	1000.	600.00
27	Fritz Ostermueller	18.00	9.00	6.00
28	Syl Johnson	18.00	9.00	6.00
29	Jack Wilson	18.00	9.00	6.00
30	Bill Dickey	135.00	67.00	40.00
31	Sammy West	18.00	9.00	6.00
32	Bob Seeds	18.00	9.00	6.00
33	Del Young	18.00	9.00	6.00
34	Frank Demaree	18.00	9.00	6.00
35	Bill Jurges	18.00	9.00	6.00
36	Frank McCormick	18.00	9.00	6.00
37	Spud Davis	18.00	9.00	6.00
38	Billy Myers	18.00	9.00	6.00
39	Rick Ferrell	85.00	38.00	28.00
40	Jim Bagby Jr.	18.00	9.00	6.00
41	Lon Warneke	18.00	9.00	6.00
42	Arndt Jorgens	22.00	10.00	7.25
43	Mel Almada	32.00	14.50	10.50
44	Don Heffner	18.00	9.00	6.00
45	Pinky May	18.00	9.00	6.00
46	Morrie Arnovich	18.00	9.00	6.00
47	Buddy Lewis	18.00	9.00	6.00
48	Lefty Gomez	140.00	70.00	45.00
49	Eddie Miller	18.00	9.00	6.00
50	Charlie Gehringer	175.00	79.00	58.00
51	Mel Ott	155.00	70.00	51.00
52	Tommy Henrich	37.00	16.50	12.00
53	Carl Hubbell	160.00	72.00	53.00
54	Harry Gumbert	18.00	9.00	6.00
55	Arky Vaughan	100.00	50.00	30.00
56	Hank Greenberg	225.00	100.00	75.00
57	Buddy Hassett	18.00	9.00	6.00
58	Lou Chiozza	18.00	9.00	6.00
59	Ken Chase	18.00	9.00	6.00
60	Schoolboy Rowe	18.00	9.00	6.00
61	Tony Cuccinello	18.00	9.00	6.00
62	Tom Carey	18.00	9.00	6.00
63	Heinie Mueller	18.00	9.00	6.00
64	Wally Moses	18.00	9.00	6.00
65	Harry Craft	18.00	9.00	6.00
66	Jimmy Ripple	18.00	9.00	6.00
67	Eddie Joost	18.00	9.00	6.00
68	Fred Sington	18.00	9.00	6.00
69	Elbie Fletcher	18.00	9.00	6.00
70	Fred Frankhouse	18.00	9.00	6.00
71	Monte Pearson	18.00	9.00	6.00

72	Debs Garms	18.00	9.00	6.00
73	Hal Schumacher	18.00	9.00	6.00
74	Cookie Lavagetto	18.00	9.00	6.00
75	Frenchy Bordagaray	18.00	9.00	6.00
76	Goody Rosen	18.00	9.00	6.00
77	Lew Riggs	18.00	9.00	6.00
78	Moose Solters	18.00	9.00	6.00
79	Joe Moore	18.00	9.00	6.00
80	Pete Fox	18.00	9.00	6.00
81	Babe Dahlgren	18.00	9.00	6.00
82	Chuck Klein	125.00	56.00	41.00
83	Gus Suhr	18.00	9.00	6.00
84	Skeeter Newsome	18.00	9.00	6.00
85	Johnny Cooney	18.00	9.00	6.00
86	Dolph Camilli	18.00	9.00	6.00
87	Milt Shoffner	18.00	9.00	6.00
88	Charlie Keller	30.00	13.50	10.00
89	Lloyd Waner	85.00	38.00	28.00
90	Bob Klinger	18.00	9.00	6.00
91	Jack Knott	18.00	9.00	6.00
92	Ted Williams	2300.	975.00	650.00
93	Charley Gelbert	18.00	9.00	6.00
94	Heinie Manush	95.00	47.00	28.00
95	Whit Wyatt	18.00	9.00	6.00
96	Babe Phelps	18.00	9.00	6.00
97	Bob Johnson	18.00	9.00	6.00
98	Pinky Whitney	18.00	9.00	6.00
99	Wally Berger	18.00	9.00	6.00
100	Buddy Myer	18.00	9.00	6.00
101	Doc Cramer	18.00	9.00	6.00
102	Pep Young	18.00	9.00	6.00
103	Moe Berg	200.00	90.00	65.00
104	Tommy Bridges	18.00	9.00	6.00
105	Eric McNair	18.00	9.00	6.00
106	Dolly Stark	18.00	9.00	6.00
107	Joe Vosmik	18.00	9.00	6.00
108	Frankie Hayes	18.00	9.00	6.00
109	Myril Hoag	18.00	9.00	6.00
110	Freddie Fitzsimmons	18.00	9.00	6.00
111	Van Lingle Mungo	25.00	11.00	8.25
112	Paul Waner	90.00	45.00	27.00
113	Al Schacht	23.00	10.50	7.50
114	Cecil Travis	18.00	9.00	6.00
115	Red Kress	18.00	9.00	6.00
116	Gene Desautels	95.00	50.00	30.00
117	Wayne Ambler	95.00	50.00	30.00
118	Lynn Nelson	95.00	50.00	30.00
119	Will Hershberger	95.00	50.00	30.00
120	Rabbit Warstler	95.00	50.00	30.00
121	Bill Posedel	95.00	50.00	30.00
122	George McQuinn	95.00	50.00	30.00
123	Peaches Davis	95.00	50.00	30.00
124	Jumbo Brown	95.00	50.00	30.00
125	Cliff Melton	95.00	50.00	30.00
126	Not issued	18.00	9.00	6.00
127	Gil Brack	95.00	50.00	30.00
128	Joe Bowman	95.00	50.00	30.00
129	Bill Swift	95.00	50.00	30.00
130	Bill Brubaker	95.00	50.00	30.00
131	Mort Cooper	95.00	50.00	30.00
132	Jimmy Brown	95.00	50.00	30.00
133	Lynn Myers	95.00	50.00	30.00
134	Tot Pressnell	95.00	50.00	30.00
135	Mickey Owen	95.00	50.00	30.00
136	Roy Bell	95.00	50.00	30.00
137	Pete Appleton	95.00	50.00	30.00
138	George Case	95.00	50.00	30.00
139	Vito Tamulis	95.00	50.00	30.00
140	Ray Hayworth	95.00	50.00	30.00
141	Pete Coscarart	95.00	50.00	30.00
142	Ira Hutchinson	95.00	50.00	30.00
143	Earl Averill	300.00	150.00	80.00
144	Zeke Bonura	95.00	50.00	30.00
145	Hugh Mulcahy	95.00	50.00	30.00
146	Tom Sunkel	95.00	50.00	30.00
147	George Coffman	95.00	50.00	30.00
148	Bill Trotter	95.00	50.00	30.00
149	Max West	95.00	50.00	30.00
150	Jim Walkup	95.00	50.00	30.00
151	Hugh Casey	95.00	50.00	30.00
152	Roy Weatherly	95.00	50.00	30.00
153	Dizzy Trout	95.00	50.00	30.00
154	Johnny Hudson	95.00	50.00	30.00
155	Jimmy Outlaw	95.00	50.00	30.00
156	Ray Berres	95.00	50.00	30.00
157	Don Padgett	95.00	50.00	30.00
158	Bud Thomas	95.00	50.00	30.00
159	Red Evans	95.00	50.00	30.00
160	Gene Moore Jr.	95.00	50.00	30.00
161	Lonny Frey	110.00	50.00	32.00
162	Whitey Moore	225.00	70.00	35.00

1940 Play Ball

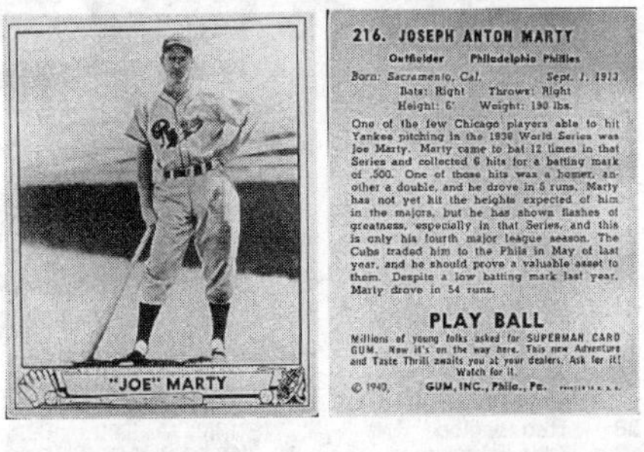

"JOE" MARTY
216. JOSEPH ANTON MARTY
Outfielder Philadelphia Phillies
Born: Sacramento, Cal. Sept. 1, 1913
Bats: Right Throws: Right
Height: 6' Weight: 190 lbs.
One of the few Chicago players able to hit Yankee pitching in the 1938 World Series was Joe Marty. Marty came to bat 12 times in that Series and collected 6 hits for a batting mark of .500. One of those hits was a homer, another a double, and he drove in 5 runs. Marty has not yet hit the heights expected of him in the majors, but he has shown flashes of greatness, especially in that Series, and this is only his fourth major league season. The Cubs traded him to the Phils in May of last year, and he should prove a valuable asset to them. Despite a low batting mark last year, Marty drove in 54 runs.
PLAY BALL
Millions of young folks asked for SUPERMAN CARD GUM. Now it's on the way here. This new Adventure and Taste Thrill awaits you at your dealers. Ask for it! Watch for it.
© 1940, GUM, INC., Phila., Pa.

Following the success of its initial effort in 1939, Gum Inc. issued a bigger and better set in 1940. The 240 black-and-white cards are once again in 2-1/2" x 3-1/8" size, but the front photos are enclosed by a frame with the player's name. Backs again offer extensive biographies and are dated. A number of former stars were issued along with contemporary players, and many Hall of Famers are included. The final 60 cards of the set are more difficult to obtain.

		NM	EX	VG
Complete Set (240):		17500.	7875.	5775.
Common Player (1-120):		22.00	10.00	5.00
Common Player (121-180):		24.00	12.00	6.00
Common Player (181-240):		70.00	32.00	20.00
1	Joe DiMaggio	2650.	1325.	795.00
2	"Art" Jorgens	22.00	10.00	5.00
3	"Babe" Dahlgren	22.00	10.00	5.00
4	"Tommy" Henrich	40.00	18.00	13.00
5	"Monte" Pearson	22.00	10.00	5.00
6	"Lefty" Gomez	180.00	90.00	54.00
7	"Bill" Dickey	155.00	70.00	50.00
8	"Twinkletoes" Selkirk	22.00	10.00	5.00
9	"Charley" Keller	35.00	15.50	11.50
10	"Red" Ruffing	90.00	40.00	30.00
11	"Jake" Powell	22.00	10.00	5.00
12	"Johnny" Schulte	22.00	10.00	5.00
13	"Jack" Knott	22.00	10.00	5.00
14	"Rabbit" McNair	22.00	10.00	5.00
15	George Case	22.00	10.00	5.00
16	Cecil Travis	22.00	10.00	5.00
17	"Buddy" Myer	22.00	10.00	5.00
18	"Charley" Gelbert	22.00	10.00	5.00
19	Ken Chase	22.00	10.00	5.00
20	"Buddy" Lewis	22.00	10.00	5.00
21	"Rick" Ferrell	90.00	40.00	30.00
22	"Sammy" West	22.00	10.00	5.00
23	"Dutch" Leonard	22.00	10.00	5.00
24	Frank "Blimp" Hayes	22.00	10.00	5.00
25	"Cherokee" Bob Johnson	22.00	10.00	5.00
26	"Wally" Moses	22.00	10.00	5.00
27	"Ted" Williams	2000.	1000.	600.00
28	"Gene" Desautels	22.00	10.00	5.00
29	"Doc" Cramer	22.00	10.00	5.00
30	"Moe" Berg	190.00	95.00	57.00
31	Jack Wilson	22.00	10.00	5.00
32	"Jim" Bagby	22.00	10.00	5.00
33	"Fritz" Ostermueller	22.00	10.00	5.00
34	John Peacock	22.00	10.00	5.00
35	"Joe" Heving	22.00	10.00	5.00
36	"Jim" Tabor	22.00	10.00	5.00
37	Emerson Dickman	22.00	10.00	5.00
38	"Bobby" Doerr	100.00	50.00	30.00
39	"Tom" Carey	22.00	10.00	5.00
40	"Hank" Greenberg	250.00	125.00	75.00
41	"Charley" Gehringer	130.00	65.00	40.00
42	"Bud" Thomas	22.00	10.00	5.00
43	Pete Fox	22.00	10.00	5.00
44	"Dizzy" Trout	22.00	10.00	5.00
45	"Red" Kress	22.00	10.00	5.00
46	Earl Averill	100.00	50.00	30.00
47	"Old Os" Vitt	22.00	10.00	5.00
48	"Luke" Sewell	22.00	10.00	5.00
49	"Stormy Weather" Weatherly	22.00	10.00	5.00
50	"Hal" Trosky	22.00	10.00	5.00
51	"Don" Heffner	22.00	10.00	5.00
52	Myril Hoag	22.00	10.00	5.00
53	"Mac" McQuinn	22.00	10.00	5.00
54	"Bill" Trotter	22.00	10.00	5.00
55	"Slick" Coffman	22.00	10.00	5.00
56	"Eddie" Miller	22.00	10.00	5.00
57	Max West	22.00	10.00	5.00
58	"Bill" Posedel	22.00	10.00	5.00
59	"Rabbit" Warstler	22.00	10.00	5.00
60	John Cooney	22.00	10.00	5.00
61	"Tony" Cuccinello	22.00	10.00	5.00
62	"Buddy" Hassett	22.00	10.00	5.00
63	"Pete" Cascarart (Coscarart)	22.00	10.00	5.00
64	"Van" Mungo	35.00	17.50	10.50
65	"Fitz" Fitzsimmons	22.00	10.00	5.00
66	"Babe" Phelps	22.00	10.00	5.00
67	"Whit" Wyatt	22.00	10.00	5.00
68	"Dolph" Camilli	22.00	10.00	5.00
69	"Cookie" Lavagetto	22.00	10.00	5.00
70	"Hot Potato" Hamlin	22.00	10.00	5.00
71	Mel Almada	32.00	14.50	10.50
72	"Chuck" Dressen	27.00	12.00	9.00
73	"Bucky" Walters	27.00	13.50	8.00
74	"Duke" Derringer	35.00	17.50	10.50
75	"Buck" McCormick	22.00	10.00	5.00
76	"Lonny" Frey	22.00	10.00	5.00
77	"Bill" Hershberger	22.00	10.00	5.00
78	"Lew" Riggs	22.00	10.00	5.00
79	"Wildfire" Craft	22.00	10.00	5.00
80	"Bill" Myers	22.00	10.00	5.00
81	"Wally" Berger	22.00	10.00	5.00
82	"Hank" Gowdy	22.00	10.00	5.00
83	"Clif" Melton (Cliff)	22.00	10.00	5.00
84	"Jo-Jo" Moore	22.00	10.00	5.00
85	"Hal" Schumacher	22.00	10.00	5.00
86	Harry Gumbert	22.00	10.00	5.00
87	Carl Hubbell	190.00	95.00	57.00
88	"Mel" Ott	200.00	100.00	60.00
89	"Bill" Jurges	22.00	10.00	5.00
90	Frank Demaree	22.00	10.00	5.00
91	Bob "Suitcase" Seeds	22.00	10.00	5.00
92	"Whitey" Whitehead	22.00	10.00	5.00
93	Harry "The Horse" Danning	22.00	10.00	5.00
94	"Gus" Suhr	22.00	10.00	5.00
95	"Mul" Mulcahy	22.00	10.00	5.00
96	"Heinie" Mueller	22.00	10.00	5.00
97	"Morry" Arnovich	22.00	10.00	5.00
98	"Pinky" May	22.00	10.00	5.00
99	"Syl" Johnson	22.00	10.00	5.00
100	"Hersh" Martin	22.00	10.00	5.00
101	"Del" Young	22.00	10.00	5.00
102	"Chuck" Klein	140.00	70.00	42.00
103	"Elbie" Fletcher	22.00	10.00	5.00
104	"Big Poison" Waner	140.00	70.00	42.00
105	"Little Poison" Waner	110.00	50.00	35.00
106	"Pep" Young	22.00	10.00	5.00
107	"Arky" Vaughan	100.00	50.00	30.00
108	"Johnny" Rizzo	22.00	10.00	5.00
109	"Don" Padgett	22.00	10.00	5.00
110	"Tom" Sunkel	22.00	10.00	5.00
111	"Mickey" Owen	22.00	10.00	5.00
112	"Jimmy" Brown	22.00	10.00	5.00
113	"Mort" Cooper	22.00	10.00	5.00
114	"Lon" Warneke	22.00	10.00	5.00
115	"Mike" Gonzales (Gonzalez)	32.00	14.50	10.50
116	"Al" Schacht	32.00	14.50	10.50
117	"Dolly" Stark	22.00	10.00	5.00
118	"Schoolboy" Hoyt	90.00	40.00	30.00
119	"Ol Pete" Alexander	165.00	74.00	54.00
120	Walter "Big Train" Johnson	255.00	125.00	76.00
121	Atley Donald	24.00	12.00	6.00
122	"Sandy" Sundra	24.00	12.00	6.00
123	"Hildy" Hildebrand	24.00	12.00	6.00
124	"Colonel" Combs	85.00	38.00	28.00
125	"Art" Fletcher	24.00	12.00	6.00
126	"Jake" Solters	24.00	12.00	6.00
127	"Muddy" Ruel	24.00	12.00	6.00
128	"Pete" Appleton	24.00	12.00	6.00
129	"Bucky" Harris	80.00	36.00	26.00
130	"Deerfoot" Milan	24.00	12.00	6.00
131	"Zeke" Bonura	24.00	12.00	6.00
132	Connie Mack	200.00	100.00	60.00
133	"Jimmie" Foxx	275.00	135.00	82.00
134	"Joe" Cronin	125.00	62.00	35.00
135	"Line Drive" Nelson	24.00	12.00	6.00
136	"Cotton" Pippen	24.00	12.00	6.00
137	"Bing" Miller	24.00	12.00	6.00
138	"Beau" Bell	24.00	12.00	6.00
139	Elden Auker (Eldon)	24.00	12.00	6.00
140	"Dick" Coffman	24.00	12.00	6.00
141	"Casey" Stengel	185.00	90.00	55.00
142	"Highpockets" Kelly	80.00	36.00	26.00
143	"Gene" Moore	24.00	12.00	6.00
144	"Joe" Vosmik	24.00	12.00	6.00
145	"Vito" Tamulis	24.00	12.00	6.00
146	"Tot" Pressnell	24.00	12.00	6.00
147	"Johnny" Hudson	24.00	12.00	6.00
148	"Hugh" Casey	24.00	12.00	6.00
149	"Pinky" Shoffner	24.00	12.00	6.00
150	"Whitey" Moore	24.00	12.00	6.00
151	Edwin Joost	24.00	12.00	6.00
152	Jimmy Wilson	24.00	12.00	6.00
153	"Bill" McKechnie	80.00	36.00	26.00
154	"Jumbo" Brown	24.00	12.00	6.00
155	"Ray" Hayworth	24.00	12.00	6.00
156	"Daffy" Dean	36.00	16.00	12.00
157	"Lou" Chiozza	24.00	12.00	6.00
158	"Stonewall" Jackson	85.00	38.00	28.00
159	"Pancho" Snyder	24.00	12.00	6.00
160	"Hans" Lobert	24.00	12.00	6.00
161	"Debs" Garms	24.00	12.00	6.00
162	Joe Bowman	24.00	12.00	6.00
163	"Spud" Davis	24.00	12.00	6.00
164	"Ray" Berres	24.00	12.00	6.00
165	"Bob" Klinger	24.00	12.00	6.00
166	"Bill" Brubaker	24.00	12.00	6.00
167	"Frankie" Frisch	100.00	45.00	33.00
168	"Honus" Wagner	325.00	145.00	105.00
169	"Gabby" Street	24.00	12.00	6.00
170	"Tris" Speaker	175.00	79.00	58.00
171	Harry Heilmann	125.00	62.00	37.00
172	"Chief" Bender	125.00	62.00	37.00
173	"Larry" Lajoie	175.00	87.00	52.00
174	"Johnny" Evers	100.00	50.00	30.00
175	"Christy" Mathewson	250.00	112.00	82.00
176	"Heinie" Manush	100.00	50.00	30.00
177	Frank "Homerun" Baker	125.00	62.00	37.00
178	Max Carey	95.00	47.00	28.00
179	George Sisler	125.00	62.00	37.00
180	"Mickey" Cochrane	160.00	80.00	48.00
181	"Spud" Chandler	70.00	32.00	20.00
182	"Knick" Knickerbocker	70.00	32.00	20.00
183	Marvin Breuer	70.00	32.00	20.00
184	"Mule" Haas	70.00	32.00	20.00
185	"Joe" Kuhel	70.00	32.00	20.00
186	Taft Wright	70.00	32.00	20.00
187	"Jimmy" Dykes	70.00	32.00	20.00
188	"Joe" Krakauskas	70.00	32.00	20.00
189	"Jim" Bloodworth	70.00	32.00	20.00
190	"Charley" Berry	70.00	32.00	20.00
191	John Babich	70.00	32.00	20.00
192	"Dick" Siebert	70.00	32.00	20.00
193	"Chubby" Dean	70.00	32.00	20.00
194	Sam Chapman	70.00	32.00	20.00
195	"Dee" Miles	70.00	32.00	20.00
196	"Nonny" Nonnenkamp	70.00	32.00	20.00
197	"Lou" Finney	70.00	32.00	20.00
198	"Denny" Galehouse	70.00	32.00	20.00
199	"Pinky" Higgins	70.00	32.00	20.00
200	"Soupy" Campbell	70.00	32.00	20.00
201	Barney McCosky	70.00	32.00	20.00
202	"Al" Milnar	70.00	32.00	20.00
203	"Bad News" Hale	70.00	32.00	20.00
204	Harry Eisenstat	70.00	32.00	20.00
205	"Rollie" Hemsley	70.00	32.00	20.00
206	"Chet" Laabs	70.00	32.00	20.00
207	"Gus" Mancuso	70.00	32.00	20.00
208	Lee Gamble	70.00	32.00	20.00
209	"Hy" Vandenberg	70.00	32.00	20.00
210	"Bill" Lohrman	70.00	32.00	20.00
211	"Pop" Joiner	70.00	32.00	20.00
212	"Babe" Young	70.00	32.00	20.00
213	John Rucker	70.00	32.00	20.00
214	"Ken" O'Dea	70.00	32.00	20.00
215	"Johnnie" McCarthy	70.00	32.00	20.00
216	"Joe" Marty	70.00	32.00	20.00
217	Walter Beck	70.00	32.00	20.00
218	"Wally" Millies	70.00	32.00	20.00
219	Russ Bauers	70.00	32.00	20.00
220	Mace Brown	70.00	32.00	20.00
221	Lee Handley	70.00	32.00	20.00

222	"Max" Butcher	70.00	32.00	20.00
223	Hugh "Ee-Yah" Jennings	165.00	82.00	49.00
224	"Pie" Traynor	225.00	110.00	65.00
225	"Shoeless Joe" Jackson	3750.	1875.	1125.
226	Harry Hooper	195.00	88.00	64.00
227	"Pop" Haines	200.00	100.00	60.00
228	"Charley" Grimm	70.00	32.00	20.00
229	"Buck" Herzog	70.00	32.00	20.00
230	"Red" Faber	195.00	88.00	64.00
231	"Dolf" Luque	90.00	40.00	30.00
232	"Goose" Goslin	200.00	100.00	60.00
233	"Moose" Earnshaw	70.00	32.00	20.00
234	Frank "Husk" Chance	225.00	110.00	55.00
235	John J. McGraw	195.00	88.00	64.00
236	"Sunny Jim" Bottomley	195.00	88.00	64.00
237	"Wee Willie" Keeler	225.00	110.00	67.00
238	"Poosh 'Em Up Tony" Lazzeri	195.00	88.00	64.00
239	George Uhle	70.00	32.00	20.00
240	"Bill" Atwood	195.00	88.00	64.00

1941 Play Ball

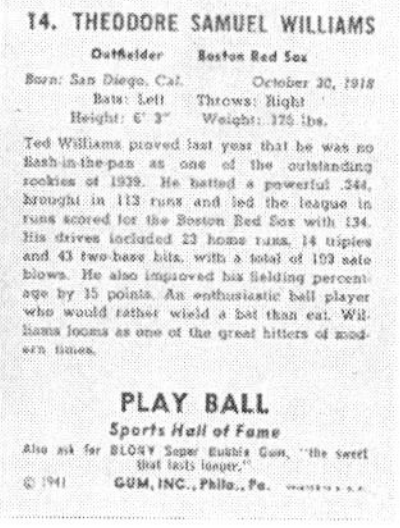

While the backs are quite similar to the black-and-white cards Gum Inc. issued in 1940, the card fronts in the 1941 set are printed in color. Many of the card photos, however, are just colorized versions of the player's 1940 card. The cards are still in the 2-1/2" x 3-1/8" size, but only 72 cards are included in the set. Card numbers 49-72 are rarer than the lower-numbered cards. The cards were printed in sheets of 12, and can still be found that way.

		NM	EX	VG
Complete Set (72):		8000.	3600.	2600.
Common Player (1-48):		55.00	27.50	18.00
Common Player (49-72):		75.00	45.00	20.00
1	"Eddie" Miller	295.00	45.00	18.00
2	Max West	55.00	27.50	18.00
3	"Bucky" Walters	55.00	27.50	18.00
4	"Duke" Derringer	55.00	27.50	18.00
5	"Buck" McCormick	55.00	27.50	18.00
6	Carl Hubbell	250.00	125.00	75.00
7	"The Horse" Danning	55.00	27.50	18.00
8	"Mel" Ott	300.00	150.00	90.00
9	"Pinky" May	55.00	27.50	18.00
10	"Arky" Vaughan	110.00	55.00	33.00
11	Debs Garms	55.00	27.50	18.00
12	"Jimmy" Brown	55.00	27.50	18.00
13	"Jimmie" Foxx	400.00	200.00	120.00
14	"Ted" Williams	2500.	900.00	600.00
15	"Joe" Cronin	125.00	56.00	41.00
16	"Hal" Trosky	55.00	27.50	18.00
17	"Stormy" Weatherly	55.00	27.50	18.00
18	"Hank" Greenberg	325.00	146.00	107.00
19	"Charley" Gehringer	250.00	125.00	75.00
20	"Red" Ruffing	165.00	80.00	50.00
21	"Charlie" Keller	80.00	36.00	26.00
22	"Indian Bob" Johnson	55.00	27.50	18.00
23	"Mac" McQuinn	55.00	27.50	18.00
24	"Dutch" Leonard	55.00	27.50	18.00
25	"Gene" Moore	55.00	27.50	18.00
26	Harry "Gunboat" Gumbert	55.00	27.50	18.00
27	"Babe" Young	55.00	27.50	18.00
28	"Joe" Marty	55.00	27.50	18.00
29	Jack Wilson	55.00	27.50	18.00
30	"Lou" Finney	55.00	27.50	18.00
31	"Joe" Kuhel	55.00	27.50	18.00
32	Taft Wright	55.00	27.50	18.00
33	"Happy" Milnar	55.00	27.50	18.00
34	"Rollie" Hemsley	55.00	27.50	18.00
35	"Pinky" Higgins	55.00	27.50	18.00
36	Barney McCosky	55.00	27.50	18.00
37	"Soupy" Campbell	55.00	27.50	18.00
38	Atley Donald	55.00	27.50	18.00
39	"Tommy" Henrich	80.00	40.00	25.00
40	"Johnny" Babich	55.00	27.50	18.00
41	Frank "Blimp" Hayes	55.00	27.50	18.00
42	"Wally" Moses	55.00	27.50	18.00
43	Albert "Bronk" Brancato	55.00	27.50	18.00
44	Sam Chapman	55.00	27.50	18.00
45	Elden Auker (Eldon)	55.00	27.50	18.00
46	"Sid" Hudson	55.00	27.50	18.00
47	"Buddy" Lewis	55.00	27.50	18.00
48	Cecil Travis	55.00	27.50	18.00
49	"Babe" Dahlgren	75.00	45.00	20.00
50	"Johnny" Cooney	75.00	45.00	20.00
51	"Dolph" Camilli	75.00	45.00	20.00
52	Kirby Higbe	75.00	45.00	20.00
53	Luke "Hot Potato" Hamlin	75.00	45.00	20.00
54	"Pee Wee" Reese	750.00	350.00	210.00
55	"Whit" Wyatt	75.00	45.00	20.00
56	"Vandy" Vander Meer	75.00	45.00	20.00
57	"Moe" Arnovich	75.00	45.00	20.00
58	"Frank" Demaree	75.00	45.00	20.00
59	"Bill" Jurges	75.00	45.00	20.00
60	"Chuck" Klein	225.00	110.00	70.00
61	"Vince" DiMaggio	150.00	67.00	49.00
62	"Elbie" Fletcher	75.00	45.00	20.00
63	"Dom" DiMaggio	175.00	79.00	58.00
64	"Bobby" Doerr	200.00	90.00	66.00
65	"Tommy" Bridges	75.00	45.00	20.00
66	Harland Clift (Harlond)	75.00	45.00	20.00
67	"Walt" Judnich	75.00	45.00	20.00
68	"Jack" Knott	75.00	45.00	20.00
69	George Case	75.00	45.00	20.00
70	"Bill" Dickey	525.00	260.00	155.00
71	"Joe" DiMaggio	3000.	1250.	650.00
72	"Lefty" Gomez	500.00	200.00	75.00

1941 Play Ball Paper Version

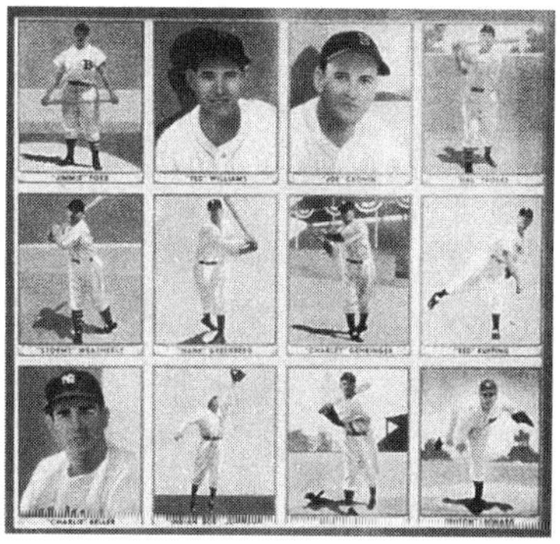

As cardboard became a critical commodity during the months prior to the United States' entry into WWII, Play Ball experimented by issuing a version of the first 24 cards in the 1941 set on blank-back sheets of 12, comprising only the top, color-printed layer of the regular cards. These paper versions, understandably, did not stand up to handling as well as the cardboard cards and survivors are much scarcer today.

		NM	EX	VG
Complete Set (24):		3125.	1100.	625.00
Common Player:		40.00	14.00	8.00
Complete Sheet 1-12:		725.00	250.00	145.00
Complete Sheet 13-24:		2475.	865.00	495.00
1	Eddie Miller	40.00	14.00	8.00
2	Max West	40.00	14.00	8.00
3	Bucky Walters	40.00	14.00	8.00
4	"Duke" Derringer	40.00	14.00	8.00
5	"Buck" McCormick	40.00	14.00	8.00
6	Carl Hubbell	145.00	51.00	29.00
7	"The Horse" Danning	40.00	14.00	8.00
8	Mel Ott	160.00	56.00	32.00
9	"Pinky" May	40.00	14.00	8.00
10	"Arky" Vaughan	100.00	35.00	20.00
11	Debs Garms	40.00	14.00	8.00
12	"Jimmy" Brown	40.00	14.00	8.00
13	Jimmie Foxx	270.00	94.00	54.00
14	Ted Williams	1600.	560.00	320.00
15	Joe Cronin	130.00	45.00	26.00
16	Hal Trosky	40.00	14.00	8.00
17	Roy Weatherly	40.00	14.00	8.00
18	Hank Greenberg	260.00	91.00	52.00
19	Charley Gehringer	160.00	56.00	32.00
20	"Red" Ruffing	120.00	42.00	24.00
21	Charlie Keller	50.00	17.50	10.00
22	Bob Johnson	40.00	14.00	8.00
23	"Mac" McQuinn	40.00	14.00	8.00
24	Dutch Leonard	40.00	14.00	8.00

1976 Playboy Press Who Was Harry Steinfeldt?

(Babe Ruth)

This 12-card set was issued in 1976 by Playboy Press to promote author Bert Randolph Sugar's book "Who Was Harry Steinfeldt? & Other Baseball Trivia Questions." (Steinfeldt was the third baseman in the Cubs' famous infield that featured Hall of Famers Tinker, Evers and Chance). The black and white cards measure the standard 2-1/2" x 3-1/2" with a player photo on the front and a trivia question and ad for the book on the back.

		NM	EX	VG
Complete Set (12):		125.00	62.00	37.00
Common Player:		2.50	1.25	.70
(1)	Frankie Baumholtz	2.50	1.25	.70
(2)	Jim Bouton	3.50	1.75	1.00
(3)	Tony Conigliaro	7.50	3.75	2.25
(4)	Don Drysdale	9.00	4.50	2.75
(5)	Hank Greenberg	11.00	5.50	3.25
(6)	Walter Johnson	18.50	9.25	5.50
(7)	Billy Loes	2.50	1.25	.70
(8)	Johnny Mize	6.00	3.00	1.75
(9)	Frank "Lefty" O'Doul	3.50	1.75	1.00
(10)	Babe Ruth	50.00	25.00	15.00
(11)	Johnny Sain	3.50	1.75	1.00
(12)	Jim Thorpe	35.00	17.50	10.50

1962 Playing Card Supers

The attributed date is approximate since none is shown on the cards; nor is a credit line to the manufacturer. Player content suggests Pittsburgh was the center of distribution. The 3-1/4" x 5-1/4" round cornered cards are printed in black-and-white, or red, black and white; they are blank-backed. Probably intended for sale in penny arcade machines, most of the card "denominations" can be found with more than one person. Besides the ballplayers listed here, the set contained TV and movie cowboys, rock-and-roll stars, boxers, wrestlers and cartoon characters.

		NM	EX	VG
Complete Set (81):		90.00	45.00	27.00
Common Player:		1.00	.50	.30
AC	Bill Mazeroski	1.25	.60	.40
2C	Whitey Ford	1.50	.70	.45
2C	Al Kaline	1.50	.70	.45
2C	Pirates logo cartoon	1.00	.50	.30
4C	Frank Robinson	1.50	.70	.45
4C	Babe Ruth	8.00	4.00	2.50
5C	Wilmer Mizell	1.00	.50	.30
5C	Mickey Mantle	12.00	6.00	3.50
5C	Honus Wagner	1.50	.70	.45
6C	Eddie Mathews	1.50	.70	.45
6C	Willie Mays	6.00	3.00	1.75
7C	Dodgers' "Bum" cartoon logo	1.00	.50	.30
7C	Eddie Mathews	1.50	.70	.45
7C	Willie Mays	6.00	3.00	1.75
8C	Walter Johnson	1.50	.70	.45
8C	Mickey Mantle	12.00	6.00	3.50
8C	Wilmer Mizell	1.00	.50	.30
9C	Hank Aaron	6.00	3.00	1.75
9C	Frank Robinson	1.50	.70	.45
10C	Lew Burdette	1.00	.50	.30
JC	Harvey Haddix	1.00	.50	.30
JC	Bill Mazeroski	1.25	.60	.40
JC	Al McBean	1.00	.50	.30
QC	Ty Cobb	4.00	2.00	1.25
QC	Whitey Ford	1.50	.70	.45
QC	Don Leppert	1.00	.50	.30
KC	Al Kaline	1.50	.70	.45
KC	Honus Wagner	1.50	.70	.45
AS	Lew Burdette	1.00	.50	.30
AS	Ty Cobb	4.00	2.00	1.25
2S	Smoky Burgess	1.00	.50	.30
3S	Don Hoak	1.00	.50	.30
4S	Roy Face	1.00	.50	.30
5S	Roberto Clemente	8.00	4.00	2.50
5S	Danny Murtaugh	1.00	.50	.30
6S	Christy Mathewson	1.50	.70	.45
6S	Dick Stuart	1.00	.50	.30
7S	Christy Mathewson	1.50	.70	.45
7S	Dick Stuart	1.00	.50	.30
8S	Danny Murtaugh	1.00	.50	.30
9S	Roy Face	1.00	.50	.30
10S	Don Hoak	1.00	.50	.30
JS	Smoky Burgess	1.00	.50	.30
QS	Walter Johnson	1.50	.70	.45
QS	Babe Ruth	8.00	4.00	2.50
KS	Hank Aaron	6.00	3.00	1.75
KS	Harvey Haddix	1.00	.50	.30
AH	Don Drysdale	1.50	.70	.45

AH	Ken Boyer	1.00	.50	.30
2H	Satchel Paige	3.00	1.50	.90
3H	Rocky Colavito	1.50	.70	.45
4H	Stan Musial	3.00	1.50	.90
4H	Bobby Richardson	1.00	.50	.30
5H	Ken Boyer	1.00	.50	.30
5H	Harmon Killebrew	1.50	.70	.45
6H	Luis Aparicio	1.50	.70	.45
6H	Ralph Kiner	1.50	.70	.45
7H	Sandy Koufax	3.00	1.50	.90
8H	Warren Spahn	1.50	.70	.45
9H	Jimmy Piersall	1.00	.50	.30
10H	Yogi Berra	1.50	.70	.45
10H	Ralph Kiner	1.50	.70	.45
JH	Orlando Cepeda	1.50	.70	.45
JH	Ken Boyer	1.00	.50	.30
QH	Roger Maris	6.00	3.00	1.75
QH	Stan Musial	3.00	1.50	.90
KH	Bob Purkey	1.00	.50	.30
AD	Don Drysdale	1.50	.70	.45
AD	Don Hoak	1.00	.50	.30
2D	Satchel Paige	3.00	1.50	.90
6D	Luis Aparicio	1.50	.70	.45
6D	Ernie Banks	1.50	.70	.45
7D	Bill Virdon	1.00	.50	.30
7D	Sandy Koufax	3.00	1.50	.90
8D	Bob Skinner	1.00	.50	.30
9D	Dick Groat	1.00	.50	.30
10D	Vernon Law	1.00	.50	.30
JD	Joe Adcock	1.00	.50	.30
JD	Orlando Cepeda	1.50	.70	.45
QD	Roger Maris	6.00	3.00	1.75
KD	Bob Friend	1.00	.50	.30

1910 Plow Boy Tobacco

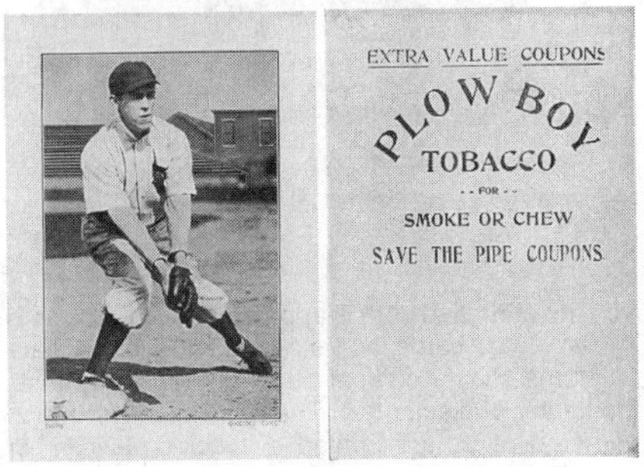

Plowboy Tobacco, a product of the Spaulding & Merrick Company, issued a set of bainet-size cards in the Chicago area featuring members of the Cubs and the White Sox. From the checklist of the 50 known cards, it appears that the bulk of the set was originally issued in 1910 with a few additional cards appearing over the next several years. The set appears to be complete at 25 Cubs and 25 White Sox players, although there is some speculation that other cards may still be discovered. Measuring approximately 5-3/4" x 8", the Plowboys are one of the largest tobacco cards of the 20th Century. They feature very nice sepia-toned player photos in poses not found on other tobacco issues. The player's name appears in the lower left corner, while the team name appears in the lower right. Two different backs are known to exist. One consists of a simple advertisement for Plowboy Tobacco, while a second more difficult variety includes a list of premiums available in exchange for coupons. The set is among the rarest of all 20th Century tobacco issues.

		NM	EX	VG
Complete Set (48):		18000.	7200.	3600.
Common Player:		400.00	160.00	80.00
(1)	Jimmy Archer	400.00	160.00	80.00
(2)	Ginger Beaumont	400.00	160.00	80.00
(3)	Lena Blackburne	400.00	160.00	80.00
(4)	Bruno Block	400.00	160.00	80.00
(5)	Ping Bodie	400.00	160.00	80.00
(6)	Mordecai Brown	700.00	280.00	140.00
(7)	Al Carson	400.00	160.00	80.00
(8)	Frank Chance	700.00	280.00	140.00
(9)	Ed Cicotte	500.00	200.00	100.00
(10)	King Cole	400.00	160.00	80.00
(11)	Shano Collins	400.00	160.00	80.00
(12)	George Davis	600.00	240.00	120.00
(13)	Patsy Dougherty	400.00	160.00	80.00
(14)	Johnny Evers	700.00	280.00	140.00
(15)	Chick Gandel (Gandil)	500.00	200.00	100.00
(16)	Ed Hahn	400.00	160.00	80.00
(17)	Solly Hoffman (Hofman)	400.00	160.00	80.00
(18)	Del Howard	400.00	160.00	80.00
(19)	Bill Jones	400.00	160.00	80.00
(20)	Johnny Kling	400.00	160.00	80.00
(21)	Rube Kroh	400.00	160.00	80.00
(22)	Frank Lange	400.00	160.00	80.00
(23)	Fred Luderus	400.00	160.00	80.00
(24)	Harry McIntyre	400.00	160.00	80.00
(25)	Ward Miller	400.00	160.00	80.00
(26)	Charlie Mullen	400.00	160.00	80.00
(27)	Tom Needham	400.00	160.00	80.00
(28)	Fred Olmstead	400.00	160.00	80.00
(29)	Orval Overall	400.00	160.00	80.00
(30)	Fred Parent	400.00	160.00	80.00
(31)	Fred Payne	400.00	160.00	80.00
(32)	Francis "Big Jeff" Pfeffer	400.00	160.00	80.00
(33)	Jake Pfeister	400.00	160.00	80.00
(34)	Billy Purtell	400.00	160.00	80.00
(35)	Ed Reulbach	400.00	160.00	80.00
(36)	Lew Richie	400.00	160.00	80.00
(37)	Jimmy Scheckard (Sheckard)	400.00	160.00	80.00
(38)	Wildfire Schulte	400.00	160.00	80.00
(39a)	Jim Scot (name incorrect)	400.00	160.00	80.00
(39b)	Jim Scott (name correct)	400.00	160.00	80.00
(40)	Frank Smith	400.00	160.00	80.00
(41)	Harry Steinfeldt	400.00	160.00	80.00
(42)	Billy Sullivan	400.00	160.00	80.00
(43)	Lee Tannehill	400.00	160.00	80.00
(44)	Joe Tinker	700.00	280.00	140.00
(45)	Ed Walsh	700.00	280.00	140.00
(46)	Doc White	400.00	160.00	80.00
(47)	Irv Young	400.00	160.00	80.00
(48)	Rollie Zeider	400.00	160.00	80.00
(49)	Heinie Zimmerman	400.00	160.00	80.00

1912 Plow's Candy (E300)

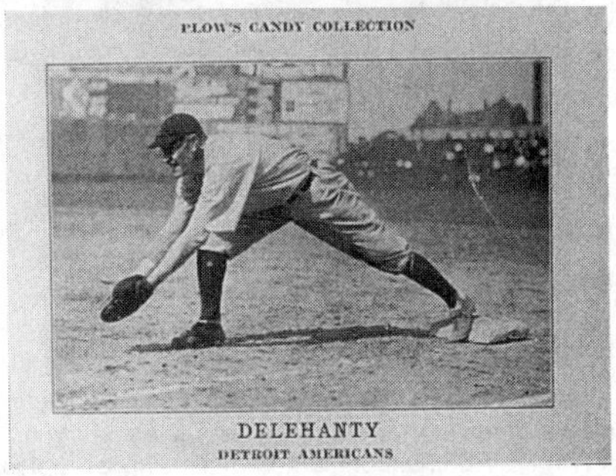

An extremely rare candy issue, cards in this 1912 set measure 3" x 4" and feature sepia-toned photos surrounded by a rather wide border. The player's name and team appear in the border below the photo, while the words "Plow's Candy Collection" appear at the top. The backs are blank. Not even known to exist until the late 1960s, this set has been assigned the designation of E300.

		NM	EX	VG
Complete Set (66):		40000.	18000.	10000.
Common Player:		500.00	225.00	125.00
(1)	Babe Adams	500.00	225.00	125.00
(2)	Home Run Baker	1100.	495.00	275.00
(3)	Cy Barger	500.00	225.00	125.00
(4)	Jack Barry	500.00	225.00	125.00
(5)	Johnny Bates	500.00	225.00	125.00
(7)	Joe Benz	500.00	225.00	125.00
(8)	Cy Berger (Barger)	500.00	225.00	125.00
(9)	Roger Bresnahan	1100.	495.00	275.00
(10)	Mordecai Brown	1100.	495.00	275.00
(11)	Donie Bush	500.00	225.00	125.00
(12)	Bobby Byrne	500.00	225.00	125.00
(13)	Nixey Callahan	500.00	225.00	125.00
(14)	Hal Chase	700.00	315.00	175.00
(15)	Fred Clarke	1100.	495.00	275.00
(16)	Ty Cobb	4500.	2025.	1125.
(17)	King Cole	500.00	225.00	125.00
(18)	Eddie Collins	1100.	495.00	275.00
(19)	Jack Coombs	500.00	225.00	125.00
(20)	Bill Dahlen	500.00	225.00	125.00
(21)	Bert Daniels	500.00	225.00	125.00
(22)	Harry Davis	500.00	225.00	125.00
(23)	Jim Delehanty	500.00	225.00	125.00
(24)	Josh Devore	500.00	225.00	125.00
(25)	Wild Bill Donovan	500.00	225.00	125.00
(26)	Red Dooin	500.00	225.00	125.00
(27)	Johnny Evers	1100.	495.00	275.00
(28)	Russ Ford	500.00	225.00	125.00
(29)	Del Gainor	500.00	225.00	125.00
(30)	Vean Gregg	500.00	225.00	125.00
(31)	Bob Harmon	500.00	225.00	125.00
(32)	Arnold Hauser	500.00	225.00	125.00
(33)	Dick Hoblitzelle (Hoblitzell)	500.00	225.00	125.00
(34)	Solly Hofman	500.00	225.00	125.00
(35)	Miller Huggins	1100.	495.00	275.00
(36)	John Hummel	500.00	225.00	125.00
(37)	Walter Johnson	3000.	1350.	750.00
(38)	Johnny Kling	500.00	225.00	125.00
(39)	Nap Lajoie	1250.	562.00	312.00
(40)	Jack Lapp	500.00	225.00	125.00
(41)	Fred Luderus	500.00	225.00	125.00
(42)	Sherry Magee	500.00	225.00	125.00
(43)	Rube Marquard	1100.	495.00	275.00
(44)	Christy Mathewson	3000.	1350.	750.00
(45)	Stuffy McInnes (McInnis)	500.00	225.00	125.00
(46)	Larry McLean	500.00	225.00	125.00
(47)	Fred Merkle	500.00	225.00	125.00
(48)	Cy Morgan	500.00	225.00	125.00
(49)	George Moriarty	500.00	225.00	125.00
(50)	Mike Mowrey	500.00	225.00	125.00
(51)	Chief Myers (Meyers)	500.00	225.00	125.00
(52)	Rube Oldring	500.00	225.00	125.00
(53)	Marty O'Toole	500.00	225.00	125.00
(54)	Nap Rucker	500.00	225.00	125.00
(55)	Slim Sallee	500.00	225.00	125.00
(56)	Boss Schmidt	500.00	225.00	125.00
(57)	Jimmy Sheckard	500.00	225.00	125.00
(58)	Tris Speaker	1100.	495.00	275.00
(59)	Billy Sullivan	500.00	225.00	125.00
(60)	Ira Thomas	500.00	225.00	125.00
(61)	Joe Tinker	1100.	495.00	275.00
(62)	John Titus	500.00	225.00	125.00
(63)	Hippo Vaughan (Vaughn)	500.00	225.00	125.00
(64)	Honus Wagner	3000.	1350.	750.00
(65)	Ed Walsh	1100.	495.00	275.00
(66)	Bob Williams	500.00	225.00	125.00

1915 PM1 Ornate-frame Pins

Little is known about these tiny (approximately 1-1/16" x 1") pins, such as who issued them, when and how they were distributed and how many are in the set. The pins feature sepia-tone player photos surrounded by ornate gilded metal frames. The player's name is printed in a black strip at the bottom of the photo. The pins were originally sold for 19¢.

		NM	EX	VG
Complete Set (15):		8750.	4500.	2600.
Common Pin:		225.00	112.00	67.00
(1)	Jimmy Archer	225.00	112.00	67.00
(2)	Frank Baker	750.00	375.00	225.00
(3)	Frank Chance	750.00	375.00	225.00
(4)	Ty Cobb	3000.	1500.	900.00
(5)	Al Demaree	225.00	112.00	67.00
(6)	Johnny Evers	750.00	375.00	225.00
(7)	Rube Foster	225.00	112.00	67.00
(8)	Dick Hoblitzell	225.00	112.00	67.00
(9)	Walter Johnson	1200.	600.00	360.00
(10)	Benny Kauff	225.00	112.00	67.00
(11)	Ed Konetchy	225.00	112.00	67.00
(12)	Nap Lajoie	750.00	375.00	225.00
(13)	Christy Mathewson	1500.	750.00	450.00
(14)	Tris Speaker	750.00	375.00	225.00
(15)	Joe Tinker	750.00	375.00	225.00

1956 PM15 Yellow Basepath Pins

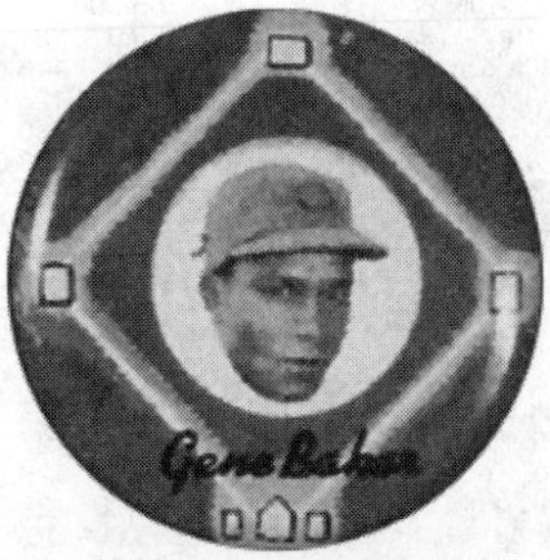

These pins were issued circa 1956; the sponsor of this 32-pin set is not indicated. The set, which has been assigned the American Card Catalog designation PM15, is commonly called "Yellow Basepaths" because of the design of the pin, which features a black-and-white player photo set inside a green infield with yellow basepaths. The unnumbered pins measure 7/8" in diameter. The names of Kluszewski and Mathews are misspelled.

		NM	EX	VG
Complete Set (32):		2950.	1350.	825.00
Common Player:		35.00	17.50	10.50
(1)	Hank Aaron	225.00	112.00	67.00
(2)	Joe Adcock	35.00	17.50	10.50
(3)	Luis Aparicio	85.00	42.00	25.00
(4)	Richie Ashburn	105.00	52.00	31.00
(5)	Gene Baker	35.00	17.50	10.50
(6)	Ernie Banks	125.00	62.00	37.00

(7)	Yogi Berra	125.00	62.00	37.00
(8)	Bill Bruton	35.00	17.50	10.50
(9)	Larry Doby	85.00	42.00	25.00
(10)	Bob Friend	35.00	17.50	10.50
(11)	Nellie Fox	65.00	32.00	19.50
(12)	Ted Greengrass (Jim)	35.00	17.50	10.50
(13)	Steve Gromek	35.00	17.50	10.50
(14)	Johnny Groth	35.00	17.50	10.50
(15)	Gil Hodges	105.00	52.00	31.00
(16)	Al Kaline	125.00	62.00	37.00
(17)	Ted Kluzewski (Kluszewski)	70.00	35.00	21.00
(18)	Johnny Logan	35.00	17.50	10.50
(19)	Dale Long	35.00	17.50	10.50
(20)	Mickey Mantle	750.00	375.00	225.00
(21)	Ed Mathews	85.00	42.00	25.00
(22)	Minnie Minoso	55.00	27.00	16.50
(23)	Stan Musial	225.00	112.00	67.00
(24)	Don Newcombe	50.00	25.00	15.00
(25)	Bob Porterfield	35.00	17.50	10.50
(26)	Pee Wee Reese	105.00	52.00	31.00
(27)	Robin Roberts	70.00	35.00	21.00
(28)	Red Schoendienst	60.00	30.00	18.00
(29)	Duke Snider	125.00	62.00	37.00
(30)	Vern Stephens	35.00	17.50	10.50
(31)	Gene Woodling	35.00	17.50	10.50
(32)	Gus Zernial	35.00	17.50	10.50

1950 Pocket Television Theatre

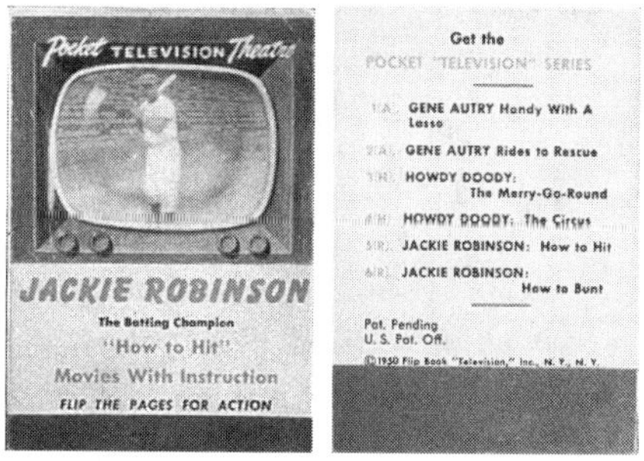

Generically known as "flip books," these 2-1/4" x 3-1/8" novelties have multiple pages stapled together which, when fanned rapidly, give the appearance of action. Each of the black-and-white pages in the book is a photo made from one frame of a movie. A photo on the red, white and black front cover shows Jackie Robinson as if on a television screen. A list on the back of the booklet shows that besides the Jackie Robinson booklets, there were two each featuring Gene Autry and Howdy Doody.

	NM	EX	VG
Complete Set (2):	600.00	300.00	175.00
5 (R) How to Hit (Jackie Robinson)	300.00	150.00	90.00
6 (R) How to Bunt (Jackie Robinson)	300.00	150.00	90.00

1909-11 Polar Bear Tobacco

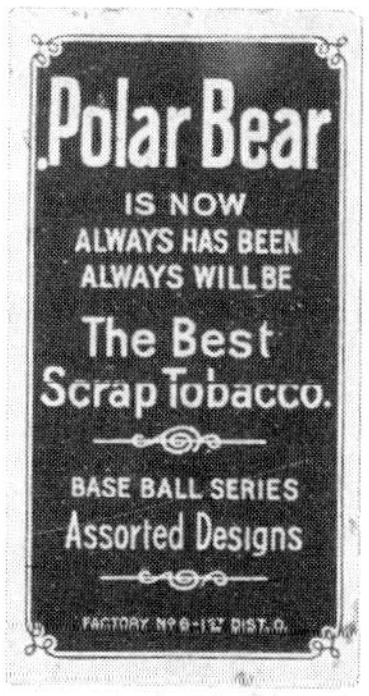

(See T205, T206. Premium: T205/T206 +30%)

1889 Police Gazette Cabinets

Issued in the late 1880s through early 1890s as a premium by Police Gazette, a popular newspaper of the day, these cabinet cards were only recently discovered and are very rare. The 4-1/2" x 6-1/2" cards consist of sepia-toned photographs mounted on cardboard of various colors. Only about two dozen players are currently known. Some photographs correspond to those used in the S.F. Hess card series and many players are depicted in suit and tie, rather than baseball uniform. All of the cards display the name of the player next to his portrait, along with the signature of "Richard K. Fox" and a line identifying him as "Editor and Proprietor/Police Gazette/Franklin Square, New York."

		NM	EX	VG
Common Player:		2500.	1250.	750.00
(1)	Hick Carpenter	2500.	1250.	750.00
(2)	Fred Carroll	2500.	1250.	750.00
(3)	Bob Clark	2500.	1250.	750.00
(4)	Roger Conner (Connor)	3750.	1875.	1125.
(5)	Pete Conway	2500.	1250.	750.00
(6)	John Corckhill	2500.	1250.	750.00
(7)	Jerry Denny	2500.	1250.	750.00
(8)	Buck Ewing	3750.	1875.	1125.
(9)	Bob Ferguson	2500.	1250.	750.00
(10)	Jocko Fields	2500.	1250.	750.00
(11)	Elmer Foster	2500.	1250.	750.00
(12)	Charlie Getzein (Getzien)	2500.	1250.	750.00
(13)	Pebbly Jack Glasscock	2500.	1250.	750.00
(14)	Bill Gleason	2500.	1250.	750.00
(15)	George Gore	2500.	1250.	750.00
(16)	Tim Keefe	3750.	1875.	1125.
(17)	Gus Krock	2500.	1250.	750.00
(18)	Tip O'Neil (O'Neill)	2850.	1425.	855.00
(19)	N. (Fred) Pfeffer	2500.	1250.	750.00
(20)	Danny Richardson	2500.	1250.	750.00
(21)	Elmer Smith	2500.	1250.	750.00
(22)	Harry Staley	2500.	1250.	750.00
(23)	William Swett (San Francisco)	2500.	1250.	750.00
(24)	George Tebeau	2500.	1250.	750.00
(25)	John Tener	2500.	1250.	750.00
(26)	Curt Welch	2500.	1250.	750.00

1914 Polo Grounds Game

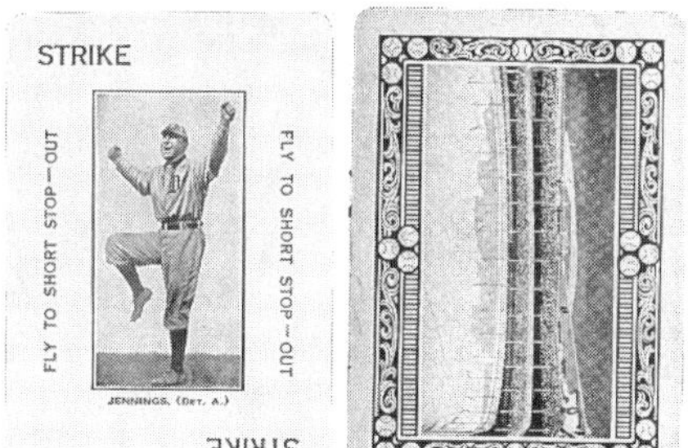

Some catalogers have attributed this set to 1910. Because many of the players depicted were not in the major leagues at that time, or had played only a handful of games, a more likely date of issue is 1914. The round-cornered 2-1/2" x 3-1/2" cards feature a green-and-white photo of the Polo Grounds on the back. Fronts have a black-and-white player photo and a baseball play scenario that is used to play a card game. The unnumbered cards are checklisted here alphabetically.

		NM	EX	VG
Complete Set (30):		2350.	1175.	705.00
Common Player:		35.00	17.50	10.50
(1)	Jimmy Archer	35.00	17.50	10.50
(2)	Frank Baker	70.00	35.00	21.00
(3)	Frank Chance	70.00	35.00	21.00
(4)	Larry Cheney	35.00	17.50	10.50
(5)	Ty Cobb	550.00	275.00	165.00
(6)	Eddie Collins	70.00	35.00	21.00
(7)	Larry Doyle	35.00	17.50	10.50
(8)	Art Fletcher	35.00	17.50	10.50
(9)	Claude Hendrix	35.00	17.50	10.50
(10)	Joe Jackson	875.00	435.00	260.00
(11)	Hughie Jennings	70.00	35.00	21.00
(12)	Nap Lajoie	75.00	37.00	22.00
(13)	Jimmy Lavender	35.00	17.50	10.50
(14)	Fritz Maisel	35.00	17.50	10.50
(15)	Rabbit Maranville	70.00	35.00	21.00
(16)	Rube Marquard	70.00	35.00	21.00
(17)	Christy Mathewson	175.00	87.00	52.00
(18)	John McGraw	70.00	35.00	21.00
(19)	Stuffy McInnis	35.00	17.50	10.50
(20)	Chief Meyers	35.00	17.50	10.50
(21)	Red Murray	35.00	17.50	10.50
(22)	Ed Plank	70.00	35.00	21.00
(23)	Nap Rucker	35.00	17.50	10.50
(24)	Reb Russell	35.00	17.50	10.50
(25)	Wildfire Schulte	35.00	17.50	10.50
(26)	Jim Scott	35.00	17.50	10.50
(27)	Tris Speaker	85.00	42.00	25.00
(28)	Honus Wagner	175.00	87.00	52.00
(29)	Ed Walsh	70.00	35.00	21.00
(30)	Joe Wood	35.00	17.50	10.50

1915 Postaco Stamps

A small find of these early stamps in complete sheets of 12 in the mid-1990s made the issue collectible, rather than impossibly rare. Individual stamps are 1-3/4" x 2-1/8" and feature black-and-white player portraits set against a bright background of either yellow or red-orange. The player name, position (in most cases), team and league are designated at the bottom of the picture. In the black frame between the picture and the perforated white border is a copyright symbol and "Postaco". Backs are, of course, blank. Stamps are checklisted here in alphabetical order within color group. The yellow stamps are scarcer than the red-orange.

		NM	EX	VG
Complete Set, Sheets (3):		2250.	1100.	725.00
Complete Set, Singles (36):		1500.	750.00	450.00
Common Player:		40.00	20.00	12.00
	Red-orange background			
(1)	Home Run Baker	95.00	47.00	28.00
(2)	Chief Bender	95.00	47.00	28.00
(3)	George Burns	40.00	20.00	12.00
(4)	John Evers	95.00	47.00	28.00
(5)	Max Flack	40.00	20.00	12.00
(6)	Hank Gawdy (Gowdy)	40.00	20.00	12.00
(7)	Claude Ray Hendrix	40.00	20.00	12.00
(8)	Walter Johnson	200.00	100.00	60.00
(9)	Nap Lajoie	95.00	47.00	28.00
(10)	Hans Lobert	40.00	20.00	12.00
(11)	Sherwood Magee	40.00	20.00	12.00
(12)	Rabbit Maranville	95.00	47.00	28.00
(13)	Christy Mathewson	250.00	125.00	75.00
(14)	George McBride	40.00	20.00	12.00
(15)	John McGraw	95.00	47.00	28.00
(16)	Fred Merkle	40.00	20.00	12.00
(17)	Jack Miller	40.00	20.00	12.00
(18)	Emiliano Palmero	100.00	50.00	30.00
(19)	Pol Perritt	40.00	20.00	12.00
(20)	Derrill Pratt	40.00	20.00	12.00
(21)	Richard Rudolph	40.00	20.00	12.00
(22)	Butch Schmidt	40.00	20.00	12.00
(23)	Joe Tinker	95.00	47.00	28.00
(24)	Honus Wagner	250.00	125.00	75.00
	Yellow background			
(25)	G.C. Alexander	95.00	47.00	28.00
(26)	J.P. Archer	40.00	20.00	12.00
(27)	Ty Cobb	600.00	300.00	180.00
(28)	Eugene Cocreham	40.00	20.00	12.00
(29)	E.S. Cottrell	40.00	20.00	12.00
(30)	Josh Devore	40.00	20.00	12.00
(31)	A. Hartzell (Roy)	40.00	20.00	12.00
(32)	Wm. H. James (middle initial actually L)	40.00	20.00	12.00
(33)	Connie Mack	95.00	47.00	28.00
(34)	M. McHale	40.00	20.00	12.00
(35)	Geo. T. Stallings	40.00	20.00	12.00
(36)	Ed. Sweeney	40.00	20.00	12.00

1930 Post Sports Stars

The year of issue is unconfirmed. Mathewson is the only baseball player from a group of cereal-box cards. The front is printed in red and yellow, the back is blank. The card measures about 2-5/8" x 3-1/2".

CHRISTY MATHEWSON (1880-1925)—Greatest of all baseball pitchers.

	NM	EX	VG
Christy Mathewson	400.00	200.00	120.00

1960 Post Cereal

MICKEY MANTLE

These cards were issued on the backs of Grape Nuts cereal and measure an oversized 7" x 8-3/4". The nine cards in the set include five baseball players (Al Kaline, Mickey Mantle, Don Drysdale, Harmon Killebrew and Ed Mathews) as well as two football and two basketball players. The full-color photos were placed on a color background and bordered by a wood frame design. The cards covered the entire back of the cereal box and were blank backed. Card fronts also include the player's name and team and a facsimile autograph. A panel on the side of the box contains player biographical information. A scarce set, the cards are very difficult to obtain in mint condition.

		NM	EX	VG
Complete Set (9):		4500.	2250.	1350.
Common Player:		300.00	150.00	90.00
(1)	Bob Cousy	450.00	225.00	135.00
(2)	Don Drysdale	400.00	200.00	120.00
(3)	Frank Gifford	300.00	150.00	90.00
(4)	Al Kaline	450.00	225.00	135.00
(5)	Harmon Killebrew	300.00	150.00	90.00
(6)	Ed Mathews	300.00	150.00	90.00
(7)	Mickey Mantle	1600.	800.00	480.00
(8)	Bob Pettit	400.00	200.00	120.00
(9)	John Unitas	400.00	200.00	120.00

1961 Post Cereal

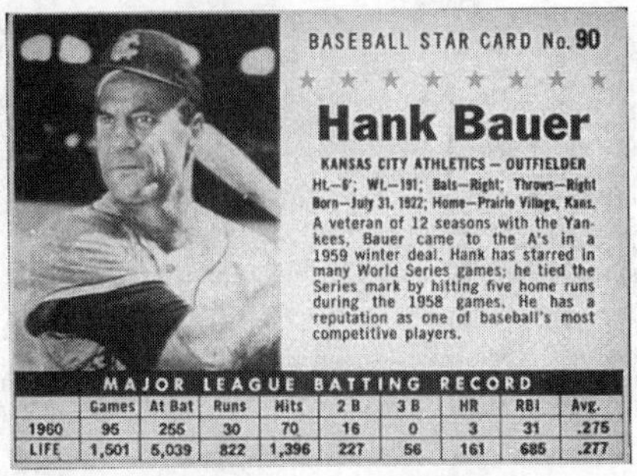
BASEBALL STAR CARD No. 90
Hank Bauer
KANSAS CITY ATHLETICS — OUTFIELDER
Ht.—6'; Wt.—191; Bats—Right; Throws—Right
Born—July 31, 1922; Home—Prairie Village, Kans.
A veteran of 12 seasons with the Yankees, Bauer came to the A's in a 1959 winter deal. Hank has starred in many World Series games; he tied the Series mark by hitting five home runs during the 1958 games. He has a reputation as one of baseball's most competitive players.
MAJOR LEAGUE BATTING RECORD
Games | At Bat | Runs | Hits | 2 B | 3 B | HR | RBI | Avg.
1960 | 95 | 255 | 30 | 70 | 16 | 0 | 3 | 31 | .275
LIFE | 1,501 | 5,039 | 822 | 1,396 | 227 | 56 | 161 | 685 | .277

Two hundred different players are included in this set, but with variations the number of different cards exceeds 350. This was the first large-scale card set by the cereal company and it proved very popular with fans. Cards were issued both singly and in various panel sizes on the thick cardboard stock of cereal boxes, as well on thinner stock, in team sheets issued directly by Post via a mail-in offer. About 10 cards in the set were issued in significantly smaller quantities, making their prices much higher than other comparable players in the set. Individual cards measure a 3-1/2" x 2-1/2", and all cards are numbered in the upper left corner. Card fronts have full-color portait photos of the player, along with biographical information and 1960 and career statistics. Card backs are blank. The complete set price includes does not include the scarcer variations.

		NM	EX	VG
Complete Set (200):		1800.	900.00	500.00
Common Player:		3.50	1.50	.90
1a	Yogi Berra (box)	33.00	15.00	8.25
1b	Yogi Berra (company)	20.00	9.00	5.00
2a	Elston Howard (box)	7.00	3.25	1.75
2b	Elston Howard (company)	4.00	1.75	1.00
3a	Bill Skowron (box)	3.50	1.50	.90
3b	Bill Skowron (company)	3.50	1.50	.90
4a	Mickey Mantle (box)	125.00	56.00	31.00
4b	Mickey Mantle (company)	105.00	47.00	26.00
5	Bob Turley (company)	27.50	12.50	7.00
6a	Whitey Ford (box)	11.50	5.25	3.00
6b	Whitey Ford (company)	11.50	5.25	3.00
7a	Roger Maris (box)	33.00	15.00	8.25
7b	Roger Maris (company)	33.00	15.00	8.25
8a	Bobby Richardson (box)	4.00	1.75	1.00
8b	Bobby Richardson (company)	4.00	1.75	1.00
9a	Tony Kubek (box)	4.00	1.75	1.00
9b	Tony Kubek (company)	4.00	1.75	1.00
10	Gil McDougald (box)	47.00	21.00	11.50
11	Cletis Boyer (box)	3.50	1.50	.90
12a	Hector Lopez (box)	3.50	1.50	.90
12b	Hector Lopez (company)	3.50	1.50	.90
13	Bob Cerv (box)	3.50	1.50	.90
14	Ryne Duren (box)	3.50	1.50	.90
15	Bobby Shantz (box)	3.50	1.50	.90
16	Art Ditmar (box)	3.50	1.50	.90
17	Jim Coates (box)	3.50	1.50	.90
18	John Blanchard (box)	3.50	1.50	.90
19a	Luis Aparicio (box)	7.00	3.25	1.75
19b	Luis Aparicio (company)	7.00	3.25	1.75
20a	Nelson Fox (box)	5.75	2.50	1.50
20b	Nelson Fox (company)	5.75	2.50	1.50
21a	Bill Pierce (box)	7.00	3.25	1.75
21b	Bill Pierce (company)	7.00	3.25	1.75
22a	Early Wynn (box)	9.25	4.25	2.25
22b	Early Wynn (company)	33.00	15.00	8.25
23	Bob Shaw (box)	115.00	52.00	29.00
24a	Al Smith (box)	4.00	1.75	1.00
24b	Al Smith (company)	3.50	1.50	.90
25a	Minnie Minoso (box)	4.50	2.00	1.25
25b	Minnie Minoso (company)	4.50	2.00	1.25
26a	Roy Sievers (box)	3.50	1.50	.90
26b	Roy Sievers (company)	3.50	1.50	.90
27a	Jim Landis (box)	3.50	1.50	.90
27b	Jim Landis (company)	3.50	1.50	.90
28a	Sherman Lollar (box)	4.00	1.75	1.00
28b	Sherman Lollar (company)	3.50	1.50	.90
29	Gerry Staley (box)	3.50	1.50	.90
30a	Gene Freese (box, White Sox)	3.50	1.50	.90
30b	Gene Freese (company, Reds)	9.00	4.00	2.25
31	Ted Kluszewski (box)	4.50	2.00	1.25
32	Turk Lown (box)	3.50	1.50	.90
33a	Jim Rivera (box)	3.50	1.50	.90
33b	Jim Rivera (company)	3.50	1.50	.90
34	Frank Baumann (box)	3.50	1.50	.90
35a	Al Kaline (box)	28.00	12.50	7.00
35b	Al Kaline (company)	28.00	12.50	7.00
36a	Rocky Colavito (box)	8.50	3.75	2.25
36b	Rocky Colavito (company)	5.00	2.25	1.25
37a	Charley Maxwell (box)	5.50	2.50	1.50
37b	Charley Maxwell (company)	3.50	1.50	.90
38a	Frank Lary (box)	3.50	1.50	.90
38b	Frank Lary (company)	3.50	1.50	.90
39a	Jim Bunning (box)	7.00	3.25	1.75
39b	Jim Bunning (company)	7.00	3.25	1.75
40a	Norm Cash (box)	3.50	1.50	.90
40b	Norm Cash (company)	3.50	1.50	.90
41a	Frank Bolling (box, Tigers)	7.50	3.50	2.00
41b	Frank Bolling (company, Braves)	7.00	3.25	1.75
42a	Don Mossi (box)	3.50	1.50	.90
42b	Don Mossi (company)	3.50	1.50	.90
43a	Lou Berberet (box)	3.50	1.50	.90
43b	Lou Berberet (company)	3.50	1.50	.90
44	Dave Sisler (box)	3.50	1.50	.90
45	Ed Yost (box)	3.50	1.50	.90
46	Pete Burnside (box)	3.50	1.50	.90
47a	Pete Runnels (box)	4.00	1.75	1.00
47b	Pete Runnels (company)	3.50	1.50	.90
48a	Frank Malzone (box)	3.50	1.50	.90
48b	Frank Malzone (company)	3.50	1.50	.90
49a	Vic Wertz (box)	7.00	3.25	1.75
49b	Vic Wertz (company)	4.00	1.75	1.00
50a	Tom Brewer (box)	3.50	1.50	.90
50b	Tom Brewer (company)	3.50	1.50	.90
51a	Willie Tasby (box, no sold line)	7.50	3.50	2.00
51b	Willie Tasby (company, sold line)	5.00	2.25	1.25
52a	Russ Nixon (box)	3.50	1.50	.90
52b	Russ Nixon (company)	3.50	1.50	.90
53a	Don Buddin (box)	3.50	1.50	.90
53b	Don Buddin (company)	3.50	1.50	.90
54a	Bill Monbouquette (box)	3.50	1.50	.90
54b	Bill Monbouquette (company)	3.50	1.50	.90
55a	Frank Sullivan (box, Red Sox)	3.50	1.50	.90
55b	Frank Sullivan (company, Phillies)	33.00	15.00	8.25
56a	Haywood Sullivan (box)	3.50	1.50	.90
56b	Haywood Sullivan (company)	3.50	1.50	.90
57a	Harvey Kuenn (box, Indians)	4.00	1.75	1.00
57b	Harvey Kuenn (company, Giants)	9.00	4.00	2.25
58a	Gary Bell (box)	7.00	3.25	1.75
58b	Gary Bell (company)	3.50	1.50	.90
59a	Jim Perry (box)	3.50	1.50	.90
59b	Jim Perry (company)	3.50	1.50	.90
60a	Jim Grant (box)	4.00	1.75	1.00
60b	Jim Grant (company)	3.50	1.50	.90
61a	Johnny Temple (box)	3.50	1.50	.90
61b	Johnny Temple (company)	3.50	1.50	.90
62a	Paul Foytack (box)	3.50	1.50	.90
62b	Paul Foytack (company)	3.50	1.50	.90
63a	Vic Power (box)	3.50	1.50	.90
63b	Vic Power (company)	3.50	1.50	.90
64a	Tito Francona (box)	3.50	1.50	.90
64b	Tito Francona (company)	3.50	1.50	.90
65a	Ken Aspromonte (box, no sold line)	8.50	3.75	2.25
65b	Ken Aspromonte (company, sold line)	8.50	3.75	2.25
66	Bob Wilson (box)	3.50	1.50	.90
67a	John Romano (box)	3.50	1.50	.90
67b	John Romano (company)	3.50	1.50	.90
68a	Jim Gentile (box)	3.50	1.50	.90
68b	Jim Gentile (company)	3.50	1.50	.90
69a	Gus Triandos (box)	4.00	1.75	1.00
69b	Gus Triandos (company)	3.50	1.50	.90
70	Gene Woodling (box)	18.50	8.25	4.75
71a	Milt Pappas (box)	4.00	1.75	1.00
71b	Milt Pappas (company)	3.50	1.50	.90
72a	Ron Hansen (box)	4.00	1.75	1.00
72b	Ron Hansen (company)	3.50	1.50	.90
73	Chuck Estrada (company)	115.00	52.00	29.00
74a	Steve Barber (box)	3.50	1.50	.90
74b	Steve Barber (company)	3.50	1.50	.90
75a	Brooks Robinson (box)	27.50	12.50	7.00
75b	Brooks Robinson (company)	27.50	12.50	7.00
76a	Jackie Brandt (box)	3.50	1.50	.90
76b	Jackie Brandt (company)	3.50	1.50	.90
77a	Marv Breeding (box)	3.50	1.50	.90
77b	Marv Breeding (company)	3.50	1.50	.90
78	Hal Brown (box)	3.50	1.50	.90
79	Billy Klaus (box)	3.50	1.50	.90
80a	Hoyt Wilhelm (box)	7.00	3.25	1.75
80b	Hoyt Wilhelm (company)	8.50	3.75	2.25
81a	Jerry Lumpe (box)	8.50	3.75	2.25
81b	Jerry Lumpe (company)	5.50	2.50	1.50
82a	Norm Siebern (box)	3.50	1.50	.90
82b	Norm Siebern (company)	3.50	1.50	.90
83a	Bud Daley (box)	3.50	1.50	.90
83b	Bud Daley (company)	3.50	1.50	.90
84a	Bill Tuttle (box)	3.50	1.50	.90
84b	Bill Tuttle (company)	3.50	1.50	.90
85a	Marv Throneberry (box)	3.50	1.50	.90
85b	Marv Throneberry (company)	3.50	1.50	.90
86a	Dick Williams (box)	3.50	1.50	.90
86b	Dick Williams (company)	3.50	1.50	.90
87a	Ray Herbert (box)	3.50	1.50	.90
87b	Ray Herbert (company)	3.50	1.50	.90
88a	Whitey Herzog (box)	3.50	1.50	.90
88b	Whitey Herzog (company)	3.50	1.50	.90
89a	Ken Hamlin (box, no sold line)	3.50	1.50	.90
89b	Ken Hamlin (company, sold line)	9.00	4.00	2.25
90a	Hank Bauer (box)	3.50	1.50	.90
90b	Hank Bauer (company)	3.50	1.50	.90
91a	Bob Allison (box, Minneapolis)	5.50	2.50	1.50
91b	Bob Allison (company, Minnesota)	7.00	3.25	1.75
92a	Harmon Killebrew (box, Minneapolis)	30.00	13.50	7.50
92b	Harmon Killebrew (company, Minnesota)	30.00	13.50	7.50
93a	Jim Lemon (box, Minneapolis)	55.00	25.00	13.50
93b	Jim Lemon (company, Minnesota)	7.00	3.25	1.75
94	Chuck Stobbs (company)	170.00	76.00	42.00
95a	Reno Bertoia (box, Minneapolis)	3.50	1.50	.90
95b	Reno Bertoia (company, Minnesota)	5.50	2.50	1.50
96a	Billy Gardner (box, Minneapolis)	3.50	1.50	.90
96b	Billy Gardner (company, Minnesota)	5.50	2.50	1.50
97a	Earl Battey (box, Minneapolis)	5.50	2.50	1.50
97b	Earl Battey (company, Minnesota)	5.50	2.50	1.50
98a	Pedro Ramos (box, Minneapolis)	3.50	1.50	.90
98b	Pedro Ramos (company, Minnesota)	5.50	2.50	1.50
99a	Camilio Pascual (Camilo) (box, Minneapolis)	3.50	1.50	.90
99b	Camilio Pascual (Camilo) (company, Minnesota)	5.50	2.50	1.50
100a	Billy Consolo (box, Minneapolis)	3.50	1.50	.90
100b	Billy Consolo (company, Minnesota)	5.50	2.50	1.50
101a	Warren Spahn (box)	20.00	9.00	5.00
101b	Warren Spahn (company)	11.00	5.00	2.75
102a	Lew Burdette (box)	3.50	1.50	.90
102b	Lew Burdette (company)	3.50	1.50	.90
103a	Bob Buhl (box)	3.50	1.50	.90
103b	Bob Buhl (company)	3.50	1.50	.90
104a	Joe Adcock (box)	5.50	2.50	1.50
104b	Joe Adcock (company)	3.50	1.50	.90

105a	John Logan (box)	5.50	2.50	1.50
105b	John Logan (company)	3.50	1.50	.90
106	Ed Mathews (company)	37.00	16.50	9.25
107a	Hank Aaron (box)	33.00	15.00	8.25
107b	Hank Aaron (company)	33.00	15.00	8.25
108a	Wes Covington (box)	3.50	1.50	.90
108b	Wes Covington (company)	3.50	1.50	.90
109a	Bill Bruton (box, Braves)	8.50	3.75	2.25
109b	Bill Bruton (company, Tigers)	7.50	3.50	2.00
110a	Del Crandall (box)	5.50	2.50	1.50
110b	Del Crandall (company)	3.50	1.50	.90
111	Red Schoendienst (box)	7.00	3.25	1.75
112	Juan Pizarro (box)	3.50	1.50	.90
113	Chuck Cottier (box)	7.50	3.50	2.00
114	Al Spangler (box)	3.50	1.50	.90
115a	Dick Farrell (box)	8.50	3.75	2.25
115b	Dick Farrell (company)	5.50	2.50	1.50
116a	Jim Owens (box)	8.50	3.75	2.25
116b	Jim Owens (company)	5.50	2.50	1.50
117a	Robin Roberts (box)	8.50	3.75	2.25
117b	Robin Roberts (company)	8.50	3.75	2.25
118a	Tony Taylor (box)	3.50	1.50	.90
118b	Tony Taylor (company)	3.50	1.50	.90
119a	Lee Walls (box)	3.50	1.50	.90
119b	Lee Walls (company)	3.50	1.50	.90
120a	Tony Curry (box)	3.50	1.50	.90
120b	Tony Curry (company)	3.50	1.50	.90
121a	Pancho Herrera (box)	3.50	1.50	.90
121b	Pancho Herrera (company)	3.50	1.50	.90
122a	Ken Walters (box)	3.50	1.50	.90
122b	Ken Walters (company)	3.50	1.50	.90
123a	John Callison (box)	3.50	1.50	.90
123b	John Callison (company)	3.50	1.50	.90
124a	Gene Conley (box, Phillies)	3.50	1.50	.90
124b	Gene Conley (company, Red Sox)	18.50	8.25	4.75
125a	Bob Friend (box)	5.50	2.50	1.50
125b	Bob Friend (company)	3.50	1.50	.90
126a	Vernon Law (box)	5.50	2.50	1.50
126b	Vernon Law (company)	3.50	1.50	.90
127a	Dick Stuart (box)	3.50	1.50	.90
127b	Dick Stuart (company)	3.50	1.50	.90
128a	Bill Mazeroski (box)	7.50	3.75	2.25
128b	Bill Mazeroski (company)	7.50	3.75	2.25
129a	Dick Groat (box)	4.00	1.75	1.00
129b	Dick Groat (company)	3.50	1.50	.90
130a	Don Hoak (box)	3.50	1.50	.90
130b	Don Hoak (company)	3.50	1.50	.90
131a	Bob Skinner (box)	3.50	1.50	.90
131b	Bob Skinner (company)	3.50	1.50	.90
132a	Bob Clemente (box)	33.00	15.00	8.25
132b	Bob Clemente (company)	33.00	15.00	8.25
133	Roy Face (box)	4.00	1.75	1.00
134	Harvey Haddix (box)	3.50	1.50	.90
135	Bill Virdon (box)	41.00	18.50	10.00
136a	Gino Cimoli (box)	3.50	1.50	.90
136b	Gino Cimoli (company)	3.50	1.50	.90
137	Rocky Nelson (box)	3.50	1.50	.90
138a	Smoky Burgess (box)	3.50	1.50	.90
138b	Smoky Burgess (company)	3.50	1.50	.90
139	Hal Smith (box)	3.50	1.50	.90
140	Wilmer Mizell (box)	3.50	1.50	.90
141a	Mike McCormick (box)	3.50	1.50	.90
141b	Mike McCormick (company)	3.50	1.50	.90
142a	John Antonelli (box, Giants)	4.00	1.75	1.00
142b	John Antonelli (company, Indians)	5.50	2.50	1.50
143a	Sam Jones (box)	5.50	2.50	1.50
143b	Sam Jones (company)	3.50	1.50	.90
144a	Orlando Cepeda (box)	7.50	3.75	2.25
144b	Orlando Cepeda (company)	7.50	3.75	2.25
145a	Willie Mays (box)	33.00	15.00	8.25
145b	Willie Mays (company)	33.00	15.00	8.25
146a	Willie Kirkland (box, Giants)	8.00	3.50	2.00
146b	Willie Kirkland (company, Indians)	8.00	3.50	2.00
147a	Willie McCovey (box)	6.50	3.00	1.75
147b	Willie McCovey (company)	28.00	12.50	7.00
148a	Don Blasingame (box)	3.50	1.50	.90
148b	Don Blasingame (company)	3.50	1.50	.90
149a	Jim Davenport (box)	3.50	1.50	.90
149b	Jim Davenport (company)	3.50	1.50	.90
150a	Hobie Landrith (box)	3.50	1.50	.90
150b	Hobie Landrith (company)	3.50	1.50	.90
151	Bob Schmidt (box)	3.50	1.50	.90
152a	Ed Bressoud (box)	3.50	1.50	.90
152b	Ed Bressoud (company)	3.50	1.50	.90
153a	Andre Rodgers (box, no traded line)	8.50	3.75	2.25
153b	Andre Rodgers (box, traded line)	3.50	1.50	.90
154	Jack Sanford (box)	3.50	1.50	.90
155	Billy O'Dell (box)	3.50	1.50	.90
156a	Norm Larker (box)	7.00	3.25	1.75
156b	Norm Larker (company)	3.50	1.50	.90
157a	Charlie Neal (box)	3.50	1.50	.90
157b	Charlie Neal (company)	3.50	1.50	.90
158a	Jim Gilliam (box)	5.50	2.50	1.50
158b	Jim Gilliam (company)	3.50	1.50	.90
159a	Wally Moon (box)	3.50	1.50	.90
159b	Wally Moon (company)	3.50	1.50	.90
160a	Don Drysdale (box)	8.00	3.50	2.00
160b	Don Drysdale (company)	9.00	4.00	2.25
161a	Larry Sherry (box)	3.50	1.50	.90
161b	Larry Sherry (company)	3.50	1.50	.90
162	Stan Williams (box)	7.00	3.25	1.75
163	Mel Roach (box)	40.00	18.00	10.00
164a	Maury Wills (box)	5.50	2.50	1.50
164b	Maury Wills (company)	5.50	2.50	1.50
165	Tom Davis (box)	3.50	1.50	.90
166a	John Roseboro (box)	3.50	1.50	.90
166b	John Roseboro (company)	3.50	1.50	.90
167a	Duke Snider (box)	7.50	3.50	2.00
167b	Duke Snider (company)	28.00	12.50	7.00
168a	Gil Hodges (box)	7.00	3.25	1.75
168b	Gil Hodges (company)	8.50	3.75	2.25
169	John Podres (box)	3.50	1.50	.90
170	Ed Roebuck (box)	3.50	1.50	.90
171a	Ken Boyer (box)	8.50	3.75	2.25
171b	Ken Boyer (company)	5.50	2.50	1.50
172a	Joe Cunningham (box)	3.50	1.50	.90
172b	Joe Cunningham (company)	3.50	1.50	.90
173a	Daryl Spencer (box)	3.50	1.50	.90
173b	Daryl Spencer (company)	3.50	1.50	.90
174a	Larry Jackson (box)	3.50	1.50	.90
174b	Larry Jackson (company)	3.50	1.50	.90
175a	Lindy McDaniel (box)	3.50	1.50	.90
175b	Lindy McDaniel (company)	3.50	1.50	.90
176a	Bill White (box)	3.50	1.50	.90
176b	Bill White (company)	3.50	1.50	.90
177a	Alex Grammas (box)	3.50	1.50	.90
177b	Alex Grammas (company)	3.50	1.50	.90
178a	Curt Flood (box)	3.50	1.50	.90
178b	Curt Flood (company)	3.50	1.50	.90
179a	Ernie Broglio (box)	3.50	1.50	.90
179b	Ernie Broglio (company)	3.50	1.50	.90
180a	Hal Smith (box)	3.50	1.50	.90
180b	Hal Smith (company)	3.50	1.50	.90
181a	Vada Pinson (box)	3.50	1.50	.90
181b	Vada Pinson (company)	3.50	1.50	.90
182a	Frank Robinson (box)	28.00	12.50	7.00
182b	Frank Robinson (company)	28.00	12.50	7.00
183	Roy McMillan (box)	70.00	31.00	17.50
184a	Bob Purkey (box)	3.50	1.50	.90
184b	Bob Purkey (company)	3.50	1.50	.90
185a	Ed Kasko (box)	3.50	1.50	.90
185b	Ed Kasko (company)	3.50	1.50	.90
186a	Gus Bell (box)	3.50	1.50	.90
186b	Gus Bell (company)	3.50	1.50	.90
187a	Jerry Lynch (box)	3.50	1.50	.90
187b	Jerry Lynch (company)	3.50	1.50	.90
188a	Ed Bailey (box)	3.50	1.50	.90
188b	Ed Bailey (company)	3.50	1.50	.90
189a	Jim O'Toole (box)	3.50	1.50	.90
189b	Jim O'Toole (company)	3.50	1.50	.90
190a	Billy Martin (box, no sold line)	4.00	1.75	1.00
190b	Billy Martin (company, sold line)	8.50	3.75	2.25
191a	Ernie Banks (box)	8.50	3.75	2.25
191b	Ernie Banks (company)	8.50	3.75	2.25
192a	Richie Ashburn (box)	10.00	4.50	2.50
192b	Richie Ashburn (company)	10.00	4.50	2.50
193a	Frank Thomas (box)	37.00	16.50	9.25
193b	Frank Thomas (company)	7.00	3.25	1.75
194a	Don Cardwell (box)	3.50	1.50	.90
194b	Don Cardwell (company)	3.50	1.50	.90
195a	George Altman (box)	3.50	1.50	.90
195b	George Altman (company)	3.50	1.50	.90
196a	Ron Santo (box)	4.00	1.75	1.00
196b	Ron Santo (company)	4.00	1.75	1.00
197a	Glen Hobbie (box)	3.50	1.50	.90
197b	Glen Hobbie (company)	3.50	1.50	.90
198a	Sam Taylor (box)	3.50	1.50	.90
198b	Sam Taylor (company)	3.50	1.50	.90
199a	Jerry Kindall (box)	3.50	1.50	.90
199b	Jerry Kindall (company)	3.50	1.50	.90
200a	Don Elston (box)	4.00	1.75	1.00
200b	Don Elston (company)	4.00	1.75	1.00

1962 Post Cereal

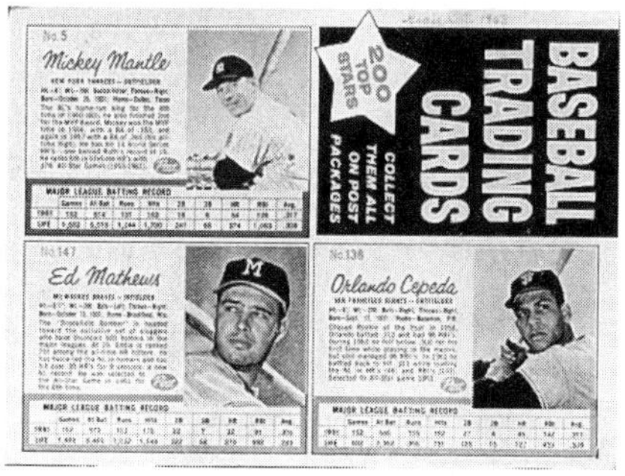

Like the 1961 Post set, there are 200 players pictured in the set of 3-1/2" x 2-1/2" cards. Differences include a Post logo on the card fronts and the player's name in script lettering. Cards are again blank backed and were issued in panels of five to seven cards on cereal boxes. American League players are numbered 1-100 and National League players 101-200. With variations there are 210 of the full-color cards known. A handful of the '62 cards were also issued in smaller quantities. The cards of Mickey Mantle and Roger Maris were reproduced in a special two-card panel for a Life magazine insert. The card stock for this insert is slightly thinner, with white margins. The 1962 Post Canadian and Jell-O sets have virtually the same checklist as this set. The complete set price does not include the scarcer variations.

		NM	EX	VG
Complete Set (200):		1100.	500.00	275.00
Common Player:		2.50	1.25	.60
1	Bill Skowron	4.25	2.00	1.00
2	Bobby Richardson	4.00	2.00	1.25
3	Cletis Boyer	2.50	1.25	.60
4	Tony Kubek	4.00	1.75	1.00
5a	Mickey Mantle (from box, no printing on back)	85.00	38.00	21.00
5b	Mickey Mantle (from ad, printing on back)	80.00	36.00	20.00
6a	Roger Maris (from box, no printing on back)	22.00	10.00	5.50
6b	Roger Maris (from ad, printing on back)	18.00	8.00	4.50
7	Yogi Berra	12.50	5.75	3.25
8	Elston Howard	4.00	1.75	1.00
9	Whitey Ford	9.00	4.00	2.25
10	Ralph Terry	2.50	1.25	.60
11	John Blanchard	2.50	1.25	.60
12	Luis Arroyo	2.50	1.25	.60
13	Bill Stafford	2.50	1.25	.60
14a	Norm Cash (Throws: Right)	18.00	8.00	4.50
14b	Norm Cash (Throws: Left)	4.00	1.75	1.00
15	Jake Wood	2.50	1.25	.60
16	Steve Boros	2.50	1.25	.60
17	Chico Fernandez	2.50	1.25	.60
18	Bill Bruton	2.50	1.25	.60
19	Rocky Colavito	5.00	2.50	1.50
20	Al Kaline	9.00	4.00	2.25
21	Dick Brown	2.50	1.25	.60
22	Frank Lary	2.50	1.25	.60
23	Don Mossi	2.50	1.25	.60
24	Phil Regan	2.50	1.25	.60
25	Charley Maxwell	2.50	1.25	.60
26	Jim Bunning	6.00	2.75	1.50
27a	Jim Gentile (Home: Baltimore)	2.50	1.25	.60
27b	Jim Gentile (Home: San Lorenzo)	5.50	2.50	1.50
28	Marv Breeding	2.50	1.25	.60
29	Brooks Robinson	9.00	4.00	2.25
30	Ron Hansen	2.50	1.25	.60
31	Jackie Brandt	2.50	1.25	.60
32	Dick Williams	2.50	1.25	.60
33	Gus Triandos	2.50	1.25	.60
34	Milt Pappas	2.50	1.25	.60
35	Hoyt Wilhelm	6.50	3.00	1.75
36	Chuck Estrada	5.50	2.50	1.50
37	Vic Power	2.50	1.25	.60
38	Johnny Temple	2.50	1.25	.60
39	Bubba Phillips	2.50	1.25	.60
40	Tito Francona	2.50	1.25	.60
41	Willie Kirkland	2.50	1.25	.60
42	John Romano	2.50	1.25	.60
43	Jim Perry	2.50	1.25	.60
44	Woodie Held	2.50	1.25	.60
45	Chuck Essegian	2.50	1.25	.60
46	Roy Sievers	2.50	1.25	.60
47	Nellie Fox	7.50	3.75	2.25
48	Al Smith	2.50	1.25	.60
49	Luis Aparicio	7.75	3.50	2.00
50	Jim Landis	2.50	1.25	.60
51	Minnie Minoso	3.75	1.75	.90
52	Andy Carey	2.50	1.25	.60
53	Sherman Lollar	2.50	1.25	.60
54	Bill Pierce	2.50	1.25	.60
55	Early Wynn	35.00	15.50	8.75
56	Chuck Schilling	2.50	1.25	.60
57	Pete Runnels	2.50	1.25	.60
58	Frank Malzone	2.50	1.25	.60
59	Don Buddin	2.50	1.25	.60
60	Gary Geiger	2.50	1.25	.60
61	Carl Yastrzemski	40.00	18.00	10.00
62	Jackie Jensen	3.75	1.75	.90
63	Jim Pagliaroni	2.50	1.25	.60
64	Don Schwall	2.50	1.25	.60
65	Dale Long	2.50	1.25	.60
66	Chuck Cottier	2.50	1.25	.60
67	Billy Klaus	2.50	1.25	.60
68	Coot Veal	2.50	1.25	.60
69	Marty Keough	33.00	15.00	8.25
70	Willie Tasby	2.50	1.25	.60
71	Gene Woodling	3.00	1.25	.70
72	Gene Green	2.50	1.25	.60
73	Dick Donovan	2.50	1.25	.60
74	Steve Bilko	2.50	1.25	.60
75	Rocky Bridges	2.50	1.25	.60
76	Eddie Yost	2.50	1.25	.60
77	Leon Wagner	2.50	1.25	.60
78	Albie Pearson	2.50	1.25	.60
79	Ken Hunt	2.50	1.25	.60
80	Earl Averill	2.50	1.25	.60
81	Ryne Duren	2.50	1.25	.60
82	Ted Kluszewski	4.00	2.00	1.25
83	Bob Allison	30.00	13.50	7.50
84	Billy Martin	4.00	2.00	1.25
85	Harmon Killebrew	8.50	3.75	2.25
86	Zoilo Versalles	2.50	1.25	.60
87	Lenny Green	2.50	1.25	.60
88	Bill Tuttle	2.50	1.25	.60
89	Jim Lemon	2.50	1.25	.60
90	Earl Battey	2.50	1.25	.60
91	Camilo Pascual	2.50	1.25	.60
92	Norm Siebern	50.00	22.00	12.50
93	Jerry Lumpe	2.50	1.25	.60
94	Dick Howser	2.50	1.25	.60
95a	Gene Stephens (Born: Jan. 5)	2.50	1.25	.60
95b	Gene Stephens (Born: Jan. 20)	5.50	2.50	1.50
96	Leo Posada	2.50	1.25	.60
97	Joe Pignatano	2.50	1.25	.60
98	Jim Archer	2.50	1.25	.60
99	Haywood Sullivan	2.50	1.25	.60
100	Art Ditmar	2.50	1.25	.60
101	Gil Hodges	55.00	25.00	13.50
102	Charlie Neal	2.50	1.25	.60
103	Daryl Spencer	20.00	9.00	5.00
104	Maury Wills	4.25	2.00	1.00
105	Tommy Davis	2.50	1.25	.60
106	Willie Davis	2.50	1.25	.60

107	John Roseboro	2.50	1.25	.60
108	John Podres	3.00	1.25	.70
109a	Sandy Koufax (blue lines around stats)	65.00	29.00	16.00
109b	Sandy Koufax (red lines around stats)	22.00	10.00	5.50
110	Don Drysdale	8.50	3.75	2.25
111	Larry Sherry	2.50	1.25	.60
112	Jim Gilliam	3.00	1.25	.70
113	Norm Larker	35.00	15.50	8.75
114	Duke Snider	10.00	4.50	2.50
115	Stan Williams	2.50	1.25	.60
116	Gordy Coleman	60.00	27.00	15.00
117	Don Blasingame	2.50	1.25	.60
118	Gene Freese	2.50	1.25	.60
119	Ed Kasko	2.50	1.25	.60
120	Gus Bell	2.50	1.25	.60
121	Vada Pinson	3.00	1.25	.70
122	Frank Robinson	21.00	9.50	5.25
123	Bob Purkey	2.50	1.25	.60
124a	Joey Jay (blue lines around stats)	15.00	6.75	3.75
124b	Joey Jay (red lines around stats)	2.50	1.25	.60
125	Jim Brosnan	20.00	9.00	5.00
126	Jim O'Toole	2.50	1.25	.60
127	Jerry Lynch	50.00	22.00	12.50
128	Wally Post	2.50	1.25	.60
129	Ken Hunt	2.50	1.25	.60
130	Jerry Zimmerman	2.50	1.25	.60
131	Willie McCovey	65.00	29.00	16.00
132	Jose Pagan	2.50	1.25	.60
133	Felipe Alou	2.50	1.25	.60
134	Jim Davenport	2.50	1.25	.60
135	Harvey Kuenn	2.50	1.25	.60
136	Orlando Cepeda	5.00	2.50	1.50
137	Ed Bailey	2.50	1.25	.60
138	Sam Jones	2.50	1.25	.60
139	Mike McCormick	2.50	1.25	.60
140	Juan Marichal	70.00	31.00	17.50
141	Jack Sanford	2.50	1.25	.60
142	Willie Mays	30.00	13.50	7.50
143	Stu Miller (photo actually Chuck Hiller)	5.00	2.25	1.25
144	Joe Amalfitano	12.50	5.75	3.25
145a	Joe Adock (name incorrect)	35.00	15.50	8.75
145b	Joe Adcock (name correct)	2.50	1.25	.60
146	Frank Bolling	2.50	1.25	.60
147	Ed Mathews	9.00	4.00	2.25
148	Roy McMillan	2.50	1.25	.60
149	Hank Aaron	38.00	17.00	9.50
150	Gino Cimoli	2.50	1.25	.60
151	Frank Thomas	2.50	1.25	.60
152	Joe Torre	4.00	2.00	1.25
153	Lou Burdette	3.00	1.25	.70
154	Bob Buhl	2.50	1.25	.60
155	Carlton Willey	2.50	1.25	.60
156	Lee Maye	2.50	1.25	.60
157	Al Spangler	2.50	1.25	.60
158	Bill White	38.00	17.00	9.50
159	Ken Boyer	4.00	2.00	1.25
160	Joe Cunningham	2.50	1.25	.60
161	Carl Warwick	2.50	1.25	.60
162	Carl Sawatski	2.50	1.25	.60
163	Lindy McDaniel	2.50	1.25	.60
164	Ernie Broglio	2.50	1.25	.60
165	Larry Jackson	2.50	1.25	.60
166	Curt Flood	3.00	1.25	.70
167	Curt Simmons	2.50	1.25	.60
168	Alex Grammas	2.50	1.25	.60
169	Dick Stuart	3.00	1.25	.70
170	Bill Mazeroski	5.00	2.50	1.50
171	Don Hoak	2.50	1.25	.60
172	Dick Groat	2.50	1.25	.60
173a	Roberto Clemente (blue lines around stats)	65.00	29.00	16.00
173b	Roberto Clemente (red lines around stats)	22.00	10.00	5.50
174	Bob Skinner	2.50	1.25	.60
175	Bill Virdon	2.50	1.25	.60
176	Smoky Burgess	2.50	1.25	.60
177	Elroy Face	2.50	1.25	.60
178	Bob Friend	2.50	1.25	.60
179	Vernon Law	2.50	1.25	.60
180	Harvey Haddix	2.50	1.25	.60
181	Hal Smith	2.50	1.25	.60
182	Ed Bouchee	2.50	1.25	.60
183	Don Zimmer	2.50	1.25	.60
184	Ron Santo	3.00	1.25	.70
185	Andre Rodgers	2.50	1.25	.60
186	Richie Ashburn	8.50	3.75	2.25
187a	George Altman (last line is "...1955).")	2.50	1.25	.60
187b	George Altman (last line is "...1955.")	3.75	1.75	.90
188	Ernie Banks	12.50	5.75	3.25
189	Sam Taylor	2.50	1.25	.60
190	Don Elston	2.50	1.25	.60
191	Jerry Kindall	2.50	1.25	.60
192	Pancho Herrera	2.50	1.25	.60
193	Tony Taylor	2.50	1.25	.60
194	Ruben Amaro	2.50	1.25	.60
195	Don Demeter	2.50	1.25	.60
196	Bobby Gene Smith	2.50	1.25	.60
197	Clay Dalrymple	2.50	1.25	.60
198	Robin Roberts	8.50	3.75	2.25
199	Art Mahaffey	2.50	1.25	.60
200	John Buzhardt	3.00	1.25	.70

1962 Post Cereal - Canadian

This Post set is scarce due to the much more limited distribution in Canada. Most cards were printed on the back of the cereal boxes and contain a full-color player photo with biography and statistics given in both French and English. Card backs are blank. Cards measure 3-1/2" x 2-1/2". This 200-card set is very similar to the Post Cereal cards printed in the United States. The Post logo appears at the upper-left corner in the Canadian issue. Several cards are scarce because of limited distribution and there are two Whitey Ford cards, the corrected version being the most scarce. The complete set price does not include the scarcer variations. Certain cereal brands had the cards packaged inside the box on perforated panels, and will be found with perforated edges on one side or other.

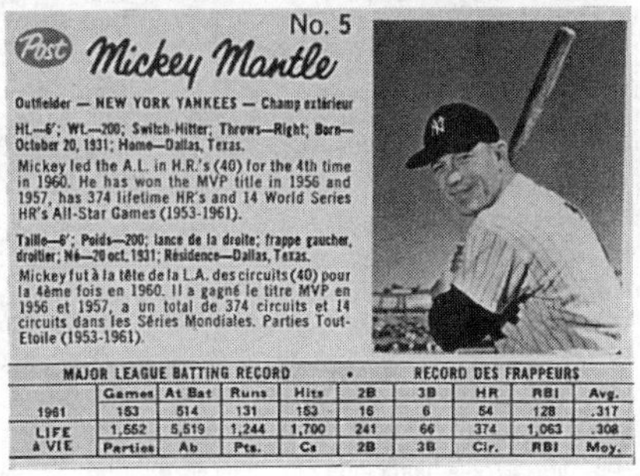

		NM	EX	VG
Complete Set (200):		2400.	1100.	600.00
Common Player:		4.00	1.75	1.00
1	Bill Skowron	12.00	6.00	3.50
2	Bobby Richardson	8.00	3.50	2.00
3	Cletis Boyer	5.00	2.25	1.25
4	Tony Kubek	8.00	3.50	2.00
5a	Mickey Mantle (stats list 153 hits)	200.00	90.00	50.00
5b	Mickey Mantle (163 hits; first line of bio ends: "4th time in")	125.00	56.00	31.00
5c	Mickey Mantle (163 hits; first line of bio ends: "4th time")	125.00	56.00	31.00
6a	Roger Maris (First line of French bio has large "P" in "Pour les circuits".)	40.00	18.00	10.00
6b	Roger Maris (French text reads, "Residence". Small "p" in "pour".)	40.00	18.00	10.00
6c	Roger Maris (French text reads, "a", not "Residence". Small "p" in "pour".)	40.00	18.00	10.00
7	Yogi Berra	30.00	13.50	7.50
8	Elston Howard	5.75	2.50	1.50
9a	Whitey Ford (Dodgers)	30.00	13.50	7.50
9b	Whitey Ford (Yankees)	55.00	25.00	13.50
10	Ralph Terry	40.00	18.00	10.00
11	John Blanchard	5.00	2.25	1.25
12	Luis Arroyo	5.00	2.25	1.25
13	Bill Stafford	5.00	2.25	1.25
14	Norm Cash	5.75	2.50	1.50
15	Jake Wood	4.00	1.75	1.00
16	Steve Boros	4.00	1.75	1.00
17	Chico Fernandez	4.00	1.75	1.00
18	Bill Bruton	4.00	1.75	1.00
19a	Rocky Colavito (script name large)	15.00	6.75	3.75
19b	Rocky Colavito (script name small)	15.00	6.75	3.75
20	Al Kaline	29.00	13.00	7.25
21	Dick Brown	9.75	4.50	2.50
22a	Frank Lary ("Residence-Northport, Alabama.")	12.50	5.75	3.25
22b	Frank Lary ("a Northport, Alabama.")	12.50	5.75	3.25
23	Don Mossi	4.00	1.75	1.00
24	Phil Regan	4.00	1.75	1.00
25	Charley Maxwell	4.00	1.75	1.00
26	Jim Bunning	24.00	11.00	6.00
27a	Jim Gentile (French bio begins "Le 8 mai, Jim ...")	10.00	4.50	2.50
27b	Jim Gentile (Begins, "Le 8 mai 1961, Jim ...")	10.00	4.50	2.50
28	Marv Breeding	4.00	1.75	1.00
29	Brooks Robinson	40.00	18.00	10.00
30	Ron Hansen	4.00	1.75	1.00
31	Jackie Brandt	4.00	1.75	1.00
32	Dick Williams	40.00	18.00	10.00
33	Gus Triandos	4.00	1.75	1.00
34	Milt Pappas	5.00	2.25	1.25
35	Hoyt Wilhelm	29.00	13.00	7.25
36	Chuck Estrada	4.00	1.75	1.00
37	Vic Power	4.00	1.75	1.00
38	Johnny Temple	4.00	1.75	1.00
39	Bubba Phillips	40.00	18.00	10.00
40	Tito Francona	11.00	5.00	2.75
41	Willie Kirkland	10.00	4.50	2.50
42	John Romano	10.00	4.50	2.50
43	Jim Perry	5.75	2.50	1.50
44	Woodie Held	4.00	1.75	1.00
45	Chuck Essegian	4.00	1.75	1.00
46	Roy Sievers	5.00	2.25	1.25
47	Nellie Fox	12.00	5.50	3.00
48	Al Smith	4.00	1.75	1.00
49	Luis Aparicio	40.00	18.00	10.00
50	Jim Landis	4.00	1.75	1.00
51	Minnie Minoso	40.00	18.00	10.00
52	Andy Carey	9.00	4.00	2.25
53	Sherman Lollar	4.00	1.75	1.00
54	Bill Pierce	5.00	2.25	1.25
55	Early Wynn	23.00	10.50	5.75
56	Chuck Schilling	4.00	1.75	1.00
57	Pete Runnels	5.00	2.25	1.25
58	Frank Malzone	4.00	1.75	1.00
59	Don Buddin	9.00	4.00	2.25
60	Gary Geiger	4.00	1.75	1.00
61	Carl Yastrzemski	55.00	25.00	13.50
62	Jackie Jensen	10.00	4.50	2.50
63	Jim Pagliaroni	4.00	1.75	1.00
64	Don Schwall	10.00	4.50	2.50
65	Dale Long	4.00	1.75	1.00
66	Chuck Cottier	4.00	1.75	1.00
67	Billy Klaus	4.00	1.75	1.00
68	Coot Veal	4.00	1.75	1.00
69	Marty Keough	4.00	1.75	1.00
70	Willie Tasby	40.00	18.00	10.00
71	Gene Woodling (photo reversed)	5.00	2.25	1.25
72	Gene Green	4.00	1.75	1.00
73	Dick Donovan	4.00	1.75	1.00
74	Steve Bilko	4.00	1.75	1.00
75	Rocky Bridges	8.00	3.50	2.00
76	Eddie Yost	4.00	1.75	1.00
77	Leon Wagner	40.00	18.00	10.00
78	Albie Pearson	10.00	4.50	2.50
79	Ken Hunt	4.00	1.75	1.00
80	Earl Averill	4.00	1.75	1.00
81	Ryne Duren	5.75	2.50	1.50
82	Ted Kluszewski	15.00	7.50	4.50
83	Bob Allison	5.00	2.25	1.25
84	Billy Martin	12.00	6.00	3.50
85	Harmon Killebrew	23.00	10.50	5.75
86	Zoilo Versalles	4.00	1.75	1.00
87	Lenny Green	40.00	18.00	10.00
88	Bill Tuttle	4.00	1.75	1.00
89	Jim Lemon	4.00	1.75	1.00
90	Earl Battey	4.00	1.75	1.00
91	Camilo Pascual	5.00	2.25	1.25
92	Norm Siebern	4.00	1.75	1.00
93	Jerry Lumpe	4.00	1.75	1.00
94	Dick Howser	40.00	18.00	10.00
95	Gene Stephens	4.00	1.75	1.00
96	Leo Posada	4.00	1.75	1.00
97	Joe Pignatano	4.00	1.75	1.00
98	Jim Archer	4.00	1.75	1.00
99	Haywood Sullivan	40.00	18.00	10.00
100	Art Ditmar	35.00	15.50	8.75
101	Gil Hodges	23.00	10.50	5.75
102	Charlie Neal	4.00	1.75	1.00
103	Daryl Spencer	4.00	1.75	1.00
104	Maury Wills	12.00	5.50	3.00
105	Tommy Davis	12.00	5.50	3.00
106	Willie Davis	5.75	2.50	1.50
107	John Rosboro (Roseboro)	5.00	2.25	1.25
108	John Podres	5.75	2.50	1.50
109	Sandy Koufax	35.00	15.50	8.75
110	Don Drysdale	30.00	13.50	7.50
111	Larry Sherry	40.00	18.00	10.00
112	Jim Gilliam	40.00	18.00	10.00
113	Norm Larker	4.00	1.75	1.00
114	Duke Snider	35.00	15.50	8.75
115	Stan Williams	4.00	1.75	1.00
116	Gordy Coleman	4.00	1.75	1.00
117	Don Blasingame	40.00	18.00	10.00
118	Gene Freese	9.00	4.00	2.25
119	Ed Kasko	4.00	1.75	1.00
120	Gus Bell	4.00	1.75	1.00
121	Vada Pinson	7.00	3.25	1.75
122	Frank Robinson	30.00	13.50	7.50
123	Bob Purkey	40.00	18.00	10.00
124	Joey Jay	4.00	1.75	1.00
125	Jim Brosnan	5.00	2.25	1.25
126	Jim O'Toole	4.00	1.75	1.00
127	Jerry Lynch	4.00	1.75	1.00
128	Wally Post	80.00	36.00	20.00
129	Ken Hunt	4.00	1.75	1.00
130	Jerry Zimmerman	4.00	1.75	1.00
131	Willie McCovey	30.00	13.50	7.50
132	Jose Pagan	4.00	1.75	1.00
133	Felipe Alou	5.00	2.25	1.25
134	Jim Davenport	4.00	1.75	1.00
135	Harvey Kuenn	5.75	2.50	1.50
136	Orlando Cepeda	10.00	5.00	3.00
137	Ed Bailey	40.00	18.00	10.00
138	Sam Jones	40.00	18.00	10.00
139	Mike McCormick	4.00	1.75	1.00
140	Juan Marichal	30.00	13.50	7.50
141	Jack Sanford	4.00	1.75	1.00
142a	Willie Mays (big head)	65.00	29.00	16.00
142b	Willie Mays (small head)	90.00	40.00	22.00
143	Stu Miller	4.00	1.75	1.00
144	Joe Amalfitano	40.00	18.00	10.00
145	Joe Adcock	5.75	2.50	1.50
146	Frank Bolling	4.00	1.75	1.00
147	Ed Mathews	23.00	10.50	5.75
148	Roy McMillan	4.00	1.75	1.00
149a	Hank Aaron (script name large)	57.00	26.00	14.00
149b	Hank Aaron (script name small)	57.00	26.00	14.00
150	Gino Cimoli	4.00	1.75	1.00
151	Frank J. Thomas	4.00	1.75	1.00
152	Joe Torre	11.00	5.50	3.25
153	Lou Burdette	7.00	3.25	1.75
154	Bob Buhl	5.00	2.25	1.25
155	Carlton Willey	4.00	1.75	1.00
156	Lee Maye	4.00	1.75	1.00
157	Al Spangler	4.00	1.75	1.00
158	Bill White	5.00	2.25	1.25
159	Ken Boyer	30.00	13.50	7.50
160	Joe Cunningham	4.00	1.75	1.00
161	Carl Warwick	9.00	4.00	2.25
162	Carl Sawatski	4.00	1.75	1.00
163	Lindy McDaniel	4.00	1.75	1.00

164	Ernie Broglio	4.00	1.75	1.00
165	Larry Jackson	4.00	1.75	1.00
166	Curt Flood	5.75	2.50	1.50
167	Curt Simmons	11.00	5.00	2.75
168	Alex Grammas	4.00	1.75	1.00
169	Dick Stuart	5.00	2.25	1.25
170	Bill Mazeroski	40.00	18.00	10.00
171	Don Hoak	4.00	1.75	1.00
172	Dick Groat	11.00	5.00	2.75
173	Roberto Clemente	75.00	34.00	18.50
174	Bob Skinner	4.00	1.75	1.00
175	Bill Virdon	5.75	2.50	1.50
176	Smoky Burgess	11.00	5.00	2.75
177	Elroy Face	11.00	5.00	2.75
178	Bob Friend	5.00	2.25	1.25
179	Vernon Law	5.00	2.25	1.25
180	Harvey Haddix	5.00	2.25	1.25
181	Hal Smith	40.00	18.00	10.00
182	Ed Bouchee	4.00	1.75	1.00
183	Don Zimmer	5.75	2.50	1.50
184	Ron Santo	7.00	3.25	1.75
185	Andre Rogers (Rodgers)	4.00	1.75	1.00
186	Richie Ashburn	22.00	10.00	5.50
187	George Altman	4.00	1.75	1.00
188	Ernie Banks	40.00	18.00	10.00
189	Sam Taylor	4.00	1.75	1.00
190	Don Elston	4.00	1.75	1.00
191	Jerry Kindall	4.00	1.75	1.00
192	Pancho Herrera	4.00	1.75	1.00
193	Tony Taylor	4.00	1.75	1.00
194	Ruben Amaro	4.00	1.75	1.00
195	Don Demeter	40.00	18.00	10.00
196	Bobby Gene Smith	4.00	1.75	1.00
197	Clay Dalrymple	4.00	1.75	1.00
198	Robin Roberts	23.00	10.50	5.75
199	Art Mahaffey	4.00	1.75	1.00
200	John Buzhardt	7.00	3.25	1.75

1963 Post Cereal

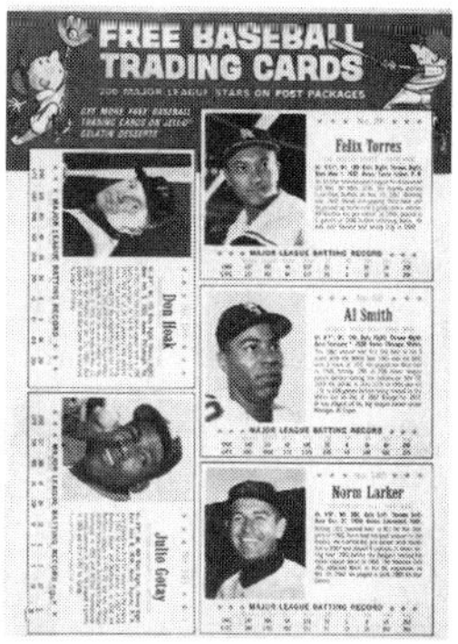

Another 200-player, 3-1/2" x 2-1/2" set that, with variations, totals more than 205 cards. Numerous color variations also exist due to the different cereal boxes on which the cards were printed. As many as 25 cards in the set are considered scarce, making it much more difficult to complete than the other major Post sets. Star cards also command higher prices than in the '61 or '62 Post cards. The 1963 Post cards are almost identical to the '63 Jell-O set, which is a slight 1/4" narrower. Cards are still blank backed, with a color player photo, biographies and statistics on the numbered card fronts. No Post logo appears on the '63 cards. The complete set price does not include the scarcer variations.

		NM	EX	VG
Complete Set (200):		3000.	1350.	750.00
Common Player:		3.00	1.50	.90
1	Vic Power	4.50	2.00	1.25
2	Bernie Allen	3.00	1.25	.70
3	Zoilo Versalles	3.00	1.25	.70
4	Rich Rollins	3.00	1.25	.70
5	Harmon Killebrew	15.00	6.75	3.75
6	Lenny Green	37.50	17.00	9.50
7	Bob Allison	3.00	1.25	.70
8	Earl Battey	3.00	1.25	.70
9	Camilo Pascual	3.00	1.25	.70
10	Jim Kaat	4.00	1.75	1.00
11	Jack Kralick	3.00	1.25	.70
12	Bill Skowron	3.50	1.50	.90
13	Bobby Richardson	4.00	1.75	1.00
14	Cletis Boyer	3.50	1.50	.90
15	Mickey Mantle	300.00	135.00	75.00
16	Roger Maris	150.00	67.00	37.00
17	Yogi Berra	15.00	6.75	3.75
18	Elston Howard	4.00	1.75	1.00
19	Whitey Ford	10.00	4.50	2.50
20	Ralph Terry	3.50	1.50	.90
21	John Blanchard	3.50	1.50	.90
22	Bill Stafford	3.50	1.50	.90
23	Tom Tresh	3.50	1.50	.90
24	Steve Bilko	3.00	1.25	.70
25	Bill Moran	3.00	1.25	.70
26a	Joe Koppe (1962 Avg. is .277)	3.00	1.25	.70
26b	Joe Koppe (1962 Avg. is .227)	12.00	5.50	3.00
27	Felix Torres	3.00	1.25	.70
28a	Leon Wagner (lifetime Avg. is .278)	3.00	1.25	.70
28b	Leon Wagner (lifetime Avg. is .272)	12.00	5.50	3.00
29	Albie Pearson	3.00	1.25	.70
30	Lee Thomas (photo actually George Thomas)	80.00	36.00	20.00
31	Bob Rodgers	3.00	1.25	.70
32	Dean Chance	3.00	1.25	.70
33	Ken McBride	3.00	1.25	.70
34	George Thomas (photo actually Lee Thomas)	3.00	1.25	.70
35	Joe Cunningham	3.00	1.25	.70
36a	Nelson Fox (no bat showing)	10.00	4.50	2.50
36b	Nelson Fox (part of bat showing)	12.00	5.50	3.00
37	Luis Aparicio	9.00	4.00	2.25
38	Al Smith	25.00	11.00	6.25
39	Floyd Robinson	80.00	36.00	20.00
40	Jim Landis	3.00	1.25	.70
41	Charlie Maxwell	3.00	1.25	.70
42	Sherman Lollar	3.00	1.25	.70
43	Early Wynn	7.50	3.50	2.00
44	Juan Pizarro	3.00	1.25	.70
45	Ray Herbert	3.00	1.25	.70
46	Norm Cash	4.00	1.75	1.00
47	Steve Boros	3.00	1.25	.70
48	Dick McAuliffe	25.00	11.00	6.25
49	Bill Bruton	3.00	1.25	.70
50	Rocky Colavito	7.50	3.50	2.00
51	Al Kaline	10.00	4.50	2.50
52	Dick Brown	3.00	1.25	.70
53	Jim Bunning	125.00	56.00	31.00
54	Hank Aguirre	3.00	1.25	.70
55	Frank Lary	3.00	1.25	.70
56	Don Mossi	3.00	1.25	.70
57	Jim Gentile	3.00	1.25	.70
58	Jackie Brandt	3.00	1.25	.70
59	Brooks Robinson	10.00	4.50	2.50
60	Ron Hansen	3.00	1.25	.70
61	Jerry Adair	150.00	67.00	37.00
62	John (Boog) Powell	4.00	1.75	1.00
63	Russ Snyder	3.00	1.25	.70
64	Steve Barber	3.00	1.25	.70
65	Milt Pappas	3.00	1.25	.70
66	Robin Roberts	7.50	3.50	2.00
67	Tito Francona	3.00	1.25	.70
68	Jerry Kindall	3.00	1.25	.70
69	Woodie Held	3.00	1.25	.70
70	Bubba Phillips	15.00	6.75	3.75
71	Chuck Essegian	3.00	1.25	.70
72	Willie Kirkland	3.00	1.25	.70
73	Al Luplow	3.00	1.25	.70
74	Ty Cline	3.00	1.25	.70
75	Dick Donovan	3.00	1.25	.70
76	John Romano	3.00	1.25	.70
77	Pete Runnels	3.00	1.25	.70
78	Ed Bressoud	3.00	1.25	.70
79	Frank Malzone	3.00	1.25	.70
80	Carl Yastrzemski	250.00	112.00	62.00
81	Gary Geiger	3.00	1.25	.70
82	Lou Clinton	3.00	1.25	.70
83	Earl Wilson	3.00	1.25	.70
84	Bill Monbouquette	3.00	1.25	.70
85	Norm Siebern	3.00	1.25	.70
86	Jerry Lumpe	80.00	36.00	20.00
87	Manny Jimenez	85.00	38.00	21.00
88	Gino Cimoli	3.00	1.25	.70
89	Ed Charles	3.00	1.25	.70
90	Ed Rakow	3.00	1.25	.70
91	Bob Del Greco	3.00	1.25	.70
92	Haywood Sullivan	3.00	1.25	.70
93	Chuck Hinton	3.00	1.25	.70
94	Ken Retzer	3.00	1.25	.70
95	Harry Bright	3.00	1.25	.70
96	Bob Johnson	3.00	1.25	.70
97	Dave Stenhouse	13.00	5.75	3.25
98	Chuck Cottier	25.00	11.00	6.25
99	Tom Cheney	3.00	1.25	.70
100	Claude Osteen	18.00	8.00	4.50
101	Orlando Cepeda	6.00	2.75	1.50
102	Charley Hiller	3.00	1.25	.70
103	Jose Pagan	3.00	1.25	.70
104	Jim Davenport	3.00	1.25	.70
105	Harvey Kuenn	3.50	1.50	.90
106	Willie Mays	25.00	11.00	6.25
107	Felipe Alou	4.00	1.75	1.00
108	Tom Haller	110.00	49.00	27.00
109	Juan Marichal	9.00	4.00	2.25
110	Jack Sanford	3.00	1.25	.70
111	Bill O'Dell	3.00	1.25	.70
112	Willie McCovey	10.00	4.50	2.50
113	Lee Walls	3.00	1.25	.70
114	Jim Gilliam	4.00	1.75	1.00
115	Maury Wills	4.00	1.75	1.00
116	Ron Fairly	3.00	1.25	.70
117	Tommy Davis	3.50	1.50	.90
118	Duke Snider	10.00	4.50	2.50
119	Willie Davis	150.00	67.00	37.00
120	John Roseboro	3.00	1.25	.70
121	Sandy Koufax	15.00	6.75	3.75
122	Stan Williams	3.00	1.25	.70
123	Don Drysdale	12.00	5.50	3.00
124a	Daryl Spencer (no arm showing)	3.00	1.25	.70
124b	Daryl Spencer (part of arm showing)	10.00	4.50	2.50
125	Gordy Coleman	3.00	1.25	.70
126	Don Blasingame	3.00	1.25	.70
127	Leo Cardenas	3.00	1.25	.70
128	Eddie Kasko	150.00	67.00	37.00
129	Jerry Lynch	15.00	6.75	3.75
130	Vada Pinson	3.50	1.50	.90
131a	Frank Robinson (no stripes on hat)	10.00	4.50	2.50
131b	Frank Robinson (stripes on hat)	15.00	6.75	3.75
132	John Edwards	3.00	1.25	.70
133	Joey Jay	3.00	1.25	.70
134	Bob Purkey	3.00	1.25	.70
135	Marty Keough	15.00	6.75	3.75
136	Jim O'Toole	3.00	1.25	.70
137	Dick Stuart	3.50	1.50	.90
138	Bill Mazeroski	7.50	3.50	2.00
139	Dick Groat	3.50	1.50	.90
140	Don Hoak	30.00	13.50	7.50
141	Bob Skinner	15.00	6.75	3.75
142	Bill Virdon	3.50	1.50	.90
143	Roberto Clemente	25.00	11.00	6.25
144	Smoky Burgess	3.00	1.25	.70
145	Bob Friend	3.00	1.25	.70
146	Al McBean	3.00	1.25	.70
147	El Roy Face (Elroy)	3.50	1.50	.90
148	Joe Adcock	3.50	1.50	.90
149	Frank Bolling	3.00	1.25	.70
150	Roy McMillan	3.00	1.25	.70
151	Eddie Mathews	10.00	4.50	2.50
152	Hank Aaron	70.00	31.00	17.50
153	Del Crandall	30.00	13.50	7.50
154a	Bob Shaw (third sentence has "In 1959" twice)	10.00	4.50	2.50
154b	Bob Shaw (third sentence has "In 1959" once)	3.00	1.25	.70
155	Lew Burdette	3.50	1.50	.90
156	Joe Torre	4.00	1.75	1.00
157	Tony Cloninger	3.00	1.25	.70
158	Bill White	3.50	1.50	.90
159	Julian Javier	3.00	1.25	.70
160	Ken Boyer	4.00	1.75	1.00
161	Julio Gotay	3.00	1.25	.70
162	Curt Flood	110.00	49.00	27.00
163	Charlie James	3.00	1.25	.70
164	Gene Oliver	3.00	1.25	.70
165	Ernie Broglio	3.00	1.25	.70
166	Bob Gibson	10.00	4.50	2.50
167a	Lindy McDaniel (asterisk before trade line)	3.00	1.25	.70
167b	Lindy McDaniel (no asterisk before trade line)	6.50	3.00	1.75
168	Ray Washburn	3.00	1.25	.70
169	Ernie Banks	10.00	4.50	2.50
170	Ron Santo	3.50	1.50	.90
171	George Altman	3.00	1.25	.70
172	Billy Williams	110.00	49.00	27.00
173	Andre Rodgers	7.50	3.50	2.00
174	Ken Hubbs	20.00	9.00	5.00
175	Don Landrum	3.00	1.25	.70
176	Dick Bertell	15.00	6.75	3.75
177	Roy Sievers	3.00	1.25	.70
178	Tony Taylor	3.00	1.25	.70
179	John Callison	3.00	1.25	.70
180	Don Demeter	3.00	1.25	.70
181	Tony Gonzalez	20.00	9.00	5.00
182	Wes Covington	20.00	9.00	5.00
183	Art Mahaffey	3.00	1.25	.70
184	Clay Dalrymple	3.00	1.25	.70
185	Al Spangler	3.00	1.25	.70
186	Roman Mejias	3.00	1.25	.70
187	Bob Aspromonte	295.00	133.00	74.00
188	Norm Larker	30.00	13.50	7.50
189	Johnny Temple	3.00	1.25	.70
190	Carl Warwick	3.00	1.25	.70
191	Bob Lillis	3.00	1.25	.70
192	Dick Farrell	3.00	1.25	.70
193	Gil Hodges	9.00	4.00	2.25
194	Marv Throneberry	4.00	1.75	1.00
195	Charlie Neal	10.00	4.50	2.50
196	Frank Thomas	145.00	65.00	36.00
197	Richie Ashburn	20.00	9.00	5.00
198	Felix Mantilla	3.00	1.25	.70
199	Rod Kanehl	20.00	9.00	5.00
200	Roger Craig	4.00	1.75	1.00

1978 Post Cereal Steve Garvey Baseball Tips

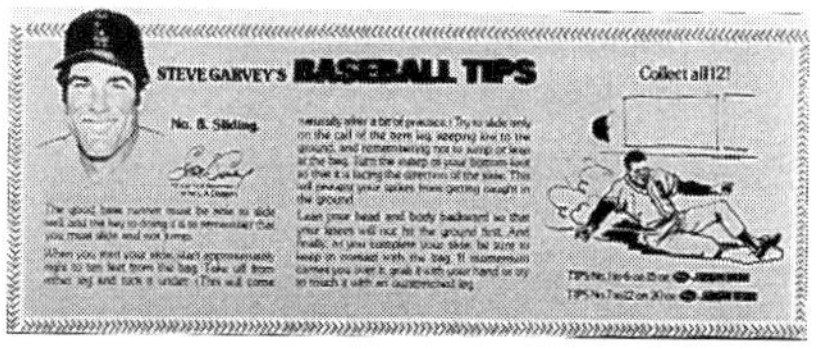

These 7-1/8" x 2-5/8" cut-out panels bordered in red "baseball" stitching were printed on the backs of 15-oz. (#1-6) and 20-oz. (#7-12) packages of Post Raisin Brand cereal. The panels have a green background with black-and-white artwork of a generic player illustrating the tip and a color portrait of Garvey.

		NM	EX	VG
Complete Set (12):		45.00	22.00	13.50
Common Panel:		4.00	2.00	1.25
1	The Batting Stance	4.00	2.00	1.25
2	Bunting	4.00	2.00	1.25
3	Rounding First Base	4.00	2.00	1.25
4	The Grip in Throwing	4.00	2.00	1.25
5	Fielding a Pop-Up	4.00	2.00	1.25
6	Proper Fielding Stances	4.00	2.00	1.25
7	On-Deck Observation	4.00	2.00	1.25
8	Sliding	4.00	2.00	1.25
9	Hitting to the Opposite Field	4.00	2.00	1.25
10	Throwing From the Outfield	4.00	2.00	1.25
11	Mental Preparation for Each Play	4.00	2.00	1.25
12	Total Conditioning	4.00	2.00	1.25

1978 Post-Intelligencer 1969 Pilot Profiles

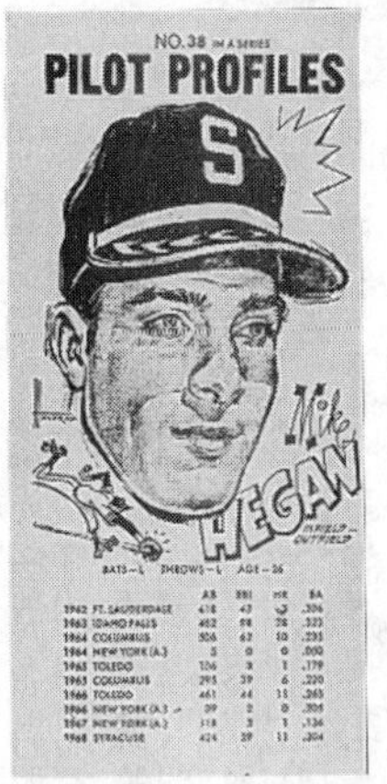

This series of cards of the one-year American League team states on its back they are reprinted from the Seattle Post-Intelligencer newspaper. The 1-3/8" x 5" cards are printed in black-and-white on semi-gloss cardboard. Fronts feature a pencil caricature of the player and include major and minor league stats. A card number is at top. Backs have the newspaper's ad. The cards were a collectors' issue produced by long-time minor league card maker Frank Caruso, with the paper's permission. The cartoons originally ran in a somewhat larger format within the pages of the newspaper, and are themselves highly collectible, with values about 2X-3X those of the reprints listed here. Reprint sets were originally sold for $6.

		NM	EX	VG
Complete Set (39):		135.00	65.00	40.00
Common Player:		4.00	3.00	1.50
1	Don Mincher	4.00	3.00	1.50
2	Tommy Harper	5.00	2.50	1.50
3	Ray Oyler	4.00	3.00	1.50
4	Jerry McNertney	4.00	3.00	1.50
5	Not issued	4.00	3.00	1.50
6	Tommy Davis	5.00	2.50	1.50
7	Gary Bell	4.00	3.00	1.50
8	Chico Salmon	4.00	3.00	1.50
9	Jack Aker	4.00	3.00	1.50
10	Rich Rollins	4.00	3.00	1.50
11	Diego Segui	4.00	3.00	1.50
12	Steve Barber	5.00	2.50	1.50
13	Wayne Comer	4.00	3.00	1.50
14	John Kennedy	4.00	3.00	1.50
15	Buzz Stephen	4.00	3.00	1.50
16	Jim Gosger	4.00	3.00	1.50
17	Mike Ferraro	4.00	3.00	1.50
18	Marty Pattin	4.00	3.00	1.50
19	Gerry Schoen	4.00	3.00	1.50
20	Steve Hovely	4.00	3.00	1.50
21	Frank Crosetti	5.00	2.50	1.50
22	Charles Bates	4.00	3.00	1.50
23	Jose Vidal	4.00	3.00	1.50
24	Bob Richmond	4.00	3.00	1.50
25	Lou Piniella	6.00	3.00	1.75
26	John Miklos	4.00	3.00	1.50
27	John Morris	4.00	3.00	1.50
28	Larry Haney	4.00	3.00	1.50
29	Mike Marshall	5.00	2.50	1.50
30	Marv Staehle	4.00	3.00	1.50
31	Gus Gil	4.00	3.00	1.50
32	Sal Maglie	5.00	2.50	1.50
33	Ron Plaza	4.00	3.00	1.50
34	Ed O'Brien	4.00	3.00	1.50
35	Jim Bouton	6.00	3.00	1.75
36	Bill Stafford	4.00	3.00	1.50
37	Darrell Brandon	4.00	3.00	1.50
38	Mike Hegan	4.00	3.00	1.50
39	Dick Baney	4.00	3.00	1.50

1975 Praeger Publishers Ty Cobb

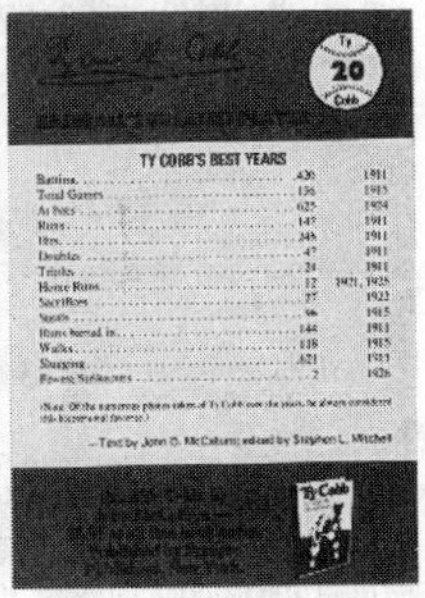

This set was produced by Washington state collector Stephen Mitchell in conjunction with Praeger Publishers of New York to promote the book "Ty Cobb" by John McCallum. Slightly larger than the current 2-1/2" x 3-1/2" standard, the cards featured black-and-white photos on front surrounded by a woodgrain-effect frame and with a plaque at bottom bearing the card title. Backs have an excerpt from the book, an ad for the book and a facsimile autograph. Cards are numbered in a baseball at upper-right. Sets originally sold for $3.25.

		NM	EX	VG
Complete Set (20):		30.00	15.00	9.00
Common Card:		2.00	1.00	.60
1	Ty Breaks In	3.00	1.50	.90
2	Four Inches of the Plate	2.00	1.00	.60
3	Slashing into Third	2.00	1.00	.60
4	Inking Another Contract	2.00	1.00	.60
5	Captain Tyrus R. Cobb	2.00	1.00	.60
6	Ty with "The Big Train" (with Walter Johnson)	4.00	2.00	1.25
7	The End of an Era (with Babe Ruth)	6.00	3.00	1.75
8	All-Time Centerfielder	2.00	1.00	.60
9	Ty Could "Walk 'em down"	2.00	1.00	.60
10	Menacing Batsman	2.00	1.00	.60
11	With Brother Paul	2.00	1.00	.60
12	Thomas Edison, Cobb Fan	3.00	1.50	.90
13	Ty Tangles with Muggsy McGraw	2.50	1.25	.70
14	Author McCallum with Cy Young	2.00	1.00	.60
15	Speaker - DiMaggio - Cobb	5.00	2.50	1.50
16	Ted Gets a Lesson (with Ted Williams)	5.00	2.50	1.50
17	Five for Five	2.00	1.00	.60
18	"I have but one regret ..."	2.00	1.00	.60
19	Excellence: The Cobb Standard	2.00	1.00	.60
20	His Favorite Photo	3.00	1.50	.90

1954 Preferred Products Milwaukee Braves

Sold as a 12-piece set in an envelope marked "Braves Team Autographed Portraits," this portfolio was one of several issued in the team's early years in Milwaukee. The artwork is apparently by Scott Douglas, whose copyright appears on the outer envelope. The same pictures can be found on Preferred Product felt patches and t-shirts. These 8" x 10" portraits are printed in sepia on cream-colored heavy textured paper and feature facsimile autographs. Backs are blank. The unnumbered portraits are checklisted here alphabetically.

		NM	EX	VG
Complete Set (12):		235.00	120.00	65.00
Common Player:		20.00	10.00	6.00
(1)	Joe Adcock	20.00	10.00	6.00
(2)	Bill Bruton	20.00	10.00	6.00
(3)	Bob Buhl	20.00	10.00	6.00
(4)	Lew Burdette	20.00	10.00	6.00
(5)	Del Crandall	20.00	10.00	6.00
(6)	Johnny Logan	20.00	10.00	6.00
(7)	Ed Mathews	35.00	17.50	10.50
(8)	Danny O'Connell	20.00	10.00	6.00
(9)	Andy Pafko	20.00	10.00	6.00
(10)	Jim Pendleton	20.00	10.00	6.00
(11)	Warren Spahn	30.00	15.00	9.00
(12)	Bob Thomson	20.00	10.00	6.00

1957-60 Preferred Products Milwaukee Braves

Similar in format to the company's 1954 issue, these 8" x 10" portraits are printed in sepia on cream-colored heavy textured paper with player names printed beneath. Backs are blank. The unnumbered portraits are checklisted here alphabetically, but the list may not be complete.

		NM	EX	VG
Common Player:		20.00	10.00	6.00
(1)	Hank Aaron	125.00	62.00	37.00
(2)	Joe Adcock	20.00	10.00	6.00
(3)	Bill Bruton	20.00	10.00	6.00
(4)	Wes Covington	20.00	10.00	6.00
(5)	Johnny Logan	20.00	10.00	6.00
(6)	Red Schoendienst	25.00	12.50	7.50
(7)	Frank Torre	20.00	10.00	6.00

1914 Pritchard Publishing Giants/Yankees Stamps

These colorful large-format (about 1-7/8" x 2-5/8") stamps are copyrighted 1914 by Pritchard Publishing Co., New York. All players currently known in the set are N.Y. Giants or Yankees. The unnumbered stamps are listed here alphabetically within teams.

		NM	EX	VG
Common Player:		150.00	75.00	45.00
	N.Y. GIANTS			
(1)	Bob Bescher	150.00	75.00	45.00
(2)	Josh Devore	150.00	75.00	45.00
(3)	Christy Mathewson	450.00	225.00	135.00
(4)	Chief Meyers	150.00	75.00	45.00
(5)	Fred Snodgrass	150.00	75.00	45.00
	N.Y. YANKEES			
(1)	Ray Caldwell	150.00	75.00	45.00
(2)	Les Channell	150.00	75.00	45.00
(3)	Roy Hartzell	150.00	75.00	45.00
(4)	Bill Holden	150.00	75.00	45.00
(5)	Fritz Maisel	150.00	75.00	45.00
(6)	Roger Peckinpaugh	150.00	75.00	45.00
(7)	Jeff Sweeney	150.00	75.00	45.00
(8)	Jimmy Walsh	150.00	75.00	45.00
(9)	Harry Williams	150.00	75.00	45.00

Vintage cards in Good condition are valued at about 50% of the Very Good value shown here. Fair cards are valued at 25% or less of VG. The ratio of Excellent and Very Good prices to Near Mint can vary depending on relative collectibility for each grade in a specific set. Current listings reflect such adjustments.

1956 Prize Frankies Cleveland Indians

Though the back of the cards says 24 Indians' cards were issued, only one player has ever been seen - and precious few of him. The 2-1/4" x 3-3/8"

cards have a black-and-white photo on front with the player's name and number in black in the white border at bottom. Backs have an Indian logo and instructions to redeem complete sets of the cards for a pair of box seats. It is unlikely this alone accounts for the scarcity of the cards. More likely this card was made as a prototype for a promotion which never materialized.

		NM	EX	VG
10	Vic Wertz	400.00	200.00	120.00

1946-47 Propagandas Montiel Los Reyes del Deporte

)pagandas MONTIEL presenta
)S REYES DEL DEPORTE
73
CARL OWEN HUBBELL
Pitcher del New York, L. N.
Nació en Carthage, Mo., el 22 de Junio de 1903. Tiene 6 pies de estatura y pesa 170 libras. Batea en ambas manos y tira con la zurda. El "Rey Carl" como se le bautizó, ha sido uno de los mejores pitchers que ha tenido la Liga Nacional. Entre sus muchas proezas está la establecida el día 10 de Julio de 1934 que en el juego de "Estrellas" de ambas Ligas struckó consecutivamente a Babe Ruth, Lou Gehrig, Foxx, Simmons y Cronin. Fué Champion Pitcher de la Liga Nacional en los años 1936 y 1937. En las Grandes Ligas ganó 253 games por sólo 154 perdidos.

The 180 athletes in this issue of "Sporting Kings" cards are featured in a couple of different styles. Most cards from #1-101 have only the athlete's photo on front, surrounded by a yellow or orange border. Most cards #100-180 also have the card number and player ID on front, with a chest-to-cap photo set a colored frame. All are roughly 2-1/8" x 3-1/8". Backs have biographical data, the issuer's name and, sometimes, an ad for a Cuban novelty store or radio program. Most examples in the hobby today were once pasted in the colorful album accompanying the issue and it is rare to find cards in better than VG condition. The set opens with a run of boxers, then a group of Cuban baseball stars of the past and present, former big league greats and contemporary major leaguers, plus a few wrestlers. Cards #100-180 (except 101) feature players from the Florida International League, a Class B circuit within Organized Baseball with teams in Havana, Miami, Miami Beach, Lakeland and Tampa included. Curiously, the West Palm Beach team is not represented.

		NM	EX	VG
Complete Set (180):				6000.
Common Baseball Player:				25.00
Album:				300.00
1	John L. Sullivan (boxer)			45.00
2	James J. Corbett (boxer)			30.00
3	Bob Fitzsimmons (boxer)			20.00
4	James J. Jeffries (boxer)			30.00
5	Tommy Burns (boxer)			20.00
6	Jack Johnson (boxer)			30.00
7	Jess Willard (boxer)			25.00
8	Jack Dempsey (boxer)			45.00
9	Gene Tunney (boxer)			25.00
10	Max Schmeling (boxer)			20.00
11	Jack Sharkey (boxer)			20.00
12	Primo Carnera (boxer)			20.00
13	Max Baer (boxer)			20.00
14	James J. Braddock (boxer)			30.00
15	Joe Louis (boxer)			45.00
16	Georges Carpentier (boxer)			20.00
17	Tommy Loughran (boxer)			20.00
18	Tony Zale (boxer)			20.00
19	Johnny Dundee (boxer)			20.00
20	Billy Conn (boxer)			20.00
21	Holman Williams (boxer)			20.00
22	Kid Tunero (boxer)			20.00
23	Lazaro Salazar			25.00
24	Napoleon Reyes			40.00
25	Roberto Estalella			40.00
26	Juan Oliva (boxer)			20.00
27	Gilberto Torres			30.00
28	Heberto Blanco			25.00
29	Adolfo Luque			65.00
30	Luis Galvani (boxer)			20.00
31	Miguel Angel Gonzalez			65.00
32	Chuck Klein			50.00
33	Joe Legon (boxer)			20.00
34	Carlos Blanco			20.00
35	Santos Amaro			20.00
36	Kid Chocolate (boxer)			30.00
37	Henry Armstrong (boxer)			20.00
38	Silvio Garcia			30.00
39	Martin Dihigo			150.00
40	Fermin Guerra			40.00
41	Babe Ruth			250.00
42	Ty Cobb			150.00
43	Alejandro Crespo			25.00
44	Ted Williams			150.00
45	Jose Maria Fernandez			30.00
46	Dom DiMaggio			45.00
47	Julio Rojo			25.00
48	Armando Marsans			40.00
49	Dick Sisler			25.00
50	Antonio Rodriguez			25.00
51	Joscito Rodriguez			25.00
52	Antonio Ordenana			30.00
53	Armandito Pi (boxer)			20.00
54	Paul Derringer			25.00
55	Bob Feller			100.00
56	Bill Dickey			75.00
57	Lou Gehrig			350.00
58	Joe DiMaggio			200.00
59	Hank Greenberg			75.00
60	Red Ruffing			50.00
61	Tex Hughson			25.00
62	Bucky Walters			25.00
63	Stanley Hack			25.00
64	Stanley Musial			150.00
65	Melvin Ott			50.00
66	Dutch Leonard			25.00
67	Frank Overmire			25.00
68	Mort Cooper			25.00
69	Edward Miller			25.00
70	Jimmie Foxx			50.00
71	Joseph Cronin			50.00
72	James Vernon			25.00
73	Carl Hubbell			50.00
74	Andrew Pafko			25.00
75	David Ferris			25.00
76	John Mize			50.00
77	Spud Chandler			25.00
78	Joseph Medwick			50.00
79	Christy Mathewson			75.00
80	Nelson Potter			25.00
81	James Tabor			25.00
82	Martin Marion			25.00
83	Rip Sewell			25.00
84	Philip Cavaretta (Cavarretta)			25.00
85	Al Lopez			50.00
86	Rudy York			25.00
87	Walter Masterson			25.00
88	Roger Wolff			25.00
89	Jacob Early			25.00
90	Oswald Bluege			25.00
91	Zoco Godoy (wrestler)			15.00
92	John Kelly Lewis			25.00
93	Well Stewart (wrestler)			15.00
94	Bruce Campbell			25.00
95	Sherrod Robertson			25.00
96	Rose Evans (wrestler)			15.00
97	Maurice "El Angel" Tillet (wrestler)			15.00
98	Nicholas Altrock			25.00
99	Helen Willis (tennis)			15.00
100	Borrest Smith			15.00
101	Merito Acosta			30.00
102	Oscar Rodriguez			15.00
103	Octavio Rubert			15.00
104	Antonio Lorenzo			15.00
105	Agustin del Toro			15.00
106	Hector Arago			15.00
107	Agustin de la Ville			15.00
108	Valeriano (Lilo) Fano			15.00
109	Orlando Moreno			15.00
110	"Bicho" Dunabeitia			15.00
111	Rafael Rivas			15.00
112	Jose Traspuestro			15.00
113	Mario Diaz			15.00
114	Armando Valdes			15.00
115	Alberto Matos			15.00
116	Humberto Baez			15.00
117	Orlando (Tango) Suarez			15.00
118	Manuel (Chino) Hidalgo			15.00
119	Fernando Rodriguez			30.00
120	Jose Cendan			15.00
121	Francisco Gallardo			15.00
122	Orlando Mejido			15.00
123	Julio (Jiqui) Moreno			30.00
124	Efrain Vinajcras			15.00
125	Luis Suarez			30.00
126	Oscar del Calvo			15.00
127	Julio Gomez			15.00
128	Ernesto Morillas			15.00
129	Leonardo Goicochea			15.00
130	Max Rosenfeld			15.00
131	Oscar Garmendia			15.00
132	Fernando Solis			15.00
133	Oliverio Ortiz			30.00
134	Osmaro Blanco			15.00
135	Oral Ratliff			15.00
136	Deo Grose			15.00
137	Homer Daugherty			15.00
138	Frank Matthews			15.00
139	Roger LaFrance			15.00
140	Harold Cowan			15.00
141	Richard Henton			15.00
142	Banks McDowell			15.00
143	Harold Graham			15.00
144	Jack Sweeting			15.00
145	Bill Wixted			15.00
146	Larry Graham			15.00
147	Ralph Brown			15.00
148	Felipe Jimenez			15.00
149	John Ippolito			15.00
150	Joe Benito			15.00
151	Bernardo Fernandez			15.00
152	Buckey Winkler			15.00
153	Carl Armstrong			15.00
154	Jack Bearden			15.00
155	George Bucci			15.00
156	John Pere (Pare)			15.00
157	Mickey O'Brien			15.00
158	Lamar Murphy			15.00
159	Devon Chaptman (Choptman)			15.00
160	Hal Johnson			15.00
161	"Bitsy" Mott			15.00
162	Charles Cuellar			15.00
163	Chester Covington			15.00
164	Howard Ermisch			15.00
165	Bill Lewis			15.00
166	Roy Knepper			15.00
167	Bull Enos			15.00
168	Joe Wilder			15.00
169	Jake Baker			15.00
170	Joe Bodner			15.00
171	Jackie Myer			15.00
172	Mel Fisher			15.00
173	Larry Baldwin			15.00
174	Richard Farkas			15.00
175	Alston McGahgin			15.00
176	Ray Weiss			15.00
177	Paul Waner			50.00
178	Frank Miller			15.00
179	John Sabatie			15.00
180	John Maire			15.00

1966 Pro's Pizza Chicago Cubs

These black-and-white player cards were printed on boxes in which frozen pizzas were sold. The panel measures 6" x 6" and has a black-and-white player photo at left, with his name in a white strip at bottom. At right are drawn sports action scenes and toward the top is a black box with "the pro's PIZZA" in white. The panels are blank. The unnumbered pieces are listed here alphabetically. The example pictured was autographed by the player, no facsimile signature was printed originally.

		NM	EX	VG
Complete Set (15):		175.00	85.00	50.00
Common Player:		10.00	5.00	3.00
(1)	Ted Abernathy	10.00	5.00	3.00
(2)	Joe Amalfitano	10.00	5.00	3.00
(3)	George Altman	10.00	5.00	3.00
(4)	Ernie Banks	40.00	20.00	12.00
(5)	Ernie Broglio	10.00	5.00	3.00
(6)	Billy Connors	10.00	5.00	3.00
(7)	Dick Ellsworth	10.00	5.00	3.00
(8)	Bill Hoeft	10.00	5.00	3.00
(9)	Ken Holtzman	10.00	5.00	3.00
(10)	Randy Hundley	10.00	5.00	3.00
(11)	Ferguson Jenkins	20.00	10.00	6.00
(12)	Chris Krug	10.00	5.00	3.00
(13)	Ron Santo	15.00	7.50	4.50
(14)	Carl Warwick	10.00	5.00	3.00
(15)	Billy Williams	25.00	12.50	7.50

1967 Pro's Pizza - b & w

For a second year, Chicago players - Cubs and White Sox - were featured on boxes of frozen pizza. The panel on which the player photos (black-and-white) were printed measures 4-3/4" x 5-3/4" and is similar in design to the 1966 issue, except there is a vertical perforation allowing most of the player photo to be torn away in a 3-1/16" x 5-3/4" size. Cards are unnumbered and listed here alphabetically. Values are for unseparated panels. Those separated at the perforation line are worth 60-75%.

		NM	EX	VG
Complete Set (9):		75.00	35.00	20.00
Common Player:		8.00	4.00	2.50
(1)	Ernie Banks	30.00	15.00	9.00
(2)	Glenn Beckert	8.00	4.00	2.50
(3)	Byron Browne	8.00	4.00	2.50
(4)	Don Buford	8.00	4.00	2.50
(5)	Joel Horlen	8.00	4.00	2.50
(6)	Randy Hundley	8.00	4.00	2.50
(7)	Don Kessinger	8.00	4.00	2.50
(8)	Gary Peters	8.00	4.00	2.50
(9)	Ron Santo	10.00	5.00	3.00

1967 Pro's Pizza - color

Only Chicago Cubs are included in this set of cards printed on the top of frozen pizza boxes. The color player poses are printed in a 4-3/4" diameter circle on top of the box, with the player's name in a white panel at bottom. The player's name was also printed in large black letters on one side of the box, presumably to make selection easy in a grocery store's freezer. Values of the unnumbered cards are for the round player picture only; complete box top would bring 2-3X. A similar issue of Chicago Bears players was also produced.

		NM	EX	VG
Complete Set (12):		90.00	45.00	27.00
Common Player:		7.50	3.75	2.25
(1)	Joe Amalfitano	7.50	3.75	2.25
(2)	Ernie Banks	20.00	10.00	6.00
(3)	Glenn Beckert	7.50	3.75	2.25
(4)	John Boccabella	7.50	3.75	2.25
(5)	Bill Hands	7.50	3.75	2.25
(6)	Ken Holtzman	7.50	3.75	2.25
(7)	Randy Hundley	7.50	3.75	2.25
(8)	Ferguson Jenkins	12.00	6.00	3.50
(9)	Don Kessinger	7.50	3.75	2.25
(10)	Adolfo Phillips	7.50	3.75	2.25
(11)	Ron Santo	9.00	4.50	2.75
(12)	Billy Williams	15.00	7.50	4.50

1972 Pro Star Promotions

This set of postcard-sized (3-1/2" x 5-1/2") color photocards features players from 14 major league teams, with a heavy emphasis on Montreal Expos. Uniforms in the photos have had team logos removed. Cards have a facsimile autograph on front. In the white border at bottom is the player name, league, copyright notice and "Printed in Canada." The unnumbered cards are checklisted here in alphabetical order.

		NM	EX	VG
Complete Set (39):		450.00	225.00	135.00
Common Player:		6.00	3.00	1.75
(1)	Hank Aaron	35.00	17.50	10.50
(2)	Bob Bailey	6.00	3.00	1.75
(3)	Johnny Bench	25.00	12.50	7.50
(4)	John Boccabella	6.00	3.00	1.75
(5)	Roberto Clemente	40.00	20.00	12.00
(6)	Boots Day	6.00	3.00	1.75
(7)	Jim Fairey	6.00	3.00	1.75
(8)	Tim Foli	6.00	3.00	1.75
(9)	Ron Hunt	6.00	3.00	1.75
(10)	Catfish Hunter	15.00	7.50	4.50
(11)	Reggie Jackson	25.00	12.50	7.50
(12)	Fergy Jenkins	20.00	10.00	6.00
(13)	Mike Jorgensen	6.00	3.00	1.75
(14)	Al Kaline	25.00	12.50	7.50
(15)	Harmon Killebrew	20.00	10.00	6.00
(16)	Mickey Lolich	6.00	3.00	1.75
(17)	Juan Marichal	15.00	7.50	4.50
(18)	Willie Mays	35.00	17.50	10.50
(19)	Willie McCovey	20.00	10.00	6.00
(20)	Ernie McAnally	6.00	3.00	1.75
(21)	Dave McNally	6.00	3.00	1.75
(22)	Bill Melton	6.00	3.00	1.75
(23)	Carl Morton	6.00	3.00	1.75
(24)	Bobby Murcer	6.00	3.00	1.75
(25)	Fritz Peterson	6.00	3.00	1.75
(26)	Boog Powell	12.00	6.00	3.50
(27)	Steve Renko	6.00	3.00	1.75
(28)	Merv Rettenmund	6.00	3.00	1.75
(29)	Brooks Robinson	25.00	12.50	7.50
(30)	Frank Robinson	25.00	12.50	7.50
(31)	Pete Rose	30.00	15.00	9.00
(32)	Tom Seaver	25.00	12.50	7.50
(33)	Ken Singleton	6.00	3.00	1.75
(34)	Willie Stargell	20.00	10.00	6.00
(35)	Bill Stoneman	6.00	3.00	1.75
(36)	Joe Torre	12.00	6.00	3.50
(37)	Checklist - American League	3.00	1.50	.90
(38)	Checklist - National League	3.00	1.50	.90
(39)	Checklist - Montreal Expos	3.00	1.50	.90

1930 PR4 Cracker Jack Pins

Although no manufacturer is indicated on the pins themselves, this 25-player set was apparently issued by Cracker Jack in the early 1930s. Each pin measures 13/16" in diameter and features a line drawing of a player portrait. The unnumbered pins are printed in blue and gray with backgrounds found in either yellow or gray.

		NM	EX	VG
Complete Set (25):		750.00	375.00	220.00
Common Player:		17.00	8.50	5.00
(1)	Charles Berry	17.00	8.50	5.00
(2)	Bill Cissell	17.00	8.50	5.00
(3)	KiKi Cuyler	30.00	15.00	9.00
(4)	Dizzy Dean	50.00	25.00	15.00
(5)	Wesley Ferrell	17.00	8.50	5.00
(6)	Frank Frisch	30.00	15.00	9.00
(7)	Lou Gehrig	125.00	62.00	37.00
(8)	Vernon Gomez	30.00	15.00	9.00
(9)	Goose Goslin	30.00	15.00	9.00
(10)	George Grantham	17.00	8.50	5.00
(11)	Charley Grimm	17.00	8.50	5.00
(12)	Lefty Grove	30.00	15.00	9.00
(13)	Gabby Hartnett	30.00	15.00	9.00
(14)	Travis Jackson	30.00	15.00	9.00
(15)	Tony Lazzeri	30.00	15.00	9.00
(16)	Ted Lyons	30.00	15.00	9.00
(17)	Rabbit Maranville	30.00	15.00	9.00
(18)	Carl Reynolds	17.00	8.50	5.00
(19)	Charles Ruffing	30.00	15.00	9.00
(20)	Al Simmons	30.00	15.00	9.00
(21)	Gus Suhr	17.00	8.50	5.00
(22)	Bill Terry	30.00	15.00	9.00
(23)	Dazzy Vance	30.00	15.00	9.00
(24)	Paul Waner	30.00	15.00	9.00
(25)	Lon Warneke	17.00	8.50	5.00

1948 Puerto Rican Sports Action

These 2-1/2" x 3-1/2" cards are part of a set of about 150 covering many different sports. The pictures are colorized photographs and the cards are blank-backed, intended to be glued into an album. The number of baseball subjects is not known.

		NM	EX	VG
Common Baseball Card:				
9	(Artie) Wilson safe en terecera	60.00	30.00	18.00
115	(Jim) Gilliam dio out a Casanovas	60.00	30.00	18.00

1953 Puerto Rican League

Little is known of this issue. The 1-11/16" x 2-1/2" cards have colorized portrait photos with blank backs, probably intended to be glued into an album. Cards are unnumbered and this checklist is surely incomplete. Black and white reprints of the cards are known.

	NM	EX	VG
Common Card:	35.00	17.50	10.50
Luis Arroyo	35.00	17.50	10.50
Carlos Bernier	35.00	17.50	10.50
Hiram Bithorn	35.00	17.50	10.50
Willard Brown	40.00	20.00	12.00
Jim Davis	35.00	17.50	10.50
Leon Day	60.00	30.00	18.00
Luicius Easter	45.00	22.00	13.50
Ruben Gomez	35.00	17.50	10.50
Johnny Logan	35.00	17.50	10.50
Emilio Navarro	35.00	17.50	10.50
Arnie Portocarrero	35.00	17.50	10.50
Vic Power	45.00	22.00	13.50
Miguel A. Rivera	35.00	17.50	10.50
Jose Santiago	35.00	17.50	10.50
Bob Thurman	35.00	17.50	10.50

1972 Puerto Rican League Stickers

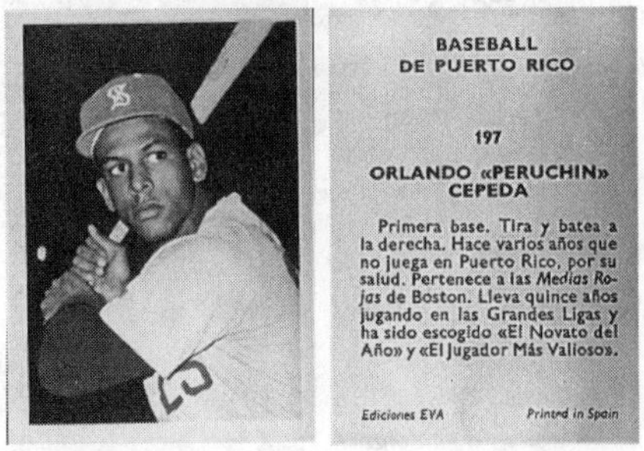

Often mistakenly called "minor league" cards, this issue consists of 231 ungummed stickers pertinent to the Puerto Rican winter baseball league. A colorful album was available in which to paste the stickers, though obviously stickers that have evidence of glue or torn paper have little collector value. Besides individual player photos, there are stickers of "old-timers" and groups of stickers which make up composite photos of all-star teams and of the island's god of baseball, Roberto Clemente. Team emblem stickers are also included. Many big league stars who were either beginning or ending their pro careers can be found in the set, including some current and future Hall of Famers. Stickers have color photos on the front, with backs printed in Spanish. They measure 2-1/4" x 3".

		NM	EX	VG
Complete Set w/Album:		900.00	650.00	350.00
Common Player:		5.00	2.50	1.50
1	Santurce All-Star Team Composite Photo	10.00	5.00	3.00
2	Santurce All-Star Team Composite Photo	10.00	5.00	3.00
3	Santurce All-Star Team Composite Photo	10.00	5.00	3.00
4	Santurce All-Star Team Composite Photo	10.00	5.00	3.00
5	Santurce All-Star Team Composite Photo	10.00	5.00	3.00
6	Santurce All-Star Team Composite Photo	10.00	5.00	3.00
7	Santurce All-Star Team Composite Photo	10.00	5.00	3.00
8	Santurce All-Star Team Composite Photo	10.00	5.00	3.00
9	Santurce All-Star Team Composite Photo	10.00	5.00	3.00
10	Ponce All-Star Team Composite Photo	10.00	5.00	3.00
11	Ponce All-Star Team Composite Photo	10.00	5.00	3.00
12	Ponce All-Star Team Composite Photo	10.00	5.00	3.00
13	Ponce All-Star Team Composite Photo	10.00	5.00	3.00
14	Ponce All-Star Team Composite Photo	10.00	5.00	3.00
15	Ponce All-Star Team Composite Photo	10.00	5.00	3.00
16	Ponce All-Star Team Composite Photo	10.00	5.00	3.00
17	Ponce All-Star Team Composite Photo	10.00	5.00	3.00
18	Ponce All-Star Team Composite Photo	10.00	5.00	3.00
19	Arecibo Team Emblem	5.00	2.50	1.50
20	Caguas-Guayana Team Emblem	5.00	2.50	1.50
21	Mayaguez Team Emblem	5.00	2.50	1.50
22	Ponce Team Emblem	5.00	2.50	1.50
23	San Juan Team Emblem	5.00	2.50	1.50
24	Santurce Team Emblem	5.00	2.50	1.50
25	Steve Boros	5.00	2.50	1.50
26	Luis Isaac	5.00	2.50	1.50
27	Emmanuel Toledo	5.00	2.50	1.50
28	Gregorio Perez	5.00	2.50	1.50
29	Rosario Llanos	5.00	2.50	1.50
30	Jose Geigel	5.00	2.50	1.50
31	Eduardo Figueroa	5.00	2.50	1.50
32	Julian Muniz	5.00	2.50	1.50
33	Fernando Gonzalez	5.00	2.50	1.50
34	Bennie Ayala	5.00	2.50	1.50
35	Miguel Villaran	5.00	2.50	1.50
36	Efrain Vazquez	5.00	2.50	1.50
37	Ramon Ariles	5.00	2.50	1.50
38	Angel Alcaraz	5.00	2.50	1.50
39	Henry Cruz	5.00	2.50	1.50
40	Jose Silva	5.00	2.50	1.50
41	Jose Alcaide	5.00	2.50	1.50
42	Pepe Mangual	5.00	2.50	1.50
43	Mike Jackson	5.00	2.50	1.50
44	Lynn McGlothen	5.00	2.50	1.50
45	Frank Ortenzio	5.00	2.50	1.50
46	Norm Angelini	5.00	2.50	1.50
47	Richard Coggins	5.00	2.50	1.50
48	Lance Clemons	5.00	2.50	1.50
49	Mike Kelleher	5.00	2.50	1.50
50	Ken Wright	5.00	2.50	1.50
51	Buck Martinez	5.00	2.50	1.50
52	Billy De Mars	5.00	2.50	1.50
53	Elwood Huyke	5.00	2.50	1.50
54	Pedro Garcia	5.00	2.50	1.50
55	Bob Boone	20.00	10.00	6.00
56	Jose Laboy	5.00	2.50	1.50
57	Eduardo Rodriguez	5.00	2.50	1.50
58	Jesus Hernaiz	5.00	2.50	1.50
59	Joaquin Quintana	5.00	2.50	1.50
60	Domingo Figueroa	5.00	2.50	1.50
61	Juan Lopez	5.00	2.50	1.50
62	Luis Alvarado	5.00	2.50	1.50
63	Otoniel Velez	5.00	2.50	1.50
64	Mike Schmidt	350.00	175.00	105.00
65	Felix Millan	5.00	2.50	1.50
66	Guillermo Montanez	5.00	2.50	1.50
67	Ivan de Jesus	7.50	3.75	2.25
68	Sixto Lezcano	5.00	2.50	1.50
69	Jerry Morales	5.00	2.50	1.50
70	Bombo Rivera	5.00	2.50	1.50
71	Mike Ondina	5.00	2.50	1.50
72	Grant Jackson	5.00	2.50	1.50
73	Roger Freed	5.00	2.50	1.50
74	Steve Rogers	5.00	2.50	1.50
75	Mac Scarce	5.00	2.50	1.50
76	Mike Jorgensen	5.00	2.50	1.50
77	Jerry Crider	5.00	2.50	1.50
78	Fred Beene	5.00	2.50	1.50
79	Carl Ermer	5.00	2.50	1.50
80	Luis Marquez	5.00	2.50	1.50
81	Hector Valle	5.00	2.50	1.50
82	Ramon Vega	5.00	2.50	1.50
83	Cirito Cruz	5.00	2.50	1.50
84	Fernando Vega	5.00	2.50	1.50
85	Porfiro Sanchez	5.00	2.50	1.50
86	Jose Sevillano	5.00	2.50	1.50
87	Felix Roque	5.00	2.50	1.50
88	Enrique Rivera	5.00	2.50	1.50
89	Wildredo Rios	5.00	2.50	1.50
90	Javier Andino	5.00	2.50	1.50
91	Milton Ramirez	5.00	2.50	1.50
92	Max Oliveras	5.00	2.50	1.50
93	Jose Calero	5.00	2.50	1.50
94	Esteban Vazquez	5.00	2.50	1.50
95	Hector Cruz	5.00	2.50	1.50
96	Felix Arce	5.00	2.50	1.50
97	Gilberto Rivera	5.00	2.50	1.50
98	Rafael Rodriguez	5.00	2.50	1.50
99	Julio Gonzalez	5.00	2.50	1.50
100	Rosendo Cedeno	5.00	2.50	1.50
101	Pedro Cintron	5.00	2.50	1.50
102	Osvaldo Ortiz	5.00	2.50	1.50
103	Frank Verdi	5.00	2.50	1.50
104	Carlos Santiago	5.00	2.50	1.50
105	Ramon Conde	5.00	2.50	1.50
106	Pat Corrales	5.00	2.50	1.50
107	Jose Morales	5.00	2.50	1.50
108	Jack Whillock	5.00	2.50	1.50
109	Raul Mercado	5.00	2.50	1.50
110	Bonifacio Aponte	5.00	2.50	1.50
111	Angel Alicea	5.00	2.50	1.50
112	Santos Alomar	10.00	5.00	3.00
113	Francisco Libran	5.00	2.50	1.50
114	Edwin Pacheco	5.00	2.50	1.50
115	Luis Gonzalez	5.00	2.50	1.50
116	Juan Rios	5.00	2.50	1.50
117	Jorge Roque	5.00	2.50	1.50
118	Carlos Velez	5.00	2.50	1.50
119	David Gonzalez	5.00	2.50	1.50
120	Jose Cruz	7.50	3.75	2.25
121	Luis Melendez	5.00	2.50	1.50
122	Jose Ortiz	5.00	2.50	1.50
123	David Rosello	5.00	2.50	1.50
124	Juan Veintidos	5.00	2.50	1.50
125	Arnaldo Nazario	5.00	2.50	1.50
126	Dave Lemonds	5.00	2.50	1.50
127	Jim Magnuson	5.00	2.50	1.50
128	Tom Kelley	7.50	3.75	2.25
129	Chris Zachary	5.00	2.50	1.50
130	Hal Breeden	5.00	2.50	1.50
131	Jackie Hernandez	5.00	2.50	1.50
132	Rick Gossage	10.00	5.00	3.00
133	Frank Luchessi	5.00	2.50	1.50
134	Nino Escalera	5.00	2.50	1.50
135	Julio Navarro	5.00	2.50	1.50
136	Manny Sanguillen	7.50	3.75	2.25
137	Bob Johnson	5.00	2.50	1.50
138	Chuck Coggins	5.00	2.50	1.50
139	Orlando Gomez	5.00	2.50	1.50
140	William Melendez	5.00	2.50	1.50
141	Jose Del Moral	5.00	2.50	1.50
142	Jacinto Camacho	5.00	2.50	1.50
143	Emiliano Rivera	5.00	2.50	1.50
144	Luis Peraza	5.00	2.50	1.50
145	Carlos Velazquez	5.00	2.50	1.50
146	Luis Raul Garcia	5.00	2.50	1.50
147	Eliseo Rodriguez	5.00	2.50	1.50
148	Santiago Rosario	5.00	2.50	1.50
149	Ruben Castillo	5.00	2.50	1.50
150	Sergio Ferrer	5.00	2.50	1.50
151	Jose Pagan	5.00	2.50	1.50
152	Raul Colon	5.00	2.50	1.50
153	Robert Rauch	5.00	2.50	1.50
154	Luis Rosado	5.00	2.50	1.50
155	Francisco Lopez	5.00	2.50	1.50
156	Richard Zisk	5.00	2.50	1.50
157	Orlando Alvarez	5.00	2.50	1.50
158	Jaime Rosario	5.00	2.50	1.50
159	Rosendo Torres	5.00	2.50	1.50
160	Jim McKee	5.00	2.50	1.50
161	Mike Nagy	5.00	2.50	1.50
162	Brent Strom	5.00	2.50	1.50
163	Tom Walker	5.00	2.50	1.50
164	Angel Davila	5.00	2.50	1.50
165	Jose Cruz	5.00	2.50	1.50
166	Frank Robinson	30.00	15.00	9.00
167	German Rivera	5.00	2.50	1.50
168	Reinaldo Oliver	5.00	2.50	1.50
169	Geraldo Rodriguez	5.00	2.50	1.50
170	Elrod Hendricks	5.00	2.50	1.50
171	Gilberto Flores	5.00	2.50	1.50
172	Ruben Gomez	5.00	2.50	1.50
173	Juan Pizarro	5.00	2.50	1.50
174	William De Jesus	5.00	2.50	1.50
175	Rogelio Morel	5.00	2.50	1.50
176	Victor Agosto	5.00	2.50	1.50
177	Esteban Texidor	5.00	2.50	1.50
178	Ramon Hernandez	5.00	2.50	1.50
179	Gilberto Rondon Olivo	5.00	2.50	1.50
180	Juan Beniquez	5.00	2.50	1.50
181	Arturo Miranda	5.00	2.50	1.50
182	Manuel Ruiz	5.00	2.50	1.50
183	Julio Gotay	5.00	2.50	1.50
184	Arsenio Rodriguez	5.00	2.50	1.50
185	Luis Delgado	5.00	2.50	1.50
186	Jorge Rivera	5.00	2.50	1.50
187	Willie Crawford	5.00	2.50	1.50
188	Angel Mangual	5.00	2.50	1.50
189	Mike Strahler	5.00	2.50	1.50
190	Doyle Alexander	5.00	2.50	1.50
191	Bob Reynolds	5.00	2.50	1.50
192	Ron Cey	10.00	5.00	3.00
193	Jerr Da Vanon	5.00	2.50	1.50
194	Don Baylor	20.00	10.00	6.00
195	Tony Perez	20.00	10.00	6.00
196	Lloyd Allen	5.00	2.50	1.50
197	Orlando Cepeda	30.00	15.00	9.00
198	Roberto Clemente Composite Photo	25.00	12.50	7.50
199	Roberto Clemente Composite Photo	25.00	12.50	7.50
200	Roberto Clemente Composite Photo	25.00	12.50	7.50
201	Roberto Clemente Composite Photo	25.00	12.50	7.50
202	Roberto Clemente Composite Photo	25.00	12.50	7.50
203	Roberto Clemente Composite Photo	25.00	12.50	7.50
204	Roberto Clemente Composite Photo	25.00	12.50	7.50
205	Roberto Clemente Composite Photo	25.00	12.50	7.50
206	Roberto Clemente Composite Photo	25.00	12.50	7.50
207	Jaime Almendro	5.00	2.50	1.50
208	Jose R. Santiago	5.00	2.50	1.50
209	Luis Cabrera	5.00	2.50	1.50
210	Jorge Tirado	5.00	2.50	1.50
211	Radames Lopez	5.00	2.50	1.50
212	Juan Vargas	5.00	2.50	1.50
213	Francisco Coimbre	5.00	2.50	1.50
214	Freddie Thon	5.00	2.50	1.50
215	Manuel Alvarez	5.00	2.50	1.50
216	Luis Olmo	5.00	2.50	1.50
217	Jose Santiago	7.50	3.75	2.25
218	Hiram Bithorn	7.50	3.75	2.25
219	Willard Brown	7.50	3.75	2.25
220	Robert Thurman	7.50	3.75	2.25
221	Buster Clarkson	7.50	3.75	2.25
222	Satchel Paige	40.00	20.00	12.00
223	Raymond Brown	7.50	3.75	2.25
224	Alonso Perry	7.50	3.75	2.25
225	Quincy Trouppe	10.00	5.00	3.00
226	Santiago Muratti	5.00	2.50	1.50
227	Johnny Davis	5.00	2.50	1.50
228	Lino Suarez	5.00	2.50	1.50
229	Demetrio Pesante	5.00	2.50	1.50
230	Luis Arroyo	5.00	2.50	1.50
231	Jose Garcia	5.00	2.50	1.50

1966 Pure Oil Atlanta Braves

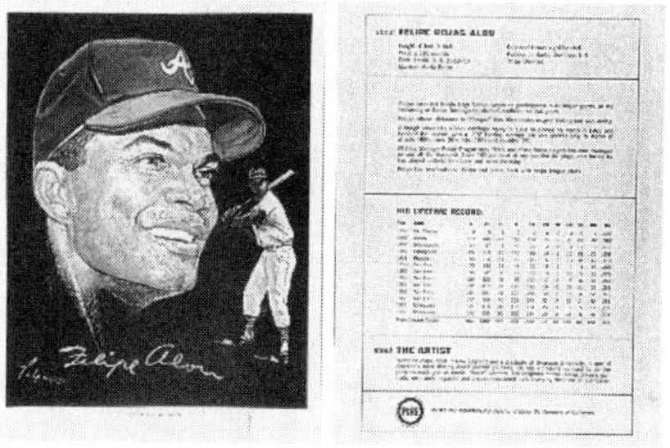

In their first year in Atlanta a set of Braves premium pictures done by noted portrait artist Nicholas Volpe was sponsored by Pure Oil. The 8-1/2" x 11" pictures were given away with gas purchases. Fronts featured a large pastel portrait and smaller full-figure action picture of the player set against a black background. A facsimile player autograph was pencilled at the bottom, along with the artist's signature. The player's name was printed in black in the white bottom border. Backs are printed in black-and-white and include biographical and career notes, full major and minor league stats, a short biography of the artist and the sponsoring company's logo. The unnumbered cards are checklisted here alphabetically.

		NM	EX	VG
Complete Set (12):		175.00	85.00	50.00
Common Player:		9.00	4.50	2.75
(1)	Hank Aaron	50.00	25.00	15.00
(2)	Felipe Alou	12.00	6.00	3.50
(3)	Frank Bolling	9.00	4.50	2.75
(4)	Bobby Bragan	9.00	4.50	2.75
(5)	Rico Carty	11.00	5.50	3.25
(6)	Tony Cloninger	9.00	4.50	2.75
(7)	Mack Jones	9.00	4.50	2.75
(8)	Denny Lemaster	9.00	4.50	2.75
(9)	Eddie Mathews	30.00	15.00	9.00
(10)	Denis Menke	9.00	4.50	2.75
(11)	Lee Thomas	9.00	4.50	2.75
(12)	Joe Torre	15.00	7.50	4.50

1933 PX3 Double Header Pins

Issued by Gum Inc. circa 1933, this unnumbered set consists of 43 metal discs approximately 1-1/4" in diameter. The front of the pin lists the player's name and team beneath his picture. The numbers "1" or "2" also appear inside a small circle at the bottom of the disc, and the wrapper advised collectors to "put 1 and 2 together and make a double header." The set is designated as PX3 in the American Card Catalog.

		NM	EX	VG
Complete Set (43):		1100.	550.00	330.00
Common Player:		25.00	12.50	7.50
(1)	Sparky Adams	25.00	12.50	7.50
(2)	Dale Alexander	25.00	12.50	7.50
(3)	Earl Averill	45.00	22.00	13.50
(4)	Dick Bartell	25.00	12.50	7.50
(5)	Walter Berger	25.00	12.50	7.50
(6)	Jim Bottomley	45.00	22.00	13.50
(7)	Lefty Brandt	25.00	12.50	7.50
(8)	Owen Carroll	25.00	12.50	7.50
(9)	Lefty Clark	25.00	12.50	7.50
(10)	Mickey Cochrane	45.00	22.00	13.50
(11)	Joe Cronin	45.00	22.00	13.50
(12)	Jimmy Dykes	25.00	12.50	7.50
(13)	George Earnshaw	25.00	12.50	7.50
(14)	Wes Ferrell	25.00	12.50	7.50
(15)	Neal Finn	25.00	12.50	7.50
(16)	Lew Fonseca	25.00	12.50	7.50
(17)	Jimmy Foxx	65.00	32.00	19.50
(18)	Frankie Frisch	45.00	22.00	13.50
(19)	Chick Fullis	25.00	12.50	7.50
(20)	Charley Gehringer	45.00	22.00	13.50
(21)	Goose Goslin	45.00	22.00	13.50
(22)	Johnny Hodapp	25.00	12.50	7.50
(23)	Frank Hogan	25.00	12.50	7.50
(24)	Si Johnson	25.00	12.50	7.50
(25)	Joe Judge	25.00	12.50	7.50
(26)	Chuck Klein	45.00	22.00	13.50
(27)	Al Lopez	45.00	22.00	13.50
(28)	Ray Lucas	25.00	12.50	7.50
(29)	Red Lucas	25.00	12.50	7.50
(30)	Ted Lyons	45.00	22.00	13.50
(31)	Firpo Marberry	25.00	12.50	7.50
(32)	Oscar Melillo	25.00	12.50	7.50
(33)	Lefty O'Doul	30.00	15.00	9.00
(34)	George Pipgras	25.00	12.50	7.50
(35)	Flint Rhem	25.00	12.50	7.50
(36)	Sam Rice	45.00	22.00	13.50
(37)	Muddy Ruel	25.00	12.50	7.50
(38)	Harry Seibold	25.00	12.50	7.50
(39)	Al Simmons	45.00	22.00	13.50
(40)	Joe Vosmik	25.00	12.50	7.50
(41)	Gerald Walker	25.00	12.50	7.50
(42)	Pinky Whitney	25.00	12.50	7.50
(43)	Hack Wilson	45.00	22.00	13.50

R

1888 R & S Artistic Series Baseball

This series of die-cut color lithographed player figures does not represent actual players, but rather generic figures in late 19th Century uniforms labeled with the names of various major league teams of the era. The actual date of issue is unknown. The cardboard figures were issued in a sheet of 20 with duplicates. Individual figures vary in size with a typical piece about 1-1/2" wide and 2-3/4". Players are shown in batting, throwing and fielding poses.

		NM	EX	VG
Complete Set (10):		2000.	1000.	600.00
Common Card:		200.00	100.00	60.00
(1)	Baltimore	200.00	100.00	60.00
(2)	Boston	200.00	100.00	60.00
(3)	Brooklyn	200.00	100.00	60.00
(4)	Chicago	200.00	100.00	60.00
(5)	Detroit	200.00	100.00	60.00
(6)	Indianapolis	200.00	100.00	60.00
(7)	New York	200.00	100.00	60.00
(8)	Philadelphia	200.00	100.00	60.00
(9)	Pittsburgh	200.00	100.00	60.00
(10)	St. Louis	200.00	100.00	60.00

1909 Ramly Cigarettes (T204)

While issued with both Ramly and T.T.T. brand Turkish tobacco cigarettes, the cards in this set take their name from the more common of the two brands. By whatever name, the set is one of the more interesting and attractive of the early 20th Century. The 2" x 2-1/2" cards carry black-and-white photographic portraits with impressive gold embossed frames and borders on the front. Toward the bottom appears the player's last name, position, team and league. The backs carry only the most basic information on the cigarette company. The complete set price does not include the scarce variations.

		NM	EX	VG
Complete Set (121):		62000.	25000.	12500.
Common Player:		450.00	180.00	90.00
(1)	Whitey Alperman	450.00	180.00	90.00
(2)	John Anderson	450.00	180.00	90.00
(3)	Jimmy Archer	450.00	180.00	90.00
(4)	Frank Arrelanes (Arellanes)	450.00	180.00	90.00
(5)	Jim Ball	450.00	180.00	90.00
(6)	Neal Ball	450.00	180.00	90.00
(7a)	Frank C. Bancroft (photo inside oval frame)	450.00	180.00	90.00
(7b)	Frank C. Bancroft (photo inside square frame)	4250.	1700.	850.00
(8)	Johnny Bates	450.00	180.00	90.00
(9)	Fred Beebe	450.00	180.00	90.00
(10)	George Bell	450.00	180.00	90.00
(11)	Chief Bender	1500.	600.00	300.00
(12)	Walter Blair	450.00	180.00	90.00
(13)	Cliff Blankenship	450.00	180.00	90.00
(14)	Frank Bowerman	450.00	180.00	90.00
(15a)	Wm. Bransfield (photo inside oval frame)	450.00	180.00	90.00
(15b)	Wm. Bransfield (photo inside square frame)	3250.	1300.	650.00
(16)	Roger Bresnahan	1500.	600.00	300.00
(17)	Al Bridwell	450.00	180.00	90.00
(18)	Mordecai Brown	1500.	600.00	300.00
(19)	Fred Burchell	450.00	180.00	90.00
(20a)	Jesse C. Burkett (photo inside oval frame)	1500.	600.00	300.00
(20b)	Jesse C. Burkett (photo inside square frame)	6000.	2400.	1200.
(21)	Bobby Byrnes (Byrne)	450.00	180.00	90.00
(22)	Bill Carrigan	450.00	180.00	90.00
(23)	Frank Chance	1500.	600.00	300.00
(24)	Charlie Chech	450.00	180.00	90.00
(25)	Ed Cicolte (Cicotte)	600.00	240.00	120.00
(26)	Otis Clymer	450.00	180.00	90.00
(27)	Andy Coakley	450.00	180.00	90.00
(28)	Jimmy Collins	1500.	600.00	300.00
(29)	Ed. Collins	1500.	600.00	300.00
(30)	Wid Conroy	450.00	180.00	90.00
(31)	Jack Coombs	450.00	180.00	90.00
(32)	Doc Crandall	450.00	180.00	90.00
(33)	Lou Criger	450.00	180.00	90.00
(34)	Harry Davis	450.00	180.00	90.00
(35)	Art Devlin	450.00	180.00	90.00
(36a)	Wm. H. Dineen (Dinneen) (photo inside oval frame)	450.00	180.00	90.00
(36b)	Wm. H. Dineen (Dinneen) (photo inside square frame)	3250.	1300.	650.00
(37)	Jiggs Donahue	450.00	180.00	90.00
(38)	Mike Donlin	450.00	180.00	90.00
(39)	Wild Bill Donovan	450.00	180.00	90.00
(40)	Gus Dorner	450.00	180.00	90.00
(41)	Joe Dunn	450.00	180.00	90.00
(42)	Kid Elberfield (Elberfeld)	450.00	180.00	90.00
(43)	Johnny Evers	1500.	600.00	300.00
(44)	Bob Ewing	450.00	180.00	90.00
(45)	Cecil Ferguson	450.00	180.00	90.00
(46)	Hobe Ferris	450.00	180.00	90.00
(47)	Jerry Freeman	450.00	180.00	90.00
(48)	Art Fromme	450.00	180.00	90.00
(49)	Bob Ganley	450.00	180.00	90.00
(50)	Doc Gessler	450.00	180.00	90.00
(51)	Peaches Graham	450.00	180.00	90.00
(52)	Clark Griffith	1500.	600.00	300.00
(53)	Roy Hartzell	450.00	180.00	90.00
(54)	Charlie Hemphill	450.00	180.00	90.00
(55)	Dick Hoblitzel (Hoblitzell)	450.00	180.00	90.00
(56)	Geo. Howard	450.00	180.00	90.00
(57)	Harry Howell	450.00	180.00	90.00
(58)	Miller Huggins	1500.	600.00	300.00
(59)	John Hummell (Hummel)	450.00	180.00	90.00
(60)	Walter Johnson	8000.	3200.	1600.
(61)	Thos. Jones	450.00	180.00	90.00
(62)	Mike Kahoe	450.00	180.00	90.00
(63)	Ed Kargar	450.00	180.00	90.00
(64)	Wee Willie Keeler	1500.	600.00	300.00
(65)	Red Kleinon (Kleinow)	450.00	180.00	90.00
(66)	Jack Knight	450.00	180.00	90.00
(67)	Ed Konetchey	450.00	180.00	90.00
(68)	Vive Lindaman	450.00	180.00	90.00
(69)	Hans Loebert (Lobert)	450.00	180.00	90.00
(70)	Harry Lord	450.00	180.00	90.00
(71)	Harry Lumley	450.00	180.00	90.00
(72)	Johnny Lush	450.00	180.00	90.00
(73)	Rube Manning	450.00	180.00	90.00
(74)	Jimmy McAleer	450.00	180.00	90.00
(75)	Amby McConnell	450.00	180.00	90.00
(76)	Moose McCormick	450.00	180.00	90.00
(77)	Harry McIntyre	450.00	180.00	90.00
(78)	Larry McLean	450.00	180.00	90.00
(79)	Fred Merkle	450.00	180.00	90.00
(80)	Clyde Milan	450.00	180.00	90.00
(81)	Mike Mitchell	450.00	180.00	90.00
(82a)	Pat Moran (photo inside oval frame)	450.00	180.00	90.00
(82b)	Pat Moran (photo inside square frame)	3250.	1300.	650.00
(83)	Cy Morgan	450.00	180.00	90.00
(84)	Tim Murname (Murnane)	450.00	180.00	90.00
(85)	Danny Murphy	450.00	180.00	90.00
(86)	Red Murray	450.00	180.00	90.00
(87)	Doc Newton	450.00	180.00	90.00
(88)	Simon Nichols (Nicholls)	450.00	180.00	90.00
(89)	Harry Niles	450.00	180.00	90.00
(90)	Bill O'Hare (O'Hara)	450.00	180.00	90.00
(91)	Charley O'Leary	450.00	180.00	90.00
(92)	Dode Paskert	450.00	180.00	90.00
(93)	Barney Pelty	450.00	180.00	90.00
(94)	Jake Pfeister	450.00	180.00	90.00
(95)	Ed Plank	1500.	600.00	300.00
(96)	Jack Powell	450.00	180.00	90.00
(97)	Bugs Raymond	450.00	180.00	90.00
(98)	Tom Reilly	450.00	180.00	90.00
(99)	Claude Ritchey	450.00	180.00	90.00
(100)	Nap Rucker	450.00	180.00	90.00
(101)	Ed Ruelbach (Reulbach)	450.00	180.00	90.00
(102)	Slim Sallee	450.00	180.00	90.00
(103)	Germany Schaefer	450.00	180.00	90.00
(104)	Jimmy Schekard (Sheckard)	450.00	180.00	90.00
(105)	Admiral Schlei	450.00	180.00	90.00
(106)	Wildfire Schulte	450.00	180.00	90.00
(107)	Jimmy Sebring	450.00	180.00	90.00
(108)	Bill Shipke	450.00	180.00	90.00
(109)	Charlie Smith	450.00	180.00	90.00
(110)	Tubby Spencer	450.00	180.00	90.00
(111)	Jake Stahl	450.00	180.00	90.00
(112)	Jim Stephens	450.00	180.00	90.00
(113)	Harry Stienfeldt (Steinfeldt)	450.00	180.00	90.00
(114)	Gabby Street	450.00	180.00	90.00
(115)	Bill Sweeney	450.00	180.00	90.00
(116)	Fred Tenney	450.00	180.00	90.00
(117)	Ira Thomas	450.00	180.00	90.00
(118)	Joe Tinker	1500.	600.00	300.00
(119)	Bob Unglane (Unglaub)	450.00	180.00	90.00
(120)	Heinie Wagner	450.00	180.00	90.00
(121)	Bobby Wallace	1500.	600.00	300.00

1950s-70s Rawlings Advisory Staff Photos

Advisory staff photos were a promtional item which debuted in the early 1950s, flourished in the Sixties and died in the early 1970s. Generally 8" x 10" (sometimes a little larger), these black-and-white (a few later were color) glossy photos picture players who had contracted with a major baseball equipment company to endorse and use their product. Usually the product - most often a glove - was prominently displayed in the photo. The pictures were often displayed in the windows of sporting goods stores or the walls of sports departments and were sometimes made available to customers. Because the companies tended to stick with players over the years, some photos were reissued, sometimes with and sometimes without a change of team, pose or style. All advisory staff photos of the era are checklisted here in alphabetical order. A pose description is given for each known picture. The photos are checklisted here in alphabetical order. It is unlikely this list is complete. In general,

Rawlings advisory staff photos feature a white box within the photo which contains the glove-company logo and a facsimile autograph of the player. Gaps have been left in the checklist numbering to accommodate possible additions.

		NM	EX	VG
	Common Player:	12.00	6.00	3.50
(1)	Joe Adcock (Braves, kneeling)	12.00	6.00	3.50
(2)	Joe Adcock (Braves, locker room)	12.00	6.00	3.50
(3)	Joe Adcock (Braves, upper body)	12.00	6.00	3.50
(4)	Hank Aguirre (Tigers, glove on knee)	12.00	6.00	3.50
(5)	Bobby Avila (Indians, upper body)	12.00	6.00	3.50
(6)	Bob Bailey (Pirates, kneeling)	12.00	6.00	3.50
(7)	Ed Bailey (Reds, dugout)	12.00	6.00	3.50
(8)	Ed Bailey (Giants, catching crouch)	12.00	6.00	3.50
(9)	Earl Battey (Twins, catching crouch)	12.00	6.00	3.50
(10)	Earl Battey (Twins, kneeling w/bat)	12.00	6.00	3.50
(11)	Johnny Bench (crouching, no catcher's gear)	30.00	15.00	9.00
(12)	Dick Bertell (Cubs, catching crouch)	12.00	6.00	3.50
(13)	John Blanchard (Yankees, catching crouch)	12.00	6.00	3.50
(14)	John Blanchard (Yankees, dugout step)	12.00	6.00	3.50
(16)	Clete Boyer (Yankees, fielding)	12.00	6.00	3.50
(17)	Ken Boyer (Cardinals, b/w, kneeling)	15.00	7.50	4.50
(19)	Ken Boyer (White Sox, upper body)	15.00	7.50	4.50
(20)	Ken Boyer (Mets, color, leaning on bat)	12.00	6.00	3.50
(21)	Lew Burdette (Braves, beginning windup)	12.00	6.00	3.50
(22)	Lew Burdette (Braves, upper body w/ball)	12.00	6.00	3.50
(23)	Bob Cerv (A's, at bat rack)	12.00	6.00	3.50
(24)	Gordon Coleman (Reds, kneeling w/bat)	12.00	6.00	3.50
(25)	Tony Conigliaro (Red Sox, glove at chest)	24.00	12.00	7.25
(26)	Wes Covington (Braves, upper body)	12.00	6.00	3.50
(27)	Joe Cunningham (White Sox, glove at knee)	12.00	6.00	3.50
(28)	Joe Cunningham (Cardinals, upper body)	12.00	6.00	3.50
(29)	Tommy Davis (Dodgers, dugout step)	12.00	6.00	3.50
(31)	Don Demeter (Dodgers, upper body)	12.00	6.00	3.50
(32)	Don Demeter (Phillies, hands on knees)	12.00	6.00	3.50
(33)	Tito Francona (Indians, sitting w/glove)	12.00	6.00	3.50
(34)	Steve Garvey (Dodgers, horizontal, pose and action)	16.00	8.00	4.75
(35)	Mudcat Grant (Indians, horizontal, upper body)	12.00	6.00	3.50
(36)	Dick Groat (Pirates, b/w, upper body)	12.00	6.00	3.50
(38)	Dick Groat (Cardinals, b/w, kneeling w/bat)	12.00	6.00	3.50
(39)	Dick Groat (Cardinals, b/w, kneeling)	12.00	6.00	3.50
(41)	Harvey Haddix (Pirates, kneeling)	12.00	6.00	3.50
(42)	Harvey Haddix (Pirates, locker room)	12.00	6.00	3.50
(43)	Ken Holtzman (Cubs, hands on knees)	12.00	6.00	3.50
(44)	Ken Holtzman (A's, horizontal, two poses)	12.00	6.00	3.50
(45)	Elston Howard (Yankees, catching crouch)	17.50	8.75	5.25
(46)	Al Hrabosky (Cardinals, upper body)	12.00	6.00	3.50
(47)	Larry Jackson (Cubs, kneeling)	12.00	6.00	3.50
(48)	Larry Jackson (Cardinals, fielding)	12.00	6.00	3.50
(49)	Reggie Jackson (A's, full-length)	27.50	13.50	8.25
(51)	Joey Jay (Reds, dugout step, glove on rail)	12.00	6.00	3.50
(52)	Fergie Jenkins (Cubs, hands on knees)	17.50	8.75	5.25
(53)	Ed Kranepool (Mets, color, batting)	12.00	6.00	3.50
(54)	Tony Kubek (kneeling, no bat)	16.00	8.00	4.75
(55)	Tony Kubek (kneeling w/bat)	16.00	8.00	4.75
(56)	Tony Kubek (horizontal, upper body)	16.00	8.00	4.75
(57)	Vern Law (locker room)	12.00	6.00	3.50
(58)	Jim Lefebvre (Dodgers, kneeling, bat on shoulder)	12.00	6.00	3.50
(59)	Sherman Lollar (White Sox, catching crouch)	12.00	6.00	3.50
(60)	Art Mahaffey (Phillies, upper body)	12.00	6.00	3.50
(61)	Mickey Mantle (upper body, road uniform)	100.00	50.00	30.00
(62)	Mickey Mantle (leaning, hands on knees)	100.00	50.00	30.00
(63)	Mickey Mantle (seated w/bat, glove on knee)	100.00	50.00	30.00
(64)	Mickey Mantle (kneeling)	100.00	50.00	30.00
(65)	Mickey Mantle (seated at locker, pointing to glove)	100.00	50.00	30.00
(66)	Eddie Mathews (Braves, full-length)	30.00	15.00	9.00
(67)	Eddie Mathews (Braves, sepia, upper body)	30.00	15.00	9.00
(68)	Eddie Mathews (Braves, upper body, glove in front)	30.00	15.00	9.00
(69)	Eddie Mathews (Braves, upper body, looking at glove)	30.00	15.00	9.00
(70)	Dal Maxvill (Cardinals, bat on shoulder)	12.00	6.00	3.50
(71)	Dal Maxvill (Cardinals, fielding)	12.00	6.00	3.50
(72)	Charlie Maxwell (Tigers, horizontal, upper body)	12.00	6.00	3.50
(74)	Tim McCarver (Cardinals, catching crouch)	16.00	8.00	4.75
(75)	Dave McNally (Orioles, upper body)	12.00	6.00	3.50
(76)	Wilmer Mizell (Cardinals, upper body)	12.00	6.00	3.50
(77)	Wally Moon (Dodgers, kneeling)	12.00	6.00	3.50
(78)	Wally Moon (Dodgers, standing)	12.00	6.00	3.50
(79)	Stan Musial (upper body)	35.00	17.50	10.50
(80)	Stan Musial (horizontal, batting)	35.00	17.50	10.50
(81)	Stan Musial (full-length holding glove and bat)	35.00	17.50	10.50
(82)	Stan Musial (kneeling on bat)	35.00	17.50	10.50
(83)	Stan Musial (kneeling on bat, glove on ground)	35.00	17.50	10.50
(84)	Stan Musial (kneeling, glove in front, Busch Stadium)	35.00	17.50	10.50
(85)	Stan Musial (full-length, glove on knee)	35.00	17.50	10.50
(86)	Charlie Neal (Dodgers, kneeling)	12.00	6.00	3.50
(87)	Charlie Neal (Dodgers, upper body)	12.00	6.00	3.50
(88)	Rocky Nelson (Pirates, kneeling)	12.00	6.00	3.50
(89)	Rocky Nelson (Pirates, fielding)	12.00	6.00	3.50
(91)	Amos Otis (Royals, upper body)	12.00	6.00	3.50
(92)	Jim Perry (Indians, pitching)	12.00	6.00	3.50
(93)	Boog Powell (Orioles, full-length)	17.50	8.75	5.25
(94)	Rick Reichardt (Angels, full-length)	12.00	6.00	3.50
(95)	Brooks Robinson (dugout step)	30.00	15.00	9.00
(96)	Brooks Robinson (throwing)	30.00	15.00	9.00
(97)	Brooks Robinson (tying shoe)	30.00	15.00	9.00
(99)	John Romano (Indians, adjusting shinguard)	12.00	6.00	3.50
(101)	Manny Sanguillen (Pirates, catching crouch)	12.00	6.00	3.50
(102)	Chuck Schilling (full-length)	12.00	6.00	3.50
(103)	Herb Score (Indians, pitching)	15.00	7.50	4.50
(104)	Norm Siebern (A's, vest)	12.00	6.00	3.50
(105)	Norm Siebern (A's, jersey)	12.00	6.00	3.50
(106)	Roy Sievers (Senators, full-length)	12.00	6.00	3.50
(107)	Roy Sievers (White Sox, drinking fountain)	12.00	6.00	3.50
(108)	Roy Sievers (Phillies, kneeling)	12.00	6.00	3.50
(109)	Bob Skinner (Pirates, upper body)	12.00	6.00	3.50
(110)	Duke Snider (Brooklyn Dodgers, full-length)	30.00	15.00	9.00
(111)	Duke Snider (L.A. Dodgers, upper body)	30.00	15.00	9.00
(112)	Warren Spahn (Braves, b/w, pitching)	30.00	15.00	9.00
(114)	Willie Stargell (upper body)	25.00	12.50	7.50
(115)	Willie Stargell (full-length)	25.00	12.50	7.50
(116)	Tom Tresh (Yankees, fielding)	15.00	7.50	4.50
(117)	Tom Tresh (Yankees, full-length)	15.00	7.50	4.50
(119)	Bob Turley (Yankees, upper body)	12.50	6.25	3.75
(121)	Bill White (Cardinals, glove over rail)	12.00	6.00	3.50
(122)	Bill White (Phillies, b/w, full-length)	12.00	6.00	3.50
(123)	Bill White (Phillies, color, full-length)	12.00	6.00	3.50
(124)	Billy Williams (Cubs, full-length)	24.00	12.00	7.25
(126)	Steve Yeager (Dodgers, upper body)	12.00	6.00	3.50

1930 Ray-O-Print Photo Kits

This was one of several contemporary kits for do-it-yourself production of photo prints. The outfits were produced by M.P. & Co., of New York. The novelty kit consists of a 4-1/8" x 2-1/2" kraft paper envelope with production instructions printed on the outside and the name of the subject rubber-stamped on one end. Inside was a film negative, a piece of light-sensitive photo paper (each 1-7/8" x 2-15/16") and a tin stand for exposing and displaying the photo. Values shown are for complete kits. Individual components would be pro-rated, with the negative being the most valuable of the pieces. Anyone with a negative could make unlimited prints today, and even make them look old; collectors should use caution in purchasing prints alone.

		NM	EX	VG
	Complete Set (8):	1000.	500.00	300.00
	Common Kit:	125.00	67.00	38.00
(1)	Lou Gehrig	250.00	125.00	75.00
(2)	Babe Ruth	400.00	200.00	120.00
(3)	Jack Dempsey (boxer)	100.00	50.00	30.00
(4)	Herbert Hoover (president)	75.00	37.00	22.00
(5)	Charles Lindbergh (aviator)	150.00	75.00	45.00
(6)	Mary Pickford (actress)	50.00	25.00	15.00
(7)	Will Rogers (humorist)	50.00	25.00	15.00
(8)	We (Charles Lindbergh) (w/ plane, Spirit of St. Louis)	150.00	75.00	45.00

1954 Rawlings Stan Musial

The date of issue is speculation although the picture is certainly from 1955 or earlier. This 5-1/2" x 7-1/2" colorized photo is actually part of a cardboard Rawlings glove box. The panel at lower-right of the card identifies it as "A GENUINE RAWLINGS FACSIMILE AUTOGRAPH PICTURE". Back is blank.

	NM	EX	VG
Stan Musial	300.00	150.00	90.00

1955 Rawlings Stan Musial

Though missing from Topps and Bowman card sets from 1954-57, Cardinals superstar Stan Musial wasn't entirely unavailable on baseball cards. About 1955 he appeared on a series of six cards found on boxes of Rawlings baseball gloves carrying Musial's endorsement. The cards feature black-and-white photos of Musial set against a blue background. Because the cards were part of a display box, they are blank-backed. Depending on the position on the box, the cards measure approximately 2" x 3" (#1A and 2A) or 2-1/2" x 3-3/4" (#1-4). Cards are numbered in a yellow star at upper left.

		NM	EX	VG
Complete Set (6):		900.00	450.00	270.00
Complete Box:		2500.	1250.	750.00
Common Card:		150.00	75.00	45.00
1	Stan Musial (portrait)	150.00	75.00	45.00
1A	Stan Musial (portrait with bat)	150.00	75.00	45.00
2	Stan Musial (kneeling)	150.00	75.00	45.00
2A	Stan Musial (portrait)	150.00	75.00	45.00
3	Stan Musial (swinging, horizontal)	150.00	75.00	45.00
4	Stan Musial (batting pose)	150.00	75.00	45.00

1964 Rawlings Glove Box

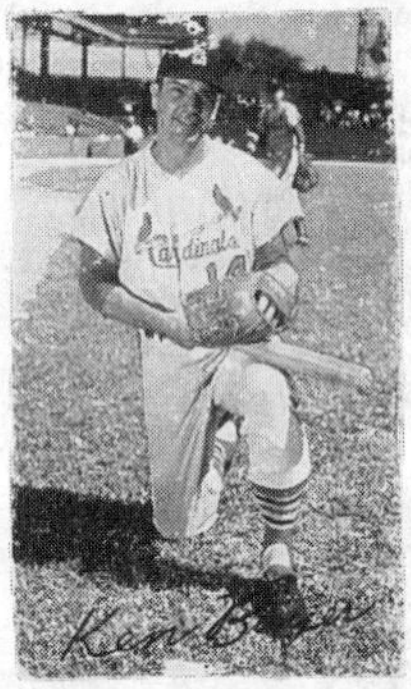

Measuring about 2-3/8" x 4" when properly cut off the glove boxes on which they were printed, these full-color cards show stars of the day posing with their Rawlings glove prominently displayed. The blank-backed unnumbered cards are checklisted here alphabetically. The quality of cutting should be considered in grading these cards. In actuality, the cards were not meant to be cut from the boxes, but rather to show which premium photo was packed inside the glove box.

		NM	EX	VG
Complete Set (8):		450.00	225.00	135.00
Common Player:		25.00	12.50	7.50
(1)	Ken Boyer	35.00	17.50	10.50
(2)	Tommy Davis	25.00	12.50	7.50
(3)	Dick Groat	25.00	12.50	7.50
(4)	Mickey Mantle	200.00	100.00	60.00
(5)	Brooks Robinson	60.00	30.00	18.00
(6)	Warren Spahn	50.00	25.00	15.00
(7)	Tom Tresh	25.00	12.50	7.50
(8)	Billy Williams	45.00	22.00	13.50

1964-66 Rawlings Premium Photos

One premium photo was inserted into each baseball glove box sold by Rawlings in 1964. The 8" x 9-1/2" full-color photos were advertised on the outside of the boxes in miniature form. Each of the photos pictures a player posed with his Rawlings leather prominently displayed. A black facsimile autograph is printed on the front.

		NM	EX	VG
Complete Set (8):		450.00	225.00	135.00
Common Player:		15.00	7.50	4.50
(1)	Ken Boyer	25.00	12.50	7.50
(2)	Tommy Davis	15.00	7.50	4.50
(3)	Dick Groat	15.00	7.50	4.50
(4)	Mickey Mantle	200.00	100.00	60.00
(5a)	Brooks Robinson (full-bird cap)	60.00	30.00	18.00
(5b)	Brooks Robinson (bird's-head cap)	75.00	37.00	22.00
(6)	Warren Spahn	65.00	32.00	19.50
(7)	Tom Tresh	15.00	7.50	4.50
(8)	Billy Williams	45.00	22.00	13.50

1969 Rawlings Reggie Jackson

How this card was distributed is not certain today. If there are any other cards in the series they are not known. This black-and-white card of Reggie Jackson measures 3" x 5" and features a close-up portrait on front, with a white strip at bottom which holds a facsimile autograph. The back has Jackson's minor league stats, career highlights and a Rawlings ad.

	NM	EX	VG
Reggie Jackson	90.00	67.00	36.00

1899 Henry Reccius Cigars Honus Wagner

The date of this card's issue is probable, though it could have been issued anytime between 1897-99 during Wagner's stay in Louisville. The 3-3/8" x 4-3/4" card is printed in black-and-white with an oval photograph of Wagner at center. Advertising for the cigar company which marketed cigars under his name is around the border. The back has a lengthy pro-trade union poem. Only one example of the card is known, having been auctioned in early 1998. A slightly earlier cigar box when the price was a nickel a smoke, sold in the same auction for $9,000.

	NM	EX	VG
Honus Wagner			15000.

1912 Recruit Little Cigars

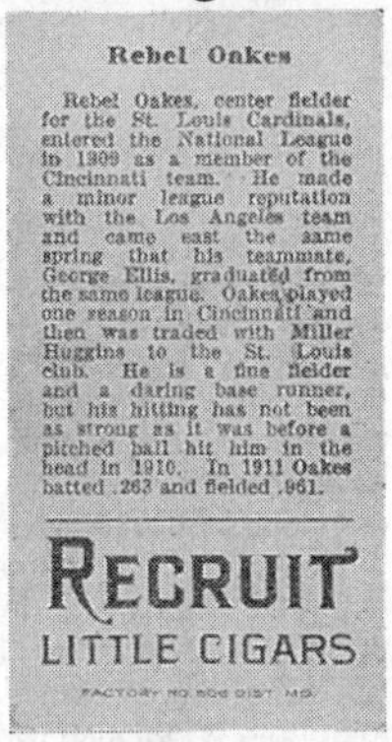

(See T207)

1976 Red Barn discs

The scarcest among the several regional sponsors of player disc sets issued in 1976 are those of the Red Barn family restaurant chain in Southeastern Wisconsin. The discs are 3-3/8" diameter with a black-and-white player portrait photo in the center of the baseball design. A line of red stars is above, while the left and right panels feature one of several bright colors. Produced by Michael Schecter Associates under license from the Major League Baseball Players Association, the player photos have had uniform and cap logos removed. Backs are printed in red and purple. The unnumbered checklist here is presented in alphabetical order.

		NM	EX	VG
Complete Set:		400.00	200.00	120.00
Common Player:		4.00	2.00	1.25
(1)	Henry Aaron	65.00	32.00	19.50
(2)	Johnny Bench	35.00	17.50	10.50
(3)	Vida Blue	4.00	2.00	1.25
(4)	Larry Bowa	4.00	2.00	1.25
(5)	Lou Brock	20.00	10.00	6.00
(6)	Jeff Burroughs	4.00	2.00	1.25
(7)	John Candelaria	4.00	2.00	1.25
(8)	Jose Cardenal	4.00	2.00	1.25
(9)	Rod Carew	20.00	10.00	6.00
(10)	Steve Carlton	20.00	10.00	6.00
(11)	Dave Cash	4.00	2.00	1.25
(12)	Cesar Cedeno	4.00	2.00	1.25
(13)	Ron Cey	4.00	2.00	1.25
(14)	Carlton Fisk	20.00	10.00	6.00
(15)	Tito Fuentes	4.00	2.00	1.25
(16)	Steve Garvey	18.00	9.00	5.50
(17)	Ken Griffey	4.00	2.00	1.25
(18)	Don Gullett	4.00	2.00	1.25
(19)	Willie Horton	4.00	2.00	1.25
(20)	Al Hrabosky	4.00	2.00	1.25
(21)	Catfish Hunter	20.00	10.00	6.00
(22)	Reggie Jackson	40.00	20.00	12.00
(23)	Randy Jones	4.00	2.00	1.25
(24)	Jim Kaat	4.00	2.00	1.25
(25)	Don Kessinger	4.00	2.00	1.25
(26)	Dave Kingman	11.00	5.50	3.25
(27)	Jerry Koosman	4.00	2.00	1.25
(28)	Mickey Lolich	9.50	4.75	2.75
(29)	Greg Luzinski	4.00	2.00	1.25
(30)	Fred Lynn	6.00	3.00	1.75
(31)	Bill Madlock	4.00	2.00	1.25
(32)	Carlos May	4.00	2.00	1.25
(33)	John Mayberry	4.00	2.00	1.25
(34)	Bake McBride	4.00	2.00	1.25
(35)	Doc Medich	4.00	2.00	1.25
(36)	Andy Messersmith	4.00	2.00	1.25
(37)	Rick Monday	4.00	2.00	1.25
(38)	John Montefusco	4.00	2.00	1.25
(39)	Jerry Morales	4.00	2.00	1.25
(40)	Joe Morgan	20.00	10.00	6.00
(41)	Thurman Munson	25.00	12.50	7.50
(42)	Bobby Murcer	4.00	2.00	1.25
(43)	Al Oliver	4.00	2.00	1.25
(44)	Jim Palmer	20.00	10.00	6.00
(45)	Dave Parker	10.00	5.00	3.00
(46)	Tony Perez	20.00	10.00	6.00
(47)	Jerry Reuss	4.00	2.00	1.25
(48)	Brooks Robinson	25.00	12.50	7.50
(49)	Frank Robinson	25.00	12.50	7.50
(50)	Steve Rogers	4.00	2.00	1.25
(51)	Pete Rose	50.00	25.00	15.00
(52)	Nolan Ryan	100.00	50.00	30.00
(53)	Manny Sanguillen	4.00	2.00	1.25
(54)	Mike Schmidt	45.00	22.00	13.50
(55)	Tom Seaver	25.00	12.50	7.50
(56)	Ted Simmons	4.00	2.00	1.25
(57)	Reggie Smith	4.00	2.00	1.25
(58)	Willie Stargell	20.00	10.00	6.00
(59)	Rusty Staub	6.00	3.00	1.75
(60)	Rennie Stennett	4.00	2.00	1.25
(61)	Don Sutton	20.00	10.00	6.00
(62)	Andy Thornton	4.00	2.00	1.25
(63)	Luis Tiant	4.00	2.00	1.25
(64)	Joe Torre	6.00	3.00	1.75
(65)	Mike Tyson	4.00	2.00	1.25
(66)	Bob Watson	4.00	2.00	1.25
(67)	Wilbur Wood	4.00	2.00	1.25
(68)	Jimmy Wynn	4.00	2.00	1.25
(69)	Carl Yastrzemski	25.00	12.50	7.50
(70)	Richie Zisk	4.00	2.00	1.25

1910-12 Red Cross Tobacco Type 1 (T215)

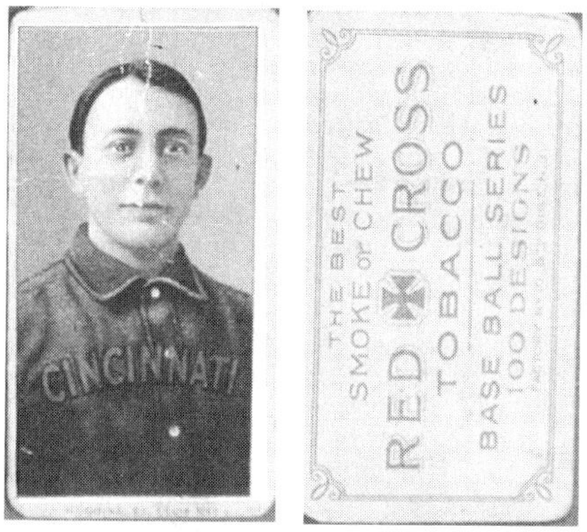

The T215 set issued by Red Cross Tobacco is another of the Louisana area sets closely related to the popular T206 "White Border" tobacco cards. Very similar to the T213 Coupon cards, the Red Cross Tobacco cards are found in two distinct types, both featuring color player lithographs and measuring approximately 1-1/2" x 2-5/8", the standard tobacco card size. Type I Red Cross cards, issued from 1910 to 1912, have brown captions; while Type II cards, most of which appear to be from 1912-13, have blue printing. The backs of both types are identical, displaying the Red Cross name and emblem which can be used to positively identify the set and differentiate it from the other Louisana sets of the same period. Numerous variations have been found, most of them involving caption changes.

		NM	EX	VG
Complete Set (87):		20000.	8000.	4000.
Common Player:		200.00	80.00	40.00
(1)	Red Ames	200.00	80.00	40.00
(2)	Home Run Baker	500.00	200.00	100.00
(3)	Neal Ball	200.00	80.00	40.00
(4)	Chief Bender (no trees in background)	500.00	200.00	100.00
(5)	Chief Bender (trees in background)	500.00	200.00	100.00
(6)	Al Bridwell	200.00	80.00	40.00
(7)	Bobby Byrne	200.00	80.00	40.00
(8)	Howie Camnitz	200.00	80.00	40.00
(9)	Frank Chance	500.00	200.00	100.00
(10)	Hal Chase	200.00	80.00	40.00
(11)	Ty Cobb	2750.	1100.	550.00
(12)	Eddie Collins	500.00	200.00	100.00
(13)	Wid Conroy	200.00	80.00	40.00
(14)	Doc Crandall	200.00	80.00	40.00
(15)	Sam Crawford	500.00	200.00	100.00
(16)	Birdie Cree	200.00	80.00	40.00
(17)	Harry Davis	200.00	80.00	40.00
(18)	Josh Devore	200.00	80.00	40.00
(19)	Mike Donlin	200.00	80.00	40.00
(20)	Mickey Doolan	200.00	80.00	40.00
(21)	Patsy Dougherty	200.00	80.00	40.00
(22)	Larry Doyle (batting)	200.00	80.00	40.00
(23)	Larry Doyle (portrait)	200.00	80.00	40.00
(24)	Kid Elberfeld	200.00	80.00	40.00
(25)	Russ Ford	200.00	80.00	40.00
(26)	Art Fromme	200.00	80.00	40.00
(27)	Clark Griffith	500.00	200.00	100.00
(28)	Topsy Hartsel	200.00	80.00	40.00
(29)	Dick Hoblitzell	200.00	80.00	40.00
(30)	Solly Hofman	200.00	80.00	40.00
(31)	Del Howard	200.00	80.00	40.00
(32)	Miller Huggins	500.00	200.00	100.00
(33)	John Hummel	200.00	80.00	40.00
(34)	Hughie Jennings (both hands showing)	500.00	200.00	100.00
(35)	Hughie Jennings (one hand showing)	500.00	200.00	100.00
(36)	Walter Johnson	625.00	250.00	125.00
(37)	Ed Konetchy	200.00	80.00	40.00
(38)	Harry Krause	200.00	80.00	40.00
(39)	Nap Lajoie	500.00	200.00	100.00
(40)	Arlie Latham	200.00	80.00	40.00
(41)	Tommy Leach	200.00	80.00	40.00
(42)	Lefty Leifield	200.00	80.00	40.00
(43)	Harry Lord	200.00	80.00	40.00
(44)	Sherry Magee	200.00	80.00	40.00
(45)	Rube Marquard (pitching)	500.00	200.00	100.00
(46)	Rube Marquard (portrait)	500.00	200.00	100.00
(47)	Christy Mathewson (dark cap)	625.00	250.00	125.00
(48)	Christy Mathewson (white cap)	625.00	250.00	125.00
(49)	Joe McGinnity	500.00	200.00	100.00
(50)	John McGraw (glove at hip)	500.00	200.00	100.00
(51)	John McGraw (portrait)	500.00	200.00	100.00
(52)	Harry McIntyre	200.00	80.00	40.00
(53)	Fred Merkle	200.00	80.00	40.00
(54)	Chief Meyers	200.00	80.00	40.00
(55)	Dots Miller	200.00	80.00	40.00
(56)	Mike Mowrey	200.00	80.00	40.00
(57)	Danny Murphy	200.00	80.00	40.00
(58)	Red Murray	200.00	80.00	40.00
(59)	Rebel Oakes	200.00	80.00	40.00
(60)	Charley O'Leary	200.00	80.00	40.00
(61)	Dode Paskert	200.00	80.00	40.00
(62)	Barney Pelty	200.00	80.00	40.00
(63)	Jack Quinn	200.00	80.00	40.00
(64)	Ed Reulbach	200.00	80.00	40.00
(65)	Nap Rucker	200.00	80.00	40.00
(66)	Germany Schaefer	200.00	80.00	40.00
(67)	Wildfire Schulte	200.00	80.00	40.00
(68)	Jimmy Sheckard	200.00	80.00	40.00
(69a)	Frank Smith	200.00	80.00	40.00
(69b)	Frank Smither (Smith)	200.00	80.00	40.00
(70)	Tris Speaker	500.00	200.00	100.00
(71)	Jake Stahl	200.00	80.00	40.00
(72)	Harry Steinfeldt	200.00	80.00	40.00
(73)	Gabby Street (catching)	200.00	80.00	40.00
(74)	Gabby Street (portrait)	200.00	80.00	40.00
(75)	Jeff Sweeney	200.00	80.00	40.00
(76)	Lee Tannehill	200.00	80.00	40.00
(77)	Joe Tinker (bat off shoulder)	500.00	200.00	100.00
(78)	Joe Tinker (bat on shoulder)	500.00	200.00	100.00
(79)	Heinie Wagner	200.00	80.00	40.00
(80)	Jack Warhop	200.00	80.00	40.00
(81)	Zach Wheat	500.00	200.00	100.00
(82)	Doc White	200.00	80.00	40.00
(83)	Ed Willetts (Willett)	200.00	80.00	40.00
(84)	Owen Wilson	200.00	80.00	40.00
(85)	Hooks Wiltse (pitching)	200.00	80.00	40.00
(86)	Hooks Wiltse (portrait)	200.00	80.00	40.00
(87)	Cy Young	600.00	240.00	120.00

1912-13 Red Cross Tobacco Type 2 (T215)

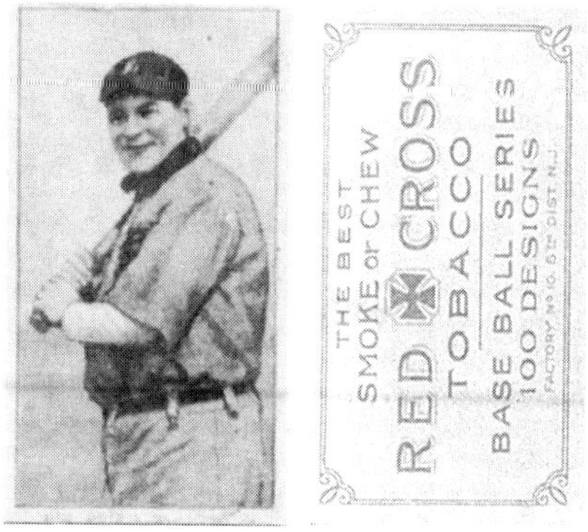

		NM	EX	VG
Complete Set (83):		17500.	7000.	3500.
Common Player:		200.00	80.00	40.00
(1)	Red Ames	200.00	80.00	40.00
(2)	Chief Bender (no trees in background)	400.00	160.00	80.00
(3)	Chief Bender (trees in background)	400.00	160.00	80.00
(4)	Roger Bresnahan	325.00	130.00	65.00
(5)	Al Bridwell	200.00	80.00	40.00
(6)	Mordecai Brown	325.00	130.00	65.00
(7)	Bobby Byrne	200.00	80.00	40.00
(8)	Howie Camnitz	200.00	80.00	40.00
(9)	Frank Chance	325.00	130.00	65.00
(10)	Hal Chase	250.00	100.00	50.00
(11)	Ty Cobb	2000.	800.00	400.00
(12)	Eddie Collins	325.00	130.00	65.00
(13)	Doc Crandall	200.00	80.00	40.00
(14)	Sam Crawford	500.00	200.00	100.00
(15)	Birdie Cree	200.00	80.00	40.00
(16)	Harry Davis	200.00	80.00	40.00
(17)	Josh Devore	200.00	80.00	40.00
(18)	Mike Donlin	200.00	80.00	40.00
(19)	Mickey Doolan (batting)	200.00	80.00	40.00
(20)	Mickey Doolan (fielding)	200.00	80.00	40.00
(21)	Patsy Dougherty	200.00	80.00	40.00
(22)	Larry Doyle (batting)	200.00	80.00	40.00
(23)	Larry Doyle (portrait)	200.00	80.00	40.00
(24)	Jean Dubuc	200.00	80.00	40.00
(25)	Kid Elberfeld	200.00	80.00	40.00
(26)	Johnny Evers	325.00	130.00	65.00
(27)	Russ Ford	200.00	80.00	40.00
(28)	Art Fromme	200.00	80.00	40.00
(29)	Clark Griffith	325.00	130.00	65.00
(30)	Bob Groom	200.00	80.00	40.00
(31)	Topsy Hartsel	200.00	80.00	40.00
(32)	Duck Herzog	200.00	80.00	40.00
(33)	Dick Hoblitzell	200.00	80.00	40.00
(34)	Solly Hofman	200.00	80.00	40.00
(35)	Miller Huggins (hands at mouth)	325.00	130.00	65.00
(36)	Miller Huggins (portrait)	325.00	130.00	65.00
(37)	John Hummel	200.00	80.00	40.00
(38)	Hughie Jennings	325.00	130.00	65.00
(39)	Walter Johnson	800.00	320.00	160.00
(40)	Joe Kelley	325.00	130.00	65.00
(41)	Ed Konetchy	200.00	80.00	40.00
(42)	Harry Krause	200.00	80.00	40.00
(43)	Nap Lajoie	325.00	130.00	65.00
(44)	Joe Lake	200.00	80.00	40.00
(45)	Tommy Leach	200.00	80.00	40.00
(46)	Lefty Leifield	200.00	80.00	40.00
(47)	Harry Lord	200.00	80.00	40.00
(48)	Sherry Magee	200.00	80.00	40.00
(49)	Rube Marquard	325.00	130.00	65.00
(50)	Christy Mathewson	800.00	320.00	160.00
(51)	John McGraw (glove at side)	350.00	140.00	70.00
(52)	John McGraw (portrait)	350.00	140.00	70.00
(53)	Larry McLean	200.00	80.00	40.00
(54)	Fred Merkle	200.00	80.00	40.00
(55)	Dots Miller	200.00	80.00	40.00
(56)	Mike Mitchell	200.00	80.00	40.00
(57)	Mike Mowrey	200.00	80.00	40.00
(58)	George Mullin	200.00	80.00	40.00
(59)	Danny Murphy	200.00	80.00	40.00
(60)	Red Murray	200.00	80.00	40.00
(61)	Rebel Oakes	200.00	80.00	40.00
(62)	Rube Oldring	200.00	80.00	40.00
(63)	Charley O'Leary	200.00	80.00	40.00
(64)	Dode Paskert	200.00	80.00	40.00
(65)	Barney Pelty	200.00	80.00	40.00
(66)	Billy Purtell	200.00	80.00	40.00
(67)	Ed Reulbach	200.00	80.00	40.00
(68)	Nap Rucker	200.00	80.00	40.00
(69a)	Germany Schaefer (Chicago)	200.00	80.00	40.00
(69b)	Germany Schaefer (Washington)	200.00	80.00	40.00
(70)	Wildfire Schulte	200.00	80.00	40.00
(71a)	Frank Smith	200.00	80.00	40.00
(71b)	Frank Smither (Smith)	200.00	80.00	40.00
(72)	Tris Speaker	500.00	200.00	100.00
(73)	Jake Stahl	200.00	80.00	40.00
(74)	Harry Steinfeldt	200.00	80.00	40.00
(75)	Ed Summers	200.00	80.00	40.00
(76)	Jeff Sweeney	200.00	80.00	40.00
(77)	Joe Tinker	325.00	130.00	65.00
(78)	Ira Thomas	200.00	80.00	40.00
(79)	Heinie Wagner	200.00	80.00	40.00
(80)	Jack Warhop	200.00	80.00	40.00
(81)	Doc White	200.00	80.00	40.00
(82)	Hooks Wiltse (pitching)	200.00	80.00	40.00
(83)	Hooks Wiltse (portrait)	200.00	80.00	40.00

1912 Red Cross Tobacco

(See T207. Premium. 5-7X.)

1954 Red Heart Dog Food

This set of 33 cards was issued in three color-coded series by the Red Heart Dog Food Co. Card fronts feature hand-colored photos on either a blue, green or red background. The 11 red-background cards are scarcer than the 11-card blue or green series. Backs of the 2-5/8" x 3-3/4" cards contain biographical and statistical information along with a Red Heart ad. Each 11-card series was available via a mail-in offer. As late as the early 1970s, the company was still sending cards to collectors who requested them.

		NM	EX	VG
Complete Set (33):		2200.	880.00	440.00
Common Player:		30.00	12.00	6.00
(1)	Richie Ashburn	55.00	22.00	11.00
(2)	Frankie Baumholtz	35.00	14.00	7.00
(3)	Gus Bell	40.00	16.00	8.00
(4)	Billy Cox	35.00	14.00	7.00
(5)	Alvin Dark	30.00	12.00	6.00
(6)	Carl Erskine	42.00	17.00	8.50
(7)	Ferris Fain	30.00	12.00	6.00
(8)	Dee Fondy	30.00	12.00	6.00
(9)	Nelson Fox	55.00	22.00	11.00
(10)	Jim Gilliam	40.00	16.00	8.00
(11)	Jim Hegan	35.00	14.00	7.00
(12)	George Kell	50.00	20.00	10.00
(13)	Ted Kluszewski	50.00	20.00	10.00
(14)	Ralph Kiner	55.00	22.00	11.00
(15)	Harvey Kuenn	35.00	14.00	7.00
(16)	Bob Lemon	50.00	20.00	10.00
(17)	Sherman Lollar	30.00	12.00	6.00
(18)	Mickey Mantle	600.00	240.00	120.00
(19)	Billy Martin	45.00	18.00	9.00
(20)	Gil McDougald	40.00	16.00	8.00
(21)	Roy McMillan	30.00	12.00	6.00
(22)	Minnie Minoso	37.50	15.00	7.50
(23)	Stan Musial	350.00	140.00	70.00
(24)	Billy Pierce	35.00	14.00	7.00
(25)	Al Rosen	40.00	16.00	8.00
(26)	Hank Sauer	30.00	12.00	6.00
(27)	Red Schoendienst	50.00	20.00	10.00
(28)	Enos Slaughter	50.00	20.00	10.00
(29)	Duke Snider	165.00	66.00	33.00
(30)	Warren Spahn	55.00	22.00	11.00

(31)	Sammy White	30.00	12.00	6.00
(32)	Eddie Yost	30.00	12.00	6.00
(33)	Gus Zernial	30.00	12.00	6.00

1952 Red Man Tobacco

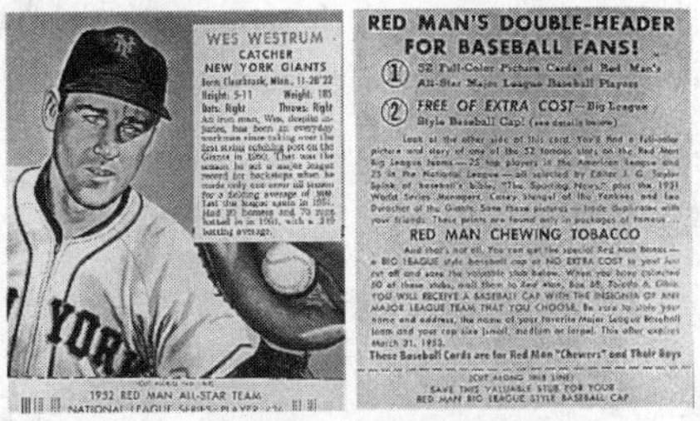

This was the first national set of tobacco cards produced since the golden days of tobacco sets in the early part of the century. There are 52 cards in the set, with 25 top players and one manager from each league. Player selection was made by editor J.G. Taylor Spink of The Sporting News. Cards measure 3-1/2" x 4", including a 1/2" tab at the bottom of each card. These tabs were redeemable for a free baseball cap from Red Man. Cards are harder to find with tabs intact, and thus more valuable in that form. Values quoted here are for cards with tabs. Cards with the tabs removed would be valued about 35-40 percent of the quoted figures. Card fronts are full color paintings of each player with biographical information inset in the portrait area. Card backs contain company advertising. Cards are numbered and dated only on the tabs. The 1952 Red Man cards can be found with either of two expiration dates on back, March 31 or June 1, 1953; neither commands a premium.

		NM	EX	VG
Complete Set (52):		2250.	1125.	675.00
Common Player:		20.00	10.00	6.00
1A	Casey Stengel	55.00	27.00	16.50
1N	Leo Durocher	50.00	25.00	15.00
2A	Roberto Avila	25.00	12.50	7.50
2N	Richie Ashburn	60.00	30.00	18.00
3A	Larry "Yogi" Berra	100.00	50.00	30.00
3N	Ewell Blackwell	30.00	15.00	9.00
4A	Gil Coan	20.00	10.00	6.00
4N	Cliff Chambers	20.00	10.00	6.00
5A	Dom DiMaggio	45.00	22.00	13.50
5N	Murry Dickson	20.00	10.00	6.00
6A	Larry Doby	55.00	27.00	16.50
6N	Sid Gordon	20.00	10.00	6.00
7A	Ferris Fain	25.00	12.50	7.50
7N	Granny Hamner	20.00	10.00	6.00
8A	Bob Feller	75.00	37.00	22.00
8N	Jim Hearn	20.00	10.00	6.00
9A	Nelson Fox	60.00	30.00	18.00
9N	Monte Irvin	55.00	27.00	16.50
10A	Johnny Groth	20.00	10.00	6.00
10N	Larry Jansen	20.00	10.00	6.00
11A	Jim Hegan	20.00	10.00	6.00
11N	Willie Jones	20.00	10.00	6.00
12A	Eddie Joost	20.00	10.00	6.00
12N	Ralph Kiner	55.00	27.00	16.50
13A	George Kell	55.00	27.00	16.50
13N	Whitey Lockman	20.00	10.00	6.00
14A	Gil McDougald	35.00	17.50	10.50
14N	Sal Maglie	25.00	12.50	7.50
15A	Orestes Minoso	30.00	15.00	9.00
15N	Willie Mays	195.00	97.00	58.00
16A	Bill Pierce	25.00	12.50	7.50
16N	Stan Musial	175.00	87.00	52.00
17A	Bob Porterfield	20.00	10.00	6.00
17N	Pee Wee Reese	75.00	37.00	22.00
18A	Eddie Robinson	20.00	10.00	6.00
18N	Robin Roberts	55.00	27.00	16.50
19A	Saul Rogovin	20.00	10.00	6.00
19N	Al Schoendienst	55.00	27.00	16.50
20A	Bobby Shantz	25.00	12.50	7.50
20N	Enos Slaughter	55.00	27.00	16.50
21A	Vern Stephens	20.00	10.00	6.00
21N	Duke Snider	120.00	60.00	36.00
22A	Vic Wertz	20.00	10.00	6.00
22N	Warren Spahn	55.00	27.00	16.50
23A	Ted Williams	195.00	97.00	58.00
23N	Eddie Stanky	20.00	10.00	6.00
24A	Early Wynn	55.00	27.00	16.50
24N	Bobby Thomson	35.00	17.50	10.50
25A	Eddie Yost	20.00	10.00	6.00
25N	Earl Torgeson	20.00	10.00	6.00
26A	Gus Zernial	20.00	10.00	6.00
26N	Wes Westrum	20.00	10.00	6.00

1953 Red Man Tobacco

This was the chewing tobacco company's second annual set of 3-1/2" x 4" cards, including the tabs at the bottom of the cards. Formats for front and back are similar to the '52 edition. The 1953 Red Man cards, however, include card numbers within the player biographical section, and the card backs are headlined "New for '53." Once again, cards with intact tabs (which were redeemable for a free cap) are more valuable. Prices below are for cards with tabs. Cards with tabs removed are worth about 35-40 percent of the stated values. Each league is represented by 25 players and a manager on the full-color cards, a total of 52. Values quoted here are for cards with tabs. Cards with the tabs removed would be valued about 35-40 percent of the quoted figures. The 1953 Red Man cards can be found with either of two expiration dates on back, March 31 or May 31, 1954; neither commands a premium.

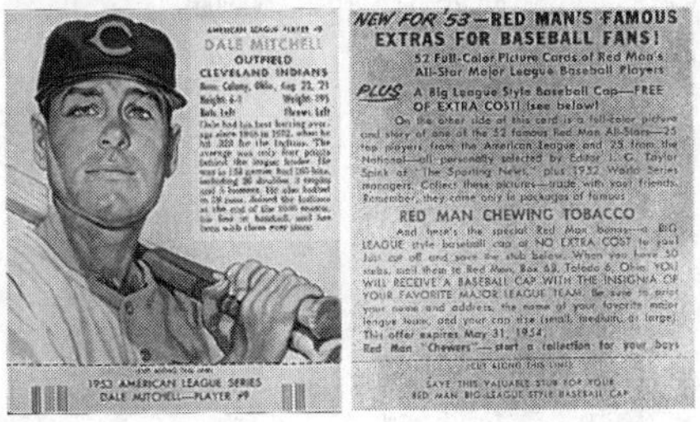

		NM	EX	VG
Complete Set (52):		1800.	900.00	550.00
Common Player:		20.00	10.00	6.00
1A	Casey Stengel	50.00	25.00	15.00
1N	Charlie Dressen	20.00	10.00	6.00
2A	Hank Bauer	25.00	12.50	7.50
2N	Bobby Adams	20.00	10.00	6.00
3A	Larry "Yogi" Berra	80.00	40.00	24.00
3N	Richie Ashburn	50.00	25.00	15.00
4A	Walt Dropo	20.00	10.00	6.00
4N	Joe Black	25.00	12.50	7.50
5A	Nelson Fox	55.00	27.00	16.50
5N	Roy Campanella	80.00	40.00	24.00
6A	Jackie Jensen	24.00	12.00	7.25
6N	Ted Kluszewski	30.00	15.00	9.00
7A	Eddie Joost	20.00	10.00	6.00
7N	Whitey Lockman	20.00	10.00	6.00
8A	George Kell	50.00	25.00	15.00
8N	Sal Maglie	20.00	10.00	6.00
9A	Dale Mitchell	20.00	10.00	6.00
9N	Andy Pafko	20.00	10.00	6.00
10A	Phil Rizzuto	55.00	27.00	16.50
10N	Pee Wee Reese	55.00	27.00	16.50
11A	Eddie Robinson	20.00	10.00	6.00
11N	Robin Roberts	50.00	25.00	15.00
12A	Gene Woodling	24.00	12.00	7.25
12N	Red Schoendienst	50.00	25.00	15.00
13A	Gus Zernial	20.00	10.00	6.00
13N	Enos Slaughter	50.00	25.00	15.00
14A	Early Wynn	50.00	25.00	15.00
14N	Edwin "Duke" Snider	100.00	50.00	30.00
15A	Joe Dobson	20.00	10.00	6.00
15N	Ralph Kiner	50.00	25.00	15.00
16A	Billy Pierce	24.00	12.00	7.25
16N	Hank Sauer	20.00	10.00	6.00
17A	Bob Lemon	50.00	25.00	15.00
17N	Del Ennis	20.00	10.00	6.00
18A	Johnny Mize	55.00	27.00	16.50
18N	Granny Hamner	20.00	10.00	6.00
19A	Bob Porterfield	20.00	10.00	6.00
19N	Warren Spahn	50.00	25.00	15.00
20A	Bobby Shantz	24.00	12.00	7.25
20N	Wes Westrum	20.00	10.00	6.00
21A	"Mickey" Vernon	20.00	10.00	6.00
21N	Hoyt Wilhelm	40.00	20.00	12.00
22A	Dom DiMaggio	35.00	17.50	10.50
22N	Murry Dickson	20.00	10.00	6.00
23A	Gil McDougald	30.00	15.00	9.00
23N	Warren Hacker	20.00	10.00	6.00
24A	Al Rosen	24.00	12.00	7.25
24N	Gerry Staley	20.00	10.00	6.00
25A	Mel Parnell	20.00	10.00	6.00
25N	Bobby Thomson	24.00	12.00	7.25
26A	Roberto Avila	20.00	10.00	6.00
26N	Stan Musial	160.00	80.00	48.00

1954 Red Man Tobacco

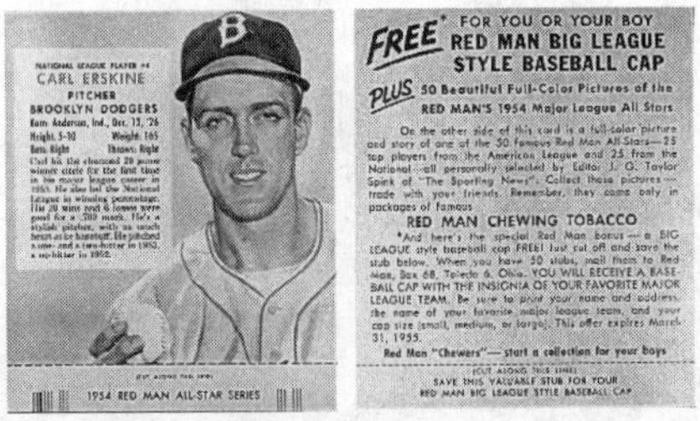

In 1954, the Red Man set eliminated managers from the set, and issued only 25 player cards for each league. There are, however, four variations which bring the total set size to 54 full-color cards. Two cards exist for Gus Bell and Enos Slaughter, while American Leaguers George Kell, Sam Mele and Dave Philley are each shown with two different teams. Complete set prices quoted below do not include the scarcer of the variation pairs. Cards measure 3-1/2" x 4" with tabs intact. Cards without tabs are worth about 35-40 per cent of the values quoted below. Formats for the cards remain virtually unchanged, with card numbers included within the player information boxes as well as on the tabs. Cards can be found with either of two expiration dates on back, March 31 or May 31, 1955; neither commands a premium.

		NM	EX	VG
Complete Set (50):		2000.	1000.	600.00
Common Player:		18.00	9.00	5.50
1A	Bobby Avila	18.00	9.00	5.50
1N	Richie Ashburn	50.00	25.00	15.00
2A	Jim Busby	18.00	9.00	5.50
2N	Billy Cox	22.00	11.00	6.50
3A	Nelson Fox	50.00	25.00	15.00
3N	Del Crandall	18.00	9.00	5.50
4Aa	George Kell (Boston)	75.00	37.00	22.00
4Ab	George Kell (Chicago)	90.00	45.00	27.00
4N	Carl Erskine	30.00	15.00	9.00
5A	Sherman Lollar	18.00	9.00	5.50
5N	Monte Irvin	50.00	25.00	15.00
6Aa	Sam Mele (Baltimore)	60.00	30.00	18.00
6Ab	Sam Mele (Chicago)	90.00	45.00	27.00
6N	Ted Kluszewski	40.00	20.00	12.00
7A	Orestes Minoso	30.00	15.00	9.00
7N	Don Mueller	18.00	9.00	5.50
8A	Mel Parnell	18.00	9.00	5.50
8N	Andy Pafko	18.00	9.00	5.50
9Aa	Dave Philley (Cleveland)	60.00	30.00	18.00
9Ab	Dave Philley (Philadelphia)	90.00	45.00	27.00
9N	Del Rice	18.00	9.00	5.50
10A	Billy Pierce	22.00	11.00	6.50
10N	Al Schoendienst	50.00	25.00	15.00
11A	Jim Piersall	27.50	13.50	8.25
11N	Warren Spahn	50.00	25.00	15.00
12A	Al Rosen	22.00	11.00	6.50
12N	Curt Simmons	18.00	9.00	5.50
13A	"Mickey" Vernon	18.00	9.00	5.50
13N	Roy Campanella	90.00	45.00	27.00
14A	Sammy White	18.00	9.00	5.50
14N	Jim Gilliam	27.50	13.50	8.25
15A	Gene Woodling	24.00	12.00	7.25
15N	"Pee Wee" Reese	75.00	37.00	22.00
16A	Ed "Whitey" Ford	80.00	40.00	24.00
16N	Edwin "Duke" Snider	100.00	50.00	30.00
17A	Phil Rizzuto	75.00	37.00	22.00
17N	Rip Repulski	18.00	9.00	5.50
18A	Bob Porterfield	18.00	9.00	5.50
18N	Robin Roberts	50.00	25.00	15.00
19A	Al "Chico" Carrasquel	18.00	9.00	5.50
19Na	Enos Slaughter	110.00	55.00	33.00
19Nb	Gus Bell	95.00	47.00	28.00
20A	Larry "Yogi" Berra	90.00	45.00	27.00
20N	Johnny Logan	18.00	9.00	5.50
21A	Bob Lemon	50.00	25.00	15.00
21N	Johnny Antonelli	18.00	9.00	5.50
22A	Ferris Fain	18.00	9.00	5.50
22N	Gil Hodges	50.00	25.00	15.00
23A	Hank Bauer	24.00	12.00	7.25
23N	Eddie Mathews	50.00	25.00	15.00
24A	Jim Delsing	18.00	9.00	5.50
24N	Lew Burdette	18.00	9.00	5.50
25A	Gil McDougald	35.00	17.50	10.50
25N	Willie Mays	160.00	80.00	48.00

1955 Red Man Tobacco

These 50 cards are quite similar to the 1954 edition, with card fronts virtually unchanged except for the data in the biographical box on the color picture area. This set of the 3-1/2" x 4" cards includes 25 players from each league, with no known variations. As with all Red Man sets, those cards complete with the redeemable tabs are more valuable. Values quoted below are for cards with tabs. Cards with the tabs removed are worth about 35-40 percent of those figures. Each card can be found with two different expiration dates on back, April 15 or June 15, 1956; neither version commands a premium.

		NM	EX	VG
Complete Set (50):		1600.	800.00	475.00
Common Player:		20.00	10.00	6.00
1A	Ray Boone	20.00	10.00	6.00
1N	Richie Ashburn	50.00	25.00	15.00
2A	Jim Busby	20.00	10.00	6.00
2N	Del Crandall	20.00	10.00	6.00
3A	Ed "Whitey" Ford	65.00	32.00	19.50
3N	Gil Hodges	50.00	25.00	15.00
4A	Nelson Fox	50.00	25.00	15.00
4N	Brooks Lawrence	20.00	10.00	6.00
5A	Bob Grim	20.00	10.00	6.00
5N	Johnny Logan	20.00	10.00	6.00
6A	Jack Harshman	20.00	10.00	6.00
6N	Sal Maglie	20.00	10.00	6.00
7A	Jim Hegan	20.00	10.00	6.00
7N	Willie Mays	145.00	72.00	43.00
8A	Bob Lemon	45.00	22.00	13.50
8N	Don Mueller	20.00	10.00	6.00
9A	Irv Noren	20.00	10.00	6.00
9N	Bill Sarni	20.00	10.00	6.00
10A	Bob Porterfield	20.00	10.00	6.00
10N	Warren Spahn	50.00	25.00	15.00
11A	Al Rosen	22.00	11.00	6.50
11N	Henry Thompson	20.00	10.00	6.00
12A	"Mickey" Vernon	20.00	10.00	6.00
12N	Hoyt Wilhelm	45.00	22.00	13.50
13A	Vic Wertz	20.00	10.00	6.00
13N	Johnny Antonelli	20.00	10.00	6.00
14A	Early Wynn	45.00	22.00	13.50
14N	Carl Erskine	30.00	15.00	9.00
15A	Bobby Avila	20.00	10.00	6.00
15N	Granny Hamner	20.00	10.00	6.00
16A	Larry "Yogi" Berra	80.00	40.00	24.00
16N	Ted Kluszewski	40.00	20.00	12.00
17A	Joe Coleman	20.00	10.00	6.00
17N	Pee Wee Reese	60.00	30.00	18.00
18A	Larry Doby	45.00	22.00	13.50
18N	Al Schoendienst	45.00	22.00	13.50
19A	Jackie Jensen	22.00	11.00	6.50
19N	Duke Snider	90.00	45.00	27.00
20A	Pete Runnels	20.00	10.00	6.00
20N	Frank Thomas	20.00	10.00	6.00
21A	Jim Piersall	22.00	11.00	6.50
21N	Ray Jablonski	20.00	10.00	6.00
22A	Hank Bauer	22.00	11.00	6.50
22N	James "Dusty" Rhodes	20.00	10.00	6.00
23A	"Chico" Carrasquel	20.00	10.00	6.00
23N	Gus Bell	20.00	10.00	6.00
24A	Orestes Minoso	32.00	16.00	9.50
24N	Curt Simmons	20.00	10.00	6.00
25A	Sandy Consuegra	20.00	10.00	6.00
25N	Marvin Grissom	20.00	10.00	6.00

1976 Redpath Sugar Expos

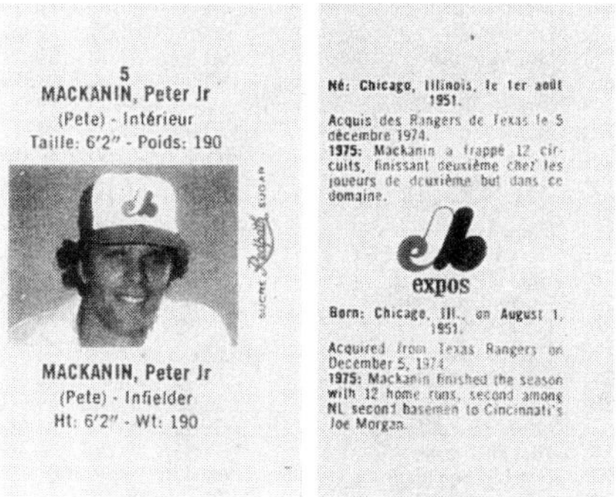

Among the more unusual baseball collectibles of the late 1970s are the Montreal Expos sugar packs produced by Redpath Sugar for distribution in Quebec. About 1-1/2" x 2-3/4" in size, the sugar packs feature color portraits of the players on front, along with bi-lingual personal information and a uniform number. Backs have a color team logo and career highlights. Uncut sheets or the packaging are known which indicate several players were double- or triple-printed. The checklist here is arranged by uniform number.

		NM	EX	VG
Complete Set (36):		75.00	37.00	22.00
Common Player:		2.00	1.00	.60
1	Osvaldo Jose Virgil	2.00	1.00	.60
5	Peter Mackanin, Jr.	2.00	1.00	.60
6	Karl Otto Kuehl	2.00	1.00	.60
8	Gary Edmund Carter	12.00	6.00	3.50
9	Barry Clifton Foote	2.00	1.00	.60
11	Jose Manuel Mangual	2.00	1.00	.60
14	Lawrence Eugene Doby	6.00	3.00	1.75
15	Larry Alton Parrish	2.00	1.00	.60
16	Michael Jorgensen	2.00	1.00	.60
17	Andre Thornton	4.00	2.00	1.25
18	Joseph Thomas Kerrigan	2.00	1.00	.60
19	Timothy John Foli (DP)	2.00	1.00	.60
20	James Lawrence Lyttle, Jr.	2.00	1.00	.60
21	Frederick John Scherman, Jr.	2.00	1.00	.60
22	Ellis Clarence Valentine	2.00	1.00	.60
26	Donald Joseph Stanhouse	2.00	1.00	.60
27	Dale Albert Murray	2.00	1.00	.60
31	Clayton Laws Kirby, Jr.	2.00	1.00	.60
33	Robert David Lang	2.00	1.00	.60
34	Jose Manuel Morales	2.00	1.00	.60
35	Woodrow Thompson Fryman	3.00	1.50	.90
36	Steven John Dunning	2.00	1.00	.60
37	Jerome Cardell White	2.00	1.00	.60
38	Jesus Maria Frias (Andujar)	2.00	1.00	.60
39	Daniel Dean Warthen	2.00	1.00	.60
40	Donald George Carrithers (3P)	2.00	1.00	.60
41	Ronald Jacques Piche	2.00	1.00	.60
43	James Edward Dwyer	2.00	1.00	.60
44	Jesus Rivera (Torres), Jr.	2.00	1.00	.60
45	Stephen Douglas Rogers (DP)	2.00	1.00	.60
46	Marion Danne Adair	2.00	1.00	.60
47	Wayne Allen Granger	2.00	1.00	.60
48	Lawrence Donald Bearnarth	2.00	1.00	.60
---	Roland Wayne Garrett	2.00	1.00	.60
---	Charles Gilbert Taylor	2.00	1.00	.60
---	Delbert Bernard Unser	2.00	1.00	.60

1977 Redpath Sugar Expos

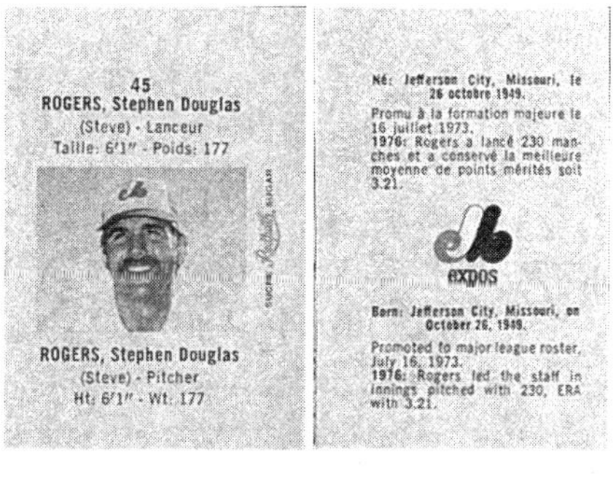

One of the more obscure regional Canadian issues, this 30-player set features members of the Expos and was printed on sugar packets distributed in the Montreal area in 1977. The front of the packet features a color photo of the player with his name, uniform number, position, height and weight listed in both English and French. A line identifying Redpath Sugar appears alongside the photo. The backs display the Expos logo and brief player highlights (again printed in both French and English). The set has been seen in uncut sheets, revealing that the packets of Steve Rogers and David Cash, Jr. were double printed.

		NM	EX	VG
Complete Set (30):		75.00	37.00	22.00
Common Player:		1.50	.70	.45
1	Osvaldo Jose Virgil	1.50	.70	.45
2	James Thomas Brewer	1.50	.70	.45
3	James Barton Vernon	1.50	.70	.45
4	Chris Edward Speier	1.50	.70	.45
5	Peter Mackanin Jr.	1.50	.70	.45
6	William Frederick Gardner	1.50	.70	.45
8	Gary Edmund Carter	12.00	6.00	3.50
9	Barry Clifton Foote	1.50	.70	.45
10	Andre Dawson	15.00	7.50	4.50
11	Ronald Wayne Garrett	1.50	.70	.45
14	Samuel Elias Mejias	1.50	.70	.45
15	Larry Alton Parrish	2.00	1.00	.60
16	Michael Jorgensen	1.50	.70	.45
17	Ellis Clarence Valentine	1.50	.70	.45
18	Joseph Thomas Kerrigan	1.50	.70	.45
20	William Henry McEnaney	1.50	.70	.45
23	Richard Hirshfield Williams	2.00	1.00	.60
24	Atanasio Rigal Perez	3.00	1.50	.90
25	Delbert Bernard Unser	1.50	.70	.45
26	Donald Joseph Stanhouse	1.50	.70	.45
30	David Cash, Jr.	1.50	.70	.45
31	Jackie Gene Brown	1.50	.70	.45
34	Jose Manual Morales	1.50	.70	.45
35	Gerald Ellis Hannahs	1.50	.70	.45
38	Jesus Maria Frias (Andujar)	1.50	.70	.45
39	Daniel Dean Warthen	1.50	.70	.45
42	William Cecil Glenn Atkinson	1.50	.70	.45
45	Stephen Douglas Rogers	2.25	1.25	.70
48	Jeffrey Michael Terpko	1.50	.70	.45
49	Warren Livingston Cromartie	1.50	.70	.45

1869 Red Stocking B.B.C. of Cincinnati

(See 1869 Peck & Snyder)

1886 Red Stocking Cigars

This set of Boston Red Stockings schedule cards was issued in 1886, and the three known cards measure 6-1/2" x 3-3/4". The cards were printed in black and red. One side carries the 1886 Boston schedule, while the other side features a full-length player drawing. Both sides include advertising for "Red Stocking" cigars. Only three different players are known.

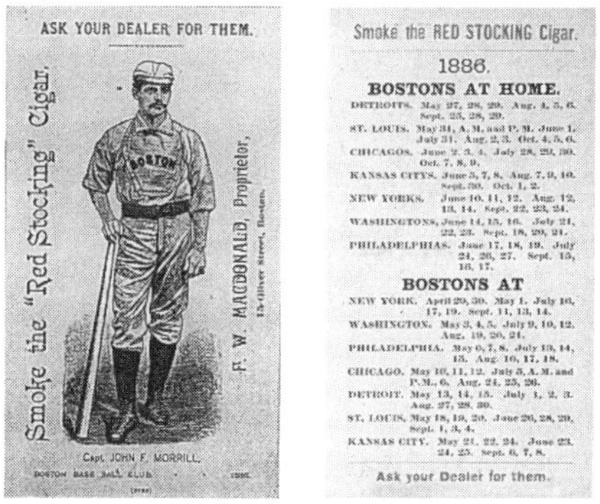

		NM	EX	VG
Complete Set (3):		13000.	5200.	2600.
Common Player:		4000.	1600.	800.00
(1)	C.G. Buffington	4000.	1600.	800.00
(2)	Capt. John F. Morrill	4000.	1600.	800.00
(3)	Charles Radbourn	5350.	2140.	1070.

1972 Regent Glove Hang Tag

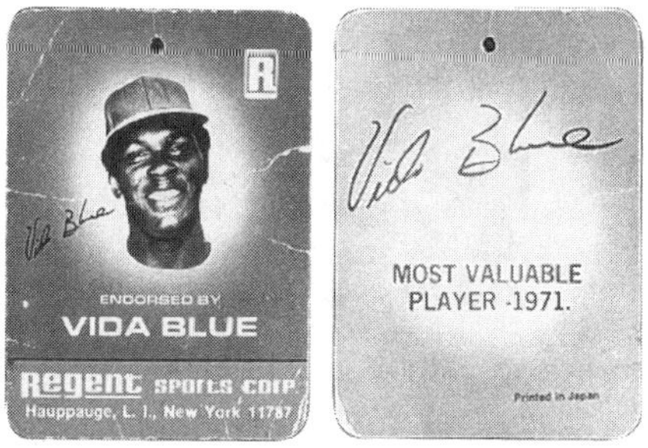

This 2-1/4" x 3" card was distributed as an attachment to baseball gloves sold at retail outlets. A hole punched at top allowed the card to be strung to the glove. Front has a blue background and black-and-white portrait photo of 1971 MVP Vida Blue. His facsimile autograph is on back.

	NM	EX	VG
Vida Blue	15.00	7.50	4.50

1964-68 Requena N.Y. Yankees Postcards

Over a period of several years in the 1960s a series of Yankee color player postcards was issued with the identifier "Photo by Requena". Similar in format, the 3-1/2" x 5-1/2" cards have borderless color photos on front. Except for facsimile autographs on some players' cards, there are no other front graphics. Backs are printed in dark green with player ID at upper-left, a "K"-within-diamond Kodachrome logo at bottom-left, a card number centered at bottom, the Requena line vertically at center and standard postcard markings at right.

	NM	EX	VG
Complete Set (17):	275.00	130.00	80.00
Common Player:	18.00	9.00	5.50
66443 Phil Linz	18.00	9.00	5.50
66880 Clete Boyer	18.00	9.00	5.50
66881 Jim Bouton	27.00	13.50	8.00
66882 Tom Tresh	22.00	11.00	6.50
66883 Joe Pepitone	27.00	13.50	8.00
66884 Tony Kubek	27.00	13.50	8.00
66885 Elston Howard	27.00	13.50	8.00
66886 Ralph Terry	18.00	9.00	5.50
66887 Bill Stafford	18.00	9.00	5.50
66888 Whitey Ford	36.00	18.00	11.00
66889 Bob Richardson	27.00	13.50	8.00
69891 Yogi Berra (signature at top)	36.00	18.00	11.00
69891 Yogi Berra (signature at bottom)	36.00	18.00	11.00
74284 John Blanchard	18.00	9.00	5.50
78909 Pedro Ramos	18.00	9.00	5.50
78910 Mel Stottlemyre	22.00	11.00	6.50
98553 Fritz Peterson	18.00	9.00	5.50
101461 Steve Barber	18.00	9.00	5.50

1964-66 Requena N.Y. Yankees 8x10s

Many of the same Yankees players and poses which appear in the standard (3-1/2" x 5-1/2") Requena postcard series can also be found, along with additional subjects, in an 8" x 10" blank-back format. The large format cards are listed here in alphabetical order.

		NM	EX	VG
Complete Set (18):		100.00	50.00	30.00
Common Player:		3.75	2.00	1.25
(1)	Yogi Berra	7.50	3.75	2.25
(2)	John Blanchard	3.75	2.00	1.25
(3)	Jim Bouton	4.50	2.25	1.25
(4)	Clete Boyer	3.75	2.00	1.25
(5)	Al Downing	3.75	2.00	1.25
(6)	Whitey Ford	7.50	3.75	2.25
(7)	Ralph Houk	3.75	2.00	1.25
(8)	Elston Howard	4.50	2.25	1.25
(9)	Tony Kubek	4.50	2.25	1.25
(10)	Phil Linz	3.75	2.00	1.25
(11)	Mickey Mantle	17.50	8.75	5.25
(12)	Mickey Mantle, Roger Maris	12.50	6.25	3.75
(13a)	Roger Maris (facsimile autograph)	10.00	5.00	3.00
(13b)	Roger Maris (no facsimile autograph)	10.00	5.00	3.00
(14)	Joe Pepitone	3.75	2.00	1.25
(15)	Pedro Ramos	3.75	2.00	1.25
(16)	Bobby Richardson	4.50	2.25	1.25
(17)	Bill Stafford	3.75	2.00	1.25
(18)	Mel Stottlemyre	3.75	2.00	1.25
(19)	Ralph Terry	3.75	2.00	1.25
(20)	Tom Tresh	3.75	2.00	1.25

1953 R.G. Dun Cigars Milwaukee Braves

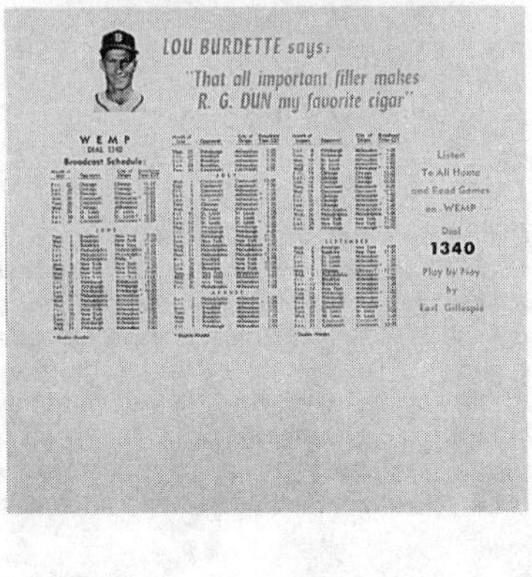

This series of counter cards was issued by a cigar company and features the radio schedule for the 1953 Braves. The cards are printed in red and black on cream cardboard and measure 10" x 9-1/2". They are unnumbered and blank-backed. The cards have vertical slits from bottom to about 1/3 the height of the cards, probably so they could be inserted into some type of counter display for Dun cigars. It's unknown how many players were represented in the series.

		NM	EX	VG
Common Player:		35.00	17.50	10.00
(1)	Lew Burdette	35.00	17.50	10.00
(2)	Jim Wilson	35.00	17.50	10.00

1920 Tex Rickard's Babe Ruth 'Headin Home'

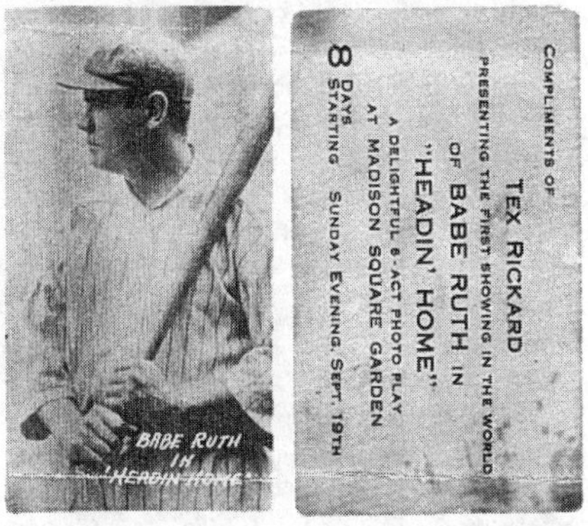

Taking advantage of the Babe's enormous popularity in the pinstripes of his new team, he was given a starring role in a 1920 silent movie titled "Headin Home." To promote the flick, a small set of cards was issued. The 1-7/8" x 3-1/4" black-and-white cards have posed photos of Ruth on front. Dropped out in white in the lower portion of the photo is his name and movie title. Backs have an ad for the movie (some cards are known with blank backs, as well). This checklist may be incomplete.

		NM	EX	VG
Common Card:		5000.	2000.	1000.
(1)	Babe Ruth (Bat on shoulder, crotch to cap)	5000.	2000.	1000.
(2)	Babe Ruth (Bat on shoulder, full-length)	5000.	2000.	1000.
(3)	Babe Ruth (Batting follow-through)	5000.	2000.	1000.

1935 Rice-Stix

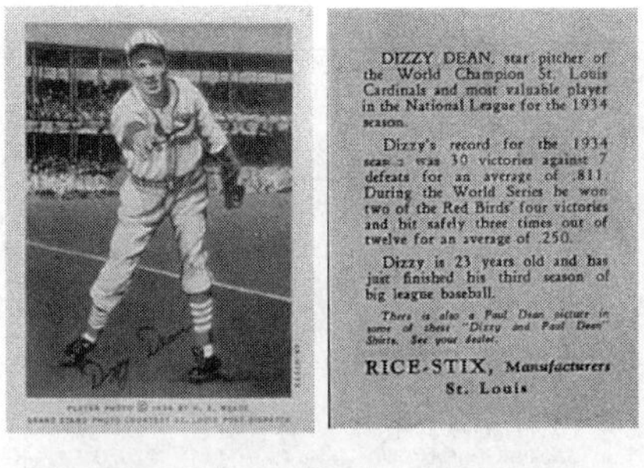

This two-card set was distributed in packages of shirts from a St. Louis firm. Measuring about 2-1/4" x 3", the cards feature color painting of the pitchers on front, along with a facsimile autograph and photo credits. Backs have a short career summary and an ad for the issuer.

		NM	EX	VG
Complete Set (2):		1600.	650.00	400.00
(1)	Dizzy Dean	1000.	400.00	250.00
(2)	Paul Dean	600.00	240.00	150.00

1933 Rittenhouse Candy (E285)

Designed to resemble a set of playing cards, this set, issued circa 1933 by the Rittenhouse Candy Company of Philadelphia, carries the ACC designation E285 and is generally considered to be the last of the E-card issues. Each card measures 1-7/16" x 2-1/4" and features a small black-and-white player photo in the center of the playing card design. The backs of the cards usually consist of just one large letter and were part of a promotion in which collectors were instructed to find enough different letters to spell "Rittenhouse Candy Co." Other backs explaining the contest and the prizes available have also been found, as have backs with numbers. Because it was designed as a deck of playing cards, the set is complete at 52 cards, featuring 46 different players (six are pictured on two cards each). Cards have been found in red, orange, green and blue.

		NM	EX	VG
Complete Set (52):		5850.	2350.	1175.
Common Player:		65.00	26.00	13.00
(1)	Dick Bartell	65.00	26.00	13.00
(2)	Walter Berger	65.00	26.00	13.00
(3)	Max Bishop	65.00	26.00	13.00
(4)	James Bottomley	130.00	52.00	26.00
(5)	Fred Brickell	65.00	26.00	13.00
(6)	Sugar Cain	65.00	26.00	13.00
(7)	Ed. Cihocki	65.00	26.00	13.00
(8)	Phil Collins	65.00	26.00	13.00
(9)	Roger Cramer	65.00	26.00	13.00
(10)	Hughie Critz	65.00	26.00	13.00
(11)	Joe Cronin	130.00	52.00	26.00
(12)	Hazen (Kiki) Cuyler	130.00	52.00	26.00
(13)	Geo. Davis	65.00	26.00	13.00
(14)	Spud Davis	65.00	26.00	13.00
(15)	Jimmy Dykes	65.00	26.00	13.00
(16)	George Earnshaw	65.00	26.00	13.00
(17)	Jumbo Elliot	65.00	26.00	13.00
(18)	Lou Finney	65.00	26.00	13.00
(19)	Jimmy Foxx	195.00	78.00	39.00
(20)	Frankie Frisch (3 of Spades)	130.00	52.00	26.00
(21)	Frankie Frisch (7 of Spades)	130.00	52.00	26.00
(22)	Robert (Lefty) Grove	150.00	60.00	30.00
(23)	Mule Haas	65.00	26.00	13.00
(24)	Chick Hafey	130.00	52.00	26.00
(25)	Chas. Leo Hartnett	130.00	52.00	26.00
(26)	Babe Herman	70.00	28.00	14.00
(27)	Wm. Herman	130.00	52.00	26.00
(28)	Kid Higgins	65.00	26.00	13.00
(29)	Rogers Hornsby	160.00	64.00	32.00
(30)	Don Hurst (Jack of Diamonds)	65.00	26.00	13.00
(31)	Don Hurst (6 of Spades)	65.00	26.00	13.00
(32)	Chuck Klein	130.00	52.00	26.00
(33)	Leroy Mahaffey	65.00	26.00	13.00
(34)	Gus Mancuso	65.00	26.00	13.00
(35)	Rabbit McNair	65.00	26.00	13.00
(36)	Bing Miller	65.00	26.00	13.00
(37)	Frank (Lefty) O'Doul	75.00	30.00	15.00
(38)	Mel Ott	130.00	52.00	26.00
(39)	Babe Ruth (Ace of Spades)	975.00	390.00	195.00
(40)	Babe Ruth (King of Clubs)	975.00	390.00	195.00
(41)	Al Simmons	130.00	52.00	26.00
(42)	Bill Terry	130.00	52.00	26.00
(43)	Pie Traynor	130.00	52.00	26.00
(44)	Rube Wallberg (Walberg)	65.00	26.00	13.00
(45)	Lloyd Waner	130.00	52.00	26.00
(46)	Paul Waner	130.00	52.00	26.00
(47)	Lloyd Warner (Waner)	130.00	52.00	26.00
(48)	Paul Warner (Warner)	130.00	52.00	26.00
(49)	Pinkey Whitney	65.00	26.00	13.00
(50)	Dib Williams	65.00	26.00	13.00
(51)	Hack Wilson (9 of Spades)	130.00	52.00	26.00
(52)	Hack Wilson (9 of Clubs)	130.00	52.00	26.00

1951 Roadmaster Photos

Black-and-white glossy photos of at least two major league stars were available as a premium from Roadmaster bicycles. Contemporary ads said that for a dime, an 8" x 10" photo could be obtained. The photos show the uniformed players seated on Roadmaster bikes inside a ballpark. There is a facsimile autograph on each. Backs are blank. It's possible other player photos may yet be seen.

		NM	EX	VG
(1)	Bob Feller	200.00	100.00	60.00
(2)	Pee Wee Reese	250.00	125.00	75.00

1975 Jb Robinson Jewelers Cleveland Indians

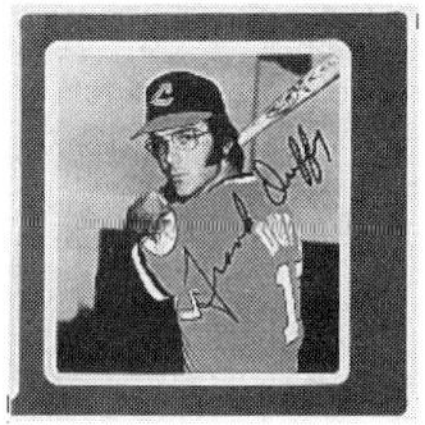

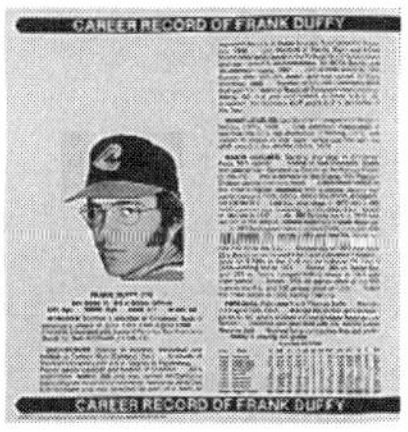

This set of color player pictures was issued in the format of an accordion-fold album sponsored by an area jewelry store chain. Individual pictures measure 8-1/2" x 8-1/2". Fronts have player poses with white trim and blue borders. There is a facsimile autograph on each picture. Black-and-white backs repeat the front photo as a portrait and add Personal data, professional stats and career highlights. The pictures are unnumbered and listed here in alphabetical order.

		NM	EX	VG
Complete Album:		40.00	20.00	12.00
Complete Set, Singles (7):		20.00	10.00	6.00
Common Player:		4.00	2.00	1.25
(1)	Buddy Bell	5.00	2.50	1.50
(2)	Jack Brohamer	4.00	2.00	1.25
(3)	Rico Carty	7.50	3.75	2.25
(4)	Frank Duffy	4.00	2.00	1.25
(5)	Oscar Gamble	4.00	2.00	1.25
(6)	Boog Powell	7.50	3.75	2.25
(7)	Frank Robinson	9.00	4.50	2.75

1911 Rochester Baking Philadelphia A's (D359)

The 1911 Rochester Baking set, an 18-card Philadelphia Athletics set, is among the scarcest of early 20th Century bakery issues. The set commemorates the Athletics' 1910 Championship season, and, except for pitcher Jack Coombs, the checklist includes nearly all key members of the club, including manager Connie Mack. The cards are the standard size for the era, 1-1/2" x 2-5/8". The front of each card features a player portrait set against a colored background. The player's name and the word "Athletics" appear at the bottom, while "World's Champions 1910" is printed along the top. The backs of the cards advertise the set as the "Athletics Series." Collectors should be aware that the same checklist was used for a similar Athletics set issued by Williams Baking and Cullivan's Fireside tobacco (T208), and also that blank-backed versions are also known to exist, but these are classified as E104 cards in the American Card Catalog.

		NM	EX	VG
Complete Set (18):		12700.	6350.	3800.
Common Player:		485.00	240.00	145.00
(1)	Home Run Baker	1150.	575.00	345.00
(2)	Jack Barry	485.00	240.00	145.00
(3)	Chief Bender	1150.	575.00	345.00
(4)	Eddie Collins	1150.	575.00	345.00
(5)	Harry Davis	485.00	240.00	145.00
(6)	Jimmy Dygert	485.00	240.00	145.00
(7)	Topsy Hartsel	485.00	240.00	145.00
(8)	Harry Krause	485.00	240.00	145.00
(9)	Jack Lapp	485.00	240.00	145.00
(10)	Paddy Livingstone (Livingston)	485.00	240.00	145.00
(11)	Bris Lord	485.00	240.00	145.00
(12)	Connie Mack	1200.	600.00	360.00
(13)	Cy Morgan	485.00	240.00	145.00
(14)	Danny Murphy	485.00	240.00	145.00
(15)	Rube Oldring	485.00	240.00	145.00
(16)	Eddie Plank	1450.	725.00	435.00
(17)	Amos Strunk	485.00	240.00	145.00
(18)	Ira Thomas	485.00	240.00	145.00

1955 Rodeo Meats Athletics

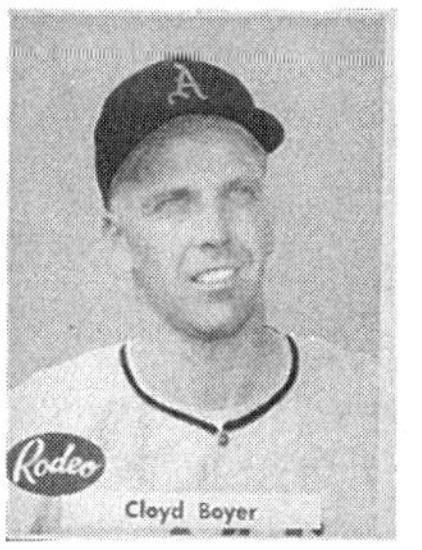

This set of 2-1/2" x 3-1/2" color cards was issued by a local meat company to commemorate the first year of the Athletics in Kansas City. There are 38 different players included in the set, with nine players known to apppear in two different variations for a total of 47 cards in the set. Most variations are in background colors, although Bobby Shantz is also listed incorrectly as "Schantz" on one variation. The cards are unnumbered, with the Rodeo logo and player name on the fronts, and an ad for a scrapbook album listed on the backs.

		NM	EX	VG
Complete Set (47):		9675.	4825.	2900.
Common Player:		200.00	100.00	60.00
Album:		525.00	250.00	155.00
(1)	Joe Astroth	200.00	100.00	60.00
(2)	Harold Bevan	265.00	130.00	79.00
(3)	Charles Bishop	265.00	130.00	79.00
(4)	Don Bollweg	265.00	130.00	79.00
(5)	Lou Boudreau	525.00	260.00	155.00
(6)	Cloyd Boyer (blue background)	265.00	130.00	79.00
(7)	Cloyd Boyer (pink background)	200.00	100.00	60.00
(8)	Ed Burtschy	265.00	130.00	79.00
(9)	Art Ceccarelli	200.00	100.00	60.00
(10)	Joe DeMaestri (pea green background)	265.00	130.00	79.00
(11)	Joe DeMaestri (light green background)	200.00	100.00	60.00
(12)	Art Ditmar	200.00	100.00	60.00
(13)	John Dixon	265.00	130.00	79.00
(14)	Jim Finigan	200.00	100.00	60.00
(15)	Marion Fricano	265.00	130.00	79.00
(16)	Tom Gorman	265.00	130.00	79.00
(17)	John Gray	200.00	100.00	60.00
(18)	Ray Herbert	200.00	100.00	60.00
(19)	Forest "Spook" Jacobs (Forrest)	265.00	130.00	79.00
(20)	Alex Kellner	265.00	130.00	79.00
(21)	Harry Kraft (Craft)	200.00	100.00	60.00
(22)	Jack Littrell	200.00	100.00	60.00
(23)	Hector Lopez	215.00	105.00	64.00
(24)	Oscar Melillo	200.00	100.00	60.00
(25)	Arnold Portocarrero (purple background)	265.00	130.00	79.00
(26)	Arnold Portocarrero (grey background)	200.00	100.00	60.00
(27)	Vic Power (pink background)	265.00	130.00	79.00
(28)	Vic Power (yellow background)	215.00	105.00	64.00
(29)	Vic Raschi	265.00	130.00	79.00
(30)	Bill Renna (dark pink background)	265.00	130.00	79.00
(31)	Bill Renna (light pink background)	200.00	100.00	60.00
(32)	Al Robertson	265.00	130.00	79.00
(33)	Johnny Sain	265.00	130.00	79.00
(34a)	Bobby Schantz (incorrect spelling)	525.00	260.00	155.00
(34b)	Bobby Shantz (correct spelling)	265.00	130.00	79.00
(35)	Wilmer Shantz (orange background)	265.00	130.00	79.00
(36)	Wilmer Shantz (purple background)	200.00	100.00	60.00
(37)	Harry Simpson	200.00	100.00	60.00
(38)	Enos Slaughter	565.00	280.00	170.00
(39)	Lou Sleater	200.00	100.00	60.00
(40)	George Susce	200.00	100.00	60.00
(41)	Bob Trice	265.00	130.00	79.00
(42)	Elmer Valo (yellow background)	265.00	130.00	79.00
(43)	Elmer Valo (green background)	200.00	100.00	60.00
(44)	Bill Wilson (yellow background)	265.00	130.00	79.00
(45)	Bill Wilson (purple background)	200.00	100.00	60.00
(46)	Gus Zernial	215.00	105.00	64.00

1956 Rodeo Meats Athletics

Rodeo Meats issued another Kansas City Athletics set in 1956, but this one was a much smaller 13-card set. The 2-1/2" x 3-1/2" cards are again unnumbered, with the player name and Rodeo logo on the fronts. Card backs feature some of the same graphics and copy as the 1955 cards, but the album offer is omitted. The full-color cards were only available in packages of Rodeo hot dogs.

		NM	EX	VG
Complete Set (12):		2425.	1200.	725.00
Common Player:		175.00	85.00	50.00
(1)	Joe Astroth	175.00	85.00	50.00
(2)	Lou Boudreau	450.00	225.00	135.00
(3)	Joe DeMaestri	175.00	85.00	50.00
(4)	Art Ditmar	175.00	85.00	50.00
(5)	Jim Finigan	175.00	85.00	50.00
(6)	Hector Lopez	195.00	97.00	58.00
(7)	Vic Power	215.00	105.00	64.00
(8)	Bobby Shantz	240.00	120.00	72.00
(9)	Harry Simpson	175.00	85.00	50.00
(10)	Enos Slaughter	475.00	235.00	140.00
(11)	Elmer Valo	175.00	85.00	50.00
(12)	Gus Zernial	195.00	97.00	58.00

1962 Roger Maris Action Baseball Game

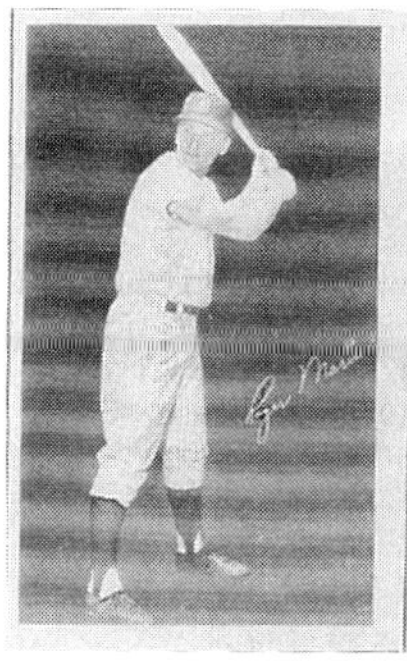

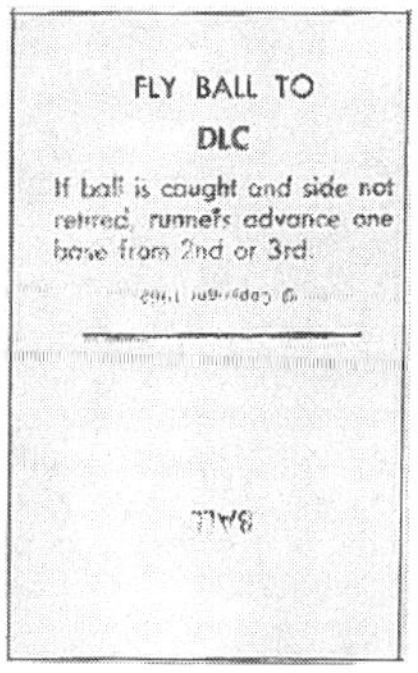
FLY BALL TO
DLC
If ball is caught and side not retired, runners advance one base from 2nd or 3rd.

Baseball's new home run king was featured in this board game by Pressman Toy Co. Besides the colorful metal game board and other pieces, the set contains 88 playing cards. Each 2-1/4" x 3-1/2" card has a black-and-white photo on front of Maris in a batting pose, along with a white facsimile autograph. Backs have two possible game action plays printed, along with a copyright line.

	NM	EX	VG
Complete Game:	150.00	75.00	45.00
Single Card:	8.00	4.00	2.50
Roger Maris			

1930s Rogers Peet Sport Album

This is one of the scarcest multi-sport issues of the 1930s. It was the promotion of a New York-Boston chain of stores (boys' clothing?) in the form of a frequent customer program. Boys visiting the store with a parent could receive a set of four cards to be placed in a 14-page 4-1/2" x 7-1/4" album. Individual cards are about 1-7/8" x 2-1/2" and feature black-and-white photos with a white border. The athlete's name and card number are printed in the bottom border. Numbers correspond to spaces in the album. Only the "Baseball Stars" from the issue are checklisted here. Others include hockey, football, track, swimming, golf, tennis, aviation, etc.

		NM	EX	VG
Complete Set (44):		8000.	4000.	2400.
Complete Set in Album:		6000.	3000.	1800.
Common Sticker:		40.00	20.00	12.00
Album:		650.00	325.00	195.00
5	Dazzy Vance	300.00	150.00	90.00
13	Walter Johnson	450.00	225.00	135.00
16	Rogers Hornsby	350.00	175.00	105.00
18	Herb Pennock	300.00	150.00	90.00
28	Lou Gehrig	1500.	750.00	450.00
34	Ty Cobb	750.00	375.00	225.00
38	Tris Speaker	350.00	175.00	105.00
48	Babe Ruth	2750.	1375.	825.00

1960s Rogers Printing Co. Postcards

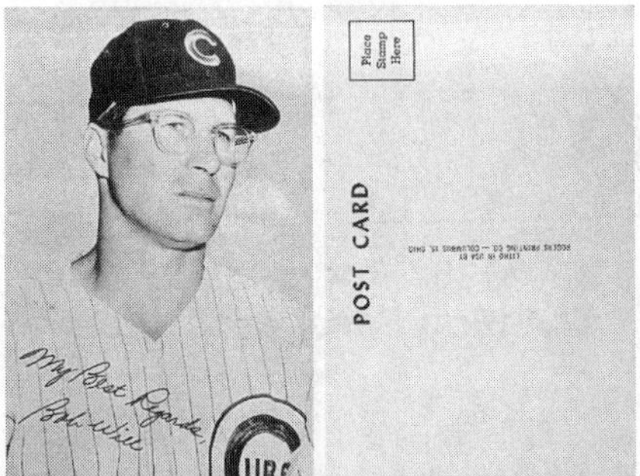

The extent to which this Columbus, Ohio, firm may have provided baseball players with postcards to answer fan mail requests is unknown. At present, only a single card is known, that of Bob Wills, who played his entire major league career (1957-63) with the Cubs. The card is printed in black-and-white on glossy stock in a 3-1/2" x 5-1/2" format. A facsimile autograph message is printed on front. Postcard-style backs have the imprint of the printer.

	NM	EX	VG
Bob Will	3.00	1.50	.90

1970 Rold Gold Pretzels

The 1970 Rold Gold Pretzels set of 15 cards honors the "Greatest Players Ever" in the first 100 years of baseball as chosen by the Baseball Writers of America. The cards, which measure 2-1/4" x 3-1/2" in size, feature a simulated 3-D effect. The set was re-released in 1972 by Kellogg's in packages of Danish-Go-Rounds. Rold Gold cards can be differentiated from the Kellogg's cards of 1972 by the 1970 copyright date found on the card reverse.

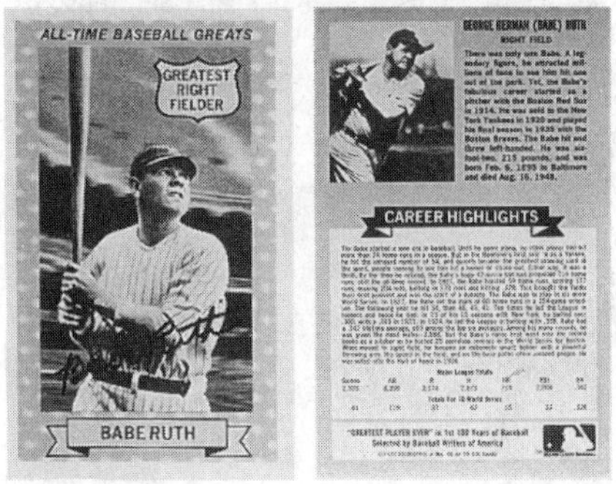

		NM	EX	VG
Complete Set (15):		120.00	60.00	36.00
Common Player:		3.00	1.50	.90
1	Walter Johnson	7.50	3.75	2.25
2	Rogers Hornsby	4.50	2.25	1.25
3	John McGraw	3.00	1.50	.90
4	Mickey Cochrane	3.00	1.50	.90
5	George Sisler	3.00	1.50	.90
6	Babe Ruth ("Greatest Ever")	35.00	17.50	10.50
7	Robert "Lefty" Grove	3.00	1.50	.90
8	Harold "Pie" Traynor	3.00	1.50	.90
9	Honus Wagner	7.50	3.75	2.25
10	Eddie Collins	3.00	1.50	.90
11	Tris Speaker	4.50	2.25	1.25
12	Cy Young	7.50	3.75	2.25
13	Lou Gehrig	20.00	10.00	6.00
14	Babe Ruth ("Greatest Right Fielder")	35.00	17.50	10.50
15	Ty Cobb	18.00	9.00	5.50

1908-1909 Rose Company Postcards

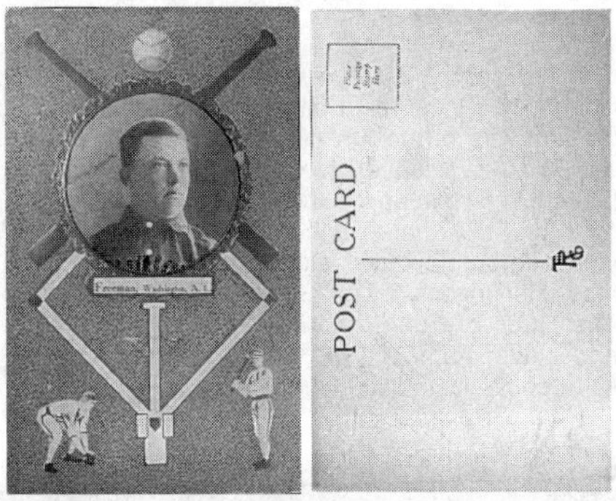

Among the most ornate and attractive baseball cards of the pre-1910 period is the set of postcards produced by The Rose Co., between 1908-09. The 3-1/2" x 5-1/2" cards feature a black-and-white player portrait photo at center, surrounded by an embossed round gold frame. The player's surname and (usually) team are in a white panel under the photo. The background of the card's front is in green and includes crossed bats and a baseball, a diamond diagram and pictures of a fielder and batter. The postcard-format back is printed in black-and-white with a TRC logo at bottom-center. The unnumbered postcards are checklisted here alphabetically; including 10 minor league players from Scranton in the New York State League. There is a card labeled "Frank Delehanty, Wash., A.L." although it was Jim Delahanty who played for Washington from 1907-1909. It is possible future discoveries will be added to this checklist.

		NM	EX	VG
Complete Set (176):		52750.	21125.	10550.
Common Player:		375.00	150.00	75.00
(1)	Whitey Alperman	375.00	150.00	75.00
(2)	Nick Altrock	375.00	150.00	75.00
(3)	John Anderson	375.00	150.00	75.00
(4)	Shad Barry	375.00	150.00	75.00
(5)	Ginger Beaumont	375.00	150.00	75.00
(6)	Fred Beebe	375.00	150.00	75.00
(7)	Harry Bemis	375.00	150.00	75.00
(8)	Chief Bender	595.00	240.00	120.00
(9)	Bills	375.00	150.00	75.00
(10)	Joe Birmingham	375.00	150.00	75.00
(11)	Bill Bradley	375.00	150.00	75.00
(12)	Kitty Bransfield	375.00	150.00	75.00
(13)	Al Bridwell	375.00	150.00	75.00
(14a)	Buster Brown (Philadelphia)	375.00	150.00	75.00
(14b)	Buster Brown (Boston)	375.00	150.00	75.00
(15)	Three Finger Brown	595.00	240.00	120.00
(16)	Bobby Byrne	375.00	150.00	75.00
(17)	Howie Camnitz	375.00	150.00	75.00
(18)	Billy Campbell	375.00	150.00	75.00
(19)	Frank Chance	685.00	275.00	135.00
(20)	Hal Chase	395.00	160.00	79.00
(21)	Jack Chesbro	595.00	240.00	120.00
(22)	Fred Clarke	595.00	240.00	120.00
(23)	Josh Clarke	375.00	150.00	75.00
(24)	Otis Clymer	375.00	150.00	75.00
(25a)	Andy Coakley (no team name)	375.00	150.00	75.00
(25b)	Andy Coakley (w/ team name)	375.00	150.00	75.00
(26)	Ty Cobb	3250.	1300.	650.00
(27)	Jimmy Collins	595.00	240.00	120.00
(28)	Wid Conroy	375.00	150.00	75.00
(29)	Jack Coombs	375.00	150.00	75.00
(30)	Frank Corridon	375.00	150.00	75.00
(31)	Sam Crawford	595.00	240.00	120.00
(32)	Bill Dahlen	375.00	150.00	75.00
(33)	Harry Davis	375.00	150.00	75.00
(34)	Joe Delahanty	395.00	160.00	79.00
(35)	Frank Delehanty (Delahanty)	395.00	160.00	79.00
(36)	Mike Donlin	375.00	150.00	75.00
(37)	Jiggs Donohue (Donahue)	375.00	150.00	75.00
(38)	Wild Bill Donovan	375.00	150.00	75.00
(39)	Red Dooin	375.00	150.00	75.00
(40)	Mickey Doolan	375.00	150.00	75.00
(41)	Larry Doyle	375.00	150.00	75.00
(42)	Jimmy Dygert	375.00	150.00	75.00
(43)	Kid Elberfeld	375.00	150.00	75.00
(44)	Johnny Evers	685.00	275.00	135.00
(45)	Bob Ewing	375.00	150.00	75.00
(46)	George Ferguson	375.00	150.00	75.00
(47)	Hobe Ferris	375.00	150.00	75.00
(48)	Jerry Freeman	375.00	150.00	75.00
(49)	Bob Ganley	375.00	150.00	75.00
(50)	John Ganzel	375.00	150.00	75.00
(51)	George Gibson	375.00	150.00	75.00
(52)	Billy Gilbert	375.00	150.00	75.00
(53)	Fred Glade	375.00	150.00	75.00
(54)	Ralph Glaze	375.00	150.00	75.00
(55)	Graham	375.00	150.00	75.00
(56)	Eddie Grant	395.00	160.00	79.00
(57)	Groh	375.00	150.00	75.00
(58)	Charley Hale (Hall)	375.00	150.00	75.00
(59)	Halligan	375.00	150.00	75.00
(60)	Topsy Hartsel	375.00	150.00	75.00
(61)	Charlie Hemphill	375.00	150.00	75.00
(62)	Bill Hinchman	375.00	150.00	75.00
(63)	Art Hoelskoetter	375.00	150.00	75.00
(64)	Danny Hoffman	375.00	150.00	75.00
(65)	Solly Hofmann	375.00	150.00	75.00
(66)	Houser	375.00	150.00	75.00
(67)	Harry Howell	375.00	150.00	75.00
(68)	Miller Huggins	595.00	240.00	120.00
(69)	Rudy Hulswitt	375.00	150.00	75.00
(70)	John Hummel	375.00	150.00	75.00
(71)	Frank Isbel (Isbell)	375.00	150.00	75.00
(72)	Walter Johnson	2175.	870.00	435.00
(73)	Fielder Jones	375.00	150.00	75.00
(74)	Tom Jones	375.00	150.00	75.00
(75)	Addie Joss	685.00	275.00	135.00
(76)	Johnny Kane	375.00	150.00	75.00
(77)	Ed Karger	375.00	150.00	75.00
(78)	Wee Willie Keeler	595.00	240.00	120.00
(79)	Kellogg	375.00	150.00	75.00
(80)	Ed Killian	375.00	150.00	75.00
(81)	Malachi Kittredge (Kittridge)	375.00	150.00	75.00
(82)	Red Kleinow	375.00	150.00	75.00
(83)	Johnny Kling	375.00	150.00	75.00
(84)	Otto Knabe	375.00	150.00	75.00
(85)	John Knight	375.00	150.00	75.00
(86)	Ed Konetchy	375.00	150.00	75.00
(87)	Nap Lajoie	685.00	275.00	135.00
(88)	Frank LaPorte	375.00	150.00	75.00
(89)	Glenn Leibhardt (Liebhardt)	375.00	150.00	75.00
(90)	Vive Lindamann (Lindaman)	375.00	150.00	75.00
(91)	Hans Lobert	375.00	150.00	75.00
(92)	Harry Lord	375.00	150.00	75.00
(93)	Harry Lumley	375.00	150.00	75.00
(94)	Johnny Lush	375.00	150.00	75.00
(95)	Nick Maddox	375.00	150.00	75.00
(96)	Sherry Magee	375.00	150.00	75.00
(97)	Billy Maloney	375.00	150.00	75.00
(98)	Christy Mathewson	2175.	870.00	435.00
(99)	George McBride	375.00	150.00	75.00
(100)	Joe McGinnity	595.00	240.00	120.00
(101)	Stoney McGlynn	375.00	150.00	75.00
(102)	Harry McIntyre	375.00	150.00	75.00
(103)	Larry McLean	375.00	150.00	75.00
(104)	George McQuillen (McQuillan)	375.00	150.00	75.00
(105)	Clyde Milan	375.00	150.00	75.00
(106)	Mike Mitchell	375.00	150.00	75.00
(107)	Moran	375.00	150.00	75.00
(108)	Mike Mowrey	375.00	150.00	75.00
(109)	George Mullin	375.00	150.00	75.00
(110)	Danny Murphy	375.00	150.00	75.00
(111)	Red Murray	375.00	150.00	75.00
(112)	Doc Newton	375.00	150.00	75.00
(113)	Simon Nicholls	375.00	150.00	75.00
(114)	Harry Niles	375.00	150.00	75.00
(115)	Rube Oldring	375.00	150.00	75.00
(116)	Charley O'Leary	375.00	150.00	75.00
(117)	Patsy O'Rourke	375.00	150.00	75.00
(118)	Al Orth	375.00	150.00	75.00
(119)	Fred Osborne (Osborn)	375.00	150.00	75.00
(120)	Orval Overall	375.00	150.00	75.00
(121)	Freddy Parent	375.00	150.00	75.00
(122)	George Paskert	375.00	150.00	75.00
(123)	Case Patten	375.00	150.00	75.00

(124)	Deacon Phillipi	375.00	150.00	75.00
(125)	Eddie Plank	595.00	240.00	120.00
(126)	Jack Powell	375.00	150.00	75.00
(127)	Tex Pruiett	375.00	150.00	75.00
(128)	Ed Reulbach	375.00	150.00	75.00
(129)	Bob Rhoades (Rhoads)	375.00	150.00	75.00
(130)	Claude Ritchey	375.00	150.00	75.00
(131)	Claude Rossman	375.00	150.00	75.00
(132)	Nap Rucker	375.00	150.00	75.00
(133)	Germany Schaefer	375.00	150.00	75.00
(134)	George Schlei	375.00	150.00	75.00
(135)	Boss Schmidt	375.00	150.00	75.00
(136)	Ossie Schreck	375.00	150.00	75.00
(137)	Wildfire Schulte	375.00	150.00	75.00
(138)	Schultz	375.00	150.00	75.00
(139)	Socks Seybold	375.00	150.00	75.00
(140)	Cy Seymour	375.00	150.00	75.00
(141)	Spike Shannon	375.00	150.00	75.00
(142)	Jimmy Sheckard	375.00	150.00	75.00
(143)	Tommy Sheehan	375.00	150.00	75.00
(144)	Bill Shipke	375.00	150.00	75.00
(145)	Jimmy Slagle	375.00	150.00	75.00
(146)	Charlie Smith	375.00	150.00	75.00
(147)	Bob Spade	375.00	150.00	75.00
(148)	Tully Sparks	375.00	150.00	75.00
(149)	Tris Speaker	685.00	275.00	135.00
(150)	Tubby Spencer	375.00	150.00	75.00
(151)	Jake Stahl	375.00	150.00	75.00
(152)	Steele	375.00	150.00	75.00
(153)	Harry Steinfeldt	375.00	150.00	75.00
(154)	George Stone	375.00	150.00	75.00
(155)	George Stovall	375.00	150.00	75.00
(156)	Billy Sullivan	375.00	150.00	75.00
(157)	Ed Summers	375.00	150.00	75.00
(158)	Dummy Taylor	395.00	160.00	79.00
(159)	Fred Tenney	375.00	150.00	75.00
(160)	Roy Thomas	375.00	150.00	75.00
(161)	Jack Thoney	375.00	150.00	75.00
(162)	Joe Tinker	685.00	275.00	135.00
(163)	John Titus	375.00	150.00	75.00
(164)	Terry Turner	375.00	150.00	75.00
(165)	Bob Unglaub	375.00	150.00	75.00
(166)	Hube Waddell	505.00	240.00	120.00
(167)	Heinie Wagner	375.00	150.00	75.00
(168)	Honus Wagner	2500.	1000.	500.00
(169)	Jack Warner	375.00	150.00	75.00
(170)	Jake Weimer	375.00	150.00	75.00
(171)	Doc White	375.00	150.00	75.00
(172)	Jimmy Williams	375.00	150.00	75.00
(173)	Hooks Wiltse	375.00	150.00	75.00
(174)	George Winter	375.00	150.00	75.00
(175)	Cy Young	875.00	350.00	175.00
(176)	Harley Young	375.00	150.00	75.00

1977 Jim Rowe 4-on-1 Exhibits

This collectors' edition set harkens back to the four-player cards issued in the 1930s by Exhibit Supply Co. The 1977 version is printed in black on yellow in a 3-1/4" x 5-1/2" format. Backs are blank. Each of the four player photos on front is identified by name. The cards are checklisted here in order of team name.

		NM	EX	VG
Complete Set (16):		75.00	37.50	22.00
Common Card:		4.00	2.00	1.25
(1)	Boston Braves (Al Lopez, Rabbit Maranville, Warren Spahn, Casey Stengel)	4.00	2.00	1.25
(2)	Boston Red Sox (Joe Cronin, Herb Pennock, Babe Ruth, Ted Williams)	12.00	6.00	3.50
(3)	Brooklyn Dodgers (Max Carey, Burleigh Grimes, Joe Medwick, Dazzy Vance)	4.00	2.00	1.25
(4)	Chicago Cubs (Kiki Cuyler, Gabby Hartnett, Billy Herman, Freddy Lindstrom)	4.00	2.00	1.25
(5)	Chicago White Sox (Luke Appling, Red Faber, Ted Lyons, Red Ruffing)	4.00	2.00	1.25
(6)	Cincinnati Reds (Chick Hafey, George Kelly, Bill McKechnie, Edd Roush)	4.00	2.00	1.25
(7)	Cleveland Indians (Earl Averill, Lou Boudreau, Bob Feller, Bob Lemon)	4.00	2.00	1.25
(8)	Detroit Tigers (Ty Cobb, Charlie Gehringer, Goose Goslin, Hank Greenberg)	9.00	4.50	2.75
(9)	New York Giants (Dave Bancroft, Carl Hubbell, Mel Ott, Bill Terry)	4.00	2.00	1.25
(10)	New York Yankees (Bill Dickey, Joe DiMaggio, Lou Gehrig, Lefty Gomez)	10.00	5.00	3.00
(11)	Philadelphia Athletics (Mickey Cochrane, Eddie Collins, Lefty Grove, Al Simmons)	4.00	2.00	1.25
(12)	Philadelphia Phillies (Grover Alexander, Jimmie Foxx, Eppa Rixey, Robin Roberts)	4.00	2.00	1.25
(13)	Pittsburgh Pirates (Pie Traynor, Honus Wagner, Lloyd Waner, Paul Waner)	5.00	2.50	1.50
(14)	St. Louis Browns (Jim Bottomley, Earle Combs, Rogers Hornsby, George Sisler)	4.00	2.00	1.25
(15)	St. Louis Cardinals (Dizzy Dean, Frankie Frisch, Jesse Haines, Stan Musial)	4.00	2.00	1.25
(16)	Washington Senators (Bucky Harris, Walter Johnson, Heinie Manush, Sam Rice)	5.00	2.50	1.50

1950 Royal Desserts

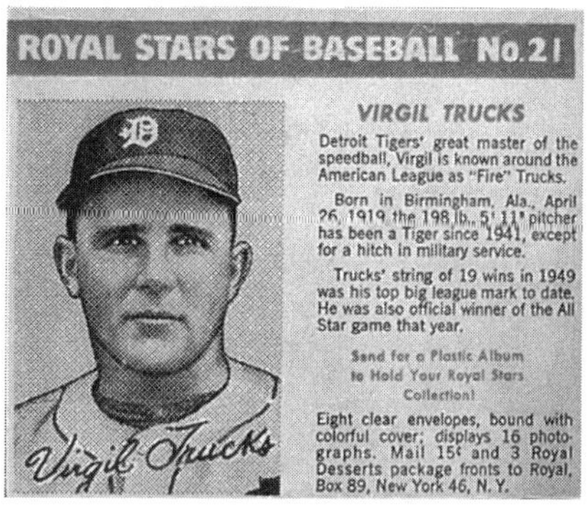

This set was issued one per box on the backs of various Royal Dessert products over a period of three years. The basic set contains 24 players, however a number of variations create the much higher total for the set. In 1950, Royal issued cards with two different tints - black and white with red, or blue and white with red. Over the next two years, various sentences of the cards' biographies were updated; up to three times in some cases. Some players from the set left the majors after 1950 and others were apparently never updated, but the 23 biography updates that do exist, added to the original 24 cards issued in 1950, give the set a total of 47 cards. The 2-1/2" x 3-1/2" cards are blank-backed with personal and playing biographies alongside the card front photos. Some sample cards can be found with advertising for the desserts on back; they are valued at about 1.5X regular card prices.

		NM	EX	VG
Complete Set (24):		1750.	775.00	350.00
Common Player:		50.00	22.00	10.00
1a	Stan Musial (2nd paragraph begins "Musial's 207...")	200.00	90.00	40.00
1b	Stan Musial (2nd paragraph begins "Musial batted...")	200.00	90.00	40.00
2a	Pee Wee Reese (2nd paragraph begins "Pee Wee's...")	160.00	72.00	32.00
2b	Pee Wee Reese (2nd paragraph begins "Captain...")	160.00	72.00	32.00
3a	George Kell (2nd paragraph ends "...in 1945, '46.")	80.00	36.00	16.00
3b	George Kell (2nd paragraph ends "...two base hits, 56.")	80.00	36.00	16.00
4a	Dom DiMaggio (2nd paragraph ends "...during 1947.")	65.00	29.00	13.00
4b	Dom DiMaggio (2nd paragraph ends "...with 11.")	65.00	29.00	13.00
5a	Warren Spahn (2nd paragraph ends "...shutouts 7.")	120.00	54.00	24.00
5b	Warren Spahn (2nd paragraph ends "...with 191.")	120.00	54.00	24.00
6a	Andy Pafko (2nd paragraph ends "...7 games.")	57.00	26.00	11.50
6b	Andy Pafko (2nd paragraph ends "...National League.")	57.00	26.00	11.50
6c	Andy Pafko (2nd paragraph ends "...weighs 190.")	57.00	26.00	11.50
7a	Andy Seminick (2nd paragraph ends "...as outfield.")	50.00	22.00	10.00
7b	Andy Seminick (2nd paragraph ends "...since 1916.")	50.00	22.00	10.00
7c	Andy Seminick (2nd paragraph ends "...in the outfield. ")	50.00	22.00	10.00
7d	Andy Seminick (2nd paragraph ends "...right handed.")	50.00	22.00	10.00
8a	Lou Brissie (2nd paragraph ends "...when pitching.")	50.00	22.00	10.00
8b	Lou Brissie (2nd paragraph ends "...weighs 215.")	50.00	22.00	10.00
9a	Ewell Blackwell (2nd paragraph begins "Despite recent illness...")	65.00	29.00	13.00
9b	Ewell Blackwell (2nd paragraph begins "Blackwell's...")	65.00	29.00	13.00
10a	Bobby Thomson (2nd paragraph begins "In 1949...")	65.00	29.00	13.00
10b	Bobby Thomson (2nd paragraph begins "Thomson is...")	65.00	29.00	13.00
11a	Phil Rizzuto (2nd paragraph ends "...one 1942 game.")	145.00	65.00	29.00
11b	Phil Rizzuto (2nd paragraph ends "...Most Valuable Player.")	145.00	65.00	29.00
12	Tommy Henrich	65.00	29.00	13.00
13	Joe Gordon	57.00	26.00	11.50
14a	Ray Scarborough (Senators)	50.00	22.00	10.00
14b	Ray Scarborough (White Sox, 2nd paragraph ends "...military service.")	50.00	22.00	10.00
14c	Ray Scarborough (White Sox, 2nd paragraph ends "...the season.")	50.00	22.00	10.00
14d	Ray Scarborough (Red Sox)	50.00	22.00	10.00
15a	Stan Rojek (Pirates)	50.00	22.00	10.00
15b	Stan Rojek (Browns)	50.00	22.00	10.00
16	Luke Appling	75.00	34.00	15.00
17	Willard Marshall	50.00	22.00	10.00
18	Alvin Dark	65.00	29.00	13.00
19a	Dick Sisler (2nd paragraph ends "...service record.")	50.00	22.00	10.00
19b	Dick Sisler (2nd paragraph ends "...National League flag.")	50.00	22.00	10.00
19c	Dick Sisler (2nd paragraph ends "...Nov. 2, 1920.")	50.00	22.00	10.00
19d	Dick Sisler (2nd paragraph ends "...from '46 to '48. ")	50.00	22.00	10.00
20a	Johnny Ostrowski (White Sox)	50.00	22.00	10.00
20b	Johnny Ostrowski (Senators)	50.00	22.00	10.00
21a	Virgil Trucks (2nd paragraph ends "...in military service.")	57.00	26.00	11.50
21b	Virgil Trucks (2nd paragraph ends "...that year.")	57.00	26.00	11.50
21c	Virgil Trucks (2nd paragraph ends "...for military service.")	57.00	26.00	11.50
22	Eddie Robinson	50.00	22.00	10.00
23	Nanny Fernandez	65.00	29.00	13.00
24	Ferris Fain	57.00	26.00	11.50

1952 Royal Desserts

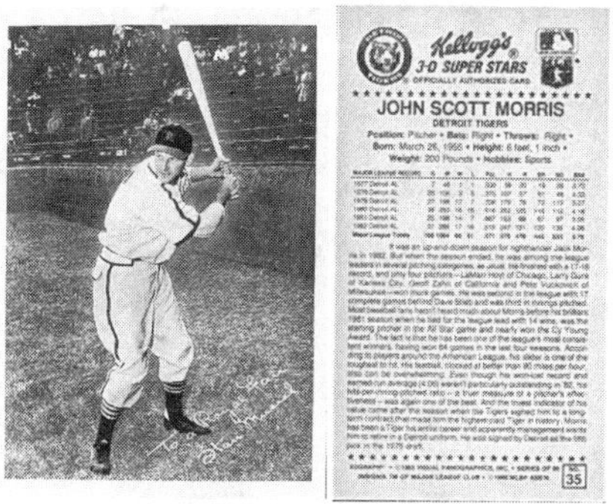

This set, issued as a premium by Royal Desserts in 1952, consists of 16 unnumbered black-and-white cards, each measuring 5" x 7". The cards include the inscription "To A Royal Fan" along with the player's facsimile autograph. Backs are blank.

		NM	EX	VG
Complete Set (16):		900.00	400.00	180.00
Common Player:		35.00	15.50	7.00
		35.00	15.50	7.00
(1)	Ewell Blackwell			
(2)	Leland V. Brissie Jr.	35.00	15.50	7.00
(3)	Alvin Dark	35.00	15.50	7.00
(4)	Dom DiMaggio	60.00	27.00	12.00
(5)	Ferris Fain	35.00	15.50	7.00
(6)	George Kell	60.00	27.00	12.00
(7)	Stan Musial	170.00	76.00	34.00
(8)	Andy Pafko	35.00	15.50	7.00
(9)	Pee Wee Reese	90.00	40.00	18.00
(10)	Phil Rizzuto	90.00	40.00	18.00
(11)	Eddie Robinson	35.00	15.50	7.00
(12)	Ray Scarborough	35.00	15.50	7.00
(13)	Andy Seminick	35.00	15.50	7.00
(14)	Dick Sisler	35.00	15.50	7.00
(15)	Warren Spahn	85.00	38.00	17.00
(16)	Bobby Thomson	45.00	20.00	9.00

1928 George Ruth Candy Co.

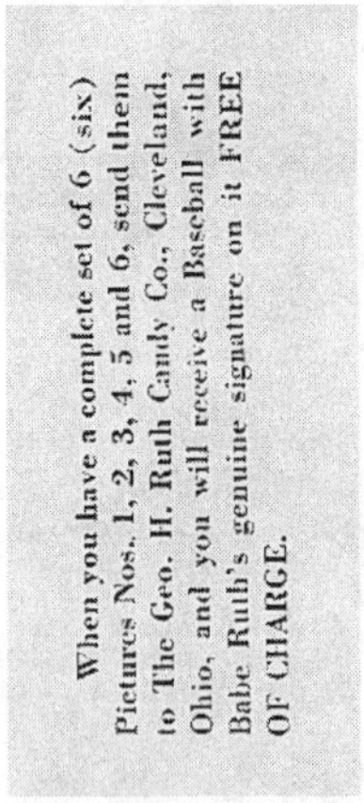
When you have a complete set of 6 (six) Pictures Nos. 1, 2, 3, 4, 5 and 6, send them to The Geo. H. Ruth Candy Co., Cleveland, Ohio, and you will receive a Baseball with Babe Ruth's genuine signature on it FREE OF CHARGE.

This obscure six-card set, issued circa 1928, features sepia-toned photos of Babe Ruth, and, according to the back of the cards, was actually issued by the Geo. H. Ruth Candy Co. The cards measure 1-7/8" by 4" and picture Ruth during a 1924 promotional West Coast tour and in scenes from the movie "Babe Comes Home." The cards are numbered and include photo captions at the bottom. The backs of the card contain an offer to exchange the six cards for an autographed baseball, which may explain their scarcity today.

		NM	EX	VG
Complete Set (6):		5250.	2400.	1050.
Common Card:		900.00	400.00	180.00
1	"Babe" Ruth (King of them all. Home Run Candy Bar. His Candy Helped Him.)	900.00	400.00	180.00
2	"Babe" Ruth (Knocked out 60 Home Runs in 1927. His C andy Helped Him.)	900.00	400.00	180.00
3	"Babe" Ruth (The only player who broke his own record. His Candy Helped Him.)	900.00	400.00	180.00
4	"Babe" Ruth (The Popular Bambino eating his Home Run Candy. His Candy Helped Him.)	900.00	400.00	180.00
5	"Babe" Ruth (A favorite with the Kiddies. Babe Ruth' s Own Candy.)	900.00	400.00	180.00
6	"Babe" Ruth (The King of Swat. Babe Ruth's Own Candy .)	900.00	400.00	180.00

1936 R311 Glossy Finish

The cards in this 28-card set, which was available as a premium in 1936, measure 6" x 8" and were printed on a glossy cardboard. The photos are either black-and-white or sepia-toned and include a facsimile autograph. The unnumbered set includes individual players and team photos. The Boston Red Sox team card can be found in two varieties; one shows the sky above the building on the card's right side, while the other does not. Some of the cards are scarcer than others in the set and command a premium. Babe Ruth is featured on the Boston Braves team card.

		NM	EX	VG
Complete Set (28):		2500.	1250.	750.00
Common Player:		50.00	25.00	15.00
(1)	Earl Averill	90.00	45.00	27.00
(2)	James L. "Jim" Bottomley	90.00	45.00	27.00
(3)	Gordon S. "Mickey" Cochrane	90.00	45.00	27.00
(4)	Joe Cronin	90.00	45.00	27.00
(5)	Jerome "Dizzy" Dean	150.00	75.00	45.00
(6)	Jimmy Dykes	50.00	25.00	15.00
(7)	Jimmy Foxx	110.00	55.00	33.00
(8)	Frankie Frisch	90.00	45.00	27.00
(9)	Henry "Hank" Greenberg	110.00	55.00	33.00
(10)	Mel Harder	50.00	25.00	15.00
(11)	Ken Keltner	50.00	25.00	15.00
(12)	Pepper Martin	65.00	32.00	19.50
(13)	Lynwood "Schoolboy" Rowe	50.00	25.00	15.00
(14)	William "Bill" Terry	90.00	45.00	27.00
(15)	Harold "Pie" Traynor	90.00	45.00	27.00
(16)	American League All-Stars - 1935	150.00	75.00	45.00
(17)	American League Pennant Winners - 1934 (Detroit Tigers)	90.00	45.00	27.00
(18)	Boston Braves - 1935	250.00	125.00	75.00
(19)	Boston Red Sox	90.00	45.00	27.00
(20)	Brooklyn Dodgers - 1935	150.00	75.00	45.00
(21)	Chicago White Sox - 1935	90.00	45.00	27.00
(22)	Columbus Red Birds (1934 Pennant Winners of American Association)	60.00	30.00	18.00
(23)	National League All-Stars - 1934	150.00	75.00	45.00
(24)	National League Champions - 1935 (Chicago Cubs)	90.00	45.00	27.00
(25)	New York Yankees - 1935	250.00	125.00	75.00
(26)	Pittsburgh Pirates - 1935	90.00	45.00	27.00
(27)	St. Louis Browns - 1935	90.00	45.00	27.00
(28)	The World Champions, 1934 (St. Louis Cardinals)	90.00	45.00	27.00

1936 R311 Leather Finish

This set of 15 unnumbered cards, issued as a premium in 1936, is distinctive because of its uneven, leather-like surface. The cards measure 6" x 8" and display a facsimilie autograph on the black and white photo surrounded by a plain border. The cards are unnumbered and include individual player photos, multi-player photos and team photos of the 1935 pennant winners.

		NM	EX	VG
Complete Set (15):		1950.	975.00	585.00
Common Player:		50.00	25.00	15.00
(1)	Frank Crosetti, Joe DiMaggio, Tony Lazzeri	400.00	200.00	120.00
(2)	Paul Derringer	50.00	25.00	15.00
(3)	Wes Ferrell	50.00	25.00	15.00
(4)	Jimmy Foxx	125.00	62.00	37.00
(5)	Charlie Gehringer	100.00	50.00	30.00
(6)	Mel Harder	50.00	25.00	15.00
(7)	Gabby Hartnett	100.00	50.00	30.00
(8)	Rogers Hornsby	150.00	75.00	45.00
(9)	Connie Mack	100.00	50.00	30.00
(10)	Van Mungo	50.00	25.00	15.00
(11)	Steve O'Neill	50.00	25.00	15.00
(12)	Charles Ruffing	100.00	50.00	30.00
(13)	Arky Vaughan, Honus Wagner	195.00	97.00	58.00
(14)	American League Pennant Winners - 1935 (Detroit Tigers)	75.00	37.00	22.00
(15)	National League Pennant Winners - 1935 (Chicago Cubs)	75.00	37.00	22.00

1936 R312

The 50 cards in this set are black-and-white photos that have been tinted in soft pastel colors. The set includes 25 individual player portraits, 14 multi-player cards and 11 action photos. Six of the action photos include facsimilie autographs, while the other five have printed legends. The Allen card is more scarce than the others in the set.

		NM	EX	VG
Complete Set (50):		5400.	2700.	1600.
Common Player:		75.00	37.00	22.00
(1)	John Thomas Allen	90.00	45.00	27.00
(2)	Nick Altrock, Al Schact	75.00	37.00	22.00
(3)	Ollie Bejma, Rolly Hemsley	75.00	37.00	22.00
(4)	Les Bell, Zeke Bonura	75.00	37.00	22.00
(5)	Cy Blanton	75.00	37.00	22.00
(6)	Cliff Bolton, Earl Whitehill	75.00	37.00	22.00
(7)	Frenchy Bordagaray, George Earnshaw	75.00	37.00	22.00
(8)	Mace Brown	75.00	37.00	22.00
(9)	Dolph Camilli	75.00	37.00	22.00
(10)	Phil Cavaretta (Cavarretta), Frank Demaree, Augie Galan, Stan Hack, Gabby Hartnett, Billy Herman, Billy Jurges,	150.00	75.00	45.00
(11)	Phil Cavaretta (Cavarretta), Stan Hack, Billy Herman, Billy Jurges	95.00	47.00	28.00
(12)	Gordon Cochrane	150.00	75.00	45.00
(13)	Jim Collins, Stan Hack	75.00	37.00	22.00
(14)	Rip Collins	75.00	37.00	22.00
(15)	Joe Cronin, Buckey Harris (Bucky)	150.00	75.00	45.00
(16)	Alvin Crowder	75.00	37.00	22.00
(17)	Kiki Cuyler	150.00	75.00	45.00
(18)	Kiki Cuyler, Tris Speaker, Danny Taylor	150.00	75.00	45.00
(19)	"Bill" Dickey	150.00	75.00	45.00
(20)	Joe DiMagio (DiMaggio)	650.00	325.00	195.00
(21)	"Chas." Dressen	75.00	37.00	22.00
(22)	Rick Ferrell, Russ Van Atta	150.00	75.00	45.00
(23)	Pete Fox, Goose Goslin, "Jo Jo" White	135.00	67.00	40.00
(24)	Jimmey Foxx (Jimmie), Luke Sewell	175.00	87.00	52.00
(25)	Benny Frey	75.00	37.00	22.00
(26)	Augie Galan, "Pie" Traynor	135.00	67.00	40.00
(27)	Lefty Gomez, Myril Hoag	135.00	67.00	40.00
(28)	"Hank" Greenberg	150.00	75.00	45.00
(29)	Lefty Grove, Connie Mack	200.00	100.00	60.00
(30)	Muel Haas (Mule), Mike Kreevich, Dixie Walker	75.00	37.00	22.00
(31)	Mel Harder	75.00	37.00	22.00
(32)	Gabby Hartnett (Mickey Cochrane, Frank Demaree, Ernie Quigley (ump) in photo)	135.00	67.00	40.00
(33)	Gabby Hartnett, Lonnie Warnecke (Warneke)	110.00	55.00	33.00
(34)	Roger Hornsby ((Rogers))	200.00	100.00	60.00
(35)	Rogers Hornsby, Allen Sothoren (Sothoron)	150.00	75.00	45.00
(36)	Ernie Lombardi	150.00	75.00	45.00
(37)	Al Lopez	150.00	75.00	45.00
(38)	Pepper Martin	90.00	45.00	27.00
(39)	"Johnny" Mize	150.00	75.00	45.00
(40)	Van L. Mungo	75.00	37.00	22.00
(41)	Bud Parmelee	75.00	37.00	22.00
(42)	Schoolboy Rowe	75.00	37.00	22.00
(43)	Chas. Ruffing	150.00	75.00	45.00
(44)	Eugene Schott	75.00	37.00	22.00
(45)	Casey Stengel	150.00	75.00	45.00
(46)	Bill Sullivan	75.00	37.00	22.00
(47)	Bill Swift	75.00	37.00	22.00
(48)	Floyd Vaughan, Hans Wagner	175.00	87.00	52.00
(49)	L. Waner, P. Waner, Big Jim Weaver	175.00	87.00	52.00
(50)	Ralph Winegarner	75.00	37.00	22.00

1936 R314

(See 1936 Goudey "Wide Pen" Premiums)

1928 R315

Issued in 1928, the 58 cards in this set can be found in either black-and-white or yellow-and-black. The unnumbered, blank-backed cards measure 3-1/4" x 5-1/4" and feature either portraits or action photos. The set includes several different types of cards, depending on the caption. Cards can be found with the player's name and team inside a white box in a lower corner; other cards add the position and team in small type in the bottom border; a third type has the player's name in hand lettering near the bottom; and the final type includes the position and team printed in small type along the bottom border.

		NM	EX	VG
Complete Set (46):		2400.	1200.	720.00
Common Player:		30.00	15.00	9.00
(1)	Earl Averill	60.00	30.00	18.00
(2)	"Benny" Bengough	30.00	15.00	9.00
(3)	Laurence Benton (Lawrence)	30.00	15.00	9.00
(4)	"Max" Bishop	30.00	15.00	9.00
(5)	"Sunny Jim" Bottomley	60.00	30.00	18.00
(6)	Bill Cissell	30.00	15.00	9.00
(7)	Bud Clancey (Clancy)	30.00	15.00	9.00
(8)	"Freddy" Fitzsimmons	30.00	15.00	9.00
(9)	"Jimmy" Foxx	90.00	45.00	27.00
(10)	"Johnny" Fredericks (Frederick)	30.00	15.00	9.00
(11)	Frank Frisch	75.00	37.00	22.00
(12)	"Lou" Gehrig	400.00	200.00	120.00
(13)	"Goose" Goslin	60.00	30.00	18.00
(14)	Burleigh Grimes	60.00	30.00	18.00
(15)	"Lefty" Grove	70.00	35.00	21.00
(16)	"Mule" Haas	30.00	15.00	9.00
(17)	Harvey Hendricks (Hendrick)	30.00	15.00	9.00
(18)	"Babe" Herman	40.00	20.00	12.00
(19)	"Roger" Hornsby (Rogers)	90.00	45.00	27.00
(20)	Karl Hubbell (Carl)	60.00	30.00	18.00
(21)	"Stonewall" Jackson	60.00	30.00	18.00
(22)	Smead Jolley	30.00	15.00	9.00
(23)	"Chuck" Klein	60.00	30.00	18.00
(24)	Mark Koenig	30.00	15.00	9.00
(25)	"Tony" Lazerri (Lazzeri)	60.00	30.00	18.00
(26)	Fred Leach	30.00	15.00	9.00
(27)	"Freddy" Lindstrom	60.00	30.00	18.00
(28)	Fred Marberry	30.00	15.00	9.00
(29)	"Bing" Miller	30.00	15.00	9.00
(30)	"Bob" O'Farrell	30.00	15.00	9.00
(31)	Frank O'Doul	40.00	20.00	12.00
(32)	"Herbie" Pennock	60.00	30.00	18.00
(33)	George Pipgras	30.00	15.00	9.00
(34)	Andrew Reese	30.00	15.00	9.00
(35)	Carl Reynolds	30.00	15.00	9.00
(36)	"Babe" Ruth	400.00	200.00	120.00
(37)	"Bob" Shawkey	30.00	15.00	9.00
(38)	Art Shires	30.00	15.00	9.00
(39)	"Al" Simmons	60.00	30.00	18.00
(40)	"Riggs" Stephenson	30.00	15.00	9.00
(41)	"Bill" Terry	60.00	30.00	18.00
(42)	"Pie" Traynor	60.00	30.00	18.00
(43)	"Dazzy" Vance	60.00	30.00	18.00
(44)	Paul Waner	60.00	30.00	18.00
(45)	Hack Wilson	60.00	30.00	18.00
(46)	"Tom" Zachary	30.00	15.00	9.00

1933 R337

(See 1933 Eclipse Import)

1948 R346 Blue Tint

Issued circa 1948-49, the cards in this set derive their name from the distinctive blue coloring used to tint the black-and-white photos. The cards have blank backs and measure 2" x 2-5/8". The set has a high percentage of New York players and was originally issued in strips of six or eight cards each and therefore would have been more appropriately cataloged as a "W" strip card set. The set includes several major variations of team desginations, black-and-white rather than blue printing, and cards which can be found either with or without numbers. The complete set price does not include the variations. Proof cards have been found with printing on the back indicating they were photographed by Al Weinstein of Brooklyn.

		NM	EX	VG
Complete Set (48):		1300.	650.00	375.00
Common Player:		15.00	7.50	4.50
1	Bill Johnson	15.00	7.50	4.50
2a	Leo Durocher (Brooklyn)	30.00	15.00	9.00
2b	Leo Durocher (New York)	30.00	15.00	9.00
3	Marty Marion	18.50	9.25	5.50
4	Ewell Blackwell	18.50	9.25	5.50
5	John Lindell	15.00	7.50	4.50
6	Larry Jansen	15.00	7.50	4.50
7	Ralph Kiner	30.00	15.00	9.00
8	Chuck Dressen	15.00	7.50	4.50
9	Bobby Brown	18.50	9.25	5.50
10	Luke Appling	30.00	15.00	9.00
11	Bill Nicholson	15.00	7.50	4.50
12	Phil Masi	15.00	7.50	4.50
13	Frank Shea	15.00	7.50	4.50
14	Bob Dillinger	15.00	7.50	4.50
15	Pete Suder	15.00	7.50	4.50
16	Joe DiMaggio	225.00	112.00	67.00
17	John Corriden	15.00	7.50	4.50
18a	Mel Ott (New York)	35.00	17.50	10.50
18b	Mel Ott (no team)	35.00	17.50	10.50
19	Warren Rosar	15.00	7.50	4.50
20	Warren Spahn	30.00	15.00	9.00
21	Allie Reynolds	20.00	10.00	6.00
22	Lou Boudreau	30.00	15.00	9.00
23	Harry Majeski (Hank) (photo actually Randy Gumpert)	15.00	7.50	4.50
24	Frank Crosetti	18.50	9.25	5.50
25	Gus Niarhos	15.00	7.50	4.50
26	Bruce Edwards	15.00	7.50	4.50
27a	Rudy York (blue)	15.00	7.50	4.50
27b	Rudy York (b/w)	15.00	7.50	4.50
28a	Don Black (blue)	15.00	7.50	4.50
28b	Don Black (b/w)	15.00	7.50	4.50
29	Lou Gehrig	225.00	112.00	67.00
30	Johnny Mize	30.00	15.00	9.00
31	Ed Stanky	18.50	9.25	5.50
32	Vic Raschi	18.50	9.25	5.50
33a	Cliff Mapes (blue)	15.00	7.50	4.50
33b	Cliff Mapes (b/w)	15.00	7.50	4.50
34	Enos Slaughter	30.00	15.00	9.00
35	Hank Greenberg	40.00	20.00	12.00
36a	Jackie Robinson (blue)	125.00	62.00	37.00
36b	Jackie Robinson (b/w)	150.00	75.00	45.00
37	Frank Hiller	15.00	7.50	4.50
38	Bob Elliot (Elliott)	15.00	7.50	4.50
39a	Harry Walker (blue)	15.00	7.50	4.50
39b	Harry Walker (b/w)	15.00	7.50	4.50
40	Ed Lopat	18.50	9.25	5.50
41	Bobby Thomson	18.50	9.25	5.50
	Bobby Thomson	18.50	9.25	5.50
42	Tommy Henrich	20.00	10.00	6.00
	Tommy Henrich	35.00	10.00	6.00
43	Bobby Feller	35.00	17.50	10.50
	Bobby Feller	35.00	17.50	10.50
44	Ted Williams	110.00	55.00	33.00
	Ted Williams	110.00	55.00	33.00
45	Dixie Walker	15.00	7.50	4.50
	Dixie Walker	15.00	7.50	4.50
46	Johnnie Vander Meer	18.50	9.25	5.50
	Johnny Vander Meer	18.50	9.25	5.50
47	Clint Hartung	15.00	7.50	4.50
	Clint Hartung	15.00	7.50	4.50
48	Charlie Keller	20.00	10.00	6.00
	Charlie Keller	20.00	10.00	6.00

1950 R423

These tiny (5/8" x 7/8") cards are numbered roughly in alphabetical order from 1 through 120, although some cards are still unknown or were never issued. The cards were available in 13-card perforated strips from vending machines in the 1950s. The black-and-white cards are printed on thin stock and include the player's name beneath his photo. The backs - most commonly printed in orange, but sometimes purple - display a rough drawing of a baseball infield with tiny figures at the various positions. It appears the cards were intended to be used to play a game of baseball. Many of the cards were printed on more than one strip, creating varying levels of scarcity.

		NM	EX	VG
Complete Set (120):		750.00	375.00	225.00
Common Player:		5.00	2.50	1.50
(1)	Richie Ashburn	20.00	10.00	6.00
(2)	Grover Alexander	10.00	5.00	3.00
(3)	Frank Baumholtz	5.00	2.50	1.50
(4)	Ralph Branca	5.00	2.50	1.50
(5)	Yogi Berra	15.00	7.50	4.50
(6)	Ewell Blackwell	5.00	2.50	1.50
(7)	Unknown			
(8)	Harry Brecheen	5.00	2.50	1.50
(9)	Chico Carrasquel	5.00	2.50	1.50
(10)	Jerry Coleman	5.00	2.50	1.50
(11)	Walker Cooper	5.00	2.50	1.50
(12)	Roy Campanella	17.50	8.75	5.25
(13)	Phil Cavaretta (Cavarretta)	5.00	2.50	1.50
(14a)	Ty Cobb (w/ facsimile autograph)	45.00	22.00	13.50
(14b)	Ty Cobb (no facsimile autograph)	45.00	22.00	13.50
(15)	Unknown			
(16)	Unknown			
(17)	Frank Crosetti	5.00	2.50	1.50
(18)	Larry Doby	10.00	5.00	3.00
(19)	Walter Dropo	5.00	2.50	1.50
(20)	Alvin Dark	5.00	2.50	1.50
(21)	Dizzy Dean	20.00	10.00	6.00
(22)	Bill Dickey	25.00	12.50	7.50
(23)	Murray Dickson (Murry)	5.00	2.50	1.50
(24)	Dom DiMaggio	8.00	4.00	2.50
(25)	Joe DiMaggio	60.00	30.00	18.00
(26)	Leo Durocher	9.00	4.50	2.75
(27)	Luke Easter	5.00	2.50	1.50
(28)	Bob Elliott	5.00	2.50	1.50
(29)	(Del Ennis)	5.00	2.50	1.50
(30)	Ferris Fain	5.00	2.50	1.50
(31)	Bob Feller	15.00	7.50	4.50
(32)	Frank Frisch	10.00	5.00	3.00
(33)	(Billy Goodman)	5.00	2.50	1.50
(34)	Lefty Gomez	12.50	6.25	3.75
(35)	Lou Gehrig	60.00	30.00	18.00
(36)	Joe Gordon	5.00	2.50	1.50
(37)	Sid Gordon	5.00	2.50	1.50
(38)	Hank Greenberg	12.50	6.25	3.75
(39)	Lefty Grove	12.50	6.25	3.75
(40)	Art Houtteman	5.00	2.50	1.50
(41)	Sid Hudson	5.00	2.50	1.50
(42)	Ken Heintzelman	5.00	2.50	1.50
(43)	Gene Hermanski	5.00	2.50	1.50
(44)	Jim Hearn	5.00	2.50	1.50
(45)	Gil Hodges	12.50	6.25	3.75
(46)	Harry Heilman (Heilmann)	9.00	4.50	2.75
(47)	Tommy Henrich	5.00	2.50	1.50
(48)	Roger Hornsby (Rogers)	10.00	5.00	3.00
(49)	(Carl Hubbell)	10.00	5.00	3.00
(50)	Edwin Joost	5.00	2.50	1.50
(51)	(John Jorgensen)	5.00	2.50	1.50
(52)	Larry Jansen	5.00	2.50	1.50
(53)	Nippy Jones	5.00	2.50	1.50
(54)	Walter Johnson	12.50	6.25	3.75
(55)	Ellis Kinder	5.00	2.50	1.50
(56)	Jim Konstanty	5.00	2.50	1.50
(57)	George Kell	8.00	4.00	2.50
(58)	Ralph Kiner	10.00	5.00	3.00
(59)	Bob Lemon	8.00	4.00	2.50
(60)	Whitey Lockman	5.00	2.50	1.50
(61)	Ed Lopat	6.50	3.25	2.00
(62)	(Tony Lazzeri)	9.00	4.50	2.75
(63)	Cass Michaels	5.00	2.50	1.50
(64)	Cliff Mapes	5.00	2.50	1.50
(65)	Willard Marshall	5.00	2.50	1.50
(66)	Clyde McCullough	5.00	2.50	1.50
(67)	Connie Mack	10.00	5.00	3.00
(68)	Christy Mathewson	12.50	6.25	3.75
(69)	Joe Medwick	9.00	4.50	2.75
(70)	Johnny Mize	10.00	5.00	3.00
(71)	Terry Moore	5.00	2.50	1.50
(72)	Stan Musial	25.00	12.50	7.50
(73)	Hal Newhouser	9.00	4.50	2.75
(74)	Don Newcombe	6.50	3.25	2.00
(75)	Lefty O'Doul	5.00	2.50	1.50
(76)	(Mel Ott)	9.00	4.50	2.75
(77)	Mel Parnell	5.00	2.50	1.50
(78)	Johnny Pesky	5.00	2.50	1.50
(79)	Gerald Priddy	5.00	2.50	1.50
(80)	Dave Philley	5.00	2.50	1.50
(81)	Bob Porterfield	5.00	2.50	1.50
(82)	Andy Pafko	5.00	2.50	1.50
(83)	Howie Pollet	5.00	2.50	1.50
(84)	Herb Pennock	5.00	2.50	1.50
(85)	Al Rosen	8.00	4.00	2.50
(86)	Pee Wee Reese	12.50	6.25	3.75
(87)	Del Rice	5.00	2.50	1.50
(88)	Vic Raschi	6.50	3.25	2.00
(89)	Allie Reynolds	6.50	3.25	2.00
(90)	(Phil Rizzuto)	12.50	6.25	3.75
(91)	(Jackie Robinson)	50.00	25.00	15.00
(92)	Babe Ruth	90.00	45.00	27.00
(93)	Casey Stengel	15.00	7.50	4.50
(94)	Vern Stephens	5.00	2.50	1.50
(95)	Duke Snider	12.50	6.25	3.75
(96)	Enos Slaughter	9.00	4.50	2.75
(97)	Al Schoendienst	9.00	4.50	2.75
(98)	Gerald Staley	5.00	2.50	1.50
(99)	Clyde Shoun	5.00	2.50	1.50
(100)	Unknown			
(101)	Hank Sauer	5.00	2.50	1.50
(102)	Al Simmons	9.00	4.50	2.75
(103)	George Sisler	8.00	4.00	2.50
(104)	Tris Speaker	12.50	6.25	3.75
(105)	Ed Stanky	5.00	2.50	1.50
(106)	Virgil Trucks	5.00	2.50	1.50
(107)	Henry Thompson	5.00	2.50	1.50
(108)	Bobby Thomson	7.50	3.75	2.25
(109)	Dazzy Vance	8.00	4.00	2.50
(110)	Lloyd Waner	8.00	4.00	2.50
(111)	Paul Waner	8.00	4.00	2.50
(112)	Gene Woodling	5.00	2.50	1.50

(113)	Ted Williams	50.00	25.00	15.00
(114)	Vic Wertz	5.00	2.50	1.50
(115)	Wes Westrom (Westrum)	5.00	2.50	1.50
(116)	Johnny Wyrostek	5.00	2.50	1.50
(117)	Eddie Yost	5.00	2.50	1.50
(118)	Allen Zarilla	5.00	2.50	1.50
(119)	Gus Zernial	5.00	2.50	1.50
(120)	Sam Zoldack (Zoldak)	5.00	2.50	1.50

S

1936 S and S Game

Small black-and-white player photos are featured on the fronts of this 52-card game set. Measuring about 2-1/4" x 3-1/2", with rounded corners, the cards feature plain green backs. Besides the player photo on front, there are a few biographical details and stats, and a pair of game scenarios. The cards are unnumbered and are checklisted here alphabetically.

		NM	EX	VG
Complete Set (52):		1000.	500.00	300.00
Complete Boxed Set:		1500.	750.00	450.00
Common Player:		30.00	15.00	9.00
(1)	Luke Appling	80.00	40.00	24.00
(2)	Earl Averill	80.00	40.00	24.00
(3)	Zeke Bonura	30.00	15.00	9.00
(4)	Dolph Camilli	30.00	15.00	9.00
(5)	Ben Cantwell	30.00	15.00	9.00
(6)	Phil Cavaretta (Cavarretta)	40.00	20.00	12.00
(7)	Rip Collins	30.00	15.00	9.00
(8)	Joe Cronin	80.00	40.00	24.00
(9)	Frank Crosetti	40.00	20.00	12.00
(10)	Kiki Cuyler	80.00	40.00	24.00
(11)	Virgil Davis	30.00	15.00	9.00
(12)	Frank Demaree	30.00	15.00	9.00
(13)	Paul Derringer	30.00	15.00	9.00
(14)	Bill Dickey	80.00	40.00	24.00
(15)	Woody English	30.00	15.00	9.00
(16)	Fred Fitzsimmons	30.00	15.00	9.00
(17)	Richard Ferrell	80.00	40.00	24.00
(18)	Pete Fox	30.00	15.00	9.00
(19)	Jimmy Foxx	90.00	45.00	27.00
(20)	Larry French	30.00	15.00	9.00
(21)	Frank Frisch	80.00	40.00	24.00
(22)	August Galan	30.00	15.00	9.00
(23)	Chas. Gehringer	80.00	40.00	24.00
(24)	John Gill	30.00	15.00	9.00
(25)	Charles Grimm	30.00	15.00	9.00
(26)	Mule Haas	30.00	15.00	9.00
(27)	Stanley Hack	40.00	20.00	12.00
(28)	Bill Hallahan	30.00	15.00	9.00
(29)	Melvin Harder	30.00	15.00	9.00
(30)	Gabby Hartnett	80.00	40.00	24.00
(31)	Ray Hayworth	30.00	15.00	9.00
(32)	Ralston Hemsley	30.00	15.00	9.00
(33)	Bill Herman	80.00	40.00	24.00
(34)	Frank Higgins	30.00	15.00	9.00
(35)	Carl Hubbell	80.00	40.00	24.00
(36)	Bill Jurges	30.00	15.00	9.00
(37)	Vernon Kennedy	30.00	15.00	9.00
(38)	Chuck Klein	80.00	40.00	24.00
(39)	Mike Kreevich	30.00	15.00	9.00
(40)	Bill Lee	30.00	15.00	9.00
(41)	Jos. Medwick	80.00	40.00	24.00
(42)	Van Mungo	30.00	15.00	9.00
(43)	James O'Dea	30.00	15.00	9.00
(44)	Mel Ott	80.00	40.00	24.00
(45)	Rip Radcliff	30.00	15.00	9.00
(46)	Pie Traynor	80.00	40.00	24.00
(47)	Arky Vaughan (Vaughn)	80.00	40.00	24.00
(48)	Joe Vosmik	30.00	15.00	9.00
(49)	Lloyd Waner	80.00	40.00	24.00
(50)	Paul Waner	80.00	40.00	24.00
(51)	Lon Warneke	30.00	15.00	9.00
(52)	Floyd Young	30.00	15.00	9.00

1948-50 Safe-T-Card

The earliest known safety issue is this series sponsored by a children's television show which was in turn sponsored by a Washington, D.C. auto dealer. Player selection and team indications on the cards point to a three-year (1948-50) range of issue dates for the cards. Minor differences in typography and information printed on the front probably differentiate the years of issue. All cards are about 2-1/2" x 3-1/2" with rounded corners. Fronts feature rather crude black-and-white drawings of the players with a facsimile autograph superimposed. A safety message is at top and, on most cards, the player's position and team are printed at bottom. Backs are printed in one of several colors and have a picture of the TV host and an ad for the program and its sponsors. The set is checklisted here alphabetically, though it's possible other cards may be added in the future. Only the baseball players from the set are listed here. Cards featuring football, basketball and other sports figures were also produced, along with cards for team executives, sports reporters and broadcasters.

		NM	EX	VG
Complete (Baseball) Set (21):		725.00	362.00	217.00
Common Player:		35.00	17.50	10.50
(1)	Ossie Bluege	35.00	17.50	10.50
(2)	Gil Coan	35.00	17.50	10.50
(3)	Sam Dente	35.00	17.50	10.50
(4)	Jake Early	35.00	17.50	10.50
(5)	Al Evans	35.00	17.50	10.50
(6)	Calvin Griffith	45.00	22.00	13.50
(7)	Clark Griffith	45.00	22.00	13.50
(8)	Bucky Harris	45.00	22.00	13.50
(9)	Sid Hudson	35.00	17.50	10.50
(10)	Joe Kuhel	35.00	17.50	10.50
(11)	Bob Lemon	45.00	22.00	13.50
(12)	Bill McGowan	45.00	22.00	13.50
(13)	George McQuinn	35.00	17.50	10.50
(14)	Don Newcombe	45.00	22.00	13.50
(15)	Joe Ostrowski	35.00	17.50	10.50
(16)	Sam Rice	45.00	22.00	13.50
(17)	Bert Shepard	45.00	22.00	13.50
(18)	Ray Scarborough	35.00	17.50	10.50
(19)	Mickey Vernon	35.00	17.50	10.50
(20)	Early Wynn	45.00	22.00	13.50
(21)	Eddie Yost	35.00	17.50	10.50

1976 Safelon discs

One of several regional sponsors of player disc sets in 1976, Safelon, of New York, advertised its "Super Star Lunch Bags" in red and purple on the backs of its discs. The discs are 3-3/8" diameter with a black-and-white player portrait photo in the center of the baseball design. A line of red stars is above, while the left and right panels feature one of several bright colors. Produced by Michael Schechter Associates under license from the Major League Baseball Players Association, the player photos have had uniform and cap logos removed. The unnumbered checklist here is presented in alphabetical order.

		NM	EX	VG
Complete Set (70):		250.00	125.00	75.00
Common Player:		4.00	2.00	1.25
(1)	Henry Aaron	35.00	17.50	10.50
(2)	Johnny Bench	20.00	10.00	6.00
(3)	Vida Blue	4.00	2.00	1.25
(4)	Larry Bowa	4.00	2.00	1.25
(5)	Lou Brock	12.00	6.00	3.50
(6)	Jeff Burroughs	4.00	2.00	1.25
(7)	John Candelaria	4.00	2.00	1.25
(8)	Jose Cardenal	4.00	2.00	1.25
(9)	Rod Carew	12.00	6.00	3.50
(10)	Steve Carlton	12.00	6.00	3.50
(11)	Dave Cash	4.00	2.00	1.25
(12)	Cesar Cedeno	4.00	2.00	1.25
(13)	Ron Cey	4.00	2.00	1.25
(14)	Carlton Fisk	12.00	6.00	3.50
(15)	Tito Fuentes	4.00	2.00	1.25
(16)	Steve Garvey	12.00	6.00	3.50
(17)	Ken Griffey	4.00	2.00	1.25
(18)	Don Gullett	4.00	2.00	1.25
(19)	Willie Horton	4.00	2.00	1.25
(20)	Al Hrabosky	4.00	2.00	1.25
(21)	Catfish Hunter	12.00	6.00	3.50
(22)	Reggie Jackson	25.00	12.50	7.50
(23)	Randy Jones	4.00	2.00	1.25
(24)	Jim Kaat	5.00	2.50	1.50
(25)	Don Kessinger	4.00	2.00	1.25
(26)	Dave Kingman	6.00	3.00	1.75
(27)	Jerry Koosman	4.00	2.00	1.25
(28)	Mickey Lolich	5.00	2.50	1.50
(29)	Greg Luzinski	4.00	2.00	1.25
(30)	Fred Lynn	5.00	2.50	1.50
(31)	Bill Madlock	4.00	2.00	1.25
(32)	Carlos May	4.00	2.00	1.25
(33)	John Mayberry	4.00	2.00	1.25
(34)	Bake McBride	4.00	2.00	1.25
(35)	Doc Medich	4.00	2.00	1.25
(36)	Andy Messersmith	4.00	2.00	1.25
(37)	Rick Monday	4.00	2.00	1.25
(38)	John Montefusco	4.00	2.00	1.25
(39)	Jerry Morales	4.00	2.00	1.25
(40)	Joe Morgan	12.00	6.00	3.50
(41)	Thurman Munson	14.00	7.00	4.25
(42)	Bobby Murcer	4.00	2.00	1.25
(43)	Al Oliver	4.00	2.00	1.25
(44)	Jim Palmer	12.00	6.00	3.50
(45)	Dave Parker	6.00	3.00	1.75
(46)	Tony Perez	12.00	6.00	3.50
(47)	Jerry Reuss	4.00	2.00	1.25
(48)	Brooks Robinson	15.00	7.50	4.50
(49)	Frank Robinson	15.00	7.50	4.50
(50)	Steve Rogers	4.00	2.00	1.25
(51)	Pete Rose	30.00	15.00	9.00
(52)	Nolan Ryan	65.00	32.00	19.50
(53)	Manny Sanguillen	4.00	2.00	1.25
(54)	Mike Schmidt	25.00	12.50	7.50
(55)	Tom Seaver	15.00	7.50	4.50
(56)	Ted Simmons	4.00	2.00	1.25
(57)	Reggie Smith	4.00	2.00	1.25
(58)	Willie Stargell	12.00	6.00	3.50
(59)	Rusty Staub	5.00	2.50	1.50
(60)	Rennie Stennett	4.00	2.00	1.25
(61)	Don Sutton	12.00	6.00	3.50
(62)	Andy Thornton	4.00	2.00	1.25
(63)	Luis Tiant	4.00	2.00	1.25
(64)	Joe Torre	4.00	2.00	1.25
(65)	Mike Tyson	4.00	2.00	1.25
(66)	Bob Watson	4.00	2.00	1.25
(67)	Wilbur Wood	4.00	2.00	1.25
(68)	Jimmy Wynn	4.00	2.00	1.25
(69)	Carl Yastrzemski	17.50	8.75	5.25
(70)	Richie Zisk	4.00	2.00	1.25

1977 Saga discs

Virtually identical in format to the several locally sponsored disc sets of the previous year, these 3-3/8" diameter player discs were given away with the purchase of school lunches in the Philadelphia area. They are the scarcest of the 1977 disc sets. Discs once again feature black-and-white player portrait photos in the center of a baseball design. The left and right panels are in one of several bright colors. Licensed by the players' association through Mike Schechter Associates, the player photos carry no uniform logos. Backs are printed in orange with background art of a sunrise over the mountains. The unnumbered discs are checklisted here alphabetically.

		NM	EX	VG
Complete Set (70):		1200.	600.00	360.00
Common Player:		15.00	7.50	4.50
(1)	Sal Bando	15.00	7.50	4.50
(2)	Buddy Bell	15.00	7.50	4.50
(3)	Johnny Bench	75.00	37.00	22.00
(4)	Larry Bowa	15.00	7.50	4.50
(5)	Steve Braun	15.00	7.50	4.50
(6)	George Brett	125.00	62.00	37.00
(7)	Lou Brock	60.00	30.00	18.00
(8)	Jeff Burroughs	15.00	7.50	4.50
(9)	Bert Campaneris	15.00	7.50	4.50

(10)	John Candelaria	15.00	7.50	4.50
(11)	Jose Cardenal	15.00	7.50	4.50
(12)	Rod Carew	60.00	30.00	18.00
(13)	Steve Carlton	60.00	30.00	18.00
(14)	Dave Cash	15.00	7.50	4.50
(15)	Cesar Cedeno	15.00	7.50	4.50
(16)	Ron Cey	15.00	7.50	4.50
(17)	Dave Concepcion	15.00	7.50	4.50
(18)	Dennis Eckersley	45.00	22.00	13.50
(19)	Mark Fidrych	40.00	20.00	12.00
(20)	Rollie Fingers	60.00	30.00	18.00
(21)	Carlton Fisk	60.00	30.00	18.00
(22)	George Foster	15.00	7.50	4.50
(23)	Wayne Garland	15.00	7.50	4.50
(24)	Ralph Garr	15.00	7.50	4.50
(25)	Steve Garvey	40.00	20.00	12.00
(26)	Cesar Geronimo	15.00	7.50	4.50
(27)	Bobby Grich	15.00	7.50	4.50
(28)	Ken Griffey Sr.	20.00	10.00	6.00
(29)	Don Gullett	15.00	7.50	4.50
(30)	Mike Hargrove	15.00	7.50	4.50
(31)	Willie Horton	15.00	7.50	4.50
(32)	Al Hrabosky	15.00	7.50	4.50
(33)	Reggie Jackson	75.00	37.00	22.00
(34)	Randy Jones	15.00	7.50	4.50
(35)	Dave Kingman	25.00	12.50	7.50
(36)	Jerry Koosman	15.00	7.50	4.50
(37)	Dave LaRoche	15.00	7.50	4.50
(38)	Greg Luzinski	15.00	7.50	4.50
(39)	Fred Lynn	15.00	7.50	4.50
(40)	Bill Madlock	15.00	7.50	4.50
(41)	Rick Manning	15.00	7.50	4.50
(42)	Jon Matlock	15.00	7.50	4.50
(43)	John Mayberry	15.00	7.50	4.50
(44)	Hal McRae	15.00	7.50	4.50
(45)	Andy Messersmith	15.00	7.50	4.50
(46)	Rick Monday	15.00	7.50	4.50
(47)	John Montefusco	15.00	7.50	4.50
(48)	Joe Morgan	60.00	30.00	18.00
(49)	Thurman Munson	75.00	37.00	22.00
(50)	Bobby Murcer	15.00	7.50	4.50
(51)	Bill North	15.00	7.50	4.50
(52)	Jim Palmer	60.00	30.00	18.00
(53)	Tony Perez	60.00	30.00	18.00
(54)	Jerry Reuss	15.00	7.50	4.50
(55)	Pete Rose	125.00	62.00	37.00
(56)	Joe Rudi	15.00	7.50	4.50
(57)	Nolan Ryan	250.00	125.00	75.00
(58)	Manny Sanguillen	15.00	7.50	4.50
(59)	Mike Schmidt	100.00	50.00	30.00
(60)	Tom Seaver	60.00	30.00	18.00
(61)	Bill Singer	15.00	7.50	4.50
(62)	Willie Stargell	60.00	30.00	18.00
(63)	Rusty Staub	18.50	9.25	5.50
(64)	Luis Tiant	15.00	7.50	4.50
(65)	Mike Tyson	15.00	7.50	4.50
(66)	Bob Watson	15.00	7.50	4.50
(67)	Butch Wynegar	15.00	7.50	4.50
(68)	Carl Yastrzemski	60.00	30.00	18.00
(69)	Robin Yount	60.00	30.00	18.00
(70)	Richie Zisk	15.00	7.50	4.50

1978 Saga discs

One player from each major league team was selected for inclusion in this disc set distributed by Saga, a provider of school lunches; discs were given one per lunch purchase at selected schools. The 3-3/8" diameter discs have a sepia-toned player portrait photo at center within a white diamond and surrounded by a brightly colored border with four colored stars at top. Licensed by the players' association through Michael Schechter Associates, the photos have had uniform logos removed. Backs are nearly identical to the previous year, but printed in red. The unnumbered Saga discs are checklisted here according to the numbers found on the Big T/Tastee Freeze versions.

		NM	EX	VG
Complete Set (26):		400.00	200.00	120.00
Common Player:		10.00	5.00	3.00
(1)	Buddy Bell	10.00	5.00	3.00
(2)	Jim Palmer	24.00	12.00	7.25
(3)	Steve Garvey	16.00	8.00	4.75
(4)	Jeff Burroughs	10.00	5.00	3.00
(5)	Greg Luzinski	10.00	5.00	3.00
(6)	Lou Brock	24.00	12.00	7.25
(7)	Thurman Munson	24.00	12.00	7.25
(8)	Rod Carew	24.00	12.00	7.25
(9)	George Brett	60.00	30.00	18.00
(10)	Tom Seaver	30.00	15.00	9.00
(11)	Willie Stargell	24.00	12.00	7.25
(12)	Jerry Koosman	10.00	5.00	3.00
(13)	Bill North	10.00	5.00	3.00
(14)	Richie Zisk	10.00	5.00	3.00
(15)	Bill Madlock	10.00	5.00	3.00
(16)	Carl Yastrzemski	30.00	15.00	9.00
(17)	Dave Cash	10.00	5.00	3.00
(18)	Bob Watson	10.00	5.00	3.00
(19)	Dave Kingman	12.50	6.25	3.75
(20)	Gene Tenance (Tenace)	10.00	5.00	3.00
(21)	Ralph Garr	10.00	5.00	3.00
(22)	Mark Fidrych	12.50	6.25	3.75
(23)	Frank Tanana	10.00	5.00	3.00
(24)	Larry Hisle	10.00	5.00	3.00
(25)	Bruce Bochte	10.00	5.00	3.00
(26)	Bob Bailor	10.00	5.00	3.00

1962 Salada-Junket Coins

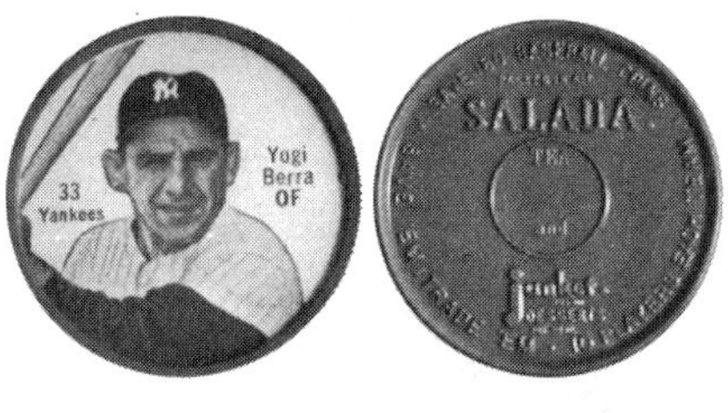

These 1-3/8" diameter plastic coins were issued in packages of Salada Tea and Junket Pudding mix. There are 221 different players available, with variations bringing the total of different coins to 261. Each coin has a paper color photo inserted in the front which contains the player's name and position plus the coin number. The plastic rims come in six different colors, coded by team. Production began with 180 coins, but the addition of the New York Mets and Houston Colt .45's to the National League allowed the company to expand the set's size. Twenty expansion players were added along with 21 other players. Several players' coins were dropped after the initial 180 run, causing some scarcities.

		NM	EX	VG
Complete Set, no variations (221):		2000.	1000.	600.00
Complete Set, w/ variations (261):		5000.	2500.	1500.
Complete Boxed Presentation Set (180):		1750.	875.00	525.00
Common Player (1-180):		3.50	1.75	1.00
Common Player (181-221):		9.00	4.50	2.75
1	Jim Gentile	5.00	2.50	1.50
2	Bill Pierce	85.00	42.00	25.00
3	Chico Fernandez	3.50	1.75	1.00
4	Tom Brewer	20.00	10.00	6.00
5	Woody Held	3.50	1.75	1.00
6	Ray Herbert	24.00	12.00	7.25
7a	Ken Aspromonte (Angels)	12.00	6.00	3.50
7b	Ken Aspromonte (Indians)	5.50	2.75	1.75
8	Whitey Ford	27.00	13.50	8.00
9	Jim Lemon	3.50	1.75	1.00
10	Billy Klaus	3.50	1.75	1.00
11	Steve Barber	38.00	19.00	11.50
12	Nellie Fox	18.00	9.00	5.50
13	Jim Bunning	12.00	6.00	3.50
14	Frank Malzone	5.50	2.75	1.75
15	Tito Francona	3.50	1.75	1.00
16	Bobby Del Greco	3.50	1.75	1.00
17a	Steve Bilko (red shirt buttons)	7.75	4.00	2.25
17b	Steve Bilko (white shirt buttons)	6.00	3.00	1.75
18	Tony Kubek	60.00	30.00	18.00
19	Earl Battey	3.50	1.75	1.00
20	Chuck Cottier	3.50	1.75	1.00
21	Willie Tasby	3.50	1.75	1.00
22	Bob Allison	4.25	2.25	1.25
23	Roger Maris	34.00	17.00	10.00
24a	Earl Averill (red shirt buttons)	7.75	4.00	2.25
24b	Earl Averill (white shirt buttons)	4.25	2.25	1.25
25	Jerry Lumpe	3.50	1.75	1.00
26	Jim Grant	20.00	10.00	6.00
27	Carl Yastrzemski	65.00	32.00	19.50
28	Rocky Colavito	14.00	7.00	4.25
29	Al Smith	3.50	1.75	1.00
30	Jim Busby	36.00	18.00	11.00
31	Dick Howser	3.50	1.75	1.00
32	Jim Perry	3.50	1.75	1.00
33	Yogi Berra	35.00	17.50	10.50
34a	Ken Hamlin (red shirt buttons)	7.75	4.00	2.25
34b	Ken Hamlin (white shirt buttons)	4.25	2.25	1.25
35	Dale Long	3.50	1.75	1.00
36	Harmon Killebrew	22.00	11.00	6.50
37	Dick Brown	3.50	1.75	1.00
38	Gary Geiger	3.50	1.75	1.00
39a	Minnie Minoso (White Sox)	27.00	13.50	8.00
39b	Minnie Minoso (Cardinals)	12.50	6.25	3.75
40	Brooks Robinson	39.00	19.50	11.50
41	Mickey Mantle	120.00	60.00	36.00
42	Bennie Daniels	3.50	1.75	1.00
43	Billy Martin	12.00	6.00	3.50
44	Vic Power	5.50	2.75	1.75
45	Joe Pignatano	3.50	1.75	1.00
46a	Ryne Duren (red shirt buttons)	7.75	4.00	2.25
46b	Ryne Duren (white shirt buttons)	5.50	2.75	1.75
47a	Pete Runnels (2B)	11.00	5.50	3.25
47b	Pete Runnels (1B)	6.50	3.25	2.00
48a	Dick Williams (name on right)	1100.	550.00	330.00
48b	Dick Williams (name on left)	4.25	2.25	1.25
49	Jim Landis	3.50	1.75	1.00
50	Steve Boros	3.50	1.75	1.00
51a	Zoilo Versalles (red shirt buttons)	7.75	4.00	2.25
51b	Zoilo Versalles (white shirt buttons)	5.50	2.75	1.75
52a	Johnny Temple (Indians)	19.00	9.50	5.75
52b	Johnny Temple (Orioles)	5.50	2.75	1.75
53a	Jackie Brandt (Oriole)	8.50	4.25	2.50
53b	Jackie Brandt (Orioles)	925.00	462.00	277.00
54	Joe McClain	3.50	1.75	1.00
55	Sherman Lollar	5.50	2.75	1.75
56	Gene Stephens	3.50	1.75	1.00
57a	Leon Wagner (red shirt buttons)	7.75	4.00	2.25
57b	Leon Wagner (white shirt buttons)	5.50	2.75	1.75
58	Frank Lary	3.50	1.75	1.00
59	Bill Skowron	7.75	4.00	2.25
60	Vic Wertz	6.50	3.25	2.00
61	Willie Kirkland	3.50	1.75	1.00
62	Leo Posada	3.50	1.75	1.00
63a	Albie Pearson (red shirt buttons)	7.75	4.00	2.25
63b	Albie Pearson (white shirt buttons)	4.25	2.25	1.25
64	Bobby Richardson	13.00	6.50	4.00
65a	Marv Breeding (SS)	14.00	7.00	4.25
65b	Marv Breeding (2B)	7.50	3.75	2.25
66	Roy Sievers	85.00	42.00	25.00
67	Al Kaline	35.00	17.50	10.50
68a	Don Buddin (Red Sox)	17.50	8.75	5.25
68b	Don Buddin (Colts)	5.00	2.50	1.50
69a	Lenny Green (red shirt buttons)	7.75	4.00	2.25
69B	Lenny Green (white shirt buttons)	5.50	2.75	1.75
70	Gene Green	35.00	17.50	10.50
71	Luis Aparicio	15.00	7.50	4.50
72	Norm Cash	7.75	4.00	2.25
73	Jackie Jensen	42.00	21.00	12.50
74	Bubba Phillips	3.50	1.75	1.00
75	Jim Archer	3.50	1.75	1.00
76a	Ken Hunt (red shirt buttons)	7.75	4.00	2.25
76b	Ken Hunt (white shirt buttons)	4.25	2.25	1.25
77	Ralph Terry	4.25	2.25	1.25
78	Camilo Pascual	3.50	1.75	1.00
79	Marty Keough	38.00	19.00	11.50
80	Cletis Boyer	5.00	2.50	1.50
81	Jim Pagliaroni	3.50	1.75	1.00
82a	Gene Leek (red shirt buttons)	7.75	4.00	2.25
82b	Gene Leek (white shirt buttons)	4.25	2.25	1.25
83	Jake Wood	3.50	1.75	1.00
84	Coot Veal	35.00	17.50	10.50
85	Norm Siebern	5.50	2.75	1.75
86a	Andy Carey (White Sox)	44.00	22.00	13.00
86b	Andy Carey (Phillies)	9.00	4.50	2.75
87a	Bill Tuttle (red shirt buttons)	8.25	4.25	2.50
87b	Bill Tuttle (white shirt buttons)	5.50	2.75	1.75
88a	Jimmy Piersall (Indians)	16.50	8.25	5.00
88b	Jimmy Piersall (Senators)	9.00	4.50	2.75
89	Ron Hansen	45.00	22.00	13.50
90a	Chuck Stobbs (red shirt buttons)	7.75	4.00	2.25
90b	Chuck Stobbs (white shirt buttons)	4.25	2.25	1.25
91a	Ken McBride (red shirt buttons)	7.75	4.00	2.25
91b	Ken McBride (white shirt buttons)	4.25	2.25	1.25
92	Bill Bruton	3.50	1.75	1.00
93	Gus Triandos	3.50	1.75	1.00
94	John Romano	3.50	1.75	1.00
95	Elston Howard	7.75	4.00	2.25
96	Gene Woodling	4.25	2.25	1.25
97a	Early Wynn (pitching pose)	75.00	37.00	22.00
97b	Early Wynn (portrait)	21.00	10.50	6.25
98	Milt Pappas	4.25	2.25	1.25
99	Bill Monbouquette	3.50	1.75	1.00
100	Wayne Causey	3.50	1.75	1.00
101	Don Elston	3.50	1.75	1.00
102a	Charlie Neal (Dodgers)	13.50	6.75	4.00
102b	Charlie Neal (Mets)	4.25	2.25	1.25
103	Don Blasingame	3.50	1.75	1.00
104	Frank Thomas	41.00	20.00	12.50
105	Wes Covington	4.25	2.25	1.25
106	Chuck Hiller	3.50	1.75	1.00
107	Don Hoak	4.25	2.25	1.25
108a	Bob Lillis (Cardinals)	33.00	16.50	10.00
108b	Bob Lillis (Colts)	4.25	2.25	1.25
109	Sandy Koufax	42.00	21.00	12.50
110	Gordy Coleman	3.50	1.75	1.00
111	Ed Matthews (Mathews)	20.00	10.00	6.00
112	Art Mahaffey	4.25	2.25	1.25
113a	Ed Bailey (red period above "i" in Giants)	12.00	6.00	3.50
113b	Ed Bailey (white period)	4.25	2.25	1.25
114	Smoky Burgess	5.50	2.75	1.75
115	Bill White	6.00	3.00	1.75
116	Ed Bouchee	27.00	13.50	8.00
117	Bob Buhl	3.50	1.75	1.00
118	Vada Pinson	4.25	2.25	1.25
119	Carl Sawatski	3.50	1.75	1.00
120	Dick Stuart	4.25	2.25	1.25
121	Harvey Kuenn	70.00	35.00	21.00
122	Pancho Herrera	3.50	1.75	1.00
123a	Don Zimmer (Cubs)	13.00	6.50	4.00
123b	Don Zimmer (Mets)	5.50	2.75	1.75
124	Wally Moon	4.25	2.25	1.25
125	Joe Adcock	5.50	2.75	1.75
126	Joey Jay	3.50	1.75	1.00
127a	Maury Wills (blue "3" on shirt)	16.00	8.00	4.75
127b	Maury Wills (red "3" on shirt)	7.50	3.75	2.25
128	George Altman	3.50	1.75	1.00

129a	John Buzhardt (Phillies)	19.00	9.50	5.75
129b	John Buzhardt (White Sox)	5.50	2.75	1.75
130	Felipe Alou	4.25	2.25	1.25
131	Bill Mazeroski	10.00	5.00	3.00
132	Ernie Broglio	3.50	1.75	1.00
133	John Roseboro	4.25	2.25	1.25
134	Mike McCormick	3.50	1.75	1.00
135a	Chuck Smith (Phillies)	20.00	10.00	6.00
135b	Chuck Smith (White Sox)	6.50	3.25	2.00
136	Ron Santo	5.50	2.75	1.75
137	Gene Freese	3.50	1.75	1.00
138	Dick Groat	5.50	2.75	1.75
139	Curt Flood	4.25	2.25	1.25
140	Frank Bolling	3.50	1.75	1.00
141	Clay Dalrymple	3.50	1.75	1.00
142	Willie McCovey	35.00	17.50	10.50
143	Bob Skinner	3.50	1.75	1.00
144	Lindy McDaniel	3.50	1.75	1.00
145	Glen Hobbie	3.50	1.75	1.00
146a	Gil Hodges (Dodgers)	37.50	18.50	11.00
146b	Gil Hodges (Mets)	30.00	15.00	9.00
147	Eddie Kasko	3.50	1.75	1.00
148	Gino Cimoli	50.00	25.00	15.00
149	Willie Mays	70.00	35.00	21.00
150	Roberto Clemente	75.00	37.00	22.00
151	Red Schoendienst	6.50	3.25	2.00
152	Joe Torre	5.00	2.50	1.50
153	Bob Purkey	3.50	1.75	1.00
154a	Tommy Davis (3B)	11.00	5.50	3.25
154b	Tommy Davis (OF)	5.50	2.75	1.75
155a	Andre Rogers (incorrect spelling)	11.00	5.50	3.25
155b	Andre Rodgers (correct spelling)	4.25	2.25	1.25
156	Tony Taylor	3.50	1.75	1.00
157	Bob Friend	3.50	1.75	1.00
158a	Gus Bell (Redlegs)	9.00	4.50	2.75
158b	Gus Bell (Mets)	4.25	2.25	1.25
159	Roy McMillan	3.50	1.75	1.00
160	Carl Warwick	3.50	1.75	1.00
161	Willie Davis	4.25	2.25	1.25
162	Sam Jones	65.00	32.00	19.50
163	Ruben Amaro	3.50	1.75	1.00
164	Sam Taylor	3.50	1.75	1.00
165	Frank Robinson	27.50	13.50	8.25
166	Lou Burdette	5.50	2.75	1.75
167	Ken Boyer	5.50	2.75	1.75
168	Bill Virdon	4.25	2.25	1.25
169	Jim Davenport	3.50	1.75	1.00
170	Don Demeter	3.50	1.75	1.00
171	Richie Ashburn	45.00	22.00	13.50
172	John Podres	4.25	2.25	1.25
173a	Joe Cunningham (Cardinals)	45.00	22.00	13.50
173b	Joe Cunningham (White Sox)	12.50	6.25	3.75
174	ElRoy Face	5.50	2.75	1.75
175	Orlando Cepeda	9.00	4.50	2.75
176a	Bobby Gene Smith (Phillies)	22.00	11.00	6.50
176b	Bobby Gene Smith (Mets)	7.00	3.50	2.00
177a	Ernie Banks (OF)	57.00	28.00	17.00
177b	Ernie Banks (SS)	27.00	13.50	8.00
178a	Daryl Spencer (3B)	16.50	8.25	5.00
178b	Daryl Spencer (1B)	4.25	2.25	1.25
179	Bob Schmidt	28.00	14.00	8.50
180	Hank Aaron	65.00	32.00	19.50
181	Hobie Landrith	9.00	4.50	2.75
182a	Ed Broussard	400.00	200.00	120.00
182b	Ed Bressoud	38.00	19.00	11.50
183	Felix Mantilla	9.00	4.50	2.75
184	Dick Farrell	9.00	4.50	2.75
185	Bob Miller	9.00	4.50	2.75
186	Don Taussig	9.00	4.50	2.75
187	Pumpsie Green	14.00	7.00	4.25
188	Bobby Shantz	11.00	5.50	3.25
189	Roger Craig	12.00	6.00	3.50
190	Hal Smith	9.00	4.50	2.75
191	John Edwards	12.00	6.00	3.50
192	John DeMerit	9.00	4.50	2.75
193	Joe Amalfitano	9.00	4.50	2.75
194	Norm Larker	9.00	4.50	2.75
195	Al Heist	9.00	4.50	2.75
196	Al Spangler	9.00	4.50	2.75
197	Alex Grammas	9.00	4.50	2.75
198	Gerry Lynch	12.00	6.00	3.50
199	Jim McKnight	9.00	4.50	2.75
200	Jose Pagen (Pagan)	9.00	4.50	2.75
201	Junior Gilliam	24.00	12.00	7.25
202	Art Ditmar	9.00	4.50	2.75
203	Pete Daley	9.00	4.50	2.75
204	Johnny Callison	28.00	14.00	8.50
205	Stu Miller	9.00	4.50	2.75
206	Russ Snyder	12.00	6.00	3.50
207	Billy Williams	30.00	15.00	9.00
208	Walter Bond	9.00	4.50	2.75
209	Joe Koppe	9.00	4.50	2.75
210	Don Schwall	33.00	16.50	10.00
211	Billy Gardner	20.00	10.00	6.00
212	Chuck Estrada	9.00	4.50	2.75
213	Gary Bell	12.00	6.00	3.50
214	Floyd Robinson	9.00	4.50	2.75
215	Duke Snider	50.00	25.00	15.00
216	Lee Maye	9.00	4.50	2.75
217	Howie Bedell	9.00	4.50	2.75
218	Bob Will	9.00	4.50	2.75
219	Dallas Green	12.00	6.00	3.50
220	Carroll Hardy	22.00	11.00	6.50
221	Danny O'Connell	12.00	6.00	3.50

1962 Salada-Junket Coins - Clip Back

A very rare version of the Salada Tea/Junket Dessert plastic coins exists in a clip-back format. An extruded tab at back center would allow the coin to be slid onto a cap bill or shirt flap as a decoration. Clip-back pieces of Earl Averill (#24 Angels) and Pete Runnels (#47 Red Sox) are confirmed to exist while other Red Sox players have reportedly been seen.

(Values undetermined)

1963 Salada-Junket Coins

A much smaller set of baseball coins was issued by Salada/Junket in 1963. The 63 coins issued were called "All-Star Baseball Coins" and included most of the top players of the day. Unlike 1962, the coins were made of metal and measured a slightly larger 1-1/2" diameter. American League players have blue rims on their coins, while National Leaguers are rimmed in red. Coin fronts contain no printing on the full-color player photos, while backs list coin number, player name, team and position, along with brief statistics and the sponsors' logos.

		NM	EX	VG
Complete Set (63):		700.00	350.00	225.00
Common Player:		4.00	2.00	1.25
1	Don Drysdale	16.50	8.25	5.00
2	Dick Farrell	4.00	2.00	1.25
3	Bob Gibson	16.50	8.25	5.00
4	Sandy Koufax	30.00	15.00	9.00
5	Juan Marichal	16.50	8.25	5.00
6	Bob Purkey	4.00	2.00	1.25
7	Bob Shaw	4.00	2.00	1.25
8	Warren Spahn	16.50	8.25	5.00
9	Johnny Podres	5.00	2.50	1.50
10	Art Mahaffey	4.00	2.00	1.25
11	Del Crandall	4.00	2.00	1.25
12	John Roseboro	4.00	2.00	1.25
13	Orlando Cepeda	15.00	7.50	4.50
14	Bill Mazeroski	12.00	6.00	3.50
15	Ken Boyer	7.50	3.75	2.25
16	Dick Groat	4.00	2.00	1.25
17	Ernie Banks	18.50	9.25	5.50
18	Frank Bolling	4.00	2.00	1.25
19	Jim Davenport	4.00	2.00	1.25
20	Maury Wills	5.50	2.75	1.75
21	Tommy Davis	4.00	2.00	1.25
22	Willie Mays	50.00	25.00	15.00
23	Roberto Clemente	60.00	30.00	18.00
24	Henry Aaron	50.00	25.00	15.00
25	Felipe Alou	5.00	2.50	1.50
26	Johnny Callison	4.00	2.00	1.25
27	Richie Ashburn	18.50	9.25	5.50
28	Eddie Mathews	18.50	9.25	5.50
29	Frank Robinson	18.50	9.25	5.50
30	Billy Williams	16.50	8.25	5.00
31	George Altman	4.00	2.00	1.25
32	Hank Aguirre	4.00	2.00	1.25
33	Jim Bunning	16.50	8.25	5.00
34	Dick Donovan	4.00	2.00	1.25
35	Bill Monbouquette	4.00	2.00	1.25
36	Camilo Pascual	4.00	2.00	1.25
37	David Stenhouse	4.00	2.00	1.25
38	Ralph Terry	4.00	2.00	1.25
39	Hoyt Wilhelm	16.50	8.25	5.00
40	Jim Kaat	6.00	3.00	1.75
41	Ken McBride	4.00	2.00	1.25
42	Ray Herbert	4.00	2.00	1.25
43	Milt Pappas	4.00	2.00	1.25
44	Earl Battey	4.00	2.00	1.25
45	Elston Howard	6.50	3.25	2.00
46	John Romano	4.00	2.00	1.25
47	Jim Gentile	4.00	2.00	1.25
48	Billy Moran	4.00	2.00	1.25
49	Rich Rollins	4.00	2.00	1.25
50	Luis Aparicio	16.50	8.25	5.00
51	Norm Siebern	4.00	2.00	1.25
52	Bobby Richardson	7.50	3.75	2.25
53	Brooks Robinson	18.50	9.25	5.50
54	Tom Tresh	5.50	2.75	1.75
55	Leon Wagner	4.00	2.00	1.25
56	Mickey Mantle	100.00	50.00	30.00
57	Roger Maris	35.00	17.50	10.50
58	Rocky Colavito	12.00	6.00	3.50
59	Lee Thomas	4.00	2.00	1.25
60	Jim Landis	4.00	2.00	1.25
61	Pete Runnels	4.00	2.00	1.25
62	Yogi Berra	18.50	9.25	5.50
63	Al Kaline	18.50	9.25	5.50

1961 Sam's Family Restaurants Roger Maris

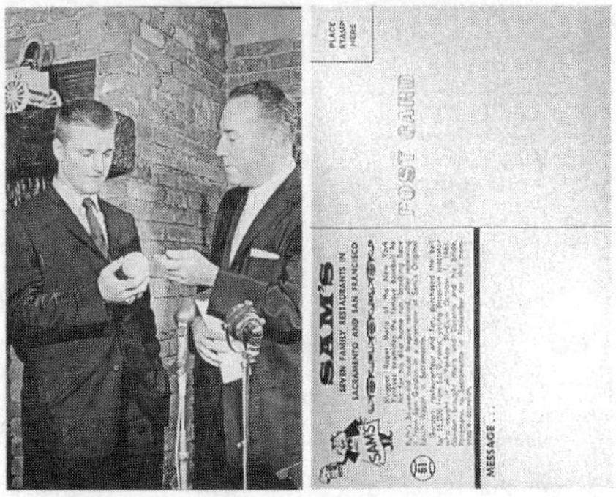

This postcard was issued to commemorate the presentation of Roger Maris' historic 61st home run ball back to the slugger. Pictured with Maris on this color 3-1/2" x 5-1/2" postcard is Sam Gordon, owner of a chain of family restaurants in northern California. Gordon purchased the ball from the fan who caught it, Sal Durante, and flew Durante and his wife, and Maris to Sacramento where he paid $5,000 for the ball and presented it to Maris, who later donated it to the Hall of Fame. On front is a borderless color photo of the presentation. Back has the historical details and the traditional postcard indicia.

		NM	EX	VG
61	Roger Maris, Sam Gordon	125.00	62.00	37.00

1969 San Diego Padres Premium Pictures

Unlike most of the contemporary large-format (8-1/2" x 11") premium pictures, this issue carries no advertising and appears to have been a team-issue in the Padres inaugural year. Fronts feature large portraits and smaller action pictures of the player against a dark background with a facsimile autograph at the bottom and the player's name printed in the white bottom border. The signature of the artist appears in the lower-left corner. The artwork was done by Nicholas Volpe, who produced many similar items for teams in all sports in the '60s, '70s and '80s. Backs have a large team logo at center and a sketch of the artist at bottom. There is evidence to suggest that the picture of Cito Gaston is scarcer than the other seven.

		NM	EX	VG
Complete Set (8):		60.00	30.00	18.00
Common Player:		7.50	3.75	2.25
(1)	Ollie Brown	7.50	3.75	2.25
(2)	Tommy Dean	7.50	3.75	2.25
(3)	Al Ferrara	7.50	3.75	2.25
(4)	Clarence Gaston	10.00	5.00	3.00
(5)	Preston Gomez	7.50	3.75	2.25
(6)	Johnny Podres	9.00	4.50	2.75
(7)	Al Santorini	7.50	3.75	2.25
(8)	Ed Spiezio	7.50	3.75	2.25

1974 San Diego Padres Photocards

This set of player photocards challenges the collector in that the pictured player is not identified anywhere on the card. Fronts of the 3-3/8" x 5-3/8" cards have borderless black-and-white poses with no extraneous graphics. Backs are blank. The unnumbered cards are checklisted here in alphabetical order.

	NM	EX	VG
Complete Set (18):	100.00	50.00	30.00
Common Player:	5.00	2.50	1.50
(1) Bob Barton	5.00	2.50	1.50
(2) Glenn Beckert	6.00	3.00	1.75
(3) Mike Corkins	5.00	2.50	1.50
(4) Dave Freisleben	5.00	2.50	1.50
(5) Bill Greif	5.00	2.50	1.50
(6) Larry Hardy	5.00	2.50	1.50
(7) Randy Jones	5.00	2.50	1.50
(8) Willie McCovey (batting)	10.00	5.00	3.00
(9) Willie McCovey (leaning on bat)	10.00	5.00	3.00
(10) Dave Roberts (catching)	5.00	2.50	1.50
(11) Dave Roberts (leaning on bat)	5.00	2.50	1.50
(12) Vicente Romo	5.00	2.50	1.50
(13) Dan Spillner	5.00	2.50	1.50
(14) Derrel Thomas	5.00	2.50	1.50
(15) Bobby Tolan	5.00	2.50	1.50
(16) Dave Tomlin	5.00	2.50	1.50
(17) Rich Troedson	5.00	2.50	1.50
(18) Dave Winfield	15.00	7.50	4.50

1977 San Diego Padres Schedule Cards

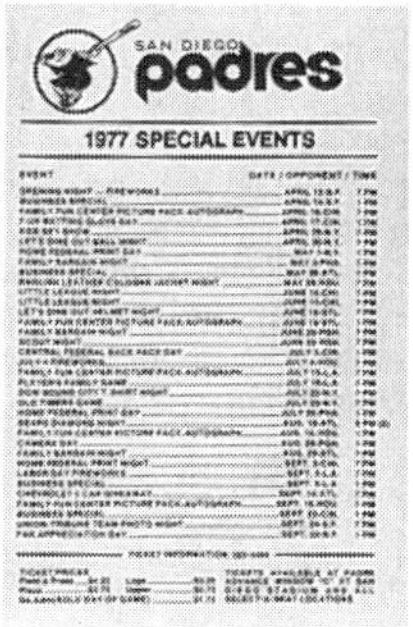

Members of the 1977 San Diego Padres, players and management, are featured in this set. The 2-1/4" x 3-3/8" cards are printed in brown on thin white stock. Fronts have a player photo with a pinstripe around and the team and player name at bottom. Backs have the team logo at top, a list of promotional dates in the center and ticket information at bottom. While some card backs state "One in a Series of 40 Player Photos," more than 80 variations are known, including some poses with blank backs. The unnumbered cards are checklisted here in alphabetical order, within three types differentiated by back printing.

	NM	EX	VG
Complete Set:	80.00	40.00	24.00
Common Player:	1.00	.50	.30
Type I - "Series of 40"			
(1) Bill Almon	1.00	.50	.30
(2) Joe Amalfitano	1.00	.50	.30
(3) Buzzy Bavasi (general manager)	1.00	.50	.30
(4) Vic Bernal	1.00	.50	.30
(5) Mike Champion	1.00	.50	.30
(7) Roger Craig	1.50	1.25	.60
(8) John D'Acquisto	1.00	.50	.30
(9) Bob Davis	1.00	.50	.30
(10) Rollie Fingers	3.00	2.25	1.25
(11) Dave Freisleben	1.00	.50	.30
(12) Tom Griffin	1.00	.50	.30
(13) George Hendrick	1.00	.50	.30
(14) Enzo Hernandez	1.00	.50	.30
(15) Mike Ivie	1.00	.50	.30
(16) Randy Jones (follow-through)	1.00	.50	.30
(17) Randy Jones (Cy Young Award)	1.00	.50	.30
(18) John McNamara	1.00	.50	.30
(19) Luis Melendez	1.00	.50	.30
(20) Butch Metzger	1.00	.50	.30
(21) Bob Owchinko	1.00	.50	.30
(22) Doug Rader	1.00	.50	.30
(23) Merv Rettenmund	1.00	.50	.30
(24) Gene Richards	1.00	.50	.30
(25) Dave Roberts	1.00	.50	.30
(26) Rick Sawyer	1.00	.50	.30
(27) Bob Shirley	1.00	.50	.30
(28) Bob Skinner	1.00	.50	.30
(29) Dan Spillner	1.00	.50	.30
(30) Brent Strom	1.00	.50	.30
(31) Gary Sutherland	1.00	.50	.30
(32) Gene Tenace	1.00	.50	.30
(33) Dave Tomlin	1.00	.50	.30
(34) Jerry Turner	1.00	.50	.30
(35) Bobby Valentine	1.00	.50	.30
(36) Dan Wehrmeister	1.00	.50	.30
(37) Whitey Wietelmann	1.00	.50	.30
(38) Don Williams	1.00	.50	.30
(39) Dave Winfield (one bat)	4.00	2.00	1.25
(40) Dave Winfield (two bats)	4.00	2.00	1.25
Type II - No "Series of 40"			
(1) Bill Almon	1.00	.50	.30
(2) Matty Alou	1.00	.50	.30
(3) Steve Arlin (glove to chest)	1.00	.50	.30
(4) Steve Arlin (follow-through)	1.00	.50	.30
(5) Bob Barton, Glenn Beckert	1.00	.50	.30
(6) Ollie Brown	1.00	.50	.30
(7) Dave Campbell (bat on shoulder)	1.00	.50	.30
(8) Dave Campbell (kneeling)	1.00	.50	.30
(9) Mike Champion, Bill Almon	1.00	.50	.30
(10) Nate Colbert	1.00	.50	.30
(11) Colbert and Friend (with child)	1.00	.50	.30
(12) Jerry Coleman (announcer)	1.00	.50	.30
(13) Willie Davis	1.00	.50	.30
(14) Jim Eakle ("TUBA MAN")	1.00	.50	.30
(15) Rollie Fingers	3.00	2.25	1.25
(16) Cito Gaston (bare hands)	1.50	1.25	.60
(17) Cito Gaston (batting gloves)	1.50	1.25	.60
(18) Johnny Grubb	1.00	.50	.30
(19) George Hendrick	1.00	.50	.30
(20) Enzo Hernandez and Note Colbert	1.00	.50	.30
(21) Mike Ivie	1.00	.50	.30
(22) Fred Kendall (batting)	1.00	.50	.30
(23) Fred Kendall (holding ball)	1.00	.50	.30
(24) Clay Kirby (follow-through)	1.00	.50	.30
(25) Clay Kirby (glove to chest)	1.00	.50	.30
(26) Dave Marshall	1.00	.50	.30
(27) Willie McCovey (moustache)	4.00	3.00	1.50
(28) John McNamara	1.00	.50	.30
(29) Bob Miller	1.00	.50	.30
(30) Fred Norman (arms above head)	1.00	.50	.30
(31) Fred Norman (kneeling)	1.00	.50	.30
(32) Gene Richards	1.00	.50	.30
(33) Ballard Smith (general manager)	1.00	.50	.30
(34) Ed Spiezio	1.00	.50	.30
(35) Derrell Thomas (glasses)	1.00	.50	.30
(36) Derrell Thomas (no glasses)	1.00	.50	.30
(37) Bobby Tolan (batting)	1.00	.50	.30
(38) Bobby Tolan (kneeling)	1.00	.50	.30
(39) Jerry Turner	1.00	.50	.30
(40) Dave Winfield	4.00	2.00	1.25
Type III - Blank back			
(1) Nate Colbert	1.00	.50	.30
(2) Dave Freisleben	1.00	.50	.30
(3) Mike Ivie	1.00	.50	.30
(4) Randy Jones and Bowie Kuhn	1.00	.50	.30
(5) Mike Kilkenny	1.00	.50	.30
(6) Ray Kroc (owner)	1.00	.50	.30
(7) Willie McCovey	4.00	3.00	1.50
(8) John McNamara (facing his right)	1.00	.50	.30
(9) Dave Winfield	4.00	2.00	1.25

1958 San Francisco Call-Bulletin Giants

These unnumbered cards, picturing members of the San Francisco Giants, were inserted in copies of the San Francisco Call-Bulletin newspaper as part of a promotional contest. The 25 cards in the set measure 2" x 4" and were printed on orange paper. The top of the card contains a black and white player photo, while the bottom contains a perforated stub with a serial number used to win prizes. (Cards without the stub intact are approximately 50 percent of the prices listed.) The contest name, "Giant Payoff", appears prominently on both sides of the stub. The back of the card contains a 1958 Giants schedule.

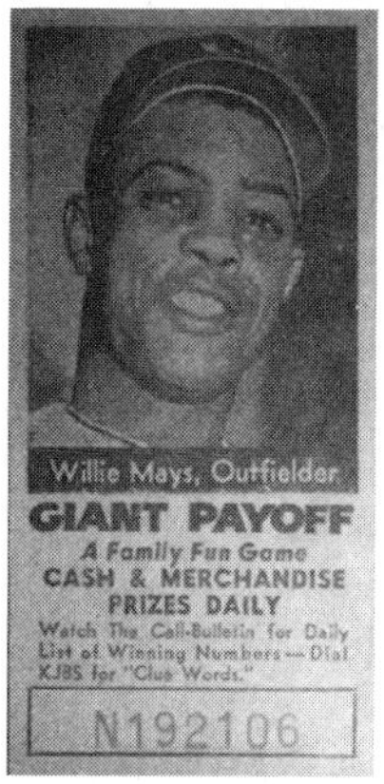

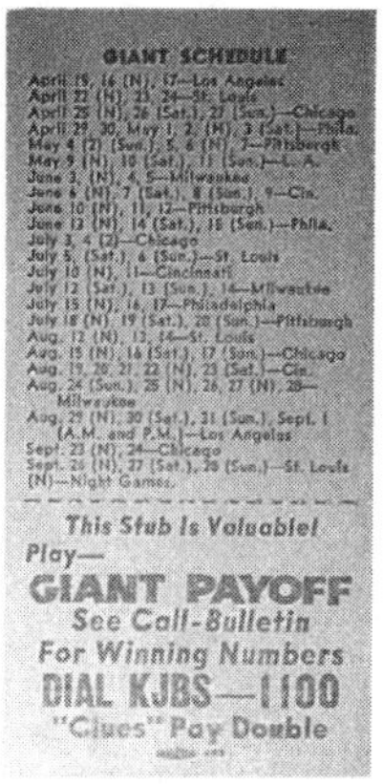

	NM	EX	VG
Complete Set (25):	1000.	500.00	300.00
Common Player:	12.50	6.25	3.75
(1) Johnny Antonelli	12.50	6.25	3.75
(2) Curt Barclay	12.50	6.25	3.75
(3) Tom Bowers	400.00	200.00	120.00
(4) Ed Bressoud	75.00	37.00	22.00
(5) Orlando Cepeda	75.00	37.00	22.00
(6) Ray Crone	12.50	6.25	3.75
(7) Jim Davenport	12.50	6.25	3.75
(8) Paul Giel	12.50	6.25	3.75
(9) Ruben Gomez	12.50	6.25	3.75
(10) Marv Grissom	12.50	6.25	3.75
(11) Ray Jablonski	75.00	37.00	22.00
(12) Willie Kirkland	80.00	40.00	24.00
(13) Whitey Lockman	12.50	6.25	3.75
(14) Willie Mays	275.00	137.00	82.00
(15) Mike McCormick	12.50	6.25	3.75
(16) Stu Miller	12.50	6.25	3.75
(17) Ramon Monzant	12.50	6.25	3.75
(18) Danny O'Connell	12.50	6.25	3.75
(19) Bill Rigney	12.50	6.25	3.75
(20) Hank Sauer	12.50	6.25	3.75
(21) Bob Schmidt	12.50	6.25	3.75
(22) Daryl Spencer	12.50	6.25	3.75
(23) Valmy Thomas	12.50	6.25	3.75
(24) Bobby Thomson	25.00	12.50	7.50
(25) Allan Worthington	12.50	6.25	3.75

1977 San Francisco Giants team issue

These 3-1/2" x 5" blank-back cards feature black-and-white player photos surrounded by an orange frame with black borders. The manager, coaches and instructors are featured along with players in the issue. The unnumbered cards are checklisted here in alphabetical order.

	NM	EX	VG
Complete Set (25):	45.00	22.00	13.50
Common Player:	2.00	1.00	.60
(1) Joe Altobelli	2.00	1.00	.60
(2) Jim Barr	2.00	1.00	.60
(3) Jack Clark	4.00	2.00	1.25
(4) Terry Cornutt	2.00	1.00	.60
(5) Rob Dressler	2.00	1.00	.60
(6) Darrell Evans	3.00	1.50	.90
(7) Frank Funk	2.00	1.00	.60
(8) Ed Halicki	2.00	1.00	.60
(9) Tom Haller	2.00	1.00	.60
(10) Marc Hill	2.00	1.00	.60
(11) Skip James	2.00	1.00	.60
(12) Bob Knepper	2.00	1.00	.60
(13) Gary Lavelle	2.00	1.00	.60
(14) Bill Madlock	2.50	1.25	.70
(15) Willie McCovey	8.00	4.00	2.50
(16) Randy Moffitt	2.00	1.00	.60
(17) John Montefusco	2.00	1.00	.60
(18) Marty Perez	2.00	1.00	.60
(19) Frank Riccelli	2.00	1.00	.60
(20) Mike Sadek	2.00	1.00	.60
(21) Hank Sauer	2.00	1.00	.60
(22) Chris Speier	2.00	1.00	.60

(23)	Gary Thomasson	2.00	1.00	.60
(24)	Tommy Toms	2.00	1.00	.60
(25)	Bobby Winkles	2.00	1.00	.60

1979 San Francisco Giants Police

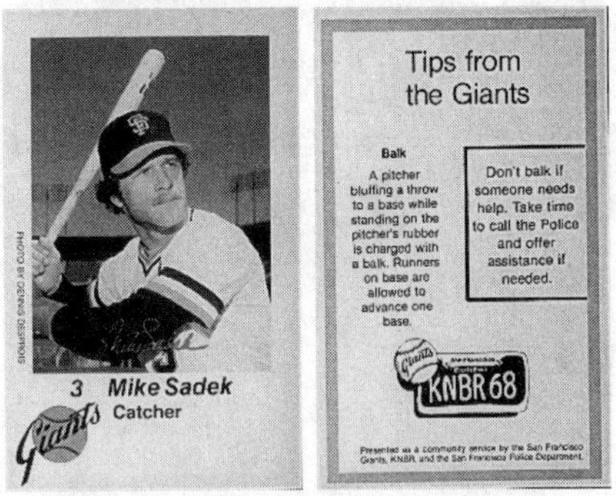

Each of the full-color cards measures 2-5/8" x 4-1/8" and is numbered by player uniform number. The set includes players and coaches. The player's name, position and facsimile autograph are on front, along with the Giants logo. Backs have a "Tip from the Giants" and sponsor logos for the Giants and radio station KNBR, all printed in orange and black. Half of the set was distributed as a ballpark promotion, while the other cards were available from police agencies in several San Francisco Bay area counties.

		NM	EX	VG
Complete Set (29):		15.00	7.50	4.50
Common Player:		.50	.25	.15
1	Dave Bristol	.50	.25	.15
2	Marc Hill	.50	.25	.15
3	Mike Sadek	.50	.25	.15
5	Tom Haller	.50	.25	.15
6	Joe Altobelli	.50	.25	.15
8	Larry Shepard	.50	.25	.15
9	Heity Cruz	.50	.25	.15
10	Johnnie LeMaster	.50	.25	.15
12	Jim Davenport	.50	.25	.15
14	Vida Blue	.75	.40	.25
15	Mike Ivie	.50	.25	.15
16	Roger Metzger	.50	.25	.15
17	Randy Moffitt	.50	.25	.15
18	Bill Madlock	.60	.30	.20
21	Rob Andrews	.50	.25	.15
22	Jack Clark	.75	.40	.25
25	Dave Roberts	.50	.25	.15
26	John Montefusco	.50	.25	.15
28	Ed Halicki	.50	.25	.15
30	John Tamargo	.50	.25	.15
31	Larry Herndon	.50	.25	.15
36	Bill North	.50	.25	.15
39	Bob Knepper	.50	.25	.15
40	John Curtis	.50	.25	.15
41	Darrell Evans	.75	.40	.25
43	Tom Griffin	.50	.25	.15
44	Willie McCovey	5.00	2.50	1.50
46	Gary Lavelle	.50	.25	.15
49	Max Venable	.50	.25	.15

1980 San Francisco Giants Police

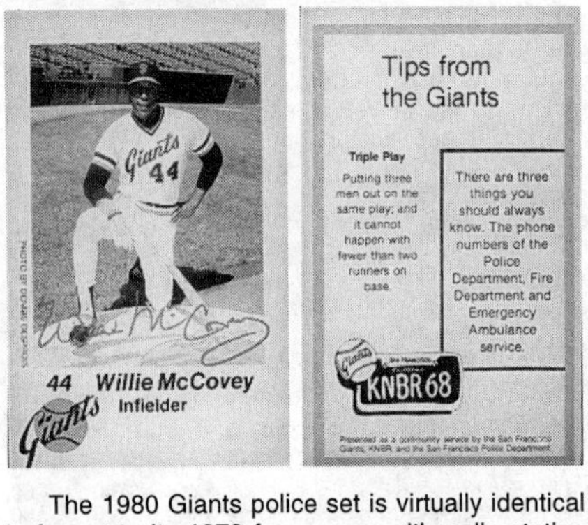

The 1980 Giants police set is virtually identical in format to its 1979 forerunner, with radio station KNBR and the San Francisco Police Department once again co-sponsors. The 2-5/8" x 4-1/8" cards feature full-color photos and facsimile autographs. Backs are in the team's orange and black colors. The set includes players and coaches, with each card numbered by uniform number. As in 1979, half the cards were distributed as a stadium promotion, with the remainder available only from police officers.

		NM	EX	VG
Complete Set (31):		10.00	5.00	3.00
Common Player:		.30	.15	.09
1	Dave Bristol	.30	.15	.09
2	Marc Hill	.30	.15	.09
3	Mike Sadek	.30	.15	.09
5	Jim Lefebvre	.30	.15	.09
6	Rennie Stennett	.30	.15	.09
7	Milt May	.30	.15	.09
8	Vern Benson	.30	.15	.09
9	Jim Wohlford	.30	.15	.09
10	Johnnie LeMaster	.30	.15	.09
12	Jim Davenport	.30	.15	.09
14	Vida Blue	.50	.25	.15
15	Mike Ivie	.30	.15	.09
16	Roger Metzger	.30	.15	.09
17	Randy Moffitt	.30	.15	.09
19	Al Holland	.30	.15	.09
20	Joe Strain	.30	.15	.09
22	Jack Clark	.60	.30	.20
26	John Montefusco	.30	.15	.09
28	Ed Halicki	.30	.15	.09
31	Larry Herndon	.30	.15	.09
32	Ed Whitson	.30	.15	.09
36	Bill North	.30	.15	.09
38	Greg Minton	.30	.15	.09
39	Bob Knepper	.30	.15	.09
41	Darrell Evans	.60	.30	.20
42	John Van Ornum	.30	.15	.09
43	Tom Griffin	.30	.15	.09
44	Willie McCovey	4.00	2.00	1.25
45	Terry Whitfield	.30	.15	.09
46	Gary Lavelle	.30	.15	.09
47	Don McMahon	.30	.15	.09

1921 Schapira Bros. Candy Babe Ruth

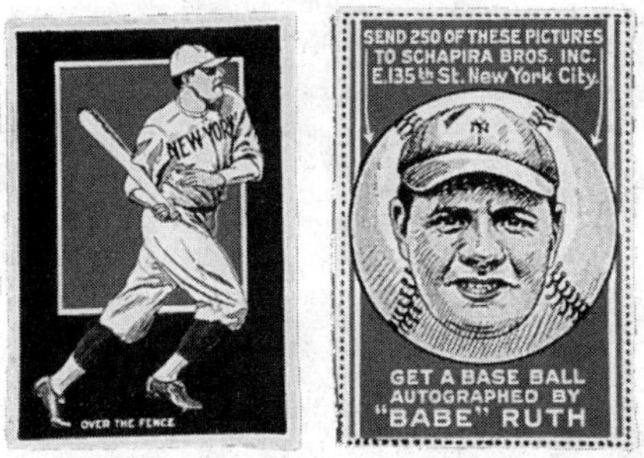

The date assigned to this rare candy issue is a best guess based on the uniform in which the Babe is shown on the various cards. The blank-back cards measure between 1-5/8" and 1-3/4" in width, and are 2-1/2" tall. Printed in red, white and blue the cards were printed on a candy box and come in two types. Apparently each box contained a portrait card of Ruth which offered "a base ball autographed by Babe Ruth" for 250 of the pictures, plus one of five action photos. The portrait card would thus be much more common than any particular action pose, unless great numbers of them were redeemed. The cards illustrated here are not front and back, but show a typical action card and the portrait card. The unnumbered cards are checklisted here in alphabetical order based on the card's caption.

		NM	EX	VG
Complete Set (6):		3750.	1500.	750.00
(1)	Cleared the Bags (Babe Ruth)	750.00	300.00	150.00
(2)	Home Run (Babe Ruth)	750.00	300.00	150.00
(3)	Over the Fence (Babe Ruth)	750.00	300.00	150.00
(4)	They Passed Him (Babe Ruth)	750.00	300.00	150.00
(5)	Waiting for a High One (Babe Ruth)	750.00	300.00	150.00
(6)	Babe Ruth (portrait)	350.00	140.00	70.00

1926-28 Schapira Bros. Big Show Candy

The few players known in this issue can reasonably pinpoint the issue date no closer than circa 1926-28, when four of the players were on New York teams. The 1-7/8" x 2-3/8" cards were one of several types of insert cards and toys found in boxes of Schapira's "Big Show" candy. The cards have black-and-white borderless photos on which the player's name is printed diagonally in white script at lower right. Most cards have an Underwood & Underwood credit line on front, as well. Backs are blank. The unnumbered cards are listed here alphabetically though the checklist may or may not be complete. Most cards are found with a horizontal crease at center, possibly to get them into the tight-fitting candy box.

		NM	EX	VG
Common Player:		200.00	100.00	60.00
(1)	Ty Cobb	2000.	1000.	600.00
(2)	Walter Johnson	400.00	160.00	80.00
(3)	Joe Judge	200.00	80.00	40.00
(4)	Rabbit Maranville	250.00	100.00	50.00
(5)	Meusel (Bob or Irish?)	200.00	80.00	40.00
(6)	O'Neil (Mickey?)	200.00	80.00	40.00
(7)	Edd Rousch (Roush)	250.00	100.00	50.00

1949 Schumacher Service Station

The date of issue on these cards has been arbitrarily fixed. Given that the two known players from this set were with their respective teams together from 1948-1952, the issue date could be anywhere in that range. It is also unknown where Schumacher Service Station was located. Measuring 2-5/8" x 3-9/16", the cards are black-and-white on the front, with backs printed in red. It is unknown whether other players were issued in this series.

		NM	EX	VG
Complete Set (2):		150.00	75.00	45.00
Common Player:		75.00	37.50	22.50
(1)	George (Red) Munger	75.00	37.50	22.50
(2)	Vernon Stephens	75.00	37.50	22.00

1935 Schutter-Johnson (R332)

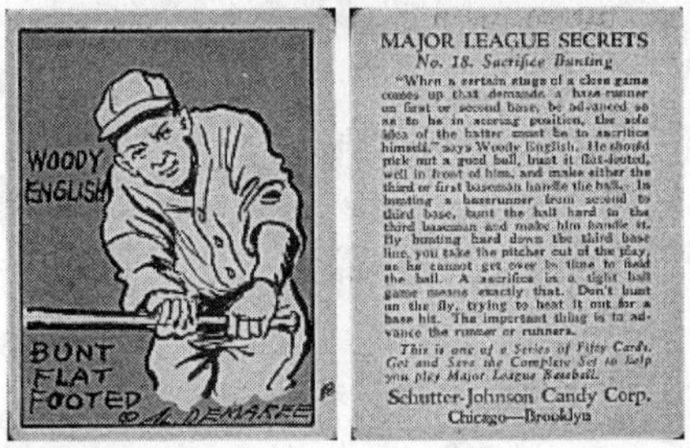

This 50-card set was issued by the Schutter-Johnson Candy Corp. of Chicago and Brooklyn circa 1930 and features drawings of major league players offering baseball playing tips. The cards measure 2-1/4" x 2-7/8". The drawings on the front are set against a red background while the backs are titled "Major League Secrets" and give the player's advice on some aspect of the game. The Scutter-Johnson name appears at the bottom.

		NM	EX	VG
Complete Set (50):		6800.	2700.	1350.
Common Player:		100.00	40.00	20.00
1	Al Simmons	125.00	50.00	25.00
2	Lloyd Waner	125.00	50.00	25.00
3	Kiki Cuyler	125.00	50.00	25.00
4	Frank Frisch	125.00	50.00	25.00
5	Chick Hafey	125.00	50.00	25.00
6	Bill Klem (umpire)	125.00	50.00	25.00
7	Rogers Hornsby	135.00	54.00	27.00
8	Carl Mays	100.00	40.00	20.00
9	Chas. Wrigley (umpire)	100.00	40.00	20.00
10	Christy Mathewson	225.00	90.00	45.00
11	Bill Dickey	125.00	50.00	25.00
12	Walter Berger	100.00	40.00	20.00
13	George Earnshaw	100.00	40.00	20.00
14	Hack Wilson	125.00	50.00	25.00
15	Charley Grimm	100.00	40.00	20.00
16	Lloyd Waner, Paul Waner	125.00	50.00	25.00
17	Chuck Klein	125.00	50.00	25.00
18	Woody English	100.00	40.00	20.00
19	Grover Alexander	150.00	60.00	30.00
20	Lou Gehrig	650.00	260.00	130.00
21	Wes Ferrell	100.00	40.00	20.00
22	Carl Hubbell	130.00	52.00	26.00
23	Pie Traynor	125.00	50.00	25.00
24	Gus Mancuso	100.00	40.00	20.00
25	Ben Cantwell	100.00	40.00	20.00
26	Babe Ruth	1100.	440.00	220.00
27	"Goose" Goslin	125.00	50.00	25.00
28	Earle Combs	125.00	50.00	25.00
29	"Kiki" Cuyler	125.00	50.00	25.00
30	Jimmy Wilson	100.00	40.00	20.00
31	Dizzy Dean	165.00	66.00	33.00
32	Mickey Cochrane	125.00	50.00	25.00
33	Ted Lyons	125.00	50.00	25.00
34	Si Johnson	100.00	40.00	20.00
35	Dizzy Dean	165.00	66.00	33.00
36	Pepper Martin	105.00	42.00	21.00
37	Joe Cronin	125.00	50.00	25.00
38	Gabby Hartnett	125.00	50.00	25.00
39	Oscar Melillo	100.00	40.00	20.00
40	Ben Chapman	100.00	40.00	20.00
41	John McGraw	125.00	50.00	25.00
42	Babe Ruth	1100.	440.00	220.00
43	"Red" Lucas	100.00	40.00	20.00
44	Charley Root	100.00	40.00	20.00
45	Dazzy Vance	125.00	50.00	25.00
46	Hugh Critz	100.00	40.00	20.00
47	"Firpo" Marberry	100.00	40.00	20.00
48	Grover Alexander	150.00	60.00	30.00
49	Lefty Grove	125.00	50.00	25.00
50	Heinie Meine	100.00	40.00	20.00

1888 Scrapps Tobacco

The origin of these die-cut, embossed player busts is not known, but they were apparently part of a book of "punch-outs" issued in the late 1880s. When out of their original album, they apparently resembled scraps of paper, presumably leading to their unusual name. An earlier theory that they were issued by "Scrapps Tobacco" has since been discounted after research indicated there never was such a company. The die-cuts include 18 different players - nine members of the American Association St. Louis Browns and nine from the National League Detroit Wolverines. Although they vary slightly in size, the player busts are generally about 2" wide and 3" high. The drawings for the St. Louis player busts were taken from the Old Judge "Brown's Champions" set. The player's name appears along the bottom.

		NM	EX	VG
Complete Set (18):		15000.	6000.	3000.
Common Player:		1050.	425.00	200.00
(1)	C.W. Bennett	1050.	425.00	200.00
(2)	D. Brouthers	1500.	600.00	300.00
(3)	A.J. Bushong	1050.	425.00	200.00
(4)	Robert L. Caruthers	1050.	425.00	200.00
(5)	Charles Comiskey	1550.	620.00	310.00
(6)	F. Dunlap	1050.	425.00	200.00
(7)	David L. Foutz	1050.	425.00	200.00
(8)	C.H. Getzen (Getzien)	1050.	425.00	200.00
(9)	Wm. Gleason	1050.	425.00	200.00
(10)	E. Hanlon	1500.	600.00	300.00
(11)	Walter A. Latham	1050.	425.00	200.00
(12)	James O'Neill	1050.	425.00	200.00
(13)	H. Richardson	1050.	425.00	200.00
(14)	Wm. Robinson	1500.	600.00	300.00
(15)	J.C. Rowe	1050.	425.00	200.00
(16)	S. Thompson	1550.	620.00	310.00
(17)	Curtis Welch	1050.	425.00	200.00
(18)	J.L. White	1050.	425.00	200.00

1949 Sealtest Phillies

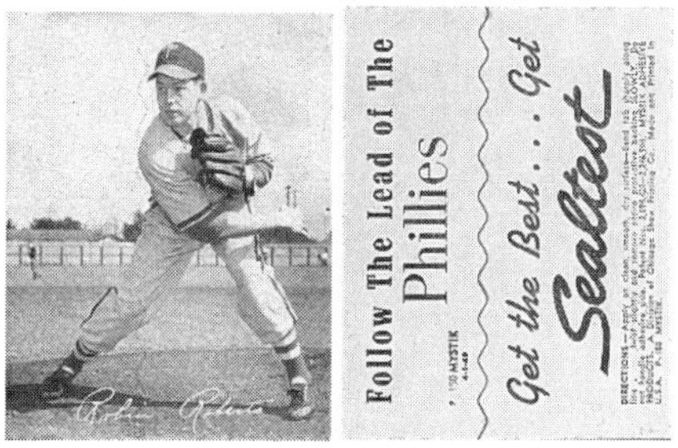

This regional Phillies set was issued in the Philadelphia area in 1949 by Sealtest Dairy. It consisted of 12 large (3-1/2" by 4-1/4") sticker cards with peel-off backs. The front of the unnumbered cards featured an action photo with facsimilie autograph, while the back has an advertisement for Sealtest products. The same format, photos and checklist were also used for the Lummis Peanut Butter card set issued in Philadelphia the same year.

		NM	EX	VG
Complete Set (12):		1400.	700.00	420.00
Common Player:		90.00	45.00	27.00
(1)	Rich Ashburn	300.00	150.00	90.00
(2)	Hank Borowy	100.00	50.00	30.00
(3)	Del Ennis	130.00	65.00	39.00
(4)	Granny Hamner	100.00	50.00	30.00
(5)	Puddinhead Jones	100.00	50.00	30.00
(6)	Russ Meyer	100.00	50.00	30.00
(7)	Bill Nicholson	100.00	50.00	30.00
(8)	Robin Roberts	300.00	150.00	90.00
(9)	"Schoolboy" Rowe	100.00	50.00	30.00
(10)	Andy Seminick	100.00	50.00	30.00
(11)	Curt Simmons	150.00	75.00	45.00
(12)	Eddie Waitkus	100.00	50.00	30.00

1946 Sears St. Louis Browns/Cardinals Postcards

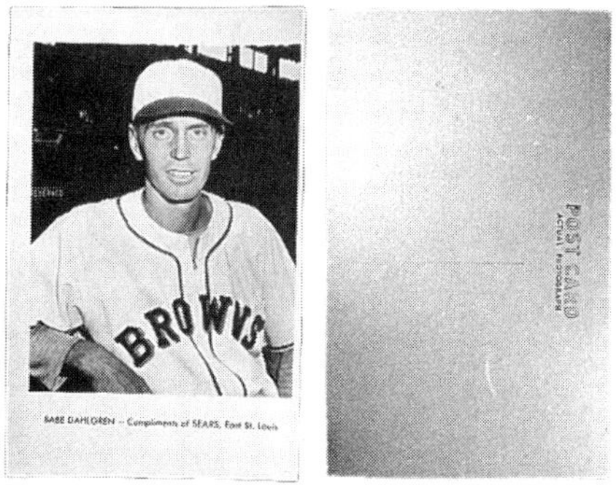

One of the more popular issues of the immediate post-war period are the black-and-white postcards of St. Louis Browns and Cardinals players issued by Sears in East St. Louis. The 3-1/2" x 5-3/8" postcards have posed player portraits on front with the player's name and Sears "Compliments of" line in the white border beneath. Backs are stamped "POST CARD / ACTUAL PHOTOGRAPH". The cards were reported to have been issued in groups of five on a bi-weekly basis, sold both at the Sears store and through the mail. The unnumbered cards are checklisted here alphabetically within team.

		NM	EX	VG
Complete Set (69):		4800.	2400.	1400.
Common Player:		80.00	40.00	24.00
	St. Louis Browns set (33):	2400.	1200.	720.00
(1)	John Berardino	125.00	62.00	37.00
(2)	Frank Biscan	80.00	40.00	24.00
(3)	Mark Christman	80.00	40.00	24.00
(4)	Babe Dahlgren	80.00	40.00	24.00
(5)	Bob Dillinger	80.00	40.00	24.00
(6)	Stanley Ferens	80.00	40.00	24.00
(7)	Denny Galehouse	80.00	40.00	24.00
(8)	Joe Grace	80.00	40.00	24.00
(9)	Jeff Heath	80.00	40.00	24.00
(10)	Henry Helf	80.00	40.00	24.00
(11)	Fred Hoffman	80.00	40.00	24.00
(12)	Walt Judnich	80.00	40.00	24.00
(13)	Ellis Kinder	80.00	40.00	24.00
(14)	Jack Kramer	80.00	40.00	24.00
(15)	Chet Laabs	80.00	40.00	24.00
(16)	Al LaMacchia	125.00	62.00	37.00
(17)	John Lucadello	80.00	40.00	24.00
(18)	Frank Mancuso	80.00	40.00	24.00
(19)	Glenn McQuillen	80.00	40.00	24.00
(20)	John Miller	80.00	40.00	24.00
(21)	Al Milnar	125.00	62.00	37.00
(22)	Bob Muncrief	80.00	40.00	24.00
(23)	Nelson Potter	80.00	40.00	24.00
(24)	Ken Sears	80.00	40.00	24.00
(25)	Len Schulte	80.00	40.00	24.00
(26)	Luke Sewell	80.00	40.00	24.00
(27)	Joe Schultz	80.00	40.00	24.00
(28)	Tex Shirley	80.00	40.00	24.00
(29)	Vern Stephens	80.00	40.00	24.00
(30)	Chuck Stevens	80.00	40.00	24.00
(31)	Zack Taylor	80.00	40.00	24.00
(32)	Al Zarilla	80.00	40.00	24.00
(33)	Sam Zoldak	80.00	40.00	24.00
	St. Louis Cardinals set (36):	3000.	1500.	900.00
(1)	Buster Adams	80.00	40.00	24.00
(2)	Red Barrett	80.00	40.00	24.00
(3)	Johnny Beazley	80.00	40.00	24.00
(4)	Al Brazle	80.00	40.00	24.00
(5)	Harry Brecheen	80.00	40.00	24.00
(6)	Ken Burkhart	80.00	40.00	24.00
(7)	Joffre Cross	80.00	40.00	24.00
(8)	Murray Dickson	80.00	40.00	24.00
(9)	George Dockins	80.00	40.00	20.00
(10)	Blix Donnelly	125.00	62.00	37.00
(11)	Erv Dusak	80.00	40.00	24.00
(12)	Eddie Dyer	80.00	40.00	24.00
(13)	Bill Endicott	80.00	40.00	24.00
(14)	Joe Garagiola	200.00	100.00	60.00
(15)	Mike Gonzales (Gonzalez)	95.00	47.00	28.00
(16)	Lou Klein	80.00	40.00	24.00
(17)	Clyde Kluttz	80.00	40.00	24.00
(18)	Howard Krist	80.00	40.00	24.00
(19)	George Kurowski	80.00	40.00	24.00
(20)	Danny Litwhiler	80.00	40.00	24.00
(21)	Marty Marion	125.00	62.00	37.00
(22)	Fred Martin	80.00	40.00	24.00
(23)	Terry Moore	95.00	47.00	28.00
(24)	Stan Musial	350.00	175.00	105.00
(25)	Ken O'Dea	80.00	40.00	24.00
(26)	Howard Pollet	80.00	40.00	24.00
(27)	Del Rice	80.00	40.00	24.00
(28)	Red Schoendienst	145.00	72.00	43.00
(29)	Walt Sessi	80.00	40.00	24.00
(30)	Dick Sisler	80.00	40.00	24.00
(31)	Enos Slaughter	145.00	72.00	43.00
(32)	Max Surkont	80.00	40.00	24.00
(33)	Harry Walker	80.00	40.00	24.00
(34)	Buzzy Wares	80.00	40.00	24.00
(35)	Ernie White	80.00	40.00	24.00
(36)	Ted Wilks	80.00	40.00	24.00

1969 Seattle Pilots Premium Pictures

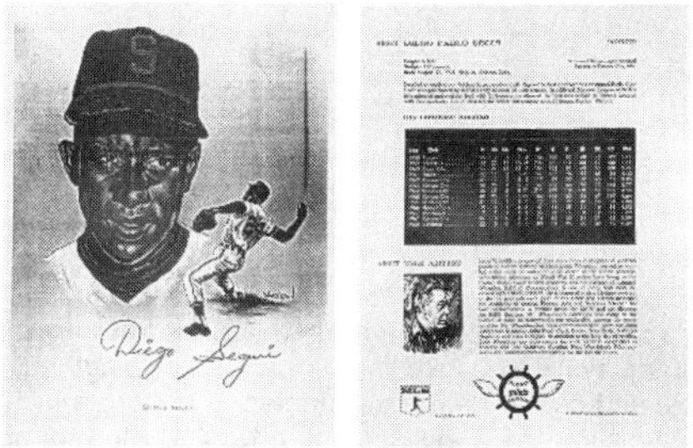

This set of 8-1/2" x 11" premium pictures is based on the artwork of John Wheeldon, who did contemporary issues for the Mets, Twins and Red Sox, as well. The pastels feature large portraits and smaller action pictures with a large facsimile autograph at bottom. Backs are in black-and-white and feature biographical data, comprehensive career summary and complete minor and major league stats. There is a self-portrait and biographical sketch of the artist on back, as well. The premiums were given away at selected Pilots home games during their lone season in Seattle. They were later sold for 25 cents each in the concession stand. The unnumbered pictures are checklisted here in alphabetical order.

		NM	EX	VG
Complete Set (8):		75.00	37.00	22.00
Common Player:		8.00	4.00	2.50
(1)	Wayne Comer	8.00	4.00	2.50

		NM	EX	VG
(2)	Tommy Harper	10.00	5.00	3.00
(3)	Mike Hegan	8.00	4.00	2.50
(4)	Jerry McNertney	8.00	4.00	2.50
(5)	Don Mincher	8.00	4.00	2.50
(6)	Ray Oyler	8.00	4.00	2.50
(7)	Marty Pattin	8.00	4.00	2.50
(8)	Diego Segui	8.00	4.00	2.50

1963 Mickey Sego S.F. Giants

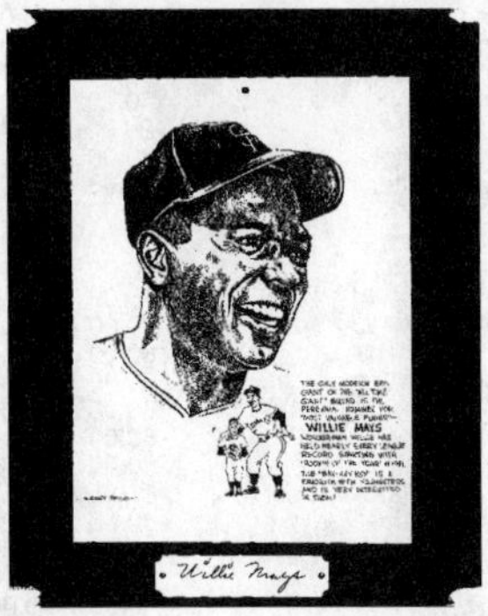

These self-framing picutres feature the artwork of Mickey Sego, but the method of their distribution is unknown. Measuring 7" x 8-1/2", the pieces have a dark frame around a large black-and-white portrait and smaller cartoon drawing of the player. There are also a few words about the player's career. A simulated plaque at the bottom of the frame bears a facsimile autograph. Each picture has a hole at top for hanging.

		NM	EX	VG
Common Player:		15.00	7.50	4.50
(1)	Chuck Hiller	15.00	7.50	4.50
(2)	Harvey Kuenn	20.00	10.00	6.00
(3)	Willie Mays	85.00	42.00	25.00
(4)	Billy Pierce	17.50	8.75	5.25

1914 Lawrence Serman Postcards

Only six players are currently known in this series, but it's possible other remain to be reported. The approximately 3-1/2" x 5-1/2" postcards feature on their fronts either portrait or action drawings of star players by Lawrence Serman. A few biographical and career details are printed at bottom, which have allowed the assignment of 1914 as the year of issue. Backs are standard postcard style. The unnumbered cards are checklisted here alphabetically.

		NM	EX	VG
Common Player:		150.00	75.00	45.00
(1)	George Burns	150.00	75.00	45.00
(2)	Frank Chance	300.00	150.00	90.00
(3)	Ty Cobb	850.00	425.00	255.00
(4)	Walter Johnson	450.00	225.00	135.00
(5)	Cornelius McGillicuddy (Connie Mack)	250.00	125.00	75.00
(6)	Richard (Rube) Marquard	250.00	125.00	75.00
(7)	John J. McGraw	250.00	125.00	75.00

1933 Senella Margarine

One of several "foreign" Babe Ruth cards issued during his prime was included in a 112-card set produced as premiums for Senella Margarine in Germany. Ruth is the only major league ballplayer in the issue. Cards are in full color, measuring 2-3/4" x 4-1/8". Backs of the unnumbered cards are printed in German. Two types of backs can be found on the Ruth card. The more common, Type 1, has the Senella name nearly centered. The scarcer Type 2 back has the brand name printed closer to the bottom of the card, with only four lines of type under it.

	NM	EX	VG
Type 1Babe Ruth	450.00	225.00	135.00
Type 2Babe Ruth	500.00	250.00	150.00

1977 Sertoma Stars

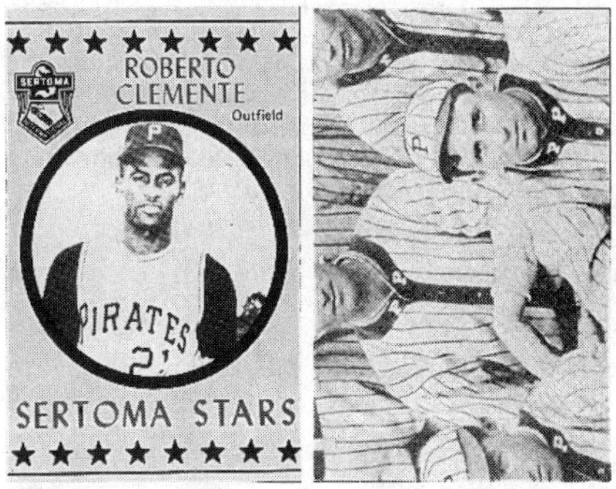

This collectors set was issued in conjunction with the Indianapolis Sports Collectors Convention in 1977. The set was sold for $3 with proceeds benefiting the local Sertoma (Service to Mankind) Club's charity works. Cards measure 2-3/4" x 4-1/8". A 2-1/2" black circle at center contains a black-and-white player photo. The background on front is yellow, with red and black printing. Backs are borderless and form an old Pittsburgh Pirates team photo puzzle. Sets were originally sold for $3.50.

		NM	EX	VG
Complete Set (25):		150.00	75.00	45.00
Common Player:		2.00	1.00	.60
(1)	Bernie Allen	2.00	1.00	.60
(2)	Home Run Baker	2.00	1.00	.60
(3)	Ted Beard	2.00	1.00	.60
(4)	Don Buford	2.00	1.00	.60
(5)	Eddie Cicotte	6.00	3.00	1.75
(6)	Roberto Clemente	35.00	17.50	10.50
(7)	Dom Dallessandro	2.00	1.00	.60
(8)	Carl Erskine	2.00	1.00	.60
(9)	Nellie Fox	6.00	3.00	1.75
(10)	Lou Gehrig	25.00	12.50	7.50
(11)	Joe Jackson	25.00	12.50	7.50
(12)	Len Johnston	2.00	1.00	.60
(13)	Benny Kauff	2.00	1.00	.60
(14)	Dick Kenworthy	2.00	1.00	.60
(15)	Harmon Killebrew	10.00	5.00	3.00
(16)	"Lefty Bob" Logan	2.00	1.00	.60
(17)	Willie Mays	20.00	10.00	6.00
(18)	Satchel Paige	15.00	7.50	4.50
(19)	Edd Roush	2.00	1.00	.60
(20)	Chico Ruiz	2.00	1.00	.60
(21)	Babe Ruth	25.00	12.50	7.50
(22)	Herb Score	6.00	3.00	1.75
(23)	George Sisler	2.00	1.00	.60
(24)	Buck Weaver	6.00	3.00	1.75
(25)	Early Wynn	2.00	1.00	.60

1961 7-11

The first of 7-11's baseball card issues was a crude attempt which was abruptly halted. The checklist for the 30-card set indicated that it was the first of planned series to be issued two weeks apart. No follow-up to the first series was ever distributed. The 2-7/16" x 3-3/8" cards are printed on pink cardboard stock, with blank backs. Small black-and-white player portraits appear in the upper-left, with the player name at top, team name at bottom and card number in the lower-right corner. There are a few biographical bits and stats to the right of the photo, and several lines of 1960 season highlights below. The cards were sold seven for a nickel in vending machines.

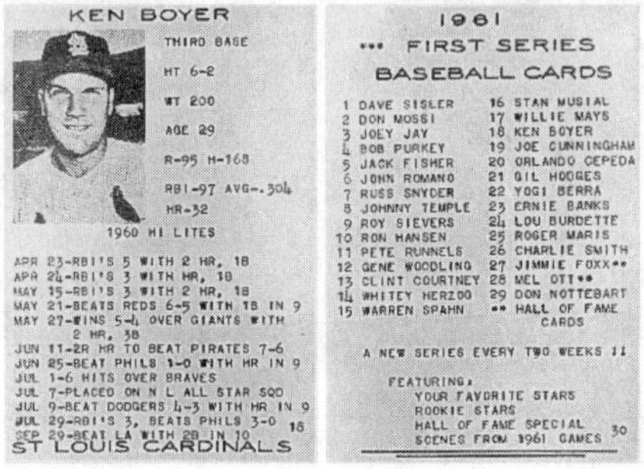

		NM	EX	VG
Complete Set (30):		450.00	225.00	135.00
Common Player:		7.50	3.75	2.25
1	Dave Sisler	7.50	3.75	2.25
2	Don Mossi	7.50	3.75	2.25
3	Joey Jay	7.50	3.75	2.25
4	Bob Purkey	7.50	3.75	2.25
5	Jack Fisher	7.50	3.75	2.25
6	John Romano	7.50	3.75	2.25
7	Russ Snyder	7.50	3.75	2.25
8	Johnny Temple	7.50	3.75	2.25
9	Roy Sievers	7.50	3.75	2.25
10	Ron Hansen	7.50	3.75	2.25
11	Pete Runnels	7.50	3.75	2.25
12	Gene Woodling	9.00	4.50	2.75
13	Clint Courtney	7.50	3.75	2.25
14	Whitey Herzog	12.00	6.00	3.50
15	Warren Spahn	25.00	12.50	7.50
16	Stan Musial	50.00	25.00	15.00
17	Willie Mays	100.00	50.00	30.00
18	Ken Boyer	9.00	4.50	2.75
19	Joe Cunningham	7.50	3.75	2.25
20	Orlando Cepeda	15.00	7.50	4.50
21	Gil Hodges	25.00	12.50	7.50
22	Yogi Berra	25.00	12.50	7.50
23	Ernie Banks	30.00	15.00	9.00
24	Lou Burdette	7.50	3.75	2.25
25	Roger Maris	45.00	22.00	13.50
26	Charlie Smith	7.50	3.75	2.25
27	Jimmie Foxx	9.00	4.50	2.75
28	Mel Ott	9.00	4.50	2.75
29	Don Nottebart	7.50	3.75	2.25
----	Checklist	25.00	12.50	7.50

1975 Shakey's Pizza West Coast Greats

This collectors issue was sponsored by Seattle area Shakey's Pizza restaurants in conjunction with the 1975 convention of the Washington State Sports Collectors Assn. Two thousand sets were produced featuring players who were born and/or played on the West Coast. The first 1,000 attendees at the convention were given a free sample of card #1, DiMaggio. Cards are 2-3/4" x about 3-5/8". Fronts have a black-and-white photo at center with black and red graphics. A large Shakey's logo is at lower-left. The card number, player name, position and connection to the West Coast are printed at lower-right. Backs are in red and white with the pizza chain's logo and a list of four Seattle-area locations.

		NM	EX	VG
Complete Set (18):		40.00	20.00	12.00
Common Player:		2.00	1.00	.60
1	Joe DiMaggio	8.00	4.00	2.50
2	Paul Waner	2.00	1.00	.60
3	Lefty Gomez	2.00	1.00	.60

4	Earl Averill	2.00	1.00	.60
5	Ernie Lombardi	2.00	1.00	.60
6	Joe Cronin	2.00	1.00	.60
7	George Burns	2.00	1.00	.60
8	Casey Stengel	2.00	1.00	.60
9	Wahoo Sam Crawford	2.00	1.00	.60
10	Ted Williams	6.00	3.00	1.75
11	Fred Hutchinson	2.00	1.00	.60
12	Duke Snider	3.00	1.50	.90
13	Hal Chase	2.00	1.00	.60
14	Bobby Doerr	2.00	1.00	.60
15	Arky Vaughan	2.00	1.00	.60
16	Tony Lazzeri	2.00	1.00	.60
17	Lefty O'Doul	2.00	1.00	.60
18	Stan Hack	2.00	1.00	.60

1976 Shakey's Pizza Hall of Fame

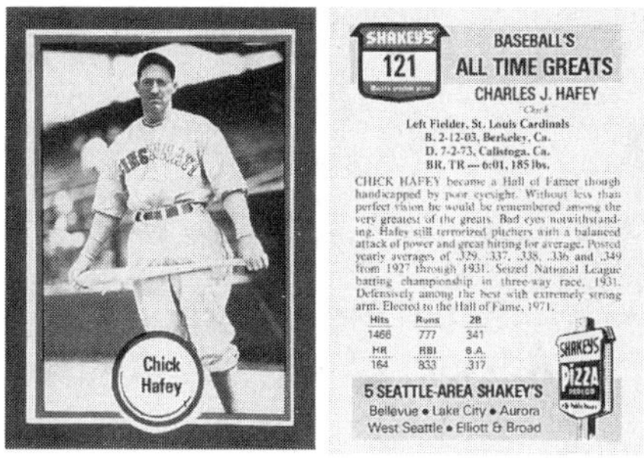

Between 1975-77 the Washington State Sports Collectors Assn. worked with the Shakey's pizza chain in the Seattle area to produce and distribute several sets of "old timers" cards. Generally one card from the set was given away to hobbyists attending the club's annual convention, with other cards available at the pizza places. Complete sets were also widely sold within the hobby. Interpretation of whether these are "legitimate" cards or a collector issue is up to each collector. The 1976 cards were issued in four series: Hall of Fame, Greatest Players, Immortals and All-Time Greats. The format was identical, with the (approximately) 2-1/2" x 3-1/2" cards featuring black-and-white player photos on front, surrounded by a red frame and bright blue border. Backs are in red, black and white with large Shakey ads at top and bottom. Also on back are player biographies and career stats. The cards were issued in order of the players' induction into the Hall of Fame. All four series are skip-numbered. Cards of Sam Thompson and Robin Roberts were re-issued in Series 2 to correct errors.

		NM	EX	VG
Complete Set (160):		300.00	150.00	90.00
Common Player:		2.00	1.00	.60
	Series 1 - Baseball's Hall of Fame	90.00	45.00	27.00
A	Earl Averill ($1 off pizza coupon on back; card show giveaway)	4.00	2.00	1.25
1	Ty Cobb	7.50	3.75	2.25
3	Walter Johnson	3.00	1.50	.90
12	Connie Mack	2.00	1.00	.60
18	Lou Gehrig	8.00	4.00	2.50
20	George Sisler	2.00	1.00	.60
21	Cap Anson	2.00	1.00	.60
36	Mike "King" Kelly	2.00	1.00	.60
41	Jack Chesbro	2.00	1.00	.60
50	Mickey Cochrane	2.00	1.00	.60
52	Lefty Grove	2.00	1.00	.60
54	Herb Pennock	2.00	1.00	.60
55	Pie Traynor	2.00	1.00	.60
56	Charlie Gehringer	2.00	1.00	.60
57	Three-Finger Brown	2.00	1.00	.60
58	Kid Nichols	2.00	1.00	.60
59	Jimmie Foxx	2.00	1.00	.60
64	Al Simmons	2.00	1.00	.60
72	Rabbit Maranville	2.00	1.00	.60
73	Bill Terry	2.00	1.00	.60
80	Joe Cronin	2.00	1.00	.60
83	Joe McCarthy	2.00	1.00	.60
86	Bill Hamilton	2.00	1.00	.60
88	Jackie Robinson	8.00	4.00	2.50
89	Bill McKechnie	2.00	1.00	.60
93	Sam Rice	2.00	1.00	.60
95	Luke Appling	2.00	1.00	.60
103	Ted Williams	8.00	4.00	2.50
104	Casey Stengel	2.00	1.00	.60
107	Lloyd Waner	2.00	1.00	.60
108	Joe Medwick	2.00	1.00	.60
115	Lou Boudreau	2.00	1.00	.60
122	Harry Hooper	2.00	1.00	.60
127	Yogi Berra	3.00	1.50	.90
129	Lefty Gomez	2.00	1.00	.60
131	Sandy Koufax	5.00	2.50	1.50
143	Jocko Conlan	2.00	1.00	.60
144	Whitey Ford	2.00	1.00	.60
146	Sam Thompson	2.00	1.00	.60
147	Earl Averill	2.00	1.00	.60
149	Billy Herman	2.00	1.00	.60
154	Cal Hubbard	2.00	1.00	.60
156	Fred Lindstrom	2.00	1.00	.60
157	Robin Roberts	2.00	1.00	.60
	Series 2 - Baseball's Greatest Players	90.00	45.00	27.00
A	Earl Averill (card show giveaway, coupon on back)	2.00	1.00	.60
4	Christy Mathewson	3.00	1.50	.90
6	Nap Lajoie	2.00	1.00	.60
7	Tris Speaker	2.00	1.00	.60
9	Morgan Bulkeley	2.00	1.00	.60
10	Ban Johnson	2.00	1.00	.60
11	John McGraw	2.00	1.00	.60
14	Grover Alexander	2.00	1.00	.60
17	Eddie Collins	2.00	1.00	.60
19	Willie Keeler	2.00	1.00	.60
22	Charles Comiskey	2.00	1.00	.60
24	Buck Ewing	2.00	1.00	.60
31	Fred Clarke	2.00	1.00	.60
32	Jimmy Collins	2.00	1.00	.60
34	Hugh Duffy	2.00	1.00	.60
35	Hugh Jennings	2.00	1.00	.60
38	Wilbert Robinson	2.00	1.00	.60
40	Frank Chance	2.00	1.00	.60
42	John Evers	2.00	1.00	.60
43	Clark Griffith	2.00	1.00	.60
47	Joe Tinker	2.00	1.00	.60
51	Frank Frisch	2.00	1.00	.60
53	Carl Hubbell	2.00	1.00	.60
65	Ed Barrow	2.00	1.00	.60
66	Chief Bender	2.00	1.00	.60
67	Tommy Connolly	2.00	1.00	.60
74	Joe DiMaggio	12.00	6.00	3.50
75	Gabby Hartnett	2.00	1.00	.60
78	Home Run Baker	2.00	1.00	.60
81	Hank Greenberg	3.00	1.50	.90
87	Bob Feller	2.00	1.00	.60
90	Edd Roush	2.00	1.00	.60
109	Kiki Cuyler	2.00	1.00	.60
111	Roy Campanella	4.00	2.00	1.25
113	Stan Coveleski	2.00	1.00	.60
116	Earle Combs	2.00	1.00	.60
120	Jake Beckley	2.00	1.00	.60
125	Satchel Paige	4.00	2.00	1.25
128	Josh Gibson	3.00	1.50	.90
135	Roberto Clemente	10.00	5.00	3.00
141	Cool Papa Bell	2.00	1.00	.60
142	Jim Bottomley	2.00	1.00	.60
146	Sam Thompson	2.00	1.00	.60
150	Judy Johnson	2.00	1.00	.60
152	Oscar Charleston	2.00	1.00	.60
157	Robin Roberts	2.00	1.00	.60
	Series 3 - Baseball's Immortals	72.00	36.00	22.00
5	Honus Wagner	3.00	1.50	.90
13	George Wright	2.00	1.00	.60
15	Alexander Cartwright	2.00	1.00	.60
16	Henry Chadwick	2.00	1.00	.60
23	Candy Cummings	2.00	1.00	.60
25	Old Hoss Radbourne	2.00	1.00	.60
26	Al Spalding	2.00	1.00	.60
28	Judge Landis	2.00	1.00	.60
29	Roger Bresnahan	2.00	1.00	.60
30	Dan Brouthers	2.00	1.00	.60
33	Ed Delahanty	2.00	1.00	.60
37	Jim O'Rourke	2.00	1.00	.60
39	Jesse Burkett	2.00	1.00	.60
44	Tommy McCarthy	2.00	1.00	.60
45	Joe McGinnity	2.00	1.00	.60
46	Eddie Plank	2.00	1.00	.60
49	Ed Walsh	2.00	1.00	.60
61	Harry Heilmann	2.00	1.00	.60
68	Bill Klem	2.00	1.00	.60
70	Harry Wright	2.00	1.00	.60
85	Max Carey	2.00	1.00	.60
91	John Clarkson	2.00	1.00	.60
92	Elmer Flick	2.00	1.00	.60
96	Red Faber	2.00	1.00	.60
97	Burleigh Grimes	2.00	1.00	.60
98	Miller Huggins	2.00	1.00	.60
99	Tim Keefe	2.00	1.00	.60
101	Monte Ward	2.00	1.00	.60
102	Pud Galvin	2.00	1.00	.60
110	Goose Goslin	2.00	1.00	.60
114	Waite Hoyt	2.00	1.00	.60
117	Ford Frick	2.00	1.00	.60
118	Jesse Haines	2.00	1.00	.60
126	George Weiss	2.00	1.00	.60
130	William Harridge	2.00	1.00	.60
132	Buck Leonard	2.00	1.00	.60
133	Early Wynn	2.00	1.00	.60
136	Billy Evans	2.00	1.00	.60
137	Monte Irvin	2.00	1.00	.60
138	George Kelly	2.00	1.00	.60
140	Mickey Welch	2.00	1.00	.60
148	Bucky Harris	2.00	1.00	.60
151	Ralph Kiner	2.00	1.00	.60
153	Roger Connor	2.00	1.00	.60
	Series 4 - Ball's All-Time Greats	64.00	32.00	19.00
2	Babe Ruth	10.00	5.00	3.00
8	Cy Young	2.50	1.25	.70
27	Rogers Hornsby	2.00	1.00	.60
48	Rube Waddell	2.00	1.00	.60
62	Paul Waner	2.00	1.00	.60
63	Dizzy Dean	2.50	1.25	.70
69	Bobby Wallace	2.00	1.00	.60
71	Bill Dickey	2.00	1.00	.60
77	Dazzy Vance	2.00	1.00	.60
79	Ray Schalk	2.00	1.00	.60
82	Sam Crawford	2.00	1.00	.60
84	Zack Wheat	2.00	1.00	.60
94	Eppa Rixey	2.00	1.00	.60
100	Heinie Manush	2.00	1.00	.60
105	Red Ruffing	2.00	1.00	.60
106	Branch Rickey	2.00	1.00	.60
112	Stan Musial	5.00	2.50	1.50
119	Dave Bancroft	2.00	1.00	.60
121	Chick Hafey	2.00	1.00	.60
123	Joe Kelley	2.00	1.00	.60
124	Rube Marquard	2.00	1.00	.60
134	Ross Youngs	2.00	1.00	.60
139	Warren Spahn	2.00	1.00	.60
145	Mickey Mantle	16.00	8.00	4.75
155	Bob Lemon	2.00	1.00	.60

1977 Shakey's All-Time Superstars

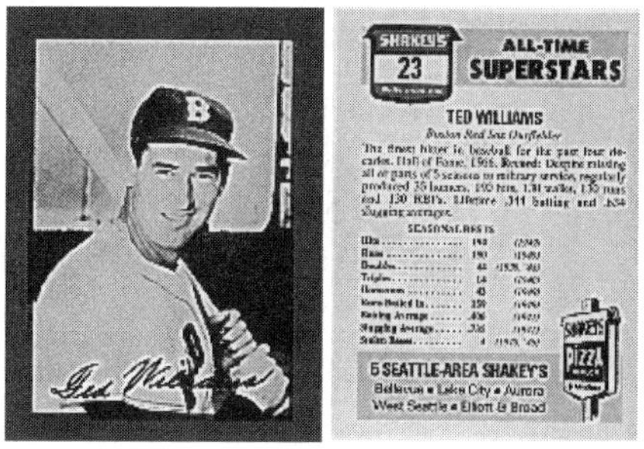

This set of baseball's all-time greatest (at least through the 1950s) was the final production of the Washington State Sports Collectors Assn. and local Shakey's restaurants. About 2-3/8" x 3", the cards feature black-and-white player photos at center with a red border around. A facsimile autograph appears in blue on the photo. Backs are similar to earlier Shakey's issues, with large logos for the pizza chain, player information and "Seasonal Bests" stats, all printed in red and black on white. Several special cards were produced for distribution at the 1977 annual convention and other venues.

		NM	EX	VG
Complete Set (28):		35.00	17.50	10.50
Common Player:		1.00	.50	.30
---	Welcome to WSSCA Show card (collectibles collage)	3.00	1.50	.90
A	Earl Averill	1.50	.70	.45
B	John Mize ($1 coupon on back)	2.00	1.00	.60
C	Robert Lee Johnson	1.50	.70	.45
1	Connie Mack	1.00	.50	.30
2	John J. McGraw	1.00	.50	.30
3	Denton T. (Cy) Young	2.00	1.00	.60
4	Walter Johnson	2.00	1.00	.60
5	G.C. Alexander	1.00	.50	.30
6	Christy Mathewson	2.00	1.00	.60
7	Lefty Grove	1.00	.50	.30
8	Mickey Cochrane	1.00	.50	.30
9	Bill Dickey	1.00	.50	.30
10	Lou Gehrig	5.00	2.50	1.50
11	George Sisler	1.00	.50	.30
12	Cap Anson	1.00	.50	.30
13	Jimmie Foxx	1.00	.50	.30
14	Rogers Hornsby	1.00	.50	.30
15	Nap Lajoie	1.00	.50	.30
16	Eddie Collins	1.00	.50	.30
17	Pie Traynor	1.00	.50	.30
18	Honus Wagner	1.50	.70	.45
19	Ty Cobb	4.00	2.00	1.25
20	Babe Ruth	7.50	3.75	2.25
21	Joe Jackson	7.50	3.75	2.25
22	Tris Speaker	1.00	.50	.30
23	Ted Williams	3.00	1.50	.90
24	Joe DiMaggio	5.00	2.50	1.50
25	Stan Musial	2.50	1.25	.70
---	WSSCA club information card	2.00	1.00	.60

1952 Shelby Bicycles

The year of issue stated is conjectural, based on the familiar picture of Berra used for this promotional photo. The photo shows Yogi kneeling in full catcher's gear, except mask, ready to throw the ball; it is seen on his '50 Bowman card, among others. The blank-back, black-and-white photo is 5" x 7" with a white border all around. Scripted at bottom is, "Ride Shelby / The Winner's Bike / Sincerely / Yogi Berra".

	NM	EX	VG
Yogi Berra	35.00	17.50	10.50

1962 Shirriff Coins

This is a Canadian version of the better-known Salada-Junket plastic player coins issued in the U.S. Backs specify an issue of 200, packed in potato chip bags.

(See 1962 Salada for checklist. Sherriff coins valued about 50% of Salada.)

1957 Sohio Gas Indians/Reds

In 1957 Sohio (Standard Oil of Ohio) gas stations in Ohio issued sets of Cleveland Indians and Cincinnati Reds photocards and team albums. The blank-backed cards are 5" x 7" and printed in black-and-white with one perforated edge. The cards have a facsimile autograph as the only identification. The unnumbered cards are checklisted here alphabetically within team.

		NM	EX	VG
Complete Set (36):		725.00	360.00	215.00
Common Player:		12.00	6.00	3.50
CLEVELAND INDIANS				
	Complete set (18):	475.00	237.00	142.00
(1)	Bob Avila	12.00	6.00	3.50
(2)	Jim Busby	12.00	6.00	3.50
(3)	Chico Carrasquel	12.00	6.00	3.50
(4)	Rocky Colavito	145.00	72.00	43.00
(5)	Mike Garcia	12.00	6.00	3.50
(6)	Jim Hegan	12.00	6.00	3.50
(7)	Bob Lemon	24.00	12.00	7.25
(8)	Roger Maris	225.00	112.00	67.00
(9)	Don Mossi	12.00	6.00	3.50
(10)	Ray Narleski	12.00	6.00	3.50
(11)	Russ Nixon	12.00	6.00	3.50
(12)	Herb Score	18.00	9.00	5.50
(13)	Al Smith	12.00	6.00	3.50
(14)	George Strickland	12.00	6.00	3.50
(15)	Bob Usher	12.00	6.00	3.50
(16)	Vic Wertz	12.00	6.00	3.50
(17)	Gene Woodling	12.00	6.00	3.50
(18)	Early Wynn	24.00	12.00	7.25
----	Cleveland Indians album	75.00	37.00	22.00
CINCINNATI REDS				
	Complete set (18):	275.00	137.00	82.00
(1)	Ed Bailey	12.00	6.00	3.50
(2)	Gus Bell	12.00	6.00	3.50
(3)	Rocky Bridges	12.00	6.00	3.50
(4)	Smoky Burgess	12.00	6.00	3.50
(5)	Hersh Freeman	12.00	6.00	3.50
(6)	Alex Grammas	12.00	6.00	3.50
(7)	Don Gross	12.00	6.00	3.50
(8)	Warren Hacker	12.00	6.00	3.50
(9)	Don Hoak	12.00	6.00	3.50
(10)	Hal Jeffcoat	12.00	6.00	3.50
(11)	Johnny Klippstein	12.00	6.00	3.50
(12)	Ted Kluszewski	50.00	25.00	15.00
(13)	Brooks Lawrence	12.00	6.00	3.50
(14)	Roy McMillan	12.00	6.00	3.50
(15)	Joe Nuxhall	12.00	6.00	3.50
(16)	Wally Post	12.00	6.00	3.50
(17)	Frank Robinson	75.00	37.00	22.00
(18)	Johnny Temple	12.00	6.00	3.50
----	Cincinnati Redlegs album	75.00	37.00	22.00

Suffix letters after a card number indicate a variation card.

1969 Solon Kansas City Royals

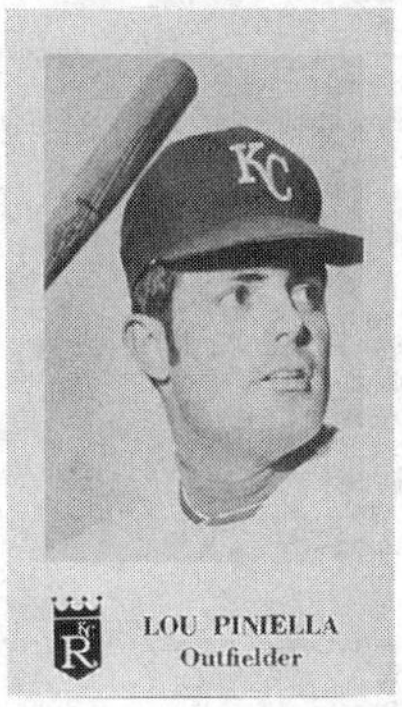

This collectors' issue is believed to have originated with Illinois hobbyist Bob Solon. The black-and-white, blank-back cards feature members of the expansion Royals. The border beneath the posed photos features a team logo and player identification at bottom. Cards measure 2-1/8" x 3-5/8". The checklist here is arranged alphabetically, as the cards are unnumbered.

		NM	EX	VG
Complete Set (15):		16.00	8.00	4.75
Common Player:		1.00	.50	.30
(1)	Jerry Adair	1.00	.50	.30
(2)	Wally Bunker	1.00	.50	.30
(3)	Moe Drabowsky	1.50	.50	.30
(4)	Dick Drago	1.00	.50	.30
(5)	Joe Foy	1.00	.50	.30
(6)	Joe Gordon	1.00	.50	.30
(7)	Chuck Harrison	1.00	.50	.30
(8)	Mike Hedlund	1.00	.50	.30
(9)	Jack Hernandez	1.00	.50	.30
(10)	Pat Kelly	1.00	.50	.30
(11)	Roger Nelson	1.00	.50	.30
(12)	Bob Oliver	1.00	.50	.30
(13)	Lou Piniella	3.00	1.50	1.00
(14)	Ellie Rodriguez	1.00	.50	.30
(15)	Dave Wickersham	1.00	.50	.30

1905 Souvenir Post Card Shop of Cleveland

Formal portraits of the 1905 Cleveland Naps are featured in this set of black-and-white postcards. The 3-1/4" x 5-1/2" cards have a wide white border at bottom which carries the legend, "SOUVENIR POST CARD SHOP OF CLEVELAND". The player's name is in white at the bottom of the photo. Backs have postage rate information and the notice, "NOTHING BUT ADDRESS ON THIS SIDE".

		NM	EX	VG
Complete Set (18):				
Common Player:		225.00	110.00	65.00
(1)	Harry Bay	225.00	110.00	65.00
(2)	Harry Bemis	225.00	110.00	65.00
(3)	Bill Bernhard	225.00	110.00	65.00
(4)	Bill Bradley	225.00	110.00	65.00
(5)	Fred Buelow	225.00	110.00	65.00
(6)	Charles C. Carr	225.00	110.00	65.00
(7)	Frank Donahue	225.00	110.00	65.00
(8)	Elmer Flick	300.00	150.00	90.00
(9)	Otto Hess	225.00	110.00	65.00
(10)	Jay Jackson	225.00	110.00	65.00
(11)	Addie Joss	350.00	175.00	105.00
(12)	Nick Kahl	225.00	110.00	65.00
(13)	Napoleon Lajoie	600.00	300.00	180.00
(14)	Earl Moore	225.00	110.00	65.00
(15)	Robert Rhoads	225.00	110.00	65.00
(16)	George Stovall	225.00	110.00	65.00
(17)	Terry Turner	225.00	110.00	65.00
(18)	Ernest Vinson	225.00	110.00	65.00

1909-11 Sovereign Cigarettes

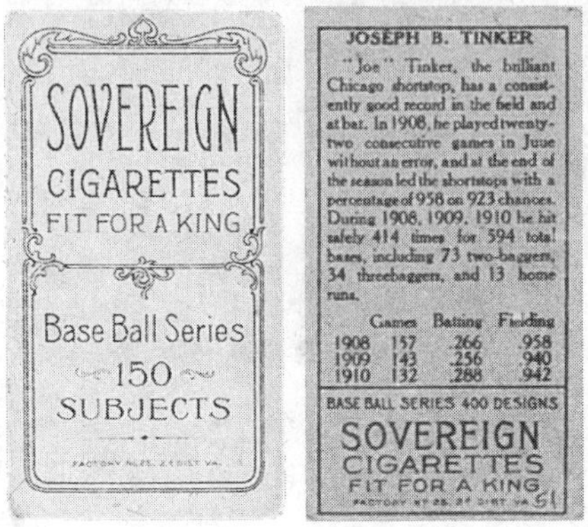

(See T205, T206. Premium: T205/T206: +30%)

1950s-70s Spalding Advisory Staff Photos

Advisory staff photos were a promotional item which debuted in the early 1950s, flourished in the sixties and died in the early 1970s. Generally 8" x 10" (sometimes a little larger), these black-and-white (a few later were color) glossy photos picture players who had contracted with a major baseball equipment company to endorse and use their product. Usually the product - most often a glove - was prominently displayed in the photo. The pictures were often displayed in the windows of sporting goods stores or the walls of sports departments and were sometimes made available to customers. Because the companies tended to stick with players over the years, some photos were reissued, sometimes with and sometimes without a change of team, pose or typography. All Spalding staff photos of the era are checklisted here in alphabetical order. Team designation and pose description is given for each known picture. The photos are checklisted here in alphabetical order. It is unlikely this list is complete. Several arrangements of typography in the bottom border are seen for Spalding advisory staff pictures.

		NM	EX	VG
Common Player:		12.00	6.00	3.50
(1)	Richie Allen (Phillies, batting helmet)	18.00	9.00	5.50
(2)	Gene Alley (Pirates, upper body)	12.00	6.00	3.50
(3)	Mike Andrews (Red Sox, upper body)	12.00	6.00	3.50
(4)	Bob Aspromonte (Dodgers, upper body)	12.00	6.00	3.50
(5)	Sal Bando (A's, upper body)	12.00	6.00	3.50
(6)	John Bateman (Colt .45s, upper body)	12.00	6.00	3.50
(7)	Yogi Berra (Yankees, batting)	30.00	15.00	9.00
(8)	Yogi Berra (Mets, upper body)	30.00	15.00	9.00
(9)	Jim Bouton (Yankees, upper body)	15.00	7.50	4.50
(11)	Jim Bunning (Phillies, upper body)	20.00	10.00	6.00
(12)	John Callison (Phillies, batson shoulder)	12.00	6.00	3.50
(13)	Rocky Colavito (Tigers, batting)	25.00	12.50	7.50
(14)	Roger Craig (Dodgers, on mound)	12.00	6.00	3.50

(15)	Clay Dalrymple (Phillies, upper body)	12.00	6.00	3.50
(16)	Don Drysdale (Dodgers, pitching follow-through)	25.00	12.50	7.50
(17)	Ron Fairly (Dodgers, upper body)	12.00	6.00	3.50
(18)	Whitey Ford (Yankees, hands over head)	30.00	15.00	9.00
(19)	Jim Fregosi (L.A. Angels, upper body)	15.00	7.50	4.50
(20)	Jim Fregosi (California Angels, upper body, looking front)	15.00	7.50	4.50
(21)	Jim Fregosi (California Angels, upper body, looking right)	15.00	7.50	4.50
(22)	Jim Fregosi (Angels, green borders, b/w portrait)	15.00	7.50	4.50
(23)	Bob Gibson (color, stretch position)	25.00	12.50	7.50
(24)	Tom Haller (Giants, catching crouch)	12.00	6.00	3.50
(25)	Richie Hebner (Pirates, full-length)	12.00	6.00	3.50
(26)	Mike Hegan (Brewers, upper body)	12.00	6.00	3.50
(27)	Jim Hickman (Mets, upper body)	12.00	6.00	3.50
(28)	Jerry Koosman (Mets, ready to pitch)	15.00	7.50	4.50
(29)	Jerry Koosman (Mets, upper body)	15.00	7.50	4.50
(30)	Charlie Lau (Braves, upper body)	15.00	7.50	4.50
(31)	Mickey Lolich (Tigers, upper body, ready to pitch)	15.00	7.50	4.50
(32)	Jerry Lumpe (Tigers, upper body)	12.00	6.00	3.50
(33)	Roger Maris (Yankees, batting)	30.00	15.00	9.00
(34)	Roger Maris (Yankees, full length)	30.00	15.00	9.00
(35)	Roger Maris (Cardinals, rust borders, b/w photo)	30.00	15.00	9.00
(36)	Dick McAuliffe (Tigers, portrait)	12.00	6.00	3.50
(37)	Bobby Murcer (Yankees, upper body)	12.00	6.00	3.50
(38)	Jim Northrup (Tigers, batting)	12.00	6.00	3.50
(39)	Jim Pagliaroni (Pirates, batting)	12.00	6.00	3.50
(40)	Jim Palmer (upper body)	25.00	12.50	7.50
(41)	Joe Pepitone (Yankees, batting)	15.00	7.50	4.50
(42)	Gary Peters (White Sox, green borders, b/w portrait)	12.00	6.00	3.50
(43)	Rico Petrocelli (Red Sox, upper body)	12.00	6.00	3.50
(44)	Joe Pignatano (A's, waist-to-cap)	12.00	6.00	3.50
(45)	Bob Rodgers (Angels, portrait)	12.00	6.00	3.50
(46)	Rich Rollins (Twins, arms crossed)	12.00	6.00	3.50
(47)	Nolan Ryan (Angels, color, pitching)	75.00	37.00	22.00
(48)	Tom Seaver (Mets, waist-to-cap)	30.00	15.00	9.00
(49)	Tom Seaver (Mets, color, pitching)	30.00	15.00	9.00
(50)	Mel Stottlemyre (Yankees, rust borders, b/w pitching pose)	12.00	6.00	3.50
(51)	Dick Stuart (Pirates, batting)	15.00	7.50	4.50
(52)	Joe Torre (Braves, upper body)	15.00	7.50	4.50
(53)	Joe Torre (Cardinals, red borders, b/w portrait)	15.00	7.50	4.50
(54)	Pete Ward (White Sox, portrait)	12.00	6.00	3.50
(55)	Fred Whitfield (Indians, portrait)	12.00	6.00	3.50
(56)	Maury Wills (Dodgers, chest-to-cap)	15.00	7.50	4.50
(57)	Carl Yastrzemski (kneeling w/ bats)	30.00	15.00	9.00
(58)	Carl Yastrzemski (rust borders, b/w portrait)	30.00	15.00	9.00

1948 Speedway 79 Tiger of the Week Photos

This set of blank-back, black-and-white 8" x 10" photos was issued by one of the Tigers radio sponsors. One photo, bearing a facsimile autograph on front, was given away each week to honor the outstanding Tigers performer. The photos have no markings identifying the issuer and they are unnumbered. They are checklisted here alphabetically.

		NM	EX	VG
Complete Set (14):		180.00	90.00	55.00
Common Player:		15.00	7.50	4.50
(1)	Neil Berry	15.00	7.50	4.50
(2)	"Hoot" Evers	15.00	7.50	4.50
(3)	Ted Gray	15.00	7.50	4.50
(4)	Art Houtteman	15.00	7.50	4.50
(5)	Fred Hutchinson	15.00	7.50	4.50
(6)	George Kell	25.00	12.50	7.50
(7)	Eddie Lake	15.00	7.50	4.50
(8)	Johnny Lipon	15.00	7.50	4.50
(9)	Hal Newhouser	25.00	12.50	7.50
(10)	Dizzy Trout	15.00	7.50	4.50
(11)	Virgil Trucks	15.00	7.50	4.50
(12)	George Vico	15.00	7.50	4.50
(13)	Dick Wakefield	15.00	7.50	4.50
(14)	Bill Wertz	15.00	7.50	4.50

1953-55 Spic and Span Braves

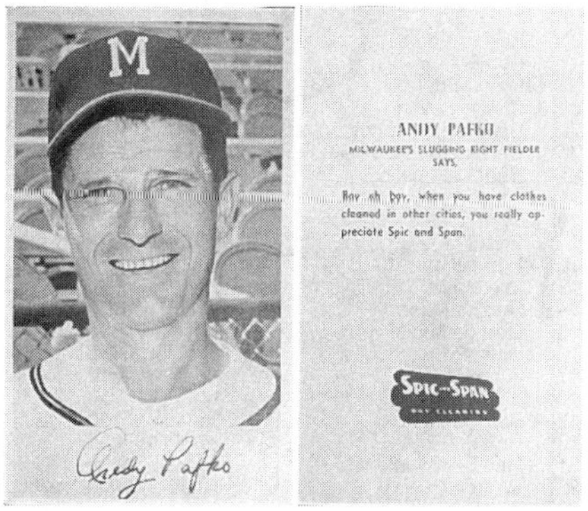

The first of several regional issues from a Milwaukee dry cleaner, the 1953-55 Spic and Span Braves set consists of black-and-white cards, 3-1/4" x 5-1/2". The front of the cards have a facsimilie autograph beneath the player photo. Cards are found with blank backs or with a Spic and Span advertising message on the back. Blank-backed cards are believed to have been issued by Wisco gas stations.

		NM	EX	VG
Complete Set (29):		900.00	450.00	275.00
Common Player:		25.00	12.50	7.50
(1)	Hank Aaron	300.00	150.00	90.00
(2)	Joe Adcock	25.00	12.50	7.50
(3)	John Antonelli	25.00	12.50	7.50
(4)	Vern Bickford	25.00	12.50	7.50
(5)	Bill Bruton	25.00	12.50	7.50
(6)	Bob Buhl	25.00	12.50	7.50
(7)	Lew Burdette	25.00	12.50	7.50
(8)	Dick Cole	25.00	12.50	7.50
(9)	Walker Cooper	25.00	12.50	7.50
(10)	Del Crandall	25.00	12.50	7.50
(11)	George Crowe	25.00	12.50	7.50
(12)	Jack Dittmer	25.00	12.50	7.50
(13)	Sid Gordon	25.00	12.50	7.50
(14)	Ernie Johnson	25.00	12.50	7.50
(15)	Dave Jolly	25.00	12.50	7.50
(16)	Don Liddle	25.00	12.50	7.50
(17)	John Logan	25.00	12.50	7.50
(18)	Ed Mathews	100.00	50.00	30.00
(19)	Chet Nichols	25.00	12.50	7.50
(20)	Dan O'Connell	25.00	12.50	7.50
(21)	Andy Pafko	25.00	12.50	7.50
(22)	Jim Pendleton	25.00	12.50	7.50
(23)	Ebba St. Claire	25.00	12.50	7.50
(24)	Warren Spahn	100.00	50.00	30.00
(25)	Max Surkont	25.00	12.50	7.50
(26)	Bob Thomson	35.00	17.50	10.50
(27)	Bob Thorpe	25.00	12.50	7.50
(28)	Roberto Vargas	25.00	12.50	7.50
(29)	Jim Wilson	25.00	12.50	7.50

1953-57 Spic and Span Braves 7x10 Photos

This regional set was issued by Spic and Span Dry Cleaners of Milwaukee over a four-year period and consists of large (7" x 10") photos of Braves players. Of all the various Spic and Span sets, this one seems to be the easiest to find. The fronts feature a player photo with a facsimilie autograph below. The Spic and Span logo also appears on the fronts, while the backs are blank. A photo of Milwaukee County Stadium also exists but is not generally considered to be part of the set.

		NM	EX	VG
Complete Set (13):		335.00	165.00	100.00
Common Player:		22.00	11.00	6.50
(1)	Joe Adcock	22.00	11.00	6.50
(2)	William H. Bruton	22.00	11.00	6.50
(3)	Robert Buhl	22.00	11.00	6.50
(4)	Lou Burdette	22.00	11.00	6.50
(5)	Del Crandall	22.00	11.00	6.50
(6)	Jack Dittmer	22.00	11.00	6.50
(7)	Johnny Logan	22.00	11.00	6.50
(8)	Edwin L. Mathews, Jr.	75.00	37.00	22.00
(9)	Chet Nichols	22.00	11.00	6.50
(10)	Danny O'Connell	22.00	11.00	6.50
(11)	Andy Pafko	22.00	11.00	6.50
(12)	Warren E. Spahn	75.00	37.00	22.00
(13)	Bob Thomson	35.00	17.50	10.50

1954-56 Spic and Span Braves

Issued during the three-year period from 1954-1956, this Spic and Span set consists of 18 post-card-size (4" x 6") cards. The front of the cards include a facsimilie autograph printed in white and the Spic and Span logo.

		NM	EX	VG
Complete Set (18):		450.00	340.00	180.00
Common Player:		12.00	6.00	3.50
(1)	Hank Aaron	175.00	87.00	52.00
(2)	Joe Adcock	12.00	6.00	3.50
(3)	William H. Bruton	12.00	6.00	3.50
(4)	Robert Buhl	12.00	6.00	3.50
(5)	Lou Burdette	12.00	6.00	3.50
(6)	Gene Conley	12.00	6.00	3.50
(7)	Del Crandall	12.00	6.00	3.50
(8)	Ray Crone	12.00	6.00	3.50
(9)	Jack Dittmer	12.00	6.00	3.50
(10)	Ernie Johnson	12.00	6.00	3.50
(11)	Dave Jolly	12.00	6.00	3.50
(12)	Johnny Logan	12.00	6.00	3.50
(13)	Edwin L. Mathews, Jr.	75.00	37.00	22.00
(14)	Chet Nichols	12.00	6.00	3.50
(15)	Danny O'Connell	12.00	6.00	3.50
(16)	Andy Pafko	12.00	6.00	3.50
(17)	Warren E. Spahn	75.00	37.00	22.00
(18)	Bob Thomson	20.00	10.00	6.00

1955 Spic and Span Braves Die-cuts

This 17-card, die-cut set is the rarest of all the Spic and Span issues. The stand-ups, which measure approximately 7-1/2" x 7", picture the players in action poses and were designed to be punched out, allowing them to stand up. Most cards were used in this fashion, making better-condition cards very rare today. The front of the card includes a facsimilie autograph and the Spic and Span logo.

		NM	EX	VG
Complete Set (18):		4225.	2100.	1275.
Common Player:		180.00	90.00	50.00
(1)	Hank Aaron	950.00	475.00	285.00
(2)	Joe Adcock	180.00	90.00	50.00
(3)	Bill Bruton	180.00	90.00	50.00
(4)	Bob Buhl	180.00	90.00	50.00
(5)	Lew Burdette	180.00	90.00	50.00
(6)	Gene Conley	180.00	90.00	50.00
(7)	Del Crandall	180.00	90.00	50.00
(8)	Jack Dittmer	180.00	90.00	50.00
(9)	Ernie Johnson	180.00	90.00	50.00
(10)	Dave Jolly	180.00	90.00	50.00
(11)	John Logan	180.00	90.00	50.00
(12)	Ed Mathews	425.00	210.00	125.00
(13)	Chet Nichols	180.00	90.00	50.00
(14)	Dan O'Connell	180.00	90.00	50.00
(15)	Andy Pafko	180.00	90.00	50.00
(16)	Warren Spahn	425.00	210.00	125.00
(17)	Bob Thomson	225.00	110.00	67.00
(18)	Jim Wilson	180.00	90.00	50.00

1957 Spic and Span Braves

This 20-card set was issued in 1957, the year the Braves were World Champions and is a highly desirable set. The cards measure 4" x 5" and have a wide white border surrounding the player photo. A blue Spic and Span logo appears in the lower-right corner and the card includes a salutation and facsimile autograph, also in blue.

		NM	EX	VG
Complete Set (20):		750.00	350.00	175.00
Common Player:		15.00	7.50	4.50
(1)	Hank Aaron	350.00	175.00	105.00
(2)	Joe Adcock	15.00	7.50	4.50
(3)	Bill Bruton	15.00	7.50	4.50
(4)	Bob Buhl	15.00	7.50	4.50
(5)	Lew Burdette	15.00	7.50	4.50
(6)	Gene Conley	15.00	7.50	4.50
(7)	Wes Covington (SP)	30.00	15.00	9.00
(8)	Del Crandall	15.00	7.50	4.50
(9)	Ray Crone	15.00	7.50	4.50
(10)	Fred Haney	15.00	7.50	4.50
(11)	Ernie Johnson	15.00	7.50	4.50
(12)	John Logan	15.00	7.50	4.50
(13)	Felix Mantilla (SP)	30.00	15.00	9.00
(14)	Ed Mathews	50.00	25.00	15.00
(15)	Dan O'Connell	15.00	7.50	4.50
(16)	Andy Pafko	15.00	7.50	4.50
(17)	Red Schoendienst (SP)	65.00	32.00	19.50
(18)	Warren Spahn	50.00	25.00	15.00
(19)	Bob Thomson	25.00	12.50	7.50
(20)	Bob Trowbridge (SP)	30.00	15.00	9.00

1960 Spic and Span Braves

Spic and Span's final Milwaukee Braves issue consists of 26 cards, each measuring 2-3/4" x 3-1/8". The fronts contain a white-bordered photo with no printing, while the backs include a facsimilie autograph and the words "Photographed and Autographed Exclusively for Spic and Span." The 1960 set includes the only known variation in the Spic and Span sets; a "flopped" negative error showing catcher Del Crandell batting left-handed was later corrected.

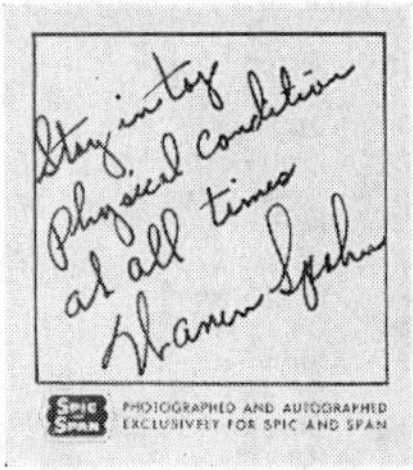

		NM	EX	VG
Complete Set (26):		750.00	375.00	220.00
Common Player:		15.00	7.50	4.50
(1)	Hank Aaron	350.00	175.00	105.00
(2)	Joe Adcock	15.00	7.50	4.50
(3)	Bill Bruton	15.00	7.50	4.50
(4)	Bob Buhl	15.00	7.50	4.50
(5)	Lew Burdette	15.00	7.50	4.50
(6)	Chuck Cottier	15.00	7.50	4.50
(7a)	Del Crandall (photo reversed)	30.00	15.00	9.00
(7b)	Del Crandall (correct photo)	18.00	9.00	5.50
(8)	Chuck Dressen	15.00	7.50	4.50
(9)	Joey Jay	15.00	7.50	4.50
(10)	John Logan	15.00	7.50	4.50
(11)	Felix Mantilla	15.00	7.50	4.50
(12)	Ed Mathews	60.00	30.00	18.00
(13)	Lee Maye	15.00	7.50	4.50
(14)	Don McMahon	15.00	7.50	4.50
(15)	George Myatt	15.00	7.50	4.50
(16)	Andy Pafko	15.00	7.50	4.50
(17)	Juan Pizarro	15.00	7.50	4.50
(18)	Mel Roach	15.00	7.50	4.50
(19)	Bob Rush	15.00	7.50	4.50
(20)	Bob Scheffing	15.00	7.50	4.50
(21)	Red Schoendienst	45.00	22.00	13.50
(22)	Warren Spahn	60.00	30.00	18.00
(23)	Al Spangler	15.00	7.50	4.50
(24)	Frank Torre	15.00	7.50	4.50
(25)	Carl Willey	15.00	7.50	4.50
(26)	Whit Wyatt	15.00	7.50	4.50

1964-67 Sport Hobbyist Famous Card Series

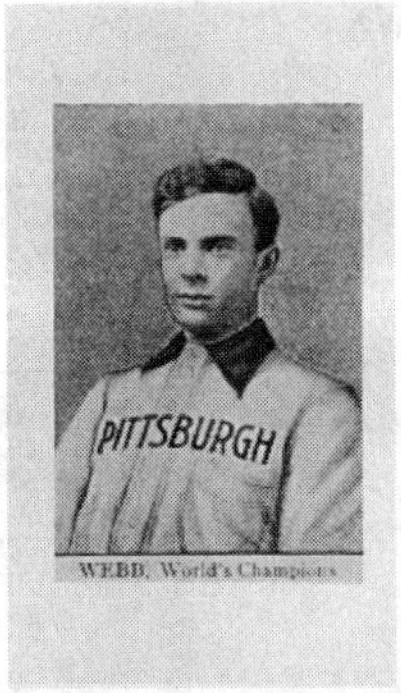

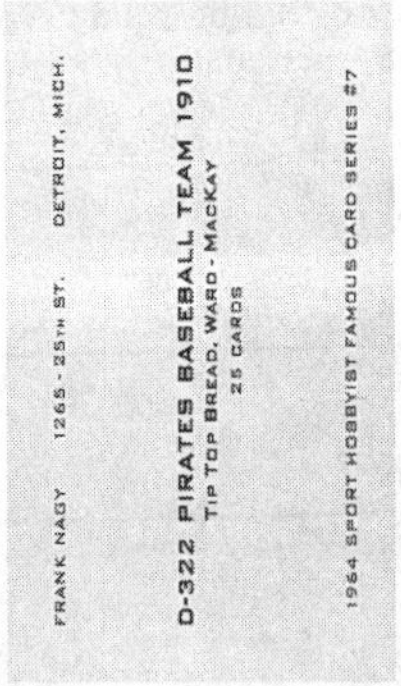

These very early collectors issues were produced over a period of several years in the mid-1960s during Frank Nagy's ownership of the "Sport Hobbyist" magazine. The 2-1/4" x 3-3/4" black-and-white cards picture on their fronts reproductions of rare and famous baseball cards from Nagy's unequaled collection, including eight of the very rare Tarzan Bread issue of the mid-1930s which few collectors even today have seen. Backs have identification of the pictured card, utilizing the then-standard "American Card Catalog" set designations.

		NM	EX	VG
Complete Set (30):		50.00	25.00	15.00
Common Player:		2.00	1.00	.60
1	T206 Honus Wagner	5.00	2.50	1.50
2	Not known			
3	C46 Simmons	2.00	1.00	.60
4	M116 Christy Mathewson	2.00	1.00	.60
5	M101-5 Jack Barry	2.00	1.00	.60
6	T204 Mordecai Brown	2.00	1.00	.60
7	D322 Tip Top Bread Webb	2.00	1.00	.60
8	S74 Lou Criger	2.00	1.00	.60
9	R333 DeLong Kiki Cuyler	2.00	1.00	.60
10	R319 Nap Lajoie	2.50	1.25	.70
11	T205 John McGraw	2.00	1.00	.60
12	E107 Addie Joss	2.00	1.00	.60
13	W502 George Sisler	2.00	1.00	.60
14	Allen & Ginter N29 Buck Ewing	2.00	1.00	.60
15	E90 Chief Bender	2.00	1.00	.60
16	E104 George Mullin	2.00	1.00	.60
17	E95 Fred Merkle	2.00	1.00	.60
18	E121 Walter Schang	2.00	1.00	.60
19	Allen & Ginter N28 Tim Keefe	2.00	1.00	.60
20	E120 Harold (Muddy) Ruel	2.00	1.00	.60
21	D382 Irving (Jack) Burns	2.00	1.00	.60
22	D382 George Connally	2.00	1.00	.60
23	D382 Myril Hoag	2.00	1.00	.60
24	D382 Willie Kamm	2.00	1.00	.60
25	D382 Dutch Leonard	2.00	1.00	.60
26	D382 Clyde Manion	2.00	1.00	.60
27	D382 Johnny Vergez	2.00	1.00	.60
28	D382 Tom Zachary	2.00	1.00	.60
29	E145 Ty Cobb	2.50	1.25	.70
30	Playing Card, Richardson	2.00	1.00	.60

1971 Sport Hobbyist Famous Card Series

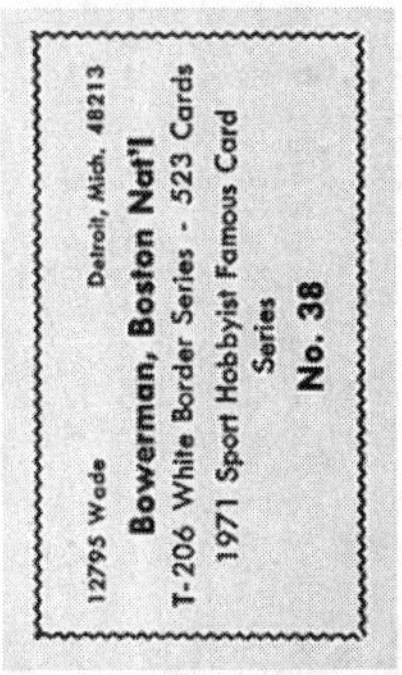

A new series of collector cards, designed as the first-ever attempt to reproduce the T206 tobacco set, was begun under the hobby paper's new ownership but quickly abandoned. The 2" x 3" cards have a black-and-white picture of a card at center, surrounded by a red frame. Backs identify the card and include a card number. It is unknown whether the second series was skip-numbered or whether there are cards extant for the missing numbers.

		NM	EX	VG
Complete Set (18):		25.00	12.50	7.50
Common Card:		2.00	1.00	.60
31	T206 Abbaticchio	2.00	1.00	.60
32	T206 Barbeau	2.00	1.00	.60
33	T206 Burch	2.00	1.00	.60
34	T206 M. Brown	2.00	1.00	.60
35	T206 Chase	2.00	1.00	.60
36	T206 Ball	2.00	1.00	.60
37	T206 Abstein	2.00	1.00	.60
38	T206 Bowerman	2.00	1.00	.60
39	T206 Chase	2.00	1.00	.60
40	T206 Criss	2.00	1.00	.60
41	T206 Beck	2.00	1.00	.60
43	T206 Bradley	2.00	1.00	.60
45	T206 Bransfield	2.00	1.00	.60
47	T206 Bell	2.00	1.00	.60
48	T206 Bergen	2.00	1.00	.60
49	T206 Bender	2.00	1.00	.60
50	T206 Bush	2.00	1.00	.60
51	T206 Chesbro	2.00	1.00	.60

1975 Sport Hobbyist

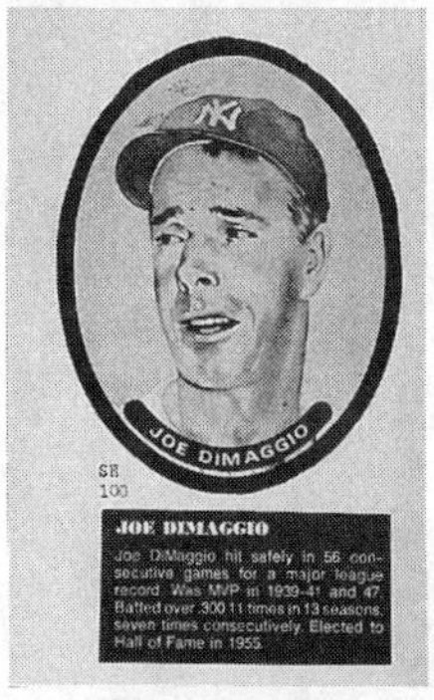

This was one of several series of collectors issues produced in the 1960s and 1970s by the Sport Hobbyist, one of the card hobby's earliest periodicals. This series features the past greats of the game in postcard size (3-1/2" x 5-1/2"). Cards are found either blank-backed or with an ad offering vendor boxes of 1975 Topps football cards. Fronts have sepia watercolor portraits in an oval frame. A box below offers a career summary. Cards are numbered with an SH prefix. The checklist here is not complete. Complete sets of 18 were originally sold at $1.50.

		NM	EX	VG
Common Player:		3.00	1.50	.90
100	Joe DiMaggio	9.00	4.50	2.75
101	Mel Ott	3.00	1.50	.90
102				
103	Babe Ruth	12.00	6.00	3.50
104				
105				
106				
107	Jimmy Foxx	3.00	1.50	.90
108	Ted Williams	9.00	4.50	2.75
109	Mickey Cochrane	3.00	1.50	.90
110				
111				
112	George Sissler (Sisler)	3.00	1.50	.90
113	Honus Wagner	3.00	1.50	.90
114	Lefty Grove	3.00	1.50	.90
115	Dizzy Dean	3.00	1.50	.90
?	Lou Gehrig	9.00	4.50	2.75

1902 Sporting Life Team Composites (W601)

Printed on heavy 13" x 14" paper and featuring a composite of player photos arranged around that of the manager and a notice of league championship status, these prints were offered to readers of the weekly sports paper for six cents in postage stamps or 50 cents per dozen. The art was often found on the covers of "Sporting Life." While the prints were issued in 1902, they specify the teams as champions "for 1903". The Buck Weaver shown on the Butte composite is not the future Black Sox shortstop.

		NM	EX	VG
Complete Set:		4500.	2200.	1350.
Common Team:		300.00	150.00	90.00
(1)	Philadelphia, American League	500.00	250.00	150.00
(2)	Pittsburgh, National League	500.00	250.00	150.00
(3)	Albany, New York State League	300.00	150.00	90.00
(4)	Butte, Pacific Northwest League	400.00	200.00	120.00
(5)	Indianapolis, American Association	400.00	200.00	120.00
(6)	Kansas City, Western League	400.00	200.00	120.00
(7)	Manchester, New England League	300.00	150.00	90.00
(8)	Nashville, Southern League	350.00	175.00	105.00
(9)	New Haven, Connecticut League	300.00	150.00	90.00
(10)	Rockford, Illinois-Indiana-Iowa League	300.00	150.00	90.00
(11)	Toronto, Eastern League	400.00	200.00	120.00

1903 Sporting Life Team Composites (W601)

Portraits of the individual players, usually identified by name and position, surround the manager's portrait in this series of team composites sold by Sporting Life newspaper. The 1903 series is the first in which all major league team composites were available. The 13" x 14" pictures are printed on heavy enamel paper and were sold for six cents in postage stamps, 50 cents per dozen. In some years bound portfolio complete sets were also offered, as were some of the more popular minor league teams. Notations of league and World Championships were incorporated into the design where appropriate.

		NM	EX	VG
Complete Set (25):		5550.	2700.	1650.
Common (Major League) Team:		400.00	200.00	120.00
(1)	Boston, National League	400.00	200.00	120.00
(2)	Brooklyn, National League	400.00	200.00	120.00
(3)	Chicago, National League	600.00	300.00	180.00
(4)	Cincinnati, National League	400.00	200.00	120.00
(5)	New York, National League	500.00	250.00	150.00
(6)	Philadelphia, National League	400.00	200.00	120.00
(7)	Pittsburgh, National League	500.00	250.00	150.00
(8)	St. Louis, National League	400.00	200.00	120.00
(9)	Boston, American League	450.00	225.00	135.00
(10)	Chicago, American League	400.00	200.00	120.00
(11)	Cleveland, American League	400.00	200.00	120.00
(12)	Detroit, American League	400.00	200.00	120.00
(13)	New York, American League	450.00	225.00	135.00
(14)	Philadelphia, American League	450.00	225.00	135.00
(15)	St. Louis, American League	400.00	200.00	120.00
(16)	Washington, American League	400.00	200.00	120.00
(17)	Ft. Wayne, Central League	250.00	125.00	75.00
(18)	Holyoke, Connecticut League	250.00	125.00	75.00
(19)	Jersey City, Eastern League	300.00	150.00	90.00
(20)	Los Angeles, Pacific Coast League	300.00	150.00	90.00
(21)	Lowell, New England League	250.00	125.00	75.00
(22)	Memphis, Southern League	250.00	125.00	75.00
(23)	Schenectady, New York State League	250.00	125.00	75.00
(24)	Sedalia, Missouri Valley League	250.00	125.00	75.00
(25)	St. Paul, American Association	300.00	150.00	90.00

1904 Sporting Life Team Composites (W601)

Portraits of the individual players, usually identified by name and position, surround the manager's portrait in this series of team composites sold by Sporting Life newspaper. The 13" x 14" pictures are printed on heavy enamel paper and were sold for a dime apiece postpaid. In some years bound portfolio complete sets were also offered, as were some of the more popular minor league teams. Notations of league and World Championships were incorporated into the design where appropriate.

		NM	EX	VG
Complete Set (24):		5550.	2700.	1650.
Common (Major League) Team:		400.00	200.00	120.00
(1)	Boston, National League	400.00	200.00	120.00
(2)	Brooklyn, National League	400.00	200.00	120.00
(3)	Chicago, National League	600.00	300.00	180.00
(4)	Cincinnati, National League	400.00	200.00	120.00
(5)	New York, National League	500.00	250.00	150.00
(6)	Philadelphia, National League	400.00	200.00	120.00
(7)	Pittsburgh, National League	550.00	275.00	165.00
(8)	St. Louis, National League	400.00	200.00	120.00
(9)	Boston, American League	450.00	225.00	135.00
(10)	Chicago, American League	400.00	200.00	120.00
(11)	Cleveland, American League	400.00	200.00	120.00
(12)	Detroit, American League	400.00	200.00	120.00
(13)	New York, American League	450.00	225.00	135.00
(14)	Philadelphia, American League	450.00	225.00	135.00
(15)	St. Louis, American League	400.00	200.00	120.00
(16)	Washington, American League	400.00	200.00	120.00
(17)	Buffalo, Eastern League	300.00	150.00	90.00
(18)	Ft. Wayne, Central League	200.00	100.00	60.00
(19)	Haverhill, New England League	200.00	100.00	60.00
(20)	Macon, South Atlantic League	200.00	100.00	60.00
(21)	Memphis, Southern League	200.00	100.00	60.00
(22)	Springfield, Indiana-Illinois-Iowa League	200.00	100.00	60.00
(23)	St. Paul, American Association	250.00	125.00	75.00
(24)	Syracuse, New York League (1903 Indiana-Illinois-Iowa League Champs)	200.00	100.00	60.00

1905 Sporting Life Team Composites (W601)

Portraits of the individual players, usually identified by name and position, surround the manager's portrait in this series of team composites sold by Sporting Life newspaper. The 13" x 14" pictures are printed on heavy enamel paper and were sold for a dime apiece postpaid. In some years bound portfolio complete sets were also offered, as were some of the more popular minor league teams. Notations of league and World Championships were incorporated into the design where appropriate.

		NM	EX	VG
Complete Set (23):		5500.	2700.	1650.
Common (Major League) Team:		400.00	200.00	120.00
(1)	Boston, National League	400.00	200.00	120.00
(2)	Brooklyn, National League	400.00	200.00	120.00
(3)	Chicago, National League	500.00	250.00	150.00
(4)	Cincinnati, National League	400.00	200.00	120.00
(5)	New York, National League	450.00	225.00	135.00
(6)	Philadelphia, National League	400.00	200.00	120.00
(7)	Pittsburgh, National League	500.00	250.00	150.00
(8)	St. Louis, National League	400.00	200.00	120.00
(9)	Boston, American League	400.00	200.00	120.00
(10)	Chicago, American League	400.00	200.00	120.00
(11)	Cleveland, American League	400.00	200.00	120.00
(12)	Detroit, American League	400.00	200.00	120.00
(13)	New York, American League	450.00	225.00	135.00
(14)	Philadelphia, American League	500.00	250.00	150.00
(15)	St. Louis, American League	400.00	200.00	120.00
(16)	Washington, American League	400.00	200.00	120.00
(17)	A., J. & G., New York League	200.00	100.00	60.00
(18)	Columbus, American Association	250.00	125.00	75.00
(19)	Concord, New England League	200.00	100.00	60.00
(20)	Des Moines, Western League	250.00	125.00	75.00
(21)	Macon, South Atlantic League	200.00	100.00	60.00
(22)	New Orleans, Southern League	250.00	125.00	75.00
(23)	Providence, Eastern League	250.00	125.00	75.00

1906-07 Sporting Life Team Composite Postcards

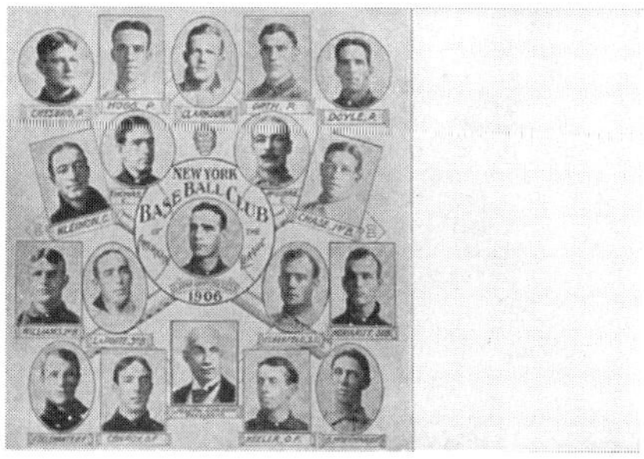

A miniature version of the Sporting Life's team composite lithographs was utilized to create a postcard set. In 3-5/8" x 5-7/16" format, the postcards have a composite of player portraits surrounding that of the manager, with a wide white right margin. Backs have standard postcard indicia.

		NM	EX	VG
Complete Set (16):		10000.	5000.	3000.
Common Team:		600.00	300.00	180.00
(1)	Boston, National League	600.00	300.00	180.00
(2)	Brooklyn, National League	600.00	300.00	180.00
(3)	Chicago, National League	800.00	400.00	240.00
(4)	Cincinnati, National League	600.00	300.00	180.00
(5)	New York, National League	650.00	325.00	195.00
(6)	Philadelphia, National League	600.00	300.00	180.00
(7)	Pittsburgh, National League	650.00	325.00	195.00
(8)	St. Louis, National League	600.00	300.00	180.00
(9)	Boston, American League	800.00	400.00	240.00
(10)	Chicago, American League	650.00	325.00	195.00
(11)	Cleveland, American League	1000.	500.00	300.00
(12)	Detroit, American League	1000.	500.00	300.00
(13)	New York, American League	800.00	400.00	240.00
(14)	Philadelphia, American League	800.00	400.00	240.00
(15)	St. Louis, American League	600.00	300.00	180.00
(16)	Washington, American League	600.00	300.00	180.00

1906 Sporting Life Team Composites (W601)

Originally sold as a string-bound "Premier Art Portfolio" containing 24 major and minor league team composite pictures, single pieces from this premium issue are not uncommonly found as they were later offered individually for 10 cents apiece. The individual pieces measure 13" x 14" and are printed in black-and-white on heavy enameled paper. Individual player pictures are arranged around a baseball containing the manager's picture. Each player is identified beneath his photo by name and position.

		NM	EX	VG
Complete Set (24):		6500.	3200.	1950.
Common Major League Team:		352.00	176.00	106.00
Common Minor League Team:		220.00	110.00	66.00
(1)	Boston, National League	350.00	175.00	105.00
(2)	Brooklyn, National League	350.00	175.00	105.00
(3)	Chicago, National League	525.00	262.00	157.00
(4)	Cincinnati, National League	350.00	175.00	105.00
(5)	New York, National League	440.00	220.00	132.00
(6)	Philadelphia, National League	350.00	175.00	105.00
(7)	Pittsburgh, National League	440.00	220.00	132.00
(8)	St. Louis, National League	350.00	175.00	105.00
(9)	Boston, American League	525.00	262.00	157.00
(10)	Chicago, American League	440.00	220.00	132.00
(11)	Cleveland, American League	795.00	395.00	238.00
(12)	Detroit, American League	795.00	395.00	238.00
(13)	New York, American League	525.00	265.00	157.00
(14)	Philadelphia, American League	525.00	265.00	157.00
(15)	St. Louis, American League	350.00	175.00	105.00
(16)	Washington, American League	350.00	175.00	105.00
(17)	National League president, managers	350.00	175.00	105.00
(18)	American League president, managers	350.00	175.00	105.00
(19)	Birmingham, Southern League (Amsterdam, Johnstown and Gloversville)	175.00	87.00	52.00
(20)	Buffalo, Eastern League	220.00	110.00	66.00
(21)	Columbus, American Association	220.00	110.00	66.00
(22)	Grand Rapids, Central League	175.00	87.00	52.00
(23)	Norwich, Connecticut League	175.00	87.00	52.00
(24)	Scranton, New York League	175.00	87.00	52.00

1907 Sporting Life Team Composites (W601)

Portraits of the individual players, usually identified by name and position, surround the manager's portrait in this series of team composites sold by Sporting Life newspaper. The 13" x 14" pictures are printed on heavy enamel paper and were sold for a dime apiece postpaid. In some years bound portfolio complete sets were also offered, as were some of the more popular minor league teams. Notations of league and World Championships were incorporated into the design where appropriate.

		NM	EX	VG
Complete Set (20):		5500.	2700.	1600.
Common (Major League) Team:		400.00	200.00	120.00
(1)	Boston, National League	400.00	200.00	120.00
(2)	Brooklyn, National League	400.00	200.00	120.00
(3)	Chicago, National League	500.00	250.00	150.00
(4)	Cincinnati, National League	400.00	200.00	120.00
(5)	New York, National League	450.00	225.00	135.00
(6)	Philadelphia, National League	400.00	200.00	120.00
(7)	Pittsburgh, National League	450.00	225.00	135.00
(8)	St. Louis, National League	400.00	200.00	120.00
(9)	Boston, American League	400.00	200.00	120.00
(10)	Chicago, American League	400.00	200.00	120.00
(11)	Cleveland, American League	400.00	200.00	120.00
(12)	Detroit, American League	600.00	300.00	180.00
(13)	New York, American League	450.00	225.00	135.00
(14)	Philadelphia, American League	400.00	200.00	120.00
(15)	St. Louis, American League	400.00	200.00	120.00
(16)	Washington, American League	500.00	250.00	150.00
(17)	Toronto, Eastern League	300.00	150.00	90.00
(18)	Columbus, American Association	300.00	150.00	90.00
(19)	Williamsport, Tri-State League	200.00	100.00	60.00
(20)	Albany, New York League	200.00	100.00	60.00
(21)	Atlanta, Southern League	200.00	100.00	60.00
(22)	Holyoke, Connecticut League	200.00	100.00	60.00
(23)	Norfolk, Virginia League	200.00	100.00	60.00

1908 Sporting Life Team Composites (W601)

Portraits of the individual players, usually identified by name and position, surround the manager's portrait in this series of team composites sold by Sporting Life newspaper. The 13" x 14" pictures are printed on heavy enamel paper and were sold for a dime apiece postpaid. In some years bound portfolio complete sets were also offered, as were some of the more popular minor league teams. Notations of league and World Championships were incorporated into the design where appropriate.

		NM	EX	VG
Complete Set (16):		4500.	2250.	1350.
Common Team:		400.00	200.00	120.00
(1)	Boston, National League	400.00	200.00	120.00
(2)	Brooklyn, National League	400.00	200.00	120.00
(3)	Chicago, National League	500.00	250.00	150.00
(4)	Cincinnati, National League	400.00	200.00	120.00
(5)	New York, National League	450.00	225.00	135.00
(6)	Philadelphia, National League	400.00	200.00	120.00
(7)	Pittsburgh, National League	450.00	225.00	135.00
(8)	St. Louis, National League	400.00	200.00	120.00
(9)	Boston, American League	400.00	200.00	120.00
(10)	Chicago, American League	400.00	200.00	120.00
(11)	Cleveland, American League	400.00	200.00	120.00
(12)	Detroit, American League	600.00	300.00	180.00
(13)	New York, American League	450.00	225.00	135.00
(14)	Philadelphia, American League	400.00	200.00	120.00
(15)	St. Louis, American League	400.00	200.00	120.00
(16)	Washington, American League	450.00	225.00	135.00

1909 Sporting Life Team Composites (W601)

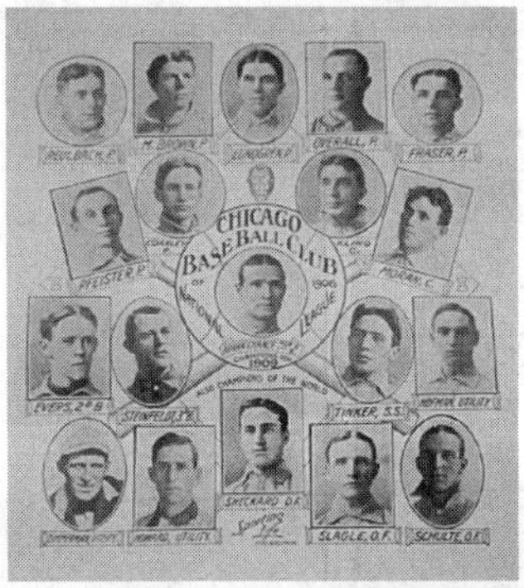

Portraits of the individual players, usually identified by name and position, surround the manager's portrait in this series of team composites sold by Sporting Life newspaper. The 13" x 14" pictures are printed on heavy enamel paper and were sold for a dime apiece postpaid. In some years bound portfolio complete sets were also offered, as were some of the more popular minor league teams. Notations of league and World Championships were incorporated into the design where appropriate.

		NM	EX	VG
Complete Set (16):		4500.	2250.	1350.
Common Team:		400.00	200.00	120.00
(1)	Boston, National League	400.00	200.00	120.00
(2)	Brooklyn, National League	400.00	200.00	120.00
(3)	Chicago, National League	500.00	250.00	150.00
(4)	Cincinnati, National League	400.00	200.00	120.00
(5)	New York, National League	450.00	225.00	135.00
(6)	Philadelphia, National League	400.00	200.00	120.00
(7)	Pittsburgh, National League	500.00	250.00	150.00
(8)	St. Louis, National League	400.00	200.00	120.00
(9)	Boston, American League	400.00	200.00	120.00
(10)	Chicago, American League	400.00	200.00	120.00
(11)	Cleveland, American League	400.00	200.00	120.00
(12)	Detroit, American League	600.00	300.00	180.00
(13)	New York, American League	450.00	225.00	135.00
(14)	Philadelphia, American League	400.00	200.00	120.00
(15)	St. Louis, American League	400.00	200.00	120.00
(16)	Washington, American League	450.00	225.00	135.00

1910-11 Sporting Life (M116)

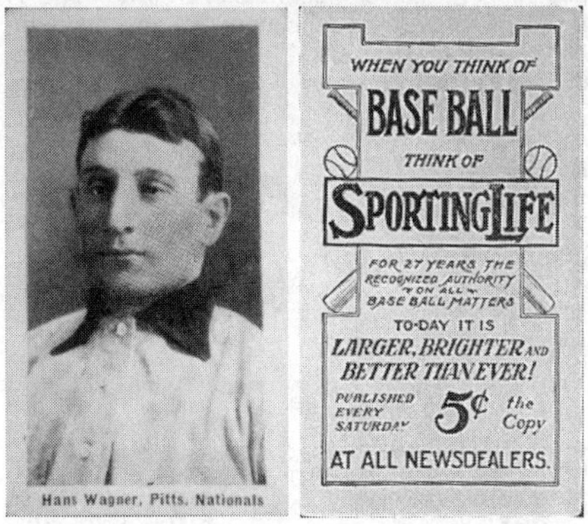

This set of 1-1/2" x 2-3/4" cards was offered to subscribers to "Sporting Life," a major competitor of "The Sporting News" in the early part of the century. The cards were issued in 24 series of 12 cards each, sold by mail for four cents per series. Card fronts feature hand-tinted black-and-white portrait photos with the name and team printed below. Backs have various ads for the weekly paper. The last 72 cards issued are scarcer than the earlier cards. The scarce blue-background cards appear to have been a second printing of the first two 12-card series which no doubt sold out quickly in the original pastel-background version due to the popularity of the players included. The 12 players in the Third Series can be found in an original printing with the ad on back printed in black, and a later reprinting with a blue ad. Each of the Third Series cards also exhibits on front subtle differences in the size and coloring of the player portrait. The complete set price does not include variations.

		NM	EX	VG
Complete Set (287):		45000.	20000.	10000.
Common Player:		75.00	37.00	22.00
(1)	Ed Abbaticchio	65.00	32.00	19.50
(2a)	Babe Adams (black back)	450.00	225.00	135.00
(2b)	Babe Adams (blue back)	325.00	162.00	97.00
(3)	Red Ames	225.00	112.00	67.00
(4)	Jimmy Archer	225.00	112.00	67.00
(5)	Frank Arrelanes (Arellanes)	65.00	32.00	19.50
(6)	Tommy Atkins	225.00	112.00	67.00
(7)	Jimmy Austin	225.00	112.00	67.00
(8)	Les Bachman (Backman)	65.00	32.00	19.50
(9)	Bill Bailey	65.00	32.00	19.50
(10a)	Home Run Baker (black back)	450.00	225.00	135.00
(10b)	Home Run Baker (blue back)	325.00	162.00	97.00
(11)	Cy Barger	65.00	32.00	19.50
(12)	Jack Barry	65.00	32.00	19.50
(13)	Johnny Bates	65.00	32.00	19.50
(14)	Ginger Beaumont	65.00	32.00	19.50
(15)	Fred Beck	65.00	32.00	19.50
(16)	Heinie Beckendorf	65.00	32.00	19.50
(17)	Fred Beebe	65.00	32.00	19.50
(18)	George Bell	65.00	32.00	19.50
(19)	Harry Bemis	65.00	32.00	19.50
(20a)	Chief Bender (blue background)	600.00	300.00	180.00
(21b)	Chief Bender (pastel background)	325.00	162.00	97.00
(21)	Bill Bergen	65.00	32.00	19.50
(22)	Heinie Berger	65.00	32.00	19.50
(23)	Bob Bescher	65.00	32.00	19.50
(24)	Joe Birmingham	65.00	32.00	19.50
(25)	Lena Blackburn (Blackburne)	65.00	32.00	19.50
(26)	John Bliss	225.00	112.00	67.00
(27)	Bruno Block	225.00	112.00	67.00
(28)	Bill Bradley	65.00	32.00	19.50
(29)	Kitty Bransfield	65.00	32.00	19.50
(30a)	Roger Bresnahan (blue)	400.00	200.00	120.00
(30b)	Roger Bresnahan (pastel)	325.00	162.00	97.00
(31)	Al Bridwell	65.00	32.00	19.50
(32)	Buster Brown (Boston)	65.00	32.00	19.50
(33a)	Mordecai Brown (blue, Chicago)	400.00	200.00	120.00
(33b)	Mordecai Brown (pastel, Chicago)	325.00	162.00	97.00
(34)	Al Burch	65.00	32.00	19.50
(35)	Donie Bush	65.00	32.00	19.50
(36)	Bobby Byrne	65.00	32.00	19.50
(37)	Howie Camnitz	65.00	32.00	19.50
(38)	Vin Campbell	225.00	112.00	67.00
(39)	Bill Carrigan	65.00	32.00	19.50
(40a)	Frank Chance (blue)	600.00	300.00	180.00
(40b)	Frank Chance (pastel)	325.00	162.00	97.00
(41)	Chappy Charles	65.00	32.00	19.50
(42a)	Hal Chase (blue)	400.00	200.00	120.00
(42b)	Hal Chase (pastel)	245.00	122.00	73.00
(43)	Ed Cicotte	250.00	125.00	75.00
(44a)	Fred Clarke (Pittsburgh, black back)	450.00	225.00	135.00
(44b)	Fred Clarke (Pittsburgh, blue back)	325.00	162.00	97.00
(45)	Nig Clarke (Cleveland)	65.00	32.00	19.50
(46)	Tommy Clarke (Cincinnati)	225.00	112.00	67.00

(47a)	Ty Cobb (blue)	2750.	1375.	825.00
(47b)	Ty Cobb (pastel)	1500.	750.00	450.00
(48a)	Eddie Collins (blue)	675.00	337.00	202.00
(48b)	Eddie Collins (pastel)	350.00	175.00	105.00
(49)	Ray Collins	225.00	112.00	67.00
(50)	Wid Conroy	65.00	32.00	19.50
(51)	Jack Coombs	65.00	32.00	19.50
(52)	Frank Corridon	65.00	32.00	19.50
(53)	Harry Coveleskie (Coveleski)	325.00	162.00	97.00
(54)	Doc Crandall	65.00	32.00	19.50
(55a)	Sam Crawford (blue)	400.00	200.00	120.00
(55b)	Sam Crawford (pastel)	325.00	162.00	97.00
(56)	Birdie Cree	65.00	32.00	19.50
(57)	Lou Criger	65.00	32.00	19.50
(58)	Dode Criss	225.00	112.00	67.00
(59)	Cliff Curtis	225.00	112.00	67.00
(60)	Bill Dahlen	65.00	32.00	19.50
(62)	Bill Davidson	225.00	112.00	67.00
(62a)	Harry Davis (blue)	225.00	112.00	67.00
(62b)	Harry Davis (pastel)	65.00	32.00	19.50
(63)	Jim Delehanty (Delahanty)	65.00	32.00	19.50
(64)	Ray Demmitt	225.00	112.00	67.00
(65)	Rube Dessau	225.00	112.00	67.00
(66a)	Art Devlin (black back)	110.00	55.00	33.00
(66b)	Art Devlin (blue back)	65.00	32.00	19.50
(67)	Josh Devore	225.00	112.00	67.00
(68)	Pat Donahue	65.00	32.00	19.50
(69)	Patsy Donovan	225.00	112.00	67.00
(70a)	Wild Bill Donovan (blue)	200.00	100.00	60.00
(70b)	Wild Bill Donovan (pastel)	65.00	32.00	19.50
(71a)	Red Dooin (blue)	225.00	112.00	67.00
(71b)	Red Dooin (pastel)	65.00	32.00	19.50
(72)	Mickey Doolan	65.00	32.00	19.50
(73)	Patsy Dougherty	65.00	32.00	19.50
(74)	Tom Downey	65.00	32.00	19.50
(75)	Jim Doyle	65.00	32.00	19.50
(76a)	Larry Doyle (blue)	225.00	112.00	67.00
(76b)	Larry Doyle (pastel)	65.00	32.00	19.50
(77)	Hugh Duffy	390.00	195.00	117.00
(78)	Jimmy Dygert	65.00	32.00	19.50
(79)	Dick Eagan (Egan)	65.00	32.00	19.50
(80)	Kid Elborfold	65.00	32.00	19.50
(81)	Rube Ellis	65.00	32.00	19.50
(82)	Clyde Engle	65.00	32.00	19.50
(83)	Tex Erwin	225.00	112.00	67.00
(84)	Steve Evans	225.00	112.00	67.00
(85a)	Johnny Evers (black back)	450.00	225.00	135.00
(85b)	Johnny Evers (blue back)	325.00	162.00	97.00
(86)	Bob Ewing	65.00	32.00	19.50
(87)	Cy Falkenberg	65.00	32.00	19.50
(88)	George Ferguson	65.00	32.00	19.50
(89)	Art Fletcher	225.00	112.00	67.00
(90)	Elmer Flick	325.00	162.00	97.00
(91)	John Flynn	225.00	112.00	67.00
(92)	Russ Ford	225.00	112.00	67.00
(93)	Eddie Foster	225.00	112.00	67.00
(94)	Bill Foxen	65.00	32.00	19.50
(95)	John Frill	225.00	112.00	67.00
(96)	Sam Frock	225.00	112.00	67.00
(97)	Art Fromme	65.00	32.00	19.50
(98)	Earl Gardner (New York)	225.00	112.00	67.00
(99)	Larry Gardner (Boston)	225.00	112.00	67.00
(100)	Harry Gaspar	225.00	112.00	67.00
(101)	Doc Gessler	65.00	32.00	19.50
(102a)	George Gibson (blue)	200.00	100.00	60.00
(102b)	George Gibson (pastel)	65.00	32.00	19.50
(103)	Bill Graham (St. Louis)	65.00	32.00	19.50
(104)	Peaches Graham (Boston)	65.00	32.00	19.50
(105)	Eddie Grant	65.00	32.00	19.50
(106)	Clark Griffith	300.00	150.00	90.00
(107)	Ed Hahn	65.00	32.00	19.50
(108)	Charley Hall	65.00	32.00	19.50
(109)	Bob Harmon	225.00	112.00	67.00
(110)	Topsy Hartsel	65.00	32.00	19.50
(111)	Roy Hartzell	65.00	32.00	19.50
(112)	Heinie Heitmuller	65.00	32.00	19.50
(113)	Buck Herzog	65.00	32.00	19.50
(114)	Dick Hoblitzel (Hoblitzell)	65.00	32.00	19.50
(115)	Danny Hoffman	65.00	32.00	19.50
(116)	Solly Hofman	65.00	32.00	19.50
(117)	Harry Hooper	400.00	200.00	120.00
(118)	Harry Howell	65.00	32.00	19.50
(119)	Miller Huggins	325.00	162.00	97.00
(120)	Long Tom Hughes	225.00	112.00	67.00
(121)	Rudy Hulswitt	65.00	32.00	19.50
(122)	John Hummel	65.00	32.00	19.50
(123)	George Hunter	65.00	32.00	19.50
(124)	Ham Hyatt	65.00	32.00	19.50
(125)	Fred Jacklitsch	65.00	32.00	19.50
(126a)	Hughie Jennings (blue)	500.00	250.00	150.00
(126b)	Hughie Jennings (pastel)	325.00	162.00	97.00
(127)	Walter Johnson	850.00	425.00	255.00
(128a)	Davy Jones (blue)	200.00	100.00	60.00
(128b)	Davy Jones (pastel)	65.00	32.00	19.50
(129)	Tom Jones	65.00	32.00	19.50
(130a)	Tim Jordan (blue)	200.00	100.00	60.00
(130b)	Tim Jordan (pastel)	65.00	32.00	19.50
(131)	Addie Joss	350.00	175.00	105.00
(132)	Johnny Kane	65.00	32.00	19.50
(133)	Ed Karger	65.00	32.00	19.50
(134)	Red Killifer (Killefer)	225.00	112.00	67.00
(135)	Johnny Kling	65.00	32.00	19.50
(136)	Otto Knabe	65.00	32.00	19.50
(137)	John Knight	225.00	112.00	67.00
(138)	Ed Konetchy	65.00	32.00	19.50
(139)	Harry Krause	65.00	32.00	19.50
(140)	Rube Kroh	65.00	32.00	19.50
(141)	Art Krueger	400.00	200.00	120.00
(142a)	Nap Lajoie (blue)	600.00	300.00	180.00
(142b)	Nap Lajoie (pastel)	450.00	225.00	135.00
(143)	Fred Lake (Boston)	65.00	32.00	19.50
(144)	Joe Lake (St. Louis)	225.00	112.00	67.00
(145)	Frank LaPorte	65.00	32.00	19.50
(146)	Jack Lapp	225.00	112.00	67.00
(147)	Chick Lathers	225.00	112.00	67.00
(148a)	Tommy Leach (blue)	200.00	100.00	60.00
(148b)	Tommy Leach (pastel)	65.00	32.00	19.50
(149)	Sam Leever	65.00	32.00	19.50
(150)	Lefty Leifeld	65.00	32.00	19.50
(151)	Ed Lennox	65.00	32.00	19.50
(152)	Fred Linke (Link)	225.00	112.00	67.00
(153)	Paddy Livingstone (Livingston)	65.00	32.00	19.50
(154)	Hans Lobert	65.00	32.00	19.50
(155)	Bris Lord	65.00	32.00	19.50
(156a)	Harry Lord (blue)	200.00	100.00	60.00
(156b)	Harry Lord (pastel)	65.00	32.00	19.50
(157)	Johnny Lush	65.00	32.00	19.50
(158)	Connie Mack	350.00	175.00	105.00
(159)	Tom Madden	225.00	112.00	67.00
(160)	Nick Maddox	65.00	32.00	19.50
(161)	Sherry Magee	90.00	45.00	27.00
(162a)	Christy Mathewson (blue)	1600.	800.00	480.00
(162b)	Christy Mathewson (pastel)	900.00	450.00	270.00
(163)	Al Mattern	65.00	32.00	19.50
(164)	Jimmy McAleer	65.00	32.00	19.50
(165)	George McBride	225.00	112.00	67.00
(166a)	Amby McConnell (Boston)	65.00	32.00	19.50
(166b)	Amby McConnell (Chicago)	2750.	1375.	825.00
(167)	Pryor McElveen	65.00	32.00	19.50
(168)	John McGraw	350.00	175.00	105.00
(169)	Deacon McGuire	65.00	32.00	19.50
(170)	Stuffy McInnes (McInnis)	225.00	112.00	67.00
(171)	Harry McIntire (McIntyre)	65.00	32.00	19.50
(172)	Matty McIntyre	65.00	32.00	19.50
(173)	Larry McLean	65.00	32.00	19.50
(174)	Tommy McMillan	65.00	32.00	19.50
(175a)	George McQuillan (blue, Philadelphia)	225.00	112.00	67.00
(175b)	George McQuillan (pastel, Philadelphia)	65.00	32.00	19.50
(175c)	George McQuillan (Cincinnati)	2200.	1100.	660.00
(176)	Paul Meloan	225.00	112.00	67.00
(177)	Fred Merkle	65.00	32.00	19.50
(178)	Clyde Milan	65.00	32.00	19.50
(179)	Dots Miller (Pittsburgh)	65.00	32.00	19.50
(180)	Warren Miller (Washington)	225.00	112.00	67.00
(181)	Fred Mitchell	225.00	112.00	67.00
(182)	Mike Mitchell	65.00	32.00	19.50
(183)	Earl Moore	65.00	32.00	19.50
(184)	Pat Moran	65.00	32.00	19.50
(185a)	Lew Moren (black back)	110.00	55.00	33.00
(185b)	Lew Moren (blue back)	65.00	32.00	19.50
(186)	Cy Morgan	65.00	32.00	19.50
(187)	George Moriarty	65.00	32.00	19.50
(188)	Mike Mowrey	225.00	112.00	67.00
(189a)	George Mullin (black back)	110.00	55.00	33.00
(189b)	George Mullin (blue back)	65.00	32.00	19.50
(190)	Danny Murphy	65.00	32.00	19.50
(191)	Red Murray	65.00	32.00	19.50
(192)	Chief Myers (Meyers)	225.00	112.00	67.00
(193)	Tom Needham	65.00	32.00	19.50
(194)	Harry Niles	65.00	32.00	19.50
(195)	Rebel Oakes	225.00	112.00	67.00
(196)	Jack O'Connor	65.00	32.00	19.50
(197)	Paddy O'Connor	65.00	32.00	19.50
(198)	Bill O'Hara	150.00	75.00	45.00
(199)	Rube Oldring	65.00	32.00	19.50
(200)	Charley O'Leary	65.00	32.00	19.50
(201)	Orval Overall	65.00	32.00	19.50
(202)	Freddy Parent	65.00	32.00	19.50
(203)	Dode Paskert	225.00	112.00	67.00
(204)	Fred Payne	225.00	112.00	67.00
(205)	Barney Pelty	65.00	32.00	19.50
(206)	Hub Pernoll	225.00	112.00	67.00
(207)	George Perring	225.00	112.00	67.00
(208)	Big Jeff Pfeffer	225.00	112.00	67.00
(209)	Jack Pfiester	65.00	32.00	19.50
(210)	Art Phelan	225.00	112.00	67.00
(211)	Ed Phelps	65.00	32.00	19.50
(212)	Deacon Phillippe	65.00	32.00	19.50
(213)	Eddie Plank	350.00	175.00	105.00
(214)	Jack Powell	65.00	32.00	19.50
(215)	Billy Purtell	65.00	32.00	19.50
(216)	Farmer Ray	225.00	112.00	67.00
(217)	Bugs Raymond	65.00	32.00	19.50
(218)	Doc Reisling	65.00	32.00	19.50
(219)	Ed Reulbach	65.00	32.00	19.50
(220)	Lew Richie	65.00	32.00	19.50
(221)	Jack Rowan	65.00	32.00	19.50
(222a)	Nap Rucker (black back)	110.00	55.00	33.00
(222b)	Nap Rucker (blue back)	65.00	32.00	19.50
(223)	Slim Sallee	65.00	32.00	19.50
(224)	Doc Scanlon	65.00	32.00	19.50
(225)	Germany Schaefer	65.00	32.00	19.50
(226)	Lou Schettler	225.00	112.00	67.00
(227)	Admiral Schlei	65.00	32.00	19.50
(228)	Boss Schmidt	65.00	32.00	19.50
(229)	Wildfire Schulte	65.00	32.00	19.50
(230)	Al Schweitzer	65.00	32.00	19.50
(231)	Jim Scott	225.00	112.00	67.00
(232)	Cy Seymour	65.00	32.00	19.50
(233)	Tillie Shafer	65.00	32.00	19.50
(234)	Bud Sharpe	225.00	112.00	67.00
(235)	Dave Shean	225.00	112.00	67.00
(236)	Jimmy Sheckard	65.00	32.00	19.50
(237)	Mike Simon	225.00	112.00	67.00
(238)	Charlie Smith (Boston)	225.00	112.00	67.00
(239)	Frank Smith (Chicago)	65.00	32.00	19.50
(240)	Harry Smith (Boston)	65.00	32.00	19.50
(241)	Fred Snodgrass	65.00	32.00	19.50
(242)	Bob Spade	65.00	32.00	19.50
(243)	Tully Sparks	65.00	32.00	19.50
(244)	Tris Speaker	600.00	300.00	180.00
(245)	Jake Stahl	65.00	32.00	19.50
(246)	George Stallings	65.00	32.00	19.50
(247)	Oscar Stanage	65.00	32.00	19.50
(248)	Harry Steinfeldt	65.00	32.00	19.50
(249)	Jim Stephens	65.00	32.00	19.50
(250)	George Stone	65.00	32.00	19.50
(251)	George Stovall	65.00	32.00	19.50
(252)	Gabby Street	65.00	32.00	19.50
(253)	Sailor Stroud	225.00	112.00	67.00
(254)	Amos Strunk	225.00	112.00	67.00
(255)	George Suggs	65.00	32.00	19.50
(256)	Billy Sullivan	65.00	32.00	19.50
(257a)	Ed Summers (black back)	110.00	55.00	33.00
(257b)	Ed Summers (blue back)	65.00	32.00	19.50
(258)	Bill Sweeney (Boston)	65.00	32.00	19.50
(259)	Jeff Sweeney (New York)	225.00	112.00	67.00
(260)	Lee Tannehill	65.00	32.00	19.50
(261a)	Fred Tenney (blue)	200.00	100.00	60.00
(261b)	Fred Tenney (pastel)	65.00	32.00	19.50
(262a)	Ira Thomas (blue)	200.00	100.00	60.00
(262b)	Ira Thomas (pastel)	65.00	32.00	19.50
(263)	Jack Thoney	65.00	32.00	19.50
(264a)	Joe Tinker (black back)	450.00	225.00	135.00
(264b)	Joe Tinker (blue back)	325.00	162.00	97.00
(265)	John Titus	225.00	112.00	67.00
(266)	Terry Turner	65.00	32.00	19.50
(267)	Bob Unglaub	65.00	32.00	19.50
(268a)	Rube Waddell (black back)	325.00	162.00	97.00
(268b)	Rube Waddell (blue back)	250.00	125.00	75.00
(269a)	Hans Wagner (Pittsburgh, blue)	1950.	975.00	585.00
(269b)	Hans Wagner (Pittsburgh, pastel)	1150.	575.00	345.00
(270)	Heinie Wagner (Boston)	65.00	32.00	19.50
(271)	Bobby Wallace	325.00	162.00	97.00
(272)	Ed Walsh (Chicago)	325.00	162.00	97.00
(273a)	Jimmy Walsh (gray background, Philadelphia)	300.00	150.00	90.00
(273b)	Jimmy Walsh (white background, Philadelphia)	300.00	150.00	90.00
(274)	Doc White	65.00	32.00	19.50
(275)	Kaiser Wilhelm	65.00	32.00	19.50
(276)	Ed Willett	65.00	32.00	19.50
(277)	Vic Willis	325.00	162.00	97.00
(278)	Art Wilson (New York)	225.00	112.00	67.00
(279)	Owen Wilson (Pittsburgh)	65.00	32.00	19.50
(280)	Hooks Wiltse	65.00	32.00	19.50
(281)	Harry Wolter	65.00	32.00	19.50
(282)	Smoky Joe Wood	250.00	125.00	75.00
(283)	Ralph Works	65.00	32.00	19.50
(284a)	Cy Young (black back)	750.00	375.00	225.00
(284b)	Cy Young (blue back)	550.00	275.00	165.00
(285)	Irv Young	65.00	32.00	19.50
(286)	Heinie Zimmerman	225.00	112.00	67.00
(287)	Dutch Zwilling	65.00	32.00	19.50

1910 Sporting Life Team Composites (W601)

After several years of issuing composite team photos for all major league teams (and some minor league teams), Sporting Life in 1910 began issuing them only for the league and World's Champions. Like the others, they are 13" x 14", printed on heavy enamel paper with individual player portrait photos surrounding the manager at center.

		NM	EX	VG
Complete Set:		600.00	300.00	180.00
Common Team:		300.00	150.00	90.00
(1)	Chicago Cubs (N.L. champs)	300.00	150.00	90.00
(2)	Philadelphia Athletics (World's Champions)	300.00	150.00	90.00

1911 Sporting Life Cabinets (M110)

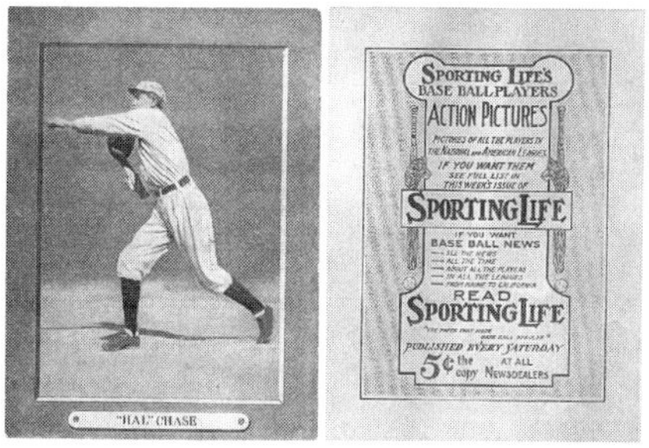

This set of 5-5/8" x 7-1/2" premium photos is similar to, but much scarcer than, the contemporary T3 Turkey Red cabinets. Like those, the Sporting Life cabinets feature a pastel player picture surrounded by a gray frame with a "gold" nameplate at bottom. Backs have advertising for the weekly sports paper printed in blue.

		NM	EX	VG
Complete Set (6):		20000.	10000.	6000.
Common Player:		2775.	1100.	555.00
(1)	Frank Chance	3000.	1200.	600.00
(2)	Hal Chase	2750.	1100.	550.00
(3)	Ty Cobb	7500.	3000.	1500.
(4)	Napoleon Lajoie	3000.	1200.	600.00
(5)	Christy Mathewson	2000.	800.00	400.00
(6)	Honus Wagner	6500.	2600.	1300.

Suffix letters after a card number indicate a variation card.

1911 Sporting Life Team Composites (W601)

		NM	EX	VG
Complete Set:		600.00	300.00	180.00
Common Team:		300.00	150.00	90.00
(1)	New York Giants (N.L. champs)	300.00	150.00	90.00
(2)	Philadelphia Athletics (World's Champions)	300.00	150.00	90.00

1899-1900 Sporting News Supplements (M101-1)

For much of 1899 and 1900, the weekly issues of The Sporting News included a baseball player portrait supplement. About 10" x 13", the pictures offered vignetted photos of the era's stars on a glossy paper stock. Virtually all pictures were formal head-and-shoulders portraits; some in uniform, some in civilian clothes. A handful of players are depicted in full-length poses. The pictures were produced for the sports paper by National Copper Plate Co., (which issued its own set of prints listed elsewhere in this catalog). The TSN supplements have a logotype above the photo and the date in which it was included in the paper. Full player name and team/year are printed at bottom. Backs have a small box offering career information. Besides offering the pictures with weekly issues, portfolios of 50 could be had by starting or renewing a subscription for $2 a year.

		NM	EX	VG
Complete Set (62):		21250.	10600.	6350.
Common Player:		400.00	200.00	120.00
	1899			
(1)	William Lange (Apr. 22)	400.00	200.00	120.00
(2)	Hugh Duffy (Apr. 29)	525.00	262.00	157.00
(3)	Charles A. Nichols (May 6)	525.00	262.00	157.00
(4)	Martin Bergen (May 13)	400.00	200.00	120.00
(5)	Michael Griffin (May 20)	400.00	200.00	120.00
(6)	Wilbert Robinson (May 27)	525.00	262.00	157.00
(7)	Clark C. Griffith (June 3)	525.00	262.00	157.00
(8)	John J. Doyle (June 10)	400.00	200.00	120.00
(9)	R.J. Wallace (June 17)	525.00	262.00	157.00
(10)	John O'Connor (June 24)	400.00	200.00	120.00
(11)	Louis Criger (July 1)	400.00	200.00	120.00
(12)	Jerry H. Nops (July 8)	400.00	200.00	120.00
(13)	William Kennedy (July 15)	400.00	200.00	120.00
(14)	P.J. Donovan (July 22)	400.00	200.00	120.00
(15)	William H. Keeler (July 29)	525.00	262.00	157.00
(16)	John J. McGraw (Aug. 5)	525.00	262.00	157.00
(17)	James Hughes (Aug. 12)	400.00	200.00	120.00
(18)	John Wagner (Aug. 19)	850.00	425.00	255.00
(19)	Victor G. Willis (Aug. 26)	525.00	262.00	157.00
(20)	James J. Collins (Sept. 2)	525.00	262.00	157.00
(21)	Eugene DeMontreville (Sept. 9)	400.00	200.00	120.00
(22)	Joseph J. Kelley (Sept. 16)	525.00	262.00	157.00
(23)	Frank L. Donahue (Francis R. "Red") (Sept. 23)	400.00	200.00	120.00
(24)	Edward J. Delehanty (Delahanty) (Sept. 30)	400.00	200.00	120.00
(25)	Fred C. Clark (Clarke) (Oct. 7)	525.00	262.00	157.00
(26)	Napoleon Lajoie (Oct. 14)	600.00	300.00	180.00
(27)	Edward Hanlon (Oct. 21)	525.00	262.00	157.00
(28)	Charles Stahl (Oct. 28)	400.00	200.00	120.00
(29)	Lave N. Cross (Nov. 4)	400.00	200.00	120.00
(30)	Elmer H. Flick (Nov. 11)	525.00	262.00	157.00
(31)	Frank LeRoy Chance (Nov. 18)	525.00	262.00	157.00
(32)	George S. Davis (Nov. 25)	450.00	225.00	135.00
(33)	Hugh J. Jennings (Dec. 2)	525.00	262.00	157.00
(34)	Denton T. Young (Dec. 9)	675.00	337.00	202.00
	1900			
(35)	George E. Waddell (Apr. 14)	525.00	262.00	157.00
(36)	John Dunn (Apr. 21)	400.00	200.00	120.00
(37)	Clarence Beaumont (Apr. 28)	400.00	200.00	120.00
(38)	James T. McGuire (May 5)	400.00	200.00	120.00
(39)	William H. Dineen (May 12)	400.00	200.00	120.00
(40)	James T. Williams (May 19)	400.00	200.00	120.00
(41)	Thomas W. Corcoran (May 26)	400.00	200.00	120.00
(42)	John Freeman (June 2)	400.00	200.00	120.00
(43)	Henry Peitz (June 9)	400.00	200.00	120.00
(44)	Charles Phillippe (June 16)	400.00	200.00	120.00
(45)	Frank Hahn (June 23)	400.00	200.00	120.00
(46)	J. Emmet Heidrick (June 30)	400.00	200.00	120.00
(47)	Joseph McGinnity (July 7)	525.00	262.00	157.00
(48)	John D. Chesbro (July 14)	525.00	262.00	157.00
(49)	William R. Hamilton (July 21)	400.00	200.00	120.00
(50)	Samuel Leever (July 28)	400.00	200.00	120.00
(51)	Mike Donlin (Aug. 4)	400.00	200.00	120.00
(52)	William F. Dahlen (Aug. 11)	400.00	200.00	120.00
(53)	Frederick Tenney (Aug. 18)	400.00	200.00	120.00
(54)	Edward P. Scott (Aug. 25)	400.00	200.00	120.00
(55)	Edward M. Lewis (Sept. 1)	400.00	200.00	120.00
(56)	Theodore Breitenstein (Sept. 8)	400.00	200.00	120.00
(57)	Herman C. Long (Sept. 15)	400.00	200.00	120.00
(58)	Jesse Tannehill (Sept. 22)	400.00	200.00	120.00
(59)	Burt E. Jones (Albert Edward "Cowboy") (Sept. 29)	425.00	212.00	127.00
(60)	J. Callahan (Nixey) (Oct. 6)	400.00	200.00	120.00
(61)	Claude Ritchey (Oct. 13)	400.00	200.00	120.00
(62)	Roy Thomas (Oct. 20)	400.00	200.00	120.00

1909-1913 Sporting News Supplements (M101-2)

Among the finest large-format baseball collectibles published in the early part of the 20th Century was the 100-piece series of sepia-toned supplements issued by The Sporting News. Generally 8" x 10" (though there was some size variation over the years), the series was begun with the insertion of a supplement in the July 22, 1909, issue of TSN. One supplement was issued with each week's paper through April 7, 1910. There were several gaps over the course of the next several years, until the final piece was issued with the TSN dated Dec. 11, 1913. Most of the supplements feature full-length poses of the players. Each is labeled "Supplement to The Sporting News" with the issue date at top. At bottom is a box with the player's name and team. Backs are blank. The TSN supplements were printed on heavy paper and are usually found with corner creases or other signs of wear.

		NM	EX	VG
Complete Set (100):		6500.	2600.	1300.
Common Player:		30.00	12.00	6.00
	1909			
(1)	Roger Bresnahan (7/22)	90.00	36.00	18.00
(2)	Denton Young, Louis Criger (7/29)	120.00	48.00	24.00
(3)	Christopher Mathewson (8/5)	200.00	80.00	40.00
(4)	Tyrus R. Cobb (8/12)	400.00	160.00	80.00
(5)	Napoleon Lajoie (8/19)	150.00	60.00	30.00
(6)	Sherwood N. Magee (8/26)	30.00	12.00	6.00
(7)	Frank L. Chance (9/2)	150.00	60.00	30.00
(8)	Edward Walsh (9/9)	120.00	48.00	24.00
(9)	Nap Rucker (9/16)	30.00	12.00	6.00
(10)	Honus Wagner (9/23)	200.00	100.00	60.00
(11)	Hugh Jennings (9/30)	120.00	48.00	24.00
(12)	Fred C. Clarke (10/7)	120.00	48.00	24.00
(13)	Byron Bancroft Johnson (10/14)	150.00	60.00	30.00
(14)	Charles A. Comiskey (10/21)	150.00	60.00	30.00
(15)	Edward Collins (10/28)	120.00	48.00	24.00
(16)	James A. McAleer (11/4)	30.00	12.00	6.00
(17)	Pittsburgh Team (11/11)	48.00	19.00	9.50
(18)	Detroit Team (11/18)	70.00	28.00	14.00
(19)	George Bell (11/25)	30.00	12.00	6.00
(20)	Tris Speaker (12/2)	150.00	60.00	30.00
(21)	Mordecai Brown (12/9)	120.00	48.00	24.00
(22)	Hal Chase (12/16)	100.00	40.00	20.00
(23)	Thomas W. Leach (12/23)	30.00	12.00	6.00
(24)	Owen Bush (12/30)	30.00	12.00	6.00
	1910			
(25)	John J. Evers (1/6)	150.00	60.00	30.00
(26)	Harry Krause (1/13)	30.00	12.00	6.00
(27)	Chas. B. Adams (1/20)	30.00	12.00	6.00
(28)	Addie Joss (1/27)	150.00	60.00	30.00
(29)	Orval Overall (2/3)	30.00	12.00	6.00
(30)	Samuel E. Crawford (2/10)	120.00	48.00	24.00
(31)	Fred Merkle (2/17)	35.00	14.00	7.00
(32)	George Mullin (2/24)	30.00	12.00	6.00
(33)	Edward Konetchy (3/3)	30.00	12.00	6.00
(34)	George Gibson, Arthur Raymond (3/10)	30.00	12.00	6.00
(35)	Ty Cobb, Hans Wagner (3/17)	650.00	325.00	195.00
(36)	Connie Mack (3/24)	150.00	60.00	30.00
(37)	Wm. Evans, "Silk" O'Loughlin, William Klem, Wm. Johnston (3/31)	150.00	60.00	30.00
(38)	Edward Plank (4/7)	120.00	48.00	24.00
(39)	Walter Johnson, Charles E. Street (9/1)	150.00	60.00	30.00
(40)	John C. Kling (9/8)	30.00	12.00	6.00
(41)	Frank Baker (9/15)	120.00	48.00	24.00
(42)	Charles S. Dooin (9/22)	30.00	12.00	6.00
(43)	Wm. F. Carrigan (9/29)	30.00	12.00	6.00
(44)	John B. McLean (10/6)	30.00	12.00	6.00
(45)	John W. Coombs (10/13)	30.00	12.00	6.00
(46)	Jos. B. Tinker (10/20)	150.00	60.00	30.00
(47)	John I. Taylor (10/27)	30.00	12.00	6.00
(48)	Russell Ford (11/3)	30.00	12.00	6.00
(49)	Leonard L. Cole (11/10)	30.00	12.00	6.00
(50)	Harry Lord (11/17)	30.00	12.00	6.00
(51)	Philadelphia-A Team (11/24)	40.00	16.00	8.00
(52)	Chicago-N Team (12/1)	40.00	16.00	8.00
(53)	Charles A. Bender (12/8)	120.00	48.00	24.00
(54)	Arthur Hofman (12/15)	30.00	12.00	6.00
(55)	Bobby Wallace (12/21)	120.00	48.00	24.00
(56)	Jno. J. McGraw (12/28)	120.00	48.00	24.00
	1911			
(57)	Harry H. Davis (1/5)	30.00	12.00	6.00
(58)	James P. Archer (1/12)	30.00	12.00	6.00
(59)	Ira Thomas (1/19)	30.00	12.00	6.00
(60)	Robert Byrnes (1/26)	30.00	12.00	6.00
(61)	Clyde Milan (2/2)	30.00	12.00	6.00
(62)	John T. Meyer (2/9) (Meyers)	30.00	12.00	6.00
(63)	Robert Bescher (2/16)	30.00	12.00	6.00
(64)	John J. Barry (2/23)	30.00	12.00	6.00
(65)	Frank Schulte (3/2)	30.00	12.00	6.00
(66)	C. Harris White (3/9)	30.00	12.00	6.00
(67)	Lawrence Doyle (3/16)	30.00	12.00	6.00
(68)	Joe Jackson (3/23)	1200.	480.00	240.00
(69)	Martin O'Toole, William Kelly (10/26)	30.00	12.00	6.00
(70)	Vean Gregg (11/2)	30.00	12.00	6.00
(71)	Richard W. Marquard (11/9)	120.00	48.00	24.00
(72)	John E. McInnis (11/16)	30.00	12.00	6.00
(73)	Grover C. Alexander (11/23)	125.00	62.00	37.00
(74)	Del Gainor (11/30)	30.00	12.00	6.00
(75)	Fred Snodgrass (12/7)	30.00	12.00	6.00
(76)	James J. Callahan (12/14)	30.00	12.00	6.00
(77)	Robert Harmon (12/21)	30.00	12.00	6.00
(78)	George Stovall (12/28)	30.00	12.00	6.00
	1912			
(79)	Zack D. Wheat (1/4)	120.00	48.00	24.00
(80)	Frank "Ping" Bodie (1/11)	30.00	12.00	6.00
(81)	Boston-A Team (10/10)	40.00	16.00	8.00
(82)	New York-N Team (10/17)	48.00	19.00	9.50
(83)	Jake Stahl (10/24)	30.00	12.00	6.00
(84)	Joe Wood (10/31)	30.00	12.00	6.00
(85)	Charles Wagner (11/7)	30.00	12.00	6.00
(86)	Lew Ritchie (11/14)	30.00	12.00	6.00
(87)	Clark Griffith (11/21)	120.00	48.00	24.00
(88)	Arnold Hauser (11/28)	30.00	12.00	6.00
(89)	Charles Herzog (12/5)	30.00	12.00	6.00
(90)	James Lavender (12/12)	30.00	12.00	6.00
(91)	Jeff Tesreau (12/19)	30.00	12.00	6.00
(92)	August Herrmann (12/26)	48.00	19.00	9.50
	1913			
(93)	Jake Daubert (10/23)	30.00	12.00	6.00
(94)	Heinie Zimmerman (10/30)	30.00	12.00	6.00
(95)	Ray Schalk (11/6)	120.00	48.00	24.00
(96)	Hans Lobert (11/13)	30.00	12.00	6.00
(97)	Albert W. Demaree (11/20)	30.00	12.00	6.00
(98)	Arthur Fletcher (11/27)	30.00	12.00	6.00
(99)	Charles A. Somers (12/4)	30.00	12.00	6.00
(100)	Joe Birmingham (12/11)	30.00	12.00	6.00

1915 Sporting News Postcards (M101-3)

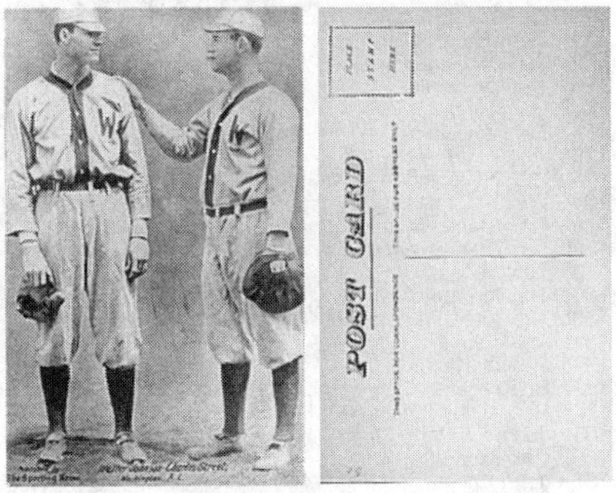

This six-card set was issued as a premium by the weekly sports newspaper in the first half of the 1910s. The generally accepted date of issue is 1915, though it may actually have been a few years earlier. The 3-1/2" x 5-1/2" cards have borderless front photos printed in duotone color. Along with the player and team names at bottom is a "Published by The Sporting News" tag line. Postcard-format backs are in black-and-white. The unnumbered cards are checklisted here alphabetically.

		NM	EX	VG
Complete Set (6):		2500.	1250.	750.00
Common Player:		125.00	50.00	25.00
(1)	Roger Bresnahan	450.00	225.00	135.00
(2)	Ty Cobb	1200.	480.00	240.00
(3)	Eddie Collins	400.00	200.00	120.00
(4)	Vean Gregg	175.00	87.00	52.00
(5)	Walter Johnson, Gabby Street	450.00	225.00	135.00
(6)	Rube Marquard	250.00	125.00	75.00

1915 The Sporting News (M101-5)

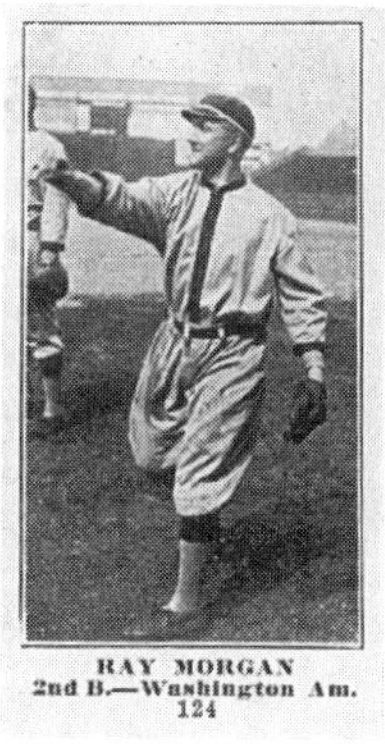

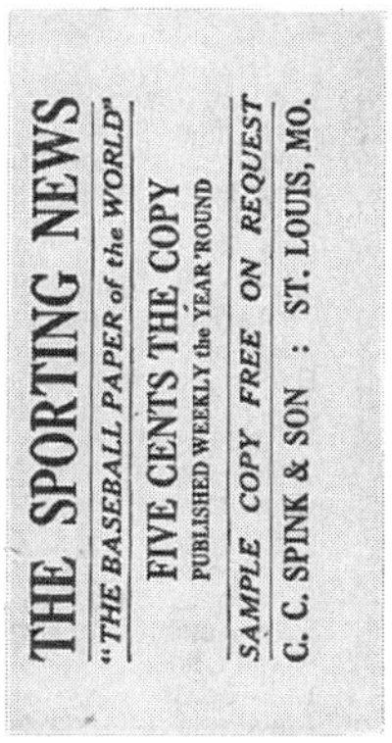

This 200-card set was issued as a premium by The Sporting News and was also used by a number of regional companies which placed their advertising on the backs. The 1-5/8" x 3" cards have black-and-white photos on the fronts, with the player name, position and team, as well as a card number. Card backs are in a horizontal format and show an advertisement for the sponsoring sports weekly. Most of the day's top players and many Hall of Famers are included in the set, with the Babe Ruth card carrying the highest value. The complete set price does not include variations.

		NM	EX	VG
Complete Set (200):		20000.	10000.	6000.
Common Player:		60.00	30.00	18.00
1	Babe Adams	80.00	30.00	18.00
2	Sam Agnew	60.00	30.00	18.00
3	Eddie Ainsmith	60.00	30.00	18.00
4	Grover Alexander	170.00	85.00	51.00
5	Leon Ames	60.00	30.00	18.00
6	Jimmy Archer	60.00	30.00	18.00
7	Jimmy Austin	60.00	30.00	18.00
8	J. Franklin Baker	125.00	62.00	37.00
9	Dave Bancroft	125.00	62.00	37.00
10	Jack Barry	60.00	30.00	18.00
11	Zinn Beck	60.00	30.00	18.00
12	Lute Boone	60.00	30.00	18.00
13	Joe Benz	60.00	30.00	18.00
14	Bob Bescher	60.00	30.00	18.00
15	Al Betzel	60.00	30.00	18.00
16	Roger Bresnahan	125.00	62.00	37.00
17	Eddie Burns	60.00	30.00	18.00
18	Geo. J. Burns	60.00	30.00	18.00
19	Joe Bush	60.00	30.00	18.00
20	Owen Bush	60.00	30.00	18.00
21	Art Butler	60.00	30.00	18.00
22	Bobbie Byrne	60.00	30.00	18.00
23a	Forrest Cady	180.00	90.00	54.00
23b	Mordecai Brown	145.00	72.00	43.00
24	Jimmy Callahan	60.00	30.00	18.00
25	Ray Caldwell	60.00	30.00	18.00
26	Max Carey	125.00	62.00	37.00
27	George Chalmers	60.00	30.00	18.00
28	Frank Chance	125.00	62.00	37.00
29	Ray Chapman	80.00	40.00	24.00
30	Larry Cheney	60.00	30.00	18.00
31	Eddie Cicotte	110.00	55.00	33.00
32	Tom Clarke	60.00	30.00	18.00
33	Eddie Collins	125.00	62.00	37.00
34	"Shauno" Collins	60.00	30.00	18.00
35	Charles Comisky (Comiskey)	125.00	62.00	37.00
36	Joe Connolly	60.00	30.00	18.00
37	Luther Cook	60.00	30.00	18.00
38	Jack Coombs	60.00	30.00	18.00
39	Dan Costello	60.00	30.00	18.00
40	Harry Coveleskie (Coveleski)	60.00	30.00	18.00
41	Gavvy Cravath	60.00	30.00	18.00
42	Sam Crawford	125.00	62.00	37.00
43	Jean Dale	60.00	30.00	18.00
44	Jake Daubert	60.00	30.00	18.00
45	Geo. A. Davis Jr.	60.00	30.00	18.00
46	Charles Deal	60.00	30.00	18.00
47	Al Demaree	60.00	30.00	18.00
48	William Doak	60.00	30.00	18.00
49	Bill Donovan	60.00	30.00	18.00
50	Charles Dooin	60.00	30.00	18.00
51	Mike Doolan	60.00	30.00	18.00
52	Larry Doyle	60.00	30.00	18.00
53	Jean Dubuc	60.00	30.00	18.00
54	Oscar Dugey	60.00	30.00	18.00
55	Johnny Evers	125.00	62.00	37.00
56	Urban Faber	125.00	62.00	37.00
57	"Hap" Felsch	120.00	60.00	36.00
58	Bill Fischer	60.00	30.00	18.00
59	Ray Fisher	60.00	30.00	18.00
60	Max Flack	60.00	30.00	18.00
61	Art Fletcher	60.00	30.00	18.00
62	Eddie Foster	60.00	30.00	18.00
63	Jacques Fournier	60.00	30.00	18.00
64	Del Gainer (Gainor)	60.00	30.00	18.00
65	Larry Gardner	60.00	30.00	18.00
66	Joe Gedeon	60.00	30.00	18.00
67	Gus Getz	60.00	30.00	18.00
68	Geo. Gibson	60.00	30.00	18.00
69	Wilbur Good	60.00	30.00	18.00
70	Hank Gowdy	60.00	30.00	18.00
71	John Graney	60.00	30.00	18.00
72	Tom Griffith	60.00	30.00	18.00
73	Heinie Groh	60.00	30.00	18.00
74	Earl Hamilton	60.00	30.00	18.00
75	Bob Harmon	60.00	30.00	18.00
76	Roy Hartzell	60.00	30.00	18.00
77	Claude Hendrix	60.00	30.00	18.00
78	Olaf Henriksen	60.00	30.00	18.00
79	John Henry	60.00	30.00	18.00
80	"Buck" Herzog	60.00	30.00	18.00
81	Hugh High	60.00	30.00	18.00
82	Dick Hoblitzell	60.00	30.00	18.00
83	Harry Hooper	125.00	62.00	37.00
84	Ivan Howard	60.00	30.00	18.00
85	Miller Huggins	125.00	62.00	37.00
86	Joe Jackson	3250.	1625.	975.00
87	William James	60.00	30.00	18.00
88	Harold Janvrin	60.00	30.00	18.00
89	Hugh Jennings	125.00	62.00	37.00
90	Walter Johnson	440.00	220.00	132.00
91	Fielder Jones	60.00	30.00	18.00
92	Bennie Kauff	60.00	30.00	18.00
93	Wm. Killefer Jr.	60.00	30.00	18.00
94	Ed. Konetchy	60.00	30.00	18.00
95	Napoleon Lajoie	175.00	87.00	52.00
96	Jack Lapp	60.00	30.00	18.00
97a	John Lavan (correct spelling)	80.00	40.00	24.00
97b	John Lavin (incorrect spelling)	80.00	40.00	24.00
98	Jimmy Lavender	60.00	30.00	18.00
99	"Nemo" Leibold	60.00	30.00	18.00
100	H.B. Leonard	60.00	30.00	18.00
101	Duffy Lewis	60.00	30.00	18.00
102	Hans Lobert	60.00	30.00	18.00
103	Tom Long	60.00	30.00	18.00
104	Fred Luderus	60.00	30.00	18.00
105	Connie Mack	125.00	62.00	37.00
106	Lee Magee	60.00	30.00	18.00
107	Al. Mamaux	60.00	30.00	18.00
108	Leslie Mann	60.00	30.00	18.00
109	"Rabbit" Maranville	125.00	62.00	37.00
110	Rube Marquard	125.00	62.00	37.00
111	Armando Marsans	85.00	42.00	25.00
112	J. Erskine Mayer	60.00	30.00	18.00
113	George McBride	60.00	30.00	18.00
114	John J. McGraw	125.00	62.00	37.00
115	Jack McInnis	60.00	30.00	18.00
116	Fred Merkle	60.00	30.00	18.00
117	Chief Meyers	60.00	30.00	18.00
118	Clyde Milan	60.00	30.00	18.00
119	Otto Miller	60.00	30.00	18.00
120	Willie Mitchel (Mitchell)	60.00	30.00	18.00
121	Fred Mollwitz	60.00	30.00	18.00
122	J. Herbert Moran	60.00	30.00	18.00
123	Pat Moran	60.00	30.00	18.00
124	Ray Morgan	60.00	30.00	18.00
125	Geo. Moriarty	60.00	30.00	18.00
126	Guy Morton	60.00	30.00	18.00
127	Ed. Murphy (photo actually Danny Murphy)	60.00	30.00	18.00
128	John Murray	60.00	30.00	18.00
129	"Hy" Myers	60.00	30.00	18.00
130	J.A. Niehoff	60.00	30.00	18.00
131	Leslie Nunamaker	60.00	30.00	18.00
132	Rube Oldring	60.00	30.00	18.00
133	Oliver O'Mara	60.00	30.00	18.00
134	Steve O'Neill	60.00	30.00	18.00
135	"Dode" Paskert	60.00	30.00	18.00
136	Roger Peckinpaugh (photo actually Gavvy Cravath)	60.00	30.00	18.00
137	E.J. Pfeffer (photo actually Jeff Pfeffer)	60.00	30.00	18.00
138	Geo. Pierce (Pearce)	60.00	30.00	18.00
139	Walter Pipp	80.00	40.00	24.00
140	Derril Pratt (Derrill)	60.00	30.00	18.00
141	Bill Rariden	60.00	30.00	18.00
142	Eppa Rixey	125.00	62.00	37.00
143	Davey Robertson	60.00	30.00	18.00
144	Wilbert Robinson	125.00	62.00	37.00
145	Bob Roth	60.00	30.00	18.00
146	Ed. Roush	125.00	62.00	37.00
147	Clarence Rowland	60.00	30.00	18.00
148	"Nap" Rucker	60.00	30.00	18.00
149	Dick Rudolph	60.00	30.00	18.00
150	Reb Russell	60.00	30.00	18.00
151	Babe Ruth	3750.	1875.	1125.
152	Vic Saier	60.00	30.00	18.00
153	"Slim" Sallee	60.00	30.00	18.00
154	"Germany" Schaefer	60.00	30.00	18.00
155	Ray Schalk	125.00	62.00	37.00
156	Walter Schang	60.00	30.00	18.00
157	Chas. Schmidt	60.00	30.00	18.00
158	Frank Schulte	60.00	30.00	18.00
159	Jim Scott	60.00	30.00	18.00
160	Everett Scott	60.00	30.00	18.00
161	Tom Seaton	60.00	30.00	18.00
162	Howard Shanks	60.00	30.00	18.00
163	Bob Shawkey (photo actually Jack McInnis)	60.00	30.00	18.00
164	Ernie Shore	60.00	30.00	18.00
165	Burt Shotton	60.00	30.00	18.00
166	George Sisler	125.00	62.00	37.00
167	J. Carlisle Smith	60.00	30.00	18.00
168	Fred Snodgrass	60.00	30.00	18.00
169	Geo. Stallings	60.00	30.00	18.00
170	Oscar Stanage (photo actually Chas. Schmidt)	60.00	30.00	18.00
171	Charles Stengel	200.00	100.00	60.00
172	Milton Stock	60.00	30.00	18.00
173	Amos Strunk (photo actually Olaf Henriksen)	60.00	30.00	18.00
174	Billy Sullivan	60.00	30.00	18.00
175	Chas. Tesreau	60.00	30.00	18.00
176	Jim Thorpe	3500.	1750.	1050.
177	Joe Tinker	125.00	62.00	37.00
178	Fred Toney	60.00	30.00	18.00
179	Terry Turner	60.00	30.00	18.00
180	Jim Vaughn	60.00	30.00	18.00
181	Bob Veach	60.00	30.00	18.00
182	James Voix	60.00	30.00	18.00
183	Oscar Vitt	60.00	30.00	18.00
184	Hans Wagner	700.00	350.00	210.00
185	Clarence Walker (photo not Walker)	60.00	30.00	18.00
186	Zach Wheat	125.00	62.00	37.00
187	Ed. Walsh	125.00	62.00	37.00
188	Buck Weaver	100.00	50.00	30.00
189	Carl Weilman	60.00	30.00	18.00
190	Geo. Whitted	60.00	30.00	18.00
191	Fred Williams	60.00	30.00	18.00
192	Art Wilson	60.00	30.00	18.00
193	J. Owen Wilson	60.00	30.00	18.00
194	Ivy Wingo	60.00	30.00	18.00
195	"Mel" Wolfgang	60.00	30.00	18.00
196	Joe Wood	60.00	30.00	18.00
197	Steve Yerkes	60.00	30.00	18.00
198	Rollie Zeider	60.00	30.00	18.00
199	Heiny Zimmerman	60.00	30.00	18.00
200	Ed. Zwilling	60.00	30.00	18.00

1916 The Sporting News (M101-4)

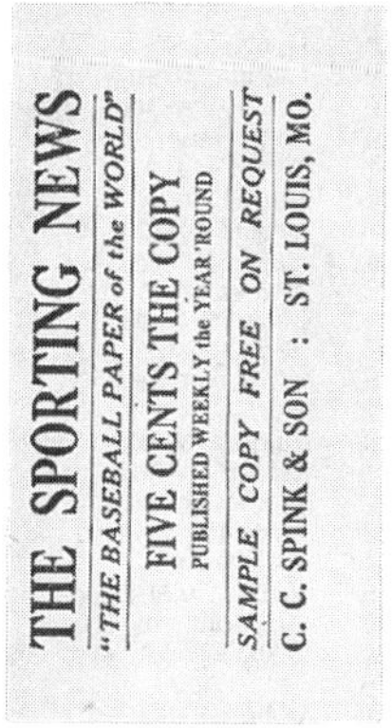

The second annual set issued as a promotional premium by The Sporting News is nearly identical to the 1915 cards. The 200 black-and-white cards once again are printed with player photo, name, position, team and card number on front and advertising on the backs. The set checklist, and, generally, values are the same for sets issued by several other businesses around the country. Most of the players included on the 1-5/8" x 3" cards also appear in the prior The Sporting News edition. The complete set price does not include variations.

		NM	EX	VG
Complete Set (200):		23000.	11500.	6500.
Common Player:		65.00	32.00	19.50
1	Babe Adams	75.00	35.00	20.00
2	Sam Agnew	65.00	32.00	19.50
3	Eddie Ainsmith	65.00	32.00	19.50
4	Grover Alexander	175.00	87.00	52.00
5	Leon Ames	65.00	32.00	19.50
6	Jimmy Archer	65.00	32.00	19.50
7	Jimmy Austin	65.00	32.00	19.50
8	H.D. Baird	65.00	32.00	19.50
9	J. Franklin Baker	150.00	75.00	45.00
10	Dave Bancroft	150.00	75.00	45.00
11	Jack Barry	65.00	32.00	19.50
12	Zinn Beck	65.00	32.00	19.50
13	"Chief" Bender	150.00	75.00	45.00
14	Joe Benz	65.00	32.00	19.50
15	Bob Bescher	65.00	32.00	19.50
16	Al Betzel	65.00	32.00	19.50
17	Mordecai Brown	150.00	75.00	45.00
18	Eddie Burns	65.00	32.00	19.50
19	George Burns	65.00	32.00	19.50
20	Geo. J. Burns	65.00	32.00	19.50
21	Joe Bush	65.00	32.00	19.50
22	"Donie" Bush	65.00	32.00	19.50
23	Art Butler	65.00	32.00	19.50
24	Bobbie Byrne	65.00	32.00	19.50
25	Forrest Cady	65.00	32.00	19.50
26	Jimmy Callahan	65.00	32.00	19.50
27	Ray Caldwell	65.00	32.00	19.50
28	Max Carey	150.00	75.00	45.00
29	George Chalmers	65.00	32.00	19.50
30	Ray Chapman	80.00	40.00	24.00
31	Larry Cheney	65.00	32.00	19.50
32	Eddie Cicotte	120.00	60.00	36.00
33	Tom Clarke	65.00	32.00	19.50
34	Eddie Collins	150.00	75.00	45.00

35	"Shauno" Collins	65.00	32.00	19.50
36	Charles Comiskey	175.00	87.00	52.00
37	Joe Connolly	65.00	32.00	19.50
38	Ty Cobb	2200.	1100.	550.00
39	Harry Coveleskie (Coveleski)	65.00	32.00	19.50
40	Gavvy Cravath	65.00	32.00	19.50
41	Sam Crawford	150.00	75.00	45.00
42	Jean Dale	65.00	32.00	19.50
43	Jake Daubert	65.00	32.00	19.50
44	Charles Deal	65.00	32.00	19.50
45	Al Demaree	65.00	32.00	19.50
46	Josh Devore	65.00	32.00	19.50
47	William Doak	65.00	32.00	19.50
48	Bill Donovan	65.00	32.00	19.50
49	Charles Dooin	65.00	32.00	19.50
50	Mike Doolan	65.00	32.00	19.50
51	Larry Doyle	65.00	32.00	19.50
52	Jean Dubuc	65.00	32.00	19.50
53	Oscar Dugey	65.00	32.00	19.50
54	Johnny Evers	150.00	75.00	45.00
55	Urban Faber	150.00	75.00	45.00
56	"Hap" Felsch	100.00	50.00	30.00
57	Bill Fischer	65.00	32.00	19.50
58	Ray Fisher	65.00	32.00	19.50
59	Max Flack	65.00	32.00	19.50
60	Art Fletcher	65.00	32.00	19.50
61	Eddie Foster	65.00	32.00	19.50
62	Jacques Fournier	65.00	32.00	19.50
63	Del Gainer (Gainor)	65.00	32.00	19.50
64	"Chic" Gandil	150.00	75.00	45.00
65	Larry Gardner	65.00	32.00	19.50
66	Joe Gedeon	65.00	32.00	19.50
67	Gus Getz	65.00	32.00	19.50
68	Geo. Gibson	65.00	32.00	19.50
69	Wilbur Good	65.00	32.00	19.50
70	Hank Gowdy	65.00	32.00	19.50
71	John Graney	65.00	32.00	19.50
72	Clark Griffith	150.00	75.00	45.00
73	Tom Griffith	65.00	32.00	19.50
74	Heinie Groh	65.00	32.00	19.50
75	Earl Hamilton	65.00	32.00	19.50
76	Bob Harmon	65.00	32.00	19.50
77	Roy Hartzell	65.00	32.00	19.50
78	Claude Hendrix	65.00	32.00	19.50
79	Olaf Henriksen	65.00	32.00	19.50
80	John Henry	65.00	32.00	19.50
81	"Buck" Herzog	65.00	32.00	19.50
82	Hugh High	65.00	32.00	19.50
83	Dick Hoblitzell	65.00	32.00	19.50
84	Harry Hooper	150.00	75.00	45.00
85	Ivan Howard	65.00	32.00	19.50
86	Miller Huggins	150.00	75.00	45.00
87	Joe Jackson	4250.	2100.	1100.
88	William James	65.00	32.00	19.50
89	Harold Janvrin	65.00	32.00	19.50
90	Hugh Jennings	150.00	75.00	45.00
91	Walter Johnson	650.00	325.00	195.00
92	Fielder Jones	65.00	32.00	19.50
93	Joe Judge	65.00	32.00	19.50
94	Bennie Kauff	65.00	32.00	19.50
95	Wm. Killefer Jr.	65.00	32.00	19.50
96	Ed. Konetchy	65.00	32.00	19.50
97	Napoleon Lajoie	200.00	100.00	60.00
98	Jack Lapp	65.00	32.00	19.50
99	John Lavan	65.00	32.00	19.50
100	Jimmy Lavender	65.00	32.00	19.50
101	"Nemo" Leibold	65.00	32.00	19.50
102	H.B. Leonard	65.00	32.00	19.50
103	Duffy Lewis	65.00	32.00	19.50
104	Hans Lobert	65.00	32.00	19.50
105	Tom Long	65.00	32.00	19.50
106	Fred Luderus	65.00	32.00	19.50
107	Connie Mack	150.00	75.00	45.00
108	Lee Magee	65.00	32.00	19.50
109	Sherwood Magee	65.00	32.00	19.50
110	Al. Mamaux	65.00	32.00	19.50
111	Leslie Mann	65.00	32.00	19.50
112	"Rabbit" Maranville	150.00	75.00	45.00
113	Rube Marquard	150.00	75.00	45.00
114	J. Erskine Mayer	65.00	32.00	19.50
115	George McBride	65.00	32.00	19.50
116	John J. McGraw	150.00	75.00	45.00
117	Jack McInnis	65.00	32.00	19.50
118	Fred Merkle	65.00	32.00	19.50
119	Chief Meyers	65.00	32.00	19.50
120	Clyde Milan	65.00	32.00	19.50
121	John Miller	65.00	32.00	19.50
122	Otto Miller	65.00	32.00	19.50
123	Willie Mitchell	65.00	32.00	19.50
124	Fred Mollwitz	65.00	32.00	19.50
125	Pat Moran	65.00	32.00	19.50
126	Ray Morgan	65.00	32.00	19.50
127	Geo. Moriarty	65.00	32.00	19.50
128	Guy Morton	65.00	32.00	19.50
129	Mike Mowrey	65.00	32.00	19.50
130	Ed. Murphy	65.00	32.00	19.50
131	"Hy" Myers	65.00	32.00	19.50
132	J.A. Niehoff	65.00	32.00	19.50
133	Rube Oldring	65.00	32.00	19.50
134	Oliver O'Mara	65.00	32.00	19.50
135	Steve O'Neill	65.00	32.00	19.50
136	"Dode" Paskert	65.00	32.00	19.50
137	Roger Peckinpaugh	65.00	32.00	19.50
138	Walter Pipp	80.00	40.00	24.00
139	Derril Pratt (Derrill)	65.00	32.00	19.50
140	Pat Ragan	65.00	32.00	19.50
141	Bill Rariden	65.00	32.00	19.50
142	Eppa Rixey	150.00	75.00	45.00
143	Davey Robertson	65.00	32.00	19.50
144	Wilbert Robinson	150.00	75.00	45.00
145	Bob Roth	65.00	32.00	19.50
146	Ed. Roush	150.00	75.00	45.00
147	Clarence Rowland	65.00	32.00	19.50
148	"Nap" Rucker	65.00	32.00	19.50
149	Dick Rudolph	65.00	32.00	19.50
150	Reb Russell	65.00	32.00	19.50
151	Babe Ruth	5250.	2625.	1200.
152	Vic Saier	65.00	32.00	19.50
153	"Slim" Sallee	65.00	32.00	19.50
154	Ray Schalk	150.00	75.00	45.00
155	Walter Schang	65.00	32.00	19.50
156	Frank Schulte	65.00	32.00	19.50
157	Everett Scott	65.00	32.00	19.50
158	Jim Scott	65.00	32.00	19.50
159	Tom Seaton	65.00	32.00	19.50
160	Howard Shanks	65.00	32.00	19.50
161	Bob Shawkey	65.00	32.00	19.50
162	Ernie Shore	65.00	32.00	19.50
163	Burt Shotton	65.00	32.00	19.50
164	Geo. Sisler	150.00	75.00	45.00
165	J. Carlisle Smith	65.00	32.00	19.50
166	Fred Snodgrass	65.00	32.00	19.50
167	Geo. Stallings	65.00	32.00	19.50
168a	Oscar Stanage (catching)	80.00	40.00	24.00
168b	Oscar Stanage (portrait to waist)	80.00	40.00	24.00
169	Charles Stengel	250.00	125.00	75.00
170	Milton Stock	65.00	32.00	19.50
171	Amos Strunk	65.00	32.00	19.50
172	Billy Sullivan	65.00	32.00	19.50
173	"Jeff" Tesreau	65.00	32.00	19.50
174	Joe Tinker	150.00	75.00	45.00
175	Fred Toney	65.00	32.00	19.50
176	Terry Turner	65.00	32.00	19.50
177	George Tyler	65.00	32.00	19.50
178	Jim Vaughn	65.00	32.00	19.50
179	Bob Veach	65.00	32.00	19.50
180	James Viox	65.00	32.00	19.50
181	Oscar Vitt	65.00	32.00	19.50
182	Hans Wagner	525.00	262.00	157.00
183	Clarence Walker	65.00	32.00	19.50
184	Ed. Walsh	150.00	75.00	45.00
185	W. Wambsganss (photo actually Fritz Coumbe)	65.00	32.00	19.50
186	Buck Weaver	115.00	57.00	34.00
187	Carl Weilman	65.00	32.00	19.50
188	Zach Wheat	150.00	75.00	45.00
189	Geo. Whitted	65.00	32.00	19.50
190	Fred Williams	65.00	32.00	19.50
191	Art Wilson	65.00	32.00	19.50
192	J. Owen Wilson	65.00	32.00	19.50
193	Ivy Wingo	65.00	32.00	19.50
194	"Mel" Wolfgang	65.00	32.00	19.50
195	Joe Wood	65.00	32.00	19.50
196	Steve Yerkes	65.00	32.00	19.50
197	"Pep" Young	65.00	32.00	19.50
198	Rollie Zeider	65.00	32.00	19.50
199	Heiny Zimmerman	65.00	32.00	19.50
200	Ed. Zwilling	65.00	32.00	19.50

1919 Sporting News Supplements (M101-6)

This set of glossy black-and-white player photos is generally attributed to The Sporting News, even though the only clue to the issuer are the initials "F.M." beneath the copyright logo. The photos measure 4-1/2" x 6-1/2" and feature action shots of the player whose name, position and team appear at the bottom of the borderless pictures. Four of the players in the checklist appear with two different teams, but since the trades spanned the years 1915-20, it gives rise to speculation these photos were issued over a period of several seasons, rather than the generally attributed 1919. The Sporting News itself carries no advertisements for these photos in its 1919 issues.

		NM	EX	VG
Complete Set (95):		10000.	4000.	2000.
Common Player:		45.00	22.00	13.50
(1)	Grover C. Alexander (Philadelphia)	90.00	36.00	18.00
(2)	Grover C. Alexander (Chicago)	90.00	36.00	18.00
(3)	Jim Bagby	55.00	22.00	11.00
(4)	Franklin Baker	75.00	30.00	15.00
(5)	Dave Bancroft	75.00	30.00	15.00
(6)	Jack Barry	55.00	22.00	11.00
(7)	Johnny Bates	55.00	22.00	11.00
(8)	Carson Bigbee	55.00	22.00	11.00
(9)	George Burns	55.00	22.00	11.00
(10)	Owen Bush	55.00	22.00	11.00
(11)	Max Carey	75.00	30.00	15.00
(12)	Ray Chapman	60.00	24.00	12.00
(13)	Hal Chase	60.00	24.00	12.00
(14)	Eddie Cicotte	75.00	37.00	22.00
(15)	Ty Cobb	950.00	380.00	190.00
(16)	Eddie Collins	75.00	30.00	15.00
(17)	"Gavvy" Cravath	55.00	22.00	11.00
(18)	Walton Cruise	55.00	22.00	11.00
(19)	George Cutshaw	55.00	22.00	11.00
(20)	George Dauss	55.00	22.00	11.00
(21)	Dave Davenport	55.00	22.00	11.00
(22)	Bill Doak	55.00	22.00	11.00
(23)	Larry Doyle	55.00	22.00	11.00
(24)	Howard Ehmke	55.00	22.00	11.00
(25)	Urban Faber	75.00	30.00	15.00
(26)	Happy Felsch	75.00	30.00	15.00
(27)	Del Gainer (Gainor)	55.00	22.00	11.00
(28)	Chick Gandil	75.00	30.00	15.00
(29)	Larry Gardner	55.00	22.00	11.00
(30)	Mike Gonzales (Gonzalez)	65.00	26.00	13.00
(31)	Jack Graney	55.00	22.00	11.00
(32)	Heinie Groh	55.00	22.00	11.00
(33)	Earl Hamilton	55.00	22.00	11.00
(34)	Harry Heilmann	75.00	30.00	15.00
(35)	Hugh High (New York, photo actually Bob Shawkey)	55.00	22.00	11.00
(36)	Hugh High (Detroit, correct photo)	55.00	22.00	11.00
(37)	Bill Hinchman	55.00	22.00	11.00
(38)	Walter Holke (New York)	55.00	22.00	11.00
(39)	Walter Holke (Boston)	55.00	22.00	11.00
(40)	Harry Hooper	75.00	30.00	15.00
(41)	Rogers Hornsby	100.00	50.00	30.00
(42)	Joe Jackson	2000.	800.00	400.00
(43)	Bill Jacobson	55.00	22.00	11.00
(44)	Walter Johnson	400.00	160.00	80.00
(45)	Sam Jones	55.00	22.00	11.00
(46)	Joe Judge	55.00	22.00	11.00
(47)	Benny Kauff	55.00	22.00	11.00
(48)	Ed Konetchy (Boston)	55.00	22.00	11.00
(49)	Ed Konetchy (Brooklyn)	55.00	22.00	11.00
(50)	Nemo Leibold	55.00	22.00	11.00
(51)	Duffy Lewis	55.00	22.00	11.00
(52)	Fred Luderas (Luderus)	55.00	22.00	11.00
(53)	Les Mann	55.00	22.00	11.00
(54)	"Rabbit" Maranville	75.00	30.00	15.00
(55)	John McGraw	75.00	30.00	15.00
(56)	Fred Merkle	55.00	22.00	11.00
(57)	Clyde Milan	55.00	22.00	11.00
(58)	Otto Miller	55.00	22.00	11.00
(59)	Guy Morton	55.00	22.00	11.00
(60)	Hy Myers	55.00	22.00	11.00
(61)	Greasy Neale	60.00	24.00	12.00
(62)	Dode Paskert	55.00	22.00	11.00
(63)	Roger Peckinpaugh	55.00	22.00	11.00
(64)	Jeff Pfeffer	55.00	22.00	11.00
(65)	Walter Pipp	60.00	24.00	12.00
(66)	Johnny Rawlings	55.00	22.00	11.00
(67)	Sam Rice	75.00	30.00	15.00
(68)	Edd Roush	75.00	30.00	15.00
(69)	Dick Rudolph	55.00	22.00	11.00
(70)	Babe Ruth (Red Sox)	1950.	780.00	390.00
(71)	Babe Ruth (New York)	1750.	700.00	350.00
(72)	Ray Schalk	75.00	30.00	15.00
(73)	Hank Severeid	55.00	22.00	11.00
(74)	Burt Shotton	55.00	22.00	11.00
(75)	George Sisler	75.00	30.00	15.00
(76)	Jack Smith	55.00	22.00	11.00
(77)	Frank Snyder	55.00	22.00	11.00
(78)	Tris Speaker	90.00	36.00	18.00
(79)	Oscar Stanage	55.00	22.00	11.00
(80)	Casey Stengel	90.00	36.00	18.00
(81)	Amos Strunk	55.00	22.00	11.00
(82)	Fred Toney	55.00	22.00	11.00
(83)	Jim Vaughn	55.00	22.00	11.00
(84)	Bobby Veach	55.00	22.00	11.00
(85)	Oscar Vitt	55.00	22.00	11.00
(86)	"Honus" Wagner	250.00	100.00	50.00
(87)	Tilly Walker	55.00	22.00	11.00
(88)	Bill Wambsganss	55.00	22.00	11.00
(89)	"Buck" Weaver	75.00	30.00	15.00
(90)	Zack Wheat	75.00	30.00	15.00
(91)	George Whitted	55.00	22.00	11.00
(92)	Cy Williams	55.00	22.00	11.00
(93)	Ivy Wingo	55.00	22.00	11.00
(94)	Pep ("Pep" Young)	55.00	22.00	11.00
(95)	Heinie Zimmerman	55.00	22.00	11.00

1926 Sporting News Supplements (M101-7)

This set of 11 player photos was issued as a supplement by The Sporting News in 1926. The sepia-toned portrait photos were enclosed inside an oval on the 7" x 10" supplements. The player's name and team are printed at the bottom, while a line indentifying The Sporting News and the date appear in the upper left corner. The unnumbered set includes a half-dozen Hall of Famers.

		NM	EX	VG
Complete Set (11):		1750.	700.00	350.00
Common Player:		60.00	24.00	12.00
(1)	Hazen "Kiki" Cuyler	160.00	64.00	32.00
(2)	Rogers Hornsby	175.00	70.00	35.00
(3)	Tony Lazzeri	160.00	64.00	32.00
(4)	Harry E. Manush (Henry)	160.00	64.00	32.00
(5)	John Mostil	60.00	24.00	12.00
(6)	Harry Rice	60.00	24.00	12.00
(7)	George Herman Ruth	650.00	260.00	130.00
(8)	Al Simmons	160.00	64.00	32.00
(9)	Harold "Pie" Traynor	160.00	64.00	32.00
(10)	George Uhle	60.00	24.00	12.00
(11)	Glenn Wright	60.00	24.00	12.00

1939 Sporting News Supplements (M101-9)

These dated supplements feature a trio of team photos and two star players as individuals. The team pictures are about 15" x 10-1/2" and comprise double-page spreads; the single players are 7-1/2" x 10".

		NM	EX	VG
Complete Set (5):		300.00	150.00	90.00
Common:		50.00	25.00	15.00
(1)	Joe DiMaggio	150.00	75.00	45.00
(2)	Bob Feller	50.00	25.00	15.00
(3)	Cincinnati Reds team	50.00	25.00	15.00
(4)	N.Y. Yankees team	100.00	50.00	30.00
(5)	St. Louis Cardinals team	50.00	25.00	15.00

1888 Sporting Times (M117)

Examples of these cards, issued in 1888 and 1889 by the Sporting Times weekly newspaper, are very rare. The complete set price includes all variations. The cabinet-size cards (7-1/4" x 4-1/2") feature line drawings of players in action poses on soft cardboard stock. The cards came in a variety of pastel colors surrounded by a 1/4" white border. The player's last name is printed on each drawing, as are the words "Courtesy Sporting Times New York." A pair of crossed bats and a baseball appear along the bottom of the card. Twenty-seven different players are known to exist. The drawing of Cap Anson is the same one used in the N28 Allen & Ginter series, and some of the other drawings are based on photos used in the popular Old Judge series.

		NM	EX	VG
Common Player:		3150.	1575.	945.00
(1)	Cap Anson	9500.	4750.	2850.
(2)	Jersey Bakely	3150.	1575.	945.00
(3)	Dan Brouthers	6300.	3150.	1900.
(4)	Doc Bushong	3150.	1575.	945.00
(5)	Jack Clements	3150.	1575.	945.00
(6)	Commy Comiskey	6300.	3150.	1900.
(7)	Jerry Denny	3150.	1575.	945.00
(8)	Buck Ewing	6300.	3150.	1900.
(9)	Dude Esterbrook	3150.	1575.	945.00
(10)	Jay Faatz	3150.	1575.	945.00
(11)	Pud Galvin	6300.	3150.	1900.
(12)	Pebbly Jack Glasscock	3150.	1575.	945.00
(13)	Tim Keefe	6300.	3150.	1900.
(14)	King Kelly	6300.	3150.	1900.
(15)	Matt Kilroy	3150.	1575.	945.00
(16)	Arlie Latham	3150.	1575.	945.00
(17)	Doggie Miller	3150.	1575.	945.00
(18)	Hank O'Day	3150.	1575.	945.00
(19)	Fred Pfeffer	3150.	1575.	945.00
(20)	Henry Porter	3150.	1575.	945.00
(21)	Toad Ramsey	3150.	1575.	945.00
(22)	Long John Reilly	3150.	1575.	945.00
(23)	Mike Smith	3150.	1575.	945.00
(24)	Harry Stovey	3150.	1575.	945.00
(25)	Big Sam Thompson	6300.	3150.	1900.
(26)	Monte Ward	6300.	3150.	1900.
(27)	Mickey Welch	6300.	3150.	1900.

1888 Sporting Times Cigar N.Y. Giants

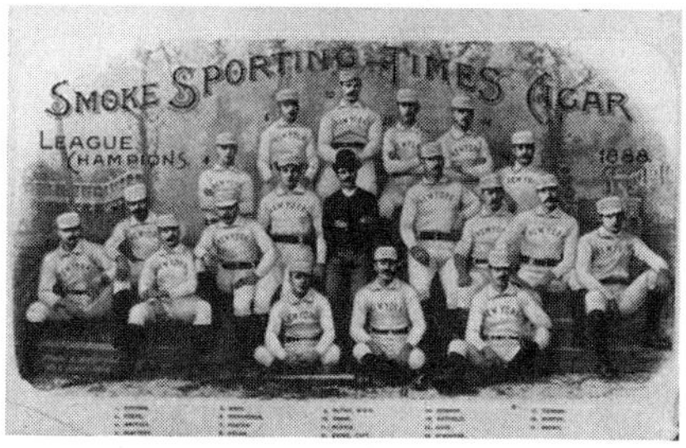

The National League champion N.Y. Giants of 1888 are featured in this team-picture advertising card. About 7-1/4" x 4-5/16", the card features a sepia engraving of the team keyed by numbers and identified at bottom. The photo from which the engraving was made and copyright of the card itself is by Joseph Hall, who produced a contemporary series of team cabinet photo cards.

	NM	EX	VG
1888 New York Giants team picture	3000.	1500.	900.00

1933 Sport Kings

This 48-card set was issued by the Goudey Gum Company. Participants in 18 different sports are included in the set, which honors the top sports figures of the era. Three baseball players are pictured on the 2-3/8" x 2-7/8" cards. The card fronts are color portraits and include the player's name and silhouette representations of the respective sport. The card backs are numbered and list biographical information and a company ad.

		NM	EX	VG
Complete Set (48):		18500.	8325.	4625.
Common Player (1-24):		90.00	40.00	22.00
Common Player (25-48):		200.00	90.00	50.00
Advertising Poster:		7500.	4000.	2400.
1	Ty Cobb	2500.	1150.	500.00
2	Babe Ruth	3550.	1600.	885.00
3	Nat Holman (basketball)	550.00	245.00	135.00
4	Red Grange (football)	950.00	425.00	235.00
5	Ed Wachter (basketball)	275.00	125.00	70.00
6	Jim Thorpe (football)	1100.	495.00	275.00
7	Bobby Walthour, Sr. (bicycling)	110.00	50.00	27.00
8	Walter Hagen (golf)	425.00	190.00	105.00
9	Ed Blood (skiiing)	150.00	65.00	35.00
10	Anston Lekang (skiing)	140.00	65.00	35.00
11	Charles Jewtraw (ice skating)	130.00	58.00	32.00
12	Bobby McLean (ice skating)	130.00	58.00	32.00
13	Laverne Fator (jockey)	125.00	56.00	31.00
14	Jim Londos (wrestling)	90.00	40.00	22.00
15	Reggie McNamara (bicycling)	90.00	40.00	22.00
16	Bill Tilden (tennis)	225.00	100.00	55.00
17	Jack Dempsey (boxing)	425.00	190.00	105.00
18	Gene Tunney (boxing)	400.00	180.00	100.00
19	Eddie Shore (hockey)	350.00	155.00	85.00
20	Duke Kahanamoku (surfing/swimming)	350.00	155.00	85.00
21	Johnny Weissmuller (swimming/ "Tarzan")	375.00	170.00	94.00
22	Gene Sarazen (golf)	300.00	135.00	75.00
23	Vincent Richards (tennis)	175.00	80.00	45.00
24	Howie Morenz (hockey)	600.00	275.00	150.00
25	Ralph Snoddy (speedboating)	200.00	90.00	50.00
26	James Wedell (aviator)	200.00	90.00	50.00
27	Roscoe Turner (aviator)	250.00	110.00	60.00
28	James Doolittle (aviator)	450.00	202.00	112.00
29	Ace Bailey (hockey)	550.00	247.00	137.00
30	Irvin Johnson (hockey)	350.00	157.00	87.00
31	Bobby Walthour, Jr. (bicycling)	200.00	90.00	50.00
32	Joe Lopchick (basketball)	325.00	145.00	80.00
33	Eddie Burke (basketball)	300.00	135.00	75.00
34	Irving Jaffee (ice skating)	200.00	90.00	50.00
35	Knute Rockne (football)	1000.	450.00	250.00
36	Willie Hoppe (billiards)	600.00	275.00	150.00
37	Helene Madison (swimming)	200.00	90.00	50.00
38	Bobby Jones (golf)	950.00	425.00	235.00
39	Jack Westrope (jockey)	200.00	90.00	50.00
40	Don George (wrestling)	200.00	90.00	50.00
41	Jim Browning (wrestling)	225.00	100.00	55.00
42	Carl Hubbell	575.00	260.00	145.00
43	Primo Carnera (boxing)	350.00	155.00	85.00
44	Max Baer (boxing)	375.00	170.00	95.00
45	Babe Didrickson (track)	975.00	435.00	245.00
46	Ellsworth Vines (tennis)	275.00	125.00	70.00
47	J.H. Stevens (bobsled)	200.00	90.00	50.00
48	Leonard Seppala (dog sled)	300.00	125.00	70.00

1953 Sport Magazine All-Star Portfolio

This set of 5-3/8" x 7" glossy color pictures was used by Sport Magazine as a subscription premium. Featuring the outstanding photography of Ozzie Sweet, all but the Bob Mathias pictures are portraits, surrounded with a white border and the player name at bottom. Backs are blank. The heavy cardboard mailing envelope contains short athlete biographies.

		NM	EX	VG
Complete Set (10):		115.00	57.00	33.00
Common Player:		9.00	4.50	2.75
(1)	Joe Black	12.00	6.00	3.50
(2)	Robert Cousy (basketball)	12.00	6.00	3.50
(3)	Elroy Hirsch (football)	12.00	6.00	3.50
(4)	Rocky Marciano (boxing)	15.00	7.50	4.50
(5)	Robert Bruce Mathias (track and field)	9.00	4.50	2.75
(6)	Stanley Frank Musial	18.00	9.00	5.50
(7)	John Olszewski (football)	9.00	4.50	2.75
(8)	Allie Pierce Reynolds	12.00	6.00	3.50
(9)	Robin Evan Roberts	15.00	7.50	4.50
(10)	Robert Clayton Shantz	12.00	6.00	3.50

1977-79 Sportscaster

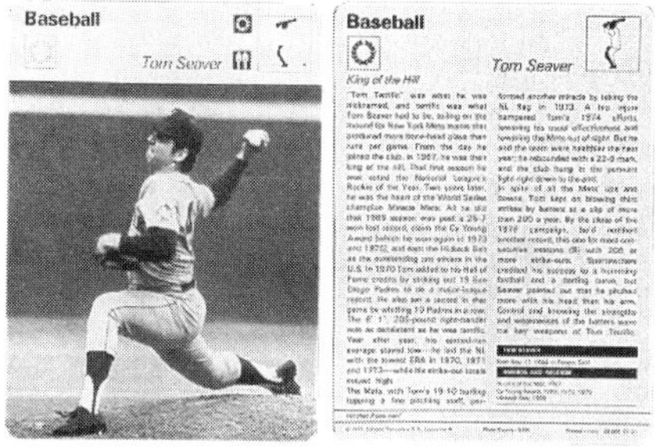

This massive set of full-color cards includes players from dozens of different sports - some of them very obscure - among more than 2,000 different subjects, making it one of the biggest sets of trading cards ever issued. Available by mail subscription from 1977 through 1979, the Sportscaster cards are large, measuring 4-3/4" x 6-1/4". Subscribers were mailed one series of 24 cards for $1.89 plus postage every month or so. The set has an international flavor to it, including such sports as rugby, soccer, lawn bowling, fencing, karate, bicycling, curling, skiing, bullfighting, auto racing, mountain climbing, hang gliding, yachting, sailing, badminton, bobsledding, etc. Each card has a series of icons in the upper-right corner to assist collectors in the various methods of sorting. Most popular among American collectors are the baseball, football and basketball stars in the set, which includes the 140 baseball subjects listed here. The checklist includes many Hall of Famers. Backs contain detailed write-ups of the player featured. Because the set was issued in series, and many collectors dropped out of the program before the end, cards in the higher series are especially scarce. This accounts for prices on some of the superstar cards, issued in early series, being lower than for some of the lesser-known players. The cards of Aaron and Bench are quite common because they were mailed to large numbers of persons as samples to introduce the program. The cards were also sold in several European countries and can be found with backs printed in French, Swedish and other languages.

		NM	EX	VG
Complete (Baseball) Set (140):		1000.	500.00	300.00
Common Player:		3.00	1.50	.90
(1)	Henry Aaron	12.00	6.00	3.50
(2)	Danny Ainge	100.00	50.00	30.00
(3)	Emmett Ashford (umpire)	7.50	3.75	2.25
(4)	Ernie Banks	8.00	4.00	2.50
(5)	Johnny Bench	9.00	4.50	2.75
(6)	Vida Blue	5.00	2.50	1.50
(7)	Bert Blyleven	4.00	2.00	1.25
(8)	Bobby Bonds	10.00	5.00	3.00
(9)	Lyman Bostock	4.00	2.00	1.25
(10)	George Brett	15.00	7.50	4.50
(11)	Lou Brock	10.00	5.00	3.00
(12)	Jeff Burroughs	4.00	2.00	1.25
(13)	Roy Campanella	25.00	12.50	7.50
(14)	John Candelaria	4.00	2.00	1.25
(15)	Rod Carew	10.00	5.00	3.00
(16)	Steve Carlton	12.00	6.00	3.50
(17)	Ron Cey	3.00	1.50	.90
(18)	Roberto Clemente	35.00	17.50	10.50
(19)	Steve Dembowski	7.00	3.50	2.00
(20)	Joe DiMaggio	20.00	10.00	6.00
(21)	Dennis Eckersley	8.00	4.00	2.50
(22)	Mark Fidrych	5.00	2.50	1.50
(23)	Carlton Fisk	25.00	12.50	7.50
(24)	Mike Flanagan	9.00	4.50	2.75
(25)	Steve Garvey	15.00	7.50	4.50
(26)	Ron Guidry	9.00	4.50	2.75
(27)	Gil Hodges	12.00	6.00	3.50
(28)	Catfish Hunter	12.00	6.00	3.50
(29)	Tommy John	4.00	2.00	1.25
(30)	Randy Jones	3.00	1.50	.90
(31)	Dave Kingman	5.00	2.50	1.50
(32)	Sandy Koufax	25.00	12.50	7.50
(33)	Tommy Lasorda	20.00	10.00	6.00
(34)	Ron LeFlore	4.00	2.00	1.25
(35)	Greg Luzinski	3.00	1.50	.90
(36)	Billy Martin	10.00	5.00	3.00
(37)	Willie Mays	12.00	6.00	3.50
(38)	Lee Mazzilli	6.00	3.00	1.75
(39)	Willie McCovey	11.00	5.50	3.25
(40)	Joe Morgan	8.00	4.00	2.50
(41)	Thurman Munson	12.00	6.00	3.50
(42)	Stan Musial	15.00	7.50	4.50
(43)	Phil Niekro	12.00	6.00	3.50
(44)	Jim Palmer	9.00	4.50	2.75
(45)	Dave Parker	5.00	2.50	1.50
(46)	Freddie Patek	4.00	2.00	1.25
(47)	Gaylord Perry	7.00	3.50	2.00
(48)	Jim Piersall	8.00	4.00	2.50
(49)	Vada Pinson	4.00	2.00	1.25
(50)	Rick Reuschel	4.00	2.00	1.25
(51)	Jim Rice	4.00	2.00	1.25
(52)	J.R. Richard	7.00	3.50	2.00
(53)	Brooks Robinson	11.00	5.50	3.25
(54)	Frank Robinson	15.00	7.50	4.50
(55)	Jackie Robinson	20.00	10.00	6.00
(56)	Pete Rose	11.00	5.50	3.25
(57)	Joe Rudi	3.00	1.50	.90
(58)	Babe Ruth	18.00	9.00	5.50
(59)	Nolan Ryan	35.00	17.50	10.50
(60)	Tom Seaver	11.00	5.50	3.25
(61)	Warren Spahn	11.00	5.50	3.25
(62)	Monty Stratton	7.00	3.50	2.00
(63)	Craig Swan	5.00	2.50	1.50
(64)	Frank Tanana	3.00	1.50	.90
(65)	Ron Taylor	7.00	3.50	2.00
(66)	Garry Templeton	3.00	1.50	.90
(67)	Gene Tenace	3.00	1.50	.90
(68)	Bobby Thomson	5.00	2.50	1.50
(69)	Andre Thornton	4.00	2.00	1.25
(70)	Johnny VanderMeer	5.00	2.50	1.50
(71)	Ted Williams	15.00	7.50	4.50
(72)	Maury Wills	3.00	1.50	.90
(73)	Hack Wilson	10.00	5.00	3.00
(74)	Dave Winfield (hitting)	25.00	12.50	7.50
(75)	Dave Winfield (portrait)	12.00	6.00	3.50
(76)	Cy Young	8.00	4.00	2.50
(77)	The 1927 Yankees	8.00	4.00	2.50
(78)	1969 Mets	20.00	10.00	6.00
(79)	All-Star Game (Steve Garvey, Joe Morgan)	8.00	4.00	2.50
(80)	Amateur Draft (Rick Monday)	4.00	2.00	1.25
(81)	At-A-Glance Reference (Tom Seaver)	15.00	7.50	4.50
(82)	Babe Ruth Baseball (Ed Figueroa)	10.00	5.00	3.00
(83)	Baltimore Memorial Stadium	9.00	4.50	2.75
(84)	Boston's Fenway Park	15.00	7.50	4.50
(85)	Brother vs. Brother (Joe Niekro)	8.00	4.00	2.50
(86)	Busch Memorial Stadium	7.50	3.75	2.25
(87)	Candlestick Park	6.00	3.00	1.75
(88)	Cape Cod League (Jim Beattie)	6.00	3.00	1.75
(89)	A Century and a Half of Baseball (Johnny Bench)	5.00	2.50	1.50
(90)	Cy Young Award (Tom Seaver)	8.00	4.00	2.50
(91)	The Dean Brothers (Dizzy Dean, Paul Dean)	15.00	7.50	4.50
(92)	Designated Hitter (Rusty Staub)	7.00	3.50	2.00
(93)	Dodger Stadium	8.00	4.00	2.50
(94)	Perfect Game (Don Larsen)	10.00	5.00	3.00
(95)	The Double Steal (Davey Lopes)	3.00	1.50	.90
(96)	Fenway Park	12.00	6.00	3.50
(97)	The Firemen (Goose Gossage)	12.00	6.00	3.50
(98)	Forever Blowing Bubbles (Davey Lopes)	6.00	3.00	1.75
(99)	The Forsch Brothers (Bob Forsch, Ken Forsch)	8.00	4.00	2.50
(100)	Four Home Runs In A Game (Mike Schmidt)	20.00	10.00	6.00
(101)	400-Homer Club (Duke Snider)	15.00	7.50	4.50
(102)	Great Moments (Bob Gibson)	10.00	5.00	3.00
(103)	Great Moments (Ferguson Jenkins)	7.00	3.50	2.00
(104)	Great Moments (Mickey Lolich)	5.00	2.50	1.50
(105)	Great Moments (Carl Yastrzemski)	10.00	5.00	3.00
(106)	Hidden Ball Trick (Carl Yastrzemski)	8.00	4.00	2.50
(107)	Hit And Run (George Foster)	4.00	2.00	1.25
(108)	Hitting The Cutoff Man	3.00	1.50	.90
(109)	Hitting Pitchers (Don Drysdale)	10.00	5.00	3.00
(110)	Infield Fly Rule (Bobby Grich)	4.00	2.00	1.25
(111)	Instruction (Rod Carew)	8.00	4.00	2.50
(112)	Interference (Johnny Bench)	8.00	4.00	2.50
(113)	Iron Mike (Pitching Machine)	8.00	4.00	2.50
(114)	Keeping Score	5.00	2.50	1.50
(115)	Like Father, Like Son (Roy Smalley)	11.00	5.50	3.25
(116)	Lingo I (Gary Carter)	5.00	2.50	1.50
(117)	Lingo II (Earl Weaver)	8.00	4.00	2.50
(118)	Little Leagues To Big Leagues (Hector Torres)	5.00	2.50	1.50
(119)	Maris and Mantle (Mickey Mantle, Roger Maris)	35.00	17.50	10.50
(120)	Measurements (Memorial Stadium)	3.00	1.50	.90
(121)	The Money Game (Dennis Eckersley)	15.00	7.50	4.50
(122)	NCAA Tournament (Aggies-Longhorns)	5.00	2.50	1.50
(123)	The Oakland A's, 1971-75	9.00	4.50	2.75
(124)	The Perfect Game (Sandy Koufax)	15.00	7.50	4.50
(125)	Pickoff (Luis Tiant)	4.00	2.00	1.25
(126)	The Presidential Ball (William Howard Taft)	5.00	2.50	1.50
(127)	Relief Pitching (Mike Marshall)	4.00	2.00	1.25
(128)	The Rules (Hank Aaron)	8.00	4.00	2.50
(129)	Rundown (Mets vs. Astros)	5.00	2.50	1.50
(130)	7th Game of the World Series (Bert Campaneris)	7.00	3.50	2.00
(131)	Shea Stadium	8.00	4.00	2.50
(132)	The 3000 Hit Club (Roberto Clemente)	25.00	12.50	7.50
(133)	Training Camps (Orioles)	8.00	4.00	2.50
(134)	Triple Crown (Carl Yastrzemski)	15.00	7.50	4.50
(135)	Triple Play (Rick Burleson)	8.00	4.00	2.50
(136)	Triple Play (Bill Wambsganss)	5.00	2.50	1.50
(137)	Umpires Strike	5.00	2.50	1.50
(138)	Veterans Stadium	9.00	4.50	2.75
(139)	Wrigley Marathon (Mike Schmidt)	25.00	12.50	7.50
(140)	Yankee Stadium	3.00	1.50	.90
Beyond Sports (Baseball) Set: (6):				
(1)	Clemente Award (Andre Thornton)	15.00	7.50	4.50
(2)	Clowns (Al Schact, Nick Altrock)	12.00	6.00	3.50
(3)	Fellowship of Christian Athletes (Don Kessinger)	12.00	6.00	3.50
(4)	High School Record Book (David Clyde)	8.00	4.00	2.50
(5)	Hutchinson Award (Al Kaline)	15.00	7.50	4.50
(6)	Walkie-Talkie (Yogi Berra)	16.00	8.00	4.75

1977 Sports Challenge Records

Taped highlights and an interview with the player are featured on this series of 33-1/3 RPM records. The 6" diameter records have a center hole to be punched out to play the record. Fronts have a stylized picture of the player, his name and a title. Backs describe the highlight and give other career details.

		NM	EX	VG
Complete Set (4):		45.00	22.00	13.50
Common Player:		11.00	5.50	3.25
(1)	Johnny Bench (Beats Pirates in '72 Playoff)	18.00	9.00	5.50
(2)	Don Larsen ('56 World Series Perfect Game)	11.00	5.50	3.25
(3)	Bill Mazeroski (Wins 1960 World Series)	15.00	7.50	4.50
(4)	Fred Lynn (Has Incredible Day in Detroit)	11.00	5.50	3.25

1926 Sports Co. of America Champions

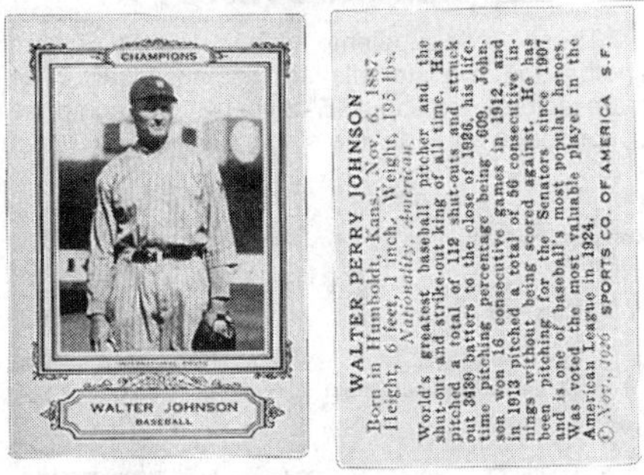

Little was known of these small (1-1/2" x 2-1/4") black-and-white cards until an original store display was discovered in the late 1980s. Carrying a copyright date of Nov., 1926, from Sports Co. of America, a San Francisco publishing firm, these cards were produced for A.G. Spalding & Bros., the sporting goods firm. Each card was issued in a wax paper baggie with a like-sized red, white and blue "SportScrip" which was serial numbered for use in a candy prize drawing at the store or could be redeemed for 10 cents on Spalding equipment. The cards themselves feature ornately framed photos at center, with "CHAMPIONS" in a cartouche at top and the player's name and sport in a second ornate frame at bottom. Nearly 50 baseball players are known from a list of over 175 male and female athletes from sports as diverse as fishing, chess and balloon racing. The unnumbered baseball players from the set are checklisted here in alphabetical order.

		NM	EX	VG
Complete Baseball Set (49):		5000.	2000.	1000.
Common Baseball Player:		30.00	12.00	6.00
(1)	"Babe" Adams	30.00	12.00	6.00
(2)	Grover Alexander	150.00	60.00	30.00
(3)	Nick Altrock	30.00	12.00	6.00
(4)	Dave Bancroft	125.00	50.00	25.00
(5)	Jesse Barnes	30.00	12.00	6.00
(6)	Oswald Bluege	30.00	12.00	6.00
(7)	Jim Bottomley	125.00	50.00	25.00
(8)	Max Carey	125.00	50.00	25.00
(9)	Ty Cobb	900.00	360.00	180.00
(10)	Mickey Cochrane	125.00	50.00	25.00
(11)	Eddie Collins	125.00	50.00	25.00
(12)	Stan Coveleskie (Coveleski)	125.00	50.00	25.00
(13)	Kiki Cuyler	125.00	50.00	25.00
(14)	Hank DeBerry	30.00	12.00	6.00
(15)	Jack Fournier	30.00	12.00	6.00
(16)	Goose Goslin	125.00	50.00	25.00
(17)	Charlie Grimm	30.00	12.00	6.00
(18)	Bucky Harris	125.00	50.00	25.00
(19)	Gabby Hartnett	125.00	50.00	25.00
(20)	Fred Hofmann	30.00	12.00	6.00
(21)	Rogers Hornsby	150.00	60.00	30.00
(22)	Waite Hoyt	125.00	50.00	25.00
(23)	Walter Johnson	225.00	90.00	45.00
(24)	Joe Judge	30.00	12.00	6.00
(25)	Willie Kamm	30.00	12.00	6.00
(26)	Tony Lazzeri	125.00	50.00	25.00
(27)	Rabbit Maranville	125.00	50.00	25.00
(28)	Fred Marberry	30.00	12.00	6.00
(29)	Rube Marquard	125.00	50.00	25.00
(30)	"Stuffy" McInnis	30.00	12.00	6.00
(31)	"Babe" Pinelli	30.00	12.00	6.00
(32)	Wally Pipp	35.00	14.00	7.00
(33)	Sam Rice	125.00	50.00	25.00
(34)	Emory Rigney	30.00	12.00	6.00
(35)	Dutch Ruether	30.00	12.00	6.00
(36)	Babe Ruth	1200.	480.00	240.00
(37)	Ray Schalk	125.00	50.00	25.00
(38)	Joe Sewell	125.00	50.00	25.00
(39)	Urban Shocker	30.00	12.00	6.00
(40)	Al Simmons	125.00	50.00	25.00
(41)	George Sisler	125.00	50.00	25.00
(42)	Tris Speaker	150.00	60.00	30.00
(43)	Pie Traynor	125.00	50.00	25.00
(44)	George Uhle	30.00	12.00	6.00

		NM	EX	VG
(45)	Paul Waner	125.00	50.00	25.00
(46)	Aaron L. Ward	30.00	12.00	6.00
(47)	Ken Williams	30.00	12.00	6.00
(48)	Glenn Wright	30.00	12.00	6.00
(49)	Emil Yde	30.00	12.00	6.00

1946-49 Sports Exchange All-Star Picture File

Produced and sold (originally at 50 cents per series) by "The Trading Post," one of the first card collectors' publications, over a period which spanned several years in the late 1940s, this 113-card set was issued in 12 series. Most of the series were nine cards each, printed in black-and-white, unnumbered and blank-backed in a 7" x 10" format. The first 27 cards carry no series designation but were advertised as Series 1A and 1B and Series 2. Series 3 features 11 cards and is printed in sepia tones rather than black-and-white. The fourth series is also unmarked. The final two series consist of 12 cards each, printed two per sheet in smaller format. The photos are labeled as originating with the International News Service. Most of the same players and photos appearing in this set are also found in the Sports Exchange Baseball Miniatures set. Because this was one of the first baseball card sets issued after World War II, it contains cards of several players not found in other issues. The set carries a W603 designation in the "American Card Catalog." Cards are listed alphabetically within series in the checklist which follows.

		NM	EX	VG
Complete Set (113):		2000.	1000.	600.00
Common Card:		10.00	5.00	3.00
SERIES 1A				
(1)	Phil Cavaretta	12.50	6.25	3.75
(2)	Walker Cooper	10.00	5.00	3.00
(3)	Dave Ferriss	10.00	5.00	3.00
(4)	Les Fleming	10.00	5.00	3.00
(5)	Whitey Kurowski	10.00	5.00	3.00
(6)	Marty Marion	12.50	6.25	3.75
(7)	Rip Sewell	10.00	5.00	3.00
(8)	Eddie Stanky	12.50	6.25	3.75
(9)	Dixie Walker	10.00	5.00	3.00
SERIES 1B				
(10)	Bill Dickey	27.00	13.50	8.00
(11)	Bobby Doerr	20.00	10.00	6.00
(12)	Bob Feller	27.00	13.50	8.00
(13)	Hank Greenberg	32.00	16.00	9.50
(14)	George McQuinn	10.00	5.00	3.00
(15)	Ray Mueller	10.00	5.00	3.00
(16)	Hal Newhouser	20.00	10.00	6.00
(17)	Dick Wakefield	10.00	5.00	3.00
(18)	Ted Williams	100.00	50.00	30.00
SERIES 2				
(19)	Al Benton	10.00	5.00	3.00
(20)	Lou Boudreau	20.00	10.00	6.00
(21)	Spud Chandler	10.00	5.00	3.00
(22)	Jeff Heath	10.00	5.00	3.00
(23)	Kirby Higbe	10.00	5.00	3.00
(24)	Tex Hughson	10.00	5.00	3.00
(25)	Stan Musial	85.00	42.00	25.00
(26)	Howie Pollet	10.00	5.00	3.00
(27)	Enos Slaughter	20.00	10.00	6.00
SERIES 3				
(28)	Harry Brecheen	10.00	5.00	3.00
(29)	Dom DiMaggio	20.00	10.00	6.00
(30)	Del Ennis	10.00	5.00	3.00
(31)	Al Evans	10.00	5.00	3.00
(32)	Johnny Lindell	10.00	5.00	3.00
(33)	Johnny Mize	20.00	10.00	6.00
(34)	Johnny Pesky	10.00	5.00	3.00
(35)	Pete Reiser	10.00	5.00	3.00
(36)	Aaron Robinson	10.00	5.00	3.00
(37)	1946 Boston Red Sox Team	15.00	7.50	4.50
(38)	1946 St. Louis Cardinals Team	15.00	7.50	4.50
SERIES 4				
(39)	Jimmie Foxx	27.00	13.50	8.00
(40)	Frank Frisch	20.00	10.00	6.00
(41)	Lou Gehrig	150.00	75.00	45.00
(42)	Lefty Grove	24.00	12.00	7.25
(43)	Bill Hallahan	10.00	5.00	3.00
(44)	Rogers Hornsby	30.00	15.00	9.00
(45)	Carl Hubbell	30.00	15.00	9.00
(46)	Babe Ruth	300.00	150.00	90.00
(47)	Hack Wilson	20.00	10.00	6.00
SERIES 5				
(48)	Eddie Dyer	10.00	5.00	3.00
(49)	Charlie Grimm	10.00	5.00	3.00
(50)	Billy Herman	20.00	10.00	6.00
(51)	Ted Lyons	20.00	10.00	6.00
(52)	Lefty O'Doul	12.50	6.25	3.75
(53)	Steve O'Neill	10.00	5.00	3.00
(54)	Herb Pennock	20.00	10.00	6.00
(55)	Luke Sewell	10.00	5.00	3.00
(56)	Billy Southworth	10.00	5.00	3.00
SERIES 6				
(57)	Ewell Blackwell	10.00	5.00	3.00
(58)	Jimmy Outlaw	10.00	5.00	3.00
(59)	Andy Pafko	10.00	5.00	3.00
(60)	Pee Wee Reese	25.00	12.50	7.50
(61)	Phil Rizzuto	25.00	12.50	7.50
(62)	Buddy Rosar	10.00	5.00	3.00
(63)	Johnny Sain	12.50	6.25	3.75
(64)	Dizzy Trout	10.00	5.00	3.00
(65)	Harry Walker	10.00	5.00	3.00
SERIES 7				
(66)	Floyd Bevens	10.00	5.00	3.00
(67)	Hugh Casey	10.00	5.00	3.00
(68)	Sam Chapman	10.00	5.00	3.00
(69)	Joe DiMaggio	150.00	75.00	45.00
(70)	Tommy Henrich	12.50	6.25	3.75
(71)	Ralph Kiner	20.00	10.00	6.00
(72)	Cookie Lavagetto	10.00	5.00	3.00
(73)	Vic Lombardi	10.00	5.00	3.00
(74)	Cecil Travis	10.00	5.00	3.00
SERIES 8				
(75)	Nick Altrock	10.00	5.00	3.00
(76)	Mark Christman	10.00	5.00	3.00
(77)	Earle Combs	20.00	10.00	6.00
(78)	Travis Jackson	20.00	10.00	6.00
(79)	Bob Muncrief	10.00	5.00	3.00
(80)	Earl Neale	12.50	6.25	3.75
(81)	Joe Page	10.00	5.00	3.00
(82)	Honus Wagner	35.00	17.50	10.50
(83)	Mickey Witek	10.00	5.00	3.00
SERIES 9				
(84)	George Case	10.00	5.00	3.00
(85)	Jake Early	10.00	5.00	3.00
(86)	Carl Furillo	12.50	6.25	3.75
(87)	Augie Galan	10.00	5.00	3.00
(88)	Bert Haas	10.00	5.00	3.00
(89)	Johnny Hopp	10.00	5.00	3.00
(90)	Ray Lamanno	10.00	5.00	3.00
(91)	Buddy Lewis	10.00	5.00	3.00
(92)	Warren Spahn	20.00	10.00	6.00
SERIES 10				
(93)	Lu Blue	10.00	5.00	3.00
(94)	Bruce Edwards	10.00	5.00	3.00
(95)	Elbie Fletcher	10.00	5.00	3.00
(96)	Joe Gordon	10.00	5.00	3.00
(97)	Tommy Holmes	10.00	5.00	3.00
(98)	Billy Johnson	10.00	5.00	3.00
(99)	Phil Masi	10.00	5.00	3.00
(100)	Red Munger	10.00	5.00	3.00
(101)	Vern Stephens	10.00	5.00	3.00
SERIES 11				
(102)	Ralph Branca, Ken Keltner	15.00	7.50	4.50
(103)	Mickey Cochrane, Bob Dillinger	20.00	10.00	6.00
(104)	Dizzy Dean, Eddie Joost	35.00	17.50	10.50
(105)	Joe Jackson, Wally Westlake	275.00	137.00	82.00
(106)	Larry Jansen, Yogi Berra	35.00	17.50	10.50
(107)	Peanuts Lowrey, Heinie Manush	20.00	10.00	6.00
SERIES 12				
(108)	Gene Bearden, Dale Mitchell	27.00	13.50	8.00
(109)	Steve Gromek, Earl Torgeson	27.00	13.50	8.00
(110)	Jim Hegan, Mickey Vernon	27.00	13.50	8.00
(111)	Bob Lemon, Red Rolfe	40.00	20.00	12.00
(112)	Billy Meyer, Ben Chapman	27.00	13.50	8.00
(113)	Sibbi Sisti, Zach Taylor	27.00	13.50	8.00

1947 Sports Exchange Baseball Miniatures

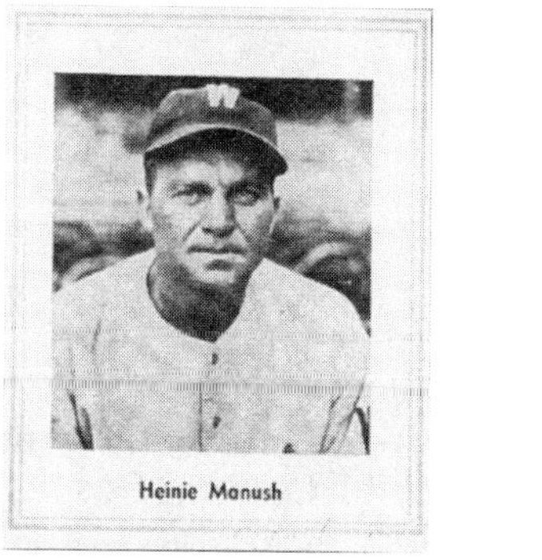

Produced and sold (originally at $1 per series) by one of the hobby's first periodicals, "The Trading Post," this 118 card set was released in three series, designated by red, green and gold borders. The blank-back, unnumbered cards are printed in black-and-white and were sold in sheets of six. When cut from the sheets, individual cards in the red- and green-bordered series measure 2-1/2" x 3," while the gold-bordered cards measure 2-1/2" x 3-1/8". The set is checklisted here alphabetically within series. The set carries an "American Card Catalog" designation of W602.

		NM	EX	VG
Complete Set (108):		2400.	1200.	725.00
Common Player:		12.00	6.00	3.50
GREEN BORDER SERIES				
(1)	Nick Altrock	12.00	6.00	3.50
(2)	Floyd Bevens	12.00	6.00	3.50
(3)	Ewell Blackwell	12.00	6.00	3.50
(4)	Lou Boudreau	24.00	12.00	7.25
(5)	Harry Brecheen	12.00	6.00	3.50
(6)	Hugh Casey	12.00	6.00	3.50
(7)	Phil Cavaretta	15.00	7.50	4.50
(8)	Sam Chapman	12.00	6.00	3.50
(9)	Mark Christman	12.00	6.00	3.50
(10)	Bill Dickey	25.00	12.50	7.50
(11)	Dom DiMaggio	20.00	10.00	6.00
(12)	Joe DiMaggio	175.00	87.00	52.00
(13)	Eddie Dyer	12.00	6.00	3.50
(14)	Frank Frisch	25.00	12.50	7.50
(15)	Lou Gehrig	175.00	87.00	52.00
(16)	Charlie Grimm	12.00	6.00	3.50
(17)	Lefty Grove	25.00	12.50	7.50
(18)	Tommy Henrich	15.00	7.50	4.50
(19)	Ralph Kiner	24.00	12.00	7.25
(20)	Cookie Lavagetto	12.00	6.00	3.50
(21)	Vic Lombardi	12.00	6.00	3.50
(22)	Ted Lyons	24.00	12.00	7.25
(23)	Bob Muncrief	12.00	6.00	3.50
(24)	Stan Musial	100.00	50.00	30.00
(25)	Steve O'Neill	12.00	6.00	3.50
(26)	Jimmy Outlaw	12.00	6.00	3.50
(27)	Joe Page	15.00	7.50	4.50
(28)	Pee Wee Reese	36.00	18.00	11.00
(29)	Phil Rizzuto	40.00	20.00	12.00
(30)	Buddy Rosar	12.00	6.00	3.50
(31)	Johnny Sain	18.00	9.00	5.50
(32)	Billy Southworth	12.00	6.00	3.50
(33)	Cecil Travis	12.00	6.00	3.50
(34)	Honus Wagner	48.00	24.00	14.50
(35)	Harry Walker	12.00	6.00	3.50
(36)	Mickey Witek	12.00	6.00	3.50
RED BORDER SERIES				
(37)	Yogi Berra	48.00	24.00	14.50
(38)	Lu Blue	12.00	6.00	3.50
(39)	Ben Chapman	15.00	7.50	4.50
(40)	Mickey Cochrane	24.00	12.00	7.25
(41)	Earle Combs	24.00	12.00	7.25
(42)	Dizzy Dean	60.00	30.00	18.00
(43)	Bob Dillinger	12.00	6.00	3.50
(44)	Bobby Doerr	24.00	12.00	7.25
(45)	Al Evans	12.00	6.00	3.50
(46)	Jimmie Foxx	36.00	18.00	11.00
(47)	Joe Gordon	12.00	6.00	3.50
(48)	Bill Hallahan	12.00	6.00	3.50
(49)	Tommy Holmes	12.00	6.00	3.50
(50)	Rogers Hornsby	48.00	24.00	14.50
(51)	Carl Hubbell	48.00	24.00	14.50
(52)	Travis Jackson	24.00	12.00	7.25
(53)	Bill Johnson	12.00	6.00	3.50
(54)	Ken Keltner	12.00	6.00	3.50
(55)	Whitey Kurowski	12.00	6.00	3.50
(56)	Ray Lamanno	12.00	6.00	3.50
(57)	Johnny Lindell	12.00	6.00	3.50
(58)	Peanuts Lowrey	12.00	6.00	3.50
(59)	Phil Masi	12.00	6.00	3.50
(60)	Earl Neale	15.00	7.50	4.50
(61)	Hal Newhouser	24.00	12.00	7.25
(62)	Lefty O'Doul	18.00	9.00	5.50
(63)	Herb Pennock	24.00	12.00	7.25
(64)	Red Rolfe	24.00	12.00	7.25
(65)	Babe Ruth	300.00	150.00	90.00
(66)	Luke Sewell	12.00	6.00	3.50
(67)	Rip Sewell	12.00	6.00	3.50
(68)	Warren Spahn	30.00	15.00	9.00
(69)	Vern Stephens	12.00	6.00	3.50
(70)	Dizzy Trout	15.00	7.50	4.50
(71)	Wally Westlake	12.00	6.00	3.50
(72)	Hack Wilson	24.00	12.00	7.25
GOLD BORDER SERIES				
(73)	Al Benton	12.00	6.00	3.50
(74)	Ralph Branca	15.00	7.50	4.50
(75)	George Case	12.00	6.00	3.50
(76)	Spud Chandler	12.00	6.00	3.50
(77)	Jake Early	12.00	6.00	3.50
(78)	Bruce Edwards	12.00	6.00	3.50
(79)	Del Ennis	12.00	6.00	3.50
(80)	Bob Feller	30.00	15.00	9.00
(81)	Dave Ferriss	12.00	6.00	3.50
(82)	Les Fleming	12.00	6.00	3.50
(83)	Carl Furillo	18.00	9.00	5.50
(84)	Augie Galan	12.00	6.00	3.50
(85)	Hank Greenberg	36.00	18.00	11.00
(86)	Bert Haas	12.00	6.00	3.50
(87)	Jeff Heath	12.00	6.00	3.50
(88)	Billy Herman	24.00	12.00	7.25
(89)	Kirby Higbe	12.00	6.00	3.50
(90)	Tex Hughson	12.00	6.00	3.50
(91)	Johnny Hopp	12.00	6.00	3.50
(92)	Joe Jackson	350.00	175.00	105.00
(93)	Larry Jansen	12.00	6.00	3.50
(94)	Eddie Joost	12.00	6.00	3.50
(95)	Buddy Lewis	12.00	6.00	3.50
(96)	Heinie Manush	24.00	12.00	7.25
(97)	Marty Marion	15.00	7.50	4.50
(98)	George McQuinn	12.00	6.00	3.50
(99)	Johnny Mize	24.00	12.00	7.25
(100)	Red Munger	12.00	6.00	3.50
(101)	Andy Pafko	12.00	6.00	3.50
(102)	Johnny Pesky	12.00	6.00	3.50
(103)	Howie Pollet	12.00	6.00	3.50
(104)	Pete Reiser	12.00	6.00	3.50
(105)	Aaron Robinson	12.00	6.00	3.50
(106)	Enos Slaughter	24.00	12.00	7.25
(107)	Dixie Walker	12.00	6.00	3.50
(108)	Ted Williams (photo actually Bobby Doerr)	120.00	60.00	36.00

1963 Sports "Hall of Fame" Busts

Licensed by the National Baseball Hall of Fame, this set of 20 plastic player busts was produced by Sports "Hall of Fame," Inc., of New York. Each six-inch statue has a white player figure atop a wood-look pedestal with a plaque providing career details. The busts were sold in a red, white and gold display box with photos of the players on the back. Though the box back promised "Many More," only the 20 players pictured were ever issued. Retail price at issue was $1-1.25. The first 12 busts are more common than the final eight, with Foxx and Greenberg especially scarce. Values quoted are for busts alone, add $25 for accompanying box and $50 or more for unopened box with cellophane.

		NM	EX	VG
Complete Set (20):		1700.	850.00	450.00
Common Player:		75.00	37.00	22.00
(1)	Babe Ruth	60.00	30.00	18.00
(2)	Ty Cobb	35.00	17.50	10.50
(3)	Joe DiMaggio	50.00	25.00	15.00
(4)	Rogers Hornsby	30.00	15.00	9.00
(5)	Lou Gehrig	60.00	30.00	18.00
(6)	Pie Traynor	25.00	12.50	7.50
(7)	Honus Wagner	40.00	20.00	12.00
(8)	Bill Dickey	25.00	12.50	7.50
(9)	Walter Johnson	30.00	15.00	9.00
(10)	Christy Mathewson	30.00	15.00	9.00
(11)	Jimmie Foxx	200.00	100.00	60.00
(12)	Tris Speaker	30.00	15.00	9.00
(13)	Joe Cronin	75.00	37.00	22.00
(14)	Paul Waner	75.00	37.00	22.00
(15)	Bobby Feller	75.00	37.00	22.00
(16)	Hank Greenberg	95.00	47.00	28.00
(17)	Jackie Robinson	150.00	75.00	45.00
(18)	George Sisler	125.00	62.00	37.00
(19)	John McGraw	125.00	62.00	37.00
(20)	Mickey Cochrane	125.00	62.00	37.00

1954 Sports Illustrated Topps Foldouts

To illustrate a feature about baseball card collecting in its very first issue, Sports Illustrated included a three-page foldout featuring 27 contemporary Topps cards. Printed on glossy paper stock in full color, the paper cards are exact front and back reproductions of the real thing. The foldout panel is found in the Aug. 16, 1954, issue of SI which features on its cover a photo of Eddie Mathews at bat during a night game. The magazine's second issue also contains a 27-card foldout of New York Yankees. The insert reproduces all of Topps' 1954 Yankees cards in full color, and supplements them with black-and-white "cards" in the general style of '54 Topps for those Yankees who appeared only on Bowman cards or on no cards in 1954. The Aug. 23 issue of SI features a stand of golf clubs on its cover. Survivng examples of SI issue #2 are actually scarcer than the debut issue. Singles of the paper cards are rarely encountered.

		NM	EX	VG
	Aug. 16, 1954 issue	350.00	175.00	105.00
1	Ted Williams	100.00	50.00	30.00
2	Gus Zernial	12.00	6.00	3.50
4	Hank Sauer	12.00	6.00	3.50
6	Pete Runnels	12.00	6.00	3.50
7	Ted Kluszewski	15.00	7.50	4.50
9	Harvey Haddix	12.00	6.00	3.50
10	Jackie Robinson	75.00	37.00	22.00
15	Al Rosen	12.00	6.00	3.50
24	Granny Hamner	12.00	6.00	3.50
25	Harvey Kuenn	15.00	7.50	4.50
26	Ray Jablonski	12.00	6.00	3.50
27	Ferris Fain	12.00	6.00	3.50
29	Jim Hegan	12.00	6.00	3.50
30	Ed Mathews	30.00	15.00	9.00
32	Duke Snider	35.00	17.50	10.50
34	Jim Rivera	12.00	6.00	3.50
40	Mel Parnell	12.00	6.00	3.50
45	Richie Ashburn	30.00	15.00	9.00
70	Larry Doby	21.00	10.50	6.25
77	Ray Boone	12.00	6.00	3.50
85	Bob Turley	15.00	7.50	4.50
90	Willie Mays	75.00	37.00	22.00
100	Bob Keegan	12.00	6.00	3.50
102	Gil Hodges	30.00	15.00	9.00
119	Johnny Antonelli	12.00	6.00	3.50
137	Wally Moon	15.00	7.50	4.50
235	Vern Law	12.00	6.00	3.50
	Aug. 23, 1954 issue	200.00	100.00	60.00
5	Ed Lopat	10.00	5.00	3.00
17	Phil Rizzuto	30.00	15.00	9.00
37	Whitey Ford	30.00	15.00	9.00
50	Yogi Berra	35.00	17.50	10.50
56	Willie Miranda	10.00	5.00	3.00
62	Eddie Robinson	10.00	5.00	3.00
83	Joe Collins	10.00	5.00	3.00
96	Charlie Silvera	10.00	5.00	3.00
101	Gene Woodling	10.00	5.00	3.00
105	Andy Carey	10.00	5.00	3.00
130	Hank Bauer	10.00	5.00	3.00
175	Frank Leja	10.00	5.00	3.00
205	Johnny Sain	12.00	6.00	3.50
230	Bob Kuzava	10.00	5.00	3.00
239	Bill Skowron	15.00	7.50	4.50
----	Harry Byrd	6.00	3.00	1.75
----	Bob Cerv	6.00	3.00	1.75
----	Jerry Coleman	6.00	3.00	1.75
----	Tom Gorman	6.00	3.00	1.75
----	Bob Grim	6.00	3.00	1.75
----	Mickey Mantle	125.00	62.00	37.00
----	Jim McDonald	6.00	3.00	1.75
----	Gil McDougald	7.50	3.75	2.25
----	Tom Morgan	6.00	3.00	1.75
----	Irv Noren	6.00	3.00	1.75
----	Allie Reynolds	7.50	3.75	2.25
----	Enos Slaughter	9.00	4.50	2.75

1955 Sports Illustrated Topps Foldouts

SI kicked off the 1955 baseball season by including a page of 1955 Topps card reproductions in its April 11 and April 18 issues. Unlike the tri-fold panels of 1954, the 1955 issues contain only eight reproductions per magazine. Printed in full size in full color on glossy magazine paper, the pages are exact front and back replicas of regular-issue 1955 Topps cards. The April 11 issue features on its cover Willie Mays, Leo Durocher and Lorraine Day (Mrs. D.); the April 18 issue has Al Rosen at bat. Survivng examples of these 1955 SI issues are scarce and the paper cards are seldom seen as singles.

		NM	EX	VG
	April 11, 1955 issue	75.00	37.00	22.00
1	Dusty Rhodes	12.00	6.00	3.50
26	Dick Groat	12.00	6.00	3.50
28	Ernie Banks	25.00	12.50	7.50
31	Warren Spahn	20.00	10.00	6.00
56	Ray Jablonski	8.00	4.00	2.50
67	Wally Moon	10.00	5.00	3.00
79	Danny Schell	8.00	4.00	2.50
90	Karl Spooner	10.00	5.00	3.00
	April 18, 1955 issue	60.00	30.00	18.00
8	Hal Smith	8.00	4.00	2.50
10	Bob Keegan	8.00	4.00	2.50
11	Ferris Fain	8.00	4.00	2.50
16	Roy Sievers	8.00	4.00	2.50
38	Bob Turley	10.00	5.00	3.00
70	Al Rosen	12.00	6.00	3.50
77	Arnie Portocarrero	8.00	4.00	2.50
106	Frank Sullivan	8.00	4.00	2.50

1968-70 Sports Illustrated Major League Posters

Between 1968-70, Sports Illustrated issued a series of baseball player posters. The 2' x 3' blank-back posters have borderless color action or posed photos. In the upper corners are the player identification, copyright, poster number, etc., in small type. Values for the posters issued in 1969 and 1970 are higher than those produced in 1968. Current market values reflect the fact that many superstars' posters were sold in larger quantities than those of journeyman players and survive in greater numbers. The posters are listed here alphabetically within year of issue. Original selling price of the posters was $1.50 each, plus postage.

		NM	EX	VG
Complete Set (86):		2200.	1100.	700.00
Common Player:		15.00	7.50	4.50
	1968			
(1)	Hank Aaron	75.00	37.00	22.00
(2)	Rich Allen	40.00	20.00	12.00
(3)	Gene Alley	15.00	7.50	4.50
(4)	Felipe Alou	25.00	12.50	7.50
(5)	Max Alvis	15.00	7.50	4.50
(6)	Bob Aspromonte	15.00	7.50	4.50
(7)	Ernie Banks (photo actually Billy Williams)	50.00	25.00	15.00
(8)	Clete Boyer	15.00	7.50	4.50
(9)	Lou Brock	30.00	15.00	9.00
(10)	John Callison	20.00	10.00	6.00
(11)	Campy Campaneris	20.00	10.00	6.00
(12)	Leo Cardenas	15.00	7.50	4.50
(13)	Paul Casanova	25.00	12.50	7.50
(14)	Orlando Cepeda	25.00	12.50	7.50
(15)	Roberto Clemente	250.00	125.00	75.00
(16)	Tony Conigliaro	30.00	15.00	9.00
(17)	Willie Davis	20.00	10.00	6.00
(18)	Don Drysdale	40.00	20.00	12.00
(19)	Al Ferrara	15.00	7.50	4.50
(20)	Curt Flood	20.00	10.00	6.00
(21)	Bill Freehan	40.00	20.00	12.00
(22)	Jim Fregosi	16.00	8.00	4.75
(23)	Bob Gibson	27.50	13.50	8.25
(24)	Bud Harrelson (photo actually Ken Harrelson)	18.00	9.00	5.50
(25)	Joe Horlen	15.00	7.50	4.50
(26)	Tony Horton	15.00	7.50	4.50
(27)	Tommy John	20.00	10.00	6.00
(28)	Al Kaline	60.00	30.00	18.00
(29)	Harmon Killebrew	35.00	17.50	10.50
(30)	Jim Lonborg	25.00	12.50	7.50
(31)	Jim Maloney	15.00	7.50	4.50
(32)	Mickey Mantle	250.00	125.00	75.00
(33)	Juan Marichal	45.00	22.00	13.50
(34)	Willie Mays	150.00	75.00	45.00
(35)	Bill Mazeroski	30.00	15.00	9.00
(36)	Tim McCarver	20.00	10.00	6.00
(37)	Mike McCormack	20.00	10.00	6.00
(38)	Willie McCovey	60.00	30.00	18.00
(39a)	Don Mincher (Angels)	15.00	7.50	4.50
(39b)	Don Mincher (Pilots)	30.00	15.00	9.00
(40)	Rick Monday	20.00	10.00	6.00
(41)	Tony Oliva	22.00	11.00	6.50
(42)	Rick Reichardt	15.00	7.50	4.50
(43)	Brooks Robinson	175.00	87.00	52.00
(44)	Frank Robinson	75.00	37.00	22.00
(45)	Pete Rose	150.00	75.00	45.00
(46)	Ron Santo	25.00	12.50	7.50
(47)	Tom Seaver	200.00	100.00	60.00
(48)	Chris Short	15.00	7.50	4.50
(49)	Reggie Smith	20.00	10.00	6.00
(50)	Rusty Staub	24.00	12.00	7.25
(51)	Mel Stottlemyre	30.00	15.00	9.00
(52)	Ron Swoboda	30.00	15.00	9.00
(53)	Cesar Tovar	20.00	10.00	6.00
(54)	Earl Wilson	20.00	10.00	6.00
(55)	Jim Wynn	16.00	8.00	4.75
(56)	Carl Yastrzemski	45.00	22.00	13.50
	1969			
(1)	Tommie Agee	25.00	12.50	7.50
(2)	Mike Andrews	15.00	7.50	4.50
(3)	Ernie Banks (batting)	27.50	13.50	8.25
(4a)	Gary Bell (Indians)	30.00	15.00	9.00
(4b)	Gary Bell (Pilots)	30.00	15.00	9.00
(5a)	Tommy Davis (White Sox)	25.00	12.50	7.50
(5b)	Tommy Davis (Pilots)	35.00	17.50	10.50
(6)	Frank Howard	25.00	12.50	7.50
(7)	Reggie Jackson	125.00	62.00	37.00
(8)	Fergie Jenkins	60.00	30.00	18.00
(9)	Let's Go Mets (Tommie Agee, Jerry Grote, Cleon Jones, Jerry Koosman, Ed Kranepool, Tom Seaver, Ron	35.00	17.50	10.50
(10)	Denny McLain	30.00	15.00	9.00
(11)	Bobby Murcer	60.00	30.00	18.00
(12)	John Odom	25.00	12.50	7.50
(13)	Rico Petrocelli	30.00	15.00	9.00
(14)	Boog Powell	30.00	15.00	9.00
(15)	Roy White	25.00	12.50	7.50
	1970			
(1)	Glenn Beckert	25.00	12.50	7.50
(2)	Bobby Bonds	30.00	15.00	9.00
(3)	Rod Carew	60.00	30.00	18.00
(4)	Mike Cuellar	25.00	12.50	7.50
(5)	Mike Epstein	20.00	10.00	6.00
(6)	Ken Holtzman	15.00	7.50	4.50

(7)	Cleon Jones	20.00	10.00	6.00
(8)	Mickey Lolich	20.00	10.00	6.00
(9)	Sam McDowell	20.00	10.00	6.00
(10)	Phil Niekro	50.00	25.00	15.00
(11)	Wes Parker	25.00	12.50	7.50
(12)	Tony Perez	35.00	17.50	10.50
(13)	Bill Singer	15.00	7.50	4.50
(14)	Walt Williams	15.00	7.50	4.50

1968 Sports Memorabilia All Time Baseball Team

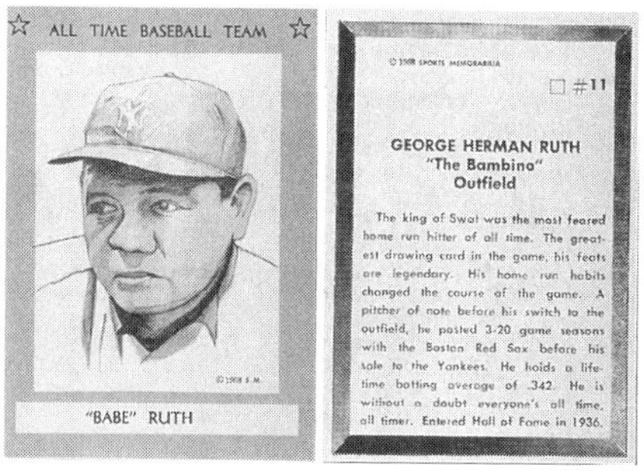

This is one of the earliest collectors' issue baseball card sets created for distribution solely within the hobby. The 2-1/2" x 3-1/2" cards feature the artwork of Art Oulette done in sepia tones on a white background and surrounded by a yellow border. Backs have career information, copyright and player identification. Issue price was $2.50.

		NM	EX	VG
Complete Set (15):		80.00	40.00	24.00
Common Player:		3.00	1.50	.90
1	Checklist	1.50	.70	.45
2	Connie Mack	3.00	1.50	.90
3	Walter Johnson	6.00	3.00	1.75
4	Warren Spahn	3.00	1.50	.90
5	Christy Mathewson	6.00	3.00	1.75
6	Lefty Grove	3.00	1.50	.90
7	Mickey Cochrane	3.00	1.50	.90
8	Bill Dickey	3.00	1.50	.90
9	Tris Speaker	5.00	2.50	1.50
10	Ty Cobb	9.00	4.50	2.75
11	Babe Ruth	15.00	7.50	4.50
12	Lou Gehrig	10.00	5.00	3.00
13	Rogers Hornsby	4.00	2.00	1.25
14	Honus Wagner	7.50	3.75	2.25
15	Pie Traynor	3.00	1.50	.90

1960 Sports Novelties Inc. Genuine Baseball Photos

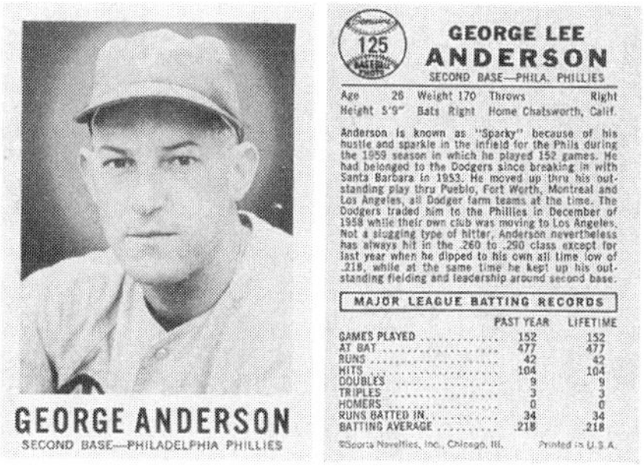

(See 1960 Leaf for checklist and price guide.)

1976 Sportstix

These peel-off player stickers were sold in five-piece plastic packs, with specific contents noted on the header. Stickers are found in three formats: 3-1/2" square, 3-1/2" square with clipped corners and 3" diameter round. The set includes 10 numbered current players and three retired baseball superstars identified as A, B and D. Stickers have full-color player pictures on front with no border. The player's name and sticker number are printed in black. Backs are blank. Besides the baseball players, there were stickers for football and basketball players, in a total issue of 30.

		NM	EX	VG
Complete Set (13):		160.00	80.00	47.50
Common Player:		6.00	3.00	1.75
A	Willie Mays	35.00	17.50	10.50
C	Roberto Clemente	45.00	22.00	13.50
D	Mickey Mantle	60.00	30.00	18.00
1	Dave Kingman	9.00	4.50	2.75
2	Steve Busby	6.00	3.00	1.75
3	Bill Madlock	6.00	3.00	1.75
4	Jeff Burroughs	6.00	3.00	1.75
5	Ted Simmons	6.00	3.00	1.75
6	Randy Jones	6.00	3.00	1.75
7	Buddy Bell	6.00	3.00	1.75
8	Dave Cash	6.00	3.00	1.75
9	Jerry Grote	6.00	3.00	1.75
10	Davey Lopes	6.00	3.00	1.75

1980 Squirt Cello Pack Header

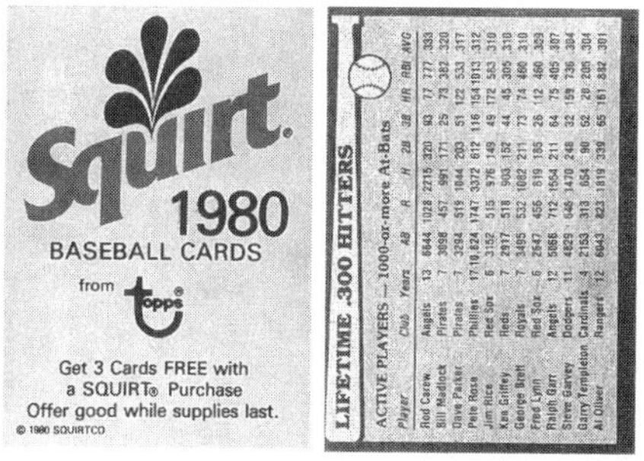

Kmart was one of several businesses in 1980 which used four-card cello packs of Topps (or, in Canada, O-Pee-Chee) baseball cards as a promotional premium. Besides the three regular-issue 1980 cards in each pack, there was a header card with the sponsor's advertising in full color on front. On back of the header card is a chart of some major league records list. This card has on back a list of players with 3,000 or more hits.

	NM	EX	VG
Squirt/.300 hitters	2.00	1.00	.60

1975 SSPC Promo Cards

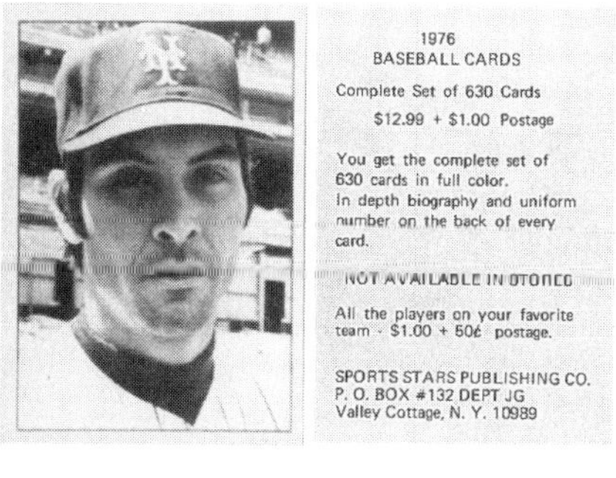

The six players in this sample set can each be found with three different backs. Some backs are similar to the cards issued in 1976, with player data and career summary. Some cards will have an ad message on back offering the complete 1976 SSPC set and team sets. Still others have blank backs. All cards are in 2-1/2" x 3-1/2" format with color photos on front surrounded by a white border and no extraneous graphics. Blank-back versions are worth 2-4X the values quoted here.

		NM	EX	VG
Complete Set (6):		10.00	5.00	3.00
Common Player:		1.00	.50	.30
(1)	Hank Aaron	2.50	1.25	.70
(2)	Catfish Hunter	1.25	.60	.40
(3)	Dave Kingman	1.00	.50	.30
(4)	Mickey Mantle	5.00	2.50	1.50
(5)	Willie Mays	2.50	1.25	.70
(6)	Tom Seaver	2.00	1.00	.60

1975 SSPC

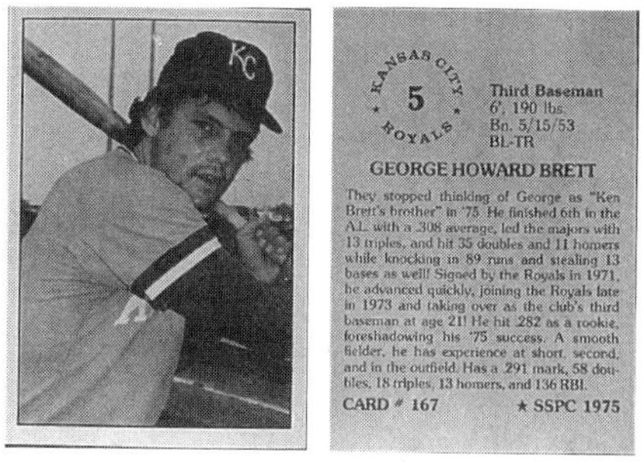

This set, produced by the Sport Star Publishing Company in 1975 as a collectors' issue (though not actually issued until 1976), was withdrawn from the market because of legal entanglements. Because SSPC agreed never to reprint the issue, some collectors feel it has an air of legitimacy. The complete set contains 630 full-color cards, each 2-1/2" x 3-1/2" in size. The cards look similar to 1953 Bowmans, with only the player picture (no identification) on the fronts. Card backs are in a vertical format, with personal stats, brief biographies, uniform and card numbers printed in a variety of colors.

		NM	EX	VG
Complete Set (630):		125.00	65.00	45.00
Common Player:		.15	.08	.05
1	Lee William (Buzz) Capra	.15	.08	.05
2	Thomas Ross House	.15	.08	.05
3	Maximino Leon	.15	.08	.05
4	Carl Wendle Morton	.15	.08	.05
5	Philip Henry Niekro	3.00	1.50	.90
6	Michael Wayne Thompson	.15	.08	.05
7	Elias Sosa (Martinez)	.15	.08	.05
8	Larvell Blanks	.15	.08	.05
9	Darrell Wayne Evans	.15	.08	.05
10	Rodney Joe Gilbreath	.15	.08	.05
11	Michael Ken-Wai Lum	.15	.08	.05
12	Craig George Robinson	.15	.08	.05
13	Earl Craig Williams, Jr.	.15	.08	.05
14	Victor Crosby Correll	.15	.08	.05
15	Biff Pocoroba	.15	.08	.05
16	Johnny B. (Dusty) Baker, Jr.	.20	.10	.06
17	Ralph Allen Garr	.15	.08	.05
18	Clarence Edward (Cito) Gaston	.25	.13	.08
19	David LaFrance May	.15	.08	.05
20	Rowland Johnnie Office	.15	.08	.05
21	Robert Brooks Beall	.15	.08	.05
22	George Lee (Sparky) Anderson	.75	.40	.25
23	John Eugene Billingham	.15	.08	.05
24	Pedro Rodriguez Borbon	.15	.08	.05
25	Clay Palmer Carroll	.15	.08	.05
26	Patrick Leonard Darcy	.15	.08	.05
27	Donald Edward Gullett	.15	.08	.05
28	Clayton Laws Kirby	.15	.08	.05
29	Gary Lynn Nolan	.15	.08	.05
30	Fredie Hubert Norman	.15	.08	.05
31	Johnny Lee Bench	7.50	3.75	2.25
32	William Francis Plummer	.15	.08	.05
33	Darrel Lee Chaney	.15	.08	.05
34	David Ismael Concepcion	.15	.08	.05
35	Terrence Michael Crowley	.15	.08	.05
36	Daniel Driessen	.15	.08	.05
37	Robert Douglas Flynn, Jr.	.15	.08	.05
38	Joe Leonard Morgan	3.00	1.50	.90
39	Atanasio Rigal (Tony) Perez	.80	.40	.25
40	George Kenneth (Ken) Griffey	.30	.15	.09
41	Peter Edward Rose	12.00	6.00	3.50
42	Edison Rosanda Armbrister	.15	.08	.05
43	John Christopher Vukovich	.15	.08	.05
44	George Arthur Foster	.15	.08	.05
45	Cesar Francisco Geronimo	.15	.08	.05
46	Mervin Weldon Rettenmund	.15	.08	.05
47	James Frederick Crawford	.15	.08	.05
48	Kenneth Roth Forsch	.15	.08	.05
49	Douglas James Konieczny	.15	.08	.05
50	Joseph Franklin Niekro	.25	.13	.08
51	Clifford Johnson	.15	.08	.05
52	Alfred Henry (Skip) Jutze	.15	.08	.05
53	Milton Scott May	.15	.08	.05
54	Robert Patrick Andrews	.15	.08	.05
55	Kenneth George Boswell	.15	.08	.05

56	Tommy Vann Helms	.15	.08	.05
57	Roger Henry Metzger	.15	.08	.05
58	Lawrence William Milbourne	.15	.08	.05
59	Douglas Lee Rader	.15	.08	.05
60	Robert Jose Watson	.15	.08	.05
61	Enos Milton Cabell, Jr.	.15	.08	.05
62	Jose Delan Cruz	.25	.13	.08
63	Cesar Cedeno	.20	.10	.06
64	Gregory Eugene Gross	.15	.08	.05
65	Wilbur Leon Howard	.15	.08	.05
66	Alphonso Erwin Downing	.15	.08	.05
67	Burt Carlton Hooton	.15	.08	.05
68	Charles Oliver Hough	.15	.08	.05
69	Thomas Edward John	.50	.25	.15
70	John Alexander Messersmith	.15	.08	.05
71	Douglas James Rau	.15	.08	.05
72	Richard Alan Rhoden	.15	.08	.05
73	Donald Howard Sutton	2.50	1.25	.70
74	Frederick Steven Auerbach	.15	.08	.05
75	Ronald Charles Cey	.25	.13	.08
76	Ivan De Jesus	.15	.08	.05
77	Steven Patrick Garvey	3.00	1.50	.90
78	Leonadus Lacy	.15	.08	.05
79	David Earl Lopes	.15	.08	.05
80	Kenneth Lee McMullen	.15	.08	.05
81	Joseph Vance Ferguson	.15	.08	.05
82	Paul Ray Powell	.15	.08	.05
83	Stephen Wayne Yeager	.15	.08	.05
84	Willie Murphy Crawford	.15	.08	.05
85	Henry Cruz	.15	.08	.05
86	Charles Fuqua Manuel	.15	.08	.05
87	Manuel Mota	.15	.08	.05
88	Thomas Marian Paciorek	.15	.08	.05
89	James Sherman Wynn	.15	.08	.05
90	Walter Emmons Alston	.45	.25	.14
91	William Joseph Buckner	.20	.10	.06
92	James Leland Barr	.15	.08	.05
93	Ralph Michael (Mike) Caldwell	.15	.08	.05
94	John Francis D'Acquisto	.15	.08	.05
95	David Wallace Heaverlo	.15	.08	.05
96	Gary Robert Lavelle	.15	.08	.05
97	John Joseph Montefusco, Jr.	.15	.08	.05
98	Charles Prosek Williams	.15	.08	.05
99	Christopher Paul Arnold	.15	.08	.05
100	Mark Kevin Hill (Marc)	.15	.08	.05
101	David Martin Rader	.15	.08	.05
102	Charles Bruce Miller	.15	.08	.05
103	Guillermo Naranjo (Willie) Montanez	.15	.08	.05
104	Steven Robert Ontiveros	.15	.08	.05
105	Chris Edward Speier	.15	.08	.05
106	Derrel Osbon Thomas	.15	.08	.05
107	Gary Leah Thomasson	.15	.08	.05
108	Glenn Charles Adams	.15	.08	.05
109	Von Everett Joshua	.15	.08	.05
110	Gary Nathaniel Matthews	.15	.10	.06
111	Bobby Ray Murcer	.15	.13	.08
112	Horace Arthur Speed III	.15	.08	.05
113	Wesley Noreen Westrum	.15	.08	.05
114	Richard Nevin Folkers	.15	.08	.05
115	Alan Benton Foster	.15	.08	.05
116	David James Freisleben	.15	.08	.05
117	Daniel Vincent Frisella	.15	.08	.05
118	Randall Leo Jones	.15	.08	.05
119	Daniel Ray Spillner	.15	.08	.05
120	Howard Lawrence (Larry) Hardy	.15	.08	.05
121	Cecil Randolph (Randy) Hundley	.15	.08	.05
122	Fred Lyn Kendall	.15	.08	.05
123	John Francis McNamara	.15	.08	.05
124	Rigoberto (Tito) Fuentes	.15	.08	.05
125	Enzo Octavio Hernandez	.15	.08	.05
126	Stephen Michael Huntz	.15	.08	.05
127	Michael Wilson Ivie	.15	.08	.05
128	Hector Epitacio Torres	.15	.08	.05
129	Theodore Rodger Kubiak	.15	.08	.05
130	John Maywood Grubb, Jr.	.15	.08	.05
131	John Henry Scott	.15	.08	.05
132	Robert Tolan	.15	.08	.05
133	David Mark Winfield	9.00	4.50	2.75
134	William Joseph Gogolewski	.15	.08	.05
135	Danny L. Osborn	.15	.08	.05
136	James Lee Kaat	.25	.13	.08
137	Claude Wilson Osteen	.15	.08	.05
138	Cecil Lee Upshaw, Jr.	.15	.08	.05
139	Wilbur Forrester Wood, Jr.	.15	.08	.05
140	Lloyd Cecil Allen	.15	.08	.05
141	Brian Jay Downing	.15	.08	.05
142	James Sarkis Essian, Jr.	.15	.08	.05
143	Russell Earl (Bucky) Dent	.20	.10	.06
144	Jorge Orta	.15	.08	.05
145	Lee Edward Richard	.15	.08	.05
146	William Allen Stein	.15	.08	.05
147	Kenneth Joseph Henderson	.15	.08	.05
148	Carlos May	.15	.08	.05
149	Nyls Wallace Rex Nyman	.15	.08	.05
150	Robert Pasquali Coluccio, Jr.	.15	.08	.05
151	Charles William Tanner, Jr.	.15	.08	.05
152	Harold Patrick (Pat) Kelly	.15	.08	.05
153	Jerry Wayne Hairston	.15	.08	.05
154	Richard Fred (Pete) Varney, Jr.	.15	.08	.05
155	William Edwin Melton	.15	.08	.05
156	Richard Michael Gossage	.30	.15	.09
157	Terry Jay Forster	.15	.08	.05
158	Richard Michael Hinton	.15	.08	.05
159	Nelson Kelley Briles	.15	.08	.05
160	Alan James Fitzmorris	.15	.08	.05
161	Stephen Bernard Mingori	.15	.08	.05
162	Martin William Pattin	.15	.08	.05
163	Paul William Splittorff, Jr.	.15	.08	.05
164	Dennis Patrick Leonard	.15	.08	.05
165	John Albert (Buck) Martinez	.15	.08	.05
166	Gorrell Robert (Bob) Stinson III	.15	.08	.05
167	George Howard Brett	12.00	6.00	3.50
168	Harmon Clayton Killebrew, Jr.	6.00	3.00	1.75
169	John Claiborn Mayberry	.15	.08	.05
170	Freddie Joe Patek	.15	.08	.05
171	Octavio (Cookie) Rojas	.15	.08	.05
172	Rodney Darrell Scott	.15	.08	.05
173	Tolia (Tony) Solaita	.15	.08	.05
174	Frank White, Jr.	.15	.08	.05
175	Alfred Edward Cowens, Jr.	.15	.08	.05
176	Harold Abraham McRae	.15	.08	.05
177	Amos Joseph Otis	.15	.08	.05
178	Vada Edward Pinson, Jr.	.25	.13	.08
179	James Eugene Wohlford	.15	.08	.05
180	James Douglas Bird	.15	.08	.05
181	Mark Alan Littell	.15	.08	.05
182	Robert McClure	.15	.08	.05
183	Steven Lee Busby	.15	.08	.05
184	Francis Xavier Healy	.15	.08	.05
185	Dorrel Norman Elvert (Whitey) Herzog	.15	.08	.05
186	Andrew Earl Hassler	.15	.08	.05
187	Lynn Nolan Ryan, Jr.	20.00	10.00	6.00
188	William Robert Singer	.15	.08	.05
189	Frank Daryl Tanana	.15	.08	.05
190	Eduardo Figueroa	.15	.08	.05
191	David S. Collins	.15	.08	.05
192	Richard Hirshfeld Williams	.15	.08	.05
193	Eliseo Rodriguez	.15	.08	.05
194	David Lee Chalk	.15	.08	.05
195	Winston Enriquillo Llenas	.15	.08	.05
196	Rudolph Bart Meoli	.15	.08	.05
197	Orlando Ramirez	.15	.08	.05
198	Gerald Peter Remy	.15	.08	.05
199	Billy Edward Smith	.15	.08	.05
200	Bruce Anton Bochte	.15	.08	.05
201	Joseph Michael Lahoud, Jr.	.15	.08	.05
202	Morris Nettles, Jr.	.15	.08	.05
203	John Milton (Mickey) Rivers	.15	.08	.05
204	Leroy Bobby Stanton	.15	.08	.05
205	Victor Albury	.15	.08	.05
206	Thomas Henry Burgmeier	.15	.08	.05
207	William Franklin Butler	.15	.08	.05
208	William Richard Campbell	.15	.08	.05
209	Alton Ray Corbin	.15	.08	.05
210	George Henry (Joe) Decker, Jr.	.15	.08	.05
211	James Michael Hughes	.15	.08	.05
212	Edward Norman Bane (photo actually Mike Pazik)	.15	.08	.05
213	Glenn Dennis Borgmann	.15	.08	.05
214	Rodney Cline Carew	6.00	3.00	1.75
215	Stephen Robert Brye	.15	.08	.05
216	Darnell Glenn (Dan) Ford	.15	.08	.05
217	Antonio Oliva	.25	.13	.08
218	David Allan Goltz	.15	.08	.05
219	Rikalbert Blyleven	.25	.13	.08
220	Larry Eugene Hisle	.15	.08	.05
221	Stephen Russell Braun, III	.15	.08	.05
222	Jerry Wayne Terrell	.15	.08	.05
223	Eric Thane Soderholm	.15	.08	.05
224	Philip Anthony Roof	.15	.08	.05
225	Danny Leon Thompson	.15	.08	.05
226	James William Colborn	.15	.08	.05
227	Thomas Andrew Murphy	.15	.08	.05
228	Eduardo Rodriguez	.15	.08	.05
229	James Michael Slaton	.15	.08	.05
230	Edward Nelson Sprague	.15	.08	.05
231	Charles William Moore, Jr.	.15	.08	.05
232	Darrell Ray Porter	.15	.08	.05
233	Kurt Anthony Bevacqua	.15	.08	.05
234	Pedro Garcia	.15	.08	.05
235	James Michael (Mike) Hegan	.15	.08	.05
236	Donald Wayne Money	.15	.08	.05
237	George C. Scott, Jr.	.15	.08	.05
238	Robin R. Yount	9.00	4.50	2.75
239	Henry Louis Aaron	12.00	6.00	3.50
240	Robert Walker Ellis	.15	.08	.05
241	Sixto Lezcano	.15	.08	.05
242	Robert Vance Mitchell	.15	.08	.05
243	James Gorman Thomas, III	.15	.08	.05
244	William Edward Travers	.15	.08	.05
245	Peter Sven Broberg	.15	.08	.05
246	William Howard Sharp	.15	.08	.05
247	Arthur Bobby Lee Darwin	.15	.08	.05
248	Rick Gerald Austin (photo actually Larry Anderson)	.15	.08	.05
249	Lawrence Dennis Anderson (photo actually Rick Austin)	.15	.08	.05
250	Thomas Antony Bianco	.15	.08	.05
251	DeLancy LaFayette Currence	.15	.08	.05
252	Steven Raymond Foucault	.15	.08	.05
253	William Alfred Hands, Jr.	.15	.08	.05
254	Steven Lowell Hargan	.15	.08	.05
255	Ferguson Arthur Jenkins	3.00	1.50	.90
256	Bob Mitchell Sheldon	.15	.08	.05
257	James Umbarger	.15	.08	.05
258	Clyde Wright	.15	.08	.05
259	William Roger Fahey	.15	.08	.05
260	James Howard Sundberg	.15	.08	.05
261	Leonardo Alfonso Cardenas	.15	.08	.05
262	James Louis Fregosi	.15	.08	.05
263	Dudley Michael (Mike) Hargrove	.15	.08	.05
264	Colbert Dale (Toby) Harrah	.15	.08	.05
265	Roy Lee Howell	.15	.08	.05
266	Leonard Shenoff Randle	.15	.08	.05
267	Roy Frederick Smalley III	.15	.08	.05
268	James Lloyd Spencer	.15	.08	.05
269	Jeffrey Alan Burroughs	.15	.08	.05
270	Thomas Alan Grieve	.15	.08	.05
271	Joseph Lovitto, Jr.	.15	.08	.05
272	Frank Joseph Lucchesi	.15	.08	.05
273	David Earl Nelson	.15	.08	.05
274	Ted Lyle Simmons	.15	.08	.05
275	Louis Clark Brock	4.00	2.00	1.25
276	Ronald Ray Fairly	.15	.08	.05
277	Arnold Ray (Bake) McBride	.15	.08	.05
278	Carl Reginald (Reggie) Smith	.25	.13	.08
279	William Henry Davis	.15	.08	.05
280	Kenneth John Reitz	.15	.08	.05
281	Charles William (Buddy) Bradford	.15	.08	.05
282	Luis Antonio Melendez	.15	.08	.05
283	Michael Ray Tyson	.15	.08	.05
284	Ted Crawford Sizemore	.15	.08	.05
285	Mario Miguel Guerrero	.15	.08	.05
286	Larry Lintz	.15	.08	.05
287	Kenneth Victor Rudolph	.15	.08	.05
288	Richard Arlin Billings	.15	.08	.05
289	Jerry Wayne Mumphrey	.15	.08	.05
290	Michael Sherman Wallace	.15	.08	.05
291	Alan Thomas Hrabosky	.15	.08	.05
292	Kenneth Lee Reynolds	.15	.08	.05
293	Michael Douglas Garman	.15	.08	.05
294	Robert Herbert Forsch	.15	.08	.05
295	John Allen Denny	.15	.08	.05
296	Harold R. Rasmussen	.15	.08	.05
297	Lynn Everratt McGlothen (Everett)	.15	.08	.05
298	Michael Roswell Barlow	.15	.08	.05
299	Gregory John Terlecky	.15	.08	.05
300	Albert Fred (Red) Schoendienst	.50	.25	.15
301	Ricky Eugene Reuschel	.15	.13	.08
302	Steven Michael Stone	.15	.08	.05
303	William Gordon Bonham	.15	.08	.05
304	Oscar Joseph Zamora	.15	.08	.05
305	Kenneth Douglas Frailing	.15	.08	.05
306	Milton Edward Wilcox	.15	.08	.05
307	Darold Duane Knowles	.15	.08	.05
308	Rufus James (Jim) Marshall	.15	.08	.05
309	Bill Madlock, Jr.	.15	.08	.05
310	Jose Domec Cardenal	.15	.08	.05
311	Robert James (Rick) Monday, Jr.	.15	.08	.05
312	Julio Ruben (Jerry) Morales	.15	.08	.05
313	Timothy Kenneth Hosley	.15	.08	.05
314	Gene Taylor Hiser	.15	.08	.05
315	Donald Eulon Kessinger	.15	.08	.05
316	Jesus Manuel (Manny) Trillo	.15	.08	.05
317	Ralph Pierre (Pete) LaCock, Jr.	.15	.08	.05
318	George Eugene Mitterwald	.15	.08	.05
319	Steven Eugene Swisher	.15	.08	.05
320	Robert Walter Sperring	.15	.08	.05
321	Victor Lanier Harris	.15	.08	.05
322	Ronald Ray Dunn	.15	.08	.05
323	Jose Manuel Morales	.15	.08	.05
324	Peter MacKanin, Jr.	.15	.08	.05
325	James Charles Cox	.15	.08	.05
326	Larry Alton Parrish	.15	.08	.05
327	Michael Jorgensen	.15	.08	.05
328	Timothy John Foli	.15	.08	.05
329	Harold Noel Breeden	.15	.08	.05
330	Nathan Colbert, Jr.	.15	.08	.05
331	Jesus Maria (Pepe) Frias	.15	.08	.05
332	James Patrick (Pat) Scanlon	.15	.08	.05
333	Robert Sherwood Bailey	.15	.08	.05
334	Gary Edmund Carter	2.50	1.25	.70
335	Jose Mauel (Pepe) Mangual	.15	.08	.05
336	Lawrence David Biittner	.15	.08	.05
337	James Lawrence Lyttle, Jr.	.15	.08	.05
338	Gary Roenicke	.15	.08	.05
339	Anthony Scott	.15	.08	.05
340	Jerome Cardell White	.15	.08	.05
341	James Edward Dwyer	.15	.08	.05
342	Ellis Clarence Valentine	.15	.08	.05
343	Frederick John Scherman, Jr.	.15	.08	.05
344	Dennis Herman Blair	.15	.08	.05
345	Woodrow Thompson Fryman	.15	.08	.05
346	Charles Gilbert Taylor	.15	.08	.05
347	Daniel Dean Warthen	.15	.08	.05
348	Donald George Carrithers	.15	.08	.05
349	Stephen Douglas Rogers	.15	.08	.05
350	Dale Albert Murray	.15	.08	.05
351	Edwin Donald (Duke) Snider	8.00	4.00	2.50
352	Ralph George Houk	.15	.08	.05
353	John Frederick Hiller	.15	.08	.05
354	Michael Stephen Lolich	.25	.13	.08
355	David Lawrence Lemancyzk	.15	.08	.05
356	Lerrin Harris LaGrow	.15	.08	.05
357	Fred Arroyo	.15	.08	.05
358	Joseph Howard Coleman	.15	.08	.05
359	Benjamin A. Oglivie	.15	.08	.05
360	Willie Wattison Horton	.15	.08	.05
361	John Clinton Knox	.15	.08	.05
362	Leon Kauffman Roberts	.15	.08	.05
363	Ronald LeFlore	.15	.08	.05
364	Gary Lynn Sutherland	.15	.08	.05
365	Daniel Thomas Meyer	.15	.08	.05
366	Aurelio Rodriguez	.15	.08	.05
367	Thomas Martin Veryzer	.15	.08	.05
368	Lavern Jack Pierce	.15	.08	.05
369	Eugene Richard Michael	.15	.08	.05
370	Robert (Billy) Baldwin	.15	.08	.05
371	William James Gates Brown	.15	.08	.05
372	Mitchell Jack (Mickey) Stanley	.15	.08	.05
373	Terryal Gene Humphrey	.15	.08	.05
374	Doyle Lafayette Alexander	.15	.08	.05
375	Miguel Angel (Mike) Cuellar	.15	.08	.05
376	Marcus Wayne Garland	.15	.08	.05
377	Ross Albert Grimsley III	.15	.08	.05
378	Grant Dwight Jackson	.15	.08	.05
379	Dyar K. Miller	.15	.08	.05
380	James Alvin Palmer	5.00	2.50	1.50
381	Michael Augustine Torrez	.15	.08	.05
382	Michael Henry Willis	.15	.08	.05
383	David Edwin Duncan	.15	.08	.05
384	Elrod Jerome Hendricks	.15	.08	.05
385	James Neamon Hutto Jr.	.15	.08	.05
386	Robert Michael Bailor	.15	.08	.05
387	Douglas Vernon DeCinces	.15	.08	.05
388	Robert Anthony Grich	.15	.08	.05
389	Lee Andrew May	.15	.08	.05
390	Anthony Joseph Muser	.15	.08	.05

391	Timothy C. Nordbrook	.15	.08	.05
392	Brooks Calbert Robinson, Jr.	9.00	4.50	2.75
393	Royle Stillman	.15	.08	.05
394	Don Edward Baylor	.15	.08	.05
395	Paul L.D. Blair	.15	.08	.05
396	Alonza Benjamin Bumbry	.15	.08	.05
397	Larry Duane Harlow	.15	.08	.05
398	Herman Thomas (Tommy) Davis, Jr.	.15	.08	.05
399	James Thomas Northrup	.15	.08	.05
400	Kenneth Wayne Singleton	.15	.08	.05
401	Thomas Michael Shopay	.15	.08	.05
402	Fredrick Michael Lynn	.45	.25	.14
403	Carlton Ernest Fisk	5.00	2.50	1.50
404	Cecil Celester Cooper	.15	.08	.05
405	James Edward Rice	1.00	.50	.30
406	Juan Jose Beniquez	.15	.08	.05
407	Robert Dennis Doyle	.15	.08	.05
408	Dwight Michael Evans	.15	.08	.05
409	Carl Michael Yastrzemski	7.50	3.75	2.25
410	Richard Paul Burleson	.15	.08	.05
411	Bernardo Carbo	.15	.08	.05
412	Douglas Lee Griffin, Jr.	.15	.08	.05
413	Americo P. Petrocelli	.15	.08	.05
414	Robert Edward Montgomery	.15	.08	.05
415	Timothy P. Blackwell	.15	.08	.05
416	Richard Alan Miller	.15	.08	.05
417	Darrell Dean Johnson	.15	.08	.05
418	Jim Scott Burton	.15	.08	.05
419	James Arthur Willoughby	.15	.08	.05
420	Rogelio (Roger) Moret	.15	.08	.05
421	William Francis Lee, III	.15	.08	.05
422	Richard Anthony Drago	.15	.08	.05
423	Diego Pablo Segui	.15	.08	.05
424	Luis Clemente Tiant	.30	.15	.09
425	James Augustus (Catfish) Hunter	1.50	.70	.45
426	Richard Clyde Sawyer	.15	.08	.05
427	Rudolph May Jr.	.15	.08	.05
428	Richard William Tidrow	.15	.08	.05
429	Albert Walter (Sparky) Lyle	.15	.08	.05
430	George Francis (Doc) Medich	.15	.08	.05
431	Patrick Edward Dobson, Jr.	.15	.08	.05
432	David Percy Pagan	.15	.08	.05
433	Thurman Lee Munson	4.00	2.00	1.25
434	Carroll Christopher Chambliss	.15	.08	.05
435	Roy Hilton White	.15	.08	.05
436	Walter Allen Williams	.15	.08	.05
437	Graig Nettles	.15	.08	.05
438	John Rikard (Rick) Dempsey	.15	.08	.05
439	Bobby Lee Bonds	.25	.13	.08
440	Edward Martin Hermann (Herrmann)	.15	.08	.05
441	Santos Alomar	.15	.08	.05
442	Frederick Blair Stanley	.15	.08	.05
443	Terry Bertland Whitfield	.15	.08	.05
444	Richard Alan Bladt	.15	.08	.05
445	Louis Victor Piniella	.20	.10	.06
446	Richard Allen Coggins	.15	.08	.05
447	Edwin Albert Brinkman	.15	.08	.05
448	James Percy Mason	.15	.08	.05
449	Larry Murray	.15	.08	.05
450	Ronald Mark Blomberg	.15	.08	.05
451	Elliott Maddox	.15	.08	.05
452	Kerry Dineen	.15	.08	.05
453	Alfred Manuel (Billy) Martin	.30	.15	.09
454	Dave Bergman	.15	.08	.05
455	Otoniel Velez	.15	.08	.05
456	Joseph Walter Hoerner	.15	.08	.05
457	Frank Edwin (Tug) McGraw, Jr.	.15	.08	.05
458	Henry Eugene (Gene) Garber	.15	.08	.05
459	Steven Norman Carlton	7.00	3.50	2.00
460	Larry Richard Christenson	.15	.08	.05
461	Thomas Gerald Underwood	.15	.08	.05
462	James Reynold Lonborg	.15	.08	.05
463	John William (Jay) Johnstone, Jr.	.15	.08	.05
464	Lawrence Robert Bowa	.15	.08	.05
465	David Cash, Jr.	.15	.08	.05
466	Ollie Lee Brown	.15	.08	.05
467	Gregory Michael Luzinski	.25	.13	.08
468	Johnny Lane Oates	.15	.08	.05
469	Michael Allen Anderson	.15	.08	.05
470	Michael Jack Schmidt	9.00	4.50	2.75
471	Robert Raymond Boone	.15	.08	.05
472	Thomas George Hutton	.15	.08	.05
473	Richard Anthony Allen	.50	.25	.15
474	Antonio Taylor	.15	.08	.05
475	Jerry Lindsey Martin	.15	.08	.05
476	Daniel Leonard Ozark	.15	.08	.05
477	Richard David Ruthven	.15	.08	.05
478	James Richard Todd, Jr.	.15	.08	.05
479	Paul Aaron Lindblad	.15	.08	.05
480	Roland Glen Fingers	2.00	1.00	.60
481	Vida Blue, Jr.	.15	.08	.05
482	Kenneth Dale Holtzman	.15	.08	.05
483	Richard Allen Bosman	.15	.08	.05
484	Wilfred Charles (Sonny) Siebert	.15	.08	.05
485	William Glenn Abbott	.15	.08	.05
486	Stanley Raymond Bahnsen	.15	.08	.05
487	Michael Norris	.15	.08	.05
488	Alvin Ralph Dark	.15	.08	.05
489	Claudell Washington	.15	.08	.05
490	Joseph Oden Rudi	.15	.08	.05
491	William Alex North	.15	.08	.05
492	Dagoberto Blanco (Bert) Campaneris	.15	.08	.05
493	Fury Gene Tenace	.15	.08	.05
494	Reginald Martinez Jackson	8.00	4.00	2.50
495	Philip Mason Garner	.15	.08	.05
496	Billy Leo Williams	5.00	2.50	1.50
497	Salvatore Leonard Bando	.15	.08	.05
498	James William Holt	.15	.08	.05
499	Teodoro Noel Martinez	.15	.08	.05
500	Raymond Earl Fosse	.15	.08	.05
501	Matthew Alexander	.15	.08	.05
502	Wallace Larry Haney	.15	.08	.05
503	Angel Luis Mangual	.15	.08	.05
504	Fred Ray Beene	.15	.08	.05
505	Thomas William Buskey	.15	.08	.05
506	Dennis Lee Eckersley	4.00	2.00	1.25
507	Roric Edward Harrison	.15	.08	.05
508	Donald Harris Hood	.15	.08	.05
509	James Lester Kern	.15	.08	.05
510	David Eugene LaRoche	.15	.08	.05
511	Fred Ingels (Fritz) Peterson	.15	.08	.05
512	James Michael Strickland	.15	.08	.05
513	Michael Richard (Rick) Waits	.15	.08	.05
514	Alan Dean Ashby	.15	.08	.05
515	John Charles Ellis	.15	.08	.05
516	Rick Cerone	.15	.08	.05
517	David Gus (Buddy) Bell	.15	.08	.05
518	John Anthony Brohamer, Jr.	.15	.08	.05
519	Ricardo Adolfo Jacobo Carty	.15	.08	.05
520	Edward Carlton Crosby	.15	.08	.05
521	Frank Thomas Duffy	.15	.08	.05
522	Duane Eugene Kuiper (photo actually Rick Manning)	.15	.08	.05
523	Joseph Anthony Lis	.15	.08	.05
524	John Wesley (Boog) Powell	.50	.25	.15
525	Frank Robinson	7.00	3.50	2.00
526	Oscar Charles Gamble	.15	.08	.05
527	George Andrew Hendrick	.15	.08	.05
528	John Lee Lowenstein	.15	.08	.05
529	Richard Eugene Manning (photo actually Duane Kuiper)	.15	.08	.05
530	Tommy Alexander Smith	.15	.08	.05
531	Leslie Charles (Charlie) Spikes	.15	.08	.05
532	Steve Jack Kline	.15	.08	.05
533	Edward Emil Kranepool	.15	.08	.05
534	Michael Vail	.15	.08	.05
535	Delbert Bernard Unser	.15	.08	.05
536	Felix Bernardo Martinez Millan	.15	.08	.05
537	Daniel Joseph (Rusty) Staub	.40	.20	.12
538	Jesus Maria Rojas Alou	.15	.08	.05
539	Ronald Wayne Garrett	.15	.08	.05
540	Michael Dwaine Phillips	.15	.08	.05
541	Joseph Paul Torre	.15	.08	.05
542	David Arthur Kingman	.30	.15	.09
543	Eugene Anthony Clines	.15	.08	.05
544	Jack Seale Heidemann	.15	.08	.05
545	Derrel McKinley (Bud) Harrelson	.15	.08	.05
546	John Hardin Stearns	.15	.08	.05
547	John David Milner	.15	.08	.05
548	Robert John Apodaca	.15	.08	.05
549	Claude Edward (Skip) Lockwood Jr.	.15	.08	.05
550	Kenneth George Sanders	.15	.08	.05
551	George Thomas (Tom) Seaver	9.00	4.50	2.75
552	Ricky Alan Baldwin	.15	.08	.05
553	Jonathan Trumpbour Matlack	.15	.08	.05
554	Henry Gaylon Webb	.15	.08	.05
555	Randall Lee Tate	.15	.08	.05
556	Tom Edward Hall	.15	.08	.05
557	George Heard Stone Jr.	.15	.08	.05
558	Craig Steven Swan	.15	.08	.05
559	Gerald Allen Cram	.15	.08	.05
560	Roy J. Staiger	.15	.08	.05
561	Kenton C. Tekulve	.15	.08	.05
562	Jerry Reuss	.15	.08	.05
563	John R. Candelaria	.15	.08	.05
564	Lawrence C. Demery	.15	.08	.05
565	David John Giusti Jr.	.15	.08	.05
566	James Phillip Rooker	.15	.08	.05
567	Ramon Gonzalez Hernandez	.15	.08	.05
568	Bruce Eugene Kison	.15	.08	.05
569	Kenneth Alven Brett (Alvin)	.15	.08	.05
570	Robert Ralph Moose Jr.	.15	.08	.05
571	Manuel Jesus Sanguillen	.15	.08	.05
572	David Gene Parker	2.00	1.00	.60
573	Wilver Dornel Stargell	5.00	2.50	1.50
574	Richard Walter Zisk	.15	.08	.05
575	Renaldo Antonio Stennett	.15	.08	.05
576	Albert Oliver Jr.	.30	.15	.09
577	William Henry Robinson Jr.	.15	.08	.05
578	Robert Eugene Robertson	.15	.08	.05
579	Richard Joseph Hebner	.15	.08	.05
580	Edgar Leon Kirkpatrick	.15	.08	.05
581	Don Robert (Duffy) Dyer	.15	.08	.05
582	Craig Reynolds	.15	.08	.05
583	Franklin Fabian Taveras	.15	.08	.05
584	William Larry Randolph	.15	.08	.05
585	Arthur H. Howe	.15	.08	.05
586	Daniel Edward Murtaugh	.15	.08	.05
587	Charles Richard (Rich) McKinney	.15	.08	.05
588	James Edward Goodson	.15	.08	.05
589	George Brett, Al Cowans/Checklist	1.75	.90	.50
590	Keith Hernandez, Lou Brock/Checklist	.45	.25	.14
591	Jerry Koosman, Duke Snider/Checklist	.60	.30	.20
592	John Knox, Maury Wills/Checklist	.20	.10	.06
593a	Catfish Hunter, Noland Ryan/Checklist	15.00	7.50	4.50
593b	Catfish Hunter, Nolan Ryan/Checklist	1.00	.50	.30
594	Pee Wee Reese, Ralph Branca, Carl Erskine	.50	.25	.15
595	Willie Mays, Herb Score/Checklist	1.50	.70	.45
596	Larry Eugene Cox	.15	.08	.05
597	Eugene William Mauch	.15	.08	.05
598	William Frederick (Whitey) Wietelmann	.15	.08	.05
599	Wayne Kirby Simpson	.15	.08	.05
600	Melvin Erskine Thomason	.15	.08	.05
601	Issac Bernard (Ike) Hampton	.15	.08	.05
602	Kenneth S. Crosby	.15	.08	.05
603	Ralph Emanuel Rowe	.15	.08	.05
604	James Vernon Tyrone	.15	.08	.05
605	Michael Dennis Kelleher	.15	.08	.05
606	Mario Mendoza	.15	.08	.05
607	Michael George Rogodzinski	.15	.08	.05
608	Robert Collins Gallagher	.15	.08	.05
609	Jerry Martin Koosman	.15	.08	.05
610	Joseph Filmore Frazier	.15	.08	.05
611	Karl Kuehl	.15	.08	.05
612	Frank J. LaCorte	.15	.08	.05
613	Raymond Douglas Bare	.15	.08	.05
614	Billy Arnold Muffett	.15	.08	.05
615	William Harry Laxton	.15	.08	.05
616	Willie Howard Mays	12.00	6.00	3.50
617	Philip Joseph Cavaretta (Cavarretta)	.15	.08	.05
618	Theodore Bernard Kluszewski	.50	.25	.15
619	Elston Gene Howard	.30	.15	.09
620	Alexander Peter Grammas	.15	.08	.05
621	James Barton (Mickey) Vernon	.15	.08	.05
622	Richard Allan Sisler	.15	.08	.05
623	Harvey Haddix, Jr.	.15	.08	.05
624	Bobby Brooks Winkles	.15	.08	.05
625	John Michael Pesky	.15	.08	.05
626	James Houston Davenport	.15	.08	.05
627	David Allen Tomlin	.15	.08	.05
628	Roger Lee Craig	.15	.08	.05
629	John Joseph Amalfitano	.15	.08	.05
630	James Harrison Reese	.25	.13	.08

1975 SSPC Sample Cards

The Winter, 1975, issue of "Collector's Quarterly" magazine (an advertising vehicle for Mike Aronstein, SSPC's principal) contained a two-page cardboard insert previewing the 1976 SSPC set. The cards could be cut apart into singles and represented something of a traded set, as each player or manager changed teams between the end of the 1975 season and the start of 1976. The cards have the players pictured on front in their old uniforms, with their new teams identified on back. Backs of the 2-1/2" x 3-1/2" cards are printed in red and black with a player biography and uniform number. "SAMPLE CARD 1975" is printed around the uniform number. A card number is in the lower-left corner, with 1975 copyright at bottom-right.

		NM	EX	VG
Complete Set, Uncut Sheet:		25.00	12.50	7.50
Complete Set, Singles:		12.50	6.25	3.75
Common Card:		1.00	.50	.30
1	Harry Parker	1.00	.50	.30
2	Jim Bibby	1.00	.50	.30
3	Mike Wallace	1.00	.50	.30
4	Tony Muser	1.00	.50	.30
5	Yogi Berra	4.00	2.00	1.25
6	Preston Gomez	1.00	.50	.30
7	Jack McKeon	1.00	.50	.30
8	Sam McDowell	1.25	.60	.40
9	Gaylord Perry	2.00	1.00	.60
10	Fred Stanley	1.00	.50	.30
11	Willie Davis	1.25	.60	.40
12	Don Hopkins	1.00	.50	.30
13	Whitey Herzog	1.25	.60	.40
14	Ray Sadecki	1.00	.50	.30
15	Stan Bahnsen	1.00	.50	.30
16	Bob Oliver	1.00	.50	.30
17	Denny Doyle	1.00	.50	.30
18	Deron Johnson	1.25	.60	.40

1975 SSPC Mets/Yankees

Team sets of the New York clubs were issued by SSPC bearing a 1975 copyright date and in the same "pure card" format as most of the company's other issues. The 2-1/2" x 3-1/2" cards have a posed color photo on front with a thin white border and no extraneous graphics - not even the player's name. Backs are printed in red and blue with personal data and a career summary, along with the player's full formal name. The checklist lists the player as he is best known. Issue price was $1.25 per team set.

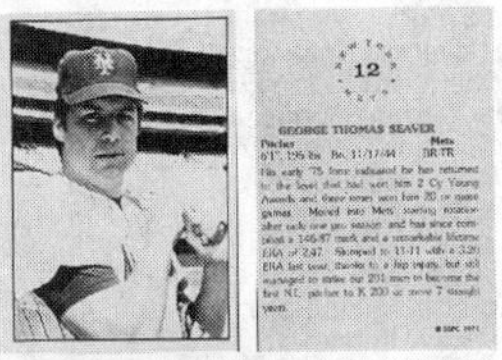

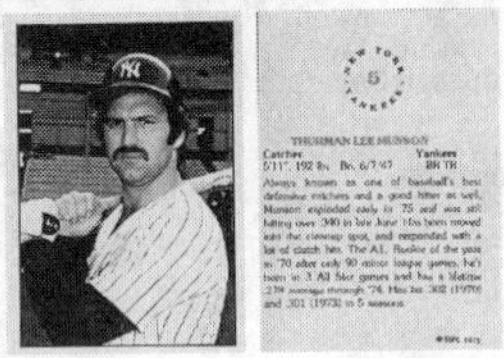

		NM	EX	VG
Complete Set (45):		60.00	30.00	18.00
Common Player:		.50	.25	.15
	New York Mets team set:	35.00	17.50	10.50
1	John Milner	.50	.25	.15
2	Henry Webb	.50	.25	.15
3	Tom Hall	.50	.25	.15
4	Del Unser	.50	.25	.15
5	Wayne Garrett	.50	.25	.15
6	Jesus Alou	.70	.35	.20
7	Rusty Staub	1.50	.70	.45
8	John Stearns	.50	.25	.15
9	Dave Kingman	3.00	1.50	.90
10	Ed Kranepool	1.50	.70	.45
11	Cleon Jones	1.50	.70	.45
12	Tom Seaver	11.00	5.50	3.25
13	George Stone	.50	.25	.15
14	Jerry Koosman	1.50	.70	.45
15	Bob Apodaca	.50	.25	.15
16	Felix Millan	.50	.25	.15
17	Gene Clines	.50	.25	.15
18	Mike Phillips	.50	.25	.15
19	Yogi Berra	8.00	4.00	2.50
20	Joe Torre	3.00	1.50	.90
21	Jon Matlack	.70	.35	.20
22	Ricky Baldwin	.50	.25	.15
	New York Yankees team set:	25.00	12.50	7.50
1	Catfish Hunter	4.00	2.00	1.25
2	Bobby Bonds	2.00	1.00	.60
3	Ed Brinkman	.70	.35	.20
4	Ron Blomberg	.70	.35	.20
5	Thurman Munson	8.00	4.00	2.50
6	Roy White	1.50	.70	.45
7	Larry Gura	.50	.25	.15
8	Ed Hermann	.50	.25	.15
9	Bill Virdon	.70	.35	.20
10	Elliott Maddox	.50	.25	.15
11	Lou Piniella	1.50	.70	.45
12	Rick Dempsey	.70	.35	.20
13	Fred Stanley	.50	.25	.15
14	Chris Chambliss	.70	.35	.20
15	Doc Medich	.70	.35	.20
16	Pat Dobson	.50	.25	.15
17	Alex Johnson	.50	.25	.15
18	Jim Mason	.50	.25	.15
19	Sandy Alomar	.70	.35	.20
20	Graig Nettles	1.50	.70	.45
21	Walt Williams	.50	.25	.15
22	Sparky Lyle	1.50	.70	.45
23	Dick Tidrow	.50	.25	.15

1975 SSPC Puzzle Backs

A large black-and-white puzzle picture of Nolan Ryan and Catfish Hunter can be assembled with the backs of these cards. Fronts of the 3-9/16" x 4-1/4" cards have a color player pose with a white border. The player's name, position and team are printed at bottom. Fronts have a glossy surface. The SSPC identification only appears around the border of the puzzle. The unnumbered cards are checklisted here alphabetically. Issue price was $2.

		NM	EX	VG
Complete Set (24):		30.00	15.00	9.00
Common Player:		.45	.25	.14
(1)	Hank Aaron	6.00	3.00	1.75
(2)	Johnny Bench	2.50	1.25	.70
(3)	Bobby Bonds	.50	.25	.15
(4)	Jeff Burroughs	.45	.25	.14
(5)	Rod Carew	2.50	1.25	.70
(6)	Dave Cash	.45	.25	.14
(7)	Cesar Cedeno	.45	.25	.14
(8)	Bucky Dent	.45	.25	.14
(9)	Rollie Fingers	2.00	1.00	.60
(10)	Steve Garvey	1.50	.70	.45
(11)	John Grubb	.45	.25	.14
(12)	Reggie Jackson	3.00	1.50	.90
(13)	Jim Kaat	.45	.25	.14
(14)	Greg Luzinski	.50	.25	.15
(15)	Fred Lynn	.75	.40	.25
(16)	Bill Madlock	.45	.25	.14
(17)	Andy Messersmith	.45	.25	.14
(18)	Thurman Munson	2.50	1.25	.70
(19)	Jim Palmer	2.00	1.00	.60
(20)	Dave Parker	.75	.40	.25
(21)	Jim Rice	.75	.40	.25
(22)	Pete Rose	6.00	3.00	1.75
(23)	Tom Seaver	2.50	1.25	.70
(24)	Chris Speier	.45	.25	.14

1975 SSPC Superstars

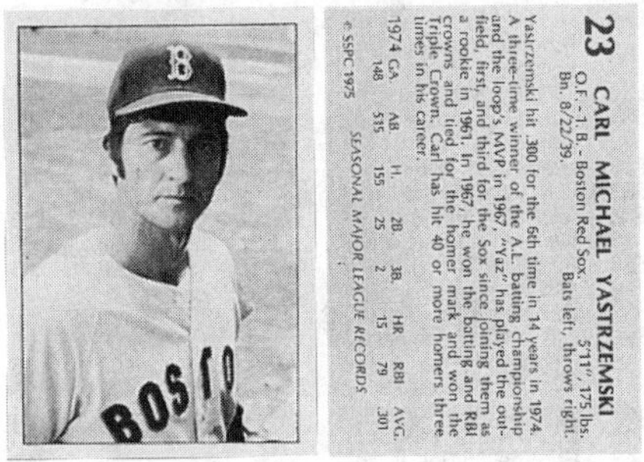

Nearly four dozen of the game's contemporary and former stars are featured in this set. Like other SSPC issues of 1975, fronts of the 2-1/2" x 3-1/2" cards have posed color photos with a white border. There are no other graphics, not even the player's name. The horizontal backs feature the player's full formal name (checklist here uses popular name) along with personal data, career summary and stats. Issue price was $4.

		NM	EX	VG
Complete Set (42):		60.00	30.00	18.00
Common Player:		.60	.30	.20
1	Wilbur Wood	.60	.30	.20
2	Johnny Sain	.60	.30	.20
3	Bill Melton	.60	.30	.20
4	Dick Allen	1.25	.60	.40
5	Jim Palmer	2.50	1.25	.70
6	Brooks Robinson	2.50	1.25	.70
7	Tommy Davis	.90	.45	.25
8	Frank Robinson	2.50	1.25	.70
9	Vada Pinson (Nolan Ryan in background of photo)	2.50	1.25	.70
10	Nolan Ryan	8.50	4.25	2.50
11	Reggie Jackson	4.50	2.25	1.25
12	Vida Blue	.60	.30	.20
13	Sal Bando	.60	.30	.20
14	Bert Campaneris	.60	.30	.20
15	Tom Seaver	5.00	2.50	1.50
16	Bud Harrelson	.90	.45	.25
17	Jerry Koosman	.90	.45	.25
18	Dave Nelson	.60	.30	.20
19	Ted Williams	6.00	3.00	1.75
20	Tony Oliva	.90	.45	.25
21	Mickey Lolich	.90	.45	.25
22	Amos Otis	.60	.30	.20
23	Carl Yastrzemski	3.50	1.75	1.00
24	Mike Cuellar	.90	.45	.25
25	Doc Medich	.60	.30	.20
26	Cesar Cedeno	.60	.30	.20
27	Jeff Burroughs	.60	.30	.20
28	Ted Williams, Sparky Lyle	1.75	.90	.50
29	Johnny Bench	5.00	2.50	1.50
30	Gaylord Perry	2.50	1.25	.70
31	John Mayberry	.60	.30	.20
32	Rod Carew	3.50	1.75	1.00
33	Whitey Ford	5.00	2.50	1.50
34	Al Kaline	5.00	2.50	1.50
35	Willie Mays	6.00	3.00	1.75
36	Warren Spahn	2.50	1.25	.70
37	Mickey Mantle	12.00	6.00	3.50
38	Norm Cash	.90	.45	.25
39	Steve Busby	.60	.30	.20
40	Yogi Berra	5.00	2.50	1.50
41	Harvey Kuenn	.90	.45	.25
42	Felipe Alou, Jesus Alou, Matty Alou	1.25	.60	.40

1976 SSPC Yankees Old Timers Day

The Spring, 1976, edition of "Collectors Quarterly" magazine contained a nine-card sheet of players who had appeared at an old timers' games in Yankee Stadium. The sheet could be cut into individual 2-1/2" x 3-1/2" cards with a color player photo and name on front. Backs form a black-and-white puzzle picture of Joe DiMaggio, Mickey Mantle, Whitey Ford and Billy Martin. Cards are checklisted here alphabetically.

		NM	EX	VG
Complete Set, Uncut Sheet:		35.00	17.50	10.50
Complete Set, Singles:		25.00	12.50	7.50
Common Player:		.50	.25	.15
(1)	Earl Averill	.50	.25	.15
(2)	Joe DiMaggio	8.00	4.00	2.50
(3)	Tommy Henrich	.50	.25	.15
(4)	Billy Herman	.50	.25	.15
(5)	Monte Irvin	.50	.25	.15
(6)	Jim Konstanty	.50	.25	.15
(7)	Mickey Mantle	10.00	5.00	3.00
(8)	Pee Wee Reese	5.00	2.50	1.50
(9)	Bobby Thompson (Thomson)	.75	.40	.25

1976 SSPC 1887 World Series

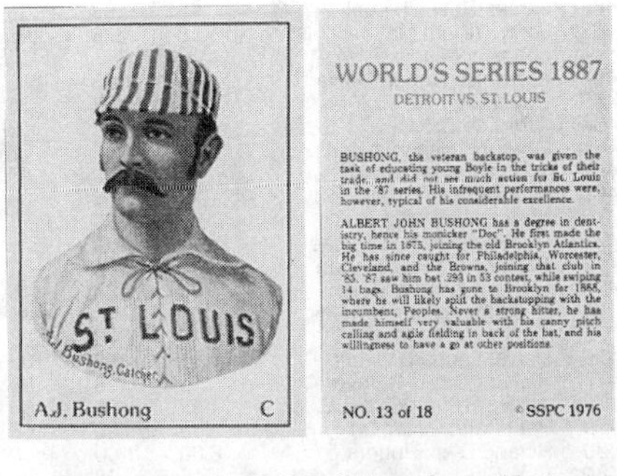

The history of the 1887 "World Series" between the Detroit Wolverines of the National League and the St. Louis Browns of the American Association is told on the backs of this collector's issue. The 2-1/2" x 3-1/2" cards were printed on a pair of uncut sheets inserted in the Fall, 1976, issue of "Collectors Quarterly" magazine. Fronts of the cards reproduce in full color the Scrapps tobacco die-cut cards originally issued in 1888. Backs recount the individual players' performances in the series as well as giving a career summary; they are printed in red and black. Detroit won the Series, a best-of-15 contest.

		NM	EX	VG
Complete Set, Uncut Sheets:		15.00	7.50	4.50
Complete Set, Singles:		12.00	6.00	3.50
Common Player:		.75	.40	.25
1	Bob Caruthers	.75	.40	.25

		NM	EX	VG
2	David Foutz	.75	.40	.25
3	W.A. Latham	.75	.40	.25
4	Charles H. Getzin (Getzien)	.75	.40	.25
5	J.C. Rowe	.75	.40	.25
6	Fred Dunlap	.75	.40	.25
7	James O'Neill	.75	.40	.25
8	Curtis Welch	.75	.40	.25
9	William Gleason	.75	.40	.25
10	Sam Thompson	.75	.40	.25
11	Ned Hanlon	.75	.40	.25
12	Dan Brothers (Brouthers)	.75	.40	.25
13	Albert Bushong	.75	.40	.25
14	Charles Comiskey	.75	.40	.25
15	Wm. Robinson	.75	.40	.25
16	Charles Bennett	.75	.40	.25
17	Hardy Richardson	.75	.40	.25
18	Deacon White	.75	.40	.25

1976 SSPC 1963 New York Mets

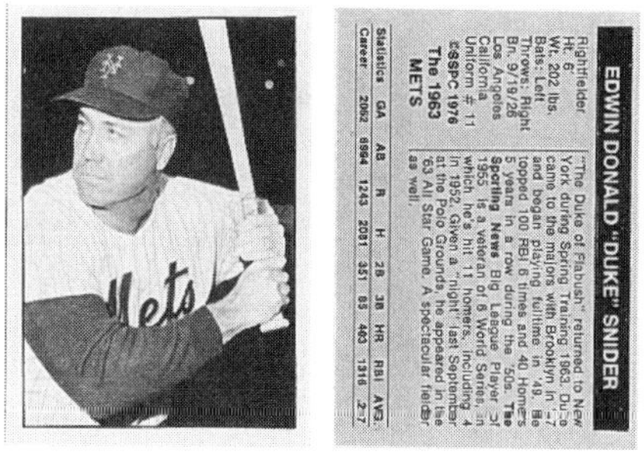

Issued in the Summer, 1976, issue of "Collectors Quarterly" magazine as a two-page uncut sheet, this 18-card issue features the 1963 Mets. Like contemporary collectors' issues from SSPC, the cards feature white-bordered color photos on front with no other graphics or player identification. Backs are printed in black-and-white, contain player biographical data, a career summary and uniform number, by which the checklist is arranged. Size is standard 2-1/2" x 3-1/2".

		NM	EX	VG
	Complete Set, Uncut Sheets:	40.00	20.00	12.00
	Complete Set, Singles (18):	35.00	17.50	10.50
	Common Player:	1.50	.75	.45
1	Duke Carmel	1.50	.75	.45
5	Norman Burt Sherry	2.00	1.00	.60
7	Casey Stengel	6.00	3.00	1.75
9	Jim Hickman	1.50	.75	.45
10	Rod Kanehl	1.50	.75	.45
11	Duke Snider	9.00	4.50	2.75
12	Jesse Gonder	2.50	1.25	.70
16	Dick Smith	1.50	.75	.45
17	Clarence Coleman	2.50	1.25	.70
18	Pumpsie Green	2.50	1.25	.70
23	Joe Christopher	1.50	.75	.45
36	Tracy Stallard	1.50	.75	.45
39	Steve Dillon	1.50	.75	.45
40	Rich Moran	1.50	.75	.45
41	Grover Powell	1.50	.75	.45
43	Ted Schreiber	1.50	.75	.45
53	Ernest White	1.50	.75	.45
56	Ed Bauta	1.50	.75	.45

1978 SSPC All-Star Gallery

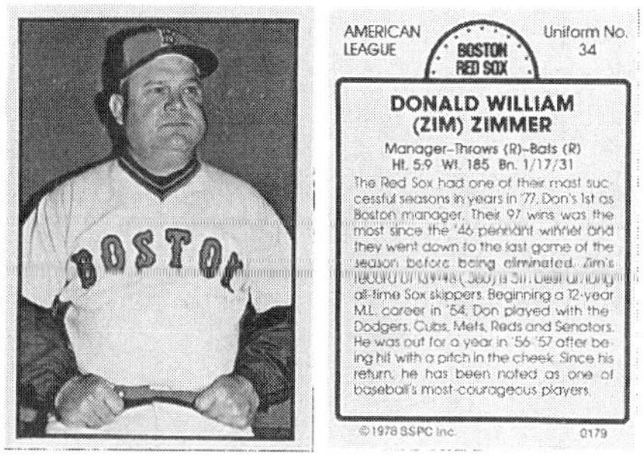

A series of team "Photo Fact Cards" was produced by Sports Stars Publishing Co., for insertion into its 48-page "All-Star Gallery" magazine, sold for $2. Fully licensed by MLB and the players' union, the 27 cards in each team set are printed on a triple-fold 24" x 10-7/8" cardboard sheet stapled into the center of the magazine. Cards are not perforated, though the back of each nine-card panel has dotted lines to guide the cutting of 2-1/2" x 3-1/2" single cards from the sheet. Fronts are full color poses with no extraneous graphics. Backs are in black-and-white with a few vital data, a career summary, uniform number and a card number from within the overall issue of 270. Only eight teams are represented in the All-Star Gallery magazine series. The Yankees (#001-027) and Phillies cards (#028-054) issued with other magazines that year may be considered part of the All-Star Gallery issue.

		NM	EX	VG
	Complete Set, Magazines:	240.00	120.00	72.00
	Complete Set, Singles:	195.00	97.00	58.00
	Common Player:	.75	.40	.25
	Los Angeles Dodgers magazine:	28.00	14.00	8.50
0055	Burt Hooton	.75	.40	.25
0056	Bill Russell	1.00	.50	.30
0057	Dusty Baker	1.50	.70	.45
0058	Reggie Smith	1.00	.50	.30
0059	Dick Rhoden	.75	.40	.25
0060	Jerry Grote	.75	.40	.25
0061	Bill Butler	.75	.40	.25
0062	Ron Cey	1.25	.60	.40
0063	Ron Cey	1.25	.60	.40
0064	Ted Martinez	.75	.40	.25
0065	Ed Goodson	.75	.40	.25
0066	Vic Davalillo	.75	.40	.25
0067	Davey Lopes	1.00	.50	.30
0068	Terry Forster	1.00	.50	.30
0069	Lee Lacy	.75	.40	.25
0070	Mike Garman	.75	.40	.25
0071	Steve Garvey	3.00	1.50	.90
0072	Johnny Oates	.75	.40	.25
0073	Steve Yaeger	.75	.40	.25
0074	Rafael Landestoy	.75	.40	.25
0075	Tommy John	1.25	.60	.40
0076	Glenn Burke	.75	.40	.25
0077	Rick Monday	1.25	.60	.40
0078	Doug Rau	.75	.40	.25
0079	Manny Mota	1.00	.50	.30
0080	Don Sutton	2.25	1.25	.70
0081	Charlie Hough	1.00	.50	.30
	Texas Rangers magazine:	24.00	12.00	7.25
0082	Mike Hargrove	1.00	.50	.30
0083	Jim Sundberg	1.00	.50	.30
0084	Fergie Jenkins	3.75	2.00	1.25
0085	Paul Lindblad	.75	.40	.25
0086	Sandy Alomar	1.25	.60	.40
0087	John Lowenstein	.75	.40	.25
0088	Claudell Washington	.75	.40	.25
0089	Toby Harrah	1.00	.50	.30
0090	Jim Umbarger	.75	.40	.25
0091	Len Barker	.75	.40	.25
0092	Dave May	.75	.40	.25
0093	Kurt Bevacqua	.75	.40	.25
0094	Jim Mason	.75	.40	.25
0095	Bump Wills	.75	.40	.25
0096	Dock Ellis	.75	.40	.25
0097	Bill Fahey	.75	.40	.25
0098	Richie Zisk	.75	.40	.25
0099	Jon Matlack	.75	.40	.25
0100	John Ellis	.75	.40	.25
0101	Bert Campaneris	1.25	.60	.40
0102	Doc Medich	.75	.40	.25
0103	Juan Beniquez	.75	.40	.25
0104	Bill Hunter	.75	.40	.25
0105	Doyle Alexander	.75	.40	.25
0106	Roger Moret	.75	.40	.25
0107	Mike Jorgensen	.75	.40	.25
0108	Al Oliver	1.25	.60	.40
	Cincinnati Reds magazine:	45.00	22.00	13.50
0109	Fred Norman	.75	.40	.25
0110	Ray Knight	1.25	.60	.40
0111	Pedro Borbon	.75	.40	.25
0112	Bill Bonham	.75	.40	.25
0113	George Foster	2.25	1.25	.70
0114	Doug Bair	.75	.40	.25
0115	Cesar Geronimo	1.00	.50	.30
0116	Tom Seaver	6.00	3.00	1.75
0117	Mario Soto	1.00	.50	.30
0118	Ken Griffey	1.50	.70	.45
0119	Mike Lum	.75	.40	.25
0120	Tom Hume	.75	.40	.25
0121	Joe Morgan	3.75	2.00	1.25
0122	Manny Sarmiento	.75	.40	.25
0123	Dan Driessen	.75	.40	.25
0124	Ed Armbrister	.75	.40	.25
0125	John Summers	.75	.40	.25
0126	Fred Auerbach	.75	.40	.25
0127	Doug Capilla	.75	.40	.25
0128	Johnny Bench	6.00	3.00	1.75
0129	Sparky Anderson	2.25	1.25	.70
0130	Raul Ferreyra	.75	.40	.25
0131	Dale Murray	.75	.40	.25
0132	Pete Rose	7.50	3.75	2.25
0133	Dave Concepcion	1.25	.60	.40
0134	Junior Kennedy	.75	.40	.25
0135	Dave Collins	1.00	.50	.30
	Chicago White Sox magazine:	27.00	13.50	8.00
0136	Mike Eden	.75	.40	.25
0137	Lamar Johnson	.75	.40	.25
0138	Ron Schueler	.75	.40	.25
0139	Bob Lemon	2.25	1.25	.70
0140	Thad Bosley	.75	.40	.25
0141	Bobby Bonds	2.25	1.25	.70
0142	Wilbur Wood	1.25	.60	.40
0143	Jorge Orta	.75	.40	.25
0144	Francisco Barrios	.75	.40	.25
0145	Greg Pryor	.75	.40	.25
0146	Chet Lemon	1.25	.60	.40
0147	Mike Squires	.75	.40	.25
0148	Eric Soderholm	.75	.40	.25
0149	Reggie Sanders	.75	.40	.25
0150	Kevin Bell	.75	.40	.25
0151	Alan Bannister	.75	.40	.25
0152	Henry Cruz	.75	.40	.25
0153	Larry Doby	2.25	1.25	.70
0154	Don Kessinger	1.25	.60	.40
0155	Ralph Garr	1.00	.50	.30
0156	Bill Nahorodny	.75	.40	.25
0157	Ron Blomberg	.75	.40	.25
0158	Bob Molinaro	.75	.40	.25
0159	Junior Moore	.75	.40	.25
0160	Minnie Minoso	2.25	1.25	.70
0161	Lerrin LaGrow	.75	.40	.25
0162	Wayne Nordhagen	.75	.40	.25
	Boston Red Sox magazine:	37.00	18.50	11.00
0163	Ramon Aviles	.75	.40	.25
0164	Bob Stanley	.75	.40	.25
0165	Reggie Cleveland	.75	.40	.25
0166	John Brohamer	.75	.40	.25
0167	Bill Lee	1.25	.60	.40
0168	Jim Burton	.75	.40	.25
0169	Bill Campbell	.75	.40	.25
0170	Mike Torrez	.75	.40	.25
0171	Dick Drago	.75	.40	.25
0172	Butch Hobson	.75	.40	.25
0173	Bob Bailey	.75	.40	.25
0174	Fred Lynn	2.00	1.00	.60
0175	Rick Burleson	.75	.40	.25
0176	Luis Tiant	1.50	.70	.45
0177	Ted Williams	7.50	3.75	2.25
0178	Dennis Eckersley	2.75	1.50	.80
0179	Don Zimmer	.75	.40	.25
0180	Carlton Fisk	3.00	1.50	.90
0181	Dwight Evans	1.00	.50	.30
0182	Fred Kendall	.75	.40	.25
0183	George Scott	1.00	.50	.30
0184	Frank Duffy	.75	.40	.25
0185	Bernie Carbo	.75	.40	.25
0186	Jerry Remy	.75	.40	.25
0187	Carl Yastrzemski	6.00	3.00	1.75
0188	Allen Ripley	.75	.40	.25
0189	Jim Rice	1.50	.70	.45
	California Angels magazine:	30.00	15.00	9.00
0190	Ken Landreaux	.75	.40	.25
0191	Paul Hartzell	.75	.40	.25
0192	Ken Brett	.75	.40	.25
0193	Dave Garcia	.75	.40	.25
0194	Bobby Grich	1.00	.50	.30
0195	Lyman Bostock	1.25	.60	.40
0196	Isaac Hampton	.75	.40	.25
0197	Dave LaRoche	.75	.40	.25
0198	Dave Chalk	.75	.40	.25
0199	Rick Miller	.75	.40	.25
0200	Floyd Rayford	.75	.40	.25
0201	Willie Aikens	1.00	.50	.30
0202	Balor Moore	.75	.40	.25
0203	Nolan Ryan	9.00	4.50	2.75
0204	Dan Goodwin	.75	.40	.25
0205	Ron Fairly	.75	.40	.25
0206	Dyar Miller	.75	.40	.25
0207	Carney Lansford	1.00	.50	.30
0208	Don Baylor	1.50	.70	.45
0209	Gil Flores	.75	.40	.25
0210	Terry Humphrey	.75	.40	.25
0211	Frank Tanana	.75	.40	.25
0212	Chris Knapp	.75	.40	.25
0213	Ron Jackson	.75	.40	.25
0214	Joe Rudi	1.00	.50	.30
0215	Tony Solaita	.75	.40	.25
0216	Steve Mulliniks	.75	.40	.25
	Kansas City Royals magazine:	27.00	13.50	8.00
0217	George Brett	6.00	3.00	1.75
0218	Doug Bird	.75	.40	.25
0219	Hal McRae	1.50	.70	.45
0220	Dennis Leonard	.75	.40	.25
0221	Darrell Porter	1.00	.50	.30
0222	Randy McGilberry	.75	.40	.25
0223	Pete LaCock	.75	.40	.25
0224	Whitey Herzog	1.25	.60	.40
0225	Andy Hassler	.75	.40	.25
0226	Joe Lahoud	.75	.40	.25
0227	Amos Otis	1.25	.60	.40
0228	Al Hrabosky	.75	.40	.25
0229	Clint Hurdle	.75	.40	.25
0230	Paul Splittorff	.75	.40	.25
0231	Marty Pattin	.75	.40	.25
0232	Frank White	1.25	.60	.40
0233	John Wathan	.75	.40	.25
0234	Freddie Patek	1.00	.50	.30
0235	Rich Gale	.75	.40	.25
0236	U.L. Washington	1.00	.50	.30
0237	Larry Gura	.75	.40	.25
0238	Jim Colburn	.75	.40	.25
0239	Tom Poquette	.75	.40	.25
0240	Al Cowens	.75	.40	.25
0241	Willie Wilson	2.25	1.25	.70
0242	Steve Mingori	.75	.40	.25
0243	Jerry Terrell	.75	.40	.25
	Chicago Cubs magazine:	24.00	12.00	7.25
0244	Larry Biitner	.75	.40	.25
0245	Rick Reuschel	1.00	.50	.30
0246	Dave Rader	.75	.40	.25
0247	Paul Reuschel	.75	.40	.25
0248	Hector Cruz	.75	.40	.25
0249	Woody Fryman	.75	.40	.25
0250	Steve Ontiveros	.75	.40	.25
0251	Mike Gordon	.75	.40	.25
0252	Dave Kingman	1.50	.70	.45
0253	Gene Clines	.75	.40	.25
0254	Bruce Sutter	1.00	.50	.30
0255	Guillermo Hernandez	1.00	.50	.30
0256	Ivan DeJesus	1.00	.50	.30
0257	Greg Gross	.75	.40	.25
0258	Larry Cox	.75	.40	.25
0259	Joe Wallis	.75	.40	.25

		NM	EX	VG
0260	Dennis Lamp	.75	.40	.25
0261	Ray Burris	.75	.40	.25
0262	Bill Caudill	.75	.40	.25
0263	Donnie Moore	.75	.40	.25
0264	Bill Buckner	1.25	.60	.40
0265	Bobby Murcer	1.00	.50	.30
0266	Dave Roberts	.75	.40	.25
0267	Mike Krukow	.75	.40	.25
0268	Herman Franks	.75	.40	.25
0269	Mike Kelleher	.75	.40	.25
0270	Rudy Meoli	.75	.40	.25

1978 SSPC Baseball the Phillies Way

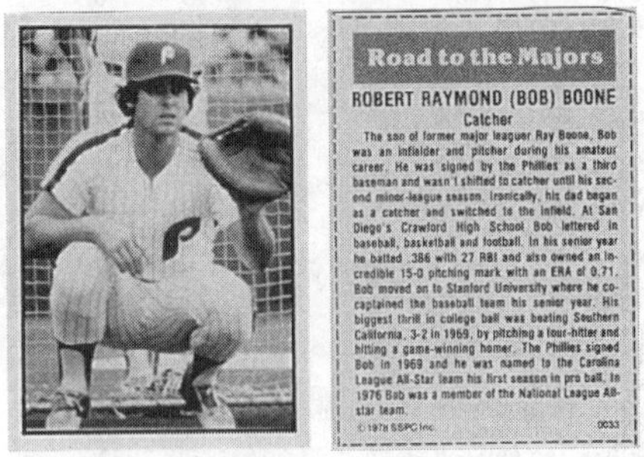

This team set was produced on a tri-fold insert in an SSPC magazine titled, "Baseball the Phillies Way." The magazine offered playing tips. Cards are in the contemporary SSPC format of a posed front photo with a white border and no other graphics. Backs are printed in red, white and black with player ID, career data and card numbers between 0028-0054, continuing the sequence begun with the Yankees yearbook team set which continues with the All-Star Gallery set. Cards could be cut from the sheets into 2-1/2" x 3-1/2" singles.

		NM	EX	VG
Complete Set, Uncut Sheets:		20.00	10.00	6.00
Complete Set, Singles:		15.00	7.50	4.50
Common Player:		.50	.25	.15
0028	Garry Maddox	.50	.25	.15
0029	Steve Carlton	1.50	.70	.45
0030	Ron Reed	.50	.25	.15
0031	Greg Luzinski	.75	.40	.25
0032	Bobby Wine	.50	.25	.15
0033	Bob Boone	1.00	.50	.30
0034	Carroll Beringer	.50	.25	.15
0035	Dick Hebner	.50	.25	.15
0036	Ray Ripplemeyer	.50	.25	.15
0037	Terry Harmon	.50	.25	.15
0038	Gene Garber	.50	.25	.15
0039	Ted Sizemore	.50	.25	.15
0040	Barry Foote	.50	.25	.15
0041	Tony Taylor	.50	.25	.15
0042	Tug McGraw	.75	.40	.25
0043	Jay Johnstone	.75	.40	.25
0044	Randy Lerch	.50	.25	.15
0045	Billy DeMars	.50	.25	.15
0046	Mike Schmidt	3.00	1.50	.90
0047	Larry Christenson	.50	.25	.15
0048	Tim McCarver	1.00	.50	.30
0049	Larry Bowa	.75	.40	.25
0050	Danny Ozark	.50	.25	.15
0051	Jerry Martin	.50	.25	.15
0052	Jim Lonborg	.75	.40	.25
0053	Bake McBride	.50	.25	.15
0054	Warren Brusstar	.50	.25	.15

1978 SSPC Yankees Yearbook

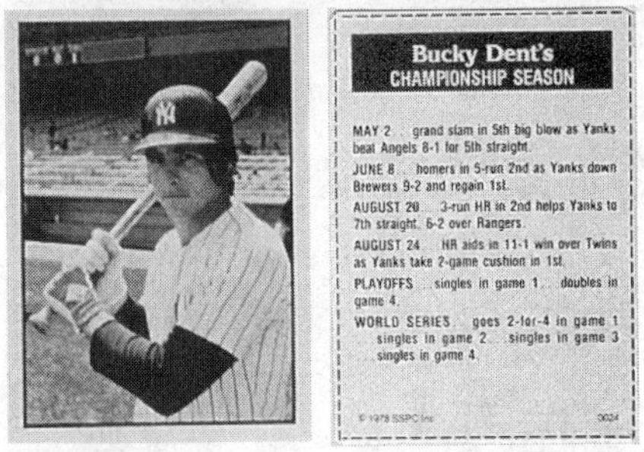

This team set was printed on a tri-fold insert found both in the 1978 Yankees yearbook and a magazine titled "Diary of a Champion Yankee," produced by SSPC. The nine cards on each sheet could be cut apart into 2-1/2" x 3-1/2" singles. Cards follow the basic SSPC format of a posed color photo on front with a white border and no graphic elements. Backs have player identification, career summary and "CHAMPIONSHIP SEASON" highlights, printed in black and blue on white. Cards are numbered from 0001-0027, and may be considered part of the larger All-Star Gallery issue.

		NM	EX	VG
Complete Set, Uncut Sheets:		17.50	8.75	5.25
Complete Set, Singles (27):		12.00	6.00	3.50
Common Player:		.50	.25	.15
0001	Thurman Munson	2.00	1.00	.60
0002	Cliff Johnson	.50	.25	.15
0003	Lou Piniella	.75	.40	.25
0004	Dell Alston	.50	.25	.15
0005	Yankee Stadium	.50	.25	.15
0006	Ken Holtzman	.50	.25	.15
0007	Chris Chambliss	.50	.25	.15
0008	Roy White	.75	.40	.25
0009	Ed Figueroa	.50	.25	.15
0010	Dick Tidrow	.50	.25	.15
0011	Sparky Lyle	.75	.40	.25
0012	Fred Stanley	.50	.25	.15
0013	Mickey Rivers	.50	.25	.15
0014	Billy Martin	1.00	.50	.30
0015	George Zeber	.50	.25	.15
0016	Ken Clay	.50	.25	.15
0017	Ron Guidry	.75	.40	.25
0018	Don Gullett	.50	.25	.15
0019	Fran Healy	.50	.25	.15
0020	Paul Blair	.50	.25	.15
0021	Mickey Klutts	.50	.25	.15
0022	Yankee team	.50	.25	.15
0023	Catfish Hunter	1.00	.50	.30
0024	Bucky Dent	.75	.40	.25
0025	Graig Nettles	.75	.40	.25
0026	Reggie Jackson	1.50	.70	.45
0027	Willie Randolph	.75	.40	.25

1953 Stahl-Meyer Franks

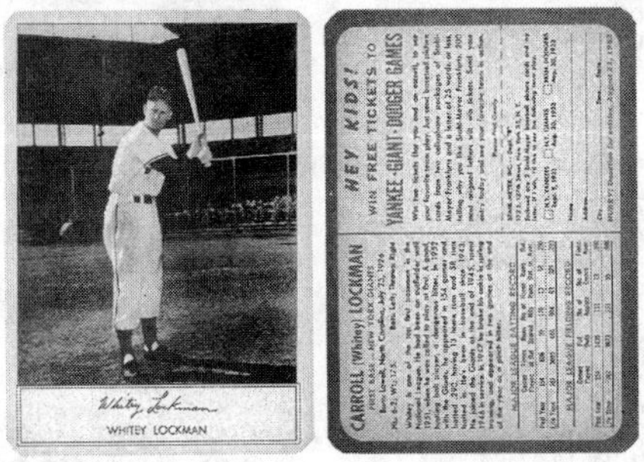

These nine cards, issued in packages of hot dogs by a New York area meat company, feature three players from each of the New York teams of the day - Dodgers, Giants and Yankees. Cards in the set measure 3-1/4" x 4-1/2". The card fronts in this unnumbered set feature color photos with player name and facsimile autograph. The backs list both biographical and statistical information on half the card and a ticket offer promotion on the other half. The card corners are cut diagonally, although some cards (apparently cut from sheets) with square corners have been seen. Cards are white-bordered.

		NM	EX	VG
Complete Set (9):		5000.	2250.	1000.
Common Player:		125.00	56.00	25.00
(1)	Hank Bauer	150.00	67.00	30.00
(2)	Roy Campanella	500.00	225.00	100.00
(3)	Gil Hodges	300.00	135.00	60.00
(4)	Monte Irvin	200.00	90.00	40.00
(5)	Whitey Lockman	125.00	56.00	25.00
(6)	Mickey Mantle	3000.	1350.	600.00
(7)	Phil Rizzuto	350.00	157.00	70.00
(8)	Duke Snider	500.00	225.00	100.00
(9)	Bobby Thomson	200.00	90.00	40.00

1954 Stahl-Meyer Franks

The 1954 set of Stahl-Meyer Franks was increased to 12 cards which retained the 3-1/4" x 4-1/2" size. The most prominent addition to the '54 set was New York Giants slugger Willie Mays. The card fronts are identical in format to the previous year's set. However, the backs are different as they are designed on a vertical format. The backs also contain an advertisement for a "Johnny Stahl-Meyer Baseball Kit." The cards in the set are unnumbered.

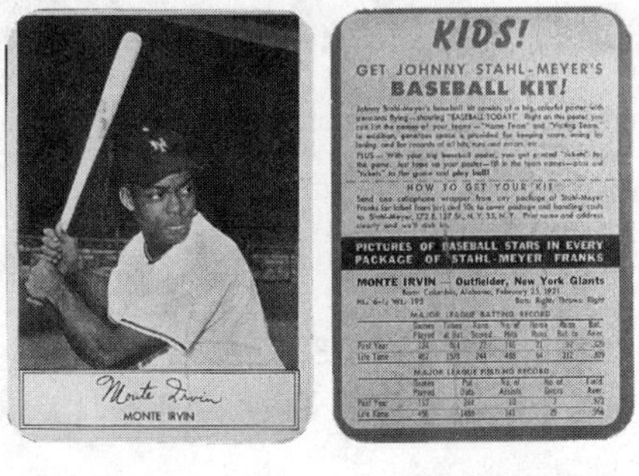

		NM	EX	VG
Complete Set (12):		6000.	2700.	1200.
Common Player:		125.00	56.00	25.00
(1)	Hank Bauer	150.00	67.00	30.00
(2)	Carl Erskine	150.00	67.00	30.00
(3)	Gil Hodges	300.00	135.00	60.00
(4)	Monte Irvin	200.00	90.00	40.00
(5)	Whitey Lockman	125.00	56.00	25.00
(6)	Gil McDougald	150.00	67.00	30.00
(7)	Mickey Mantle	2400.	1080.	480.00
(8)	Willie Mays	1500.	675.00	300.00
(9)	Don Mueller	125.00	56.00	25.00
(10)	Don Newcombe	150.00	67.00	30.00
(11)	Phil Rizzuto	350.00	157.00	70.00
(12)	Duke Snider	450.00	202.00	90.00

1955 Stahl-Meyer Franks

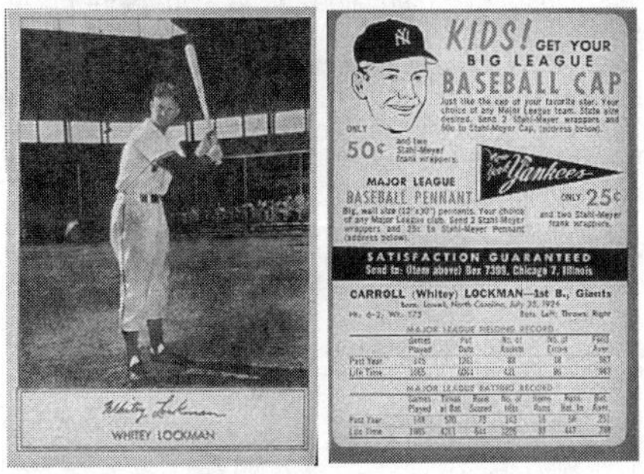

Eleven of the 12 players in the 1955 set are the same as those featured in 1954. The exception is the New York Giants Dusty Rhodes, who replaced Willie Mays on the 3-1/4" x 4-1/2" cards. The card fronts are again full-color photos bordered in yellow with diagonal corners, and four players from each of the three New York teams are featured. The backs offer a new promotion, with a drawing of Mickey Mantle and advertisements selling pennants and caps. Player statistics are still included on the vertical card backs. The cards in the set are unnumbered.

		NM	EX	VG
Complete Set (12):		4000.	1800.	800.00
Common Player:		105.00	53.00	32.00
(1)	Hank Bauer	125.00	56.00	25.00
(2)	Carl Erskine	125.00	56.00	25.00
(3)	Gil Hodges	250.00	112.00	50.00
(4)	Monte Irvin	170.00	76.00	34.00
(5)	Whitey Lockman	105.00	47.00	21.00
(6)	Mickey Mantle	2400.	1100.	480.00
(7)	Gil McDougald	125.00	56.00	25.00
(8)	Don Mueller	105.00	47.00	21.00
(9)	Don Newcombe	125.00	56.00	25.00
(10)	Jim Rhodes	105.00	47.00	21.00
(11)	Phil Rizzuto	295.00	133.00	59.00
(12)	Duke Snider	450.00	202.00	90.00

Near Mint-Mint and Mint examples of vintage cards carry a significant premium over the Near Mint values quoted here. This premium reflects availability of the highest-grade cards as well as demand for a particular card or set in top grade. Premiums of 2X to 3X are not uncommon and many are even higher.

1960-70s Stan Musial & Biggie's Restaurant

These 5" x 7" black-and-white photos were evidently prepared for Musial's use while glad-handing patrons at his St. Louis eatery. The pictures have a facsimile autograph. A "Compliments of . . ." message is printed in the bottom border. Backs are blank.

		NM	EX	VG
(1)	Stan Musial (batting pose)	8.00	4.00	2.50
(2)	Stan Musial (standing w/glove)	8.00	4.00	2.50

1915 Standard Biscuit

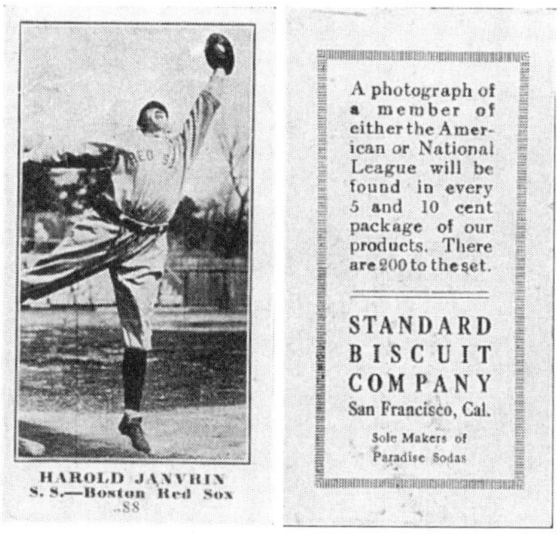

The 200 cards in this issue are more commonly found with advertising on back for The Sporting News. The 1-5/8" x 3" black-and-white cards share the checklist and pricing structure with the TSN version, though a collector may pay a small premium for a Standard Biscuit card to enhance a type collection or superstar collection. This version was listed as D350-2 in the American Card Catalog.

(See 1915 Sporting News for checklist; star card values slightly higher.)

1916 Standard Biscuit

The 200 cards in this set are usually found with the advertising of San Francisco's Collins-McCarthy Candy Co. on the back. The cards were also made available for use by other advertisers, including Standard Biscuit Co. Though the Standard Biscuit cards are much scarcer than the Collins-McCarthy version, collectors do not attach much premium to them.

(See 1916 Collins-McCarthy for checklist; star card values slightly higher)

1910 Standard Caramel Co. (E93)

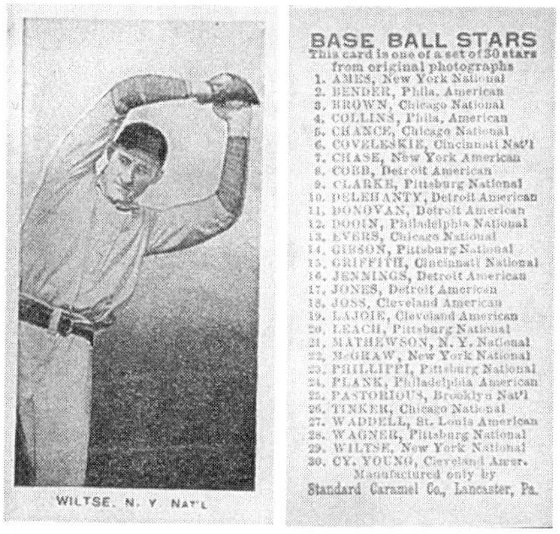

This 30-card set issued in 1910 by Standard Caramel Co. of Lancaster, Pa., is closely related to several other candy sets from this period which share the same format and, in many cases, the same player poses. The cards measure 1-1/2" x 2-3/4" and utilize tinted black-and-white player photos. The back of each card contains an alphabetical checklist of the set plus a line indicating it was manufactured by Standard Caramel Co., Lancaster, Pa. The set carries the ACC designation of E93.

		NM	EX	VG
Complete Set (30):		10000.	4000.	2000.
Common Player:		125.00	50.00	25.00
(1)	Red Ames	125.00	50.00	25.00
(2)	Chief Bender	375.00	150.00	75.00
(3)	Mordecai Brown	375.00	150.00	75.00
(4)	Frank Chance	375.00	150.00	75.00
(5)	Hal Chase	175.00	70.00	35.00
(6)	Fred Clarke	375.00	150.00	75.00
(7)	Ty Cobb	2000.	800.00	400.00
(8)	Eddie Collins	375.00	150.00	75.00
(9)	Harry Coveleskie (Coveleski)	125.00	50.00	25.00
(10)	Jim Delehanty	125.00	50.00	25.00
(11)	Wild Bill Donovan	125.00	50.00	25.00
(12)	Red Dooin	125.00	50.00	25.00
(13)	Johnny Evers	375.00	150.00	75.00
(14)	George Gibson	125.00	50.00	25.00
(15)	Clark Griffith	375.00	150.00	75.00
(16)	Hugh Jennings	375.00	150.00	75.00
(17)	Davy Jones	125.00	50.00	25.00
(18)	Addie Joss	375.00	150.00	75.00
(19)	Nap Lajoie	400.00	160.00	80.00
(20)	Tommy Leach	125.00	50.00	25.00
(21)	Christy Mathewson	650.00	260.00	130.00
(22)	John McGraw	375.00	150.00	75.00
(23)	Jim Pastorious	125.00	50.00	25.00
(24)	Deacon Phillippi (Phillippe)	125.00	50.00	25.00
(25)	Eddie Plank	375.00	150.00	75.00
(26)	Joe Tinker	375.00	150.00	75.00
(27)	Honus Wagner	1100.	440.00	220.00
(28)	Rube Waddell	375.00	150.00	75.00
(29)	Hooks Wiltse	125.00	50.00	25.00
(30)	Cy Young	650.00	260.00	130.00

1952 Star-Cal Decals - Type 1

The Meyercord Co., of Chicago issued two sets of baseball player decals in 1952. The Type I Star-Cal Decal set consists of 68 different major leaguers, each pictured on a large (4-1/8" x 6-1/8") decal. The player's name and facsimile autograph appear on the decal, along with the decal number listed on the checklist here. Values shown are for decals complete with outer directions envelope.

		NM	EX	VG
Complete Set (68):		4000.	2000.	1200.
Common Player:		25.00	12.50	7.50
70A	Allie Reynolds	27.50	13.50	8.25
70B	Ed Lopat	27.50	13.50	8.25
70C	Yogi Berra	65.00	32.00	19.50
70D	Vic Raschi	27.50	13.50	8.25
70E	Jerry Coleman	27.50	13.50	8.25
70F	Phil Rizzuto	65.00	32.00	19.50
70G	Mickey Mantle	1250.	625.00	375.00
71A	Mel Parnell	25.00	12.50	7.50
71B	Ted Williams	235.00	117.00	70.00
71C	Ted Williams	235.00	117.00	70.00
71D	Vern Stephens	25.00	12.50	7.50
71E	Billy Goodman	25.00	12.50	7.50
71F	Dom DiMaggio	25.00	12.50	7.50
71G	Dick Gernert	25.00	12.50	7.50
71H	Hoot Evers	25.00	12.50	7.50
72A	George Kell	30.00	15.00	9.00
72B	Hal Newhouser	30.00	15.00	9.00
72C	Hoot Evers	25.00	12.50	7.50
72D	Vic Wertz	25.00	12.50	7.50
72E	Fred Hutchinson	25.00	12.50	7.50
72F	Johnny Groth	25.00	12.50	7.50
73A	Al Zarilla	25.00	12.50	7.50
73B	Billy Pierce	25.00	12.50	7.50
73C	Eddie Robinson	25.00	12.50	7.50
73D	Chico Carrasquel	25.00	12.50	7.50
73E	Minnie Minoso	25.00	12.50	7.50
73F	Jim Busby	25.00	12.50	7.50
73G	Nellie Fox	30.00	15.00	9.00
73H	Sam Mele	25.00	12.50	7.50
74A	Larry Doby	30.00	15.00	9.00
74B	Al Rosen	25.00	12.50	7.50
74C	Bob Lemon	30.00	15.00	9.00
74D	Jim Hegan	25.00	12.50	7.50
74E	Bob Feller	50.00	25.00	15.00
74F	Dale Mitchell	25.00	12.50	7.50
75A	Ned Garver	25.00	12.50	7.50
76A	Gus Zernial	25.00	12.50	7.50
76B	Ferris Fain	25.00	12.50	7.50
76C	Bobby Shantz	25.00	12.50	7.50
77A	Richie Ashburn	35.00	17.50	10.50
77B	Ralph Kiner	30.00	15.00	9.00
77C	Curt Simmons	25.00	12.50	7.50
78A	Bobby Thomson	25.00	12.50	7.50
78B	Alvin Dark	25.00	12.50	7.50
78C	Sal Maglie	25.00	12.50	7.50
78D	Larry Jansen	25.00	12.50	7.50
78E	Willie Mays	300.00	150.00	90.00
78F	Monte Irvin	30.00	15.00	9.00
78G	Whitey Lockman	25.00	12.50	7.50
79A	Gil Hodges	45.00	22.00	13.50
79B	Pee Wee Reese	50.00	25.00	15.00
79C	Roy Campanella	65.00	32.00	19.50
79D	Don Newcombe	25.00	12.50	7.50
79E	Duke Snider	65.00	32.00	19.50
79F	Preacher Roe	25.00	12.50	7.50
79G	Jackie Robinson	150.00	75.00	45.00
80A	Eddie Miksis	25.00	12.50	7.50
80B	Dutch Leonard	25.00	12.50	7.50
80C	Randy Jackson	25.00	12.50	7.50
80D	Bob Rush	25.00	12.50	7.50
80E	Hank Sauer	25.00	12.50	7.50
80F	Phil Cavarretta	25.00	12.50	7.50
80G	Warren Hacker	25.00	12.50	7.50
81A	Red Schoendienst	30.00	15.00	9.00
81B	Wally Westlake	25.00	12.50	7.50
81C	Cliff Chambers	25.00	12.50	7.50
81D	Enos Slaughter	30.00	15.00	9.00
81E	Stan Musial	175.00	87.00	52.00
81F	Stan Musial	175.00	87.00	52.00
81G	Jerry Staley	25.00	12.50	7.50

1952 Star-Cal Decals - Type 2

Also produced by Chicago's Meyercord Company in 1952, these Star-Cal decals are similar to the Type I variety, except the decal sheets are smaller, measuring 4-1/8" x 3-1/16", and each sheet features two players instead of one.

		NM	EX	VG
Complete Set (32):		2200.	1100.	650.00
Common Player:		25.00	12.50	7.50
84A	Vic Raschi, Allie Reynolds	40.00	20.00	12.00
84B	Yogi Berra, Ed Lopat	95.00	47.00	28.00
84C	Jerry Coleman, Phil Rizzuto	80.00	40.00	24.00
85A	Ted Williams, Ted Williams	350.00	175.00	105.00
85B	Dom DiMaggio, Mel Parnell	30.00	15.00	9.00
85C	Billy Goodman, Vern Stephens	25.00	12.50	7.50
86A	George Kell, Hal Newhouser	50.00	25.00	15.00
86B	Hoot Evers, Vic Wertz	25.00	12.50	7.50
86C	Johnny Groth, Fred Hutchinson	25.00	12.50	7.50
87A	Eddie Robinson, Eddie Robinson	25.00	12.50	7.50
87B	Chico Carrasquel, Minnie Minoso	30.00	15.00	9.00
87C	Nellie Fox, Billy Pierce	40.00	20.00	12.00
87D	Jim Busby, Al Zarilla	25.00	12.50	7.50
88A	Jim Hegan, Bob Lemon	40.00	20.00	12.00
88B	Larry Doby, Bob Feller	95.00	47.00	28.00
88C	Dale Mitchell, Al Rosen	30.00	15.00	9.00
89A	Ned Garver, Ned Garver	25.00	12.50	7.50
89B	Ferris Fain, Gus Zernial	25.00	12.50	7.50
89C	Richie Ashburn, Richie Ashburn	45.00	22.00	13.50
89D	Ralph Kiner, Ralph Kiner	45.00	22.00	13.50
90A	Monty Irvin, Willie Mays (Monte)	250.00	125.00	75.00
90B	Larry Jansen, Sal Maglie	25.00	12.50	7.50
90C	Al Dark, Bobby Thomson	30.00	15.00	9.00
91A	Gil Hodges, Pee Wee Reese	100.00	50.00	30.00
91B	Roy Campanella, Jackie Robinson	200.00	100.00	60.00
91C	Preacher Roe, Duke Snider	115.00	57.00	34.00
92A	Phil Cavarretta, Dutch Leonard	25.00	12.50	7.50
92B	Randy Jackson, Eddie Miksis	25.00	12.50	7.50
92C	Bob Rush, Hank Sauer	25.00	12.50	7.50
93A	Stan Musial, Stan Musial	200.00	100.00	60.00
93B	Red Schoendienst, Enos Slaughter	40.00	20.00	12.00
93C	Cliff Chambers, Wally Westlake	25.00	12.50	7.50

1976 Star Market Red Sox

Only Red Sox are featured in this set issued by the Star Market chain in the Boston area. Players are photographed hatless in jerseys which feature the Massachusetts Bicentennial logo. Pictures measure 5-7/8" x 9" and have a 3-16" white border all around. A facsimile autograph is printed on the front in black. Backs are blank. The unnumbered pictures are checklisted here alphabetically.

		NM	EX	VG
Complete Set (16):		50.00	25.00	15.00
Common Player:		2.00	1.00	.60
(1)	Rick Burleson	2.00	1.00	.60
(2)	Reggie Cleveland	2.00	1.00	.60
(3)	Cecil Cooper	3.00	1.50	.90
(4)	Denny Doyle	2.00	1.00	.60
(5)	Dwight Evans	3.00	1.50	.90
(6)	Carlton Fisk	6.00	3.00	1.75
(7)	Tom House	2.00	1.00	.60
(8)	Fergie Jenkins	4.00	2.00	1.25
(9)	Bill Lee	2.00	1.00	.60
(10)	Fred Lynn	4.00	2.00	1.25
(11)	Rick Miller	2.00	1.00	.60
(12)	Rico Petrocelli	3.00	1.50	.90
(13)	Jim Rice	4.00	2.00	1.25
(14)	Luis Tiant	3.00	1.50	.90
(15)	Rick Wise	2.00	1.00	.60
(16)	Carl Yastrzemski	12.00	6.00	3.50

1928 Star Player Candy

This somewhat confusing issue can be dated to 1928, although little is known about its origin. The producer of the set is not identified, but experienced collectors generally refer to it as the Star Player Candy set, apparently because it was distributed with a product of that name. The cards measure 1-7/8" by 2-7/8", are sepia-toned and blank-backed. The player's name (but no team designation) appears in the border below the photo in brown capital letters. To date the checklist of baseball players numbers 72, but more may exist, and cards of football players have also been found.

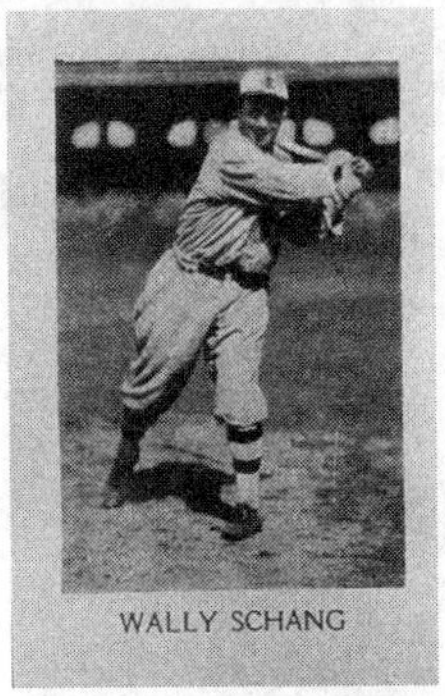
WALLY SCHANG

		NM	EX	VG
Complete Set (72):		18000.	7200.	3600.
Common Player:		150.00	60.00	30.00
(1)	Dave Bancroft	250.00	100.00	50.00
(2)	Emile Barnes	150.00	60.00	30.00
(3)	L.A. Blue	150.00	60.00	30.00
(4)	Garland Buckeye	150.00	60.00	30.00
(5)	George Burns	150.00	60.00	30.00
(6)	Guy T. Bush	150.00	60.00	30.00
(7)	Owen T. Carroll	150.00	60.00	30.00
(8)	Chalmer Cissell	150.00	60.00	30.00
(9)	Ty Cobb	2750.	1100.	550.00
(10)	Gordon Cochrane	250.00	100.00	50.00
(11)	Richard Coffman	150.00	60.00	30.00
(12)	Eddie Collins	250.00	100.00	50.00
(13)	Stanley Coveleskie (Coveleski)	250.00	100.00	50.00
(14)	Hugh Critz	150.00	60.00	30.00
(15)	Hazen Cuyler	250.00	100.00	50.00
(16)	Charles Dressen	150.00	60.00	30.00
(17)	Joe Dugan	150.00	60.00	30.00
(18)	Elwood English	150.00	60.00	30.00
(19)	Bib Falk (Bibb)	150.00	60.00	30.00
(20)	Ira Flagstead	150.00	60.00	30.00
(21)	Bob Fothergill	150.00	60.00	30.00
(22)	Frank T. Frisch	250.00	100.00	50.00
(23)	Foster Ganzel	150.00	60.00	30.00
(24)	Lou Gehrig	3000.	1200.	600.00
(25)	Chas. Gihringer (Gehringer)	250.00	100.00	50.00
(26)	George Gerken	150.00	60.00	30.00
(27)	Grant Gillis	150.00	60.00	30.00
(28)	Miguel Gonzales (Gonzalez)	175.00	70.00	35.00
(29)	Sam Gray	150.00	60.00	30.00
(30)	Chas. J. Grimm	150.00	60.00	30.00
(31)	Robert M. Grove	250.00	100.00	50.00
(32)	Chas. J. Hafey	250.00	100.00	50.00
(33)	Jesse Haines	250.00	100.00	50.00
(34)	Chas. L. Hartnett	250.00	100.00	50.00
(35)	Clifton Heathcote	150.00	60.00	30.00
(36)	Harry Heilmann	250.00	100.00	50.00
(37)	John Heving	150.00	60.00	30.00
(38)	Waite Hoyt	250.00	100.00	50.00
(39)	Chas. Jamieson	150.00	60.00	30.00
(40)	Joe Judge	150.00	60.00	30.00
(41)	Willie Kamm	150.00	60.00	30.00
(42)	George Kelly	250.00	100.00	50.00
(43)	Tony Lazzeri	250.00	100.00	50.00
(44)	Adolfo Luque	175.00	70.00	35.00
(45)	Ted Lyons	250.00	100.00	50.00
(46)	Hugh McMullen	150.00	60.00	30.00
(47)	Bob Meusel	150.00	60.00	30.00
(48)	Wilcey Moore (Wilcy)	150.00	60.00	30.00
(49)	Ed C. Morgan	150.00	60.00	30.00
(50)	Herb Pennock	250.00	100.00	50.00
(51)	Everett Purdy	150.00	60.00	30.00
(52)	William Regan	150.00	60.00	30.00
(53)	Eppa Rixey	250.00	100.00	50.00
(54)	Charles Root	150.00	60.00	30.00
(55)	Jack Rothrock	150.00	60.00	30.00
(56)	Harold Ruel (Herold)	150.00	60.00	30.00
(57)	Babe Ruth	3750.	1500.	750.00
(58)	Wally Schang	150.00	60.00	30.00
(59)	Joe Sewell	250.00	100.00	50.00
(60)	Luke Sewell	150.00	60.00	30.00
(61)	Joe Shaute	150.00	60.00	30.00
(62)	George Sisler	250.00	100.00	50.00
(63)	Tris Speaker	300.00	120.00	60.00
(64)	Riggs Stephenson	150.00	60.00	30.00
(65)	Jack Tavener	150.00	60.00	30.00
(66)	Al Thomas	150.00	60.00	30.00
(67)	Harold J. Traynor	250.00	100.00	50.00
(68)	George Uhle	150.00	60.00	30.00
(69)	Dazzy Vance	250.00	100.00	50.00
(70)	Cy Williams	150.00	60.00	30.00
(71)	Ken Williams	150.00	60.00	30.00
(72)	Lewis R. Wilson	250.00	100.00	50.00

1929 Star Player Candy

The actual year of issue can only be approximated from the write-ups on the cards' backs. Only two players can be checklisted thus far, though the numbers on the backs would seem to indicate an issue of at least 32. The 1-7/8" x 2-7/8" cards are printed in sepia with wide borders on front and player name below the photo. Unlike the 1928 Star Candy issue, this series has printed and numbered backs.

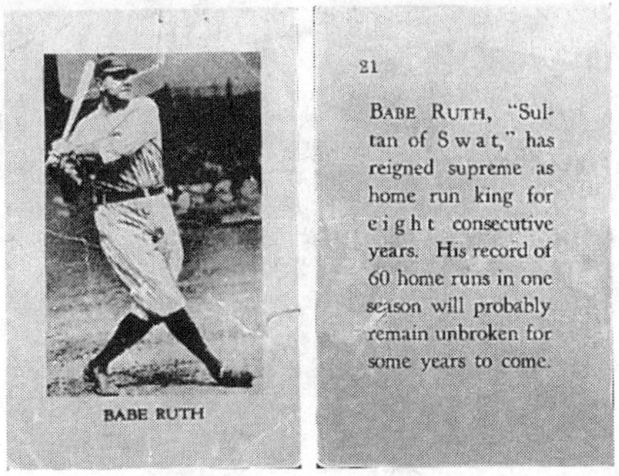
BABE RUTH
21
BABE RUTH, "Sultan of Swat," has reigned supreme as home run king for eight consecutive years. His record of 60 home runs in one season will probably remain unbroken for some years to come.

	NM	EX	VG
Lou Gehrig	3000.	1200.	600.00
Babe Ruth	3750.	1500.	750.00

1920s Stars of the Diamond Notebooks

One of several contemporary series of notebooks, this is in an 8" x 10" top-bound format. At center on the cover is a fancy frame with bats, balls and gloves surrounding a 4" x 5" photo of the player. At top is a large diamond with the series title. Beneath the player photo is his name, team and league.

	NM	EX	VG
Grover Alexander	200.00	100.00	60.00
Burleigh Grimes	200.00	100.00	60.00
Rogers Hornsby	300.00	150.00	90.00
Babe Ruth	600.00	300.00	180.00
George Sisler	200.00	100.00	60.00

1909-16 Max Stein Postcards

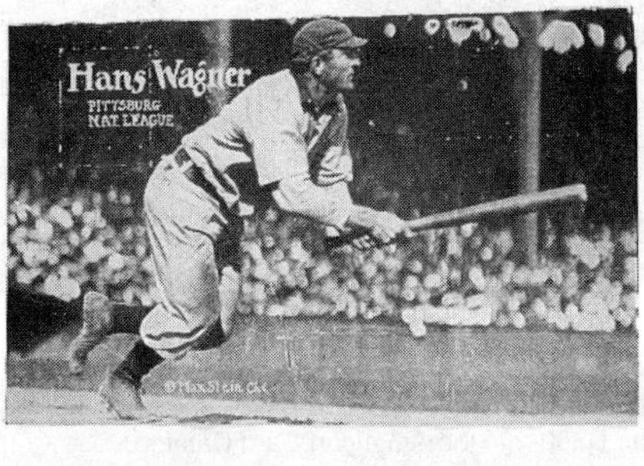
Hans Wagner
PITTSBURG
NAT LEAGUE

Issued over a period of several years these sepia-toned photo postcards depict most of the stars of the day. In standard 3-1/2" x 5-1/2" format they have typical postcard indicia on the back. Some cards have been seen with a "United States Pub." legend on the back. Most of the subjects played in Stein's Chicago location. Besides the baseball players listed here, the series also included "Statesmen, etc., Aeroplanes and Flyers, Fighters, etc.," and, "Dancing Girls," according to advertising found on the back of some cards. Wholesale prices when issued were 35¢ per hundred, $2.75 per thousand.

		NM	EX	VG
Complete Set (26):		7000.	2800.	1400.
Common Player:		150.00	75.00	45.00
(1)	Ping Bodie	150.00	60.00	30.00
(2)	Frank Chance	300.00	120.00	60.00
(3)	Ty Cobb	800.00	320.00	160.00
(4)	Johnny Evers	300.00	120.00	60.00
(5)	Rube Marquard	300.00	120.00	60.00
(6)	Christy Mathewson	500.00	200.00	100.00
(7)	John McGraw	300.00	120.00	60.00
(8)	Chief Meyers	150.00	60.00	30.00
(9)	Marty O'Toole	150.00	60.00	30.00
(10)	Wildfire Schulte	150.00	60.00	30.00
(11)	Tris Speaker	300.00	120.00	60.00
(12)	Jake Stahl	150.00	60.00	30.00
(13)	Jim Thorpe	900.00	360.00	180.00
(14)	Joe Tinker	300.00	120.00	60.00
(15)	Honus Wagner	400.00	160.00	80.00

(16)	Ed Walsh	300.00	120.00	60.00
(17)	Buck Weaver	250.00	100.00	50.00
(18)	Joe Wood	150.00	60.00	30.00
(19)	Heinie Zimmerman	150.00	60.00	30.00
(20)	Chicago Cubs (Jimmy Archer, Roger Bresnahan, Johnny Evers, Mike Hechinger, Tom Needham)	150.00	60.00	30.00
(21)	Chicago Cubs (Bill Clymer, Wilbur Good, Ward Miller, Mike Mitchell, Wildfire Schulte)	150.00	60.00	30.00
(22)	Boston Americans team photo	150.00	60.00	30.00
(23)	1916 Chicago Cubs team photo	150.00	60.00	30.00
(24)	1916 Cincinnati Reds team photo	150.00	60.00	30.00
(25)	New York Nationals team photo	150.00	60.00	30.00
(26)	Johnny Coulon, Jess Willard (boxers)	150.00	60.00	30.00

1941 St. Louis Browns team issue

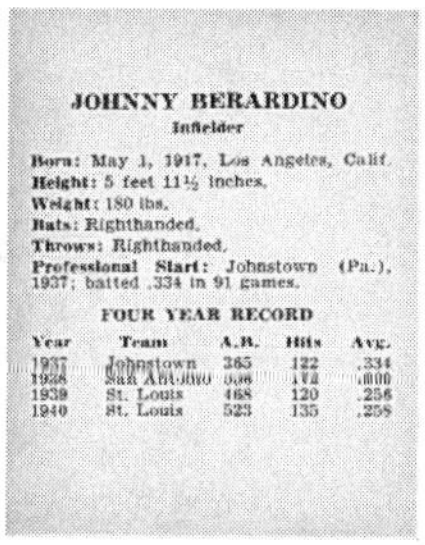
JOHNNY BERARDINO
Infielder
Born: May 1, 1917, Los Angeles, Calif.
Height: 5 feet 11½ inches.
Weight: 180 lbs.
Bats: Righthanded.
Throws: Righthanded.
Professional Start: Johnstown (Pa.), 1937; batted .334 in 91 games.

FOUR YEAR RECORD

Year	Team	A.B.	Hits	Avg.
1937	Johnstown	365	122	.334
1938	San Antonio	[illegible]	[illegible]	[illegible]
1939	St. Louis	468	120	.256
1940	St. Louis	523	135	.258

Measuring 2-1/8" x 2-5/8", this unnumbered boxed set of cards features the St. Louis Browns in black-and-white portrait photos on front. Backs have player name, position and personal and statistical information. There are also cards for coaches and one of the the club's two managers that season (Luke Sewell). As the Browns weren't much of a team in 1941 (or in most seasons for that matter) there are no major stars in the set. The issue was cataloged as W573 in the ACC.

		NM	EX	VG
Complete Set w/box (30):		600.00	300.00	180.00
Common Player:		20.00	10.00	6.00
(1)	Johnny Allen	20.00	10.00	6.00
(2)	Elden Auker (Eldon)	20.00	10.00	6.00
(3)	Donald L Barnes	20.00	10.00	6.00
(4)	Johnny Berardino	35.00	17.50	10.50
(5)	George Caster	20.00	10.00	6.00
(6)	Harlond Benton (Darky) Clift	20.00	10.00	6.00
(7)	Roy J. Cullenbine	20.00	10.00	6.00
(8)	William O. DeWitt	20.00	10.00	6.00
(9)	Roberto Estalella	20.00	10.00	6.00
(10)	Richard Benjamin (Rick) Ferrell	75.00	37.00	22.00
(11)	Dennis W. Galehouse	20.00	10.00	6.00
(12)	Joseph L. Grace	20.00	10.00	6.00
(13)	Frank Grube	20.00	10.00	6.00
(14)	Robert A. Harris	20.00	10.00	6.00
(15)	Donald Henry Heffner	20.00	10.00	6.00
(16)	Fred Hofmann	20.00	10.00	6.00
(17)	Walter Franklin Judnich	20.00	10.00	6.00
(18)	John Henry (Jack) Kramer	20.00	10.00	6.00
(19)	Chester (Chet) Laabs	20.00	10.00	6.00
(20)	John Lucadello	20.00	10.00	6.00
(21)	George Hartley McQuinn	20.00	10.00	6.00
(22)	Robert Cleveland Muncrief, Jr.	20.00	10.00	6.00
(23)	John Niggeling	20.00	10.00	6.00
(24)	Fred Raymond (Fritz) Ostermueller	20.00	10.00	6.00
(25)	James Luther (Luke) Sewell	20.00	10.00	6.00
(26)	Alan Cochran Strange (Cochrane)	20.00	10.00	6.00
(27)	Robert Virgil (Bob) Swift	20.00	10.00	6.00
(28)	James W. (Zack) Taylor	20.00	10.00	6.00
(29)	William Felix (Bill) Trotter	20.00	10.00	6.00
(30)	Presentation card/order form	15.00	7.50	4.50

1952 St. Louis Browns Postcards

This series of player postcards features black-and-white glossy photos on front with a white border. The cards bear no player identification and were evidently intended for use in honoring fan requests for autographs. The 1952 issue can be differentiated from that of 1953 by the absence of a stamp box on back. The unnumbered cards are checklisted here alphabetically and the list may not be complete. Multiple player names indicate known different poses.

		NM	EX	VG
Common Player:		50.00	25.00	15.00
(1)	Tommy Byrne	50.00	25.00	15.00
(3)	Bob Cain	50.00	25.00	15.00
(3)	Bob Cain	50.00	25.00	15.00
(4)	Jim Delsing	50.00	25.00	15.00
(5)	Jim Dyck	50.00	25.00	15.00
(6)	Jim Dyck	50.00	25.00	15.00
(7)	Ned Garver	50.00	25.00	15.00
(8)	Marty Marion	60.00	30.00	18.00
(9)	Satchel Paige	150.00	75.00	45.00
(10)	Duane Pillette	50.00	25.00	15.00
(11)	Jim Rivera	50.00	25.00	15.00
(12)	Bill Veeck	75.00	37.00	22.00
(13)	Bobby Young	50.00	25.00	15.00

1953 St. Louis Browns Postcards

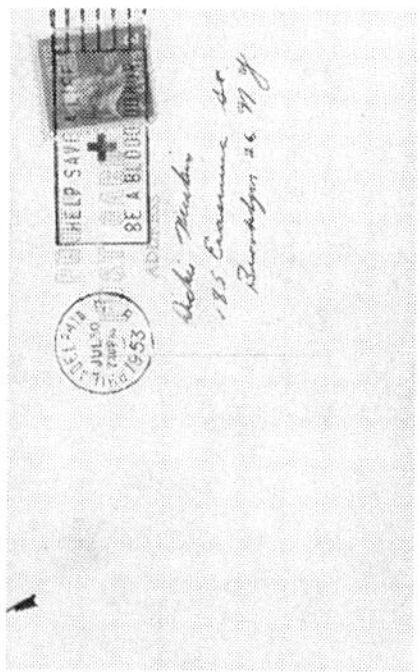

This series of player postcards from the team's final year in St. Louis features black-and-white glossy photos on front with a white border. The cards bear no player identification and were evidently intended for use in honoring fan requests for autographs. The 1953 issue can be differentiated from that of 1952 by the presence of a stamp box on back identifying the issuer as Deorite Peerless. The unnumbered cards are checklisted here alphabetically and the list may not be complete. Multiple player names indicate known different poses.

		NM	EX	VG
Common Player:		50.00	25.00	15.00
(1)	Mike Blyzka	50.00	25.00	15.00
(2)	Harry Brecheen	50.00	25.00	15.00
(3)	Jim Dyck	50.00	25.00	15.00
(4)	Bobo Holloman	50.00	25.00	15.00
(5)	Billy Hunter	50.00	25.00	15.00
(6)	Dick Kokos	50.00	25.00	15.00
(7)	Dick Kryhoski	50.00	25.00	15.00
(8)	Don Larsen	75.00	37.50	22.00
(9)	Don Lenhardt	50.00	25.00	15.00
(10)	Dick Littlefield	50.00	25.00	15.00
(11)	Satchel Paige	150.00	75.00	45.00
(12)	Satchel Paige	150.00	75.00	45.00
(13)	Bob Scheffing	50.00	25.00	15.00
(14)	Marlin Stuart	50.00	25.00	15.00
(15)	Virgil Trucks	65.00	32.00	19.50
(16)	Vic Wertz	50.00	25.00	15.00

1941 St. Louis Cardinals team issue

A companion set to W753, this time featuring the National League team in St. Louis. Cards measure 2-1/8" x 2-5/8" and are unnumbered. Like the Browns set, this issue features black-and-white portrait photos on front and the individual's name, position and personal and statistical information on back. One interesting addition to the set is a card of Branch Rickey which, coupled with cards of Enos Slaughter and Johnny Mize, gives the set a bit more appeal than the Browns set. ACC designation is W754.

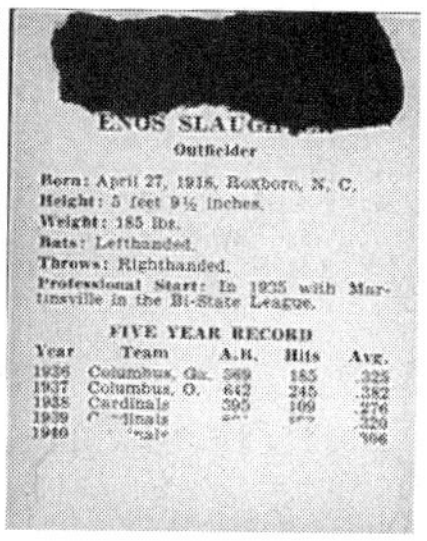
ENOS SLAUG
Outfielder
Born: April 27, 1916, Roxboro, N. C.
Height: 5 feet 9½ inches.
Weight: 185 lbs.
Bats: Lefthanded.
Throws: Righthanded.
Professional Start: In 1935 with Martinsville in the Bi-State League.

FIVE YEAR RECORD

Year	Team	A.B.	Hits	Avg.
1936	Columbus, Ga.	569	185	.325
1937	Columbus, O.	642	245	.382
1938	Cardinals	395	109	.276
1939	[illegible]	[illegible]	[illegible]	.320
1940	[illegible]	[illegible]	[illegible]	[illegible]

		NM	EX	VG
Complete Set (30):		600.00	300.00	180.00
Common Player:		20.00	10.00	6.00
(1)	Sam Breadon	20.00	10.00	6.00
(2)	James Brown	20.00	10.00	6.00
(3)	Morton Cooper	20.00	10.00	6.00
(4)	William Walker Cooper	20.00	10.00	6.00
(5)	Estel Crabtree	20.00	10.00	6.00
(6)	Frank Crespi	20.00	10.00	6.00
(7)	William Crouch	20.00	10.00	6.00
(8)	Miguel Mike Gonzalez	30.00	15.00	9.00
(9)	Harry Gumbert	20.00	10.00	6.00
(10)	John Hopp	20.00	10.00	6.00
(11)	Ira Hutchinson	20.00	10.00	6.00
(12)	Howard Krist	20.00	10.00	6.00
(13)	Edward E. Lake	20.00	10.00	6.00
(14)	Hubert Max Lanier	20.00	10.00	6.00
(15)	Gus Mancuso	20.00	10.00	6.00
(16)	Martin Marion	30.00	15.00	9.00
(17)	Steve Mesner	20.00	10.00	6.00
(18)	John Mize	75.00	37.00	22.00
(19)	Capt. Terry Moore	24.00	12.00	7.25
(20)	Sam Nahem	20.00	10.00	6.00
(21)	Don Padgett	20.00	10.00	6.00
(22)	Branch Rickey	75.00	37.00	22.00
(23)	Clyde Shoun	20.00	10.00	6.00
(24)	Enos Slaughter	75.00	37.00	22.00
(25)	William H. (Billy) Southworth	20.00	10.00	6.00
(26)	Herman Coaker Triplett	20.00	10.00	6.00
(27)	Clyde Buzzy Wares	20.00	10.00	6.00
(28)	Lon Warneke	20.00	10.00	6.00
(29)	Ernest White	20.00	10.00	6.00
(30)	Presentation card/order form	15.00	7.50	4.50

1970 St. Louis Cardinals team issue

Issued in packs of 12 and possibly over a period of more than one year, these 4-1/4" x 7" player pictures are printed in black-and-white on heavy textured paper. The poses are surrounded by white borders with a facsimile autograph in the wider bottom border. The unnumbered pictures are listed here alphabetically and there are probably other players or photo variations to be reported.

		NM	EX	VG
Common Player:		2.00	1.00	.60
(1)	Richie Allen (uniform # shows)	6.00	3.00	1.75
(2)	Richie Allen (uniform # doesn't show)	6.00	3.00	1.75
(3)	Jim Beauchamp	2.00	1.00	.60
(4)	Lou Brock	6.00	3.00	1.75
(5)	Vern Benson	2.00	1.00	.60
(6)	Sal Campisi	2.00	1.00	.60
(7)	Jose Cardenal	2.00	1.00	.60
(8)	Bob Chlupsa	2.00	1.00	.60
(9)	Ed Crosby	2.00	1.00	.60
(10)	George Culver	2.00	1.00	.60
(11)	Vic Davalillo	2.00	1.00	.60
(12)	Bob Gibson	7.50	3.75	2.25
(13)	Santiago Guzman	2.00	1.00	.60
(14)	Joe Hague	2.00	1.00	.60
(15)	Julian Javier (batting)	2.00	1.00	.60
(16)	Julian Javier (portrait)	2.00	1.00	.60

(17)	Al Hrabosky	2.00	1.00	.60
(18)	Leron Lee (uniform # shows)	2.00	1.00	.60
(19)	Leron Lee (uniform # doesn't show)	2.00	1.00	.60
(20)	Frank Linzy	2.00	1.00	.60
(21)	Dal Maxvill	2.00	1.00	.60
(22)	Milt Ramirez	2.00	1.00	.60
(23)	Jerry Reuss	2.00	1.00	.60
(24)	Cookie Rojas	2.00	1.00	.60
(25)	Red Schoendienst	6.00	3.00	1.75
(26)	Mike Shannon	4.50	2.25	1.25
(27)	Ted Simmons	3.00	1.50	.90
(28)	Dick Sisler	2.00	1.00	.60
(29)	Carl Taylor (kneeling)	2.00	1.00	.60
(30)	Carl Taylor (portrait)	2.00	1.00	.60
(31)	Joe Torre	4.00	2.00	1.25
(32)	Bart Zeller (batting)	2.00	1.00	.60
(33)	Bart Zeller (portrait)	2.00	1.00	.60

1979-80 Story of America

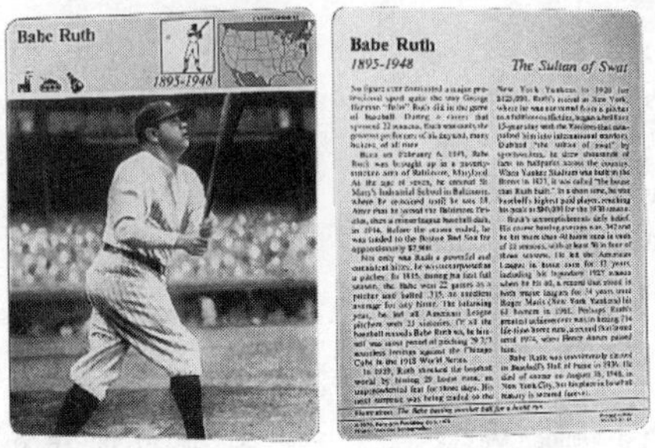

In the same size (4-3/4" x 6-1/4") and style as the better-known Sportscaster cards, these American history cards were also sold by mail in series. A number of sports topics were included in the issue. As with the Sportscaster cards, those issued in the later series are scarcer than the early releases. Only the baseball-related cards are checklisted here.

	NM	EX	VG
Common Card:	.25	.13	.08
01-16 Babe Ruth	25.00	12.50	7.50
36-08 Black Sox Scandal (1919 White Sox team photo)	25.00	12.50	7.50
46-22 Jackie Robinson	15.00	7.50	4.50
49-10 Hank Aaron	20.00	10.00	6.00

1916 Successful Farming

Best known for its use as a promotional medium for The Sporting News, this 200-card set can be found with ads on the back for several local and regional businesses. Among them is Successful Farming magazine of Des Moines, Iowa. While type card collectors and superstar collectors may pay a premium for individual cards with the magazine's advertising, prices will generally parallel the 1916 Sporting News values. Cards measure 1-5/8" x 3" and are printed in black-and-white.

	NM	EX	VG
Complete Set (200):	17500.	8500.	5000.
Common Player:	40.00	20.00	12.00

(See 1916 Sporting News for checklist and value information.)

1962 Sugardale Weiners

The Sugardale Meats set of black and white cards measure 5-1/8" x 3-3/4". The 22-card set includes 18 Cleveland Indians and four Pittsburgh Pirates players. The Indians cards are numbered from 1-19 with card number 6 not issued. The Pirates cards are lettered from A to D. The card fronts contain a relatively small player photo, with biographical information and Sugardale logo. The backs are printed in red and offer playing tips and another company logo. Card number 10 (Bob Nieman) is considerably more scarce than other cards in the set.

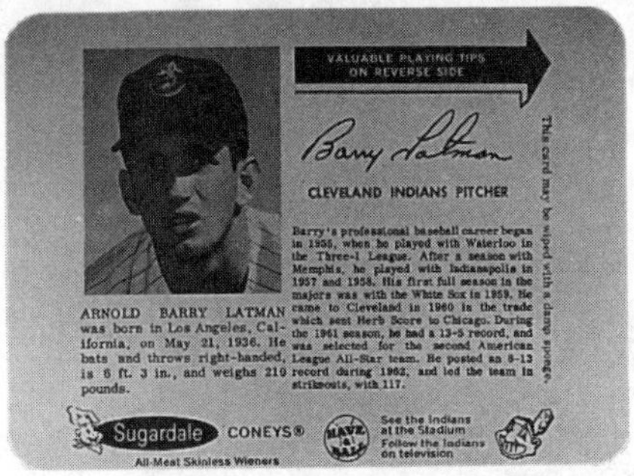

		NM	EX	VG
Complete Set (22):		2100.	1050.	625.00
Common Player:		50.00	25.00	15.00
A	Dick Groat	85.00	42.00	25.00
B	Roberto Clemente	900.00	450.00	270.00
C	Don Hoak	70.00	35.00	21.00
D	Dick Stuart	70.00	35.00	21.00
1	Barry Latman	50.00	25.00	15.00
2	Gary Bell	55.00	27.00	16.50
3	Dick Donovan	50.00	25.00	15.00
4	Frank Funk	50.00	25.00	15.00
5	Jim Perry	60.00	30.00	18.00
6	Not issued			
7	Johnny Romano	50.00	25.00	15.00
8	Ty Cline	50.00	25.00	15.00
9	Tito Francona	50.00	25.00	15.00
10	Bob Nieman	375.00	187.00	112.00
11	Willie Kirkland	50.00	25.00	15.00
12	Woodie Held	50.00	25.00	15.00
13	Jerry Kindall	50.00	25.00	15.00
14	Bubba Phillips	50.00	25.00	15.00
15	Mel Harder	50.00	25.00	15.00
16	Salty Parker	50.00	25.00	15.00
17	Ray Katt	50.00	25.00	15.00
18	Mel McGaha	50.00	25.00	15.00
19	Pedro Ramos	50.00	25.00	15.00

1963 Sugardale Weiners

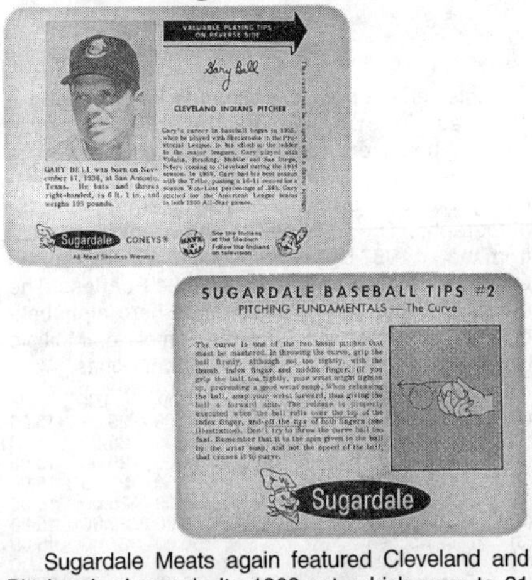

Sugardale Meats again featured Cleveland and Pittsburgh players in its 1963 set, which grew to 31 cards. The black and white cards again measure 5-1/8" x 3-3/4", and consist of 28 Indians and five Pirates players. Card formats are virtually identical to the 1962 cards, with the only real difference being the information included in the player biographies. The cards are numbered 1-38, with numbers 6, 21, 22 and 29-32 not issued. Cards for Bob Skinner (#35) and Jim Perry (#5) are scarce as these two players were traded during the season and their cards withdrawn from distribution. The red card backs again offer playing tips.

		NM	EX	VG
Complete Set (31):		1800.	900.00	550.00
Common Player:		50.00	25.00	15.00
A	Don Cardwell	50.00	25.00	15.00
B	Robert R. Skinner	200.00	100.00	60.00
C	Donald B. Schwall	50.00	25.00	15.00
D	Jim Pagliaroni	50.00	25.00	15.00
E	Dick Schofield	55.00	27.00	16.50
1	Barry Latman	50.00	25.00	15.00
2	Gary Bell	55.00	27.00	16.50
3	Dick Donovan	50.00	25.00	15.00
4	Joe Adcock	65.00	32.00	19.50
5	Jim Perry	200.00	100.00	60.00
6	Not issued			
7	Johnny Romano	50.00	25.00	15.00
8	Mike de la Hoz	50.00	25.00	15.00
9	Tito Francona	50.00	25.00	15.00
10	Gene Green	50.00	25.00	15.00
11	Willie Kirkland	50.00	25.00	15.00
12	Woodie Held	50.00	25.00	15.00
13	Jerry Kindall	50.00	25.00	15.00
14	Max Alvis	50.00	25.00	15.00
15	Mel Harder	55.00	27.00	16.50
16	George Strickland	50.00	25.00	15.00
17	Elmer Valo	50.00	25.00	15.00
18	Birdie Tebbetts	50.00	25.00	15.00
19	Pedro Ramos	50.00	25.00	15.00
20	Al Luplow	50.00	25.00	15.00
21	Not issued			
22	Not issued			
23	Jim Grant	55.00	27.00	16.50
24	Victor Davalillo	50.00	25.00	15.00
25	Jerry Walker	50.00	25.00	15.00
26	Sam McDowell	65.00	32.00	19.50
27	Fred Whitfield	50.00	25.00	15.00
28	Jack Kralick	50.00	25.00	15.00
29	Not issued			
30	Not issued			
31	Not issued			
32	Not issued			
33	Bob Allen	50.00	25.00	15.00

1974 Sun-Glo Pop Al Kaline

This 2-1/4" x 4-1/2" card was issued as an attachment to bottles of soda pop. The blank-back card features a modishly dressed portrait of the former Tigers great and his endorsement for the soda. Cards are printed in black on various brightly colored backgrounds.

	NM	EX	VG
Al Kaline	6.00	3.00	1.75

1969 Sunoco Cubs/Brewers Pins

Fans in Southern Wisconsin and Northern Illinois could acquire 1-1/8" lithographed steel baseball player pins of the Cubs and Brewers at participating Sunoco gas stations. The blue-and-white (Cubs) or red-and-white (Brewers) pins have black-and-white player portrait photos at center on which cap logos have been removed. The Brewers pins are somewhat scarcer than those of the Cubs.

	NM	EX	VG
Complete Set (18):	90.00	45.00	27.00
Common Player:	3.00	2.25	1.25
Chicago Cubs team set:	45.00	22.00	13.50

(1) Ernie Banks	12.00	6.00	3.50
(2) Glenn Beckert	3.00	2.25	1.25
(3) Jim Hickman	3.00	2.25	1.25
(4) Randy Hundley	4.50	2.25	1.25
(5) Ferguson Jenkins	6.00	3.00	1.75
(6) Don Kessinger	4.50	2.25	1.25
(7) Joe Pepitone	4.50	2.25	1.25
(8) Ron Santo	5.00	2.50	1.50
(9) Billy Williams	6.00	3.00	1.75
Milwaukee Brewers team set:	45.00	22.00	13.50
(1) Tommy Harper	5.00	2.50	1.50
(2) Mike Hegan	5.00	2.50	1.50
(3) Lew Krausse	5.00	2.50	1.50
(4) Ted Kubiak	5.00	2.50	1.50
(5) Marty Pattin	5.00	2.50	1.50
(6) Phil Roof	5.00	2.50	1.50
(7) Ken Sanders	5.00	2.50	1.50
(8) Ted Savage	5.00	2.50	1.50
(9) Danny Walton	5.00	2.50	1.50

1931 Sun Pictures Photo Kits

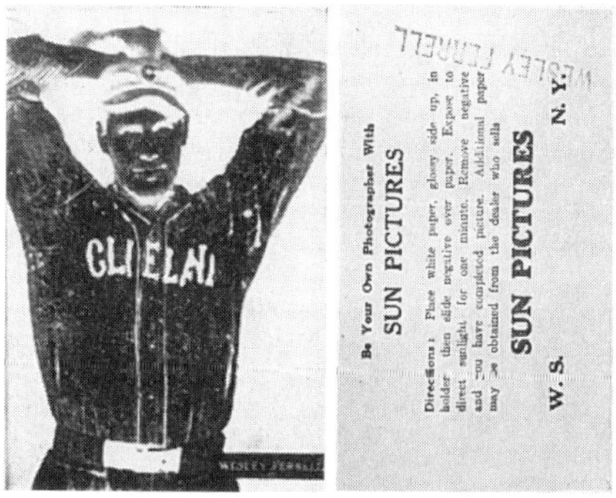

One of several contemporary kits for do-it-yourself production of photos, this issue was produced in New York City by a firm identified only as "W.S." A complete outfit consists of a 4-1/4" x 2-1/2" pink or kraft paper envelope with the name of the subject inside rubber-stamped on one end, a film negative, a piece of photo paper and a stand for producing/displaying the photo. The negative and resulting print measure 2-5/16" x 3-1/4". Listed in the American Card Catalog as W626, it is certain there are more sport and non-sport subjects in the issue. Prices shown are for complete kits; individual pieces would be pro-rated, with the negative the most valuable component.

	NM	EX	VG
Common Player Kit:	125.00	62.00	37.50
(1) Jack Dempsey (boxer)	200.00	100.00	60.00
(2) George Earnshaw	125.00	62.00	38.00
(3) Wesley Ferrell	125.00	62.00	37.00
(4) Lefty Grove	250.00	125.00	75.00
(5) Leo Hartnett	225.00	112.00	67.00
(6) Tony Lazzeri	250.00	125.00	75.00
(7) Tom Loughran (boxer)	100.00	50.00	30.00
(8) Jimmy McLarnen (boxer)	100.00	50.00	30.00
(9) Herb Pennock	225.00	112.00	67.00
(10) Babe Ruth	2400.	1200.	725.00
(11) Al Simmons	225.00	112.00	67.00
(12) Dazzy Vance	225.00	112.00	67.00
(13) Hack Wilson	225.00	112.00	67.00

1980 Superstar

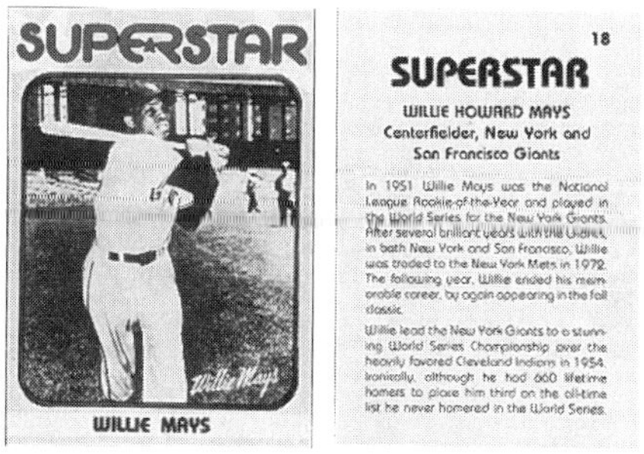

This collectors issue, probably produced by Card Collectors Closet in Springfield, Mass., included up to five cards each of the most famous former players. The 2-1/2" x 3-1/2" cards have black-and-white photos on front, with yellow, white and blue graphics. Backs are in black-and-white with career narrative. The set sold originally for $3.50.

	NM	EX	VG
Complete Set (45):	22.00	11.00	6.50
Common Player:	.50	.25	.15
1 Babe Ruth	1.00	.50	.30
2 Roberto Clemente	1.00	.50	.30
3 Roberto Clemente	1.00	.50	.30
4 Roberto Clemente	1.00	.50	.30
5 Lou Gehrig, Joe DiMaggio	.50	.25	.15
6 Mickey Mantle, Roger Maris	1.50	.70	.45
7 Roger Maris, Yogi Berra, Mickey Mantle	1.00	.50	.30
8 Whitey Ford, Sandy Koufax	.50	.25	.15
9 Babe Ruth	1.00	.50	.30
10 Roger Maris, Mickey Mantle	1.50	.70	.45
11 Ted Williams, Stan Musial, Willie Mays	.50	.25	.15
12 Mickey Mantle, Hank Aaron	1.25	.60	.40
13 Sandy Koufax	.50	.25	.15
14 Sandy Koufax	.50	.25	.15
15 Thurman Munson	.50	.25	.15
16 Sandy Koufax	.50	.25	.15
17 Sandy Koufax	.50	.25	.15
18 Willie Mays	.50	.25	.15
19 Willie Mays	.50	.25	.15
20 Willie Mays	.50	.25	.15
21 Willie Mays	.50	.25	.15
22 Ted Williams	.50	.25	.15
23 Ted Williams	.50	.25	.15
24 Ted Williams	.50	.25	.15
25 Ted Williams	.50	.25	.15
26 Lou Gehrig	.50	.25	.15
27 Lou Gehrig	.50	.25	.15
28 Lou Gehrig	.50	.25	.15
29 Lou Gehrig	.50	.25	.15
30 Mickey Mantle	2.00	1.00	.60
31 Mickey Mantle	2.00	1.00	.60
32 Mickey Mantle	2.00	1.00	.60
33 Mickey Mantle	2.00	1.00	.60
34 Hank Aaron	.50	.25	.15
35 Joe DiMaggio	.75	.40	.25
36 Joe DiMaggio	.75	.40	.25
37 Joe DiMaggio	.75	.40	.25
38 Joe DiMaggio	.75	.40	.25
39 Roberto Clemente	1.00	.50	.30
40 Babe Ruth	1.00	.50	.30
41 Babe Ruth	1.00	.50	.30
42 Babe Ruth	1.00	.50	.30
43 Hank Aaron	.50	.25	.15
44 Hank Aaron	.50	.25	.15
45 Hank Aaron	.50	.25	.15

1982 Superstar

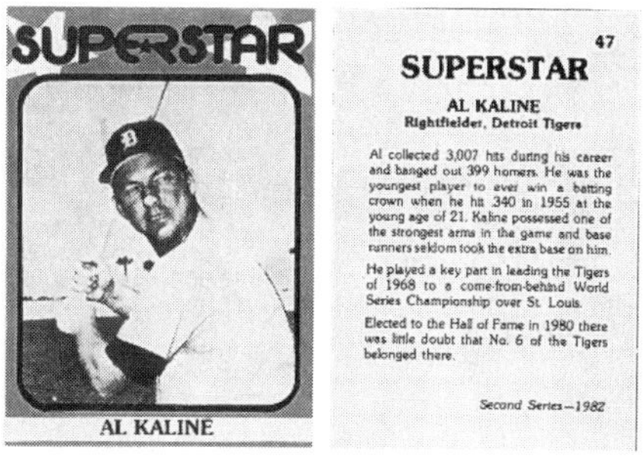

A second series of Superstar collector cards was produced in 1982. Similar in format to the 1980 issue, they also feature black-and-white photos. Surrounding graphics on the second series are in red, white and blue. Backs are numbered from 45-90 in continuation of the first series and contain career narratives. Many players are again featured on multiple cards, and the second series contains sports stars other than baseball players. Issue price was again $3.50.

	MT	NM	EX
Complete Set (45):	25.00	18.50	10.00
Common Player:	.50	.40	.20
46 Duke Snider	.50	.40	.20
47 Al Kaline	.50	.40	.20
48 Stan Musial	.50	.40	.20
49 Frank Robinson	.50	.40	.20
50 Jim Brown	.75	.60	.30
51 Bobby Orr	.75	.60	.30
52 Roger Staubach	.50	.40	.20
53 Honus Wagner	.50	.40	.20
54 Willie Mays	.50	.40	.20
55 Roy Campanella	.50	.40	.20
56 Mickey Mantle	2.00	1.50	.80
57 Hank Aaron	.50	.40	.20
58 Ernie Banks	.50	.40	.20
59 Babe Ruth, Lou Gehrig	1.00	.70	.40
60 Ted Williams	.50	.40	.20
61 Babe Ruth	1.00	.70	.40
62 Lou Gehrig	.50	.40	.20
63 Sandy Koufax	.50	.40	.20
64 Fran Tarkenton	.50	.40	.20
65 Gordie Howe	.75	.60	.30
66 Roberto Clemente	1.00	.70	.40
67 Ty Cobb	.50	.40	.20
68 Lou Brock	.50	.40	.20
69 Joe Namath	.50	.40	.20
70 O.J. Simpson	.75	.60	.30
71 Whitey Ford	.50	.40	.20
72 Jackie Robinson	.75	.60	.30
73 Bill Russell	.75	.60	.30
74 Johnny Unitas	.50	.40	.20
75 Bobby Hull	.75	.60	.30
76 Bob Cousy	.75	.60	.30
77 Walter Johnson	.50	.40	.20
78 Satchel Paige	.65	.50	.25
79 Joe DiMaggio	.75	.60	.30
80 Yogi Berra	.50	.40	.20
81 Jerry West	.75	.60	.30
82 Rod Gilbert	.75	.60	.30
83 Sadaharu Oh	.50	.40	.20
84 Wilt Chamberlain	.75	.60	.30
85 Frank Gifford	.50	.40	.20
86 Casey Stengel	.50	.40	.20
87 Eddie Mathews	.50	.40	.20
88 Hank Aaron, Sandy Koufax	.50	.40	.20
89 Ted Williams, Mickey Mantle	1.00	.70	.40
90 Casey Stengel, Mickey Mantle	.90	.70	.35

1970 Super Valu Minnesota Twins

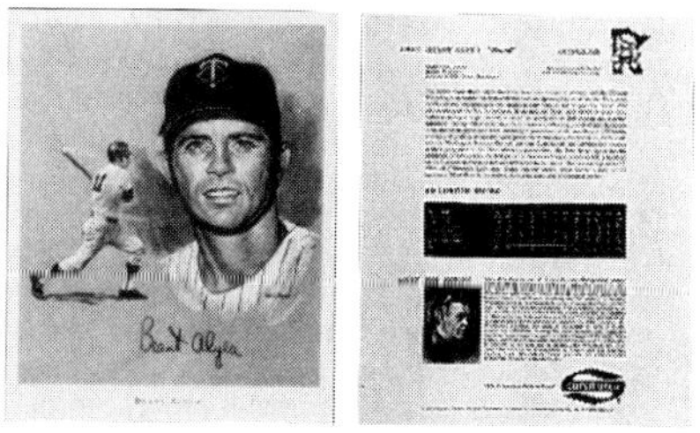

One of many Minnesota Twins regional issues from the team's first decade, this set of player portraits was painted by noted celebrity artist John Wheeldon. Individual player pictures were given away at Super Valu grocery stores. The premiums feature large portraits and smaller action pictures, painted in pastels, against a pastel background. A facsimile autograph is printed below the pictures and the player's name is printed in the bottom border. At 7-3/4" x 9-3/8", the Twins portraits are somewhat smaller than similar contemporary issues. Backs are printed in black-and-white and include a self-portrait and biography of the artist. Player information includes biographical bits, a lengthy career summary and complete major and minor league stats. Team and sponsor logo are also included on the unnumbered card backs. The set is checklisted here alphabetically.

	NM	EX	VG
Complete Set (12):	135.00	65.00	41.00
Common Player:	8.00	4.00	2.50
(1) Brant Alyea	8.00	4.00	2.50
(2) Leo Cardenas	8.00	4.00	2.50
(3) Rod Carew	24.00	12.00	7.25
(4) Jim Kaat	12.00	6.00	3.50
(5) Harmon Killebrew	24.00	12.00	7.25
(6) George Mitterwald	8.00	4.00	2.50
(7) Tony Oliva	12.00	6.00	3.50
(8) Ron Perranoski	8.00	4.00	2.50
(9) Jim Perry	8.00	4.00	2.50
(10) Rich Reese	8.00	4.00	2.50
(11) Luis Tiant	10.00	5.00	3.00
(12) Cesar Tovar	8.00	4.00	2.50

1909-11 Sweet Caporal

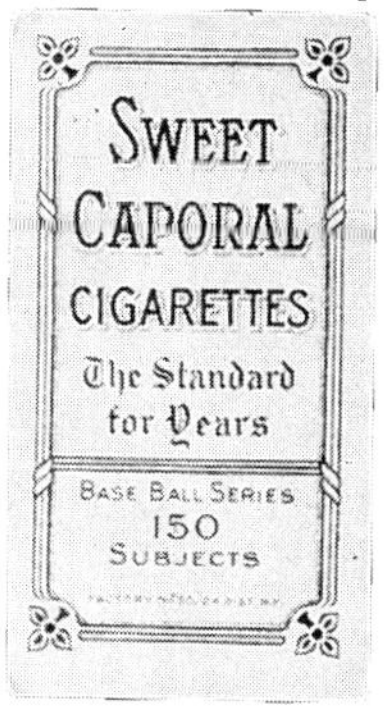

(See T205, T206)

1909-12 Sweet Caporal Domino Discs (PX7)

Domino Discs, distributed by Sweet Caporal Cigarettes from 1909 to 1912, are among the more obscure 20th Century tobacco issues. Although the disc set contains many of the same players - some even pictured in the same poses - as the later Sweet Caporal pin set, the discs have always lagged behind the pins in collector appeal. The Domino Discs, so called because each disc has a large, white domino printed on the back, measure approximately 1-1/8" in diameter and are made of thin cardboard surrounded by a metal rim. The fronts of the discs contain a player portrait set against a background of either red, green or blue. The words "Sweet Caporal Cigarettes" appear on the front along with the player's last name and team. There are 129 different major leaguers featured in the set. Each player can be found with two picture variations involving uniform or cap details, or just the size of the portrait. Also known to exist as part of the set is a disc which pictures a generic player and contains the words "Home Team" against a red background on one side and "Visiting Team" with a green background on the reverse. Because each of the players can theoretically be found in two pictures, with three different background colors and with varying numbers of dots on the dominoes, there is almost an impossible number of variations available. Collectors, however, generally collect the discs without regard to background color or domino arrangement. The Domino Disc set was assigned the designation PX7 in the American Card Catalog.

		NM	EX	VG
Complete Set (129):		8000.	4000.	2400.
Common Player:		45.00	22.00	13.00
(1)	Red Ames	45.00	22.00	13.00
(2)	Jimmy Archer	45.00	22.00	13.00
(3)	Jimmy Austin	45.00	22.00	13.00
(4)	Home Run Baker	110.00	55.00	33.00
(5)	Neal Ball	45.00	22.00	13.00
(6)	Cy Barger	45.00	22.00	13.00
(7)	Jack Barry	45.00	22.00	13.00
(8)	Johnny Bates	45.00	22.00	13.00
(9)	Beals Becker	45.00	22.00	13.00
(10)	George Bell	45.00	22.00	13.00
(11)	Chief Bender	110.00	55.00	33.00
(12)	Bill Bergen	45.00	22.00	13.00
(13)	Bob Bescher	45.00	22.00	13.00
(14)	Joe Birmingham	45.00	22.00	13.00
(15)	Roger Bresnahan	110.00	55.00	33.00
(16)	Al Bridwell	45.00	22.00	13.00
(17)	Mordecai Brown	110.00	55.00	33.00
(18)	Bobby Byrne	45.00	22.00	13.00
(19)	Nixey Callahan	45.00	22.00	13.00
(20)	Howie Camnitz	45.00	22.00	13.00
(21)	Bill Carrigan	45.00	22.00	13.00
(22)	Frank Chance	110.00	55.00	33.00
(23)	Hal Chase	55.00	27.00	16.50
(24)	Ed Cicotte	45.00	22.00	13.00
(25)	Fred Clarke	110.00	55.00	33.00
(26a)	Ty Cobb ("D" on cap)	550.00	275.00	165.00
(26b)	Ty Cobb (no "D" on cap)	550.00	275.00	165.00
(27)	Eddie Collins	110.00	55.00	33.00
(28)	Doc Crandall	45.00	22.00	13.00
(29)	Birdie Cree	45.00	22.00	13.00
(30)	Bill Dahlen	45.00	22.00	13.00
(31)	Jim Delahanty	45.00	22.00	13.00
(32)	Art Devlin	45.00	22.00	13.00
(33)	Josh Devore	45.00	22.00	13.00
(34)	Red Dooin	45.00	22.00	13.00
(35)	Mickey Doolan	45.00	22.00	13.00
(36)	Patsy Dougherty	45.00	22.00	13.00
(37)	Tom Downey	45.00	22.00	13.00
(38)	Larry Doyle	45.00	22.00	13.00
(39)	Louis Drucke	45.00	22.00	13.00
(40)	Clyde Engle	45.00	22.00	13.00
(41)	Tex Erwin	45.00	22.00	13.00
(42)	Steve Evans	45.00	22.00	13.00
(43)	Johnny Evers	110.00	55.00	33.00
(44)	Cecil Ferguson	45.00	22.00	13.00
(45)	Russ Ford	45.00	22.00	13.00
(46)	Art Fromme	45.00	22.00	13.00
(47)	Harry Gaspar	45.00	22.00	13.00
(48)	George Gibson	45.00	22.00	13.00
(49)	Eddie Grant	45.00	22.00	13.00
(50)	Clark Griffith	110.00	55.00	33.00
(51)	Bob Groom	45.00	22.00	13.00
(52)	Bob Harmon	45.00	22.00	13.00
(53)	Topsy Hartsel	45.00	22.00	13.00
(54)	Arnold Hauser	45.00	22.00	13.00
(55)	Dick Hoblitzell	45.00	22.00	13.00
(56)	Danny Hoffman	45.00	22.00	13.00
(57)	Miller Huggins	110.00	55.00	33.00
(58)	John Hummel	45.00	22.00	13.00
(59)	Hugh Jennings	110.00	55.00	33.00
(60)	Walter Johnson	225.00	110.00	67.00
(61)	Ed Karger	45.00	22.00	13.00
(62a)	Jack Knight (Yankees)	45.00	22.00	13.00
(62b)	Jack Knight (Senators)	45.00	22.00	13.00
(63)	Ed Konetchy	45.00	22.00	13.00
(64)	Harry Krause	45.00	22.00	13.00
(65)	Frank LaPorte	45.00	22.00	13.00
(66)	Nap Lajoie	110.00	55.00	33.00
(67)	Tommy Leach	45.00	22.00	13.00
(68)	Sam Leever	45.00	22.00	13.00
(69)	Lefty Leifield	45.00	22.00	13.00
(70)	Paddy Livingston	45.00	22.00	13.00
(71)	Hans Lobert	45.00	22.00	13.00
(72)	Harry Lord	45.00	22.00	13.00
(73)	Nick Maddox	45.00	22.00	13.00
(74)	Sherry Magee	45.00	22.00	13.00
(75)	Rube Marquard	110.00	55.00	33.00
(76)	Christy Mathewson	225.00	110.00	67.00
(77)	Al Mattern	45.00	22.00	13.00
(78)	George McBride	45.00	22.00	13.00
(79)	John McGraw	110.00	55.00	33.00
(80)	Harry McIntire	45.00	22.00	13.00
(81)	Matty McIntyre	45.00	22.00	13.00
(82)	Larry McLean	45.00	22.00	13.00
(83)	Fred Merkle	45.00	22.00	13.00
(84)	Chief Meyers	45.00	22.00	13.00
(85)	Clyde Milan	45.00	22.00	13.00
(86)	Dots Miller	45.00	22.00	13.00
(87)	Mike Mitchell	45.00	22.00	13.00
(88a)	Pat Moran (Cubs)	45.00	22.00	13.00
(88b)	Pat Moran (Phillies)	45.00	22.00	13.00
(89)	George Mullen (Mullin)	45.00	22.00	13.00
(90)	Danny Murphy	45.00	22.00	13.00
(91)	Red Murray	45.00	22.00	13.00
(92)	Tom Needham	45.00	22.00	13.00
(93)	Rebel Oakes	45.00	22.00	13.00
(94)	Rube Oldring	45.00	22.00	13.00
(95)	Fred Parent	45.00	22.00	13.00
(96)	Dode Paskert	45.00	22.00	13.00
(97)	Barney Pelty	45.00	22.00	13.00
(98)	Eddie Phelps	45.00	22.00	13.00
(99)	Deacon Phillippe	45.00	22.00	13.00
(100)	Jack Quinn	45.00	22.00	13.00
(101)	Ed Reulbach	45.00	22.00	13.00
(102)	Lew Richie	45.00	22.00	13.00
(103)	Jack Rowan	45.00	22.00	13.00
(104)	Nap Rucker	45.00	22.00	13.00
(105a)	Doc Scanlon (Scanlan) (Superbas)	45.00	22.00	13.00
(105b)	Doc Scanlon (Scanlan) (Phillies)	45.00	22.00	13.00
(106)	Germany Schaefer	45.00	22.00	13.00
(107)	Boss Schmidt	45.00	22.00	13.00
(108)	Wildfire Schulte	45.00	22.00	13.00
(109)	Jimmy Sheckard	45.00	22.00	13.00
(110)	Hap Smith	45.00	22.00	13.00
(111)	Tris Speaker	110.00	55.00	33.00
(112)	Harry Stovall	45.00	22.00	13.00
(113a)	Gabby Street (Senators)	45.00	22.00	13.00
(113b)	Gabby Street (Yankees)	45.00	22.00	13.00
(114)	George Suggs	45.00	22.00	13.00
(115)	Ira Thomas	45.00	22.00	13.00
(116)	Joe Tinker	110.00	55.00	33.00
(117)	John Titus	45.00	22.00	13.00
(118)	Terry Turner	45.00	22.00	13.00
(119)	Heinie Wagner	45.00	22.00	13.00
(120)	Bobby Wallace	110.00	55.00	33.00
(121)	Ed Walsh	110.00	55.00	33.00
(122)	Jack Warhop	45.00	22.00	13.00
(123)	Zach Wheat	110.00	55.00	33.00
(124)	Doc White	45.00	22.00	13.00
(125a)	Art Wilson (dark cap, Pirates)	45.00	22.00	13.00
(125b)	Art Wilson (dark cap, Giants)	45.00	22.00	13.00
(126a)	Owen Wilson (white cap, Giants)	45.00	22.00	13.00
(126b)	Owen Wilson (white cap, Pirates)	45.00	22.00	13.00
(127)	Hooks Wiltse	45.00	22.00	13.00
(128)	Harry Wolter	45.00	22.00	13.00
(129)	Cy Young	225.00	110.00	67.00

1910-12 Sweet Caporal Pins (P2)

Expanding its premiums to include more than just trading cards, the American Tobacco Co. issued a series of baseball pins circa 1910-12. The sepia-colored pins measure 7/8" in diameter. The set includes 152 different players, but because of numerous "large letter" and "small letter" variations, collectors generally consider the set complete at 205 different pins. Fifty of the players are pictured on a second pin that usually displays the same photo but has the player's name and team designation printed in larger letters. Three players (Bresnahan, Mullin and Wallace) have three pins each. It is now generally accepted that there are 153 pins with "small letters" and another 52 "large letter" variations in a complete set. Research among advanced collectors has shown that 19 of the pins, including six of the "large letter" variations, are considered more difficult to find. The back of each pin has a variously colored paper insert advertising Sweet Caporal Cigarettes. The red backings, issued only with the "large letter" pins, are generally less common. The Sweet Caporal pins are closely related to the popular T205 Gold Border tobacco cards, also issued by the American Tobacco Co. about the same time. All but nine of the players featured in the pin set were also pictured on T205 cards, and in nearly all cases the photos are identical. The Sweet Caporal pins are designated as P2 in the American Card Catalog. The complete set price includes all variations.

		NM	EX	VG
Complete Set (205):		5500.	2825.	1700.
Common Player:		20.00	10.00	6.00
(1)	Ed Abbaticchio	20.00	10.00	6.00
(2)	Red Ames	20.00	10.00	6.00
(3a)	Jimmy Archer (small letters)	20.00	10.00	6.00
(3b)	Jimmy Archer (large letters)	24.00	12.00	7.25
(4a)	Jimmy Austin (small letters)	20.00	10.00	6.00
(4b)	Jimmy Austin (large letters)	24.00	12.00	7.25
(5)	Home Run Baker	40.00	20.00	12.00
(6)	Neal Ball	20.00	10.00	6.00
(7)	Cy Barger	20.00	10.00	6.00
(8)	Jack Barry	20.00	10.00	6.00
(9)	Johnny Bates	20.00	10.00	6.00
(10)	Beals Becker	20.00	10.00	6.00
(11)	Fred Beebe	20.00	10.00	6.00
(12a)	George Bell (small letters)	20.00	10.00	6.00
(12b)	George Bell (large letters)	24.00	12.00	7.25
(13a)	"Chief" Bender (small letters)	40.00	20.00	12.00
(13b)	"Chief" Bender (large letters)	60.00	30.00	18.00
(14)	Bill Bergen	20.00	10.00	6.00
(15)	Bob Bescher	20.00	10.00	6.00
(16)	Joe Birmingham	20.00	10.00	6.00
(17)	Kitty Bransfield	45.00	22.00	13.50
(18a)	Roger Bresnahan (mouth closed, small letters)	40.00	20.00	12.00
(18b)	Roger Bresnahan (mouth closed, large letters)	60.00	30.00	18.00
(19)	Roger Bresnahan (mouth open)	40.00	20.00	12.00
(20)	Al Bridwell	20.00	10.00	6.00
(21a)	Mordecai Brown (small letters)	40.00	20.00	12.00
(21b)	Mordecai Brown (large letters)	60.00	30.00	18.00
(22)	Bobby Byrne	20.00	10.00	6.00
(23)	Nixey Callahan	20.00	10.00	6.00
(24a)	Howie Camnitz (small letters)	20.00	10.00	6.00
(24b)	Howie Camnitz (large letters)	24.00	12.00	7.25
(25a)	Bill Carrigan (small letters)	20.00	10.00	6.00
(25b)	Bill Carrigan (large letters)	24.00	12.00	7.25
(26a)	Frank Chance (small letters)	40.00	20.00	12.00
(26b)	Frank Chance (large letters)	60.00	30.00	18.00
(27)	Hal Chase (small letters)	24.00	12.00	7.25
(28)	Hal Chase (large letters)	30.00	15.00	9.00
(29)	Ed Cicotte	50.00	25.00	15.00
(30a)	Fred Clarke (small letters)	40.00	20.00	12.00
(30b)	Fred Clarke (large letters)	60.00	30.00	18.00
(31a)	Ty Cobb (small letters)	330.00	165.00	99.00
(31b)	Ty Cobb (large letters)	400.00	200.00	120.00
(32a)	Eddie Collins (small letters)	40.00	20.00	12.00
(32b)	Eddie Collins (large letters)	60.00	30.00	18.00
(33)	Doc Crandall	20.00	10.00	6.00
(34)	Birdie Cree	45.00	22.00	13.50
(35)	Bill Dahlen	20.00	10.00	6.00
(36)	Jim Delahanty	20.00	10.00	6.00
(37)	Art Devlin	20.00	10.00	6.00
(38)	Josh Devore	20.00	10.00	6.00
(39)	Wild Bill Donovan	45.00	22.00	13.50
(40a)	Red Dooin (small letters)	20.00	10.00	6.00
(40b)	Red Dooin (large letters)	24.00	12.00	7.25
(41a)	Mickey Doolan (small letters)	20.00	10.00	6.00
(41b)	Mickey Doolan (large letters)	24.00	12.00	7.25
(42)	Patsy Dougherty	20.00	10.00	6.00
(43a)	Tom Downey (small letters)	20.00	10.00	6.00
(43b)	Tom Downey (large letters)	24.00	12.00	7.25
(44a)	Larry Doyle (small letters)	20.00	10.00	6.00
(44b)	Larry Doyle (large letters)	24.00	12.00	7.25
(45)	Louis Drucke	20.00	10.00	6.00
(46a)	Hugh Duffy (small letters)	40.00	20.00	12.00
(46b)	Hugh Duffy (large letters)	60.00	30.00	18.00
(47)	Jimmy Dygert	20.00	10.00	6.00
(48a)	Kid Elberfeld (small letters)	20.00	10.00	6.00
(48b)	Kid Elberfeld (large letters)	24.00	12.00	7.25
(49a)	Clyde Engle (small letters)	20.00	10.00	6.00
(49b)	Clyde Engle (large letters)	24.00	12.00	7.25
(50)	Tex Erwin	20.00	10.00	6.00
(51)	Steve Evans	20.00	10.00	6.00
(52)	Johnny Evers	40.00	20.00	12.00
(53)	Cecil Ferguson	20.00	10.00	6.00
(54)	John Flynn	20.00	10.00	6.00
(55a)	Russ Ford (small letters)	20.00	10.00	6.00
(55b)	Russ Ford (large letters)	24.00	12.00	7.25
(56)	Art Fromme	20.00	10.00	6.00

(57)	Harry Gaspar	20.00	10.00	6.00
(58a)	George Gibson (small letters)	20.00	10.00	6.00
(58b)	George Gibson (large letters)	24.00	12.00	7.25
(59)	Eddie Grant	45.00	22.00	13.50
(60)	Dolly Gray	20.00	10.00	6.00
(61a)	Clark Griffith (small letters)	40.00	20.00	12.00
(61b)	Clark Griffith (large letters)	60.00	30.00	18.00
(62)	Bob Groom	20.00	10.00	6.00
(63)	Bob Harmon	20.00	10.00	6.00
(64)	Topsy Hartsel	20.00	10.00	6.00
(65)	Arnold Hauser	45.00	22.00	13.50
(66)	Ira Hemphill	20.00	10.00	6.00
(67a)	Buck Herzog (small letters)	20.00	10.00	6.00
(67b)	Buck Herzog (large letters)	24.00	12.00	7.25
(68)	Dick Hoblitzell	20.00	10.00	6.00
(69)	Danny Hoffman	20.00	10.00	6.00
(70)	Harry Hooper	20.00	10.00	6.00
(71a)	Miller Huggins (small letters)	40.00	20.00	12.00
(71b)	Miller Huggins (large letters)	60.00	30.00	18.00
(72)	John Hummel	20.00	10.00	6.00
(73)	Hugh Jennings (small letters)	40.00	20.00	12.00
(74)	Hugh Jennings (large letters)	60.00	30.00	18.00
(75a)	Walter Johnson (small letters)	120.00	60.00	36.00
(75b)	Walter Johnson (large letters)	165.00	82.00	49.00
(76)	Tom Jones	45.00	22.00	13.50
(77)	Ed Karger	20.00	10.00	6.00
(78)	Ed Killian	45.00	22.00	13.50
(79a)	Jack Knight (small letters)	20.00	10.00	6.00
(79b)	Jack Knight (large letters)	24.00	12.00	7.25
(80)	Ed Konetchy	20.00	10.00	6.00
(81)	Harry Krause	20.00	10.00	6.00
(82)	Rube Kroh	20.00	10.00	6.00
(83)	Nap Lajoie	60.00	30.00	18.00
(84a)	Frank LaPorte (small letters)	20.00	10.00	6.00
(84b)	Frank LaPorte (large letters)	24.00	12.00	7.25
(85)	Arlie Latham	20.00	10.00	6.00
(86a)	Tommy Leach (small letters)	20.00	10.00	6.00
(86b)	Tommy Leach (large letters)	24.00	12.00	7.25
(87)	Sam Leever	20.00	10.00	6.00
(88)	Lefty Leifield	20.00	10.00	6.00
(89)	Hans Lobert	20.00	10.00	6.00
(90a)	Harry Lord (small letters)	20.00	10.00	6.00
(90b)	Harry Lord (large letters)	24.00	12.00	7.25
(91)	Paddy Livingston	20.00	10.00	6.00
(92)	Nick Maddox	20.00	10.00	6.00
(93)	Sherry Magee	20.00	10.00	6.00
(94)	Rube Marquard	40.00	20.00	12.00
(95a)	Christy Mathewson (small letters)	120.00	60.00	36.00
(95b)	Christy Mathewson (large letters)	165.00	82.00	49.00
(96a)	Al Mattern (small letters)	20.00	10.00	6.00
(96b)	Al Mattern (large letters)	24.00	12.00	7.25
(97)	George McBride	20.00	10.00	6.00
(98a)	John McGraw (small letters)	40.00	20.00	12.00
(98b)	John McGraw (large letters)	60.00	30.00	18.00
(99)	Harry McIntire (Cubs)	20.00	10.00	6.00
(100a)	Matty McIntyre (White Sox, small letters)	20.00	10.00	6.00
(100b)	Matty McIntyre (White Sox, large letters)	24.00	12.00	7.25
(101a)	John McLean (small letters)	20.00	10.00	6.00
(101b)	John McLean (large letters)	24.00	12.00	7.25
(102)	Fred Merkle	20.00	10.00	6.00
(103)	Chief Meyers	20.00	10.00	6.00
(104)	Clyde Milan	20.00	10.00	6.00
(105)	Dots Miller	20.00	10.00	6.00
(106)	Mike Mitchell	20.00	10.00	6.00
(107)	Pat Moran	20.00	10.00	6.00
(108a)	George Mullen (Mullin) (small letters)	20.00	10.00	6.00
(108b)	George Mullen (Mullin) (large letters)	24.00	12.00	7.25
(108c)	George Mullin (large letters, white cap)	60.00	30.00	18.00
(109)	Danny Murphy	20.00	10.00	6.00
(110a)	Red Murray (small letters)	24.00	12.00	7.25
(110b)	Red Murray (large letters)	20.00	10.00	6.00
(111)	Tom Needham	45.00	22.00	13.50
(112a)	Rebel Oakes (small letters)	20.00	10.00	6.00
(112b)	Rebel Oakes (large letters)	24.00	12.00	7.25
(113)	Rube Oldring	20.00	10.00	6.00
(114)	Charley O'Leary	20.00	10.00	6.00
(115)	Orval Overall	45.00	22.00	13.50
(116)	Fred Parent	20.00	10.00	6.00
(117a)	Dode Paskert (small letters)	20.00	10.00	6.00
(117b)	Dode Paskert (large letters)	24.00	12.00	7.25
(118)	Barney Pelty	20.00	10.00	6.00
(119)	Jake Pfeister	20.00	10.00	6.00
(120)	Eddie Phelps	20.00	10.00	6.00
(121)	Deacon Phillippe	20.00	10.00	6.00
(122)	Jack Quinn	20.00	10.00	6.00
(123)	Ed Reulbach	20.00	10.00	6.00
(124)	Lew Richie	20.00	10.00	6.00
(125)	Jack Rowan	20.00	10.00	6.00
(126a)	Nap Rucker (small letters)	20.00	10.00	6.00
(126b)	Nap Rucker (large letters)	24.00	12.00	7.25
(127)	Doc Scanlon (Scanlan)	45.00	22.00	13.50
(128)	Germany Schaefer	20.00	10.00	6.00
(129)	Jimmy Scheckard (Sheckard)	20.00	10.00	6.00
(130a)	Boss Schmidt (small letters)	20.00	10.00	6.00
(130b)	Boss Schmidt (large letters)	24.00	12.00	7.25
(131)	Wildfire Schulte	20.00	10.00	6.00
(132)	Hap Smith	20.00	10.00	6.00
(133a)	Tris Speaker (small letters)	60.00	30.00	18.00
(133b)	Tris Speaker (large letters)	85.00	42.00	25.00
(134)	Oscar Stanage	20.00	10.00	6.00
(135)	Harry Steinfeldt	20.00	10.00	6.00
(136)	George Stone	20.00	10.00	6.00
(137a)	George Stoval (Stovall) (small letters)	20.00	10.00	6.00
(137b)	George Stoval (Stovall) (large letters)	24.00	12.00	7.25
(138a)	Gabby Street (small letters)	20.00	10.00	6.00
(138b)	Gabby Street (large letters)	24.00	12.00	7.25
(139)	George Suggs	20.00	10.00	6.00
(140a)	Ira Thomas (small letters)	20.00	10.00	6.00
(140b)	Ira Thomas (large letters)	24.00	12.00	7.25
(141a)	Joe Tinker (small letters)	40.00	20.00	12.00
(141b)	Joe Tinker (large letters)	60.00	30.00	18.00
(142a)	John Titus (small letters)	20.00	10.00	6.00
(142b)	John Titus (large letters)	24.00	12.00	7.25
(143)	Terry Turner	24.00	12.00	7.25
(144)	Heinie Wagner	20.00	10.00	6.00
(145a)	Bobby Wallace (with cap, small letters)	40.00	20.00	12.00
(145b)	Bobby Wallace (with cap, large letters)	60.00	30.00	18.00
(146)	Bobby Wallace (without cap)	40.00	20.00	12.00
(147)	Ed Walsh	40.00	20.00	12.00
(148)	Jack Warhop	45.00	22.00	13.50
(149a)	Zach Wheat (small letters)	40.00	20.00	12.00
(149b)	Zach Wheat (large letters)	60.00	30.00	18.00
(150)	Doc White	20.00	10.00	6.00
(151)	Art Wilson (Giants)	45.00	22.00	13.50
(152)	Owen Wilson (Pirates)	20.00	10.00	6.00
(153)	Hooks Wiltse	20.00	10.00	6.00
(154)	Harry Wolter	20.00	10.00	6.00
(155a)	Cy Young (small letters)	100.00	50.00	30.00
(155b)	Cy Young (large letters)	135.00	67.00	40.00

1928 Sweetman

(27) TY COBB
This set consists of 60 of the most prominent Baseball players in the big Leagues. We have made up an album which will hold the complete set. On receipt of 15 cents in stamps we will send a blank album to any address in the United States.
Manufactured only by the
SWEETMAN CO. INC.
1611 Cass Ave. St. Louis, Mo.

The cards of this St. Louis firm share the format - about 1-3/8" x 2-1/2", black-and-white with card number in parentheses to the left of player name on front - checklist and most, but not all of the photos of such "ice cream" issues as Yeungling's, Tharp's and Harrington's, as well as the W502 strip cards and E210 York Caramels, but are less frequently encountered. Backs of the Sweetman cards offer an album for 15 cents in stamps. The type of business is which Sweetman Co., Inc., was engaged is unknown.

(See 1928 Yeungling for checklist and values.)

1948 Swell Babe Ruth Story

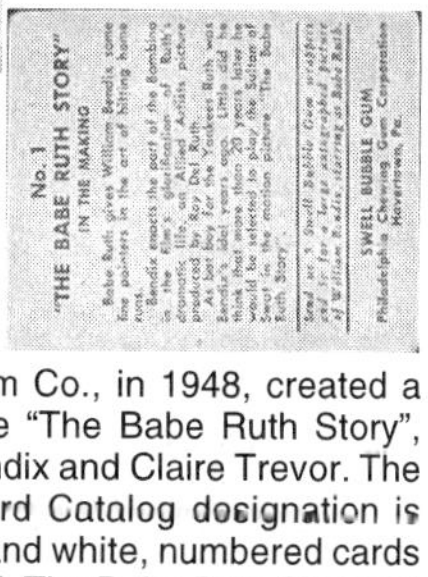

The Philadelphia Gum Co., in 1948, created a card set about the movie "The Babe Ruth Story", which starred William Bendix and Claire Trevor. The set, whose American Card Catalog designation is R421, contains 28 black and white, numbered cards which measure 2" x 2-1/2". The Babe Ruth Story set was originally intended to consist of sixteen cards. Twelve additional cards (#'s 17-28) were added when Ruth died before the release of the film. The card backs include an offer for an autographed photo of William Bendix, starring as the Babe, for five Swell Bubble Gum wrappers and five cents.

		NM	EX	VG
Complete Set (28):		1750.	785.00	435.00
Common Card (1-16):		24.00	12.00	7.00
Common Card (17-28):		75.00	35.00	20.00
1	"The Babe Ruth Story" in the Making	145.00	65.00	36.00
2	Batboy Becomes the Babe (William Bendix)	24.00	12.00	7.00
3	Claire Hodgson (Claire Trevor)	24.00	12.00	7.00
4	Babe Ruth and Claire Hodgson	24.00	12.00	7.00
5	Brother Mathias (Charles Bickford)	24.00	12.00	7.00
6	Phil Conrad (Sam Levene)	24.00	12.00	7.00
7	Nightclub Singer (Gertrude Niesen)	24.00	12.00	7.00
8	Baseball's Famous Deal, Jack Dunn (William Frawley)	24.00	12.00	7.00
9	Mr. and Mrs. Babe Ruth	24.00	12.00	7.00
10	Babe Ruth, Claire Ruth and Brother Mathias	24.00	12.00	7.00
11	Babe Ruth and Miller Huggins (Fred Lightner)	24.00	12.00	7.00
12	Babe at Bed of Ill Boy Johnny Sylvester (Gregory Marshall)	24.00	12.00	7.00
13	Sylvester Family Listening to Game	24.00	12.00	7.00
14	"When a Feller Needs a Friend" (With dog at police station)	24.00	12.00	7.00
15	Dramatic Home Run	24.00	12.00	7.00
16	The Homer That Set the Record - #60 (#60)	35.00	15.50	8.75
17	"The Slap That Started Baseball's Famous Career"	75.00	35.00	20.00
18	The Babe Plays Santa Claus	75.00	35.00	20.00
19	Meeting of Owner and Manager	75.00	35.00	20.00
20	"Broken Window Paid Off"	75.00	35.00	20.00
21	Babe in a Crowd of Autograph Collectors	100.00	45.00	25.00
22	Charley Grimm, William Bendix	75.00	35.00	20.00
23	Ted Lyons, William Bendix	100.00	45.00	25.00
24	Lefty Gomez, William Bendix, Bucky Harris	100.00	45.00	25.00
25	Babe Ruth, William Bendix	235.00	105.00	59.00
26	Babe Ruth, William Bendix	235.00	105.00	59.00
27	Babe Ruth, Claire Trevor	235.00	105.00	59.00
28	William Bendix, Babe Ruth, Claire Trevor	235.00	105.00	59.00

1948 Swell Sport Thrills

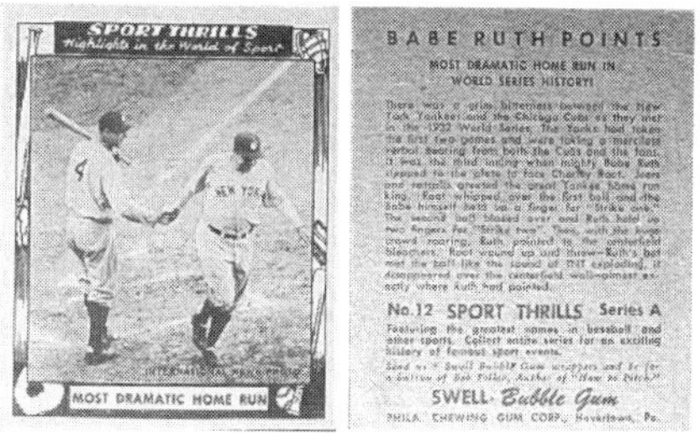

This is a set of black-and-white cards which depicts memorable events in baseball history. The cards measure 2-1/2" x 3" and have a picture frame border and event title on the card fronts. The card backs describe the event in detail. Twenty cards were produced in this set by the Swell Gum Company of Philadelphia. Each card is numbered, and card numbers 9, 11, 16 and 20 are considered more difficult to obtain.

		NM	EX	VG
Complete Set (20):		1900.	950.00	575.00
Common Player:		37.00	16.50	9.25
1	Greatest Single Inning (Mickey Cochrane, Jimmy Foxx, George Haas, Bing Miller, Al Simmons)	100.00	45.00	25.00
2	Amazing Record (Pete Reiser)	35.00	15.50	8.75
3	Dramatic Debut (Jackie Robinson)	200.00	90.00	50.00
4	Greatest Pitcher (Walter Johnson)	125.00	56.00	31.00
5	Three Strikes Not Out! (Tommy Henrich, Mickey Owen)	35.00	15.50	8.75
6	Home Run Wins Series (Bill Dickey)	40.00	18.00	10.00
7	Never Say Die Pitcher (Hal Schumacher)	35.00	15.50	8.75
8	Five Strikeouts! (Carl Hubbell)	40.00	18.00	10.00
9	Greatest Catch! (Al Gionfriddo)	60.00	27.00	15.00
10	No Hits! No Runs! (Johnny VanderMeer)	35.00	15.50	8.75
11	Bases Loaded! (Tony Lazzeri, Bob O'Farrell)	75.00	34.00	18.50
12	Most Dramatic Home Run (Lou Gehrig, Babe Ruth)	300.00	135.00	75.00
13	Winning Run (Tommy Bridges, Mickey Cochrane, Goose Goslin)	35.00	15.50	8.75
14	Great Slugging (Lou Gehrig)	250.00	112.00	62.00

15	Four Men to Stop Him! (Jim Bagby, Al Smith)	35.00	15.50	8.75
16	Three Run Homer in Ninth! (Joe DiMaggio, Joe Gordon, Ted Williams)	250.00	112.00	62.00
17	Football Block! (Whitey Kurowski, Johnny Lindell)	35.00	15.50	8.75
18	Home Run to Fame (Pee Wee Reese)	75.00	34.00	18.50
19	Strikout Record! (Bob Feller)	100.00	45.00	25.00
20	Rifle Arm! (Carl Furillo)	85.00	38.00	21.00

1957 Swift Meats

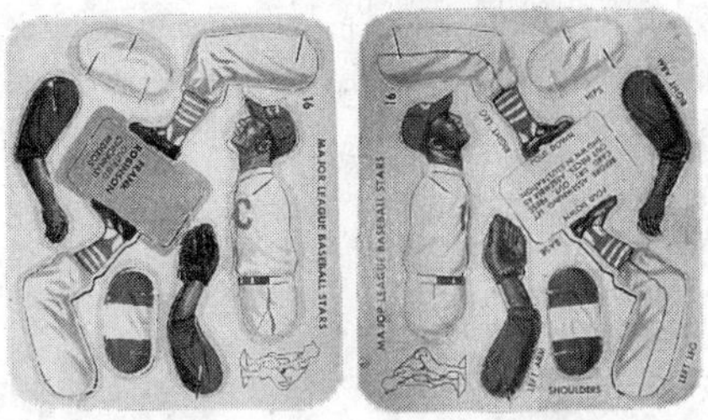

One of the really different baseball card issues of the Fifties was the set of 18 3-D baseball player figures which could be punched out and assembled from cards included in packages of hot dogs. The unpunched cards measure approximately 3-1/2" x 4". Prices below are for unpunched cards. Values for assembled figures are problematical.

		NM	EX	VG
Complete Set, Singles (18):		1200.	600.00	350.00
Complete Set w/Mailer, Playing Board:		2000.	1000.	600.00
Common Player:		75.00	37.00	22.00
1	John Podres	90.00	45.00	27.00
2	Gus Triandos	75.00	37.00	22.00
3	Dale Long	75.00	37.00	22.00
4	Billy Pierce	75.00	37.00	22.00
5	Ed Bailey	75.00	37.00	22.00
6	Vic Wertz	75.00	37.00	22.00
7	Nelson Fox	175.00	87.00	52.00
8	Ken Boyer	90.00	45.00	27.00
9	Gil McDougald	90.00	45.00	27.00
10	Junior Gilliam	90.00	45.00	27.00
11	Eddie Yost	75.00	37.00	22.00
12	Johnny Logan	75.00	37.00	22.00
13	Hank Aaron	200.00	100.00	60.00
14	Bill Tuttle	75.00	37.00	22.00
15	Jackie Jensen	75.00	37.00	22.00
16	Frank Robinson	175.00	87.00	52.00
17	Richie Ashburn	175.00	87.00	52.00
18	Rocky Colavito	200.00	100.00	60.00

1909 S74 Silks - White

Designated as S74 in the "American Card Catalog," these delicate fabric collectibles are popular with advanced collectors. The silks were issued as premiums with several different brands of cigarettes: Turkey Red, Old Mill, Helmar, and, rarely, Red Sun. The satin-like silks can be found in two different styles, either "white" or "colored." The white silks measure 1-7/8" x 3" and were originally issued with a brown paper backing that carried an advertisement for one of the cigarette brands. The backing also advised that the silks were "useful in making pillow covers and other fancy articles for home decoration." Many undoubtedly were used for such purposes, making silks with the paper backing still intact more difficult to find. White silks must have the backing intact to command top values shown here. Although similar, the S74 "colored" silks, as their name indicates, were issued in a variety of colors. They are also slightly larger, measuring 1-7/8" x 3-1/2", and were issued without a paper backing, carrying the cigarette brand name on the lower front of the fabric. (No color silks advertising the Helmar brand are known to exist.) There are 121 different players reported: six have been found in two poses, resulting in 127 different subjects. Ninety-two subjects are known in the "white" silk, while 120 have been found in the "colored." The silks feature the same players pictured in the popular T205 Gold Border tobacco card set.

		NM	EX	VG
Complete Set (92):		16000.	8000.	4750.
Common Player:		150.00	75.00	45.00
(1)	Home Run Baker	300.00	150.00	90.00
(2)	Cy Barger	150.00	75.00	45.00
(3)	Jack Barry	150.00	75.00	45.00
(4)	Johnny Bates	150.00	75.00	45.00
(5)	Fred Beck	150.00	75.00	45.00
(6)	Beals Becker	150.00	75.00	45.00
(7)	George Bell	150.00	75.00	45.00
(8)	Chief Bender	300.00	150.00	90.00
(9)	Roger Bresnahan	300.00	150.00	90.00
(10)	Al Bridwell	150.00	75.00	45.00
(11)	Mordecai Brown	300.00	150.00	90.00
(12)	Bobby Byrne	150.00	75.00	45.00
(13)	Howie Camnitz	150.00	75.00	45.00
(14)	Bill Carrigan	150.00	75.00	45.00
(15)	Frank Chance	300.00	150.00	90.00
(16)	Hal Chase	200.00	100.00	60.00
(17)	Fred Clarke	300.00	150.00	90.00
(18)	Ty Cobb	1500.	750.00	450.00
(19)	Eddie Collins	300.00	150.00	90.00
(20)	Doc Crandall	150.00	75.00	45.00
(21)	Lou Criger	150.00	75.00	45.00
(22)	Jim Delahanty	150.00	75.00	45.00
(23)	Art Devlin	150.00	75.00	45.00
(24)	Red Dooin	150.00	75.00	45.00
(25)	Mickey Doolan	150.00	75.00	45.00
(26)	Larry Doyle	150.00	75.00	45.00
(27)	Jimmy Dygert	150.00	75.00	45.00
(28)	Kid Elberfield (Elberfeld)	150.00	75.00	45.00
(29)	Steve Evans	150.00	75.00	45.00
(30)	Johnny Evers	300.00	150.00	90.00
(31)	Bob Ewing	150.00	75.00	45.00
(32)	Art Fletcher	150.00	75.00	45.00
(33)	John Flynn	150.00	75.00	45.00
(34)	Bill Foxen	150.00	75.00	45.00
(35)	George Gibson	150.00	75.00	45.00
(36)	Peaches Graham (Cubs)	150.00	75.00	45.00
(37)	Peaches Graham (Rustlers)	150.00	75.00	45.00
(38)	Clark Griffith	300.00	150.00	90.00
(39)	Topsy Hartsel	150.00	75.00	45.00
(40)	Arnold Hauser	150.00	75.00	45.00
(41)	Charlie Hemphill	150.00	75.00	45.00
(42)	Tom Jones	150.00	75.00	45.00
(43)	Jack Knight	150.00	75.00	45.00
(44)	Ed Konetchy	150.00	75.00	45.00
(45)	Harry Krause	150.00	75.00	45.00
(46)	Tommy Leach	150.00	75.00	45.00
(47)	Rube Marquard	300.00	150.00	90.00
(48)	Christy Mathewson	550.00	275.00	165.00
(49)	Al Mattern	150.00	75.00	45.00
(50)	Amby McConnell	150.00	75.00	45.00
(51)	John McGraw	300.00	150.00	90.00
(52)	Harry McIntire (McIntyre)	150.00	75.00	45.00
(53)	Fred Merkle	150.00	75.00	45.00
(54)	Chief Meyers	150.00	75.00	45.00
(55)	Dots Miller	150.00	75.00	45.00
(56)	Danny Murphy	150.00	75.00	45.00
(57)	Red Murray	150.00	75.00	45.00
(58)	Tom Needham	150.00	75.00	45.00
(59)	Rebel Oakes	150.00	75.00	45.00
(60)	Rube Oldring	150.00	75.00	45.00
(61)	Orval Overall	150.00	75.00	45.00
(62)	Fred Parent	150.00	75.00	45.00
(63)	Fred Payne	150.00	75.00	45.00
(64)	Barney Pelty	150.00	75.00	45.00
(65)	Deacon Phillippe	150.00	75.00	45.00
(66)	Jack Quinn	150.00	75.00	45.00
(67)	Bugs Raymond	150.00	75.00	45.00
(68)	Ed Reulbach	150.00	75.00	45.00
(69)	Doc Scanlon (Scanlan)	150.00	75.00	45.00
(70)	Germany Schaefer	150.00	75.00	45.00
(71)	Admiral Schlei	150.00	75.00	45.00
(72)	Wildfire Schulte	150.00	75.00	45.00
(73)	Dave Shean	150.00	75.00	45.00
(74)	Jimmy Sheckard	150.00	75.00	45.00
(75)	Hap Smith (Superbas)	150.00	75.00	45.00
(76)	Harry Smith (Rustlers)	500.00	250.00	150.00
(77)	Fred Snodgrass	150.00	75.00	45.00
(78)	Tris Speaker	400.00	200.00	120.00
(79)	Harry Steinfeldt (Cubs)	150.00	75.00	45.00
(80)	Harry Steinfeldt (Rustlers)	150.00	75.00	45.00
(81)	George Stone	150.00	75.00	45.00
(82)	Gabby Street	150.00	75.00	45.00
(83)	Ed Summers	150.00	75.00	45.00
(84)	Lee Tannehill	150.00	75.00	45.00
(85)	Joe Tinker	300.00	150.00	90.00
(86)	John Titus	150.00	75.00	45.00
(87)	Terry Turner	150.00	75.00	45.00
(88)	Bobby Wallace	300.00	150.00	90.00
(89)	Doc White	150.00	75.00	45.00
(90)	Ed Willett	150.00	75.00	45.00
(91)	Art Wilson	150.00	75.00	45.00
(92)	Harry Wolter	150.00	75.00	45.00

1910 S74 Silks - Colored

		NM	EX	VG
Complete Set (120):		17500.	8000.	5000.
Common Player:		125.00	62.00	37.00
(1)	Red Ames	125.00	62.00	37.00
(2)	Jimmy Archer	125.00	62.00	37.00
(3)	Home Run Baker	250.00	125.00	75.00
(4)	Cy Barger	125.00	62.00	37.00
(5)	Jack Barry	125.00	62.00	37.00
(6)	Johnny Bates	125.00	62.00	37.00
(7)	Beals Becker	125.00	62.00	37.00
(8)	George Bell	125.00	62.00	37.00
(9)	Chief Bender	250.00	125.00	75.00
(10)	Bill Bergen	125.00	62.00	37.00
(11)	Bob Bescher	125.00	62.00	37.00
(12)	Roger Bresnahan (mouth closed)	300.00	150.00	90.00
(13)	Roger Bresnahan (mouth open)	300.00	150.00	90.00
(14)	Al Bridwell	125.00	62.00	37.00
(15)	Mordecai Brown	250.00	125.00	75.00
(16)	Bobby Byrne	125.00	62.00	37.00
(17)	Howie Camnitz	125.00	62.00	37.00
(18)	Bill Carrigan	125.00	62.00	37.00
(19)	Frank Chance	300.00	150.00	90.00
(20)	Hal Chase	175.00	87.00	52.00
(21)	Ed Cicotte	225.00	112.00	67.00
(22)	Fred Clarke	250.00	125.00	75.00
(23)	Ty Cobb	1000.	500.00	300.00
(24)	Eddie Collins	250.00	125.00	75.00
(25)	Doc Crandall	125.00	62.00	37.00
(26)	Bill Dahlen	125.00	62.00	37.00
(27)	Jake Daubert	125.00	62.00	37.00
(28)	Jim Delahanty	125.00	62.00	37.00
(29)	Art Devlin	125.00	62.00	37.00
(30)	Josh Devore	125.00	62.00	37.00
(31)	Red Dooin	125.00	62.00	37.00
(32)	Mickey Doolan	125.00	62.00	37.00
(33)	Tom Downey	125.00	62.00	37.00
(34)	Larry Doyle	125.00	62.00	37.00
(35)	Hugh Duffy	250.00	125.00	75.00
(36)	Jimmy Dygert	125.00	62.00	37.00
(37)	Kid Elberfield (Elberfeld)	125.00	62.00	37.00
(38)	Steve Evans	125.00	62.00	37.00
(39)	Johnny Evers	250.00	125.00	75.00
(40)	Bob Ewing	125.00	62.00	37.00
(41)	Art Fletcher	125.00	62.00	37.00
(42)	John Flynn	125.00	62.00	37.00
(43)	Russ Ford	125.00	62.00	37.00
(44)	Bill Foxen	125.00	62.00	37.00
(45)	Art Fromme	125.00	62.00	37.00
(46)	George Gibson	125.00	62.00	37.00
(47)	Peaches Graham	125.00	62.00	37.00
(48)	Eddie Grant	125.00	62.00	37.00
(49)	Clark Griffith	250.00	125.00	75.00
(50)	Topsy Hartsel	125.00	62.00	37.00
(51)	Arnold Hauser	125.00	62.00	37.00
(52)	Charlie Hemphill	125.00	62.00	37.00
(53)	Dick Hoblitzell	125.00	62.00	37.00
(54)	Miller Huggins	250.00	125.00	75.00
(55)	John Hummel	125.00	62.00	37.00
(56)	Walter Johnson	500.00	250.00	150.00
(57)	Davy Jones	125.00	62.00	37.00
(58)	Johnny Kling	125.00	62.00	37.00
(59)	Jack Knight	125.00	62.00	37.00
(60)	Ed Konetchy	125.00	62.00	37.00
(61)	Harry Krause	125.00	62.00	37.00
(62)	Tommy Leach	125.00	62.00	37.00
(63)	Lefty Leifield	125.00	62.00	37.00
(64)	Hans Lobert	125.00	62.00	37.00
(65)	Rube Marquard	250.00	125.00	75.00
(66)	Christy Mathewson	500.00	250.00	150.00
(67)	Al Mattern	125.00	62.00	37.00
(68)	Amby McConnell	125.00	62.00	37.00
(69)	John McGraw	250.00	125.00	75.00
(70)	Harry McIntire (McIntyre)	125.00	62.00	37.00
(71)	Fred Merkle	125.00	62.00	37.00
(72)	Chief Meyers	125.00	62.00	37.00
(73)	Dots Miller	125.00	62.00	37.00
(74)	Mike Mitchell	125.00	62.00	37.00
(75)	Pat Moran	125.00	62.00	37.00
(76)	George Moriarty	125.00	62.00	37.00
(77)	George Mullin	125.00	62.00	37.00
(78)	Danny Murphy	125.00	62.00	37.00
(79)	Red Murray	125.00	62.00	37.00
(80)	Tom Needham	125.00	62.00	37.00
(81)	Rebel Oakes	125.00	62.00	37.00
(82)	Rube Oldring	125.00	62.00	37.00
(83)	Orval Overall	125.00	62.00	37.00
(84)	Fred Parent	125.00	62.00	37.00
(85)	Dode Paskert	125.00	62.00	37.00

		NM	EX	VG
(86)	Billy Payne	125.00	62.00	37.00
(87)	Barney Pelty	125.00	62.00	37.00
(88)	Deacon Phillippe	125.00	62.00	37.00
(89)	Jack Quinn	125.00	62.00	37.00
(90)	Bugs Raymond	125.00	62.00	37.00
(91)	Ed Reulbach	125.00	62.00	37.00
(92)	Jack Rowan	125.00	62.00	37.00
(93)	Nap Rucker	125.00	62.00	37.00
(94)	Doc Scanlon (Scanlan)	125.00	62.00	37.00
(95)	Germany Schaefer	125.00	62.00	37.00
(96)	Admiral Schlei	125.00	62.00	37.00
(97)	Wildfire Schulte	125.00	62.00	37.00
(98)	Dave Shean	125.00	62.00	37.00
(99)	Jimmy Sheckard	125.00	62.00	37.00
(100)	Happy Smith	125.00	62.00	37.00
(101)	Fred Snodgrass	125.00	62.00	37.00
(102)	Tris Speaker	400.00	200.00	120.00
(103)	Jake Stahl	125.00	62.00	37.00
(104)	Harry Steinfeldt	125.00	62.00	37.00
(105)	George Stone	125.00	62.00	37.00
(106)	Gabby Street	125.00	62.00	37.00
(107)	Ed Summers	125.00	62.00	37.00
(108)	Lee Tannehill	125.00	62.00	37.00
(109)	Joe Tinker	250.00	125.00	75.00
(110)	John Titus	125.00	62.00	37.00
(111)	Terry Turner	125.00	62.00	37.00
(112)	Bobby Wallace	250.00	125.00	75.00
(113)	Zack Wheat	250.00	125.00	75.00
(114)	Doc White (White Sox)	125.00	62.00	37.00
(115)	Kirby White (Pirates)	125.00	62.00	37.00
(116)	Ed Willett	125.00	62.00	37.00
(117)	Owen Wilson	125.00	62.00	37.00
(118)	Hooks Wiltse	125.00	62.00	37.00
(119)	Harry Wolter	125.00	62.00	37.00
(120)	Cy Young	600.00	300.00	180.00

1912 S81 Silks

The 1912 S81 "Silks," so-called because they featured pictures of baseball players on a satin-like fabric rather than paper or cardboard, are closely related to the better-known T3 Turkey Red cabinet cards of the same era. The silks, which featured 25 of the day's top baseball players among its other various subjects, were available as a premium with Helmar "Turkish Trophies" cigarettes. According to an advertising sheet, one silk could be obtained for 25 Helmar coupons. The silks measure 7" x 9" and, with a few exceptions, used the same pictures featured on the popular Turkey Red cards. Five players (Rube Marquard, Rube Benton, Marty O'Toole, Grover Alexander and Russ Ford) appear in the "Silks" set that were not included in the T3 set. In addition, an error involving the Frank Baker card was corrected for the "Silks" set. (In the T3 set, Baker's card actually pictured Jack Barry.) Several years ago a pair of New England collectors found a small stack of Christy Mathewson "Silks," making his, by far, the most common. Otherwise, the "Silks" are generally so rare that it is difficult to determine the relative scarcity of the others. Baseball enthusiasts are usually only attracted to the 25 baseball players in the "Silks" premium set, but it is interesting to note that the promotion also offered dozens of other subjects, including "beautiful women in bathing and athletic costumes, charming dancers in gorgeous attire, national flags and generals on horseback."

		NM	EX	VG
	Complete Set (25):	45000.	15750.	8550.
	Common Player:	2000.	750.00	425.00
86	Rube Marquard	2400.	840.00	455.00
87	Marty O'Toole	2000.	750.00	425.00
88	Rube Benton	2000.	750.00	425.00
89	Grover Alexander	2500.	875.00	475.00
90	Russ Ford	2100.	775.00	450.00
91	John McGraw	2400.	840.00	455.00
92	Nap Rucker	2000.	750.00	425.00
93	Mike Mitchell	2000.	750.00	425.00
94	Chief Bender	2400.	840.00	455.00
95	Home Run Baker	2400.	840.00	455.00
96	Nap Lajoie	2750.	960.00	525.00
97	Joe Tinker	2400.	840.00	455.00
98	Sherry Magee	2000.	750.00	425.00
99	Howie Camnitz	2000.	750.00	425.00
100	Eddie Collins	2400.	840.00	455.00
101	Red Dooin	2000.	750.00	425.00
102	Ty Cobb	8000.	2800.	1525.
103	Hugh Jennings	2400.	840.00	455.00
104	Roger Bresnahan	2750.	960.00	525.00
105	Jake Stahl	2000.	750.00	425.00
106	Tris Speaker	3200.	1125.	600.00
107	Ed Walsh	2400.	840.00	450.00
108	Christy Mathewson	2550.	890.00	485.00
109	Johnny Evers	2400.	840.00	455.00
110	Walter Johnson	4000.	1400.	760.00

1912 S110 Baseball Player Silks Pillow Case

Closely related to the S81 silks, and evidently issued in some fashion as a premium, this 23" x 23" pillow case shares the same designs as the individual silks of the players thereon. Cross-stich borders for the player images on the cloth pillow case would indicate the silks were meant to be sewn on as they were acquired. Besides the baseball players pillow cases, similar premiums are known for the other Turkey Red/Helmar silks -- Indians, generals, etc.

		NM	EX	VG
	Complete Set (2):	10800.	5400.	3200.
(1)	Home Run Baker, Ty Cobb, Walter Johnson, Christy Mathewson, Tris Speaker	6000.	3000.	1700.
(2)	Home Run Baker, Ty Cobb, Christy Mathewson, Marty O'Toole, Tris Speaker	5000.	2500.	1500.

T

1916 Tango Eggs

Unknown until the discovery of a hoard of "fewer than 500" cards in 1991, this 20-card set was produced for L. Frank & Company of New Orleans to be distributed in an as-yet unknown manner in connection with its Tango brand eggs. Similar in size (1-7/16" x 2-3/4") and format to contemporary caramel cards, the Tango set features familiar player pictures from those issues. In fact, several of the Tango cards have player designations which differ from the same pictures used in the E106 American Caramel issue of 1915. The Tango cards feature a glossy front surface, and are brightly colored. The hoard varied greatly in the number of each player's card. Some were found in quantities as low as one, while some were represented by more than 50 specimens. Because several of the cards exist in only a single specimen, no price for a complete set is quoted.

		NM	EX	VG
	Common Player:	175.00	87.00	52.00
(1)	Bob Bescher	375.00	150.00	75.00
(2)	Roger Bresnahan (four known)	2500.	1000.	500.00
(3)	Al Bridwell (fewer than 10 known)	900.00	360.00	180.00
(4)	Hal Chase	500.00	200.00	100.00
(5)	Ty Cobb (one known, VG)			10000.
(6)	Eddie Collins	2000.	800.00	400.00
(7)	Sam Crawford (fewer than five known)	2500.	1000.	500.00
(8)	Red Dooin	350.00	140.00	70.00
(9)	Johnny Evers (one known, G/VG)			1500.
(10)	Happy Felsch (picture actually Ray Demmitt) (2-3 known)	3000.	1200.	600.00
(11)	Hughie Jennings (20 known)	400.00	160.00	80.00
(12)	George McQuillen	225.00	90.00	45.00
(13)	Billy Meyer (picture actually Fred Jacklitsch)	300.00	120.00	60.00
(14)	Ray Morgan (picture actually Mike Doolan) (2-3 known)	2000.	800.00	400.00
(15)	Danny Murphy	375.00	150.00	75.00
(16)	Germany Schaefer (1-2 known)	2500.	1000.	500.00
(17)	Joe Tinker (1-2 known)	3000.	1200.	600.00
(18)	Honus Wagner (none confirmed)	5000.	2000.	1000.
(19)	Buck Weaver (picture actually Joe Tinker)	1500.	600.00	300.00
(20)	Heinie Zimmerman (fewer than 10 known)	900.00	360.00	180.00

1934 Tarzan Bread

Among the rarest issues of the 1930s is this set sponsored by an unusually named brand of bread from a bakery whose location is unknown. The cards are printed in black-and-white in 2-1/4" x 3-1/4" format. Borderless front photos have the player name in capital letters. Backs have the sponsor's name and a short career summary. The checklist here, almost certainly incomplete, is arranged alphabetically; the cards are unnumbered.

		NM	EX	VG
	Common Player:	600.00	300.00	180.00
(1)	Sparky Adams	600.00	300.00	180.00
(2)	Walter Betts	600.00	300.00	180.00
(3)	Ed Brandt	600.00	300.00	180.00
(4)	Tommy Bridges	600.00	300.00	180.00
(5)	Irving "Jack" Burns	600.00	300.00	180.00
(6)	Bruce Campbell	600.00	300.00	180.00
(7)	Tex Carleton	600.00	300.00	180.00
(8)	Dick Coffman	600.00	300.00	180.00
(9)	George Connally	600.00	300.00	180.00
(10)	Tony Cuccinello	600.00	300.00	180.00
(11)	Debs Garms	600.00	300.00	180.00
(12)	Milt Gaston	600.00	300.00	180.00
(13)	Bill Hallahan	600.00	300.00	180.00
(14)	Myril Hoag	600.00	300.00	180.00
(15)	Chief Hogsett	600.00	300.00	180.00
(16)	Arndt Jorgens	600.00	300.00	180.00
(17)	Willie Kamm	600.00	300.00	180.00
(18)	Dutch Leonard	600.00	300.00	180.00
(19)	Clyde Manion	600.00	300.00	180.00
(20)	Eric McNair	600.00	300.00	180.00
(21)	Oscar Melillo	600.00	300.00	180.00
(22)	Bob O'Farrell	600.00	300.00	180.00
(23)	Gus Suhr	600.00	300.00	180.00
(24)	Evar Swanson	600.00	300.00	180.00
(25)	Billy Urbanski	600.00	300.00	180.00
(26)	Johnny Vergez	600.00	300.00	180.00
(27)	Robert Worthington	600.00	300.00	180.00
(28)	Tom Zachary	600.00	300.00	180.00

1933 Tattoo Orbit (R305)

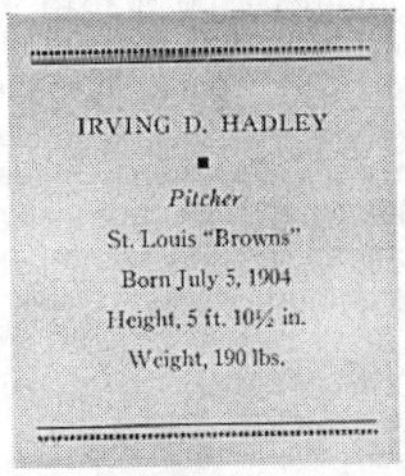

Found in 1¢ packages of Tattoo gum, these 2" x 2-1/4" cards were produced by the Orbit Gum Co., of Chicago, a sibsidiary of Wrigley's. Fronts feature a black-and-white photo which is tinted to give the skin some color. Stylized ballpark backgrounds are separated from the photograph by a black line. The rest of the background is printed in vivid red, yellow and green. Backs have player identification and vitals. Cards of Bump Hadley and George Blaeholder are the most elusive, followed by those of Ivy Andrews and Rogers Hornsby.

		NM	EX	VG
Complete Set (60):		8000.	4000.	2200.
Common Player:		95.00	45.00	25.00
(1)	Dale Alexander	160.00	72.00	40.00
(2)	Ivy Paul Andrews	325.00	145.00	80.00
(3)	Earl Averill	160.00	72.00	40.00
(4)	Richard Bartell	95.00	45.00	25.00
(5)	Walter Berger	95.00	45.00	25.00
(6)	George F. Blaeholder	255.00	115.00	64.00
(7)	Irving J. Burns	95.00	45.00	25.00
(8)	Guy T. Bush	95.00	45.00	25.00
(9)	Bruce D. Campbell	95.00	45.00	25.00
(10)	William Cissell	95.00	45.00	25.00
(11)	Lefty Clark	95.00	45.00	25.00
(12)	Mickey Cochrane	160.00	72.00	40.00
(13)	Phil Collins	95.00	45.00	25.00
(14)	Hazen Kiki Cuyler	160.00	72.00	40.00
(15)	Dizzy Dean	300.00	135.00	75.00
(16)	Jimmy Dykes	95.00	45.00	25.00
(17)	George L. Earnshaw	95.00	45.00	25.00
(18)	Woody English	95.00	45.00	25.00
(19)	Lewis A. Fonseca	95.00	45.00	25.00
(20)	Jimmy Foxx	200.00	90.00	50.00
(21)	Burleigh A. Grimes	160.00	72.00	40.00
(22)	Charles John Grimm	95.00	45.00	25.00
(23)	Robert M. Grove	160.00	72.00	40.00
(24)	Frank Grube	95.00	45.00	25.00
(25)	George W. Haas	95.00	45.00	25.00
(26)	Irving D. Hadley	250.00	112.00	62.00
(27)	Chick Hafey	160.00	72.00	40.00
(28)	Jesse Joseph Haines	160.00	72.00	40.00
(29)	William Hallahan	95.00	45.00	25.00
(30)	Melvin Harder	95.00	45.00	25.00
(31)	Gabby Hartnett	160.00	72.00	40.00
(32)	Babe Herman	85.00	38.00	21.00
(33)	William Herman	160.00	72.00	40.00
(34)	Rogers Hornsby	225.00	101.00	56.00
(35)	Roy C. Johnson	95.00	45.00	25.00
(36)	J. Smead Jolley	95.00	45.00	25.00
(37)	William Jurges	95.00	45.00	25.00
(38)	William Kamm	95.00	45.00	25.00
(39)	Mark A. Koenig	95.00	45.00	25.00
(40)	James J. Levey	95.00	45.00	25.00
(41)	Ernie Lombardi	160.00	72.00	40.00
(42)	Red Lucas	95.00	45.00	25.00
(43)	Ted Lyons	160.00	72.00	40.00
(44)	Connie Mack	175.00	79.00	44.00
(45)	Pat Malone	95.00	45.00	25.00
(46)	Pepper Martin	85.00	38.00	21.00
(47)	Marty McManus	95.00	45.00	25.00
(48)	Frank J. O'Doul	90.00	40.00	22.00
(49)	Richard Porter	95.00	45.00	25.00
(50)	Carl N. Reynolds	95.00	45.00	25.00
(51)	Charles Henry Root	95.00	45.00	25.00
(52)	Robert Seeds	95.00	45.00	25.00
(53)	Al H. Simmons	160.00	72.00	40.00
(54)	Jackson Riggs Stephenson	95.00	45.00	25.00
(55)	Bud Tinning	95.00	45.00	25.00
(56)	Joe Vosmik	95.00	45.00	25.00
(57)	Rube Walberg	95.00	45.00	25.00
(58)	Paul Waner	160.00	72.00	40.00
(59)	Lonnie Warneke	95.00	45.00	25.00
(60)	Arthur C. Whitney	95.00	45.00	25.00

1933 Tattoo Orbit (R308)

This obscure set of cards, issued with Tattoo Orbit gum, is numbered from 151 through 207, with a few of the numbers still unknown. Most surviving examples measure 1-7/8" x 1-1/4," but larger pieces (2-1/2" x 3-7/8") are also known with the same players and numbers. These are considered more of a novelty item because the player drawings on the cards actually "developed" when moistened and rubbed with a piece of blotting paper. Besides the baseball players, there were also pictures of movie stars and other celebrities.

		NM	EX	VG
Common Player:		30.00	15.00	9.00
151	Vernon Gomez	75.00	34.00	18.50
152	Kiki Cuyler	75.00	34.00	18.50
153	Jimmy Foxx	100.00	45.00	25.00
154	Al Simmons	75.00	34.00	18.50
155	Chas. J. Grimm	30.00	13.50	7.50
156	William Jurges	30.00	13.50	7.50
157	Chuck Klein	75.00	34.00	18.50
158	Richard Bartell	30.00	13.50	7.50
159	Pepper Martin	40.00	18.00	10.00
160	Earl Averill	75.00	34.00	18.50
161	William Dickey	75.00	34.00	18.50
162	Wesley Ferrell	30.00	13.50	7.50
163	Oral Hildebrand	30.00	13.50	7.50
164	Wm. Kamm	30.00	13.50	7.50
165	Earl Whitehill	30.00	13.50	7.50
166	Charles Fullis	30.00	13.50	7.50
167	Jimmy Dykes	30.00	13.50	7.50
168	Ben Cantwell	30.00	13.50	7.50
169	George Earnshaw	30.00	13.50	7.50
170	Jackson Stephenson	30.00	13.50	7.50
171	Randolph Moore	30.00	13.50	7.50
172	Ted Lyons	75.00	34.00	18.50
173	Goose Goslin	75.00	34.00	18.50
174	E. Swanson	30.00	13.50	7.50
175	Lee Roy Mahaffey	30.00	13.50	7.50
176	Joe Cronin	75.00	34.00	18.50
177	Tom Bridges	30.00	13.50	7.50
178	Henry Manush	75.00	34.00	18.50
179	Walter Stewart	30.00	13.50	7.50
180	Frank Pytlak	30.00	13.50	7.50
181	Dale Alexander	30.00	13.50	7.50
182	Robert Grove	75.00	34.00	18.50
183	Charles Gehringer	75.00	34.00	18.50
184	Lewis Fonseca	30.00	13.50	7.50
185	Alvin Crowder	30.00	13.50	7.50
186	Mickey Cochrane	75.00	34.00	18.50
187	Max Bishop	30.00	13.50	7.50
188	Connie Mack	80.00	36.00	20.00
189	Guy Bush	30.00	13.50	7.50
190	Charlie Root	30.00	13.50	7.50
191a	Burleigh Grimes	75.00	34.00	18.50
191b	Gabby Hartnett	75.00	34.00	18.50
192	Pat Malone	30.00	13.50	7.50
193	Woody English	30.00	13.50	7.50
194	Lonnie Warneke	30.00	13.50	7.50
195	Babe Herman	35.00	15.50	8.75
196	Unknown			
197	Unknown			
198	Unknown			
199	Unknown			
200	Gabby Hartnett	75.00	34.00	18.50
201	Paul Waner	75.00	34.00	18.50
202	Dizzy Dean	125.00	56.00	31.00
203	Unknown			
204	Unknown			
205	Jim Bottomley	75.00	34.00	18.50
206	Unknown			
207	Charles Hafey	75.00	34.00	18.50
208	Unknown			
209	Unknown			
210	Unknown			

1972 TCMA The 1930's

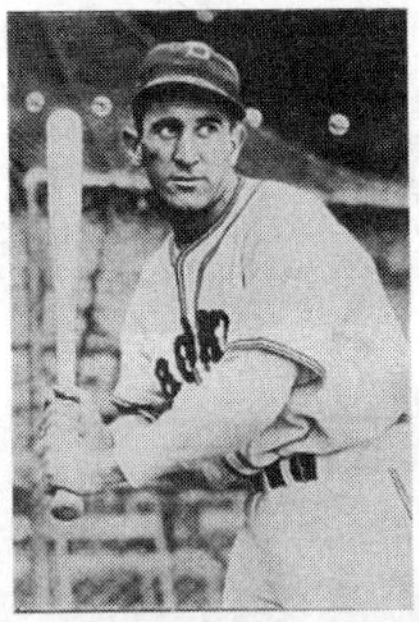

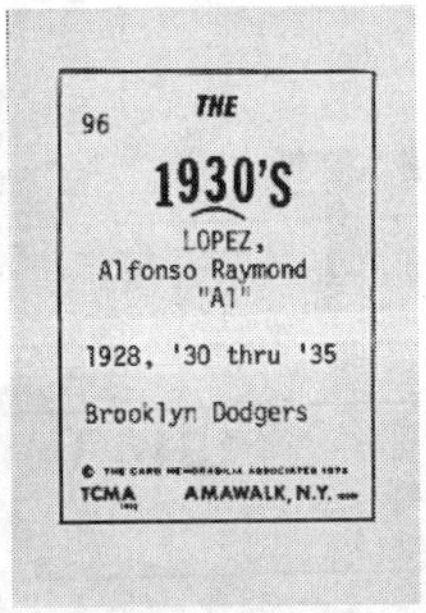

Extending to over 500 cards, this was one of TCMA's first ventures into the business of creating collectors' edition card sets of former players. Over the length of the series there were a number of size and style differences. All cards are printed in black-and-white and feature player photos on usually borderless fronts. Dimensions range from about 2" to 2-1/2" side-to-side, and 2-3/4" to 3-1/2" top-to-bottom. Except for a TCMA copyright line on some of the earlier cards, there is no other printing on front. Backs have player identification, team affiliations, TCMA copyright and, after #72, a card number.

		NM	EX	VG
Complete Set (501):		350.00	175.00	100.00
Common Player:		.50	.25	.15
(1)	Roy Bell	.50	.25	.15
(2)	Max Bishop	.50	.25	.15
(3)	Bob Boken	.50	.25	.15
(4)	Cliff Bolton	.50	.25	.15
(5)	John Broaca	.50	.25	.15
(6)	Bill Brubaker	.50	.25	.15
(7)	Slick Castleman	.50	.25	.15
(8)	Dick Coffman	.50	.25	.15
(9)	Phil Collins	.50	.25	.15
(10)	Earle Combs	.75	.40	.25
(11)	Doc Cramer	.50	.25	.15
(12)	Joe Cronin	1.00	.50	.30
(13)	Jack Crouch	.50	.25	.15
(14)	Tony Cuccinello	.50	.25	.15
(15)	Babe Dahlgren	.50	.25	.15
(16)	Spud Davis	.50	.25	.15
(17)	Dizzy Dean	2.00	1.00	.60
(18)	Paul Dean	1.00	.50	.30
(19)	Bill Dickey	1.00	.50	.30
(20)	Joe DiMaggio	6.00	3.00	1.75
(21)	George Earnshaw	.50	.25	.15
(22)	Woody English	.50	.25	.15
(23)	Woody English	.50	.25	.15
(24)	Hal Finney	.50	.25	.15
(25)	Freddie Fitzsimmons, Bump Hadley	.50	.25	.15
(26)	Tony Freitas	.50	.25	.15
(27)	Frank Frisch	.75	.40	.25
(28)	Milt Gaston	.50	.25	.15
(29)	Sid Gautreaux	.50	.25	.15
(30)	Charlie Gehringer	.75	.40	.25
(31)	Charley Gelbert	.50	.25	.15
(32)	Lefty Gomez	.75	.40	.25
(33)	Lefty Grove	.75	.40	.25
(34)	Chick Hafey	.75	.40	.25
(35)	Jesse Haines	.75	.40	.25
(36)	Bill Hallahan	.50	.25	.15
(37)	Bucky Harris	.75	.40	.25
(38)	Ed Heusser	.50	.25	.15
(39)	Carl Hubbell	.75	.40	.25
(40)	Carl Hubbell	.75	.40	.25
(41)	Jimmy Jordan	.50	.25	.15
(42)	Joe Judge	.50	.25	.15
(43)	Len Koenecke	.50	.25	.15
(44)	Mark Koenig	.50	.25	.15
(45)	Cookie Lavagetto	.50	.25	.15
(46)	Roxie Lawson	.50	.25	.15
(47)	Tony Lazzeri	.75	.40	.25
(48)	Gus Mancuso	.50	.25	.15
(49)	John McCarthy	.50	.25	.15
(50)	Joe Medwick	.75	.40	.25
(51)	Cliff Melton	.50	.25	.15
(52)	Terry Moore	.50	.25	.15
(53)	John Murphy	.50	.25	.15
(54)	Ken O'Dea	.50	.25	.15
(55)	Bob O'Farrell	.50	.25	.15
(56)	Manuel Onis	.50	.25	.15
(57)	Monte Pearson	.50	.25	.15
(58)	Paul Richards	.50	.25	.15
(59)	Max Rosenfeld	.50	.25	.15
(60)	Red Ruffing	.75	.40	.25
(61)	Red Ruffing	.75	.40	.25
(62)	Hal Schumacher	.50	.25	.15
(63)	George Selkirk	.50	.25	.15
(64)	Joe Shaute	.50	.25	.15
(65)	Gordon Slade	.50	.25	.15
(66)	Lindo Storti	.50	.25	.15
(67)	Smokey Sundra	.50	.25	.15
(68)	Bill Terry	.75	.40	.25
(69)	Jack Tising	.75	.40	.25
(70)	Sandy Vance	.50	.25	.15
(71)	Rube Walberg	.50	.25	.15
(72)	Sammy West	.50	.25	.15
73	Vito Tamulis	.50	.25	.15
74	Kemp Wicker	.50	.25	.15
75	Bob Seeds	.50	.25	.15
76	Jack Saltzgaver	.50	.25	.15
77	Walter Brown	.50	.25	.15
78	Spud Chandler	.50	.25	.15
79	Myril Hoag	.50	.25	.15
80	Joe Glenn	.50	.25	.15
81	Lefty Gomez	.75	.40	.25
82	Arndt Jorgens	.50	.25	.15
83	Jesse Hill	.50	.25	.15
84	Red Rolfe	.50	.25	.15
85	Wes Ferrell	.50	.25	.15
86	Joe Morrissey	.50	.25	.15
87	Tony Piet	.50	.25	.15
88	Fred Walker	.50	.25	.15
89	Bill Dietrich	.50	.25	.15
90	Lyn Lary	.50	.25	.15
91	Lyn Lary	.50	.25	.15
92	Lyn Lary	.50	.25	.15
93	Lyn Lary	.50	.25	.15
94	Buzz Boyle	.50	.25	.15
95	Tony Malinosky	.50	.25	.15
96	Al Lopez	.75	.40	.25
97	Linus Frey	.50	.25	.15
98	Tony Malinosky	.50	.25	.15
99	Owen Carroll	.50	.25	.15
100	Buddy Hassett	.50	.25	.15
101	Gib Brack	.50	.25	.15
102	Sam Leslie	.50	.25	.15
103	Fred Heimach	.50	.25	.15
104	Burleigh Grimes	.75	.40	.25
105	Ray Benge	.50	.25	.15
106	Joe Stripp	.50	.25	.15
107	Joe Becker	.50	.25	.15
108	Oscar Melillo	.50	.25	.15
109	Charley O'Leary, Rogers Hornsby	.75	.40	.25
110	Luke Appling	.75	.40	.25
111	Stan Hack	.60	.30	.20
112	Ray Hayworth	.50	.25	.15
113	Charles Wilson	.50	.25	.15
114	Hal Trosky	.50	.25	.15
115	Wes Ferrell	.50	.25	.15
116	Lyn Lary	.50	.25	.15
117	Milt Gaston	.50	.25	.15
118	Eldon Auker	.50	.25	.15
119	Heinie Manush	.75	.40	.25
120	Jimmie Foxx	1.00	.50	.30
121	Don Heffner	.50	.25	.15
122	George Pipgras	.50	.25	.15
123	Bump Hadley	.50	.25	.15
124	Tommy Henrich	.50	.25	.15
125	Not issued			
126	Not issued			
127	Frank Crosetti	.60	.30	.20
128	Fred Walker	.50	.25	.15
129	Ted Kleinhans	.50	.25	.15

130	Jake Powell	.50	.25	.15
131	Ben Chapman	.50	.25	.15
132	John Murphy	.50	.25	.15
133	Lon Warneke	.50	.25	.15
134	Augie Galan	.50	.25	.15
135	Gene Lillard	.50	.25	.15
136	Stan Hack	.60	.30	.20
137	Frank Demaree	.50	.25	.15
138	Tony Piet	.50	.25	.15
139	Tony Piet	.50	.25	.15
140	Don Brennan	.50	.25	.15
141	Hal Schumacher, Lefty Gomez	.65	.35	.20
142	Bump Hadley	.50	.25	.15
143	Ollie Bejma	.50	.25	.15
144	Jim Bottomley	.75	.40	.25
145	Clay Bryant	.50	.25	.15
146	Charlie Grimm	.50	.25	.15
147	Not issued			
148	Rollie Stiles	.75	.40	.25
149	Al Simmons	.75	.40	.25
150	Al Simmons	.75	.40	.25
151	Lyn Lary	.50	.25	.15
152	Roy Weatherly	.50	.25	.15
153	Whit Wyatt	.50	.25	.15
154	Oscar Vitt	.50	.25	.15
155	Jack Kroner	.50	.25	.15
156	Ted Lyons	.75	.40	.25
157	Joe Malay	.75	.40	.25
158	John McCarthy	.50	.25	.15
159	Hy Vandenberg	.50	.25	.15
160	Hank Leiber	.50	.25	.15
161	Joe Moore	.50	.25	.15
162	Cliff Melton	.50	.25	.15
163	Harry Danning	.50	.25	.15
164	Ray Harrell	.50	.25	.15
165	Bruce Ogrodowski	.50	.25	.15
166	Leo Durocher	.75	.40	.25
167	Leo Durocher	.75	.40	.25
168	William Walker	.50	.25	.15
169	Alvin Crowder	.50	.25	.15
170	Gus Suhr	.50	.25	.15
171	Monty Stratton	.75	.40	.25
172	Boze Berger	.50	.25	.15
173	John Whitehead	.50	.25	.15
174	Joe Heving	.50	.25	.15
175	Merv Shea	.50	.25	.15
176	Ed Durham	.50	.25	.15
177	Buddy Myer	.50	.25	.15
178	Earl Whitehill	.50	.25	.15
179	Joe Cronin	.75	.40	.25
180	Zeke Bonura	.50	.25	.15
181	John Knott	.50	.25	.15
182	John Allen	.50	.25	.15
183	William Knickerbocker	.50	.25	.15
184	Earl Averill	.75	.40	.25
185	Bob Feller	1.00	.50	.30
186	Steve O'Neill	.50	.25	.15
187	Bruce Campbell	.50	.25	.15
188	Ivy Andrews	.50	.25	.15
189	Ivy Andrews	.50	.25	.15
190	Muddy Ruel	.50	.25	.15
191	Art Scharein	.50	.25	.15
192	Merv Shea	.50	.25	.15
193	George Myatt	.50	.25	.15
194	Bill Werber	.50	.25	.15
195	Red Lucas	.50	.25	.15
196	Hugh Luby	.50	.25	.15
197	Vic Sorrell	.50	.25	.15
198	Mickey Cochrane	.75	.40	.25
199	Rudy York	.50	.25	.15
200	Ray Mack	.50	.25	.15
201	Vince DiMaggio	.65	.35	.20
202	Mel Ott	.75	.40	.25
203	John Lucadello	.50	.25	.15
204	Debs Garms	.50	.25	.15
205	John Murphy, Pat Malone, Bump Hadley, Kemp Wicker, John Broaca	.50	.25	.15
206	Stan Sperry	.50	.25	.15
207	Hal Schumacher	.50	.25	.15
208	Blondy Ryan	.50	.25	.15
209	Bob Seeds	.50	.25	.15
210	Danny MacFayden	.50	.25	.15
211	Fran Healy	.50	.25	.15
212	Al Spohrer	.50	.25	.15
213	Ed Linke	.50	.25	.15
214	Joe Schultz	.50	.25	.15
215	Casey Stengel	.75	.40	.25
216	Casey Stengel	.75	.40	.25
217	Phil Hensick	.50	.25	.15
218	Rollie Hemsley	.50	.25	.15
219	Ace Parker	.65	.35	.20
220	Henry Helf	.50	.25	.15
221	Bill Schuster	.50	.25	.15
222	Heinie Schuble	.50	.25	.15
223	John Salveson	.50	.25	.15
224	Robert Grace	.50	.25	.15
225	Sig Gryska	.50	.25	.15
226	Mickey Haslin	.50	.25	.15
227	Randy Gumpert	.50	.25	.15
228	Frank Gustine	.50	.25	.15
229	Marv Gudat	.50	.25	.15
230	Bob Logan	.50	.25	.15
231	Marvin Owen	.50	.25	.15
232	Bucky Walters	.50	.25	.15
233	Marty Hopkins	.50	.25	.15
234	Jimmy Dykes	.50	.25	.15
235	Lefty O'Doul	.60	.30	.20
236	Larry Rosenthal	.50	.25	.15
237	Mickey Haslin	.50	.25	.15
238	Eugene Schott	.50	.25	.15
239	Sad Sam Jones	.50	.25	.15
240	Edwin Rommel	.50	.25	.15
241	Rip Collins	.50	.25	.15
242	Rosy Ryan	.50	.25	.15
243	James Bucher	.50	.25	.15
244	Ethan Allen	.50	.25	.15
245	Dick Bartell	.50	.25	.15
246	Henry Leiber	.50	.25	.15
247	Lou Chiozza	.75	.40	.25
248	Babe Herman	.60	.30	.20
249	Tommy Henrich	.50	.25	.15
250	Thornton Lee	.50	.25	.15
251	Joe Kuhel	.50	.25	.15
252	George Pipgras	.50	.25	.15
253	Luke Sewell	.50	.25	.15
254	Tony Lazzeri	.75	.40	.25
255	Ival Goodman	.50	.25	.15
256	George Rensa	.50	.25	.15
257	Hal Newhouser	.75	.40	.25
258	Rogers Hornsby	1.00	.50	.30
259	Tuck Stainback	.50	.25	.15
260	Vance Page	.50	.25	.15
261	Art Scharein	.50	.25	.15
262	Mike Ryba	.50	.25	.15
263	James Lindsey	.50	.25	.15
264	Ed Parsons	.50	.25	.15
265	Elon Hogsett	.50	.25	.15
266	Bud Hafey	.50	.25	.15
267	John Gill	.50	.25	.15
268	Owen Bush	.50	.25	.15
269	Ethan Allen	.50	.25	.15
270	Jim Bagby	.50	.25	.15
271	Bill Atwood	.50	.25	.15
272	Phil Cavarretta	.50	.25	.15
273	Travis Jackson	.75	.40	.25
274	Ted Olson	.50	.25	.15
275	Boze Berger	.50	.25	.15
276	Norb Kleinke	.50	.25	.15
277	Rip Radcliff	.50	.25	.15
278	Mule Haas	.50	.25	.15
279	Julius Solters	.50	.25	.15
280	Ivey Shiver	.50	.25	.15
281	Wes Schulmerich	.50	.25	.15
282	Ray Kolp	.50	.25	.15
283	Si Johnson	.50	.25	.15
284	Al Hollingsworth	.50	.25	.15
285	D'Arcy Flowers	.50	.25	.15
286	Adam Comorosky	.50	.25	.15
287	Allen Cooke	.50	.25	.15
288	Clyde Kimsey	.50	.25	.15
289	Fred Ostermueller	.50	.25	.15
290	Angelo Giuliani	.50	.25	.15
291	John Wilson	.50	.25	.15
292	George Dickman	.50	.25	.15
293	Jim DeShong	.50	.25	.15
294	Red Evans	.50	.25	.15
295	Curtis Davis	.50	.25	.15
296	Charlie Berry	.50	.25	.15
297	George Gibson	.50	.25	.15
298	Fern Bell	.50	.25	.15
299	Irv Bartling	.50	.25	.15
300	Babe Barna	.50	.25	.15
301	Henry Johnson	.50	.25	.15
302	Harlond Clift	.50	.25	.15
303	Lu Blue	.50	.25	.15
304	George Hockette	.50	.25	.15
305	Walt Bashore	.50	.25	.15
306	Walter Beck	.50	.25	.15
307	Jewel Ens	.50	.25	.15
308	Doc Prothro	.50	.25	.15
309	Morrie Arnovich	.50	.25	.15
310	Bill Killefer	.50	.25	.15
311	Pete Appleton	.50	.25	.15
312	Fred Archer	.50	.25	.15
313	Bill Lohrman	.50	.25	.15
314	Fred Haney	.50	.25	.15
315	Jimmy Ripple	.50	.25	.15
316	Johnny Kerr	.50	.25	.15
317	Harry Gumbert	.50	.25	.15
318	Samuel Derringer	.50	.25	.15
319	Firpo Marberry	.50	.25	.15
320	Waite Hoyt	.75	.40	.25
321	Rick Ferrell	.75	.40	.25
322	Hank Greenberg	1.50	.70	.45
323	Carl Reynolds	.50	.25	.15
324	Roy Johnson	.50	.25	.15
325	Gil English	.50	.25	.15
326	Al Smith	.50	.25	.15
327	Dolph Camilli	.75	.40	.25
328	Oscar Grimes	.50	.25	.15
329	Ray Berres	.50	.25	.15
330	Norm Schlueter	.50	.25	.15
331	Joe Vosmik	.50	.25	.15
332	Michael Kelly	.50	.25	.15
333	Vern Washington	.50	.25	.15
334	"Bad News" Hale	.50	.25	.15
335	Lew Fonseca	.50	.25	.15
336	Mike Kreevich	.50	.25	.15
337	Bob Johnson	.50	.25	.15
338	"Jeep" Handley	.50	.25	.15
339	Gabby Hartnett	.75	.40	.25
340	Freddie Lindstrom	.75	.40	.25
341	Bert Haas	.50	.25	.15
342	Elbie Fletcher	.50	.25	.15
343	Tom Hafey	.50	.25	.15
344	Rip Collins	.50	.25	.15
345	John Babich	.50	.25	.15
346	Joe Beggs	.50	.25	.15
347	Bobo Newsom	.50	.25	.15
348	Wally Berger	.50	.25	.15
349	Bud Thomas	.50	.25	.15
350	Tom Heath	.50	.25	.15
351	Cecil Travis	.50	.25	.15
352	Jack Redmond	.75	.40	.25
353	Fred Schulte	.50	.25	.15
354	Pat Malone	.50	.25	.15
355	Hugh Critz	.50	.25	.15
356	Frank Pytlak	.50	.25	.15
357	Glenn Liebhardt	.50	.25	.15
358	Al Milnar	.50	.25	.15
359	Al Benton	.50	.25	.15
360	Moe Berg	.90	.45	.25
361	Al Brancato	.50	.25	.15
362	Mark Christman	.50	.25	.15
363	Fabian Gaffke	.50	.25	.15
364	George Gill	.50	.25	.15
365	Oral Hildebrand	.50	.25	.15
366	Lou Fette	.50	.25	.15
367	Tex Carleton	.50	.25	.15
368	Don Gutteridge	.50	.25	.15
369	Pete Fox	.50	.25	.15
370	George Blaeholder	.50	.25	.15
371	George Caster	.50	.25	.15
372	Joe Cascarella	.50	.25	.15
373	Jimmy Hitchcock	.50	.25	.15
374	Frank Croucher	.50	.25	.15
375	LeRoy Parmelee	.50	.25	.15
376	Joe Mulligan	.50	.25	.15
377	John Welch	.50	.25	.15
378	Donald McNair	.50	.25	.15
379	Frenchy Bordagaray	.50	.25	.15
380	Denny Galehouse	.50	.25	.15
381	Robert Harris	.50	.25	.15
382	Max Butcher	.50	.25	.15
383	Sam Byrd	.50	.25	.15
384	Pete Coscarart	.50	.25	.15
385	George Case	.50	.25	.15
386	John Hudson	.50	.25	.15
387	Frank Crespi	.50	.25	.15
388	Gene Desautels	.50	.25	.15
389	Bill Cissell	.50	.25	.15
390	John Burns	.50	.25	.15
391	Larry Benton	.50	.25	.15
392	James Holbrook	.50	.25	.15
393	Ernie Koy	.50	.25	.15
394	Bobby Doerr	.75	.40	.25
395	Harry Boyles	.50	.25	.15
396	Pinky Higgins	.50	.25	.15
397	Mel Almada	.60	.30	.20
398	Carl Fischer	.50	.25	.15
399	Rabbit Maranville, Johnny Evers, Hank Gowdy	.65	.35	.20
400	Lou Gehrig	6.00	3.00	1.75
401	Lincoln Blakely	.50	.25	.15
402	James Henry	.50	.25	.15
403	Ed Holley	.50	.25	.15
404	Elmer Hodgin	.50	.25	.15
405	Bob Garbark	.50	.25	.15
406	John Burnett	.50	.25	.15
407	David Harris	.50	.25	.15
408	Johnny Dickshot	.50	.25	.15
409	Ray Mueller	.50	.25	.15
410	John Welaj	.50	.25	.15
411	Les McCrabb	.50	.25	.15
412	George Uhle	.50	.25	.15
413	Leo Mangum	.50	.25	.15
414	Howard Maple	.50	.25	.15
415	Syl Johnson	.50	.25	.15
416	Hershel Martin	.50	.25	.15
417	Joe Martin	.50	.25	.15
418	Phil Masi	.50	.25	.15
419	Bobby Mattick	.50	.25	.15
420	Marshall Mauldin	.50	.25	.15
421	Frank May	.50	.25	.15
422	Merrill May	.50	.25	.15
423	Bill McAfee	.50	.25	.15
424	Benny McCoy	.50	.25	.15
425	Charlie George	.50	.25	.15
426	Roy Hughes	.50	.25	.15
427	Bill Kerksieck	.75	.40	.25
428	Wes Kingdon	.50	.25	.15
429	Lynn King	.50	.25	.15
430	Harry Kinzy	.50	.25	.15
431	Harry Kimberlin	.50	.25	.15
432	Bob Klinger	.50	.25	.15
433	Wilfred Knothe	.50	.25	.15
434	Lou Finney	.50	.25	.15
435	Roy Johnson	.50	.25	.15
436	Woody Jensen	.50	.25	.15
437	George Jeffcoat	.50	.25	.15
438	Roy Joiner	.50	.25	.15
439	Baxter Jordan	.50	.25	.15
440	Edwin Joost	.50	.25	.15
441	Bubber Jonnard	.50	.25	.15
442	Bucky Jacobs	.50	.25	.15
443	Art Jacobs	.50	.25	.15
444	Orville Jorgens	.50	.25	.15
445	Hal Kelleher	.50	.25	.15
446	Harry Kelley	.50	.25	.15
447	Ken Keltner	.50	.25	.15
448	Paul Kardon	.50	.25	.15
449	Alex Kampouris	.50	.25	.15
450	Willie Kamm	.50	.25	.15
451	Bob Kahle	.50	.25	.15
452	Billy Jurges	.50	.25	.15
453	Ken Jungles	.50	.25	.15
454	John Juelich	.50	.25	.15
455	John Marcum	.50	.25	.15
456	Walt Masterson	.50	.25	.15
457	Clint Brown	.50	.25	.15
458	Buddy Lewis	.50	.25	.15
459	Watty Clark	.50	.25	.15
460	Johnny Cooney	.50	.25	.15
461	Mel Harder	.50	.25	.15
462	Justin McLaughlin	.50	.25	.15
463	Frank Grube	.50	.25	.15
464	Jeff Heath	.50	.25	.15
465	Cliff Heathcote	.50	.25	.15
466	Harvey Hendrick	.50	.25	.15
467	Johnny Hodapp	.50	.25	.15
468	Bob Holland	.50	.25	.15
469	Otto Huber	.50	.25	.15
470	Rudy Hulswitt	.50	.25	.15
471	Roy Johnson	.50	.25	.15
472	Smead Jolley	.50	.25	.15
473	Rollie Hemsley, Bob Smith, John Moore	.50	.25	.15
474	John Jones	.50	.25	.15
475	Harry Kelley	.50	.25	.15
476	George Kelly	.50	.25	.15
477	Chuck Klein	.75	.40	.25
478	Joe Krakauskas	.50	.25	.15

479	Mike Kreevich	.50	.25	.15
480	Dick Lanahan	.50	.25	.15
481	Emil "Dutch" Leonard	.50	.25	.15
482	Harl Maggert	.50	.25	.15
483	Cyrus Malis	.50	.25	.15
484	Dario Lodigiani	.50	.25	.15
485	Walt Masterson	.50	.25	.15
486	Rabbit Maranville	.75	.40	.25
487	Ed Marshall	.50	.25	.15
488	Tim McKeithan	.75	.40	.25
489	Patrick McLaughlin	.75	.40	.25
490	Bob McNamara	.50	.25	.15
491	Steve Mesner	.50	.25	.15
492	Clarence Mitchell	.50	.25	.15
493	Mal Moss	.75	.40	.25
494	Joe Murray	.50	.25	.15
495	Pete Naktenis	.50	.25	.15
496	Bill Nicholson	.50	.25	.15
497	John Rigney	.50	.25	.15
498	Clyde Sukeforth	.50	.25	.15
499	Evar Swanson	.50	.25	.15
500	Dan Taylor	.50	.25	.15
501	Sloppy Thurston	.50	.25	.15
502	Forrest Wright	.50	.25	.15
503	Ray Lucas	.50	.25	.15
504	Nig Lipscomb	.75	.40	.25

1973-80 TCMA All-Time Greats Postcards

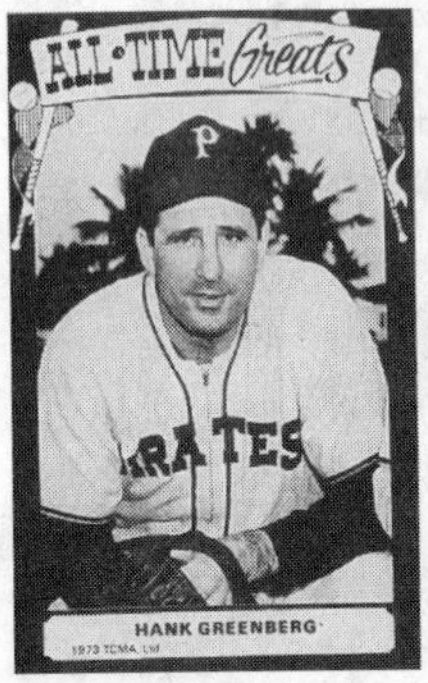

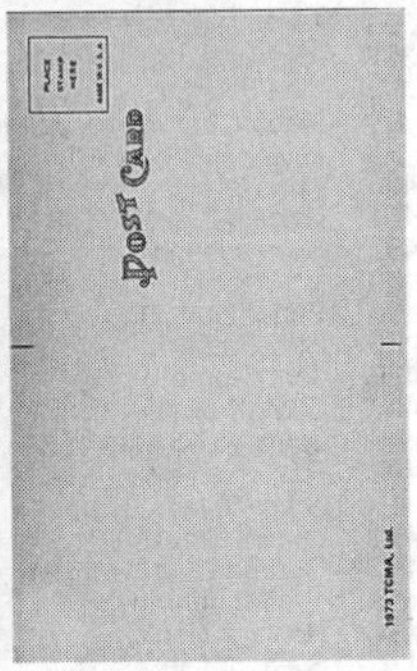

One of the longest collectors' series issued by TCMA in the 1970s was this set of player postcards. Measuring 3-1/2" x 5-1/2" the black-and-white cards have large photos on front, bordered in black and highlighted with banners and baseball equipment. Backs have postcard markings. Six series of cards were issued between 1973-80 and the unnumbered cards are checklisted here in alphabetical order within series.

		NM	EX	VG
Complete Set (156):		150.00	75.00	45.00
Common Player:		1.00	.50	.20
	SERIES 1			
(1)	Luke Appling	1.00	.50	.20
(2)	Mickey Cochrane	1.00	.50	.20
(3)	Eddie Collins	1.00	.50	.20
(4)	Kiki Cuyler	1.00	.50	.20
(5)	Bill Dickey	1.00	.50	.20
(6)	Joe DiMaggio	6.00	3.00	1.75
(7)	Bob Feller	1.00	.50	.20
(8)	Frank Frisch	1.00	.50	.20
(9)	Lou Gehrig	6.00	3.00	1.75
(10)	Goose Goslin	1.00	.50	.20
(11)	Chick Hafey	1.00	.50	.20
(12)	Gabby Hartnett	1.00	.50	.20
(13)	Rogers Hornsby	1.00	.50	.20
(14)	Ted Lyons	1.00	.50	.20
(15)	Connie Mack	1.00	.50	.20
(16)	Heinie Manush	1.00	.50	.20
(17)	Rabbit Maranville	1.00	.50	.20
(18)	Ducky Medwick	1.00	.50	.20
(19)	Al Simmons	1.00	.50	.20
(20)	Bill Terry	1.00	.50	.20
(21)	Pie Traynor	1.00	.50	.20
(22)	Dazzy Vance	1.00	.50	.20
(23)	Cy Young	2.00	1.00	.60
(24)	Gabby Hartnett, Babe Ruth	2.50	1.25	.70
	SERIES 2			
(1)	Roger Bresnahan	1.00	.50	.20
(2)	Dizzy Dean	1.50	.70	.45
(3)	Buck Ewing & mascot	1.00	.50	.20
(4)	Jimmie Foxx	1.50	.70	.45
(5)	Hank Greenberg	2.00	1.00	.60
(6)	Burleigh Grimes	1.00	.50	.20
(7)	Harry Heilmann	1.00	.50	.20
(8)	Waite Hoyt	1.00	.50	.20
(9)	Walter Johnson	2.00	1.00	.60
(10)	George Kelly	1.00	.50	.20
(11)	Christy Mathewson	2.00	1.00	.60
(12)	John McGraw	1.00	.50	.20
(13)	Stan Musial	2.50	1.25	.70
(14)	Mel Ott	1.00	.50	.20
(15)	Satchel Paige	2.50	1.25	.70
(16)	Sam Rice	1.00	.50	.20
(17)	Edd Roush	1.00	.50	.20
(18)	Red Ruffing	1.00	.50	.20
(19)	Casey Stengel	1.00	.50	.20
(20)	Honus Wagner	2.00	1.00	.60
(21)	Lloyd Waner	1.00	.50	.20
(22)	Paul Waner	1.00	.50	.20
(23)	Harry Wright	1.00	.50	.20
(24)	Ross Youngs	1.00	.50	.20
	SERIES 3			
(1)	Home Run Baker	1.00	.50	.20
(2)	Chief Bender	1.00	.50	.20
(3)	Jim Bottomley	1.00	.50	.20
(4)	Lou Boudreau	1.00	.50	.20
(5)	Mordecai Brown	1.00	.50	.20
(6)	Roy Campanella	1.50	.70	.45
(7)	Max Carey	1.00	.50	.20
(8)	Ty Cobb	2.50	1.25	.70
(9)	Earle Combs	1.00	.50	.20
(10)	Jocko Conlan	1.00	.50	.20
(11)	Hugh Duffy	1.00	.50	.20
(12)	Red Faber	1.00	.50	.20
(13)	Lefty Grove	1.00	.50	.20
(14)	Judge K.M. Landis	1.00	.50	.20
(15)	Eddie Plank	1.00	.50	.20
(16)	Hoss Radbourne	1.00	.50	.20
(17)	Eppa Rixey	1.00	.50	.20
(18)	Jackie Robinson	3.00	1.50	.90
(19)	Babe Ruth	9.00	4.50	2.75
(20)	George Sisler	1.00	.50	.20
(21)	Zack Wheat	1.00	.50	.20
(22)	Ted Williams	3.00	1.50	.90
(23)	Mel Ott, Babe Ruth	2.50	1.25	.70
(24)	Tris Speaker & (?)	1.00	.50	.20
	SERIES 4			
(1)	Grover C. Alexander	1.00	.50	.20
(2)	Cap Anson	1.00	.50	.20
(3)	Earl Averill	1.00	.50	.20
(4)	Ed Barrow	1.00	.50	.20
(5)	Yogi Berra	1.50	.70	.45
(6)	Roberto Clemente	5.00	2.50	1.50
(7)	Jimmy Collins	1.00	.50	.20
(8)	Whitey Ford	1.50	.70	.45
(9)	Ford Frick	1.00	.50	.20
(10)	Vernon Gomez	1.00	.50	.20
(11)	Bucky Harris	1.00	.50	.20
(12)	Billy Herman	1.00	.50	.20
(13)	Carl Hubbell	1.00	.50	.20
(14)	Miller Huggins	1.00	.50	.20
(15)	Monte Irvin	1.00	.50	.20
(16)	Ralph Kiner	1.00	.50	.20
(17)	Bill Klem	1.00	.50	.20
(18)	Sandy Koufax	2.50	1.25	.70
(19)	Napoleon Lajoie	1.00	.50	.20
(20)	Bob Lemon	1.00	.50	.20
(21)	Mickey Mantle	12.00	6.00	3.50
(22)	Rube Marquard	1.00	.50	.20
(23)	Joe McCarthy	1.00	.50	.20
(24)	Bill McKechnie	1.00	.50	.20
(25)	Herb Pennock	1.00	.50	.20
(26)	Warren Spahn	1.00	.50	.20
(27)	Joe Tinker	1.00	.50	.20
(28)	Early Wynn	1.00	.50	.20
(29)	Joe Cronin, Honus Wagner, Bill Terry	1.00	.50	.20
(30)	Jimmie Foxx, Lou Gehrig	2.50	1.25	.70
(31)	Hank Greenberg, Ralph Kiner	1.50	.70	.45
(32)	Walter Johnson, Connie Mack	1.00	.50	.20
(33)	Connie Mack, Bob Feller	1.00	.50	.20
(34)	Mel Ott, Lou Gehrig	2.00	1.00	.60
(35)	Al Simmons, Tris Speaker, Ty Cobb	1.50	.70	.45
(36)	Ted Williams, Lou Boudreau	1.00	.50	.20
	SERIES 5			
(1)	Dave Bancroft	1.00	.50	.20
(2)	Ernie Banks	1.50	.70	.45
(3)	Frank Chance	1.00	.50	.20
(4)	Stan Coveleski	1.00	.50	.20
(5)	Billy Evans	1.00	.50	.20
(6)	Clark Griffith	1.00	.50	.20
(7)	Jesse Haines	1.00	.50	.20
(8)	Will Harridge	1.00	.50	.20
(9)_	Harry Hooper	1.00	.50	.20
(10)	Cal Hubbard	1.00	.50	.20
(11)	Hugh Jennings	1.00	.50	.20
(12)	Wee Willie Keeler	1.00	.50	.20
(13)	Fred Lindstrom	1.00	.50	.20
(14)	Pop Lloyd	1.00	.50	.20
(15)	Al Lopez	1.00	.50	.20
(16)	Robin Roberts	1.00	.50	.20
(17)	Amos Rusie	1.00	.50	.20
(18)	Ray Schalk	1.00	.50	.20
(19)	Joe Sewell	1.00	.50	.20
(20)	Rube Waddell	1.00	.50	.20
(21)	George Weiss	1.00	.50	.20
(22)	Dizzy Dean, Gabby Hartnett	1.00	.50	.20
(23)	Joe DiMaggio, Mickey Mantle	9.00	4.50	2.75
(24)	Ted Williams, Joe DiMaggio	7.50	3.75	2.25
	SERIES 6			
(1)	Jack Chesbro	1.00	.50	.20
(2)	Tom Connolly	1.00	.50	.20
(3)	Sam Crawford	1.00	.50	.20
(4)	Elmer Flick	1.00	.50	.20
(5)	Charlie Gehringer	1.00	.50	.20
(6)	Warren Giles	1.00	.50	.20
(7)	Ban Johnson	1.00	.50	.20
(8)	Addie Joss	1.00	.50	.20
(9)	Al Kaline	1.00	.50	.20
(10)	Willie Mays	2.50	1.25	.70
(11)	Joe McGinnity	1.00	.50	.20
(12)	Larry McPhail	1.00	.50	.20
(13)	Branch Rickey	1.00	.50	.20
(14)	Wilbert Robinson	1.00	.50	.20
(15)	Duke Snider	1.50	.70	.45
(16)	Tris Speaker	1.00	.50	.20
(17)	Bobby Wallace	1.00	.50	.20
(18)	Hack Wilson	1.00	.50	.20
(19)	Yogi Berra, Casey Stengel	1.50	.70	.45
(20)	Warren Giles, Roberto Clemente	6.00	3.00	1.75
(21)	Mickey Mantle, Willie Mays	8.00	4.00	2.50
(22)	John McGraw, Babe Ruth	2.50	1.25	.70
(23)	Satchel Paige, Bob Feller	2.00	1.00	.60
(24)	Paul Waner, Lloyd Waner	2.00	1.00	.60

1973-78 TCMA League Leaders

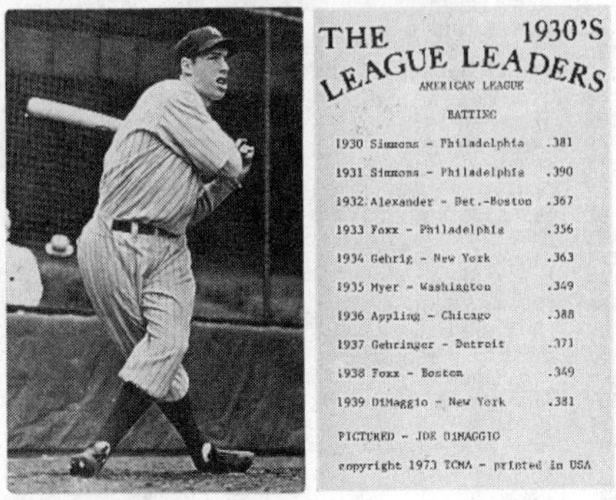

One of TCMA's earliest major series of collectors cards was this run of postcard-size (3-1/2" x 5-1/2") black-and-whites honoring various statistical leaders in each league from the 1920s through the 1950s. Backs have a list of the leaders by year within decade, with one of them pictured on the front. The unnumbered cards are checklisted here in alphabetical order within decade, as they were issued.

		NM	EX	VG
Complete Set (96):		190.00	95.00	55.00
Common Player:		5.00	2.50	1.50
	Complete set, The 1920s	50.00	25.00	15.00
(1)	Grover C. Alexander	5.00	2.50	1.50
(2)	Jim Bagby, Sr.	5.00	2.50	1.50
(3)	Jim Bottomley	5.00	2.50	1.50
(4)	Eddie Collins	5.00	2.50	1.50
(5)	Earle Combs	5.00	2.50	1.50
(6)	Kiki Cuyler	5.00	2.50	1.50
(7)	Urban "Red" Faber	5.00	2.50	1.50
(8)	Johnny Frederick	5.00	2.50	1.50
(9)	Charlie Gehringer	5.00	2.50	1.50
(10)	Goose Goslin	5.00	2.50	1.50
(11)	Rogers Hornsby	5.00	2.50	1.50
(12)	Walter Johnson	6.25	3.25	2.00
(13)	Freddie Lindstrom	5.00	2.50	1.50
(14)	Bob Meusel	5.00	2.50	1.50
(15)	Charlie Root	5.00	2.50	1.50
(16)	Babe Ruth, Rogers Hornsby	7.50	3.75	2.25
(17)	Al Simmons, Babe Ruth	7.50	3.75	2.25
(18)	Tris Speaker	5.00	2.50	1.50
(19)	Dazzy Vance	5.00	2.50	1.50
(20)	Lloyd Waner	5.00	2.50	1.50
(21)	Cy Williams	5.00	2.50	1.50
(22)	Ken Williams	5.00	2.50	1.50
(23)	Hack Wilson	5.00	2.50	1.50
(24)	Ross Youngs	5.00	2.50	1.50
	Complete set, The 1930s	50.00	25.00	15.00
(1)	Johnny Allen	5.00	2.50	1.50
(2)	Beau Bell	5.00	2.50	1.50
(3)	Cy Blanton	5.00	2.50	1.50
(4)	Ben Chapman	5.00	2.50	1.50
(5)	Joe Cronin	5.00	2.50	1.50
(6)	Dizzy Dean	7.50	3.75	2.25
(7)	Joe DiMaggio	20.00	10.00	6.00
(8)	Jimmie Foxx	5.00	2.50	1.50
(9)	Lou Gehrig	15.00	7.50	4.50
(10)	Charlie Gehringer	5.00	2.50	1.50
(11)	Lefty Gomez	5.00	2.50	1.50
(12)	Ival Goodman	5.00	2.50	1.50
(13)	Lefty Grove	5.00	2.50	1.50
(14)	Billy Herman	5.00	2.50	1.50
(15)	Ernie Lombardi	5.00	2.50	1.50
(16)	Chuck Klein	5.00	2.50	1.50
(17)	Heinie Manush	5.00	2.50	1.50
(18)	Pepper Martin	5.00	2.50	1.50
(19)	Joe Medwick	5.00	2.50	1.50
(20)	Van Mungo	5.00	2.50	1.50
(21)	Mel Ott	5.00	2.50	1.50
(22)	Bill Terry	5.00	2.50	1.50
(23)	Hal Trosky	5.00	2.50	1.50
(24)	Arky Vaughan	5.00	2.50	1.50
	Complete set, The 1940s	50.00	25.00	15.00
(1)	Gene Bearden	5.00	2.50	1.50
(2)	Lou Boudreau	5.00	2.50	1.50
(3)	George Case	5.00	2.50	1.50
(4)	Phil Cavarretta	5.00	2.50	1.50
(5)	Bob Feller	6.25	3.25	2.00
(6)	Boo Ferriss	5.00	2.50	1.50
(7)	Jeff Heath	5.00	2.50	1.50
(8)	Tommy Holmes	5.00	2.50	1.50
(9)	Hank Greenberg	8.75	4.50	2.75
(10)	Larry Jansen	5.00	2.50	1.50
(11)	George Kell	5.00	2.50	1.50
(12)	Ralph Kiner	5.00	2.50	1.50
(13)	Marty Marion	5.00	2.50	1.50
(14)	Johnny Mize	5.00	2.50	1.50
(15)	Stan Musial	10.00	5.00	3.00
(16)	Bill Nicholson	5.00	2.50	1.50
(17)	Johnny Pesky	5.00	2.50	1.50
(18)	Jackie Robinson	10.00	5.00	3.00
(19)	Enos Slaughter	5.00	2.50	1.50
(20)	Snuffy Stirnweiss	5.00	2.50	1.50
(21)	Bill Voiselle	5.00	2.50	1.50
(22)	Bucky Walters	5.00	2.50	1.50
(23)	Ted Williams	10.00	5.00	3.00
(24)	Ted Williams, Joe DiMaggio	10.00	5.00	3.00
	Complete set, The 1950s	50.00	25.00	15.00

(1)	Luis Aparicio	5.00	2.50	1.50
(2)	Ernie Banks	5.00	2.50	1.50
(3)	Bill Bruton	5.00	2.50	1.50
(4)	Lew Burdette	5.00	2.50	1.50
(5)	Rocky Colavito	5.00	2.50	1.50
(6)	Dom DiMaggio	5.00	2.50	1.50
(7)	Ferris Fain	5.00	2.50	1.50
(8)	Whitey Ford	5.00	2.50	1.50
(9)	Don Hoak	5.00	2.50	1.50
(10)	Sam Jethroe	5.00	2.50	1.50
(11)	Ted Kluszewski	5.00	2.50	1.50
(12)	Harvey Kuenn	5.00	2.50	1.50
(13)	Bob Lemon	5.00	2.50	1.50
(14)	Mickey Mantle	30.00	15.00	9.00
(15)	Willie Mays	15.00	7.50	4.50
(16)	Willie Mays, Bobby Avila	5.00	2.50	1.50
(17)	Minnie Minoso	5.00	2.50	1.50
(18)	Don Newcombe	5.00	2.50	1.50
(19)	Robin Roberts	5.00	2.50	1.50
(20)	Hank Sauer	5.00	2.50	1.50
(21)	Roy Sievers	5.00	2.50	1.50
(22)	Bobby Shantz	5.00	2.50	1.50
(23)	Duke Snider	6.25	3.25	2.00
(24)	Bill Virdon	5.00	2.50	1.50

1974-75 TCMA St. Louis Browns

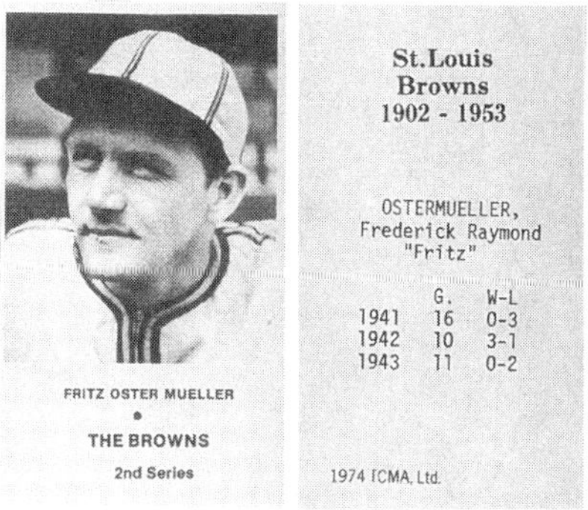

Some of baseball's most loveable losers from about the 1930s through the team's flight to Baltimore in 1953 are presented in this multi-series collectors' issue. Cards are printed in a 2-1/4" x 3-7/8" format, with brown ink used on both front and back. Some cards have player identification on front, some only on back. All cards have a TCMA copyright date line and a few player stats for his years with the Brownies. The unnumbered cards are checklisted here alphabetically without regard to series.

		NM	EX	VG
Complete Set (108):		95.00	47.00	28.00
Common Player:		1.00	.50	.30
(1)	Ethan Allen	1.00	.50	.30
(2)	Mel Almada	1.50	.70	.45
(3)	Bow-Wow Arft	1.00	.50	.30
(4)	Ed Baecht	1.00	.50	.30
(5)	Floyd Baker	1.00	.50	.30
(6)	John Bassler	1.00	.50	.30
(7)	Matt Batts	1.00	.50	.30
(8)	Ollie Bejma	1.00	.50	.30
(9)	John Berardino	3.00	1.50	.90
(10)	Hill Billy Bildilli	1.00	.50	.30
(11)	Sheriff Blake	1.00	.50	.30
(12)	Julio Bonetti	1.00	.50	.30
(13)	Jim Bottomley	2.00	1.00	.60
(14)	Willard Brown	1.00	.50	.30
(15)	Tommy Byrne	1.00	.50	.30
(16)	Skippy Byrnes	1.00	.50	.30
(17)	Teach Caldwell	1.00	.50	.30
(18)	Scoops Carey	1.00	.50	.30
(19)	Ray Coleman	1.00	.50	.30
(20)	Clint Courtney	1.00	.50	.30
(21)	Stinky Davis	1.00	.50	.30
(22)	Jim Delsing	1.00	.50	.30
(23)	Kid DeMars	1.00	.50	.30
(24)	Bob Dillinger	1.00	.50	.30
(25)	Mule Fannin	1.00	.50	.30
(26)	Tom Fine	1.00	.50	.30
(27)	Owen Friend	1.00	.50	.30
(28)	Eddie Gaedel	3.00	1.50	.90
(29)	Denny Galehouse	1.00	.50	.30
(30)	Joe Gallagher	1.00	.50	.30
(31)	Ned Garver	1.00	.50	.30
(32)	Pete Gray	3.00	1.50	.90
(33)	Fred Haney	1.00	.50	.30
(34)	Bob Harris	1.00	.50	.30
(35)	Red Hayworth	1.00	.50	.30
(36)	Jeff Heath	1.00	.50	.30
(37)	Jeep Heffner	1.00	.50	.30
(38)	Rollie Hemsley	1.00	.50	.30
(39)	Procopio Herrera	1.50	.70	.45
(40)	Oral Hildebrand	1.00	.50	.30
(41)	Fred Hoffman	1.00	.50	.30
(42)	Chief Hogsett	1.00	.50	.30
(43)	Walt Holke	1.00	.50	.30
(44)	Boots Hollingsworth	1.00	.50	.30
(45)	Hal Hudson	1.50	.70	.45
(46)	Ben Huffman	1.00	.50	.30
(47)	Jack Jakucki	1.00	.50	.30
(48)	Walt Judnich	1.00	.50	.30
(49)	Bill Kennedy	1.00	.50	.30
(50)	Bill Knickerbocker	1.00	.50	.30
(51)	John Knott	1.00	.50	.30
(52)	Dick Kokos	1.00	.50	.30
(53)	John Kramer	1.00	.50	.30
(54)	Mike Kreevich	1.00	.50	.30
(55)	Red Kress	1.00	.50	.30
(56)	Lou Kretlow	1.00	.50	.30
(57)	Dick Kryhoski	1.00	.50	.30
(58)	Chet Laabs	1.00	.50	.30
(59)	Peanuts Lehner	1.00	.50	.30
(60)	Footsie Lenhardt	1.00	.50	.30
(61)	Nig Lipscomb	1.00	.50	.30
(62)	John Lucadello	1.00	.50	.30
(63)	Joe Lutz	1.00	.50	.30
(64)	Bob Mahoney	1.00	.50	.30
(65)	Frank Mancuso	1.00	.50	.30
(66)	Cliff Mapes	1.00	.50	.30
(67)	Marty Marion	1.25	.60	.40
(68)	Mike Mazzera	1.00	.50	.30
(69)	Red McQuillen	1.00	.50	.30
(70)	George McQuinn	1.00	.50	.30
(71)	Ski Melillo	1.00	.50	.30
(72)	Cass Michaels	1.00	.50	.30
(73)	Lefty Mills	1.00	.50	.30
(74)	Les Moss	1.00	.50	.30
(75)	Bob Muncrief	1.00	.50	.30
(76)	Bobo Newsom	1.00	.50	.30
(77)	Fritz Ostermueller	1.00	.50	.30
(78)	Joe Ostrowski	1.00	.50	.30
(79)	Stubby Overmire	1.00	.50	.30
(80)	Satchel Paige	3.00	1.50	.90
(81)	Ed Pellagrini	1.00	.50	.30
(82)	Duane Pillette	1.00	.50	.30
(83)	Nelson Potter	1.00	.50	.30
(84)	Rip Radcliff	1.00	.50	.30
(85)	Harry Rice	1.00	.50	.30
(86)	Jim Rivera	1.00	.50	.30
(87)	Fred Sanford	1.00	.50	.30
(88)	Luke Sewell	1.00	.50	.30
(89)	Al Shirley	1.00	.50	.30
(90)	Roy Sievers	1.00	.50	.30
(91)	Lou Sleator	1.00	.50	.30
(92)	Dick Starr	1.00	.50	.30
(93)	Junior Stephens	1.00	.50	.30
(94)	Hank Thompson	1.00	.50	.30
(95)	Tom Turner	1.00	.50	.30
(96)	Tom Upton	1.00	.50	.30
(97)	Russ Van Atta	1.00	.50	.30
(98)	Joe Vosmik	1.00	.50	.30
(99)	Jim Walkup	1.00	.50	.30
(100)	Sam West	1.00	.50	.30
(101)	Jerome Witte	1.00	.50	.30
(102)	Ken Wood	1.00	.50	.30
(103)	Bob Young	1.00	.50	.30
(104)	Al Zarilla	1.00	.50	.30
(105)	Sam Zoldak	1.00	.50	.30
(106)	1944 Infield	1.00	.50	.30
(107)	1951 Browns	1.00	.50	.30
(108)	1952 Browns	1.00	.50	.30

1973 TCMA 1890 Base-ball Season

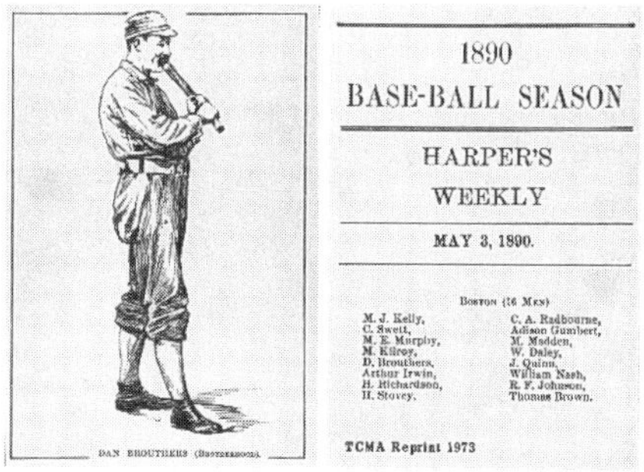

This set commemorates the baseball "war" of 1890 when many National League players - stars and journeymen alike - defected to a new player-owned league called, appropriately enough, the Players League. Fronts of these 3-1/8" x 4-1/2" black-and-white cards feature reproductions of woodcuts originally printed in Harper's Weekly. Backs have information about the teams in each league. The unnumbered cards are checklisted here in alphabetical order. Original issue price of the set was $3.

		NM	EX	VG
Complete Set (30):		48.00	24.00	14.50
Common Player:		2.00	1.00	.60
(1)	Cap Anson	2.00	1.00	.60
(2)	Dan Brouthers	2.00	1.00	.60
(3)	Thomas E. Burns	2.00	1.00	.60
(4)	John Clarkson	2.00	1.00	.60
(5)	C.A. Comiskey	2.00	1.00	.60
(6)	Roger Connor	2.00	1.00	.60
(7)	E.N. Crane	2.00	1.00	.60
(8)	Jeremiah Denny	2.00	1.00	.60
(9)	William B. Ewing	2.00	1.00	.60
(10)	D.L. Foutz	2.00	1.00	.60
(11)	John W. Glasscock	2.00	1.00	.60
(12)	W. Hallman	2.00	1.00	.60
(13)	Edward Hanlon	2.00	1.00	.60
(14)	Timothy J. Keefe	2.00	1.00	.60
(15)	M.J. Kelly	2.00	1.00	.60
(16)	M. Kilroy	2.00	1.00	.60
(17)	W.A. Latham	2.00	1.00	.60
(18)	J.A. McPhee	2.00	1.00	.60
(19)	Joseph Mulvey	2.00	1.00	.60
(20)	W.D. O'Brien	2.00	1.00	.60
(21)	David Orr	2.00	1.00	.60
(22)	John G. Reilly	2.00	1.00	.60
(23)	S.L. Thompson	2.00	1.00	.60
(24)	M. Tiernan	2.00	1.00	.60
(25)	John M. Ward	2.00	1.00	.60
(26)	M. Welsh (Welch)	2.00	1.00	.60
(27)	A. Weyhing	2.00	1.00	.60
(28)	Charles Zimmer	2.00	1.00	.60
(29)	A dive for second base	1.00	.50	.30
(30)	Brotherhood Players header card	1.00	.50	.30

1974 TCMA 1890 Brooklyn Club

The National League champion Brooklyn Bridegrooms are featured in this collectors issue. Fronts of the 3-1/2" x 3-3/4" black-and-white cards picture the players in dress suits with ornate designs around the border. The design was copied from an 1890 Brooklyn scorecard/yearbook. Backs have biographical information and career highlights, also copied from the earlier publication. The back also includes a 1974 TCMA reprint notice. The unnumbered cards are checklisted here in alphabetical order.

		NM	EX	VG
Complete Set (16):		50.00	25.00	15.50
Common Player:		4.00	2.00	1.25
(1)	Thomas P. Burns	4.00	2.00	1.25
(2)	Albert J. Bushong	4.00	2.00	1.25
(3)	Robert Lee Caruthers	4.00	2.00	1.25
(4)	Robert H. Clark	4.00	2.00	1.25
(5)	Hubbert Collins	4.00	2.00	1.25
(6)	John S. Corkhill	4.00	2.00	1.25
(7)	Thomas P. Daly	4.00	2.00	1.25
(8)	D.L. Foutz	4.00	2.00	1.25
(9)	Michael F. Hughes	4.00	2.00	1.25
(10)	Thomas J. Lovett	4.00	2.00	1.25
(11)	W.H. McGunnigle	4.00	2.00	1.25
(12)	Wm. D. O'Brien	4.00	2.00	1.25
(13)	George Burton Pinkney	4.00	2.00	1.25
(14)	George J. Smith	4.00	2.00	1.25
(15)	George T. Stallings	4.00	2.00	1.25
(16)	Wm. H. Terry	4.00	2.00	1.25

1974 TCMA 1929-31 Athletics

Stars of the Philadelphia A's dynasty which won two World Series and an A.L. pennant from 1929-31 are featured in this collectors issue. The 2-5/8" x 4" cards have black-and-white player photos at center.

Printed in green in the white border at top is "1929-31 Athletics". At bottom, also in green, is the player's name and position. Backs are in black-and-white with stats for 1929, 1930 and 1931, as appropriate. The unnumbered cards are checklisted here in alphabetical order.

		NM	EX	VG
Complete Set (25):		48.00	24.00	14.50
Common Player:		2.00	1.00	.60
(1)	Joe Boley	2.00	1.00	.60
(2)	Mickey Cochrane	2.50	1.25	.70
(3)	Eddie Collins, Lew Krausse	2.00	1.00	.60
(4)	"Doc" Cramer	2.00	1.00	.60
(5)	Jimmy Dykes	2.00	1.00	.60
(6)	George Earnshaw	2.00	1.00	.60
(7)	Howard Ehmke	2.00	1.00	.60
(8)	Lou Finney, John Heving	2.00	1.00	.60
(9)	Jimmie Foxx	3.00	1.50	.90
(10)	Walt French, Waite Hoyt	2.00	1.00	.60
(11)	"Lefty" Grove	3.00	1.50	.90
(12)	"Mule" Haas	2.00	1.00	.60
(13)	Sammy Hale	2.00	1.00	.60
(14)	"Pinky" Higgins, Phil Todt	2.00	1.00	.60
(15)	Earle Mack, Connie Mack	2.00	1.00	.60
(16)	Roy Mahaffey	2.00	1.00	.60
(17)	Eric McNair	2.00	1.00	.60
(18)	Bing Miller	2.00	1.00	.60
(19)	Jim Moore, Jim Peterson	2.00	1.00	.60
(20)	Jack Quinn	2.00	1.00	.60
(21)	Eddie Rommel	2.00	1.00	.60
(22)	Al Simmons	2.50	1.25	.70
(23)	Homer Summa	2.00	1.00	.60
(24)	Rube Walberg	2.00	1.00	.60
(25)	"Dib" Williams	2.00	1.00	.60
(26)	Team photo card (10" x 5")	10.00	5.00	3.00
(28)	Connie Mack Stadium (5-3/4" x 3-3/4")	5.00	2.50	1.50

1974 TCMA 1934 St. Louis Cardinals

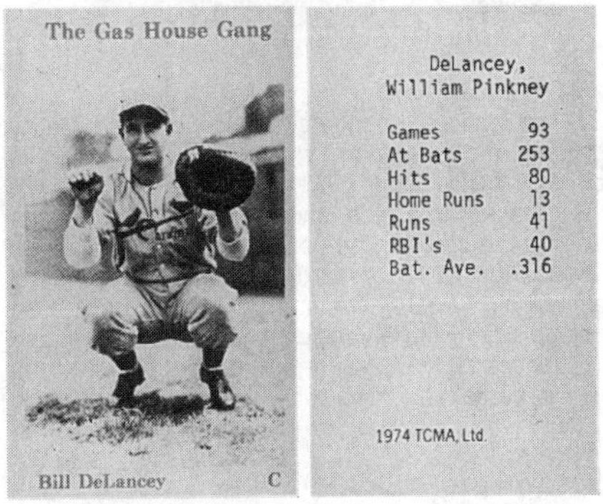

The "Gas House Gang" (as some of these cards are designated) is featured in this collectors issue. Cards are 2-1/4" x 3-5/8" (#27-31 are 4-1/2" x 3-3/4") and feature black-and-white photos on front with red typography. Backs have a few stats in black-and-white. Some cards have a title at top front reading "1934 Cardinals". The unnumbered cards are checklisted here in alphabetical order.

		NM	EX	VG
Complete Set (31):		50.00	25.00	15.00
Common Player:		2.00	1.00	.60
(1)	"Tex" Carleton	2.00	1.00	.60
(2)	"Ripper" Collins	2.00	1.00	.60
(3)	"Pat" Crawford	2.00	1.00	.60
(4)	"Spud" Davis	2.00	1.00	.60
(5)	"Daffy" Dean	2.50	1.25	.70
(6)	"Dizzy" Dean	4.00	2.00	1.25
(7)	Bill DeLancey	2.00	1.00	.60
(8)	Leo Durocher	2.50	1.25	.70
(9)	Frank Frisch	2.50	1.25	.70
(10)	"Chick" Fullis	2.00	1.00	.60
(11)	"Mike" Gonzalez	2.50	1.25	.70
(12)	"Pop" Haines	2.50	1.25	.70
(13)	Bill Hallahan	2.00	1.00	.60
(14)	Francis Healey (Healy)	2.00	1.00	.60
(15)	Jim Lindsey	2.00	1.00	.60
(16)	"Pepper" Martin	2.50	1.25	.70
(17)	"Ducky" Medwick	2.50	1.25	.70
(18)	Jim Mooney	2.00	1.00	.60
(19)	Ernie Orsatti	2.00	1.00	.60
(20)	Flint Rhem	2.00	1.00	.60
(21)	John Rothrock	2.00	1.00	.60
(22)	"Dazzy" Vance	2.50	1.25	.70
(23)	Bill Walker	2.00	1.00	.60
(24)	"Buzzy" Wares	2.00	1.00	.60
(25)	"Whitey" Whitehead	2.00	1.00	.60
(26)	Jim Winford	2.00	1.00	.60
(27)	"Daffy" & "Dizzy" (Daffy Dean, Dizzy Dean)	4.00	2.00	1.25
(28)	Dizzy & Leo Celebrate (Dizzy Dean, Leo Durocher)	2.50	1.25	.70
(29)	Durocher Scores (Leo Durocher) (1934 World Series)	2.00	1.00	.60
(30)	Medwick Out Cochrane Catcher (Mickey Cochrane, Ducky Medwick) (1934 World Series)	2.00	1.00	.60
(31)	1934 St. Louis Cardinals World Champions	2.00	1.00	.60

1974 TCMA 1934-5 Detroit Tigers

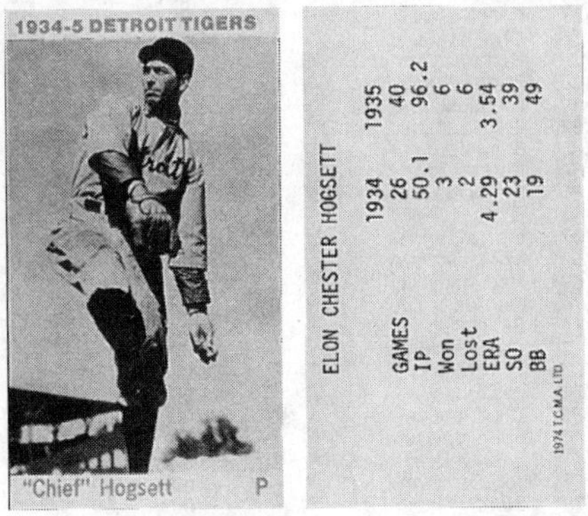

Members of the 1934 A.L. Champion and 1935 World's Champion teams are featured in this collectors issue team set. Except for a pair of large-format (4-1/4" x 3-3/4") cards, the cards measure about 2-1/8" x 3-5/8". Fronts have black-and-white photos. Above and below the photo are white stripes with the set title, player name and position. Backs are in black-and-white with 1934 and/or 1935 stats. The unnumbered cards are checklisted here alphabetically.

		NM	EX	VG
Complete Set (36):		35.00	17.50	10.50
Common Player:		1.00	.50	.30
(1)	Eldon Auker	1.00	.50	.30
(2)	Del Baker	1.00	.50	.30
(3)	Tommy Bridges	1.00	.50	.30
(4)	"Flea" Clifton	1.00	.50	.30
(5)	Mickey Cochrane	2.00	1.00	.60
(6)	"General" Crowder	1.00	.50	.30
(7)	Frank Doljack	1.00	.50	.30
(8)	Carl Fischer	1.00	.50	.30
(9)	Pete Fox	1.00	.50	.30
(10)	Vic Frasier	1.00	.50	.30
(11)	Charlie Gehringer	2.00	1.00	.60
(12)	Goose Goslin	1.00	.50	.30
(13)	Hank Greenberg	2.50	1.25	.70
(14)	Luke Hamlin	1.00	.50	.30
(15)	Clyde Hatter	1.00	.50	.30
(16)	Ray Hayworth	1.00	.50	.30
(17)	"Chief" Hogsett	1.00	.50	.30
(18)	Roxie Lawson	1.00	.50	.30
(19)	"Firpo" Marberry	1.00	.50	.30
(20)	Chet Morgan	1.00	.50	.30
(21)	Marv Owen	1.00	.50	.30
(22)	"Cy" Perkins	1.00	.50	.30
(23)	"Red" Phillips	1.00	.50	.30
(24)	Frank Reiber	1.00	.50	.30
(25)	Billy Rogell	1.00	.50	.30
(26)	"Schoolboy" Rowe	1.50	.70	.45
(27)	"Heinie" Schuble	1.00	.50	.30
(28)	Hugh Shelley	1.00	.50	.30
(29)	Vic Sorrell	1.00	.50	.30
(30)	Joe Sullivan	1.00	.50	.30
(31)	"Gee" Walker	1.00	.50	.30
(32)	"Hub" Walker	1.00	.50	.30
(33)	"Jo-Jo" White	1.00	.50	.30
(34)	Rudy York	1.00	.50	.30
(35)	1934 Pitchers (Eldon Auker, Firpo Marberry, Tommy Bridges, Schoolboy Rowe) (4-1/4" x 3-3/4")	3.00	1.50	.90
(36)	1935 Outfield (Goose Goslin, Jo-Jo White, Pete Fox) (4-1/4" x 3-3/4")	3.00	1.50	.90

1974 TCMA 1936-1939 Yankee Dynasty

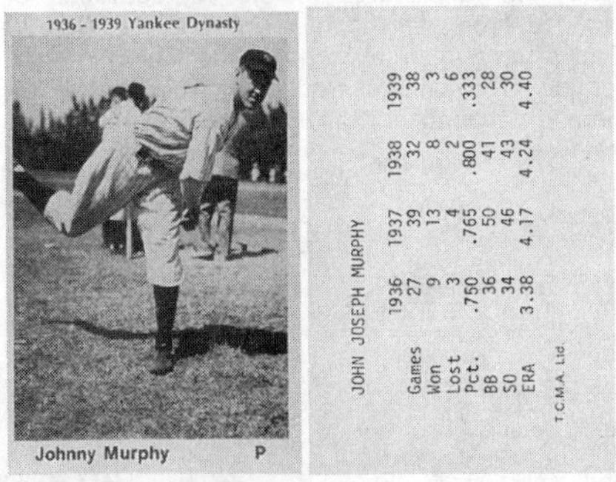

Many of the players who participated in one or more of the Yankees' four consecutive World Champion seasons in the late 1930s are included in this collectors' edition. Cards are 2-3/4" x 4" and feature black-and-white photos on front. In the white borders at top and bottom, the set name and player identification are printed in blue. Backs have stats for each season and are printed in black-and-white. The unnumbered cards are checklisted here alphabetically.

		NM	EX	VG
Complete Set (51):		65.00	32.50	19.50
Common Player:		1.00	.50	.30
(1)	"Poison Ivy" Andrews	1.00	.50	.30
(2)	Joe Beggs	1.00	.50	.30
(3)	Marv Breuer	1.00	.50	.30
(4)	Johnny Broaca	1.00	.50	.30
(5)	"Jumbo" Brown	1.00	.50	.30
(6)	"Spud" Chandler	1.00	.50	.30
(7)	Ben Chapman	1.00	.50	.30
(8)	Earle Combs	1.00	.50	.30
(9)	Frankie Crosetti	1.00	.50	.30
(10)	"Babe" Dahlgren	1.00	.50	.30
(11)	Bill Dickey	1.50	.70	.45
(12)	Joe DiMaggio	12.00	6.00	3.50
(13)	Atley Donald	1.00	.50	.30
(14)	Wes Ferrell	1.00	.50	.30
(15)	Artie Fletcher	1.00	.50	.30
(16)	Joe Gallagher	1.00	.50	.30
(17)	Lou Gehrig	12.00	6.00	3.50
(18)	Joe Glenn	1.00	.50	.30
(19)	"Lefty" Gomez	1.00	.50	.30
(20)	Joe Gordon	1.00	.50	.30
(21)	"Bump" Hadley	1.00	.50	.30
(22)	Don Heffner	1.00	.50	.30
(23)	Tommy Henrich	1.00	.50	.30
(24)	Oral Hildebrand	1.00	.50	.30
(25)	Myril Hoag	1.00	.50	.30
(26)	Roy Johnson	1.00	.50	.30
(27)	Arndt Jorgens	1.00	.50	.30
(28)	Charlie Keller	1.00	.50	.30
(29)	Ted Kleinhans	1.00	.50	.30
(30)	Billy Knickerbocker	1.00	.50	.30
(31)	Tony Lazzeri	1.00	.50	.30
(32)	Frank Makosky	1.00	.50	.30
(33)	"Pat" Malone	1.00	.50	.30
(34)	Johnny Murphy	1.00	.50	.30
(35)	"Monty" Pearson	1.00	.50	.30
(36)	"Jake" Powell	1.00	.50	.30
(37)	"Red" Rolfe	1.00	.50	.30
(38)	"Buddy" Rosar	1.00	.50	.30
(39)	"Red" Ruffing	1.00	.50	.30
(40)	Marius Russo	1.00	.50	.30
(41)	"Jack" Saltzgaver	1.00	.50	.30
(42)	Paul Schreiber	1.00	.50	.30
(43)	Johnny Schulte	1.00	.50	.30
(44)	Bob Seeds	1.00	.50	.30
(45)	"Twinkletoes" Selkirk	1.00	.50	.30
(46)	Lee Stine	1.00	.50	.30
(47)	Steve Sundra	1.00	.50	.30
(48)	"Sandy" Vance	1.00	.50	.30
(49)	"Dixie" Walker	1.00	.50	.30
(50)	Kemp Wicker	1.00	.50	.30
(51)	Joe McCarthy, Jacob Ruppert	1.00	.50	.30
	5-1/2" x 4" FEATURE CARDS			
(1)	Joe DiMaggio, Frank Crosetti, Tony Lazzeri, Bill Dickey, Lou Gehrig, Jake Powell, George Selkirk	3.00	1.50	.90
(2)	Lou Gehrig, Joe DiMaggio	5.00	2.50	1.50
(3)	Gehrig Hits Another	5.00	2.50	1.50
(4)	Red Rolfe, Tony Lazzeri, Lou Gehrig, Frank Crosetti	3.00	1.50	.90
(5)	World Champions - 1936	3.00	1.50	.90
(6)	World Champions - 1937	3.00	1.50	.90
(7)	World Champions - 1938	3.00	1.50	.90
(8)	World Champions - 1939	3.00	1.50	.90

1974 TCMA 1952 Brooklyn Dodgers

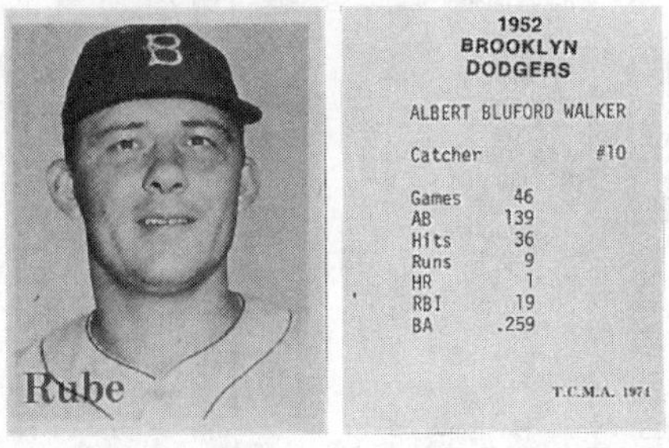

The National League champion '52 Dodgers are featured in this collectors issue. Nominally 2-3/4" x 3-3/8", the cards are often found with small variations in size. Fronts are printed in red and blue with a white border. The only identification on front is the player's first name or nickname. Backs are in black-

and-white with the player's full name, position, uniform number, 1952 stats and TCMA copyright. Cards are checklisted here in alphabetical order.

		NM	EX	VG
Complete Set (39):		55.00	27.50	15.50
Common Player:		.75	.35	.20
(1)	Header/team history card (Jackie Robinson, Gil Hodges, Roy Campanella, Billy Cox, Pee Wee Reese)	2.25	1.25	.70
(2)	Cal Abrams	.75	.35	.20
(3)	Sandy Amoros	.75	.35	.20
(4)	Joe Black	1.25	.60	.40
(5)	Ralph Branca	.75	.35	.20
(6)	Rocky Bridges	.75	.35	.20
(7)	Roy Campanella	6.00	3.00	1.75
(8)	Billy Cox	.75	.35	.20
(9)	Chuck Dressen	.75	.35	.20
(10)	Carl Erskine	1.25	.60	.40
(11)	Carl Furillo	1.50	.70	.45
(12)	Billy Herman	.90	.45	.25
(13)	Gil Hodges	4.50	2.25	1.25
(14)	Tommy Holmes	.75	.35	.20
(15)	Jim Hughes	.75	.35	.20
(16)	Clyde King	.75	.35	.20
(17)	Clem Labine	.75	.35	.20
(18)	Joe Landrum	.75	.35	.20
(19)	Cookie Lavagetto	.75	.35	.20
(20)	Ken Lehman	.75	.35	.20
(21)	Steve Lembo	.75	.35	.20
(22)	Billy Loes	.75	.35	.20
(23)	Ray Moore	.75	.35	.20
(24)	Bobby Morgan	.75	.35	.20
(25)	Ron Negray	.75	.35	.20
(26)	Rocky Nelson	.75	.35	.20
(27)	Andy Pafko	.75	.35	.20
(28)	Jake Pitler	.75	.35	.20
(29)	Bud Podbielan	.75	.35	.20
(30)	Pee Wee Reese	4.50	2.25	1.25
(31)	Jackie Robinson	12.00	6.00	3.50
(32)	Preacher Roe	.90	.45	.25
(33)	Johnny Rutherford	.75	.35	.20
(34)	Johnny Schmitz	.75	.35	.20
(35)	George Shuba	.75	.35	.20
(36)	Duke Snider	6.00	3.00	1.75
(37)	Chris Van Cuyk	.75	.35	.20
(38)	Ben Wade	.75	.35	.20
(39)	Rube Walker	.75	.35	.20
(40)	Dick Williams	.90	.45	.25

1975 TCMA All Time Brooklyn/Los Angeles Dodgers

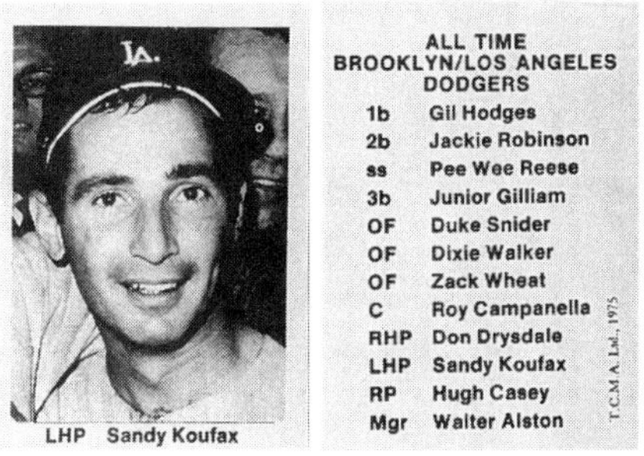
LHP Sandy Koufax
ALL TIME
BROOKLYN/LOS ANGELES
DODGERS
1b Gil Hodges
2b Jackie Robinson
ss Pee Wee Reese
3b Junior Gilliam
OF Duke Snider
OF Dixie Walker
OF Zack Wheat
C Roy Campanella
RHP Don Drysdale
LHP Sandy Koufax
RP Hugh Casey
Mgr Walter Alston
T.C.M.A. Ltd. 1975

A picked team of former Dodgers stars is featured in this collectors issue team set. Cards are in black-and-white in the standard 2-1/2" x 3-1/2" format. Fronts have player identification in the border beneath the photo. Backs have a checklist by position and a TCMA copyright line. The unnumbered cards are checklisted here in the order presented on back.

		NM	EX	VG
Complete Set (12):		25.00	12.50	7.50
Common Player:		1.50	.75	.45
(1)	Gil Hodges	2.00	1.00	.60
(2)	Jackie Robinson	9.00	4.50	2.75
(3)	Pee Wee Reese	2.00	1.00	.60
(4)	Junior Gilliam	1.50	.75	.45
(5)	Duke Snider	2.00	1.00	.60
(6)	Dixie Walker	1.50	.75	.45
(7)	Zack Wheat	1.50	.75	.45
(8)	Roy Campanella	2.50	1.25	.70
(9)	Don Drysdale	2.00	1.00	.60
(10)	Sandy Koufax	3.00	1.50	.90
(11)	Hugh Casey	1.50	.75	.45
(12)	Walter Alston	1.50	.75	.45

1975 TCMA All-Time Greats

This is a smaller - both in size and number - version of TCMA's Hall of Famer postcard set issued between 1973-80. These collectors' edition cards measure 2-3/8" x 3-3/4" and are printed in black-and-white, blank-backed. Surrounding the photo on front is a black border with baseball equipment ornamentation. The unnumbered cards are checklisted here in alphabetical order.

ALL-TIME Greats
"LUKE" APPLING

		NM	EX	VG
Complete Set (36):		35.00	17.50	10.50
Common Player:		1.00	.50	.30
(1)	"Luke" Appling	1.00	.50	.30
(2)	Roger Bresnahan	1.00	.50	.30
(3)	Mickey Cochrane	1.00	.50	.30
(4)	Eddie Collins	1.00	.50	.30
(5)	Kiki Cuyler	1.00	.50	.30
(6)	Dizzy Dean	2.00	1.00	.60
(7)	Bill Dickey	1.00	.50	.30
(8)	Joe DiMaggio	8.00	4.00	2.50
(9)	Bob Feller	1.50	.70	.45
(10)	Elmer Flick	1.00	.50	.30
(11)	Frank Frisch	1.00	.50	.30
(12)	Lou Gehrig	6.00	3.00	1.75
(13)	Hank Greenberg	2.50	1.25	.70
(14)	Goose Goslin	1.00	.50	.30
(15)	Chick Hafey	1.00	.50	.30
(16)	Gabby Hartnett	1.00	.50	.30
(17)	Harry Heilmann	1.00	.50	.30
(18)	Rogers Hornsby	1.00	.50	.30
(19)	Waite Hoyt	1.00	.50	.30
(20)	Walter Johnson	2.00	1.00	.60
(21)	George Kelly	1.00	.50	.30
(22)	Ted Lyons	1.00	.50	.30
(23)	Connie Mack	1.00	.50	.30
(24)	Rabbit Maranville	1.00	.50	.30
(25)	Mel Ott	1.00	.50	.30
(26)	Edd Roush	1.00	.50	.30
(27)	Red Ruffing	1.00	.50	.30
(28)	Babe Ruth	10.00	5.00	3.00
(29)	Al Simmons	1.00	.50	.30
(30)	Casey Stengel	1.00	.50	.30
(31)	Pie Traynor	1.00	.50	.30
(32)	Dazzy Vance	1.00	.50	.30
(33)	Honus Wagner	2.00	1.00	.60
(34)	Lloyd Waner	1.00	.50	.30
(35)	Paul Waner	1.00	.50	.30
(36)	Harry Wright	1.00	.50	.30

1975 TCMA All Time New York Giants

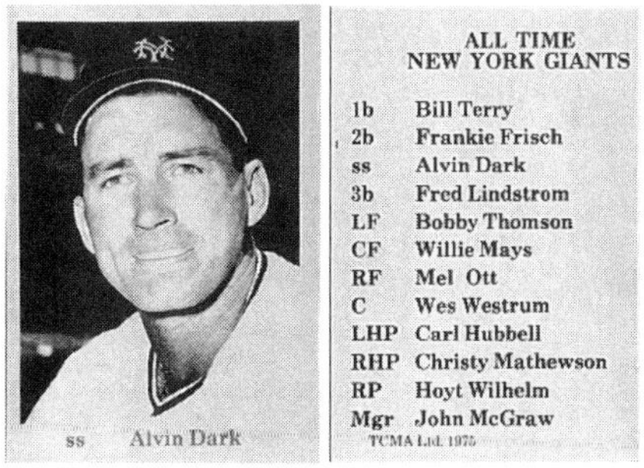
ss Alvin Dark
ALL TIME
NEW YORK GIANTS
1b Bill Terry
2b Frankie Frisch
ss Alvin Dark
3b Fred Lindstrom
LF Bobby Thomson
CF Willie Mays
RF Mel Ott
C Wes Westrum
LHP Carl Hubbell
RHP Christy Mathewson
RP Hoyt Wilhelm
Mgr John McGraw

An all-time line-up of Giants is presented in this collector issue. Fronts of the 2-1/2" x 3-1/2" cards have black-and-white player photos with the player's name and position printed in red in the white bottom border. Backs are in black-and-white and present the all-time roster. The unnumbered cards are checklisted here alphabetically.

		NM	EX	VG
Complete Set (12)_:		25.00	12.50	7.50
Common Player:		1.25	.60	.40
(1)	Alvin Dark	1.25	.60	.40
(2)	Frankie Frisch	1.25	.60	.40
(3)	Carl Hubbell	1.25	.60	.40
(4)	Freddie Lindstrom	1.25	.60	.40
(5)	Christy Mathewson	3.00	1.50	.90
(6)	Willie Mays	15.00	7.50	4.50
(7)	John McGraw	1.25	.60	.40
(8)	Mel Ott	1.25	.60	.40
(9)	Bill Terry	1.25	.60	.40
(10)	Bobby Thomson	1.25	.60	.40
(11)	Wes Westrum	1.25	.60	.40
(12)	Hoyt Wilhelm	1.25	.60	.40

1975 TCMA All Time New York Yankees

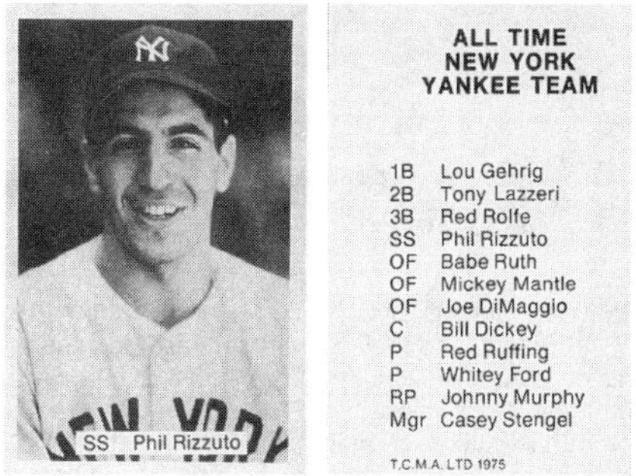
SS Phil Rizzuto
ALL TIME
NEW YORK
YANKEE TEAM
1B Lou Gehrig
2B Tony Lazzeri
3B Red Rolfe
SS Phil Rizzuto
OF Babe Ruth
OF Mickey Mantle
OF Joe DiMaggio
C Bill Dickey
P Red Ruffing
P Whitey Ford
RP Johnny Murphy
Mgr Casey Stengel
T.C.M.A. LTD 1975

The best players on the best team in baseball history are featured in this collectors' edition. Cards measure 2-1/2" x 3-3/4" and feature black-and-white photos on front, with white borders. Player name and position are printed in a white strip toward the bottom of the picture. Backs have a list of the all-time team. The unnumbered cards are listed here in that order.

		NM	EX	VG
Complete Set (12):		30.00	15.00	9.00
Common Player:		2.00	1.00	.60
(1)	Lou Gehrig	6.00	3.00	1.75
(2)	Tony Lazzeri	2.00	1.00	.60
(3)	Red Rolfe	2.00	1.00	.60
(4)	Phil Rizzuto	4.00	2.00	1.25
(5)	Babe Ruth	10.00	5.00	3.00
(6)	Mickey Mantle	12.00	6.00	3.50
(7)	Joe DiMaggio	6.00	3.00	1.75
(8)	Bill Dickey	2.00	1.00	.60
(9)	Red Ruffing	2.00	1.00	.60
(10)	Whitey Ford	3.00	1.50	.90
(11)	Johnny Murphy	2.00	1.00	.60
(12)	Casey Stengel	2.00	1.00	.60

1975 TCMA 1913 Philadelphia Athletics

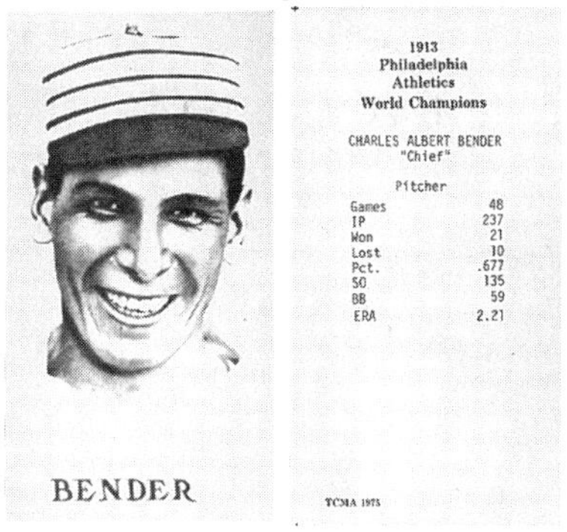
BENDER
1913
Philadelphia
Athletics
World Champions
CHARLES ALBERT BENDER
"Chief"
Pitcher
Games 48
IP 237
Won 21
Lost 10
Pct. .677
SO 135
BB 59
ERA 2.21
TCMA 1975

Members of the World Champion A's of 1913 are featured in this collectors' edition card set. In an unusual 3-1/8" x 5-11/16" format, the cards have black-and-white photos on front, with white borders and player identification at bottom. Backs feature season statistics. The unnumbered cards are checklisted here alphabetically.

		NM	EX	VG
Complete Set (16):		30.00	15.00	9.00
Common Player:		2.00	1.00	.60
(1)	Home Run Baker	2.00	1.00	.60
(2)	Jack Barry	2.00	1.00	.60
(3)	Chief Bender	2.00	1.00	.60
(4)	Joe Bush	2.00	1.00	.60
(5)	Eddie Collins	2.00	1.00	.60
(6)	Jack Coombs	2.00	1.00	.60
(7)	Jack Lapp	2.00	1.00	.60
(8)	Connie Mack	2.00	1.00	.60
(9)	Stuffy McInnis	2.00	1.00	.60
(10)	Eddie Murphy	2.00	1.00	.60
(11)	Dan Murphy	2.00	1.00	.60
(12)	Rube Oldring	2.00	1.00	.60
(13)	William Orr	2.00	1.00	.60
(14)	Ed Plank	2.00	1.00	.60
(15)	Walter Schang	2.00	1.00	.60
(16)	Amos Strunk	2.00	1.00	.60

1975 TCMA 1919 Chicago White Sox

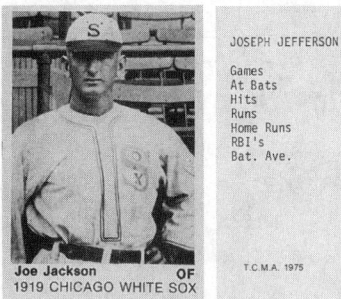

JOSEPH JEFFERSON JACKSON

Games	139
At Bats	516
Hits	181
Runs	79
Home Runs	7
RBI's	96
Bat. Ave.	.351

T.C.M.A. 1975

The infamous Black Sox who threw the 1919 World Series, and their teammates, are featured in this collectors' edition. The 2-1/2" x 3-1/2" cards are printed in black-and-white. Fronts have player photos with identification in the white border at bottom. Backs have 1919 season stats. The unnumbered cards are checklisted here alphabetically.

		NM	EX	VG
Complete Set (27):		60.00	30.00	18.00
Common Player:		1.00	.50	.30
(1)	Joe Benz	1.00	.50	.30
(2)	Eddie Cicotte	5.00	2.50	1.50
(3)	Eddie Collins	3.50	1.75	1.00
(4)	Shano Collins	1.00	.50	.30
(5)	Dave Danforth	1.00	.50	.30
(6)	Red Faber	1.50	.70	.45
(7)	Happy Felsch	5.00	2.50	1.50
(8)	Chick Gandil	7.50	3.75	2.25
(9)	Kid Gleason	1.00	.50	.30
(10)	Joe Jackson	15.00	7.50	4.50
(11)	Bill James	1.00	.50	.30
(12)	Dickie Kerr	1.00	.50	.30
(13)	Nemo Leibold	1.00	.50	.30
(14)	Byrd Lynn	1.00	.50	.30
(15)	Erskine Mayer	2.50	1.25	.70
(16)	Harvey McClellan	1.00	.50	.30
(17)	Fred McMullin	5.00	2.50	1.50
(18)	Eddie Murphy	1.00	.50	.30
(19)	Pat Ragan	1.00	.50	.30
(20)	Swede Risberg	5.00	2.50	1.50
(21)	Charlie Robertson	1.00	.50	.30
(22)	Reb Russell	1.00	.50	.30
(23)	Ray Schalk	1.50	.70	.45
(24)	Buck Weaver	9.00	4.50	2.75
(25)	Roy Wilkinson	1.00	.50	.30
(26)	Lefty Williams	5.00	2.50	1.50
(27)	Frank Shellenback, Grover Lowdermilk, Joe Jenkins, Dickie Kerr, Ray Schalk	1.00	.50	.30

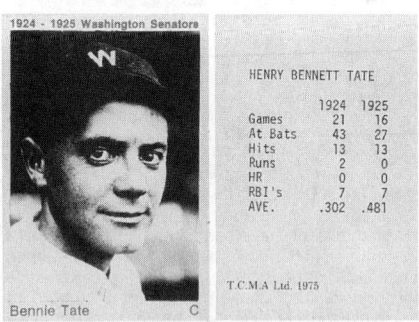

1975 TCMA 1924-1925 Washington Senators

HENRY BENNETT TATE

	1924	1925
Games	21	16
At Bats	43	27
Hits	13	13
Runs	2	0
HR	0	0
RBI's	7	7
AVE.	.302	.481

T.C.M.A Ltd. 1975

The back-to-back American League champion Senators of 1924-25 are featured in this collectors' edition card set. Cards measure 2-3/8" x 3-7/16". Fronts have black-and-white photos with blue captions and white borders. Backs have player stats for the two seasons. The unnumbered cards are checklisted here in alphabetical order.

		NM	EX	VG
Complete Set (39):		40.00	20.00	12.00
Common Player:		1.00	.50	.30
(1)	Spencer Adams	1.00	.50	.30
(2)	Nick Altrock	1.00	.50	.30
(3)	Ossie Bluege	1.00	.50	.30
(4)	Stan Coveleski	1.00	.50	.30
(5)	Alex Ferguson	1.00	.50	.30
(6)	Showboat Fisher	1.50	.70	.45
(7)	Goose Goslin	1.00	.50	.30
(8)	Bart Griffith	1.50	.70	.45
(9)	Pinky Hargrave	1.00	.50	.30
(10)	Bucky Harris	1.00	.50	.30
(11)	Joe Harris	1.00	.50	.30
(12)	Tex Jeanes	1.50	.70	.45
(13)	Walter Johnson	3.00	1.50	.90
(14)	Joe Judge	1.00	.50	.30
(15)	Wade Lefler	1.50	.70	.45
(16)	Nemo Leibold	1.00	.50	.30
(17)	Firpo Marberry	1.00	.50	.30
(18)	Joe Martina	1.50	.70	.45
(19)	Wid Matthews	1.00	.50	.30
(20)	Earl McNeely	1.00	.50	.30
(21)	Buddy Myer	1.00	.50	.30
(22)	Ralph Miller	1.00	.50	.30
(23)	George Mogridge	1.00	.50	.30
(24)	Curly Ogden	1.00	.50	.30
(25)	Roger Peckinpaugh	1.00	.50	.30
(26)	Sam Rice	1.00	.50	.30
(27)	Muddy Ruel	1.00	.50	.30
(28)	Dutch Ruether	1.00	.50	.30
(29)	Allen Russell	1.00	.50	.30
(30)	Everett Scott	1.00	.50	.30
(31)	Hank Severeid	1.00	.50	.30
(32)	Mule Shirley	1.00	.50	.30
(33)	Byron Speece	1.00	.50	.30
(34)	Benny Tate	1.00	.50	.30
(35)	Bobby Veach	1.00	.50	.30
(36)	Tom Zachary	1.00	.50	.30
(37)	Bucky Harris, Bill McKechnie	1.00	.50	.30
(38)	Ossie Bluege, Roger Peckinpaugh, Bucky Harris, Joe Judge	1.00	.50	.30
(39)	Tom Zachary, Firpo Marberry, Alex Ferguson, Walter Johnson	1.00	.50	.30

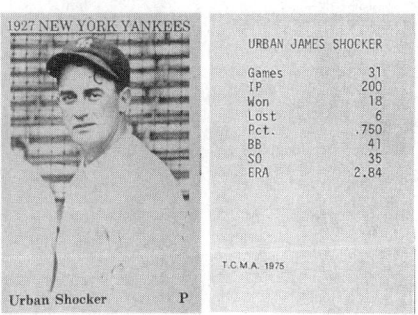

1975 TCMA 1927 New York Yankees

URBAN JAMES SHOCKER

Games	31
IP	200
Won	18
Lost	6
Pct.	.750
BB	41
SO	35
ERA	2.84

T.C.M.A. 1975

One of the greatest teams in baseball history is featured in this set of collectors' cards. The 2-1/2" x 3-1/2" cards have black-and-white photos with a white border. At top is the team identification, at bottom is player name and position. The back has the player's 1927 season stats. The unnumbered cards are checklisted here alphabetically.

		NM	EX	VG
Complete Set (28):		45.00	22.50	13.50
Common Player:		2.00	1.00	.60
(1)	Walter Beall	2.00	1.00	.60
(2)	Benny Bengough	2.00	1.00	.60
(3)	Pat Collins	2.00	1.00	.60
(4)	Earle Combs	2.00	1.00	.60
(5)	Joe Dugan	2.00	1.00	.60
(6)	Cedric Durst	2.00	1.00	.60
(7)	Mike Gazella	2.00	1.00	.60
(8)	Lou Gehrig	7.50	3.75	2.25
(9)	Joe Giard	2.00	1.00	.60
(10)	Johnny Grabowski	2.00	1.00	.60
(11)	Waite Hoyt	2.50	1.25	.70
(12)	Miller Huggins	2.00	1.00	.60
(13)	Mark Koenig	2.00	1.00	.60
(14)	Tony Lazzeri	2.00	1.00	.60
(15)	Bob Meusel	2.00	1.00	.60
(16)	Wilcy Moore	2.00	1.00	.60
(17)	Ray Morehart	2.00	1.00	.60
(18)	Ben Paschal	2.00	1.00	.60
(19)	Herb Pennock	2.00	1.00	.60
(20)	George Pipgras	2.00	1.00	.60
(21)	Dutch Ruether	2.00	1.00	.60
(22)	Jacob Ruppert	2.00	1.00	.60
(23)	Babe Ruth	12.00	6.00	3.50
(24)	Bob Shawkey	2.00	1.00	.60
(25)	Urban Shocker	2.00	1.00	.60
(26)	Myles Thomas	2.00	1.00	.60
(27)	Julie Wera	2.00	1.00	.60
(28)	Yankees infield (Lou Gehrig, Tony Lazzeri, Mark Koenig, Joe Dugan) (5" x 3-5/8")	5.00	2.50	1.50

1975 TCMA 1946 Boston Red Sox

The Red Sox American League champions of 1946 are featured in this collectors' issue. Blue-and-white player photos appear on front, with the player's name and position in black below. At bottom-front is the team name in red. Backs of the 2-1/2" x 3-1/2" cards have the player's 1946 stats. The unnumbered cards are checklisted here in alphabetical order.

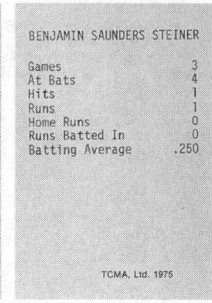

BENJAMIN SAUNDERS STEINER

Games	3
At Bats	4
Hits	1
Runs	1
Home Runs	0
Runs Batted In	0
Batting Average	.250

TCMA, Ltd. 1975

		NM	EX	VG
Complete Set (43):		45.00	22.50	13.50
Common Player:		1.00	.50	.30
(1)	Jim Bagby	1.00	.50	.30
(2)	Del Baker	1.00	.50	.30
(3)	Mace Brown	1.00	.50	.30
(4)	Bill Butland	1.00	.50	.30
(5)	Paul Campbell	1.00	.50	.30
(6)	Tom Carey	1.00	.50	.30
(7)	Joe Cronin	1.50	.70	.45
(8)	Leon Culberson	1.00	.50	.30
(9)	Tom Daly	1.00	.50	.30
(10)	Dom DiMaggio	2.50	1.25	.70
(11)	Joe Dobson	1.00	.50	.30
(12)	Bobby Doerr	1.00	.50	.30
(13)	Clem Dreisewerd	1.00	.50	.30
(14)	"Boo" Ferriss	1.00	.50	.30
(15)	Andy Gilbert	1.00	.50	.30
(16)	Don Gutteridge	1.00	.50	.30
(17)	Mickey Harris	1.00	.50	.30
(18)	Randy Heflin	1.00	.50	.30
(19)	"Pinky" Higgins	1.00	.50	.30
(20)	"Tex" Hughson	1.00	.50	.30
(21)	Earl Johnson	1.00	.50	.30
(22)	Bob Klinger	1.00	.50	.30
(23)	Johnny Lazor	1.00	.50	.30
(24)	Tom McBride	1.00	.50	.30
(25)	Ed McGah	1.00	.50	.30
(26)	"Catfish" Metkovich	1.00	.50	.30
(27)	Wally Moses	1.00	.50	.30
(28)	Roy Partee	1.00	.50	.30
(29)	Eddie Pellagrini	1.00	.50	.30
(30)	Johnny Pesky	1.00	.50	.30
(31)	Frank Pytlak	1.00	.50	.30
(32)	"Rip" Russell	1.00	.50	.30
(33)	Mike Ryba	1.00	.50	.30
(34)	Ben Steiner	1.50	.70	.45
(35)	Charlie Wagner	1.00	.50	.30
(36)	Hal Wagner	1.00	.50	.30
(37)	Ted Williams	7.00	3.50	2.00
(38)	Larry Woodall	1.00	.50	.30
(39)	Rudy York	1.00	.50	.30
(40)	Bill Zuber	1.00	.50	.30
(41)	Team photo	1.00	.50	.30
(42)	Larry Woodall, Hal Wagner, Del Baker	1.00	.50	.30
(43)	Rudy York, Wally Moses, Dom DiMaggio, Bobby Doerr, Charlie Wagner (5" x 3-1/2")	2.50	1.25	.70

1975 TCMA 1950 Philadelphia Phillies/Whiz Kids

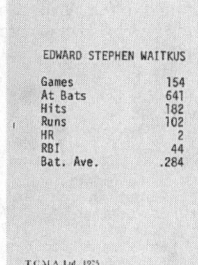

EDWARD STEPHEN WAITKUS

Games	154
At Bats	641
Hits	182
Runs	102
HR	2
RBI	44
Bat. Ave.	.284

T.C.M.A. Ltd. 1975

The National League Champion "Whiz Kids" are featured in this collectors issue. The 2-1/2" x 3-1/2" cards have black-and-white photos on front with the player's name and position in red at bottom and either "Whiz Kids" or "1950 Philadelphia Phillies" in red at top. Black-and-white backs have 1950 season stats. The unnumbered cards are checklisted here alphabetically. The large-format multiple-player card which was issued coincidentally with the set is not factored into the complete-set price.

	NM	EX	VG
Complete Set (31):	55.00	27.50	16.00
Common Player:	2.00	1.00	.60
(1) Richie Ashburn	11.00	5.50	3.25
(2) Benny Bengough	2.00	1.00	.60
(3) Jimmy Bloodworth	2.00	1.00	.60
(4) Hank Borowy	2.00	1.00	.60
(5) "Putsy" Caballero	2.00	1.00	.60
(6) "Bubba" Church	2.00	1.00	.60
(7) Dusty Cooke	2.00	1.00	.60
(8) Blix Donnelly	2.00	1.00	.60
(9) Del Ennis	2.00	1.00	.60
(10) Mike Goliat	2.00	1.00	.60
(11) Granny Hamner	2.00	1.00	.60
(12) Ken Heintzelman	2.00	1.00	.60
(13) Stan Hollmig	2.00	1.00	.60
(14) Ken Johnson	2.00	1.00	.60
(15) "Puddin-Head" Jones	2.00	1.00	.60
(16) Jim Konstanty	2.00	1.00	.60
(17) Stan Lopata	2.00	1.00	.60
(18) Jackie Mayo	2.00	1.00	.60
(19) Russ Meyer	2.00	1.00	.60
(20) Bob Miller	2.00	1.00	.60
(21) Bill Nicholson	2.00	1.00	.60
(22) Cy Perkins	2.00	1.00	.60
(23) Robin Roberts	11.00	5.50	3.25
(24) Eddie Sawyer	2.00	1.00	.60
(25) Andy Seminick	2.00	1.00	.60
(26) Ken Silvestri	2.00	1.00	.60
(27) Curt Simmons	2.00	1.00	.60
(28) Dick Sisler	2.00	1.00	.60
(29) "Jocko" Thompson	2.00	1.00	.60
(30) Eddie Waitkus	2.00	1.00	.60
(31) Dick Whitman	2.00	1.00	.60
(---) Russ Meyer, Hank Borowy, Bill Nicholson, Willie Jones (4-7/8" x 3-1/2")	15.00	7.50	4.50

1975 TCMA 1951 New York Giants

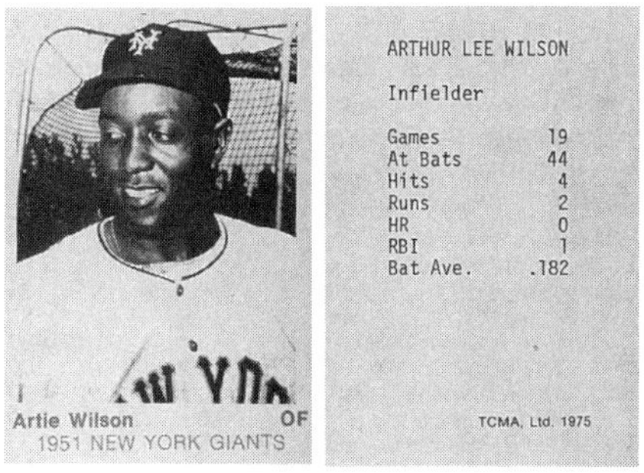
ARTHUR LEE WILSON
Infielder
Games 19
At Bats 44
Hits 4
Runs 2
HR 0
RBI 1
Bat Ave. .182
Artie Wilson OF
1951 NEW YORK GIANTS
TCMA, Ltd. 1975

The National League Champion Giants of 1951 are honored in this collectors' issue card set. The 2-1/2" x 3-1/2" cards have black-and-white photos on front, with player name, team and position in the bottom border in red-orange ink. Backs are black-and-white with 1951 stats. The unnumbered cards are listed here in alphabetical order.

	NM	EX	VG
Complete Set (34):	50.00	25.00	15.00
Common Player:	1.00	.50	.30
(1) George Bamberger	1.00	.50	.30
(2) Roger Bowman	1.00	.50	.30
(3) Al Corwin	1.00	.50	.30
(4) Alvin Dark	1.50	.70	.45
(5) Allen Gettel	1.00	.50	.30
(6) Clint Hartung	1.00	.50	.30
(7) Jim Hearn	1.00	.50	.30
(8) Monte Irvin	2.00	1.00	.60
(9) Larry Jansen	1.00	.50	.30
(10) Sheldon Jones	1.00	.50	.30
(11) "Spider" Jorgensen	1.00	.50	.30
(12) Monte Kennedy	1.00	.50	.30
(13) Alex Konikowski	1.50	.70	.45
(14) Dave Koslo	1.00	.50	.30
(15) Jack Kramer	1.00	.50	.30
(16) Whitey Lockman	1.00	.50	.30
(17) "Lucky" Lohrke	1.00	.50	.30
(18) Sal Maglie	1.50	.70	.45
(19) Jack Maguire	1.50	.70	.45
(20) Willie Mays	10.00	5.00	3.00
(21) Don Mueller	1.00	.50	.30
(22) Ray Noble	1.00	.50	.30
(23) Earl Rapp	1.00	.50	.30
(24) Bill Rigney	1.00	.50	.30
(25) George Spencer	1.00	.50	.30
(26) Eddie Stanky	1.50	.70	.45
(27) Bobby Thomson	2.50	1.25	.70
(28) Hank Thompson	1.00	.50	.30
(29) Wes Westrum	1.00	.50	.30
(30) Davey Williams	1.00	.50	.30
(31) Artie Wilson	1.00	.50	.30
(32) Sal Yvars	1.00	.50	.30
(33) Leo Durocher, Willie Mays (3-5/8" x 5")	7.00	3.50	2.00
(34) Durocher and coaches (3-5/8" x 5")	3.00	1.50	.90

1975 TCMA 1954 Cleveland Indians

Art Houtteman P
1954 CLEVELAND INDIANS
ARTHUR JOSEPH HOUTTEMAN
Games 32
IP 188
Won 15
Lost 7
Pct. 6.82
BB 59
SO 68
ERA 3.35
T.C.M.A. 1975

Pope, Philley, Westlake, Doby, Smith

The American League Champions of 1954 are featured in this collectors issue. Individual player cards are 2-1/2" x 3-1/2" printed in black-and-white. Backs have 1954 season stats. Three large-format (3-3/4" x 5-1/8") multi-player cards which were issued coincident to the small cards are not considered part of the complete set. The unnumbered cards are checklisted here alphabetically.

	NM	EX	VG
Complete Set (36):	65.00	32.00	19.50
Common Player:	2.50	1.25	.70
(1) Bobby Avila	3.50	1.75	1.00
(2) Bob Chakales	2.50	1.25	.70
(3) Tony Cuccinello	2.50	1.25	.70
(4) Sam Dente	2.50	1.25	.70
(5) Larry Doby	5.50	2.75	1.75
(6) Luke Easter	3.00	1.50	.90
(7) Bob Feller	10.00	5.00	3.00
(8) Mike Garcia	3.00	1.50	.90
(9) Joe Ginsberg	2.50	1.25	.70
(10) Bill Glynn	2.50	1.25	.70
(11) Mickey Grasso	2.50	1.25	.70
(12) Mel Harder	2.50	1.25	.70
(13) Jim Hegan	2.50	1.25	.70
(14) Bob Hooper	2.50	1.25	.70
(15) Dave Hoskins	2.50	1.25	.70
(16) Art Houtteman	2.50	1.25	.70
(17) Bob Kennedy	2.50	1.25	.70
(18) Bob Lemon	4.00	2.00	1.25
(19) Al Lopez	4.00	2.00	1.25
(20) Hank Majeski	2.50	1.25	.70
(21) Dale Mitchell	2.50	1.25	.70
(22) Don Mossi	2.50	1.25	.70
(23) Hal Naragon	2.50	1.25	.70
(24) Ray Narleski	2.50	1.25	.70
(25) Rocky Nelson	2.50	1.25	.70
(26) Hal Newhouser	4.00	2.00	1.25
(27) Dave Philley	2.50	1.25	.70
(28) Dave Pope	2.50	1.25	.70
(29) Rudy Regaldo	2.50	1.25	.70
(30) Al Rosen	3.00	1.50	.90
(31) Jose Santiago	2.50	1.25	.70
(32) Al Smith	2.50	1.25	.70
(33) George Strickland	2.50	1.25	.70
(34) Vic Wertz	2.50	1.25	.70
(35) Wally Westlake	2.50	1.25	.70
(36) Early Wynn	5.00	2.50	1.50
Large format cards	2.50	1.25	.70
--- Al Lopez and coaches	25.00	12.50	7.50
--- Al Lopez and pitchers	25.00	12.50	7.50
--- Indians outfielders	25.00	12.50	7.50

1976 TCMA Umpires

Three of the better-known umpires of the era apparently commissioned TCMA to produce cards for them. The cards are black-and-white in the standard 2-1/2" x 3-1/2" format.

	NM	EX	VG
Complete Set (3):	40.00	20.00	12.00
Common Card:	15.00	7.50	4.50
(1) Larry Barnett	15.00	7.50	4.50
(2) Don Denkinger	15.00	7.50	4.50
(3) Marty Springstead	15.00	7.50	4.50

1976 TCMA 1938 Chicago Cubs

Augie Galan OF
AUGUST JOHN GALAN
Games 110
At Bats 395
Hits 113
Runs 52
Home Runs 6
RBI 69
Bat. Ave. .286
1938 CHICAGO CUBS
NATIONAL LEAGUE CHAMPIONS
1976 TCMA LTD.

The National League Champion Chicago Cubs of 1938 are featured in this collectors issue. The 2-1/2" x 3-1/2" cards have black-and-white player photos on front with the player's name and position in blue at bottom. Backs are in black-and-white with season stats. The unnumbered cards are checklisted here alphabetically.

	NM	EX	VG
Complete Set (33):	60.00	30.00	18.00
Common Player:	2.00	1.00	.60
(1) Jim Asbell	2.00	1.00	.60
(2) Clay Bryant	2.00	1.00	.60
(3) Tex Carleton	2.00	1.00	.60
(4) Phil Cavarretta	2.00	1.00	.60
(5) Ripper Collins	2.00	1.00	.60
(6) "Red" Corriden	2.00	1.00	.60
(7) Dizzy Dean	15.00	7.50	4.50
(8) Frank Demaree	2.00	1.00	.60
(9) Al Epperly	2.00	1.00	.60
(10) Larry French	2.00	1.00	.60
(11) Augie Galan	2.00	1.00	.60
(12) Bob Garbark	2.00	1.00	.60
(13) Charlie Grimm	2.00	1.00	.60
(14) Stan Hack	2.00	1.00	.60
(15) Gabby Hartnett	3.00	1.50	.90
(16) Billy Herman	3.00	1.50	.90
(17) Kirby Higbe	2.00	1.00	.60
(18) Hardrock Johnson	2.00	1.00	.60
(19) Billy Jurges	2.00	1.00	.60
(20) Newt Kimball	2.00	1.00	.60
(21) Tony Lazzeri	3.00	1.50	.90
(22) Bill Lee	2.00	1.00	.60
(23) Bob Logan	2.00	1.00	.60
(24) Joe Marty	2.00	1.00	.60
(25) Bobby Mattick	2.00	1.00	.60
(26) Steve Mesner	2.00	1.00	.60
(27) Ken O'Dea	2.00	1.00	.60
(28) Vance Page	2.00	1.00	.60
(29) Carl Reynolds	2.00	1.00	.60
(30) Charlie Root	2.00	1.00	.60
(31) Jack Russell	2.00	1.00	.60
(32) Coaker Triplett	2.00	1.00	.60
(33) Team history card	.90	.45	.25

1977 TCMA All-Time White Sox

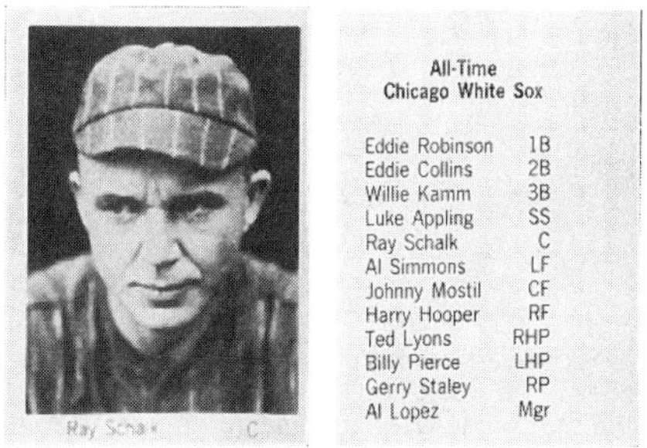
Ray Schalk C
All-Time
Chicago White Sox
Eddie Robinson 1B
Eddie Collins 2B
Willie Kamm 3B
Luke Appling SS
Ray Schalk C
Al Simmons LF
Johnny Mostil CF
Harry Hooper RF
Ted Lyons RHP
Billy Pierce LHP
Gerry Staley RP
Al Lopez Mgr

Because this is one of the few early TCMA issues not to have a date printed on the back, the quoted year of issue is approximate. Fronts of the 2-1/2" x 3-1/2" cards have black-and-white player photos with name and position printed in red in the bottom border. Black-and-white backs have an all-time team roster of position players, pitchers and manager. The unnumbered cards are checklisted here in alphabetical order.

	NM	EX	VG
Complete Set (12):	24.00	12.00	7.25
Common Player:	2.00	1.00	.60
(1) Luke Appling	2.50	1.25	.70
(2) Eddie Collins	2.50	1.25	.70

		NM	EX	VG
(3)	Harry Hooper	2.00	1.00	.60
(4)	Willie Kamm	2.00	1.00	.60
(5)	Al Lopez	2.00	1.00	.60
(6)	Ted Lyons	2.00	1.00	.00
(7)	Johnny Mostil	2.00	1.00	.60
(8)	Billy Pierce	2.00	1.00	.60
(9)	Eddie Robinson	2.00	1.00	.60
(10)	Ray Schalk	2.00	1.00	.60
(11)	Al Simmons	2.00	1.00	.60
(12)	Gerry Staley	2.00	1.00	.60

1977 TCMA Chicago Cubs All Time Team

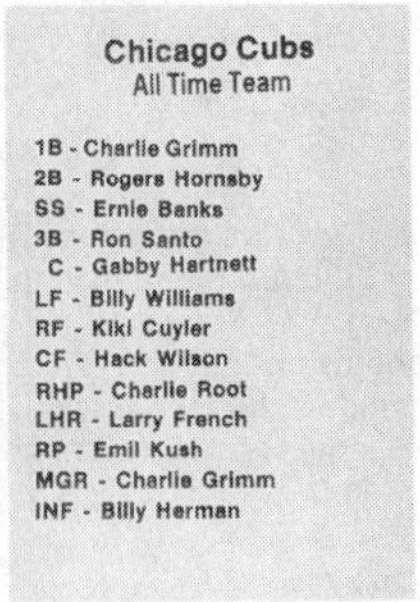

The best of the Cubs are presented in this collectors issue. An all-time great at each position is featured on the 2-1/2" x 3-1/2" card. Fronts have black-and-white photos with orange graphics. Backs are in black-and-white and list the team by position. The unnumbered cards are checklisted here in that order.

		NM	EX	VG
Complete Set (12):		24.00	12.00	7.25
Common Player:		2.00	1.00	.60
(1)	Charlie Grimm	2.00	1.00	.60
(2)	Rogers Hornsby	2.50	1.25	.70
(3)	Ernie Banks	2.50	1.25	.70
(4)	Ron Santo	2.00	1.00	.60
(5)	Gabby Hartnett	2.00	1.00	.60
(6)	Billy Williams	2.00	1.00	.60
(7)	Kiki Cuyler	2.00	1.00	.60
(8)	Hack Wilson	2.50	1.25	.70
(9)	Charlie Root	2.00	1.00	.60
(10)	Larry French	2.00	1.00	.60
(11)	Emil Kush	2.00	1.00	.60
(12)	Billy Herman	2.00	1.00	.60

1977 TCMA Stars of the Twenties

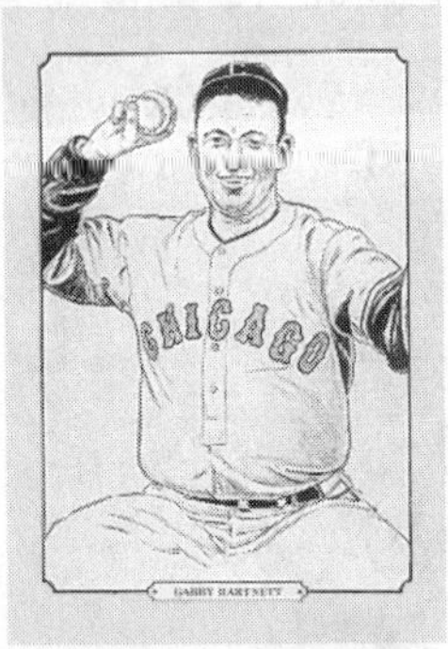

Six players are featured on this 22" x 11" triple-folder which was glued into issues of the Summer, 1977, "Baseball Quarterly" magazine from TCMA. The pictures feature artwork by John Anderson in sepia tones on heavy cream-colored textured paper stock. The pictures are back-to-back in pairs as listed here, with individual pictures varying in width from 7-1/4" to 7-1/2".

		NM	EX	VG
Complete Foldout:		10.00	5.00	3.00
Common Pair:		3.00	1.50	.90
(1/2)	Joe Bush, Gabby Hartnett	3.00	1.50	.90
(3/4)	Jim Bottomley, "Mule" Haas	3.00	1.50	.90
(5/6)	Sam Rice, Buddy Myer	3.00	1.50	.90

1977 TCMA The War Years

The decimated major league rosters circa 1942-46 are reflected in this collectors' card set. The 2-1/2" x 3-1/2" cards have black-and-white player photos on front, with a white border around. There is no typography on front. Backs have player identification, stats and the set title. Issue price was about $7.

		NM	EX	VG
Complete Set (90):		75.00	37.50	22.00
Common Player:		.75	.40	.25
1	Samuel Narron	.75	.40	.25
2	Raymond Mack	.75	.40	.25
3	Arnold (Mickey) Owen	.75	.40	.25
4	John Peacock	.75	.40	.25
5	Paul (Dizzy) Trout	.75	.40	.25
6	George (Birdie) Tebbetts	.75	.40	.25
7	Alfred Todd	.75	.40	.25
8	Harlond Clift	.75	.40	.25
9	Don G.N. (Gil) Torres	.75	.40	.25
10	Alfonso Lopez	1.00	.50	.30
11	Ulysses (Tony) Lupien	.75	.40	.25
12	Lucius Appling	1.00	.50	.30
13	James (Pat) Seery	.75	.40	.25
14	Phil Masi	.75	.40	.25
15	Thomas Turner	.75	.40	.25
16	Nicholas Piccuito	.75	.40	.25
17	Mel Ott	1.50	.70	.45
18	Thadford Treadway	3.00	1.50	.90
19	Sam Naham (Neham)	.75	.40	.25
20	Truett (Rip) Sewell	.75	.40	.25
21	Roy Partee	.75	.40	.25
22	Richard Siebert	.75	.40	.25
23	Francis (Red) Barrett	.75	.40	.25
24	Paul O'Dea	.75	.40	.25
25	Lou Parisse	.75	.40	.25
26	Martin Marion	1.25	.60	.40
27	Eugene Moore	.75	.40	.25
28	Walter Beck	.75	.40	.25
29	Donald Manno	.75	.40	.25
30	Harold Newhouser	1.25	.60	.40
31	August Mancuso	.75	.40	.25
32	Merrill May	.75	.40	.25
33	Gerald Priddy	.75	.40	.25
34	Herman Besse	.75	.40	.25
35	Luis Olmo	.75	.40	.25
36	Robert O'Neill	.75	.40	.25
37	John Barrett	.75	.40	.25
38	Gordon Maltzberger	.75	.40	.25
39	William Nicholson	.75	.40	.25
40	Ron Northey	.75	.40	.25
41	Howard Pollet	.75	.40	.25
42	Aloysius Piechota	.75	.40	.25
43	Albert Shepard	3.50	1.75	1.00
44	Alfred Anderson	.75	.40	.25
45	Damon Phillips	.75	.40	.25
46	Herman Franks	.75	.40	.25
47	Aldon Wilke	.75	.40	.25
48	Max Macon	.75	.40	.25
49	Lester Webber	.75	.40	.25
50	Robert Swift	.75	.40	.25
51	Philip Weintraub	.75	.40	.25
52	Nicholas Strincevich	.75	.40	.25
53	Michael Tresh	.75	.40	.25
54	William Trotter	.75	.40	.25
55	1943 Yankees (Spud Chandler, Frank Crosetti, Bill Dickey, Nick Etten, Joe Gordon, Billy Johnson), , (Bud Metheny)	1.50	.70	.45
56	John Sturm	.75	.40	.25
57	Silas Johnson	.75	.40	.25
58	Donald Kolloway	.75	.40	.25
59	Cecil Vaughn (Vaughan)	.75	.40	.25
60	St. Louis Browns Bombers (Harlond Clift, Walt Judnich, Chet Laabs)	1.25	.60	.40
61	Harold Wagner	.75	.40	.25
62	Alva Javery	.75	.40	.25
63	1941 Boston Bees Pitchers (George Barnicle, Ed Carnett, Art Johnson, Frank LaManna, Casey Stengel, Bob	1.25	.60	.40
64	Adolph Camilli	.75	.40	.25
65	Myron McCormick	.75	.40	.25
66	Richard Wakefield	.75	.40	.25
67	James (Mickey) Vernon	1.00	.50	.30
68	John Vander Meer	1.00	.50	.30
69	James McDonnell	3.00	1.50	.90
70	Thomas Jordan	.75	.40	.25
71	Maurice Van Robays	.75	.40	.25
72	Charles Stanceau	.75	.40	.25
73	Samuel Zoldak	.75	.40	.25
74	Raymond Starr	.75	.40	.25
75	Roger Wolff	.75	.40	.25
76	Cecil Travis	.75	.40	.25
77	Arthur Johnson	.75	.40	.25
78	Louis (Lewis) Riggs	.75	.40	.25
79	Peter Suder	.75	.40	.25
80	Thomas Warren	.75	.40	.25
81	John Welaj	.75	.40	.25
82	Gerald Walker	.75	.40	.25
83	Dewey Williams	.75	.40	.25
84	Leonard Merullo	.75	.40	.25
85	John Johnson	.75	.40	.25
86	Eugene Thompson	.75	.40	.25
87	William Zuber	.75	.40	.25
88	Earl Johnson	.75	.40	.25
89	Norman Young	.75	.40	.25
90	James Wallace	.75	.40	.25

1977 1927 Yankees 50th Anniversary

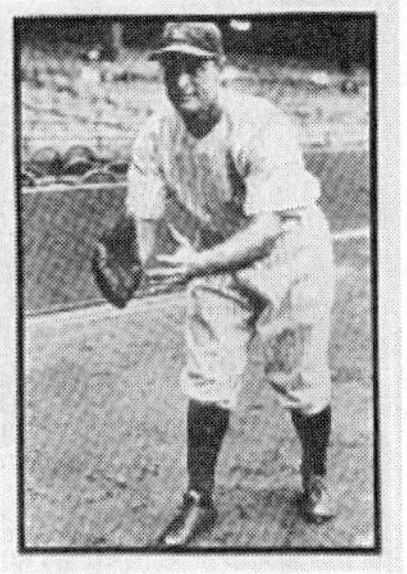

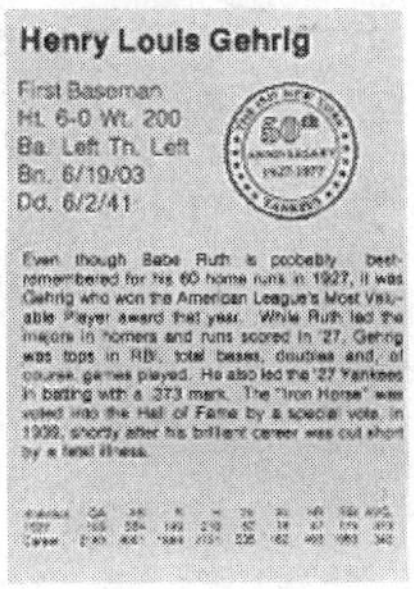

As an insert in its inaugural issue of "Baseball Quarterly" magazine dated Winter, 1977, TCMA included a 16-3/4" x 11" cardboard panel with 18 black-and-white cards featuring members of the 1927 N.Y. Yankees. Measuring about 2-1/2" x 3-3/8" if cut apart, the individual cards have unadorned photos on front framed in black with a white border. Backs have player identification, a 50th anniversary logo, career summary and 1927 and career stats. The unnumbered cards are listed here in alphabetical order.

		NM	EX	VG
Complete Panel:		35.00	17.50	10.50
Complete Set (18):		25.00	12.50	7.50
Common Player:		1.00	.50	.30
(1)	Bernard Oliver Bengough	1.00	.50	.30
(2)	Tharon Patrick Collins	1.00	.50	.30
(3)	Earle Bryan Combs	1.00	.50	.30
(4)	Joseph Anthony Dugan	1.00	.50	.30
(5)	Henry Louis Gehrig	5.00	2.50	1.50
(6)	John Patrick Grabowski	1.00	.50	.30
(7)	Waite Charles Hoyt	1.00	.50	.30
(8)	Miller James Huggins	1.00	.50	.30
(9)	Mark Anthony Koenig	1.00	.50	.30
(10)	Anthony Michael Lazzeri	1.00	.50	.30
(11)	Robert Williams Meusel	1.00	.50	.30
(12)	William Wilcy Moore	1.00	.50	.30
(13)	Herbert Jeffries Pennock	1.00	.50	.30
(14)	George William Pipgras	1.00	.50	.30
(15)	Walter Henry Ruether	1.00	.50	.30
(16)	George Herman Ruth	8.00	4.00	2.50
(17)	James Robert Shawkey	1.00	.50	.30
(18)	Urban James Shocker	1.00	.50	.30

1977 TCMA 1939-40 Cincinnati Reds

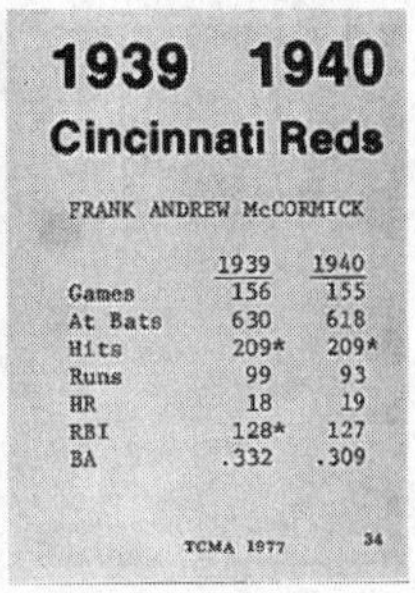

The National League Champion Reds of 1939 and the World's Champion team of 1940 are featured in this collectors issue. The 2-1/2" x 3-1/2" cards have black-and-white photos on front surrounded by red borders. Backs, also in black-and-white, have 1939 and/or 1940 season stats. The set is checklisted here in alphabetical order.

		NM	EX	VG
Complete Set (45):		44.00	22.00	13.00
Common Player:		1.00	.50	.30
(1)	Morrie Arnovich	1.00	.50	.30
(2)	Bill Baker	1.00	.50	.30
(3)	Joe Beggs	1.00	.50	.30
(4)	Wally Berger	1.00	.50	.30
(5)	Nino Bongiovanni	1.00	.50	.30
(6)	Frenchy Bordagaray	1.00	.50	.30
(7)	Harry Craft	1.00	.50	.30
(8)	Peaches Davis	1.00	.50	.30
(9)	Mike Dejan	1.00	.50	.30
(10)	Paul Derringer	1.00	.50	.30
(11)	Vince DiMaggio	2.00	1.00	.60
(12)	Lonny Frey	1.00	.50	.30
(13)	Milt Galatzer	1.00	.50	.30
(14)	Lee Gamble	1.00	.50	.30
(15)	Ival Goodman	1.00	.50	.30
(16)	Lee Grissom	1.00	.50	.30
(17)	Willard Hershberger	1.50	.70	.45
(18)	Johnny Hutchings	1.00	.50	.30
(19)	Art Jacobs	1.00	.50	.30
(20)	Hank Johnson	1.00	.50	.30
(21)	Eddie Joost	1.00	.50	.30
(22)	Wes Livengood	1.00	.50	.30
(23)	Ernie Lombardi	1.50	.70	.45
(24)	Frank McCormick	1.00	.50	.30
(25)	Mike McCormick	1.00	.50	.30
(26)	Bill McKechnie	1.25	.60	.40
(27)	Whitey Moore	1.00	.50	.30
(28)	Billy Myers	1.00	.50	.30
(29)	Johnny Niggeling	1.00	.50	.30
(30)	Pete Naktenis	1.00	.50	.30
(31)	Nolen Richardson	1.50	.70	.45
(32)	Lew Riggs	1.00	.50	.30
(33)	Jimmy Ripple	1.00	.50	.30
(34)	Johnny Rizzo	1.00	.50	.30
(35)	Les Scarsella	1.00	.50	.30
(36)	Milt Shofner	1.00	.50	.30
(37)	Al Simmons	1.50	.70	.45
(38)	Junior Thompson	1.00	.50	.30
(39)	Jim Turner	1.00	.50	.30
(40)	Johnny Vander Meer	1.25	.60	.40
(41)	Bucky Walters	1.00	.50	.30
(42)	Jim Weaver	1.00	.50	.30
(43)	Bill Werber	1.00	.50	.30
(44)	Dick West	1.00	.50	.30
(45)	Jimmy Wilson	1.00	.50	.30

1977 TCMA 1960 Pittsburgh Pirates

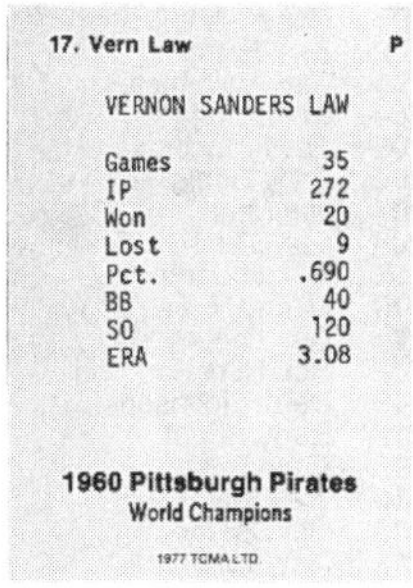

The World Champion Pirates are featured on this collector issue. The 2-1/2" x 3-1/2" cards have black-and-white photos on front surrounded by orange borders. Backs, also in black-and-white, have a card number, player name and position at top and season stats.

		NM	EX	VG
Complete Set (42):		70.00	35.00	22.00
Common Player:		1.50	.70	.45
1	Danny Murtaugh	1.50	.70	.45
2	Dick Stuart	2.50	1.25	.70
3	Bill Mazeroski	5.00	2.50	1.50
4	Dick Groat	2.50	1.25	.70
5	Don Hoak	2.00	1.00	.60
6	Roberto Clemente	12.00	6.00	3.50
7	Bill Virdon	1.50	.70	.45
8	Bob Skinner	1.50	.70	.45
9	Smoky Burgess	1.50	.70	.45
10	Gino Cimoli	1.50	.70	.45
11	Rocky Nelson	1.50	.70	.45
12	Hal Smith	1.50	.70	.45
13	Dick Schofield	1.50	.70	.45
14	Joe Christopher	1.50	.70	.45
15	Gene Baker	1.50	.70	.45
16	Bob Oldis	1.50	.70	.45
17	Vern Law	1.50	.70	.45
18	Bob Friend	1.50	.70	.45
19	Wilmer Mizell	1.50	.70	.45
20	Harvey Haddix	1.50	.70	.45
21	Roy Face	1.50	.70	.45
22	Fred Green	1.50	.70	.45
23	Joe Gibbon	1.50	.70	.45
24	Clem Labine	1.50	.70	.45
25	Paul Giel	1.50	.70	.45
26	Tom Cheney	1.50	.70	.45
27	Earl Francis	1.50	.70	.45
28	Jim Umbricht	1.50	.70	.45
29	George Witt	1.50	.70	.45
30	Bennie Daniels	1.50	.70	.45
31	Don Gross	1.50	.70	.45
32	Diomedes Olivo	2.50	1.25	.70
33	Roman Mejias	1.50	.70	.45
34	R.C. Stevens	1.50	.70	.45
35	Mickey Vernon	1.50	.70	.45
36	Danny Kravitz	1.50	.70	.45
37	Harry Bright	1.50	.70	.45
38	Dick Barone	1.50	.70	.45
39	Bill Burwell	1.50	.70	.45
40	Lenny Levy	2.00	1.00	.60
41	Sam Narron	1.50	.70	.45
42	Team card (Bob Friend)	1.50	.70	.45

1977-81 TCMA/ Renata Galasso

This issue of five series is in similar format but with different players, checklists and copyright dates produced by TCMA and marketed by Renata Galasso. In 2-1/2" x 3-1/2" format the cards have black-and-white photos on front. Backs are printed in red and blue and include a career summary, large Galasso ad and TCMA dateline.

		NM	EX	VG
Complete Set (224):		65.00	32.00	19.50
Common Player:		.25	.13	.08
	SERIES 1			
1	Joe DiMaggio	1.50	.70	.45
2	Ralph Kiner	.25	.13	.08
3	Don Larsen	.25	.13	.08
4	Robin Roberts	.25	.13	.08
5	Roy Campanella	.50	.25	.15
6	Smoky Burgess	.25	.13	.08
7	Mickey Mantle	3.00	1.50	.90
8	Willie Mays	1.00	.50	.30
9	George Kell	.25	.13	.08
10	Ted Williams	1.00	.50	.30
11	Carl Furillo	.25	.13	.08
12	Bob Feller	.35	.20	.11
13	Casey Stengel	.25	.13	.08
14	Richie Ashburn	.35	.20	.11
15	Gil Hodges	.35	.20	.11
16	Stan Musial	1.00	.50	.30
17	Don Newcombe	.25	.13	.08
18	Jackie Jensen	.25	.13	.08
19	Lou Boudreau	.25	.13	.08
20	Jackie Robinson	.75	.40	.25
21	Billy Goodman	.25	.13	.08
22	Satchel Paige	.50	.25	.15
23	Hoyt Wilhelm	.25	.13	.08
24	Duke Snider	.35	.20	.11
25	Whitey Ford	.35	.20	.11
26	Monte Irvin	.25	.13	.08
27	Hank Sauer	.25	.13	.08
28	Sal Maglie	.25	.13	.08
29	Ernie Banks	.35	.20	.11
30	Billy Pierce	.25	.13	.08
31	Pee Wee Reese	.35	.20	.11
32	Al Lopez	.25	.13	.08
33	Allie Reynolds	.25	.13	.08
34	Eddie Mathews	.35	.20	.11
35	Al Rosen	.25	.13	.08
36	Early Wynn	.25	.13	.08
37	Phil Rizzuto	.35	.20	.11
38	Warren Spahn	.35	.20	.11
39	Bobby Thomson	.25	.13	.08
40	Enos Slaughter	.25	.13	.08
41	Roberto Clemente	2.00	1.00	.60
42	Luis Aparicio	.25	.13	.08
43	Roy Sievers	.25	.13	.08
44	Hank Aaron	1.50	.70	.45
45	Mickey Vernon	.25	.13	.08
	SERIES 2			
46	Lou Gehrig	.75	.40	.25
47	Lefty O'Doul	.25	.13	.08
48	Chuck Klein	.25	.13	.08
49	Paul Waner	.25	.13	.08
50	Mel Ott	.25	.13	.08
51	Riggs Stephenson	.25	.13	.08
52	Dizzy Dean	.35	.20	.11
53	Frankie Frisch	.25	.13	.08
54	Red Ruffing	.25	.13	.08
55	Lefty Grove	.25	.13	.08
56	Heinie Manush	.25	.13	.08
57	Jimmie Foxx	.25	.13	.08
58	Al Simmons	.25	.13	.08
59	Charlie Root	.25	.13	.08
60	Goose Goslin	.25	.13	.08
61	Mickey Cochrane	.25	.13	.08
62	Gabby Hartnett	.25	.13	.08
63	Ducky Medwick	.25	.13	.08
64	Ernie Lombardi	.25	.13	.08
65	Joe Cronin	.25	.13	.08
66	Pepper Martin	.25	.13	.08
67	Jim Bottomley	.25	.13	.08
68	Bill Dickey	.25	.13	.08
69	Babe Ruth	2.00	1.00	.60
70	Joe McCarthy	.25	.13	.08
71	Doc Cramer	.25	.13	.08
72	Kiki Cuyler	.25	.13	.08
73	Johnny Vander Meer	.25	.13	.08
74	Paul Derringer	.25	.13	.08
75	Freddie Fitzsimmons	.25	.13	.08
76	Lefty Gomez	.25	.13	.08
77	Arky Vaughan	.25	.13	.08
78	Stan Hack	.25	.13	.08
79	Earl Averill	.25	.13	.08
80	Luke Appling	.25	.13	.08
81	Mel Harder	.25	.13	.08
82	Hank Greenberg	.35	.20	.11
83	Schoolboy Rowe	.25	.13	.08
84	Billy Herman	.25	.13	.08
85	Gabby Street	.25	.13	.08
86	Lloyd Waner	.25	.13	.08
87	Jocko Conlan	.25	.13	.08
88	Carl Hubbell	.25	.13	.08
89	Series 1 checklist	.25	.13	.08
90	Series 2 checklist	.25	.13	.08
	SERIES 3			
91	Babe Ruth	2.00	1.00	.60
92	Rogers Hornsby	.35	.20	.11
93	Edd Roush	.25	.13	.08
94	George Sisler	.25	.13	.08
95	Harry Heilmann	.25	.13	.08
96	Tris Speaker	.35	.20	.11
97	Burleigh Grimes	.25	.13	.08
98	John McGraw	.25	.13	.08
99	Eppa Rixey	.25	.13	.08
100	Ty Cobb	1.00	.50	.30
101	Zack Wheat	.25	.13	.08
102	Pie Traynor	.25	.13	.08
103	Max Carey	.25	.13	.08
104	Dazzy Vance	.25	.13	.08
105	Walter Johnson	.35	.20	.11
106	Herb Pennock	.25	.13	.08
107	Joe Sewell	.25	.13	.08
108	Sam Rice	.25	.13	.08
109	Earle Combs	.25	.13	.08
110	Ted Lyons	.25	.13	.08
111	Eddie Collins	.25	.13	.08
112	Bill Terry	.25	.13	.08
113	Hack Wilson	.25	.13	.08
114	Rabbit Maranville	.25	.13	.08
115	Charlie Grimm	.25	.13	.08
116	Tony Lazzeri	.25	.13	.08
117	Waite Hoyt	.25	.13	.08
118	Stan Coveleski	.25	.13	.08
119	George Kelly	.25	.13	.08
120	Jimmy Dykes	.25	.13	.08
121	Red Faber	.25	.13	.08
122	Dave Bancroft	.25	.13	.08
123	Judge Landis	.25	.13	.08
124	Branch Rickey	.25	.13	.08
125	Jesse Haines	.25	.13	.08
126	Carl Mays	.25	.13	.08
127	Fred Lindstrom	.25	.13	.08
128	Miller Huggins	.25	.13	.08
129	Sad Sam Jones	.25	.13	.08
130	Joe Judge	.25	.13	.08
131	Ross Young (Youngs)	.25	.13	.08
132	Bucky Harris	.25	.13	.08
133	Bob Meusel	.25	.13	.08
134	Billy Evans	.25	.13	.08
135	1927 N.Y. Yankees team photo/checklist	.25	.13	.08
	SERIES 4			
136	Ty Cobb	1.00	.50	.30
137	Nap Lajoie	.25	.13	.08
138	Tris Speaker	.25	.13	.08
139	Heinie Groh	.25	.13	.08
140	Sam Crawford	.25	.13	.08
141	Clyde Milan	.25	.13	.08
142	Chief Bender	.25	.13	.08
143	Big Ed Walsh	.25	.13	.08
144	Walter Johnson	.35	.20	.11
145	Connie Mack	.25	.13	.08
146	Hal Chase	.25	.13	.08
147	Hugh Duffy	.25	.13	.08
148	Honus Wagner	.65	.35	.20
149	Tom Connolly	.25	.13	.08
150	Clark Griffith	.25	.13	.08
151	Zack Wheat	.25	.13	.08
152	Christy Mathewson	.35	.20	.11
153	Grover C. Alexander	.25	.13	.08
154	Joe Jackson	2.00	1.00	.60
155	Home Run Baker	.25	.13	.08
156	Ed Plank	.25	.13	.08
157	Larry Doyle	.25	.13	.08
158	Rube Marquard	.25	.13	.08
159	Johnny Evers	.25	.13	.08
160	Joe Tinker	.25	.13	.08
161	Frank Chance	.25	.13	.08
162	Wilbert Robinson	.25	.13	.08
163	Roger Peckinpaugh	.25	.13	.08
164	Fred Clarke	.25	.13	.08
165	Babe Ruth	2.00	1.00	.60
166	Wilbur Cooper	.25	.13	.08
167	Germany Schaefer	.25	.13	.08
168	Addie Joss	.25	.13	.08
169	Cy Young	.50	.25	.15
170	Ban Johnson	.25	.13	.08
171	Joe Judge	.25	.13	.08
172	Harry Hooper	.25	.13	.08
173	Bill Klem	.25	.13	.08
174	Ed Barrow	.25	.13	.08
175	Ed Cicotte	.25	.13	.08
176	Hughie Jennings	.25	.13	.08
177	Ray Schalk	.25	.13	.08

178	Nick Altrock	.25	.13	.08
179	Roger Bresnahan	.25	.13	.08
180	$100,000 Infield	.25	.13	.08
	SERIES 5			
181	Lou Gehrig	1.00	.50	.30
182	Eddie Collins	.25	.13	.08
183	Art Fletcher	.25	.13	.08
184	Jimmie Foxx	.35	.20	.11
185	Lefty Gomez	.25	.13	.08
186	Oral Hildebrand	.25	.13	.08
187	General Crowder	.25	.13	.08
188	Bill Dickey	.25	.13	.08
189	Wes Ferrell	.25	.13	.08
190	Al Simmons	.25	.13	.08
191	Tony Lazzeri	.25	.13	.08
192	Sam West	.25	.13	.08
193	Babe Ruth	2.00	1.00	.60
194	Connie Mack	.25	.13	.08
195	Lefty Grove	.25	.13	.08
196	Eddie Rommel	.25	.13	.08
197	Ben Chapman	.25	.13	.08
198	Joe Cronin	.25	.13	.08
199	Rich Ferrell (Rick)	.25	.13	.08
200	Charlie Gehringer	.25	.13	.08
201	Jimmy Dykes	.25	.13	.08
202	Earl Averill	.25	.13	.08
203	Pepper Martin	.25	.13	.08
204	Bill Terry	.25	.13	.08
205	Pie Traynor	.25	.13	.08
206	Gabby Hartnett	.25	.13	.08
207	Frank Frisch	.25	.13	.08
208	Carl Hubbell	.25	.13	.08
209	Paul Waner	.25	.13	.08
210	Woody English	.25	.13	.08
211	Bill Hallahan	.25	.13	.08
212	Dick Bartell	.25	.13	.08
213	Bill McKechnie	.25	.13	.08
214	Max Carey	.25	.13	.08
215	John McGraw	.25	.13	.08
216	Jimmie Wilson	.25	.13	.08
217	Chick Hafey	.25	.13	.08
218	Chuck Klein	.25	.13	.08
219	Lefty O'Doul	.25	.13	.08
220	Wally Berger	.25	.13	.08
221	Hal Schumacher	.25	.13	.08
222	Lon Warneke	.25	.13	.08
---	1933 A.L. All-Stars	.25	.13	.08
---	1933 N.L. All-Stars	.25	.13	.08

1978 TCMA The 1960's

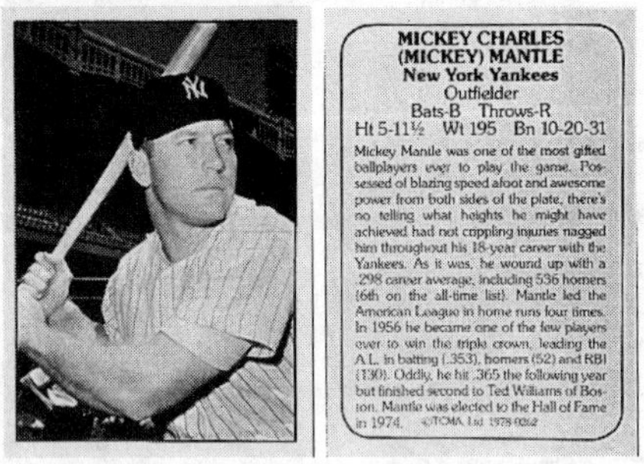
MICKEY CHARLES (MICKEY) MANTLE
New York Yankees
Outfielder
Bats-B Throws-R
Ht 5-11½ Wt 195 Bn 10-20-31
Mickey Mantle was one of the most gifted ballplayers ever to play the game. Possessed of blazing speed afoot and awesome power from both sides of the plate, there's no telling what heights he might have achieved had not crippling injuries nagged him throughout his 18-year career with the Yankees. As it was, he wound up with a .298 career average, including 536 homers (6th on the all-time list). Mantle led the American League in home runs four times. In 1956 he became one of the few players ever to win the triple crown, leading the A.L. in batting (.353), homers (52) and RBI (130). Oddly, he hit .365 the following year but finished second to Ted Williams of Boston. Mantle was elected to the Hall of Fame in 1974. ©TCMA Ltd 1978 0062

Nearly 300 players of the 1960s are featured in this collectors issue. Fronts of the 2-1/2" x 3-1/2" cards have a color photo with a black frameline and white border. There are no other graphics. Backs are printed in green and include a lengthy career summary. On some cards the set's title, "The 1960's" is printed at top. Several mistakes in card numbering are noted in the accompanying checklist.

		NM	EX	VG
Complete Set (293):		70.00	35.00	21.00
Common Player:		.30	.15	.09
1	Smoky Burgess	.30	.15	.09
2	Juan Marichal	.90	.45	.25
3	Don Drysdale	.90	.45	.25
4	Jim Gentile	.30	.15	.09
5	Roy Face	.30	.15	.09
6	Joe Pepitone	.30	.15	.09
7	Joe Christopher	.30	.15	.09
8	Wayne Causey	.30	.15	.09
9	Frank Bolling	.30	.15	.09
10	Jim Maloney	.30	.15	.09
11	Roger Maris	4.00	2.00	1.25
12	Bill White	.30	.15	.09
13	Roberto Clemente	7.50	3.75	2.25
14	Bob Saverine	.30	.15	.09
15	Barney Schultz	.30	.15	.09
16	Albie Pearson	.30	.15	.09
17	Denny Lemaster	.30	.15	.09
18	Ernie Broglio	.30	.15	.09
19	Bobby Klaus	.30	.15	.09
20	Tony Cloninger	.30	.15	.09
21	Whitey Ford	2.00	1.00	.60
22	Ron Santo	.45	.25	.14
23	Jim Duckworth	.30	.15	.09
24	Willie Davis	.30	.15	.09
25	Ed Charles	.30	.15	.09
26	Bob Allison	.30	.15	.09
27	Fritz Ackley	.30	.15	.09
28	Ruben Amaro	.30	.15	.09
29	Johnny Callison	.30	.15	.09
30	Greg Bollo	.30	.15	.09
31	Felix Millan	.30	.15	.09
32	Camilo Pascual	.30	.15	.09
33	Jackie Brandt	.30	.15	.09
34	Don Lock	.30	.15	.09
35	Chico Ruiz	.30	.15	.09
36	Joe Azcue	.30	.15	.09
37	Ed Bailey	.30	.15	.09
38	Pete Ramos	.30	.15	.09
39	Eddie Bressoud	.30	.15	.09
40	Al Kaline	2.00	1.00	.60
41	Ron Brand	.30	.15	.09
42	Bob Lillis	.30	.15	.09
43	Not issued (see #125)			
44	Buster Narum	.30	.15	.09
45	Jim Gilliam	.30	.15	.09
46	Claude Raymond	.30	.15	.09
47	Billy Bryan	.30	.15	.09
48	Marshall Bridges	.30	.15	.09
49	Norm Cash	.45	.25	.14
50	Orlando Cepeda	.90	.45	.25
51	Lee Maye	.30	.15	.09
52	Andre Rodgers	.30	.15	.09
53	Ken Berry	.30	.15	.09
54	Don Mincher	.30	.15	.09
55	Jerry Lumpe	.30	.15	.09
56	Milt Pappas	.30	.15	.09
57	Steve Barber	.30	.15	.09
58	Denis Menke	.30	.15	.09
59	Larry Maxie	.30	.15	.09
60	Bob Gibson	.90	.45	.25
61	Larry Bearnarth	.30	.15	.09
62	Bill Mazeroski	.75	.40	.25
63	Bob Rodgers	.30	.15	.09
64	Jerry Arrigo	.30	.15	.09
65	Joe Nuxhall	.30	.15	.09
66	Dean Chance	.30	.15	.09
67	Ken Boyer	.60	.30	.20
68	John Odom	.30	.15	.09
69	Chico Cardenas	.30	.15	.09
70	Maury Wills	.45	.25	.14
71	Tony Oliva	.45	.25	.14
72	Don Nottebart	.30	.15	.09
73	Joe Adcock	.30	.15	.09
74	Felipe Alou	.30	.15	.09
75	Matty Alou	.30	.15	.09
76	Dick Radatz	.30	.15	.09
77	Jim Bouton	.30	.15	.09
78	John Blanchard	.30	.15	.09
79	Juan Pizarro	.30	.15	.09
80	Boog Powell	.45	.25	.14
81	Earl Robinson	.30	.15	.09
82	Bob Chance	.30	.15	.09
83	Max Alvis	.30	.15	.09
84	Don Blasingame	.30	.15	.09
85	Tom Cheney	.30	.15	.09
86	Jerry Arrigo	.30	.15	.09
87	Tommy Davis	.30	.15	.09
88	Steve Boros	.30	.15	.09
89	Don Cardwell	.30	.15	.09
90	Harmon Killebrew	.90	.45	.25
91	Jim Pagliaroni	.30	.15	.09
92	Jim O'Toole	.30	.15	.09
93	Dennis Bennett	.30	.15	.09
94	Dick McAuliffe	.30	.15	.09
95	Dick Brown	.30	.15	.09
96	Joe Amalfitano	.30	.15	.09
97	Phil Linz	.30	.15	.09
98	Not issued (see #165)			
99	Dave Nicholson	.30	.15	.09
100	Hoyt Wilhelm	.90	.45	.25
101	Don Leppert	.30	.15	.09
102	Jose Pagan	.30	.15	.09
103	Sam McDowell	.30	.15	.09
104	Jack Baldschun	.30	.15	.09
105	Jim Perry	.30	.15	.09
106	Hal Reniff	.30	.15	.09
107	Lee Maye	.30	.15	.09
108	Joe Adcock	.30	.15	.09
109	Bob Bolin	.30	.15	.09
110	Don Leppert	.30	.15	.09
111	Bill Monbouquette	.30	.15	.09
112	Bobby Richardson	.45	.25	.14
113	Earl Battey	.30	.15	.09
114	Bob Veale	.30	.15	.09
115	Lou Jackson	.30	.15	.09
116	Frank Kreutzer	.30	.15	.09
117	Jerry Zimmerman	.30	.15	.09
118	Don Schwall	.30	.15	.09
119	Rich Rollins	.30	.15	.09
120	Pete Ward	.30	.15	.09
121	Moe Drabowsky	.30	.15	.09
122	Jesse Gonder	.30	.15	.09
123	Hal Woodeshick	.30	.15	.09
124	John Herrnstein	.30	.15	.09
125a	Gary Peters (should be #43)	.30	.15	.09
125b	Leon Wagner	.30	.15	.09
126	Dwight Siebler	.30	.15	.09
127	Gary Kroll	.30	.15	.09
128	Tony Horton	.30	.15	.09
129	John DeMerit	.30	.15	.09
130	Sandy Koufax	5.00	2.50	1.50
131	Jim Davenport	.30	.15	.09
132	Wes Covington	.30	.15	.09
133	Tony Taylor	.30	.15	.09
134	Jack Kralick	.30	.15	.09
135	Bill Pleis	.30	.15	.09
136	Russ Snyder	.30	.15	.09
137	Joe Torre	.50	.25	.15
138	Ted Wills	.30	.15	.09
139	Wes Stock	.30	.15	.09
140	Frank Robinson	2.00	1.00	.60
141	Dave Stenhouse	.30	.15	.09
142	Ron Hansen	.30	.15	.09
143	Don Elston	.30	.15	.09
144	Del Crandall	.30	.15	.09
145	Bennie Daniels	.30	.15	.09
146	Vada Pinson	.45	.25	.14
147	Bill Spanswick	.30	.15	.09
148	Earl Wilson	.30	.15	.09
149	Ty Cline	.30	.15	.09
150	Dick Groat	.30	.15	.09
151	Jim Duckworth	.30	.15	.09
152	Jimmie Schaffer	.30	.15	.09
153	George Thomas	.30	.15	.09
154	Wes Stock	.30	.15	.09
155	Mike White	.30	.15	.09
156	John Podres	.30	.15	.09
157	Willie Crawford	.30	.15	.09
158	Fred Gladding	.30	.15	.09
159	John Wyatt	.30	.15	.09
160	Bob Friend	.30	.15	.09
161	Ted Uhlaender	.30	.15	.09
162	Dick Stigman	.30	.15	.09
163	Don Wert	.30	.15	.09
164	Eddie Bressoud	.30	.15	.09
165a	Ed Roebuck (should be #98)	.30	.15	.09
165b	Leon Wagner	.30	.15	.09
166	Al Spangler	.30	.15	.09
167	Bob Sadowski	.30	.15	.09
168	Ralph Terry	.30	.15	.09
169	Jimmie Schaffer	.30	.15	.09
170a	Jim Fregosi (should be #180)	.30	.15	.09
170b	Dick Hall	.30	.15	.09
171	Al Spangler	.30	.15	.09
172	Bob Tillman	.30	.15	.09
173	Ed Bailey	.30	.15	.09
174	Cesar Tovar	.30	.15	.09
175	Morrie Stevens	.30	.15	.09
176	Floyd Weaver	.30	.15	.09
177	Frank Malzone	.30	.15	.09
178	Norm Siebern	.30	.15	.09
179	Dick Phillips	.30	.15	.09
180	Not issued (see #170)			
181	Bobby Wine	.30	.15	.09
182	Masanori Murakami	.50	.25	.15
183	Chuck Schilling	.30	.15	.09
184	Jimmie Schaffer	.30	.15	.09
185	John Roseboro	.30	.15	.09
186	Jake Wood	.30	.15	.09
187	Dallas Green	.30	.15	.09
188	Tom Haller	.30	.15	.09
189	Chuck Cottier	.30	.15	.09
190	Brooks Robinson	2.00	1.00	.60
191	Ty Cline	.30	.15	.09
192	Bubba Phillips	.30	.15	.09
193	Al Jackson	.30	.15	.09
194	Herm Starrette	.30	.15	.09
195	Dave Wickersham	.30	.15	.09
196	Vic Power	.30	.15	.09
197	Ray Culp	.30	.15	.09
198	Don Demeter	.30	.15	.09
199	Dick Schofield	.30	.15	.09
200	Stephen Grant	.30	.15	.09
201	Roger Craig	.30	.15	.09
202	Dick Farrell	.30	.15	.09
203	Clay Dalrymple	.30	.15	.09
204	Jim Duffalo	.30	.15	.09
205	Tito Francona	.30	.15	.09
206	Tony Conigliaro	.45	.25	.14
207	Jim King	.30	.15	.09
208	Joe Gibbon	.30	.15	.09
209	Arnold Earley	.30	.15	.09
210	Denny McLain	.45	.25	.14
211	Don Larsen	.30	.15	.09
212	Ron Hunt	.30	.15	.09
213	Deron Johnson	.30	.15	.09
214	Harry Bright	.30	.15	.09
215	Ernie Fazio	.30	.15	.09
216	Joey Jay	.30	.15	.09
217	Jim Coates	.30	.15	.09
218	Jerry Kindall	.30	.15	.09
219	Joe Gibbon	.30	.15	.09
220	Frank Howard	.45	.25	.14
221	Howie Koplitz	.30	.15	.09
222	Larry Jackson	.30	.15	.09
223	Dale Long	.30	.15	.09
224	Jimmy Dykes	.30	.15	.09
225	Hank Aguirre	.30	.15	.09
226	Earl Francis	.30	.15	.09
227	Vic Wertz	.30	.15	.09
228	Larry Haney	.30	.15	.09
229	Tony LaRussa	.45	.25	.14
230	Moose Skowron	.45	.25	.14
231a	Tito Francona (should be #235)	.30	.15	.09
231b	Lee Thomas	.30	.15	.09
232	Ken Johnson	.30	.15	.09
233	Dick Howser	.30	.15	.09
234	Bobby Knoop	.30	.15	.09
235	Not issued (see #231)			
236	Elston Howard	.45	.25	.14
237	Donn Clendenon	.30	.15	.09
238	Jesse Gonder	.30	.15	.09
239	Vern Law	.30	.15	.09
240	Curt Flood	.30	.15	.09
241	Dal Maxvill	.30	.15	.09
242	Roy Sievers	.30	.15	.09
243	Jim Brewer	.30	.15	.09
244	Harry Craft	.30	.15	.09
245	Dave Eilers	.30	.15	.09
246	Dave DeBusschere	.30	.15	.09
247	Ken Harrelson	.30	.15	.09
248	(Eddie Kasko) (see #249)	.30	.15	.09
249	Jim Duffalo	.30	.15	.09
250	Luis Aparicio	.90	.45	.25
251	Ron Kline	.30	.15	.09
252	Chuck Hinton	.30	.15	.09
253	Frank Lary	.30	.15	.09
254	Stu Miller	.30	.15	.09
255	Ernie Banks	2.50	1.25	.70
256	Dick Farrell	.30	.15	.09
257	Bud Daley	.30	.15	.09
258	Luis Arroyo	.30	.15	.09
259	Bob Del Greco	.30	.15	.09
260	Ted Williams	6.00	3.00	1.75

261	Mike Epstein	.30	.15	.09
262	Mickey Mantle	15.00	7.50	4.50
263	Jim LeFebvre	.30	.15	.09
264	Pat Jarvis	.30	.15	.09
265	Chuck Hinton	.30	.15	.09
266	Don Larsen	.30	.15	.09
267	Jim Coates	.30	.15	.09
268	Gary Kolb	.30	.15	.09
269	Jim Ray Hart	.30	.15	.09
270	Dave McNally	.30	.15	.09
271	Jerry Kindall	.30	.15	.09
272	Hector Lopez	.30	.15	.09
273	Claude Osteen	.30	.15	.09
274	Jack Aker	.30	.15	.09
275	Mike Shannon	.30	.15	.09
276	Lew Burdette	.30	.15	.09
277	Mack Jones	.30	.15	.09
278	Art Shamsky	.30	.15	.09
279	Bob Johnson	.30	.15	.09
280	Willie Mays	6.00	3.00	1.75
281	Rich Nye	.30	.15	.09
282	Bill Cowan	.30	.15	.09
283	Gary Kolb	.30	.15	.09
284	Woody Held	.30	.15	.09
285	Bill Freehan	.30	.15	.09
286	Larry Jackson	.30	.15	.09
287	Mike Hershberger	.30	.15	.09
288	Julian Javier	.30	.15	.09
289	Charley Smith	.30	.15	.09
290	Hank Aaron	6.00	3.00	1.75
291	John Boccabella	.30	.15	.09
292	Charley James	.30	.15	.09
293	Sammy Ellis	.30	.15	.09

1978 TCMA 1941 Brooklyn Dodgers

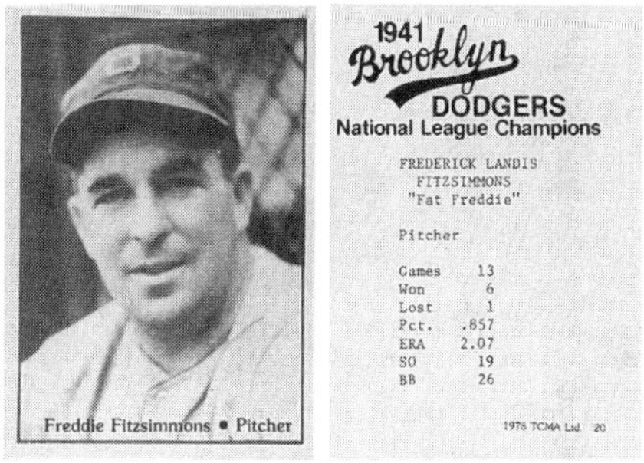

The National League Champion Brooklyn Dodgers are featured in the collectors' edition card set. Measuring 2-1/2" x 3-1/2", the cards have blue duotone player photos on front with the name and position overprinted in black at bottom. A white border surrounds the photo. Backs are in black-and-white with a large championship logo and a few stats from the 1941 season.

		NM	EX	VG
Complete Set (43):		65.00	32.00	18.00
Common Player:		1.25	.60	.40
1	Mickey Owen	2.00	1.00	.60
2	Pee Wee Reese	6.00	3.00	1.75
3	Hugh Casey	1.25	.60	.40
4	Larry French	1.25	.60	.40
5	Tom Drake	1.25	.60	.40
6	Ed Albosta	1.25	.60	.40
7	Tommy Tatum	1.25	.60	.40
8	Paul Waner	3.00	1.50	.90
9	Van Lingle Mungo	2.00	1.00	.60
10	Bill Swift	1.25	.60	.40
11	Dolph Camilli	2.00	1.00	.60
12	Pete Coscarart	1.25	.60	.40
13	Vito Tamulis	1.25	.60	.40
14	John Allen	1.25	.60	.40
15	Lee Grissom	1.25	.60	.40
16	Billy Herman	2.00	1.00	.60
17	Joe Vosmik	1.25	.60	.40
18	Babe Phelps	1.25	.60	.40
19	Mace Brown	1.25	.60	.40
20	Freddie Fitzsimmons	1.25	.60	.40
21	Angelo Guiliani	1.25	.60	.40
22	Lewis Riggs	1.25	.60	.40
23	Jimmy Wasdell	1.25	.60	.40
24	Herman Franks	1.25	.60	.40
25	Alex Kampouris	1.25	.60	.40
26	Kirby Higbe	1.25	.60	.40
27	Joe Medwick	2.00	1.00	.60
28	Newt Kimball	1.25	.60	.40
29	Curt Davis	1.25	.60	.40
30	Augie Galan	1.25	.60	.40
31	Luke Hamlin	1.25	.60	.40
32	Cookie Lavagetto	1.25	.60	.40
33	Joe Gallagher	1.25	.60	.40
34	Whitlow Wyatt	1.25	.60	.40
35	Dixie Walker	1.25	.60	.40
36	Pete Reiser	1.25	.60	.40
37	Leo Durocher	2.00	1.00	.60
38	Pee Wee Reese, Joe Medwick (3" x 5")	2.50	1.25	.70
39	Dixie Walker, Joe Medwick, Dolph Camilli, Pete Reiser (3" x 5")	2.50	1.25	.70
40	Team photo	2.00	1.00	.60
41	Kemp Wicker	1.25	.60	.40
42	George Pfister	2.00	1.00	.60
43	Chuck Dressen	1.25	.60	.40

1979 TCMA All Time Tigers

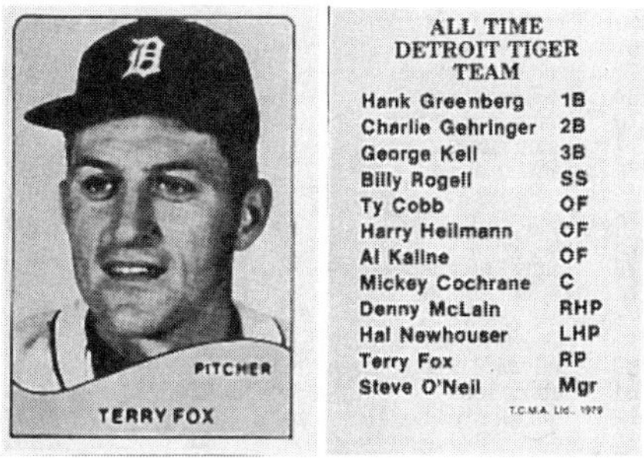

PITCHER
TERRY FOX
ALL TIME DETROIT TIGER TEAM
Hank Greenberg 1B
Charlie Gehringer 2B
George Kell 3B
Billy Rogell SS
Ty Cobb OF
Harry Heilmann OF
Al Kaline OF
Mickey Cochrane C
Denny McLain RHP
Hal Newhouser LHP
Terry Fox RP
Steve O'Neil Mgr
T.C.M.A. Ltd. 1979

Utilizing a format similar to its several minor league team sets of the same year, this collectors issue from TCMA features an "All Time" Tigers team selection of position players, pitchers and manager. The 2-1/2" x 3-1/2" cards have black-and-white photos on front with the player's name and position in an orange "wave" at bottom; the whole is surrounded by a white border. Backs are in black-and-white and detail the all-time line-up. The unnumbered cards are checklisted here alphabetically.

		NM	EX	VG
Complete Set (12):		24.00	12.00	7.25
Common Player:		1.50	.70	.45
(1)	Ty Cobb	6.00	3.00	1.75
(2)	Mickey Cochrane	1.50	.70	.45
(3)	Terry Fox	1.50	.70	.45
(4)	Charlie Gehringer	2.25	1.25	.70
(5)	Hank Greenberg	4.50	2.25	1.25
(6)	Harry Heilmann	1.50	.70	.45
(7)	Al Kaline	4.50	2.25	1.25
(8)	George Kell	1.50	.70	.45
(9)	Denny McLain	2.25	1.25	.70
(10)	Hal Newhouser	1.50	.70	.45
(11)	Steve O'Neil (O'Neill)	1.50	.70	.45
(12)	Billy Rogell	1.50	.70	.45

1979 TCMA Baseball History Series

The "pure" format of the 1953 Bowman set was borrowed in this collectors issue featuring the stars and journeymen of baseball in the 1950s. The 2-1/2" x 3-1/2" cards have color photos on front with white borders. Backs are in red and black with personal data and career summary and stats.

		NM	EX	VG
Complete Set (291):		70.00	35.00	21.00
Common Player:		.25	.13	.08
1	Joe DiMaggio	10.00	5.00	3.00
2	Yogi Berra	2.00	1.00	.60
3	Warren Spahn	2.00	1.00	.60
4	Robin Roberts	1.00	.50	.30
5	Ernie Banks	2.00	1.00	.60
6	Willie Mays	5.00	2.50	1.50
7	Mickey Mantle	15.00	7.50	4.50
8	Roy Campanella	2.50	1.25	.70
9	Stan Musial	5.00	2.50	1.50
10	Ted Williams	5.00	2.50	1.50
11	Ed Bailey	.25	.13	.08
12	Ted Kluszewski	.75	.40	.25
13	Ralph Kiner	.75	.40	.25
14	Dick Littlefield	.25	.13	.08
15	Nellie Fox	.60	.30	.20
16	Billy Pierce	.25	.13	.08
17	Richie Ashburn	.75	.40	.25
18	Del Ennis	.25	.13	.08
19	Bob Lemon	.75	.40	.25
20	Early Wynn	.75	.40	.25
21	Joe Collins	.25	.13	.08
22	Hank Bauer	.25	.13	.08
23	Roberto Clemente	7.50	3.75	2.25
24	Frank Thomas	.25	.13	.08
25	Alvin Dark	.25	.13	.08
26	Whitey Lockman	.25	.13	.08
27	Larry Doby	.75	.40	.25
28	Bob Feller	.75	.40	.25
29	Willie Jones	.25	.13	.08
30	Granny Hamner	.25	.13	.08
31	Clem Labine	.25	.13	.08
32	Ralph Branca	.25	.13	.08
33	Jack Harshman	.25	.13	.08
34	Dick Donovan	.25	.13	.08
35	Tommy Henrich	.25	.13	.08
36	Jerry Coleman	.25	.13	.08
37	Billy Hoeft	.25	.13	.08
38	Johnny Groth	.25	.13	.08
39	Harvey Haddix	.25	.13	.08
40	Gerry Staley	.25	.13	.08
41	Dale Long	.25	.13	.08
42	Vern Law	.25	.13	.08
43	Dodger Power	1.50	.70	.45
44	Sam Jethroe	.25	.13	.08
45	Vic Wertz	.25	.13	.08
46	Wes Westrum	.25	.13	.08
47	Dee Fondy	.25	.13	.08
48	Gene Baker	.25	.13	.08
49	Sandy Koufax	4.00	2.00	1.25
50	Billy Loes	.25	.13	.08
51	Chuck Diering	.25	.13	.08
52	Joe Ginsberg	.25	.13	.08
53	Jim Konstanty	.25	.13	.08
54	Curt Simmons	.25	.13	.08
55	Alex Kellner	.25	.13	.08
56	Charlie Dressen	.25	.13	.08
57	Frank Sullivan	.25	.13	.08
58	Mel Parnell	.25	.13	.08
59	Bobby Hofman	.25	.13	.08
60	Bill Connelly	.25	.13	.08
61	Corky Valentine	.25	.13	.08
62	Johnny Klippstein	.25	.13	.08
63	Chuck Tanner	.25	.13	.08
64	Dick Drott	.25	.13	.08
65	Dean Stone	.25	.13	.08
66	Jim Busby	.25	.13	.08
67	Sid Gordon	.25	.13	.08
68	Del Crandall	.25	.13	.08
69	Walker Cooper	.25	.13	.08
70	Hank Sauer	.25	.13	.08
71	Gil Hodges	.75	.40	.25
72	Duke Snider	2.00	1.00	.60
73	Sherman Lollar	.25	.13	.08
74	Chico Carrasquel	.25	.13	.08
75	Gus Triandos	.25	.13	.08
76	Bob Harrison	.25	.13	.08
77	Eddie Waitkus	.25	.13	.08
78	Ken Heintzelman	.25	.13	.08
79	Harry Simpson	.25	.13	.08
80	Luke Easter	.25	.13	.08
81	Ed Dick	.25	.13	.08
82	Jim DePaola	.25	.13	.08
83	Billy Cox	.25	.13	.08
84	Pee Wee Reese	1.50	.70	.45
85	Virgil Trucks	.25	.13	.08
86	George Kell	.75	.40	.25
87	Mickey Vernon	.25	.13	.08
88	Eddie Yost	.25	.13	.08
89	Gus Bell	.25	.13	.08
90	Wally Post	.25	.13	.08
91	Ed Lopat	.25	.13	.08
92	Dick Wakefield	.25	.13	.08
93	Solly Hemus	.25	.13	.08
94	Al "Red" Schoendienst	.75	.40	.25
95	Sammy White	.25	.13	.08
96	Billy Goodman	.25	.13	.08
97	Jim Hearn	.25	.13	.08
98	Ruben Gomez	.25	.13	.08
99	Marty Marion	.25	.13	.08
100	Bill Virdon	.25	.13	.08
101	Chuck Stobbs	.25	.13	.08
102	Ron Samford	.25	.13	.08
103	Bill Tuttle	.25	.13	.08
104	Harvey Kuenn	.25	.13	.08
105	Joe Cunningham	.25	.13	.08
106	Bill Sarni	.25	.13	.08
107	Jack Kramer	.25	.13	.08
108	Eddie Stanky	.25	.13	.08
109	Carmen Mauro	.25	.13	.08
110	Wayne Belardi	.25	.13	.08
111	Preston Ward	.25	.13	.08
112	Jack Shepard	.25	.13	.08
113	Buddy Kerr	.25	.13	.08
114	Vern Bickford	.25	.13	.08
115	Ellis Kinder	.25	.13	.08
116	Walt Dropo	.25	.13	.08
117	Duke Maas	.25	.13	.08
118	Billy Hunter	.25	.13	.08
119	Ewell Blackwell	.25	.13	.08
120	Hershell Freeman	.25	.13	.08
121	Freddie Martin	.25	.13	.08
122	Erv Dusak	.25	.13	.08
123	Roy Hartsfield	.25	.13	.08
124	Willard Marshall	.25	.13	.08
125	Jack Sanford	.25	.13	.08
126	Herm Wehmeier	.25	.13	.08
127	Hal Smith	.25	.13	.08
128	Jim Finigan	.25	.13	.08
129	Bob Hale	.25	.13	.08
130	Jim Wilson	.25	.13	.08
131	Bill Wight	.25	.13	.08
132	Mike Fornieles	.25	.13	.08
133	Steve Gromek	.25	.13	.08
134	Herb Score	.35	.20	.11
135	Ryne Duren	.25	.13	.08

136	Bob Turley	.25	.13	.08
137	Wally Moon	.25	.13	.08
138	Fred Hutchinson	.25	.13	.08
139	Jim Hegan	.25	.13	.08
140	Dale Mitchell	.25	.13	.08
141	Walt Moryn	.25	.13	.08
142	Cal Neeman	.25	.13	.08
143	Billy Martin	.50	.25	.15
144	Phil Rizzuto	1.50	.70	.45
145	Preacher Roe	.25	.13	.08
146	Carl Erskine	.25	.13	.08
147	Vic Power	.25	.13	.08
148	Elmer Valo	.25	.13	.08
149	Don Mueller	.25	.13	.08
150	Hank Thompson	.25	.13	.08
151	Stan Lopata	.25	.13	.08
152	Dick Sisler	.25	.13	.08
153	Willard Schmidt	.25	.13	.08
154	Roy McMillan	.25	.13	.08
155	Gil McDougald	.25	.13	.08
156	Gene Woodling	.25	.13	.08
157	Eddie Mathews	2.00	1.00	.60
158	Johnny Logan	.25	.13	.08
159	Dan Bankhead	.25	.13	.08
160	Joe Black	.25	.13	.08
161	Roger Maris	4.00	2.00	1.25
162	Bob Cerv	.25	.13	.08
163	Paul Minner	.25	.13	.08
164	Bob Rush	.25	.13	.08
165	Gene Hermanski	.25	.13	.08
166	Harry Brecheen	.25	.13	.08
167	Davey Williams	.25	.13	.08
168	Monte Irvin	.75	.40	.25
169	Clint Courtney	.25	.13	.08
170	Sandy Consuegra	.25	.13	.08
171	Bobby Shantz	.25	.13	.08
172	Harry Byrd	.25	.13	.08
173	Marv Throneberry	.25	.13	.08
174	Woody Held	.25	.13	.08
175	Al Rosen	.25	.13	.08
176	Rance Pless	.25	.13	.08
177	Steve Bilko	.25	.13	.08
178	Joe Presko	.25	.13	.08
179	Ray Boone	.25	.13	.08
180	Jim Lemon	.25	.13	.08
181	Andy Pafko	.25	.13	.08
182	Don Newcombe	.35	.20	.11
183	Frank Lary	.25	.13	.08
184	Al Kaline	1.50	.70	.45
185	Allie Reynolds	.25	.13	.08
186	Vic Raschi	.25	.13	.08
187	Dodger Braintrust	1.00	.50	.30
188	Jim Piersall	.25	.13	.08
189	George Wilson	.25	.13	.08
190	Jim "Dusty" Rhodes	.25	.13	.08
191	Duane Pillette	.25	.13	.08
192	Dave Philley	.25	.13	.08
193	Bobby Morgan	.25	.13	.08
194	Russ Meyer	.25	.13	.08
195	Hector Lopez	.25	.13	.08
196	Arnie Portocarrero	.25	.13	.08
197	Joe Page	.25	.13	.08
198	Tommy Byrne	.25	.13	.08
199	Ray Monzant	.25	.13	.08
200	John "Windy" McCall	.25	.13	.08
201	Leo Durocher	.75	.40	.25
202	Bobby Thomson	.35	.20	.11
203	Jack Banta	.25	.13	.08
204	Joe Pignatano	.25	.13	.08
205	Carlos Paula	.25	.13	.08
206	Roy Sievers	.25	.13	.08
207	Mickey McDermott	.25	.13	.08
208	Ray Scarborough	.25	.13	.08
209	Bill Miller	.25	.13	.08
210	Bill Skowron	.35	.20	.11
211	Bob Nieman	.25	.13	.08
212	Al Pilarcik	.25	.13	.08
213	Jerry Priddy	.25	.13	.08
214	Frank House	.25	.13	.08
215	Don Mossi	.25	.13	.08
216	Rocky Colavito	.60	.30	.20
217	Brooks Lawrence	.25	.13	.08
218	Ted Wilks	.25	.13	.08
219	Zack Monroe	.25	.13	.08
220	Art Ditmar	.25	.13	.08
221	Cal McLish	.25	.13	.08
222	Gene Bearden	.25	.13	.08
223	Norm Siebern	.25	.13	.08
224	Bob Wiesler	.25	.13	.08
225	Foster Castleman	.25	.13	.08
226	Daryl Spencer	.25	.13	.08
227	Dick Williams	.25	.13	.08
228	Don Zimmer	.25	.13	.08
229	Jackie Jensen	.25	.13	.08
230	Billy Johnson	.25	.13	.08
231	Dave Koslo	.25	.13	.08
232	Al Corwin	.25	.13	.08
233	Erv Palica	.25	.13	.08
234	Bob Milliken	.25	.13	.08
235	Ray Katt	.25	.13	.08
236	Sammy Calderone	.25	.13	.08
237	Don Demeter	.25	.13	.08
238	Karl Spooner	.25	.13	.08
239	The Veteran and The Rookie	.50	.25	.15
240	Enos Slaughter	.75	.40	.25
241	Dick Kryhoski	.25	.13	.08
242	Art Houtteman	.25	.13	.08
243	Andy Carey	.25	.13	.08
244	Tony Kubek	.35	.20	.11
245	Mike McCormick	.25	.13	.08
246	Bob Schmidt	.25	.13	.08
247	Nelson King	.25	.13	.08
248	Bob Skinner	.25	.13	.08
249	Dick Bokelmann	.25	.13	.08
250	Eddie Kazak	.25	.13	.08
251	Billy Klaus	.25	.13	.08
252	Norm Zauchin	.25	.13	.08
253	Art Schult	.25	.13	.08
254	Bob Martyn	.25	.13	.08
255	Larry Jansen	.25	.13	.08
256	Sal Maglie	.25	.13	.08
257	Bob Darnell	.25	.13	.08
258	Ken Lehman	.25	.13	.08
259	Jim Blackburn	.25	.13	.08
260	Bob Purkey	.25	.13	.08
261	Harry Walker	.25	.13	.08
262	Joe Garagiola	.35	.20	.11
263	Gus Zernial	.25	.13	.08
264	Walter "Hoot" Evers	.25	.13	.08
265	Mark Freeman	.25	.13	.08
266	Charlie Silvera	.25	.13	.08
267	Johnny Podres	.25	.13	.08
268	Jim Hughes	.25	.13	.08
269	Al Worthington	.25	.13	.08
270	Hoyt Wilhelm	.75	.40	.25
271	Elston Howard	.25	.13	.08
272	Don Larsen	.40	.20	.12
273	Don Hoak	.25	.13	.08
274	Chico Fernandez	.25	.13	.08
275	Gail Harris	.25	.13	.08
276	Valmy Thomas	.25	.13	.08
277	George Shuba	.25	.13	.08
278	Al "Rube" Walker	.25	.13	.08
279	Willard Ramsdell	.25	.13	.08
280	Lindy McDaniel	.25	.13	.08
281	Bob Wilson	.25	.13	.08
282	Chuck Templeton	.25	.13	.08
283	Eddie Robinson	.25	.13	.08
284	Bob Porterfield	.25	.13	.08
285	Larry Miggins	.25	.13	.08
286	Minnie Minoso	.35	.20	.11
287	Lou Boudreau	.50	.25	.15
288	Jim Davenport	.25	.13	.08
289	Bob Miller	.25	.13	.08
290	Jim Gilliam	.25	.13	.08
291	Jackie Robinson	3.00	1.50	.90

1979 TCMA Japan Pro Baseball

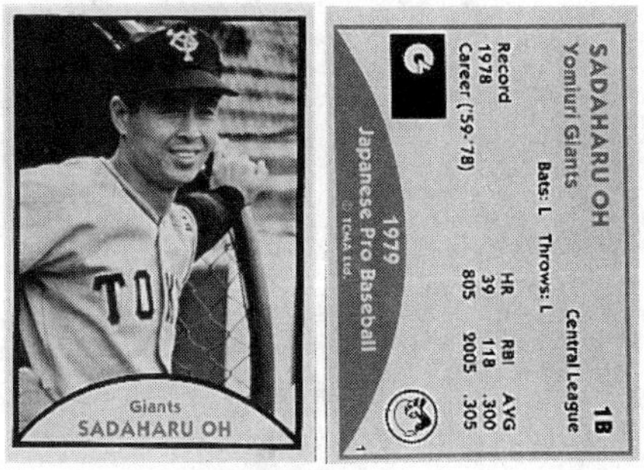

Stars of Japan's Pacific and Central "major" leagues are featured in this collectors issue. More than a dozen Americans playing or managing in Japan at the time are included in the set, as well as several Japanese Hall of Famers including home-run king Sadaharu Oh. Cards feature a color posed portrait with a light blue semi-circle at bottom containing the team and player name in royal blue. Backs are printed in red and black on white and have a few personal data, 1978 and career stats, plus league and team logos and TCMA copyright. Cards are nominally standard 2-1/2" x 3-1/2" in size, but actual size varies a bit due to cutting discrepancies.

		NM	EX	VG
Complete Set (90):		90.00	45.00	27.00
Common Player:		.50	.25	.15
1	Sadaharu Oh	16.00	8.00	4.75
2	Jinten Haku	.50	.25	.15
3	Toshizo Sakamoto	.50	.25	.15
4	Tony Muser	1.00	.50	.30
5	Makoto Matsubara	.50	.25	.15
6	Masayuki Nakaysuka	.50	.25	.15
7	Daisuke Yamashita	.50	.25	.15
8	Koji Yamamoto	.50	.25	.15
9	Sachio Kinugasa	5.00	2.50	1.50
10	Bernie Williams	1.00	.50	.30
11	Bobby Marcano	1.00	.50	.30
12	Koichi Tabuchi	.50	.25	.15
13	Katsuya Nomura	4.00	2.00	1.25
14	Jack Maloof	1.00	.50	.30
15	Masahiro Doi	.50	.25	.15
16	Hiroyuki Yamazaki	.50	.25	.15
17	Vernon Law	2.50	1.25	.70
18	Dave Hilton	1.00	.50	.30
19	Katsuo Osugi	.50	.25	.15
20	Tsutomu Wakamatsu	.50	.25	.15
21	John Scott	1.00	.50	.30
22	Toru Sugiura	.50	.25	.15
23	Akihiko Kondo	.50	.25	.15
24	Shintaro Mizutani	.50	.25	.15
25	Tatsuro Hirooka	.50	.25	.15
26	Kojiro Ikegaya	.50	.25	.15
27	Yutaka Enatsu	4.00	2.00	1.25
28	Tomehiro Kaneda	.50	.25	.15
29	Yoshihiko Takahashi	.50	.25	.15
30	Jitsuo Mizutani	.50	.25	.15
31	Adrian Garrett	1.00	.50	.30
32	Jim Lyttle	1.00	.50	.30
33	Takeshi Koba	.50	.25	.15
34	Sam Ewing	1.00	.50	.30
35	Kazumi Takahashi	.50	.25	.15
36	Kazushi Saeki	.50	.25	.15
37	Masanori Murakami	10.00	5.00	3.00
38	Toshiro Kato	.50	.25	.15
39	Junichi Kashiwabara	.50	.25	.15
40	Masaru Tomita	.50	.25	.15
41	Bobby Mitchell	1.00	.50	.30
42	Mikio Sendoh	.50	.25	.15
43	Chris Arnold	1.00	.50	.30
44	Charlie Manuel	1.00	.50	.30
45	Keiji Suzuki	.50	.25	.15
46	Toru Ogawa	.50	.25	.15
47	Shigeru Ishiwata	.50	.25	.15
48	Kyosuke Sasaki	.50	.25	.15
49	Iwao Ikebe	.50	.25	.15
50	Kaoru Betto	.50	.25	.15
51	Gene Martin	1.00	.50	.30
52	Felix Millan	2.00	1.00	.60
53	Mitsuo Motoi	.50	.25	.15
54	Tomio Tashiro	.50	.25	.15
55	Shigeo Nagashima	10.00	5.00	3.00
56	Yoshikazu Takagi	.50	.25	.15
57	Keiichi Nagasaki	.50	.25	.15
58	Rick Krueger	1.00	.50	.30
59	John Sipin	1.00	.50	.30
60	Osao Shibata	.50	.25	.15
61	Isao Harimoto	.50	.25	.15
62	Shigeru Takada	.50	.25	.15
63	Michiyo Arito	.50	.25	.15
64	Hisao Niura	.50	.25	.15
65	Teruhide Sakurai	.50	.25	.15
66	Yoshito Oda	.50	.25	.15
67	Leron Lee	1.00	.50	.30
68	Carlos May	1.00	.50	.30
69	Frank Ortenzio	1.00	.50	.30
70	Leon Lee	1.00	.50	.30
71	Mitsuru Fujiwara	.50	.25	.15
72	Senichi Hoshino	.50	.25	.15
73	Tatsuhiko Kimata	.50	.25	.15
74	Morimichi Takagi	.50	.25	.15
75	Yasunori Oshima	.50	.25	.15
76	Yasushi Tao	.50	.25	.15
77	Wayne Garrett	1.00	.50	.30
78	Bob Jones	1.00	.50	.30
79	Toshiro Naka	.50	.25	.15
80	Don Blasingame	4.00	2.00	1.25
81	Mike Reinbach	1.00	.50	.30
82	Masashi Takenouchi	.50	.25	.15
83	Masayuki Kakefu	.50	.25	.15
84	Katsuhiro Nakamura	.50	.25	.15
85	Shigeru Kobayashi	.50	.25	.15
86	Lee Stanton	1.00	.50	.30
87	Takenori Emoto	.50	.25	.15
88	Sohachi Aniya	.50	.25	.15
89	Wally Yonamine	4.00	2.00	1.25
90	Kazuhiro Yamauchi	.50	.25	.15

1979 TCMA 1927 New York Yankees

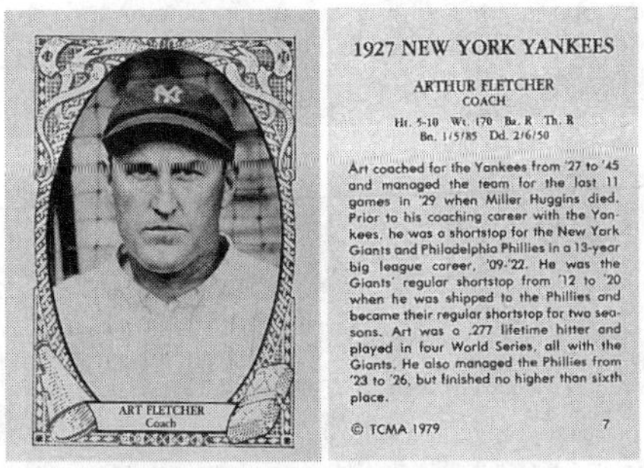

Perhaps the finest baseball team of all time is featured in this collectors' set. The sepia oval photos at center are surrounded by black-and-white graphics of baseball equipment and other ornamentation. Player name and position are in a strip beneath the photo. Backs have personal data and a career summary. The cards are in standard 2-1/2" x 3-1/2".

		NM	EX	VG
Complete Set (32):		60.00	30.00	18.00
Common Player:		1.75	.90	.50
1	Babe Ruth	13.00	6.50	4.00
2	Lou Gehrig	8.50	4.25	2.50
3	Tony Lazzeri	1.75	.90	.50
4	Mark Koenig	1.75	.90	.50
5	Julie Wera	1.75	.90	.50
6	Ray Morehart	1.75	.90	.50
7	Art Fletcher	1.75	.90	.50
8	Joe Dugan	1.75	.90	.50
9	Charley O'Leary	1.75	.90	.50
10	Bob Meusel	1.75	.90	.50
11	Earle Combs	1.75	.90	.50
12	Cedric Durst	1.75	.90	.50
13	Johnny Grabowski	1.75	.90	.50
14	Mike Gazella	1.75	.90	.50

15	Pat Collins	1.75	.90	.50
16	Waite Hoyt	2.50	1.25	.70
17	Myles Thomas	1.75	.90	.50
18	Benny Bengough	1.75	.90	.50
19	Herb Pennock	1.75	.90	.50
20	Wilcy Moore	1.75	.90	.50
21	Urban Shocker	1.75	.90	.50
22	Dutch Ruether	1.75	.90	.50
23	George Pipgras	1.75	.90	.50
24	Jacob Ruppert	1.75	.90	.50
25	Eddie Bennett	1.75	.90	.50
26	Ed Barrow	1.75	.90	.50
27	Ben Paschal	1.75	.90	.50
28	Miller Huggins	1.75	.90	.50
29	Joe Giard	1.75	.90	.50
30	Bob Shawkey	1.75	.90	.50
31	Walter Beall	1.75	.90	.50
32	Don Miller	1.75	.90	.50

1980 TCMA All-Time Teams

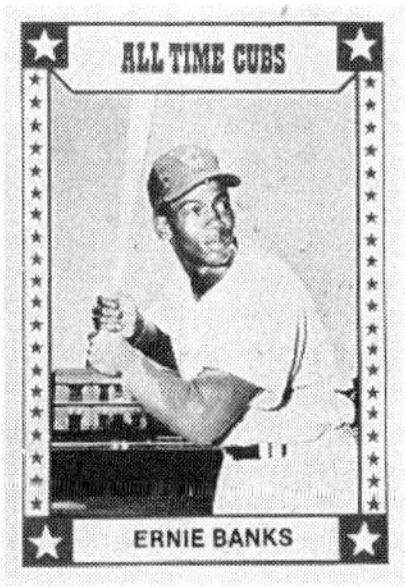

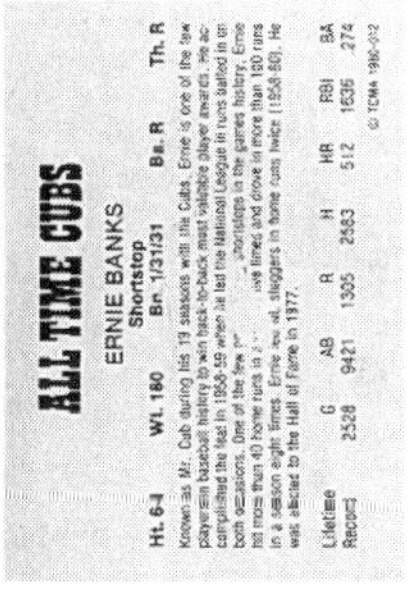

In 1980, TCMA began a new series of sets featuring 11 all-time great players and a manager from several of the 26 teams. In standard 2-1/2" x 3-1/2" format, most of the cards utilize black-and-white player photos, though some more recent stars are pictured in color. Several decorative borders, varying by team, surround the front photos. On most team sets there is an "All Time" designation at top, with the player name and (usually) position at bottom. Backs are fairly uniform, printed in blue or black, and offering a few biographical details and career highlights or a checklist. Besides hobby sales, these old-timers' sets were also sold in several major retail chains.

(Team sets listed individually)

1980 TCMA All Time Brooklyn Dodgers

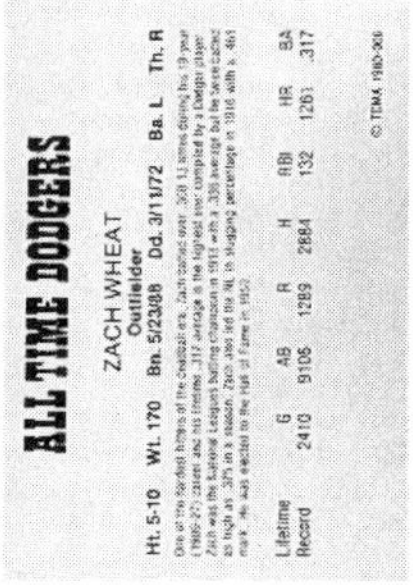

		NM	EX	VG
Complete Set (12):		20.00	10.00	6.00
Common Player:		.75	.40	.25
1	Gil Hodges	1.75	.90	.50
2	Jim Gilliam	.75	.40	.25
3	Pee Wee Reese	2.00	1.00	.60
4	Jackie Robinson	6.00	3.00	1.75
5	Sandy Koufax	4.00	2.00	1.25
6	Zach Wheat	.75	.40	.25
7	Dixie Walker	.75	.40	.25
8	Hugh Casey	.75	.40	.25
9	Dazzy Vance	.75	.40	.25
10	Duke Snider	2.00	1.00	.60
11	Roy Campanella	3.00	1.50	.90
12	Walter Alston	1.00	.50	.30

1980 TCMA All Time Cubs

		NM	EX	VG
Complete Set (12):		15.00	7.50	4.50
Common Player:		.75	.40	.25
1	Billy Williams	2.50	1.25	.70
2	Charlie Root	.75	.40	.25
3	Ron Santo	2.25	1.25	.70
4	Larry French	.75	.40	.25
5	Gabby Hartnett	.75	.40	.25
6	Emil Kush	.75	.40	.25
7	Charlie Grimm	.75	.40	.25
8	Kiki Cuyler	.75	.40	.25
9	Billy Herman	1.25	.60	.40
10	Hack Wilson	1.25	.60	.40
11	Rogers Hornsby	2.25	1.25	.70
12	Ernie Banks	6.00	3.00	1.75

1980 TCMA All Time N.Y. Giants

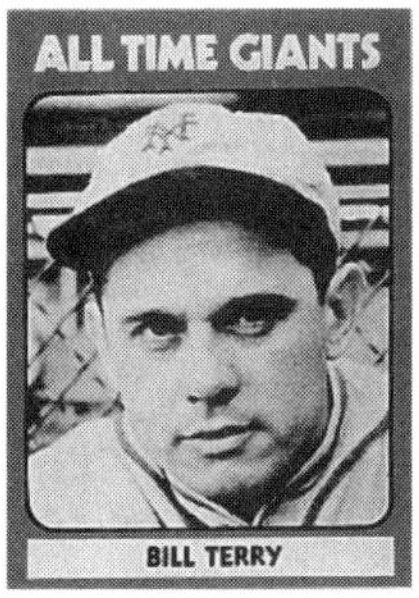

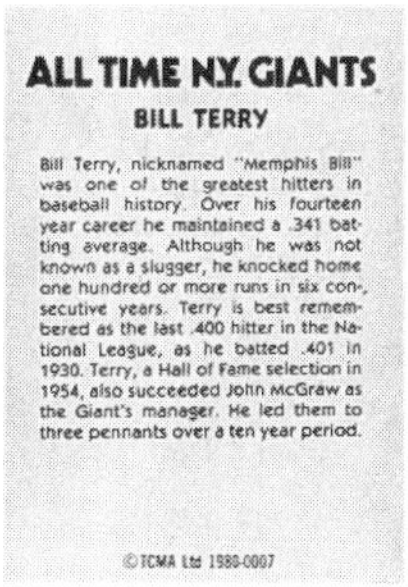

		NM	EX	VG
Complete Set (12):		15.00	7.50	4.50
Common Player:		.50	.25	.15
1	Willie Mays	6.00	3.00	1.75
2	Wes Westrum	.50	.25	.15
3	Carl Hubbell	.90	.45	.25
4	Hoyt Wilhelm	.50	.25	.15
5	Bobby Thomson	.70	.35	.20
6	Frankie Frisch	.70	.35	.20
7	Bill Terry	.50	.25	.15
8	Alvin Dark	.50	.25	.15
9	Mel Ott	.70	.35	.20
10	Christy Mathewson	1.50	.70	.45
11	Freddie Lindstrom	.50	.25	.15
12	John McGraw	.50	.25	.15

1980 TCMA All Time Tigers

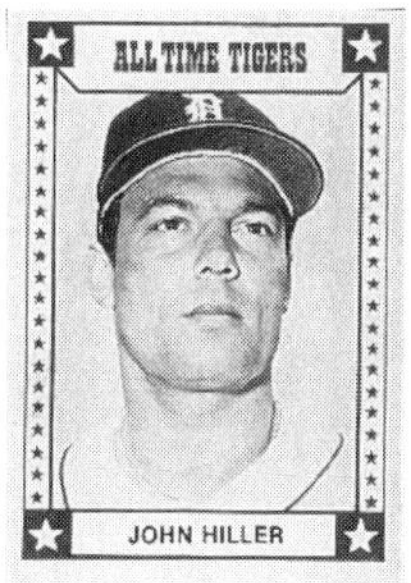

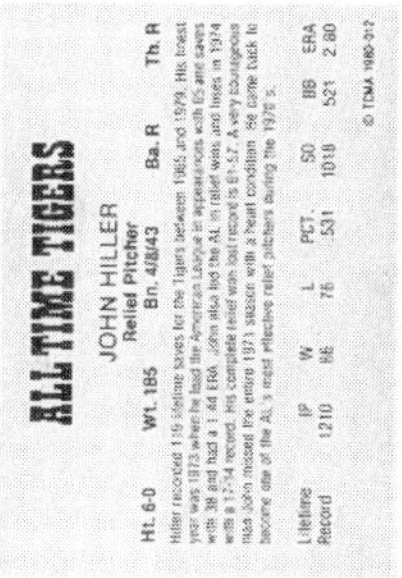

		NM	EX	VG
Complete Set (12):		22.00	11.00	6.50
Common Player:		.75	.40	.25
1	George Kell	.75	.40	.25
2	Billy Rogell	.75	.40	.25
3	Ty Cobb	9.00	4.50	2.75
4	Hank Greenberg	4.50	2.25	1.25
5	Al Kaline	3.00	1.50	.90
6	Charlie Gehringer	1.50	.70	.45
7	Harry Heilmann	.75	.40	.25
8	Hal Newhouser	.75	.40	.25
9	Steve O'Neill	.75	.40	.25
10	Denny McLain	1.25	.60	.40
11	Mickey Cochrane	.75	.40	.25
12	John Hiller	.75	.40	.25

1980 TCMA All Time White Sox

		NM	EX	VG
Complete Set (12):		15.00	7.50	4.50
Common Player:		1.25	.60	.40
1	Ted Lyons	1.25	.60	.40
2	Eddie Collins	1.75	.90	.50
3	Al Lopez	1.25	.60	.40
4	Luke Appling	1.75	.90	.50
5	Billy Pierce	1.25	.60	.40
6	Willie Kamm	1.25	.60	.40
7	Johnny Mostil	1.25	.60	.40
8	Al Simmons	1.25	.60	.40
9	Ray Schalk	1.25	.60	.40
10	Gerry Staley	1.25	.60	.40
11	Harry Hooper	1.25	.60	.40
12	Eddie Robinson	1.25	.60	.40

1980 TCMA All Time Yankees

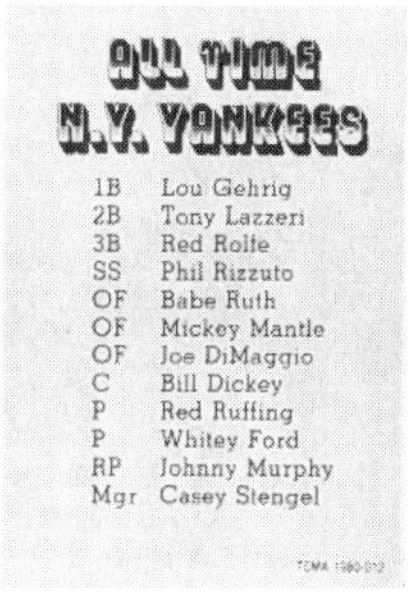

		NM	EX	VG
Complete Set (12):		37.00	18.50	11.00
Common Player:		.60	.30	.20
1	Lou Gehrig	9.00	4.50	2.75
2	Tony Lazzeri	.60	.30	.20
3	Red Rolfe	.60	.30	.20
4	Phil Rizzuto	1.25	.60	.40
5	Babe Ruth	12.00	6.00	3.50
6	Mickey Mantle	13.50	6.75	4.00
7	Joe DiMaggio	10.00	5.00	3.00
8	Bill Dickey	.70	.35	.20
9	Red Ruffing	.60	.30	.20
10	Whitey Ford	1.25	.60	.40
11	Johnny Murphy	.60	.30	.20
12	Casey Stengel	.70	.35	.20

1980 TCMA 1950 Philadelphia Phillies/Whiz Kids

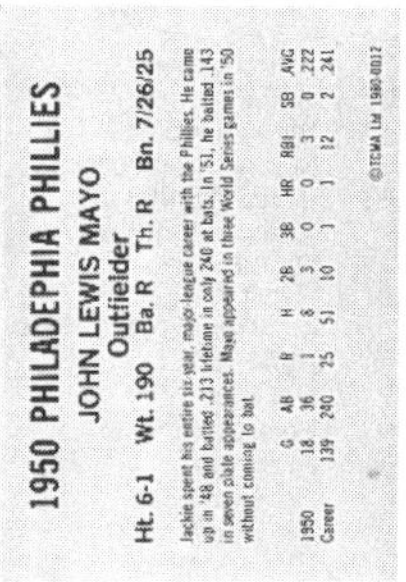

The National League Champions of 1950 are featured in this collectors issue team-set. The 2-1/2" x 3-1/2" cards have black-and-white player photo surrounded by red borders. Backs are in black-and-white with player personal data, career summary and 1950 and lifetime stats.

		NM	EX	VG
Complete Set (31):		22.00	11.00	6.50
Common Player:		.75	.40	.25
1	Ken Silvestri	.75	.40	.25
2	Hank Borowy	.75	.40	.25
3	Bob Miller	.75	.40	.25
4	Jocko Thompson	.75	.40	.25
5	Curt Simmons	.75	.40	.25
6	Dick Sisler	.75	.40	.25
7	Eddie Waitkus	.75	.40	.25
8	Dick Whitman	.75	.40	.25
9	Andy Seminick	.75	.40	.25
10	Richie Ashburn	5.00	2.50	1.50
11	Bubba Church	.75	.40	.25
12	Jackie Mayo	.75	.40	.25
13	Eddie Sawyer	.75	.40	.25
14	Benny Bengough	.75	.40	.25
15	Jim Konstanty	.75	.40	.25
16	Robin Roberts	5.00	2.50	1.50
17	Del Ennis	.75	.40	.25
18	Dusty Cooke	.75	.40	.25
19	Mike Goliat	.75	.40	.25
20	Russ Meyer	.75	.40	.25
21	Granny Hamner	.75	.40	.25
22	Stan Lopata	.75	.40	.25
23	Willie Jones	.75	.40	.25
24	Stan Hollmig	.75	.40	.25
25	Jimmy Bloodworth	.75	.40	.25
26	Ken Johnson	.75	.40	.25
27	Bill Nicholson	.75	.40	.25
28	Ken Heintzelman	.75	.40	.25
29	Blix Donnelly	.75	.40	.25
30	Putsy Caballero	.75	.40	.25
31	Cy Perkins	.75	.40	.25

Suffix letters after a card number indicate a variation card.

1980 TCMA 1957 Milwaukee Braves

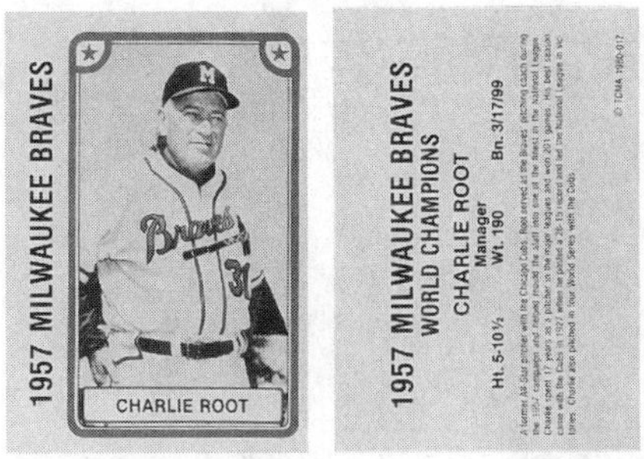

The World Champion Milwaukee Braves are featured in this collectors' issue. The 2-1/2" x 3-1/2" cards have blue-and-white player photos with white borders, blue typography and red graphics. Backs are in blue-and-white with a few bits of player data, career information and stats, along with a TCMA copyright line.

		NM	EX	VG
Complete Set (42):		27.50	12.50	7.50
Common Player:		.50	.25	.15
1	Don McMahon	.50	.25	.15
2	Joey Jay	.50	.25	.15
3	Phil Paine	.50	.25	.15
4	Bob Trowbridge	.50	.25	.15
5	Bob Buhl	.50	.25	.15
6	Lew Burdette	.65	.35	.20
7	Ernie Johnson	.65	.35	.20
8	Ray Crone	.50	.25	.15
9	Taylor Phillips	.50	.25	.15
10	Johnny Logan	.50	.25	.15
11	Frank Torre	.50	.25	.15
12	John DeMerit	.50	.25	.15
13	Red Murff	.50	.25	.15
14	Nippy Jones	.50	.25	.15
15	Bobby Thomson	.50	.25	.15
16	Chuck Tanner	.50	.25	.15
17	Charlie Root	.50	.25	.15
18	Juan Pizarro	.50	.25	.15
19	Hawk Taylor	.50	.25	.15
20	Mel Roach	.50	.25	.15
21	Bob Hazle	.50	.25	.15
22	Del Rice	.50	.25	.15
23	Felix Mantilla	.50	.25	.15
24	Andy Pafko	.50	.25	.15
25	Del Crandall	.65	.35	.20
26	Wes Covington	.50	.25	.15
27	Eddie Mathews	2.00	1.00	.60
28	Joe Adcock	.75	.40	.25
29	Dick Cole	.50	.25	.15
30	Carl Sawatski	.50	.25	.15
31	Warren Spahn	2.00	1.00	.60
32	Hank Aaron	6.00	3.00	1.75
33	Bob Keely	.50	.25	.15
34	Johnny Riddle	.50	.25	.15
35	Connie Ryan	.50	.25	.15
36	Harry Hanebrink	.50	.25	.15
37	Danny O'Connell	.50	.25	.15
38	Fred Haney	.50	.25	.15
39	Dave Jolly	.50	.25	.15
40	Red Schoendienst	1.00	.50	.30
41	Gene Conley	.50	.25	.15
42	Bill Bruton	.50	.25	.15

1980 TCMA 1959 L.A. Dodgers

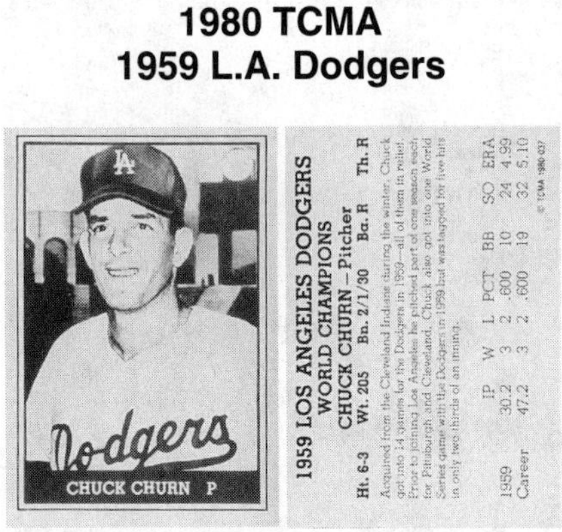

This collectors' issue features the members of the 1959 World Champion L.A. Dodgers. The 2-1/2" x 3-1/2" cards are printed in black-and-white on front and back. Fronts have player photos with white borders. Backs have personal data, 1959 and career stats and a few sentences about the player's performance in the championship season.

		NM	EX	VG
Complete Set (40):		48.00	24.00	14.50
Common Player:		1.00	.50	.30
1	Joe Pignatano	1.25	.60	.40
2	Carl Furillo	1.50	.70	.45
3	Bob Lillis	1.25	.60	.40
4	Chuck Essegian	1.25	.60	.40
5	Dick Gray	1.25	.60	.40
6	Rip Repulski	1.25	.60	.40
7	Jim Baxes	1.25	.60	.40
8	Frank Howard	2.25	1.25	.70
9	Solly Drake	1.25	.60	.40
10	Sandy Amoros	1.50	.70	.45
11	Norm Sherry	1.25	.60	.40
12	Tommy Davis	1.50	.70	.45
13	Jim Gilliam	1.50	.70	.45
14	Duke Snider	4.50	2.25	1.25
15	Maury Wills	2.25	1.25	.70
16	Don Demeter	1.25	.60	.40
17	Wally Moon	1.25	.60	.40
18	John Roseboro	1.25	.60	.40
19	Ron Fairly	1.25	.60	.40
20	Norm Larker	1.25	.60	.40
21	Charlie Neal	1.25	.60	.40
22	Don Zimmer	1.25	.60	.40
23	Chuck Dressen	1.25	.60	.40
24	Gil Hodges	4.00	2.00	1.25
25	Joe Becker	1.25	.60	.40
26	Walter Alston	1.50	.70	.45
27	Greg Mulleavy	1.25	.60	.40
28	Don Drysdale	3.50	1.75	1.00
29	Johnny Podres	1.50	.70	.45
30	Sandy Koufax	6.00	3.00	1.75
31	Roger Craig	1.25	.60	.40
32	Danny McDevitt	1.25	.60	.40
33	Bill Harris	1.25	.60	.40
34	Larry Sherry	1.25	.60	.40
35	Stan Williams	1.25	.60	.40
36	Clem Labine	1.25	.60	.40
37	Chuck Churn	1.25	.60	.40
38	Johnny Klippstein	1.25	.60	.40
39	Carl Erskine	1.50	.70	.45
40	Fred Kipp	1.25	.60	.40

1980 TCMA 1960 Pittsburgh Pirates

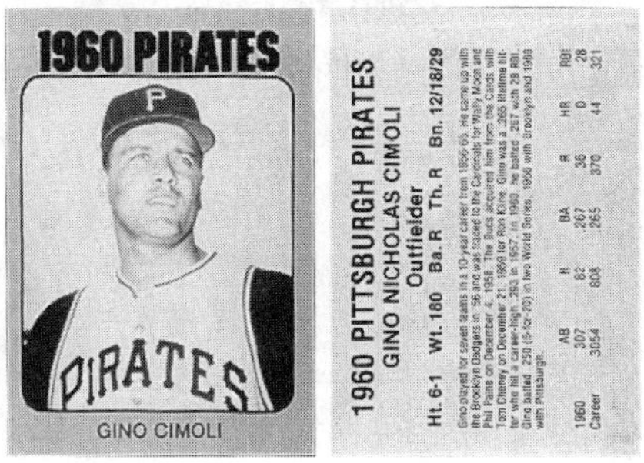

The World Champion 1960 Pirates are featured in this collectors issue team-set. Black-and-white player photos are bordered in gold on the fronts of the 2-1/2" x 3-1/2" cards. Backs are in black-and-white with personal data, career summary and stats for the 1960 season and career.

		NM	EX	VG
Complete Set (42):		55.00	27.00	16.00
Common Player:		1.00	.50	.30
1	Clem Labine	1.00	.50	.30
2	Bob Friend	1.00	.50	.30
3	Roy Face	1.00	.50	.30
4	Vern Law	1.00	.50	.30
5	Harvey Haddix	1.00	.50	.30
6	Vinegar Bend Mizell	1.00	.50	.30
7	Bill Burwell	1.00	.50	.30
8	Diomedes Olivo	1.00	.50	.30
9	Don Gross	1.00	.50	.30
10	Fred Green	1.00	.50	.30
11	Jim Umbricht	1.00	.50	.30
12	George Witt	1.00	.50	.30
13	Tom Cheney	1.00	.50	.30
14	Bennie Daniels	1.00	.50	.30
15	Earl Francis	1.00	.50	.30
16	Joe Gibbon	1.00	.50	.30
17	Paul Giel	1.00	.50	.30
18	Danny Kravitz	1.00	.50	.30
19	R.C. Stevens	1.00	.50	.30
20	Roman Mejias	1.00	.50	.30
21	Dick Barone	1.00	.50	.30
22	Sam Narron	1.00	.50	.30
23	Harry Bright	1.00	.50	.30
24	Mickey Vernon	1.00	.50	.30
25	Bob Skinner	1.00	.50	.30
26	Smokey Burgess (Smoky)	1.00	.50	.30
27	Bill Virdon	1.00	.50	.30
28	Roberto Clemente	16.00	8.00	4.75
29	Don Hoak	1.00	.50	.30
30	Bill Mazeroski	4.00	2.00	1.25
31	Dick Stuart	2.00	1.00	.60
32	Dick Groat	2.00	1.00	.60
33	Bob Oldis	1.00	.50	.30
34	Gene Baker	1.00	.50	.30
35	Joe Christopher	1.00	.50	.30
36	Dick Schofield	1.00	.50	.30
37	Hal Smith	1.00	.50	.30
38	Rocky Nelson	1.00	.50	.30
39	Gino Cimoli	1.00	.50	.30
40	Danny Murtaugh	1.00	.50	.30
41	Lenny Levy	1.00	.50	.30
(42)	Gino Cimoli	1.00	.50	.30

1980 TCMA 1961 Cincinnati Reds

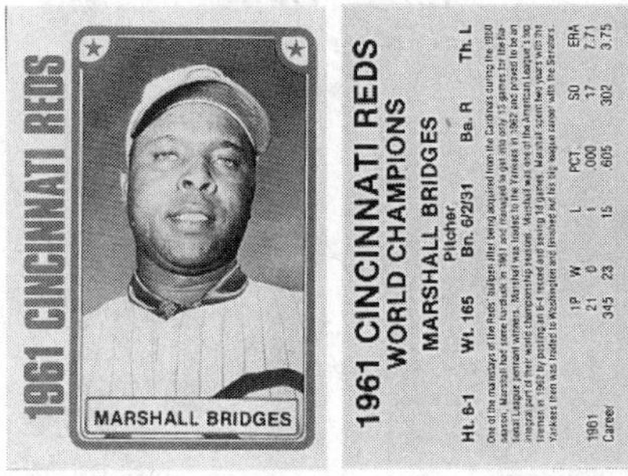

Virtually every member of the World Champion Cincinnati Reds team of 1961 is included in this collector's issue. Fronts of the 2-1/2" x 3-1/2" cards feature black-and-white player poses with red graphics. Backs are in black-and-white with personal data, 1961 and career stats and a short career summary.

		NM	EX	VG
Complete Set (41):		45.00	22.00	13.50
Common Player:		1.00	.50	.30
1	Eddie Kasko	1.00	.50	.30
2	Wally Post	1.00	.50	.30
3	Vada Pinson	3.00	1.50	.90
4	Frank Robinson	6.00	3.00	1.75
5	Pete Whisenant	1.00	.50	.30
6	Reggie Otero	1.00	.50	.30
7	Dick Sisler	1.00	.50	.30
8	Jim Turner	1.00	.50	.30
9	Fred Hutchinson	1.00	.50	.30
10	Gene Freese	1.00	.50	.30
11	Gordy Coleman	1.00	.50	.30
12	Don Blasingame	1.00	.50	.30
13	Gus Bell	2.00	1.00	.60
14	Leo Cardenas	1.00	.50	.30
15	Elio Chacon	1.00	.50	.30
16	Dick Gernert	1.00	.50	.30
17	Jim Baumer	1.00	.50	.30
18	Willie Jones	1.00	.50	.30
19	Joe Gaines	1.00	.50	.30
20	Cliff Cook	1.00	.50	.30
21	Harry Anderson	1.00	.50	.30
22	Jerry Zimmerman	1.00	.50	.30
23	Johnny Edwards	1.00	.50	.30
24	Bob Schmidt	1.00	.50	.30
25	Darrell Johnson	1.00	.50	.30
26	Ed Bailey	2.00	1.00	.60
27	Joey Jay	1.00	.50	.30
28	Jim O'Toole	1.00	.50	.30
29	Bob Purkey	1.00	.50	.30
30	Jim Brosnan	1.00	.50	.30
31	Ken Hunt	1.00	.50	.30
32	Ken Johnson	1.00	.50	.30
33	Jim Mahoney	1.00	.50	.30
34	Bill Henry	1.00	.50	.30
35	Jerry Lynch	1.00	.50	.30
36	Hal Bevan	1.00	.50	.30
37	Howie Nunn	1.00	.50	.30
38	Sherman Jones	1.00	.50	.30
39	Jay Hook	1.00	.50	.30
40	Claude Osteen	1.00	.50	.30
41	Marshall Bridges	1.00	.50	.30

1980 TCMA/ Renata Galasso

Another series of baseball superstar collectors cards was produced by TCMA for distribution by Renata Galasso. The 2-1/2" x 3-1/2" cards have black-and-white photos on front with the player name, position and team in black in the wide white bottom border. Backs are printed in red and blue with a short player history, a large Galasso ad and a TCMA dateline. Virtually every card in the series is a Hall of Famer.

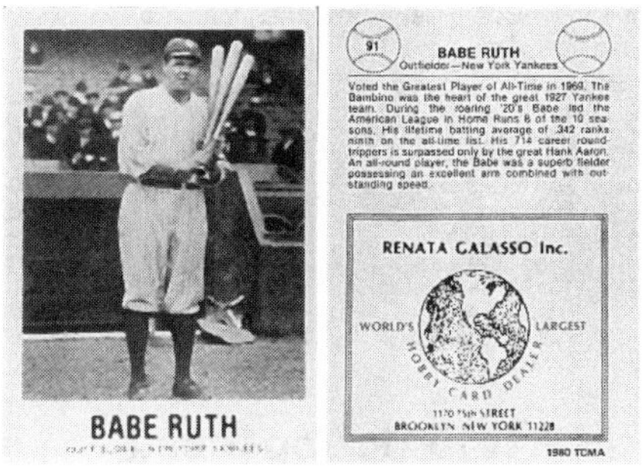

		NM	EX	VG
Complete Set (45):		10.00	5.00	3.00
Common Player:		.50	.25	.15
91	Babe Ruth	2.00	1.00	.60
92	Rogers Hornsby	.65	.35	.20
93	Edd Roush	.50	.25	.15
94	George Sisler	.50	.25	.15
95	Harry Heilmann	.50	.25	.15
96	Tris Speaker	.65	.35	.20
97	Burleigh Grimes	.50	.25	.15
98	John McGraw	.50	.25	.15
99	Eppa Rixey	.50	.25	.15
100	Ty Cobb	1.00	.50	.30
101	Zack Wheat	.50	.25	.15
102	Pie Traynor	.50	.25	.15
103	Max Carey	.50	.25	.15
104	Dazzy Vance	.50	.25	.15
105	Walter Johnson	.50	.25	.15
106	Herb Pennock	.50	.25	.15
107	Joe Sewell	.50	.25	.15
108	Sam Rice	.50	.25	.15
109	Earle Combs	.50	.25	.15
110	Ted Lyons	.50	.25	.15
111	Eddie Collins	.50	.25	.15
112	Bill Terry	.50	.25	.15
113	Hack Wilson	.50	.25	.15
114	Rabbit Maranville	.50	.25	.15
115	Charlie Grimm	.50	.25	.15
116	Tony Lazzeri	.50	.25	.15
117	Waite Hoyt	.50	.25	.15
118	Stan Coveleski	.50	.25	.15
119	George Kelly	.50	.25	.15
120	Jimmy Dykes	.50	.25	.15
121	Red Faber	.50	.25	.15
122	Dave Bancroft	.50	.25	.15
123	Judge Landis	.50	.25	.15
124	Branch Rickey	.50	.25	.15
125	Jesse Haines	.50	.25	.15
126	Carl Mays	.50	.25	.15
127	Fred Lindstrom	.50	.25	.15
128	Miller Huggins	.50	.25	.15
129	Sad Sam Jones	.50	.25	.15
130	Joe Judge	.50	.25	.15
131	Ross Young (Youngs)	.50	.25	.15
132	Bucky Harris	.50	.25	.15
133	Bob Meusel	.50	.25	.15
134	Billy Evans	.50	.25	.15
135	1927 N.Y. Yankees team photo/checklist	.50	.25	.15

1978 Allen P. Terach Immortals of Baseball

These souvenir cards were issued as the first of what was intended to be a series honoring baseball's greatest players. No succeeding issues were forthcoming. The images on the 9" x 6-1/2" blank-back cards are printed in black-and-white and sepia. Fine print at the bottom states the card is part of an edition of 3,500. Issue price was just under $5 apiece.

		NM	EX	VG
Souvenir Card:				
1	Babe Ruth, Joe DiMaggio	9.00	4.50	2.75
2	Ty Cobb, Stan Musial	6.00	3.00	1.75

1914 Texas Tommy Type I (E224)

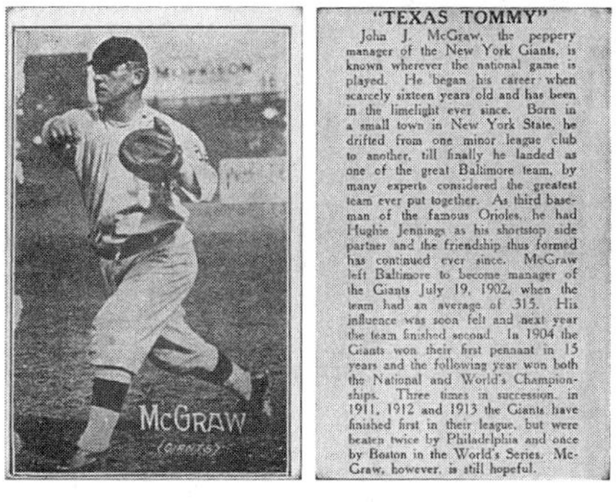

Little is known about the origin of this 50-card set issued in 1914 and designated as E224 in the American Card Catalog. Measuring 2-3/8" x 3-1/2", card fronts feature sepia-toned action photos with the player's name in capital letters and his team below in parenthesis. The back carries a lengthy player biography and most cards, although not all, include year-by-year statistics at the bottom. The words "Texas Tommy" appear at the top, apparently referring to the sponsor of the set, although it is still unclear who or what "Texas Tommy" was, and despite its name, most examples of this set have been found in northern California. There is also a second variety of the set, smaller in size (1-7/8" x 3"), which are borderless pictures with a glossy finish.

		NM	EX	VG
Complete Set (50):		37500.	18500.	11000.
Common Player:		500.00	250.00	150.00
(1)	Jimmy Archer	500.00	250.00	150.00
(2)	Jimmy Austin	500.00	250.00	150.00
(3)	Home Run Baker	800.00	400.00	240.00
(4)	Chief Bender	800.00	400.00	240.00
(5)	Bob Bescher	500.00	250.00	150.00
(6)	Ping Bodie	500.00	250.00	150.00
(7)	Donie Bush	500.00	250.00	150.00
(8)	Bobby Byrne	500.00	250.00	150.00
(9)	Nixey Callanan (Callahan)	500.00	250.00	150.00
(10)	Howie Camnitz	500.00	250.00	150.00
(11)	Frank Chance	800.00	400.00	240.00
(12)	Hal Chase	550.00	275.00	165.00
(13)	Ty Cobb	3500.	1750.	1050.
(14)	Jack Coombs	500.00	250.00	150.00
(15)	Sam Crawford	800.00	400.00	240.00
(16)	Birdie Cree	500.00	250.00	150.00
(17)	Al DeMaree (Demaree)	500.00	250.00	150.00
(18)	Red Dooin	500.00	250.00	150.00
(19)	Larry Doyle	500.00	250.00	150.00
(20)	Johnny Evers	800.00	400.00	240.00
(21)	Vean Gregg	500.00	250.00	150.00
(22)	Bob Harmon	500.00	250.00	150.00
(23)	Shoeless Joe Jackson	4500.	2250.	1350.
(24)	Walter Johnson	1250.	625.00	375.00
(25)	Otto Knabe	500.00	250.00	150.00
(26)	Nap Lajoie	900.00	450.00	270.00
(27)	Harry Lord	500.00	250.00	150.00
(28)	Connie Mack	800.00	400.00	240.00
(29)	Armando Marsans	550.00	275.00	165.00
(30)	Christy Mathewson	1200.	600.00	360.00
(31)	George McBride	500.00	250.00	150.00
(32)	John McGraw	800.00	400.00	240.00
(33)	Stuffy McInnis	500.00	250.00	150.00
(34)	Chief Meyers	500.00	250.00	150.00
(35)	Earl Moore	500.00	250.00	150.00
(36)	Mike Mowrey	500.00	250.00	150.00
(37)	Marty O'Toole	500.00	250.00	150.00
(38)	Eddie Plank	800.00	400.00	240.00
(39)	Bud Ryan	500.00	250.00	150.00
(40)	Tris Speaker	900.00	450.00	270.00
(41)	Jake Stahl	500.00	250.00	150.00
(42)	Oscar Strange (Stanage)	500.00	250.00	150.00
(43)	Bill Sweeney	500.00	250.00	150.00
(44)	Honus Wagner	1800.	900.00	540.00
(45)	Ed Walsh	800.00	400.00	240.00
(46)	Zach Wheat	800.00	400.00	240.00
(47)	Harry Wolter	500.00	250.00	150.00
(48)	Joe Wood	500.00	250.00	150.00
(49)	Steve Yerkes	500.00	250.00	150.00
(50)	Heinie Zimmerman	500.00	250.00	150.00

Vintage cards in Good condition are valued at about 50% of the Very Good value shown here. Fair cards are valued at 25% or less of VG.
The ratio of Excellent and Very Good prices to Near Mint can vary depending on relative collectibility for each grade in a specific set. Current listings reflect such adjustments.

1914 Texas Tommy Type II (E224)

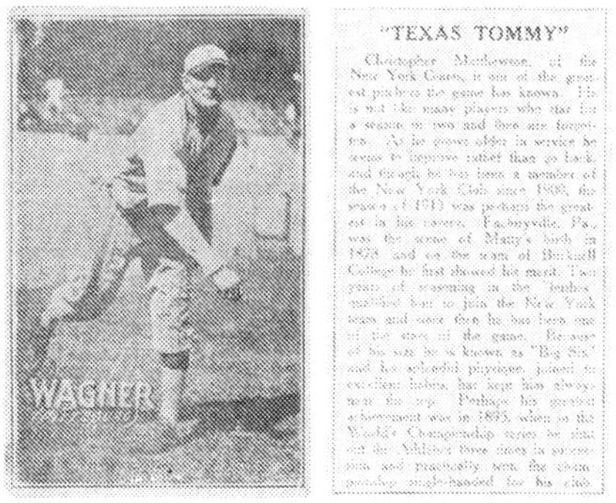

		NM	EX	VG
Complete Set (15):		22000.	11000.	6500.
Common Player:		1000.	500.00	300.00
(1)	Ping Bodie	1000.	500.00	300.00
(2)	Larry Doyle	1000.	500.00	300.00
(3)	Vean Gregg	1000.	500.00	300.00
(4)	Harry Hooper	1600.	800.00	480.00
(5)	Walter Johnson	2500.	1250.	750.00
(6)	Connie Mack	1600.	800.00	480.00
(7)	Rube Marquard	1600.	800.00	480.00
(8)	Christy Mathewson	2500.	1250.	750.00
(9)	John McGraw	1600.	800.00	480.00
(10)	Chief Meyers	1000.	500.00	300.00
(11)	Fred Snodgrass	1000.	500.00	300.00
(12)	Jake Stahl	1000.	500.00	300.00
(13)	Honus Wagner	5000.	2500.	1500.
(14)	Joe Wood	1100.	550.00	330.00
(15)	Steve Yerkes	1000.	500.00	300.00

1928 Tharp's Ice Cream

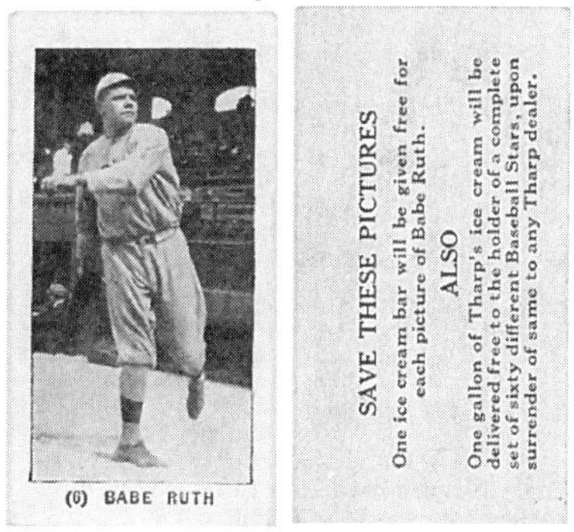

(6) BABE RUTH
SAVE THESE PICTURES
One ice cream bar will be given free for each picture of Babe Ruth.
ALSO
One gallon of Tharp's ice cream will be delivered free to the holder of a complete set of sixty different Baseball Stars, upon surrender of same to any Tharp dealer.

Sharing the same format and checklist with several other contemporary ice cream sets this 60-card set includes all of the top stars of the day. Cards are printed in black-and-white on a 1-3/8" x 2-1/2" format. There appears to have been two different types issued, but the extent of each version is unknown. The variations are found in the player's name and card number which can appear either in a strip within the frame of the photo, or printed in the border beneath the photo. Card backs have a redemption offer that includes an ice cream bar in exchange for a Babe Ruth card, or a gallon of ice cream for a complete set of 60.

		NM	EX	VG
Complete Set (60):		3500.	1400.	700.00
Common Player:		30.00	12.00	6.00
1	Burleigh Grimes	50.00	20.00	10.00
2	Walter Reuther	30.00	12.00	6.00
3	Joe Dugan	30.00	12.00	6.00
4	Red Faber	50.00	20.00	10.00
5	Gabby Hartnett	50.00	20.00	10.00
6	Babe Ruth	750.00	300.00	150.00
7	Bob Meusel	30.00	12.00	6.00
8	Herb Pennock	50.00	20.00	10.00
9	George Burns	30.00	12.00	6.00
10	Joe Sewell	50.00	20.00	10.00
11	George Uhle	30.00	12.00	6.00
12	Bob O'Farrell	30.00	12.00	6.00
13	Rogers Hornsby	55.00	22.00	11.00
14	"Pie" Traynor	50.00	20.00	10.00
15	Clarence Mitchell	30.00	12.00	6.00
16a	Eppa Jepha Rixey	50.00	20.00	10.00
16b	Eppa Rixey	50.00	20.00	10.00
17	Carl Mays	30.00	12.00	6.00
18	Adolfo Luque	40.00	16.00	8.00
19	Dave Bancroft	50.00	20.00	10.00
20	George Kelly	50.00	20.00	10.00
21	Earl (Earle) Combs	50.00	20.00	10.00
22	Harry Heilmann	50.00	20.00	10.00
23a	Ray W. Schalk	50.00	20.00	10.00
23b	Ray Schalk	50.00	20.00	10.00

24	Johnny Mostil	30.00	12.00	6.00
25	Hack Wilson	50.00	20.00	10.00
26	Lou Gehrig	500.00	200.00	100.00
27	Ty Cobb	500.00	200.00	100.00
28	Tris Speaker	55.00	22.00	11.00
29	Tony Lazzeri	50.00	20.00	10.00
30	Waite Hoyt	50.00	20.00	10.00
31	Sherwood Smith	30.00	12.00	6.00
32	Max Carey	50.00	20.00	10.00
33	Eugene Hargrave	30.00	12.00	6.00
34	Miguel L. Gonzalez (Middle initial A.)	40.00	16.00	8.00
35	Joe Judge	30.00	12.00	6.00
36	E.C. (Sam) Rice	50.00	20.00	10.00
37	Earl Sheely	30.00	12.00	6.00
38	Sam Jones	30.00	12.00	6.00
39	Bib (Bibb) A. Falk	30.00	12.00	6.00
40	Willie Kamm	30.00	12.00	6.00
41	Stanley Harris	50.00	20.00	10.00
42	John J. McGraw	50.00	20.00	10.00
43	Artie Nehf	30.00	12.00	6.00
44	Grover Alexander	55.00	22.00	11.00
45	Paul Waner	50.00	20.00	10.00
46	William H. Terry	50.00	20.00	10.00
47	Glenn Wright	30.00	12.00	6.00
48	Earl Smith	30.00	12.00	6.00
49	Leon (Goose) Goslin	50.00	20.00	10.00
50	Frank Frisch	50.00	20.00	10.00
51	Joe Harris	30.00	12.00	6.00
52	Fred (Cy) Williams	30.00	12.00	6.00
53	Eddie Roush	50.00	20.00	10.00
54	George Sisler	50.00	20.00	10.00
55	Ed. Rommel	30.00	12.00	6.00
56	Rogers Peckinpaugh (Roger)	30.00	12.00	6.00
57	Stanley Coveleskie (Coveleski)	50.00	20.00	10.00
58	Lester Bell	30.00	12.00	6.00
59	L. Waner	50.00	20.00	10.00
60	John P. McInnis	30.00	12.00	6.00

1978 The Card Coach Milwaukee Braves Greats

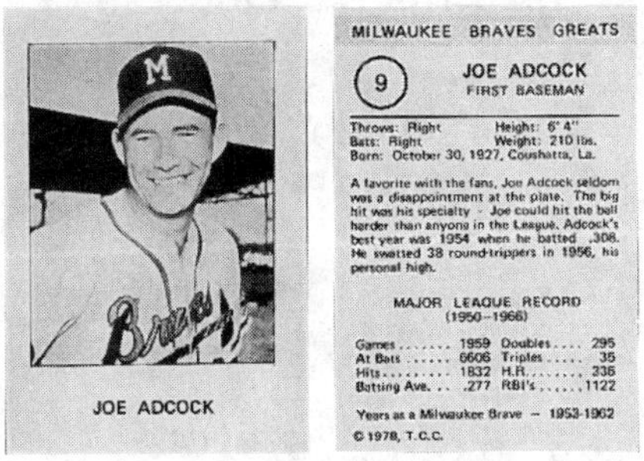

Stars of the Milwaukee Braves from the early 1950s through the early 1960s are featured in this collectors issue. The 2-1/2" x 3-1/2" cards have black-and-white player photos on front with the player name in the white border at bottom. Backs are also in black-and-white with personal data, career summary and stats. Cards are numbered by uniform number.

		NM	EX	VG
Complete Set (15):		9.00	4.50	2.75
Common Player:		.50	.25	.15
1	Del Crandall	.50	.25	.15
4	Red Schoendienst	.50	.25	.15
8	Bob Uecker	.65	.35	.20
9	Joe Adcock	.50	.25	.15
10	Bob Buhl	.50	.25	.15
15	Joe Torre	.50	.25	.15
16	Carlton Willey	.50	.25	.15
21	Warren Spahn	.75	.40	.25
22	Johnny Logan	.50	.25	.15
33	Lew Burdette	.50	.25	.15
34	Billy Bruton	.50	.25	.15
41	Eddie Mathews	.75	.40	.25
43	Wes Covington	.50	.25	.15
44	Hank Aaron	2.00	1.00	.60
48	Andy Pafko (checklist)	.50	.25	.15

1971 Ticketron L.A. Dodgers/S.F. Giants

Essentially large team schedule cards with promotional dates noted and an ad for the ticket service, the Ticketron Dodgers/Giants cards of 1971 are similar in format. Each has a color photo on front with facsimile autograph. The Dodgers cards are 4" x 6" with no borders on fronts; the 3-3/4" x 5-3/4" Giants cards have a white border. Backs are white with red and blue printing. The unnumbered cards are checklisted here alphabetically within team.

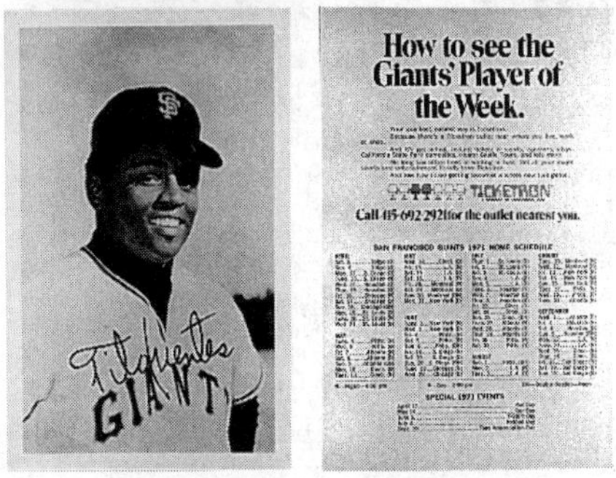

		NM	EX	VG
Complete Dodgers Set (20):		75.00	37.00	22.00
Complete Giants Set (10):		110.00	55.00	33.00
Common Dodger Player:		2.00	1.00	.60
Common Giant Player:		4.00	2.00	1.25
	LOS ANGELES DODGERS			
(1)	Richie Allen	10.00	5.00	3.00
(2)	Walter Alston	4.00	2.00	1.25
(3)	Jim Brewer	2.00	1.00	.60
(4)	Willie Crawford	2.00	1.00	.60
(5)	Willie Davis	3.00	1.50	.90
(6)	Steve Garvey	12.00	6.00	3.50
(7)	Bill Grabarkewitz	2.00	1.00	.60
(8)	Jim Lefebvre	2.00	1.00	.60
(9)	Pete Mikkelsen	2.00	1.00	.60
(10)	Joe Moeller	2.00	1.00	.60
(11)	Manny Mota	3.00	1.50	.90
(12)	Claude Osteen	2.00	1.00	.60
(13)	Wes Parker	2.00	1.00	.60
(14)	Bill Russell	3.00	1.50	.90
(15)	Duke Sims	2.00	1.00	.60
(16)	Bill Singer	2.00	1.00	.60
(17)	Bill Sudakis	2.00	1.00	.60
(18)	Don Sutton	15.00	7.50	4.50
(19)	Maury Wills	5.00	2.50	1.50
(20)	Jerry Doggett, Vin Scully	2.00	1.00	.60
	SAN FRANSICO GIANTS			
(1)	Bobby Bonds	8.00	4.00	2.50
(2)	Dick Dietz	4.00	2.00	1.25
(3)	Charles Fox	4.00	2.00	1.25
(4)	Tito Fuentes	4.00	2.00	1.25
(5)	Ken Henderson	4.00	2.00	1.25
(6)	Juan Marichal	15.00	7.50	4.50
(7)	Willie Mays	45.00	22.00	13.50
(8)	Willie McCovey	18.00	9.00	5.50
(9)	Don McMahon	2.00	1.00	.60
(10)	Gaylord Perry	10.00	5.00	3.00

1972 Ticketron Phillies

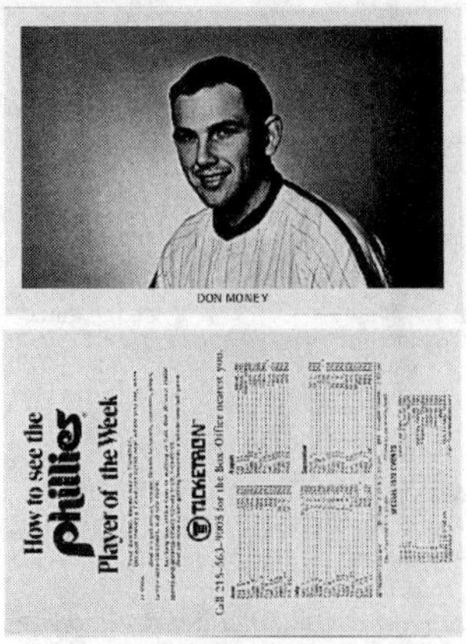

The Phillies' main off-site ticket outlet produced this set of schedule cards. Fronts are in horizontal 6" x 3-7/8" format with a color player photo at center. Backs are in black-and-white and include a Phillies home schedule and sponsor advertising. Because he was traded to the Expos in mid-season, the card of Tim McCarver is scarcer than the others.

		NM	EX	VG
Complete Set (10):		95.00	47.00	28.00
Common Player:		8.00	4.00	2.50
(1)	Mike Anderson	8.00	4.00	2.50
(2)	Larry Bowa	8.00	4.00	2.50
(3)	Steve Carlton	15.00	7.50	4.50
(4)	Deron Johnson	8.00	4.00	2.50
(5)	Frank Lucchesi	8.00	4.00	2.50
(6)	Greg Luzinski	10.00	5.00	3.00
(7)	Tim McCarver	35.00	17.50	10.50
(8)	Don Money	8.00	4.00	2.50
(9)	Willie Montanez	8.00	4.00	2.50
(10)	Dick Selma	8.00	4.00	2.50

1910 Tip-Top Bread Pittsburgh Pirates

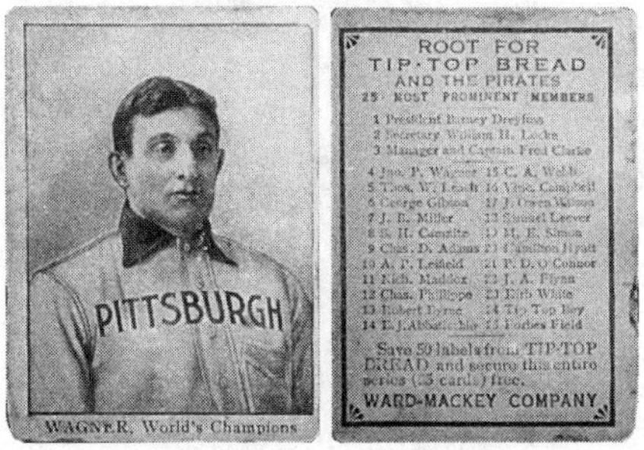

The previous season's World Champion Pittsburgh Pirates are featured in this issue. The cards have an unusual - for the era - nearly square (1-13/16" x 2-3/8") format. Fronts have pastel paintings of the subjects with identification in the white border below as "World's Champions". Backs have a checklist, ad for the bakery and offer to send the complete set of cards for 50 bread labels.

		NM	EX	VG
Complete Set (25):		12000.	4800.	2400.
Common Player:		399.00	160.00	80.00
1	Barney Dreyfuss (President)	600.00	240.00	120.00
2	William H. Locke (Secretary)	400.00	160.00	80.00
3	Fred Clarke	750.00	300.00	150.00
4	Honus Wagner	3000.	1200.	600.00
5	Tom Leach	400.00	160.00	80.00
6	George Gibson	400.00	160.00	80.00
7	Dots Miller	400.00	160.00	80.00
8	Howie Camnitz	400.00	160.00	80.00
9	Babe Adams	400.00	160.00	80.00
10	Lefty Leifield	400.00	160.00	80.00
11	Nick Maddox	400.00	160.00	80.00
12	Deacon Philippe	400.00	160.00	80.00
13	Bobby Byrne	400.00	160.00	80.00
14	Ed Abbaticchio	400.00	160.00	80.00
15	Lefty Webb	400.00	160.00	80.00
16	Vin Campbell	400.00	160.00	80.00
17	Owen Wilson	400.00	160.00	80.00
18	Sam Leever	400.00	160.00	80.00
19	Mike Simon	400.00	160.00	80.00
20	Ham Hyatt	400.00	160.00	80.00
21	Paddy O'Connor	400.00	160.00	80.00
22	John Flynn	400.00	160.00	80.00
23	Kirby White	400.00	160.00	80.00
24	Tip Top Boy Mascot	400.00	160.00	80.00
25	Forbes Field	400.00	160.00	80.00

1947 Tip Top Bread

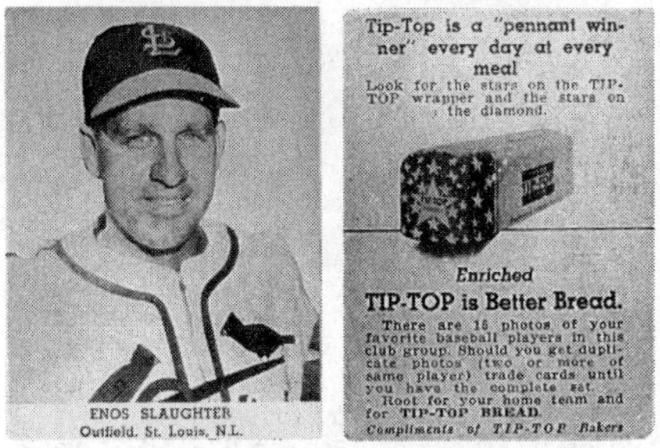

This 163-card set actually consists of a group of regional issues, some of which are scarcer than others. The 2-1/4" x 3" cards are borderless at top and sides, with a black-and-white player photo below which is a white strip containing the player identification. Backs carry an illustrated advertisement. The set is known for a quantity of obscure players, many of whom played during the talent-lean World War II seasons.

		NM	EX	VG
Complete Set (163):		12000.	6000.	2400.
Common Player:		60.00	24.00	12.00
(1)	Bill Ayers	60.00	24.00	12.00
(2)	Floyd Baker	90.00	36.00	18.00
(3)	Charles Barrett	90.00	36.00	18.00
(4)	Eddie Basinski	60.00	24.00	12.00
(5)	John Berardino	95.00	38.00	19.00
(6)	Larry Berra	500.00	200.00	100.00
(7)	Bill Bevens	90.00	36.00	18.00
(8)	Robert Blattner	60.00	24.00	12.00
(9)	Ernie Bonham	60.00	24.00	12.00
(10)	Bob Bragan	75.00	30.00	15.00
(11)	Ralph Branca	120.00	48.00	24.00
(12)	Alpha Brazle	60.00	24.00	12.00
(13)	Bobbie Brown (Bobby)	95.00	38.00	19.00
(14)	Mike Budnick	60.00	24.00	12.00
(15)	Ken Burkhart	60.00	24.00	12.00
(16)	Thomas Byrne	90.00	36.00	18.00
(17)	Earl Caldwell	90.00	36.00	18.00
(18)	"Hank" Camelli	90.00	36.00	18.00
(19)	Hugh Casey	75.00	30.00	15.00
(20)	Phil Cavarretta	105.00	42.00	21.00
(21)	Bob Chipman	90.00	36.00	18.00
(22)	Lloyd Christopher	90.00	36.00	18.00
(23)	Bill Cox	60.00	24.00	12.00
(24)	Bernard Creger	60.00	24.00	12.00
(25)	Frank Crosetti	105.00	42.00	21.00
(26)	Joffre Cross	60.00	24.00	12.00
(27)	Leon Culberson	90.00	36.00	18.00
(28)	Dick Culler	90.00	36.00	18.00
(29)	Dom DiMaggio	300.00	120.00	60.00
(30)	George Dickey	105.00	42.00	21.00
(31)	Chas. E. Diering	60.00	24.00	12.00
(32)	Joseph Dobson	90.00	36.00	18.00
(33)	Bob Doerr	350.00	140.00	70.00
(34)	Ervin Dusak	60.00	24.00	12.00
(35)	Bruce Edwards	65.00	26.00	13.00
(36)	Walter "Hoot" Evers	90.00	36.00	18.00
(37)	Clifford Fannin	60.00	24.00	12.00
(38)	"Nanny" Fernandez	90.00	36.00	18.00
(39)	Dave "Boo" Ferriss	90.00	36.00	18.00
(40)	Elbie Fletcher	60.00	24.00	12.00
(41)	Dennis Galehouse	60.00	24.00	12.00
(42)	Joe Garagiola	300.00	120.00	60.00
(43)	Sid Gordon	60.00	24.00	12.00
(44)	John Gorsica	90.00	36.00	18.00
(45)	Hal Gregg	65.00	26.00	13.00
(46)	Frank Gustine	60.00	24.00	12.00
(47)	Stanley Hack	105.00	42.00	21.00
(48)	Mickey Harris	90.00	36.00	18.00
(49)	Clinton Hartung	60.00	24.00	12.00
(50)	Joe Hatten	65.00	26.00	13.00
(51)	Frank Hayes	90.00	36.00	18.00
(52)	"Jeff" Heath	60.00	24.00	12.00
(53)	Tom Henrich	120.00	48.00	24.00
(54)	Gene Hermanski	65.00	26.00	13.00
(55)	Kirby Higbe	60.00	24.00	12.00
(56)	Ralph Hodgin	90.00	36.00	18.00
(57)	Tex Hughson	90.00	36.00	18.00
(58)	Fred Hutchinson	120.00	48.00	24.00
(59)	LeRoy Jarvis	60.00	24.00	12.00
(60)	"Si" Johnson	90.00	36.00	18.00
(61)	Don Johnson	90.00	36.00	18.00
(62)	Earl Johnson	90.00	36.00	18.00
(63)	John Jorgensen	65.00	26.00	13.00
(64)	Walter Judnick (Judnich)	60.00	24.00	12.00
(65)	Tony Kaufmann	60.00	24.00	12.00
(66)	George Kell	350.00	140.00	70.00
(67)	Charlie Keller	115.00	46.00	23.00
(68)	Bob Kennedy	90.00	36.00	18.00
(69)	Montia Kennedy	60.00	24.00	12.00
(70)	Ralph Kiner	130.00	52.00	26.00
(71)	Dave Koslo	60.00	24.00	12.00
(72)	Jack Kramer	60.00	24.00	12.00
(73)	Joe Kuhel	90.00	36.00	18.00
(74)	George Kurowski	60.00	24.00	12.00
(75)	Emil Kush	90.00	36.00	18.00
(76)	"Eddie" Lake	90.00	36.00	18.00
(77)	Harry Lavagetto	75.00	30.00	15.00
(78)	Bill Lee	90.00	36.00	18.00
(79)	Thornton Lee	90.00	36.00	18.00
(80)	Paul Lehner	60.00	24.00	12.00
(81)	John Lindell	90.00	36.00	18.00
(82)	Danny Litwhiler	90.00	36.00	18.00
(83)	"Mickey" Livingston	90.00	36.00	18.00
(84)	Carroll Lockman	60.00	24.00	12.00
(85)	Jack Lohrke	60.00	24.00	12.00
(86)	Ernie Lombardi	130.00	52.00	26.00
(87)	Vic Lombardi	65.00	26.00	13.00
(88)	Edmund Lopat	105.00	42.00	21.00
(89)	Harry Lowrey	90.00	36.00	18.00
(90)	Marty Marion	90.00	36.00	18.00
(91)	Willard Marshall	60.00	24.00	12.00
(92)	Phil Masi	90.00	36.00	18.00
(93)	Edward J. Mayo	90.00	36.00	18.00
(94)	Clyde McCullough	90.00	36.00	18.00
(95)	Frank Melton	65.00	26.00	13.00
(96)	Cass Michaels	90.00	36.00	18.00
(97)	Ed Miksis	65.00	26.00	13.00
(98)	Arthur Mills	90.00	36.00	18.00
(99)	Johnny Mize	130.00	52.00	26.00
(100)	Lester Moss	60.00	24.00	12.00
(101)	"Pat" Mullin	90.00	36.00	18.00
(102)	"Bob" Muncrief	60.00	24.00	12.00
(103)	George Munger	60.00	24.00	12.00
(104)	Fritz Ostermueller	60.00	24.00	12.00
(105)	James P. Outlaw	90.00	36.00	18.00
(106)	Frank "Stub" Overmire	90.00	36.00	18.00
(107)	Andy Pafko	95.00	38.00	19.00
(108)	Joe Page	90.00	36.00	18.00
(109)	Roy Partee	90.00	36.00	18.00
(110)	Johnny Pesky	95.00	38.00	19.00
(111)	Nelson Potter	60.00	24.00	12.00
(112)	Mel Queen	90.00	36.00	18.00
(113)	Marion Rackley	65.00	26.00	13.00
(114)	Al Reynolds	125.00	50.00	25.00
(115)	Del Rice	60.00	24.00	12.00
(116)	Marv Rickert	90.00	36.00	18.00
(117)	John Rigney	90.00	36.00	18.00
(118)	Phil Rizzuto	400.00	160.00	80.00
(119)	Aaron Robinson	90.00	36.00	18.00
(120)	"Preacher" Roe	75.00	30.00	15.00
(121)	Carvel Rowell	90.00	36.00	18.00
(122)	Jim Russell	60.00	24.00	12.00
(123)	Rip Russell	90.00	36.00	18.00
(124)	Connie Ryan	90.00	36.00	18.00
(125)	John Sain	145.00	58.00	29.00
(126)	Ray Sanders	90.00	36.00	18.00
(127)	Fred Sanford	60.00	24.00	12.00
(128)	Johnny Schmitz	90.00	36.00	18.00
(129)	Joe Schultz	60.00	24.00	12.00
(130)	"Rip" Sewell	60.00	24.00	12.00
(131)	Dick Sisler	60.00	24.00	12.00
(132)	"Sibby" Sisti	90.00	36.00	18.00
(133)	Enos Slaughter	130.00	52.00	26.00
(134)	"Billy" Southworth	90.00	36.00	18.00
(135)	Warren Spahn	500.00	200.00	100.00
(136)	Verne Stephens (Vern)	60.00	24.00	12.00
(137)	George Sternweiss (Stirnweiss)	90.00	36.00	18.00
(138)	Ed Stevens	65.00	26.00	13.00
(139)	Nick Strincevich	60.00	24.00	12.00
(140)	"Bobby" Sturgeon	90.00	36.00	18.00
(141)	Robt. "Bob" Swift	90.00	36.00	18.00
(142)	Geo. "Birdie" Tibbetts (Tebbetts)	95.00	38.00	19.00
(143)	"Mike" Tresh	95.00	38.00	19.00
(144)	Ken Trinkle	60.00	24.00	12.00
(145)	Paul "Diz" Trout	95.00	38.00	19.00
(146)	Virgil "Fire" Trucks	95.00	38.00	19.00
(147)	Thurman Tucker	90.00	36.00	18.00
(148)	Bill Voiselle	60.00	24.00	12.00
(149)	Hal Wagner	90.00	36.00	18.00
(150)	Honus Wagner	500.00	200.00	100.00
(151)	Eddy Waitkus	90.00	36.00	18.00
(152)	Richard "Dick" Wakefield	90.00	36.00	18.00
(153)	Jack Wallaesa	90.00	36.00	18.00
(154)	Charles Wensloff	90.00	36.00	18.00
(155)	Ted Wilks	60.00	24.00	12.00
(156)	Mickey Witek	60.00	24.00	12.00
(157)	"Jerry" Witte	60.00	24.00	12.00
(158)	Ed Wright	90.00	36.00	18.00
(159)	Taft Wright	90.00	36.00	18.00
(160)	Henry Wyse	90.00	36.00	18.00
(161)	"Rudy" York	90.00	36.00	18.00
(162)	Al Zarilla	60.00	24.00	12.00
(163)	Bill Zuber	90.00	36.00	18.00

1952 Tip Top Bread Labels

This unnumbered set of bread end-labels consists of 48 different labels, including two of Phil Rizzuto. The player's photo, name and team appear inside a star, with the words "Tip Top" printed above. The labels measure approximately 2-1/2" x 2-3/4".

		NM	EX	VG
Complete Set (48):		6500.	2900.	1600.
Common Player:		80.00	40.00	24.00
(1)	Hank Bauer	95.00	43.00	24.00
(2)	Yogi Berra	250.00	112.00	62.00
(3)	Ralph Branca	95.00	43.00	24.00
(4)	Lou Brissie	90.00	40.00	22.00
(5)	Roy Campanella	300.00	135.00	75.00
(6)	Phil Cavarreta (Cavarretta)	90.00	40.00	22.00
(7)	Murray Dickson (Murry)	90.00	40.00	22.00
(8)	Ferris Fain	90.00	40.00	22.00
(9)	Carl Furillo	95.00	43.00	24.00
(10)	Ned Garver	90.00	40.00	22.00
(11)	Sid Gordon	90.00	40.00	22.00
(12)	John Groth	90.00	40.00	22.00
(13)	Gran Hamner	90.00	40.00	22.00
(14)	Jim Hearn	90.00	40.00	22.00
(15)	Gene Hermanski	90.00	40.00	22.00
(16)	Gil Hodges	135.00	61.00	34.00
(17)	Larry Jansen	90.00	40.00	22.00
(18)	Eddie Joost	90.00	40.00	22.00
(19)	George Kell	120.00	54.00	30.00
(20)	Dutch Leonard	90.00	40.00	22.00
(21)	Whitey Lockman	90.00	40.00	22.00
(22)	Ed Lopat	95.00	43.00	24.00
(23)	Sal Maglie	90.00	40.00	22.00
(24)	Mickey Mantle	2250.	1000.	550.00
(25)	Gil McDougald	95.00	43.00	24.00
(26)	Dale Mitchell	90.00	40.00	22.00
(27)	Don Mueller	90.00	40.00	22.00
(28)	Andy Pafko	90.00	40.00	22.00
(29)	Bob Porterfield	90.00	40.00	22.00
(30)	Ken Raffensberger	90.00	40.00	22.00
(31)	Allie Reynolds	95.00	43.00	24.00
(32a)	Phil Rizzuto (Rizzuto) ("NY" shows on shirt)	135.00	61.00	34.00
(32b)	Phil Rizzuto (Rizzuto) (no "NY" visible on shirt)	135.00	61.00	34.00
(33)	Robin Roberts	120.00	54.00	30.00
(34)	Saul Rogovin	90.00	40.00	22.00
(35)	Ray Scarborough	90.00	40.00	22.00
(36)	Red Schoendienst	95.00	43.00	24.00
(37)	Dick Sisler	90.00	40.00	22.00
(38)	Enos Slaughter	95.00	43.00	24.00
(39)	Duke Snider	175.00	79.00	44.00
(40)	Warren Spahn	120.00	54.00	30.00
(41)	Vern Stephens	90.00	40.00	22.00
(42)	Earl Torgeson	90.00	40.00	22.00
(43)	Mickey Vernon	90.00	40.00	22.00
(44)	Ed Waitkus	90.00	40.00	22.00
(45)	Wes Westrum	90.00	40.00	22.00
(46)	Eddie Yost	90.00	40.00	22.00
(47)	Al Zarilla	90.00	40.00	22.00

1887 Tobin Lithographs (H891)

The Tobin lithographs, measuring 3" x 4-1/2", are typical of the "trade" cards that were popular advertising vehicles in the late 19th Century. Found in both black-and-white and color, the lithos include 10 cards depicting caricature action drawings of popular baseball players of the era. Each cartoon-like drawing is accompanied by a colorful caption along with the player's name in parenthesis below. The team affiliation is printed in the upper-left corner, while a large space in the upper-right corner was left blank to accomodate advertising messages. As a result, Tobin cards can be found with ads for various cigarettes and other products or left blank. Similarly the backs of the cards are also found either blank or with advertising. The set takes its name from the manufacturer, whose name ("Tobin N.Y.") appears in the lower-right corner of each card.

		NM	EX	VG
Complete Set (10):		2950.	1175.	550.00
Common Player:		250.00	100.00	50.00
(1)	"Go It Old Boy" (Ed Andrews)	250.00	100.00	50.00
(2)	"Oh, Come Off!" (Cap Anson)	850.00	340.00	170.00
(3)	"Watch Me Soak it" (Dan Brouthers)	335.00	135.00	67.00
(4)	"Not Onto It" (Charlie Ferguson)	250.00	100.00	50.00
(5)	"Struck By A Cyclone" (Pebbly Jack Glasscock)	250.00	100.00	50.00
(6)	"An Anxious Moment" (Paul Hines)	250.00	100.00	50.00
(7)	"Where'l You Have It?" (Tim Keefe)	335.00	135.00	67.00
(8)	"The Flower Of The Flock" (Our Own Kelly)	335.00	135.00	67.00
(9)	"A Slide For Home" (Jim M'Cormick) (McCormick)	250.00	100.00	50.00
(10)	"Ain't It A Daisy?" (Smiling Mickey Welch)	335.00	135.00	67.00

Near Mint-Mint and Mint examples of vintage cards carry a significant premium over the Near Mint values quoted here. This premium reflects availability of the highest-grade cards as well as demand for a particular card or set in top grade. Premiums of 2X to 3X are not uncommon and many are even higher.

1909-11 Tolstoi Cigarettes

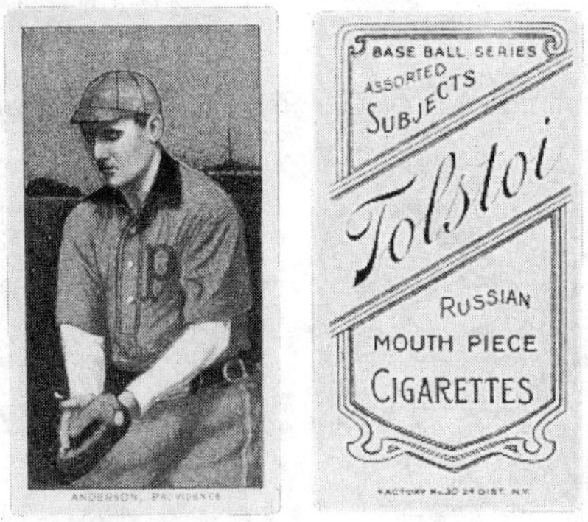

(See T206. Premium: +75%)

1953 Top Taste Bread Labels

(See 1953 Northland Bread Labels for checklist and price guide.)

1953 Top Taste Bread Milwaukee Braves

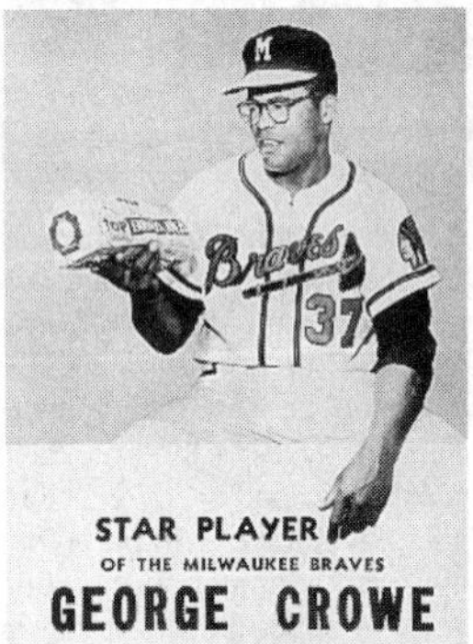

This series of black-and-white mini-posters (8-1/2" x 11-1/4") depicts members of the 1953 Braves holding loaves of bread. They were probably intended for grocery store window or bakery aisle display. Backs are blank. It's unknown how many players are in the set.

		NM	EX	VG
Common Player:		45.00	22.50	13.50
(1)	Lew Burdette	45.00	22.50	13.50
(2)	George Crowe	45.00	22.50	13.50

1909 Topping & Co. Detroit Tigers Postcards

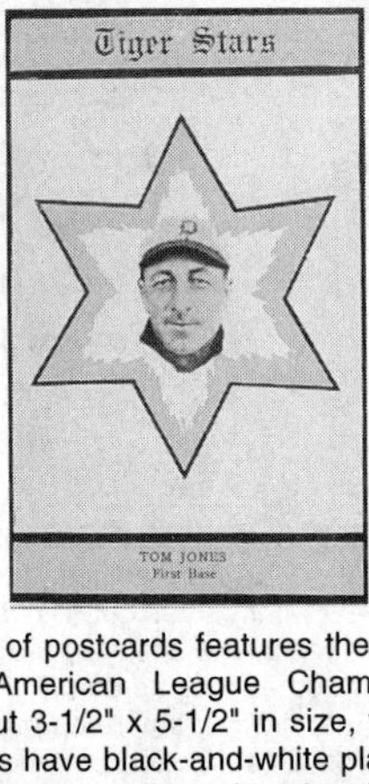

This set of postcards features the members of the 1909 American League Champion Detroit Tigers. About 3-1/2" x 5-1/2" in size, vertically formatted fronts have black-and-white player portraits at center within a yellow six-pointed star. "Tiger Stars" appears in script in a yellow stripe at top, while the player name and position are in a similar strip at bottom. Black trim surrounds the design elements. Backs are black-and-white with standard postcard markings and a credit line for Topping and Publishers Co., Detroit. The unnumbered cards are listed here alphabetically.

		NM	EX	VG
Complete Set (21):		3525.	1750.	1050.
Common Player:		200.00	100.00	60.00
(1)	Henry Beckendorf	200.00	100.00	60.00
(2)	Donie Bush	200.00	100.00	60.00
(3)	Ty Cobb	1400.	700.00	420.00
(4)	Sam Crawford	275.00	135.00	82.00
(5)	Jim Delehanty	200.00	100.00	60.00
(6)	Bill Donovan	200.00	100.00	60.00
(7)	Hughie Jennings	275.00	135.00	82.00
(8)	Davy Jones	200.00	100.00	60.00
(9)	Tom Jones	200.00	100.00	60.00
(10)	Ed Killian	200.00	100.00	60.00
(11)	Matty McIntyre	200.00	100.00	60.00
(12)	George Moriarty	200.00	100.00	60.00
(13)	George Mullin	200.00	100.00	60.00
(14)	Charley O'Leary	200.00	100.00	60.00
(15)	Germany Schaefer	200.00	100.00	60.00
(16)	Charlie Schmidt	200.00	100.00	60.00
(17)	George Speer	200.00	100.00	60.00
(18)	Oscar Stanage	200.00	100.00	60.00
(19)	Eddie Summers	200.00	100.00	60.00
(20)	Ed Willett	200.00	100.00	60.00
(21)	Ralph Works	200.00	100.00	60.00

1948 Topps Magic Photos

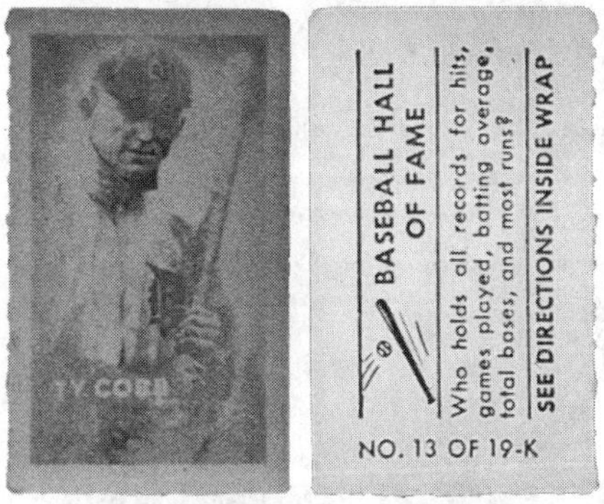

The first Topps baseball cards appeared as a subset of 19 cards from an issue of 252 "Magic Photos." The set takes its name from the self-developing nature of the cards. The cards were blank on the front when first taken from the wrapper. By spitting on the wrapper and holding it to the card while exposing it to light the black-and-white photo appeared. Measuring 7/8" x 1-1/2," the cards are very similar to Topps 1956 "Hocus Focus" issue.

		NM	EX	VG
Complete Set (19):		2200.	1100.	650.00
Common Player:		55.00	27.50	16.50
(1)	Lou Boudreau	110.00	55.00	33.00
(2)	Cleveland Indians	55.00	27.50	16.50
(3)	Bob Eliott	55.00	27.50	16.50
(4)	Cleveland Indians 4-3	55.00	27.50	16.50
(5)	Cleveland Indians 4-1 (Lou Boudreau) (scoring)	80.00	40.00	24.00
(6)	Babe Ruth (714)	450.00	225.00	135.00
(7)	Tris Speaker (793)	125.00	62.00	37.00
(8)	Rogers Hornsby	150.00	75.00	45.00
(9)	Connie Mack	125.00	62.00	37.00
(10)	Christy Mathewson	160.00	80.00	48.00
(11)	Hans Wagner	175.00	87.00	52.00
(12)	Grover Alexander	125.00	62.00	37.00
(13)	Ty Cobb	225.00	112.00	67.00
(14)	Lou Gehrig	350.00	175.00	105.00
(15)	Walter Johnson	175.00	87.00	52.00
(16)	Cy Young	150.00	75.00	45.00
(17)	George Sisler (257)	110.00	55.00	33.00
(18)	Tinker and Evers (Joe Tinker, Johnny Evers)	110.00	55.00	33.00
(19)	Third Base Cleveland Indians	55.00	27.50	16.50

1951 Topps Red Backs

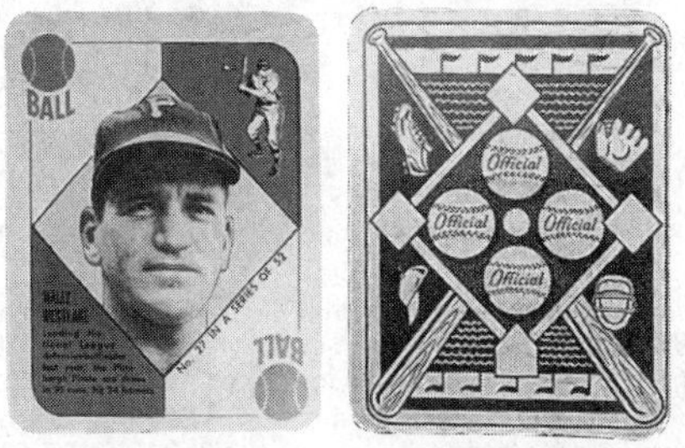

Like the Blue Backs, the Topps Red Backs which were sold at the same time came two to a package for 1¢. Their black-and-white photographs appear on a red, white, blue and yellow background. The back printing is red on white. Their 2" x 2-5/8" size is the same as Blue Backs. Also identical is the set size (52 cards) and the game situations to be found on the fronts of the cards, for use in playing a card game of baseball. Red Backs are more common than the Blue Backs by virtue of a 1980s discovery of a large hoard of unopened boxes.

		NM	EX	VG
Complete Set (52):		850.00	425.00	250.00
Common Player:		10.00	5.00	3.00
1	Yogi Berra	90.00	45.00	27.00
2	Sid Gordon	10.00	5.00	3.00
3	Ferris Fain	10.00	5.00	3.00
4	Vern Stephens	10.00	5.00	3.00
5	Phil Rizzuto	45.00	22.00	13.50
6	Allie Reynolds	14.00	7.00	4.25
7	Howie Pollet	10.00	5.00	3.00
8	Early Wynn	24.00	12.00	7.25
9	Roy Sievers	10.00	5.00	3.00
10	Mel Parnell	10.00	5.00	3.00
11	Gene Hermanski	10.00	5.00	3.00
12	Jim Hegan	10.00	5.00	3.00
13	Dale Mitchell	10.00	5.00	3.00
14	Wayne Terwilliger	10.00	5.00	3.00
15	Ralph Kiner	24.00	12.00	7.25
16	Preacher Roe	12.00	6.00	3.50
17	Gus Bell	12.00	6.00	3.50
18	Gerry Coleman	12.00	6.00	3.50
19	Dick Kokos	10.00	5.00	3.00
20	Dom DiMaggio	17.50	8.75	5.25
21	Larry Jansen	10.00	5.00	3.00
22	Bob Feller	50.00	25.00	15.00
23	Ray Boone	12.00	6.00	3.50
24	Hank Bauer	15.00	7.50	4.50
25	Cliff Chambers	10.00	5.00	3.00
26	Luke Easter	10.00	5.00	3.00
27	Wally Westlake	10.00	5.00	3.00
28	Elmer Valo	10.00	5.00	3.00
29	Bob Kennedy	10.00	5.00	3.00
30	Warren Spahn	50.00	25.00	15.00
31	Gil Hodges	40.00	20.00	12.00
32	Henry Thompson	10.00	5.00	3.00
33	William Werle	10.00	5.00	3.00
34	Grady Hatton	10.00	5.00	3.00
35	Al Rosen	12.00	6.00	3.50
36a	Gus Zernial (Chicago in bio)	35.00	17.50	10.50
36b	Gus Zernial (Philadelphia in bio)	20.00	10.00	6.00
37	Wes Westrum	10.00	5.00	3.00
38	Duke Snider	65.00	32.00	19.50
39	Ted Kluszewski	20.00	10.00	6.00
40	Mike Garcia	10.00	5.00	3.00
41	Whitey Lockman	10.00	5.00	3.00
42	Ray Scarborough	10.00	5.00	3.00
43	Maurice McDermott	10.00	5.00	3.00
44	Sid Hudson	10.00	5.00	3.00
45	Andy Seminick	10.00	5.00	3.00
46	Billy Goodman	10.00	5.00	3.00
47	Tommy Glaviano	10.00	5.00	3.00
48	Eddie Stanky	10.00	5.00	3.00
49	Al Zarilla	10.00	5.00	3.00
50	Monte Irvin	45.00	22.00	13.50
51	Eddie Robinson	10.00	5.00	3.00
52a	Tommy Holmes (Boston in bio)	35.00	17.50	10.50
52b	Tommy Holmes (Hartford in bio)	22.00	11.00	6.50

1951 Topps Blue Backs

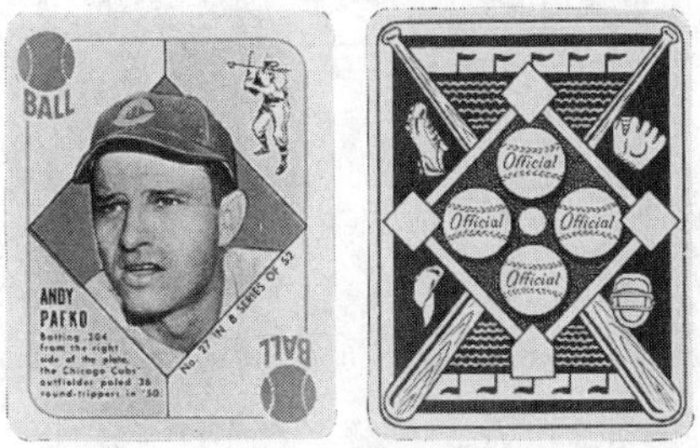

Sold two cards in a package with a piece of candy for 1¢, the Topps Blue Backs are considerably scarcer than their Red Back counterparts. The 2" x 2-5/8" cards carry a black-and-white player photograph on a red, white, yellow and green background along with the player's name and other information including their 1950 record on the front. The back is printed in blue on a white background. The 52-card set has varied baseball situations on them, making the playing of a rather elementary game of baseball possible. Although scarce, Blue Backs were printed on thick cardboard and have survived quite well over the years. There are, however, few stars in the set, and despite being a Topps product, Blue Backs do not currently enjoy great popularity.

		NM	EX	VG
Complete Set (52):		1600.	800.00	475.00
Common Player:		30.00	15.00	9.00
1	Eddie Yost	30.00	15.00	9.00
2	Henry Majeski	30.00	15.00	9.00
3	Richie Ashburn	110.00	55.00	33.00
4	Del Ennis	30.00	15.00	9.00
5	Johnny Pesky	30.00	15.00	9.00
6	Red Schoendienst	85.00	42.00	25.00
7	Gerry Staley	30.00	15.00	9.00
8	Dick Sisler	30.00	15.00	9.00
9	Johnny Sain	45.00	22.00	13.50
10	Joe Page	40.00	20.00	12.00
11	Johnny Groth	30.00	15.00	9.00
12	Sam Jethroe	30.00	15.00	9.00
13	Mickey Vernon	30.00	15.00	9.00
14	Red Munger	30.00	15.00	9.00
15	Eddie Joost	30.00	15.00	9.00
16	Murry Dickson	30.00	15.00	9.00
17	Roy Smalley	30.00	15.00	9.00
18	Ned Garver	30.00	15.00	9.00
19	Phil Masi	30.00	15.00	9.00
20	Ralph Branca	40.00	20.00	12.00
21	Billy Johnson	30.00	15.00	9.00
22	Bob Kuzava	30.00	15.00	9.00
23	Dizzy Trout	30.00	15.00	9.00
24	Sherman Lollar	30.00	15.00	9.00
25	Sam Mele	30.00	15.00	9.00
26	Chico Carrasquel	30.00	15.00	9.00
27	Andy Pafko	30.00	15.00	9.00
28	Harry (The Cat) Brecheen	30.00	15.00	9.00
29	Granny Hamner	30.00	15.00	9.00
30	Enos Slaughter	75.00	37.00	22.00
31	Lou Brissie	30.00	15.00	9.00
32	Bob Elliott	30.00	15.00	9.00
33	Don Lenhardt	30.00	15.00	9.00
34	Earl Torgeson	30.00	15.00	9.00
35	Tommy Byrne	30.00	15.00	9.00
36	Cliff Fannin	30.00	15.00	9.00
37	Bobby Doerr	75.00	37.00	22.00
38	Irv Noren	30.00	15.00	9.00
39	Ed Lopat	35.00	17.50	10.50
40	Vic Wertz	30.00	15.00	9.00
41	Johnny Schmitz	30.00	15.00	9.00
42	Bruce Edwards	30.00	15.00	9.00
43	Willie Jones	30.00	15.00	9.00
44	Johnny Wyrostek	30.00	15.00	9.00
45	Bill Pierce	35.00	17.50	10.50
46	Gerry Priddy	30.00	15.00	9.00
47	Herman Wehmeier	30.00	15.00	9.00
48	Billy Cox	30.00	15.00	9.00
49	Hank Sauer	30.00	15.00	9.00
50	Johnny Mize	95.00	47.00	28.00
51	Eddie Waitkus	30.00	15.00	9.00
52	Sam Chapman	30.00	15.00	9.00

1951 Topps Connie Mack's All-Stars

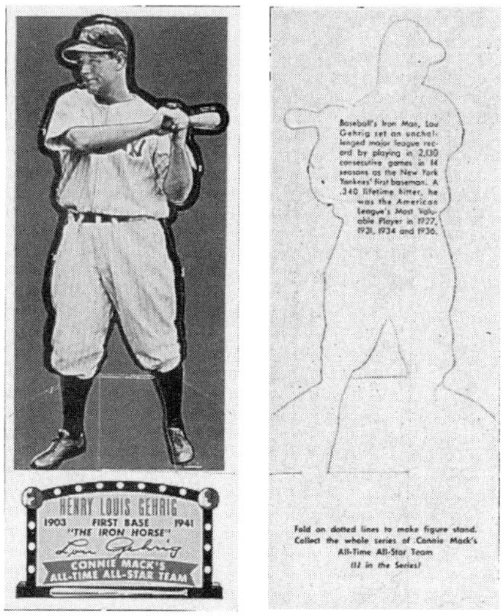

A set of die-cut, 2-1/16" x 5-1/4" cards, all 11 players are Hall of Famers. The cards feature a black-and-white action player photograph printed on a red background with a colored name plaque underneath. Like the "Current All-Stars," with which they were issued, the background could be folded, making it possible for the card to stand up. This practice, however, resulted in the card's mutilation and lowers its condition in the eyes of today's collectors. Connie Mack All-Stars are scarce today and, despite being relatively expensive, retain a certain popularity as one of Topps first issues.

		NM	EX	VG
Complete Set (11):		6000.	3000.	1800.
Common Player:		300.00	150.00	90.00
(1)	Grover Cleveland Alexander	525.00	260.00	155.00
(2)	Gordon Stanley Cochrane	375.00	185.00	110.00
(3)	Edward Trowbridge Collins	300.00	150.00	90.00
(4)	James J. Collins	300.00	150.00	90.00
(5)	Lou Gehrig	2250.	1125.	675.00
(6)	Walter Johnson	750.00	375.00	225.00
(7)	Connie Mack	375.00	185.00	110.00
(8)	Christopher Mathewson	750.00	375.00	225.00
(9)	George Herman Ruth	2500.	1250.	750.00
(10)	Tris Speaker	525.00	260.00	155.00
(11)	Honus Wagner	600.00	300.00	180.00

1951 Topps Major League All-Stars

The Topps Major League All-Stars are very similar to the Connie Mack All-Stars of the same year. The 2-1/16" x 5-1/4" cards have a black-and-white photograph on a red die-cut background. Most of the background could be folded over so that the card would stand up. A plaque at the base carries brief biographical information. The set was to contain 11 cards, but only eight were actually issued in gum packs. Those of Konstanty, Roberts and Stanky were not issued and are very rare, with only a handful of each known. A big problem with the set is that if the card was used as it was intended it was folded and, thus, damaged from a collector's viewpoint. That makes top quality examples of any players difficult to find and quite expensive.

		NM	EX	VG
Complete Set (8):		5500.	2750.	1650.
Common Player:		350.00	175.00	100.00
(1)	Yogi Berra	1100.	550.00	330.00
(2)	Larry Doby	700.00	350.00	210.00
(3)	Walt Dropo	550.00	275.00	165.00
(4)	"Hoot" Evers	350.00	175.00	100.00
(5)	George Clyde Kell	600.00	300.00	180.00
(6)	Ralph Kiner	600.00	300.00	180.00
(7)	Jim Konstanty	30000.	15000.	9000.
(8)	Bob Lemon	600.00	300.00	180.00
(9)	Phil Rizzuto	1100.	550.00	330.00
(10)	Robin Roberts	35000.	17500.	10500.
(11)	Ed Stanky	30000.	15000.	9000.

1951 Topps Teams

An innovative issue for 1951, the Topps team cards were a nine-card set, 5-1/4" x 2-1/16," which carry a black-and-white picture of a major league team surrounded by a yellow border on the front. The back identifies team members with red printing on white cardboard. There are two versions of each card, with and without the date "1950" in the banner that carries the team name. Undated versions are valued slightly higher than the cards with dates. Strangely only nine teams were issued. Scarcity varies, with the Cardinals and Red Sox being the most difficult to obtain. The complete set price does not include the scarcer variations.

		NM	EX	VG
Common Team (Dated):		160.00	80.00	48.00
(1a)	Boston Red Sox (1950)	260.00	130.00	78.00
(1b)	Boston Red Sox (undated)	325.00	162.00	97.00
(2a)	Brooklyn Dodgers (1950)	345.00	172.00	103.00
(2b)	Brooklyn Dodgers (undated)	385.00	192.00	115.00
(3a)	Chicago White Sox (1950)	160.00	80.00	48.00
(3b)	Chicago White Sox (undated)	215.00	107.00	64.00
(4a)	Cincinnati Reds (1950)	160.00	80.00	48.00
(4b)	Cincinnati Reds (undated)	215.00	107.00	64.00
(5a)	New York Giants (1950)	260.00	130.00	78.00
(5b)	New York Giants (undated)	325.00	162.00	97.00
(6a)	Philadelphia Athletics (1950)	160.00	80.00	48.00
(6b)	Philadelphia Athletics (undated)	215.00	107.00	64.00
(7a)	Philadelphia Phillies (1950)	160.00	80.00	48.00
(7b)	Philadelphia Phillies (undated)	215.00	107.00	64.00
(8a)	St. Louis Cardinals (1950)	250.00	125.00	75.00
(8b)	St. Louis Cardinals (undated)	300.00	150.00	90.00
(9a)	Washington Senators (1950)	170.00	85.00	51.00
(9b)	Washington Senators (undated)	215.00	107.00	64.00

1952 Topps

At 407 cards, the 1952 Topps set was the largest set of its day, both in number of cards and physical dimensions of the cards. Cards are 2-5/8" x 3-3/4" with a hand-colored black and white photo on front. Major baseball card innovations presented in the set include the first-ever use of color team logos as part of the design, and the inclusion of stats for the previous season and overall career on the backs. A major variety in the set is that the first 80 cards can be found with backs printed entirely in black or black and red. Backs entirely in black command a $10-15 premium. Cards #311-407 were distributed in limited supplies and are extremely rare.

		NM	EX	VG
Complete Set (407):		55000.	24000.	12500.
Common Player (1-80):		40.00	20.00	10.00
Common Player (81-250):		30.00	15.00	7.50
Common Player (251-310):		40.00	20.00	10.00
Common Player (311-407):		220.00	110.00	55.00
1	Andy Pafko	3500.	850.00	400.00
2	*Pete Runnels*	125.00	27.00	13.50
3	Hank Thompson	40.00	20.00	10.00
4	Don Lenhardt	40.00	20.00	10.00
5	Larry Jansen	40.00	20.00	10.00
6	Grady Hatton	40.00	20.00	10.00
7	Wayne Terwilliger	40.00	20.00	10.00
8	Fred Marsh	40.00	20.00	10.00
9	Bobby Hogue	40.00	20.00	10.00
10	Al Rosen	60.00	30.00	15.00
11	Phil Rizzuto	225.00	112.00	56.00
12	Monty Basgall	40.00	20.00	10.00
13	Johnny Wyrostek	40.00	20.00	10.00
14	Bob Elliott	40.00	20.00	10.00
15	Johnny Pesky	40.00	20.00	10.00
16	Gene Hermanski	40.00	20.00	10.00
17	Jim Hegan	40.00	20.00	10.00
18	Merrill Combs	40.00	20.00	10.00
19	Johnny Bucha	40.00	20.00	10.00
20	*Billy Loes*	85.00	42.00	21.00
21	Ferris Fain	40.00	20.00	10.00
22	Dom DiMaggio	75.00	37.00	18.50
23	Billy Goodman	40.00	20.00	10.00
24	Luke Easter	40.00	20.00	10.00
25	Johnny Groth	40.00	20.00	10.00
26	Monte Irvin	65.00	32.00	16.00
27	Sam Jethroe	40.00	20.00	10.00
28	Jerry Priddy	40.00	20.00	10.00
29	Ted Kluszewski	80.00	40.00	20.00
30	Mel Parnell	40.00	20.00	10.00
31	Gus Zernial	80.00	40.00	20.00
32	Eddie Robinson	40.00	20.00	10.00
33	Warren Spahn	250.00	125.00	62.00
34	Elmer Valo	40.00	20.00	10.00
35	Hank Sauer	40.00	20.00	10.00

36	Gil Hodges	140.00	70.00	35.00
37	Duke Snider	250.00	125.00	62.00
38	Wally Westlake	40.00	20.00	10.00
39	"Dizzy" Trout	40.00	20.00	10.00
40	Irv Noren	40.00	20.00	10.00
41	Bob Wellman	40.00	20.00	10.00
42	Lou Kretlow	40.00	20.00	10.00
43	Ray Scarborough	40.00	20.00	10.00
44	Con Dempsey	40.00	20.00	10.00
45	Eddie Joost	40.00	20.00	10.00
46	Gordon Goldsberry	40.00	20.00	10.00
47	Willie Jones	40.00	20.00	10.00
48a	Joe Page (wrong (Sain) back)	1100.	550.00	275.00
48b	Joe Page (correct back)	70.00	35.00	17.50
49a	Johnny Sain (wrong (Page) back)	1100.	550.00	275.00
49b	Johnny Sain (correct back)	75.00	37.00	18.50
50	Marv Rickert	40.00	20.00	10.00
51	Jim Russell	40.00	20.00	10.00
52	Don Mueller	40.00	20.00	10.00
53	Chris Van Cuyk	40.00	20.00	10.00
54	Leo Kiely	40.00	20.00	10.00
55	Ray Boone	40.00	20.00	10.00
56	Tommy Glaviano	40.00	20.00	10.00
57	Ed Lopat	80.00	40.00	20.00
58	Bob Mahoney	40.00	20.00	10.00
59	Robin Roberts	125.00	62.00	31.00
60	Sid Hudson	40.00	20.00	10.00
61	"Tookie" Gilbert	40.00	20.00	10.00
62	Chuck Stobbs	40.00	20.00	10.00
63	Howie Pollet	40.00	20.00	10.00
64	Roy Sievers	40.00	20.00	10.00
65	Enos Slaughter	125.00	62.00	31.00
66	Preacher Roe	80.00	40.00	20.00
67	Allie Reynolds	70.00	35.00	17.50
68	Cliff Chambers	40.00	20.00	10.00
69	Virgil Stallcup	40.00	20.00	10.00
70	Al Zarilla	40.00	20.00	10.00
71	Tom Upton	40.00	20.00	10.00
72	Karl Olson	40.00	20.00	10.00
73	William Werle	40.00	20.00	10.00
74	Andy Hansen	40.00	20.00	10.00
75	Wes Westrum	40.00	20.00	10.00
76	Eddie Stanky	40.00	20.00	10.00
77	Bob Kennedy	40.00	20.00	10.00
78	Ellis Kinder	40.00	20.00	10.00
79	Gerald Staley	40.00	20.00	10.00
80	Herman Wehmeier	40.00	20.00	10.00
81	Vernon Law	30.00	15.00	7.50
82	Duane Pillette	30.00	15.00	7.50
83	Billy Johnson	30.00	15.00	7.50
84	Vern Stephens	30.00	15.00	7.50
85	Bob Kuzava	30.00	15.00	7.50
86	Ted Gray	30.00	15.00	7.50
87	Dale Coogan	30.00	15.00	7.50
88	Bob Feller	175.00	87.00	44.00
89	Johnny Lipon	30.00	15.00	7.50
90	Mickey Grasso	30.00	15.00	7.50
91	Red Schoendienst	90.00	45.00	22.00
92	Dale Mitchell	30.00	15.00	7.50
93	Al Sima	30.00	15.00	7.50
94	Sam Mele	30.00	15.00	7.50
95	Ken Holcombe	30.00	15.00	7.50
96	Willard Marshall	30.00	15.00	7.50
97	Earl Torgeson	30.00	15.00	7.50
98	Bill Pierce	30.00	15.00	7.50
99	Gene Woodling	50.00	25.00	12.50
100	Del Rice	30.00	15.00	7.50
101	Max Lanier	30.00	15.00	7.50
102	Bill Kennedy	30.00	15.00	7.50
103	Cliff Mapes	30.00	15.00	7.50
104	Don Kolloway	30.00	15.00	7.50
105	John Pramesa	30.00	15.00	7.50
106	Mickey Vernon	30.00	15.00	7.50
107	Connie Ryan	30.00	15.00	7.50
108	Jim Konstanty	30.00	15.00	7.50
109	Ted Wilks	30.00	15.00	7.50
110	Dutch Leonard	30.00	15.00	7.50
111	Harry Lowrey	30.00	15.00	7.50
112	Henry Majeski	30.00	15.00	7.50
113	Dick Sisler	30.00	15.00	7.50
114	Willard Ramsdell	30.00	15.00	7.50
115	George Munger	30.00	15.00	7.50
116	Carl Scheib	30.00	15.00	7.50
117	Sherman Lollar	30.00	15.00	7.50
118	Ken Raffensberger	30.00	15.00	7.50
119	Maurice McDermott	30.00	15.00	7.50
120	Bob Chakales	30.00	15.00	7.50
121	Gus Niarhos	30.00	15.00	7.50
122	Jack Jensen	55.00	27.00	13.50
123	Eddie Yost	30.00	15.00	7.50
124	Monte Kennedy	30.00	15.00	7.50
125	Bill Rigney	30.00	15.00	7.50
126	Fred Hutchinson	30.00	15.00	7.50
127	Paul Minner	30.00	15.00	7.50
128	Don Bollweg	30.00	15.00	7.50
129	Johnny Mize	100.00	50.00	25.00
130	Sheldon Jones	30.00	15.00	7.50
131	Morrie Martin	30.00	15.00	7.50
132	Clyde Kluttz	30.00	15.00	7.50
133	Al Widmar	30.00	15.00	7.50
134	Joe Tipton	30.00	15.00	7.50
135	Dixie Howell	30.00	15.00	7.50
136	Johnny Schmitz	30.00	15.00	7.50
137	*Roy McMillan*	30.00	15.00	7.50
138	Bill MacDonald	30.00	15.00	7.50
139	Ken Wood	30.00	15.00	7.50
140	John Antonelli	30.00	15.00	7.50
141	Clint Hartung	30.00	15.00	7.50
142	Harry Perkowski	30.00	15.00	7.50
143	Les Moss	30.00	15.00	7.50
144	Ed Blake	30.00	15.00	7.50
145	Joe Haynes	30.00	15.00	7.50
146	Frank House	30.00	15.00	7.50
147	Bob Young	30.00	15.00	7.50
148	Johnny Klippstein	30.00	15.00	7.50
149	Dick Kryhoski	30.00	15.00	7.50
150	Ted Beard	30.00	15.00	7.50
151	Wally Post	30.00	15.00	7.50
152	Al Evans	30.00	15.00	7.50
153	Bob Rush	30.00	15.00	7.50
154	Joe Muir	30.00	15.00	7.50
155	Frank Overmire	30.00	15.00	7.50
156	Frank Hiller	30.00	15.00	7.50
157	Bob Usher	30.00	15.00	7.50
158	Eddie Waitkus	30.00	15.00	7.50
159	Saul Rogovin	30.00	15.00	7.50
160	Owen Friend	30.00	15.00	7.50
161	Bud Byerly	30.00	15.00	7.50
162	Del Crandall	30.00	15.00	7.50
163	Stan Rojek	30.00	15.00	7.50
164	Walt Dubiel	30.00	15.00	7.50
165	Eddie Kazak	30.00	15.00	7.50
166	Paul LaPalme	30.00	15.00	7.50
167	Bill Howerton	30.00	15.00	7.50
168	*Charlie Silvera*	32.00	16.00	8.00
169	Howie Judson	30.00	15.00	7.50
170	Gus Bell	30.00	15.00	7.50
171	Ed Erautt	30.00	15.00	7.50
172	Eddie Miksis	30.00	15.00	7.50
173	Roy Smalley	30.00	15.00	7.50
174	Clarence Marshall	30.00	15.00	7.50
175	*Billy Martin*	275.00	137.00	69.00
176	Hank Edwards	30.00	15.00	7.50
177	Bill Wight	30.00	15.00	7.50
178	Cass Michaels	30.00	15.00	7.50
179	Frank Smith	30.00	15.00	7.50
180	*Charley Maxwell*	30.00	15.00	7.50
181	Bob Swift	30.00	15.00	7.50
182	Billy Hitchcock	30.00	15.00	7.50
183	Erv Dusak	30.00	15.00	7.50
184	Bob Ramazzotti	30.00	15.00	7.50
185	Bill Nicholson	30.00	15.00	7.50
186	Walt Masterson	30.00	15.00	7.50
187	Bob Miller	30.00	15.00	7.50
188	Clarence Podbielan	30.00	15.00	7.50
189	Pete Reiser	30.00	15.00	7.50
190	Don Johnson	30.00	15.00	7.50
191	Yogi Berra	550.00	275.00	137.00
192	Myron Ginsberg	30.00	15.00	7.50
193	Harry Simpson	30.00	15.00	7.50
194	Joe Hatten	30.00	15.00	7.50
195	*Minnie Minoso*	125.00	62.00	31.00
196	Solly Hemus	30.00	15.00	7.50
197	George Strickland	30.00	15.00	7.50
198	Phil Haugstad	30.00	15.00	7.50
199	George Zuverink	30.00	15.00	7.50
200	Ralph Houk	60.00	30.00	15.00
201	Alex Kellner	30.00	15.00	7.50
202	Joe Collins	30.00	15.00	7.50
203	Curt Simmons	30.00	15.00	7.50
204	Ron Northey	30.00	15.00	7.50
205	Clyde King	30.00	15.00	7.50
206	Joe Ostrowski	30.00	15.00	7.50
207	Mickey Harris	30.00	15.00	7.50
208	Marlin Stuart	30.00	15.00	7.50
209	Howie Fox	30.00	15.00	7.50
210	Dick Fowler	30.00	15.00	7.50
211	Ray Coleman	30.00	15.00	7.50
212	Ned Garver	30.00	15.00	7.50
213	Nippy Jones	30.00	15.00	7.50
214	Johnny Hopp	30.00	15.00	7.50
215	Hank Bauer	60.00	30.00	15.00
216	Richie Ashburn	150.00	75.00	37.00
217	George Stirnweiss	30.00	15.00	7.50
218	Clyde McCullough	30.00	15.00	7.50
219	Bobby Shantz	30.00	15.00	7.50
220	Joe Presko	30.00	15.00	7.50
221	Granny Hamner	30.00	15.00	7.50
222	"Hoot" Evers	30.00	15.00	7.50
223	Del Ennis	30.00	15.00	7.50
224	Bruce Edwards	30.00	15.00	7.50
225	Frank Baumholtz	30.00	15.00	7.50
226	Dave Philley	30.00	15.00	7.50
227	Joe Garagiola	80.00	40.00	20.00
228	Al Brazle	30.00	15.00	7.50
229	Gene Bearden	30.00	15.00	7.50
230	Matt Batts	30.00	15.00	7.50
231	Sam Zoldak	30.00	15.00	7.50
232	Billy Cox	36.00	18.00	9.00
233	*Bob Friend*	40.00	20.00	10.00
234	Steve Souchock	30.00	15.00	7.50
235	Walt Dropo	30.00	15.00	7.50
236	Ed Fitz Gerald	30.00	15.00	7.50
237	Jerry Coleman	40.00	20.00	10.00
238	Art Houtteman	30.00	15.00	7.50
239	*Rocky Bridges*	30.00	15.00	7.50
240	Jack Phillips	30.00	15.00	7.50
241	Tommy Byrne	30.00	15.00	7.50
242	Tom Poholsky	30.00	15.00	7.50
243	Larry Doby	70.00	35.00	17.50
244	Vic Wertz	30.00	15.00	7.50
245	Sherry Robertson	30.00	15.00	7.50
246	George Kell	80.00	40.00	20.00
247	Randy Gumpert	30.00	15.00	7.50
248	Frank Shea	30.00	15.00	7.50
249	Bobby Adams	30.00	15.00	7.50
250	Carl Erskine	70.00	35.00	17.50
251	Chico Carrasquel	40.00	20.00	10.00
252	Vern Bickford	40.00	20.00	10.00
253	Johnny Berardino	50.00	25.00	12.50
254	Joe Dobson	40.00	20.00	10.00
255	Clyde Vollmer	40.00	20.00	10.00
256	Pete Suder	40.00	20.00	10.00
257	Bobby Avila	40.00	20.00	10.00
258	Steve Gromek	40.00	20.00	10.00
259	Bob Addis	40.00	20.00	10.00
260	Pete Castiglione	40.00	20.00	10.00
261	Willie Mays	2000.	900.00	500.00
262	Virgil Trucks	40.00	20.00	10.00
263	Harry Brecheen	40.00	20.00	10.00
264	Roy Hartsfield	40.00	20.00	10.00
265	Chuck Diering	40.00	20.00	10.00
266	Murry Dickson	40.00	20.00	10.00
267	Sid Gordon	40.00	20.00	10.00
268	Bob Lemon	125.00	62.00	31.00
269	Willard Nixon	40.00	20.00	10.00
270	Lou Brissie	40.00	20.00	10.00
271	Jim Delsing	40.00	20.00	10.00
272	Mike Garcia	40.00	20.00	10.00
273	Erv Palica	40.00	20.00	10.00
274	Ralph Branca	80.00	40.00	20.00
275	Pat Mullin	40.00	20.00	10.00
276	Jim Wilson	40.00	20.00	10.00
277	Early Wynn	135.00	67.00	34.00
278	Al Clark	40.00	20.00	10.00
279	Ed Stewart	40.00	20.00	10.00
280	Cloyd Boyer	40.00	20.00	10.00
281	Tommy Brown	40.00	20.00	10.00
282	Birdie Tebbetts	40.00	20.00	10.00
283	Phil Masi	40.00	20.00	10.00
284	Hank Arft	40.00	20.00	10.00
285	Cliff Fannin	40.00	20.00	10.00
286	Joe DeMaestri	40.00	20.00	10.00
287	Steve Bilko	40.00	20.00	10.00
288	Chet Nichols	40.00	20.00	10.00
289	Tommy Holmes	40.00	20.00	10.00
290	Joe Astroth	40.00	20.00	10.00
291	Gil Coan	40.00	20.00	10.00
292	Floyd Baker	40.00	20.00	10.00
293	Sibby Sisti	40.00	20.00	10.00
294	Walker Cooper	40.00	20.00	10.00
295	Phil Cavarretta	40.00	20.00	10.00
296	Red Rolfe	40.00	20.00	10.00
297	Andy Seminick	40.00	20.00	10.00
298	Bob Ross	40.00	20.00	10.00
299	Ray Murray	40.00	20.00	10.00
300	Barney McCosky	40.00	20.00	10.00
301	Bob Porterfield	40.00	20.00	10.00
302	Max Surkont	40.00	20.00	10.00
303	Harry Dorish	40.00	20.00	10.00
304	Sam Dente	40.00	20.00	10.00
305	Paul Richards	40.00	20.00	10.00
306	Lou Sleator	40.00	20.00	10.00
307	Frank Campos	40.00	20.00	10.00
308	Luis Aloma	40.00	20.00	10.00
309	Jim Busby	40.00	20.00	10.00
310	George Metkovich	40.00	20.00	10.00
311	Mickey Mantle	15000.	7500.	3750.
312	Jackie Robinson	1800.	950.00	450.00
313	Bobby Thomson	300.00	150.00	75.00
314	Roy Campanella	1750.	875.00	435.00
315	Leo Durocher	400.00	200.00	100.00
316	Davey Williams	250.00	125.00	60.00
317	Connie Marrero	220.00	110.00	55.00
318	Hal Gregg	220.00	110.00	55.00
319	Al Walker	220.00	110.00	55.00
320	John Rutherford	260.00	130.00	65.00
321	*Joe Black*	275.00	135.00	69.00
322	Randy Jackson	220.00	110.00	55.00
323	Bubba Church	220.00	110.00	55.00
324	Warren Hacker	220.00	110.00	55.00
325	Bill Serena	220.00	110.00	55.00
326	George Shuba	250.00	125.00	62.00
327	Archie Wilson	220.00	110.00	55.00
328	Bob Borkowski	220.00	110.00	55.00
329	Ike Delock	220.00	110.00	55.00
330	Turk Lown	220.00	110.00	55.00
331	Tom Morgan	220.00	110.00	55.00
332	Tony Bartirome	220.00	110.00	55.00
333	Pee Wee Reese	1500.	650.00	375.00
334	Wilmer Mizell	245.00	122.00	61.00
335	Ted Lepcio	220.00	110.00	55.00
336	Dave Koslo	220.00	110.00	55.00
337	Jim Hearn	220.00	110.00	55.00
338	Sal Yvars	220.00	110.00	55.00
339	Russ Meyer	220.00	110.00	55.00
340	Bob Hooper	220.00	110.00	55.00
341	Hal Jeffcoat	220.00	110.00	55.00
342	*Clem Labine*	275.00	137.00	69.00
343	Dick Gernert	220.00	110.00	55.00
344	Ewell Blackwell	220.00	110.00	55.00
345	Sam White	220.00	110.00	55.00
346	George Spencer	220.00	110.00	55.00
347	Joe Adcock	260.00	130.00	65.00
348	Bob Kelly	220.00	110.00	55.00
349	Bob Cain	220.00	110.00	55.00
350	Cal Abrams	220.00	110.00	55.00
351	Al Dark	220.00	110.00	55.00
352	Karl Drews	220.00	110.00	55.00
353	Bob Del Greco	220.00	110.00	55.00
354	Fred Hatfield	220.00	110.00	55.00
355	Bobby Morgan	240.00	120.00	60.00
356	Toby Atwell	220.00	110.00	55.00
357	Smoky Burgess	245.00	122.00	61.00
358	John Kucab	220.00	110.00	55.00
359	Dee Fondy	220.00	110.00	55.00
360	George Crowe	220.00	110.00	55.00
361	Bill Posedel	220.00	110.00	55.00
362	Ken Heintzelman	220.00	110.00	55.00
363	Dick Rozek	220.00	110.00	55.00
364	Clyde Sukeforth	220.00	110.00	55.00
365	Cookie Lavagetto	240.00	120.00	60.00
366	Dave Madison	220.00	110.00	55.00
367	Bob Thorpe	220.00	110.00	55.00
368	Ed Wright	220.00	110.00	55.00
369	*Dick Groat*	360.00	180.00	90.00
370	Billy Hoeft	220.00	110.00	55.00
371	Bob Hofman	220.00	110.00	55.00
372	*Gil McDougald*	350.00	175.00	87.00
373	Jim Turner	275.00	137.00	69.00
374	Al Benton	220.00	110.00	55.00
375	Jack Merson	220.00	110.00	55.00
376	Faye Throneberry	220.00	110.00	55.00
377	Chuck Dressen	300.00	150.00	75.00
378	Les Fusselman	220.00	110.00	55.00
379	Joe Rossi	220.00	110.00	55.00
380	Clem Koshorek	220.00	110.00	55.00
381	Milton Stock	220.00	110.00	55.00
382	Sam Jones	220.00	110.00	55.00
383	Del Wilber	220.00	110.00	55.00
384	Frank Crosetti	325.00	162.00	81.00
385	Herman Franks	220.00	110.00	55.00
386	Eddie Yuhas	220.00	110.00	55.00

387	Billy Meyer	220.00	110.00	55.00
388	Bob Chipman	220.00	110.00	55.00
389	Ben Wade	220.00	110.00	55.00
390	Rocky Nelson	260.00	130.00	65.00
391	Ben Chapman (photo actually Sam Chapman)	220.00	110.00	55.00
392	*Hoyt Wilhelm*	675.00	337.00	169.00
393	Ebba St. Claire	220.00	110.00	55.00
394	Billy Herman	300.00	150.00	75.00
395	Jake Pitler	220.00	110.00	55.00
396	*Dick Williams*	300.00	150.00	75.00
397	Forrest Main	220.00	110.00	55.00
398	Hal Rice	220.00	110.00	55.00
399	Jim Fridley	220.00	110.00	55.00
400	Bill Dickey	650.00	325.00	162.00
401	Bob Schultz	220.00	110.00	55.00
402	Earl Harrist	220.00	110.00	55.00
403	Bill Miller	220.00	110.00	55.00
404	Dick Brodowski	220.00	110.00	55.00
405	Eddie Pellagrini	220.00	110.00	55.00
406	*Joe Nuxhall*	350.00	175.00	87.00
407	*Eddie Mathews*	4500.	1600.	800.00

1953 Topps

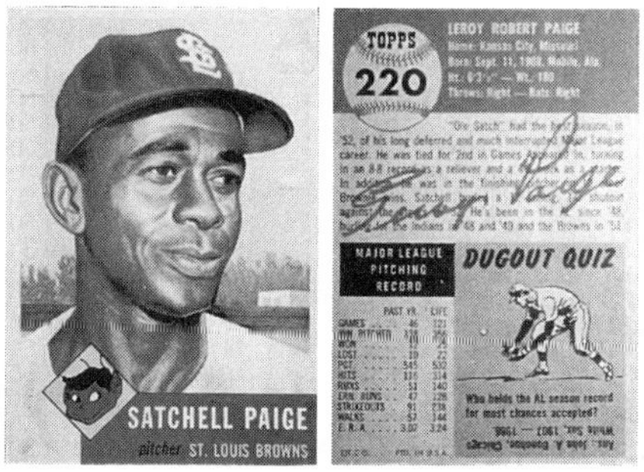

The 1953 Topps set reflects the company's continuing legal battles with Bowman. The set, originally intended to consist of 280 cards, is lacking six numbers (#'s 253, 261, 267, 268, 271 and 275) which probably represent players whose contracts were lost to the competition. The 2-5/8" x 3-3/4" cards feature painted player pictures. A color team logo appears at a bottom panel (red for American league and black for National.) Card backs contain the first baseball trivia questions along with brief statistics and player biographies. In the red panel at the top which lists the player's personal data, cards from the 2nd Series (#'s 86-165 plus 10, 44, 61, 72 and 81) can be found with that data printed in either black or white, black being the scarcer variety. Cards 221-280 are the scarce high numbers, with even scarcer short-printed cards interspersed in the series.

		NM	EX	VG
Complete Set (274):		9500.	5000.	3000.
Common Player (1-220):		20.00	10.00	6.00
Common Player (221-280):		40.00	20.00	12.00
Short-print Player (221-280):		80.00	40.00	24.00
1	Jackie Robinson	600.00	150.00	90.00
2	Luke Easter	20.00	10.00	6.00
3	George Crowe	20.00	10.00	6.00
4	Ben Wade	20.00	10.00	6.00
5	Joe Dobson	20.00	10.00	6.00
6	Sam Jones	20.00	10.00	6.00
7	Bob Borkowski	20.00	10.00	6.00
8	Clem Koshorek	20.00	10.00	6.00
9	Joe Collins	20.00	10.00	6.00
10	Smoky Burgess (SP)	55.00	27.00	16.50
11	Sal Yvars	20.00	10.00	6.00
12	Howie Judson	20.00	10.00	6.00
13	Connie Marrero	20.00	10.00	6.00
14	Clem Labine	27.50	13.50	8.25
15	Bobo Newsom	20.00	10.00	6.00
16	Harry Lowrey	20.00	10.00	6.00
17	Billy Hitchcock	20.00	10.00	6.00
18	Ted Lepcio	20.00	10.00	6.00
19	Mel Parnell	20.00	10.00	6.00
20	Hank Thompson	20.00	10.00	6.00
21	Billy Johnson	20.00	10.00	6.00
22	Howie Fox	20.00	10.00	6.00
23	Toby Atwell	20.00	10.00	6.00
24	Ferris Fain	20.00	10.00	6.00
25	Ray Boone	20.00	10.00	6.00
26	Dale Mitchell	20.00	10.00	6.00
27	Roy Campanella	175.00	87.00	52.00
28	Eddie Pellagrini	20.00	10.00	6.00
29	Hal Jeffcoat	20.00	10.00	6.00
30	Willard Nixon	20.00	10.00	6.00
31	Ewell Blackwell	40.00	20.00	12.00
32	Clyde Vollmer	20.00	10.00	6.00
33	Bob Kennedy	20.00	10.00	6.00
34	George Shuba	20.00	10.00	6.00
35	Irv Noren	20.00	10.00	6.00
36	Johnny Groth	20.00	10.00	6.00
37	Eddie Mathews	125.00	62.00	37.00
38	Jim Hearn	20.00	10.00	6.00
39	Eddie Miksis	20.00	10.00	6.00
40	John Lipon	20.00	10.00	6.00
41	Enos Slaughter	90.00	45.00	27.00
42	Gus Zernial	20.00	10.00	6.00
43	Gil McDougald	40.00	20.00	12.00
44	Ellis Kinder (SP)	30.00	15.00	9.00
45	Grady Hatton	20.00	10.00	6.00
46	Johnny Klippstein	20.00	10.00	6.00
47	Bubba Church	20.00	10.00	6.00
48	Bob Del Greco	20.00	10.00	6.00
49	Faye Throneberry	20.00	10.00	6.00
50	Chuck Dressen	30.00	15.00	9.00
51	Frank Campos	20.00	10.00	6.00
52	Ted Gray	20.00	10.00	6.00
53	Sherman Lollar	20.00	10.00	6.00
54	Bob Feller	90.00	45.00	27.00
55	Maurice McDermott	20.00	10.00	6.00
56	Gerald Staley	20.00	10.00	6.00
57	Carl Scheib	20.00	10.00	6.00
58	George Metkovich	20.00	10.00	6.00
59	Karl Drews	20.00	10.00	6.00
60	Cloyd Boyer	20.00	10.00	6.00
61	Early Wynn (SP)	110.00	55.00	33.00
62	Monte Irvin	35.00	17.50	10.50
63	Gus Niarhos	20.00	10.00	6.00
64	Dave Philley	20.00	10.00	6.00
65	Earl Harrist	20.00	10.00	6.00
66	Minnie Minoso	40.00	20.00	9.25
67	Roy Sievers	20.00	10.00	6.00
68	Del Rice	20.00	10.00	6.00
69	Dick Brodowski	20.00	10.00	6.00
70	Ed Yuhas	20.00	10.00	6.00
71	Tony Bartirome	20.00	10.00	6.00
72	Fred Hutchinson (SP)	40.00	20.00	12.00
73	Eddie Robinson	20.00	10.00	6.00
74	Joe Rossi	20.00	10.00	6.00
75	Mike Garcia	20.00	10.00	6.00
76	Pee Wee Reese	140.00	70.00	42.00
77	Johnny Mize	55.00	27.00	16.50
78	Red Schoendienst	55.00	27.00	16.50
79	Johnny Wyrostek	20.00	10.00	6.00
80	Jim Hegan	20.00	10.00	6.00
81	Joe Black (SP)	75.00	37.00	22.00
82	Mickey Mantle	2600.	1300.	700.00
83	Howie Pollet	20.00	10.00	6.00
84	Bob Hooper	20.00	10.00	6.00
85	Bobby Morgan	20.00	10.00	6.00
86	Billy Martin	100.00	50.00	30.00
87	Ed Lopat	35.00	17.50	10.50
88	Willie Jones	20.00	10.00	6.00
89	Chuck Stobbs	20.00	10.00	6.00
90	Hank Edwards	20.00	10.00	6.00
91	Ebba St. Claire	20.00	10.00	6.00
92	Paul Minner	20.00	10.00	6.00
93	Hal Rice	20.00	10.00	6.00
94	William Kennedy	20.00	10.00	6.00
95	Willard Marshall	20.00	10.00	6.00
96	Virgil Trucks	20.00	10.00	6.00
97	Don Kolloway	20.00	10.00	6.00
98	Cal Abrams	20.00	10.00	6.00
99	Dave Madison	20.00	10.00	6.00
100	Bill Miller	20.00	10.00	6.00
101	Ted Wilks	20.00	10.00	6.00
102	Connie Ryan	20.00	10.00	6.00
103	Joe Astroth	20.00	10.00	6.00
104	Yogi Berra	225.00	110.00	67.00
105	Joe Nuxhall	21.00	10.50	6.25
106	Johnny Antonelli	20.00	10.00	6.00
107	Danny O'Connell	20.00	10.00	6.00
108	Bob Porterfield	20.00	10.00	6.00
109	Alvin Dark	20.00	10.00	6.00
110	Herman Wehmeier	20.00	10.00	6.00
111	Hank Sauer	20.00	10.00	6.00
112	Ned Garver	20.00	10.00	6.00
113	Jerry Priddy	20.00	10.00	6.00
114	Phil Rizzuto	125.00	62.00	37.00
115	George Spencer	20.00	10.00	6.00
116	Frank Smith	20.00	10.00	6.00
117	Sid Gordon	20.00	10.00	6.00
118	Gus Bell	20.00	10.00	6.00
119	Johnny Sain	42.00	21.00	12.50
120	Davey Williams	20.00	10.00	6.00
121	Walt Dropo	20.00	10.00	6.00
122	Elmer Valo	20.00	10.00	6.00
123	Tommy Byrne	20.00	10.00	6.00
124	Sibby Sisti	20.00	10.00	6.00
125	Dick Williams	20.00	10.00	6.00
126	Bill Connelly	20.00	10.00	6.00
127	Clint Courtney	20.00	10.00	6.00
128	Wilmer Mizell	20.00	10.00	6.00
129	Keith Thomas	20.00	10.00	6.00
130	Turk Lown	20.00	10.00	6.00
131	Harry Byrd	20.00	10.00	6.00
132	Tom Morgan	20.00	10.00	6.00
133	Gil Coan	20.00	10.00	6.00
134	Rube Walker	20.00	10.00	6.00
135	Al Rosen	28.00	14.00	8.50
136	Ken Heintzelman	20.00	10.00	6.00
137	John Rutherford	20.00	10.00	6.00
138	George Kell	45.00	22.00	13.50
139	Sammy White	20.00	10.00	6.00
140	Tommy Glaviano	20.00	10.00	6.00
141	Allie Reynolds	40.00	20.00	12.00
142	Vic Wertz	20.00	10.00	6.00
143	Billy Pierce	30.00	15.00	9.00
144	Bob Schultz	20.00	10.00	6.00
145	Harry Dorish	20.00	10.00	6.00
146	Granny Hamner	20.00	10.00	6.00
147	Warren Spahn	150.00	75.00	45.00
148	Mickey Grasso	20.00	10.00	6.00
149	Dom DiMaggio	50.00	25.00	15.00
150	Harry Simpson	20.00	10.00	6.00
151	Hoyt Wilhelm	60.00	30.00	18.00
152	Bob Adams	20.00	10.00	6.00
153	Andy Seminick	20.00	10.00	6.00
154	Dick Groat	24.00	12.00	7.25
155	Dutch Leonard	20.00	10.00	6.00
156	Jim Rivera	20.00	10.00	6.00
157	Bob Addis	20.00	10.00	6.00
158	*Johnny Logan*	20.00	10.00	6.00
159	Wayne Terwilliger	20.00	10.00	6.00
160	Bob Young	20.00	10.00	6.00
161	Vern Bickford	20.00	10.00	6.00
162	Ted Kluszewski	48.00	24.00	14.50
163	Fred Hatfield	20.00	10.00	6.00
164	Frank Shea	20.00	10.00	6.00
165	Billy Hoeft	20.00	10.00	6.00
166	Bill Hunter	20.00	10.00	6.00
167	Art Schult	20.00	10.00	6.00
168	Willard Schmidt	20.00	10.00	6.00
169	Dizzy Trout	20.00	10.00	6.00
170	Bill Werle	20.00	10.00	6.00
171	Bill Glynn	20.00	10.00	6.00
172	Rip Repulski	20.00	10.00	6.00
173	Preston Ward	20.00	10.00	6.00
174	Billy Loes	20.00	10.00	6.00
175	Ron Kline	20.00	10.00	6.00
176	*Don Hoak*	25.00	12.50	5.75
177	Jim Dyck	20.00	10.00	6.00
178	Jim Waugh	20.00	10.00	6.00
179	Gene Hermanski	20.00	10.00	6.00
180	Virgil Stallcup	20.00	10.00	6.00
181	Al Zarilla	20.00	10.00	6.00
182	Bob Hofman	20.00	10.00	6.00
183	*Stu Miller*	20.00	10.00	6.00
184	*Hal Brown*	20.00	10.00	6.00
185	*Jim Pendleton*	20.00	10.00	6.00
186	Charlie Bishop	20.00	10.00	6.00
187	Jim Fridley	20.00	10.00	6.00
188	*Andy Carey*	20.00	10.00	6.00
189	Ray Jablonski	20.00	10.00	6.00
190	Dixie Walker	20.00	10.00	6.00
191	Ralph Kiner	80.00	40.00	24.00
192	Wally Westlake	20.00	10.00	6.00
193	Mike Clark	20.00	10.00	6.00
194	Eddie Kazak	20.00	10.00	6.00
195	Ed McGhee	20.00	10.00	6.00
196	Bob Keegan	20.00	10.00	6.00
197	Del Crandall	20.00	10.00	6.00
198	Forrest Main	20.00	10.00	6.00
199	Marion Fricano	20.00	10.00	6.00
200	Gordon Goldsberry	20.00	10.00	6.00
201	Paul LaPalme	20.00	10.00	6.00
202	Carl Sawatski	20.00	10.00	6.00
203	Cliff Fannin	20.00	10.00	6.00
204	Dick Bokelmann	20.00	10.00	6.00
205	Vern Benson	20.00	10.00	6.00
206	*Ed Bailey*	20.00	10.00	6.00
207	Whitey Ford	150.00	75.00	45.00
208	Jim Wilson	20.00	10.00	6.00
209	Jim Greengrass	20.00	10.00	6.00
210	*Bob Cerv*	20.00	10.00	6.00
211	J.W. Porter	20.00	10.00	6.00
212	Jack Dittmer	20.00	10.00	6.00
213	Ray Scarborough	20.00	10.00	6.00
214	*Bill Bruton*	20.00	10.00	6.00
215	*Gene Conley*	20.00	10.00	6.00
216	Jim Hughes	20.00	10.00	6.00
217	Murray Wall	20.00	10.00	6.00
218	Les Fusselman	20.00	10.00	6.00
219	Pete Runnels (picture actually Don Johnson)	20.00	10.00	6.00
220	Satchel Paige	400.00	150.00	90.00
221	Bob Milliken	90.00	45.00	27.00
222	Vic Janowicz	50.00	25.00	11.50
223	John O'Brien	50.00	25.00	15.00
224	Lou Sleater	50.00	25.00	15.00
225	Bobby Shantz	90.00	45.00	27.00
226	Ed Erautt	90.00	45.00	27.00
227	Morris Martin	50.00	25.00	15.00
228	Hal Newhouser	130.00	65.00	39.00
229	Rocky Krsnich	90.00	45.00	27.00
230	Johnny Lindell	50.00	25.00	15.00
231	Solly Hemus	50.00	25.00	15.00
232	Dick Kokos	90.00	45.00	27.00
233	Al Aber	90.00	45.00	27.00
234	Ray Murray	50.00	25.00	15.00
235	John Hetki	50.00	25.00	15.00
236	Harry Perkowski	50.00	25.00	15.00
237	Clarence Podbielan	50.00	25.00	15.00
238	Cal Hogue	50.00	25.00	15.00
239	Jim Delsing	90.00	45.00	27.00
240	Freddie Marsh	50.00	25.00	15.00
241	Al Sima	50.00	25.00	15.00
242	Charlie Silvera	120.00	60.00	36.00
243	Carlos Bernier	50.00	25.00	15.00
244	Willie Mays	2400.	750.00	525.00
245	Bill Norman	90.00	45.00	27.00
246	*Roy Face*	85.00	42.00	25.00
247	Mike Sandlock	50.00	25.00	15.00
248	Gene Stephens	50.00	25.00	15.00
249	Ed O'Brien	90.00	45.00	27.00
250	Bob Wilson	90.00	45.00	27.00
251	Sid Hudson	90.00	45.00	27.00
252	Henry Foiles	90.00	45.00	27.00
253	Not issued			
254	Preacher Roe	90.00	45.00	27.00
255	Dixie Howell	90.00	45.00	27.00
256	Les Peden	90.00	45.00	27.00
257	Bob Boyd	90.00	45.00	27.00
258	*Jim Gilliam*	235.00	117.00	70.00
259	Roy McMillan	50.00	25.00	15.00
260	Sam Calderone	90.00	45.00	27.00
261	Not issued			
262	Bob Oldis	90.00	45.00	27.00
263	*Johnny Podres*	250.00	125.00	57.00
264	Gene Woodling	55.00	27.00	16.50
265	Jackie Jensen	110.00	55.00	33.00
266	Bob Cain	90.00	45.00	27.00
267	Not issued			
268	Not issued			
269	Duane Pillette	90.00	45.00	27.00
270	Vern Stephens	90.00	45.00	27.00
271	Not issued			
272	Bill Antonello	90.00	45.00	27.00
273	*Harvey Haddix*	110.00	55.00	33.00
274	John Riddle	90.00	45.00	27.00
275	Not issued			

276	Ken Raffensberger	90.00	45.00	27.00
277	Don Lund	90.00	45.00	27.00
278	Willie Miranda	90.00	45.00	27.00
279	Joe Coleman	50.00	25.00	15.00
280	*Milt Bolling*	400.00	75.00	30.00

1954 Topps

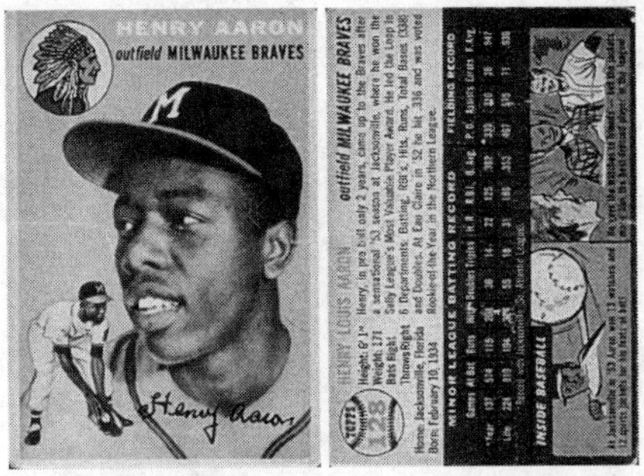

The first issue to use two player pictures on the front, the 1954 Topps set is very popular today. Solid color backgrounds frame both color head and shoulders and black and white action pictures of the player. The player's name, position, team and team logo appear at the top. Backs include an "Inside Baseball" cartoon regarding the player as well as statistics and biography. The 250-card, 2-5/8" x 3-3/4", set includes manager and coaches cards, and the first use by Topps of two players together on a card; the players were, appropriately, the O'Brien twins.

		NM	EX	VG
Complete Set (250):		6000.	3000.	1800.
Common Player (1-50):		15.00	7.50	4.50
Common Player (51-75):		24.00	12.00	7.25
Common Player (76-250):		15.00	7.50	4.50
1	Ted Williams	800.00	250.00	150.00
2	Gus Zernial	15.00	7.50	4.50
3	Monte Irvin	35.00	17.50	10.50
4	Hank Sauer	15.00	7.50	4.50
5	Ed Lopat	16.00	8.00	4.75
6	Pete Runnels	15.00	7.50	4.50
7	Ted Kluszewski	33.00	16.50	10.00
8	Bobby Young	15.00	7.50	4.50
9	Harvey Haddix	15.00	7.50	4.50
10	Jackie Robinson	225.00	112.00	67.00
11	Paul Smith	15.00	7.50	4.50
12	Del Crandall	15.00	7.50	4.50
13	Billy Martin	50.00	25.00	15.00
14	Preacher Roe	18.00	9.00	5.50
15	Al Rosen	16.00	8.00	4.75
16	Vic Janowicz	16.00	8.00	4.75
17	Phil Rizzuto	60.00	30.00	18.00
18	Walt Dropo	15.00	7.50	4.50
19	Johnny Lipon	15.00	7.50	4.50
20	Warren Spahn	65.00	32.00	19.50
21	Bobby Shantz	16.00	8.00	4.75
22	Jim Greengrass	15.00	7.50	4.50
23	Luke Easter	15.00	7.50	4.50
24	Granny Hamner	15.00	7.50	4.50
25	*Harvey Kuenn*	35.00	17.50	10.50
26	Ray Jablonski	15.00	7.50	4.50
27	Ferris Fain	15.00	7.50	4.50
28	Paul Minner	15.00	7.50	4.50
29	Jim Hegan	15.00	7.50	4.50
30	Eddie Mathews	70.00	35.00	21.00
31	Johnny Klippstein	15.00	7.50	4.50
32	Duke Snider	150.00	75.00	45.00
33	Johnny Schmitz	15.00	7.50	4.50
34	Jim Rivera	15.00	7.50	4.50
35	Junior Gilliam	30.00	15.00	9.00
36	Hoyt Wilhelm	40.00	20.00	12.00
37	Whitey Ford	80.00	40.00	24.00
38	Eddie Stanky	20.00	10.00	6.00
39	Sherman Lollar	15.00	7.50	4.50
40	Mel Parnell	15.00	7.50	4.50
41	Willie Jones	15.00	7.50	4.50
42	Don Mueller	15.00	7.50	4.50
43	Dick Groat	16.00	8.00	4.75
44	Ned Garver	15.00	7.50	4.50
45	Richie Ashburn	65.00	32.00	19.50
46	Ken Raffensberger	15.00	7.50	4.50
47	Ellis Kinder	15.00	7.50	4.50
48	Billy Hunter	15.00	7.50	4.50
49	Ray Murray	15.00	7.50	4.50
50	Yogi Berra	175.00	87.00	52.00
51	Johnny Lindell	24.00	12.00	7.25
52	Vic Power	24.00	12.00	7.25
53	Jack Dittmer	24.00	12.00	7.25
54	Vern Stephens	24.00	12.00	7.25
55	Phil Cavarretta	24.00	12.00	7.25
56	Willie Miranda	24.00	12.00	7.25
57	Luis Aloma	24.00	12.00	7.25
58	Bob Wilson	24.00	12.00	7.25
59	Gene Conley	24.00	12.00	7.25
60	Frank Baumholtz	24.00	12.00	7.25
61	Bob Cain	24.00	12.00	7.25
62	Eddie Robinson	24.00	12.00	7.25
63	Johnny Pesky	24.00	12.00	7.25
64	Hank Thompson	24.00	12.00	7.25
65	Bob Swift	24.00	12.00	7.25
66	Ted Lepcio	24.00	12.00	7.25
67	Jim Willis	24.00	12.00	7.25
68	Sam Calderone	24.00	12.00	7.25
69	Bud Podbielan	24.00	12.00	7.25
70	Larry Doby	65.00	32.00	19.50
71	Frank Smith	24.00	12.00	7.25
72	Preston Ward	24.00	12.00	7.25
73	Wayne Terwilliger	24.00	12.00	7.25
74	Bill Taylor	24.00	12.00	7.25
75	Fred Haney	24.00	12.00	7.25
76	Bob Scheffing	15.00	7.50	4.50
77	Ray Boone	15.00	7.50	4.50
78	Ted Kazanski	15.00	7.50	4.50
79	Andy Pafko	15.00	7.50	4.50
80	Jackie Jensen	24.00	12.00	7.25
81	Dave Hoskins	15.00	7.50	4.50
82	Milt Bolling	15.00	7.50	4.50
83	Joe Collins	15.00	7.50	4.50
84	Dick Cole	15.00	7.50	4.50
85	*Bob Turley*	27.50	13.50	8.25
86	Billy Herman	24.00	12.00	7.25
87	Roy Face	15.00	7.50	4.50
88	Matt Batts	15.00	7.50	4.50
89	Howie Pollet	15.00	7.50	4.50
90	Willie Mays	400.00	175.00	100.00
91	Bob Oldis	15.00	7.50	4.50
92	Wally Westlake	15.00	7.50	4.50
93	Sid Hudson	15.00	7.50	4.50
94	*Ernie Banks*	700.00	400.00	200.00
95	Hal Rice	15.00	7.50	4.50
96	Charlie Silvera	15.00	7.50	4.50
97	Jerry Lane	15.00	7.50	4.50
98	Joe Black	27.50	13.50	8.25
99	Bob Hofman	15.00	7.50	4.50
100	Bob Keegan	15.00	7.50	4.50
101	Gene Woodling	16.00	8.00	4.75
102	Gil Hodges	70.00	35.00	21.00
103	*Jim Lemon*	15.00	7.50	4.50
104	Mike Sandlock	15.00	7.50	4.50
105	Andy Carey	15.00	7.50	4.50
106	Dick Kokos	15.00	7.50	4.50
107	Duane Pillette	15.00	7.50	4.50
108	Thornton Kipper	15.00	7.50	4.50
109	Bill Bruton	15.00	7.50	4.50
110	Harry Dorish	15.00	7.50	4.50
111	Jim Delsing	15.00	7.50	4.50
112	Bill Renna	15.00	7.50	4.50
113	Bob Boyd	15.00	7.50	4.50
114	Dean Stone	15.00	7.50	4.50
115	"Rip" Repulski	15.00	7.50	4.50
116	Steve Bilko	15.00	7.50	4.50
117	Solly Hemus	15.00	7.50	4.50
118	Carl Scheib	15.00	7.50	4.50
119	Johnny Antonelli	15.00	7.50	4.50
120	Roy McMillan	15.00	7.50	4.50
121	Clem Labine	16.00	8.00	4.75
122	Johnny Logan	15.00	7.50	4.50
123	Bobby Adams	15.00	7.50	4.50
124	Marion Fricano	15.00	7.50	4.50
125	Harry Perkowski	15.00	7.50	4.50
126	Ben Wade	15.00	7.50	4.50
127	Steve O'Neill	15.00	7.50	4.50
128	*Hank Aaron*	1200.	450.00	250.00
129	Forrest Jacobs	15.00	7.50	4.50
130	Hank Bauer	24.00	12.00	7.25
131	Reno Bertoia	15.00	7.50	4.50
132	*Tom Lasorda*	145.00	72.00	43.00
133	Del Baker	15.00	7.50	4.50
134	Cal Hogue	15.00	7.50	4.50
135	Joe Presko	15.00	7.50	4.50
136	Connie Ryan	15.00	7.50	4.50
137	*Wally Moon*	27.50	13.50	8.25
138	Bob Borkowski	15.00	7.50	4.50
139	Ed O'Brien, Johnny O'Brien	35.00	17.50	10.50
140	Tom Wright	15.00	7.50	4.50
141	*Joe Jay*	15.00	7.50	4.50
142	Tom Poholsky	15.00	7.50	4.50
143	Rollie Hemsley	15.00	7.50	4.50
144	Bill Werle	15.00	7.50	4.50
145	Elmer Valo	15.00	7.50	4.50
146	Don Johnson	15.00	7.50	4.50
147	John Riddle	15.00	7.50	4.50
148	Bob Trice	15.00	7.50	4.50
149	Jim Robertson	15.00	7.50	4.50
150	Dick Kryhoski	15.00	7.50	4.50
151	Alex Grammas	15.00	7.50	4.50
152	Mike Blyzka	15.00	7.50	4.50
153	Rube Walker	15.00	7.50	4.50
154	Mike Fornieles	15.00	7.50	4.50
155	Bob Kennedy	15.00	7.50	4.50
156	Joe Coleman	15.00	7.50	4.50
157	Don Lenhardt	15.00	7.50	4.50
158	Peanuts Lowrey	15.00	7.50	4.50
159	Dave Philley	15.00	7.50	4.50
160	Red Kress	15.00	7.50	4.50
161	John Hetki	15.00	7.50	4.50
162	Herman Wehmeier	15.00	7.50	4.50
163	Frank House	15.00	7.50	4.50
164	Stu Miller	15.00	7.50	4.50
165	Jim Pendleton	15.00	7.50	4.50
166	Johnny Podres	24.00	12.00	7.25
167	Don Lund	15.00	7.50	4.50
168	Morrie Martin	15.00	7.50	4.50
169	Jim Hughes	15.00	7.50	4.50
170	*Dusty Rhodes*	17.50	8.75	5.25
171	Leo Kiely	15.00	7.50	4.50
172	Hal Brown	15.00	7.50	4.50
173	Jack Harshman	15.00	7.50	4.50
174	Tom Qualters	15.00	7.50	4.50
175	Frank Leja	15.00	7.50	4.50
176	Bob Keely	15.00	7.50	4.50
177	Bob Milliken	15.00	7.50	4.50
178	Bill Gylnn (Glynn)	15.00	7.50	4.50
179	Gair Allie	15.00	7.50	4.50
180	Wes Westrum	15.00	7.50	4.50
181	Mel Roach	15.00	7.50	4.50
182	Chuck Harmon	15.00	7.50	4.50
183	Earle Combs	20.00	10.00	6.00
184	Ed Bailey	15.00	7.50	4.50
185	Chuck Stobbs	15.00	7.50	4.50
186	Karl Olson	15.00	7.50	4.50
187	Heinie Manush	20.00	10.00	6.00
188	Dave Jolly	15.00	7.50	4.50
189	Bob Ross	15.00	7.50	4.50
190	Ray Herbert	15.00	7.50	4.50
191	*Dick Schofield*	22.00	11.00	6.50
192	Cot Deal	15.00	7.50	4.50
193	Johnny Hopp	15.00	7.50	4.50
194	Bill Sarni	15.00	7.50	4.50
195	Bill Consolo	15.00	7.50	4.50
196	Stan Jok	15.00	7.50	4.50
197	Schoolboy Rowe	15.00	7.50	4.50
198	Carl Sawatski	15.00	7.50	4.50
199	Rocky Nelson	15.00	7.50	4.50
200	Larry Jansen	15.00	7.50	4.50
201	*Al Kaline*	550.00	275.00	165.00
202	*Bob Purkey*	15.00	7.50	4.50
203	Harry Brecheen	15.00	7.50	4.50
204	Angel Scull	15.00	7.50	4.50
205	Johnny Sain	25.00	12.50	7.50
206	Ray Crone	15.00	7.50	4.50
207	Tom Oliver	15.00	7.50	4.50
208	Grady Hatton	15.00	7.50	4.50
209	Charlie Thompson	15.00	7.50	4.50
210	*Bob Buhl*	15.00	7.50	4.50
211	Don Hoak	15.00	7.50	4.50
212	Mickey Micelotta	15.00	7.50	4.50
213	John Fitzpatrick	15.00	7.50	4.50
214	Arnold Portocarrero	15.00	7.50	4.50
215	Ed McGhee	15.00	7.50	4.50
216	Al Sima	15.00	7.50	4.50
217	Paul Schreiber	15.00	7.50	4.50
218	Fred Marsh	15.00	7.50	4.50
219	Charlie Kress	15.00	7.50	4.50
220	Ruben Gomez	15.00	7.50	4.50
221	Dick Brodowski	15.00	7.50	4.50
222	Bill Wilson	15.00	7.50	4.50
223	Joe Haynes	15.00	7.50	4.50
224	Dick Weik	15.00	7.50	4.50
225	Don Liddle	15.00	7.50	4.50
226	Jehosie Heard	15.00	7.50	4.50
227	Buster Mills	15.00	7.50	4.50
228	Gene Hermanski	15.00	7.50	4.50
229	Bob Talbot	15.00	7.50	4.50
230	Bob Kuzava	15.00	7.50	4.50
231	Roy Smalley	15.00	7.50	4.50
232	Lou Limmer	15.00	7.50	4.50
233	Augie Galan	15.00	7.50	4.50
234	*Jerry Lynch*	15.00	7.50	4.50
235	Vern Law	15.00	7.50	4.50
236	Paul Penson	15.00	7.50	4.50
237	Mike Ryba	15.00	7.50	4.50
238	Al Aber	15.00	7.50	4.50
239	*Bill Skowron*	85.00	42.00	25.00
240	Sam Mele	15.00	7.50	4.50
241	Bob Miller	15.00	7.50	4.50
242	Curt Roberts	15.00	7.50	4.50
243	Ray Blades	15.00	7.50	4.50
244	Leroy Wheat	15.00	7.50	4.50
245	Roy Sievers	15.00	7.50	4.50
246	Howie Fox	15.00	7.50	4.50
247	Eddie Mayo	15.00	7.50	4.50
248	*Al Smith*	15.00	7.50	4.50
249	Wilmer Mizell	15.00	7.50	4.50
250	Ted Williams	750.00	225.00	150.00

1954 Topps Look 'N See

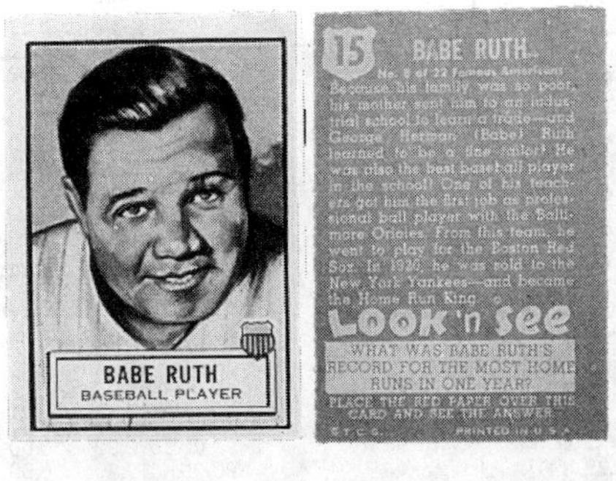

Among the 135 historical figures in this set is only one baseball player - Babe Ruth. These 2-1/16" x 2-15/16" cards feature colorful portrait paintings on the front and biographies on the back. The answer to a trivia question on back can be discovered by laying a piece of red cellophane over the question box.

		NM	EX	VG
Complete Set (135):		1000.	500.00	300.00
Common Card:		4.00	2.00	1.25
15	Babe Ruth	150.00	75.00	45.00

Check lists with card numbers in parentheses ( ) indicates the numbers do not appear on the cards.

1954 Topps Scoops

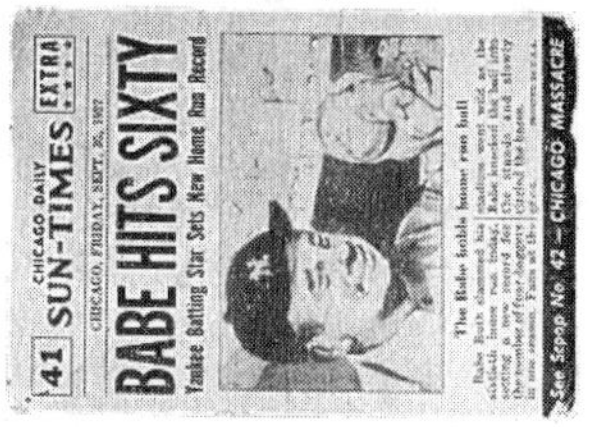

World - and sports - history from the mid-18th Century through Oct., 1953, is chronicled in this 156-card set. Three baseball subjects are presented in the set. Cards are 2-1/16" x 2-15/16" and feature on the front a color painting with a dated caption box at bottom. Originally a black scratch-off ink covered the caption box (cards with the black ink removed can still be considered Mint as those with the ink currently command little premium value). Backs feature a simulated newspaper front page with banner headline and picture, along with a description of the event.

		NM	EX	VG
Complete Set (156):		1750.	875.00	525.00
Common Player:		6.00	3.00	1.75
27	Bob Feller Strikeout King, Oct. 2, 1938 (Bob Feller)	80.00	40.00	24.00
41	Babe Ruth Sets Record, Sept. 30, 1927 (Babe Ruth)	200.00	100.00	60.00
130	Braves Go to Milwaukee	40.00	20.00	12.00

1955 Topps

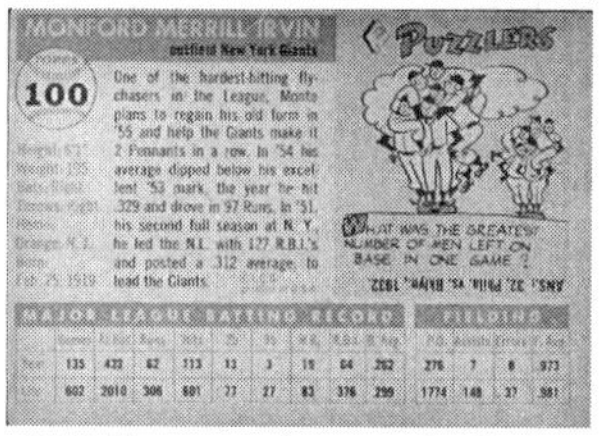

The 1955 Topps set is numerically the smallest of the regular annual issues. The 3-3/4" x 2-5/8" cards mark the first time that Topps used a horizontal format for the entire set. While that format was new, the design was not; they are very similar to the 1954 cards to the point many pictures appeared in both years. Although it was slated for a 210-card set, the 1955 Topps set turned out to be only 206 cards with numbers 175, 186, 203 and 209 never being released. The scarce high numbers in this set begin with #161.

		NM	EX	VG
Complete Set (206):		6000.	2750.	1650.
Common Player (1-150):		12.00	6.00	3.50
Common Player (151-160):		20.00	10.00	6.00
Common Player (161-210):		30.00	15.00	9.00
1	Dusty Rhodes	75.00	10.00	4.00
2	Ted Williams	400.00	175.00	100.00
3	Art Fowler	12.00	6.00	3.50
4	Al Kaline	165.00	82.00	49.00
5	Jim Gilliam	20.00	10.00	6.00
6	Stan Hack	12.00	6.00	3.50
7	Jim Hegan	12.00	6.00	3.50
8	Hal Smith	12.00	6.00	3.50
9	Bob Miller	12.00	6.00	3.50
10	Bob Keegan	12.00	6.00	3.50
11	Ferris Fain	12.00	6.00	3.50
12	"Jake" Thies	12.00	6.00	3.50
13	Fred Marsh	12.00	6.00	3.50
14	Jim Finigan	12.00	6.00	3.50
15	Jim Pendleton	12.00	6.00	3.50
16	Roy Sievers	12.00	6.00	3.50
17	Bobby Hofman	12.00	6.00	3.50
18	Russ Kemmerer	12.00	6.00	3.50
19	Billy Herman	15.00	7.50	4.50
20	Andy Carey	12.00	6.00	3.50
21	Alex Grammas	12.00	6.00	3.50
22	Bill Skowron	20.00	10.00	6.00
23	Jack Parks	12.00	6.00	3.50
24	Hal Newhouser	22.00	11.00	6.50
25	Johnny Podres	25.00	12.50	7.50
26	Dick Groat	12.00	6.00	3.50
27	Billy Gardner	12.00	6.00	3.50
28	Ernie Banks	175.00	80.00	50.00
29	Herman Wehmeier	12.00	6.00	3.50
30	Vic Power	12.00	6.00	3.50
31	Warren Spahn	75.00	37.00	22.00
32	Ed McGhee	12.00	6.00	3.50
33	Tom Qualters	12.00	6.00	3.50
34	Wayne Terwilliger	12.00	6.00	3.50
35	Dave Jolly	12.00	6.00	3.50
36	Leo Kiely	12.00	6.00	3.50
37	*Joe Cunningham*	12.00	6.00	3.50
38	Bob Turley	15.00	7.50	4.50
39	Bill Glynn	12.00	6.00	3.50
40	Don Hoak	12.00	6.00	3.50
41	Chuck Stobbs	12.00	6.00	3.50
42	Windy McCall	12.00	6.00	3.50
43	Harvey Haddix	12.00	6.00	3.50
44	Corky Valentine	12.00	6.00	3.50
45	Hank Sauer	12.00	6.00	3.50
46	Ted Kazanski	12.00	6.00	3.50
47	Hank Aaron	290.00	125.00	80.00
48	Bob Kennedy	12.00	6.00	3.50
49	J.W. Porter	12.00	6.00	3.50
50	Jackie Robinson	245.00	110.00	65.00
51	Jim Hughes	12.00	6.00	3.50
52	Bill Tremel	12.00	6.00	3.50
53	Bill Taylor	12.00	6.00	3.50
54	Lou Limmer	12.00	6.00	3.50
55	"Rip" Repulski	12.00	6.00	3.50
56	Ray Jablonski	12.00	6.00	3.50
57	*Billy O'Dell*	12.00	6.00	3.50
58	Jim Rivera	12.00	6.00	3.50
59	Gair Allie	12.00	6.00	3.50
60	Dean Stone	12.00	6.00	3.50
61	"Spook" Jacobs	12.00	6.00	3.50
62	Thornton Kipper	12.00	6.00	3.50
63	Joe Collins	12.00	6.00	3.50
64	*Gus Triandos*	12.00	6.00	3.50
65	Ray Boone	12.00	6.00	3.50
66	Ron Jackson	12.00	6.00	3.50
67	Wally Moon	12.00	6.00	3.50
68	Jim Davis	12.00	6.00	3.50
69	Ed Bailey	12.00	6.00	3.50
70	Al Rosen	15.00	7.50	4.50
71	Ruben Gomez	12.00	6.00	3.50
72	Karl Olson	12.00	6.00	3.50
73	Jack Shepard	12.00	6.00	3.50
74	Bob Borkowski	12.00	6.00	3.50
75	*Sandy Amoros*	20.00	10.00	6.00
76	Howie Pollet	12.00	6.00	3.50
77	Arnold Portocarrero	12.00	6.00	3.50
78	Gordon Jones	12.00	6.00	3.50
79	Danny Schell	12.00	6.00	3.50
80	Bob Grim	12.00	6.00	3.50
81	Gene Conley	12.00	6.00	3.50
82	Chuck Harmon	12.00	6.00	3.50
83	Tom Brewer	12.00	6.00	3.50
84	*Camilo Pascual*	15.00	7.50	4.50
85	*Don Mossi*	15.00	7.50	4.50
86	Bill Wilson	12.00	6.00	3.50
87	Frank House	12.00	6.00	3.50
88	*Bob Skinner*	12.00	6.00	3.50
89	*Joe Frazier*	12.00	6.00	3.50
90	*Karl Spooner*	12.00	6.00	3.50
91	Milt Bolling	12.00	6.00	3.50
92	*Don Zimmer*	25.00	12.50	7.50
93	Steve Bilko	12.00	6.00	3.50
94	Reno Bertoia	12.00	6.00	3.50
95	Preston Ward	12.00	6.00	3.50
96	Charlie Bishop	12.00	6.00	3.50
97	Carlos Paula	12.00	6.00	3.50
98	Johnny Riddle	12.00	6.00	3.50
99	Frank Leja	12.00	6.00	3.50
100	Monte Irvin	25.00	12.50	7.50
101	Johnny Gray	12.00	6.00	3.50
102	Wally Westlake	12.00	6.00	3.50
103	Charlie White	12.00	6.00	3.50
104	Jack Harshman	12.00	6.00	3.50
105	Chuck Diering	12.00	6.00	3.50
106	*Frank Sullivan*	12.00	6.00	3.50
107	Curt Roberts	12.00	6.00	3.50
108	Rube Walker	12.00	6.00	3.50
109	Ed Lopat	12.00	6.00	3.50
110	Gus Zernial	12.00	6.00	3.50
111	Bob Milliken	12.00	6.00	3.50
112	Nelson King	12.00	6.00	3.50
113	Harry Brecheen	12.00	6.00	3.50
114	Lou Ortiz	12.00	6.00	3.50
115	Ellis Kinder	12.00	6.00	3.50
116	Tom Hurd	12.00	6.00	3.50
117	Mel Roach	12.00	6.00	3.50
118	Bob Purkey	12.00	6.00	3.50
119	Bob Lennon	12.00	6.00	3.50
120	Ted Kluszewski	30.00	15.00	9.00
121	Bill Renna	12.00	6.00	3.50
122	Carl Sawatski	12.00	6.00	3.50
123	*Sandy Koufax*	675.00	335.00	200.00
124	*Harmon Killebrew*	225.00	112.00	67.00
125	*Ken Boyer*	60.00	30.00	18.00
126	*Dick Hall*	12.00	6.00	3.50
127	*Dale Long*	12.00	6.00	3.50
128	Ted Lepcio	12.00	6.00	3.50
129	Elvin Tappe	12.00	6.00	3.50
130	Mayo Smith	12.00	6.00	3.50
131	Grady Hatton	12.00	6.00	3.50
132	Bob Trice	12.00	6.00	3.50
133	Dave Hoskins	12.00	6.00	3.50
134	Joe Jay	12.00	6.00	3.50
135	Johnny O'Brien	12.00	6.00	3.50
136	"Bunky" Stewart	12.00	6.00	3.50
137	Harry Elliott	12.00	6.00	3.50
138	Ray Herbert	12.00	6.00	3.50
139	Steve Kraly	12.00	6.00	3.50
140	Mel Parnell	12.00	6.00	3.50
141	Tom Wright	12.00	6.00	3.50
142	Jerry Lynch	12.00	6.00	3.50
143	Dick Schofield	12.00	6.00	3.50
144	Joe Amalfitano	12.00	6.00	3.50
145	Elmer Valo	12.00	6.00	3.50
146	*Dick Donovan*	12.00	6.00	3.50
147	Laurin Pepper	12.00	6.00	3.50
148	Hal Brown	12.00	6.00	3.50
149	Ray Crone	12.00	6.00	3.50
150	Mike Higgins	12.00	6.00	3.50
151	Red Kress	20.00	10.00	6.00
152	*Harry Agganis*	60.00	25.00	15.00
153	Bud Podbielan	20.00	10.00	6.00
154	Willie Miranda	20.00	10.00	6.00
155	Eddie Mathews	85.00	42.00	25.00
156	Joe Black	24.00	12.00	7.25
157	Bob Miller	20.00	10.00	6.00
158	Tom Carroll	20.00	10.00	6.00
159	Johnny Schmitz	20.00	10.00	6.00
160	Ray Narleski	20.00	10.00	6.00
161	*Chuck Tanner*	30.00	15.00	9.00
162	Joe Coleman	30.00	15.00	9.00
163	Faye Throneberry	30.00	15.00	9.00
164	*Roberto Clemente*	1750.	875.00	525.00
165	Don Johnson	30.00	15.00	9.00
166	Hank Bauer	40.00	20.00	12.00
167	Tom Casagrande	30.00	15.00	9.00
168	Duane Pillette	30.00	15.00	9.00
169	Bob Oldis	30.00	15.00	9.00
170	Jim Pearce	30.00	15.00	9.00
171	Dick Brodowski	30.00	15.00	9.00
172	Frank Baumholtz	30.00	15.00	9.00
173	Bob Kline	30.00	15.00	9.00
174	Rudy Minarcin	30.00	15.00	9.00
175	Not issued			
176	Norm Zauchin	30.00	15.00	9.00
177	Jim Robertson	30.00	15.00	9.00
178	Bobby Adams	30.00	15.00	9.00
179	Jim Bolger	30.00	15.00	9.00
180	Clem Labine	35.00	17.50	10.50
181	Roy McMillan	30.00	15.00	9.00
182	Humberto Robinson	30.00	15.00	9.00
183	Tony Jacobs	30.00	15.00	9.00
184	Harry Perkowski	30.00	15.00	9.00
185	Don Ferrarese	30.00	15.00	9.00
186	Not issued			
187	Gil Hodges	130.00	65.00	39.00
188	Charlie Silvera	35.00	17.50	10.50
189	Phil Rizzuto	125.00	62.00	37.00
190	Gene Woodling	37.50	18.50	11.00
191	Ed Stanky	30.00	15.00	9.00
192	Jim Delsing	30.00	15.00	9.00
193	Johnny Sain	35.00	17.50	10.50
194	Willie Mays	425.00	200.00	125.00
195	Ed Roebuck	30.00	15.00	9.00
196	Gale Wade	30.00	15.00	9.00
197	Al Smith	30.00	15.00	9.00
198	Yogi Berra	175.00	90.00	45.00
199	Bert Hamric	30.00	15.00	9.00
200	Jack Jensen	32.50	16.00	9.75
201	Sherman Lollar	30.00	15.00	9.00
202	Jim Owens	30.00	15.00	9.00
203	Not issued			
204	Frank Smith	30.00	15.00	9.00
205	Gene Freese	30.00	15.00	9.00
206	Pete Daley	30.00	15.00	9.00
207	Bill Consolo	30.00	15.00	9.00
208	Ray Moore	30.00	15.00	9.00
209	Not issued			
210	Duke Snider	375.00	165.00	90.00

1955 Topps Doubleheaders

This set is a throwback to the 1911 T201 Mecca Double Folders. The cards are perforated through the middle, allowing them to be folded. Open, there is a color painting of a player set against a stadium background. When folded, a different player and stadium appears; both players share the same lower legs and feet. Backs have abbreviated career histories and stats. Placed side by side in reverse numerical order, the backgrounds form a continuous stadium scene. When open the cards measure 2-1/16" x 4-7/8". The 66 cards in the set mean 132 total players, all of whom also appeared in the lower numbers of the regular 1955 Topps set.

		NM	EX	VG
Complete Set (66):		3000.	1500.	900.00
Common Player:		32.50	16.00	9.75
1-2	Al Rosen, Chuck Diering	35.00	17.50	10.50
3-4	Monte Irvin, Russ Kemmerer	55.00	27.00	16.50
5-6	Ted Kazanski, Gordon Jones	35.00	17.50	10.50
7-8	Bill Taylor, Billy O'Dell	35.00	17.50	10.50
9-10	J.W. Porter, Thornton Kipper	35.00	17.50	10.50
11-12	Curt Roberts, Arnie Portocarrero	35.00	17.50	10.50
13-14	Wally Westlake, Frank House	35.00	17.50	10.50
15-16	Rube Walker, Lou Limmer	35.00	17.50	10.50
17-18	Dean Stone, Charlie White	35.00	17.50	10.50
19-20	Karl Spooner, Jim Hughes	35.00	17.50	10.50
21-22	Bill Skowron, Frank Sullivan	45.00	22.00	13.50
23-24	Jack Shepard, Stan Hack	35.00	17.50	10.50
25-26	Jackie Robinson, Don Hoak	325.00	162.00	97.00
27-28	Dusty Rhodes, Jim Davis	35.00	17.50	10.50
29-30	Vic Power, Ed Bailey	35.00	17.50	10.50
31-32	Howie Pollet, Ernie Banks	145.00	72.00	43.00
33-34	Jim Pendleton, Gene Conley	35.00	17.50	10.50
35-36	Karl Olson, Andy Carey	35.00	17.50	10.50
37-38	Wally Moon, Joe Cunningham	35.00	17.50	10.50
39-40	Fred Marsh, "Jake" Thies	35.00	17.50	10.50
41-42	Ed Lopat, Harvey Haddix	35.00	17.50	10.50
43-44	Len Kiely, Chuck Stobbs	35.00	17.50	10.50
45-46	Al Kaline, "Corky" Valentine	300.00	150.00	90.00
47-48	"Spook" Jacobs, Johnny Gray	35.00	17.50	10.50
49-50	Ron Jackson, Jim Finigan	35.00	17.50	10.50
51-52	Ray Jablonski, Bob Keegan	35.00	17.50	10.50
53-54	Billy Herman, Sandy Amoros	35.00	17.50	10.50
55-56	Chuck Harmon, Bob Skinner	35.00	17.50	10.50
57-58	Dick Hall, Bob Grim	35.00	17.50	10.50
59-60	Bill Glynn, Bob Miller	35.00	17.50	10.50
61-62	Billy Gardner, John Hetki	35.00	17.50	10.50
63-64	Bob Borkowski, Bob Turley	35.00	17.50	10.50
65-66	Joe Collins, Jack Harshman	35.00	17.50	10.50
67-68	Jim Hegan, Jack Parks	35.00	17.50	10.50
69-70	Ted Williams, Hal Smith	400.00	200.00	120.00
71-72	Gair Allie, Grady Hatton	35.00	17.50	10.50
73-74	Jerry Lynch, Harry Brecheen	35.00	17.50	10.50
75-76	Tom Wright, "Bunky" Stewart	35.00	17.50	10.50
77-78	Dave Hoskins, Ed McGhee	35.00	17.50	10.50
79-80	Roy Sievers, Art Fowler	35.00	17.50	10.50
81-82	Danny Schell, Gus Triandos	35.00	17.50	10.50
83-84	Joe Frazier, Don Mossi	35.00	17.50	10.50
85-86	Elmer Valo, Hal Brown	35.00	17.50	10.50
87-88	Bob Kennedy, "Windy" McCall	35.00	17.50	10.50
89-90	Ruben Gomez, Jim Rivera	35.00	17.50	10.50
91-92	Lou Ortiz, Milt Bolling	35.00	17.50	10.50
93-94	Carl Sawatski, Elvin Tappe	35.00	17.50	10.50
95-96	Dave Jolly, Bobby Hofman	35.00	17.50	10.50
97-98	Preston Ward, Don Zimmer	35.00	17.50	10.50
99-100	Bill Renna, Dick Groat	35.00	17.50	10.50
101-102	Bill Wilson, Bill Tremel	35.00	17.50	10.50
103-104	Hank Sauer, Camilo Pascual	35.00	17.50	10.50
105-106	Hank Aaron, Ray Herbert	350.00	175.00	105.00
107-108	Alex Grammas, Tom Qualters	35.00	17.50	10.50
109-110	Hal Newhouser, Charlie Bishop	55.00	27.00	16.50
111-112	Harmon Killebrew, John Podres	250.00	125.00	75.00
113-114	Ray Boone, Bob Purkey	35.00	17.50	10.50
115-116	Dale Long, Ferris Fain	35.00	17.50	10.50
117-118	Steve Bilko, Bob Milliken	35.00	17.50	10.50
119-120	Mel Parnell, Tom Hurd	35.00	17.50	10.50
121-122	Ted Kluszewski, Jim Owens	35.00	17.50	10.50
123-124	Gus Zernial, Bob Trice	35.00	17.50	10.50
125-126	"Rip" Repulski, Ted Lepcio	35.00	17.50	10.50
127-128	Warren Spahn, Tom Brewer	160.00	80.00	48.00
129-130	Jim Gilliam, Ellis Kinder	35.00	17.50	10.50
131-132	Herm Wehmeier, Wayne Terwilliger	35.00	17.50	10.50

1955 Topps Hocus Focus

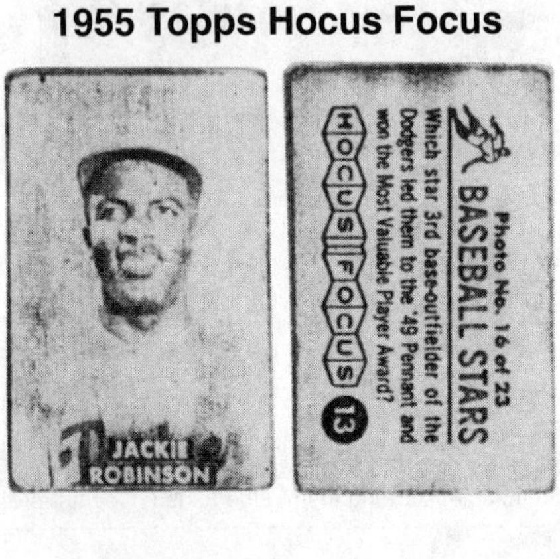

This set is a direct descendant of the 1948 "Topps Magic Photo" issue. Again, the baseball players were part of a larger overall series covering several topical areas. The cards, 7/8 x 1-3/8", state on the back that they are a series of 23, though only 14 are known. The photos on these cards were developed by wetting the card's surface and exposing to light. Prices below are for cards with well-developed pictures. Cards with poorly developed photos are worth significantly less.

		NM	EX	VG
Common Player:		85.00	42.00	25.00
1	Babe Ruth	950.00	475.00	285.00
2	Unknown			
3	Dick Groat	125.00	62.00	37.00
4	Unknown			
5	Unknown (Hank Sauer)	85.00	42.00	25.00
6	"Dusty" Rhodes	85.00	42.00	25.00
7	Ted Williams	750.00	375.00	225.00
8	Harvey Haddix	85.00	42.00	25.00
9	Ray Boone	85.00	42.00	25.00
10	Unknown			
11	Unknown			
12	Warren Spahn	275.00	137.00	82.00
13	Jim Rivera	85.00	42.00	25.00
14	Ted Kluszewski	195.00	97.00	58.00
15	Gus Zernial	85.00	42.00	25.00
16	Jackie Robinson	800.00	400.00	240.00
17	Unknown			
18	Johnny Schmitz	85.00	42.00	25.00
19	Unknown			
20	Karl Spooner	95.00	47.00	28.00
21	Ed Mathews	300.00	150.00	90.00
22	Unknown			
23	Unknown			

1955 Topps Test Stamps

An extremely rare and enigmatic test issue, only a handful of specimens have been cataloged to date. The stamps are the same size as Topps' 1955 card issue and have a blank, gummed back. Most of the specimens currently known are imperforate along one of the sides. All of the known examples have counterparts in the regular set which range from card #6 through 108. The unnumbered stamps are checklisted here alphabetically.

		NM	EX	VG
Common Player:		350.00	175.00	105.00
(1)	Joe Cunningham	350.00	175.00	105.00
(2)	Jim Davis	350.00	175.00	105.00
(3)	Chuck Diering	350.00	175.00	105.00
(4)	Ruben Gomez	350.00	175.00	105.00
(5)	Alex Grammas	350.00	175.00	105.00
(6)	Stan Hack	350.00	175.00	105.00
(7)	Harvey Haddix	350.00	175.00	105.00
(8)	Bobby Hofman	350.00	175.00	105.00
(9)	Dave Jolly	350.00	175.00	105.00
(10)	Ted Kazanski	350.00	175.00	105.00
(11)	Don Mossi	350.00	175.00	105.00
(12)	Jim Pendleton	350.00	175.00	105.00
(13)	Bob Skinner	350.00	175.00	105.00
(14)	Bill Skowron	400.00	200.00	120.00
(15)	Karl Spooner	375.00	185.00	110.00
(16)	Rube Walker	375.00	185.00	110.00
(17)	Charlie White	350.00	175.00	105.00

1956 Topps

This 340-card set is quite similar in design to the 1955 Topps set, again using both a portrait and an "action" picture. Some portraits are the same as those used in 1955 (and even 1954). Innovations found in the 1956 Topps set of 2-5/8" x 3-3/4" cards include team cards introduced as part of a regular set. Additionally, there are two unnumbered checklist cards (the complete set price quoted below does not include the checklist cards). Finally, there are cards of the two league presidents, William Harridge and Warren Giles. On the backs, a three-panel cartoon depicts big moments from the player's career while biographical information appears above the cartoon and the statistics below. Card backs for numbers 1-180 can be found with either white or grey cardboard. Some dealers charge a premium for grey backs (#'s 1-100) and white backs (#'s 101-180).

		NM	EX	VG
Complete Set (340):		5750.	2750.	1750.
Common Player (1-100):		8.00	4.00	2.50
Common Player (101-180):		9.00	4.50	2.75
Common Player (181-260):		12.00	6.00	3.50
Common Player (261-340):		9.00	4.50	2.75
1	William Harridge	90.00	35.00	22.00
2	Warren Giles	40.00	10.00	6.00
3	Elmer Valo	8.00	4.00	2.50
4	Carlos Paula	8.00	4.00	2.50
5	Ted Williams	325.00	160.00	97.00
6	Ray Boone	8.00	4.00	2.50
7	Ron Negray	8.00	4.00	2.50
8	Walter Alston	40.00	20.00	12.00
9	Ruben Gomez	8.00	4.00	2.50
10	Warren Spahn	70.00	35.00	21.00
11a	Cubs team (with date)	75.00	37.00	22.00
11b	Cubs team (no date, name centered)	25.00	12.50	7.50
11c	Cubs team (no date, name at left)	30.00	15.00	9.00
12	Andy Carey	12.50	6.25	3.75
13	Roy Face	8.00	4.00	2.50
14	Ken Boyer	18.00	9.00	5.50
15	Ernie Banks	80.00	40.00	24.00
16	*Hector Lopez*	8.00	4.00	2.50
17	Gene Conley	8.00	4.00	2.50
18	Dick Donovan	8.00	4.00	2.50
19	Chuck Diering	8.00	4.00	2.50
20	Al Kaline	100.00	50.00	30.00
21	Joe Collins	8.00	4.00	2.50
22	Jim Finigan	8.00	4.00	2.50
23	Freddie Marsh	8.00	4.00	2.50
24	Dick Groat	8.00	4.00	2.50
25	Ted Kluszewski	24.00	12.00	7.25
26	Grady Hatton	8.00	4.00	2.50
27	Nelson Burbrink	8.00	4.00	2.50
28	Bobby Hofman	8.00	4.00	2.50
29	Jack Harshman	8.00	4.00	2.50
30	Jackie Robinson	175.00	87.00	52.00
31	Hank Aaron	235.00	90.00	50.00
32	Frank House	8.00	4.00	2.50
33	Roberto Clemente	300.00	150.00	90.00
34	Tom Brewer	8.00	4.00	2.50
35	Al Rosen	12.00	6.00	3.50
36	Rudy Minarcin	8.00	4.00	2.50
37	Alex Grammas	8.00	4.00	2.50
38	Bob Kennedy	8.00	4.00	2.50
39	Don Mossi	8.00	4.00	2.50
40	Bob Turley	11.00	5.50	3.25
41	Hank Sauer	8.00	4.00	2.50
42	Sandy Amoros	12.00	6.00	3.50
43	Ray Moore	8.00	4.00	2.50
44	"Windy" McCall	8.00	4.00	2.50
45	Gus Zernial	8.00	4.00	2.50
46	Gene Freese	8.00	4.00	2.50
47	Art Fowler	8.00	4.00	2.50
48	Jim Hegan	8.00	4.00	2.50
49	*Pedro Ramos*	8.00	4.00	2.50
50	"Dusty" Rhodes	8.00	4.00	2.50
51	Ernie Oravetz	8.00	4.00	2.50
52	Bob Grim	8.00	4.00	2.50
53	Arnold Portocarrero	8.00	4.00	2.50
54	Bob Keegan	8.00	4.00	2.50
55	Wally Moon	8.00	4.00	2.50
56	Dale Long	8.00	4.00	2.50
57	"Duke" Maas	8.00	4.00	2.50
58	Ed Roebuck	8.00	4.00	2.50
59	Jose Santiago	8.00	4.00	2.50
60	Mayo Smith	8.00	4.00	2.50
61	Bill Skowron	17.50	8.75	5.25
62	Hal Smith	8.00	4.00	2.50
63	*Roger Craig*	12.50	6.25	3.75
64	Luis Arroyo	8.00	4.00	2.50
65	Johnny O'Brien	8.00	4.00	2.50
66	Bob Speake	8.00	4.00	2.50
67	Vic Power	8.00	4.00	2.50
68	Chuck Stobbs	8.00	4.00	2.50
69	Chuck Tanner	8.00	4.00	2.50
70	Jim Rivera	8.00	4.00	2.50
71	Frank Sullivan	8.00	4.00	2.50
72a	Phillies team (with date)	65.00	32.00	19.50
72b	Phillies team (no date, name centered)	32.50	16.00	9.75
72c	Philadelphia Phillies (no date, name at left)	24.00	12.00	7.25
73	Wayne Terwilliger	8.00	4.00	2.50

74	Jim King	8.00	4.00	2.50
75	Roy Sievers	8.00	4.00	2.50
76	Ray Crone	8.00	4.00	2.50
77	Harvey Haddix	8.00	4.00	2.50
78	Herman Wehmeier	8.00	4.00	2.50
79	Sandy Koufax	250.00	125.00	75.00
80	Gus Triandos	8.00	4.00	2.50
81	Wally Westlake	8.00	4.00	2.50
82	Bill Renna	8.00	4.00	2.50
83	Karl Spooner	8.00	4.00	2.50
84	Babe Birrer	8.00	4.00	2.50
85a	Indians team (with date)	75.00	37.00	22.00
85b	Indians team (no date, name centered)	27.00	13.50	8.00
85c	Indians team (no date, name at left)	30.00	15.00	9.00
86	Ray Jablonski	8.00	4.00	2.50
87	Dean Stone	8.00	4.00	2.50
88	Johnny Kucks	8.00	4.00	2.50
89	Norm Zauchin	8.00	4.00	2.50
90a	Redlegs team (with date)	80.00	40.00	24.00
90b	Redlegs team (no date, name centered)	27.00	13.50	8.00
90c	Redlegs team (no date, name at left)	32.00	16.00	9.50
91	Gail Harris	8.00	4.00	2.50
92	Red Wilson	8.00	4.00	2.50
93	George Susce, Jr.	10.00	5.00	3.00
94	Ronnie Kline	10.00	5.00	3.00
95a	Braves Team (with date)	75.00	37.00	22.00
95b	Braves Team (no date, name centered)	40.00	20.00	12.00
95c	Braves Team (no date, name at left)	28.00	14.00	8.50
96	Bill Tremel	10.00	5.00	3.00
97	Jerry Lynch	10.00	5.00	3.00
98	Camilo Pascual	10.00	5.00	3.00
99	Don Zimmer	12.00	6.00	3.50
100a	Orioles team (with date)	75.00	37.00	22.00
100b	Orioles team (no date, name centered)	35.00	17.50	10.50
100c	Orioles team (no date, name at left)	28.00	14.00	8.50
101	Roy Campanella	135.00	67.00	40.00
102	Jim Davis	9.00	4.50	2.75
103	Willie Miranda	9.00	4.50	2.75
104	Bob Lennon	9.00	4.50	2.75
105	Al Smith	9.00	4.50	2.75
106	Joe Astroth	9.00	4.50	2.75
107	Eddie Mathews	55.00	27.00	16.50
108	Laurin Pepper	9.00	4.50	2.75
109	Enos Slaughter	35.00	17.50	10.50
110	Yogi Berra	125.00	62.00	37.00
111	Red Sox team	30.00	15.00	9.00
112	Dee Fondy	9.00	4.50	2.75
113	Phil Rizzuto	80.00	40.00	24.00
114	Jim Owens	9.00	4.50	2.75
115	Jackie Jensen	12.00	6.00	3.50
116	Eddie O'Brien	9.00	4.50	2.75
117	Virgil Trucks	9.00	4.50	2.75
118	Nellie Fox	35.00	17.50	10.50
119	*Larry Jackson*	9.00	4.50	2.75
120	Richie Ashburn	50.00	25.00	15.00
121	Pirates team	30.00	15.00	9.00
122	Willard Nixon	9.00	4.50	2.75
123	Roy McMillan	9.00	4.50	2.75
124	Don Kaiser	9.00	4.50	2.75
125	Minnie Minoso	24.00	12.00	7.25
126	Jim Brady	9.00	4.50	2.75
127	Willie Jones	9.00	4.50	2.75
128	Eddie Yost	9.00	4.50	2.75
129	Jake Martin	9.00	4.50	2.75
130	Willie Mays	275.00	135.00	82.00
131	Bob Roselli	9.00	4.50	2.75
132	Bobby Avila	9.00	4.50	2.75
133	Ray Narleski	9.00	4.50	2.75
134	Cardinals Team	30.00	15.00	9.00
135	Mickey Mantle	1100.	550.00	300.00
136	Johnny Logan	9.00	4.50	2.75
137	Al Silvera	9.00	4.50	2.75
138	Johnny Antonelli	9.00	4.50	2.75
139	Tommy Carroll	9.00	4.50	2.75
140	*Herb Score*	50.00	25.00	15.00
141	Joe Frazier	9.00	4.50	2.75
142	Gene Baker	9.00	4.50	2.75
143	Jim Piersall	9.00	4.50	2.75
144	Leroy Powell	9.00	4.50	2.75
145	Gil Hodges	45.00	22.00	13.50
146	Washington Nationals team	30.00	15.00	9.00
147	Earl Torgeson	9.00	4.50	2.75
148	Alvin Dark	12.00	6.00	3.50
149	Dixie Howell	9.00	4.50	2.75
150	Duke Snider	115.00	57.00	34.00
151	Spook Jacobs	9.00	4.50	2.75
152	Billy Hoeft	9.00	4.50	2.75
153	Frank Thomas	9.00	4.50	2.75
154	Dave Pope	9.00	4.50	2.75
155	Harvey Kuenn	15.00	7.50	4.50
156	Wes Westrum	9.00	4.50	2.75
157	Dick Brodowski	9.00	4.50	2.75
158	Wally Post	9.00	4.50	2.75
159	Clint Courtney	9.00	4.50	2.75
160	Billy Pierce	12.00	6.00	3.50
161	Joe DeMaestri	9.00	4.50	2.75
162	Gus Bell	9.00	4.50	2.75
163	Gene Woodling	16.00	8.00	4.75
164	Harmon Killebrew	90.00	45.00	27.00
165	Red Schoendienst	30.00	15.00	9.00
166	Dodgers Team	200.00	100.00	60.00
167	Harry Dorish	9.00	4.50	2.75
168	Sammy White	9.00	4.50	2.75
169	Bob Nelson	9.00	4.50	2.75
170	Bill Virdon	12.00	6.00	3.50
171	Jim Wilson	9.00	4.50	2.75
172	*Frank Torre*	9.00	4.50	2.75
173	Johnny Podres	15.00	7.50	4.50
174	Glen Gorbous	9.00	4.50	2.75
175	Del Crandall	9.00	4.50	2.75
176	Alex Kellner	9.00	4.50	2.75
177	Hank Bauer	20.00	10.00	6.00
178	Joe Black	12.00	6.00	3.50
179	Harry Chiti	9.00	4.50	2.75
180	Robin Roberts	40.00	20.00	12.00
181	Billy Martin	50.00	25.00	15.00
182	Paul Minner	12.00	6.00	3.50
183	Stan Lopata	12.00	6.00	3.50
184	Don Bessent	12.00	6.00	3.50
185	Bill Bruton	12.00	6.00	3.50
186	Ron Jackson	12.00	6.00	3.50
187	Early Wynn	45.00	22.00	13.50
188	White Sox team	40.00	20.00	12.00
189	Ned Garver	12.00	6.00	3.50
190	Carl Furillo	24.00	12.00	7.25
191	Frank Lary	12.00	6.00	3.50
192	Smoky Burgess	12.00	6.00	3.50
193	Wilmer Mizell	12.00	6.00	3.50
194	Monte Irvin	30.00	15.00	9.00
195	George Kell	28.00	14.00	8.50
196	Tom Poholsky	12.00	6.00	3.50
197	Granny Hamner	12.00	6.00	3.50
198	Ed Fitzgerald (Fitz Gerald)	12.00	6.00	3.50
199	Hank Thompson	12.00	6.00	3.50
200	Bob Feller	100.00	50.00	30.00
201	Rip Repulski	12.00	6.00	3.50
202	Jim Hearn	12.00	6.00	3.50
203	Bill Tuttle	12.00	6.00	3.50
204	Art Swanson	12.00	6.00	3.50
205	"Whitey" Lockman	12.00	6.00	3.50
206	Erv Palica	12.00	6.00	3.50
207	Jim Small	12.00	6.00	3.50
208	Elston Howard	24.00	12.00	7.25
209	Max Surkont	12.00	6.00	3.50
210	Mike Garcia	12.00	6.00	3.50
211	Murry Dickson	12.00	6.00	3.50
212	Johnny Temple	12.00	6.00	3.50
213	Tigers team	50.00	25.00	15.00
214	Bob Rush	12.00	6.00	3.50
215	Tommy Byrne	12.00	6.00	3.50
216	Jerry Schoonmaker	12.00	6.00	3.50
217	Billy Klaus	12.00	6.00	3.50
218	Joe Nuxall (Nuxhall)	12.00	6.00	3.50
219	Lew Burdette	12.00	6.00	3.50
220	Del Ennis	12.00	6.00	3.50
221	Bob Friend	12.00	6.00	3.50
222	Dave Philley	12.00	6.00	3.50
223	Randy Jackson	12.00	6.00	3.50
224	Bud Podbielan	12.00	6.00	3.50
225	Gil McDougald	20.00	10.00	6.00
226	Giants team	70.00	35.00	21.00
227	Russ Meyer	12.00	6.00	3.50
228	Mickey Vernon	12.00	6.00	3.50
229	Harry Brecheen	12.00	6.00	3.50
230	Chico Carrasquel	12.00	6.00	3.50
231	Bob Hale	12.00	6.00	3.50
232	Toby Atwell	12.00	6.00	3.50
233	Carl Erskine	20.00	10.00	6.00
234	Pete Runnels	12.00	6.00	3.50
235	Don Newcombe	20.00	10.00	6.00
236	Athletics Team	35.00	17.50	10.50
237	Jose Valdivielso	12.00	6.00	3.50
238	Walt Dropo	12.00	6.00	3.50
239	Harry Simpson	12.00	6.00	3.50
240	Whitey Ford	110.00	55.00	33.00
241	Don Mueller	12.00	6.00	3.50
242	Hershell Freeman	12.00	6.00	3.50
243	Sherman Lollar	12.00	6.00	3.50
244	Bob Buhl	12.00	6.00	3.50
245	Billy Goodman	12.00	6.00	3.50
246	Tom Gorman	12.00	6.00	3.50
247	Bill Sarni	12.00	6.00	3.50
248	Bob Porterfield	12.00	6.00	3.50
249	Johnny Klippstein	15.00	7.50	4.50
250	Larry Doby	30.00	15.00	9.00
251	Yankees team	200.00	100.00	60.00
252	Vernon Law	15.00	7.50	4.50
253	Irv Noren	15.00	7.50	4.50
254	George Crowe	15.00	7.50	4.50
255	Bob Lemon	30.00	15.00	9.00
256	Tom Hurd	15.00	7.50	4.50
257	Bobby Thomson	15.00	7.50	4.50
258	Art Ditmar	15.00	7.50	4.50
259	Sam Jones	15.00	7.50	4.50
260	Pee Wee Reese	100.00	50.00	30.00
261	Bobby Shantz	15.00	7.50	4.50
262	Howie Pollet	9.00	4.50	2.75
263	Bob Miller	9.00	4.50	2.75
264	Ray Monzant	9.00	4.50	2.75
265	Sandy Consuegra	9.00	4.50	2.75
266	Don Ferrarese	9.00	4.50	2.75
267	Bob Nieman	9.00	4.50	2.75
268	Dale Mitchell	9.00	4.50	2.75
269	Jack Meyer	9.00	4.50	2.75
270	Billy Loes	12.00	6.00	3.50
271	Foster Castleman	9.00	4.50	2.75
272	Danny O'Connell	9.00	4.50	2.75
273	Walker Cooper	9.00	4.50	2.75
274	Frank Baumholtz	9.00	4.50	2.75
275	Jim Greengrass	9.00	4.50	2.75
276	George Zuverink	9.00	4.50	2.75
277	Daryl Spencer	9.00	4.50	2.75
278	Chet Nichols	9.00	4.50	2.75
279	Johnny Groth	9.00	4.50	2.75
280	Jim Gilliam	15.00	7.50	4.50
281	Art Houtteman	9.00	4.50	2.75
282	Warren Hacker	9.00	4.50	2.75
283	Hal Smith	9.00	4.50	2.75
284	Ike Delock	9.00	4.50	2.75
285	Eddie Miksis	9.00	4.50	2.75
286	Bill Wight	9.00	4.50	2.75
287	Bobby Adams	9.00	4.50	2.75
288	Bob Cerv	27.50	13.50	8.25
289	Hal Jeffcoat	9.00	4.50	2.75
290	Curt Simmons	9.00	4.50	2.75
291	Frank Kellert	9.00	4.50	2.75
292	*Luis Aparicio*	120.00	60.00	36.00
293	Stu Miller	9.00	4.50	2.75
294	Ernie Johnson	9.00	4.50	2.75
295	Clem Labine	12.00	6.00	3.50
296	Andy Seminick	9.00	4.50	2.75
297	Bob Skinner	9.00	4.50	2.75
298	Johnny Schmitz	9.00	4.50	2.75
299	Charley Neal	25.00	12.50	7.50
300	Vic Wertz	9.00	4.50	2.75
301	Marv Grissom	9.00	4.50	2.75
302	Eddie Robinson	9.00	4.50	2.75
303	Jim Dyck	9.00	4.50	2.75
304	Frank Malzone	17.50	8.75	5.25
305	Brooks Lawrence	9.00	4.50	2.75
306	Curt Roberts	9.00	4.50	2.75
307	Hoyt Wilhelm	32.50	16.00	9.75
308	Chuck Harmon	9.00	4.50	2.75
309	*Don Blasingame*	9.00	4.50	2.75
310	Steve Gromek	9.00	4.50	2.75
311	Hal Naragon	9.00	4.50	2.75
312	Andy Pafko	9.00	4.50	2.75
313	Gene Stephens	9.00	4.50	2.75
314	Hobie Landrith	9.00	4.50	2.75
315	Milt Bolling	9.00	4.50	2.75
316	Jerry Coleman	9.00	4.50	2.75
317	Al Aber	9.00	4.50	2.75
318	Fred Hatfield	9.00	4.50	2.75
319	Jack Crimian	9.00	4.50	2.75
320	Joe Adcock	9.00	4.50	2.75
321	Jim Konstanty	12.00	6.00	3.50
322	Karl Olson	9.00	4.50	2.75
323	Willard Schmidt	9.00	4.50	2.75
324	"Rocky" Bridges	9.00	4.50	2.75
325	Don Liddle	9.00	4.50	2.75
326	Connie Johnson	9.00	4.50	2.75
327	Bob Wiesler	9.00	4.50	2.75
328	Preston Ward	9.00	4.50	2.75
329	Lou Berberet	9.00	4.50	2.75
330	Jim Busby	9.00	4.50	2.75
331	Dick Hall	9.00	4.50	2.75
332	Don Larsen	50.00	25.00	15.00
333	Rube Walker	9.00	4.50	2.75
334	Bob Miller	9.00	4.50	2.75
335	Don Hoak	9.00	4.50	2.75
336	Ellis Kinder	9.00	4.50	2.75
337	Bobby Morgan	9.00	4.50	2.75
338	Jim Delsing	9.00	4.50	2.75
339	Rance Pless	9.00	4.50	2.75
340	Mickey McDermott	55.00	15.00	8.00
----	Checklist 1/3	235.00	115.00	70.00
----	Checklist 2/4	275.00	135.00	82.00

1956 Topps Hocus Focus

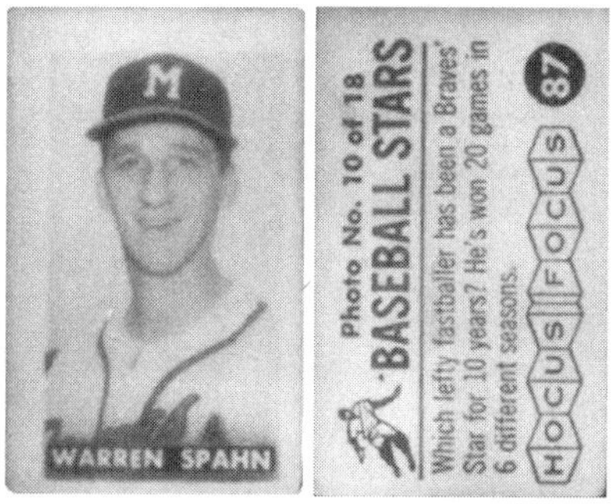

Following its 1955 issue with a somewhat larger format (1" x 1-5/8") the following year, the baseball players in this set are part of a larger overall series covering several topical areas. Cards backs specify an issue of 18 baseball stars. The black-and-white photos on these cards were developed by wetting the card's surface and exposing to light. Prices below are for cards with well-developed pictures. Cards with poorly developed photos are worth significantly less.

		NM	EX	VG
Complete Set (18):		2800.	1400.	850.00
Common Player:		90.00	45.00	27.00
1	Dick Groat	195.00	97.00	58.00
2	Ed Lopat	125.00	62.00	37.00
3	Hank Sauer	90.00	45.00	27.00
4	"Dusty" Rhodes	90.00	45.00	27.00
5	Ted Williams	850.00	425.00	255.00
6	Harvey Haddix	100.00	50.00	30.00
7	Ray Boone	90.00	45.00	27.00
8	Al Rosen	95.00	47.00	28.00
9	Mayo Smith	90.00	45.00	27.00
10	Warren Spahn	275.00	137.00	82.00
11	Jim Rivera	90.00	45.00	27.00
12	Ted Kluszewski	195.00	97.00	58.00
13	Gus Zernial	90.00	45.00	27.00
14	Jackie Robinson	700.00	350.00	210.00
15	Hal Smith	90.00	45.00	27.00
16	Johnny Schmitz	90.00	45.00	27.00
17	"Spook" Jacobs	90.00	45.00	27.00
18	Mel Parnell	90.00	45.00	27.00

Check lists with card numbers in parentheses ( ) indicates the numbers do not appear on the cards.

1956 Topps Pins

One of Topps first specialty issues, the 60-pin set of ballplayers issued in 1956 contains a high percentage of big-name stars which, combined with the scarcity of the pins, makes collecting a complete set extremely challenging. Compounding the situation is the fact that some pins are seen far less often than others, though the reason is unknown. Chuck Stobbs, Hector Lopez and Chuck Diering are unaccountably scarce. Measuring 1-1/8" in diameter, the pins utilize the same portraits found on 1956 Topps baseball cards. The photos are set against a solid color background.

		NM	EX	VG
Complete Set (60):		3000.	1500.	900.00
Common Player:		18.00	9.00	5.50
(1)	Hank Aaron	125.00	62.00	37.00
(2)	Sandy Amoros	24.00	12.00	7.25
(3)	Luis Arroyo	20.00	10.00	6.00
(4)	Ernie Banks	60.00	30.00	18.00
(5)	Yogi Berra	80.00	40.00	24.00
(6)	Joe Black	20.00	10.00	6.00
(7)	Ray Boone	20.00	10.00	6.00
(8)	Ken Boyer	22.00	11.00	6.50
(9)	Joe Collins	20.00	10.00	6.00
(10)	Gene Conley	20.00	10.00	6.00
(11)	Chuck Diering	225.00	112.00	67.00
(12)	Dick Donovan	20.00	10.00	6.00
(13)	Jim Finigan	20.00	10.00	6.00
(14)	Art Fowler	20.00	10.00	6.00
(15)	Ruben Gomez	20.00	10.00	6.00
(16)	Dick Groat	20.00	10.00	6.00
(17)	Harvey Haddix	20.00	10.00	6.00
(18)	Jack Harshman	20.00	10.00	6.00
(19)	Grady Hatton	20.00	10.00	6.00
(20)	Jim Hegan	20.00	10.00	6.00
(21)	Gil Hodges	45.00	22.00	13.50
(22)	Bobby Hofman	20.00	10.00	6.00
(23)	Frank House	20.00	10.00	6.00
(24)	Jackie Jensen	20.00	10.00	6.00
(25)	Al Kaline	65.00	32.00	19.50
(26)	Bob Kennedy	20.00	10.00	6.00
(27)	Ted Kluszewski	35.00	17.50	10.50
(28)	Dale Long	20.00	10.00	6.00
(29)	Hector Lopez	200.00	100.00	60.00
(30)	Ed Mathews	60.00	30.00	18.00
(31)	Willie Mays	125.00	62.00	37.00
(32)	Roy McMillan	20.00	10.00	6.00
(33)	Willie Miranda	20.00	10.00	6.00
(34)	Wally Moon	20.00	10.00	6.00
(35)	Don Mossi	20.00	10.00	6.00
(36)	Ron Negray	20.00	10.00	6.00
(37)	Johnny O'Brien	20.00	10.00	6.00
(38)	Carlos Paula	20.00	10.00	6.00
(39)	Vic Power	20.00	10.00	6.00
(40)	Jim Rivera	20.00	10.00	6.00
(41)	Phil Rizzuto	75.00	37.00	22.00
(42)	Jackie Robinson	125.00	62.00	37.00
(43)	Al Rosen	20.00	10.00	6.00
(44)	Hank Sauer	20.00	10.00	6.00
(45)	Roy Sievers	20.00	10.00	6.00
(46)	Bill Skowron	20.00	10.00	6.00
(47)	Al Smith	20.00	10.00	6.00
(48)	Hal Smith	20.00	10.00	6.00
(49)	Mayo Smith	20.00	10.00	6.00
(50)	Duke Snider	80.00	40.00	24.00
(51)	Warren Spahn	60.00	30.00	18.00
(52)	Karl Spooner	20.00	10.00	6.00
(53)	Chuck Stobbs	175.00	87.00	52.00
(54)	Frank Sullivan	20.00	10.00	6.00
(55)	Bill Tremel	20.00	10.00	6.00
(56)	Gus Triandos	20.00	10.00	6.00
(57)	Bob Turley	25.00	12.50	7.50
(58)	Herman Wehmeier	20.00	10.00	6.00
(59)	Ted Williams	150.00	75.00	45.00
(60)	Gus Zernial	20.00	10.00	6.00

1957 Topps

For 1957, Topps reduced the size of its cards to the now-standard 2-1/2" x 3-1/2." Set size was increased to 407 cards. Another change came in the form of the use of real color photographs as opposed to the hand-colored black and whites of previous years. For the first time since 1954, there were also cards with more than one player. The two, "Dodger Sluggers" and "Yankees' Power Hitters" began a trend toward the increased use of multiple-player cards. Another first-time innovation, found on the backs, is complete players statistics. The scarce cards in the set are not the highest numbers, but rather numbers 265-352. Four unnumbered checklist cards were issued along with the set. They are quite expensive and are not included in the complete set prices quoted below.

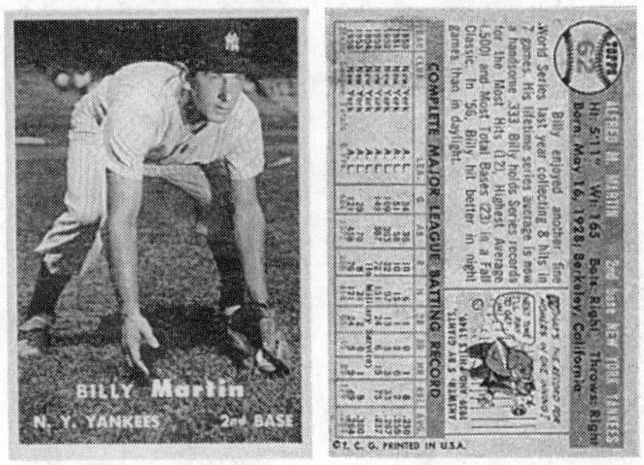

		NM	EX	VG
Complete Set (407):		6500.	3000.	1650.
Common Player (1-88):		8.00	4.00	2.50
Common Player (89-264):		7.00	3.50	2.00
Common Player (265-352):		17.00	8.50	5.00
Common Player (353-407):		7.00	3.50	2.00
1	Ted Williams	450.00	175.00	100.00
2	Yogi Berra	115.00	57.00	34.00
3	Dale Long	8.00	4.00	2.50
4	Johnny Logan	8.00	4.00	2.50
5	Sal Maglie	9.00	4.50	2.75
6	Hector Lopez	8.00	4.00	2.50
7	Luis Aparicio	32.00	16.00	9.50
8	Don Mossi	8.00	4.00	2.50
9	Johnny Temple	8.00	4.00	2.50
10	Willie Mays	195.00	97.00	58.00
11	George Zuverink	8.00	4.00	2.50
12	Dick Groat	8.00	4.00	2.50
13	Wally Burnette	8.00	4.00	2.50
14	Bob Nieman	8.00	4.00	2.50
15	Robin Roberts	33.00	16.50	10.00
16	Walt Moryn	8.00	4.00	2.50
17	Billy Gardner	8.00	4.00	2.50
18	*Don Drysdale*	175.00	87.00	52.00
19	Bob Wilson	8.00	4.00	2.50
20	Hank Aaron (photo reversed)	190.00	95.00	57.00
21	Frank Sullivan	8.00	4.00	2.50
22	Jerry Snyder (photo actually Ed Fitz Gerald)	8.00	4.00	2.50
23	Sherman Lollar	8.00	4.00	2.50
24	*Bill Mazeroski*	60.00	30.00	18.00
25	Whitey Ford	70.00	35.00	21.00
26	Bob Boyd	8.00	4.00	2.50
27	Ted Kazanski	8.00	4.00	2.50
28	Gene Conley	8.00	4.00	2.50
29	*Whitey Herzog*	24.00	12.00	7.25
30	Pee Wee Reese	60.00	30.00	18.00
31	Ron Northey	8.00	4.00	2.50
32	Hersh Freeman	8.00	4.00	2.50
33	Jim Small	8.00	4.00	2.50
34	Tom Sturdivant	8.00	4.00	2.50
35	*Frank Robinson*	180.00	90.00	54.00
36	Bob Grim	8.00	4.00	2.50
37	Frank Torre	8.00	4.00	2.50
38	Nellie Fox	30.00	15.00	9.00
39	Al Worthington	8.00	4.00	2.50
40	Early Wynn	30.00	15.00	9.00
41	Hal Smith	8.00	4.00	2.50
42	Dee Fondy	8.00	4.00	2.50
43	Connie Johnson	8.00	4.00	2.50
44	Joe DeMaestri	8.00	4.00	2.50
45	Carl Furillo	18.00	9.00	5.50
46	Bob Miller	8.00	4.00	2.50
47	Don Blasingame	8.00	4.00	2.50
48	Bill Bruton	8.00	4.00	2.50
49	Daryl Spencer	8.00	4.00	2.50
50	Herb Score	14.00	7.00	4.25
51	Clint Courtney	8.00	4.00	2.50
52	Lee Walls	8.00	4.00	2.50
53	Clem Labine	10.00	5.00	3.00
54	Elmer Valo	8.00	4.00	2.50
55	Ernie Banks	100.00	50.00	30.00
56	Dave Sisler	8.00	4.00	2.50
57	Jim Lemon	8.00	4.00	2.50
58	Ruben Gomez	8.00	4.00	2.50
59	Dick Williams	9.00	4.50	2.75
60	Billy Hoeft	8.00	4.00	2.50
61	Dusty Rhodes	8.00	4.00	2.50
62	Billy Martin	35.00	17.50	10.50
63	Ike Delock	8.00	4.00	2.50
64	Pete Runnels	8.00	4.00	2.50
65	Wally Moon	8.00	4.00	2.50
66	Brooks Lawrence	8.00	4.00	2.50
67	Chico Carrasquel	8.00	4.00	2.50
68	Ray Crone	8.00	4.00	2.50
69	Roy McMillan	8.00	4.00	2.50
70	Richie Ashburn	35.00	17.50	10.50
71	Murry Dickson	8.00	4.00	2.50
72	Bill Tuttle	8.00	4.00	2.50
73	George Crowe	8.00	4.00	2.50
74	Vito Valentinetti	8.00	4.00	2.50
75	Jim Piersall	10.00	5.00	3.00
76	Roberto Clemente	265.00	110.00	60.00
77	Paul Foytack	8.00	4.00	2.50
78	Vic Wertz	8.00	4.00	2.50
79	*Lindy McDaniel*	12.00	6.00	3.50
80	Gil Hodges	40.00	20.00	12.00
81	Herm Wehmeier	8.00	4.00	2.50
82	Elston Howard	17.00	8.50	5.00
83	Lou Skizas	8.00	4.00	2.50
84	Moe Drabowsky	8.00	4.00	2.50
85	Larry Doby	25.00	12.50	7.50
86	Bill Sarni	8.00	4.00	2.50
87	Tom Gorman	8.00	4.00	2.50
88	Harvey Kuenn	8.00	4.00	2.50
89	Roy Sievers	7.00	3.50	2.00
90	Warren Spahn	60.00	30.00	18.00
91	Mack Burk	7.00	3.50	2.00
92	Mickey Vernon	7.00	3.50	2.00
93	Hal Jeffcoat	7.00	3.50	2.00
94	Bobby Del Greco	7.00	3.50	2.00
95	Mickey Mantle	900.00	450.00	250.00
96	*Hank Aguirre*	7.00	3.50	2.00
97	Yankees team	72.00	36.00	22.00
98	Al Dark	7.00	3.50	2.00
99	Bob Keegan	7.00	3.50	2.00
100	League Presidents (Warren Giles, William Harridge)	13.00	6.50	4.00
101	Chuck Stobbs	7.00	3.50	2.00
102	Ray Boone	7.00	3.50	2.00
103	Joe Nuxhall	7.00	3.50	2.00
104	Hank Foiles	7.00	3.50	2.00
105	Johnny Antonelli	7.00	3.50	2.00
106	Ray Moore	7.00	3.50	2.00
107	Jim Rivera	7.00	3.50	2.00
108	Tommy Byrne	7.00	3.50	2.00
109	Hank Thompson	7.00	3.50	2.00
110	Bill Virdon	7.00	3.50	2.00
111	Hal Smith	7.00	3.50	2.00
112	Tom Brewer	7.00	3.50	2.00
113	Wilmer Mizell	7.00	3.50	2.00
114	Braves Team	18.00	9.00	5.50
115	Jim Gilliam	12.00	6.00	3.50
116	Mike Fornieles	7.00	3.50	2.00
117	Joe Adcock	7.00	3.50	2.00
118	Bob Porterfield	7.00	3.50	2.00
119	Stan Lopata	7.00	3.50	2.00
120	Bob Lemon	24.00	12.00	7.25
121	*Cletis Boyer*	20.00	10.00	6.00
122	Ken Boyer	12.00	6.00	3.50
123	Steve Ridzik	7.00	3.50	2.00
124	Dave Philley	7.00	3.50	2.00
125	Al Kaline	90.00	45.00	27.00
126	Bob Wiesler	7.00	3.50	2.00
127	Bob Buhl	7.00	3.50	2.00
128	Ed Bailey	7.00	3.50	2.00
129	Saul Rogovin	7.00	3.50	2.00
130	Don Newcombe	15.00	7.50	4.50
131	Milt Bolling	7.00	3.50	2.00
132	Art Ditmar	7.00	3.50	2.00
133	Del Crandall	7.00	3.50	2.00
134	Don Kaiser	7.00	3.50	2.00
135	Bill Skowron	17.50	8.75	5.25
136	Jim Hegan	7.00	3.50	2.00
137	Bob Rush	7.00	3.50	2.00
138	Minnie Minoso	17.50	8.75	5.25
139	Lou Kretlow	7.00	3.50	2.00
140	Frank J. Thomas	7.00	3.50	2.00
141	Al Aber	7.00	3.50	2.00
142	Charley Thompson	7.00	3.50	2.00
143	Andy Pafko	7.00	3.50	2.00
144	Ray Narleski	7.00	3.50	2.00
145	Al Smith	7.00	3.50	2.00
146	Don Ferrarese	7.00	3.50	2.00
147	Al Walker	7.00	3.50	2.00
148	Don Mueller	7.00	3.50	2.00
149	Bob Kennedy	7.00	3.50	2.00
150	Bob Friend	7.00	3.50	2.00
151	Willie Miranda	7.00	3.50	2.00
152	Jack Harshman	7.00	3.50	2.00
153	Karl Olson	7.00	3.50	2.00
154	Red Schoendienst	24.00	12.00	7.25
155	Jim Brosnan	7.00	3.50	2.00
156	Gus Triandos	7.00	3.50	2.00
157	Wally Post	7.00	3.50	2.00
158	Curt Simmons	7.00	3.50	2.00
159	Solly Drake	7.00	3.50	2.00
160	Billy Pierce	7.00	3.50	2.00
161	Pirates team	15.00	7.50	4.50
162	Jack Meyer	7.00	3.50	2.00
163	Sammy White	7.00	3.50	2.00
164	Tommy Carroll	7.00	3.50	2.00
165	Ted Kluszewski	50.00	25.00	15.00
166	Roy Face	7.00	3.50	2.00
167	Vic Power	7.00	3.50	2.00
168	Frank Lary	7.00	3.50	2.00
169	Herb Plews	7.00	3.50	2.00
170	Duke Snider	100.00	50.00	30.00
171	Red Sox team	14.00	7.00	4.25
172	Gene Woodling	7.00	3.50	2.00
173	Roger Craig	9.00	4.50	2.75
174	Willie Jones	7.00	3.50	2.00
175	Don Larsen	20.00	10.00	6.00
176	Gene Baker	7.00	3.50	2.00
177	Eddie Yost	7.00	3.50	2.00
178	Don Bessent	7.00	3.50	2.00
179	Ernie Oravetz	7.00	3.50	2.00
180	Gus Bell	7.00	3.50	2.00
181	Dick Donovan	7.00	3.50	2.00
182	Hobie Landrith	7.00	3.50	2.00
183	Cubs team	13.00	6.50	4.00
184	*Tito Francona*	7.00	3.50	2.00
185	Johnny Kucks	7.00	3.50	2.00
186	Jim King	7.00	3.50	2.00
187	Virgil Trucks	7.00	3.50	2.00
188	Felix Mantilla	7.00	3.50	2.00
189	Willard Nixon	7.00	3.50	2.00
190	Randy Jackson	7.00	3.50	2.00
191	Joe Margoneri	7.00	3.50	2.00
192	Jerry Coleman	7.00	3.50	2.00
193	Del Rice	7.00	3.50	2.00

194	Hal Brown	7.00	3.50	2.00
195	Bobby Avila	7.00	3.50	2.00
196	Larry Jackson	7.00	3.50	2.00
197	Hank Sauer	7.00	3.50	2.00
198	Tigers team	12.00	6.00	3.50
199	Vernon Law	7.00	3.50	2.00
200	Gil McDougald	15.00	7.50	4.50
201	Sandy Amoros	7.00	3.50	2.00
202	Dick Gernert	7.00	3.50	2.00
203	Hoyt Wilhelm	24.00	12.00	7.25
204	Athletics Team	14.00	7.00	4.25
205	Charley Maxwell	7.00	3.50	2.00
206	Willard Schmidt	7.00	3.50	2.00
207	Billy Hunter	7.00	3.50	2.00
208	Lew Burdette	7.00	3.50	2.00
209	Bob Skinner	7.00	3.50	2.00
210	Roy Campanella	100.00	50.00	30.00
211	Camilo Pascual	7.00	3.50	2.00
212	*Rocky Colavito*	125.00	62.00	37.00
213	Les Moss	7.00	3.50	2.00
214	Phillies Team	15.00	7.50	4.50
215	Enos Slaughter	24.00	12.00	7.25
216	Marv Grissom	7.00	3.50	2.00
217	Gene Stephens	7.00	3.50	2.00
218	Ray Jablonski	7.00	3.50	2.00
219	Tom Acker	7.00	3.50	2.00
220	Jackie Jensen	9.00	4.50	2.75
221	Dixie Howell	7.00	3.50	2.00
222	Alex Grammas	7.00	3.50	2.00
223	Frank House	7.00	3.50	2.00
224	Marv Blaylock	7.00	3.50	2.00
225	Harry Simpson	7.00	3.50	2.00
226	Preston Ward	7.00	3.50	2.00
227	Jerry Staley	7.00	3.50	2.00
228	Smoky Burgess	7.00	3.50	2.00
229	George Susce	7.00	3.50	2.00
230	George Kell	20.00	10.00	6.00
231	Solly Hemus	7.00	3.50	2.00
232	Whitey Lockman	7.00	3.50	2.00
233	Art Fowler	7.00	3.50	2.00
234	Dick Cole	7.00	3.50	2.00
235	Tom Poholsky	7.00	3.50	2.00
236	Joe Ginsberg	7.00	3.50	2.00
237	Foster Castleman	7.00	3.50	2.00
238	Eddie Robinson	7.00	3.50	2.00
239	Tom Morgan	7.00	3.50	2.00
240	Hank Bauer	12.00	6.00	3.50
241	Joe Lonnett	7.00	3.50	2.00
242	Charley Neal	7.00	3.50	2.00
243	Cardinals Team	15.00	7.50	4.50
244	Billy Loes	7.00	3.50	2.00
245	Rip Repulski	7.00	3.50	2.00
246	Jose Valdivielso	7.00	3.50	2.00
247	Turk Lown	7.00	3.50	2.00
248	Jim Finigan	7.00	3.50	2.00
249	Dave Pope	7.00	3.50	2.00
250	Eddie Mathews	45.00	22.00	13.50
251	Orioles Team	15.00	7.50	4.50
252	Carl Erskine	11.00	5.50	3.25
253	Gus Zernial	7.00	3.50	2.00
254	Ron Negray	7.00	3.50	2.00
255	Charlie Silvera	7.00	3.50	2.00
256	Ronnie Kline	7.00	3.50	2.00
257	Walt Dropo	7.00	3.50	2.00
258	Steve Gromek	7.00	3.50	2.00
259	Eddie O'Brien	7.00	3.50	2.00
260	Del Ennis	7.00	3.50	2.00
261	Bob Chakales	7.00	3.50	2.00
262	Bobby Thomson	10.00	5.00	3.00
263	George Strickland	7.00	3.50	2.00
264	Bob Turley	11.00	5.50	3.25
265	Harvey Haddix	20.00	10.00	6.00
266	Ken Kuhn	17.00	8.50	5.00
267	Danny Kravitz	17.00	8.50	5.00
268	Jackie Collum	17.00	8.50	5.00
269	Bob Cerv	17.00	8.50	5.00
270	Senators Team	50.00	25.00	15.00
271	Danny O'Connell	17.00	8.50	5.00
272	Bobby Shantz	18.00	9.00	5.50
273	Jim Davis	17.00	8.50	5.00
274	Don Hoak	17.00	8.50	5.00
275	Indians Team	35.00	17.50	10.50
276	Jim Pyburn	17.00	8.50	5.00
277	Johnny Podres	32.00	16.00	9.50
278	Fred Hatfield	17.00	8.50	5.00
279	Bob Thurman	17.00	8.50	5.00
280	Alex Kellner	17.00	8.50	5.00
281	Gail Harris	17.00	8.50	5.00
282	Jack Dittmer	17.00	8.50	5.00
283	*Wes Covington*	17.00	8.50	5.00
284	Don Zimmer	25.00	12.50	7.50
285	Ned Garver	17.00	8.50	5.00
286	*Bobby Richardson*	110.00	55.00	33.00
287	Sam Jones	17.00	8.50	5.00
288	Ted Lepcio	17.00	8.50	5.00
289	Jim Bolger	17.00	8.50	5.00
290	Andy Carcy	17.00	8.50	5.00
291	Windy McCall	17.00	8.50	5.00
292	Billy Klaus	17.00	8.50	5.00
293	Ted Abernathy	17.00	8.50	5.00
294	Rocky Bridges	17.00	8.50	5.00
295	Joe Collins	17.00	8.50	5.00
296	Johnny Klippstein	17.00	8.50	5.00
297	Jack Crimian	17.00	8.50	5.00
298	Irv Noren	17.00	8.50	5.00
299	Chuck Harmon	17.00	8.50	5.00
300	Mike Garcia	17.00	8.50	5.00
301	Sam Esposito	17.00	8.50	5.00
302	Sandy Koufax	275.00	150.00	82.00
303	Billy Goodman	17.00	8.50	5.00
304	Joe Cunningham	17.00	8.50	5.00
305	Chico Fernandez	17.00	8.50	5.00
306	Darrell Johnson	18.00	9.00	5.50
307	Jack Phillips	17.00	8.50	5.00
308	Dick Hall	17.00	8.50	5.00
309	Jim Busby	17.00	8.50	5.00
310	Max Surkont	17.00	8.50	5.00
311	Al Pilarcik	17.00	8.50	5.00

312	*Tony Kubek*	65.00	32.00	19.50
313	Mel Parnell	17.00	8.50	5.00
314	Ed Bouchee	17.00	8.50	5.00
315	Lou Berberet	17.00	8.50	5.00
316	Billy O'Dell	17.00	8.50	5.00
317	Giants Team	60.00	30.00	18.00
318	Mickey McDermott	17.00	8.50	5.00
319	*Gino Cimoli*	19.00	9.50	5.75
320	Neil Chrisley	17.00	8.50	5.00
321	Red Murff	17.00	8.50	5.00
322	Redlegs Team	60.00	30.00	18.00
323	Wes Westrum	17.00	8.50	5.00
324	Dodgers Team	100.00	50.00	30.00
325	Frank Bolling	17.00	8.50	5.00
326	Pedro Ramos	17.00	8.50	5.00
327	Jim Pendleton	17.00	8.50	5.00
328	*Brooks Robinson*	350.00	175.00	105.00
329	White Sox Team	50.00	25.00	15.00
330	Jim Wilson	17.00	8.50	5.00
331	Ray Katt	17.00	8.50	5.00
332	Bob Bowman	17.00	8.50	5.00
333	Ernie Johnson	17.00	8.50	5.00
334	Jerry Schoonmaker	17.00	8.50	5.00
335	Granny Hamner	17.00	8.50	5.00
336	*Haywood Sullivan*	17.00	8.50	5.00
337	Rene Valdes (Valdez)	17.00	8.50	5.00
338	*Jim Bunning*	120.00	60.00	36.00
339	Bob Speake	17.00	8.50	5.00
340	Bill Wight	17.00	8.50	5.00
341	Don Gross	17.00	8.50	5.00
342	Gene Mauch	17.00	8.50	5.00
343	Taylor Phillips	17.00	8.50	5.00
344	Paul LaPalme	17.00	8.50	5.00
345	Paul Smith	17.00	8.50	5.00
346	Dick Littlefield	17.00	8.50	5.00
347	Hal Naragon	17.00	8.50	5.00
348	Jim Hearn	17.00	8.50	5.00
349	Nelson King	17.00	8.50	5.00
350	Eddie Miksis	17.00	8.50	5.00
351	Dave Hillman	17.00	8.50	5.00
352	Ellis Kinder	17.00	8.50	5.00
353	Cal Neeman	7.00	3.50	2.00
354	Rip Coleman	7.00	3.50	2.00
355	Frank Malzone	7.00	3.50	2.00
356	Faye Throneberry	7.00	3.50	2.00
357	Earl Torgeson	7.00	3.50	2.00
358	Jerry Lynch	7.00	3.50	2.00
359	Tom Cheney	7.00	3.50	2.00
360	Johnny Groth	7.00	3.50	2.00
361	Curt Barclay	7.00	3.50	2.00
362	Roman Mejias	7.00	3.50	2.00
363	Eddie Kasko	7.00	3.50	2.00
364	Cal McLish	7.00	3.50	2.00
365	Ossie Virgil	7.00	3.50	2.00
366	Ken Lehman	7.00	3.50	2.00
367	Ed Fitz Gerald	7.00	3.50	2.00
368	Bob Purkey	7.00	3.50	2.00
369	Milt Graff	7.00	3.50	2.00
370	Warren Hacker	7.00	3.50	2.00
371	Bob Lennon	7.00	3.50	2.00
372	Norm Zauchin	7.00	3.50	2.00
373	Pete Whisenant	7.00	3.50	2.00
374	Don Cardwell	7.00	3.50	2.00
375	*Jim Landis*	7.00	3.50	2.00
376	Don Elston	7.00	3.50	2.00
377	Andre Rodgers	7.00	3.50	2.00
378	Elmer Singleton	7.00	3.50	2.00
379	Don Lee	7.00	3.50	2.00
380	Walker Cooper	7.00	3.50	2.00
381	Dean Stone	7.00	3.50	2.00
382	Jim Brideweser	7.00	3.50	2.00
383	*Juan Pizarro*	7.00	3.50	2.00
384	Bobby Gene Smith	7.00	3.50	2.00
385	Art Houtteman	7.00	3.50	2.00
386	Lyle Luttrell	7.00	3.50	2.00
387	*Jack Sanford*	7.00	3.50	2.00
388	Pete Daley	7.00	3.50	2.00
389	Dave Jolly	7.00	3.50	2.00
390	Reno Bertoia	7.00	3.50	2.00
391	*Ralph Terry*	9.00	4.50	2.75
392	Chuck Tanner	7.00	3.50	2.00
393	Raul Sanchez	7.00	3.50	2.00
394	Luis Arroyo	7.00	3.50	2.00
395	Bubba Phillips	7.00	3.50	2.00
396	Casey Wise	7.00	3.50	2.00
397	Roy Smalley	7.00	3.50	2.00
398	Al Cicotte	7.00	3.50	2.00
399	Billy Consolo	7.00	3.50	2.00
400	Dodgers' Sluggers (Roy Campanella, Carl Furillo, Gil Hodges, Duke Snider)	200.00	100.00	60.00
401	*Earl Battey*	9.00	4.50	2.75
402	Jim Pisoni	7.00	3.50	2.00
403	Dick Hyde	7.00	3.50	2.00
404	Harry Anderson	7.00	3.50	2.00
405	Duke Maas	7.00	3.50	2.00
406	Bob Hale	7.00	3.50	2.00
407	Yankees' Power Hitters (Mickey Mantle, Yogi Berra)	375.00	185.00	110.00
----	Checklist Series 1-2 (Big Blony ad on back)	250.00	125.00	75.00
----	Checklist Series 1-2 (Bazooka ad on back)	250.00	125.00	75.00
----	Checklist Series 2-3 (Big Blony)	275.00	137.00	82.00
----	Checklist Series 2-3 (Bazooka)	275.00	137.00	82.00
----	Checklist Series 3-4 (Big Blony)	600.00	300.00	180.00
----	Checklist Series 3-4 (Bazooka)	600.00	300.00	180.00
----	Checklist Series 4-5 (Big Blony)	900.00	450.00	270.00
----	Checklist Series 4-5 (Bazooka)	900.00	450.00	270.00
----	Contest May 4	40.00	30.00	15.00
----	Contest May 25	40.00	30.00	15.00
----	Contest June 22	50.00	35.00	20.00
----	Contest July 19	60.00	30.00	20.00
----	Lucky Penny insert card	15.00	7.50	4.50

1958 Topps

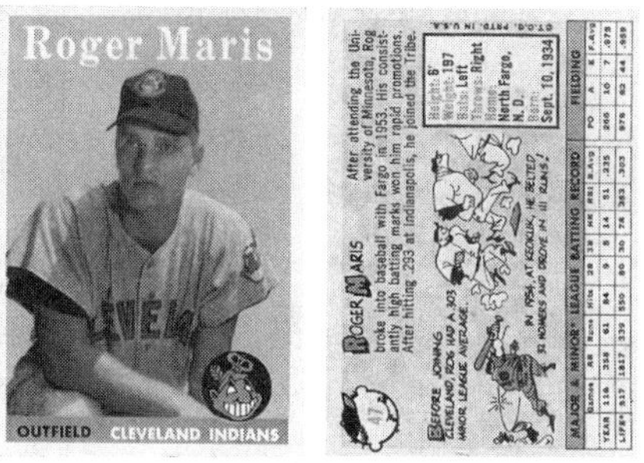

Topps continued to expand its set size in 1958 with the release of a 494-card set. One card (#145) was not issued after Ed Bouchee was suspended from baseball. Cards retained the 2-1/2" x 3-1/2" size. There are a number of variations, including yellow or white lettering on 33 cards between numbers 2-108 (higher priced yellow letter variations checklisted below are not included in the complete set prices). The number of multiple-player cards was increased. A major innovation is the addition of 20 "All-Star" cards. For the first time, checklists were incorporated into the numbered series, as the backs of team cards.

		NM	EX	VG
Complete Set (495):		4500.	2250.	1300.
Common Player (1-110):		11.00	5.50	3.25
Common Player (111-474):		7.50	3.75	2.25
All-Stars: (475-495):		10.00	5.00	3.00
1	Ted Williams	400.00	150.00	95.00
2a	Bob Lemon (yellow team letters)	45.00	22.00	13.50
2b	Bob Lemon (white team letters)	22.00	11.00	6.50
3	Alex Kellner	11.00	5.50	3.25
4	Hank Foiles	11.00	5.50	3.25
5	Willie Mays	180.00	90.00	54.00
6	George Zuverink	11.00	5.50	3.25
7	Dale Long	11.00	5.50	3.25
8a	Eddie Kasko (yellow name)	28.00	14.00	8.50
8b	Eddie Kasko (white name)	11.00	5.50	3.25
9	Hank Bauer	11.00	5.50	3.25
10	Lou Burdette	11.00	5.50	3.25
11a	Jim Rivera (yellow team letters)	28.00	14.00	8.50
11b	Jim Rivera (white team letters)	11.00	5.50	3.25
12	George Crowe	11.00	5.50	3.25
13a	Billy Hoeft (yellow name)	30.00	15.00	9.00
13b	Billy Hoeft (white name, orange triangle by foot)	11.00	5.50	3.25
13c	Billy Hoeft (white name, red triangle by foot)	11.00	5.50	3.25
14	Rip Repulski	11.00	5.50	3.25
15	Jim Lemon	11.00	5.50	3.25
16	Charley Neal	12.50	6.25	3.75
17	Felix Mantilla	11.00	5.50	3.25
18	Frank Sullivan	11.00	5.50	3.25
19	Giants team/Checklist 1-88	35.00	17.50	10.50
20a	Gil McDougald (yellow name)	40.00	20.00	12.00
20b	Gil McDougald (white name)	12.50	6.25	3.75
21	Curt Barclay	11.00	5.50	3.25
22	Hal Naragon	11.00	5.50	3.25
23a	Bill Tuttle (yellow name)	28.00	14.00	8.50
23b	Bill Tuttle (white name)	11.00	5.50	3.25
24a	Hobie Landrith (yellow name)	28.00	14.00	8.50
24b	Hobie Landrith (white name)	11.00	5.50	3.25
25	Don Drysdale	65.00	32.00	19.50
26	Ron Jackson	11.00	5.50	3.25
27	Bud Freeman	11.00	5.50	3.25
28	Jim Busby	11.00	5.50	3.25
29	Ted Lepcio	11.00	5.50	3.25
30a	Hank Aaron (yellow name)	295.00	147.00	88.00
30b	Hank Aaron (white name)	150.00	75.00	45.00
31	Tex Clevenger	11.00	5.50	3.25
32a	J.W. Porter (yellow name)	28.00	14.00	8.50
32b	J.W. Porter (white name)	11.00	5.50	3.25
33a	Cal Neeman (yellow team letters)	20.00	14.00	8.50
33b	Cal Neeman (white team letters)	11.00	5.50	3.25
34	Bob Thurman	11.00	5.50	3.25
35a	Don Mossi (yellow team letters)	28.00	14.00	8.50
35b	Don Mossi (white team letters)	11.00	5.50	3.25
36	Ted Kazanski	11.00	5.50	3.25
37	*Mike McCormick* (photo actually Ray Monzant)	11.00	5.50	3.25
38	Dick Gernert	11.00	5.50	3.25
39	Bob Martyn	11.00	5.50	3.25
40	George Kell	15.00	7.50	4.50
41	Dave Hillman	11.00	5.50	3.25
42	*John Roseboro*	17.50	8.75	5.25
43	Sal Maglie	12.50	6.25	3.75

44	Senators Team/Checklist 1-88	15.00	7.50	4.50
45	Dick Groat	12.50	6.25	3.75
46a	Lou Sleater (yellow name)	28.00	14.00	8.50
46b	Lou Sleater (white name)	11.00	5.50	3.25
47	*Roger Maris*	315.00	155.00	94.00
48	Chuck Harmon	11.00	5.50	3.25
49	Smoky Burgess	11.00	5.50	3.25
50a	Billy Pierce (yellow team letters)	32.00	16.00	9.50
50b	Billy Pierce (white team letters)	11.00	5.50	3.25
51	Del Rice	11.00	5.50	3.25
52a	Roberto Clemente (yellow team letters)	425.00	212.00	127.00
52b	Roberto Clemente (white team letters)	260.00	130.00	78.00
53a	Morrie Martin (yellow name)	28.00	14.00	8.50
53b	Morrie Martin (white name)	11.00	5.50	3.25
54	*Norm Siebern*	11.00	5.50	3.25
55	Chico Carrasquel	11.00	5.50	3.25
56	Bill Fischer	11.00	5.50	3.25
57a	Tim Thompson (yellow name)	28.00	14.00	8.50
57b	Tim Thompson (white name)	11.00	5.50	3.25
58a	Art Schult (yellow team letters)	28.00	14.00	8.50
58b	Art Schult (white team letters)	11.00	5.50	3.25
59	Dave Sisler	11.00	5.50	3.25
60a	Del Ennis (yellow name)	36.00	18.00	11.00
60b	Del Ennis (white name)	11.00	5.50	3.25
61a	Darrell Johnson (yellow name)	42.00	21.00	12.50
61b	Darrell Johnson (white name)	12.50	6.25	3.75
62	Joe DeMaestri	11.00	5.50	3.25
63	Joe Nuxhall	11.00	5.50	3.25
64	Joe Lonnett	11.00	5.50	3.25
65a	Von McDaniel (yellow name)	28.00	14.00	8.50
65b	Von McDaniel (white name)	11.00	5.50	3.25
66	Lee Walls	11.00	5.50	3.25
67	Joe Ginsberg	11.00	5.50	3.25
68	Daryl Spencer	11.00	5.50	3.25
69	Wally Burnette	11.00	5.50	3.25
70a	Al Kaline (yellow name)	185.00	92.00	55.00
70b	Al Kaline (white name)	75.00	37.00	22.00
71	Dodgers team	50.00	25.00	15.00
72	Bud Byerly	11.00	5.50	3.25
73	Pete Daley	11.00	5.50	3.25
74	Roy Face	11.00	5.50	3.25
75	Gus Bell	11.00	5.50	3.25
76a	Dick Farrell (yellow team letters)	28.00	14.00	8.50
76b	Dick Farrell (white team letters)	11.00	5.50	3.25
77a	Don Zimmer (yellow team letters)	30.00	15.00	9.00
77b	Don Zimmer (white team letters)	15.00	7.50	4.50
78a	Ernie Johnson (yellow name)	28.00	14.00	8.50
78b	Ernie Johnson (white name)	11.00	5.50	3.25
79a	Dick Williams (yellow team letters)	28.00	14.00	8.50
79b	Dick Williams (white team letters)	11.00	5.50	3.25
80	Dick Drott	11.00	5.50	3.25
81a	*Steve Boros* (yellow team letters)	28.00	14.00	8.50
81b	*Steve Boros* (white team letters)	11.00	5.50	3.25
82	Ronnie Kline	11.00	5.50	3.25
83	*Bob Hazle*	11.00	5.50	3.25
84	Billy O'Dell	11.00	5.50	3.25
85a	Luis Aparicio (yellow team letters)	75.00	37.00	22.00
85b	Luis Aparicio (white team letters)	25.00	12.50	7.50
86	Valmy Thomas	11.00	5.50	3.25
87	Johnny Kucks	11.00	5.50	3.25
88	Duke Snider	70.00	35.00	21.00
89	Billy Klaus	11.00	5.50	3.25
90	Robin Roberts	25.00	12.50	7.50
91	Chuck Tanner	11.00	5.50	3.25
92a	Clint Courtney (yellow name)	28.00	14.00	8.50
92b	Clint Courtney (white name)	11.00	5.50	3.25
93	Sandy Amoros	12.00	6.00	3.50
94	Bob Skinner	11.00	5.50	3.25
95	Frank Bolling	11.00	5.50	3.25
96	Joe Durham	11.00	5.50	3.25
97a	Larry Jackson (yellow name)	28.00	14.00	8.50
97b	Larry Jackson (white name)	11.00	5.50	3.25
98a	Billy Hunter (yellow name)	28.00	14.00	8.50
98b	Billy Hunter (white name)	11.00	5.50	3.25
99	Bobby Adams	11.00	5.50	3.25
100a	Early Wynn (yellow team letters)	50.00	25.00	15.00
100b	Early Wynn (white team letters)	18.00	9.00	5.50
101a	Bobby Richardson (yellow name)	50.00	25.00	15.00
101b	Bobby Richardson (white name)	25.00	12.50	7.50
102	George Strickland	11.00	5.50	3.25
103	Jerry Lynch	11.00	5.50	3.25
104	Jim Pendleton	11.00	5.50	3.25
105	Billy Gardner	11.00	5.50	3.25
106	Dick Schofield	11.00	5.50	3.25
107	Ossie Virgil	11.00	5.50	3.25
108a	Jim Landis (yellow team letters)	28.00	14.00	8.50
108b	Jim Landis (white team letters)	11.00	5.50	3.25
109	Herb Plews	11.00	5.50	3.25
110	Johnny Logan	11.00	5.50	3.25
111	Stu Miller	7.50	3.75	2.25
112	Gus Zernial	7.50	3.75	2.25
113	Jerry Walker	7.50	3.75	2.25
114	Irv Noren	7.50	3.75	2.25
115	Jim Bunning	24.00	12.00	7.25
116	Dave Philley	7.50	3.75	2.25

117	Frank Torre	7.50	3.75	2.25
118	Harvey Haddix	7.50	3.75	2.25
119	Harry Chiti	7.50	3.75	2.25
120	Johnny Podres	12.50	6.25	3.75
121	Eddie Miksis	7.50	3.75	2.25
122	Walt Moryn	7.50	3.75	2.25
123	Dick Tomanek	7.50	3.75	2.25
124	Bobby Usher	7.50	3.75	2.25
125	Al Dark	7.50	3.75	2.25
126	Stan Palys	7.50	3.75	2.25
127	Tom Sturdivant	7.50	3.75	2.25
128	*Willie Kirkland*	7.50	3.75	2.25
129	Jim Derrington	7.50	3.75	2.25
130	Jackie Jensen	8.00	4.00	2.50
131	Bob Henrich	7.50	3.75	2.25
132	Vernon Law	7.50	3.75	2.25
133	Russ Nixon	7.50	3.75	2.25
134	Phillies Team/Checklist 89-176	13.00	6.50	4.00
135	Mike Drabowsky	7.50	3.75	2.25
136	Jim Finigan	7.50	3.75	2.25
137	Russ Kemmerer	7.50	3.75	2.25
138	Earl Torgeson	7.50	3.75	2.25
139	George Brunet	7.50	3.75	2.25
140	Wes Covington	7.50	3.75	2.25
141	Ken Lehman	7.50	3.75	2.25
142	Enos Slaughter	20.00	10.00	6.00
143	Billy Muffett	7.50	3.75	2.25
144	Bobby Morgan	7.50	3.75	2.25
145	Not issued			
146	Dick Gray	7.50	3.75	2.25
147	*Don McMahon*	7.50	3.75	2.25
148	Billy Consolo	7.50	3.75	2.25
149	Tom Acker	7.50	3.75	2.25
150	Mickey Mantle	650.00	325.00	195.00
151	Buddy Pritchard	7.50	3.75	2.25
152	Johnny Antonelli	7.50	3.75	2.25
153	Les Moss	7.50	3.75	2.25
154	Harry Byrd	7.50	3.75	2.25
155	Hector Lopez	7.50	3.75	2.25
156	Dick Hyde	7.50	3.75	2.25
157	Dee Fondy	7.50	3.75	2.25
158	Indians Team/Checklist 177-264	13.00	6.50	4.00
159	Taylor Phillips	7.50	3.75	2.25
160	Don Hoak	7.50	3.75	2.25
161	Don Larsen	13.00	6.50	4.00
162	Gil Hodges	27.50	13.50	8.25
163	Jim Wilson	7.50	3.75	2.25
164	Bob Taylor	7.50	3.75	2.25
165	Bob Nieman	7.50	3.75	2.25
166	Danny O'Connell	7.50	3.75	2.25
167	Frank Baumann	7.50	3.75	2.25
168	Joe Cunningham	7.50	3.75	2.25
169	Ralph Terry	7.50	3.75	2.25
170	Vic Wertz	7.50	3.75	2.25
171	Harry Anderson	7.50	3.75	2.25
172	Don Gross	7.50	3.75	2.25
173	Eddie Yost	7.50	3.75	2.25
174	A's Team/Checklist 89-176	12.00	6.00	3.50
175	*Marv Throneberry*	12.00	6.00	3.50
176	Bob Buhl	7.50	3.75	2.25
177	Al Smith	7.50	3.75	2.25
178	Ted Kluszewski	14.00	7.00	4.25
179	Willy Miranda	7.50	3.75	2.25
180	Lindy McDaniel	7.50	3.75	2.25
181	Willie Jones	7.50	3.75	2.25
182	Joe Caffie	7.50	3.75	2.25
183	Dave Jolly	7.50	3.75	2.25
184	Elvin Tappe	7.50	3.75	2.25
185	Ray Boone	7.50	3.75	2.25
186	Jack Meyer	7.50	3.75	2.25
187	Sandy Koufax	175.00	87.00	52.00
188	Milt Bolling (photo actually Lou Berberet)	7.50	3.75	2.25
189	George Susce	7.50	3.75	2.25
190	Red Schoendienst	18.00	9.00	5.50
191	Art Ceccarelli	7.50	3.75	2.25
192	Milt Graff	7.50	3.75	2.25
193	*Jerry Lumpe*	7.50	3.75	2.25
194	Roger Craig	9.00	4.50	2.75
195	Whitey Lockman	7.50	3.75	2.25
196	Mike Garcia	7.50	3.75	2.25
197	Haywood Sullivan	7.50	3.75	2.25
198	Bill Virdon	7.50	3.75	2.25
199	Don Blasingame	7.50	3.75	2.25
200	Bob Keegan	7.50	3.75	2.25
201	Jim Bolger	7.50	3.75	2.25
202	*Woody Held*	7.50	3.75	2.25
203	Al Walker	7.50	3.75	2.25
204	Leo Kiely	7.50	3.75	2.25
205	Johnny Temple	7.50	3.75	2.25
206	Bob Shaw	7.50	3.75	2.25
207	Solly Hemus	7.50	3.75	2.25
208	Cal McLish	7.50	3.75	2.25
209	Bob Anderson	7.50	3.75	2.25
210	Wally Moon	7.50	3.75	2.25
211	Pete Burnside	7.50	3.75	2.25
212	Bubba Phillips	7.50	3.75	2.25
213	Red Wilson	7.50	3.75	2.25
214	Willard Schmidt	7.50	3.75	2.25
215	Jim Gilliam	11.00	5.50	3.25
216	Cards Team/Checklist 177-264	12.00	6.00	3.50
217	Jack Harshman	7.50	3.75	2.25
218	Dick Rand	7.50	3.75	2.25
219	Camilo Pascual	7.50	3.75	2.25
220	Tom Brewer	7.50	3.75	2.25
221	Jerry Kindall	7.50	3.75	2.25
222	Bud Daley	7.50	3.75	2.25
223	Andy Pafko	7.50	3.75	2.25
224	Bob Grim	7.50	3.75	2.25
225	Billy Goodman	7.50	3.75	2.25
226	Bob Smith (photo actually Bobby Gene Smith)	7.50	3.75	2.25
227	Gene Stephens	7.50	3.75	2.25
228	Duke Maas	7.50	3.75	2.25
229	Frank Zupo	7.50	3.75	2.25

230	Richie Ashburn	30.00	15.00	9.00
231	Lloyd Merritt	7.50	3.75	2.25
232	Reno Bertoia	7.50	3.75	2.25
233	Mickey Vernon	7.50	3.75	2.25
234	Carl Sawatski	7.50	3.75	2.25
235	Tom Gorman	7.50	3.75	2.25
236	Ed Fitz Gerald	7.50	3.75	2.25
237	Bill Wight	7.50	3.75	2.25
238	Bill Mazeroski	24.00	12.00	7.25
239	Chuck Stobbs	7.50	3.75	2.25
240	Moose Skowron	16.00	8.00	4.75
241	Dick Littlefield	7.50	3.75	2.25
242	Johnny Klippstein	7.50	3.75	2.25
243	Larry Raines	7.50	3.75	2.25
244	*Don Demeter*	7.50	3.75	2.25
245	*Frank Lary*	7.50	3.75	2.25
246	Yankees Team	75.00	37.00	22.00
247	Casey Wise	7.50	3.75	2.25
248	Herm Wehmeier	7.50	3.75	2.25
249	Ray Moore	7.50	3.75	2.25
250	Roy Sievers	7.50	3.75	2.25
251	Warren Hacker	7.50	3.75	2.25
252	Bob Trowbridge	7.50	3.75	2.25
253	Don Mueller	7.50	3.75	2.25
254	Alex Grammas	7.50	3.75	2.25
255	Bob Turley	7.50	3.75	2.25
256	White Sox Team/Checklist 265-352	12.00	6.00	3.50
257	Hal Smith	7.50	3.75	2.25
258	Carl Erskine	12.50	6.25	3.75
259	Al Pilarcik	7.50	3.75	2.25
260	Frank Malzone	7.50	3.75	2.25
261	Turk Lown	7.50	3.75	2.25
262	Johnny Groth	7.50	3.75	2.25
263	Eddie Bressoud	7.50	3.75	2.25
264	Jack Sanford	7.50	3.75	2.25
265	Pete Runnels	7.50	3.75	2.25
266	Connie Johnson	7.50	3.75	2.25
267	Sherman Lollar	7.50	3.75	2.25
268	Granny Hamner	7.50	3.75	2.25
269	Paul Smith	7.50	3.75	2.25
270	Warren Spahn	50.00	25.00	15.00
271	Billy Martin	15.00	7.50	4.50
272	Ray Crone	7.50	3.75	2.25
273	Hal Smith	7.50	3.75	2.25
274	Rocky Bridges	7.50	3.75	2.25
275	Elston Howard	11.00	5.50	3.25
276	Bobby Avila	7.50	3.75	2.25
277	Virgil Trucks	7.50	3.75	2.25
278	Mack Burk	7.50	3.75	2.25
279	Bob Boyd	7.50	3.75	2.25
280	Jim Piersall	7.50	3.75	2.25
281	Sam Taylor	7.50	3.75	2.25
282	Paul Foytack	7.50	3.75	2.25
283	Ray Shearer	9.00	4.50	2.75
284	Ray Katt	7.50	3.75	2.25
285	Frank Robinson	80.00	40.00	24.00
286	Gino Cimoli	7.50	3.75	2.25
287	Sam Jones	7.50	3.75	2.25
288	Harmon Killebrew	70.00	35.00	21.00
289	Series Hurling Rivals (Lou Burdette, Bobby Shantz)	9.00	4.50	2.75
290	Dick Donovan	7.50	3.75	2.25
291	Don Landrum	7.50	3.75	2.25
292	Ned Garver	7.50	3.75	2.25
293	Gene Freese	7.50	3.75	2.25
294	Hal Jeffcoat	7.50	3.75	2.25
295	Minnie Minoso	8.00	4.00	2.50
296	*Ryne Duren*	12.00	6.00	3.50
297	Don Buddin	7.50	3.75	2.25
298	Jim Hearn	7.50	3.75	2.25
299	Harry Simpson	7.50	3.75	2.25
300	League Presidents (Warren Giles, William Harridge)	9.00	4.50	2.75
301	Randy Jackson	7.50	3.75	2.25
302	Mike Baxes	7.50	3.75	2.25
303	Neil Chrisley	7.50	3.75	2.25
304	Tigers' Big Bats (Al Kaline, Harvey Kuenn)	18.00	9.00	5.50
305	Clem Labine	9.00	4.50	2.75
306	Whammy Douglas	7.50	3.75	2.25
307	Brooks Robinson	95.00	47.00	28.00
308	Paul Giel	7.50	3.75	2.25
309	Gail Harris	7.50	3.75	2.25
310	Ernie Banks	95.00	47.00	28.00
311	Bob Purkey	7.50	3.75	2.25
312	Red Sox Team	12.00	6.00	3.50
313	Bob Rush	7.50	3.75	2.25
314	Dodgers' Boss & Power (Duke Snider, Walter Alston)	22.00	11.00	6.50
315	Bob Friend	7.50	3.75	2.25
316	Tito Francona	7.50	3.75	2.25
317	*Albie Pearson*	7.50	3.75	2.25
318	Frank House	7.50	3.75	2.25
319	Lou Skizas	7.50	3.75	2.25
320	Whitey Ford	45.00	22.00	13.50
321	Sluggers Supreme (Ted Kluszewski, Ted Williams)	70.00	35.00	21.00
322	Harding Peterson	7.50	3.75	2.25
323	Elmer Valo	7.50	3.75	2.25
324	Hoyt Wilhelm	17.00	8.50	5.00
325	Joe Adcock	7.50	3.75	2.25
326	Bob Miller	7.50	3.75	2.25
327	Cubs Team/Checklist 265-352	15.00	7.50	4.50
328	Ike Delock	7.50	3.75	2.25
329	Bob Cerv	7.50	3.75	2.25
330	Ed Bailey	7.50	3.75	2.25
331	Pedro Ramos	7.50	3.75	2.25
332	Jim King	7.50	3.75	2.25
333	Andy Carey	7.50	3.75	2.25
334	Mound Aces (Bob Friend, Billy Pierce)	8.00	4.00	2.50
335	Ruben Gomez	7.50	3.75	2.25
336	Bert Hamric	7.50	3.75	2.25
337	Hank Aguirre	7.50	3.75	2.25
338	Walt Dropo	7.50	3.75	2.25
339	Fred Hatfield	7.50	3.75	2.25

340	Don Newcombe	11.00	5.50	3.25
341	Pirates Team/Checklist 265-352	14.00	7.00	4.25
342	Jim Brosnan	7.50	3.75	2.25
343	*Orlando Cepeda*	90.00	45.00	27.00
344	Bob Porterfield	7.50	3.75	2.25
345	Jim Hegan	7.50	3.75	2.25
346	Steve Bilko	7.50	3.75	2.25
347	Don Rudolph	7.50	3.75	2.25
348	Chico Fernandez	7.50	3.75	2.25
349	Murry Dickson	7.50	3.75	2.25
350	Ken Boyer	14.00	7.00	4.25
351	Braves' Fence Busters (Hank Aaron, Joe Adcock, Del Crandall, Eddie Mathews)	35.00	17.50	10.50
352	Herb Score	13.00	6.50	4.00
353	Stan Lopata	7.50	3.75	2.25
354	Art Ditmar	7.50	3.75	2.25
355	Bill Bruton	7.50	3.75	2.25
356	Bob Malkmus	7.50	3.75	2.25
357	Danny McDevitt	7.50	3.75	2.25
358	Gene Baker	7.50	3.75	2.25
359	Billy Loes	7.50	3.75	2.25
360	Roy McMillan	7.50	3.75	2.25
361	Mike Fornieles	7.50	3.75	2.25
362	Ray Jablonski	7.50	3.75	2.25
363	Don Elston	7.50	3.75	2.25
364	Earl Battey	7.50	3.75	2.25
365	Tom Morgan	7.50	3.75	2.25
366	Gene Green	7.50	3.75	2.25
367	Jack Urban	7.50	3.75	2.25
368	Rocky Colavito	45.00	22.00	13.50
369	Ralph Lumenti	7.50	3.75	2.25
370	Yogi Berra	70.00	35.00	21.00
371	Marty Keough	7.50	3.75	2.25
372	Don Cardwell	7.50	3.75	2.25
373	Joe Pignatano	7.50	3.75	2.25
374	Brooks Lawrence	7.50	3.75	2.25
375	Pee Wee Reese	45.00	22.00	13.50
376	Charley Rabe	7.50	3.75	2.25
377a	Braves Team (alphabetical checklist on back)	13.00	6.50	4.00
377b	Braves Team (numerical checklist on back)	75.00	37.00	22.00
378	Hank Sauer	7.50	3.75	2.25
379	Ray Herbert	7.50	3.75	2.25
380	Charley Maxwell	7.50	3.75	2.25
381	Hal Brown	7.50	3.75	2.25
382	Al Cicotte	7.50	3.75	2.25
383	Lou Berberet	7.50	3.75	2.25
384	John Goryl	7.50	3.75	2.25
385	Wilmer Mizell	7.50	3.75	2.25
386	Birdie's Young Sluggers (Ed Bailey, Frank Robinson, Birdie Tebbetts)	11.00	5.50	3.25
387	Wally Post	7.50	3.75	2.25
388	Billy Moran	7.50	3.75	2.25
389	Bill Taylor	7.50	3.75	2.25
390	Del Crandall	7.50	3.75	2.25
391	Dave Melton	7.50	3.75	2.25
392	Bennie Daniels	7.50	3.75	2.25
393	Tony Kubek	11.00	5.50	3.25
394	*Jim Grant*	7.50	3.75	2.25
395	Willard Nixon	7.50	3.75	2.25
396	Dutch Dotterer	7.50	3.75	2.25
397a	Tigers team (alphabetical checklist on back)	12.00	6.00	3.50
397b	Tigers team (numerical checklist on back)	70.00	35.00	21.00
398	Gene Woodling	7.50	3.75	2.25
399	Marv Grissom	7.50	3.75	2.25
400	Nellie Fox	24.00	12.00	7.25
401	Don Bessent	7.50	3.75	2.25
402	Bobby Gene Smith	7.50	3.75	2.25
403	Steve Korcheck	7.50	3.75	2.25
404	Curt Simmons	7.50	3.75	2.25
405	Ken Aspromonte	7.50	3.75	2.25
406	Vic Power	7.50	3.75	2.25
407	Carlton Willey	7.50	3.75	2.25
408a	Orioles team (alphabetical checklist on back)	12.50	6.25	3.75
408b	Orioles team (numerical checklist on back)	70.00	35.00	21.00
409	Frank Thomas	7.50	3.75	2.25
410	Murray Wall	7.50	3.75	2.25
411	*Tony Taylor*	7.50	3.75	2.25
412	Jerry Staley	7.50	3.75	2.25
413	*Jim Davenport*	7.50	3.75	2.25
414	Sammy White	7.50	3.75	2.25
415	Bob Bowman	7.50	3.75	2.25
416	Foster Castleman	7.50	3.75	2.25
417	Carl Furillo	12.50	6.25	3.75
418	World Series Foes (Hank Aaron, Mickey Mantle)	240.00	120.00	72.00
419	Bobby Shantz	7.50	3.75	2.25
420	*Vada Pinson*	27.50	13.50	8.25
421	Dixie Howell	7.50	3.75	2.25
422	Norm Zauchin	7.50	3.75	2.25
423	Phil Clark	7.50	3.75	2.25
424	Larry Doby	16.00	8.00	4.75
425	Sam Esposito	7.50	3.75	2.25
426	Johnny O'Brien	7.50	3.75	2.25
427	Al Worthington	7.50	3.75	2.25
428a	Redlegs Team (alphabetical checklist on back)	16.00	8.00	4.75
428b	Redlegs Team (numerical checklist on back)	75.00	37.00	22.00
429	Gus Triandos	7.50	3.75	2.25
430	Bobby Thomson	7.50	3.75	2.25
431	Gene Conley	7.50	3.75	2.25
432	John Powers	7.50	3.75	2.25
433	Pancho Herrera	7.50	3.75	2.25
433a	Pancho Herrera (printing error, no "a" in Herrera)	1200.	600.00	360.00
434	Harvey Kuenn	7.50	3.75	2.25
435	Ed Roebuck	7.50	3.75	2.25
436	Rival Fence Busters (Willie Mays, Duke Snider)	65.00	32.00	19.50
437	Bob Speake	10.00	5.00	3.00
438	Whitey Herzog	10.00	5.00	3.00
439	Ray Narleski	10.00	5.00	3.00
440	Eddie Mathews	35.00	17.50	10.50
441	Jim Marshall	10.00	5.00	3.00
442	Phil Paine	10.00	5.00	3.00
443	Billy Harrell (SP)	15.00	7.50	4.50
444	Danny Kravitz	10.00	5.00	3.00
445	Bob Smith	10.00	5.00	3.00
446	Carroll Hardy (SP)	15.00	7.50	4.50
447	Ray Monzant	10.00	5.00	3.00
448	*Charlie Lau*	12.00	6.00	3.50
449	Gene Fodge	10.00	5.00	3.00
450	Preston Ward (SP)	15.00	7.50	4.50
451	Joe Taylor	10.00	5.00	3.00
452	Roman Mejias	10.00	5.00	3.00
453	Tom Qualters	10.00	5.00	3.00
454	Harry Hanebrink	10.00	5.00	3.00
455	Hal Griggs	10.00	5.00	3.00
456	Dick Brown	10.00	5.00	3.00
457	*Milt Pappas*	10.00	5.00	3.00
458	Julio Becquer	10.00	5.00	3.00
459	Ron Blackburn	10.00	5.00	3.00
460	Chuck Essegian	10.00	5.00	3.00
461	Ed Mayer	10.00	5.00	3.00
462	Gary Geiger (SP)	15.00	7.50	4.50
463	Vito Valentinetti	10.00	5.00	3.00
464	*Curt Flood*	25.00	12.50	7.50
465	Arnie Portocarrero	10.00	5.00	3.00
466	Pete Whisenant	10.00	5.00	3.00
467	Glen Hobbie	10.00	5.00	3.00
468	Bob Schmidt	10.00	5.00	3.00
469	Don Ferrarese	10.00	5.00	3.00
470	R.C. Stevens	10.00	5.00	3.00
471	Lenny Green	10.00	5.00	3.00
472	Joe Jay	10.00	5.00	3.00
473	Bill Renna	10.00	5.00	3.00
474	Roman Semproch	10.00	5.00	3.00
475	All-Star Managers (Fred Haney, Casey Stengel)	17.00	8.50	5.00
476	Stan Musial (All-Star)	35.00	17.50	10.50
477	Bill Skowron (All-Star)	12.50	6.25	3.75
478	Johnny Temple (All-Star)	10.00	5.00	3.00
479	Nellie Fox (All-Star)	11.00	5.50	3.25
480	Eddie Mathews (All-Star)	12.50	6.25	3.75
481	Frank Malzone (All-Star)	10.00	5.00	3.00
482	Ernie Banks (All-Star)	27.50	13.50	8.25
483	Luis Aparicio (All-Star)	16.00	8.00	4.75
484	Frank Robinson (All-Star)	22.00	11.00	6.50
485	Ted Williams (All-Star)	105.00	52.00	31.00
486	Willie Mays (All-Star)	50.00	25.00	15.00
487	Mickey Mantle (All-Star) (Triple Print)	150.00	75.00	45.00
488	Hank Aaron (All-Star)	45.00	22.00	13.50
489	Jackie Jensen (All-Star)	10.00	5.00	3.00
490	Ed Bailey (All-Star)	10.00	5.00	3.00
491	Sherman Lollar (All-Star)	10.00	5.00	3.00
492	Bob Friend (All-Star)	10.00	5.00	3.00
493	Bob Turley (All-Star)	10.00	5.00	3.00
494	Warren Spahn (All-Star)	20.00	10.00	6.00
495	Herb Score (All-Star)	15.00	7.50	4.50
----	Contest Card (All-Star Game, July 8)	20.00	10.00	6.00
----	Felt Emblems Insert Card	20.00	10.00	6.00

1959 Topps

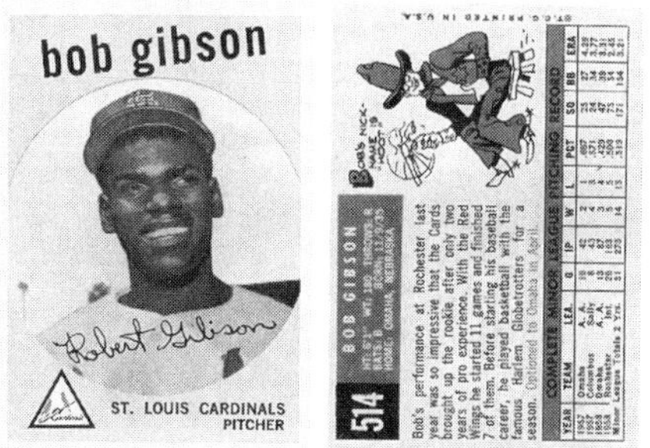

These 2-1/2" x 3-1/2" cards have a round photograph at the center of the front with a solid-color background and white border. A facsimile autograph is found across the photo. The 572-card set marks the largest set issued to that time. Card numbers below 507 have red and green printing with the card number in white in a green box. On high number cards beginning with #507, the printing is black and red and the card number is in a black box. Specialty cards include multiple-player cards, team cards with checklists, "All-Star" cards, highlights from previous season, and 31 "Rookie Stars." There is also a card of the commissioner, Ford Frick, and one of Roy Campanella in a wheelchair. A handful of cards can be found with and without lines added to the biographies on back indicating trades or demotions; those without the added lines are considerably more rare and valuable and are not included in the complete set price. Card numbers 199-286 can be found with either white or grey backs, with the grey stock being the less common.

		NM	EX	VG
	Complete Set (572):	5250.	1750.	1125.
	Common Player (1-110):	6.00	3.00	1.75
	Common Player (111-506):	4.00	2.00	1.25
	Common Player (507-572):	15.00	7.50	4.50
1	Ford Frick	50.00	19.00	9.00
2	Eddie Yost	6.00	3.00	1.75
3	Don McMahon	6.00	3.00	1.75
4	Albie Pearson	6.00	3.00	1.75
5	Dick Donovan	6.00	3.00	1.75
6	Alex Grammas	6.00	3.00	1.75
7	Al Pilarcik	6.00	3.00	1.75
8	Phillies Team	50.00	25.00	15.00
9	Paul Giel	6.00	3.00	1.75
10	Mickey Mantle	525.00	200.00	125.00
11	Billy Hunter	6.00	3.00	1.75
12	Vern Law	6.00	3.00	1.75
13	Dick Gernert	6.00	3.00	1.75
14	Pete Whisenant	6.00	3.00	1.75
15	Dick Drott	6.00	3.00	1.75
16	Joe Pignatano	6.00	3.00	1.75
17	Danny's All-Stars (Ted Kluszewski, Danny Murtaugh, Frank J. Thomas)	7.50	3.75	2.25
18	Jack Urban	6.00	3.00	1.75
19	Ed Bressoud	6.00	3.00	1.75
20	Duke Snider	50.00	25.00	15.00
21	Connie Johnson	6.00	3.00	1.75
22	Al Smith	6.00	3.00	1.75
23	Murry Dickson	6.00	3.00	1.75
24	Red Wilson	6.00	3.00	1.75
25	Don Hoak	6.00	3.00	1.75
26	Chuck Stobbs	6.00	3.00	1.75
27	Andy Pafko	6.00	3.00	1.75
28	Red Worthington	6.00	3.00	1.75
29	Jim Bolger	6.00	3.00	1.75
30	Nellie Fox	16.00	8.00	4.75
31	Ken Lehman	6.00	3.00	1.75
32	Don Buddin	6.00	3.00	1.75
33	Ed Fitz Gerald	6.00	3.00	1.75
34	Pitchers Beware (Al Kaline, Charlie Maxwell)	15.00	7.50	4.50
35	Ted Kluszewski	15.00	7.50	4.50
36	Hank Aguirre	6.00	3.00	1.75
37	Gene Green	6.00	3.00	1.75
38	Morrie Martin	6.00	3.00	1.75
39	Ed Bouchee	6.00	3.00	1.75
40a	Warren Spahn (Born 1931)	70.00	35.00	21.00
40b	Warren Spahn (Born 1931, "3" partially obscured)	95.00	47.00	28.00
40c	Warren Spahn (Born 1921)	50.00	25.00	15.00
41	Bob Martyn	6.00	3.00	1.75
42	Murray Wall	6.00	3.00	1.75
43	Steve Bilko	6.00	3.00	1.75
44	Vito Valentinetti	6.00	3.00	1.75
45	Andy Carey	6.00	3.00	1.75
46	Bill Henry	6.00	3.00	1.75
47	Jim Finigan	6.00	3.00	1.75
48	Orioles Team/Checklist 1-88	22.00	11.00	6.50
49	Bill Hall	6.00	3.00	1.75
50	Willie Mays	110.00	55.00	33.00
51	Rip Coleman	6.00	3.00	1.75
52	Coot Veal	6.00	3.00	1.75
53	Stan Williams	6.00	3.00	1.75
54	Mel Roach	6.00	3.00	1.75
55	Tom Brewer	6.00	3.00	1.75
56	Carl Sawatski	6.00	3.00	1.75
57	Al Cicotte	6.00	3.00	1.75
58	Eddie Miksis	6.00	3.00	1.75
59	Irv Noren	6.00	3.00	1.75
60	Bob Turley	6.00	3.00	1.75
61	Dick Brown	6.00	3.00	1.75
62	Tony Taylor	6.00	3.00	1.75
63	Jim Hearn	6.00	3.00	1.75
64	Joe DeMaestri	6.00	3.00	1.75
65	Frank Torre	6.00	3.00	1.75
66	Joe Ginsberg	6.00	3.00	1.75
67	Brooks Lawrence	6.00	3.00	1.75
68	Dick Schofield	6.00	3.00	1.75
69	Giants Team/Checklist 89-176	16.00	8.00	4.75
70	Harvey Kuenn	6.00	3.00	1.75
71	Don Bessent	6.00	3.00	1.75
72	Bill Renna	6.00	3.00	1.75
73	Ron Jackson	6.00	3.00	1.75
74	Directing the Power (Cookie Lavagetto, Jim Lemon, Roy Sievers)	9.00	4.50	2.75
75	Sam Jones	6.00	3.00	1.75
76	Bobby Richardson	19.00	9.50	5.75
77	John Goryl	6.00	3.00	1.75
78	Pedro Ramos	6.00	3.00	1.75
79	Harry Chiti	6.00	3.00	1.75
80	Minnie Minoso	8.00	4.00	2.50
81	Hal Jeffcoat	6.00	3.00	1.75
82	Bob Boyd	6.00	3.00	1.75
83	Bob Smith	6.00	3.00	1.75
84	Reno Bertoia	6.00	3.00	1.75
85	Harry Anderson	6.00	3.00	1.75
86	Bob Keegan	6.00	3.00	1.75
87	Danny O'Connell	6.00	3.00	1.75
88	Herb Score	8.00	4.00	2.50
89	Billy Gardner	6.00	3.00	1.75
90	Bill Skowron (SP)	16.00	8.00	4.75
91	Herb Moford	6.00	3.00	1.75
92	Dave Philley	6.00	3.00	1.75
93	Julio Becquer	6.00	3.00	1.75
94	White Sox Team	30.00	15.00	9.00
95	Carl Willey	6.00	3.00	1.75
96	Lou Berberet	6.00	3.00	1.75
97	Jerry Lynch	6.00	3.00	1.75
98	Arnie Portocarrero	6.00	3.00	1.75
99	Ted Kazanski	6.00	3.00	1.75

100	Bob Cerv	6.00	3.00	1.75
101	Alex Kellner	6.00	3.00	1.75
102	*Felipe Alou*	29.00	14.50	8.75
103	Billy Goodman	6.00	3.00	1.75
104	Del Rice	6.00	3.00	1.75
105	Lee Walls	6.00	3.00	1.75
106	Hal Woodeshick	6.00	3.00	1.75
107	Norm Larker	6.00	3.00	1.75
108	Zack Monroe	6.00	3.00	1.75
109	Bob Schmidt	6.00	3.00	1.75
110	George Witt	6.00	3.00	1.75
111	Redlegs Team/Checklist 89-176	15.00	7.50	4.50
112	Billy Consolo	4.00	2.00	1.25
113	Taylor Phillips	4.00	2.00	1.25
114	Earl Battey	4.00	2.00	1.25
115	Mickey Vernon	4.00	2.00	1.25
116	*Bob Allison*	8.00	4.00	2.50
117	*John Blanchard*	7.50	3.75	2.25
118	John Buzhardt	4.00	2.00	1.25
119	*John Callison*	8.00	4.00	2.50
120	Chuck Coles	4.00	2.00	1.25
121	Bob Conley	4.00	2.00	1.25
122	Bennie Daniels	4.00	2.00	1.25
123	Don Dillard	4.00	2.00	1.25
124	Dan Dobbek	4.00	2.00	1.25
125	*Ron Fairly*	6.00	3.00	1.75
126	Eddie Haas	4.00	2.00	1.25
127	Kent Hadley	4.00	2.00	1.25
128	Bob Hartman	4.00	2.00	1.25
129	Frank Herrera	4.00	2.00	1.25
130	Lou Jackson	4.00	2.00	1.25
131	*Deron Johnson*	8.00	4.00	2.50
132	Don Lee	4.00	2.00	1.25
133	*Bob Lillis*	4.00	2.00	1.25
134	Jim McDaniel	4.00	2.00	1.25
135	Gene Oliver	4.00	2.00	1.25
136	*Jim O'Toole*	4.00	2.00	1.25
137	Dick Ricketts	4.00	2.00	1.25
138	John Romano	4.00	2.00	1.25
139	Ed Sadowski	4.00	2.00	1.25
140	Charlie Secrest	4.00	2.00	1.25
141	Joe Shipley	4.00	2.00	1.25
142	Dick Stigman	4.00	2.00	1.25
143	Willie Tasby	4.00	2.00	1.25
144	Jerry Walker	4.00	2.00	1.25
145	Dom Zanni	4.00	2.00	1.25
146	Jerry Zimmerman	4.00	2.00	1.25
147	Cubs' Clubbers (Ernie Banks, Dale Long, Walt Moryn)	20.00	10.00	6.00
148	Mike McCormick	4.00	2.00	1.25
149	Jim Bunning	15.00	7.50	4.50
150	Stan Musial	100.00	50.00	30.00
151	Bob Malkmus	4.00	2.00	1.25
152	Johnny Klippstein	4.00	2.00	1.25
153	Jim Marshall	4.00	2.00	1.25
154	Ray Herbert	4.00	2.00	1.25
155	Enos Slaughter	16.00	8.00	4.75
156	Ace Hurlers (Billy Pierce, Robin Roberts)	11.00	5.50	3.25
157	Felix Mantilla	4.00	2.00	1.25
158	Walt Dropo	4.00	2.00	1.25
159	Bob Shaw	4.00	2.00	1.25
160	Dick Groat	4.00	2.00	1.25
161	Frank Baumann	4.00	2.00	1.25
162	Bobby G. Smith	4.00	2.00	1.25
163	Sandy Koufax	130.00	65.00	39.00
164	Johnny Groth	4.00	2.00	1.25
165	Bill Bruton	4.00	2.00	1.25
166	Destruction Crew (Rocky Colavito, Larry Doby, Minnie Minoso)	16.00	8.00	4.75
167	Duke Maas	4.00	2.00	1.25
168	Carroll Hardy	4.00	2.00	1.25
169	Ted Abernathy	4.00	2.00	1.25
170	Gene Woodling	4.00	2.00	1.25
171	Willard Schmidt	4.00	2.00	1.25
172	A's Team/Checklist 177-242	13.00	6.50	4.00
173	*Bill Monbouquette*	4.00	2.00	1.25
174	Jim Pendleton	4.00	2.00	1.25
175	Dick Farrell	4.00	2.00	1.25
176	Preston Ward	4.00	2.00	1.25
177	Johnny Briggs	4.00	2.00	1.25
178	Ruben Amaro	4.00	2.00	1.25
179	Don Rudolph	4.00	2.00	1.25
180	Yogi Berra	65.00	32.00	19.50
181	Bob Porterfield	4.00	2.00	1.25
182	Milt Graff	4.00	2.00	1.25
183	Stu Miller	4.00	2.00	1.25
184	Harvey Haddix	4.00	2.00	1.25
185	Jim Busby	4.00	2.00	1.25
186	Mudcat Grant	4.00	2.00	1.25
187	Bubba Phillips	4.00	2.00	1.25
188	Juan Pizarro	4.00	2.00	1.25
189	Neil Chrisley	4.00	2.00	1.25
190	Bill Virdon	4.00	2.00	1.25
191	Russ Kemmerer	4.00	2.00	1.25
192	Charley Beamon	4.00	2.00	1.25
193	Sammy Taylor	4.00	2.00	1.25
194	Jim Brosnan	4.00	2.00	1.25
195	Rip Repulski	4.00	2.00	1.25
196	Billy Moran	4.00	2.00	1.25
197	Ray Semproch	4.00	2.00	1.25
198	Jim Davenport	4.00	2.00	1.25
199	Leo Kiely	4.00	2.00	1.25
200	Warren Giles	7.00	3.50	2.00
201	Tom Acker	4.00	2.00	1.25
202	Roger Maris	90.00	45.00	27.00
203	Ozzie Virgil	4.00	2.00	1.25
204	Casey Wise	4.00	2.00	1.25
205	Don Larsen	7.50	3.75	2.25
206	Carl Furillo	6.00	3.00	1.75
207	George Strickland	4.00	2.00	1.25
208	Willie Jones	4.00	2.00	1.25
209	Lenny Green	4.00	2.00	1.25
210	Ed Bailey	4.00	2.00	1.25
211	Bob Blaylock	4.00	2.00	1.25
212	Fence Busters (Hank Aaron, Eddie Mathews)	65.00	32.00	19.50
213	Jim Rivera	4.00	2.00	1.25
214	Marcelino Solis	4.00	2.00	1.25
215	Jim Lemon	4.00	2.00	1.25
216	Andre Rodgers	4.00	2.00	1.25
217	Carl Erskine	7.00	3.50	2.00
218	Roman Mejias	4.00	2.00	1.25
219	George Zuverink	4.00	2.00	1.25
220	Frank Malzone	4.00	2.00	1.25
221	Bob Bowman	4.00	2.00	1.25
222	Bobby Shantz	4.00	2.00	1.25
223	Cards Team/Checklist 265-352	11.00	5.50	3.25
224	*Claude Osteen*	6.00	3.00	1.75
225	Johnny Logan	4.00	2.00	1.25
226	Art Ceccarelli	4.00	2.00	1.25
227	Hal Smith	4.00	2.00	1.25
228	Don Gross	4.00	2.00	1.25
229	Vic Power	4.00	2.00	1.25
230	Bill Fischer	4.00	2.00	1.25
231	Ellis Burton	4.00	2.00	1.25
232	Eddie Kasko	4.00	2.00	1.25
233	Paul Foytack	4.00	2.00	1.25
234	Chuck Tanner	4.00	2.00	1.25
235	Valmy Thomas	4.00	2.00	1.25
236	Ted Bowsfield	4.00	2.00	1.25
237	Run Preventers (Gil McDougald, Bobby Richardson, Bob Turley)	11.00	5.50	3.25
238	Gene Baker	4.00	2.00	1.25
239	Bob Trowbridge	4.00	2.00	1.25
240	Hank Bauer	6.50	3.25	2.00
241	Billy Muffett	4.00	2.00	1.25
242	Ron Samford	4.00	2.00	1.25
243	Marv Grissom	4.00	2.00	1.25
244	Dick Gray	4.00	2.00	1.25
245	Ned Garver	4.00	2.00	1.25
246	J.W. Porter	4.00	2.00	1.25
247	Don Ferrarese	4.00	2.00	1.25
248	Red Sox Team/Checklist 177-264	15.00	7.50	4.50
249	Bobby Adams	4.00	2.00	1.25
250	Billy O'Dell	4.00	2.00	1.25
251	Cletis Boyer	7.00	3.50	2.00
252	Ray Boone	4.00	2.00	1.25
253	Seth Morehead	4.00	2.00	1.25
254	Zeke Bella	4.00	2.00	1.25
255	Del Ennis	4.00	2.00	1.25
256	Jerry Davie	4.00	2.00	1.25
257	*Leon Wagner*	7.00	3.50	2.00
258	Fred Kipp	4.00	2.00	1.25
259	Jim Pisoni	4.00	2.00	1.25
260	Early Wynn	16.00	8.00	4.75
261	Gene Stephens	4.00	2.00	1.25
262	Hitters' Foes (Don Drysdale, Clem Labine, Johnny Podres)	15.00	7.50	4.50
263	Buddy Daley	4.00	2.00	1.25
264	Chico Carrasquel	4.00	2.00	1.25
265	Ron Kline	4.00	2.00	1.25
266	Woody Held	4.00	2.00	1.25
267	John Romonosky	4.00	2.00	1.25
268	Tito Francona	4.00	2.00	1.25
269	Jack Meyer	4.00	2.00	1.25
270	Gil Hodges	17.50	8.75	5.25
271	*Orlando Pena*	4.00	2.00	1.25
272	Jerry Lumpe	4.00	2.00	1.25
273	Joe Jay	4.00	2.00	1.25
274	Jerry Kindall	4.00	2.00	1.25
275	Jack Sanford	4.00	2.00	1.25
276	Pete Daley	4.00	2.00	1.25
277	Turk Lown	4.00	2.00	1.25
278	Chuck Essegian	4.00	2.00	1.25
279	Ernie Johnson	4.00	2.00	1.25
280	Frank Bolling	4.00	2.00	1.25
281	Walt Craddock	4.00	2.00	1.25
282	R.C. Stevens	4.00	2.00	1.25
283	Russ Heman	4.00	2.00	1.25
284	Steve Korcheck	4.00	2.00	1.25
285	Joe Cunningham	4.00	2.00	1.25
286	Dean Stone	4.00	2.00	1.25
287	Don Zimmer	4.50	2.25	1.25
288	Dutch Dotterer	4.00	2.00	1.25
289	Johnny Kucks	4.00	2.00	1.25
290	Wes Covington	4.00	2.00	1.25
291	Pitching Partners (Camilo Pascual, Pedro Ramos)	6.00	3.00	1.75
292	Dick Williams	4.00	2.00	1.25
293	Ray Moore	4.00	2.00	1.25
294	Hank Foiles	4.00	2.00	1.25
295	Billy Martin	15.00	7.50	4.50
296	*Ernie Broglio*	4.00	2.00	1.25
297	*Jackie Brandt*	4.00	2.00	1.25
298	Tex Clevenger	4.00	2.00	1.25
299	Billy Klaus	4.00	2.00	1.25
300	Richie Ashburn	18.00	9.00	5.50
301	Earl Averill	4.00	2.00	1.25
302	Don Mossi	4.00	2.00	1.25
303	Marty Keough	4.00	2.00	1.25
304	Cubs Team/Checklist 265-352	15.00	7.50	4.50
305	Curt Raydon	4.00	2.00	1.25
306	Jim Gilliam	7.00	3.50	2.00
307	Curt Barclay	4.00	2.00	1.25
308	Norm Siebern	4.00	2.00	1.25
309	Sal Maglie	4.00	2.00	1.25
310	Luis Aparicio	19.00	9.50	5.75
311	Norm Zauchin	4.00	2.00	1.25
312	Don Newcombe	5.00	2.50	1.50
313	Frank House	4.00	2.00	1.25
314	Don Cardwell	4.00	2.00	1.25
315	Joe Adcock	4.00	2.00	1.25
316a	Ralph Lumenti (no optioned statement)	80.00	40.00	24.00
316b	Ralph Lumenti (optioned statement)	4.00	2.00	1.25
317	N.L. Hitting Kings (Richie Ashburn, Willie Mays)	45.00	22.00	13.50
318	Rocky Bridges	4.00	2.00	1.25
319	Dave Hillman	4.00	2.00	1.25
320	Bob Skinner	4.00	2.00	1.25
321a	Bob Giallombardo (no optioned statement)	80.00	40.00	24.00
321b	Bob Giallombardo (optioned statement)	4.00	2.00	1.25
322a	Harry Hanebrink (no trade statement)	80.00	40.00	24.00
322b	Harry Hanebrink (trade statement)	4.00	2.00	1.25
323	Frank Sullivan	4.00	2.00	1.25
324	Don Demeter	4.00	2.00	1.25
325	Ken Boyer	8.00	4.00	2.50
326	Marv Throneberry	5.00	2.50	1.50
327	*Gary Bell*	4.00	2.00	1.25
328	Lou Skizas	4.00	2.00	1.25
329	Tigers Team/Checklist 353-429	15.00	7.50	4.50
330	Gus Triandos	4.00	2.00	1.25
331	Steve Boros	4.00	2.00	1.25
332	Ray Monzant	4.00	2.00	1.25
333	Harry Simpson	4.00	2.00	1.25
334	Glen Hobbie	4.00	2.00	1.25
335	Johnny Temple	4.00	2.00	1.25
336a	Billy Loes (no trade statement)	80.00	40.00	24.00
336b	Billy Loes (trade statement)	4.00	2.00	1.25
337	George Crowe	4.00	2.00	1.25
338	*Sparky Anderson*	65.00	32.00	19.50
339	Roy Face	4.00	2.00	1.25
340	Roy Sievers	4.00	2.00	1.25
341	Tom Qualters	4.00	2.00	1.25
342	Ray Jablonski	4.00	2.00	1.25
343	Billy Hoeft	4.00	2.00	1.25
344	Russ Nixon	4.00	2.00	1.25
345	Gil McDougald	7.50	3.75	2.25
346	Batter Bafflers (Tom Brewer, Dave Sisler)	4.00	2.00	1.25
347	Bob Buhl	4.00	2.00	1.25
348	Ted Lepcio	4.00	2.00	1.25
349	Hoyt Wilhelm	14.00	7.00	4.25
350	Ernie Banks	70.00	35.00	21.00
351	Earl Torgeson	4.00	2.00	1.25
352	Robin Roberts	17.50	8.75	5.25
353	Curt Flood	6.00	3.00	1.75
354	Pete Burnside	4.00	2.00	1.25
355	Jim Piersall	4.00	2.00	1.25
356	Bob Mabe	4.00	2.00	1.25
357	*Dick Stuart*	6.00	3.00	1.75
358	Ralph Terry	4.00	2.00	1.25
359	*Bill White*	16.00	8.00	4.75
360	Al Kaline	60.00	30.00	18.00
361	Willard Nixon	4.00	2.00	1.25
362a	Dolan Nichols (no optioned statement)	80.00	40.00	24.00
362b	Dolan Nichols (optioned statement)	4.00	2.00	1.25
363	Bobby Avila	4.00	2.00	1.25
364	Danny McDevitt	4.00	2.00	1.25
365	Gus Bell	4.00	2.00	1.25
366	Humberto Robinson	4.00	2.00	1.25
367	Cal Neeman	4.00	2.00	1.25
368	Don Mueller	4.00	2.00	1.25
369	Dick Tomanek	4.00	2.00	1.25
370	Pete Runnels	4.00	2.00	1.25
371	Dick Brodowski	4.00	2.00	1.25
372	Jim Hegan	4.00	2.00	1.25
373	Herb Plews	4.00	2.00	1.25
374	Art Ditmar	4.00	2.00	1.25
375	Bob Nieman	4.00	2.00	1.25
376	Hal Naragon	4.00	2.00	1.25
377	Johnny Antonelli	4.00	2.00	1.25
378	Gail Harris	4.00	2.00	1.25
379	Bob Miller	4.00	2.00	1.25
380	Hank Aaron	95.00	47.00	28.00
381	Mike Baxes	4.00	2.00	1.25
382	Curt Simmons	4.00	2.00	1.25
383	Words of Wisdom (Don Larsen, Casey Stengel)	9.00	4.50	2.75
384	Dave Sisler	4.00	2.00	1.25
385	Sherman Lollar	4.00	2.00	1.25
386	Jim Delsing	4.00	2.00	1.25
387	Don Drysdale	40.00	20.00	12.00
388	Bob Will	4.00	2.00	1.25
389	Joe Nuxhall	4.00	2.00	1.25
390	Orlando Cepeda	24.00	12.00	7.25
391	Milt Pappas	4.00	2.00	1.25
392	Whitey Herzog	5.50	2.75	1.75
393	Frank Lary	4.00	2.00	1.25
394	Randy Jackson	4.00	2.00	1.25
395	Elston Howard	10.00	5.00	3.00
396	Bob Rush	4.00	2.00	1.25
397	Senators Team/Checklist 430-495	15.00	7.50	4.50
398	Wally Post	4.00	2.00	1.25
399	Larry Jackson	4.00	2.00	1.25
400	Jackie Jensen	6.00	3.00	1.75
401	Ron Blackburn	4.00	2.00	1.25
402	Hector Lopez	4.00	2.00	1.25
403	Clem Labine	4.00	2.00	1.25
404	Hank Sauer	4.00	2.00	1.25
405	Roy McMillan	4.00	2.00	1.25
406	Solly Drake	4.00	2.00	1.25
407	Moe Drabowsky	4.00	2.00	1.25
408	Keystone Combo (Luis Aparicio, Nellie Fox)	20.00	10.00	6.00
409	Gus Zernial	4.00	2.00	1.25
410	Billy Pierce	4.00	2.00	1.25
411	Whitey Lockman	4.00	2.00	1.25
412	Stan Lopata	4.00	2.00	1.25
413	Camillo (Camilo) Pascual	4.00	2.00	1.25
414	Dale Long	4.00	2.00	1.25
415	Bill Mazeroski	12.50	6.25	3.75
416	Haywood Sullivan	4.00	2.00	1.25
417	Virgil Trucks	4.00	2.00	1.25
418	Gino Cimoli	4.00	2.00	1.25

419	Braves Team/Checklist 353-429	15.00	7.50	4.50
420	Rocky Colavito	29.00	14.50	8.75
421	Herm Wehmeier	4.00	2.00	1.25
422	Hobie Landrith	4.00	2.00	1.25
423	Bob Grim	4.00	2.00	1.25
424	Ken Aspromonte	4.00	2.00	1.25
425	Del Crandall	4.00	2.00	1.25
426	Jerry Staley	4.00	2.00	1.25
427	Charlie Neal	4.00	2.00	1.25
428	Buc Hill Aces (Roy Face, Bob Friend, Ron Kline, Vern Law)	6.00	3.00	1.75
429	Bobby Thomson	4.00	2.00	1.25
430	Whitey Ford	55.00	27.00	16.50
431	Whammy Douglas	4.00	2.00	1.25
432	Smoky Burgess	4.00	2.00	1.25
433	Billy Harrell	4.00	2.00	1.25
434	Hal Griggs	4.00	2.00	1.25
435	Frank Robinson	40.00	20.00	12.00
436	Granny Hamner	4.00	2.00	1.25
437	Ike Delock	4.00	2.00	1.25
438	Sam Esposito	4.00	2.00	1.25
439	Brooks Robinson	35.00	17.50	10.50
440	Lou Burdette	7.00	3.50	2.00
441	John Roseboro	5.00	2.50	1.50
442	Ray Narleski	4.00	2.00	1.25
443	Daryl Spencer	4.00	2.00	1.25
444	*Ronnie Hansen*	4.00	2.00	1.25
445	Cal McLish	4.00	2.00	1.25
446	Rocky Nelson	4.00	2.00	1.25
447	Bob Anderson	4.00	2.00	1.25
448	Vada Pinson	7.00	3.50	2.00
449	Tom Gorman	4.00	2.00	1.25
450	Eddie Mathews	25.00	12.50	7.50
451	Jimmy Constable	4.00	2.00	1.25
452	Chico Fernandez	4.00	2.00	1.25
453	Les Moss	4.00	2.00	1.25
454	Phil Clark	4.00	2.00	1.25
455	Larry Doby	14.00	7.00	4.25
456	Jerry Casale	4.00	2.00	1.25
457	Dodgers Team	22.00	11.00	6.50
458	Gordon Jones	4.00	2.00	1.25
459	Bill Tuttle	4.00	2.00	1.25
460	Bob Friend	4.00	2.00	1.25
461	Mantle Hits 42nd Homer For Crown (Mickey Mantle)	100.00	50.00	30.00
462	Colavito's Great Catch Saves Game (Rocky Colavito)	15.00	7.50	4.50
463	Kaline Becomes Youngest Batting Champ (Al Kaline)	24.00	12.00	7.25
464	Mays' Catch Makes Series History (Willie Mays)	38.00	19.00	11.50
465	Sievers Sets Homer Mark (Roy Sievers)	6.00	3.00	1.75
466	Pierce All-Star Starter (Billy Pierce)	6.00	3.00	1.75
467	Aaron Clubs World Series Homer (Hank Aaron)	30.00	15.00	9.00
468	Snider's Play Brings L.A. Victory (Duke Snider)	18.00	9.00	5.50
469	Hustler Banks Wins M.V.P. Award (Ernie Banks)	18.00	9.00	5.50
470	Musial Raps Out 3,000th Hit (Stan Musial)	22.00	11.00	6.50
471	Tom Sturdivant	4.00	2.00	1.25
472	Gene Freese	4.00	2.00	1.25
473	Mike Fornieles	4.00	2.00	1.25
474	Moe Thacker	4.00	2.00	1.25
475	Jack Harshman	4.00	2.00	1.25
476	Indians Team/Checklist 496-572	15.00	7.50	4.50
477	Barry Latman	4.00	2.00	1.25
478	Roberto Clemente	180.00	90.00	54.00
479	Lindy McDaniel	4.00	2.00	1.25
480	Red Schoendienst	14.50	7.25	4.25
481	Charley Maxwell	4.00	2.00	1.25
482	Russ Meyer	4.00	2.00	1.25
483	Clint Courtney	4.00	2.00	1.25
484	Willie Kirkland	4.00	2.00	1.25
485	Ryne Duren	7.00	3.50	2.00
486	Sammy White	4.00	2.00	1.25
487	Hal Brown	4.00	2.00	1.25
488	Walt Moryn	4.00	2.00	1.25
489	John C. Powers	4.00	2.00	1.25
490	Frank Thomas	4.00	2.00	1.25
491	Don Blasingame	4.00	2.00	1.25
492	Gene Conley	4.00	2.00	1.25
493	Jim Landis	4.00	2.00	1.25
494	Don Pavletich	4.00	2.00	1.25
495	Johnny Podres	5.00	2.50	1.50
496	Wayne Terwilliger	4.00	2.00	1.25
497	Hal R. Smith	4.00	2.00	1.25
498	Dick Hyde	4.00	2.00	1.25
499	Johnny O'Brien	4.00	2.00	1.25
500	Vic Wertz	4.00	2.00	1.25
501	Bobby Tiefenauer	4.00	2.00	1.25
502	Al Dark	4.00	2.00	1.25
503	Jim Owens	4.00	2.00	1.25
504	Ossie Alvarez	4.00	2.00	1.25
505	Tony Kubek	9.00	4.50	2.75
506	Bob Purkey	4.00	2.00	1.25
507	Bob Hale	15.00	7.50	4.50
508	Art Fowler	15.00	7.50	4.50
509	*Norm Cash*	55.00	27.00	16.50
510	Yankees Team	90.00	45.00	27.00
511	George Susce	15.00	7.50	4.50
512	George Altman	15.00	7.50	4.50
513	Tom Carroll	15.00	7.50	4.50
514	*Bob Gibson*	225.00	110.00	67.00
515	Harmon Killebrew	115.00	57.00	34.00
516	Mike Garcia	15.00	7.50	4.50
517	Joe Koppe	15.00	7.50	4.50
518	*Mike Cuellar*	27.50	13.50	8.25
519	Infield Power (Dick Gernert, Frank Malzone, Pete Runnels)	18.00	9.00	5.50
520	Don Elston	15.00	7.50	4.50
521	Gary Geiger	15.00	7.50	4.50
522	Gene Snyder	15.00	7.50	4.50
523	Harry Bright	15.00	7.50	4.50
524	Larry Osborne	15.00	7.50	4.50
525	Jim Coates	15.00	7.50	4.50
526	Bob Speake	15.00	7.50	4.50
527	Solly Hemus	15.00	7.50	4.50
528	Pirates Team	65.00	32.00	19.50
529	*George Bamberger*	15.00	7.50	4.50
530	Wally Moon	15.00	7.50	4.50
531	Ray Webster	15.00	7.50	4.50
532	Mark Freeman	15.00	7.50	4.50
533	Darrell Johnson	15.00	7.50	4.50
534	Faye Throneberry	15.00	7.50	4.50
535	Ruben Gomez	15.00	7.50	4.50
536	Dan Kravitz	15.00	7.50	4.50
537	Rodolfo Arias	15.00	7.50	4.50
538	Chick King	15.00	7.50	4.50
539	Gary Blaylock	15.00	7.50	4.50
540	Willy Miranda	15.00	7.50	4.50
541	Bob Thurman	15.00	7.50	4.50
542	*Jim Perry*	24.00	12.00	7.25
543	Corsair Outfield Trio (Roberto Clemente, Bob Skinner, Bill Virdon)	105.00	52.00	31.00
544	Lee Tate	15.00	7.50	4.50
545	Tom Morgan	15.00	7.50	4.50
546	Al Schroll	15.00	7.50	4.50
547	Jim Baxes	15.00	7.50	4.50
548	Elmer Singleton	15.00	7.50	4.50
549	Howie Nunn	15.00	7.50	4.50
550	Roy Campanella (Symbol of Courage)	150.00	75.00	45.00
551	Fred Haney (All-Star)	16.00	8.00	4.75
552	Casey Stengel (All-Star)	24.00	12.00	7.25
553	Orlando Cepeda (All-Star)	25.00	12.50	7.50
554	Bill Skowron (All-Star)	22.00	11.00	6.50
555	Bill Mazeroski (All-Star)	24.00	12.00	7.25
556	Nellie Fox (All-Star)	27.50	13.50	8.25
557	Ken Boyer (All-Star)	24.00	12.00	7.25
558	Frank Malzone (All-Star)	14.00	7.00	4.25
559	Ernie Banks (All-Star)	60.00	30.00	18.00
560	Luis Aparicio (All-Star)	27.50	13.50	8.25
561	Hank Aaron (All-Star)	115.00	57.00	34.00
562	Al Kaline (All-Star)	65.00	32.00	19.50
563	Willie Mays (All-Star)	100.00	50.00	30.00
564	Mickey Mantle (All-Star)	250.00	125.00	75.00
565	Wes Covington (All-Star)	15.00	7.50	4.50
566	Roy Sievers (All-Star)	15.00	7.50	4.50
567	Del Crandall (All-Star)	15.00	7.50	4.50
568	Gus Triandos (All-Star)	15.00	7.50	4.50
569	Bob Friend (All-Star)	15.00	7.50	4.50
570	Bob Turley (All-Star)	17.00	8.50	5.00
571	Warren Spahn (All-Star)	30.00	15.00	9.00
572	Billy Pierce (All-Star)	18.00	9.00	5.50
----	Elect Your Favorite Rookie Insert (paper stock, September 29 date on back)	13.50	6.75	4.00
----	Felt Pennants Insert (paper stock)	13.50	6.75	4.00

1960 Topps

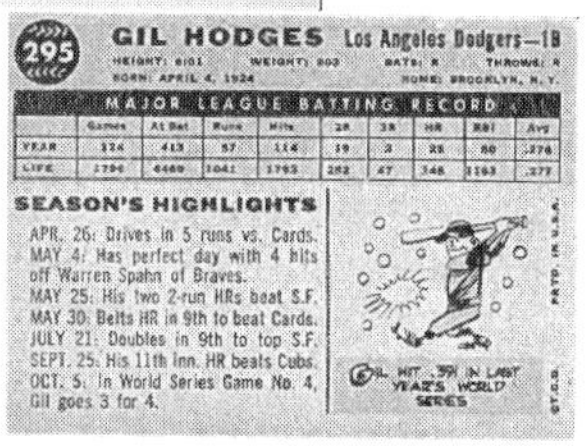

In 1960, Topps returned to a horizontal format (3-1/2" x 2-1/2") with a color portrait and a black-and-white action photograph on the front. After a one-year hiatus, backs returned to the use of lifetime statistics along with a cartoon and short career summary or previous season highlights. Specialty cards in the 572-card set are multi-player cards, managers and coaches cards, and highlights of the 1959 World Series. Two groups of rookie cards are included. The first are numbers 117-148, which are the Sport Magazine rookies. The second group is called "Topps All-Star Rookies." Finally, there is a run of All-Star cards to close out the set in the scarcer high numbers. Cards #375-440 can be found with backs printed on either white or grey cardboard, with the white stock being the less common.

		NM	EX	VG
	Complete Set (572):	3500.	1750.	975.00
	Common Player (1-440):	3.50	1.75	1.00
	Common Player (441-506):	6.00	3.00	1.75
	Common Player (507-572):	14.00	7.00	4.25
1	Early Wynn	27.00	9.00	4.00
2	Roman Mejias	3.50	1.75	1.00
3	Joe Adcock	3.50	1.75	1.00
4	Bob Purkey	3.50	1.75	1.00
5	Wally Moon	4.00	2.00	1.25
6	Lou Berberet	3.50	1.75	1.00
7	Master and Mentor (Willie Mays, Bill Rigney)	24.00	12.00	7.25
8	Bud Daley	3.50	1.75	1.00
9	Faye Throneberry	3.50	1.75	1.00
10	Ernie Banks	32.00	16.00	9.50
11	Norm Siebern	3.50	1.75	1.00
12	Milt Pappas	3.50	1.75	1.00
13	Wally Post	3.50	1.75	1.00
14	Jim Grant	3.50	1.75	1.00
15	Pete Runnels	3.50	1.75	1.00
16	Ernie Broglio	3.50	1.75	1.00
17	Johnny Callison	3.50	1.75	1.00
18	Dodgers Team/Checklist 1-88	35.00	17.50	10.50
19	Felix Mantilla	3.50	1.75	1.00
20	Roy Face	3.50	1.75	1.00
21	Dutch Dotterer	3.50	1.75	1.00
22	Rocky Bridges	3.50	1.75	1.00
23	Eddie Fisher	3.50	1.75	1.00
24	Dick Gray	3.50	1.75	1.00
25	Roy Sievers	3.50	1.75	1.00
26	Wayne Terwilliger	3.50	1.75	1.00
27	Dick Drott	3.50	1.75	1.00
28	Brooks Robinson	48.00	24.00	14.50
29	Clem Labine	3.50	1.75	1.00
30	Tito Francona	3.50	1.75	1.00
31	Sammy Esposito	3.50	1.75	1.00
32	Sophomore Stalwarts (Jim O'Toole, Vada Pinson)	5.50	2.75	1.75
33	Tom Morgan	3.50	1.75	1.00
34	Sparky Anderson	24.00	12.00	7.25
35	Whitey Ford	45.00	22.00	13.50
36	Russ Nixon	3.50	1.75	1.00
37	Bill Bruton	3.50	1.75	1.00
38	Jerry Casale	3.50	1.75	1.00
39	Earl Averill	3.50	1.75	1.00
40	Joe Cunningham	3.50	1.75	1.00
41	Barry Latman	3.50	1.75	1.00
42	Hobie Landrith	3.50	1.75	1.00
43	Senators Team/Checklist 1-88	9.00	4.50	2.75
44	Bobby Locke	3.50	1.75	1.00
45	Roy McMillan	3.50	1.75	1.00
46	Jack Fisher	3.50	1.75	1.00
47	Don Zimmer	4.00	2.00	1.25
48	Hal Smith	3.50	1.75	1.00
49	Curt Raydon	3.50	1.75	1.00
50	Al Kaline	37.50	18.50	11.00
51	Jim Coates	3.50	1.75	1.00
52	Dave Philley	3.50	1.75	1.00
53	Jackie Brandt	3.50	1.75	1.00
54	Mike Fornieles	3.50	1.75	1.00
55	Bill Mazeroski	10.00	5.00	3.00
56	Steve Korcheck	3.50	1.75	1.00
57	Win-Savers (Turk Lown, Gerry Staley)	4.00	2.00	1.25
58	Gino Cimoli	3.50	1.75	1.00
59	Juan Pizarro	3.50	1.75	1.00
60	Gus Triandos	3.50	1.75	1.00
61	Eddie Kasko	3.50	1.75	1.00
62	Roger Craig	3.50	1.75	1.00
63	George Strickland	3.50	1.75	1.00
64	Jack Meyer	3.50	1.75	1.00
65	Elston Howard	6.50	3.25	2.00
66	Bob Trowbridge	3.50	1.75	1.00
67	*Jose Pagan*	3.50	1.75	1.00
68	Dave Hillman	3.50	1.75	1.00
69	Billy Goodman	3.50	1.75	1.00
70	Lou Burdette	3.50	1.75	1.00
71	Marty Keough	3.50	1.75	1.00
72	Tigers Team/Checklist 89-176	15.00	7.50	4.50
73	Bob Gibson	37.50	18.50	11.00
74	Walt Moryn	3.50	1.75	1.00
75	Vic Power	3.50	1.75	1.00
76	Bill Fischer	3.50	1.75	1.00
77	Hank Foiles	3.50	1.75	1.00
78	Bob Grim	3.50	1.75	1.00
79	Walt Dropo	3.50	1.75	1.00
80	Johnny Antonelli	3.50	1.75	1.00
81	Russ Snyder	3.50	1.75	1.00
82	Ruben Gomez	3.50	1.75	1.00
83	Tony Kubek	6.00	3.00	1.75
84	Hal Smith	3.50	1.75	1.00
85	Frank Lary	3.50	1.75	1.00
86	Dick Gernert	3.50	1.75	1.00
87	John Romonosky	3.50	1.75	1.00
88	John Roseboro	3.50	1.75	1.00
89	Hal Brown	3.50	1.75	1.00
90	Bobby Avila	3.50	1.75	1.00
91	Bennie Daniels	3.50	1.75	1.00
92	Whitey Herzog	4.00	2.00	1.25
93	Art Schult	3.50	1.75	1.00
94	Leo Kiely	3.50	1.75	1.00
95	Frank Thomas	3.50	1.75	1.00
96	Ralph Terry	3.50	1.75	1.00
97	Ted Lepcio	3.50	1.75	1.00
98	Gordon Jones	3.50	1.75	1.00
99	Lenny Green	3.50	1.75	1.00
100	Nellie Fox	10.00	5.00	3.00
101	Bob Miller	3.50	1.75	1.00
102	Kent Hadley	3.50	1.75	1.00
103	Dick Farrell	3.50	1.75	1.00
104	Dick Schofield	3.50	1.75	1.00
105	*Larry Sherry*	5.50	2.75	1.75
106	Billy Gardner	3.50	1.75	1.00
107	Carl Willey	3.50	1.75	1.00

108	Pete Daley	3.50	1.75	1.00
109	Cletis Boyer	6.00	3.00	1.75
110	Cal McLish	3.50	1.75	1.00
111	Vic Wertz	3.50	1.75	1.00
112	Jack Harshman	3.50	1.75	1.00
113	Bob Skinner	3.50	1.75	1.00
114	Ken Aspromonte	3.50	1.75	1.00
115	Fork and Knuckler (Roy Face, Hoyt Wilhelm)	5.50	2.75	1.75
116	Jim Rivera	3.50	1.75	1.00
117	Tom Borland	3.50	1.75	1.00
118	Bob Bruce	3.50	1.75	1.00
119	*Chico Cardenas*	3.50	1.75	1.00
120	Duke Carmel	3.50	1.75	1.00
121	Camilo Carreon	3.50	1.75	1.00
122	Don Dillard	3.50	1.75	1.00
123	Dan Dobbek	3.50	1.75	1.00
124	Jim Donohue	3.50	1.75	1.00
125	*Dick Ellsworth*	3.50	1.75	1.00
126	*Chuck Estrada*	3.50	1.75	1.00
127	Ronnie Hansen	3.50	1.75	1.00
128	Bill Harris	3.50	1.75	1.00
129	Bob Hartman	3.50	1.75	1.00
130	Frank Herrera	3.50	1.75	1.00
131	Ed Hobaugh	3.50	1.75	1.00
132	*Frank Howard*	18.00	9.00	5.50
133	*Manuel Javier*	4.00	2.00	1.25
134	Deron Johnson	5.00	2.50	1.50
135	Ken Johnson	3.50	1.75	1.00
136	*Jim Kaat*	30.00	15.00	9.00
137	Lou Klimchock	3.50	1.75	1.00
138	*Art Mahaffey*	3.50	1.75	1.00
139	Carl Mathias	3.50	1.75	1.00
140	Julio Navarro	3.50	1.75	1.00
141	Jim Proctor	3.50	1.75	1.00
142	Bill Short	3.50	1.75	1.00
143	Al Spangler	3.50	1.75	1.00
144	Al Stieglitz	3.50	1.75	1.00
145	Jim Umbricht	3.50	1.75	1.00
146	Ted Wieand	3.50	1.75	1.00
147	Bob Will	3.50	1.75	1.00
148	*Carl Yastrzemski*	120.00	60.00	36.00
149	Bob Nieman	3.50	1.75	1.00
150	Billy Pierce	3.50	1.75	1.00
151	Giants Team/Checklist 177-264	6.00	3.00	1.75
152	Gail Harris	3.50	1.75	1.00
153	Bobby Thomson	4.00	2.00	1.25
154	Jim Davenport	3.50	1.75	1.00
155	Charlie Neal	3.50	1.75	1.00
156	Art Ceccarelli	3.50	1.75	1.00
157	Rocky Nelson	3.50	1.75	1.00
158	Wes Covington	3.50	1.75	1.00
159	Jim Piersall	4.00	2.00	1.25
160	Rival All-Stars (Ken Boyer, Mickey Mantle)	80.00	40.00	24.00
161	Ray Narleski	3.50	1.75	1.00
162	Sammy Taylor	3.50	1.75	1.00
163	Hector Lopez	3.50	1.75	1.00
164	Reds Team/Checklist 89-176	7.00	3.50	2.00
165	Jack Sanford	3.50	1.75	1.00
166	Chuck Essegian	3.50	1.75	1.00
167	Valmy Thomas	3.50	1.75	1.00
168	Alex Grammas	3.50	1.75	1.00
169	Jake Striker	3.50	1.75	1.00
170	Del Crandall	3.50	1.75	1.00
171	Johnny Groth	3.50	1.75	1.00
172	Willie Kirkland	3.50	1.75	1.00
173	Billy Martin	11.00	5.50	3.25
174	Indians Team/Checklist 89-176	7.00	3.50	2.00
175	Pedro Ramos	3.50	1.75	1.00
176	Vada Pinson	4.00	2.00	1.25
177	Johnny Kucks	3.50	1.75	1.00
178	Woody Held	3.50	1.75	1.00
179	Rip Coleman	3.50	1.75	1.00
180	Harry Simpson	3.50	1.75	1.00
181	Billy Loes	3.50	1.75	1.00
182	Glen Hobbie	3.50	1.75	1.00
183	Eli Grba	3.50	1.75	1.00
184	Gary Geiger	3.50	1.75	1.00
185	Jim Owens	3.50	1.75	1.00
186	Dave Sisler	3.50	1.75	1.00
187	Jay Hook	3.50	1.75	1.00
188	Dick Williams	3.50	1.75	1.00
189	Don McMahon	3.50	1.75	1.00
190	Gene Woodling	3.50	1.75	1.00
191	Johnny Klippstein	3.50	1.75	1.00
192	Danny O'Connell	3.50	1.75	1.00
193	Dick Hyde	3.50	1.75	1.00
194	Bobby Gene Smith	3.50	1.75	1.00
195	Lindy McDaniel	3.50	1.75	1.00
196	Andy Carey	3.50	1.75	1.00
197	Ron Kline	3.50	1.75	1.00
198	Jerry Lynch	3.50	1.75	1.00
199	Dick Donovan	3.50	1.75	1.00
200	Willie Mays	85.00	42.00	25.00
201	Larry Osborne	3.50	1.75	1.00
202	Fred Kipp	3.50	1.75	1.00
203	Sammy White	3.50	1.75	1.00
204	Ryne Duren	3.50	1.75	1.00
205	Johnny Logan	3.50	1.75	1.00
206	Claude Osteen	3.50	1.75	1.00
207	Bob Boyd	3.50	1.75	1.00
208	White Sox Team/Checklist 177-264	8.00	4.00	2.50
209	Ron Blackburn	3.50	1.75	1.00
210	Harmon Killebrew	22.00	11.00	6.50
211	Taylor Phillips	3.50	1.75	1.00
212	Walt Alston	9.00	4.50	2.75
213	Chuck Dressen	3.50	1.75	1.00
214	Jimmie Dykes	3.50	1.75	1.00
215	Bob Elliott	3.50	1.75	1.00
216	Joe Gordon	3.50	1.75	1.00
217	Charley Grimm	3.50	1.75	1.00
218	Solly Hemus	3.50	1.75	1.00
219	Fred Hutchinson	3.50	1.75	1.00
220	Billy Jurges	3.50	1.75	1.00
221	Cookie Lavagetto	3.50	1.75	1.00
222	Al Lopez	4.50	2.25	1.25
223	Danny Murtaugh	3.50	1.75	1.00
224	Paul Richards	3.50	1.75	1.00
225	Bill Rigney	3.50	1.75	1.00
226	Eddie Sawyer	3.50	1.75	1.00
227	Casey Stengel	15.00	7.50	4.50
228	Ernie Johnson	3.50	1.75	1.00
229	Joe M. Morgan	3.50	1.75	1.00
230	Mound Magicians (Bob Buhl, Lou Burdette, Warren Spahn)	9.00	4.50	2.75
231	Hal Naragon	3.50	1.75	1.00
232	Jim Busby	3.50	1.75	1.00
233	Don Elston	3.50	1.75	1.00
234	Don Demeter	3.50	1.75	1.00
235	Gus Bell	3.50	1.75	1.00
236	Dick Ricketts	3.50	1.75	1.00
237	Elmer Valo	3.50	1.75	1.00
238	Danny Kravitz	3.50	1.75	1.00
239	Joe Shipley	3.50	1.75	1.00
240	Luis Aparicio	13.00	6.50	4.00
241	Albie Pearson	3.50	1.75	1.00
242	Cards Team/Checklist 265-352	9.00	4.50	2.75
243	Bubba Phillips	3.50	1.75	1.00
244	Hal Griggs	3.50	1.75	1.00
245	Eddie Yost	3.50	1.75	1.00
246	Lee Maye	3.50	1.75	1.00
247	Gil McDougald	4.50	2.25	1.25
248	Del Rice	3.50	1.75	1.00
249	*Earl Wilson*	4.00	2.00	1.25
250	Stan Musial	70.00	35.00	21.00
251	Bobby Malkmus	3.50	1.75	1.00
252	Ray Herbert	3.50	1.75	1.00
253	Eddie Bressoud	3.50	1.75	1.00
254	Arnie Portocarrero	3.50	1.75	1.00
255	Jim Gilliam	4.00	2.00	1.25
256	Dick Brown	3.50	1.75	1.00
257	Gordy Coleman	3.50	1.75	1.00
258	Dick Groat	4.00	2.00	1.25
259	George Altman	3.50	1.75	1.00
260	Power Plus (Rocky Colavito, Tito Francona)	12.50	6.25	3.75
261	Pete Burnside	3.50	1.75	1.00
262	Hank Bauer	3.50	1.75	1.00
263	Darrell Johnson	3.50	1.75	1.00
264	Robin Roberts	12.50	6.25	3.75
265	Rip Repulski	3.50	1.75	1.00
266	Joe Jay	3.50	1.75	1.00
267	Jim Marshall	3.50	1.75	1.00
268	Al Worthington	3.50	1.75	1.00
269	Gene Green	3.50	1.75	1.00
270	Bob Turley	3.50	1.75	1.00
271	Julio Becquer	3.50	1.75	1.00
272	Fred Green	3.50	1.75	1.00
273	Neil Chrisley	3.50	1.75	1.00
274	Tom Acker	3.50	1.75	1.00
275	Curt Flood	5.00	2.50	1.50
276	Ken McBride	3.50	1.75	1.00
277	Harry Bright	3.50	1.75	1.00
278	Stan Williams	3.50	1.75	1.00
279	Chuck Tanner	3.50	1.75	1.00
280	Frank Sullivan	3.50	1.75	1.00
281	Ray Boone	3.50	1.75	1.00
282	Joe Nuxhall	3.50	1.75	1.00
283	John Blanchard	4.00	2.00	1.25
284	Don Gross	3.50	1.75	1.00
285	Harry Anderson	3.50	1.75	1.00
286	Ray Semproch	3.50	1.75	1.00
287	Felipe Alou	5.00	2.50	1.50
288	Bob Mabe	3.50	1.75	1.00
289	Willie Jones	3.50	1.75	1.00
290	Jerry Lumpe	3.50	1.75	1.00
291	Bob Keegan	3.50	1.75	1.00
292	Dodger Backstops (Joe Pignatano, John Roseboro)	5.50	2.75	1.75
293	Gene Conley	3.50	1.75	1.00
294	Tony Taylor	3.50	1.75	1.00
295	Gil Hodges	17.50	8.75	5.25
296	Nelson Chittum	3.50	1.75	1.00
297	Reno Bertoia	3.50	1.75	1.00
298	George Witt	3.50	1.75	1.00
299	Earl Torgeson	3.50	1.75	1.00
300	Hank Aaron	75.00	37.00	22.00
301	Jerry Davie	3.50	1.75	1.00
302	Phillies Team/Checklist 353-429	6.00	3.00	1.75
303	Billy O'Dell	3.50	1.75	1.00
304	Joe Ginsberg	3.50	1.75	1.00
305	Richie Ashburn	12.50	6.25	3.75
306	Frank Baumann	3.50	1.75	1.00
307	Gene Oliver	3.50	1.75	1.00
308	Dick Hall	3.50	1.75	1.00
309	Bob Hale	3.50	1.75	1.00
310	Frank Malzone	3.50	1.75	1.00
311	Raul Sanchez	3.50	1.75	1.00
312	Charlie Lau	3.50	1.75	1.00
313	Turk Lown	3.50	1.75	1.00
314	Chico Fernandez	3.50	1.75	1.00
315	Bobby Shantz	4.00	2.00	1.25
316	*Willie McCovey*	100.00	50.00	30.00
317	Pumpsie Green	3.50	1.75	1.00
318	Jim Baxes	3.50	1.75	1.00
319	Joe Koppe	3.50	1.75	1.00
320	Bob Allison	3.50	1.75	1.00
321	Ron Fairly	3.50	1.75	1.00
322	Willie Tasby	3.50	1.75	1.00
323	Johnny Romano	3.50	1.75	1.00
324	Jim Perry	3.50	1.75	1.00
325	Jim O'Toole	3.50	1.75	1.00
326	Roberto Clemente	125.00	65.00	40.00
327	*Ray Sadecki*	3.50	1.75	1.00
328	Earl Battey	3.50	1.75	1.00
329	Zack Monroe	3.50	1.75	1.00
330	Harvey Kuenn	4.00	2.00	1.25
331	Henry Mason	3.50	1.75	1.00
332	Yankees Team/Checklist 265-352	55.00	27.00	16.50
333	Danny McDevitt	3.50	1.75	1.00
334	Ted Abernathy	3.50	1.75	1.00
335	Red Schoendienst	10.00	5.00	3.00
336	Ike Delock	3.50	1.75	1.00
337	Cal Neeman	3.50	1.75	1.00
338	Ray Monzant	3.50	1.75	1.00
339	Harry Chiti	3.50	1.75	1.00
340	Harvey Haddix	3.50	1.75	1.00
341	Carroll Hardy	3.50	1.75	1.00
342	Casey Wise	3.50	1.75	1.00
343	Sandy Koufax	105.00	52.00	31.00
344	Clint Courtney	3.50	1.75	1.00
345	Don Newcombe	4.00	2.00	1.25
346	J.C. Martin (photo actually Gary Peters)	3.50	1.75	1.00
347	Ed Bouchee	3.50	1.75	1.00
348	Barry Shetrone	3.50	1.75	1.00
349	Moe Drabowsky	3.50	1.75	1.00
350	Mickey Mantle	350.00	175.00	105.00
351	Don Nottebart	3.50	1.75	1.00
352	Cincy Clouters (Gus Bell, Jerry Lynch, Frank Robinson)	6.00	3.00	1.75
353	Don Larsen	4.50	2.25	1.25
354	Bob Lillis	3.50	1.75	1.00
355	Bill White	3.50	1.75	1.00
356	Joe Amalfitano	3.50	1.75	1.00
357	Al Schroll	3.50	1.75	1.00
358	Joe DeMaestri	3.50	1.75	1.00
359	Buddy Gilbert	3.50	1.75	1.00
360	Herb Score	4.00	2.00	1.25
361	Bob Oldis	3.50	1.75	1.00
362	Russ Kemmerer	3.50	1.75	1.00
363	Gene Stephens	3.50	1.75	1.00
364	Paul Foytack	3.50	1.75	1.00
365	Minnie Minoso	6.00	3.00	1.75
366	*Dallas Green*	5.00	2.50	1.50
367	Bill Tuttle	3.50	1.75	1.00
368	Daryl Spencer	3.50	1.75	1.00
369	Billy Hoeft	3.50	1.75	1.00
370	Bill Skowron	4.50	2.25	1.25
371	Bud Byerly	3.50	1.75	1.00
372	Frank House	3.50	1.75	1.00
373	Don Hoak	3.50	1.75	1.00
374	Bob Buhl	3.50	1.75	1.00
375	Dale Long	3.50	1.75	1.00
376	Johnny Briggs	3.50	1.75	1.00
377	Roger Maris	75.00	37.00	22.00
378	Stu Miller	3.50	1.75	1.00
379	Red Wilson	3.50	1.75	1.00
380	Bob Shaw	3.50	1.75	1.00
381	Braves Team/Checklist 353-429	8.50	4.25	2.50
382	Ted Bowsfield	3.50	1.75	1.00
383	Leon Wagner	3.50	1.75	1.00
384	Don Cardwell	3.50	1.75	1.00
385	World Series Game 1 (Neal Steals Second)	5.00	2.50	1.50
386	World Series Game 2 (Neal Belts 2nd Homer)	5.00	2.50	1.50
387	World Series Game 3 (Furillo Breaks Up Game)	5.00	2.50	1.50
388	World Series Game 4 (Hodges' Winning Homer)	9.50	4.75	2.75
389	World Series Game 5 (Luis Swipes Base)	12.00	6.00	3.50
390	World Series Game 6 (Scrambling After Ball)	4.00	2.00	1.25
391	World Series Summary (The Champs Celebrate)	6.00	2.50	1.45
392	Tex Clevenger	3.50	1.75	1.00
393	Smoky Burgess	3.50	1.75	1.00
394	Norm Larker	3.50	1.75	1.00
395	Hoyt Wilhelm	12.50	6.25	3.75
396	Steve Bilko	3.50	1.75	1.00
397	Don Blasingame	3.50	1.75	1.00
398	Mike Cuellar	3.50	1.75	1.00
399	Young Hill Stars (Jack Fisher, Milt Pappas, Jerry Walker)	3.50	1.75	1.00
400	Rocky Colavito	20.00	10.00	6.00
401	Bob Duliba	3.50	1.75	1.00
402	Dick Stuart	4.00	2.00	1.25
403	Ed Sadowski	3.50	1.75	1.00
404	Bob Rush	3.50	1.75	1.00
405	Bobby Richardson	13.00	6.50	4.00
406	Billy Klaus	3.50	1.75	1.00
407	*Gary Peters* (photo actually J.C. Martin)	3.50	1.75	1.00
408	Carl Furillo	5.50	2.75	1.75
409	Ron Samford	3.50	1.75	1.00
410	Sam Jones	3.50	1.75	1.00
411	Ed Bailey	3.50	1.75	1.00
412	Bob Anderson	3.50	1.75	1.00
413	A's Team/Checklist 430-495	9.00	4.50	2.75
414	Don Williams	3.50	1.75	1.00
415	Bob Cerv	3.50	1.75	1.00
416	Humberto Robinson	3.50	1.75	1.00
417	Chuck Cottier	3.50	1.75	1.00
418	Don Mossi	3.50	1.75	1.00
419	George Crowe	3.50	1.75	1.00
420	Eddie Mathews	25.00	12.50	7.50
421	Duke Maas	3.50	1.75	1.00
422	Johnny Powers	3.50	1.75	1.00
423	Ed Fitz Gerald	3.50	1.75	1.00
424	Pete Whisenant	3.50	1.75	1.00
425	Johnny Podres	6.00	3.00	1.75
426	Ron Jackson	3.50	1.75	1.00
427	Al Grunwald	3.50	1.75	1.00
428	Al Smith	3.50	1.75	1.00
429	American League Kings (Nellie Fox, Harvey Kuenn)	7.50	3.75	2.25
430	Art Ditmar	3.50	1.75	1.00
431	Andre Rodgers	3.50	1.75	1.00
432	Chuck Stobbs	3.50	1.75	1.00
433	Irv Noren	3.50	1.75	1.00
434	Brooks Lawrence	3.50	1.75	1.00
435	Gene Freese	3.50	1.75	1.00
436	Marv Throneberry	4.50	2.25	1.25
437	Bob Friend	3.50	1.75	1.00

438	Jim Coker	3.50	1.75	1.00
439	Tom Brewer	3.50	1.75	1.00
440	Jim Lemon	3.50	1.75	1.00
441	Gary Bell	6.00	3.00	1.75
442	Joe Pignatano	6.00	3.00	1.75
443	Charlie Maxwell	6.00	3.00	1.75
444	Jerry Kindall	6.00	3.00	1.75
445	Warren Spahn	45.00	22.00	13.50
446	Ellis Burton	6.00	3.00	1.75
447	Ray Moore	6.00	3.00	1.75
448	*Jim Gentile*	12.50	6.25	3.75
449	Jim Brosnan	6.00	3.00	1.75
450	Orlando Cepeda	15.00	7.50	4.50
451	Curt Simmons	6.00	3.00	1.75
452	Ray Webster	6.00	3.00	1.75
453	Vern Law	6.00	3.00	1.75
454	Hal Woodeshick	6.00	3.00	1.75
455	Orioles Coaches (Harry Brecheen, Lum Harris, Eddie Robinson)	6.00	3.00	1.75
456	Red Sox Coaches (Del Baker, Billy Herman, Sal Maglie, Rudy York)	7.00	3.50	2.00
457	Cubs Coaches (Lou Klein, Charlie Root, Elvin Tappe)	6.00	3.00	1.75
458	White Sox Coaches (Ray Berres, Johnny Cooney, Tony Cuccinello, Don Gutteridge)	6.00	3.00	1.75
459	Reds Coaches (Cot Deal, Wally Moses, Reggie Otero)	6.00	3.00	1.75
460	Indians Coaches (Mel Harder, Red Kress, Bob Lemon, Jo-Jo White)	7.00	3.50	2.00
461	Tigers Coaches (Luke Appling, Tom Ferrick, Billy Hitchcock)	6.00	3.00	1.75
462	A's Coaches (Walker Cooper, Fred Fitzsimmons, Don Heffner)	6.00	3.00	1.75
463	Dodgers Coaches (Joe Becker, Bobby Bragan, Greg Mulleavy, Pete Reiser)	6.00	3.00	1.75
464	Braves Coaches (George Myatt, Andy Pafko, Bob Scheffing, Whitlow Wyatt)	6.00	3.00	1.75
465	Yankees Coaches (Frank Crosetti, Bill Dickey, Ralph Houk, Ed Lopat)	12.00	6.00	3.50
466	Phillies Coaches (Dick Carter, Andy Cohen, Ken Silvestri)	6.00	3.00	1.75
467	Pirates Coaches (Bill Burwell, Sam Narron, Frank Oceak, Mickey Vernon)	6.00	3.00	1.75
468	Cardinals Coaches (Ray Katt, Johnny Keane, Howie Pollet, Harry Walker)	6.00	3.00	1.75
469	Giants Coaches (Salty Parker, Bill Posedel, Wes Westrum)	6.00	3.00	1.75
470	Senators Coaches (Ellis Clary, Sam Mele, Bob Swift)	6.00	3.00	1.75
471	Ned Garver	6.00	3.00	1.75
472	Al Dark	6.00	3.00	1.75
473	Al Cicotte	6.00	3.00	1.75
474	Haywood Sullivan	6.00	3.00	1.75
475	Don Drysdale	30.00	15.00	9.00
476	Lou Johnson	6.00	3.00	1.75
477	Don Ferrarese	6.00	3.00	1.75
478	Frank Torre	6.00	3.00	1.75
479	Georges Maranda	6.00	3.00	1.75
480	Yogi Berra	55.00	27.00	16.50
481	Wes Stock	6.00	3.00	1.75
482	Frank Bolling	6.00	3.00	1.75
483	Camilo Pascual	6.00	3.00	1.75
484	Pirates Team/Checklist 430-495	35.00	20.00	12.00
485	Ken Boyer	14.00	7.00	4.25
486	Bobby Del Greco	6.00	3.00	1.75
487	Tom Sturdivant	6.00	3.00	1.75
488	Norm Cash	12.50	6.25	3.75
489	Steve Ridzik	6.00	3.00	1.75
490	Frank Robinson	36.00	18.00	11.00
491	Mel Roach	6.00	3.00	1.75
492	Larry Jackson	6.00	3.00	1.75
493	Duke Snider	45.00	22.00	13.50
494	Orioles Team/Checklist 496-572	12.50	6.25	3.75
495	Sherman Lollar	6.00	3.00	1.75
496	Bill Virdon	6.00	3.00	1.75
497	John Tsitouris	6.00	3.00	1.75
498	Al Pilarcik	6.00	3.00	1.75
499	Johnny James	6.00	3.00	1.75
500	Johnny Temple	6.00	3.00	1.75
501	Bob Schmidt	6.00	3.00	1.75
502	Jim Bunning	16.00	8.00	4.75
503	Don Lee	6.00	3.00	1.75
504	Seth Morehead	6.00	3.00	1.75
505	Ted Kluszewski	16.00	8.00	4.75
506	Lee Walls	6.00	3.00	1.75
507	Dick Stigman	14.00	7.00	4.25
508	Billy Consolo	14.00	7.00	4.25
509	*Tommy Davis*	25.00	12.50	7.50
510	Jerry Staley	14.00	7.00	4.25
511	Ken Walters	14.00	7.00	4.25
512	Joe Gibbon	14.00	7.00	4.25
513	Cubs Team/Checklist 496-572	24.00	12.00	7.25
514	*Steve Barber*	17.50	8.75	5.25
515	Stan Lopata	14.00	7.00	4.25
516	Marty Kutyna	14.00	7.00	4.25
517	Charley James	14.00	7.00	4.25
518	*Tony Gonzalez*	14.00	7.00	4.25
519	Ed Roebuck	14.00	7.00	4.25
520	Don Buddin	14.00	7.00	4.25
521	Mike Lee	14.00	7.00	4.25
522	Ken Hunt	14.00	7.00	4.25
523	*Clay Dalrymple*	14.00	7.00	4.25
524	Bill Henry	14.00	7.00	4.25
525	Marv Breeding	14.00	7.00	4.25
526	Paul Giel	14.00	7.00	4.25
527	Jose Valdivielso	14.00	7.00	4.25
528	Ben Johnson	14.00	7.00	4.25
529	Norm Sherry	14.00	7.00	4.25
530	Mike McCormick	14.00	7.00	4.25
531	Sandy Amoros	14.00	7.00	4.25
532	Mike Garcia	14.00	7.00	4.25
533	Lu Clinton	14.00	7.00	4.25
534	Ken MacKenzie	14.00	7.00	4.25
535	Whitey Lockman	14.00	7.00	4.25
536	Wynn Hawkins	14.00	7.00	4.25
537	Red Sox Team/Checklist 496-572	25.00	12.50	7.50
538	Frank Barnes	14.00	7.00	4.25
539	Gene Baker	14.00	7.00	4.25
540	Jerry Walker	14.00	7.00	4.25
541	Tony Curry	14.00	7.00	4.25
542	Ken Hamlin	14.00	7.00	4.25
543	Elio Chacon	14.00	7.00	4.25
544	Bill Monbouquette	14.00	7.00	4.25
545	Carl Sawatski	14.00	7.00	4.25
546	Hank Aguirre	14.00	7.00	4.25
547	*Bob Aspromonte*	14.00	7.00	4.25
548	*Don Mincher*	14.00	7.00	4.25
549	John Buzhardt	14.00	7.00	4.25
550	Jim Landis	14.00	7.00	4.25
551	Ed Rakow	14.00	7.00	4.25
552	Walt Bond	14.00	7.00	4.25
553	Bill Skowron (All-Star)	22.00	11.00	6.50
554	Willie McCovey (All-Star)	27.50	13.50	8.25
555	Nellie Fox (All-Star)	27.50	13.50	8.25
556	Charlie Neal (All-Star)	16.00	8.00	4.75
557	Frank Malzone (All-Star)	16.00	8.00	4.75
558	Eddie Mathews (All-Star)	25.00	12.50	7.50
559	Luis Aparicio (All-Star)	25.00	12.50	7.50
560	Ernie Banks (All-Star)	50.00	25.00	15.00
561	Al Kaline (All-Star)	50.00	25.00	15.00
562	Joe Cunningham (All-Star)	16.00	8.00	4.75
563	Mickey Mantle (All-Star)	225.00	110.00	67.00
564	Willie Mays (All-Star)	100.00	50.00	30.00
565	Roger Maris (All-Star)	80.00	40.00	24.00
566	Hank Aaron (All-Star)	85.00	42.00	25.00
567	Sherman Lollar (All-Star)	16.00	8.00	4.75
568	Del Crandall (All-Star)	16.00	8.00	4.75
569	Camilo Pascual (All-Star)	16.00	8.00	4.75
570	Don Drysdale (All-Star)	27.50	13.50	8.25
571	Billy Pierce (All-Star)	16.00	8.00	4.75
572	Johnny Antonelli (All-Star)	24.00	12.00	7.25
----	Elect Your Favorite Rookie Insert (paper stock, no date on back)	15.00	7.50	4.50
----	Hot Iron Transfer Insert (paper stock)	15.00	7.50	4.50

1960 Topps Proofs

Subsequent to a pair of December, 1959, trades, the 1960 Topps cards of three players were significantly changed. Whether the change occurred prior to regular production printing and packaging or while the cards were still in the proof-ing stage is unknown. The changes affect the cards of Gino Cimoli, Kent Hadley and, reportedly, Marv Throneberry. In the very rare versions each player's card has at bottom left the logo of his team prior to the trade. The common regular-issue version has the new team logo. The front of Hadley's rare card names his team as the Yankees, while Cimoli's rare version says Cardinals.

58	Gino Cimoli (Cardinals logo) (No recent sales)	
102	Kent Hadley (A's logo) (Nov., 1999 auction record)	13500.
436	Marv Throneberry (Yankees logo) (Existence not conmfirmed)	

1960 Topps Tattoos

Probably the least popular of all Topps products among parents and teachers, the Topps Tattoos were delightful little items on the reverse of the wrappers of Topps "Tattoo Bubble Gum." The entire wrapper was 1-9/16" x 3-1/2." The happy owner simply moistened his skin and applied the back of the wrapper to the wet spot. Presto, out came a "tat-too" in color (although often blurred by running col-ors). The set offered 96 tattoo possibilities of which 55 were players, 16 teams, 15 action shots and 10 autographed balls. Surviving specimens are very rare today.

		NM	EX	VG
Complete Set (96):		1200.	600.00	350.00
Common Player:		11.00	5.50	3.25
Common Non-player:		8.50	4.25	2.50
(1)	Hank Aaron	55.00	27.00	16.50
(2)	Bob Allison	11.00	5.50	3.25
(3)	John Antonelli	11.00	5.50	3.25
(4)	Richie Ashburn	26.00	12.50	7.50
(5)	Ernie Banks	35.00	17.50	10.50
(6)	Yogi Berra	40.00	20.00	12.00
(7)	Lew Burdette	11.00	5.50	3.25
(8)	Orlando Cepeda	20.00	10.00	6.00
(9)	Rocky Colavito	18.00	9.00	5.50
(10)	Joe Cunningham	11.00	5.50	3.25
(11)	Buddy Daley	11.00	5.50	3.25
(12)	Don Drysdale	25.00	12.50	7.50
(13)	Ryne Duren	11.00	5.50	3.25
(14)	Roy Face	11.00	5.50	3.25
(15)	Whitey Ford	30.00	15.00	9.00
(16)	Nellie Fox	20.00	10.00	6.00
(17)	Tito Francona	11.00	5.50	3.25
(18)	Gene Freese	11.00	5.50	3.25
(19)	Jim Gilliam	13.00	6.50	4.00
(20)	Dick Groat	12.00	6.00	3.50
(21)	Ray Herbert	11.00	5.50	3.25
(22)	Glen Hobbie	11.00	5.50	3.25
(23)	Jackie Jensen	11.00	5.50	3.25
(24)	Sam Jones	11.00	5.50	3.25
(25)	Al Kaline	25.00	12.50	7.50
(26)	Harmon Killebrew	25.00	12.50	7.50
(27)	Harvey Kuenn	11.00	5.50	3.25
(28)	Frank Lary	11.00	5.50	3.25
(29)	Vernon Law	11.00	5.50	3.25
(30)	Frank Malzone	11.00	5.50	3.25
(31)	Mickey Mantle	125.00	62.00	37.00
(32)	Roger Maris	45.00	22.00	13.50
(33)	Ed Mathews	22.00	11.00	6.50
(34)	Willie Mays	55.00	27.00	16.50
(35)	Cal Mclish	11.00	5.50	3.25
(36)	Wally Moon	11.00	5.50	3.25
(37)	Walt Moryn	11.00	5.50	3.25
(38)	Don Mossi	11.00	5.50	3.25
(39)	Stan Musial	50.00	25.00	15.00
(40)	Charlie Neal	11.00	5.50	3.25
(41)	Don Newcombe	12.00	6.00	3.50
(42)	Milt Pappas	11.00	5.50	3.25
(43)	Camilo Pascual	11.00	5.50	3.25
(44)	Billie (Billy) Pierce	11.00	5.50	3.25
(45)	Robin Roberts	20.00	10.00	6.00
(46)	Frank Robinson	24.00	12.00	7.25
(47)	Pete Runnels	11.00	5.50	3.25
(48)	Herb Score	12.00	6.00	3.50
(49)	Warren Spahn	20.00	10.00	6.00
(50)	Johnny Temple	11.00	5.50	3.25
(51)	Gus Triandos	11.00	5.50	3.25
(52)	Jerry Walker	11.00	5.50	3.25
(53)	Bill White	11.00	5.50	3.25
(54)	Gene Woodling	11.00	5.50	3.25
(55)	Early Wynn	20.00	10.00	6.00
(56)	Chicago Cubs Logo	8.50	4.25	2.50
(57)	Cincinnati Reds Logo	8.50	4.25	2.50
(58)	Los Angeles Dodgers Logo	8.50	4.25	2.50
(59)	Milwaukee Braves Logo	8.50	4.25	2.50
(60)	Philadelphia Phillies Logo	8.50	4.25	2.50
(61)	Pittsburgh Pirates Logo	11.00	5.50	3.25
(62)	San Francisco Giants Logo	8.50	4.25	2.50
(63)	St. Louis Cardinals Logo	8.50	4.25	2.50
(64)	Baltimore Orioles Logo	8.50	4.25	2.50
(65)	Boston Red Sox Logo	8.50	4.25	2.50
(66)	Chicago White Sox Logo	8.50	4.25	2.50
(67)	Cleveland Indians Logo	8.50	4.25	2.50
(68)	Detroit Tigers Logo	8.50	4.25	2.50
(69)	Kansas City Athletics Logo	8.50	4.25	2.50
(70)	New York Yankees Logo	11.00	5.50	3.25
(71)	Washington Senators Logo	8.50	4.25	2.50
(72)	Autograph (Richie Ashburn)	12.00	6.00	3.50
(73)	Autograph (Rocky Colavito)	15.00	7.50	4.50
(74)	Autograph (Roy Face)	8.50	4.25	2.50
(75)	Autograph (Jackie Jensen)	8.50	4.25	2.50
(76)	Autograph (Harmon Killebrew)	15.00	7.50	4.50
(77)	Autograph (Mickey Mantle)	60.00	30.00	18.00

		NM	EX	VG
(78)	Autograph (Willie Mays)	25.00	12.50	7.50
(79)	Autograph (Stan Musial)	25.00	12.50	7.50
(80)	Autograph (Billy Pierce)	8.50	4.25	2.50
(81)	Autograph (Jerry Walker)	8.50	4.25	2.50
(82)	Run-Down	8.50	4.25	2.50
(83)	Out At First	8.50	4.25	2.50
(84)	The Final Word	8.50	4.25	2.50
(85)	Twisting Foul	8.50	4.25	2.50
(86)	Out At Home	8.50	4.25	2.50
(87)	Circus Catch	8.50	4.25	2.50
(88)	Great Catch	8.50	4.25	2.50
(89)	Stolen Base	8.50	4.25	2.50
(90)	Grand Slam Homer	8.50	4.25	2.50
(91)	Double Play	8.50	4.25	2.50
(92)	Right-Handed Follow Thru	8.50	4.25	2.50
(93)	Right-Handed High Leg Kick	8.50	4.25	2.50
(94)	Left-handed pitcher	8.50	4.25	2.50
(95)	Right-handed batter	8.50	4.25	2.50
(96)	Left-handed batter	8.50	4.25	2.50

1961 Topps

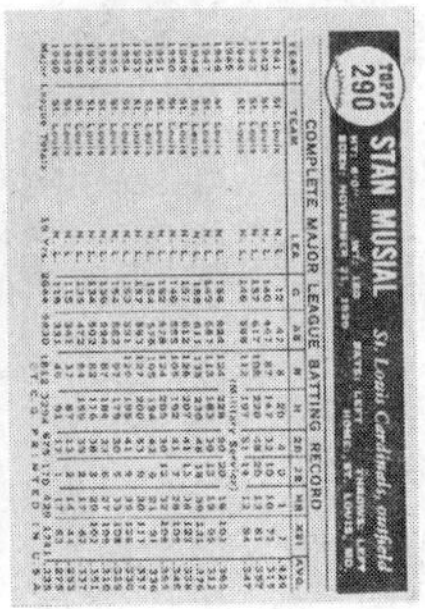

Except for some of the specialty cards, Topps returned to a vertical format with their 1961 cards. The set is numbered through 598, however only 587 cards were printed. No numbers 426, 587 and 588 were issued. Two cards numbered 463 exist (one a Braves team card and one a player card of Jack Fisher). Actually, the Braves team card is checklisted as #426. Designs for 1961 are basically large color portraits; the backs return to extensive statistics. A three-panel cartoon highlighting the player's career appears on the card backs. Innovations include numbered checklists, cards for statistical leaders, and 10 "Baseball Thrills" cards. The scarce high numbers are card numbers 523-589.

		NM	EX	VG
Complete Set (587):		4000.	2000.	1200.
Common Player (1-370):		2.50	1.25	.70
Common Player (371-446):		3.00	1.50	.90
Common Player (447-522):		5.00	2.50	1.50
Common Player (523-589):		24.00	12.00	7.25
1	Dick Groat	25.00	8.00	5.00
2	Roger Maris	110.00	58.00	35.00
3	John Buzhardt	2.50	1.25	.70
4	Lenny Green	2.50	1.25	.70
5	Johnny Romano	2.50	1.25	.70
6	Ed Roebuck	2.50	1.25	.70
7	White Sox team	6.00	3.00	1.75
8	Dick Williams	2.50	1.25	.70
9	Bob Purkey	2.50	1.25	.70
10	Brooks Robinson	32.00	16.00	9.50
11	Curt Simmons	2.50	1.25	.70
12	Moe Thacker	2.50	1.25	.70
13	Chuck Cottier	2.50	1.25	.70
14	Don Mossi	2.50	1.25	.70
15	Willie Kirkland	2.50	1.25	.70
16	Billy Muffett	2.50	1.25	.70
17	Checklist 1-88	8.00	4.00	2.50
18	Jim Grant	2.50	1.25	.70
19	Cletis Boyer	4.00	2.00	1.25
20	Robin Roberts	11.00	5.50	3.25
21	*Zoilo Versalles*	4.00	2.00	1.25
22	Clem Labine	3.50	1.75	1.00
23	Don Demeter	2.50	1.25	.70
24	Ken Johnson	2.50	1.25	.70
25	Reds' Heavy Artillery (Gus Bell, Vada Pinson, Frank Robinson)	7.00	3.50	2.00
26	Wes Stock	2.50	1.25	.70
27	Jerry Kindall	2.50	1.25	.70
28	Hector Lopez	2.50	1.25	.70
29	Don Nottebart	2.50	1.25	.70
30	Nellie Fox	9.00	4.50	2.75
31	Bob Schmidt	2.50	1.25	.70
32	Ray Sadecki	2.50	1.25	.70
33	Gary Geiger	2.50	1.25	.70
34	Wynn Hawkins	2.50	1.25	.70
35	*Ron Santo*	40.00	20.00	12.00
36	Jack Kralick	2.50	1.25	.70
37	Charlie Maxwell	2.50	1.25	.70
38	Bob Lillis	2.50	1.25	.70
39	Leo Posada	2.50	1.25	.70
40	Bob Turley	3.50	1.75	1.00
41	N.L. Batting Leaders (Roberto Clemente, Dick Groat, Norm Larker, Willie Mays)	25.00	12.50	7.50
42	A.L. Batting Leaders (Minnie Minoso, Pete Runnels, Bill Skowron, Al Smith)	5.50	2.75	1.75
43	N.L. Home Run Leaders (Hank Aaron, Ernie Banks, Ken Boyer, Eddie Mathews)	19.00	9.50	5.75
44	A.L. Home Run Leaders (Rocky Colavito, Jim Lemon, Mickey Mantle, Roger Maris)	85.00	42.00	25.00
45	N.L. E.R.A. Leaders (Ernie Broglio, Don Drysdale, Bob Friend, Mike McCormick, Stan Williams)	5.50	2.75	1.75
46	A.L. E.R.A. Leaders (Frank Baumann, Hal Brown, Jim Bunning, Art Ditmar)	5.00	2.50	1.50
47	N.L. Pitching Leaders (Ernie Broglio, Lou Burdette, Vern Law, Warren Spahn)	6.00	3.00	1.50
48	A.L. Pitching Leaders (Bud Daley, Art Ditmar, Chuck Estrada, Frank Lary, Milt Pappas, Jim Perry)	6.00	3.00	1.50
49	N.L. Strikeout Leaders (Ernie Broglio, Don Drysdale, Sam Jones, Sandy Koufax)	12.50	6.25	3.75
50	A.L. Strikeout Leaders (Jim Bunning, Frank Lary, Pedro Ramos, Early Wynn)	7.00	3.50	2.00
51	Tigers team	7.00	3.50	2.00
52	George Crowe	2.50	1.25	.70
53	Russ Nixon	2.50	1.25	.70
54	Earl Francis	2.50	1.25	.70
55	Jim Davenport	2.50	1.25	.70
56	Russ Kemmerer	2.50	1.25	.70
57	Marv Throneberry	3.50	1.75	1.00
58	Joe Schaffernoth	2.50	1.25	.70
59	Jim Woods	2.50	1.25	.70
60	Woodie Held	2.50	1.25	.70
61	Ron Piche	2.50	1.25	.70
62	Al Pilarcik	2.50	1.25	.70
63	Jim Kaat	6.50	3.25	2.00
64	Alex Grammas	2.50	1.25	.70
65	Ted Kluszewski	6.50	3.25	2.00
66	Bill Henry	2.50	1.25	.70
67	Ossie Virgil	2.50	1.25	.70
68	Deron Johnson	2.50	1.25	.70
69	Earl Wilson	2.50	1.25	.70
70	Bill Virdon	2.50	1.25	.70
71	Jerry Adair	2.50	1.25	.70
72	Stu Miller	2.50	1.25	.70
73	Al Spangler	2.50	1.25	.70
74	Joe Pignatano	2.50	1.25	.70
75	Lindy Shows Larry (Larry Jackson, Lindy McDaniel)	5.00	2.50	1.50
76	Harry Anderson	2.50	1.25	.70
77	Dick Stigman	2.50	1.25	.70
78	Lee Walls	2.50	1.25	.70
79	Joe Ginsberg	2.50	1.25	.70
80	Harmon Killebrew	17.50	8.75	5.25
81	Tracy Stallard	2.50	1.25	.70
82	Joe Christopher	2.50	1.25	.70
83	Bob Bruce	2.50	1.25	.70
84	Lee Maye	2.50	1.25	.70
85	Jerry Walker	2.50	1.25	.70
86	Dodgers Team	8.00	4.00	2.50
87	Joe Amalfitano	2.50	1.25	.70
88	Richie Ashburn	11.00	5.50	3.25
89	Billy Martin	9.00	4.50	2.75
90	Jerry Staley	2.50	1.25	.70
91	Walt Moryn	2.50	1.25	.70
92	Hal Naragon	2.50	1.25	.70
93	Tony Gonzalez	2.50	1.25	.70
94	Johnny Kucks	2.50	1.25	.70
95	Norm Cash	4.00	2.00	1.25
96	Billy O'Dell	2.50	1.25	.70
97	Jerry Lynch	2.50	1.25	.70
98a	Checklist 89-176 ("Checklist" in red on front)	9.00	4.50	2.75
98b	Checklist 89-176 ("Checklist" in yellow, 98 on back in black)	7.50	3.75	2.25
98c	Checklist 89-176 ("Checklist" in yellow, 98 on back in white)	9.00	4.50	2.75
99	Don Buddin	2.50	1.25	.70
100	Harvey Haddix	2.50	1.25	.70
101	Bubba Phillips	2.50	1.25	.70
102	Gene Stephens	2.50	1.25	.70
103	Ruben Amaro	2.50	1.25	.70
104	John Blanchard	2.50	1.25	.70
105	Carl Willey	2.50	1.25	.70
106	Whitey Herzog	2.50	1.25	.70
107	Seth Morehead	2.50	1.25	.70
108	Dan Dobbek	2.50	1.25	.70
109	Johnny Podres	2.50	1.25	.70
110	Vada Pinson	4.50	2.25	1.25
111	Jack Meyer	2.50	1.25	.70
112	Chico Fernandez	2.50	1.25	.70
113	Mike Fornieles	2.50	1.25	.70
114	Hobie Landrith	2.50	1.25	.70
115	Johnny Antonelli	2.50	1.25	.70
116	Joe DeMaestri	2.50	1.25	.70
117	Dale Long	2.50	1.25	.70
118	Chris Cannizzaro	2.50	1.25	.70
119	A's Big Armor (Hank Bauer, Jerry Lumpe, Norm Siebern)	4.50	2.25	1.25
120	Eddie Mathews	18.00	9.00	5.50
121	Eli Grba	2.50	1.25	.70
122	Cubs team	6.50	3.25	2.00
123	Billy Gardner	2.50	1.25	.70
124	J.C. Martin	2.50	1.25	.70
125	Steve Barber	2.50	1.25	.70
126	Dick Stuart	2.50	1.25	.70
127	Ron Kline	2.50	1.25	.70
128	Rip Repulski	2.50	1.25	.70
129	Ed Hobaugh	2.50	1.25	.70
130	Norm Larker	2.50	1.25	.70
131	Paul Richards	2.50	1.25	.70
132	Al Lopez	3.50	1.75	1.00
133	Ralph Houk	3.50	1.75	1.00
134	Mickey Vernon	2.50	1.25	.70
135	Fred Hutchinson	2.50	1.25	.70
136	Walt Alston	4.00	2.00	1.25
137	Chuck Dressen	2.50	1.25	.70
138	Danny Murtaugh	2.50	1.25	.70
139	Solly Hemus	2.50	1.25	.70
140	Gus Triandos	2.50	1.25	.70
141	*Billy Williams*	42.00	21.00	12.50
142	Luis Arroyo	2.50	1.25	.70
143	Russ Snyder	2.50	1.25	.70
144	Jim Coker	2.50	1.25	.70
145	Bob Buhl	2.50	1.25	.70
146	Marty Keough	2.50	1.25	.70
147	Ed Rakow	2.50	1.25	.70
148	Julian Javier	2.50	1.25	.70
149	Bob Oldis	2.50	1.25	.70
150	Willie Mays	85.00	42.00	25.00
151	Jim Donohue	2.50	1.25	.70
152	Earl Torgeson	2.50	1.25	.70
153	Don Lee	2.50	1.25	.70
154	Bobby Del Greco	2.50	1.25	.70
155	Johnny Temple	2.50	1.25	.70
156	Ken Hunt	2.50	1.25	.70
157	Cal McLish	2.50	1.25	.70
158	Pete Daley	2.50	1.25	.70
159	Orioles team	6.00	3.00	1.75
160	Whitey Ford	35.00	17.50	10.50
161	Sherman Jones (photo actually Eddie Fisher)	2.50	1.25	.70
162	Jay Hook	2.50	1.25	.70
163	Ed Sadowski	2.50	1.25	.70
164	Felix Mantilla	2.50	1.25	.70
165	Gino Cimoli	2.50	1.25	.70
166	Danny Kravitz	2.50	1.25	.70
167	Giants team	6.00	3.00	1.75
168	Tommy Davis	6.00	3.00	1.75
169	Don Elston	2.50	1.25	.70
170	Al Smith	2.50	1.25	.70
171	Paul Foytack	2.50	1.25	.70
172	Don Dillard	2.50	1.25	.70
173	Beantown Bombers (Jackie Jensen, Frank Malzone, Vic Wertz)	4.00	2.00	1.25
174	Ray Semproch	2.50	1.25	.70
175	Gene Freese	2.50	1.25	.70
176	Ken Aspromonte	2.50	1.25	.70
177	Don Larsen	4.50	2.25	1.25
178	Bob Nieman	2.50	1.25	.70
179	Joe Koppe	2.50	1.25	.70
180	Bobby Richardson	9.00	4.50	2.75
181	Fred Green	2.50	1.25	.70
182	Dave Nicholson	2.50	1.25	.70
183	Andre Rodgers	2.50	1.25	.70
184	Steve Bilko	2.50	1.25	.70
185	Herb Score	3.50	1.75	1.00
186	Elmer Valo	2.50	1.25	.70
187	Billy Klaus	2.50	1.25	.70
188	Jim Marshall	2.50	1.25	.70
189	Checklist 177-264	8.00	4.00	2.50
190	Stan Williams	2.50	1.25	.70
191	Mike de la Hoz	2.50	1.25	.70
192	Dick Brown	2.50	1.25	.70
193	Gene Conley	2.50	1.25	.70
194	Gordy Coleman	2.50	1.25	.70
195	Jerry Casale	2.50	1.25	.70
196	Ed Bouchee	2.50	1.25	.70
197	Dick Hall	2.50	1.25	.70
198	Carl Sawatski	2.50	1.25	.70
199	Bob Boyd	2.50	1.25	.70
200	Warren Spahn	24.00	12.00	7.25
201	Pete Whisenant	2.50	1.25	.70
202	Al Neiger	2.50	1.25	.70
203	Eddie Bressoud	2.50	1.25	.70
204	Bob Skinner	2.50	1.25	.70
205	Bill Pierce	2.50	1.25	.70
206	Gene Green	2.50	1.25	.70
207	Dodger Southpaws (Sandy Koufax, Johnny Podres)	25.00	12.50	7.50
208	Larry Osborne	2.50	1.25	.70
209	Ken McBride	2.50	1.25	.70
210	Pete Runnels	2.50	1.25	.70
211	Bob Gibson	30.00	15.00	9.00
212	Haywood Sullivan	2.50	1.25	.70
213	*Bill Stafford*	3.25	1.75	1.00
214	Danny Murphy	2.50	1.25	.70
215	Gus Bell	2.50	1.25	.70
216	Ted Bowsfield	2.50	1.25	.70
217	Mel Roach	2.50	1.25	.70
218	Hal Brown	2.50	1.25	.70
219	Gene Mauch	2.50	1.25	.70
220	Al Dark	2.50	1.25	.70
221	Mike Higgins	2.50	1.25	.70
222	Jimmie Dykes	2.50	1.25	.70
223	Bob Scheffing	2.50	1.25	.70
224	Joe Gordon	2.50	1.25	.70
225	Bill Rigney	2.50	1.25	.70
226	Harry Lavagetto	2.50	1.25	.70
227	Juan Pizarro	2.50	1.25	.70
228	Yankees team	42.00	21.00	12.50
229	Rudy Hernandez	2.50	1.25	.70
230	Don Hoak	2.50	1.25	.70
231	Dick Drott	2.50	1.25	.70
232	Bill White	3.50	1.75	1.00
233	Joe Jay	2.50	1.25	.70
234	Ted Lepcio	2.50	1.25	.70
235	Camilo Pascual	2.50	1.25	.70
236	Don Gile	2.50	1.25	.70
237	Billy Loes	2.50	1.25	.70
238	Jim Gilliam	4.00	2.00	1.25
239	Dave Sisler	2.50	1.25	.70
240	Ron Hansen	2.50	1.25	.70
241	Al Cicotte	2.50	1.25	.70
242	Hal W. Smith	2.50	1.25	.70
243	Frank Lary	2.50	1.25	.70
244	Chico Cardenas	2.50	1.25	.70
245	Joe Adcock	2.50	1.25	.70
246	Bob Davis	2.50	1.25	.70

247	Billy Goodman	2.50	1.25	.70
248	Ed Keegan	2.50	1.25	.70
249	Reds team	7.50	3.75	2.25
250	Buc Hill Aces (Roy Face, Vern Law)	6.00	3.00	1.50
251	Bill Bruton	2.50	1.25	.70
252	Bill Short	2.50	1.25	.70
253	Sammy Taylor	2.50	1.25	.70
254	Ted Sadowski	2.50	1.25	.70
255	Vic Power	2.50	1.25	.70
256	Billy Hoeft	2.50	1.25	.70
257	Carroll Hardy	2.50	1.25	.70
258	Jack Sanford	2.50	1.25	.70
259	John Schaive	2.50	1.25	.70
260	Don Drysdale	24.00	12.00	7.25
261	Charlie Lau	2.50	1.25	.70
262	Tony Curry	2.50	1.25	.70
263	Ken Hamlin	2.50	1.25	.70
264	Glen Hobbie	2.50	1.25	.70
265	Tony Kubek	7.50	3.75	2.25
266	Lindy McDaniel	2.50	1.25	.70
267	Norm Siebern	2.50	1.25	.70
268	Ike DeLock (Delock)	2.50	1.25	.70
269	Harry Chiti	2.50	1.25	.70
270	Bob Friend	2.50	1.25	.70
271	Jim Landis	2.50	1.25	.70
272	Tom Morgan	2.50	1.25	.70
273	Checklist 265-352	8.00	4.00	2.50
274	Gary Bell	2.50	1.25	.70
275	Gene Woodling	3.50	1.75	1.00
276	Ray Rippelmeyer	2.50	1.25	.70
277	Hank Foiles	2.50	1.25	.70
278	Don McMahon	2.50	1.25	.70
279	Jose Pagan	2.50	1.25	.70
280	Frank Howard	4.50	2.25	1.25
281	Frank Sullivan	2.50	1.25	.70
282	Faye Throneberry	2.50	1.25	.70
283	Bob Anderson	2.50	1.25	.70
284	Dick Gernert	2.50	1.25	.70
285	Sherman Lollar	2.50	1.25	.70
286	George Witt	2.50	1.25	.70
287	Carl Yastrzemski	40.00	20.00	12.00
288	Albie Pearson	2.50	1.25	.70
289	Ray Moore	2.50	1.25	.70
290	Stan Musial	70.00	35.00	21.00
291	Tex Clevenger	2.50	1.25	.70
292	Jim Baumer	2.50	1.25	.70
293	Tom Sturdivant	2.50	1.25	.70
294	Don Blasingame	2.50	1.25	.70
295	Milt Pappas	2.50	1.25	.70
296	Wes Covington	2.50	1.25	.70
297	Athletics Team	7.50	3.75	2.25
298	Jim Golden	2.50	1.25	.70
299	Clay Dalrymple	2.50	1.25	.70
300	Mickey Mantle	375.00	185.00	110.00
301	Chet Nichols	2.50	1.25	.70
302	Al Heist	2.50	1.25	.70
303	Gary Peters	2.50	1.25	.70
304	Rocky Nelson	2.50	1.25	.70
305	Mike McCormick	2.50	1.25	.70
306	World Series Game 1 (Virdon Saves Game)	7.50	3.75	2.25
307	World Series Game 2 (Mantle Slams 2 Homers)	85.00	42.00	25.00
308	World Series Game 3 (Richardson is Hero)	7.50	3.75	2.25
309	World Series Game 4 (Cimoli is Safe in Crucial Play)	6.50	3.25	2.00
310	World Series Game 5 (Face Saves the Day)	7.50	3.75	2.25
311	World Series Game 6 (Ford Pitches Second Shutout)	14.00	7.00	4.25
312	World Series Game 7 (Mazeroski's Homer Wins Itl)	17.50	8.75	5.25
313	World Series Summary (The Winners Celebrate)	13.00	6.50	4.00
314	Bob Miller	2.50	1.25	.70
315	Earl Battey	2.50	1.25	.70
316	Bobby Gene Smith	2.50	1.25	.70
317	*Jim Brewer*	2.50	1.25	.70
318	Danny O'Connell	2.50	1.25	.70
319	Valmy Thomas	2.50	1.25	.70
320	Lou Burdette	2.50	1.25	.70
321	Marv Breeding	2.50	1.25	.70
322	Bill Kunkel	2.50	1.25	.70
323	Sammy Esposito	2.50	1.25	.70
324	Hank Aguirre	2.50	1.25	.70
325	Wally Moon	2.50	1.25	.70
326	Dave Hillman	2.50	1.25	.70
327	*Matty Alou*	7.00	3.50	2.00
328	Jim O'Toole	2.50	1.25	.70
329	Julio Becquer	2.50	1.25	.70
330	Rocky Colavito	17.50	8.75	5.25
331	Ned Garver	2.50	1.25	.70
332	Dutch Dotterer (photo actually Tommy Dotterer)	2.50	1.25	.70
333	Fritz Brickell	2.50	1.25	.70
334	Walt Bond	2.50	1.25	.70
335	Frank Bolling	2.50	1.25	.70
336	Don Mincher	2.50	1.25	.70
337	Al's Aces (Al Lopez, Herb Score, Early Wynn)	6.00	3.00	1.75
338	Don Landrum	2.50	1.25	.70
339	Gene Baker	2.50	1.25	.70
340	Vic Wertz	2.50	1.25	.70
341	Jim Owens	2.50	1.25	.70
342	Clint Courtney	2.50	1.25	.70
343	Earl Robinson	2.50	1.25	.70
344	Sandy Koufax	80.00	40.00	24.00
345	Jim Piersall	4.00	2.00	1.25
346	Howie Nunn	2.50	1.25	.70
347	Cardinals Team	7.00	3.50	2.00
348	Steve Boros	2.50	1.25	.70
349	Danny McDevitt	2.50	1.25	.70
350	Ernie Banks	37.50	18.50	11.00
351	Jim King	2.50	1.25	.70
352	Bob Shaw	2.50	1.25	.70
353	Howie Bedell	2.50	1.25	.70
354	Billy Harrell	2.50	1.25	.70
355	Bob Allison	2.50	1.25	.70
356	Ryne Duren	2.50	1.25	.70
357	Daryl Spencer	2.50	1.25	.70
358	Earl Averill	2.50	1.25	.70
359	Dallas Green	3.50	1.75	1.00
360	Frank Robinson	28.00	14.00	8.50
361a	Checklist 353-429 ("Topps Baseball" in black on front)	8.00	4.00	2.50
361b	Checklist 353-429 ("Topps Baseball" in yellow)	9.00	4.50	2.75
362	Frank Funk	2.50	1.25	.70
363	John Roseboro	2.50	1.25	.70
364	Moe Drabowsky	2.50	1.25	.70
365	Jerry Lumpe	2.50	1.25	.70
366	Eddie Fisher	2.50	1.25	.70
367	Jim Rivera	2.50	1.25	.70
368	Bennie Daniels	3.00	1.50	.90
369	Dave Philley	3.00	1.50	.90
370	Roy Face	3.00	1.50	.90
371	Bill Skowron (SP)	50.00	25.00	15.00
372	Bob Hendley	3.00	1.50	.90
373	Red Sox team	7.00	3.50	2.00
374	Paul Giel	3.00	1.50	.90
375	Ken Boyer	10.00	5.00	3.00
376	Mike Roarke	3.00	1.50	.90
377	Ruben Gomez	3.00	1.50	.90
378	Wally Post	3.00	1.50	.90
379	Bobby Shantz	3.00	1.50	.90
380	Minnie Minoso	5.00	2.50	1.50
381	Dave Wickersham	3.00	1.50	.90
382	Frank Thomas	3.00	1.50	.90
383	Frisco First Liners (Mike McCormick, Billy O'Dell, Jack Sanford)	3.00	1.50	.90
384	Chuck Essegian	3.00	1.50	.90
385	Jim Perry	3.00	1.50	.90
386	Joe Hicks	3.00	1.50	.90
387	Duke Maas	3.00	1.50	.90
388	Roberto Clemente	115.00	57.00	34.00
389	Ralph Terry	4.50	2.25	1.25
390	Del Crandall	3.00	1.50	.90
391	Winston Brown	3.00	1.50	.90
392	Reno Bertoia	3.00	1.50	.90
393	Batter Bafflers (Don Cardwell, Glen Hobbie)	3.00	1.50	.90
394	Ken Walters	3.00	1.50	.90
395	Chuck Estrada	3.00	1.50	.90
396	Bob Aspromonte	3.00	1.50	.90
397	Hal Woodeshick	3.00	1.50	.90
398	Hank Bauer	4.50	2.25	1.25
399	Cliff Cook	3.00	1.50	.90
400	Vern Law	3.00	1.50	.90
401	Babe Ruth Hits 60th Homer	45.00	22.00	13.50
402	Larsen Pitches Perfect Game (SP)	24.00	12.00	7.25
403	Brooklyn-Boston Play 26-Inning Tie	5.00	2.50	1.50
404	Hornsby Tops N.L. with .424 Average	7.50	3.75	2.25
405	Gehrig Benched After 2,130 Games	60.00	30.00	18.00
406	Mantle Blasts 565 ft. Home Run	70.00	35.00	21.00
407	Jack Chesbro Wins 41st Game	3.00	1.50	.90
408	Mathewson Strikes Out 267 Batters (SP)	18.00	9.00	5.50
409	Johnson Hurls 3rd Shutout in 4 Days	9.00	4.50	2.75
410	Haddix Pitches 12 Perfect Innings	5.00	2.50	1.50
411	Tony Taylor	3.00	1.50	.90
412	Larry Sherry	3.00	1.50	.90
413	Eddie Yost	3.00	1.50	.90
414	Dick Donovan	3.00	1.50	.90
415	Hank Aaron	90.00	45.00	27.00
416	*Dick Howser* (SP)	7.00	3.50	2.00
417	*Juan Marichal*	80.00	40.00	24.00
418	Ed Bailey	3.00	1.50	.90
419	Tom Borland	3.00	1.50	.90
420	Ernie Broglio	3.00	1.50	.90
421	Ty Cline (SP)	13.00	6.50	4.00
422	Bud Daley	3.00	1.50	.90
423	Charlie Neal (SP)	15.00	7.50	4.50
424	Turk Lown	3.00	1.50	.90
425	Yogi Berra	65.00	32.00	19.50
426	Not issued			
427	Dick Ellsworth	3.00	1.50	.90
428	Ray Barker (SP)	12.00	6.00	3.50
429	Al Kaline	35.00	17.50	10.50
430	Bill Mazeroski (SP)	50.00	25.00	15.00
431	Chuck Stobbs	3.00	1.50	.90
432	Coot Veal	3.00	1.50	.90
433	Art Mahaffey	3.00	1.50	.90
434	Tom Brewer	3.00	1.50	.90
435	Orlando Cepeda	11.00	5.50	3.25
436	*Jim Maloney* (SP)	17.50	8.75	5.25
437a	Checklist 430-506 (#440 is Louis Aparicio)	14.00	7.00	4.25
437b	Checklist 430-506 (#440 is Luis Aparicio)	10.00	5.00	3.00
438	Curt Flood	6.00	3.00	1.75
439	*Phil Regan*	5.00	2.50	1.50
440	Luis Aparicio	13.00	6.50	4.00
441	Dick Bertell	3.00	1.50	.90
442	Gordon Jones	3.00	1.50	.90
443	Duke Snider	35.00	17.50	10.50
444	Joe Nuxhall	4.00	2.00	1.25
445	Frank Malzone	4.00	2.00	1.25
446	Bob "Hawk" Taylor	4.00	2.00	1.25
447	Harry Bright	5.00	2.50	1.50
448	Del Rice	5.00	2.50	1.50
449	*Bobby Bolin*	5.00	2.50	1.50
450	Jim Lemon	5.00	2.50	1.50
451	Power For Ernie (Ernie Broglio, Daryl Spencer, Bill White)	6.00	3.00	1.50
452	Bob Allen	5.00	2.50	1.50
453	Dick Schofield	5.00	2.50	1.50
454	Pumpsie Green	5.00	2.50	1.50
455	Early Wynn	9.00	4.50	2.75
456	Hal Bevan	5.00	2.50	1.50
457	Johnny James	5.00	2.50	1.50
458	Willie Tasby	5.00	2.50	1.50
459	Terry Fox	5.00	2.50	1.50
460	Gil Hodges	14.00	7.00	4.25
461	Smoky Burgess	5.00	2.50	1.50
462	Lou Klimchock	5.00	2.50	1.50
463a	Braves Team (should be card #426)	8.00	4.00	2.50
463b	Jack Fisher	5.00	2.50	1.50
464	*Leroy Thomas*	5.00	2.50	1.50
465	Roy McMillan	5.00	2.50	1.50
466	Ron Moeller	5.00	2.50	1.50
467	Indians team	9.00	4.50	2.75
468	Johnny Callison	5.00	2.50	1.50
469	Ralph Lumenti	5.00	2.50	1.50
470	Roy Sievers	5.00	2.50	1.50
471	Phil Rizzuto (MVP)	15.00	7.50	4.50
472	Yogi Berra (MVP)	55.00	27.00	16.50
473	Bobby Shantz (MVP)	5.00	2.50	1.50
474	Al Rosen (MVP)	5.00	2.50	1.50
475	Mickey Mantle (MVP)	165.00	82.00	49.00
476	Jackie Jensen (MVP)	7.00	3.50	2.00
477	Nellie Fox (MVP)	11.00	5.50	3.25
478	Roger Maris (MVP)	47.50	24.00	14.00
479	Jim Konstanty (MVP)	5.00	2.50	1.50
480	Roy Campanella (MVP)	32.50	16.00	9.75
481	Hank Sauer (MVP)	5.00	2.50	1.50
482	Willie Mays (MVP)	45.00	22.00	13.50
483	Don Newcombe (MVP)	10.00	5.00	3.00
484	Hank Aaron (MVP)	45.00	22.00	13.50
485	Ernie Banks (MVP)	27.50	13.50	8.25
486	Dick Groat (MVP)	7.50	3.75	2.25
487	Gene Oliver	5.00	2.50	1.50
488	Joe McClain	5.00	2.50	1.50
489	Walt Dropo	5.00	2.50	1.50
490	Jim Bunning	11.00	5.50	3.25
491	Phillies team	9.00	4.50	2.75
492	Ron Fairly	5.00	2.50	1.50
493	Don Zimmer	5.00	2.50	1.50
494	Tom Cheney	5.00	2.50	1.50
495	Elston Howard	9.00	4.50	2.75
496	Ken MacKenzie	5.00	2.50	1.50
497	Willie Jones	5.00	2.50	1.50
498	Ray Herbert	5.00	2.50	1.50
499	Chuck Schilling	5.00	2.50	1.50
500	Harvey Kuenn	7.00	3.50	2.00
501	John DeMerit	5.00	2.50	1.50
502	Clarence Coleman	5.00	2.50	1.50
503	Tito Francona	5.00	2.50	1.50
504	Billy Consolo	5.00	2.50	1.50
505	Red Schoendienst	9.00	4.50	2.75
506	*Willie Davis*	11.00	5.50	3.25
507	Pete Burnside	5.00	2.50	1.50
508	Rocky Bridges	5.00	2.50	1.50
509	Camilo Carreon	5.00	2.50	1.50
510	Art Ditmar	5.00	2.50	1.50
511	Joe M. Morgan	5.00	2.50	1.50
512	Bob Will	5.00	2.50	1.50
513	Jim Brosnan	5.00	2.50	1.50
514	Jake Wood	5.00	2.50	1.50
515	Jackie Brandt	5.00	2.50	1.50
516	Checklist 507-587	11.00	5.50	3.25
517	Willie McCovey	45.00	22.00	13.50
518	Andy Carey	6.50	3.25	2.00
519	Jim Pagliaroni	6.50	3.25	2.00
520	Joe Cunningham	6.50	3.25	2.00
521	Brother Battery (Larry Sherry, Norm Sherry)	7.00	3.50	2.00
522	Dick Farrell	6.50	3.25	2.00
523	Joe Gibbon	24.00	12.00	7.25
524	Johnny Logan	24.00	12.00	7.25
525	*Ron Perranoski*	32.00	16.00	9.50
526	R.C. Stevens	24.00	12.00	7.25
527	Gene Leek	24.00	12.00	7.25
528	Pedro Ramos	24.00	12.00	7.25
529	Bob Roselli	24.00	12.00	7.25
530	Bobby Malkmus	24.00	12.00	7.25
531	Jim Coates	24.00	12.00	7.25
532	Bob Hale	24.00	12.00	7.25
533	Jack Curtis	24.00	12.00	7.25
534	Eddie Kasko	24.00	12.00	7.25
535	Larry Jackson	24.00	12.00	7.25
536	Bill Tuttle	24.00	12.00	7.25
537	Bobby Locke	24.00	12.00	7.25
538	Chuck Hiller	24.00	12.00	7.25
539	Johnny Klippstein	24.00	12.00	7.25
540	Jackie Jensen	25.00	12.50	7.50
541	Roland Sheldon	24.00	12.00	7.25
542	Twins team	60.00	30.00	18.00
543	Roger Craig	30.00	15.00	9.00
544	George Thomas	24.00	12.00	7.25
545	Hoyt Wilhelm	42.50	21.00	12.50
546	Marty Kutyna	24.00	12.00	7.25
547	Leon Wagner	24.00	12.00	7.25
548	Ted Wills	24.00	12.00	7.25
549	Hal R. Smith	24.00	12.00	7.25
550	Frank Baumann	24.00	12.00	7.25
551	George Altman	24.00	12.00	7.25
552	Jim Archer	24.00	12.00	7.25
553	Bill Fischer	24.00	12.00	7.25
554	Pirates team	55.00	27.00	16.50
555	Sam Jones	24.00	12.00	7.25
556	Ken R. Hunt	24.00	12.00	7.25
557	Jose Valdivielso	24.00	12.00	7.25
558	Don Ferrarese	24.00	12.00	7.25
559	Jim Gentile	39.00	19.50	11.50
560	Barry Latman	24.00	12.00	7.25
561	Charley James	24.00	12.00	7.25
562	Bill Monbouquette	24.00	12.00	7.25
563	Bob Cerv	24.00	12.00	7.25
564	Don Cardwell	24.00	12.00	7.25
565	Felipe Alou	35.00	17.50	10.50
566	Paul Richards (All-Star)	24.00	12.00	7.25

567	Danny Murtaugh (All-Star)	24.00	12.00	7.25
568	Bill Skowron (All-Star)	40.00	20.00	12.00
569	Frank Herrera (All-Star)	24.00	12.00	7.25
570	Nellie Fox (All-Star)	35.00	17.50	10.50
571	Bill Mazeroski (All-Star)	32.00	16.00	9.50
572	Brooks Robinson (All-Star)	75.00	37.00	22.00
573	Ken Boyer (All-Star)	28.00	14.00	8.50
574	Luis Aparicio (All-Star)	37.50	18.50	11.00
575	Ernie Banks (All-Star)	60.00	30.00	18.00
576	Roger Maris (All-Star)	135.00	67.00	40.00
577	Hank Aaron (All-Star)	125.00	62.00	37.00
578	Mickey Mantle (All-Star)	325.00	160.00	97.00
579	Willie Mays (All-Star)	125.00	62.00	37.00
580	Al Kaline (All-Star)	70.00	35.00	21.00
581	Frank Robinson (All-Star)	80.00	40.00	24.00
582	Earl Battey (All-Star)	24.00	12.00	7.25
583	Del Crandall (All-Star)	24.00	12.00	7.25
584	Jim Perry (All-Star)	24.00	12.00	7.25
585	Bob Friend (All-Star)	24.00	12.00	7.25
586	Whitey Ford (All-Star)	90.00	45.00	27.00
587	Not issued			
588	Not issued			
589	Warren Spahn (All-Star)	90.00	45.00	27.00

1961 Topps Dice Game

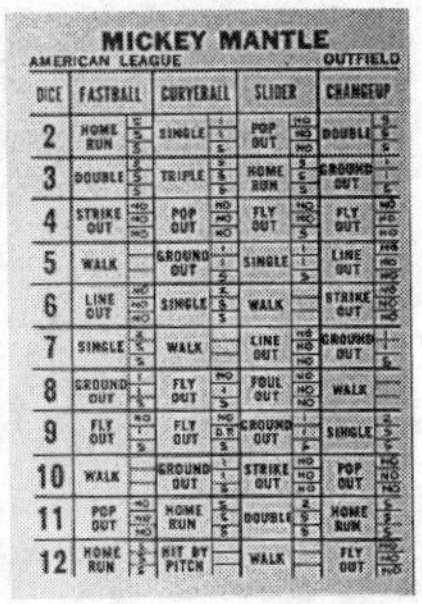

One of the more obscure Topps test issues that may have never actually been issued is the 1961 Topps Dice Game. Eighteen black and white cards, each measuring 2-1/2" x 3-1/2" in size, comprise the set. Interestingly, there are no identifying marks, such as copyrights or trademarks, to indicate the set was produced by Topps. The card backs contain various baseball plays that occur when a certain pitch is called and a specific number of the dice is rolled.

		NM	EX	VG
Complete Set (18):		27500.	13500.	8250.
Common Player:		250.00	125.00	75.00
(1)	Earl Battey	250.00	125.00	75.00
(2)	Del Crandall	250.00	125.00	75.00
(3)	Jim Davenport	250.00	125.00	75.00
(4)	Don Drysdale	1500.	750.00	450.00
(5)	Dick Groat	300.00	150.00	90.00
(6)	Al Kaline	2200.	1100.	660.00
(7)	Tony Kubek	750.00	375.00	225.00
(8)	Mickey Mantle	9000.	4500.	2700.
(9)	Willie Mays	6500.	3250.	1950.
(10)	Bill Mazeroski	900.00	450.00	270.00
(11)	Stan Musial	3750.	1875.	1125.
(12)	Camilo Pascual	250.00	125.00	75.00
(13)	Bobby Richardson	650.00	325.00	195.00
(14)	Brooks Robinson	2200.	1100.	660.00
(15)	Frank Robinson	2200.	1100.	660.00
(16)	Norm Siebern	250.00	125.00	75.00
(17)	Leon Wagner	250.00	125.00	75.00
(18)	Bill White	250.00	125.00	75.00

1961 Topps Magic Rub-Offs

Not too different in concept from the tattoos of the previous year, the Topps Magic Rub-Off was designed to leave impressions of team themes or individual players when properly applied. Measuring 2-1/16" x 3-1/16," the Magic Rub-Off was not designed specifically for application to the owner's skin. The set of 36 Rub-Offs seems to almost be a tongue-in-cheek product as the team themes were a far cry from official logos, and the players seem to have been included for their nicknames. Among the players (one representing each team) the best known and most valuable are Yogi Berra and Ernie Banks.

		NM	EX	VG
Complete Set (36):		160.00	80.00	45.00
Common Player:		6.00	3.00	1.75
(1)	Baltimore Orioles Pennant	6.00	3.00	1.75
(2)	Ernie "Bingo" Banks	18.00	9.00	5.50
(3)	Yogi Berra	18.00	9.00	5.50
(4)	Boston Red Sox Pennant	6.00	3.00	1.75
(5)	Jackie "Ozark" Brandt	6.00	3.00	1.75
(6)	Jim "Professor" Brosnan	6.00	3.00	1.75
(7)	Chicago Cubs Pennant	6.00	3.00	1.75
(8)	Chicago White Sox Pennant	6.00	3.00	1.75
(9)	Cincinnati Red Legs Pennant	6.00	3.00	1.75
(10)	Cleveland Indians Pennant	6.00	3.00	1.75
(11)	Detroit Tigers Pennant	6.00	3.00	1.75
(12)	Henry "Dutch" Dotterer	6.00	3.00	1.75
(13)	Joe "Flash" Gordon	6.00	3.00	1.75
(14)	Harvey "The Kitten" Haddix	6.00	3.00	1.75
(15)	Frank "Pancho" Hererra	6.00	3.00	1.75
(16)	Frank "Tower" Howard	7.50	3.75	2.25
(17)	"Sad" Sam Jones	6.00	3.00	1.75
(18)	Kansas City Athletics Pennant	6.00	3.00	1.75
(19)	Los Angeles Angels Pennant	6.00	3.00	1.75
(20)	Los Angeles Dodgers Pennant	6.00	3.00	1.75
(21)	Omar "Turk" Lown	6.00	3.00	1.75
(22)	Billy "The Kid" Martin	12.50	6.25	3.75
(23)	Duane "Duke" Mass (Maas)	6.00	3.00	1.75
(24)	Charlie "Paw Paw" Maxwell	6.00	3.00	1.75
(25)	Milwaukee Braves Pennant	6.00	3.00	1.75
(26)	Minnesota Twins Pennant	6.00	3.00	1.75
(27)	"Farmer" Ray Moore	6.00	3.00	1.75
(28)	Walt "Moose" Moryn	6.00	3.00	1.75
(29)	New York Yankees Pennant	11.00	5.50	3.25
(30)	Philadelphia Phillies Pennant	6.00	3.00	1.75
(31)	Pittsburgh Pirates Pennant	6.00	3.00	1.75
(32)	John "Honey" Romano	6.00	3.00	1.75
(33)	"Pistol Pete" Runnels	6.00	3.00	1.75
(34)	St. Louis Cardinals Pennant	6.00	3.00	1.75
(35)	San Francisco Giants Pennant	6.00	3.00	1.75
(36)	Washington Senators Pennant	8.50	4.25	2.50

1961 Topps Stamps

Issued as an added insert to 1961 Topps wax packs these 1-3/8" x 1-3/16" stamps were desigend to be collected and placed in an album which could be bought for an additional 10Û. Packs of cards contained two stamps. There are 208 stamps in a complete set which depict 207 different players (Al Kaline appears twice). There are 104 players on brown stamps and 104 on green. While there are many Hall of Famers on the stamps, prices remain low because there is relatively little interest in what is a non-card set.

		NM	EX	VG
Complete Set (208):		335.00	160.00	98.00
Stamp Album:		40.00	20.00	12.00
Common Player:		1.50	.70	.45
(1)	Hank Aaron	15.00	7.50	4.50
(2)	Joe Adcock	1.50	.70	.45
(3)	Hank Aguirre	1.50	.70	.45
(4)	Bob Allison	1.50	.70	.45
(5)	George Altman	1.50	.70	.45
(6)	Bob Anderson	1.50	.70	.45
(7)	Johnny Antonelli	1.50	.70	.45
(8)	Luis Aparicio	9.00	4.50	2.75
(9)	Luis Arroyo	1.50	.70	.45
(10)	Richie Ashburn	9.00	4.50	2.75
(11)	Ken Aspromonte	1.50	.70	.45
(12)	Ed Bailey	1.50	.70	.45
(13)	Ernie Banks	10.00	5.00	3.00
(14)	Steve Barber	1.50	.70	.45
(15)	Earl Battey	1.50	.70	.45
(16)	Hank Bauer	1.50	.70	.45
(17)	Gus Bell	1.50	.70	.45
(18)	Yogi Berra	10.00	5.00	3.00
(19)	Reno Bertoia	1.50	.70	.45
(20)	John Blanchard	1.50	.70	.45
(21)	Don Blasingame	1.50	.70	.45
(22)	Frank Bolling	1.50	.70	.45
(23)	Steve Boros	1.50	.70	.45
(24)	Ed Bouchee	1.50	.70	.45
(25)	Bob Boyd	1.50	.70	.45
(26)	Cletis Boyer	1.50	.70	.45
(27)	Ken Boyer	2.50	1.25	.70
(28)	Jackie Brandt	1.50	.70	.45
(29)	Marv Breeding	1.50	.70	.45
(30)	Eddie Bressoud	1.50	.70	.45
(31)	Jim Brewer	1.50	.70	.45
(32)	Tom Brewer	1.50	.70	.45
(33)	Jim Brosnan	1.50	.70	.45
(34)	Bill Bruton	1.50	.70	.45
(35)	Bob Buhl	1.50	.70	.45
(36)	Jim Bunning	7.50	3.75	2.25
(37)	Smoky Burgess	1.50	.70	.45
(38)	John Buzhardt	1.50	.70	.45
(39)	Johnny Callison	1.50	.70	.45
(40)	Chico Cardenas	1.50	.70	.45
(41)	Andy Carey	1.50	.70	.45
(42)	Jerry Casale	1.50	.70	.45
(43)	Norm Cash	3.00	1.50	.90
(44)	Orlando Cepeda	7.50	3.75	2.25
(45)	Bob Cerv	1.50	.70	.45
(46)	Harry Chiti	1.50	.70	.45
(47)	Gene Conley	1.50	.70	.45
(48)	Wes Covington	1.50	.70	.45
(49)	Del Crandall	1.50	.70	.45
(50)	Tony Curry	1.50	.70	.45
(51)	Bud Daley	1.50	.70	.45
(52)	Pete Daley	1.50	.70	.45
(53)	Clay Dalrymple	1.50	.70	.45
(54)	Jim Davenport	1.50	.70	.45
(55)	Tommy Davis	1.50	.70	.45
(56)	Bobby Del Greco	1.50	.70	.45
(57)	Ike Delock	1.50	.70	.45
(58)	Art Ditmar	1.50	.70	.45
(59)	Dick Donovan	1.50	.70	.45
(60)	Don Drysdale	10.00	5.00	3.00
(61)	Dick Ellsworth	1.50	.70	.45
(62)	Don Elston	1.50	.70	.45
(63)	Chuck Estrada	1.50	.70	.45
(64)	Roy Face	1.50	.70	.45
(65)	Dick Farrell	1.50	.70	.45
(66)	Chico Fernandez	1.50	.70	.45
(67)	Curt Flood	1.50	.70	.45
(68)	Whitey Ford	10.00	5.00	3.00
(69)	Tito Francona	1.50	.70	.45
(70)	Gene Freese	1.50	.70	.45
(71)	Bob Friend	1.50	.70	.45
(72)	Billy Gardner	1.50	.70	.45
(73)	Ned Garver	1.50	.70	.45
(74)	Gary Geiger	1.50	.70	.45
(75)	Jim Gentile	1.50	.70	.45
(76)	Dick Gernert	1.50	.70	.45
(77)	Tony Gonzalez	1.50	.70	.45
(78)	Alex Grammas	1.50	.70	.45
(79)	Jim Grant	1.50	.70	.45
(80)	Dick Groat	1.50	.70	.45
(81)	Dick Hall	1.50	.70	.45
(82)	Ron Hansen	1.50	.70	.45
(83)	Bob Hartman	1.50	.70	.45
(84)	Woodie Held	1.50	.70	.45
(85)	Ray Herbert	1.50	.70	.45
(86)	Frank Herrera	1.50	.70	.45
(87)	Whitey Herzog	2.00	1.00	.60
(88)	Don Hoak	1.50	.70	.45
(89)	Elston Howard	4.00	2.00	1.25
(90)	Frank Howard	3.00	1.50	.90
(91)	Ken Hunt	1.50	.70	.45
(92)	Larry Jackson	1.50	.70	.45
(93)	Julian Javier	1.50	.70	.45
(94)	Joe Jay	1.50	.70	.45
(95)	Jackie Jensen	1.50	.70	.45
(96)	Jim Kaat	2.50	1.25	.70
(97a)	Al Kaline (green)	15.00	7.50	4.50
(97b)	Al Kaline (brown)	12.50	6.25	3.75
(98)	Eddie Kasko	1.50	.70	.45
(99)	Russ Kemmerer	1.50	.70	.45
(100)	Harmon Killebrew	10.00	5.00	3.00
(101)	Billy Klaus	1.50	.70	.45
(102)	Ron Kline	1.50	.70	.45
(103)	Johnny Klippstein	1.50	.70	.45
(104)	Ted Kluszewski	7.50	3.75	2.25
(105)	Tony Kubek	4.00	2.00	1.25
(106)	Harvey Kuenn	2.00	1.00	.60
(107)	Jim Landis	1.50	.70	.45
(108)	Hobie Landrith	1.50	.70	.45
(109)	Norm Larker	1.50	.70	.45
(110)	Frank Lary	1.50	.70	.45
(111)	Barry Latman	1.50	.70	.45
(112)	Vern Law	1.50	.70	.45
(113)	Jim Lemon	1.50	.70	.45
(114)	Sherman Lollar	1.50	.70	.45
(115)	Dale Long	1.50	.70	.45
(116)	Jerry Lumpe	1.50	.70	.45
(117)	Jerry Lynch	1.50	.70	.45
(118)	Art Mahaffey	1.50	.70	.45
(119)	Frank Malzone	1.50	.70	.45
(120)	Felix Mantilla	1.50	.70	.45
(121)	Mickey Mantle	75.00	37.00	22.00
(122)	Juan Marichal	9.00	4.50	2.75
(123)	Roger Maris	15.00	7.50	4.50
(124)	Billy Martin	4.00	2.00	1.25
(125)	J.C. Martin	1.50	.70	.45
(126)	Ed Mathews	10.00	5.00	3.00
(127)	Charlie Maxwell	1.50	.70	.45
(128)	Willie Mays	15.00	7.50	4.50
(129)	Bill Mazeroski	7.50	3.75	2.25
(130)	Mike McCormick	1.50	.70	.45
(131)	Willie McCovey	10.00	5.00	3.00
(132)	Lindy McDaniel	1.50	.70	.45
(133)	Roy McMillan	1.50	.70	.45
(134)	Minnie Minoso	2.00	1.00	.60
(135)	Bill Monbouquette	1.50	.70	.45

(136) Wally Moon	1.50	.70	.45
(137) Stan Musial	15.00	7.50	4.50
(138) Charlie Neal	1.50	.70	.45
(139) Rocky Nelson	1.50	.70	.45
(140) Russ Nixon	1.50	.70	.45
(141) Billy O'Dell	1.50	.70	.45
(142) Jim O'Toole	1.50	.70	.45
(143) Milt Pappas	1.50	.70	.45
(144) Camilo Pascual	1.50	.70	.45
(145) Jim Perry	1.50	.70	.45
(146) Bubba Phillips	1.50	.70	.45
(147) Bill Pierce	1.50	.70	.45
(148) Jim Piersall	2.00	1.00	.60
(149) Vada Pinson	2.00	1.00	.60
(150) Johnny Podres	2.00	1.00	.60
(151) Wally Post	1.50	.70	.45
(152) Vic Powers (Power)	1.50	.70	.45
(153) Pedro Ramos	1.50	.70	.45
(154) Robin Roberts	7.50	3.75	2.25
(155) Brooks Robinson	10.00	5.00	3.00
(156) Frank Robinson	10.00	5.00	3.00
(157) Ed Roebuck	1.50	.70	.45
(158) John Romano	1.50	.70	.45
(159) John Roseboro	1.50	.70	.45
(160) Pete Runnels	1.50	.70	.45
(161) Ed Sadowski	1.50	.70	.45
(162) Jack Sanford	1.50	.70	.45
(163) Ron Santo	1.50	.70	.45
(164) Ray Semproch	1.50	.70	.45
(165) Bobby Shantz	2.00	1.00	.60
(166) Bob Shaw	1.50	.70	.45
(167) Larry Sherry	1.50	.70	.45
(168) Norm Siebern	1.50	.70	.45
(169) Roy Sievers	1.50	.70	.45
(170) Curt Simmons	1.50	.70	.45
(171) Dave Sisler	1.50	.70	.45
(172) Bob Skinner	1.50	.70	.45
(173) Al Smith	1.50	.70	.45
(174) Hal Smith	1.50	.70	.45
(175) Hal Smith	1.50	.70	.45
(176) Duke Snider	10.00	5.00	3.00
(177) Warren Spahn	10.00	5.00	3.00
(178) Daryl Spencer	1.50	.70	.45
(179) Bill Stafford	1.50	.70	.45
(180) Jerry Staley	1.50	.70	.45
(181) Gene Stephens	1.50	.70	.45
(182) Chuck Stobbs	1.50	.70	.45
(183) Dick Stuart	1.50	.70	.45
(184) Willie Tasby	1.50	.70	.45
(185) Sammy Taylor	1.50	.70	.45
(186) Tony Taylor	1.50	.70	.45
(187) Johnny Temple	1.50	.70	.45
(188) Marv Throneberry	1.50	.70	.45
(189) Gus Triandos	1.50	.70	.45
(190) Bob Turley	1.50	.70	.45
(191) Bill Tuttle	1.50	.70	.45
(192) Zoilo Versalles	1.50	.70	.45
(193) Bill Virdon	1.50	.70	.45
(194) Lee Walls	1.50	.70	.45
(195) Vic Wertz	1.50	.70	.45
(196) Pete Whisenant	1.50	.70	.45
(197) Bill White	1.50	.70	.45
(198) Hoyt Wilhelm	7.50	3.75	2.25
(199) Bob Will	1.50	.70	.45
(200) Carl Willey	1.50	.70	.45
(201) Billy Williams	9.00	4.50	2.75
(202) Dick Williams	1.50	.70	.45
(203) Stan Williams	1.50	.70	.45
(204) Gene Woodling	1.50	.70	.45
(205) Early Wynn	7.50	3.75	2.25
(206) Carl Yastrzemski	10.00	5.00	3.00
(207) Eddie Yost	1.50	.70	.45

1961 Topps Stamps Panels

Some advanced collectors pursue the 1961 Topps stamps in the form of the two-stamp panels in which they were issued. The 208 different stamps which make up the issue can be found on 182 different two-stamp panels. The unnumbered stamps are listed here alphabetically according to the name of the player which appears on the left end of the panel. Values shown are for complete panels of two players stamps plus the attached tab at left.

	NM	EX	VG
Complete Panel Set (182):	1400.	700.00	425.00
Common Panel:	4.00	2.00	1.20
(1) Hank Aguirre/Bob Boyd	4.00	2.00	1.20
(2) Bob Allison/Orlando Cepeda	12.00	6.00	3.50
(3) Bob Allison/Early Wynn	12.00	6.00	3.50
(4) George Altman/Andy Carey	4.00	2.00	1.20
(5) George Altman/Lindy McDaniel	4.00	2.00	1.20
(6) Johnny Antonelli/Ken Hunt	5.00	2.50	1.50
(7) Richie Ashburn/Don Drysdale	25.00	12.50	7.50
(8) Richie Ashburn/Joe Jay	12.00	6.00	3.50
(9) Ken Aspromonte/Chuck Estrada	4.00	2.00	1.20
(10) Ken Aspromonte/Jerry Lynch	4.00	2.00	1.20
(11) Ed Bailey/Marv Breeding	4.00	2.00	1.20
(12) Ed Bailey/Smoky Burgess	5.00	2.50	1.50
(13) Ernie Banks/Chico Fernandez	20.00	10.00	6.00
(14) Ernie Banks/Pedro Ramos	20.00	10.00	6.00
(15) Steve Barber/Eddie Kasko	4.00	2.00	1.20
(16) Steve Barber/Roy Sievers	5.00	2.50	1.50
(17) Earl Battey/Art Ditmar	5.00	2.50	1.50
(18) Earl Battey/Bill White	7.00	3.50	2.00
(19) Gus Bell/Gary Geiger	4.00	2.00	1.20
(20) Gus Bell/Early Wynn	12.00	6.00	3.50
(21) John Blanchard/Dick Donovan	5.00	2.50	1.50
(22) John Blanchard/Ray Semproch	5.00	2.50	1.50
(23) Don Blasingame/Elston Howard	8.00	4.00	2.50
(24) Don Blasingame/Charlie Maxwell	4.00	2.00	1.20
(25) Frank Bolling/Luis Aparicio	12.00	6.00	3.50
(26) Frank Bolling/Whitey Herzog	7.00	3.50	2.00
(27) Steve Boros/Ike Delock	4.00	2.00	1.20
(28) Steve Boros/Russ Nixon	4.00	2.00	1.20
(29) Ed Bouchee/Larry Sherry	4.00	2.00	1.20
(30) Ed Bouchee/Willie Tasby	4.00	2.00	1.20
(31) Cletis Boyer/Johnny Klippstein	6.00	3.00	1.75
(32) Jim Brewer/Vern Law	6.00	3.00	1.75
(33) Jim Brewer/Camilo Pascual	5.00	2.50	1.50
(34) Tom Brewer/Tommy Davis	5.00	2.50	1.50
(35) Tom Brewer/Larry Sherry	4.00	2.00	1.20
(36) Jim Brosnan/Roy McMillan	4.00	2.00	1.20
(37) Jim Brosnan/Calr Willey	4.00	2.00	1.20
(38) Bill Bruton/Ken Boyer	7.00	3.50	2.00
(39) Bill Bruton/Mickey Mantle	100.00	50.00	30.00
(40) Bob Buhl/Willie Mays	50.00	25.00	15.00
(41) Bob Buhl/Roy Sievers	5.00	2.50	1.50
(42) Jim Bunning/Bob Boyd	12.00	6.00	3.50
(43) Jim Bunning/Ron Hansen	12.00	6.00	3.50
(44) John Buzhardt/Brooks Robinson	25.00	12.50	7.50
(45) John Buzhardt/Dick Williams	6.00	3.00	1.75
(46) Johnny Callison/Jim Landis	5.00	2.50	1.50
(47) Johnny Callison/Ed Roebuck	5.00	2.50	1.50
(48) Harry Chiti/Jackie Brandt	4.00	2.00	1.20
(49) Harry Chiti/Gene Conley	4.00	2.00	1.20
(50) Del Crandall/Billy Gardner	5.00	2.50	1.50
(51) Bud Daley/Al Kaline	20.00	10.00	6.00
(52) Bud Daley/Dave Sisler	4.00	2.00	1.20
(53) Pete Daley/Dick Ellsworth	4.00	2.00	1.20
(54) Pete Daley/Hal (R.) Smith	4.00	2.00	1.20
(55) Clay Dalrymple/Norm Larker	4.00	2.00	1.20
(56) CLay Dalrymple/Stan Williams	4.00	2.00	1.20
(57) Jim Davenport/Reno Bertoia	4.00	2.00	1.20
(58) Jim Davenport/Jerry Lynch	4.00	2.00	1.20
(59) Bobby Del Greco/Roy Face	5.00	2.50	1.50
(60) Bobby Del Greco/Frank Howard	10.00	5.00	3.00
(61) Gene Freese/Wes Covington	4.00	2.00	1.20
(62) Gene Freese/Vada Pinson	5.00	2.50	1.50
(63) Bob Friend/Hank Aaron	50.00	25.00	15.00
(64) Bob Friend/Lee Walls	5.00	2.50	1.50
(65) Jim Gentile/Chuck Estrada	4.00	2.00	1.20
(66) Jim Gentile/Billy O'Dell	4.00	2.00	1.20
(67) Dick Gernert/Russ Nixon	4.00	2.00	1.20
(68) Alex Grammas/Eddie Bressoud	4.00	2.00	1.20
(69) Frank Herrera/Joe Jay	4.00	2.00	1.20
(70) Frank Herrera/Jim Landis	4.00	2.00	1.20
(71) Julian Javier/Eddie Kasko	4.00	2.00	1.20
(72) Jackie Jensen/Hank Bauer	10.00	5.00	3.00
(73) Jackie Jensen/Mickey Mantle	100.00	50.00	30.00
(74) Al Kaline/Dick Hall	20.00	10.00	6.00
(75) Al Kaline/Ray Herbert	20.00	10.00	6.00
(76) Russ Kemmerer/Ed Sadowski	4.00	2.00	1.20
(77) Harmon Killebrew/Bill Stafford	20.00	10.00	6.00
(78) Harmon Killebrew/Bill White	20.00	10.00	6.00
(79) Billy Klaus/Bob Anderson	4.00	2.00	1.20
(80) Ron Kline/Juan Marichal	15.00	7.50	4.50
(81) Ron Kline/Curt Simmons	5.00	2.50	1.50
(82) Tony Kubek/Reno Bertoia	8.00	4.00	2.50
(83) Frank Lary/Andy Carey	4.00	2.00	1.20
(84) Barry Latman/Hank Bauer	5.00	2.50	1.50
(85) Jim Lemon/Tony Curry	4.00	2.00	1.20
(86) Jim Lemon/Dick Williams	5.00	2.50	1.50
(87) Sherm Lollar/Willie Mays	50.00	25.00	15.00
(88) Sherm Lollar/Duke Snider	25.00	12.50	7.50
(89) Dale Long/Bob Anderson	4.00	2.00	1.20
(90) Dale Long/Don Elston	4.00	2.00	1.20
(91) Art Mahaffey/Vada Pinson	5.00	2.50	1.50
(92) Art Mahaffey/Robin Roberts	12.00	6.00	3.50
(93) Frank Malzone/Dick Hall	4.00	2.00	1.20
(94) Frank Malzone/Bob Hartman	[illegible]	2.00	1.20
(95) Felix Mantilla/Billy Gardner	4.00	2.00	1.20
(96)_ Felix Mantilla/Gary Geiger	4.00	2.00	1.20
(97) Roger Maris/Johnny Klippstein	30.00	15.00	9.00
(98) Roger Maris/Ray Semproch	30.00	15.00	9.00
(99) Billy Martin/Hank Aaron	50.00	25.00	15.00
(100) Billy Martin/Whitey Herzog	12.00	6.00	3.50
(101) J.C. Martin/Bob Cerv	4.00	2.00	1.20
(102) J.C. Martin/Eddie Yost	4.00	2.00	1.20
(103) Ed Mathews/Chico Cardenas	15.00	7.50	4.50
(104) Bill Mazeroski/Joe Adcock	10.00	5.00	3.00
(105) Bill Mazeroski/Elston Howard	12.00	6.00	3.50
(106) Mike McCormick/Rocky Nelson	4.00	2.00	1.20
(107) Mike McCormick/Curt Simmons	5.00	2.50	1.50
(108) Wille McCovey/Smoky Burgess	20.00	10.00	6.00
(109) Minnie Minoso/Ted Kluszewski	10.00	5.00	3.00
(110) Minnie Minoso/Eddie Yost	8.00	4.00	2.50
(111) Bikli Monbouquette/Tony Curry	4.00	2.00	1.20
(112) Bill Monbouquette/Sammy Taylor	4.00	2.00	1.20
(113) Wally Moon/Roy Face	6.00	3.00	1.75
(114) Stan Musial/Rocky Nelson	50.00	25.00	15.00
(115) Charlie Neal/Marv Breeding	4.00	2.00	1.20
(116) Charlie Neal/Jim Grant	4.00	2.00	1.20
(117) Jim O'Toole/Chico Cardenas	4.00	2.00	1.20
(118) Jim O'Toole/Roy McMillan	4.00	2.00	1.20
(119) Milt Pappas/Tito Francona	5.00	2.50	1.50
(120) Milt Pappas/Jim Piersall	6.00	3.00	1.75
(121) Jim Perry/Bob Cerv	5.00	2.50	1.50
(122) Jim Perry/Ken Hunt	5.00	2.50	1.50
(123) Bubba Phillips/Art Ditmar	4.00	2.00	1.20
(124) Bubba Phillips/Jim Kaat	10.00	5.00	3.00
(125) Johnny Podres/Dick Farrell	5.00	2.50	1.50
(126) Wally Post/Dick Farrell	4.00	2.00	1.20
(127) Wally Post/Robin Roberts	12.00	6.00	3.50
(128) Frank Robinson/Jim Grant	20.00	10.00	6.00
(129) Frank Robinson/Don Hoak	20.00	10.00	6.00
(130) John Romano/Al Kaline	20.00	10.00	6.00
(131) John Roseboro/Dick Groat	6.00	3.00	1.75
(132) Pete Runnels/Larry Jackson	4.00	2.00	1.20
(133) Jack Sanford/Whitey Ford	20.00	10.00	6.00
(134) Jack Sanford/Pedro Ramos	4.00	2.00	1.20
(135) Ron Santo/Harvey Kuenn	10.00	5.00	3.00
(136) Ron Santo/Vern Law	10.00	5.00	3.00
(137) Bobby Shantz/Joe Adcock	5.00	2.50	1.50
(138) Bobby Shantz/Dick Groat	5.00	2.50	1.50
(139) Bob Shaw/Jerry Casale	4.00	2.00	1.20
(140) Bob Shaw/Ned Garver	4.00	2.00	1.20
(141) Norm Siebern/Tony Gonzalez	4.00	2.00	1.20
(142) Norm Siebern/Woodie Held	4.00	2.00	1.20
(143) Bob Skinner/Hobie Landrith	4.00	2.00	1.20
(144) Bob Skinner/Juan Marichal	15.00	7.50	4.50
(145) Al Smith/Don Drysdale	15.00	7.50	4.50
(146) Hal (W.) Smith/Eddie Bressoud	4.00	2.00	1.20
(147) Hal (W.) Smith/Harvey Kuenn	5.00	2.50	1.50
(148) Daryl Spencer/Norm Cash	5.00	2.50	1.50
(149) Daryl Spencer/Vic Powers (Power)	4.00	2.00	1.20
(150) Jerry Staley/Ned Garver	4.00	2.00	1.20
(151) Jerry Staley/Ed Sadowski	4.00	2.00	1.20
(152) Gene Stephens/Gene Conley	4.00	2.00	1.20
(153) Gene Stephens/Ike Delock	4.00	2.00	1.20
(154) Chuck Stobbs/Ken Boyer	8.00	4.00	2.50
(155) Chuck Stobbs/Curt Flood	6.00	3.00	1.75
(156) Dick Stuart/Whitey Ford	20.00	10.00	6.00
(157) Dick Stuart/Larry Jackson	5.00	2.50	1.50
(158) Tony Taylor/Frank Howard	8.00	4.00	2.50
(159) Tony Taylor/Norm Larker	4.00	2.00	1.20
(160) Johnny Temple/Norm Cash	5.00	2.50	1.50
(161) Johnny Temple/Dave Sisler	4.00	2.00	1.20
(162) Marv Throneberry/Yogi Berra	30.00	15.00	9.00
(163) Marv Throneberry/Tommy Davis	7.00	3.50	2.00
(164) Gus Triandos/Sammy Taylor	4.00	2.00	1.20
(165) Bob Turley/Luis Aparicio	12.00	6.00	3.50
(166) Bill Tuttle/Jerry Casale	4.00	2.00	1.20
(167) Bill Tuttle/Bill Pierce	5.00	2.50	1.50
(168) Zoilo Versalles/Bill Stafford	5.00	2.50	1.50
(169) Bill Virdon/Yogi Berra	25.00	12.50	7.50
(170) Vic Wertz/Bob Hartman	5.00	2.50	1.50
(171) Vic Wertz/Jerry Lumpe	5.00	2.50	1.50
(172) Pete Whisenant/Luis Arroyo	4.00	2.00	1.20
(173) Pete Whisenant/Dick Donovan	4.00	2.00	1.20
(174) Hoyt Wilhelm/Ron Hansen	12.00	6.00	3.50
(175) Hoyt Wilhelm/Jim Piersall	12.00	6.00	3.50
(176) Bob Will/Tony Gonzalez	4.00	2.00	1.20
(177) Bob Will/Lindy McDaniel	4.00	2.00	1.20
(178) Billy Williams/Warren Spahn	25.00	12.50	7.50
(179) Billy Williams/Carl Willey	18.00	9.00	5.50
(180) Gene Woodling/Don Elston	5.00	2.50	1.50
(181) Gene Woodling/Hal (R.) Smith	5.00	2.50	1.50
(182) Carl Yastrzemski/Jerry Lumpe	75.00	37.00	22.00

1962 Topps

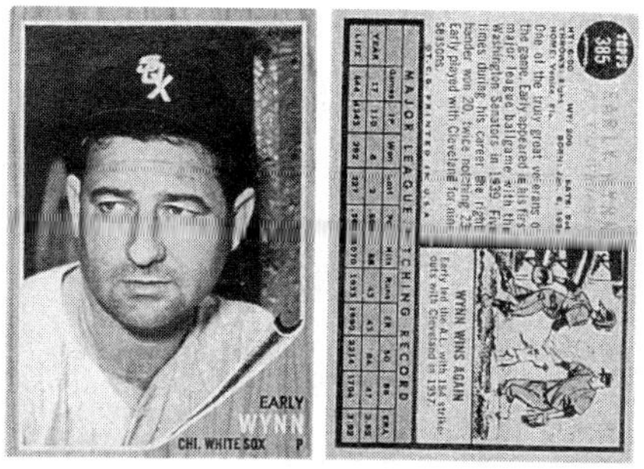

The 1962 Topps set established another plateau for set size with 598 cards. The 2-1/2" x 3-1/2" cards feature a photograph set against a woodgrain background. The lower-right corner has been made to look like it is curling away. Many established specialty cards dot the set including statistical leaders, multi-player cards, team cards, checklists, World Series cards and All-Stars. Of note is that 1962 was the first year of the multi-player rookie card. There is a 9-card "In Action" subset and a 10-card run of special Babe Ruth cards. Photo variations of several cards in the 2nd Series (#110-196) exist. All cards in the 2nd Series can be found with two distinct printing variations, an early printing with the cards containing a very noticeable greenish tint, having been corrected to clear photos in subsequent print runs. The complete set price in the checklist that follows does not include the higher-priced variations. Among the high numbers (#523-598) certain cards were "short-printed," produced in lesser quantities. These cards carry a higher value and are indicated in the checklist by the notation (SP) after the player name.

		NM	EX	VG
	Complete Set (598):	5500.	1900.	1200.
	Common Player (1-370):	3.75	2.00	1.25
	Common Player (371-446):	4.50	2.25	1.25
	Common Player (447-522):	8.00	4.00	2.50
	Common Player (523-598):	15.00	7.50	4.50
1	Roger Maris	160.00	70.00	45.00
2	Jim Brosnan	3.50	1.75	1.00
3	Pete Runnels	3.50	1.75	1.00
4	John DeMerit	3.50	1.75	1.00
5	Sandy Koufax	110.00	55.00	33.00
6	Marv Breeding	3.50	1.75	1.00
7	Frank Thomas	3.50	1.75	1.00
8	Ray Herbert	3.50	1.75	1.00
9	Jim Davenport	3.50	1.75	1.00
10	Roberto Clemente	140.00	70.00	42.00
11	Tom Morgan	3.50	1.75	1.00
12	Harry Craft	3.50	1.75	1.00
13	Dick Howser	3.50	1.75	1.00
14	Bill White	3.50	1.75	1.00
15	Dick Donovan	3.50	1.75	1.00
16	Darrell Johnson	3.50	1.75	1.00
17	Johnny Callison	3.50	1.75	1.00
18	Managers' Dream (Mickey Mantle, Willie Mays)	150.00	75.00	45.00
19	*Ray Washburn*	3.50	1.75	1.00
20	Rocky Colavito	13.00	6.50	4.00
21	Jim Kaat	6.50	3.25	2.00
22a	Checklist 1-88 (numbers 121-176 on back)	7.00	3.50	2.00
22b	Checklist 1-88 (numbers 33-88 on back)	7.00	3.50	2.00
23	Norm Larker	3.50	1.75	1.00
24	Tigers team	6.50	3.25	2.00
25	Ernie Banks	32.50	16.00	9.75
26	Chris Cannizzaro	3.50	1.75	1.00
27	Chuck Cottier	3.50	1.75	1.00
28	Minnie Minoso	5.50	2.75	1.75
29	Casey Stengel	12.50	6.25	3.75
30	Eddie Mathews	18.00	9.00	5.50
31	*Tom Tresh*	17.50	8.75	5.25
32	John Roseboro	3.50	1.75	1.00
33	Don Larsen	3.50	1.75	1.00
34	Johnny Temple	3.50	1.75	1.00
35	*Don Schwall*	3.50	1.75	1.00
36	Don Leppert	3.50	1.75	1.00
37	Tribe Hill Trio (Barry Latman, Jim Perry, Dick Stigman)	4.50	2.25	1.25
38	Gene Stephens	3.50	1.75	1.00
39	Joe Koppe	3.50	1.75	1.00
40	Orlando Cepeda	15.00	7.50	4.50
41	Cliff Cook	3.50	1.75	1.00
42	Jim King	3.50	1.75	1.00
43	Dodgers team	7.50	3.75	2.25
44	Don Taussig	3.50	1.75	1.00
45	Brooks Robinson	35.00	17.50	10.50
46	*Jack Baldschun*	3.50	1.75	1.00
47	Bob Will	3.50	1.75	1.00
48	Ralph Terry	3.50	1.75	1.00
49	Hal Jones	3.50	1.75	1.00
50	Stan Musial	70.00	35.00	21.00
51	A.L. Batting Leaders (Norm Cash, Elston Howard, Al Kaline, Jim Piersall)	7.00	3.50	2.00
52	N.L. Batting Leaders (Ken Boyer, Roberto Clemente, Wally Moon, Vada Pinson)	12.00	6.00	3.50
53	A.L. Home Run Leaders (Jim Gentile, Harmon Killebrew, Mickey Mantle, Roger Maris)	80.00	40.00	24.00
54	N.L. Home Run Leaders (Orlando Cepeda, Willie Mays, Frank Robinson)	12.00	6.00	3.50
55	A.L. E.R.A. Leaders (Dick Donovan, Don Mossi, Milt Pappas, Bill Stafford)	6.50	3.25	2.00
56	N.L. E.R.A. Leaders (Mike McCormick, Jim O'Toole, Curt Simmons, Warren Spahn)	7.00	3.50	2.00
57	A.L. Win Leaders (Steve Barber, Jim Bunning, Whitey Ford, Frank Lary)	9.00	4.50	2.75
58	N.L. Win Leaders (Joe Jay, Jim O'Toole, Warren Spahn)	6.50	3.25	2.00
59	A.L. Strikeout Leaders (Jim Bunning, Whitey Ford, Camilo Pascual, Juan Pizzaro)	6.50	3.25	2.00
60	N.L. Strikeout Leaders (Don Drysdale, Sandy Koufax, Jim O'Toole, Stan Williams)	10.00	5.00	3.00
61	Cardinals Team	6.50	3.25	2.00
62	Steve Boros	3.50	1.75	1.00
63	*Tony Cloninger*	5.00	2.50	1.50
64	Russ Snyder	3.50	1.75	1.00
65	Bobby Richardson	12.00	6.00	3.50
66	Cuno Barragon (Barragan)	3.50	1.75	1.00
67	Harvey Haddix	3.50	1.75	1.00
68	Ken L. Hunt	3.50	1.75	1.00
69	Phil Ortega	3.50	1.75	1.00
70	Harmon Killebrew	18.00	9.00	5.50
71	Dick LeMay	3.50	1.75	1.00
72	Bob's Pupils (Steve Boros, Bob Scheffing, Jake Wood)	4.50	2.25	1.25
73	Nellie Fox	12.00	6.00	3.50
74	Bob Lillis	3.50	1.75	1.00
75	Milt Pappas	3.50	1.75	1.00
76	Howie Bedell	3.50	1.75	1.00
77	Tony Taylor	3.50	1.75	1.00
78	Gene Green	3.50	1.75	1.00
79	Ed Hobaugh	3.50	1.75	1.00
80	Vada Pinson	5.00	2.50	1.50
81	Jim Pagliaroni	3.50	1.75	1.00
82	Deron Johnson	3.50	1.75	1.00
83	Larry Jackson	3.50	1.75	1.00
84	Lenny Green	3.50	1.75	1.00
85	Gil Hodges	15.00	7.50	4.50
86	*Donn Clendenon*	5.50	2.75	1.75
87	Mike Roarke	3.50	1.75	1.00
88	Ralph Houk	3.50	1.75	1.00
89	Barney Schultz	3.50	1.75	1.00
90	Jim Piersall	4.50	2.25	1.25
91	J.C. Martin	3.50	1.75	1.00
92	Sam Jones	3.50	1.75	1.00
93	John Blanchard	3.50	1.75	1.00
94	Jay Hook	3.50	1.75	1.00
95	Don Hoak	3.50	1.75	1.00
96	Eli Grba	3.50	1.75	1.00
97	Tito Francona	3.50	1.75	1.00
98	Checklist 89-176	9.00	4.50	2.75
99	*Boog Powell*	24.00	12.00	7.25
100	Warren Spahn	21.00	10.50	6.25
101	Carroll Hardy	3.50	1.75	1.00
102	Al Schroll	3.50	1.75	1.00
103	Don Blasingame	3.50	1.75	1.00
104	Ted Savage	3.50	1.75	1.00
105	Don Mossi	3.50	1.75	1.00
106	Carl Sawatski	3.50	1.75	1.00
107	Mike McCormick	3.50	1.75	1.00
108	Willie Davis	5.00	2.50	1.50
109	Bob Shaw	3.50	1.75	1.00
110	Bill Skowron	5.00	2.50	1.50
111	Dallas Green	4.50	2.25	1.25
112	Hank Foiles	3.50	1.75	1.00
113	White Sox team	5.00	2.50	1.50
114	Howie Koplitz	3.50	1.75	1.00
115	Bob Skinner	3.50	1.75	1.00
116	Herb Score	4.50	2.25	1.25
117	Gary Geiger	3.50	1.75	1.00
118	Julian Javier	3.50	1.75	1.00
119	Danny Murphy	3.50	1.75	1.00
120	Bob Purkey	3.50	1.75	1.00
121	Billy Hitchcock	3.50	1.75	1.00
122	Norm Bass	3.50	1.75	1.00
123	Mike de la Hoz	3.50	1.75	1.00
124	Bill Pleis	3.50	1.75	1.00
125	Gene Woodling	3.50	1.75	1.00
126	Al Cicotte	3.50	1.75	1.00
127	Pride of the A's (Hank Bauer, Jerry Lumpe, Norm Siebern)	4.50	2.25	1.25
128	Art Fowler	3.50	1.75	1.00
129a	Lee Walls (pinstriped jersey)	22.00	11.00	6.50
129b	Lee Walls (plain jersey)	3.50	1.75	1.00
130	Frank Bolling	3.50	1.75	1.00
131	*Pete Richert*	3.50	1.75	1.00
132a	Angels Team (with inset photos)	20.00	10.00	6.00
132b	Angels Team (no inset photos)	7.00	3.50	2.00
133	Felipe Alou	6.00	3.00	1.75
134a	Billy Hoeft (green sky)	24.00	12.00	7.25
134b	Billy Hoeft (blue sky)	3.50	1.75	1.00
135	Babe as a Boy (Babe Ruth)	20.00	10.00	6.00
136	Babe Joins Yanks (Babe Ruth)	16.00	8.00	4.75
137	Babe and Mgr. Huggins (Babe Ruth)	15.00	7.50	4.50
138	The Famous Slugger (Babe Ruth)	17.50	8.75	5.25
139a	Hal Reniff (pitching)	55.00	27.00	16.50
139b	Hal Reniff (portrait)	9.00	4.50	2.75
139c	Babe Hits 60 (Babe Ruth) (pole in background at left)	22.00	11.00	6.50
139d	Babe Hits 60 (Babe Ruth) (no pole)	22.00	11.00	6.50
140	Gehrig and Ruth (Babe Ruth)	37.50	18.50	11.00
141	Twilight Years (Babe Ruth)	16.00	8.00	4.75
142	Coaching for the Dodgers (Babe Ruth)	16.00	8.00	4.75
143	Greatest Sports Hero (Babe Ruth)	15.00	7.50	4.50
144	Farewell Speech (Babe Ruth)	15.00	7.50	4.50
145	Barry Latman	3.50	1.75	1.00
146	Don Demeter	3.50	1.75	1.00
147a	Bill Kunkel (pitching)	24.00	12.00	7.25
147b	Bill Kunkel (portrait)	3.50	1.75	1.00
148	Wally Post	3.50	1.75	1.00
149	Bob Duliba	3.50	1.75	1.00
150	Al Kaline	33.00	16.50	10.00
151	Johnny Klippstein	3.50	1.75	1.00
152	Mickey Vernon	3.50	1.75	1.00
153	Pumpsie Green	3.50	1.75	1.00
154	Lee Thomas	3.50	1.75	1.00
155	Stu Miller	3.50	1.75	1.00
156	Merritt Ranew	3.50	1.75	1.00
157	Wes Covington	3.50	1.75	1.00
158	Braves Team	5.50	2.75	1.75
159	Hal Reniff	3.50	1.75	1.00
160	Dick Stuart	3.50	1.75	1.00
161	Frank Baumann	3.50	1.75	1.00
162	Sammy Drake	3.50	1.75	1.00
163	Hot Corner Guardians (Cletis Boyer, Billy Gardner)	4.50	2.25	1.25
164	Hal Naragon	3.50	1.75	1.00
165	Jackie Brandt	3.50	1.75	1.00
166	Don Lee	3.50	1.75	1.00
167	*Tim McCarver*	20.00	10.00	6.00
168	Leo Posada	3.50	1.75	1.00
169	Bob Cerv	3.50	1.75	1.00
170	Ron Santo	12.50	6.25	3.75
171	Dave Sisler	3.50	1.75	1.00
172	Fred Hutchinson	3.50	1.75	1.00
173	Chico Fernandez	3.50	1.75	1.00
174a	Carl Willey (with cap)	17.50	8.75	5.25
174b	Carl Willey (no cap)	3.50	1.75	1.00
175	Frank Howard	4.50	2.25	1.25
176a	Eddie Yost (batting)	22.00	11.00	6.50
176b	Eddie Yost (portrait)	3.50	1.75	1.00
177	Bobby Shantz	3.50	1.75	1.00
178	Camilo Carreon	3.50	1.75	1.00
179	Tom Sturdivant	3.50	1.75	1.00
180	Bob Allison	3.50	1.75	1.00
181	Paul Brown	3.50	1.75	1.00
182	Bob Nieman	3.50	1.75	1.00
183	Roger Craig	3.50	1.75	1.00
184	Haywood Sullivan	3.50	1.75	1.00
185	Roland Sheldon	3.50	1.75	1.00
186	*Mack Jones*	3.50	1.75	1.00
187	Gene Conley	3.50	1.75	1.00
188	Chuck Hiller	3.50	1.75	1.00
189	Dick Hall	3.50	1.75	1.00
190a	Wally Moon (with cap)	22.50	11.00	6.75
190b	Wally Moon (no cap)	3.50	1.75	1.00
191	Jim Brewer	3.50	1.75	1.00
192a	Checklist 177-264 (192 is Check List, 3)	9.00	4.50	2.75
192b	Checklist 177-264 (192 is Check List 3)	7.00	3.50	2.00
193	Eddie Kasko	3.50	1.75	1.00
194	*Dean Chance*	5.00	2.50	1.50
195	Joe Cunningham	3.50	1.75	1.00
196	Terry Fox	3.50	1.75	1.00
197	Daryl Spencer	3.50	1.75	1.00
198	Johnny Keane	3.50	1.75	1.00
199	*Gaylord Perry*	70.00	35.00	21.00
200	Mickey Mantle	400.00	200.00	115.00
201	Ike Delock	3.50	1.75	1.00
202	Carl Warwick	3.50	1.75	1.00
203	Jack Fisher	3.50	1.75	1.00
204	Johnny Weekly	3.50	1.75	1.00
205	Gene Freese	3.50	1.75	1.00
206	Senators team	5.50	2.75	1.75
207	Pete Burnside	3.50	1.75	1.00
208	Billy Martin	12.00	6.00	3.50
209	*Jim Fregosi*	9.00	4.50	2.75
210	Roy Face	3.50	1.75	1.00
211	Midway Masters (Frank Bolling, Roy McMillan)	4.50	2.25	1.25
212	Jim Owens	3.50	1.75	1.00
213	Richie Ashburn	13.00	6.50	4.00
214	Dom Zanni	3.50	1.75	1.00
215	Woody Held	3.50	1.75	1.00
216	Ron Kline	3.50	1.75	1.00
217	Walt Alston	5.50	2.75	1.75
218	*Joe Torre*	35.00	17.50	10.50
219	*Al Downing*	4.50	2.25	1.25
220	Roy Sievers	3.50	1.75	1.00
221	Bill Short	3.50	1.75	1.00
222	Jerry Zimmerman	3.50	1.75	1.00
223	Alex Grammas	3.50	1.75	1.00
224	Don Rudolph	3.50	1.75	1.00
225	Frank Malzone	3.50	1.75	1.00
226	Giants team	5.50	2.75	1.75
227	Bobby Tiefenauer	3.50	1.75	1.00
228	Dale Long	3.50	1.75	1.00
229	Jesus McFarlane	3.50	1.75	1.00
230	Camlio Pascual	3.50	1.75	1.00
231	Ernie Bowman	3.50	1.75	1.00
232	World Series Game 1 (Yanks Win Opener)	5.00	2.50	1.50
233	World Series Game 2 (Jay Ties It Up)	6.00	3.00	1.75
234	World Series Game 3 (Maris Wins It In the 9th)	24.00	12.00	7.25
235	World Series Game 4 (Ford Sets New Mark)	9.00	4.50	2.75
236	World Series Game 5 (Yanks Crush Reds in Finale)	6.00	3.00	1.75
237	World Series Summary (The Winners Celebrate)	5.00	2.50	1.50
238	Norm Sherry	3.50	1.75	1.00
239	Cecil Butler	3.50	1.75	1.00
240	George Altman	3.50	1.75	1.00
241	Johnny Kucks	3.50	1.75	1.00
242	Mel McGaha	3.50	1.75	1.00
243	Robin Roberts	12.00	6.00	3.50
244	Don Gile	3.50	1.75	1.00
245	Ron Hansen	3.50	1.75	1.00
246	Art Ditmar	3.50	1.75	1.00
247	Joe Pignatano	3.50	1.75	1.00
248	Bob Aspromonte	3.50	1.75	1.00
249	Ed Keegan	3.50	1.75	1.00
250	Norm Cash	9.00	4.50	2.75
251	Yankees team	55.00	27.00	16.50
252	Earl Francis	3.50	1.75	1.00
253	Harry Chiti	3.50	1.75	1.00
254	Gordon Windhorn	3.50	1.75	1.00
255	Juan Pizarro	3.50	1.75	1.00
256	Elio Chacon	3.50	1.75	1.00
257	Jack Spring	3.50	1.75	1.00
258	Marty Keough	3.50	1.75	1.00
259	Lou Klimchock	3.50	1.75	1.00
260	Bill Pierce	3.50	1.75	1.00
261	George Alusik	3.50	1.75	1.00
262	Bob Schmidt	3.50	1.75	1.00
263	The Right Pitch (Joe Jay, Bob Purkey, Jim Turner)	4.50	2.25	1.25
264	Dick Ellsworth	3.50	1.75	1.00

265	Joe Adcock	3.50	1.75	1.00
266	John Anderson	3.50	1.75	1.00
267	Dan Dobbek	3.50	1.75	1.00
268	Ken McBride	3.50	1.75	1.00
269	Bob Oldis	3.50	1.75	1.00
270	Dick Groat	3.50	1.75	1.00
271	Ray Rippelmeyer	3.50	1.75	1.00
272	Earl Robinson	3.50	1.75	1.00
273	Gary Bell	3.50	1.75	1.00
274	Sammy Taylor	3.50	1.75	1.00
275	Norm Siebern	3.50	1.75	1.00
276	Hal Kostad	3.50	1.75	1.00
277	Checklist 265-352	9.00	4.50	2.75
278	Ken Johnson	3.50	1.75	1.00
279	Hobie Landrith	3.50	1.75	1.00
280	Johnny Podres	4.50	2.25	1.25
281	*Jake Gibbs*	3.50	1.75	1.00
282	Dave Hillman	3.50	1.75	1.00
283	Charlie Smith	3.50	1.75	1.00
284	Ruben Amaro	3.50	1.75	1.00
285	Curt Simmons	3.50	1.75	1.00
286	Al Lopez	4.50	2.25	1.25
287	George Witt	3.50	1.75	1.00
288	Billy Williams	26.00	13.00	7.75
289	Mike Krsnich	3.50	1.75	1.00
290	Jim Gentile	3.50	1.75	1.00
291	Hal Stowe	3.50	1.75	1.00
292	Jerry Kindall	3.50	1.75	1.00
293	Bob Miller	3.50	1.75	1.00
294	Phillies team	7.50	3.75	2.25
295	Vern Law	3.50	1.75	1.00
296	Ken Hamlin	3.50	1.75	1.00
297	Ron Perranoski	3.50	1.75	1.00
298	Bill Tuttle	3.50	1.75	1.00
299	*Don Wert*	3.50	1.75	1.00
300	Willie Mays	100.00	50.00	30.00
301	Galen Cisco	3.50	1.75	1.00
302	*John Edwards*	3.50	1.75	1.00
303	Frank Torre	3.50	1.75	1.00
304	Dick Farrell	3.50	1.75	1.00
305	Jerry Lumpe	3.50	1.75	1.00
306	Redbird Rippers (Larry Jackson, Lindy McDaniel)	4.50	2.25	1.25
307	Jim Grant	3.50	1.75	1.00
308	Neil Chrisley	3.50	1.75	1.00
309	Moe Morhardt	3.50	1.75	1.00
310	Whitey Ford	35.00	17.50	10.50
311	Kubek Makes The Double Play (Tony Kubek)	6.00	3.00	1.75
312	Spahn Shows No-Hit Form (Warren Spahn)	11.00	5.50	3.25
313	Maris Blasts 61st (Roger Maris)	32.50	16.00	9.75
314	Colavito's Power (Rocky Colavito)	9.50	4.75	2.75
315	Ford Tosses a Curve (Whitey Ford)	10.00	5.00	3.00
316	Killebrew Sends One into Orbit (Harmon Killebrew)	12.50	6.25	3.75
317	Musial Plays 21st Season (Stan Musial)	17.50	8.75	5.25
318	The Switch Hitter Connects (Mickey Mantle)	120.00	60.00	36.00
319	McCormick Shows His Stuff (Mike McCormick)	6.00	3.00	1.75
320	Hank Aaron	95.00	47.00	28.00
321	Lee Stange	3.50	1.75	1.00
322	Al Dark	3.50	1.75	1.00
323	Don Landrum	3.50	1.75	1.00
324	Joe McClain	3.50	1.75	1.00
325	Luis Aparicio	12.50	6.25	3.75
326	Tom Parsons	3.50	1.75	1.00
327	Ozzie Virgil	3.50	1.75	1.00
328	Ken Walters	3.50	1.75	1.00
329	Bob Bolin	3.50	1.75	1.00
330	Johnny Romano	3.50	1.75	1.00
331	Moe Drabowsky	3.50	1.75	1.00
332	Don Buddin	3.50	1.75	1.00
333	Frank Cipriani	3.50	1.75	1.00
334	Red Sox team	7.50	3.75	2.25
335	Bill Bruton	3.50	1.75	1.00
336	Billy Muffett	3.50	1.75	1.00
337	Jim Marshall	3.50	1.75	1.00
338	Billy Gardner	3.50	1.75	1.00
339	Jose Valdivielso	3.50	1.75	1.00
340	Don Drysdale	30.00	15.00	9.00
341	Mike Hershberger	3.50	1.75	1.00
342	Ed Rakow	3.50	1.75	1.00
343	Albie Pearson	3.50	1.75	1.00
344	Ed Bauta	3.50	1.75	1.00
345	Chuck Schilling	3.50	1.75	1.00
346	Jack Kralick	3.50	1.75	1.00
347	Chuck Hinton	3.50	1.75	1.00
348	Larry Burright	3.50	1.75	1.00
349	Paul Foytack	3.50	1.75	1.00
350	Frank Robinson	35.00	17.50	10.50
351	Braves' Backstops (Del Crandall, Joe Torre)	6.50	3.25	2.00
352	Frank Sullivan	3.50	1.75	1.00
353	Bill Mazeroski	10.00	5.00	3.00
354	Roman Mejias	3.50	1.75	1.00
355	Steve Barber	3.50	1.75	1.00
356	Tom Haller	3.50	1.75	1.00
357	Jerry Walker	3.50	1.75	1.00
358	Tommy Davis	5.00	2.50	1.50
359	Bobby Locke	4.00	2.00	1.25
360	Yogi Berra	70.00	35.00	21.00
361	Bob Hendley	4.00	2.00	1.25
362	Ty Cline	4.00	2.00	1.25
363	Bob Roselli	4.00	2.00	1.25
364	Ken Hunt	4.00	2.00	1.25
365	Charley Neal	4.00	2.00	1.25
366	Phil Regan	4.00	2.00	1.25
367	Checklist 353-429	9.00	4.50	2.75
368	Bob Tillman	4.00	2.00	1.25
369	Ted Bowsfield	4.00	2.00	1.25
370	Ken Boyer	4.50	2.25	1.25
371	Earl Battey	4.50	2.25	1.25
372	Jack Curtis	4.50	2.25	1.25
373	Al Heist	4.50	2.25	1.25
374	Gene Mauch	4.50	2.25	1.25
375	Ron Fairly	4.50	2.25	1.25
376	Bud Daley	4.50	2.25	1.25
377	Johnny Orsino	4.50	2.25	1.25
378	Bennie Daniels	4.50	2.25	1.25
379	Chuck Essegian	4.50	2.25	1.25
380	Lou Burdette	4.50	2.25	1.25
381	Chico Cardenas	4.50	2.25	1.25
382	Dick Williams	4.50	2.25	1.25
383	Ray Sadecki	4.50	2.25	1.25
384	Athletics Team	9.00	4.50	2.75
385	Early Wynn	14.00	7.00	4.25
386	Don Mincher	4.50	2.25	1.25
387	*Lou Brock*	110.00	55.00	33.00
388	Ryne Duren	4.50	2.25	1.25
389	Smoky Burgess	5.00	2.50	1.50
390	Orlando Cepeda (All-Star)	10.00	5.00	3.00
391	Bill Mazeroski (All-Star)	9.00	4.50	2.75
392	Ken Boyer (All-Star)	6.00	3.00	1.75
393	Roy McMillan (All-Star)	4.50	2.25	1.25
394	Hank Aaron (All-Star)	40.00	20.00	12.00
395	Willie Mays (All-Star)	40.00	20.00	12.00
396	Frank Robinson (All-Star)	15.00	7.50	4.50
397	John Roseboro (All-Star)	6.00	3.00	1.75
398	Don Drysdale (All-Star)	12.00	6.00	3.50
399	Warren Spahn (All-Star)	14.00	7.00	4.25
400	Elston Howard	7.50	3.75	2.25
401	AL & NL Homer Kings (Roger Maris, Orlando Cepeda)	50.00	25.00	15.00
402	Gino Cimoli	4.50	2.25	1.25
403	Chet Nichols	4.50	2.25	1.25
404	Tim Harkness	4.50	2.25	1.25
405	Jim Perry	4.50	2.25	1.25
406	Bob Taylor	4.50	2.25	1.25
407	Hank Aguirre	4.50	2.25	1.25
408	Gus Bell	4.50	2.25	1.25
409	Pirates team	9.00	4.50	2.75
410	Al Smith	4.50	2.25	1.25
411	Danny O'Connell	4.50	2.25	1.25
412	Charlie James	4.50	2.25	1.25
413	Matty Alou	4.50	2.25	1.25
414	Joe Gaines	4.50	2.25	1.25
415	Bill Virdon	5.00	2.50	1.50
416	Bob Scheffing	4.50	2.25	1.25
417	Joe Azcue	4.50	2.25	1.25
418	Andy Carey	4.50	2.25	1.25
419	Bob Bruce	4.50	2.25	1.25
420	Gus Triandos	4.50	2.25	1.25
421	Ken MacKenzie	4.50	2.25	1.25
422	Steve Bilko	4.50	2.25	1.25
423	Rival League Relief Aces (Roy Face, Hoyt Wilhelm)	6.50	3.25	2.00
424	Al McBean	4.50	2.25	1.25
425	Carl Yastrzemski	90.00	45.00	27.00
426	Bob Farley	4.50	2.25	1.25
427	Jake Wood	4.50	2.25	1.25
428	Joe Hicks	4.50	2.25	1.25
429	Bill O'Dell	4.50	2.25	1.25
430	Tony Kubek	9.00	4.50	2.75
431	*Bob Rodgers*	4.50	2.25	1.25
432	Jim Pendleton	4.50	2.25	1.25
433	Jim Archer	4.50	2.25	1.25
434	Clay Dalrymple	4.50	2.25	1.25
435	Larry Sherry	5.00	2.50	1.50
436	Felix Mantilla	5.00	2.50	1.50
437	Ray Moore	5.00	2.50	1.50
438	Dick Brown	5.00	2.50	1.50
439	Jerry Buchek	5.00	2.50	1.50
440	Joe Jay	5.00	2.50	1.50
441	Checklist 430-506	11.00	5.50	3.25
442	Wes Stock	5.00	2.50	1.50
443	Del Crandall	5.00	2.50	1.50
444	Ted Wills	5.00	2.50	1.50
445	Vic Power	5.00	2.50	1.50
446	Don Elston	5.00	2.50	1.50
447	Willie Kirkland	7.00	3.50	2.00
448	Joe Gibbon	7.00	3.50	2.00
449	Jerry Adair	7.00	3.50	2.00
450	Jim O'Toole	7.00	3.50	2.00
451	*Jose Tartabull*	7.00	3.50	2.00
452	Earl Averill	7.00	3.50	2.00
453	Cal McLish	7.00	3.50	2.00
454	Floyd Robinson	7.00	3.50	2.00
455	Luis Arroyo	7.00	3.50	2.00
456	Joe Amalfitano	7.00	3.50	2.00
457	Lou Clinton	7.00	3.50	2.00
458a	Bob Buhl ("M" on cap)	7.00	3.50	2.00
458b	Bob Buhl (plain cap)	40.00	20.00	12.00
459	Ed Bailey	7.00	3.50	2.00
460	Jim Bunning	12.50	6.25	3.75
461	*Ken Hubbs*	28.00	14.00	8.50
462a	Willie Tasby ("W" on cap)	7.00	3.50	2.00
462b	Willie Tasby (plain cap)	45.00	22.00	13.50
463	Hank Bauer	11.00	5.50	3.25
464	*Al Jackson*	7.00	3.50	2.00
465	Reds team	11.00	5.50	3.25
466	Norm Cash (All-Star)	12.50	6.25	3.75
467	Chuck Schilling (All-Star)	7.00	3.50	2.00
468	Brooks Robinson (All-Star)	15.00	7.50	4.50
469	Luis Aparicio (All-Star)	12.50	6.25	3.75
470	Al Kaline (All-Star)	16.00	8.00	4.75
471	Mickey Mantle (All-Star)	145.00	72.00	43.00
472	Rocky Colavito (All-Star)	14.00	7.00	4.25
473	Elston Howard (All-Star)	11.00	5.50	3.25
474	Frank Lary (All-Star)	7.00	3.50	2.00
475	Whitey Ford (All-Star)	14.00	7.00	4.25
476	Orioles team	12.50	6.25	3.75
477	Andre Rodgers	7.00	3.50	2.00
478	Don Zimmer	7.00	3.50	2.00
479	*Joel Horlen*	7.00	3.50	2.00
480	Harvey Kuenn	7.00	3.50	2.00
481	Vic Wertz	7.00	3.50	2.00
482	Sam Mele	7.00	3.50	2.00
483	Don McMahon	7.00	3.50	2.00
484	Dick Schofield	7.00	3.50	2.00
485	Pedro Ramos	7.00	3.50	2.00
486	Jim Gilliam	7.00	3.50	2.00
487	Jerry Lynch	7.00	3.50	2.00
488	Hal Brown	7.00	3.50	2.00
489	Julio Gotay	7.00	3.50	2.00
490	Clete Boyer	7.00	3.50	2.00
491	Leon Wagner	7.00	3.50	2.00
492	Hal Smith	7.00	3.50	2.00
493	Danny McDevitt	7.00	3.50	2.00
494	Sammy White	7.00	3.50	2.00
495	Don Cardwell	7.00	3.50	2.00
496	Wayne Causey	7.00	3.50	2.00
497	Ed Bouchee	7.00	3.50	2.00
498	Jim Donohue	7.00	3.50	2.00
499	Zoilo Versalles	7.00	3.50	2.00
500	Duke Snider	40.00	20.00	12.00
501	Claude Osteen	7.00	3.50	2.00
502	Hector Lopez	7.00	3.50	2.00
503	Danny Murtaugh	10.00	5.00	3.00
504	Eddie Bressoud	7.00	3.50	2.00
505	Juan Marichal	35.00	17.50	10.50
506	Charley Maxwell	7.00	3.50	2.00
507	Ernie Broglio	7.00	3.50	2.00
508	Gordy Coleman	7.00	3.50	2.00
509	*Dave Giusti*	7.00	3.50	2.00
510	Jim Lemon	7.00	3.50	2.00
511	Bubba Phillips	7.00	3.50	2.00
512	Mike Fornieles	7.00	3.50	2.00
513	Whitey Herzog	10.00	5.00	3.00
514	Sherman Lollar	7.00	3.50	2.00
515	Stan Williams	7.00	3.50	2.00
516	Checklist 507-598	12.00	6.00	3.50
517	Dave Wickersham	7.00	3.50	2.00
518	Lee Maye	7.00	3.50	2.00
519	Bob Johnson	7.00	3.50	2.00
520	Bob Friend	9.00	4.50	2.75
521	Jacke Davis	7.00	3.50	2.00
522	Lindy McDaniel	7.00	3.50	2.00
523	Russ Nixon (SP)	22.00	11.00	6.50
524	Howie Nunn (SP)	22.00	11.00	6.50
525	George Thomas	15.00	7.50	4.50
526	Hal Woodeshick (SP)	22.00	11.00	6.50
527	*Dick McAuliffe*	18.00	9.00	5.50
528	Turk Lown	15.00	7.50	4.50
529	John Schaive (SP)	22.00	11.00	6.50
530	Bob Gibson (SP)	110.00	55.00	33.00
531	Bobby G. Smith	15.00	7.50	4.50
532	Dick Stigman	15.00	7.50	4.50
533	Charley Lau (SP)	25.00	12.50	7.50
534	Tony Gonzalez (SP)	22.00	11.00	6.50
535	Ed Roebuck	15.00	7.50	4.50
536	Dick Gernert	15.00	7.50	4.50
537	Indians team	42.00	21.00	12.50
538	Jack Sanford	15.00	7.50	4.50
539	Billy Moran	15.00	7.50	4.50
540	Jim Landis (SP)	22.00	11.00	6.50
541	Don Nottebart (SP)	22.00	11.00	6.50
542	Dave Philley	15.00	7.50	4.50
543	Bob Allen (SP)	22.00	11.00	6.50
544	Willie McCovey (SP)	125.00	62.00	37.00
545	Hoyt Wilhelm (SP)	35.00	17.50	10.50
546	Moe Thacker (SP)	22.00	11.00	6.50
547	Don Ferrarese	15.00	7.50	4.50
548	Bobby Del Greco	15.00	7.50	4.50
549	Bill Rigney (SP)	22.00	11.00	6.50
550	Art Mahaffey (SP)	22.00	11.00	6.50
551	Harry Bright	15.00	7.50	4.50
552	Cubs team (SP)	45.00	22.00	13.50
553	Jim Coates	15.00	7.50	4.50
554	Bubba Morton (SP)	22.00	11.00	6.50
555	John Buzhardt (SP)	22.00	11.00	6.50
556	Al Spangler	15.00	7.50	4.50
557	Bob Anderson (SP)	22.00	11.00	6.50
558	John Goryl	15.00	7.50	4.50
559	Mike Higgins	15.00	7.50	4.50
560	Chuck Estrada (SP)	22.00	11.00	6.50
561	Gene Oliver (SP)	22.00	11.00	6.50
562	Bill Henry	15.00	7.50	4.50
563	Ken Aspromonte	15.00	7.50	4.50
564	Bob Grim	15.00	7.50	4.50
565	Jose Pagan	15.00	7.50	4.50
566	Marty Kutyna (SP)	22.00	11.00	6.50
567	Tracy Stallard (SP)	22.00	11.00	6.50
568	Jim Golden	15.00	7.50	4.50
569	Ed Sadowski (SP)	22.00	11.00	6.50
570	Bill Stafford	15.00	7.50	4.50
571	Billy Klaus (SP)	22.00	11.00	6.50
572	Bob Miller (SP)	22.00	11.00	6.50
573	Johnny Logan	15.00	7.50	4.50
574	Dean Stone	15.00	7.50	4.50
575	Red Schoendienst	40.00	20.00	12.00
576	Russ Kemmerer (SP)	22.00	11.00	6.50
577	Dave Nicholson (SP)	22.00	11.00	6.50
578	Jim Duffalo	15.00	7.50	4.50
579	Jim Schaffer (SP)	22.00	11.00	6.50
580	Bill Monbouquette	15.00	7.50	4.50
581	Mel Roach	15.00	7.50	4.50
582	Ron Piche	15.00	7.50	4.50
583	Larry Osborne	15.00	7.50	4.50
584	Twins team (SP)	45.00	22.00	13.50
585	Glen Hobbie (SP)	22.00	11.00	6.50
586	Sammy Esposito (SP)	22.00	11.00	6.50
587	Frank Funk (SP)	22.00	11.00	6.50
588	Birdie Tebbetts	15.00	7.50	4.50
589	Bob Turley	15.00	7.50	4.50
590	Curt Flood	25.00	12.50	7.50
591	Rookie Parade Pitchers *(Sam McDowell), (Ron Nischwitz),* Art Quirk), *(Dick Radatz), (Ron Taylor)*	60.00	30.00	18.00
592	Rookie Parade Pitchers *(Bo Belinsky,* Joe Bonikowski), *(Jim Bouton,* Dan Pfister, Dave Stenhouse)	70.00	35.00	21.00
593	Rookie Parade Pitchers (Craig Anderson), *(Jack Hamilton,* Jack Lamabe, Bob Moorhead), *(Bob Veale)*	39.00	19.50	11.50

594	Rookie Parade Catchers *(Doug Camilli), (Doc Edwards), (Don Pavletich), (Ken Retzer), (Bub Uecker)*	60.00	30.00	18.00
595	Rookie Parade Infielders *(Ed Charles,* Marlin Coughtry, Bob Sadowski, Felix Torres)	42.00	21.00	12.50
596	Rookie Parade Infielders *(Bernie Allen), (Phil Linz), (Joe Pepitone), (Rich Rollins)*	65.00	32.00	19.50
597	Rookie Parade Infielders (Rod Kanehl, Jim McKnight), *(Denis Menke,* Amado Samuel)	42.00	21.00	12.50
598	Rookie Parade Outfielders *(Howie Goss), (Jim Hickman), (Manny Jimenez), (Al Luplow), (Ed Olivares)*	75.00	37.00	22.00

1962 Topps Baseball Bucks

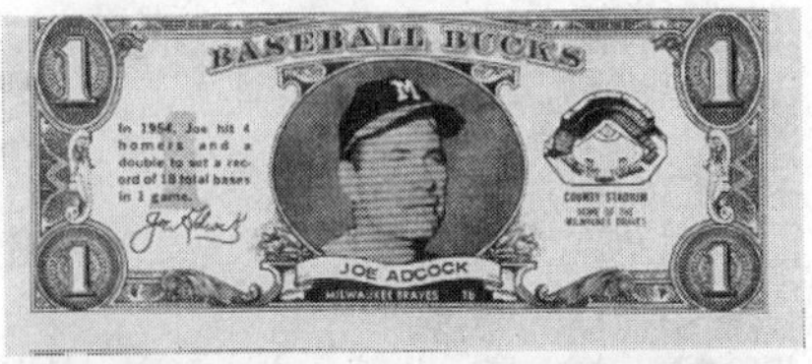

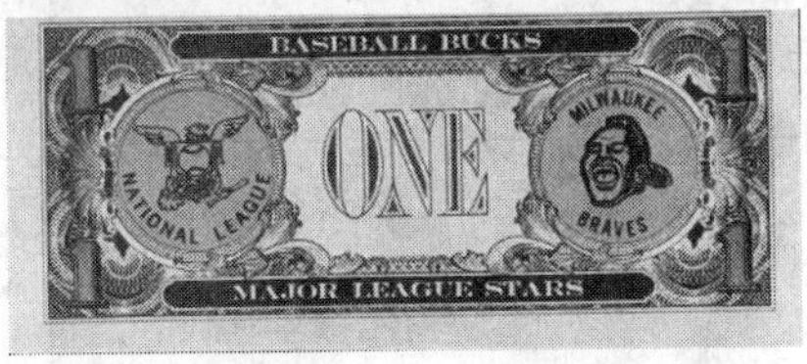

Issued in their own 1Û package, the 1962 Topps "Baseball Bucks" were another in the growing list of specialty Topps items. The 96 Baseball Bucks in the set measure 4-1/8" x 1-3/4," were printed in black on green paper and designed to resemble dollar bills. The center player portrait has a banner underneath with the player's name. His home park is shown on the right and there is some biographical information on the left. The back features a large denomination, with the player's league and team logo on either side. Poorly centered examples of this issue are the rule, rather than the exception. Sixty-two of the players appear on facsimile $1 notes. There are 24 $5 stars and 10 $10 superstars.

	NM	EX	VG
Complete Set (96):	1750.	875.00	525.00
Common Player:	9.00	4.50	2.75
(1) Hank Aaron ($5)	80.00	40.00	24.00
(2) Joe Adcock	9.00	4.50	2.75
(3) George Altman	9.00	4.50	2.75
(4) Jim Archer	9.00	4.50	2.75
(5) Richie Ashburn ($5)	40.00	20.00	12.00
(6) Ernie Banks ($10)	55.00	27.00	16.50
(7) Earl Battey	9.00	4.50	2.75
(8) Gus Bell	9.00	4.50	2.75
(9) Yogi Berra ($5)	55.00	27.00	16.50
(10) Ken Boyer ($10)	12.00	6.00	3.50
(11) Jackie Brandt	9.00	4.50	2.75
(12) Jim Bunning	35.00	17.50	10.50
(13) Lou Burdette ($5)	9.00	4.50	2.75
(14) Don Cardwell	9.00	4.50	2.75
(15) Norm Cash ($5)	12.00	6.00	3.50
(16) Orlando Cepeda ($5)	30.00	15.00	9.00
(17) Roberto Clemente ($5)	100.00	50.00	30.00
(18) Rocky Colavito ($5)	30.00	15.00	9.00
(19) Chuck Cottier	9.00	4.50	2.75
(20) Roger Craig	9.00	4.50	2.75
(21) Bennie Daniels	9.00	4.50	2.75
(22) Don Demeter	9.00	4.50	2.75
(23) Don Drysdale	40.00	20.00	12.00
(24) Chuck Estrada	9.00	4.50	2.75
(25) Dick Farrell	9.00	4.50	2.75
(26) Whitey Ford ($10)	50.00	25.00	15.00
(27) Nellie Fox ($5)	40.00	20.00	12.00
(28) Tito Francona	9.00	4.50	2.75
(29) Bob Friend	9.00	4.50	2.75
(30) Jim Gentile ($5)	9.00	4.50	2.75
(31) Dick Gernert	9.00	4.50	2.75
(32) Lenny Green	9.00	4.50	2.75
(33) Dick Groat	9.00	4.50	2.75
(34) Woody Held	9.00	4.50	2.75
(35) Don Hoak	9.00	4.50	2.75
(36) Gil Hodges ($5)	30.00	15.00	9.00
(37) Frank Howard	12.00	6.00	3.50
(38) Elston Howard	12.00	6.00	3.50
(39) Dick Howser	9.00	4.50	2.75
(40) Ken Hunt	9.00	4.50	2.75
(41) Larry Jackson	9.00	4.50	2.75
(42) Joe Jay	9.00	4.50	2.75
(43) Al Kaline	50.00	25.00	15.00
(44) Harmon Killebrew ($5)	40.00	20.00	12.00
(45) Sandy Koufax ($5)	75.00	37.00	22.00
(46) Harvey Kuenn	9.00	4.50	2.75
(47) Jim Landis	9.00	4.50	2.75
(48) Norm Larker	9.00	4.50	2.75
(49) Frank Lary ($5)	9.00	4.50	2.75
(50) Jerry Lumpe	9.00	4.50	2.75
(51) Art Mahaffey	9.00	4.50	2.75
(52) Frank Malzone	9.00	4.50	2.75
(53) Felix Mantilla	9.00	4.50	2.75
(54) Mickey Mantle ($10)	200.00	100.00	60.00
(55) Roger Maris ($10)	50.00	25.00	15.00
(56) Ed Mathews ($10)	40.00	20.00	12.00
(57) Willie Mays ($10)	80.00	40.00	24.00
(58) Ken McBride	9.00	4.50	2.75
(59) Mike McCormick	9.00	4.50	2.75
(60) Stu Miller	9.00	4.50	2.75
(61) Minnie Minoso	12.00	6.00	3.50
(62) Wally Moon ($5)	9.00	4.50	2.75
(63) Stan Musial ($10)	70.00	35.00	21.00
(64) Danny O'Connell	9.00	4.50	2.75
(65) Jim O'Toole	9.00	4.50	2.75
(66) Camilo Pascual ($5)	9.00	4.50	2.75
(67) Jim Perry	9.00	4.50	2.75
(68) Jimmy Piersall ($5)	12.00	6.00	3.50
(69) Vada Pinson ($5)	11.00	5.50	3.25
(70) Juan Pizarro	9.00	4.50	2.75
(71) Johnny Podres	11.00	5.50	3.25
(72) Vic Power ($5)	9.00	4.50	2.75
(73) Bob Purkey	9.00	4.50	2.75
(74) Pedro Ramos	9.00	4.50	2.75
(75) Brooks Robinson ($5)	50.00	25.00	15.00
(76) Floyd Robinson	9.00	4.50	2.75
(77) Frank Robinson ($10)	50.00	25.00	15.00
(78) Johnny Romano	9.00	4.50	2.75
(79) Pete Runnels ($5)	9.00	4.50	2.75
(80) Don Schwall	9.00	4.50	2.75
(81) Bobby Shantz ($5)	9.00	4.50	2.75
(82) Norm Siebern	9.00	4.50	2.75
(83) Roy Sievers ($5)	9.00	4.50	2.75
(84) Hal (W.) Smith	9.00	4.50	2.75
(85) Warren Spahn ($10)	40.00	20.00	12.00
(86) Dick Stuart	9.00	4.50	2.75
(87) Tony Taylor	9.00	4.50	2.75
(88) Lee Thomas	9.00	4.50	2.75
(89) Gus Triandos	9.00	4.50	2.75
(90) Leon Wagner	9.00	4.50	2.75
(91) Jerry Walker	9.00	4.50	2.75
(92) Bill White	9.00	4.50	2.75
(93) Billy Williams	40.00	20.00	12.00
(94) Gene Woodling	9.00	4.50	2.75
(95) Early Wynn ($5)	30.00	15.00	9.00
(96) Carl Yastrzemski	50.00	25.00	15.00

1962 Topps Stamps

An artistic improvement over the somewhat drab Topps stamps of the previous year, the 1962 stamps, 1-3/8" x 1-7/8," had color player photographs set on red or yellow backgrounds. As in 1961, they were issued in two-stamp panels as insert with Topps baseball cards. A change from 1961 was the inclusion of team emblems in the set. A complete set consists of 201 stamps; Roy Sievers was originally portrayed on the wrong team - Athletics - and was later corrected to the Phillies.

	NM	EX	VG
Complete Set (200):	350.00	175.00	100.00
Stamp Album:	40.00	20.00	12.00
Common Player:	1.25	.60	.40
(1) Hank Aaron	18.00	9.00	5.50
(2) Jerry Adair	1.25	.60	.40
(3) Joe Adcock	1.25	.60	.40
(4) Bob Allison	1.25	.60	.40
(5) Felipe Alou	2.00	1.00	.60
(6) George Altman	1.25	.60	.40
(7) Joe Amalfitano	1.25	.60	.40
(8) Ruben Amaro	1.25	.60	.40
(9) Luis Aparicio	5.00	2.50	1.50
(10) Jim Archer	1.25	.60	.40
(11) Bob Aspromonte	1.25	.60	.40
(12) Ed Bailey	1.25	.60	.40
(13) Jack Baldschun	1.25	.60	.40
(14) Ernie Banks	11.00	5.50	3.25
(15) Earl Battey	1.25	.60	.40
(16) Gus Bell	1.25	.60	.40
(17) Yogi Berra	12.00	6.00	3.50
(18) Dick Bertell	1.25	.60	.40
(19) Steve Bilko	1.25	.60	.40
(20) Frank Bolling	1.25	.60	.40
(21) Steve Boros	1.25	.60	.40
(22) Ted Bowsfield	1.25	.60	.40
(23) Clete Boyer	1.25	.60	.40
(24) Ken Boyer	1.50	.70	.45
(25) Jackie Brandt	1.25	.60	.40
(26) Bill Bruton	1.25	.60	.40
(27) Jim Bunning	5.00	2.50	1.50
(28) Lou Burdette	1.25	.60	.40
(29) Smoky Burgess	1.25	.60	.40
(30) Johnny Callizon (Callison)	1.25	.60	.40
(31) Don Cardwell	1.25	.60	.40
(32) Camilo Carreon	1.25	.60	.40
(33) Norm Cash	2.00	1.00	.60
(34) Orlando Cepeda	5.00	2.50	1.50
(35) Roberto Clemente	20.00	10.00	6.00
(36) Ty Cline	1.25	.60	.40
(37) Rocky Colavito	5.00	2.50	1.50
(38) Gordon Coleman	1.25	.60	.40
(39) Chuck Cottier	1.25	.60	.40
(40) Roger Craig	1.25	.60	.40
(41) Del Crandall	1.25	.60	.40
(42) Pete Daley	1.25	.60	.40
(43) Clay Dalrymple	1.25	.60	.40
(44) Bennie Daniels	1.25	.60	.40
(45) Jim Davenport	1.25	.60	.40
(46) Don Demeter	1.25	.60	.40
(47) Dick Donovan	1.25	.60	.40
(48) Don Drysdale	10.00	5.00	3.00
(49) John Edwards	1.25	.60	.40
(50) Dick Ellsworth	1.25	.60	.40
(51) Chuck Estrada	1.25	.60	.40
(52) Roy Face	1.25	.60	.40
(53) Ron Fairly	1.25	.60	.40
(54) Dick Farrell	1.25	.60	.40
(55) Whitey Ford	9.00	4.50	2.75
(56) Mike Fornieles	1.25	.60	.40
(57) Nellie Fox	7.00	3.50	2.00
(58) Tito Francona	1.25	.60	.40
(59) Gene Freese	1.25	.60	.40
(60) Bob Friend	1.25	.60	.40
(61) Gary Geiger	1.25	.60	.40
(62) Jim Gentile	1.25	.60	.40
(63) Tony Gonzalez	1.25	.60	.40
(64) Lenny Green	1.25	.60	.40
(65) Dick Groat	1.25	.60	.40
(66) Ron Hansen	1.25	.60	.40
(67) Al Heist	1.25	.60	.40
(68) Woody Held	1.25	.60	.40
(69) Ray Herbert	1.25	.60	.40
(70) Chuck Hinton	1.25	.60	.40
(71) Don Hoak	1.25	.60	.40
(72) Glen Hobbie	1.25	.60	.40
(73) Gil Hodges	5.00	2.50	1.50
(74) Jay Hook	1.25	.60	.40
(75) Elston Howard	2.00	1.00	.60
(76) Frank Howard	1.25	.60	.40
(77) Dick Howser	1.25	.60	.40
(78) Ken Hunt	1.25	.60	.40
(79) Larry Jackson	1.25	.60	.40
(80) Julian Javier	1.25	.60	.40
(81) Joe Jay	1.25	.60	.40
(82) Bob Johnson	1.25	.60	.40
(83) Sam Jones	1.25	.60	.40
(84) Al Kaline	10.00	5.00	3.00
(85) Eddie Kasko	1.25	.60	.40
(86) Harmon Killebrew	9.00	4.50	2.75
(87) Sandy Koufax	18.00	9.00	5.50
(88) Jack Kralick	1.25	.60	.40
(89) Tony Kubek	1.50	.70	.45
(90) Harvey Kuenn	1.25	.60	.40
(91) Jim Landis	1.25	.60	.40
(92) Hobie Landrith	1.25	.60	.40
(93) Frank Lary	1.25	.60	.40
(94) Barry Latman	1.25	.60	.40
(95) Jerry Lumpe	1.25	.60	.40
(96) Art Mahaffey	1.25	.60	.40
(97) Frank Malzone	1.25	.60	.40
(98) Felix Mantilla	1.25	.60	.40
(99) Mickey Mantle	65.00	32.00	19.50
(100) Juan Marichal	5.00	2.50	1.50
(101) Roger Maris	10.00	5.00	3.00
(102) J.C. Martin	1.25	.60	.40
(103) Ed Mathews	7.00	3.50	2.00
(104) Willie Mays	18.00	9.00	5.50
(105) Bill Mazeroski	5.00	2.50	1.50
(106) Ken McBride	1.25	.60	.40
(107) Tim McCarver	1.25	.60	.40
(108) Joe McClain	1.25	.60	.40
(109) Mike McCormick	1.25	.60	.40
(110) Lindy McDaniel	1.25	.60	.40
(111) Roy McMillan	1.25	.60	.40
(112) Bob L. Miller	1.25	.60	.40
(113) Stu Miller	1.25	.60	.40
(114) Minnie Minoso	2.50	1.25	.70
(115) Bill Monbouquette	1.25	.60	.40
(116) Wally Moon	1.25	.60	.40
(117) Don Mossi	1.25	.60	.40
(118) Stan Musial	18.00	9.00	5.50
(119) Russ Nixon	1.25	.60	.40
(120) Danny O'Connell	1.25	.60	.40
(121) Jim O'Toole	1.25	.60	.40
(122) Milt Pappas	1.25	.60	.40
(123) Camilo Pascual	1.25	.60	.40
(124) Albie Pearson	1.25	.60	.40
(125) Jim Perry	1.25	.60	.40
(126) Bubba Phillips	1.25	.60	.40
(127) Jimmy Piersall	1.25	.60	.40
(128) Vada Pinson	1.25	.60	.40
(129) Juan Pizarro	1.25	.60	.40
(130) Johnny Podres	1.25	.60	.40
(131) Leo Posada	1.25	.60	.40
(132) Vic Power	1.25	.60	.40
(133) Bob Purkey	1.25	.60	.40
(134) Pedro Ramos	1.25	.60	.40
(135) Bobby Richardson	1.25	.60	.40
(136) Brooks Robinson	10.00	5.00	3.00
(137) Floyd Robinson	1.25	.60	.40
(138) Frank Robinson	9.00	4.50	2.75
(139) Bob Rodgers	1.25	.60	.40
(140) Johnny Romano	1.25	.60	.40
(141) John Roseboro	1.25	.60	.40

(142)	Pete Runnels	1.25	.60	.40
(143)	Ray Sadecki	1.25	.60	.40
(144)	Ron Santo	1.25	.60	.40
(145)	Chuck Schilling	1.25	.60	.40
(146)	Barney Schultz	1.25	.60	.40
(147)	Don Schwall	1.25	.60	.40
(148)	Bobby Shantz	1.25	.60	.40
(149)	Bob Shaw	1.25	.60	.40
(150)	Norm Siebern	1.25	.60	.40
(151a)	Roy Sievers (Kansas City)	1.25	.60	.40
(151b)	Roy Sievers (Philadelphia)	1.25	.60	.40
(152)	Bill Skowron	1.50	.70	.45
(153)	Hal (W.) Smith	1.25	.60	.40
(154)	Duke Snider	11.00	5.50	3.25
(155)	Warren Spahn	9.00	4.50	2.75
(156)	Al Spangler	1.25	.60	.40
(157)	Daryl Spencer	1.25	.60	.40
(158)	Gene Stephens	1.25	.60	.40
(159)	Dick Stuart	1.25	.60	.40
(160)	Haywood Sullivan	1.25	.60	.40
(161)	Tony Taylor	1.25	.60	.40
(162)	George Thomas	1.25	.60	.40
(163)	Lee Thomas	1.25	.60	.40
(164)	Bob Tiefenauer	1.25	.60	.40
(165)	Joe Torre	1.25	.60	.40
(166)	Gus Triandos	1.25	.60	.40
(167)	Bill Tuttle	1.25	.60	.40
(168)	Zoilo Versalles	1.25	.60	.40
(169)	Bill Virdon	1.25	.60	.40
(170)	Leon Wagner	1.25	.60	.40
(171)	Jerry Walker	1.25	.60	.40
(172)	Lee Walls	1.25	.60	.40
(173)	Bill White	1.25	.60	.40
(174)	Hoyt Wilhelm	4.00	2.00	1.25
(175)	Billy Williams	7.00	3.50	2.00
(176)	Jake Wood	1.25	.60	.40
(177)	Gene Woodling	1.25	.60	.40
(178)	Early Wynn	4.00	2.00	1.25
(179)	Carl Yastrzemski	9.00	4.50	2.75
(180)	Don Zimmer	1.25	.60	.40
(181)	Baltimore Orioles Logo	1.25	.60	.40
(182)	Boston Red Sox Logo	1.25	.60	.40
(183)	Chicago Cubs Logo	1.25	.60	.40
(184)	Chicago White Sox Logo	1.25	.60	.40
(185)	Cincinnati Reds Logo	1.25	.60	.40
(186)	Cleveland Indians Logo	1.25	.60	.40
(187)	Detroit Tigers Logo	1.25	.60	.40
(188)	Houston Colts Logo	1.25	.60	.40
(189)	Kansas City Athletics Logo	1.25	.60	.40
(190)	Los Angeles Angels Logo	1.25	.60	.40
(191)	Los Angeles Dodgers Logo	1.25	.60	.40
(192)	Milwaukee Braves Logo	1.25	.60	.40
(193)	Minnesota Twins Logo	1.25	.60	.40
(194)	New York Mets Logo	1.25	.60	.40
(195)	New York Yankees Logo	1.50	.70	.45
(196)	Philadelphia Phillies Logo	1.25	.60	.40
(197)	Pittsburgh Pirates Logo	1.25	.60	.40
(198)	St. Louis Cardinals Logo	1.25	.60	.40
(199)	San Francisco Giants Logo	1.25	.60	.40
(200)	Washington Senators Logo	1.25	.60	.40

1962 Topps Stamps Panels

Some advanced collectors pursue the 1962 Topps stamps in the form of the two-stamp panels in which they were issued. The 200 different stamps which make up the issue can be found on 245 different two-stamp panels, flanked at left by a smaller tab advertising the accompanying album. The unnumbered stamps are listed here alphabetically according to the name of the player or team which apears on the left end of the panel. Values shown are for full three-piece panels.

		NM	EX	VG
Complete Panel Set (245):		1750.	875.00	525.00
Common Panel:		3.00	1.50	.90
(1)	Hank Aaron/Ted Bowsfield	50.00	25.00	15.00
(2)	Jerry Adair/Tony Gonzalez	3.00	1.50	.90
(3)	Joe Adcock/George Thomas	3.00	1.50	.90
(4)	Bob Allison/Jim Davenport	3.00	1.50	.90
(5)	Felipe Alou/Mickey Mantle	100.00	50.00	30.00
(6)	Felipe Alou/Chuck Schilling	8.00	4.00	2.50
(7)	George Altman/Rocky Colavito	12.00	6.00	3.50
(8)	George Altman/Don Schwall	3.00	1.50	.90
(9)	Joe Amalfitano/Jim Gentile	3.00	1.50	.90
(10)	Joe Amalfitano/Vic Power	3.00	1.50	.90
(11)	Ruben Amaro/Carl Yastrzemski	50.00	25.00	15.00
(12)	Luis Aparicio/Dick Farrell	12.00	6.00	3.50
(13)	Luis Aparicio/Al Heist	12.00	6.00	3.50
(14)	Bob Aspromonte/Al Kaline	20.00	10.00	6.00
(15)	Ed Bailey/Jim Piersall	4.50	2.25	1.25
(16)	Ernie Banks/Milt Pappas	20.00	10.00	6.00
(17)	Earl Battey/Bob Clemente	50.00	25.00	15.00
(18)	Earl Battey/Ed Mathews	15.00	7.50	4.50
(19)	Gus Bell/Steve Boros	3.00	1.50	.90
(20)	Gus Bell/Ty Cline	3.00	1.50	.90
(21)	Yogi Berra/Roy Face	20.00	10.00	6.00
(22)	Yogi Berra/Jack Kralick	20.00	10.00	6.00
(23)	Dick Bertell/Hoyt Wilhelm	12.00	6.00	3.50
(24)	Dick Bertell/Don Zimmer	4.50	2.25	1.25
(25)	Steve Bilko/Ruben Amaro	3.00	1.50	.90
(26)	Steve Bilko/Roy Sievers	3.00	1.50	.90
(27)	Frank Bolling/Nellie Fox	12.00	6.00	3.50
(28)	Steve Boros/Art Mahaffey	3.00	1.50	.90
(29)	Clete Boyer/Chuck Cottier	4.00	2.00	1.25
(30)	Ken Boyer/Bob Friend	6.00	3.00	1.75
(31)	Jackie Brandt/Frank Robinson	20.00	10.00	6.00
(32)	Bill Bruton/Ernie Banks	20.00	10.00	6.00
(33)	Bill Bruton/Jay Hook	3.00	1.50	.90
(34)	Jim Bunning/Bob Miller	12.00	6.00	3.50
(35)	Jim Bunning/Jim O'Toole	12.00	6.00	3.50
(36)	Jim Bunning/Daryl Spencer	12.00	6.00	3.50
(37)	Lou Burdette/Ed Mathews	15.00	7.50	4.50
(38)	Lou Burdette/Willie Mays	50.00	25.00	15.00
(39)	Smoky Burgess/Bobby Richardson	6.00	3.00	1.75
(40)	Johnny Callizon (Callison)/Barry Latman	4.50	2.25	1.25
(41)	Johnny Callizon (Callison)/Frank Malzone	4.50	2.25	1.25
(42)	Johnny Callizon (Callison)/Willie Mays	50.00	25.00	15.00
(43)	Don Cardwell/Hoyt Wilhelm	12.00	6.00	3.50
(44)	Norm Cash/Dick Bertell	5.00	2.50	1.50
(45)	Norm Cash/Don Cardwell	5.00	2.50	1.50
(46)	Norm Cash/Dick Howser	5.00	2.50	1.50
(47)	Ty Cline/Art Mahaffey	3.00	1.50	.90
(48)	Rocky Colavito/Sam Jones	12.00	6.00	3.50
(49)	Gordon Coleman/Pete Daley	3.00	1.50	.90
(50)	Gordon Coleman/Danny O'Connell	3.00	1.50	.90
(51)	Roger Craig/Tod Bowsfield	3.00	1.50	.90
(52)	Roger Craig/Minnie Minoso	6.00	3.00	1.75
(53)	Del Crandall/Clete Boyer	4.50	2.25	1.25
(54)	Del Crandall/Ray Sadecki	3.00	1.50	.90
(55)	Pete Daley/Bob Friend	3.00	1.50	.90
(56)	Pete Daley/Mike McCormick	3.00	1.50	.90
(57)	Clay Dalrymple/Woody Held	3.00	1.50	.90
(58)	Clay Dalrymple/Pedro Ramos	3.00	1.50	.90
(59)	Bennie Daniels/Jerry Walker	3.00	1.50	.90
(60)	Jim Davenport/Harmon Killebrew	20.00	10.00	6.00
(61)	Don Demeter/Haywood Sullivan	3.00	1.50	.90
(62)	Don Demeter/Gus Triandos	3.00	1.50	.90
(63)	Don Demeter/Lee Walls	3.00	1.50	.90
(64)	Dick Donovan/Jerry Adair	3.00	1.50	.90
(65)	Dick Donovan/Jim Perry	3.00	1.50	.90
(66)	Dick Donovan/Vada Pinson	4.00	2.00	1.25
(67)	John Edwards/Jerry Walker	3.00	1.50	.90
(68)	Dick Ellsworth/Glen Hobbie	3.00	1.50	.90
(69)	Dick Ellsworth/Pete Runnels	3.00	1.50	.90
(70)	Chuck Estrada/Don Drysdale	15.00	7.50	4.50
(71)	Chuck Estrada/Al Kaline	20.00	10.00	6.00
(72)	Roy Face/Minnie Minoso	6.00	3.00	1.75
(73)	Ron Fairly/Jim Landis	3.00	1.50	.90
(74)	Dick Farrell/Frank Lary	3.00	1.50	.90
(75)	Whitey Ford/Joe Torre	20.00	10.00	6.00
(76)	Nellie Fox/Willie Mays	60.00	30.00	18.00
(77)	Tito Francona/Ken Boyer	5.00	2.50	1.50
(78)	Tito Francona/Bob Johnson	3.00	1.50	.90
(79)	Gene Freese/Bob Allison	3.00	1.50	.90
(80)	Gene Freese/Ernie Banks	20.00	10.00	6.00
(81)	Gary Geiger/Bobby Richardson	5.00	2.50	1.50
(82)	Jim Gentile/Hal W. Smith	3.00	1.50	.90
(83)	Dick Groat/Joe McClain	3.00	1.50	.90
(84)	Al Heist/Frank Lary	3.00	1.50	.90
(85)	Woody Held/Orlando Cepeda	12.00	6.00	3.50
(86)	Ray Herbert/Frank Bolling	3.00	1.50	.90
(87)	Ray Herbert/Eddie Kasko	3.00	1.50	.90
(88)	Chuck Hinton/Dick Groat	3.00	1.50	.90
(89)	Chuck Hinton/Stu Miller	3.00	1.50	.90
(90)	Don Hoak/Bob Allison	3.00	1.50	.90
(91)	Gil Hodges/Bennie Daniels	12.00	6.00	3.50
(92)	Gil Hodges/John Edwards	12.00	6.00	3.50
(93)	Elston Howard/Bob Clemente	60.00	30.00	18.00
(94)	Dick Howser/Don Zimmer	4.50	2.25	1.25
(95)	Ken Hunt/Lenny Green	3.00	1.50	.90
(96)	Larry Jackson/Smoky Burgess	3.00	1.50	.90
(97)	Larry Jackson/Gary Geiger	3.00	1.50	.90
(98)	Joe Jay/Johnny Romano	3.00	1.50	.90
(99)	Bob Johnson/Bob Friend	3.00	1.50	.90
(100)	Al Kaline/Don Hoak	20.00	10.00	6.00
(101)	Eddie Kasko/Nellie Fox	12.00	6.00	3.50
(102)	Sandy Koufax/Joe Adcock	30.00	15.00	9.00
(103)	Sandy Koufax/Hobie Landrith	30.00	15.00	9.00
(104)	Sandy Koufax/Bob Shaw	30.00	15.00	9.00
(105)	Jack Kralick/Minnie Minoso	4.50	2.25	1.25
(106)	Harvey Kuenn/Ken Hunt	3.00	1.50	.90
(107)	Havey Kuenn/Gene Woodling	3.00	1.50	.90
(108)	Hobie Landrith/Mike Fornieles	3.00	1.50	.90
(109)	Barry Latman/Tony Kubek	4.50	2.25	1.25
(110)	Barry Latman/Johnny Podres	3.00	1.50	.90
(111)	Frank Malzone/Johnny Podres	3.00	1.50	.90
(112)	Frank Malzone/Duke Snider	20.00	10.00	6.00
(113)	Felix Mantilla/Camilo Carreon	3.00	1.50	.90
(114)	Mickey Mantle/Hank Aaron	125.00	62.00	37.00
(115)	Mickey Mantle/Dick Stuart	100.00	50.00	30.00
(116)	Juan Marichal/Bill Bruton	15.00	7.50	4.50
(117)	Juan Marichal/Gene Freese	15.00	7.50	4.50
(118)	Juan Marichal/Don Hoak	15.00	7.50	4.50
(119)	Roger Maris/Lou Burdette	30.00	15.00	9.00
(120)	Roger Maris/Nellie Fox	35.00	17.50	10.50
(121)	Roger Maris/Lee Thomas	30.00	15.00	9.00
(122)	J.C. Martin/Felix Mantilla	3.00	1.50	.90
(123)	J.C. Martin/Barney Schultz	3.00	1.50	.90
(124)	Willie Mays/Tony Kubek	60.00	30.00	18.00
(125)	Bill Mazeroski/Earl Battey	8.00	4.00	2.50
(126)	Bill Mazeroski/Elston Howard	10.00	5.00	3.00
(127)	Bill Mazeroski/Early Wynn	15.00	7.50	4.50
(128)	Ken McBride/Joe Torre	8.00	4.00	2.50
(129)	Tim McCarver/Bill Tuttle	8.00	4.00	2.50
(130)	Lindy McDaniel/Jim Piersall	4.50	2.25	1.25
(131)	Roy McMillan/Bob Allison	3.00	1.50	.90
(132)	Roy McMillan/Albie Pearson	3.00	1.50	.90
(133)	Roy McMillan/Leon Wagner	3.00	1.50	.90
(134)	Bob Miller/Ron Hansen	3.00	1.50	.90
(135)	Stu Miller/Joe McCain	3.00	1.50	.90
(136)	Bill Monbouquette/Don Hoak	3.00	1.50	.90
(137)	Bill Monbouquette/Joe Torre	8.00	4.00	2.50
(138)	Wally Moon/Frank Malzone	3.00	1.50	.90
(139)	Wally Moon/Juan Pizarro	3.00	1.50	.90
(140)	Wally Moon/Brooks Robinson	20.00	10.00	6.00
(141)	Don Mossi/Bill Bruton	3.00	1.50	.90
(142)	Don Mossi/Johnny Podres	3.00	1.50	.90
(143)	Don Mossi/Al Spangler	3.00	1.50	.90
(144)	Stan Musial/Whitey Ford	60.00	30.00	18.00
(145)	Stan Musial/Joe Torre	60.00	30.00	18.00
(146)	Russ Nixon/Ed Bailey	3.00	1.50	.90
(147)	Russ Nixon/Lindy McDaniel	3.00	1.50	.90
(148)	Danny O'Connell/Mike McCormick	3.00	1.50	.90
(149)	Jim O'Toole/Ron Hansen	3.00	1.50	.90
(150)	Jim O'Toole/Gene Stephens	3.00	1.50	.90
(151)	Camilo Pascual/Pete Daley	3.00	1.50	.90
(152)	Camilo Pascual/Tim McCarver	4.50	2.25	1.25
(153)	Camilo Pascual/Bill Virdon	3.00	1.50	.90
(154)	Albie Pearson/Julian Javier	3.00	1.50	.90
(155)	Jim Perry/Frank Howard	6.00	3.00	1.75
(156)	Bubba Phillips/Don Drsydale	15.00	7.50	4.50
(157)	Vada Pinson/Tony Gonzalez	4.50	2.25	1.25
(158)	Vada Pinson/Frank Howard	6.00	3.00	1.75
(159)	Juan Pizarro/Jack Baldschun	3.00	1.50	.90
(160)	Johnny Podres/Jim Archer	3.00	1.50	.90
(161)	Leo Posada/Milt Pappas	3.00	1.50	.90
(162)	Leo Posada/Johnny Romano	3.00	1.50	.90
(163)	Vic Power/Hal W. Smith	3.00	1.50	.90
(164)	Bob Purkey/Harmon Killebrew	20.00	10.00	6.00
(165)	Pedro Ramos/Orlando Cepeda	12.00	6.00	3.50
(166)	Brooks Robinson/Jack Baldschun	20.00	10.00	6.00
(167)	Brooks Robinson/Duke Snider	30.00	15.00	9.00
(168)	Floyd Robinson/Ron Fairly	3.00	1.50	.90
(169)	Floyd Robinson/Tony Taylor	3.00	1.50	.90
(170)	Bob Rodgers/Hank Aaron	50.00	25.00	15.00
(171)	Bob Rodgers/Roger Craig	3.00	1.50	.90
(172)	Bob Rodgers/Johnny Romano	3.00	1.50	.90
(173)	Johnny Romano/Minnie Minoso	4.50	2.25	1.25
(174)	John Roseboro/Bob Aspromonte	3.00	1.50	.90
(175)	John Roseboro/Chuck Estrada	3.00	1.50	.90
(176)	John Roseboro/Bubba Phillips	3.00	1.50	.90
(177)	Ray Sadecki/Chuck Cottier	3.00	1.50	.90
(178)	Ron Santo/Ernie Banks	30.00	15.00	9.00
(179)	Ron Santo/Joe Jay	10.00	5.00	3.00
(180)	Ron Santo/Leo Posada	10.00	5.00	3.00
(181)	Chuck Schilling/Hank Aaron	50.00	25.00	15.00
(182)	Chuck Schilling/Dick Stuart	3.00	1.50	.90
(183)	Barney Schultz/Camilo Carreon	3.00	1.50	.90
(184)	Don Schwall/Sam Jones	3.00	1.50	.90
(185)	Bobby Shantz/Pete Runnels	3.00	1.50	.90
(186)	Bob Shaw/Mike Fornieles	3.00	1.50	.90
(187)	Bob Shaw/George Thomas	3.00	1.50	.90
(188)	Norm Siebern/Dick Ellsworth	3.00	1.50	.90
(189)	Norm Siebern/Bobby Shantz	3.00	1.50	.90
(190)	Norm Siebern/Early Wynn	12.00	6.00	3.50
(191)	Roy Sievers/Carl Yastrzemski	50.00	25.00	15.00
(192)	Bill Skowron/Jim Davenport	5.00	2.50	1.50
(193)	Bill Skowron/Bob Purkey	5.00	2.50	1.50
(194)	Warren Spahn/Whitey Ford	30.00	15.00	9.00
(195)	Al Spangler/Jim Archer	3.00	1.50	.90
(196)	Al Spangler/Jay Hook	3.00	1.50	.90
(197)	Daryl Spencer/Gene Stephens	3.00	1.50	.90
(198)	Haywood Sullivan/Jerry Lumpe	3.00	1.50	.90
(199)	Haywood Sullivan/Billy Williams	12.00	6.00	3.50
(200)	Tony Taylor/Jim Landis	3.00	1.50	.90
(201)	Lee Thomas/Ed Mathews	15.00	7.50	4.50
(202)	Bob Tiefenauer/Jackie Brandt	3.00	1.50	.90
(203)	Bob Tiefenauer/Jake Wood	3.00	1.50	.90
(204)	Gus Triandos/Billy Williams	12.00	6.00	3.50
(205)	Zoilo Versalles/Whitey Ford	15.00	7.50	4.50
(206)	Zoilo Versalles/Stan Musial	50.00	25.00	15.00
(207)	Zoilo Veraalles/Warren Spahn	15.00	7.50	4.50
(208)	Bill Virdon/Bob Friend	3.00	1.50	.90
(209)	Bill Virdon/Bill Tuttle	3.00	1.50	.90
(210)	Leon Wagner/Jim Davenport	3.00	1.50	.90
(211)	Leon Wagner/Julian Javier	3.00	1.50	.90
(212)	Lee Walls/Jerry Lumpe	3.00	1.50	.90
(213)	Bill White/Al Kaline	20.00	10.00	6.00
(214)	Bill White/Ken McBride	3.00	1.50	.90
(215)	Bill White/Bill Monbouquette	3.00	1.50	.90
(216)	Jake Wood/Frank Robinson	15.00	7.50	4.50
(217)	Gene Woodling/Lenny Green	3.00	1.50	.90
(218)	Early Wynn/Glen Hobbie	12.00	6.00	3.50
(219)	Early Wynn/Ed Mathews	25.00	12.50	7.50

(220)	Angels/Athletics	3.00	1.50	.90
(221)	Angels/Colts	3.00	1.50	.90
(222)	Angels/Orioles	3.00	1.50	.90
(223)	Athletics/Mets	5.00	2.50	1.50
(224)	Athletics/Pirates	3.00	1.50	.90
(225)	Cardinals/Indians	3.00	1.50	.90
(226)	Colts/Mets	6.00	3.00	1.75
(227)	Colts/Twins	3.00	1.50	.90
(228)	Cubs/Senators	3.00	1.50	.90
(229)	Giants/Red Sox	4.00	2.00	1.25
(230)	Giants/Tigers	4.00	2.00	1.25
(231)	Giants/White Sox	4.00	2.00	1.25
(232)	Indians/Reds	3.00	1.50	.90
(233)	Mets/Dodgers	5.00	2.50	1.50
(234)	Orioles/Pirates	3.00	1.50	.90
(235)	Phillies/Senators	3.00	1.50	.90
(236)	Red Sox/Braves	4.00	2.00	1.25
(237)	Red Sox/Phillies	4.00	2.00	1.25
(238)	Reds/Indians	3.00	1.50	.90
(239)	Reds/Yankees	8.00	4.00	2.50
(240)	Tigers/Braves	4.00	2.00	1.25
(241)	Twins/Dodgers	4.00	2.00	1.25
(242)	White Sox/Cubs	5.00	2.50	1.50
(243)	White Sox/Phillies	3.00	1.50	.90
(244)	Yankees/Cardinals	8.00	4.00	2.50
(245)	Yankees/Reds	8.00	4.00	2.50

1963 Topps

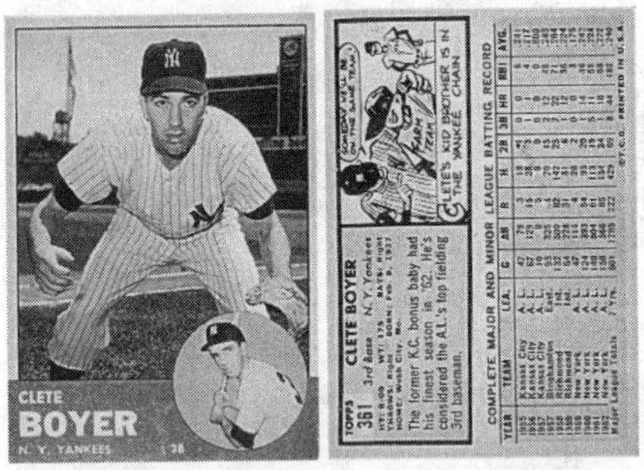

Although the number of cards dropped to 576, the 1963 Topps set is among the most popular of the 1960s. A color photo dominates the 2-1/2" x 3-1/2" card, but a colored circle at the bottom carries a black and white portrait as well. A colored band gives the player's name, team and position. The backs again feature career statistics and a cartoon, career summary and brief biographical details. The set is somewhat unlike those immediately preceding it in that there are fewer specialty cards. The major groupings are statistical leaders, World Series highlights and rookies. It is one rookie which makes the set special - Pete Rose. As one of most avidly sought cards in history and a high-numbered card at that, the Rose rookie card accounts for much of the value of a complete set.

		NM	EX	VG
	Complete Set (576):	4500.	2000.	1250.
	Common Player (1-283):	3.00	1.50	.90
	Common Player (284-446):	4.00	2.00	1.25
	Common Player (447-522):	16.00	8.00	4.75
	Common Player (523-576):	11.00	5.50	3.25
1	N.L. Batting Leaders (Hank Aaron, Bill White, Frank Robinson, Tommy Davis, Stan Musial)	35.00	17.50	10.50
2	A.L. Batting Leaders (Chuck Hinton, Mickey Mantle, Floyd Robinson, Pete Runnels, Norm Siebern)	40.00	20.00	12.00
3	N.L. Home Run Leaders (Hank Aaron, Ernie Banks, Orlando Cepeda, Willie Mays, Frank Robinson)	30.00	15.00	9.00
4	A.L. Home Run Leaders (Norm Cash, Rocky Colavito, Jim Gentile, Harmon Killebrew, Roger Maris, Leon	15.00	7.50	4.50
5	N.L. E.R.A. Leaders (Don Drysdale, Bob Gibson, Sandy Koufax, Bob Shaw, Bob Purkey)	20.00	10.00	6.00
6	A.L. E.R.A. Leaders (Hank Aguirre, Dean Chance, Eddie Fisher, Whitey Ford, Robin Roberts)	7.00	3.50	2.00
7	N.L. Pitching Leaders (Don Drysdale, Joe Jay, Art Mahaffey, Billy O'Dell, Bob Purkey, Jack Sanford)	6.00	3.00	1.75
8	A.L. Pitching Leaders (Jim Bunning, Dick Donovan, Ray Herbert, Camilo Pascual, Ralph Terry)	5.00	2.50	1.50
9	N.L. Strikeout Leaders (Don Drysdale, Dick Farrell, Bob Gibson, Sandy Koufax, Billy O'Dell)	15.00	7.50	4.50
10	A.L. Strikeout Leaders (Jim Bunning, Jim Kaat, Camilo Pascual, Juan Pizarro, Ralph Terry)	5.00	2.50	1.50
11	Lee Walls	3.00	1.50	.90
12	Steve Barber	3.00	1.50	.90
13	Phillies team	5.00	2.50	1.50
14	Pedro Ramos	3.00	1.50	.90
15	Ken Hubbs	5.00	2.50	1.50
16	Al Smith	3.00	1.50	.90
17	Ryne Duren	3.00	1.50	.90
18	Buc Blasters (Smoky Burgess, Roberto Clemente, Bob Skinner, Dick Stuart)	45.00	22.00	13.50
19	Pete Burnside	3.00	1.50	.90
20	Tony Kubek	5.00	2.50	1.50
21	Marty Keough	3.00	1.50	.90
22	Curt Simmons	3.00	1.50	.90
23	Ed Lopat	3.00	1.50	.90
24	Bob Bruce	3.00	1.50	.90
25	Al Kaline	37.50	18.50	11.00
26	Ray Moore	3.00	1.50	.90
27	Choo Choo Coleman	3.00	1.50	.90
28	Mike Fornieles	3.00	1.50	.90
29a	1962 Rookie Stars (Sammy Ellis, Ray Culp), *(John Boozer, Jesse Gonder)*	6.00	3.00	1.75
29b	1963 Rookie Stars (Sammy Ellis), *(Ray Culp,* John Boozer, Jesse Gonder)	3.50	1.75	1.00
30	Harvey Kuenn	3.50	1.50	.90
31	Cal Koonce	3.00	1.50	.90
32	Tony Gonzalez	3.00	1.50	.90
33	Bo Belinsky	3.00	1.50	.90
34	Dick Schofield	3.00	1.50	.90
35	John Buzhardt	3.00	1.50	.90
36	Jerry Kindall	3.00	1.50	.90
37	Jerry Lynch	3.00	1.50	.90
38	Bud Daley	3.00	1.50	.90
39	Angels Team	4.25	2.25	1.25
40	Vic Power	3.00	1.50	.90
41	Charlie Lau	3.00	1.50	.90
42	Stan Williams	3.00	1.50	.90
43	Veteran Masters (Casey Stengel, Gene Woodling)	4.50	2.25	1.25
44	Terry Fox	3.00	1.50	.90
45	Bob Aspromonte	3.00	1.50	.90
46	*Tommie Aaron*	3.50	1.75	1.00
47	Don Lock	3.00	1.50	.90
48	Birdie Tebbetts	3.00	1.50	.90
49	*Dal Maxvill*	3.00	1.50	.90
50	Bill Pierce	3.00	1.50	.90
51	George Alusik	3.00	1.50	.90
52	Chuck Schilling	3.00	1.50	.90
53	Joe Moeller	3.00	1.50	.90
54a	1962 Rookie Stars *(Nelson Mathews), (Harry Fanok), (Jack Cullen), (Dave*	15.00	7.50	4.50
54b	1963 Rookie Stars *(Jack Cullen), (Dave DeBusschere), (Harry Fanok), (Nelson*	6.00	3.00	1.75
55	Bill Virdon	3.00	1.50	.90
56	Dennis Bennett	3.00	1.50	.90
57	Billy Moran	3.00	1.50	.90
58	Bob Will	3.00	1.50	.90
59	Craig Anderson	3.00	1.50	.90
60	Elston Howard	4.00	2.00	1.25
61	Ernie Bowman	3.00	1.50	.90
62	Bob Hendley	3.00	1.50	.90
63	Reds team	4.50	2.25	1.25
64	Dick McAuliffe	3.00	1.50	.90
65	Jackie Brandt	3.00	1.50	.90
66	Mike Joyce	3.00	1.50	.90
67	Ed Charles	3.00	1.50	.90
68	Friendly Foes (Gil Hodges, Duke Snider)	17.00	8.50	5.00
69	Bud Zipfel	3.00	1.50	.90
70	Jim O'Toole	3.00	1.50	.90
71	*Bobby Wine*	3.00	1.50	.90
72	Johnny Romano	3.00	1.50	.90
73	Bobby Bragan	3.00	1.50	.90
74	*Denver Lemaster*	3.00	1.50	.90
75	Bob Allison	3.00	1.50	.90
76	Earl Wilson	3.00	1.50	.90
77	Al Spangler	3.00	1.50	.90
78	Marv Throneberry	3.00	1.50	.90
79	Checklist 1-88	7.50	3.75	2.25
80	Jim Gilliam	4.00	2.00	1.25
81	Jimmie Schaffer	3.00	1.50	.90
82	Ed Rakow	3.00	1.50	.90
83	Charley James	3.00	1.50	.90
84	Ron Kline	3.00	1.50	.90
85	Tom Haller	3.00	1.50	.90
86	Charley Maxwell	3.00	1.50	.90
87	Bob Veale	3.00	1.50	.90
88	Ron Hansen	3.00	1.50	.90
89	Dick Stigman	3.00	1.50	.90
90	Gordy Coleman	3.00	1.50	.90
91	Dallas Green	3.00	1.50	.90
92	Hector Lopez	3.00	1.50	.90
93	Galen Cisco	3.00	1.50	.90
94	Bob Schmidt	3.00	1.50	.90
95	Larry Jackson	3.00	1.50	.90
96	Lou Clinton	3.00	1.50	.90
97	Bob Duliba	3.00	1.50	.90
98	George Thomas	3.00	1.50	.90
99	Jim Umbricht	3.00	1.50	.90
100	Joe Cunningham	3.00	1.50	.90
101	Joe Gibbon	3.00	1.50	.90
102a	Checklist 89-176 ("Checklist" in red on front)	7.00	3.50	2.00
102b	Checklist 89-176 ("Checklist" in white)	11.00	5.50	3.25
103	Chuck Essegian	3.00	1.50	.90
104	Lew Krausse	3.00	1.50	.90
105	Ron Fairly	3.00	1.50	.90
106	Bob Bolin	3.00	1.50	.90
107	Jim Hickman	3.00	1.50	.90
108	Hoyt Wilhelm	7.50	3.75	2.25
109	Lee Maye	3.00	1.50	.90
110	Rich Rollins	3.00	1.50	.90
111	Al Jackson	3.00	1.50	.90
112	Dick Brown	3.00	1.50	.90
113	Don Landrum (photo actally Ron Santo)	3.00	1.50	.90
114	Dan Osinski	3.00	1.50	.90
115	Carl Yastrzemski	40.00	20.00	12.00
116	Jim Brosnan	3.00	1.50	.90
117	Jacke Davis	3.00	1.50	.90
118	Sherman Lollar	3.00	1.50	.90
119	Bob Lillis	3.00	1.50	.90
120	Roger Maris	42.50	21.00	12.50
121	Jim Hannan	3.00	1.50	.90
122	Julio Gotay	3.00	1.50	.90
123	Frank Howard	3.75	2.00	1.25
124	Dick Howser	3.00	1.50	.90
125	Robin Roberts	11.00	5.50	3.25
126	Bob Uecker	11.00	5.50	3.25
127	Bill Tuttle	3.00	1.50	.90
128	Matty Alou	3.00	1.50	.90
129	Gary Bell	3.00	1.50	.90
130	Dick Groat	3.50	1.75	1.00
131	Senators team	5.00	2.50	1.50
132	Jack Hamilton	3.00	1.50	.90
133	Gene Freese	3.00	1.50	.90
134	Bob Scheffing	3.00	1.50	.90
135	Richie Ashburn	11.00	5.50	3.25
136	Ike Delock	3.00	1.50	.90
137	Mack Jones	3.00	1.50	.90
138	Pride of N.L. (Willie Mays, Stan Musial)	60.00	30.00	18.00
139	Earl Averill	3.00	1.50	.90
140	Frank Lary	3.00	1.50	.90
141	*Manny Mota*	5.50	2.75	1.75
142	World Series Game 1 (Yanks' Ford Wins Series Opener)	6.00	3.00	1.75
143	World Series Game 2 (Sanford Flashes Shutout Magic)	5.00	2.50	1.50
144	World Series Game 3 (Maris Sparks Yankee Rally)	12.00	6.00	3.50
145	World Series Game 4 (Hiller Blasts Grand Slammer)	5.50	2.75	1.75
146	World Series Game 5 (Tresh's Homer Defeats Giants)	5.50	2.75	1.75
147	World Series Game 6 (Pierce Stars in 3-Hit Victory)	5.00	2.50	1.50
148	World Series Game 7 (Yanks Celebrate as Terry Wins)	5.00	2.50	1.50
149	Marv Breeding	3.00	1.50	.90
150	Johnny Podres	3.50	1.75	1.00
151	Pirates team	5.00	2.50	1.50
152	Ron Nischwitz	3.00	1.50	.90
153	Hal Smith	3.00	1.50	.90
154	Walt Alston	6.00	3.00	1.75
155	Bill Stafford	3.00	1.50	.90
156	Roy McMillan	3.00	1.50	.90
157	*Diego Segui*	3.00	1.50	.90
158	1963 Rookie Stars (Rogelio Alvarez), *(Tommy Harper,* Dave Roberts, Bob Saverine)	5.00	2.50	1.50
159	Jim Pagliaroni	3.00	1.50	.90
160	Juan Pizarro	3.00	1.50	.90
161	Frank Torre	3.00	1.50	.90
162	Twins team	4.50	2.25	1.25
163	Don Larsen	3.00	1.50	.90
164	Bubba Morton	3.00	1.50	.90
165	Jim Kaat	4.50	2.25	1.25
166	Johnny Keane	3.00	1.50	.90
167	Jim Fregosi	3.50	1.75	1.00
168	Russ Nixon	3.00	1.50	.90
169	1963 Rookie Stars *(Dick Egan), (Julio Navarro), (Gaylord Perry), (Tommie*	18.00	9.00	5.50
170	Joe Adcock	3.00	1.50	.90
171	Steve Hamilton	3.00	1.50	.90
172	Gene Oliver	3.00	1.50	.90
173	Bombers' Best (Tom Tresh, Mickey Mantle, Bobby Richardson)	120.00	60.00	36.00
174	Larry Burright	3.00	1.50	.90
175	Bob Buhl	3.00	1.50	.90
176	Jim King	3.00	1.50	.90
177	Bubba Phillips	3.00	1.50	.90
178	Johnny Edwards	3.00	1.50	.90
179	Ron Piche	3.00	1.50	.90
180	Bill Skowron	4.00	2.00	1.25
181	Sammy Esposito	3.00	1.50	.90
182	Albie Pearson	3.00	1.50	.90
183	Joe Pepitone	4.00	2.00	1.25
184	Vern Law	3.00	1.50	.90
185	Chuck Hiller	3.00	1.50	.90
186	Jerry Zimmerman	3.00	1.50	.90
187	Willie Kirkland	3.00	1.50	.90
188	Eddie Bressoud	3.00	1.50	.90
189	Dave Giusti	3.00	1.50	.90
190	Minnie Minoso	4.00	2.00	1.25
191	Checklist 177-264	8.00	4.00	2.50
192	Clay Dalrymple	3.00	1.50	.90
193	Andre Rodgers	3.00	1.50	.90
194	Joe Nuxhall	3.00	1.50	.90
195	Manny Jimenez	3.00	1.50	.90
196	Doug Camilli	3.00	1.50	.90
197	Roger Craig	3.00	1.50	.90
198	Lenny Green	3.00	1.50	.90
199	Joe Amalfitano	3.00	1.50	.90
200	Mickey Mantle	400.00	200.00	120.00
201	Cecil Butler	3.00	1.50	.90
202	Red Sox team	6.00	3.00	1.75
203	Chico Cardenas	3.00	1.50	.90
204	Don Nottebart	3.00	1.50	.90
205	Luis Aparicio	13.00	6.50	4.00
206	Ray Washburn	3.00	1.50	.90
207	Ken Hunt	3.00	1.50	.90

208	1963 Rookie Stars (Ron Herbel, John Miller, Ron Taylor, Wally Wolf)	3.00	1.50	.90
209	Hobie Landrith	3.00	1.50	.90
210	Sandy Koufax	120.00	60.00	36.00
211	Fred Whitfield	3.00	1.50	.90
212	Glen Hobbie	3.00	1.50	.90
213	Billy Hitchcock	3.00	1.50	.90
214	Orlando Pena	3.00	1.50	.90
215	Bob Skinner	3.00	1.50	.90
216	Gene Conley	3.00	1.50	.90
217	Joe Christopher	3.00	1.50	.90
218	Tiger Twirlers (Jim Bunning, Frank Lary, Don Mossi)	6.00	3.00	1.75
219	Chuck Cottier	3.00	1.50	.90
220	Camilo Pascual	3.00	1.50	.90
221	*Cookie Rojas*	5.50	2.75	1.75
222	Cubs team	6.00	3.00	1.75
223	Eddie Fisher	3.00	1.50	.90
224	Mike Roarke	3.00	1.50	.90
225	Joe Jay	3.00	1.50	.90
226	Julian Javier	3.00	1.50	.90
227	Jim Grant	3.00	1.50	.90
228	1963 Rookie Stars (*Max Alvis*), (*Bob Bailey*), (*Ed Kranepool*), (*Tony*	40.00	20.00	12.00
229	Willie Davis	3.00	1.50	.90
230	Pete Runnels	3.00	1.50	.90
231	Eli Grba (photo actually Ryne Duren)	3.00	1.50	.90
232	Frank Malzone	3.00	1.50	.90
233	Casey Stengel	16.00	8.00	4.75
234	Dave Nicholson	3.00	1.50	.90
235	Billy O'Dell	3.00	1.50	.90
236	Bill Bryan	3.00	1.50	.90
237	Jim Coates	3.00	1.50	.90
238	Lou Johnson	3.00	1.50	.90
239	Harvey Haddix	3.00	1.50	.90
240	Rocky Colavito	12.00	6.00	3.50
241	Billy Smith	3.00	1.50	.90
242	Power Plus (Hank Aaron, Ernie Banks)	48.00	24.00	14.50
243	Don Leppert	3.00	1.50	.90
244	John Tsitouris	3.00	1.50	.90
245	Gil Hodges	13.00	6.50	4.00
246	Lee Stange	3.00	1.50	.90
247	Yankees team	27.50	13.50	8.25
248	Tito Francona	3.00	1.50	.90
249	Leo Burke	3.00	1.50	.90
250	Stan Musial	95.00	47.00	28.00
251	Jack Lamabe	3.00	1.50	.90
252	Ron Santo	10.00	5.00	3.00
253	1963 Rookie Stars (Len Gabrielson, Pete Jernigan, Deacon Jones, John Wojcik)	3.00	1.50	.90
254	Mike Hershberger	3.00	1.50	.90
255	Bob Shaw	3.00	1.50	.90
256	Jerry Lumpe	3.00	1.50	.90
257	Hank Aguirre	3.00	1.50	.90
258	Alvin Dark	3.00	1.50	.90
259	Johnny Logan	3.00	1.50	.90
260	Jim Gentile	3.00	1.50	.90
261	Bob Miller	3.00	1.50	.90
262	Ellis Burton	3.00	1.50	.90
263	Dave Stenhouse	3.00	1.50	.90
264	Phil Linz	3.00	1.50	.90
265	Vada Pinson	5.00	2.50	1.50
266	Bob Allen	3.00	1.50	.90
267	Carl Sawatski	3.00	1.50	.90
268	Don Demeter	3.00	1.50	.90
269	Don Mincher	3.00	1.50	.90
270	Felipe Alou	4.50	2.25	1.25
271	Dean Stone	3.00	1.50	.90
272	Danny Murphy	3.00	1.50	.90
273	Sammy Taylor	3.00	1.50	.90
274	Checklist 265-352	8.00	4.00	2.50
275	Eddie Mathews	16.50	8.25	5.00
276	Barry Shetrone	3.00	1.50	.90
277	Dick Farrell	3.00	1.50	.90
278	Chico Fernandez	3.00	1.50	.90
279	Wally Moon	3.00	1.50	.90
280	Bob Rodgers	3.00	1.50	.90
281	Tom Sturdivant	3.00	1.50	.90
282	Bob Del Greco	3.00	1.50	.90
283	Roy Sievers	3.00	1.50	.90
284	Dave Sisler	4.00	2.00	1.25
285	Dick Stuart	4.00	2.00	1.25
286	Stu Miller	4.00	2.00	1.25
287	Dick Bertell	4.00	2.00	1.25
288	White Sox team	8.00	4.00	2.50
289	Hal Brown	4.00	2.00	1.25
290	Bill White	4.00	2.00	1.25
291	Don Rudolph	4.00	2.00	1.25
292	Pumpsie Green	4.00	2.00	1.25
293	Bill Pleis	4.00	2.00	1.25
294	Bill Rigney	4.00	2.00	1.25
295	Ed Roebuck	4.00	2.00	1.25
296	Doc Edwards	4.00	2.00	1.25
297	Jim Golden	4.00	2.00	1.25
298	Don Dillard	4.00	2.00	1.25
299	1963 Rookie Stars (Tom Butters, Bob Dustal, Dave Morehead, Dan Schneider)	5.00	2.50	1.50
300	Willie Mays	120.00	60.00	36.00
301	Bill Fischer	4.00	2.00	1.25
302	Whitey Herzog	5.00	2.50	1.50
303	Earl Francis	4.00	2.00	1.25
304	Harry Bright	4.00	2.00	1.25
305	Don Hoak	4.00	2.00	1.25
306	Star Receivers (Earl Battey, Elston Howard)	5.00	2.50	1.50
307	Chet Nichols	4.00	2.00	1.25
308	Camilo Carreon	4.00	2.00	1.25
309	Jim Brewer	4.00	2.00	1.25
310	Tommy Davis	4.50	2.25	1.25
311	Joe McClain	4.00	2.00	1.25
312	Colt .45s team	18.00	9.00	5.50
313	Ernie Broglio	4.00	2.00	1.25
314	John Goryl	4.00	2.00	1.25
315	Ralph Terry	4.00	2.00	1.25
316	Norm Sherry	4.00	2.00	1.25
317	Sam McDowell	5.00	2.50	1.50
318	Gene Mauch	4.00	2.00	1.25
319	Joe Gaines	4.00	2.00	1.25
320	Warren Spahn	30.00	15.00	9.00
321	Gino Cimoli	4.00	2.00	1.25
322	Bob Turley	4.00	2.00	1.25
323	Bill Mazeroski	10.00	5.00	3.00
324	1963 Rookie Stars (*Vic Davalillo*, Phil Roof), (*Pete Ward*, George Williams)	6.00	3.00	1.75
325	Jack Sanford	4.00	2.00	1.25
326	Hank Foiles	4.00	2.00	1.25
327	Paul Foytack	4.00	2.00	1.25
328	Dick Williams	4.00	2.00	1.25
329	Lindy McDaniel	4.00	2.00	1.25
330	Chuck Hinton	4.00	2.00	1.25
331	Series Foes (Bill Pierce, Bill Stafford)	4.00	2.00	1.25
332	Joel Horlen	4.00	2.00	1.25
333	Carl Warwick	4.00	2.00	1.25
334	Wynn Hawkins	4.00	2.00	1.25
335	Leon Wagner	4.00	2.00	1.25
336	Ed Bauta	4.00	2.00	1.25
337	Dodgers team	16.00	8.00	4.75
338	Russ Kemmerer	4.00	2.00	1.25
339	Ted Bowsfield	4.00	2.00	1.25
340	Yogi Berra	50.00	25.00	15.00
341a	Jack Baldschun (white slash across body in inset photo)	4.00	2.00	1.25
341b	Jack Baldschun (slash repaired with red/mottling)	4.00	2.00	1.25
342	Gene Woodling	4.00	2.00	1.25
343	Johnny Pesky	4.00	2.00	1.25
344	Don Schwall	4.00	2.00	1.25
345	Brooks Robinson	50.00	25.00	15.00
346	Billy Hoeft	4.00	2.00	1.25
347	Joe Torre	9.00	4.50	2.75
348	Vic Wertz	4.00	2.00	1.25
349	Zoilo Versalles	4.00	2.00	1.25
350	Bob Purkey	4.00	2.00	1.25
351	Al Luplow	4.00	2.00	1.25
352	Ken Johnson	4.00	2.00	1.25
353	Billy Williams	25.00	12.50	7.50
354	Dom Zanni	4.00	2.00	1.25
355	Dean Chance	4.00	2.00	1.25
356	John Schaive	4.00	2.00	1.25
357	George Altman	4.00	2.00	1.25
358	Milt Pappas	4.00	2.00	1.25
359	Haywood Sullivan	4.00	2.00	1.25
360	Don Drysdale	35.00	17.50	10.50
361	Clete Boyer	5.00	2.50	1.50
362	Checklist 353-429	9.00	4.50	2.75
363	Dick Radatz	4.00	2.00	1.25
364	Howie Goss	4.00	2.00	1.25
365	Jim Bunning	12.00	6.00	3.50
366	Tony Taylor	4.00	2.00	1.25
367	Tony Cloninger	4.00	2.00	1.25
368	Ed Bailey	4.00	2.00	1.25
369	Jim Lemon	4.00	2.00	1.25
370	Dick Donovan	4.00	2.00	1.25
371	Rod Kanehl	4.00	2.00	1.25
372	Don Lee	4.00	2.00	1.25
373	Jim Campbell	4.00	2.00	1.25
374	Claude Osteen	4.00	2.00	1.25
375	Ken Boyer	8.00	4.00	2.50
376	Johnnie Wyatt	4.00	2.00	1.25
377	Orioles team	9.00	4.50	2.75
378	Bill Henry	4.00	2.00	1.25
379	Bob Anderson	4.00	2.00	1.25
380	Ernie Banks	65.00	32.00	19.50
381	Frank Baumann	4.00	2.00	1.25
382	Ralph Houk	4.00	2.00	1.25
383	Pete Richert	4.00	2.00	1.25
384	Bob Tillman	4.00	2.00	1.25
385	Art Mahaffey	4.00	2.00	1.25
386	1963 Rookie Stars (*John Bateman*, Larry Bearnarth), (*Ed Kirkpatrick*, Garry Roggenburk)	4.00	2.00	1.25
387	Al McBean	4.00	2.00	1.25
388	Jim Davenport	4.00	2.00	1.25
389	Frank Sullivan	4.00	2.00	1.25
390	Hank Aaron	120.00	60.00	36.00
391	Bill Dailey	4.00	2.00	1.25
392	Tribe Thumpers (Tito Francona, Johnny Romano)	4.50	2.25	1.25
393	Ken MacKenzie	4.00	2.00	1.25
394	Tim McCarver	9.00	4.50	2.75
395	Don McMahon	4.00	2.00	1.25
396	Joe Koppe	4.00	2.00	1.25
397	Athletics Team	9.00	4.50	2.75
398	Boog Powell	18.00	9.00	5.50
399	Dick Ellsworth	4.00	2.00	1.25
400	Frank Robinson	55.00	27.00	16.50
401	Jim Bouton	15.00	7.50	4.50
402	Mickey Vernon	4.00	2.00	1.25
403	Ron Perranoski	4.00	2.00	1.25
404	Bob Oldis	4.00	2.00	1.25
405	Floyd Robinson	4.00	2.00	1.25
406	Howie Koplitz	4.00	2.00	1.25
407	1963 Rookie Stars (Larry Elliot, Frank Kostro, Chico Ruiz, Dick Simpson)	4.00	2.00	1.25
408	Billy Gardner	4.00	2.00	1.25
409	Roy Face	4.00	2.00	1.25
410	Earl Battey	4.00	2.00	1.25
411	Jim Constable	4.00	2.00	1.25
412	Dodgers' Big Three (Johnny Podres, Don Drysdale, Sandy Koufax)	35.00	17.50	10.50
413	Jerry Walker	4.00	2.00	1.25
414	Ty Cline	4.00	2.00	1.25
415	Bob Gibson	45.00	22.00	13.50
416	Alex Grammas	4.00	2.00	1.25
417	Giants team	8.00	4.00	2.50
418	Johnny Orsino	4.00	2.00	1.25
419	Tracy Stallard	4.00	2.00	1.25
420	Bobby Richardson	9.00	4.50	2.75
421	Tom Morgan	4.00	2.00	1.25
422	Fred Hutchinson	4.00	2.00	1.25
423	Ed Hobaugh	4.00	2.00	1.25
424	Charley Smith	4.00	2.00	1.25
425	Smoky Burgess	4.00	2.00	1.25
426	Barry Latman	4.00	2.00	1.25
427	Bernie Allen	4.00	2.00	1.25
428	Carl Boles	4.00	2.00	1.25
429	Lou Burdette	4.00	2.00	1.25
430	Norm Siebern	4.00	2.00	1.25
431a	Checklist 430-506 ("Checklist" in black on front)	8.00	4.00	2.50
431b	Checklist 430-506 ("Checklist" in white)	20.00	10.00	6.00
432	Roman Mejias	4.00	2.00	1.25
433	Denis Menke	4.00	2.00	1.25
434	Johnny Callison	4.00	2.00	1.25
435	Woody Held	4.00	2.00	1.25
436	Tim Harkness	4.00	2.00	1.25
437	Bill Bruton	4.00	2.00	1.25
438	Wes Stock	4.00	2.00	1.25
439	Don Zimmer	4.00	2.00	1.25
440	Juan Marichal	24.00	12.00	7.25
441	Lee Thomas	4.00	2.00	1.25
442	J.C. Hartman	4.00	2.00	1.25
443	Jim Piersall	5.00	2.50	1.50
444	Jim Maloney	4.00	2.00	1.25
445	Norm Cash	4.50	2.25	1.25
446	Whitey Ford	37.50	18.50	11.00
447	Felix Mantilla	16.00	8.00	4.75
448	Jack Kralick	16.00	8.00	4.75
449	Jose Tartabull	16.00	8.00	4.75
450	Bob Friend	16.00	8.00	4.75
451	Indians team	35.00	17.50	10.50
452	Barney Schultz	16.00	8.00	4.75
453	Jake Wood	16.00	8.00	4.75
454a	Art Fowler (card # on orange background)	16.00	8.00	4.75
454b	Art Fowler (card # on white background)	27.50	13.50	8.25
455	Ruben Amaro	16.00	8.00	4.75
456	Jim Coker	16.00	8.00	4.75
457	Tex Clevenger	16.00	8.00	4.75
458	Al Lopez	18.00	9.00	5.50
459	Dick LeMay	16.00	8.00	4.75
460	Del Crandall	16.00	8.00	4.75
461	Norm Bass	16.00	8.00	4.75
462	Wally Post	16.00	8.00	4.75
463	Joe Schaffernoth	16.00	8.00	4.75
464	Ken Aspromonte	16.00	8.00	4.75
465	Chuck Estrada	16.00	8.00	4.75
466	1963 Rookie Stars (*Bill Freehan*, Tony Martinez, Nate Oliver, Jerry Robinson)	47.50	24.00	14.00
467	Phil Ortega	16.00	8.00	4.75
468	Carroll Hardy	16.00	8.00	4.75
469	Jay Hook	16.00	8.00	4.75
470	Tom Tresh (SP)	55.00	27.00	16.50
471	Ken Retzer	16.00	8.00	4.75
472	Lou Brock	80.00	40.00	24.00
473	Mets team	87.50	44.00	26.00
474	Jack Fisher	16.00	8.00	4.75
475	Gus Triandos	16.00	8.00	4.75
476	Frank Funk	16.00	8.00	4.75
477	Donn Clendenon	16.00	8.00	4.75
478	Paul Brown	16.00	8.00	4.75
479	*Ed Brinkman*	16.00	8.00	4.75
480	Bill Monbouquette	16.00	8.00	4.75
481	Bob Taylor	16.00	8.00	4.75
482	Felix Torres	16.00	8.00	4.75
483	Jim Owens	16.00	8.00	4.75
484	Dale Long (SP)	19.00	9.50	5.75
485	Jim Landis	16.00	8.00	4.75
486	Ray Sadecki	16.00	8.00	4.75
487	John Roseboro	16.00	8.00	4.75
488	Jerry Adair	16.00	8.00	4.75
489	Paul Toth	16.00	8.00	4.75
490	Willie McCovey	95.00	47.00	28.00
491	Harry Craft	16.00	8.00	4.75
492	Dave Wickersham	16.00	8.00	4.75
493	Walt Bond	16.00	8.00	4.75
494	Phil Regan	16.00	8.00	4.75
495	Frank Thomas (SP)	19.00	9.50	5.75
496	1963 Rookie Stars (Carl Bouldin), (*Steve Dalkowski*), (*Fred Newman*, Jack Smith)	18.00	9.00	5.50
497	Bennie Daniels	16.00	8.00	4.75
498	Eddie Kasko	16.00	8.00	4.75
499	J.C. Martin	16.00	8.00	4.75
500	Harmon Killebrew (SP)	115.00	57.00	34.00
501	Joe Azcue	16.00	8.00	4.75
502	Daryl Spencer	16.00	8.00	4.75
503	Braves Team	35.00	17.50	10.50
504	Bob Johnson	16.00	8.00	4.75
505	Curt Flood	18.00	9.00	5.50
506	Gene Green	16.00	8.00	4.75
507	Roland Sheldon	16.00	8.00	4.75
508	Ted Savage	16.00	8.00	4.75
509a	Checklist 507-576 (copyright centered)	19.00	9.50	5.75
509b	Checklist 509-576 (copyright to right)	19.00	9.50	5.75
510	Ken McBride	16.00	8.00	4.75
511	Charlie Neal	16.00	8.00	4.75
512	Cal McLish	16.00	8.00	4.75
513	Gary Geiger	16.00	8.00	4.75
514	Larry Osborne	16.00	8.00	4.75
515	Don Elston	16.00	8.00	4.75
516	Purnal Goldy	16.00	8.00	4.75
517	Hal Woodeshick	16.00	8.00	4.75
518	Don Blasingame	16.00	8.00	4.75
519	Claude Raymond	16.00	8.00	4.75
520	Orlando Cepeda	30.00	15.00	9.00
521	Dan Pfister	16.00	8.00	4.75

522	1963 Rookie Stars (Mel Nelson, Gary Peters, Art Quirk, Jim Roland)	16.00	8.00	4.75
523	Bill Kunkel	11.00	5.50	3.25
524	Cardinals Team	22.00	11.00	6.50
525	Nellie Fox	35.00	17.50	10.50
526	Dick Hall	11.00	5.50	3.25
527	Ed Sadowski	11.00	5.50	3.25
528	Carl Willey	11.00	5.50	3.25
529	Wes Covington	11.00	5.50	3.25
530	Don Mossi	11.00	5.50	3.25
531	Sam Mele	11.00	5.50	3.25
532	Steve Boros	11.00	5.50	3.25
533	Bobby Shantz	11.00	5.50	3.25
534	Ken Walters	11.00	5.50	3.25
535	Jim Perry	11.00	5.50	3.25
536	Norm Larker	11.00	5.50	3.25
537	1963 Rookie Stars *(Pedro Gonzalez), (Ken McMullen), (Pete Rose), (Al*	750.00	375.00	225.00
538	George Brunet	11.00	5.50	3.25
539	Wayne Causey	11.00	5.50	3.25
540	Roberto Clemente	225.00	110.00	67.00
541	Ron Moeller	11.00	5.50	3.25
542	Lou Klimchock	11.00	5.50	3.25
543	Russ Snyder	11.00	5.50	3.25
544	1963 Rookie Stars *(Duke Carmel), (Bill Haas), (Dick Phillips), (Rusty*	32.00	16.00	9.50
545	Jose Pagan	11.00	5.50	3.25
546	Hal Reniff	11.00	5.50	3.25
547	Gus Bell	11.00	5.50	3.25
548	Tom Satriano	11.00	5.50	3.25
549	1963 Rookie Stars *(Marcelino Lopez*, Pete Lovrich, Elmo Plaskett, Paul Ratliff)	11.00	5.50	3.25
550	Duke Snider	75.00	37.00	22.00
551	Billy Klaus	11.00	5.50	3.25
552	Tigers team	40.00	20.00	12.00
553	1963 Rookie Stars *(Brock Davis), (Jim Gosger), (John Herrnstein), (Willie*	80.00	40.00	24.00
554	Hank Fischer	11.00	5.50	3.25
555	John Blanchard	11.00	5.50	3.25
556	Al Worthington	11.00	5.50	3.25
557	Cuno Barragan	11.00	5.50	3.25
558	1963 Rookie Stars *(Bill Faul), (Ron Hunt), (Bob Lipski), (Al Moran)*	14.00	7.00	4.25
559	Danny Murtaugh	11.00	5.50	3.25
560	Ray Herbert	11.00	5.50	3.25
561	Mike de la Hoz	11.00	5.50	3.25
562	1963 Rookie Stars *(Randy Cardinal), (Dave McNally), (Don Rowe), (Ken*	21.00	10.50	6.25
563	Mike McCormick	11.00	5.50	3.25
564	George Banks	11.00	5.50	3.25
565	Larry Sherry	11.00	5.50	3.25
566	Cliff Cook	11.00	5.50	3.25
567	Jim Duffalo	11.00	5.50	3.25
568	Bob Sadowski	11.00	5.50	3.25
569	Luis Arroyo	11.00	5.50	3.25
570	Frank Bolling	11.00	5.50	3.25
571	Johnny Klippstein	11.00	5.50	3.25
572	Jack Spring	11.00	5.50	3.25
573	Coot Veal	11.00	5.50	3.25
574	Hal Kolstad	11.00	5.50	3.25
575	Don Cardwell	11.00	5.50	3.25
576	Johnny Temple	15.00	5.50	3.25

1963 Topps Mickey Mantle Plaque

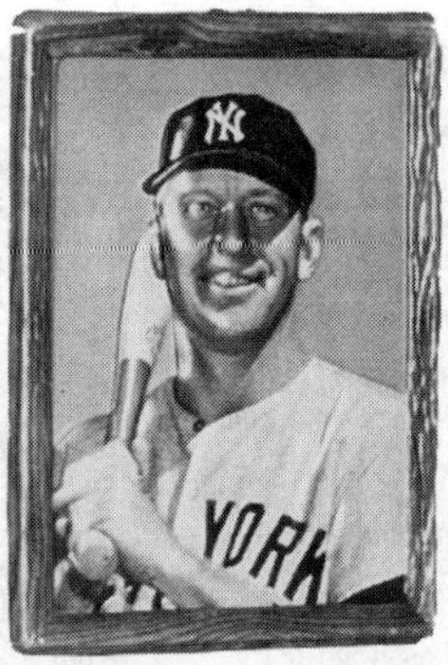

Advertised as a "mask" on high-number 1963 Topps wax wrappers, this is actually a plastic plaque. About 6" x 8", the plaque features a color picture of Mantle in embossed plastic with a faux wood frame, also embossed plastic, around it. A holed tab at top allows hanging.

	NM	EX	VG
Mickey Mantle	900.00	450.00	275.00

Many vintage-section card sets are indexed under both their common name and their American Card Catalog designation.

1963 Topps Peel-Offs

Measuring 1-1/4" x 2-3/4," Topps Peel-Offs were an insert with 1963 Topps baseball cards. There are 46 players in the unnumbered set, each pictured in a color photo inside an oval with the player's name, team and position in a band below. The back of the Peel-Off is removable, leaving a sticky surface that made the Peel-Off a popular decorative item among youngsters of the day. Naturally, that makes them quite scarce today, but as a non-card Topps issue, demand is not particularly strong.

		NM	EX	VG
Complete Set (46):		250.00	125.00	75.00
Common Player:		2.25	1.25	.70
(1)	Hank Aaron	16.50	8.25	5.00
(2)	Luis Aparicio	5.50	2.75	1.75
(3)	Richie Ashburn	6.50	3.25	2.00
(4)	Bob Aspromonte	2.25	1.25	.70
(5)	Ernie Banks	10.00	5.00	3.00
(6)	Ken Boyer	2.75	1.50	.80
(7)	Jim Bunning	4.50	2.25	1.25
(8)	Johnny Callison	2.75	1.50	.80
(9)	Orlando Cepeda	5.00	2.50	1.50
(10)	Roberto Clemente	18.00	9.00	5.50
(11)	Rocky Colavito	4.50	2.25	1.25
(12)	Tommy Davis	2.75	1.50	.80
(13)	Dick Donovan	2.25	1.25	.70
(14)	Don Drysdale	6.50	3.25	2.00
(15)	Dick Farrell	2.25	1.25	.70
(16)	Jim Gentile	2.25	1.25	.70
(17)	Ray Herbert	2.25	1.25	.70
(18)	Chuck Hinton	2.25	1.25	.70
(19)	Ken Hubbs	3.50	1.75	1.00
(20)	Al Jackson	2.25	1.25	.70
(21)	Al Kaline	10.00	5.00	3.00
(22)	Harmon Killebrew	7.50	3.75	2.25
(23)	Sandy Koufax	16.00	8.00	4.75
(24)	Jerry Lumpe	2.25	1.25	.70
(25)	Art Mahaffey	2.25	1.25	.70
(26)	Mickey Mantle	40.00	20.00	12.00
(27)	Willie Mays	16.50	8.25	5.00
(28)	Bill Mazeroski	5.50	2.75	1.75
(29)	Bill Monbouquette	2.25	1.25	.70
(30)	Stan Musial	16.00	8.00	4.75
(31)	Camilo Pascual	2.25	1.25	.70
(32)	Bob Purkey	2.25	1.25	.70
(33)	Bobby Richardson	4.00	2.00	1.25
(34)	Brooks Robinson	10.00	5.00	3.00
(35)	Floyd Robinson	2.25	1.25	.70
(36)	Frank Robinson	10.00	5.00	3.00
(37)	Bob Rodgers	2.25	1.25	.70
(38)	Johnny Romano	2.25	1.25	.70
(39)	Jack Sanford	2.25	1.25	.70
(40)	Norm Siebern	2.25	1.25	.70
(41)	Warren Spahn	9.00	4.50	2.75
(42)	Dave Stenhouse	2.25	1.25	.70
(43)	Ralph Terry	2.25	1.25	.70
(44)	Lee Thomas	2.25	1.25	.70
(45)	Bill White	2.25	1.25	.70
(46)	Carl Yastrzemski	10.00	5.00	3.00

Vintage cards in Good condition are valued at about 50% of the Very Good value shown here. Fair cards are valued at 25% or less of VG.
The ratio of Excellent and Very Good prices to Near Mint can vary depending on relative collectibility for each grade in a specific set. Current listings reflect such adjustments.

1963 Topps Valentine Foldees

Featuring the artwork of 1960s cartoonist Jack Davis, this set of specialty cards had the left and right panels of the 4-1/2" x 2-3/8" pieces slit to allow either the top or the bottom half of the portrait to be folded over the central panel to create funny combinations. There were 55 cards in the series; Babe Ruth is the only baseball player included.

		NM	EX	VG
Complete Set (55):		150.00	75.00	45.00
6	Babe Ruth	35.00	17.50	10.50

1964 Topps

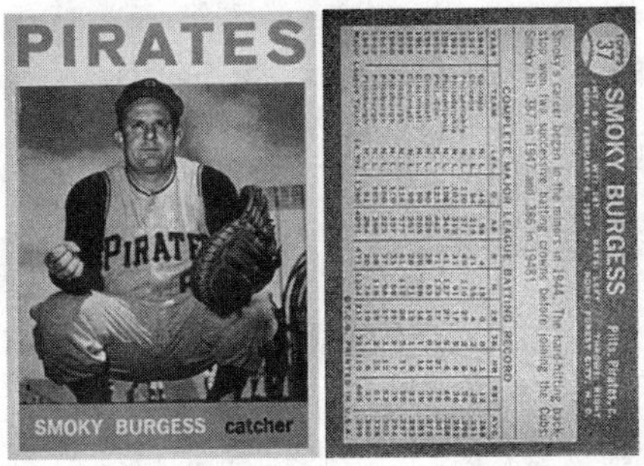

The 1964 Topps set is a 587-card issue of 2-1/2" x 3-1/2" cards which is considered by many as being among the company's best efforts. Card fronts feature a large color photo which blends into a top panel which contains the team name, while a panel below the picture carries the player's name and position. An interesting innovation on the back is a baseball quiz question which required the rubbing of a white panel to reveal the answer. As in 1963, specialty cards remained modest in number with a 12-card set of statistical leaders, a few multi-player cards, rookies and World Series highlights. An interesting card is an "In Memoriam" card for Ken Hubbs who was killed in an airplane crash.

		NM	EX	VG
Complete Set (587):		2550.	1300.	700.00
Common Player (1-196):		2.00	1.00	.60
Common Player (197-370):		3.00	1.50	.90
Common Player (371-522):		7.00	3.50	2.00
Common Player (523-587):		12.50	6.25	3.75
1	N.L. E.R.A. Leaders (Dick Ellsworth, Bob Friend, Sandy Koufax)	20.00	10.00	5.50
2	A.L. E.R.A. Leaders (Camilo Pascual, Gary Peters, Juan Pizarro)	4.75	2.50	1.50
3	N.L. Pitching Leaders (Sandy Koufax, Jim Maloney, Juan Marichal, Warren Spahn)	15.00	7.50	4.50
4a	A.L. Pitching Leaders (Jim Bouton, Whitey Ford, Camilo Pascual) (apostrophe after "Pitching" on back)	7.50	3.75	2.25
4b	A.L. Pitching Leaders (Jim Bouton, Whitey Ford, Camilo Pascual) (no apostrophe)	7.00	3.50	2.00
5	N.L. Strikeout Leaders (Don Drysdale, Sandy Koufax, Jim Maloney)	14.00	7.00	4.25
6	A.L. Strikeout Leaders (Jim Bunning, Camilo Pascual, Dick Stigman)	7.00	3.50	2.00
7	N.L. Batting Leaders (Hank Aaron, Roberto Clemente, Tommy Davis, Dick Groat)	15.00	7.50	4.50
8	A.L. Batting Leaders (Al Kaline, Rich Rollins, Carl Yastrzemski)	9.00	4.50	2.75
9	N.L. Home Run Leaders (Hank Aaron, Orlando Cepeda, Willie Mays, Willie McCovey)	26.00	13.00	7.75

10	A.L. Home Run Leaders (Bob Allison, Harmon Killebrew, Dick Stuart)	7.00	3.50	2.00
11	N.L. R.B.I. Leaders (Hank Aaron, Ken Boyer, Bill White)	9.00	4.50	2.75
12	A.L. R.B.I. Leaders (Al Kaline, Harmon Killebrew, Dick Stuart)	7.50	3.75	2.25
13	Hoyt Wilhelm	7.00	3.50	2.00
14	Dodgers Rookies (Dick Nen, Nick Willhite)	2.00	1.00	.60
15	Zoilo Versalles	2.00	1.00	.60
16	John Boozer	2.00	1.00	.60
17	Willie Kirkland	2.00	1.00	.60
18	Billy O'Dell	2.00	1.00	.60
19	Don Wart	2.00	1.00	.60
20	Bob Friend	2.00	1.00	.60
21	Yogi Berra	25.00	12.50	7.50
22	Jerry Adair	2.00	1.00	.60
23	Chris Zachary	2.00	1.00	.60
24	Carl Sawatski	2.00	1.00	.60
25	Bill Monbouquette	2.00	1.00	.60
26	Gino Cimoli	2.00	1.00	.60
27	Mets Team	6.50	3.25	2.00
28	Claude Osteen	2.00	1.00	.60
29	Lou Brock	30.00	15.00	9.00
30	Ron Perranoski	2.00	1.00	.60
31	Dave Nicholson	2.00	1.00	.60
32	Dean Chance	2.00	1.00	.60
33	Reds Rookies (Sammy Ellis, Mel Queen)	2.00	1.00	.60
34	Jim Perry	2.00	1.00	.60
35	Eddie Mathews	19.00	9.50	5.75
36	Hal Reniff	2.00	1.00	.60
37	Smoky Burgess	2.00	1.00	.60
38	*Jim Wynn*	5.00	2.50	1.50
39	Hank Aguirre	2.00	1.00	.60
40	Dick Groat	2.00	1.00	.60
41	Friendly Foes (Willie McCovey, Leon Wagner)	6.50	3.25	2.00
42	Moe Drabowsky	2.00	1.00	.60
43	Roy Sievers	2.00	1.00	.60
44	Duke Carmel	2.00	1.00	.60
45	Milt Pappas	2.00	1.00	.60
46	Ed Brinkman	2.00	1.00	.60
47	Giants Rookies (*Jesus Alou*, Ron Herbel)	5.00	2.50	1.75
48	Bob Perry	2.00	1.00	.60
49	Bill Henry	2.00	1.00	.60
50	Mickey Mantle	250.00	125.00	75.00
51	Pete Richert	2.00	1.00	.60
52	Chuck Hinton	2.00	1.00	.60
53	Denis Menke	2.00	1.00	.60
54	Sam Mele	2.00	1.00	.60
55	Ernie Banks	33.00	16.50	10.00
56	Hal Brown	2.00	1.00	.60
57	Tim Harkness	2.00	1.00	.60
58	Don Demeter	2.00	1.00	.60
59	Ernie Broglio	2.00	1.00	.60
60	Frank Malzone	2.00	1.00	.60
61	Angel Backstops (Bob Rodgers, Ed Sadowski)	2.00	1.00	.60
62	Ted Savage	2.00	1.00	.60
63	Johnny Orsino	2.00	1.00	.60
64	Ted Abernathy	2.00	1.00	.60
65	Felipe Alou	3.50	1.75	1.00
66	Eddie Fisher	2.00	1.00	.60
67	Tigers Team	5.00	2.50	1.50
68	Willie Davis	3.00	1.50	.90
69	Clete Boyer	4.00	2.00	1.25
70	Joe Torre	5.00	2.50	1.50
71	Jack Spring	2.00	1.00	.60
72	Chico Cardenas	2.00	1.00	.60
73	*Jimmie Hall*	2.00	1.00	.60
74	Pirates Rookies (Tom Butters, Bob Priddy)	2.00	1.00	.60
75	Wayne Causey	2.00	1.00	.60
76	Checklist 1-88	6.50	3.25	2.00
77	Jerry Walker	2.00	1.00	.60
78	Merritt Ranew	2.00	1.00	.60
79	Bob Heffner	2.00	1.00	.60
80	Vada Pinson	4.50	2.25	1.25
81	All-Star Vets (Nellie Fox, Harmon Killebrew)	11.00	5.50	3.25
82	Jim Davenport	2.00	1.00	.60
83	Gus Triandos	2.00	1.00	.60
84	Carl Willey	2.00	1.00	.60
85	Pete Ward	2.00	1.00	.60
86	Al Downing	2.00	1.00	.60
87	Cardinals Team	7.00	3.50	2.00
88	John Roseboro	2.00	1.00	.60
89	Boog Powell	5.00	2.50	1.75
90	Earl Battey	2.00	1.00	.60
91	Bob Bailey	2.00	1.00	.60
92	Steve Ridzik	2.00	1.00	.60
93	Gary Geiger	2.00	1.00	.60
94	Braves Rookies (Jim Britton, Larry Maxie)	2.00	1.00	.60
95	George Altman	2.00	1.00	.60
96	Bob Buhl	2.00	1.00	.60
97	Jim Fregosi	2.00	1.00	.60
98	Bill Bruton	2.00	1.00	.60
99	Al Stanek	2.00	1.00	.60
100	Elston Howard	4.00	2.00	1.25
101	Walt Alston	5.00	2.50	1.50
102	Checklist 89-176	8.00	4.00	2.50
103	Curt Flood	3.00	1.50	.90
104	Art Mahaffey	2.00	1.00	.60
105	Woody Held	2.00	1.00	.60
106	Joe Nuxhall	2.00	1.00	.60
107	White Sox Rookies (Bruce Howard, Frank Kreutzer)	2.00	1.00	.60
108	John Wyatt	2.00	1.00	.60
109	Rusty Staub	4.00	2.00	1.25
110	Albie Pearson	2.00	1.00	.60
111	Don Elston	2.00	1.00	.60
112	Bob Tillman	2.00	1.00	.60
113	Grover Powell	2.00	1.00	.60
114	Don Lock	2.00	1.00	.60
115	Frank Bolling	2.00	1.00	.60
116	Twins Rookies (Tony Oliva, Jay Ward)	10.00	5.00	3.00
117	Earl Francis	2.00	1.00	.60
118	John Blanchard	2.00	1.00	.60
119	Gary Kolb	2.00	1.00	.60
120	Don Drysdale	18.00	9.00	5.50
121	Pete Runnels	2.00	1.00	.60
122	Don McMahon	2.00	1.00	.60
123	Jose Pagan	2.00	1.00	.60
124	Orlando Pena	2.00	1.00	.60
125	Pete Rose	120.00	60.00	36.00
126	Russ Snyder	2.00	1.00	.60
127	Angels Rookies (Aubrey Gatewood, Dick Simpson)	2.00	1.00	.60
128	*Mickey Lolich*	20.00	10.00	6.00
129	Amado Samuel	2.00	1.00	.60
130	Gary Peters	2.00	1.00	.60
131	Steve Boros	2.00	1.00	.60
132	Braves Team	5.50	2.75	1.75
133	Jim Grant	2.00	1.00	.60
134	Don Zimmer	2.00	1.00	.60
135	Johnny Callison	2.00	1.00	.60
136	World Series Game 1 (Koufax Strikes Out 15)	15.00	7.50	4.50
137	World Series Game 2 (Davis Sparks Rally)	4.50	2.25	1.25
138	World Series Game 3 (L.A. Takes 3rd Straight)	4.50	2.25	1.25
139	World Series Game 4 (Sealing Yanks' Doom)	5.00	2.50	1.50
140	World Series Summary (The Dodgers Celebrate)	5.50	2.75	1.75
141	Danny Murtaugh	2.00	1.00	.60
142	John Bateman	2.00	1.00	.60
143	Bubba Phillips	2.00	1.00	.60
144	Al Worthington	2.00	1.00	.60
145	Norm Siebern	2.00	1.00	.60
146	Indians Rookies (*Bob Chance*), (*Tommy John*)	22.50	11.00	6.75
147	Ray Sadecki	2.00	1.00	.60
148	J.C. Martin	2.00	1.00	.60
149	Paul Foytack	2.00	1.00	.60
150	Willie Mays	75.00	37.00	22.00
151	Athletics Team	5.50	2.75	1.75
152	Denver Lemaster	2.00	1.00	.60
153	Dick Williams	2.00	1.00	.60
154	Dick Tracewski	2.00	1.00	.60
155	Duke Snider	25.00	12.50	7.50
156	Bill Dailey	2.00	1.00	.60
157	Gene Mauch	2.00	1.00	.60
158	Ken Johnson	2.00	1.00	.60
159	Charlie Dees	2.00	1.00	.60
160	Ken Boyer	4.50	2.25	1.25
161	Dave McNally	2.00	1.00	.60
162	Hitting Area (Vada Pinson, Dick Sisler)	2.00	1.00	.60
163	Donn Clendenon	2.00	1.00	.60
164	Bud Daley	2.00	1.00	.60
165	Jerry Lumpe	2.00	1.00	.60
166	Marty Keough	2.00	1.00	.60
167	Senators Rookies (*Mike Brumley*), (*Lou Piniella*)	24.00	12.00	7.25
168	Al Weis	2.00	1.00	.60
169	Del Crandall	2.00	1.00	.60
170	Dick Radatz	2.00	1.00	.60
171	Ty Cline	2.00	1.00	.60
172	Indians Team	5.50	2.75	1.75
173	Ryne Duren	2.00	1.00	.60
174	Doc Edwards	2.00	1.00	.60
175	Billy Williams	12.50	6.25	3.75
176	Tracy Stallard	2.00	1.00	.60
177	Harmon Killebrew	17.00	8.50	5.00
178	Hank Bauer	2.00	1.00	.60
179	Carl Warwick	2.00	1.00	.60
180	Tommy Davis	2.00	1.00	.60
181	Dave Wickersham	2.00	1.00	.60
182	Sox Sockers (Chuck Schilling, Carl Yastrzemski)	12.00	6.00	3.50
183	Ron Taylor	2.00	1.00	.60
184	Al Luplow	2.00	1.00	.60
185	Jim O'Toole	2.00	1.00	.60
186	Roman Mejias	2.00	1.00	.60
187	Ed Roebuck	2.00	1.00	.60
188	Checklist 177-264	6.50	3.25	2.00
189	Bob Hendley	2.00	1.00	.60
190	Bobby Richardson	5.50	2.75	1.75
191	Clay Dalrymple	2.00	1.00	.60
192	Cubs Rookies (John Boccabella, Billy Cowan)	2.00	1.00	.60
193	Jerry Lynch	2.00	1.00	.60
194	John Goryl	2.00	1.00	.60
195	Floyd Robinson	2.00	1.00	.60
196	Jim Gentile	3.00	1.50	.90
197	Frank Lary	3.00	3.50	.90
198	Len Gabrielson	3.00	1.50	.90
199	Joe Azcue	3.00	1.50	.90
200	Sandy Koufax	75.00	37.00	22.00
201	Orioles Rookies (Sam Bowens), (*Wally Bunker*)	3.00	1.50	.90
202	Galen Cisco	3.00	1.50	.90
203	John Kennedy	3.00	1.50	.90
204	Matty Alou	3.00	1.50	.90
205	Nellie Fox	12.00	6.00	3.50
206	Steve Hamilton	3.00	1.50	.90
207	Fred Hutchinson	3.00	1.50	.90
208	Wes Covington	3.00	1.50	.90
209	Bob Allen	3.00	1.50	.90
210	Carl Yastrzemski	32.50	16.00	9.75
211	Jim Coker	3.00	1.50	.90
212	Pete Lovrich	3.00	1.50	.90
213	Angels Team	5.50	2.75	1.75
214	Ken McMullen	3.00	1.50	.90
215	Ray Herbert	3.00	1.50	.90
216	Mike de la Hoz	3.00	1.50	.90
207	Jim King	3.00	1.50	.90
218	Hank Fischer	3.00	1.50	.90
219	Young Aces (Jim Bouton, Al Downing)	5.00	2.50	1.50
220	Dick Ellsworth	3.00	1.50	.90
221	Bob Saverine	3.00	1.50	.90
222	Bill Pierce	3.00	1.50	.90
223	George Banks	3.00	1.50	.90
224	Tommie Sisk	3.00	1.50	.90
225	Roger Maris	55.00	27.00	16.50
226	Colts Rookies (*Gerald Grote*, Larry Yellen)	7.00	3.50	2.00
227	Barry Latman	3.00	1.50	.90
228	Felix Mantilla	3.00	1.50	.90
229	Charley Lau	3.00	1.50	.90
230	Brooks Robinson	27.50	13.50	8.25
231	Dick Calmus	3.00	1.50	.90
232	Al Lopez	4.50	2.25	1.25
233	Hal Smith	3.00	1.50	.90
234	Gary Bell	3.00	1.50	.90
235	Ron Hunt	3.00	1.50	.90
236	Bill Faul	3.00	1.50	.90
237	Cubs Team	6.50	3.25	2.00
238	Roy McMillan	3.00	1.50	.90
239	Herm Starrette	3.00	1.50	.90
240	Bill White	3.00	1.50	.90
241	Jim Owens	3.00	1.50	.90
242	Harvey Kuenn	3.00	1.50	.90
243	Phillies Rookies (*Richie Allen*, John Herrnstein)	27.00	13.50	8.00
244	*Tony LaRussa*	24.00	12.00	7.25
245	Dick Stigman	3.00	1.50	.90
246	Manny Mota	3.00	1.50	.90
247	Dave DeBusschere	5.00	2.50	1.50
248	Johnny Pesky	3.00	1.50	.90
249	Doug Camilli	3.00	1.50	.90
250	Al Kaline	35.00	17.50	10.50
251	Choo Choo Coleman	3.00	1.50	.90
252	Ken Aspromonte	3.00	1.50	.90
253	Wally Post	3.00	1.50	.90
254	Don Hoak	3.00	1.50	.90
255	Lee Thomas	3.00	1.50	.90
256	Johnny Weekly	3.00	1.50	.90
257	Giants Team	5.00	2.50	1.50
258	Garry Roggenburk	3.00	1.50	.90
259	Harry Bright	3.00	1.50	.90
260	Frank Robinson	25.00	12.50	7.50
261	Jim Hannan	3.00	1.50	.90
262	Cardinals Rookies (Harry Fanok), (*Mike Shannon*)	7.00	3.50	2.00
263	Chuck Estrada	3.00	1.50	.90
264	Jim Landis	3.00	1.50	.90
265	Jim Bunning	9.00	4.50	2.75
266	Gene Freese	3.00	1.50	.90
267	*Wilbur Wood*	7.00	3.50	2.00
268	Bill's Got It (Danny Murtaugh, Bill Virdon)	3.00	1.50	.90
269	Ellis Burton	3.00	1.50	.90
270	Rich Rollins	3.00	1.50	.90
271	Bob Sadowski	3.00	1.50	.90
272	Jake Wood	3.00	1.50	.90
273	Mel Nelson	3.00	1.50	.90
274	Checklist 265-352	8.00	4.00	2.50
275	John Tsitouris	3.00	1.50	.90
276	Jose Tartabull	3.00	1.50	.90
277	Ken Retzer	3.00	1.50	.90
278	Bobby Shantz	3.00	1.50	.90
279	Joe Koppe	3.00	1.50	.90
280	Juan Marichal	12.50	6.25	3.75
281	Yankees Rookies (Jake Gibbs, Tom Metcalf)	7.00	3.50	2.00
282	Bob Bruce	3.00	1.50	.90
283	*Tommy McCraw*	3.00	1.50	.90
284	Dick Schofield	3.00	1.50	.90
285	Robin Roberts	10.00	5.00	3.00
286	Don Landrum	3.00	1.50	.90
287	Red Sox Rookies (*Tony Conigliaro*, Bill Spanswick)	42.50	21.00	12.50
288	Al Moran	3.00	1.50	.90
289	Frank Funk	3.00	1.50	.90
290	Bob Allison	3.00	1.50	.90
291	Phil Ortega	3.00	1.50	.90
292	Mike Roarke	3.00	1.50	.90
293	Phillies Team	5.00	2.50	1.50
294	Ken Hunt	3.00	1.50	.90
295	Roger Craig	3.00	1.50	.90
296	Ed Kirkpatrick	3.00	1.50	.90
297	Ken MacKenzie	3.00	1.50	.90
298	Harry Craft	3.00	1.50	.90
299	Bill Stafford	3.00	1.50	.90
300	Hank Aaron	85.00	42.00	25.00
301	Larry Brown	3.00	1.50	.90
302	Dan Pfister	3.00	1.50	.90
303	Jim Campbell	3.00	1.50	.90
304	Bob Johnson	3.00	1.50	.90
305	Jack Lamabe	3.00	1.50	.90
306	Giant Gunners (Orlando Cepeda, Willie Mays)	32.00	16.00	9.50
307	Joe Gibbon	3.00	1.50	.90
308	Gene Stephens	3.00	1.50	.90
309	Paul Toth	3.00	1.50	.90
010	Jim Gilliam	3.50	1.75	1.00
311	Tom Brown	3.00	1.50	.90
312	Tigers Rookies (Fritz Fisher, Fred Gladding)	3.00	1.50	.90
313	Chuck Hiller	3.00	1.50	.90
314	Jerry Buchek	3.00	1.50	.90
315	Bo Belinsky	3.00	1.50	.90
316	Gene Oliver	3.00	1.50	.90
317	Al Smith	3.00	1.50	.90
318	Twins Team	5.50	2.75	1.75
319	Paul Brown	3.00	1.50	.90
320	Rocky Colavito	12.50	6.25	3.75
321	Bob Lillis	3.00	1.50	.90
322	George Brunet	3.00	1.50	.90
323	John Buzhardt	3.00	1.50	.90
324	Casey Stengel	14.00	7.00	4.25
325	Hector Lopez	3.00	1.50	.90
326	Ron Brand	3.00	1.50	.90
327	Don Blasingame	3.00	1.50	.90

328	Bob Shaw	3.00	1.50	.90
329	Russ Nixon	3.00	1.50	.90
330	Tommy Harper	3.00	1.50	.90
331	A.L. Bombers (Norm Cash, Al Kaline, Mickey Mantle, Roger Maris)	135.00	67.00	40.00
332	Ray Washburn	3.00	1.50	.90
333	Billy Moran	3.00	1.50	.90
334	Lew Krausse	3.00	1.50	.90
335	Don Mossi	3.00	1.50	.90
336	Andre Rodgers	3.00	1.50	.90
337	Dodgers Rookies (*Al Ferrara*), (*Jeff Torborg*)	6.00	3.00	1.75
338	Jack Kralick	3.00	1.50	.90
339	Walt Bond	3.00	1.50	.90
340	Joe Cunningham	3.00	1.50	.90
341	Jim Roland	3.00	1.50	.90
342	Willie Stargell	27.50	13.50	8.25
343	Senators Team	5.50	2.75	1.75
344	Phil Linz	3.00	1.50	.90
345	Frank Thomas	3.00	1.50	.90
346	Joe Jay	3.00	1.50	.90
347	Bobby Wine	3.00	1.50	.90
348	Ed Lopat	3.00	1.50	.90
349	Art Fowler	3.00	1.50	.90
350	Willie McCovey	21.00	10.50	6.25
351	Dan Schneider	3.00	1.50	.90
352	Eddie Bressoud	3.00	1.50	.90
353	Wally Moon	3.00	1.50	.90
354	Dave Giusti	3.00	1.50	.90
355	Vic Power	3.00	1.50	.90
356	Reds Rookies (Bill McCool, Chico Ruiz)	3.00	1.50	.90
357	Charley James	3.00	1.50	.90
358	Ron Kline	3.00	1.50	.90
359	Jim Schaffer	3.00	1.50	.90
360	Joe Pepitone	3.00	1.50	.90
361	Jay Hook	3.00	1.50	.90
362	Checklist 353-429	8.00	4.00	2.50
363	Dick McAuliffe	3.00	1.50	.90
364	Joe Gaines	3.00	1.50	.90
365	Cal McLish	3.00	1.50	.90
366	Nelson Mathews	3.00	1.50	.90
367	Fred Whitfield	3.00	1.50	.90
368	White Sox Rookies (Fritz Ackley), (*Don Buford*)	5.50	2.75	1.75
369	Jerry Zimmerman	3.00	1.50	.90
370	Hal Woodeshick	3.00	1.50	.90
371	Frank Howard	6.00	3.00	1.75
372	Howie Koplitz	6.00	3.00	1.75
373	Pirates Team	10.00	5.00	3.00
374	Bobby Bolin	6.00	3.00	1.75
375	Ron Santo	11.00	5.50	3.25
376	Dave Morehead	6.00	3.00	1.75
377	Bob Skinner	6.00	3.00	1.75
378	Braves Rookies (Jack Smith), (*Woody Woodward*)	6.00	3.00	1.75
379	Tony Gonzalez	6.00	3.00	1.75
380	Whitey Ford	27.50	13.50	8.25
381	Bob Taylor	6.00	3.00	1.75
382	Wes Stock	6.00	3.00	1.75
383	Bill Rigney	6.00	3.00	1.75
384	Ron Hansen	6.00	3.00	1.75
385	Curt Simmons	6.00	3.00	1.75
386	Lenny Green	6.00	3.00	1.75
387	Terry Fox	6.00	3.00	1.75
388	Athletics Rookies (John O'Donoghue, George Williams)	6.00	3.00	1.75
389	Jim Umbricht	6.00	3.00	1.75
390	Orlando Cepeda	18.00	9.00	5.50
391	Sam McDowell	6.00	3.00	1.75
392	Jim Pagliaroni	6.00	3.00	1.75
393	Casey Teaches (Ed Kranepool, Casey Stengel)	10.00	5.00	3.00
394	Bob Miller	6.00	3.00	1.75
395	Tom Tresh	7.50	3.75	2.25
396	Dennis Bennett	6.00	3.00	1.75
397	Chuck Cottier	6.00	3.00	1.75
398	Mets Rookies (Bill Haas, Dick Smith)	6.00	3.00	1.75
399	Jackie Brandt	6.00	3.00	1.75
400	Warren Spahn	32.50	16.00	9.75
401	Charlie Maxwell	6.00	3.00	1.75
402	Tom Sturdivant	6.00	3.00	1.75
403	Reds Team	10.00	5.00	3.00
404	Tony Martinez	6.00	3.00	1.75
405	Ken McBride	6.00	3.00	1.75
406	Al Spangler	6.00	3.00	1.75
407	Bill Freehan	7.50	3.75	2.25
408	Cubs Rookies (Fred Burdette, Jim Stewart)	6.00	3.00	1.75
409	Bill Fischer	6.00	3.00	1.75
410	Dick Stuart	6.00	3.00	1.75
411	Lee Walls	6.00	3.00	1.75
412	Ray Culp	6.00	3.00	1.75
413	Johnny Keane	6.00	3.00	1.75
414	Jack Sanford	6.00	3.00	1.75
415	Tony Kubek	8.00	4.00	2.50
416	Lee Maye	6.00	3.00	1.75
417	Don Cardwell	6.00	3.00	1.75
418	Orioles Rookies (*Darold Knowles*, Les Narum)	6.00	3.00	1.75
419	*Ken Harrelson*	9.00	4.50	2.75
420	Jim Maloney	6.00	3.00	1.75
421	Camilo Carreon	6.00	3.00	1.75
422	Jack Fisher	6.00	3.00	1.75
423	Tops in N.L. (Hank Aaron, Willie Mays)	100.00	50.00	30.00
424	Dick Bertell	6.00	3.00	1.75
425	Norm Cash	7.50	3.75	2.25
426	Bob Rodgers	6.00	3.00	1.75
427	Don Rudolph	6.00	3.00	1.75
428	Red Sox Rookies (Archie Skeen, Pete Smith)	6.00	3.00	1.75
429	Tim McCarver	8.00	4.00	2.50
430	Juan Pizarro	6.00	3.00	1.75
431	George Alusik	6.00	3.00	1.75
432	Ruben Amaro	6.00	3.00	1.75
433	Yankees Team	27.50	13.50	8.25
434	Don Nottebart	6.00	3.00	1.75
435	Vic Davalillo	6.00	3.00	1.75
436	Charlie Neal	6.00	3.00	1.75
437	Ed Bailey	6.00	3.00	1.75
438	Checklist 430-506	14.00	7.00	4.25
439	Harvey Haddix	6.00	3.00	1.75
440	Roberto Clemente	180.00	90.00	54.00
441	Bob Duliba	6.00	3.00	1.75
442	Pumpsie Green	6.00	3.00	1.75
443	Chuck Dressen	6.00	3.00	1.75
444	Larry Jackson	6.00	3.00	1.75
445	Bill Skowron	8.00	4.00	2.50
446	Julian Javier	6.00	3.00	1.75
447	Ted Bowsfield	6.00	3.00	1.75
448	Cookie Rojas	6.00	3.00	1.75
449	Deron Johnson	6.00	3.00	1.75
450	Steve Barber	6.00	3.00	1.75
451	Joe Amalfitano	6.00	3.00	1.75
452	Giants Rookies (Gil Garrido), (*Jim Hart*)	6.00	3.00	1.75
453	Frank Baumann	6.00	3.00	1.75
454	Tommie Aaron	6.00	3.00	1.75
455	Bernie Allen	6.00	3.00	1.75
456	Dodgers Rookies (*Wes Parker*, John Werhas)	6.00	3.00	1.75
457	Jesse Gonder	6.00	3.00	1.75
458	Ralph Terry	6.00	3.00	1.75
459	Red Sox Rookies (Pete Charton, Dalton Jones)	6.00	3.00	1.75
460	Bob Gibson	32.50	16.00	9.75
461	George Thomas	6.00	3.00	1.75
462	Birdie Tebbetts	6.00	3.00	1.75
463	Don Leppert	6.00	3.00	1.75
464	Dallas Green	6.00	3.00	1.75
465	Mike Hershberger	6.00	3.00	1.75
466	Athletics Rookies (*Dick Green*, Aurelio Monteagudo)	6.00	3.00	1.75
467	Bob Aspromonte	6.00	3.00	1.75
468	Gaylord Perry	32.50	16.00	9.75
469	Cubs Rookies (Fred Norman, Sterling Slaughter)	6.00	3.00	1.75
470	Jim Bouton	7.50	3.75	2.25
471	*Gates Brown*	6.50	3.25	2.00
472	Vern Law	6.00	3.00	1.75
473	Orioles Team	9.00	4.50	3.75
474	Larry Sherry	6.00	3.00	1.75
475	Ed Charles	6.00	3.00	1.75
476	Braves Rookies (*Rico Carty*, Dick Kelley)	13.50	6.75	4.00
477	Mike Joyce	6.00	3.00	1.75
478	Dick Howser	6.00	3.00	1.75
479	Cardinals Rookies (Dave Bakenhaster, Johnny Lewis)	6.00	3.00	1.75
480	Bob Purkey	6.00	3.00	1.75
481	Chuck Schilling	6.00	3.00	1.75
482	Phillies Rookies (*John Briggs*), (*Danny Cater*)	6.00	3.00	1.75
483	Fred Valentine	6.00	3.00	1.75
484	Bill Pleis	6.00	3.00	1.75
485	Tom Haller	6.00	3.00	1.75
486	Bob Kennedy	6.00	3.00	1.75
487	Mike McCormick	6.00	3.00	1.75
488	Yankees Rookies (Bob Meyer, Pete Mikkelsen)	6.00	3.00	1.75
489	Julio Navarro	6.00	3.00	1.75
490	Ron Fairly	6.00	3.00	1.75
491	Ed Rakow	6.00	3.00	1.75
492	Colts Rookies (Jim Beauchamp, Mike White)	6.00	3.00	1.75
493	Don Lee	6.00	3.00	1.75
494	Al Jackson	6.00	3.00	1.75
495	Bill Virdon	6.00	3.00	1.75
496	White Sox Team	9.50	4.75	2.75
497	Jeoff Long	6.00	3.00	1.75
498	Dave Stenhouse	6.00	3.00	1.75
499	Indians Rookies (Chico Salmon, Gordon Seyfried)	6.00	3.00	1.75
500	Camilo Pascual	6.00	3.00	1.75
501	Bob Veale	6.00	3.00	1.75
502	Angels Rookies (*Bobby Knoop*, Bob Lee)	6.00	3.00	1.75
503	Earl Wilson	6.00	3.00	1.75
504	Claude Raymond	6.00	3.00	1.75
505	Stan Williams	6.00	3.00	1.75
506	Bobby Bragan	6.00	3.00	1.75
507	John Edwards	6.00	3.00	1.75
508	Diego Segui	6.00	3.00	1.75
509	Pirates Rookies (*Gene Alley*, Orlando McFarlane)	6.00	3.00	1.75
510	Lindy McDaniel	6.00	3.00	1.75
511	Lou Jackson	6.00	3.00	1.75
512	Tigers Rookies (*Willie Horton*), (*Joe Sparma*)	12.50	6.25	3.75
513	Don Larsen	6.00	3.00	1.75
514	Jim Hickman	6.00	3.00	1.75
515	Johnny Romano	6.00	3.00	1.75
516	Twins Rookies (Jerry Arrigo, Dwight Siebler)	6.00	3.00	1.75
517a	Checklist 507-587 (wrong numbering on back)	15.00	7.50	4.50
517b	Checklist 507-587 (correct numbering on back)	11.00	5.50	3.25
518	Carl Bouldin	6.00	3.00	1.75
519	Charlie Smith	6.00	3.00	1.75
520	Jack Baldschun	6.00	3.00	1.75
521	Tom Satriano	6.00	3.00	1.75
522	Bobby Tiefenauer	6.00	3.00	1.75
523	Lou Burdette	12.50	6.25	3.75
524	Reds Rookies (Jim Dickson, Bobby Klaus)	12.50	6.25	3.75
525	Al McBean	12.50	6.25	3.75
526	Lou Clinton	12.50	6.25	3.75
527	Larry Bearnarth	12.50	6.25	3.75
528	Athletics Rookies (*Dave Duncan*, Tom Reynolds)	12.50	6.25	3.75
529	Al Dark	12.50	6.25	3.75
530	Leon Wagner	12.50	6.25	3.75
531	Dodgers Team	22.00	11.00	6.50
532	Twins Rookies (Bud Bloomfield, Joe Nossek)	12.50	6.25	3.75
533	Johnny Klippstein	12.50	6.25	3.75
534	Gus Bell	12.50	6.25	3.75
535	Phil Regan	12.50	6.25	3.75
536	Mets Rookies (Larry Elliot, John Stephenson)	12.50	6.25	3.75
537	Dan Osinski	12.50	6.25	3.75
538	Minnie Minoso	15.00	7.50	4.50
539	Roy Face	12.50	6.25	3.75
540	Luis Aparicio	24.00	12.00	7.25
541	Braves Rookies (*Phil Niekro*, Phil Roof)	70.00	35.00	21.00
542	Don Mincher	12.50	6.25	3.75
543	Bob Uecker	35.00	17.50	10.50
544	Colts Rookies (Steve Hertz, Joe Hoerner)	12.50	6.25	3.75
545	Max Alvis	12.50	6.25	3.75
546	Joe Christopher	12.50	6.25	3.75
547	Gil Hodges	20.00	10.00	6.00
548	N.L. Rookies (Wayne Schurr, Paul Speckenbach)	12.50	6.25	3.75
549	Joe Moeller	12.50	6.25	3.75
550	Ken Hubbs Memorial	28.00	14.00	8.50
551	Billy Hoeft	12.50	6.25	3.75
552	Indians Rookies (Tom Kelley), (*Sonny Siebert*)	15.00	7.50	4.50
553	Jim Brewer	12.50	6.25	3.75
554	Hank Foiles	12.50	6.25	3.75
555	Lee Stange	12.50	6.25	3.75
556	Mets Rookies (Steve Dillon, Ron Locke)	12.50	6.25	3.75
557	Leo Burke	12.50	6.25	3.75
558	Don Schwall	12.50	6.25	3.75
559	Dick Phillips	12.50	6.25	3.75
560	Dick Farrell	12.50	6.25	3.75
561	Phillies Rookies (*Dave Bennett*), (*Rick Wise*)	15.00	7.50	4.50
562	Pedro Ramos	12.50	6.25	3.75
563	Dal Maxvill	12.50	6.25	3.75
564	A.L. Rookies (Joe McCabe, Jerry McNertney)	12.50	6.25	3.75
565	Stu Miller	12.50	6.25	3.75
566	Ed Kranepool	12.50	6.25	3.75
567	Jim Kaat	16.00	8.00	4.75
568	N.L. Rookies (Phil Gagliano, Cap Peterson)	12.50	6.25	3.75
569	Fred Newman	12.50	6.25	3.75
570	Bill Mazeroski	20.00	10.00	6.00
571	Gene Conley	12.50	6.25	3.75
572	A.L. Rookies (Dick Egan, Dave Gray)	12.50	6.25	3.75
573	Jim Duffalo	12.50	6.25	3.75
574	Manny Jimenez	12.50	6.25	3.75
575	Tony Cloninger	12.50	6.25	3.75
576	Mets Rookies (Jerry Hinsley, Bill Wakefield)	12.50	6.25	3.75
577	Gordy Coleman	12.50	6.25	3.75
578	Glen Hobbie	12.50	6.25	3.75
579	Red Sox Team	20.00	10.00	6.00
580	Johnny Podres	14.00	7.00	4.25
581	Yankees Rookies (Pedro Gonzalez, Archie Moore)	12.50	6.25	3.75
582	Rod Kanehl	12.50	6.25	3.75
583	Tito Francona	12.50	6.25	3.75
584	Joel Horlen	12.50	6.25	3.75
585	Tony Taylor	12.50	6.25	3.75
586	Jim Piersall	15.00	7.50	4.50
587	Bennie Daniels	17.50	6.25	3.75

1964 Topps Coins

The 164 metal coins in this set were issued by Topps as inserts in the company's baseball card wax packs. The series is divided into two principal types, 120 "regular" coins and 44 All-Star coins. The 1 1/2" diameter coins feature a full-color background for the player photos in the "regular" series, while the players in the All-Star series are featured against plain red or blue backgrounds. There are two variations each of the Mantle, Causey and Hinton coins among the All-Star subset.

		NM	EX	VG
Complete Set (164):		800.00	400.00	240.00
Common Player:		2.50	1.25	.70
1	Don Zimmer	2.50	1.25	.70
2	Jim Wynn	2.50	1.25	.70
3	Johnny Orsino	2.50	1.25	.70
4	Jim Bouton	3.00	1.50	.90
5	Dick Groat	3.00	1.50	.90
6	Leon Wagner	2.50	1.25	.70
7	Frank Malzone	2.50	1.25	.70
8	Steve Barber	2.50	1.25	.70
9	Johnny Romano	2.50	1.25	.70

10	Tom Tresh	3.00	1.50	.90
11	Felipe Alou	3.50	1.75	1.00
12	Dick Stuart	2.50	1.25	.70
13	Claude Osteen	2.50	1.25	.70
14	Juan Pizarro	2.50	1.25	.70
15	Donn Clendenon	2.50	1.25	.70
16	Jimmie Hall	2.50	1.25	.70
17	Larry Jackson	2.50	1.25	.70
18	Brooks Robinson	12.50	6.25	3.75
19	Bob Allison	2.50	1.25	.70
20	Ed Roebuck	2.50	1.25	.70
21	Pete Ward	2.50	1.25	.70
22	Willie McCovey	8.00	4.00	2.50
23	Elston Howard	3.00	1.50	.90
24	Diego Segui	2.50	1.25	.70
25	Ken Boyer	3.00	1.50	.90
26	Carl Yastrzemski	15.00	7.50	4.50
27	Bill Mazeroski	6.00	3.00	1.75
28	Jerry Lumpe	2.50	1.25	.70
29	Woody Held	2.50	1.25	.70
30	Dick Radatz	2.50	1.25	.70
31	Luis Aparicio	8.00	4.00	2.50
32	Dave Nicholson	2.50	1.25	.70
33	Ed Mathews	12.00	6.00	3.50
34	Don Drysdale	12.00	6.00	3.50
35	Ray Culp	2.50	1.25	.70
36	Juan Marichal	8.00	4.00	2.50
37	Frank Robinson	12.50	6.25	3.75
38	Chuck Hinton	2.50	1.25	.70
39	Floyd Robinson	2.50	1.25	.70
40	Tommy Harper	2.50	1.25	.70
41	Ron Hansen	2.50	1.25	.70
42	Ernie Banks	15.00	7.50	4.50
43	Jesse Gonder	2.50	1.25	.70
44	Billy Williams	8.00	4.00	2.50
45	Vada Pinson	3.00	1.50	.90
46	Rocky Colavito	6.00	3.00	1.75
47	Bill Monbouquette	2.50	1.25	.70
48	Max Alvis	2.50	1.25	.70
49	Norm Siebern	2.50	1.25	.70
50	John Callison	2.50	1.25	.70
51	Rich Rollins	2.50	1.25	.70
52	Ken McBride	2.50	1.25	.70
53	Don Lock	2.50	1.25	.70
54	Ron Fairly	2.50	1.25	.70
55	Roberto Clemente	25.00	12.50	7.50
56	Dick Ellsworth	2.50	1.25	.70
57	Tommy Davis	2.50	1.25	.70
58	Tony Gonzalez	2.50	1.25	.70
59	Bob Gibson	12.00	6.00	3.50
60	Jim Maloney	2.50	1.25	.70
61	Frank Howard	3.00	1.50	.90
62	Jim Pagliaroni	2.50	1.25	.70
63	Orlando Cepeda	8.00	4.00	2.50
64	Ron Perranoski	2.50	1.25	.70
65	Curt Flood	2.50	1.25	.70
66	Al McBean	2.50	1.25	.70
67	Dean Chance	2.50	1.25	.70
68	Ron Santo	3.50	1.75	1.00
69	Jack Baldschun	2.50	1.25	.70
70	Milt Pappas	2.50	1.25	.70
71	Gary Peters	2.50	1.25	.70
72	Bobby Richardson	3.00	1.50	.90
73	Lee Thomas	2.50	1.25	.70
74	Hank Aguirre	2.50	1.25	.70
75	Carl Willey	2.50	1.25	.70
76	Camilo Pascual	2.50	1.25	.70
77	Bob Friend	2.50	1.25	.70
78	Bill White	2.50	1.25	.70
79	Norm Cash	3.00	1.50	.90
80	Willie Mays	25.00	12.50	7.50
81	Duke Carmel	2.50	1.25	.70
82	Pete Rose	25.00	12.50	7.50
83	Hank Aaron	25.00	12.50	7.50
84	Bob Aspromonte	2.50	1.25	.70
85	Jim O'Toole	2.50	1.25	.70
86	Vic Davalillo	2.50	1.25	.70
87	Bill Freehan	2.50	1.25	.70
88	Warren Spahn	10.00	5.00	3.00
89	Ron Hunt	2.50	1.25	.70
90	Denis Menke	2.50	1.25	.70
91	Turk Farrell	2.50	1.25	.70
92	Jim Hickman	2.50	1.25	.70
93	Jim Bunning	6.00	3.00	1.75
94	Bob Hendley	2.50	1.25	.70
95	Ernie Broglio	2.50	1.25	.70
96	Rusty Staub	3.00	1.50	.90
97	Lou Brock	8.00	4.00	2.50
98	Jim Fregosi	2.50	1.25	.70
99	Jim Grant	2.50	1.25	.70
100	Al Kaline	15.00	7.50	4.50
101	Earl Battey	2.50	1.25	.70
102	Wayne Causey	2.50	1.25	.70
103	Chuck Schilling	2.50	1.25	.70
104	Boog Powell	3.50	1.75	1.00
105	Dave Wickersham	2.50	1.25	.70
106	Sandy Koufax	18.00	9.00	5.50
107	John Bateman	2.50	1.25	.70
108	Ed Brinkman	2.50	1.25	.70
109	Al Downing	2.50	1.25	.70
110	Joe Azcue	2.50	1.25	.70
111	Albie Pearson	2.50	1.25	.70
112	Harmon Killebrew	12.00	6.00	3.50
113	Tony Taylor	2.50	1.25	.70
114	Alvin Jackson	2.50	1.25	.70
115	Billy O'Dell	2.50	1.25	.70
116	Don Demeter	2.50	1.25	.70
117	Ed Charles	2.50	1.25	.70
118	Joe Torre	4.00	2.00	1.25
119	Don Nottebart	2.50	1.25	.70
120	Mickey Mantle	50.00	25.00	15.00
121	Joe Pepitone (All-Star)	2.50	1.25	.70
122	Dick Stuart (All-Star)	3.00	1.50	.90
123	Bobby Richardson (All-Star)	2.50	1.25	.70
124	Jerry Lumpe (All-Star)	2.50	1.25	.70
125	Brooks Robinson (All-Star)	12.00	6.00	3.50
126	Frank Malzone (All-Star)	2.50	1.25	.70
127	Luis Aparicio (All-Star)	8.00	4.00	2.50
128	Jim Fregosi (All-Star)	2.50	1.25	.70
129	Al Kaline (All-Star)	15.00	7.50	4.50
130	Leon Wagner (All-Star)	2.50	1.25	.70
131a	Mickey Mantle (All-Star, lefthanded)	70.00	35.00	21.00
131b	Mickey Mantle (All-Star, righthanded)	40.00	20.00	12.00
132	Albie Pearson (All-Star)	2.50	1.25	.70
133	Harmon Killebrew (All-Star)	12.00	6.00	3.50
134	Carl Yastrzemski (All-Star)	15.00	7.50	4.50
135	Elston Howard (All-Star)	3.00	1.50	.90
136	Earl Battey (All-Star)	2.50	1.25	.70
137	Camilo Pascual (All-Star)	2.50	1.25	.70
138	Jim Bouton (All-Star)	3.00	1.50	.90
139	Whitey Ford (All-Star)	10.00	5.00	3.00
140	Gary Peters (All-Star)	2.50	1.25	.70
141	Bill White (All-Star)	2.50	1.25	.70
142	Orlando Cepeda (All-Star)	5.00	2.50	1.50
143	Bill Mazeroski (All-Star)	5.00	2.50	1.50
144	Tony Taylor (All-Star)	2.50	1.25	.70
145	Ken Boyer (All-Star)	3.00	1.50	.90
146	Ron Santo (All-Star)	3.00	1.50	.90
147	Dick Groat (All-Star)	2.50	1.25	.70
148	Roy McMillan (All-Star)	2.50	1.25	.70
149	Hank Aaron (All-Star)	22.00	11.00	6.50
150	Roberto Clemente (All-Star)	30.00	15.00	9.00
151	Willie Mays (All-Star)	22.00	11.00	6.50
152	Vada Pinson (All-Star)	3.00	1.50	.90
153	Tommy Davis (All-Star)	2.50	1.25	.70
154	Frank Robinson (All-Star)	12.50	6.25	3.75
155	Joe Torre (All-Star)	3.00	1.50	.90
156	Tim McCarver (All-Star)	2.50	1.25	.70
157	Juan Marichal (All-Star)	8.00	4.00	2.50
158	Jim Maloney (All-Star)	2.50	1.25	.70
159	Sandy Koufax (All-Star)	18.00	9.00	5.50
160	Warren Spahn (All-Star)	12.00	6.00	3.50
161a	Wayne Causey (All-Star, N.L. on back)	15.00	7.50	4.50
161b	Wayne Causey (All-Star, A.L. on back)	2.50	1.25	.70
162a	Chuck Hinton (All-Star, N.L. on back)	15.00	7.50	4.50
162b	Chuck Hinton (All-Star, A.L. on back)	2.50	1.25	.70
163	Bob Aspromonte (All-Star)	2.50	1.25	.70
164	Ron Hunt (All-Star)	2.50	1.25	.70

1964 Topps Giants

Measuring 3-1/8" x 5-1/4" the Topps Giants were the company's first postcard-size issue. The cards feature large color photographs surrounded by white borders with a white baseball containing the player's name, position and team. Card backs carry another photo of the player surrounded by a newspaper-style explanation of the depicted career highlight. The 60-card set contains primarily stars which means it's an excellent place to find inexpensive cards of Hall of Famers. The '64 Giants were not printed in equal quantity and seven of the cards, including Sandy Koufax and Willie Mays, are significantly scarcer than the remainder of the set.

		NM	EX	VG
Complete Set (60):		150.00	75.00	45.00
Common Player:		1.50	.75	.45
1	Gary Peters	1.50	.75	.45
2	Ken Johnson	1.50	.75	.45
3	Sandy Koufax (Short-print)	50.00	25.00	15.00
4	Bob Bailey	1.50	.75	.45
5	Milt Pappas	1.50	.75	.45
6	Ron Hunt	1.50	.75	.45
7	Whitey Ford	7.50	3.75	2.25
8	Roy McMillan	1.50	.75	.45
9	Rocky Colavito	5.00	2.50	1.50
10	Jim Bunning	5.00	2.50	1.50
11	Roberto Clemente	20.00	10.00	6.00
12	Al Kaline	6.00	3.00	1.75
13	Nellie Fox	6.00	3.00	1.80
14	Tony Gonzalez	1.50	.75	.45
15	Jim Gentile	1.50	.75	.45
16	Dean Chance	1.50	.75	.45
17	Dick Ellsworth	1.50	.75	.45
18	Jim Fregosi	2.00	1.00	.60
19	Dick Groat	1.50	.75	.45
20	Chuck Hinton	1.50	.75	.45
21	Elston Howard	4.00	2.00	1.25
22	Dick Farrell	1.50	.75	.45
23	Albie Pearson	1.50	.75	.45
24	Frank Howard	3.00	1.50	.90
25	Mickey Mantle	30.00	15.00	9.00
26	Joe Torre	3.00	1.50	.90
27	Ed Brinkman	1.50	.75	.45
28	Bob Friend (SP)	14.00	7.00	4.25
29	Frank Robinson	6.00	3.00	1.75
30	Bill Freehan	1.50	.75	.45
31	Warren Spahn	6.00	3.00	1.75
32	Camilo Pascual	1.50	.75	.45
33	Pete Ward	1.50	.75	.45
34	Jim Maloney	1.50	.75	.45
35	Dave Wickersham	1.50	.75	.45
36	Johnny Callison	1.50	.75	.45
37	Juan Marichal	6.00	3.00	1.75
38	Harmon Killebrew	6.00	3.00	1.75
39	Luis Aparicio	6.00	3.00	1.75
40	Dick Radatz	1.50	.75	.45
41	Bob Gibson	6.00	3.00	1.75
42	Dick Stuart (SP)	14.00	7.00	4.25
43	Tommy Davis	1.50	.75	.45
44	Tony Oliva	3.00	1.50	.90
45	Wayne Causey (SP)	14.00	7.00	4.25
46	Max Alvis	1.50	.75	.45
47	Galen Cisco (SP)	14.00	7.00	4.25
48	Carl Yastrzemski	9.00	4.50	2.75
49	Hank Aaron	11.00	5.50	3.25
50	Brooks Robinson	7.50	3.75	2.25
51	Willie Mays (SP)	45.00	22.00	13.50
52	Billy Williams	6.00	3.00	1.75
53	Juan Pizarro	1.50	.75	.45
54	Leon Wagner	1.50	.75	.45
55	Orlando Cepeda	6.00	3.00	1.75
56	Vada Pinson	3.00	1.50	.90
57	Ken Boyer	3.00	1.50	.90
58	Ron Santo	3.00	1.50	.90
59	John Romano	1.50	.75	.45
60	Bill Skowron (SP)	17.50	8.75	5.25

1964 Topps Photo Tatoos

Apparently not content to leave the skin of American children without adornment, Topps jumped back into the tattoo field in 1964 with the release of a new series. Measuring 1-9/16" x 3-1/2," there were 75 tattoos in a complete set. The picture side for the 20 team tattoos gives the team logo and name. For the player tattoos, the picture side has the player's face, name and team.

		NM	EX	VG
Complete Set (75):		1250.	625.00	375.00
Common Player:		8.00	4.00	2.50
(1)	Hank Aaron	70.00	35.00	21.00
(2)	Hank Aguirre	8.00	4.00	2.50
(3)	Max Alvis	8.00	4.00	2.50
(4)	Ernie Banks	40.00	20.00	12.00
(5)	Steve Barber	8.00	4.00	2.50
(6)	Ken Boyer	9.50	4.75	2.75
(7)	Johnny Callison	8.00	4.00	2.50
(8)	Norm Cash	9.50	4.75	2.75
(9)	Wayne Causey	8.00	4.00	2.50
(10)	Orlando Cepeda	20.00	10.00	6.00
(11)	Rocky Colavito	24.00	12.00	7.25
(12)	Ray Culp	8.00	4.00	2.50
(13)	Vic Davalillo	8.00	4.00	2.50
(14)	Moc Drabowsky	8.00	4.00	2.50
(15)	Dick Ellsworth	8.00	4.00	2.50
(16)	Curt Flood	8.00	4.00	2.50
(17)	Bill Freehan	8.00	4.00	2.50
(18)	Jim Fregosi	8.00	4.00	2.50
(19)	Bob Friend	8.00	4.00	2.50
(20)	Dick Groat	9.50	4.75	2.75
(21)	Woody Held	8.00	4.00	2.50
(22)	Frank Howard	8.00	4.00	2.50
(23)	Al Jackson	8.00	4.00	2.50
(24)	Larry Jackson	8.00	4.00	2.50
(25)	Ken Johnson	8.00	4.00	2.50
(26)	Al Kaline	35.00	17.50	10.50
(27a)	Harmon Killebrew (green background)	45.00	22.00	13.50
(27b)	Harmon Killebrew (red background)	45.00	22.00	13.50
(28a)	Sandy Koufax (horizontal band)	65.00	32.00	19.50
(28b)	Sandy Koufax (diagonal band)	65.00	32.00	19.50

(29)	Don Lock	8.00	4.00	2.50
(30)	Frank Malzone	8.00	4.00	2.50
(31a)	Mickey Mantle (diagonal yellow band)	160.00	80.00	48.00
(31b)	Mickey Mantle (red triangle)	160.00	80.00	48.00
(32)	Eddie Mathews	28.00	14.00	8.50
(33a)	Willie Mays (yellow background encompasses head)	70.00	35.00	21.00
(33b)	Willie Mays (yellow background ears-to-chin)	70.00	35.00	21.00
(34)	Bill Mazeroski	24.00	12.00	7.25
(35)	Ken McBride	8.00	4.00	2.50
(36)	Bill Monbouquette	8.00	4.00	2.50
(37)	Dave Nicholson	8.00	4.00	2.50
(38)	Claude Osteen	8.00	4.00	2.50
(39)	Milt Pappas	8.00	4.00	2.50
(40)	Camilio Pascual	8.00	4.00	2.50
(41)	Albie Pearson	8.00	4.00	2.50
(42)	Ron Perranoski	8.00	4.00	2.50
(43)	Gary Peters	8.00	4.00	2.50
(44)	Boog Powell	10.00	5.00	3.00
(45)	Frank Robinson	32.00	16.00	9.50
(46)	John Romano	8.00	4.00	2.50
(47)	Norm Siebern	8.00	4.00	2.50
(48)	Warren Spahn	32.00	16.00	9.50
(49)	Dick Stuart	8.00	4.00	2.50
(50)	Lee Thomas	8.00	4.00	2.50
(51)	Joe Torre	15.00	7.50	4.50
(52)	Pete Ward	8.00	4.00	2.50
(53)	Carlton Willey	8.00	4.00	2.50
(54)	Billy Williams	32.00	16.00	9.50
(55)	Carl Yastrzemski	40.00	20.00	12.00
(56)	Baltimore Orioles Logo	6.50	3.25	2.00
(57)	Boston Red Sox Logo	6.50	3.25	2.00
(58)	Chicago Cubs Logo	6.50	3.25	2.00
(59)	Chicago White Sox Logo	6.50	3.25	2.00
(60)	Cincinnati Reds Logo	6.50	3.25	2.00
(61)	Cleveland Indians Logo	6.50	3.25	2.00
(62)	Detroit Tigers Logo	6.50	3.25	2.00
(63)	Houston Colts Logo	6.50	3.25	2.00
(64)	Kansas City Athletics Logo	6.50	3.25	2.00
(65)	Los Angeles Angels Logo	6.50	3.25	2.00
(66)	Los Angeles Dodgers Logo	6.50	3.25	2.00
(67)	Milwaukee Braves Logo	6.50	3.25	2.00
(68)	Minnesota Twins Logo	6.50	3.25	2.00
(69)	New York Mets Logo	6.50	3.25	2.00
(70)	New York Yankees Logo	10.00	5.00	3.00
(71)	Philadelphia Phillies Logo	6.50	3.25	2.00
(72)	Pittsburgh Pirates Logo	6.50	3.25	2.00
(73)	St. Louis Cardinals Logo	6.50	3.25	2.00
(74)	San Francisco Giants Logo	6.50	3.25	2.00
(75)	Washington Senators Logo	6.50	3.25	2.00

1964 Topps Rookie All-Star Banquet

Since 1959 Topps has sponsored a formal post-season banquet to honor its annual all-star rookie team. In 1964, the gum company deviated from the tradition dinner program by issuing a 35-card boxed set. Each of the cards is printed in black-and-white, with red or light blue graphic highlights. The first seven cards in the set feature Topps staff and baseball dignitaries involved in the selection of the rookie team. Cards #8-12 are composite photos of the 1959-63 Rookie All-Star team. Cards #13-34A showcase the '64 honorees. Each player's card is matched with a card from the team's public relations officer extolling the rookie's virtues. Each card in this unique dinner program measures 3" x 5-1/4" and is numbered as a "PAGE" in the lower-right corner.

		NM	EX	VG
Complete Boxed Set (35):		600.00	300.00	180.00
Common Player:		5.00	2.50	1.50
1	"6th Annual Topps Rookie All-Star Team Awards" header card	5.00	2.50	1.50
2	The Baseball World Votes (Tommy Davis, Jeff Torborg, Ron Santo, Billy Williams)	5.00	2.50	1.50
3	The Baseball World Votes (Six more clubhouse scenes)	5.00	2.50	1.50
4	Topps Rookie All-Star Team Honorary Election Committee (photos of media and Hall of Famers Hank Greenberg and Fran	12.00	6.00	3.50
5	Topps Rookie All-Star Team Honorary Election Committee (photos of five media, Topps' VP Joel Shorin and Jackie	25.00	12.50	7.50
6	Executive Director of the Committee and His Associates (Topps' Cy Berger, three others)	5.00	2.50	1.50
7	Topps Salutes Joe Garagiola (Joe Garagiola)	20.00	10.00	6.00
8	The 1959 Topps Rookie All-Star Team (Willie McCovey, Pumpsie Green, Joe Koppe, Jim Baxes, Bobby Allison), , (John Romano, Jim Perry, Jim O'Toole)	50.00	25.00	15.00
9	The 1960 Topps Rookie All-Star Team (Jim Gentile, Julian Javier, Ron Hansen, Ron Santo, Tommy Davis, Frank , (Jimmie Coker, Chuck Estrada, Dick Stigman)	45.00	22.00	13.50
10	The 1961 Topps Rookie All-Star Team (J.C. Martin, Jake Wood, Dick Howser, Charlie Smith, Billy Williams), , (Joe Torre, Don Schwall, Jack Curtis)	40.00	20.00	12.00
11	The 1962 Topps Rookie All-Star Team (Fred Whitfield, Bernie Allen, Tom Tresh, Ed Charles, Manny Jiminez), , (Buck Rodgers, Dean Chance, Al Jackson)	40.00	20.00	12.00
12	The 1963 Topps Rookie All-Star Team (Pete Rose, Rusty Staub, Al Weis, Pete Ward, Jimmie Hall, Vic , (Jesse Gonder, Ray Culp, Gary Peters)	300.00	150.00	90.00
13	1964 Topps Rookie All-Star Team header card	5.00	2.50	1.50
14	Ed Uhas, Cleveland Indians PR	5.00	2.50	1.50
15	Bob Chance	30.00	15.00	9.00
16	Garry Schumacher, S.F. Giants PR	5.00	2.50	1.50
17	Hal Lanier	30.00	15.00	9.00
18	Larry Shenk, Phillies PR	5.00	2.50	1.50
19	Richie Allen	65.00	32.00	19.50
20	Jim Schaaf, Athletics PR	5.00	2.50	1.50
21	Bert Campaneris	35.00	17.50	10.50
22	Ernie Johnson, Braves PR	5.00	2.50	1.50
23	Rico Carty	35.00	17.50	10.50
24	Bill Crowley, Red Sox PR	5.00	2.50	1.50
25	Tony Conigliaro	75.00	37.00	22.00
26	Tom Mee, Twins PR	5.00	2.50	1.50
27	Tony Oliva	45.00	22.00	13.50
28	Burt Hawkins, Senators PR	5.00	2.50	1.50
29	Mike Brumley	30.00	15.00	9.00
30	Hank Zureick, Reds PR	5.00	2.50	1.50
31	Bill McCool	30.00	15.00	9.00
32	Rob Brown, Orioles PR	5.00	2.50	1.50
33	Wally Bunker	30.00	15.00	9.00
34	"5th Annual Topps Minor League Player of the Year" header card	5.00	2.50	1.50
34A	Luis Tiant (Minor League Player of the Year)	35.00	17.50	10.50

1964 Topps Stand-Ups

These 2-1/2" x 3-1/2" cards were the first since the All-Star sets of 1951 to be die-cut. This made it possible for a folded card to stand on display. The 77-cards in the set feature color photographs of the player with yellow and green backgrounds. Directions for folding are on the yellow top background, and when folded only the green background remains. Of the 77 cards, 55 were double-printed while 22 were single-printed, making them twice as scarce.

		NM	EX	VG
Complete Set (77):		2000.	1000.	600.00
Common Player:		10.00	5.00	3.00
(1)	Hank Aaron	125.00	62.00	37.00
(2)	Hank Aguirre	10.00	5.00	3.00
(3)	George Altman	10.00	5.00	3.00
(4)	Max Alvis	10.00	5.00	3.00
(5)	Bob Aspromonte	10.00	5.00	3.00
(6)	Jack Baldschun (SP)	22.00	11.00	6.50
(7)	Ernie Banks	70.00	35.00	21.00
(8)	Steve Barber	10.00	5.00	3.00
(9)	Earl Battey	10.00	5.00	3.00
(10)	Ken Boyer	12.00	6.00	3.50
(11)	Ernie Broglio	10.00	5.00	3.00
(12)	Johnny Callison	10.00	5.00	3.00
(13)	Norm Cash (SP)	35.00	17.50	10.50
(14)	Wayne Causey	10.00	5.00	3.00
(15)	Orlando Cepeda	30.00	15.00	9.00
(16)	Ed Charles	10.00	5.00	3.00
(17)	Roberto Clemente	125.00	62.00	37.00
(18)	Donn Clendenon (SP)	25.00	12.50	7.50
(19)	Rocky Colavito	25.00	12.50	7.50
(20)	Ray Culp (SP)	22.00	11.00	6.50
(21)	Tommy Davis	12.00	6.00	3.50
(22)	Don Drysdale (SP)	145.00	72.00	43.00
(23)	Dick Ellsworth	10.00	5.00	3.00
(24)	Dick Farrell	10.00	5.00	3.00
(25)	Jim Fregosi	10.00	5.00	3.00
(26)	Bob Friend	10.00	5.00	3.00
(27)	Jim Gentile	10.00	5.00	3.00
(28)	Jesse Gonder (SP)	22.00	11.00	6.50
(29)	Tony Gonzalez (SP)	22.00	11.00	6.50
(30)	Dick Groat	10.00	5.00	3.00
(31)	Woody Held	10.00	5.00	3.00
(32)	Chuck Hinton	10.00	5.00	3.00
(33)	Elston Howard	12.00	6.00	3.50
(34)	Frank Howard (SP)	25.00	12.50	7.50
(35)	Ron Hunt	10.00	5.00	3.00
(36)	Al Jackson	10.00	5.00	3.00
(37)	Ken Johnson	10.00	5.00	3.00
(38)	Al Kaline	45.00	22.00	13.50
(39)	Harmon Killebrew	40.00	20.00	12.00
(40)	Sandy Koufax	125.00	62.00	37.00
(41)	Don Lock (SP)	22.00	11.00	6.50
(42)	Jerry Lumpe (SP)	22.00	11.00	6.50
(43)	Jim Maloney	10.00	5.00	3.00
(44)	Frank Malzone	10.00	5.00	3.00
(45)	Mickey Mantle	440.00	220.00	132.00
(46)	Juan Marichal (SP)	110.00	55.00	33.00
(47)	Ed Mathews (SP)	110.00	55.00	33.00
(48)	Willie Mays	125.00	62.50	37.50
(49)	Bill Mazeroski	16.00	8.00	4.75
(50)	Ken McBride	10.00	5.00	3.00
(51)	Willie McCovey (SP)	110.00	55.00	33.00
(52)	Claude Osteen	10.00	5.00	3.00
(53)	Jim O'Toole	10.00	5.00	3.00
(54)	Camilo Pascual	10.00	5.00	3.00
(55)	Albie Pearson (SP)	25.00	12.50	7.50
(56)	Gary Peters	10.00	5.00	3.00
(57)	Vada Pinson	12.00	6.00	3.50
(58)	Juan Pizarro	10.00	5.00	3.00
(59)	Boog Powell	12.00	6.00	3.50
(60)	Bobby Richardson	12.00	6.00	3.50
(61)	Brooks Robinson	50.00	25.00	15.00
(62)	Floyd Robinson	10.00	5.00	3.00
(63)	Frank Robinson	48.00	24.00	14.50
(64)	Ed Roebuck (SP)	25.00	12.50	7.50
(65)	Rich Rollins	10.00	5.00	3.00
(66)	Johnny Romano	10.00	5.00	3.00
(67)	Ron Santo (SP)	28.00	14.00	8.50
(68)	Norm Siebern	10.00	5.00	3.00
(69)	Warren Spahn (SP)	110.00	55.00	33.00
(70)	Dick Stuart (SP)	25.00	12.50	7.50
(71)	Lee Thomas	10.00	5.00	3.00
(72)	Joe Torre	25.00	12.50	7.50
(73)	Pete Ward	10.00	5.00	3.00
(74)	Bill White (SP)	25.00	12.50	7.50
(75)	Billy Williams (SP)	110.00	55.00	33.00
(76)	Hal Woodeshick (SP)	28.00	14.00	8.50
(77)	Carl Yastrzemski (SP)	325.00	160.00	97.00

1965 Topps

The 1965 Topps set features a large color photograph of the player surrounded by a colored, round-cornered frame and a white border. The bottom of the 2-1/2" x 3-1/2" cards includes a pennant with a color team logo and name over the left side of a rectangle which features the player's name and position. Backs feature statistics and, if space allowed, a cartoon and headline about the player. There are no multi-player cards in the 1965 set other than the usual team cards and World Series highlights. Rookie cards include team, as well as league groupings from two to four players per card. Also present in the 598-card set are statistical leaders. Certain cards in the high-number series (#523-

598) were produced in lesser quantities than the rest of the series. Known as "short-prints," and valued somewhat higher than the other high numbers, they are indicated in the checklist by an (SP) after the player name.

		NM	EX	VG
	Complete Set (598):	3000.	1500.	900.00
	Common Player (1-283):	2.00	1.00	.60
	Common Player (284-370):	3.00	1.50	.90
	Common Player (371-598):	5.00	2.50	1.50
1	A.L. Batting Leaders (Elston Howard, Tony Oliva, Brooks Robinson)	20.00	6.00	4.00
2	N.L. Batting Leaders (Hank Aaron, Rico Carty, Roberto Clemente)	20.00	10.00	6.00
3	A.L. Home Run Leaders (Harmon Killebrew, Mickey Mantle, Boog Powell)	40.00	20.00	12.00
4	N.L. Home Run Leaders (Johnny Callison, Orlando Cepeda, Jim Hart, Willie Mays, Billy Williams)	12.50	6.25	3.75
5	A.L. RBI Leaders (Harmon Killebrew, Mickey Mantle, Brooks Robinson, Dick Stuart)	32.00	16.00	9.50
6	N.L. RBI Leaders (Ken Boyer, Willie Mays, Ron Santo)	9.00	4.50	2.75
7	A.L. ERA Leaders (Dean Chance, Joel Horlen)	3.00	1.50	.90
8	N.L. ERA Leaders (Don Drysdale, Sandy Koufax)	15.00	7.50	4.50
9	A.L. Pitching Leaders (Wally Bunker, Dean Chance, Gary Peters, Juan Pizarro, Dave Wickersham)	3.00	1.50	.90
10	N.L. Pitching Leaders (Larry Jackson, Juan Marichal, Ray Sadecki)	3.00	1.50	.90
11	A.L. Strikeout Leaders (Dean Chance, Al Downing, Camilo Pascual)	3.00	1.50	.90
12	N.L. Strikeout Leaders (Don Drysdale, Bob Gibson, Bob Veale)	7.00	3.50	2.00
13	Pedro Ramos	2.00	1.00	.60
14	Len Gabrielson	2.00	1.00	.60
15	Robin Roberts	8.00	4.00	2.50
16	Astros Rookies *(Sonny Jackson)*, *(Joe Morgan)*	55.00	27.00	16.50
17	Johnny Romano	2.00	1.00	.60
18	Bill McCool	2.00	1.00	.60
19	Gates Brown	2.00	1.00	.60
20	Jim Bunning	6.00	3.00	1.75
21	Don Blasingame	2.00	1.00	.60
22	Charlie Smith	2.00	1.00	.60
23	Bob Tiefenauer	2.00	1.00	.60
24	Twins Team	5.00	2.50	1.50
25	Al McBean	2.00	1.00	.60
26	Bobby Knoop	2.00	1.00	.60
27	Dick Bertell	2.00	1.00	.60
28	Barney Schultz	2.00	1.00	.60
29	Felix Mantilla	2.00	1.00	.60
30	Jim Bouton	3.00	1.50	.90
31	Mike White	2.00	1.00	.60
32	Herman Franks	2.00	1.00	.60
33	Jackie Brandt	2.00	1.00	.60
34	Cal Koonce	2.00	1.00	.60
35	Ed Charles	2.00	1.00	.60
36	Bobby Wine	2.00	1.00	.60
37	Fred Gladding	2.00	1.00	.60
38	Jim King	2.00	1.00	.60
39	Gerry Arrigo	2.00	1.00	.60
40	Frank Howard	2.50	1.25	.70
41	White Sox Rookies (Bruce Howard, Marv Staehle)	2.00	1.00	.60
42	Earl Wilson	2.00	1.00	.60
43	Mike Shannon	2.00	1.00	.60
44	Wade Blasingame	2.00	1.00	.60
45	Roy McMillan	2.00	1.00	.60
46	Bob Lee	2.00	1.00	.60
47	Tommy Harper	2.00	1.00	.60
48	Claude Raymond	2.00	1.00	.60
49	Orioles Rookies *(Curt Blefary)*, John Miller)	3.00	1.50	.90
50	Juan Marichal	8.00	4.00	2.50
51	Billy Bryan	2.00	1.00	.60
52	Ed Roebuck	2.00	1.00	.60
53	Dick McAuliffe	2.00	1.00	.60
54	Joe Gibbon	2.00	1.00	.60
55	Tony Conigliaro	12.50	6.25	3.75
56	Ron Kline	2.00	1.00	.60
57	Cardinals Team	4.50	2.25	1.25
58	Fred Talbot	2.00	1.00	.60
59	Nate Olivor	2.00	1.00	.60
60	Jim O'Toole	2.00	1.00	.60
61	Chris Cannizzaro	2.00	1.00	.60
62	Jim Katt (Kaat)	4.00	[illegible]	[illegible]
63	Ty Cline	2.00	1.00	.60
64	Lou Burdette	2.00	1.00	.60
65	Tony Kubek	3.50	1.75	1.00
66	Bill Rigney	2.00	1.00	.60
67	Harvey Haddix	2.00	1.00	.60
68	Del Crandall	2.00	1.00	.60
69	Bill Virdon	2.00	1.00	.60
70	Bill Skowron	3.00	1.50	.90
71	John O'Donoghue	2.00	1.00	.60
72	Tony Gonzalez	2.00	1.00	.60
73	Dennis Ribant	2.00	1.00	.60
74	Red Sox Rookies *(Rico Petrocelli)*, Jerry Stephenson)	8.00	4.00	2.50
75	Deron Johnson	2.00	1.00	.60
76	Sam McDowell	2.00	1.00	.60
77	Doug Camilli	2.00	1.00	.60
78	Dal Maxvill	2.00	1.00	.60
79a	Checklist 1-88 (61 is C. Cannizzaro)	4.50	2.25	1.25
79b	Checklist 1-88 (61 is Cannizzaro)	9.50	4.75	2.75
80	Turk Farrell	2.00	1.00	.60
81	Don Buford	2.00	1.00	.60
82	Braves Rookies *(Santos Alomar)*, John Braun)	4.50	2.25	1.25
83	George Thomas	2.00	1.00	.60
84	Ron Herbel	2.00	1.00	.60
85	Willie Smith	2.00	1.00	.60
86	Les Narum	2.00	1.00	.60
87	Nelson Mathews	2.00	1.00	.60
88	Jack Lamabe	2.00	1.00	.60
89	Mike Hershberger	2.00	1.00	.60
90	Rich Rollins	2.00	1.00	.60
91	Cubs Team	4.50	2.25	1.25
92	Dick Howser	2.00	1.00	.60
93	Jack Fisher	2.00	1.00	.60
94	Charlie Lau	2.00	1.00	.60
95	Bill Mazeroski	6.00	3.00	1.75
96	Sonny Siebert	2.00	1.00	.60
97	Pedro Gonzalez	2.00	1.00	.60
98	Bob Miller	2.00	1.00	.60
99	Gil Hodges	6.50	3.25	2.00
100	Ken Boyer	4.00	2.00	1.25
101	Fred Newman	2.00	1.00	.60
102	Steve Boros	2.00	1.00	.60
103	Harvey Kuenn	2.00	1.00	.60
104	Checklist 89-176	5.00	2.50	1.50
105	Chico Salmon	2.00	1.00	.60
106	Gene Oliver	2.00	1.00	.60
107	Phillies Rookies *(Pat Corrales)*, Costen Shockley)	3.50	1.75	1.00
108	Don Mincher	2.00	1.00	.60
109	Walt Bond	2.00	1.00	.60
110	Ron Santo	4.50	2.25	1.25
111	Lee Thomas	2.00	1.00	.60
112	Derrell Griffith	2.00	1.00	.60
113	Steve Barber	2.00	1.00	.60
114	Jim Hickman	2.00	1.00	.60
115	Bobby Richardson	3.50	1.75	1.00
116	Cardinals Rookies (Dave Dowling), *(Bob Tolan)*	2.00	1.00	.60
117	Wes Stock	2.00	1.00	.60
118	*Hal Lanier*	2.00	1.00	.60
119	John Kennedy	2.00	1.00	.60
120	Frank Robinson	25.00	12.50	7.50
121	Gene Alley	2.00	1.00	.60
122	Bill Pleis	2.00	1.00	.60
123	Frank J. Thomas	2.00	1.00	.60
124	Tom Satriano	2.00	1.00	.60
125	Juan Pizarro	2.00	1.00	.60
126	Dodgers Team	5.00	2.50	1.50
127	Frank Lary	2.00	1.00	.60
128	Vic Davalillo	2.00	1.00	.60
129	Bennie Daniels	2.00	1.00	.60
130	Al Kaline	30.00	15.00	9.00
131	Johnny Keane	2.00	1.00	.60
132	World Series Game 1 (Cards Take Opener)	4.00	2.00	1.25
133	World Series Game 2 (Stottlemyre Wins)	4.00	2.00	1.25
134	World Series Game 3 (Mantle's Clutch HR)	60.00	30.00	18.00
135	World Series Game 4 (Boyer's Grand-Slam)	4.00	2.00	1.25
136	World Series Game 5 (10th Inning Triumph)	4.00	2.00	1.25
137	World Series Game 6 (Bouton Wins Again)	4.00	2.00	1.25
138	World Series Game 7 (Gibson Wins Finale)	10.00	5.00	3.00
139	World Series Summary (The Cards Celebrate)	4.00	2.00	1.25
140	Dean Chance	2.00	1.00	.60
141	Charlie James	2.00	1.00	.60
142	Bill Monbouquette	2.00	1.00	.60
143	Pirates Rookies (John Gelnar, Jerry May)	2.00	1.00	.60
144	Ed Kranepool	2.00	1.00	.60
145	*Luis Tiant*	16.00	8.00	4.75
146	Ron Hansen	2.00	1.00	.60
147	Dennis Bennett	2.00	1.00	.60
148	Willie Kirkland	2.00	1.00	.60
149	Wayne Schurr	2.00	1.00	.60
150	Brooks Robinson	28.00	14.00	8.50
151	Athletics Team	5.50	2.75	1.75
152	Phil Ortega	2.00	1.00	.60
153	Norm Cash	2.50	1.25	.70
154	Bob Humphreys	2.00	1.00	.60
155	Roger Maris	45.00	22.00	13.50
156	Bob Sadowski	2.00	1.00	.60
157	Zoilo Versalles	2.00	1.00	.60
158	Dick Sisler	2.00	1.00	.60
159	Jim Duffalo	2.00	1.00	.60
160	Roberto Clemente	125.00	62.00	37.00
161	Frank Baumann	2.00	1.00	.60
162	Russ Nixon	2.00	1.00	.60
163	John Briggs	2.00	1.00	.60
164	Al Spangler	2.00	1.00	.60
165	Dick Ellsworth	2.00	1.00	.60
166	Indians Rookies *(Tommie Agee)*, George Culver)	[illegible]	[illegible]	[illegible]
167	Bill Wakefield	2.00	1.00	.60
168	Dick Green	2.00	1.00	.60
169	Dave Vineyard	2.00	1.00	.60
170	Hank Aaron	70.00	35.00	21.00
171	Jim Roland	2.00	1.00	.60
172	Jim Piersall	2.00	1.00	.60
173	Tigers Team	4.50	2.25	1.25
174	Joe Jay	2.00	1.00	.60
175	Bob Aspromonte	2.00	1.00	.60
176	Willie McCovey	16.00	8.00	4.75
177	Pete Mikkelsen	2.00	1.00	.60
178	Dalton Jones	2.00	1.00	.60
179	Hal Woodeshick	2.00	1.00	.60
180	Bob Allison	2.00	1.00	.60
181	Senators Rookies (Don Loun, Joe McCabe)	2.00	1.00	.60
182	Mike de la Hoz	2.00	1.00	.60
183	Dave Nicholson	2.00	1.00	.60
184	John Boozer	2.00	1.00	.60
185	Max Alvis	2.00	1.00	.60
186	Billy Cowan	2.00	1.00	.60
187	Casey Stengel	12.50	6.25	3.75
188	Sam Bowens	2.00	1.00	.60
189	Checklist 177-264	6.50	3.25	2.00
190	Bill White	2.00	1.00	.60
191	Phil Regan	2.00	1.00	.60
192	Jim Coker	2.00	1.00	.60
193	Gaylord Perry	12.50	6.25	3.75
194	Angels Rookies (Bill Kelso), *(Rick Reichardt)*	2.00	1.00	.60
195	Bob Veale	2.00	1.00	.60
196	Ron Fairly	2.00	1.00	.60
197	Diego Segui	2.00	1.00	.60
198	Smoky Burgess	2.00	1.00	.60
199	Bob Heffner	2.00	1.00	.60
200	Joe Torre	4.00	2.00	1.25
201	Twins Rookies *(Cesar Tovar)*, Sandy Valdespino)	3.00	1.50	.90
202	Leo Burke	2.00	1.00	.60
203	Dallas Green	2.50	1.25	.70
204	Russ Snyder	2.00	1.00	.60
205	Warren Spahn	24.00	12.00	7.25
206	Willie Horton	2.50	1.25	.70
207	Pete Rose	115.00	57.00	34.00
208	Tommy John	6.50	3.25	2.00
209	Pirates Team	5.00	2.50	1.50
210	Jim Fregosi	2.00	1.00	.60
211	Steve Ridzik	2.00	1.00	.60
212	Ron Brand	2.00	1.00	.60
213	Jim Davenport	2.00	1.00	.60
214	Bob Purkey	2.00	1.00	.60
215	Pete Ward	2.00	1.00	.60
216	Al Worthington	2.00	1.00	.60
217	Walt Alston	4.00	2.00	1.25
218	Dick Schofield	2.00	1.00	.60
219	Bob Meyer	2.00	1.00	.60
220	Billy Williams	8.00	4.00	2.50
221	John Tsitouris	2.00	1.00	.60
222	Bob Tillman	2.00	1.00	.60
223	Dan Osinski	2.00	1.00	.60
224	Bob Chance	2.00	1.00	.60
225	Bo Belinsky	2.00	1.00	.60
226	Yankees Rookies (Jake Gibbs, Elvio Jimenez)	2.00	1.00	.60
227	Bobby Klaus	2.00	1.00	.60
228	Jack Sanford	2.00	1.00	.60
229	Lou Clinton	2.00	1.00	.60
230	Ray Sadecki	2.00	1.00	.60
231	Jerry Adair	2.00	1.00	.60
232	*Steve Blass*	2.00	1.00	.60
233	Don Zimmer	2.00	1.00	.60
234	White Sox Team	5.00	2.50	1.50
235	Chuck Hinton	2.00	1.00	.60
236	*Dennis McLain*	18.00	9.00	5.50
237	Bernie Allen	2.00	1.00	.60
238	Joe Moeller	2.00	1.00	.60
239	Doc Edwards	2.00	1.00	.60
240	Bob Bruce	2.00	1.00	.60
241	Mack Jones	2.00	1.00	.60
242	George Brunet	2.00	1.00	.60
243	Reds Rookies (Ted Davidson), *(Tommy Helms)*	3.00	1.50	.90
244	Lindy McDaniel	2.00	1.00	.60
245	Joe Pepitone	2.00	1.00	.60
246	Tom Butters	2.00	1.00	.60
247	Wally Moon	2.00	1.00	.60
248	Gus Triandos	2.00	1.00	.60
249	Dave McNally	2.00	1.00	.60
250	Willie Mays	80.00	40.00	24.00
251	Billy Herman	4.00	2.00	1.25
252	Pete Richert	2.00	1.00	.60
253	Danny Cater	2.00	1.00	.60
254	Roland Sheldon	2.00	1.00	.60
255	Camilo Pascual	2.00	1.00	.60
256	Tito Francona	2.00	1.00	.60
257	Jim Wynn	2.00	1.00	.60
258	Larry Bearnarth	2.00	1.00	.60
259	Tigers Rookies *(Jim Northrup)*, *(Ray Oyler)*	5.00	2.50	1.50
260	Don Drysdale	19.00	9.50	5.75
261	Duke Carmel	2.00	1.00	.60
262	Bud Daley	2.00	1.00	.60
263	Marty Keough	2.00	1.00	.60
264	Bob Buhl	2.00	1.00	.60
265	Jim Pagliaroni	2.00	1.00	.60
266	*Bert Campaneris*	7.50	3.75	2.25
267	Senators Team	4.00	2.00	1.25
268	Ken McBride	2.00	1.00	.60
269	Frank Bolling	2.00	1.00	.60
270	Milt Pappas	2.00	1.00	.60
271	Don Wert	2.00	1.00	.60
272	Chuck Schilling	2.00	1.00	.60
273	Checklist 265-352	7.50	3.75	2.25
274	Lum Harris	2.00	1.00	.60
275	Dick Groat	2.00	1.00	.60
276	Hoyt Wilhelm	7.50	3.75	2.25
277	Johnny Lewis	2.00	1.00	.60
278	Ken Rotzer	2.00	1.00	.60
279	Dick Tracewski	2.00	1.00	.60
280	Dick Stuart	2.00	1.00	.60
281	Bill Stafford	2.00	1.00	.60
282	Giants Rookies (Dick Estelle), *(Masanori Murakami)*	30.00	15.00	9.00
283	Fred Whitfield	2.00	1.00	.60
284	Nick Willhite	3.00	1.50	.90
285	Ron Hunt	3.00	1.50	.90
286	Athletic Rookies (Jim Dickson, Aurelio Monteagudo)	3.00	1.50	.90
287	Gary Kolb	3.00	1.50	.90
288	Jack Hamilton	3.00	1.50	.90
289	Gordy Coleman	3.00	1.50	.90
290	Wally Bunker	3.00	1.50	.90
291	Jerry Lynch	3.00	1.50	.90
292	Larry Yellen	3.00	1.50	.90
293	Angels Team	5.00	2.50	1.50

294	Tim McCarver	5.00	2.50	1.50
295	Dick Radatz	3.00	1.50	.90
296	Tony Taylor	3.00	1.50	.90
297	Dave DeBusschere	4.00	2.00	1.25
298	Jim Stewart	3.00	1.50	.90
299	Jerry Zimmerman	3.00	1.50	.90
300	Sandy Koufax	100.00	50.00	30.00
301	Birdie Tebbetts	3.00	1.50	.90
302	Al Stanek	3.00	1.50	.90
303	Johnny Orsino	3.00	1.50	.90
304	Dave Stenhouse	3.00	1.50	.90
305	Rico Carty	3.00	1.50	.90
306	Bubba Phillips	3.00	1.50	.90
307	Barry Latman	3.00	1.50	.90
308	Mets Rookies (*Cleon Jones*, Tom Parsons)	8.00	4.00	2.50
309	Steve Hamilton	3.00	1.50	.90
310	Johnny Callison	3.00	1.50	.90
311	Orlando Pena	3.00	1.50	.90
312	Joe Nuxhall	3.00	1.50	.90
313	Jimmie Schaffer	3.00	1.50	.90
314	Sterling Slaughter	3.00	1.50	.90
315	Frank Malzone	3.00	1.50	.90
316	Reds Team	7.00	3.50	2.00
317	Don McMahon	3.00	1.50	.90
318	Matty Alou	3.00	1.50	.90
319	Ken McMullen	3.00	1.50	.90
320	Bob Gibson	35.00	17.50	10.50
321	Rusty Staub	5.00	2.50	1.50
322	Rick Wise	3.00	1.50	.90
323	Hank Bauer	3.00	1.50	.90
324	Bobby Locke	3.00	1.50	.90
325	Donn Clendenon	3.00	1.50	.90
326	Dwight Siebler	3.00	1.50	.90
327	Denis Menke	3.00	1.50	.90
328	Eddie Fisher	3.00	1.50	.90
329	Hawk Taylor	3.00	1.50	.90
330	Whitey Ford	35.00	17.50	10.50
331	Dodgers Rookies (Al Ferrara, John Purdin)	3.00	1.50	.90
332	Ted Abernathy	3.00	1.50	.90
333	Tommie Reynolds	3.00	1.50	.90
334	Vic Roznovsky	3.00	1.50	.90
335	Mickey Lolich	5.00	2.50	1.50
336	Woody Held	3.00	1.50	.90
337	Mike Cuellar	3.00	1.50	.90
338	Phillies Team	6.00	3.00	1.75
339	Ryne Duren	3.00	1.50	.90
340	Tony Oliva	9.00	4.50	2.75
341	Bobby Bolin	3.00	1.50	.90
342	Bob Rodgers	3.00	1.50	.90
343	Mike McCormick	3.00	1.50	.90
344	Wes Parker	3.00	1.50	.90
345	Floyd Robinson	3.00	1.50	.90
346	Bobby Bragan	3.00	1.50	.90
347	Roy Face	3.00	1.50	.90
348	George Banks	3.00	1.50	.90
349	Larry Miller	3.00	1.50	.90
350	Mickey Mantle	400.00	200.00	120.00
351	Jim Perry	3.00	1.50	.90
352	*Alex Johnson*	4.00	2.00	1.25
353	Jerry Lumpe	3.00	1.50	.90
354	Cubs Rookies (Billy Ott, Jack Warner)	3.00	1.50	.90
355	Vada Pinson	5.00	2.50	1.50
356	Bill Spanswick	3.00	1.50	.90
357	Carl Warwick	3.00	1.50	.90
358	Albie Pearson	3.00	1.50	.90
359	Ken Johnson	3.00	1.50	.90
360	Orlando Cepeda	15.00	7.50	4.50
361	Checklist 353-429	8.50	4.25	2.50
362	Don Schwall	3.00	1.50	.90
363	Bob Johnson	3.00	1.50	.90
364	Galen Cisco	3.00	1.50	.90
365	Jim Gentile	3.00	1.50	.90
366	Dan Schneider	3.00	1.50	.90
367	Leon Wagner	3.00	1.50	.90
368	White Sox Rookies (*Ken Berry*, Joel Gibson)	3.00	1.50	.90
369	Phil Linz	3.00	1.50	.90
370	Tommy Davis	3.00	1.50	.90
371	Frank Kreutzer	5.00	2.50	1.50
372	Clay Dalrymple	5.00	2.50	1.50
373	Curt Simmons	5.00	2.50	1.50
374	Angels Rookies (*Jose Cardenal*, Dick Simpson)	7.50	3.75	2.25
375	Dave Wickersham	5.00	2.50	1.50
376	Jim Landis	5.00	2.50	1.50
377	Willie Stargell	20.00	10.00	6.00
378	Chuck Estrada	5.00	2.50	1.50
379	Giants Team	8.00	4.00	2.50
380	Rocky Colavito	12.00	6.00	3.50
381	Al Jackson	5.00	2.50	1.50
382	J.C. Martin	5.00	2.50	1.50
383	Felipe Alou	7.50	3.75	2.25
384	Johnny Klippstein	5.00	2.50	1.50
385	Carl Yastrzemski	55.00	27.00	16.50
386	Cubs Rookies (Paul Jaeckel, Fred Norman)	5.00	2.50	1.50
387	Johnny Podres	6.50	3.25	2.00
388	John Blanchard	5.00	2.50	1.50
389	Don Larsen	5.00	2.50	1.50
390	Bill Freehan	5.00	2.50	1.50
391	Mel McGaha	5.00	2.50	1.50
392	Bob Friend	5.00	2.50	1.50
393	Ed Kirkpatrick	5.00	2.50	1.50
394	Jim Hannan	5.00	2.50	1.50
395	Jim Hart	5.00	2.50	1.50
396	Frank Bertaina	5.00	2.50	1.50
397	Jerry Buchek	5.00	2.50	1.50
398	Reds Rookies (Dan Neville), (*Art Shamsky*)	5.00	2.50	1.50
399	Ray Herbert	5.00	2.50	1.50
400	Harmon Killebrew	35.00	17.50	10.50
401	Carl Willey	5.00	2.50	1.50
402	Joe Amalfitano	5.00	2.50	1.50
403	Red Sox Team	7.50	3.75	2.25
404	Stan Williams	5.00	2.50	1.50
405	John Roseboro	5.00	2.50	1.50
406	Ralph Terry	5.00	2.50	1.50
407	Lee Maye	5.00	2.50	1.50
408	Larry Sherry	5.00	2.50	1.50
409	Astros Rookies (Jim Beauchamp), (*Larry Dierker*)	7.00	3.50	2.00
410	Luis Aparicio	10.00	5.00	3.00
411	Roger Craig	5.00	2.50	1.50
412	Bob Bailey	5.00	2.50	1.50
413	Hal Reniff	5.00	2.50	1.50
414	Al Lopez	6.00	3.00	1.75
415	Curt Flood	7.50	3.75	2.25
416	Jim Brewer	5.00	2.50	1.50
417	Ed Brinkman	5.00	2.50	1.50
418	Johnny Edwards	5.00	2.50	1.50
419	Ruben Amaro	5.00	2.50	1.50
420	Larry Jackson	5.00	2.50	1.50
421	Twins Rookies (Gary Dotter, Jay Ward)	5.00	2.50	1.50
422	Aubrey Gatewood	5.00	2.50	1.50
423	Jesse Gonder	5.00	2.50	1.50
424	Gary Bell	5.00	2.50	1.50
425	Wayne Causey	5.00	2.50	1.50
426	Braves Team	8.00	4.00	2.50
427	Bob Saverine	5.00	2.50	1.50
428	Bob Shaw	5.00	2.50	1.50
429	Don Demeter	5.00	2.50	1.50
430	Gary Peters	5.00	2.50	1.50
431	Cardinals Rookies (*Nelson Briles*, Wayne Spiezio)	7.00	3.50	2.00
432	Jim Grant	5.00	2.50	1.50
433	John Bateman	5.00	2.50	1.50
434	Dave Morehead	5.00	2.50	1.50
435	Willie Davis	5.00	2.50	1.50
436	Don Elston	5.00	2.50	1.50
437	Chico Cardenas	5.00	2.50	1.50
438	Harry Walker	5.00	2.50	1.50
439	Moe Drabowsky	5.00	2.50	1.50
440	Tom Tresh	7.50	3.75	2.25
441	Denver Lemaster	5.00	2.50	1.50
442	Vic Power	5.00	2.50	1.50
443	Checklist 430-506	9.00	4.50	2.75
444	Bob Hendley	5.00	2.50	1.50
445	Don Lock	5.00	2.50	1.50
446	Art Mahaffey	5.00	2.50	1.50
447	Julian Javier	5.00	2.50	1.50
448	Lee Stange	5.00	2.50	1.50
449	Mets Rookies (Jerry Hinsley, Gary Kroll)	5.00	2.50	1.50
450	Elston Howard	8.00	4.00	2.50
451	Jim Owens	5.00	2.50	1.50
452	Gary Geiger	5.00	2.50	1.50
453	Dodgers Rookies (*Willie Crawford*, John Werhas)	5.00	2.50	1.50
454	Ed Rakow	5.00	2.50	1.50
455	Norm Siebern	5.00	2.50	1.50
456	Bill Henry	5.00	2.50	1.50
457	Bob Kennedy	5.00	2.50	1.50
458	John Buzhardt	5.00	2.50	1.50
459	Frank Kostro	5.00	2.50	1.50
460	Richie Allen	30.00	15.00	9.00
461	Braves Rookies (*Clay Carroll*, *Phil Niekro*)	42.50	21.00	12.50
462	Lew Krausse (photo actually Pete Lovrich)	5.00	2.50	1.50
463	Manny Mota	5.00	2.50	1.50
464	Ron Piche	5.00	2.50	1.50
465	Tom Haller	5.00	2.50	1.50
466	Senators Rookies (Pete Craig, Dick Nen)	5.00	2.50	1.50
467	Ray Washburn	5.00	2.50	1.50
468	Larry Brown	5.00	2.50	1.50
469	Don Nottebart	5.00	2.50	1.50
470	Yogi Berra	40.00	20.00	12.00
471	Billy Hoeft	5.00	2.50	1.50
472	Don Pavletich	5.00	2.50	1.50
473	Orioles Rookies (*Paul Blair*), (*Dave Johnson*)	12.00	6.00	3.50
474	Cookie Rojas	5.00	2.50	1.50
475	Clete Boyer	8.00	4.00	2.50
476	Billy O'Dell	5.00	2.50	1.50
477	Cardinals Rookies (*Fritz Ackley*), (*Steve Carlton*)	130.00	65.00	39.00
478	Wilbur Wood	5.00	2.50	1.50
479	Ken Harrelson	5.00	2.50	1.50
480	Joel Horlen	5.00	2.50	1.50
481	Indians Team	10.00	5.00	3.00
482	Bob Priddy	5.00	2.50	1.50
483	George Smith	5.00	2.50	1.50
484	Ron Perranoski	5.00	2.50	1.50
485	Nellie Fox	17.50	8.75	5.25
486	Angels Rookies (Tom Egan, Pat Rogan)	5.00	2.50	1.50
487	Woody Woodward	5.00	2.50	1.50
488	Ted Wills	5.00	2.50	1.50
489	Gene Mauch	5.00	2.50	1.50
490	Earl Battey	5.00	2.50	1.50
491	Tracy Stallard	5.00	2.50	1.50
492	Gene Freese	5.00	2.50	1.50
493	Tigers Rookies (Bruce Brubaker, Bill Roman)	5.00	2.50	1.50
494	Jay Ritchie	5.00	2.50	1.50
495	Joe Christopher	5.00	2.50	1.50
496	Joe Cunningham	5.00	2.50	1.50
497	Giants Rookies (*Ken Henderson*, Jack Hiatt)	5.00	2.50	1.50
498	Gene Stephens	5.00	2.50	1.50
499	Stu Miller	5.00	2.50	1.50
500	Eddie Mathews	29.00	14.50	8.75
501	Indians Rookies (Ralph Gagliano, Jim Rittwage)	5.00	2.50	1.50
502	Don Cardwell	5.00	2.50	1.50
503	Phil Gagliano	5.00	2.50	1.50
504	Jerry Grote	5.00	2.50	1.50
505	Ray Culp	5.00	2.50	1.50
506	Sam Mele	5.00	2.50	1.50
507	Sammy Ellis	5.00	2.50	1.50
508a	Checklist 507-598 (large print on front)	10.00	5.00	3.00
508b	Checklist 507-598 (small print on front)	10.00	5.00	3.00
509	Red Sox Rookies (Bob Guindon, Gerry Vezendy)	5.00	2.50	1.50
510	Ernie Banks	65.00	32.00	19.50
511	Ron Locke	5.00	2.50	1.50
512	Cap Peterson	5.00	2.50	1.50
513	Yankees Team	32.50	16.00	9.75
514	Joe Azcue	5.00	2.50	1.50
515	Vern Law	5.00	2.50	1.50
516	Al Weis	5.00	2.50	1.50
517	Angels Rookies (Paul Schaal, Jack Warner)	5.00	2.50	1.50
518	Ken Rowe	5.00	2.50	1.50
519	Bob Uecker	24.00	12.00	7.25
520	Tony Cloninger	5.00	2.50	1.50
521	Phillies Rookies (Dave Bennett, Morrie Stevens)	5.00	2.50	1.50
522	Hank Aguirre	5.00	2.50	1.50
523	Mike Brumley (SP)	10.00	5.00	3.00
524	Dave Giusti (SP)	10.00	5.00	3.00
525	Eddie Bressoud	5.00	2.50	1.50
526	Athletics Rookies (*Catfish Hunter*), (*Rene Lachemann*), (*Skip Lockwood*), (*Johnny*	65.00	32.00	19.50
527	Jeff Torborg	8.00	4.00	2.50
528	George Altman	5.00	2.50	1.50
529	Jerry Fosnow (SP)	10.00	5.00	3.00
530	Jim Maloney	5.00	2.50	1.50
531	Chuck Hiller	5.00	2.50	1.50
532	Hector Lopez	5.00	2.50	1.50
533	Mets Rookies (Jim Bethke), (*Tug McGraw*, Dan Napolean), (*Ron Swoboda*)	22.00	11.00	6.50
534	John Herrnstein	5.00	2.50	1.50
535	Jack Kralick (SP)	10.00	5.00	3.00
536	Andre Rodgers (SP)	10.00	5.00	3.00
537	Angels Rookies (Marcelino Lopez), (*Rudy May*, Phil Roof)	8.00	4.00	2.50
538	Chuck Dressen (SP)	10.00	5.00	3.00
539	Herm Starrette	5.00	2.50	1.50
540	Lou Brock	40.00	20.00	12.00
541	White Sox Rookies (Greg Bollo, Bob Locker)	5.00	2.50	1.50
542	Lou Klimchock	5.00	2.50	1.50
543	Ed Connolly (SP)	10.00	5.00	3.00
544	Howie Reed	5.00	2.50	1.50
545	Jesus Alou (SP)	10.00	5.00	3.00
546	Indians Rookies (Ray Barker, Bill Davis, Mike Hedlund, Floyd Weaver)	5.00	2.50	1.50
547	Jake Wood (SP)	10.00	5.00	3.00
548	Dick Stigman	5.00	2.50	1.50
549	Cubs Rookies (*Glenn Beckert*, Roberto Pena)	16.00	8.00	4.75
550	*Mel Stottlemyre*	24.00	12.00	7.25
551	Mets Team	22.50	11.00	6.75
552	Julio Gotay	5.00	2.50	1.50
553	Houston Rookies (Dan Coombs, Jack McClure, Gene Ratliff)	5.00	2.50	1.50
554	Chico Ruiz (SP)	10.00	5.00	3.00
555	Jack Baldschun (SP)	10.00	5.00	3.00
556	Red Schoendienst	16.00	8.00	4.75
557	Jose Santiago	5.00	2.50	1.50
558	Tommie Sisk	5.00	2.50	1.50
559	Ed Bailey (SP)	10.00	5.00	3.00
560	Boog Powell	17.50	8.75	5.25
561	Dodgers Rookies (Dennis Daboll), (*Mike Kekich*), (*Jim Lefebvre*, Hector Valle)	7.00	3.50	2.00
562	Billy Moran	5.00	2.50	1.50
563	Julio Navarro	5.00	2.50	1.50
564	Mel Nelson	5.00	2.50	1.50
565	Ernie Broglio (SP)	10.00	5.00	3.00
566	Yankees Rookies (Gil Blanco, Art Lopez, Ross Moschitto) (SP)	12.00	6.00	3.50
567	Tommie Aaron	5.00	2.50	1.50
568	Ron Taylor (SP)	10.00	5.00	3.00
569	Gino Cimoli (SP)	10.00	5.00	3.00
570	Claude Osteen (SP)	10.00	5.00	3.00
571	Ossie Virgil (SP)	10.00	5.00	3.00
572	Orioles Team	22.50	11.00	6.75
573	Red Sox Rookies (*Jim Lonborg*, Gerry Moses, Mike Ryan, Bill Schlesinger)	16.00	8.00	4.75
574	Roy Sievers	5.00	2.50	1.50
575	Jose Pagan	5.00	2.50	1.50
576	Terry Fox (SP)	10.00	5.00	3.00
577	A.L. Rookies (Jim Buschhorn, Darold Knowles, Richie Scheinblum) (SP)	10.00	5.00	3.00
578	Camilo Carreon (SP)	10.00	5.00	3.00
579	Dick Smith (SP)	10.00	5.00	3.00
580	Jimmie Hall (SP)	10.00	5.00	3.00
581	N.L. Rookies (Kevin Collins), (*Tony Perez*, Dave Ricketts)	55.00	27.00	16.50
582	Bob Schmidt (SP)	10.00	5.00	3.00
583	Wes Covington (SP)	10.00	5.00	3.00
584	Harry Bright	5.00	2.50	1.50
585	Hank Fischer	5.00	2.50	1.50
586	Tommy McCraw (SP)	10.00	5.00	3.00
587	Joe Sparma	5.00	2.50	1.50
588	Lenny Green	5.00	2.50	1.50
589	Giants Rookies (Frank Linzy, Bob Schroder) (SP)	10.00	5.00	3.00
590	Johnnie Wyatt	10.00	5.00	1.75
591	Bob Skinner (SP)	10.00	5.00	3.00
592	Frank Bork (SP)	10.00	5.00	3.00
593	Tigers Rookies (Jackie Moore, John Sullivan)	7.00	3.50	2.00
594	Joe Gaines	5.00	2.50	1.50
595	Don Lee	5.00	2.50	1.50
596	Don Landrum (SP)	10.00	5.00	3.00
597	Twins Rookies (Joe Nossek, Dick Reese, John Sevcik)	7.00	3.50	2.00
598	Al Downing	20.00	4.00	2.00

1965 Topps Embossed

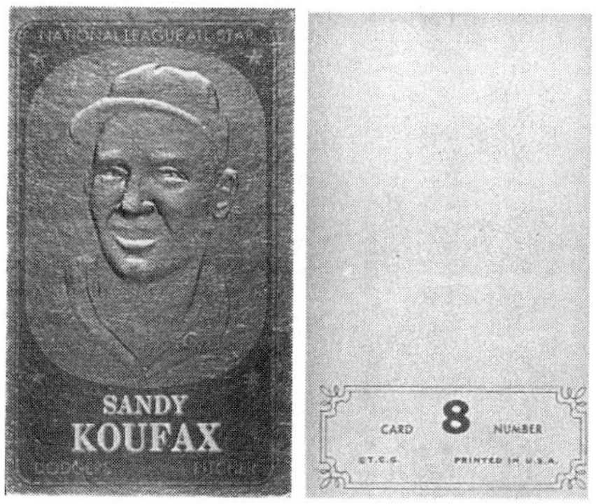

Inserted in regular packs, the 2-1/8" x 3-1/2" Topps Embossed cards are one of the more fascinating issues of the company. The fronts feature an embossed profile portrait on gold foil-like cardboard (some collectors report finding the cards with silver cardboard). The player's name, team and position are below the portrait - which is good, because most of the embossed portraits are otherwise unrecognizeable. There is a gold border with American players framed in blue and National Leaguers in red. The set contains 72 cards divided equally between the leagues. The set provides an inexpensive way to add some interesting cards to a collection. Being special cards, many stars appear in the set.

		NM	EX	VG
Complete Set (72):		410.00	205.00	125.00
Common Player:		3.00	1.50	.90
1	Carl Yastrzemski	12.00	6.00	3.50
2	Ron Fairly	3.00	1.50	.90
3	Max Alvis	3.00	1.50	.90
4	Jim Ray Hart	3.00	1.50	.90
5	Bill Skowron	4.50	2.25	1.25
6	Ed Kranepool	3.00	1.50	.90
7	Tim McCarver	4.50	2.25	1.25
8	Sandy Koufax	25.00	12.50	7.50
9	Donn Clendenon	3.00	1.50	.90
10	John Romano	3.00	1.50	.90
11	Mickey Mantle	40.00	20.00	12.00
12	Joe Torre	4.50	2.25	1.25
13	Al Kaline	12.00	6.00	3.50
14	Al McBean	3.00	1.50	.90
15	Don Drysdale	12.00	6.00	3.50
16	Brooks Robinson	13.50	6.75	4.00
17	Jim Bunning	9.00	4.50	2.75
18	Gary Peters	3.00	1.50	.90
19	Roberto Clemente	30.00	15.00	9.00
20	Milt Pappas	3.00	1.50	.90
21	Wayne Causey	3.00	1.50	.90
22	Frank Robinson	12.00	6.00	3.50
23	Bill Mazeroski	7.50	3.75	2.25
24	Diego Segui	3.00	1.50	.90
25	Jim Bouton	3.75	2.00	1.25
26	Ed Mathews	12.00	6.00	3.50
27	Willie Mays	25.00	12.50	7.50
28	Ron Santo	6.00	3.00	1.75
29	Boog Powell	4.50	2.25	1.25
30	Ken McBride	3.00	1.50	.90
31	Leon Wagner	3.00	1.50	.90
32	John Callison	3.00	1.50	.90
33	Zoilo Versalles	3.00	1.50	.90
34	Jack Baldschun	3.00	1.50	.90
35	Ron Hunt	3.00	1.50	.90
36	Richie Allen	6.00	3.00	1.75
37	Frank Malzone	3.00	1.50	.90
38	Bob Allison	3.00	1.50	.90
39	Jim Fregosi	3.00	1.50	.90
40	Billy Williams	9.00	4.50	2.75
41	Bill Freehan	3.00	1.50	.90
42	Vada Pinson	3.75	2.00	1.25
43	Bill White	3.00	1.50	.90
44	Roy McMillan	3.00	1.50	.90
45	Orlando Cepeda	9.00	4.50	2.75
46	Rocky Colavito	7.50	3.75	2.25
47	Ken Boyer	3.75	2.00	1.25
48	Dick Radatz	3.00	1.50	.90
49	Tommy Davis	3.00	1.50	.90
50	Wall Bond	3.00	1.50	.90
51	John Orsino	3.00	1.50	.90
52	Joe Christopher	3.00	1.50	.90
53	Al Spangler	3.00	1.50	.90
54	Jim King	3.00	1.50	.90
55	Mickey Lolich	3.75	2.00	1.25
56	Harmon Killebrew	10.00	5.00	3.00
57	Bob Shaw	3.00	1.50	.90
58	Ernie Banks	12.00	6.00	3.50
59	Hank Aaron	25.00	12.50	7.50
60	Chuck Hinton	3.00	1.50	.90
61	Bob Aspromonte	3.00	1.50	.90
62	Lee Maye	3.00	1.50	.90
63	Joe Cunningham	3.00	1.50	.90
64	Pete Ward	3.00	1.50	.90
65	Bobby Richardson	3.75	2.00	1.25
66	Dean Chance	3.00	1.50	.90
67	Dick Ellsworth	3.00	1.50	.90
68	Jim Maloney	3.00	1.50	.90
69	Bob Gibson	9.00	4.50	2.75
70	Earl Battey	3.00	1.50	.90
71	Tony Kubek	3.75	2.00	1.25
72	Jack Kralick	3.00	1.50	.90

1965 Topps Push-Pull

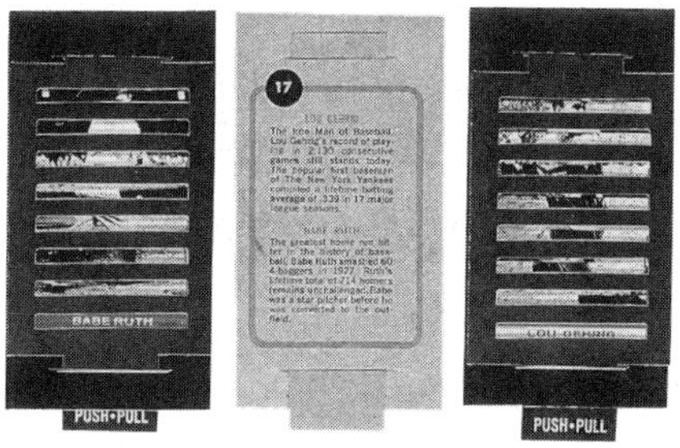

Part of a 36-card set combining sports and non-sport subjects, the Push-Pull novelties have a louvered shutter attached to a tab at the bottom. When the tab is moved, from position to position, each of the underlying photos is revealed in turn. The cards measure 2-1/2" x 4-11/16". Backs are printed in black-and-white and contain biographical data. Three of the cards in the set feature baseball players.

		NM	EX	VG
Complete Set (36):		1600.	800.00	475.00
Common Player:		10.00	5.00	3.00
(1)	Lou Gehrig, Babe Ruth	600.00	300.00	180.00
(2)	Casey Stengel Wins/Casey Stengel Loses (Casey Stengel) (smiling Casey/frowning Casey)	60.00	30.00	18.00
(3)	Yogi Berra, Mickey Mantle	800.00	400.00	240.00

1965 Topps Transfers

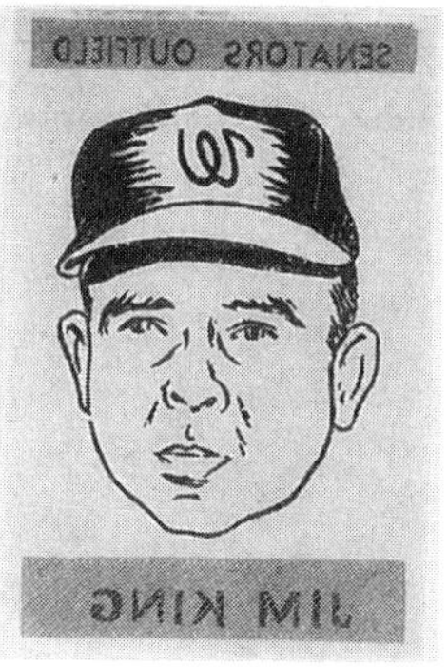

Issued as strips of three players each as inserts in 1965, the Topps Transfers were 2" x 3" portraits of players. The transfers have blue or red bands at the top and bottom with the team name and position in the top band and the player's name in the bottom. As is so often the case, the superstars in the transfer set can be quite expensive, but like many of Topps non-card products, the common transfers are neither terribly expensive or popular today.

		NM	EX	VG
Complete Set (72):		600.00	300.00	180.00
Common Player:		6.00	3.00	1.75
(1)	Hank Aaron	42.00	21.00	12.50
(2)	Richie Allen	12.00	6.00	3.50
(3)	Bob Allison	6.00	3.00	1.75
(4)	Max Alvis	6.00	3.00	1.75
(5)	Luis Aparicio	16.00	8.00	4.75
(6)	Bob Aspromonte	6.00	3.00	1.75
(7)	Walt Bond	6.00	3.00	1.75
(8)	Jim Bouton	9.00	4.50	2.75
(9)	Ken Boyer	10.00	5.00	3.00
(10)	Jim Bunning	17.50	8.75	5.25
(11)	John Callison	6.00	3.00	1.75
(12)	Rico Carty	6.00	3.00	1.75
(13)	Wayne Causey	6.00	3.00	1.75
(14)	Orlando Cepeda	18.00	9.00	5.50
(15)	Bob Chance	6.00	3.00	1.75
(16)	Dean Chance	6.00	3.00	1.75
(17)	Joe Christopher	6.00	3.00	1.75
(18)	Roberto Clemente	45.00	22.00	13.50
(19)	Rocky Colavito	15.00	7.50	4.50
(20)	Tony Conigliaro	10.00	5.00	3.00
(21)	Tommy Davis	6.00	3.00	1.75
(22)	Don Drysdale	18.00	9.00	5.50
(23)	Bill Freehan	6.00	3.00	1.75
(24)	Jim Fregosi	6.00	3.00	1.75
(25)	Bob Gibson	18.00	9.00	5.50
(26)	Dick Groat	6.00	3.00	1.75
(27)	Tom Haller	6.00	3.00	1.75
(28)	Chuck Hinton	6.00	3.00	1.75
(29)	Elston Howard	9.00	4.50	2.75
(30)	Ron Hunt	6.00	3.00	1.75
(31)	Al Jackson	6.00	3.00	1.75
(32)	Al Kaline	22.00	11.00	6.50
(33)	Harmon Killebrew	18.00	9.00	5.50
(34)	Jim King	6.00	3.00	1.75
(35)	Ron Kline	6.00	3.00	1.75
(36)	Bobby Knoop	6.00	3.00	1.75
(37)	Sandy Koufax	40.00	20.00	12.00
(38)	Ed Kranepool	6.00	3.00	1.75
(39)	Jim Maloney	6.00	3.00	1.75
(40)	Mickey Mantle	90.00	45.00	27.00
(41)	Juan Marichal	18.00	9.00	5.50
(42)	Lee Maye	6.00	3.00	1.75
(43)	Willie Mays	42.00	21.00	12.50
(44)	Bill Mazeroski	15.00	7.50	4.50
(45)	Tony Oliva	8.00	4.00	2.50
(46)	Jim O'Toole	6.00	3.00	1.75
(47)	Milt Pappas	6.00	3.00	1.75
(48)	Camilo Pascual	6.00	3.00	1.75
(49)	Gary Peters	6.00	3.00	1.75
(50)	Vada Pinson	6.00	3.00	1.75
(51)	Juan Pizarro	6.00	3.00	1.75
(52)	Boog Powell	10.00	5.00	3.00
(53)	Dick Radatz	6.00	3.00	1.75
(54)	Bobby Richardson	10.00	5.00	3.00
(55)	Brooks Robinson	22.00	11.00	6.50
(56)	Frank Robinson	18.00	9.00	5.50
(57)	Bob Rodgers	6.00	3.00	1.75
(58)	John Roseboro	6.00	3.00	1.75
(59)	Ron Santo	12.00	6.00	3.50
(60)	Diego Segui	6.00	3.00	1.75
(61)	Bill Skowron	10.00	5.00	3.00
(62)	Al Spangler	6.00	3.00	1.75
(63)	Dick Stuart	6.00	3.00	1.75
(64)	Luis Tiant	6.00	3.00	1.75
(65)	Joe Torre	10.00	5.00	3.00
(66)	Bob Veale	6.00	3.00	1.75
(67)	Leon Wagner	6.00	3.00	1.75
(68)	Pete Ward	6.00	3.00	1.75
(69)	Bill White	6.00	3.00	1.75
(70)	Dave Wickersham	6.00	3.00	1.75
(71)	Billy Williams	17.50	8.75	5.25
(72)	Carl Yastrzemski	22.00	11.00	6.50

1966 Topps

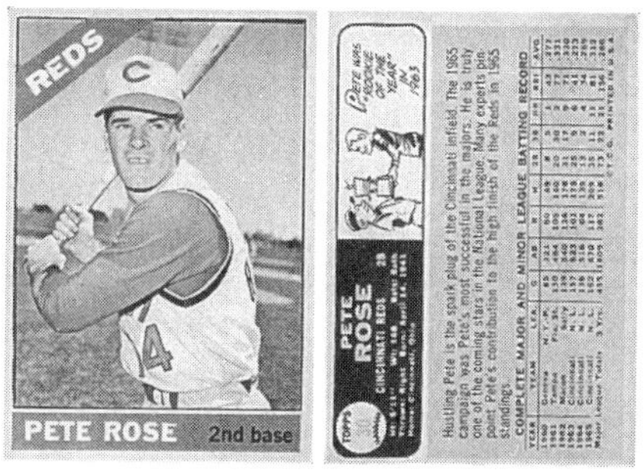

In 1966, Topps produced another 598-card set. The 2-1/2" x 3-1/2" cards feature the traditional color photograph with a diagonal strip in the upper left-hand corner carrying the team name. A band at the bottom carries the player's name and position. Multi-player cards returned in 1966 after a year's hiatus. The statistical leader cards feature the categorical leader and two runners-up. Most team managers have cards as well. The 1966 set features a handful of cards found with or without a notice of the player's sale or trade to another team. Cards without the notice bring higher prices and are not included in the complete set prices. Some cards in the high series (#523-598) were short-printed - produced in lesser quantities than the rest of the series. They are valued somewhat higher than the others and are indicated in the checklist by an (SP) notation following the player name.

		NM	EX	VG
Complete Set (598):		2750.	1350.	825.00
Common Player (1-109):		1.50	.75	.45
Common Player (110-283):		2.00	1.00	.60
Common Player (284-370):		2.50	1.25	.75
Common Player (371-446):		5.00	2.50	1.50
Common Player (447-522):		8.00	4.00	2.50
Common Player (523-598):		12.50	6.25	3.75
1	Willie Mays	95.00	45.00	25.00
2	Ted Abernathy	1.50	.70	.45
3	Sam Mele	1.50	.70	.45
4	Ray Culp	1.50	.70	.45
5	Jim Fregosi	1.50	.70	.45
6	Chuck Schilling	1.50	.70	.45
7	Tracy Stallard	1.50	.70	.45
8	Floyd Robinson	1.50	.70	.45

9	Clete Boyer	2.00	1.00	.60
10	Tony Cloninger	1.50	.70	.45
11	Senators Rookies (Brant Alyea, Pete Craig)	1.50	.70	.45
12	John Tsitouris	1.50	.70	.45
13	Lou Johnson	1.50	.70	.45
14	Norm Siebern	1.50	.70	.45
15	Vern Law	1.50	.70	.45
16	Larry Brown	1.50	.70	.45
17	Johnny Stephenson	1.50	.70	.45
18	Roland Sheldon	1.50	.70	.45
19	Giants Team	3.00	1.50	.90
20	Willie Horton	1.50	.70	.45
21	Don Nottebart	1.50	.70	.45
22	Joe Nossek	1.50	.70	.45
23	Jack Sanford	1.50	.70	.45
24	*Don Kessinger*	4.50	2.25	1.25
25	Pete Ward	1.50	.70	.45
26	Ray Sadecki	1.50	.70	.45
27	Orioles Rookies (*Andy Etchebarren*, Darold Knowles)	2.00	1.00	.60
28	Phil Niekro	14.50	7.25	4.25
29	Mike Brumley	1.50	.70	.45
30	Pete Rose	32.50	16.00	9.75
31	Jack Cullen	1.50	.70	.45
32	Adolfo Phillips	1.50	.70	.45
33	Jim Pagliaroni	1.50	.70	.45
34	Checklist 1-88	6.00	3.00	1.75
35	Ron Swoboda	1.50	.70	.45
36	Catfish Hunter	15.00	7.50	4.50
37	Billy Herman	2.50	1.25	.70
38	Ron Nischwitz	1.50	.70	.45
39	Ken Henderson	1.50	.70	.45
40	Jim Grant	1.50	.70	.45
41	Don LeJohn	1.50	.70	.45
42	Aubrey Gatewood	1.50	.70	.45
43	Don Landrum	1.50	.70	.45
44	Indians Rookies (Bill Davis, Tom Kelley)	1.50	.70	.45
45	Jim Gentile	1.50	.70	.45
46	Howie Koplitz	1.50	.70	.45
47	J.C. Martin	1.50	.70	.45
48	Paul Blair	1.50	.70	.45
49	Woody Woodward	1.50	.70	.45
50	Mickey Mantle	225.00	100.00	65.00
51	Gordon Richardson	1.50	.70	.45
52	Power Plus (Johnny Callison, Wes Covington)	2.00	1.00	.60
53	Bob Duliba	1.50	.70	.45
54	Jose Pagan	1.50	.70	.45
55	Ken Harrelson	1.50	.70	.45
56	Sandy Valdespino	1.50	.70	.45
57	Jim Lefebvre	1.50	.70	.45
58	Dave Wickersham	1.50	.70	.45
59	Reds Team	3.50	1.75	1.00
60	Curt Flood	2.00	1.00	.60
61	Bob Bolin	1.50	.70	.45
62a	Merritt Ranew (no sold statement)	36.00	18.00	11.00
62b	Merritt Ranew (with sold statement)	1.50	.70	.45
63	Jim Stewart	1.50	.70	.45
64	Bob Bruce	1.50	.70	.45
65	Leon Wagner	1.50	.70	.45
66	Al Weis	1.50	.70	.45
67	Mets Rookies (Cleon Jones, Dick Selma)	2.00	1.00	.60
68	Hal Reniff	1.50	.70	.45
69	Ken Hamlin	1.50	.70	.45
70	Carl Yastrzemski	22.00	11.00	6.50
71	Frank Carpin	1.50	.70	.45
72	Tony Perez	20.00	10.00	6.00
73	Jerry Zimmerman	1.50	.70	.45
74	Don Mossi	1.50	.70	.45
75	Tommy Davis	1.50	.70	.45
76	Red Schoendienst	3.50	1.75	1.00
77	Johnny Orsino	1.50	.70	.45
78	Frank Linzy	1.50	.70	.45
79	Joe Pepitone	1.50	.70	.45
80	Richie Allen	5.00	2.50	1.50
81	Ray Oyler	1.50	.70	.45
82	Bob Hendley	1.50	.70	.45
83	Albie Pearson	1.50	.70	.45
84	Braves Rookies (Jim Beauchamp, Dick Kelley)	1.50	.70	.45
85	Eddie Fisher	1.50	.70	.45
86	John Bateman	1.50	.70	.45
87	Dan Napoleon	1.50	.70	.45
88	Fred Whitfield	1.50	.70	.45
89	Ted Davidson	1.50	.70	.45
90	Luis Aparicio	6.00	3.00	1.75
91a	Bob Uecker (no trade statement)	48.00	24.00	14.50
91b	Bob Uecker (with trade statement)	10.00	5.00	3.00
92	Yankees Team	8.50	4.25	2.50
93	Jim Lonborg	1.50	.70	.45
94	Matty Alou	1.50	.70	.45
95	Pete Richert	1.50	.70	.45
96	Felipe Alou	3.00	1.50	.90
97	Jim Merritt	1.50	.70	.45
98	Don Demeter	1.50	.70	.45
99	Buc Belters (Donn Clendenon, Willie Stargell)	5.00	2.50	1.50
100	Sandy Koufax	70.00	35.00	21.00
101a	Checklist 89-176 (115 is Spahn)	11.00	5.50	3.25
101b	Checklist 89-176 (115 is Henry)	5.00	2.50	1.50
102	Ed Kirkpatrick	1.50	.70	.45
103a	Dick Groat (no trade statement)	25.00	12.50	7.50
103b	Dick Groat (with trade statement)	3.00	1.50	.90
104a	Alex Johnson (no trade statement)	32.00	16.00	9.50
104b	Alex Johnson (with trade statement)	1.50	.70	.45
105	Milt Pappas	2.00	1.00	.60
106	Rusty Staub	4.00	2.00	1.25
107	Athletics Rookies (Larry Stahl, Ron Tompkins)	2.00	1.00	.60
108	Bobby Klaus	2.00	1.00	.60
109	Ralph Terry	2.00	1.00	.60
110	Ernie Banks	26.00	13.00	7.75
111	Gary Peters	2.00	1.00	.60
112	Manny Mota	2.00	1.00	.60
113	Hank Aguirre	2.00	1.00	.60
114	Jim Gosger	2.00	1.00	.60
115	Bill Henry	2.00	1.00	.60
116	Walt Alston	4.00	2.00	1.25
117	Jake Gibbs	2.00	1.00	.60
118	Mike McCormick	2.00	1.00	.60
119	Art Shamsky	2.00	1.00	.60
120	Harmon Killebrew	13.00	6.50	4.00
121	Ray Herbert	2.00	1.00	.60
122	Joe Gaines	2.00	1.00	.60
123	Pirates Rookies (Frank Bork, Jerry May)	2.00	1.00	.60
124	Tug McGraw	3.00	1.50	.90
125	Lou Brock	17.50	8.75	5.25
126	*Jim Palmer*	75.00	37.00	22.00
127	Ken Berry	2.00	1.00	.60
128	Jim Landis	2.00	1.00	.60
129	Jack Kralick	2.00	1.00	.60
130	Joe Torre	4.00	2.00	1.25
131	Angels Team	3.50	1.75	1.00
132	Orlando Cepeda	16.00	8.00	4.75
133	Don McMahon	2.00	1.00	.60
134	Wes Parker	2.00	1.00	.60
135	Dave Morehead	2.00	1.00	.60
136	Woody Held	2.00	1.00	.60
137	Pat Corrales	2.00	1.00	.60
138	Roger Repoz	2.00	1.00	.60
139	Cubs Rookies (Byron Browne, Don Young)	2.00	1.00	.60
140	Jim Maloney	2.00	1.00	.60
141	Tom McCraw	2.00	1.00	.60
142	Don Dennis	2.00	1.00	.60
143	Jose Tartabull	2.00	1.00	.60
144	Don Schwall	2.00	1.00	.60
145	Bill Freehan	2.50	1.25	.70
146	George Altman	2.00	1.00	.60
147	Lum Harris	2.00	1.00	.60
148	Bob Johnson	2.00	1.00	.60
149	Dick Nen	2.00	1.00	.60
150	Rocky Colavito	7.50	3.75	2.25
151	Gary Wagner	2.00	1.00	.60
152	Frank Malzone	2.00	1.00	.60
153	Rico Carty	2.00	1.00	.60
154	Chuck Hiller	2.00	1.00	.60
155	Marcelino Lopez	2.00	1.00	.60
156	D P Combo (Hal Lanier, Dick Schofield)	2.50	1.25	.70
157	Rene Lachemann	2.00	1.00	.60
158	Jim Brewer	2.00	1.00	.60
159	Chico Ruiz	2.00	1.00	.60
160	Whitey Ford	24.00	12.00	7.25
161	Jerry Lumpe	2.00	1.00	.60
162	Lee Maye	2.00	1.00	.60
163	Tito Francona	2.00	1.00	.60
164	White Sox Rookies (Tommie Agee, Marv Staehle)	2.50	1.25	.70
165	Don Lock	2.00	1.00	.60
166	Chris Krug	2.00	1.00	.60
167	Boog Powell	3.50	1.75	1.00
168	Dan Osinski	2.00	1.00	.60
169	Duke Sims	2.00	1.00	.60
170	Cookie Rojas	2.00	1.00	.60
171	Nick Willhite	2.00	1.00	.60
172	Mets Team	4.50	2.25	1.25
173	Al Spangler	2.00	1.00	.60
174	Ron Taylor	2.00	1.00	.60
175	Bert Campaneris	2.50	1.25	.70
176	Jim Davenport	2.00	1.00	.60
177	Hector Lopez	2.00	1.00	.60
178	Bob Tillman	2.00	1.00	.60
179	Cardinals Rookies (Dennis Aust, Bob Tolan)	2.00	1.00	.60
180	Vada Pinson	2.50	1.25	.70
181	Al Worthington	2.00	1.00	.60
182	Jerry Lynch	2.00	1.00	.60
183a	Checklist 177-264 (large print on front)	6.00	3.00	1.75
183b	Checklist 177-264 (small print on front)	9.00	4.50	2.75
184	Denis Menke	2.00	1.00	.60
185	Bob Buhl	2.00	1.00	.60
186	Ruben Amaro	2.00	1.00	.60
187	Chuck Dressen	2.00	1.00	.60
188	Al Luplow	2.00	1.00	.60
189	John Roseboro	2.00	1.00	.60
190	Jimmie Hall	2.00	1.00	.60
191	Darrell Sutherland	2.00	1.00	.60
192	Vic Power	2.00	1.00	.60
193	Dave McNally	2.00	1.00	.60
194	Senators Team	6.00	3.00	1.75
195	Joe Morgan	12.00	6.00	3.50
196	Don Pavletich	2.00	1.00	.60
197	Sonny Siebert	2.00	1.00	.60
198	*Mickey Stanley*	3.00	1.50	.90
199	Chisox Clubbers (Floyd Robinson, Johnny Romano, Bill Skowron)	2.50	1.25	.70
200	Eddie Mathews	12.50	6.25	3.75
201	Jim Dickson	2.00	1.00	.60
202	Clay Dalrymple	2.00	1.00	.60
203	Jose Santiago	2.00	1.00	.60
204	Cubs Team	5.00	2.50	1.50
205	Tom Tresh	3.50	1.75	1.00
206	Alvin Jackson	2.00	1.00	.60
207	Frank Quilici	2.00	1.00	.60
208	Bob Miller	2.00	1.00	.60
209	Tigers Rookies (Fritz Fisher), (*John Hiller*)	2.00	1.00	.60
210	Bill Mazeroski	8.00	4.00	2.50
211	Frank Kreutzer	2.00	1.00	.60
212	Ed Kranepool	2.00	1.00	.60
213	Fred Newman	2.00	1.00	.60
214	Tommy Harper	2.00	1.00	.60
215	N.L. Batting Leaders (Hank Aaron, Roberto Clemente, Willie Mays)	40.00	20.00	12.00
216	A.L. Batting Leaders (Vic Davalillo, Tony Oliva, Carl Yastrzemski)	6.00	3.00	1.75
217	N.L. Home Run Leaders (Willie Mays, Willie McCovey, Billy Williams)	19.00	9.50	5.75
218	A.L. Home Run Leaders (Norm Cash, Tony Conigliaro, Willie Horton)	4.50	2.25	1.25
219	N.L. RBI Leaders (Deron Johnson, Willie Mays, Frank Robinson)	11.00	5.50	3.25
220	A.L. RBI Leaders (Rocky Colavito, Willie Horton, Tony Oliva)	5.00	2.50	1.50
221	N.L. ERA Leaders (Sandy Koufax, Vern Law, Juan Marichal)	9.00	4.50	2.75
222	A.L. ERA Leaders (Eddie Fisher, Sam McDowell, Sonny Siebert)	5.00	2.50	1.50
223	N.L. Pitching Leaders (Tony Cloninger, Don Drysdale, Sandy Koufax)	12.00	6.00	3.50
224	A.L. Pitching Leaders (Jim Grant, Jim Kaat, Mel Stottlemyre)	5.00	2.50	1.50
225	N.L. Strikeout Leaders (Bob Gibson, Sandy Koufax, Bob Veale)	11.00	5.50	3.25
226	A.L. Strikeout Leaders (Mickey Lolich, Sam McDowell, Denny McLain, Sonny Siebert)	4.50	2.25	1.25
227	Russ Nixon	2.00	1.00	.60
228	Larry Dierker	2.00	1.00	.60
229	Hank Bauer	2.00	1.00	.60
230	Johnny Callison	2.00	1.00	.60
231	Floyd Weaver	2.00	1.00	.60
232	Glenn Beckert	2.00	1.00	.60
233	Dom Zanni	2.00	1.00	.60
234	Yankees Rookies (Rich Beck), (*Roy White*)	6.00	3.00	1.75
235	Don Cardwell	2.00	1.00	.60
236	Mike Hershberger	2.00	1.00	.60
237	Billy O'Dell	2.00	1.00	.60
238	Dodgers Team	6.00	3.00	1.75
239	Orlando Pena	2.00	1.00	.60
240	Earl Battey	2.00	1.00	.60
241	Dennis Ribant	2.00	1.00	.60
242	Jesus Alou	2.00	1.00	.60
243	Nelson Briles	2.00	1.00	.60
244	Astros Rookies (Chuck Harrison, Sonny Jackson)	2.00	1.00	.60
245	John Buzhardt	2.00	1.00	.60
246	Ed Bailey	2.00	1.00	.60
247	Carl Warwick	2.00	1.00	.60
248	Pete Mikkelsen	2.00	1.00	.60
249	Bill Rigney	2.00	1.00	.60
250	Sam Ellis	2.00	1.00	.60
251	Ed Brinkman	2.00	1.00	.60
252	Denver Lemaster	2.00	1.00	.60
253	Don Wert	2.00	1.00	.60
254	Phillies Rookies (*Fergie Jenkins*, Bill Sorrell)	60.00	30.00	18.00
255	Willie Stargell	17.00	8.50	5.00
256	Lew Krausse	2.00	1.00	.60
257	Jeff Torborg	2.00	1.00	.60
258	Dave Giusti	2.00	1.00	.60
259	Red Sox Team	5.00	2.50	1.50
260	Bob Shaw	2.00	1.00	.60
261	Ron Hansen	2.00	1.00	.60
262	Jack Hamilton	2.00	1.00	.60
263	Tom Egan	2.00	1.00	.60
264	Twins Rookies (Andy Kosco, Ted Uhlaender)	2.00	1.00	.60
265	Stu Miller	2.00	1.00	.60
266	Pedro Gonzalez	2.00	1.00	.60
267	Joe Sparma	2.00	1.00	.60
268	John Blanchard	2.00	1.00	.60
269	Don Heffner	2.00	1.00	.60
270	Claude Osteen	2.00	1.00	.60
271	Hal Lanier	2.00	1.00	.60
272	Jack Baldschun	2.00	1.00	.60
273	Astro Aces (Bob Aspromonte, Rusty Staub)	7.50	3.75	2.25
274	Buster Narum	2.00	1.00	.60
275	Tim McCarver	3.50	1.75	1.00
276	Jim Bouton	2.00	1.00	.60
277	George Thomas	2.00	1.00	.60
278	Calvin Koonce	2.50	1.25	.70
279a	Checklist 265-352 (player's cap black)	8.00	4.00	2.50
279b	Checklist 265-352 (player's cap red)	5.00	2.50	1.50
280	Bobby Knoop	2.50	1.25	.70
281	Bruce Howard	2.50	1.25	.70
282	Johnny Lewis	2.50	1.25	.70
283	Jim Perry	3.00	1.50	.90
284	Bobby Wine	2.50	1.25	.70
285	Luis Tiant	5.00	2.50	1.50
286	Gary Geiger	2.50	1.25	.70
287	Jack Aker	2.50	1.25	.70
288	Dodgers Rookies (*Bill Singer*), (*Don Sutton*)	65.00	32.00	19.50
289	Larry Sherry	2.50	1.25	.70
290	Ron Santo	9.00	4.50	2.75
291	Moe Drabowsky	2.50	1.25	.70
292	Jim Coker	2.50	1.25	.70
293	Mike Shannon	2.50	1.25	.70
294	Steve Ridzik	2.50	1.25	.70

295	Jim Hart	2.50	1.25	.70
296	Johnny Keane	2.50	1.25	.70
297	Jim Owens	2.50	1.25	.70
298	Rico Petrocelli	2.50	1.25	.70
299	Lou Burdette	2.50	1.25	.70
300	Roberto Clemente	95.00	45.00	28.00
301	Greg Bollo	2.50	1.25	.70
302	Ernie Bowman	2.50	1.25	.70
303	Indians Team	6.00	3.00	1.75
304	John Herrnstein	2.50	1.25	.70
305	Camilo Pascual	2.50	1.25	.70
306	Ty Cline	2.50	1.25	.70
307	Clay Carroll	2.50	1.25	.70
308	Tom Haller	2.50	1.25	.70
309	Diego Segui	2.50	1.25	.70
310	Frank Robinson	25.00	12.50	7.50
311	Reds Rookies (Tommy Helms, Dick Simpson)	2.50	1.25	.70
312	Bob Saverine	2.50	1.25	.70
313	Chris Zachary	2.50	1.25	.70
314	Hector Valle	2.50	1.25	.70
315	Norm Cash	3.00	1.50	.90
316	Jack Fisher	2.50	1.25	.70
317	Dalton Jones	2.50	1.25	.70
318	Harry Walker	2.50	1.25	.70
319	Gene Freese	2.50	1.25	.70
320	Bob Gibson	22.00	11.00	6.50
321	Rick Reichardt	2.50	1.25	.70
322	Bill Faul	2.50	1.25	.70
323	Ray Barker	2.50	1.25	.70
324	John Boozer	2.50	1.25	.70
325	Vic Davalillo	2.50	1.25	.70
326	Braves Team	5.00	2.50	1.50
327	Bernie Allen	2.50	1.25	.70
328	Jerry Grote	2.50	1.25	.70
329	Pete Charton	2.50	1.25	.70
330	Ron Fairly	2.50	1.25	.70
331	Ron Herbel	2.50	1.25	.70
332	Billy Bryan	2.50	1.25	.70
333	Senators Rookies (*Joe Coleman*, Jim French)	2.50	1.25	.70
334	Marty Keough	2.50	1.25	.70
335	Juan Pizarro	2.50	1.25	.70
336	Gene Alley	2.50	1.25	.70
337	Fred Gladding	2.50	1.25	.70
338	Dal Maxvill	2.50	1.25	.70
339	Del Crandall	2.50	1.25	.70
340	Dean Chance	2.50	1.25	.70
341	Wes Westrum	2.50	1.25	.70
342	Bob Humphreys	2.50	1.25	.70
343	Joe Christopher	2.50	1.25	.70
344	Steve Blass	2.50	1.25	.70
345	Bob Allison	2.50	1.25	.70
346	Mike de la Hoz	2.50	1.25	.70
347	Phil Regan	2.50	1.25	.70
348	Orioles Team	6.00	3.00	1.75
349	Cap Peterson	2.50	1.25	.70
350	Mel Stottlemyre	2.50	1.25	.70
351	Fred Valentine	2.50	1.25	.70
352	Bob Aspromonte	2.50	1.25	.70
353	Al McBean	2.50	1.25	.70
354	Smoky Burgess	2.50	1.25	.70
355	Wade Blasingame	2.50	1.25	.70
356	Red Sox Rookies (Owen Johnson, Ken Sanders)	2.50	1.25	.70
357	Gerry Arrigo	2.50	1.25	.70
358	Charlie Smith	2.50	1.25	.70
359	Johnny Briggs	2.50	1.25	.70
360	Ron Hunt	2.50	1.25	.70
361	Tom Satriano	2.50	1.25	.70
362	Gates Brown	2.50	1.25	.70
363	Checklist 353-429	8.00	4.00	2.50
364	Nate Oliver	2.50	1.25	.70
365	Roger Maris	45.00	22.00	13.50
366	Wayne Causey	2.50	1.25	.70
367	Mel Nelson	2.50	1.25	.70
368	Charlie Lau	2.50	1.25	.70
369	Jim King	2.50	1.25	.70
370	Chico Cardenas	2.50	1.25	.70
371	Lee Stange	5.00	2.50	1.50
372	Harvey Kuenn	5.00	2.50	1.50
373	Giants Rookies (Dick Estelle, Jack Hiatt)	5.00	2.50	1.50
374	Bob Locker	5.00	2.50	1.50
375	Donn Clendenon	5.00	2.50	1.50
376	Paul Schaal	5.00	2.50	1.50
377	Turk Farrell	5.00	2.50	1.50
378	Dick Tracewski	5.00	2.50	1.50
379	Cardinals Team	8.50	4.25	2.50
380	Tony Conigliaro	10.00	5.00	3.00
381	Hank Fischer	5.00	2.50	1.50
382	Phil Roof	5.00	2.50	1.50
383	Jackie Brandt	5.00	2.50	1.50
384	Al Downing	5.00	2.50	1.50
385	Ken Boyer	5.00	2.50	1.50
386	Gil Hodges	12.00	6.00	3.50
387	Howie Reed	5.00	2.50	1.50
388	Don Mincher	5.00	2.50	1.50
389	Jim O'Toole	5.00	2.50	1.50
390	Brooks Robinson	40.00	20.00	12.00
391	Chuck Hinton	5.00	2.50	1.50
392	Cubs Rookies (*Bill Hands*), (*Randy Hundley*)	6.50	3.25	2.00
393	George Brunet	5.00	2.50	1.50
394	Ron Brand	5.00	2.50	1.50
395	Len Gabrielson	5.00	2.50	1.50
396	Jerry Stephenson	5.00	2.50	1.50
397	Bill White	5.00	2.50	1.50
398	Danny Cater	5.00	2.50	1.50
399	Ray Washburn	5.00	2.50	1.50
400	Zoilo Versalles	5.00	2.50	1.50
401	Ken McMullen	5.00	2.50	1.50
402	Jim Hickman	5.00	2.50	1.50
403	Fred Talbot	5.00	2.50	1.50
404	Pirates Team	9.00	4.50	2.75
405	Elston Howard	6.00	3.00	1.75
406	Joe Jay	5.00	2.50	1.50
407	John Kennedy	5.00	2.50	1.50
408	Lee Thomas	5.00	2.50	1.50
409	Billy Hoeft	5.00	2.50	1.50
410	Al Kaline	28.00	14.00	8.50
411	Gene Mauch	5.00	2.50	1.50
412	Sam Bowens	5.00	2.50	1.50
413	John Romano	5.00	2.50	1.50
414	Dan Coombs	5.00	2.50	1.50
415	Max Alvis	5.00	2.50	1.50
416	Phil Ortega	5.00	2.50	1.50
417	Angels Rookies (Jim McGlothlin, Ed Sukla)	5.00	2.50	1.50
418	Phil Gagliano	5.00	2.50	1.50
419	Mike Ryan	5.00	2.50	1.50
420	Juan Marichal	14.00	7.00	4.25
421	Roy McMillan	5.00	2.50	1.50
422	Ed Charles	5.00	2.50	1.50
423	Ernie Broglio	5.00	2.50	1.50
424	Reds Rookies (*Lee May*, Darrell Osteen)	8.00	4.00	2.50
425	Bob Veale	5.00	2.50	1.50
426	White Sox Team	8.00	4.00	2.50
427	John Miller	5.00	2.50	1.50
428	Sandy Alomar	5.50	2.75	1.75
429	Bill Monbouquette	5.00	2.50	1.50
430	Don Drysdale	18.00	9.00	5.50
431	Walt Bond	5.00	2.50	1.50
432	Bob Heffner	5.00	2.50	1.50
433	Alvin Dark	5.00	2.50	1.50
434	Willie Kirkland	5.00	2.50	1.50
435	Jim Bunning	12.00	6.00	3.50
436	Julian Javier	5.00	2.50	1.50
437	Al Stanek	5.00	2.50	1.50
438	Willie Smith	5.00	2.50	1.50
439	Pedro Ramos	5.00	2.50	1.50
440	Deron Johnson	5.00	2.50	1.50
441	Tommie Sisk	5.00	2.50	1.50
442	Orioles Rookies (Ed Barnowski, Eddie Watt)	5.00	2.50	1.50
443	Bill Wakefield	5.00	2.50	1.50
444a	Checklist 430-506 (456 is R. Sox Rookies)	5.00	2.50	1.50
444b	Checklist 430-506 (456 is Red Sox Rookies)	8.00	4.00	2.50
445	Jim Kaat	8.00	4.00	2.50
446	Mack Jones	5.00	2.50	1.50
447	Dick Ellsworth (photo actually Ken Hubbs)	10.00	5.00	3.00
448	Eddie Stanky	8.00	4.00	2.50
449	Joe Moeller	8.00	4.00	2.50
450	Tony Oliva	10.00	5.00	3.00
451	Barry Latman	8.00	4.00	2.50
452	Joe Azcue	8.00	4.00	2.50
453	Ron Kline	8.00	4.00	2.50
454	Jerry Buchek	8.00	4.00	2.50
455	Mickey Lolich	10.00	5.00	3.00
456	Red Sox Rookies (Darrell Brandon, Joe Foy)	8.00	4.00	2.50
457	Joe Gibbon	8.00	4.00	2.50
458	Manny Jiminez (Jimenez)	8.00	4.00	2.50
459	Bill McCool	8.00	4.00	2.50
460	Curt Blefary	8.00	4.00	2.50
461	Roy Face	8.00	4.00	2.50
462	Bob Rodgers	8.00	4.00	2.50
463	Phillies Team	11.00	5.50	3.25
464	Larry Bearnarth	8.00	4.00	2.50
465	Don Buford	8.00	4.00	2.50
466	Ken Johnson	8.00	4.00	2.50
467	Vic Roznovsky	8.00	4.00	2.50
468	Johnny Podres	8.00	4.00	2.50
469	Yankees Rookies (*Bobby Murcer*, Dooley Womack)	24.00	12.00	7.25
470	Sam McDowell	8.00	4.00	2.50
471	Bob Skinner	8.00	4.00	2.50
472	Terry Fox	8.00	4.00	2.50
473	Rich Rollins	8.00	4.00	2.50
474	Dick Schofield	8.00	4.00	2.50
475	Dick Radatz	8.00	4.00	2.50
476	Bobby Bragan	8.00	4.00	2.50
477	Steve Barber	8.00	4.00	2.50
478	Tony Gonzalez	8.00	4.00	2.50
479	Jim Hannan	8.00	4.00	2.50
480	Dick Stuart	8.00	4.00	2.50
481	Bob Lee	8.00	4.00	2.50
482	Cubs Rookies (John Boccabella, Dave Dowling)	8.00	4.00	2.50
483	Joe Nuxhall	8.00	4.00	2.50
484	Wes Covington	8.00	4.00	2.50
485	Bob Bailey	8.00	4.00	2.50
486	Tommy John	9.00	4.50	2.75
487	Al Ferrara	8.00	4.00	2.50
488	George Banks	8.00	4.00	2.50
489	Curt Simmons	8.00	4.00	2.50
490	Bobby Richardson	14.00	7.00	4.25
491	Dennis Bennett	8.00	4.00	2.50
492	Athletics Team	12.00	6.00	3.50
493	Johnny Klippstein	8.00	4.00	2.50
494	Gordon Coleman	8.00	4.00	2.50
495	Dick McAuliffe	8.00	4.00	2.50
496	Lindy McDaniel	8.00	4.00	2.50
497	Chris Cannizzaro	8.00	4.00	2.50
498	Pirates Rookies (*Woody Fryman*, Luke Walker)	8.00	4.00	2.50
499	Wally Bunker	8.00	4.00	2.50
500	Hank Aaron	100.00	50.00	30.00
501	John O'Donoghue	8.00	4.00	2.50
502	Lenny Green	8.00	4.00	2.50
503	Steve Hamilton	8.00	4.00	2.50
504	Grady Hatton	8.00	4.00	2.50
505	Jose Cardenal	8.00	4.00	2.50
506	Bo Belinsky	8.00	4.00	2.50
507	John Edwards	8.00	4.00	2.50
508	*Steve Hargan*	8.00	4.00	2.50
509	Jake Wood	8.00	4.00	2.50
510	Hoyt Wilhelm	12.00	6.00	3.50
511	Giants Rookies (Bob Barton), (*Tito Fuentes*)	8.00	4.00	2.50
512	Dick Stigman	8.00	4.00	2.50
513	Camilo Carreon	8.00	4.00	2.50
514	Hal Woodeshick	8.00	4.00	2.50
515	Frank Howard	10.00	5.00	3.00
516	Eddie Bressoud	8.00	4.00	2.50
517a	Checklist 507-598 (529 is W. Sox Rookies)	12.00	6.00	3.50
517b	Checklist 506-598 (529 is White Sox Rookies)	15.00	7.50	4.50
518	Braves Rookies (Herb Hippauf, Arnie Umbach)	8.00	4.00	2.50
519	Bob Friend	8.00	4.00	2.50
520	Jim Wynn	8.00	4.00	2.50
521	John Wyatt	8.00	4.00	2.50
522	Phil Linz	8.00	4.00	2.50
523	Bob Sadowski	12.50	6.25	3.75
524	Giants Rookies (Ollie Brown, Don Mason) (SP)	22.50	11.00	6.75
525	Gary Bell (SP)	22.50	11.00	6.75
526	Twins Team	75.00	37.00	22.00
527	Julio Navarro	12.50	6.25	3.75
528	Jesse Gonder (SP)	22.50	11.00	6.75
529	White Sox Rookies (*Lee Elia*, Dennis Higgins, Bill Voss)	12.50	6.25	3.75
530	Robin Roberts	44.00	22.00	13.00
531	Joe Cunningham	12.50	6.25	3.75
532	Aurelio Monteagudo (SP)	22.50	11.00	6.75
533	Jerry Adair (SP)	22.50	11.00	6.75
534	Mets Rookies (Dave Eilers, Rob Gardner)	12.50	6.25	3.75
535	Willie Davis	20.00	10.00	6.00
536	Dick Egan	12.50	6.25	3.75
537	Herman Franks	12.50	6.25	3.75
538	Bob Allen (SP)	22.50	11.00	6.75
539	Astros Rookies (Bill Heath, Carroll Sembera)	12.50	6.25	3.75
540	Denny McLain (SP)	70.00	35.00	21.00
541	Gene Oliver (SP)	22.50	11.00	6.75
542	George Smith	12.50	6.25	3.75
543	Roger Craig	17.50	8.75	5.25
544	Cardinals Rookies (Joe Hoerner, George Kernek, Jimmy Williams) (SP)	22.50	11.00	6.75
545	Dick Green (SP)	22.50	11.00	6.75
546	Dwight Siebler	12.50	6.25	3.75
547	*Horace Clarke* (SP)	36.00	18.00	11.00
548	Gary Kroll (SP)	22.50	11.00	6.75
549	Senators Rookies (Al Closter, Casey Cox)	12.50	6.25	3.75
550	Willie McCovey (SP)	70.00	35.00	21.00
551	Bob Purkey (SP)	22.50	11.00	6.75
552	Birdie Tebbetts (SP)	22.50	11.00	6.75
553	Major League Rookies (Pat Garrett, Jackie Warner)	12.50	6.25	3.75
554	Jim Northrup (SP)	22.50	11.00	6.75
555	Ron Perranoski (SP)	25.00	12.50	7.50
556	Mel Queen (SP)	22.50	11.00	6.75
557	Felix Mantilla (SP)	22.50	11.00	6.75
558	Red Sox Rookies (Guido Grilli, Pete Magrini), (*George Scott*)	25.00	12.50	7.50
559	Roberto Pena (SP)	22.50	11.00	6.75
560	Joel Horlen	12.50	6.25	3.75
561	Choo Choo Coleman	30.00	15.00	9.00
562	Russ Snyder	12.50	6.25	3.75
563	Twins Rookies (Pete Cimino, Cesar Tovar)	12.50	6.25	3.75
564	Bob Chance (SP)	22.50	11.00	6.75
565	Jimmy Piersall	30.00	15.00	9.00
566	Mike Cuellar	22.00	11.00	6.50
567	Dick Howser	25.00	12.50	7.50
568	Athletics Rookies (Paul Lindblad, Ron Stone)	12.50	6.25	3.75
569	Orlando McFarlane (SP)	22.50	11.00	6.75
570	Art Mahaffey (SP)	22.50	11.00	6.75
571	Dave Roberts (SP)	22.50	11.00	6.75
572	Bob Priddy	12.50	6.25	3.75
573	Derrell Griffith	12.50	6.25	3.75
574	Mets Rookies (Bill Hepler, Bill Murphy)	12.50	6.25	3.75
575	Earl Wilson	12.50	6.25	3.75
576	Dave Nicholson (SP)	22.50	11.00	6.75
577	Jack Lamabe (SP)	22.50	11.00	6.75
578	Chi Chi Olivo (SP)	22.50	11.00	6.75
579	Orioles Rookies (Frank Bertaina, Gene Brabender, Dave Johnson)	15.00	7.50	4.50
580	Billy Williams (SP)	60.00	30.00	18.00
581	Tony Martinez	12.50	6.25	3.75
582	Garry Roggenburk	12.50	6.25	3.75
583	Tigers Team	100.00	50.00	30.00
584	Yankees Rookies (Frank Fernandez), (*Fritz Peterson*)	12.50	6.25	3.75
585	Tony Taylor	12.50	6.25	3.75
586	Claude Raymond (SP)	22.50	11.00	6.75
587	Dick Bertell	12.50	6.25	3.75
588	Athletics Rookies (Chuck Dobson, Ken Suarez)	12.50	6.25	3.75
589	Lou Klimchock (SP)	22.50	11.00	6.75
590	Bill Skowron (SP)	35.00	17.50	10.50
591	N.L. Rookies (*Grant Jackson*, Bart Shirley) (SP)	32.00	16.00	9.50
592	Andre Rodgers	12.50	6.25	3.75
593	Doug Camilli (SP)	22.50	11.00	6.75
594	Chico Salmon	12.50	6.25	3.75
595	Larry Jackson	12.50	6.25	3.75
596	Astros Rookies (*Nate Colbert*, Greg Sims)	25.00	12.50	7.50
597	John Sullivan	12.50	6.25	3.75
598	Gaylord Perry	175.00	70.00	40.00

1966 Topps Comic Book Foldees

Comic book heroes and other fictional characters were the focus of this set of 44 "foldees." The pictures on the left and right ends of the 4-1/2" x 2-3/8" cards were cut through the middle to allow them to be folded over the central picture and each other to create funny combinations. Babe Ruth, in a rather generic drawing, is the only baseball player represented in the issue.

		NM	EX	VG
Complete Set (44):		100.00	50.00	30.00
12	Babe Ruth	20.00	10.00	7.25

1966 Topps Rub-Offs

Returning to a concept last tried in 1961, Topps tried an expanded version of Rub-Offs in 1966. Measuring 2-1/16" x 3," the Rub-Offs are in vertical format for the 100 players and horizontal for the 20 team pennants. The player Rub-Offs feature a color photo.

		NM	EX	VG
Complete Set (120):		600.00	300.00	180.00
Common Player:		3.00	1.50	.90
(1)	Hank Aaron	20.00	10.00	6.00
(2)	Jerry Adair	3.00	1.50	.90
(3)	Richie Allen	3.75	2.00	1.25
(4)	Jesus Alou	3.00	1.50	.90
(5)	Max Alvis	3.00	1.50	.90
(6)	Bob Aspromonte	3.00	1.50	.90
(7)	Ernie Banks	9.00	4.50	2.75
(8)	Earl Battey	3.00	1.50	.90
(9)	Curt Blefary	3.00	1.50	.90
(10)	Ken Boyer	3.75	2.00	1.25
(11)	Bob Bruce	3.00	1.50	.90
(12)	Jim Bunning	6.00	3.00	1.75
(13)	Johnny Callison	3.00	1.50	.90
(14)	Bert Campaneris	3.00	1.50	.90
(15)	Jose Cardenal	3.00	1.50	.90
(16)	Dean Chance	3.00	1.50	.90
(17)	Ed Charles	3.00	1.50	.90
(18)	Bob Clemente	30.00	15.00	9.00
(19)	Tony Cloninger	3.00	1.50	.90
(20)	Rocky Colavito	6.00	3.00	1.75
(21)	Tony Conigliaro	4.50	2.25	1.25
(22)	Vic Davillilo	3.00	1.50	.90
(23)	Willie Davis	3.00	1.50	.90
(24)	Don Drysdale	7.50	3.75	2.25
(25)	Sammy Ellis	3.00	1.50	.90
(26)	Dick Ellsworth	3.00	1.50	.90
(27)	Ron Fairly	3.00	1.50	.90
(28)	Dick Farrell	3.00	1.50	.90
(29)	Eddie Fisher	3.00	1.50	.90
(30)	Jack Fisher	3.00	1.50	.90
(31)	Curt Flood	3.00	1.50	.90
(32)	Whitey Ford	9.00	4.50	2.75
(33)	Bill Freehan	3.00	1.50	.90
(34)	Jim Fregosi	3.00	1.50	.90
(35)	Bob Gibson	7.50	3.75	2.25
(36)	Jim Grant	3.00	1.50	.90
(37)	Jimmie Hall	3.00	1.50	.90
(38)	Ken Harrelson	3.00	1.50	.90
(39)	Jim Hart	3.00	1.50	.90
(40)	Joel Horlen	3.00	1.50	.90
(41)	Willie Horton	3.00	1.50	.90
(42)	Frank Howard	3.75	2.00	1.25
(43)	Deron Johnson	3.00	1.50	.90
(44)	Al Kaline	9.00	4.50	2.75
(45)	Harmon Killebrew	7.50	3.75	2.25
(46)	Bobby Knoop	3.00	1.50	.90
(47)	Sandy Koufax	20.00	10.00	6.00
(48)	Ed Kranepool	3.00	1.50	.90
(49)	Gary Kroll	3.00	1.50	.90
(50)	Don Landrum	3.00	1.50	.90
(51)	Vernon Law	3.00	1.50	.90
(52)	Johnny Lewis	3.00	1.50	.90
(53)	Don Lock	3.00	1.50	.90
(54)	Mickey Lolich	3.75	2.00	1.25
(55)	Jim Maloney	3.00	1.50	.90
(56)	Felix Mantilla	3.00	1.50	.90
(57)	Mickey Mantle	80.00	40.00	24.00
(58)	Juan Marichal	7.50	3.75	2.25
(59)	Ed Mathews	7.50	3.75	2.25
(60)	Willie Mays	20.00	10.00	6.00
(61)	Bill Mazeroski	6.00	3.00	1.75
(62)	Dick McAuliffe	3.00	1.50	.90
(63)	Tim McCarver	3.75	2.00	1.25
(64)	Willie McCovey	7.50	3.75	2.25
(65)	Sammy McDowell	3.00	1.50	.90
(66)	Ken McMullen	3.00	1.50	.90
(67)	Denis Menke	3.00	1.50	.90
(68)	Bill Monbouquette	3.00	1.50	.90
(69)	Joe Morgan	7.50	3.75	2.25
(70)	Fred Newman	3.00	1.50	.90
(71)	John O'Donoghue	3.00	1.50	.90
(72)	Tony Oliva	3.50	1.75	1.00
(73)	Johnny Orsino	3.00	1.50	.90
(74)	Phil Ortega	3.00	1.50	.90
(75)	Milt Pappas	3.00	1.50	.90
(76)	Dick Radatz	3.00	1.50	.90
(77)	Bobby Richardson	4.50	2.25	1.25
(78)	Pete Richert	3.00	1.50	.90
(79)	Brooks Robinson	12.00	6.00	3.50
(80)	Floyd Robinson	3.00	1.50	.90
(81)	Frank Robinson	9.00	4.50	2.75
(82)	Cookie Rojas	3.00	1.50	.90
(83)	Pete Rose	25.00	12.50	7.50
(84)	John Roseboro	3.00	1.50	.90
(85)	Ron Santo	4.50	2.25	1.25
(86)	Bill Skowron	3.75	2.00	1.25
(87)	Willie Stargell	7.50	3.75	2.25
(88)	Mel Stottlemyre	3.00	1.50	.90
(89)	Dick Stuart	3.00	1.50	.90
(90)	Ron Swoboda	3.00	1.50	.90
(91)	Fred Talbot	3.00	1.50	.90
(92)	Ralph Terry	3.00	1.50	.90
(93)	Joe Torre	4.50	2.25	1.25
(94)	Tom Tresh	3.00	1.50	.90
(95)	Bob Veale	3.00	1.50	.90
(96)	Pete Ward	3.00	1.50	.90
(97)	Bill White	3.00	1.50	.90
(98)	Billy Williams	7.50	3.75	2.25
(99)	Jim Wynn	3.00	1.50	.90
(100)	Carl Yastrzemski	12.00	6.00	3.50
(101)	Angels Pennant	3.00	1.50	.90
(102)	Astros Pennant	3.00	1.50	.90
(103)	Athletics Pennant	3.00	1.50	.90
(104)	Braves Pennant	3.00	1.50	.90
(105)	Cards Pennant	3.00	1.50	.90
(106)	Cubs Pennant	3.00	1.50	.90
(107)	Dodgers Pennant	3.00	1.50	.90
(108)	Giants Pennant	3.00	1.50	.90
(109)	Indians Pennant	3.00	1.50	.90
(110)	Mets Pennant	3.00	1.50	.90
(111)	Orioles Pennant	3.00	1.50	.90
(112)	Phillies Pennant	3.00	1.50	.90
(113)	Pirates Pennant	3.00	1.50	.90
(114)	Red Sox Pennant	3.00	1.50	.90
(115)	Reds Pennant	3.00	1.50	.90
(116)	Senators Pennant	3.00	1.50	.90
(117)	Tigers Pennant	3.00	1.50	.90
(118)	Twins Pennant	3.00	1.50	.90
(119)	White Sox Pennant	3.00	1.50	.90
(120)	Yankees Pennant	3.00	1.50	.90

1967 Topps

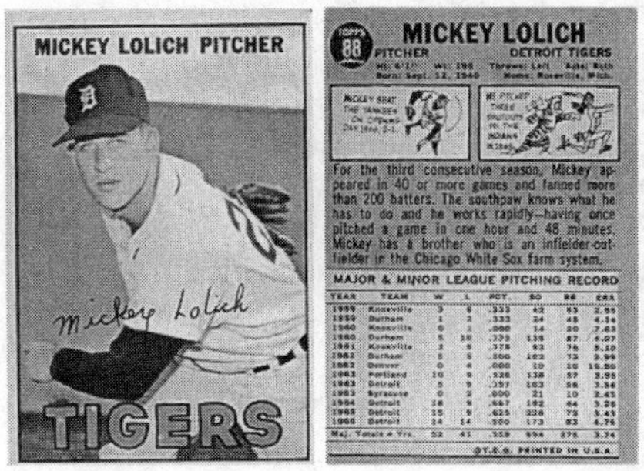

This 609-card set of 2-1/2" x 3-1/2" cards marked the largest set up to that time for Topps. Card fronts feature large color photographs bordered by white. The player's name and position are printed at the top with the team at the bottom. Across the front of the card with the exception of #254 (Milt Pappas) there is a facsimile autograph. The backs were the first to be done vertically, although they continued to carry familiar statistical and biographical information. The only subsets are statistical leaders and World Series highlights. Rookie cards are done by team or league with two players per card. The high numbers (#534-609) in '67 are quite scarce, and while it is known that some are even scarcer, by virtue of having been short-printed in relation to the rest of the series, there is no general agreement on which cards are involved. Cards in the high series which are generally believed to have been double-printed - and thus worth somewhat less than the other cards in the series - are indicated in the checklist by a (DP) notation following the player name.

		NM	EX	VG
Complete Set (609):		3600.	1750.	1000.
Common Player (1-370):		1.50	.70	.45
Common Player (371-457):		3.00	1.50	.90
Common Player (458-533):		5.00	2.50	1.50
Common Player (534-609):		12.00	6.00	3.50
1	The Champs (Hank Bauer, Brooks Robinson, Frank Robinson)	17.50	8.75	5.25
2	Jack Hamilton	1.50	.70	.45
3	Duke Sims	1.50	.70	.45
4	Hal Lanier	1.50	.70	.45
5	Whitey Ford	17.50	8.75	5.25
6	Dick Simpson	1.50	.70	.45
7	Don McMahon	1.50	.70	.45
8	Chuck Harrison	1.50	.70	.45
9	Ron Hansen	1.50	.70	.45
10	Matty Alou	1.50	.70	.45
11	Barry Moore	1.50	.70	.45
12	Dodgers Rookies (Jimmy Campanis, Bill Singer)	1.50	.70	.45
13	Joe Sparma	1.50	.70	.45
14	Phil Linz	1.50	.70	.45
15	Earl Battey	1.50	.70	.45
16	Bill Hands	1.50	.70	.45
17	Jim Gosger	1.50	.70	.45
18	Gene Oliver	1.50	.70	.45
19	Jim McGlothlin	1.50	.70	.45
20	Orlando Cepeda	9.00	4.50	2.75
21	Dave Bristol	1.50	.70	.45
22	Gene Brabender	1.50	.70	.45
23	Larry Elliot	1.50	.70	.45
24	Bob Allen	1.50	.70	.45
25	Elston Howard	3.00	1.50	.90
26a	Bob Priddy (no trade statement)	35.00	17.50	10.50
26b	Bob Priddy (with trade statement)	1.50	.70	.45
27	Bob Saverine	1.50	.70	.45
28	Barry Latman	1.50	.70	.45
29	Tommy McCraw	1.50	.70	.45
30	Al Kaline	12.50	6.25	3.75
31	Jim Brewer	1.50	.70	.45
32	Bob Bailey	1.50	.70	.45
33	Athletics Rookies *(Sal Bando,* Randy Schwartz)	3.00	1.50	.90
34	Pete Cimino	1.50	.70	.45
35	Rico Carty	1.50	.70	.45
36	Bob Tillman	1.50	.70	.45
37	Rick Wise	1.50	.70	.45
38	Bob Johnson	1.50	.70	.45
39	Curt Simmons	1.50	.70	.45
40	Rick Reichardt	1.50	.70	.45
41	Joe Hoerner	1.50	.70	.45
42	Mets Team	8.00	4.00	2.50
43	Chico Salmon	1.50	.70	.45
44	Joe Nuxhall	1.50	.70	.45
45a	Roger Maris (Cards on front)	32.00	16.00	9.50
45b	Roger Maris (Yankees on front, blank-back proof)	1750.	875.00	525.00
46	Lindy McDaniel	1.50	.70	.45
47	Ken McMullen	1.50	.70	.45
48	Bill Freehan	1.50	.70	.45
49	Roy Face	1.50	.70	.45
50	Tony Oliva	3.00	1.50	.90
51	Astros Rookies (Dave Adlesh, Wes Bales)	1.50	.70	.45
52	Dennis Higgins	1.50	.70	.45
53	Clay Dalrymple	1.50	.70	.45
54	Dick Green	1.50	.70	.45
55	Don Drysdale	12.00	6.00	3.50
56	Jose Tartabull	1.50	.70	.45
57	*Pat Jarvis*	1.50	.70	.45
58	Paul Schaal	1.50	.70	.45
59	Ralph Terry	1.50	.70	.45
60	Luis Aparicio	8.00	4.00	2.50
61	Gordy Coleman	1.50	.70	.45
62a	Checklist 1-109 (Frank Robinson) (copyright symbol beneath T of Tribe)	5.00	2.50	1.50
62b	Checklist 1-109 (Frank Robinson) (copyright symbol beneath r of Tribe)	5.00	2.50	1.50
63	Cards Clubbers (Lou Brock, Curt Flood)	8.50	4.25	2.50
64	Fred Valentine	1.50	.70	.45
65	Tom Haller	1.50	.70	.45
66	Manny Mota	1.50	.70	.45
67	Ken Berry	1.50	.70	.45
68	Bob Buhl	1.50	.70	.45
69	Vic Davalillo	1.50	.70	.45
70	Ron Santo	3.50	1.75	1.00
71	Camilo Pascual	1.50	.70	.45
72	Tigers Rookies (George Korince, John Matchick) (Korince photo actually James M. Brown)	1.50	.70	.45
73	Rusty Staub	3.50	1.75	1.00
74	Wes Stock	1.50	.70	.45
75	George Scott	1.50	.70	.45

76	Jim Barbieri	1.50	.70	.45
77	Dooley Womack	1.50	.70	.45
78	Pat Corrales	1.50	.70	.45
79	Bubba Morton	1.50	.70	.45
80	Jim Maloney	1.50	.70	.45
81	Eddie Stanky	1.50	.70	.45
82	Steve Barber	1.50	.70	.45
83	Ollie Brown	1.50	.70	.45
84	Tommie Sisk	1.50	.70	.45
85	Johnny Callison	1.50	.70	.45
86a	Mike McCormick (no trade statement)	30.00	15.00	9.00
86b	Mike McCormick (with trade statement)	1.50	.70	.45
87	George Altman	1.50	.70	.45
88	Mickey Lolich	2.50	1.25	.70
89	*Felix Millan*	1.50	.70	.45
90	Jim Nash	1.50	.70	.45
91	Johnny Lewis	1.50	.70	.45
92	Ray Washburn	1.50	.70	.45
93	Yankees Rookies *(Stan Bahnsen), (Bobby Murcer)*	3.50	1.75	1.00
94	Ron Fairly	1.50	.70	.45
95	Sonny Siebert	1.50	.70	.45
96	Art Shamsky	1.50	.70	.45
97	Mike Cuellar	1.50	.70	.45
98	Rich Rollins	1.50	.70	.45
99	Lee Stange	1.50	.70	.45
100	Frank Robinson	13.00	6.50	4.00
101	Ken Johnson	1.50	.70	.45
102	Phillies Team	3.50	1.75	1.00
103a	Checklist 110-196 (Mickey Mantle) (170 is D McAuliffe)	14.00	7.00	4.25
103b	Checklist 110-196 (Mickey Mantle) (170 is D. McAuliffe)	10.00	5.00	3.00
104	Minnie Rojas	1.50	.70	.45
105	Ken Boyer	3.00	1.50	.90
106	Randy Hundley	1.50	.70	.45
107	Joel Horlen	1.50	.70	.45
108	Alex Johnson	1.50	.70	.45
109	Tribe Thumpers (Rocky Colavito, Leon Wagner)	5.50	2.75	1.75
110	Jack Aker	1.50	.70	.45
111	John Kennedy	1.50	.70	.45
112	Dave Wickersham	1.50	.70	.45
113	Dave Nicholson	1.50	.70	.45
114	Jack Baldschun	1.50	.70	.45
115	Paul Casanova	1.50	.70	.45
116	Herman Franks	1.50	.70	.45
117	Darrell Brandon	1.50	.70	.45
118	Bernie Allen	1.50	.70	.45
119	Wade Blasingame	1.50	.70	.45
120	Floyd Robinson	1.50	.70	.45
121	Ed Bressoud	1.50	.70	.45
122	George Brunet	1.50	.70	.45
123	Pirates Rookies (Jim Price, Luke Walker)	1.50	.70	.45
124	Jim Stewart	1.50	.70	.45
125	Moe Drabowsky	1.50	.70	.45
126	Tony Taylor	1.50	.70	.45
127	John O'Donoghue	1.50	.70	.45
128	Ed Spiezio	1.50	.70	.45
129	Phil Roof	1.50	.70	.45
130	Phil Regan	1.50	.70	.45
131	Yankees Team	9.00	4.50	2.75
132	Ozzie Virgil	1.50	.70	.45
133	Ron Kline	1.50	.70	.45
134	Gates Brown	1.50	.70	.45
135	Deron Johnson	1.50	.70	.45
136	Carroll Sembera	1.50	.70	.45
137	Twins Rookies (Ron Clark, Jim Ollom)	1.50	.70	.45
138	Dick Kelley	1.50	.70	.45
139	Dalton Jones	1.50	.70	.45
140	Willie Stargell	16.00	8.00	4.75
141	John Miller	1.50	.70	.45
142	Jackie Brandt	1.50	.70	.45
143	Sox Sockers (Don Buford, Pete Ward)	1.50	.70	.45
144	Bill Hepler	1.50	.70	.45
145	Larry Brown	1.50	.70	.45
146	Steve Carlton	45.00	22.00	13.50
147	Tom Egan	1.50	.70	.45
148	Adolfo Phillips	1.50	.70	.45
149	Joe Moeller	1.50	.70	.45
150	Mickey Mantle	220.00	110.00	66.00
151	World Series Game 1 (Moe Mows Down 11)	3.50	1.75	1.00
152	World Series Game 2 (Palmer Blanks Dodgers)	7.50	3.75	2.25
153	World Series Game 3 (Blair's Homer Defeats L.A.)	3.50	1.75	1.00
154	World Series Game 4 (Orioles Win 4th Straight)	3.50	1.75	1.00
155	World Series Summary (The Winners Celebrate)	3.50	1.75	1.00
156	Ron Herbel	1.50	.70	.45
157	Danny Cater	1.50	.70	.45
158	Jimmy Coker	1.50	.70	.45
159	Bruce Howard	1.50	.70	.45
160	Willie Davis	1.50	.70	.45
161	Dick Williams	1.50	.70	.45
162	Billy O'Dell	1.50	.70	.45
163	Vic Roznovsky	1.50	.70	.45
164	Dwight Siebler	1.50	.70	.45
165	Cleon Jones	1.50	.70	.45
166	Eddie Mathews	14.00	7.00	4.25
167	Senators Rookies (Joe Coleman, Tim Cullen)	1.50	.70	.45
168	Ray Culp	1.50	.70	.45
169	Horace Clarke	1.50	.70	.45
170	Dick McAuliffe	1.50	.70	.45
171	Calvin Koonce	1.50	.70	.45
172	Bill Heath	1.50	.70	.45
173	Cardinals Team	4.00	2.00	1.25
174	Dick Radatz	1.50	.70	.45
175	Bobby Knoop	1.50	.70	.45
176	Sammy Ellis	1.50	.70	.45

177	Tito Fuentes	1.50	.70	.45
178	John Buzhardt	1.50	.70	.45
179	Braves Rookies (Cecil Upshaw, Chas. Vaughan)	1.50	.70	.45
180	Curt Blefary	1.50	.70	.45
181	Terry Fox	1.50	.70	.45
182	Ed Charles	1.50	.70	.45
183	Jim Pagliaroni	1.50	.70	.45
184	George Thomas	1.50	.70	.45
185	*Ken Holtzman*	4.00	2.00	1.25
186	Mets Maulers (Ed Kranepool, Ron Swoboda)	3.50	1.75	1.00
187	Pedro Ramos	1.50	.70	.45
188	Ken Harrelson	1.50	.70	.45
189	Chuck Hinton	1.50	.70	.45
190	Turk Farrell	1.50	.70	.45
191a	Checklist 197-283 (Willie Mays) (214 is Dick Kelley)	7.50	3.75	2.25
191b	Checklist 197-283 (Willie Mays) (214 is Tom Kelley)	9.00	4.50	2.75
192	Fred Gladding	1.50	.70	.45
193	Jose Cardenal	1.50	.70	.45
194	Bob Allison	1.50	.70	.45
195	Al Jackson	1.50	.70	.45
196	Johnny Romano	1.50	.70	.45
197	Ron Perranoski	1.50	.70	.45
198	Chuck Hiller	1.50	.70	.45
199	Billy Hitchcock	1.50	.70	.45
200	Willie Mays	65.00	32.00	19.50
201	Hal Reniff	1.50	.70	.45
202	Johnny Edwards	1.50	.70	.45
203	Al McBean	1.50	.70	.45
204	Orioles Rookies *(Mike Epstein*, Tom Phoebus)	1.50	.70	.45
205	Dick Groat	1.50	.70	.45
206	Dennis Bennett	1.50	.70	.45
207	John Orsino	1.50	.70	.45
208	Jack Lamabe	1.50	.70	.45
209	Joe Nossek	1.50	.70	.45
210	Bob Gibson	16.00	8.00	4.75
211	Twins Team	5.50	2.75	1.75
212	Chris Zachary	1.50	.70	.45
213	*Jay Johnstone*	4.00	2.00	1.25
214	Tom Kelley	1.50	.70	.45
215	Ernie Banks	18.00	9.00	5.50
216	Bengal Belters (Norm Cash, Al Kaline)	7.50	3.75	2.25
217	Rob Gardner	1.50	.70	.45
218	Wes Parker	1.50	.70	.45
219	Clay Carroll	1.50	.70	.45
220	Jim Hart	1.50	.70	.45
221	Woody Fryman	1.50	.70	.45
222	Reds Rookies (Lee May, Darrell Osteen)	1.50	.70	.45
223	Mike Ryan	1.50	.70	.45
224	Walt Bond	1.50	.70	.45
225	Mel Stottlemyre	1.50	.70	.45
226	Julian Javier	1.50	.70	.45
227	Paul Lindblad	1.50	.70	.45
228	Gil Hodges	5.00	2.50	1.50
229	Larry Jackson	1.50	.70	.45
230	Boog Powell	3.00	1.50	.90
231	John Bateman	1.50	.70	.45
232	Don Buford	1.50	.70	.45
233	A.L. ERA Leaders (Steve Hargan, Joel Horlen, Gary Peters)	3.00	1.50	.90
234	N.L. ERA Leaders (Mike Cuellar, Sandy Koufax, Juan Marichal)	14.00	7.00	4.25
235	A.L. Pitching Leaders (Jim Kaat, Denny McLain, Earl Wilson)	3.50	1.75	1.00
236	N.L. Pitching Leaders (Bob Gibson, Sandy Koufax, Juan Marichal, Gaylord Perry)	24.00	12.00	7.25
237	A.L. Strikeout Leaders (Jim Kaat, Sam McDowell, Earl Wilson)	3.50	1.75	1.00
238	N.L. Strikeout Leaders (Jim Bunning, Sandy Koufax, Bob Veale)	12.00	6.00	3.50
239	A.L. Batting Leaders (Al Kaline, Tony Oliva, Frank Robinson)	7.50	3.75	2.25
240	N.L. Batting Leaders (Felipe Alou, Matty Alou, Rico Carty)	4.00	2.00	1.25
241	A.L. RBI Leaders (Harmon Killebrew, Boog Powell, Frank Robinson)	8.00	4.00	2.50
242	N.L. RBI Leaders (Hank Aaron, Richie Allen, Bob Clemente)	18.00	9.00	5.50
243	A.L. Home Run Leaders (Harmon Killebrew, Boog Powell, Frank Robinson)	8.50	4.25	2.50
244	N.L. Home Run Leaders (Hank Aaron, Richie Allen, Willie Mays)	18.00	9.00	5.50
245	Curt Flood	2.50	1.25	.70
246	Jim Perry	1.50	.70	.45
247	Jerry Lumpe	1.50	.70	.45
248	Gene Mauch	1.50	.70	.45
249	Nick Willhite	1.50	.70	.45
250	Hank Aaron	65.00	32.00	19.50
251	Woody Held	1.50	.70	.45
252	Bob Bolin	1.50	.70	.45
253	Indians Rookies (Bill Davis, Gus Gil)	1.50	.70	.45
254	Milt Pappas	1.50	.70	.45
255	Frank Howard	2.50	1.25	.70
256	Bob Hendley	1.50	.70	.45
257	Charley Smith	1.50	.70	.45
258	Lee Maye	1.50	.70	.45
259	Don Dennis	1.50	.70	.45
260	Jim Lefebvre	1.50	.70	.45
261	John Wyatt	1.50	.70	.45
262	Athletics Team	5.50	2.75	1.75

263	Hank Aguirre	1.50	.70	.45
264	Ron Swoboda	1.50	.70	.45
265	Lou Burdette	1.50	.70	.45
266	Pitt Power (Donn Clendenon, Willie Stargell)	4.00	2.00	1.25
267	Don Schwall	1.50	.70	.45
268	John Briggs	1.50	.70	.45
269	Don Nottebart	1.50	.70	.45
270	Zoilo Versalles	1.50	.70	.45
271	Eddie Watt	1.50	.70	.45
272	Cubs Rookies (Bill Connors, Dave Dowling)	1.50	.70	.45
273	Dick Lines	1.50	.70	.45
274	Bob Aspromonte	1.50	.70	.45
275	Fred Whitfield	1.50	.70	.45
276	Bruce Brubaker	1.50	.70	.45
277	Steve Whitaker	1.50	.70	.45
278	Checklist 284-370 (Jim Kaat)	5.00	2.50	1.50
279	Frank Linzy	1.50	.70	.45
280	Tony Conigliaro	5.00	2.50	1.50
281	Bob Rodgers	1.50	.70	.45
282	Johnny Odom	1.50	.70	.45
283	Gene Alley	1.50	.70	.45
284	Johnny Podres	2.50	1.25	.70
285	Lou Brock	16.00	8.00	4.75
286	Wayne Causey	1.50	.70	.45
287	Mets Rookies (Greg Goossen, Bart Shirley)	1.50	.70	.45
288	Denver Lemaster	1.50	.70	.45
289	Tom Tresh	3.00	1.50	.90
290	Bill White	1.50	.70	.45
291	Jim Hannan	1.50	.70	.45
292	Don Pavletich	1.50	.70	.45
293	Ed Kirkpatrick	1.50	.70	.45
294	Walt Alston	4.00	2.00	1.25
295	Sam McDowell	2.50	1.25	.70
296	Glenn Beckert	1.50	.70	.45
297	Dave Morehead	1.50	.70	.45
298	Ron Davis	1.50	.70	.45
299	Norm Siebern	1.50	.70	.45
300	Jim Kaat	4.00	2.00	1.25
301	Jesse Gonder	1.50	.70	.45
302	Orioles Team	5.50	2.75	1.75
303	Gil Blanco	1.50	.70	.45
304	Phil Gagliano	1.50	.70	.45
305	Earl Wilson	1.50	.70	.45
306	*Bud Harrelson*	5.00	2.50	1.50
307	Jim Beauchamp	1.50	.70	.45
308	Al Downing	1.50	.70	.45
309	Hurlers Beware (Richie Allen, Johnny Callison)	4.00	2.00	1.25
310	Gary Peters	1.50	.70	.45
311	Ed Brinkman	1.50	.70	.45
312	Don Mincher	1.50	.70	.45
313	Bob Lee	1.50	.70	.45
314	Red Sox Rookies *(Mike Andrews), (Reggie Smith)*	5.00	2.50	1.50
315	Billy Williams	12.00	6.00	3.50
316	Jack Kralick	1.50	.70	.45
317	Cesar Tovar	1.50	.70	.45
318	Dave Giusti	1.50	.70	.45
319	Paul Blair	1.50	.70	.45
320	Gaylord Perry	11.00	5.50	3.25
321	Mayo Smith	1.50	.70	.45
322	Jose Pagan	1.50	.70	.45
323	Mike Hershberger	1.50	.70	.45
324	Hal Woodeshick	1.50	.70	.45
325	Chico Cardenas	1.50	.70	.45
326	Bob Uecker	9.00	4.50	2.75
327	Angels Team	5.00	2.50	1.50
328	Clete Boyer	1.50	.70	.45
329	Charlie Lau	1.50	.70	.45
330	Claude Osteen	1.50	.70	.45
331	Joe Foy	1.50	.70	.45
332	Jesus Alou	1.50	.70	.45
333	Fergie Jenkins	11.00	5.50	3.25
334	Twin Terrors (Bob Allison, Harmon Killebrew)	7.50	3.75	2.25
335	Bob Veale	1.50	.70	.45
336	Joe Azcue	1.50	.70	.45
337	Joe Morgan	12.00	6.00	3.50
338	Bob Locker	1.50	.70	.45
339	Chico Ruiz	1.50	.70	.45
340	Joe Pepitone	1.50	.70	.45
341	Giants Rookies *(Dick Dietz*, Bill Sorrell)	1.50	.70	.45
342	Hank Fischer	1.50	.70	.45
343	Tom Satriano	1.50	.70	.45
344	Ossie Chavarria	1.50	.70	.45
345	Stu Miller	1.50	.70	.45
346	Jim Hickman	1.50	.70	.45
347	Grady Hatton	1.50	.70	.45
348	Tug McGraw	2.00	1.00	.60
349	Bob Chance	1.50	.70	.45
350	Joe Torre	4.50	2.25	1.25
351	Vern Law	1.50	.70	.45
352	Ray Oyler	1.50	.70	.45
353	Bill McCool	1.50	.70	.45
354	Cubs Team	5.00	2.50	1.50
355	Carl Yastrzemski	35.00	17.50	10.50
356	Larry Jaster	1.50	.70	.45
357	Bill Skowron	1.50	.70	.45
358	Ruben Amaro	1.50	.70	.45
359	Dick Ellsworth	1.50	.70	.45
360	Leon Wagner	1.50	.70	.45
361	Checklist 371-457 (Roberto Clemente)	12.00	6.00	3.50
362	Darold Knowles	1.50	.70	.45
363	Dave Johnson	1.50	.70	.45
364	Claude Raymond	1.50	.70	.45
365	John Roseboro	1.50	.70	.45
366	Andy Kosco	1.50	.70	.45
367	Angels Rookies (Bill Kelso, Don Wallace)	1.50	.70	.45
368	Jack Hiatt	1.50	.70	.45
369	Catfish Hunter	12.00	6.00	3.50
370	Tommy Davis	1.50	.70	.45
371	Jim Lonborg	2.50	1.25	.70

372	Mike de la Hoz	3.00	1.50	.90
373	White Sox Rookies (Duane Josephson, Fred Klages)	3.00	1.50	.90
374	Mel Queen	3.00	1.50	.90
375	Jake Gibbs	3.00	1.50	.90
376	Don Lock	3.00	1.50	.90
377	Luis Tiant	4.00	2.00	1.25
378	Tigers Team	7.00	3.50	2.00
379	Jerry May	3.00	1.50	.90
380	Dean Chance	3.00	1.50	.90
381	Dick Schofield	3.00	1.50	.90
382	Dave McNally	3.00	1.50	.90
383	Ken Henderson	3.00	1.50	.90
384	Cardinals Rookies (Jim Cosman, Dick Hughes)	3.00	1.50	.90
385	Jim Fregosi	3.00	1.50	.90
386	Dick Selma	3.00	1.50	.90
387	Cap Peterson	3.00	1.50	.90
388	Arnold Earley	3.00	1.50	.90
389	Al Dark	3.00	1.50	.90
390	Jim Wynn	3.00	1.50	.90
391	Wilbur Wood	3.00	1.50	.90
392	Tommy Harper	3.00	1.50	.90
393	Jim Bouton	3.00	1.50	.90
394	Jake Wood	3.00	1.50	.90
395	Chris Short	3.00	1.50	.90
396	Atlanta Aces (Tony Cloninger, Denis Menke)	3.00	1.50	.90
397	Willie Smith	3.00	1.50	.90
398	Jeff Torborg	3.00	1.50	.90
399	Al Worthington	3.00	1.50	.90
400	Roberto Clemente	75.00	37.00	22.00
401	Jim Coates	3.00	1.50	.90
402	Phillies Rookies (Grant Jackson, Billy Wilson)	3.00	1.50	.90
403	Dick Nen	3.00	1.50	.90
404	Nelson Briles	3.00	1.50	.90
405	Russ Snyder	3.00	1.50	.90
406	Lee Elia	3.00	1.50	.90
407	Reds Team	6.00	3.00	1.75
408	Jim Northrup	3.00	1.50	.90
409	Ray Sadecki	3.00	1.50	.90
410	Lou Johnson	3.00	1.50	.90
411	Dick Howser	3.00	1.50	.90
412	Astros Rookies (Norm Miller), *(Doug Rader)*	4.50	2.25	1.25
413	Jerry Grote	3.00	1.50	.90
414	Casey Cox	3.00	1.50	.90
415	Sonny Jackson	3.00	1.50	.90
416	Roger Repoz	3.00	1.50	.90
417a	Bob Bruce (BRAVES on back)	30.00	15.00	9.00
417b	Bob Bruce (corrected)	3.00	1.50	.90
418	Sam Mele	3.00	1.50	.90
419	Don Kessinger	3.00	1.50	.90
420	Denny McLain	5.00	2.50	1.50
421	Dal Maxvill	3.00	1.50	.90
422	Hoyt Wilhelm	8.00	4.00	2.50
423	Fence Busters (Willie Mays, Willie McCovey)	27.50	13.50	8.25
424	Pedro Gonzalez	3.00	1.50	.90
425	Pete Mikkelsen	3.00	1.50	.90
426	Lou Clinton	3.00	1.50	.90
427	Ruben Gomez	3.00	1.50	.90
428	Dodgers Rookies (Tom Hutton), *(Gene Michael)*	3.00	1.50	.90
429	Garry Roggenburk	3.00	1.50	.90
430	Pete Rose	60.00	30.00	18.00
431	Ted Uhlaender	3.00	1.50	.90
432	Jimmie Hall	3.00	1.50	.90
433	Al Luplow	3.00	1.50	.90
434	Eddie Fisher	3.00	1.50	.90
435	Mack Jones	3.00	1.50	.90
436	Pete Ward	3.00	1.50	.90
437	Senators Team	5.00	2.50	1.50
438	Chuck Dobson	3.00	1.50	.90
439	Byron Browne	3.00	1.50	.90
440	Steve Hargan	3.00	1.50	.90
441	Jim Davenport	3.00	1.50	.90
442	Yankees Rookies *(Bill Robinson*, Joe Verbanic)	3.00	1.50	.90
443	Tito Francona	3.00	1.50	.90
444	George Smith	3.00	1.50	.90
445	Don Sutton	16.00	8.00	4.75
446	Russ Nixon	3.00	1.50	.90
447	Bo Belinsky	3.00	1.50	.90
448	Harry Walker	3.00	1.50	.90
449	Orlando Pena	3.00	1.50	.90
450	Richie Allen	8.00	4.00	2.50
451	Fred Newman	3.50	1.75	1.00
452	Ed Kranepool	3.50	1.75	1.00
453	Aurelio Monteagudo	3.50	1.75	1.00
454a	Checklist 458-533 (Juan Marichal) (left ear shows)	7.50	3.75	2.25
454b	Checklist 458-533 (Juan Marichal) (no left ear)	8.00	4.00	2.50
455	Tommie Agee	3.50	1.75	1.00
456	Phil Niekro	10.00	5.00	3.00
457	Andy Etchebarren	3.50	1.75	1.00
458	Lee Thomas	5.00	2.50	1.50
459	Senators Rookies *(Dick Bosman*, Pete Craig)	5.00	2.50	1.50
460	Harmon Killebrew	32.50	16.00	9.75
461	Bob Miller	5.00	2.50	1.50
462	Bob Barton	5.00	2.50	1.50
463	Hill Aces (Sam McDowell, Sonny Siebert)	9.00	4.50	2.75
464	Dan Coombs	5.00	2.50	1.50
465	Willie Horton	8.00	4.00	2.50
466	Bobby Wine	5.00	2.50	1.50
467	Jim O'Toole	5.00	2.50	1.50
468	Ralph Houk	6.00	3.00	1.75
469	Len Gabrielson	5.00	2.50	1.50
470	Bob Shaw	5.00	2.50	1.50
471	Rene Lachemann	5.00	2.50	1.50
472	Pirates Rookies (John Gelnar, George Spriggs)	5.00	2.50	1.50
473	Jose Santiago	5.00	2.50	1.50

474	Bob Tolan	5.00	2.50	1.50
475	Jim Palmer	55.00	27.00	16.50
476	Tony Perez (SP)	55.00	27.00	16.50
477	Braves Team	12.00	6.00	3.50
478	Bob Humphreys	5.00	2.50	1.50
479	Gary Bell	5.00	2.50	1.50
480	Willie McCovey	29.00	14.50	8.75
481	Leo Durocher	11.00	5.50	3.25
482	Bill Monbouquette	5.00	2.50	1.50
483	Jim Landis	5.00	2.50	1.50
484	Jerry Adair	5.00	2.50	1.50
485	Tim McCarver	8.00	4.00	2.50
486	Twins Rookies (Rich Reese, Bill Whitby)	5.00	2.50	1.50
487	Tom Reynolds	5.00	2.50	1.50
488	Gerry Arrigo	5.00	2.50	1.50
489	Doug Clemens	5.00	2.50	1.50
490	Tony Cloninger	5.00	2.50	1.50
491	Sam Bowens	5.00	2.50	1.50
492	Pirates Team	12.00	6.00	3.50
493	Phil Ortega	5.00	2.50	1.50
494	Bill Rigney	5.00	2.50	1.50
495	Fritz Peterson	5.00	2.50	1.50
496	Orlando McFarlane	5.00	2.50	1.50
497	Ron Campbell	5.00	2.50	1.50
498	Larry Dierker	5.00	2.50	1.50
499	Indians Rookies (George Culver, Jose Vidal)	5.00	2.50	1.50
500	Juan Marichal	21.00	10.50	6.25
501	Jerry Zimmerman	5.00	2.50	1.50
502	Derrell Griffith	5.00	2.50	1.50
503	Dodgers Team	17.50	8.75	5.25
504	Orlando Martinez	5.00	2.50	1.50
505	Tommy Helms	5.00	2.50	1.50
506	Smoky Burgess	5.00	2.50	1.50
507	Orioles Rookies (Ed Barnowski, Larry Haney)	5.00	2.50	1.50
508	Dick Hall	5.00	2.50	1.50
509	Jim King	5.00	2.50	1.50
510	Bill Mazeroski	16.00	8.00	4.75
511	Don Wert	5.00	2.50	1.50
512	Red Schoendienst	13.00	6.50	4.00
513	Marcelino Lopez	5.00	2.50	1.50
514	John Werhas	5.00	2.50	1.50
515	Bert Campaneris	6.00	3.00	1.75
516	Giants Team	13.50	6.75	4.00
517	Fred Talbot	5.00	2.50	1.50
518	Denis Menke	5.00	2.50	1.50
519	Ted Davidson	5.00	2.50	1.50
520	Max Alvis	5.00	2.50	1.50
521	Bird Bombers (Curt Blefary, Boog Powell)	7.50	3.75	2.25
522	John Stephenson	5.00	2.50	1.50
523	Jim Merritt	5.00	2.50	1.50
524	Felix Mantilla	5.00	2.50	1.50
525	Ron Hunt	5.00	2.50	1.50
526	Tigers Rookies *(Pat Dobson*, George Korince)	9.00	4.50	2.75
527	Dennis Ribant	5.50	2.75	1.75
528	Rico Petrocelli	7.50	3.75	2.25
529	Gary Wagner	5.50	2.75	1.75
530	Felipe Alou	8.00	4.00	2.50
531	Checklist 534-609 (Brooks Robinson)	9.00	4.50	2.75
532	Jim Hicks	5.50	2.75	1.75
533	Jack Fisher	5.50	2.75	1.75
534	Hank Bauer (DP)	12.00	6.00	3.50
535	Donn Clendenon	12.00	6.00	3.50
536	Cubs Rookies *(Joe Niekro*, Paul Popovich)	32.00	16.00	9.50
537	Chuck Estrada (DP)	12.00	6.00	3.50
538	J.C. Martin	12.00	6.00	3.50
539	Dick Egan (DP)	12.00	6.00	3.50
540	Norm Cash	25.00	12.50	7.50
541	Joe Gibbon	12.00	6.00	3.50
542	Athletics Rookies *(Rick Monday*, Tony Pierce) (DP)	14.00	7.00	4.25
543	Dan Schneider	12.00	6.00	3.50
544	Indians Team	21.00	10.50	6.25
545	Jim Grant	12.00	6.00	3.50
546	Woody Woodward	12.00	6.00	3.50
547	Red Sox Rookies (Russ Gibson, Bill Rohr) (DP)	12.00	6.00	3.50
548	Tony Gonzalez (DP)	12.00	6.00	3.50
549	Jack Sanford	12.00	6.00	3.50
550	Vada Pinson (DP)	12.00	6.00	3.50
551	Doug Camilli (DP)	12.00	6.00	3.50
552	Ted Savage	12.00	6.00	3.50
553	Yankees Rookies (Mike Hegan, Thad Tillotson)	30.00	15.00	9.00
554	Andre Rodgers (DP)	12.00	6.00	3.50
555	Don Cardwell	12.00	6.00	3.50
556	Al Weis (DP)	12.00	6.00	3.50
557	Al Ferrara	12.00	6.00	3.50
558	Orioles Rookies *(Mark Belanger*, Bill Dillman)	45.00	22.00	13.50
559	Dick Tracewski (DP)	12.00	6.00	3.50
560	Jim Bunning	50.00	25.00	15.00
561	Sandy Alomar	16.00	8.00	4.75
562	Steve Blass (DP)	12.00	6.00	3.50
563	Joe Adcock	21.00	10.50	6.25
564	Astros Rookies (Alonzo Harris, Aaron Pointer) (DP)	12.00	6.00	3.50
565	Lew Krausse	12.00	6.00	3.50
566	Gary Geiger (DP)	12.00	6.00	3.50
567	Steve Hamilton	12.00	6.00	3.50
568	John Sullivan	12.00	6.00	3.50
569	A.L. Rookies *(Hank Allen)*, *(Rod Carew)* (DP)	190.00	95.00	57.00
570	Maury Wills	77.00	38.00	23.00
571	Larry Sherry	12.00	6.00	3.50
572	Don Demeter	12.00	6.00	3.50
573	White Sox Team	30.00	15.00	9.00
574	Jerry Buchek	12.00	6.00	3.50
575	*Dave Boswell*	12.00	6.00	3.50
576	N.L. Rookies (Norm Gigon, Ramon Hernandez)	12.00	6.00	3.50
577	Bill Short	12.00	6.00	3.50

578	John Boccabella	12.00	6.00	3.50
579	Bill Henry	12.00	6.00	3.50
580	Rocky Colavito	80.00	40.00	24.00
581	Mets Rookies *(Bill Denehy)*, *(Tom Seaver)*	535.00	265.00	160.00
582	Jim Owens (DP)	12.00	6.00	3.50
583	Ray Barker	12.00	6.00	3.50
584	Jim Piersall	17.50	8.75	5.25
585	Wally Bunker	12.00	6.00	3.50
586	Manny Jimenez	12.00	6.00	3.50
587	N.L. Rookies (Don Shaw, Gary Sutherland)	20.00	10.00	6.00
588	Johnny Klippstein (DP)	12.00	6.00	3.50
589	Dave Ricketts (DP)	12.00	6.00	3.50
590	Pete Richert	12.00	6.00	3.50
591	Ty Cline	12.00	6.00	3.50
592	N.L. Rookies (Jim Shellenback, Ron Willis)	12.00	6.00	3.50
593	Wes Westrum	12.00	6.00	3.50
594	Dan Osinski	12.00	6.00	3.50
595	Cookie Rojas	12.00	6.00	3.50
596	Galen Cisco (DP)	12.00	6.00	3.50
597	Ted Abernathy	12.00	6.00	3.50
598	White Sox Rookies (Ed Stroud, Walt Williams)	12.00	6.00	3.50
599	Bob Duliba (DP)	12.00	6.00	3.50
600	Brooks Robinson	235.00	100.00	65.00
601	Bill Bryan (DP)	12.00	6.00	3.50
602	Juan Pizarro	12.00	6.00	3.50
603	Athletics Rookies (Tim Talton, Ramon Webster)	12.00	6.00	3.50
604	Red Sox Team	100.00	50.00	30.00
605	Mike Shannon	35.00	17.50	10.50
606	Ron Taylor	12.00	6.00	3.50
607	Mickey Stanley	27.50	13.50	8.25
608	Cubs Rookies (Rich Nye, John Upham) (DP)	12.00	6.00	3.50
609	Tommy John	68.00	22.00	12.00

1967 Topps Pin-Ups

The 5" x 7" "All Star Pin-ups" were inserts to regular 1967 Topps baseball cards. They feature a full color picture with the player's name, position and team in a circle on the lower left side of the front. The numbered set consists of 32 players (generally big names). Even so, they are rather inexpensive. Because the large paper pin-ups had to be folded several times to fit into the wax packs, they are almost never found in true "Mint" condition.

		NM	EX	VG
Complete Set (32):		80.00	40.00	24.00
Common Player:		1.00	.50	.30
1	Boog Powell	1.50	.70	.45
2	Bert Campaneris	1.00	.50	.30
3	Brooks Robinson	6.00	3.00	1.75
4	Tommie Agee	1.00	.50	.30
5	Carl Yastrzemski	6.00	3.00	1.75
6	Mickey Mantle	20.00	10.00	6.00
7	Frank Howard	1.50	.70	.45
8	Sam McDowell	1.00	.50	.30
9	Orlando Cepeda	4.00	2.00	1.25
10	Chico Cardenas	1.00	.50	.30
11	Roberto Clemente	12.00	6.00	3.50
12	Willie Mays	10.00	5.00	3.00
13	Cleon Jones	1.00	.50	.30
14	John Callison	1.00	.50	.30
15	Hank Aaron	10.00	5.00	3.00
16	Don Drysdale	6.00	3.00	1.75
17	Bobby Knoop	1.00	.50	.30
18	Tony Oliva	1.50	.70	.45
19	Frank Robinson	6.00	3.00	1.75
20	Denny McLain	1.50	.70	.45
21	Al Kaline	6.00	3.00	1.75
22	Joe Pepitone	1.00	.50	.30
23	Harmon Killebrew	5.00	2.50	1.50
24	Leon Wagner	1.00	.50	.30
25	Joe Morgan	5.00	2.50	1.50
26	Ron Santo	2.00	1.00	.60
27	Joe Torre	3.00	1.50	.90
28	Juan Marichal	4.00	2.00	1.25
29	Matty Alou	1.00	.50	.30
30	Felipe Alou	2.00	1.00	.60
31	Ron Hunt	1.00	.50	.30
32	Willie McCovey	5.00	2.50	1.50

1967 Topps Punch-outs

This little-known Topps test issue was reportedly issued around Maryland in cello packs containing two perforated strips of three game cards each. Cards are printed in black, white and red and measure 2-1/2" x 4-2/3". Backs have instructions on how to play a baseball game by punching out the small squares. Only the "Team Captain" is pictured on the card, and the same captain can be found with different line-ups on his team, creating a large number of collectible variations. Cropping variations in some player photos have been noted, also. The unnumbered issue is checklisted here in alphabetical order.

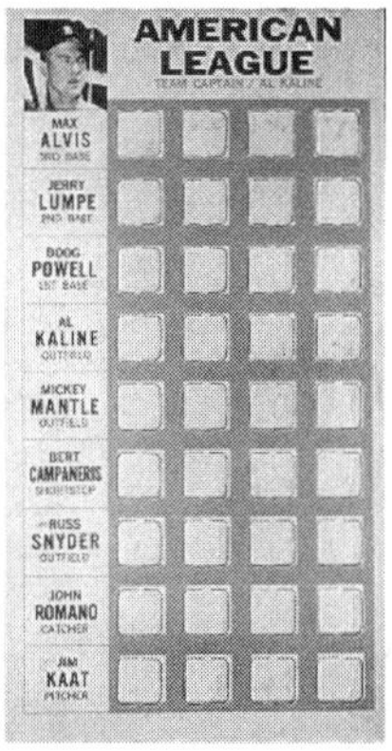

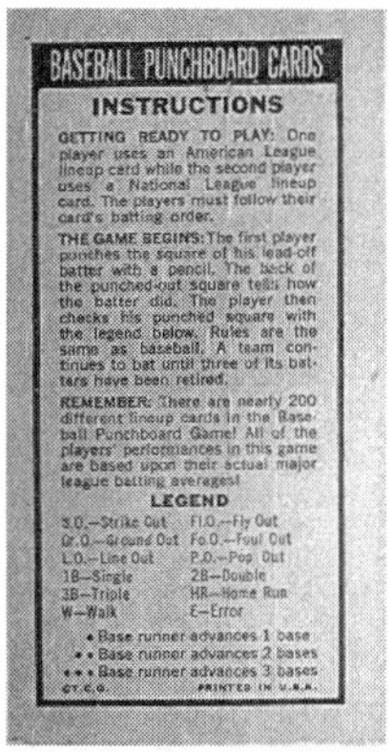

	NM	EX	VG
Complete Set (90):	5000.	2500.	1500.
Common Player:	45.00	22.00	13.50
(1) Hank Aaron	200.00	100.00	60.00
(2) Richie Allen	80.00	40.00	24.00
(3) Gene Alley	45.00	22.00	13.50
(4) Felipe Alou	45.00	22.00	13.50
(5) Matty Alou	45.00	22.00	13.50
(6) Max Alvis	45.00	22.00	13.50
(7) Luis Aparicio	100.00	50.00	30.00
(8) Steve Barber	45.00	22.00	13.50
(9) Earl Battey	45.00	22.00	13.50
(10) Clete Boyer	45.00	22.00	13.50
(11) Ken Boyer	60.00	30.00	18.00
(12) Lou Brock	100.00	50.00	30.00
(13) Jim Bunning	90.00	45.00	27.00
(14) Johnny Callison	45.00	22.00	13.50
(15) Bert Campaneris	45.00	22.00	13.50
(16) Leo Cardenas	45.00	22.00	13.50
(17) Rico Carty	45.00	22.00	13.50
(18) Norm Cash	45.00	22.00	13.50
(19) Orlando Cepeda	90.00	45.00	27.00
(20) Ed Charles	45.00	22.00	13.50
(21) Roberto Clemente	250.00	125.00	75.00
(22) Donn Clendenon	45.00	22.00	13.50
(23) Rocky Colavito	75.00	37.00	22.00
(24) Tony Conigliaro	60.00	30.00	18.00
(25) Willie Davis	45.00	22.00	13.50
(26) Johnny Edwards	45.00	22.00	13.50
(27) Andy Etchebarren	45.00	22.00	13.50
(28) Curt Flood	45.00	22.00	13.50
(29) Bill Freehan	45.00	22.00	13.50
(30) Jim Fregosi	45.00	22.00	13.50
(31) Bob Gibson	100.00	50.00	30.00
(32) Dick Green	45.00	22.00	13.50
(33) Dick Groat	45.00	22.00	13.50
(34) Jerry Grote	45.00	22.00	13.50
(35) Tom Haller	45.00	22.00	13.50
(36) Jim Ray Hart	45.00	22.00	13.50
(37) Mike Hershberger	45.00	22.00	13.50
(38) Elston Howard	65.00	32.00	19.50
(39) Frank Howard	75.00	37.00	22.00
(40) Ron Hunt	45.00	22.00	13.50
(41) Sonny Jackson	45.00	22.00	13.50
(42) Cleon Jones	45.00	22.00	13.50
(43) Jim Kaat	60.00	30.00	18.00
(44) Al Kaline	125.00	62.00	37.00
(45) Harmon Killebrew	100.00	50.00	30.00
(46) Bobby Knoop	45.00	22.00	13.50
(47) Sandy Koufax	200.00	100.00	60.00
(48) Ed Kranepool	45.00	22.00	13.50
(49) Jim Lefebvre	45.00	22.00	13.50
(50) Don Lock	45.00	22.00	13.50
(51) Jerry Lumpe	45.00	22.00	13.50
(52) Mickey Mantle	550.00	275.00	165.00
(53) Juan Marichal	90.00	45.00	27.00
(54) Willie Mays	200.00	100.00	60.00
(55) Bill Mazeroski	75.00	37.00	22.00
(56) Dick McAuliffe	45.00	22.00	13.50
(57) Tim McCarver	50.00	25.00	15.00
(58) Willie McCovey	110.00	55.00	33.00
(59) Denny McLain	45.00	22.00	13.50
(60) Roy McMillan	45.00	22.00	13.50
(61) Denis Menke	45.00	22.00	13.50
(62) Joe Morgan	90.00	45.00	27.00
(63) Tony Oliva	50.00	25.00	15.00
(64) Joe Pepitone	45.00	22.00	13.50
(65) Gaylord Perry	90.00	45.00	27.00
(66) Vada Pinson	45.00	22.00	13.50
(67) Boog Powell	55.00	27.00	16.50
(68) Rick Reichardt	45.00	22.00	13.50
(69) Brooks Robinson	125.00	62.00	37.00
(70) Floyd Robinson	45.00	22.00	13.50
(71) Frank Robinson	120.00	60.00	36.00
(72) Johnny Romano	45.00	22.00	13.50
(73) Pete Rose	175.00	87.00	52.00
(74) John Roseboro	45.00	22.00	13.50
(75) Ron Santo	60.00	30.00	18.00
(76) Chico Salmon	45.00	22.00	13.50
(77) George Scott	45.00	22.00	13.50
(78) Sonny Siebert	45.00	22.00	13.50
(79) Russ Snyder	45.00	22.00	13.50
(80) Willie Stargell	100.00	50.00	30.00
(81) Mel Stottlemyre	45.00	22.00	13.50
(82) Joe Torre	60.00	30.00	18.00
(83) Cesar Tovar	45.00	22.00	13.50
(84) Tom Tresh	45.00	22.00	13.50
(85) Zoilo Versalles	45.00	22.00	13.50
(86) Leon Wagner	45.00	22.00	13.50
(87) Bill White	45.00	22.00	13.50
(88) Fred Whitfield	45.00	22.00	13.50
(89) Billy Williams	90.00	45.00	27.00
(90) Jimmy Wynn	45.00	22.00	13.50
(91) Carl Yastrzemski	125.00	62.00	37.00

1967 Topps Stand-Ups

Never actually issued, no more than a handful of each of these rare test issues has made their way into the hobby market. Designed so that the color photo of the player's head could be popped out of the black background, and the top folded over to create a stand-up display, examples of these 3-1/8" x 5-1/4" cards can be found either die-cut around the portrait or without the cutting. Blank-backed, there are 24 cards in the set, numbered on the front at bottom left. The cards are popular with advanced superstar collectors.

	NM	EX	VG
Complete Set (24):	8000.	4000.	2400.
Common Player:	75.00	37.00	22.00
1 Pete Rose	800.00	400.00	240.00
2 Gary Peters	75.00	37.00	22.00
3 Frank Robinson	250.00	125.00	75.00
4 Jim Lonborg	75.00	37.00	22.00
5 Ron Swoboda	75.00	37.00	22.00
6 Harmon Killebrew	250.00	125.00	75.00
7 Roberto Clemente	1000.	500.00	300.00
8 Mickey Mantle	1800.	900.00	540.00
9 Jim Fregosi	75.00	37.00	22.00
10 Al Kaline	350.00	175.00	105.00
11 Don Drysdale	300.00	150.00	90.00
12 Dean Chance	75.00	37.00	22.00
13 Orlando Cepeda	200.00	100.00	60.00
14 Tim McCarver	90.00	45.00	27.00
15 Frank Howard	90.00	45.00	27.00
16 Max Alvis	75.00	37.00	22.00
17 Rusty Staub	75.00	37.00	22.00
18 Richie Allen	90.00	45.00	27.00
19 Willie Mays	950.00	475.00	285.00
20 Hank Aaron	950.00	475.00	285.00
21 Carl Yastrzemski	450.00	225.00	135.00
22 Ron Santo	90.00	45.00	27.00
23 Catfish Hunter	200.00	100.00	60.00
24 Jim Wynn	75.00	37.00	22.00

1967 Topps Pirates Stickers

Considered a "test" issue, this 33-sticker set of 2-1/2" x 3-1/2" stickers is very similar to the Red Sox stickers which were produced the same year. Player stickers have a color picture (often just the player's head) and the player's name in large "comic book" letters. Besides the players, there are other topics such as "I Love the Pirates," "Bob Clemente for Mayor," and a number of similar sentiments. The stickers have blank backs and are rather scarce.

	NM	EX	VG
Complete Set (33):	400.00	200.00	120.00
Common Player:	5.00	2.50	1.50
1 Gene Alley	5.00	2.50	1.50
2 Matty Alou	6.00	3.00	1.75
3 Dennis Ribant	5.00	2.50	1.50
4 Steve Blass	5.00	2.50	1.50
5 Juan Pizarro	5.00	2.50	1.50
6 Bob Clemente	125.00	62.00	37.00
7 Donn Clendenon	9.00	4.50	2.75
8 Roy Face	6.00	3.00	1.75
9 Woody Fryman	5.00	2.50	1.50
10 Jesse Gonder	5.00	2.50	1.50
11 Vern Law	7.50	3.75	2.25
12 Al McBean	5.00	2.50	1.50
13 Jerry May	5.00	2.50	1.50
14 Bill Mazeroski	25.00	12.50	7.50
15 Pete Mikkelsen	5.00	2.50	1.50
16 Manny Mota	7.00	3.50	2.00
17 Billy O'Dell	5.00	2.50	1.50
18 Jose Pagan	5.00	2.50	1.50
19 Jim Pagliaroni	5.00	2.50	1.50
20 Johnny Pesky	5.00	2.50	1.50
21 Tommie Sisk	5.00	2.50	1.50
22 Willie Stargell	50.00	25.00	15.00
23 Bob Veale	5.00	2.50	1.50
24 Harry Walker	5.00	2.50	1.50
25 I Love The Pirates	5.00	2.50	1.50
26 Let's Go Pirates	5.00	2.50	1.50
27 Bob Clemente For Mayor	50.00	25.00	15.00
28 National League Batting Champion (Matty Alou)	5.50	2.75	1.75
29 Happiness Is A Pirate Win	5.00	2.50	1.50
30 Donn Clendenon Is My Hero	6.00	3.00	1.75
31 Pirates' Home Run Champion (Willie Stargell)	24.00	12.00	7.25
32 Pirates Logo	5.00	2.50	1.50
33 Pirates Pennant	5.00	2.50	1.50

1967 Topps Red Sox Stickers

Like the 1967 Pirates Stickers, the Red Sox Stickers were part of the same test procedure. The Red Sox Stickers have the same 2-1/2" x 3-1/2" dimensions, color picture and large player's name on the front. A set is complete at 33 stickers. The majority are players, but themes such as "Let's Go Red Sox" are also included.

	NM	EX	VG
Complete Set (33):	375.00	185.00	110.00
Common Player:	5.00	2.50	1.50
1 Dennis Bennett	5.00	2.50	1.50
2 Darrell Brandon	5.00	2.50	1.50
3 Tony Conigliaro	45.00	22.00	13.50
4 Don Demeter	5.00	2.50	1.50
5 Hank Fischer	5.00	2.50	1.50
6 Joe Foy	5.00	2.50	1.50
7 Mike Andrews	5.00	2.50	1.50
8 Dalton Jones	5.00	2.50	1.50
9 Jim Lonborg	15.00	7.50	4.50
10 Don McMahon	5.00	2.50	1.50
11 Dave Morehead	5.00	2.50	1.50
12 George Smith	5.00	2.50	1.50
13 Rico Petrocelli	12.50	6.25	3.75
14 Mike Ryan	5.00	2.50	1.50
15 Jose Santiago	5.00	2.50	1.50
16 George Scott	9.00	4.50	2.75
17 Sal Maglie	9.00	4.50	2.75
18 Reggie Smith	9.00	4.50	2.75
19 Lee Stange	5.00	2.50	1.50
20 Jerry Stephenson	5.00	2.50	1.50
21 Jose Tartabull	5.00	2.50	1.50
22 George Thomas	5.00	2.50	1.50
23 Bob Tillman	5.00	2.50	1.50
24 Johnnie Wyatt	5.00	2.50	1.50
25 Carl Yastrzemski	75.00	37.00	22.00
26 Dick Williams	7.00	3.50	2.00

27	I Love The Red Sox	5.00	2.50	1.50
28	Let's Go Red Sox	5.00	2.50	1.50
29	Carl Yastrzemski For Mayor	35.00	17.50	10.50
30	Tony Conigliaro Is My Hero	20.00	10.00	6.00
31	Happiness Is A Boston Win	5.00	2.50	1.50
32	Red Sox Logo	5.00	2.50	1.50
33	Red Sox Pennant	5.00	2.50	1.50

1967 Topps Test Discs

Similar to the more common 28-piece set of 1968, this set of all-stars is known only in proof form, evidently intended to be pressed onto a pin-back button issue which never materialized. Printed on blank-backed silver foil about 2-3/8" square, the pieces have a 2-1/4" diameter center with color player portrait with name and position printed in black across the chest. Some pieces have a team name to the left and right of the player's picture. "JAPAN" is printed in tiny black letters at top-left, apparently intended to be folded under the rim of the button. The unnumbered discs are checklisted here alphabetically.

		NM	EX	VG
Complete Set (24):		3250.	1600.	975.00
Common Player:		40.00	20.00	12.00
(1)	Hank Aaron	300.00	150.00	90.00
(2)	Johnny Callison	40.00	20.00	12.00
(3)	Bert Campaneris	40.00	20.00	12.00
(4)	Leo Cardenas	40.00	20.00	12.00
(5)	Orlando Cepeda	125.00	62.00	37.00
(6)	Roberto Clemente	400.00	200.00	120.00
(7)	Frank Howard	45.00	22.00	13.50
(8)	Cleon Jones	40.00	20.00	12.00
(9)	Bobby Knoop	40.00	20.00	12.00
(10)	Sandy Koufax	250.00	125.00	75.00
(11)	Mickey Mantle	600.00	300.00	180.00
(12)	Juan Marichal	125.00	62.00	37.00
(13)	Willie Mays	300.00	150.00	90.00
(14)	Sam McDowell	40.00	20.00	12.00
(15)	Denny McLain	45.00	22.00	13.50
(17)	Joe Morgan	125.00	62.00	37.00
(18)	Tony Oliva	40.00	20.00	12.00
(19)	Boog Powell	50.00	25.00	15.00
(20)	Brooks Robinson	200.00	100.00	60.00
(21)	Frank Robinson	200.00	100.00	60.00
(22)	Ron Santo	45.00	22.00	13.50
(23)	Joe Torre	65.00	32.00	19.50
(24)	Carl Yastrzemski	200.00	100.00	60.00

1967 Topps S.F. Giants Test Discs

One of several prototypes for pinback button sets which were never issued. Generally found in the form of a silver-foil cardboard square, about 2-3/8" a side, the 2-1/4" round center features color player photos or team booster slogans. The player's name and position are printed across his chest, the team name at top. At top-left is a tiny black "JAPAN". The unnumbered discs are checklisted here alphabetically.

		NM	EX	VG
Complete Set (24):		1500.	750.00	450.00
Common Player:		40.00	20.00	12.00
(1)	Jesus Alou	40.00	20.00	12.00
(2)	Bob Bolin	40.00	20.00	12.00
(3)	Ollie Brown	40.00	20.00	12.00
(4)	Jim Davenport	40.00	20.00	12.00
(5)	Herman Franks	40.00	20.00	12.00
(6)	Len Gabrielson	40.00	20.00	12.00
(7)	Joe Gibbon	40.00	20.00	12.00
(8)	Tom Haller	40.00	20.00	12.00
(9)	Jim Ray Hart	40.00	20.00	12.00
(10)	Ron Herbel	40.00	20.00	12.00
(11)	Hal Lanier	40.00	20.00	12.00
(12)	Frank Linzy	40.00	20.00	12.00
(13)	Juan Marichal	200.00	100.00	60.00
(14)	Willie Mays	350.00	175.00	105.00
(15)	Willie McCovey	200.00	100.00	60.00
(16)	Lindy McDaniel	40.00	20.00	12.00
(17)	Gaylord Perry	175.00	87.00	52.00
(18)	Cap Peterson	40.00	20.00	12.00
(19)	Bob Priddy	40.00	20.00	12.00
(20)	Happiness is a Giant Win	25.00	12.50	7.50
(21)	I Love the Giants	25.00	12.50	7.50
(22)	Let's Go Giants	25.00	12.50	7.50
(23)	Willie Mays for Mayor (Willie Mays)	150.00	75.00	45.00
(24)	S.F. Giants logo	25.00	12.50	7.50

1967 Topps Who Am I?

A cartoon caption and goofy facial features were printed on the front of these 2-1/2" x 3-1/2" cards and were designed to be scratched off to reveal the portrait, name and claim to fame of the person beneath. This 44-card set includes all manner of U.S. and international historical figures, including four baseball players. Backs are printed in red and have a large question mark with several hints printed thereon. Unscratched cards are much rarer than scratched cards, though they carry only about a 50% premium.

		NM	EX	VG
Complete Set (44):		500.00	250.00	150.00
Common Player:		1.00	.50	.30
12	Babe Ruth	140.00	70.00	42.00
22	Mickey Mantle	160.00	80.00	48.00
33	Willie Mays	95.00	47.00	28.00
41	Sandy Koufax	125.00	62.00	37.00

1968 Topps

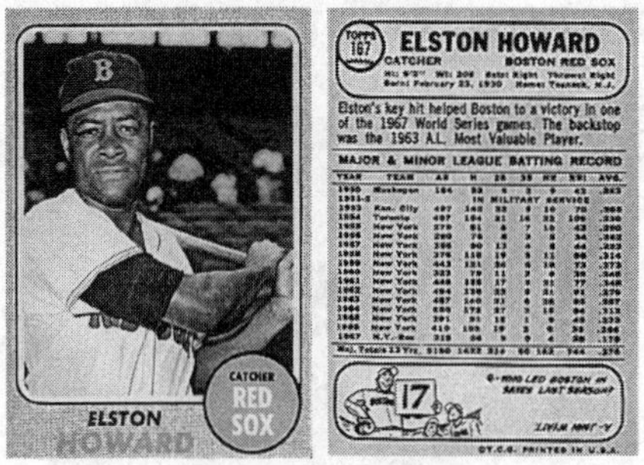

In 1968, Topps returned to a 598-card set of 2-1/2" x 3-1/2" cards. It is not, however, more of the same by way of appearance as the cards feature a color photograph on a background of what appears to be a burlap fabric. The player's name is below the photo but on the unusual background. A colored circle on the lower right carries the team and position. Backs were also changed, while retaining the vertical format introduced the previous year, with stats in the middle and cartoon at the bottom. The set features many of the old favorite subsets, including statistical leaders, World Series highlights, multi-player cards, checklists, rookie cards and the return of All-Star cards.

		NM	EX	VG
Complete Set (598):		2750.	1200.	700.00
Common Player (1-457):		1.50	.70	.45
Common Player (458-533):		3.00	1.50	.90
Common Player (534-598):		3.50	1.75	1.00
1	N.L. Batting Leaders (Matty Alou, Roberto Clemente, Tony Gonzalez)	22.00	11.00	6.50
2	A.L. Batting Leaders (Al Kaline, Frank Robinson, Carl Yastrzemski)	10.00	5.00	3.00
3	N.L. RBI Leaders (Hank Aaron, Orlando Cepeda, Roberto Clemente)	16.00	8.00	4.75
4	A.L. RBI Leaders (Harmon Killebrew, Frank Robinson, Carl Yastrzemski)	11.00	5.50	3.25
5	N.L. Home Run Leaders (Hank Aaron, Willie McCovey, Ron Santo, Jim Wynn)	7.50	3.75	2.25
6	A.L. Home Run Leaders (Frank Howard, Harmon Killebrew, Carl Yastrzemski)	7.00	3.50	2.00
7	N.L. ERA Leaders (Jim Bunning, Phil Niekro, Chris Short)	3.50	1.75	1.00
8	A.L. ERA Leaders (Joe Horlen, Gary Peters, Sonny Siebert)	3.50	1.75	1.00
9	N.L. Pitching Leaders (Jim Bunning, Fergie Jenkins, Mike McCormick, Claude Osteen)	4.50	2.25	1.25
10a	A.L. Pitching Leaders (Dean Chance, Jim Lonborg, Earl Wilson) ("Lonberg" on back)	3.75	2.00	1.25
10b	A.L. Pitching Leaders (Dean Chance, Jim Lonborg, Earl Wilson) ("Lonborg" on back)	2.50	1.25	.70
11	N.L. Strikeout Leaders (Jim Bunning, Fergie Jenkins, Gaylord Perry)	4.50	2.25	1.25
12	A.L. Strikeout Leaders (Dean Chance, Jim Lonborg, Sam McDowell)	3.50	1.75	1.00
13	Chuck Hartenstein	1.50	.70	.45
14	Jerry McNertney	1.50	.70	.45
15	Ron Hunt	1.50	.70	.45
16	Indians Rookies (Lou Piniella, Richie Scheinblum)	3.00	1.50	.90
17	Dick Hall	1.50	.70	.45
18	Mike Hershberger	1.50	.70	.45
19	Juan Pizarro	1.50	.70	.45
20	Brooks Robinson	20.00	10.00	6.00
21	Ron Davis	1.50	.70	.45
22	Pat Dobson	1.50	.70	.45
23	Chico Cardenas	1.50	.70	.45
24	Bobby Locke	1.50	.70	.45
25	Julian Javier	1.50	.70	.45
26	Darrell Brandon	1.50	.70	.45
27	Gil Hodges	6.50	3.25	2.00
28	Ted Uhlaender	1.50	.70	.45
29	Joe Verbanic	1.50	.70	.45
30	Joe Torre	4.50	2.25	1.25
31	Ed Stroud	1.50	.70	.45
32	Joe Gibbon	1.50	.70	.45
33	Pete Ward	1.50	.70	.45
34	Al Ferrara	1.50	.70	.45
35	Steve Hargan	1.50	.70	.45
36	Pirates Rookies (Bob Moose), *(Bob Robertson)*	1.50	.70	.45
37	Billy Williams	8.00	4.00	2.50
38	Tony Pierce	1.50	.70	.45
39	Cookie Rojas	1.50	.70	.45
40	Denny McLain	6.00	3.00	1.75
41	Julio Gotay	1.50	.70	.45
42	Larry Haney	1.50	.70	.45
43	Gary Bell	1.50	.70	.45
44	Frank Kostro	1.50	.70	.45
45	Tom Seaver	40.00	20.00	12.00
46	Dave Ricketts	1.50	.70	.45
47	Ralph Houk	1.50	.70	.45
48	Ted Davidson	1.50	.70	.45
49a	Ed Brinkman (yellow team)	75.00	37.00	22.00
49b	Ed Brinkman (white team)	1.50	.70	.45
50	Willie Mays	60.00	30.00	18.00
51	Bob Locker	1.50	.70	.45
52	Hawk Taylor	1.50	.70	.45
53	Gene Alley	1.50	.70	.45
54	Stan Williams	1.50	.70	.45
55	Felipe Alou	2.00	1.00	.60
56	Orioles Rookies (Dave Leonhard, Dave May)	2.00	1.00	.60
57	Dan Schneider	1.50	.70	.45
58	Eddie Mathews	14.00	7.00	4.25
59	Don Lock	1.50	.70	.45
60	Ken Holtzman	1.50	.70	.45
61	Reggie Smith	2.00	1.00	.60
62	Chuck Dobson	1.50	.70	.45
63	Dick Kenworthy	1.50	.70	.45
64	Jim Merritt	1.50	.70	.45
65	John Roseboro	1.50	.70	.45
66a	Casey Cox (yellow team)	75.00	37.00	22.00
66b	Casey Cox (white team)	1.50	.70	.45
67	Checklist 1-109 (Jim Kaat)	5.00	2.50	1.50
68	Ron Willis	1.50	.70	.45
69	Tom Tresh	2.25	1.25	.70
70	Bob Veale	1.50	.70	.45
71	Vern Fuller	1.50	.70	.45
72	Tommy John	3.50	1.75	1.00
73	Jim Hart	1.50	.70	.45
74	Milt Pappas	1.50	.70	.45

75	Don Mincher	1.50	.70	.45
76	Braves Rookies (Jim Britton), *(Ron Reed)*	2.00	1.00	.60
77	*Don Wilson*	1.50	.70	.45
78	Jim Northrup	1.50	.70	.45
79	Ted Kubiak	1.50	.70	.45
80	Rod Carew	45.00	22.00	13.50
81	Larry Jackson	1.50	.70	.45
82	Sam Bowens	1.50	.70	.45
83	John Stephenson	1.50	.70	.45
84	Bob Tolan	1.50	.70	.45
85	Gaylord Perry	7.00	3.50	2.00
86	Willie Stargell	9.00	4.50	2.75
87	Dick Williams	1.50	.70	.45
88	Phil Regan	1.50	.70	.45
89	Jake Gibbs	1.50	.70	.45
90	Vada Pinson	2.50	1.25	.70
91	Jim Ollom	1.50	.70	.45
92	Ed Kranepool	1.50	.70	.45
93	Tony Cloninger	1.50	.70	.45
94	Lee Maye	1.50	.70	.45
95	Bob Aspromonte	1.50	.70	.45
96	Senators Rookies (Frank Coggins, Dick Nold)	1.50	.70	.45
97	Tom Phoebus	1.50	.70	.45
98	Gary Sutherland	1.50	.70	.45
99	Rocky Colavito	6.00	3.00	1.75
100	Bob Gibson	21.00	10.50	6.25
101	Glenn Beckert	1.50	.70	.45
102	Jose Cardenal	1.50	.70	.45
103	Don Sutton	8.00	4.00	2.50
104	Dick Dietz	1.50	.70	.45
105	Al Downing	1.50	.70	.45
106	Dalton Jones	1.50	.70	.45
107	Checklist 110-196 (Juan Marichal)	4.50	2.25	1.25
108	Don Pavletich	1.50	.70	.45
109	Bert Campaneris	1.50	.70	.45
110	Hank Aaron	50.00	25.00	15.00
111	Rich Reese	1.50	.70	.45
112	Woody Fryman	1.50	.70	.45
113	Tigers Rookies (Tom Matchick, Daryl Patterson)	1.50	.70	.45
114	Ron Swoboda	1.50	.70	.45
115	Sam McDowell	1.50	.70	.45
116	Ken McMullen	1.50	.70	.45
117	Larry Jaster	1.50	.70	.45
118	Mark Belanger	1.50	.70	.45
119	Ted Savage	1.50	.70	.45
120	Mel Stottlemyre	1.50	.70	.45
121	Jimmie Hall	1.50	.70	.45
122	Gene Mauch	1.50	.70	.45
123	Jose Santiago	1.50	.70	.45
124	Nate Oliver	1.50	.70	.45
125	Joe Horlen	1.50	.70	.45
126	Bobby Etheridge	1.50	.70	.45
127	Paul Lindblad	1.50	.70	.45
128	Astros Rookies (Tom Dukes, Alonzo Harris)	1.50	.70	.45
129	Mickey Stanley	1.50	.70	.45
130	Tony Perez	9.00	4.50	2.75
131	Frank Bertaina	1.50	.70	.45
132	Bud Harrelson	1.50	.70	.45
133	Fred Whitfield	1.50	.70	.45
134	Pat Jarvis	1.50	.70	.45
135	Paul Blair	1.50	.70	.45
136	Randy Hundley	1.50	.70	.45
137	Twins Team	3.00	1.50	.90
138	Ruben Amaro	1.50	.70	.45
139	Chris Short	1.50	.70	.45
140	Tony Conigliaro	4.50	2.25	1.25
141	Dal Maxvill	1.50	.70	.45
142	White Sox Rookies (Buddy Bradford, Bill Voss)	1.50	.70	.45
143	Pete Cimino	1.50	.70	.45
144	Joe Morgan	10.00	5.00	3.00
145	Don Drysdale	10.00	5.00	3.00
146	Sal Bando	1.50	.70	.45
147	Frank Linzy	1.50	.70	.45
148	Dave Bristol	1.50	.70	.45
149	Bob Saverine	1.50	.70	.45
150	Roberto Clemente	65.00	32.00	19.50
151	World Series Game 1 (Brock Socks 4 Hits in Opener)	7.00	3.50	2.00
152	World Series Game 2 (Yaz Smashes Two Homers)	7.00	3.50	2.00
153	World Series Game 3 (Briles Cools Off Boston)	3.50	1.75	1.00
154	World Series Game 4 (Gibson Hurls Shutout)	7.00	3.50	2.00
155	World Series Game 5 (Lonborg Wins Again)	3.50	1.75	1.00
156	World Series Game 6 (Petrocelli Socks Two Homers)	3.00	1.50	.90
157	World Series Game 7 (St. Louis Wins It)	3.50	1.75	1.00
158	World Series Summary (The Cardinals Celebrate)	3.00	1.50	.90
159	Don Kessinger	1.50	.70	.45
160	Earl Wilson	1.50	.70	.45
161	Norm Miller	1.50	.70	.45
162	Cardinals Rookies (Hal Gilson), *(Mike Torrez)*	2.00	1.00	.60
163	Gene Brabender	1.50	.70	.45
164	Ramon Webster	1.50	.70	.45
165	Tony Oliva	2.50	1.25	.70
166	Claude Raymond	1.50	.70	.45
167	Elston Howard	2.50	1.25	.70
168	Dodgers Team	3.00	1.50	.90
169	Bob Bolin	1.50	.70	.45
170	Jim Fregosi	1.50	.70	.45
171	Don Nottebart	1.50	.70	.45
172	Walt Williams	1.50	.70	.45
173	John Boozer	1.50	.70	.45
174	Bob Tillman	1.50	.70	.45
175	Maury Wills	2.50	1.25	.70
176	Bob Allen	1.50	.70	.45

177	Mets Rookies *(Jerry Koosman)*, *(Nolan Ryan)*	665.00	330.00	200.00
178	Don Wert	1.50	.70	.45
179	Bill Stoneman	1.50	.70	.45
180	Curt Flood	2.50	1.25	.70
181	Jerry Zimmerman	1.50	.70	.45
182	Dave Giusti	1.50	.70	.45
183	Bob Kennedy	1.50	.70	.45
184	Lou Johnson	1.50	.70	.45
185	Tom Haller	1.50	.70	.45
186	Eddie Watt	1.50	.70	.45
187	Sonny Jackson	1.50	.70	.45
188	Cap Peterson	1.50	.70	.45
189	Bill Landis	1.50	.70	.45
190	Bill White	1.50	.70	.45
191	Dan Frisella	1.50	.70	.45
192a	Checklist 197-283 (Carl Yastrzemski) ("To increase the..." on back)	5.50	2.75	1.75
192b	Checklist 197-283 (Carl Yastrzemski) ("To increase your..." on back)	6.00	3.00	1.75
193	Jack Hamilton	1.50	.70	.45
194	Don Buford	1.50	.70	.45
195	Joe Pepitone	1.50	.70	.45
196	Gary Nolan	1.50	.70	.45
197	Larry Brown	1.50	.70	.45
198	Roy Face	1.50	.70	.45
199	A's Rookies (Darrell Osteen, Roberto Rodriguez)	2.00	1.00	.60
200	Orlando Cepeda	9.00	4.50	2.75
201	*Mike Marshall*	3.00	1.50	.90
202	Adolfo Phillips	1.50	.70	.45
203	Dick Kelley	1.50	.70	.45
204	Andy Etchebarren	1.50	.70	.45
205	Juan Marichal	6.50	3.25	2.00
206	Cal Ermer	1.50	.70	.45
207	Carroll Sembera	1.50	.70	.45
208	Willie Davis	1.50	.70	.45
209	Tim Cullen	1.50	.70	.45
210	Gary Peters	1.50	.70	.45
211	J.C. Martin	1.50	.70	.45
212	Dave Morehead	1.50	.70	.45
213	Chico Ruiz	1.50	.70	.45
214	Yankees Rookies (Stan Bahnsen, Frank Fernandez)	2.00	1.00	.60
215	Jim Bunning	6.00	3.00	1.75
216	Bubba Morton	1.50	.70	.45
217	Turk Farrell	1.50	.70	.45
218	Ken Suarez	1.50	.70	.45
219	Rob Gardner	1.50	.70	.45
220	Harmon Killebrew	11.00	5.50	3.25
221	Braves Team	3.00	1.50	.90
222	Jim Hardin	1.50	.70	.45
223	Ollie Brown	1.50	.70	.45
224	Jack Aker	1.50	.70	.45
225	Richie Allen	3.00	1.50	.90
226	Jimmie Price	1.50	.70	.45
227	Joe Hoerner	1.50	.70	.45
228	Dodgers Rookies *(Jack Billingham)*, Jim Fairey)	1.50	.70	.45
229	Fred Klages	1.50	.70	.45
230	Pete Rose	40.00	20.00	12.00
231	Dave Baldwin	1.50	.70	.45
232	Denis Menke	1.50	.70	.45
233	George Scott	1.50	.70	.45
234	Bill Monbouquette	1.50	.70	.45
235	Ron Santo	3.75	2.00	1.25
236	Tug McGraw	1.50	.70	.45
237	Alvin Dark	1.50	.70	.45
238	Tom Satriano	1.50	.70	.45
239	Bill Henry	1.50	.70	.45
240	Al Kaline	20.00	10.00	6.00
241	Felix Millan	1.50	.70	.45
242	Moe Drabowsky	1.50	.70	.45
243	Rich Rollins	1.50	.70	.45
244	John Donaldson	1.50	.70	.45
245	Tony Gonzalez	1.50	.70	.45
246	Fritz Peterson	1.50	.70	.45
247	Reds Rookies *(Johnny Bench)*, Ron Tompkins)	105.00	52.00	31.00
248	Fred Valentine	1.50	.70	.45
249	Bill Singer	1.50	.70	.45
250	Carl Yastrzemski	24.00	12.00	7.25
251	*Manny Sanguillen*	4.50	2.25	1.25
252	Angels Team	3.00	1.50	.90
253	Dick Hughes	1.50	.70	.45
254	Cleon Jones	1.50	.70	.45
255	Dean Chance	1.50	.70	.45
256	Norm Cash	3.00	1.50	.90
257	Phil Niekro	7.50	3.75	2.25
258	Cubs Rookies (Jose Arcia, Bill Schlesinger)	1.50	.70	.45
259	Ken Boyer	3.00	1.50	.90
260	Jim Wynn	1.50	.70	.45
261	Dave Duncan	1.50	.70	.45
262	Rick Wise	1.50	.70	.45
263	Horace Clarke	1.50	.70	.45
264	Ted Abernathy	1.50	.70	.45
265	Tommy Davis	2.00	1.00	.60
266	Paul Popovich	1.50	.70	.45
267	Herman Franks	1.50	.70	.45
268	Bob Humphreys	1.50	.70	.45
269	Bob Tiefenauer	1.50	.70	.45
270	Matty Alou	1.50	.70	.45
271	Bobby Knoop	1.50	.70	.45
272	Ray Culp	1.50	.70	.45
273	Dave Johnson	1.50	.70	.45
274	Mike Cuellar	1.50	.70	.45
275	Tim McCarver	2.50	1.25	.70
276	Jim Roland	1.50	.70	.45
277	Jerry Buchek	1.50	.70	.45
278a	Checklist 284-370 (Orlando Cepeda) (copyright at right)	5.00	2.50	1.50
278b	Checklist 284-370 (Orlando Cepeda) (copyright at left)	5.50	2.75	1.75
279	Bill Hands	1.50	.70	.45
280	Mickey Mantle	220.00	110.00	66.00

281	Jim Campanis	1.50	.70	.45
282	Rick Monday	1.50	.70	.45
283	Mel Queen	1.50	.70	.45
284	John Briggs	1.50	.70	.45
285	Dick McAuliffe	1.50	.70	.45
286	Cecil Upshaw	1.50	.70	.45
287	White Sox Rookies (Mickey Abarbanel, Cisco Carlos)	1.50	.70	.45
288	Dave Wickersham	1.50	.70	.45
289	Woody Held	1.50	.70	.45
290	Willie McCovey	9.00	4.50	2.75
291	Dick Lines	1.50	.70	.45
292	Art Shamsky	1.50	.70	.45
293	Bruce Howard	1.50	.70	.45
294	Red Schoendienst	4.50	2.25	1.25
295	Sonny Siebert	1.50	.70	.45
296	Byron Browne	1.50	.70	.45
297	Russ Gibson	1.50	.70	.45
298	Jim Brewer	1.50	.70	.45
299	Gene Michael	1.50	.70	.45
300	Rusty Staub	2.50	1.25	.70
301	Twins Rookies (George Mitterwald, Rick Renick)	1.50	.70	.45
302	Gerry Arrigo	1.50	.70	.45
303	Dick Green	1.50	.70	.45
304	Sandy Valdespino	1.50	.70	.45
305	Minnie Rojas	1.50	.70	.45
306	Mike Ryan	1.50	.70	.45
307	John Hiller	1.50	.70	.45
308	Pirates Team	3.00	1.50	.90
309	Ken Henderson	1.50	.70	.45
310	Luis Aparicio	6.00	3.00	1.75
311	Jack Lamabe	1.50	.70	.45
312	Curt Blefary	1.50	.70	.45
313	Al Weis	1.50	.70	.45
314	Red Sox Rookies (Bill Rohr, George Spriggs)	1.50	.70	.45
315	Zoilo Versalles	1.50	.70	.45
316	Steve Barber	1.50	.70	.45
317	Ron Brand	1.50	.70	.45
318	Chico Salmon	1.50	.70	.45
319	George Culver	1.50	.70	.45
320	Frank Howard	2.00	1.00	.60
321	Leo Durocher	4.50	2.25	1.25
322	Dave Boswell	1.50	.70	.45
323	Deron Johnson	1.50	.70	.45
324	Jim Nash	1.50	.70	.45
325	Manny Mota	1.50	.70	.45
326	Dennis Ribant	1.50	.70	.45
327	Tony Taylor	1.50	.70	.45
328	Angels Rookies (Chuck Vinson, Jim Weaver)	1.50	.70	.45
329	Duane Josephson	1.50	.70	.45
330	Roger Maris	35.00	17.50	10.50
331	Dan Osinski	1.50	.70	.45
332	Doug Rader	1.50	.70	.45
333	Ron Herbel	1.50	.70	.45
334	Orioles Team	3.00	1.50	.90
335	Bob Allison	1.50	.70	.45
336	John Purdin	1.50	.70	.45
337	Bill Robinson	1.50	.70	.45
338	Bob Johnson	1.50	.70	.45
339	Rich Nye	1.50	.70	.45
340	Max Alvis	1.50	.70	.45
341	Jim Lemon	1.50	.70	.45
342	Ken Johnson	1.50	.70	.45
343	Jim Gosger	1.50	.70	.45
344	Donn Clendenon	1.50	.70	.45
345	Bob Hendley	1.50	.70	.45
346	Jerry Adair	1.50	.70	.45
347	George Brunet	1.50	.70	.45
348	Phillies Rookies (Larry Colton, Dick Thoenen)	1.50	.70	.45
349	Ed Spiezio	1.50	.70	.45
350	Hoyt Wilhelm	6.00	3.00	1.75
351	Bob Barton	1.50	.70	.45
352	Jackie Hernandez	1.50	.70	.45
353	Mack Jones	1.50	.70	.45
354	Pete Richert	1.50	.70	.45
355	Ernie Banks	22.00	11.00	6.50
356	Checklist 371-457 (Ken Holtzman)	4.00	2.00	1.25
357	Len Gabrielson	1.50	.70	.45
358	Mike Epstein	1.50	.70	.45
359	Joe Moeller	1.50	.70	.45
360	Willie Horton	1.50	.70	.45
361	Harmon Killebrew (All-Star)	6.00	3.00	1.75
362	Orlando Cepeda (All-Star)	4.50	2.25	1.25
363	Rod Carew (All-Star)	6.00	3.00	1.75
364	Joe Morgan (All-Star)	5.50	2.75	1.75
365	Brooks Robinson (All-Star)	7.00	3.50	2.00
366	Ron Santo (All-Star)	4.00	2.00	1.25
367	Jim Fregosi (All-Star)	2.00	1.00	.60
368	Gene Alley (All-Star)	2.00	1.00	.60
369	Carl Yastrzemski (All-Star)	7.00	3.50	2.00
370	Hank Aaron (All-Star)	16.00	8.00	4.75
371	Tony Oliva (All-Star)	3.00	1.50	.90
372	Lou Brock (All-Star)	6.00	3.00	1.75
373	Frank Robinson (All-Star)	7.00	3.50	2.00
374	Roberto Clemente (All-Star)	17.50	8.75	5.25
375	Bill Freehan (All-Star)	2.00	1.00	.60
376	Tim McCarver (All-Star)	[illegible]	1.50	.90
377	Joe Horlen (All-Star)	2.00	1.00	.60
378	Bob Gibson (All-Star)	6.00	3.00	1.75
379	Gary Peters (All-Star)	2.00	1.00	.60
380	Ken Holtzman (All-Star)	2.00	1.00	.60
381	Boog Powell	3.00	1.50	.90
382	Ramon Hernandez	1.50	.70	.45
383	Steve Whitaker	1.50	.70	.45
384	Red Rookies (Bill Henry), *(Hal McRae)*	6.00	3.00	1.75
385	Catfish Hunter	9.00	4.50	2.75
386	Greg Goossen	1.50	.70	.45
387	Joe Foy	1.50	.70	.45
388	Ray Washburn	1.50	.70	.45
389	Jay Johnstone	1.50	.70	.45
390	Bill Mazeroski	4.50	2.25	1.25
391	Bob Priddy	1.50	.70	.45

392	Grady Hatton	1.50	.70	.45
393	Jim Perry	1.50	.70	.45
394	Tommie Aaron	1.50	.70	.45
395	Camilo Pascual	1.50	.70	.45
396	Bobby Wine	1.50	.70	.45
397	Vic Davalillo	1.50	.70	.45
398	Jim Grant	1.50	.70	.45
399	Ray Oyler	1.50	.70	.45
400a	Mike McCormick (white team)	80.00	40.00	24.00
400b	Mike McCormick (yellow team)	1.50	.70	.45
401	Mets Team	4.00	2.00	1.25
402	Mike Hegan	1.50	.70	.45
403	John Buzhardt	1.50	.70	.45
404	Floyd Robinson	1.50	.70	.45
405	Tommy Helms	1.50	.70	.45
406	Dick Ellsworth	1.50	.70	.45
407	Gary Kolb	1.50	.70	.45
408	Steve Carlton	24.00	12.00	7.25
409	Orioles Rookies (Frank Peters, Ron Stone)	1.50	.70	.45
410	Fergie Jenkins	10.00	5.00	3.00
411	Ron Hansen	1.50	.70	.45
412	Clay Carroll	1.50	.70	.45
413	Tommy McCraw	1.50	.70	.45
414	Mickey Lolich	2.00	1.00	.60
415	Johnny Callison	1.50	.70	.45
416	Bill Rigney	1.50	.70	.45
417	Willie Crawford	1.50	.70	.45
418	Eddie Fisher	1.50	.70	.45
419	Jack Hiatt	1.50	.70	.45
420	Cesar Tovar	1.50	.70	.45
421	Ron Taylor	1.50	.70	.45
422	Rene Lachemann	1.50	.70	.45
423	Fred Gladding	1.50	.70	.45
424	White Sox Team	3.00	1.50	.90
425	Jim Maloney	1.50	.70	.45
426	Hank Allen	1.50	.70	.45
427	Dick Calmus	1.50	.70	.45
428	Vic Roznovsky	1.50	.70	.45
429	Tommie Sisk	1.50	.70	.45
430	Rico Petrocelli	1.50	.70	.45
431	Dooley Womack	1.50	.70	.45
432	Indians Rookies (Bill Davis, Jose Vidal)	1.50	.70	.45
433	Bob Rodgers	1.50	.70	.45
434	Ricardo Joseph	1.50	.70	.45
435	Ron Perranoski	1.50	.70	.45
436	Hal Lanier	1.50	.70	.45
437	Don Cardwell	1.50	.70	.45
438	Lee Thomas	1.50	.70	.45
439	Luman Harris	1.50	.70	.45
440	Claude Osteen	1.50	.70	.45
441	Alex Johnson	1.50	.70	.45
442	Dick Bosman	1.50	.70	.45
443	Joe Azcue	1.50	.70	.45
444	Jack Fisher	1.50	.70	.45
445	Mike Shannon	2.00	1.00	.60
446	Ron Kline	1.50	.70	.45
447	Tigers Rookies (George Korince, Fred Lasher)	1.50	.70	.45
448	Gary Wagner	1.50	.70	.45
449	Gene Oliver	1.50	.70	.45
450	Jim Kaat	4.00	2.00	1.25
451	Al Spangler	1.50	.70	.45
452	Jesus Alou	1.50	.70	.45
453	Sammy Ellis	1.50	.70	.45
454	Checklist 458-533 (Frank Robinson)	6.00	3.00	1.75
455	Rico Carty	1.50	.70	.45
456	John O'Donoghue	1.50	.70	.45
457	Jim Lefebvre	1.50	.70	.45
458	Lew Krausse	3.00	1.50	.90
459	Dick Simpson	3.00	1.50	.90
460	Jim Lonborg	3.00	1.50	.90
461	Chuck Hiller	3.00	1.50	.90
462	Barry Moore	3.00	1.50	.90
463	Jimmie Schaffer	3.00	1.50	.90
464	Don McMahon	3.00	1.50	.90
465	Tommie Agee	3.00	1.50	.90
466	Bill Dillman	3.00	1.50	.90
467	Dick Howser	3.00	1.50	.90
468	Larry Sherry	3.00	1.50	.90
469	Ty Cline	3.00	1.50	.90
470	Bill Freehan	3.50	1.75	1.00
471	Orlando Pena	3.00	1.50	.90
472	Walt Alston	4.75	2.50	1.50
473	Al Worthington	3.00	1.50	.90
474	Paul Schaal	3.00	1.50	.90
475	Joe Niekro	3.00	1.50	.90
476	Woody Woodward	3.00	1.50	.90
477	Phillies Team	4.00	2.00	1.25
478	Dave McNally	3.00	1.50	.90
479	Phil Gagliano	3.00	1.50	.90
480	Manager's Dream (Chico Cardenas, Roberto Clemente, Tony Oliva)	65.00	32.00	19.50
481	John Wyatt	3.00	1.50	.90
482	Jose Pagan	3.00	1.50	.90
483	Darold Knowles	3.00	1.50	.90
484	Phil Roof	3.00	1.50	.90
485	Ken Berry	3.00	1.50	.90
486	Cal Koonce	3.00	1.50	.90
487	Lee May	3.00	1.50	.90
488	Dick Tracewski	3.00	1.50	.90
489	Wally Bunker	3.00	1.50	.90
490	Super Stars (Harmon Killebrew, Mickey Mantle, Willie Mays)	150.00	75.00	45.00
491	Denny Lemaster	3.00	1.50	.90
492	Jeff Torborg	3.00	1.50	.90
493	Jim McGlothlin	3.00	1.50	.90
494	Ray Sadecki	3.00	1.50	.90
495	Leon Wagner	3.00	1.50	.90
496	Steve Hamilton	3.00	1.50	.90
497	Cards Team	4.00	2.00	1.25
498	Bill Bryan	3.00	1.50	.90
499	Steve Blass	3.00	1.50	.90

500	Frank Robinson	25.00	12.50	7.50
501	John Odom	3.00	1.50	.90
502	Mike Andrews	3.00	1.50	.90
503	Al Jackson	3.00	1.50	.90
504	Russ Snyder	3.00	1.50	.90
505	Joe Sparma	3.00	1.50	.90
506	Clarence Jones	3.00	1.50	.90
507	Wade Blasingame	3.00	1.50	.90
508	Duke Sims	3.00	1.50	.90
509	Dennis Higgins	3.00	1.50	.90
510	Ron Fairly	3.00	1.50	.90
511	Bill Kelso	3.00	1.50	.90
512	Grant Jackson	3.00	1.50	.90
513	Hank Bauer	3.00	1.50	.90
514	Al McBean	3.00	1.50	.90
515	Russ Nixon	3.00	1.50	.90
516	Pete Mikkelsen	3.00	1.50	.90
517	Diego Segui	3.00	1.50	.90
518a	Checklist 534-598 (Clete Boyer) (539 is Maj. L. Rookies)	7.00	3.50	2.00
518b	Checklist 534-598 (Clete Boyer) (539 is Amer. L. Rookies)	9.00	4.50	2.75
519	Jerry Stephenson	3.00	1.50	.90
520	Lou Brock	20.00	10.00	6.00
521	Don Shaw	3.00	1.50	.90
522	Wayne Causey	3.00	1.50	.90
523	John Tsitouris	3.00	1.50	.90
524	Andy Kosco	3.00	1.50	.90
525	Jim Davenport	3.00	1.50	.90
526	Bill Denehy	3.00	1.50	.90
527	Tito Francona	3.00	1.50	.90
528	Tigers Team	55.00	27.00	16.50
529	Bruce Von Hoff	3.00	1.50	.90
530	Bird Belters (Brooks Robinson, Frank Robinson)	27.50	13.50	8.25
531	Chuck Hinton	3.00	1.50	.90
532	Luis Tiant	4.00	2.00	1.25
533	Wes Parker	3.00	1.50	.90
534	Bob Miller	3.50	1.75	1.00
535	Danny Cater	3.50	1.75	1.00
536	Bill Short	3.50	1.75	1.00
537	Norm Siebern	3.50	1.75	1.00
538	Manny Jimenez	3.50	1.75	1.00
539	Major League Rookies (Mike Ferraro, Jim Ray)	3.50	1.75	1.00
540	Nelson Briles	3.50	1.75	1.00
541	Sandy Alomar	3.50	1.75	1.00
542	John Boccabella	3.50	1.75	1.00
543	Bob Lee	3.50	1.75	1.00
544	Mayo Smith	3.50	1.75	1.00
545	Lindy McDaniel	3.50	1.75	1.00
546	Roy White	3.50	1.75	1.00
547	Dan Coombs	3.50	1.75	1.00
548	Bernie Allen	3.50	1.75	1.00
549	Orioles Rookies (Curt Motton, Roger Nelson)	3.50	1.75	1.00
550	Clete Boyer	4.00	2.00	1.25
551	Darrell Sutherland	3.50	1.75	1.00
552	Ed Kirkpatrick	3.50	1.75	1.00
553	Hank Aguirre	3.50	1.75	1.00
554	A's Team	6.00	3.00	1.75
555	Jose Tartabull	3.50	1.75	1.00
556	Dick Selma	3.50	1.75	1.00
557	Frank Quilici	3.50	1.75	1.00
558	John Edwards	3.50	1.75	1.00
559	Pirates Rookies (Carl Taylor, Luke Walker)	3.50	1.75	1.00
560	Paul Casanova	3.50	1.75	1.00
561	Lee Elia	3.50	1.75	1.00
562	Jim Bouton	3.50	1.75	1.00
563	Ed Charles	3.50	1.75	1.00
564	Eddie Stanky	3.50	1.75	1.00
565	Larry Dierker	3.50	1.75	1.00
566	Ken Harrelson	3.50	1.75	1.00
567	Clay Dalrymple	3.50	1.75	1.00
568	Willie Smith	3.50	1.75	1.00
569	N.L. Rookies (Ivan Murrell, Les Rohr)	3.50	1.75	1.00
570	Rick Reichardt	3.50	1.75	1.00
571	Tony LaRussa	8.00	4.00	2.50
572	Don Bosch	3.50	1.75	1.00
573	Joe Coleman	3.50	1.75	1.00
574	Reds Team	6.50	3.25	2.00
575	Jim Palmer	30.00	15.00	9.00
576	Dave Adlesh	3.50	1.75	1.00
577	Fred Talbot	3.50	1.75	1.00
578	Orlando Martinez	3.50	1.75	1.00
579	N.L. Rookies *(Larry Hisle), (Mike Lum)*	4.00	2.00	1.25
580	Bob Bailey	3.50	1.75	1.00
581	Garry Roggenburk	3.50	1.75	1.00
582	Jerry Grote	3.50	1.75	1.00
583	Gates Brown	3.50	1.75	1.00
584	Larry Shepard	3.50	1.75	1.00
585	Wilbur Wood	3.50	1.75	1.00
586	Jim Pagliaroni	3.50	1.75	1.00
587	Roger Repoz	3.50	1.75	1.00
588	Dick Schofield	3.50	1.75	1.00
589	Twins Rookies (Ron Clark, Moe Ogier)	3.50	1.75	1.00
590	Tommy Harper	3.50	1.75	1.00
591	Dick Nen	3.50	1.75	1.00
592	John Bateman	3.50	1.75	1.00
593	Lee Stange	3.50	1.75	1.00
594	Phil Linz	3.50	1.75	1.00
595	Phil Ortega	3.50	1.75	1.00
596	Charlie Smith	3.50	1.75	1.00
597	Bill McCool	3.50	1.75	1.00
598	Jerry May	5.50	2.00	1.00

1968 Topps Action All-Star Stickers

Another of the many Topps test issues of the late 1960s, Action All-Star stickers were sold in a strip of three, with bubble gum, for 10¢. The strip is comprised of three 3-1/4" x 5-1/4" panels, perforated at the joints for separation. The numbered central panel contain a large photo of a star player. The top and bottom panels contains smaller pictures of three players each. While there are 16 numbered center panels, only 12 of them are different; panels 13-16 show players previously used. Similarly, the triple-player panels at top and bottom of stickers 13-16 repeat panels from #1-4. Prices below are for stickers which have all three panels still joined. Individual panels are priced significantly lower.

		NM	EX	VG
Complete Set (16):		4250.	2100.	1275.
Common Panel:		90.00	45.00	27.00
1	Orlando Cepeda, Joe Horlen, Al Kaline, Bill Mazeroski, Claude Osteen, Mel Stottlemyre, Carl Yastrzemski	300.00	150.00	90.00
2	Don Drysdale, Harmon Killebrew, Mike McCormick, Tom Phoebus, George Scott, Ron Swoboda, Pete Ward	90.00	45.00	27.00
3	Hank Aaron, Paul Casanova, Jim Maloney, Joe Pepitone, Rick Reichardt, Frank Robinson, Tom Seaver	120.00	60.00	36.00
4	Bob Aspromonte, Johnny Callison, Dean Chance, Jim Lefebvre, Jim Lonborg, Frank Robinson, Ron Santo	150.00	75.00	45.00
5	Bert Campaneris, Al Downing, Willie Horton, Ed Kranepool, Willie Mays, Pete Rose, Ron Santo	450.00	225.00	135.00
6	Max Alvis, Ernie Banks, Al Kaline, Tim McCarver, Rusty Staub, Walt Williams, Carl Yastrzemski	200.00	100.00	60.00
7	Rod Carew, Tony Gonzalez, Steve Hargan, Mickey Mantle, Willie McCovey, Rick Monday, Billy Williams	750.00	375.00	225.00
8	Clete Boyer, Jim Bunning, Tony Conigliaro, Mike Cuellar, Joe Horlen, Ken McMullen, Don Mincher	60.00	30.00	18.00
9	Orlando Cepeda, Bob Clemente, Jim Fregosi, Harmon Killebrew, Willie Mays, Chris Short, Earl Wilson	350.00	175.00	105.00
10	Hank Aaron, Bob Gibson, Bud Harrelson, Jim Hunter, Mickey Mantle, Gary Peters, Vada Pinson	300.00	150.00	90.00
11	Don Drysdale, Bill Freehan, Frank Howard, Ferguson Jenkins, Tony Oliva, Bob Veale, Jim Wynn	180.00	90.00	54.00
12	Richie Allen, Bob Clemente, Sam McDowell, Jim McGlothlin, Tony Perez, Brooks Robinson, Joe Torre	700.00	350.00	210.00
13	Dean Chance, Don Drysdale, Jim Lefebvre, Tom Phoebus, Frank Robinson, George Scott, Carl Yastrzemski	300.00	150.00	90.00
14	Paul Casanova, Orlando Cepeda, Joe Horlen, Harmon Killebrew, Bill Mazeroski, Rick Reichardt, Tom Seaver	120.00	60.00	36.00

		NM	EX	VG
15	Bob Aspromonte, Johnny Callison, Jim Lonborg, Mike McCormick, Frank Robinson, Ron Swoboda, Pete Ward	90.00	45.00	27.00
16	Hank Aaron, Al Kaline, Jim Maloney, Claude Osteen, Joe Pepitone, Ron Santo, Mel Stottlemyre	180.00	90.00	54.00

1968 Topps Deckle Edge Test Proofs

While most Topps proofs are so rare as to preclude their listing in this catalog, the 1968 Deckle Edge test set is an exception. Usually found in the form of a 7-3/4" x 11" uncut sheet of nine black-and-white cards, single cards are sometimes encountered. The blank-backed sheet and cards can be found with the players' facsimile autographs printed in red, black or blue. Unnumbered cards are checklisted here alphabetically.

		NM	EX	VG
Complete Set, Singles (9):		400.00	200.00	120.00
Uncut Sheet:		600.00	300.00	180.00
Common Player:		30.00	15.00	9.00
(1)	Dave Adlesh	30.00	15.00	9.00
(2)	Hank Aguire	30.00	15.00	9.00
(3)	Sandy Alomar	50.00	25.00	15.00
(4)	Sonny Jackson	30.00	15.00	9.00
(5)	Bob Johnson	30.00	15.00	9.00
(6)	Claude Osteen	30.00	15.00	9.00
(7)	Juan Pizarro	30.00	15.00	9.00
(8)	Hal Woodeshick	30.00	15.00	9.00
(9)	Carl Yastrzemski	250.00	125.00	75.00

1968 Topps Discs

One of the scarcer Topps baseball collectibles, this set was apparently a never-completed test issue. These full-color, cardboard discs, which measure approximately 2-1/4" in diameter, were probably intended to be made into a pin set but production was never completed and no actual pins are known to exist. Uncut sheets of the player discs have been found. The discs include a player portrait photo with the name beneath and the city and team nickname along the sides.

		NM	EX	VG
Complete Set (28):		3250.	1600.	975.00
Common Player:		40.00	20.00	12.00
(1)	Hank Aaron	350.00	175.00	105.00
(2)	Richie Allen	60.00	30.00	18.00
(3)	Gene Alley	40.00	20.00	12.00
(4)	Rod Carew	200.00	100.00	60.00
(5)	Orlando Cepeda	150.00	75.00	45.00
(6)	Dean Chance	40.00	20.00	12.00
(7)	Roberto Clemente	450.00	225.00	135.00
(8)	Tommy Davis	40.00	20.00	12.00
(9)	Bill Freehan	40.00	20.00	12.00
(10)	Jim Fregosi	40.00	20.00	12.00
(11)	Steve Hargan	40.00	20.00	12.00
(12)	Frank Howard	45.00	22.00	13.50
(13)	Al Kaline	200.00	100.00	60.00
(14)	Harmon Killebrew	200.00	100.00	60.00
(15)	Mickey Mantle	700.00	350.00	210.00
(16)	Willie Mays	350.00	175.00	105.00
(17)	Mike McCormick	40.00	20.00	12.00
(18)	Rick Monday	40.00	20.00	12.00
(19)	Claude Osteen	40.00	20.00	12.00
(20)	Gary Peters	40.00	20.00	12.00
(21)	Brooks Robinson	200.00	100.00	60.00
(22)	Frank Robinson	200.00	100.00	60.00
(23)	Pete Rose	300.00	150.00	90.00
(24)	Ron Santo	60.00	30.00	18.00
(25)	Rusty Staub	45.00	22.00	13.50
(26)	Joe Torre	75.00	37.00	22.00
(27)	Carl Yastrzemski	200.00	100.00	60.00
(28)	Bob Veale	40.00	20.00	12.00

1968 Topps Game

A throwback to the Red and Blue Back sets of 1951, the 33-cards in the 1968 Topps Game set, inserted into packs of regular '68 Topps cards or purchased as a complete boxed set, enable the owner to play a game of baseball based on the game situations on each card. Also on the 2-1/4" x 3-1/4" cards was a color photograph of a player and his facsimile autograph. One redeeming social value of the set (assuming you're not mesmerized by the game) is that it affords an inexpensive way to get big-name cards as the set is loaded with stars, but not at all popular with collectors.

		NM	EX	VG
Complete Set (33):		90.00	45.00	27.00
Common Player:		2.00	1.00	.60
1	Mateo Alou	2.00	1.00	.60
2	Mickey Mantle	32.50	16.00	9.75
3	Carl Yastrzemski	7.00	3.50	2.00
4	Henry Aaron	12.50	6.25	3.75
5	Harmon Killebrew	6.00	3.00	1.75
6	Roberto Clemente	15.00	7.50	4.50
7	Frank Robinson	6.00	3.00	1.75
8	Willie Mays	12.50	6.25	3.75
9	Brooks Robinson	7.00	3.50	2.00
10	Tommy Davis	2.00	1.00	.60
11	Bill Freehan	2.00	1.00	.60
12	Claude Osteen	2.00	1.00	.60
13	Gary Peters	2.00	1.00	.60
14	Jim Lonborg	2.00	1.00	.60
15	Steve Hargan	2.00	1.00	.60
16	Dean Chance	2.00	1.00	.60
17	Mike McCormick	2.00	1.00	.60
18	Tim McCarver	2.50	1.25	.70
19	Ron Santo	3.00	1.50	.90
20	Tony Gonzalez	2.00	1.00	.60
21	Frank Howard	2.50	1.25	.70
22	George Scott	2.00	1.00	.60
23	Rich Allen	3.00	1.50	.90
24	Jim Wynn	2.00	1.00	.60
25	Gene Alley	2.00	1.00	.60
26	Rick Monday	2.00	1.00	.60
27	Al Kaline	7.00	3.50	2.00
28	Rusty Staub	3.00	1.50	.90
29	Rod Carew	7.00	3.50	2.00
30	Pete Rose	12.00	6.00	3.50
31	Joe Torre	4.00	2.00	1.25
32	Orlando Cepeda	6.00	3.00	1.75
33	Jim Fregosi	2.00	1.00	.60

1968 Topps Plaks

Among the scarcest Topps test issues of the late 1960s, the "All Star Baseball Plaks" were plastic busts of two dozen stars of the era which came packaged like model airplane parts. The busts had to be snapped off a sprue and could be inserted into a base which carried the player's name. Packed with the plastic plaks was one of two checklist cards which featured six color photos per side. The 2-1/8" x 4" checklist cards are popular with superstar collectors and are considerably easier to find today than the actual plaks.

		NM	EX	VG
Complete Set (24):		6500.	3250.	1950.
Common Player:		40.00	20.00	12.00
1	Max Alvis	40.00	20.00	12.00
2	Dean Chance	40.00	20.00	12.00
3	Jim Fregosi	40.00	20.00	12.00
4	Frank Howard	60.00	30.00	18.00
5	Jim Hunter	150.00	75.00	45.00
6	Al Kaline	350.00	175.00	105.00
7	Harmon Killebrew	200.00	100.00	60.00
8	Jim Lonborg	50.00	25.00	15.00
9	Mickey Mantle	2000.	1000.	600.00
10	Gary Peters	40.00	20.00	12.00
11	Frank Robinson	350.00	175.00	105.00
12	Carl Yastrzemski	125.00	62.00	37.00
13	Hank Aaron	750.00	375.00	225.00
14	Richie Allen	75.00	37.00	22.00
15	Orlando Cepeda	200.00	100.00	60.00
16	Roberto Clemente	1750.	875.00	525.00
17	Tommy Davis	60.00	30.00	18.00
18	Don Drysdale	120.00	60.00	36.00
19	Willie Mays	750.00	375.00	225.00
20	Tim McCarver	60.00	30.00	18.00
21	Ron Santo	60.00	30.00	18.00
22	Rusty Staub	50.00	25.00	15.00
23	Pete Rose	750.00	375.00	225.00
24	Jim Wynn	40.00	20.00	12.00
---	Checklist Card 1-12	600.00	300.00	180.00
---	Checklist Card 13-24	600.00	300.00	180.00

1968 Topps Posters

Yet another innovation from the creative minds at Topps appeared in 1968; a set of color player posters. Measuring 9-3/4" x 18-1/8," each poster was sold separately with its own piece of gum, rather than as an insert. The posters feature a large color photograph with a star at the bottom containing the player's name, position and team. There are 24 different posters which were folded numerous times to fit into the package they were sold in.

		NM	EX	VG
Complete Set (24):		500.00	250.00	150.00
Common Player:		7.50	3.75	2.25
1	Dean Chance	7.50	3.75	2.25
2	Max Alvis	7.50	3.75	2.25
3	Frank Howard	8.00	4.00	2.50
4	Jim Fregosi	7.50	3.75	2.25
5	Catfish Hunter	12.50	6.25	3.75
6	Roberto Clemente	50.00	25.00	15.00
7	Don Drysdale	18.50	9.25	5.50
8	Jim Wynn	7.50	3.75	2.25
9	Al Kaline	22.00	11.00	6.50
10	Harmon Killebrew	22.00	11.00	6.50
11	Jim Lonborg	7.50	3.75	2.25
12	Orlando Cepeda	15.00	7.50	4.50
13	Gary Peters	7.50	3.75	2.25
14	Hank Aaron	40.00	20.00	12.00
15	Richie Allen	11.00	5.50	3.25
16	Carl Yastrzemski	22.00	11.00	6.50
17	Ron Swoboda	7.50	3.75	2.25
18	Mickey Mantle	80.00	40.00	24.00

		NM	EX	VG
19	Tim McCarver	8.00	4.00	2.50
20	Willie Mays	40.00	20.00	12.00
21	Ron Santo	11.00	5.50	3.25
22	Rusty Staub	8.00	4.00	2.50
23	Pete Rose	40.00	20.00	12.00
24	Frank Robinson	22.00	11.00	6.50

1968 Topps 3-D

These are very rare pioneer issues on the part of Topps. The cards measure 2-1/4" x 3-1/2" and were specially printed to simulate a three-dimensional effect. Backgrounds are a purposely blurred stadium scene, in front of which was a normally sharp color player photograph. The outer layer is a thin coating of ribbed plastic. The special process gives the picture the illusion of depth when the card is moved or tilted. As this was done two years before Kellogg's began its 3-D cards, this 12-card test issue really was breaking new ground. Unfortunately, production and distribution were limited making the cards very tough to find.

		NM	EX	VG
Complete Set (12):		9000.	4500.	2750.
Common Player:		600.00	300.00	180.00
Wrapper:		1500.	750.00	450.00
(1)	Bob Clemente	4000.	2000.	1200.
(2)	Willie Davis	600.00	300.00	180.00
(3)	Ron Fairly	600.00	300.00	180.00
(4)	Curt Flood	850.00	425.00	255.00
(5)	Jim Lonborg	600.00	300.00	180.00
(6)	Jim Maloney	600.00	300.00	180.00
(7)	Tony Perez	800.00	400.00	240.00
(8)	Boog Powell	800.00	400.00	240.00
(9)	Bill Robinson	600.00	300.00	180.00
(10)	Rusty Staub	800.00	400.00	240.00
(11)	Mel Stottlemyre	600.00	300.00	180.00
(12)	Ron Swoboda	600.00	300.00	180.00

1969 Topps

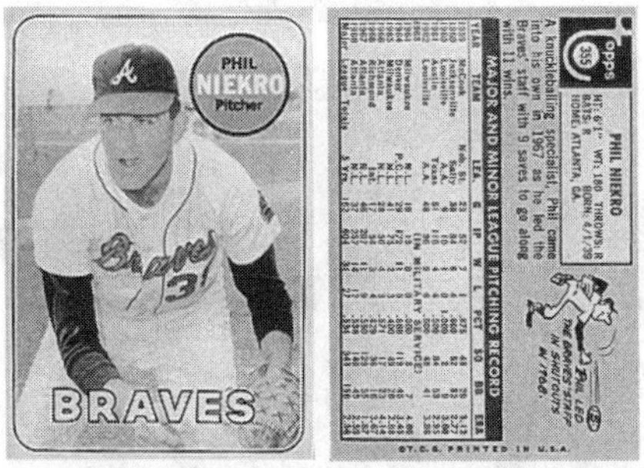

The 1969 Topps set broke yet another record for quantity as the issue is officially a whopping 664 cards. With substantial numbers of variations, the number of possible cards runs closer to 700. The design of the 2-1/2" x 3-1/2" cards in the set feature a color photo with the team name printed in block letters underneath. A circle contains the player's name and position. Card backs returned to a horizontal format. Despite the size of the set, it contains no team cards. It does, however, have multi-player cards, All-Stars, statistical leaders, and World Series highlights. Most significant among the varieties are white and yellow letter cards from the run of #'s 440-511. The complete set prices below do not include the scarcer and more expensive "white letter" variations.

		NM	EX	VG
Complete Set (664):		2000.	900.00	650.00
Common Player (1-218):		1.50	.70	.45
Common Player (219-327):		2.50	1.25	.70
Common Player (328-512):		1.50	.70	.45
Common Player (513-588):		2.50	1.25	.70
Common Player (589-664):		3.00	1.50	.90
1	A.L. Batting Leaders (Danny Cater, Tony Oliva, Carl Yastrzemski)	10.00	5.00	3.00
2	N.L. Batting Leaders (Felipe Alou, Matty Alou, Pete Rose)	7.00	3.50	2.00
3	A.L. RBI Leaders (Ken Harrelson, Frank Howard, Jim Northrup)	3.00	1.50	.90
4	N.L. RBI Leaders (Willie McCovey, Ron Santo, Billy Williams)	6.00	3.00	1.75
5	A.L. Home Run Leaders (Ken Harrelson, Willie Horton, Frank Howard)	3.00	1.50	.90
6	N.L. Home Run Leaders (Richie Allen, Ernie Banks, Willie McCovey)	6.00	3.00	1.75
7	A.L. ERA Leaders (Sam McDowell, Dave McNally, Luis Tiant)	3.00	1.50	.90
8	N.L. ERA Leaders (Bobby Bolin, Bob Gibson, Bob Veale)	3.00	1.50	.90
9	A.L. Pitching Leaders (Denny McLain, Dave McNally, Mel Stottlemyre, Luis Tiant)	3.00	1.50	.90
10	N.L. Pitching Leaders (Bob Gibson, Fergie Jenkins, Juan Marichal)	6.00	3.00	1.75
11	A.L. Strikeout Leaders (Sam McDowell, Denny McLain, Luis Tiant)	3.00	1.50	.90
12	N.L. Strikeout Leaders (Bob Gibson, Fergie Jenkins, Bill Singer)	4.00	2.00	1.25
13	Mickey Stanley	1.50	.70	.45
14	Al McBean	1.50	.70	.45
15	Boog Powell	2.50	1.25	.70
16	Giants Rookies (Cesar Gutierrez, Rich Robertson)	1.50	.70	.45
17	Mike Marshall	1.50	.70	.45
18	Dick Schofield	1.50	.70	.45
19	Ken Suarez	1.50	.70	.45
20	Ernie Banks	16.00	8.00	4.75
21	Jose Santiago	1.50	.70	.45
22	Jesus Alou	1.50	.70	.45
23	Lew Krausse	1.50	.70	.45
24	Walt Alston	3.00	1.50	.90
25	Roy White	1.50	.70	.45
26	Clay Carroll	1.50	.70	.45
27	Bernie Allen	1.50	.70	.45
28	Mike Ryan	1.50	.70	.45
29	Dave Morehead	1.50	.70	.45
30	Bob Allison	1.50	.70	.45
31	Mets Rookies *(Gary Gentry)*, *(Amos Otis)*	2.50	1.25	.70
32	Sammy Ellis	1.50	.70	.45
33	Wayne Causey	1.50	.70	.45
34	Gary Peters	1.50	.70	.45
35	Joe Morgan	8.50	4.25	2.50
36	Luke Walker	1.50	.70	.45
37	Curt Motton	1.50	.70	.45
38	Zoilo Versalles	1.50	.70	.45
39	Dick Hughes	1.50	.70	.45
40	Mayo Smith	1.50	.70	.45
41	Bob Barton	1.50	.70	.45
42	Tommy Harper	1.50	.70	.45
43	Joe Niekro	2.00	1.00	.60
44	Danny Cater	1.50	.70	.45
45	Maury Wills	2.00	1.00	.60
46	Fritz Peterson	1.50	.70	.45
47a	Paul Popovich (emblem visible thru airbrush)	25.00	12.50	7.50
47b	Paul Popovich (helmet emblem completely airbrushed)	1.50	.70	.45
48	Brant Alyea	1.50	.70	.45
49a	Royals Rookies (Steve Jones, Eliseo Rodriguez) (Rodriguez on front)	22.00	11.00	6.50
49b	Royals Rookies (Steve Jones, Eliseo Rodriguez) (Rodriguez on front)	1.50	.70	.45
50	Roberto Clemente	45.00	22.00	13.50
51	Woody Fryman	1.50	.70	.45
52	Mike Andrews	1.50	.70	.45
53	Sonny Jackson	1.50	.70	.45
54	Cisco Carlos	1.50	.70	.45
55	Jerry Grote	1.50	.70	.45
56	Rich Reese	1.50	.70	.45
57	Checklist 1-109 (Denny McLain)	4.50	2.25	1.25
58	Fred Gladding	1.50	.70	.45
59	Jay Johnstone	1.50	.70	.45
60	Nelson Briles	1.50	.70	.45
61	Jimmie Hall	1.50	.70	.45
62	Chico Salmon	1.50	.70	.45
63	Jim Hickman	1.50	.70	.45
64	Bill Monbouquette	1.50	.70	.45
65	Willie Davis	1.50	.70	.45
66	Orioles Rookies (Mike Adamson), *(Merv Rettenmund)*	1.50	.70	.45
67	Bill Stoneman	1.50	.70	.45
68	Dave Duncan	1.50	.70	.45
69	Steve Hamilton	1.50	.70	.45
70	Tommy Helms	1.50	.70	.45
71	Steve Whitaker	1.50	.70	.45
72	Ron Taylor	1.50	.70	.45
73	Johnny Briggs	1.50	.70	.45
74	Preston Gomez	1.50	.70	.45
75	Luis Aparicio	4.00	2.00	1.25
76	Norm Miller	1.50	.70	.45
77a	Ron Perranoski (LA visible thru airbrush)	18.00	9.00	5.50
77b	Ron Perranoski (cap emblem completely airbrushed)	1.50	.70	.45
78	Tom Satriano	1.50	.70	.45
79	Milt Pappas	1.50	.70	.45
80	Norm Cash	2.50	1.25	.70
81	Mel Queen	1.50	.70	.45
82	Pirates Rookies *(Rich Hebner)*, *(Al Oliver)*	9.00	4.50	2.75
83	Mike Ferraro	1.50	.70	.45
84	Bob Humphreys	1.50	.70	.45
85	Lou Brock	15.00	7.50	4.50
86	Pete Richert	1.50	.70	.45
87	Horace Clarke	1.50	.70	.45
88	Rich Nye	1.50	.70	.45
89	Russ Gibson	1.50	.70	.45
90	Jerry Koosman	2.50	1.25	.70
91	Al Dark	1.50	.70	.45
92	Jack Billingham	1.50	.70	.45
93	Joe Foy	1.50	.70	.45
94	Hank Aguirre	1.50	.70	.45
95	Johnny Bench	45.00	22.00	13.50
96	Denver Lemaster	1.50	.70	.45
97	Buddy Bradford	1.50	.70	.45
98	Dave Giusti	1.50	.70	.45
99a	Twins Rookies (Danny Morris), *(Graig Nettles)* (black loop above "Twins")	17.00	8.50	5.00
99b	Twins Rookies (Danny Morris), *(Graig Nettles)* (no black loop)	19.00	9.50	5.75
100	Hank Aaron	40.00	20.00	12.00
101	Daryl Patterson	1.50	.70	.45
102	Jim Davenport	1.50	.70	.45
103	Roger Repoz	1.50	.70	.45
104	Steve Blass	1.50	.70	.45
105	Rick Monday	1.50	.70	.45
106	Jim Hannan	1.50	.70	.45
107a	Checklist 110-218 (Bob Gibson) (161 is Jim Purdin)	4.00	2.00	1.25
107b	Checklist 110-218 (Bob Gibson) (161 is John Purdin)	6.00	3.00	1.75
108	Tony Taylor	1.50	.70	.45
109	Jim Lonborg	1.50	.70	.45
110	Mike Shannon	1.50	.70	.45
111	Johnny Morris	1.50	.70	.45
112	J.C. Martin	1.50	.70	.45
113	Dave May	1.50	.70	.45
114	Yankees Rookies (Alan Closter, John Cumberland)	1.50	.70	.45
115	Bill Hands	1.50	.70	.45
116	Chuck Harrison	1.50	.70	.45
117	Jim Fairey	1.50	.70	.45
118	Stan Williams	1.50	.70	.45
119	Doug Rader	1.50	.70	.45
120	Pete Rose	25.00	12.50	7.50
121	Joe Grzenda	1.50	.70	.45
122	Ron Fairly	1.50	.70	.45
123	Wilbur Wood	1.50	.70	.45
124	Hank Bauer	1.50	.70	.45
125	Ray Sadecki	1.50	.70	.45
126	Dick Tracewski	1.50	.70	.45
127	Kevin Collins	1.50	.70	.45
128	Tommie Aaron	1.50	.70	.45
129	Bill McCool	1.50	.70	.45
130	Carl Yastrzemski	16.00	8.00	4.75
131	Chris Cannizzaro	1.50	.70	.45
132	Dave Baldwin	1.50	.70	.45
133	Johnny Callison	1.50	.70	.45
134	Jim Weaver	1.50	.70	.45
135	Tommy Davis	2.00	1.00	.60
136	Cards Rookies (Steve Huntz, Mike Torrez)	1.50	.70	.45
137	Wally Bunker	1.50	.70	.45
138	John Bateman	1.50	.70	.45
139	Andy Kosco	1.50	.70	.45
140	Jim Lefebvre	1.50	.70	.45
141	Bill Dillman	1.50	.70	.45
142	Woody Woodward	1.50	.70	.45
143	Joe Nossek	1.50	.70	.45
144	Bob Hendley	1.50	.70	.45
145	Max Alvis	1.50	.70	.45
146	Jim Perry	1.50	.70	.45
147	Leo Durocher	3.00	1.50	.90
148	Lee Stange	1.50	.70	.45
149	Ollie Brown	1.50	.70	.45
150	Denny McLain	2.00	1.00	.60
151a	Clay Dalrymple (Phillies)	17.00	8.50	5.00
151b	Clay Dalrymple (Orioles)	1.50	.70	.45
152	Tommie Sisk	1.50	.70	.45
153	Ed Brinkman	1.50	.70	.45
154	Jim Britton	1.50	.70	.45
155	Pete Ward	1.50	.70	.45
156	Astros Rookies (Hal Gilson, Leon McFadden)	1.50	.70	.45
157	Bob Rodgers	1.50	.70	.45
158	Joe Gibbon	1.50	.70	.45
159	Jerry Adair	1.50	.70	.45
160	Vada Pinson	2.50	1.25	.70
161	John Purdin	1.50	.70	.45
162	World Series Game 1 (Gibson Fans 17; Sets New Record)	4.25	2.25	1.25
163	World Series Game 2 (Tiger Homers Deck The Cards)	4.00	2.00	1.25
164	World Series Game 3 (McCarver's Homer Puts St. Louis Ahead)	5.00	2.50	1.50
165	World Series Game 4 (Brock's Lead-Off HR Starts Cards' Romp)	5.00	2.50	1.50
166	World Series Game 5 (Kaline's Key Hit Sparks Tiger Rally)	4.50	2.25	1.25

167	World Series Game 6 (Tiger 10-Run Inning Ties Mark)	4.00	2.00	1.25
168	World Series Game 7 (Lolich Series Hero Outduels Gibson)	6.00	3.00	1.75
169	World Series Summary (Tigers Celebrate Their Victory)	4.00	2.00	1.25
170	Frank Howard	2.00	1.00	.60
171	Glenn Beckert	1.50	.70	.45
172	Jerry Stephenson	1.50	.70	.45
173	White Sox Rookies (Bob Christian, Gerry Nyman)	1.50	.70	.45
174	Grant Jackson	1.50	.70	.45
175	Jim Bunning	4.25	2.25	1.25
176	Joe Azcue	1.50	.70	.45
177	Ron Reed	1.50	.70	.45
178	Ray Oyler	1.50	.70	.45
179	Don Pavletich	1.50	.70	.45
180	Willie Horton	1.50	.70	.45
181	Mel Nelson	1.50	.70	.45
182	Bill Rigney	1.50	.70	.45
183	Don Shaw	1.50	.70	.45
184	Roberto Pena	1.50	.70	.45
185	Tom Phoebus	1.50	.70	.45
186	John Edwards	1.50	.70	.45
187	Leon Wagner	1.50	.70	.45
188	Rick Wise	1.50	.70	.45
189	Red Sox Rookies (Joe Lahoud, John Thibdeau)	1.50	.70	.45
190	Willie Mays	45.00	22.00	13.50
191	Lindy McDaniel	1.50	.70	.45
192	Jose Pagan	1.50	.70	.45
193	Don Cardwell	1.50	.70	.45
194	Ted Uhlaender	1.50	.70	.45
195	John Odom	1.50	.70	.45
196	Lum Harris	1.50	.70	.45
197	Dick Selma	1.50	.70	.45
198	Willie Smith	1.50	.70	.45
199	Jim French	1.50	.70	.45
200	Bob Gibson	11.50	5.75	3.50
201	Russ Snyder	1.50	.70	.45
202	Don Wilson	1.50	.70	.45
203	Dave Johnson	1.50	.70	.45
204	Jack Hiatt	1.50	.70	.45
205	Rick Reichardt	1.50	.70	.45
206	Phillies Rookies (Larry Hisle, Barry Lersch)	1.50	.70	.45
207	Roy Face	1.50	.70	.45
208a	Donn Clendenon (Expos)	16.00	8.00	4.75
208b	Donn Clendenon (Houston)	1.50	.70	.45
209	Larry Haney (photo reversed)	1.50	.70	.45
210	Felix Millan	1.50	.70	.45
211	Galen Cisco	1.50	.70	.45
212	Tom Tresh	1.50	.70	.45
213	Gerry Arrigo	1.50	.70	.45
214	Checklist 219-327	5.00	2.50	1.50
215	Rico Petrocelli	1.50	.70	.45
216	Don Sutton	5.00	2.50	1.50
217	John Donaldson	1.50	.70	.45
218	John Roseboro	1.50	.70	.45
219	*Freddie Patek*	2.50	1.25	.70
220	Sam McDowell	2.50	1.25	.70
221	Art Shamsky	2.50	1.25	.70
222	Duane Josephson	2.50	1.25	.70
223	Tom Dukes	2.50	1.25	.70
224	Angels Rookies (Bill Harrelson, Steve Kealey)	2.50	1.25	.70
225	Don Kessinger	2.50	1.25	.70
226	Bruce Howard	2.50	1.25	.70
227	Frank Johnson	2.50	1.25	.70
228	Dave Leonhard	2.50	1.25	.70
229	Don Lock	2.50	1.25	.70
230	Rusty Staub	3.00	1.50	.90
231	Pat Dobson	2.50	1.25	.70
232	Dave Ricketts	2.50	1.25	.70
233	Steve Barber	2.50	1.25	.70
234	Dave Bristol	2.50	1.25	.70
235	Catfish Hunter	9.00	4.50	2.75
236	Manny Mota	2.50	1.25	.70
237	*Bobby Cox*	8.00	4.00	2.50
238	Ken Johnson	2.50	1.25	.70
239	Bob Taylor	2.50	1.25	.70
240	Ken Harrelson	2.50	1.25	.70
241	Jim Brewer	2.50	1.25	.70
242	Frank Kostro	2.50	1.25	.70
243	Ron Kline	2.50	1.25	.70
244	Indians Rookies *(Ray Fosse,* George Woodson)	4.00	2.00	1.25
245	Ed Charles	2.50	1.25	.70
246	Joe Coleman	2.50	1.25	.70
247	Gene Oliver	2.50	1.25	.70
248	Bob Priddy	2.50	1.25	.70
249	Ed Spiezio	2.50	1.25	.70
250	Frank Robinson	30.00	15.00	9.00
251	Ron Herbel	2.50	1.25	.70
252	Chuck Cottier	2.50	1.25	.70
253	Jerry Johnson	2.50	1.25	.70
254	Joe Schultz	2.50	1.25	.70
255	Steve Carlton	30.00	15.00	[illegible]
256	Gates Brown	2.50	1.25	.70
257	Jim Ray	2.50	1.25	.70
258	Jackie Hernandez	2.50	1.25	.70
259	Bill Short	2.50	1.25	.70
260	*Reggie Jackson*	160.00	80.00	48.00
261	Bob Johnson	2.50	1.25	.70
262	Mike Kekich	2.50	1.25	.70
263	Jerry May	2.50	1.25	.70
264	Bill Landis	2.50	1.25	.70
265	Chico Cardenas	2.50	1.25	.70
266	Dodgers Rookies (Alan Foster, Tom Hutton)	2.50	1.25	.70
267	Vicente Romo	2.50	1.25	.70
268	Al Spangler	2.50	1.25	.70
269	Al Weis	2.50	1.25	.70
270	Mickey Lolich	3.00	1.50	.90
271	Larry Stahl	2.50	1.25	.70
272	Ed Stroud	2.50	1.25	.70

273	Ron Willis	2.50	1.25	.70
274	Clyde King	2.50	1.25	.70
275	Vic Davalillo	2.50	1.25	.70
276	Gary Wagner	2.50	1.25	.70
277	*Rod Hendricks*	2.50	1.25	.70
278	Gary Geiger	2.50	1.25	.70
279	Roger Nelson	2.50	1.25	.70
280	Alex Johnson	2.50	1.25	.70
281	Ted Kubiak	2.50	1.25	.70
282	Pat Jarvis	2.50	1.25	.70
283	Sandy Alomar	2.50	1.25	.70
284	Expos Rookies (Jerry Robertson, Mike Wegener)	2.50	1.25	.70
285	Don Mincher	2.50	1.25	.70
286	*Dock Ellis*	3.00	1.50	.90
287	Jose Tartabull	2.50	1.25	.70
288	Ken Holtzman	2.50	1.25	.70
289	Bart Shirley	2.50	1.25	.70
290	Jim Kaat	4.50	2.25	1.25
291	Vern Fuller	2.50	1.25	.70
292	Al Downing	2.50	1.25	.70
293	Dick Dietz	2.50	1.25	.70
294	Jim Lemon	2.50	1.25	.70
295	Tony Perez	12.00	6.00	3.50
296	*Andy Messersmith*	3.00	1.50	.90
297	Deron Johnson	2.50	1.25	.70
298	Dave Nicholson	2.50	1.25	.70
299	Mark Belanger	2.50	1.25	.70
300	Felipe Alou	4.00	2.00	1.25
301	Darrell Brandon	2.50	1.25	.70
302	Jim Pagliaroni	2.50	1.25	.70
303	Cal Koonce	2.50	1.25	.70
304	Padres Rookies (Bill Davis), *(Cito Gaston)*	6.00	3.00	1.75
305	Dick McAuliffe	2.50	1.25	.70
306	Jim Grant	2.50	1.25	.70
307	Gary Kolb	2.50	1.25	.70
308	Wade Blasingame	2.50	1.25	.70
309	Walt Williams	2.50	1.25	.70
310	Tom Haller	2.50	1.25	.70
311	*Sparky Lyle*	7.50	3.75	2.25
312	Lee Elia	2.50	1.25	.70
313	Bill Robinson	2.50	1.25	.70
314	Checklist 328-425 (Don Drysdale)	5.00	2.50	1.50
315	Eddie Fisher	2.50	1.25	.70
316	Hal Lanier	2.50	1.25	.70
317	Bruce Look	2.50	1.25	.70
318	Jack Fisher	2.50	1.25	.70
319	Ken McMullen	2.50	1.25	.70
320	Dal Maxvill	2.50	1.25	.70
321	Jim McAndrew	2.50	1.25	.70
322	Jose Vidal	2.50	1.25	.70
323	Larry Miller	2.50	1.25	.70
324	Tigers Rookies (Les Cain, Dave Campbell)	2.50	1.25	.70
325	Jose Cardenal	2.50	1.25	.70
326	Gary Sutherland	2.50	1.25	.70
327	Willie Crawford	2.50	1.25	.70
328	Joe Horlen	1.50	.70	.45
329	Rick Joseph	1.50	.70	.45
330	Tony Conigliaro	3.50	1.75	1.00
331	Braves Rookies (Gil Garrido), *(Tom House)*	1.50	.70	.45
332	Fred Talbot	1.50	.70	.45
333	Ivan Murrell	1.50	.70	.45
334	Phil Roof	1.50	.70	.45
335	Bill Mazeroski	4.00	2.00	1.25
336	Jim Roland	1.50	.70	.45
337	Marty Martinez	1.50	.70	.45
338	*Del Unser*	1.50	.70	.45
339	Reds Rookies (Steve Mingori, Jose Pena)	1.50	.70	.45
340	Dave McNally	1.50	.70	.45
341	Dave Adlesh	1.50	.70	.45
342	Bubba Morton	1.50	.70	.45
343	Dan Frisella	1.50	.70	.45
344	Tom Matchick	1.50	.70	.45
345	Frank Linzy	1.50	.70	.45
346	Wayne Comer	1.50	.70	.45
347	Randy Hundley	1.50	.70	.45
348	Steve Hargan	1.50	.70	.45
349	Dick Williams	1.50	.70	.45
350	Richie Allen	4.00	2.00	1.25
351	Carroll Sembera	1.50	.70	.45
352	Paul Schaal	1.50	.70	.45
353	Jeff Torborg	1.50	.70	.45
354	Nate Oliver	1.50	.70	.45
355	Phil Niekro	6.00	3.00	1.75
356	Frank Quilici	1.50	.70	.45
357	Carl Taylor	1.50	.70	.45
358	Athletics Rookies (George Lauzerique, Roberto Rodriguez)	1.50	.70	.45
359	Dick Kelley	1.50	.70	.45
360	Jim Wynn	1.50	.70	.45
361	Gary Holman	1.50	.70	.45
362	Jim Maloney	1.50	.70	.45
363	Russ Nixon	1.50	.70	.45
364	Tommie Agee	1.50	.70	.45
365	Jim Fregosi	1.50	.70	.45
366	Bo Belinsky	1.50	.70	.45
367	Lou Johnson	1.50	.70	.45
368	Vic Roznovsky	1.50	.70	.45
369	Bob Skinner	1.50	.70	.45
370	Juan Marichal	6.00	3.00	1.75
371	Sal Bando	1.50	.70	.45
372	Adolfo Phillips	1.50	.70	.45
373	Fred Lasher	1.50	.70	.45
374	Bob Tillman	1.50	.70	.45
375	Harmon Killebrew	15.00	7.50	4.50
376	Royals Rookies (Mike Fiore), *(Jim Rooker)*	1.50	.70	.45
377	Gary Bell	1.50	.70	.45
378	Jose Herrera	1.50	.70	.45
379	Ken Boyer	2.50	1.25	.70
380	Stan Bahnsen	1.50	.70	.45
381	Ed Kranepool	1.50	.70	.45

382	Pat Corrales	1.50	.70	.45
383	Casey Cox	1.50	.70	.45
384	Larry Shepard	1.50	.70	.45
385	Orlando Cepeda	12.00	6.00	3.50
386	Jim McGlothlin	1.50	.70	.45
387	Bobby Klaus	1.50	.70	.45
388	Tom McCraw	1.50	.70	.45
389	Dan Coombs	1.50	.70	.45
390	Bill Freehan	2.00	1.00	.60
391	Ray Culp	1.50	.70	.45
392	Bob Burda	1.50	.70	.45
393	Gene Brabender	1.50	.70	.45
394	Pilots Rookies (Lou Piniella, Marv Staehle)	3.00	1.50	.90
395	Chris Short	1.50	.70	.45
396	Jim Campanis	1.50	.70	.45
397	Chuck Dobson	1.50	.70	.45
398	Tito Francona	1.50	.70	.45
399	Bob Bailey	1.50	.70	.45
400	Don Drysdale	12.00	6.00	3.50
401	Jake Gibbs	1.50	.70	.45
402	Ken Boswell	1.50	.70	.45
403	Bob Miller	1.50	.70	.45
404	Cubs Rookies (Vic LaRose, Gary Ross)	1.50	.70	.45
405	Lee May	1.50	.70	.45
406	Phil Ortega	1.50	.70	.45
407	Tom Egan	1.50	.70	.45
408	Nate Colbert	1.50	.70	.45
409	Bob Moose	1.50	.70	.45
410	Al Kaline	22.00	11.00	6.50
411	Larry Dierker	1.50	.70	.45
412	Checklist 426-512 (Mickey Mantle)	10.00	5.00	3.00
413	Roland Sheldon	1.50	.70	.45
414	Duke Sims	1.50	.70	.45
415	Ray Washburn	1.50	.70	.45
416	Willie McCovey (All-Star)	4.75	2.50	1.50
417	Ken Harrelson (All-Star)	1.50	.70	.45
418	Tommy Helms (All-Star)	1.50	.70	.45
419	Rod Carew (All-Star)	8.00	4.00	2.50
420	Ron Santo (All-Star)	2.50	1.25	.70
421	Brooks Robinson (All-Star)	5.00	2.50	1.50
422	Don Kessinger (All-Star)	1.50	.70	.45
423	Bert Campaneris (All-Star)	1.50	.70	.45
424	Pete Rose (All-Star)	12.00	6.00	3.50
425	Carl Yastrzemski (All-Star)	9.00	7.00	2.75
426	Curt Flood (All-Star)	1.50	.70	.45
427	Tony Oliva (All-Star)	2.50	1.25	.70
428	Lou Brock (All-Star)	4.00	2.00	1.25
429	Willie Horton (All-Star)	1.50	.70	.45
430	Johnny Bench (All-Star)	10.00	5.00	3.00
431	Bill Freehan (All-Star)	1.50	.70	.45
432	Bob Gibson (All-Star)	4.00	2.00	1.25
433	Denny McLain (All-Star)	2.50	1.25	.70
434	Jerry Koosman (All-Star)	1.50	.70	.45
435	Sam McDowell (All-Star)	1.50	.70	.45
436	Gene Alley	1.50	.70	.45
437	Luis Alcaraz	1.50	.70	.45
438	Gary Waslewski	1.50	.70	.45
439	White Sox Rookies (Ed Herrmann, Dan Lazar)	1.50	.70	.45
440a	Willie McCovey (last name in white)	80.00	40.00	24.00
440b	Willie McCovey (last name in yellow)	16.00	8.00	4.75
441a	Dennis Higgins (last name in white)	24.00	12.00	7.25
441b	Dennis Higgins (last name in yellow)	1.50	.70	.45
442	Ty Cline	1.50	.70	.45
443	Don Wert	1.50	.70	.45
444a	Joe Moeller (last name in white)	24.00	12.00	7.25
444b	Joe Moeller (last name in yellow)	1.50	.70	.45
445	Bobby Knoop	1.50	.70	.45
446	Claude Raymond	1.50	.70	.45
447a	Ralph Houk (last name in white)	29.00	14.50	8.75
447b	Ralph Houk (last name in yellow)	2.50	1.25	.70
448	Bob Tolan	1.50	.70	.45
449	Paul Lindblad	1.50	.70	.45
450	Billy Williams	10.00	5.00	3.00
451a	Rich Rollins (first name in white)	24.00	12.00	7.25
451b	Rich Rollins (first name in yellow)	1.50	.70	.45
452a	Al Ferrara (first name in white)	24.00	12.00	7.25
452b	Al Ferrara (first name in yellow)	1.50	.70	.45
453	Mike Cuellar	1.50	.70	.45
454a	Phillies Rookies (Larry Colton), *(Don Money)* (names in white)	24.00	12.00	7.25
454b	Phillies Rookies (Larry Colton), *(Don Money)* (names in yellow)	1.50	.70	.45
455	Sonny Siebert	1.50	.70	.45
456	Bud Harrelson	1.50	.70	.45
457	Dalton Jones	1.50	.70	.45
458	Curt Blefary	1.50	.70	.45
459	Dave Boswell	1.50	.70	.45
460	Joe Torre	4.00	2.00	1.25
461a	Mike Epstein (last name in white)	24.00	12.00	7.25
461b	Mike Epstein (last name in yellow)	1.50	.70	.45
462	Red Schoendienst	4.00	2.00	1.25
463	Dennis Ribant	1.50	.70	.45
464a	Dave Marshall (last name in white)	24.00	12.00	7.25
464b	Dave Marshall (last name in yellow)	1.50	.70	.45
465	Tommy John	3.00	1.50	.90
466	John Boccabella	1.50	.70	.45

467	Tom Reynolds	1.50	.70	.45
468a	Pirates Rookies (Bruce Dal Canton, Bob Robertson) (names in white)	24.00	12.00	7.25
468b	Pirates Rookies (Bruce Dal Canton, Bob Robertson) (names in yellow)	1.50	.70	.45
469	Chico Ruiz	1.50	.70	.45
470a	Mel Stottlemyre (last name in white)	24.00	12.00	7.25
470b	Mel Stottlemyre (last name in yellow)	2.50	1.25	.70
471a	Ted Savage (last name in white)	24.00	12.00	7.25
471b	Ted Savage (last name in yellow)	1.50	.70	.45
472	Jim Price	1.50	.70	.45
473a	Jose Arcia (first name in white)	24.00	12.00	7.25
473b	Jose Arcia (first name in yellow)	1.50	.70	.45
474	Tom Murphy	1.50	.70	.45
475	Tim McCarver	2.50	1.25	.70
476a	Red Sox Rookies (*Ken Brett*, Gerry Moses) (names in white)	24.00	12.00	7.25
476b	Red Sox Rookies (*Ken Brett*, Gerry Moses) (names in yellow)	1.50	.70	.45
477	Jeff James	1.50	.70	.45
478	Don Buford	1.50	.70	.45
479	Richie Scheinblum	1.50	.70	.45
480	Tom Seaver	60.00	30.00	18.00
481	*Bill Melton*	1.50	.70	.45
482a	Jim Gosger (first name in white)	24.00	12.00	7.25
482b	Jim Gosger (first name in yellow)	1.50	.70	.45
483	Ted Abernathy	1.50	.70	.45
484	Joe Gordon	1.50	.70	.45
485a	Gaylord Perry (last name in white)	75.00	37.00	22.00
485b	Gaylord Perry (last name in yellow)	9.00	4.50	2.75
486a	Paul Casanova (last name in white)	24.00	12.00	7.25
486b	Paul Casanova (last name in yellow)	1.50	.70	.45
487	Denis Menke	1.50	.70	.45
488	Joe Sparma	1.50	.70	.45
489	Clete Boyer	1.50	.70	.45
490	Matty Alou	1.50	.70	.45
491a	Twins Rookies (Jerry Crider, George Mitterwald) (names in white)	24.00	12.00	7.25
491b	Twins Rookies (Jerry Crider, George Mitterwald) (names in yellow)	1.50	.70	.45
492	Tony Cloninger	1.50	.70	.45
493a	Wes Parker (last name in white)	24.00	12.00	7.25
493b	Wes Parker (last name in yellow)	1.50	.70	.45
494	Ken Berry	1.50	.70	.45
495	Bert Campaneris	1.50	.70	.45
496	Larry Jaster	1.50	.70	.45
497	Julian Javier	1.50	.70	.45
498	Juan Pizarro	1.50	.70	.45
499	Astros Rookies (Don Bryant, Steve Shea)	1.50	.70	.45
500a	Mickey Mantle (last name in white)	1200.	600.00	360.00
500b	Mickey Mantle (last name in yellow)	235.00	115.00	70.00
501a	Tony Gonzalez (first name in white)	24.00	12.00	7.25
501b	Tony Gonzalez (first name in yellow)	1.50	.70	.45
502	Minnie Rojas	1.50	.70	.45
503	Larry Brown	1.50	.70	.45
504	Checklist 513-588 (Brooks Robinson)	6.00	3.00	1.75
505a	Bobby Bolin (last name in white)	24.00	12.00	7.25
505b	Bobby Bolin (last name in yellow)	1.50	.70	.45
506	Paul Blair	1.50	.70	.45
507	Cookie Rojas	1.50	.70	.45
508	Moe Drabowsky	1.50	.70	.45
509	Manny Sanguillen	1.50	.70	.45
510	Rod Carew	30.00	15.00	9.00
511a	Diego Segui (first name in white)	24.00	12.00	7.25
511b	Diego Segui (first name in yellow)	1.50	.70	.45
512	Cleon Jones	1.50	.70	.45
513	Camilo Pascual	2.50	1.25	.70
514	Mike Lum	2.50	1.25	.70
515	Dick Green	2.50	1.25	.70
516	Earl Weaver	13.00	6.50	4.00
517	Mike McCormick	2.50	1.25	.70
518	Fred Whitfield	2.50	1.25	.70
519	Yankees Rookies (Len Boehmer, Gerry Kenney)	2.50	1.25	.70
520	Bob Veale	2.50	1.25	.70
521	George Thomas	2.50	1.25	.70
522	Joe Hoerner	2.50	1.25	.70
523	Bob Chance	2.50	1.25	.70
524	Expos Rookies (Jose Laboy, Floyd Wicker)	2.50	1.25	.70
525	Earl Wilson	2.50	1.25	.70
526	Hector Torres	2.50	1.25	.70
527	Al Lopez	3.50	1.75	1.00
528	Claude Osteen	2.50	1.25	.70
529	Ed Kirkpatrick	2.50	1.25	.70
530	Cesar Tovar	2.50	1.25	.70
531	Dick Farrell	2.50	1.25	.70
532	Bird Hill Aces (Mike Cuellar, Jim Hardin, Dave McNally, Tom Phoebus)	3.50	1.75	1.00
533	Nolan Ryan	215.00	105.00	64.00
534	Jerry McNertney	2.50	1.25	.70
535	Phil Regan	2.50	1.25	.70
536	Padres Rookies (Danny Breeden), (*Dave Roberts*)	2.50	1.25	.70
537	Mike Paul	2.50	1.25	.70
538	Charlie Smith	2.50	1.25	.70
539	Ted Shows How (Mike Epstein, Ted Williams)	6.00	3.00	1.75
540	Curt Flood	3.00	1.50	.90
541	Joe Verbanic	2.50	1.25	.70
542	Bob Aspromonte	2.50	1.25	.70
543	Fred Newman	2.50	1.25	.70
544	Tigers Rookies (Mike Kilkenny, Ron Woods)	2.50	1.25	.70
545	Willie Stargell	12.00	6.00	3.50
546	Jim Nash	2.50	1.25	.70
547	Billy Martin	4.00	2.00	1.25
548	Bob Locker	2.50	1.25	.70
549	Ron Brand	2.50	1.25	.70
550	Brooks Robinson	25.00	12.50	7.50
551	Wayne Granger	2.50	1.25	.70
552	Dodgers Rookies (*Ted Sizemore*), (*Bill Sudakis*)	3.00	1.50	.90
553	Ron Davis	2.50	1.25	.70
554	Frank Bertaina	2.50	1.25	.70
555	Jim Hart	2.50	1.25	.70
556	A's Stars (Sal Bando, Bert Campaneris, Danny Cater)	3.00	1.50	.90
557	Frank Fernandez	2.50	1.25	.70
558	*Tom Burgmeier*	2.50	1.25	.70
559	Cards Rookies (Joe Hague, Jim Hicks)	2.50	1.25	.70
560	Luis Tiant	3.00	1.50	.90
561	Ron Clark	2.50	1.25	.70
562	*Bob Watson*	4.00	2.00	1.25
563	Marty Pattin	2.50	1.25	.70
564	Gil Hodges	7.50	3.75	2.25
565	Hoyt Wilhelm	8.00	4.00	2.50
566	Ron Hansen	2.50	1.25	.70
567	Pirates Rookies (Elvio Jimenez, Jim Shellenback)	2.50	1.25	.70
568	Cecil Upshaw	2.50	1.25	.70
569	Billy Harris	2.50	1.25	.70
570	Ron Santo	4.50	2.25	1.25
571	Cap Peterson	2.50	1.25	.70
572	Giants Heroes (Juan Marichal, Willie McCovey)	13.00	6.50	4.00
573	Jim Palmer	25.00	12.50	7.50
574	George Scott	2.50	1.25	.70
575	Bill Singer	2.50	1.25	.70
576	Phillies Rookies (Ron Stone, Bill Wilson)	2.50	1.25	.70
577	Mike Hegan	2.50	1.25	.70
578	Don Bosch	2.50	1.25	.70
579	*Dave Nelson*	2.50	1.25	.70
580	Jim Northrup	2.50	1.25	.70
581	Gary Nolan	2.50	1.25	.70
582a	Checklist 589-664 (Tony Oliva) (red circle on back)	4.50	2.25	1.25
582b	Checklist 589-664 (Tony Oliva) (white circle on back)	3.00	1.50	.90
583	*Clyde Wright*	2.50	1.25	.70
584	Don Mason	2.50	1.25	.70
585	Ron Swoboda	2.50	1.25	.70
586	Tim Cullen	2.50	1.25	.70
587	*Joe Rudi*	5.00	2.50	1.50
588	Bill White	2.50	1.25	.70
589	Joe Pepitone	3.00	1.50	.90
590	Rico Carty	3.00	1.50	.90
591	Mike Hedlund	3.00	1.50	.90
592	Padres Rookies (Rafael Robles, Al Santorini)	3.00	1.50	.90
593	Don Nottebart	3.00	1.50	.90
594	Dooley Womack	3.00	1.50	.90
595	Lee Maye	3.00	1.50	.90
596	Chuck Hartenstein	3.00	1.50	.90
597	A.L. Rookies (Larry Burchart), (*Rollie Fingers*, Bob Floyd)	30.00	15.00	9.00
598	Ruben Amaro	3.00	1.50	.90
599	John Boozer	3.00	1.50	.90
600	Tony Oliva	4.00	2.00	1.25
601	Tug McGraw	3.50	1.75	1.00
602	Cubs Rookies (Alec Distaso, Jim Qualls, Don Young)	3.00	1.50	.90
603	Joe Keough	3.00	1.50	.90
604	Bobby Etheridge	3.00	1.50	.90
605	Dick Ellsworth	3.00	1.50	.90
606	Gene Mauch	3.00	1.50	.90
607	Dick Bosman	3.00	1.50	.90
608	Dick Simpson	3.00	1.50	.90
609	Phil Gagliano	3.00	1.50	.90
610	Jim Hardin	3.00	1.50	.90
611	Braves Rookies (Bob Didier, Walt Hriniak, Gary Neibauer)	3.00	1.50	.90
612	Jack Aker	3.00	1.50	.90
613	Jim Beauchamp	3.00	1.50	.90
614	Astros Rookies (Tom Griffin, Skip Guinn)	3.00	1.50	.90
615	Len Gabrielson	3.00	1.50	.90
616	Don McMahon	3.00	1.50	.90
617	Jesse Gonder	3.00	1.50	.90
618	Ramon Webster	3.00	1.50	.90
619	Royals Rookies (Bill Butler), (*Pat Kelly*, Juan Rios)	3.00	1.50	.90
620	Dean Chance	3.00	1.50	.90
621	Bill Voss	3.00	1.50	.90
622	Dan Osinski	3.00	1.50	.90
623	Hank Allen	3.00	1.50	.90
624	N.L. Rookies (Darrel Chaney, Duffy Dyer, Terry Harmon)	3.00	1.50	.90
625	Mack Jones	3.00	1.50	.90
626	Gene Michael	3.00	1.50	.90
627	George Stone	3.00	1.50	.90
628	Red Sox Rookies (*Bill Conigliaro*, Syd O'Brien, Fred Wenz)	4.00	2.00	1.25
629	Jack Hamilton	3.00	1.50	.90
630	*Bobby Bonds*	30.00	15.00	9.00
631	John Kennedy	3.00	1.50	.90
632	Jon Warden	3.00	1.50	.90
633	Harry Walker	3.00	1.50	.90
634	Andy Etchebarren	3.00	1.50	.90
635	George Culver	3.00	1.50	.90
636	Woodie Held	3.00	1.50	.90
637	Padres Rookies (Jerry DaVanon), (*Clay Kirby*, Frank Reberger)	3.00	1.50	.90
638	Ed Sprague	3.00	1.50	.90
639	Barry Moore	3.00	1.50	.90
640	Fergie Jenkins	15.00	7.50	4.50
641	N.L. Rookies (Bobby Darwin, Tommy Dean, John Miller)	3.00	1.50	.90
642	John Hiller	3.00	1.50	.90
643	Billy Cowan	3.00	1.50	.90
644	Chuck Hinton	3.00	1.50	.90
645	George Brunet	3.00	1.50	.90
646	Expos Rookies (Dan McGinn), (*Carl Morton*)	3.00	1.50	.90
647	Dave Wickersham	3.00	1.50	.90
648	Bobby Wine	3.00	1.50	.90
649	Al Jackson	3.00	1.50	.90
650	Ted Williams	20.00	10.00	6.00
651	Gus Gil	3.00	1.50	.90
652	Eddie Watt	3.00	1.50	.90
653	*Aurelio Rodriguez* (photo actually batboy Leonard Garcia)	4.00	2.00	1.25
654	White Sox Rookies (*Carlos May*, Rich Morales, Don Secrist)	3.50	1.75	1.00
655	Mike Hershberger	3.00	1.50	.90
656	Dan Schneider	3.00	1.50	.90
657	Bobby Murcer	3.00	1.50	.90
658	A.L. Rookies (Bill Burbach, Tom Hall, Jim Miles)	3.00	1.50	.90
659	Johnny Podres	3.50	1.75	1.00
660	Reggie Smith	3.00	1.50	.90
661	Jim Merritt	3.00	1.50	.90
662	Royals Rookies (Dick Drago, Bob Oliver, George Spriggs)	3.00	1.50	.90
663	Dick Radatz	3.00	1.50	.90
664	Ron Hunt	4.50	2.00	.90

1969 Topps Decals

Designed as an insert for 1969 regular issue card packs, these decals are virtually identical in format to the '69 cards. The 48 decals in the set measure 1" x 2-1/2," although they are mounted on white paper backing which measures 1-3/4" x 2-1/8."

		NM	EX	VG
Complete Set (48):		400.00	200.00	120.00
Common Player:		4.00	2.00	1.25
(1)	Hank Aaron	40.00	20.00	12.00
(2)	Richie Allen	7.00	3.50	2.00
(3)	Felipe Alou	6.00	3.00	1.75
(4)	Matty Alou	4.00	2.00	1.25
(5)	Luis Aparicio	10.00	5.00	3.00
(6)	Bob Clemente	50.00	25.00	15.00
(7)	Donn Clendenon	4.00	2.00	1.25
(8)	Tommy Davis	4.00	2.00	1.25
(9)	Don Drysdale	10.00	5.00	3.00
(10)	Joe Foy	4.00	2.00	1.25
(11)	Jim Fregosi	4.00	2.00	1.25
(12)	Bob Gibson	10.00	5.00	3.00
(13)	Tony Gonzalez	4.00	2.00	1.25
(14)	Tom Haller	4.00	2.00	1.25
(15)	Ken Harrelson	4.00	2.00	1.25
(16)	Tommy Helms	4.00	2.00	1.25
(17)	Willie Horton	4.00	2.00	1.25
(18)	Frank Howard	4.00	2.00	1.25
(19)	Reggie Jackson	60.00	30.00	18.00
(20)	Fergie Jenkins	9.00	4.50	2.75
(21)	Harmon Killebrew	10.00	5.00	3.00
(22)	Jerry Koosman	4.00	2.00	1.25
(23)	Mickey Mantle	80.00	40.00	24.00
(24)	Willie Mays	40.00	20.00	12.00
(25)	Tim McCarver	4.50	2.25	1.25
(26)	Willie McCovey	10.00	5.00	3.00
(27)	Sam McDowell	4.00	2.00	1.25
(28)	Denny McLain	4.00	2.00	1.25
(29)	Dave McNally	4.00	2.00	1.25
(30)	Don Mincher	4.00	2.00	1.25
(31)	Rick Monday	4.00	2.00	1.25
(32)	Tony Oliva	4.50	2.25	1.25

(33)	Camilo Pascual	4.00	2.00	1.25
(34)	Rick Reichardt	4.00	2.00	1.25
(35)	Frank Robinson	10.00	5.00	3.00
(36)	Pete Rose	35.00	17.50	10.50
(37)	Ron Santo	5.00	2.50	1.50
(38)	Tom Seaver	20.00	10.00	6.00
(39)	Dick Selma	4.00	2.00	1.25
(40)	Chris Short	4.00	2.00	1.25
(41)	Rusty Staub	4.00	2.00	1.25
(42)	Mel Stottlemyre	4.00	2.00	1.25
(43)	Luis Tiant	4.00	2.00	1.25
(44)	Pete Ward	4.00	2.00	1.25
(45)	Hoyt Wilhelm	7.50	3.75	2.25
(46)	Maury Wills	4.00	2.00	1.25
(47)	Jim Wynn	4.00	2.00	1.25
(48)	Carl Yastrzemski	12.00	6.00	3.50

1969 Topps Deckle Edge

These 2-1/4" x 3-1/4" inch cards take their name from their borders which have a scalloped effect. Fronts have a black-and-white player photo along with a blue facsimile autograph. Backs have the player's name and the card number in light blue ink in a small box at the bottom of the card. While there are only 33 numbered cards, there are actually 35 possible players; both Jim Wynn and Hoyt Wilhelm cards are found as #11 while cards of Joe Foy and Rusty Staub as #22. Cards are sometimes found with straight-cut edges, but these were never formally issued; they carry a 50% premium.

		NM	EX	VG
Complete Set (33):		100.00	50.00	30.00
Common Player:		1.00	.50	.30
1	Brooks Robinson	12.00	6.00	3.50
2	Boog Powell	2.00	1.00	.60
3	Ken Harrelson	1.00	.50	.30
4	Carl Yastrzemski	12.00	6.00	3.50
5	Jim Fregosi	1.00	.50	.30
6	Luis Aparicio	9.00	4.50	2.75
7	Luis Tiant	2.00	1.00	.60
8	Denny McLain	2.00	1.00	.60
9	Willie Horton	1.00	.50	.30
10	Bill Freehan	1.00	.50	.30
11a	Hoyt Wilhelm	9.00	4.50	2.75
11b	Jim Wynn	11.00	5.50	3.25
12	Rod Carew	11.00	5.50	3.25
13	Mel Stottlemyre	1.00	.50	.30
14	Rick Monday	1.00	.50	.30
15	Tommy Davis	1.00	.50	.30
16	Frank Howard	2.00	1.00	.60
17	Felipe Alou	2.00	1.00	.60
18	Don Kessinger	1.00	.50	.30
19	Ron Santo	2.00	1.00	.60
20	Tommy Helms	1.00	.50	.30
21	Pete Rose	17.50	8.75	5.25
22a	Rusty Staub	3.50	1.75	1.00
22b	Joe Foy	6.50	3.25	2.00
23	Tom Haller	1.00	.50	.30
24	Maury Wills	1.75	.90	.50
25	Jerry Koosman	1.00	.50	.30
26	Richie Allen	4.00	2.00	1.25
27	Roberto Clemente	20.00	10.00	6.00
28	Curt Flood	1.00	.50	.30
29	Bob Gibson	10.00	5.00	3.00
30	Al Ferrara	1.00	.50	.30
31	Willie McCovey	9.00	4.50	2.75
32	Juan Marichal	8.00	4.00	2.50
33	Willie Mays	17.50	8.75	5.25

Suffix letters after a card number indicate a variation card.

1969 Topps Stamps

Topps continued to refine its efforts at baseball stamps in 1969 with the release of 240 player stamps, each measuring 1" x 1-7/16." Each stamp has a color photo along with the player's name, position and team. Unlike prior stamp issues, the 1969 stamps have 24 separate albums (one per team). The stamps were issued in strips of 12.

		NM	EX	VG
Complete Sheet Set (24):		250.00	125.00	75.00
Common Sheet:		3.00	1.50	.90
Complete Stamp Album Set (24):		30.00	15.00	9.00
Single Stamp Album:		2.00	1.00	.60
(1)	Tommie Agee, Sandy Alomar, Jose Cardenal, Dean Chance, Joe Foy, Jim Grant, Don Kessinger, Mickey Mantle, Jerry May, Bob Rodgers, Cookie Rojas, Gary Sutherland	40.00	20.00	12.00
(2)	Jesus Alou, Mike Andrews, Larry Brown, Moe Drabowsky, Alex Johnson, Lew Krausse, Jim Lefebvre, Dal Maxvill, John Odom, Claude Osteen, Rick Reichardt, Luis Tiant	3.00	1.50	.90
(3)	Hank Aaron, Matty Alou, Max Alvis, Nelson Briles, Eddie Fisher, Bud Harrelson, Willie Horton, Randy Hundley, Larry Jaster, Jim Kaat, Gary Peters, Pete Ward	15.00	7.50	4.50
(4)	Don Buford, John Callison, Tommy Davis, Jackie Hernandez, Fergie Jenkins, Lee May, Denny McLain, Bob Oliver, Roberto Pena, Tony Perez, Joe Torre, Tom Tresh	6.50	3.25	2.00
(5)	Jim Bunning, Dean Chance, Joe Foy, Sonny Jackson, Don Kessinger, Rick Monday, Gaylord Perry, Roger Repoz, Cookie Rojas, Mel Stottlemyre, Leon Wagner, Jim Wynn	8.00	4.00	2.50
(6)	Felipe Alou, Gerry Arrigo, Bob Aspromonte, Gary Bell, Clay Dalrymple, Jim Fregosi, Tony Gonzalez, Duane Josephson, Dick McAuliffe, Tony Olvia, Brooks Robinson, Willie Stargell	12.00	6.00	3.50
(7)	Steve Barber, Donn Clendenon, Joe Coleman, Vic Davalillo, Russ Gibson, Jerry Grote, Tom Haller, Andy Kosco, Willie McCovey, Don Mincher, Joe Morgan, Don Wilson	9.00	4.50	2.75
(8)	George Brunet, Don Buford, John Callison, Danny Cater, Tommy Davis, Willie Davis, John Edwards, Jim Hart, Mickey Lolich, Willie May, Roberto Pena, Mickey Stanley	15.00	7.50	4.50
(9)	Ernie Banks, Glenn Beckert, Ken Berry, Horace Clarke, Roberto Clemente, Larry Dierker, Len Gabrielson, Jake Gibbs, Jerry Koosman, Sam McDowell, Tom Satriano, Bill Singer	13.50	6.75	4.00
(10)	Gene Alley, Lou Brock, Larry Brown, Moe Drabowsky, Frank Howard, Tommie John, Roger Nelson, Claude Osteen, Phil Regan, Rlce Reichardt, Tony Taylor, Roy White	7.50	3.75	2.25
(11)	Bob Allison, John Bateman, Don Drysdale, Dave Johnson, Harmon Killebrew, Jim Maloney, Bill Mazeroski, Gerry McNertney, Ron Perranoski, Rico Petrocelli, Pete Rose, Billy Williams	36.00	18.00	11.00
(12)	Bernie Allen, Jose Arcia, Stan Bahnsen, Sal Bando, Jim Davenport, Tito Francona, Dick Green, Ron Hunt, Mack Jones, Vada Pinson, George Scott, Don Wert	3.00	1.50	.90
(13)	Gerry Arrigo, Bob Aspromonte, Joe Azcue, Curt Blefary, Orlando Cepeda, Bill Freehan, Jim Fregosi, Dave Giusti, Duane Josephson, Tim McCarver, Jose Santiago, Bob Tolan	4.00	2.00	1.25
(14)	Jerry Adair, Johnny Bench, Clete Boyer, John Briggs, Bert Campaneris, Woody Fryman, Ron Kline, Bobby Knoop, Ken McMuellen, Adolfo Phillips, John Roseboro, Tom Seaver	15.00	7.50	4.50
(15)	Norm Cash, Ron Fairly, Bob Gibson, Bill Hands, Cleon Jones, Al Kaline, Paul Schaal, Mike Shannon, Duke Sims, Reggie Smith, Steve Whitaker, Carl Yastrzemski	24.00	12.00	7.25
(16)	Steve Barber, Paul Casanova, Dick Dietz, Russ Gibson, Jerry Grote, Tom Haller, Ed Kranepool, Juan Marichal, Denis Menke, Jim Nash, Bill Robinson, Frank Robinson	9.00	4.50	2.75
(17)	Bobby Bolin, Ollie Brown, Rod Carew, Mike Epstein, Bud Harrelson, Larry Jaster, Dave McNally, Willie Norton, Milt Pappas, Gary Peters, Paul Popovich, Stan Williams	9.00	4.50	2.75
(18)	Ted Abernathy, Bob Allison, Ed Brinkman, Don Drysdale, Jim Hardin, Julian Javier, Hal Lanier, Jim McGlothlin, Ron Perranoski, Rich Rollins, Ron Santo, Billy Williams	5.50	2.75	1.75
(19)	Richie Allen, Luis Aparicio, Wally Bunker, Curt Flood, Ken Harrelson, Catfish Hunter, Denver Lemaster, Felix Millan, Jim Northrop (Northrup), Art Shamsky, Larry Stahl, Ted Uhlaender	6.50	3.25	2.00
(20)	Bob Bailey, Johnny Bench, Woody Fryman, Jim Hannan, Ron Kline, Al McBean, Camilo Pascual, Joe Pepitone, Doug Rader, Ron Reed, John Roseboro, Sonny Siebert	8.00	4.00	2.50
(21)	Jack Aker, Tommy Harper, Tommy Helms, Dennis Higgins, Jim Hunter, Don Lock, Lee Maye, Felix Millan, Jim Northrop (Northrup), Larry Stahl, Don Sutton, Zoilo Versalles	6.50	3.25	2.00
(22)	Norm Cash, Ed Charles, Joe Horlen, Pat Jarvis, Jim Lonborg, Manny Mota, Boog Powell, Dick Selma, Mike Shannon, Duke Sims, Steve Whitaker, Hoyt Wilhelm	5.50	2.75	1.75
(23)	Bernie Allen, Ray Culp, Al Ferrara, Tito Francona, Dick Green, Ron Hunt, Ray Oyler, Tom Phoebus, Rusty Staub, Bob Veale, Maury Wills, Wilbur Wood	3.50	1.75	1.00
(24)	Ernie Banks, Mark Belanger, Steve Blass, Horace Clarke, Bob Clemente, Larry Dierker, Dave Duncan, Chico Salmon, Chris Short, Ron Swoboda, Cesar Tovar, Rick Wise	12.00	6.00	3.50

1969 Topps Super

These 2-1/4" x 3-1/4" cards are not the bigger "Super" cards which would be seen in following years. Rather, what enabled Topps to dub them "Super Baseball Cards" is their high-gloss finish which enhances the bright color photograph used on their fronts. The only other design element on the front is a facsimile autograph. The backs contain a box at the bottom which carries the player's name, team, position, a copyright line and the card number. Another unusual feature is that the cards have rounded corners. The 66-card set saw limited production, meaning supplies are tight today. Considering the quality of the cards and the fact that many big names are represented, it's easy to understand why the set is quite expensive and desirable.

		NM	EX	VG
Complete Set (66):		7000.	3500.	2100.
Common Player:		22.00	11.00	6.50
1	Dave McNally	22.00	11.00	6.50
2	Frank Robinson	250.00	125.00	75.00
3	Brooks Robinson	250.00	125.00	75.00
4	Ken Harrelson	22.00	11.00	6.50
5	Carl Yastrzemski	250.00	125.00	75.00
6	Ray Culp	22.00	11.00	6.50
7	James Fregosi	22.00	11.00	6.50
8	Rick Reichardt	22.00	11.00	6.50
9	Vic Davalillo	22.00	11.00	6.50
10	Luis Aparicio	100.00	50.00	30.00
11	Pete Ward	22.00	11.00	6.50
12	Joe Horlen	22.00	11.00	6.50
13	Luis Tiant	24.00	12.00	7.25
14	Sam McDowell	24.00	12.00	7.25
15	Jose Cardenal	22.00	11.00	6.50
16	Willie Horton	22.00	11.00	6.50
17	Denny McLain	24.00	12.00	7.25
18	Bill Freehan	22.00	11.00	6.50
19	Harmon Killebrew	200.00	100.00	60.00
20	Tony Oliva	22.00	11.00	6.50
21	Dean Chance	22.00	11.00	6.50
22	Joe Foy	22.00	11.00	6.50
23	Roger Nelson	22.00	11.00	6.50
24	Mickey Mantle	1500.	750.00	450.00
25	Mel Stottlemyre	22.00	11.00	6.50
26	Roy White	22.00	11.00	6.50
27	Rick Monday	22.00	11.00	6.50
28	Reggie Jackson	500.00	250.00	150.00
29	Bert Campaneris	22.00	11.00	6.50
30	Frank Howard	24.00	12.00	7.25
31	Camilo Pascual	22.00	11.00	6.50
32	Tommy Davis	22.00	11.00	6.50
33	Don Mincher	22.00	11.00	6.50
34	Henry Aaron	550.00	275.00	165.00
35	Felipe Alou	35.00	17.50	10.50
36	Joe Torre	50.00	25.00	15.00
37	Fergie Jenkins	90.00	45.00	27.00
38	Ronald Santo	35.00	17.50	10.50
39	Billy Williams	100.00	50.00	30.00
40	Tommy Helms	22.00	11.00	6.50
41	Pete Rose	450.00	225.00	135.00
42	Joe Morgan	150.00	75.00	45.00
43	Jim Wynn	22.00	11.00	6.50
44	Curt Blefary	22.00	11.00	6.50
45	Willie Davis	22.00	11.00	6.50
46	Don Drysdale	200.00	100.00	60.00
47	Tom Haller	22.00	11.00	6.50
48	Rusty Staub	25.00	12.50	7.50
49	Maurice Wills	24.00	12.00	7.25
50	Cleon Jones	22.00	11.00	6.50
51	Jerry Koosman	22.00	11.00	6.50
52	Tom Seaver	250.00	125.00	75.00
53	Rich Allen	75.00	37.00	22.00
54	Chris Short	22.00	11.00	6.50
55	Cookie Rojas	22.00	11.00	6.50
56	Mateo Alou	22.00	11.00	6.50
57	Steve Blass	22.00	11.00	6.50
58	Roberto Clemente	750.00	375.00	225.00
59	Curt Flood	22.00	11.00	6.50
60	Bob Gibson	150.00	75.00	45.00
61	Tim McCarver	25.00	12.50	7.50
62	Dick Selma	22.00	11.00	6.50
63	Ollie Brown	22.00	11.00	6.50
64	Juan Marichal	125.00	62.00	37.00
65	Willie Mays	550.00	275.00	165.00
66	Willie McCovey	200.00	100.00	60.00

1969 Topps Team Posters

Picking up where the 1968 posters left off, the 1969 poster is larger at about 12" x 20". The posters, 24 in number like the previous year, are very different in style. Each has a team focus with a large pennant carrying the team name, along with nine or ten photos of players. Each of the photos carries a name and a facsimile autograph. Unfortunately, the bigger size of 1969 posters meant they had to be folded to fit in their packages as was the case in 1968. That means that collectors today will have a tough job finding them without fairly heavy creases from the folding.

		NM	EX	VG
Complete Set (24):		1600.	800.00	475.00
Common Poster:		75.00	37.50	22.00
1	Detroit Tigers (Norm Cash, Bill Freehan, Willie Horton, Al Kaline, Mickey Lolich, Dick McAuliffe, Denny McLain, Jim Northrup, (Mickey Stanley, Don Wert, Earl Wilson)	105.00	52.00	31.00
2	Atlanta Braves (Hank Aaron, Felipe Alou, Clete Boyer, Rico Carty, Tito Francona, Sonny Jackson, Pat Jarvis, Felix Millan, (Phil Niekro, Milt Pappas, Joe Torre)	100.00	50.00	30.00
3	Boston Red Sox (Mike Andrews, Tony Conigliaro, Ray Culp, Russ Gibson, Ken Harrelson, Jim Lonborg, Rico Petrocelli, Jose Santiago, (George Scott, Reggie Smith, Carl Yastrzemski)	120.00	60.00	36.00
4	Chicago Cubs (Ernie Banks, Glenn Beckert, Bill Hands, Jim Hickman, Ken Holtzman, Randy Hundley, Fergie Jenkins, Don Kessinger, (Adolfo Phillips, Ron Santo, Billy Williams)	105.00	52.00	31.00
5	Baltimore Orioles (Mark Belanger, Paul Blair, Don Buford, Andy Etchebarren, Jim Hardin, Dave Johnson), Dave McNally, Tom Phoebus, (Boog Powell, Brooks Robinson, Frank Robinson)	105.00	52.00	31.00
6	Houston Astros (Curt Blefary, Donn Clendenon, Larry Dierker, John Edwards, Denny Lemaster, Denis Menke), Norm Miller, Joe Morgan, (Doug Rader, Don Wilson, Jim Wynn)	75.00	37.00	22.00
7	Kansas City Royals (Jerry Adair, Wally Bunker, Mike Fiore, Joe Foy, Jackie Hernandez, Pat Kelly, Dave Morehead, Roger Nelson, (Dave Nicholson, Eliseo Rodriguez, Steve Whitaker)	75.00	37.50	22.00
8	Philadelphia Phillies (Richie Allen, Johnny Callison, Woody Fryman, Larry Hisle, Don Money, Cookie Rojas, Mike Ryan, Chris Short, (Tony Taylor, Bill White, Rick Wise)	80.00	40.00	24.00
9	Seattle Pilots (Jack Aker, Steve Barber, Gary Bell, Tommy Davis, Jim Gosger, Tommy Harper, Gerry McNertney, Don Mincher, (Ray Oyler, Rich Rollins, Chico Salmon)	160.00	80.00	48.00
10	Montreal Expos (Bob Bailey, John Bateman, Jack Billingham, Jim Grant, Larry Jaster, Mack Jones, Manny Mota, Rusty Staub, (Gary Sutherland, Jim Williams, Maury Wills)	75.00	37.50	22.00
11	Chicago White Sox (Sandy Alomar, Luis Aparicio, Ken Berry, Buddy Bradford, Joe Horlen, Tommy John), Duane Josephson, Tom McCraw, (Bill Melton, Pete Ward, Wilbur Wood)	85.00	42.00	25.00
12	San Diego Padres (Jose Arcia, Danny Breeden, Ollie Brown, Bill Davis, Ron Davis, Tony Gonzalez, Dick Kelley, Al McBean, (Roberto Pena, Dick Selma, Ed Spiezio)	75.00	37.50	22.00
13	Cleveland Indians (Max Alvis, Joe Azcue, Jose Cardenal, Vern Fuller, Lou Johnson, Sam McDowell, Sonny Siebert, Duke Sims, (Russ Snyder, Luis Tiant, Zoilo Versalles)	75.00	37.50	22.00
14	San Francisco Giants (Bobby Bolin, Jim Davenport, Dick Dietz, Jim Hart, Ron Hunt, Hal Lanier, Juan Marichal, Willie Mays, (Willie McCovey, Gaylord Perry, Charlie Smith)	150.00	75.00	45.00
15	Minnesota Twins (Bob Allison, Chico Cardenas, Rod Carew, Dean Chance, Jim Kaat, Harmon Killebrew, Tony Oliva, Jim Perry, (John Roseboro, Cesar Tovar, Ted Uhlaender)	120.00	60.00	36.00
16	Pittsburgh Pirates (Gene Alley, Matty Alou, Steve Blass, Jim Bunning, Bob Clemente, Rich Hebner, Jerry May, Bill Mazeroski, (Bob Robertson, Willie Stargell, Bob Veale)	175.00	87.00	52.00
17	California Angels (Ruben Amaro, George Brunet, Bob Chance, Vic Davalillo, Jim Fregosi, Bobby Knoop, Jim McGlothlin, Rick Reichardt, (Roger Repoz, Bob Rodgers, Hoyt Wilhelm)	80.00	40.00	24.00
18	St. Louis Cardinals (Nelson Briles, Lou Brock, Orlando Cepeda, Curt Flood, Bob Gibson, Julian Javier), Dal Maxvill, Tim McCarver, Vada Pinson, Mike Shannon, Ray Washburn)	85.00	42.00	25.00
19	New York Yankees (Stan Bahnsen, Horace Clarke, Bobby Cox, Jake Gibbs, Mickey Mantle, Joe Pepitone), Fritz Peterson, Bill Robinson, (Mel Stottlemyre, Tom Tresh, Roy White)	200.00	100.00	60.00
20	Cincinnati Reds (Gerry Arrigo, Johnny Bench, Tommy Helms, Alex Johnson, Jim Maloney, Lee May, Gary Nolan, Tony Perez, Pete Rose, (Bob Tolan, Woody Woodward)	135.00	67.00	40.00
21	Oakland Athletics (Sal Bando, Bert Campaneris, Danny Cater, Dick Green, Mike Hershberger, Jim Hunter), Reggie Jackson, Rick Monday, (Jim Nash, John Odom, Jim Pagliaroni)	125.00	62.00	37.00
22	Los Angeles Dodgers (Willie Crawford, Willie Davis, Don Drysdale, Ron Fairly, Tom Haller, Andy Kosco), Jim Lefebvre, Claude Osteen, (Paul Popovich, Bill Singer, Bill Sudakis)	100.00	50.00	30.00
23	Washington Senators (Bernie Allen, Brant Alyea, Ed Brinkman, Paul Casanova, Joe Coleman, Mike Epstein), Jim Hannan, Frank Howard, (Ken McMullen, Camilo Pascual, Del Unser)	80.00	40.00	24.00
24	New York Mets (Tommie Agee, Ken Boswell, Ed Charles, Jerry Grote, Bud Harrelson, Cleon Jones, Jerry Koosman, Ed Kranepool, (Jim McAndrew, Tom Seaver, Ron Swoboda)	185.00	92.00	55.00

1969 Topps 4-On-1 Mini Stickers

Another in the long line of Topps test issues, the 4-on-1s are 2-1/2" x 3-1/2" cards with blank backs featuring a quartet of miniature stickers in the design of the same cards from the 1969 Topps regular set. There are 25 different cards, for a total of 100 different stickers. As they are not common, Mint cards bring fairly strong prices on today's market. As the set was drawn from the 3rd Series of the regular cards, it includes some rookie stickers and World Series highlight stickers.

		NM	EX	VG
Complete Set (25):		1500.	750.00	450.00
Common 4-in-1:		40.00	20.00	12.00
(1)	Jerry Adair, Willie Mays, Johnny Morris, Don Wilson	200.00	100.00	60.00
(2)	Tommie Aaron, Jim Britton, Donn Clendenon, Woody Woodward	40.00	20.00	12.00
(3)	Tommy Davis, Don Pavletich, Vada Pinson, World Series Game 4 (Lou Brock)	45.00	22.00	13.50
(4)	Max Alvis, Glenn Beckert, Ron Fairly, Rick Wise	40.00	20.00	12.00
(5)	Johnny Callison, Jim French, Lum Harris, Dick Selma	40.00	20.00	12.00
(6)	Bob Gibson, Larry Haney, Rick Reichardt, World Series Game 3 (Tim McCarver)	85.00	42.00	25.00
(7)	Wally Bunker, Don Cardwell, Joe Gibbon, Astros Rookies (Gilsen, McFadden)	40.00	20.00	12.00
(8)	Ollie Brown, Jim Bunning, Andy Kosco, Ron Reed	50.00	25.00	15.00

(9)	Bill Dillman, Jim Lefebvre, John Purdin, John Roseboro	40.00	20.00	12.00
(10)	Bill Hands, Chuck Harrison, Lindy McDaniel, Felix Millan	40.00	20.00	12.00
(11)	Jack Hiatt, Dave Johnson, Mel Nelson, Tommie Sisk	40.00	20.00	12.00
(12)	Clay Dalrymple, Leo Durocher, John Odom, Wilbur Wood	40.00	20.00	12.00
(13)	Hank Bauer, Kevin Collins, Ray Oyler, Russ Snyder	40.00	20.00	12.00
(14)	Gerry Arrigo, Jim Perry, Red Sox Rookies (Lahoud, Thibdeau), World Series Game 7 (Mickey Lolich)	40.00	20.00	12.00
(15)	Bill McCool, Roberto Pena, Doug Rader, World Series Game 2 (Willie Horton)	40.00	20.00	12.00
(16)	Ed Brinkman, Roy Face, Willie Horton, Bob Rodgers	40.00	20.00	12.00
(17)	Dave Baldwin, J.C. Martin, Dave May, Ray Sadecki	40.00	20.00	12.00
(18)	Jose Pagan, Tom Phoebus, Mike Shannon, World Series Game 1 (Bob Gibson)	40.00	20.00	12.00
(19)	Pete Rose, Lee Stange, Don Sutton, Ted Uhlaender	550.00	275.00	165.00
(20)	Joe Grzenda, Frank Howard, Dick Tracewski, Jim Weaver	40.00	20.00	12.00
(21)	Joe Azcue, Grant Jackson, Denny McLain, White Sox Rookies (Christman, Nyman)	40.00	20.00	12.00
(22)	John Edwards, Jim Fairey, Phillies Rookies, Stan Williams	40.00	20.00	12.00
(23)	John Bateman, Willie Smith, Leon Wagner, World Series Summary	40.00	20.00	12.00
(24)	Chris Cannizzaro, Bob Hendley, World Series Game 5 (Al Kaline), Yankees Rookies (Closter, Cumberland)	40.00	20.00	12.00
(25)	Joe Nossek, Rico Petrocelli, Carl Yastrzemski, Cardinals Rookies (Huntz, Torrez)	350.00	175.00	105.00

1970 Topps

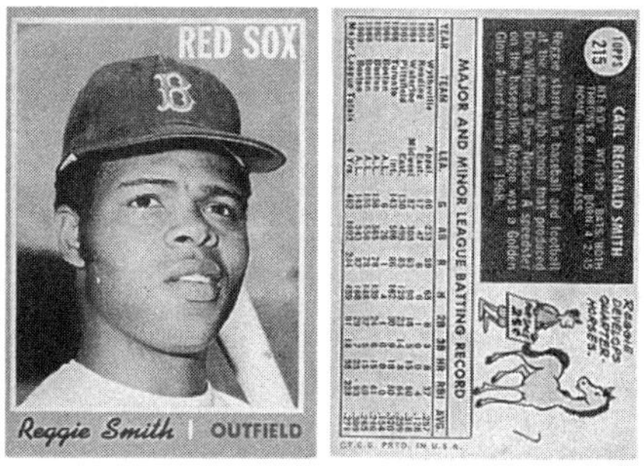

Topps established another set size record by coming out with 720 cards in 1970. The 2-1/2" x 3-1/2" cards have a color photo with a thin white frame. The photos have the player's team overprinted at the top, while the player's name in script and his position are at the bottom. A gray border surrounds the front. Card backs follow the normal design pattern, although they are more readable than some issues of the past. Team cards returned and were joined with many of the usual specialty cards. The World Series highlights were joined by cards with playoff highlights. Statistical leaders and All-Stars are also included in the set. High-numbered cards provide the most expensive cards in the set.

		NM	EX	VG
Complete Set (720):		1350.	600.00	350.00
Common Player (1-372):		1.00	.50	.30
Common Player (373-546):		1.25	.60	.40
Common Player (547-633):		3.50	1.75	1.00
Common Player (634-720):		7.50	3.75	2.25
1	World Champions (Mets Team)	10.00	[illegible]	[illegible]
2	Diego Segui	1.00	.50	.30
3	Darrel Chaney	1.00	.50	.30
4	Tom Egan	1.00	.50	.30
5	Wes Parker	1.00	.50	.30
6	Grant Jackson	1.00	.50	.30
7	Indians Rookies (Gary Boyd, Russ Nagelson)	1.00	.50	.30
8	Jose Martinez	1.00	.50	.30
9	Checklist 1-132	7.00	3.50	2.00
10	Carl Yastrzemski	12.50	6.25	3.75
11	Nate Colbert	1.00	.50	.30
12	John Hiller	1.00	.50	.30
13	Jack Hiatt	1.00	.50	.30
14	Hank Allen	1.00	.50	.30
15	Larry Dierker	1.00	.50	.30
16	Charlie Metro	1.00	.50	.30
17	Hoyt Wilhelm	3.00	1.50	.90
18	Carlos May	1.00	.50	.30
19	John Boccabella	1.00	.50	.30
20	Dave McNally	1.00	.50	.30
21	Athletics Rookies *(Vida Blue)*, *(Gene Tenace)*	6.00	3.00	1.75
22	Ray Washburn	1.00	.50	.30
23	Bill Robinson	1.00	.50	.30
24	Dick Selma	1.00	.50	.30
25	Cesar Tovar	1.00	.50	.30
26	Tug McGraw	1.50	.70	.45
27	Chuck Hinton	1.00	.50	.30
28	Billy Wilson	1.00	.50	.30
29	Sandy Alomar	1.00	.50	.30
30	Matty Alou	1.00	.50	.30
31	Marty Pattin	1.00	.50	.30
32	Harry Walker	1.00	.50	.30
33	Don Wert	1.00	.50	.30
34	Willie Crawford	1.00	.50	.30
35	Joe Horlen	1.00	.50	.30
36	Reds Rookies (Danny Breeden), *(Bernie Carbo)*	1.00	.50	.30
37	Dick Drago	1.00	.50	.30
38	Mack Jones	1.00	.50	.30
39	Mike Nagy	1.00	.50	.30
40	Rich Allen	2.50	1.25	.70
41	George Lauzerique	1.00	.50	.30
42	Tito Fuentes	1.00	.50	.30
43	Jack Aker	1.00	.50	.30
44	Roberto Pena	1.00	.50	.30
45	Dave Johnson	1.00	.50	.30
46	Ken Rudolph	1.00	.50	.30
47	Bob Miller	1.00	.50	.30
48	Gill Garrido (Gil)	1.00	.50	.30
49	Tim Cullen	1.00	.50	.30
50	Tommie Agee	1.00	.50	.30
51	Bob Christian	1.00	.50	.30
52	Bruce Dal Canton	1.00	.50	.30
53	John Kennedy	1.00	.50	.30
54	Jeff Torborg	1.00	.50	.30
55	John Odom	1.00	.50	.30
56	Phillies Rookies (Joe Lis, Scott Reid)	1.00	.50	.30
57	Pat Kelly	1.00	.50	.30
58	Dave Marshall	1.00	.50	.30
59	Dick Ellsworth	1.00	.50	.30
60	Jim Wynn	1.00	.50	.30
61	N.L. Batting Leaders (Roberto Clemente, Cleon Jones, Pete Rose)	14.00	7.00	4.25
62	A.L. Batting Leaders (Rod Carew, Tony Oliva, Reggie Smith)	2.50	1.25	.70
63	N.L. RBI Leaders (Willie McCovey, Tony Perez, Ron Santo)	3.50	1.75	1.00
64	A.L. RBI Leaders (Reggie Jackson, Harmon Killebrew, Boog Powell)	5.50	2.75	1.75
65	N.L. Home Run Leaders (Hank Aaron, Lee May, Willie McCovey)	6.00	3.00	1.75
66	A.L. Home Run Leaders (Frank Howard, Reggie Jackson, Harmon Killebrew)	6.00	3.00	1.75
67	N.L. ERA Leaders (Steve Carlton, Bob Gibson, Juan Marichal)	6.00	3.00	1.75
68	A.L. ERA Leaders (Dick Bosman, Mike Cuellar, Jim Palmer)	3.00	1.50	.90
69	N.L. Pitching Leaders (Fergie Jenkins, Juan Marichal, Phil Niekro, Tom Seaver)	6.50	3.25	2.00
70	A.L. Pitching Leaders (Dave Boswell, Mike Cuellar, Dennis McLain, Dave McNally, Jim Perry, Mel	2.50	1.25	.70
71	N.L. Strikeout Leaders (Bob Gibson, Fergie Jenkins, Bill Singer)	3.75	2.00	1.25
72	A.L. Strikeout Leaders (Mickey Lolich, Sam McDowell, Andy Messersmith)	2.50	1.25	.70
73	Wayne Granger	1.00	.50	.30
74	Angels Rookies (Greg Washburn, Wally Wolf)	1.00	.50	.30
75	Jim Kaat	1.50	.70	.45
76	Carl Taylor	1.00	.50	.30
77	Frank Linzy	1.00	.50	.30
78	Joe Lahoud	1.00	.50	.30
79	Clay Kirby	1.00	.50	.30
80	Don Kessinger	1.00	.50	.30
81	Dave May	1.00	.50	.30
82	Frank Fernandez	1.00	.50	.30
83	Don Cardwell	1.00	.50	.30
84	Paul Casanova	1.00	.50	.30
85	Max Alvis	1.00	.50	.30
86	Lum Harris	1.00	.50	.30
87	[illegible]	1.00	.50	.30
88	Pilots Rookies (Dick Baney, Miguel Fuentes)	1.00	.50	.30
89	Juan Rios	1.00	.50	.30
90	Tim McCarver	1.50	.70	.45
91	Rich Morales	1.00	.50	.30
92	George Culver	1.00	.50	.30
93	Rick Renick	1.00	.50	.30
94	Fred Patek	1.00	.50	.30
95	Earl Wilson	1.00	.50	.30
96	Cards Rookies (Leron Lee), *(Jerry Reuss)*	3.00	1.50	.90
97	Joe Moeller	1.00	.50	.30
98	Gates Brown	1.00	.50	.30
99	Bobby Pfeil	1.00	.50	.30
100	Mel Stottlemyre	1.00	.50	.30
101	Bobby Floyd	1.00	.50	.30
102	Joe Rudi	1.00	.50	.30
103	Frank Reberger	1.00	.50	.30
104	Gerry Moses	1.00	.50	.30
105	Tony Gonzalez	1.00	.50	.30
106	Darold Knowles	1.00	.50	.30
107	Bobby Etheridge	1.00	.50	.30
108	Tom Burgmeier	1.00	.50	.30
109	Expos Rookies (Garry Jestadt, Carl Morton)	1.00	.50	.30
110	Bob Moose	1.00	.50	.30
111	Mike Hegan	1.00	.50	.30
112	Dave Nelson	1.00	.50	.30
113	Jim Ray	1.00	.50	.30
114	Gene Michael	1.00	.50	.30
115	Alex Johnson	1.00	.50	.30
116	Sparky Lyle	1.00	.50	.30
117	Don Young	1.00	.50	.30
118	George Mitterwald	1.00	.50	.30
119	Chuck Taylor	1.00	.50	.30
120	Sal Bando	1.00	.50	.30
121	Orioles Rookies (Fred Beene), *(Terry Crowley)*	1.00	.50	.30
122	George Stone	1.00	.50	.30
123	Don Gutteridge	1.00	.50	.30
124	Larry Jaster	1.00	.50	.30
125	Deron Johnson	1.00	.50	.30
126	Marty Martinez	1.00	.50	.30
127	Joe Coleman	1.00	.50	.30
128a	Checklist 133-263 (226 is R Perranoski)	5.00	2.50	1.50
128b	Checklist 133-263 (226 is R. Perranoski)	5.00	2.50	1.50
129	Jimmie Price	1.00	.50	.30
130	Ollie Brown	1.00	.50	.30
131	Dodgers Rookies (Ray Lamb, Bob Stinson)	1.00	.50	.30
132	Jim McGlothlin	1.00	.50	.30
133	Clay Carroll	1.00	.50	.30
134	Danny Walton	1.00	.50	.30
135	Dick Dietz	1.00	.50	.30
136	Steve Hargan	1.00	.50	.30
137	Art Shamsky	1.00	.50	.30
138	Joe Foy	1.00	.50	.30
139	Rich Nye	1.00	.50	.30
140	Reggie Jackson	40.00	20.00	12.00
141	Pirates Rookies *(Dave Cash*, Johnny Jeter)	1.00	.50	.30
142	Fritz Peterson	1.00	.50	.30
143	Phil Gagliano	1.00	.50	.30
144	Ray Culp	1.00	.50	.30
145	Rico Carty	1.00	.50	.30
146	Danny Murphy	1.00	.50	.30
147	Angel Hermoso	1.00	.50	.30
148	Earl Weaver	4.00	2.00	1.25
149	Billy Champion	1.00	.50	.30
150	Harmon Killebrew	7.00	3.50	2.00
151	Dave Roberts	1.00	.50	.30
152	Ike Brown	1.00	.50	.30
153	Gary Gentry	1.00	.50	.30
154	Senators Rookies (Jan Dukes, Jim Miles)	1.00	.50	.30
155	Denis Menke	1.00	.50	.30
156	Eddie Fisher	1.00	.50	.30
157	Manny Mota	1.00	.50	.30
158	Jerry McNertney	1.00	.50	.30
159	Tommy Helms	1.00	.50	.30
160	Phil Niekro	4.50	2.25	1.25
161	Richie Scheinblum	1.00	.50	.30
162	Jerry Johnson	1.00	.50	.30
163	Syd O'Brien	1.00	.50	.30
164	Ty Cline	1.00	.50	.30
165	Ed Kirkpatrick	1.00	.50	.30
166	Al Oliver	1.50	.70	.45
167	Bill Burbach	1.00	.50	.30
168	Dave Watkins	1.00	.50	.30
169	Tom Hall	1.00	.50	.30
170	Billy Williams	5.00	2.50	1.50
171	Jim Nash	1.00	.50	.30
172	Braves Rookies *(Ralph Garr*, Garry Hill)	2.00	1.00	.60
173	Jim Hicks	1.00	.50	.30
174	Ted Sizemore	1.00	.50	.30
175	Dick Bosman	1.00	.50	.30
176	Jim Hart	1.00	.50	.30
177	Jim Northrup	1.00	.50	.30
178	Denny Lemaster	1.00	.50	.30
179	Ivan Murrell	1.00	.50	.30
180	Tommy John	1.50	.70	.45
181	Sparky Anderson	5.00	2.50	1.50
182	Dick Hall	1.00	.50	.30
183	Jerry Grote	1.00	.50	.30
184	Ray Fosse	1.00	.50	.30
185	Don Mincher	1.00	.50	.30
186	Rick Joseph	1.00	.50	.30
187	Mike Hedlund	1.00	.50	.30
188	Manny Sanguillen	1.00	.50	.30
189	Yankees Rookies *(Dave McDonald)*, *(Thurman Munson)*	45.00	22.00	13.50
190	Joe Torre	3.00	1.50	.90
191	Vicente Romo	1.00	.50	.30
192	Jim [illegible]	1.00	.50	.30
193	Mike Wegener	1.00	.50	.30
194	Chuck Manuel	1.00	.50	.30
195	N.L.C.S. Game 1 (Seaver Wins Opener!)	10.00	5.00	3.00
196	N.L.C.S. Game 2 (Mets Show Muscle!)	4.00	2.00	1.25
197	N.L.C.S. Game 3 (Ryan Saves the Day!)	30.00	15.00	9.00
198	N.L. Playoffs Summary (We're Number One!) (Nolan Ryan)	12.50	6.25	3.75
199	A.L.C.S. Game 1 (Orioles Win A Squeaker!)	4.00	2.00	1.25
200	A.L.C.S. Game 2 (Powell Scores Winning Run!)	4.00	2.00	1.25
201	A.L.C.S. Game 3 (Birds Wrap It Up!)	3.50	1.75	1.00

202	A.L.C.S. Summary (Sweep Twins In Three!)	3.50	1.75	1.00
203	Rudy May	1.00	.50	.30
204	Len Gabrielson	1.00	.50	.30
205	Bert Campaneris	1.00	.50	.30
206	Clete Boyer	1.25	.60	.40
207	Tigers Rookies (Norman McRae, Bob Reed)	1.00	.50	.30
208	Fred Gladding	1.00	.50	.30
209	Ken Suarez	1.00	.50	.30
210	Juan Marichal	6.00	3.00	1.75
211	Ted Williams	12.00	6.00	3.50
212	Al Santorini	1.00	.50	.30
213	Andy Etchebarren	1.00	.50	.30
214	Ken Boswell	1.00	.50	.30
215	Reggie Smith	1.50	.70	.45
216	Chuck Hartenstein	1.00	.50	.30
217	Ron Hansen	1.00	.50	.30
218	Ron Stone	1.00	.50	.30
219	Jerry Kenney	1.00	.50	.30
220	Steve Carlton	12.00	6.00	3.50
221	Ron Brand	1.00	.50	.30
222	Jim Rooker	1.00	.50	.30
223	Nate Oliver	1.00	.50	.30
224	Steve Barber	1.00	.50	.30
225	Lee May	1.00	.50	.30
226	Ron Perranoski	1.00	.50	.30
227	Astros Rookies (*John Mayberry*, Bob Watkins)	1.25	.60	.40
228	Aurelio Rodriguez	1.00	.50	.30
229	Rich Robertson	1.00	.50	.30
230	Brooks Robinson	12.00	6.00	3.50
231	Luis Tiant	1.75	.90	.50
232	Bob Didier	1.00	.50	.30
233	Lew Krausse	1.00	.50	.30
234	Tommy Dean	1.00	.50	.30
235	Mike Epstein	1.00	.50	.30
236	Bob Veale	1.00	.50	.30
237	Russ Gibson	1.00	.50	.30
238	Jose Laboy	1.00	.50	.30
239	Ken Berry	1.00	.50	.30
240	Fergie Jenkins	5.00	2.50	1.50
241	Royals Rookies (Al Fitzmorris, Scott Northey)	1.00	.50	.30
242	Walter Alston	2.00	1.00	.60
243	Joe Sparma	1.00	.50	.30
244a	Checklist 264-372 (red bat on front)	5.00	2.50	1.50
244b	Checklist 264-372 (brown bat on front)	5.00	2.50	1.50
245	Leo Cardenas	1.00	.50	.30
246	Jim McAndrew	1.00	.50	.30
247	Lou Klimchock	1.00	.50	.30
248	Jesus Alou	1.00	.50	.30
249	Bob Locker	1.00	.50	.30
250	Willie McCovey	7.50	3.75	2.25
251	Dick Schofield	1.00	.50	.30
252	Lowell Palmer	1.00	.50	.30
253	Ron Woods	1.00	.50	.30
254	Camilo Pascual	1.00	.50	.30
255	*Jim Spencer*	1.00	.50	.30
256	Vic Davalillo	1.00	.50	.30
257	Dennis Higgins	1.00	.50	.30
258	Paul Popovich	1.00	.50	.30
259	Tommie Reynolds	1.00	.50	.30
260	Claude Osteen	1.00	.50	.30
261	Curt Motton	1.00	.50	.30
262	Padres Rookies (Jerry Morales, Jim Williams)	1.00	.50	.30
263	Duane Josephson	1.00	.50	.30
264	Rich Hebner	1.00	.50	.30
265	Randy Hundley	1.00	.50	.30
266	Wally Bunker	1.00	.50	.30
267	Twins Rookies (Herman Hill, Paul Ratliff)	1.00	.50	.30
268	Claude Raymond	1.00	.50	.30
269	Cesar Gutierrez	1.00	.50	.30
270	Chris Short	1.00	.50	.30
271	Greg Goossen	1.00	.50	.30
272	Hector Torres	1.00	.50	.30
273	Ralph Houk	1.00	.50	.30
274	Gerry Arrigo	1.00	.50	.30
275	Duke Sims	1.00	.50	.30
276	Ron Hunt	1.00	.50	.30
277	Paul Doyle	1.00	.50	.30
278	Tommie Aaron	1.00	.50	.30
279	*Bill Lee*	1.25	.60	.40
280	Donn Clendenon	1.00	.50	.30
281	Casey Cox	1.00	.50	.30
282	Steve Huntz	1.00	.50	.30
283	Angel Bravo	1.00	.50	.30
284	Jack Baldschun	1.00	.50	.30
285	Paul Blair	1.00	.50	.30
286	Dodgers Rookies (*Bill Buckner*, Jack Jenkins)	5.50	2.75	1.75
287	Fred Talbot	1.00	.50	.30
288	Larry Hisle	1.00	.50	.30
289	Gene Brabender	1.00	.50	.30
290	Rod Carew	12.00	6.00	3.50
291	Leo Durocher	3.00	1.50	.90
292	Eddie Leon	1.00	.50	.30
293	Bob Bailey	1.00	.50	.30
294	Jose Azcue	1.00	.50	.30
295	Cecil Upshaw	1.00	.50	.30
296	Woody Woodward	1.00	.50	.30
297	Curt Blefary	1.00	.50	.30
298	Ken Henderson	1.00	.50	.30
299	Buddy Bradford	1.00	.50	.30
300	Tom Seaver	30.00	15.00	9.00
301	Chico Salmon	1.00	.50	.30
302	Jeff James	1.00	.50	.30
303	Brant Alyea	1.00	.50	.30
304	*Bill Russell*	4.00	2.00	1.25
305	World Series Game 1 (Buford Belts Leadoff Homer!)	4.00	2.00	1.25
306	World Series Game 2 (Clendenon's HR Breaks Ice!)	4.00	2.00	1.25

307	World Series Game 3 (Agee's Catch Saves The Day!)	4.00	2.00	1.25
308	World Series Game 4 (Martin's Bunt Ends Deadlock!)	4.00	2.00	1.25
309	World Series Game 5 (Koosman Shuts The Door!)	4.00	2.00	1.25
310	World Series Summary (Mets Whoop It Up!)	3.50	1.75	1.00
311	Dick Green	1.00	.50	.30
312	Mike Torrez	1.00	.50	.30
313	Mayo Smith	1.00	.50	.30
314	Bill McCool	1.00	.50	.30
315	Luis Aparicio	5.50	2.75	1.75
316	Skip Guinn	1.00	.50	.30
317	Red Sox Rookies (Luis Alvarado, Billy Conigliaro)	1.00	.50	.30
318	Willie Smith	1.00	.50	.30
319	Clayton Dalrymple	1.00	.50	.30
320	Jim Maloney	1.00	.50	.30
321	Lou Piniella	1.50	.70	.45
322	Luke Walker	1.00	.50	.30
323	Wayne Comer	1.00	.50	.30
324	Tony Taylor	1.00	.50	.30
325	Dave Boswell	1.00	.50	.30
326	Bill Voss	1.00	.50	.30
327	Hal King	1.00	.50	.30
328	George Brunet	1.00	.50	.30
329	Chris Cannizzaro	1.00	.50	.30
330	Lou Brock	8.00	4.00	2.50
331	Chuck Dobson	1.00	.50	.30
332	Bobby Wine	1.00	.50	.30
333	Bobby Murcer	1.50	.70	.45
334	Phil Regan	1.00	.50	.30
335	Bill Freehan	1.25	.60	.40
336	Del Unser	1.00	.50	.30
337	Mike McCormick	1.00	.50	.30
338	Paul Schaal	1.00	.50	.30
339	Johnny Edwards	1.00	.50	.30
340	Tony Conigliaro	2.00	1.00	.60
341	Bill Sudakis	1.00	.50	.30
342	Wilbur Wood	1.00	.50	.30
343a	Checklist 373-459 (red bat on front)	5.00	2.50	1.50
343b	Checklist 373-459 (brown bat on front)	5.00	2.50	1.50
344	Marcelino Lopez	1.00	.50	.30
345	Al Ferrara	1.00	.50	.30
346	Red Schoendienst	3.00	1.50	.90
347	Russ Snyder	1.00	.50	.30
348	Mets Rookies (Jesse Hudson, Mike Jorgensen)	1.00	.50	.30
349	Steve Hamilton	1.00	.50	.30
350	Roberto Clemente	45.00	22.00	13.50
351	Tom Murphy	1.00	.50	.30
352	Bob Barton	1.00	.50	.30
353	Stan Williams	1.00	.50	.30
354	Amos Otis	1.00	.50	.30
355	Doug Rader	1.00	.50	.30
356	Fred Lasher	1.00	.50	.30
357	Bob Burda	1.00	.50	.30
358	*Pedro Borbon*	1.00	.50	.30
359	Phil Roof	1.00	.50	.30
360	Curt Flood	1.25	.60	.40
361	Ray Jarvis	1.00	.50	.30
362	Joe Hague	1.00	.50	.30
363	Tom Shopay	1.00	.50	.30
364	Dan McGinn	1.00	.50	.30
365	Zoilo Versalles	1.00	.50	.30
366	Barry Moore	1.00	.50	.30
367	Mike Lum	1.00	.50	.30
368	Ed Herrmann	1.00	.50	.30
369	Alan Foster	1.00	.50	.30
370	Tommy Harper	1.00	.50	.30
371	Rod Gaspar	1.00	.50	.30
372	Dave Giusti	1.00	.50	.30
373	Roy White	1.50	.70	.45
374	Tommie Sisk	1.50	.70	.45
375	Johnny Callison	1.50	.70	.45
376	Lefty Phillips	1.50	.70	.45
377	Bill Butler	1.50	.70	.45
378	Jim Davenport	1.50	.70	.45
379	Tom Tischinski	1.50	.70	.45
380	Tony Perez	7.50	3.75	2.25
381	Athletics Rookies (Bobby Brooks, Mike Olivo)	1.50	.70	.45
382	Jack DiLauro	1.50	.70	.45
383	Mickey Stanley	1.50	.70	.45
384	Gary Neibauer	1.50	.70	.45
385	George Scott	1.50	.70	.45
386	Bill Dillman	1.50	.70	.45
387	Orioles Team	3.00	1.50	.90
388	Byron Browne	1.50	.70	.45
389	Jim Shellenback	1.50	.70	.45
390	Willie Davis	2.00	1.00	.60
391	Larry Brown	1.50	.70	.45
392	Walt Hriniak	1.50	.70	.45
393	John Gelnar	1.50	.70	.45
394	Gil Hodges	4.00	2.00	1.25
395	Walt Williams	1.50	.70	.45
396	Steve Blass	1.50	.70	.45
397	Roger Repoz	1.50	.70	.45
398	Bill Stoneman	1.50	.70	.45
399	Yankees Team	5.00	2.50	1.50
400	Denny McLain	2.00	1.00	.60
401	Giants Rookies (John Harrell, Bernie Williams)	1.50	.70	.45
402	Ellie Rodriguez	1.50	.70	.45
403	Jim Bunning	5.00	2.50	1.50
404	Rich Reese	1.50	.70	.45
405	Bill Hands	1.50	.70	.45
406	Mike Andrews	1.50	.70	.45
407	Bob Watson	1.50	.70	.45
408	Paul Lindblad	1.50	.70	.45
409	Bob Tolan	1.50	.70	.45
410	Boog Powell	2.75	1.50	.80
411	Dodgers Team	5.50	2.75	1.75
412	Larry Burchart	1.50	.70	.45

413	Sonny Jackson	1.50	.70	.45
414	Paul Edmondson	1.50	.70	.45
415	Julian Javier	1.50	.70	.45
416	Joe Verbanic	1.50	.70	.45
417	John Bateman	1.50	.70	.45
418	John Donaldson	1.50	.70	.45
419	Ron Taylor	1.50	.70	.45
420	Ken McMullen	1.50	.70	.45
421	Pat Dobson	1.50	.70	.45
422	Royals Team	3.00	1.50	.90
423	Jerry May	1.50	.70	.45
424	Mike Kilkenny	1.50	.70	.45
425	Bobby Bonds	4.00	2.00	1.25
426	Bill Rigney	1.50	.70	.45
427	Fred Norman	1.50	.70	.45
428	Don Buford	1.50	.70	.45
429	Cubs Rookies (Randy Bobb, Jim Cosman)	1.50	.70	.45
430	Andy Messersmith	1.50	.70	.45
431	Ron Swoboda	1.50	.70	.45
432a	Checklist 460-546 ("Baseball" on front in yellow)	5.00	2.50	1.50
432b	Checklist 460-546 ("Baseball" on front in white)	5.00	2.50	1.50
433	Ron Bryant	1.50	.70	.45
434	Felipe Alou	2.00	1.00	.60
435	Nelson Briles	1.50	.70	.45
436	Phillies Team	3.00	1.50	.90
437	Danny Cater	1.50	.70	.45
438	Pat Jarvis	1.50	.70	.45
439	Lee Maye	1.50	.70	.45
440	Bill Mazeroski	4.50	2.25	1.25
441	John O'Donoghue	1.50	.70	.45
442	Gene Mauch	1.50	.70	.45
443	Al Jackson	1.50	.70	.45
444	White Sox Rookies (Bill Farmer, John Matias)	1.50	.70	.45
445	Vada Pinson	2.00	1.00	.60
446	*Billy Grabarkewitz*	1.50	.70	.45
447	Lee Stange	1.50	.70	.45
448	Astros Team	3.00	1.50	.90
449	Jim Palmer	10.00	5.00	3.00
450	Willie McCovey (All-Star)	4.50	2.25	1.25
451	Boog Powell (All-Star)	1.50	.70	.45
452	Felix Millan (All-Star)	1.50	.70	.45
453	Rod Carew (All-Star)	5.50	2.75	1.75
454	Ron Santo (All-Star)	1.50	.70	.45
455	Brooks Robinson (All-Star)	6.50	3.25	2.00
456	Don Kessinger (All-Star)	1.50	.70	.45
457	Rico Petrocelli (All-Star)	1.50	.70	.45
458	Pete Rose (All-Star)	11.00	5.50	3.25
459	Reggie Jackson (All-Star)	10.00	5.00	3.00
460	Matty Alou (All-Star)	1.50	.70	.45
461	Carl Yastrzemski (All-Star)	7.50	3.75	2.25
462	Hank Aaron (All-Star)	13.50	6.75	4.00
463	Frank Robinson (All-Star)	5.50	2.75	1.75
464	Johnny Bench (All-Star)	9.00	4.50	2.75
465	Bill Freehan (All-Star)	1.50	.70	.45
466	Juan Marichal (All-Star)	2.50	1.25	.70
467	Denny McLain (All-Star)	1.50	.70	.45
468	Jerry Koosman (All-Star)	1.50	.70	.45
469	Sam McDowell (All-Star)	1.50	.70	.45
470	Willie Stargell	8.00	4.00	2.50
471	Chris Zachary	1.50	.70	.45
472	Braves Team	3.00	1.50	.90
473	Don Bryant	1.50	.70	.45
474	Dick Kelley	1.50	.70	.45
475	Dick McAuliffe	1.50	.70	.45
476	Don Shaw	1.50	.70	.45
477	Orioles Rookies (Roger Freed, Al Severinsen)	1.50	.70	.45
478	Bob Heise	1.50	.70	.45
479	Dick Woodson	1.50	.70	.45
480	Glenn Beckert	1.50	.70	.45
481	Jose Tartabull	1.50	.70	.45
482	Tom Hilgendorf	1.50	.70	.45
483	Gail Hopkins	1.50	.70	.45
484	Gary Nolan	1.50	.70	.45
485	Jay Johnstone	1.50	.70	.45
486	Terry Harmon	1.50	.70	.45
487	Cisco Carlos	1.50	.70	.45
488	J.C. Martin	1.50	.70	.45
489	Eddie Kasko	1.50	.70	.45
490	Bill Singer	1.50	.70	.45
491	Graig Nettles	3.00	1.50	.90
492	Astros Rookies (Keith Lampard, Scipio Spinks)	1.50	.70	.45
493	Lindy McDaniel	1.50	.70	.45
494	Larry Stahl	1.50	.70	.45
495	Dave Morehead	1.50	.70	.45
496	Steve Whitaker	1.50	.70	.45
497	Eddie Watt	1.50	.70	.45
498	Al Weis	1.50	.70	.45
499	Skip Lockwood	1.50	.70	.45
500	Hank Aaron	35.00	17.50	10.50
501	White Sox Team	3.00	1.50	.90
502	Rollie Fingers	7.50	3.75	2.25
503	Dal Maxvill	1.50	.70	.45
504	Don Pavletich	1.50	.70	.45
505	Ken Holtzman	1.50	.70	.45
506	Ed Stroud	1.50	.70	.45
507	Pat Corrales	1.50	.70	.45
508	Joe Niekro	2.00	1.00	.60
509	Expos Team	3.00	1.50	.90
510	Tony Oliva	2.00	1.00	.60
511	Joe Hoerner	1.50	.70	.45
512	Billy Harris	1.50	.70	.45
513	Preston Gomez	1.50	.70	.45
514	Steve Hovley	1.50	.70	.45
515	Don Wilson	1.50	.70	.45
516	Yankees Rookies (John Ellis, Jim Lyttle)	1.50	.70	.45
517	Joe Gibbon	1.50	.70	.45
518	Bill Melton	1.50	.70	.45
519	Don McMahon	1.50	.70	.45
520	Willie Horton	1.75	.90	.50
521	Cal Koonce	1.50	.70	.45
522	Angels Team	3.00	1.50	.90

523	Jose Pena	1.50	.70	.45
524	Alvin Dark	1.50	.70	.45
525	Jerry Adair	1.50	.70	.45
526	Ron Herbel	1.50	.70	.45
527	Don Bosch	1.50	.70	.45
528	Elrod Hendricks	1.50	.70	.45
529	Bob Aspromonte	1.50	.70	.45
530	Bob Gibson	12.00	6.00	3.50
531	Ron Clark	1.50	.70	.45
532	Danny Murtaugh	1.50	.70	.45
533	Buzz Stephen	1.50	.70	.45
534	Twins Team	3.00	1.50	.90
535	Andy Kosco	1.50	.70	.45
536	Mike Kekich	1.50	.70	.45
537	Joe Morgan	7.00	3.50	2.00
538	Bob Humphreys	1.50	.70	.45
539	Phillies Rookies *(Larry Bowa,* Dennis Doyle)	4.00	2.00	1.25
540	Gary Peters	1.50	.70	.45
541	Bill Heath	1.50	.70	.45
542a	Checklist 547-633 (grey bat on front)	5.00	2.50	1.50
542b	Checklist 547-633 (brown bat on front)	5.00	2.50	1.50
543	Clyde Wright	1.50	.70	.45
544	Reds Team	3.00	1.50	.90
545	Ken Harrelson	1.50	.70	.45
546	Ron Reed	1.50	.70	.45
547	Rick Monday	3.75	2.00	1.25
548	Howie Reed	3.75	2.00	1.25
549	Cardinals Team	7.00	3.50	2.00
550	Frank Howard	5.00	2.50	1.50
551	Dock Ellis	3.75	2.00	1.25
552	Royals Rookies (Don O'Riley, Dennis Paepke, Fred Rico)	3.75	2.00	1.25
553	Jim Lefebvre	3.75	2.00	1.25
554	Tom Timmermann	3.75	2.00	1.25
555	Orlando Cepeda	9.00	4.50	2.75
556	Dave Bristol	3.75	2.00	1.25
557	Ed Kranepool	3.75	2.00	1.25
558	Vern Fuller	3.75	2.00	1.25
559	Tommy Davis	4.00	2.00	1.25
560	Gaylord Perry	8.00	4.00	2.50
561	Tom McCraw	3.75	2.00	1.25
562	Ted Abernathy	3.75	2.00	1.25
563	Red Sox Team	7.00	3.50	2.00
564	Johnny Briggs	3.75	2.00	1.25
565	Catfish Hunter	8.00	4.00	2.50
566	Gene Alley	3.75	2.00	1.25
567	Bob Oliver	3.75	2.00	1.25
568	Stan Bahnsen	3.75	2.00	1.25
569	Cookie Rojas	3.75	2.00	1.25
570	Jim Fregosi	3.75	2.00	1.25
571	Jim Brewer	3.75	2.00	1.25
572	Frank Quilici	3.75	2.00	1.25
573	Padres Rookies (Mike Corkins, Rafael Robles, Ron Slocum)	3.75	2.00	1.25
574	Bobby Bolin	3.75	2.00	1.25
575	Cleon Jones	3.75	2.00	1.25
576	Milt Pappas	3.75	2.00	1.25
577	Bernie Allen	3.75	2.00	1.25
578	Tom Griffin	3.75	2.00	1.25
579	Tigers Team	7.00	3.50	2.00
580	Pete Rose	40.00	20.00	12.00
581	Tom Satriano	3.75	2.00	1.25
582	Mike Paul	3.75	2.00	1.25
583	Hal Lanier	3.75	2.00	1.25
584	Al Downing	3.75	2.00	1.25
585	Rusty Staub	4.50	2.25	1.25
586	Rickey Clark	3.75	2.00	1.25
587	Jose Arcia	3.75	2.00	1.25
588a	Checklist 634-720 (666 is Adolpho Phillips)	5.00	2.50	1.50
588b	Checklist 634-720 (666 is Adolfo Phillips)	5.00	2.50	1.50
589	Joe Keough	3.75	2.00	1.25
590	Mike Cuellar	3.75	2.00	1.25
591	Mike Ryan	3.75	2.00	1.25
592	Daryl Patterson	3.75	2.00	1.25
593	Cubs Team	7.00	3.50	2.00
594	Jake Gibbs	3.75	2.00	1.25
595	Maury Wills	3.75	2.00	1.25
596	Mike Hershberger	3.75	2.00	1.25
597	Sonny Siebert	3.75	2.00	1.25
598	Joe Pepitone	3.75	2.00	1.25
599	Senators Rookies (Gene Martin, Dick Stelmaszek, Dick Such)	3.75	2.00	1.25
600	Willie Mays	55.00	27.00	16.50
601	Pete Richert	3.75	2.00	1.25
602	Ted Savage	3.75	2.00	1.25
603	Ray Oyler	3.75	2.00	1.25
604	Cito Gaston	3.75	2.00	1.25
605	Rick Wise	3.75	2.00	1.25
606	Chico Ruiz	3.75	2.00	1.25
607	Gary Waslewski	3.75	2.00	1.25
608	Pirates Team	7.00	3.50	2.00
609	*Buck Martinez*	3.75	2.00	1.25
610	Jerry Koosman	3.75	2.00	[illegible]
611	Norm Cash	4.50	2.25	1.25
612	Jim Hickman	3.75	2.00	1.25
613	Dave Baldwin	3.75	2.00	1.25
614	Mike Shannon	3.75	2.00	1.25
615	Mark Belanger	3.75	2.00	1.25
616	Jim Merritt	3.75	2.00	1.25
617	Jim French	3.75	2.00	1.25
618	Billy Wynne	3.75	2.00	1.25
619	Norm Miller	3.75	2.00	1.25
620	Jim Perry	3.75	2.00	1.25
621	Braves Rookies *(Darrell Evans,* Rick Kester, Mike McQueen)	9.00	4.50	2.75
622	Don Sutton	9.00	4.50	2.75
623	Horace Clarke	3.75	2.00	1.25
624	Clyde King	3.75	2.00	1.25
625	Dean Chance	3.75	2.00	1.25
626	Dave Ricketts	3.75	2.00	1.25
627	Gary Wagner	3.75	2.00	1.25
628	Wayne Garrett	3.75	2.00	1.25
629	Merv Rettenmund	3.75	2.00	1.25
630	Ernie Banks	30.00	15.00	9.00
631	Athletics Team	7.00	3.50	2.00
632	Gary Sutherland	3.75	2.00	1.25
633	Roger Nelson	3.75	2.00	1.25
634	Bud Harrelson	9.00	4.50	2.75
635	Bob Allison	9.00	4.50	2.75
636	Jim Stewart	9.00	4.50	2.75
637	Indians Team	15.00	7.50	4.50
638	Frank Bertaina	9.00	4.50	2.75
639	Dave Campbell	9.00	4.50	2.75
640	Al Kaline	45.00	22.00	13.50
641	Al McBean	9.00	4.50	2.75
642	Angels Rookies (Greg Garrett, Gordon Lund, Jarvis Tatum)	9.00	4.50	2.75
643	Jose Pagan	9.00	4.50	2.75
644	Gerry Nyman	9.00	4.50	2.75
645	Don Money	9.00	4.50	2.75
646	Jim Britton	9.00	4.50	2.75
647	Tom Matchick	9.00	4.50	2.75
648	Larry Haney	9.00	4.50	2.75
649	Jimmie Hall	9.00	4.50	2.75
650	Sam McDowell	9.00	4.50	2.75
651	Jim Gosger	9.00	4.50	2.75
652	Rich Rollins	9.00	4.50	2.75
653	Moe Drabowsky	9.00	4.50	2.75
654	N.L. Rookies (Boots Day), *(Oscar Gamble,* Angel Mangual)	10.00	5.00	3.00
655	John Roseboro	9.00	4.50	2.75
656	Jim Hardin	9.00	4.50	2.75
657	Padres Team	13.00	6.50	4.00
658	Ken Tatum	9.00	4.50	2.75
659	Pete Ward	9.00	4.50	2.75
660	Johnny Bench	90.00	45.00	27.00
661	Jerry Robertson	9.00	4.50	2.75
662	Frank Lucchesi	9.00	4.50	2.75
663	Tito Francona	9.00	4.50	2.75
664	Bob Robertson	9.00	4.50	2.75
665	Jim Lonborg	9.00	4.50	2.75
666	Adolfo Phillips	9.00	4.50	2.75
667	Bob Meyer	9.00	4.50	2.75
668	Bob Tillman	9.00	4.50	2.75
669	White Sox Rookies (Bart Johnson, Dan Lazar, Mickey Scott)	9.00	4.50	2.75
670	Ron Santo	12.00	6.00	3.50
671	Jim Campanis	9.00	4.50	2.75
672	Leon McFadden	9.00	4.50	2.75
673	Ted Uhlaender	9.00	4.50	2.75
674	Dave Leonhard	9.00	4.50	2.75
675	Jose Cardenal	9.00	4.50	2.75
676	Senators Team	13.00	6.50	4.00
677	Woodie Fryman	9.00	4.50	2.75
678	Dave Duncan	9.00	4.50	2.75
679	Ray Sadecki	9.00	4.50	2.75
680	Rico Petrocelli	9.00	4.50	2.75
681	Bob Garibaldi	9.00	4.50	2.75
682	Dalton Jones	9.00	4.50	2.75
683	Reds Rookies (Vern Geishert, Hal McRae, Wayne Simpson)	9.00	4.50	2.75
684	Jack Fisher	9.00	4.50	2.75
685	Tom Haller	9.00	4.50	2.75
686	Jackie Hernandez	9.00	4.50	2.75
687	Bob Priddy	9.00	4.50	2.75
688	Ted Kubiak	9.00	4.50	2.75
689	Frank Tepedino	9.00	4.50	2.75
690	Ron Fairly	9.00	4.50	2.75
691	Joe Grzenda	9.00	4.50	2.75
692	Duffy Dyer	9.00	4.50	2.75
693	Bob Johnson	9.00	4.50	2.75
694	Gary Ross	9.00	4.50	2.75
695	Bobby Knoop	9.00	4.50	2.75
696	Giants Team	13.00	6.50	4.00
697	Jim Hannan	9.00	4.50	2.75
698	Tom Tresh	12.00	6.00	3.50
699	Hank Aguirre	9.00	4.50	2.75
700	Frank Robinson	45.00	22.00	13.50
701	Jack Billingham	9.00	4.50	2.75
702	A.L. Rookies (Bob Johnson, Ron Klimkowski, Bill Zepp)	9.00	4.50	2.75
703	Lou Marone	9.00	4.50	2.75
704	Frank Baker	9.00	4.50	2.75
705	Tony Cloninger	9.00	4.50	2.75
706	John McNamara	9.00	4.50	2.75
707	Kevin Collins	9.00	4.50	2.75
708	Jose Santiago	9.00	4.50	2.75
709	Mike Fiore	9.00	4.50	2.75
710	Felix Millan	9.00	4.50	2.75
711	Ed Brinkman	9.00	4.50	2.75
712	Nolan Ryan	190.00	95.00	57.00
713	Pilots Team	20.00	10.00	6.00
714	Al Spangler	9.00	4.50	2.75
715	Mickey Lolich	11.00	5.50	3.25
716	Cards Rookies (Sal Campisi), *(Reggie Cleveland,* Santiago Guzman)	9.00	4.50	2.75
717	Tom Phoebus	9.00	4.50	2.75
718	Ed Spiezio	9.00	4.50	2.75
719	Jim Roland	9.00	4.50	2.75
720	Rick Reichardt	9.00	4.50	2.75

1970 Topps Candy Lids

The 1970 Topps Candy Lids are a test issue that was utilized again in 1973. The set is made up of 24 lids that measure 1-7/8" in diameter and were the tops of small 1.1 oz. tubs of "Baseball Stars Candy." Unlike the 1973 versions, the 1970 lids have no border surrounding the full-color photos. Frank Howard, Tom Seaver and Carl Yastrzemski photos are found on the top (outside) of the candy lid.

		NM	EX	VG
Complete Set (24):		1600.	800.00	475.00
Common Player:		30.00	15.00	9.00
(1)	Hank Aaron	200.00	100.00	60.00
(2)	Rich Allen	65.00	32.00	19.50
(3)	Luis Aparicio	80.00	40.00	24.00
(4)	Johnny Bench	150.00	75.00	45.00
(5)	Ollie Brown	30.00	15.00	9.00
(6)	Willie Davis	30.00	15.00	9.00
(7)	Jim Fregosi	30.00	15.00	9.00
(8)	Mike Hegan	30.00	15.00	9.00
(9)	Frank Howard	45.00	22.00	13.50
(10)	Reggie Jackson	150.00	75.00	45.00
(11)	Fergie Jenkins	75.00	37.00	22.00
(12)	Harmon Killebrew	80.00	40.00	24.00
(13)	Juan Marichal	80.00	40.00	24.00
(14)	Bill Mazeroski	65.00	32.00	19.50
(15)	Tim McCarver	40.00	20.00	12.00
(16)	Sam McDowell	30.00	15.00	9.00
(17)	Denny McLain	50.00	25.00	15.00
(18)	Lou Piniella	30.00	15.00	9.00
(19)	Frank Robinson	100.00	50.00	30.00
(20)	Tom Seaver	150.00	75.00	45.00
(21)	Rusty Staub	50.00	25.00	15.00
(22)	Mel Stottlemyre	30.00	15.00	9.00
(23)	Jim Wynn	30.00	15.00	9.00
(24)	Carl Yastrzemski	125.00	62.00	37.00

1970 Topps Cloth Stickers

The earliest and rarest of the Topps cloth sticker test issues, only 15 subjects are known, and only a single specimen apiece is known for many of them. In the same 2-1/2" x 3-1/2" size, and with the same design as the 1970 Topps baseball cards, the stickers are blank-backed. The stickers of Denny Lemaster, Dennis Higgins and Rich Nye use photos that are different from their '70 Topps cards. It is quite likely that the checklist presented here is incomplete. The stickers are unnumbered and are checklisted alphabetically.

		NM	EX	VG
Common Player:		75.00	37.00	22.00
(1)	A.L. Playoff Game 2 (Boog Powell)	90.00	45.00	27.00
(2)	Bill Burbach	75.00	37.00	22.00
(3)	Tom Hall	75.00	37.00	22.00
(4)	Chuck Hartenstein	75.00	37.00	22.00
(5)	Dennis Higgins	75.00	37.00	22.00
(6)	Jose Laboy	75.00	37.00	22.00
(7)	Denny Lemaster	75.00	37.00	22.00
(8)	Juan Marichal	300.00	150.00	90.00
(9)	Jerry McNertney	75.00	37.00	22.00
(10)	Ivan Murrell	75.00	37.00	22.00
(11)	N.L. Playoff Game 1 (Tom Seaver)	335.00	165.00	100.00
(12)	N.L. Playoff Game 3 (Nolan Ryan)	525.00	260.00	155.00
(13)	Phil Niekro	125.00	62.00	37.00
(14)	Jim Northrup	75.00	37.00	22.00
(15)	Rich Nye	75.00	37.00	22.00
(16)	Ron Perranoski	75.00	37.00	22.00
(17)	Al Santorini	75.00	37.00	22.00

1970 Topps Posters

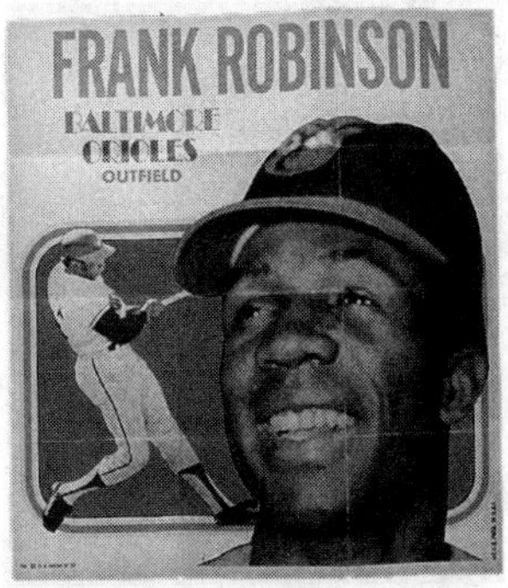

Helping to ease a price increase, Topps included extremely fragile 8-11/16" x 9-5/8" posters in packs of regular cards. The posters feature color portraits and a smaller black and white "action" pose as well as the player's name, team and position at the top. Although there are Hall of Famers in the 24-poster set, all the top names are not represented. Once again, due to folding, heavy creases are a fact of life for today's collector.

		NM	EX	VG
Complete Set (24):		75.00	37.00	22.00
Common Player:		2.00	1.00	.60
1	Joe Horlen	2.00	1.00	.60
2	Phil Niekro	4.50	2.25	1.25
3	Willie Davis	2.00	1.00	.60
4	Lou Brock	5.00	2.50	1.50
5	Ron Santo	3.50	1.75	1.00
6	Ken Harrelson	2.00	1.00	.60
7	Willie McCovey	6.00	3.00	1.75
8	Rick Wise	2.00	1.00	.60
9	Andy Messersmith	2.00	1.00	.60
10	Ron Fairly	2.00	1.00	.60
11	Johnny Bench	10.00	5.00	3.00
12	Frank Robinson	7.50	3.75	2.25
13	Tommie Agee	2.00	1.00	.60
14	Roy White	2.00	1.00	.60
15	Larry Dierker	2.00	1.00	.60
16	Rod Carew	7.00	3.50	2.00
17	Don Mincher	2.00	1.00	.60
18	Ollie Brown	2.00	1.00	.60
19	Ed Kirkpatrick	2.00	1.00	.60
20	Reggie Smith	2.00	1.00	.60
21	Roberto Clemente	15.00	7.50	4.50
22	Frank Howard	2.50	1.25	.70
23	Bert Campaneris	2.00	1.00	.60
24	Denny McLain	2.50	1.25	.70

1970-71 Topps Scratch-Offs

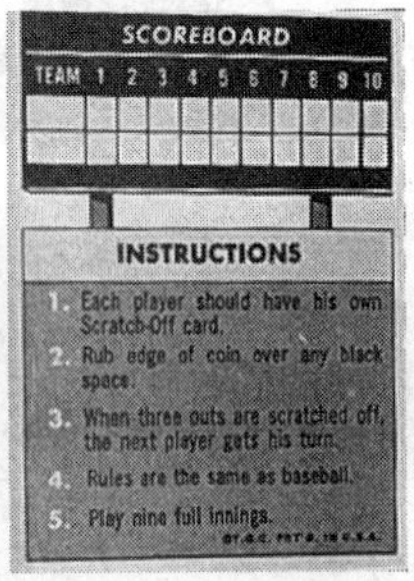

Needing inserts, and having not given up on the idea of a game which could be played with baseball cards, Topps provided a new game - the baseball scratch-off. The set consists of 24 cards. Unfolded, they measure 3-3/8" x 5", and reveal a baseball game of sorts which was played by rubbing the black ink off playing squares which then determined the "action." Fronts of the cards have a player picture as "captain," while backs have instructions and a scoreboard. Inserts with white centers are from 1970 while those with red centers are from 1971.

		NM	EX	VG
Complete Set (24):		70.00	35.00	21.00
Common Player:		2.00	1.00	.60
(1)	Hank Aaron	15.00	7.50	4.50
(2)	Rich Allen	5.00	2.50	1.50
(3)	Luis Aparicio	8.00	4.00	2.50
(4)	Sal Bando	2.00	1.00	.60
(5)	Glenn Beckert	2.00	1.00	.60
(6)	Dick Bosman	2.00	1.00	.60
(7)	Nate Colbert	2.00	1.00	.60
(8)	Mike Hegan	2.00	1.00	.60
(9)	Mack Jones	2.00	1.00	.60
(10)	Al Kaline	10.00	5.00	3.00
(11)	Harmon Killebrew	8.00	4.00	2.50
(12)	Juan Marichal	8.00	4.00	2.50
(13)	Tim McCarver	3.00	1.50	.90
(14)	Sam McDowell	2.00	1.00	.60
(15)	Claude Osteen	2.00	1.00	.60
(16)	Tony Perez	6.00	3.00	1.75
(17)	Lou Piniella	2.00	1.00	.60
(18)	Boog Powell	2.50	1.25	.70
(19)	Tom Seaver	10.00	5.00	3.00
(20)	Jim Spencer	2.00	1.00	.60
(21)	Willie Stargell	8.00	4.00	2.50
(22)	Mel Stottlemyre	2.00	1.00	.60
(23)	Jim Wynn	2.00	1.00	.60
(24)	Carl Yastrzemski	10.00	5.00	3.00

1970 Topps Story Booklets

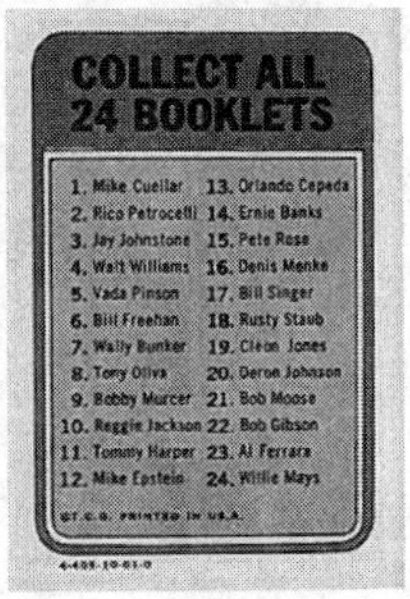

Measuring 2-1/2" x 3-7/16," the Topps Story Booklet was a 1970 regular pack insert. The booklet feature a photo, title and booklet number on the "cover." Inside are six pages of comic book story. The backs give a checklist of other available booklets. Not every star had a booklet as the set is only 24 in number.

		NM	EX	VG
Complete Set (24):		75.00	37.00	22.00
Common Player:		2.00	1.00	.60
1	Mike Cuellar	2.00	1.00	.60
2	Rico Petrocelli	2.00	1.00	.60
3	Jay Johnstone	2.00	1.00	.60
4	Walt Williams	2.00	1.00	.60
5	Vada Pinson	2.50	1.25	.70
6	Bill Freehan	2.00	1.00	.60
7	Wally Bunker	2.00	1.00	.60
8	Tony Oliva	2.50	1.25	.70
9	Bobby Murcer	2.00	1.00	.60
10	Reggie Jackson	12.00	6.00	3.50
11	Tommy Harper	2.00	1.00	.60
12	Mike Epstein	2.00	1.00	.60
13	Orlando Cepeda	5.00	2.50	1.50
14	Ernie Banks	8.50	4.25	2.50
15	Pete Rose	15.00	7.50	4.50
16	Denis Menke	2.00	1.00	.60
17	Bill Singer	2.00	1.00	.60
18	Rusty Staub	2.50	1.25	.70
19	Cleon Jones	2.00	1.00	.60
20	Deron Johnson	2.00	1.00	.60
21	Bob Moose	2.00	1.00	.60
22	Bob Gibson	6.50	3.25	2.00
23	Al Ferrara	2.00	1.00	.60
24	Willie Mays	13.50	6.75	4.00

1970 Topps Super

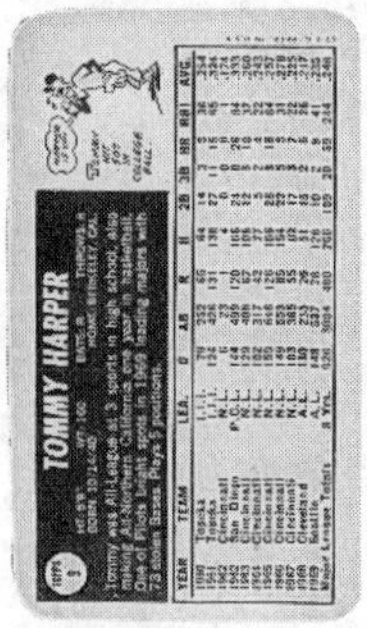

Representing a refinement of the concept begun in 1969, the 1970 Topps Supers had a new 3-1/8" x 5-1/4" postcard size. Printed on heavy stock with rounded corners, card fronts feature a borderless color photograph and facsimile autograph. Card backs are simply an enlarged back from the player's regular 1970 Topps card. The Topps Supers set numbers 42 cards. Probably due to the press sheet configuration, eight of the 42 had smaller printings. The most elusive is card #38 (Boog Powell). The set was more widely produced than was the case in 1969, meaning collectors stand a much better chance of affording it.

		NM	EX	VG
Complete Set (42):		200.00	100.00	60.00
Common Player:		2.50	1.25	.70
1	Claude Osteen (SP)	6.00	3.00	1.75
2	Sal Bando (SP)	6.00	3.00	1.75
3	Luis Aparicio	5.00	2.50	1.50
4	Harmon Killebrew	6.00	3.00	1.75
5	Tom Seaver (SP)	40.00	20.00	12.00
6	Larry Dierker	2.50	1.25	.70
7	Bill Freehan	2.50	1.25	.70
8	Johnny Bench	15.00	7.50	4.50
9	Tommy Harper	2.50	1.25	.70
10	Sam McDowell	2.50	1.25	.70
11	Lou Brock	7.00	3.50	2.00
12	Roberto Clemente	30.00	15.00	9.00
13	Willie McCovey	7.00	3.50	2.00
14	Rico Petrocelli	2.50	1.25	.70
15	Phil Niekro	5.00	2.50	1.50
16	Frank Howard	3.00	1.50	.90
17	Denny McLain	3.00	1.50	.90
18	Willie Mays	20.00	10.00	6.00
19	Willie Stargell	7.00	3.50	2.00
20	Joe Horlen	2.50	1.25	.70
21	Ron Santo	3.00	1.50	.90
22	Dick Bosman	2.50	1.25	.70
23	Tim McCarver	3.00	1.50	.90
24	Henry Aaron	20.00	10.00	6.00
25	Andy Messersmith	2.50	1.25	.70
26	Tony Oliva	3.00	1.50	.90
27	Mel Stottlemyre	2.50	1.25	.70
28	Reggie Jackson	17.50	8.75	5.25
29	Carl Yastrzemski	15.00	7.50	4.50
30	James Fregosi	2.50	1.25	.70
31	Vada Pinson	3.00	1.50	.90
32	Lou Piniella	2.50	1.25	.70
33	Robert Gibson	6.00	3.00	1.75
34	Pete Rose	20.00	10.00	6.00
35	Jim Wynn	2.50	1.25	.70
36	Ollie Brown (SP)	6.00	3.00	1.75
37	Frank Robinson (SP)	22.00	11.00	6.50
38	Boog Powell (SP)	45.00	22.00	13.50
39	Willie Davis (SP)	6.00	3.00	1.75
40	Billy Williams (SP)	12.00	6.00	3.50
41	Rusty Staub	3.00	1.50	.90
42	Tommie Agee	2.50	1.25	.70

1971 Topps

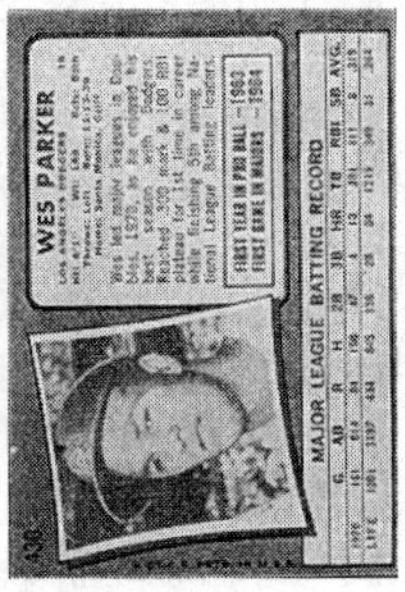

In 1971, Topps again increased the size of its set to 752 cards. These well-liked cards, measuring 2-1/2" x 3-1/2," feature a large color photo which has a thin white frame. Above the picture, in the card's overall black border, is the player's name, team and position. A facsimile autograph completes the front. Backs feature a major change as a black and white "snapshot" of the player appears. Abbreviated statistics, a line giving the player's first pro and major-league games and a short biography complete the back of these innovative cards. Specialty cards in this issue are limited. There are statistical leaders as well as World Series and playoff highlights. High numbered cards #644-752 are scarce, with about half of the cards being short-printed.

		NM	EX	VG
Complete Set (752):		1950.	800.00	500.00
Common Player (1-393):		1.50	.75	.45
Common Player (394-523):		2.00	1.00	.60
Common Player (524-643):		3.50	1.75	1.00
Common Player (644-752):		6.00	3.00	1.75
1	World Champions (Orioles Team)	12.00	6.00	3.50
2	Dock Ellis	1.50	.70	.45
3	Dick McAuliffe	1.50	.70	.45
4	Vic Davalillo	1.50	.70	.45
5	Thurman Munson	20.00	10.00	6.00
6	Ed Spiezio	1.50	.70	.45
7	Jim Holt	1.50	.70	.45
8	Mike McQueen	1.50	.70	.45
9	George Scott	1.50	.70	.45
10	Claude Osteen	1.50	.70	.45
11	*Elliott Maddox*	1.50	.70	.45
12	Johnny Callison	1.50	.70	.45
13	White Sox Rookies (Charlie Brinkman, Dick Moloney)	1.50	.70	.45

14	*Dave Concepcion*	15.00	7.50	4.50
15	Andy Messersmith	1.50	.70	.45
16	*Ken Singleton*	3.50	1.75	1.00
17	Billy Sorrell	1.50	.70	.45
18	Norm Miller	1.50	.70	.45
19	Skip Pitlock	1.50	.70	.45
20	Reggie Jackson	24.00	12.00	7.25
21	Dan McGinn	1.50	.70	.45
22	Phil Roof	1.50	.70	.45
23	Oscar Gamble	1.50	.70	.45
24	Rich Hand	1.50	.70	.45
25	Cito Gaston	1.50	.70	.45
26	*Bert Blyleven*	9.00	4.50	2.75
27	Pirates Rookies (Fred Cambria, Gene Clines)	1.50	.70	.45
28	Ron Klimkowski	1.50	.70	.45
29	Don Buford	1.50	.70	.45
30	Phil Niekro	5.00	2.50	1.50
31	Eddie Kasko	1.50	.70	.45
32	Jerry DaVanon	1.50	.70	.45
33	Del Unser	1.50	.70	.45
34	Sandy Vance	1.50	.70	.45
35	Lou Piniella	2.00	1.00	.60
36	Dean Chance	1.50	.70	.45
37	Rich McKinney	1.50	.70	.45
38	*Jim Colborn*	1.50	.70	.45
39	Tigers Rookies (Gene Lamont), *(Lerrin LaGrow)*	1.50	.70	.45
40	Lee May	1.50	.70	.45
41	Rick Austin	1.50	.70	.45
42	Boots Day	1.50	.70	.45
43	Steve Kealey	1.50	.70	.45
44	Johnny Edwards	1.50	.70	.45
45	Catfish Hunter	5.50	2.75	1.75
46	Dave Campbell	1.50	.70	.45
47	Johnny Jeter	1.50	.70	.45
48	Dave Baldwin	1.50	.70	.45
49	Don Money	1.50	.70	.45
50	Willie McCovey	6.50	3.25	2.00
51	Steve Kline	1.50	.70	.45
52	Braves Rookies (Oscar Brown), *(Earl Williams)*	1.50	.70	.45
53	Paul Blair	1.50	.70	.45
54	Checklist 1-132	3.25	1.75	1.00
55	Steve Carlton	14.00	7.00	4.25
56	Duane Josephson	1.50	.70	.45
57	Von Joshua	1.50	.70	.45
58	Bill Lee	1.50	.70	.45
59	Gene Mauch	1.50	.70	.45
60	Dick Bosman	1.50	.70	.45
61	A.L. Batting Leaders (Alex Johnson, Tony Oliva, Carl Yastrzemski)	3.00	1.50	.90
62	N.L. Batting Leaders (Rico Carty, Manny Sanguillen, Joe Torre)	2.50	1.25	.70
63	A.L. RBI Leaders (Tony Conigliaro, Frank Howard, Boog Powell)	2.25	1.25	.70
64	N.L. RBI Leaders (Johnny Bench, Tony Perez, Billy Williams)	4.75	2.50	1.50
65	A.L. Home Run Leaders (Frank Howard, Harmon Killebrew, Carl Yastrzemski)	4.00	2.00	1.25
66	N.L. Home Run Leaders (Johnny Bench, Tony Perez, Billy Williams)	5.50	2.75	1.75
67	A.L. ERA Leaders (Jim Palmer, Diego Segui, Clyde Wright)	3.00	1.50	.90
68	N.L. ERA Leaders (Tom Seaver, Wayne Simpson, Luke Walker)	3.50	1.75	1.00
69	A.L. Pitching Leaders (Mike Cuellar, Dave McNally, Jim Perry)	1.75	.90	.50
70	N.L. Pitching Leaders (Bob Gibson, Fergie Jenkins, Gaylord Perry)	4.50	2.25	1.25
71	A.L. Strikeout Leaders (Bob Johnson, Mickey Lolich, Sam McDowell)	2.00	1.00	.60
72	N.L. Strikeout Leaders (Bob Gibson, Fergie Jenkins, Tom Seaver)	5.50	2.75	1.75
73	George Brunet	1.50	.70	.45
74	Twins Rookies (Pete Hamm, Jim Nettles)	1.50	.70	.45
75	Gary Nolan	1.50	.70	.45
76	Ted Savage	1.50	.70	.45
77	Mike Compton	1.50	.70	.45
78	Jim Spencer	1.50	.70	.45
79	Wade Blasingame	1.50	.70	.45
80	Bill Melton	1.50	.70	.45
81	Felix Millan	1.50	.70	.45
82	Casey Cox	1.50	.70	.45
83	Mets Rookies (Randy Bobb), *(Tim Foli)*	1.50	.70	.45
84	Marcel Lachemann	1.50	.70	.45
85	Billy Grabarkewitz	1.50	.70	.45
86	Mike Kilkenny	1.50	.70	.45
87	Jack Heidemann	1.50	.70	.45
88	Hal King	1.50	.70	.45
89	Ken Brett	1.50	.70	.45
90	Joe Pepitone	1.50	.70	.45
91	Bob Lemon	3.00	1.50	.90
92	Fred Wenz	1.50	.70	.45
93	Senators Rookies (Norm McRae, Denny Riddleberger)	1.50	.70	.45
94	Don Hahn	1.50	.70	.45
95	Luis Tiant	1.50	.70	.45
96	Joe Hague	1.50	.70	.45
97	Floyd Wicker	1.50	.70	.45
98	Joe Decker	1.50	.70	.45
99	Mark Belanger	1.50	.70	.45
100	Pete Rose	35.00	17.50	10.50
101	Les Cain	1.50	.70	.45
102	Astros Rookies *(Ken Forsch,* Larry Howard)	1.50	.70	.45
103	Rich Severson	1.50	.70	.45
104	Dan Frisella	1.50	.70	.45
105	Tony Conigliaro	3.00	1.50	.90
106	Tom Dukes	1.50	.70	.45
107	Roy Foster	1.50	.70	.45
108	John Cumberland	1.50	.70	.45
109	Steve Hovley	1.50	.70	.45
110	Bill Mazeroski	4.00	2.00	1.25
111	Yankees Rookies (Loyd Colson, Bobby Mitchell)	1.50	.70	.45
112	Manny Mota	1.50	.70	.45
113	Jerry Crider	1.50	.70	.45
114	Billy Conigliaro	1.50	.70	.45
115	Donn Clendenon	1.50	.70	.45
116	Ken Sanders	1.50	.70	.45
117	*Ted Simmons*	7.50	3.75	2.25
118	Cookie Rojas	1.50	.70	.45
119	Frank Lucchesi	1.50	.70	.45
120	Willie Horton	1.50	.70	.45
121	Cubs Rookies (Jim Dunegan, Roe Skidmore)	1.50	.70	.45
122	Eddie Watt	1.50	.70	.45
123a	Checklist 133-263 (card # on right, orange helmet)	3.25	1.75	1.00
123b	Checklist 133-263 (card # on right, red helmet)	3.25	1.75	1.00
123c	Checklist 133-263 (card # centered)	3.50	1.75	1.00
124	*Don Gullett*	1.50	.70	.45
125	Ray Fosse	1.50	.70	.45
126	Danny Coombs	1.50	.70	.45
127	*Danny Thompson*	1.50	.70	.45
128	Frank Johnson	1.50	.70	.45
129	Aurelio Monteagudo	1.50	.70	.45
130	Denis Menke	1.50	.70	.45
131	Curt Blefary	1.50	.70	.45
132	Jose Laboy	1.50	.70	.45
133	Mickey Lolich	2.00	1.00	.60
134	Jose Arcia	1.50	.70	.45
135	Rick Monday	1.50	.70	.45
136	Duffy Dyer	1.50	.70	.45
137	Marcelino Lopez	1.50	.70	.45
138	Phillies Rookies (Joe Lis), *(Willie Montanez)*	1.50	.70	.45
139	Paul Casanova	1.50	.70	.45
140	Gaylord Perry	5.50	2.75	1.75
141	Frank Quilici	1.50	.70	.45
142	Mack Jones	1.50	.70	.45
143	Steve Blass	1.50	.70	.45
144	Jackie Hernandez	1.50	.70	.45
145	Bill Singer	1.50	.70	.45
146	Ralph Houk	1.50	.70	.45
147	Bob Priddy	1.50	.70	.45
148	John Mayberry	1.50	.70	.45
149	Mike Hershberger	1.50	.70	.45
150	Sam McDowell	1.50	.70	.45
151	Tommy Davis	1.50	.70	.45
152	Angels Rookies (Lloyd Allen, Winston Llenas)	1.50	.70	.45
153	Gary Ross	1.50	.70	.45
154	Cesar Gutierrez	1.50	.70	.45
155	Ken Henderson	1.50	.70	.45
156	Bart Johnson	1.50	.70	.45
157	Bob Bailey	1.50	.70	.45
158	Jerry Reuss	1.50	.70	.45
159	Jarvis Tatum	1.50	.70	.45
160	Tom Seaver	15.00	7.50	4.50
161	Coins Checklist	3.25	1.75	1.00
162	Jack Billingham	1.50	.70	.45
163	Buck Martinez	1.50	.70	.45
164	Reds Rookies (Frank Duffy), *(Milt Wilcox)*	1.50	.70	.45
165	Cesar Tovar	1.50	.70	.45
166	Joe Hoerner	1.50	.70	.45
167	Tom Grieve	1.50	.70	.45
168	Bruce Dal Canton	1.50	.70	.45
169	Ed Herrmann	1.50	.70	.45
170	Mike Cuellar	1.50	.70	.45
171	Bobby Wine	1.50	.70	.45
172	Duke Sims	1.50	.70	.45
173	Gil Garrido	1.50	.70	.45
174	*Dave LaRoche*	1.50	.70	.45
175	Jim Hickman	1.50	.70	.45
176	Red Sox Rookies (Doug Griffin, Bob Montgomery)	1.50	.70	.45
177	Hal McRae	2.00	1.00	.60
178	Dave Duncan	1.50	.70	.45
179	Mike Corkins	1.50	.70	.45
180	Al Kaline	13.00	6.50	4.00
181	Hal Lanier	1.50	.70	.45
182	Al Downing	1.50	.70	.45
183	Gil Hodges	4.00	2.00	1.25
184	Stan Bahnsen	1.50	.70	.45
185	Julian Javier	1.50	.70	.45
186	Bob Spence	1.50	.70	.45
187	Ted Abernathy	1.50	.70	.45
188	Dodgers Rookies (Mike Strahler), *(Bob Valentine)*	3.50	1.75	1.00
189	George Mitterwald	1.50	.70	.45
190	Bob Tolan	1.50	.70	.45
191	Mike Andrews	1.50	.70	.45
192	Billy Wilson	1.50	.70	.45
193	*Bob Grich*	3.50	1.75	1.00
194	Mike Lum	1.50	.70	.45
195	A.L. Playoff Game 1 (Powell Muscles Twins!)	2.00	1.00	.60
196	A.L. Playoff Game 2 (McNally Makes It Two Straight!)	2.00	1.00	.60
197	A.L. Playoff Game 3 (Palmer Mows 'Em Down!)	4.00	2.00	1.25
198	A.L. Playoffs Summary (A Team Effort!)	2.00	1.00	.60
199	N.L. Playoff Game 1 (Cline Pinch-Triple Decides It!)	2.00	1.00	.60
200	N.L. Playoff Game 2 (Tolan Scores For Third Time!)	2.00	1.00	.60
201	N.L. Playoff Game 3 (Cline Scores Winning Run!)	2.00	1.00	.60
202	N.L. Playoffs Summary (World Series Bound!)	2.00	1.00	.60
203	*Larry Gura*	1.50	.70	.45
204	Brewers Rookies (George Kopacz, Bernie Smith)	1.50	.70	.45
205	Gerry Moses	1.50	.70	.45
206a	Checklist 264-393 (orange helmet)	4.50	2.25	1.25
206b	Checklist 264-393 (red helmet)	4.00	2.00	1.25
207	Alan Foster	1.50	.70	.45
208	Billy Martin	4.00	2.00	1.25
209	Steve Renko	1.50	.70	.45
210	Rod Carew	16.00	8.00	4.75
211	Phil Hennigan	1.50	.70	.45
212	Rich Hebner	1.50	.70	.45
213	Frank Baker	1.50	.70	.45
214	Al Ferrara	1.50	.70	.45
215	Diego Segui	1.50	.70	.45
216	Cards Rookies (Reggie Cleveland, Luis Melendez)	1.50	.70	.45
217	Ed Stroud	1.50	.70	.45
218	Tony Cloninger	1.50	.70	.45
219	Elrod Hendricks	1.50	.70	.45
220	Ron Santo	4.00	2.00	1.25
221	Dave Morehead	1.50	.70	.45
222	Bob Watson	1.50	.70	.45
223	Cecil Upshaw	1.50	.70	.45
224	Alan Gallagher	1.50	.70	.45
225	Gary Peters	1.50	.70	.45
226	Bill Russell	1.50	.70	.45
227	Floyd Weaver	1.50	.70	.45
228	Wayne Garrett	1.50	.70	.45
229	Jim Hannan	1.50	.70	.45
230	Willie Stargell	7.50	3.75	2.25
231	Indians Rookies (Vince Colbert), *(John Lowenstein)*	1.50	.70	.45
232	John Strohmayer	1.50	.70	.45
233	Larry Bowa	2.00	1.00	.60
234	Jim Lyttle	1.50	.70	.45
235	Nate Colbert	1.50	.70	.45
236	Bob Humphreys	1.50	.70	.45
237	*Cesar Cedeno*	3.00	1.50	.90
238	Chuck Dobson	1.50	.70	.45
239	Red Schoendienst	3.00	1.50	.90
240	Clyde Wright	1.50	.70	.45
241	Dave Nelson	1.50	.70	.45
242	Jim Ray	1.50	.70	.45
243	Carlos May	1.50	.70	.45
244	Bob Tillman	1.50	.70	.45
245	Jim Kaat	2.50	1.25	.70
246	Tony Taylor	1.50	.70	.45
247	Royals Rookies (Jerry Cram), *(Paul Splittorff)*	1.50	.70	.45
248	Hoyt Wilhelm	5.00	2.50	1.50
249	Chico Salmon	1.50	.70	.45
250	Johnny Bench	20.00	10.00	6.00
251	Frank Reberger	1.50	.70	.45
252	Eddie Leon	1.50	.70	.45
253	Bill Sudakis	1.50	.70	.45
254	Cal Koonce	1.50	.70	.45
255	Bob Robertson	1.50	.70	.45
256	Tony Gonzalez	1.50	.70	.45
257	Nelson Briles	1.50	.70	.45
258	Dick Green	1.50	.70	.45
259	Dave Marshall	1.50	.70	.45
260	Tommy Harper	1.50	.70	.45
261	Darold Knowles	1.50	.70	.45
262	Padres Rookies (Dave Robinson, Jim Williams)	1.50	.70	.45
263	John Ellis	1.50	.70	.45
264	Joe Morgan	7.00	3.50	2.00
265	Jim Northrup	1.50	.70	.45
266	Bill Stoneman	1.50	.70	.45
267	Rich Morales	1.50	.70	.45
268	Phillies Team	3.00	1.50	.90
269	Gail Hopkins	1.50	.70	.45
270	Rico Carty	1.50	.70	.45
271	Bill Zepp	1.50	.70	.45
272	Tommy Helms	1.50	.70	.45
273	Pete Richert	1.50	.70	.45
274	Ron Slocum	1.50	.70	.45
275	Vada Pinson	2.00	1.00	.60
276	Giants Rookies *(Mike Davison), (George Foster)*	6.00	3.00	1.75
277	Gary Waslewski	1.50	.70	.45
278	Jerry Grote	1.50	.70	.45
279	Lefty Phillips	1.50	.70	.45
280	Fergie Jenkins	6.50	3.25	2.00
281	Danny Walton	1.50	.70	.45
282	Jose Pagan	1.50	.70	.45
283	Dick Such	1.50	.70	.45
284	Jim Gosger	1.50	.70	.45
285	Sal Bando	1.50	.70	.45
286	Jerry McNertney	1.50	.70	.45
287	Mike Fiore	1.50	.70	.45
288	Joe Moeller	1.50	.70	.45
289	White Sox Team	3.00	1.50	.90
290	Tony Oliva	2.00	[illegible]	[illegible]
291	George Culver	1.50	.70	.45
292	Jay Johnstone	1.50	.70	.45
293	Pat Corrales	1.50	.70	.45
294	Steve Dunning	1.50	.70	.45
295	Bobby Bonds	2.50	1.25	.70
296	Tom Timmermann	1.50	.70	.45
297	Johnny Briggs	1.50	.70	.45
298	Jim Nelson	1.50	.70	.45
299	Ed Kirkpatrick	1.50	.70	.45
300	Brooks Robinson	17.50	8.75	5.25
301	Earl Wilson	1.50	.70	.45
302	Phil Gagliano	1.50	.70	.45
303	Lindy McDaniel	1.50	.70	.45
304	Ron Brand	1.50	.70	.45
305	Reggie Smith	1.50	.70	.45
306a	Jim Nash (black blob, left center)	1.50	.70	.45

306b	Jim Nash (blob airbrushed away)	1.50	.70	.45
307	Don Wert	1.50	.70	.45
308	Cards Team	3.00	1.50	.90
309	Dick Ellsworth	1.50	.70	.45
310	Tommie Agee	1.50	.70	.45
311	Lee Stange	1.50	.70	.45
312	Harry Walker	1.50	.70	.45
313	Tom Hall	1.50	.70	.45
314	Jeff Torborg	1.50	.70	.45
315	Ron Fairly	1.50	.70	.45
316	Fred Scherman	1.50	.70	.45
317	Athletics Rookies (Jim Driscoll, Angel Mangual)	1.50	.70	.45
318	Rudy May	1.50	.70	.45
319	Ty Cline	1.50	.70	.45
320	Dave McNally	1.50	.70	.45
321	Tom Matchick	1.50	.70	.45
322	Jim Beauchamp	1.50	.70	.45
323	Billy Champion	1.50	.70	.45
324	Graig Nettles	1.50	.70	.45
325	Juan Marichal	5.50	2.75	1.75
326	Richie Scheinblum	1.50	.70	.45
327	World Series Game 1 (Powell Homers To Opposite Field!)	3.00	1.50	.90
328	World Series Game 2 (Buford Goes 2-For-4!)	2.00	1.00	.60
329	World Series Game 3 (F. Robinson Shows Muscle!)	4.50	2.25	1.25
330	World Series Game 4 (Reds Stay Alive!)	2.00	1.00	.60
331	World Series Game 5 (B. Robinson Commits Robbery!)	4.50	2.25	1.25
332	World Series Summary (Convincing Performance!)	2.00	1.00	.60
333	Clay Kirby	1.50	.70	.45
334	Roberto Pena	1.50	.70	.45
335	Jerry Koosman	1.50	.70	.45
336	Tigers Team	3.00	1.50	.90
337	Jesus Alou	1.50	.70	.45
338	Gene Tenace	1.50	.70	.45
339	Wayne Simpson	1.50	.70	.45
340	Rico Petrocelli	1.50	.70	.45
341	*Steve Garvey*	25.00	12.50	7.50
342	Frank Tepedino	1.50	.70	.45
343	Pirates Rookies (Ed Acosta), *(Milt May)*	1.50	.70	.45
344	Ellie Rodriguez	1.50	.70	.45
345	Joe Horlen	1.50	.70	.45
346	Lum Harris	1.50	.70	.45
347	Ted Uhlaender	1.50	.70	.45
348	Fred Norman	1.50	.70	.45
349	Rich Reese	1.50	.70	.45
350	Billy Williams	6.00	3.00	1.75
351	Jim Shellenback	1.50	.70	.45
352	Denny Doyle	1.50	.70	.45
353	Carl Taylor	1.50	.70	.45
354	Don McMahon	1.50	.70	.45
355	Bud Harrelson	2.50	1.25	.70
356	Bob Locker	1.50	.70	.45
357	Reds Team	3.50	1.75	1.00
358	Danny Cater	1.50	.70	.45
359	Ron Reed	1.50	.70	.45
360	Jim Fregosi	1.50	.70	.45
361	Don Sutton	7.00	3.50	2.00
362	Orioles Rookies (Mike Adamson, Roger Freed)	1.50	.70	.45
363	Mike Nagy	1.50	.70	.45
364	Tommy Dean	1.50	.70	.45
365	Bob Johnson	1.50	.70	.45
366	Ron Stone	1.50	.70	.45
367	Dalton Jones	1.50	.70	.45
368	Bob Veale	1.50	.70	.45
369a	Checklist 394-523 (orange helmet)	4.00	2.00	1.25
369b	Checklist 394-523 (red helmet, black line above ear)	4.00	2.00	1.25
369c	Checklist 394-523 (red helmet, no line)	4.00	2.00	1.25
370	Joe Torre	4.00	2.00	1.25
371	Jack Hiatt	1.50	.70	.45
372	Lew Krausse	1.50	.70	.45
373	Tom McCraw	1.50	.70	.45
374	Clete Boyer	2.00	1.00	.60
375	Steve Hargan	1.50	.70	.45
376	Expos Rookies (Clyde Mashore, Ernie McAnally)	1.50	.70	.45
377	Greg Garrett	1.50	.70	.45
378	Tito Fuentes	1.50	.70	.45
379	Wayne Granger	1.50	.70	.45
380	Ted Williams	12.00	6.00	3.50
381	Fred Gladding	1.50	.70	.45
382	Jake Gibbs	1.50	.70	.45
383	Rod Gaspar	1.50	.70	.45
384	Rollie Fingers	6.00	3.00	1.75
385	Maury Wills	1.50	.70	.45
386	Red Sox Team	3.00	1.50	.90
387	Ron Herbel	1.50	.70	.45
388	Al Oliver	1.50	.70	.45
389	Ed Brinkman	1.50	.70	.45
390	Glenn Beckert	1.50	.70	.45
391	Twins Rookies (Steve Brye, Cotton Nash)	1.50	.70	.45
392	Grant Jackson	1.50	.70	.45
393	Merv Rettenmund	1.50	.70	.45
394	Clay Carroll	2.25	1.25	.70
395	Roy White	2.25	1.25	.70
396	Dick Schofield	2.25	1.25	.70
397	Alvin Dark	2.25	1.25	.70
398	Howie Reed	2.25	1.25	.70
399	Jim French	2.25	1.25	.70
400	Hank Aaron	42.00	21.00	12.50
401	Tom Murphy	2.25	1.25	.70
402	Dodgers Team	3.50	1.75	1.00
403	Joe Coleman	2.25	1.25	.70
404	Astros Rookies (Buddy Harris, Roger Metzger)	2.25	1.25	.70
405	Leo Cardenas	2.25	1.25	.70
406	Ray Sadecki	2.25	1.25	.70
407	Joe Rudi	2.25	1.25	.70
408	Rafael Robles	2.25	1.25	.70
409	Don Pavletich	2.25	1.25	.70
410	Ken Holtzman	2.25	1.25	.70
411	George Spriggs	2.25	1.25	.70
412	Jerry Johnson	2.25	1.25	.70
413	Pat Kelly	2.25	1.25	.70
414	Woodie Fryman	2.25	1.25	.70
415	Mike Hegan	2.25	1.25	.70
416	Gene Alley	2.25	1.25	.70
417	Dick Hall	2.25	1.25	.70
418	Adolfo Phillips	2.25	1.25	.70
419	Ron Hansen	2.25	1.25	.70
420	Jim Merritt	2.25	1.25	.70
421	John Stephenson	2.25	1.25	.70
422	Frank Bertaina	2.25	1.25	.70
423	Tigers Rookies (Tim Marting, Dennis Saunders)	2.25	1.25	.70
424	Roberto Rodriquez (Rodriguez)	2.25	1.25	.70
425	Doug Rader	2.25	1.25	.70
426	Chris Cannizzaro	2.25	1.25	.70
427	Bernie Allen	2.25	1.25	.70
428	Jim McAndrew	2.25	1.25	.70
429	Chuck Hinton	2.25	1.25	.70
430	Wes Parker	2.25	1.25	.70
431	Tom Burgmeier	2.25	1.25	.70
432	Bob Didier	2.25	1.25	.70
433	Skip Lockwood	2.25	1.25	.70
434	Gary Sutherland	2.25	1.25	.70
435	Jose Cardenal	2.25	1.25	.70
436	Wilbur Wood	2.25	1.25	.70
437	Danny Murtaugh	2.25	1.25	.70
438	Mike McCormick	2.25	1.25	.70
439	Phillies Rookies (*Greg Luzinski*, Scott Reid)	4.50	2.25	1.25
440	Bert Campaneris	2.25	1.25	.70
441	Milt Pappas	2.25	1.25	.70
442	Angels Team	3.50	1.75	1.00
443	Rich Robertson	2.25	1.25	.70
444	Jimmie Price	2.25	1.25	.70
445	Art Shamsky	2.25	1.25	.70
446	Bobby Bolin	2.25	1.25	.70
447	*Cesar Geronimo*	2.25	1.25	.70
448	Dave Roberts	2.25	1.25	.70
449	Brant Alyea	2.25	1.25	.70
450	Bob Gibson	15.00	7.50	4.50
451	Joe Keough	2.25	1.25	.70
452	John Boccabella	2.25	1.25	.70
453	Terry Crowley	2.25	1.25	.70
454	Mike Paul	2.25	1.25	.70
455	Don Kessinger	2.25	1.25	.70
456	Bob Meyer	2.25	1.25	.70
457	Willie Smith	2.25	1.25	.70
458	White Sox Rookies (Dave Lemonds, Ron Lolich)	2.25	1.25	.70
459	Jim Lefebvre	2.25	1.25	.70
460	Fritz Peterson	2.25	1.25	.70
461	Jim Hart	2.25	1.25	.70
462	Senators Team	3.00	1.50	.90
463	Tom Kelley	2.25	1.25	.70
464	Aurelio Rodriguez	2.25	1.25	.70
465	Tim McCarver	3.25	1.75	1.00
466	Ken Berry	2.25	1.25	.70
467	Al Santorini	2.25	1.25	.70
468	Frank Fernandez	2.25	1.25	.70
469	Bob Aspromonte	2.25	1.25	.70
470	Bob Oliver	2.25	1.25	.70
471	Tom Griffin	2.25	1.25	.70
472	Ken Rudolph	2.25	1.25	.70
473	Gary Wagner	2.25	1.25	.70
474	Jim Fairey	2.25	1.25	.70
475	Ron Perranoski	2.25	1.25	.70
476	Dal Maxvill	2.25	1.25	.70
477	Earl Weaver	4.00	2.00	1.25
478	Bernie Carbo	2.25	1.25	.70
479	Dennis Higgins	2.25	1.25	.70
480	Manny Sanguillen	2.25	1.25	.70
481	Daryl Patterson	2.25	1.25	.70
482	Padres Team	4.00	2.00	1.25
483	Gene Michael	2.25	1.25	.70
484	Don Wilson	2.25	1.25	.70
485	Ken McMullen	2.25	1.25	.70
486	Steve Huntz	2.25	1.25	.70
487	Paul Schaal	2.25	1.25	.70
488	Jerry Stephenson	2.25	1.25	.70
489	Luis Alvarado	2.25	1.25	.70
490	Deron Johnson	2.25	1.25	.70
491	Jim Hardin	2.25	1.25	.70
492	Ken Boswell	2.25	1.25	.70
493	Dave May	2.25	1.25	.70
494	Braves Rookies (Ralph Garr, Rick Kester)	2.25	1.25	.70
495	Felipe Alou	3.50	1.75	1.00
496	Woody Woodward	2.25	1.25	.70
497	Horacio Pina	2.25	1.25	.70
498	John Kennedy	2.25	1.25	.70
499	Checklist 524-643	4.50	2.25	1.25
500	Jim Perry	2.25	1.25	.70
501	Andy Etchebarren	2.25	1.25	.70
502	Cubs Team	3.00	1.50	.90
503	Gates Brown	2.25	1.25	.70
504	Ken Wright	2.25	1.25	.70
505	Ollie Brown	2.25	1.25	.70
506	Bobby Knoop	2.25	1.25	.70
507	George Stone	2.25	1.25	.70
508	Roger Repoz	2.25	1.25	.70
509	Jim Grant	2.25	1.25	.70
510	Ken Harrelson	2.25	1.25	.70
511	Chris Short	2.25	1.25	.70
512	Red Sox Rookies (Mike Garman, Dick Mills)	2.25	1.25	.70
513	Nolan Ryan	120.00	60.00	36.00
514	Ron Woods	2.25	1.25	.70
515	Carl Morton	2.25	1.25	.70
516	Ted Kubiak	2.25	1.25	.70
517	Charlie Fox	2.25	1.25	.70
518	Joe Grzenda	2.25	1.25	.70
519	Willie Crawford	2.25	1.25	.70
520	Tommy John	3.50	1.75	1.00
521	Leron Lee	2.25	1.25	.70
522	Twins Team	4.00	2.00	1.25
523	John Odom	2.25	1.25	.70
524	Mickey Stanley	4.00	2.00	1.25
525	Ernie Banks	40.00	20.00	12.00
526	Ray Jarvis	4.00	2.00	1.25
527	Cleon Jones	4.00	2.00	1.25
528	Wally Bunker	4.00	2.00	1.25
529	N.L. Rookies (Bill Buckner, Enzo Hernandez, Marty Perez)	8.00	4.00	2.50
530	Carl Yastrzemski	27.50	13.50	8.25
531	Mike Torrez	4.00	2.00	1.25
532	Bill Rigney	4.00	2.00	1.25
533	Mike Ryan	4.00	2.00	1.25
534	Luke Walker	4.00	2.00	1.25
535	Curt Flood	5.00	2.50	1.50
536	Claude Raymond	4.00	2.00	1.25
537	Tom Egan	4.00	2.00	1.25
538	Angel Bravo	4.00	2.00	1.25
539	Larry Brown	4.00	2.00	1.25
540	Larry Dierker	4.00	2.00	1.25
541	Bob Burda	4.00	2.00	1.25
542	Bob Miller	4.00	2.00	1.25
543	Yankees Team	9.00	4.50	2.75
544	Vida Blue	4.00	2.00	1.25
545	Dick Dietz	4.00	2.00	1.25
546	John Matias	4.00	2.00	1.25
547	Pat Dobson	4.00	2.00	1.25
548	Don Mason	4.00	2.00	1.25
549	Jim Brewer	4.00	2.00	1.25
550	Harmon Killebrew	22.50	11.00	6.75
551	Frank Linzy	4.00	2.00	1.25
552	Buddy Bradford	4.00	2.00	1.25
553	Kevin Collins	4.00	2.00	1.25
554	Lowell Palmer	4.00	2.00	1.25
555	Walt Williams	4.00	2.00	1.25
556	Jim McGlothlin	4.00	2.00	1.25
557	Tom Satriano	4.00	2.00	1.25
558	Hector Torres	4.00	2.00	1.25
559	A.L. Rookies (Terry Cox, Bill Gogolewski, Gary Jones)	4.00	2.00	1.25
560	Rusty Staub	4.50	2.25	1.25
561	Syd O'Brien	4.00	2.00	1.25
562	Dave Giusti	4.00	2.00	1.25
563	Giants Team	7.00	3.50	2.00
564	Al Fitzmorris	4.00	2.00	1.25
565	Jim Wynn	4.00	2.00	1.25
566	Tim Cullen	4.00	2.00	1.25
567	Walt Alston	6.00	3.00	1.75
568	Sal Campisi	4.00	2.00	1.25
569	Ivan Murrell	4.00	2.00	1.25
570	Jim Palmer	22.00	11.00	6.50
571	Ted Sizemore	4.00	2.00	1.25
572	Jerry Kenney	4.00	2.00	1.25
573	Ed Kranepool	4.00	2.00	1.25
574	Jim Bunning	8.00	4.00	2.50
575	Bill Freehan	4.00	2.00	1.25
576	Cubs Rookies (Brock Davis, Adrian Garrett, Garry Jestadt)	4.00	2.00	1.25
577	Jim Lonborg	4.00	2.00	1.50
578	Ron Hunt	4.00	2.00	1.25
579	Marty Pattin	4.00	2.00	1.25
580	Tony Perez	12.00	6.00	3.50
581	Roger Nelson	4.00	2.00	1.25
582	Dave Cash	4.00	2.00	1.25
583	Ron Cook	4.00	2.00	1.25
584	Indians Team	7.50	3.75	2.25
585	Willie Davis	4.00	2.00	1.25
586	Dick Woodson	4.00	2.00	1.25
587	Sonny Jackson	4.00	2.00	1.25
588	Tom Bradley	4.00	2.00	1.25
589	Bob Barton	4.00	2.00	1.25
590	Alex Johnson	4.00	2.00	1.25
591	Jackie Brown	4.00	2.00	1.25
592	Randy Hundley	4.00	2.00	1.25
593	Jack Aker	4.00	2.00	1.25
594	Cards Rookies (Bob Chlupsa), *(Al Hrabosky*, Bob Stinson)	4.00	2.00	1.25
595	Dave Johnson	4.00	2.00	1.25
596	Mike Jorgensen	4.00	2.00	1.25
597	Ken Suarez	4.00	2.00	1.25
598	Rick Wise	4.00	2.00	1.25
599	Norm Cash	5.00	2.50	1.50
600	Willie Mays	85.00	42.00	25.00
601	Ken Tatum	4.00	2.00	1.25
602	Marty Martinez	4.00	2.00	1.25
603	Pirates Team	12.00	6.00	3.50
604	John Gelnar	4.00	2.00	1.25
605	Orlando Cepeda	9.00	4.50	2.75
606	Chuck Taylor	4.00	2.00	1.25
607	Paul Ratliff	4.00	2.00	1.25
608	Mike Wegener	4.00	2.00	1.25
609	Leo Durocher	4.00	2.00	1.25
610	Amos Otis	4.00	2.00	1.25
611	Tom Phoebus	4.00	2.00	1.25
612	Indians Rookies (Lou Camilli, Ted Ford, Steve Mingori)	4.00	2.00	1.25
613	Pedro Borbon	4.00	2.00	1.25
614	Billy Cowan	4.00	2.00	1.25
615	Mel Stottlemyre	4.00	2.00	1.25
616	Larry Hisle	4.00	2.00	1.25
617	Clay Dalrymple	4.00	2.00	1.25
618	Tug McGraw	5.00	2.50	1.50
619a	Checklist 644-752 (no copyright on back)	5.50	2.75	1.75
619b	Checklist 644-752 (with copyright, no wavy line on helmet brim)	4.00	2.00	1.25
619c	Checklist 644-752 (with copyright, wavy line on helmet brim)	4.00	2.00	1.25
620	Frank Howard	4.75	2.50	1.50
621	Ron Bryant	4.00	2.00	1.25

622	Joe Lahoud	4.00	2.00	1.25
623	Pat Jarvis	4.00	2.00	1.25
624	Athletics Team	7.00	3.50	2.00
625	Lou Brock	30.00	15.00	9.00
626	Freddie Patek	4.00	2.00	1.25
627	Steve Hamilton	4.00	2.00	1.25
628	John Bateman	4.00	2.00	1.25
629	John Hiller	4.00	2.00	1.25
630	Roberto Clemente	90.00	45.00	27.00
631	Eddie Fisher	4.00	2.00	1.25
632	Darrel Chaney	4.00	2.00	1.25
633	A.L. Rookies (Bobby Brooks, Pete Koegel, Scott Northey)	4.00	2.00	1.25
634	Phil Regan	4.00	2.00	1.25
635	Bobby Murcer	4.00	2.00	1.25
636	Denny Lemaster	4.00	2.00	1.25
637	Dave Bristol	4.00	2.00	1.25
638	Stan Williams	4.00	2.00	1.25
639	Tom Haller	4.00	2.00	1.25
640	Frank Robinson	30.00	15.00	9.00
641	Mets Team	11.00	5.50	3.25
642	Jim Roland	4.00	2.00	1.25
643	Rick Reichardt	4.00	2.00	1.25
644	Jim Stewart (SP)	9.00	4.50	2.75
645	Jim Maloney (SP)	9.00	4.50	2.75
646	Bobby Floyd (SP)	9.00	4.50	2.75
647	Juan Pizarro	7.00	3.50	2.00
648	Mets Rookies (Rich Folkers, Ted Martinez), *(Jon Matlack)* (SP)	13.00	6.50	4.00
649	Sparky Lyle (SP)	9.00	4.50	2.75
650	Rich Allen (SP)	32.50	16.00	9.75
651	Jerry Robertson	7.00	3.50	2.00
652	Braves Team	8.00	4.00	2.50
653	Russ Snyder (SP)	9.00	4.50	2.75
654	Don Shaw (SP)	9.00	4.50	2.75
655	Mike Epstein (SP)	9.00	4.50	2.75
656	Gerry Nyman (SP)	9.00	4.50	2.75
657	Jose Azcue	7.00	3.50	2.00
658	Paul Lindblad (SP)	9.00	4.50	2.75
659	Byron Browne (SP)	9.00	4.50	2.75
660	Ray Culp	7.00	3.50	2.00
661	Chuck Tanner (SP)	9.00	4.50	2.75
662	Mike Hedlund (SP)	9.00	4.50	2.75
663	Marv Staehle	7.00	3.50	2.00
664	Major League Rookies (Archie Reynolds, Bob Reynolds, Ken Reynolds) (SP)	9.00	4.50	2.75
665	Ron Swoboda	9.00	4.50	2.75
666	Gene Brabender (SP)	9.00	4.50	2.75
667	Pete Ward	7.00	3.50	2.00
668	Gary Neibauer	7.00	3.50	2.00
669	Ike Brown (SP)	9.00	4.50	2.75
670	Bill Hands	7.00	3.50	2.00
671	Bill Voss (SP)	9.00	4.50	2.75
672	Ed Crosby (SP)	9.00	4.50	2.75
673	Gerry Janeski (SP)	9.00	4.50	2.75
674	Expos Team	8.00	4.00	2.50
675	Dave Boswell	7.00	3.50	2.00
676	Tommie Reynolds	7.00	3.50	2.00
677	Jack DiLauro (SP)	9.00	4.50	2.75
678	George Thomas	7.00	3.50	2.00
679	Don O'Riley	7.00	3.50	2.00
680	Don Mincher (SP)	9.00	4.50	2.75
681	Bill Butler	7.00	3.50	2.00
682	Terry Harmon	7.00	3.50	2.00
683	Bill Burbach (SP)	9.00	4.50	2.75
684	Curt Motton	7.00	3.50	2.00
685	Moe Drabowsky	7.00	3.50	2.00
686	Chico Ruiz (SP)	9.00	4.50	2.75
687	Ron Taylor (SP)	9.00	4.50	2.75
688	Sparky Anderson (SP)	32.50	16.00	9.75
689	Frank Baker	7.00	3.50	2.00
690	Bob Moose	7.00	3.50	2.00
691	Bob Heise	7.00	3.50	2.00
692	A.L. Rookies (Hal Haydel, Rogelio Moret, Wayne Twitchell) (SP)	9.00	4.50	2.75
693	Jose Pena (SP)	9.00	4.50	2.75
694	Rick Renick (SP)	9.00	4.50	2.75
695	Joe Niekro	7.00	3.50	2.00
696	Jerry Morales	7.00	3.50	2.00
697	Rickey Clark (SP)	9.00	4.50	2.75
698	Brewers Team (SP)	16.00	8.00	4.75
699	Jim Britton	7.00	3.50	2.00
700	Boog Powell (SP)	16.00	8.00	4.75
701	Bob Garibaldi	7.00	3.50	2.00
702	Milt Ramirez	7.00	3.50	2.00
703	Mike Kekich	7.00	3.50	2.00
704	J.C. Martin (SP)	9.00	4.50	2.75
705	Dick Selma (SP)	9.00	4.50	2.75
706	Joe Foy (SP)	9.00	4.50	2.75
707	Fred Lasher	7.00	3.50	2.00
708	Russ Nagelson (SP)	9.00	4.50	2.75
709	Major League Rookies *(Dusty Baker)*, *(Don Baylor)*, *(Tom [illegible])* (SP)	85.00	42.00	25.00
710	Sonny Siebert	7.00	3.50	2.00
711	Larry Stahl (SP)	9.00	4.50	2.75
712	Jose Martinez	7.00	3.50	2.00
713	Mike Marshall (SP)	9.00	4.50	2.75
714	Dick Williams (SP)	9.00	4.50	2.75
715	Horace Clarke (SP)	9.00	4.50	2.75
716	Dave Leonhard	7.00	3.50	2.00
717	Tommie Aaron (SP)	9.00	4.50	2.75
718	Billy Wynne	7.00	3.50	2.00
719	Jerry May (SP)	9.00	4.50	2.75
720	Matty Alou	7.00	3.50	2.00
721	John Morris	7.00	3.50	2.00
722	Astros Team	10.00	5.00	3.00
723	Vicente Romo (SP)	9.00	4.50	2.75
724	Tom Tischinski (SP)	9.00	4.50	2.75
725	Gary Gentry (SP)	9.00	4.50	2.75
726	Paul Popovich	7.00	3.50	2.00
727	Ray Lamb (SP)	9.00	4.50	2.75
728	N.L. Rookies (Keith Lampard, Wayne Redmond, Bernie Williams)	7.00	3.50	2.00
729	Dick Billings	7.00	3.50	2.00
730	Jim Rooker	7.00	3.50	2.00
731	Jim Qualls (SP)	9.00	4.50	2.75
732	Bob Reed	7.00	3.50	2.00
733	Lee Maye (SP)	9.00	4.50	2.75
734	Rob Gardner (SP)	9.00	4.50	2.75
735	Mike Shannon (SP)	9.00	4.50	2.75
736	Mel Queen (SP)	9.00	4.50	2.75
737	Preston Gomez (SP)	9.00	4.50	2.75
738	Russ Gibson (SP)	9.00	4.50	2.75
739	Barry Lersch (SP)	9.00	4.50	2.75
740	Luis Aparicio (SP)	25.00	12.50	7.50
741	Skip Guinn	7.00	3.50	2.00
742	Royals Team	8.00	4.00	2.50
743	John O'Donoghue (SP)	9.00	4.50	2.75
744	Chuck Manuel (SP)	9.00	4.50	2.75
745	Sandy Alomar (SP)	9.00	4.50	2.75
746	Andy Kosco	7.00	3.50	2.00
747	N.L. Rookies (Balor Moore, Al Severinsen, Scipio Spinks)	7.00	3.50	2.00
748	John Purdin (SP)	9.00	4.50	2.75
749	Ken Szotkiewicz	7.00	3.50	2.00
750	Denny McLain (SP)	20.00	10.00	6.00
751	Al Weis	7.00	3.50	2.00
752	Dick Drago	12.50	6.25	3.75

1971 Topps Coins

Measuring 1-1/2" in diameter, the latest edition of the Topps coins was a 153-piece set. The coins feature a color photograph surrounded by a colored band on the front. The band carries the player's name, team, position and several stars. Backs have a short biography, the coin number and encouragement to collect the entire set. Back colors differ, with #s 1-51 having a brass back, #s 52-102 chrome backs, and the rest have blue backs. Most of the stars of the period are included in the set.

		NM	EX	VG
Complete Set (153):		350.00	175.00	100.00
Common Player:		1.25	.60	.40
1	Cito Gaston	1.25	.60	.40
2	Dave Johnson	1.25	.60	.40
3	Jim Bunning	5.00	2.50	1.50
4	Jim Spencer	1.25	.60	.40
5	Felix Millan	1.25	.60	.40
6	Gerry Moses	1.25	.60	.40
7	Fergie Jenkins	5.00	2.50	1.50
8	Felipe Alou	2.50	1.25	.70
9	Jim McGlothlin	1.25	.60	.40
10	Dick McAuliffe	1.25	.60	.40
11	Joe Torre	3.00	1.50	.90
12	Jim Perry	1.25	.60	.40
13	Bobby Bonds	2.00	1.00	.60
14	Danny Cater	1.25	.60	.40
15	Bill Mazeroski	5.00	2.50	1.50
16	Luis Aparicio	6.00	3.00	1.75
17	Doug Rader	1.25	.60	.40
18	Vada Pinson	2.00	1.00	.60
19	John Bateman	1.25	.60	.40
20	Lew Krausse	1.25	.60	.40
21	Billy Grabarkewitz	1.25	.60	.40
22	Frank Howard	1.50	.70	.45
23	Jerry Koosman	1.25	.60	.40
24	Rod Carew	8.00	4.00	2.50
25	Al Ferrara	1.25	.60	.40
26	Dave McNally	1.25	.60	.40
27	Jim Hickman	1.25	.60	.40
28	Sandy Alomar	1.25	.60	.40
29	Lee May	1.25	.60	.40
30	Rico Petrocelli	1.25	.60	.40
31	Don Money	1.25	.60	.40
32	Jlm Rooker	1.25	.60	.40
33	Dick Dietz	1.25	.60	.40
34	Roy White	1.25	.60	.40
35	Carl Morton	1.25	.60	.40
36	Walt Williams	1.25	.60	.40
37	Phil Niekro	5.00	2.50	1.50
38	Bill Freehan	1.25	.60	.40
39	Julian Javier	1.25	.60	.40
40	Rick Monday	1.25	.60	.40
41	Don Wilson	1.25	.60	.40
42	Ray Fosse	1.25	.60	.40
43	Art Shamsky	1.25	.60	.40
44	Ted Savage	1.25	.60	.40
45	Claude Osteen	1.25	.60	.40
46	Ed Brinkman	1.25	.60	.40
47	Matty Alou	1.25	.60	.40
48	Bob Oliver	1.25	.60	.40
49	Danny Coombs	1.25	.60	.40
50	Frank Robinson	8.00	4.00	2.50
51	Randy Hundley	1.25	.60	.40
52	Cesar Tovar	1.25	.60	.40
53	Wayne Simpson	1.25	.60	.40
54	Bobby Murcer	1.25	.60	.40
55	Tony Taylor	1.25	.60	.40
56	Tommy John	1.50	.70	.45
57	Willie McCovey	8.00	4.00	2.50
58	Carl Yastrzemski	11.50	5.75	3.50
59	Bob Bailey	1.25	.60	.40
60	Clyde Wright	1.25	.60	.40
61	Orlando Cepeda	5.00	2.50	1.50
62	Al Kaline	9.00	4.50	2.75
63	Bob Gibson	8.00	4.00	2.50
64	Bert Campaneris	1.25	.60	.40
65	Ted Sizemore	1.25	.60	.40
66	Duke Sims	1.25	.60	.40
67	Bud Harrelson	1.25	.60	.40
68	Jerry McNertney	1.25	.60	.40
69	Jim Wynn	1.25	.60	.40
70	Dick Bosman	1.25	.60	.40
71	Roberto Clemente	20.00	10.00	6.00
72	Rich Reese	1.25	.60	.40
73	Gaylord Perry	5.00	2.50	1.50
74	Boog Powell	1.50	.70	.45
75	Billy Williams	6.00	3.00	1.75
76	Bill Melton	1.25	.60	.40
77	Nate Colbert	1.25	.60	.40
78	Reggie Smith	1.25	.60	.40
79	Deron Johnson	1.25	.60	.40
80	Catfish Hunter	5.00	2.50	1.50
81	Bob Tolan	1.25	.60	.40
82	Jim Northrup	1.25	.60	.40
83	Ron Fairly	1.25	.60	.40
84	Alex Johnson	1.25	.60	.40
85	Pat Jarvis	1.25	.60	.40
86	Sam McDowell	1.25	.60	.40
87	Lou Brock	7.00	3.50	2.00
88	Danny Walton	1.25	.60	.40
89	Denis Menke	1.25	.60	.40
90	Jim Palmer	7.00	3.50	2.00
91	Tommie Agee	1.25	.60	.40
92	Duane Josephson	1.25	.60	.40
93	Willie Davis	1.25	.60	.40
94	Mel Stottlemyre	1.25	.60	.40
95	Ron Santo	2.00	1.00	.60
96	Amos Otis	1.25	.60	.40
97	Ken Henderson	1.25	.60	.40
98	George Scott	1.25	.60	.40
99	Dock Ellis	1.25	.60	.40
100	Harmon Killebrew	7.00	3.50	2.00
101	Pete Rose	17.50	8.75	5.25
102	Rick Reichardt	1.25	.60	.40
103	Cleon Jones	1.25	.60	.40
104	Ron Perranoski	1.25	.60	.40
105	Tony Perez	5.00	2.50	1.50
106	Mickey Lolich	1.50	.70	.45
107	Tim McCarver	1.50	.70	.45
108	Reggie Jackson	11.50	5.75	3.50
109	Chris Cannizzaro	1.25	.60	.40
110	Steve Hargan	1.25	.60	.40
111	Rusty Staub	1.50	.70	.45
112	Andy Messersmith	1.25	.60	.40
113	Rico Carty	1.25	.60	.40
114	Brooks Robinson	8.00	4.00	2.50
115	Steve Carlton	7.00	3.50	2.00
116	Mike Hegan	1.25	.60	.40
117	Joe Morgan	6.00	3.00	1.75
118	Thurman Munson	7.00	3.50	2.00
119	Don Kessinger	1.25	.60	.40
120	Joe Horlen	1.25	.60	.40
121	Wes Parker	1.25	.60	.40
122	Sonny Siebert	1.25	.60	.40
123	Willie Stargell	6.00	3.00	1.75
124	Ellie Rodriguez	1.25	.60	.40
125	Juan Marichal	6.00	3.00	1.75
126	Mike Epstein	1.25	.60	.40
127	Tom Seaver	8.00	4.00	2.50
128	Tony Oliva	1.50	.70	.45
129	Jim Merritt	1.25	.60	.40
130	Willie Horton	1.25	.60	.40
131	Rick Wise	1.25	.60	.40
132	Sal Bando	1.25	.60	.40
133	Ollie Brown	1.25	.60	.40
134	Ken Harrelson	1.25	.60	.40
135	Mack Jones	1.25	.60	.40
136	Jim Fregosi	1.25	.60	.40
137	Hank Aaron	17.50	8.75	5.25
138	Fritz Peterson	1.25	.60	.40
139	Joe Hague	1.25	.60	.40
140	Tommy Harper	1.25	.60	.40
141	Larry Dierker	1.25	.60	.40
142	Tony Conigliaro	2.50	1.25	.70
143	Glenn Beckert	1.25	.60	.40
144	Carlos May	1.25	.60	.40
145	Don Sutton	5.00	2.50	1.50
146	Paul Casanova	1.25	.60	.40
147	Bob Moose	1.25	.60	.40
148	Leo Cardenas	1.25	.60	.40
149	Johnny Bench	11.50	5.75	3.50
150	Mike Cuellar	1.25	.60	.40
151	Donn Clendenon	1.25	.60	.40
152	Lou Piniella	1.50	.70	.45
153	Willie Mays	17.50	8.75	5.25

Vintage cards in Good condition are valued at about 50% of the Very Good value shown here. Fair cards are valued at 25% or less of VG.

The ratio of Excellent and Very Good prices to Near Mint can vary depending on relative collectibility for each grade in a specific set. Current listings reflect such adjustments.

1971 Topps Greatest Moments

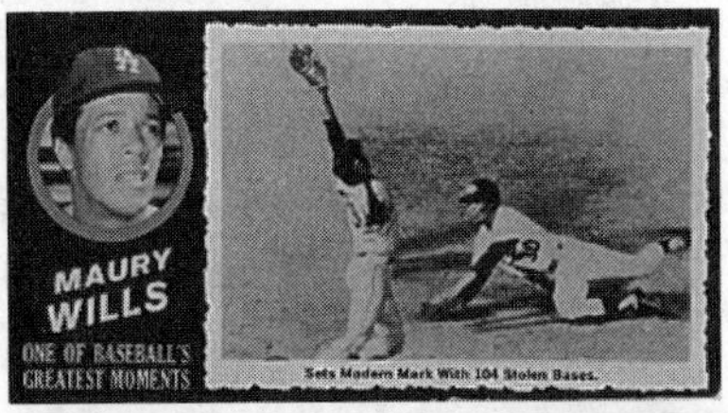

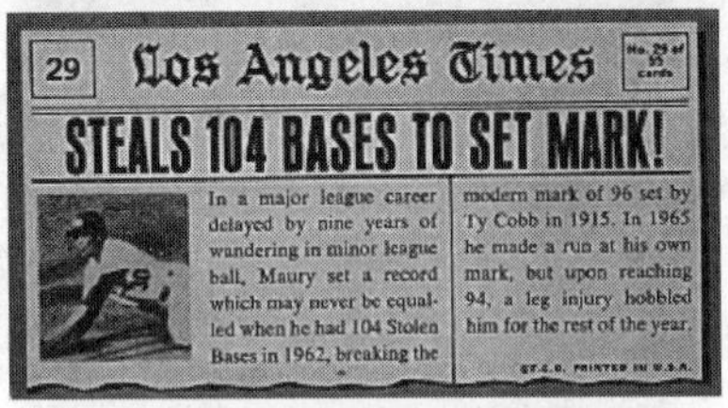

This 55-card set features highlights from the careers of top players of the day. The front of the 2-1/2" x 4-3/4" cards features a portrait photo of the player at left and deckle-edge action photo at right. There is a small headline on the white border of the action photo. The player's name and "One of Baseball's Greatest Moments" along with a black border complete the front. The back features a detail from the front photo and the story of the event. The newspaper style presentation includes the name of real newspapers. Relatively scarce, virtually every card in this set is a star or at least an above-average player. Twenty-two of the cards were double-printed, sometimes resulting in unusual pricing structures.

		NM	EX	VG
Complete Set (55):		1950.	975.00	585.00
Common Player:		8.00	4.00	2.50
1	Thurman Munson	80.00	40.00	24.00
2	Hoyt Wilhelm	40.00	20.00	12.00
3	Rico Carty	18.50	9.25	5.50
4	Carl Morton	8.00	4.00	2.50
5	Sal Bando	8.00	4.00	2.50
6	Bert Campaneris	8.00	4.00	2.50
7	Jim Kaat	30.00	15.00	9.00
8	Harmon Killebrew	80.00	40.00	24.00
9	Brooks Robinson	145.00	72.00	43.00
10	Jim Perry	24.00	12.00	7.25
11	Tony Oliva	37.00	18.50	11.00
12	Vada Pinson	37.00	18.50	11.00
13	Johnny Bench	215.00	107.00	64.00
14	Tony Perez	37.00	18.50	11.00
15	Pete Rose	110.00	55.00	33.00
16	Jim Fregosi	8.00	4.00	2.50
17	Alex Johnson	8.00	4.00	2.50
18	Clyde Wright	8.00	4.00	2.50
19	Al Kaline	50.00	25.00	15.00
20	Denny McLain	30.00	15.00	9.00
21	Jim Northrup	18.50	9.25	5.50
22	Bill Freehan	24.00	12.00	7.25
23	Mickey Lolich	30.00	15.00	9.00
24	Bob Gibson	40.00	20.00	12.00
25	Tim McCarver	12.00	6.00	3.50
26	Orlando Cepeda	22.00	11.00	6.50
27	Lou Brock	50.00	25.00	15.00
28	Nate Colbert	8.00	4.00	2.50
29	Maury Wills	27.00	13.50	8.00
30	Wes Parker	24.00	12.00	7.25
31	Jim Wynn	22.00	11.00	6.50
32	Larry Dierker	21.00	10.50	6.25
33	Bill Melton	17.00	8.50	5.00
34	Joe Morgan	70.00	35.00	21.00
35	Rusty Staub	35.00	17.50	10.50
36	Ernie Banks	60.00	30.00	18.00
37	Billy Williams	60.00	30.00	18.00
38	Lou Piniella	32.00	16.00	9.50
39	Rico Petrocelli	11.00	5.50	3.25
40	Carl Yastrzemski	75.00	37.00	22.00
41	Willie Mays	60.00	30.00	18.00
42	Tommy Harper	17.00	8.50	5.00
43	Jim Bunning	24.00	12.00	7.25
44	Fritz Peterson	27.00	13.50	8.00
45	Roy White	22.00	11.00	6.50
46	Bobby Murcer	35.00	17.50	10.50
47	Reggie Jackson	275.00	137.00	82.00
48	Frank Howard	35.00	17.50	10.50
49	Dick Bosman	19.50	9.75	5.75
50	Sam McDowell	11.00	5.50	3.25
51	Luis Aparicio	24.00	12.00	7.25
52	Willie McCovey	27.00	13.50	8.00
53	Joe Pepitone	27.00	13.50	8.00
54	Jerry Grote	27.00	13.50	8.00
55	Bud Harrelson	24.00	12.00	7.25

1971 Topps Super

Topps continued to produce its special oversized cards in 1971. The cards, measuring 3-1/8" x 5-1/4," carry a large color photograph with a facsimile autograph on the front. Backs are basically enlargements of the player's regular Topps card. The set size was enlarged to 63 cards in 1971, so there are no short-printed cards as in 1970. Again, Topps included almost every major star who was active at the time, so the set of oversized cards with rounded corners remains an interesting source for those seeking the big names of the era.

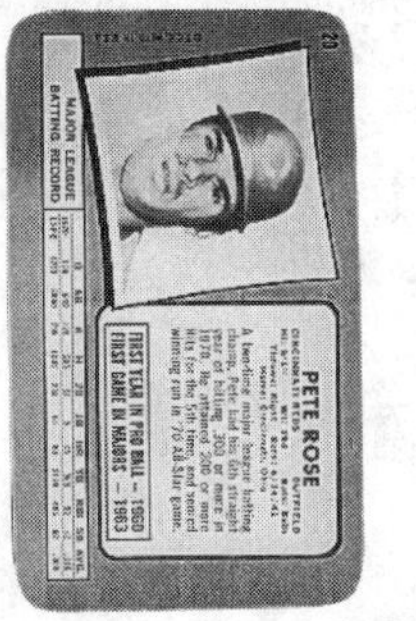

		NM	EX	VG
Complete Set (63):		200.00	100.00	60.00
Common Player:		2.00	1.00	.60
1	Reggie Smith	2.00	1.00	.60
2	Gaylord Perry	5.00	2.50	1.50
3	Ted Savage	2.00	1.00	.60
4	Donn Clendenon	2.00	1.00	.60
5	Boog Powell	3.00	1.50	.90
6	Tony Perez	5.00	2.50	1.50
7	Dick Bosman	2.00	1.00	.60
8	Alex Johnson	2.00	1.00	.60
9	Rusty Staub	2.00	1.00	.60
10	Mel Stottlemyre	2.00	1.00	.60
11	Tony Oliva	2.00	1.00	.60
12	Bill Freehan	2.00	1.00	.60
13	Fritz Peterson	2.00	1.00	.60
14	Wes Parker	2.00	1.00	.60
15	Cesar Cedeno	2.00	1.00	.60
16	Sam McDowell	2.00	1.00	.60
17	Frank Howard	2.50	1.25	.70
18	Dave McNally	2.00	1.00	.60
19	Rico Petrocelli	2.00	1.00	.60
20	Pete Rose	20.00	10.00	6.00
21	Luke Walker	2.00	1.00	.60
22	Nate Colbert	2.00	1.00	.60
23	Luis Aparicio	5.00	2.50	1.50
24	Jim Perry	2.00	1.00	.60
25	Louis Brock	6.00	3.00	1.75
26	Roy White	2.00	1.00	.60
27	Claude Osteen	2.00	1.00	.60
28	Carl W. Morton	2.00	1.00	.60
29	Rico Carty	2.00	1.00	.60
30	Larry Dierker	2.00	1.00	.60
31	Bert Campaneris	2.00	1.00	.60
32	Johnny Bench	9.00	4.50	2.75
33	Felix Millan	2.00	1.00	.60
34	Tim McCarver	2.50	1.25	.70
35	Ronald Santo	3.00	1.50	.90
36	Tommie Agee	2.00	1.00	.60
37	Roberto Clemente	25.00	12.50	7.50
38	Reggie Jackson	12.00	6.00	3.50
39	Clyde Wright	2.00	1.00	.60
40	Rich Allen	4.00	2.00	1.25
41	Curt Flood	2.50	1.25	.70
42	Fergie Jenkins	5.00	2.50	1.50
43	Willie Stargell	6.00	3.00	1.75
44	Henry Aaron	15.00	7.50	4.50
45	Amos Otis	2.00	1.00	.60
46	Willie McCovey	6.00	3.00	1.75
47	William Melton	2.00	1.00	.60
48	Bob Gibson	6.00	3.00	1.75
49	Carl Yastrzemski	12.00	6.00	3.50
50	Glenn Beckert	2.00	1.00	.60
51	Ray Fosse	2.00	1.00	.60
52	Clarence Gaston	2.00	1.00	.60
53	Tom Seaver	12.00	6.00	3.50
54	Al Kaline	8.00	4.00	2.50
55	Jim Northrup	2.00	1.00	.60
56	Willie Mays	15.00	7.50	4.50
57	Sal Bando	2.00	1.00	.60
58	Deron Johnson	2.00	1.00	.60
59	Brooks Robinson	10.00	5.00	3.00
60	Harmon Killebrew	7.00	3.50	2.00
61	Joseph Torre	3.00	1.50	.90
62	Lou Piniella	2.00	1.00	.60
63	Tommy Harper	2.00	1.00	.60

1971 Topps Tattoos

Topps once again produced baseball tattoos in 1971. This time, the tattoos came in a variety of sizes, shapes and themes. The sheets of tattoos measure 3-1/2" x 14-1/4." Each sheet contains an assortment of tattoos in two sizes, 1-3/4" x 2-3/8," or 1-3/16" x 1-3/4." There are players, facsimile autographed baseballs, team pennants and assorted baseball cartoon figures carried on the 16 different sheets. Listings below are for complete sheets; with the exception of the biggest-name stars, individual tattoos have little or no collector value.

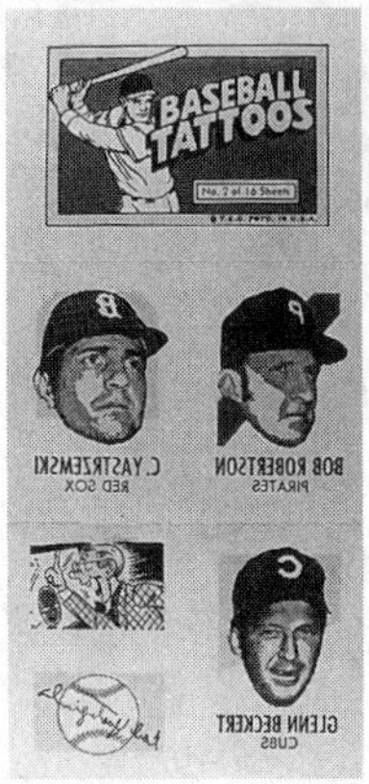

		NM	EX	VG
Complete Sheet Set (16):		300.00	150.00	90.00
Common Sheet:		15.00	7.50	4.50
1	Brooks Robinson Autograph Montreal Expos Pennant San Francisco Giants Pennant (Sal Bando, Dick Bosman, Nate Colbert, Cleon Jones, (Juan Marichal)	30.00	15.00	9.00
2	Red Sox Pennant Carl Yastrzemski Autograph New York Mets Pennant (Glenn Beckert, Tommy Harper, Ken Henderson), Fritz Peterson, Bob Robertson, (Carl Yastrzemski)	42.00	21.00	12.50
3	Jim Fregosi Autograph New York Yankees Pennant Philadelphia Phillies Pennant (Orlando Cepeda, Jim Fregosi, Randy Hundley, Reggie Jackson, (Jerry Koosman, Jim Palmer)	42.00	21.00	12.50
4	Kansas City Royals Pennant Oakland Athletics Pennant Sam McDowell Autograph (Dick Dietz, Cito Gaston, Dave Johnson, Sam McDowell, (Gary Nolan, Amos Otis)	15.00	7.50	4.50
5	Al Kaline Autograph Braves Pennant L.A. Dodgers Pennant (Bill Grabarkewitz, Al Kaline, Lee May, Tom Murphy), Vada Pinson, Manny Sanguillen	24.00	12.00	7.25
6	Chicago Cubs Pennant Cincinnati Reds Pennant Harmon Killebrew Autograph (Luis Aparicio, Paul Blair, Chris Cannizzaro, Donn Clendenon, (Larry Dieker, Harmon Killebrew)	30.00	15.00	9.00
7	Boog Powell Autograph Cleveland Indians Pennant Milwaukee Brewers Pennant (Rich Allen, Bert Campaneris, Don Money, Boog Powell, Ted Savage, (Rusty Staub)	18.00	9.00	5.50
8	Chicago White Sox Pennant Frank Howard Autograph San Diego Padres Pennant (Leo Cardenas, Bill Hands, Frank Howard, Wes Parker, Reggie Smith, (Willie Stargell)	15.00	7.50	4.50
9	Detroit Tigers Pennant Henry Aaron Autograph (Hank Aaron, Tommy Agee, Jim Hunter, Dick McAuliffe, Tony Perez, Lou Piniella)	42.00	21.00	12.50
10	Baltimore Orioles Pennant Fergie Jenkins Autograph (Roberto Clemente, Tony Conigliaro, Fergie Jenkins), Thurman Munson, Gary Peters, (Joe Torre)	60.00	30.00	18.00
11	Johnny Bench Autograph Washington Senators Pennant (Johnny Bench, Rico Carty, Bill Mazeroski, Bob Oliver), Rico Petrocelli, Frank Robinson	42.00	21.00	12.50
12	Billy Williams Autograph Houston Astros Pennant (Bill Freehan, Dave McNally, Felix Millan, Mel Stottlemyre), Bob Tolan, Billy Williams	18.00	9.00	5.50
13	Pittsburgh Pirates Pennant Willie McCovey Autograph (Ray Culp, Bud Harrelson, Mickey Lolich, Willie McCovey, Ron Santo, Roy White)	24.00	12.00	7.25

14	Minnesota Twins Pennant Tom Seaver Autograph (Bill Melton, Jim Perry, Pete Rose, Tom Seaver, Maury Wills), Clyde Wright	48.00	24.00	14.50
15	Robert Gibson Autograph St. Louis Cardinals Pennant (Rod Carew, Bob Gibson, Alex Johnson, Don Kessinger), Jim Merritt, Rick Monday	24.00	12.00	7.25
16	Angels Pennant Willie Mays Autograph (Larry Bowa, Mike Cuellar, Ray Fosse, Willie Mays, Carl Morton, Tony Oliva)	30.00	15.00	9.00

1972 Topps

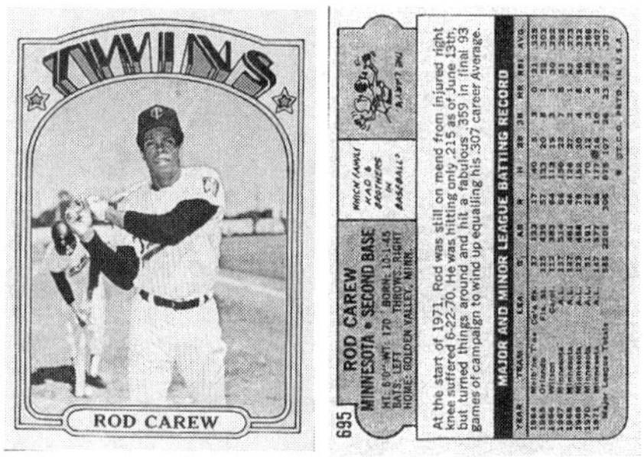

The largest Topps issue of its time appeared in 1972, with the set size reaching the 787 mark. The 2-1/2" x 3-1/2" cards are something special as well. Their fronts have a color photo which is shaped into an arch and surrounded by two different color borders, all of which is inside the overall white border. The player's name is in a white panel below the picture while the team name is above the picture in what might best be described as "superhero" type in a variety of colors. No mention of the player's position appears on the front. Card backs are tame by comparison, featuring statistics and a trivia question. The set features a record number of specialty cards including more than six dozen "In Action" (shown as "IA" in checklists below) cards featuring action shots of popular players. There are the usual statistical leaders, playoff and World Series highlights. Other innovations are 16 "Boyhood Photo" cards which depict scrapbook black-and-white photos of 1972's top players, and a group of cards depicting the trophies which comprise baseball's major awards. Finally, a group of seven "Traded" cards was included which feature a large "Traded" across the front of the card.

		NM	EX	VG
	Complete Set (787):	1650.	800.00	500.00
	Common Player (1-132):	.75	.40	.25
	Common Player (133-263):	1.25	.60	.40
	Common Player (264-394):	1.50	.70	.45
	Common Player (395-525):	1.75	.90	.50
	Common Player (526-656):	2.50	1.25	.70
	Common Player (657-787):	10.00	5.00	3.00
1	World Champions (Pirates Team)	7.50	3.75	2.25
2	Ray Culp	.75	.40	.25
3	Bob Tolan	.75	.40	.25
4	Checklist 1-132	2.00	1.00	.60
5	John Bateman	.75	.40	.25
6	Fred Scherman	.75	.40	.25
7	Enzo Hernandez	.75	.40	.25
8	Ron Swoboda	.75	.40	.25
9	Stan Williams	.75	.40	.25
10	Amos Otis	.75	.40	.25
11	Bobby Valentine	.75	.40	.25
12	Jose Cardenal	.75	.40	.25
13	Joe Grzenda	.75	.40	.25
14	Phillies Rookies (Mike Anderson, Pete Koegel, Wayne Twitchell)	.75	.40	.25
15	Walt Williams	.75	.40	.25
16	Mike Jorgensen	.75	.40	.25
17	Dave Duncan	.75	.40	.25
18a	Juan Pizarro (green under "C" and "S")	3.50	1.75	1.00
18b	Juan Pizarro (yellow under "C" and "S")	.75	.40	.25
19	Billy Cowan	.75	.40	.25
20	Don Wilson	.75	.40	.25
21	Braves Team	2.00	1.00	.60
22	Rob Gardner	.75	.40	.25
23	Ted Kubiak	.75	.40	.25
24	Ted Ford	.75	.40	.25
25	Bill Singer	.75	.40	.25
26	Andy Etchebarren	.75	.40	.25
27	Bob Johnson	.75	.40	.25
28	Twins Rookies (Steve Brye, Bob Gebhard, Hal Haydel)	.75	.40	.25
29a	Bill Bonham (green under "C" and "S")	3.50	1.75	1.00
29b	Bill Bonham (yellow under "C" and "S")	.75	.40	.25
30	Rico Petrocelli	.75	.40	.25
31	Cleon Jones	.75	.40	.25
32	Cleon Jones (In Action)	.75	.40	.25
33	Billy Martin	3.00	1.50	.90
34	Billy Martin (In Action)	2.00	1.00	.60
35	Jerry Johnson	.75	.40	.25
36	Jerry Johnson (In Action)	.75	.40	.25
37	Carl Yastrzemski	10.00	5.00	3.00
38	Carl Yastrzemski (In Action)	5.50	2.75	1.75
39	Bob Barton	.75	.40	.25
40	Bob Barton (In Action)	.75	.40	.25
41	Tommy Davis	.75	.40	.25
42	Tommy Davis (In Action)	.75	.40	.25
43	Rick Wise	.75	.40	.25
44	Rick Wise (In Action)	.75	.40	.25
45a	Glenn Beckert (green under "C" and "S")	3.50	1.75	1.00
45b	Glenn Beckert (yellow under "C" and "S")	.75	.40	.25
46	Glenn Beckert (In Action)	.75	.40	.25
47	John Ellis	.75	.40	.25
48	John Ellis (In Action)	.75	.40	.25
49	Willie Mays	22.50	11.00	6.75
50	Willie Mays (In Action)	12.50	6.25	3.75
51	Harmon Killebrew	7.50	3.75	2.25
52	Harmon Killebrew (In Action)	3.50	1.75	1.00
53	Bud Harrelson	.75	.40	.25
54	Bud Harrelson (In Action)	.75	.40	.25
55	Clyde Wright	.75	.40	.25
56	Rich Chiles	.75	.40	.25
57	Bob Oliver	.75	.40	.25
58	Ernie McAnally	.75	.40	.25
59	*Fred Stanley*	.90	.45	.25
60	Manny Sanguillen	.75	.40	.25
61	Cubs Rookies (Gene Hiser), *(Burt Hooton*, Earl Stephenson)	1.00	.50	.30
62	Angel Mangual	.75	.40	.25
63	Duke Sims	.75	.40	.25
64	Pete Broberg	.75	.40	.25
65	Cesar Cedeno	.75	.40	.25
66	Ray Corbin	.75	.40	.25
67	Red Schoendienst	2.00	1.00	.60
68	Jim York	.75	.40	.25
69	Roger Freed	.75	.40	.25
70	Mike Cuellar	.75	.40	.25
71	Angels Team	3.00	1.50	.90
72	*Bruce Kison*	.75	.40	.25
73	Steve Huntz	.75	.40	.25
74	Cecil Upshaw	.75	.40	.25
75	Bert Campaneris	.75	.40	.25
76	Don Carrithers	.75	.40	.25
77	Ron Theobald	.75	.40	.25
78	Steve Arlin	.75	.40	.25
79	Red Sox Rookies *(Cecil Cooper)*, *(Carlton Fisk*, Mike Garman)	55.00	27.00	16.50
80	Tony Perez	6.00	3.00	1.75
81	Mike Hedlund	.75	.40	.25
82	Ron Woods	.75	.40	.25
83	Dalton Jones	.75	.40	.25
84	Vince Colbert	.75	.40	.25
85	N.L. Batting Leaders (Glenn Beckert, Ralph Garr, Joe Torre)	2.00	1.00	.60
86	A.L. Batting Leaders (Bobby Murcer, Tony Oliva, Merv Rettenmund)	1.00	.50	.30
87	N.L. R.B.I. Leaders (Hank Aaron, Willie Stargell, Joe Torre)	4.00	2.00	1.25
88	A.L. R.B.I. Leaders (Harmon Killebrew, Frank Robinson, Reggie Smith)	4.00	2.00	1.25
89	N.L. Home Run Leaders (Hank Aaron, Lee May, Willie Stargell)	4.00	2.00	1.25
90	A.L. Home Run Leaders (Norm Cash, Reggie Jackson, Bill Melton)	3.50	1.75	1.00
91	N.L. E.R.A. Leaders (Dave Roberts, Tom Seaver, Don Wilson)	2.00	1.00	.60
92	A.L. E.R.A. Leaders (Vida Blue, Jim Palmer, Wilbur Wood)	2.00	1.00	.60
93	N.L. Pitching Leaders (Steve Carlton, Al Downing, Fergie Jenkins, Tom Seaver)	3.75	2.00	1.25
94	A.L. Pitching Leaders (Vida Blue, Mickey Lolich, Wilbur Wood)	1.50	.70	.45
95	N.L. Strikeout Leaders (Fergie Jenkins, Tom Seaver, Bill Stoneman)	3.50	1.75	1.00
96	A.L. Strikeout Leaders (Vida Blue, Joe Coleman, Mickey Lolich)	1.50	.70	.45
97	Tom Kelley	.75	.40	.25
98	Chuck Tanner	.75	.40	.25
99	*Ross Grimsley*	.75	.40	.25
100	Frank Robinson	8.00	4.00	2.50
101	Astros Rookies (Ray Busse, Bill Grief), *(J.R. Richard)*	2.00	1.00	.60
102	Lloyd Allen	.75	.40	.25
103	Checklist 133-263	3.50	1.75	1.00
104	*Toby Harrah*	1.50	.70	.45
105	Gary Gentry	.75	.40	.25
106	Brewers Team	3.00	1.50	.90
107	*Jose Cruz*	2.00	1.00	.60
108	Gary Waslewski	.75	.40	.25
109	Jerry May	.75	.40	.25
110	Ron Hunt	.75	.40	.25
111	Jim Grant	.75	.40	.25
112	Greg Luzinski	1.00	.50	.30
113	Rogelio Moret	.75	.40	.25
114	Bill Buckner	1.50	.70	.45
115	Jim Fregosi	.75	.40	.25
116	*Ed Farmer*	.75	.40	.25
117a	Cleo James (green under "C" and "S")	3.50	1.75	1.00
117b	Cleo James (yellow under "C" and "S")	.75	.40	.25
118	Skip Lockwood	.75	.40	.25
119	Marty Perez	.75	.40	.25
120	Bill Freehan	.75	.40	.25
121	Ed Sprague	.75	.40	.25
122	Larry Biittner	.75	.40	.25
123	Ed Acosta	.75	.40	.25
124	Yankees Rookies (Alan Closter, Roger Hambright, Rusty Torres)	.75	.40	.25
125	Dave Cash	.75	.40	.25
126	Bart Johnson	.75	.40	.25
127	Duffy Dyer	.75	.40	.25
128	Eddie Watt	.75	.40	.25
129	Charlie Fox	.75	.40	.25
130	Bob Gibson	7.00	3.50	2.00
131	Jim Nettles	.75	.40	.25
132	Joe Morgan	5.00	2.50	1.50
133	Joe Keough	1.25	.60	.40
134	Carl Morton	1.25	.60	.40
135	Vada Pinson	1.75	.90	.50
136	Darrel Chaney	1.25	.60	.40
137	Dick Williams	1.25	.60	.40
138	Mike Kekich	1.25	.60	.40
139	Tim McCarver	1.75	.90	.50
140	Pat Dobson	1.25	.60	.40
141	Mets Rookies (Buzz Capra, Jon Matlack, Leroy Stanton)	1.25	.60	.40
142	*Chris Chambliss*	3.25	1.75	1.00
143	Garry Jestadt	1.25	.60	.40
144	Marty Pattin	1.25	.60	.40
145	Don Kessinger	1.50	.70	.45
146	Steve Kealey	1.25	.60	.40
147	*Dave Kingman*	4.50	2.25	1.25
148	Dick Billings	1.25	.60	.40
149	Gary Neibauer	1.25	.60	.40
150	Norm Cash	1.75	.90	.50
151	Jim Brewer	1.25	.60	.40
152	Gene Clines	1.25	.60	.40
153	Rick Auerbach	1.25	.60	.40
154	Ted Simmons	1.25	.60	.40
155	Larry Dierker	1.25	.60	.40
156	Twins Team	3.00	1.50	.90
157	Don Gullett	1.25	.60	.40
158	Jerry Kenney	1.25	.60	.40
159	John Boccabella	1.25	.60	.40
160	Andy Messersmith	1.25	.60	.40
161	Brock Davis	1.25	.60	.40
162	Brewers Rookies (Jerry Bell), *(Darrell Porter*, Bob Reynolds)	1.25	.60	.40
163	Tug McGraw	1.25	.60	.40
164	Tug McGraw (In Action)	1.25	.60	.40
165	*Chris Speier*	1.25	.60	.40
166	Chris Speier (In Action)	1.25	.60	.40
167	Deron Johnson	1.25	.60	.40
168	Deron Johnson (In Action)	1.25	.60	.40
169	Vida Blue	1.25	.60	.40
170	Vida Blue (In Action)	1.25	.60	.40
171	Darrell Evans	1.75	.90	.50
172	Darrell Evans (In Action)	1.25	.60	.40
173	Clay Kirby	1.25	.60	.40
174	Clay Kirby (In Action)	1.25	.60	.40
175	Tom Haller	1.25	.60	.40
176	Tom Haller (In Action)	1.25	.60	.40
177	Paul Schaal	1.25	.60	.40
178	Paul Schaal (In Action)	1.25	.60	.40
179	Dock Ellis	1.25	.60	.40
180	Dock Ellis (In Action)	1.25	.60	.40
181	Ed Kranepool	1.25	.60	.40
182	Ed Kranepool (In Action)	1.25	.60	.40
183	Bill Melton	1.25	.60	.40
184	Bill Melton (In Action)	1.25	.60	.40
185	Ron Bryant	1.25	.60	.40
186	Ron Bryant (In Action)	1.25	.60	.40
187	Gates Brown	1.25	.60	.40
188	Frank Lucchesi	1.25	.60	.40
189	Gene Tenace	1.25	.60	.40
190	Dave Giusti	1.25	.60	.40
191	*Jeff Burroughs*	1.75	.90	.50
192	Cubs Team	3.00	1.50	.90
193	*Kurt Bevacqua*	1.25	.60	.40
194	Fred Norman	1.25	.60	.40
195	Orlando Cepeda	6.00	3.00	1.75
196	Mel Queen	1.25	.60	.40
197	Johnny Briggs	1.25	.60	.40
198	Dodgers Rookies *(Charlie Hough*, Bob O'Brien, Mike Strahler)	4.00	2.00	1.25
199	Mike Fiore	1.25	.60	.40
200	Lou Brock	6.00	3.00	1.75
201	Phil Roof	1.25	.60	.40
202	Scipio Spinks	1.25	.60	.40
203	*Ron Blomberg*	1.25	.60	.40
204	Tommy Helms	1.25	.60	.40
205	Dick Drago	1.25	.60	.40
206	Dal Maxvill	1.25	.60	.40
207	Tom Egan	1.25	.60	.40
208	Milt Pappas	1.25	.60	.40
209	Joe Rudi	1.25	.60	.40
210	Denny McLain	1.75	.90	.50
211	Gary Sutherland	1.25	.60	.40
212	Grant Jackson	1.25	.60	.40
213	Angels Rookies (Art Kusnyer, Billy Parker, Tom Silverio)	1.25	.60	.40
214	Mike McQueen	1.25	.60	.40
215	Alex Johnson	1.25	.60	.40
216	Joe Niekro	1.25	.60	.40
217	Roger Metzger	1.25	.60	.40
218	Eddie Kasko	1.25	.60	.40
219	*Rennie Stennett*	1.25	.60	.40

220	Jim Perry	1.25	.60	.40
221	N.L. Playoffs (Bucs Champs)	2.00	1.00	.60
222	A.L. Playoffs (Orioles Champs)	3.00	1.50	.90
223	World Series Game 1	2.00	1.00	.60
224	World Series Game 2	2.00	1.00	.60
225	World Series Game 3	2.00	1.00	.60
226	World Series Game 4 (Roberto Clemente)	9.00	4.50	2.75
227	World Series Game 5	3.00	1.50	.90
228	World Series Game 6	3.00	1.50	.90
229	World Series Game 7	3.00	1.50	.90
230	World Series Summary (Series Celebration)	2.00	1.00	.60
231	Casey Cox	1.25	.60	.40
232	Giants Rookies (Chris Arnold, Jim Barr, Dave Rader)	1.25	.60	.40
233	Jay Johnstone	1.25	.60	.40
234	Ron Taylor	1.25	.60	.40
235	Merv Rettenmund	1.25	.60	.40
236	Jim McGlothlin	1.25	.60	.40
237	Yankees Team	4.00	2.00	1.25
238	Leron Lee	1.25	.60	.40
239	Tom Timmermann	1.25	.60	.40
240	Rich Allen	3.50	1.75	1.00
241	Rollie Fingers	5.00	2.50	1.50
242	Don Mincher	1.25	.60	.40
243	Frank Linzy	1.25	.60	.40
244	Steve Braun	1.25	.60	.40
245	Tommie Agee	1.25	.60	.40
246	Tom Burgmeier	1.25	.60	.40
247	Milt May	1.25	.60	.40
248	Tom Bradley	1.25	.60	.40
249	Harry Walker	1.25	.60	.40
250	Boog Powell	2.00	1.00	.60
251a	Checklist 264-394 (small print on front)	4.00	2.00	1.25
251b	Checklist 264-394 (large print on front)	4.00	2.00	1.25
252	Ken Reynolds	1.25	.60	.40
253	Sandy Alomar	1.25	.60	.40
254	Boots Day	1.25	.60	.40
255	Jim Lonborg	1.50	.70	.45
256	George Foster	1.75	.90	.50
257	Tigers Rookies (Jim Foor, Tim Hosley, Paul Jata)	1.25	.60	.40
258	Randy Hundley	1.25	.60	.40
259	Sparky Lyle	1.25	.60	.40
260	Ralph Garr	1.25	.60	.40
261	Steve Mingori	1.25	.60	.40
262	Padres Team	3.00	1.50	.90
263	Felipe Alou	2.00	1.00	.60
264	Tommy John	1.50	.70	.45
265	Wes Parker	1.50	.70	.45
266	Bobby Bolin	1.50	.70	.45
267	Dave Concepcion	2.00	1.00	.60
268	A's Rookies (Dwain Anderson, Chris Floethe)	1.50	.70	.45
269	Don Hahn	1.50	.70	.45
270	Jim Palmer	7.50	3.75	2.25
271	Ken Rudolph	1.50	.70	.45
272	*Mickey Rivers*	2.00	1.00	.60
273	Bobby Floyd	1.50	.70	.45
274	Al Severinsen	1.50	.70	.45
275	Cesar Tovar	1.50	.70	.45
276	Gene Mauch	1.50	.70	.45
277	Elliott Maddox	1.50	.70	.45
278	Dennis Higgins	1.50	.70	.45
279	Larry Brown	1.50	.70	.45
280	Willie McCovey	7.00	3.50	2.00
281	Bill Parsons	1.50	.70	.45
282	Astros Team	3.00	1.50	.90
283	Darrell Brandon	1.50	.70	.45
284	Ike Brown	1.50	.70	.45
285	Gaylord Perry	5.00	2.50	1.50
286	Gene Alley	1.50	.70	.45
287	Jim Hardin	1.50	.70	.45
288	Johnny Jeter	1.50	.70	.45
289	Syd O'Brien	1.50	.70	.45
290	Sonny Siebert	1.50	.70	.45
291	Hal McRae	2.00	1.00	.60
292	Hal McRae (In Action)	1.50	.70	.45
293	Danny Frisella	1.50	.70	.45
294	Danny Frisella (In Action)	1.50	.70	.45
295	Dick Dietz	1.50	.70	.45
296	Dick Dietz (In Action)	1.50	.70	.45
297	Claude Osteen	1.50	.70	.45
298	Claude Osteen (In Action)	1.50	.70	.45
299	Hank Aaron	32.00	16.00	9.50
300	Hank Aaron (In Action)	15.00	7.50	4.50
301	George Mitterwald	1.50	.70	.45
302	George Mitterwald (In Action)	1.50	.70	.45
303	Joe Pepitone	1.50	.70	.45
304	Joe Pepitone (In Action)	1.50	.70	.45
305	Ken Boswell	1.50	.70	.45
306	Ken Boswell (In Action)	1.50	.70	.45
307	Steve Renko	1.50	.70	.45
308	Steve Renko (In Action)	1.50	.70	.45
309	Roberto Clemente	50.00	25.00	15.00
310	Roberto Clemente (In Action)	25.00	12.50	7.50
311	Clay Carroll	1.50	.70	.45
312	Clay Carroll (In Action)	1.50	.70	.45
313	Luis Aparicio	5.00	2.50	1.50
314	Luis Aparicio (In Action)	2.50	1.25	.70
315	Paul Splittorff	1.50	.70	.45
316	Cardinals Rookies *(Jim Bibby*, Santiago Guzman, Jorge Roque)	1.50	.70	.45
317	Rich Hand	1.50	.70	.45
318	Sonny Jackson	1.50	.70	.45
319	Aurelio Rodriguez	1.50	.70	.45
320	Steve Blass	1.50	.70	.45
321	Joe Lahoud	1.50	.70	.45
322	Jose Pena	1.50	.70	.45
323	Earl Weaver	3.00	1.50	.90
324	Mike Ryan	1.50	.70	.45
325	Mel Stottlemyre	1.50	.70	.45
326	Pat Kelly	1.50	.70	.45
327	*Steve Stone*	3.00	1.50	.90
328	Red Sox Team	4.00	2.00	1.25
329	Roy Foster	1.50	.70	.45
330	Catfish Hunter	4.00	2.00	1.25
331	Stan Swanson	1.50	.70	.45
332	Buck Martinez	1.50	.70	.45
333	Steve Barber	1.50	.70	.45
334	Rangers Rookies (Bill Fahey, Jim Mason, Tom Ragland)	1.50	.70	.45
335	Bill Hands	1.50	.70	.45
336	Marty Martinez	1.50	.70	.45
337	Mike Kilkenny	1.50	.70	.45
338	Bob Grich	1.50	.70	.45
339	Ron Cook	1.50	.70	.45
340	Roy White	1.50	.70	.45
341	Joe Torre (Boyhood Photo)	1.75	.90	.50
342	Wilbur Wood (Boyhood Photo)	1.50	.70	.45
343	Willie Stargell (Boyhood Photo)	2.00	1.00	.60
344	Dave McNally (Boyhood Photo)	1.50	.70	.45
345	Rick Wise (Boyhood Photo)	1.50	.70	.45
346	Jim Fregosi (Boyhood Photo)	1.50	.70	.45
347	Tom Seaver (Boyhood Photo)	3.00	1.50	.90
348	Sal Bando (Boyhood Photo)	1.50	.70	.45
349	Al Fitzmorris	1.50	.70	.45
350	Frank Howard	2.00	1.00	.60
351	Braves Rookies (Jimmy Britton, Tom House, Rick Kester)	1.50	.70	.45
352	Dave LaRoche	1.50	.70	.45
353	Art Shamsky	1.50	.70	.45
354	Tom Murphy	1.50	.70	.45
355	Bob Watson	1.50	.70	.45
356	Gerry Moses	1.50	.70	.45
357	Woodie Fryman	1.50	.70	.45
358	Sparky Anderson	4.00	2.00	1.25
359	Don Pavletich	1.50	.70	.45
360	Dave Roberts	1.50	.70	.45
361	Mike Andrews	1.50	.70	.45
362	Mets Team	4.00	2.00	1.25
363	Ron Klimkowski	1.50	.70	.45
364	Johnny Callison	1.50	.70	.45
365	Dick Bosman	1.50	.70	.45
366	Jimmy Rosario	1.50	.70	.45
367	Ron Perranoski	1.50	.70	.45
368	Danny Thompson	1.50	.70	.45
369	Jim Lefebvre	1.50	.70	.45
370	Don Buford	1.50	.70	.45
371	Denny Lemaster	1.50	.70	.45
372	Royals Rookies (Lance Clemons, Monty Montgomery)	1.50	.70	.45
373	John Mayberry	1.50	.70	.45
374	Jack Heidemann	1.50	.70	.45
375	Reggie Cleveland	1.50	.70	.45
376	Andy Kosco	1.50	.70	.45
377	Terry Harmon	1.50	.70	.45
378	Checklist 395-525	4.50	2.25	1.25
379	Ken Berry	1.50	.70	.45
380	Earl Williams	1.50	.70	.45
381	White Sox Team	3.00	1.50	.90
382	Joe Gibbon	1.50	.70	.45
383	Brant Alyea	1.50	.70	.45
384	Dave Campbell	1.50	.70	.45
385	Mickey Stanley	1.50	.70	.45
386	Jim Colborn	1.50	.70	.45
387	Horace Clarke	1.50	.70	.45
388	Charlie Williams	1.50	.70	.45
389	Bill Rigney	1.50	.70	.45
390	Willie Davis	1.50	.70	.45
391	Ken Sanders	1.50	.70	.45
392	Pirates Rookies (Fred Cambria), *(Richie Zisk)*	2.00	1.00	.60
393	Curt Motton	1.50	.70	.45
394	Ken Forsch	1.50	.70	.45
395	Matty Alou	1.75	.90	.50
396	Paul Lindblad	1.75	.90	.50
397	Phillies Team	4.00	2.00	1.25
398	Larry Hisle	1.75	.90	.50
399	Milt Wilcox	1.75	.90	.50
400	Tony Oliva	2.25	1.25	.70
401	Jim Nash	1.75	.90	.50
402	Bobby Heise	1.75	.90	.50
403	John Cumberland	1.75	.90	.50
404	Jeff Torborg	1.75	.90	.50
405	Ron Fairly	1.75	.90	.50
406	*George Hendrick*	2.00	1.00	.60
407	Chuck Taylor	1.75	.90	.50
408	Jim Northrup	1.75	.90	.50
409	Frank Baker	1.75	.90	.50
410	Fergie Jenkins	6.00	3.00	1.75
411	Bob Montgomery	1.75	.90	.50
412	Dick Kelley	1.75	.90	.50
413	White Sox Rookies (Don Eddy, Dave Lemonds)	1.75	.90	.50
414	Bob Miller	1.75	.90	.50
415	Cookie Rojas	1.75	.90	.50
416	Johnny Edwards	1.75	.90	.50
417	Tom Hall	1.75	.90	.50
418	Tom Shopay	1.75	.90	.50
419	Jim Spencer	1.75	.90	.50
420	Steve Carlton	17.50	8.75	5.25
421	Ellie Rodriguez	1.75	.90	.50
422	Ray Lamb	1.75	.90	.50
423	Oscar Gamble	1.75	.90	.50
424	Bill Gogolewski	1.75	.90	.50
425	Ken Singleton	1.75	.90	.50
426	Ken Singleton (In Action)	1.75	.90	.50
427	Tito Fuentes	1.75	.90	.50
428	Tito Fuentes (In Action)	1.75	.90	.50
429	Bob Robertson	1.75	.90	.50
430	Bob Robertson (In Action)	1.75	.90	.50
431	Cito Gaston	1.75	.90	.50
432	Cito Gaston (In Action)	1.75	.90	.50
433	Johnny Bench	20.00	10.00	6.00
434	Johnny Bench (In Action)	10.00	5.00	3.00
435	Reggie Jackson	25.00	12.50	7.50
436	Reggie Jackson (In Action)	12.00	6.00	3.50
437	Maury Wills	1.75	.90	.50
438	Maury Wills (In Action)	1.75	.90	.50
439	Billy Williams	6.00	3.00	1.75
440	Billy Williams (In Action)	3.00	1.50	.90
441	Thurman Munson	13.50	6.75	4.00
442	Thurman Munson (In Action)	6.75	3.50	2.00
443	Ken Henderson	1.75	.90	.50
444	Ken Henderson (In Action)	1.75	.90	.50
445	Tom Seaver	20.00	10.00	6.00
446	Tom Seaver (In Action)	13.50	6.75	4.00
447	Willie Stargell	6.00	3.00	1.75
448	Willie Stargell (In Action)	3.00	1.50	.90
449	Bob Lemon	3.00	1.50	.90
450	Mickey Lolich	2.00	1.00	.60
451	Tony LaRussa	3.00	1.50	.90
452	Ed Herrmann	1.75	.90	.50
453	Barry Lersch	1.75	.90	.50
454	A's Team	4.00	2.00	1.25
455	Tommy Harper	1.75	.90	.50
456	Mark Belanger	1.75	.90	.50
457	Padres Rookies (Darcy Fast, Mike Ivie), *(Derrel Thomas)*	1.75	.90	.50
458	Aurelio Monteagudo	1.75	.90	.50
459	Rick Renick	1.75	.90	.50
460	Al Downing	1.75	.90	.50
461	Tim Cullen	1.75	.90	.50
462	Rickey Clark	1.75	.90	.50
463	Bernie Carbo	1.75	.90	.50
464	Jim Roland	1.75	.90	.50
465	Gil Hodges	3.00	1.50	.90
466	Norm Miller	1.75	.90	.50
467	Steve Kline	1.75	.90	.50
468	Richie Scheinblum	1.75	.90	.50
469	Ron Herbel	1.75	.90	.50
470	Ray Fosse	1.75	.90	.50
471	Luke Walker	1.75	.90	.50
472	Phil Gagliano	1.75	.90	.50
473	Dan McGinn	1.75	.90	.50
474	Orioles Rookies (Don Baylor), *(Roric Harrison)*, *(Johnny Oates)*	12.00	6.00	3.50
475	Gary Nolan	1.75	.90	.50
476	Lee Richard	1.75	.90	.50
477	Tom Phoebus	1.75	.90	.50
478a	Checklist 526-656 (small print on front)	2.50	1.25	.70
478b	Checklist 526-656 (large printing on front)	2.50	1.25	.70
479	Don Shaw	1.75	.90	.50
480	Lee May	1.75	.90	.50
481	Billy Conigliaro	1.75	.90	.50
482	Joe Hoerner	1.75	.90	.50
483	Ken Suarez	1.75	.90	.50
484	Lum Harris	1.75	.90	.50
485	Phil Regan	1.75	.90	.50
486	John Lowenstein	1.75	.90	.50
487	Tigers Team	4.00	2.00	1.25
488	Mike Nagy	1.75	.90	.50
489	Expos Rookies (Terry Humphrey, Keith Lampard)	1.75	.90	.50
490	Dave McNally	1.75	.90	.50
491	Lou Piniella (Boyhood Photo)	1.75	.90	.50
492	Mel Stottlemyre (Boyhood Photo)	1.75	.90	.50
493	Bob Bailey (Boyhood Photo)	1.75	.90	.50
494	Willie Horton (Boyhood Photo)	1.75	.90	.50
495	Bill Melton (Boyhood Photo)	1.75	.90	.50
496	Bud Harrelson (Boyhood Photo)	1.75	.90	.50
497	Jim Perry (Boyhood Photo)	1.75	.90	.50
498	Brooks Robinson (Boyhood Photo)	2.50	1.25	.70
499	Vicente Romo	1.75	.90	.50
500	Joe Torre	4.00	2.00	1.25
501	Pete Hamm	1.75	.90	.50
502	Jackie Hernandez	1.75	.90	.50
503	Gary Peters	1.75	.90	.50
504	Ed Spiezio	1.75	.90	.50
505	Mike Marshall	1.75	.90	.50
506	Indians Rookies (Terry Ley, Jim Moyer), *(Dick Tidrow)*	1.75	.90	.50
507	Fred Gladding	1.75	.90	.50
508	Ellie Hendricks	1.75	.90	.50
509	Don McMahon	1.75	.90	.50
510	Ted Williams	12.00	6.00	3.50
511	Tony Taylor	1.75	.90	.50
512	Paul Popovich	1.75	.90	.50
513	Lindy McDaniel	1.75	.90	.50
514	Ted Sizemore	1.75	.90	.50
515	Bert Blyleven	2.50	1.25	.70
516	Oscar Brown	1.75	.90	.50
517	Ken Brett	1.75	.90	.50
518	Wayne Garrett	1.75	.90	.50
519	Ted Abernathy	1.75	.90	.50
520	Larry Bowa	1.75	.90	.50
521	Alan Foster	1.75	.90	.50
522	Dodgers Team	4.50	2.25	1.25
523	Chuck Dobson	1.75	.90	.50
524	Reds Rookies (Ed Armbrister, Mel Behney)	1.75	.90	.50
525	Carlos May	1.75	.90	.50
526	Bob Bailey	3.50	1.75	1.00
527	Dave Leonhard	3.50	1.75	1.00
528	Ron Stone	3.50	1.75	1.00
529	Dave Nelson	3.50	1.75	1.00
530	Don Sutton	8.00	4.00	2.50
531	Freddie Patek	3.50	1.75	1.00
532	Fred Kendall	3.50	1.75	1.00
533	Ralph Houk	3.50	1.75	1.00
534	Jim Hickman	3.50	1.75	1.00
535	Ed Brinkman	3.50	1.75	1.00
536	Doug Rader	3.50	1.75	1.00
537	Bob Locker	3.50	1.75	1.00
538	Charlie Sands	3.50	1.75	1.00

539	*Terry Forster*	3.50	1.75	1.00
540	Felix Millan	3.50	1.75	1.00
541	Roger Repoz	3.50	1.75	1.00
542	Jack Billingham	3.50	1.75	1.00
543	Duane Josephson	3.50	1.75	1.00
544	Ted Martinez	3.50	1.75	1.00
545	Wayne Granger	3.50	1.75	1.00
546	Joe Hague	3.50	1.75	1.00
547	Indians Team	6.50	3.25	2.00
548	Frank Reberger	3.50	1.75	1.00
549	Dave May	3.50	1.75	1.00
550	Brooks Robinson	20.00	10.00	6.00
551	Ollie Brown	3.50	1.75	1.00
552	Ollie Brown (In Action)	3.50	1.75	1.00
553	Wilbur Wood	3.50	1.75	1.00
554	Wilbur Wood (In Action)	3.50	1.75	1.00
555	Ron Santo	6.00	3.00	1.75
556	Ron Santo (In Action)	3.50	1.75	1.00
557	John Odom	3.50	1.75	1.00
558	John Odom (In Action)	3.50	1.75	1.00
559	Pete Rose	35.00	17.50	10.50
560	Pete Rose (In Action)	20.00	10.00	6.00
561	Leo Cardenas	3.50	1.75	1.00
562	Leo Cardenas (In Action)	3.50	1.75	1.00
563	Ray Sadecki	3.50	1.75	1.00
564	Ray Sadecki (In Action)	3.50	1.75	1.00
565	Reggie Smith	3.50	1.75	1.00
566	Reggie Smith (In Action)	3.50	1.75	1.00
567	Juan Marichal	9.00	4.50	2.75
568	Juan Marichal (In Action)	4.50	2.25	1.25
569	Ed Kirkpatrick	3.50	1.75	1.00
570	Ed Kirkpatrick (In Action)	3.50	1.75	1.00
571	Nate Colbert	3.50	1.75	1.00
572	Nate Colbert (In Action)	3.50	1.75	1.00
573	Fritz Peterson	3.50	1.75	1.00
574	Fritz Peterson (In Action)	3.50	1.75	1.00
575	Al Oliver	4.00	2.00	1.25
576	Leo Durocher	5.00	2.50	1.50
577	Mike Paul	3.50	1.75	1.00
578	Billy Grabarkewitz	3.50	1.75	1.00
579	*Doyle Alexander*	3.50	1.75	1.00
580	Lou Piniella	5.00	2.50	1.50
581	Wade Blasingame	3.50	1.75	1.00
582	Expos Team	5.00	2.50	1.50
583	Darold Knowles	3.50	1.75	1.00
584	Jerry McNertney	3.50	1.75	1.00
585	George Scott	3.50	1.75	1.00
586	Denis Menke	3.50	1.75	1.00
587	Billy Wilson	3.50	1.75	1.00
588	Jim Holt	3.50	1.75	1.00
589	Hal Lanier	3.50	1.75	1.00
590	Graig Nettles	3.50	1.75	1.00
591	Paul Casanova	3.50	1.75	1.00
592	Lew Krausse	3.50	1.75	1.00
593	Rich Morales	3.50	1.75	1.00
594	Jim Beauchamp	3.50	1.75	1.00
595	Nolan Ryan	90.00	45.00	27.00
596	Manny Mota	3.50	1.75	1.00
597	Jim Magnuson	3.50	1.75	1.00
598	Hal King	3.50	1.75	1.00
599	Billy Champion	3.50	1.75	1.00
600	Al Kaline	22.00	11.00	6.50
601	George Stone	3.50	1.75	1.00
602	Dave Bristol	3.50	1.75	1.00
603	Jim Ray	3.50	1.75	1.00
604a	Checklist 657-787 (copyright on right)	8.00	4.00	2.50
604b	Checklist 657-787 (copyright on left)	8.00	4.00	2.50
605	Nelson Briles	3.50	1.75	1.00
606	Luis Melendez	3.50	1.75	1.00
607	Frank Duffy	3.50	1.75	1.00
608	Mike Corkins	3.50	1.75	1.00
609	Tom Grieve	3.50	1.75	1.00
610	Bill Stoneman	3.50	1.75	1.00
611	Rich Reese	3.50	1.75	1.00
612	Joe Decker	3.50	1.75	1.00
613	Mike Ferraro	3.50	1.75	1.00
614	Ted Uhlaender	3.50	1.75	1.00
615	Steve Hargan	3.50	1.75	1.00
616	*Joe Ferguson*	3.50	1.75	1.00
617	Royals Team	5.00	2.50	1.50
618	Rich Robertson	3.50	1.75	1.00
619	Rich McKinney	3.50	1.75	1.00
620	Phil Niekro	8.00	4.00	2.50
621	Commissioners Award	3.50	1.75	1.00
622	MVP Award	3.50	1.75	1.00
623	Cy Young Award	3.50	1.75	1.00
624	Minor League Player Of The Year Award	3.50	1.75	1.00
625	Rookie of the Year Award	3.50	1.75	1.00
626	Babe Ruth Award	3.50	1.75	1.00
627	Moe Drabowsky	3.50	1.75	1.00
628	Terry Crowley	3.50	1.75	1.00
629	Paul Doyle	3.50	1.75	1.00
630	Rich Hebner	3.50	1.75	1.00
631	John Strohmayer	3.50	1.75	1.00
632	Mike Hegan	3.50	1.75	1.00
633	Jack Hiatt	3.50	1.75	1.00
634	Dick Woodson	3.50	1.75	1.00
635	Don Money	3.50	1.75	1.00
636	Bill Lee	3.50	1.75	1.00
637	Preston Gomez	3.50	1.75	1.00
638	Ken Wright	3.50	1.75	1.00
639	J.C. Martin	3.50	1.75	1.00
640	Joe Coleman	3.50	1.75	1.00
641	Mike Lum	3.50	1.75	1.00
642	Denny Riddleberger	3.50	1.75	1.00
643	Russ Gibson	3.50	1.75	1.00
644	Bernie Allen	3.50	1.75	1.00
645	Jim Maloney	3.50	1.75	1.00
646	Chico Salmon	3.50	1.75	1.00
647	Bob Moose	3.50	1.75	1.00
648	Jim Lyttle	3.50	1.75	1.00
649	Pete Richert	3.50	1.75	1.00
650	Sal Bando	3.50	1.75	1.00
651	Reds Team	7.00	3.50	2.00
652	Marcelino Lopez	3.50	1.75	1.00
653	Jim Fairey	3.50	1.75	1.00
654	Horacio Pina	3.50	1.75	1.00
655	Jerry Grote	3.50	1.75	1.00
656	Rudy May	3.50	1.75	1.00
657	Bobby Wine	11.00	5.50	3.25
658	Steve Dunning	11.00	5.50	3.25
659	Bob Aspromonte	11.00	5.50	3.25
660	Paul Blair	11.00	5.50	3.25
661	Bill Virdon	11.00	5.50	3.25
662	Stan Bahnsen	11.00	5.50	3.25
663	Fran Healy	11.00	5.50	3.25
664	Bobby Knoop	11.00	5.50	3.25
665	Chris Short	11.00	5.50	3.25
666	Hector Torres	11.00	5.50	3.25
667	Ray Newman	11.00	5.50	3.25
668	Rangers Team	22.00	11.00	6.50
669	Willie Crawford	11.00	5.50	3.25
670	Ken Holtzman	11.00	5.50	3.25
671	Donn Clendenon	11.00	5.50	3.25
672	Archie Reynolds	11.00	5.50	3.25
673	Dave Marshall	11.00	5.50	3.25
674	John Kennedy	11.00	5.50	3.25
675	Pat Jarvis	11.00	5.50	3.25
676	Danny Cater	11.00	5.50	3.25
677	Ivan Murrell	11.00	5.50	3.25
678	Steve Luebber	11.00	5.50	3.25
679	Astros Rookies (Bob Fenwick, Bob Stinson)	11.00	5.50	3.25
680	Dave Johnson	11.00	5.50	3.25
681	Bobby Pfeil	11.00	5.50	3.25
682	Mike McCormick	11.00	5.50	3.25
683	Steve Hovley	11.00	5.50	3.25
684	Hal Breeden	11.00	5.50	3.25
685	Joe Horlen	11.00	5.50	3.25
686	Steve Garvey	35.00	17.50	10.50
687	Del Unser	11.00	5.50	3.25
688	Cardinals Team	14.00	7.00	4.25
689	Eddie Fisher	11.00	5.50	3.25
690	Willie Montanez	11.00	5.50	3.25
691	Curt Blefary	11.00	5.50	3.25
692	Curt Blefary (In Action)	11.00	5.50	3.25
693	Alan Gallagher	11.00	5.50	3.25
694	Alan Gallagher (In Action)	11.00	5.50	3.25
695	Rod Carew	40.00	20.00	12.00
696	Rod Carew (In Action)	20.00	10.00	6.00
697	Jerry Koosman	12.00	6.00	3.50
698	Jerry Koosman (In Action)	11.00	5.50	3.25
699	Bobby Murcer	15.00	7.50	4.50
700	Bobby Murcer (In Action)	11.00	5.50	3.25
701	Jose Pagan	11.00	5.50	3.25
702	Jose Pagan (In Action)	11.00	5.50	3.25
703	Doug Griffin	11.00	5.50	3.25
704	Doug Griffin (In Action)	11.00	5.50	3.25
705	Pat Corrales	11.00	5.50	3.25
706	Pat Corrales (In Action)	11.00	5.50	3.25
707	Tim Foli	11.00	5.50	3.25
708	Tim Foli (In Action)	11.00	5.50	3.25
709	Jim Kaat	14.00	7.00	4.25
710	Jim Kaat (In Action)	11.00	5.50	3.25
711	Bobby Bonds	12.50	6.25	3.75
712	Bobby Bonds (In Action)	11.00	5.50	3.25
713	Gene Michael	11.00	5.50	3.25
714	Gene Michael (In Action)	11.00	5.50	3.25
715	Mike Epstein	11.00	5.50	3.25
716	Jesus Alou	11.00	5.50	3.25
717	Bruce Dal Canton	11.00	5.50	3.25
718	Del Rice	11.00	5.50	3.25
719	Cesar Geronimo	11.00	5.50	3.25
720	Sam McDowell	11.00	5.50	3.25
721	Eddie Leon	11.00	5.50	3.25
722	Bill Sudakis	11.00	5.50	3.25
723	Al Santorini	11.00	5.50	3.25
724	A.L. Rookies (John Curtis, Rich Hinton, Mickey Scott)	11.00	5.50	3.25
725	Dick McAuliffe	11.00	5.50	3.25
726	Dick Selma	11.00	5.50	3.25
727	Jose Laboy	11.00	5.50	3.25
728	Gail Hopkins	11.00	5.50	3.25
729	Bob Veale	11.00	5.50	3.25
730	Rick Monday	11.00	5.50	3.25
731	Orioles Team	15.00	7.50	4.50
732	George Culver	11.00	5.50	3.25
733	Jim Hart	11.00	5.50	3.25
734	Bob Burda	11.00	5.50	3.25
735	Diego Segui	11.00	5.50	3.25
736	Bill Russell	11.00	5.50	3.25
737	*Lenny Randle*	11.00	5.50	3.25
738	Jim Merritt	11.00	5.50	3.25
739	Don Mason	11.00	5.50	3.25
740	Rico Carty	11.00	5.50	3.25
741	Major League Rookies (Tom Hutton), *(Rick Miller)*, *(John Milner)*	11.00	5.50	3.25
742	Jim Rooker	11.00	5.50	3.25
743	Cesar Gutierrez	11.00	5.50	3.25
744	*Jim Slaton*	11.00	5.50	3.25
745	Julian Javier	11.00	5.50	3.25
746	Lowell Palmer	11.00	5.50	3.25
747	Jim Stewart	11.00	5.50	3.25
748	Phil Hennigan	11.00	5.50	3.25
749	Walter Alston	11.00	5.50	3.25
750	Willie Horton	11.00	5.50	3.25
751	Steve Carlton (Traded)	40.00	20.00	12.00
752	Joe Morgan (Traded)	25.00	12.50	7.50
753	Denny McLain (Traded)	15.00	7.50	4.50
754	Frank Robinson (Traded)	30.00	15.00	9.00
755	Jim Fregosi (Traded)	11.00	5.50	3.25
756	Rick Wise (Traded)	11.00	5.50	3.25
757	Jose Cardenal (Traded)	11.00	5.50	3.25
758	Gil Garrido	11.00	5.50	3.25
759	Chris Cannizzaro	11.00	5.50	3.25
760	Bill Mazeroski	18.00	9.00	5.50
761	A.L.-N.L. Rookies *(Ron Cey)*, *(Ben Oglivie)*, Bernie Williams)	22.00	11.00	6.50
762	Wayne Simpson	11.00	5.50	3.25
763	Ron Hansen	11.00	5.50	3.25
764	Dusty Baker	16.00	8.00	4.75
765	Ken McMullen	11.00	5.50	3.25
766	Steve Hamilton	11.00	5.50	3.25
767	Tom McCraw	11.00	5.50	3.25
768	Denny Doyle	11.00	5.50	3.25
769	Jack Aker	11.00	5.50	3.25
770	Jim Wynn	11.00	5.50	3.25
771	Giants Team	14.00	7.00	4.25
772	Ken Tatum	11.00	5.50	3.25
773	Ron Brand	11.00	5.50	3.25
774	Luis Alvarado	11.00	5.50	3.25
775	Jerry Reuss	11.00	5.50	3.25
776	Bill Voss	11.00	5.50	3.25
777	Hoyt Wilhelm	18.00	9.00	5.50
778	Twins Rookies (Vic Albury), *(Rick Dempsey*, Jim Strickland)	12.50	6.25	3.75
779	Tony Cloninger	11.00	5.50	3.25
780	Dick Green	11.00	5.50	3.25
781	Jim McAndrew	11.00	5.50	3.25
782	Larry Stahl	11.00	5.50	3.25
783	Les Cain	11.00	5.50	3.25
784	Ken Aspromonte	11.00	5.50	3.25
785	Vic Davalillo	11.00	5.50	3.25
786	Chuck Brinkman	11.00	5.50	3.25
787	Ron Reed	12.50	5.50	3.25

1972 Topps Cloth Stickers

Despite the fact they were never actually issued, examples of this test issue can readily be found within the hobby. The set of 33 contains stickers with designs identical to cards found in three contiguous rows of a regular Topps card sheet that year; thus the inclusion of a meaningless checklist card. Sometimes found in complete 33-sticker strips, or 132-piece sheets, individual stickers nominally measure 2-1/2" x 3-1/2," though dimensions vary according to the care with which they were cut. Stickers are unnumbered and blank-backed; most are found without the original paper backing as the glue used did not hold up well over the years. Eleven of the stickers are prone to miscutting and are identified with an (SP) in the checklist.

		NM	EX	VG
Complete Set (33):		480.00	240.00	145.00
Common Player:		6.50	3.25	2.00
(1)	Hank Aaron	75.00	37.00	22.00
(2)	Luis Aparicio (In Action) (SP)	25.00	12.50	7.50
(3)	Ike Brown	6.50	3.25	2.00
(4)	Johnny Callison	8.00	4.00	2.50
(5)	Checklist 264-319	6.50	3.25	2.00
(6)	Roberto Clemente (In Action)	110.00	55.00	33.00
(7)	Dave Concepcion (SP)	16.00	8.00	4.75
(8)	Ron Cook	6.50	3.25	2.00
(9)	Willie Davis	8.00	4.00	2.50
(10)	Al Fitzmorris	6.50	3.25	2.00
(11)	Bobby Floyd	6.50	3.25	2.00
(12)	Roy Foster	6.50	3.25	2.00
(13)	Jim Fregosi (Boyhood Photo)	8.00	4.00	2.50
(14)	Danny Frisella (In Action)	6.50	3.25	2.00
(15)	Woody Fryman (SP)	9.50	4.75	2.75
(16)	Terry Harmon	6.50	3.25	2.00
(17)	Frank Howard (SP)	16.00	8.00	4.75
(18)	Ron Klimkowski	6.50	3.25	2.00
(19)	Joe Lahoud	6.50	3.25	2.00
(20)	Jim Lefebvre	6.50	3.25	2.00
(21)	Elliott Maddox	6.50	3.25	2.00
(22)	Marty Martinez	6.50	3.25	2.00
(23)	Willie McCovey (SP)	35.00	17.50	10.50
(24)	Hal McRae (SP)	16.00	8.00	4.75
(25)	Syd O'Brien (SP)	9.50	4.75	2.75
(26)	Red Sox Team	8.00	4.00	2.50
(27)	Aurelio Rodriguez	6.50	3.25	2.00
(28)	Al Severinsen	6.50	3.25	2.00
(29)	Art Shamsky (SP)	9.50	4.75	2.75
(30)	Steve Stone (SP)	13.00	6.50	4.00
(31)	Stan Swanson (SP)	9.50	4.75	2.75
(32)	Bob Watson	6.50	3.25	2.00
(33)	Roy White (SP)	13.00	6.50	4.00

1972 Topps Posters

Issued as a separate set, rather than as a wax pack insert, these 9-7/16" x 18" posters feature a borderless full-color picture on the front with the player's name, team and position. Printed on very thin paper, the posters, as happened with earlier issues, were folded for packaging, causing large creases which cannot be removed. Even so, they are good display items for they feature many top stars of the period.

		NM	EX	VG
Complete Set (24):		450.00	225.00	135.00
Common Player:		9.00	4.50	2.75
1	Dave McNally	9.00	4.50	2.75
2	Carl Yastrzemski	30.00	15.00	9.00
3	Bill Melton	9.00	4.50	2.75
4	Ray Fosse	9.00	4.50	2.75
5	Mickey Lolich	10.00	5.00	3.00
6	Amos Otis	9.00	4.50	2.75
7	Tony Oliva	10.00	5.00	3.00
8	Vida Blue	9.00	4.50	2.75
9	Hank Aaron	45.00	22.00	13.50
10	Fergie Jenkins	15.00	7.50	4.50
11	Pete Rose	45.00	22.00	13.50
12	Willie Davis	9.00	4.50	2.75
13	Tom Seaver	30.00	15.00	9.00
14	Rick Wise	9.00	4.50	2.75
15	Willie Stargell	22.00	11.00	6.50
16	Joe Torre	10.00	5.00	3.00
17	Willie Mays	45.00	22.00	13.50
18	Andy Messersmith	9.00	4.50	2.75
19	Wilbur Wood	9.00	4.50	2.75
20	Harmon Killebrew	25.00	12.50	7.50
21	Billy Williams	18.00	9.00	5.50
22	Bud Harrelson	9.00	4.50	2.75
23	Roberto Clemente	50.00	25.00	15.00
24	Willie McCovey	18.00	9.00	5.50

1973 Topps

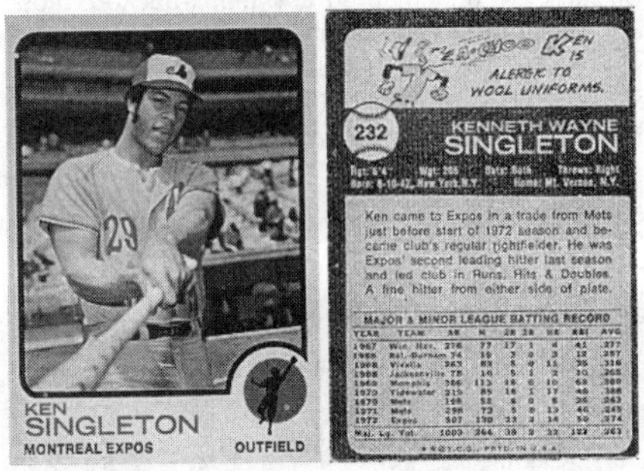

Topps cut back to 660 cards in 1973. The set is interesting for it marks the last time cards were issued by series, a procedure which had produced many a scarce high number card over the years. These 2-1/2" x 3-1/2" cards have a color photo, accented by a silhouette of a player on the front, indicative of his position. Card backs are vertical for the first time since 1968, with the usual statistical and biographical information. Specialty cards begin with card number 1, which depicted Ruth, Mays and Aaron as the all-time home run leaders. It was followed by statistical leaders, although there also were additional all-time leader cards. Also present are playoff and World Series highlights. From the age-and-youth department, the 1973 Topps set has coaches and managers as well as more "Boyhood Photos."

		NM	EX	VG
Complete Set (660):		1000.	375.00	225.00
Common Player (1-264):		.40	.20	.12
Common Player (265-396)		.60	.30	.20
Common Player (397-528):		.90	.45	.25
Common Player (529-660):		2.50	1.25	.70
1	All Time Home Run Leaders (Hank Aaron, Willie Mays, Babe Ruth)	30.00	15.00	9.00
2	Rich Hebner	.40	.20	.12
3	Jim Lonborg	.50	.25	.15
4	John Milner	.40	.20	.12
5	Ed Brinkman	.40	.20	.12
6	Mac Scarce	.40	.20	.12
7	Rangers Team	1.00	.50	.30
8	Tom Hall	.40	.20	.12
9	Johnny Oates	.40	.20	.12
10	Don Sutton	2.00	1.00	.60
11	Chris Chambliss	.40	.20	.12
12a	Padres Mgr./Coaches (Dave Garcia, Johnny Podres, Bob Skinner, Whitey Wietelmann, Don Zimmer) (Coaches background brown)	.75	.40	.25
12b	Padres Mgr./Coaches (Dave Garcia, Johnny Podres, Bob Skinner, Whitey Wietelmann, Don Zimmer) (Coaches background orange)	.75	.40	.25
13	George Hendrick	.40	.20	.12
14	Sonny Siebert	.40	.20	.12
15	Ralph Garr	.40	.20	.12
16	Steve Braun	.40	.20	.12
17	Fred Gladding	.40	.20	.12
18	Leroy Stanton	.40	.20	.12
19	Tim Foli	.40	.20	.12
20a	Stan Bahnsen (small gap in left border)	.90	.45	.25
20b	Stan Bahnsen (no gap)	.40	.20	.12
21	Randy Hundley	.40	.20	.12
22	Ted Abernathy	.40	.20	.12
23	Dave Kingman	.90	.45	.25
24	Al Santorini	.40	.20	.12
25	Roy White	.40	.20	.12
26	Pirates Team	2.00	1.00	.60
27	Bill Gogolewski	.40	.20	.12
28	Hal McRae	.60	.30	.20
29	Tony Taylor	.40	.20	.12
30	Tug McGraw	.50	.25	.15
31a	*Buddy Bell* (small gap in right border)	4.00	2.00	1.25
31b	*Buddy Bell* (no gap)	4.00	2.00	1.25
32	Fred Norman	.40	.20	.12
33	Jim Breazeale	.40	.20	.12
34	Pat Dobson	.40	.20	.12
35	Willie Davis	.40	.20	.12
36	Steve Barber	.40	.20	.12
37	Bill Robinson	.40	.20	.12
38	Mike Epstein	.40	.20	.12
39	Dave Roberts	.40	.20	.12
40	Reggie Smith	.40	.20	.12
41	Tom Walker	.40	.20	.12
42	Mike Andrews	.40	.20	.12
43	*Randy Moffitt*	.40	.20	.12
44	Rick Monday	.40	.20	.12
45	Ellie Rodriguez (photo actually Paul Ratliff)	.40	.20	.12
46	Lindy McDaniel	.40	.20	.12
47	Luis Melendez	.40	.20	.12
48	Paul Splittorff	.40	.20	.12
49a	Twins Mgr./Coaches (Vern Morgan, Frank Quilici, Bob Rodgers, Ralph Rowe, Al Worthington) (Coaches background brown)	.50	.25	.15
49b	Twins Mgr./Coaches (Vern Morgan, Frank Quilici, Bob Rodgers, Ralph Rowe, Al Worthington) (Coaches	.50	.25	.15
50	Roberto Clemente	40.00	20.00	12.00
51	Chuck Seelbach	.40	.20	.12
52	Denis Menke	.40	.20	.12
53	Steve Dunning	.40	.20	.12
54	Checklist 1-132	1.00	.50	.30
55	Jon Matlack	.40	.20	.12
56	Merv Rettenmund	.40	.20	.12
57	Derrel Thomas	.40	.20	.12
58	Mike Paul	.40	.20	.12
59	*Steve Yeager*	.65	.35	.20
60	Ken Holtzman	.40	.20	.12
61	Batting Leaders (Rod Carew, Billy Williams)	2.00	1.00	.60
62	Home Run Leaders (Dick Allen, Johnny Bench)	1.50	.70	.45
63	Runs Batted In Leaders (Dick Allen, Johnny Bench)	1.50	.70	.45
64	Stolen Base Leaders (Lou Brock, Bert Campaneris)	1.00	.50	.30
65	Earned Run Average Leaders (Steve Carlton, Luis Tiant)	1.00	.50	.30
66	Victory Leaders (Steve Carlton, Gaylord Perry, Wilbur Wood)	1.00	.50	.30
67	Strikeout Leaders (Steve Carlton, Nolan Ryan)	18.00	9.00	5.50
68	Leading Firemen (Clay Carroll, Sparky Lyle)	.60	.30	.20
69	Phil Gagliano	.40	.20	.12
70	Milt Pappas	.40	.20	.12
71	Johnny Briggs	.40	.20	.12
72	Ron Reed	.40	.20	.12
73	Ed Herrmann	.40	.20	.12
74	Billy Champion	.40	.20	.12
75	Vada Pinson	.75	.40	.25
76	Doug Rader	.40	.20	.12
77	Mike Torrez	.40	.20	.12
78	Richie Scheinblum	.40	.20	.12
79	Jim Willoughby	.40	.20	.12
80	Tony Oliva	.75	.40	.25
81a	Cubs Mgr./Coaches (Hank Aguirre, Ernie Banks, Larry Jansen, Whitey Lockman, Pete Reiser) (Trees in coaches background)	1.25	.60	.40
81b	Cubs Mgr./Coaches (Hank Aguirre, Ernie Banks, Larry Jansen, Whitey Lockman, Pete Reiser) (solid orange background)	1.25	.60	.40
82	Fritz Peterson	.40	.20	.12
83	Leron Lee	.40	.20	.12
84	Rollie Fingers	3.00	1.50	.90
85	Ted Simmons	.40	.20	.12
86	Tom McCraw	.40	.20	.12
87	Ken Boswell	.40	.20	.12
88	Mickey Stanley	.40	.20	.12
89	Jack Billingham	.40	.20	.12
90	Brooks Robinson	6.00	3.00	1.75
91	Dodgers Team	2.50	1.25	.70
92	Jerry Bell	.40	.20	.12
93	Jesus Alou	.40	.20	.12
94	Dick Billings	.40	.20	.12
95	Steve Blass	.40	.20	.12
96	Doug Griffin	.40	.20	.12
97	Willie Montanez	.40	.20	.12
98	Dick Woodson	.40	.20	.12
99	Carl Taylor	.40	.20	.12
100	Hank Aaron	25.00	12.50	7.50
101	Ken Henderson	.40	.20	.12
102	Rudy May	.40	.20	.12
103	Celerino Sanchez	.40	.20	.12
104	Reggie Cleveland	.40	.20	.12
105	Carlos May	.40	.20	.12
106	Terry Humphrey	.40	.20	.12
107	Phil Hennigan	.40	.20	.12
108	Bill Russell	.40	.20	.12
109	Doyle Alexander	.40	.20	.12
110	Bob Watson	.40	.20	.12
111	Dave Nelson	.40	.20	.12
112	Gary Ross	.40	.20	.12
113	Jerry Grote	.40	.20	.12
114	Lynn McGlothen	.40	.20	.12
115	Ron Santo	.75	.40	.25
116a	Yankees Mgr./Coaches (Jim Hegan, Ralph Houk, Elston Howard, Dick Howser, Jim Turner) (Coaches background brown)	2.00	1.00	.60
116b	Yankees Mgr./Coaches (Jim Hegan, Ralph Houk, Elston Howard, Dick Howser, Jim Turner) (Coaches background orange)	2.00	1.00	.60
117	Ramon Hernandez	.40	.20	.12
118	John Mayberry	.40	.20	.12
119	Larry Bowa	.40	.20	.12
120	Joe Coleman	.40	.20	.12
121	Dave Rader	.40	.20	.12
122	Jim Strickland	.40	.20	.12
123	Sandy Alomar	.40	.20	.12
124	Jim Hardin	.40	.20	.12
125	Ron Fairly	.40	.20	.12
126	Jim Brewer	.40	.20	.12
127	Brewers Team	2.00	1.00	.60
128	Ted Sizemore	.40	.20	.12
129	Terry Forster	.40	.20	.12
130	Pete Rose	20.00	10.00	6.00
131a	Red Sox Mgr./Coaches (Doug Camilli, Eddie Kasko, Don Lenhardt, Eddie Popowski, Lee Stange) (Coaches background brown)	.50	.25	.15
131b	Red Sox Mgr./Coaches (Doug Camilli, Eddie Kasko, Don Lenhardt, Eddie Popowski, Lee Stange) (Coaches background orange)	.50	.25	.15
132	Matty Alou	.40	.20	.12
133	Dave Roberts	.40	.20	.12
134	Milt Wilcox	.40	.20	.12
135	Lee May	.40	.20	.12
136a	Orioles Mgr./Coaches (George Bamberger, Jim Frey, Billy Hunter, George Staller, Earl Weaver) (Coaches background brown)	2.25	1.25	.70
136b	Orioles Mgr./Coaches (George Bamberger, Jim Frey, Billy Hunter, George Staller, Earl Weaver) (Coaches background orange)	2.25	1.25	.70
137	Jim Beauchamp	.40	.20	.12
138	Horacio Pina	.40	.20	.12
139	Carmen Fanzone	.40	.20	.12
140	Lou Piniella	.60	.30	.25
141	Bruce Kison	.40	.20	.12
142	Thurman Munson	6.00	3.00	1.75
143	John Curtis	.40	.20	.12
144	Marty Perez	.40	.20	.12
145	Bobby Bonds	.75	.40	.25
146	Woodie Fryman	.40	.20	.12
147	Mike Anderson	.40	.20	.12
148	*Dave Goltz*	.40	.20	.12
149	Ron Hunt	.40	.20	.12
150	Wilbur Wood	.40	.20	.12
151	Wes Parker	.40	.20	.12
152	Dave May	.40	.20	.12
153	Al Hrabosky	.40	.20	.12
154	Jeff Torborg	.40	.20	.12
155	Sal Bando	.40	.20	.12
156	Cesar Geronimo	.40	.20	.12
157	Denny Riddleberger	.40	.20	.12
158	Astros Team	2.00	1.00	.60
159	Cito Gaston	.40	.20	.12
160	Jim Palmer	6.00	3.00	1.75
161	Ted Martinez	.40	.20	.12
162	Pete Broberg	.40	.20	.12
163	Vic Davalillo	.40	.20	.12
164	Monty Montgomery	.40	.20	.12
165	Luis Aparicio	4.00	2.00	1.25

166	Terry Harmon	.40	.20	.12
167	Steve Stone	.45	.25	.14
168	Jim Northrup	.40	.20	.12
169	Ron Schueler	.40	.20	.12
170	Harmon Killebrew	4.00	2.00	1.25
171	Bernie Carbo	.40	.20	.12
172	Steve Kline	.40	.20	.12
173	Hal Breeden	.40	.20	.12
174	*Rich Gossage*	7.50	3.75	2.25
175	Frank Robinson	7.00	3.50	2.00
176	Chuck Taylor	.40	.20	.12
177	Bill Plummer	.40	.20	.12
178	Don Rose	.40	.20	.12
179a	A's Mgr./Coaches (Jerry Adair, Vern Hoscheit, Irv Noren, Wes Stock, Dick Williams) (Coaches background brown)	1.00	.50	.30
179b	A's Mgr./Coaches (Jerry Adair, Vern Hoscheit, Irv Noren, Wes Stock, Dick Williams) (Coaches background orange)	1.00	.50	.30
180	Fergie Jenkins	3.50	1.75	1.00
181	Jack Brohamer	.40	.20	.12
182	*Mike Caldwell*	.40	.20	.12
183	Don Buford	.40	.20	.12
184	Jerry Koosman	.40	.20	.12
185	Jim Wynn	.40	.20	.12
186	Bill Fahey	.40	.20	.12
187	Luke Walker	.40	.20	.12
188	Cookie Rojas	.40	.20	.12
189	Greg Luzinski	.50	.25	.15
190	Bob Gibson	5.00	2.50	1.50
191	Tigers Team	2.00	1.00	.60
192	Pat Jarvis	.40	.20	.12
193	Carlton Fisk	19.00	9.50	5.75
194	*Jorge Orta*	.40	.20	.12
195	Clay Carroll	.40	.20	.12
196	Ken McMullen	.40	.20	.12
197	Ed Goodson	.40	.20	.12
198	Horace Clarke	.40	.20	.12
199	Bert Blyleven	.65	.35	.20
200	Billy Williams	3.50	1.75	1.00
201	A.L. Playoffs (Hendrick Scores Winning Run.)	1.50	.70	.45
202	N.L. Playoffs (Foster's Run Decides It.)	1.50	.70	.45
203	World Series Game 1 (Tenace The Menace.)	1.50	.70	.45
204	World Series Game 2 (A's Make It Two Straight.)	1.50	.70	.45
205	World Series Game 3 (Reds Win Squeeker.)	1.50	.70	.45
206	World Series Game 4 (Tenace Singles In Ninth.)	1.50	.70	.45
207	World Series Game 5 (Odom Out At Plate.)	1.50	.70	.45
208	World Series Game 6 (Reds' Slugging Ties Series.)	1.50	.70	.45
209	World Series Game 7 (Campy Starts Winning Rally.)	1.50	.70	.45
210	World Series Summary (World Champions.)	1.50	.70	.45
211	Balor Moore	.40	.20	.12
212	Joe Lahoud	.40	.20	.12
213	Steve Garvey	4.00	2.00	1.25
214	Dave Hamilton	.40	.20	.12
215	Dusty Baker	1.25	.60	.40
216	Toby Harrah	.40	.20	.12
217	Don Wilson	.40	.20	.12
218	Aurelio Rodriguez	.40	.20	.12
219	Cardinals Team	2.00	1.00	.60
220	Nolan Ryan	55.00	27.00	16.50
221	Fred Kendall	.40	.20	.12
222	Rob Gardner	.40	.20	.12
223	Bud Harrelson	.40	.20	.12
224	Bill Lee	.40	.20	.12
225	Al Oliver	.75	.40	.25
226	Ray Fosse	.40	.20	.12
227	Wayne Twitchell	.40	.20	.12
228	Bobby Darwin	.40	.20	.12
229	Roric Harrison	.40	.20	.12
230	Joe Morgan	4.50	2.25	1.25
231	Bill Parsons	.40	.20	.12
232	Ken Singleton	.40	.20	.12
233	Ed Kirkpatrick	.40	.20	.12
234	*Bill North*	.40	.20	.12
235	Catfish Hunter	3.50	1.75	1.00
236	Tito Fuentes	.40	.20	.12
237a	Braves Mgr./Coaches (Lew Burdette, Jim Busby, Roy Hartsfield, Eddie Mathews, Ken Silvestri) (Coaches background brown)	1.25	.60	.40
237b	Braves Mgr./Coaches (Lew Burdette, Jim Busby, Roy Hartsfield, Eddie Mathews, Ken Silvestri) (Coaches background orange)	1.25	.60	.40
238	Tony Muser	.40	.20	.12
239	Pete Richert	.40	.20	.12
240	Bobby Murcer	.60	.30	.25
241	Dwain Anderson	.40	.20	.12
242	George Culver	.40	.20	.12
243	Angels Team	2.00	1.00	.60
244	Ed Acosta	.40	.20	.12
245	Carl Yastrzemski	10.00	5.00	3.00
246	Ken Sanders	.40	.20	.12
247	Del Unser	.40	.20	.12
248	Jerry Johnson	.40	.20	.12
249	Larry Biittner	.40	.20	.12
250	Manny Sanguillen	.40	.20	.12
251	Roger Nelson	.40	.20	.12
252a	Giants Mgr./Coaches (Joe Amalfitano, Charlie Fox, Andy Gilbert, Don McMahon, John McNamara) (Coaches background brown)	.50	.25	.15
252b	Giants Mgr./Coaches (Joe Amalfitano, Charlie Fox, Andy Gilbert, Don McMahon, John McNamara) (Coaches background orange)	.50	.25	.15
253	Mark Belanger	.40	.20	.12
254	Bill Stoneman	.40	.20	.12
255	Reggie Jackson	12.50	6.25	3.75
256	Chris Zachary	.40	.20	.12
257a	Mets Mgr./Coaches (Yogi Berra, Roy McMillan, Joe Pignatano, Rube Walker, Eddie Yost) (Coaches background brown)	1.50	.70	.45
257b	Mets Mgr./Coaches (Yogi Berra, Roy McMillan, Joe Pignatano, Rube Walker, Eddie Yost) (Coaches background orange)	2.00	1.00	.60
258	Tommy John	1.00	.50	.30
259	Jim Holt	.40	.20	.12
260	Gary Nolan	.40	.20	.12
261	Pat Kelly	.40	.20	.12
262	Jack Aker	.40	.20	.12
263	George Scott	.40	.20	.12
264	Checklist 133-264	1.00	.50	.30
265	Gene Michael	.60	.30	.25
266	Mike Lum	.60	.30	.25
267	Lloyd Allen	.60	.30	.25
268	Jerry Morales	.60	.30	.25
269	Tim McCarver	.75	.40	.25
270	Luis Tiant	.75	.40	.25
271	Tom Hutton	.60	.30	.25
272	Ed Farmer	.60	.30	.25
273	Chris Speier	.60	.30	.25
274	Darold Knowles	.60	.30	.25
275	Tony Perez	6.00	3.00	1.75
276	Joe Lovitto	.60	.30	.25
277	Bob Miller	.60	.30	.25
278	Orioles Team	3.00	1.50	.90
279	Mike Strahler	.60	.30	.25
280	Al Kaline	7.50	3.75	2.25
281	Mike Jorgensen	.60	.30	.25
282	Steve Hovley	.60	.30	.25
283	Ray Sadecki	.60	.30	.25
284	Glenn Borgmann	.60	.30	.25
285	Don Kessinger	.60	.30	.25
286	Frank Linzy	.60	.30	.25
287	Eddie Leon	.60	.30	.25
288	Gary Gentry	.60	.30	.25
289	Bob Oliver	.60	.30	.25
290	Cesar Cedeno	.60	.30	.25
291	Rogelio Moret	.60	.30	.25
292	Jose Cruz	.60	.30	.20
293	Bernie Allen	.60	.30	.25
294	Steve Arlin	.60	.30	.25
295	Bert Campaneris	.60	.30	.20
296	Reds Mgr./Coaches (Sparky Anderson, Alex Grammas, Ted Kluszewski, George Scherger, Larry Shepard)	2.50	1.25	.70
297	Walt Williams	.60	.30	.25
298	Ron Bryant	.60	.30	.25
299	Ted Ford	.60	.30	.25
300	Steve Carlton	9.00	4.50	2.75
301	Billy Grabarkewitz	.60	.30	.25
302	Terry Crowley	.60	.30	.25
303	Nelson Briles	.60	.30	.25
304	Duke Sims	.60	.30	.25
305	Willie Mays	30.00	15.00	9.00
306	Tom Burgmeier	.60	.30	.25
307	Boots Day	.60	.30	.25
308	Skip Lockwood	.60	.30	.25
309	Paul Popovich	.60	.30	.25
310	Dick Allen	1.50	.70	.45
311	Joe Decker	.60	.30	.25
312	Oscar Brown	.60	.30	.25
313	Jim Ray	.60	.30	.25
314	Ron Swoboda	.60	.30	.25
315	John Odom	.60	.30	.25
316	Padres Team	2.00	1.00	.60
317	Danny Cater	.60	.30	.25
318	Jim McGlothlin	.60	.30	.25
319	Jim Spencer	.60	.30	.25
320	Lou Brock	6.00	3.00	1.75
321	Rich Hinton	.60	.30	.25
322	*Garry Maddox*	1.00	.50	.30
323	Tigers Mgr./Coaches (Art Fowler, Billy Martin, Joe Schultz, Charlie Silvera, Dick Tracewski)	1.50	.70	.45
324	Al Downing	.60	.30	.25
325	Boog Powell	.75	.40	.25
326	Darrell Brandon	.60	.30	.25
327	John Lowenstein	.60	.30	.25
328	Bill Bonham	.60	.30	.25
329	Ed Kranepool	.60	.30	.25
330	Rod Carew	7.00	3.50	2.00
331	Carl Morton	.60	.30	.25
332	*John Felske*	.60	.30	.25
333	Gene Clines	.60	.30	.25
334	Freddie Patek	.60	.30	.25
335	Bob Tolan	.60	.30	.25
336	Tom Bradley	.60	.30	.25
337	Dave Duncan	.60	.30	.25
338	Checklist 265-396	1.00	.50	.30
339	Dick Tidrow	.60	.30	.25
340	Nate Colbert	.60	.30	.25
341	Jim Palmer (Boyhood Photo)	1.00	.50	.30
342	Sam McDowell (Boyhood Photo)	.60	.30	.25
343	Bobby Murcer (Boyhood Photo)	.60	.30	.25
344	Catfish Hunter (Boyhood Photo)	.75	.40	.25
345	Chris Speier (Boyhood Photo)	.60	.30	.25
346	Gaylord Perry (Boyhood Photo)	.75	.40	.25
347	Royals Team	2.00	1.00	.60
348	Rennie Stennett	.60	.30	.25
349	Dick McAuliffe	.60	.30	.25
350	Tom Seaver	10.00	5.00	3.00
351	Jimmy Stewart	.60	.30	.25
352	*Don Stanhouse*	.60	.30	.25
353	Steve Brye	.60	.30	.25
354	Billy Parker	.60	.30	.25
355	Mike Marshall	.60	.30	.25
356	White Sox Mgr./Coaches (Joe Lonnett, Jim Mahoney, Al Monchak, Johnny Sain, Chuck Tanner)	.75	.40	.25
357	Ross Grimsley	.60	.30	.25
358	Jim Nettles	.60	.30	.25
359	Cecil Upshaw	.60	.30	.25
360	Joe Rudi (photo actually Gene Tenace)	.60	.30	.25
361	Fran Healy	.60	.30	.25
362	Eddie Watt	.60	.30	.25
363	Jackie Hernandez	.60	.30	.25
364	Rick Wise	.60	.30	.25
365	Rico Petrocelli	.60	.30	.25
366	Brock Davis	.60	.30	.25
367	Burt Hooton	.60	.30	.25
368	Bill Buckner	.75	.40	.25
369	Lerrin LaGrow	.60	.30	.25
370	Willie Stargell	5.00	2.50	1.50
371	Mike Kekich	.60	.30	.25
372	Oscar Gamble	.60	.30	.25
373	Clyde Wright	.60	.30	.25
374	Darrell Evans	.75	.40	.25
375	Larry Dierker	.60	.30	.25
376	Frank Duffy	.60	.30	.25
377	Expos Mgr./Coaches (Dave Bristol, Larry Doby, Gene Mauch, Cal McLish, Jerry Zimmerman)	1.00	.50	.30
378	Lenny Randle	.60	.30	.25
379	Cy Acosta	.60	.30	.25
380	Johnny Bench	9.00	4.50	2.75
381	Vicente Romo	.60	.30	.25
382	Mike Hegan	.60	.30	.25
383	Diego Segui	.60	.30	.25
384	Don Baylor	1.75	.90	.50
385	Jim Perry	.60	.30	.25
386	Don Money	.60	.30	.25
387	Jim Barr	.60	.30	.25
388	Ben Oglivie	.60	.30	.25
389	Mets Team	2.50	1.25	.70
390	Mickey Lolich	.90	.45	.25
391	*Lee Lacy*	.60	.30	.25
392	Dick Drago	.60	.30	.25
393	Jose Cardenal	.60	.30	.25
394	Sparky Lyle	.60	.30	.25
395	Roger Metzger	.60	.30	.25
396	Grant Jackson	.60	.30	.25
397	Dave Cash	.90	.45	.25
398	Rich Hand	.90	.45	.25
399	George Foster	1.50	.70	.45
400	Gaylord Perry	6.00	3.00	1.75
401	Clyde Mashore	.90	.45	.25
402	Jack Hiatt	.90	.45	.25
403	Sonny Jackson	.90	.45	.25
404	Chuck Brinkman	.90	.45	.25
405	Cesar Tovar	.90	.45	.25
406	Paul Lindblad	.90	.45	.25
407	Felix Millan	.90	.45	.25
408	Jim Colborn	.90	.45	.25
409	Ivan Murrell	.90	.45	.25
410	Willie McCovey	7.00	3.50	2.00
411	Ray Corbin	.90	.45	.25
412	Manny Mota	.90	.45	.25
413	Tom Timmermann	.90	.45	.25
414	Ken Rudolph	.90	.45	.25
415	Marty Pattin	.90	.45	.25
416	Paul Schaal	.90	.45	.25
417	Scipio Spinks	.90	.45	.25
418	Bobby Grich	.90	.45	.25
419	Casey Cox	.90	.45	.25
420	Tommie Agee	.90	.45	.25
421	Angels Mgr./Coaches (Tom Morgan, Salty Parker, Jimmie Reese, John Roseboro, Bobby Winkles)	1.00	.50	.30
422	Bob Robertson	.90	.45	.25
423	Johnny Jeter	.90	.45	.25
424	Denny Doyle	.90	.45	.25
425	Alex Johnson	.90	.45	.25
426	Dave LaRoche	.90	.45	.25
427	Rick Auerbach	.90	.45	.25
428	Wayne Simpson	.90	.45	.25
429	Jim Fairey	.90	.45	.25
430	Vida Blue	.90	.45	.25
431	Gerry Moses	.90	.45	.25
432	Dan Frisella	.90	.45	.25
433	Willie Horton	.90	.45	.25
434	Giants Team	4.00	2.00	1.25
435	Rico Carty	.90	.45	.25
436	Jim McAndrew	.90	.45	.25
437	John Kennedy	.90	.45	.25
438	Enzo Hernandez	.90	.45	.25
439	Eddie Fisher	.90	.45	.25
440	Glenn Beckert	.90	.45	.25
441	Gail Hopkins	.90	.45	.25
442	Dick Dietz	.90	.45	.25
443	Danny Thompson	.90	.45	.25
444	Ken Brett	.90	.45	.25
445	Ken Berry	.90	.45	.25
446	Jerry Reuss	.90	.45	.25
447	Joe Hague	.90	.45	.25
448	John Hiller	.90	.45	.25

449a	Indians Mgr./Coaches (Ken Aspromonte, Rocky Colavito, Joe Lutz, Warren Spahn) (Spahn's ear pointed)	1.50	.70	.45
449b	Indians Mgr./Coaches (Ken Aspromonte, Rocky Colavito, Joe Lutz, Warren Spahn) (Spahn's ear round)	2.50	1.25	.70
450	Joe Torre	2.50	1.25	.70
451	John Vukovich	.90	.45	.25
452	Paul Casanova	.90	.45	.25
453	Checklist 397-528	1.25	.60	.40
454	Tom Haller	.90	.45	.25
455	Bill Melton	.90	.45	.25
456	Dick Green	.90	.45	.25
457	John Strohmayer	.90	.45	.25
458	Jim Mason	.90	.45	.25
459	Jimmy Howarth	.90	.45	.25
460	Bill Freehan	.90	.45	.25
461	Mike Corkins	.90	.45	.25
462	Ron Blomberg	.90	.45	.25
463	Ken Tatum	.90	.45	.25
464	Cubs Team	4.00	2.00	1.25
465	Dave Giusti	.90	.45	.25
466	Jose Arcia	.90	.45	.25
467	Mike Ryan	.90	.45	.25
468	Tom Griffin	.90	.45	.25
469	Dan Monzon	.90	.45	.25
470	Mike Cuellar	.90	.45	.25
471	All-Time Hit Leader (Ty Cobb)	7.00	3.50	2.00
472	All-Time Grand Slam Leader (Lou Gehrig)	12.00	6.00	3.50
473	All-Time Total Base Leader (Hank Aaron)	12.00	6.00	3.50
474	All-Time RBI Leader (Babe Ruth)	15.00	7.50	4.50
475	All-Time Batting Leader (Ty Cobb)	7.00	3.50	2.00
476	All-Time Shutout Leader (Walter Johnson)	2.00	1.00	.60
477	All-Time Victory Leader (Cy Young)	2.00	1.00	.60
478	All-Time Strikeout Leader (Walter Johnson)	2.00	1.00	.60
479	Hal Lanier	.90	.45	.25
480	Juan Marichal	6.00	3.00	1.75
481	White Sox Team	4.00	2.00	1.25
482	*Rick Reuschel*	1.50	.70	.45
483	Dal Maxvill	.90	.45	.25
484	Ernie McAnally	.90	.45	.25
485	Norm Cash	1.50	.70	.45
486a	Phillies Mgr./Coaches (Carroll Berringer, Billy DeMars, Danny Ozark, Ray Rippelmeyer, Bobby Wine) (Coaches background brown-red)	.90	.45	.25
486b	Phillies Mgr./Coaches (Carroll Beringer, Billy DeMars, Danny Ozark, Ray Rippelmeyer, Bobby Wine) (Coaches background orange)	.90	.45	.25
487	Bruce Dal Canton	.90	.45	.25
488	Dave Campbell	.90	.45	.25
489	Jeff Burroughs	.90	.45	.25
490	Claude Osteen	.90	.45	.25
491	Bob Montgomery	.90	.45	.25
492	Pedro Borbon	.90	.45	.25
493	Duffy Dyer	.90	.45	.25
494	Rich Morales	.90	.45	.25
495	Tommy Helms	.90	.45	.25
496	Ray Lamb	.90	.45	.25
497	Cardinals Mgr./Coaches (Vern Benson, George Kissell, Red Schoendienst, Barney Schultz)	1.50	.70	.45
498	Graig Nettles	.90	.45	.25
499	Bob Moose	.90	.45	.25
500	A's Team	4.00	2.00	1.25
501	Larry Gura	.90	.45	.25
502	Bobby Valentine	.90	.45	.25
503	Phil Niekro	6.00	3.00	1.75
504	Earl Williams	.90	.45	.25
505	Bob Bailey	.90	.45	.25
506	Bart Johnson	.90	.45	.25
507	Darrel Chaney	.90	.45	.25
508	Gates Brown	.90	.45	.25
509	Jim Nash	.90	.45	.25
510	Amos Otis	.90	.45	.25
511	Sam McDowell	.90	.45	.25
512	Dalton Jones	.90	.45	.25
513	Dave Marshall	.90	.45	.25
514	Jerry Kenney	.90	.45	.25
515	Andy Messersmith	.90	.45	.25
516	Danny Walton	.90	.45	.25
517a	Pirates Mgr./Coaches (Don Leppert, Bill Mazeroski, Dave Ricketts, Bill Virdon, Mel Wright) (Coaches background brown)	2.00	1.00	.60
517b	Pirates Mgr./Coaches (Don Leppert, Bill Mazeroski, Dave Ricketts, Bill Virdon, Mel Wright) (Coaches background orange)	2.00	1.00	.60
518	Bob Veale	.90	.45	.25
519	John Edwards	.90	.45	.25
520	Mel Stottlemyre	.90	.45	.25
521	Braves Team	4.00	2.00	1.25
522	Leo Cardenas	.90	.45	.25
523	Wayne Granger	.90	.45	.25
524	Gene Tenace	.90	.45	.25
525	Jim Fregosi	.90	.45	.25
526	Ollie Brown	.90	.45	.25
527	Dan McGinn	.90	.45	.25
528	Paul Blair	.90	.45	.25
529	Milt May	2.50	1.25	.70
530	Jim Kaat	3.00	1.50	.90
531	Ron Woods	2.50	1.25	.70
532	Steve Mingori	2.50	1.25	.70
533	Larry Stahl	2.50	1.25	.70
534	Dave Lemonds	2.50	1.25	.70
535	John Callison	2.50	1.25	.70
536	Phillies Team	6.00	3.00	1.75
537	Bill Slayback	2.50	1.25	.70
538	Jim Hart	2.50	1.25	.70
539	Tom Murphy	2.50	1.25	.70
540	Cleon Jones	2.50	1.25	.70
541	Bob Bolin	2.50	1.25	.70
542	Pat Corrales	2.50	1.25	.70
543	Alan Foster	2.50	1.25	.70
544	Von Joshua	2.50	1.25	.70
545	Orlando Cepeda	12.00	6.00	3.50
546	Jim York	2.50	1.25	.70
547	Bobby Heise	2.50	1.25	.70
548	Don Durham	2.50	1.25	.70
549	Rangers Mgr./Coaches (Chuck Estrada, Whitey Herzog, Chuck Hiller, Jackie Moore)	2.50	1.25	.70
550	Dave Johnson	2.50	1.25	.70
551	Mike Kilkenny	2.50	1.25	.70
552	J.C. Martin	2.50	1.25	.70
553	Mickey Scott	2.50	1.25	.70
554	Dave Concepcion	2.50	1.25	.70
555	Bill Hands	2.50	1.25	.70
556	Yankees Team	6.50	3.25	2.00
557	Bernie Williams	2.50	1.25	.70
558	Jerry May	2.50	1.25	.70
559	Barry Lersch	2.50	1.25	.70
560	Frank Howard	3.00	1.50	.90
561	Jim Geddes	2.50	1.25	.70
562	Wayne Garrett	2.50	1.25	.70
563	Larry Haney	2.50	1.25	.70
564	Mike Thompson	2.50	1.25	.70
565	Jim Hickman	2.50	1.25	.70
566	Lew Krausse	2.50	1.25	.70
567	Bob Fenwick	2.50	1.25	.70
568	Ray Newman	2.50	1.25	.70
569	Dodgers Mgr./Coaches (Red Adams, Walt Alston, Monty Basgall, Jim Gilliam, Tom Lasorda)	5.00	2.50	1.50
570	Bill Singer	2.50	1.25	.70
571	Rusty Torres	2.50	1.25	.70
572	Gary Sutherland	2.50	1.25	.70
573	Fred Beene	2.50	1.25	.70
574	Bob Didier	2.50	1.25	.70
575	Dock Ellis	2.50	1.25	.70
576	Expos Team	4.50	2.25	1.25
577	*Eric Soderholm*	2.50	1.25	.70
578	Ken Wright	2.50	1.25	.70
579	Tom Grieve	2.50	1.25	.70
580	Joe Pepitone	2.50	1.25	.70
581	Steve Kealey	2.50	1.25	.70
582	Darrell Porter	2.50	1.25	.70
583	Bill Greif	2.50	1.25	.70
584	Chris Arnold	2.50	1.25	.70
585	Joe Niekro	3.00	1.50	.90
586	Bill Sudakis	2.50	1.25	.70
587	Rich McKinney	2.50	1.25	.70
588	Checklist 529-660	3.00	1.50	.90
589	Ken Forsch	2.50	1.25	.70
590	Deron Johnson	2.50	1.25	.70
591	Mike Hedlund	2.50	1.25	.70
592	John Boccabella	2.50	1.25	.70
593	Royals Mgr./Coaches (Galen Cisco, Harry Dunlop, Charlie Lau, Jack McKeon)	3.50	1.75	1.00
594	Vic Harris	2.50	1.25	.70
595	Don Gullett	2.50	1.25	.70
596	Red Sox Team	4.50	2.25	1.25
597	Mickey Rivers	2.50	1.25	.70
598	Phil Roof	2.50	1.25	.70
599	Ed Crosby	2.50	1.25	.70
600	Dave McNally	2.50	1.25	.70
601	Rookie Catchers (George Pena, Sergio Robles, Rick Stelmaszek)	2.50	1.25	.70
602	Rookie Pitchers (Mel Behney, Ralph Garcia), *(Doug Rau)*	2.50	1.25	.70
603	Rookie Third Basemen (Terry Hughes, Bill McNulty), *(Ken Reitz)*	2.50	1.25	.70
604	Rookie Pitchers (Jesse Jefferson, Dennis O'Toole, Bob Strampe)	2.50	1.25	.70
605	Rookie First Basemen (Pat Bourque), *(Enos Cabell,* Gonzalo Marquez)	2.50	1.25	.70
606	Rookie Outfielders *(Gary Matthews,* Tom Paciorek, Jorge Roque)	3.00	1.50	.90
607	Rookie Shortstops (Ray Busse, Pepe Frias, Mario Guerrero)	2.50	1.25	.70
608	Rookie Pitchers *(Steve Busby,* Dick Colpaert), *(George Medich)*	3.00	1.50	.90
609	Rookie Second Basemen *(Larvell Blanks), (Pedro Garcia), (Dave Lopes)*	4.00	2.00	1.25
610	Rookie Pitchers (Jimmy Freeman, Charlie Hough, Hank Webb)	3.00	1.50	.90
611	Rookie Outfielders (Rich Coggins, Jim Wohlford, Richie Zisk)	2.50	1.25	.70
612	Rookie Pitchers (Steve Lawson, Bob Reynolds, Brent Strom)	2.50	1.25	.70
613	Rookie Catchers *(Bob Boone,* Mike Ivie, Skip Jutze)	24.00	12.00	7.25
614	Rookie Outfielders *(Al Bumbry), (Dwight Evans,* Charlie Spikes)	25.00	12.50	7.50
615	Rookie Third Basemen *(Ron Cey), (John Hilton), (Mike Schmidt)*	140.00	70.00	42.00
616	Rookie Pitchers (Norm Angelini, Steve Blateric, Mike Garman)	2.50	1.25	.70
617	Rich Chiles	2.50	1.25	.70
618	Andy Etchebarren	2.50	1.25	.70
619	Billy Wilson	2.50	1.25	.70
620	Tommy Harper	2.50	1.25	.70
621	Joe Ferguson	2.50	1.25	.70
622	Larry Hisle	2.50	1.25	.70
623	Steve Renko	2.50	1.25	.70
624	Astros Mgr./Coaches (Leo Durocher, Preston Gomez, Grady Hatton, Hub Kittle, Jim Owens)	3.00	1.50	.90
625	Angel Mangual	2.50	1.25	.70
626	Bob Barton	2.50	1.25	.70
627	Luis Alvarado	2.50	1.25	.70
628	Jim Slaton	2.50	1.25	.70
629	Indians Team	4.50	2.25	1.25
630	Denny McLain	3.00	1.50	.90
631	Tom Matchick	2.50	1.25	.70
632	Dick Selma	2.50	1.25	.70
633	Ike Brown	2.50	1.25	.70
634	Alan Closter	2.50	1.25	.70
635	Gene Alley	2.50	1.25	.70
636	Rick Clark	2.50	1.25	.70
637	Norm Miller	2.50	1.25	.70
638	Ken Reynolds	2.50	1.25	.70
639	Willie Crawford	2.50	1.25	.70
640	Dick Bosman	2.50	1.25	.70
641	Reds Team	6.00	3.00	1.75
642	Jose Laboy	2.50	1.25	.70
643	Al Fitzmorris	2.50	1.25	.70
644	Jack Heidemann	2.50	1.25	.70
645	Bob Locker	2.50	1.25	.70
646	Brewers Mgr./Coaches (Del Crandall, Harvey Kuenn, Joe Nossek, Bob Shaw, Jim Walton)	3.00	1.50	.90
647	George Stone	2.50	1.25	.70
648	Tom Egan	2.50	1.25	.70
649	Rich Folkers	2.50	1.25	.70
650	Felipe Alou	4.00	2.00	1.25
651	Don Carrithers	2.50	1.25	.70
652	Ted Kubiak	2.50	1.25	.70
653	Joe Hoerner	2.50	1.25	.70
654	Twins Team	4.00	2.00	1.25
655	Clay Kirby	2.50	1.25	.70
656	John Ellis	2.50	1.25	.70
657	Bob Johnson	2.50	1.25	.70
658	Elliott Maddox	2.50	1.25	.70
659	Jose Pagan	2.50	1.25	.70
660	Fred Scherman	2.50	1.25	.70

1973 Topps Candy Lids

A bit out of the ordinary, the Topps Candy Lids were the top of a product called "Baseball Stars Bubble Gum." The bottom (inside) of the lids carry a color photo of a player with a ribbon containing the name, position and team. The lids are 1-7/8" in diameter. A total of 55 different lids were made, featuring most of the stars of the day.

		NM	EX	VG
Complete Set (55):		800.00	400.00	250.00
Common Player:		7.50	3.75	2.25
(1)	Hank Aaron	55.00	27.00	16.50
(2)	Dick Allen	15.00	7.50	4.50
(3)	Dusty Baker	7.50	3.75	2.25
(4)	Sal Bando	7.50	3.75	2.25
(5)	Johnny Bench	35.00	17.50	10.50
(6)	Bobby Bonds	9.00	4.50	2.75
(7)	Dick Bosman	7.50	3.75	2.25
(8)	Lou Brock	30.00	15.00	9.00
(9)	Rod Carew	30.00	15.00	9.00
(10)	Steve Carlton	30.00	15.00	9.00
(11)	Nate Colbert	7.50	3.75	2.25
(12)	Willie Davis	7.50	3.75	2.25
(13)	Larry Dierker	7.50	3.75	2.25
(14)	Mike Epstein	7.50	3.75	2.25
(15)	Carlton Fisk	25.00	12.50	7.50
(16)	Tim Foli	7.50	3.75	2.25
(17)	Ray Fosse	7.50	3.75	2.25
(18)	Bill Freehan	7.50	3.75	2.25
(19)	Bob Gibson	30.00	15.00	9.00
(20)	Bud Harrelson	7.50	3.75	2.25
(21)	Catfish Hunter	25.00	12.50	7.50
(22)	Reggie Jackson	35.00	17.50	10.50

(23)	Fergie Jenkins	25.00	12.50	7.50
(24)	Al Kaline	35.00	17.50	10.50
(25)	Harmon Killebrew	35.00	17.50	10.50
(26)	Clay Kirby	7.50	3.75	2.25
(27)	Mickey Lolich	9.00	4.50	2.75
(28)	Greg Luzinski	7.50	3.75	2.25
(29)	Mike Marshall	7.50	3.75	2.25
(30)	Lee May	7.50	3.75	2.25
(31)	John Mayberry	7.50	3.75	2.25
(32)	Willie Mays	55.00	27.00	16.50
(33)	Willie McCovey	30.00	15.00	9.00
(34)	Thurman Munson	35.00	17.50	10.50
(35)	Bobby Murcer	7.50	3.75	2.25
(36)	Gary Nolan	7.50	3.75	2.25
(37)	Amos Otis	7.50	3.75	2.25
(38)	Jim Palmer	25.00	12.50	7.50
(39)	Gaylord Perry	25.00	12.50	7.50
(40)	Lou Piniella	7.50	3.75	2.25
(41)	Brooks Robinson	35.00	17.50	10.50
(42)	Frank Robinson	35.00	17.50	10.50
(43)	Ellie Rodriguez	7.50	3.75	2.25
(44)	Pete Rose	55.00	27.00	16.50
(45)	Nolan Ryan	150.00	75.00	45.00
(46)	Manny Sanguillen	7.50	3.75	2.25
(47)	George Scott	7.50	3.75	2.25
(48)	Tom Seaver	35.00	17.50	10.50
(49)	Chris Speier	7.50	3.75	2.25
(50)	Willie Stargell	30.00	15.00	9.00
(51)	Don Sutton	25.00	12.50	7.50
(52)	Joe Torre	15.00	7.50	4.50
(53)	Billy Williams	30.00	15.00	9.00
(54)	Wilbur Wood	7.50	3.75	2.25
(55)	Carl Yastrzemski	35.00	17.50	10.50

1973 Topps Comics

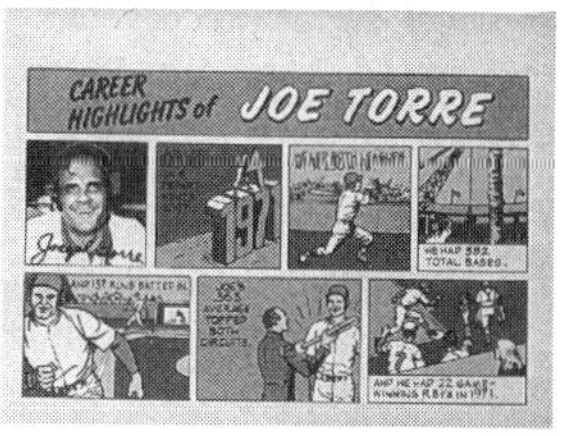

Strictly a test issue, if ever publicly distributed at all (most are found without any folding which would have occurred had they actually been used to wrap a piece of bubblegum), the 24 players in the 1973 Topps Comics issue appear on 4-5/8" x 3-7/16" waxed paper wrappers. The inside of the wrapper combines a color photo and facsimile autograph with a comic-style presentation of the player's career highlights. The Comics share a checklist with the 1973 Topps Pin-Ups, virtually all star players.

		NM	EX	VG
Complete Set (24):		4150.	2000.	1200.
Common Player:		100.00	50.00	30.00
(1)	Hank Aaron	275.00	137.00	82.00
(2)	Dick Allen	125.00	62.00	37.00
(3)	Johnny Bench	215.00	107.00	64.00
(4)	Steve Carlton	175.00	87.00	52.00
(5)	Nate Colbert	100.00	50.00	30.00
(6)	Willie Davis	100.00	50.00	30.00
(7)	Mike Epstein	100.00	50.00	30.00
(8)	Reggie Jackson	215.00	107.00	64.00
(9)	Harmon Killebrew	175.00	87.00	52.00
(10)	Mickey Lolich	110.00	55.00	33.00
(11)	Mike Marshall	100.00	50.00	30.00
(12)	Lee May	100.00	50.00	30.00
(13)	Willie McCovey	150.00	75.00	45.00
(14)	Bobby Murcer	100.00	50.00	30.00
(15)	Gaylord Perry	150.00	75.00	45.00
(16)	Lou Piniella	100.00	50.00	30.00
(17)	Brooks Robinson	175.00	87.00	52.00
(18)	Nolan Ryan	300.00	150.00	90.00
(19)	George Scott	100.00	50.00	30.00
(20)	Tom Seaver	200.00	100.00	60.00
(21)	Willie Stargell	150.00	75.00	45.00
(22)	Joe Torre	125.00	62.00	37.00
(23)	Billy Williams	150.00	75.00	45.00
(24)	Carl Yastrzemski	215.00	105.00	64.00

1973 Topps Pin-Ups

Another test issue of 1973, the 24 Topps Pin-Ups include the same basic format and the same checklist of star-caliber players as the Comics test issue of the same year. The 3-7/16" x 4-5/8" Pin-Ups are actually the inside of a wrapper for a piece of bubble gum. The color player photo features a decorative lozenge inserted at bottom with the player's name, team and position. There is also a facsimile autograph. Curiously, neither the Pin-Ups nor the Comics of 1973 bear team logos on the players' caps.

		NM	EX	VG
Complete Set (24):		2000.	1000.	600.00
Common Player:		90.00	45.00	27.00
(1)	Hank Aaron	250.00	125.00	75.00
(2)	Dick Allen	100.00	50.00	30.00
(3)	Johnny Bench	200.00	100.00	60.00
(4)	Steve Carlton	150.00	75.00	45.00
(5)	Nate Colbert	90.00	45.00	27.00
(6)	Willie Davis	90.00	45.00	27.00
(7)	Mike Epstein	90.00	45.00	27.00
(8)	Reggie Jackson	200.00	100.00	60.00
(9)	Harmon Killebrew	150.00	75.00	45.00
(10)	Mickey Lolich	100.00	50.00	30.00
(11)	Mike Marshall	90.00	45.00	27.00
(12)	Lee May	90.00	45.00	27.00
(13)	Willie McCovey	125.00	62.00	37.00
(14)	Bobby Murcer	90.00	45.00	27.00
(15)	Gaylord Perry	125.00	62.00	37.00
(16)	Lou Piniella	90.00	45.00	27.00
(17)	Brooks Robinson	150.00	75.00	45.00
(18)	Nolan Ryan	300.00	150.00	90.00
(19)	George Scott	90.00	45.00	27.00
(20)	Tom Seaver	200.00	100.00	60.00
(21)	Willie Stargell	125.00	62.00	37.00
(22)	Joe Torre	100.00	50.00	30.00
(23)	Billy Williams	135.00	67.00	40.00
(24)	Carl Yastrzemski	200.00	100.00	60.00

1973 Topps Team Checklists

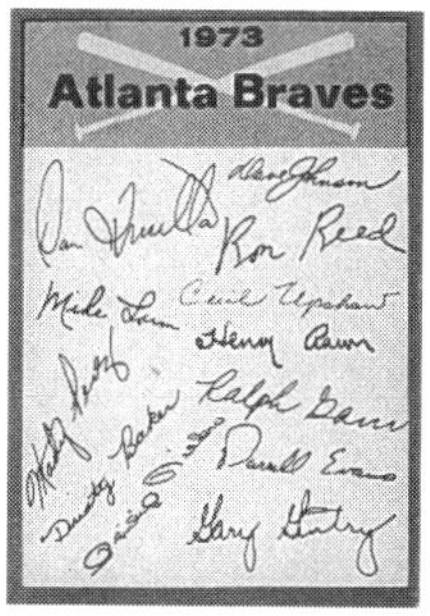

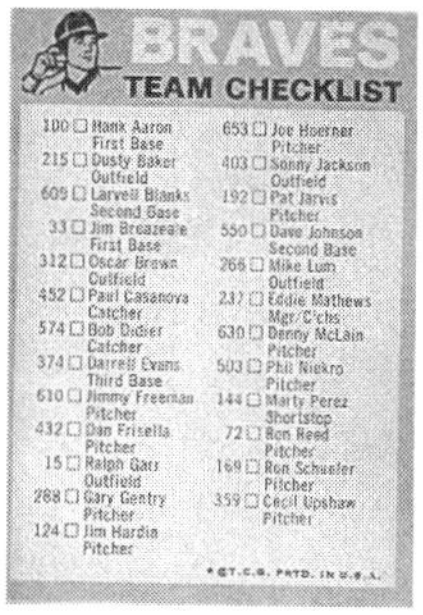

This is a 24-card unnumbered set of 2-1/2" x 3-1/2" cards that is generally believed to have been included with the high-numbered series in 1973, while also being made available in a mail-in offer. The front of the cards have the team name at the top and a white panel with various facsimile autographs takes up the rest of the space except for a blue border. Backs feature the team name and checklist. Relatively scarce, these somewhat mysterious cards are not included by many in their collections despite their obvious relationship to the regular set.

		NM	EX	VG
Complete Set (24):		75.00	37.00	22.00
Common Checklist:		3.00	1.50	.90
(1)	Atlanta Braves	3.00	1.50	.90
(2)	Baltimore Orioles	3.00	1.50	.90
(3)	Boston Red Sox	3.00	1.50	.90
(4)	California Angels	3.00	1.50	.90
(5)	Chicago Cubs	3.00	1.50	.90
(6)	Chicago White Sox	3.00	1.50	.90
(7)	Cincinnati Reds	3.00	1.50	.90
(8)	Cleveland Indians	3.00	1.50	.90
(9)	Detroit Tigers	3.50	1.75	1.00
(10)	Houston Astros	3.00	1.50	.90
(11)	Kansas City Royals	3.00	1.50	.90
(12)	Los Angeles Dodgers	3.00	1.50	.90
(13)	Milwaukee Brewers	3.00	1.50	.90
(14)	Minnesota Twins	3.00	1.50	.90
(15)	Montreal Expos	3.00	1.50	.90
(16)	New York Mets	3.50	1.75	1.00
(17)	New York Yankees	3.50	1.75	1.00
(18)	Oakland A's	3.50	1.75	1.00
(19)	Philadelphia Phillies	3.00	1.50	.90
(20)	Pittsburgh Pirates	3.00	1.50	.90
(21)	St. Louis Cardinals	3.00	1.50	.90
(22)	San Diego Padres	3.00	1.50	.90
(23)	San Francisco Giants	3.00	1.50	.90
(24)	Texas Rangers	3.00	1.50	.90

1973 Topps 1953 Reprints

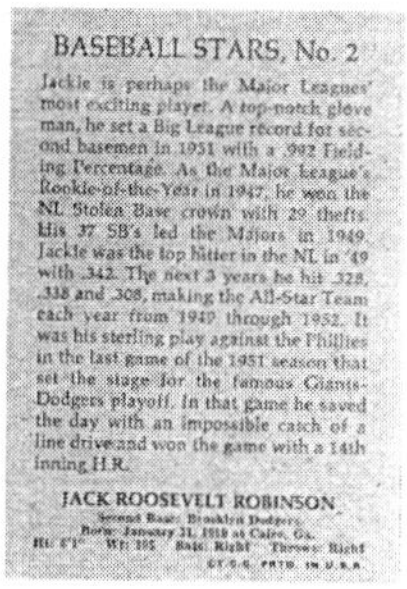

Long before Topps reprinted virtually the entire 1953 set in its "Archives" program in 1991, selected cards from the '53 set had been reprinted in a rare eight-card issue. Some sources say the cards were produced as table favors at a Topps banquet, while at least one contemporary hobby periodical said they were sold on a test-issue basis in Brooklyn. It was said only 300 of the sets were made. Unlike the original cards in 2-5/8" x 3-3/4" format, the test issue cards are modern standard 2-1/2" x 3-1/2". Three of the players in the issue were misidentified. Card backs feature a career summary written as though in 1953; the backs are formatted differently than original 1953 Topps cards and are printed in black-and-white.

		NM	EX	VG
Complete Set (8):		575.00	275.00	165.00
Common Player:		24.00	12.00	7.25
1	Satchell Paige	175.00	87.00	52.00
2	Jackie Robinson	250.00	125.00	75.00
3	Carl Furillo (picture actually Bill Antonello)	40.00	20.00	12.00
4	Al Rosen (picture actually Jim Fridley)	30.00	15.00	9.00
5	Hal Newhouser	40.00	20.00	12.00
6	Clyde McCullough (picture actually Vic Janowicz)	24.00	12.00	7.25
7	"Peanuts Lowrey	24.00	12.00	7.25
8	Johnny Mize	75.00	37.00	22.00

1974 Topps

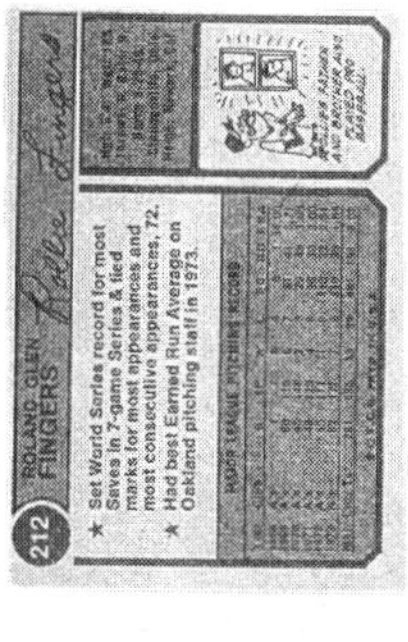

Issued all at once at the beginning of the year, rather than by series throughout the baseball season as had been done since 1952, this 660-card '74 Topps set features a famous group of error cards. At the time the cards were printed, it was uncertain whether the San Diego Padres would move to Washington, D.C., and by the time a decision was made some Padres cards had appeared with a "Washington, Nat'l League" designation on the front. A total of 15 cards were affected, and those with the Washington designation bring prices well in excess of regular cards of the same players (the Washington variations are not included in the complete set prices quoted below). The 2-1/2" x 3-1/2" cards feature color photos (frequently game-action shots) along with the player's name, team and position. Specialty cards abound, starting with a Hank Aaron tribute and running through the usual managers, statistical leaders, playoff and World Series highlights, multi-player rookie cards and All-Stars.

		NM	EX	VG
	Complete Set (660):	500.00	200.00	120.00
	Common Player:	.30	.15	.09
1	Hank Aaron (All-Time Home Run King)	35.00	17.50	10.50
2	Hank Aaron (Aaron Special 1954-57)	5.00	2.50	1.50
3	Hank Aaron (Aaron Special 1958-61)	4.00	2.00	1.25
4	Hank Aaron (Aaron Special 1962-65)	4.00	2.00	1.25
5	Hank Aaron (Aaron Special 1966-69)	4.00	2.00	1.25
6	Hank Aaron (Aaron Special 1970-73)	4.00	2.00	1.25
7	Catfish Hunter	2.50	1.25	.70
8	George Theodore	.30	.15	.09
9	Mickey Lolich	.60	.30	.20
10	Johnny Bench	10.00	5.00	3.00
11	Jim Bibby	.30	.15	.09
12	Dave May	.30	.15	.09
13	Tom Hilgendorf	.30	.15	.09
14	Paul Popovich	.30	.15	.09
15	Joe Torre	.75	.40	.25
16	Orioles Team	2.00	1.00	.60
17	Doug Bird	.30	.15	.09
18	Gary Thomasson	.30	.15	.09
19	Gerry Moses	.30	.15	.09
20	Nolan Ryan	35.00	17.50	10.50
21	Bob Gallagher	.30	.15	.09
22	Cy Acosta	.30	.15	.09
23	Craig Robinson	.30	.15	.09
24	John Hiller	.30	.15	.09
25	Ken Singleton	.30	.15	.09
26	*Bill Campbell*	.30	.15	.09
27	George Scott	.30	.15	.09
28	Manny Sanguillen	.30	.15	.09
29	Phil Niekro	2.00	1.00	.60
30	Bobby Bonds	.50	.25	.15
31	Astros Mgr./Coaches (Roger Craig, Preston Gomez, Grady Hatton, Hub Kittle, Bob Lillis)	.50	.25	.15
32a	John Grubb (Washington)	3.50	1.75	1.00
32b	John Grubb (San Diego)	.30	.15	.09
33	Don Newhauser	.30	.15	.09
34	Andy Kosco	.30	.15	.09
35	Gaylord Perry	2.50	1.25	.70
36	Cardinals Team	1.00	.50	.30
37	Dave Sells	.30	.15	.09
38	Don Kessinger	.30	.15	.09
39	Ken Suarez	.30	.15	.09
40	Jim Palmer	4.00	2.00	1.25
41	Bobby Floyd	.30	.15	.09
42	Claude Osteen	.30	.15	.09
43	Jim Wynn	.30	.15	.09
44	Mel Stottlemyre	.30	.15	.09
45	Dave Johnson	.30	.15	.09
46	Pat Kelly	.30	.15	.09
47	*Dick Ruthven*	.30	.15	.09
48	Dick Sharon	.30	.15	.09
49	Steve Renko	.30	.15	.09
50	Rod Carew	5.00	2.50	1.50
51	Bobby Heise	.30	.15	.09
52	Al Oliver	.60	.30	.20
53a	Fred Kendall (Washington)	3.50	1.75	1.00
53b	Fred Kendall (San Diego)	.30	.15	.09
54	*Elias Sosa*	.30	.15	.09
55	Frank Robinson	6.00	3.00	1.75
56	Mets Team	1.50	.70	.45
57	Darold Knowles	.30	.15	.09
58	Charlie Spikes	.30	.15	.09
59	Ross Grimsley	.30	.15	.09
60	Lou Brock	4.50	2.25	1.25
61	Luis Aparicio	4.00	2.00	1.25
62	Bob Locker	.30	.15	.09
63	Bill Sudakis	.30	.15	.09
64	Doug Rau	.30	.15	.09
65	Amos Otis	.30	.15	.09
66	Sparky Lyle	.30	.15	.09
67	Tommy Helms	.30	.15	.09
68	Grant Jackson	.30	.15	.09
69	Del Unser	.30	.15	.09
70	Dick Allen	.75	.40	.25
71	Danny Frisella	.30	.15	.09
72	Aurelio Rodriguez	.30	.15	.09
73	Mike Marshall	.30	.15	.09
74	Twins Team	1.00	.50	.30
75	Jim Colborn	.30	.15	.09
76	Mickey Rivers	.30	.15	.09
77a	Rich Troedson (Washington)	3.50	1.75	1.00
77b	Rich Troedson (San Diego)	.30	.15	.09
78	Giants Mgr./Coaches (Joe Amalfitano, Charlie Fox, Andy Gilbert, Don McMahon, John McNamara)	.50	.25	.15
79	Gene Tenace	.30	.15	.09
80	Tom Seaver	9.00	4.50	2.75
81	Frank Duffy	.30	.15	.09
82	Dave Giusti	.30	.15	.09
83	Orlando Cepeda	5.00	2.50	1.50
84	Rick Wise	.30	.15	.09
85	Joe Morgan	4.00	2.00	1.25
86	Joe Ferguson	.30	.15	.09
87	Fergie Jenkins	3.00	1.50	.90
88	Freddie Patek	.30	.15	.09
89	Jackie Brown	.30	.15	.09
90	Bobby Murcer	.40	.20	.12
91	Ken Forsch	.30	.15	.09
92	Paul Blair	.30	.15	.09
93	Rod Gilbreath	.30	.15	.09
94	Tigers Team	1.00	.50	.30
95	Steve Carlton	6.00	3.00	1.75
96	*Jerry Hairston*	.30	.15	.09
97	Bob Bailey	.30	.15	.09
98	Bert Blyleven	.45	.25	.14
99	Brewers Mgr./Coaches (Del Crandall, Harvey Kuenn, Joe Nossek, Jim Walton, Al Widmar)	.50	.25	.15
100	Willie Stargell	4.50	2.25	1.25
101	Bobby Valentine	.30	.15	.09
102a	Bill Greif (Washington)	3.50	1.75	1.00
102b	Bill Greif (San Diego)	.30	.15	.09
103	Sal Bando	.30	.15	.09
104	Ron Bryant	.30	.15	.09
105	Carlton Fisk	9.00	4.50	2.75
106	Harry Parker	.30	.15	.09
107	Alex Johnson	.30	.15	.09
108	Al Hrabosky	.30	.15	.09
109	Bob Grich	.30	.15	.09
110	Billy Williams	4.00	2.00	1.25
111	Clay Carroll	.30	.15	.09
112	Dave Lopes	.30	.15	.09
113	Dick Drago	.30	.15	.09
114	Angels Team	1.00	.50	.30
115	Willie Horton	.30	.15	.09
116	Jerry Reuss	.30	.15	.09
117	Ron Blomberg	.30	.15	.09
118	Bill Lee	.30	.15	.09
119	Phillies Mgr./Coaches (Carroll Beringer, Bill DeMars, Danny Ozark, Ray Ripplemeyer, Bobby Wine)	.50	.25	.15
120	Wilbur Wood	.30	.15	.09
121	Larry Lintz	.30	.15	.09
122	Jim Holt	.30	.15	.09
123	Nelson Briles	.30	.15	.09
124	Bob Coluccio	.30	.15	.09
125a	Nate Colbert (Washington)	3.50	1.75	1.00
125b	Nate Colbert (San Diego)	.30	.15	.09
126	Checklist 1-132	.50	.25	.15
127	Tom Paciorek	.30	.15	.09
128	John Ellis	.30	.15	.09
129	Chris Speier	.30	.15	.09
130	Reggie Jackson	12.00	6.00	3.50
131	Bob Boone	1.75	.90	.50
132	Felix Millan	.30	.15	.09
133	*David Clyde*	.30	.15	.09
134	Denis Menke	.30	.15	.09
135	Roy White	.30	.15	.09
136	Rick Reuschel	.30	.15	.09
137	Al Bumbry	.30	.15	.09
138	Ed Brinkman	.30	.15	.09
139	Aurelio Monteagudo	.30	.15	.09
140	Darrell Evans	.45	.25	.14
141	Pat Bourque	.30	.15	.09
142	Pedro Garcia	.30	.15	.09
143	Dick Woodson	.30	.15	.09
144	Dodgers Mgr./Coaches (Red Adams, Walter Alston, Monty Basgall, Jim Gilliam, Tom Lasorda) (Mgr.)	1.50	.70	.45
145	Dock Ellis	.30	.15	.09
146	Ron Fairly	.30	.15	.09
147	Bart Johnson	.30	.15	.09
148a	Dave Hilton (Washington)	3.50	1.75	1.00
148b	Dave Hilton (San Diego)	.30	.15	.09
149	Mac Scarce	.30	.15	.09
150	John Mayberry	.30	.15	.09
151	Diego Segui	.30	.15	.09
152	Oscar Gamble	.30	.15	.09
153	Jon Matlack	.30	.15	.09
154	Astros Team	1.00	.50	.30
155	Bert Campaneris	.30	.15	.09
156	Randy Moffitt	.30	.15	.09
157	Vic Harris	.30	.15	.09
158	Jack Billingham	.30	.15	.09
159	Jim Ray Hart	.30	.15	.09
160	Brooks Robinson	7.00	3.50	2.00
161	*Ray Burris*	.30	.15	.09
162	Bill Freehan	.30	.15	.09
163	Ken Berry	.30	.15	.09
164	Tom House	.30	.15	.09
165	Willie Davis	.30	.15	.09
166	Royals Mgr./Coaches (Galen Cisco, Harry Dunlop, Charlie Lau, Jack McKeon)	.50	.25	.15
167	Luis Tiant	.40	.20	.12
168	Danny Thompson	.30	.15	.09
169	*Steve Rogers*	.30	.15	.09
170	Bill Melton	.30	.15	.09
171	Eduardo Rodriguez	.30	.15	.09
172	Gene Clines	.30	.15	.09
173a	*Randy Jones* (Washington)	3.50	1.75	1.00
173b	*Randy Jones* (San Diego)	.30	.15	.09
174	Bill Robinson	.30	.15	.09
175	Reggie Cleveland	.30	.15	.09
176	John Lowenstein	.30	.15	.09
177	Dave Roberts	.30	.15	.09
178	Garry Maddox	.30	.15	.09
179	Mets Mgr./Coaches (Yogi Berra, Roy McMillan, Joe Pignatano, Rube Walker, Eddie Yost)	1.50	.70	.45
180	Ken Holtzman	.30	.15	.09
181	Cesar Geronimo	.30	.15	.09
182	Lindy McDaniel	.30	.15	.09
183	Johnny Oates	.30	.15	.09
184	Rangers Team	1.00	.50	.30
185	Jose Cardenal	.30	.15	.09
186	Fred Scherman	.30	.15	.09
187	Don Baylor	.90	.45	.25
188	Rudy Meoli	.30	.15	.09
189	Jim Brewer	.30	.15	.09
190	Tony Oliva	.50	.25	.15
191	Al Fitzmorris	.30	.15	.09
192	Mario Guerrero	.30	.15	.09
193	Tom Walker	.30	.15	.09
194	Darrell Porter	.30	.15	.09
195	Carlos May	.30	.15	.09
196	Jim Fregosi	.30	.15	.09
197a	Vicente Romo (Washington)	3.50	1.75	1.00
197b	Vicente Romo (San Diego)	.30	.15	.09
198	Dave Cash	.30	.15	.09
199	Mike Kekich	.30	.15	.09
200	Cesar Cedeno	.30	.15	.09
201	Batting Leaders (Rod Carew, Pete Rose)	4.00	2.00	1.25
202	Home Run Leaders (Reggie Jackson, Willie Stargell)	3.00	1.50	.90
203	RBI Leaders (Reggie Jackson, Willie Stargell)	3.00	1.50	.90
204	Stolen Base Leaders (Lou Brock, Tommy Harper)	1.00	.50	.30
205	Victory Leaders (Ron Bryant, Wilbur Wood)	.40	.20	.12
206	Earned Run Average Leaders (Jim Palmer, Tom Seaver)	3.00	1.50	.90
207	Strikeout Leaders (Nolan Ryan, Tom Seaver)	16.00	8.00	4.75
208	Leading Firemen (John Hiller, Mike Marshall)	.30	.15	.09
209	Ted Sizemore	.30	.15	.09
210	Bill Singer	.30	.15	.09
211	Cubs Team	1.00	.50	.30
212	Rollie Fingers	2.50	1.25	.70
213	Dave Rader	.30	.15	.09
214	Billy Grabarkewitz	.30	.15	.09
215	Al Kaline	6.00	3.00	1.75
216	Ray Sadecki	.30	.15	.09
217	Tim Foli	.30	.15	.09
218	Johnny Briggs	.30	.15	.09
219	Doug Griffin	.30	.15	.09
220	Don Sutton	2.50	1.25	.70
221	White Sox Mgr./Coaches (Joe Lonnett, Jim Mahoney, Alex Monchak, Johnny Sain, Chuck Tanner)	.50	.25	.15
222	Ramon Hernandez	.30	.15	.09
223	Jeff Burroughs	.30	.15	.09
224	Roger Metzger	.30	.15	.09
225	Paul Splittorff	.30	.15	.09
226a	Washington Nat'l. Team	7.50	3.75	2.25
226b	Padres Team	2.00	1.00	.60
227	Mike Lum	.30	.15	.09
228	Ted Kubiak	.30	.15	.09
229	Fritz Peterson	.30	.15	.09
230	Tony Perez	4.50	2.25	1.25
231	Dick Tidrow	.30	.15	.09
232	Steve Brye	.30	.15	.09
233	Jim Barr	.30	.15	.09
234	John Milner	.30	.15	.09
235	Dave McNally	.30	.15	.09
236	Cardinals Mgr./Coaches (Vern Benson, George Kissell, Johnny Lewis, Red Schoendienst, Barney	.50	.25	.15
237	Ken Brett	.30	.15	.09
238	Fran Healy	.30	.15	.09
239	Bill Russell	.30	.15	.09
240	Joe Coleman	.30	.15	.09
241a	Glenn Beckert (Washington)	3.50	1.75	1.00
241b	Glenn Beckert (San Diego)	2.50	1.25	.70
242	Bill Gogolewski	.30	.15	.09
243	Bob Oliver	.30	.15	.09
244	Carl Morton	.30	.15	.09
245	Cleon Jones	.30	.15	.09
246	A's Team	2.00	1.00	.60
247	Rick Miller	.30	.15	.09
248	Tom Hall	.30	.15	.09
249	George Mitterwald	.30	.15	.09
250a	Willie McCovey (Washington)	24.00	12.00	7.25
250b	Willie McCovey (San Diego)	5.00	2.50	1.50
251	Graig Nettles	.30	.15	.09
252	*Dave Parker*	10.00	5.00	3.00
253	John Boccabella	.30	.15	.09
254	Stan Bahnsen	.30	.15	.09
255	Larry Bowa	.30	.15	.09
256	Tom Griffin	.30	.15	.09
257	Buddy Bell	.30	.15	.09
258	Jerry Morales	.30	.15	.09
259	Bob Reynolds	.30	.15	.09
260	Ted Simmons	.30	.15	.09
261	Jerry Bell	.30	.15	.09
262	Ed Kirkpatrick	.30	.15	.09
263	Checklist 133-264	.50	.25	.15
264	Joe Rudi	.30	.15	.09
265	Tug McGraw	.30	.15	.09
266	Jim Northrup	.30	.15	.09
267	Andy Messersmith	.30	.15	.09
268	Tom Grieve	.30	.15	.09
269	Bob Johnson	.30	.15	.09
270	Ron Santo	.50	.25	.15
271	Bill Hands	.30	.15	.09
272	Paul Casanova	.30	.15	.09
273	Checklist 265-396	.50	.25	.15
274	Fred Beene	.30	.15	.09
275	Ron Hunt	.30	.15	.09
276	Angels Mgr./Coaches (Tom Morgan, Salty Parker, Jimmie Reese, John Roseboro, Bobby Winkles)	.50	.25	.15
277	Gary Nolan	.30	.15	.09
278	Cookie Rojas	.30	.15	.09
279	Jim Crawford	.30	.15	.09
280	Carl Yastrzemski	7.50	3.75	2.25
281	Giants Team	1.00	.50	.30
282	Doyle Alexander	.30	.15	.09
283	Mike Schmidt	30.00	15.00	9.00
284	Dave Duncan	.30	.15	.09
285	Reggie Smith	.30	.15	.09
286	Tony Muser	.30	.15	.09
287	Clay Kirby	.30	.15	.09
288	*Gorman Thomas*	.30	.15	.09
289	Rick Auerbach	.30	.15	.09
290	Vida Blue	.30	.15	.09
291	Don Hahn	.30	.15	.09

292	Chuck Seelbach	.30	.15	.09
293	Milt May	.30	.15	.09
294	Steve Foucault	.30	.15	.09
295	Rick Monday	.30	.15	.09
296	Ray Corbin	.30	.15	.09
297	Hal Breeden	.30	.15	.09
298	Roric Harrison	.30	.15	.09
299	Gene Michael	.30	.15	.09
300	Pete Rose	20.00	10.00	6.00
301	Bob Montgomery	.30	.15	.09
302	Rudy May	.30	.15	.09
303	George Hendrick	.30	.15	.09
304	Don Wilson	.30	.15	.09
305	Tito Fuentes	.30	.15	.09
306	Orioles Mgr./Coaches (George Bamberger, Jim Frey, Billy Hunter, George Staller, Earl Weaver)	1.50	.70	.45
307	Luis Melendez	.30	.15	.09
308	Bruce Dal Canton	.30	.15	.09
309a	Dave Roberts (Washington)	3.50	1.75	1.00
309b	Dave Roberts (San Diego)	.30	.15	.09
310	Terry Forster	.30	.15	.09
311	Jerry Grote	.30	.15	.09
312	Deron Johnson	.30	.15	.09
313	Berry Lersch	.30	.15	.09
314	Brewers Team	1.00	.50	.30
315	Ron Cey	.30	.15	.09
316	Jim Perry	.30	.15	.09
317	Richie Zisk	.30	.15	.09
318	Jim Merritt	.30	.15	.09
319	Randy Hundley	.30	.15	.09
320	Dusty Baker	.40	.20	.12
321	Steve Braun	.30	.15	.09
322	Ernie McAnally	.30	.15	.09
323	Richie Scheinblum	.30	.15	.09
324	Steve Kline	.30	.15	.09
325	Tommy Harper	.30	.15	.09
326	Reds Mgr./Coaches (Sparky Anderson, Alex Grammas, Ted Kluszewski, George Scherger, Larry Shepard)	1.50	.70	.45
327	Tom Timmermann	.30	.15	.09
328	Skip Jutze	.30	.15	.09
329	Mark Belanger	.30	.15	.09
330	Juan Marichal	3.50	1.75	1.00
331	All-Star Catchers (Johnny Bench, Carlton Fisk)	4.00	2.00	1.25
332	All-Star First Basemen (Hank Aaron, Dick Allen)	3.50	1.75	1.00
333	All-Star Second Basemen (Rod Carew, Joe Morgan)	3.00	1.50	.90
334	All-Star Third Basemen (Brooks Robinson, Ron Santo)	3.00	1.50	.90
335	All-Star Shortstops (Bert Campaneris, Chris Speier)	.40	.20	.12
336	All-Star Left Fielders (Bobby Murcer, Pete Rose)	2.50	1.25	.70
337	All-Star Center Fielders (Cesar Cedeno, Amos Otis)	.40	.20	.12
338	All-Star Right Fielders (Reggie Jackson, Billy Williams)	3.00	1.50	.90
339	All-Star Pitchers (Catfish Hunter, Rick Wise)	.80	.40	.25
340	Thurman Munson	5.00	2.50	1.50
341	*Dan Driessen*	.30	.15	.09
342	Jim Lonborg	.30	.15	.09
343	Royals Team	1.00	.50	.30
344	Mike Caldwell	.30	.15	.09
345	Bill North	.30	.15	.09
346	Ron Reed	.30	.15	.09
347	Sandy Alomar	.30	.15	.09
348	Pete Richert	.30	.15	.09
349	John Vukovich	.30	.15	.09
350	Bob Gibson	5.00	2.50	1.50
351	Dwight Evans	.75	.40	.25
352	Bill Stoneman	.30	.15	.09
353	Rich Coggins	.30	.15	.09
354	Cubs Mgr./Coaches (Hank Aguirre, Whitey Lockman, Jim Marshall, J.C. Martin, Al Spangler)	.50	.25	.15
355	Dave Nelson	.30	.15	.09
356	Jerry Koosman	.30	.15	.09
357	Buddy Bradford	.30	.15	.09
358	Dal Maxvill	.30	.15	.09
359	Brent Strom	.30	.15	.09
360	Greg Luzinski	.30	.15	.09
361	Don Carrithers	.30	.15	.09
362	Hal King	.30	.15	.09
363	Yankees Team	2.00	1.00	.60
364a	Cito Gaston (Washington)	3.50	1.75	1.00
364b	Cito Gaston (San Diego)	.30	.15	.09
365	Steve Busby	.30	.15	.09
366	Larry Hisle	.30	.15	.09
367	Norm Cash	.45	.25	.14
368	Manny Mota	.30	.15	.09
369	Paul Lindblad	.30	.15	.09
370	Bob Watson	.30	.15	.09
371	Jim Slaton	.30	.15	.09
372	Ken Reitz	.30	.15	.09
373	John Curtis	.30	.15	.09
374	Marty Perez	.30	.15	.09
375	Earl Williams	.30	.15	.09
376	Jorge Orta	.30	.15	.09
377	Ron Woods	.30	.15	.09
378	Burt Hooton	.30	.15	.09
379	Rangers Mgr./Coaches (Art Fowler, Frank Lucchesi, Billy Martin, Jackie Moore, Charlie Silvera)	.50	.25	.15
380	Bud Harrelson	.30	.15	.09
381	Charlie Sands	.30	.15	.09
382	Bob Moose	.30	.15	.09
383	Phillies Team	1.00	.50	.30
384	Chris Chambliss	.30	.15	.09
385	Don Gullett	.30	.15	.09
386	Gary Matthews	.30	.15	.09
387a	Rich Morales (Washington)	3.50	1.75	1.00
387b	Rich Morales (San Diego)	.30	.15	.09
388	Phil Roof	.30	.15	.09
389	Gates Brown	.30	.15	.09
390	Lou Piniella	.40	.20	.12
391	Billy Champion	.30	.15	.09
392	Dick Green	.30	.15	.09
393	Orlando Pena	.30	.15	.09
394	Ken Henderson	.30	.15	.09
395	Doug Rader	.30	.15	.09
396	Tommy Davis	.30	.15	.09
397	George Stone	.30	.15	.09
398	Duke Sims	.30	.15	.09
399	Mike Paul	.30	.15	.09
400	Harmon Killebrew	5.00	2.50	1.50
401	Elliott Maddox	.30	.15	.09
402	Jim Rooker	.30	.15	.09
403	Red Sox Mgr./Coaches (Don Bryant, Darrell Johnson, Eddie Popowski, Lee Stange, Don Zimmer)	.50	.25	.15
404	Jim Howarth	.30	.15	.09
405	Ellie Rodriguez	.30	.15	.09
406	Steve Arlin	.30	.15	.09
407	Jim Wohlford	.30	.15	.09
408	Charlie Hough	.30	.15	.09
409	Ike Brown	.30	.15	.09
410	Pedro Borbon	.30	.15	.09
411	Frank Baker	.30	.15	.09
412	Chuck Taylor	.30	.15	.09
413	Don Money	.30	.15	.09
414	Checklist 397-528	.50	.25	.15
415	Gary Gentry	.30	.15	.09
416	White Sox Team	1.00	.50	.30
417	Rich Folkers	.30	.15	.09
418	Walt Williams	.30	.15	.09
419	Wayne Twitchell	.30	.15	.09
420	Ray Fosse	.30	.15	.09
421	Dan Fife	.30	.15	.09
422	Gonzalo Marquez	.30	.15	.09
423	Fred Stanley	.30	.15	.09
424	Jim Beauchamp	.30	.15	.09
425	Pete Broberg	.30	.15	.09
426	Rennie Stennett	.30	.15	.09
427	Bobby Bolin	.30	.15	.09
428	Gary Sutherland	.30	.15	.09
429	Dick Lange	.30	.15	.09
430	Matty Alou	.30	.15	.09
431	*Gene Garber*	.30	.15	.09
432	Chris Arnold	.30	.15	.09
433	Lerrin LaGrow	.30	.15	.09
434	Ken McMullen	.30	.15	.09
435	Dave Concepcion	.50	.25	.15
436	Don Hood	.30	.15	.09
437	Jim Lyttle	.30	.15	.09
438	Ed Herrmann	.30	.15	.09
439	Norm Miller	.30	.15	.09
440	Jim Kaat	.50	.25	.15
441	Tom Ragland	.30	.15	.09
442	Alan Foster	.30	.15	.09
443	Tom Hutton	.30	.15	.09
444	Vic Davalillo	.30	.15	.09
445	George Medich	.30	.15	.09
446	Len Randle	.30	.15	.09
447	Twins Mgr./Coaches (Vern Morgan, Frank Quilici, Bob Rodgers, Ralph Rowe)	.50	.25	.15
448	Ron Hodges	.30	.15	.09
449	Tom McCraw	.30	.15	.09
450	Rich Hebner	.30	.15	.09
451	Tommy John	.60	.30	.20
452	Gene Hiser	.30	.15	.09
453	Balor Moore	.30	.15	.09
454	Kurt Bevacqua	.30	.15	.09
455	Tom Bradley	.30	.15	.09
456	*Dave Winfield*	45.00	22.00	13.50
457	Chuck Goggin	.30	.15	.09
458	Jim Ray	.30	.15	.09
459	Reds Team	1.00	.50	.30
460	Boog Powell	.75	.40	.25
461	John Odom	.30	.15	.09
462	Luis Alvarado	.30	.15	.09
463	Pat Dobson	.30	.15	.09
464	Jose Cruz	.30	.15	.09
465	Dick Bosman	.30	.15	.09
466	Dick Billings	.30	.15	.09
467	Winston Llenas	.30	.15	.09
468	Pepe Frias	.30	.15	.09
469	Joe Decker	.30	.15	.09
470	A.L. Playoffs (Reggie Jackson)	5.00	2.50	1.50
471	N.L. Playoffs	.80	.40	.25
472	World Series Game 1 (Rollie Fingers)	.80	.40	.25
473	World Series Game 2 (Willie Mays)	5.00	2.50	1.50
474	World Series Game 3	.80	.40	.25
475	World Series Game 4	.80	.40	.25
476	World Series Game 5	.80	.40	.25
477	World Series Game 6 (Reggie Jackson)	5.00	2.50	1.50
478	World Series Game 7	.80	.40	.25
479	World Series Summary (A's Celebrate)	.80	.40	.25
480	Willie Crawford	.30	.15	.09
481	Jerry Terrell	.30	.15	.09
482	Bob Didier	.30	.15	.09
483	Braves Team	1.00	.50	.30
484	Carmen Fanzone	.30	.15	.09
485	Felipe Alou	.50	.25	.15
486	Steve Stone	.30	.15	.09
487	Ted Martinez	.30	.15	.09
488	Andy Etchebarren	.30	.15	.09
489	Pirates Mgr./Coaches (Don Leppert, Bill Mazeroski, Danny Murtaugh, Don Osborn, Bob Skinner)	.75	.40	.25
490	Vada Pinson	.60	.30	.20
491	Roger Nelson	.30	.15	.09
492	Mike Rogodzinski	.30	.15	.09
493	Joe Hoerner	.30	.15	.09
494	Ed Goodson	.30	.15	.09
495	Dick McAuliffe	.30	.15	.09
496	Tom Murphy	.30	.15	.09
497	Bobby Mitchell	.30	.15	.09
498	Pat Corrales	.30	.15	.09
499	Rusty Torres	.30	.15	.09
500	Lee May	.30	.15	.09
501	Eddie Leon	.30	.15	.09
502	Dave LaRoche	.30	.15	.09
503	Eric Soderholm	.30	.15	.09
504	Joe Niekro	.30	.15	.09
505	Bill Buckner	.30	.15	.09
506	Ed Farmer	.30	.15	.09
507	Larry Stahl	.30	.15	.09
508	Expos Team	1.00	.50	.30
509	Jesse Jefferson	.30	.15	.09
510	Wayne Garrett	.30	.15	.09
511	Toby Harrah	.30	.15	.09
512	Joe Lahoud	.30	.15	.09
513	Jim Campanis	.30	.15	.09
514	Paul Schaal	.30	.15	.09
515	Willie Montanez	.30	.15	.09
516	Horacio Pina	.30	.15	.09
517	Mike Hegan	.30	.15	.09
518	Derrel Thomas	.30	.15	.09
519	Bill Sharp	.30	.15	.09
520	Tim McCarver	.45	.25	.14
521	Indians Mgr./Coaches (Ken Aspromonte, Clay Bryant, Tony Pacheco)	.50	.25	.15
522	J.R. Richard	.50	.25	.15
523	Cecil Cooper	.35	.20	.11
524	Bill Plummer	.30	.15	.09
525	Clyde Wright	.30	.15	.09
526	Frank Tepedino	.30	.15	.09
527	Bobby Darwin	.30	.15	.09
528	Bill Bonham	.30	.15	.09
529	Horace Clarke	.30	.15	.09
530	Mickey Stanley	.30	.15	.09
531	Expos Mgr./Coaches (Dave Bristol, Larry Doby, Gene Mauch, Cal McLish, Jerry Zimmerman)	.90	.45	.25
532	Skip Lockwood	.30	.15	.09
533	Mike Phillips	.30	.15	.09
534	Eddie Watt	.30	.15	.09
535	Bob Tolan	.30	.15	.09
536	Duffy Dyer	.30	.15	.09
537	Steve Mingori	.30	.15	.09
538	Cesar Tovar	.30	.15	.09
539	Lloyd Allen	.30	.15	.09
540	Bob Robertson	.30	.15	.09
541	Indians Team	1.00	.50	.30
542	Rich Gossage	1.00	.50	.30
543	Danny Cater	.30	.15	.09
544	Ron Schueler	.30	.15	.09
545	Billy Conigliaro	.30	.15	.09
546	Mike Corkins	.30	.15	.09
547	Glenn Borgmann	.30	.15	.09
548	Sonny Siebert	.30	.15	.09
549	Mike Jorgensen	.30	.15	.09
550	Sam McDowell	.30	.15	.09
551	Von Joshua	.30	.15	.09
552	Denny Doyle	.30	.15	.09
553	Jim Willoughby	.30	.15	.09
554	Tim Johnson	.30	.15	.09
555	Woodie Fryman	.30	.15	.09
556	Dave Campbell	.30	.15	.09
557	Jim McGlothlin	.30	.15	.09
558	Bill Fahey	.30	.15	.09
559	Darrel Chaney	.30	.15	.09
560	Mike Cuellar	.30	.15	.09
561	Ed Kranepool	.30	.15	.09
562	Jack Aker	.30	.15	.09
563	Hal McRae	.30	.15	.09
564	Mike Ryan	.30	.15	.09
565	Milt Wilcox	.30	.15	.09
566	Jackie Hernandez	.30	.15	.09
567	Red Sox Team	1.50	.70	.45
568	Mike Torrez	.30	.15	.09
569	Rick Dempsey	.30	.15	.09
570	Ralph Garr	.30	.15	.09
571	Rich Hand	.30	.15	.09
572	Enzo Hernandez	.30	.15	.09
573	Mike Adams	.30	.15	.09
574	Bill Parsons	.30	.15	.09
575	Steve Garvey	4.50	2.25	1.25
576	Scipio Spinks	.30	.15	.09
577	Mike Sadek	.30	.15	.09
578	Ralph Houk	.30	.15	.09
579	Cecil Upshaw	.30	.15	.09
580	Jim Spencer	.30	.15	.09
581	Fred Norman	.30	.15	.09
582	*Bucky Dent*	1.50	.70	.45
583	Marty Pattin	.30	.15	.09
584	Ken Rudolph	.30	.15	.09
585	Merv Rettenmund	.30	.15	.09
586	Jack Brohamer	.30	.15	.09
587	*Larry Christenson*	.30	.15	.09
588	Hal Lanier	.30	.15	.09
589	Boots Day	.30	.15	.09
590	Rogelio Moret	.30	.15	.09
591	Sonny Jackson	.30	.15	.09
592	Ed Bane	.30	.15	.09
593	Steve Yeager	.30	.15	.09
594	Leroy Stanton	.30	.15	.09
595	Steve Blass	.30	.15	.09
596	Rookie Pitchers (*Wayne Garland*, Fred Holdsworth), (*Mark Littell*, Dick Pole)	.30	.15	.09
597	Rookie Shortstops (Dave Chalk, John Gamble, Pete Mackanin), (*Manny Trillo*)	.80	.40	.25

		NM	EX	VG
598	Rookie Outfielders *(Dave Augustine), (Ken Griffey), (Steve Ontiveros), (Jim Tyrone)*	10.00	5.00	3.00
599a	Rookie Pitchers (Ron Diorio, Dave Freisleben, Frank Riccelli, Greg Shanahan) (Freisleben- Washington)	.80	.40	.25
599b	Rookie Pitchers (Ron Diorio, Dave Freisleben, Frank Riccelli, Greg Shanahan) (Freisleben- San Diego large print)	3.50	1.75	1.00
599c	Rookie Pitchers (Ron Diorio, Dave Freisleben, Frank Riccelli, Greg Shanahan) (Freisleben- San Diego small print)	6.00	3.00	1.75
600	Rookie Infielders *(Ron Cash), (Jim Cox), (Bill Madlock), (Reggie Sanders)*	4.00	2.00	1.25
601	Rookie Outfielders *(Ed Armbrister), (Rich Bladt), (Brian Downing), (Bake McBride)*	3.00	1.50	.90
602	Rookie Pitchers (Glenn Abbott, Rick Henninger, Craig Swan, Dan Vossler)	.30	.15	.09
603	Rookie Catchers (Barry Foote, Tom Lundstedt), *(Charlie Moore*, Sergio Robles)	.30	.15	.09
604	Rookie Infielders *(Terry Hughes), (John Knox), (Andy Thornton), (Frank White)*	4.00	2.00	1.25
605	Rookie Pitchers *(Vic Albury), (Ken Frailing), (Kevin Kobel), (Frank Tanana)*	3.00	1.50	.90
606	Rookie Outfielders (Jim Fuller, Wilbur Howard, Tommy Smith, Otto Velez)	.30	.15	.09
607	Rookie Shortstops (Leo Foster, Tom Heintzelman, Dave Rosello), *(Frank Taveras)*	.30	.15	.09
608a	Rookie Pitchers (Bob Apodaco, Dick Baney, John D'Acquisto, Mike Wallace) (Apodaca incorrect)	2.00	1.00	.60
608b	Rookie Pitchers (Bob Apodaca, Dick Baney, John D'Acquisto, Mike Wallace) (corrected)	.30	.15	.09
609	Rico Petrocelli	.30	.15	.09
610	Dave Kingman	.45	.25	.14
611	Rick Stelmaszek	.30	.15	.09
612	Luke Walker	.30	.15	.09
613	Dan Monzon	.30	.15	.09
614	Adrian Devine	.30	.15	.09
615	Johnny Jeter	.30	.15	.09
616	Larry Gura	.30	.15	.09
617	Ted Ford	.30	.15	.09
618	Jim Mason	.30	.15	.09
619	Mike Anderson	.30	.15	.09
620	Al Downing	.30	.15	.09
621	Bernie Carbo	.30	.15	.09
622	Phil Gagliano	.30	.15	.09
623	Celerino Sanchez	.30	.15	.09
624	Bob Miller	.30	.15	.09
625	Ollie Brown	.30	.15	.09
626	Pirates Team	1.00	.50	.30
627	Carl Taylor	.30	.15	.09
628	Ivan Murrell	.30	.15	.09
629	Rusty Staub	.50	.25	.15
630	Tommie Agee	.30	.15	.09
631	Steve Barber	.30	.15	.09
632	George Culver	.30	.15	.09
633	Dave Hamilton	.30	.15	.09
634	Braves Mgr./Coaches (Jim Busby, Eddie Mathews, Connie Ryan, Ken Silvestri, Herm Starrette)	1.00	.50	.30
635	John Edwards	.30	.15	.09
636	Dave Goltz	.30	.15	.09
637	Checklist 529-660	.50	.25	.15
638	Ken Sanders	.30	.15	.09
639	Joe Lovitto	.30	.15	.09
640	Milt Pappas	.30	.15	.09
641	Chuck Brinkman	.30	.15	.09
642	Terry Harmon	.30	.15	.09
643	Dodgers Team	2.50	1.25	.70
644	Wayne Granger	.30	.15	.09
645	Ken Boswell	.30	.15	.09
646	George Foster	.60	.30	.20
647	*Juan Beniquez*	.30	.15	.09
648	Terry Crowley	.30	.15	.09
649	Fernando Gonzalez	.30	.15	.09
650	Mike Epstein	.30	.15	.09
651	Leron Lee	.30	.15	.09
652	Gail Hopkins	.30	.15	.09
653	Bob Stinson	.30	.15	.09
654a	Jesus Alou (no position)	8.00	4.00	2.50
654b	Jesus Alou ("Outfield")	.30	.15	.09
655	Mike Tyson	.30	.15	.09
656	Adrian Garrett	.30	.15	.09
657	Jim Shellenback	.30	.15	.09
658	Lee Lacy	.30	.15	.09
659	Joe Lis	.30	.15	.09
660	Larry Dierker	.30	.15	.09

1974 Topps Traded

Appearing late in the season, these 2-1/2" x 3-1/2" cards share the format of the regular-issue Topps cards. The major change is a large red panel with the word "Traded" which was added below the player photo. Backs feature a "Baseball News" newspaper which contains the details of the trade. Card numbers correspond to the player's regular card number in 1974 except that the suffix "T" is added after the number. The set consists of 43 player cards and a checklist. In most cases, Topps did not obtain pictures of the players in their new uniforms. Instead the Topps artists simply provided the needed changes to existing photos.

		NM	EX	VG
Complete Set (44):		8.00	4.00	2.50
Common Player:		.15	.08	.05
23T	Craig Robinson	.15	.08	.05
42T	Claude Osteen	.15	.08	.05
43T	Jim Wynn	.15	.08	.05
51T	Bobby Heise	.15	.08	.05
59T	Ross Grimsley	.15	.08	.05
62T	Bob Locker	.15	.08	.05
63T	Bill Sudakis	.15	.08	.05
73T	Mike Marshall	.15	.08	.05
123T	Nelson Briles	.15	.08	.05
139T	Aurelio Monteagudo	.15	.08	.05
151T	Diego Segui	.15	.08	.05
165T	Willie Davis	.15	.08	.05
175T	Reggie Cleveland	.15	.08	.05
182T	Lindy McDaniel	.15	.08	.05
186T	Fred Scherman	.15	.08	.05
249T	George Mitterwald	.15	.08	.05
262T	Ed Kirkpatrick	.15	.08	.05
269T	Bob Johnson	.15	.08	.05
270T	Ron Santo	.75	.40	.25
313T	Barry Lersch	.15	.08	.05
319T	Randy Hundley	.25	.13	.08
330T	Juan Marichal	1.50	.70	.45
348T	Pete Richert	.15	.08	.05
373T	John Curtis	.15	.08	.05
390T	Lou Piniella	.35	.20	.11
428T	Gary Sutherland	.15	.08	.05
454T	Kurt Bevacqua	.15	.08	.05
458T	Jim Ray	.15	.08	.05
485T	Felipe Alou	.50	.25	.15
486T	Steve Stone	.25	.13	.08
496T	Tom Murphy	.15	.08	.05
516T	Horacio Pina	.15	.08	.05
534T	Eddie Watt	.15	.08	.05
538T	Cesar Tovar	.15	.08	.05
544T	Ron Schueler	.15	.08	.05
579T	Cecil Upshaw	.15	.08	.05
585T	Merv Rettenmund	.15	.08	.05
612T	Luke Walker	.15	.08	.05
616T	Larry Gura	.15	.08	.05
618T	Jim Mason	.15	.08	.05
630T	Tommie Agee	.15	.08	.05
648T	Terry Crowley	.15	.08	.05
649T	Fernando Gonzalez	.15	.08	.05
----	Traded Checklist	.20	.10	.06

1974 Topps Action Emblem Cloth Stickers

This enigmatic Topps test issue has never found favor with collectors because no actual ballplayers are pictured. In fact, official team logos are not used either, negating the necessity of licensing from either Major League Baseball or the players' association. The 2-1/2" x 3-1/2" cloth stickers were sold with a rub-off baseball game card in a Topps white test wrapper with a sticker describing them as "Topps Baseball Action Emblems Cloth Stickers." Each sticker features a generic ballplayer on front with a city (not team) name. At bottom is a pennant with another major league city named and a generic baseball symbol at its left. Backs are blank. This issue can be found in either a cloth sticker version or cardboard version. The cloth pieces are worth about twice the cardboard type.

		NM	EX	VG
Complete Set (24):		300.00	150.00	90.00
Common Sticker:		15.00	7.50	4.50
(1)	Atlanta/Baltimore	15.00	7.50	4.50
(2)	Baltimore/Montreal	15.00	7.50	4.50
(3)	Boston/Oakland	15.00	7.50	4.50
(4)	California/St. Louis	15.00	7.50	4.50
(5)	Chicago/Houston	15.00	7.50	4.50
(6)	Chicago/Pittsburgh	15.00	7.50	4.50
(7)	Cincinnati/Minnesota	15.00	7.50	4.50
(8)	Cleveland/San Diego	15.00	7.50	4.50
(9)	Detroit/New York	15.00	7.50	4.50
(10)	Houston/Chicago	15.00	7.50	4.50
(11)	Kansas City/Philadelphia	15.00	7.50	4.50
(12)	Los Angeles/Milwaukee	15.00	7.50	4.50
(13)	Milwaukee/New York	15.00	7.50	4.50
(14)	Minnesota/California	15.00	7.50	4.50
(15)	Montreal/San Francisco	15.00	7.50	4.50
(16)	New York/Cincinnati	15.00	7.50	4.50
(17)	New York/Texas	15.00	7.50	4.50
(18)	Oakland/Boston	15.00	7.50	4.50
(19)	Philadelphia/Los Angeles	15.00	7.50	4.50
(20)	Pittsburgh/Cleveland	15.00	7.50	4.50
(21)	St. Louis/Kansas City	15.00	7.50	4.50
(22)	San Diego/Detroit	15.00	7.50	4.50
(23)	San Francisco/Chicago	15.00	7.50	4.50
(24)	Texas/Atlanta	15.00	7.50	4.50

1974 Topps Deckle Edge

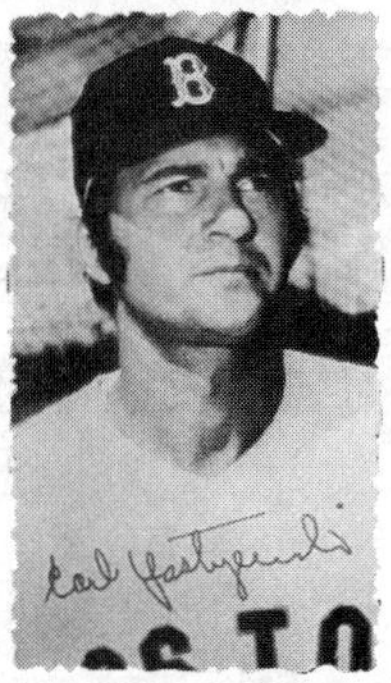

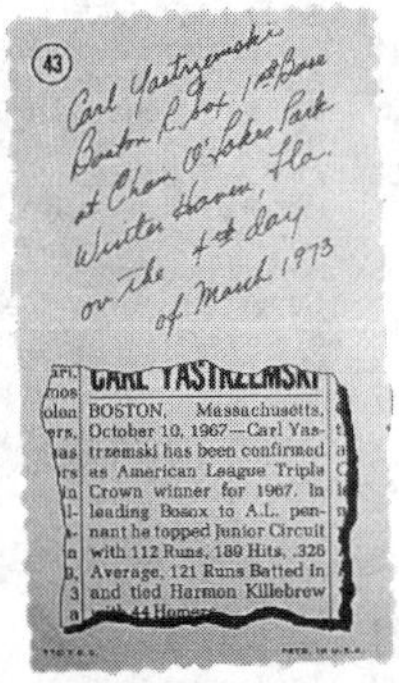

These borderless 2-7/8" x 5" cards feature a black-and-white photograph with a blue facsimile autograph on the front. The backs have in handwritten script the player's name, team, position and the date and location of the picture. Below is a mock newspaper clipping providing a detail from the player's career. Backs can be found in either gray or white. The cards take their names from their specially cut edges which give them a scalloped appearance. The 72-card set was a test issue and received rather limited distribution around Massachusetts. The cards were sold three per pack for five cents with a piece of gum, or in two-card packs with no gum.

		NM	EX	VG
Complete Set (72):		3250.	1600.	975.00
Common Player:		25.00	12.50	7.50
1	Amos Otis	25.00	12.50	7.50
2	Darrell Evans	25.00	12.50	7.50
3	Bob Gibson	125.00	62.00	37.00
4	David Nelson	25.00	12.50	7.50
5	Steve Carlton	125.00	62.00	37.00
6	Catfish Hunter	125.00	62.00	37.00
7	Thurman Munson	125.00	62.00	37.00
8	Bob Grich	25.00	12.50	7.50
9	Tom Seaver	150.00	75.00	45.00
10	Ted Simmons	25.00	12.50	7.50
11	Bobby Valentine	25.00	12.50	7.50
12	Don Sutton	125.00	62.00	37.00
13	Wilbur Wood	25.00	12.50	7.50
14	Doug Rader	25.00	12.50	7.50
15	Chris Chambliss	25.00	12.50	7.50
16	Pete Rose	250.00	125.00	75.00
17	John Hiller	25.00	12.50	7.50
18	Burt Hooton	25.00	12.50	7.50
19	Tim Foli	25.00	12.50	7.50
20	Lou Brock	125.00	62.00	37.00
21	Ron Bryant	25.00	12.50	7.50
22	Manuel Sanguillen	25.00	12.50	7.50
23	Bobby Tolan	25.00	12.50	7.50
24	Greg Luzinski	25.00	12.50	7.50
25	Brooks Robinson	150.00	75.00	45.00

26	Felix Millan	25.00	12.50	7.50
27	Luis Tiant	25.00	12.50	7.50
28	Willie McCovey	125.00	62.00	37.00
29	Chris Speier	25.00	12.50	7.50
30	George Scott	25.00	12.50	7.50
31	Willie Stargell	125.00	62.00	37.00
32	Rod Carew	125.00	62.00	37.00
33	Charlie Spikes	25.00	12.50	7.50
34	Nate Colbert	25.00	12.50	7.50
35	Richie Hebner	25.00	12.50	7.50
36	Bobby Bonds	25.00	12.50	7.50
37	Buddy Bell	25.00	12.50	7.50
38	Claude Osteen	25.00	12.50	7.50
39	Rich Allen	60.00	30.00	18.00
40	Bill Russell	25.00	12.50	7.50
41	Nolan Ryan	900.00	450.00	270.00
42	Willie Davis	25.00	12.50	7.50
43	Carl Yastrzemski	140.00	70.00	42.00
44	Jon Matlack	25.00	12.50	7.50
45	Jim Palmer	125.00	62.00	37.00
46	Bert Campaneris	25.00	12.50	7.50
47	Bert Blyleven	25.00	12.50	7.50
48	Jeff Burroughs	25.00	12.50	7.50
49	Jim Colborn	25.00	12.50	7.50
50	Dave Johnson	25.00	12.50	7.50
51	John Mayberry	25.00	12.50	7.50
52	Don Kessinger	25.00	12.50	7.50
53	Joe Coleman	25.00	12.50	7.50
54	Tony Perez	100.00	50.00	30.00
55	Jose Cardenal	25.00	12.50	7.50
56	Paul Splittorff	25.00	12.50	7.50
57	Henry Aaron	250.00	125.00	75.00
58	David May	25.00	12.50	7.50
59	Fergie Jenkins	125.00	62.00	37.00
60	Ron Blomberg	25.00	12.50	7.50
61	Reggie Jackson	175.00	87.00	52.00
62	Tony Oliva	45.00	22.00	13.50
63	Bobby Murcer	25.00	12.50	7.50
64	Carlton Fisk	100.00	50.00	30.00
65	Steve Rogers	25.00	12.50	7.50
66	Frank Robinson	145.00	72.00	43.00
67	Joe Ferguson	25.00	12.50	7.50
68	Bill Melton	25.00	12.50	7.50
69	Bob Watson	25.00	12.50	7.50
70	Larry Bowa	25.00	12.50	7.50
71	Johnny Bench	175.00	87.00	52.00
72	Willie Horton	25.00	12.50	7.50

1974 Topps Puzzles

One of many test issues by Topps in the mid-1970s, the 12-player jigsaw puzzle set was an innovation which never caught on with collectors. The 40-piece puzzles (4-3/4" x 7-1/2") feature color photos with a decorative lozenge at bottom naming the player, team and position. The puzzles came in individual wrappers picturing Tom Seaver. The Ryan puzzle is almost always found off-center. Well-centered Ryan puzzles will command a significant premium.

		NM	EX	VG
Complete Set (12):		1650.	850.00	500.00
Common Player:		45.00	22.00	13.50
(1)	Hank Aaron	250.00	125.00	75.00
(2)	Dick Allen	100.00	50.00	30.00
(3)	Johnny Bench	175.00	87.00	52.00
(4)	Bobby Bonds	45.00	22.00	13.50
(5)	Bob Gibson	125.00	62.00	37.00
(6)	Reggie Jackson	175.00	87.00	52.00
(7)	Bobby Murcer	45.00	22.00	13.50
(8)	Jim Palmer	125.00	62.00	37.00
(9)	Nolan Ryan	700.00	350.00	210.00
(10)	Tom Seaver	150.00	75.00	45.00
(11)	Willie Stargell	125.00	62.00	37.00
(12)	Carl Yastrzemski	150.00	75.00	45.00

1974 Topps Stamps

Topps continued to market baseball stamps in 1974 through the release of 240 unnumbered stamps featuring color player portraits. The player's name, team and position are found in an oval at the bottom of the 1" x 1-1/2" stamps. The stamps, sold separately rather than issued as an insert, came in strips of six which were then pasted in an appropriate team album designed to hold 10 stamps.

		NM	EX	VG
Complete Sheet Set (24):		150.00	75.00	45.00
Common Sheet:		2.00	1.00	.60
Complete Stamp Album Set (24):		200.00	100.00	60.00
Single Stamp Album:		4.00	2.00	1.20
(1)	Hank Aaron, Luis Aparicio, Bob Bailey, Johnny Bench, Ron Blomberg, Bob Boone, Lou Brock, Bud Harrelson, Randy Jones, Dave Rader, Nolan Ryan, Joe Torre	15.00	7.50	4.50
(2)	Buddy Bell, Steve Braun, Jerry Grote, Tommy Helms, Bill Lee, Mike Lum, Dave May, Brooks Robinson, Bill Russell, Del Unser, Wilber Wood, Carl Yastrzemski	9.00	4.50	2.75
(3)	Jerry Bell, Jerry Bell, Jim Colborn, Toby Harrah, Ken Henderson, John Hiller, Randy Hundley, Don Kessinger, Jerry Kooseman, Dave Lopes, Felix Millan, Thurman Munson, Ted Simmons	6.00	3.00	1.75
(4)	Jerry Bell, Bill Buckner, Jim Colborn, Ken Henderson, Don Kessinger, Felix Millan, George Mitterwald, Dave Roberts, Ted Simmons, Jim Slaton, Charlie Spikes, Paul Splittorff	2.00	1.00	.60
(5)	Glenn Beckert, Jim Bibby, Bill Buckner, Jim Lonborg, George Mitterwald, Dave Parker, Dave Roberts, Jim Slaton, Reggie Smith, Charlie Spikes, Paul Splittorff, Bob Watson	2.00	1.00	.60
(6)	Paul Blair, Bobby Bonds, Ed Brinkman, Norm Cash, Mike Epstein, Tommy Harper, Mike Marshall, Phil Niekro, Cookie Rojas, George Scott, Mel Stottlemyre, Jim Wynn	2.25	1.25	.70
(7)	Jack Billingham, Reggie Cleveland, Bobby Darwin, Dave Duncan, Tim Foli, Ed Goodson, Cleon Jones, Mickey Lolich, George Medich, John Milner, Rick Monday, Bobby Murcer	2.00	1.00	.60
(8)	Steve Carlton, Orlando Cepeda, Joe Decker, Reggie Jackson, Dave Johnson, John Mayberry, Bill Melton, Roger Metzger, Dave Nelson, Jerry Reuss, Jim Spencer, Bobby Valentine	10.00	5.00	3.00
(9)	Dan Driessen, Pedro Garcia, Grant Jackson, Al Kaline, Clay Kirby, Carlos May, Willie Montanez, Rogelio Moret, Jim Palmer, Doug Rader, J. R. Richard, Frank Robinson	8.00	4.00	2.50
(10)	Pedro Garcia, Ralph Garr, Wayne Garrett, Ron Hunt, Al Kaline, Fred Kendall, Carlos May, Jim Palmer, Doug Rader, Frank Robinson, Rick Wise, Richie Zisk	8.00	4.00	2.50
(11)	Dusty Baker, Larry Bowa, Steve Busby, Chris Chambliss, Dock Ellis, Cesar Geronimo, Fran Healy, Deron Johnson, Jorge Orta, Joe Rudi, , Mickey Stanley, Rennie Stennett	2.00	1.00	.60
(12)	Bob Coluccio, Ray Corbin, John Ellis, Oscar Gamble, Dave Giusti, Bill Greif, Alex Johnson, Mike Jorgensen, Andy Messersmith, Bill Robinson, Elias Sosa, Willie Stargell	2.50	1.25	.70
(13)	Ron Bryant, Nate Colbert, Jose Cruz, Dan Driessen, Billy Grabarkewitz, Don Gullett, Willie Horton, Grant Jackson, Clay Kirby, Willie Montanez, Rogelio Moret, J. R. Richard	2.00	1.00	.60
(14)	Carlton Fisk, Bill Freehan, Bobby Grich, Vic Harris, George Hendrick, Ed Herrmann, Jim Holt, Ken Holtzman, Fergie Jenkins, Lou Piniella, Steve Rogers, Ken Singleton	4.00	2.00	1.25
(15)	Stan Bahnsen, Sal Bando, Mark Belanger, David Clyde, Willie Crawford, Burt Hooton, Jon Matlack, Tim McCarver, Joe Morgan, Gene Tenace, Dick Tidrow, Dave Winfield	8.00	4.00	2.50
(16)	Hank Aaron, Stan Bahnsen, Bob Bailey, Johnny Bench, Bob Boone, Jon Matlack, Tim McCarver, Joe Morgan, Dave Rader, Gene Tenace, Dick Tidrow, Joe Torre	10.00	5.00	3.00
(17)	John Boccabella, Frank Duffy, Darrell Evans, Sparky Lyle, Lee May, Don Money, Bill North, Ted Sizemore, Chris Speier, Wayne Twitchell, Billy Williams, Earl Williams	2.00	1.00	.60
(18)	John Boccabella, Bobby Darwin, Frank Duffy, Dave Duncan, Tim Foli, Cleon Jones, Mickey Lolich, Sparky Lyle, Lee May, Rick Monday, Bill North, Billy Williams	2.00	1.00	.60
(19)	Don Baylor, Vida Blue, Tom Bradley, Jose Cardenal, Ron Cey, Greg Luzinski, Johnny Oates, Tony Oliva, Al Oliver, Tony Perez, Darrell Porter, Roy White	3.00	1.50	.90
(20)	Pedro Borbon, Rod Carew, Roric Harrison, Jim Hunter, Ed Kirkpatrick, Garry Maddox, Gene Michael, Rick Miller, Claude Osteen, Amos Otis, Rich Reuschel, Mike Tyson	5.00	2.50	1.50
(21)	Sandy Alomar, Bert Campaneris, Dave Concepcion, Tommy Davis, Joe Ferguson, Tito Fuentes, Jerry Morales, Carl Morton, Gaylord Perry, Vada Pinson, Dave Roberts, Ellie Rodriguez	2.00	1.00	.60
(22)	Dick Allen, Jeff Burroughs, Joe Coleman, Terry Forster, Bob Gibson, Harmon Killebrew, Tug McGraw, Bob Oliver, Steve Renko, Pete Rose, Luis Tiant, Otto Velez	10.00	5.00	3.00
(23)	Johnny Briggs, Willie Davis, Jim Fregosi, Rich Hebner, Pat Kelly, Dave Kingman, Willie McCovey, Graig Nettles, Freddie Patek, Marty Pattin, Manny Sanguillen, Richie Scheinblum	4.00	2.00	1.25
(24)	Bert Blyleven, Nelson Briles, Cesar Cedeno, Ron Fairly, Johnny Grubb, Dave McNally, Aurelio Rodriguez, Ron Santo, Tom Seaver, Bill Singer, Bill Sudakis, Don Sutton	6.00	3.00	1.75

1974 Topps Team Checklists

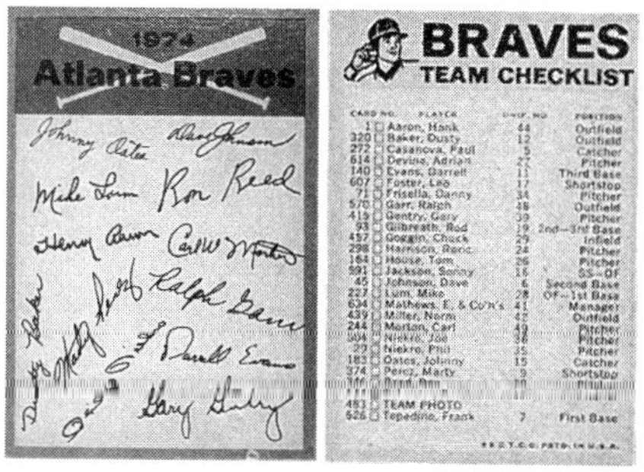

This set is a repeat of the 1973 mystery set in the form of 24 unnumbered 2-1/2" x 3-1/2" checklist cards. As with the 1973 set, the 1974s feature a team name on the front at the top with a white panel and a number of facsimile autographs below. Backs feature the team name and a checklist. The big difference between the 1973 and 1974 checklists is that the 1973s have blue borders while the 1974s have a red border. The 1974s were inserted into packages of the regular issue Topps cards.

		NM	EX	VG
Complete Set (24):		12.00	6.00	3.50
Common Checklist:		.50	.25	.15
(1)	Atlanta Braves	.50	.25	.15
(2)	Baltimore Orioles	.50	.25	.15
(3)	Boston Red Sox	.50	.25	.15
(4)	California Angels	.50	.25	.15
(5)	Chicago Cubs	.50	.25	.15
(6)	Chicago White Sox	.50	.25	.15
(7)	Cincinnati Reds	.50	.25	.15
(8)	Cleveland Indians	.50	.25	.15
(9)	Detroit Tigers	.50	.25	.15
(10)	Houston Astros	.50	.25	.15
(11)	Kansas City Royals	.50	.25	.15
(12)	Los Angeles Dodgers	.50	.25	.15
(13)	Milwaukee Brewers	.50	.25	.15
(14)	Minnesota Twins	.50	.25	.15
(15)	Montreal Expos	.50	.25	.15
(16)	New York Mets	.50	.25	.15
(17)	New York Yankees	.50	.25	.15
(18)	Oakland A's	.50	.25	.15
(19)	Philadelphia Phillies	.50	.25	.15
(20)	Pittsburgh Pirates	.50	.25	.15
(21)	St. Louis Cardinals	.50	.25	.15
(22)	San Diego Padres	.50	.25	.15
(23)	San Francisco Giants	.50	.25	.15
(24)	Texas Rangers	.50	.25	.15

1975 Topps

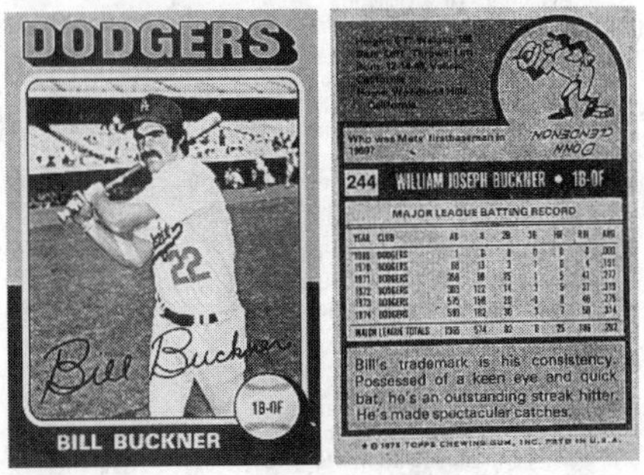

What was once seen as the strongest rookie card crop of any modern card set made this a collector favorite from the outset. As several of the superstar prospects faded into merely outstanding ball players by the ends of their careers, however, demand has leveled. Featuring the most colorful designs since 1972, which Topps has yet to top into the mid 1990s, cards feature large front photos with facsimile autographs, and red-and-green backs which include a cartoon trivia fact and complete stats. A subset of 1951-74 MVP cards which reproduces or creates contemporary cards of past stars is one of several special features of the set, as are a group of four-on-one rookie cards. While the cards were all issued at one time, the first 132 cards have been discovered to have been printed in noticeably lesser quantities than the rest of the issue. This scarcity is not noted among the mini-version of the set which was produced as a test issue. Team/manager cards are sometimes found on thinner, white cardboard stock; these are a special version produced for a mail-in offer.

		NM	EX	VG
Complete Set (660):		600.00	275.00	165.00
Common Player (1-132):		.35	.20	.11
Common Player (133-660):		.30	.15	.09
Mini Stars: 1x to 1.5x				
Mini Rookies: 1x		.40	.20	.12
1	Hank Aaron ('74 Highlights)	25.00	12.50	7.50
2	Lou Brock ('74 Highlights)	2.00	1.00	.60
3	Bob Gibson ('74 Highlights)	2.25	1.25	.70
4	Al Kaline ('74 Highlights)	2.50	1.25	.70
5	Nolan Ryan ('74 Highlights)	20.00	10.00	6.00
6	Mike Marshall ('74 Highlights)	.35	.20	.11
7	Dick Bosman, Steve Busby, Nolan Ryan ('74 Highlights)	6.50	3.25	2.00
8	Rogelio Moret	.35	.20	.11
9	Frank Tepedino	.35	.20	.11
10	Willie Davis	.35	.20	.11
11	Bill Melton	.35	.20	.11
12	David Clyde	.35	.20	.11
13	Gene Locklear	.35	.20	.11
14	Milt Wilcox	.35	.20	.11
15	Jose Cardenal	.35	.20	.11
16	Frank Tanana	.35	.20	.11
17	Dave Concepcion	.35	.20	.11
18	Tigers Team (Ralph Houk)	1.00	.50	.30
19	Jerry Koosman	.35	.20	.11
20	Thurman Munson	5.00	2.50	1.50
21	Rollie Fingers	3.00	1.50	.90
22	Dave Cash	.35	.20	.11
23	Bill Russell	.35	.20	.11
24	Al Fitzmorris	.35	.20	.11
25	Lee May	.35	.20	.11
26	Dave McNally	.35	.20	.11
27	Ken Reitz	.35	.20	.11
28	Tom Murphy	.35	.20	.11
29	Dave Parker	1.50	.70	.45
30	Bert Blyleven	.50	.25	.15
31	Dave Rader	.35	.20	.11
32	Reggie Cleveland	.35	.20	.11
33	Dusty Baker	.40	.20	.12
34	Steve Renko	.35	.20	.11
35	Ron Santo	.65	.35	.20
36	Joe Lovitto	.35	.20	.11
37	Dave Freisleben	.35	.20	.11
38	Buddy Bell	.35	.20	.11
39	Andy Thornton	.40	.20	.12
40	Bill Singer	.35	.20	.11
41	Cesar Geronimo	.35	.20	.11
42	Joe Coleman	.35	.20	.11
43	Cleon Jones	.35	.20	.11
44	Pat Dobson	.35	.20	.11
45	Joe Rudi	.35	.20	.11
46	Phillies Team (Danny Ozark)	1.00	.50	.30
47	Tommy John	.90	.45	.25
48	Freddie Patek	.35	.20	.11
49	Larry Dierker	.35	.20	.11
50	Brooks Robinson	5.00	2.50	1.50
51	*Bob Forsch*	.80	.40	.25
52	Darrell Porter	.35	.20	.11
53	Dave Giusti	.35	.20	.11
54	Eric Soderholm	.35	.20	.11
55	Bobby Bonds	.50	.25	.15
56	Rick Wise	.35	.20	.11
57	Dave Johnson	.35	.20	.11
58	Chuck Taylor	.35	.20	.11
59	Ken Henderson	.35	.20	.11
60	Fergie Jenkins	3.00	1.50	.90
61	Dave Winfield	20.00	10.00	6.00
62	Fritz Peterson	.35	.20	.11
63	Steve Swisher	.35	.20	.11
64	Dave Chalk	.35	.20	.11
65	Don Gullett	.35	.20	.11
66	Willie Horton	.35	.20	.11
67	Tug McGraw	.35	.20	.11
68	Ron Blomberg	.35	.20	.11
69	John Odom	.35	.20	.11
70	Mike Schmidt	30.00	15.00	9.00
71	Charlie Hough	.35	.20	.11
72	Royals Team (Jack McKeon)	1.00	.50	.30
73	J.R. Richard	.45	.25	.14
74	Mark Belanger	.35	.20	.11
75	Ted Simmons	.35	.20	.11
76	Ed Sprague	.35	.20	.11
77	Richie Zisk	.35	.20	.11
78	Ray Corbin	.35	.20	.11
79	Gary Matthews	.35	.20	.11
80	Carlton Fisk	9.00	4.50	2.75
81	Ron Reed	.35	.20	.11
82	Pat Kelly	.35	.20	.11
83	Jim Merritt	.35	.20	.11
84	Enzo Hernandez	.35	.20	.11
85	Bill Bonham	.35	.20	.11
86	Joe Lis	.35	.20	.11
87	George Foster	.35	.20	.11
88	Tom Egan	.35	.20	.11
89	Jim Ray	.35	.20	.11
90	Rusty Staub	.45	.25	.14
91	Dick Green	.35	.20	.11
92	Cecil Upshaw	.35	.20	.11
93	Dave Lopes	.35	.20	.11
94	Jim Lonborg	.35	.20	.11
95	John Mayberry	.35	.20	.11
96	Mike Cosgrove	.35	.20	.11
97	Earl Williams	.35	.20	.11
98	Rich Folkers	.35	.20	.11
99	Mike Hegan	.35	.20	.11
100	Willie Stargell	3.50	1.75	1.00
101	Expos Team (Gene Mauch)	1.00	.50	.30
102	Joe Decker	.35	.20	.11
103	Rick Miller	.35	.20	.11
104	Bill Madlock	.60	.30	.20
105	Buzz Capra	.35	.20	.11
106	*Mike Hargrove*	.75	.40	.25
107	Jim Barr	.35	.20	.11
108	Tom Hall	.35	.20	.11
109	George Hendrick	.35	.20	.11
110	Wilbur Wood	.35	.20	.11
111	Wayne Garrett	.35	.20	.11
112	Larry Hardy	.35	.20	.11
113	Elliott Maddox	.35	.20	.11
114	Dick Lange	.35	.20	.11
115	Joe Ferguson	.35	.20	.11
116	Lerrin LaGrow	.35	.20	.11
117	Orioles Team (Earl Weaver)	2.25	1.25	.70
118	Mike Anderson	.35	.20	.11
119	Tommy Helms	.35	.20	.11
120	Steve Busby (photo actually Fran Healy)	.35	.20	.11
121	Bill North	.35	.20	.11
122	Al Hrabosky	.35	.20	.11
123	Johnny Briggs	.35	.20	.11
124	Jerry Reuss	.35	.20	.11
125	Ken Singleton	.35	.20	.11
126	Checklist 1-132	.45	.25	.14
127	Glen Borgmann	.35	.20	.11
128	Bill Lee	.35	.20	.11
129	Rick Monday	.35	.20	.11
130	Phil Niekro	2.50	1.25	.70
131	Toby Harrah	.35	.20	.11
132	Randy Moffitt	.35	.20	.11
133	Dan Driessen	.30	.15	.09
134	Ron Hodges	.30	.15	.09
135	Charlie Spikes	.30	.15	.09
136	Jim Mason	.30	.15	.09
137	Terry Forster	.30	.15	.09
138	Del Unser	.30	.15	.09
139	Horacio Pina	.30	.15	.09
140	Steve Garvey	5.00	2.50	1.50
141	Mickey Stanley	.30	.15	.09
142	Bob Reynolds	.30	.15	.09
143	*Cliff Johnson*	.30	.15	.09
144	Jim Wohlford	.30	.15	.09
145	Ken Holtzman	.30	.15	.09
146	Padres Team (John McNamara)	1.00	.50	.30
147	Pedro Garcia	.30	.15	.09
148	Jim Rooker	.30	.15	.09
149	Tim Foli	.30	.15	.09
150	Bob Gibson	4.50	2.25	1.25
151	Steve Brye	.30	.15	.09
152	Mario Guerrero	.30	.15	.09
153	Rick Reuschel	.30	.15	.09
154	Mike Lum	.30	.15	.09
155	Jim Bibby	.30	.15	.09
156	Dave Kingman	.45	.25	.14
157	Pedro Borbon	.30	.15	.09
158	Jerry Grote	.30	.15	.09
159	Steve Arlin	.30	.15	.09
160	Graig Nettles	.30	.15	.09
161	Stan Bahnsen	.30	.15	.09
162	Willie Montanez	.30	.15	.09
163	Jim Brewer	.30	.15	.09
164	Mickey Rivers	.30	.15	.09
165	Doug Rader	.30	.15	.09
166	Woodie Fryman	.30	.15	.09
167	Rich Coggins	.30	.15	.09
168	Bill Greif	.30	.15	.09
169	Cookie Rojas	.30	.15	.09
170	Bert Campaneris	.30	.15	.09
171	Ed Kirkpatrick	.30	.15	.09
172	Red Sox Team (Darrell Johnson)	1.50	.70	.45
173	Steve Rogers	.30	.15	.09
174	Bake McBride	.30	.15	.09
175	Don Money	.30	.15	.09
176	Burt Hooton	.30	.15	.09
177	Vic Correll	.30	.15	.09
178	Cesar Tovar	.30	.15	.09
179	Tom Bradley	.30	.15	.09
180	Joe Morgan	4.00	2.00	1.25
181	Fred Beene	.30	.15	.09
182	Don Hahn	.30	.15	.09
183	Mel Stottlemyre	.30	.15	.09
184	Jorge Orta	.30	.15	.09
185	Steve Carlton	6.00	3.00	1.75
186	Willie Crawford	.30	.15	.09
187	Denny Doyle	.30	.15	.09
188	Tom Griffin	.30	.15	.09
189	1951-MVPs (Yogi Berra, Roy Campanella)	2.00	1.00	.60
190	1952-MVPs (Hank Sauer, Bobby Shantz)	.40	.20	.12
191	1953-MVPs (Roy Campanella, Al Rosen)	1.00	.50	.30
192	1954-MVPs (Yogi Berra, Willie Mays)	3.00	1.50	.90
193	1955-MVPs (Yogi Berra, Roy Campanella)	2.50	1.25	.70
194	1956-MVPs (Mickey Mantle, Don Newcombe)	10.00	5.00	3.00
195	1957-MVPs (Hank Aaron, Mickey Mantle)	17.50	8.75	5.25
196	1958-MVPs (Ernie Banks, Jackie Jensen)	1.00	.50	.30
197	1959-MVPs (Ernie Banks, Nellie Fox)	1.50	.70	.45
198	1960-MVPs (Dick Groat, Roger Maris)	1.50	.70	.45
199	1961-MVPs (Roger Maris, Frank Robinson)	1.50	.70	.45
200	1962-MVPs (Mickey Mantle, Maury Wills)	12.00	6.00	3.50
201	1963-MVPs (Elston Howard, Sandy Koufax)	1.50	.70	.45
202	1964-MVPs (Ken Boyer, Brooks Robinson)	1.25	.60	.40
203	1965-MVPs (Willie Mays, Zoilo Versalles)	1.50	.70	.45
204	1966-MVPs (Roberto Clemente, Frank Robinson)	3.50	1.75	1.00
205	1967-MVPs (Orlando Cepeda, Carl Yastrzemski)	1.25	.60	.40
206	1968-MVPs (Bob Gibson, Denny McLain)	1.25	.60	.40
207	1969-MVPs (Harmon Killebrew, Willie McCovey)	1.25	.60	.40
208	1970-MVPs (Johnny Bench, Boog Powell)	1.25	.60	.40
209	1971-MVPs (Vida Blue, Joe Torre)	.50	.25	.15
210	1972-MVPs (Rich Allen, Johnny Bench)	1.25	.60	.40
211	1973-MVPs (Reggie Jackson, Pete Rose)	5.00	2.50	1.50
212	1974-MVPs (Jeff Burroughs, Steve Garvey)	.60	.30	.20
213	Oscar Gamble	.30	.15	.09
214	Harry Parker	.30	.15	.09
215	Bobby Valentine	.30	.15	.09
216	Giants Team (Wes Westrum)	1.00	.50	.30
217	Lou Piniella	.45	.25	.14
218	Jerry Johnson	.30	.15	.09
219	Ed Herrmann	.30	.15	.09
220	Don Sutton	3.00	1.50	.90
221	Aurelio Rodriquez (Rodriguez)	.30	.15	.09
222	Dan Spillner	.30	.15	.09
223	*Robin Yount*	45.00	22.00	13.50
224	Ramon Hernandez	.30	.15	.09
225	Bob Grich	.30	.15	.09
226	Bill Campbell	.30	.15	.09
227	Bob Watson	.30	.15	.09
228	*George Brett*	95.00	47.00	28.00
229	Barry Foote	.30	.15	.09
230	Catfish Hunter	2.50	1.25	.70
231	Mike Tyson	.30	.15	.09
232	Diego Segui	.30	.15	.09
233	Billy Grabarkewitz	.30	.15	.09
234	Tom Grieve	.30	.15	.09
235	Jack Billingham	.30	.15	.09

236	Angels Team (Dick Williams)	1.00	.50	.30
237	Carl Morton	.30	.15	.09
238	Dave Duncan	.30	.15	.09
239	George Stone	.30	.15	.09
240	Garry Maddox	.30	.15	.09
241	Dick Tidrow	.30	.15	.09
242	Jay Johnstone	.30	.15	.09
243	Jim Kaat	.75	.40	.25
244	Bill Buckner	.30	.15	.09
245	Mickey Lolich	.40	.20	.12
246	Cardinals Team (Red Schoendienst)	1.00	.50	.30
247	Enos Cabell	.30	.15	.09
248	Randy Jones	.30	.15	.09
249	Danny Thompson	.30	.15	.09
250	Ken Brett	.30	.15	.09
251	Fran Healy	.30	.15	.09
252	Fred Scherman	.30	.15	.09
253	Jesus Alou	.30	.15	.09
254	Mike Torrez	.30	.15	.09
255	Dwight Evans	.75	.40	.25
256	Billy Champion	.30	.15	.09
257	Checklist 133-264	.45	.25	.14
258	Dave LaRoche	.30	.15	.09
259	Len Randle	.30	.15	.09
260	Johnny Bench	10.00	5.00	3.00
261	Andy Hassler	.30	.15	.09
262	Rowland Office	.30	.15	.09
263	Jim Perry	.30	.15	.09
264	John Milner	.30	.15	.09
265	Ron Bryant	.30	.15	.09
266	Sandy Alomar	.30	.15	.09
267	Dick Ruthven	.30	.15	.09
268	Hal McRae	.30	.15	.09
269	Doug Rau	.30	.15	.09
270	Ron Fairly	.30	.15	.09
271	Jerry Moses	.30	.15	.09
272	Lynn McGlothen	.30	.15	.09
273	Steve Braun	.30	.15	.09
274	Vicente Romo	.30	.15	.09
275	Paul Blair	.30	.15	.09
276	White Sox Team (Chuck Tanner)	1.00	.50	.30
277	Frank Taveras	.30	.15	.09
278	Paul Lindblad	.30	.15	.09
279	Milt May	.30	.15	.09
280	Carl Yastrzemski	7.00	3.50	2.00
281	Jim Slaton	.30	.15	.09
282	Jerry Morales	.30	.15	.09
283	Steve Foucault	.30	.15	.09
284	Ken Griffey	.50	.25	.15
285	Ellie Rodriguez	.30	.15	.09
286	Mike Jorgensen	.30	.15	.09
287	Roric Harrison	.30	.15	.09
288	Bruce Ellingsen	.30	.15	.09
289	Ken Rudolph	.30	.15	.09
290	Jon Matlack	.30	.15	.09
291	Bill Sudakis	.30	.15	.09
292	Ron Schueler	.30	.15	.09
293	Dick Sharon	.30	.15	.09
294	*Geoff Zahn*	.30	.15	.09
295	Vada Pinson	.45	.25	.14
296	Alan Foster	.30	.15	.09
297	Craig Kusick	.30	.15	.09
298	Johnny Grubb	.30	.15	.09
299	Bucky Dent	.30	.15	.09
300	Reggie Jackson	12.00	6.00	3.50
301	Dave Roberts	.30	.15	.09
302	*Rick Burleson*	.30	.15	.09
303	Grant Jackson	.30	.15	.09
304	Pirates Team (Danny Murtaugh)	1.00	.50	.30
305	Jim Colborn	.30	.15	.09
306	Batting Leaders (Rod Carew, Ralph Garr)	.50	.25	.15
307	Home Run Leaders (Dick Allen, Mike Schmidt)	.90	.45	.25
308	Runs Batted In Leaders (Johnny Bench, Jeff Burroughs)	.75	.40	.25
309	Stolen Base Leaders (Lou Brock, Bill North)	.40	.20	.12
310	Victory Leaders (Jim Hunter, Fergie Jenkins, Andy Messersmith, Phil Niekro)	.75	.40	.25
311	Earned Run Average Leaders (Buzz Capra, Catfish Hunter)	.45	.25	.14
312	Strikeout Leaders (Steve Carlton, Nolan Ryan)	15.00	7.50	4.50
313	Leading Firemen (Terry Forster, Mike Marshall)	.30	.15	.09
314	Buck Martinez	.30	.15	.09
315	Don Kessinger	.30	.15	.09
316	Jackie Brown	.30	.15	.09
317	Joe Lahoud	.30	.15	.09
318	Ernie McAnally	.30	.15	.09
319	Johnny Oates	.30	.15	.09
320	Pete Rose	24.00	12.00	7.25
321	Rudy May	.30	.15	.09
322	Ed Goodson	.30	.15	.09
323	Fred Holdsworth	.30	.15	.09
324	Ed Kranepool	.30	.15	.09
325	Tony Oliva	.45	.25	.14
326	Wayne Twitchell	.30	.15	.09
327	Jerry Hairston	.30	.15	.09
328	Sonny Siebert	.30	.15	.09
329	Ted Kubiak	.30	.15	.09
330	Mike Marshall	.30	.15	.09
331	Indians Team (Frank Robinson)	1.50	.70	.45
332	Fred Kendall	.30	.15	.09
333	Dick Drago	.30	.15	.09
334	*Greg Gross*	.30	.15	.09
335	Jim Palmer	4.00	2.00	1.25
336	Rennie Stennett	.30	.15	.09
337	Kevin Kobel	.30	.15	.09
338	Rick Stelmaszek	.30	.15	.09
339	Jim Fregosi	.30	.15	.09
340	Paul Splittorff	.30	.15	.09
341	Hal Breeden	.30	.15	.09
342	Leroy Stanton	.30	.15	.09
343	Danny Frisella	.30	.15	.09
344	Ben Oglivie	.30	.15	.09
345	Clay Carroll	.30	.15	.09
346	Bobby Darwin	.30	.15	.09
347	Mike Caldwell	.30	.15	.09
348	Tony Muser	.30	.15	.09
349	Ray Sadecki	.30	.15	.09
350	Bobby Murcer	.30	.15	.09
351	Bob Boone	.40	.20	.12
352	Darold Knowles	.30	.15	.09
353	Luis Melendez	.30	.15	.09
354	Dick Bosman	.30	.15	.09
355	Chris Cannizzaro	.30	.15	.09
356	Rico Petrocelli	.30	.15	.09
357	Ken Forsch	.30	.15	.09
358	Al Bumbry	.30	.15	.09
359	Paul Popovich	.30	.15	.09
360	George Scott	.30	.15	.09
361	Dodgers Team (Walter Alston)	1.50	.70	.45
362	Steve Hargan	.30	.15	.09
363	Carmen Fanzone	.30	.15	.09
364	Doug Bird	.30	.15	.09
365	Bob Bailey	.30	.15	.09
366	Ken Sanders	.30	.15	.09
367	Craig Robinson	.30	.15	.09
368	Vic Albury	.30	.15	.09
369	Merv Rettenmund	.30	.15	.09
370	Tom Seaver	9.00	4.50	2.75
371	Gates Brown	.30	.15	.09
372	John D'Acquisto	.30	.15	.09
373	Bill Sharp	.30	.15	.09
374	Eddie Watt	.30	.15	.09
375	Roy White	.30	.15	.09
376	Steve Yeager	.30	.15	.09
377	Tom Hilgendorf	.30	.15	.09
378	Derrel Thomas	.30	.15	.09
379	Bernie Carbo	.30	.15	.09
380	Sal Bando	.30	.15	.09
381	John Curtis	.30	.15	.09
382	Don Baylor	.75	.40	.25
383	Jim York	.30	.15	.09
384	Brewers Team (Del Crandall)	1.00	.50	.30
385	Dock Ellis	.30	.15	.09
386	Checklist 265-396	.45	.25	.14
387	Jim Spencer	.30	.15	.09
388	Steve Stone	.30	.15	.09
389	Tony Solaita	.30	.15	.09
390	Ron Cey	.30	.15	.09
391	Don DeMola	.30	.15	.09
392	Bruce Bochte	.30	.15	.09
393	Gary Gentry	.30	.15	.09
394	Larvell Blanks	.30	.15	.09
395	Bud Harrelson	.30	.15	.09
396	Fred Norman	.30	.15	.09
397	Bill Freehan	.30	.15	.09
398	Elias Sosa	.30	.15	.09
399	Terry Harmon	.30	.15	.09
400	Dick Allen	.80	.40	.25
401	Mike Wallace	.30	.15	.09
402	Bob Tolan	.30	.15	.09
403	Tom Buskey	.30	.15	.09
404	Ted Sizemore	.30	.15	.09
405	John Montague	.30	.15	.09
406	Bob Gallagher	.30	.15	.09
407	*Herb Washington*	.50	.25	.15
408	Clyde Wright	.30	.15	.09
409	Bob Robertson	.30	.15	.09
410	Mike Cueller (Cuellar)	.30	.15	.09
411	George Mitterwald	.30	.15	.09
412	Bill Hands	.30	.15	.09
413	Marty Pattin	.30	.15	.09
414	Manny Mota	.30	.15	.09
415	John Hiller	.30	.15	.09
416	Larry Lintz	.30	.15	.09
417	Skip Lockwood	.30	.15	.09
418	Leo Foster	.30	.15	.09
419	Dave Goltz	.30	.15	.09
420	Larry Bowa	.30	.15	.09
421	Mets Team (Yogi Berra)	2.00	1.00	.60
422	Brian Downing	.30	.15	.09
423	Clay Kirby	.30	.15	.09
424	John Lowenstein	.30	.15	.09
425	Tito Fuentes	.30	.15	.09
426	George Medich	.30	.15	.09
427	Clarence Gaston	.30	.15	.09
428	Dave Hamilton	.30	.15	.09
429	*Jim Dwyer*	.30	.15	.09
430	Luis Tiant	.30	.15	.09
431	Rod Gilbreath	.30	.15	.09
432	Ken Berry	.30	.15	.09
433	Larry Demery	.30	.15	.09
434	Bob Locker	.30	.15	.09
435	Dave Nelson	.30	.15	.09
436	Ken Frailing	.30	.15	.09
437	*Al Cowens*	.30	.15	.09
438	Don Carrithers	.30	.15	.09
439	Ed Brinkman	.30	.15	.09
440	Andy Messersmith	.30	.15	.09
441	Bobby Heise	.30	.15	.09
442	Maximino Leon	.30	.15	.09
443	Twins Team (Frank Quilici)	1.00	.50	.30
444	Gene Garber	.30	.15	.09
445	Felix Millan	.30	.15	.09
446	Bart Johnson	.30	.15	.09
447	Terry Crowley	.30	.15	.09
448	Frank Duffy	.30	.15	.09
449	Charlie Williams	.30	.15	.09
450	Willie McCovey	4.50	2.25	1.25
451	Rick Dempsey	.30	.15	.09
452	Angel Mangual	.30	.15	.09
453	Claude Osteen	.30	.15	.09
454	Doug Griffin	.30	.15	.09
455	Don Wilson	.30	.15	.09
456	Bob Coluccio	.30	.15	.09
457	Mario Mendoza	.30	.15	.09
458	Ross Grimsley	.30	.15	.09
459	A.L. Championships (Frank Robinson)	.80	.40	.25
460	N.L. Championships (Steve Garvey)	.80	.40	.25
461	World Series Game 1 (Reggie Jackson)	1.50	.70	.45
462	World Series Game 2	.80	.40	.25
463	World Series Game 3 (Rollie Fingers)	.90	.45	.25
464	World Series Game 4	.80	.40	.25
465	World Series Game 5	.80	.40	.25
466	A's Do It Again!	.80	.40	.25
467	Ed Halicki	.30	.15	.09
468	Bobby Mitchell	.30	.15	.09
469	Tom Dettore	.30	.15	.09
470	Jeff Burroughs	.30	.15	.09
471	Bob Stinson	.30	.15	.09
472	Bruce Dal Canton	.30	.15	.09
473	Ken McMullen	.30	.15	.09
474	Luke Walker	.30	.15	.09
475	Darrell Evans	.45	.25	.14
476	*Ed Figueroa*	.30	.15	.09
477	Tom Hutton	.30	.15	.09
478	Tom Burgmeier	.30	.15	.09
479	Ken Boswell	.30	.15	.09
480	Carlos May	.30	.15	.09
481	*Will McEnaney*	.30	.15	.09
482	Tom McCraw	.30	.15	.09
483	Steve Ontiveros	.30	.15	.09
484	Glenn Beckert	.30	.15	.09
485	Sparky Lyle	.30	.15	.09
486	Ray Fosse	.30	.15	.09
487	Astros Team (Preston Gomez)	1.00	.50	.30
488	Bill Travers	.30	.15	.09
489	Cecil Cooper	.30	.15	.09
490	Reggie Smith	.30	.15	.09
491	Doyle Alexander	.30	.15	.09
492	Rich Hebner	.30	.15	.09
493	Don Stanhouse	.30	.15	.09
494	*Pete LaCock*	.30	.15	.09
495	Nelson Briles	.30	.15	.09
496	Pepe Frias	.30	.15	.09
497	Jim Nettles	.30	.15	.09
498	Al Downing	.30	.15	.09
499	Marty Perez	.30	.15	.09
500	Nolan Ryan	45.00	22.00	13.50
501	Bill Robinson	.30	.15	.09
502	Pat Bourque	.30	.15	.09
503	Fred Stanley	.30	.15	.09
504	Buddy Bradford	.30	.15	.09
505	Chris Speier	.30	.15	.09
506	Leron Lee	.30	.15	.09
507	Tom Carroll	.30	.15	.09
508	Bob Hansen	.30	.15	.09
509	Dave Hilton	.30	.15	.09
510	Vida Blue	.30	.15	.09
511	Rangers Team (Billy Martin)	1.50	.70	.45
512	Larry Milbourne	.30	.15	.09
513	Dick Pole	.30	.15	.09
514	Jose Cruz	.30	.15	.09
515	Manny Sanguillen	.30	.15	.09
516	Don Hood	.30	.15	.09
517	Checklist 397-528	.45	.25	.14
518	Leo Cardenas	.30	.15	.09
519	Jim Todd	.30	.15	.09
520	Amos Otis	.30	.15	.09
521	Dennis Blair	.30	.15	.09
522	Gary Sutherland	.30	.15	.09
523	Tom Paciorek	.30	.15	.09
524	John Doherty	.30	.15	.09
525	Tom House	.30	.15	.09
526	Larry Hisle	.30	.15	.09
527	Mac Scarce	.30	.15	.09
528	Eddie Leon	.30	.15	.09
529	Gary Thomasson	.30	.15	.09
530	Gaylord Perry	2.50	1.25	.70
531	Reds Team (Sparky Anderson)	3.00	1.50	.90
532	Gorman Thomas	.30	.15	.09
533	Rudy Meoli	.30	.15	.09
534	Alex Johnson	.30	.15	.09
535	Gene Tenace	.30	.15	.09
536	Bob Moose	.30	.15	.09
537	Tommy Harper	.30	.15	.09
538	Duffy Dyer	.30	.15	.09
539	Jesse Jefferson	.30	.15	.09
540	Lou Brock	4.00	2.00	1.25
541	Roger Metzger	.30	.15	.09
542	Pete Broberg	.30	.15	.09
543	Larry Biittner	.30	.15	.09
544	Steve Mingori	.30	.15	.09
545	Billy Williams	4.00	2.00	1.25
546	John Knox	.30	.15	.09
547	Von Joshua	.30	.15	.09
548	Charlie Sands	.30	.15	.09
549	Bill Butler	.30	.15	.09
550	Ralph Garr	.30	.15	.09
551	Larry Christenson	.30	.15	.09
552	Jack Brohamer	.30	.15	.09
553	John Boccabella	.30	.15	.09
554	Rich Gossage	.40	.20	.12
555	Al Oliver	.45	.25	.14
556	Tim Johnson	.30	.15	.09
557	Larry Gura	.30	.15	.09
558	Dave Roberts	.30	.15	.09
559	Bob Montgomery	.30	.15	.09
560	Tony Perez	4.00	2.00	1.25
561	A's Team (Alvin Dark)	1.00	.50	.30
562	Gary Nolan	.30	.15	.09
563	Wilbur Howard	.30	.15	.09
564	Tommy Davis	.30	.15	.09
565	Joe Torre	.75	.40	.25
566	Ray Burris	.30	.15	.09
567	*Jim Sundberg*	.45	.25	.14

568	Dale Murray	.30	.15	.09
569	Frank White	.30	.15	.09
570	Jim Wynn	.30	.15	.09
571	Dave Lemanczyk	.30	.15	.09
572	Roger Nelson	.30	.15	.09
573	Orlando Pena	.30	.15	.09
574	Tony Taylor	.30	.15	.09
575	Gene Clines	.30	.15	.09
576	Phil Roof	.30	.15	.09
577	John Morris	.30	.15	.09
578	Dave Tomlin	.30	.15	.09
579	Skip Pitlock	.30	.15	.09
580	Frank Robinson	6.50	3.25	2.00
581	Darrel Chaney	.30	.15	.09
582	Eduardo Rodriguez	.30	.15	.09
583	Andy Etchebarren	.30	.15	.09
584	Mike Garman	.30	.15	.09
585	Chris Chambliss	.30	.15	.09
586	Tim McCarver	.35	.20	.11
587	Chris Ward	.30	.15	.09
588	Rick Auerbach	.30	.15	.09
589	Braves Team (Clyde King)	1.00	.50	.30
590	Cesar Cedeno	.30	.15	.09
591	Glenn Abbott	.30	.15	.09
592	Balor Moore	.30	.15	.09
593	Gene Lamont	.30	.15	.09
594	Jim Fuller	.30	.15	.09
595	Joe Niekro	.30	.15	.09
596	Ollie Brown	.30	.15	.09
597	Winston Llenas	.30	.15	.09
598	Bruce Kison	.30	.15	.09
599	Nate Colbert	.30	.15	.09
600	Rod Carew	6.50	3.25	2.00
601	Juan Beniquez	.30	.15	.09
602	John Vukovich	.30	.15	.09
603	Lew Krausse	.30	.15	.09
604	Oscar Zamora	.30	.15	.09
605	John Ellis	.30	.15	.09
606	Bruce Miller	.30	.15	.09
607	Jim Holt	.30	.15	.09
608	Gene Michael	.30	.15	.09
609	Ellie Hendricks	.30	.15	.09
610	Ron Hunt	.30	.15	.09
611	Yankees Team (Bill Virdon)	1.50	.70	.45
612	Terry Hughes	.30	.15	.09
613	Bill Parsons	.30	.15	.09
614	Rookie Pitchers (Jack Kucek, Dyar Miller, Vern Ruhle, Paul Siebert)	.30	.15	.09
615	Rookie Pitchers (Pat Darcy), *(Dennis Leonard)*, *(Tom Underwood*, Hank Webb)	.30	.15	.09
616	Rookie Outfielders *(Dave Augustine)*, *(Pepe Mangual)*, *(Jim Rice)*, *(John Scott)*	10.00	5.00	3.00
617	Rookie Infielders (Mike Cubbage), *(Doug DeCinces*, Reggie Sanders, Manny Trillo)	1.75	.90	.50
618	Rookie Pitchers *(Jamie Easterly*, Tom Johnson), *(Scott McGregor)*, *(Rick Rhoden)*	2.25	1.25	.70
619	Rookie Outfielders (Benny Ayala, Nyls Nyman, Tommy Smith, Jerry Turner)	.30	.15	.09
620	Rookie Catchers-Outfielders *(Gary Carter)*, *(Marc Hill)*, *(Danny Meyer)*, *(Leon Roberts)*	22.00	11.00	6.50
621	Rookie Pitchers *(John Denny)*, *(Rawly Eastwick)*, *(Jim Kern*, Juan Veintidos)	.60	.30	.20
622	Rookie Outfielders *(Ed Armbrister)*, *(Fred Lynn)*, *(Tom Poquette)*, *(Terry Whitfield)*	6.00	3.00	1.75
623	Rookie Infielders *(Phil Garner)*, *(Keith Hernandez)*, *(Bob Sheldon)*, *(Tom Veryzer)*	4.00	2.00	1.25
624	Rookie Pitchers (Doug Konieczny), *(Gary Lavelle*, Jim Otten, Eddie Solomon)	.30	.15	.09
625	Boog Powell	.45	.25	.14
626	Larry Haney	.30	.15	.09
627	Tom Walker	.30	.15	.09
628	*Ron LeFlore*	.80	.40	.25
629	Joe Hoerner	.30	.15	.09
630	Greg Luzinski	.30	.15	.09
631	Lee Lacy	.30	.15	.09
632	Morris Nettles	.30	.15	.09
633	Paul Casanova	.30	.15	.09
634	Cy Acosta	.30	.15	.09
635	Chuck Dobson	.30	.15	.09
636	Charlie Moore	.30	.15	.09
637	Ted Martinez	.30	.15	.09
638	Cubs Team (Jim Marshall)	1.00	.50	.30
639	Steve Kline	.30	.15	.09
640	Harmon Killebrew	6.00	3.00	1.75
641	Jim Northrup	.30	.15	.09
642	Mike Phillips	.30	.15	.09
643	Brent Strom	.30	.15	.09
644	Bill Fahey	.30	.15	.09
645	Danny Cater	.30	.15	.09
646	Checklist 529-660	.45	.25	.14
647	*Claudell Washington*	.80	.40	.25
648	Dave Pagan	.30	.15	.09
649	Jack Heidemann	.30	.15	.09
650	Dave May	.30	.15	.09
651	John Morlan	.30	.15	.09
652	Lindy McDaniel	.30	.15	.09
653	Lee Richards	.30	.15	.09
654	Jerry Terrell	.30	.15	.09
655	Rico Carty	.30	.15	.09
656	Bill Plummer	.30	.15	.09
657	Bob Oliver	.30	.15	.09
658	Vic Harris	.30	.15	.09
659	Bob Apodaca	.30	.15	.09
660	Hank Aaron	20.00	10.00	6.00

1975 Topps Mini

This popular set was actually a test issue to see how collectors would react to cards which were 20% smaller than the standard 2-1/2" x 3-1/2". Other than their 2-1/4" x 3-1/8" size, they are exactly the same, front and back as the regular-issue '75 Topps. The experimental cards were sold in Michigan and on the West Coast, where they were quickly gobbled up by collectors, dealers and speculators. While the minis for many years enjoyed a 2X premium over regular 1975 Topps values, that differential has shrunk in recent years.

	NM	EX	VG
Complete Set (660):	800.00	400.00	240.00
Common Player:	.50	.25	.15
(Stars and rookies valued about 125% to 150% of regular 1975 Topps version)			

1975 Topps Team Checklist Sheet

Via a mail-in wrapper redemption, collectors could receive an uncut sheet of the 24 team photo/checklist cards from the 1975 Topps baseball set. Measuring about 10-1/2" x 20-1/8", the sheet could be cut into individual team cards of standard size.

	NM	EX	VG
Complete Sheet:	25.00	12.50	7.50

1976 Topps

These 2-1/2" x 3-1/2" cards begin a design trend for Topps. The focus was more on the photo quality than in past years with a corresponding trend toward simplicity in the borders. The front of the card has the player's name and team in two strips while his position is in the lower-left corner under a drawing of a player representing that position. The backs have a bat and ball with the card number on the left; statistics and personal information and career highlights on the right. The 660-card set features a number of specialty sets including record-setting performances, statistical leaders, playoff and World Series highlights, the Sporting News All-Time All-Stars and father and son combinations.

		NM	EX	VG
Complete Set (660):		275.00	135.00	85.00
Common Player:		.30	.15	.09
Wax Box:		850.00		
1	Hank Aaron (Record Breaker)	15.00	7.50	4.50
2	Bobby Bonds (Record Breaker)	.30	.15	.09
3	Mickey Lolich (Record Breaker)	.30	.15	.09
4	Dave Lopes (Record Breaker)	.30	.15	.09
5	Tom Seaver (Record Breaker)	2.00	1.00	.60
6	Rennie Stennett (Record Breaker)	.30	.15	.09
7	Jim Umbarger	.30	.15	.09
8	Tito Fuentes	.30	.15	.09
9	Paul Lindblad	.30	.15	.09
10	Lou Brock	3.50	1.75	1.00
11	Jim Hughes	.30	.15	.09
12	Richie Zisk	.30	.15	.09
13	Johnny Wockenfuss	.30	.15	.09
14	Gene Garber	.30	.15	.09
15	George Scott	.30	.15	.09
16	Bob Apodaca	.30	.15	.09
17	Yankees Team (Billy Martin)	1.25	.60	.40
18	Dale Murray	.30	.15	.09
19	George Brett	30.00	15.00	9.00
20	Bob Watson	.30	.15	.09
21	Dave LaRoche	.30	.15	.09
22	Bill Russell	.30	.15	.09
23	Brian Downing	.30	.15	.09
24	Cesar Geronimo	.30	.15	.09
25	Mike Torrez	.30	.15	.09
26	Andy Thornton	.30	.15	.09
27	Ed Figueroa	.30	.15	.09
28	Dusty Baker	.60	.30	.20
29	Rick Burleson	.30	.15	.09
30	*John Montefusco*	.30	.15	.09
31	Len Randle	.30	.15	.09
32	Danny Frisella	.30	.15	.09
33	Bill North	.30	.15	.09
34	Mike Garman	.30	.15	.09
35	Tony Oliva	.40	.20	.12
36	Frank Taveras	.30	.15	.09
37	John Hiller	.30	.15	.09
38	Garry Maddox	.30	.15	.09
39	Pete Broberg	.30	.15	.09
40	Dave Kingman	.35	.20	.11
41	*Tippy Martinez*	.30	.15	.09
42	Barry Foote	.30	.15	.09
43	Paul Splittorff	.30	.15	.09
44	Doug Rader	.30	.15	.09
45	Boog Powell	.35	.20	.11
46	Dodgers Team (Walter Alston)	1.00	.50	.30
47	Jesse Jefferson	.30	.15	.09
48	Dave Concepcion	.30	.15	.09
49	Dave Duncan	.30	.15	.09
50	Fred Lynn	.90	.45	.25
51	Ray Burris	.30	.15	.09
52	Dave Chalk	.30	.15	.09
53	Mike Beard	.30	.15	.09
54	Dave Rader	.30	.15	.09
55	Gaylord Perry	1.75	.90	.50
56	Bob Tolan	.30	.15	.09
57	Phil Garner	.30	.15	.09
58	Ron Reed	.30	.15	.09
59	Larry Hisle	.30	.15	.09
60	Jerry Reuss	.30	.15	.09
61	Ron LeFlore	.30	.15	.09
62	Johnny Oates	.30	.15	.09
63	Bobby Darwin	.30	.15	.09
64	Jerry Koosman	.30	.15	.09
65	Chris Chambliss	.30	.15	.09
66	Father & Son (Buddy Bell, Gus Bell)	.30	.15	.09
67	Father & Son (Bob Boone, Ray Boone)	.40	.20	.12
68	Father & Son (Joe Coleman, Joe Coleman, Jr.)	.30	.15	.09
69	Father & Son (Jim Hegan, Mike Hegan)	.30	.15	.09
70	Father & Son (Roy Smalley, III, Roy Smalley, Jr.)	.30	.15	.09
71	Steve Rogers	.30	.15	.09
72	Hal McRae	.30	.15	.09
73	Orioles Team (Earl Weaver)	.90	.45	.25
74	Oscar Gamble	.30	.15	.09
75	Larry Dierker	.30	.15	.09
76	Willie Crawford	.30	.15	.09
77	Pedro Borbon	.30	.15	.09
78	Cecil Cooper	.30	.15	.09
79	Jerry Morales	.30	.15	.09
80	Jim Kaat	.60	.30	.20
81	Darrell Evans	.40	.20	.12
82	Von Joshua	.30	.15	.09
83	Jim Spencer	.30	.15	.09
84	Brent Strom	.30	.15	.09
85	Mickey Rivers	.30	.15	.09
86	Mike Tyson	.30	.15	.09
87	Tom Burgmeier	.30	.15	.09
88	Duffy Dyer	.30	.15	.09
89	Vern Ruhle	.30	.15	.09
90	Sal Bando	.30	.15	.09
91	Tom Hutton	.30	.15	.09
92	Eduardo Rodriguez	.30	.15	.09
93	Mike Phillips	.30	.15	.09
94	Jim Dwyer	.30	.15	.09
95	Brooks Robinson	5.00	2.50	1.50
96	Doug Bird	.30	.15	.09
97	Wilbur Howard	.30	.15	.09
98	*Dennis Eckersley*	20.00	10.00	6.00
99	Lee Lacy	.30	.15	.09
100	Catfish Hunter	2.00	1.00	.60
101	Pete LaCock	.30	.15	.09
102	Jim Willoughby	.30	.15	.09
103	Biff Pocoroba	.30	.15	.09
104	Reds Team (Sparky Anderson)	1.00	.50	.30
105	Gary Lavelle	.30	.15	.09
106	Tom Grieve	.30	.15	.09
107	Dave Roberts	.30	.15	.09
108	Don Kirkwood	.30	.15	.09
109	Larry Lintz	.30	.15	.09
110	Carlos May	.30	.15	.09
111	Danny Thompson	.30	.15	.09
112	*Kent Tekulve*	.60	.30	.20
113	Gary Sutherland	.30	.15	.09
114	Jay Johnstone	.30	.15	.09
115	Ken Holtzman	.30	.15	.09
116	Charlie Moore	.30	.15	.09
117	Mike Jorgensen	.30	.15	.09
118	Red Sox Team (Darrell Johnson)	.50	.25	.15
119	Checklist 1-132	.35	.20	.11
120	Rusty Staub	.35	.20	.11
121	Tony Solaita	.30	.15	.09
122	Mike Cosgrove	.30	.15	.09
123	Walt Williams	.30	.15	.09
124	Doug Rau	.30	.15	.09
125	Don Baylor	.60	.30	.20
126	Tom Dettore	.30	.15	.09
127	Larvell Blanks	.30	.15	.09
128	Ken Griffey	.35	.20	.11
129	Andy Etchebarren	.30	.15	.09
130	Luis Tiant	.30	.15	.09
131	Bill Stein	.30	.15	.09

132	Don Hood	.30	.15	.09
133	Gary Matthews	.30	.15	.09
134	Mike Ivie	.30	.15	.09
135	Bake McBride	.30	.15	.09
136	Dave Goltz	.30	.15	.09
137	Bill Robinson	.30	.15	.09
138	Lerrin LaGrow	.30	.15	.09
139	Gorman Thomas	.30	.15	.09
140	Vida Blue	.30	.15	.09
141	*Larry Parrish*	.50	.25	.15
142	Dick Drago	.30	.15	.09
143	Jerry Grote	.30	.15	.09
144	Al Fitzmorris	.30	.15	.09
145	Larry Bowa	.30	.15	.09
146	George Medich	.30	.15	.09
147	Astros Team (Bill Virdon)	.50	.25	.15
148	Stan Thomas	.30	.15	.09
149	Tommy Davis	.30	.15	.09
150	Steve Garvey	3.00	1.50	.90
151	Bill Bonham	.30	.15	.09
152	Leroy Stanton	.30	.15	.09
153	Buzz Capra	.30	.15	.09
154	Bucky Dent	.30	.15	.09
155	Jack Billingham	.30	.15	.09
156	Rico Carty	.30	.15	.09
157	Mike Caldwell	.30	.15	.09
158	Ken Reitz	.30	.15	.09
159	Jerry Terrell	.30	.15	.09
160	Dave Winfield	15.00	7.50	4.50
161	Bruce Kison	.30	.15	.09
162	Jack Pierce	.30	.15	.09
163	Jim Slaton	.30	.15	.09
164	Pepe Mangual	.30	.15	.09
165	Gene Tenace	.30	.15	.09
166	Skip Lockwood	.30	.15	.09
167	Freddie Patek	.30	.15	.09
168	Tom Hilgendorf	.30	.15	.09
169	Graig Nettles	.30	.15	.09
170	Rick Wise	.30	.15	.09
171	Greg Gross	.30	.15	.09
172	Rangers Team (Frank Lucchesi)	.50	.25	.15
173	Steve Swisher	.30	.15	.09
174	Charlie Hough	.30	.15	.09
175	Ken Singleton	.30	.15	.09
176	Dick Lange	.30	.15	.09
177	Marty Perez	.30	.15	.09
178	Tom Buskey	.30	.15	.09
179	George Foster	.45	.25	.14
180	Rich Gossage	.90	.45	.25
181	Willie Montanez	.30	.15	.09
182	Harry Rasmussen	.30	.15	.09
183	Steve Braun	.30	.15	.09
184	Bill Greif	.30	.15	.09
185	Dave Parker	1.00	.50	.30
186	Tom Walker	.30	.15	.09
187	Pedro Garcia	.30	.15	.09
188	Fred Scherman	.30	.15	.09
189	Claudell Washington	.30	.15	.09
190	Jon Matlack	.30	.15	.09
191	N.L. Batting Leaders (Bill Madlock, Manny Sanguillen, Ted Simmons)	.35	.20	.11
192	A.L. Batting Leaders (Rod Carew, Fred Lynn, Thurman Munson)	1.00	.50	.30
193	N.L. Home Run Leaders (Dave Kingman, Greg Luzinski, Mike Schmidt)	1.00	.50	.30
194	A.L. Home Run Leaders (Reggie Jackson, John Mayberry, George Scott)	1.00	.50	.30
195	N.L. RBI Leaders (Johnny Bench, Greg Luzinski, Tony Perez)	1.00	.50	.30
196	A.L. RBI Leaders (Fred Lynn, John Mayberry, George Scott)	.35	.20	.11
197	N.L. Stolen Base Leaders (Lou Brock, Dave Lopes, Joe Morgan)	.40	.20	.12
198	A.L. Stolen Base Leaders (Amos Otis, Mickey Rivers, Claudell Washington)	.30	.15	.09
199	N.L. Victory Leaders (Randy Jones, Andy Messersmith, Tom Seaver)	1.00	.50	.30
200	A.L. Victory Leaders (Vida Blue, Catfish Hunter, Jim Palmer)	.75	.40	.25
201	N.L. ERA Leaders (Randy Jones, Andy Messersmith, Tom Seaver)	1.00	.50	.30
202	A.L. ERA Leaders (Dennis Eckersley, Catfish Hunter, Jim Palmer)	3.50	1.75	1.00
203	N.L. Strikeout Leaders (Andy Messersmith, John Montefusco, Tom Seaver)	1.00	.50	.30
204	A.L. Strikeout Leaders (Bert Blyleven, Gaylord Perry, Frank Tanana)	.60	.30	.20
205	Major League Leading Firemen (Rich Gossage, Al Hrabosky)	.30	.15	.09
206	Manny Trillo	.30	.15	.09
207	Andy Hassler	.30	.15	.09
208	Mike Lum	.30	.15	.09
209	Alan Ashby	.30	.15	.09
210	Lee May	.30	.15	.09
211	Clay Carroll	.30	.15	.09
212	Pat Kelly	.30	.15	.09
213	Dave Heaverlo	.30	.15	.09
214	Eric Soderholm	.30	.15	.09
215	Reggie Smith	.30	.15	.09
216	Expos Team (Karl Kuehl)	.50	.25	.15
217	Dave Freisleben	.30	.15	.09
218	John Knox	.30	.15	.09
219	Tom Murphy	.30	.15	.09
220	Manny Sanguillen	.30	.15	.09
221	Jim Todd	.30	.15	.09
222	Wayne Garrett	.30	.15	.09
223	Ollie Brown	.30	.15	.09
224	Jim York	.30	.15	.09
225	Roy White	.30	.15	.09
226	Jim Sundberg	.30	.15	.09
227	Oscar Zamora	.30	.15	.09
228	John Hale	.30	.15	.09
229	*Jerry Remy*	.30	.15	.09
230	Carl Yastrzemski	5.00	2.50	1.50
231	Tom House	.30	.15	.09
232	Frank Duffy	.30	.15	.09
233	Grant Jackson	.30	.15	.09
234	Mike Sadek	.30	.15	.09
235	Bert Blyleven	.30	.15	.09
236	Royals Team (Whitey Herzog)	.80	.40	.25
237	Dave Hamilton	.30	.15	.09
238	Larry Biittner	.30	.15	.09
239	John Curtis	.30	.15	.09
240	Pete Rose	15.00	7.50	4.50
241	Hector Torres	.30	.15	.09
242	Dan Meyer	.30	.15	.09
243	Jim Rooker	.30	.15	.09
244	Bill Sharp	.30	.15	.09
245	Felix Millan	.30	.15	.09
246	Cesar Tovar	.30	.15	.09
247	Terry Harmon	.30	.15	.09
248	Dick Tidrow	.30	.15	.09
249	Cliff Johnson	.30	.15	.09
250	Fergie Jenkins	1.75	.90	.50
251	Rick Monday	.30	.15	.09
252	Tim Nordbrook	.30	.15	.09
253	Bill Buckner	.30	.15	.09
254	Rudy Meoli	.30	.15	.09
255	Fritz Peterson	.30	.15	.09
256	Rowland Office	.30	.15	.09
257	Ross Grimsley	.30	.15	.09
258	Nyls Nyman	.30	.15	.09
259	Darrel Chaney	.30	.15	.09
260	Steve Busby	.30	.15	.09
261	Gary Thomasson	.30	.15	.09
262	Checklist 133-264	.35	.20	.11
263	*Lyman Bostock*	.60	.30	.20
264	Steve Renko	.30	.15	.09
265	Willie Davis	.30	.15	.09
266	Alan Foster	.30	.15	.09
267	Aurelio Rodriguez	.30	.15	.09
268	Del Unser	.30	.15	.09
269	Rick Austin	.30	.15	.09
270	Willie Stargell	2.50	1.25	.70
271	Jim Lonborg	.30	.15	.09
272	Rick Dempsey	.30	.15	.09
273	Joe Niekro	.30	.15	.09
274	Tommy Harper	.30	.15	.09
275	*Rick Manning*	.35	.20	.11
276	Mickey Scott	.30	.15	.09
277	Cubs Team (Jim Marshall)	.50	.25	.15
278	Bernie Carbo	.30	.15	.09
279	Roy Howell	.30	.15	.09
280	Burt Hooton	.30	.15	.09
281	Dave May	.30	.15	.09
282	Dan Osborn	.30	.15	.09
283	Merv Rettenmund	.30	.15	.09
284	Steve Ontiveros	.30	.15	.09
285	Mike Cuellar	.30	.15	.09
286	Jim Wohlford	.30	.15	.09
287	Pete Mackanin	.30	.15	.09
288	Bill Campbell	.30	.15	.09
289	Enzo Hernandez	.30	.15	.09
290	Ted Simmons	.30	.15	.09
291	Ken Sanders	.30	.15	.09
292	Leon Roberts	.30	.15	.09
293	Bill Castro	.30	.15	.09
294	Ed Kirkpatrick	.30	.15	.09
295	Dave Cash	.30	.15	.09
296	Pat Dobson	.30	.15	.09
297	Roger Metzger	.30	.15	.09
298	Dick Bosman	.30	.15	.09
299	Champ Summers	.30	.15	.09
300	Johnny Bench	6.00	3.00	1.75
301	Jackie Brown	.30	.15	.09
302	Rick Miller	.30	.15	.09
303	Steve Foucault	.30	.15	.09
304	Angels Team (Dick Williams)	.50	.25	.15
305	Andy Messersmith	.30	.15	.09
306	Rod Gilbreath	.30	.15	.09
307	Al Bumbry	.30	.15	.09
308	Jim Barr	.30	.15	.09
309	Bill Melton	.30	.15	.09
310	Randy Jones	.30	.15	.09
311	Cookie Rojas	.30	.15	.09
312	Don Carrithers	.30	.15	.09
313	*Dan Ford*	.30	.15	.09
314	Ed Kranepool	.30	.15	.09
315	Al Hrabosky	.30	.15	.09
316	Robin Yount	15.00	7.50	4.50
317	*John Candelaria*	2.00	1.00	.60
318	Bob Boone	.30	.15	.09
319	Larry Gura	.30	.15	.09
320	Willie Horton	.30	.15	.09
321	Jose Cruz	.30	.15	.09
322	Glenn Abbott	.30	.15	.09
323	Rob Sperring	.30	.15	.09
324	Jim Bibby	.30	.15	.09
325	Tony Perez	4.50	2.25	1.25
326	Dick Pole	.30	.15	.09
327	Dave Moates	.30	.15	.09
328	Carl Morton	.30	.15	.09
329	Joe Ferguson	.30	.15	.09
330	Nolan Ryan	30.00	15.00	9.00
331	Padres Team (John McNamara)	.50	.25	.15
332	Charlie Williams	.30	.15	.09
333	Bob Coluccio	.30	.15	.09
334	Dennis Leonard	.30	.15	.09
335	Bob Grich	.30	.15	.09
336	Vic Albury	.30	.15	.09
337	Bud Harrelson	.30	.15	.09
338	Bob Bailey	.30	.15	.09
339	John Denny	.30	.15	.09
340	Jim Rice	2.00	1.00	.60
341	Lou Gehrig (All Time 1B)	9.00	4.50	2.75
342	Rogers Hornsby (All Time 2B)	1.00	.50	.30
343	Pie Traynor (All Time 3B)	.30	.15	.09
344	Honus Wagner (All Time SS)	2.25	1.25	.70
345	Babe Ruth (All Time OF)	11.00	5.50	3.25
346	Ty Cobb (All Time OF)	5.00	2.50	1.50
347	Ted Williams (All Time OF)	8.00	4.00	2.50
348	Mickey Cochrane (All Time C)	.30	.15	.09
349	Walter Johnson (All Time RHP)	.75	.40	.25
350	Lefty Grove (All Time LHP)	.35	.20	.11
351	Randy Hundley	.30	.15	.09
352	Dave Giusti	.30	.15	.09
353	*Sixto Lezcano*	.30	.15	.09
354	Ron Blomberg	.30	.15	.09
355	Steve Carlton	4.00	2.00	1.25
356	Ted Martinez	.30	.15	.09
357	Ken Forsch	.30	.15	.09
358	Buddy Bell	.30	.15	.09
359	Rick Reuschel	.30	.15	.09
360	Jeff Burroughs	.30	.15	.09
361	Tigers Team (Ralph Houk)	.50	.25	.15
362	Will McEnaney	.30	.15	.09
363	*Dave Collins*	.40	.20	.12
364	Elias Sosa	.30	.15	.09
365	Carlton Fisk	4.00	2.00	1.25
366	Bobby Valentine	.30	.15	.09
367	Bruce Miller	.30	.15	.09
368	Wilbur Wood	.30	.15	.09
369	Frank White	.30	.15	.09
370	Ron Cey	.30	.15	.09
371	Ellie Hendricks	.30	.15	.09
372	Rick Baldwin	.30	.15	.09
373	Johnny Briggs	.30	.15	.09
374	Dan Warthen	.30	.15	.09
375	Ron Fairly	.30	.15	.09
376	Rich Hebner	.30	.15	.09
377	Mike Hegan	.30	.15	.09
378	Steve Stone	.30	.15	.09
379	Ken Boswell	.30	.15	.09
380	Bobby Bonds	.40	.20	.12
381	Denny Doyle	.30	.15	.09
382	Matt Alexander	.30	.15	.09
383	John Ellis	.30	.15	.09
384	Phillies Team (Danny Ozark)	.80	.40	.25
385	Mickey Lolich	.35	.20	.11
386	Ed Goodson	.30	.15	.09
387	Mike Miley	.30	.15	.09
388	Stan Perzanowski	.30	.15	.09
389	Glenn Adams	.30	.15	.09
390	Don Gullett	.30	.15	.09
391	Jerry Hairston	.30	.15	.09
392	Checklist 265-396	.35	.20	.11
393	Paul Mitchell	.30	.15	.09
394	Fran Healy	.30	.15	.09
395	Jim Wynn	.30	.15	.09
396	Bill Lee	.30	.15	.09
397	Tim Foli	.30	.15	.09
398	Dave Tomlin	.30	.15	.09
399	Luis Melendez	.30	.15	.09
400	Rod Carew	4.00	2.00	1.25
401	Ken Brett	.30	.15	.09
402	Don Money	.30	.15	.09
403	Geoff Zahn	.30	.15	.09
404	Enos Cabell	.30	.15	.09
405	Rollie Fingers	2.00	1.00	.60
406	Ed Herrmann	.30	.15	.09
407	Tom Underwood	.30	.15	.09
408	Charlie Spikes	.30	.15	.09
409	Dave Lemanczyk	.30	.15	.09
410	Ralph Garr	.30	.15	.09
411	Bill Singer	.30	.15	.09
412	Toby Harrah	.30	.15	.09
413	Pete Varney	.30	.15	.09
414	Wayne Garland	.30	.15	.09
415	Vada Pinson	.40	.20	.12
416	Tommy John	.60	.30	.20
417	Gene Clines	.30	.15	.09
418	Jose Morales	.30	.15	.09
419	Reggie Cleveland	.30	.15	.09
420	Joe Morgan	4.00	2.00	1.25
421	A's Team	.50	.25	.15
422	Johnny Grubb	.30	.15	.09
423	Ed Halicki	.30	.15	.09
424	Phil Roof	.30	.15	.09
425	Rennie Stennett	.30	.15	.09
426	Bob Forsch	.30	.15	.09
427	Kurt Bevacqua	.30	.15	.09
428	Jim Crawford	.30	.15	.09
429	Fred Stanley	.30	.15	.09
430	Jose Cardenal	.30	.15	.09
431	Dick Ruthven	.30	.15	.09
432	Tom Veryzer	.30	.15	.09
433	Rick Waits	.30	.15	.09
434	Morris Nettles	.30	.15	.09
435	Phil Niekro	2.00	1.00	.60
436	Bill Fahey	.30	.15	.09
437	Terry Forster	.30	.15	.09
438	Doug DeCinces	.30	.15	.09
439	Rick Rhoden	.30	.15	.09
440	John Mayberry	.30	.15	.09
441	Gary Carter	5.00	2.50	1.50
442	Hank Webb	.30	.15	.09
443	Giants Team	.50	.25	.15
444	Gary Nolan	.30	.15	.09
445	Rico Petrocelli	.30	.15	.09
446	Larry Haney	.30	.15	.09
447	Gene Locklear	.30	.15	.09
448	Tom Johnson	.30	.15	.09
449	Bob Robertson	.30	.15	.09

450	Jim Palmer	3.50	1.75	1.00
451	Buddy Bradford	.30	.15	.09
452	Tom Hausman	.30	.15	.09
453	Lou Piniella	.35	.20	.11
454	Tom Griffin	.30	.15	.09
455	Dick Allen	.50	.25	.15
456	Joe Coleman	.30	.15	.09
457	Ed Crosby	.30	.15	.09
458	Earl Williams	.30	.15	.09
459	Jim Brewer	.30	.15	.09
460	Cesar Cedeno	.30	.15	.09
461	NL & AL Championships	.50	.25	.15
462	1975 World Series	.50	.25	.15
463	Steve Hargan	.30	.15	.09
464	Ken Henderson	.30	.15	.09
465	Mike Marshall	.30	.15	.09
466	Bob Stinson	.30	.15	.09
467	Woodie Fryman	.30	.15	.09
468	Jesus Alou	.30	.15	.09
469	Rawly Eastwick	.30	.15	.09
470	Bobby Murcer	.30	.15	.09
471	Jim Burton	.30	.15	.09
472	Bob Davis	.30	.15	.09
473	Paul Blair	.30	.15	.09
474	Ray Corbin	.30	.15	.09
475	Joe Rudi	.30	.15	.09
476	Bob Moose	.30	.15	.09
477	Indians Team (Frank Robinson)	1.00	.50	.30
478	Lynn McGlothen	.30	.15	.09
479	Bobby Mitchell	.30	.15	.09
480	Mike Schmidt	22.00	11.00	6.50
481	Rudy May	.30	.15	.09
482	Tim Hosley	.30	.15	.09
483	Mickey Stanley	.30	.15	.09
484	Eric Raich	.30	.15	.09
485	Mike Hargrove	.30	.15	.09
486	Bruce Dal Canton	.30	.15	.09
487	Leron Lee	.30	.15	.09
488	Claude Osteen	.30	.15	.09
489	Skip Jutze	.30	.15	.09
490	Frank Tanana	.30	.15	.09
491	Terry Crowley	.30	.15	.09
492	Marty Pattin	.30	.15	.09
493	Derrel Thomas	.30	.15	.09
494	Craig Swan	.30	.15	.09
495	Nate Colbert	.30	.15	.09
496	Juan Beniquez	.30	.15	.09
497	Joe McIntosh	.30	.15	.09
498	Glenn Borgmann	.30	.15	.09
499	Mario Guerrero	.30	.15	.09
500	Reggie Jackson	11.00	5.50	3.25
501	Billy Champion	.30	.15	.09
502	Tim McCarver	.40	.20	.12
503	Elliott Maddox	.30	.15	.09
504	Pirates Team (Danny Murtaugh)	.50	.25	.15
505	Mark Belanger	.30	.15	.09
506	George Mitterwald	.30	.15	.09
507	Ray Bare	.30	.15	.09
508	*Duane Kuiper*	.30	.15	.09
509	Bill Hands	.30	.15	.09
510	Amos Otis	.30	.15	.09
511	Jamie Easterly	.30	.15	.09
512	Ellie Rodriguez	.30	.15	.09
513	Bart Johnson	.30	.15	.09
514	Dan Driessen	.30	.15	.09
515	Steve Yeager	.30	.15	.09
516	Wayne Granger	.30	.15	.09
517	John Milner	.30	.15	.09
518	*Doug Flynn*	.30	.15	.09
519	Steve Brye	.30	.15	.09
520	Willie McCovey	3.50	1.75	1.00
521	Jim Colborn	.30	.15	.09
522	Ted Sizemore	.30	.15	.09
523	Bob Montgomery	.30	.15	.09
524	Pete Falcone	.30	.15	.09
525	Billy Williams	3.50	1.75	1.00
526	Checklist 397-528	.35	.20	.11
527	Mike Anderson	.30	.15	.09
528	Dock Ellis	.30	.15	.09
529	Deron Johnson	.30	.15	.09
530	Don Sutton	2.50	1.25	.70
531	Mets Team (Joe Frazier)	.75	.40	.25
532	Milt May	.30	.15	.09
533	Lee Richard	.30	.15	.09
534	Stan Bahnsen	.30	.15	.09
535	Dave Nelson	.30	.15	.09
536	Mike Thompson	.30	.15	.09
537	Tony Muser	.30	.15	.09
538	Pat Darcy	.30	.15	.09
539	John Balaz	.30	.15	.09
540	Bill Freehan	.30	.15	.09
541	Steve Mingori	.30	.15	.09
542	Keith Hernandez	1.00	.50	.30
543	Wayne Twitchell	.30	.15	.09
544	Pepe Frias	.30	.15	.09
545	Sparky Lyle	.30	.15	.09
546	Dave Rosello	.30	.15	.09
547	Roric Harrison	.30	.15	.09
548	Manny Mota	.30	.15	.09
549	Randy Tate	.30	.15	.09
550	Hank Aaron	18.00	9.00	5.50
551	Jerry DaVanon	.30	.15	.09
552	Terry Humphrey	.30	.15	.09
553	Randy Moffitt	.30	.15	.09
554	Ray Fosse	.30	.15	.09
555	Dyar Miller	.30	.15	.09
556	Twins Team (Gene Mauch)	.30	.15	.09
557	Dan Spillner	.30	.15	.09
558	Cito Gaston	.30	.15	.09
559	Clyde Wright	.30	.15	.09
560	Jorge Orta	.30	.15	.09
561	Tom Carroll	.30	.15	.09
562	Adrian Garrett	.30	.15	.09
563	Larry Demery	.30	.15	.09
564	Kurt Bevacqua (Bubble Gum Blowing Champ)	.30	.15	.09
565	Tug McGraw	.30	.15	.09
566	Ken McMullen	.30	.15	.09
567	George Stone	.30	.15	.09
568	Rob Andrews	.30	.15	.09
569	Nelson Briles	.30	.15	.09
570	George Hendrick	.30	.15	.09
571	Don DeMola	.30	.15	.09
572	Rich Coggins	.30	.15	.09
573	Bill Travers	.30	.15	.09
574	Don Kessinger	.30	.15	.09
575	Dwight Evans	.50	.25	.15
576	Maximino Leon	.30	.15	.09
577	Marc Hill	.30	.15	.09
578	Ted Kubiak	.30	.15	.09
579	Clay Kirby	.30	.15	.09
580	Bert Campaneris	.30	.15	.09
581	Cardinals Team (Red Schoendienst)	.65	.35	.20
582	Mike Kekich	.30	.15	.09
583	Tommy Helms	.30	.15	.09
584	Stan Wall	.30	.15	.09
585	Joe Torre	.30	.15	.09
586	Ron Schueler	.30	.15	.09
587	Leo Cardenas	.30	.15	.09
588	Kevin Kobel	.30	.15	.09
589	Rookie Pitchers (Santo Alcala), (*Mike Flanagan*, Joe Pactwa, Pablo Torrealba)	1.00	.50	.30
590	Rookie Outfielders (Henry Cruz), (*Chet Lemon*), (*Ellis Valentine*, Terry Whitfield)	.75	.40	.25
591	Rookie Pitchers (Steve Grilli, Craig Mitchell, Jose Sosa, George Throop)	.30	.15	.09
592	Rookie Infielders (*Dave McKay*), (*Willie Randolph*), (*Jerry Royster*), (*Roy Staiger*)	3.00	1.50	.90
593	Rookie Pitchers (Larry Anderson, Ken Crosby, Mark Littell), (*Butch Metzger*)	.30	.15	.09
594	Rookie Catchers & Outfielders (Andy Merchant, Ed Ott, Royle Stillman, Jerry White)	.30	.15	.09
595	Rookie Pitchers (Steve Barr, Art DeFilippis, Randy Lerch, Sid Monge)	.30	.15	.09
596	Rookie Infielders (Lamar Johnson), (*Johnny LeMaster*, Jerry Manuel), (*Craig Reynolds*)	.30	.15	.09
597	Rookie Pitchers (*Don Aase*, Jack Kucek, Frank LaCorte, Mike Pazik)	.30	.15	.09
598	Rookie Outfielders (Hector Cruz), (*Jamie Quirk*, Jerry Turner, Joe Wallis)	.30	.15	.09
599	Rookie Pitchers (*Rob Dressler*), (*Ron Guidry*), (*Bob McClure*), (*Pat Zachry*)	4.00	2.00	1.25
600	Tom Seaver	6.00	3.00	1.75
601	Ken Rudolph	.30	.15	.09
602	Doug Konieczny	.30	.15	.09
603	Jim Holt	.30	.15	.09
604	Joe Lovitto	.30	.15	.09
605	Al Downing	.30	.15	.09
606	Brewers Team (Alex Grammas)	.50	.25	.15
607	Rich Hinton	.30	.15	.09
608	Vic Correll	.30	.15	.09
609	Fred Norman	.30	.15	.09
610	Greg Luzinski	.30	.15	.09
611	Rich Folkers	.30	.15	.09
612	Joe Lahoud	.30	.15	.09
613	Tim Johnson	.30	.15	.09
614	Fernando Arroyo	.30	.15	.09
615	Mike Cubbage	.30	.15	.09
616	Buck Martinez	.30	.15	.09
617	Darold Knowles	.30	.15	.09
618	Jack Brohamer	.30	.15	.09
619	Bill Butler	.30	.15	.09
620	Al Oliver	.40	.20	.12
621	Tom Hall	.30	.15	.09
622	Rick Auerbach	.30	.15	.09
623	Bob Allietta	.30	.15	.09
624	Tony Taylor	.30	.15	.09
625	J.R. Richard	.30	.15	.09
626	Bob Sheldon	.30	.15	.09
627	Bill Plummer	.30	.15	.09
628	John D'Acquisto	.30	.15	.09
629	Sandy Alomar	.30	.15	.09
630	Chris Speier	.30	.15	.09
631	Braves Team (Dave Bristol)	.50	.25	.15
632	Rogelio Moret	.30	.15	.09
633	*John Stearns*	.30	.15	.09
634	Larry Christenson	.30	.15	.09
635	Jim Fregosi	.30	.15	.09
636	Joe Decker	.30	.15	.09
637	Bruce Bochte	.30	.15	.09
638	Doyle Alexander	.30	.15	.09
639	Fred Kendall	.30	.15	.09
640	Bill Madlock	.45	.25	.14
641	Tom Paciorek	.30	.15	.09
642	Dennis Blair	.30	.15	.09
643	Checklist 529-660	.35	.20	.11
644	Tom Bradley	.30	.15	.09
645	Darrell Porter	.30	.15	.09
646	John Lowenstein	.30	.15	.09
648	Al Cowens	.30	.15	.09
649	Dave Roberts	.30	.15	.09
650	Thurman Munson	5.00	2.50	1.50
651	John Odom	.30	.15	.09
652	Ed Armbrister	.30	.15	.09
653	*Mike Norris*	.30	.15	.09
654	Doug Griffin	.30	.15	.09
655	Mike Vail	.30	.15	.09
656	White Sox Team (Chuck Tanner)	.50	.25	.15
657	*Roy Smalley*	.30	.15	.09
658	Jerry Johnson	.30	.15	.09
659	Ben Oglivie	.30	.15	.09
660	Dave Lopes	.30	.15	.09

1976 Topps Traded

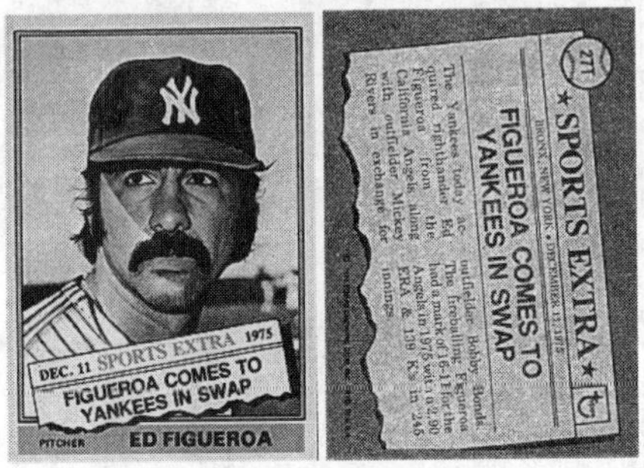

Similar to the Topps Traded set of 1974, the 2-1/2" x 3-1/2" cards feature photos of players traded after the printing deadline. The style of the cards is essentially the same as the regular issue but with a large "Sports Extra" headline announcing the trade and its date. The backs continue in newspaper style to detail the specifics of the trade. There are 43 player cards and one checklist in the set. Numbers remain the same as the player's regular card, with the addition of a "T" suffix.

		NM	EX	VG
Complete Set (44):		10.00	5.00	3.00
Common Player:		.25	.13	.08
27T	Ed Figueroa	.25	.13	.08
28T	Dusty Baker	.50	.25	.15
44T	Doug Rader	.25	.13	.08
58T	Ron Reed	.25	.13	.08
74T	Oscar Gamble	.25	.13	.08
80T	Jim Kaat	.90	.45	.25
83T	Jim Spencer	.25	.13	.08
85T	Mickey Rivers	.25	.13	.08
99T	Lee Lacy	.25	.13	.08
120T	Rusty Staub	.35	.20	.11
127T	Larvell Blanks	.25	.13	.08
146T	George Medich	.25	.13	.08
158T	Ken Reitz	.25	.13	.08
208T	Mike Lum	.25	.13	.08
211T	Clay Carroll	.25	.13	.08
231T	Tom House	.25	.13	.08
250T	Fergie Jenkins	3.00	1.50	.90
259T	Darrel Chaney	.25	.13	.08
292T	Leon Roberts	.25	.13	.08
296T	Pat Dobson	.25	.13	.08
309T	Bill Melton	.25	.13	.08
338T	Bob Bailey	.25	.13	.08
380T	Bobby Bonds	.50	.25	.15
383T	John Ellis	.25	.13	.08
385T	Mickey Lolich	.75	.40	.25
401T	Ken Brett	.25	.13	.08
410T	Ralph Garr	.25	.13	.08
411T	Bill Singer	.25	.13	.08
428T	Jim Crawford	.25	.13	.08
434T	Morris Nettles	.25	.13	.08
464T	Ken Henderson	.25	.13	.08
497T	Joe McIntosh	.25	.13	.08
524T	Pete Falcone	.25	.13	.08
527T	Mike Anderson	.25	.13	.08
528T	Dock Ellis	.25	.13	.08
532T	Milt May	.25	.13	.08
554T	Ray Fosse	.25	.13	.08
579T	Clay Kirby	.25	.13	.08
583T	Tommy Helms	.25	.13	.08
592T	Willie Randolph	.35	.20	.11
618T	Jack Brohamer	.25	.13	.08
632T	Rogelio Moret	.25	.13	.08
649T	Dave Roberts	.25	.13	.08
----	Traded Checklist	.25	.13	.08

1976 Topps Cloth Sticker Prototypes

Apparently produced to test different materials for the cloth sticker set which would be issued the following year, these prototypes were never issued. Each of the players can be found on four different types of material. The blank-backed stickers feature the card fronts as they appeared in the regular 1976 issue. It is unknown whether other players were produced for the test.

		NM	EX	VG
Common Player:		40.00	20.00	12.00
(1a)	Bob Apodaca (silk)	40.00	20.00	12.00
(1b)	Bob Apodaca (thin felt)	40.00	20.00	12.00
(1c)	Bob Apodaca (textured felt)	40.00	20.00	12.00
(1d)	Bob Apodaca (thick felt)	40.00	20.00	12.00
(2a)	Duffy Dyer (silk)	40.00	20.00	12.00
(2b)	Duffy Dyer (thin felt)	40.00	20.00	12.00
(2c)	Duffy Dyer (textured felt)	40.00	20.00	12.00
(2d)	Duffy Dyer (thick felt)	40.00	20.00	12.00

1976 Topps Team Checklist Sheet

Via a mail-in redemption (50¢ and a wrapper), collectors could receive an uncut sheet of the 24 team photo/checklist cards from the 1976 Topps baseball set. Measuring about 10-1/2" x 20-1/8", the sheet could be cut into individual team cards of standard size.

	NM	EX	VG
Complete Sheet:	25.00	12.50	7.50

1977 Topps

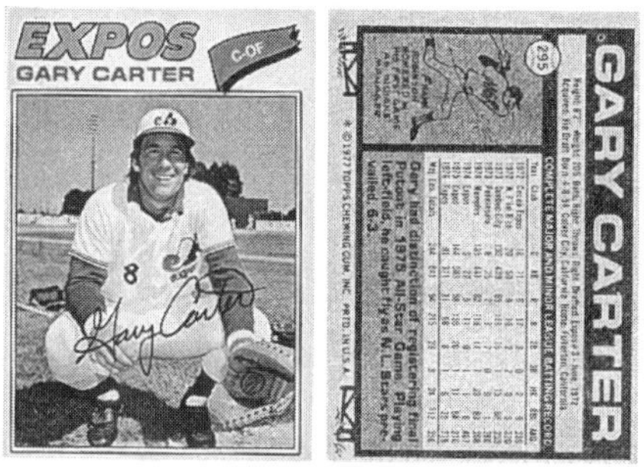

The 1977 Topps Set is a 660-card effort featuring front designs dominated by a color photograph on which there is a facsimile autograph. Above the picture are the player's name, team and position. The backs of the 2-1/2" x 3-1/2" cards include personal and career statistics along with newspaper-style highlights and a cartoon. Specialty cards include statistical leaders, record performances, a new "Turn Back The Clock" feature which highlighted great past moments and a "Big League Brothers" feature.

		NM	EX	VG
Complete Set (660):		250.00	125.00	75.00
Common Player:		.20	.10	.06
Wax Box:		450.00		
1	Batting Leaders (George Brett, Bill Madlock)	3.00	1.50	.90
2	Home Run Leaders (Graig Nettles, Mike Schmidt)	1.00	.50	.30
3	RBI Leaders (George Foster, Lee May)	.20	.10	.06
4	Stolen Base Leaders (Dave Lopes, Bill North)	.20	.10	.06
5	Victory Leaders (Randy Jones, Jim Palmer)	.40	.20	.12
6	Strikeout Leaders (Nolan Ryan, Tom Seaver)	12.00	6.00	3.50
7	ERA Leaders (John Denny, Mark Fidrych)	.20	.10	.06
8	Leading Firemen (Bill Campbell, Rawly Eastwick)	.20	.10	.06
9	Doug Rader	.20	.10	.06
10	Reggie Jackson	8.00	4.00	2.50
11	Rob Dressler	.20	.10	.06
12	Larry Haney	.20	.10	.06
13	Luis Gomez	.20	.10	.06
14	Tommy Smith	.20	.10	.06
15	Don Gullett	.20	.10	.06
16	Bob Jones	.20	.10	.06
17	Steve Stone	.25	.13	.08
18	Indians Team (Frank Robinson)	2.00	1.00	.60
19	John D'Acquisto	.20	.10	.06
20	Graig Nettles	.20	.10	.06
21	Ken Forsch	.20	.10	.06
22	Bill Freehan	.20	.10	.06
23	Dan Driessen	.20	.10	.06
24	Carl Morton	.20	.10	.06
25	Dwight Evans	.40	.20	.12
26	Ray Sadecki	.20	.10	.06
27	Bill Buckner	.25	.13	.08
28	Woodie Fryman	.20	.10	.06
29	Bucky Dent	.20	.10	.06
30	Greg Luzinski	.20	.10	.06
31	Jim Todd	.20	.10	.06
32	Checklist 1-132	.25	.13	.08
33	Wayne Garland	.20	.10	.06
34	Angels Team (Norm Sherry)	.35	.20	.11
35	Rennie Stennett	.20	.10	.06
36	John Ellis	.20	.10	.06
37	Steve Hargan	.20	.10	.06
38	Craig Kusick	.20	.10	.06
39	Tom Griffin	.20	.10	.06
40	Bobby Murcer	.20	.10	.06
41	Jim Kern	.20	.10	.06
42	Jose Cruz	.20	.10	.06
43	Ray Bare	.20	.10	.06
44	Bud Harrelson	.20	.10	.06
45	Rawly Eastwick	.20	.10	.06
46	Buck Martinez	.20	.10	.06
47	Lynn McGlothen	.20	.10	.06
48	Tom Paciorek	.20	.10	.06
49	Grant Jackson	.20	.10	.06
50	Ron Cey	.20	.10	.06
51	Brewers Team (Alex Grammas)	.35	.20	.11
52	Ellis Valentine	.20	.10	.06
53	Paul Mitchell	.20	.10	.06
54	Sandy Alomar	.20	.10	.06
55	Jeff Burroughs	.20	.10	.06
56	Rudy May	.20	.10	.06
57	Marc Hill	.20	.10	.06
58	Chet Lemon	.20	.10	.06
59	Larry Christenson	.20	.10	.06
60	Jim Rice	1.00	.50	.30
61	Manny Sanguillen	.20	.10	.06
62	Eric Raich	.20	.10	.06
63	Tito Fuentes	.20	.10	.06
64	Larry Biittner	.20	.10	.06
65	Skip Lockwood	.20	.10	.06
66	Roy Smalley	.20	.10	.06
67	*Joaquin Andujar*	.20	.10	.06
68	Bruce Bochte	.20	.10	.06
69	Jim Crawford	.20	.10	.06
70	Johnny Bench	4.50	2.25	1.25
71	Dock Ellis	.20	.10	.06
72	Mike Anderson	.20	.10	.06
73	Charlie Williams	.20	.10	.06
74	A's Team (Jack McKeon)	.35	.20	.11
75	Dennis Leonard	.20	.10	.06
76	Tim Foli	.20	.10	.06
77	Dyar Miller	.20	.10	.06
78	Bob Davis	.20	.10	.06
79	Don Money	.20	.10	.06
80	Andy Messersmith	.20	.10	.06
81	Juan Beniquez	.20	.10	.06
82	Jim Rooker	.20	.10	.06
83	Kevin Bell	.20	.10	.06
84	Ollie Brown	.20	.10	.06
85	Duane Kuiper	.20	.10	.06
86	Pat Zachry	.20	.10	.06
87	Glenn Borgmann	.20	.10	.06
88	Stan Wall	.20	.10	.06
89	*Butch Hobson*	.20	.10	.06
90	Cesar Cedeno	.20	.10	.06
91	John Verhoeven	.20	.10	.06
92	Dave Rosello	.20	.10	.06
93	Tom Poquette	.20	.10	.06
94	Craig Swan	.20	.10	.06
95	Keith Hernandez	.75	.40	.25
96	Lou Piniella	.30	.15	.09
97	Dave Heaverlo	.20	.10	.06
98	Milt May	.20	.10	.06
99	Tom Hausman	.20	.10	.06
100	Joe Morgan	2.50	1.25	.70
101	Dick Bosman	.20	.10	.06
102	Jose Morales	.20	.10	.06
103	Mike Bacsik	.20	.10	.06
104	*Omar Moreno*	.20	.10	.06
105	Steve Yeager	.20	.10	.06
106	Mike Flanagan	.20	.10	.06
107	Bill Melton	.20	.10	.06
108	Alan Foster	.20	.10	.06
109	Jorge Orta	.20	.10	.06
110	Steve Carlton	3.50	1.75	1.00
111	Rico Petrocelli	.20	.10	.06
112	Bill Greif	.20	.10	.06
113	Blue Jays Mgr./Coaches (Roy Hartsfield, Don Leppert, Bob Miller, Jackie Moore, Harry Warner)	.90	.45	.25
114	Bruce Dal Canton	.20	.10	.06
115	Rick Manning	.20	.10	.06
116	Joe Niekro	.20	.10	.06
117	Frank White	.20	.10	.06
118	Rick Jones	.20	.10	.06
119	John Stearns	.20	.10	.06
120	Rod Carew	4.00	2.00	1.25
121	Gary Nolan	.20	.10	.06
122	Ben Oglivie	.20	.10	.06
123	Fred Stanley	.20	.10	.06
124	George Mitterwald	.20	.10	.06
125	Bill Travers	.20	.10	.06
126	Rod Gilbreath	.20	.10	.06
127	Ron Fairly	.20	.10	.06
128	Tommy John	.30	.15	.09
129	Mike Sadek	.20	.10	.06
130	Al Oliver	.40	.20	.12
131	Orlando Ramirez	.20	.10	.06
132	Chip Lang	.20	.10	.06
133	Ralph Garr	.20	.10	.06
134	Padres Team (John McNamara)	.35	.20	.11
135	Mark Belanger	.20	.10	.06
136	*Jerry Mumphrey*	.20	.10	.06
137	Jeff Terpko	.20	.10	.06
138	Bob Stinson	.20	.10	.06
139	Fred Norman	.20	.10	.06
140	Mike Schmidt	12.00	6.00	3.50
141	Mark Littell	.20	.10	.06
142	Steve Dillard	.20	.10	.06
143	Ed Herrmann	.20	.10	.06
144	*Bruce Sutter*	3.00	1.50	.90
145	Tom Veryzer	.20	.10	.06
146	Dusty Baker	.25	.13	.08
147	Jackie Brown	.20	.10	.06
148	Fran Healy	.20	.10	.06
149	Mike Cubbage	.20	.10	.06
150	Tom Seaver	5.00	2.50	1.50
151	Johnnie LeMaster	.20	.10	.06
152	Gaylord Perry	2.00	1.00	.60
153	Ron Jackson	.20	.10	.06
154	Dave Giusti	.20	.10	.06
155	Joe Rudi	.20	.10	.06
156	Pete Mackanin	.20	.10	.06
157	Ken Brett	.20	.10	.06
158	Ted Kubiak	.20	.10	.06
159	Bernie Carbo	.20	.10	.06
160	Will McEnaney	.20	.10	.06
161	*Garry Templeton*	.60	.30	.20
162	Mike Cuellar	.20	.10	.06
163	Dave Hilton	.20	.10	.06
164	Tug McGraw	.20	.10	.06
165	Jim Wynn	.20	.10	.06
166	Bill Campbell	.20	.10	.06
167	Rich Hebner	.20	.10	.06
168	Charlie Spikes	.20	.10	.06
169	Darold Knowles	.20	.10	.06
170	Thurman Munson	3.50	1.75	1.00
171	Ken Sanders	.20	.10	.06
172	John Milner	.20	.10	.06
173	Chuck Scrivener	.20	.10	.06
174	Nelson Briles	.20	.10	.06
175	*Butch Wynegar*	.20	.10	.06
176	Bob Robertson	.20	.10	.06
177	Bart Johnson	.20	.10	.06
178	Bombo Rivera	.20	.10	.06
179	Paul Hartzell	.20	.10	.06
180	Dave Lopes	.20	.10	.06
181	Ken McMullen	.20	.10	.06
182	Dan Spillner	.20	.10	.06
183	Cardinals Team (Vern Rapp)	.35	.20	.11
184	Bo McLaughlin	.20	.10	.06
185	Sixto Lezcano	.20	.10	.06
186	Doug Flynn	.20	.10	.06
187	Dick Pole	.20	.10	.06
188	Bob Tolan	.20	.10	.06
189	Rick Dempsey	.20	.10	.06
190	Ray Burris	.20	.10	.06
191	Doug Griffin	.20	.10	.06
192	Clarence Gaston	.20	.10	.06
193	Larry Gura	.20	.10	.06
194	Gary Matthews	.20	.10	.06
195	Ed Figueroa	.20	.10	.06
196	Len Randle	.20	.10	.06
197	Ed Ott	.20	.10	.06
198	Wilbur Wood	.20	.10	.06
199	Pepe Frias	.20	.10	.06
200	Frank Tanana	.20	.10	.06
201	Ed Kranepool	.20	.10	.06
202	Tom Johnson	.20	.10	.06
203	Ed Armbrister	.20	.10	.06
204	Jeff Newman	.20	.10	.06
205	Pete Falcone	.20	.10	.06
206	Boog Powell	.50	.25	.15
207	Glenn Abbott	.20	.10	.06
208	Checklist 133-264	.25	.13	.08
209	Rob Andrews	.20	.10	.06
210	Fred Lynn	.25	.13	.08
211	Giants Team (Joe Altobelli)	.35	.20	.11
212	Jim Mason	.20	.10	.06
213	Maximino Leon	.20	.10	.06
214	Darrell Porter	.20	.10	.06
215	Butch Metzger	.20	.10	.06
216	Doug DeCinces	.20	.10	.06
217	Tom Underwood	.20	.10	.06
218	*John Wathan*	.20	.10	.06
219	Joe Coleman	.20	.10	.06
220	Chris Chambliss	.20	.10	.06
221	Bob Bailey	.20	.10	.06
222	Francisco Barrios	.20	.10	.06
223	Earl Williams	.20	.10	.06
224	Rusty Torres	.20	.10	.06
225	Bob Apodaca	.20	.10	.06
226	Leroy Stanton	.20	.10	.06
227	*Joe Sambito*	.20	.10	.06
228	Twins Team (Gene Mauch)	.35	.20	.11
229	Don Kessinger	.20	.10	.06
230	Vida Blue	.20	.10	.06
231	George Brett (Record Breaker)	5.00	2.50	1.50
232	Minnie Minoso (Record Breaker)	.35	.20	.11
233	Jose Morales (Record Breaker)	.20	.10	.06
234	Nolan Ryan (Record Breaker)	15.00	7.50	4.50
235	Cecil Cooper	.20	.10	.06
236	Tom Buskey	.20	.10	.06
237	Gene Clines	.20	.10	.06
238	Tippy Martinez	.20	.10	.06
239	Bill Plummer	.20	.10	.06
240	Ron LeFlore	.20	.10	.06
241	Dave Tomlin	.20	.10	.06
242	Ken Henderson	.20	.10	.06
243	Ron Reed	.20	.10	.06
244	John Mayberry	.20	.10	.06
245	Rick Rhoden	.20	.10	.06
246	Mike Vail	.20	.10	.06
247	Chris Knapp	.20	.10	.06
248	Wilbur Howard	.20	.10	.06
249	Pete Redfern	.20	.10	.06
250	Bill Madlock	.30	.15	.09
251	Tony Muser	.20	.10	.06
252	Dale Murray	.20	.10	.06
253	John Hale	.20	.10	.06
254	Doyle Alexander	.20	.10	.06
255	George Scott	.20	.10	.06
256	Joe Hoerner	.20	.10	.06
257	Mike Miley	.20	.10	.06
258	Luis Tiant	.20	.10	.06
259	Mets Team (Joe Frazier)	.50	.25	.15
260	J.R. Richard	.25	.13	.08
261	Phil Garner	.20	.10	.06
262	Al Cowens	.20	.10	.06
263	Mike Marshall	.20	.10	.06
264	Tom Hutton	.20	.10	.06
265	*Mark Fidrych*	.90	.45	.25
266	Derrel Thomas	.20	.10	.06
267	Ray Fosse	.20	.10	.06
268	Rick Sawyer	.20	.10	.06
269	Joe Lis	.20	.10	.06
270	Dave Parker	.80	.40	.25
271	Terry Forster	.20	.10	.06
272	Lee Lacy	.20	.10	.06
273	Eric Soderholm	.20	.10	.06
274	Don Stanhouse	.20	.10	.06
275	Mike Hargrove	.20	.10	.06

276	A.L. Championship (Chambliss' Dramatic Homer Decides It)	.25	.13	.08
277	N.L. Championship (Reds Sweep Phillies 3 In Row)	.25	.13	.08
278	Danny Frisella	.20	.10	.06
279	Joe Wallis	.20	.10	.06
280	Catfish Hunter	1.75	.90	.50
281	Roy Staiger	.20	.10	.06
282	Sid Monge	.20	.10	.06
283	Jerry DaVanon	.20	.10	.06
284	Mike Norris	.20	.10	.06
285	Brooks Robinson	6.00	3.00	1.75
286	Johnny Grubb	.20	.10	.06
287	Reds Team (Sparky Anderson)	1.00	.50	.30
288	Bob Montgomery	.20	.10	.06
289	Gene Garber	.20	.10	.06
290	Amos Otis	.20	.10	.06
291	*Jason Thompson*	.20	.10	.06
292	Rogelio Moret	.20	.10	.06
293	Jack Brohamer	.20	.10	.06
294	George Medich	.20	.10	.06
295	Gary Carter	2.00	1.00	.60
296	Don Hood	.20	.10	.06
297	Ken Reitz	.20	.10	.06
298	Charlie Hough	.20	.10	.06
299	Otto Velez	.20	.10	.06
300	Jerry Koosman	.20	.10	.06
301	Toby Harrah	.20	.10	.06
302	Mike Garman	.20	.10	.06
303	Gene Tenace	.20	.10	.06
304	Jim Hughes	.20	.10	.06
305	Mickey Rivers	.20	.10	.06
306	Rick Waits	.20	.10	.06
307	Gary Sutherland	.20	.10	.06
308	Gene Pentz	.20	.10	.06
309	Red Sox Team (Don Zimmer)	.35	.20	.11
310	Larry Bowa	.20	.10	.06
311	Vern Ruhle	.20	.10	.06
312	Rob Belloir	.20	.10	.06
313	Paul Blair	.20	.10	.06
314	Steve Mingori	.20	.10	.06
315	Dave Chalk	.20	.10	.06
316	Steve Rogers	.20	.10	.06
317	Kurt Bevacqua	.20	.10	.06
318	Duffy Dyer	.20	.10	.06
319	Rich Gossage	.25	.13	.08
320	Ken Griffey	.30	.15	.09
321	Dave Goltz	.20	.10	.06
322	Bill Russell	.20	.10	.06
323	Larry Lintz	.20	.10	.06
324	John Curtis	.20	.10	.06
325	Mike Ivie	.20	.10	.06
326	Jesse Jefferson	.20	.10	.06
327	Astros Team (Bill Virdon)	.35	.20	.11
328	Tommy Boggs	.20	.10	.06
329	Ron Hodges	.20	.10	.06
330	George Hendrick	.20	.10	.06
331	Jim Colborn	.20	.10	.06
332	Elliott Maddox	.20	.10	.06
333	Paul Reuschel	.20	.10	.06
334	Bill Stein	.20	.10	.06
335	Bill Robinson	.20	.10	.06
336	Denny Doyle	.20	.10	.06
337	Ron Schueler	.20	.10	.06
338	Dave Duncan	.20	.10	.06
339	Adrian Devine	.20	.10	.06
340	Hal McRae	.20	.10	.06
341	Joe Kerrigan	.20	.10	.06
342	Jerry Remy	.20	.10	.06
343	Ed Halicki	.20	.10	.06
344	Brian Downing	.20	.10	.06
345	Reggie Smith	.20	.10	.06
346	Bill Singer	.20	.10	.06
347	George Foster	.30	.15	.09
348	Brent Strom	.20	.10	.06
349	Jim Holt	.20	.10	.06
350	Larry Dierker	.20	.10	.06
351	Jim Sundberg	.20	.10	.06
352	Mike Phillips	.20	.10	.06
353	Stan Thomas	.20	.10	.06
354	Pirates Team (Chuck Tanner)	.35	.20	.11
355	Lou Brock	3.00	1.50	.90
356	Checklist 265-396	.25	.13	.08
357	Tim McCarver	.30	.15	.09
358	Tom House	.20	.10	.06
359	Willie Randolph	.20	.10	.06
360	Rick Monday	.20	.10	.06
361	Eduardo Rodriguez	.20	.10	.06
362	Tommy Davis	.20	.10	.06
363	Dave Roberts	.20	.10	.06
364	Vic Correll	.20	.10	.06
365	Mike Torrez	.20	.10	.06
366	Ted Sizemore	.20	.10	.06
367	Dave Hamilton	.20	.10	.06
368	Mike Jorgensen	.20	.10	.06
369	Terry Humphrey	.20	.10	.06
370	John Montefusco	.20	.10	.06
371	Royals Team (Whitey Herzog)	.90	.45	.25
372	Rich Folkers	.20	.10	.06
373	Bert Campaneris	.20	.10	.06
374	Kent Tekulve	.20	.10	.06
375	Larry Hisle	.20	.10	.06
376	Nino Espinosa	.20	.10	.06
377	Dave McKay	.20	.10	.06
378	Jim Umbarger	.20	.10	.06
379	Larry Cox	.20	.10	.06
380	Lee May	.20	.10	.06
381	Bob Forsch	.20	.10	.06
382	Charlie Moore	.20	.10	.06
383	Stan Bahnsen	.20	.10	.06
384	Darrel Chaney	.20	.10	.06
385	Dave LaRoche	.20	.10	.06
386	Manny Mota	.20	.10	.06
387	Yankees Team (Billy Martin)	1.00	.50	.30
388	Terry Harmon	.20	.10	.06
389	Ken Kravec	.20	.10	.06
390	Dave Winfield	6.00	3.00	1.75
391	Dan Warthen	.20	.10	.06
392	Phil Roof	.20	.10	.06
393	John Lowenstein	.20	.10	.06
394	Bill Laxton	.20	.10	.06
395	Manny Trillo	.20	.10	.06
396	Tom Murphy	.20	.10	.06
397	*Larry Herndon*	.20	.10	.06
398	Tom Burgmeier	.20	.10	.06
399	Bruce Boisclair	.20	.10	.06
400	Steve Garvey	3.00	1.50	.90
401	Mickey Scott	.20	.10	.06
402	Tommy Helms	.20	.10	.06
403	Tom Grieve	.20	.10	.06
404	Eric Rasmussen	.20	.10	.06
405	Claudell Washington	.20	.10	.06
406	Tim Johnson	.20	.10	.06
407	Dave Freisleben	.20	.10	.06
408	Cesar Tovar	.20	.10	.06
409	Pete Broberg	.20	.10	.06
410	Willie Montanez	.20	.10	.06
411	World Series Games 1 & 2 (Joe Morgan, Johnny Bench)	.75	.40	.25
412	World Series Games 3 & 4 (Johnny Bench)	.75	.40	.25
413	World Series Summary	.45	.25	.14
414	Tommy Harper	.20	.10	.06
415	Jay Johnstone	.20	.10	.06
416	Chuck Hartenstein	.20	.10	.06
417	Wayne Garrett	.20	.10	.06
418	White Sox Team (Bob Lemon)	.35	.20	.11
419	Steve Swisher	.20	.10	.06
420	Rusty Staub	.25	.13	.08
421	Doug Rau	.20	.10	.06
422	Freddie Patek	.20	.10	.06
423	Gary Lavelle	.20	.10	.06
424	Steve Brye	.20	.10	.06
425	Joe Torre	.45	.25	.14
426	Dick Drago	.20	.10	.06
427	Dave Rader	.20	.10	.06
428	Rangers Team (Frank Lucchesi)	.35	.20	.11
429	Ken Boswell	.20	.10	.06
430	Fergie Jenkins	1.75	.90	.50
431	Dave Collins	.20	.10	.06
432	Buzz Capra	.20	.10	.06
433	Nate Colbert (Turn Back The Clock)	.20	.10	.06
434	Carl Yastrzemski (Turn Back The Clock)	.90	.45	.25
435	Maury Wills (Turn Back The Clock)	.35	.20	.11
436	Bob Keegan (Turn Back The Clock)	.20	.10	.06
437	Ralph Kiner (Turn Back The Clock)	.25	.13	.08
438	Marty Perez	.20	.10	.06
439	Gorman Thomas	.20	.10	.06
440	Jon Matlack	.20	.10	.06
441	Larvell Blanks	.20	.10	.06
442	Braves Team (Dave Bristol)	.35	.20	.11
443	Lamar Johnson	.20	.10	.06
444	Wayne Twitchell	.20	.10	.06
445	Ken Singleton	.20	.10	.06
446	Bill Bonham	.20	.10	.06
447	Jerry Turner	.20	.10	.06
448	Ellie Rodriguez	.20	.10	.06
449	Al Fitzmorris	.20	.10	.06
450	Pete Rose	10.00	5.00	3.00
451	Checklist 397-528	.25	.13	.08
452	Mike Caldwell	.20	.10	.06
453	Pedro Garcia	.20	.10	.06
454	Andy Etchebarren	.20	.10	.06
455	Rick Wise	.20	.10	.06
456	Leon Roberts	.20	.10	.06
457	Steve Luebber	.20	.10	.06
458	Leo Foster	.20	.10	.06
459	Steve Foucault	.20	.10	.06
460	Willie Stargell	2.00	1.00	.60
461	Dick Tidrow	.20	.10	.06
462	Don Baylor	.30	.15	.09
463	Jamie Quirk	.20	.10	.06
464	Randy Moffitt	.20	.10	.06
465	Rico Carty	.20	.10	.06
466	Fred Holdsworth	.20	.10	.06
467	Phillies Team (Danny Ozark)	.50	.25	.15
468	Ramon Hernandez	.20	.10	.06
469	Pat Kelly	.20	.10	.06
470	Ted Simmons	.20	.10	.06
471	Del Unser	.20	.10	.06
472	Rookie Pitchers (Don Aase, Bob McClure, Gil Patterson, Dave Wehrmeister)	.20	.10	.06
473	Rookie Outfielders *(Andre Dawson)*, *(Gene Richards)*, *(John Scott)*, *(Denny Walling)*	20.00	10.00	6.00
474	Rookie Shortstops (Bob Bailor, Kiko Garcia, Craig Reynolds, Alex Taveras)	.20	.10	.06
475	Rookie Pitchers (Chris Batton, Rick Camp, Scott McGregor, Manny Sarmiento)	.20	.10	.06
476	Rookie Catchers *(Gary Alexander)*, *(Rick Cerone)*, *(Dale Murphy)*, *(Kevin Pasley)*	18.00	9.00	5.50
477	Rookie Infielders (Doug Ault), *(Rich Dauer*, Orlando Gonzalez, Phil Mankowski)	.20	.10	.06
478	Rookie Pitchers (Jim Gideon, Leon Hooten, Dave Johnson, Mark Lemongello)	.20	.10	.06
479	Rookie Outfielders (Brian Asselstine), *(Wayne Gross*, Sam Mejias, Alvis Woods)	.20	.10	.06
480	Carl Yastrzemski	5.00	2.50	1.50
481	Roger Metzger	.20	.10	.06
482	Tony Solaita	.20	.10	.06
483	Richie Zisk	.20	.10	.06
484	Burt Hooton	.20	.10	.06
485	Roy White	.20	.10	.06
486	Ed Bane	.20	.10	.06
487	Rookie Pitchers (Larry Anderson, Ed Glynn, Joe Henderson, Greg Terlecky)	.20	.10	.06
488	Rookie Outfielders *(Jack Clark)*, *(Ruppert Jones)*, *(Lee Mazzilli)*, *(Dan Thomas)*	4.00	2.00	1.25
489	Rookie Pitchers *(Len Barker*, Randy Lerch), *(Greg Minton*, Mike Overy)	.40	.20	.12
490	Rookie Shortstops *(Billy Almon*, Mickey Klutts, Tommy McMillan, Mark Wagner)	.20	.10	.06
491	Rookie Pitchers *(Mike Dupree)*, *(Dennis Martinez)*, *(Craig Mitchell)*, *(Bob Sykes)*	10.00	5.00	3.00
492	Rookie Outfielders *(Tony Armas)*, *(Steve Kemp)*, *(Carlos Lopez)*, *(Gary Woods)*	.80	.40	.25
493	Rookie Pitchers *(Mike Krukow*, Jim Otten, Gary Wheelock, Mike Willis)	.30	.15	.09
494	Rookie Infielders (Juan Bernhardt, Mike Champion), *(Jim Gantner)*, *(Bump Wills)*	.35	.20	.11
495	Al Hrabosky	.20	.10	.06
496	Gary Thomasson	.20	.10	.06
497	Clay Carroll	.20	.10	.06
498	Sal Bando	.20	.10	.06
499	Pablo Torrealba	.20	.10	.06
500	Dave Kingman	.30	.15	.09
501	Jim Bibby	.20	.10	.06
502	Randy Hundley	.20	.10	.06
503	Bill Lee	.20	.10	.06
504	Dodgers Team (Tom Lasorda)	1.50	.70	.45
505	Oscar Gamble	.20	.10	.06
506	Steve Grilli	.20	.10	.06
507	Mike Hegan	.20	.10	.06
508	Dave Pagan	.20	.10	.06
509	Cookie Rojas	.20	.10	.06
510	John Candelaria	.20	.10	.06
511	Bill Fahey	.20	.10	.06
512	Jack Billingham	.20	.10	.06
513	Jerry Terrell	.20	.10	.06
514	Cliff Johnson	.20	.10	.06
515	Chris Speier	.20	.10	.06
516	Bake McBride	.20	.10	.06
517	*Pete Vuckovich*	.35	.20	.11
518	Cubs Team (Herman Franks)	.35	.20	.11
519	Don Kirkwood	.20	.10	.06
520	Garry Maddox	.20	.10	.06
521	Bob Grich	.20	.10	.06
522	Enzo Hernandez	.20	.10	.06
523	Rollie Fingers	2.00	1.00	.60
524	Rowland Office	.20	.10	.06
525	Dennis Eckersley	4.00	2.00	1.25
526	Larry Parrish	.20	.10	.06
527	Dan Meyer	.20	.10	.06
528	Bill Castro	.20	.10	.06
529	Jim Essian	.20	.10	.06
530	Rick Reuschel	.20	.10	.06
531	Lyman Bostock	.20	.10	.06
532	Jim Willoughby	.20	.10	.06
533	Mickey Stanley	.20	.10	.06
534	Paul Splittorff	.20	.10	.06
535	Cesar Geronimo	.20	.10	.06
536	Vic Albury	.20	.10	.06
537	Dave Roberts	.20	.10	.06
538	Frank Taveras	.20	.10	.06
539	Mike Wallace	.20	.10	.06
540	Bob Watson	.20	.10	.06
541	John Denny	.20	.10	.06
542	Frank Duffy	.20	.10	.06
543	Ron Blomberg	.20	.10	.06
544	Gary Ross	.20	.10	.06
545	Bob Boone	.30	.15	.09
546	Orioles Team (Earl Weaver)	1.00	.50	.30
547	Willie McCovey	3.50	1.75	1.00
548	*Joel Youngblood*	.20	.10	.06
549	Jerry Royster	.20	.10	.06
550	Randy Jones	.20	.10	.06
551	Bill North	.20	.10	.06
552	Pepe Mangual	.20	.10	.06
553	Jack Heidemann	.20	.10	.06
554	Bruce Kimm	.20	.10	.06
555	Dan Ford	.20	.10	.06
556	Doug Bird	.20	.10	.06
557	Jerry White	.20	.10	.06
558	Elias Sosa	.20	.10	.06
559	Alan Bannister	.20	.10	.06
560	Dave Concepcion	.20	.10	.06
561	Pete LaCock	.20	.10	.06
562	Checklist 529-660	.25	.13	.08
563	Bruce Kison	.20	.10	.06
564	Alan Ashby	.20	.10	.06
565	Mickey Lolich	.25	.13	.08
566	Rick Miller	.20	.10	.06
567	Enos Cabell	.20	.10	.06
568	Carlos May	.20	.10	.06
569	Jim Lonborg	.20	.10	.06
570	Bobby Bonds	.30	.15	.09
571	Darrell Evans	.35	.20	.11
572	Ross Grimsley	.20	.10	.06
573	Joe Ferguson	.20	.10	.06
574	Aurelio Rodriguez	.20	.10	.06
575	Dick Ruthven	.20	.10	.06
576	Fred Kendall	.20	.10	.06
577	Jerry Augustine	.20	.10	.06
578	Bob Randall	.20	.10	.06
579	Don Carrithers	.20	.10	.06
580	George Brett	20.00	10.00	6.00
581	Pedro Borbon	.20	.10	.06

582	Ed Kirkpatrick	.20	.10	.06
583	Paul Lindblad	.20	.10	.06
584	Ed Goodson	.20	.10	.06
585	Rick Burleson	.20	.10	.06
586	Steve Renko	.20	.10	.06
587	Rick Baldwin	.20	.10	.06
588	Dave Moates	.20	.10	.06
589	Mike Cosgrove	.20	.10	.06
590	Buddy Bell	.20	.10	.06
591	Chris Arnold	.20	.10	.06
592	Dan Briggs	.20	.10	.06
593	Dennis Blair	.20	.10	.06
594	Biff Pocoroba	.20	.10	.06
595	John Hiller	.20	.10	.06
596	*Jerry Martin*	.20	.10	.06
597	Mariners Mgr./Coaches (Don Bryant, Jim Busby, Darrell Johnson, Vada Pinson, Wes Stock)	1.25	.60	.40
598	Sparky Lyle	.20	.10	.06
599	Mike Tyson	.20	.10	.06
600	Jim Palmer	3.00	1.50	.90
601	Mike Lum	.20	.10	.06
602	Andy Hassler	.20	.10	.06
603	Willie Davis	.20	.10	.06
604	Jim Slaton	.20	.10	.06
605	Felix Millan	.20	.10	.06
606	Steve Braun	.20	.10	.06
607	Larry Demery	.20	.10	.06
608	Roy Howell	.20	.10	.06
609	Jim Barr	.20	.10	.06
610	Jose Cardenal	.20	.10	.06
611	Dave Lemanczyk	.20	.10	.06
612	Barry Foote	.20	.10	.06
613	Reggie Cleveland	.20	.10	.06
614	Greg Gross	.20	.10	.06
615	Phil Niekro	2.00	1.00	.60
616	Tommy Sandt	.20	.10	.06
617	Bobby Darwin	.20	.10	.06
618	Pat Dobson	.20	.10	.06
619	Johnny Oates	.20	.10	.06
620	Don Sutton	2.00	1.00	.60
621	Tigers Team (Ralph Houk)	.45	.25	.14
622	Jim Wohlford	.20	.10	.06
623	Jack Kucek	.20	.10	.06
624	Hector Cruz	.20	.10	.06
625	Ken Holtzman	.20	.10	.06
626	Al Bumbry	.20	.10	.06
627	Bob Myrick	.20	.10	.06
628	Mario Guerrero	.20	.10	.06
629	Bobby Valentine	.20	.10	.06
630	Bert Blyleven	.25	.13	.08
631	Big League Brothers (George Brett, Ken Brett)	5.00	2.50	1.50
632	Big League Brothers (Bob Forsch, Ken Forsch)	.20	.10	.06
633	Big League Brothers (Carlos May, Lee May)	.20	.10	.06
634	Big League Brothers (Paul Reuschel, Rick Reuschel) (names switched)	.20	.10	.06
635	Robin Yount	20.00	10.00	6.00
636	Santo Alcala	.20	.10	.06
637	Alex Johnson	.20	.10	.06
638	Jim Kaat	.35	.20	.11
639	Jerry Morales	.20	.10	.06
640	Carlton Fisk	4.00	2.00	1.25
641	Dan Larson	.20	.10	.06
642	Willie Crawford	.20	.10	.06
643	Mike Pazik	.20	.10	.06
644	Matt Alexander	.20	.10	.06
645	Jerry Reuss	.20	.10	.06
646	Andres Mora	.20	.10	.06
647	Expos Team (Dick Williams)	.35	.20	.11
648	Jim Spencer	.20	.10	.06
649	Dave Cash	.20	.10	.06
650	Nolan Ryan	25.00	12.50	7.50
651	Von Joshua	.20	.10	.06
652	Tom Walker	.20	.10	.06
653	Diego Segui	.20	.10	.06
654	Ron Pruitt	.20	.10	.06
655	Tony Perez	3.00	1.50	.90
656	Ron Guidry	.35	.20	.11
657	Mick Kelleher	.20	.10	.06
658	Marty Pattin	.20	.10	.06
659	Merv Rettenmund	.20	.10	.06
660	Willie Horton	.20	.10	.06

1977 Topps Cloth Stickers

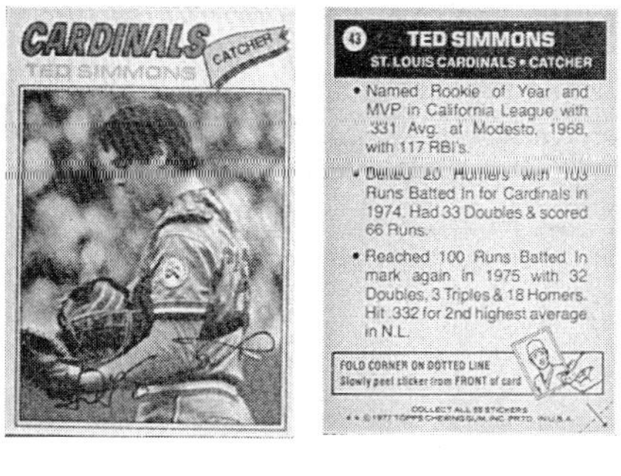

One of the few Topps specialty issues of the late 1970s, the 73-piece set of cloth stickers issued in 1977 includes 55 player stickers and 18 puzzle cards which could be joined to form a photo of the American League or National League All-Star teams. Issued as a separate issue, the 2-1/2" x 3-1/2" stickers have a paper backing which could be removed to allow the cloth to be adhered to a jacket, notebook, etc.

		NM	EX	VG
Complete Set (73):		200.00	100.00	60.00
Common Player:		1.25	.60	.40
1	Alan Ashby	1.25	.60	.40
2	Buddy Bell	1.25	.60	.40
3	Johnny Bench	12.00	6.00	3.50
4	Vida Blue	1.25	.60	.40
5	Bert Blyleven	1.25	.60	.40
6	Steve Braun	1.25	.60	.40
7	George Brett	25.00	12.50	7.50
8	Lou Brock	9.00	4.50	2.75
9	Jose Cardenal	1.25	.60	.40
10	Rod Carew	9.00	4.50	2.75
11	Steve Carlton	9.00	4.50	2.75
12	Dave Cash	1.25	.60	.40
13	Cesar Cedeno	1.25	.60	.40
14	Ron Cey	1.25	.60	.40
15	Mark Fidrych	3.50	1.75	1.00
16	Dan Ford	1.25	.60	.40
17	Wayne Garland	1.25	.60	.40
18	Ralph Garr	1.25	.60	.40
19	Steve Garvey	6.00	3.00	1.75
20	Mike Hargrove	1.25	.60	.40
21	Catfish Hunter	8.00	4.00	2.50
22	Reggie Jackson	12.00	6.00	3.50
23	Randy Jones	1.25	.60	.40
24	Dave Kingman	2.00	1.00	.60
25	Bill Madlock	1.25	.60	.40
26	Lee May	1.25	.60	.40
27	John Mayberry	1.25	.60	.40
28	Andy Messersmith	1.25	.60	.40
29	Willie Montanez	1.25	.60	.40
30	John Montefusco	1.25	.60	.40
31	Joe Morgan	9.00	4.50	2.75
32	Thurman Munson	11.00	5.50	3.25
33	Bobby Murcer	1.25	.60	.40
34	Al Oliver	1.25	.60	.40
35	Dave Pagan	1.25	.60	.40
36	Jim Palmer	9.00	4.50	2.75
37	Tony Perez	6.00	3.00	1.75
38	Pete Rose	35.00	17.50	10.50
39	Joe Rudi	1.25	.60	.40
40	Nolan Ryan	75.00	37.00	22.00
41	Mike Schmidt	25.00	12.50	7.50
42	Tom Seaver	15.00	7.50	4.50
43	Ted Simmons	1.25	.60	.40
44	Bill Singer	1.25	.60	.40
45	Willie Stargell	9.00	4.50	2.75
46	Rusty Staub	1.50	.70	.45
47	Don Sutton	8.00	4.00	2.50
48	Luis Tiant	1.50	.70	.45
49	Bill Travers	1.25	.60	.40
50	Claudell Washington	1.25	.60	.40
51	Bob Watson	1.25	.60	.40
52	Dave Winfield	9.00	4.50	2.75
53	Carl Yastrzemski	12.00	6.00	3.50
54	Robin Yount	12.00	6.00	3.50
55	Richie Zisk	1.25	.60	.40
----	American League 9-piece puzzle	7.50	3.75	2.25
----	National League 9-piece puzzle	7.50	3.75	2.25

1977 Topps Dale Murphy Aluminum

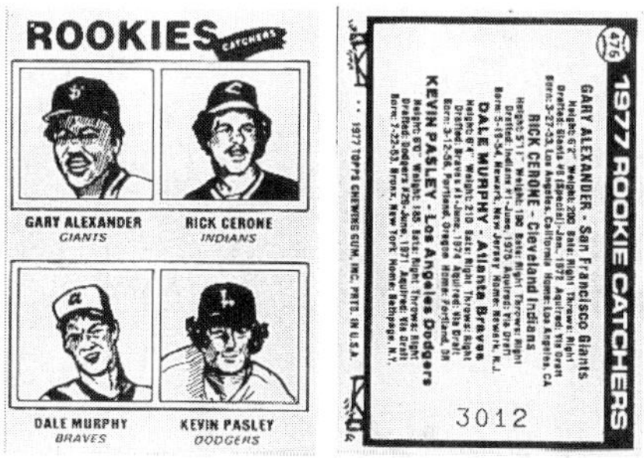

Authorized by Topps to be issued in 1984 as a fundraiser for Huntington's Disease research, this aluminum card is a full size replica of 1977 Topps card #476, Dale Murphy's rookie card. Front features rather crude black etchings of the player portraits found on the cardboard version, while back reproduces the biographical data and includes a serial number. The cards were originally sold for $10.

		NM	EX	VG
Dale Murphy aluminum replica		8.00	4.00	2.50
476	Rookie Catchers (Gary Alexander, Rick Cerone, Dale Murphy, Kevin Pasley)			

1978 Topps

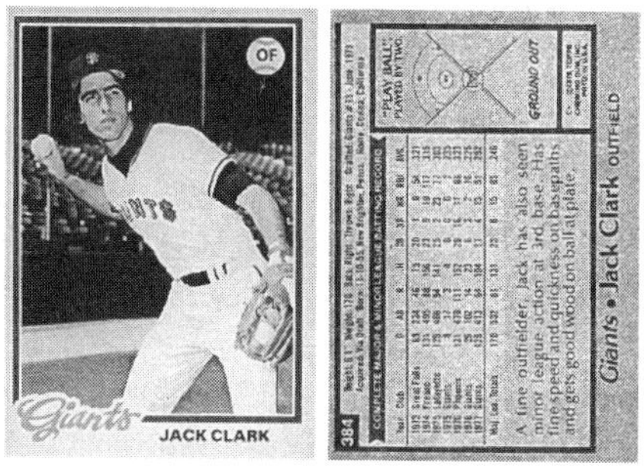

At 726 cards, this was the largest issue from Topps since 1972. In design, the color player photo is slightly larger than usual, with the player's name and team at the bottom. In the upper right-hand corner of the 2-1/2" x 3-1/2" cards there is a small white baseball with the player's position. Most of the starting All-Stars from the previous year had a red, white and blue shield instead of the baseball. Backs feature statistics and a baseball situation which made a card game of baseball possible. Specialty cards include baseball records, statistical leaders and the World Series and playoffs. As one row of cards per sheet had to be double-printed to accommodate the 720-card set size, some cards are more common, yet that seems to have no serious impact on their prices.

		NM	EX	VG
Complete Set (726):		150.00	75.00	45.00
Common Player:		.20	.10	.06
Wax Box:		400.00		
1	Lou Brock (Record Breaker)	1.25	.60	.40
2	Sparky Lyle (Record Breaker)	.20	.10	.06
3	Willie McCovey (Record Breaker)	.75	.40	.25
4	Brooks Robinson (Record Breaker)	1.50	.70	.45
5	Pete Rose (Record Breaker)	3.00	1.50	.90
6	Nolan Ryan (Record Breaker)	12.50	6.25	3.75
7	Reggie Jackson (Record Breaker)	2.00	1.00	.60
8	Mike Sadek	.20	.10	.06
9	Doug DeCinces	.20	.10	.06
10	Phil Niekro	1.50	.70	.45
11	Rick Manning	.20	.10	.06
12	Don Aase	.20	.10	.06
13	Art Howe	.20	.10	.06
14	Lerrin LaGrow	.20	.10	.06
15	Tony Perez	3.00	1.50	.90
16	Roy White	.20	.10	.06
17	Mike Krukow	.20	.10	.06
18	Bob Grich	.20	.10	.06
19	Darrell Porter	.20	.10	.06
20	Pete Rose	8.00	4.00	2.50
21	Steve Kemp	.20	.10	.06
22	Charlie Hough	.20	.10	.06
23	Bump Wills	.20	.10	.06
24	Don Money	.20	.10	.06
25	Jon Matlack	.20	.10	.06
26	Rich Hebner	.20	.10	.06
27	Geoff Zahn	.20	.10	.06
28	Ed Ott	.20	.10	.06
29	Bob Lacey	.20	.10	.06
30	George Hendrick	.20	.10	.06
31	Glenn Abbott	.20	.10	.06
32	Garry Templeton	.20	.10	.06
33	Dave Lemanczyk	.20	.10	.06
34	Willie McCovey	4.00	2.00	1.25
35	Sparky Lyle	.20	.10	.06
36	*Eddie Murray*	35.00	17.50	10.50
37	Rick Waits	.20	.10	.06
38	Willie Montanez	.20	.10	.06
39	*Floyd Bannister*	.60	.30	.20
40	Carl Yastrzemski	4.00	2.00	1.25
41	Burt Hooton	.20	.10	.06
42	Jorge Orta	.20	.10	.06
43	Bill Atkinson	.20	.10	.06
44	Toby Harrah	.20	.10	.06
45	Mark Fidrych	.25	.13	.08
46	Al Cowens	.20	.10	.06
47	Jack Billingham	.20	.10	.06
48	Don Baylor	.30	.15	.09
49	Ed Kranepool	.20	.10	.06
50	Rick Reuschel	.20	.10	.06
51	Charlie Moore	.20	.10	.06
52	Jim Lonborg	.20	.10	.06
53	Phil Garner	.20	.10	.06
54	Tom Johnson	.20	.10	.06
55	Mitchell Page	.20	.10	.06
56	Randy Jones	.20	.10	.06
57	Dan Meyer	.20	.10	.06
58	Bob Forsch	.20	.10	.06
59	Otto Velez	.20	.10	.06
60	Thurman Munson	4.00	2.00	1.25
61	Larvell Blanks	.20	.10	.06
62	Jim Barr	.20	.10	.06
63	Don Zimmer	.20	.10	.06
64	Gene Pentz	.20	.10	.06

65	Ken Singleton	.20	.10	.06
66	White Sox Team	.25	.13	.08
67	Claudell Washington	.20	.10	.06
68	Steve Foucault	.20	.10	.06
69	Mike Vail	.20	.10	.06
70	Rich Gossage	.20	.10	.06
71	Terry Humphrey	.20	.10	.06
72	Andre Dawson	6.00	3.00	1.75
73	Andy Hassler	.20	.10	.06
74	Checklist 1-121	.20	.10	.06
75	Dick Ruthven	.20	.10	.06
76	Steve Ontiveros	.20	.10	.06
77	Ed Kirkpatrick	.20	.10	.06
78	Pablo Torrealba	.20	.10	.06
79	Darrell Johnson (DP)	.20	.10	.06
80	Ken Griffey	.25	.13	.08
81	Pete Redfern	.20	.10	.06
82	Giants Team	.25	.13	.08
83	Bob Montgomery	.20	.10	.06
84	Kent Tekulve	.20	.10	.06
85	Ron Fairly	.20	.10	.06
86	Dave Tomlin	.20	.10	.06
87	John Lowenstein	.20	.10	.06
88	Mike Phillips	.20	.10	.06
89	Ken Clay	.20	.10	.06
90	Larry Bowa	.20	.10	.06
91	Oscar Zamora	.20	.10	.06
92	Adrian Devine	.20	.10	.06
93	Bobby Cox	.25	.13	.08
94	Chuck Scrivener	.20	.10	.06
95	Jamie Quirk	.20	.10	.06
96	Orioles Team	.25	.13	.08
97	Stan Bahnsen	.20	.10	.06
98	Jim Essian	.20	.10	.06
99	*Willie Hernandez*	.30	.15	.09
100	George Brett	10.00	5.00	3.00
101	Sid Monge	.20	.10	.06
102	Matt Alexander	.20	.10	.06
103	Tom Murphy	.20	.10	.06
104	Lee Lacy	.20	.10	.06
105	Reggie Cleveland	.20	.10	.06
106	Bill Plummer	.20	.10	.06
107	Ed Halicki	.20	.10	.06
108	Von Joshua	.20	.10	.06
109	Joe Torre	.50	.25	.15
110	Richie Zisk	.20	.10	.06
111	Mike Tyson	.20	.10	.06
112	Astros Team	.25	.13	.08
113	Don Carrithers	.20	.10	.06
114	Paul Blair	.20	.10	.06
115	Gary Nolan	.20	.10	.06
116	Tucker Ashford	.20	.10	.06
117	John Montague	.20	.10	.06
118	Terry Harmon	.20	.10	.06
119	Denny Martinez	.30	.15	.09
120	Gary Carter	1.50	.70	.45
121	Alvis Woods	.20	.10	.06
122	Dennis Eckersley	2.50	1.25	.70
123	Manny Trillo	.20	.10	.06
124	*Dave Rozema*	.20	.10	.06
125	George Scott	.20	.10	.06
126	Paul Moskau	.20	.10	.06
127	Chet Lemon	.20	.10	.06
128	Bill Russell	.20	.10	.06
129	Jim Colborn	.20	.10	.06
130	Jeff Burroughs	.20	.10	.06
131	Bert Blyleven	.20	.10	.06
132	Enos Cabell	.20	.10	.06
133	Jerry Augustine	.20	.10	.06
134	*Steve Henderson*	.20	.10	.06
135	Ron Guidry	.20	.10	.06
136	Ted Sizemore	.20	.10	.06
137	Craig Kusick	.20	.10	.06
138	Larry Demery	.20	.10	.06
139	Wayne Gross	.20	.10	.06
140	Rollie Fingers	2.00	1.00	.60
141	Ruppert Jones	.20	.10	.06
142	John Montefusco	.20	.10	.06
143	Keith Hernandez	.60	.30	.20
144	Jesse Jefferson	.20	.10	.06
145	Rick Monday	.20	.10	.06
146	Doyle Alexander	.20	.10	.06
147	Lee Mazzilli	.20	.10	.06
148	Andre Thornton	.20	.10	.06
149	Dale Murray	.20	.10	.06
150	Bobby Bonds	.20	.10	.06
151	Milt Wilcox	.20	.10	.06
152	*Ivan DeJesus*	.20	.10	.06
153	Steve Stone	.20	.10	.06
154	Cecil Cooper	.20	.10	.06
155	Butch Hobson	.20	.10	.06
156	Andy Messersmith	.20	.10	.06
157	Pete LaCock	.20	.10	.06
158	Joaquin Andujar	.20	.10	.06
159	Lou Piniella	.30	.15	.09
160	Jim Palmer	3.00	1.50	.90
161	Bob Boone	.20	.10	.06
162	Paul Thormodsgard	.20	.10	.06
163	Bill North	.20	.10	.06
164	Bob Owchinko	.20	.10	.06
165	Rennie Stennett	.20	.10	.06
166	Carlos Lopez	.20	.10	.06
167	Tim Foli	.20	.10	.06
168	Reggie Smith	.20	.10	.06
169	Jerry Johnson	.20	.10	.06
170	Lou Brock	3.00	1.50	.90
171	Pat Zachry	.20	.10	.06
172	Mike Hargrove	.20	.10	.06
173	Robin Yount	10.00	5.00	3.00
174	Wayne Garland	.20	.10	.06
175	Jerry Morales	.20	.10	.06
176	Milt May	.20	.10	.06
177	Gene Garber	.20	.10	.06
178	Dave Chalk	.20	.10	.06
179	Dick Tidrow	.20	.10	.06
180	Dave Concepcion	.25	.13	.08
181	Ken Forsch	.20	.10	.06
182	Jim Spencer	.20	.10	.06
183	Doug Bird	.20	.10	.06
184	Checklist 122-242	.20	.10	.06
185	Ellis Valentine	.20	.10	.06
186	*Bob Stanley*	.20	.10	.06
187	Jerry Royster	.20	.10	.06
188	Al Bumbry	.20	.10	.06
189	Tom Lasorda	.55	.30	.15
190	John Candelaria	.20	.10	.06
191	Rodney Scott	.20	.10	.06
192	Padres Team	.25	.13	.08
193	Rich Chiles	.20	.10	.06
194	Derrel Thomas	.20	.10	.06
195	Larry Dierker	.20	.10	.06
196	Bob Bailor	.20	.10	.06
197	Nino Espinosa	.20	.10	.06
198	Ron Pruitt	.20	.10	.06
199	Craig Reynolds	.20	.10	.06
200	Reggie Jackson	6.00	3.00	1.75
201	Batting Leaders (Rod Carew, Dave Parker)	.50	.25	.15
202	Home Run Leaders (George Foster, Jim Rice)	.25	.13	.08
203	RBI Leaders (George Foster, Larry Hisle)	.20	.10	.06
204	Stolen Base Leaders (Freddie Patek, Frank Taveras)	.20	.10	.06
205	Victory Leaders (Steve Carlton, Dave Goltz, Dennis Leonard, Jim Palmer)	.65	.35	.20
206	Strikeout Leaders (Phil Niekro, Nolan Ryan)	2.50	1.25	.70
207	ERA Leaders (John Candelaria, Frank Tanana)	.20	.10	.06
208	Leading Firemen (Bill Campbell, Rollie Fingers)	.25	.13	.08
209	Dock Ellis	.20	.10	.06
210	Jose Cardenal	.20	.10	.06
211	Earl Weaver (DP)	.50	.25	.15
212	Mike Caldwell	.20	.10	.06
213	Alan Bannister	.20	.10	.06
214	Angels Team	.25	.13	.08
215	Darrell Evans	.30	.15	.09
216	Mike Paxton	.20	.10	.06
217	Rod Gilbreath	.20	.10	.06
218	Marty Pattin	.20	.10	.06
219	Mike Cubbage	.20	.10	.06
220	Pedro Borbon	.20	.10	.06
221	Chris Speier	.20	.10	.06
222	Jerry Martin	.20	.10	.06
223	Bruce Kison	.20	.10	.06
224	Jerry Tabb	.20	.10	.06
225	Don Gullett	.20	.10	.06
226	Joe Ferguson	.20	.10	.06
227	Al Fitzmorris	.20	.10	.06
228	Manny Mota	.20	.10	.06
229	Leo Foster	.20	.10	.06
230	Al Hrabosky	.20	.10	.06
231	Wayne Nordhagen	.20	.10	.06
232	Mickey Stanley	.20	.10	.06
233	Dick Pole	.20	.10	.06
234	Herman Franks	.20	.10	.06
235	Tim McCarver	.30	.15	.09
236	Terry Whitfield	.20	.10	.06
237	Rich Dauer	.20	.10	.06
238	Juan Beniquez	.20	.10	.06
239	Dyar Miller	.20	.10	.06
240	Gene Tenace	.20	.10	.06
241	Pete Vuckovich	.20	.10	.06
242	Barry Bonnell	.20	.10	.06
243	Bob McClure	.20	.10	.06
244	Expos Team	.25	.13	.08
245	Rick Burleson	.20	.10	.06
246	Dan Driessen	.20	.10	.06
247	Larry Christenson	.20	.10	.06
248	Frank White	.20	.10	.06
249	Dave Goltz	.20	.10	.06
250	Graig Nettles	.20	.10	.06
251	Don Kirkwood	.20	.10	.06
252	Steve Swisher	.20	.10	.06
253	Jim Kern	.20	.10	.06
254	Dave Collins	.20	.10	.06
255	Jerry Reuss	.20	.10	.06
256	Joe Altobelli	.20	.10	.06
257	Hector Cruz	.20	.10	.06
258	John Hiller	.20	.10	.06
259	Dodgers Team	.50	.25	.15
260	Bert Campaneris	.20	.10	.06
261	Tim Hosley	.20	.10	.06
262	Rudy May	.20	.10	.06
263	Danny Walton	.20	.10	.06
264	Jamie Easterly	.20	.10	.06
265	Sal Bando	.20	.10	.06
266	*Bob Shirley*	.20	.10	.06
267	Doug Ault	.20	.10	.06
268	Gil Flores	.20	.10	.06
269	Wayne Twitchell	.20	.10	.06
270	Carlton Fisk	4.00	2.00	1.25
271	Randy Lerch	.20	.10	.06
272	Royle Stillman	.20	.10	.06
273	Fred Norman	.20	.10	.06
274	Freddie Patek	.20	.10	.06
275	Dan Ford	.20	.10	.06
276	Bill Bonham	.20	.10	.06
277	Bruce Boisclair	.20	.10	.06
278	Enrique Romo	.20	.10	.06
279	Bill Virdon	.20	.10	.06
280	Buddy Bell	.20	.10	.06
281	Eric Rasmussen	.20	.10	.06
282	Yankees Team	.75	.40	.25
283	Omar Moreno	.20	.10	.06
284	Randy Moffitt	.20	.10	.06
285	Steve Yeager	.20	.10	.06
286	Ben Oglivie	.20	.10	.06
287	Kiko Garcia	.20	.10	.06
288	Dave Hamilton	.20	.10	.06
289	Checklist 243-363	.20	.10	.06
290	Willie Horton	.20	.10	.06
291	Gary Ross	.20	.10	.06
292	Gene Richard	.20	.10	.06
293	Mike Willis	.20	.10	.06
294	Larry Parrish	.20	.10	.06
295	Bill Lee	.20	.10	.06
296	Biff Pocoroba	.20	.10	.06
297	Warren Brusstar	.20	.10	.06
298	Tony Armas	.20	.10	.06
299	Whitey Herzog	.20	.10	.06
300	Joe Morgan	2.50	1.25	.70
301	Buddy Schultz	.20	.10	.06
302	Cubs Team	.25	.13	.08
303	Sam Hinds	.20	.10	.06
304	John Milner	.20	.10	.06
305	Rico Carty	.20	.10	.06
306	Joe Niekro	.20	.10	.06
307	Glenn Borgmann	.20	.10	.06
308	Jim Rooker	.20	.10	.06
309	Cliff Johnson	.20	.10	.06
310	Don Sutton	2.00	1.00	.60
311	Jose Baez	.20	.10	.06
312	Greg Minton	.20	.10	.06
313	Andy Etchebarren	.20	.10	.06
314	Paul Lindblad	.20	.10	.06
315	Mark Belanger	.20	.10	.06
316	Henry Cruz	.20	.10	.06
317	Dave Johnson	.20	.10	.06
318	Tom Griffin	.20	.10	.06
319	Alan Ashby	.20	.10	.06
320	Fred Lynn	.20	.10	.06
321	Santo Alcala	.20	.10	.06
322	Tom Paciorek	.20	.10	.06
323	Jim Fregosi (DP)	.20	.10	.06
324	Vern Rapp	.20	.10	.06
325	Bruce Sutter	.20	.10	.06
326	Mike Lum	.20	.10	.06
327	Rick Langford	.20	.10	.06
328	Brewers Team	.25	.13	.08
329	John Verhoeven	.20	.10	.06
330	Bob Watson	.20	.10	.06
331	Mark Littell	.20	.10	.06
332	Duane Kuiper	.20	.10	.06
333	Jim Todd	.20	.10	.06
334	John Stearns	.20	.10	.06
335	Bucky Dent	.20	.10	.06
336	Steve Busby	.20	.10	.06
337	Tom Grieve	.20	.10	.06
338	Dave Heaverlo	.20	.10	.06
339	Mario Guerrero	.20	.10	.06
340	Bake McBride	.20	.10	.06
341	Mike Flanagan	.20	.10	.06
342	Aurelio Rodriguez	.20	.10	.06
343	John Wathan (DP)	.20	.10	.06
344	Sam Ewing	.20	.10	.06
345	Luis Tiant	.20	.10	.06
346	Larry Biittner	.20	.10	.06
347	Terry Forster	.20	.10	.06
348	Del Unser	.20	.10	.06
349	Rick Camp (DP)	.20	.10	.06
350	Steve Garvey	2.50	1.25	.70
351	Jeff Torborg	.20	.10	.06
352	Tony Scott	.20	.10	.06
353	Doug Bair	.20	.10	.06
354	Cesar Geronimo	.20	.10	.06
355	Bill Travers	.20	.10	.06
356	Mets Team	.60	.30	.20
357	Tom Poquette	.20	.10	.06
358	Mark Lemongello	.20	.10	.06
359	Marc Hill	.20	.10	.06
360	Mike Schmidt	10.00	5.00	3.00
361	Chris Knapp	.20	.10	.06
362	Dave May	.20	.10	.06
363	Bob Randall	.20	.10	.06
364	Jerry Turner	.20	.10	.06
365	Ed Figueroa	.20	.10	.06
366	Larry Milbourne (DP)	.20	.10	.06
367	Rick Dempsey	.20	.10	.06
368	Balor Moore	.20	.10	.06
369	Tim Nordbrook	.20	.10	.06
370	Rusty Staub	.25	.13	.08
371	Ray Burris	.20	.10	.06
372	Brian Asselstine	.20	.10	.06
373	Jim Willoughby	.20	.10	.06
374	Jose Morales	.20	.10	.06
375	Tommy John	.30	.15	.09
376	Jim Wohlford	.20	.10	.06
377	Manny Sarmiento	.20	.10	.06
378	Bobby Winkles	.20	.10	.06
379	Skip Lockwood	.20	.10	.06
380	Ted Simmons	.20	.10	.06
381	Phillies Team	.35	.20	.11
382	Joe Lahoud	.20	.10	.06
383	Mario Mendoza	.20	.10	.06
384	Jack Clark	.35	.20	.11
385	Tito Fuentes	.20	.10	.06
386	Bob Gorinski	.20	.10	.06
387	Ken Holtzman	.20	.10	.06
388	Bill Fahey (DP)	.20	.10	.06
389	Julio Gonzalez	.20	.10	.06
390	Oscar Gamble	.20	.10	.06
391	Larry Haney	.20	.10	.06
392	Billy Almon	.20	.10	.06
393	Tippy Martinez	.20	.10	.06
394	Roy Howell	.20	.10	.06
395	Jim Hughes	.20	.10	.06
396	Bob Stinson	.20	.10	.06
397	Greg Gross	.20	.10	.06
398	Don Hood	.20	.10	.06
399	Pete Mackanin	.20	.10	.06
400	Nolan Ryan	25.00	12.50	7.50
401	Sparky Anderson	.55	.30	.15
402	Dave Campbell	.20	.10	.06
403	Bud Harrelson	.20	.10	.06
404	Tigers Team	.25	.13	.08
405	Rawly Eastwick	.20	.10	.06
406	Mike Jorgensen	.20	.10	.06
407	Odell Jones	.20	.10	.06
408	Joe Zdeb	.20	.10	.06

409	Ron Schueler	.20	.10	.06
410	Bill Madlock	.20	.10	.06
411	A.L. Championships (Yankees Rally To Defeat Royals)	.70	.35	.20
412	N.L. Championships (Dodgers Overpower Phillies In Four)	.50	.25	.15
413	World Series (Reggie & Yankees Reign Supreme)	2.50	1.25	.70
414	Darold Knowles (DP)	.20	.10	.06
415	Ray Fosse	.20	.10	.06
416	Jack Brohamer	.20	.10	.06
417	Mike Garman	.20	.10	.06
418	Tony Muser	.20	.10	.06
419	Jerry Garvin	.20	.10	.06
420	Greg Luzinski	.20	.10	.06
421	Junior Moore	.20	.10	.06
422	Steve Braun	.20	.10	.06
423	Dave Rosello	.20	.10	.06
424	Red Sox Team	.45	.25	.14
425	Steve Rogers	.20	.10	.06
426	Fred Kendall	.20	.10	.06
427	*Mario Soto*	.40	.20	.12
428	Joel Youngblood	.20	.10	.06
429	Mike Barlow	.20	.10	.06
430	Al Oliver	.30	.15	.09
431	Butch Metzger	.20	.10	.06
432	Terry Bulling	.20	.10	.06
433	Fernando Gonzalez	.20	.10	.06
434	Mike Norris	.20	.10	.06
435	Checklist 364-484	.20	.10	.06
436	Vic Harris (DP)	.20	.10	.06
437	Bo McLaughlin	.20	.10	.06
438	John Ellis	.20	.10	.06
439	Ken Kravec	.20	.10	.06
440	Dave Lopes	.20	.10	.06
441	Larry Gura	.20	.10	.06
442	Elliott Maddox	.20	.10	.06
443	Darrel Chaney	.20	.10	.06
444	Roy Hartsfield	.20	.10	.06
445	Mike Ivie	.20	.10	.06
446	Tug McGraw	.20	.10	.06
447	Leroy Stanton	.20	.10	.06
448	Bill Castro	.20	.10	.06
449	Tim Blackwell	.20	.10	.06
450	Tom Seaver	6.00	3.00	1.75
451	Twins Team	.25	.13	.08
452	Jerry Mumphrey	.20	.10	.06
453	Doug Flynn	.20	.10	.06
454	Dave LaRoche	.20	.10	.06
455	Bill Robinson	.20	.10	.06
456	Vern Ruhle	.20	.10	.06
457	Bob Bailey	.20	.10	.06
458	Jeff Newman	.20	.10	.06
459	Charlie Spikes	.20	.10	.06
460	Catfish Hunter	2.00	1.00	.60
461	Rob Andrews	.20	.10	.06
462	Rogelio Moret	.20	.10	.06
463	Kevin Bell	.20	.10	.06
464	Jerry Grote	.20	.10	.06
465	Hal McRae	.20	.10	.06
466	Dennis Blair	.20	.10	.06
467	Alvin Dark	.20	.10	.06
468	*Warren Cromartie*	.20	.10	.06
469	Rick Cerone	.20	.10	.06
470	J.R. Richard	.20	.10	.06
471	Roy Smalley	.20	.10	.06
472	Ron Reed	.20	.10	.06
473	Bill Buckner	.20	.10	.06
474	Jim Slaton	.20	.10	.06
475	Gary Matthews	.20	.10	.06
476	Bill Stein	.20	.10	.06
477	Doug Capilla	.20	.10	.06
478	Jerry Remy	.20	.10	.06
479	Cardinals Team	.25	.13	.08
480	Ron LeFlore	.20	.10	.06
481	Jackson Todd	.20	.10	.06
482	Rick Miller	.20	.10	.06
483	Ken Macha	.20	.10	.06
484	Jim Norris	.20	.10	.06
485	Chris Chambliss	.20	.10	.06
486	John Curtis	.20	.10	.06
487	Jim Tyrone	.20	.10	.06
488	Dan Spillner	.20	.10	.06
489	Rudy Meoli	.20	.10	.06
490	Amos Otis	.20	.10	.06
491	Scott McGregor	.20	.10	.06
492	Jim Sundberg	.20	.10	.06
493	Steve Renko	.20	.10	.06
494	Chuck Tanner	.20	.10	.06
495	Dave Cash	.20	.10	.06
496	*Jim Clancy*	.20	.10	.06
497	Glenn Adams	.20	.10	.06
498	Joe Sambito	.20	.10	.06
499	Mariners Team	.25	.13	.08
500	George Foster	.30	.15	.09
501	Dave Roberts	.20	.10	.06
502	Pat Rockett	.20	.10	.06
503	Ike Hampton	[illegible]	.10	.06
504	Roger Freed	.20	.10	.06
505	Felix Millan	.20	.10	.06
506	Ron Blomberg	.20	.10	.06
507	Willie Crawford	.20	.10	.06
508	Johnny Oates	.20	.10	.06
509	Brent Strom	.20	.10	.06
510	Willie Stargell	2.50	1.25	.70
511	Frank Duffy	.20	.10	.06
512	Larry Herndon	.20	.10	.06
513	Barry Foote	.20	.10	.06
514	Rob Sperring	.20	.10	.06
515	Tim Corcoran	.20	.10	.06
516	Gary Beare	.20	.10	.06
517	Andres Mora	.20	.10	.06
518	Tommy Boggs (DP)	.20	.10	.06
519	Brian Downing	.20	.10	.06
520	Larry Hisle	.20	.10	.06
521	Steve Staggs	.20	.10	.06
522	Dick Williams	.20	.10	.06
523	*Donnie Moore*	.20	.10	.06
524	Bernie Carbo	.20	.10	.06
525	Jerry Terrell	.20	.10	.06
526	Reds Team	.45	.25	.14
527	Vic Correll	.20	.10	.06
528	Rob Picciolo	.20	.10	.06
529	Paul Hartzell	.20	.10	.06
530	Dave Winfield	4.00	2.00	1.25
531	Tom Underwood	.20	.10	.06
532	Skip Jutze	.20	.10	.06
533	Sandy Alomar	.20	.10	.06
534	Wilbur Howard	.20	.10	.06
535	Checklist 485-605	.20	.10	.06
536	Roric Harrison	.20	.10	.06
537	Bruce Bochte	.20	.10	.06
538	Johnnie LeMaster	.20	.10	.06
539	Vic Davalillo	.20	.10	.06
540	Steve Carlton	4.00	2.00	1.25
541	Larry Cox	.20	.10	.06
542	Tim Johnson	.20	.10	.06
543	Larry Harlow	.20	.10	.06
544	Len Randle	.20	.10	.06
545	Bill Campbell	.20	.10	.06
546	Ted Martinez	.20	.10	.06
547	John Scott	.20	.10	.06
548	Billy Hunter (DP)	.20	.10	.06
549	Joe Kerrigan	.20	.10	.06
550	John Mayberry	.20	.10	.06
551	Braves Team	.25	.13	.08
552	Francisco Barrios	.20	.10	.06
553	*Terry Puhl*	.25	.13	.08
554	Joe Coleman	.20	.10	.06
555	Butch Wynegar	.20	.10	.06
556	Ed Armbrister	.20	.10	.06
557	Tony Solaita	.20	.10	.06
558	Paul Mitchell	.20	.10	.06
559	Phil Mankowski	.20	.10	.06
560	Dave Parker	.75	.40	.25
561	Charlie Williams	.20	.10	.06
562	Glenn Burke	.20	.10	.06
563	Dave Rader	.20	.10	.06
564	Mick Kelleher	.20	.10	.06
565	Jerry Koosman	.20	.10	.06
566	Merv Rettenmund	.20	.10	.06
567	Dick Drago	.20	.10	.06
568	Tom Hutton	.20	.10	.06
569	*Lary Sorensen*	.20	.10	.06
570	Dave Kingman	.30	.15	.09
571	Buck Martinez	.20	.10	.06
572	Rick Wise	.20	.10	.06
573	Luis Gomez	.20	.10	.06
574	Bob Lemon	.45	.25	.14
575	Pat Dobson	.20	.10	.06
576	Sam Mejias	.20	.10	.06
577	A's Team	.25	.13	.08
578	Buzz Capra	.20	.10	.06
579	*Rance Mulliniks*	.25	.13	.08
580	Rod Carew	4.00	2.00	1.25
581	Lynn McGlothen	.20	.10	.06
582	Fran Healy	.20	.10	.06
583	George Medich	.20	.10	.06
584	John Hale	.20	.10	.06
585	Woodie Fryman	.20	.10	.06
586	Ed Goodson	.20	.10	.06
587	John Urrea	.20	.10	.06
588	Jim Mason	.20	.10	.06
589	*Bob Knepper*	.40	.20	.12
590	Bobby Murcer	.20	.10	.06
591	George Zeber	.20	.10	.06
592	Bob Apodaca	.20	.10	.06
593	Dave Skaggs	.20	.10	.06
594	Dave Freisleben	.20	.10	.06
595	Sixto Lezcano	.20	.10	.06
596	Gary Wheelock	.20	.10	.06
597	Steve Dillard	.20	.10	.06
598	Eddie Solomon	.20	.10	.06
599	Gary Woods	.20	.10	.06
600	Frank Tanana	.20	.10	.06
601	Gene Mauch	.20	.10	.06
602	Eric Soderholm	.20	.10	.06
603	Will McEnaney	.20	.10	.06
604	Earl Williams	.20	.10	.06
605	Rick Rhoden	.20	.10	.06
606	Pirates Team	.25	.13	.08
607	Fernando Arroyo	.20	.10	.06
608	Johnny Grubb	.20	.10	.06
609	John Denny	.20	.10	.06
610	Garry Maddox	.20	.10	.06
611	Pat Scanlon	.20	.10	.06
612	Ken Henderson	.20	.10	.06
613	Marty Perez	.20	.10	.06
614	Joe Wallis	.20	.10	.06
615	Clay Carroll	.20	.10	.06
616	Pat Kelly	.20	.10	.06
617	Joe Nolan	.20	.10	.06
618	Tommy Helms	.20	.10	.06
619	*Thad Bosley*	.20	.10	.06
620	Willie Randolph	.20	.10	.06
621	Craig Swan	.20	.10	.06
622	Champ Summers	.20	.10	.06
623	Eduardo Rodriguez	.20	.10	.06
624	Gary Alexander	.20	.10	.06
625	Jose Cruz	.20	.10	.06
626	Blue Jays Team	.25	.13	.08
627	Dave Johnson	.20	.10	.06
628	Ralph Garr	.20	.10	.06
629	Don Stanhouse	.20	.10	.06
630	Ron Cey	.20	.10	.06
631	Danny Ozark	.20	.10	.06
632	Rowland Office	.20	.10	.06
633	Tom Veryzer	.20	.10	.06
634	Len Barker	.20	.10	.06
635	Joe Rudi	.20	.10	.06
636	Jim Bibby	.20	.10	.06
637	Duffy Dyer	.20	.10	.06
638	Paul Splittorff	.20	.10	.06
639	Gene Clines	.20	.10	.06
640	Lee May	.20	.10	.06
641	Doug Rau	.20	.10	.06
642	Denny Doyle	.20	.10	.06
643	Tom House	.20	.10	.06
644	Jim Dwyer	.20	.10	.06
645	Mike Torrez	.20	.10	.06
646	Rick Auerbach	.20	.10	.06
647	Steve Dunning	.20	.10	.06
648	Gary Thomasson	.20	.10	.06
649	*Moose Haas*	.20	.10	.06
650	Cesar Cedeno	.20	.10	.06
651	Doug Rader	.20	.10	.06
652	Checklist 606-726	.20	.10	.06
653	Ron Hodges	.20	.10	.06
654	Pepe Frias	.20	.10	.06
655	Lyman Bostock	.20	.10	.06
656	Dave Garcia	.20	.10	.06
657	Bombo Rivera	.20	.10	.06
658	Manny Sanguillen	.20	.10	.06
659	Rangers Team	.25	.13	.08
660	Jason Thompson	.20	.10	.06
661	Grant Jackson	.20	.10	.06
662	Paul Dade	.20	.10	.06
663	Paul Reuschel	.20	.10	.06
664	Fred Stanley	.20	.10	.06
665	Dennis Leonard	.20	.10	.06
666	Billy Smith	.20	.10	.06
667	Jeff Byrd	.20	.10	.06
668	Dusty Baker	.25	.13	.08
669	Pete Falcone	.20	.10	.06
670	Jim Rice	.75	.40	.25
671	Gary Lavelle	.20	.10	.06
672	Don Kessinger	.20	.10	.06
673	Steve Brye	.20	.10	.06
674	*Ray Knight*	1.00	.50	.30
675	Jay Johnstone	.20	.10	.06
676	Bob Myrick	.20	.10	.06
677	Ed Herrmann	.20	.10	.06
678	Tom Burgmeier	.20	.10	.06
679	Wayne Garrett	.20	.10	.06
680	Vida Blue	.20	.10	.06
681	Rob Belloir	.20	.10	.06
682	Ken Brett	.20	.10	.06
683	Mike Champion	.20	.10	.06
684	Ralph Houk	.20	.10	.06
685	Frank Taveras	.20	.10	.06
686	Gaylord Perry	2.00	1.00	.60
687	*Julio Cruz*	.25	.13	.08
688	George Mitterwald	.20	.10	.06
689	Indians Team	.25	.13	.08
690	Mickey Rivers	.20	.10	.06
691	Ross Grimsley	.20	.10	.06
692	Ken Reitz	.20	.10	.06
693	Lamar Johnson	.20	.10	.06
694	Elias Sosa	.20	.10	.06
695	Dwight Evans	.25	.13	.08
696	Steve Mingori	.20	.10	.06
697	Roger Metzger	.20	.10	.06
698	Juan Bernhardt	.20	.10	.06
699	Jackie Brown	.20	.10	.06
700	Johnny Bench	5.00	2.50	1.50
701	Rookie Pitchers *(Tom Hume*, Larry Landreth), *(Steve McCatty*, Bruce Taylor)	.20	.10	.06
702	Rookie Catchers (Bill Nahorodny, Kevin Pasley, Rick Sweet, Don Werner)	.20	.10	.06
703	Rookie Pitchers *(Larry Andersen), (Tim Jones), (Mickey Mahler), (Jack Morris)*	3.50	1.75	1.00
704	Rookie 2nd Basemen *(Garth Iorg*, Dave Oliver, Sam Perlozzo), *(Lou Whitaker)*	12.00	6.00	3.50
705	Rookie Outfielders *(Dave Bergman*, Miguel Dilone), *(Clint Hurdle*, Willie Norwood)	.20	.10	.06
706	Rookie 1st Basemen (Wayne Cage, Ted Cox), *(Pat Putnam), (Dave Revering)*	.20	.10	.06
707	Rookie Shortstops *(Mickey Klutts), (Paul Molitor), (Alan Trammell), (U.L. Washington)*	40.00	20.00	12.00
708	Rookie Catchers *(Bo Diaz*, Dale Murphy), *(Lance Parrish), (Ernie Whitt)*	12.00	6.00	3.50
709	Rookie Pitchers (Steve Burke), *(Matt Keough*, Lance Rautzhan), *(Dan Schatzeder)*	.20	.10	.06
710	Rookie Outfielders (Dell Alston, Rick Bosetti), *(Mike Easler*, Keith Smith)	.20	.10	.06
711	Rookie Pitchers (Cardell Camper, Dennis Lamp, Craig Mitchell, Roy Thomas)	.20	.10	.06
712	Bobby Valentine	.20	.10	.06
713	Bob Davis	.20	.10	.06
714	Mike Anderson	.20	.10	.06
715	Jim Kaat	.35	.20	.11
716	Cito Gaston	.20	.10	.06
717	Nelson Briles	.20	.10	.06
718	Ron Jackson	.20	.10	.06
719	Randy Elliott	.20	.10	.06
720	Fergie Jenkins	2.00	1.00	.60
721	Billy Martin	.45	.25	.14
722	Pete Broberg	.20	.10	.06
723	Johnny Wockenfuss	.20	.10	.06
724	Royals Team	.25	.13	.08
725	Kurt Bevacqua	.20	.10	.06
726	Wilbur Wood	.20	.10	.06

Check lists with card numbers in parentheses ( ) indicates the numbers do not appear on the cards.

1978 Topps Team/Checklist Uncut Sheet

A redemption offer on packs of 1978 Topps cards offered an uncut sheet of the 26 team/checklist cards by mail. Besides the team cards, the 10-1/2" x 22-1/2" sheet has a card offering collectors card boxes. The cards on the sheet are identical to the single team/checklist cards issued in packs.

	NM	EX	VG
Uncut Sheet	36.00	18.00	10.00

1979 Topps

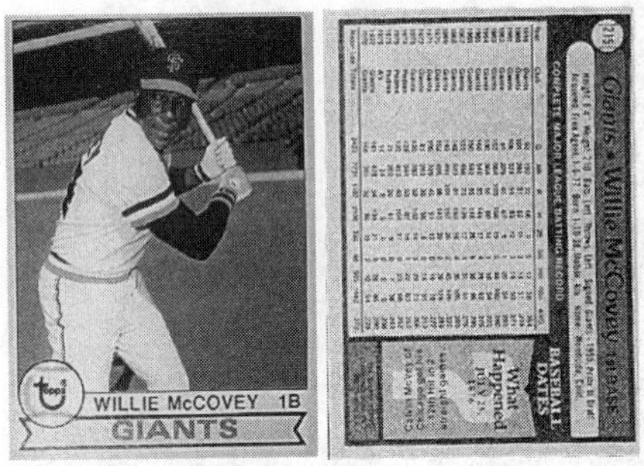

The size of this issue remained the same as in 1978 with 726 cards making their appearance. Actually, the 2-1/2" x 3-1/2" cards have a relatively minor design change from the previous year. The large color photo still dominates the front, with the player's name, team and position below it. The baseball with the player's position was moved to the lower left and the position replaced by a Topps logo. On the back, the printing color was changed and the game situation was replaced by a quiz called "Baseball Dates". Specialty cards include statistical leaders, major league records set during the season and eight cards devoted to career records. For the first time, rookies were arranged by teams under the heading of "Prospects." The key Ozzie Smith rookie card is usually seen with very poor centering.

		NM	EX	VG
Complete Set (726):		125.00	65.00	35.00
Common Player:		.15	.08	.05
Wax Box:		250.00		
1	Batting Leaders (Rod Carew, Dave Parker)	1.50	.70	.45
2	Home Run Leaders (George Foster, Jim Rice)	.15	.08	.05
3	RBI Leaders (George Foster, Jim Rice)	.15	.08	.05
4	Stolen Base Leaders (Ron LeFlore, Omar Moreno)	.15	.08	.05
5	Victory Leaders (Ron Guidry, Gaylord Perry)	.15	.08	.05
6	Strikeout Leaders (J.R. Richard, Nolan Ryan)	4.50	2.25	1.25
7	ERA Leaders (Ron Guidry, Craig Swan)	.15	.08	.05
8	Leading Firemen (Rollie Fingers, Rich Gossage)	.20	.10	.06
9	Dave Campbell	.15	.08	.05
10	Lee May	.15	.08	.05
11	Marc Hill	.15	.08	.05
12	Dick Drago	.15	.08	.05
13	Paul Dade	.15	.08	.05
14	Rafael Landestoy	.15	.08	.05
15	Ross Grimsley	.15	.08	.05
16	Fred Stanley	.15	.08	.05
17	Donnie Moore	.15	.08	.05
18	Tony Solaita	.15	.08	.05
19	Larry Gura	.15	.08	.05
20	Joe Morgan	1.25	.60	.40
21	Kevin Kobel	.15	.08	.05
22	Mike Jorgensen	.15	.08	.05
23	Terry Forster	.15	.08	.05
24	Paul Molitor	15.00	7.50	4.50
25	Steve Carlton	3.00	1.50	.90
26	Jamie Quirk	.15	.08	.05
27	Dave Goltz	.15	.08	.05
28	Steve Brye	.15	.08	.05
29	Rick Langford	.15	.08	.05
30	Dave Winfield	6.00	3.00	1.75
31	Tom House	.15	.08	.05
32	Jerry Mumphrey	.15	.08	.05
33	Dave Rozema	.15	.08	.05
34	Rob Andrews	.15	.08	.05
35	Ed Figueroa	.15	.08	.05
36	Alan Ashby	.15	.08	.05
37	Joe Kerrigan	.15	.08	.05
38	Bernie Carbo	.15	.08	.05
39	Dale Murphy	6.00	3.00	1.75
40	Dennis Eckersley	2.00	1.00	.60

41	Twins Team (Gene Mauch)	.25	.13	.08
42	Ron Blomberg	.15	.08	.05
43	Wayne Twitchell	.15	.08	.05
44	Kurt Bevacqua	.15	.08	.05
45	Al Hrabosky	.15	.08	.05
46	Ron Hodges	.15	.08	.05
47	Fred Norman	.15	.08	.05
48	Merv Rettenmund	.15	.08	.05
49	Vern Ruhle	.15	.08	.05
50	Steve Garvey	.90	.45	.25
51	Ray Fosse	.15	.08	.05
52	Randy Lerch	.15	.08	.05
53	Mick Kelleher	.15	.08	.05
54	Dell Alston	.15	.08	.05
55	Willie Stargell	2.00	1.00	.60
56	John Hale	.15	.08	.05
57	Eric Rasmussen	.15	.08	.05
58	Bob Randall	.15	.08	.05
59	John Denny	.15	.08	.05
60	Mickey Rivers	.15	.08	.05
61	Bo Diaz	.15	.08	.05
62	Randy Moffitt	.15	.08	.05
63	Jack Brohamer	.15	.08	.05
64	Tom Underwood	.15	.08	.05
65	Mark Belanger	.15	.08	.05
66	Tigers Team (Les Moss)	.25	.13	.08
67	Jim Mason	.15	.08	.05
68	Joe Niekro	.15	.08	.05
69	Elliott Maddox	.15	.08	.05
70	John Candelaria	.15	.08	.05
71	Brian Downing	.15	.08	.05
72	Steve Mingori	.15	.08	.05
73	Ken Henderson	.15	.08	.05
74	*Shane Rawley*	.15	.08	.05
75	Steve Yeager	.15	.08	.05
76	Warren Cromartie	.15	.08	.05
77	Dan Briggs	.15	.08	.05
78	Elias Sosa	.15	.08	.05
79	Ted Cox	.15	.08	.05
80	Jason Thompson	.15	.08	.05
81	Roger Erickson	.15	.08	.05
82	Mets Team (Joe Torre)	.50	.25	.15
83	Fred Kendall	.15	.08	.05
84	Greg Minton	.15	.08	.05
85	Gary Matthews	.15	.08	.05
86	Rodney Scott	.15	.08	.05
87	Pete Falcone	.15	.08	.05
88	Bob Molinaro	.15	.08	.05
89	Dick Tidrow	.15	.08	.05
90	Bob Boone	.15	.08	.05
91	Terry Crowley	.15	.08	.05
92	Jim Bibby	.15	.08	.05
93	Phil Mankowski	.15	.08	.05
94	Len Barker	.15	.08	.05
95	Robin Yount	8.00	4.00	2.50
96	Indians Team (Jeff Torborg)	.25	.13	.08
97	Sam Mejias	.15	.08	.05
98	Ray Burris	.15	.08	.05
99	John Wathan	.15	.08	.05
100	Tom Seaver	3.50	1.75	1.00
101	Roy Howell	.15	.08	.05
102	Mike Anderson	.15	.08	.05
103	Jim Todd	.15	.08	.05
104	Johnny Oates	.15	.08	.05
105	Rick Camp	.15	.08	.05
106	Frank Duffy	.15	.08	.05
107	Jesus Alou	.15	.08	.05
108	Eduardo Rodriguez	.15	.08	.05
109	Joel Youngblood	.15	.08	.05
110	Vida Blue	.15	.08	.05
111	Roger Freed	.15	.08	.05
112	Phillies Team (Danny Ozark)	.25	.13	.08
113	Pete Redfern	.15	.08	.05
114	Cliff Johnson	.15	.08	.05
115	Nolan Ryan	15.00	7.50	4.50
116	*Ozzie Smith*	45.00	22.00	13.50
117	Grant Jackson	.15	.08	.05
118	Bud Harrelson	.15	.08	.05
119	Don Stanhouse	.15	.08	.05
120	Jim Sundberg	.15	.08	.05
121	Checklist 1-121	.15	.08	.05
122	Mike Paxton	.15	.08	.05
123	Lou Whitaker	2.00	1.00	.60
124	Dan Schatzeder	.15	.08	.05
125	Rick Burleson	.15	.08	.05
126	Doug Bair	.15	.08	.05
127	Thad Bosley	.15	.08	.05
128	Ted Martinez	.15	.08	.05
129	Marty Pattin	.15	.08	.05
130	Bob Watson	.15	.08	.05
131	Jim Clancy	.15	.08	.05
132	Rowland Office	.15	.08	.05
133	Bill Castro	.15	.08	.05
134	Alan Bannister	.15	.08	.05
135	Bobby Murcer	.15	.08	.05
136	Jim Kaat	.25	.13	.08
137	Larry Wolfe	.15	.08	.05
138	Mark Lee	.15	.08	.05
139	Luis Pujols	.15	.08	.05
140	Don Gullett	.15	.08	.05
141	Tom Paciorek	.15	.08	.05
142	Charlie Williams	.15	.08	.05
143	Tony Scott	.15	.08	.05
144	Sandy Alomar	.15	.08	.05
145	Rick Rhoden	.15	.08	.05
146	Duane Kuiper	.15	.08	.05
147	Dave Hamilton	.15	.08	.05
148	Bruce Boisclair	.15	.08	.05
149	Manny Sarmiento	.15	.08	.05
150	Wayne Cage	.15	.08	.05
151	John Hiller	.15	.08	.05
152	Rick Cerone	.15	.08	.05
153	Dennis Lamp	.15	.08	.05
154	Jim Gantner	.15	.08	.05
155	Dwight Evans	.25	.13	.08
156	Buddy Solomon	.15	.08	.05
157	U.L. Washington	.15	.08	.05
158	Joe Sambito	.15	.08	.05

159	Roy White	.15	.08	.05
160	Mike Flanagan	.15	.08	.05
161	Barry Foote	.15	.08	.05
162	Tom Johnson	.15	.08	.05
163	Glenn Burke	.15	.08	.05
164	Mickey Lolich	.20	.10	.06
165	Frank Taveras	.15	.08	.05
166	Leon Roberts	.15	.08	.05
167	Roger Metzger	.15	.08	.05
168	Dave Freisleben	.15	.08	.05
169	Bill Nahorodny	.15	.08	.05
170	Don Sutton	1.50	.70	.45
171	Gene Clines	.15	.08	.05
172	Mike Bruhert	.15	.08	.05
173	John Lowenstein	.15	.08	.05
174	Rick Auerbach	.15	.08	.05
175	George Hendrick	.15	.08	.05
176	Aurelio Rodriguez	.15	.08	.05
177	Ron Reed	.15	.08	.05
178	Alvis Woods	.15	.08	.05
179	Jim Beattie	.15	.08	.05
180	Larry Hisle	.15	.08	.05
181	Mike Garman	.15	.08	.05
182	Tim Johnson	.15	.08	.05
183	Paul Splittorff	.15	.08	.05
184	Darrel Chaney	.15	.08	.05
185	Mike Torrez	.15	.08	.05
186	Eric Soderholm	.15	.08	.05
187	Mark Lemongello	.15	.08	.05
188	Pat Kelly	.15	.08	.05
189	*Eddie Whitson*	.25	.13	.08
190	Ron Cey	.15	.08	.05
191	Mike Norris	.15	.08	.05
192	Cardinals Team (Ken Boyer)	.25	.13	.08
193	Glenn Adams	.15	.08	.05
194	Randy Jones	.15	.08	.05
195	Bill Madlock	.15	.08	.05
196	Steve Kemp	.15	.08	.05
197	Bob Apodaca	.15	.08	.05
198	Johnny Grubb	.15	.08	.05
199	Larry Milbourne	.15	.08	.05
200	Johnny Bench	3.00	1.50	.90
201	Mike Edwards (Record Breaker)	.15	.08	.05
202	Ron Guidry (Record Breaker)	.15	.08	.05
203	J.R. Richard (Record Breaker)	.15	.08	.05
204	Pete Rose (Record Breaker)	1.00	.50	.30
205	John Stearns (Record Breaker)	.15	.08	.05
206	Sammy Stewart (Record Breaker)	.15	.08	.05
207	Dave Lemanczyk	.15	.08	.05
208	Cito Gaston	.15	.08	.05
209	Reggie Cleveland	.15	.08	.05
210	Larry Bowa	.15	.08	.05
211	Denny Martinez	.25	.13	.08
212	*Carney Lansford*	.75	.40	.25
213	Bill Travers	.15	.08	.05
214	Red Sox Team (Don Zimmer)	.35	.20	.11
215	Willie McCovey	2.00	1.00	.60
216	Wilbur Wood	.15	.08	.05
217	Steve Dillard	.15	.08	.05
218	Dennis Leonard	.15	.08	.05
219	Roy Smalley	.15	.08	.05
220	Cesar Geronimo	.15	.08	.05
221	Jesse Jefferson	.15	.08	.05
222	Bob Beall	.15	.08	.05
223	Kent Tekulve	.15	.08	.05
224	Dave Revering	.15	.08	.05
225	Rich Gossage	.15	.08	.05
226	Ron Pruitt	.15	.08	.05
227	Steve Stone	.15	.08	.05
228	Vic Davalillo	.15	.08	.05
229	Doug Flynn	.15	.08	.05
230	Bob Forsch	.15	.08	.05
231	Johnny Wockenfuss	.15	.08	.05
232	Jimmy Sexton	.15	.08	.05
233	Paul Mitchell	.15	.08	.05
234	Toby Harrah	.15	.08	.05
235	Steve Rogers	.15	.08	.05
236	Jim Dwyer	.15	.08	.05
237	Billy Smith	.15	.08	.05
238	Balor Moore	.15	.08	.05
239	Willie Horton	.15	.08	.05
240	Rick Reuschel	.15	.08	.05
241	Checklist 122-242	.15	.08	.05
242	Pablo Torrealba	.15	.08	.05
243	Buck Martinez	.15	.08	.05
244	Pirates Team (Chuck Tanner)	.50	.25	.15
245	Jeff Burroughs	.15	.08	.05
246	Darrell Jackson	.15	.08	.05
247	Tucker Ashford	.15	.08	.05
248	Pete LaCock	.15	.08	.05
249	Paul Thormodsgard	.15	.08	.05
250	Willie Randolph	.15	.08	.05
251	Jack Morris	.50	.25	.15
252	Bob Stinson	.15	.08	.05
253	Rick Wise	.15	.08	.05
254	Luis Gomez	.15	.08	.05
255	Tommy John	.35	.20	.11
256	Mike Sadek	.15	.08	.05
257	Adrian Devine	.15	.08	.05
258	Mike Phillips	.15	.08	.05
259	Reds Team (Sparky Anderson)	1.00	.50	.30
260	Richie Zisk	.15	.08	.05
261	Mario Guerrero	.15	.08	.05
262	Nelson Briles	.15	.08	.05
263	Oscar Gamble	.15	.08	.05
264	*Don Robinson*	.15	.08	.05
265	Don Money	.15	.08	.05
266	Jim Willoughby	.15	.08	.05
267	Joe Rudi	.15	.08	.05
268	Julio Gonzalez	.15	.08	.05
269	Woodie Fryman	.15	.08	.05
270	Butch Hobson	.15	.08	.05
271	Rawly Eastwick	.15	.08	.05

272	Tim Corcoran	.15	.08	.05
273	Jerry Terrell	.15	.08	.05
274	Willie Norwood	.15	.08	.05
275	Junior Moore	.15	.08	.05
276	Jim Colborn	.15	.08	.05
277	Tom Grieve	.15	.08	.05
278	Andy Messersmith	.15	.08	.05
279	Jerry Grote	.15	.08	.05
280	Andre Thornton	.15	.08	.05
281	Vic Correll	.15	.08	.05
282	Blue Jays Team (Roy Hartsfield)	.25	.13	.08
283	Ken Kravec	.15	.08	.05
284	Johnnie LeMaster	.15	.08	.05
285	Bobby Bonds	.15	.08	.05
286	Duffy Dyer	.15	.08	.05
287	Andres Mora	.15	.08	.05
288	Milt Wilcox	.15	.08	.05
289	Jose Cruz	.15	.08	.05
290	Dave Lopes	.15	.08	.05
291	Tom Griffin	.15	.08	.05
292	Don Reynolds	.15	.08	.05
293	Jerry Garvin	.15	.08	.05
294	Pepe Frias	.15	.08	.05
295	Mitchell Page	.15	.08	.05
296	Preston Hanna	.15	.08	.05
297	Ted Sizemore	.15	.08	.05
298	Rich Gale	.15	.08	.05
299	Steve Ontiveros	.15	.08	.05
300	Rod Carew	3.50	1.75	1.00
301	Tom Hume	.15	.08	.05
302	Braves Team (Bobby Cox)	.35	.20	.11
303	Lary Sorensen	.15	.08	.05
304	Steve Swisher	.15	.08	.05
305	Willie Montanez	.15	.08	.05
306	Floyd Bannister	.15	.08	.05
307	Larvell Blanks	.15	.08	.05
308	Bert Blyleven	.15	.08	.05
309	Ralph Garr	.15	.08	.05
310	Thurman Munson	3.00	1.50	.90
311	Gary Lavelle	.15	.08	.05
312	Bob Robertson	.15	.08	.05
313	Dyar Miller	.15	.08	.05
314	Larry Harlow	.15	.08	.05
315	Jon Matlack	.15	.08	.05
316	Milt May	.15	.08	.05
317	Jose Cardenal	.15	.08	.05
318	*Bob Welch*	2.50	1.25	.70
319	Wayne Garrett	.15	.08	.05
320	Carl Yastrzemski	4.00	2.00	1.25
321	Gaylord Perry	1.75	.90	.50
322	Danny Goodwin	.15	.08	.05
323	Lynn McGlothen	.15	.08	.05
324	Mike Tyson	.15	.08	.05
325	Cecil Cooper	.15	.08	.05
326	Pedro Borbon	.15	.08	.05
327	Art Howe	.15	.08	.05
328	A's Team (Jack McKeon)	.25	.13	.08
329	Joe Coleman	.15	.08	.05
330	George Brett	10.00	5.00	3.00
331	Mickey Mahler	.15	.08	.05
332	Gary Alexander	.15	.08	.05
333	Chet Lemon	.15	.08	.05
334	Craig Swan	.15	.08	.05
335	Chris Chambliss	.15	.08	.05
336	Bobby Thompson	.15	.08	.05
337	John Montague	.15	.08	.05
338	Vic Harris	.15	.08	.05
339	Ron Jackson	.15	.08	.05
340	Jim Palmer	1.50	.70	.45
341	*Willie Upshaw*	.20	.10	.06
342	Dave Roberts	.15	.08	.05
343	Ed Glynn	.15	.08	.05
344	Jerry Royster	.15	.08	.05
345	Tug McGraw	.15	.08	.05
346	Bill Buckner	.15	.08	.05
347	Doug Rau	.15	.08	.05
348	Andre Dawson	3.00	1.50	.90
349	Jim Wright	.15	.08	.05
350	Garry Templeton	.15	.08	.05
351	Wayne Nordhagen	.15	.08	.05
352	Steve Renko	.15	.08	.05
353	Checklist 243-363	.15	.08	.05
354	Bill Bonham	.15	.08	.05
355	Lee Mazzilli	.15	.08	.05
356	Giants Team (Joe Altobelli)	.25	.13	.08
357	Jerry Augustine	.15	.08	.05
358	Alan Trammell	4.00	2.00	1.25
359	Dan Spillner	.15	.08	.05
360	Amos Otis	.15	.08	.05
361	Tom Dixon	.15	.08	.05
362	Mike Cubbage	.15	.08	.05
363	Craig Skok	.15	.08	.05
364	Gene Richards	.15	.08	.05
365	Sparky Lyle	.15	.08	.05
366	Juan Bernhardt	.15	.08	.05
367	Dave Skaggs	.15	.08	.05
368	Don Aase	.15	.08	.05
369a	Bump Wills (Blue Jays)	2.00	1.00	.60
369b	Bump Wills (Rangers)	[illegible]	[illegible]	[illegible]
370	Dave Kingman	.25	.13	.08
371	Jeff Holly	.15	.08	.05
372	Lamar Johnson	.15	.08	.05
373	Lance Rautzhan	.15	.08	.05
374	Ed Herrmann	.15	.08	.05
375	Bill Campbell	.15	.08	.05
376	Gorman Thomas	.15	.08	.05
377	Paul Moskau	.15	.08	.05
378	Rob Picciolo	.15	.08	.05
379	Dale Murray	.15	.08	.05
380	John Mayberry	.15	.08	.05
381	Astros Team (Bill Virdon)	.25	.13	.08
382	Jerry Martin	.15	.08	.05
383	Phil Garner	.15	.08	.05
384	Tommy Boggs	.15	.08	.05
385	Dan Ford	.15	.08	.05
386	Francisco Barrios	.15	.08	.05
387	Gary Thomasson	.15	.08	.05
388	Jack Billingham	.15	.08	.05
389	Joe Zdeb	.15	.08	.05
390	Rollie Fingers	1.75	.90	.50
391	Al Oliver	.30	.15	.09
392	Doug Ault	.15	.08	.05
393	Scott McGregor	.15	.08	.05
394	Randy Stein	.15	.08	.05
395	Dave Cash	.15	.08	.05
396	Bill Plummer	.15	.08	.05
397	Sergio Ferrer	.15	.08	.05
398	Ivan DeJesus	.15	.08	.05
399	David Clyde	.15	.08	.05
400	Jim Rice	.40	.20	.12
401	Ray Knight	.25	.13	.08
402	Paul Hartzell	.15	.08	.05
403	Tim Foli	.15	.08	.05
404	White Sox Team (Don Kessinger)	.25	.13	.08
405	Butch Wynegar	.15	.08	.05
406	Joe Wallis	.15	.08	.05
407	Pete Vuckovich	.15	.08	.05
408	Charlie Moore	.15	.08	.05
409	*Willie Wilson*	2.00	1.00	.60
410	Darrell Evans	.25	.13	.08
411	All-Time Hits Leaders (Ty Cobb, George Sisler)	.50	.25	.15
412	All-Time RBI Leaders (Hank Aaron, Hack Wilson)	.50	.25	.15
413	All-Time Home Run Leaders (Hank Aaron, Roger Maris)	3.00	1.50	.90
414	All-Time Batting Average Leaders (Ty Cobb, Roger Hornsby)	.50	.25	.15
415	All-Time Stolen Bases Leader (Lou Brock)	.35	.20	.11
416	All-Time Wins Leaders (Jack Chesbro, Cy Young)	.30	.15	.09
417	All-Time Strikeout Leaders (Walter Johnson, Nolan Ryan)	4.00	2.00	1.25
418	All-Time ERA Leaders (Walter Johnson, Dutch Leonard)	.20	.10	.06
419	Dick Ruthven	.15	.08	.05
420	Ken Griffey	.25	.13	.08
421	Doug DeCinces	.15	.08	.05
422	Ruppert Jones	.15	.08	.05
423	Bob Montgomery	.15	.08	.05
424	Angels Team (Jim Fregosi)	.25	.13	.08
425	Rick Manning	.15	.08	.05
426	Chris Speier	.15	.08	.05
427	Andy Replogle	.15	.08	.05
428	Bobby Valentine	.15	.08	.05
429	John Urrea	.15	.08	.05
430	Dave Parker	.40	.20	.12
431	Glenn Borgmann	.15	.08	.05
432	Dave Heaverlo	.15	.08	.05
433	Larry Biittner	.15	.08	.05
434	Ken Clay	.15	.08	.05
435	Gene Tenace	.15	.08	.05
436	Hector Cruz	.15	.08	.05
437	Rick Williams	.15	.08	.05
438	Horace Speed	.15	.08	.05
439	Frank White	.15	.08	.05
440	Rusty Staub	.15	.08	.05
441	Lee Lacy	.15	.08	.05
442	Doyle Alexander	.15	.08	.05
443	Bruce Bochte	.15	.08	.05
444	*Aurelio Lopez*	.15	.08	.05
445	Steve Henderson	.15	.08	.05
446	Jim Lonborg	.15	.08	.05
447	Manny Sanguillen	.15	.08	.05
448	Moose Haas	.15	.08	.05
449	Bombo Rivera	.15	.08	.05
450	Dave Concepcion	.15	.08	.05
451	Royals Team (Whitey Herzog)	.25	.13	.08
452	Jerry Morales	.15	.08	.05
453	Chris Knapp	.15	.08	.05
454	Len Randle	.15	.08	.05
455	Bill Lee	.15	.08	.05
456	Chuck Baker	.15	.08	.05
457	Bruce Sutter	.15	.08	.05
458	Jim Essian	.15	.08	.05
459	Sid Monge	.15	.08	.05
460	Graig Nettles	.15	.08	.05
461	Jim Barr	.15	.08	.05
462	Otto Velez	.15	.08	.05
463	Steve Comer	.15	.08	.05
464	Joe Nolan	.15	.08	.05
465	Reggie Smith	.15	.08	.05
466	Mark Littell	.15	.08	.05
467	Don Kessinger	.15	.08	.05
468	Stan Bahnsen	.15	.08	.05
469	Lance Parrish	.40	.20	.12
470	Garry Maddox	.15	.08	.05
471	Joaquin Andujar	.15	.08	.05
472	Craig Kusick	.15	.08	.05
473	Dave Roberts	.15	.08	.05
474	Dick Davis	.15	.08	.05
475	Dan Driessen	.15	.08	.05
476	Tom Poquette	.15	.08	.05
477	Bob Grich	.15	.08	.05
478	Juan Beniquez	.15	.08	.05
479	Padres Team (Roger Craig)	.25	.13	.08
480	Fred Lynn	.15	.08	.05
481	Skip Lockwood	.15	.08	.05
482	Craig Reynolds	.15	.08	.05
483	Checklist 364-484	.15	.08	.05
484	Rick Waits	.15	.08	.05
485	Bucky Dent	.15	.08	.05
486	Bob Knepper	.15	.08	.05
487	Miguel Dilone	.15	.08	.05
488	Bob Owchinko	.15	.08	.05
489	Larry Cox (photo actually Dave Rader)	.15	.08	.05
490	Al Cowens	.15	.08	.05
491	Tippy Martinez	.15	.08	.05
492	Bob Bailor	.15	.08	.05
493	Larry Christenson	.15	.08	.05
494	Jerry White	.15	.08	.05
495	Tony Perez	.30	.15	.09
496	Barry Bonnell	.15	.08	.05
497	Glenn Abbott	.15	.08	.05
498	Rich Chiles	.15	.08	.05
499	Rangers Team (Pat Corrales)	.25	.13	.08
500	Ron Guidry	.20	.10	.06
501	Junior Kennedy	.15	.08	.05
502	Steve Braun	.15	.08	.05
503	Terry Humphrey	.15	.08	.05
504	*Larry McWilliams*	.15	.08	.05
505	Ed Kranepool	.15	.08	.05
506	John D'Acquisto	.15	.08	.05
507	Tony Armas	.15	.08	.05
508	Charlie Hough	.15	.08	.05
509	Mario Mendoza	.15	.08	.05
510	Ted Simmons	.15	.08	.05
511	Paul Reuschel	.15	.08	.05
512	Jack Clark	.15	.08	.05
513	Dave Johnson	.15	.08	.05
514	Mike Proly	.15	.08	.05
515	Enos Cabell	.15	.08	.05
516	Champ Summers	.15	.08	.05
517	Al Bumbry	.15	.08	.05
518	Jim Umbarger	.15	.08	.05
519	Ben Oglivie	.15	.08	.05
520	Gary Carter	1.75	.90	.50
521	Sam Ewing	.15	.08	.05
522	Ken Holtzman	.15	.08	.05
523	John Milner	.15	.08	.05
524	Tom Burgmeier	.15	.08	.05
525	Freddie Patek	.15	.08	.05
526	Dodgers Team (Tom Lasorda)	.60	.30	.20
527	Lerrin LaGrow	.15	.08	.05
528	Wayne Gross	.15	.08	.05
529	Brian Asselstine	.15	.08	.05
530	Frank Tanana	.15	.08	.05
531	Fernando Gonzalez	.15	.08	.05
532	Buddy Schultz	.15	.08	.05
533	Leroy Stanton	.15	.08	.05
534	Ken Forsch	.15	.08	.05
535	Ellis Valentine	.15	.08	.05
536	Jerry Reuss	.15	.08	.05
537	Tom Veryzer	.15	.08	.05
538	Mike Ivie	.15	.08	.05
539	John Ellis	.15	.08	.05
540	Greg Luzinski	.15	.08	.05
541	Jim Slaton	.15	.08	.05
542	Rick Bosetti	.15	.08	.05
543	Kiko Garcia	.15	.08	.05
544	Fergie Jenkins	1.75	.90	.50
545	John Stearns	.15	.08	.05
546	Bill Russell	.15	.08	.05
547	Clint Hurdle	.15	.08	.05
548	Enrique Romo	.15	.08	.05
549	Bob Bailey	.15	.08	.05
550	Sal Bando	.15	.08	.05
551	Cubs Team (Herman Franks)	.25	.13	.08
552	Jose Morales	.15	.08	.05
553	Denny Walling	.15	.08	.05
554	Matt Keough	.15	.08	.05
555	Biff Pocoroba	.15	.08	.05
556	Mike Lum	.15	.08	.05
557	Ken Brett	.15	.08	.05
558	Jay Johnstone	.15	.08	.05
559	Greg Pryor	.15	.08	.05
560	John Montefusco	.15	.08	.05
561	Ed Ott	.15	.08	.05
562	Dusty Baker	.25	.13	.08
563	Roy Thomas	.15	.08	.05
564	Jerry Turner	.15	.08	.05
565	Rico Carty	.15	.08	.05
566	Nino Espinosa	.15	.08	.05
567	Rich Hebner	.15	.08	.05
568	Carlos Lopez	.15	.08	.05
569	Bob Sykes	.15	.08	.05
570	Cesar Cedeno	.15	.08	.05
571	Darrell Porter	.15	.08	.05
572	Rod Gilbreath	.15	.08	.05
573	Jim Kern	.15	.08	.05
574	Claudell Washington	.15	.08	.05
575	Luis Tiant	.15	.08	.05
576	Mike Parrott	.15	.08	.05
577	Brewers Team (George Bamberger)	.25	.13	.08
578	Pete Broberg	.15	.08	.05
579	Greg Gross	.15	.08	.05
580	Ron Fairly	.15	.08	.05
581	Darold Knowles	.15	.08	.05
582	Paul Blair	.15	.08	.05
583	Julio Cruz	.15	.08	.05
584	Jim Rooker	.15	.08	.05
585	Hal McRae	.15	.08	.05
586	*Bob Horner*	.90	.45	.25
587	Ken Reitz	.15	.08	.05
588	Tom Murphy	.15	.08	.05
589	Terry Whitfield	.15	.08	.05
590	J.R. Richard	.15	.08	.05
591	Mike Hargrove	.15	.08	.05
592	Mike Krukow	.15	.08	.05
593	Rick Dempsey	.15	.08	.05
594	Bob Shirley	.15	.08	.05
595	Phil Niekro	1.75	.90	.50
596	Jim Wohlford	.15	.08	.05
597	Bob Stanley	.15	.08	.05
598	Mark Wagner	.15	.08	.05
599	Jim Spencer	.15	.08	.05
600	George Foster	.15	.08	.05
601	Dave LaRoche	.15	.08	.05
602	Checklist 485-605	.15	.08	.05
603	Rudy May	.15	.08	.05
604	Jeff Newman	.15	.08	.05
605	Rick Monday	.15	.08	.05
606	Expos Team (Dick Williams)	.25	.13	.08
607	Omar Moreno	.15	.08	.05

608	Dave McKay	.15	.08	.05
609	Silvio Martinez	.15	.08	.05
610	Mike Schmidt	7.50	3.75	2.25
611	Jim Norris	.15	.08	.05
612	*Rick Honeycutt*	.25	.13	.08
613	Mike Edwards	.15	.08	.05
614	Willie Hernandez	.15	.08	.05
615	Ken Singleton	.15	.08	.05
616	Billy Almon	.15	.08	.05
617	Terry Puhl	.15	.08	.05
618	Jerry Remy	.15	.08	.05
619	*Ken Landreaux*	.15	.08	.05
620	Bert Campaneris	.15	.08	.05
621	Pat Zachry	.15	.08	.05
622	Dave Collins	.15	.08	.05
623	Bob McClure	.15	.08	.05
624	Larry Herndon	.15	.08	.05
625	Mark Fidrych	.15	.08	.05
626	Yankees Team (Bob Lemon)	.50	.25	.15
627	Gary Serum	.15	.08	.05
628	Del Unser	.15	.08	.05
629	Gene Garber	.15	.08	.05
630	Bake McBride	.15	.08	.05
631	Jorge Orta	.15	.08	.05
632	Don Kirkwood	.15	.08	.05
633	Rob Wilfong	.15	.08	.05
634	Paul Lindblad	.15	.08	.05
635	Don Baylor	.25	.13	.08
636	Wayne Garland	.15	.08	.05
637	Bill Robinson	.15	.08	.05
638	Al Fitzmorris	.15	.08	.05
639	Manny Trillo	.15	.08	.05
640	Eddie Murray	12.50	6.25	3.75
641	*Bobby Castillo*	.15	.08	.05
642	Wilbur Howard	.15	.08	.05
643	Tom Hausman	.15	.08	.05
644	Manny Mota	.15	.08	.05
645	George Scott	.15	.08	.05
646	Rick Sweet	.15	.08	.05
647	Bob Lacey	.15	.08	.05
648	Lou Piniella	.20	.10	.06
649	John Curtis	.15	.08	.05
650	Pete Rose	8.00	4.00	2.50
651	Mike Caldwell	.15	.08	.05
652	Stan Papi	.15	.08	.05
653	Warren Brusstar	.15	.08	.05
654	Rick Miller	.15	.08	.05
655	Jerry Koosman	.15	.08	.05
656	Hosken Powell	.15	.08	.05
657	George Medich	.15	.08	.05
658	Taylor Duncan	.15	.08	.05
659	Mariners Team (Darrell Johnson)	.25	.13	.08
660	Ron LeFlore	.15	.08	.05
661	Bruce Kison	.15	.08	.05
662	Kevin Bell	.15	.08	.05
663	Mike Vail	.15	.08	.05
664	Doug Bird	.15	.08	.05
665	Lou Brock	2.00	1.00	.60
666	Rich Dauer	.15	.08	.05
667	Don Hood	.15	.08	.05
668	Bill North	.15	.08	.05
669	Checklist 606-726	.15	.08	.05
670	Catfish Hunter	1.75	.90	.50
671	Joe Ferguson	.15	.08	.05
672	Ed Halicki	.15	.08	.05
673	Tom Hutton	.15	.08	.05
674	Dave Tomlin	.15	.08	.05
675	Tim McCarver	.25	.13	.08
676	Johnny Sutton	.15	.08	.05
677	Larry Parrish	.15	.08	.05
678	Geoff Zahn	.15	.08	.05
679	Derrel Thomas	.15	.08	.05
680	Carlton Fisk	2.50	1.25	.70
681	*John Henry Johnson*	.15	.08	.05
682	Dave Chalk	.15	.08	.05
683	Dan Meyer	.15	.08	.05
684	Jamie Easterly	.15	.08	.05
685	Sixto Lezcano	.15	.08	.05
686	Ron Schueler	.15	.08	.05
687	Rennie Stennett	.15	.08	.05
688	Mike Willis	.15	.08	.05
689	Orioles Team (Earl Weaver)	.60	.30	.20
690	Buddy Bell	.15	.08	.05
691	Dock Ellis	.15	.08	.05
692	Mickey Stanley	.15	.08	.05
693	Dave Rader	.15	.08	.05
694	Burt Hooton	.15	.08	.05
695	Keith Hernandez	.20	.10	.06
696	Andy Hassler	.15	.08	.05
697	Dave Bergman	.15	.08	.05
698	Bill Stein	.15	.08	.05
699	Hal Dues	.15	.08	.05
700	Reggie Jackson	4.00	2.00	1.25
701	Orioles Prospects (Mark Corey, John Flinn), *(Sammy Stewart)*	.15	.08	.05
702	Red Sox Prospects (Joel Finch, Garry Hancock, Allen Ripley)	.15	.08	.05
703	Angels Prospects (Jim Anderson, Dave Frost, Bob Slater)	.15	.08	.05
704	White Sox Prospects (Ross Baumgarten, Mike Colbern), *(Mike Squires)*	.15	.08	.05
705	Indians Prospects *(Alfredo Griffin*, Tim Norrid, Dave Oliver)	.25	.13	.08
706	Tigers Prospects (Dave Stegman, Dave Tobik, Kip Young)	.15	.08	.05
707	Royals Prospects (Randy Bass, Jim Gaudet, Randy McGilberry)	.15	.08	.05
708	Brewers Prospects *(Kevin Bass)*, *(Eddie Romero*, Ned Yost)	.25	.13	.08
709	Twins Prospects (Sam Perlozzo, Rick Sofield, Kevin Stanfield)	.15	.08	.05
710	Yankees Prospects (Brian Doyle), *(Mike Heath*, Dave Rajsich)	.20	.10	.06
711	A's Prospects *(Dwayne Murphy*, Bruce Robinson, Alan Wirth)	.15	.08	.05
712	Mariners Prospects (Bud Anderson, Greg Biercevicz, Byron McLaughlin)	.15	.08	.05
713	Rangers Prospects *(Danny Darwin*, Pat Putnam), *(Billy Sample)*	.25	.13	.08
714	Blue Jays Prospects (Victor Cruz, Pat Kelly, Ernie Whitt)	.15	.08	.05
715	Braves Prospects *(Bruce Benedict)*, *(Glenn Hubbard*, Larry Whisenton)	.25	.13	.08
716	Cubs Prospects (Dave Geisel, Karl Pagel), *(Scot Thompson)*	.15	.08	.05
717	Reds Prospects *(Mike LaCoss)*, *(Ron Oester)*, *(Harry Spilman)*	.15	.08	.05
718	Astros Prospects (Bruce Bochy, Mike Fischlin, Don Pisker)	.15	.08	.05
719	Dodgers Prospects *(Pedro Guerrero)*, *(Rudy Law*, Joe Simpson)	2.00	1.00	.60
720	Expos Prospects *(Jerry Fry)*, *(Jerry Pirtle)*, *(Scott Sanderson)*	.60	.30	.20
721	Mets Prospects *(Juan Berenguer*, Dwight Bernard, Dan Norman)	.15	.08	.05
722	Phillies Prospects *(Jim Morrison)*, *(Lonnie Smith)*, *(Jim Wright)*	.50	.25	.15
723	Pirates Prospects *(Dale Berra*, Eugenio Cotes, Ben Wiltbank)	.15	.08	.05
724	Cardinals Prospects (Tom Bruno), *(George Frazier)*, *(Terry Kennedy)*	.20	.10	.06
725	Padres Prospects (Jim Beswick, Steve Mura, Broderick Perkins)	.15	.08	.05
726	Giants Prospects (Greg Johnston, Joe Strain, John Tamargo)	.15	.08	.05

1979 Topps Comics

Issued as the 3" x 3-3/4" wax wrapper for a piece of bubblegum, this "test" issue was bought up in great quantities by speculators and remains rather common. It is also inexpensive, because the comic-style player representations were not popular with collectors. The set is complete at 33 pieces.

		NM	EX	VG
Complete Set (33):		10.00	5.00	3.00
Common Player:		.12	.06	.04
1	Eddie Murray	.80	.40	.25
2	Jim Rice	.15	.08	.05
3	Carl Yastrzemski	.80	.40	.25
4	Nolan Ryan	2.50	1.25	.70
5	Chet Lemon	.12	.06	.04
6	Andre Thornton	.12	.06	.04
7	Rusty Staub	.12	.06	.04
8	Ron LeFlore	.12	.06	.04
9	George Brett	1.50	.70	.45
10	Larry Hisle	.12	.06	.04
11	Rod Carew	.50	.25	.15
12	Reggie Jackson	.60	.30	.20
13	Ron Guidry	.12	.06	.04
14	Mitchell Page	.12	.06	.04
15	Leon Roberts	.12	.06	.04
16	Al Oliver	.12	.06	.04
17	John Mayberry	.12	.06	.04
18	Bob Horner	.12	.06	.04
19	Phil Niekro	.50	.25	.15
20	Dave Kingman	.15	.08	.05
21	John Bench	.80	.40	.25
22	Tom Seaver	.80	.40	.25
23	J.R. Richard	.15	.08	.05
24	Steve Garvey	.50	.25	.15
25	Reggie Smith	.12	.06	.04
26	Ross Grimsley	.12	.06	.04
27	Craig Swan	.12	.06	.04
28	Pete Rose	1.75	.90	.50
29	Dave Parker	.15	.08	.05
30	Ted Simmons	.12	.06	.04
31	Dave Winfield	.50	.25	.15
32	Jack Clark	.12	.06	.04
33	Vida Blue	.12	.06	.04

1979 Topps Team/Checklist Sheet

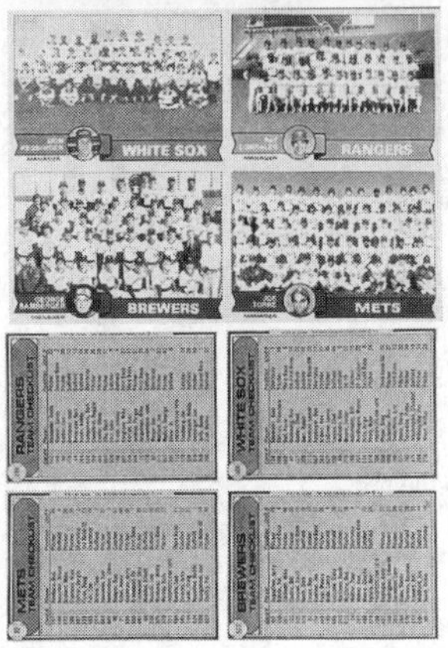

This uncut sheet of 26 team card/checklists was available via a mail-in offer. The sheet was mailed with two folds.

	NM	EX	VG
Uncut Sheet:	20.00	10.00	6.00

1980 Topps

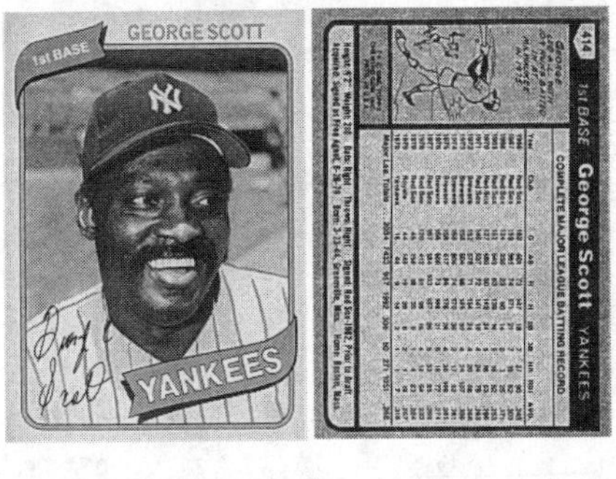

Again numbering 726 cards measuring 2-1/2" x 3-1/2", Topps did make some design changes in 1980. Fronts have the usual color picture with a facsimile autograph. The player's name appears above the picture, while his position is on a pennant at the upper left and his team on another pennant in the lower right. Backs no longer feature games, returning instead to statistics, personal information, a few headlines and a cartoon about the player. Specialty cards include statistical leaders, and previous season highlights. Many rookies again appear in team threesomes.

		NM	EX	VG
Complete Set (726):		175.00	85.00	50.00
Common Player:		.12	.06	.04
Wax Box:		200.00		
1	Lou Brock, Carl Yastrzemski (Highlights)	1.00	.50	.30
2	Willie McCovey (Highlights)	.40	.20	.12
3	Manny Mota (Highlights)	.12	.06	.04
4	Pete Rose (Highlights)	2.00	1.00	.60
5	Garry Templeton (Highlights)	.12	.06	.04
6	Del Unser (Highlights)	.12	.06	.04
7	Mike Lum	.12	.06	.04
8	Craig Swan	.12	.06	.04
9	Steve Braun	.12	.06	.04
10	Denny Martinez	.20	.10	.06
11	Jimmy Sexton	.12	.06	.04
12	John Curtis	.12	.06	.04
13	Ron Pruitt	.12	.06	.04
14	Dave Cash	.12	.06	.04
15	Bill Campbell	.12	.06	.04
16	Jerry Narron	.12	.06	.04
17	Bruce Sutter	.12	.06	.04
18	Ron Jackson	.12	.06	.04
19	Balor Moore	.12	.06	.04
20	Dan Ford	.12	.06	.04
21	Manny Sarmiento	.12	.06	.04
22	Pat Putnam	.12	.06	.04
23	Derrel Thomas	.12	.06	.04
24	Jim Slaton	.12	.06	.04
25	Lee Mazzilli	.12	.06	.04

26	Marty Pattin	.12	.06	.04
27	Del Unser	.12	.06	.04
28	Bruce Kison	.12	.06	.04
29	Mark Wagner	.12	.06	.04
30	Vida Blue	.12	.06	.04
31	Jay Johnstone	.12	.06	.04
32	Julio Cruz	.12	.06	.04
33	Tony Scott	.12	.06	.04
34	Jeff Newman	.12	.06	.04
35	Luis Tiant	.15	.08	.05
36	Rusty Torres	.12	.06	.04
37	Kiko Garcia	.12	.06	.04
38	Dan Spillner	.12	.06	.04
39	Rowland Office	.12	.06	.04
40	Carlton Fisk	3.00	1.50	.90
41	Rangers Team (Pat Corrales)	.25	.13	.08
42	*Dave Palmer*	.12	.06	.04
43	Bombo Rivera	.12	.06	.04
44	Bill Fahey	.12	.06	.04
45	Frank White	.12	.06	.04
46	Rico Carty	.12	.06	.04
47	Bill Bonham	.12	.06	.04
48	Rick Miller	.12	.06	.04
49	Mario Guerrero	.12	.06	.04
50	J.R. Richard	.20	.10	.06
51	Joe Ferguson	.12	.06	.04
52	Warren Brusstar	.12	.06	.04
53	Ben Oglivie	.12	.06	.04
54	Dennis Lamp	.12	.06	.04
55	Bill Madlock	.12	.06	.04
56	Bobby Valentine	.12	.06	.04
57	Pete Vuckovich	.12	.06	.04
58	Doug Flynn	.12	.06	.04
59	Eddy Putman	.12	.06	.04
60	Bucky Dent	.12	.06	.04
61	Gary Serum	.12	.06	.04
62	Mike Ivie	.12	.06	.04
63	Bob Stanley	.12	.06	.04
64	Joe Nolan	.12	.06	.04
65	Al Bumbry	.12	.06	.04
66	Royals Team (Jim Frey)	.25	.13	.08
67	Doyle Alexander	.12	.06	.04
68	Larry Harlow	.12	.06	.04
69	Rick Williams	.12	.06	.04
70	Gary Carter	1.50	.70	.45
71	John Milner	.12	.06	.04
72	Fred Howard	.12	.06	.04
73	Dave Collins	.12	.06	.04
74	Sid Monge	.12	.06	.04
75	Bill Russell	.12	.06	.04
76	John Stearns	.12	.06	.04
77	*Dave Stieb*	1.00	.50	.30
78	Ruppert Jones	.12	.06	.04
79	Bob Owchinko	.12	.06	.04
80	Ron LeFlore	.12	.06	.04
81	Ted Sizemore	.12	.06	.04
82	Astros Team (Bill Virdon)	.25	.13	.08
83	*Steve Trout*	.15	.08	.05
84	Gary Lavelle	.12	.06	.04
85	Ted Simmons	.12	.06	.04
86	Dave Hamilton	.12	.06	.04
87	Pepe Frias	.12	.06	.04
88	Ken Landreaux	.12	.06	.04
89	Don Hood	.12	.06	.04
90	Manny Trillo	.12	.06	.04
91	Rick Dempsey	.12	.06	.04
92	Rick Rhoden	.12	.06	.04
93	Dave Roberts	.12	.06	.04
94	*Neil Allen*	.12	.06	.04
95	Cecil Cooper	.12	.06	.04
96	A's Team (Jim Marshall)	.25	.13	.08
97	Bill Lee	.12	.06	.04
98	Jerry Terrell	.12	.06	.04
99	Victor Cruz	.12	.06	.04
100	Johnny Bench	3.00	1.50	.90
101	Aurelio Lopez	.12	.06	.04
102	Rich Dauer	.12	.06	.04
103	*Bill Caudill*	.15	.08	.05
104	Manny Mota	.12	.06	.04
105	Frank Tanana	.12	.06	.04
106	*Jeff Leonard*	.25	.13	.08
107	Francisco Barrios	.12	.06	.04
108	Bob Horner	.12	.06	.04
109	Bill Travers	.12	.06	.04
110	Fred Lynn	.12	.06	.04
111	Bob Knepper	.12	.06	.04
112	White Sox Team (Tony LaRussa)	.40	.20	.12
113	Geoff Zahn	.12	.06	.04
114	Juan Beniquez	.12	.06	.04
115	Sparky Lyle	.12	.06	.04
116	Larry Cox	.12	.06	.04
117	Dock Ellis	.12	.06	.04
118	Phil Garner	.12	.06	.04
119	Sammy Stewart	.12	.06	.04
120	Greg Luzinski	.12	.06	.04
121	Checklist 1-121	.12	.06	.04
122	Dave Rosello	.12	.06	.04
123	Lynn Jones	.12	.06	.04
124	Dave Lemanczyk	.12	.06	.04
125	Tony Perez	2.00	1.00	.60
126	Dave Tomlin	.12	.06	.04
127	Gary Thomasson	.12	.06	.04
128	Tom Burgmeier	.12	.06	.04
129	Craig Reynolds	.12	.06	.04
130	Amos Otis	.12	.06	.04
131	Paul Mitchell	.12	.06	.04
132	Biff Pocoroba	.12	.06	.04
133	Jerry Turner	.12	.06	.04
134	Matt Keough	.12	.06	.04
135	Bill Buckner	.15	.08	.05
136	Dick Ruthven	.12	.06	.04
137	*John Castino*	.12	.06	.04
138	Ross Baumgarten	.12	.06	.04
139	*Dane Iorg*	.12	.06	.04
140	Rich Gossage	.15	.08	.05
141	Gary Alexander	.12	.06	.04
142	Phil Huffman	.12	.06	.04
143	Bruce Bochte	.12	.06	.04
144	Steve Comer	.12	.06	.04
145	Darrell Evans	.15	.08	.05
146	Bob Welch	.12	.06	.04
147	Terry Puhl	.12	.06	.04
148	Manny Sanguillen	.12	.06	.04
149	Tom Hume	.12	.06	.04
150	Jason Thompson	.12	.06	.04
151	Tom Hausman	.12	.06	.04
152	John Fulgham	.12	.06	.04
153	Tim Blackwell	.12	.06	.04
154	Lary Sorensen	.12	.06	.04
155	Jerry Remy	.12	.06	.04
156	Tony Brizzolara	.12	.06	.04
157	Willie Wilson	.12	.06	.04
158	Rob Picciolo	.12	.06	.04
159	Ken Clay	.12	.06	.04
160	Eddie Murray	6.00	3.00	1.75
161	Larry Christenson	.12	.06	.04
162	Bob Randall	.12	.06	.04
163	Steve Swisher	.12	.06	.04
164	Greg Pryor	.12	.06	.04
165	Omar Moreno	.12	.06	.04
166	Glenn Abbott	.12	.06	.04
167	Jack Clark	.12	.06	.04
168	Rick Waits	.12	.06	.04
169	Luis Gomez	.12	.06	.04
170	Burt Hooton	.12	.06	.04
171	Fernando Gonzalez	.12	.06	.04
172	Ron Hodges	.12	.06	.04
173	John Henry Johnson	.12	.06	.04
174	Ray Knight	.12	.06	.04
175	Rick Reuschel	.12	.06	.04
176	Champ Summers	.12	.06	.04
177	Dave Heaverlo	.12	.06	.04
178	Tim McCarver	.15	.08	.05
179	*Ron Davis*	.15	.08	.05
180	Warren Cromartie	.12	.06	.04
181	Moose Haas	.12	.06	.04
182	Ken Reitz	.12	.06	.04
183	Jim Anderson	.12	.06	.04
184	Steve Renko	.12	.06	.04
185	Hal McRae	.12	.06	.04
186	Junior Moore	.12	.06	.04
187	Alan Ashby	.12	.06	.04
188	Terry Crowley	.12	.06	.04
189	Kevin Kobel	.12	.06	.04
190	Buddy Bell	.12	.06	.04
191	Ted Martinez	.12	.06	.04
192	Braves Team (Bobby Cox)	.40	.20	.12
193	Dave Goltz	.12	.06	.04
194	Mike Easler	.12	.06	.04
195	John Montefusco	.12	.06	.04
196	Lance Parrish	.12	.06	.04
197	Byron McLaughlin	.12	.06	.04
198	Dell Alston	.12	.06	.04
199	Mike LaCoss	.12	.06	.04
200	Jim Rice	.25	.13	.08
201	Batting Leaders (Keith Hernandez, Fred Lynn)	.12	.06	.04
202	Home Run Leaders (Dave Kingman, Gorman Thomas)	.12	.06	.04
203	Runs Batted In Leaders (Don Baylor, Dave Winfield)	.45	.25	.14
204	Stolen Base Leaders (Omar Moreno, Willie Wilson)	.12	.06	.04
205	Victory Leaders (Mike Flanagan, Joe Niekro, Phil Niekro)	.25	.13	.08
206	Strikeout Leaders (J.R. Richard, Nolan Ryan)	3.00	1.50	.90
207	ERA Leaders (Ron Guidry, J.R. Richard)	.25	.13	.08
208	Wayne Cage	.12	.06	.04
209	Von Joshua	.12	.06	.04
210	Steve Carlton	2.00	1.00	.60
211	Dave Skaggs	.12	.06	.04
212	Dave Roberts	.12	.06	.04
213	Mike Jorgensen	.12	.06	.04
214	Angels Team (Jim Fregosi)	.35	.20	.11
215	Sixto Lezcano	.12	.06	.04
216	Phil Mankowski	.12	.06	.04
217	Ed Halicki	.12	.06	.04
218	Jose Morales	.12	.06	.04
219	Steve Mingori	.12	.06	.04
220	Dave Concepcion	.12	.06	.04
221	Joe Cannon	.12	.06	.04
222	*Ron Hassey*	.25	.13	.08
223	Bob Sykes	.12	.06	.04
224	Willie Montanez	.12	.06	.04
225	Lou Piniella	.15	.08	.05
226	Bill Stein	.12	.06	.04
227	Len Barker	.12	.06	.04
228	Johnny Oates	.12	.06	.04
229	Jim Bibby	.12	.06	.04
230	Dave Winfield	4.00	2.00	1.25
231	Steve McCatty	.12	.06	.04
232	Alan Trammell	1.00	.50	.30
233	LaRue Washington	.12	.06	.04
234	Vern Ruhle	.12	.06	.04
235	Andre Dawson	1.50	.70	.45
236	Marc Hill	.12	.06	.04
237	Scott McGregor	.12	.06	.04
238	Rob Wilfong	.12	.06	.04
239	Don Aase	.12	.06	.04
240	Dave Kingman	.15	.08	.05
241	Checklist 122-242	.12	.06	.04
242	Lamar Johnson	.12	.06	.04
243	Jerry Augustine	.12	.06	.04
244	Cardinals Team (Ken Boyer)	.25	.13	.08
245	Phil Niekro	1.50	.70	.45
246	Tim Foli	.12	.06	.04
247	Frank Riccelli	.12	.06	.04
248	Jamie Quirk	.12	.06	.04
249	Jim Clancy	.12	.06	.04
250	Jim Kaat	.30	.15	.09
251	Kip Young	.12	.06	.04
252	Ted Cox	.12	.06	.04
253	John Montague	.12	.06	.04
254	Paul Dade	.12	.06	.04
255	Dusty Baker	.12	.06	.04
256	Roger Erickson	.12	.06	.04
257	Larry Herndon	.12	.06	.04
258	Paul Moskau	.12	.06	.04
259	Mets Team (Joe Torre)	.50	.25	.15
260	Al Oliver	.15	.08	.05
261	Dave Chalk	.12	.06	.04
262	Benny Ayala	.12	.06	.04
263	Dave LaRoche	.12	.06	.04
264	Bill Robinson	.12	.06	.04
265	Robin Yount	5.00	2.50	1.50
266	Bernie Carbo	.12	.06	.04
267	Dan Schatzeder	.12	.06	.04
268	Rafael Landestoy	.12	.06	.04
269	Dave Tobik	.12	.06	.04
270	Mike Schmidt	4.00	2.00	1.25
271	Dick Drago	.12	.06	.04
272	Ralph Garr	.12	.06	.04
273	Eduardo Rodriguez	.12	.06	.04
274	Dale Murphy	2.00	1.00	.60
275	Jerry Koosman	.12	.06	.04
276	Tom Veryzer	.12	.06	.04
277	Rick Bosetti	.12	.06	.04
278	Jim Spencer	.12	.06	.04
279	Rob Andrews	.12	.06	.04
280	Gaylord Perry	1.50	.70	.45
281	Paul Blair	.12	.06	.04
282	Mariners Team (Darrell Johnson)	.25	.13	.08
283	John Ellis	.12	.06	.04
284	Larry Murray	.12	.06	.04
285	Don Baylor	.20	.10	.06
286	Darold Knowles	.12	.06	.04
287	John Lowenstein	.12	.06	.04
288	Dave Rozema	.12	.06	.04
289	Bruce Bochy	.12	.06	.04
290	Steve Garvey	1.25	.60	.40
291	Randy Scarbery	.12	.06	.04
292	Dale Berra	.12	.06	.04
293	Elias Sosa	.12	.06	.04
294	Charlie Spikes	.12	.06	.04
295	Larry Gura	.12	.06	.04
296	Dave Rader	.12	.06	.04
297	Tim Johnson	.12	.06	.04
298	Ken Holtzman	.12	.06	.04
299	Steve Henderson	.12	.06	.04
300	Ron Guidry	.25	.13	.08
301	Mike Edwards	.12	.06	.04
302	Dodgers Team (Tom Lasorda)	.60	.30	.20
303	Bill Castro	.12	.06	.04
304	Butch Wynegar	.12	.06	.04
305	Randy Jones	.12	.06	.04
306	Denny Walling	.12	.06	.04
307	Rick Honeycutt	.12	.06	.04
308	Mike Hargrove	.12	.06	.04
309	Larry McWilliams	.12	.06	.04
310	Dave Parker	.30	.15	.09
311	Roger Metzger	.12	.06	.04
312	Mike Barlow	.12	.06	.04
313	Johnny Grubb	.12	.06	.04
314	*Tim Stoddard*	.12	.06	.04
315	Steve Kemp	.12	.06	.04
316	Bob Lacey	.12	.06	.04
317	Mike Anderson	.12	.06	.04
318	Jerry Reuss	.12	.06	.04
319	Chris Speier	.12	.06	.04
320	Dennis Eckersley	1.00	.50	.30
321	Keith Hernandez	.25	.13	.08
322	Claudell Washington	.12	.06	.04
323	Mick Kelleher	.12	.06	.04
324	Tom Underwood	.12	.06	.04
325	Dan Driessen	.12	.06	.04
326	Bo McLaughlin	.12	.06	.04
327	Ray Fosse	.12	.06	.04
328	Twins Team (Gene Mauch)	.25	.13	.08
329	Bert Roberge	.12	.06	.04
330	Al Cowens	.12	.06	.04
331	Rich Hebner	.12	.06	.04
332	Enrique Romo	.12	.06	.04
333	Jim Norris	.12	.06	.04
334	Jim Beattie	.12	.06	.04
335	Willie McCovey	2.00	1.00	.60
336	George Medich	.12	.06	.04
337	Carney Lansford	.12	.06	.04
338	Johnny Wockenfuss	.12	.06	.04
339	John D'Acquisto	.12	.06	.04
340	Ken Singleton	.12	.06	.04
341	Jim Essian	.12	.06	.04
342	Odell Jones	.12	.06	.04
343	Mike Vail	.12	.06	.04
344	Randy Lerch	.12	.06	.04
345	Larry Parrish	.12	.06	.04
346	Buddy Solomon	.12	.06	.04
347	*Harry Chappas*	.12	.06	.04
348	Checklist 243-363	.12	.06	.04
349	Jack Brohamer	.12	.06	.04
350	George Hendrick	.12	.06	.04
351	Bob Davis	.12	.06	.04
352	Dan Briggs	.12	.06	.04
353	Andy Hassler	.12	.06	.04
354	Rick Auerbach	.12	.06	.04
355	Gary Matthews	.12	.06	.04
356	Padres Team (Jerry Coleman)	.25	.13	.08
357	Bob McClure	.12	.06	.04
358	Lou Whitaker	.35	.20	.11
359	Randy Moffitt	.12	.06	.04
360	Darrell Porter	.12	.06	.04
361	Wayne Garland	.12	.06	.04
362	Danny Goodwin	.12	.06	.04
363	Wayne Gross	.12	.06	.04
364	Ray Burris	.12	.06	.04
365	Bobby Murcer	.12	.06	.04
366	Rob Dressler	.12	.06	.04
367	Billy Smith	.12	.06	.04

368	*Willie Aikens*	.20	.10	.06
369	Jim Kern	.12	.06	.04
370	Cesar Cedeno	.12	.06	.04
371	Jack Morris	.20	.10	.06
372	Joel Youngblood	.12	.06	.04
373	*Dan Petry*	.20	.10	.06
374	Jim Gantner	.12	.06	.04
375	Ross Grimsley	.12	.06	.04
376	Gary Allenson	.12	.06	.04
377	Junior Kennedy	.12	.06	.04
378	Jerry Mumphrey	.12	.06	.04
379	Kevin Bell	.12	.06	.04
380	Garry Maddox	.12	.06	.04
381	Cubs Team (Preston Gomez)	.25	.13	.08
382	Dave Freisleben	.12	.06	.04
383	Ed Ott	.12	.06	.04
384	Joey McLaughlin	.12	.06	.04
385	Enos Cabell	.12	.06	.04
386	Darrell Jackson	.12	.06	.04
387a	Fred Stanley (name in red)	.12	.06	.04
387b	Fred Stanley (name in yellow)	3.00	1.50	.90
388	Mike Paxton	.12	.06	.04
389	Pete LaCock	.12	.06	.04
390	Fergie Jenkins	1.50	.70	.45
391	Tony Armas	.12	.06	.04
392	Milt Wilcox	.12	.06	.04
393	Ozzie Smith	12.00	6.00	3.50
394	Reggie Cleveland	.12	.06	.04
395	Ellis Valentine	.12	.06	.04
396	Dan Meyer	.12	.06	.04
397	Roy Thomas	.12	.06	.04
398	Barry Foote	.12	.06	.04
399	Mike Proly	.12	.06	.04
400	George Foster	.15	.08	.05
401	Pete Falcone	.12	.06	.04
402	Merv Rettenmund	.12	.06	.04
403	Pete Redfern	.12	.06	.04
404	Orioles Team (Earl Weaver)	.50	.25	.15
405	Dwight Evans	.25	.13	.08
406	Paul Molitor	6.00	3.00	1.75
407	Tony Solaita	.12	.06	.04
408	Bill North	.12	.06	.04
409	Paul Splittorff	.12	.06	.04
410	Bobby Bonds	.20	.10	.06
411	Frank LaCorte	.12	.06	.04
412	Thad Bosley	.12	.06	.04
413	Allen Ripley	.12	.06	.04
414	George Scott	.12	.06	.04
415	Bill Atkinson	.12	.06	.04
416	*Tom Brookens*	.12	.06	.04
417	Craig Chamberlain	.12	.06	.04
418	Roger Freed	.12	.06	.04
419	Vic Correll	.12	.06	.04
420	Butch Hobson	.12	.06	.04
421	Doug Bird	.12	.06	.04
422	Larry Milbourne	.12	.06	.04
423	Dave Frost	.12	.06	.04
424	Yankees Team (Dick Howser)	.45	.25	.14
425	Mark Belanger	.12	.06	.04
426	Grant Jackson	.12	.06	.04
427	Tom Hutton	.12	.06	.04
428	Pat Zachry	.12	.06	.04
429	Duane Kuiper	.12	.06	.04
430	Larry Hisle	.12	.06	.04
431	Mike Krukow	.12	.06	.04
432	Willie Norwood	.12	.06	.04
433	Rich Gale	.12	.06	.04
434	Johnnie LeMaster	.12	.06	.04
435	Don Gullett	.12	.06	.04
436	Billy Almon	.12	.06	.04
437	Joe Niekro	.12	.06	.04
438	Dave Revering	.12	.06	.04
439	Mike Phillips	.12	.06	.04
440	Don Sutton	1.50	.70	.45
441	Eric Soderholm	.12	.06	.04
442	Jorge Orta	.12	.06	.04
443	Mike Parrott	.12	.06	.04
444	Alvis Woods	.12	.06	.04
445	Mark Fidrych	.20	.10	.06
446	Duffy Dyer	.12	.06	.04
447	Nino Espinosa	.12	.06	.04
448	Jim Wohlford	.12	.06	.04
449	Doug Bair	.12	.06	.04
450	George Brett	9.00	4.50	2.75
451	Indians Team (Dave Garcia)	.25	.13	.08
452	Steve Dillard	.12	.06	.04
453	Mike Bacsik	.12	.06	.04
454	Tom Donohue	.12	.06	.04
455	Mike Torrez	.12	.06	.04
456	Frank Taveras	.12	.06	.04
457	Bert Blyleven	.12	.06	.04
458	Billy Sample	.12	.06	.04
459	Mickey Lolich	.12	.06	.04
460	Willie Randolph	.12	.06	.04
461	Dwayne Murphy	.12	.06	.04
462	Mike Sadek	.12	.06	.04
463	Jerry Royster	.12	.06	.04
464	John Denny	.12	.06	.04
465	Rick Monday	.12	.06	.04
466	Mike Squires	.12	.06	.04
467	Jesse Jefferson	.12	.06	.04
468	Aurelio Rodriguez	.12	.06	.04
469	Randy Niemann	.12	.06	.04
470	Bob Boone	.12	.06	.04
471	Hosken Powell	.12	.06	.04
472	Willie Hernandez	.12	.06	.04
473	Bump Wills	.12	.06	.04
474	Steve Busby	.12	.06	.04
475	Cesar Geronimo	.12	.06	.04
476	Bob Shirley	.12	.06	.04
477	Buck Martinez	.12	.06	.04
478	Gil Flores	.12	.06	.04
479	Expos Team (Dick Williams)	.25	.13	.08
480	Bob Watson	.12	.06	.04
481	Tom Paciorek	.12	.06	.04
482	*Rickey Henderson*	30.00	15.00	9.00
483	Bo Diaz	.12	.06	.04
484	Checklist 364-484	.12	.06	.04
485	Mickey Rivers	.12	.06	.04
486	Mike Tyson	.12	.06	.04
487	Wayne Nordhagen	.12	.06	.04
488	Roy Howell	.12	.06	.04
489	Preston Hanna	.12	.06	.04
490	Lee May	.12	.06	.04
491	Steve Mura	.12	.06	.04
492	Todd Cruz	.12	.06	.04
493	Jerry Martin	.12	.06	.04
494	Craig Minetto	.12	.06	.04
495	Bake McBride	.12	.06	.04
496	Silvio Martinez	.12	.06	.04
497	Jim Mason	.12	.06	.04
498	Danny Darwin	.12	.06	.04
499	Giants Team (Dave Bristol)	.25	.13	.08
500	Tom Seaver	3.00	1.50	.90
501	Rennie Stennett	.12	.06	.04
502	Rich Wortham	.12	.06	.04
503	Mike Cubbage	.12	.06	.04
504	Gene Garber	.12	.06	.04
505	Bert Campaneris	.12	.06	.04
506	Tom Buskey	.12	.06	.04
507	Leon Roberts	.12	.06	.04
508	U.L. Washington	.12	.06	.04
509	Ed Glynn	.12	.06	.04
510	Ron Cey	.12	.06	.04
511	Eric Wilkins	.12	.06	.04
512	Jose Cardenal	.12	.06	.04
513	Tom Dixon	.12	.06	.04
514	Steve Ontiveros	.12	.06	.04
515	Mike Caldwell	.12	.06	.04
516	Hector Cruz	.12	.06	.04
517	Don Stanhouse	.12	.06	.04
518	Nelson Norman	.12	.06	.04
519	Steve Nicosia	.12	.06	.04
520	Steve Rogers	.12	.06	.04
521	Ken Brett	.12	.06	.04
522	Jim Morrison	.12	.06	.04
523	Ken Henderson	.12	.06	.04
524	Jim Wright	.12	.06	.04
525	Clint Hurdle	.12	.06	.04
526	Phillies Team (Dallas Green)	.60	.30	.20
527	Doug Rau	.12	.06	.04
528	Adrian Devine	.12	.06	.04
529	Jim Barr	.12	.06	.04
530	Jim Sundberg	.12	.06	.04
531	Eric Rasmussen	.12	.06	.04
532	Willie Horton	.12	.06	.04
533	Checklist 485-605	.12	.06	.04
534	Andre Thornton	.12	.06	.04
535	Bob Forsch	.12	.06	.04
536	Lee Lacy	.12	.06	.04
537	*Alex Trevino*	.12	.06	.04
538	Joe Strain	.12	.06	.04
539	Rudy May	.12	.06	.04
540	Pete Rose	9.00	4.50	2.75
541	Miguel Dilone	.12	.06	.04
542	Joe Coleman	.12	.06	.04
543	Pat Kelly	.12	.06	.04
544	*Rick Sutcliffe*	2.00	1.00	.60
545	Jeff Burroughs	.12	.06	.04
546	Rick Langford	.12	.06	.04
547	John Wathan	.12	.06	.04
548	Dave Rajsich	.12	.06	.04
549	Larry Wolfe	.12	.06	.04
550	Ken Griffey	.15	.08	.05
551	Pirates Team (Chuck Tanner)	.25	.13	.08
552	Bill Nahorodny	.12	.06	.04
553	Dick Davis	.12	.06	.04
554	Art Howe	.12	.06	.04
555	Ed Figueroa	.12	.06	.04
556	Joe Rudi	.12	.06	.04
557	Mark Lee	.12	.06	.04
558	Alfredo Griffin	.12	.06	.04
559	Dale Murray	.12	.06	.04
560	Dave Lopes	.12	.06	.04
561	Eddie Whitson	.12	.06	.04
562	Joe Wallis	.12	.06	.04
563	Will McEnaney	.12	.06	.04
564	Rick Manning	.12	.06	.04
565	Dennis Leonard	.12	.06	.04
566	Bud Harrelson	.12	.06	.04
567	Skip Lockwood	.12	.06	.04
568	*Gary Roenicke*	.12	.06	.04
569	Terry Kennedy	.12	.06	.04
570	Roy Smalley	.12	.06	.04
571	Joe Sambito	.12	.06	.04
572	Jerry Morales	.12	.06	.04
573	Kent Tekulve	.12	.06	.04
574	Scot Thompson	.12	.06	.04
575	Ken Kravec	.12	.06	.04
576	Jim Dwyer	.12	.06	.04
577	Blue Jays Team (Bobby Mattick)	.25	.13	.08
578	Scott Sanderson	.12	.06	.04
579	Charlie Moore	.12	.06	.04
580	Nolan Ryan	12.50	6.25	3.75
581	Bob Bailor	.12	.06	.04
582	Brian Doyle	.12	.06	.04
583	Bob Stinson	.12	.06	.04
584	Kurt Bevacqua	.12	.06	.04
585	Al Hrabosky	.12	.06	.04
586	Mitchell Page	.12	.06	.04
587	Garry Templeton	.12	.06	.04
588	Greg Minton	.12	.06	.04
589	Chet Lemon	.12	.06	.04
590	Jim Palmer	2.00	1.00	.60
591	Rick Cerone	.12	.06	.04
592	Jon Matlack	.12	.06	.04
593	Jesus Alou	.12	.06	.04
594	Dick Tidrow	.12	.06	.04
595	Don Money	.12	.06	.04
596	Rick Matula	.12	.06	.04
597	Tom Poquette	.12	.06	.04
598	Fred Kendall	.12	.06	.04
599	Mike Norris	.12	.06	.04
600	Reggie Jackson	6.00	3.00	1.75
601	Buddy Schultz	.12	.06	.04
602	Brian Downing	.12	.06	.04
603	Jack Billingham	.12	.06	.04
604	Glenn Adams	.12	.06	.04
605	Terry Forster	.12	.06	.04
606	Reds Team (John McNamara)	.35	.20	.11
607	Woodie Fryman	.12	.06	.04
608	Alan Bannister	.12	.06	.04
609	Ron Reed	.12	.06	.04
610	Willie Stargell	2.00	1.00	.60
611	Jerry Garvin	.12	.06	.04
612	Cliff Johnson	.12	.06	.04
613	Randy Stein	.12	.06	.04
614	John Hiller	.12	.06	.04
615	Doug DeCinces	.12	.06	.04
616	Gene Richards	.12	.06	.04
617	Joaquin Andujar	.12	.06	.04
618	Bob Montgomery	.12	.06	.04
619	Sergio Ferrer	.12	.06	.04
620	Richie Zisk	.12	.06	.04
621	Bob Grich	.12	.06	.04
622	Mario Soto	.12	.06	.04
623	Gorman Thomas	.12	.06	.04
624	Lerrin LaGrow	.12	.06	.04
625	Chris Chambliss	.12	.06	.04
626	Tigers Team (Sparky Anderson)	.80	.40	.25
627	Pedro Borbon	.12	.06	.04
628	Doug Capilla	.12	.06	.04
629	Jim Todd	.12	.06	.04
630	Larry Bowa	.12	.06	.04
631	Mark Littell	.12	.06	.04
632	Barry Bonnell	.12	.06	.04
633	Bob Apodaca	.12	.06	.04
634	Glenn Borgmann	.12	.06	.04
635	John Candelaria	.12	.06	.04
636	Toby Harrah	.12	.06	.04
637	Joe Simpson	.12	.06	.04
638	*Mark Clear*	.12	.06	.04
639	Larry Biittner	.12	.06	.04
640	Mike Flanagan	.12	.06	.04
641	Ed Kranepool	.12	.06	.04
642	Ken Forsch	.12	.06	.04
643	John Mayberry	.12	.06	.04
644	Charlie Hough	.12	.06	.04
645	Rick Burleson	.12	.06	.04
646	Checklist 606-726	.12	.06	.04
647	Milt May	.12	.06	.04
648	Roy White	.12	.06	.04
649	Tom Griffin	.12	.06	.04
650	Joe Morgan	2.00	1.00	.60
651	Rollie Fingers	1.50	.70	.45
652	Mario Mendoza	.12	.06	.04
653	Stan Bahnsen	.12	.06	.04
654	Bruce Boisclair	.12	.06	.04
655	Tug McGraw	.15	.08	.05
656	Larvell Blanks	.12	.06	.04
657	Dave Edwards	.12	.06	.04
658	Chris Knapp	.12	.06	.04
659	Brewers Team (George Bamberger)	.25	.13	.08
660	Rusty Staub	.15	.08	.05
661	Orioles Future Stars (Mark Corey, Dave Ford, Wayne Krenchicki)	.12	.06	.04
662	Red Sox Future Stars (Joel Finch, Mike O'Berry, Chuck Rainey)	.12	.06	.04
663	Angels Future Stars (Ralph Botting, Bob Clark), *(Dickie Thon)*	.25	.13	.08
664	White Sox Future Stars (Mike Colbern), *(Guy Hoffman*, Dewey Robinson)	.12	.06	.04
665	Indians Future Stars (Larry Andersen, Bobby Cuellar, Sandy Wihtol)	.12	.06	.04
666	Tigers Future Stars (Mike Chris, Al Greene, Bruce Robbins)	.12	.06	.04
667	Royals Future Stars (Renie Martin, Bill Paschall), *(Dan Quisenberry)*	1.50	.70	.45
668	Brewers Future Stars (Danny Boitano, Willie Mueller, Lenn Sakata)	.12	.06	.04
669	Twins Future Stars (Dan Graham, Rick Sofield), *(Gary Ward)*	.25	.13	.08
670	Yankees Future Stars (Bobby Brown, Brad Gulden, Darryl Jones)	.12	.06	.04
671	A's Future Stars (Derek Bryant, Brian Kingman), *(Mike Morgan)*	.60	.30	.20
672	Mariners Future Stars (Charlie Beamon, Rodney Craig, Rafael Vasquez)	.12	.06	.04
673	Rangers Future Stars (Brian Allard, Jerry Don Gleaton, Greg Mahlberg)	.12	.06	.04
674	Blue Jays Future Stars (Butch Edge, Pat Kelly, Ted Wilborn)	.12	.06	.04
675	Braves Future Stars (Bruce Benedict, Larry Bradford, Eddie Miller)	.12	.06	.04
676	Cubs Future Stars (Dave Geisel, Steve Macko, Karl Pagel)	.12	.06	.04
677	Reds Future Stars (Art DeFreites), *(Frank Pastore*, Harry Spilman)	.12	.06	.04
678	Astros Future Stars (Reggie Baldwin, Alan Knicely), *(Pete Ladd)*	.12	.06	.04

679	Dodgers Future Stars (Joe Beckwith), *(Mickey Hatcher,* Dave Patterson)	.25	.13	.08
680	Expos Future Stars *(Tony Bernazard,* Randy Miller, John Tamargo)	.12	.06	.04
681	Mets Future Stars (Dan Norman), *(Jesse Orosco), (Mike Scott)*	1.00	.50	.30
682	Phillies Future Stars (Ramon Aviles), *(Dickie Noles,* Kevin Saucier)	.12	.06	.04
683	Pirates Future Stars (Dorian Boyland, Alberto Lois, Harry Saferight)	.12	.06	.04
684	Cardinals Future Stars (George Frazier), *(Tom Herr,* Dan O'Brien)	.30	.15	.09
685	Padres Future Stars (Tim Flannery, Brian Greer, Jim Wilhelm)	.12	.06	.04
686	Giants Future Stars (Greg Johnston, Dennis Littlejohn, Phil Nastu)	.12	.06	.04
687	Mike Heath	.12	.06	.04
688	Steve Stone	.12	.06	.04
689	Red Sox Team (Don Zimmer)	.25	.13	.08
690	Tommy John	.25	.13	.08
691	Ivan DeJesus	.12	.06	.04
692	Rawly Eastwick	.12	.06	.04
693	Craig Kusick	.12	.06	.04
694	Jim Rooker	.12	.06	.04
695	Reggie Smith	.12	.06	.04
696	Julio Gonzalez	.12	.06	.04
697	David Clyde	.12	.06	.04
698	Oscar Gamble	.12	.06	.04
699	Floyd Bannister	.12	.06	.04
700	Rod Carew	2.00	1.00	.60
701	*Ken Oberkfell*	.12	.06	.04
702	Ed Farmer	.12	.06	.04
703	Otto Velez	.12	.06	.04
704	Gene Tenace	.12	.06	.04
705	Freddie Patek	.12	.06	.04
706	Tippy Martinez	.12	.06	.04
707	Elliott Maddox	.12	.06	.04
708	Bob Tolan	.12	.06	.04
709	Pat Underwood	.12	.06	.04
710	Graig Nettles	.12	.06	.04
711	Bob Galasso	.12	.06	.04
712	Rodney Scott	.12	.06	.04
713	Terry Whitfield	.12	.06	.04
714	Fred Norman	.12	.06	.04
715	Sal Bando	.12	.06	.04
716	Lynn McGlothen	.12	.06	.04
717	Mickey Klutts	.12	.06	.04
718	Greg Gross	.12	.06	.04
719	Don Robinson	.12	.06	.04
720	Carl Yastrzemski	3.00	1.50	.90
721	Paul Hartzell	.12	.06	.04
722	Jose Cruz	.15	.08	.05
723	Shane Rawley	.12	.06	.04
724	Jerry White	.12	.06	.04
725	Rick Wise	.12	.06	.04
726	Steve Yeager	.12	.06	.04

1980 Topps Superstar 5x7 Photos

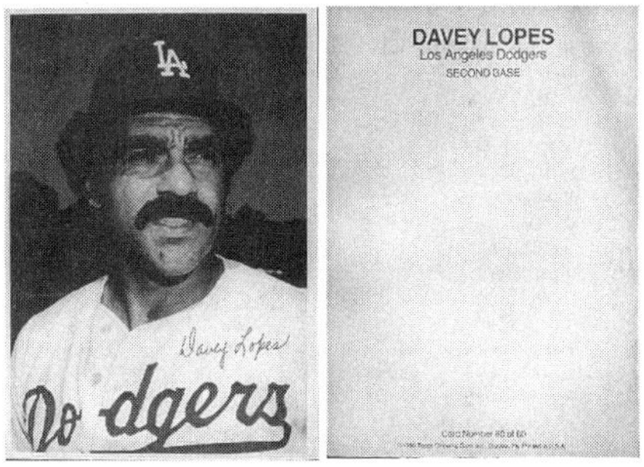

In actuality, these cards measure 4-7/8" x 6-7/8". These were another Topps "test" issue that was bought out almost entirely by speculators. The 60 cards have a color photo on the front and a blue ink facsimile autograph. Backs have the player's name, team, position and card number. The issue was printed on different cardboard stocks, with the first on thick cardboard with a white back and the second on thinner cardboard with a gray back. Prices below are for the more common gray backs; white backs are valued 2.5X-3X the figures shown, except for triple-print cards (indicated by "3P" in checklist), which are valued at about 7.5x the gray-back price in the white-back version. The white backs were test marketed in three-card cello packs in selected geographical areas.

		NM	EX	VG
Complete Set, Gray Backs (60):		10.00	5.00	3.00
Complete Set, White Backs (60):		25.00	12.50	7.50
Common Player, Gray Back:		.25	.13	.08
Common Player, White Back:		.75	.40	.25
1	Willie Stargell	.75	.40	.25
2	Mike Schmidt (3P)	1.00	.50	.30
3	Johnny Bench	1.50	.70	.45
4	Jim Palmer	.75	.40	.25
5	Jim Rice	.50	.25	.15
6	Reggie Jackson (3P)	1.50	.70	.45
7	Ron Guidry	.45	.25	.14
8	Lee Mazzilli	.25	.13	.08
9	Don Baylor	.35	.20	.11
10	Fred Lynn	.35	.20	.11
11	Ken Singleton	.25	.13	.08
12	Rod Carew (3P)	1.50	.70	.45
13	Steve Garvey (3P)	.90	.45	.25
14	George Brett (3P)	1.50	.70	.45
15	Tom Seaver	1.50	.70	.45
16	Dave Kingman	.25	.13	.08
17	Dave Parker (3P)	.25	.13	.08
18	Dave Winfield	1.25	.60	.40
19	Pete Rose	2.00	1.00	.60
20	Nolan Ryan	4.00	2.00	1.25
21	Graig Nettles	.25	.13	.08
22	Carl Yastrzemski	1.50	.70	.45
23	Tommy John	.40	.20	.12
24	George Foster	.25	.13	.08
25	J.R. Richard	.35	.20	.11
26	Keith Hernandez	.25	.13	.08
27	Bob Horner	.25	.13	.08
28	Eddie Murray	1.50	.70	.45
29	Steve Kemp	.25	.13	.08
30	Gorman Thomas	.25	.13	.08
31	Sixto Lezcano	.25	.13	.08
32	Bruce Sutter	.25	.13	.08
33	Cecil Cooper	.25	.13	.08
34	Larry Bowa	.25	.13	.08
35	Al Oliver	.35	.20	.11
36	Ted Simmons	.25	.13	.08
37	Garry Templeton	.25	.13	.08
38	Jerry Koosman	.25	.13	.08
39	Darrell Porter	.25	.13	.08
40	Roy Smalley	.25	.13	.08
41	Craig Swan	.25	.13	.08
42	Jason Thompson	.25	.13	.08
43	Andre Thornton	.25	.13	.08
44	Rick Manning	.25	.13	.08
45	Kent Tekulve	.25	.13	.08
46	Phil Niekro	1.25	.60	.40
47	Buddy Bell	.25	.13	.08
48	Randy Jones	.25	.13	.08
49	Brian Downing	.25	.13	.08
50	Amos Otis	.25	.13	.08
51	Rick Bosetti	.25	.13	.08
52	Gary Carter	.75	.40	.25
53	Larry Parrish	.25	.13	.08
54	Jack Clark	.25	.13	.08
55	Bruce Bochte	.25	.13	.08
56	Cesar Cedeno	.25	.13	.08
57	Chet Lemon	.25	.13	.08
58	Dave Revering	.25	.13	.08
59	Vida Blue	.25	.13	.08
60	Davey Lopes	.25	.13	.08

1980 Topps Team/Checklist Sheet

This uncut sheet of 26 1980 Topps team cards was available via a mail-in offer. The sheet was mailed with two folds and includes an offer to picture yourself on a baseball card.

	NM	EX	VG
Uncut Sheet	20.00	10.00	6.00

1909 T.T.T. Cigarettes (T204)

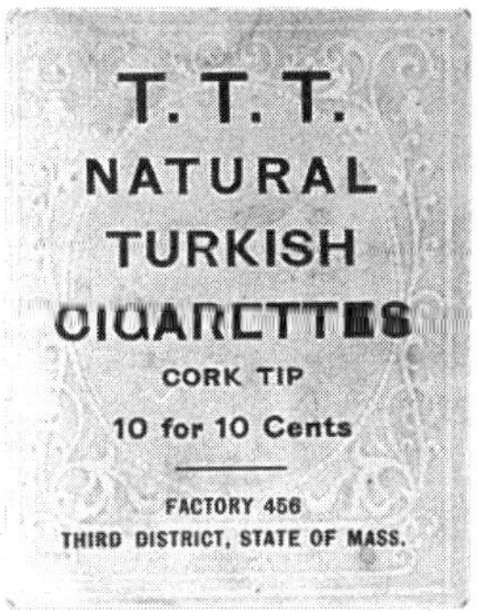

This is one of two brands of cigarette advertising found on the backs of the ornate, gold-trimmed T204 cards. The initials stand for T.T. Tinayens, the Boston firm which also produced Ramly cigarettes, more commonly found mentioned on the cards' backs. Because of the scarcity of all T204 cards, there is little or no premium attached to the T.T.T. versions.

(See checklist under Ramly Cigarettes listing.)

1978 Toronto Blue Jays Photocards

This set of 3-1/2" x 5-1/2" black-and-white, blank-back photocards features the Blue Jays in their second season. The wide white border at bottom has team identification and logo and the player name. The unnumbered cards are checklisted here in alphabetical order.

		NM	EX	VG
Complete Set (34):		65.00	32.00	19.50
Common Player:		2.00	1.00	.60
(1)	Alan Ashby	2.00	1.00	.60
(2)	Doug Ault	2.00	1.00	.60
(3)	Bob Bailor	2.00	1.00	.60
(4)	Rick Bosetti	2.00	1.00	.60
(5)	Rico Carty	3.00	1.50	.90
(6)	Rick Cerone	3.00	1.50	.90
(7)	Jim Clancy	2.00	1.00	.60
(8)	Joe Coleman	2.00	1.00	.60
(9)	Victor Cruz	2.00	1.00	.60
(10)	Sam Ewing	2.00	1.00	.60
(11)	Ron Fairly	2.00	1.00	.60
(12)	Jerry Garvin	2.00	1.00	.60
(13)	Luis Gomez	2.00	1.00	.60
(14)	Roy Hartsfield	2.00	1.00	.60
(15)	Roy Howell	2.00	1.00	.60
(16)	Jesse Jefferson	2.00	1.00	.60
(17)	Tim Johnson	2.00	1.00	.60
(18)	Don Kirkwood	2.00	1.00	.60
(19)	Dave Lemanczyk	2.00	1.00	.60
(20)	John Mayberry	2.00	1.00	.60
(21)	Dave McKay	2.00	1.00	.60
(22)	Bob Miller	2.00	1.00	.60
(23)	Balor Moore	2.00	1.00	.60
(24)	Jackie Moore	2.00	1.00	.60
(25)	Tom Murphy	2.00	1.00	.60
(26)	Phil Roof	2.00	1.00	.60
(27)	Bill Singer	2.00	1.00	.60
(28)	Hector Torres	2.00	1.00	.60
(29)	Tom Underwood	2.00	1.00	.60
(30)	Willie Upshaw	3.00	1.50	.90
(31)	Otto Velez	2.00	1.00	.60
(32)	Harry Warner	2.00	1.00	.60
(33)	Mike Willis	2.00	1.00	.60
(34)	Alvis Woods	2.00	1.00	.60

1976 Towne Club discs

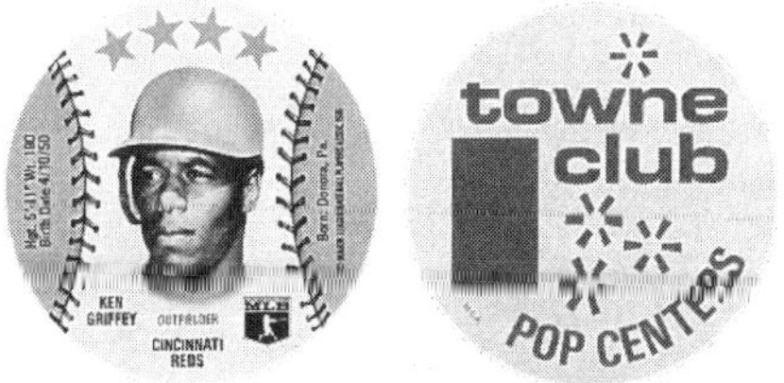

One of several regional sponsors of player disc sets in 1976 was the Towne Club Pop Centers chain. The discs are 3-3/8" diameter with a black-and-white player portrait photo in the center of the baseball design. A line of red stars is above, while the left and right panels feature one of several bright colors. Produced by Michael Schecter Associates under license from the Major League Baseball Players Association, the player photos have had uniform and cap logos removed. Backs are printed in red. The unnumbered checklist here is presented in alphabetical order.

		NM	EX	VG
Complete Set (70):		90.00	45.00	25.00
Common Player:		1.00	.50	.30
(1)	Henry Aaron	12.00	6.00	3.50
(2)	Johnny Bench	6.00	3.00	1.75
(3)	Vida Blue	1.00	.50	.30
(4)	Larry Bowa	1.00	.50	.30
(5)	Lou Brock	4.50	2.25	1.25
(6)	Jeff Burroughs	1.00	.50	.30
(7)	John Candelaria	1.00	.50	.30
(8)	Jose Cardenal	1.00	.50	.30
(9)	Rod Carew	4.50	2.25	1.25
(10)	Steve Carlton	4.50	2.25	1.25
(11)	Dave Cash	1.00	.50	.30
(12)	Cesar Cedeno	1.00	.50	.30
(13)	Ron Cey	1.00	.50	.30
(14)	Carlton Fisk	4.50	2.25	1.25
(15)	Tito Fuentes	1.00	.50	.30
(16)	Steve Garvey	4.50	2.25	1.25
(17)	Ken Griffey	1.50	.70	.45
(18)	Don Gullett	1.00	.50	.30
(19)	Willie Horton	1.00	.50	.30
(20)	Al Hrabosky	1.00	.50	.30
(21)	Catfish Hunter	4.50	2.25	1.25
(22)	Reggie Jackson	10.00	5.00	3.00
(23)	Randy Jones	1.00	.50	.30
(24)	Jim Kaat	1.50	.70	.45
(25)	Don Kessinger	1.00	.50	.30
(26)	Dave Kingman	2.00	1.00	.60
(27)	Jerry Koosman	1.00	.50	.30
(28)	Mickey Lolich	2.00	1.00	.60
(29)	Greg Luzinski	1.50	.70	.45
(30)	Fred Lynn	1.50	.70	.45
(31)	Bill Madlock	1.00	.50	.30
(32)	Carlos May	1.00	.50	.30
(33)	John Mayberry	1.00	.50	.30
(34)	Bake McBride	1.00	.50	.30
(35)	Doc Medich	1.00	.50	.30
(36)	Andy Messersmith	1.00	.50	.30
(37)	Rick Monday	1.00	.50	.30
(38)	John Montefusco	1.00	.50	.30
(39)	Jerry Morales	1.00	.50	.30
(40)	Joe Morgan	4.50	2.25	1.25
(41)	Thurman Munson	6.00	3.00	1.75
(42)	Bobby Murcer	1.00	.50	.30
(43)	Al Oliver	1.00	.50	.30
(44)	Jim Palmer	4.50	2.25	1.25
(45)	Dave Parker	2.00	1.00	.60
(46)	Tony Perez	4.50	2.25	1.25
(47)	Jerry Reuss	1.00	.50	.30
(48)	Brooks Robinson	6.00	3.00	1.75
(49)	Frank Robinson	6.00	3.00	1.75
(50)	Steve Rogers	1.00	.50	.30
(51)	Pete Rose	12.00	6.00	3.50
(52)	Nolan Ryan	25.00	12.50	7.50
(53)	Manny Sanguillen	1.00	.50	.30
(54)	Mike Schmidt	8.00	4.00	2.50
(55)	Tom Seaver	6.00	3.00	1.75
(56)	Ted Simmons	1.00	.50	.30
(57)	Reggie Smith	1.00	.50	.30
(58)	Willie Stargell	4.50	2.25	1.25
(59)	Rusty Staub	2.00	1.00	.60
(60)	Rennie Stennett	1.00	.50	.30
(61)	Don Sutton	4.50	2.25	1.25
(62)	Andy Thornton	1.00	.50	.30
(63)	Luis Tiant	1.00	.50	.30
(64)	Joe Torre	2.00	1.00	.60
(65)	Mike Tyson	1.00	.50	.30
(66)	Bob Watson	1.00	.50	.30
(67)	Wilbur Wood	1.00	.50	.30
(68)	Jimmy Wynn	1.00	.50	.30
(69)	Carl Yastrzemski	6.00	3.00	1.75
(70)	Richie Zisk	1.00	.50	.30

1910 Toy Town Post Office

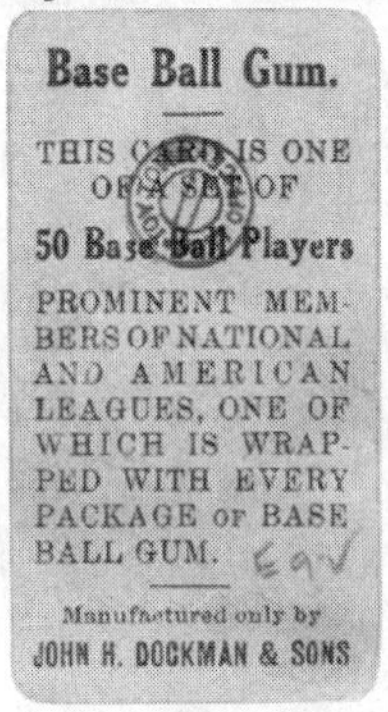
Base Ball Gum.

THIS CARD IS ONE OF A SET OF 50 Base Ball Players PROMINENT MEMBERS OF NATIONAL AND AMERICAN LEAGUES, ONE OF WHICH IS WRAPPED WITH EVERY PACKAGE OF BASE BALL GUM.

Manufactured only by JOHN H. DOCKMAN & SONS

Rather than a card issuer, this enigmatic rubber-stamp has been found on the backs of dozens of 1910-era baseball cards. Measuring 1/2" in diameter the seal is in purple ink. At center is a barred circle with "TOY TOWN" above and "POST OFFICE" below. Whether the cards were sold pre-stamped as part of a toy set or were defaced by a youngster and eventually made their way into the hobby is unknown. Because the cards are low-grade the addition of the stamp neither adds nor detracts from the value of the card on which it is placed.

(See individual card issuers for base values.)

1965 Trade Bloc Minnesota Twins

These cards were produced as part of a baseball game which was marketed at Metropolitan Stadium for $1. The blank-back cards measure 2-1/4" x 3-1/2" and are printed in either blue or sepia tones. Besides Twins players and staff, the set includes cards of various team souvenir items as well as old Met Stadium. Besides the player photo, cards include a facsimile autograph, stats and personal data. The unnumbered cards are checklisted here in alphabetical order.

		NM	EX	VG
Complete Set (52):		225.00	110.00	65.00
Common Player:		6.00	3.00	1.75
Common No-player Card:		2.00	1.00	.60
(1)	Bernard Allen	6.00	3.00	1.75
(2)	Bob Allison	6.00	3.00	1.75
(3)	Earl Battey	6.00	3.00	1.75
(4)	Dave Boswell	6.00	3.00	1.75
(5)	Gerald Fosnow	6.00	3.00	1.75
(6)	James Grant	6.00	3.00	1.75
(7)	Calvin Griffith	7.50	3.75	2.25
(8)	Jimmie Hall	6.00	3.00	1.75
(9)	Jim Kaat	8.00	4.00	2.50
(10)	Harmon Killebrew	15.00	7.50	4.50
(11)	Jerry Kindall	6.00	3.00	1.75
(12)	Johnny Klippstein	6.00	3.00	1.75
(13)	Frank Kostro	6.00	3.00	1.75
(14)	James Lemon	6.00	3.00	1.75
(15)	George "Doc" Lentz	6.00	3.00	1.75
(16)	Alfred Martin (Billy)	9.00	4.50	2.75
(17)	Sam Mele	6.00	3.00	1.75
(18)	Donald Mincher	6.00	3.00	1.75
(19)	Harold Naragon	6.00	3.00	1.75
(20)	Melvin Nelson	6.00	3.00	1.75
(21)	Joseph Nossek	6.00	3.00	1.75
(22)	Pedro Oliva (Tony)	11.00	5.50	3.25
(23)	Camilo Pascual	6.00	3.00	1.75
(24)	James Perry	6.00	3.00	1.75
(25)	Bill Pleis	6.00	3.00	1.75
(26)	Richard Rollins	6.00	3.00	1.75
(27)	John Sain	6.00	3.00	1.75
(28)	John Sevcik	6.00	3.00	1.75
(29)	Richard Stigman	6.00	3.00	1.75
(30)	Sandy Valdespino	6.00	3.00	1.75
(31)	Zoilo Versalles	5.00	2.50	1.50
(32)	Allan Worthington	6.00	3.00	1.75
(33)	Gerald Zimmerman	6.00	3.00	1.75
(34)	Metropolitan Stadium	4.00	2.00	1.25
(35)	L.A. Angels logo	2.00	1.00	.60
(36)	K.C. Athletics logo	2.00	1.00	.60
(37)	Cleveland Indians logo	2.00	1.00	.60
(38)	Baltimore Orioles logo	2.00	1.00	.60
(39)	Boston Red Sox logo	2.00	1.00	.60
(40)	Washington Senators logo	2.00	1.00	.60
(41)	Detroit Tigers logo	2.00	3.00	.60
(42)	Minnesota Twins logo	2.00	1.00	.60
(43)	Chicago White Sox logo	2.00	1.00	.60
(44)	N.Y. Yankees logo	2.00	1.00	.60
(45)	Twins autographed ball	2.00	1.00	.60
(46)	Twins autographed bat	2.00	1.00	.60
(47)	Twins bobbin' head doll	2.00	1.00	.60
(48)	Twins cap	2.00	1.00	.60
(49)	Twins pennant	2.00	1.00	.60
(50)	Twins scorebook	2.00	1.00	.60
(51)	Twins warmup jacket	2.00	1.00	.60
(52)	Twins yearbook	2.00	1.00	.60

1969 Transogram

These 2-1/2" x 3-1/2" cards were printed on the bottom of toy baseball player statue boxes. The cards feature a color photo of the player surrounded by a rounded white border. Below the photo is the player's name in red and his team and other personal details all printed in black. The overall background is yellow. The cards were designed to be cut off the box, but collectors prefer to find the box intact and better still, with the statue inside. Prices shown are for cards cut from the box. While the cards themselves are not numbered, there is a number on each box's end flap, which is the order in which the cards are checklisted here. Three-player boxes were also sold.

		NM	EX	VG
Complete Set (60):		750.00	375.00	225.00
Common Player:		4.00	2.00	1.25
(1)	Joe Azcue	4.00	2.00	1.25
(2)	Willie Horton	5.00	2.50	1.50
(3)	Luis Tiant	5.00	2.50	1.50
(4)	Denny McLain	6.00	3.00	1.75
(5)	Jose Cardenal	4.00	2.00	1.25
(6)	Al Kaline	25.00	12.50	7.50
(7)	Tony Oliva	6.00	3.00	1.75
(8)	Blue Moon Odom	4.00	2.00	1.25
(9)	Cesar Tovar	4.00	2.00	1.25
(10)	Rick Monday	4.00	2.00	1.25
(11)	Harmon Killebrew	20.00	10.00	6.00
(12)	Danny Cater	4.00	2.00	1.25
(13)	Brooks Robinson	25.00	12.50	7.50
(14)	Jim Fregosi	4.00	2.00	1.25
(15)	Dave McNally	4.00	2.00	1.25
(16)	Frank Robinson	25.00	12.50	7.50
(17)	Bobby Knoop	4.00	2.00	1.25
(18)	Rick Reichardt	4.00	2.00	1.25
(19)	Carl Yastrzemski	25.00	12.50	7.50
(20)	Pete Ward	4.00	2.00	1.25
(21)	Rico Petrocelli	4.00	2.00	1.25
(22)	Tommy John	7.50	3.75	2.25
(23)	Ken Harrelson	5.00	2.50	1.50
(24)	Luis Aparicio	20.00	10.00	6.00
(25)	Mike Epstein	4.00	2.00	1.25
(26)	Roy White	4.00	2.00	1.25
(27)	Camilo Pascual	4.00	2.00	1.25
(28)	Mel Stottlemyre	4.00	2.00	1.25
(29)	Frank Howard	5.00	2.50	1.50
(30)	Mickey Mantle	125.00	62.00	37.00
(31)	Lou Brock	20.00	10.00	6.00
(32)	Juan Marichal	20.00	10.00	6.00
(33)	Bob Gibson	20.00	10.00	6.00
(34)	Willie Mays	45.00	22.00	13.50
(35)	Tim McCarver	6.00	3.00	1.75
(36)	Willie McCovey	20.00	10.00	6.00
(37)	Don Wilson	4.00	2.00	1.25
(38)	Billy Williams	20.00	10.00	6.00
(39)	Dan Staub (Rusty)	5.00	2.50	1.50
(40)	Ernie Banks	25.00	12.50	7.50
(41)	Jim Wynn	4.00	2.00	1.25
(42)	Ron Santo	9.00	4.50	2.75
(43)	Tom Haller	4.00	2.00	1.25
(44)	Ron Swoboda	4.00	2.00	1.25
(45)	Willie Davis	4.00	2.00	1.25
(46)	Jerry Koosman	4.00	2.00	1.25
(47)	Jim Lefebvre	4.00	2.00	1.25
(48)	Tom Seaver	25.00	12.50	7.50
(49)	Joe Torre (Atlanta)	6.00	3.00	1.75
(50)	Tony Perez	20.00	10.00	6.00
(51)	Felipe Alou	5.00	2.50	1.50
(52)	Lee May	4.00	2.00	1.25
(53)	Hank Aaron	45.00	22.00	13.50
(54)	Pete Rose	40.00	20.00	12.00
(55)	Cookie Rojas	4.00	2.00	1.25
(56)	Roberto Clemente	50.00	25.00	15.00
(57)	Richie Allen	9.00	4.50	2.75
(58)	Matty Alou	4.00	2.00	1.25
(59)	Johnny Callison	4.00	2.00	1.25
(60)	Bill Mazeroski	12.00	6.00	3.50

1970 Transogram

Like the 1969 cards, the 1970 Transogram cards were available on boxes of three Transogram baseball statues. The individual player cards are slightly larger at 2-9/16" x 3-1/2". The 30-card set has the same pictures as the 1969 set except for Joe Torre. All players in the '70 set were included in the '69 Transogram issue except for Reggie Jackson, Sam McDowell and Boog Powell. Each box contains a side panel with a series number and 1" x 1-1/4" portrait photos of the players in the series. Prices shown are for cards cut from the box.

		NM	EX	VG
Complete Set (30):		325.00	162.00	97.00
Complete Set, Boxes/Statues (10):		1700.	875.00	525.00
Common Player:		4.00	2.00	1.25
	Series 1 (Complete boxed set:)	240.00	120.00	72.50
(1)	Pete Rose	30.00	15.00	9.00
(2)	Willie Mays	45.00	22.00	13.50
(3)	Cleon Jones	4.00	2.00	1.25
	Series 2 (Complete Boxed Set:)	150.00	75.00	45.00
(4)	Ron Santo	9.00	4.50	2.75
(5)	Willie Davis	4.00	2.00	1.25
(6)	Willie McCovey	20.00	10.00	6.00
	Series 3 (Complete Boxed Set:)	260.00	130.00	80.00
(7)	Juan Marichal	20.00	10.00	6.00
(8)	Joe Torre (St. Louis)	9.00	4.50	2.75
(9)	Ernie Banks	30.00	15.00	9.00
	Series 4 (Complete Boxed Set:)	350.00	175.00	105.00
(10)	Hank Aaron	45.00	22.00	13.50
(11)	Jim Wynn	4.00	2.00	1.25
(12)	Tom Seaver	22.00	11.00	6.50
	Series 5 (Complete Boxed Set:)	350.00	175.00	105.00
(13)	Bob Gibson	20.00	10.00	6.00
(14)	Roberto Clemente	50.00	25.00	15.00
(15)	Jerry Koosman	4.00	2.00	1.25
	Series 11 (Complete Boxed Set:)	240.00	120.00	72.50
(16)	Denny McLain	6.00	3.00	1.75
(17)	Reggie Jackson	30.00	15.00	9.00
(18)	Boog Powell	6.00	3.00	1.75
	Series 12 (Complete Boxed Set:)	140.00	70.00	42.50
(19)	Frank Robinson	20.00	10.00	6.00
(20)	Frank Howard	4.00	2.00	1.25
(21)	Rick Reichardt	4.00	2.00	1.25
	Series 13 (Complete Boxed Set:)	150.00	75.00	45.00
(22)	Carl Yastrzemski	20.00	10.00	6.00
(23)	Tony Oliva	6.00	3.00	1.75
(24)	Mel Stottlemyre	4.00	2.00	1.25
	Series 14 (Complete Boxed Set:)	140.00	70.00	42.50
(25)	Al Kaline	20.00	10.00	6.00
(26)	Jim Fregosi	4.00	2.00	1.25
(27)	Sam McDowell	4.00	2.00	1.25
	Series 15 (Complete Boxed Set:)	140.00	70.00	42.50
(28)	Blue Moon Odom	4.00	2.00	1.25
(29)	Harmon Killebrew	20.00	10.00	6.00
(30)	Rico Petrocelli	1.00	[illegible]	[illegible]

1970 Transogram Mets

This Transogram set features members of the World Champion N.Y. Mets. Like the other 1970 Transograms, the issue was packaged in a three-statue cardboard box with cellophane front panel and cards printed on the back. Player cards are 2-9/16" x 3-1/2" and retain the basic format of Transogram cards of 1969-70: a color photo with player name in red and team, position and biographical details in black. Backs are blank. As with the other Transogram sets, the cards are most valuable when they are still part of their original box with the statues. Values shown here are for cards cut from the box.

		NM	EX	VG
Complete Set (15):		275.00	125.00	80.00
Common Player:		5.00	2.50	1.50
	Series 21			
(1)	Ed Kranepool	5.00	2.50	1.50
(2)	Al Weis	5.00	2.50	1.50
(3)	Tom Seaver	30.00	15.00	9.00
	Series 22			
(4)	Ken Boswell	5.00	2.50	1.50
(5)	Jerry Koosman	5.00	2.50	1.50
(6)	Jerry Grote	5.00	2.50	1.50
	Series 23			
(7)	Art Shamsky	5.00	2.50	1.50
(8)	Gary Gentry	5.00	2.50	1.50
(9)	Tommie Agee	5.00	2.50	1.50
	Series 24			
(10)	Nolan Ryan	225.00	110.00	67.00
(11)	Tug McGraw	5.00	2.50	1.50
(12)	Cleon Jones	5.00	2.50	1.50
	Series 25			
(13)	Ron Swoboda	5.00	2.50	1.50
(14)	Bud Harrelson	5.00	2.50	1.50
(15)	Donn Clendenon	5.00	2.50	1.50

1925 Turf Cigarettes

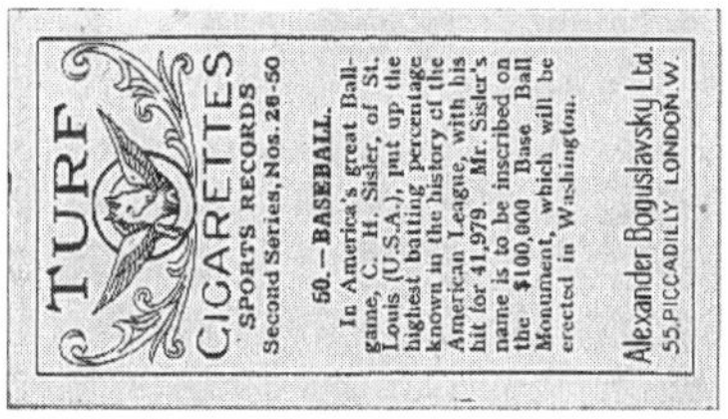

"Sports Records" is the name of a two-series, 50-card issue by Turf Cigarettes. The last card in the set depicts George Sisler (though not named) on the front in a color action scene. Black-and-white back of the card describes Sisler's batting prowess. Like other British tobacco cards of the era, size is 2-5/8" x 1-3/8".

		NM	EX	VG
50	Baseball (George Sisler)	60.00	30.00	18.00

1909-11 Turkey Red Cigarettes

(See S74, T3)

1909-11 Ty Cobb Tobacco (T206)

Much rarer than the famed Honus Wagner card from the related cigarette card series known collectively as T206, the Ty Cobb brand tobacco back was known in only about half a dozen collections until June, 1997, when a find of five lower-grade specimens was auctioned. Because T206 was generally collected by front design, rather than back, however, through most of the hobby's history, it has only been in recent years that the value of the "Ty Cobb-back" T206 has begun to approach the other great rarities of the series. To date, the only front known with a Cobb tobacco back is the red-background portrait.

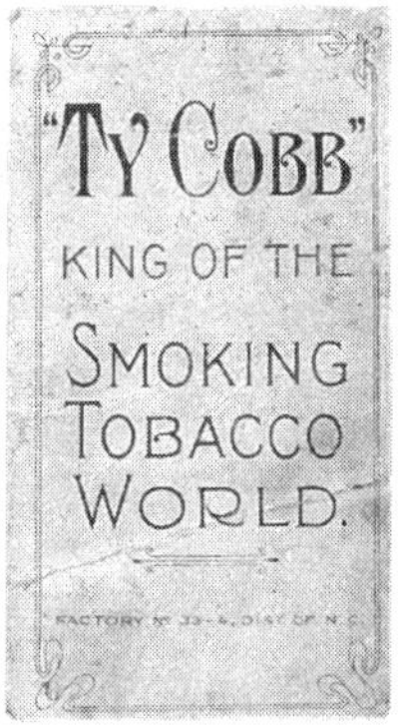

(See T206, #95b. Approximately 11 known)

1911 T3 Turkey Red Cabinets

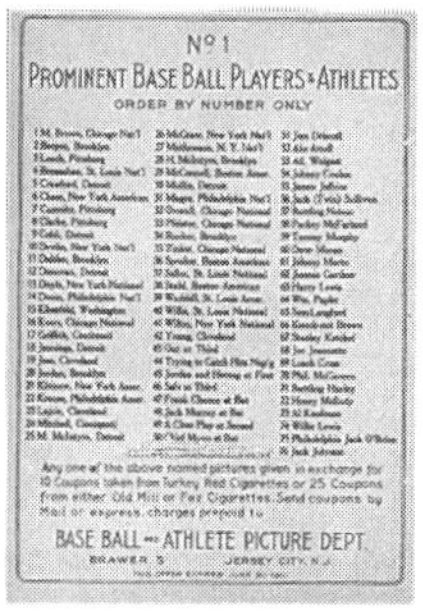

Turkey Reds are the only cabinet cards the average collector can have a realistic chance to complete. Obtained by mailing in coupons found in Turkey Red, Fez and Old Mill brand cigarettes, the Turkey Reds measure 5-3/4" x 8", a size known to collectors as "cabinet cards." Turkey Reds feature full color lithograph fronts with wide gray frames. Backs carried either a numbered ordering list or an ad for Turkey Red cigarettes. The Turkey Red series consists of 25 boxers and 100 baseball players. Despite their cost, Turkey Reds remain very popular today as the most attractive of the cabinet sets.

		NM	EX	VG
Complete (Baseball) Set (100):		65000.	35000.	21000.
Common Player:		350.00	200.00	100.00
1	Mordecai Brown	900.00	450.00	270.00
2	Bill Bergen	350.00	200.00	100.00
3	Tommy Leach	350.00	200.00	100.00
4	Roger Bresnahan	950.00	475.00	285.00
5	Sam Crawford	900.00	425.00	270.00
6	Hal Chase	425.00	240.00	120.00
7	Howie Camnitz	350.00	200.00	100.00
8	Fred Clarke	900.00	450.00	270.00
9	Ty Cobb	7000.	3500.	2100.
10	Art Devlin	350.00	200.00	100.00
11	Bill Dahlen	350.00	200.00	100.00
12	Wild Bill Donovan	350.00	200.00	100.00
13	Larry Doyle	350.00	200.00	100.00
14	Red Dooin	350.00	200.00	100.00
15	Kid Elberfeld	350.00	200.00	100.00
16	Johnny Evers	900.00	450.00	270.00
17	Clark Griffith	900.00	450.00	270.00
18	Hughie Jennings	900.00	450.00	270.00
19	Addie Joss	900.00	450.00	270.00
20	Tim Jordan	350.00	200.00	100.00
21	Red Kleinow	350.00	200.00	100.00
22	Harry Krause	350.00	200.00	100.00
23	Nap Lajoie	1600.	900.00	425.00
24	Mike Mitchell	350.00	200.00	100.00
25	Matty McIntyre	350.00	200.00	100.00
26	John McGraw	900.00	450.00	270.00
27	Christy Mathewson	2500.	1400.	750.00
28a	Harry McIntyre (Brooklyn)	350.00	200.00	100.00
28b	Harry McIntyre (Brooklyn and Chicago)	350.00	200.00	100.00
29	Amby McConnell	350.00	200.00	100.00
30	George Mullin	350.00	200.00	100.00
31	Sherry Magee	350.00	200.00	100.00

32	Orval Overall	350.00	200.00	100.00
33	Jake Pfeister	350.00	200.00	100.00
34	Nap Rucker	350.00	200.00	100.00
35	Joe Tinker	1000.	500.00	300.00
36	Tris Speaker	2200.	1200.	550.00
37	Slim Sallee	350.00	200.00	100.00
38	Jake Stahl	350.00	200.00	100.00
39	Rube Waddell	900.00	450.00	270.00
40a	Vic Willis (Pittsburgh)	900.00	450.00	270.00
40b	Vic Willis (Pittsburgh and St. Louis)	1000.	500.00	300.00
41	Hooks Wiltse	350.00	200.00	100.00
42	Cy Young	2500.	1425.	725.00
43	Out At Third	300.00	175.00	90.00
44	Trying To Catch Him Napping	300.00	175.00	90.00
45	Jordan & Herzog At First	350.00	200.00	100.00
46	Safe At Third	300.00	175.00	90.00
47	Frank Chance At Bat	900.00	450.00	270.00
48	Jack Murray At Bat	350.00	200.00	100.00
49	A Close Play At Second	350.00	200.00	100.00
50	Chief Myers At Bat	350.00	200.00	100.00
77	Red Ames	350.00	200.00	100.00
78	Home Run Baker	900.00	450.00	270.00
79	George Bell	350.00	200.00	100.00
80	Chief Bender	900.00	450.00	270.00
81	Bob Bescher	350.00	200.00	100.00
82	Kitty Bransfield	350.00	200.00	100.00
83	Al Bridwell	350.00	200.00	100.00
84	George Browne	350.00	200.00	100.00
85	Bill Burns	350.00	200.00	100.00
86	Bill Carrigan	350.00	200.00	100.00
87	Eddie Collins	900.00	450.00	270.00
88	Harry Coveleski	350.00	200.00	100.00
89	Lou Criger	350.00	200.00	100.00
90a	Mickey Doolin (Doolan)	450.00	250.00	125.00
90b	Mickey Doolan (name correct)	350.00	200.00	100.00
91	Tom Downey	350.00	200.00	100.00
92	Jimmy Dygert	350.00	200.00	100.00
93	Art Fromme	350.00	200.00	100.00
94	George Gibson	350.00	200.00	100.00
95	Peaches Graham	350.00	200.00	100.00
96	Bob Groom	350.00	200.00	100.00
97	Dick Hoblitzell	350.00	200.00	100.00
98	Solly Hofman	350.00	200.00	100.00
99	Walter Johnson	2650.	1500.	700.00
100	Davy Jones	350.00	200.00	100.00
101	Wee Willie Keeler	900.00	450.00	270.00
102	Johnny Kling	350.00	200.00	100.00
103	Ed Konetchy	350.00	200.00	100.00
104	Ed Lennox	350.00	200.00	100.00
105	Hans Lobert	350.00	200.00	100.00
106	Harry Lord	350.00	200.00	100.00
107	Rube Manning	350.00	200.00	100.00
108	Fred Merkle	350.00	200.00	100.00
109	Pat Moran	350.00	200.00	100.00
110	George McBride	350.00	200.00	100.00
111	Harry Niles	350.00	200.00	100.00
112a	Dode Paskert (Cincinnati)	350.00	200.00	100.00
112b	Dode Paskert (Cincinnati and Philadelphia)	350.00	200.00	100.00
113	Bugs Raymond	400.00	200.00	120.00
114	Bob Rhoades (Rhoads)	350.00	200.00	100.00
115	Admiral Schlei	350.00	200.00	100.00
116	Boss Schmidt	350.00	200.00	100.00
117	Wildfire Schulte	350.00	200.00	100.00
118	Frank Smith	350.00	200.00	100.00
119	George Stone	350.00	200.00	100.00
120	Gabby Street	350.00	200.00	100.00
121	Billy Sullivan	350.00	200.00	100.00
122a	Fred Tenney (New York)	350.00	200.00	100.00
122b	Fred Tenney (New York and Boston)	350.00	200.00	100.00
123	Ira Thomas	350.00	200.00	100.00
124	Bobby Wallace	900.00	450.00	270.00
125	Ed Walsh	900.00	450.00	270.00
126	Owen Wilson	350.00	200.00	100.00

1911 T5 Pinkerton Cabinets

Because they were photographs affixed to a cardboard backing, the cards in the 1911 Pinkerton set are considered "true" cabinet cards. The Pinkerton cabinets are a rather obscure issue, and because of their original method of distribution, it would be virtually impossible to assemble a complete set today. It remains uncertain how many subjects exist in the set. Pinkerton, the parent of Red Man and other tobacco products, offered the cabinets in exchange for coupons found in cigarette packages. According to an original advertising sheet, some 376 different photos were available. A consumer could exchange ten coupons for the card of his choice. The photos available included players from the 16 major league teams plus five teams from the American Association. Pinkertons have been found which vary in both size and type of mount. The most desirable combination is a 3-3/8" x 5-1/2" photograph affixed to a thick, cardboard mount measuring approximately 4-3/4" x 7-3/4". But original Pinkerton cabinets have also been found in slightly different sizes with less substantial backings. The most attractive mounts are embossed around the picture, but some Pinkertons have a white border surrounding the photograph. Prices listed are for cards with cardboard mounts. Cards with paper mounts are worth about 3/4 of listed prices. Collectors should be aware that some of the Pinkerton photos were reproduced in postcard size issues in later years. Because of the rarity of the T5s, no complete set price is given.

		NM	EX	VG
	Common Player:	300.00	150.00	90.00
101	Jim Stephens	300.00	150.00	90.00
102	Bobby Wallace	775.00	387.00	232.00
103	Joe Lake	300.00	150.00	90.00
104	George Stone	300.00	150.00	90.00
105	Jack O'Connor	300.00	150.00	90.00
106	Bill Abstein	300.00	150.00	90.00
107	Rube Waddell	775.00	387.00	232.00
108	Roy Hartzell	300.00	150.00	90.00
109	Danny Hoffman	300.00	150.00	90.00
110	Dode Cris	300.00	150.00	90.00
111	Al Schweitzer	300.00	150.00	90.00
112	Art Griggs	300.00	150.00	90.00
113	Bill Bailey	300.00	150.00	90.00
114	Pat Newman	300.00	150.00	90.00
115	Harry Howell	300.00	150.00	90.00
117	Hobe Ferris	300.00	150.00	90.00
118	John McAleese	300.00	150.00	90.00
119	Ray Demmitt	300.00	150.00	90.00
120	Red Fisher	300.00	150.00	90.00
121	Frank Truesdale	300.00	150.00	90.00
122	Barney Pelty	300.00	150.00	90.00
123	Ed Killifer (Killefer)	300.00	150.00	90.00
151	Matty McIntyre	300.00	150.00	90.00
152	Jim Delahanty	300.00	150.00	90.00
153	Hughey Jennings	775.00	387.00	232.00
154	Ralph Works	300.00	150.00	90.00
155	George Moriarity (Moriarty)	300.00	150.00	90.00
156	Sam Crawford	775.00	387.00	232.00
157	Boss Schmidt	300.00	150.00	90.00
158	Owen Bush	300.00	150.00	90.00
159	Ty Cobb	4500.	2250.	1350.
160	Bill Donovan	300.00	150.00	90.00
161	Oscar Stanage	300.00	150.00	90.00
162	George Mullin	300.00	150.00	90.00
163	Davy Jones	300.00	150.00	90.00
164	Charley O'Leary	300.00	150.00	90.00
165	Tom Jones	300.00	150.00	90.00
166	Joe Casey	300.00	150.00	90.00
167	Ed Willetts (Willett)	300.00	150.00	90.00
168	Ed Lafeite (Lafitte)	300.00	150.00	90.00
169	Ty Cobb	4500.	2250.	1350.
170	Ty Cobb	4500.	2250.	1350.
201	John Evers	775.00	387.00	232.00
202	Mordecai Brown	775.00	387.00	232.00
203	King Cole	300.00	150.00	90.00
204	Johnny Cane	300.00	150.00	90.00
205	Heinie Zimmerman	300.00	150.00	90.00
206	Wildfire Schulte	300.00	150.00	90.00
207	Frank Chance	775.00	387.00	232.00
208	Joe Tinker	775.00	387.00	232.00
209	Orvall Overall	300.00	150.00	90.00
210	Jimmy Archer	300.00	150.00	90.00
211	Johnny Kling	300.00	150.00	90.00
212	Jimmy Sheckard	300.00	150.00	90.00
213	Harry McIntyre	300.00	150.00	90.00
214	Lew Richie	300.00	150.00	90.00
215	Ed Ruelbach	300.00	150.00	90.00
216	Artie Hoffman (Hofman)	300.00	150.00	90.00
217	Jake Pfeister	300.00	150.00	90.00
218	Harry Steinfeldt	300.00	150.00	90.00
219	Tom Needham	300.00	150.00	90.00
220	Ginger Beaumont	300.00	150.00	90.00
251	Christy Mathewson	2750.	1375.	825.00
252	Fred Merkle	300.00	150.00	90.00
253	Hooks Wiltsie	300.00	150.00	90.00
254	Art Devlin	300.00	150.00	90.00
255	Fred Snodgrass	300.00	150.00	90.00
256	Josh Devore	300.00	150.00	90.00
257	Red Murray	300.00	150.00	90.00
258	Cy Seymour	300.00	150.00	90.00
259	Al Bridwell	300.00	150.00	90.00
260	Larry Doyle	300.00	150.00	90.00
261	Bugs Raymond	300.00	150.00	90.00
262	Doc Crandall	300.00	150.00	90.00
263	Admiral Schlei	300.00	150.00	90.00
264	Chief Myers (Meyers)	300.00	150.00	90.00
265	Bill Dahlen	300.00	150.00	90.00
266	Beals Becker	300.00	150.00	90.00
267	Louis Drucke	300.00	150.00	90.00
301	Fred Luderus	300.00	150.00	90.00
302	John Titus	300.00	150.00	90.00
303	Red Dooin	300.00	150.00	90.00
304	Eddie Stack	300.00	150.00	90.00
305	Kitty Bransfield	300.00	150.00	90.00
306	Sherry Magee	300.00	150.00	90.00
307	Otto Knabe	300.00	150.00	90.00
308	Jimmy "Runt" Walsh	300.00	150.00	90.00
309	Earl Moore	300.00	150.00	90.00
310	Mickey Doolan	300.00	150.00	90.00
311	Ad Brennan	300.00	150.00	90.00
312	Bob Ewing	300.00	150.00	90.00
313	Lou Schettler	300.00	150.00	90.00
351	Joe Willis	300.00	150.00	90.00
352	Rube Ellis	300.00	150.00	90.00
353	Steve Evans	300.00	150.00	90.00
354	Miller Huggins	775.00	387.00	232.00
355	Arnold Hauser	300.00	150.00	90.00
356	Frank Corridon	300.00	150.00	90.00
357	Roger Bresnahan	775.00	387.00	232.00
358	Slim Sallee	300.00	150.00	90.00
359	Mike Mowrey	300.00	150.00	90.00
360	Ed Konetchy	300.00	150.00	90.00
361	Beckman	300.00	150.00	90.00
362	Rebel Oakes	300.00	150.00	90.00
363	Johnny Lush	300.00	150.00	90.00
364	Eddie Phelps	300.00	150.00	90.00
365	Robert Harmon	300.00	150.00	90.00
401	Lew Moren	300.00	150.00	90.00
402	George McQuillian (McQuillan)	300.00	150.00	90.00
403	Johnny Bates	300.00	150.00	90.00
404	Eddie Grant	325.00	162.00	97.00
405	Tommy McMillan	300.00	150.00	90.00
406	Tommy Clark (Clarke)	300.00	150.00	90.00
407	Jack Rowan	300.00	150.00	90.00
408	Bob Bescher	300.00	150.00	90.00
409	Fred Beebe	300.00	150.00	90.00
410	Tom Downey	300.00	150.00	90.00
411	George Suggs	300.00	150.00	90.00
412	Hans Lobert	300.00	150.00	90.00
413	Jimmy Phelan	300.00	150.00	90.00
414	Dode Paskert	300.00	150.00	90.00
415	Ward Miller	300.00	150.00	90.00
416	Dick Egan	300.00	150.00	90.00
417	Art Fromme	300.00	150.00	90.00
418	Bill Burns	300.00	150.00	90.00
419	Clark Griffith	775.00	387.00	232.00
420	Dick Hoblitzell	300.00	150.00	90.00
421	Harry Gasper	300.00	150.00	90.00
422	Dave Altizer	300.00	150.00	90.00
423	Larry McLean	300.00	150.00	90.00
424	Mike Mitchell	300.00	150.00	90.00
451	John Hummel	300.00	150.00	90.00
452	Tony Smith	300.00	150.00	90.00
453	Bill Davidson	300.00	150.00	90.00
454	Ed Lennox	300.00	150.00	90.00
455	Zach Wheat	775.00	387.00	232.00
457	Elmer Knetzer	300.00	150.00	90.00
458	Rube Dessau	300.00	150.00	90.00
459	George Bell	300.00	150.00	90.00
460	Jake Daubert	300.00	150.00	90.00
461	Doc Scanlan	300.00	150.00	90.00
462	Nap Rucker	300.00	150.00	90.00
463	Cy Barger	300.00	150.00	90.00
464	Kaiser Wilhelm	300.00	150.00	90.00
465	Bill Bergen	300.00	150.00	90.00
466	Tex Erwin	300.00	150.00	90.00
501	Chief Bender	775.00	387.00	232.00
502	John Coombs	300.00	150.00	90.00
503	Eddie Plank	775.00	387.00	232.00
504	Amos Strunk	300.00	150.00	90.00
505	Connie Mack	775.00	387.00	232.00
506	Ira Thomas	300.00	150.00	90.00
507	Biscoe Lord (Briscoe)	300.00	150.00	90.00
508	Stuffy McInnis	300.00	150.00	90.00
509	Jimmy Dygert	300.00	150.00	90.00
510	Rube Oldring	300.00	150.00	90.00
511	Eddie Collins	775.00	387.00	232.00
512	Home Run Baker	775.00	387.00	232.00
513	Harry Krause	300.00	150.00	90.00
514	Harry Davis	300.00	150.00	90.00
515	Jack Barry	300.00	150.00	90.00
516	Jack Lapp	300.00	150.00	90.00
517	Cy Morgan	300.00	150.00	90.00
518	Danny Murphy	300.00	150.00	90.00
519	Topsy Hartsell	300.00	150.00	90.00
520	Paddy Livingston	300.00	150.00	90.00
521	P. Adkins	300.00	150.00	90.00
522	Eddie Collins	775.00	387.00	232.00
523	Paddy Livingston	300.00	150.00	90.00
551	Doc Gessler	300.00	150.00	90.00
552	Bill Cunningham	300.00	150.00	90.00
554	John Henry	300.00	150.00	90.00
555	Jack Lelivelt	300.00	150.00	90.00
556	Bobby Groome	300.00	150.00	90.00
557	Doc Ralston	300.00	150.00	90.00
558	Kid Elberfelt (Elberfeld)	300.00	150.00	90.00
559	Doc Reisling	300.00	150.00	90.00
560	Herman Schaefer	300.00	150.00	90.00
561	Walter Johnson	2750.	1375.	825.00
562	Dolly Gray	300.00	150.00	90.00
563	Wid Conroy	300.00	150.00	90.00
564	Charley Street	300.00	150.00	90.00
565	Bob Unglaub	300.00	150.00	90.00
566	Clyde Milan	300.00	150.00	90.00
567	George Browne	300.00	150.00	90.00
568	George McBride	300.00	150.00	90.00
569	Red Killifer (Killefer)	300.00	150.00	90.00
601	Addie Joss	775.00	387.00	232.00
602	Addie Joss	775.00	387.00	232.00
603	Napoleon Lajoie	1000.	500.00	300.00
604	Nig Clark (Clarke)	300.00	150.00	90.00
605	Cy Falkenberg	300.00	150.00	90.00
606	Harry Bemis	300.00	150.00	90.00
607	George Stovall	300.00	150.00	90.00
608	Fred Blanding	300.00	150.00	90.00
609	Elmer Koestner	300.00	150.00	90.00
610	Ted Easterly	300.00	150.00	90.00
611	Willie Mitchell	300.00	150.00	90.00
612	Hornhorst	300.00	150.00	90.00

613	Elmer Flick	775.00	387.00	232.00
614	Speck Harkness	300.00	150.00	90.00
615	Tuck Turner	300.00	150.00	90.00
616	Joe Jackson	6000.	3000.	1800.
617	Grover Land	300.00	150.00	90.00
618	Gladstone Graney	300.00	150.00	90.00
619	Dave Callahan	300.00	150.00	90.00
620	Ben DeMott	300.00	150.00	90.00
621	Neill Ball (Neal)	300.00	150.00	90.00
622	Dode Birmingham	300.00	150.00	90.00
623	George Kaler (Kahler)	300.00	150.00	90.00
624	Sid Smith	300.00	150.00	90.00
625	Bert Adams	300.00	150.00	90.00
626	Bill Bradley	300.00	150.00	90.00
627	Napoleon Lajoie	1000.	500.00	300.00
651	Bill Corrigan (Carrigan)	300.00	150.00	90.00
652	Joe Wood	300.00	150.00	90.00
653	Heinie Wagner	300.00	150.00	90.00
654	Billy Purtell	300.00	150.00	90.00
655	Frank Smith	300.00	150.00	90.00
656	Harry Lord	300.00	150.00	90.00
657	Patsy Donovan	300.00	150.00	90.00
658	Duffy Lewis	300.00	150.00	90.00
659	Jack Kleinow	300.00	150.00	90.00
660	Ed Karger	300.00	150.00	90.00
661	Clyde Engle	300.00	150.00	90.00
662	Ben Hunt	300.00	150.00	90.00
663	Charlie Smith	300.00	150.00	90.00
664	Tris Speaker	1100.	550.00	330.00
665	Tom Madden	300.00	150.00	90.00
666	Larry Gardner	300.00	150.00	90.00
667	Harry Hooper	775.00	387.00	232.00
668	Marty McHale	300.00	150.00	90.00
669	Ray Collins	300.00	150.00	90.00
670	Jake Stahl	300.00	150.00	90.00
701	Dave Shean	300.00	150.00	90.00
702	Roy Miller	300.00	150.00	90.00
703	Fred Beck	300.00	150.00	90.00
704	Bill Collings (Collins)	300.00	150.00	90.00
705	Bill Sweeney	300.00	150.00	90.00
706	Buck Herzog	300.00	150.00	90.00
707	Bud Sharp (Sharpe)	300.00	150.00	90.00
708	Cliff Curtis	300.00	150.00	90.00
709	Al Mattern	300.00	150.00	90.00
710	Buster Brown	300.00	150.00	90.00
711	Bill Rariden	300.00	150.00	90.00
712	Grant	300.00	150.00	90.00
713	Ed Abbaticchio	300.00	150.00	90.00
714	Cecil Ferguson	300.00	150.00	90.00
715	Billy Burke	300.00	150.00	90.00
716	Sam Frock	300.00	150.00	90.00
717	Wilbur Goode (Good)	300.00	150.00	90.00
751	Charlie French	300.00	150.00	90.00
752	Patsy Dougherty	300.00	150.00	90.00
753	Shano Collins	300.00	150.00	90.00
754	Fred Parent	300.00	150.00	90.00
755	Willis Cole	300.00	150.00	90.00
756	Billy Sullivan	300.00	150.00	90.00
757	Rube Sutor (Suter)	300.00	150.00	90.00
758	Chick Gandil	600.00	300.00	180.00
759	Jim Scott	300.00	150.00	90.00
760	Ed Walsh	775.00	387.00	232.00
761	Gavvy Cravath	300.00	150.00	90.00
762	Bobby Messenger	300.00	150.00	90.00
763	Doc White	300.00	150.00	90.00
764	Rollie Zeider	300.00	150.00	90.00
765	Fred Payne	300.00	150.00	90.00
766	Lee Tannehill	300.00	150.00	90.00
767	Eddie Hahn	300.00	150.00	90.00
768	Hugh Duffy	775.00	387.00	232.00
769	Fred Olmstead	300.00	150.00	90.00
770	Lena Blackbourne (Blackburne)	300.00	150.00	90.00
771	Young "Cy" Young	300.00	150.00	90.00
801	Lew Brockett	300.00	150.00	90.00
802	Frank Laporte (LaPorte)	300.00	150.00	90.00
803	Bert Daniels	300.00	150.00	90.00
804	Walter Blair	300.00	150.00	90.00
805	Jack Knight	300.00	150.00	90.00
806	Jimmy Austin	300.00	150.00	90.00
807	Hal Chase	350.00	175.00	105.00
808	Birdie Cree	300.00	150.00	90.00
809	Jack Quinn	300.00	150.00	90.00
810	Walter Manning	300.00	150.00	90.00
811	Jack Warhop	300.00	150.00	90.00
812	Jeff Sweeney	300.00	150.00	90.00
813	Charley Hemphill	300.00	150.00	90.00
814	Harry Wolters	300.00	150.00	90.00
815	Tom Hughes	300.00	150.00	90.00
816	Earl Gardiner (Gardner)	300.00	150.00	90.00
851	John Flynn	300.00	150.00	90.00
852	Bill Powell	300.00	150.00	90.00
853	Honus Wagner	2000.	1000.	600.00
854	Bill Powell	300.00	150.00	90.00
855	Fred Clarke	775.00	387.00	232.00
856	Owen Wilson	300.00	150.00	90.00
857	George Gibson	300.00	150.00	90.00
858	Mike Simon	300.00	150.00	90.00
859	Tommy Leach	300.00	150.00	90.00
860	Lefty Leifield ([illegible])	300.00	150.00	90.00
861	Nick Maddox	300.00	150.00	90.00
862	Dots Miller	300.00	150.00	90.00
863	Howard Camnitz	300.00	150.00	90.00
864	Deacon Phillippi (Phillippe)	300.00	150.00	90.00
865	Babe Adams	300.00	150.00	90.00
866	Ed Abbaticchio	300.00	150.00	90.00
867	Paddy O'Connor	300.00	150.00	90.00
868	Bobby Byrne	300.00	150.00	90.00
869	Vin Campbell	300.00	150.00	90.00
870	Ham Hyatt	300.00	150.00	90.00
871	Sam Leever	300.00	150.00	90.00
872	Hans Wagner	2000.	1000.	600.00
873	Hans Wagner	2000.	1000.	600.00
874	Bill McKecknie (McKechnie)	775.00	387.00	232.00
875	Kirby White	300.00	150.00	90.00
901	Jimmie Burke	300.00	150.00	90.00
902	Charlie Carr	300.00	150.00	90.00
903	Larry Cheney	300.00	150.00	90.00
904	Chet Chadbourne	300.00	150.00	90.00
905	Dan Howley	300.00	150.00	90.00
906	Jimmie Burke	300.00	150.00	90.00
907	Ray Mowe	300.00	150.00	90.00
908	Billy Milligan	300.00	150.00	90.00
909	Frank Oberlin	300.00	150.00	90.00
910	Ralph Glaze	300.00	150.00	90.00
911	O'Day	300.00	150.00	90.00
912	Kerns	300.00	150.00	90.00
913	Jim Duggan	300.00	150.00	90.00
914	Simmy Murch	300.00	150.00	90.00
915	Frank Delehanty	300.00	150.00	90.00
916	Craig	300.00	150.00	90.00
917	Jack Coffee (Coffey)	300.00	150.00	90.00
918	Lefty George	300.00	150.00	90.00
919	Otto Williams	300.00	150.00	90.00
920	M. Hayden	300.00	150.00	90.00
951	Joe Cantillion	300.00	150.00	90.00
952	Smith	300.00	150.00	90.00
953	Claud Rossman (Claude)	300.00	150.00	90.00
1001	Tony James	300.00	150.00	90.00
1002	Jack Powell	300.00	150.00	90.00
1003	Wm. J. Harbeau	300.00	150.00	90.00
1004	Homer Smoot	300.00	150.00	90.00
1051	Bill Friel	300.00	150.00	90.00
1052	Bill Friel	300.00	150.00	90.00
1053	Fred Odwell	300.00	150.00	90.00
1054	Alex Reilley	300.00	150.00	90.00
1055	Eugene Packard	300.00	150.00	90.00
1056	Irve Wrattan	300.00	150.00	90.00
1057	"Red" Nelson	300.00	150.00	90.00
1058	George Perring	300.00	150.00	90.00
1059	Glen Liebhardt	300.00	150.00	90.00
1060	Jimmie O'Rourke	300.00	150.00	90.00
1061	Fred Cook	300.00	150.00	90.00
1062	Charles Arbogast	300.00	150.00	90.00
1063	Jerry Downs	300.00	150.00	90.00
1064	"Bunk" Congalton	300.00	150.00	90.00
1065	Fred Carisch	300.00	150.00	90.00
1066	"Red" Sitton	300.00	150.00	90.00
1067	George Kaler (Kahler)	300.00	150.00	90.00
1068	Arthur Kruger	300.00	150.00	90.00
1102	Earl Yingling	300.00	150.00	90.00
1103	Jerry Freeman	300.00	150.00	90.00
1104	Harry Hinchman	300.00	150.00	90.00
1105	Jim Baskette	300.00	150.00	90.00
1106	Denny Sullivan	300.00	150.00	90.00
1107	Carl Robinson	300.00	150.00	90.00
1108	Bill Rodgers	300.00	150.00	90.00
1109	Hi West	300.00	150.00	90.00
1110	Billy Hallman	300.00	150.00	90.00
1111	Wm. Elwert	300.00	150.00	90.00
1112	Piano Legs Hickman	300.00	150.00	90.00
1113	Joe McCarthy	775.00	387.00	232.00
1114	Fred Abbott	300.00	150.00	90.00
1115	Jack Gilligan	300.00	150.00	90.00

1913 T200 Fatima Team Cards

(See 1913 Fatima Team Cards)

1911 T201 Mecca Double Folders

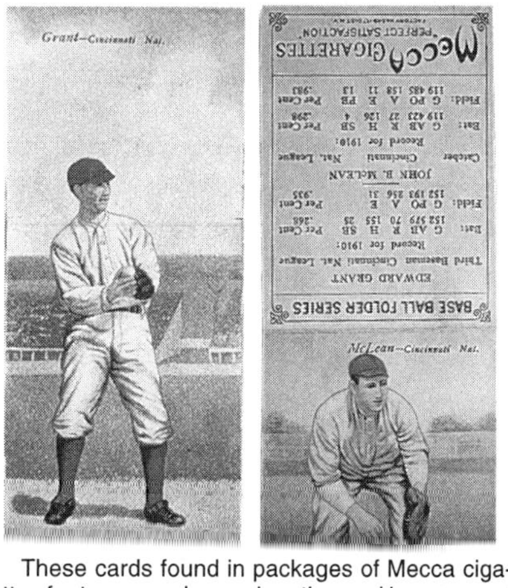

These cards found in packages of Mecca cigarettes feature one player when the card is open, and another when the card is folded; two players sharing the same pair of legs. Mecca Double Folders measure 2-1/4" x 4-11/16." The fronts are color lithographs with the player's name appearing in black script in the upper left. The backs are printed in red and contain an innovation in the form of player statistics. The 50-card set contains 100 different players including a number of Hall of Famers. The Mecca Double Folders, with two players (Topps "borrowed" the idea in 1955) and statistics, were one of the most innovative of the tobacco card era.

		NM	EX	VG
	Complete Set (50):	5650.	2750.	1500.
	Common Player:	80.00	35.00	22.00
(1)	William Abstein, John Butler	80.00	35.00	22.00
(2)	Frank Baker, Edward Collins	260.00	145.00	90.00
(3)	Harry Baker, Thomas Downie (Downey)	80.00	35.00	22.00
(4)	James Barrett, Grant McGlynn	80.00	35.00	22.00
(5)	John Barry, John Lapp	80.00	35.00	22.00
(6)	Charles Bender, Reuben Oldring	170.00	95.00	60.00
(7)	William Bergen, Zack Wheat	170.00	95.00	60.00
(8)	Walter Blair, Roy Hartzell	80.00	35.00	22.00
(9)	Roger Bresnahan, Miller Huggins	260.00	145.00	90.00
(10)	Albert Bridwell, Christy Matthewson (Mathewson)	475.00	260.00	165.00
(11)	Mordecai Brown, Arthur Hofman	170.00	95.00	60.00
(12)	Robert Byrne, Fred Clarke	180.00	95.00	60.00
(13)	Frank Chance, John Evers	260.00	145.00	90.00
(14)	Harold Chase, Edward Sweeney	90.00	50.00	30.00
(15)	Edward Cicotte, John Thoney	150.00	80.00	50.00
(16)	Thomas Clarke, Harry Gaspar	80.00	35.00	22.00
(17)	Ty Cobb, Sam Crawford	1100.	600.00	385.00
(18)	Leonard Cole, John Kling	80.00	35.00	22.00
(19)	John Coombs, Ira Thomas	80.00	35.00	22.00
(20)	Jake Daubert, Nap Rucker	80.00	35.00	22.00
(21)	Bill Donovan, Ralph Stroud	80.00	35.00	22.00
(22)	Charles Dooin, John Titus	80.00	35.00	22.00
(23)	Patsy Dougherty, Harry Lord	275.00	150.00	95.00
(24)	Jerry Downs, Fred Odwell	80.00	35.00	22.00
(25)	Larry Doyle, Chief Meyers	80.00	35.00	22.00
(26)	James Dygert, Cy Seymour	80.00	35.00	22.00
(27)	Norman Elberfeld, George McBride	80.00	35.00	22.00
(28)	Fred Falkenberg, Napoleon Lajoie	325.00	180.00	115.00
(29)	Edward Fitzpatrick, Ed Killian	80.00	35.00	22.00
(30)	Russell Ford, Otis Johnson	80.00	35.00	22.00
(31)	Edward Foster, Joseph Ward	80.00	35.00	22.00
(32)	Earl Gardner, Tris Speaker	225.00	125.00	70.00
(33)	George Gibson, Thomas Leach	80.00	35.00	22.00
(34)	George Graham, Al Mattern	80.00	35.00	22.00
(35)	Edward Grant, John McLean	80.00	35.00	22.00
(36)	Arnold Hauser, Ernest Lush	80.00	35.00	22.00
(37)	Charles Herzog, Roy Miller	80.00	35.00	22.00
(38)	Charles Hickman, Harry Hinchman	80.00	35.00	22.00
(39)	Hugh Jennings, Edgar Summers	185.00	100.00	65.00
(40)	Walter Johnson, Charles Street	450.00	245.00	145.00
(41)	Frank LaPorte, James Stephens	80.00	35.00	22.00
(42)	Joseph Lake, Robert Wallace	170.00	95.00	60.00
(43)	Albert Leifield, Mike Simon	80.00	35.00	22.00
(44)	John Lobert, Earl Moore	80.00	35.00	22.00
(45)	Arthur McCabe, Charles Starr	80.00	35.00	22.00
(46)	Lewis McCarty, Joseph McGinnity	170.00	95.00	60.00
(47)	Fred Merkle, George Wiltse	80.00	35.00	22.00
(48)	Frederick Payne, Edward Walsh	170.00	95.00	60.00
(49)	George Stovall, Terrence Turner	80.00	35.00	22.00
(50)	Otto Williams, Orville Woodruff	80.00	35.00	22.00

1912 T202 Hassan Triple Folders

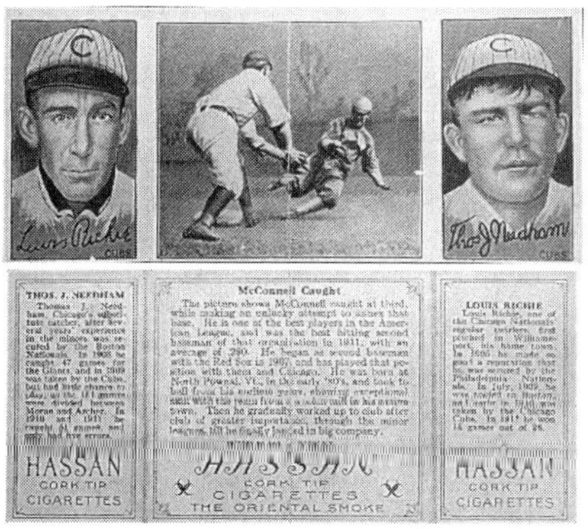

Measuring 5-1/2" x 2-1/4", Hassan cigarette cards carried the concept of multiple-player cards even further than the innovative Mecca set of the previous year. Scored so that the two end cards - which are full-color and very close to exact duplicates of T205 "Gold Borders" - can fold over the black and white center panel, the Hassan Triple Folder appears like a booklet when closed. The two end cards are individual player cards, while the larger center panel contains an action scene. Usually the two player cards are not related to the action scene. The unique Hassan Triple Folders feature player biographies on the back of the two individual cards with a description of the action on the back of the center panel. Values depend on the player featured in the center panel, as well as the players featured on the end cards.

		NM	EX	VG
	Complete Set (132):	40000.	20000.	11000.
	Common Player:	225.00	95.00	55.00
(1)	A Close Play At The Home Plate (LaPorte, Wallace)	275.00	110.00	70.00
(2)	A Close Play At The Home Plate (Pelty, Wallace)	275.00	110.00	70.00
(3)	A Desperate Slide For Third (Ty Cobb, O'Leary)	2100.	900.00	550.00
(4)	A Great Batsman (Barger, Bergen)	225.00	95.00	55.00
(5)	A Great Batsman (Bergen, Rucker)	225.00	95.00	55.00
(6)	Ambrose McConnell At Bat (Blair, Quinn)	225.00	95.00	55.00
(7)	A Wide Throw Saves Crawford (George Mullin, Stanage)	225.00	95.00	55.00
(8)	Baker Gets His Man (Frank Baker, Eddie Collins)	350.00	140.00	85.00
(9)	Birmingham Gets To Third (Johnson, Street)	595.00	240.00	150.00
(10)	Birmingham's Home Run (Birmingham, Turner)	500.00	200.00	125.00
(11)	Bush Just Misses Austin (Magee, Moran)	225.00	95.00	55.00
(12)	Carrigan Blocks His Man (Gaspar, McLean)	225.00	95.00	55.00
(13)	Carrigan Blocks His Man (Carrigan, Wagner)	225.00	95.00	55.00
(14)	Catching Him Napping (Bresnahan, Oakes)	350.00	145.00	85.00
(15)	Caught Asleep Off First (Bresnahan, Harmon)	350.00	150.00	90.00
(16)	Chance Beats Out A Hit (Chance, Foxen)	350.00	140.00	85.00
(17)	Chance Beats Out A Hit (Archer, McIntyre)	225.00	95.00	55.00
(18)	Chance Beats Out A Hit (Archer, Overall)	225.00	95.00	55.00
(19)	Chance Beats Out A Hit (Archer, Rowan)	225.00	95.00	55.00
(20)	Chance Beats Out A Hit (Chance, Shean)	350.00	140.00	85.00
(21)	Chase Dives Into Third (Chase, Wolter)	250.00	100.00	60.00
(22)	Chase Dives Into Third (Clarke, Gibson)	250.00	100.00	60.00
(23)	Chase Dives Into Third (Gibson, Deacon Phillippe)	250.00	100.00	60.00
(24)	Chase Gets Ball Too Late (Egan, Mitchell)	250.00	100.00	60.00
(25)	Chase Gets Ball Too Late (Chase, Wolter)	250.00	100.00	60.00
(26)	Chase Guarding First (Chase, Wolter)	250.00	100.00	60.00
(27)	Chase Guarding First (Clarke, Gibson)	250.00	100.00	60.00
(28)	Chase Guarding First (Gibson, Leifield)	250.00	100.00	60.00
(29)	Chase Ready For The Squeeze Play (Magee, Paskert)	250.00	100.00	60.00
(30)	Chase Safe At Third (Baker, Barry)	300.00	120.00	75.00
(31)	Chief Bender Waiting For A Good One (Bender, Thomas)	350.00	140.00	85.00
(32)	Clarke Hikes For Home (Bridwell, Kling)	225.00	95.00	55.00
(33)	Close At First (Neal Ball, George Stovall)	225.00	120.00	75.00
(34)	Close At The Plate (Payne, Walsh)	300.00	120.00	75.00
(35)	Close At The Plate (Payne, White)	225.00	95.00	55.00
(36)	Close At Third - Speaker (Speaker, Wood)	500.00	200.00	125.00
(37)	Close At Third - Wagner (Carrigan, Wagner)	250.00	100.00	60.00
(38)	Collins Easily Safe (Byrne, Clarke)	275.00	110.00	70.00
(39)	Collins Easily Safe (Frank Baker, Eddie Collins)	350.00	140.00	85.00
(40)	Collins Easily Safe (Eddie Collins, Danny Murphy)	300.00	120.00	75.00
(41)	Crawford About To Smash One (Stanage, Summers)	225.00	95.00	55.00
(42)	Cree Rolls Home (Jake Daubert, Hummel)	225.00	95.00	55.00
(43)	Davy Jones' Great Slide (Delahanty, Jones)	225.00	95.00	55.00
(44)	Devlin Gets His Man (Devlin (Giants), Mathewson)	800.00	320.00	200.00
(45)	Devlin Gets His Man (Devlin (Rustlers), Mathewson)	575.00	230.00	145.00
(46)	Devlin Gets His Man (Fletcher, Mathewson)	595.00	240.00	150.00
(47)	Devlin Gets His Man (Mathewson, Meyers)	595.00	240.00	150.00
(48)	Donlin Out At First (Camnitz, Gibson)	225.00	95.00	55.00
(49)	Donlin Out At First (Doyle, Merkle)	225.00	95.00	55.00
(50)	Donlin Out At First (Leach, Wilson)	225.00	95.00	55.00
(51)	Donlin Out At First (Dooin, Magee)	225.00	95.00	55.00
(52)	Donlin Out At First (Gibson, Deacon Phillippe)	225.00	95.00	55.00
(53)	Dooin Gets His Man (Red Dooin, Mickey Doolan)	225.00	95.00	55.00
(54)	Dooin Gets His Man (Dooin, Lobert)	225.00	95.00	55.00
(55)	Dooin Gets His Man (Dooin, Titus)	225.00	95.00	55.00
(56)	Easy For Larry (Doyle, Merkle)	225.00	95.00	55.00
(57)	Elberfeld Beats The Throw (Elberfeld, Milan)	225.00	95.00	55.00
(58)	Elberfeld Gets His Man (Elberfeld, Milan)	225.00	95.00	55.00
(59)	Engle In A Close Play (Engle, Speaker)	375.00	150.00	95.00
(60)	Evers Makes A Safe Slide (Archer, Evers)	350.00	140.00	85.00
(61)	Evers Makes A Safe Slide (Chance, Evers)	400.00	160.00	100.00
(62)	Evers Makes A Safe Slide (Archer, Overall)	225.00	95.00	55.00
(63)	Evers Makes A Safe Slide (Archer, Reulbach)	225.00	95.00	55.00
(64)	Evers Makes A Safe Slide (Chance, Tinker)	550.00	220.00	175.00
(65)	Fast Work At Third (Cobb, O'Leary)	2000.	800.00	500.00
(66)	Ford Putting Over A Spitter (Ford, Vaughn)	225.00	95.00	55.00
(67)	Ford Putting Over A Spitter (Jeff Sweeney, Russ Ford)	225.00	95.00	55.00
(68)	Good Play At Third (Cobb, Moriarity) (Moriarty)	2100.	840.00	525.00
(69)	Grant Gets His Man (Grant, Hoblitzell)	225.00	95.00	55.00
(70)	Hal Chase Too Late (McConnell, McIntyre)	225.00	95.00	55.00
(71)	Hal Chase Too Late (McLean, Suggs)	225.00	95.00	55.00
(72)	Harry Lord At Third (Lennox, Tinker)	250.00	100.00	60.00
(73)	Hartzell Covering Third (Dahlen, Scanlan)	225.00	95.00	55.00
(74)	Hartsel Strikes Out (Gray, Groom)	225.00	95.00	55.00
(75)	Held At Third (Lord, Tannehill)	225.00	95.00	55.00
(76)	Jake Stahl Guarding First (Cicotte, Stahl)	225.00	95.00	55.00
(77)	Jim Delahanty At Bat (Delahanty, Jones)	225.00	95.00	55.00
(78)	Just Before The Battle (Ames, Meyers)	225.00	95.00	55.00
(79)	Just Before The Battle (Bresnahan, McGraw)	300.00	120.00	75.00
(80)	Just Before The Battle (Crandall, Meyers)	225.00	95.00	55.00
(81)	Just Before The Battle (Becker, Devore)	225.00	95.00	55.00
(82)	Just Before The Battle (Fletcher, Mathewson)	595.00	240.00	150.00
(83)	Just Before The Battle (Marquard, Meyers)	300.00	120.00	75.00
(84)	Just Before The Battle (Jennings, McGraw)	350.00	140.00	85.00
(85)	Just Before The Battle (Mathewson, Meyers)	575.00	230.00	145.00
(86)	Just Before The Battle (Murray, Snodgrass)	225.00	95.00	55.00
(87)	Just Before The Battle (Meyers, Wiltse)	225.00	95.00	55.00
(88)	Knight Catches A Runner (Johnson, Knight)	750.00	300.00	185.00
(89)	Lobert Almost Caught (Bridwell, Kling)	225.00	95.00	55.00
(90)	Lobert Almost Caught (Kling, Young)	550.00	220.00	135.00
(91)	Lobert Almost Caught (Kling, Mattern)	250.00	100.00	60.00
(92)	Lobert Almost Caught (Kling, Steinfeldt)	225.00	95.00	55.00
(93)	Lobert Gets Tenney (Dooin, Lobert)	225.00	95.00	55.00
(94)	Lord Catches His Man (Lord, Tannehil)	225.00	95.00	55.00
(95)	McConnell Caught (Needham, Richie)	225.00	95.00	55.00
(96)	McIntyre At Bat (McConnell, McIntyre)	225.00	95.00	55.00
(97)	Moriarty Spiked (Stanage, Willett)	225.00	95.00	55.00
(98)	Nearly Caught (Bates, Bescher)	225.00	95.00	55.00
(99)	Oldring Almost Home (Lord, Oldring)	225.00	95.00	55.00
(100)	Schaefer On First (McBride, Milan)	225.00	95.00	55.00
(101)	Schaefer Steals Second (Clark Griffith, McBride)	300.00	120.00	80.00
(102)	Scoring From Second (Lord, Oldring)	225.00	95.00	55.00
(103)	Scrambling Back To First (Barger, Bergen)	225.00	95.00	55.00
(104)	Scrambling Back To First (Chase, Wolter)	225.00	95.00	55.00
(105)	Speaker Almost Caught (Clarke, Miller)	350.00	145.00	90.00
(106)	Speaker Rounding Third (Speaker, Wood)	425.00	170.00	105.00
(107)	Speaker Scores (Engle, Speaker)	425.00	170.00	105.00
(108)	Stahl Safe (Austin, Stovall)	225.00	95.00	55.00
(109)	Stone About To Swing (Schulte, Sheckard)	225.00	95.00	55.00
(110)	Sullivan Puts Up A High One (Evans, Huggins)	300.00	120.00	75.00
(111)	Sullivan Puts Up A High One (Gray, Groom)	225.00	95.00	55.00
(112)	Sweeney Gets Stahl (Ford, Vaughn)	225.00	95.00	55.00
(113)	Sweeney Gets Stahl (Ford, Sweeney)	225.00	95.00	55.00
(114)	Tenney Lands Safely (Latham, Raymond)	225.00	95.00	55.00
(115)	The Athletic Infield (Baker, Barry)	300.00	120.00	75.00
(116)	The Athletic Infield (Brown, Graham)	300.00	120.00	75.00
(117)	The Athletic Infield (Hauser, Konetchy)	225.00	95.00	55.00
(118)	The Athletic Infield (Krause, Thomas)	225.00	95.00	55.00
(119)	The Pinch Hitter (Egan, Hoblitzell)	225.00	95.00	55.00
(120)	The Scissors Slide (Birmingham, Turner)	225.00	95.00	55.00
(121)	Tom Jones At Bat (Fromme, McLean)	225.00	95.00	55.00
(122)	Tom Jones At Bat (Gaspar, McLean)	225.00	95.00	55.00
(123)	Too Late For Devlin (Ames, Meyers)	225.00	95.00	55.00
(124)	Too Late For Devlin (Crandall, Meyers)	225.00	95.00	55.00
(125)	Too Late For Devlin (Devlin (Giants), Mathewson)	800.00	320.00	200.00
(126)	Too Late For Devlin (Devlin (Rustlers), Mathewson)	575.00	230.00	145.00
(127)	Too Late For Devlin (Marquard, Meyers)	300.00	120.00	75.00
(128)	Too Late For Devlin (Meyers, Wiltse)	225.00	95.00	55.00
(129)	Ty Cobb Steals Third (Cobb, Jennings)	2100.	840.00	525.00
(130)	Ty Cobb Steals Third (Cobb, Moriarty)	2250.	900.00	600.00
(131)	Ty Cobb Steals Third (Austin, Stovall)	1075.	430.00	270.00
(132)	Wheat Strikes Out (Dahlen, Wheat)	350.00	140.00	85.00

1900 T203

(See 1900 Mayo's Baseball Comics.)

1909 T204

(See 1909 Ramly Cigarettes, 1909 T.T.T. Cigarettes.)

1911 T205 Gold Border

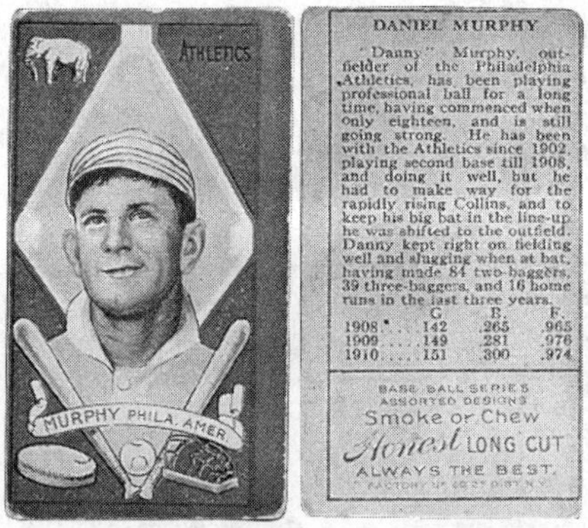

Taking their hobby nickname from their gold-leaf borders, these cards were issued in a number of different cigarette brands. The cards measure 1-7/16" x 2-5/8". American League cards feature a color lithograph of the player inside a stylized baseball diamond. National League cards have head and shoulders portraits and a plain background, plus the first-ever use of a facsimile autograph in a major card set. The 12 minor league players in the set feature three-quarter length portraits or action pictures in an elaborate frame of columns and other devices. Card backs of the major leaguers carry the player's full name (another first) and statistics. Card backs of the minor leaguers lack the statistics. The complete set price does not include the scarcer variations. Values shown are for cards with the most common cigarette advertising on back: Piedmont and Sweet Caporal; cards of other brands may carry a premium (see listings under brand name). The condition of the fragile gold leaf on the borders is an important grading consideration.

		NM	EX	VG
	Complete Set (208):	32000.	16000.	8000.
	Common Player:	80.00	35.00	18.00
(1)	Edward J. Abbaticchio	80.00	35.00	18.00
(2)	Doc Adkins	275.00	140.00	70.00
(3)	Leon K. Ames	80.00	35.00	18.00
(4)	Jas. P. Archer	80.00	35.00	18.00
(5)	Jimmy Austin	80.00	35.00	18.00
(6)	Bill Bailey	80.00	35.00	18.00
(7)	Home Run Baker	290.00	140.00	70.00
(8)	Neal Ball	80.00	35.00	18.00
(9)	E.B. Barger (full "B" on cap)	80.00	45.00	25.00
(10)	E.B. Barger (partial "B" on cap)	400.00	200.00	100.00
(11)	Jack Barry	80.00	35.00	18.00
(12)	Emil Batch	265.00	130.00	65.00
(13)	John W. Bates	80.00	35.00	18.00
(14)	Fred Beck	80.00	35.00	18.00
(15)	B. Becker	80.00	35.00	18.00
(16)	George G. Bell	80.00	35.00	18.00
(17)	Chas. Bender	395.00	190.00	105.00
(18)	William Bergen	80.00	45.00	22.00
(19)	Bob Bescher	80.00	35.00	18.00
(20)	Joe Birmingham	80.00	35.00	18.00
(21)	Lena Blackburne	80.00	35.00	18.00
(22)	William E. Bransfield	80.00	35.00	18.00
(23)	Roger P. Bresnahan (mouth closed)	350.00	175.00	90.00
(24)	Roger P. Bresnahan (mouth open)	525.00	260.00	125.00
(25)	A.H. Bridwell	80.00	35.00	18.00
(26)	Mordecai Brown	275.00	120.00	60.00
(27)	Robert Byrne	80.00	35.00	18.00
(28)	Hick Cady	230.00	115.00	60.00
(29)	H. Camnitz	80.00	35.00	18.00
(30)	Bill Carrigan	80.00	35.00	18.00
(31)	Frank J. Chance	300.00	150.00	75.00
(32a)	Hal Chase (both ears show, gold diamond frame extends below shoulders)	115.00	60.00	30.00
(32b)	Hal Chase (both ears show, gold diamond frame ends at shoulders)	115.00	60.00	30.00
(33)	Hal Chase (only left ear shows)	375.00	190.00	95.00
(34)	Ed Cicotte	190.00	95.00	50.00
(35)	Fred C. Clarke	200.00	100.00	50.00
(36)	Ty Cobb	4250.	1800.	800.00
(37)	Eddie Collins (mouth closed)	350.00	150.00	75.00
(38)	Eddie Collins (mouth open)	450.00	230.00	115.00
(39)	Jimmy Collins	500.00	260.00	130.00
(40)	Frank J. Corridon	80.00	35.00	18.00
(41a)	Otis Crandall ("t" not crossed in name)	80.00	35.00	18.00
(41b)	Otis Crandall ("t" crossed in name)	80.00	35.00	18.00
(42)	Lou Criger	80.00	35.00	18.00
(43)	W.F. Dahlen	185.00	95.00	45.00
(44)	Jake Daubert	80.00	35.00	18.00
(45)	Jim Delahanty	80.00	35.00	18.00
(46)	Arthur Devlin	80.00	35.00	18.00
(47)	Josh Devore	80.00	35.00	18.00
(48)	W.R. Dickson	80.00	35.00	18.00
(49)	Jiggs Donohue (Donahue)	350.00	180.00	90.00
(50)	Chas. S. Dooin	80.00	35.00	18.00
(51)	Michael J. Doolan	80.00	35.00	18.00
(52a)	Patsy Dougherty (red sock for team emblem)	80.00	35.00	18.00
(52b)	Patsy Dougherty (white sock for team emblem)	250.00	125.00	65.00
(53)	Thomas Downey	80.00	35.00	18.00
(54)	Larry Doyle	80.00	35.00	18.00
(55)	Hugh Duffy	400.00	200.00	100.00
(56)	Jack Dunn	300.00	150.00	75.00
(57)	Jimmy Dygert	80.00	35.00	18.00
(58)	R. Egan	80.00	35.00	18.00
(59)	Kid Elberfeld	80.00	35.00	18.00
(60)	Clyde Engle	80.00	35.00	18.00
(61)	Louis Evans	80.00	35.00	18.00
(62)	John J. Evers	300.00	175.00	85.00
(63)	Robert Ewing	80.00	35.00	18.00
(64)	G.C. Ferguson	80.00	35.00	18.00
(65)	Ray Fisher	300.00	150.00	75.00
(66)	Arthur Fletcher	80.00	35.00	18.00
(67)	John A. Flynn	80.00	35.00	18.00
(68)	Russ Ford (black cap)	80.00	35.00	18.00
(69)	Russ Ford (white cap)	300.00	150.00	75.00
(70)	Wm. A. Foxen	80.00	35.00	18.00
(71)	Jimmy Frick	230.00	150.00	75.00
(72)	Arthur Fromme	80.00	35.00	18.00
(73)	Earl Gardner	80.00	35.00	18.00
(74)	H.L. Gaspar	80.00	35.00	18.00
(75)	George Gibson	80.00	35.00	18.00
(76)	Wilbur Goode	80.00	35.00	18.00
(77)	George F. Graham (Rustlers)	80.00	35.00	18.00
(78)	George F. Graham (Cubs)	440.00	225.00	115.00
(79)	Edward L. Grant	225.00	120.00	55.00
(80a)	Dolly Gray (no stats on back)	80.00	35.00	18.00
(80b)	Dolly Gray (stats on back)	150.00	75.00	40.00
(81)	Clark Griffith	[illegible]	[illegible]	70.00
(82)	Bob Groom	80.00	35.00	18.00
(83)	Charlie Hanford	275.00	140.00	70.00
(84)	Bob Harmon (both ears show)	80.00	35.00	18.00
(85)	Bob Harmon (only left ear shows)	375.00	190.00	95.00
(86)	Topsy Hartsel	80.00	35.00	18.00
(87)	Arnold J. Hauser	80.00	35.00	18.00
(88)	Charlie Hemphill	80.00	35.00	18.00
(89)	C.L. Herzog	80.00	35.00	18.00
(90a)	R. Hoblitzell (no stats on back)	465.00	235.00	120.00
(90b)	R. Hoblitzell ("Cin." after 2nd 1908 in stats)	200.00	100.00	50.00
(90c)	R. Hoblitzel (name incorrect, no "Cin." after 1908 in stats)	80.00	35.00	18.00
(90d)	R. Hoblitzell (name correct, no "Cin." after 1908 in stats)	175.00	90.00	45.00
(91)	Danny Hoffman	80.00	35.00	18.00
(92)	Miller J. Huggins	235.00	120.00	60.00
(93)	John E. Hummel	80.00	35.00	18.00
(94)	Fred Jacklitsch	80.00	35.00	18.00
(95)	Hughie Jennings	475.00	240.00	120.00
(96)	Walter Johnson	1250.	700.00	345.00
(97)	D. Jones	80.00	35.00	18.00
(98)	Tom Jones	80.00	35.00	18.00
(99)	Addie Joss	600.00	300.00	150.00
(100)	Ed Karger	275.00	140.00	70.00
(101)	Ed Killian	80.00	35.00	18.00
(102)	Red Kleinow	275.00	140.00	70.00
(103)	John G. Kling	80.00	35.00	18.00
(104)	Jack Knight	80.00	35.00	18.00
(105)	Ed Konetchy	80.00	35.00	18.00
(106)	Harry Krause	80.00	35.00	18.00
(107)	Floyd M. Kroh	80.00	35.00	18.00
(108)	Frank LaPorte	80.00	35.00	18.00
(109)	Frank Lang (Lange)	80.00	35.00	18.00
(110a)	A. Latham (A. Latham on back)	80.00	35.00	18.00
(110b)	A. Latham (W.A. Latham on back)	80.00	35.00	18.00
(111)	Thomas W. Leach	80.00	35.00	18.00
(112)	Watty Lee	225.00	105.00	55.00
(113)	Sam Leever	80.00	35.00	18.00
(114a)	A. Leifield (initial "A." on front)	80.00	35.00	18.00
(114b)	A.P. Leifield (initials "A.P." on front)	80.00	35.00	18.00
(115)	Edgar Lennox	80.00	35.00	18.00
(116)	Paddy Livingston	80.00	35.00	18.00
(117)	John B. Lobert	80.00	35.00	18.00
(118)	Bris Lord (Athletics)	80.00	35.00	18.00
(119)	Harry Lord (White Sox)	80.00	35.00	18.00
(120)	Jno. C. Lush	80.00	35.00	18.00
(121)	Nick Maddox	80.00	35.00	18.00
(122)	Sherwood R. Magee	80.00	35.00	18.00
(123)	R.W. Marquard	325.00	160.00	80.00
(124)	C. Mathewson	1250.	600.00	325.00
(125)	A.A. Mattern	80.00	35.00	18.00
(126)	Sport McAllister	230.00	110.00	55.00
(127)	George McBride	80.00	35.00	18.00
(128)	Amby McConnell	80.00	35.00	18.00
(129)	P.M. McElveen	80.00	35.00	18.00
(130)	J.J. McGraw	400.00	180.00	90.00
(131)	Harry McIntire (Cubs)	80.00	35.00	18.00
(132)	Matty McIntyre (White Sox)	80.00	35.00	18.00
(133)	M.A. McLean (initials actually J.B.)	80.00	35.00	18.00
(134)	Fred Merkle	80.00	35.00	18.00
(135)	George Merritt	260.00	140.00	60.00
(136)	J.T. Meyers	80.00	35.00	18.00
(137)	Clyde Milan	80.00	35.00	18.00
(138)	J.D. Miller	80.00	35.00	18.00
(139)	M.F. Mitchell	80.00	35.00	18.00
(140a)	P.J. Moran (stray line of type below stats)	80.00	35.00	18.00
(140b)	P.J. Moran (no stray line)	80.00	35.00	18.00
(141)	George Moriarty	80.00	35.00	18.00
(142)	George Mullin	80.00	35.00	18.00
(143)	Danny Murphy	80.00	35.00	18.00
(144)	Jack Murray	80.00	35.00	18.00
(145)	John Nee	260.00	140.00	60.00
(146)	Thomas J. Needham	80.00	35.00	18.00
(147)	Rebel Oakes	80.00	35.00	18.00
(148)	Rube Oldring	80.00	35.00	18.00
(149)	Charley O'Leary	80.00	35.00	18.00
(150)	Fred Olmstead	80.00	35.00	18.00
(151)	Orval Overall	80.00	35.00	18.00
(152)	Freddy Parent	80.00	35.00	18.00
(153)	George Paskert	80.00	35.00	18.00
(154)	Billy Payne	80.00	35.00	18.00
(155)	Barney Pelty	80.00	35.00	18.00
(156)	John Pfeister	80.00	35.00	18.00
(157)	Jimmy Phelan	245.00	125.00	60.00
(158)	E.J. Phelps	80.00	35.00	18.00
(159)	C. Phillippe	80.00	35.00	18.00
(160)	Jack Quinn	80.00	35.00	18.00
(161)	A.L. Raymond	300.00	150.00	75.00
(162)	E.M. Reulbach	80.00	35.00	18.00
(163)	Lewis Richie	80.00	35.00	18.00
(164)	John A. Rowan	275.00	140.00	70.00
(165)	George N. Rucker	80.00	35.00	18.00
(166)	W.D. Scanlan	230.00	115.00	60.00
(167)	Germany Schaefer	80.00	35.00	18.00
(168)	George Schlei	80.00	35.00	18.00
(169)	Boss Schmidt	80.00	35.00	18.00
(170)	F.M. Schulte	80.00	35.00	18.00
(171)	Jim Scott	80.00	35.00	18.00
(172)	B.H. Sharpe	80.00	35.00	18.00
(173)	David Shean (Rustlers)	80.00	35.00	18.00
(174)	David Shean (Cubs)	375.00	190.00	95.00
(175)	Jas. T. Sheckard	80.00	35.00	18.00
(176)	Hack Simmons	80.00	35.00	18.00
(177)	Tony Smith	80.00	35.00	18.00
(178)	Fred C. Snodgrass	80.00	35.00	18.00
(179)	Tris Speaker	550.00	300.00	165.00
(180)	Jake Stahl	80.00	35.00	18.00
(181)	Oscar Stanage	80.00	35.00	18.00
(182)	Harry Steinfeldt	80.00	35.00	18.00
(183)	George Stone	80.00	35.00	18.00
(184)	George Stovall	80.00	35.00	18.00
(185)	Gabby Street	80.00	35.00	18.00
(186)	George F. Suggs	350.00	175.00	90.00
(187)	Ed Summers	80.00	35.00	18.00
(188)	Jeff Sweeney	230.00	115.00	60.00
(189)	Lee Tannehill	80.00	35.00	18.00
(190)	Ira Thomas	80.00	35.00	18.00
(191)	Joe Tinker	325.00	160.00	80.00
(192)	John Titus	80.00	35.00	18.00
(193)	Terry Turner	400.00	220.00	110.00
(194)	James Vaughn	295.00	145.00	75.00
(195)	Heinie Wagner	230.00	115.00	60.00
(196)	Bobby Wallace (with cap)	275.00	140.00	70.00
(197a)	Bobby Wallace (no cap, one line of 1910 stats)	450.00	225.00	115.00
(197b)	Bobby Wallace (no cap, two lines of 1910 stats)	345.00	175.00	85.00
(198)	Ed Walsh	450.00	180.00	90.00
(199)	Z.D. Wheat	375.00	190.00	95.00
(200)	Doc White (White Sox)	80.00	35.00	18.00
(201)	Kirb. White (Pirates)	230.00	115.00	60.00
(202)	Irvin K. Wilhelm	345.00	170.00	85.00
(203)	Ed Willett	80.00	35.00	18.00
(204)	J. Owen Wilson	80.00	35.00	18.00
(205)	George R. Wiltse (both ears show)	80.00	35.00	18.00
(206)	George R. Wiltse (only right ear shows)	345.00	170.00	85.00
(207)	Harry Wolter	80.00	35.00	18.00
(208)	Cy Young	1100.	550.00	275.00

1909-11 T206 White Border

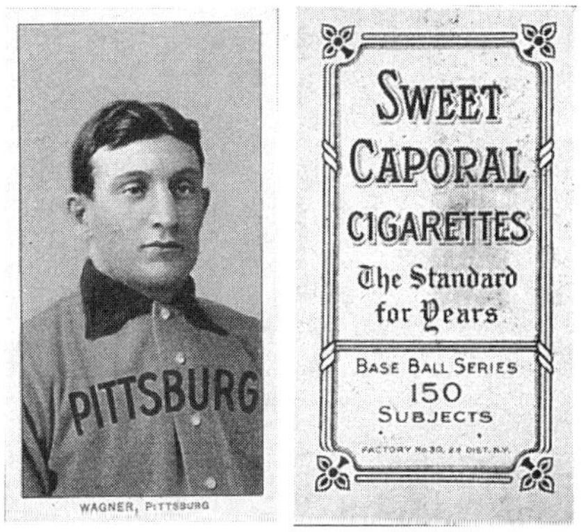

The nearly 525 cards which make up the T206 set are the most popular of the early tobacco card issues. Players are depicted in color lithographs surrounded by a white border. The player's last name on the 1-7/16" x 2-5/8" cards appear at the bottom with the city and league, when a city had more than one team. Backs contain an ad for one of 16 brands of cigarettes. There are 389 major leaguer cards and 134 minor leaguer cards in the set, but with front/back varieties the number of potentially different cards runs into the thousands. The set features many expensive cards including a number of pose and/or team variations. Values shown are for cards with the most common advertising on back: Piedmont and Sweet Caporal. Other backs carry a premium depending on scarcity (see listings under brand names). Several popularly collected printing errors have been included in the listings.

		NM	EX	VG
	Common Player:	90.00	36.00	18.00
	Common Minor Leaguer:	90.00	36.00	18.00
	Common Southern Leaguer:	225.00	90.00	45.00
(1)	Ed Abbaticchio (blue sleeves)	100.00	40.00	20.00
(2)	Ed Abbaticchio (brown sleeves)	90.00	36.00	18.00
(3)	Fred Abbott	90.00	36.00	18.00
(4)	Bill Abstein	90.00	36.00	18.00
(5)	Doc Adkins	90.00	36.00	18.00
(6)	Whitey Alperman	90.00	36.00	18.00
(7)	Red Ames (hands at chest)	90.00	36.00	18.00
(8)	Red Ames (hands above head)	90.00	36.00	18.00
(9)	Red Ames (portrait)	90.00	36.00	18.00
(10)	John Anderson	90.00	36.00	18.00
(11)	Frank Arellanes	90.00	36.00	18.00
(12)	Herman Armbruster	90.00	36.00	18.00
(13)	Harry Arndt	90.00	36.00	18.00
(14)	Jake Atz	90.00	36.00	18.00
(15)	Home Run Baker	365.00	170.00	80.00
(16)	Neal Ball (New York)	90.00	36.00	18.00
(17)	Neal Ball (Cleveland)	90.00	36.00	18.00
(18)	Jap Barbeau	90.00	36.00	18.00
(19)	Cy Barger	90.00	36.00	18.00
(20)	Jack Barry (Philadelphia)	90.00	36.00	18.00
(21)	Shad Barry (Milwaukee)	90.00	36.00	18.00
(22)	Jack Bastian	225.00	90.00	45.00
(23)	Emil Batch	90.00	36.00	18.00
(24)	Johnny Bates	90.00	[illegible]	18.00
(25)	Harry Bay	225.00	90.00	45.00
(26)	Ginger Beaumont	90.00	36.00	18.00
(27)	Fred Beck	90.00	36.00	18.00
(28)	Beals Becker	90.00	36.00	18.00
(29)	Jake Beckley	300.00	120.00	60.00
(30)	George Bell (hands above head)	90.00	36.00	18.00
(31)	George Bell (pitching follow thru)	90.00	36.00	18.00
(32)	Chief Bender (pitching, no trees in background)	325.00	130.00	65.00
(33)	Chief Bender (pitching, trees in background)	310.00	125.00	62.00
(34)	Chief Bender (portrait)	300.00	120.00	60.00
(35)	Bill Bergen (batting)	90.00	36.00	18.00
(36)	Bill Bergen (catching)	90.00	36.00	18.00
(37)	Heinie Berger	90.00	36.00	18.00

(38)	Bill Bernhard	225.00	90.00	45.00
(39)	Bob Bescher (hands in air)	90.00	36.00	18.00
(40)	Bob Bescher (portrait)	90.00	36.00	18.00
(41)	Joe Birmingham	90.00	36.00	18.00
(42)	Lena Blackburne	90.00	36.00	18.00
(43)	Jack Bliss	90.00	36.00	18.00
(44)	Frank Bowerman	90.00	36.00	18.00
(45)	Bill Bradley (portrait)	90.00	36.00	18.00
(46)	Bill Bradley (with bat)	90.00	36.00	18.00
(47)	Dave Brain	90.00	36.00	18.00
(48)	Kitty Bransfield	90.00	36.00	18.00
(49)	Roy Brashear	90.00	36.00	18.00
(50)	Ted Breitenstein	225.00	90.00	45.00
(51)	Roger Bresnahan (portrait)	375.00	160.00	80.00
(52)	Roger Bresnahan (with bat)	275.00	115.00	65.00
(53)	Al Bridwell (portrait, no cap)	90.00	36.00	18.00
(54)	Al Bridwell (portrait, with cap)	90.00	36.00	18.00
(55a)	George Brown (Browne) (Chicago)	110.00	50.00	25.00
(55b)	George Brown (Browne) (Washington)	675.00	275.00	140.00
(56)	Mordecai Brown (Chicago on shirt)	275.00	110.00	55.00
(57)	Mordecai Brown (Cubs on shirt)	400.00	160.00	80.00
(58)	Mordecai Brown (portrait)	300.00	120.00	65.00
(59)	Al Burch (batting)	185.00	75.00	37.00
(60)	Al Burch (fielding)	90.00	36.00	18.00
(61)	Fred Burchell	90.00	36.00	18.00
(62)	Jimmy Burke	90.00	36.00	18.00
(63)	Bill Burns	90.00	36.00	18.00
(64)	Donie Bush	90.00	36.00	18.00
(65)	John Butler	90.00	36.00	18.00
(66)	Bobby Byrne	90.00	36.00	18.00
(67)	Howie Camnitz (arm at side)	90.00	36.00	18.00
(68)	Howie Camnitz (arms folded)	90.00	36.00	18.00
(69)	Howie Camnitz (hands above head)	90.00	36.00	18.00
(70)	Billy Campbell	90.00	36.00	18.00
(71)	Scoops Carey	225.00	90.00	45.00
(72)	Charley Carr	90.00	36.00	18.00
(73)	Bill Carrigan	90.00	36.00	18.00
(74)	Doc Casey	90.00	36.00	18.00
(75)	Peter Cassidy	90.00	36.00	18.00
(76)	Frank Chance (batting)	310.00	125.00	65.00
(77)	Frank Chance (portrait, red background)	400.00	175.00	90.00
(78)	Frank Chance (portrait, yellow background)	425.00	180.00	90.00
(79)	Bill Chappelle	90.00	36.00	18.00
(80)	Chappie Charles	90.00	36.00	18.00
(81)	Hal Chase (holding trophy)	195.00	78.00	39.00
(82)	Hal Chase (portrait, blue background)	190.00	90.00	45.00
(83)	Hal Chase (portrait, pink background)	260.00	120.00	60.00
(84)	Hal Chase (throwing, dark cap)	175.00	70.00	35.00
(85)	Hal Chase (throwing, white cap)	250.00	100.00	50.00
(86)	Jack Chesbro	425.00	170.00	85.00
(87)	Ed Cicotte	250.00	100.00	50.00
(88)	Bill Clancy (Clancey)	90.00	36.00	18.00
(89)	Josh Clark (Columbus) (Clarke)	90.00	36.00	18.00
(90)	Fred Clarke (Pittsburgh, holding bat)	300.00	120.00	60.00
(91)	Fred Clarke (Pittsburgh, portrait)	285.00	115.00	60.00
(92)	J.J. Clarke (Nig) (Cleveland)	90.00	36.00	18.00
(93)	Bill Clymer	90.00	36.00	18.00
(94)	Ty Cobb (portrait, green background)	3750.	1400.	700.00
(95a)	Ty Cobb (portrait, red background)	2300.	1100.	500.00
(95b)	Ty Cobb (portrait, red background, Ty Cobb brand back)	100000.	40000.	20000.
(96)	Ty Cobb (bat off shoulder)	2750.	1200.	600.00
(97)	Ty Cobb (bat on shoulder)	2500.	1250.	625.00
(98)	Cad Coles	225.00	90.00	45.00
(99)	Eddie Collins (Philadelphia)	325.00	125.00	75.00
(100)	Jimmy Collins (Minneapolis)	250.00	100.00	50.00
(101)	Bunk Congalton	90.00	36.00	18.00
(102)	Wid Conroy (fielding)	90.00	36.00	18.00
(103)	Wid Conroy (with bat)	90.00	36.00	18.00
(104)	Harry Covaleski (Coveleski)	90.00	36.00	18.00
(105)	Doc Crandall (portrait, no cap)	90.00	36.00	18.00
(106)	Doc Crandall (portrait, with cap)	90.00	36.00	18.00
(107)	Bill Cranston	175.00	70.00	35.00
(108)	Gavvy Cravath	125.00	50.00	25.00
(109)	Sam Crawford (throwing)	375.00	160.00	90.00
(110)	Sam Crawford (with bat)	350.00	140.00	70.00
(111)	Birdie Cree	90.00	36.00	18.00
(112)	Lou Criger	90.00	36.00	18.00
(113)	Dode Criss	90.00	36.00	18.00
(114)	Monte Cross	90.00	36.00	18.00
(115a)	Bill Dahlen (Boston)	110.00	45.00	22.00
(115b)	Bill Dahlen (Brooklyn)	475.00	200.00	100.00
(116)	Paul Davidson	90.00	36.00	18.00
(117)	George Davis (Chicago)	250.00	100.00	50.00
(118)	Harry Davis (Philadelphia, Davis on front)	90.00	36.00	18.00
(119)	Harry Davis (Philadelphia, H. Davis on front)	90.00	36.00	18.00
(120)	Frank Delehanty (Delahanty) (Louisville)	115.00	45.00	22.00
(121)	Jim Delehanty (Delahanty) (Washington)	90.00	36.00	18.00
(122a)	Ray Demmitt (New York)	90.00	36.00	18.00
(122b)	Ray Demmitt (St. Louis)	6000.	2750.	1500.
(123)	Rube Dessau	90.00	36.00	18.00
(124)	Art Devlin	90.00	36.00	18.00
(125)	Josh Devore	90.00	36.00	18.00
(126)	Bill Dineen (Dinneen)	90.00	36.00	18.00
(127)	Mike Donlin (fielding)	250.00	100.00	50.00
(128)	Mike Donlin (seated)	90.00	36.00	18.00
(129)	Mike Donlin (with bat)	90.00	36.00	18.00
(130)	Jiggs Donohue (Donahue)	90.00	36.00	18.00
(131)	Wild Bill Donovan (portrait)	90.00	36.00	18.00
(132)	Wild Bill Donovan (throwing)	90.00	36.00	18.00
(133)	Red Dooin	90.00	36.00	18.00
(134)	Mickey Doolan (batting)	90.00	36.00	18.00
(135)	Mickey Doolan (fielding)	90.00	36.00	18.00
(136)	Mickey Doolin (Doolan)	90.00	36.00	18.00
(137)	Gus Dorner	90.00	36.00	18.00
(138)	Patsy Dougherty (arm in air)	90.00	36.00	18.00
(139)	Patsy Dougherty (portrait)	90.00	36.00	18.00
(140)	Tom Downey (batting)	90.00	36.00	18.00
(141)	Tom Downey (fielding)	90.00	36.00	18.00
(142)	Jerry Downs	90.00	36.00	18.00
(143a)	Joe Doyle (N.Y. Natl., hands above head)	75000.	40000.	20000.
(143b)	Joe Doyle (N.Y., hands above head)	90.00	36.00	18.00
(144)	Larry Doyle (N.Y. Nat'l., portrait)	90.00	36.00	18.00
(145)	Larry Doyle (N.Y. Nat'l., throwing)	125.00	50.00	25.00
(146)	Larry Doyle (N.Y. Nat'l., with bat)	90.00	36.00	18.00
(147)	Jean Dubuc	90.00	36.00	18.00
(148)	Hugh Duffy	300.00	120.00	60.00
(149)	Jack Dunn (Baltimore)	90.00	36.00	18.00
(150)	Joe Dunn (Brooklyn)	90.00	36.00	18.00
(151)	Bull Durham	125.00	50.00	25.00
(152)	Jimmy Dygert	90.00	36.00	18.00
(153)	Ted Easterly	90.00	36.00	18.00
(154)	Dick Egan	90.00	36.00	18.00
(155a)	Kid Elberfeld (New York)	90.00	36.00	18.00
(155b)	Kid Elberfeld (Washington, portrait)	1800.	900.00	360.00
(156)	Kid Elberfeld (Washington, fielding)	90.00	36.00	18.00
(157)	Roy Ellam	225.00	90.00	45.00
(158)	Clyde Engle	90.00	36.00	18.00
(159)	Steve Evans	90.00	36.00	18.00
(160)	Johnny Evers (portrait)	525.00	215.00	105.00
(161)	Johnny Evers (with bat, Chicago on shirt)	400.00	160.00	75.00
(162)	Johnny Evers (with bat, Cubs on shirt)	350.00	140.00	70.00
(163)	Bob Ewing	90.00	36.00	18.00
(164)	Cecil Ferguson	90.00	36.00	18.00
(165)	Hobe Ferris	90.00	36.00	18.00
(166)	Lou Fiene (portrait)	90.00	36.00	18.00
(167)	Lou Fiene (throwing)	90.00	36.00	18.00
(168)	Steamer Flanagan	90.00	36.00	18.00
(169)	Art Fletcher	90.00	36.00	18.00
(170)	Elmer Flick	375.00	175.00	90.00
(171)	Russ Ford	90.00	36.00	18.00
(172)	Ed Foster	225.00	90.00	45.00
(173)	Jerry Freeman	90.00	36.00	18.00
(174)	John Frill	90.00	36.00	18.00
(175)	Charlie Fritz	225.00	90.00	45.00
(176)	Art Fromme	90.00	36.00	18.00
(177)	Chick Gandil	275.00	110.00	55.00
(178)	Bob Ganley	90.00	36.00	18.00
(179)	John Ganzel	90.00	36.00	18.00
(180)	Harry Gasper	90.00	36.00	18.00
(181)	Rube Geyer	90.00	36.00	18.00
(182)	George Gibson	90.00	36.00	18.00
(183)	Billy Gilbert	90.00	36.00	18.00
(184)	Wilbur Goode (Good)	90.00	36.00	18.00
(185)	Bill Graham (St. Louis)	90.00	36.00	18.00
(186)	Peaches Graham (Boston)	90.00	36.00	18.00
(187)	Dolly Gray	90.00	36.00	18.00
(188)	Ed Greminger	225.00	90.00	45.00
(189)	Clark Griffith (batting)	300.00	120.00	60.00
(190)	Clark Griffith (portrait)	375.00	160.00	80.00
(191)	Moose Grimshaw	90.00	36.00	18.00
(192)	Bob Groom	90.00	36.00	18.00
(193)	Tom Guiheen	175.00	70.00	35.00
(194)	Ed Hahn	90.00	36.00	18.00
(195)	Bob Hall	90.00	36.00	18.00
(196)	Bill Hallman	90.00	36.00	18.00
(197)	Jack Hannifan (Hannifin)	90.00	36.00	18.00
(198)	Bill Hart (Little Rock)	225.00	90.00	45.00
(199)	Jimmy Hart (Montgomery)	225.00	90.00	45.00
(200)	Topsy Hartsel	90.00	36.00	18.00
(201)	Jack Hayden	90.00	36.00	18.00
(202)	J. Ross Helm	225.00	90.00	45.00
(203)	Charlie Hemphill	90.00	36.00	18.00
(204)	Buck Herzog (Boston)	90.00	36.00	18.00
(205)	Buck Herzog (New York)	90.00	36.00	18.00
(206)	Gordon Hickman	225.00	90.00	45.00
(207)	Bill Hinchman (Cleveland)	90.00	36.00	18.00
(208)	Harry Hinchman (Toledo)	90.00	36.00	18.00
(209)	Dick Hoblitzell	90.00	36.00	18.00
(210)	Danny Hoffman (St. Louis)	90.00	36.00	18.00
(211)	Izzy Hoffman (Providence)	90.00	36.00	18.00
(212)	Solly Hofman	90.00	36.00	18.00
(213)	Bock Hooker	225.00	90.00	45.00
(214)	Del Howard (Chicago)	90.00	36.00	18.00
(215)	Ernie Howard (Savannah)	225.00	90.00	45.00
(216)	Harry Howell (hand at waist)	90.00	36.00	18.00
(217)	Harry Howell (portrait)	90.00	36.00	18.00
(218)	Miller Huggins (hands at mouth)	350.00	140.00	75.00
(219)	Miller Huggins (portrait)	375.00	165.00	80.00
(220)	Rudy Hulswitt	90.00	36.00	18.00
(221)	John Hummel	90.00	36.00	18.00
(222)	George Hunter	90.00	36.00	18.00
(223)	Frank Isbell	90.00	36.00	18.00
(224)	Fred Jacklitsch	90.00	36.00	18.00
(225)	Jimmy Jackson	90.00	36.00	18.00
(226)	Hughie Jennings (one hand showing)	275.00	115.00	60.00
(227)	Hughie Jennings (both hands showing)	275.00	110.00	60.00
(228)	Hughie Jennings (portrait)	275.00	115.00	60.00
(229)	Walter Johnson (pitching)	1100.	440.00	210.00
(230)	Walter Johnson (portrait)	1250.	500.00	250.00
(231)	Fielder Jones (Chicago, hands at hips)	90.00	36.00	18.00
(232)	Fielder Jones (Chicago, portrait)	90.00	36.00	18.00
(233)	Davy Jones (Detroit)	90.00	36.00	18.00
(234)	Tom Jones (St. Louis)	90.00	36.00	18.00
(235)	Dutch Jordan (Atlanta)	225.00	90.00	45.00
(236)	Tim Jordan (Brooklyn, batting)	90.00	36.00	18.00
(237)	Tim Jordan (Brooklyn, portrait)	90.00	36.00	18.00
(238)	Addie Joss (pitching)	400.00	160.00	80.00
(239)	Addie Joss (portrait)	500.00	200.00	100.00
(240)	Ed Karger	90.00	36.00	18.00
(241)	Willie Keeler (portrait)	475.00	185.00	95.00
(242)	Willie Keeler (batting)	525.00	210.00	105.00
(243)	Joe Kelley	350.00	130.00	70.00
(244)	J.F. Kiernan	225.00	90.00	45.00
(245)	Ed Killian (pitching)	90.00	36.00	18.00
(246)	Ed Killian (portrait)	90.00	36.00	18.00
(247)	Frank King	225.00	90.00	45.00
(248)	Rube Kisinger (Kissinger)	90.00	36.00	18.00
(249a)	Red Kleinow (Boston)	475.00	150.00	90.00
(249b)	Red Kleinow (New York, catching)	90.00	36.00	18.00
(250)	Red Kleinow (New York, with bat)	90.00	36.00	18.00
(251)	Johnny Kling	90.00	36.00	18.00
(252)	Otto Knabe	90.00	36.00	18.00
(253)	Jack Knight (portrait)	90.00	36.00	18.00
(254)	Jack Knight (with bat)	90.00	36.00	18.00
(255)	Ed Konetchy (glove above head)	90.00	36.00	18.00
(256)	Ed Konetchy (glove near ground)	90.00	36.00	18.00
(257)	Harry Krause (pitching)	90.00	36.00	18.00
(258)	Harry Krause (portrait)	90.00	36.00	18.00
(259)	Rube Kroh	90.00	36.00	18.00
(260)	Otto Kruger (Krueger)	90.00	36.00	18.00
(261)	James Lafitte	225.00	90.00	45.00
(262)	Nap Lajoie (portrait)	800.00	350.00	160.00
(263)	Nap Lajoie (throwing)	475.00	190.00	95.00
(264)	Nap Lajoie (with bat)	550.00	220.00	110.00
(265)	Joe Lake (New York)	90.00	36.00	18.00
(266)	Joe Lake (St. Louis, ball in hand)	90.00	36.00	18.00
(267)	Joe Lake (St. Louis, no ball in hand)	90.00	36.00	18.00
(268)	Frank LaPorte	90.00	36.00	18.00
(269)	Arlie Latham	90.00	36.00	18.00
(270)	Bill Lattimore	90.00	36.00	18.00
(271)	Jimmy Lavender	90.00	36.00	18.00
(272)	Tommy Leach (bending over)	90.00	36.00	18.00
(273)	Tommy Leach (portrait)	90.00	36.00	18.00
(274)	Lefty Leifield (batting)	90.00	36.00	18.00
(275)	Lefty Leifield (pitching)	90.00	36.00	18.00
(276)	Ed Lennox	90.00	36.00	18.00
(277)	Harry Lentz (Sentz)	225.00	90.00	45.00
(278)	Glenn Liebhardt	90.00	36.00	18.00
(279)	Vive Lindaman	90.00	36.00	18.00
(280)	Perry Lipe	225.00	90.00	45.00
(281)	Paddy Livingstone (Livingston)	90.00	36.00	18.00
(282)	Hans Lobert	90.00	36.00	18.00
(283)	Harry Lord	90.00	36.00	18.00
(284)	Harry Lumley	90.00	36.00	18.00
(285a)	Carl Lundgren (Chicago)	500.00	200.00	100.00
(285b)	Carl Lundgren (Kansas City)	90.00	36.00	18.00
(286)	Nick Maddox	90.00	36.00	18.00
(287a)	Sherry Magie (Magee)	30000.	12000.	6000.
(287b)	Sherry Magee (portrait)	110.00	44.00	22.00
(288)	Sherry Magee (with bat)	90.00	36.00	18.00
(289)	Bill Malarkey	90.00	36.00	18.00
(290)	Billy Maloney	90.00	36.00	18.00
(291)	George Manion	225.00	90.00	45.00
(292)	Rube Manning (batting)	90.00	36.00	18.00
(293)	Rube Manning (pitching)	90.00	36.00	18.00
(294)	Rube Marquard (hands at thighs)	375.00	150.00	75.00
(295)	Rube Marquard (pitching follow-through)	325.00	130.00	65.00
(296)	Rube Marquard (portrait)	375.00	150.00	75.00
(297)	Doc Marshall	90.00	36.00	18.00
(298)	Christy Mathewson (dark cap)	950.00	380.00	190.00
(299)	Christy Mathewson (portrait)	1650.	625.00	300.00
(300)	Christy Mathewson (white cap)	900.00	360.00	180.00
(301)	Al Mattern	90.00	36.00	18.00
(302)	John McAleese	90.00	36.00	18.00
(303)	George McBride	90.00	36.00	18.00
(304)	Pat McCauley	225.00	90.00	45.00
(305)	Moose McCormick	90.00	36.00	18.00
(306)	Pryor McElveen	90.00	36.00	18.00
(307)	Dan McGann	90.00	36.00	18.00
(308)	Jim McGinley	90.00	36.00	18.00
(309)	Iron Man McGinnity	220.00	90.00	45.00
(310)	Stoney McGlynn	90.00	36.00	18.00
(311)	John McGraw (finger in air)	375.00	150.00	80.00
(312)	John McGraw (glove at hip)	425.00	180.00	90.00
(313)	John McGraw (portrait, no cap)	450.00	180.00	90.00
(314)	John McGraw (portrait, with cap)	375.00	140.00	70.00
(315)	Harry McIntyre (Brooklyn)	90.00	36.00	18.00
(316)	Harry McIntyre (Brooklyn & Chicago)	90.00	36.00	18.00
(317)	Matty McIntyre (Detroit)	90.00	36.00	18.00
(318)	Larry McLean	90.00	36.00	18.00
(319)	George McQuillan (ball in hand)	90.00	36.00	18.00
(320)	George McQuillan (with bat)	90.00	36.00	18.00
(321)	Fred Merkle (portrait)	110.00	44.00	22.00
(322)	Fred Merkle (throwing)	90.00	36.00	18.00
(323)	George Merritt	90.00	36.00	18.00
(324)	Chief Meyers	90.00	36.00	18.00
(325)	Clyde Milan	90.00	36.00	18.00
(326)	Dots Miller (Pittsburgh)	90.00	36.00	18.00

(327)	Molly Miller (Dallas)	225.00	90.00	45.00
(328)	Bill Milligan	90.00	36.00	18.00
(329)	Fred Mitchell (Toronto)	90.00	36.00	18.00
(330)	Mike Mitchell (Cincinnati)	90.00	36.00	18.00
(331)	Dan Moeller	90.00	36.00	18.00
(332)	Carlton Molesworth	225.00	90.00	45.00
(333)	Herbie Moran (Providence)	90.00	36.00	18.00
(334)	Pat Moran (Chicago)	90.00	36.00	18.00
(335)	George Moriarty	90.00	36.00	18.00
(336)	Mike Mowrey	90.00	36.00	18.00
(337)	Dom Mullaney	225.00	90.00	45.00
(338)	George Mullen (Mullin)	90.00	36.00	18.00
(339)	George Mullin (throwing)	90.00	36.00	18.00
(340)	George Mullin (with bat)	90.00	36.00	18.00
(341)	Danny Murphy (batting)	90.00	36.00	18.00
(342)	Danny Murphy (throwing)	90.00	36.00	18.00
(343)	Red Murray (batting)	90.00	36.00	18.00
(344)	Red Murray (portrait)	90.00	36.00	18.00
(345)	Chief Myers (Meyers) (batting)	90.00	36.00	18.00
(346)	Chief Myers (Meyers) (fielding)	90.00	36.00	18.00
(347)	Billy Nattress	90.00	36.00	18.00
(348)	Tom Needham	90.00	36.00	18.00
(349)	Simon Nicholls (hands on knees)	90.00	36.00	18.00
(350)	Simon Nichols (Nicholls) (batting)	90.00	36.00	18.00
(351)	Harry Niles	90.00	36.00	18.00
(352)	Rebel Oakes	90.00	36.00	18.00
(353)	Frank Oberlin	90.00	36.00	18.00
(354)	Peter O'Brien	90.00	36.00	18.00
(355a)	Bill O'Hara (New York)	90.00	36.00	18.00
(355b)	Bill O'Hara (St. Louis)	6500.	2600.	1200.
(356)	Rube Oldring (batting)	90.00	36.00	18.00
(357)	Rube Oldring (fielding)	90.00	36.00	18.00
(358)	Charley O'Leary (hands on knees)	90.00	36.00	18.00
(359)	Charley O'Leary (portrait)	90.00	36.00	18.00
(360)	William J. O'Neil	90.00	36.00	18.00
(361)	Al Orth	225.00	90.00	45.00
(362)	William Otey	225.00	90.00	45.00
(363)	Orval Overall (hand face level)	90.00	36.00	18.00
(364)	Orval Overall (hands waist level)	90.00	36.00	18.00
(365)	Orval Overall (portrait)	90.00	36.00	18.00
(366)	Frank Owen	90.00	36.00	18.00
(367)	George Paige	225.00	90.00	45.00
(368)	Fred Parent	90.00	36.00	18.00
(369)	Dode Paskert	90.00	36.00	18.00
(370)	Jim Pastorius	90.00	36.00	18.00
(371)	Harry Pattee	335.00	125.00	65.00
(372)	Billy Payne	90.00	36.00	18.00
(373)	Barney Pelty (horizontal photo)	225.00	90.00	45.00
(374)	Barney Pelty (vertical photo)	90.00	36.00	18.00
(375)	Hub Perdue	225.00	90.00	45.00
(376)	George Perring	90.00	36.00	18.00
(377)	Arch Persons	225.00	90.00	45.00
(378)	Francis (Big Jeff) Pfeffer	90.00	36.00	18.00
(379)	Jake Pfeister (Pfiester) (seated)	90.00	36.00	18.00
(380)	Jake Pfeister (Pfiester) (throwing)	90.00	36.00	18.00
(381)	Jimmy Phelan	90.00	36.00	18.00
(382)	Eddie Phelps	90.00	36.00	18.00
(383)	Deacon Phillippe	90.00	36.00	18.00
(384)	Ollie Pickering	90.00	36.00	18.00
(385)	Eddie Plank	65000.	26000.	13000.
(386)	Phil Poland	90.00	36.00	18.00
(387)	Jack Powell	90.00	36.00	18.00
(388)	Mike Powers	250.00	100.00	50.00
(389)	Billy Purtell	90.00	36.00	18.00
(390)	Ambrose Puttman (Puttmann)	90.00	36.00	18.00
(391)	Lee Quillen (Quillin)	90.00	36.00	18.00
(392)	Jack Quinn	90.00	36.00	18.00
(393)	Newt Randall	90.00	36.00	18.00
(394)	Bugs Raymond	90.00	36.00	18.00
(395)	Ed Reagan	225.00	90.00	45.00
(396)	Ed Reulbach (glove showing)	235.00	100.00	50.00
(397)	Ed Reulbach (no glove showing)	90.00	36.00	18.00
(398)	Dutch Revelle	225.00	90.00	45.00
(399)	Bob Rhoades (Rhoads) (hands at chest)	90.00	36.00	18.00
(400)	Bob Rhoades (Rhoads) (right arm extended)	90.00	36.00	18.00
(401)	Charlie Rhodes	90.00	36.00	18.00
(402)	Claude Ritchey	90.00	36.00	18.00
(403)	Lou Ritter	90.00	36.00	18.00
(404)	Ike Rockenfeld	225.00	90.00	45.00
(405)	Claude Rossman	90.00	36.00	18.00
(406)	Nap Rucker (portrait)	90.00	36.00	18.00
(407)	Nap Rucker (throwing)	90.00	36.00	18.00
(408)	Dick Rudolph	90.00	36.00	18.00
(409)	Ray Ryan	225.00	90.00	45.00
(410)	Germany Schaefer (Detroit)	225.00	90.00	45.00
(411)	Germany Schaefer (Washington)	90.00	36.00	18.00
(412)	George Schirm	90.00	36.00	18.00
(413)	Larry Schlafly	90.00	36.00	18.00
(414)	Admiral Schlei (batting)	90.00	36.00	18.00
(415)	Admiral Schlei (catching)	90.00	36.00	18.00
(416)	Admiral Schlei (portrait)	90.00	36.00	18.00
(417)	Boss Schmidt (portrait)	90.00	36.00	18.00
(418)	Boss Schmidt (throwing)	90.00	36.00	18.00
(419)	Ossee Schreck (Schreckengost)	90.00	36.00	18.00
(420)	Wildfire Schulte (front view)	90.00	36.00	18.00
(421)	Wildfire Schulte (back view)	90.00	36.00	18.00
(422)	Jim Scott	90.00	36.00	18.00
(423)	Charles Seitz	225.00	90.00	45.00
(424)	Cy Seymour (batting)	90.00	36.00	18.00
(425)	Cy Seymour (portrait)	90.00	36.00	18.00
(426)	Cy Seymour (throwing)	90.00	36.00	18.00
(427)	Spike Shannon	90.00	36.00	18.00
(428)	Bud Sharpe	90.00	36.00	18.00
(429)	Shag Shaughnessy	225.00	90.00	45.00
(430)	Al Shaw (St. Louis)	90.00	36.00	18.00
(431)	Hunky Shaw (Providence)	90.00	36.00	18.00
(432)	Jimmy Sheckard (glove showing)	90.00	36.00	18.00
(433)	Jimmy Sheckard (no glove showing)	90.00	36.00	18.00
(434)	Bill Shipke	90.00	36.00	18.00
(435)	Jimmy Slagle	90.00	36.00	18.00
(436)	Carlos Smith (Shreveport)	225.00	90.00	45.00
(437)	Frank Smith (Chicago, F. Smith on front)	125.00	50.00	25.00
(438a)	Frank Smith (Chicago, white cap)	90.00	36.00	18.00
(438b)	Frank Smith (Chicago & Boston)	700.00	280.00	140.00
(439)	Happy Smith (Brooklyn)	90.00	36.00	18.00
(440)	Heinie Smith (Buffalo)	90.00	36.00	18.00
(441)	Sid Smith (Atlanta)	225.00	90.00	45.00
(442)	Fred Snodgrass (batting)	90.00	36.00	18.00
(443)	Fred Snodgrass (catching)	90.00	36.00	18.00
(444)	Bob Spade	90.00	36.00	18.00
(445)	Tris Speaker	850.00	350.00	165.00
(446)	Tubby Spencer	90.00	36.00	18.00
(447)	Jake Stahl (glove shows)	90.00	36.00	18.00
(448)	Jake Stahl (no glove shows)	90.00	36.00	18.00
(449)	Oscar Stanage	90.00	36.00	18.00
(450)	Dolly Stark	225.00	90.00	45.00
(451)	Charlie Starr	90.00	36.00	18.00
(452)	Harry Steinfeldt (portrait)	110.00	44.00	22.00
(453)	Harry Steinfeldt (with bat)	90.00	36.00	18.00
(454)	Jim Stephens	90.00	36.00	18.00
(455)	George Stone	90.00	36.00	18.00
(456)	George Stovall (batting)	90.00	36.00	18.00
(457)	George Stovall (portrait)	90.00	36.00	18.00
(458)	Sam Strang	90.00	36.00	18.00
(459)	Gabby Street (catching)	90.00	36.00	18.00
(460)	Gabby Street (portrait)	90.00	36.00	18.00
(461)	Billy Sullivan	90.00	36.00	18.00
(462)	Ed Summers	90.00	36.00	18.00
(463)	Bill Sweeney (Boston)	90.00	36.00	18.00
(464)	Jeff Sweeney (New York)	90.00	36.00	18.00
(465)	Jesse Tannehill (Washington)	90.00	36.00	18.00
(466)	Lee Tannehill (Chicago, L. Tannehill on front)	90.00	36.00	18.00
(467)	Lee Tannehill (Chicago, Tannehill on front)	90.00	36.00	18.00
(468)	Dummy Taylor	90.00	36.00	18.00
(469)	Fred Tenney	90.00	36.00	18.00
(470)	Tony Thebo	225.00	90.00	45.00
(471)	Jake Thielman	90.00	36.00	18.00
(472)	Ira Thomas	90.00	36.00	18.00
(473)	Woodie Thornton	225.00	90.00	45.00
(474)	Joe Tinker (bat off shoulder)	345.00	138.00	69.00
(475)	Joe Tinker (bat on shoulder)	345.00	140.00	70.00
(476)	Joe Tinker (hands on knees)	330.00	135.00	66.00
(477)	Joe Tinker (portrait)	360.00	145.00	75.00
(478)	John Titus	90.00	36.00	18.00
(479)	Terry Turner	90.00	36.00	18.00
(480)	Bob Unglaub	90.00	36.00	18.00
(481)	Juan Violat (Viola)	250.00	100.00	50.00
(482)	Rube Waddell (portrait)	340.00	136.00	68.00
(483)	Rube Waddell (throwing)	350.00	140.00	70.00
(484)	Heinie Wagner (bat on left shoulder)	90.00	36.00	18.00
(485)	Heinie Wagner (bat on right shoulder)	90.00	36.00	18.00
(486)	Honus Wagner	640000.	350000.	150000.
(487)	Bobby Wallace	350.00	140.00	70.00
(488)	Ed Walsh	350.00	140.00	70.00
(489)	Jack Warhop	90.00	36.00	18.00
(490)	Jake Weimer	90.00	36.00	18.00
(491)	James Westlake	225.00	90.00	45.00
(492)	Zack Wheat	330.00	135.00	70.00
(493)	Doc White (Chicago, pitching)	90.00	36.00	18.00
(494)	Doc White (Chicago, portrait)	90.00	36.00	18.00
(495)	Foley White (Houston)	225.00	90.00	45.00
(496)	Jack White (Buffalo)	90.00	36.00	18.00
(497)	Kaiser Wilhelm (hands at chest)	90.00	36.00	18.00
(498)	Kaiser Wilhelm (with bat)	90.00	36.00	18.00
(499)	Ed Willett	90.00	36.00	18.00
(500)	Ed Willetts (Willett)	90.00	36.00	18.00
(501)	Jimmy Williams	90.00	36.00	18.00
(502)	Vic Willis (portrait)	350.00	140.00	70.00
(503)	Vic Willis (throwing)	275.00	110.00	55.00
(504)	Vic Willis (with bat)	325.00	130.00	65.00
(505)	Owen Wilson	90.00	36.00	18.00
(506)	Hooks Wiltse (pitching)	90.00	36.00	18.00
(507)	Hooks Wiltse (portrait, no cap)	90.00	36.00	18.00
(508)	Hooks Wiltse (portrait, with cap)	90.00	36.00	18.00
(509)	Lucky Wright	90.00	36.00	18.00
(510)	Cy Young (Cleveland, glove shows)	800.00	300.00	150.00
(511)	Cy Young (Cleveland, bare hand shows)	850.00	340.00	170.00
(512)	Cy Young (Cleveland, portrait)	1250.	450.00	195.00
(513)	Irv Young (Minneapolis)	90.00	36.00	18.00
(514)	Heinie Zimmerman	90.00	36.00	18.00

1909-11 T206 Errors

Because of the complexity of the lithographic process by which cards of the T206 series were printed, a number of significant printing errors - missing colors, broken or missing type, etc. - are known. Early in the hobby history some of these errors were collected alongside such true design variation cards such as the Magie misspelling and Joe Doyle "N.Y. Nat'l". Because of the continued popularity of T206, these errors remain in demand today and can command significant premium values. It should be noted, however, that not all similar errors within T206 bring such high prices; value seems dependent on the length of time the errors have been known in the hobby.

		NM	EX	VG
(428)	Shappe, Newark (should be Sharpe)	850.00	350.00	175.00
(442)	Nodgrass - batting (should be Snodgrass)	6500.	3250.	1950.
(443)	Nodgrass - catching (should be Snodgrass)	6500.	3250.	1950.
(463)	Sweeney, no "B" (missing magenta ink)	9000.	4500.	2700.

1912 T207 Brown Background

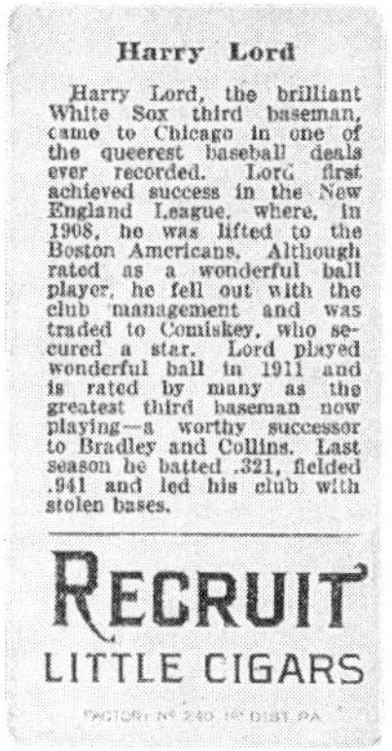

These 1-7/16" x 2-5/8" cards take their name from the background color which frames the rather drab sepia and white player drawings. They have tan borders making them less colorful than the more popular issues of their era. Player pictures are also on the dull side, with a white strip containing the player's last name, team and league. The card backs have the player's full name, a baseball biography and an ad for one of several brands of cigarettes. The set features 200 players including stars and three classic rarities: Irving Lewis (Boston-Nat.), Ward Miller (Chicago-Nat.) and Louis Lowdermilk (St. Louis-Nat.). There are a number of other scarce cards in the set, including a higher than usual number of obscure players.

		NM	EX	VG
	Common Player:	80.00	50.00	25.00
(1)	John B. Adams	100.00	50.00	35.00
(2)	Edward Ainsmith	80.00	50.00	25.00
(3)	Rafael Almeida	150.00	75.00	52.00
(4a)	James Austin (insignia on shirt)	110.00	55.00	38.00
(4b)	James Austin (no insignia on shirt)	100.00	50.00	35.00
(5)	Neal Ball	80.00	50.00	25.00
(6)	Eros Barger	80.00	50.00	25.00
(7)	Jack Barry	80.00	50.00	25.00
(8)	Charles Bauman	100.00	50.00	35.00
(9)	Beals Becker	80.00	50.00	25.00
(10)	Chief (Albert) Bender	375.00	187.00	130.00
(11)	Joseph Benz	100.00	50.00	35.00
(12)	Robert Bescher	80.00	50.00	25.00

(13)	Joe Birmingham	100.00	50.00	35.00
(14)	Russell Blackburne	100.00	50.00	35.00
(15)	Fred Blanding	100.00	50.00	35.00
(16)	Jimmy Block	80.00	50.00	25.00
(17)	Ping Bodie	80.00	50.00	25.00
(18)	Hugh Bradley	80.00	50.00	25.00
(19)	Roger Bresnahan	450.00	225.00	157.00
(20)	J.F. Bushelman	100.00	50.00	35.00
(21)	Henry (Hank) Butcher	100.00	50.00	35.00
(22)	Robert M. Byrne	80.00	50.00	25.00
(23)	John James Callahan	80.00	50.00	25.00
(24)	Howard Camnitz	80.00	50.00	25.00
(25)	Max Carey	325.00	162.00	114.00
(26a)	William Carrigan (Heinie Wagner back)	80.00	50.00	25.00
(26b)	Bill Carrigan (correct back)	80.00	50.00	25.00
(27)	George Chalmers	80.00	50.00	25.00
(28)	Frank Leroy Chance	450.00	225.00	140.00
(29)	Edward Cicotte	100.00	50.00	35.00
(30)	Tom Clarke	80.00	50.00	25.00
(31)	Leonard Cole	80.00	50.00	25.00
(32)	John Collins	100.00	50.00	35.00
(33)	Robert Coulson	80.00	50.00	25.00
(34)	Tex Covington	80.00	50.00	25.00
(35)	Otis Crandall	80.00	50.00	25.00
(36)	William Cunningham	100.00	50.00	35.00
(37)	Dave Danforth	80.00	50.00	25.00
(38)	Bert Daniels	80.00	50.00	25.00
(39)	John Daubert (Jake)	100.00	50.00	35.00
(40a)	Harry Davis (brown "C" on cap)	110.00	55.00	38.00
(40b)	Harry Davis (blue "C" on cap)	110.00	55.00	38.00
(41)	Jim Delehanty	80.00	50.00	25.00
(42)	Claude Derrick	80.00	50.00	25.00
(43)	Arthur Devlin	80.00	50.00	25.00
(44)	Joshua Devore	80.00	50.00	25.00
(45)	Mike Donlin	100.00	50.00	35.00
(46)	Edward Donnelly	100.00	50.00	35.00
(47)	Charles Dooin	80.00	50.00	25.00
(48)	Tom Downey	100.00	50.00	35.00
(49)	Lawrence Doyle	80.00	50.00	25.00
(50)	Del Drake	80.00	50.00	25.00
(51)	Ted Easterly	80.00	50.00	25.00
(52)	George Ellis	80.00	50.00	25.00
(53)	Clyde Engle	80.00	50.00	25.00
(54)	R.E. Erwin	80.00	50.00	25.00
(55)	Louis Evans	80.00	50.00	25.00
(56)	John Ferry	80.00	50.00	25.00
(57a)	Ray Fisher (blue cap)	110.00	55.00	38.00
(57b)	Ray Fisher (white cap)	110.00	55.00	38.00
(58)	Arthur Fletcher	80.00	50.00	25.00
(59)	Jacques Fournier	100.00	50.00	35.00
(60)	Arthur Fromme	80.00	50.00	25.00
(61)	Del Gainor	80.00	50.00	25.00
(62)	William Lawrence Gardner	80.00	50.00	25.00
(63)	Lefty George	80.00	50.00	25.00
(64)	Roy Golden	80.00	50.00	25.00
(65)	Harry Gowdy	80.00	50.00	25.00
(66)	George Graham	100.00	50.00	35.00
(67)	J.G. Graney	80.00	50.00	25.00
(68)	Vean Gregg	100.00	50.00	35.00
(69)	Casey Hageman	80.00	50.00	25.00
(70)	Charlie Hall	80.00	50.00	25.00
(71)	E.S. Hallinan	80.00	50.00	25.00
(72)	Earl Hamilton	80.00	50.00	25.00
(73)	Robert Harmon	80.00	50.00	25.00
(74)	Grover Hartley	100.00	50.00	35.00
(75)	Olaf Henriksen	80.00	50.00	25.00
(76)	John Henry	100.00	50.00	35.00
(77)	Charles Herzog	100.00	50.00	35.00
(78)	Robert Higgins	80.00	50.00	25.00
(79)	Chester Hoff	100.00	50.00	35.00
(80)	William Hogan	80.00	50.00	25.00
(81)	Harry Hooper	450.00	225.00	155.00
(82)	Ben Houser	100.00	50.00	35.00
(83)	Hamilton Hyatt	100.00	50.00	35.00
(84)	Walter Johnson	800.00	400.00	280.00
(85)	George Kaler	80.00	50.00	25.00
(86)	William Kelly	100.00	50.00	35.00
(87)	Jay Kirke	100.00	50.00	35.00
(88)	John Kling	80.00	50.00	25.00
(89)	Otto Knabe	80.00	50.00	25.00
(90)	Elmer Knetzer	80.00	50.00	25.00
(91)	Edward Konetchy	80.00	50.00	25.00
(92)	Harry Krause	80.00	50.00	25.00
(93)	"Red" Kuhn	100.00	50.00	35.00
(94)	Joseph Kutina	100.00	50.00	35.00
(95)	F.H. (Bill) Lange	100.00	50.00	35.00
(96)	Jack Lapp	80.00	50.00	25.00
(97)	W. Arlington Latham	80.00	50.00	25.00
(98)	Thomas W. Leach	80.00	50.00	25.00
(99)	Albert Leifield	80.00	50.00	25.00
(100)	Edgar Lennox	80.00	50.00	25.00
(101)	Duffy Lewis	80.00	50.00	25.00
(102a)	Irving Lewis (no emblem on sleeve)	4000.	2000.	1400.
(102b)	Irving Lewis (emblem on sleeve)	3500.	1750.	1225.
(103)	Jack Lively	80.00	50.00	25.00
(104a)	Paddy Livingston ("A" on shirt)	450.00	225.00	157.00
(104b)	Paddy Livingston (big "C" on shirt)	350.00	175.00	122.00
(104c)	Paddy Livingston (little "C" on shirt)	110.00	55.00	38.00
(105)	Briscoe Lord (Philadelphia)	80.00	50.00	25.00
(106)	Harry Lord (Chicago)	80.00	50.00	25.00
(107)	Louis Lowdermilk	3500.	1775.	800.00
(108)	Richard Marquard	395.00	180.00	100.00
(109)	Armando Marsans	150.00	75.00	52.00
(110)	George McBride	80.00	50.00	25.00
(111)	Alexander McCarthy	110.00	55.00	38.00
(112)	Edward McDonald	80.00	50.00	25.00
(113)	John J. McGraw	500.00	250.00	175.00
(114)	Harry McIntire	80.00	50.00	25.00
(115)	Matthew McIntyre	80.00	50.00	25.00
(116)	William McKechnie	325.00	162.00	114.00
(117)	Larry McLean	80.00	50.00	25.00
(118)	Clyde Milan	80.00	50.00	25.00
(119)	John B. Miller (Pittsburg)	80.00	50.00	25.00
(120)	Otto Miller (Brooklyn)	100.00	50.00	35.00
(121)	Roy Miller (Boston)	100.00	50.00	35.00
(122)	Ward Miller (Chicago)	1750.	875.00	550.00
(123)	Mike Mitchell (Cleveland, front depicts Willie Mitchell)	100.00	50.00	35.00
(124)	Mike Mitchell (Cincinnati)	80.00	50.00	25.00
(125)	Geo. Mogridge	100.00	50.00	35.00
(126)	Earl Moore	100.00	50.00	35.00
(127)	Patrick J. Moran	80.00	50.00	25.00
(128)	Cy Morgan (Philadelphia)	80.00	50.00	25.00
(129)	Ray Morgan (Washington)	80.00	50.00	25.00
(130)	George Moriarty	100.00	50.00	35.00
(131a)	George Mullin ("D" on cap)	110.00	55.00	38.00
(131b)	George Mullin (no "D" on cap)	110.00	55.00	38.00
(132)	Thomas Needham	80.00	50.00	25.00
(133)	Red Nelson	100.00	50.00	35.00
(134)	Herbert Northen (Hubbard)	80.00	50.00	25.00
(135)	Leslie Nunamaker	80.00	50.00	25.00
(136)	Rebel Oakes	80.00	50.00	25.00
(137)	Buck O'Brien	80.00	50.00	25.00
(138)	Rube Oldring	80.00	50.00	25.00
(139)	Ivan Olson	80.00	50.00	25.00
(140)	Martin J. O'Toole	80.00	50.00	25.00
(141)	George Paskart (Paskert)	80.00	50.00	25.00
(142)	Barney Pelty	100.00	50.00	35.00
(143)	Herbert Perdue	80.00	50.00	25.00
(144)	O.C. Peters	100.00	50.00	35.00
(145)	Arthur Phelan	100.00	50.00	35.00
(146)	Jack Quinn	80.00	50.00	25.00
(147)	Don Carlos Ragan	225.00	112.00	79.00
(148)	Arthur Rasmussen	225.00	112.00	79.00
(149)	Morris Rath	100.00	50.00	35.00
(150)	Edward Reulbach	80.00	50.00	25.00
(151)	Napoleon Rucker	80.00	50.00	25.00
(152)	J.B. Ryan	100.00	50.00	35.00
(153)	Victor Saier	1200.	600.00	420.00
(154)	William Scanlon	80.00	50.00	25.00
(155)	Germany Schaefer	80.00	50.00	25.00
(156)	Wilbur Schardt	80.00	50.00	25.00
(157)	Frank Schulte	80.00	50.00	25.00
(158)	Jim Scott	80.00	50.00	25.00
(159)	Henry Severoid (Severeid)	80.00	50.00	25.00
(160)	Mike Simon	80.00	50.00	25.00
(161)	Frank E. Smith (Cincinnati)	80.00	50.00	25.00
(162)	Wallace Smith (St. Louis)	80.00	50.00	25.00
(163)	Fred Snodgrass	80.00	50.00	25.00
(164)	Tristam Speaker	1250.	625.00	435.00
(165)	Harry Lee Spratt	80.00	50.00	25.00
(166)	Edward Stack	80.00	50.00	25.00
(167)	Oscar Stanage	80.00	50.00	25.00
(168)	William Steele	80.00	50.00	25.00
(169)	Harry Steinfeldt	80.00	50.00	25.00
(170)	George Stovall	80.00	50.00	25.00
(171)	Charles (Gabby) Street	80.00	50.00	25.00
(172)	Amos Strunk	80.00	50.00	25.00
(173)	William Sullivan	80.00	50.00	25.00
(174)	William J. Sweeney	100.00	50.00	35.00
(175)	Leeford Tannehill	80.00	50.00	25.00
(176)	C.D. Thomas	80.00	50.00	25.00
(177)	Joseph Tinker	400.00	175.00	125.00
(178)	Bert Tooley	80.00	50.00	25.00
(179)	Terence Turner (Terrence)	80.00	50.00	25.00
(180)	George Tyler	265.00	132.00	93.00
(181)	Jim Vaughn	80.00	50.00	25.00
(182a)	Chas. (Heinie) Wagner (William Carrigan back)	80.00	50.00	25.00
(182b)	Heinie Wagner (correct back)	80.00	50.00	25.00
(183)	Ed (Dixie) Walker	80.00	50.00	25.00
(184)	Robert Wallace	325.00	162.00	114.00
(185)	John Warhop	80.00	50.00	25.00
(186)	George Weaver	800.00	450.00	250.00
(187)	Zach Wheat	325.00	162.00	114.00
(188)	G. Harris White	110.00	55.00	38.00
(189)	Ernest Wilie	100.00	50.00	35.00
(190)	Bob Williams	80.00	50.00	25.00
(191)	Arthur Wilson (New York)	100.00	50.00	35.00
(192)	Owen Wilson (Pittsburg)	80.00	50.00	25.00
(193)	George Wiltse	80.00	50.00	25.00
(194)	Ivey Wingo	80.00	50.00	25.00
(195)	Harry Wolverton	80.00	50.00	25.00
(196)	Joe Wood	195.00	97.00	68.00
(197)	Eugene Woodburn	100.00	50.00	35.00
(198)	Ralph Works	100.00	50.00	35.00
(199)	Stanley Yerkes	80.00	50.00	25.00
(200)	Rollie Zeider	100.00	50.00	35.00

1914 T216 Peoples Tobacco

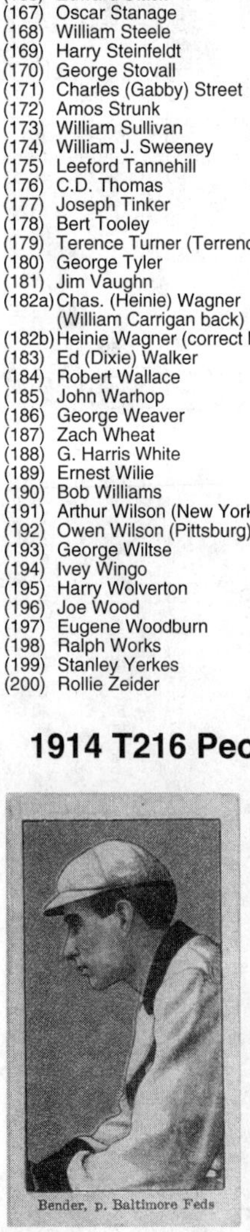
Bender, p. Baltimore Feds

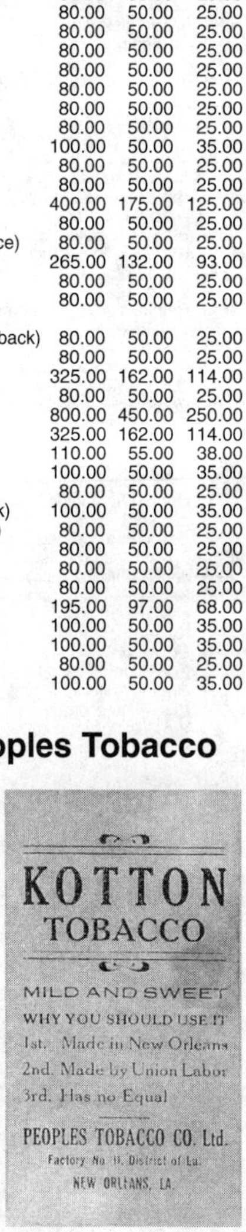
KOTTON
TOBACCO
MILD AND SWEET
WHY YOU SHOULD USE IT
1st. Made in New Orleans
2nd. Made by Union Labor
3rd. Has no Equal
PEOPLES TOBACCO CO. Ltd.
NEW ORLEANS, LA.

The T216 baseball card set, issued by several brands of the Peoples Tobacco Co., is the last of the Louisana cigarette sets and the most confusing. Apparently issued over a period of several years between 1911 and 1916, the set employs the same pictures as several contemporary caramel and bakery sets. Positive identification can be made by the back of the cards. The Peoples Tobacco cards carry advertising for one of three brands of cigarettes: Kotton, Mino or Virginia Extra. The Kotton brand is the most common, while the Virginia Extra and Mino backs command a 50-100% premium. T216 cards are found in two types; one has a glossy front finish, while a second scarcer type is printed on a thin paper. The thin paper cards command an additional 15% premium. The cards represent players from the American, National and Federal Leagues. The complete set price includes only the least expensive of each variation.

		NM	EX	VG
Complete Set (73):		19500.	8800.	4800.
Common Player:		250.00	110.00	65.00
(1)	Jack Barry (batting)	250.00	110.00	65.00
(2)	Jack Barry (fielding)	250.00	110.00	65.00
(3)	Harry Bemis	250.00	110.00	65.00
(4a)	Chief Bender (Philadelphia, striped cap)	500.00	225.00	125.00
(4b)	Chief Bender (Baltimore, striped cap)	500.00	225.00	125.00
(5a)	Chief Bender (Philadelphia, white cap)	500.00	225.00	125.00
(5b)	Chief Bender (Baltimore, white cap)	500.00	225.00	125.00
(6)	Bill Bergen	250.00	110.00	65.00
(7a)	Bob Bescher (Cincinnati)	250.00	110.00	65.00
(7b)	Bob Bescher (St. Louis)	250.00	110.00	65.00
(8)	Roger Bresnahan	500.00	225.00	125.00
(9)	Al Bridwell (batting)	250.00	110.00	65.00
(10a)	Al Bridwell (New York, sliding)	250.00	110.00	65.00
(10b)	Al Bridwell (St. Louis, sliding)	250.00	110.00	65.00
(11)	Donie Bush	250.00	110.00	65.00
(12)	Doc Casey	250.00	110.00	65.00
(13)	Frank Chance	500.00	225.00	125.00
(14a)	Hal Chase (New York, fielding)	250.00	112.00	62.00
(14b)	Hal Chase (Buffalo, fielding)	250.00	112.00	62.00
(15)	Hal Chase (portrait)	250.00	112.00	62.00
(16a)	Ty Cobb (Detroit Am., standing)	3500.	1575.	875.00
(16b)	Ty Cobb (Detroit Americans, standing)	3500.	1575.	875.00
(17)	"Ty" Cobb (batting)	3500.	1575.	875.00
(18a)	Eddie Collins (Phila. Am.)	500.00	225.00	125.00
(18b)	Eddie Collins (Phila. Amer.)	500.00	225.00	125.00
(19)	Eddie Collins (Chicago)	500.00	225.00	125.00
(20a)	Sam Crawford (small print)	500.00	225.00	125.00
(20b)	Sam Crawford (large print)	500.00	225.00	125.00
(21)	Harry Davis	250.00	110.00	65.00
(22)	Ray Demmitt	250.00	110.00	65.00
(23a)	Wild Bill Donovan (Detroit)	250.00	110.00	65.00
(23b)	Wild Bill Donovan (New York)	250.00	110.00	65.00
(24a)	Red Dooin (Philadelphia)	250.00	110.00	65.00
(24b)	Red Dooin (Cincinnati)	250.00	110.00	65.00
(25a)	Mickey Doolan (Philadelphia)	250.00	110.00	65.00
(25b)	Mickey Doolan (Baltimore)	250.00	110.00	65.00
(26)	Patsy Dougherty	250.00	110.00	65.00
(27a)	Larry Doyle, Larry Doyle (N.Y. Nat'l, batting)	250.00	110.00	65.00
(27b)	Larry Doyle (New York Nat'l, batting)	250.00	110.00	65.00
(28)	Larry Doyle (throwing)	250.00	110.00	65.00
(29)	Clyde Engle	250.00	110.00	65.00
(30a)	Johnny Evers (Chicago)	500.00	225.00	125.00
(30b)	Johnny Evers (Boston)	500.00	225.00	125.00
(31)	Art Fromme	250.00	110.00	65.00
(32a)	George Gibson (Pittsburg Nat'l, back view)	250.00	110.00	65.00
(32b)	George Gibson (Pittsburgh Nat'l., back view)	250.00	110.00	65.00
(33a)	George Gibson (Pittsburg Nat'l, front view)	250.00	110.00	65.00
(33b)	George Gibson (Pittsburgh Nat'l., front view)	250.00	110.00	65.00
(34a)	Topsy Hartsel (Phila. Am.)	250.00	110.00	65.00
(34b)	Topsy Hartsel (Phila. Amer.)	250.00	110.00	65.00
(35)	Roy Hartzell (batting)	250.00	110.00	65.00
(36)	Roy Hartzell (catching)	250.00	110.00	65.00
(37a)	Fred Jacklitsch (Philadelphia)	250.00	110.00	65.00
(37b)	Fred Jacklitsch (Baltimore)	250.00	110.00	65.00
(38a)	Hughie Jennings (orange background)	500.00	225.00	125.00
(38b)	Hughie Jennings (red background)	500.00	225.00	125.00
(39)	Red Kleinow	250.00	110.00	65.00
(40a)	Otto Knabe (Philadelphia)	250.00	110.00	65.00
(40b)	Otto Knabe (Baltimore)	250.00	110.00	65.00
(41)	Jack Knight	250.00	110.00	65.00
(42a)	Nap Lajoie (Philadelphia, fielding)	550.00	247.00	137.00
(42b)	Nap Lajoie (Cleveland, fielding)	550.00	247.00	137.00
(43)	Nap Lajoie (portrait)	550.00	247.00	137.00
(44a)	Hans Lobert (Cincinnati)	250.00	110.00	65.00
(44b)	Hans Lobert (New York)	250.00	110.00	65.00
(45)	Sherry Magee	250.00	110.00	65.00
(46)	Rube Marquard	500.00	225.00	125.00
(47a)	Christy Matthewson (Mathewson) (large print)	950.00	425.00	235.00
(47b)	Christy Matthewson (Mathewson) (small print)	950.00	425.00	235.00

		NM	EX	VG
(48a)	John McGraw (large print)	500.00	225.00	125.00
(48b)	John McGraw (small print)	500.00	225.00	125.00
(49)	Larry McLean	250.00	110.00	65.00
(50)	George McQuillan	250.00	110.00	65.00
(51)	Dots Miller (batting)	250.00	110.00	65.00
(52a)	Dots Miller (Pittsburg, fielding)	250.00	110.00	65.00
(52b)	Dots Miller (St. Louis, fielding)	250.00	110.00	65.00
(53a)	Danny Murphy (Philadelphia)	250.00	110.00	65.00
(53b)	Danny Murphy (Brooklyn)	250.00	110.00	65.00
(54)	Rebel Oakes	250.00	110.00	65.00
(55)	Bill O'Hara	250.00	110.00	65.00
(56)	Eddie Plank	500.00	225.00	125.00
(57a)	Germany Schaefer (Washington)	250.00	110.00	65.00
(57b)	Germany Schaefer (Newark)	250.00	110.00	65.00
(58)	Admiral Schlei	250.00	110.00	65.00
(59)	Boss Schmidt	250.00	110.00	65.00
(60)	Johnny Seigle	250.00	110.00	65.00
(61)	Dave Shean	250.00	110.00	65.00
(62)	Boss Smith (Schmidt)	250.00	110.00	65.00
(63)	Tris Speaker	650.00	292.00	162.00
(64)	Oscar Stanage	250.00	110.00	65.00
(65)	George Stovall	250.00	110.00	65.00
(66)	Jeff Sweeney	250.00	110.00	65.00
(67a)	Joe Tinker (Chicago Nat'l, batting)	500.00	225.00	125.00
(67b)	Joe Tinker (Chicago Feds, batting)	500.00	225.00	125.00
(68)	Joe Tinker (portrait)	500.00	225.00	125.00
(69a)	Honus Wagner (batting, S.S.)	1500.	675.00	375.00
(69b)	Honus Wagner (batting, 2b.)	1500.	675.00	375.00
(70a)	Honus Wagner (throwing, S.S.)	1500.	675.00	375.00
(70b)	Honus Wagner (throwing, 2b.)	1500.	675.00	375.00
(71)	Hooks Wiltse	250.00	110.00	65.00
(72)	Cy Young	600.00	270.00	150.00
(73a)	Heinie Zimmerman (2b.)	250.00	110.00	65.00
(73b)	Heinie Zimmerman (3b.)	250.00	110.00	65.00

1914 T222 Fatima Cigarettes

(See 1914 Fatima)

1912 T227 Series Of Champions

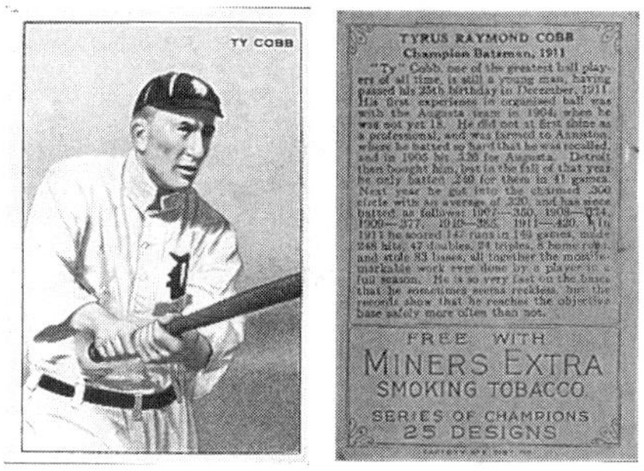

The 1912 "Series of Champions" card set issued by the "Honest Long Cut" and "Miners Extra" tobacco brands features several baseball stars among its 25 famous athletes of the day. Larger than a standard-size tobacco issue, each card in the "Champions" series measures 3-3/8" x 2-5/16". The back includes a relatively lengthy player biography, while the front features a lithograph of the player in action. Although the set includes only four baseball players, these attractive cards are popular among collectors because of the stature of the four players selected. The "Champions" series holds additional significance because it includes the only known baseball cards issued under the "Miners Extra" brand name. The set carries the American Card Catalog designation of T227.

		NM	EX	VG
Complete Set (4):		5500.	2475.	1375.
Common Player:		850.00	425.00	255.00
(1)	"Home Run" Baker	850.00	380.00	210.00
(2)	"Chief" Bender	850.00	380.00	210.00
(3)	Ty Cobb	3300.	1475.	825.00
(4)	Rube Marquard	850.00	380.00	210.00

Check lists with card numbers in parentheses ( ) indicates the numbers do not appear on the cards.

U

1923 U & U

(See 1923 W515-1, W515-2)

1906 Ullman Postcards

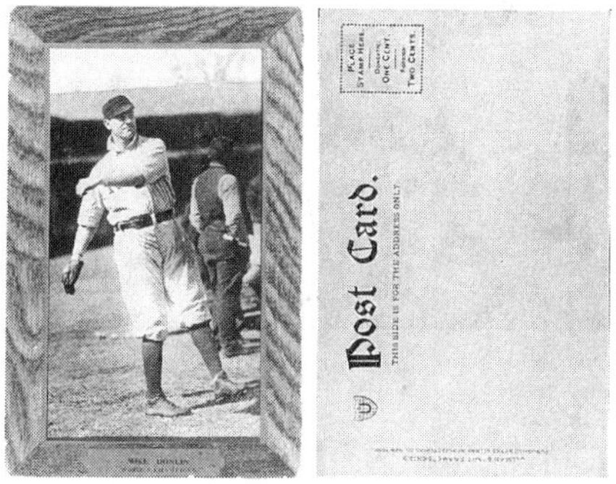

The designation of Giants' players as "World's Champions" dates this issue to 1906. The 3-1/2" x 5-1/2" cards have a black-and-white photo at center, surrounded by a gold-tone frame with a plaque printed in the bottom border. Backs are printed in brown with typical postcard markings and include mention of "Ullman's 'Art Frame' Series". This checklist is likely not complete. The card of "Harry" (name actually Henry) Mathewson is the only known baseball card appearance of Christy's kid brother.

	NM	EX	VG
Leon Ames	600.00	300.00	180.00
Mike Donlin	600.00	300.00	180.00
Christy Mathewson	4000.	2000.	1200.
Harry (Henry) Mathewson	800.00	400.00	240.00
Dan McGann (McGann on 1st Base)	600.00	300.00	180.00
Iron Man McGinnity	800.00	400.00	240.00

1933 Uncle Jacks Candy

One of the lesser-known candy issues of the early 1930s was this New England regional set sponsored by Uncle Jacks, Inc., of Springfield, Mass. and Newport, R.I. The 1-7/8" x 2-7/8" red or blue duotone, blank-backed cards were sold in a see-through wax paper wrapper with a piece of candy and a coupon which could be redeemed (in quantities of 100) for a "league baseball" and a chance at a trip to the 1933 World Series. The set is among those listed in the American Card Catalog under the catchall number R317. The unnumbered cards are checklisted here alphabetically.

		NM	EX	VG
Complete Set (30):		3800.	1900.	1150.
Common Player:		75.00	37.00	22.00
(1)	Earl Averill	145.00	72.00	43.00
(2)	James L. Bottomley	145.00	72.00	43.00
(3)	Ed Brandt	75.00	37.00	22.00
(4)	Ben Chapman	85.00	42.00	25.00
(5)	Gordon Cochrane	145.00	72.00	43.00
(6)	Joe Cronin	145.00	72.00	43.00
(7)	Hazen Cuyler	145.00	72.00	43.00
(8)	George Earnshaw	75.00	37.00	22.00
(9)	Wesley Ferrell	75.00	37.00	22.00
(10)	Jimmie Foxx	175.00	87.00	52.00
(11)	Frank Frisch	145.00	72.00	43.00
(12)	Burleigh Grimes	145.00	72.00	43.00
(13)	"Lefty" Grove	150.00	75.00	45.00
(14)	"Wild Bill" Hallahan	75.00	37.00	22.00
(15)	Leo Hartnett	145.00	72.00	43.00
(16)	"Babe" Herman	75.00	37.00	22.00
(17)	Rogers Hornsby	175.00	87.00	52.00
(18)	Charles Klein	145.00	72.00	43.00
(19)	Tony Lazzeri	145.00	72.00	43.00
(20)	Fred Lindstrom	145.00	72.00	43.00
(21)	Ted Lyons	145.00	72.00	43.00
(22)	"Pepper" Martin	90.00	45.00	27.00
(23)	Herb Pennock	145.00	72.00	43.00
(24)	"Babe" Ruth ("King of Swat")	925.00	460.00	275.00
(25)	Al Simmons	145.00	72.00	43.00
(26)	"Bill" Terry	145.00	72.00	43.00
(27)	"Dazzy" Vance	145.00	72.00	43.00
(28)	Lloyd Waner	145.00	72.00	43.00
(29)	Paul Waner	145.00	72.00	43.00
(30)	Hack Wilson	145.00	72.00	43.00

1958 Union 76 Sports Club Booklets

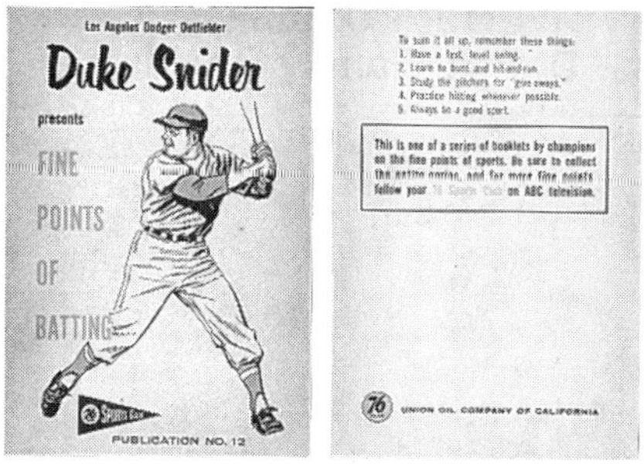

This series of sports instructional booklets was issued by Union Oil in conjunction with its Sports Club television program for youngsters. Besides seven baseball players, the series featured football, track, bowling, skiing and other stars. The booklets are 12 pages and measure about 4" x 5-1/2". Fronts have a drawing of the player and are printed in Union Oil logo colors of orange and blue. The sports tips inside are well illustrated. Books are numbered on front.

		NM	EX	VG
Complete (Baseball) Set (7):		100.00	50.00	30.00
Common Player:		10.00	5.00	3.00
12	Duke Snider	25.00	12.50	7.50
14	Bob Lemon	15.00	7.50	4.50
15	Red Schoendienst	15.00	7.50	4.50
20	Bill Rigney	10.00	5.00	3.00
38	Jackie Jensen	10.00	5.00	3.00
39	Warren Spahn	15.00	7.50	4.50
41	Ernie Banks	22.00	11.00	6.50

1960 Union Oil Dodger Family Booklets

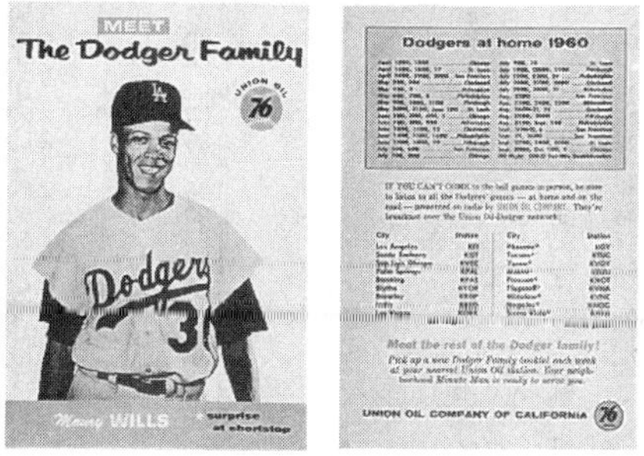

For its first major issue of Dodgers memorabilia, Union 76 gas stations in Southern California distributed a series of booklets profiling players and staff. Each 5-1/2" x 7-1/2" booklet has 16 black-and-white pages highlighted with red graphics. The covers have action poses with many other photos on the inside pages, along with a biography, personal information, career highlights, playing tips, etc. On back is a Dodgers schedule and Union 76 ad. The booklets were distributed on a one-per-week basis. They are listed here in alphabetical order.

		NM	EX	VG
Complete Set (23):		100.00	50.00	30.00
Common Player:				
(1)	Walter Alston	6.00	3.00	1.75
(2)	Roger Craig	4.00	2.00	1.25
(3)	Tom Davis	4.00	2.00	1.25
(4)	Don Demeter	4.00	2.00	1.25
(5)	Don Drysdale	10.00	5.00	3.00
(6)	Chuck Essegian	4.00	2.00	1.25
(7)	Jim Gilliam	6.00	3.00	1.75
(8)	Gil Hodges	10.00	5.00	3.00
(9)	Frank Howard	5.00	2.50	1.50
(10)	Sandy Koufax	25.00	12.50	7.50
(11)	Norm Larker	4.00	2.00	1.25
(12)	Wally Moon	4.50	2.25	1.25
(13)	Charlie Neal	4.00	2.00	1.25
(14)	Johnny Podres	4.50	2.25	1.25
(15)	Ed Roebuck	4.00	2.00	1.25
(16)	John Roseboro	4.00	2.00	1.25
(17)	Larry Sherry	4.00	2.00	1.25
(18)	Norm Sherry	4.00	2.00	1.25
(19)	Duke Snider	10.00	5.00	3.00
(20)	Stan Williams	4.00	2.00	1.25
(21)	Maury Wills	4.50	2.25	1.25
(22)	Coaches (Joe Becker, Bobby Bragan, Greg Mulleavy, Pete Reiser)	4.00	2.00	1.25
(23)	Jerry Doggett, Vin Scully (announcers)	4.00	2.00	1.25

1961 Union Oil Dodger Family Booklets

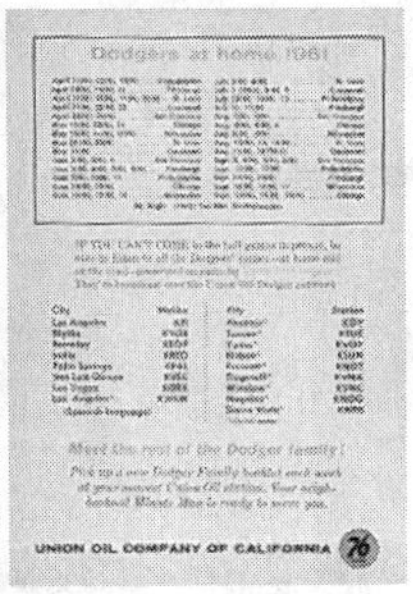

For a second consecutive year, Union 76 gas stations in Southern California distributed a series of booklets profiling team members and staff. The 5-1/2" x 7-1/2" booklets have 16 black-and-white pages highlighted with red graphics. The covers have large portraits while there are many photos on the inside pages, along with a biography, personal information, career highlights, playing tips, etc. On back is a Dodgers schedule and radio network information. The booklets were distributed on a one-per-week basis. They are listed here in alphabetical order.

		NM	EX	VG
Complete Set (24):		225.00	110.00	65.00
Common Player:		8.00	4.00	2.50
(1)	Walter Alston	12.00	6.00	3.50
(2)	Roger Craig	8.00	4.00	2.50
(3)	Tommy Davis	8.00	4.00	2.50
(4)	Willie Davis	8.00	4.00	2.50
(5)	Don Drysdale	20.00	10.00	6.00
(6)	Dick Farrell	8.00	4.00	2.50
(7)	Ron Fairly	8.00	4.00	2.50
(8)	Jim Gilliam	12.00	6.00	3.50
(9)	Gil Hodges	20.00	10.00	6.00
(10)	Frank Howard	8.00	4.00	2.50
(11)	Sandy Koufax	25.00	12.50	7.50
(12)	Norm Larker	8.00	4.00	2.50
(13)	Wally Moon	8.00	4.00	2.50
(14)	Charlie Neal	8.00	4.00	2.50
(15)	Ron Perranoski	8.00	4.00	2.50
(16)	Johnny Podres	8.00	4.00	2.50
(17)	John Roseboro	8.00	4.00	2.50
(18)	Larry Sherry	8.00	4.00	2.50
(19)	Norm Sherry	8.00	4.00	2.50
(20)	Duke Snider	20.00	10.00	6.00
(21)	Daryl Spencer	8.00	4.00	2.50
(22)	Stan Williams	8.00	4.00	2.50
(23)	Maury Wills	8.00	4.00	2.50
(24)	Jerry Doggett, Vin Scully (announcers)	8.00	4.00	2.50

1962 Union Oil Dodgers Premium Pictures

One of many premiums issued by Union Oil during the Dodgers' early years in Los Angeles, this set of player pictures is the most popular with collectors. The 8-1/2" x 11" pictures feature a large color pastel portrait of the player on front, along with a smaller action picture. The player's name is printed in the white border below. The artist's signature and a 1962 copyright are printed below the portrait. Backs are printed in black-and-white and include a career summary and complete minor and major league stats, a profile of sports artist Nicholas Volpe and an ad at bottom for Union Oil and its Union 76 brand of gasoline. The unnumbered pictures are checklisted here alphabetically. It was reported that 200,000 of each picture were produced.

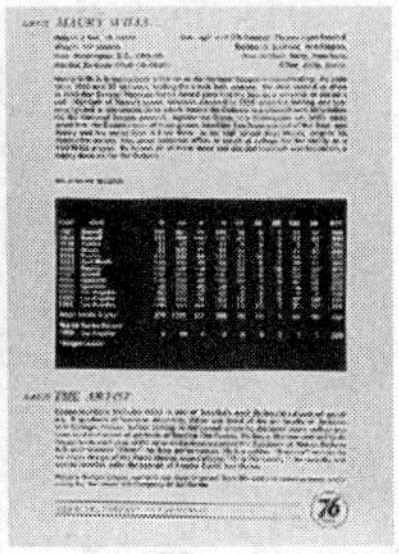

		NM	EX	VG
Complete Set (24):		125.00	62.00	37.00
Common Player:		6.00	3.00	1.75
(1)	Larry Burright	6.00	3.00	1.75
(2)	Doug Camilli	6.00	3.00	1.75
(3)	Andy Carey	6.00	3.00	1.75
(4)	Tom Davis	7.50	3.75	2.25
(5)	Willie Davis	7.50	3.75	2.25
(6)	Don Drysdale	15.00	7.50	4.50
(7)	Ron Fairly	6.00	3.00	1.75
(8)	Jim Gilliam	7.50	3.75	2.25
(9)	Tim Harkness	6.00	3.00	1.75
(10)	Frank Howard	8.00	4.00	2.50
(11)	Sandy Koufax	30.00	15.00	9.00
(12)	Joe Moeller	6.00	3.00	1.75
(13)	Wally Moon	6.00	3.00	1.75
(14)	Ron Perranoski	6.00	3.00	1.75
(15)	Johnny Podres	7.50	3.75	2.25
(16)	Ed Roebuck	6.00	3.00	1.75
(17)	John Roseboro	6.00	3.00	1.75
(18)	Larry Sherry	6.00	3.00	1.75
(19)	Norm Sherry	6.00	3.00	1.75
(20)	Duke Snider	18.00	9.00	5.50
(21)	Daryl Spencer	6.00	3.00	1.75
(22)	Lee Walls	6.00	3.00	1.75
(23)	Stan Williams	6.00	3.00	1.75
(24)	Maury Wills	9.00	4.50	2.75

1964 Union Oil Dodgers Premium Pictures

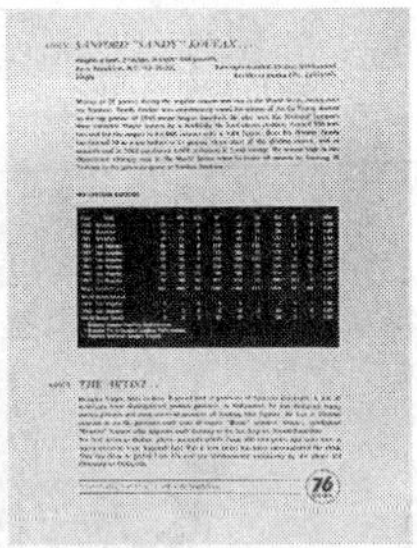

Paired pastel portraits, one in uniform and one in mufti, from sports artist Nicholas Volpe are featured on these large-format (8-1/2" x 11") premium pictures sponsored by Union Oil. The player's name is printed in the bottom border while the artist's signature and copyright date are printed beneath the portraits. Backs are in black-and-white and feature personal data about the player and artist, complete minor and major league stats and Union Oil/Union 76 logos. The unnumbered pictures are checklisted here alphabetically.

		NM	EX	VG
Complete Set (18):		90.00	45.00	27.00
Common Player:		6.00	3.00	1.75
(1)	Tommy Davis	7.50	3.75	2.25
(2)	Willie Davis	7.50	3.75	2.25
(3)	Don Drysdale	16.00	8.00	4.75
(4)	Ron Fairly	6.00	3.00	1.75
(5)	Jim Gilliam	7.50	3.75	2.25
(6)	Frank Howard	8.00	4.00	2.50
(7)	Sandy Koufax	22.00	11.00	6.50
(8)	Bob Miller	6.00	3.00	1.75
(9)	Joe Moeller	6.00	3.00	1.75
(10)	Wally Moon	6.00	3.00	1.75
(11)	Phil Ortega	6.00	3.00	1.75
(12)	Wes Parker	6.00	3.00	1.75
(13)	Ron Perranoski	6.00	3.00	1.75
(14)	John Podres	7.00	3.50	2.00
(15)	John Roseboro	6.00	3.00	1.75
(16)	Dick Tracewski	6.00	3.00	1.75
(17)	Lee Walls	6.00	3.00	1.75
(18)	Maury Wills	7.50	3.75	2.25

1969 Union Oil Dodgers Premium Pictures

These 8-1/2" x 11" cards were given to fans attending week night "Player Portrait Night" promotional games. The premiums are similar in format to earlier and later sets sponsored by Union Oil and created by sports artist Nicholas Volpe. Fronts have pastel player portraits and action drawings against a black background. Backs are in black-and-white and have player biographies, stats and a career summary, along with a word about the artist and an ad for Union Oil/Union 76. The unnumbered pictures are checklisted here alphabetically.

		NM	EX	VG
Complete Set (13):		75.00	37.00	22.00
Common Player:		6.00	3.00	1.75
(1)	Walt Alston	9.00	4.50	2.75
(2)	Jim Brewer	6.00	3.00	1.75
(3)	Willie Davis	7.50	3.75	2.25
(4)	Don Drysdale	17.50	8.75	5.25
(5)	Ron Fairly	6.00	3.00	1.75
(6)	Tom Haller	6.00	3.00	1.75
(7)	Jim Lefebvre	6.00	3.00	1.75
(8)	Claude Osteen	6.00	3.00	1.75
(9)	Wes Parker	6.00	3.00	1.75
(10)	Paul Popovich	6.00	3.00	1.75
(11)	Bill Singer	6.00	3.00	1.75
(12)	Bill Sudakis	6.00	3.00	1.75
(13)	Don Sutton	10.00	5.00	3.00

1925 Universal Toy & Novelty Brooklyn Dodgers

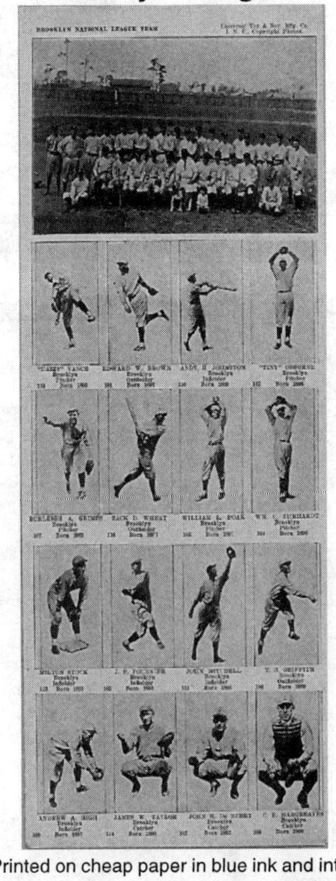

Printed on cheap paper in blue ink and intended to be cut apart into a team photo and 16 individual player cards, this set was originally issued on a 5-1/2" x 13" sheet. Single cut cards measure about 1-3/8" x 2-3/8," with the team picture about 5" x 3-1/2". Cards are blank-backed. Player cards are numbered in alphabetical order beneath the photo, where the name, team, position and birth year are also printed.

		NM	EX	VG
Complete Sheet:		750.00	370.00	225.00
Complete Set, Singles (17):		450.00	225.00	135.00
Common Player:		25.00	12.50	7.50
101	Edward W. Brown	25.00	12.50	7.50
102	John H. DeBerry	25.00	12.50	7.50
103	William L. Doak	25.00	12.50	7.50
104	Wm. C. Ehrhardt (first name Welton)	25.00	12.50	7.50
105	J.F. Fournier	25.00	12.50	7.50
106	Tommy Griffith	25.00	12.50	7.50
107	Burleigh A. Grimes	45.00	22.00	13.50
108	C.P. Hargreaves	25.00	12.50	7.50
109	Andrew A. High	25.00	12.50	7.50
110	Andy. H. Johnston (first name Jimmy)	25.00	12.50	7.50
111	Johnny Mitchell	25.00	12.50	7.50
112	"Tiny" Osborne	25.00	12.50	7.50
113	Milton Stock	25.00	12.50	7.50
114	James W. Taylor	25.00	12.50	7.50
115	"Dazzy" Vance	45.00	22.00	13.50
116	Zack D. Wheat	45.00	22.00	13.50
---	Brooklyn National League team photo	175.00	85.00	50.00

1925 Universal Toy & Novelty N.Y. Yankees

Printed on thick cardboard and intended to be cut apart into a team photo and 16 individual player cards, this set was originally issued on a 5-1/2" x 13" sheet. Single cut cards measure about 1-3/8" x 2-3/8", with the team picture about 5" x 3-1/2". Cards are blank-backed. Player cards are numbered in alphabetical order beneath the photo, where the name, team, position and birth year are also printed.

		NM	EX	VG
Complete Sheet:				
Complete Set (17):				
Common Player:		30.00	15.00	9.00
117				
118				
119				
120				
121	Robert Meusel	30.00	15.00	9.00
122				
123	Babe Ruth	300.00	150.00	90.00
124				
125	Robert J. Shawkey	30.00	15.00	9.00
126				
127	Urban Shocker	30.00	15.00	9.00
128				
129				
130				
131	Miller Huggins	45.00	22.00	13.50
132				
----	New York American League Team Photo	200.00	100.00	60.00

1932 U.S. Caramel

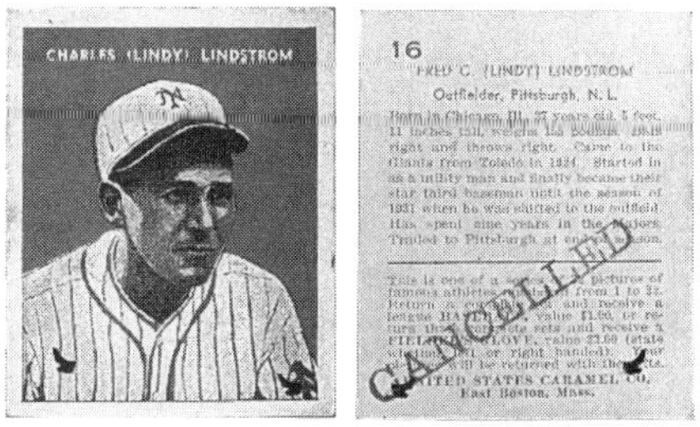

Produced by a Boston confectioner, this set is not limited to baseball, but is a set of 32 "Famous Athletes" of which 27 are baseball players. The 2-1/2" x 3" cards have a black-and-white picture on the front with a red background and white border. The player's name appears in white above the picture. Backs feature the player's name, position, team and league as well as a redemption ad and card number. The cards were among the last of the caramel card sets and are very scarce today. The cards could be redeemed for a baseball and baseball glove. Card #16 was discovered in the late 1980s and is not included in the complete set price; only two examples are currently known.

		NM	EX	VG
Complete Set, No #16 (31):		22000.	9900.	5500.
Common Player:		425.00	191.00	106.00
1	Edward T. (Eddie) Collins	695.00	313.00	174.00
2	Paul (Big Poison) Waner	550.00	247.00	137.00
3	Robert T. (Bobby) Jones (golfer)	695.00	313.00	174.00
4	William (Bill) Terry	550.00	247.00	137.00
5	Earl B. Combs (Earle)	550.00	247.00	137.00
6	William (Bill) Dickey	725.00	326.00	181.00
7	Joseph (Joe) Cronin	695.00	313.00	174.00
8	Charles (Chick) Hafey	550.00	247.00	137.00
9	Gene Sarazen (golfer)	600.00	270.00	150.00
10	Walter (Rabbit) Maranville	550.00	247.00	137.00
11	Rogers (Rajah) Hornsby	875.00	395.00	220.00
12	Gordon (Mickey) Cochrane	550.00	247.00	137.00
13	Lloyd (Little Poison) Waner	550.00	247.00	137.00
14	Tyrus (Ty) Cobb	2750.	1200.	650.00
15	Eugene (Gene) Tunney (boxer)	600.00	270.00	150.00
16	Charles (Lindy) Lindstrom (2 known)	90000.	35000.	17500.
17	Al. Simmons	550.00	247.00	137.00
18	Anthony (Tony) Lazzeri	550.00	247.00	137.00
19	Walter (Wally) Berger	425.00	191.00	106.00
20	Charles (Large Charlie) Ruffing	550.00	247.00	137.00
21	Charles (Chuck) Klein	550.00	247.00	137.00
22	John (Jack) Dempsey (boxer)	825.00	371.00	206.00
23	James (Jimmy) Foxx	875.00	395.00	220.00
24	Frank J. (Lefty) O'Doul	425.00	190.00	105.00
25	Jack (Sailor Jack) Sharkey (boxer)	300.00	135.00	75.00
26	Henry (Lou) Gehrig	3500.	1575.	875.00
27	Robert (Lefty) Grove	800.00	360.00	200.00
28	Edward Brant (Brandt)	435.00	196.00	109.00
29	George Earnshaw	435.00	196.00	109.00
30	Frank (Frankie) Frisch	695.00	313.00	174.00
31	Vernon (Lefty) Gomez	725.00	326.00	181.00
32	George (Babe) Ruth	4750.	2000.	1100.

1973 U.S. Playing Card Ruth/Gehrig

These decks of playing cards were produced for sale by the Smithsonian Institution in Washington, D.C. The 2-1/4" x 3-1/2" cards were sold as a pair. Backs have colorized pictures of the Yankees greats; Ruth on an orange background and Gehrig on red.

	NM	EX	VG
Complete Set, Ruth (54):	25.00	12.50	7.50
Single Card, Ruth:	1.50	.75	.45
Complete Set, Gehrig (54):	15.00	7.50	4.50
Single Card, Gehrig:	.75	.40	.25

(A 50% premium attaches to a complete boxed pair of decks.)

1909-11 Uzit Cigarettes

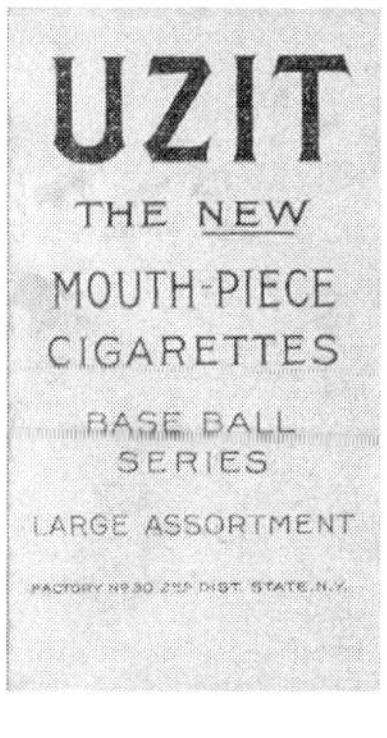

(See T206. Premium: 3-5X.)

Many vintage-section card sets are indexed under both their common name and their American Card Catalog designation.

V

1938-39 Val Decker Packing Co. Cincinnati Reds postcards

(See 1937-39 Orcajo Cincinnati Reds postcards for checklist and values.)

1966 Van Heusen Phillies

Not a great deal is known about these 8"x 10" black-and-white player portraits. The year of issue is conjectural based on the players thus far known. It is possible the checklist here is not complete. The photos are bordered in white. At lower-right is the logo of the clothing manufacturer.

		NM
Common Player:		8.00
(1)	Bo Belinsky	12.00
(2)	Jim Bunning	15.00
(3)	Wes Covington	8.00
(4)	Dick Groat	12.00
(5)	Chris Short	8.00
(6)	Bill White	8.00

1959 Venezuela Topps

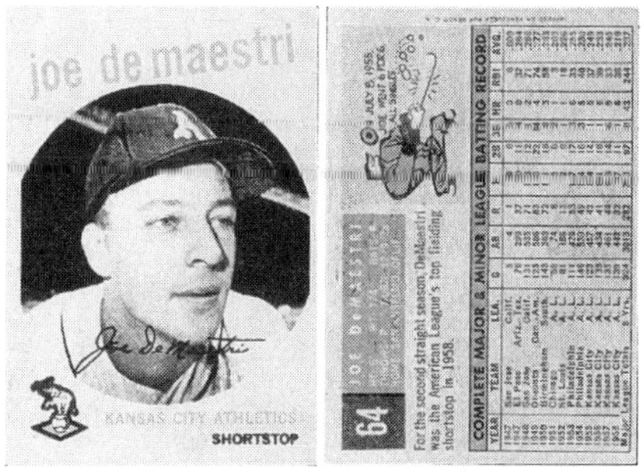

Beginning in 1959, Topps began marketing baseball cards in Venezuela, always a hotbed of baseball fandom. In most years, such as the debut set in 1959, the cards destined for the South American market represented a parallel of the first couple of series of Topps' regular U.S. issue. Print quality (usually lack of gloss on front) is the major difference between the two issues. Backs of some of the 1959 Venezuelan cards carry the credit line: "Impreso en Venezuela por Benco C.A." A reality of the Venezuelan cards is that they tend to survive in low-grade condition due to the local custom of gluing cards into albums and scrapbooks. After its 1959 issue, Topps produced Venezuelan cards only in the even numbered years, except for 1967, until the last of the sets was issued in 1968.

		NM	EX	VG
Complete Set (196):		10000.	4000.	2400.
Common Player:		45.00	18.00	11.00
1	Ford Frick	60.00	24.00	14.50
2	Eddie Yost	45.00	18.00	11.00
3	Don McMahon	45.00	18.00	11.00
4	Albie Pearson	45.00	18.00	11.00
5	Dick Donovan	45.00	18.00	11.00
6	Alex Grammas	45.00	18.00	11.00
7	Al Pilarcik	45.00	18.00	11.00
8	Phillies Team	75.00	30.00	18.00
9	Paul Giel	45.00	18.00	11.00
10	Mickey Mantle	2000.	800.00	500.00
11	Billy Hunter	45.00	18.00	11.00
12	Vern Law	45.00	18.00	11.00
13	Dick Gernert	45.00	18.00	11.00
14	Pete Whisenant	45.00	18.00	11.00
15	Dick Drott	45.00	18.00	11.00
16	Joe Pignatano	45.00	18.00	11.00
17	Danny's All-Stars (Ted Kluszewski, Danny Murtaugh, Frank Thomas)	50.00	20.00	12.00
18	Jack Urban	45.00	18.00	11.00
19	Ed Bressoud	45.00	18.00	11.00
20	Duke Snider	200.00	80.00	48.00
21	Connie Johnson	45.00	18.00	11.00
22	Al Smith	45.00	18.00	11.00
23	Murry Dickson	45.00	18.00	11.00
24	Red Wilson	45.00	18.00	11.00
25	Don Hoak	45.00	18.00	11.00
26	Chuck Stobbs	45.00	18.00	11.00
27	Andy Pafko	45.00	18.00	11.00
28	Red Worthington	45.00	18.00	11.00
29	Jim Bolger	45.00	18.00	11.00
30	Nellie Fox	100.00	40.00	24.00
31	Ken Lehman	45.00	18.00	11.00
32	Don Buddin	45.00	18.00	11.00
33	Ed Fitz Gerald	45.00	18.00	11.00
34	Pitchers Beware (Al Kaline, Charlie Maxwell)	90.00	36.00	22.00
35	Ted Kluszewski	60.00	24.00	14.50
36	Hank Aguirre	45.00	18.00	11.00
37	Gene Green	45.00	18.00	11.00
38	Morrie Martin	45.00	18.00	11.00
39	Ed Bouchee	45.00	18.00	11.00
40	Warren Spahn	125.00	50.00	30.00
41	Bob Martyn	45.00	18.00	11.00
42	Murray Wall	45.00	18.00	11.00
43	Steve Bilko	45.00	18.00	11.00
44	Vito Valentinetti	45.00	18.00	11.00
45	Andy Carey	45.00	18.00	11.00
46	Bill Henry	45.00	18.00	11.00
47	Jim Finigan	45.00	18.00	11.00
48	Orioles Team/Checklist 1-88	75.00	30.00	18.00
49	Bill Hall	45.00	18.00	11.00
50	Willie Mays	450.00	180.00	108.00
51	Rip Coleman	45.00	18.00	11.00
52	Coot Veal	45.00	18.00	11.00
53	Stan Williams	45.00	18.00	11.00
54	Mel Roach	45.00	18.00	11.00
55	Tom Brewer	45.00	18.00	11.00
56	Carl Sawatski	45.00	18.00	11.00
57	Al Cicotte	45.00	18.00	11.00
58	Eddie Miksis	45.00	18.00	11.00
59	Irv Noren	45.00	18.00	11.00
60	Bob Turley	45.00	18.00	11.00
61	Dick Brown	45.00	18.00	11.00
62	Tony Taylor	45.00	18.00	11.00
63	Jim Hearn	45.00	18.00	11.00
64	Joe DeMaestri	45.00	18.00	11.00
65	Frank Torre	45.00	18.00	11.00
66	Joe Ginsberg	45.00	18.00	11.00
67	Brooks Lawrence	45.00	18.00	11.00
68	Dick Schofield	45.00	18.00	11.00
69	Giants Team/Checklist 89-176	75.00	30.00	18.00
70	Harvey Kuenn	50.00	20.00	12.00
71	Don Bessent	45.00	18.00	11.00
72	Bill Renna	45.00	18.00	11.00
73	Ron Jackson	45.00	18.00	11.00
74	Directing the Power (Cookie Lavagetto, Jim Lemon, Roy Sievers)	45.00	18.00	11.00
75	Sam Jones	45.00	18.00	11.00
76	Bobby Richardson	50.00	20.00	12.00
77	John Goryl	45.00	18.00	11.00
78	Pedro Ramos	45.00	18.00	11.00
79	Harry Chiti	45.00	18.00	11.00
80	Minnie Minoso	55.00	22.00	13.00
81	Hal Jeffcoat	45.00	18.00	11.00
82	Bob Boyd	45.00	18.00	11.00
83	Bob Smith	45.00	18.00	11.00
84	Reno Bertoia	45.00	18.00	11.00
85	Harry Anderson	45.00	18.00	11.00
86	Bob Keegan	45.00	18.00	11.00
87	Danny O'Connell	45.00	18.00	11.00
88	Herb Score	45.00	18.00	11.00
89	Billy Gardner	45.00	18.00	11.00
90	Bill Skowron	55.00	22.00	13.00
91	Herb Moford	45.00	18.00	11.00
92	Dave Philley	45.00	18.00	11.00
93	Julio Becquer	45.00	18.00	11.00
94	White Sox Team	100.00	40.00	24.00
95	Carl Willey	45.00	18.00	11.00
96	Lou Berberet	45.00	18.00	11.00
97	Jerry Lynch	45.00	18.00	11.00
98	Arnie Portocarrero	45.00	18.00	11.00
99	Ted Kazanski	45.00	18.00	11.00
100	Bob Cerv	45.00	18.00	11.00
101	Alex Kellner	45.00	18.00	11.00
102	Felipe Alou	60.00	24.00	14.50
103	Billy Goodman	45.00	18.00	11.00
104	Del Rice	45.00	18.00	11.00
105	Lee Walls	45.00	18.00	11.00
106	Hal Woodeshick	45.00	18.00	11.00
107	Norm Larker	45.00	18.00	11.00
108	Zack Monroe	45.00	18.00	11.00
109	Bob Schmidt	45.00	18.00	11.00
110	George Witt	45.00	18.00	11.00
111	Redlegs Team/Checklist 89-176	75.00	30.00	18.00
112	Billy Consolo	45.00	18.00	11.00
113	Taylor Phillips	45.00	18.00	11.00
114	Earl Battey	45.00	18.00	11.00
115	Mickey Vernon	45.00	18.00	11.00
116	Bob Allison	45.00	18.00	11.00
117	John Blanchard	45.00	18.00	11.00
118	John Buzhardt	45.00	18.00	11.00
119	John Callison	45.00	18.00	11.00
120	Chuck Coles	45.00	18.00	11.00
121	Bob Conley	45.00	18.00	11.00
122	Bennie Daniels	45.00	18.00	11.00
123	Don Dillard	45.00	18.00	11.00
124	Dan Dobbek	45.00	18.00	11.00
125	Ron Fairly	45.00	18.00	11.00
126	Eddie Haas	45.00	18.00	11.00
127	Kent Hadley	45.00	18.00	11.00
128	Bob Hartman	45.00	18.00	11.00
129	Frank Herrera	45.00	18.00	11.00
130	Lou Jackson	45.00	18.00	11.00
131	Deron Johnson	50.00	20.00	12.00
132	Don Lee	45.00	18.00	11.00
133	Bob Lillis	45.00	18.00	11.00
134	Jim McDaniel	45.00	18.00	11.00
135	Gene Oliver	45.00	18.00	11.00
136	Jim O'Toole	45.00	18.00	11.00
137	Dick Ricketts	45.00	18.00	11.00
138	John Romano	45.00	18.00	11.00
139	Ed Sadowski	45.00	18.00	11.00
140	Charlie Secrest	45.00	18.00	11.00
141	Joe Shipley	45.00	18.00	11.00
142	Dick Stigman	45.00	18.00	11.00
143	Willie Tasby	45.00	18.00	11.00
144	Jerry Walker	45.00	18.00	11.00
145	Dom Zanni	45.00	18.00	11.00
146	Jerry Zimmerman	45.00	18.00	11.00
147	Cubs' Clubbers (Ernie Banks, Dale Long, Walt Moryn)	90.00	36.00	22.00
148	Mike McCormick	45.00	18.00	11.00
149	Jim Bunning	100.00	40.00	24.00
150	Stan Musial	400.00	160.00	100.00
151	Bob Malkmus	45.00	18.00	11.00
152	Johnny Klippstein	45.00	18.00	11.00
153	Jim Marshall	45.00	18.00	11.00
154	Ray Herbert	45.00	18.00	11.00
155	Enos Slaughter	90.00	36.00	22.00
156	Ace Hurlers (Billy Pierce, Robin Roberts)	65.00	26.00	15.50
157	Felix Mantilla	45.00	18.00	11.00
158	Walt Dropo	45.00	18.00	11.00
159	Bob Shaw	45.00	18.00	11.00
160	Dick Groat	45.00	18.00	11.00
161	Frank Baumann	45.00	18.00	11.00
162	Bobby G. Smith	45.00	18.00	11.00
163	Sandy Koufax	350.00	140.00	85.00
164	Johnny Groth	45.00	18.00	11.00
165	Bill Bruton	45.00	18.00	11.00
166	Destruction Crew (Rocky Colavito, Larry Doby, Minnie Minoso)	125.00	50.00	30.00
167	Duke Maas	45.00	18.00	11.00
168	Carroll Hardy	45.00	18.00	11.00
169	Ted Abernathy	45.00	18.00	11.00
170	Gene Woodling	45.00	18.00	11.00
171	Willard Schmidt	45.00	18.00	11.00
172	A's Team/Checklist 177-242	75.00	30.00	18.00
173	Bill Monbouquette	45.00	18.00	11.00
174	Jim Pendleton	45.00	18.00	11.00
175	Dick Farrell	45.00	18.00	11.00
176	Preston Ward	45.00	18.00	11.00
177	Johnny Briggs	45.00	18.00	11.00
178	Ruben Amaro	45.00	18.00	11.00
179	Don Rudolph	45.00	18.00	11.00
180	Yogi Berra	200.00	80.00	48.00
181	Bob Porterfield	45.00	18.00	11.00
182	Milt Graff	45.00	18.00	11.00
183	Stu Miller	45.00	18.00	11.00
184	Harvey Haddix	45.00	18.00	11.00
185	Jim Busby	45.00	18.00	11.00
186	Mudcat Grant	45.00	18.00	11.00
187	Bubba Phillips	45.00	18.00	11.00
188	Juan Pizarro	45.00	18.00	11.00
189	Neil Chrisley	45.00	18.00	11.00
190	Bill Virdon	45.00	18.00	11.00
191	Russ Kemmerer	45.00	18.00	11.00
192	Charley Beamon	45.00	18.00	11.00
193	Sammy Taylor	45.00	18.00	11.00
194	Jim Brosnan	45.00	18.00	11.00
195	Rip Repulski	45.00	18.00	11.00
196	Billy Moran	45.00	18.00	11.00

1960 Venezuela Topps

Unlike its 1959 issue, which had a printed-in-Venezuela notice on the backs, Topps' 1960 issue for that South American market is virtually identical, front and back to the company's U.S. product. Only a difference in cardboard stock differentiates the two; the Venezuelan cards have no gloss on the front. The Latin American version is a parallel of the first 198 cards from Topps' set. As usual with Latin American cards, low-grade examples are the norm due to the local collecting custom of pasting cards into albums and scrapbooks.

		NM	EX	VG
Complete Set (198):		7900.	3150.	1900.
Common Player:		40.00	16.00	9.50
1	Early Wynn	95.00	30.00	20.00
2	Roman Mejias	40.00	16.00	9.50
3	Joe Adcock	40.00	16.00	9.50
4	Bob Purkey	40.00	16.00	9.50
5	Wally Moon	40.00	16.00	9.50
6	Lou Berberet	40.00	16.00	9.50
7	Master and Mentor (Willie Mays, Bill Rigney)	125.00	50.00	30.00
8	Bud Daley	40.00	16.00	9.50
9	Faye Throneberry	40.00	16.00	9.50
10	Ernie Banks	150.00	60.00	36.00
11	Norm Siebern	40.00	16.00	9.50
12	Milt Pappas	40.00	16.00	9.50
13	Wally Post	40.00	16.00	9.50
14	Jim Grant	40.00	16.00	9.50
15	Pete Runnels	40.00	16.00	9.50
16	Ernie Broglio	40.00	16.00	9.50
17	Johnny Callison	40.00	16.00	9.50
18	Dodgers Team/Checklist 1-88	100.00	40.00	24.00
19	Felix Mantilla	40.00	16.00	9.50
20	Roy Face	40.00	16.00	9.50
21	Dutch Dotterer	40.00	16.00	9.50
22	Rocky Bridges	40.00	16.00	9.50
23	Eddie Fisher	40.00	16.00	9.50
24	Dick Gray	40.00	16.00	9.50
25	Roy Sievers	40.00	16.00	9.50
26	Wayne Terwilliger	40.00	16.00	9.50
27	Dick Drott	40.00	16.00	9.50
28	Brooks Robinson	150.00	60.00	36.00
29	Clem Labine	40.00	16.00	9.50
30	Tito Francona	40.00	16.00	9.50
31	Sammy Esposito	40.00	16.00	9.50
32	Sophomore Stalwarts (Jim O'Toole, Vada Pinson)	40.00	16.00	9.50
33	Tom Morgan	40.00	16.00	9.50
34	Sparky Anderson	90.00	45.00	27.00
35	Whitey Ford	150.00	60.00	36.00
36	Russ Nixon	40.00	16.00	9.50
37	Bill Bruton	40.00	16.00	9.50
38	Jerry Casale	40.00	16.00	9.50
39	Earl Averill	40.00	16.00	9.50
40	Joe Cunningham	40.00	16.00	9.50
41	Barry Latman	40.00	16.00	9.50
42	Hobie Landrith	40.00	16.00	9.50
43	Senators Team/Checklist 1-88	75.00	30.00	18.00
44	Bobby Locke	40.00	16.00	9.50
45	Roy McMillan	40.00	16.00	9.50
46	Jack Fisher	40.00	16.00	9.50
47	Don Zimmer	40.00	16.00	9.50
48	Hal Smith	40.00	16.00	9.50
49	Curt Raydon	40.00	16.00	9.50
50	Al Kaline	150.00	60.00	36.00
51	Jim Coates	40.00	16.00	9.50
52	Dave Philley	40.00	16.00	9.50
53	Jackie Brandt	40.00	16.00	9.50
54	Mike Fornieles	40.00	16.00	9.50
55	Bill Mazeroski	80.00	40.00	24.00
56	Steve Korcheck	40.00	16.00	9.50
57	Win-Savers (Turk Lown, Gerry Staley)	40.00	16.00	9.50
58	Gino Cimoli	40.00	16.00	9.50
59	Juan Pizarro	40.00	16.00	9.50
60	Gus Triandos	40.00	16.00	9.50
61	Eddie Kasko	40.00	16.00	9.50
62	Roger Craig	40.00	16.00	9.50
63	George Strickland	40.00	16.00	9.50
64	Jack Meyer	40.00	16.00	9.50
65	Elston Howard	45.00	18.00	11.00
66	Bob Trowbridge	40.00	16.00	9.50
67	Jose Pagan	40.00	16.00	9.50
68	Dave Hillman	40.00	16.00	9.50
69	Billy Goodman	40.00	16.00	9.50
70	Lou Burdette	40.00	16.00	9.50
71	Marty Keough	40.00	16.00	9.50
72	Tigers Team/Checklist 89-176	75.00	30.00	18.00
73	Bob Gibson	100.00	40.00	24.00
74	Walt Moryn	40.00	16.00	9.50
75	Vic Power	40.00	16.00	9.50
76	Bill Fischer	40.00	16.00	9.50
77	Hank Foiles	40.00	16.00	9.50
78	Bob Grim	40.00	16.00	9.50
79	Walt Dropo	40.00	16.00	9.50
80	Johnny Antonelli	40.00	16.00	9.50
81	Russ Snyder	40.00	16.00	9.50
82	Ruben Gomez	40.00	16.00	9.50
83	Tony Kubek	40.00	16.00	9.50
84	Hal Smith	40.00	16.00	9.50
85	Frank Lary	40.00	16.00	9.50
86	Dick Gernert	40.00	16.00	9.50
87	John Romonosky	40.00	16.00	9.50
88	John Roseboro	40.00	16.00	9.50
89	Hal Brown	40.00	16.00	9.50
90	Bobby Avila	40.00	16.00	9.50
91	Bennie Daniels	40.00	16.00	9.50
92	Whitey Herzog	45.00	18.00	11.00
93	Art Schult	40.00	16.00	9.50
94	Leo Kiely	40.00	16.00	9.50
95	Frank Thomas	40.00	16.00	9.50
96	Ralph Terry	40.00	16.00	9.50

97	Ted Lepcio	40.00	16.00	9.50
98	Gordon Jones	40.00	16.00	9.50
99	Lenny Green	40.00	16.00	9.50
100	Nellie Fox	90.00	36.00	22.00
101	Bob Miller	40.00	16.00	9.50
102	Kent Hadley	40.00	16.00	9.50
103	Dick Farrell	40.00	16.00	9.50
104	Dick Schofield	40.00	16.00	9.50
105	Larry Sherry	40.00	16.00	9.50
106	Billy Gardner	40.00	16.00	9.50
107	Carl Willey	40.00	16.00	9.50
108	Pete Daley	40.00	16.00	9.50
109	Cletis Boyer	40.00	16.00	9.50
110	Cal McLish	40.00	16.00	9.50
111	Vic Wertz	40.00	16.00	9.50
112	Jack Harshman	40.00	16.00	9.50
113	Bob Skinner	40.00	16.00	9.50
114	Ken Aspromonte	40.00	16.00	9.50
115	Fork and Knuckler (Roy Face, Hoyt Wilhelm)	45.00	18.00	11.00
116	Jim Rivera	40.00	16.00	9.50
117	Tom Borland	40.00	16.00	9.50
118	Bob Bruce	40.00	16.00	9.50
119	Chico Cardenas	40.00	16.00	9.50
120	Duke Carmel	40.00	16.00	9.50
121	Camilo Carreon	40.00	16.00	9.50
122	Don Dillard	40.00	16.00	9.50
123	Dan Dobbek	40.00	16.00	9.50
124	Jim Donohue	40.00	16.00	9.50
125	Dick Ellsworth	40.00	16.00	9.50
126	Chuck Estrada	40.00	16.00	9.50
127	Ronnie Hansen	40.00	16.00	9.50
128	Bill Harris	40.00	16.00	9.50
129	Bob Hartman	40.00	16.00	9.50
130	Frank Herrera	40.00	16.00	9.50
131	Ed Hobaugh	40.00	16.00	9.50
132	Frank Howard	50.00	20.00	12.00
133	Manuel Javier	40.00	16.00	9.50
134	Deron Johnson	45.00	18.00	11.00
135	Ken Johnson	40.00	16.00	9.50
136	Jim Kaat	60.00	24.00	14.50
137	Lou Klimchock	40.00	16.00	9.50
138	Art Mahaffey	40.00	16.00	9.50
139	Carl Mathias	40.00	16.00	9.50
140	Julio Navarro	40.00	16.00	9.50
141	Jim Proctor	40.00	16.00	9.50
142	Bill Short	40.00	16.00	9.50
143	Al Spangler	40.00	16.00	9.50
144	Al Stieglitz	40.00	16.00	9.50
145	Jim Umbricht	40.00	16.00	9.50
146	Ted Wieand	40.00	16.00	9.50
147	Bob Will	40.00	16.00	9.50
148	Carl Yastrzemski	450.00	225.00	135.00
149	Bob Nieman	40.00	16.00	9.50
150	Billy Pierce	40.00	16.00	9.50
151	Giants Team/Checklist 177-264	75.00	30.00	18.00
152	Gail Harris	40.00	16.00	9.50
153	Bobby Thomson	40.00	16.00	9.50
154	Jim Davenport	40.00	16.00	9.50
155	Charlie Neal	40.00	16.00	9.50
156	Art Ceccarelli	40.00	16.00	9.50
157	Rocky Nelson	40.00	16.00	9.50
158	Wes Covington	40.00	16.00	9.50
159	Jim Piersall	45.00	18.00	11.00
160	Rival All-Stars (Ken Boyer, Mickey Mantle)	600.00	250.00	150.00
161	Ray Narleski	40.00	16.00	9.50
162	Sammy Taylor	40.00	16.00	9.50
163	Hector Lopez	40.00	16.00	9.50
164	Reds Team/Checklist 89-176	75.00	30.00	18.00
165	Jack Sanford	40.00	16.00	9.50
166	Chuck Essegian	40.00	16.00	9.50
167	Valmy Thomas	40.00	16.00	9.50
168	Alex Grammas	40.00	16.00	9.50
169	Jake Striker	40.00	16.00	9.50
170	Del Crandall	40.00	16.00	9.50
171	Johnny Groth	40.00	16.00	9.50
172	Willie Kirkland	40.00	16.00	9.50
173	Billy Martin	45.00	18.00	11.00
174	Indians Team/Checklist 89-176	75.00	30.00	18.00
175	Pedro Ramos	40.00	16.00	9.50
176	Vada Pinson	45.00	18.00	11.00
177	Johnny Kucks	40.00	16.00	9.50
178	Woody Held	40.00	16.00	9.50
179	Rip Coleman	40.00	16.00	9.50
180	Harry Simpson	40.00	16.00	9.50
181	Billy Loes	40.00	16.00	9.50
182	Glen Hobbie	40.00	16.00	9.50
183	Eli Grba	40.00	16.00	9.50
184	Gary Geiger	40.00	16.00	9.50
185	Jim Owens	40.00	16.00	9.50
186	Dave Sisler	40.00	16.00	9.50
187	Jay Hook	40.00	16.00	9.50
188	Dick Williams	40.00	16.00	9.50
189	Don McMahon	40.00	16.00	9.50
190	Gene Woodling	40.00	16.00	9.50
191	Johnny Klippstein	40.00	16.00	9.50
192	Danny O'Connell	40.00	16.00	9.50
193	Dick Hyde	40.00	16.00	9.50
194	Bobby Gene Smith	40.00	16.00	9.50
195	Lindy McDaniel	40.00	16.00	9.50
196	Andy Carey	40.00	16.00	9.50
197	Ron Kline	40.00	16.00	9.50
198	Jerry Lynch	40.00	16.00	9.50

1962 Venezuela Topps

For the first time in its short history of producing baseball cards for the Venezuelan market, Topps in 1962 reprinted virtually the entire back of each card in Spanish. The player personal data, career summary and even the cartoon are En Espanol; only the stats are in English. There is no Topps credit or copyright line on the backs. Otherwise identical in format to the 1962 Topps North American issue, the Venezuelan set comprises the first 198 cards of the Topps issue, though cards #197 (Daryl Spencer) and 198 (Johnny Keane) have been replaced with two local Major Leaguers. Survivors of this issue tend to be in lower grades due to the common practice of gluing cards into albums or scrapbooks.

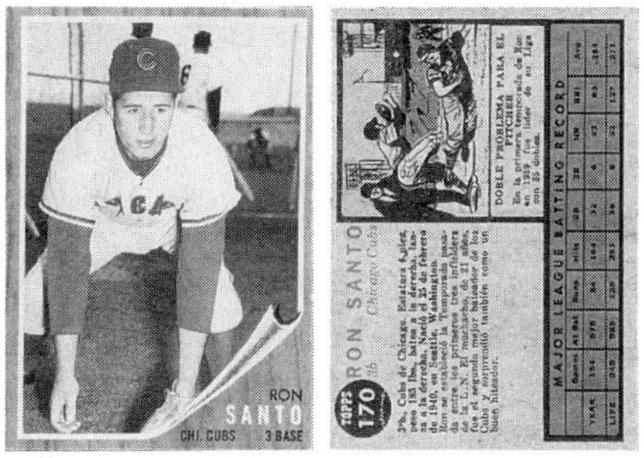

		NM	EX	VG
Complete Set (198):		8500.	3400.	2000.
Common Player:		35.00	14.00	8.50
1	Roger Maris	600.00	240.00	145.00
2	Jim Brosnan	35.00	14.00	8.50
3	Pete Runnels	35.00	14.00	8.50
4	John DeMerit	35.00	14.00	8.50
5	Sandy Koufax	350.00	140.00	85.00
6	Marv Breeding	35.00	14.00	8.50
7	Frank Thomas	35.00	14.00	8.50
8	Ray Herbert	35.00	14.00	8.50
9	Jim Davenport	35.00	14.00	8.50
10	Roberto Clemente	650.00	260.00	160.00
11	Tom Morgan	35.00	14.00	8.50
12	Harry Craft	35.00	14.00	8.50
13	Dick Howser	35.00	14.00	8.50
14	Bill White	35.00	14.00	8.50
15	Dick Donovan	35.00	14.00	8.50
16	Darrell Johnson	35.00	14.00	8.50
17	Johnny Callison	35.00	14.00	8.50
18	Managers' Dream (Mickey Mantle, Willie Mays)	600.00	240.00	145.00
19	Ray Washburn	35.00	14.00	8.50
20	Rocky Colavito	75.00	30.00	18.00
21	Jim Kaat	45.00	18.00	11.00
22	Checklist 1-88	35.00	14.00	8.50
23	Norm Larker	35.00	14.00	8.50
24	Tigers team	125.00	50.00	30.00
25	Ernie Banks	200.00	80.00	48.00
26	Chris Cannizzaro	35.00	14.00	8.50
27	Chuck Cottier	35.00	14.00	8.50
28	Minnie Minoso	50.00	20.00	12.00
29	Casey Stengel	150.00	60.00	36.00
30	Eddie Mathews	150.00	60.00	36.00
31	Tom Tresh	45.00	18.00	11.00
32	John Roseboro	35.00	14.00	8.50
33	Don Larsen	35.00	14.00	8.50
34	Johnny Temple	35.00	14.00	8.50
35	Don Schwall	35.00	14.00	8.50
36	Don Leppert	35.00	14.00	8.50
37	Tribe Hill Trio (Barry Latman, Jim Perry, Dick Stigman)	35.00	14.00	8.50
38	Gene Stephens	35.00	14.00	8.50
39	Joe Koppe	35.00	14.00	8.50
40	Orlando Cepeda	75.00	37.00	22.00
41	Cliff Cook	35.00	14.00	8.50
42	Jim King	35.00	14.00	8.50
43	Dodgers team	150.00	60.00	36.00
44	Don Taussig	35.00	14.00	8.50
45	Brooks Robinson	225.00	90.00	55.00
46	Jack Baldschun	35.00	14.00	8.50
47	Bob Will	35.00	14.00	8.50
48	Ralph Terry	35.00	14.00	8.50
49	Hal Jones	35.00	14.00	8.50
50	Stan Musial	300.00	120.00	75.00
51	A.L. Batting Leaders (Norm Cash, Elston Howard, Al Kaline, Jim Piersall)	100.00	40.00	24.00
52	N.L. Batting Leaders (Ken Boyer, Roberto Clemente, Wally Moon, Vada Pinson)	275.00	110.00	65.00
53	A.L. Home Run Leaders (Jim Gentile, Harmon Killebrew, Mickey Mantle, Roger Maris)	450.00	180.00	110.00
54	N.L. Home Run Leaders (Orlando Cepeda, Willie Mays, Frank Robinson)	150.00	60.00	36.00
55	A.L. E.R.A. Leaders (Dick Donovan, Don Mossi, Milt Pappas, Bill Stafford)	35.00	14.00	8.50
56	N.L. E.R.A. Leaders (Mike McCormick, Jim O'Toole, Curt Simmons, Warren Spahn)	50.00	20.00	12.00
57	A.L. Win Leaders (Steve Barber, Jim Bunning, Whitey Ford, Frank Lary)	60.00	24.00	14.50
58	N.L. Win Leaders (Joe Jay, Jim O'Toole, Warren Spahn)	50.00	20.00	12.00
59	A.L. Strikeout Leaders (Jim Bunning, Whitey Ford, Camilo Pascual, Juan Pizzaro)	60.00	24.00	14.50
60	N.L. Strikeout Leaders (Don Drysdale, Sandy Koufax, Jim O'Toole, Stan Williams)	75.00	30.00	18.00
61	Cardinals Team	125.00	50.00	30.00
62	Steve Boros	35.00	14.00	8.50
63	Tony Cloninger	35.00	14.00	8.50
64	Russ Snyder	35.00	14.00	8.50
65	Bobby Richardson	40.00	16.00	9.50
66	Cuno Barragon (Barragan)	35.00	14.00	8.50
67	Harvey Haddix	35.00	14.00	8.50
68	Ken Hunt	35.00	14.00	8.50
69	Phil Ortega	35.00	14.00	8.50
70	Harmon Killebrew	150.00	60.00	36.00
71	Dick LeMay	35.00	14.00	8.50
72	Bob's Pupils (Steve Boros, Bob Scheffing, Jake Wood)	35.00	14.00	8.50
73	Nellie Fox	150.00	60.00	36.00
74	Bob Lillis	35.00	14.00	8.50
75	Milt Pappas	35.00	14.00	8.50
76	Howie Bedell	35.00	14.00	8.50
77	Tony Taylor	35.00	14.00	8.50
78	Gene Green	35.00	14.00	8.50
79	Ed Hobaugh	35.00	14.00	8.50
80	Vada Pinson	45.00	18.00	11.00
81	Jim Pagliaroni	35.00	14.00	8.50
82	Deron Johnson	35.00	14.00	8.50
83	Larry Jackson	35.00	14.00	8.50
84	Lenny Green	35.00	14.00	8.50
85	Gil Hodges	100.00	50.00	30.00
86	Donn Clendenon	35.00	14.00	8.50
87	Mike Roarke	35.00	14.00	8.50
88	Ralph Houk	35.00	14.00	8.50
89	Barney Schultz	35.00	14.00	8.50
90	Jim Piersall	40.00	16.00	9.50
91	J.C. Martin	35.00	14.00	8.50
92	Sam Jones	35.00	14.00	8.50
93	John Blanchard	35.00	14.00	8.50
94	Jay Hook	35.00	14.00	8.50
95	Don Hoak	35.00	14.00	8.50
96	Eli Grba	35.00	14.00	8.50
97	Tito Francona	35.00	14.00	8.50
98	Checklist 89-176	35.00	14.00	8.50
99	Boog Powell	90.00	36.00	22.00
100	Warren Spahn	150.00	60.00	36.00
101	Carroll Hardy	35.00	14.00	8.50
102	Al Schroll	35.00	14.00	8.50
103	Don Blasingame	35.00	14.00	8.50
104	Ted Savage	35.00	14.00	8.50
105	Don Mossi	35.00	14.00	8.50
106	Carl Sawatski	35.00	14.00	8.50
107	Mike McCormick	35.00	14.00	8.50
108	Willie Davis	35.00	14.00	8.50
109	Bob Shaw	35.00	14.00	8.50
110	Bill Skowron	45.00	18.00	11.00
111	Dallas Green	35.00	14.00	8.50
112	Hank Foiles	35.00	14.00	8.50
113	White Sox team	125.00	50.00	30.00
114	Howie Koplitz	35.00	14.00	8.50
115	Bob Skinner	35.00	14.00	8.50
116	Herb Score	35.00	14.00	8.50
117	Gary Geiger	35.00	14.00	8.50
118	Julian Javier	35.00	14.00	8.50
119	Danny Murphy	35.00	14.00	8.50
120	Bob Purkey	35.00	14.00	8.50
121	Billy Hitchcock	35.00	14.00	8.50
122	Norm Bass	35.00	14.00	8.50
123	Mike de la Hoz	35.00	14.00	8.50
124	Bill Pleis	35.00	14.00	8.50
125	Gene Woodling	35.00	14.00	8.50
126	Al Cicotte	35.00	14.00	8.50
127	Pride of the A's (Hank Bauer, Jerry Lumpe, Norm Siebern)	35.00	14.00	8.50
128	Art Fowler	35.00	14.00	8.50
129	Lee Walls	35.00	14.00	8.50
130	Frank Bolling	35.00	14.00	8.50
131	Pete Richert	35.00	14.00	8.50
132	Angels Team	125.00	50.00	30.00
133	Felipe Alou	40.00	16.00	9.50
134	Billy Hoeft	35.00	14.00	8.50
135	Babe as a Boy (Babe Ruth)	100.00	40.00	24.00
136	Babe Joins Yanks (Babe Ruth)	125.00	50.00	30.00
137	Babe and Mgr. Huggins (Babe Ruth)	100.00	40.00	24.00
138	The Famous Slugger (Babe Ruth)	125.00	50.00	30.00
139	Babe Hits 60 (Babe Ruth)	150.00	60.00	36.00
140	Gehrig and Ruth (Babe Ruth)	150.00	60.00	36.00
141	Twilight Years (Babe Ruth)	100.00	40.00	24.00
142	Coaching for the Dodgers (Babe Ruth)	100.00	40.00	24.00
143	Greatest Sports Hero (Babe Ruth)	100.00	40.00	24.00
144	Farewell Speech (Babe Ruth)	100.00	40.00	24.00
145	Barry Latman	35.00	14.00	8.50
146	Don Demeter	35.00	14.00	8.50
147	Bill Kunkel	35.00	14.00	8.50
148	Wally Post	35.00	14.00	8.50
149	Bob Duliba	35.00	14.00	8.50
150	Al Kaline	160.00	65.00	40.00
151	Johnny Klippstein	35.00	14.00	8.50
152	Mickey Vernon	35.00	14.00	8.50
153	Pumpsie Green	35.00	14.00	8.50
154	Lee Thomas	35.00	14.00	8.50
155	Stu Miller	35.00	14.00	8.50
156	Merritt Ranew	35.00	14.00	8.50
157	Wes Covington	35.00	14.00	8.50
158	Braves Team	125.00	50.00	30.00
159	Hal Reniff	35.00	14.00	8.50
160	Dick Stuart	35.00	14.00	8.50
161	Frank Baumann	35.00	14.00	8.50
162	Sammy Drake	35.00	14.00	8.50
163	Hot Corner Guardians (Cletis Boyer, Billy Gardner)	35.00	14.00	8.50
164	Hal Naragon	35.00	14.00	8.50
165	Jackie Brandt	35.00	14.00	8.50
166	Don Lee	35.00	14.00	8.50
167	Tim McCarver	150.00	90.00	36.00

168	Leo Posada	35.00	14.00	8.50
169	Bob Cerv	35.00	14.00	8.50
170	Ron Santo	45.00	18.00	11.00
171	Dave Sisler	35.00	14.00	8.50
172	Fred Hutchinson	35.00	14.00	8.50
173	Chico Fernandez	35.00	14.00	8.50
174	Carl Willey	35.00	14.00	8.50
175	Frank Howard	40.00	16.00	9.50
176	Eddie Yost	35.00	14.00	8.50
177	Bobby Shantz	35.00	14.00	8.50
178	Camilo Carreon	35.00	14.00	8.50
179	Tom Sturdivant	35.00	14.00	8.50
180	Bob Allison	35.00	14.00	8.50
181	Paul Brown	35.00	14.00	8.50
182	Bob Nieman	35.00	14.00	8.50
183	Roger Craig	35.00	14.00	8.50
184	Haywood Sullivan	35.00	14.00	8.50
185	Roland Sheldon	35.00	14.00	8.50
186	Mack Jones	35.00	14.00	8.50
187	Gene Conley	35.00	14.00	8.50
188	Chuck Hiller	35.00	14.00	8.50
189	Dick Hall	35.00	14.00	8.50
190	Wally Moon	35.00	14.00	8.50
191	Jim Brewer	35.00	14.00	8.50
192	Checklist 177-264	35.00	14.00	8.50
193	Eddie Kasko	35.00	14.00	8.50
194	Dean Chance	35.00	14.00	8.50
195	Joe Cunningham	35.00	14.00	8.50
196	Terry Fox	35.00	14.00	8.50
199	Elio Chacon	80.00	35.00	20.00
200	Luis Aparicio	300.00	125.00	75.00

1964 Venezuela Topps

The first 370 cards of Topps' baseball set were issued in a parallel version for sale in Venezuela. Printed on cardboard with no front gloss, the cards are differentiated from the U.S. version by the use of a black border on back. Survivors of the issue are usually in low grade because of the common Latin American practice of collectors gluing the cards into albums or scrapbooks.

		NM	EX	VG
	Complete Set (370):	12000.	4800.	2875.
	Common Player:	40.00	16.00	9.50
1	N.L. E.R.A. Leaders (Dick Ellsworth, Bob Friend, Sandy Koufax)	90.00	36.00	22.00
2	A.L. E.R.A. Leaders (Camilo Pascual, Gary Peters, Juan Pizarro)	40.00	16.00	9.50
3	N.L. Pitching Leaders (Sandy Koufax, Jim Maloney, Juan Marichal, Warren Spahn)	90.00	36.00	22.00
4	A.L. Pitching Leaders (Jim Bouton, Whitey Ford, Camilo Pascual)	60.00	24.00	14.50
5	N.L. Strikeout Leaders (Don Drysdale, Sandy Koufax, Jim Maloney)	60.00	24.00	14.50
6	A.L. Strikeout Leaders (Jim Bunning, Camilo Pascual, Dick Stigman)	45.00	18.00	11.00
7	N.L. Batting Leaders (Hank Aaron, Roberto Clemente, Tommy Davis, Dick Groat)	125.00	50.00	30.00
8	A.L. Batting Leaders (Al Kaline, Rich Rollins, Carl Yastrzemski)	75.00	30.00	18.00
9	N.L. Home Run Leaders (Hank Aaron, Orlando Cepeda, Willie Mays, Willie McCovey)	100.00	40.00	24.00
10	A.L. Home Run Leaders (Bob Allison, Harmon Killebrew, Dick Stuart)	60.00	24.00	14.50
11	N.L. R.B.I. Leaders (Hank Aaron, Ken Boyer, Bill White)	75.00	30.00	18.00
12	A.L. R.B.I. Leaders (Al Kaline, Harmon Killebrew, Dick Stuart)	60.00	24.00	14.50
13	Hoyt Wilhelm	75.00	30.00	18.00
14	Dodgers Rookies (Dick Nen, Nick Willhite)	40.00	16.00	9.50
15	Zoilo Versalles	40.00	16.00	9.50
16	John Boozer	40.00	16.00	9.50
17	Willie Kirkland	40.00	16.00	9.50
18	Billy O'Dell	40.00	16.00	9.50
19	Don Wart	40.00	16.00	9.50
20	Bob Friend	40.00	16.00	9.50
21	Yogi Berra	125.00	50.00	30.00
22	Jerry Adair	40.00	16.00	9.50
23	Chris Zachary	40.00	16.00	9.50
24	Carl Sawatski	40.00	16.00	9.50
25	Bill Monbouquette	40.00	16.00	9.50
26	Gino Cimoli	40.00	16.00	9.50
27	Mets Team	95.00	38.00	23.00
28	Claude Osteen	40.00	16.00	9.50
29	Lou Brock	100.00	40.00	24.00
30	Ron Perranoski	40.00	16.00	9.50
31	Dave Nicholson	40.00	16.00	9.50
32	Dean Chance	40.00	16.00	9.50
33	Reds Rookies (Sammy Ellis, Mel Queen)	40.00	16.00	9.50
34	Jim Perry	40.00	16.00	9.50
35	Eddie Mathews	100.00	40.00	24.00
36	Hal Reniff	40.00	16.00	9.50
37	Smoky Burgess	40.00	16.00	9.50
38	Jim Wynn	40.00	16.00	9.50
39	Hank Aguirre	40.00	16.00	9.50
40	Dick Groat	40.00	16.00	9.50
41	Friendly Foes (Willie McCovey, Leon Wagner)	45.00	18.00	11.00
42	Moe Drabowsky	40.00	16.00	9.50
43	Roy Sievers	40.00	16.00	9.50
44	Duke Carmel	40.00	16.00	9.50
45	Milt Pappas	40.00	16.00	9.50
46	Ed Brinkman	40.00	16.00	9.50
47	Giants Rookies (Jesus Alou, Ron Herbel)	40.00	16.00	9.50
48	Bob Perry	40.00	16.00	9.50
49	Bill Henry	40.00	16.00	9.50
50	Mickey Mantle	1200.	475.00	300.00
51	Pete Richert	40.00	16.00	9.50
52	Chuck Hinton	40.00	16.00	9.50
53	Denis Menke	40.00	16.00	9.50
54	Sam Mele	40.00	16.00	9.50
55	Ernie Banks	100.00	40.00	24.00
56	Hal Brown	40.00	16.00	9.50
57	Tim Harkness	40.00	16.00	9.50
58	Don Demeter	40.00	16.00	9.50
59	Ernie Broglio	40.00	16.00	9.50
60	Frank Malzone	40.00	16.00	9.50
61	Angel Backstops (Bob Rodgers, Ed Sadowski)	40.00	16.00	9.50
62	Ted Savage	40.00	16.00	9.50
63	Johnny Orsino	40.00	16.00	9.50
64	Ted Abernathy	40.00	16.00	9.50
65	Felipe Alou	45.00	18.00	11.00
66	Eddie Fisher	40.00	16.00	9.50
67	Tigers Team	65.00	26.00	15.50
68	Willie Davis	40.00	16.00	9.50
69	Clete Boyer	45.00	18.00	11.00
70	Joe Torre	50.00	25.00	15.00
71	Jack Spring	40.00	16.00	9.50
72	Chico Cardenas	40.00	16.00	9.50
73	Jimmie Hall	40.00	16.00	9.50
74	Pirates Rookies (Tom Butters, Bob Priddy)	40.00	16.00	9.50
75	Wayne Causey	40.00	16.00	9.50
76	Checklist 1-88	40.00	16.00	9.50
77	Jerry Walker	40.00	16.00	9.50
78	Merritt Ranew	40.00	16.00	9.50
79	Bob Heffner	40.00	16.00	9.50
80	Vada Pinson	55.00	22.00	13.00
81	All-Star Vets (Nellie Fox, Harmon Killebrew)	55.00	22.00	13.00
82	Jim Davenport	40.00	16.00	9.50
83	Gus Triandos	40.00	16.00	9.50
84	Carl Willey	40.00	16.00	9.50
85	Pete Ward	40.00	16.00	9.50
86	Al Downing	40.00	16.00	9.50
87	Cardinals Team	125.00	50.00	30.00
88	John Roseboro	40.00	16.00	9.50
89	Boog Powell	45.00	18.00	11.00
90	Earl Battey	40.00	16.00	9.50
91	Bob Bailey	40.00	16.00	9.50
92	Steve Ridzik	40.00	16.00	9.50
93	Gary Geiger	40.00	16.00	9.50
94	Braves Rookies (Jim Britton, Larry Maxie)	40.00	16.00	9.50
95	George Altman	40.00	16.00	9.50
96	Bob Buhl	40.00	16.00	9.50
97	Jim Fregosi	40.00	16.00	9.50
98	Bill Bruton	40.00	16.00	9.50
99	Al Stanek	40.00	16.00	9.50
100	Elston Howard	45.00	18.00	11.00
101	Walt Alston	75.00	30.00	18.00
102	Checklist 89-176	40.00	16.00	9.50
103	Curt Flood	45.00	18.00	11.00
104	Art Mahaffey	40.00	16.00	9.50
105	Woody Held	40.00	16.00	9.50
106	Joe Nuxhall	40.00	16.00	9.50
107	White Sox Rookies (Bruce Howard, Frank Kreutzer)	40.00	16.00	9.50
108	John Wyatt	40.00	16.00	9.50
109	Rusty Staub	50.00	20.00	12.00
110	Albie Pearson	40.00	16.00	9.50
111	Don Elston	40.00	16.00	9.50
112	Bob Tillman	40.00	16.00	9.50
113	Grover Powell	40.00	16.00	9.50
114	Don Lock	40.00	16.00	9.50
115	Frank Bolling	40.00	16.00	9.50
116	Twins Rookies (Tony Oliva, Jay Ward)	60.00	24.00	14.50
117	Earl Francis	40.00	16.00	9.50
118	John Blanchard	40.00	16.00	9.50
119	Gary Kolb	40.00	16.00	9.50
120	Don Drysdale	100.00	40.00	24.00
121	Pete Runnels	40.00	16.00	9.50
122	Don McMahon	40.00	16.00	9.50
123	Jose Pagan	40.00	16.00	9.50
124	Orlando Pena	40.00	16.00	9.50
125	Pete Rose	400.00	160.00	100.00
126	Russ Snyder	40.00	16.00	9.50
127	Angels Rookies (Aubrey Gatewood, Dick Simpson)	40.00	16.00	9.50
128	Mickey Lolich	50.00	20.00	12.00
129	Amado Samuel	40.00	16.00	9.50
130	Gary Peters	40.00	16.00	9.50
131	Steve Boros	40.00	16.00	9.50
132	Braves Team	75.00	30.00	18.00
133	Jim Grant	40.00	16.00	9.50
134	Don Zimmer	40.00	16.00	9.50
135	Johnny Callison	40.00	16.00	9.50
136	World Series Game 1 (Koufax Strikes Out 15)	45.00	18.00	11.00
137	World Series Game 2 (Davis Sparks Rally)	45.00	18.00	11.00
138	World Series Game 3 (L.A. Takes 3rd Straight)	45.00	18.00	11.00
139	World Series Game 4 (Sealing Yanks' Doom)	45.00	18.00	11.00
140	World Series Summary (The Dodgers Celebrate)	45.00	18.00	11.00
141	Danny Murtaugh	40.00	16.00	9.50
142	John Bateman	40.00	16.00	9.50
143	Bubba Phillips	40.00	16.00	9.50
144	Al Worthington	40.00	16.00	9.50
145	Norm Siebern	40.00	16.00	9.50
146	Indians Rookies (Bob Chance, Tommy John)	65.00	26.00	15.50
147	Ray Sadecki	40.00	16.00	9.50
148	J.C. Martin	40.00	16.00	9.50
149	Paul Foytack	40.00	16.00	9.50
150	Willie Mays	300.00	125.00	75.00
151	Athletics Team	75.00	30.00	18.00
152	Denver Lemaster	40.00	16.00	9.50
153	Dick Williams	40.00	16.00	9.50
154	Dick Tracewski	40.00	16.00	9.50
155	Duke Snider	125.00	50.00	30.00
156	Bill Dailey	40.00	16.00	9.50
157	Gene Mauch	40.00	16.00	9.50
158	Ken Johnson	40.00	16.00	9.50
159	Charlie Dees	40.00	16.00	9.50
160	Ken Boyer	45.00	18.00	11.00
161	Dave McNally	40.00	16.00	9.50
162	Hitting Area (Vada Pinson, Dick Sisler)	40.00	16.00	9.50
163	Donn Clendenon	40.00	16.00	9.50
164	Bud Daley	40.00	16.00	9.50
165	Jerry Lumpe	40.00	16.00	9.50
166	Marty Keough	40.00	16.00	9.50
167	Senators Rookies (Mike Brumley, Lou Piniella)	45.00	18.00	11.00
168	Al Weis	40.00	16.00	9.50
169	Del Crandall	40.00	16.00	9.50
170	Dick Radatz	40.00	16.00	9.50
171	Ty Cline	40.00	16.00	9.50
172	Indians Team	75.00	30.00	18.00
173	Ryne Duren	40.00	16.00	9.50
174	Doc Edwards	40.00	16.00	9.50
175	Billy Williams	75.00	30.00	18.00
176	Tracy Stallard	40.00	16.00	9.50
177	Harmon Killebrew	100.00	40.00	24.00
178	Hank Bauer	40.00	16.00	9.50
179	Carl Warwick	40.00	16.00	9.50
180	Tommy Davis	40.00	16.00	9.50
181	Dave Wickersham	40.00	16.00	9.50
182	Sox Sockers (Chuck Schilling, Carl Yastrzemski)	65.00	26.00	15.50
183	Ron Taylor	40.00	16.00	9.50
184	Al Luplow	40.00	16.00	9.50
185	Jim O'Toole	40.00	16.00	9.50
186	Roman Mejias	40.00	16.00	9.50
187	Ed Roebuck	40.00	16.00	9.50
188	Checklist 177-264	40.00	16.00	9.50
189	Bob Hendley	40.00	16.00	9.50
190	Bobby Richardson	45.00	18.00	11.00
191	Clay Dalrymple	40.00	16.00	9.50
192	Cubs Rookies (John Boccabella, Billy Cowan)	40.00	16.00	9.50
193	Jerry Lynch	40.00	16.00	9.50
194	John Goryl	40.00	16.00	9.50
195	Floyd Robinson	40.00	16.00	9.50
196	Jim Gentile	40.00	16.00	9.50
197	Frank Lary	40.00	16.00	9.50
198	Len Gabrielson	40.00	16.00	9.50
199	Joe Azcue	40.00	16.00	9.50
200	Sandy Koufax	200.00	100.00	60.00
201	Orioles Rookies (Sam Bowens, Wally Bunker)	40.00	16.00	9.50
202	Galen Cisco	40.00	16.00	9.50
203	John Kennedy	40.00	16.00	9.50
204	Matty Alou	40.00	16.00	9.50
205	Nellie Fox	95.00	38.00	23.00
206	Steve Hamilton	40.00	16.00	9.50
207	Fred Hutchinson	40.00	16.00	9.50
208	Wes Covington	40.00	16.00	9.50
209	Bob Allen	40.00	16.00	9.50
210	Carl Yastrzemski	125.00	50.00	30.00
211	Jim Coker	40.00	16.00	9.50
212	Pete Lovrich	40.00	16.00	9.50
213	Angels Team	75.00	30.00	18.00
214	Ken McMullen	40.00	16.00	9.50
215	Ray Herbert	40.00	16.00	9.50
216	Mike de la Hoz	40.00	16.00	9.50
217	Jim King	40.00	16.00	9.50
218	Hank Fischer	40.00	16.00	9.50
219	Young Aces (Jim Bouton, Al Downing)	45.00	18.00	11.00
220	Dick Ellsworth	40.00	16.00	9.50
221	Bob Saverine	40.00	16.00	9.50
222	Bill Pierce	40.00	16.00	9.50
223	George Banks	40.00	16.00	9.50
224	Tommie Sisk	40.00	16.00	9.50
225	Roger Maris	150.00	60.00	36.00
226	Colts Rookies (Gerald Grote, Larry Yellen)	40.00	16.00	9.50
227	Barry Latman	40.00	16.00	9.50
228	Felix Mantilla	40.00	16.00	9.50
229	Charley Lau	40.00	16.00	9.50
230	Brooks Robinson	150.00	60.00	36.00
231	Dick Calmus	40.00	16.00	9.50
232	Al Lopez	75.00	30.00	18.00
233	Hal Smith	40.00	16.00	9.50
234	Gary Bell	40.00	16.00	9.50
235	Ron Hunt	40.00	16.00	9.50
236	Bill Faul	40.00	16.00	9.50
237	Cubs Team	75.00	30.00	18.00
238	Roy McMillan	40.00	16.00	9.50
239	Herm Starrette	40.00	16.00	9.50
240	Bill White	40.00	16.00	9.50
241	Jim Owens	40.00	16.00	9.50
242	Harvey Kuenn	40.00	16.00	9.50
243	Phillies Rookies (Richie Allen, John Herrnstein)	65.00	26.00	15.50
244	Tony LaRussa	45.00	18.00	11.00
245	Dick Stigman	40.00	16.00	9.50
246	Manny Mota	40.00	16.00	9.50
247	Dave DeBusschere	40.00	16.00	9.50
248	Johnny Pesky	40.00	16.00	9.50
249	Doug Camilli	40.00	16.00	9.50
250	Al Kaline	150.00	60.00	36.00
251	Choo Choo Coleman	40.00	16.00	9.50
252	Ken Aspromonte	40.00	16.00	9.50
253	Wally Post	40.00	16.00	9.50
254	Don Hoak	40.00	16.00	9.50

255	Lee Thomas	40.00	16.00	9.50
256	Johnny Weekly	40.00	16.00	9.50
257	Giants Team	75.00	30.00	18.00
258	Garry Roggenburk	40.00	16.00	9.50
259	Harry Bright	40.00	16.00	9.50
260	Frank Robinson	125.00	50.00	30.00
261	Jim Hannan	40.00	16.00	9.50
262	Cardinals Rookies (Harry Fanok, Mike Shannon)	45.00	18.00	11.00
263	Chuck Estrada	40.00	16.00	9.50
264	Jim Landis	40.00	16.00	9.50
265	Jim Bunning	75.00	30.00	18.00
266	Gene Freese	40.00	16.00	9.50
267	Wilbur Wood	40.00	16.00	9.50
268	Bill's Got It (Danny Murtaugh, Bill Virdon)	40.00	16.00	9.50
269	Ellis Burton	40.00	16.00	9.50
270	Rich Rollins	40.00	16.00	9.50
271	Bob Sadowski	40.00	16.00	9.50
272	Jake Wood	40.00	16.00	9.50
273	Mel Nelson	40.00	16.00	9.50
274	Checklist 265-352	40.00	16.00	9.50
275	John Tsitouris	40.00	16.00	9.50
276	Jose Tartabull	40.00	16.00	9.50
277	Ken Retzer	40.00	16.00	9.50
278	Bobby Shantz	40.00	16.00	9.50
279	Joe Koppe	40.00	16.00	9.50
280	Juan Marichal	90.00	36.00	22.00
281	Yankees Rookies (Jake Gibbs, Tom Metcalf)	40.00	16.00	9.50
282	Bob Bruce	40.00	16.00	9.50
283	Tommy McCraw	40.00	16.00	9.50
284	Dick Schofield	40.00	16.00	9.50
285	Robin Roberts	90.00	36.00	22.00
286	Don Landrum	40.00	16.00	9.50
287	Red Sox Rookies (Tony Conigliaro, Bill Spanswick)	50.00	20.00	12.00
288	Al Moran	40.00	16.00	9.50
289	Frank Funk	40.00	16.00	9.50
290	Bob Allison	40.00	16.00	9.50
291	Phil Ortega	40.00	16.00	9.50
292	Mike Roarke	40.00	16.00	9.50
293	Phillies Team	75.00	30.00	18.00
294	Ken Hunt	40.00	16.00	9.50
295	Roger Craig	40.00	16.00	9.50
296	Ed Kirkpatrick	40.00	16.00	9.50
297	Ken MacKenzie	40.00	16.00	9.50
298	Harry Craft	40.00	16.00	9.50
299	Bill Stafford	40.00	16.00	9.50
300	Hank Aaron	300.00	125.00	75.00
301	Larry Brown	40.00	16.00	9.50
302	Dan Pfister	40.00	16.00	9.50
303	Jim Campbell	40.00	16.00	9.50
304	Bob Johnson	40.00	16.00	9.50
305	Jack Lamabe	40.00	16.00	9.50
306	Giant Gunners (Orlando Cepeda, Willie Mays)	75.00	30.00	18.00
307	Joe Gibbon	40.00	16.00	9.50
308	Gene Stephens	40.00	16.00	9.50
309	Paul Toth	40.00	16.00	9.50
310	Jim Gilliam	40.00	16.00	9.50
311	Tom Brown	40.00	16.00	9.50
312	Tigers Rookies (Fritz Fisher, Fred Gladding)	40.00	16.00	9.50
313	Chuck Hiller	40.00	16.00	9.50
314	Jerry Buchek	40.00	16.00	9.50
315	Bo Belinsky	40.00	16.00	9.50
316	Gene Oliver	40.00	16.00	9.50
317	Al Smith	40.00	16.00	9.50
318	Twins Team	75.00	30.00	18.00
319	Paul Brown	40.00	16.00	9.50
320	Rocky Colavito	75.00	30.00	18.00
321	Bob Lillis	40.00	16.00	9.50
322	George Brunet	40.00	16.00	9.50
323	John Buzhardt	40.00	16.00	9.50
324	Casey Stengel	75.00	30.00	18.00
325	Hector Lopez	40.00	16.00	9.50
326	Ron Brand	40.00	16.00	9.50
327	Don Blasingame	40.00	16.00	9.50
328	Bob Shaw	40.00	16.00	9.50
329	Russ Nixon	40.00	16.00	9.50
330	Tommy Harper	40.00	16.00	9.50
331	A.L. Bombers (Norm Cash, Al Kaline, Mickey Mantle, Roger Maris)	400.00	160.00	95.00
332	Ray Washburn	40.00	16.00	9.50
333	Billy Moran	40.00	16.00	9.50
334	Lew Krausse	40.00	16.00	9.50
335	Don Mossi	40.00	16.00	9.50
336	Andre Rodgers	40.00	16.00	9.50
337	Dodgers Rookies (Al Ferrara, Jeff Torborg)	40.00	16.00	9.50
338	Jack Kralick	40.00	16.00	9.50
339	Walt Bond	40.00	16.00	9.50
340	Joe Cunningham	40.00	16.00	9.50
341	Jim Roland	40.00	16.00	9.50
342	Willie Stargell	95.00	38.00	23.00
343	Senators Team	75.00	30.00	18.00
344	Phil Linz	40.00	16.00	9.50
345	Frank Thomas	40.00	16.00	9.50
346	Joe Jay	40.00	16.00	9.50
347	Bobby Wine	40.00	16.00	9.50
348	Ed Lopat	40.00	16.00	9.50
349	Art Fowler	40.00	16.00	9.50
350	Willie McCovey	100.00	40.00	24.00
351	Dan Schneider	40.00	16.00	9.50
352	Eddie Bressoud	40.00	16.00	9.50
353	Wally Moon	40.00	16.00	9.50
354	Dave Giusti	40.00	16.00	9.50
355	Vic Power	40.00	16.00	9.50
356	Reds Rookies (Bill McCool, Chico Ruiz)	40.00	16.00	9.50
357	Charley James	40.00	16.00	9.50
358	Ron Kline	40.00	16.00	9.50
359	Jim Schaffer	40.00	16.00	9.50
360	Joe Pepitone	40.00	16.00	9.50
361	Jay Hook	40.00	16.00	9.50
362	Checklist 353-429	40.00	16.00	9.50
363	Dick McAuliffe	40.00	16.00	9.50
364	Joe Gaines	40.00	16.00	9.50
365	Cal McLish	40.00	16.00	9.50
366	Nelson Mathews	40.00	16.00	9.50
367	Fred Whitfield	40.00	16.00	9.50
368	White Sox Rookies (Fritz Ackley, Don Buford)	40.00	16.00	9.50
369	Jerry Zimmerman	40.00	16.00	9.50
370	Hal Woodeshick	40.00	16.00	9.50

1966 Venezuela Topps

The first 370 cards on Topps' 1966 baseball set were reprinted for sale in the Venezuelan market. Identical in design to those cards, the South American version is printed on cardboard that has virtually no gloss on front and is a brighter pink-orange on the backs. Low-grade cards are the norm for this and other Venezuelan issues as it is common collector practice south of the border to mount cards in scrapbooks and albums.

		NM	EX	VG
Complete Set (370):		12000.	4800.	2850.
Common Player:		30.00	12.00	7.00
1	Willie Mays	400.00	150.00	90.00
2	Ted Abernathy	30.00	12.00	7.25
3	Sam Mele	30.00	12.00	7.25
4	Ray Culp	30.00	12.00	7.25
5	Jim Fregosi	30.00	12.00	7.25
6	Chuck Schilling	30.00	12.00	7.25
7	Tracy Stallard	30.00	12.00	7.25
8	Floyd Robinson	30.00	12.00	7.25
9	Clete Boyer	35.00	14.00	8.50
10	Tony Cloninger	30.00	12.00	7.25
11	Senators Rookies (Brant Alyea, Pete Craig)	30.00	12.00	7.25
12	John Tsitouris	30.00	12.00	7.25
13	Lou Johnson	30.00	12.00	7.25
14	Norm Siebern	30.00	12.00	7.25
15	Vern Law	30.00	12.00	7.25
16	Larry Brown	30.00	12.00	7.25
17	Johnny Stephenson	30.00	12.00	7.25
18	Roland Sheldon	30.00	12.00	7.25
19	Giants Team	75.00	30.00	18.00
20	Willie Horton	30.00	12.00	7.25
21	Don Nottebart	30.00	12.00	7.25
22	Joe Nossek	30.00	12.00	7.25
23	Jack Sanford	30.00	12.00	7.25
24	Don Kessinger	35.00	14.00	8.50
25	Pete Ward	30.00	12.00	7.25
26	Ray Sadecki	30.00	12.00	7.25
27	Orioles Rookies (Andy Etchebarren, Darold Knowles)	30.00	12.00	7.25
28	Phil Niekro	95.00	38.00	23.00
29	Mike Brumley	30.00	12.00	7.25
30	Pete Rose	350.00	140.00	85.00
31	Jack Cullen	30.00	12.00	7.25
32	Adolfo Phillips	30.00	12.00	7.25
33	Jim Pagliaroni	30.00	12.00	7.25
34	Checklist 1-88	30.00	12.00	7.25
35	Ron Swoboda	30.00	12.00	7.25
36	Catfish Hunter	95.00	38.00	23.00
37	Billy Herman	95.00	38.00	23.00
38	Ron Nischwitz	30.00	12.00	7.25
39	Ken Henderson	30.00	12.00	7.25
40	Jim Grant	30.00	12.00	7.25
41	Don LeJohn	30.00	12.00	7.25
42	Aubrey Gatewood	30.00	12.00	7.25
43	Don Landrum	30.00	12.00	7.25
44	Indians Rookies (Bill Davis, Tom Kelley)	30.00	12.00	7.25
45	Jim Gentile	30.00	12.00	7.25
46	Howie Koplitz	30.00	12.00	7.25
47	J.C. Martin	30.00	12.00	7.25
48	Paul Blair	30.00	12.00	7.25
49	Woody Woodward	30.00	12.00	7.25
50	Mickey Mantle	1200.	500.00	300.00
51	Gordon Richardson	30.00	12.00	7.25
52	Power Plus (Johnny Callison, Wes Covington)	30.00	12.00	7.25
53	Bob Duliba	30.00	12.00	7.25
54	Jose Pagan	30.00	12.00	7.25
55	Ken Harrelson	30.00	12.00	7.25
56	Sandy Valdespino	30.00	12.00	7.25
57	Jim Lefebvre	30.00	12.00	7.25
58	Dave Wickersham	30.00	12.00	7.25
59	Reds Team	75.00	30.00	18.00
60	Curt Flood	35.00	14.00	8.50
61	Bob Bolin	30.00	12.00	7.25
62	Merritt Ranew	30.00	12.00	7.25
63	Jim Stewart	30.00	12.00	7.25
64	Bob Bruce	30.00	12.00	7.25
65	Leon Wagner	30.00	12.00	7.25
66	Al Weis	30.00	12.00	7.25
67	Mets Rookies (Cleon Jones, Dick Selma)	35.00	14.00	8.50
68	Hal Reniff	30.00	12.00	7.25
69	Ken Hamlin	30.00	12.00	7.25
70	Carl Yastrzemski	150.00	60.00	36.00
71	Frank Carpin	30.00	12.00	7.25
72	Tony Perez	150.00	75.00	45.00
73	Jerry Zimmerman	30.00	12.00	7.25
74	Don Mossi	30.00	12.00	7.25
75	Tommy Davis	30.00	12.00	7.25
76	Red Schoendienst	95.00	38.00	23.00
77	Johnny Orsino	30.00	12.00	7.25
78	Frank Linzy	30.00	12.00	7.25
79	Joe Pepitone	30.00	12.00	7.25
80	Richie Allen	45.00	18.00	11.00
81	Ray Oyler	30.00	12.00	7.25
82	Bob Hendley	30.00	12.00	7.25
83	Albie Pearson	30.00	12.00	7.25
84	Braves Rookies (Jim Beauchamp, Dick Kelley)	30.00	12.00	7.25
85	Eddie Fisher	30.00	12.00	7.25
86	John Bateman	30.00	12.00	7.25
87	Dan Napoleon	30.00	12.00	7.25
88	Fred Whitfield	30.00	12.00	7.25
89	Ted Davidson	30.00	12.00	7.25
90	Luis Aparicio	250.00	100.00	60.00
91	Bob Uecker	40.00	16.00	9.50
92	Yankees Team	125.00	50.00	30.00
93	Jim Lonborg	30.00	12.00	7.25
94	Matty Alou	30.00	12.00	7.25
95	Pete Richert	30.00	12.00	7.25
96	Felipe Alou	35.00	14.00	8.50
97	Jim Merritt	30.00	12.00	7.25
98	Don Demeter	30.00	12.00	7.25
99	Buc Belters (Donn Clendenon, Willie Stargell)	60.00	24.00	14.50
100	Sandy Koufax	250.00	100.00	60.00
101	Checklist 89-176	30.00	12.00	7.25
102	Ed Kirkpatrick	30.00	12.00	7.25
103	Dick Groat	30.00	12.00	7.25
104	Alex Johnson	30.00	12.00	7.25
105	Milt Pappas	30.00	12.00	7.25
106	Rusty Staub	40.00	16.00	9.50
107	Athletics Rookies (Larry Stahl, Ron Tompkins)	30.00	12.00	7.25
108	Bobby Klaus	30.00	12.00	7.25
109	Ralph Terry	30.00	12.00	7.25
110	Ernie Banks	200.00	80.00	50.00
111	Gary Peters	30.00	12.00	7.25
112	Manny Mota	30.00	12.00	7.25
113	Hank Aguirre	30.00	12.00	7.25
114	Jim Gosger	30.00	12.00	7.25
115	Bill Henry	30.00	12.00	7.25
116	Walt Alston	95.00	38.00	23.00
117	Jake Gibbs	30.00	12.00	7.25
118	Mike McCormick	30.00	12.00	7.25
119	Art Shamsky	30.00	12.00	7.25
120	Harmon Killebrew	150.00	60.00	36.00
121	Ray Herbert	30.00	12.00	7.25
122	Joe Gaines	30.00	12.00	7.25
123	Pirates Rookies (Frank Bork, Jerry May)	30.00	12.00	7.25
124	Tug McGraw	30.00	12.00	7.25
125	Lou Brock	125.00	50.00	30.00
126	Jim Palmer	200.00	80.00	48.00
127	Ken Berry	30.00	12.00	7.25
128	Jim Landis	30.00	12.00	7.25
129	Jack Kralick	30.00	12.00	7.25
130	Joe Torre	45.00	22.00	13.50
131	Angels Team	75.00	30.00	18.00
132	Orlando Cepeda	100.00	50.00	30.00
133	Don McMahon	30.00	12.00	7.25
134	Wes Parker	30.00	12.00	7.25
135	Dave Morehead	30.00	12.00	7.25
136	Woody Held	30.00	12.00	7.25
137	Pat Corrales	30.00	12.00	7.25
138	Roger Repoz	30.00	12.00	7.25
139	Cubs Rookies (Byron Browne, Don Young)	30.00	12.00	7.25
140	Jim Maloney	30.00	12.00	7.25
141	Tom McCraw	30.00	12.00	7.25
142	Don Dennis	30.00	12.00	7.25
143	Jose Tartabull	30.00	12.00	7.25
144	Don Schwall	30.00	12.00	7.25
145	Bill Freehan	30.00	12.00	7.25
146	George Altman	30.00	12.00	7.25
147	Lum Harris	30.00	12.00	7.25
148	Bob Johnson	30.00	12.00	7.25
149	Dick Nen	30.00	12.00	7.25
150	Rocky Colavito	75.00	30.00	18.00
151	Gary Wagner	30.00	12.00	7.25
152	Frank Malzone	30.00	12.00	7.25
153	Rico Carty	30.00	12.00	7.25
154	Chuck Hiller	30.00	12.00	7.25
155	Marcelino Lopez	30.00	12.00	7.25
156	D P Combo (Hal Lanier, Dick Schofield)	30.00	12.00	7.25
157	Rene Lachemann	30.00	12.00	7.25
158	Jim Brewer	30.00	12.00	7.25
159	Chico Ruiz	30.00	12.00	7.25
160	Whitey Ford	150.00	60.00	36.00
161	Jerry Lumpe	30.00	12.00	7.25
162	Lee Maye	30.00	12.00	7.25
163	Tito Francona	30.00	12.00	7.25
164	White Sox Rookies (Tommie Agee, Marv Staehle)	30.00	12.00	7.25
165	Don Lock	30.00	12.00	7.25
166	Chris Krug	30.00	12.00	7.25
167	Boog Powell	35.00	14.00	8.50
168	Dan Osinski	30.00	12.00	7.25
169	Duke Sims	30.00	12.00	7.25
170	Cookie Rojas	30.00	12.00	7.25
171	Nick Willhite	30.00	12.00	7.25
172	Mets Team	150.00	60.00	36.00
173	Al Spangler	30.00	12.00	7.25
174	Ron Taylor	30.00	12.00	7.25
175	Bert Campaneris	35.00	14.00	8.50
176	Jim Davenport	30.00	12.00	7.25
177	Hector Lopez	30.00	12.00	7.25
178	Bob Tillman	30.00	12.00	7.25
179	Cardinals Rookies (Dennis Aust, Bob Tolan)	30.00	12.00	7.25
180	Vada Pinson	35.00	14.00	8.50
181	Al Worthington	30.00	12.00	7.25
182	Jerry Lynch	30.00	12.00	7.25
183	Checklist 177-264	30.00	12.00	7.25
184	Denis Menke	30.00	12.00	7.25
185	Bob Buhl	30.00	12.00	7.25
186	Ruben Amaro	30.00	12.00	7.25
187	Chuck Dressen	30.00	12.00	7.25
188	Al Luplow	30.00	12.00	7.25
189	John Roseboro	30.00	12.00	7.25
190	Jimmie Hall	30.00	12.00	7.25
191	Darrell Sutherland	30.00	12.00	7.25
192	Vic Power	30.00	12.00	7.25
193	Dave McNally	30.00	12.00	7.25

194	Senators Team	75.00	30.00	18.00
195	Joe Morgan	125.00	50.00	30.00
196	Don Pavletich	30.00	12.00	7.25
197	Sonny Siebert	30.00	12.00	7.25
198	Mickey Stanley	30.00	12.00	7.25
199	Chisox Clubbers (Floyd Robinson, Johnny Romano, Bill Skowron)	30.00	12.00	7.25
200	Eddie Mathews	125.00	50.00	30.00
201	Jim Dickson	30.00	12.00	7.25
202	Clay Dalrymple	30.00	12.00	7.25
203	Jose Santiago	30.00	12.00	7.25
204	Cubs Team	90.00	36.00	22.00
205	Tom Tresh	30.00	12.00	7.25
206	Alvin Jackson	30.00	12.00	7.25
207	Frank Quilici	30.00	12.00	7.25
208	Bob Miller	30.00	12.00	7.25
209	Tigers Rookies (Fritz Fisher, John Hiller)	30.00	12.00	7.25
210	Bill Mazeroski	60.00	30.00	18.00
211	Frank Kreutzer	30.00	12.00	7.25
212	Ed Kranepool	30.00	12.00	7.25
213	Fred Newman	30.00	12.00	7.25
214	Tommy Harper	30.00	12.00	7.25
215	N.L. Batting Leaders (Hank Aaron, Roberto Clemente, Willie Mays)	300.00	125.00	75.00
216	A.L. Batting Leaders (Vic Davalillo, Tony Oliva, Carl Yastrzemski)	150.00	60.00	36.00
217	N.L. Home Run Leaders (Willie Mays, Willie McCovey, Billy Williams)	150.00	60.00	36.00
218	A.L. Home Run Leaders (Norm Cash, Tony Conigliaro, Willie Horton)	60.00	24.00	14.50
219	N.L. RBI Leaders (Deron Johnson, Willie Mays, Frank Robinson)	90.00	36.00	22.00
220	A.L. RBI Leaders (Rocky Colavito, Willie Horton, Tony Oliva)	60.00	24.00	14.50
221	N.L. ERA Leaders (Sandy Koufax, Vern Law, Juan Marichal)	75.00	30.00	18.00
222	A.L. ERA Leaders (Eddie Fisher, Sam McDowell, Sonny Siebert)	35.00	14.00	8.50
223	N.L. Pitching Leaders (Tony Cloninger, Don Drysdale, Sandy Koufax)	75.00	30.00	18.00
224	A.L. Pitching Leaders (Jim Grant, Jim Kaat, Mel Stottlemyre)	35.00	14.00	8.50
225	N.L. Strikeout Leaders (Bob Gibson, Sandy Koufax, Bob Veale)	60.00	24.00	14.50
226	A.L. Strikeout Leaders (Mickey Lolich, Sam McDowell, Denny McLain, Sonny Siebert)	45.00	18.00	11.00
227	Russ Nixon	30.00	12.00	7.25
228	Larry Dierker	30.00	12.00	7.25
229	Hank Bauer	30.00	12.00	7.25
230	Johnny Callison	30.00	12.00	7.25
231	Floyd Weaver	30.00	12.00	7.25
232	Glenn Beckert	30.00	12.00	7.25
233	Dom Zanni	30.00	12.00	7.25
234	Yankees Rookies (Rich Beck, Roy White)	35.00	14.00	8.50
235	Don Cardwell	30.00	12.00	7.25
236	Mike Hershberger	30.00	12.00	7.25
237	Billy O'Dell	30.00	12.00	7.25
238	Dodgers Team	100.00	40.00	24.00
239	Orlando Pena	30.00	12.00	7.25
240	Earl Battey	30.00	12.00	7.25
241	Dennis Ribant	30.00	12.00	7.25
242	Jesus Alou	30.00	12.00	7.25
243	Nelson Briles	30.00	12.00	7.25
244	Astros Rookies (Chuck Harrison, Sonny Jackson)	30.00	12.00	7.25
245	John Buzhardt	30.00	12.00	7.25
246	Ed Bailey	30.00	12.00	7.25
247	Carl Warwick	30.00	12.00	7.25
248	Pete Mikkelsen	30.00	12.00	7.25
249	Bill Rigney	30.00	12.00	7.25
250	Sam Ellis	30.00	12.00	7.25
251	Ed Brinkman	30.00	12.00	7.25
252	Denver Lemaster	30.00	12.00	7.25
253	Don Wert	30.00	12.00	7.25
254	Phillies Rookies (Fergie Jenkins, Bill Sorrell)	100.00	40.00	24.00
255	Willie Stargell	125.00	50.00	30.00
256	Lew Krausse	30.00	12.00	7.25
257	Jeff Torborg	30.00	12.00	7.25
258	Dave Giusti	30.00	12.00	7.25
259	Red Sox Team	75.00	30.00	18.00
260	Bob Shaw	30.00	12.00	7.25
261	Ron Hansen	30.00	12.00	7.25
262	Jack Hamilton	30.00	12.00	7.25
263	Tom Egan	30.00	12.00	7.25
264	Twins Rookies (Andy Kosco, Ted Uhlaender)	30.00	12.00	7.25
265	Stu Miller	30.00	12.00	7.25
266	Pedro Gonzalez	30.00	12.00	7.25
267	Joe Sparma	30.00	12.00	7.25
268	John Blanchard	30.00	12.00	7.25
269	Don Heffner	30.00	12.00	7.25
270	Claude Osteen	30.00	12.00	7.25
271	Hal Lanier	30.00	12.00	7.25
272	Jack Baldschun	30.00	12.00	7.25
273	Astro Aces (Bob Aspromonte, Rusty Staub)	30.00	12.00	7.25
274	Buster Narum	30.00	12.00	7.25
275	Tim McCarver	35.00	14.00	8.50
276	Jim Bouton	35.00	14.00	8.50
277	George Thomas	30.00	12.00	7.25
278	Calvin Koonce	30.00	12.00	7.25
279	Checklist 265-352	30.00	12.00	7.25
280	Bobby Knoop	30.00	12.00	7.25
281	Bruce Howard	30.00	12.00	7.25
282	Johnny Lewis	30.00	12.00	7.25
283	Jim Perry	30.00	12.00	7.25
284	Bobby Wine	30.00	12.00	7.25
285	Luis Tiant	45.00	18.00	11.00
286	Gary Geiger	30.00	12.00	7.25
287	Jack Aker	30.00	12.00	7.25
288	Dodgers Rookies (Bill Singer, Don Sutton)	125.00	50.00	30.00
289	Larry Sherry	30.00	12.00	7.25
290	Ron Santo	35.00	14.00	8.50
291	Moe Drabowsky	30.00	12.00	7.25
292	Jim Coker	30.00	12.00	7.25
293	Mike Shannon	30.00	12.00	7.25
294	Steve Ridzik	30.00	12.00	7.25
295	Jim Hart	30.00	12.00	7.25
296	Johnny Keane	30.00	12.00	7.25
297	Jim Owens	30.00	12.00	7.25
298	Rico Petrocelli	30.00	12.00	7.25
299	Lou Burdette	30.00	12.00	7.25
300	Roberto Clemente	650.00	325.00	195.00
301	Greg Bollo	30.00	12.00	7.25
302	Ernie Bowman	30.00	12.00	7.25
303	Indians Team	75.00	30.00	18.00
304	John Herrnstein	30.00	12.00	7.25
305	Camilo Pascual	30.00	12.00	7.25
306	Ty Cline	30.00	12.00	7.25
307	Clay Carroll	30.00	12.00	7.25
308	Tom Haller	30.00	12.00	7.25
309	Diego Segui	30.00	12.00	7.25
310	Frank Robinson	125.00	50.00	30.00
311	Reds Rookies (Tommy Helms, Dick Simpson)	30.00	12.00	7.25
312	Bob Saverine	30.00	12.00	7.25
313	Chris Zachary	30.00	12.00	7.25
314	Hector Valle	30.00	12.00	7.25
315	Norm Cash	30.00	12.00	7.25
316	Jack Fisher	30.00	12.00	7.25
317	Dalton Jones	30.00	12.00	7.25
318	Harry Walker	30.00	12.00	7.25
319	Gene Freese	30.00	12.00	7.25
320	Bob Gibson	125.00	50.00	30.00
321	Rick Reichardt	30.00	12.00	7.25
322	Bill Faul	30.00	12.00	7.25
323	Ray Barker	30.00	12.00	7.25
324	John Boozer	30.00	12.00	7.25
325	Vic Davalillo	95.00	40.00	25.00
326	Braves Team	75.00	30.00	18.00
327	Bernie Allen	30.00	12.00	7.25
328	Jerry Grote	30.00	12.00	7.25
329	Pete Charton	30.00	12.00	7.25
330	Ron Fairly	30.00	12.00	7.25
331	Ron Herbel	30.00	12.00	7.25
332	Billy Bryan	30.00	12.00	7.25
333	Senators Rookies (Joe Coleman, Jim French)	30.00	12.00	7.25
334	Marty Keough	30.00	12.00	7.25
335	Juan Pizarro	30.00	12.00	7.25
336	Gene Alley	30.00	12.00	7.25
337	Fred Gladding	30.00	12.00	7.25
338	Dal Maxvill	30.00	12.00	7.25
339	Del Crandall	30.00	12.00	7.25
340	Dean Chance	30.00	12.00	7.25
341	Wes Westrum	30.00	12.00	7.25
342	Bob Humphreys	30.00	12.00	7.25
343	Joe Christopher	30.00	12.00	7.25
344	Steve Blass	30.00	12.00	7.25
345	Bob Allison	30.00	12.00	7.25
346	Mike de la Hoz	30.00	12.00	7.25
347	Phil Regan	30.00	12.00	7.25
348	Orioles Team	125.00	50.00	30.00
349	Cap Peterson	30.00	12.00	7.25
350	Mel Stottlemyre	30.00	12.00	7.25
351	Fred Valentine	30.00	12.00	7.25
352	Bob Aspromonte	30.00	12.00	7.25
353	Al McBean	30.00	12.00	7.25
354	Smoky Burgess	30.00	12.00	7.25
355	Wade Blasingame	30.00	12.00	7.25
356	Red Sox Rookies (Owen Johnson, Ken Sanders)	30.00	12.00	7.25
357	Gerry Arrigo	30.00	12.00	7.25
358	Charlie Smith	30.00	12.00	7.25
359	Johnny Briggs	30.00	12.00	7.25
360	Ron Hunt	30.00	12.00	7.25
361	Tom Satriano	30.00	12.00	7.25
362	Gates Brown	30.00	12.00	7.25
363	Checklist 353-429	30.00	12.00	7.25
364	Nate Oliver	30.00	12.00	7.25
365	Roger Maris	200.00	80.00	50.00
366	Wayne Causey	30.00	12.00	7.25
367	Mel Nelson	30.00	12.00	7.25
368	Charlie Lau	30.00	12.00	7.25
369	Jim King	30.00	12.00	7.25
370	Chico Cardenas	30.00	12.00	7.25

1967 Venezuelan Topps

Cards numbered #189-338 in the 1967 Venezuelan issue feature then-current major leaguers. Card fronts are taken from Topps' 1967 baseball series, but are borderless, making them somewhat smaller than 2-1/2" x 3-1/2". Backs of the South American cards are horizontal and printed in black on two shades of green and offer a few bits of personal data and a one-paragraph career summary. Like most Venezuelan cards of the era, these are crudely printed on cheap cardboard and seldom found in condition better than Ex. Many will show evidence on back of having been glued into an album or scrapbook.

		NM	EX	VG
Complete Set (150):		6500.	3500.	2000.
Common Player:		42.00	17.00	10.00
189	Luis Aparicio	200.00	80.00	48.00
190	Vic Davalillo	42.00	17.00	10.00
191	Cesar Tovar	42.00	17.00	10.00
192	Mickey Mantle	1200.	600.00	360.00
193	Carl Yastrzemski	160.00	64.00	38.00
194	Frank Robinson	160.00	64.00	38.00
195	Willie Horton	42.00	17.00	10.00
196	Gary Peters	42.00	17.00	10.00
197	Bert Campaneris	45.00	18.00	11.00
198	Norm Cash	45.00	18.00	11.00
199	Boog Powell	45.00	18.00	11.00
200	George Scott	42.00	17.00	10.00
201	Frank Howard	45.00	18.00	11.00
202	Rick Reichardt	42.00	17.00	10.00
203	Jose Cardenal	42.00	17.00	10.00
204	Rico Petrocelli	42.00	17.00	10.00
205	Lew Krausse	42.00	17.00	10.00
206	Harmon Killebrew	160.00	64.00	38.00
207	Leon Wagner	42.00	17.00	10.00
208	Joe Foy	42.00	17.00	10.00
209	Joe Pepitone	45.00	18.00	11.00
210	Al Kaline	175.00	70.00	42.00
211	Brooks Robinson	175.00	70.00	42.00
212	Bill Freehan	42.00	17.00	10.00
213	Jim Lonborg	42.00	17.00	10.00
214	Ed Mathews	160.00	64.00	38.00
215	Dick Green	42.00	17.00	10.00
216	Tom Tresh	45.00	18.00	11.00
217	Dean Chance	42.00	17.00	10.00
218	Paul Blair	42.00	17.00	10.00
219	Larry Brown	42.00	17.00	10.00
220	Fred Valentine	42.00	17.00	10.00
221	Al Downing	42.00	17.00	10.00
222	Earl Battey	42.00	17.00	10.00
223	Don Mincher	42.00	17.00	10.00
224	Tommie Agee	42.00	17.00	10.00
225	Jim McGlothlin	42.00	17.00	10.00
226	Zoilo Versalles	42.00	17.00	10.00
227	Curt Blefary	42.00	17.00	10.00
228	Joel Horlen	42.00	17.00	10.00
229	Stu Miller	42.00	17.00	10.00
230	Tony Oliva	55.00	22.00	13.00
231	Paul Casanova	42.00	17.00	10.00
232	Orlando Pena	42.00	17.00	10.00
233	Ron Hansen	42.00	17.00	10.00
234	Earl Wilson	42.00	17.00	10.00
235	Ken Boyer	45.00	18.00	11.00
236	Jim Kaat	45.00	18.00	11.00
237	Dalton Jones	42.00	17.00	10.00
238	Pete Ward	42.00	17.00	10.00
239	Mickey Lolich	45.00	18.00	11.00
240	Jose Santiago	42.00	17.00	10.00
241	Dick McAuliffe	42.00	17.00	10.00
242	Mel Stottlemyre	42.00	17.00	10.00
243	Camilo Pascual	42.00	17.00	10.00
244	Jim Fregosi	42.00	17.00	10.00
245	Tony Conigliaro	45.00	18.00	11.00
246	Sonny Siebert	42.00	17.00	10.00
247	Jim Perry	42.00	17.00	10.00
248	Dave McNally	42.00	17.00	10.00
249	Fred Whitfield	42.00	17.00	10.00
250	Ken Berry	42.00	17.00	10.00
251	Jim Grant	42.00	17.00	10.00
252	Hank Aguirre	42.00	17.00	10.00
253	Don Wert	42.00	17.00	10.00
254	Wally Bunker	42.00	17.00	10.00
255	Elston Howard	45.00	18.00	11.00
256	Dave Johnson	42.00	17.00	10.00
257	Hoyt Wilhelm	125.00	50.00	30.00
258	Don Buford	42.00	17.00	10.00
259	Sam McDowell	45.00	18.00	11.00
260	Bobby Knoop	42.00	17.00	10.00
261	Denny McLain	45.00	18.00	11.00
262	Steve Hargan	42.00	17.00	10.00
263	Jim Nash	42.00	17.00	10.00
264	Jerry Adair	42.00	17.00	10.00
265	Tony Gonzalez	42.00	17.00	10.00
266	Mike Shannon	42.00	17.00	10.00
267	Bob Gibson	160.00	64.00	38.00
268	John Roseboro	42.00	17.00	10.00
269	Bob Aspromonte	42.00	17.00	10.00
270	Pete Rose	300.00	120.00	72.00
271	Rico Carty	45.00	18.00	11.00
272	Juan Pizarro	42.00	17.00	10.00
273	Willie Mays	300.00	120.00	72.00
274	Jim Bunning	125.00	50.00	30.00
275	Ernie Banks	175.00	70.00	42.00
276	Curt Flood	45.00	18.00	11.00
277	Mack Jones	42.00	17.00	10.00
278	Roberto Clemente	450.00	180.00	108.00
279	Sammy Ellis	42.00	17.00	10.00
280	Willie Stargell	150.00	60.00	36.00
281	Felipe Alou	45.00	18.00	11.00
282	Ed Kranepool	42.00	17.00	10.00
283	Nelson Briles	42.00	17.00	10.00
284	Hank Aaron	300.00	120.00	72.00
285	Vada Pinson	55.00	22.00	13.00
286	Jim LeFebvre	42.00	17.00	10.00
287	Hal Lanier	42.00	17.00	10.00
288	Ron Swoboda	42.00	17.00	10.00
289	Mike McCormick	42.00	17.00	10.00
290	Lou Johnson	42.00	17.00	10.00
291	Orlando Cepeda	125.00	62.00	37.00
292	Rusty Staub	45.00	18.00	11.00
293	Manny Mota	42.00	17.00	10.00
294	Tommy Harper	42.00	17.00	10.00
295	Don Drysdale	160.00	64.00	38.00
296	Mel Queen	42.00	17.00	10.00
297	Red Schoendienst	125.00	50.00	30.00
298	Matty Alou	42.00	17.00	10.00
299	Johnny Callison	42.00	17.00	10.00
300	Juan Marichal	160.00	64.00	38.00
301	Al McBean	42.00	17.00	10.00
302	Claude Osteen	42.00	17.00	10.00
303	Willie McCovey	175.00	70.00	42.00

304	Jim Owens	42.00	17.00	10.00
305	Chico Ruiz	42.00	17.00	10.00
306	Ferguson Jenkins	125.00	50.00	30.00
307	Lou Brock	125.00	50.00	30.00
308	Joe Morgan	150.00	60.00	36.00
309	Ron Santo	65.00	26.00	15.50
310	Chico Cardenas	42.00	17.00	10.00
311	Richie Allen	45.00	18.00	11.00
312	Gaylord Perry	125.00	50.00	30.00
313	Bill Mazeroski	65.00	26.00	15.50
314	Tony Taylor	42.00	17.00	10.00
315	Tommy Helms	42.00	17.00	10.00
316	Jim Wynn	42.00	17.00	10.00
317	Don Sutton	90.00	45.00	27.00
318	Mike Cuellar	45.00	18.00	11.00
319	Willie Davis	42.00	17.00	10.00
320	Julian Javier	42.00	17.00	10.00
321	Maury Wills	45.00	18.00	11.00
322	Gene Alley	42.00	17.00	10.00
323	Ray Sadecki	42.00	17.00	10.00
324	Joe Torre	50.00	25.00	15.00
325	Jim Maloney	42.00	17.00	10.00
326	Jim Davenport	42.00	17.00	10.00
327	Tony Perez	125.00	62.00	37.00
328	Roger Maris	200.00	80.00	48.00
329	Chris Short	42.00	17.00	10.00
330	Jesus Alou	42.00	17.00	10.00
331	Darron Johnson	42.00	17.00	10.00
332	Tommy Davis	42.00	17.00	10.00
333	Bob Veale	42.00	17.00	10.00
334	Bill McCool	42.00	17.00	10.00
335	Jim Hart	42.00	17.00	10.00
336	Roy Face	42.00	17.00	10.00
337	Billy Williams	125.00	50.00	30.00
338	Dick Groat	45.00	18.00	11.00

1967 Venezuela Retirado

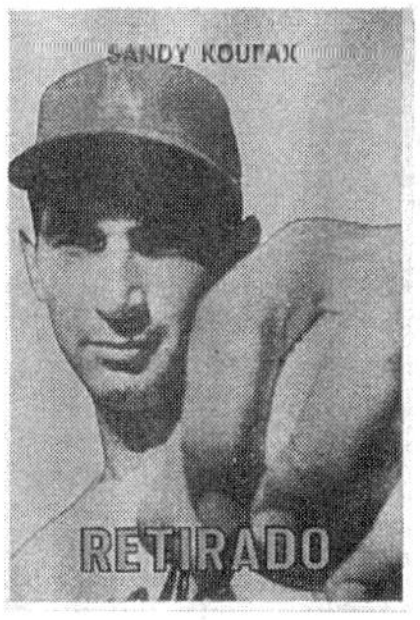

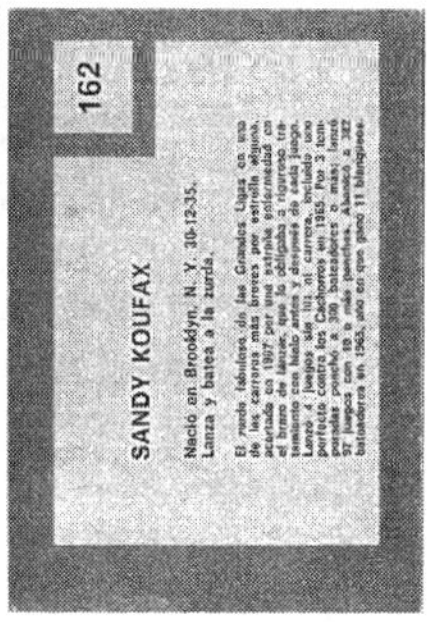

Three distinct series of baseball cards were issued in 1967 for sale in Venezuela, contiguously numbered. Cards #1-138 are minor leaguers and Hispanic players active in Latin Winter League ball. Cards #189-338 are contemporary Major League players and cards #139-188 are former big league stars. The series share a common back design printed horizontally in black on green with a few biographical data and a one paragraph career summary. Fronts of the contemporary player cards are almost identical to 1967 Topps. The fronts of the Retirado cards, however, have a blue background with the player's name in black at top and "RETIRADO" in red block letters at bottom. Player photos on the Retirado cards are sepia. Like most of the Venezuelan cards of the era, these are crudely printed on cheap cardboard. Also like most Venezuelan cards, they are virtually impossible to find in any condition above Ex. Many are found with back damage due to having been glued into an album or scrapbook.

		NM	EX	VG
Complete Set (50):		7250.	3600.	2100.
Common Player:		75.00	37.50	22.00
139	Walter Johnson	300.00	150.00	90.00
140	Bill Dickey	150.00	75.00	45.00
141	Lou Gehrig	550.00	275.00	165.00
142	Rogers Hornsby	175.00	87.00	52.00
143	Honus Wagner	225.00	112.00	67.00
144	Paul Traynor	125.00	62.00	37.00
145	Joe DiMaggio	550.00	275.00	165.00
146	Ty Cobb	450.00	225.00	135.00
147	Babe Ruth	750.00	375.00	225.00
148	Ted Williams	450.00	225.00	135.00
149	Mel Ott	125.00	62.00	37.00
150	Cy Young	175.00	87.00	52.00
151	Christy Mathewson	350.00	175.00	105.00
152	Warren Spahn	175.00	87.00	52.00
153	Mickey Cochrane	125.00	62.00	37.00
154	George Sisler	150.00	75.00	45.00
155	Jimmy Collins	125.00	62.00	37.00
156	Tris Speaker	150.00	75.00	45.00
157	Stan Musial	350.00	175.00	105.00
158	Luke Appling	125.00	62.00	37.00
159	Nap Lajoie	125.00	62.00	37.00
160	Bill Terry	125.00	62.00	37.00
161	Bob Feller	150.00	75.00	45.00
162	Sandy Koufax	250.00	125.00	75.00
163	Jimmie Foxx	125.00	62.00	37.00
164	Joe Cronin	125.00	62.00	37.00
165	Frankie Frisch	125.00	62.00	37.00
166	Paul Waner	125.00	62.00	37.00
167	Lloyd Waner	125.00	62.00	37.00
168	Lefty Grove	125.00	62.00	37.00
169	Bobby Doerr	125.00	62.00	37.00
170	Al Simmons	125.00	62.00	37.00
171	Grover Alexander	150.00	75.00	45.00
172	Carl Hubbell	125.00	62.00	37.00
173	Mordecai Brown	125.00	62.00	37.00
174	Ted Lyons	125.00	62.00	37.00
175	Johnny Vander Meer	75.00	37.50	22.00
176	Alex Carrasquel	75.00	37.50	22.00
177	Satchel Paige	300.00	150.00	90.00
178	Whitey Ford	150.00	75.00	45.00
179	Yogi Berra	150.00	75.00	45.00
180	Roy Campanella	150.00	75.00	45.00
181	Chico Carrasquel	75.00	37.50	22.00
182	Johnny Mize	125.00	62.00	37.00
183	Ted Kluszewski (photo actually Gene Bearden)	75.00	37.50	22.00
184	Jackie Robinson	350.00	175.00	105.00
185	Bobby Avila	75.00	37.50	22.00
186	Phil Rizzuto	150.00	75.00	45.00
187	Minnie Minoso	90.00	45.00	27.00
188	Connie Marrero	75.00	37.50	22.00

1968 Venezuelan Topps

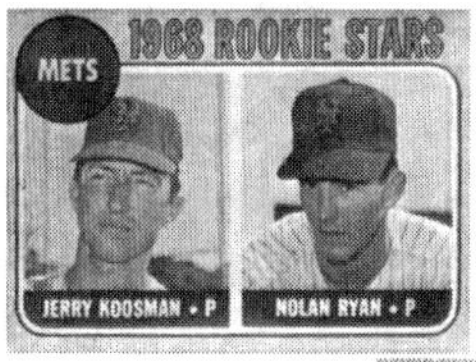

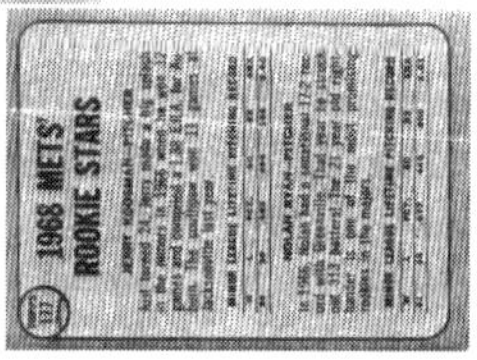

The first 370 cards of Topps' 1968 baseball card set were reproduced in South America for sale in Venezuela. Besides being rather crudely printed on cheaper, non-gloss cardboard, the cards are virtually identical to the Topps U.S. version. The only difference is a tiny line of yellow type on back which reads: "Hecho en Venezuela - C.A. Litoven". Like most contemporary Venezuelan issues, these cards are seldom found in condition better than Excellent, and often with evidence on back of having been glued into an album or scrapbook.

		NM	EX	VG
Complete Set (370):		11500.	5500.	3250.
Common Player:		20.00	8.00	4.75
1	N.L. Batting Leaders (Matty Alou, Roberto Clemente, Tony Gonzalez)	125.00	50.00	30.00
2	A.L. Batting Leaders (Al Kaline, Frank Robinson, Carl Yastrzemski)	65.00	26.00	15.50
3	N.L. RBI Leaders (Hank Aaron, Orlando Cepeda, Roberto Clemente)	100.00	40.00	24.00
4	A.L. RBI Leaders (Harmon Killebrew, Frank Robinson, Carl Yastrzemski)	80.00	32.00	19.00
5	N.L. Home Run Leaders (Hank Aaron, Willie McCovey, Ron Santo, Jim Wynn)	60.00	24.00	14.50
6	A.L. Home Run Leaders (Frank Howard, Harmon Killebrew, Carl Yastrzemski)	55.00	22.00	13.00
7	N.L. ERA Leaders (Jim Bunning, Phil Niekro, Chris Short)	25.00	10.00	6.00
8	A.L. ERA Leaders (Joe Horlen, Gary Peters, Sonny Siebert)	20.00	8.00	4.75
9	N.L. Pitching Leaders (Jim Bunning, Fergie Jenkins, Mike McCormick, Claude Osteen)	25.00	10.00	6.00
10	A.L. Pitching Leaders (Dean Chance, Jim Lonborg, Earl Wilson)	20.00	8.00	4.75
11	N.L. Strikeout Leaders (Jim Bunning, Fergie Jenkins, Gaylord Perry)	30.00	12.00	7.25
12	A.L. Strikeout Leaders (Dean Chance, Jim Lonborg, Sam McDowell)	20.00	8.00	4.75
13	Chuck Hartenstein	20.00	8.00	4.75
14	Jerry McNertney	20.00	8.00	4.75
15	Ron Hunt	20.00	8.00	4.75
16	Indians Rookies (Lou Piniella, Richie Scheinblum)	25.00	10.00	6.00
17	Dick Hall	20.00	8.00	4.75
18	Mike Hershberger	20.00	8.00	4.75
19	Juan Pizarro	20.00	8.00	4.75
20	Brooks Robinson	150.00	60.00	36.00
21	Ron Davis	20.00	8.00	4.75
22	Pat Dobson	20.00	8.00	4.75
23	Chico Cardenas	20.00	8.00	4.75
24	Bobby Locke	20.00	8.00	4.75
25	Julian Javier	20.00	8.00	4.75
26	Darrell Brandon	20.00	8.00	4.75
27	Gil Hodges	45.00	18.00	11.00
28	Ted Uhlaender	20.00	8.00	4.75
29	Joe Verbanic	20.00	8.00	4.75
30	Joe Torre	25.00	10.00	6.00
31	Ed Stroud	20.00	8.00	4.75
32	Joe Gibbon	20.00	8.00	4.75
33	Pete Ward	20.00	8.00	4.75
34	Al Ferrara	20.00	8.00	4.75
35	Steve Hargan	20.00	8.00	4.75
36	Pirates Rookies (Bob Moose, Bob Robertson)	20.00	8.00	4.75
37	Billy Williams	125.00	50.00	30.00
38	Tony Pierce	20.00	8.00	4.75
39	Cookie Rojas	20.00	8.00	4.75
40	Denny McLain	35.00	14.00	8.50
41	Julio Gotay	20.00	8.00	4.75
42	Larry Haney	20.00	8.00	4.75
43	Gary Bell	20.00	8.00	4.75
44	Frank Kostro	20.00	8.00	4.75
45	Tom Seaver	350.00	140.00	84.00
46	Dave Ricketts	20.00	8.00	4.75
47	Ralph Houk	20.00	8.00	4.75
48	Ted Davidson	20.00	8.00	4.75
49	Ed Brinkman	20.00	8.00	4.75
50	Willie Mays	450.00	180.00	108.00
51	Bob Locker	20.00	8.00	4.75
52	Hawk Taylor	20.00	8.00	4.75
53	Gene Alley	20.00	8.00	4.75
54	Stan Williams	20.00	8.00	4.75
55	Felipe Alou	25.00	10.00	6.00
56	Orioles Rookies (Dave Leonhard, Dave May)	20.00	8.00	4.75
57	Dan Schneider	20.00	8.00	4.75
58	Eddie Mathews	125.00	50.00	30.00
59	Don Lock	20.00	8.00	4.75
60	Ken Holtzman	20.00	8.00	4.75
61	Reggie Smith	20.00	8.00	4.75
62	Chuck Dobson	20.00	8.00	4.75
63	Dick Kenworthy	20.00	8.00	4.75
64	Jim Merritt	20.00	8.00	4.75
65	John Roseboro	20.00	8.00	4.75
66	Casey Cox	20.00	8.00	4.75
67	Checklist 1-109 (Jim Kaat)	30.00	12.00	7.25
68	Ron Willis	20.00	8.00	4.75
69	Tom Tresh	20.00	8.00	4.75
70	Bob Veale	20.00	8.00	4.75
71	Vern Fuller	20.00	8.00	4.75
72	Tommy John	25.00	10.00	6.00
73	Jim Hart	20.00	8.00	4.75
74	Milt Pappas	20.00	8.00	4.75
75	Don Mincher	20.00	8.00	4.75
76	Braves Rookies (Jim Britton, Ron Reed)	20.00	8.00	4.75
77	Don Wilson	20.00	8.00	4.75
78	Jim Northrup	20.00	8.00	4.75
79	Ted Kubiak	20.00	8.00	4.75
80	Rod Carew	150.00	60.00	36.00
81	Larry Jackson	20.00	8.00	4.75
82	Sam Bowens	20.00	8.00	4.75
83	John Stephenson	20.00	8.00	4.75
84	Bob Tolan	20.00	8.00	4.75
85	Gaylord Perry	100.00	40.00	24.00
86	Willie Stargell	125.00	50.00	30.00
87	Dick Williams	20.00	8.00	4.75
88	Phil Regan	20.00	8.00	4.75
89	Jake Gibbs	20.00	8.00	4.75
90	Vada Pinson	35.00	14.00	8.50
91	Jim Ollom	20.00	8.00	4.75
92	Ed Kranepool	20.00	8.00	4.75
93	Tony Cloninger	20.00	8.00	4.75
94	Lee Maye	20.00	8.00	4.75
95	Bob Aspromonte	20.00	8.00	4.75
96	Senators Rookies (Frank Coggins, Dick Nold)	20.00	8.00	4.75
97	Tom Phoebus	20.00	8.00	4.75
98	Gary Sutherland	20.00	8.00	4.75
99	Rocky Colavito	60.00	24.00	14.50
100	Bob Gibson	125.00	50.00	30.00
101	Glenn Beckert	20.00	8.00	4.75
102	Jose Cardenal	20.00	8.00	4.75
103	Don Sutton	90.00	45.00	27.00
104	Dick Dietz	20.00	8.00	4.75
105	Al Downing	20.00	8.00	4.75
106	Dalton Jones	20.00	8.00	4.75
107	Checklist 110-196 (Juan Marichal)	35.00	14.00	8.50
108	Don Pavletich	20.00	8.00	4.75
109	Bert Campaneris	25.00	10.00	6.00
110	Hank Aaron	450.00	180.00	108.00
111	Rich Reese	20.00	8.00	4.75
112	Woody Fryman	20.00	8.00	4.75
113	Tigers Rookies (Tom Matchick, Daryl Patterson)	20.00	8.00	4.75
114	Ron Swoboda	20.00	8.00	4.75
115	Sam McDowell	20.00	0.00	4.75
116	Ken McMullen	20.00	8.00	4.75
117	Larry Jaster	20.00	8.00	4.75
118	Mark Belanger	20.00	8.00	4.75
119	Ted Savage	20.00	8.00	4.75
120	Mel Stottlemyre	20.00	8.00	4.75
121	Jimmie Hall	20.00	8.00	4.75
122	Gene Mauch	20.00	8.00	4.75
123	Jose Santiago	20.00	8.00	4.75
124	Nate Oliver	20.00	8.00	4.75
125	Joe Horlen	20.00	8.00	4.75
126	Bobby Etheridge	20.00	8.00	4.75
127	Paul Lindblad	20.00	8.00	4.75
128	Astros Rookies (Tom Dukes, Alonzo Harris)	20.00	8.00	4.75
129	Mickey Stanley	20.00	8.00	4.75
130	Tony Perez	100.00	50.00	30.00
131	Frank Bertaina	20.00	8.00	4.75

132	Bud Harrelson	20.00	8.00	4.75
133	Fred Whitfield	20.00	8.00	4.75
134	Pat Jarvis	20.00	8.00	4.75
135	Paul Blair	20.00	8.00	4.75
136	Randy Hundley	20.00	8.00	4.75
137	Twins Team	30.00	12.00	7.25
138	Ruben Amaro	20.00	8.00	4.75
139	Chris Short	20.00	8.00	4.75
140	Tony Conigliaro	40.00	16.00	9.50
141	Dal Maxvill	20.00	8.00	4.75
142	White Sox Rookies (Buddy Bradford, Bill Voss)	20.00	8.00	4.75
143	Pete Cimino	20.00	8.00	4.75
144	Joe Morgan	100.00	40.00	24.00
145	Don Drysdale	125.00	50.00	30.00
146	Sal Bando	20.00	8.00	4.75
147	Frank Linzy	20.00	8.00	4.75
148	Dave Bristol	20.00	8.00	4.75
149	Bob Saverine	20.00	8.00	4.75
150	Roberto Clemente	500.00	200.00	120.00
151	World Series Game 1 (Brock Socks 4 Hits in Opener)	30.00	12.00	7.25
152	World Series Game 2 (Yaz Smashes Two Homers)	35.00	14.00	8.50
153	World Series Game 3 (Briles Cools Off Boston)	20.00	8.00	4.75
154	World Series Game 4 (Gibson Hurls Shutout)	35.00	14.00	8.50
155	World Series Game 5 (Lonborg Wins Again)	20.00	8.00	4.75
156	World Series Game 6 (Petrocelli Socks Two Homers)	20.00	8.00	4.75
157	World Series Game 7 (St. Louis Wins It)	20.00	8.00	4.75
158	World Series Summary (The Cardinals Celebrate)	20.00	8.00	4.75
159	Don Kessinger	20.00	8.00	4.75
160	Earl Wilson	20.00	8.00	4.75
161	Norm Miller	20.00	8.00	4.75
162	Cardinals Rookies (Hal Gilson, Mike Torrez)	20.00	8.00	4.75
163	Gene Brabender	20.00	8.00	4.75
164	Ramon Webster	20.00	8.00	4.75
165	Tony Oliva	35.00	14.00	8.50
166	Claude Raymond	20.00	8.00	4.75
167	Elston Howard	25.00	10.00	6.00
168	Dodgers Team	35.00	14.00	8.50
169	Bob Bolin	20.00	8.00	4.75
170	Jim Fregosi	20.00	8.00	4.75
171	Don Nottebart	20.00	8.00	4.75
172	Walt Williams	20.00	8.00	4.75
173	John Boozer	20.00	8.00	4.75
174	Bob Tillman	20.00	8.00	4.75
175	Maury Wills	25.00	10.00	6.00
176	Bob Allen	20.00	8.00	4.75
177	Mets Rookies *(Jerry Koosman), (Nolan Ryan)*	3000.	1500.	900.00
178	Don Wert	20.00	8.00	4.75
179	Bill Stoneman	20.00	8.00	4.75
180	Curt Flood	20.00	8.00	4.75
181	Jerry Zimmerman	20.00	8.00	4.75
182	Dave Giusti	20.00	8.00	4.75
183	Bob Kennedy	20.00	8.00	4.75
184	Lou Johnson	20.00	8.00	4.75
185	Tom Haller	20.00	8.00	4.75
186	Eddie Watt	20.00	8.00	4.75
187	Sonny Jackson	20.00	8.00	4.75
188	Cap Peterson	20.00	8.00	4.75
189	Bill Landis	20.00	8.00	4.75
190	Bill White	20.00	8.00	4.75
191	Dan Frisella	20.00	8.00	4.75
192	Checklist 197-283 (Carl Yastrzemski)	35.00	14.00	8.50
193	Jack Hamilton	20.00	8.00	4.75
194	Don Buford	20.00	8.00	4.75
195	Joe Pepitone	20.00	8.00	4.75
196	Gary Nolan	20.00	8.00	4.75
197	Larry Brown	20.00	8.00	4.75
198	Roy Face	20.00	8.00	4.75
199	A's Rookies (Darrell Osteen, Roberto Rodriguez)	20.00	8.00	4.75
200	Orlando Cepeda	125.00	62.00	37.00
201	Mike Marshall	20.00	8.00	4.75
202	Adolfo Phillips	20.00	8.00	4.75
203	Dick Kelley	20.00	8.00	4.75
204	Andy Etchebarren	20.00	8.00	4.75
205	Juan Marichal	125.00	50.00	30.00
206	Cal Ermer	20.00	8.00	4.75
207	Carroll Sembera	20.00	8.00	4.75
208	Willie Davis	20.00	8.00	4.75
209	Tim Cullen	20.00	8.00	4.75
210	Gary Peters	20.00	8.00	4.75
211	J.C. Martin	20.00	8.00	4.75
212	Dave Morehead	20.00	8.00	4.75
213	Chico Ruiz	20.00	8.00	4.75
214	Yankees Rookies (Stan Bahnsen, Frank Fernandez)	20.00	8.00	4.75
215	Jim Bunning	100.00	40.00	24.00
216	Bubba Morton	20.00	8.00	4.75
217	Turk Farrell	20.00	8.00	4.75
218	Ken Suarez	20.00	8.00	4.75
219	Rob Gardner	20.00	8.00	4.75
220	Harmon Killebrew	125.00	50.00	30.00
221	Braves Team	30.00	12.00	7.25
222	Jim Hardin	20.00	8.00	4.75
223	Ollie Brown	20.00	8.00	4.75
224	Jack Aker	20.00	8.00	4.75
225	Richie Allen	35.00	14.00	8.50
226	Jimmie Price	20.00	8.00	4.75
227	Joe Hoerner	20.00	8.00	4.75
228	Dodgers Rookies (Jack Billingham, Jim Fairey)	20.00	8.00	4.75
229	Fred Klages	20.00	8.00	4.75
230	Pete Rose	400.00	160.00	96.00
231	Dave Baldwin	20.00	8.00	4.75
232	Denis Menke	20.00	8.00	4.75
233	George Scott	20.00	8.00	4.75
234	Bill Monbouquette	20.00	8.00	4.75
235	Ron Santo	35.00	14.00	8.50
236	Tug McGraw	20.00	8.00	4.75
237	Alvin Dark	20.00	8.00	4.75
238	Tom Satriano	20.00	8.00	4.75
239	Bill Henry	20.00	8.00	4.75
240	Al Kaline	150.00	60.00	36.00
241	Felix Millan	20.00	8.00	4.75
242	Moe Drabowsky	20.00	8.00	4.75
243	Rich Rollins	20.00	8.00	4.75
244	John Donaldson	20.00	8.00	4.75
245	Tony Gonzalez	20.00	8.00	4.75
246	Fritz Peterson	20.00	8.00	4.75
247	Reds Rookies (Johnny Bench, Ron Tompkins)	300.00	120.00	72.00
248	Fred Valentine	20.00	8.00	4.75
249	Bill Singer	20.00	8.00	4.75
250	Carl Yastrzemski	150.00	60.00	36.00
251	Manny Sanguillen	25.00	10.00	6.00
252	Angels Team	30.00	12.00	7.25
253	Dick Hughes	20.00	8.00	4.75
254	Cleon Jones	20.00	8.00	4.75
255	Dean Chance	20.00	8.00	4.75
256	Norm Cash	25.00	10.00	6.00
257	Phil Niekro	100.00	40.00	24.00
258	Cubs Rookies (Jose Arcia, Bill Schlesinger)	20.00	8.00	4.75
259	Ken Boyer	45.00	18.00	11.00
260	Jim Wynn	20.00	8.00	4.75
261	Dave Duncan	20.00	8.00	4.75
262	Rick Wise	20.00	8.00	4.75
263	Horace Clarke	20.00	8.00	4.75
264	Ted Abernathy	20.00	8.00	4.75
265	Tommy Davis	20.00	8.00	4.75
266	Paul Popovich	20.00	8.00	4.75
267	Herman Franks	20.00	8.00	4.75
268	Bob Humphreys	20.00	8.00	4.75
269	Bob Tiefenauer	20.00	8.00	4.75
270	Matty Alou	20.00	8.00	4.75
271	Bobby Knoop	20.00	8.00	4.75
272	Ray Culp	20.00	8.00	4.75
273	Dave Johnson	20.00	8.00	4.75
274	Mike Cuellar	20.00	8.00	4.75
275	Tim McCarver	25.00	10.00	6.00
276	Jim Roland	20.00	8.00	4.75
277	Jerry Buchek	20.00	8.00	4.75
278	Checklist 284-370 (Orlando Cepeda)	35.00	14.00	8.50
279	Bill Hands	20.00	8.00	4.75
280	Mickey Mantle	1100.	440.00	264.00
281	Jim Campanis	20.00	8.00	4.75
282	Rick Monday	20.00	8.00	4.75
283	Mel Queen	20.00	8.00	4.75
284	John Briggs	20.00	8.00	4.75
285	Dick McAuliffe	20.00	8.00	4.75
286	Cecil Upshaw	20.00	8.00	4.75
287	White Sox Rookies (Mickey Abarbanel, Cisco Carlos)	20.00	8.00	4.75
288	Dave Wickersham	20.00	8.00	4.75
289	Woody Held	20.00	8.00	4.75
290	Willie McCovey	125.00	50.00	30.00
291	Dick Lines	20.00	8.00	4.75
292	Art Shamsky	20.00	8.00	4.75
293	Bruce Howard	20.00	8.00	4.75
294	Red Schoendienst	75.00	30.00	18.00
295	Sonny Siebert	20.00	8.00	4.75
296	Byron Browne	20.00	8.00	4.75
297	Russ Gibson	20.00	8.00	4.75
298	Jim Brewer	20.00	8.00	4.75
299	Gene Michael	20.00	8.00	4.75
300	Rusty Staub	25.00	10.00	6.00
301	Twins Rookies (George Mitterwald, Rick Renick)	20.00	8.00	4.75
302	Gerry Arrigo	20.00	8.00	4.75
303	Dick Green	20.00	8.00	4.75
304	Sandy Valdespino	20.00	8.00	4.75
305	Minnie Rojas	20.00	8.00	4.75
306	Mike Ryan	20.00	8.00	4.75
307	John Hiller	20.00	8.00	4.75
308	Pirates Team	35.00	14.00	8.50
309	Ken Henderson	20.00	8.00	4.75
310	Luis Aparicio	200.00	80.00	48.00
311	Jack Lamabe	20.00	8.00	4.75
312	Curt Blefary	20.00	8.00	4.75
313	Al Weis	20.00	8.00	4.75
314	Red Sox Rookies (Bill Rohr, George Spriggs)	20.00	8.00	4.75
315	Zoilo Versalles	20.00	8.00	4.75
316	Steve Barber	20.00	8.00	4.75
317	Ron Brand	20.00	8.00	4.75
318	Chico Salmon	20.00	8.00	4.75
319	George Culver	20.00	8.00	4.75
320	Frank Howard	25.00	10.00	6.00
321	Leo Durocher	75.00	30.00	18.00
322	Dave Boswell	20.00	8.00	4.75
323	Deron Johnson	20.00	8.00	4.75
324	Jim Nash	20.00	8.00	4.75
325	Manny Mota	20.00	8.00	4.75
326	Dennis Ribant	20.00	8.00	4.75
327	Tony Taylor	20.00	8.00	4.75
328	Angels Rookies (Chuck Vinson, Jim Weaver)	20.00	8.00	4.75
329	Duane Josephson	20.00	8.00	4.75
330	Roger Maris	150.00	60.00	36.00
331	Dan Osinski	20.00	8.00	4.75
332	Doug Rader	20.00	8.00	4.75
333	Ron Herbel	20.00	8.00	4.75
334	Orioles Team	35.00	14.00	8.50
335	Bob Allison	20.00	8.00	4.75
336	John Purdin	20.00	8.00	4.75
337	Bill Robinson	20.00	8.00	4.75
338	Bob Johnson	20.00	8.00	4.75
339	Rich Nye	20.00	8.00	4.75
340	Max Alvis	20.00	8.00	4.75
341	Jim Lemon	20.00	8.00	4.75
342	Ken Johnson	20.00	8.00	4.75
343	Jim Gosger	20.00	8.00	4.75
344	Donn Clendenon	20.00	8.00	4.75
345	Bob Hendley	20.00	8.00	4.75
346	Jerry Adair	20.00	8.00	4.75
347	George Brunet	20.00	8.00	4.75
348	Phillies Rookies (Larry Colton, Dick Thoenen)	20.00	8.00	4.75
349	Ed Spiezio	20.00	8.00	4.75
350	Hoyt Wilhelm	75.00	30.00	18.00
351	Bob Barton	20.00	8.00	4.75
352	Jackie Hernandez	20.00	8.00	4.75
353	Mack Jones	20.00	8.00	4.75
354	Pete Richert	20.00	8.00	4.75
355	Ernie Banks	150.00	60.00	36.00
356	Checklist 371-457 (Ken Holtzman)	30.00	12.00	7.25
357	Len Gabrielson	20.00	8.00	4.75
358	Mike Epstein	20.00	8.00	4.75
359	Joe Moeller	20.00	8.00	4.75
360	Willie Horton	20.00	8.00	4.75
361	Harmon Killebrew (All-Star)	50.00	20.00	12.00
362	Orlando Cepeda (All-Star)	30.00	12.00	7.25
363	Rod Carew (All-Star)	50.00	20.00	12.00
364	Joe Morgan (All-Star)	40.00	16.00	9.50
365	Brooks Robinson (All-Star)	60.00	24.00	14.50
366	Ron Santo (All-Star)	35.00	14.00	8.50
367	Jim Fregosi (All-Star)	20.00	8.00	4.75
368	Gene Alley (All-Star)	20.00	8.00	4.75
369	Carl Yastrzemski (All-Star)	60.00	24.00	14.50
370	Hank Aaron (All-Star)	100.00	40.00	24.00

1972 Venezuelan Baseball Stamps

Utilizing most of the same photos as the 1972 Topps baseball cards, the 242 player stamps in this set feature only Major Leaguers, though with an overrepresentation of Hispanics, rather than the usual mix of U.S. and local talent. Stamps measure 2" x 2-9/16" and feature tombstone-shaped color photos at center, surrounded by a green background. The only printing is the player name, team name (in Spanish) and stamp number, all in black. A white border surrounds the whole. Backs are blank as the stamps were meant to be mounted in an album. Because stamps are seldom seen in higher grade, only a VG price is presented here. Stamps in Good should be valued at 50% of the price shown, and stamps grading Fair at 25%.

		VG
Complete Set (242):		2100.
Common Player:		10.00
Album:		75.00
1	Vic Davalillo	10.00
2	Doug Griffin	10.00
3	Rod Carew	100.00
4	Joel Horlen	10.00
5	Jim Fregosi	15.00
6	Rod Carew ("en acion" - In Action)	75.00
7	Billy Champion	10.00
8	Ron Hansen	10.00
9	Bobby Murcer	10.00
10	Nellie Briles	10.00
11	Fred Patek	10.00
12	Mike Epstein	10.00
13	Dave Marshall	10.00
14	Steve Hargan	10.00
15	Duane Josephson	10.00
16	Steve Garvey	45.00
17	Eddie Fisher	10.00
18	Jack Aker	10.00
19	Ron Brand	10.00
20	Del Rice	10.00
21	Ollie Brown	10.00
22	Jamie McAndrew	10.00
23	Willie Horton	10.00
24	Eddie Leon	10.00
25	Steve Hovley	10.00
26	Moe Drabowsky	10.00
27	Dick Selma	10.00
28	Jim Lyttle	10.00
29	Sal Bando	10.00
30	Bill Lee	10.00
31	Al Kaline	125.00
32	Mike Lum	10.00
33	Les Cain	10.00
34	Richie Hebner	10.00
35	Donn Clendenon	15.00
36	Ralph Houk	10.00

37	Luis Melendez	10.00
38	Jim Hickman	10.00
39	Manny Mota	10.00
40	Bob Locker	10.00
41	Ron Santo	15.00
42	Tony Cloninger	10.00
43	Joe Ferguson	10.00
44	Mike McCormick	10.00
45	Bobby Wine	10.00
46	Preston Gomez	10.00
47	Pat Corrales (In Action)	10.00
48	Hector Torres	10.00
49	Fritz Peterson	10.00
50	Jim Rooker	10.00
51	Chris Short	10.00
52	Juan Marichal (In Action)	35.00
53	Teddy Martinez	10.00
54	Ken Aspromonte	10.00
55	Bobby Bonds	15.00
56	Rich Robertson	10.00
57	Nate Colbert (In Action)	10.00
58	Jose Pagan (In Action)	10.00
59	Curt Blefary (In Action)	10.00
60	Bill Mazeroski	40.00
61	John Odom	10.00
62	George Stone	10.00
63	Lew Krausse	10.00
64	Bobby Knoop	10.00
65	Pete Rose (In Action)	95.00
66	Steve Luebber	10.00
67	Bill Voss	10.00
68	Chico Salmon	10.00
69	Ivan Murrell	10.00
70	Gil Garrido	10.00
71	Terry Crowley	10.00
72	Bill Russell	10.00
73	Steve Dunning	10.00
74	Ray Sadecki (In Action)	10.00
75	Al Gallagher (In Action)	10.00
76	Cesar Gutierrez	10.00
77	John Kennedy	10.00
78	Joe Hague	10.00
79	Bruce Del Canton	10.00
80	Ken Holtzman	10.00
81	Rico Carty	10.00
82	Roger Repoz	10.00
83	Fran Healy	10.00
84	Al Gallagher	10.00
85	Rich McKinney	10.00
86	Lowell Palmer	10.00
87	Jose Cardenal	10.00
88	Ed Kirkpatrick (In Action)	10.00
89	Steve Carlton	100.00
90	Gail Hopkins	10.00
91	Reggie Smith	10.00
92	Denny Riddleberger	10.00
93	Don Sutton	45.00
94	Bob Moose	10.00
95	Joe Decker	10.00
96	Bill Wilson	10.00
97	Mike Ferraro	10.00
98	Jack Hiatt	10.00
99	Bill Grabarkewitz	10.00
100	Larry Stahl	10.00
101	Jim Slaton	10.00
102	Jim Wynn	10.00
103	Phil Niekro	40.00
104	Danny Cater	10.00
105	Ray Sadecki	10.00
106	Jack Billingham	10.00
107	Dave Nelson	10.00
108	Rudy May	10.00
109	Don Money	10.00
110	Diego Segui	10.00
111	Jose Pagan	10.00
112	John Strohmayer	10.00
113	Wade Blasingame	10.00
114	Ken Wright	10.00
115	Ken Tatum	10.00
116	Mike Paul	10.00
117	Tom McCraw	10.00
118	Bob Gibson	60.00
119	Al Santorini	10.00
120	Leo Cardenas	10.00
121	Jimmy Stewart	10.00
122	Willie Crawford	10.00
123	Bob Aspromonte	10.00
124	Frank Duffy	10.00
125	Hal Lanier	10.00
126	Nate Colbert	10.00
127	Russ Gibson	10.00
128	Cesar Geronimo	10.00
129	Pat Kelly	10.00
130	Horacio Pina	10.00
131	Charlie Brinkman	10.00
132	Bill Virdon	10.00
133	Hal McRae	12.50
134	Tony Oliva (In Action)	12.50
135	Gonzalo Marquez	10.00
136	Willie Montanez	10.00
137	Dick Green	10.00
138	Jim Ray	10.00
139	Denis Menke	10.00
140	Fred Kendall	10.00
141	Vida Blue	10.00
142	Tom Grieve	10.00
143	Ed Kirkpatrick (In Action)	10.00
144	George Scott	10.00
145	Hal Breeden	10.00
146	Ken McMullen	10.00
147	Jim Perry (In Action)	10.00
148	Wayne Granger	10.00
149	Mike Hegan	10.00
150	Al Oliver	10.00
151	Frank Robinson (In Action)	90.00
152	Paul Blair	10.00
153	Phil Hennigan	10.00
154	Ron Stone	10.00
155	Gene Michael	10.00
156	Jerry McNertney	10.00
157	Marcelino Lopez	10.00
158	Dave May	10.00
159	Jim Hart	10.00
160	Joe Coleman	10.00
161	Rick Reichardt	10.00
162	Ed Brinkman	10.00
163	Dick McAuliffe	10.00
164	Paul Doyle	10.00
165	Terry Forster	10.00
166	Steve Hamilton	10.00
167	Mike Corkins	10.00
168	Dave Concepcion	12.50
169	Bill Sudakis	10.00
170	Juan Marichal	55.00
171	Harmon Killebrew	75.00
172	Luis Tiant	15.00
173	Ted Uhlaender	10.00
174	Tim Foli	10.00
175	Luis Aparicio (In Action)	35.00
176	Bert Campaneris	10.00
177	Charlie Sands	10.00
178	Darold Knowles	10.00
179	Jerry Koosman	10.00
180	Leo Cardenas (In Action)	10.00
181	Luis Alvarado	10.00
182	Graig Nettles	10.00
183	Walter Alston	25.00
184	Nolan Ryan	300.00
185	Ed Sprague	10.00
186	Rich Reese	10.00
187	Pete Rose	150.00
188	Bernie Allen	10.00
189	Lou Piniella	12.50
190	Jerry Reuss	10.00
191	Bob Pfeil	10.00
192	Bob Burda	10.00
193	Walt Williams	10.00
194	Dusty Baker	12.50
195	Rich Morales	10.00
196	Bill Stoneman	10.00
197	Hal King	10.00
198	Julian Javier	10.00
199	Dave Mason	10.00
200	Bob Veale	10.00
201	Jim Beauchamp	10.00
202	Ron Santo (In Action)	12.50
203	Tom Seaver	125.00
204	Jim Merritt	10.00
205	Jerry Koosman (In Action)	10.00
206	Dick Woodson	10.00
207	Wayne Simpson	10.00
208	Jose Laboy	10.00
209	Sam McDowell	12.50
210	Bob Bailey	10.00
211	Jim Fairey	10.00
212	Felipe Alou	15.00
213	Dave Concepcion (In Action)	10.00
214	Wilbur Wood (In Action)	10.00
215	Enzo Hernandez	10.00
216	Ron Reed	10.00
217	Stan Bahnsen	10.00
218	Ollie Brown (In Action)	10.00
219	Pat Jarvis	10.00
220	Tim Foli (In Action)	10.00
221	Denny McLain	15.00
222	Jerry Grote	10.00
223	Davey Johnson	10.00
224	John Odom (In Action)	10.00
225	Paul Casanova	10.00
226	George Culver	10.00
227	Pat Corrales	10.00
228	Jim Kaat	12.50
229	Archie Reynolds	10.00
230	Frank Reberger	10.00
231	Carl Yastrzemski	125.00
232	Jim Holt	10.00
233	Lenny Randle	10.00
234	Doug Griffin (In Action)	10.00
235	Doug Rader	10.00
236	Jesus Alou	10.00
237	Wilbur Wood (In Action)	10.00
238	Jim Kaat (In Action)	10.00
239	Fritz Peterson (In Action)	10.00
240	Dennis Leonard	10.00
241	Brooks Robinson	125.00
242	Felix Millan	10.00

1977 Venezuelan League Baseball Stickers

More than 400 pieces comprise this set of 2-3/8" x 3-1/8" blank-back stickers. The majority have color photos of winter league players with the team name, logo and position printed above, and the sticker number and name beneath the picture. There are many former and future Major League players in this group. A subset of some 50 stickers of American Major Leaguers is printed in reproduction of their 1977 Topps cards. Other stickers include group pictures, action photos, puzzle pieces, etc. The album issued to house the stickers has a player write-up in each space. Printed on very thin paper, and often removed from albums, these stickers are generally not found in condition above Very Good. For Good condition pieces, figure value at 50% of the price shown here; stickers in Fair condition should be valued at 25%. Many of the stickers have player names misspelled.

		VG
Complete Set (402):		1950.
Common Player:		10.00
Album:		125.00
1	Aragua Tigers logo	10.00
2	Ozzie Virgil Sr.	12.50
3	Jesus Avila	10.00
4	Raul Ortega	10.00
5	Simon Barreto	10.00
6	Gustavo Quiroz	10.00
7	Jerry Cram	10.00
8	Pat Cristelli	10.00
9	Preston Hanna	10.00
10	Angel Hernandez	10.00
11	John M'Callen	10.00
12	Randy Miller	10.00
13	Dale Murray	10.00
14	Mike Nagy	10.00
15	Stan Perzanowski	10.00
16	Juan Quiroz	10.00
17	Graciano Parra	10.00
18	Larry Cox	10.00
19	Lenn Sakata	10.00
20	Lester Straker	10.00
21	Nelson Torres	10.00
22	Carlos Avila	10.00
23	Orlando Galindo	10.00
24	Dave Wagner	10.00
25	Dave Concepcion	15.00
26	Alfredo Ortiz	10.00
27	Mike Lum, Dave Concepcion, Larry Parrish	12.50
28	Jesus Padron	10.00
29	Larry Parrish	10.00
30	Rob Picciolo	10.00
31	Luis Rivas	10.00
32	Bob Slater	10.00
33	Larry Murray	10.00
34	Dave Soderholm	10.00
35	Luis Benitez	10.00
36	Cesar Tovar, Victor Davalillo	10.00
37	Luis Bravo	10.00
38	William Castillo	10.00
39	Terry Whitfield	10.00
40	Victor Davalillo	10.00
41	Mike Lum	10.00
42	Willie Norwood	10.00
43	Cesar Tovar	10.00
44	Joe Zdeb	10.00
45	Focion, Ozzie Virgil Sr.	10.00
46	Caracas Lions logo	10.00
47	Felipe Alou	20.00
48	Alfonso Carrasquel (Chico)	15.00
49	Antonio Torres	10.00
50	Len Barker	10.00
51	Gary Beare	10.00
52	Cardell Camper	10.00
53	Juan Gonzalez	10.00
54	Paul Mirabella	10.00
55	Carney Lansford	10.00
56	Ubaldo Heredia	10.00
57	Elias Lugo	10.00
58	Oswaldo Troconis	10.00
59	Diego Segui	10.00
60	Lary Sorensen	10.00
61	Pablo Torrealba	10.00
62	Gustavo Bastardo	10.00
63	Luis Sanz	10.00
64	Steve Bowling	10.00
65	Tim Corcoran	10.00
66	Antonio Armas (Tony)	15.00
67	Toribio Garboza	10.00
68	Bob Molinaro	10.00
69	Willibaldo Quintana	10.00
70	Luis Turnes	10.00
71	Chuck Baker	10.00
72	Rob Belloir	10.00
73	Tom Brookens	10.00
74	Ron Hassey	10.00
75	Gonzalo Marquez	10.00
76	Bob Clark	10.00
77	Marcano Trillo (Manny)	15.00
78	Angel Vargas	10.00
79	Flores Bolivar	10.00
80	Baudilo Diaz (Bo)	12.50
81	Camilo Pascual	15.00
82	La Guaira Sharks logo	10.00
83	Pompeyo Davalillo	10.00
84	Jose Martinez	10.00
85	Jim Willoughby	10.00
86	Romo Blanco	10.00
87	Mark Daly	10.00
88	Tom House	10.00

89	Danny Osborne	10.00
90	David Clyde	10.00
91	Luis Lunar	10.00
92	Randy McGilberry	10.00
93	Greg Minton	10.00
94	Aurelio Monteagudo	10.00
95	Carlos Moreno	10.00
96	Luis M. Sanchez	10.00
97	George Throop	10.00
98	Victor Colina	10.00
99	Edwin Verheist	10.00
100	John Wathan	10.00
101	Ruben Alcala	10.00
102	Ossie Blanco	10.00
103	Dave Cripe	10.00
104	Bob Marcano	10.00
105	Rudy Meoli	10.00
106	Pastor Perez	10.00
107	Milton Ramirez	10.00
108	Luis Salazar	10.00
109	Angel Bravo	10.00
110	Gene Clines	10.00
111	Jose Cardenal	10.00
112	Gabriel Ferrerc	10.00
113	Clint Hurdle	10.00
114	Juan Monasterio	10.00
115	Lester Morales	10.00
116	Carlos Hernandez	10.00
117	Nelo Lira	10.00
118	Raul Perez	10.00
119	Marcos Lunar	10.00
120	Franklin Moreno	10.00
121	Jerry Manuel	10.00
122	Ossie Blanco, Raul Perez	10.00
123	Tom McMillan	10.00
124	Roric Harrison	10.00
125	Tom Griffin	10.00
126	Juan Berenguer	10.00
127	Puzzle piece (Reggie Jackson)	12.50
128	Puzzle piece (Reggie Jackson)	12.50
129	Puzzle piece (Reggie Jackson)	12.50
130	Puzzle piece (Reggie Jackson)	12.50
131	Puzzle piece (Reggie Jackson)	12.50
132	Puzzle piece (Reggie Jackson)	12.50
133	Puzzle piece (Reggie Jackson)	12.50
134	Puzzle piece (Reggie Jackson)	12.50
135	Puzzle piece (Reggie Jackson)	12.50
136	Reggie Jackson	150.00
137	Rod Carew	100.00
138	Dave Concepcion	25.00
139	Joe Morgan	75.00
140	Dave Parker	50.00
141	Carlton Fisk	75.00
142	Garry Maddox	10.00
143	George Foster	15.00
144	Fred Lynn	20.00
145	Lou Piniella	25.00
146	Mark Fidrych	25.00
147	Lou Brock	75.00
148	Mitchell Page	10.00
149	Sparky Lyle	20.00
150	Manny Sanguillen	10.00
151	Steve Carlton	100.00
152	Al Oliver	15.00
153	Davey Lopes	12.50
154	Johnny Bench	100.00
155	Richie Hebner	10.00
156	Cesar Cedeno	10.00
157	Manny Trillo	15.00
158	Nolan Ryan	350.00
159	Tom Seaver	125.00
160	Jim Palmer	100.00
161	Randy Jones	10.00
162	George Brett	165.00
163	Bill Madlock	12.50
164	Cesar Geronimo	15.00
165	Vida Blue	12.50
166	Tony Armas	15.00
167	Bill Campbell	10.00
168	Graig Nettles	10.00
169	Mike Schmidt	165.00
170	Willie Stargell	100.00
171	Ron Cey	15.00
172	Victor Davalillo	10.00
173	Pete Rose	200.00
174	Steve Yaeger	10.00
175	Frank Tanana	10.00
176	Carl Yastrzemski	125.00
177	Willie McCovey	100.00
178	Thurman Munson	150.00
179	Chris Chambliss	10.00
180	Bill Russell	12.50
181	Lara Cardinals logo	10.00
182	Leo Posada	10.00
183	Lucio Celis	10.00
184	Enrique Gonzalez	10.00
185	Brian Abraham	10.00
186	Luis Aponte	10.00
187	Jose Lopez	10.00
188	Bobby Ramos	10.00
189	Tom Dixon	10.00
190	Gary Melson	10.00
191	Mark Budaska	10.00
192	Mark Fischlin	10.00
193	Garth Iorg	10.00
194	Mike Rowland	10.00
195	Dennis DeBarr	10.00
196	Gary Wilson	10.00
197	Dave McKay	10.00
198	Roberto Munoz	10.00
199	Roger Polanco	10.00
200	Pat Kelly	10.00
201	Hernan Silva	10.00
202	Francisco Navas	10.00
203	Pedro Lobaton	10.00
204	Pete Mackanin	10.00
205	Jose Caldera	10.00
206	Carlos Rodriguez (In Action)	10.00
207	Eddy Baez	10.00
208	Gary Metzeger	10.00
209	Rafael Sandoval	10.00
210	Arturo Sanchez	10.00
211	Franklin Tua	10.00
212	Teolindo Acosta	10.00
213	Arnaldo Alvarado	10.00
214	Orlando Gonzalez	10.00
215	Nelson Garcia	10.00
216	Terry Puhl	10.00
217	David Torres	10.00
218	Teolindo Acosta, Roberto Munoz	10.00
219	Terry Puhl, Mark Budaska	10.00
220	Gary Gray	10.00
221	Gustavo Gil	10.00
222	Epi Guerrero	10.00
223	Bobby Ramos, Enrique Gonzalez	10.00
224	Rick Sawyer	10.00
225	S. Byre	10.00
226	Magallanes Navigators logo	10.00
227	Alex Monchak	10.00
228	Manuel Gonzalez	10.00
229	Olinto Rojas	10.00
230	Gregorio Machado	10.00
231	Ali Arape	10.00
232	Miguel Barreto	10.00
233	Manny Sarmiento	10.00
234	Jesus Aristimuno, Alexis Ramirez, Felix Rodriguez	10.00
235	Ed Glynn	10.00
236	Luis Jiminez	10.00
237	Bob Adams	10.00
238	Edito Arteaga	10.00
239	Rafael Cariel	10.00
240	Eddie Solomon	10.00
241	Rick Williams	10.00
242	Miguel Nava	10.00
243	Rod Scurry	10.00
244	Mike Eduards (Edwards)	10.00
245	Earl Stephenson	10.00
246	Alfonso Collazo	10.00
247	Ruben Cabrera	10.00
248	Alfredo Torres	10.00
249	John Valle	10.00
250	Jesus Aristimuno	10.00
251	Joe Cannon	10.00
252	John Pacella	10.00
253	Oswaldo Olivares	10.00
254	Gary Hargis	10.00
255	Nelson Paiva	10.00
256	Bob Oliver	10.00
257	Alexis Ramirez	10.00
258	Larry Wolfe	10.00
259	Don Boyland (Doe)	10.00
260	Mark Wagner	10.00
261	Jim Wright	10.00
262	Mitchell Page	10.00
263	Felix Rodriguez	10.00
264	Willie Aaron	10.00
265	Justo Massaro	10.00
266	Norm Angelini	10.00
267	Fred Breining	10.00
268	Bill Sample	10.00
269	Than Smith	10.00
270	Harry Doris (Dorish)	10.00
271	Zulia Eagles logo	10.00
272	Luis Aparicio	75.00
273	Toni Taylor (Tony)	10.00
274	Teodoro Obregon	10.00
275	Gilberto Marcano	10.00
276	Jose Alfaro	10.00
277	Danny Boitano	10.00
278	Jesus Reyes	10.00
279	Johel Chourio	10.00
280	Scott Sanderson	15.00
281	Charles Kiffin	10.00
282	Bill Dancy	10.00
283	Tim Johnson	10.00
284	Norman Shiera	10.00
285	Lonnie Smith	15.00
286	Manny Seoane	10.00
287	David Wallace	10.00
288	Lareu Whashington (LaRue Washington)	10.00
289	Danny Warthen	10.00
290	Sebastian Martinez	10.00
291	Warren Brusstar	10.00
292	Steven Waterburry (Waterbury)	10.00
293	Gustavo Sposito	10.00
294	Billy Connors	10.00
295	Bod Reece (Bob)	10.00
296	Al Velasquez	10.00
297	Jesus Alfaro	10.00
298	Todd Cruz	10.00
299	Efren Chourio	10.00
300	Tim Norrid	10.00
301	Leonel Carrion	10.00
302	Dario Chirinos	10.00
303	Bobby Darwin	10.00
304	Levy Ochoa	10.00
305	Orlando Reyez (Reyes)	10.00
306	Antonio Garcia	10.00
307	Fred Andrews	10.00
308	Domingo Barboza	10.00
309	Emilio Rodriguez	10.00
310	Roger Brown (Rogers "Bobby")	10.00
311	Nelson Munoz	10.00
312	Unknown	10.00
313	Greg Pryor	10.00
314	Early Espina	10.00
315	Leonel Carrion, Dario Chirinos	10.00
316	Luis Aparicio	125.00
317	Alfonso Carrasquel (Chico)	15.00
318	Dave Concepcion	15.00
319	Antonio Armas (Tony)	15.00
320	Marcano Trillo (Manny)	15.00
321	Pablo Torrealba	10.00
322	Manny Sarmiento	10.00
323	Baudilo Diaz (Bo)	12.50
324	Victor Davalillo	10.00
325	Puzzle piece (Dave Parker)	10.00
326	Puzzle piece (Dave Parker)	10.00
327	Puzzle piece (Dave Parker)	10.00
328	Puzzle piece (Dave Parker)	10.00
329	Puzzle piece (Dave Parker)	10.00
330	Puzzle piece (Dave Parker)	10.00
331	Puzzle piece (Dave Parker)	10.00
332	Puzzle piece (Dave Parker)	10.00
333	Puzzle piece (Dave Parker)	10.00
334	Dave Parker	45.00
335	Steve Bowling	10.00
336	Jose Herrera	10.00
337	Mitchell Page	10.00
338	Enos Cabell	12.50
339	Orlando Reyes	10.00
340	Felix Rodriguez	10.00
341	Baudilo Diaz (Bo)	12.50
342	Gonzalo Marquez	10.00
343	Mike Kelleher	10.00
344	Juan Monasterio	10.00
345	Diego Segui	10.00
346	Steve Lueber (Luebber)	10.00
347	Mike Scott	15.00
348	Angel Bravo	10.00
349	Terry Whitfield	10.00
350	Bob Oliver	10.00
351	Tim Jonhson (Johnson)	10.00
352	Gustavo Sposito	10.00
353	Jim Norris	10.00
354	Marcano Trillo (Manny)	12.50
355	Gary Woods	10.00
356	Felix Rodriguez	10.00
357	Dave May	10.00
358	Don Lepper (Leppert)	10.00
359	Magallanes team photo	10.00
360	Magallanes team photo	10.00
361	Action photo	5.00
362	Action photo	5.00
363	Antonio Torres, Leo Posada	10.00
364	Action photo	5.00
365	Action photo	5.00
366	Action photo	5.00
367	Action photo	5.00
368	Action photo	5.00
369	Action photo	5.00
370	Action photo	5.00
371	Action photo	5.00
372	Action photo	5.00
373	Action photo	5.00
374	Action photo	5.00
375	Action photo	5.00
376	Action photo	5.00
377	Action photo	5.00
378	Action photo	5.00
399	Action photo (misnumbered)	5.00
380	Action photo	5.00
381	Action photo	5.00
382	Action photo	5.00
383	Action photo	5.00
384	Action photo	5.00
385	Action photo	5.00
386	Action photo	5.00
387	Action photo	5.00
388	Action photo	5.00
389	Antonio Torres, Franklin Parra	10.00
390	Action photo	5.00
391	Angel Bravo, Luis Aparicio	20.00
392	Action photo	5.00
393	Action photo	5.00
394	Action photo	5.00
395	Action photo	5.00
396	Action photo	5.00
397	Action photo	5.00
398	Action photo	5.00
399	Action photo	5.00
400	Action photo	5.00
401	Action photo	5.00
402	Tony Armas, Manny Trillo, Gonzalo Marquez	10.00

Vintage cards in Good condition are valued at about 50% of the Very Good value shown here. Fair cards are valued at 25% or less of VG.
The ratio of Excellent and Very Good prices to Near Mint can vary depending on relative collectibility for each grade in a specific set. Current listings reflect such adjustments.

1915 Victory Tobacco (T214)

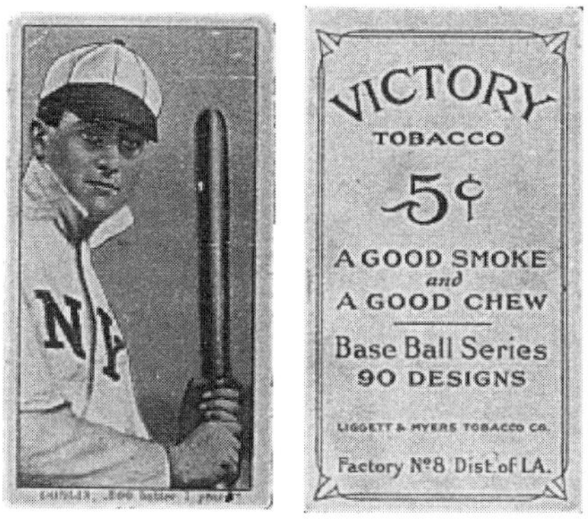

The T214 Victory set of 1915 is another obscure series of tobacco cards that is sometimes mistaken for the better-known T206 "White Border" set. The confusion is understandable because identical player poses were used for both sets. The Victory Tobacco set can be easily identified, however, by the advertising for the Victory brand on the back of the cards. The set features players from the Federal League, both major leagues and at least one minor leaguer. While card backs advertise "90 Designs," little more than half that number of subjects have surfaced to date. The set had such limited distribution - apparently restricted to just the Louisiana area - and the cards are so rare that it may be virtually impossible to ever checklist the set completely. Except for the advertising on the backs, the Victory cards are almost identical to the "Type II" Coupon cards (T213), another obscure Louisiana tobacco set issued during the same period. Of the several tobacco sets issued in Louisana in the early part of the 20th Century, the T214 Victory cards are considered the most difficult to find. Gaps have been left in the numbering sequence to accommodate future additions.

		NM	EX	VG
Common Player:		1200.	475.00	240.00
(1)	Red Ames	1200.	475.00	240.00
(2)	Chief Bender	2000.	800.00	400.00
(3)	Roger Bresnahan	2000.	800.00	400.00
(4)	Al Bridwell	1200.	475.00	240.00
(5)	Howie Camnitz	1200.	475.00	240.00
(6)	Hal Chase (portrait)	1400.	560.00	280.00
(7)	Hal Chase (throwing)	1400.	560.00	280.00
(8)	Ty Cobb	4000.	1600.	800.00
(9)	Doc Crandall	1200.	475.00	240.00
(10)	Birdie Cree	1200.	475.00	240.00
(11)	Josh Devore	1200.	475.00	240.00
(12)	Ray Demmitt	1200.	475.00	240.00
(13)	Mickey Doolan	1200.	475.00	240.00
(14)	Mike Donlin	1200.	475.00	240.00
(15)	Tom Downey	1200.	475.00	240.00
(16)	Kid Elberfeld	1200.	475.00	240.00
(17)	Johnny Evers	2000.	800.00	400.00
(18)	Russ Ford	1200.	475.00	240.00
(20)	Art Fromme	1200.	475.00	240.00
(21)	Chick Gandil	1950.	780.00	390.00
(22)	Rube Geyer	1200.	475.00	240.00
(23)	Clark Griffith	2000.	800.00	400.00
(24)	Bob Groom	1200.	475.00	240.00
(25)	Hughie Jennings	2000.	800.00	400.00
(26)	Walter Johnson	2600.	1040.	520.00
(27)	Ed Konetchy	1200.	475.00	240.00
(28)	Nap Lajoie	2000.	800.00	400.00
(30)	Ed Lennox	1200.	475.00	240.00
(31)	Sherry Magee	1200.	475.00	240.00
(32)	Rube Marquard	2000.	800.00	400.00
(33)	Chief Meyers (catching)	1200.	475.00	240.00
(34)	Chief Meyers (portrait)	1200.	475.00	240.00
(35)	George Mullin	1200.	475.00	240.00
(36)	Red Murray	1200.	475.00	240.00
(37)	Tom Needham	1200.	475.00	240.00
(38)	Rebel Oakes	1200.	475.00	240.00
(40)	Dode Paskert	1200.	475.00	240.00
(41)	Jack Quinn	1200.	475.00	240.00
(42)	Nap Rucker	1200.	475.00	240.00
(43)	Germany Schaefer	1200.	475.00	240.00
(44)	Wildfire Schulte	1200.	475.00	240.00
(45)	Frank Smith	1200.	475.00	240.00
(46)	Tris Speaker	2200.	880.00	440.00
(47)	Ed Summers	1200.	475.00	240.00
(48)	Bill Sweeney	1200.	475.00	240.00
(50)	Jeff Sweeney	1200.	475.00	240.00
(51)	Ira Thomas	1200.	475.00	240.00
(52)	Joe Tinker	2000.	800.00	400.00
(53)	Heinie Wagner	1200.	475.00	240.00
(54)	Zack Wheat	2000.	800.00	400.00
(55)	Kaiser Wilhelm	1200.	475.00	240.00
(56)	Hooks Wiltse	1200.	475.00	240.00

1909-1912 Violet/Mint Chips

(See Colgan's Chips)

1914 Virginia Extra Cigarettes

(See 1914 T216 Peoples Tobacco for checklist, Virginia Extra values 1.5X-2X)

1949 Vis-Ed Cleveland Indian Magic Dials

Similar in concept to a Viewmaster, these hand-held "Magic Dial Big League Viewers" feature the members of the World Champion 1948 Cleveland Indians, plus Mickey Vernon, who joined the team in 1949, and, inexplicably, Pittsburgh Pirate Ralph Kiner. Each of the players is pictured on six single frames of 8 mm movie film (once in color, but now usually faded to sepia tones) mounted on a 2" cardboard circle within a red, white and blue 2-1/4" x 2" rectangular frame; the whole is held together by a metal rivet. The pictures can be viewed by turning the round cardboard dial. The dials came with a playing tips instructional pamphlet. Original price was 29 cents apiece.

		NM	EX	VG
Complete Set:		700.00	350.00	210.00
Common Player:		45.00	22.00	13.50
(1)	Gene Bearden	45.00	22.00	13.50
(2)	Lou Boudreau (batting)	50.00	25.00	15.00
(3)	Lou Boudreau (double play)	50.00	25.00	15.00
(4)	Lou Boudreau (shortstop)	50.00	25.00	15.00
(5)	Larry Doby	60.00	30.00	18.00
(6)	Bob Feller	75.00	37.00	22.00
(7)	Joe Gordon (double play)	45.00	22.00	13.50
(8)	Joe Gordon (second base)	45.00	22.00	13.50
(9)	Jim Hegan	45.00	22.00	13.50
(10)	Ken Keltner	45.00	22.00	13.50
(11)	Ralph Kiner	60.00	30.00	18.00
(12)	Bob Lemon	50.00	25.00	15.00
(13)	Dale Mitchell	45.00	22.00	13.50
(14)	Satchel Paige	200.00	100.00	60.00
(15)	Mickey Vernon	45.00	22.00	13.50

1949 Vis-Ed Cleveland Indian Slide-cards

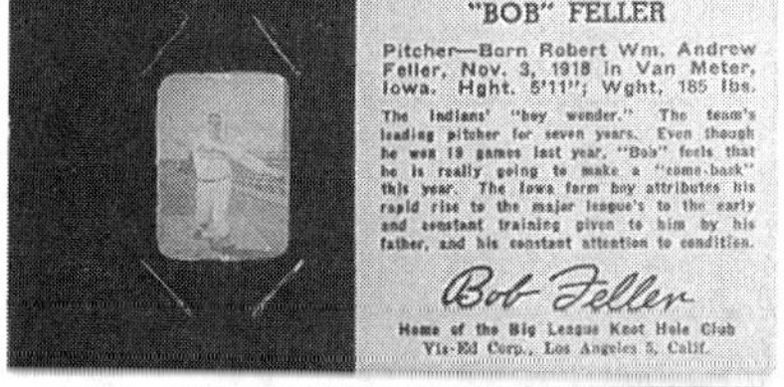

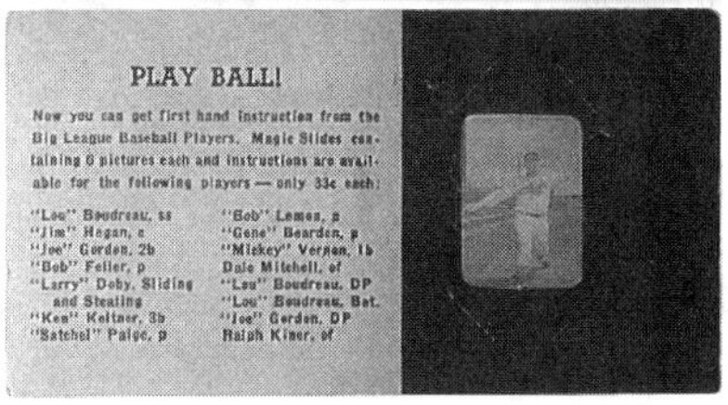

These unique novelties feature the members of the World Champion 1948 Cleveland Indians. The players are pictured on a single frame of 16mm film which has been inserted into slits cut on one end of the cardboard. The cardboard holders are dark blue and yellow, with blue printing. Fronts have player personal data, career highlights, the player's name in script and identification of the issuer. Backs have a list of "Magic Slides" which could be ordered for 33 cents each. It is likely that a slide-card exists for each of the players on that list, but only those which have been confirmed to date are checklisted here, in alphabetical order. Complete slide-cards measure 3-3/4" x 2".

		NM	EX	VG
Common Player:		35.00	17.50	10.50
(1)	Lou Boudreau	45.00	22.00	13.50
(2)	Larry Doby	45.00	22.00	13.50
(3)	Bob Feller	60.00	30.00	18.00
(4)	Joe Gordon	35.00	17.50	10.50
(5)	Jim Hegan	35.00	17.50	10.50
(6)	Ken Keltner	35.00	17.50	10.50

1913 Voskamp's Coffee Pittsburgh Pirates

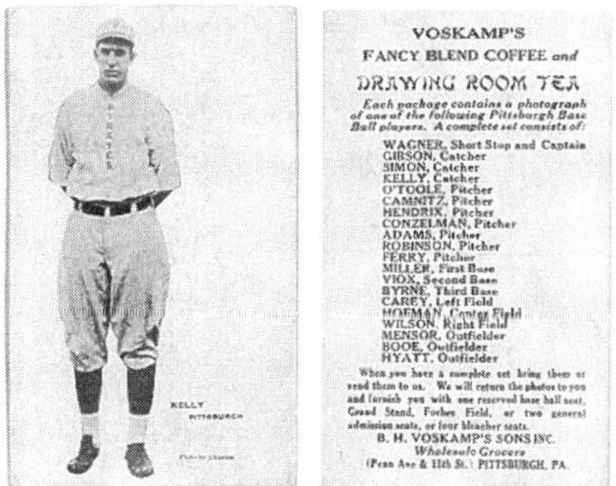

The 1913 Pittsburgh Pirates are featured in this set of cards given away in packages of coffee and tea and redeemable for seats at Pirates games. The 2-1/4" x 3-5/8" cards have black-and-white player photos on a plain white background, along with ID and a "Photo by Johnston" credit line. The black-and-white back has a checklist of the set and details of the ticket redemption program. Pose variations of the Hofman and O'Toole cards are reported to exist. The checklist for the unnumbered cards is presented here alphabetically. Because the set was issued just after the great tobacco card era, several of the Pirates in this set are not found on any other cards.

		NM	EX	VG
Complete Set (20):		5350.	2675.	1600.
Common Player:		450.00	225.00	135.00
(1)	Babe Adams	450.00	225.00	135.00
(2)	Everitt Booe	450.00	225.00	135.00
(3)	Bobby Byrne	450.00	225.00	135.00
(4)	Howie Camnitz	450.00	225.00	135.00
(5)	Max Carey	665.00	330.00	200.00
(6)	Joe Conzelman	450.00	225.00	135.00
(7)	Jack Ferry	450.00	225.00	135.00
(8)	George Gibson	450.00	225.00	135.00
(9)	Claude Hendrix	450.00	225.00	135.00
(10)	Solly Hofman	450.00	225.00	135.00
(11)	Ham Hyatt	450.00	225.00	135.00
(12)	Bill Kelly	450.00	225.00	135.00
(13)	Ed Mensor	450.00	225.00	135.00
(14)	Dots Miller	450.00	225.00	135.00
(15)	Marty O'Toole	450.00	225.00	135.00
(16)	Hank Robinson	450.00	225.00	135.00
(17)	Mike Simon	450.00	225.00	135.00
(18)	Jim Viox	450.00	225.00	135.00
(19)	Honus Wagner	3000.	1500.	900.00
(20)	Owen Wilson	450.00	225.00	135.00

W

1979 Wallin Diamond Greats

Card collector, dealer and later Donruss photographer, Jack Wallin produced this collectors' issue. Cards are in the 2-1/2" x 3-1/2" format, printed in black-and-white and blank-backed. Besides the player photo on front, there is identification and a line of career stats. Four 100-card series were issued. Series 1 concentrates on Yankees, Giants, Senators and Dodgers. Series 2 comprises the Cubs, White Sox, Cardinals and Browns. The third series features Braves, Red Sox, Reds and Indians. Series 4 concentrates on the Phillies, A's, Pirates and Tigers.

		NM	EX	VG
Complete Set (400):		125.00	62.50	37.50
Series 1 (1-100):		30.00	15.00	9.00
Series 2 (101-200):		25.00	12.50	7.50
Series 3 (201-300):		25.00	12.50	7.50
Series 4 (301-400):		25.00	12.50	7.50
Common Player:				
1	Joe DiMaggio	4.00	2.00	1.25
2	Ben Chapman	.50	.25	.15
3	Joe Dugan	.50	.25	.15
4	Bobby Shawkey	.50	.25	.15
5	Joe Sewell	.50	.25	.15
6	George Pipgras	.50	.25	.15
7	George Selkirk	.50	.25	.15
8	Babe Dahlgren	.50	.25	.15
9	Spud Chandler	.50	.25	.15
10	Duffy Lewis	.50	.25	.15
11	Lefty Gomez	.65	.35	.20
12	Atley Donald	.50	.25	.15
13	Whitey Witt	.50	.25	.15
14	Marius Russo	.50	.25	.15
15	Buddy Rosar	.50	.25	.15
16	Russ Van Atta	.50	.25	.15
17	Johnny Lindell	.50	.25	.15
18	Bobby Brown	.50	.25	.15
19	Tony Kubek	.65	.35	.20
20	Joe Beggs	.50	.25	.15
21	Don Larsen	.65	.35	.20
22	Andy Carey	.50	.25	.15
23	Johnny Kucks	.50	.25	.15
24	Elston Howard	.65	.35	.20
25	Roger Maris	2.50	1.25	.70
26	Rube Marquard	.75	.40	.25
27	Sam Leslie	.50	.25	.15
28	Freddy Leach	.50	.25	.15
29	Fred Fitzsimmons	.50	.25	.15
30	Bill Terry	.75	.40	.25
31	Joe Moore	.50	.25	.15
32	Waite Hoyt	.50	.25	.15
33	Travis Jackson	.50	.25	.15
34	Gus Mancuso	.50	.25	.15
35	Carl Hubbell	.75	.40	.25
36	Bill Voiselle	.50	.25	.15
37	Hank Leiber	.50	.25	.15
38	Burgess Whitehead	.50	.25	.15
39	Johnny Mize	.75	.40	.25
40	Bill Lohrman	.50	.25	.15
41	Bill Rigney	.50	.25	.15
42	Cliff Melton	.50	.25	.15
43	Willard Marshall	.50	.25	.15
44	Wes Westrum	.50	.25	.15
45	Monte Irvin	.65	.35	.20
46	Marv Grissom	.50	.25	.15
47	Clyde Castleman	.50	.25	.15
48	Harry Gumbert	.50	.25	.15
49	Daryl Spencer	.50	.25	.15
50	Willie Mays	2.00	1.00	.60
51	Sam West	.50	.25	.15
52	Fred Schulte	.50	.25	.15
53	Cecil Travis	.50	.25	.15
54	Tommy Thomas	.50	.25	.15
55	Dutch Leonard	.50	.25	.15
56	Jimmy Wasdell	.50	.25	.15
57	Doc Cramer	.50	.25	.15
58	Harland Clift (Harlond)	.50	.25	.15
59	Ken Chase	.50	.25	.15
60	Buddy Lewis	.50	.25	.15
61	Ossie Bluege	.50	.25	.15
62	Chuck Stobbs	.50	.25	.15
63	Jimmy DeShong	.50	.25	.15
64	Roger Wolff	.50	.25	.15
65	Luke Sewell	.50	.25	.15
66	Sid Hudson	.50	.25	.15
67	Jack Russell	.50	.25	.15
68	Walt Masterson	.50	.25	.15
69	George Myatt	.50	.25	.15
70	Monte Weaver	.50	.25	.15
71	Cliff Bolton	.50	.25	.15
72	Ray Scarborough	.50	.25	.15
73	Albie Pearson	.50	.25	.15
74	Gil Coan	.50	.25	.15
75	Roy Sievers	.50	.25	.15
76	Burleigh Grimes	.50	.25	.15
77	Charlie Hargreaves	.50	.25	.15
78	Babe Herman	.50	.25	.15
79	Fred Frankhouse	.50	.25	.15
80	Al Lopez	.50	.25	.15
81	Lonny Frey	.50	.25	.15
82	Dixie Walker	.50	.25	.15
83	Kirby Higbe	.50	.25	.15
84	Bobby Bragan	.50	.25	.15
85	Leo Durocher	.50	.25	.15
86	Woody English	.50	.25	.15
87	Preacher Roe	.50	.25	.15
88	Vic Lombardi	.50	.25	.15
89	Clyde Sukeforth	.50	.25	.15
90	Pee Wee Reese	1.00	.50	.30
91	Joe Hatten	.50	.25	.15
92	Gene Hermanski	.50	.25	.15
93	Ray Benge	.50	.25	.15
94	Duke Snider	1.50	.70	.45
95	Walter Alston	.50	.25	.15
96	Don Drysdale	.75	.40	.25
97	Andy Pafko	.50	.25	.15
98	Don Zimmer	.50	.25	.15
99	Carl Erskine	.50	.25	.15
100	Dick Williams	.50	.25	.15
101	Charlie Grimm	.50	.25	.15
102	Clarence Blair	.50	.25	.15
103	Johnny Moore	.50	.25	.15
104	Clay Bryant	.50	.25	.15
105	Billy Herman	.50	.25	.15
106	Hy Vandenberg	.50	.25	.15
107	Lennie Merullo	.50	.25	.15
108	Hank Wyse	.50	.25	.15
109	Dom Dallessandro	.50	.25	.15
110	Al Epperly	.50	.25	.15
111	Bill Nicholson	.50	.25	.15
112	Vern Olsen	.50	.25	.15
113	Johnny Schmitz	.50	.25	.15
114	Bob Scheffing	.50	.25	.15
115	Bob Rush	.50	.25	.15
116	Roy Smalley	.50	.25	.15
117	Ransom Jackson	.50	.25	.15
118	Cliff Chambers	.50	.25	.15
119	Harry Chiti	.50	.25	.15
120	Johnny Klippstein	.50	.25	.15
121	Gene Baker	.50	.25	.15
122	Walt Moryn	.50	.25	.15
123	Dick Littlefield	.50	.25	.15
124	Bob Speake	.50	.25	.15
125	Hank Sauer	.50	.25	.15
126	Monty Stratton	.65	.35	.20
127	Johnny Kerr	.50	.25	.15
128	Milt Gaston	.50	.25	.15
129	Eddie Smith	.50	.25	.15
130	Larry Rosenthal	.50	.25	.15
131	Orval Grove	.50	.25	.15
132	Johnny Hodapp	.50	.25	.15
133	Johnny Rigney	.50	.25	.15
134	Willie Kamm	.50	.25	.15
135	Ed Lopat	.50	.25	.15
136	Smead Jolley	.50	.25	.15
137	Ralph Hodgin	.50	.25	.15
138	Ollie Bejma	.50	.25	.15
139	Zeke Bonura	.50	.25	.15
140	Al Hollingsworth	.50	.25	.15
141	Thurman Tucker	.50	.25	.15
142	Cass Michaels	.50	.25	.15
143	Bill Wight	.50	.25	.15
144	Don Lenhardt	.50	.25	.15
145	Sammy Esposito	.50	.25	.15
146	Jack Harshman	.50	.25	.15
147	Turk Lown	.50	.25	.15
148	Jim Landis	.50	.25	.15
149	Bob Shaw	.50	.25	.15
150	Minnie Minoso	.65	.35	.20
151	Les Bell	.50	.25	.15
152	Taylor Douthit	.50	.25	.15
153	Jack Rothrock	.50	.25	.15
154	Terry Moore	.50	.25	.15
155	Max Lanier	.50	.25	.15
156	Don Gutteridge	.50	.25	.15
157	Stu Martin	.50	.25	.15
158	Stan Musial	1.50	.70	.45
159	Frank Crespi	.50	.25	.15
160	Johnny Hopp	.50	.25	.15
161	Ernie Koy	.50	.25	.15
162	Joe Garagiola	.75	.40	.25
163	Ed Kazak	.50	.25	.15
164	Joe Orengo	.50	.25	.15
165	Howie Krist	.50	.25	.15
166	Enos Slaughter	.65	.35	.20
167	Ray Sanders	.50	.25	.15
168	Walker Cooper	.50	.25	.15
169	Nippy Jones	.50	.25	.15
170	Dick Sisler	.50	.25	.15
171	Harvey Haddix	.50	.25	.15
172	Solly Hemus	.50	.25	.15
173	Ray Jablonski	.50	.25	.15
174	Alex Grammas	.50	.25	.15
175	Joe Cunningham	.50	.25	.15
176	Debs Garms	.50	.25	.15
177	Chief Hogsett	.50	.25	.15
178	Alan Strange	.50	.25	.15
179	Rick Ferrell	.50	.25	.15
180	Jack Kramer	.50	.25	.15
181	Jack Knott	.50	.25	.15
182	Bob Harris	.50	.25	.15
183	Billy Hitchcock	.50	.25	.15
184	Jim Walkup	.50	.25	.15
185	Roy Cullenbine	.50	.25	.15
186	Bob Muncrief	.50	.25	.15
187	Chet Laabs	.50	.25	.15
188	Vern Kennedy	.50	.25	.15
189	Bill Trotter	.50	.25	.15
190	Denny Galehouse	.50	.25	.15
191	Al Zarilla	.50	.25	.15
192	Hank Arft	.50	.25	.15
193	Nelson Potter	.50	.25	.15
194	Ray Coleman	.50	.25	.15
195	Bob Dillinger	.50	.25	.15
196	Dick Kokos	.50	.25	.15
197	Bob Cain	.50	.25	.15
198	Virgil Trucks	.60	.30	.20
199	Duane Pillette	.50	.25	.15
200	Bob Turley	.60	.30	.20
201	Wally Berger	.50	.25	.15
202	John Lanning	.50	.25	.15
203	Buck Jordan	.50	.25	.15
204	Jim Turner	.50	.25	.15
205	Johnny Cooney	.50	.25	.15
206	Hank Majeski	.50	.25	.15
207	Phil Masi	.50	.25	.15
208	Tony Cuccinello	.50	.25	.15
209	Whitey Wietelmann	.50	.25	.15
210	Lou Fette	.50	.25	.15
211	Vince DiMaggio	.75	.40	.25
212	Huck Betts	.50	.25	.15
213	Red Barrett	.50	.25	.15
214	Pinkey Whitney	.50	.25	.15
215	Tommy Holmes	.50	.25	.15
216	Ray Berres	.50	.25	.15
217	Mike Sandlock	.50	.25	.15
218	Max Macon	.50	.25	.15
219	Sibby Sisti	.50	.25	.15
220	Johnny Beazley	.50	.25	.15
221	Bill Posedel	.50	.25	.15
222	Connie Ryan	.50	.25	.15
223	Del Crandall	.50	.25	.15
224	Bob Addis	.50	.25	.15
225	Warren Spahn	1.00	.50	.30
226	Johnny Pesky	.50	.25	.15
227	Dom DiMaggio	.75	.40	.25
228	Emerson Dickman	.50	.25	.15
229	Bobby Doerr	.50	.25	.15
230	Tony Lupien	.50	.25	.15
231	Roy Partee	.50	.25	.15
232	Stan Spence	.50	.25	.15
233	Jim Bagby	.50	.25	.15
234	Buster Mills	.50	.25	.15
235	Fabian Gaffke	.50	.25	.15
236	George Metkovich	.50	.25	.15
237	Tom McBride	.50	.25	.15
238	Charlie Wagner	.50	.25	.15
239	Eddie Pellagrini	.50	.25	.15
240	Harry Dorish	.50	.25	.15
241	Ike Delock	.50	.25	.15
242	Mel Parnell	.50	.25	.15
243	Matt Batts	.50	.25	.15
244	Gene Stephens	.50	.25	.15
245	Milt Bolling	.50	.25	.15
246	Charlie Maxwell	.50	.25	.15
247	Willard Nixon	.50	.25	.15
248	Sammy White	.50	.25	.15
249	Dick Gernert	.50	.25	.15
250	Rico Petrocelli	.50	.25	.15
251	Edd Roush	.50	.25	.15
252	Mark Koenig	.50	.25	.15
253	Jimmy Outlaw	.50	.25	.15
254	Ethan Allen	.50	.25	.15
255	Tony Freitas	.50	.25	.15
256	Frank McCormick	.50	.25	.15
257	Bucky Walters	.50	.25	.15
258	Harry Craft	.50	.25	.15
259	Nate Andrews	.50	.25	.15
260	Ed Lukon	.50	.25	.15
261	Elmer Riddle	.50	.25	.15
262	Lee Grissom	.50	.25	.15
263	Johnny Vander Meer	.50	.25	.15
264	Eddie Joost	.50	.25	.15
265	Kermit Wahl	.50	.25	.15
266	Ival Goodman	.50	.25	.15
267	Clyde Vollmer	.50	.25	.15
268	Grady Hatton	.50	.25	.15
269	Ted Kluszewski	.75	.40	.25
270	Johnny Pramesa	.50	.25	.15
271	Joe Black	.60	.30	.20
272	Roy McMillan	.50	.25	.15
273	Wally Post	.50	.25	.15
274	Joe Nuxhall	.50	.25	.15
275	Jerry Lynch	.50	.25	.15
276	Stan Coveleski	.50	.25	.15
277	Bill Wambsganss	.50	.25	.15
278	Bruce Campbell	.50	.25	.15
279	George Uhle	.50	.25	.15
280	Earl Averill	.50	.25	.15
281	Whit Wyatt	.50	.25	.15
282	Oscar Grimes	.50	.25	.15
283	Roy Weatherly	.50	.25	.15
284	Joe Dobson	.50	.25	.15
285	Bob Feller	.75	.40	.25
286	Jim Hegan	.50	.25	.15
287	Mel Harder	.50	.25	.15
288	Ken Keltner	.50	.25	.15
289	Red Embree	.50	.25	.15
290	Al Milnar	.50	.25	.15
291	Lou Boudreau	.50	.25	.15
292	Ed Klieman	.50	.25	.15
293	Steve Gromek	.50	.25	.15
294	George Strickland	.50	.25	.15
295	Gene Woodling	.50	.25	.15
296	Hank Edwards	.50	.25	.15
297	Don Mossi	.50	.25	.15
298	Eddie Robinson	.50	.25	.15
299	Sam Dente	.50	.25	.15
300	Herb Score	.50	.25	.15
301	Dolf Camilli	.50	.25	.15
302	Jack Warner	.50	.25	.15
303	Ike Pearson	.50	.25	.15
304	Johnny Peacock	.50	.25	.15
305	Gene Corbett	.50	.25	.15
306	Walt Millies	.50	.25	.15
307	Vance Dinges	.50	.25	.15
308	Joe Marty	.50	.25	.15
309	Hugh Mulcahey	.50	.25	.15
310	Boom Boom Beck	.50	.25	.15
311	Charley Schanz	.50	.25	.15
312	John Bolling	.50	.25	.15
313	Danny Litwhiler	.50	.25	.15
314	Emil Verban	.50	.25	.15
315	Andy Semenick	.50	.25	.15
316	John Antonelli	.50	.25	.15

317	Robin Roberts	.75	.40	.25
318	Richie Ashburn	.75	.40	.25
319	Curt Simmons	.50	.25	.15
320	Murry Dickson	.50	.25	.15
321	Jim Greengrass	.50	.25	.15
322	Gene Freese	.50	.25	.15
323	Bobby Morgan	.50	.25	.15
324	Don Demeter	.50	.25	.15
325	Eddie Sawyer	.50	.25	.15
326	Bob Johnson	.50	.25	.15
327	Ace Parker	.65	.35	.20
328	Joe Hauser	.50	.25	.15
329	Walt French	.50	.25	.15
330	Tom Ferrick	.50	.25	.15
331	Bill Werber	.50	.25	.15
332	Walt Masters	.50	.25	.15
333	Les McCrabb	.50	.25	.15
334	Ben McCoy	.50	.25	.15
335	Eric Tipton	.50	.25	.15
336	Al Rubeling	.50	.25	.15
337	Nick Etten	.50	.25	.15
338	Carl Scheib	.50	.25	.15
339	Dario Lodigiani	.50	.25	.15
340	Earle Brucker	.50	.25	.15
341	Al Brancato	.50	.25	.15
342	Lou Limmer	.50	.25	.15
343	Elmer Valo	.50	.25	.15
344	Bob Hooper	.50	.25	.15
345	Joe Astroth	.50	.25	.15
346	Pete Suder	.50	.25	.15
347	Dave Philley	.50	.25	.15
348	Gus Zernial	.50	.25	.15
349	Bobby Shantz	.60	.30	.20
350	Joe DeMaestri	.50	.25	.15
351	Fred Lindstrom	.50	.25	.15
352	Red Lucas	.50	.25	.15
353	Clyde Barnhart	.50	.25	.15
354	Nick Strincevich	.50	.25	.15
355	Lloyd Waner	.50	.25	.15
356	Guy Bush	.50	.25	.15
357	Joe Bowman	.50	.25	.15
358	Al Todd	.50	.25	.15
359	Mace Brown	.50	.25	.15
360	Larry French	.50	.25	.15
361	Elbie Fletcher	.50	.25	.15
362	Woody Jensen	.50	.25	.15
363	Rip Sewell	.50	.25	.15
364	Johnny Dickshot	.50	.25	.15
365	Pete Coscarart	.50	.25	.15
366	Bud Hafey	.50	.25	.15
367	Ken Heintzelman	.50	.25	.15
368	Wally Westlake	.50	.25	.15
369	Frank Gustine	.50	.25	.15
370	Smoky Burgess	.50	.25	.15
371	Dick Groat	.50	.25	.15
372	Vern Law	.50	.25	.15
373	Bob Skinner	.50	.25	.15
374	Don Cardwell	.50	.25	.15
375	Bob Friend	.50	.25	.15
376	Frank O'Rourke	.50	.25	.15
377	Birdie Tebbetts	.50	.25	.15
378	Charlie Gehringer	.65	.35	.20
379	Eldon Auker	.50	.25	.15
380	Tuck Stainback	.50	.25	.15
381	Chet Morgan	.50	.25	.15
382	Johnny Lipon	.50	.25	.15
383	Paul Richards	.50	.25	.15
384	Johnny Gorsica	.50	.25	.15
385	Ray Hayworth	.50	.25	.15
386	Jimmy Bloodworth	.50	.25	.15
387	Gene Desautels	.50	.25	.15
388	Jo Jo White	.50	.25	.15
389	Boots Poffenberger	.50	.25	.15
390	Barney McCosky	.50	.25	.15
391	Dick Wakefield	.50	.25	.15
392	Johnny Groth	.50	.25	.15
393	Steve Souchock	.50	.25	.15
394	George Vico	.50	.25	.15
395	Hal Newhouser	.50	.25	.15
396	Ray Herbert	.50	.25	.15
397	Jim Bunning	.50	.25	.15
398	Frank Lary	.50	.25	.15
399	Harvey Kuenn	.50	.25	.15
400	Eddie Mathews	.75	.40	.25

1934 Ward's Sporties Pins

The date of issue can only be approximated for this issue of 1-1/4" diameter celluloid pin-back buttons. Ward's Sporties was evidently some kind of food product; at the center of each button is a black-and-white or blue-and-white portrait photo of a player with his name above and "Eats" below the picture. Printed around the photo portion in white on a red background is: "Good Sports Enjoy / WARD'S SPORTIES". Ward's bakeries issue several type of baseball cards and collectibles over the years, such as the 1947 Tip-Top bread cards. The checklist is in alphabetical order, and may not yet be complete.

		NM	EX	VG
Complete Set (8):		1800.	1350.	725.00
Common Player:		200.00	100.00	60.00
(1)	Dizzy Dean	350.00	175.00	105.00
(2)	Jimmy Dykes	200.00	100.00	60.00
(3)	Jimmie Foxx	300.00	150.00	90.00
(4)	Frank Frisch	300.00	150.00	90.00
(5)	Charlie Gehringer	300.00	150.00	90.00
(6)	Charlie Grimm	200.00	100.00	60.00
(7)	Schoolboy Rowe	200.00	100.00	60.00
(8)	Jimmie Wilson	200.00	100.00	60.00

1916 Ware's

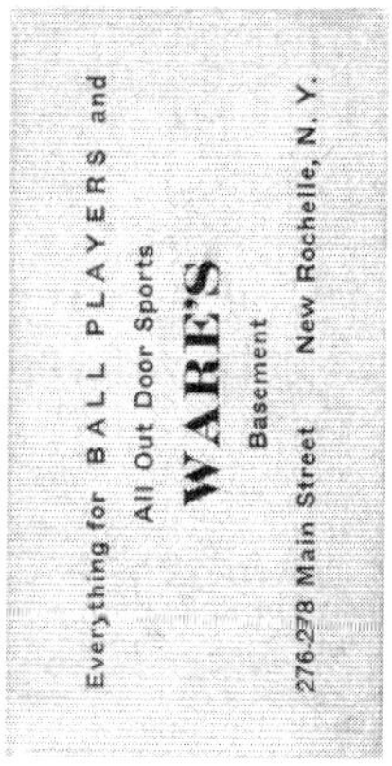

One of several regional advertisers to use this 200-card set as a promotional medium was this New Rochelle, N.Y., store's sporting goods department. Checklist and pricing will be found in these pages under the 1916 Sporting News listings. Collectors may pay a premium for individual cards to enhance a type card or superstar card collection. The American Card Catalog listed these 1-9/16" xy 3" black-and-white cards as H801-9.

(See 1916 Sporting News)

1964 Washington Senators Photo Pack

These 8-1/2" x 11" player pictures are printed in black-and-white on semi-gloss, blank-back paper. Most of the pictures are chest-to-cap portrait poses taken at spring training. The player name is printed in all-caps in the white bottom border, with position in upper- and lower-case to the right. The unnumbered pictures are checklisted here in alphabetical order.

		NM	EX	VG
Complete Set (26):		75.00	37.50	22.00
Common Player:		5.00	2.50	1.50
(1)	Don Blasingame	5.00	2.50	1.50
(2)	Carl Bouldin	5.00	2.50	1.50
(3)	Marshall Bridges	5.00	2.50	1.50
(4)	Ed Brinkman	5.00	2.50	1.50
(5)	Mike Brumley	5.00	2.50	1.50
(6)	Chuck Cottier	5.00	2.50	1.50
(7)	Bennie Daniels	5.00	2.50	1.50
(8)	Jim Duckworth	5.00	2.50	1.50
(9)	Jim Hannan	5.00	2.50	1.50
(10)	Chuck Hinton	5.00	2.50	1.50
(11)	Gil Hodges	10.00	5.00	3.00
(12)	Ken Hunt	5.00	2.50	1.50
(13)	John Kennedy	5.00	2.50	1.50
(14)	Jim King	5.00	2.50	1.50
(15)	Ron Kline	5.00	2.50	1.50
(16)	Don Leppert	5.00	2.50	1.50
(17)	Don Lock	5.00	2.50	1.50
(18)	Claude Osteen	5.00	2.50	1.50
(19)	Dick Phillips	5.00	2.50	1.50
(20)	Ken Retzer	5.00	2.50	1.50
(21)	Steve Ridzik	5.00	2.50	1.50
(22)	Ed Roebuck	5.00	2.50	1.50
(23)	Bill Skowron	7.50	3.75	2.25
(24)	Dave Stenhouse	5.00	2.50	1.50
(25)	Fred Valentine	5.00	2.50	1.50
(26)	Don Zimmer	5.00	2.50	1.50

1967 Washington Senators Picture Pack

This set of black-and-white player pictures was sold at stadium concession stands in a white paper window envelope. Blank-back pictures are 4-7/8" x 7" with portrait or posed photos surrounded by a white border. At bottom is the player and team name. The unnumbered pictures are listed here in alphabetical order.

		NM	EX	VG
Complete Set (12):		18.00	9.00	5.50
Common Player:		1.00	.50	.30
(1)	Bernie Allen	1.00	.50	.30
(2)	Ed Brinkman	1.50	.70	.45
(3)	Paul Casanova	1.00	.50	.30
(4)	Ken Harrelson	2.00	1.00	.60
(5)	Gil Hodges	7.50	3.75	2.25
(6)	Frank Howard	2.50	1.25	.70
(7)	Jim King	1.00	.50	.30
(8)	Ken McMullen	1.00	.50	.30
(9)	Phil Ortega	1.00	.50	.30
(10)	Camilo Pascual	1.50	.70	.45
(11)	Pete Richert	1.00	.50	.30
(12)	Fred Valentine	1.00	.50	.30

1967 Washington Senators team issue

About postcard size (3-1/2" x 5-7/8"), these team issued player photocards feature black-and-white photos which are borderless at the top and sides. At bottom is a wide white strip with the player's facsimile autograph. Backs are blank. The unnumbered cards are checklisted here in alphabetical order.

		NM	EX	VG
Complete Set (22):		35.00	17.50	10.00
Common Player:		2.00	1.00	.60
(1)	Bernie Allen	2.00	1.00	.60
(2)	Hank Allen	2.00	1.00	.60
(3)	Dave Baldwin	2.00	1.00	.60
(4)	Frank Bertaina	2.00	1.00	.60
(5)	Ed Brinkman	2.00	1.00	.60
(6)	Doug Camilli	2.00	1.00	.60
(7)	Paul Casanova	2.00	1.00	.60
(8)	Joe Coleman	2.00	1.00	.60
(9)	Tim Cullen	2.00	1.00	.60
(10)	Mike Epstein	2.50	1.25	.70
(11)	Frank Howard	4.00	2.00	1.25
(12)	Bob Humphreys	2.00	1.00	.60
(13)	Darold Knowles	2.00	1.00	.60
(14)	Dick Lines	2.00	1.00	.60
(15)	Ken McMullen	2.00	1.00	.60
(16)	Dick Nen	2.00	1.00	.60
(17)	Phil Ortega	2.00	1.00	.60
(18)	Camilo Pascual	3.00	1.50	.90
(19)	Cap Peterson	2.00	1.00	.60
(20)	Bob Priddy	2.00	1.00	.60
(21)	Bob Saverine	2.00	1.00	.60
(22)	Fred Valentine	2.00	1.00	.60

1970 Washington Senators Traffic Safety

Distributed in 1970 by the Washington, D.C. Department of Motor Vehicles, this issue promoting traffic safety was one of the first police sets ever issued. Featuring black-and-white player photos, the cards measure 2-1/2" x 3-7/8" and have large borders surrounding the pictures with the player's name and position below. The team name appears in smaller type at the bottom. The 1970 set can be found on either pink card stock, used for the original print run, or on bright yellow stock, used for two subsequent printings. The additional print runs resulted in a scarce card of Dave Nelson, who is found only on pink stock. Aurelio Rodriguez, who joined the team after the season began, is known only in yellow; all other players can be found in both yellow and pink. The pink varieties carry a higher value. The backs of the cards offer traffic safety tips.

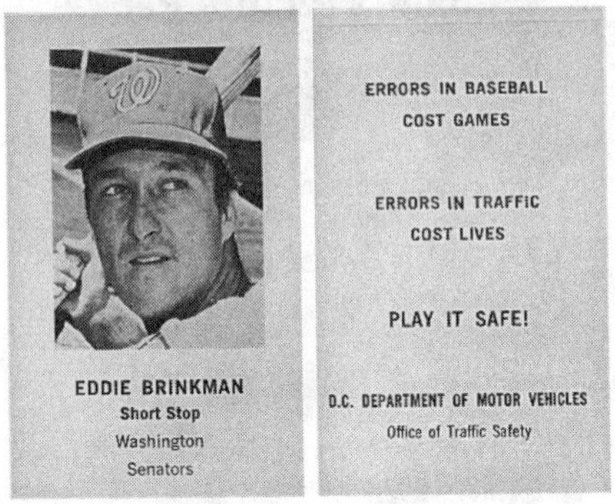

	NM	EX	VG
Complete Set, Pink (10):	300.00	150.00	90.00
Common Player, Pink:	7.00	3.50	2.00
Complete Set, Yellow (10):	125.00	62.50	37.50
Common Player, Yellow:	2.50	1.25	.70
(1a) Dick Bosman (pink)	7.00	3.50	2.00
(1b) Dick Bosman (yellow)	2.50	1.25	.70
(2a) Eddie Brinkman (pink)	7.00	3.50	2.00
(2b) Eddie Brinkman (yellow)	2.50	1.25	.70
(3a) Paul Casanova (pink)	7.00	3.50	2.00
(3b) Paul Casanova (yellow)	2.50	1.25	.70
(4a) Mike Epstein (pink)	7.00	3.50	2.00
(4b) Mike Epstein (yellow)	2.50	1.25	.70
(5a) Frank Howard (pink)	18.00	9.00	5.50
(5b) Frank Howard (yellow)	7.00	3.50	2.00
(6a) Darold Knowles (pink)	7.00	3.50	2.00
(6b) Darold Knowles (yellow)	2.50	1.25	.70
(7a) Lee Maye (pink)	7.00	3.50	2.00
(7b) Lee Maye (yellow)	2.50	1.25	.70
(8) Dave Nelson (pink)	250.00	125.00	75.00
(9) Aurelio Rodriguez (yellow)	5.00	2.50	1.50
(10a) John Roseboro (pink)	7.00	3.50	2.00
(10b) John Roseboro (yellow)	2.50	1.25	.70
(11a) Ed Stroud (pink)	7.00	3.50	2.00
(11b) Ed Stroud (yellow)	2.50	1.25	.70

1971 Washington Senators Traffic Safety

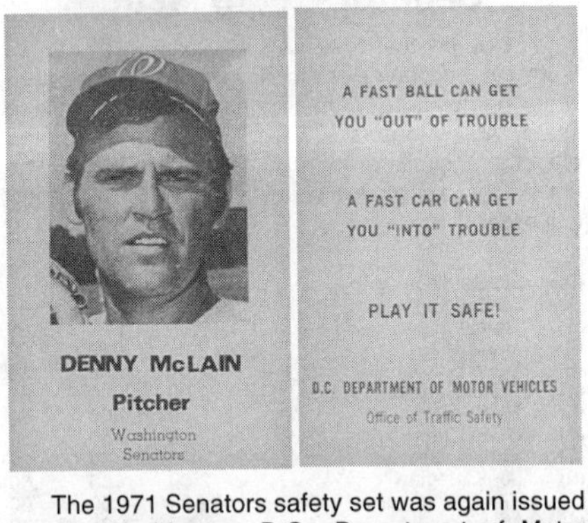

The 1971 Senators safety set was again issued by the Washington, D.C., Department of Motor Vehicles and was similar in design and size (2-1/2" x 3-7/8") to the previous year, except that it was printed on a pale yellow stock. The set, which features several new players, contains no scarce cards. The backs contain traffic safety messages.

	NM	EX	VG
Complete Set (10):	12.00	6.00	3.50
Common Player:	1.25	.60	.40
(1) Dick Bosman	1.25	.60	.40
(2) Paul Casanova	1.25	.60	.40
(3) Tim Cullen	1.25	.60	.40
(4) Joe Foy	1.25	.60	.40
(5) Toby Harrah	2.00	1.00	.60
(6) Frank Howard	6.00	3.00	1.75
(7) Elliott Maddox	1.25	.60	.40
(8) Tom McCraw	1.25	.60	.40
(9) Denny McLain	3.50	1.75	1.00
(10) Don Wert	1.25	.60	.40

1910 Washington Times

Only American League players have so far been found in this issue by the Washington Times newspaper. The 2-9/16" x 3-9/16" cards have portrait or action photos of the players within a wide border. A white panel at bottom has the player name and team at left and "Washington Times Series" at right. All printing is in dark red. Backs are blank. The manner in which these cards were distributed is unknown, as is the extent of the checklist. The unnumbered cards are checklisted here in alphabetical order.

	NM	EX	VG
Common Player:	250.00	125.00	75.00
(1) Wid Conroy	250.00	125.00	75.00
(2) Harry Davis	250.00	125.00	75.00
(3) Bob Groom	250.00	125.00	75.00
(4) George McBride	250.00	125.00	75.00
(5) Frank Oberlin	250.00	125.00	75.00
(6) Rube Oldring	250.00	125.00	75.00
(7) Freddie Parent (Freddy)	250.00	125.00	75.00
(8) Doc Reisling	250.00	125.00	75.00
(9) Gabby Street	250.00	125.00	75.00
(10) Lee Tannehill	250.00	125.00	75.00
(11) Bob Unglaub	250.00	125.00	75.00
(12) Dixie Walker	250.00	125.00	75.00
(13) Ed. Walsh	350.00	175.00	105.00
(14) Joe Wood	300.00	150.00	90.00
(15) Cy Young	450.00	225.00	135.00

1911-14 Weber Bakery (D304)

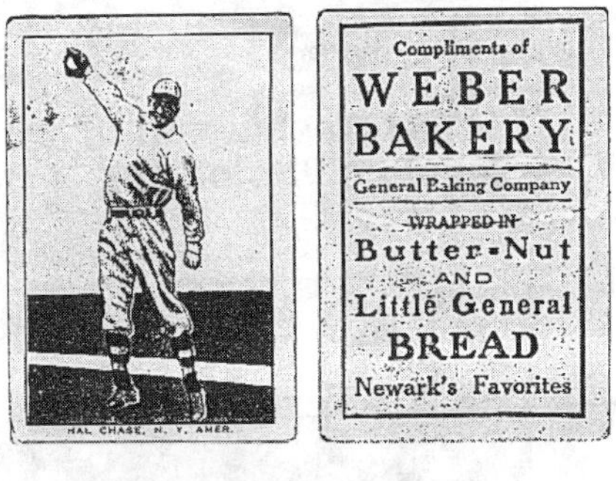

(See 1911-14 General Baking Co. for checklist and price information.)

1916 Weil Baking Co. (1)

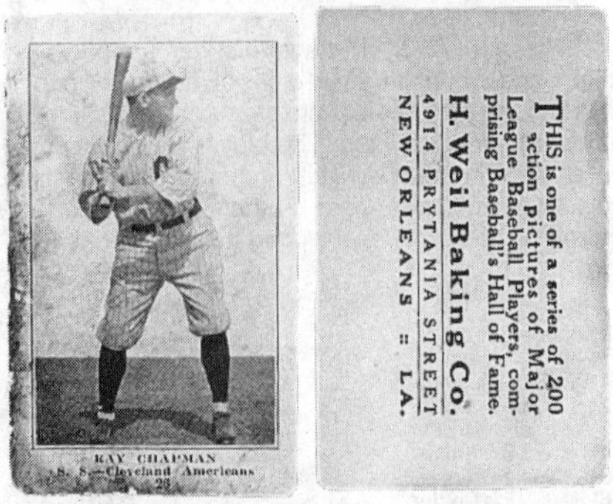

One of several issues by the New Orleans bakery, this 1-3/8" x 3" black-and-white set of 200 shares a checklist and basic values with the 1916 Sporting News set. Collectors are sometimes willing to pay a small premium for a card with the Weil Baking ad on back to add to a type collection or superstar collection. The American Card Catalog lists this issue as D329.

(See 1916 Sporting News)

1916 Weil Baking Co. (2)

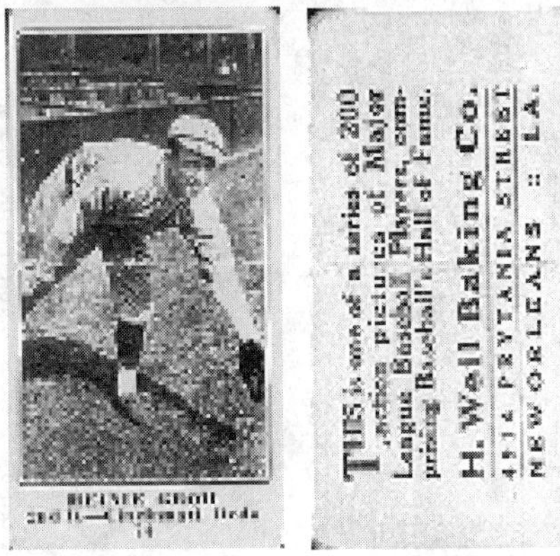

This set comprises one of several regional advertisers' use of the 200-card issue for promotional purposes. These cards are most often seen with the advertising of the Collins-McCarthy Candy Co. of San Francisco; checklist and relative values for the cards will be found under that listing elsewhere in these pages. Cards measure 2" x 3-1/4" and are printed in black-and-white. Type card collectors or superstar collectors may be willing to pay a premium for individual cards. This set was listed as D328 in the American Card Catalog.

(See 1916 Collins-McCarthy)

1886 Welton Cigars New York Giants

NM	EX	VG
27000.	12000.	6500.

(See "1886 New York Base Ball Club" for checklist and values.)

1977 Wendy's Discs

Virtually identical in format to the several locally sponsored disc sets of the previous year, these 3-3/8" diameter player discs were given away at participating stores in the fast-food hamburger chain. Discs once again feature black-and-white player portrait photos in the center of a baseball design.

The left and right panels are in one of several bright colors. Licensed by the players' association through Mike Schechter Associates, the player photos carry no uniform logos. Backs are printed in green. The unnumbered discs are checklisted here alphabetically.

		NM	EX	VG
Complete Set (70):		550.00	275.00	150.00
Common Player:		5.00	2.50	1.50
(1)	Sal Bando	5.00	2.50	1.50
(2)	Buddy Bell	5.00	2.50	1.50
(3)	Johnny Bench	30.00	15.00	9.00
(4)	Larry Bowa	5.00	2.50	1.50
(5)	Steve Braun	5.00	2.50	1.50
(6)	George Brett	65.00	32.00	19.50
(7)	Lou Brock	20.00	10.00	6.00
(8)	Jeff Burroughs	5.00	2.50	1.50
(9)	Bert Campaneris	5.00	2.50	1.50
(10)	John Candelaria	5.00	2.50	1.50
(11)	Jose Cardenal	5.00	2.50	1.50
(12)	Rod Carew	24.00	12.00	7.25
(13)	Steve Carlton	24.00	12.00	7.25
(14)	Dave Cash	5.00	2.50	1.50
(15)	Cesar Cedeno	5.00	2.50	1.50
(16)	Ron Cey	5.00	2.50	1.50
(17)	Dave Concepcion	5.00	2.50	1.50
(18)	Dennis Eckersley	16.00	8.00	4.75
(19)	Mark Fidrych	15.00	7.50	4.50
(20)	Rollie Fingers	20.00	10.00	6.00
(21)	Carlton Fisk	24.00	12.00	7.25
(22)	George Foster	5.00	2.50	1.50
(23)	Wayne Garland	5.00	2.50	1.50
(24)	Ralph Garr	5.00	2.50	1.50
(25)	Steve Garvey	15.00	7.50	4.50
(26)	Cesar Geronimo	5.00	2.50	1.50
(27)	Bobby Grich	5.00	2.50	1.50
(28)	Ken Griffey Sr.	7.50	3.75	2.25
(29)	Don Gullett	5.00	2.50	1.50
(30)	Mike Hargrove	5.00	2.50	1.50
(31)	Willie Horton	5.00	2.50	1.50
(32)	Al Hrabosky	5.00	2.50	1.50
(33)	Reggie Jackson	35.00	17.50	10.50
(34)	Randy Jones	5.00	2.50	1.50
(35)	Dave Kingman	7.50	3.75	2.25
(36)	Jerry Koosman	5.00	2.50	1.50
(37)	Dave LaRoche	5.00	2.50	1.50
(38)	Greg Luzinski	5.00	2.50	1.50
(39)	Fred Lynn	6.00	3.00	1.75
(40)	Bill Madlock	5.00	2.50	1.50
(41)	Rick Manning	5.00	2.50	1.50
(42)	Jon Matlock	5.00	2.50	1.50
(43)	John Mayberry	5.00	2.50	1.50
(44)	Hal McRae	5.00	2.50	1.50
(45)	Andy Messersmith	5.00	2.50	1.50
(46)	Rick Monday	5.00	2.50	1.50
(47)	John Montefusco	5.00	2.50	1.50
(48)	Joe Morgan	20.00	10.00	6.00
(49)	Thurman Munson	24.00	12.00	7.25
(50)	Bobby Murcer	5.00	2.50	1.50
(51)	Bill North	5.00	2.50	1.50
(52)	Jim Palmer	20.00	10.00	6.00
(53)	Tony Perez	24.00	12.00	7.25
(54)	Jerry Reuss	5.00	2.50	1.50
(55)	Pete Rose	45.00	22.00	13.50
(56)	Joe Rudi	5.00	2.50	1.50
(57)	Nolan Ryan	100.00	50.00	30.00
(58)	Manny Sanguillen	5.00	2.50	1.50
(59)	Mike Schmidt	36.00	18.00	11.00
(60)	Tom Seaver	30.00	15.00	9.00
(61)	Bill Singer	5.00	2.50	1.50
(62)	Willie Stargell	22.00	11.00	6.50
(63)	Rusty Staub	7.50	3.75	2.25
(64)	Luis Tiant	5.00	2.50	1.50
(65)	Mike Tyson	5.00	2.50	1.50
(66)	Bob Watson	5.00	2.50	1.50
(67)	Butch Wynegar	5.00	2.50	1.50
(68)	Carl Yastrzemski	25.00	12.50	7.50
(69)	Robin Yount	25.00	12.50	7.50
(70)	Richie Zisk	5.00	2.50	1.50

1963 Western Oil Minnesota Twins

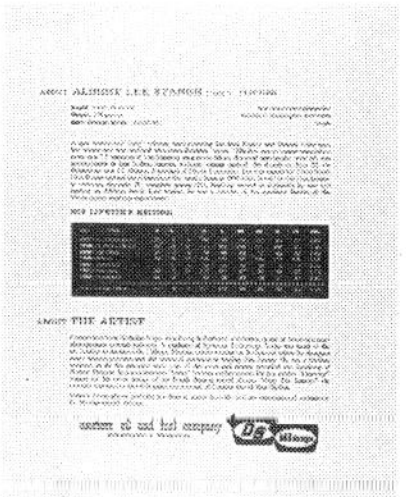

Issued by Mileage and DS gas stations, these 8-1/2" x 11" heavy paper portraits are the work of sports/entertainment artist Nicholas Volpe, who had done a similar series earlier for the Los Angeles Dodgers, and would do several more in the future for other baseball and NFL teams. The 1963 Twins issue features pastel portrait and action renderings against a black background on front. The player's name appears as a facsimile autograph in white on the painting and is printed in black in the white bottom border. Backs have biographical data and a career summary of the player at top. At center is a black box with complete major and minor league stats. At lower center is a biography of the artist, and, on most pictures, his portrait. The DS and Mileage logos of the Western Oil and Fuel Co. appear at bottom.

		NM	EX	VG
Complete Set (24):		75.00	37.00	22.00
Common Player:		5.00	2.50	1.50
(1)	Bernie Allen	5.00	2.50	1.50
(2)	Bob Allison	8.00	4.00	2.50
(3)	George Banks	5.00	2.50	1.50
(4)	Earl Battey	6.00	3.00	1.75
(5)	Bill Dailey	5.00	2.50	1.50
(6)	John Goryl	5.00	2.50	1.50
(7)	Lenny Green	5.00	2.50	1.50
(8)	Jimmie Hall	5.00	2.50	1.50
(9)	Jim Kaat	8.00	4.00	2.50
(10)	Harmon Killebrew	15.00	7.50	4.50
(11)	Sam Mele	5.00	2.50	1.50
(12)	Don Mincher	5.00	2.50	1.50
(13)	Ray Moore	5.00	2.50	1.50
(14)	Camilo Pascual	6.00	3.00	1.75
(15)	Jim Perry	5.00	2.50	1.50
(16)	Bill Pleis	5.00	2.50	1.50
(17)	Vic Power	6.00	3.00	1.75
(18)	Garry Roggenburk	5.00	2.50	1.50
(19)	Jim Roland	5.00	2.50	1.50
(20)	Rich Rollins	5.00	2.50	1.50
(21)	Lee Stange	5.00	2.50	1.50
(22)	Dick Stigman	5.00	2.50	1.50
(23)	Zoilo Versalles	6.00	3.00	1.75
(24)	Jerry Zimmerman	5.00	2.50	1.50

1964 Western Oil Minnesota Twins

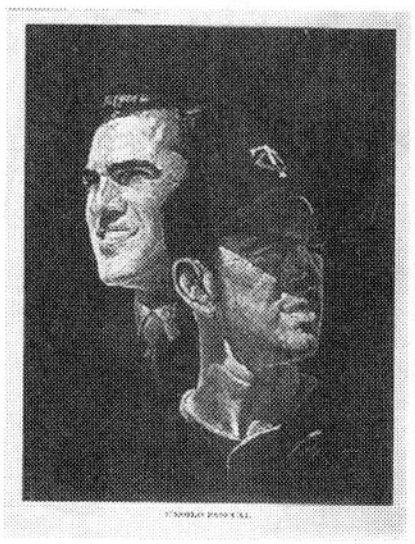

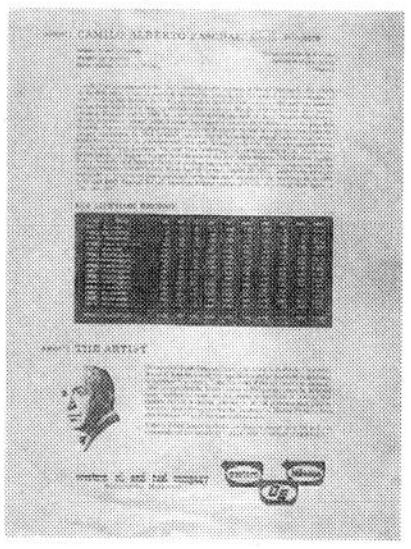

Identical in format to the previous year's issue, the 1964 set of Twins pictures features the use of a second portrait of the player in civilian dress rather than an action picture. The 1964 issue also has background of pastel colors, rather than all-black, and, on back, an oval/arrow logo for Western brand gas, along with the Mileage and DS logos.

		NM	EX	VG
Complete Set (15):		60.00	30.00	18.00
Common Player:		5.00	2.50	1.50
(1)	Bernie Allen	5.00	2.50	1.50
(2)	Bob Allison	6.00	3.00	1.75
(3)	Earl Battey	6.00	3.00	1.75
(4)	Bill Dailey	5.00	2.50	1.50
(5)	Jimmie Hall	5.00	2.50	1.50
(6)	Jim Kaat	7.50	3.75	2.25
(7)	Harmon Killebrew	15.00	7.50	4.50
(8)	Don Mincher	5.00	2.50	1.50
(9)	Tony Oliva	12.00	6.00	3.50
(10)	Camilo Pascual	6.00	3.00	1.75
(11)	Bill Pleis	5.00	2.50	1.50
(12)	Jim Roland	5.00	2.50	1.50
(13)	Rich Rollins	5.00	2.50	1.50
(14)	Dick Stigman	5.00	2.50	1.50
(15)	Zoilo Versalles	6.00	3.00	1.75

Many vintage-section card sets are indexed under both their common name and their American Card Catalog designation.

1974 Weston Expos

This 10-card set features members of the Montreal Expos. Each full-color card measures 3-1/2" x 5-1/2" and includes a facsimile autograph in black ink with the player's name printed along the bottom. The backs are distinct because they are divided in half. The top of the card lists player data and 1973 statistics in English, while the bottom carries the same information in French. The cards are numbered according to the player's uniform number.

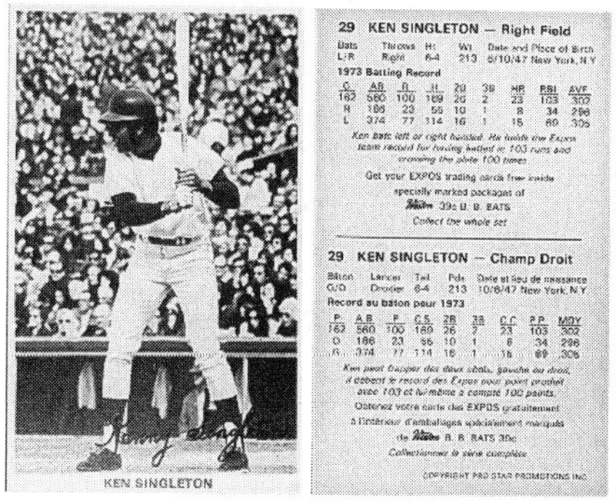

		NM	EX	VG
Complete Set (10):		24.00	12.00	7.25
Common Player:		3.00	1.50	.90
3	Bob Bailey	3.00	1.50	.90
8	Boots Day	3.00	1.50	.90
12	John Boccabella	3.00	1.50	.90
16	Mike Jorgensen	3.00	1.50	.90
18	Steve Renko	3.00	1.50	.90
19	Tim Foli	3.00	1.50	.90
21	Ernie McAnally	3.00	1.50	.90
26	Bill Stoneman	3.00	1.50	.90
29	Ken Singleton	4.00	2.00	1.25
33	Ron Hunt	3.00	1.50	.90

1935 Wheaties - Series 1

This set of major leaguers (plus fictional sports hero Jack Armstrong) was issued on the back of Wheaties cereal boxes in 1935 and because of its design, is known as "Fancy Frame with Script Signature." The unnumbered cards measure 6" x 6-1/4" with frame, and 5" x 5-1/2" without the frame. The player photo is tinted blue, while the background is blue and orange. A facsimile autograph appears at the bottom of the photo. Illinois high school track star Herman "Jack" Waddlington posed for the photos of fictional Jack Armstrong "All-American Boy".

		NM	EX	VG
Complete Set (26):		2000.	1000.	600.00
Common Player:		40.00	20.00	12.00
(1)	Jack Armstrong (batting)	40.00	20.00	12.00
(2)	Jack Armstrong (throwing)	40.00	20.00	12.00
(3)	Wally Berger	40.00	20.00	12.00
(4)	Tommy Bridges	40.00	20.00	12.00
(5a)	Mickey Cochrane (black hat)	75.00	37.00	22.00
(5b)	Michey Cochrane (white hat)	375.00	187.00	112.00
(6)	James "Rip" Collins	40.00	20.00	12.00
(7)	Dizzy Dean	200.00	100.00	60.00
(8)	Dizzy Dean, Paul Dean	200.00	100.00	60.00
(9)	Paul Dean	45.00	22.00	13.50
(10)	William Delancey	40.00	20.00	12.00
(11)	"Jimmie" Foxx	150.00	75.00	45.00
(12)	Frank Frisch	60.00	30.00	18.00
(13)	Lou Gehrig	525.00	262.00	157.00
(14)	Goose Goslin	60.00	30.00	18.00
(15)	Lefty Grove	65.00	32.00	19.50
(16)	Carl Hubbell	65.00	32.00	19.50
(17)	Travis C. Jackson	60.00	30.00	18.00
(18)	"Chuck" Klein	60.00	30.00	18.00
(19)	Gus Mancuso	40.00	20.00	12.00
(20)	Pepper Martin (batting)	45.00	22.00	13.50
(21)	Pepper Martin (portrait)	45.00	22.00	13.50
(22)	Joe Medwick	60.00	30.00	18.00
(23)	Melvin Ott	75.00	37.00	22.00
(24)	Harold Schumacher	40.00	20.00	12.00
(25)	Al Simmons	60.00	30.00	18.00
(26)	"Jo Jo" White	40.00	20.00	12.00

1936 Wheaties - Series 3

Consisting of 12 unnumbered cards, this set is similar in size (6" x 6-1/4" with frame) and design to the Wheaties of the previous year, but is known as

"Fancy Frame with Printed Name and Data" because the cards also include a few printed words describing the player.

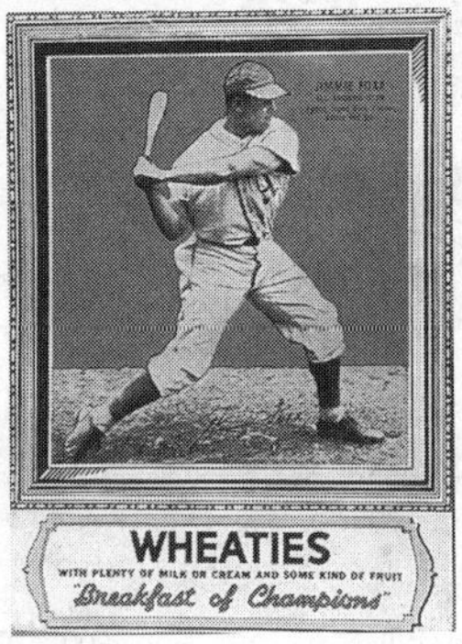

	NM	EX	VG
Complete Set (12):	1100.	550.00	330.00
Common Player:	40.00	20.00	12.00
(1) Earl Averill	60.00	30.00	18.00
(2) Mickey Cochrane	70.00	35.00	21.00
(3) Jimmy Foxx	90.00	45.00	27.00
(4) Lou Gehrig	525.00	262.00	157.00
(5) Hank Greenberg	75.00	37.00	22.00
(6) "Gabby" Hartnett	60.00	30.00	18.00
(7) Carl Hubbell	65.00	32.00	19.50
(8) "Pepper" Martin	45.00	22.00	13.50
(9) Van L. Mungo	40.00	20.00	12.00
(10) "Buck" Newsom	40.00	20.00	12.00
(11) "Arky" Vaughan	60.00	30.00	18.00
(12) Jimmy Wilson	40.00	20.00	12.00

1936 Wheaties - Series 4

This larger size (8-1/2" x 6") card also made up the back of a Wheaties box, and because of its distinctive border which featured drawings of small athletic figures, it is referred to as "Thin Orange Border/Figures in Border." Twelve major leaguers are pictured in the unnumbered set. The photos are enclosed in a 4" x 6-1/2" box. Below the photo is an endorsement for Wheaties, the "Breakfast of Champions," and a facsimile autograph.

	NM	EX	VG
Complete Set (12):	925.00	460.00	275.00
Common Player:	35.00	17.50	10.50
(1) Curt Davis	35.00	17.50	10.50
(2) Lou Gehrig	450.00	225.00	135.00
(3) Charley Gehringer	55.00	27.00	16.50
(4) Lefty Grove	55.00	27.00	16.50
(5) Rollie Hemsley	35.00	17.50	10.50
(6) Billy Herman	50.00	25.00	15.00
(7) Joe Medwick	50.00	25.00	15.00
(8) Mel Ott	60.00	30.00	18.00
(9) Schoolboy Rowe	35.00	17.50	10.50
(10) Arky Vaughan	50.00	25.00	15.00
(11) Joe Vosmik	35.00	17.50	10.50
(12) Lon Warneke	35.00	17.50	10.50

1936 Wheaties - Series 5

Often referred to as "How to Play Winning Baseball", this 12-card set features a large player photo surrounded by blue and white drawings that illustrate various playing tips. Different major leaguers offer advice on different aspects of the game. The cards again made up the back panel of a Wheaties box and measure 8-1/2" x 6-1/2". The cards are numbered from 1 through 12, and some of the panels are also found with a small number "28" followed by a letter from "A" through "L."

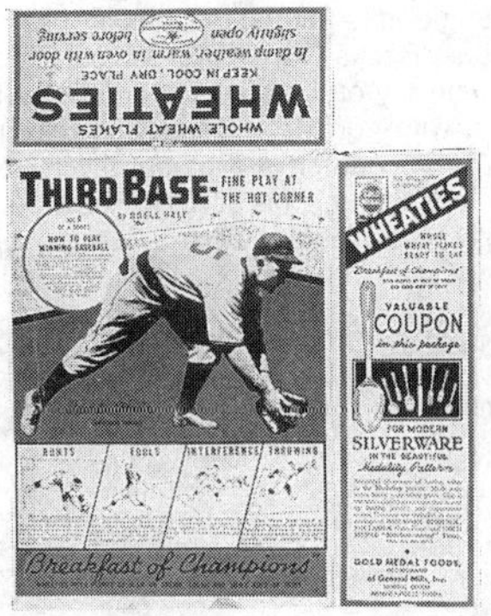

	NM	EX	VG
Complete Set (12)	600.00	300.00	180.00
Common Player:	30.00	15.00	9.00
1 Lefty Gomez	55.00	27.00	16.50
2 Billy Herman	50.00	25.00	15.00
3a Luke Appling (28C)	50.00	25.00	15.00
3b Luke Appling (no 28C)	50.00	25.00	15.00
4 Jimmie Foxx	60.00	30.00	18.00
5 Joe Medwick	50.00	25.00	15.00
6 Charles Gehringer	50.00	25.00	15.00
7a Mel Ott (tips in vertical sequence)	65.00	32.00	19.50
7b Mel Ott (tips in two horizontal rows)	65.00	32.00	19.50
8a Odell Hale (28B)	30.00	15.00	9.00
8b Odell Hale (no 28B)	30.00	15.00	9.00
9 Bill Dickey	65.00	32.00	19.50
10 "Lefty" Grove	55.00	27.00	16.50
11 Carl Hubbell	55.00	27.00	16.50
12 Earl Averill	50.00	25.00	15.00

1937 Wheaties - Series 6

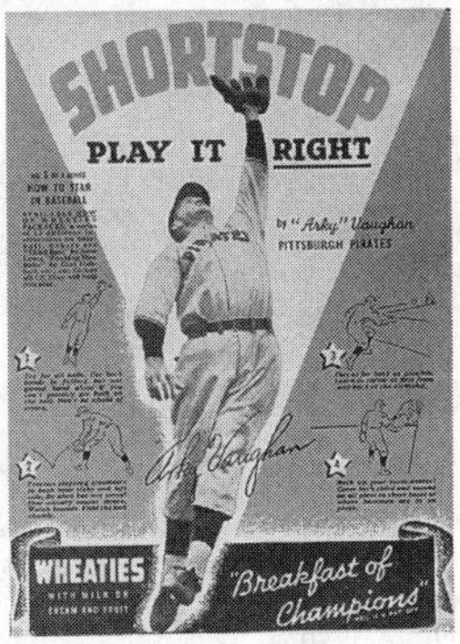

Similar to the Series 5 set, this numbered, 12-card series is known as "How to Star in Baseball" and again includes a large player photo with small instructional drawings to illustrate playing tips. The cards measure 8-1/4" x 6" and include a facsimile autograph.

	NM	EX	VG
Complete Set (12):	1000.	500.00	300.00
Common Player:	35.00	17.50	10.50
1 Bill Dickey	65.00	32.00	19.50
2 Red Ruffing	55.00	27.00	16.50
3 Zeke Bonura	35.00	17.50	10.50
4 Charlie Gehringer	55.00	27.00	16.50
5 "Arky" Vaughn (Vaughan)	55.00	27.00	16.50
6 Carl Hubbell	60.00	30.00	18.00
7 John Lewis	35.00	17.50	10.50
8 Heinie Manush	55.00	27.00	16.50
9 "Lefty" Grove	65.00	32.00	19.50
10 Billy Herman	55.00	27.00	16.50
11 Joe DiMaggio	450.00	225.00	135.00
12 Joe Medwick	55.00	27.00	16.50

1937 Wheaties - Series 7

This set of 6" x 8-1/4" panels contains several different card designs. One style (picturing Lombardi, Travis and Mungo) has a white background with an orange border and a large orange circle behind the player. Another design (showing Bonura, DiMaggio and Bridges) has the player outlined against a bright orange background with a Wheaties endorsement along the bottom. A third format (picturing Moore, Radcliff and Martin) has a distinctive red, white and blue border. And a fourth design (featuring Trosky, Demaree and Vaughan) has a tilted picture against an orange background framed in blue and white. The set also includes four Pacific Coast League Players (#29M-29P). The cards are numbered with a small "29" followed by a letter from "A" through "P".

	NM	EX	VG
Complete Set (16):	1600.	800.00	475.00
Common Player:	40.00	20.00	12.00
29A "Zeke" Bonura	40.00	20.00	12.00
29B Cecil Travis	40.00	20.00	12.00
29C Frank Demaree	40.00	20.00	12.00
29D Joe Moore	40.00	20.00	12.00
29E Ernie Lombardi	60.00	30.00	18.00
29F John L. "Pepper" Martin	45.00	22.00	13.50
29G Harold Trosky	40.00	20.00	12.00
29H Raymond Radcliff	40.00	20.00	12.00
29I Joe DiMaggio	475.00	237.00	142.00
29J Tom Bridges	40.00	20.00	12.00
29K Van L. Mungo	40.00	20.00	12.00
29L "Arky" Vaughn (Vaughan)	60.00	30.00	18.00
29M Arnold Statz	200.00	100.00	60.00
29N (Wes Schulmerich)	200.00	100.00	60.00
29O Fred Mueller	200.00	100.00	60.00
29P Gene Lillard	200.00	100.00	60.00

1937 Wheaties - Series 8

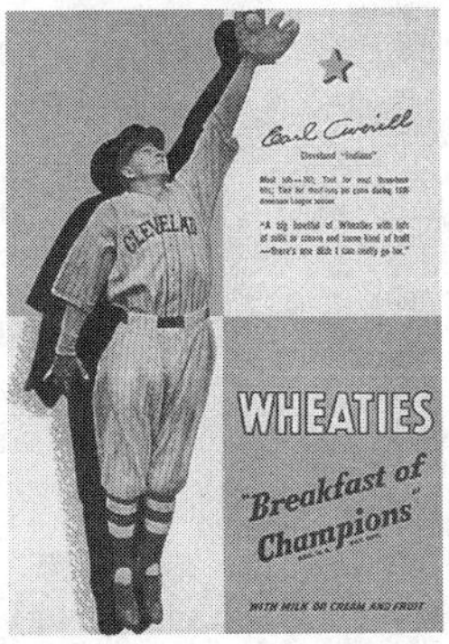

Another series printed on the back of Wheaties boxes in 1937, the eight cards in this set are unnumbered and measure 8-1/2" x 6". There are several different designs, but in all of them the player photo is surrounded by speckles of color, causing this series to be known as the "Speckled Orange, White and Blue" series. A facsimile autograph is included, along with brief printed 1936 season statistics.

	NM	EX	VG
Complete Set (8):	1000.	500.00	300.00
Common Player:	60.00	30.00	18.00
(1) Luke Appling	60.00	30.00	18.00
(2) Earl Averill	60.00	30.00	18.00
(3) Joe DiMaggio	500.00	250.00	150.00
(4) Robert Feller	165.00	82.00	49.00
(5) Chas. Gehringer	65.00	32.00	19.50
(6) Lefty Grove	70.00	35.00	21.00
(7) Carl Hubbell	65.00	32.00	19.50
(8) Joe Medwick	60.00	30.00	18.00

1937 Wheaties - Series 9

This unnumbered set includes one player from each of the 16 major league teams and is generally referred to as the "Color Series." The cards measure 8-1/2" x 6" and were the back panels of Wheaties boxes. The player photos are shown inside or against large stars, circles, "V" shapes, rectangles and other geometric designs. A facsimile autograph and team designation are printed near the photo, while a Wheaties endorsement and a line of player stats appear along the bottom.

Suffix letters after a card number indicate a variation card.

	NM	EX	VG
Complete Set (16):	1100.	550.00	330.00
Common Player:	40.00	20.00	12.00
(1) Zeke Bonura	40.00	20.00	12.00
(2) Tom Bridges	40.00	20.00	12.00
(3) Harland Clift (Harlond)	40.00	20.00	12.00
(4) Kiki Cuyler	60.00	30.00	18.00
(5) Joe DiMaggio	350.00	175.00	105.00
(6) Robert Feller	165.00	82.00	49.00
(7) Lefty Grove	65.00	32.00	19.50
(8) Billy Herman	60.00	30.00	18.00
(9) Carl Hubbell	65.00	32.00	19.50
(10) Buck Jordan	40.00	20.00	12.00
(11) "Pepper" Martin	45.00	22.00	13.50
(12) John Moore	40.00	20.00	12.00
(13) Wally Moses	40.00	20.00	12.00
(14) Van L. Mungo	40.00	20.00	12.00
(15) Cecil Travis	40.00	20.00	12.00
(16) Arky Vaughan	60.00	30.00	18.00

1937 Wheaties - Series 14

Much reduced in size (2-5/8" x 3-7/8"), these unnumbered cards made up the back panels of single-serving size Wheaties boxes. The player photo (which is sometimes identical to the photos used in the larger series) is set against an orange or white background. The player's name appears in large capital letters with hisposition and team in smaller capitals. A facsimile autograph and Wheaties endorsement are also included. Some cards are also found with the number "29" followed by a letter.

	NM	EX	VG
Complete Set (16):	1900.	950.00	575.00
Common Player:	75.00	37.00	22.00
(1) "Zeke" Bonura	75.00	37.00	22.00
(2) Tom Bridges	75.00	37.00	22.00
(3) Dolph Camilli	75.00	37.00	22.00
(4) Frank Demaree	75.00	37.00	22.00
(5) Joe DiMaggio	650.00	325.00	195.00
(6) Billy Herman	100.00	50.00	30.00
(7) Carl Hubbell	125.00	62.00	37.00
(8) Ernie Lombardi	100.00	50.00	30.00
(9) "Pepper" Martin	80.00	40.00	24.00
(10) Joe Moore	75.00	37.00	22.00
(11) Van Mungo	75.00	37.00	22.00
(12) Mel Ott	100.00	50.00	30.00
(13) Raymond Radcliff	75.00	37.00	22.00
(14) Cecil Travis	75.00	37.00	22.00
(15) Harold Trosky	75.00	37.00	22.00
(16a) "Arky" Vaughan (29L on card)	125.00	62.00	37.00
(16b) "Arky" Vaughan (no 29L on card)	125.00	62.00	37.00

1938 Wheaties - Series 10

One player from each major league team is included in this 16-card set, referred to as the "Biggest Thrills in Baseball" series. Measuring 8-1/2" x 6", each numbered card was the back panel of a Wheaties box and pictures a player along with a printed description of his biggest thrill in baseball and facsimile autograph. All 16 cards in this series have also been found on paper stock.

	NM	EX	VG
Complete Set (16):	1400.	700.00	425.00
Common Player:	40.00	20.00	12.00
1 Bob Feller	165.00	82.00	49.00
2 Cecil Travis	40.00	20.00	12.00
3 Joe Medwick	60.00	30.00	18.00
4 Gerald Walker	40.00	20.00	12.00
5 Carl Hubbell	65.00	32.00	19.50
6 Bob Johnson	40.00	20.00	12.00
7 Beau Bell	40.00	20.00	12.00
8 Ernie Lombardi	60.00	30.00	18.00
9 Lefty Grove	65.00	32.00	19.50
10 Lou Fette	40.00	20.00	12.00
11 Joe DiMaggio	475.00	237.00	142.00
12 Art Whitney	40.00	20.00	12.00
13 Dizzy Dean	175.00	87.00	52.00
14 Charley Gehringer	65.00	32.00	19.50
15 Paul Waner	60.00	30.00	18.00
16 Dolf Camilli	40.00	20.00	12.00

1938 Wheaties - Series 11

Cards in this unnumbered, eight-card series measure 8-1/2" x 6" and show the players in street clothes either eating or getting ready to enjoy a bowl of Wheaties. Sometimes a waitress or other person also appears in the photo. The set is sometimes called the "Dress Clothes" or "Civies" series.

	NM	EX	VG
Complete Set (8):	500.00	250.00	150.00
Common Player:	40.00	20.00	12.00
(1) Lou Fette	40.00	20.00	12.00
(2) Jimmie Foxx	100.00	50.00	30.00
(3) Charlie Gehringer	75.00	37.00	22.00
(4) Lefty Grove	75.00	37.00	22.00
(5) Hank Greenberg, Roxie Lawson	75.00	37.00	22.00
(6) Lee Grissom, Ernie Lombardi	60.00	30.00	18.00
(7) Joe Medwick	60.00	30.00	18.00
(8) Lon Warneke	40.00	20.00	12.00

1938 Wheaties - Series 15

Another set of small (2-5/8" x 3-7/8") cards, the photos in this unnumbered series made up the back panels of single-serving size Wheaties boxes. The panels have orange, blue and white backgrounds. Some of the photos are the same as those used in the larger Wheaties panels.

	NM	EX	VG
Complete Set (11):	1400.	700.00	425.00
Common Player:	50.00	25.00	15.00
(1) "Zeke" Bonura	50.00	25.00	15.00
(2) Joe DiMaggio	450.00	225.00	135.00
(3) Charles Gehringer (batting)	125.00	62.00	37.00
(4) Chas. Gehringer (leaping)	125.00	62.00	37.00
(5) Hank Greenberg	150.00	75.00	45.00
(6) Lefty Grove	100.00	50.00	30.00
(7) Carl Hubbell	100.00	50.00	30.00
(8) John (Buddy) Lewis	50.00	25.00	15.00
(9) Heinie Manush	90.00	45.00	27.00
(10) Joe Medwick	90.00	45.00	27.00
(11) Arky Vaughan	90.00	45.00	27.00

1939 Wheaties - Series 12

The nine cards in this numbered series, known as the "Personal Pointers" series, measure 8-1/4" x 6" and feature an instructional format similar to earlier Wheaties issues. The cards feature a player photo along with printed tips on various aspects of hitting and pitching.

	NM	EX	VG
Complete Set (9):	550.00	275.00	165.00
Common Player:	40.00	20.00	12.00
1 Ernie Lombardi	60.00	30.00	18.00
2 Johnny Allen	40.00	20.00	12.00
3 Lefty Gomez	65.00	32.00	19.50
4 Bill Lee	40.00	20.00	12.00
5 Jimmie Foxx	90.00	45.00	27.00
6 Joe Medwick	60.00	30.00	18.00
7 Hank Greenberg	90.00	45.00	27.00
8 Mel Ott	70.00	35.00	21.00
9 Arky Vaughn (Vaughan)	60.00	30.00	18.00

1939 Wheaties - Series 13

Issued in baseball's centennial year of 1939, this set of eight 6" x 6-3/4" cards commemorates "100 Years of Baseball". Each of the numbered panels illustrates a significant event in baseball history.

	NM	EX	VG
Complete Set (8):	175.00	875.00	525.00
Common Panel:	25.00	12.50	7.50
1 Design of First Diamond - 1838 (Abner Doubleday)	25.00	12.50	7.50
2 Gets News of Nomination on Field - 1860 (Abraham Lincoln)	45.00	22.00	13.50
3 Crowd Boos First Baseball Glove - 1869	25.00	12.50	7.50
4 Curve Ball Just an Illusion - 1877	25.00	12.50	7.50
5 Fencer's Mask is Pattern - 1877	25.00	12.50	7.50
6 Baseball Gets "All Dressed Up" - 1895	25.00	12.50	7.50

		NM	EX	VG
7	Modern Bludgeon Enters Game - 1895	25.00	12.50	7.50
8	"Casey at the Bat"	35.00	17.50	10.50

1940 Wheaties Champs of the USA

This set consists of 13 numbered panels (plus seven variations). Each pictures three athletes, including one, two or three baseball players; the others include football stars, golfers, skaters, racers, etc. The entire panel measures approximately 8-1/4" x 6", while the actual card measures approximately 6" square. Each athlete is pictured in what looks like a postage stamp with a serrated edge. A brief biography appears alongside the "stamp." Some variations are known to exist among the first nine panels. The cards are numbered in the upper right corner.

		NM	EX	VG
Complete Set (20):		1500.	750.00	450.00
Common Panel:		40.00	20.00	12.00
1A	Bob Feller, Lynn Patrick, Charles "Red" Ruffing	110.00	55.00	33.00
1B	Leo Durocher, Lynn Patrick, Charles "Red" Ruffing	75.00	37.00	22.00
2A	Joe DiMaggio, Don Duge, Hank Greenberg	350.00	175.00	105.00
2B	Joe DiMaggio, Mel Ott, Ellsworth Vines	325.00	162.00	97.00
3	Bernie Bierman, Bill Dickey, Jimmie Foxx	100.00	50.00	30.00
4	Morris Arnovich, Capt R.K. Baker, Earl "Dutch" Clark	40.00	20.00	12.00
5	Madison (Matty) Bell, Ab Jenkins, Joe Medwick	40.00	20.00	12.00
6A	Ralph Guldahl, John Mize, Davey O'Brien	40.00	20.00	12.00
6B	Bob Feller, John Mize, Rudy York	75.00	37.00	22.00
6C	Ralph Guldahl, Gabby Hartnett, Davey O'Brien	40.00	20.00	12.00
7A	Joe Cronin, Cecil Isbell, Byron Nelson	40.00	20.00	12.00
7B	Joe Cronin, Hank Greenberg, Byron Nelson	60.00	30.00	18.00
7C	Paul Derringer, Cecil Isbell, Byron Nelson	40.00	20.00	12.00
8A	Ernie Lombardi, Jack Manders, George I. Myers	40.00	20.00	12.00
8B	Paul Derringer, Ernie Lombardi, George I. Myers	40.00	20.00	12.00
9	Bob Bartlett, Captain R.C. Hanson, Terrell Jacobs	40.00	20.00	12.00
10	Lowell "Red" Dawson, Billy Herman, Adele Inge	40.00	20.00	12.00
11	Dolph Camilli, Antoinette Concello, Wallace Wade	40.00	20.00	12.00
12	Luke Appling, Stanley Hack, Hugh McManus	40.00	20.00	12.00
13	Felix Adler, Hal Trosky, Mabel Vinson	40.00	20.00	12.00

1941 Wheaties Champs of the USA

This eight-card series is actually a continuation of the previous year's Wheaties set, and the format is identical. The set begins with number 14, starting where the 1940 set ended.

		NM	EX	VG
Complete Set (8):		750.00	375.00	225.00
Common Panel:		40.00	20.00	12.00
14	Felix Adler, Jimmie Foxx, Capt. R.G. Hanson	70.00	35.00	21.00
15	Bernie Bierman, Bob Feller, Jessie McLeod	70.00	35.00	21.00
16	Lowell "Red" Dawson, Hank Greenberg, J.W. Stoker	55.00	27.00	16.50
17	Antoniette Concello, Joe DiMaggio, Byron Nelson	300.00	150.00	90.00
18	Capt. R.L. Baker, Frank "Buck" McCormick, Harold "Pee Wee" Reese	75.00	37.00	22.00
19	William W. Robbins, Gene Sarazen, Gerald "Gee" Walker	40.00	20.00	12.00
20	Harry Danning, Barney McCosky, Bucky Walters	40.00	20.00	12.00
21	Joe "Flash" Gordon, Stan Hack, George I. Myers	40.00	20.00	12.00

1951 Wheaties

Printed as the backs of single-serving size boxes of Wheaties, the six-card 1951 set includes three baseball players and one football player, basketball player and golfer. Well-trimmed cards measure 2-1/2" x 3-1/4". The cards feature blue line drawings of the athletes with a facsimile autograph and descriptive title below. There is a wide white border. A small hoard of complete sets of unused boxes made its way into the hobby in the early 1990s. Complete boxes should be priced at 1.5X the values shown here.

		NM	EX	VG
Complete Set (6):		450.00	225.00	135.00
Common Player:		58.00	29.00	17.50
(1)	Bob Feller (baseball)	65.00	32.00	19.50
(2)	John Lujack (football)	35.00	17.50	10.50
(3)	George Mikan (basketball)	75.00	37.00	22.00
(4)	Stan Musial (baseball)	95.00	47.00	28.00
(5)	Sam Snead (golfer)	45.00	22.00	13.50
(6)	Ted Williams (baseball)	135.00	67.00	40.00

1952 Wheaties

These 2" x 2-3/4" cards appeared on the back of the popular cereal boxes. Actually, sports figures had been appearing on the backs of the boxes for many years, but in 1952, of the 30 athletes depicted, 10 were baseball players. That means there are 20 baseball cards, as each player appears in both a portrait and an action drawing. The cards have a blue line drawing on an orange background with a white border. The player's name, team, and position appear at the bottom. The cards have rounded corners, but are often found poorly cut from the boxes.

		NM	EX	VG
Complete (Baseball) Set (20):		1200.	600.00	350.00
Common Player:		20.00	10.00	6.00
(1)	Larry "Yogi" Berra (portrait)	75.00	37.00	22.00
(2)	Larry "Yogi" Berra (action)	75.00	37.00	22.00
(3)	Roy Campanella (portrait)	75.00	37.00	22.00
(4)	Roy Campanella (action)	75.00	37.00	22.00
(5)	Bob Feller (portrait)	60.00	30.00	18.00
(6)	Bob Feller (action)	60.00	30.00	18.00
(7)	George Kell (portrait)	25.00	12.50	7.50
(8)	George Kell (action)	25.00	12.50	7.50
(9)	Ralph Kiner (portrait)	35.00	17.50	10.50
(10)	Ralph Kiner (action)	35.00	17.50	10.50
(11)	Bob Lemon (portrait)	35.00	17.50	10.50
(12)	Bob Lemon (action)	35.00	17.50	10.50
(13)	Stan Musial (portrait)	115.00	57.00	34.00
(14)	Stan Musial (action)	115.00	57.00	34.00
(15)	Phil Rizzuto (portrait)	55.00	27.00	16.50
(16)	Phil Rizzuto (action)	55.00	27.00	16.50
(17)	Elwin "Preacher" Roe (portrait)	20.00	10.00	6.00
(18)	Elwin "Preacher" Roe (action)	20.00	10.00	6.00
(19)	Ted Williams (portrait)	150.00	75.00	45.00
(20)	Ted Williams (action)	150.00	75.00	45.00

1952 Wheaties Tin Trays

This unique cereal box premium took the shape of a 4-7/8" x 5-1/8" tin tray which was glued to the back of Wheaties boxes. A cream-colored border surrounded the 3" x 4" color photo debossed at center. A black facsimile autograph appears across the photo. At top a small hole was punched for hanging the plaque. Backs were blank, and are often found with glue and paper residue on the gold-tone metal. Most of the plates have acquired numerous scratches and dings over the years, making true Nr. Mt. examples very scarce. The unnumbered trays are checklisted alphabetically. The George Kell tray listed in earlier editions has never been verified.

		NM	EX	VG
Complete Set (4):		1250.	625.00	350.00
Common Player:		60.00	30.00	18.00
(1)	Ralph Kiner	60.00	30.00	18.00
(2)	Stan Musial	110.00	55.00	33.00
(3)	Phil Rizzuto	75.00	37.00	22.00
(4)	Jackie Robinson	750.00	375.00	225.00
	George Kell (unverified)			

1964 Wheaties Stamps

This General Mills' promotion included 50 player stamps and a 48-page orange album called "Wheaties Major League All-Star Baseball Player Stamp Album". The 2-1/2" x 2-3/4" stamps have a color player photo at center with a facsimile autograph and surrounded by a white border. Backs are blank. The unnumbered set is checklisted here in alphabetical order.

	NM	EX	VG
Complete Set (50):	400.00	200.00	120.00
Common Player:	4.50	2.25	1.25
(1) Hank Aaron	30.00	15.00	9.00
(2) Bob Allison	4.50	2.25	1.25
(3) Luis Aparicio	12.00	6.00	3.50
(4) Ed Bailey	4.50	2.25	1.25
(5) Steve Barber	4.50	2.25	1.25
(6) Earl Battey	4.50	2.25	1.25
(7) Jim Bouton	6.00	3.00	1.75
(8) Ken Boyer	6.00	3.00	1.75
(9) Jim Bunning	9.00	4.50	2.75
(10) Orlando Cepeda	12.00	6.00	3.50
(11) Roberto Clemente	45.00	22.00	13.50
(12) Ray Culp	4.50	2.25	1.25
(13) Tommy Davis	4.50	2.25	1.25
(14) John Edwards	4.50	2.25	1.25
(15) Whitey Ford	18.00	9.00	5.50
(16) Nellie Fox	11.00	5.50	3.25
(17) Bob Friend	4.50	2.25	1.25
(18) Jim Gilliam	6.00	3.00	1.75
(19) Jim Grant	4.50	2.25	1.25
(20) Dick Groat	4.50	2.25	1.25
(21) Elston Howard	6.00	3.00	1.75
(22) Larry Jackson	4.50	2.25	1.25
(23) Julian Javier	4.50	2.25	1.25
(24) Al Kaline	18.00	9.00	5.50
(25) Harmon Killebrew	16.00	8.00	4.75
(26) Don Leppert	4.50	2.25	1.25
(27) Frank Malzone	4.50	2.25	1.25
(28) Juan Marichal	9.00	4.50	2.75
(29) Willie Mays	30.00	15.00	9.00
(30) Ken McBride	4.50	2.25	1.25
(31) Willie McCovey	14.00	7.00	4.25
(32) Jim O'Toole	4.50	2.25	1.25
(33) Albie Pearson	4.50	2.25	1.25
(34) Joe Pepitone	4.50	2.25	1.25
(35) Ron Perranoski	4.50	2.25	1.25
(36) Juan Pizzaro	4.50	2.25	1.25
(37) Dick Radatz	4.50	2.25	1.25
(38) Bobby Richardson	5.00	2.50	1.50
(39) Brooks Robinson	18.00	0.00	5.50
(40) Ron Santo	7.00	3.50	2.00
(41) Norm Siebern	4.50	2.25	1.25
(42) Duke Snider	18.00	9.00	5.50
(43) Warren Spahn	12.00	6.00	3.50
(44) Joe Torre	8.00	4.00	2.50
(45) Tom Tresh	5.00	2.50	1.50
(46) Zoilo Versailles (Versalles)	4.50	2.25	1.25
(47) Leon Wagner	4.50	2.25	1.25
(48) Bill White	4.50	2.25	1.25
(49) Hal Woodeshick	4.50	2.25	1.25
(50) Carl Yastrzemski	18.00	9.00	5.50

1937 WHIO-Sy Burick Cincinnati Reds postcards

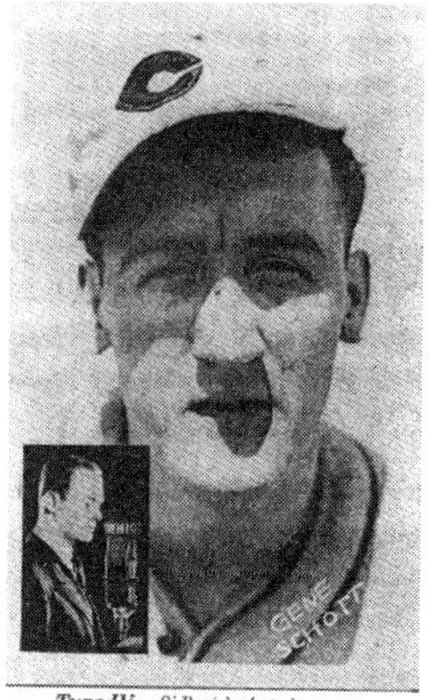

Type IV — Si Burick photo in corner

(See 1937-39 Orcajo Cincinnati Reds postcards for checklist, values.)

1889 C.S. White & Co. Boston N.L.

(See 1889 Number 7 Cigars for checklist and value information.)

1976 Wiffle discs

Similar in concept and format to the many contemporary MSA baseball player disc sets, the pieces inserted within and upon Wiffle brand baseball, softball and bat boxes differ in that they are smaller, at 2-3/8" diameter, and feature a larger checklist. The discs feature black-and-white player portrait photos in the center of a baseball design. The left and right panels are in one of several bright colors. Licensed by the players' association through Mike Schechter Associates, the player photos carry no uniform logos. Backs are printed in black and orange. The unnumbered discs are checklisted here alphabetically.

	NM	EX	VG
Complete Set (88):	325.00	160.00	97.00
Common Player:	2.50	1.25	.70
(1) Sal Bando	2.50	1.25	.70
(2) Buddy Bell	2.50	1.25	.70
(3) Johnny Bench	10.00	5.00	3.00
(4) Vida Blue	2.50	1.25	.70
(5) Bert Blyleven	3.00	1.50	.90
(6) Bobby Bonds	3.00	1.50	.90
(7) George Brett	15.00	7.50	4.50
(8) Lou Brock	7.50	3.75	2.25
(9) Bill Buckner	2.50	1.25	.70
(10) Ray Burris	2.50	1.25	.70
(11) Jeff Burroughs	2.50	1.25	.70
(12) Bert Campaneris	2.50	1.25	.70
(13) John Candelaria	2.50	1.25	.70
(14) Jose Cardenal	2.50	1.25	.70
(15) Rod Carew	10.00	5.00	3.00
(16) Steve Carlton	10.00	5.00	3.00
(17) Dave Cash	2.50	1.25	.70
(18) Cesar Cedeno	2.50	1.25	.70
(19) Ron Cey	2.50	1.25	.70
(20) Chris Chambliss	2.50	1.25	.70
(21) Dave Concepcion	2.50	1.25	.70
(22) Dennis Eckersley	6.00	3.00	1.75
(23) Mark Fidrych	3.50	1.75	1.00
(24) Rollie Fingers	7.50	3.75	2.25
(25) Carlton Fisk	7.50	3.75	2.25
(26) George Foster	2.50	1.25	.70
(27) Wayne Garland	2.50	1.25	.70
(28) Ralph Garr	2.50	1.25	.70
(29) Steve Garvey	5.00	2.50	1.50
(30) Don Gullett	2.50	1.25	.70
(31) Larry Hisle	2.50	1.25	.70
(32) Al Hrabosky	2.50	1.25	.70
(33) Catfish Hunter	7.50	3.75	2.25
(34) Reggie Jackson	10.00	5.00	3.00
(35) Randy Jones	2.50	1.25	.70
(36) Von Joshua	2.50	1.25	.70
(37) Dave Kingman	3.00	1.50	.90
(38) Jerry Koosman	2.50	1.25	.70
(39) Ed Kranepool	2.50	1.25	.70
(40) Ron LeFlore	2.50	1.25	.70
(41) Sixto Lezcano	2.50	1.25	.70
(42) Davey Lopes	2.50	1.25	.70
(43) Greg Luzinski	2.50	1.25	.70
(44) Fred Lynn	3.00	1.50	.90
(45) Garry Maddox	2.50	1.25	.70
(46) Jon Matlock	2.50	1.25	.70
(47) Gary Matthews	2.50	1.25	.70
(48) Lee May	2.50	1.25	.70
(49) John Mayberry	2.50	1.25	.70
(50) Bake McBride	2.50	1.25	.70
(51) Tug McGraw	2.50	1.25	.70
(52) Hal McRae	2.50	1.25	.70
(53) Andy Messersmith	2.50	1.25	.70
(54) Randy Moffitt	2.50	1.25	.70
(55) John Montefusco	2.50	1.25	.70
(56) Joe Morgan	7.50	3.75	2.25
(57) Thurman Munson	9.00	4.50	2.75
(58) Graig Nettles	2.50	1.25	.70
(59) Bill North	2.50	1.25	.70
(60) Al Oliver	2.50	1.25	.70
(61) Jorge Orta	2.50	1.25	.70
(62) Jim Palmer	9.00	4.50	2.75
(63) Dave Parker	3.50	1.75	1.00
(64) Tony Perez	7.50	3.75	2.25
(65) Gaylord Perry	7.50	3.75	2.25
(66) Jim Rice	4.00	2.00	1.25
(67) Ellie Rodriguez	2.50	1.25	.70
(68) Steve Rogers	2.50	1.25	.70
(69) Pete Rose	25.00	12.50	7.50
(70) Joe Rudi	2.50	1.25	.70
(71) Nolan Ryan	50.00	25.00	15.00
(72) Manny Sanguillen	2.50	1.25	.70
(73) Mike Schmidt	15.00	7.50	4.50
(74) Tom Seaver	12.00	6.00	3.50
(75) Ted Simmons	2.50	1.25	.70
(76) Reggie Smith	2.50	1.25	.70
(77) Jim Spencer	2.50	1.25	.70
(78) Willie Stargell	10.00	5.00	3.00
(79) Rusty Staub	3.00	1.50	.90
(80) Rennie Stennett	2.50	1.25	.70
(81) Frank Tanana	2.50	1.25	.70
(82) Gene Tenace	2.50	1.25	.70
(83) Luis Tiant	2.50	1.25	.70
(84) Manny Trillo	2.50	1.25	.70
(85) Bob Watson	2.50	1.25	.70
(86) Butch Wynegar	2.50	1.25	.70
(87) Carl Yastrzemski	12.00	6.00	3.50
(88) Richie Zisk	2.50	1.25	.70

1922 Willard's Chocolates Premium

Details on distribution of this 7-1/8" x 11-1/4" premium are unclear, likely involving some sort of wrapper or coupon redemption. The blank-back piece has a central photo of Babe Ruth in action. A facsimile autograph appears in a panel at bottom.

	NM	EX	VG
Babe Ruth	4000.	2000.	1200.

1923 Willard's Chocolate (V100)

Issued circa 1923, this set was produced by the Willard Chocolate Company of Canada and features sepia-toned photographs on cards measuring about 2" x 3-1/4". The cards are blank-backed and feature the player's name in script on the front, along with a tiny credit line: "Photo by International". The set is complete at 180 cards and nearly one-fourth of the photos used in the set are identical to the better known E120 American Caramel set. The Willard set is identified as V100 in the American Card Catalog.

	NM	EX	VG
Complete Set (180):	17500.	7000.	3500.
Common Player:	75.00	30.00	15.00
(1) Chas. B. Adams	75.00	30.00	15.00
(2) Grover C. Alexander	225.00	90.00	45.00
(3) J.P. Austin	75.00	30.00	15.00
(4) J.C. Bagby	75.00	30.00	15.00
(5) J. Franklin Baker	200.00	80.00	40.00
(6) David J. Bancroft	200.00	80.00	40.00
(7) Turner Barber	75.00	30.00	15.00
(8) Jesse L. Barnes	75.00	30.00	15.00
(9) J.C. Bassler	75.00	30.00	15.00
(10) L.A. Blue	75.00	30.00	15.00
(11) Norman D. Boeckel	75.00	30.00	15.00
(12) F.L. Brazil (Brazill)	75.00	30.00	15.00
(13) G.H. Burns	75.00	30.00	15.00
(14) Geo. J. Burns	75.00	30.00	15.00
(15) Leon Cadore	75.00	30.00	15.00
(16) Max G. Carey	200.00	00.00	10.00
(17) Harold G. Carlson	75.00	30.00	15.00
(18) Lloyd R Christenberry (Christenbury)	75.00	30.00	15.00
(19) Vernon J. Clemons	75.00	30.00	15.00
(20) T.R. Cobb	1500.	600.00	300.00
(21) Bert Cole	75.00	30.00	15.00
(22) John F. Collins	75.00	30.00	15.00
(23) S. Coveleskie (Coveleski)	200.00	80.00	40.00
(24) Walton E. Cruise	75.00	30.00	15.00
(25) G.W. Cutshaw	75.00	30.00	15.00
(26) Jacob E. Daubert	75.00	30.00	15.00
(27) Geo. Dauss	75.00	30.00	15.00
(28) F.T. Davis	75.00	30.00	15.00
(29) Chas. A. Deal	75.00	30.00	15.00
(30) William L. Doak	75.00	30.00	15.00

(31)	William E. Donovan	75.00	30.00	15.00
(32)	Hugh Duffy	200.00	80.00	40.00
(33)	J.A. Dugan	75.00	30.00	15.00
(34)	Louis B. Duncan	75.00	30.00	15.00
(35)	James Dykes	75.00	30.00	15.00
(36)	H.J. Ehmke	75.00	30.00	15.00
(37)	F.R. Ellerbe	75.00	30.00	15.00
(38)	E.G. Erickson	75.00	30.00	15.00
(39)	John J. Evers	200.00	80.00	40.00
(40)	U.C. Faber	200.00	80.00	40.00
(41)	B.A. Falk	75.00	30.00	15.00
(42)	Max Flack	75.00	30.00	15.00
(43)	Lee Fohl	75.00	30.00	15.00
(44)	Jacques F. Fournier	75.00	30.00	15.00
(45)	Frank F. Frisch	200.00	80.00	40.00
(46)	C.E. Galloway	75.00	30.00	15.00
(47)	W.C. Gardner	75.00	30.00	15.00
(48)	E.P. Gharrity	75.00	30.00	15.00
(49)	Geo. Gibson	75.00	30.00	15.00
(50)	Wm. Gleason	75.00	30.00	15.00
(51)	William Gleason	75.00	30.00	15.00
(52)	Henry M. Gowdy	75.00	30.00	15.00
(53)	I.M. Griffin	75.00	30.00	15.00
(54)	Tom Griffith	75.00	30.00	15.00
(55)	Burleigh A. Grimes	200.00	80.00	40.00
(56)	Charles J. Grimm	75.00	30.00	15.00
(57)	Jesse J. Haines	200.00	80.00	40.00
(58)	S.R. Harris	200.00	80.00	40.00
(59)	W.B. Harris	75.00	30.00	15.00
(60)	R.K. Hasty	75.00	30.00	15.00
(61)	H.E. Heilman (Heilmann)	200.00	80.00	40.00
(62)	Walter J. Henline	75.00	30.00	15.00
(63)	Walter L. Holke	75.00	30.00	15.00
(64)	Charles J. Hollocher	75.00	30.00	15.00
(65)	H.B. Hooper	200.00	80.00	40.00
(66)	Rogers Hornsby	250.00	100.00	50.00
(67)	W.C. Hoyt	200.00	80.00	40.00
(68)	Miller Huggins	200.00	80.00	40.00
(69)	W.C. Jacobsen (Jacobson)	75.00	30.00	15.00
(70)	C.D. Jamieson	75.00	30.00	15.00
(71)	Ernest Johnson	75.00	30.00	15.00
(72)	W.P. Johnson	500.00	200.00	100.00
(73)	James H. Johnston	75.00	30.00	15.00
(74)	R.W. Jones	75.00	30.00	15.00
(75)	Samuel Pond Jones	75.00	30.00	15.00
(76)	J.I. Judge	75.00	30.00	15.00
(77)	James W. Keenan	75.00	30.00	15.00
(78)	Geo. L. Kelly	200.00	80.00	40.00
(79)	Peter J. Kilduff	75.00	30.00	15.00
(80)	William Killefer	75.00	30.00	15.00
(81)	Lee King	75.00	30.00	15.00
(82)	Ray Kolp	75.00	30.00	15.00
(83)	John Lavan	75.00	30.00	15.00
(84)	H.L. Leibold	75.00	30.00	15.00
(85)	Connie Mack	200.00	80.00	40.00
(86)	J.W. Mails	75.00	30.00	15.00
(87)	Walter J. Maranville	200.00	80.00	40.00
(88)	Richard W. Marquard	200.00	80.00	40.00
(89)	C.W. Mays	80.00	32.00	16.00
(90)	Geo. F. McBride	75.00	30.00	15.00
(91)	H.M. McClellan	75.00	30.00	15.00
(92)	John J. McGraw	200.00	80.00	40.00
(93)	Austin B. McHenry	75.00	30.00	15.00
(94)	J. McInnis	75.00	30.00	15.00
(95)	Douglas McWeeney (McWeeny)	75.00	30.00	15.00
(96)	M. Menosky	75.00	30.00	15.00
(97)	Emil F. Meusel	75.00	30.00	15.00
(98)	R. Meusel	75.00	30.00	15.00
(99)	Henry W. Meyers	75.00	30.00	15.00
(100)	J.C. Milan	75.00	30.00	15.00
(101)	John K. Miljus	75.00	30.00	15.00
(102)	Edmund J. Miller	75.00	30.00	15.00
(103)	Elmer Miller	75.00	30.00	15.00
(104)	Otto L. Miller	75.00	30.00	15.00
(105)	Fred Mitchell	75.00	30.00	15.00
(106)	Geo. Mogridge	75.00	30.00	15.00
(107)	Patrick J. Moran	75.00	30.00	15.00
(108)	John D. Morrison	75.00	30.00	15.00
(109)	J.A. Mostil	75.00	30.00	15.00
(110)	Clarence F. Mueller	75.00	30.00	15.00
(111)	A. Earle Neale	95.00	38.00	19.00
(112)	Joseph Oeschger	75.00	30.00	15.00
(113)	Robert J. O'Farrell	75.00	30.00	15.00
(114)	J.C. Oldham	75.00	30.00	15.00
(115)	I.M. Olson	75.00	30.00	15.00
(116)	Geo. M. O'Neil	75.00	30.00	15.00
(117)	S.F. O'Neill	75.00	30.00	15.00
(118)	Frank J. Parkinson	75.00	30.00	15.00
(119)	Geo. H. Paskert	75.00	30.00	15.00
(120)	R.T. Peckinpaugh	75.00	30.00	15.00
(121)	H.J. Pennock	200.00	80.00	40.00
(122)	Ralph Perkins	75.00	30.00	15.00
(123)	Edw. J. Pfeffer	75.00	30.00	15.00
(124)	W.C. Pipp	80.00	32.00	16.00
(125)	Charles Elmer Ponder	75.00	30.00	15.00
(126)	Raymond R. Powell	75.00	30.00	15.00
(127)	D.B. Pratt	75.00	30.00	15.00
(128)	Joseph Rapp	75.00	30.00	15.00
(129)	John H. Rawlings	75.00	30.00	15.00
(130)	E.S. Rice (should be E.C.)	200.00	80.00	40.00
(131)	Branch Rickey	225.00	90.00	45.00
(132)	James J. Ring	75.00	30.00	15.00
(133)	Eppa J. Rixey	200.00	80.00	40.00
(134)	Davis A. Robertson	75.00	30.00	15.00
(135)	Edwin Rommel	75.00	30.00	15.00
(136)	Edd J. Roush	200.00	80.00	40.00
(137)	Harold Ruel (Herold)	75.00	30.00	15.00
(138)	Allen Russell	75.00	30.00	15.00
(139)	G.H. Ruth	2000.	800.00	400.00
(140)	Wilfred D. Ryan	75.00	30.00	15.00
(141)	Henry F. Sallee	75.00	30.00	15.00
(142)	W.H. Schang	75.00	30.00	15.00
(143)	Raymond H. Schmandt	75.00	30.00	15.00
(144)	Everett Scott	75.00	30.00	15.00
(145)	Henry Severeid	75.00	30.00	15.00
(146)	Jos. W. Sewell	200.00	80.00	40.00
(147)	Howard S. Shanks	75.00	30.00	15.00
(148)	E.H. Sheely	75.00	30.00	15.00
(149)	Ralph Shinners	75.00	30.00	15.00
(150)	U.J. Shocker	75.00	30.00	15.00
(151)	G.H. Sisler	200.00	80.00	40.00
(152)	Earl L. Smith	75.00	30.00	15.00
(153)	Earl S. Smith	75.00	30.00	15.00
(154)	Geo. A. Smith	75.00	30.00	15.00
(155)	J.W. Smith	75.00	30.00	15.00
(156)	Tris E. Speaker	225.00	90.00	45.00
(157)	Arnold Staatz (Statz)	75.00	30.00	15.00
(158)	J.R. Stephenson	75.00	30.00	15.00
(159)	Milton J. Stock	75.00	30.00	15.00
(160)	John L. Sullivan	75.00	30.00	15.00
(161)	H.F. Tormahlen	75.00	30.00	15.00
(162)	Jas. A. Tierney	75.00	30.00	15.00
(163)	J.T. Tobin	75.00	30.00	15.00
(164)	Jas. L. Vaughn	75.00	30.00	15.00
(165)	R.H. Veach	75.00	30.00	15.00
(166)	C.W. Walker	75.00	30.00	15.00
(167)	A.L. Ward	75.00	30.00	15.00
(168)	Zack D. Wheat	200.00	80.00	40.00
(169)	George B. Whitted	75.00	30.00	15.00
(170)	Irvin K. Wilhelm	75.00	30.00	15.00
(171)	Roy H. Wilkinson	75.00	30.00	15.00
(172)	Fred C. Williams	75.00	30.00	15.00
(173)	K.R. Williams	75.00	30.00	15.00
(174)	Sam'l W. Wilson	75.00	30.00	15.00
(175)	Ivy B. Wingo	75.00	30.00	15.00
(176)	L.W. Witt	75.00	30.00	15.00
(177)	Joseph Wood	75.00	30.00	15.00
(178)	E. Yaryan	75.00	30.00	15.00
(179)	R.S. Young	75.00	30.00	15.00
(180)	Ross Young (Youngs)	200.00	80.00	40.00

1924 Willard's Chocolate Sports Champions (V122)

Three baseball players are featured among this 56-card Canadian set. The black-and-white cards are printed on thin paper measuring 1-3/8" x 3-3/8". Backs are blank. The set features male and female athletes from many different sports, with a distinct Canadian flavor. The candy company was headquartered in Toronto.

		NM	EX	VG
Complete Set (54):		5500.	2750.	1650.
Common Player:		125.00	62.50	37.50
2	Eddie Collins	400.00	200.00	120.00
5	Babe Ruth	2000.	1200.	600.00
39	Ty Cobb	750.00	375.00	220.00

1911 Williams Baking Philadelphia A's (D359)

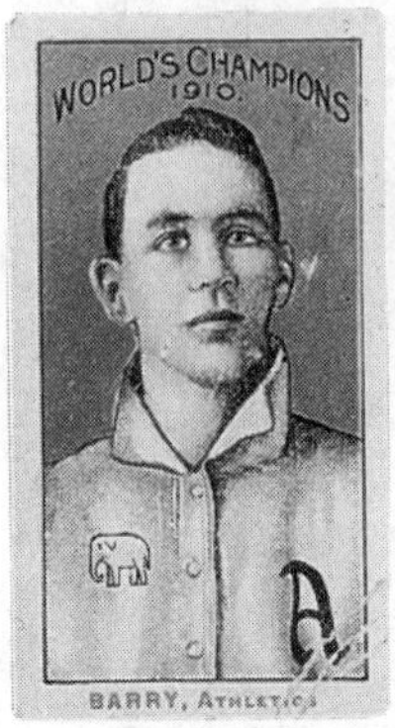

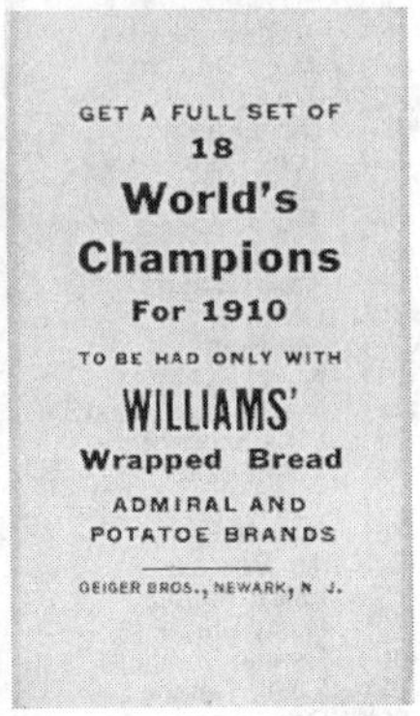

This Philadelphia Athletics team set is among the scarcest early 20th Century baking company issues. It commemorates the A's 1910 Championship season, and, except for pitcher Jack Coombs, the checklist includes nearly all key members of the club, including manager Connie Mack. The cards are the standard size for the era, 1-1/2" x 2-5/8". Fronts feature a player portrait set against a colored background. The player's name and the word "Athletics" appear at the bottom, while "World's Champions 1910" is printed along the top. Backs of the cards advertise the set as the "Athletics Series." Collectors should be aware that the same checklist was used for a similar Athletics set issued by Rochester Baking and Cullivan's Fireside tobacco (T208) and also that blank-backed versions are also known to exist, cataloged as E104 in the American Card Catalog.

		NM	EX	VG
Complete Set (18):		9000.	3600.	1800.
Common Player:		375.00	150.00	75.00
(1)	Home Run Baker	900.00	360.00	180.00
(2)	Jack Barry	375.00	150.00	75.00
(3)	Chief Bender	1100.	440.00	220.00
(4)	Eddie Collins	1100.	440.00	220.00
(5)	Harry Davis	375.00	150.00	75.00
(6)	Jimmy Dygert	375.00	150.00	75.00
(7)	Topsy Hartsel	375.00	150.00	75.00
(8)	Harry Krause	375.00	150.00	75.00
(9)	Jack Lapp	375.00	150.00	75.00
(10)	Paddy Livingstone (Livingston)	375.00	150.00	75.00
(11)	Bris Lord	375.00	150.00	75.00
(12)	Connie Mack	1000.	400.00	200.00
(13)	Cy Morgan	375.00	150.00	75.00
(14)	Danny Murphy	375.00	150.00	75.00
(15)	Rube Oldring	375.00	150.00	75.00
(16)	Eddie Plank	1100.	440.00	220.00
(17)	Amos Strunk	375.00	150.00	75.00
(18a)	Ira Thomas (1910 at top)	375.00	150.00	75.00
(18b)	Ira Thomas (1910 at right)	375.00	150.00	75.00

1910 Williams Caramels (E103)

This 30-card set issued by the Williams Caramel Co. of Oxford, Pa., in 1910 can be differentiated from other similar sets because it was printed on a thin paper stock rather than cardboard. Measuring approximately 1-1/2" x 2-3/4", each card features a player portrait set against a red background. The bottom of the card lists the player's last name, position and team; beneath that is the line, "The Williams Caramel Co. Oxford Pa." Nearly all of the photos in the set, which is designated E103 by the ACC, are identical to those in the M116 Sporting Life set.

		NM	EX	VG
Complete Set (30):		18000.	7200.	3600.
Common Player:		250.00	100.00	50.00
(1)	Chas. Bender	650.00	260.00	130.00
(2)	Roger Bresnahan	650.00	260.00	130.00
(3)	Mordecai Brown	650.00	260.00	130.00
(4)	Frank Chance	650.00	260.00	130.00
(5)	Hal Chase	500.00	200.00	100.00
(6)	Ty Cobb	4500.	1800.	900.00
(7)	Edward Collins	650.00	260.00	130.00
(8)	Sam Crawford	650.00	260.00	130.00
(9)	Harry Davis	250.00	100.00	50.00
(10)	Arthur Devlin	250.00	100.00	50.00
(11)	William Donovan	250.00	100.00	50.00
(12)	Chas. Dooin	250.00	100.00	50.00
(13)	L. Doyle	250.00	100.00	50.00
(14)	John Ewing	250.00	100.00	50.00
(15)	George Gibson	250.00	100.00	50.00
(16)	Hugh Jennings	650.00	260.00	130.00
(17)	David Jones	250.00	100.00	50.00
(18)	Tim Jordan	250.00	100.00	50.00
(19)	N. Lajoie	800.00	320.00	160.00
(20)	Thomas Leach	250.00	100.00	50.00
(21)	Harry Lord	250.00	100.00	50.00
(22)	Chris. Mathewson	2400.	950.00	475.00
(23)	John McLean	250.00	100.00	50.00
(24)	Geo. W. McQuillan	250.00	100.00	50.00

		NM	EX	VG
(25)	Pastorius	250.00	100.00	50.00
(26)	N. Rucker	250.00	100.00	50.00
(27)	Fred Tenny (Tenney)	250.00	100.00	50.00
(28)	Ira Thomas	250.00	100.00	50.00
(29)	Hans Wagner	4000.	1600.	800.00
(30)	Robert Wood	250.00	100.00	50.00

1889 E.R. Williams Card Game

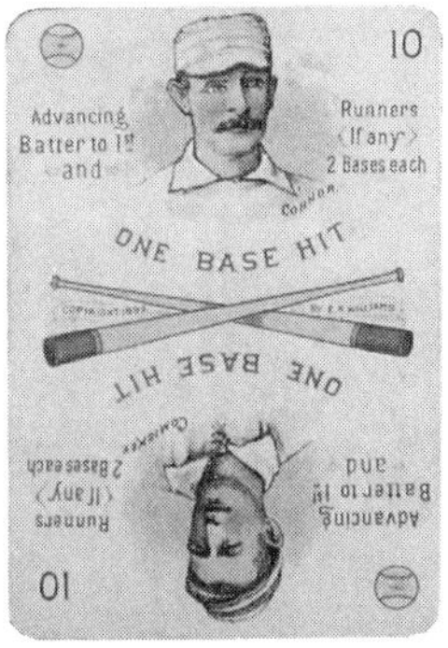

This set of 52 playing cards came packed in its own box that advertised the set as the "Egerton R. Williams Popular Indoor Base Ball Game." Designed to look like a conventional deck of playing cards, the set included various players from the National League and the American Association. Although the set contains 52 cards (like a typical deck of playing cards) only 19 actually feature color drawings of players. Each of these cards pictures two different players (one at the top and a second at the bottom, separated by sepia-colored crossed bats in the middle), resulting in 38 different players. The remaining 33 cards in the deck are strictly game cards showing a specific baseball play (such as "Batter Out on Fly" or "Two Base Hit," etc.). The cards have green-tinted backs and measure 2-7/16" x 3-1/2". Each one carries an 1889 copyright line by E.R. Williams.

		NM	EX	VG
	Complete Boxed Set:	9500.	4750.	2800.
	Common Player Card:	250.00	125.00	75.00
(1)	Cap Anson, Buck Ewing	1200.	600.00	360.00
(2)	Dan Brouthers, Arlie Latham	375.00	187.00	112.00
(3)	Charles Buffinton, Parisian Bob Carruthers	250.00	125.00	75.00
(4)	Hick Carpenter, Cliff Carroll	250.00	125.00	75.00
(5)	Charles Comiskey, Roger Connor	750.00	375.00	225.00
(6)	Pop Corkhill, Jim Fogarty	250.00	125.00	75.00
(7)	John Clarkson, Tim Keefe	600.00	300.00	180.00
(8)	Jerry Denny, Silent Mike Tiernan	250.00	125.00	75.00
(9)	Dave Foutz, King Kelly	500.00	250.00	150.00
(10)	Pud Galvin, Dave Orr	375.00	187.00	112.00
(11)	Pebbly Jack Glasscock, Foghorn Tucker	250.00	125.00	75.00
(12)	Mike Griffin, Ed McKean	250.00	125.00	75.00
(13)	Dummy Hoy, Long John Reilley (Reilly)	250.00	125.00	75.00
(14)	Arthur Irwin, Ned Williamson	250.00	125.00	75.00
(15)	Silver King, John Tener	250.00	125.00	75.00
(16)	Al Myers, Cub Stricker	250.00	125.00	75.00
(17)	Fred Pfeffer, Chicken Wolf	250.00	125.00	75.00
(18)	Toad Ramsey, Gus Weyhing	250.00	125.00	75.00
(19)	Monte Ward, Curt Welch	375.00	187.00	112.00

1908 R.C. Williams Cy Young Postcard

A mature Cy Young, about age 42, is pictured on this postcard bearing the imprint of R.C. Williams. No other contemporary cards with this imprint have been reported.

	NM	EX	VG
Cy Young	300.00	150.00	90.00

1950s-70s Wilson Advisory Staff Photos

Advisory staff photos were a promtional item which debuted in the early 1950s, flourished in the Sixties and died in the early 1970s. Generally 8" x 10" (sometimes a little larger), these black-and-white (a few later were color) glossy photos picture players who had contracted with a major baseball equipment company to endorse and use their product. Usually the product - most often a glove - was prominently displayed in the photo. The pictures were often displayed in the windows of sporting goods stores or the walls of sports departments and were sometimes made available to customers. Because the companies tended to stick with players over the years, some photos were reissued, sometimes with and sometimes without a change of team, pose or style. All advisory staff photos of the era are checklisted here in alphabetical order. A pose description is given for each known picture. The photos are checklisted here in alphabetical order. It is unlikely this list is complete. In general, Wilson advisory staff photos feature the player name and a line of type indicating the player's status as an advisory staffer in the bottom border.

		NM	EX	VG
	Common Player:	12.00	6.00	3.50
(1)	Bob Allison (Twins, full-length)	12.00	6.00	3.50
(2)	Felipe Alou (Braves, upper body)	15.00	7.50	4.50
(3)	Max Alvis (Indians, upper body)	12.00	6.00	3.50
(4)	Luis Aparicio (White Sox, full-length)	25.00	12.50	7.50
(5)	Luis Aparicio (Orioles, full-length)	25.00	12.50	7.50
(6)	Gerry Arrigo (Reds, full-length pitching)	12.00	6.00	3.50
(7)	Ernie Banks (batting)	30.00	15.00	9.00
(8)	Ernie Banks (horizontal, fielding)	27.50	13.50	8.25
(9)	Glenn Beckert (Cubs, fielding, ball in hand)	12.00	6.00	3.50
(10)	Glenn Beckert (Cubs, fielding, no ball)	12.00	6.00	3.50
(12)	Paul Blair (Orioles, full-length)	12.00	6.00	3.50
(13)	Bob Bolin (Giants, pitching follow-through)	12.00	6.00	3.50
(14)	Dave Boswell (Twins, full-length)	12.00	6.00	3.50
(15)	Dave Boswell (Twins, waist-up, stretch position)	12.00	6.00	3.50
(16)	Jackie Brandt (Orioles, full-length)	12.00	6.00	3.50
(17)	Smoky Burgess (Pirates, sitting on step w/3 bats)	12.00	6.00	3.50
(18)	Rico Carty (Milwaukee Braves, batting)	12.00	6.00	3.50
(19)	Rico Carty (Milwaukee Braves, dugout step)	12.00	6.00	3.50
(20)	Rico Carty (Atlanta Braves, batting)	12.00	6.00	3.50
(21)	Paul Casanova (Senators, catching crouch)	12.00	6.00	3.50
(22)	Norm Cash (Tigers, batting)	15.00	7.50	4.50
(23)	Orlando Cepeda (Cardinals, dugout step)	12.50	6.25	3.75
(24)	Orlando Cepeda (Cardinals, fielding)	12.50	6.25	3.75
(25)	Jim Davenport (Giants, fielding)	12.00	6.00	3.50
(26)	Vic Davalillo (Indians, upper body)	12.00	6.00	3.50
(27)	Willie Davis (Dodgers, full-length)	12.00	6.00	3.50
(28)	Chuck Dobson (A's, full-length)	12.00	6.00	3.50
(29)	Dick Ellsworth (Cubs, pitching follow-through)	12.00	6.00	3.50
(30)	Dick Ellsworth (Phillies, full-length)	12.00	6.00	3.50
(31)	Del Ennis (Cardinals, upper body)	12.00	6.00	3.50
(32)	Nelson Fox (White Sox, seated)	25.00	12.50	7.50
(33)	Nelson Fox (Colt .45s, batting)	30.00	15.00	9.00
(34)	Bill Freehan (catching crouch)	12.00	6.00	3.50
(35)	Bill Freehan (two pictures)	12.00	6.00	3.50
(36)	Phil Gagliano (Cardinals, full-length, photo actually Ed Spiezio)	12.00	6.00	3.50
(37)	Vernon "Lefty" Gomez (w/ glasses)	15.00	7.50	4.50
(38)	Lefty Gomez (no glasses)	15.00	7.50	4.50
(39)	Jim Hall (Angels, fielding)	12.00	6.00	3.50
(40)	Don Hoak (Pirates, full-length)	12.00	6.00	3.50
(41)	Willie Horton (Tigers, full-length)	12.00	6.00	3.50
(42)	Bruce Howard (White Sox, pitching follow-through)	12.00	6.00	3.50
(43)	Jim Hunter (K.C. A's, beginning wind-up)	24.00	12.00	7.25
(44)	Jim Hunter (Oakland A's, full-length, photo actually Chuck Dobson)	17.50	8.75	5.25
(45)	Mack Jones (Reds, full-length)	12.00	6.00	3.50
(46)	Duane Josephson (White Sox, catching crouch)	12.00	6.00	3.50
(47)	Jim Kaat (Twins, upper body)	16.00	8.00	4.75
(48)	Al Kaline (full-length, batting)	27.50	13.50	8.25
(49)	Al Kaline (upper body, batting)	27.50	13.50	8.25
(50)	Al Kaline (upper body, hands on knees)	27.50	13.50	8.25
(51)	Al Kaline (upper body)	27.50	13.50	8.25
(52)	Al Kaline (upper body, looking right)	27.50	13.50	8.25
(53)	Harmon Killebrew (Twins, upper body, batting)	25.00	12.50	7.50
(54)	Harmon Killebrew (Twins, batting, looking front)	25.00	12.50	7.50
(55)	Harmon Killebrew (Twins, kneeling)	25.00	12.50	7.50
(56)	Cal Koonce (Cubs, pitching follow-through)	12.00	6.00	3.50
(57)	Harvey Kuenn (Tigers, batting)	15.00	7.50	4.50
(58)	Harvey Kuenn (Tigers, upper body)	15.00	7.50	4.50
(59)	Hal Lanier (Giants, throwing)	12.00	6.00	3.50
(61)	Juan Marichal (Giants, upper body)	24.00	12.00	7.25
(62)	Willie McCovey (Giants, batting)	24.00	12.00	7.25
(63)	Sam McDowell (Indians, upper body, no cap)	15.00	7.50	4.50
(64)	Denny McLain (Tigers, pitching)	15.00	7.50	4.50
(65)	Roy McMillan (Reds, upper body)	12.00	6.00	3.50
(66)	Denis Menke (Braves, fielding)	12.00	6.00	3.50
(67)	Denis Menke (Braves, upper body)	12.00	6.00	3.50
(68)	Don Mincher (Angels, full-length)	12.00	6.00	3.50
(70)	Joe Morgan (Astros, fielding)	25.00	12.50	7.50
(72)	Jim Nash (A's, pitching)	12.00	6.00	3.50
(73)	Rich Nye (Cubs, pitching)	12.00	6.00	3.50
(74)	John Odom (Kansas City A's, pitching)	12.00	6.00	3.50
(75)	John Odom (Oakland A's, belt-up pose)	12.00	6.00	3.50
(76)	John Orsino (Orioles, kneeling)	12.00	6.00	3.50
(77)	Jim O'Toole (Reds, upper body, warm-up jacket)	12.00	6.00	3.50
(78)	Jim O'Toole (White Sox, upper body)	12.00	6.00	3.50
(79)	Ray Oyler (Tigers, fielding)	12.00	6.00	3.50
(81)	Milt Pappas (Orioles, pitching, full-length)	12.00	6.00	3.50
(82)	Milt Pappas (Orioles, pitching, knees up)	12.00	6.00	3.50
(83)	Don Pavletich (Reds, full-length)	12.00	6.00	3.50
(84)	Albie Pearson (Angels, glove under left arm)	12.00	6.00	3.50
(85)	Ron Perranoski (Dodgers, upper body)	12.00	6.00	3.50
(86)	Ron Perranoski (Twins, belt-up from side)	12.00	6.00	3.50
(87)	Ron Perranoski (Twins, pitching)	12.00	6.00	3.50
(88)	Gaylord Perry (Giants, pitching)	24.00	12.00	7.25
(89)	Doug Rader (Astros, fielding)	12.00	6.00	3.50
(90)	Dick Rodatz (Radatz) (Red Sox, upper body)	12.00	6.00	3.50
(91)	Dick Radatz (Red Sox, upper body)	12.00	6.00	3.50
(93)	Ron Santo (Cubs, fielding)	18.00	9.00	5.50

(94) George Scott (Red Sox, upper body)	12.00	6.00	3.50
(95) Chris Short (Phillies, upper body)	12.00	6.00	3.50
(96) Mickey Stanley (Tigers, full-length)	12.00	6.00	3.50
(97) Tony Taylor (Phillies, bat on shoulder)	12.00	6.00	3.50
(98) Frank Thomas (Pirates, upper body)	12.00	6.00	3.50
(99) Frank Thomas (Cubs, batting)	12.00	6.00	3.50
(100) Jeff Torborg (Dodgers, holding mask)	12.00	6.00	3.50
(101) Al Weis (White Sox, ready to throw)	12.00	6.00	3.50
(102) Al Weis (Mets, fielding)	12.00	6.00	3.50
(103) Ted Williams (batting)	65.00	32.00	19.50
(105) Bobby Wine (Phillies, ready to throw)	12.00	6.00	3.50
(106) Rick Wise (Phillies, upper body)	12.00	6.00	3.50
(107) Early Wynn (White Sox, full-length)	24.00	12.00	7.25
(108) Jim Wynn (Colt .45s, batting, upper body)	12.50	6.25	3.75
(109) Jim Wynn (Astros, batting, full-length)	12.00	6.00	3.50
(110) Don Zimmer (Cubs, waist-up batting)	12.50	6.25	3.75

1961 Wilson Advisory Staff Cards

Similar in format to the contemporary 8x10" photos, these 2-1/4" x 4" cards have black-and-white player poses on front, prominently displaying a Wilson glove. In the white bottom border is: "Member-Advisory Staff, Wilson Sporting Goods Co.". A facsimile autograph is printed across the picture. Backs are blank. The checklist, presented here alphabetically, may not be complete.

	NM	EX	VG
Common Player:	10.00	5.00	3.00
(1) Dick Ellsworth	10.00	5.00	3.00
(2) Don Hoak	12.00	6.00	3.50
(3) Harvey Kuenn	12.00	6.00	3.50
(4) Roy McMillan	10.00	5.00	3.00
(5) Jim Piersall	12.00	6.00	3.50
(6) Ron Santo	16.00	8.00	4.75

1954 Wilson Franks

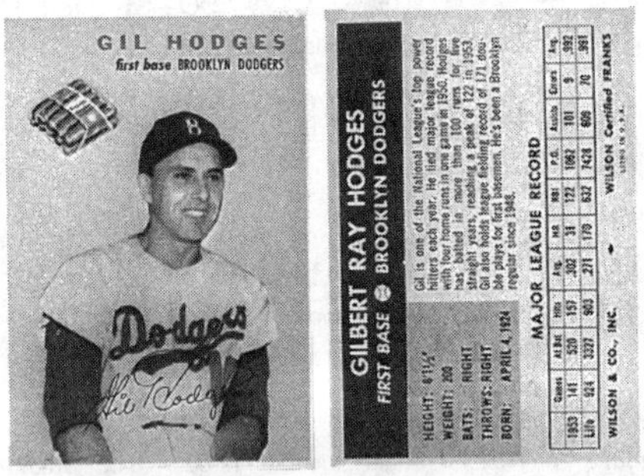

The 2-5/8" x 3-3/4" cards are among the most popular and difficult to find baseball card sets issued with hot dogs during the 1950s. The cards feature color-added photos on the front where the player's name, team and position appear at the top. The front also has a facsimile autograph and a color picture of a package of Wilson's frankfurters. The card backs feature personal information, a short career summary and 1953 and career statistics. The 20-card set includes players from a number of teams and was distributed nationally in the frankfurter packages. The problem with such distribution is that the cards are very tough to find without grease stains from the hot dogs.

	NM	EX	VG
Complete Set (20):	8900.	4200.	2550.
Common Player:	165.00	85.00	50.00
(1) Roy Campanella	800.00	400.00	240.00
(2) Del Ennis	165.00	85.00	50.00
(3) Carl Erskine	325.00	162.00	97.00
(4) Ferris Fain	165.00	85.00	50.00
(5) Bob Feller	600.00	300.00	180.00
(6) Nelson Fox	325.00	162.00	97.00
(7) Johnny Groth	165.00	85.00	50.00
(8) Stan Hack	165.00	85.00	50.00
(9) Gil Hodges	550.00	275.00	165.00
(10) Ray Jablonski	165.00	85.00	50.00
(11) Harvey Kuenn	300.00	150.00	90.00
(12) Roy McMillan	165.00	85.00	50.00
(13) Andy Pafko	165.00	85.00	50.00
(14) Paul Richards	165.00	85.00	50.00
(15) Hank Sauer	165.00	85.00	50.00
(16) Red Schoendienst	325.00	162.00	97.00
(17) Enos Slaughter	425.00	212.00	127.00
(18) Vern Stephens	165.00	85.00	50.00
(19) Sammy White	165.00	85.00	50.00
(20) Ted Williams	3500.	1750.	1050.

1958 Wilson Meats Gil Hodges

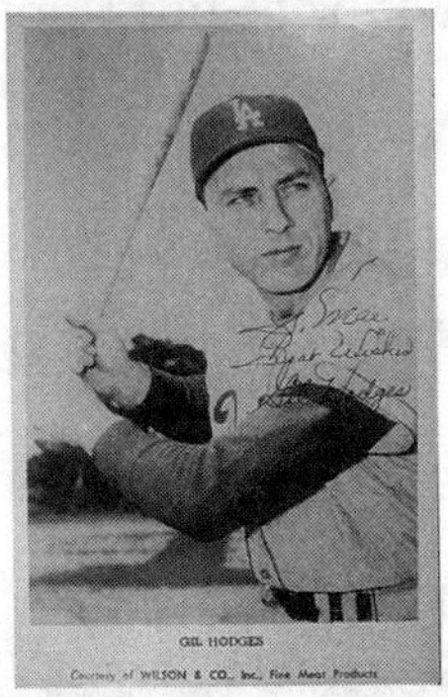

It is likely these 5-1/2" x 8-1/2" photos were prepared for promotional appearances by the popular Dodgers first baseman following the team's move to L.A. Hodges is pictured in a 1958 Dodgers road uniform. His name appears beneath the photo and the sponsor's message appears at bottom, "Courtesy of WILSON & CO., Inc., Fine Meat Products". Backs are blank. The pictures are often found with Hodges' autograph, another indicator of their use at personal appearances.

	NM	EX	VG
Gil Hodges	65.00	32.00	19.00
Gil Hodges (autographed)	125.00	62.00	37.00

1955 Don Wingfield Washington Nationals Postcards

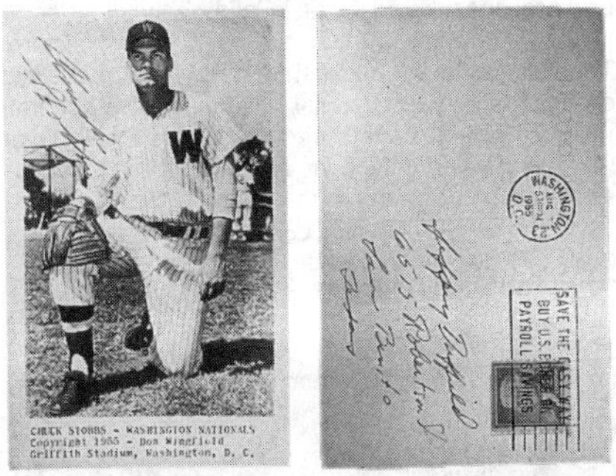

This series of 3-1/2" x 5-1/2" black-and-white postcards provided Nationals' players with a vehicle for accommodating fan requests. Player poses are bordered in white with three lines of type at bottom identifying the player, team and copyright holder. The unnumbered cards are checklisted here in alphabetical order.

	NM	EX	VG
Complete Set (11):	675.00	335.00	200.00
Common Player:	75.00	37.00	22.00
(1) Jim Busby	75.00	37.00	22.00
(2) Chuck Dressen	75.00	37.00	22.00
(3) Ed Fitz Gerald	75.00	37.00	22.00
(4) Jim Lemon	90.00	45.00	27.00
(5) Bob Porterfield	75.00	37.00	22.00
(6) Pete Runnels	75.00	37.00	22.00
(7) Roy Sievers	90.00	45.00	27.00
(8) Chuck Stobbs	75.00	37.00	22.00
(9) Dean Stone	75.00	37.00	22.00
(10) Mickey Vernon	90.00	45.00	27.00
(11) Ed Yost	75.00	37.00	22.00

1959 Don Wingfield Photocards

Possibly a predecessor to his 1960 postcard issues, these glossy photocards are usually blank-back, evidently for use as in-person handouts, rather than by mail. In 3-1/2" x 5-1/2" size, the black-and-white player photos are bordered in white with an especially wide white bottom border for affixing an autograph. Other than the autograph which may appear, the player is not identified on the card. Wingfield's name may appear in white letters in the lower-right corner of the photo, may be on a credit line on back or may not appear at all.

	NM	EX	VG
Common Player:			
(1) Bobby Allison	40.00	20.00	12.00
(2) Tex Clevenger	40.00	20.00	12.00
(3) Russ Kemmerer	40.00	20.00	12.00
(4) Harmon Killebrew	75.00	37.00	22.00
(5) Bob Usher	40.00	20.00	12.00
(6) Hal Woodeshick	40.00	20.00	12.00

1960 Don Wingfield Postcards - b/w

A second type of player photo postcards was produced by Alexandria, Va., photographer Don Wingfield beginning in 1960. Also black-and-white, the 3-1/2" x 5-1/2" cards have (usually) borderless poses on front with no extraneous graphics. Backs have standard postcard indicia plus the player name and team and a copyright line. Washington Senators players dominate the checklist which also includes stars of other teams. The autograph on the pictured card was added by the player after printing and is not part of the design. The checklist is presented here alphabetically.

	NM	EX	VG
Complete Set (35):	650.00	325.00	195.00
Common Player:	12.00	6.00	3.50
(1) Bob Allison	16.00	8.00	4.75
(2) Ernie Banks	70.00	35.00	21.00
(3a) Earl Battey (batting, chest to cap)	12.00	6.00	3.50
(4) Norm Cash	18.00	9.00	5.50
(5) Jim Coates	12.00	6.00	3.50
(6) Rocky Colavito	24.00	12.00	7.25
(7) Chuck Cottier	12.00	6.00	3.50
(8) Bennie Daniels	12.00	6.00	3.50
(9) Dan Dobbek	12.00	6.00	3.50
(10) Nellie Fox	30.00	15.00	9.00
(11) Jim Gentile	12.00	6.00	3.50
(12) Gene Green	12.00	6.00	3.50
(13) Steve Hamilton	16.00	8.00	4.75
(14) Ken Hamlin	12.00	6.00	3.50
(15) Rudy Hernandez	12.00	6.00	3.50
(16) Ed Hobaugh	12.00	6.00	3.50
(17) Elston Howard	16.00	8.00	4.75
(18) Bob Johnson	12.00	6.00	3.50
(19) Russ Kemmerer	12.00	6.00	3.50
(20) Harmon Killebrew	24.00	12.00	7.25
(21) Dale Long	12.00	6.00	3.50
(22) Mickey Mantle	250.00	125.00	75.00
(23) Roger Maris	120.00	60.00	36.00
(24) Willie Mays	150.00	75.00	45.00
(25) Stan Musial	130.00	65.00	39.00
(26) Claude Osteen	12.00	6.00	3.50
(27) Ken Retzer	12.00	6.00	3.50
(28) Brooks Robinson	70.00	35.00	21.00

		NM	EX	VG
(29)	Don Rudolph	12.00	6.00	3.50
(30)	Bill Skowron	24.00	12.00	7.25
(31)	Dave Stenhouse	12.00	6.00	3.50
(32)	Jose Valdivielso	12.00	6.00	3.50
(33)	Gene Woodling	16.00	8.00	4.75
(34)	Bud Zipfel	12.00	6.00	3.50
(35)	Unidentified Senator fielding grounder	12.00	6.00	3.50

1960 Don Wingfield Postcards - color

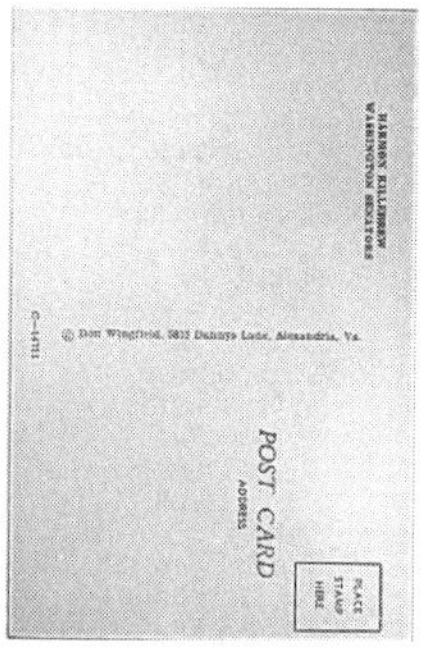

Similar in format to the contemporary series of black-and-white player photo postcards, only a single player is known to have been issued in color by Alexandria, Va., photographer Don Wingfield. The card is 3-1/2" x 5-1/2" with standard postcard indicia on back.

	NM	EX	VG
C14711Harmon Killebrew	40.00	20.00	12.00

1922 Witmor Candy Co.

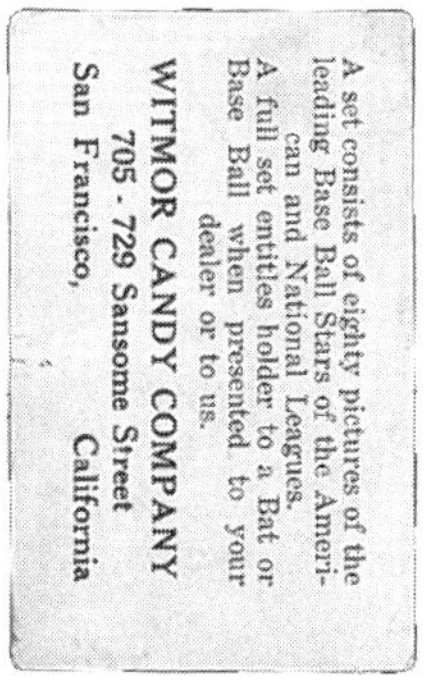

Two types of Witmor issues are known, both of which utilize the player photos from the 1921 American Caramel Co. Series of 80 (E121). The two types of Witmor issues are differentiated by the ads on back for the San Francisco candy company. One type has the advertising in a horizontal format, the other has the advertising in a vertical design. Values of Witmor Candy cards are considerably higher than the more common American Caramel versions, commanding a premium of 1.5x to 2x.

(See 1921 American Caramel Co. Series of 80 for checklist and value information)

1908 Wolverine News Co. Detroit Tigers

This series of postcards depicts members of the A.L. champ Tigers. The 3-5/16" x 5-5/16" black-and-white cards have poses or posed action photos on front, with a narrow white border at bottom carrying player identification. Backs are standard postcard format with a credit line to Wolverine News Co.

		NM	EX	VG
Complete Set (19):		3200.	1600.	900.00
Common Player:		100.00	50.00	30.00
(1)	Ty Cobb (batting)	750.00	375.00	225.00
(2)	Ty Cobb (portrait)	750.00	375.00	225.00
(3)	Bill Coughlin	100.00	50.00	30.00
(4)	Sam Crawford (bunting)	200.00	100.00	60.00
(5)	Sam Crawford (other pose?)	200.00	100.00	60.00
(6)	"Wild Bill" Donovan (pitching)	100.00	50.00	30.00
(7)	"Wild Bill" Donovan ("at the Water Wagon")	150.00	75.00	45.00
(8)	Jerry Downs	100.00	50.00	30.00
(9)	Hughie Jennings	200.00	100.00	60.00
(10)	Davy Jones	100.00	50.00	30.00
(11)	Ed Killian	100.00	50.00	30.00
(12)	George Mullin	100.00	50.00	30.00
(13)	Charley O'Leary	100.00	50.00	30.00
(14)	Fred Payne	100.00	50.00	30.00
(15)	Claude Rossman	100.00	50.00	30.00
(16)	Herman Schaefer	100.00	50.00	30.00
(17)	Herman Schaefer, Charley O'Leary	100.00	50.00	30.00
(18)	Charlie Schmidt	100.00	50.00	30.00
(19)	Eddie Siever	100.00	50.00	30.00

1933 Worch Cigar

This set of unnumbered postcard-size (3-7/16" x 5-7/16") cards, utilizing photos from the Minneapolis Star and St. Paul Dispatch newspapers, was used as a promotion by Worch Cigar Co. of St. Paul, Minn. Although there is no advertising for Worch Cigars on the cards themselves, the cards were mailed in envelopes bearing the Worch name. The cards feature portrait or action photos with the player's name and team appearing in hand-lettered type near the bottom.

		NM	EX	VG
Complete Set (146):		9750.	4750.	2750.
Common Player:		40.00	18.00	10.00
(1)	Sparky Adams	40.00	18.00	10.00
(2)	Dale Alexander	40.00	18.00	10.00
(3)	Ivy Paul Andrews	40.00	18.00	10.00
(4a)	Earl Averill (Cleveland)	80.00	36.00	20.00
(4b)	Earl Averill (no team designation)	80.00	36.00	20.00
(5)	Richard Bartell	40.00	18.00	10.00
(6)	Herman Bell	40.00	18.00	10.00
(7)	Walter Berger	40.00	18.00	10.00
(8)	Huck Betts	40.00	18.00	10.00
(9)	Max Bishop	40.00	18.00	10.00
(10)	Jim Bottomley	80.00	36.00	20.00
(11a)	Tom Bridges (name and team in box)	40.00	18.00	10.00
(11b)	Tom Bridges (no box)	40.00	18.00	10.00
(12)	Clint Brown	40.00	18.00	10.00
(13)	Donie Bush	40.00	18.00	10.00
(14a)	Max Carey (Brooklyn)	80.00	36.00	20.00
(14b)	Max Carey (no team designation)	80.00	36.00	20.00
(15)	Tex Carlton	40.00	18.00	10.00
(16)	Ben Chapman	40.00	18.00	10.00
(17)	Chalmer Cissell	40.00	18.00	10.00
(18)	Mickey Cochrane	80.00	36.00	20.00
(19)	Ripper Collins	40.00	18.00	10.00
(20)	Earle Combs	80.00	36.00	20.00
(21)	Adam Comorosky	40.00	18.00	10.00
(22)	Estel Crabtree	40.00	18.00	10.00
(23)	Rodger Cramer (Roger)	40.00	18.00	10.00
(24)	Pat Crawford	40.00	18.00	10.00
(25)	Hugh Critz	40.00	18.00	10.00
(26)	Frank Crosetti	45.00	20.00	11.00
(27a)	Joe Cronin (name and team in box)	80.00	36.00	20.00
(27b)	Joe Cronin (no box)	80.00	36.00	20.00
(28)	Alvin Crowder	40.00	18.00	10.00
(29a)	Tony Cuccinello (photo background)	40.00	18.00	10.00
(29b)	Tony Cuccinello (blank background)	40.00	20.00	12.00
(30)	KiKi Cuyler	80.00	36.00	20.00
(31)	Geo. Davis	40.00	18.00	10.00
(32)	Dizzy Dean	175.00	79.00	44.00
(33)	Wm. Dickey	100.00	45.00	25.00
(34)	Leo Durocher	85.00	38.00	21.00
(35)	James Dykes	40.00	18.00	10.00
(36)	George Earnshaw	40.00	18.00	10.00
(37)	Woody English	40.00	18.00	10.00
(38a)	Richard Ferrell (name and team in box)	80.00	36.00	20.00
(38b)	Richard Ferrell (no box)	80.00	36.00	20.00
(39a)	Wesley Ferrell (name and team in box)	40.00	18.00	10.00
(39b)	Wesley Ferrell (no box)	40.00	18.00	10.00
(40)	Fred Fitzsimmons	40.00	18.00	10.00
(41)	Lew Fonseca	40.00	18.00	10.00
(42)	Bob Fothergill	40.00	18.00	10.00
(43)	James Foxx	110.00	49.00	27.00
(44)	Fred Frankhouse	40.00	18.00	10.00
(45)	Frank Frisch	80.00	36.00	20.00
(46a)	Leon Gaslin (name incorrect)	80.00	36.00	20.00
(46b)	Leon Goslin (name correct)	80.00	36.00	20.00
(47)	Lou Gehrig	650.00	292.00	162.00
(48)	Charles Gehringer	80.00	36.00	20.00
(49)	George Gibson	40.00	18.00	10.00
(50)	Vernon Gomez	80.00	36.00	20.00
(51)	George Grantham	40.00	18.00	10.00
(52)	Grimes The Lord Of Burleigh (Burleigh Grimes)	80.00	36.00	20.00
(53)	Charlie Grimm	40.00	18.00	10.00
(54)	Robert Grove	85.00	38.00	21.00
(55)	Frank Grube	40.00	18.00	10.00
(56)	Chic Hafey (Chick)	80.00	36.00	20.00
(57)	Jess Haines	80.00	36.00	20.00
(58)	Bill Hallahan	40.00	18.00	10.00
(59)	Mel Harder	40.00	18.00	10.00
(60)	Dave Harris	40.00	18.00	10.00
(61)	Gabby Hartnett	80.00	36.00	20.00
(62)	George Hass (Haas)	40.00	18.00	10.00
(63)	Ray Hayworth	40.00	18.00	10.00
(64)	Harvey Hendrick	40.00	18.00	10.00
(65)	Dutch Henry	40.00	18.00	10.00
(66)	"Babe" Herman	50.00	22.00	12.50
(67)	Bill Herman	80.00	36.00	20.00
(68)	Frank Higgins	40.00	18.00	10.00
(69)	Oral Hildebrand	40.00	18.00	10.00
(70)	"Shanty" Hogan	40.00	18.00	10.00
(71)	Roger Hornsby (Rogers)	140.00	63.00	35.00
(72)	Carl Hubbell	85.00	38.00	21.00
(73)	Travis Jackson	80.00	36.00	20.00
(74)	Hank Johnson	40.00	18.00	10.00
(75)	Syl Johnson	40.00	18.00	10.00
(76)	Smead Jolley	40.00	18.00	10.00
(77)	Wm. Kamm	40.00	18.00	10.00
(78)	Wes Kingdon	40.00	18.00	10.00
(79a)	Charles Klein (Philadelphia, N.L.)	80.00	36.00	20.00
(79b)	Charles Klein (Chicago, N.L.)	90.00	40.00	22.00
(80)	Jos. Kuhel	40.00	18.00	10.00
(81a)	Tony Lazzeri (name and team in box)	80.00	36.00	20.00
(81b)	Tony Lazzeri (no box)	80.00	40.00	24.00
(82)	Sam Leslie	40.00	18.00	10.00
(83)	Ernie Lombardi	80.00	36.00	20.00
(84)	Al Lopez	80.00	36.00	20.00
(85)	Red Lucas	40.00	18.00	10.00
(86)	Adolfo Luque	60.00	27.00	15.00
(87)	Ted Lyons	80.00	36.00	20.00
(88)	Connie Mack	80.00	36.00	20.00
(89)	Gus Mancuso	40.00	18.00	10.00
(90)	Henry Manush	80.00	36.00	20.00
(91)	Fred Marberry	40.00	18.00	10.00
(92)	Pepper Martin	45.00	20.00	11.00
(93)	Wm. McKechnie	80.00	36.00	20.00
(94)	Joe Medwick	80.00	36.00	20.00
(95)	Jim Mooney	40.00	18.00	10.00
(96)	Joe Moore	40.00	18.00	10.00
(97)	Joe Mowry	40.00	18.00	10.00
(98)	Van Mungo	40.00	18.00	10.00
(99)	Buddy Myer	40.00	18.00	10.00
(100)	"Lefty" O'Doul	50.00	22.00	12.50
(101)	Bob O'Farrell	40.00	18.00	10.00
(102)	Ernie Orsatti	40.00	18.00	10.00
(103)	Melvin Ott	80.00	36.00	20.00
(104)	Roy Parmelee	40.00	18.00	10.00
(105)	Homer Peel	40.00	18.00	10.00
(106)	George Pipgras	40.00	18.00	10.00
(107)	Harry Rice	40.00	18.00	10.00
(108)	Paul Richards	40.00	18.00	10.00
(109)	Eppa Rixey	80.00	36.00	20.00
(110)	Charles Ruffing	80.00	36.00	20.00
(111)	Jack Russell	40.00	18.00	10.00
(112)	Babe Ruth	1400.	630.00	350.00
(113)	"Blondy" Ryan	40.00	18.00	10.00
(114)	Wilfred Ryan	40.00	18.00	10.00
(115)	Fred Schulte	40.00	18.00	10.00
(116)	Hal Schumacher	40.00	18.00	10.00
(117)	Luke Sewel (Sewell)	40.00	18.00	10.00
(118)	Al Simmons	80.00	36.00	20.00
(119)	Ray Spencer	40.00	18.00	10.00
(120)	Casey Stengel	100.00	45.00	25.00
(121)	Riggs Stephenson	40.00	18.00	10.00
(122)	Walter Stewart	40.00	18.00	10.00
(123)	John T. Stone	40.00	18.00	10.00
(124)	Gabby Street	40.00	10.00	10.00
(125)	Gus Suhr	40.00	18.00	10.00
(126)	Evar Swanson	40.00	18.00	10.00
(127)	Dan Taylor	40.00	18.00	10.00
(128)	Bill Terry	80.00	36.00	20.00
(129)	Al Todd	40.00	18.00	10.00
(130)	Pie Traynor	80.00	36.00	20.00
(131)	William Urbanski	40.00	18.00	10.00
(132)	Dazzy Vance	80.00	36.00	20.00
(133)	Lloyd (Floyd) Vaughan	80.00	36.00	20.00
(134)	Johnny Vergez	40.00	18.00	10.00
(135)	George Walberg	40.00	18.00	10.00
(136)	Bill Walker	40.00	18.00	10.00
(137)	Gerald Walker	40.00	18.00	10.00
(138a)	Lloyd Waner (photo background)	80.00	36.00	20.00

		NM	EX	VG
(138b)	Lloyd Waner (blank background)	80.00	36.00	20.00
(139a)	Paul Waner (photo background)	80.00	36.00	20.00
(139b)	Paul Waner (blank background)	80.00	36.00	20.00
(140)	Lon Warneke	40.00	18.00	10.00
(141)	George Watkins	40.00	18.00	10.00
(142)	Monte Weaver	40.00	18.00	10.00
(143)	Sam West	40.00	18.00	10.00
(144)	Earl Whitehill	40.00	18.00	10.00
(145)	Hack Wilson	80.00	36.00	20.00
(146)	Jimmy Wilson	40.00	18.00	10.00

1933 World Wide Gum (Canadian Goudey, V353)

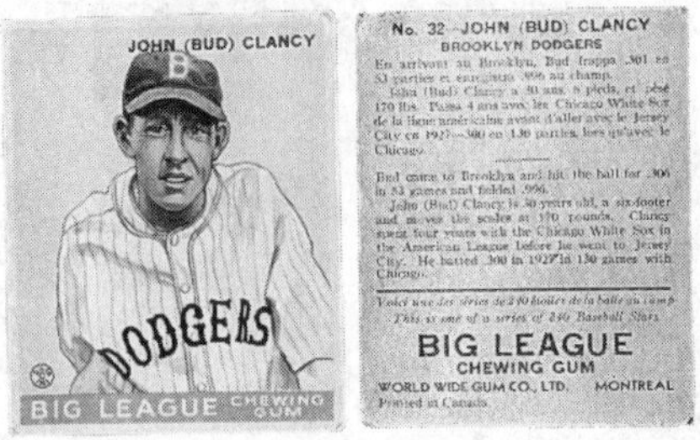

Also known as "Canadian Goudeys," this 94-card set drew heavily on its U.S. contemporary. Card fronts are identical to the '33 Goudeys and the backs are nearly so. The first 52 cards in the set carry the same card numbers as their American counterparts, while cards #53-94 have different numbers than the U.S. version. Card backs can be found printed entirely in English, or in English and French; the former being somewhat scarcer. Cards measure approximately 2-3/8" x 2-7/8".

		NM	EX	VG
Complete Set (94):		20000.	9000.	5500.
Common Player:		90.00	40.00	22.00
1	Benny Bengough	850.00	150.00	40.00
2	Arthur (Dazzy) Vance	295.00	133.00	74.00
3	Hugh Critz	90.00	40.00	22.00
4	Henry (Heinie) Schuble	90.00	40.00	22.00
5	Floyd (Babe) Herman	125.00	56.00	31.00
6	Jimmy Dykes	90.00	40.00	22.00
7	Ted Lyons	295.00	133.00	74.00
8	Roy Johnson	90.00	40.00	22.00
9	Dave Harris	90.00	40.00	22.00
10	Glenn Myatt	90.00	40.00	22.00
11	Billy Rogell	90.00	40.00	22.00
12	George Pipgras	90.00	40.00	22.00
13	Lafayette Thompson	90.00	40.00	22.00
14	Henry Johnson	90.00	40.00	22.00
15	Victor Sorrell	90.00	40.00	22.00
16	George Blaeholder	90.00	40.00	22.00
17	Watson Clark	90.00	40.00	22.00
18	Herold (Muddy) Ruel	90.00	40.00	22.00
19	Bill Dickey	300.00	135.00	75.00
20	Bill Terry	295.00	133.00	74.00
21	Phil Collins	90.00	40.00	22.00
22	Harold (Pie) Traynor	295.00	133.00	74.00
23	Hazen (Ki-Ki) Cuyler	295.00	133.00	74.00
24	Horace Ford	90.00	40.00	22.00
25	Paul Waner	295.00	133.00	74.00
26	Chalmer Cissell	90.00	40.00	22.00
27	George Connally	90.00	40.00	22.00
28	Dick Bartell	90.00	40.00	22.00
29	Jimmy Foxx	325.00	146.00	81.00
30	Frank Hogan	90.00	40.00	22.00
31	Tony Lazzeri	295.00	133.00	74.00
32	John (Bud) Clancy	90.00	40.00	22.00
33	Ralph Kress	90.00	40.00	22.00
34	Bob O'Farrell	90.00	40.00	22.00
35	Al Simmons	295.00	133.00	74.00
36	Tommy Thevenow	90.00	40.00	22.00
37	Jimmy Wilson	90.00	40.00	22.00
38	Fred Brickell	90.00	40.00	22.00
39	Mark Koenig	90.00	40.00	22.00
40	Taylor Douthit	90.00	40.00	22.00
41	Gus Mancuso	90.00	40.00	22.00
42	Eddie Collins	295.00	133.00	74.00
43	Lew Fonseca	90.00	40.00	22.00
44	Jim Bottomley	295.00	133.00	74.00
45	Larry Benton	90.00	40.00	22.00
46	Ethan Allen	90.00	40.00	22.00
47	Henry "Heinie" Manush	295.00	133.00	74.00
48	Marty McManus	90.00	40.00	22.00
49	Frank Frisch	295.00	133.00	74.00
50	Ed Brandt	90.00	40.00	22.00
51	Charlie Grimm	90.00	40.00	22.00
52	Andy Cohen	90.00	40.00	22.00
53	Jack Quinn	90.00	40.00	22.00
54	Urban (Red) Faber	295.00	133.00	74.00
55	Lou Gehrig	3250.	1450.	810.00
56	John Welch	90.00	40.00	22.00
57	Bill Walker	90.00	40.00	22.00
58	Frank (Lefty) O'Doul	125.00	56.00	31.00
59	Edmund (Bing) Miller	90.00	40.00	22.00
60	Waite Hoyt	295.00	133.00	74.00
61	Max Bishop	90.00	40.00	22.00
62	"Pepper" Martin	125.00	56.00	31.00
63	Joe Cronin	295.00	133.00	74.00
64	Burleigh Grimes	295.00	133.00	74.00
65	Milton Gaston	90.00	40.00	22.00
66	George Grantham	90.00	40.00	22.00
67	Guy Bush	90.00	40.00	22.00
68	Willie Kamm	90.00	40.00	22.00
69	Gordon (Mickey) Cochrane	295.00	133.00	74.00
70	Adam Comorosky	90.00	40.00	22.00
71	Alvin Crowder	90.00	40.00	22.00
72	Willis Hudlin	90.00	40.00	22.00
73	Eddie Farrell	90.00	40.00	22.00
74	Leo Durocher	295.00	133.00	74.00
75	Walter Stewart	90.00	40.00	22.00
76	George Walberg	90.00	40.00	22.00
77	Glenn Wright	90.00	40.00	22.00
78	Charles (Buddy) Myer	90.00	40.00	22.00
79	James (Zack) Taylor	90.00	40.00	22.00
80	George Herman (Babe) Ruth	5500.	2475.	1375.
81	D'Arcy (Jake) Flowers	90.00	40.00	22.00
82	Ray Kolp	90.00	40.00	22.00
83	Oswald Bluege	90.00	40.00	22.00
84	Morris (Moe) Berg	275.00	124.00	69.00
85	Jimmy Foxx	300.00	135.00	75.00
86	Sam Byrd	90.00	40.00	22.00
87	Danny Mcfayden (McFayden)	90.00	40.00	22.00
88	Joe Judge	90.00	40.00	22.00
89	Joe Sewell	295.00	133.00	74.00
90	Lloyd Waner	295.00	133.00	74.00
91	Luke Sewell	90.00	40.00	22.00
92	Leo Mangum	90.00	40.00	22.00
93	George Herman (Babe) Ruth	4500.	2000.	1125.
94	Al Spohrer	90.00	40.00	22.00

1934 World Wide Gum (Canadian Goudey, V354)

Again a near-clone of the American issue, the '34 "Canadian Goudeys" feature the same number (96) and size (2-3/8" x 2-7/8") of cards. Player selection is considerably different, however. Cards #1-48 feature the same front design as the '33 World Wide/Goudey sets. Cards #49-96 have the "Lou Gehrig says..." graphic on the front. Backs can be found in either all-English or English and French.

		NM	EX	VG
Complete Set (96):		14750.	7250.	4000.
Common Player:		80.00	36.00	20.00
1	Rogers Hornsby	600.00	270.00	150.00
2	Eddie Morgan	80.00	36.00	20.00
3	Valentine J. (Val) Picinich	80.00	36.00	20.00
4	Rabbit Maranville	185.00	83.00	46.00
5	Flint Rhem	80.00	36.00	20.00
6	Jim Elliott	80.00	36.00	20.00
7	Fred (Red) Lucas	80.00	36.00	20.00
8	Fred Marberry	80.00	36.00	20.00
9	Clifton Heathcote	80.00	36.00	20.00
10	Bernie Friberg	80.00	36.00	20.00
11	Elwood (Woody) English	80.00	36.00	20.00
12	Carl Reynolds	80.00	36.00	20.00
13	Ray Benge	80.00	36.00	20.00
14	Ben Cantwell	80.00	36.00	20.00
15	Irvin (Bump) Hadley	80.00	36.00	20.00
16	Herb Pennock	185.00	83.00	46.00
17	Fred Lindstrom	185.00	83.00	46.00
18	Edgar (Sam) Rice	185.00	83.00	46.00
19	Fred Frankhouse	80.00	36.00	20.00
20	Fred Fitzsimmons	80.00	36.00	20.00
21	Earl Combs (Earle)	185.00	83.00	46.00
22	George Uhle	80.00	36.00	20.00
23	Richard Coffman	80.00	36.00	20.00
24	Travis C. Jackson	185.00	83.00	46.00
25	Robert J. Burke	80.00	36.00	20.00
26	Randy Moore	80.00	36.00	20.00
27	John Henry (Heinie) Sand	80.00	36.00	20.00
28	George Herman (Babe) Ruth	4550.	2047.	1137.
29	Tris Speaker	225.00	101.00	56.00
30	Perce (Pat) Malone	80.00	36.00	20.00
31	Sam Jones	80.00	36.00	20.00
32	Eppa Rixey	185.00	83.00	46.00
33	Floyd (Pete) Scott	80.00	36.00	20.00
34	Pete Jablonowski	80.00	36.00	20.00
35	Clyde Manion	80.00	36.00	20.00
36	Dibrell Williams	80.00	36.00	20.00
37	Glenn Spencer	80.00	36.00	20.00
38	Ray Kremer	80.00	36.00	20.00
39	Phil Todt	80.00	36.00	20.00
40	Russell Rollings	80.00	36.00	20.00
41	Earl Clark	80.00	36.00	20.00
42	Jess Petty	80.00	36.00	20.00
43	Frank O'Rourke	80.00	36.00	20.00
44	Jesse Haines	185.00	83.00	46.00
45	Horace Lisenbee	80.00	36.00	20.00
46	Owen Carroll	80.00	36.00	20.00
47	Tom Zachary	80.00	36.00	20.00
48	Charlie Ruffing	185.00	83.00	46.00
49	Ray Benge	80.00	36.00	20.00
50	Elwood (Woody) English	80.00	36.00	20.00
51	Ben Chapman	80.00	36.00	20.00
52	Joe Kuhel	80.00	36.00	20.00
53	Bill Terry	185.00	83.00	46.00
54	Robert (Lefty) Grove	185.00	83.00	46.00
55	Jerome (Dizzy) Dean	245.00	110.00	61.00
56	Charles (Chuck) Klein	185.00	83.00	46.00
57	Charley Gehringer	210.00	94.00	52.00
58	Jimmy Foxx	225.00	101.00	56.00
59	Gordon (Mickey) Cochrane	185.00	83.00	46.00
60	Willie Kamm	80.00	36.00	20.00
61	Charlie Grimm	80.00	36.00	20.00
62	Ed Brandt	80.00	36.00	20.00
63	Tony Piet	80.00	36.00	20.00
64	Frank Frisch	185.00	83.00	46.00
65	Alvin Crowder	80.00	36.00	20.00
66	Frank Hogan	80.00	36.00	20.00
67	Paul Waner	185.00	83.00	46.00
68	Henry (Heinie) Manush	185.00	83.00	46.00
69	Leo Durocher	185.00	83.00	46.00
70	Floyd Vaughan	185.00	83.00	46.00
71	Carl Hubbell	200.00	90.00	50.00
72	Hugh Critz	80.00	36.00	20.00
73	John (Blondy) Ryan	80.00	36.00	20.00
74	Roger Cramer	80.00	36.00	20.00
75	Baxter Jordan	80.00	36.00	20.00
76	Ed Coleman	80.00	36.00	20.00
77	Julius Solters	80.00	36.00	20.00
78	Charles (Chick) Hafey	185.00	83.00	46.00
79	Larry French	80.00	36.00	20.00
80	Frank (Don) Hurst	80.00	36.00	20.00
81	Gerald Walker	80.00	36.00	20.00
82	Ernie Lombardi	185.00	83.00	46.00
83	Walter (Huck) Betts	80.00	36.00	20.00
84	Luke Appling	185.00	83.00	46.00
85	John Frederick	80.00	36.00	20.00
86	Fred Walker	80.00	36.00	20.00
87	Tom Bridges	80.00	36.00	20.00
88	Dick Porter	80.00	36.00	20.00
89	John Stone	80.00	36.00	20.00
90	James (Tex) Carleton	80.00	36.00	20.00
91	Joe Stripp	80.00	36.00	20.00
92	Lou Gehrig	3000.	1350.	750.00
93	George Earnshaw	80.00	36.00	20.00
94	Oscar Melillo	80.00	36.00	20.00
95	Oral Hildebrand	80.00	36.00	20.00
96	John Allen	80.00	36.00	20.00

1936 World Wide Gum (Canadian Goudey, V355)

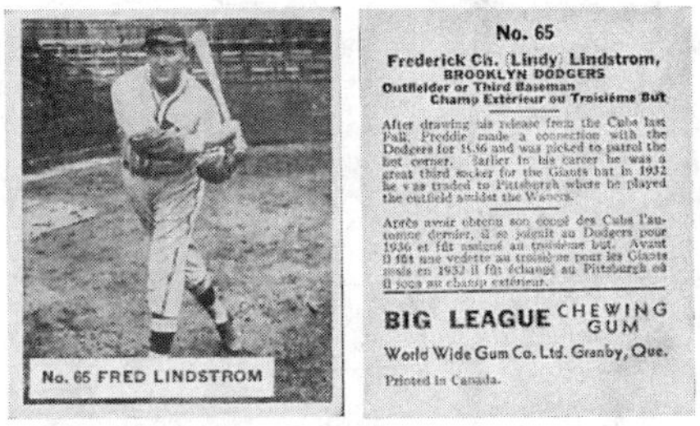

This black and white Canadian set was issued by World Wide Gum in 1936. The cards measure approximately 2-1/2" x 2-7/8", and the set includes both portrait and action photos. The card number and player's name (appearing in all capital letters) are printed inside a white box below the photo.

		NM	EX	VG
Complete Set (134):		18000.	8100.	4500.
Common Player:		95.00	47.00	28.00
1	Jimmy Dykes	300.00	100.00	50.00
2	Paul Waner	225.00	100.00	55.00
3	Cy Blanton	95.00	43.00	24.00
4	Sam Leslie	95.00	43.00	24.00
5	Johnny Louis Vergez	95.00	43.00	24.00
6	Arky Vaughan	225.00	100.00	55.00
7	Bill Terry	225.00	100.00	55.00
8	Joe Moore	95.00	43.00	24.00
9	Gus Mancuso	95.00	43.00	24.00
10	Fred Marberry	95.00	43.00	24.00
11	George Selkirk	95.00	43.00	24.00
12	Spud Davis	95.00	43.00	24.00
13	Chuck Klein	225.00	100.00	55.00
14	Fred Fitzsimmons	95.00	43.00	24.00
15	Bill Delancey	95.00	43.00	24.00
16	Billy Herman	225.00	100.00	55.00
17	George Davis	95.00	43.00	24.00
18	Rip Collins	95.00	43.00	24.00
19	Dizzy Dean	400.00	180.00	100.00
20	Roy Parmelee	95.00	43.00	24.00
21	Vic Sorrell	95.00	43.00	24.00
22	Harry Danning	95.00	43.00	24.00
23	Hal Schumacher	95.00	43.00	24.00
24	Cy Perkins	95.00	43.00	24.00
25	Speedy Durocher	225.00	100.00	55.00
26	Glenn Myatt	95.00	43.00	24.00
27	Bob Seeds	95.00	43.00	24.00
28	Jimmy Ripple	95.00	43.00	24.00
29	Al Schacht	95.00	43.00	24.00
30	Pete Fox	95.00	43.00	24.00
31	Del Baker	95.00	43.00	24.00

32	Flea Clifton	95.00	43.00	24.00
33	Tommy Bridges	95.00	43.00	24.00
34	Bill Dickey	250.00	110.00	60.00
35	Wally Berger	95.00	43.00	24.00
36	Slick Castleman	95.00	43.00	24.00
37	Dick Bartell	95.00	43.00	24.00
38	Red Rolfe	95.00	43.00	24.00
39	Waite Hoyt	225.00	100.00	55.00
40	Wes Ferrell	95.00	43.00	24.00
41	Hank Greenberg	285.00	128.00	71.00
42	Charlie Gehringer	225.00	100.00	55.00
43	Goose Goslin	225.00	100.00	55.00
44	Schoolboy Rowe	95.00	43.00	24.00
45	Mickey Cochrane	225.00	100.00	55.00
46	Joe Cronin	225.00	100.00	55.00
47	Jimmie Foxx	275.00	124.00	69.00
48	Jerry Walker	95.00	43.00	24.00
49	Charlie Gelbert	95.00	43.00	24.00
50	Roy Hayworth (Ray)	95.00	43.00	24.00
51	Joe DiMaggio	3000.	1350.	750.00
52	Billy Rogell	95.00	43.00	24.00
53	Joe McCarthy	225.00	100.00	55.00
54	Phil Cavaretta (Cavarretta)	95.00	43.00	24.00
55	Kiki Cuyler	225.00	100.00	55.00
56	Lefty Gomez	225.00	100.00	55.00
57	Gabby Hartnett	225.00	100.00	55.00
58	Johnny Marcum	95.00	43.00	24.00
59	Burgess Whitehead	95.00	43.00	24.00
60	Whitey Whitehill	95.00	43.00	24.00
61	Buckey Walters	95.00	43.00	24.00
62	Luke Sewell	95.00	43.00	24.00
63	Joey Kuhel	95.00	43.00	24.00
64	Lou Finney	95.00	43.00	24.00
65	Fred Lindstrom	225.00	100.00	55.00
66	Paul Derringer	95.00	43.00	24.00
67	Steve O'Neil (O'Neill)	95.00	43.00	24.00
68	Mule Haas	95.00	43.00	24.00
69	Freck Owen	95.00	43.00	24.00
70	Wild Bill Hallahan	95.00	43.00	24.00
71	Bill Urbanski	95.00	43.00	24.00
72	Dan Taylor	95.00	43.00	24.00
73	Heinie Manush	225.00	100.00	55.00
74	Jo-Jo White	95.00	43.00	24.00
75	Mickey Medwick (Ducky)	225.00	100.00	55.00
76	Joe Vosmik	95.00	43.00	24.00
77	Al Simmons	225.00	100.00	55.00
78	Shag Shaughnessy	95.00	43.00	24.00
79	Harry Smythe	95.00	43.00	24.00
80	Benny Tate	95.00	43.00	24.00
81	Billy Rhiel	95.00	43.00	24.00
82	Lauri Myllykangas	95.00	43.00	24.00
83	Ben Sankey	95.00	43.00	24.00
84	Crip Polli	95.00	43.00	24.00
85	Jim Bottomley	225.00	100.00	55.00
86	William Clark	95.00	43.00	24.00
87	Ossie Bluege	95.00	43.00	24.00
88	Lefty Grove	225.00	100.00	55.00
89	Charlie Grimm	95.00	43.00	24.00
90	Ben Chapman	95.00	43.00	24.00
91	Frank Crosetti	125.00	55.00	30.00
92	John Pomorski	95.00	43.00	24.00
93	Jesse Haines	225.00	100.00	55.00
94	Chick Hafey	225.00	100.00	55.00
95	Tony Piet	95.00	43.00	24.00
96	Lou Gehrig	3500.	1575.	875.00
97	Bill Jurges	95.00	43.00	24.00
98	Smead Jolley	95.00	43.00	24.00
99	Jimmy Wilson	95.00	43.00	24.00
100	Lonnie Warneke	95.00	43.00	24.00
101	Lefty Tamulis	95.00	43.00	24.00
102	Charlie Ruffing	225.00	100.00	55.00
103	Earl Grace	95.00	43.00	24.00
104	Rox Lawson	95.00	43.00	24.00
105	Stan Hack	95.00	43.00	24.00
106	August Galan	95.00	43.00	24.00
107	Frank Frisch	225.00	100.00	55.00
108	Bill McKechnie	225.00	100.00	55.00
109	Bill Lee	95.00	43.00	24.00
110	Connie Mack	225.00	100.00	55.00
111	Frank Reiber	95.00	43.00	24.00
112	Zeke Bonura	95.00	43.00	24.00
113	Luke Appling	225.00	100.00	55.00
114	Monte Pearson	95.00	43.00	24.00
115	Bob O'Farrell	95.00	43.00	24.00
116	Marvin Duke	95.00	43.00	24.00
117	Paul Florence	95.00	43.00	24.00
118	John Berley	95.00	43.00	24.00
119	Tom Oliver	95.00	43.00	24.00
120	Norman Kies	95.00	43.00	24.00
121	Hal King	95.00	43.00	24.00
122	Tom Abernathy	95.00	43.00	24.00
123	Phil Hensick	95.00	43.00	24.00
124	Roy Schalk (Ray)	225.00	100.00	55.00
125	Paul Dunlap	95.00	43.00	24.00
126	Benny Bates	95.00	43.00	24.00
127	George Puccinelli	95.00	43.00	24.00
128	Stevie Stevenson	95.00	43.00	24.00
129	Rabbit Maranville	225.00	100.00	55.00
130	Bucky Harris	225.00	100.00	55.00
131	Al Lopez	225.00	100.00	55.00
132	Buddy Myer	95.00	43.00	24.00
133	Cliff Bolton	95.00	43.00	24.00
134	Estel Crabtree	95.00	43.00	24.00

1939 World Wide Gum (Canadian Goudey V351)

These premium pictures are analogous to the R303-A issue in the U.S. The 4" x 5-3/4" pictures were given away with the purchase of World Wide gum. The pictures are printed in sepia on cream-colored paper. Fronts have a bordered photo with facsimile autograph. Backs have a "How to . . . " baseball playing tip illustrated with drawings. Backs of the Canadian version differ from the U.S. pieces in the absence of a border line around the playing tip, and the use of a "Lithographed in Canada" notice at lower-right. The unnumbered pictures are checklisted here in alphabetical order.

		NM	EX	VG
Complete Set (25):				
Common Player:		50.00	25.00	15.00
(1)	Morris Arnovich	50.00	25.00	15.00
(2)	Sam Bell	65.00	32.00	19.50
(3)	Zeke Bonura	50.00	25.00	15.00
(4)	Earl Caldwell	50.00	25.00	15.00
(5)	Flea Clifton	50.00	25.00	15.00
(6)	Frank Crosetti	70.00	35.00	21.00
(7)	Harry Danning	50.00	25.00	15.00
(8)	Dizzy Dean	125.00	62.00	37.00
(9)	Emile De Jonghe	65.00	32.00	19.50
(10)	Paul Derringer	50.00	25.00	15.00
(11)	Joe DiMaggio	750.00	375.00	225.00
(12)	Vince DiMaggio	50.00	25.00	15.00
(13)	Charlie Gehringer	100.00	50.00	30.00
(14)	Gene Hasson	65.00	32.00	19.50
(15)	Tommy Henrich	75.00	37.00	22.00
(16)	Fred Hutchinson	50.00	25.00	15.00
(17)	Phil Marchildon	50.00	25.00	15.00
(18)	Mike Meola	50.00	25.00	15.00
(19)	Arnold Mosey	65.00	32.00	19.50
(20)	Frank Pytlak	50.00	25.00	15.00
(21)	Frank Reiber	50.00	25.00	15.00
(22)	Lee Rogers	50.00	25.00	15.00
(23)	Cecil Travis	50.00	25.00	15.00
(24)	Hal Trosky	50.00	25.00	15.00
(25)	Ted Williams	750.00	375.00	225.00

1888 WG1 Base Ball Playing Cards

This little-known set of playing cards featuring drawings of real baseball players in action poses was issued in 1888 and includes members of the eight National League teams of the day. Each club is represented by nine players - one at each position - making the set complete at 72 cards. The cards measure 2-1/2" x 3-1/2" and have a blue-patterned design on the back. The cards were sold as a boxed set. They were designed to resemble a deck of regular playing cards, and the various positions were all assigned the same denomination (for example, all of the pitchers were kings, catchers were aces, etc.). There are no cards numbered either two, three, four or five; and rather than the typical hearts, clubs, diamonds and spades, each team represents a different "suit." The American Card Catalog designation is WG1.

		NM	EX	VG
Complete Set (72):		30000.	12000.	6000.
Common Player:		300.00	120.00	60.00
Box:		5000.	2500.	1500.
(1)	Ed Andrews	300.00	120.00	60.00
(2)	Cap Anson	2400.	960.00	480.00
(3)	Charles Bassett	300.00	120.00	60.00
(4)	Charles Bastian	300.00	120.00	60.00
(5)	Charles Bennett	300.00	120.00	60.00
(6)	Handsome Boyle	300.00	120.00	60.00
(7)	Dan Brouthers	1200.	480.00	240.00
(8)	Thomas Brown	300.00	120.00	60.00
(9)	Thomas Burns	300.00	120.00	60.00
(10)	Frederick Carroll	300.00	120.00	60.00
(11)	Daniel Casey	300.00	120.00	60.00
(12)	John Clarkson	1200.	480.00	240.00
(13)	Jack Clements	300.00	120.00	60.00
(14)	John Coleman	300.00	120.00	60.00
(15)	Roger Connor	1200.	480.00	240.00
(16)	Abner Dalrymple	300.00	120.00	60.00
(17)	Jerry Denny	300.00	120.00	60.00
(18)	Jim Donelly	300.00	120.00	60.00
(19)	Sure Shot Dunlap	300.00	120.00	60.00
(20)	Dude Esterbrook	300.00	120.00	60.00
(21)	Buck Ewing	1200.	480.00	240.00
(22)	Sid Farrar	300.00	120.00	60.00
(23)	Silver Flint	300.00	120.00	60.00
(24)	Jim Fogarty	300.00	120.00	60.00
(25)	Elmer Foster	300.00	120.00	60.00
(26)	Pud Galvin	1200.	480.00	240.00
(27)	Charlie Getzein (Getzien)	300.00	120.00	60.00
(28)	Pebbly Jack Glasscock	300.00	120.00	60.00
(29)	Piano Legs Gore	300.00	120.00	60.00
(30)	Ned Hanlon	1200.	480.00	240.00
(31)	Paul Hines	300.00	120.00	60.00
(32)	Joe Hornung	300.00	120.00	60.00
(33)	Dummy Hoy	600.00	240.00	120.00
(34)	Cutrate Irwin (Philadelphia)	300.00	120.00	60.00
(35)	John Irwin (Washington)	300.00	120.00	60.00
(36)	Dick Johnston	300.00	120.00	60.00
(37)	Tim Keefe	1200.	480.00	240.00
(38)	King Kelly	1600.	640.00	320.00
(39)	Willie Kuehne	300.00	120.00	60.00
(40)	Connie Mack	1400.	560.00	280.00
(41)	Smiling Al Maul	300.00	120.00	60.00
(42)	Al Meyers (Myers) (Washington)	300.00	120.00	60.00
(43)	George Meyers (Myers) (Indianapolis)	300.00	120.00	60.00
(44)	Honest John Morrill	300.00	120.00	60.00
(45)	Joseph Mulvey	300.00	120.00	60.00
(46)	Billy Nash	300.00	120.00	60.00
(47)	Billy O'Brien	300.00	120.00	60.00
(48)	Orator Jim O'Rourke	1200.	480.00	240.00
(49)	Bob Pettit	300.00	120.00	60.00
(50)	Fred Pfeffer	300.00	120.00	60.00
(51)	Danny Richardson (New York)	300.00	120.00	60.00
(52)	Hardy Richardson (Detroit)	300.00	120.00	60.00
(53)	Jack Rowe	300.00	120.00	60.00
(54)	Jimmy Ryan	300.00	120.00	60.00
(55)	Emmett Seery	300.00	120.00	60.00
(56)	George Shoch	300.00	120.00	60.00
(57)	Otto Shomberg (Schomberg)	300.00	120.00	60.00
(58)	Pap Smith	300.00	120.00	60.00
(59)	Marty Sullivan	300.00	120.00	60.00
(60)	Billy Sunday	1200.	480.00	240.00
(61)	Ezra Sutton	300.00	120.00	60.00
(62)	Big Sam Thompson	1200.	480.00	240.00
(63)	Silent Mike Tiernan	300.00	120.00	60.00
(64)	Larry Twitchell	300.00	120.00	60.00
(65)	Rip Van Haltren	300.00	120.00	60.00
(66)	Monte Ward	1200.	480.00	240.00
(67)	Deacon White	300.00	120.00	60.00
(68)	Grasshopper Whitney	300.00	120.00	60.00
(69)	Ned Williamson	300.00	120.00	60.00
(70)	Watt Wilmot	300.00	120.00	60.00
(71)	Medoc Wise	300.00	120.00	60.00
(72)	George "Dandy" Wood	300.00	120.00	60.00

1910 W-UNC Strip Cards

Considerably earlier than most known strip cards, it is possible these pieces were cut from a notebook cover, candy box or advertising poster. The known players point to an issue date 1910. Crudely printed on flimsy stock, the cards feature familiar colorized portraits of players on brightly colored backgrounds. The format is about 1-3/8" x 2-3/8" and some cards have evidence of a 1-16th" yellow strip around the outside of the black border. Player name and city are printed in the white border at bottom. Backs are blank. The unnumbered cards are listed here in alphabetical order, though the checklist may or may not be complete at 25.

		NM	EX	VG
Complete Set (26):		4000.	2000.	1200.
Common Player:		125.00	62.00	35.00
(1)	Babe Adams	125.00	62.00	35.00
(2)	Chief Bender	200.00	100.00	60.00
(3)	Roger Bresnahan	200.00	100.00	60.00
(4)	Donie Bush	125.00	62.00	35.00
(5)	Bobby Byrne	125.00	62.00	35.00
(6)	Bill Carrigan	125.00	62.00	35.00
(7)	Frank Chance	200.00	100.00	60.00
(8)	Hal Chase	150.00	75.00	45.00
(9)	Ty Cobb	600.00	300.00	180.00
(10)	Willis Cole	125.00	62.00	35.00
(11)	Eddie Collins	200.00	100.00	60.00
(12)	Jack Coombs	125.00	62.00	35.00
(13)	Sam Crawford	200.00	100.00	60.00
(14)	Johnny Evers	200.00	100.00	60.00
(15)	Solly Hoffman	125.00	62.00	35.00
(16)	Hughie Jennings	200.00	100.00	60.00
(17)	Walter Johnston (Johnson)	400.00	200.00	120.00
(18)	Johnny Kling	125.00	62.00	35.00
(19)	Ed Konetchy	125.00	62.00	35.00
(20)	Harry Lord	125.00	62.00	35.00
(21)	Sherry Magee	125.00	62.00	35.00
(22)	Christy Mathewson	400.00	200.00	120.00
(23)	Mike Mitchell	125.00	62.00	35.00
(24)	Tris Speaker	250.00	125.00	75.00
(25)	Oscar Stanage	125.00	62.00	35.00
(26)	Honus Wagner	450.00	225.00	135.00

1916-20 W-UNC "Big Head" Strip Cards

Given the known player content (certainly not complete as listed here) and the fact that no team designations are printed on the cards, it is impossible to more accurately date this blank-back strip card issue. The 1-3/8" x 2-1/2" cards have color artwork of the players in full-body poses. The pictures are unusual in that the players' heads are out of proportion to the rest of the body. Whether the portraits were meant to be accurate portrayals is conjecture. Player names given here are as printed on the cards.

		NM	EX	VG
Common Player:		150.00	75.00	45.00
(1)	Jim Bagby	150.00	75.00	45.00
(2)	Home Run Baker	300.00	150.00	90.00
(3)	Ping Bodie	150.00	75.00	45.00
(4)	Geo. Burns	300.00	150.00	90.00
(5)	Ty Cobb	450.00	225.00	135.00
(6)	Larry Doyle	150.00	75.00	45.00
(7)	Hinie Groh	150.00	75.00	45.00
(8)	R. Hornsby	350.00	175.00	105.00
(9)	Johnston (Walter Johnson)	375.00	185.00	110.00
(10)	Joe Judge	150.00	75.00	45.00
(11)	Carl Mays	150.00	75.00	45.00
(12)	Babe Ruth	800.00	400.00	240.00
(13)	Ray Schalk	300.00	150.00	90.00
(14)	Wally Schang	150.00	75.00	45.00
(15)	Geo. Sisler	300.00	150.00	90.00

1924 W UNC Strip Cards

The actual year of issue is conjectural based on the other nine athletic, cinematic and historical subjects found on the 10-card strip with this Ruth card. The approximately 1-1/2" x 2-1/2" black-and-white, blank-backed card identifies the player, position and team typographically within the photo and has the card number and name in the bottom border. The card has also been seen with the number 52, possibly from a later strip configuration.

		NM	EX	VG
1	Babe Ruth	400.00	200.00	120.00

1931 W-UNC Strip Cards

This issue, presumably of 60 cards, is virtually identical in format to the various 1928 issues cataloged as W502, York Caramel, Yeungling Ice Cream, etc. The black-and-white, blank-back cards measure about 1-3/8" (give or take a 1/16") x 2-1/2". Player photos are bordered in white with the name printed in capital letters at bottom; at bottom-left is a card number in parentheses. While the checklist for this set is considerably different than the 1928 version, some of the photos used are the same. Cards missing from the checklist here are presumed to have been issued, but have not yet been reported. One veteran collector recalls these cards were received with the purchase of a caramel sucker.

		NM	EX	VG
Common Player:		45.00	22.00	13.50
1	Muddy Ruel	45.00	22.00	13.50
2	John Grabowski	45.00	22.00	13.50
3	Mickey Cochrane	75.00	37.00	22.00
4	Bill Cissell	45.00	22.00	13.50
5	Carl Reynolds	45.00	22.00	13.50
6	Luke Sewell	45.00	22.00	13.50
7	Ted Lyons	75.00	37.00	22.00
8	Harvey Walker	45.00	22.00	13.50
9	Gerald Walker	45.00	22.00	13.50
10	Sam Byrd	45.00	22.00	13.50
11	Joe Vosmik	45.00	22.00	13.50
12	Dan MacFayden	45.00	22.00	13.50
13	William Dickey	75.00	37.00	22.00
14	Robert Grove	75.00	37.00	22.00
15	Al Simmons	75.00	37.00	22.00
16	Jimmy Foxx	75.00	37.00	22.00
18	Charlie Grimm	45.00	22.00	13.50
19	Bill Terry	75.00	37.00	22.00
20	Clifton Heathcote	45.00	22.00	13.50
23	Gabby Hartnett	75.00	37.00	22.00
26	Stanley Harris	75.00	37.00	22.00
27	John J. McGraw	75.00	37.00	22.00
28	Paul Waner	75.00	37.00	22.00
29	Babe Ruth	800.00	400.00	240.00
33	Tony Lazzeri	75.00	37.00	22.00
35	Glenn Wright	45.00	22.00	13.50
38	George Uhle	45.00	37.00	22.00
40	Rogers Hornsby	75.00	37.00	22.00
48	E.C. (Sam) Rice	75.00	37.00	22.00
50	Sam Jones	45.00	22.00	13.50
52	Willie Kamm	45.00	22.00	13.50
54	Lester Bell	45.00	22.00	13.50
55	L. Waner	75.00	37.00	22.00
58	Earl Smith	45.00	22.00	13.50

1922 W501

This "strip card" set, known as W501 in the American Card Catalog, is closely connected to the more popular E121 American Caramel set of 1921 and 1922. Measuring the same 2" x 3-1/2", the cards are actually reproductions of the E121 120-card series distributed as strip cards. The W501 cards are numbered in the upper-right corner and have the notation "G-4-22" in the upper-left corner, apparrently indicating the cards were issued in April of 1922.

		NM	EX	VG
Complete Set (121):		6500.	2600.	1300.
Common Player:		37.00	15.00	7.50
1	Ed Rounnel (Rommel)	37.00	15.00	7.50
2	Urban Shocker	37.00	15.00	7.50
3	Dixie Davis	37.00	15.00	7.50
4	George Sisler	60.00	24.00	12.00
5	Bob Veach	37.00	15.00	7.50
6	Harry Heilman (Heilmann)	60.00	24.00	12.00
7a	Ira Falgstead (name incorrect)	37.00	15.00	7.50
7b	Ira Flagstead (name correct)	37.00	15.00	7.50
8	Ty Cobb	1050.	420.00	210.00
9	Oscar Vitt	37.00	15.00	7.50
10	Muddy Ruel	37.00	15.00	7.50
11	Derrill Pratt	37.00	15.00	7.50
12	Ed Gharrity	37.00	15.00	7.50
13	Joe Judge	37.00	15.00	7.50
14	Sam Rice	60.00	24.00	12.00
15	Clyde Milan	37.00	15.00	7.50
16	Joe Sewell	60.00	24.00	12.00
17	Walter Johnson	300.00	120.00	60.00
18	Jack McInnis	37.00	15.00	7.50
19	Tris Speaker	75.00	30.00	15.00
20	Jim Bagby	37.00	15.00	7.50
21	Stanley Coveleskie (Coveleski)	60.00	24.00	12.00
22	Bill Wambsganss	37.00	15.00	7.50
23	Walter Mails	37.00	15.00	7.50
24	Larry Gardner	37.00	15.00	7.50
25	Aaron Ward	37.00	15.00	7.50
26	Miller Huggins	60.00	24.00	12.00
27	Wally Schang	37.00	15.00	7.50
28	Tom Rogers	37.00	15.00	7.50
29	Carl Mays	45.00	18.00	9.00
30	Everett Scott	37.00	15.00	7.50
31	Robert Shawkey	37.00	15.00	7.50
32	Waite Hoyt	60.00	24.00	12.00
33	Mike McNally	37.00	15.00	7.50
34	Joe Bush	37.00	15.00	7.50
35	Bob Meusel	37.00	15.00	7.50
36	Elmer Miller	37.00	15.00	7.50
37	Dick Kerr	37.00	15.00	7.50
38	Eddie Collins	60.00	24.00	12.00
39	Kid Gleason	37.00	15.00	7.50
40	Johnny Mostil	37.00	15.00	7.50
41	Bib Falk (Bibb)	37.00	15.00	7.50
42	Clarence Hodge	37.00	15.00	7.50
43	Ray Schalk	60.00	24.00	12.00
44	Amos Strunk	37.00	15.00	7.50
45	Eddie Mulligan	37.00	15.00	7.50
46	Earl Sheely	37.00	15.00	7.50
47	Harry Hooper	60.00	24.00	12.00
48	Urban Faber	60.00	24.00	12.00
49	Babe Ruth	1375.	550.00	275.00
50	Ivy B. Wingo	37.00	15.00	7.50
51	Earle Neale	45.00	18.00	9.00
52	Jake Daubert	37.00	15.00	7.50
53	Ed Roush	60.00	24.00	12.00
54	Eppa J. Rixey	60.00	24.00	12.00
55	Elwood Martin	37.00	15.00	7.50
56	Bill Killifer (Killefer)	37.00	15.00	7.50
57	Charles Hollocher	37.00	15.00	7.50
58	Zeb Terry	37.00	15.00	7.50
59	Grover Alexander	75.00	30.00	15.00
60	Turner Barber	37.00	15.00	7.50
61	John Rawlings	37.00	15.00	7.50
62	Frank Frisch	60.00	24.00	12.00
63	Pat Shea	37.00	15.00	7.50
64	Dave Bancroft	60.00	24.00	12.00
65	Cecil Causey	37.00	15.00	7.50
66	Frank Snyder	37.00	15.00	7.50
67	Heinie Groh	37.00	15.00	7.50
68	Ross Young (Youngs)	60.00	24.00	12.00
69	Fred Toney	37.00	15.00	7.50
70	Arthur Nehf	37.00	15.00	7.50
71	Earl Smith	37.00	15.00	7.50
72	George Kelly	60.00	24.00	12.00
73	John J. McGraw	60.00	24.00	12.00
74	Phil Douglas	37.00	15.00	7.50
75	Bill Ryan	37.00	15.00	7.50
76	Jess Haines	60.00	24.00	12.00
77	Milt Stock	37.00	15.00	7.50
78	William Doak	37.00	15.00	7.50
79	George Toporcer	37.00	15.00	7.50
80	Wilbur Cooper	37.00	15.00	7.50
81	George Whitted	37.00	15.00	7.50
82	Chas. Grimm	37.00	15.00	7.50
83	Rabbit Maranville	60.00	24.00	12.00
84	Babe Adams	37.00	15.00	7.50

85	Carson Bigbee	37.00	15.00	7.50
86	Max Carey	60.00	24.00	12.00
87	Whitey Glazner	37.00	15.00	7.50
88	George Gibson	37.00	15.00	7.50
89	Bill Southworth	37.00	15.00	7.50
90	Hank Gowdy	37.00	15.00	7.50
91	Walter Holke	37.00	15.00	7.50
92	Joe Oeschger	37.00	15.00	7.50
93	Pete Kilduff	37.00	15.00	7.50
94	Hy Myers	37.00	15.00	7.50
95	Otto Miller	37.00	15.00	7.50
96	Wilbert Robinson	60.00	24.00	12.00
97	Zach Wheat	60.00	24.00	12.00
98	Walter Ruether	37.00	15.00	7.50
99	Curtis Walker	37.00	15.00	7.50
100	Fred Williams	37.00	15.00	7.50
101	Dave Danforth	37.00	15.00	7.50
102	Ed Rounnel (Rommel)	37.00	15.00	7.50
103	Carl Mays	45.00	18.00	9.00
104	Frank Frisch	60.00	24.00	12.00
105	Lou DeVormer	37.00	15.00	7.50
106	Tom Griffith	37.00	15.00	7.50
107	Harry Harper	37.00	15.00	7.50
108a	John Lavan	37.00	15.00	7.50
108b	John J. McGraw	60.00	24.00	12.00
109	Elmer Smith	37.00	15.00	7.50
110	George Dauss	37.00	15.00	7.50
111	Alexander Gaston	37.00	15.00	7.50
112	John Graney	37.00	15.00	7.50
113	Emil Muesel	37.00	15.00	7.50
114	Rogers Hornsby	95.00	38.00	19.00
115	Leslie Nunamaker	37.00	15.00	7.50
116	Steve O'Neill	37.00	15.00	7.50
117	Max Flack	37.00	15.00	7.50
118	Bill Southworth	37.00	15.00	7.50
119	Arthur Nehf	37.00	15.00	7.50
120	Chick Fewster	37.00	15.00	7.50

1928 W502

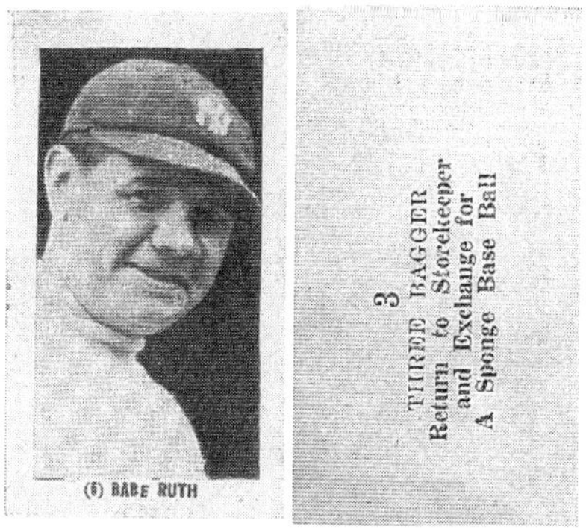

Issued in 1927, this 63-card set is closely related to the York Caramel set (E210) of the same year. The black-and-white cards measure 1-3/8" x 2-1/2" and display the player's name at the bottom in capital letters preceded by a number in parentheses. The backs of the cards read either "One Bagger," "Three Bagger" or "Home Run", and were apparently designed to be used as part of a baseball game. There are two cards known to exist for numbers 26, 38, 40, 55 and 59. The set carries the American Card Catalog designation W502.

		NM	EX	VG
Complete Set (61):		5670.	2268.	1134.
Common Player:		30.00	12.00	6.00
1	Burleigh Grimes	65.00	26.00	13.00
2	Walter Reuther	30.00	12.00	6.00
3	Joe Dugan	30.00	12.00	6.00
4	Red Faber	65.00	26.00	13.00
5	Gabby Hartnett	65.00	26.00	13.00
6	Babe Ruth	1100.	440.00	220.00
7	Bob Meusel	30.00	12.00	6.00
8	Herb Pennock	65.00	26.00	13.00
9	George Burns (photo is George J., not George H. Burns)	30.00	12.00	6.00
10	Joe Sewell	65.00	26.00	13.00
11	George Uhle	30.00	12.00	6.00
12	Bob O'Farrell	30.00	12.00	6.00
13	Rogers Hornsby	75.00	30.00	15.00
14	"Pie" Traynor	65.00	26.00	13.00
15	Clarence Mitchell	30.00	12.00	6.00
16	Eppa Jepha Rixey	65.00	26.00	13.00
17	Carl Mays	35.00	14.00	7.00
18	Adolfo Luque	45.00	18.00	9.00
19	Dave Bancroft	65.00	26.00	13.00
20	George Kelly	65.00	26.00	13.00
21	Earl Combs (Earle)	65.00	26.00	13.00
22	Harry Heilmann	65.00	26.00	13.00
23	Ray W. Schalk	65.00	26.00	13.00
24	Johnny Mostil	30.00	12.00	6.00
25	Hack Wilson (photo actually Art Wilson)	65.00	26.00	13.00
26a	Lou Gehrig	900.00	360.00	180.00
26b	Stanley Harris	30.00	12.00	6.00
27	Ty Cobb	900.00	360.00	180.00
28	Tris Speaker	75.00	30.00	15.00
29	Tony Lazzeri	65.00	26.00	13.00
30	Waite Hoyt	65.00	26.00	13.00
31	Sherwood Smith	30.00	12.00	6.00
32	Max Carey	65.00	26.00	13.00
33	Eugene Hargrave	30.00	12.00	6.00
34	Miguel L. Gonzales (Miguel A. Gonzalez)	45.00	18.00	9.00
35	Joe Judge	30.00	12.00	6.00
36	E.C. (Sam) Rice	65.00	26.00	13.00
37	Earl Sheely	30.00	12.00	6.00
38a	Sam Jones	30.00	12.00	6.00
38b	Emory E. Rigney	30.00	12.00	6.00
39	Bib A. Falk (Bibb)	30.00	12.00	6.00
40a	Nick Altrock	30.00	12.00	6.00
40b	Willie Kamm	30.00	12.00	6.00
41	Stanley Harris	65.00	26.00	13.00
42	John J. McGraw	65.00	26.00	13.00
43	Artie Nehf	30.00	12.00	6.00
44	Grover Alexander	75.00	30.00	15.00
45	Paul Waner	65.00	26.00	13.00
46	William H. Terry	65.00	26.00	13.00
47	Glenn Wright	30.00	12.00	6.00
48	Earl Smith	30.00	12.00	6.00
49	Leon (Goose) Goslin	65.00	26.00	13.00
50	Frank Frisch	65.00	26.00	13.00
51	Joe Harris	30.00	12.00	6.00
52	Fred (Cy) Williams	30.00	12.00	6.00
53	Eddie Roush	65.00	26.00	13.00
54	George Sisler	65.00	26.00	13.00
55a	Ed Rommel	30.00	12.00	6.00
55b	L. Waner (photo actually Paul Waner)	65.00	26.00	13.00
56	Rogers Peckinpaugh (Roger)	30.00	12.00	6.00
57	Stanley Coveleskie (Coveleski)	65.00	26.00	13.00
58	Lester Bell	30.00	12.00	6.00
59a	Dave Bancroft	65.00	26.00	13.00
59b	L. Waner	65.00	26.00	13.00
60	John P. McInnis	30.00	12.00	6.00

1922 W503

Issued circa 1923, this 64-card set of blank-backed cards, measuring 1-3/4" x 2-3/4", feature black and white player photos surrounded by a white border. The player's name and team appear on the card, along with a card number in either the left or right bottom corner. There is no indication of the set's producer, although it is believed the cards were issued with candy or gum. The set carries a W503 American Card Catalog designation.

		NM	EX	VG
Complete Set (64):		8000.	3200.	1600.
Common Player:		90.00	36.00	18.00
1	Joe Bush	90.00	36.00	18.00
2	Wally Schang	90.00	36.00	18.00
3	Dave Robertson	90.00	36.00	18.00
4	Wally Pipp	110.00	45.00	22.00
5	Bill Ryan	90.00	36.00	18.00
6	George Kelly	200.00	80.00	40.00
7	Frank Snyder	90.00	36.00	18.00
8	Jimmy O'Connell	90.00	36.00	18.00
9	Bill Cunningham	90.00	36.00	18.00
10	Norman McMillan	90.00	36.00	18.00
11	Waite Hoyt	200.00	80.00	40.00
12	Art Nehf	90.00	36.00	18.00
13	George Sisler	200.00	80.00	40.00
14	Al DeVormer	90.00	36.00	18.00
15	Casey Stengel	225.00	90.00	45.00
16	Ken Williams	90.00	36.00	18.00
17	Joe Dugan	90.00	36.00	18.00
18	"Irish" Meusel	90.00	36.00	18.00
19	Bob Meusel	90.00	36.00	18.00
20	Carl Mays	100.00	40.00	20.00
21	Frank Frisch	200.00	80.00	40.00
22	Jess Barnes	90.00	36.00	18.00
23	Walter Johnson	350.00	140.00	70.00
24	Claude Jonnard	90.00	36.00	18.00
25	Dave Bancroft	200.00	80.00	40.00
26	Johnny Rawlings	90.00	36.00	18.00
27	"Pep" Young	90.00	36.00	18.00
28	Earl Smith	90.00	36.00	18.00
29	Willie Kamm	90.00	36.00	18.00
30	Art Fletcher	90.00	36.00	18.00
31	"Kid" Gleason	90.00	36.00	18.00
32	"Babe" Ruth	1900.	800.00	380.00
33	Guy Morton	90.00	36.00	18.00
34	Heinie Groh	90.00	36.00	18.00
35	Leon Cadore	90.00	36.00	18.00
36	Joe Tobin	90.00	36.00	18.00
37	"Rube" Marquard	200.00	80.00	40.00
38	Grover Alexander	225.00	90.00	45.00
39	George Burns	90.00	36.00	18.00
40	Joe Oeschger	90.00	36.00	18.00
41	"Chick" Shorten	90.00	36.00	18.00
42	Roger Hornsby (Rogers)	225.00	90.00	45.00
43	Adolfo Luque	125.00	50.00	25.00
44	Zack Wheat	200.00	80.00	40.00
45	Herb Pruett (Hub)	90.00	36.00	18.00
46	Rabbit Maranville	200.00	80.00	40.00
47	Jimmy Ring	90.00	36.00	18.00
48	Sherrod Smith	90.00	36.00	18.00
49	Lea Meadows (Lee)	90.00	36.00	18.00
50	Aaron Ward	90.00	36.00	18.00
51	Herb Pennock	200.00	80.00	40.00
52	Carlson Bigbee (Carson)	90.00	36.00	18.00
53	Max Carey	200.00	80.00	40.00
54	Charles Robertson	90.00	36.00	18.00
55	Urban Shocker	90.00	36.00	18.00
56	Dutch Ruether	90.00	36.00	18.00
57	Jake Daubert	90.00	36.00	18.00
58	Louis Guisto	90.00	36.00	18.00
59	Ivy Wingo	90.00	36.00	18.00
60	Bill Pertica	90.00	36.00	18.00
61	Luke Sewell	90.00	36.00	18.00
62	Hank Gowdy	90.00	36.00	18.00
63	Jack Scott	90.00	36.00	18.00
64	Stan Coveleskie (Coveleski)	200.00	80.00	40.00

1926 W512

One of the many "strip card" sets of the period (so-called because the cards were sold in strips), the W512 set was issued in 1926 and includes 10 baseball players among its 60 cards. Also featured are boxers, golfers, tennis players, aviators, movie stars and other celebrities. The 1-3/8" x 2-1/4" cards feature crude color drawings of the subjects with their names below. A card number appears in the lower-left corner. Baseball players lead off the set and are numbered from 1 to 10. Like most strip cards, they have blank backs. Reprints of Ruth, Cobb, Johnson and Speaker are known.

		NM	EX	VG
Complete (Baseball) Set (10):		600.00	240.00	120.00
Common Player:		25.00	10.00	5.00
1	Dave Bancroft	40.00	16.00	8.00
2	Grover Alexander	45.00	18.00	9.00
3	"Ty" Cobb	200.00	80.00	40.00
4	Tris Speaker	45.00	18.00	9.00
5	Glen Wright (Glenn)	25.00	10.00	5.00
6	"Babe" Ruth	300.00	120.00	60.00
7a	Everett Scott (Yankees)	30.00	12.00	6.00
7b	Everett Scott (White Sox)	25.00	10.00	5.00
8	Frank Frisch	40.00	16.00	8.00
9	Rogers Hornsby	45.00	18.00	9.00
10	Dazzy Vance	40.00	16.00	8.00

1928 W513

This "strip card" set, issued in 1928 was actually a continuation of the W512 set issued two years earlier and is numbered starting with number 61 where the W512 set ended. The blank-backed cards measure 1-3/8" x 2-1/4" and display color drawings of the athletes, which include 14 boxers and the 26 baseball palyers listed here. The cards are numbered in the lower-left corner.

	NM	EX	VG
Complete (Baseball) Set (26):	600.00	240.00	120.00
Common Player:	25.00	12.50	7.50
61 Eddie Roush	40.00	16.00	8.00
62 Waite Hoyt	40.00	16.00	8.00
63 "Gink" Hendrick	25.00	10.00	5.00
64 "Jumbo" Elliott	25.00	10.00	5.00
65 John Miljus	25.00	10.00	5.00
66 Jumping Joe Dugan	25.00	10.00	5.00
67 Smiling Bill Terry	40.00	16.00	8.00
68 Herb Pennock	40.00	16.00	8.00
69 Rube Benton	25.00	10.00	5.00
70 Paul Waner	40.00	16.00	8.00
71 Adolfo Luque	30.00	12.00	6.00
72 Burleigh Grimes	40.00	16.00	8.00
73 Lloyd Waner	40.00	16.00	8.00
74 Hack Wilson	40.00	16.00	8.00
75 Hal Carlson	25.00	10.00	5.00
76 L. Grantham	25.00	10.00	5.00
77 Wilcey Moore (Wilcy)	25.00	10.00	5.00
78 Jess Haines	40.00	16.00	8.00
79 Tony Lazzeri	40.00	16.00	8.00
80 Al DeVormer	25.00	10.00	5.00
81 Joe Harris	25.00	10.00	5.00
82 Pie Traynor	40.00	16.00	8.00
83 Mark Koenig	25.00	10.00	5.00
84 Babe Herman	30.00	12.00	6.00
85 George Harper	25.00	10.00	5.00
86 Earl Coombs (Earle Combs)	40.00	16.00	8.00

1919-21 W514

Consisting of 120 cards, the W514 set is the largest of the various "strip card" issues of its era. Issued between 1919-1921, it is also one of the earliest and most widely-collected. The 1-3/8" x 2-1/2" cards feature color drawings of the players and display the card number in the lower-left corner. The player's name, position and team appear in the bottom border of the blank-backed cards. The set holds special interest for baseball historians because it includes seven of the eight Chicago "Black Sox" who were banned from baseball for their alleged role in throwing the 1919 World Series. The most famous of them, "Shoeless" Joe Jackson, makes his only strip card appearance in this set.

	NM	EX	VG
Complete Set (120):	6975.	2800.	1400.
Common Player:	40.00	16.00	8.00
1 Ira Flagstead	40.00	16.00	8.00
2 Babe Ruth	700.00	280.00	140.00
3 Happy Felsch	165.00	66.00	33.00
4 Doc Lavan	40.00	16.00	8.00
5 Phil Douglas	40.00	16.00	8.00
6 Earle Neale	50.00	20.00	10.00
7 Leslie Nunamaker	40.00	16.00	8.00
8 Sam Jones	40.00	16.00	8.00
9 Claude Hendrix	40.00	16.00	8.00
10 Frank Schulte	40.00	16.00	8.00
11 Cactus Cravath	40.00	16.00	8.00
12 Pat Moran	40.00	16.00	8.00
13 Dick Rudolph	40.00	16.00	8.00
14 Arthur Fletcher	40.00	16.00	8.00
15 Joe Jackson	1650.	660.00	330.00
16 Bill Southworth	40.00	16.00	8.00
17 Ad Luque	45.00	18.00	9.00
18 Charlie Deal	40.00	16.00	8.00
19 Al Mamaux	40.00	16.00	8.00
20 Stuffy McInness (McInnis)	40.00	16.00	8.00
21a Rabbit Maranville (Braves)	65.00	26.00	13.00
21b Rabbit Maranville (Pirates)	65.00	26.00	13.00
22 Max Carey	65.00	26.00	13.00
23 Dick Kerr	40.00	16.00	8.00
24 George Burns	40.00	16.00	8.00
25 Eddie Collins	65.00	26.00	13.00
26 Steve O'Neil (O'Neill)	40.00	16.00	8.00
27 Bill Fisher	40.00	16.00	8.00
28 Rube Bressler	40.00	16.00	8.00
29 Bob Shawkey	40.00	16.00	8.00
30 Donie Bush	40.00	16.00	8.00
31 Chick Gandil	125.00	50.00	25.00
32 Ollie Zeider	40.00	16.00	8.00
33 Vean Gregg	40.00	16.00	8.00
34 Miller Huggins	66.00	26.00	13.00
35 Lefty Williams	165.00	66.00	33.00
36 Tub Spencer	40.00	16.00	8.00
37 Lew McCarty	40.00	16.00	8.00
38 Hod Eller	40.00	16.00	8.00
39 Joe Gedeon	40.00	16.00	8.00
40a Dave Bancroft (Quakers)	66.00	26.00	13.00
40b Dave Bancroft (Giants)	66.00	26.00	13.00
41 Clark Griffith	66.00	26.00	13.00
42 Wilbur Cooper	40.00	16.00	8.00
43 Ty Cobb	500.00	200.00	100.00
44 Roger Peckinpaugh	40.00	16.00	8.00
45 Nic Carter (Nick)	40.00	16.00	8.00
46 Heinie Groh	40.00	16.00	8.00
47a Bob Roth (Indians)	40.00	16.00	8.00
47b Bob Roth (Yankees)	40.00	16.00	8.00
48 Frank Davis	40.00	16.00	8.00
49 Leslie Mann	40.00	16.00	8.00
50 Fielder Jones	40.00	16.00	8.00
51 Bill Doak	40.00	16.00	8.00
52 John J. McGraw	66.00	26.00	13.00
53 Charles Hollocher	40.00	16.00	8.00
54 Babe Adams	40.00	16.00	8.00
55 Dode Paskert	40.00	16.00	8.00
56 Roger Hornsby (Rogers)	70.00	28.00	14.00
57 Max Rath	40.00	16.00	8.00
58 Jeff Pfeffer	40.00	16.00	8.00
59 Nick Cullop	40.00	16.00	8.00
60 Ray Schalk	66.00	26.00	13.00
61 Bill Jacobson	40.00	16.00	8.00
62 Nap Lajoie	66.00	26.00	13.00
63 George Gibson	40.00	16.00	8.00
64 Harry Hooper	66.00	26.00	13.00
65 Grover Alexander	66.00	26.00	13.00
66 Ping Bodie	40.00	16.00	8.00
67 Hank Gowdy	40.00	16.00	8.00
68 Jake Daubert	40.00	16.00	8.00
69 Red Faber	66.00	26.00	13.00
70 Ivan Olson	40.00	16.00	8.00
71 Pickles Dilhoefer	40.00	16.00	8.00
72 Christy Mathewson	150.00	60.00	30.00
73 Ira Wingo (Ivy)	40.00	16.00	8.00
74 Fred Merkle	40.00	16.00	8.00
75 Frank Baker	66.00	26.00	13.00
76 Bert Gallia	40.00	16.00	8.00
77 Milton Watson	40.00	16.00	8.00
78 Bert Shotten (Shotton)	40.00	16.00	8.00
79 Sam Rice	66.00	26.00	13.00
80 Dan Greiner	40.00	16.00	8.00
81 Larry Doyle	40.00	16.00	8.00
82 Eddie Cicotte	100.00	40.00	20.00
83 Hugo Bezdek	40.00	16.00	8.00
84 Wally Pipp	45.00	18.00	9.00
85 Eddie Rousch (Roush)	66.00	26.00	13.00
86 Slim Sallee	40.00	16.00	8.00
87 Bill Killifer (Killefer)	40.00	16.00	8.00
88 Bob Veach	40.00	16.00	8.00
89 Jim Burke	40.00	16.00	8.00
90 Everett Scott	40.00	16.00	8.00
91 Buck Weaver	135.00	54.00	27.00
92 George Whitted	40.00	16.00	8.00
93 Ed Konetchy	40.00	16.00	8.00
94 Walter Johnson	135.00	54.00	27.00
95 Sam Crawford	66.00	26.00	13.00
96 Fred Mitchell	40.00	16.00	8.00
97 Ira Thomas	40.00	16.00	8.00
98 Jimmy Ring	40.00	16.00	8.00
99 Wally Shange (Schang)	40.00	16.00	8.00
100 Benny Kauff	40.00	16.00	8.00
101 George Sisler	66.00	26.00	13.00
102 Tris Speaker	70.00	28.00	14.00
103 Carl Mays	45.00	18.00	9.00
104 Buck Herzog	40.00	16.00	8.00
105 Swede Risberg	165.00	66.00	33.00
106a Hugh Jennings (Tigers)	65.00	26.00	13.00
106b Hughie Jennings (Giants)	65.00	26.00	13.00
107 Pep Young	40.00	16.00	8.00
108 Walter Reuther	40.00	16.00	8.00
109 Joe Gharrity (Ed)	40.00	16.00	8.00
110 Zach Wheat	66.00	26.00	13.00
111 Jim Vaughn	40.00	16.00	8.00
112 Kid Gleason	40.00	16.00	8.00
113 Casey Stengel	70.00	28.00	14.00
114 Hal Chase	45.00	18.00	9.00
115 Oscar Stange (Stanage)	40.00	16.00	8.00
116 Larry Shean	40.00	16.00	8.00
117 Steve Pendergast	40.00	16.00	8.00
118 Larry Kopf	40.00	16.00	8.00
119 Charles Whiteman	40.00	16.00	8.00
120 Jess Barnes	40.00	16.00	8.00

1923 W515-1

Cards in the 60-card "strip set" measure about 1-3/8" x 2-1/4" and feature color drawings. Backs are blank. The card number along with the player's name, position and team appear in the bottom border. Most cards also display a "U&U" copyright line, indicating that the photos on which the drawings were based were provided by Underwood & Underwood, a major news photo service of the day. The set has a heavy emphasis on New York players with 39 of the 60 cards depicting members of the Yankees, Dodgers or Giants. Babe Ruth appears on two cards and two other cards picture two players each.

	NM	EX	VG
Complete Set (60):	2600.	1050.	575.00
Common Player:	30.00	15.00	9.00
1 Bill Cunningham	30.00	12.00	6.00
2 Al Mamaux	30.00	12.00	6.00
3 "Babe" Ruth	300.00	120.00	60.00
4 Dave Bancroft	50.00	20.00	10.00
5 Ed Rommel	30.00	12.00	6.00
6 "Babe" Adams	30.00	12.00	6.00
7 Clarence Walker	30.00	12.00	6.00
8 Waite Hoyt	50.00	20.00	10.00
9 Bob Shawkey	30.00	12.00	6.00
10 "Ty" Cobb	200.00	80.00	40.00
11 George Sisler	50.00	20.00	10.00
12 Jack Bentley	30.00	12.00	6.00
13 Jim O'Connell	30.00	12.00	6.00
14 Frank Frisch	50.00	20.00	10.00
15 Frank Baker	50.00	20.00	10.00
16 Burleigh Grimes	50.00	20.00	10.00
17 Wally Schang	30.00	12.00	6.00
18 Harry Heilman (Heilmann)	50.00	20.00	10.00
19 Aaron Ward	30.00	12.00	6.00
20 Carl Mays	35.00	14.00	7.00
21 The Meusel Bros. (Bob Meusel, Irish Meusel)	35.00	14.00	7.00
22 Arthur Nehf	30.00	12.00	6.00
23 Lee Meadows	30.00	12.00	6.00
24 "Casey" Stengel	50.00	20.00	10.00
25 Jack Scott	30.00	12.00	6.00
26 Kenneth Williams	30.00	12.00	6.00
27 Joe Bush	30.00	12.00	6.00
28 Tris Speaker	55.00	22.00	11.00
29 Ross Young (Youngs)	50.00	20.00	10.00
30 Joe Dugan	30.00	12.00	6.00
31 The Barnes Bros. (Jesse Barnes, Virgil Barnes)	35.00	14.00	7.00
32 George Kelly	50.00	20.00	10.00
33 Hugh McQuillen (McQuillan)	30.00	12.00	6.00
34 Hugh Jennings	50.00	20.00	10.00
35 Tom Griffith	30.00	12.00	6.00
36 Miller Huggins	50.00	20.00	10.00
37 "Whitey" Witt	30.00	12.00	6.00
38 Walter Johnson	100.00	40.00	20.00
39 "Wally" Pipp	32.00	13.00	6.50
40 "Dutch" Reuther	30.00	12.00	6.00
41 Jim Johnston	30.00	12.00	6.00
42 Willie Kamm	30.00	12.00	6.00
43 Sam Jones	30.00	12.00	6.00
44 Frank Snyder	30.00	12.00	6.00
45 John McGraw	50.00	20.00	10.00
46 Everett Scott	30.00	12.00	6.00
47 "Babe" Ruth	300.00	120.00	60.00
48 Urban Shocker	30.00	12.00	6.00
49 Grover Alexander	50.00	20.00	10.00
50 "Rabbit" Maranville	50.00	20.00	10.00
51 Ray Schalk	50.00	20.00	10.00
52 "Heinie" Groh	30.00	12.00	6.00
53 Wilbert Robinson	50.00	20.00	10.00
54 George Burns	30.00	12.00	6.00
55 Rogers Hornsby	55.00	22.00	11.00
56 Zack Wheat	50.00	20.00	10.00
57 Eddie Roush	50.00	20.00	10.00
58 Eddie Collins	50.00	20.00	10.00
59 Charlie Hollocher	30.00	12.00	6.00
60 Red Faber	50.00	20.00	10.00

1923 W515-2

A near duplicate of the W515-1 set in every respect except size, the W515-2 strip cards are larger in format, at about 1-1/2" x 2-1/2". Placement of the U&U copyright also differs between some players' cards in each set. Cards may be found with letters in the top border from the title, "THE LITTLE WONDER PICTURE SERIES".

(See W515-1 for checklist, value guide)

1920 W516-1

This "strip card" set consists of 30 cards featuring colored drawings - either portraits or full-length action poses. The blank-backed cards measure 1-1/2" x 2-1/2". The player's name, position and team appear beneath the picture in hand-printed style. To the right of the name is the card number. The set can be identified by an "IFS" copyright symbol. representing International Feature Service.

		NM	EX	VG
Complete Set (30):		1500.	600.00	300.00
Common Player:		25.00	10.00	5.00
1	Babe Ruth	400.00	160.00	80.00
2	Heinie Groh	25.00	10.00	5.00
3	Ping Bodie	25.00	10.00	5.00
4	Ray Shalk (Schalk)	50.00	20.00	10.00
5	Tris Speaker	55.00	22.00	11.00
6	Ty Cobb	300.00	120.00	60.00
7	Roger Hornsby (Rogers)	55.00	22.00	11.00
8	Walter Johnson	100.00	40.00	20.00
9	Grover Alexander	50.00	20.00	10.00
10	George Burns	25.00	10.00	5.00
11	Jimmy Ring	25.00	10.00	5.00
12	Jess Barnes	25.00	10.00	5.00
13	Larry Doyle	25.00	10.00	5.00
14	Arty Fletcher	25.00	10.00	5.00
15	Dick Rudolph	25.00	10.00	5.00
16	Benny Kauf (Kauff)	25.00	10.00	5.00
17	Art Nehf	25.00	10.00	5.00
18	Babe Adams	25.00	10.00	5.00
19	Will Cooper	25.00	10.00	5.00
20	R. Peckinpaugh	25.00	10.00	5.00
21	Eddie Cicotte	45.00	18.00	9.00
22	Hank Gowdy	25.00	10.00	5.00
23	Eddie Collins	50.00	20.00	10.00
24	Christy Mathewson	100.00	40.00	20.00
25	Clyde Milan	25.00	10.00	5.00
26	M. Kelley (should be G. Kelly)	40.00	16.00	8.00
27	Ed Hooper (Harry)	40.00	16.00	8.00
28	Pep. Young	25.00	10.00	5.00
29	Eddie Rousch (Roush)	40.00	16.00	8.00
30	Geo. Bancroft (Dave)	40.00	16.00	8.00

1921 W516-2-2

This set is essentially a re-issue of the W516-1 set of the previous year with one major change. The card numbers have been changed and the pictures have all been reversed. The blank-backed cards measure about 1-1/2" x 2-1/4" and feature color drawings with the player's name, position and team beneath the picture in hand-printed san-serif style, along with the card number (#1-20 on the left, #21-30 on the right). The cards display a backwards "IFC" copyright symbol.

		NM	EX	VG
Complete Set (30):		1800.	900.00	550.00
Common Player:		30.00	15.00	9.00
1	George Burns	30.00	15.00	9.00
2	Grover Alexander	65.00	32.00	19.50
3	Walter Johnson	150.00	75.00	45.00
4	Roger Hornsby (Rogers)	70.00	35.00	21.00
5	Ty Cobb	300.00	150.00	90.00
6	Tris Speaker	70.00	35.00	21.00
7	Ray Shalk (Schalk)	60.00	30.00	18.00
8	Ping Bodie	30.00	15.00	9.00
9	Heinie Groh	30.00	15.00	9.00
10	Babe Ruth	450.00	225.00	135.00
11	R. Peckinpaugh	30.00	15.00	9.00
12	Will. Cooper	30.00	15.00	9.00
13	Babe Adams	30.00	15.00	9.00
14	Art Nehf	30.00	15.00	9.00
15	Benny Kauf (Kauff)	30.00	15.00	9.00
16	Dick Rudolph	30.00	15.00	9.00
17	Arty. Fletcher	30.00	15.00	9.00
18	Larry Doyle	30.00	15.00	9.00
19	Jess Barnes	30.00	15.00	9.00
20	Jimmy Ring	30.00	15.00	9.00
21	George Bancroft (Dave)	60.00	30.00	18.00
22	Eddie Rousch (Roush)	60.00	30.00	18.00
23	Pep Young	30.00	15.00	9.00
24	Ed Hooper (Harry)	60.00	30.00	18.00
25	M. Kelley (should be G. Kelly)	60.00	30.00	18.00
26	Clyde Milan	30.00	15.00	9.00
27	Christy Mathewson	150.00	75.00	45.00
28	Eddie Collins	60.00	30.00	18.00
29	Hank Gowdy	30.00	15.00	9.00
30	Eddie Cicotte	60.00	30.00	18.00

1921 W516-2-1

This set is essentially a re-issue of the W516-1 set, with several changes: The pictures are reverse images of W516-1, and are printed only in red and blue. Cards have been renumbered and have player identification in in typeset serifed style. The blank-backed cards measure about 1-1/2" x 2-3/8". The cards display a backwards "IFC" copyright symbol.

		NM	EX	VG
Complete Set (30):		1500.	600.00	300.00
Common Player:		25.00	10.00	5.00
1	George Burns	25.00	10.00	5.00
2	Grover Alexander	55.00	22.00	11.00
3	Walter Johnson	125.00	50.00	25.00
4	Roger Hornsby (Rogers)	60.00	24.00	12.00
5	Ty Cobb	250.00	100.00	50.00
6	Tris Speaker	60.00	24.00	12.00
7	Ray Shalk (Schalk)	50.00	20.00	10.00
8	Ping Bodie	25.00	10.00	5.00
9	Heinie Groh	25.00	10.00	5.00
10	Babe Ruth	375.00	150.00	75.00
11	R. Peckinpaugh	25.00	10.00	5.00
12	Will. Cooper	25.00	10.00	5.00
13	Babe Adams	25.00	10.00	5.00
14	Art Nehf	25.00	10.00	5.00
15	Benny Kauf (Kauff)	25.00	10.00	5.00
16	Dick Rudolph	25.00	10.00	5.00
17	Arty. Fletcher	25.00	10.00	5.00
18	Larry Doyle	25.00	10.00	5.00
19	Jess Barnes	25.00	10.00	5.00
20	Jimmy Ring	25.00	10.00	5.00
21	George Bancroft (Dave)	50.00	20.00	10.00
22	Eddie Rousch (Roush)	50.00	20.00	10.00
23	Pep Young	25.00	10.00	5.00
24	Ed Hooper (Harry)	50.00	20.00	10.00
25	M. Kelley (should be G. Kelly)	50.00	20.00	10.00
26	Clyde Milan	25.00	10.00	5.00
27	Christy Mathewson	125.00	50.00	25.00
28	Eddie Collins	50.00	20.00	10.00
29	Hank Gowdy	25.00	10.00	5.00
30	Eddie Cicotte	55.00	22.00	11.00

1931 W517

The 54-player W517 set is a scarce issue of 3" x 4" cards which are generally found in a sepia color. There are, however, other known colors of W517s, which bring higher prices from specialists. The cards feature a player photo as well as his name and team. The card number appears in a small circle on the front, while the backs are blank. The set is heavy in stars of the period including two Babe Ruths (#4 and 20). The cards were sold in vertical strips of three cards; some cards are found with baseball plays in a line at top. Complete set prices do not include variations.

		NM	EX	VG
Complete Set (54):		8250.	3700.	2050.
Common Player:		70.00	35.00	21.00
1	Earl Combs (Earle)	150.00	67.00	37.00
2	Pie Traynor	150.00	67.00	37.00
3	Eddie Rausch (Roush)	150.00	67.00	37.00
4	Babe Ruth	1250.	562.00	312.00
5a	Chalmer Cissell (Chicago)	70.00	31.00	17.50
5b	Chalmer Cissell (Cleveland)	70.00	31.00	17.50
6	Bill Sherdel	70.00	31.00	17.50
7	Bill Shore	70.00	31.00	17.50
8	Geo. Earnshaw	70.00	31.00	17.50
9	Bucky Harris	150.00	67.00	37.00
10	Charlie Klein	150.00	67.00	37.00
11a	Geo. Kelly (Reds)	70.00	31.00	17.50
11b	Geo. Kelly (Brooklyn)	70.00	31.00	17.50
12	Travis Jackson	150.00	67.00	37.00
13	Willie Kamm	70.00	31.00	17.50
14	Harry Heilman (Heilmann)	150.00	67.00	37.00
15	Grover Alexander	150.00	67.00	37.00
16	Frank Frisch	150.00	67.00	37.00
17	Jack Quinn	70.00	31.00	17.50
18	Cy Williams	70.00	31.00	17.50
19	Kiki Cuyler	150.00	67.00	37.00
20	Babe Ruth	1250.	562.00	312.00
21	Jimmie Foxx	160.00	72.00	40.00
22	Jimmy Dykes	70.00	31.00	17.50
23	Bill Terry	150.00	67.00	37.00
24	Freddy Lindstrom	150.00	67.00	37.00
25	Hughey Critz	70.00	31.00	17.50
26	Pete Donahue	70.00	31.00	17.50
27	Tony Lazzeri	150.00	67.00	37.00
28	Heine Manush (Heinie)	150.00	67.00	37.00
29a	Chick Hafey (Cardinals)	150.00	67.00	37.00
29b	Chick Hafey (Cincinnati)	150.00	67.00	37.00
30	Melvin Ott	150.00	67.00	37.00
31	Bing Miller	70.00	31.00	17.50
32	Geo. Haas	70.00	31.00	17.50
33a	Lefty O'Doul (Phillies)	90.00	40.00	22.00
33b	Lefty O'Doul (Brooklyn)	90.00	40.00	22.00
34	Paul Waner	150.00	67.00	37.00
35	Lou Gehrig	1200.	600.00	300.00
36	Dazzy Vance	150.00	67.00	37.00
37	Mickey Cochrane	150.00	67.00	37.00
38	Rogers Hornsby	160.00	72.00	40.00
39	Lefty Grove	150.00	67.00	37.00
40	Al Simmons	150.00	67.00	37.00
41	Rube Walberg	70.00	31.00	17.50
42	Hack Wilson	150.00	67.00	37.00
43	Art Shires	70.00	31.00	17.50
44	Sammy Hale	70.00	31.00	17.50
45	Ted Lyons	150.00	67.00	37.00
46	Joe Sewell	150.00	67.00	37.00
47	Goose Goslin	150.00	67.00	37.00
48	Lou Fonseca (Lew)	70.00	31.00	17.50
49	Bob Muesel (Meusel)	70.00	31.00	17.50
50	Lu Blue	70.00	31.00	17.50
51	Earl Averill	150.00	67.00	37.00
52	Eddy Collins (Eddie)	150.00	67.00	37.00
53	Joe Judge	70.00	31.00	17.50
54	Mickey Cochrane	150.00	67.00	37.00

1931 W517 Mini

Little is known about these smaller-format (1-3/4" x 2-3/4") versions of the W517 strip cards. They are identical in design to the more common 3" x 4" cards. It is presumed, though not confirmed, that all 54 of the regular versions can be found in the mini size, as well as several color variations.

VALUES UNDETERMINED
(See W517 for checklist.)

1920 W519 - Numbered

Cards in this 20-card "strip set" measure 1-1/2" x 2-1/2" and feature player drawings set against a brightly colored background. A card number appears in the lower-left corner followed by the player's name, printed in capital letters. The player drawings are all posed portraits, except for Joe Murphy and Ernie Kreuger, who are shown catching. Like all strip cards, the cards were sold in strips and have blank backs. The date of issue may be approximate.

		NM	EX	VG
	Complete Set (20):	1000.	400.00	200.00
	Common Player:	30.00	12.00	6.00
1	Guy Morton	30.00	12.00	6.00
2	Rube Marquard	60.00	24.00	12.00
3	Gabby Cravath (Gavvy)	30.00	12.00	6.00
4	Ernie Krueger	30.00	12.00	6.00
5	Babe Ruth	400.00	160.00	80.00
6	George Sisler	60.00	24.00	12.00
7	Rube Benton	30.00	12.00	6.00
8	Jimmie Johnston	30.00	12.00	6.00
9	Wilbur Robinson (Wilbert)	60.00	24.00	12.00
10	Johnny Griffith	30.00	12.00	6.00
11	Frank Baker	60.00	24.00	12.00
12	Bob Veach	30.00	12.00	6.00
13	Jesse Barnes	30.00	12.00	6.00
14	Leon Cadore	30.00	12.00	6.00
15	Ray Schalk	60.00	24.00	12.00
16	Kid Gleasen (Gleason)	30.00	12.00	6.00
17	Joe Murphy	30.00	12.00	6.00
18	Frank Frisch	60.00	24.00	12.00
19	Eddie Collins	60.00	24.00	12.00
20	Wallie Schang	30.00	12.00	6.00

1920 W519 - Unnumbered

Cards in this 10-card set are identical in design and size (1-1/2" x 2-1/2") to the W519 Numbered set, except the player drawings are all set against a blue background and the cards are not numbered. With the lone exception of Eddie Ciotte, all of the subjects in the unnumbered set also appear in the numbered set.

		NM	EX	VG
	Complete Set (10):	700.00	280.00	140.00
	Common Player:	30.00	12.00	6.00
(1)	Eddie Cicotte	60.00	24.00	12.00
(2)	Eddie Collins	60.00	24.00	12.00
(3)	Gabby Cravath (Gavvy)	30.00	12.00	6.00
(4)	Frank Frisch	60.00	24.00	12.00
(5)	Kid Gleasen (Gleason)	30.00	12.00	6.00
(6)	Ernie Kreuger	30.00	12.00	6.00
(7)	Rube Marquard	60.00	24.00	12.00
(8)	Guy Morton	30.00	12.00	6.00
(9)	Joe Murphy	30.00	12.00	6.00
(10)	Babe Ruth	400.00	160.00	80.00

1920 W520

Another "strip card" set issued circa 1920, cards in this set measure 1-3/8" x 2-1/4" and are numbered in the lower-right corner. The first nine cards in the set display portrait poses, while the rest are full-length action poses. Some of the poses in this set are the same as those in the W516 issue with the pictures reversed. The player's last name appears in the border beneath the picture. The cards are blank-backed.

		NM	EX	VG
	Complete Set (20):	1500.	600.00	300.00
	Common Player:	32.00	13.00	6.50
1	Dave Bancroft	90.00	36.00	18.00
2	Christy Mathewson	225.00	90.00	45.00
3	Larry Doyle	32.00	13.00	6.50
4	Jess Barnes	32.00	13.00	6.50
5	Art Fletcher	32.00	13.00	6.50
6	Wilbur Cooper	32.00	13.00	6.50
7	Mike Gonzales (Gonzalez)	50.00	20.00	10.00
8	Zach Wheat	90.00	36.00	18.00
9	Tris Speaker	100.00	40.00	20.00
10	Benny Kauff	32.00	13.00	6.50
11	Zach Wheat	90.00	36.00	18.00
12	Phil Douglas	32.00	13.00	6.50
13	Babe Ruth	500.00	200.00	100.00
14	Stan Koveleski (Coveleski)	90.00	36.00	18.00
15	Goldie Rapp	32.00	13.00	6.50
16	Pol Perritt	32.00	13.00	6.50
17	Otto Miller	32.00	13.00	6.50
18	George Kelly	90.00	36.00	18.00
19	Mike Gonzales (Gonzalez)	50.00	20.00	10.00
20	Les Nunamaker	32.00	13.00	6.50

1921 W521

This issue is closely related to the W519 Numbered set. In fact, it uses the same color drawings as that set with the pictures reversed, resulting in a mirror-image of the W519 cards. The player poses and the numbering system are identical, as are the various background colors. The W521 cards are blank-backed and were sold in strips.

		NM	EX	VG
	Complete Set (20):	1000.	400.00	200.00
	Common Player:	30.00	12.00	6.00
1	Guy Morton	30.00	12.00	6.00
2	Rube Marquard	60.00	24.00	12.00
3	Gabby Cravath (Gavvy)	30.00	12.00	6.00
4	Ernie Krueger	30.00	12.00	6.00
5	Babe Ruth	400.00	160.00	80.00
6	George Sisler	60.00	24.00	12.00
7	Rube Benton	30.00	12.00	6.00
8	Jimmie Johnston	30.00	12.00	6.00
9	Wilbur Robinson (Wilbert)	60.00	24.00	12.00
10	Johnny Griffith	30.00	12.00	6.00
11	Frank Baker	60.00	24.00	12.00
12	Bob Veach	30.00	12.00	6.00
13	Jesse Barnes	30.00	12.00	6.00
14	Leon Cadore	30.00	12.00	6.00
15	Ray Schalk	60.00	24.00	12.00
16	Kid Gleasen (Gleason)	30.00	12.00	6.00
17	Joe Murphy	30.00	12.00	6.00
18	Frank Frisch	60.00	24.00	12.00
19	Eddie Collins	60.00	24.00	12.00
20	Wallie Schang	30.00	12.00	6.00

1920 W522

The 20 cards in this "strip card" set, issued circa 1920, are numbered from 31-50 and use the same players and drawings as the W520 set, issued about the same time. The cards measure 1-3/8" x 2-1/4" and are numbered in the lower left corner followed by the player's name. The cards have blank backs.

		NM	EX	VG
	Complete Set (20):	1300.	520.00	260.00
	Common Player:	30.00	12.00	6.00
31	Benny Kauf (Kauff)	30.00	12.00	6.00
32	Tris Speaker	85.00	34.00	17.00
33	Zach Wheat	80.00	32.00	16.00
34	Mike Gonzales (Gonzalez)	55.00	22.00	11.00
35	Wilbur Cooper	30.00	12.00	6.00
36	Art Fletcher	30.00	12.00	6.00
37	Jess Barnes	30.00	12.00	6.00
38	Larry Doyle	30.00	12.00	6.00
39	Christy Mathewson	200.00	80.00	40.00
40	Dave Bancroft	80.00	32.00	16.00
41	Les Nunamaker	30.00	12.00	6.00
42	Mike Gonzales (Gonzalez)	55.00	22.00	11.00
43	George Kelly	80.00	32.00	16.00
44	Otto Miller	30.00	12.00	6.00
45	Pol Perritt	30.00	12.00	6.00
46	Goldie Rapp	30.00	12.00	6.00
47	Stan Koveleski (Coveleski)	80.00	32.00	16.00
48	Babe Ruth	450.00	180.00	90.00
49	Phil Douglas	30.00	12.00	6.00
50	Zach Wheat	80.00	32.00	16.00

1921 W551

Another "strip set" issued circa 1920, these ten cards measure 1-3/8" x 2-1/4" and feature color drawings. The cards are unnumbered and blank-backed.

		NM	EX	VG
	Complete Set (10):	850.00	325.00	175.00
	Complete Set, Uncut Strip:	900.00	350.00	190.00
	Common Player:	30.00	12.00	6.00
(1)	Frank Baker	65.00	26.00	13.00
(2)	Dave Bancroft	65.00	26.00	13.00
(3)	Jess Barnes	30.00	12.00	6.00
(4)	Ty Cobb	190.00	76.00	38.00
(5)	Walter Johnson	90.00	36.00	18.00
(6)	Wally Pipp	30.00	12.00	6.00
(7)	Babe Ruth	375.00	150.00	75.00
(8)	George Sisler	65.00	26.00	13.00
(9)	Tris Speaker	75.00	30.00	15.00
(10)	Casey Stengel	75.00	30.00	15.00

1929 W553

One of the more obscure strip card sets, and one of the last of the genre, this issue also is one of the most attractive. Player photos - the same pictures used in the contemporary Kashin Publications (R316) boxed set and anonymous W554 strip cards - are printed in either black on white on black on magenta, with an ornate frame. Cards measure 1-3/4" x 2-3/4". There is a facsimile autograph on front and the player's team and league are also spelled out. Backs are blank. According to "The Sports Collectors Bible," about a dozen different cards are known, so this list is obviously incomplete.

	NM	EX	VG
Burleigh Grimes	125.00	50.00	24.00
Babe Ruth	900.00	350.00	175.00

1930 W554

This unidentified set of black-and-photos features most of the era's stars in action poses. A facsimile autograph appears on the front of each of the blank-back 5" x 7" pictures. Player names and teams are spelled out in all-capital letters in the bottom white border, with the position in upper- and lower-case between. The unnumbered pictures are checklisted here in alphabetical order.

	NM	EX	VG
Complete Set (18):	2100.	840.00	420.00
Common Player:	60.00	30.00	18.00
(1) Gordon S. (Mickey) Cochrane	90.00	36.00	18.00
(2) Lewis A. Fonseca	60.00	24.00	12.00
(3) Jimmy Foxx (Jimmie)	100.00	40.00	20.00
(4) Lou Gehrig	350.00	140.00	70.00
(5) Burleigh Grimes	90.00	36.00	18.00
(6) Robert M. Grove	90.00	36.00	18.00
(7) Waite Hoyt	90.00	36.00	18.00
(8) Joe Judge	60.00	24.00	12.00
(9) Charles (Chuck) Klein	90.00	36.00	18.00
(10) Douglas McWeeny	60.00	24.00	12.00
(11) Frank O'Doul	75.00	30.00	15.00
(12) Melvin Ott	100.00	40.00	20.00
(13) Herbert Pennock	90.00	36.00	18.00
(14) Eddie Rommel	60.00	24.00	12.00
(15) Babe Ruth	700.00	280.00	140.00
(16) Al Simmons	90.00	36.00	18.00
(17) Lloyd Waner	90.00	36.00	18.00
(18) Hack Wilson	100.00	40.00	20.00

1907 W555

Designated as W555 in the American Card Catalog, very little is known about this obscure set. The nearly sqaure cards measure only 1-1/8" x 1-3-16" and feature a sepia-colored player photo. Sixty-six different cards have been discovered to date, but others may exist. The manufacturer of the set is unknown, but the sets appear to be related to a series of contemporary candy cards (E93, E94, E97 and E98) because, with only two exceptions, the players and poses are the same. It is not known how the cards were issued. There is speculation that they may have been issued as "strip" cards or as part of a candy box.

	NM	EX	VG
Complete Set (66):	8625.	3450.	1725.
Common Player:	75.00	30.00	15.00
(1) Red Ames	75.00	30.00	15.00
(2) Jimmy Austin	75.00	30.00	15.00
(3) Johnny Bates	75.00	30.00	15.00
(4) Chief Bender	225.00	90.00	45.00
(5) Bob Bescher	75.00	30.00	15.00
(6) Joe Birmingham	75.00	30.00	15.00
(7) Bill Bradley	75.00	30.00	15.00
(8) Kitty Bransfield	75.00	30.00	15.00
(9) Mordecai Brown	225.00	90.00	45.00
(10) Bobby Byrne	75.00	30.00	15.00
(11) Frank Chance	225.00	90.00	45.00
(12) Hal Chase	100.00	40.00	20.00
(13) Ed Cicotte	150.00	60.00	30.00
(14) Fred Clarke	225.00	90.00	45.00
(15) Ty Cobb	900.00	360.00	180.00
(16) Eddie Collins (dark uniform)	225.00	90.00	45.00
(17) Eddie Collins (light uniform)	225.00	90.00	45.00
(18) Harry Coveleskie (Coveleski)	75.00	30.00	15.00
(19) Sam Crawford	225.00	90.00	45.00
(20) Harry Davis	75.00	30.00	15.00
(21) Jim Delehanty (Delahanty)	75.00	30.00	15.00
(22) Art Devlin	75.00	30.00	15.00
(23) Josh Devore	75.00	30.00	15.00
(24) Wild Bill Donovan	75.00	30.00	15.00
(25) Red Dooin	75.00	30.00	15.00
(26) Mickey Doolan	75.00	30.00	15.00
(27) Bull Durham	75.00	30.00	15.00
(28) Jimmy Dygert	75.00	30.00	15.00
(29) Johnny Evers	225.00	90.00	45.00
(30) Russ Ford	75.00	30.00	15.00
(31) George Gibson	75.00	30.00	15.00
(32) Clark Griffith	225.00	90.00	45.00
(33) Topsy Hartsell (Hartsel)	75.00	30.00	15.00
(34) Bill Heinchman (Hinchman)	75.00	30.00	15.00
(35) Ira Hemphill	75.00	30.00	15.00
(36) Hughie Jennings	225.00	90.00	45.00
(37) Davy Jones	75.00	30.00	15.00
(38) Addie Joss	250.00	100.00	50.00
(39) Wee Willie Keeler	225.00	90.00	45.00
(40) Red Kleinow	75.00	30.00	15.00
(41) Nap Lajoie	250.00	100.00	50.00
(42) Joe Lake	75.00	30.00	15.00
(43) Tommy Leach	75.00	30.00	15.00
(44) Sherry Magee	75.00	30.00	15.00
(45) Christy Mathewson	375.00	150.00	75.00
(46) Amby McConnell	75.00	30.00	15.00
(47) John McGraw	225.00	90.00	45.00
(48) Chief Meyers	75.00	30.00	15.00
(49) Earl Moore	75.00	30.00	15.00
(50) Mike Mowery	75.00	30.00	15.00
(51) George Mullin	75.00	30.00	15.00
(52) Red Murray	75.00	30.00	15.00
(53) Nichols	75.00	30.00	15.00
(54) Jim Pastorious (Pastorius)	75.00	30.00	15.00
(55) Deacon Phillippi (Phillippe)	75.00	30.00	15.00
(56) Eddie Plank	225.00	90.00	45.00
(57) Fred Snodgrass	75.00	30.00	15.00
(58) Harry Steinfeldt	75.00	30.00	15.00
(59) Joe Tinker	225.00	90.00	45.00
(60) Hippo Vaughn	75.00	30.00	15.00
(61) Honus Wagner	975.00	390.00	195.00
(62) Rube Waddell	225.00	90.00	45.00
(63) Hooks Wiltse	75.00	30.00	15.00
(64a) Cy Young (standing, full name on front)	300.00	120.00	60.00
(64b) Cy Young (standing, last name on front)	300.00	120.00	60.00
(65) Cy Young (portrait)	300.00	120.00	60.00

1927 W560

Although assigned a "W" number by the American Card Catalog, this is not a "strip card" issue in the same sense as most other "W" sets, although W560 cards are frequently found in uncut sheets of 16 cards, in four rows of four cards each. Cards in the W560 set measure 1-3/4" x 2-3/4" and are designed like a deck of playing cards, with the pictures on the various suits. The set includes aviators and other athletes in addition to baseball players. Because they are designed as a deck of playing cards, the cards are printed in either red or black.

	NM	EX	VG
Complete (Baseball) Set (49):	2300.	950.00	475.00
Common Player:	30.00	12.00	6.00
(1) Vic Aldridge	30.00	12.00	6.00
(2) Lester Bell	30.00	12.00	6.00
(3) Larry Benton	30.00	12.00	6.00
(4) Max Bishop	30.00	12.00	6.00
(5) Del Bissonette	30.00	12.00	6.00
(6) Jim Bottomley	55.00	22.00	11.00
(7) Guy Bush	30.00	12.00	6.00
(8) W. Clark	30.00	12.00	6.00
(9) Andy Cohen	30.00	12.00	6.00
(10) Mickey Cochrane	55.00	22.00	11.00
(11) Hugh Critz	30.00	12.00	6.00
(12) Kiki Cuyler	55.00	22.00	11.00
(13) Taylor Douthit	30.00	12.00	6.00
(14) Fred Fitzsimmons	30.00	12.00	6.00
(15) Jim Foxx	75.00	30.00	15.00
(16) Lou Gehrig	500.00	200.00	100.00
(17) Goose Goslin	55.00	22.00	11.00
(18) Sam Gray	30.00	12.00	6.00
(19) Lefty Grove	55.00	22.00	11.00
(20) Jesse Haines	55.00	22.00	11.00
(21) Babe Herman	35.00	14.00	7.00
(22) Roger Hornsby (Rogers)	75.00	30.00	15.00
(23) Waite Hoyt	55.00	22.00	11.00
(24) Henry Johnson	30.00	12.00	6.00
(25) Walter Johnson	175.00	70.00	35.00
(26) Willie Kamm	30.00	12.00	6.00
(27) Remy Kremer	30.00	12.00	6.00
(28) Fred Lindstrom	55.00	22.00	11.00
(29) Fred Maguire	30.00	12.00	6.00
(30) Fred Marberry	30.00	12.00	6.00
(31) Johnny Mostil	30.00	12.00	6.00
(32) Buddy Myer	30.00	12.00	6.00
(33) Herb Pennock	55.00	22.00	11.00
(34) George Pipgras	30.00	12.00	6.00
(35) Flint Rhem	30.00	12.00	6.00
(36) Babe Ruth	600.00	240.00	120.00
(37) Luke Sewell	30.00	12.00	6.00
(38) Willie Sherdel	30.00	12.00	6.00
(39) Al Simmons	55.00	22.00	11.00
(40) Thomas Thevenow	30.00	12.00	6.00
(41) Fresco Thompson	30.00	12.00	6.00
(42) George Uhle	30.00	12.00	6.00
(43) Dazzy Vance	55.00	22.00	11.00
(44) Rube Walberg	30.00	12.00	6.00
(45) Lloyd Waner	55.00	22.00	11.00
(46) Paul Waner	55.00	22.00	11.00
(47) Fred "Cy" Williams	30.00	12.00	6.00
(48) Jim Wilson	30.00	12.00	6.00
(49) Glen Wright (Glenn)	30.00	12.00	6.00

1928 W565

Similar in concept to W560, the 50 cards comprising this set were printed on two 7" x 10-1/2" sheets of cheap cardboard, one in black-and-white and one in red-and-white, each with navy blue backs. Most of the cards in the issue are of movie stars, with a few boxers, ballplayers and other notables included. While most of the cards depict the person in the center of a playing card format, it is interesting to note that a full deck of cards cannot be made up by cutting the sheets. Individual cards are 1-1/4" x 2-1/8". Only the baseball players are listed here.

	NM	EX	VG
Complete Set (50):	1850.	740.00	375.00
Common Player:	35.00	14.00	7.00
(1) Lou Gehrig	200.00	80.00	40.00
(2) Harry Heilmann	35.00	14.00	7.00
(3) Tony Lazzeri	35.00	14.00	7.00
(4) Al Simmons	35.00	14.00	7.00

1923 W572

These cards, designated as W572 by the American Card Catalog, measure 1-5/16" x 2-1/2" and are blank-backed. Fronts feature black-and-white or sepia player photos. The set is closely related to the popular E120 American Caramel set issued in 1922 and, with the exception of Ty Cobb, it uses the same photos. The cards were originally issued as strips of ten, with five baseball players and five boxers. They are found on either a white, slick stock or a dark, coarser cardboard. The player's name on the front of the cards appears in script. All cards have on front a copyright symbol and one of several alphabetical combinations indicating the source of the photo. The baseball players from the set are checklisted here in alphabetical order.

		NM	EX	VG
Complete (Baseball) Set (121):		6500.	2600.	1300.
Common Player:		35.00	14.00	7.00
(1)	Eddie Ainsmith	35.00	14.00	7.00
(2)	Vic Aldridge	35.00	14.00	7.00
(3)	Grover Alexander	90.00	36.00	18.00
(4)	Dave Bancroft	80.00	32.00	16.00
(5)	Walt Barbare	35.00	14.00	7.00
(6)	Jess Barnes	35.00	14.00	7.00
(7)	John Bassler	35.00	14.00	7.00
(8)	Lu Blue	35.00	14.00	7.00
(9)	Norman Boeckel	35.00	14.00	7.00
(10)	George Burns	35.00	14.00	7.00
(11)	Joe Bush	35.00	14.00	7.00
(12)	Leon Cadore	35.00	14.00	7.00
(13)	Virgil Cheevers (Cheeves)	35.00	14.00	7.00
(14)	Ty Cobb	1100.	440.00	220.00
(15)	Eddie Collins	80.00	32.00	16.00
(16)	John Collins	35.00	14.00	7.00
(17)	Wilbur Cooper	35.00	14.00	7.00
(18)	Stanley Coveleski	80.00	32.00	16.00
(19)	Walton Cruise	35.00	14.00	7.00
(20)	Dave Danforth	35.00	14.00	7.00
(21)	Jake Daubert	35.00	14.00	7.00
(22)	Hank DeBerry	35.00	14.00	7.00
(23)	Lou DeVormer	35.00	14.00	7.00
(24)	Bill Doak	35.00	14.00	7.00
(25)	Pete Donohue	35.00	14.00	7.00
(26)	Pat Duncan	35.00	14.00	7.00
(27)	Jimmy Dykes	35.00	14.00	7.00
(28)	Urban Faber	80.00	32.00	16.00
(29)	Bib Falk (Bibb)	35.00	14.00	7.00
(30)	Frank Frisch	80.00	32.00	16.00
(31)	C. Galloway	35.00	14.00	7.00
(32)	Ed Gharrity	35.00	14.00	7.00
(33)	Chas. Glazner	35.00	14.00	7.00
(34)	Hank Gowdy	35.00	14.00	7.00
(35)	Tom Griffith	35.00	14.00	7.00
(36)	Burleigh Grimes	80.00	32.00	16.00
(37)	Ray Grimes	35.00	14.00	7.00
(38)	Heinie Groh	35.00	14.00	7.00
(39)	Joe Harris	35.00	14.00	7.00
(40)	Stanley Harris	80.00	32.00	16.00
(41)	Joe Hauser	40.00	16.00	8.00
(42)	Harry Heilmann	80.00	32.00	16.00
(43)	Walter Henline	35.00	14.00	7.00
(44)	Chas. Hollocher	35.00	14.00	7.00
(45)	Harry Hooper	80.00	32.00	16.00
(46)	Rogers Hornsby	90.00	36.00	18.00
(47)	Waite Hoyt	80.00	32.00	16.00
(48)	Wilbur Hubbell	35.00	14.00	7.00
(49)	Wm. Jacobson	35.00	14.00	7.00
(50)	Chas. Jamieson	35.00	14.00	7.00
(51)	S. Johnson	35.00	14.00	7.00
(52)	Walter Johnson	250.00	100.00	50.00
(53)	Jimmy Johnston	35.00	14.00	7.00
(54)	Joe Judge	35.00	14.00	7.00
(55)	Geo. Kelly	80.00	32.00	16.00
(56)	Lee King	35.00	14.00	7.00
(57)	Larry Kopff (Kopf)	35.00	14.00	7.00
(58)	Geo. Leverette	35.00	14.00	7.00
(59)	Al Mamaux	35.00	14.00	7.00
(60)	"Rabbit" Maranville	80.00	32.00	16.00
(61)	"Rube" Marquard	80.00	32.00	16.00
(62)	Martin McManus	35.00	14.00	7.00
(63)	Lee Meadows	35.00	14.00	7.00
(64)	Mike Menosky	35.00	14.00	7.00
(65)	Bob Meusel	40.00	16.00	8.00
(66)	Emil Meusel	35.00	14.00	7.00
(67)	Geo. Mogridge	35.00	14.00	7.00
(68)	John Morrison	35.00	14.00	7.00
(69)	Johnny Mostil	35.00	14.00	7.00
(70)	Roliene Naylor	35.00	14.00	7.00
(71)	Art Nehf	35.00	14.00	7.00
(72)	Joe Oeschger	35.00	14.00	7.00
(73)	Bob O'Farrell	35.00	14.00	7.00
(74)	Steve O'Neill	35.00	14.00	7.00
(75)	Frank Parkinson	35.00	14.00	7.00
(76)	Ralph Perkins	35.00	14.00	7.00
(77)	H. Pillette	35.00	14.00	7.00
(78)	Ralph Pinelli	35.00	14.00	7.00
(79)	Wallie Pipp (Wally)	40.00	16.00	8.00
(80)	Ray Powell	35.00	14.00	7.00
(81)	Jack Quinn	35.00	14.00	7.00
(82)	Goldie Rapp	35.00	14.00	7.00
(83)	Walter Reuther	35.00	14.00	7.00
(84)	Sam Rice	80.00	32.00	16.00
(85)	Emory Rigney	35.00	14.00	7.00
(86)	Eppa Rixey	80.00	32.00	16.00
(87)	Ed Rommel	35.00	14.00	7.00
(88)	Eddie Roush	80.00	32.00	16.00
(89)	Babe Ruth	1200.	480.00	240.00
(90)	Ray Schalk	80.00	32.00	16.00
(91)	Wallie Schang (Wally)	35.00	14.00	7.00
(92)	Walter Schmidt	35.00	14.00	7.00
(93)	Joe Schultz	35.00	14.00	7.00
(94)	Hank Severeid	35.00	14.00	7.00
(95)	Joe Sewell	80.00	32.00	16.00
(96)	Bob Shawkey	35.00	14.00	7.00
(97)	Earl Sheely	35.00	14.00	7.00
(98)	Will Sherdel	35.00	14.00	7.00
(99)	Urban Shocker	35.00	14.00	7.00
(100)	George Sisler	80.00	32.00	16.00
(101)	Earl Smith	35.00	14.00	7.00
(102)	Elmer Smith	35.00	14.00	7.00
(103)	Jack Smith	35.00	14.00	7.00
(104)	Bill Southworth	35.00	14.00	7.00
(105)	Tris Speaker	90.00	36.00	18.00
(106)	Arnold Statz	45.00	18.00	9.00
(107)	Milton Stock	35.00	14.00	7.00
(108)	Jim Tierney	35.00	14.00	7.00
(109)	Harold Traynor	80.00	32.00	16.00
(110)	Geo. Uhle	35.00	14.00	7.00
(111)	Bob Veach	35.00	14.00	7.00
(112)	Clarence Walker	35.00	14.00	7.00
(113)	Curtis Walker	35.00	14.00	7.00
(114)	Bill Wambsganss	35.00	14.00	7.00
(115)	Aaron Ward	35.00	14.00	7.00
(116)	Zach Wheat	80.00	32.00	16.00
(117)	Fred Williams	35.00	14.00	7.00
(118)	Ken Williams	35.00	14.00	7.00
(119)	Ivy Wingo	35.00	14.00	7.00
(120)	Joe Wood	35.00	14.00	7.00
(121)	J.T. Zachary	35.00	14.00	7.00

1922 W573

These cards, identified as W573 in the American Card Catalog, appear to be blank-backed versions of the popular E120 American Caramel set. In reality they are "strip cards," produced in 1922 and sold in strips of 10 for a penny. The cards feature black-and-white photos. To date 144 different subjects have been found, but it is possible that all 240 poses from the E120 set may exist.

		NM	EX	VG
Complete Set (144):		6500.	2600.	1300.
Common Player:		40.00	16.00	8.00
(1)	Babe Adams	40.00	16.00	8.00
(2)	Eddie Ainsmith	40.00	16.00	8.00
(3)	Vic Aldridge	40.00	16.00	8.00
(4)	Grover Alexander	90.00	36.00	18.00
(5)	Home Run Baker	90.00	36.00	18.00
(6)	Dave Bancroft	90.00	36.00	18.00
(7)	Walt Barbare	40.00	16.00	8.00
(8)	Turner Barber	40.00	16.00	8.00
(9)	Jess Barnes	40.00	16.00	8.00
(10)	John Bassler	40.00	16.00	8.00
(11)	Carson Bigbee	40.00	16.00	8.00
(12)	Lu Blue	40.00	16.00	8.00
(13)	Norman Boeckel	40.00	16.00	8.00
(14)	Geo. Burns (Boston)	40.00	16.00	8.00
(15)	Geo. Burns (Cincinnati)	40.00	16.00	8.00
(16)	Marty Callaghan	40.00	16.00	8.00
(17)	Max Carey	90.00	36.00	18.00
(18)	Jimmy Caveney	40.00	16.00	8.00
(19)	Virgil Cheeves	40.00	16.00	8.00
(20)	Vern Clemons	40.00	16.00	8.00
(21)	Ty Cobb	675.00	270.00	135.00
(22)	Bert Cole	40.00	16.00	8.00
(23)	Eddie Collins	90.00	36.00	18.00
(24)	Pat Collins	40.00	16.00	8.00
(25)	Wilbur Cooper	40.00	16.00	8.00
(26)	Elmer Cox	40.00	16.00	8.00
(27)	Bill Cunningham	40.00	16.00	8.00
(28)	George Cutshaw	40.00	16.00	8.00
(29)	Dave Danforth	40.00	16.00	8.00
(30)	George Dauss	40.00	16.00	8.00
(31)	Dixie Davis	40.00	16.00	8.00
(32)	Hank DeBerry	40.00	16.00	8.00
(33)	Lou DeVormer	40.00	16.00	8.00
(34)	Bill Doak	40.00	16.00	8.00
(35)	Joe Dugan	40.00	16.00	8.00
(36)	Howard Ehmke	40.00	16.00	8.00
(37)	Frank Ellerbe	40.00	16.00	8.00
(38)	Urban Faber	90.00	36.00	18.00
(39)	Bib Falk (Bibb)	40.00	16.00	8.00
(40)	Max Flack	40.00	16.00	8.00
(41)	Ira Flagstead	40.00	16.00	8.00
(42)	Art Fletcher	40.00	16.00	8.00
(43)	Horace Ford	40.00	16.00	8.00
(44)	Jack Fournier	40.00	16.00	8.00
(45)	Frank Frisch	90.00	36.00	18.00
(46)	Ollie Fuhrman	40.00	16.00	8.00
(47)	C. Galloway	40.00	16.00	8.00
(48)	Walter Gerber	40.00	16.00	8.00
(49)	Ed Gharrity	40.00	16.00	8.00
(50)	Chas. Glazner	40.00	16.00	8.00
(51)	Leon Goslin	90.00	36.00	18.00
(52)	Hank Gowdy	40.00	16.00	8.00
(53)	John Graney	40.00	16.00	8.00
(54)	Ray Grimes	40.00	16.00	8.00
(55)	Heinie Groh	40.00	16.00	8.00
(56)	Jesse Haines	90.00	36.00	18.00
(57)	Earl Hamilton	40.00	16.00	8.00
(58)	Bubbles Hargrave	40.00	16.00	8.00
(59)	Bryan Harris	40.00	16.00	8.00
(60)	Cliff Heathcote	40.00	16.00	8.00
(61)	Harry Heilmann	90.00	36.00	18.00
(62)	Clarence Hodge	40.00	16.00	8.00
(63)	Chas. Hollocher	40.00	16.00	8.00
(64)	Harry Hooper	90.00	36.00	18.00
(65)	Rogers Hornsby	90.00	36.00	18.00
(66)	Waite Hoyt	90.00	36.00	18.00
(67)	Ernie Johnson	40.00	16.00	8.00
(68)	S. Johnson	40.00	16.00	8.00
(69)	Walter Johnson	175.00	70.00	35.00
(70)	Doc Johnston	40.00	16.00	8.00
(71)	Sam Jones	40.00	16.00	8.00
(72)	Ben Karr	40.00	16.00	8.00
(73)	Johnny Lavan	40.00	16.00	8.00
(74)	Geo. Leverette	40.00	16.00	8.00
(75)	"Rabbit" Maranville	90.00	36.00	18.00
(76)	Cliff Markle	40.00	16.00	8.00
(77)	Carl Mays	50.00	20.00	10.00
(78)	Hervey McClellan	40.00	16.00	8.00
(79)	Martin McManus	40.00	16.00	8.00
(80)	Lee Meadows	40.00	16.00	8.00
(81)	Mike Menosky	40.00	16.00	8.00
(82)	Emil Meusel	40.00	16.00	8.00
(83)	Clyde Milan	40.00	16.00	8.00
(84)	Bing Miller	40.00	16.00	8.00
(85)	Elmer Miller	40.00	16.00	8.00
(86)	Lawrence Miller	40.00	16.00	8.00
(87)	Clarence Mitchell	40.00	16.00	8.00
(88)	Geo. Mogridge	40.00	16.00	8.00
(89)	John Morrison	40.00	16.00	8.00
(90)	Johnny Mostil	40.00	16.00	8.00
(91)	Elmer Meyers	40.00	16.00	8.00
(92)	Roliene Naylor	40.00	16.00	8.00
(93)	Les Nunamaker	40.00	16.00	8.00
(94)	Bob O'Farrell	40.00	16.00	8.00
(95)	George O'Neil	40.00	16.00	8.00
(96)	Steve O'Neill	40.00	16.00	8.00
(97)	Herb Pennock	90.00	36.00	18.00
(98)	Ralph Perkins	40.00	16.00	8.00
(99)	Tom Phillips	40.00	16.00	8.00
(100)	Val Picinich	40.00	16.00	8.00
(101)	H. Pillette	40.00	16.00	8.00
(102)	Ralph Pinelli	40.00	16.00	8.00
(103)	Wallie Pipp (Wally)	50.00	20.00	10.00
(104)	Clark Pittenger	40.00	16.00	8.00
(105)	Derrill Pratt	40.00	16.00	8.00
(106)	Goldie Rapp	40.00	16.00	8.00
(107)	John Rawlings	40.00	16.00	8.00
(108)	Walter Reuther	40.00	16.00	8.00
(109)	Emory Rigney	40.00	16.00	8.00
(110)	Charles Robertson	40.00	16.00	8.00
(111)	Ed Rommel	40.00	16.00	8.00
(112)	Muddy Ruel	40.00	16.00	8.00
(113)	Babe Ruth	900.00	360.00	180.00
(114)	Ray Schalk	90.00	36.00	18.00
(115)	Wallie Schang	40.00	16.00	8.00
(116)	Ray Schmidt	40.00	16.00	8.00
(117)	Walter Schmidt	40.00	16.00	8.00
(118)	Joe Schultz	40.00	16.00	8.00
(119)	Hank Severeid	40.00	16.00	8.00
(120)	Joe Sewell	90.00	36.00	18.00
(121)	Bob Shawkey	40.00	16.00	8.00
(122)	Earl Sheely	40.00	16.00	8.00
(123)	Ralph Shinner	40.00	16.00	8.00
(124)	Urban Shocker	40.00	16.00	8.00
(125)	George Sisler	90.00	36.00	18.00
(126)	Earl Smith (Washington)	40.00	16.00	8.00
(127)	Earl Smith (New York)	40.00	16.00	8.00
(128)	Jack Smith	40.00	16.00	8.00
(129)	Al Sothoron	40.00	16.00	8.00
(130)	Tris Speaker	90.00	36.00	18.00
(131)	Amos Strunk	40.00	16.00	8.00
(132)	Jim Tierney	40.00	16.00	8.00
(133)	John Tobin	40.00	16.00	8.00
(134)	George Toporcer	40.00	16.00	8.00
(135)	Harold (Pie) Traynor	90.00	36.00	18.00
(136)	Geo. Uhle	40.00	16.00	8.00
(137)	Bob Veach	40.00	16.00	8.00
(138)	John Watson	40.00	16.00	8.00
(139)	Zach Wheat	90.00	36.00	18.00
(140)	Fred Williams	45.00	18.00	9.00
(141)	Ken Williams	40.00	16.00	8.00
(142)	Lawrence Woodall	40.00	16.00	8.00
(143)	Russell Wrightstone	40.00	16.00	8.00
(144)	Ross Young (Youngs)	90.00	36.00	18.00
(145)	J.T. Zachary	40.00	16.00	8.00

1932 W574

Issued circa 1932, cards in the W574 set measure 2-1/4" x 2-7/8". They are unnumbered and are listed here in alphabetical order. The black-and-white photos have a facsimile autograph and team name at bottom.

		NM	EX	VG
Complete Set (29):		1650.	660.00	330.00
Common Player:		45.00	18.00	9.00
(1)	Dale Alexander	45.00	18.00	9.00

(2)	Ivy Paul Andrews	45.00	18.00	9.00
(3)	Luke Appling	125.00	50.00	25.00
(4)	Earl Averill	125.00	50.00	25.00
(5)	George Blaeholder	45.00	18.00	9.00
(6)	Irving Burns	45.00	18.00	9.00
(7)	Pat Caraway	45.00	18.00	9.00
(8)	Chalmer Cissell	45.00	18.00	9.00
(9)	Harry Davis	45.00	18.00	9.00
(10)	Jimmy Dykes	45.00	18.00	9.00
(11)	George Earnshaw	45.00	18.00	9.00
(12)	Urban Faber	125.00	50.00	25.00
(13)	Lewis Fonseca	45.00	18.00	9.00
(14)	Jimmy Foxx	175.00	70.00	35.00
(15)	Victor Frasier	45.00	18.00	9.00
(16)	Robert Grove	125.00	50.00	25.00
(17)	Frank Grube	45.00	18.00	9.00
(18)	Irving Hadley	45.00	18.00	9.00
(19)	Willie Kamm	45.00	18.00	9.00
(20)	Bill Killefer	45.00	18.00	9.00
(21)	Ralph Kress	45.00	18.00	9.00
(22)	Fred Marberry	45.00	18.00	9.00
(23)	Roger Peckinpaugh	45.00	18.00	9.00
(24)	Frank Reiber	45.00	18.00	9.00
(25)	Carl Reynolds	45.00	18.00	9.00
(26)	Al Simmons	125.00	50.00	25.00
(27)	Joe Vosmik	45.00	18.00	9.00
(28)	Gerald Walker	45.00	18.00	9.00
(29)	Whitlow Wyatt	45.00	18.00	9.00

1922 W575-1

Designated as W575 in the American Card Catalog, these "strip cards" are blank-backed versions of the contemporary American Caramel E121 set. Cards in W575-1 measure 2" x 3-1/4" and are printed in black-and-white. Without records of exact strip make-up of this set, it is impossible to distinguish W575-1 cards from the blank-backed Koester's Bread Yankees and Giants cards issued to commemorate the 1921 "Subway" World Series.

		NM	EX	VG
Complete Set (179):		8500.	3400.	1700.
Common Player:		30.00	12.00	6.00
(1)	Chas. "Babe" Adams	30.00	12.00	6.00
(2)	G.C. Alexander	100.00	40.00	20.00
(3)	Grover Alexander	100.00	40.00	20.00
(4)	Jim Bagby	30.00	12.00	6.00
(5)	J. Franklin Baker	85.00	34.00	17.00
(6)	Frank Baker	85.00	34.00	17.00
(7)	Dave Bancroft (batting)	85.00	34.00	17.00
(8)	Dave Bancroft (fielding)	85.00	34.00	17.00
(9)	Jesse Barnes	30.00	12.00	6.00
(10)	Howard Berry	30.00	12.00	6.00
(11)	L. Bigbee (should be C.)	30.00	12.00	6.00
(12)	Ping Bodie	30.00	12.00	6.00
(13)	"Ed" Brown	30.00	12.00	6.00
(14)	George Burns	30.00	12.00	6.00
(15)	Geo. J. Burns	30.00	12.00	6.00
(16)	"Bullet Joe" Bush	30.00	12.00	6.00
(17)	Owen Bush	30.00	12.00	6.00
(18)	Max Carey (batting)	85.00	34.00	17.00
(19)	Max Carey (hands on hips)	85.00	34.00	17.00
(20)	Ty Cobb	750.00	300.00	150.00
(21)	Eddie Collins	85.00	34.00	17.00
(22)	"Rip" Collins	30.00	12.00	6.00
(23)	Stanley Coveleskie (Coveleski)	85.00	34.00	17.00
(24)	Bill Cunningham	30.00	12.00	6.00
(25)	Jake Daubert	30.00	12.00	6.00
(26)	George Dauss	30.00	12.00	6.00
(27)	Dixie Davis	30.00	12.00	6.00
(28)	Charles Deal (dark uniform)	30.00	12.00	6.00
(29)	Charles Deal (light uniform)	30.00	12.00	6.00
(30)	Lou DeVormer	30.00	12.00	6.00
(31)	William Doak	30.00	12.00	6.00
(32)	Bill Donovan	30.00	12.00	6.00
(33)	"Phil" Douglas	30.00	12.00	6.00
(34)	Johnny Evers (Mgr.)	85.00	34.00	17.00
(35)	Johnny Evers (Manager)	85.00	34.00	17.00
(36)	Urban Faber (dark uniform)	85.00	34.00	17.00
(37)	Urban Faber (white uniform)	85.00	34.00	17.00
(38)	Bib Falk (Bibb)	30.00	12.00	6.00
(39)	Alex Ferguson	30.00	12.00	6.00
(40)	Wm. Fewster	30.00	12.00	6.00
(41)	Eddie Foster	30.00	12.00	6.00
(42)	Frank Frisch	85.00	34.00	17.00
(43)	W.L. Gardner	30.00	12.00	6.00
(44)	Alexander Gaston	30.00	12.00	6.00
(45)	E.P. Gharrity	30.00	12.00	6.00
(46)	Chas. "Whitey" Glazner	30.00	12.00	6.00
(47)	"Kid" Gleason	30.00	12.00	6.00
(48)	"Mike" Gonzalez	40.00	16.00	8.00
(49)	Hank Gowdy	30.00	12.00	6.00
(50)	John Graney (Util. o.f.)	30.00	12.00	6.00
(51)	John Graney (O.F.)	30.00	12.00	6.00
(52)	Tom Griffith	30.00	12.00	6.00
(53)	Chas. Grimm	30.00	12.00	6.00
(54)	Heinie Groh (Cincinnati)	30.00	12.00	6.00
(55)	Heinie Groh (New York)	30.00	12.00	6.00
(56)	Jess Haines	85.00	34.00	17.00
(57)	Harry Harper	30.00	12.00	6.00
(58)	"Chicken" Hawks	30.00	12.00	6.00
(59)	Harry Heilman (Heilmann) (holding bat)	85.00	34.00	17.00
(60)	Harry Heilman (Heilmann) (running)	85.00	34.00	17.00
(61)	Fred Hoffman	30.00	12.00	6.00
(62)	Walter Holke (1st B., portrait)	30.00	12.00	6.00
(63)	Walter Holke (1B, portrait)	30.00	12.00	6.00
(64)	Walter Holke (throwing)	30.00	12.00	6.00
(65)	Charles Hollacher (name incorrect)	30.00	12.00	6.00
(66)	Charles Hollocher (name correct)	30.00	12.00	6.00
(67)	Harry Hooper	30.00	12.00	6.00
(68)	Rogers Hornsby (2nd B.)	100.00	40.00	20.00
(69)	Rogers Hornsby (O.F.)	100.00	40.00	20.00
(70)	Waite Hoyt	85.00	34.00	17.00
(71)	Miller Huggins	85.00	34.00	17.00
(72)	Wm. C. Jacobson	30.00	12.00	6.00
(73)	Hugh Jennings	85.00	34.00	17.00
(74)	Walter Johnson (arms at chest)	200.00	80.00	40.00
(75)	Walter Johnson (throwing)	200.00	80.00	40.00
(76)	James Johnston	30.00	12.00	6.00
(77)	Joe Judge (batting)	30.00	12.00	6.00
(78)	George Kelly (1st B.)	85.00	34.00	17.00
(79)	George Kelly (1B.)	85.00	34.00	17.00
(80)	Dick Kerr	30.00	12.00	6.00
(81)	P.J. Kilduff	30.00	12.00	6.00
(82)	Bill Killefer	30.00	12.00	6.00
(83)	John Lavan	30.00	12.00	6.00
(84)	"Nemo" Leibold	30.00	12.00	6.00
(85)	Duffy Lewis	30.00	12.00	6.00
(86)	Al. Mamaux	30.00	12.00	6.00
(87)	"Rabbit" Maranville	85.00	34.00	17.00
(88)	Carl Mays (name correct)	40.00	16.00	8.00
(89)	Carl May (Mays)	40.00	16.00	8.00
(90)	John McGraw	85.00	34.00	17.00
(91)	Jack McInnis	30.00	12.00	6.00
(92)	M.J. McNally	30.00	12.00	6.00
(93)	Emil Muesel	30.00	12.00	6.00
(94)	R. Meusel	30.00	12.00	6.00
(95)	Clyde Milan	30.00	12.00	6.00
(96)	Elmer Miller	30.00	12.00	6.00
(97)	Otto Miller	30.00	12.00	6.00
(98)	John Mitchell (S.S.)	30.00	12.00	6.00
(99)	John Mitchell (3rd B.)	30.00	12.00	6.00
(100)	Guy Morton	30.00	12.00	6.00
(101)	Eddie Mulligan	30.00	12.00	6.00
(102)	Eddie Murphy	30.00	12.00	6.00
(103)	"Hy" Myers (C.F./O.F.)	30.00	12.00	6.00
(104)	Hy Myers (O.F.)	30.00	12.00	6.00
(105)	A.E. Neale	55.00	22.00	11.00
(106)	Arthur Nehf	30.00	12.00	6.00
(107)	Joe Oeschger	30.00	12.00	6.00
(108)	Chas. O'Leary	30.00	12.00	6.00
(109)	Steve O'Neill	30.00	12.00	6.00
(110)	Jeff Pfeffer (Brooklyn)	30.00	12.00	6.00
(111)	Jeff Pfeffer (St. Louis)	30.00	12.00	6.00
(112)	Roger Peckinbaugh (name incorrect)	30.00	12.00	6.00
(113)	Roger Peckinpaugh (name correct)	30.00	12.00	6.00
(114)	Walter Pipp	40.00	16.00	8.00
(115)	Jack Quinn	30.00	12.00	6.00
(116)	John Rawlings (2nd B.)	30.00	12.00	6.00
(117)	John Rawlings (2B.)	30.00	12.00	6.00
(118)	E.S. Rice (name incorrect)	85.00	34.00	17.00
(119)	E.C. Rice (name correct)	85.00	34.00	17.00
(120)	Eppa Rixey, Jr.	85.00	34.00	17.00
(121)	Wilbert Robinson	85.00	34.00	17.00
(122)	Tom Rogers	30.00	12.00	6.00
(123)	Ed Rounnel (Rommel)	30.00	12.00	6.00
(124)	Robert Roth	30.00	12.00	6.00
(125)	Ed Roush (O.F.)	85.00	34.00	17.00
(126)	Ed Roush (C.F.)	85.00	34.00	17.00
(127)	"Muddy" Ruel	30.00	12.00	6.00
(128)	"Babe" Ruth (R.F.)	900.00	360.00	180.00
(129)	Babe Ruth (L.F.)	900.00	360.00	180.00
(130)	Bill Ryan	30.00	12.00	6.00
(131)	"Slim" Sallee (ball in hand)	30.00	12.00	6.00
(132)	"Slim" Sallee (no ball in hand)	30.00	12.00	6.00
(133)	Ray Schalk (bunting)	85.00	34.00	17.00
(134)	Ray Schalk (catching)	85.00	34.00	17.00
(135)	Walter Schang	30.00	12.00	6.00
(136)	Wally Schang	30.00	12.00	6.00
(137)	Fred Schupp (name incorrect)	30.00	12.00	6.00
(138)	Ferd Schupp (name correct)	30.00	12.00	6.00
(139)	Everett Scott (Boston)	30.00	12.00	6.00
(140)	Everett Scott (New York)	30.00	12.00	6.00
(141)	Hank Severeid	30.00	12.00	6.00
(142)	Robert Shawkey	30.00	12.00	6.00
(143)	"Pat" Shea	30.00	12.00	6.00
(144)	Pat Shea	30.00	12.00	6.00
(145)	Earl Sheely	30.00	12.00	6.00
(146)	Urban Shocker	30.00	12.00	6.00
(147)	George Sisler (batting)	85.00	34.00	17.00
(148)	George Sisler (throwing)	85.00	34.00	17.00
(149)	Earl Smith	30.00	12.00	6.00
(150)	Elmer Smith	30.00	12.00	6.00
(151)	Frank Snyder	30.00	12.00	6.00
(152)	Tris Speaker (large projection)	100.00	40.00	20.00
(153)	Tris Speaker (small projection)	100.00	40.00	20.00
(154)	Charles Stengel (batting)	100.00	40.00	20.00
(155)	Charles Stengel (portrait)	100.00	40.00	20.00
(156)	Milton Stock	30.00	12.00	6.00
(157)	Amos Strunk (C.F.)	30.00	12.00	6.00
(158)	Amos Strunk (O.F.)	30.00	12.00	6.00
(159)	Zeb Terry	30.00	12.00	6.00
(160)	Chester Thomas	30.00	12.00	6.00
(161)	Fred Toney (both feet on ground)	30.00	12.00	6.00
(162)	Fred Toney (one foot in air)	30.00	12.00	6.00
(163)	George Toporcer	30.00	12.00	6.00
(164)	George Tyler	30.00	12.00	6.00
(165)	Jim Vaughn (plain uniform)	30.00	12.00	6.00
(166)	Jim Vaughn (striped uniform)	30.00	12.00	6.00
(167)	Bob Veach (arm raised)	30.00	12.00	6.00
(168)	Bob Veach (arms folded)	30.00	12.00	6.00
(169)	Oscar Vitt	30.00	12.00	6.00
(170)	Curtis Walker	30.00	12.00	6.00
(171)	W. Wambsganss	30.00	12.00	6.00
(172)	Zach Wheat	85.00	34.00	17.00
(173)	George Whitted	30.00	12.00	6.00
(174)	Fred Williams	30.00	12.00	6.00
(175)	Ivy B. Wingo	30.00	12.00	6.00
(176)	Lawton Witt	30.00	12.00	6.00
(177)	Joe Wood	30.00	12.00	6.00
(178)	Pep Young	30.00	12.00	6.00
(179)	Ross Young (Youngs)	85.00	34.00	17.00

1922 W575-2

The blank-back, black-and-white cards in this set measure 2-1/8" x 3-3/8". Because of the design of the cards the set is sometimes called the "autograph on shoulder" series.

		NM	EX	VG
Complete Set (40):		5500.	2200.	1100.
Common Player:		55.00	20.00	10.00
(1)	Dave Bancroft	125.00	50.00	25.00
(2)	Johnnie Bassler	55.00	20.00	10.00
(3)	Joe Bush	55.00	20.00	10.00
(4)	Ty Cobb	1175.	470.00	235.00
(5)	Eddie Collins	125.00	50.00	25.00
(6)	Stan Coveleskie (Coveleski)	125.00	50.00	25.00
(7)	Jake Daubert	55.00	20.00	10.00
(8)	Joe Dugan	55.00	20.00	10.00
(9)	Red Faber	125.00	50.00	25.00
(10)	Frank Frisch	125.00	50.00	25.00
(11)	Walter H. Gerber	55.00	20.00	10.00
(12)	Harry Heilmann	125.00	50.00	25.00
(13)	Harry Hooper	125.00	50.00	25.00
(14)	Rogers Hornsby	135.00	54.00	27.00
(15)	Waite Hoyt	125.00	50.00	25.00
(16)	Joe Judge	55.00	20.00	10.00
(17)	Geo. Kelly	125.00	50.00	25.00
(18)	Rabbit Maranville	125.00	50.00	25.00
(19)	Rube Marquard	125.00	50.00	25.00
(20)	Guy Morton	55.00	20.00	10.00
(21)	Art Nehf	55.00	20.00	10.00
(22)	Derrill B. Pratt	55.00	20.00	10.00
(23)	Jimmy Ring	55.00	20.00	10.00
(24)	Eppa Rixey	125.00	50.00	25.00
(25)	Gene Robertson	55.00	20.00	10.00
(26)	Ed Rommel (Rommel)	55.00	20.00	10.00
(27)	Babe Ruth	1550.	620.00	310.00
(28)	Wally Schang	55.00	20.00	10.00
(29)	Everett Scott	55.00	20.00	10.00
(30)	Henry Severeid	55.00	20.00	10.00
(31)	Joe Sewell	125.00	50.00	25.00
(32)	Geo. Sisler	125.00	50.00	25.00
(33)	Tris Speaker	135.00	54.00	27.00
(34)	Riggs Stephenson	55.00	20.00	10.00
(35)	Zeb Terry	55.00	20.00	10.00
(36)	Bobbie Veach	55.00	20.00	10.00
(37)	Clarence Walker	55.00	20.00	10.00
(38)	Johnnie Walker	55.00	20.00	10.00
(39)	Zach Wheat	125.00	50.00	25.00
(40)	Kenneth Williams	55.00	20.00	10.00

1925-31 W590 Black-and-white Photo Strip Cards

Unlisted in the original edition of the American Card Catalog, this strip card set was given the number W590 in later editions. It is part of a larger set cataloged as W580 which includes movie stars, boxers and other athletes. These cards measure approximately 1-3/8" x 2-1/2". Fronts have black-and-white player photos with a white border. In the bottom border is the player name, position, city and league. Some cards can be found with a "Former" designation before the position. Several variations are known in team designations, indicating the set was probably reissued at least once between 1928-31. Backs are blank. Only the baseball players are listed here, in alphabetical order.

		NM	EX	VG
Complete Baseball Set (41):		3250.	1600.	975.00
Common Player:		35.00	17.50	10.50
(1)	Grover C. Alexander	80.00	40.00	24.00
(2)	Dave Bancroft	75.00	37.00	22.00
(3)	Jess Barnes	35.00	17.50	10.50
(4)	Ray Blades	35.00	17.50	10.50
(5)	Pictbred Bluege (Ossie)	35.00	17.50	10.50
(6a)	George Burns (N.Y., N.L.)	35.00	17.50	10.50
(6b)	George Burns (Phil., N.L.)	35.00	17.50	10.50
(7)	George Burns (Cleveland)	35.00	17.50	10.50
(8)	Max Carey	75.00	37.00	22.00
(9)	Caveney (Jimmy)	35.00	17.50	10.50
(10)	"Ty" Cobb	450.00	225.00	135.00
(11)	Eddie Collins	80.00	40.00	24.00
(12)	George Dauss	35.00	17.50	10.50
(13)	Red Faber	75.00	37.00	22.00
(14)	Frankie Frisch	80.00	40.00	24.00
(15)	Lou Gehrig	450.00	225.00	135.00
(16)	Sam Gray	35.00	17.50	10.50
(17)	Hank Gowdy	35.00	17.50	10.50
(18)	Charley Grimm	35.00	17.50	10.50
(19)	"Buckey" Harris	75.00	37.00	22.00
(20a)	Rogers Hornsby (St. Louis)	90.00	45.00	27.00
(20b)	Rogers Hornsby (Boston)	90.00	45.00	27.00
(21)	Travis Jackson	75.00	37.00	22.00
(22)	Walter Johnson	200.00	100.00	60.00
(23)	George Kelly	75.00	37.00	22.00
(24)	Fred Lindstrom	75.00	37.00	22.00
(25)	Rabbit Maranville	75.00	37.00	22.00
(26)	Bob Meusel	35.00	17.50	10.50
(27)	Jack Quinn	35.00	17.50	10.50
(28)	Eppa Rixey	75.00	37.00	22.00
(29)	Eddie Rommel	35.00	17.50	10.50
(30)	Babe Ruth (King of the Bat)	900.00	450.00	270.00
(31)	Heinie Sand	35.00	17.50	10.50
(32)	Geo. Sisler	75.00	37.00	22.00
(33)	Earl Smith	35.00	17.50	10.50
(34)	Tris Speaker	90.00	45.00	27.00
(35)	Roy Spencer	35.00	17.50	10.50
(36)	Milton Stock	35.00	17.50	10.50
(37a)	Phil Todt (Phil., A.L.)	35.00	17.50	10.50
(37b)	Phil Todt (Bos., A.L.)	35.00	17.50	10.50
(38)	Dazzy Vance	75.00	37.00	22.00
(39a)	Kenneth Williams (St. Louis, A.L.)	35.00	17.50	10.50
(39b)	Kenneth Williams (Bos., A.L.)	35.00	17.50	10.50
(40)	Zack Wheat	75.00	37.00	22.00
(41)	Ross Youngs	75.00	37.00	22.00

1921 W9316

As crude as many of the strip cards of the era were, this issue is the worst. In the same blank-back format and size (about 1-1/2" x 2-1/2") as many contemporary strip cards, the set features 10 of the players from W519/W521. The artwork on these cards is very crudely done, almost child-like. The most striking feature about the pictures is the ruby red lips on the players. Unlisted in the American Card Catalog, this set was given the designation W9316 in John Stirling's Sports Card Catalog.

		NM	EX	VG
Complete Set (10):		175.00	90.00	50.00
Common Player:		15.00	10.00	5.00
1	Bob Veach	15.00	10.00	5.00
2	Frank Baker	25.00	12.50	7.50
3	Wilbur (Wilbert) Robinson	25.00	12.50	7.50
4	Johnny Griffith	15.00	10.00	5.00
5	Jimmie Johnston	15.00	10.00	5.00
6	Wallie Schange (Wally Schang)	15.00	10.00	5.00
7	Leon Cadore	15.00	10.00	5.00
8	George Sisler	25.00	12.50	7.50
9	Ray Schalk	25.00	12.50	7.50
10	Jesse Barnes	15.00	10.00	5.00

Y

1972 The Yawkey Red Sox

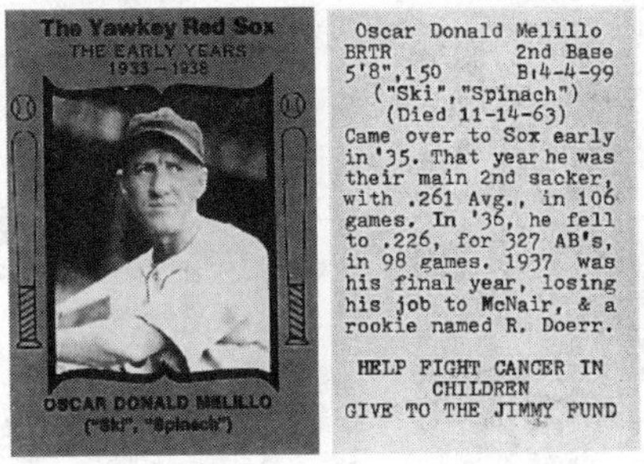

Boston Red Sox players of the 1930s are featured in this collectors issue. The issue date given is only a guess. The 2-1/2" x 3-1/2" cards have black-and-white player photos with brown borders and black graphics. Backs are also in black-and-white with personal data, a career summary and a promotion for the Red Sox long-time charity, The Jimmy Fund. The unnumbered cards are listed here alphabetically.

		NM	EX	VG
Complete Set:		22.00	11.00	6.50
Common Player:		.50	.25	.15
(1)	Mel Almada	.75	.40	.25
(2)	Moe Berg	1.50	.70	.45
(3)	Max Bishop	.50	.25	.15
(4)	Doc Bowers	.50	.25	.15
(5)	Joe Cascarella	.50	.25	.15
(6)	Ben Chapman	.50	.25	.15
(7)	Bill Cissell	.50	.25	.15
(8)	Dusty Cooke	.50	.25	.15
(9)	Doc Cramer	.50	.25	.15
(10)	Joe Cronin	.75	.40	.25
(11)	George Dickey	.50	.25	.15
(12)	Emerson Dickman	.50	.25	.15
(13)	Bobby Doerr	.75	.40	.25
(14)	Rick Ferrell	.75	.40	.25
(15)	Wes Ferrell	.50	.25	.15
(16)	Jimmie Foxx	.75	.40	.25
(17)	Joe Gonzales	.50	.25	.15
(18)	Lefty Grove	.75	.40	.25
(19)	Bucky Harris	.75	.40	.25
(20)	Jim Henry	.50	.25	.15
(21)	Pinky Higgins	.50	.25	.15
(22)	Lefty Hockette	.50	.25	.15
(23)	Roy Johnson	.50	.25	.15
(24)	John Kroner	.50	.25	.15
(25)	Heinie Manush	.75	.40	.25
(26)	Archie McKain	.50	.25	.15
(27)	Eric McNair	.50	.25	.15
(28)	Oscar Melillo	.50	.25	.15
(29)	Bing Miller	.50	.25	.15
(30)	Joe Mulligan	.50	.25	.15
(31)	Bobo Newsom	.50	.25	.15
(32)	Ted Olson	.50	.25	.15
(33)	Fritz Ostermueller	.50	.25	.15
(34)	George Pipgras	.50	.25	.15
(35)	Dusty Rhodes	.50	.25	.15
(36)	Walt Ripley	.50	.25	.15
(37)	Buck Rogers	.50	.25	.15
(38)	Jack Russell	.50	.25	.15
(39)	Tommy Thomas	.50	.25	.15
(40)	Hy Vandenberg	.50	.25	.15
(41)	Rube Walberg	.50	.25	.15
(42)	Johnny Welch	.50	.25	.15
(43)	Bill Werber	.50	.25	.15
(44)	Dib Williams	.50	.25	.15
(45)	Black Jack Wilson	.50	.25	.15

1928 Yeungling's Ice Cream

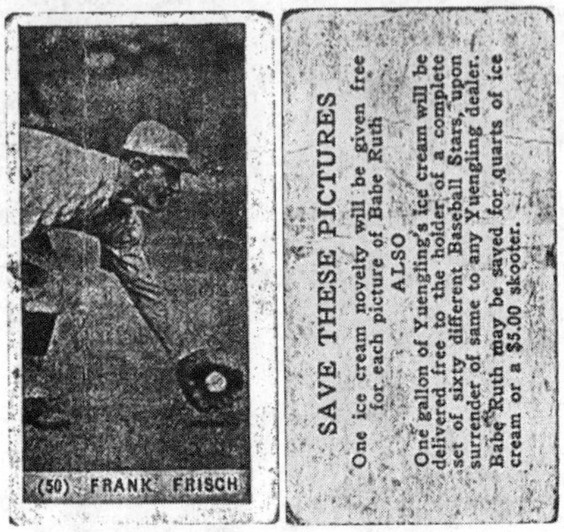

Issued in 1928, the Yeungling's Ice Cream issue consists of 60 black-and-white cards measuring 1-3/8" x 2-1/2". The photos are similar to those used in the E210 and W502 sets. Other ice cream companies such as Harrington's and Tharp's produced nearly identical cards. Two types of cards are seen, though whether either or both can be found for all players is unknown. Besides typographical placement differences on front, the back of one type mentions a "$5.00 skooter" as a redemption, while the other type has no mention of the toy. Collectors could redeem an entire set of Yeungling's cards for a gallon of ice cream.

		NM	EX	VG
Complete Set (60):		3800.	1525.	760.00
Common Player:		40.00	16.00	8.00
1	Burleigh Grimes	65.00	26.00	13.00
2	Walter Reuther	40.00	16.00	8.00
3	Joe Dugan	40.00	16.00	8.00
4	Red Faber	65.00	26.00	13.00
5	Gabby Hartnett	65.00	26.00	13.00
6	Babe Ruth	900.00	360.00	180.00
7	Bob Meusel	40.00	16.00	8.00
8	Herb Pennock	65.00	26.00	13.00
9	George Burns	40.00	16.00	8.00
10	Joe Sewell	65.00	26.00	13.00
11	George Uhle	40.00	16.00	8.00
12	Bob O'Farrell	40.00	16.00	8.00
13	Rogers Hornsby	75.00	30.00	15.00
14	"Pie" Traynor	65.00	26.00	13.00
15	Clarence Mitchell	40.00	16.00	8.00
16	Eppa Jepha Rixey	65.00	26.00	13.00
17	Carl Mays	45.00	18.00	9.00
18	Adolfo Luque	50.00	20.00	10.00
19	Dave Bancroft	65.00	26.00	13.00
20	George Kelly	65.00	26.00	13.00
21	Earl (Earle) Combs	65.00	26.00	13.00
22	Harry Heilmann	65.00	26.00	13.00
23	Ray W. Schalk	65.00	26.00	13.00
24	Johnny Mostil	40.00	16.00	8.00
25	Hack Wilson	65.00	26.00	13.00
26	Lou Gehrig	600.00	240.00	120.00
27	Ty Cobb	600.00	240.00	120.00
28	Tris Speaker	75.00	30.00	15.00
29	Tony Lazzeri	65.00	26.00	13.00
30	Waite Hoyt	65.00	26.00	13.00
31	Sherwood Smith	40.00	16.00	8.00
32	Max Carey	65.00	26.00	13.00
33	Eugene Hargrave	40.00	16.00	8.00
34	Miguel L. Gonzales (Miguel A. Gonzalez)	50.00	20.00	10.00
35	Joe Judge	40.00	16.00	8.00
36	E.C. (Sam) Rice	65.00	26.00	13.00
37	Earl Sheely	40.00	16.00	8.00
38	Sam Jones	40.00	16.00	8.00
39	Bib (Bibb) A. Falk	40.00	16.00	8.00
40	Willie Kamm	40.00	16.00	8.00
41	Stanley Harris	65.00	26.00	13.00
42	John J. McGraw	65.00	26.00	13.00
43	Artie Nehf	40.00	16.00	8.00
44	Grover Alexander	75.00	30.00	15.00
45	Paul Waner	65.00	26.00	13.00
46	William H. Terry	65.00	26.00	13.00
47	Glenn Wright	40.00	16.00	8.00
48	Earl Smith	40.00	16.00	8.00
49	Leon (Goose) Goslin	65.00	26.00	13.00
50	Frank Frisch	65.00	26.00	13.00
51	Joe Harris	40.00	16.00	8.00
52	Fred (Cy) Williams	40.00	16.00	8.00
53	Eddie Roush	65.00	26.00	13.00
54	George Sisler	65.00	26.00	13.00
55	Ed. Rommel	40.00	16.00	8.00
56	Rogers Peckinpaugh (Roger)	40.00	16.00	8.00
57	Stanley Coveleskie (Coveleski)	65.00	26.00	13.00
58	Lester Bell	40.00	16.00	8.00
59	L. Waner	65.00	26.00	13.00
60	John P. McInnis	40.00	16.00	8.00

1959 Yoo-Hoo

Issued as a promotion for Yoo-Hoo chocolate flavored soft drink (it's a New York thing), this issue features five New York Yankees players. The black-and-white blank-backed cards measure 2-7/16" x 5-1/8", including a tab at the bottom which could be redeemed for various prizes. The top of the card features a posed spring training photo and includes a facsimile autograph and "Me for Yoo-Hoo" slogan. Prices shown here are for complete cards; cards without tabs would be valued at one-half of these figures. A Mickey Mantle advertising piece in larger size is often collected as an adjunct to the set, but no card of Mantle was issued. The Berra card is considerably scarcer than the others.

CUT OFF HERE
'Me for "YOO-HOO,"
The Drink of Champions'
says Yogi Berra
Yoo-Hoo, Fans!

		NM	EX	VG
Complete Set (5):		600.00	300.00	180.00
Common Player:		60.00	30.00	18.00
(1)	Yogi Berra	325.00	162.00	97.00
(2)	Whitey Ford	125.00	62.00	37.00
(3)	Tony Kubek	60.00	30.00	18.00
(4)	Gil McDougald	60.00	30.00	18.00
(5)	Bill Skowron	65.00	32.00	19.50

1959 Yoo-Hoo Mickey Mantle

In a different format than the other contemporary Yoo-Hoo Yankees cards, the manner of original distribution of this card is unclear. The 2-5/8" x 3-5/8" black-and-white card has a portrait photo and endorsement for the product on front. Back is blank.

	NM	EX	VG
Mickey Mantle	800.00	400.00	240.00

1927 York Caramels Type I (E210)

Issued in 1927 by the York Caramel Co. of York, Pa., these black-and-white cards are among the last of the caramel issues. Measuring 1-3/8" x 2-1/2", they are similar in appearance to earlier candy and tobacco cards. Card front carries the player's name in capital letters beneath the photo preceded by a number in parentheses. The back also lists the player's name in capital letters, along with a brief phrase describing him and the line "This is one of a series of sixty of the most prominent stars in baseball." The bottom of the cards reads "York Caramel Co. York, Pa." The set includes several variations and is desgniated in the ACC as E210. It is closely related to the W502 set of the same year. The E210-2s differ from the E210-1s in that the card stock is close to being glossy as opposed to the dull appearance of E210-1.

(21) IRA FLAGSTEAD

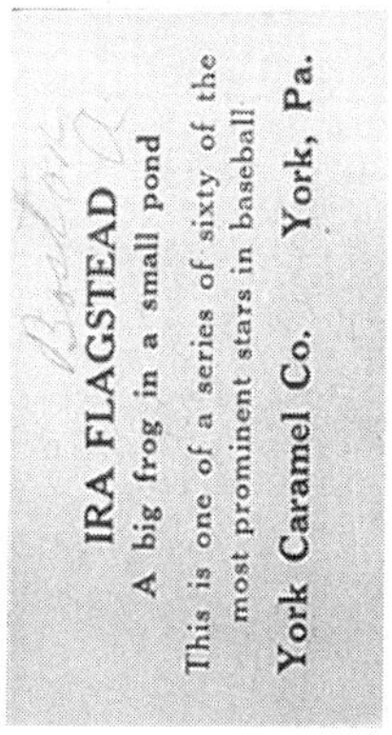
IRA FLAGSTEAD
A big frog in a small pond
This is one of a series of sixty of the most prominent stars in baseball
York Caramel Co. York, Pa.

		NM	EX	VG
Complete Set (60):		7100.	2850.	1425.
Common Player:		50.00	20.00	10.00
1	Burleigh Grimes	100.00	40.00	20.00
2	Walter Reuther (Ruether)	50.00	20.00	10.00
3	Joe Duggan (Dugan)	50.00	20.00	10.00
4	Red Faber	100.00	40.00	20.00
5	Gabby Hartnett	100.00	40.00	20.00
6	Babe Ruth	2250.	900.00	450.00
7	Bob Meusel	50.00	20.00	10.00
8	Herb Pennock	100.00	40.00	20.00
9	George Burns	50.00	20.00	10.00
10	Joe Sewell	100.00	40.00	20.00
11	George Uhle	50.00	20.00	10.00
12	Bob O'Farrel (O'Farrell)	50.00	20.00	10.00
13	Rogers Hornsby	125.00	50.00	25.00
14	Pie Traynor	100.00	40.00	20.00
15	Clarence Mitchell	50.00	20.00	10.00
16	Eppa Jepha Rixey (Jeptha)	100.00	40.00	20.00
17	Carl Mays	55.00	22.00	11.00
18	Adolph Luque (Adolfo)	70.00	28.00	14.00
19	Dave Bancroft	100.00	40.00	20.00
20	George Kelly	100.00	40.00	20.00
21	Ira Flagstead	50.00	20.00	10.00
22	Harry Heilmann	100.00	40.00	20.00
23	Raymond W. Shalk (Schalk)	100.00	40.00	20.00
24	Johnny Mostil	50.00	20.00	10.00
25	Hack Wilson (photo actually Art Wilson)	100.00	40.00	20.00
26	Tom Zachary	50.00	20.00	10.00
27	Ty Cobb	1050.	420.00	210.00
28	Tris Speaker	125.00	50.00	25.00
29	Ralph Perkins	50.00	20.00	10.00
30	Jess Haines	100.00	40.00	20.00
31	Sherwood Smith (photo actually Jack Coombs)	50.00	20.00	10.00
32	Max Carey	100.00	40.00	20.00
33	Eugene Hargraves (Hargrave)	50.00	20.00	10.00
34	Miguel L. Gonzales (Miguel A. Gonzalez)	70.00	28.00	14.00
35a	Clifton Heathcot (Heathcote)	50.00	20.00	10.00
35b	Clifton Heathcote (correct spelling)	50.00	20.00	10.00
36	E.C. (Sam) Rice	100.00	40.00	20.00
37	Earl Sheely	50.00	20.00	10.00
38	Emory E. Rigney	50.00	20.00	10.00
39	Bib A. Falk (Bibb)	50.00	20.00	10.00
40	Nick Altrock	50.00	20.00	10.00
41	Stanley Harris	100.00	40.00	20.00
42	John J. McGraw	100.00	40.00	20.00
43	Wilbert Robinson	100.00	40.00	20.00
44	Grover Alexander	115.00	46.00	23.00
45	Walter Johnson	180.00	72.00	36.00
46	William H. Terry (photo actually Zeb Terry)	100.00	40.00	20.00
47	Edward Collins	100.00	40.00	20.00
48	Marty McManus	50.00	20.00	10.00
49	Leon (Goose) Goslin	100.00	40.00	20.00
50	Frank Frisch	100.00	40.00	20.00
51	Jimmie Dykes	50.00	20.00	10.00
52	Fred (Cy) Williams	50.00	20.00	10.00
53	Eddie Roush	100.00	40.00	20.00
54	George Sisler	100.00	40.00	20.00
55	Ed Rommel	50.00	20.00	10.00
56	Rogers Peckinpaugh (Roger)	50.00	20.00	10.00
57	Stanley Coveleskie (Coveleski)	100.00	40.00	20.00
58	Clarence Gallaway (Galloway)	50.00	20.00	10.00
59	Bob Shawkey	50.00	20.00	10.00
60	John P. McInnis	50.00	20.00	10.00

Vintage cards in Good condition are valued at about 50% of the Very Good value shown here. Fair cards are valued at 25% or less of VG.
The ratio of Excellent and Very Good prices to Near Mint can vary depending on relative collectibility for each grade in a specific set. Current listings reflect such adjustments.

1927 York Caramels Type II (E210)

(3) JOE DUGAN

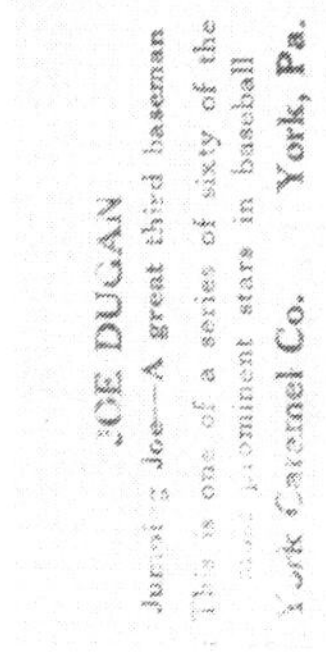
JOE DUGAN
York Caramel Co. York, Pa.

		NM	EX	VG
Common Player:		50.00	20.00	10.00
1	Burleigh Grimes	90.00	36.00	18.00
2	Walter Reuther (Ruether)	50.00	20.00	10.00
3	Joe Dugan	50.00	20.00	10.00
6	Babe Ruth	1200.	480.00	240.00
12	Bob O'Farrell	50.00	20.00	10.00
14	Pie Traynor	90.00	36.00	18.00
16	Eppa Rixey	90.00	36.00	18.00
18	Adolfo Luque	60.00	24.00	12.00
20	George Kelly	90.00	36.00	18.00
22	Harry Heilmann	90.00	36.00	18.00
23	Ray W. Schalk	90.00	36.00	18.00
24	Johnny Mostil	50.00	20.00	10.00
27	Ty Cobb	800.00	320.00	160.00
29	Tony Lazzeri	90.00	36.00	18.00
31	Sherwood Smith (photo actually Jack Coombs)	50.00	20.00	10.00
32	Max Carey	90.00	36.00	18.00
33	Eugene Hargrave (Hargraves)	50.00	20.00	10.00
34	Miguel L. Gonzales (Miguel A. Gonzalez)	60.00	24.00	12.00
35	Joe Judge	50.00	20.00	10.00
40	Willie Kamm	50.00	20.00	10.00
43	Artie Nehf	50.00	20.00	10.00
46	William H. Terry (photo actually Zeb Terry)	90.00	36.00	18.00
47	Eddie Collins	90.00	36.00	18.00
50	Frank Frisch	90.00	36.00	18.00
51	Joe Harris	50.00	20.00	10.00
54	George Sisler	90.00	36.00	18.00
55	Ed Rommel	50.00	20.00	10.00
57	Stanley Coveleskie (Coveleski)	90.00	36.00	18.00
58	Lester Bell	50.00	20.00	10.00
59	Lloyd Waner	90.00	36.00	18.00

1888 Yum Yum Tobacco

NEW YORK'S
RICHARDSON, SECOND BASE.
SMOKE AND CHEW
"YUM YUM" TOBACCO.

An extremely rare series of tobacco cards, this set was issued in 1888 by August Beck & Co., Chicago. The cards vary slightly in size but average 1-3/8" x 2-3/4". They were distributed in packages of the company's Yum Yum smoking and chewing tobacco and are found in two distinct types: photographic portraits and full-length action drawings that appear to be copied from photos used in the Old Judge sets of the same period. In both types, the player's name and position appear in capital letters below the photo, while the very bottom of the card states: "Smoke and Chew "Yum Yum" Tobacco. A. Beck & Co. Chicago, Ill." Players from all eight National League clubs, plus Brooklyn of the American Association, are included in the set.

		NM	EX	VG
Complete Set (51):		125000.	60000.	35000.
Common Line Drawing:		2400.	1200.	720.00
Common Photograph:		3000.	1500.	900.00
(1)	Cap Anson	15000.	7500.	4500.

(2)	Lady Baldwin	2400.	1200.	720.00
(3)	Dan Brouthers	2000.	1000.	600.00
(4)	Bill "California" Brown	2400.	1200.	720.00
(5)	Buffington (Buffinton)	2400.	1200.	720.00
(6)	Thomas Burns (portrait)	3000.	1500.	900.00
(7)	Thomas Burns (with bat)	2400.	1200.	720.00
(8)	John Clarkson (portrait)	7200.	3600.	2150.
(9)	John Clarkson (throwing)	2000.	1000.	600.00
(10)	John Coleman	3000.	1500.	900.00
(11)	Larry Corcoran	3000.	1500.	900.00
(12)	Tido Daily (Daly) (photo actually Billy Sunday)	3000.	1500.	900.00
(13)	Tom Deasley	3000.	1500.	900.00
(14)	Mike Dorgan	3000.	1500.	900.00
(15)	Buck Ewing (portrait)	7200.	3600.	2150.
(16)	Buck Ewing (with bat)	2000.	1000.	600.00
(17)	Silver Flint	3000.	1500.	900.00
(18)	Pud Galvin	2000.	1000.	600.00
(19)	Joe Gerhardt	3000.	1500.	900.00
(20)	Charlie Getzein (Getzien) (holding ball)	2400.	1200.	720.00
(21)	Pete Gillespie	3000.	1500.	900.00
(22)	Pebbly Jack Glasscock	2400.	1200.	720.00
(23)	Ed Greer	3000.	1500.	900.00
(24)	Tim Keefe (pitching)	2000.	1000.	600.00
(25)	Tim Keefe (portrait)	7200.	3600.	2150.
(26)	King Kelly	4800.	2400.	1450.
(27)	King Kelly (photo)	9000.	4500.	2700.
(28)	Gus Krock	3000.	1500.	900.00
(29)	Connie Mack	5600.	2800.	1675.
(30)	Kid Madden	2400.	1200.	720.00
(31)	Doggie Miller	2400.	1200.	720.00
(32)	Billy Nash (hands crossed in front)	2400.	1200.	720.00
(33)	O'Rourke (portrait)	7200.	3600.	2150.
(34)	O'Rourke (with bat)	2000.	1000.	600.00
(35)	Fred Pfeffer (bat on shoulder)	2400.	1200.	720.00
(36)	Danny Richardson	3000.	1500.	900.00
(37)	Chief Roseman	3000.	1500.	900.00
(38)	Jimmy Ryan (portrait)	3000.	1500.	900.00
(39)	Jimmy Ryan (throwing)	2400.	1200.	720.00
(40)	Little Bill Sowders	2400.	1200.	720.00
(41)	Marty Sullivan	3000.	1500.	900.00
(42)	Billy Sunday (line drawing)	3600.	1800.	1075.
(43)	Billy Sunday (portrait)	3000.	1500.	900.00
(44)	Ezra Sutton	2400.	1200.	720.00
(45)	Tiernan (portrait)	3000.	1500.	900.00
(46)	Tiernan (with bat)	2400.	1200.	720.00
(47)	Rip Van Haltren (photo not Van Haltren)	3000.	1500.	900.00
(48)	Mickey Welch (hands clasped at chest)	2000.	1000.	600.00
(49)	Mickey Welch (portrait)	7200.	3600.	2150.
(50)	Mickey Welch (right arm extended)	2000.	1000.	600.00
(51)	Grasshopper Whitney	2400.	1200.	720.00
(52)	George "Dandy" Wood	2400.	1200.	720.00

Z

1978 Zest Soap

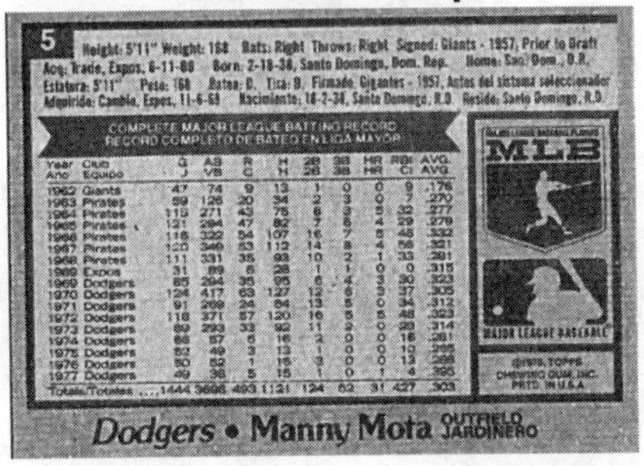

Produced by Topps for a Zest Soap promotion, the five cards in this set are almost identical to the regular 1978 Topps issue, except the backs are printed in both Spanish and English and the card numbers are different. The cards measure 2-1/2" x 3-1/2". Because of the player selection and the bilingual backs, it seems obvious that this set was aimed at the Hispanic community.

		NM	EX	VG
Complete Set (5):		12.00	6.00	3.50
Common Player:		1.50	.75	.45
1	Joaquin Andujar	2.00	1.00	.60
2	Bert Campaneris	4.00	2.00	1.25
3	Ed Figueroa	1.50	.70	.45
4	Willie Montanez	1.50	.70	.45
5	Manny Mota	4.00	2.00	1.25

1977 Zip'z discs

Virtually identical in format to the several locally sponsored disc sets of the previous year, these 3-3/8" diameter player discs were given away at the sponsor's sundae bars around the cvountry. Some are found with a black rubber-stamp on back of the specific Zip's location. Discs once again feature black-and-white player portrait photos in the center of a baseball design. The left and right panels are in one of several bright colors. Licensed by the players' association through Mike Schechter Associates, the player photos carry no uniform logos. Backs are printed in reddish-orange. The unnumbered discs are checklisted here alphabetically.

		NM	EX	VG
Complete Set (70):		250.00	125.00	75.00
Common Player:		2.00	1.00	.60
(1)	Sal Bando	2.00	1.00	.60
(2)	Buddy Bell	2.00	1.00	.60
(3)	Johnny Bench	12.00	6.00	3.50
(4)	Larry Bowa	2.00	1.00	.60
(5)	Steve Braun	2.00	1.00	.60
(6)	George Brett	20.00	10.00	6.00
(7)	Lou Brock	8.00	4.00	2.50
(8)	Jeff Burroughs	2.00	1.00	.60
(9)	Bert Campanelis	2.00	1.00	.60
(10)	John Candelaria	2.00	1.00	.60
(11)	Jose Cardenal	2.00	1.00	.60
(12)	Rod Carew	9.00	4.50	2.75
(13)	Steve Carlton	10.00	5.00	3.00
(14)	Dave Cash	2.00	1.00	.60
(15)	Cesar Cedeno	2.00	1.00	.60
(16)	Ron Cey	2.00	1.00	.60
(17)	Dave Concepcion	2.00	1.00	.60
(18)	Dennis Eckersley	7.00	3.50	2.00
(19)	Mark Fidrych	7.00	3.50	2.00
(20)	Rollie Fingers	9.00	4.50	2.75
(21)	Carlton Fisk	9.00	4.50	2.75
(22)	George Foster	2.00	1.00	.60
(23)	Wayne Garland	2.00	1.00	.60
(24)	Ralph Garr	2.00	1.00	.60
(25)	Steve Garvey	6.00	3.00	1.75
(26)	Cesar Geronimo	2.00	1.00	.60
(27)	Bobby Grich	2.00	1.00	.60
(28)	Ken Griffey Sr.	4.00	2.00	1.25
(29)	Don Gullett	2.00	1.00	.60
(30)	Mike Hargrove	2.00	1.00	.60
(31)	Willie Horton	2.00	1.00	.60
(32)	Al Hrabosky	2.00	1.00	.60
(33)	Reggie Jackson	12.00	6.00	3.50
(34)	Randy Jones	2.00	1.00	.60
(35)	Dave Kingman	3.00	1.50	.90
(36)	Jerry Koosman	2.00	1.00	.60
(37)	Dave LaRoche	2.00	1.00	.60
(38)	Greg Luzinski	2.00	1.00	.60
(39)	Fred Lynn	3.00	1.50	.90
(40)	Bill Madlock	2.00	1.00	.60
(41)	Rick Manning	2.00	1.00	.60
(42)	Jon Matlock	2.00	1.00	.60
(43)	John Mayberry	2.00	1.00	.60
(44)	Hal McRae	2.00	1.00	.60
(45)	Andy Messersmith	2.00	1.00	.60
(46)	Rick Monday	2.00	1.00	.60
(47)	John Montefusco	2.00	1.00	.60
(48)	Joe Morgan	9.00	4.50	2.75
(49)	Thurman Munson	9.00	4.50	2.75
(50)	Bobby Murcer	2.00	1.00	.60
(51)	Bill North	2.00	1.00	.60
(52)	Jim Palmer	9.00	4.50	2.75
(53)	Tony Perez	9.00	4.50	2.75
(54)	Jerry Reuss	2.00	1.00	.60
(55)	Pete Rose	24.00	12.00	7.25
(56)	Joe Rudi	2.00	1.00	.60
(57)	Nolan Ryan	60.00	30.00	18.00
(58)	Manny Sanguillen	2.00	1.00	.60
(59)	Mike Schmidt	12.00	6.00	3.50
(60)	Tom Seaver	12.00	6.00	3.50
(61)	Bill Singer	2.00	1.00	.60
(62)	Willie Stargell	9.00	4.50	2.75
(63)	Rusty Staub	3.00	1.50	.90
(64)	Luis Tiant	2.00	1.00	.60
(65)	Mike Tyson	2.00	1.00	.60
(66)	Bob Watson	2.00	1.00	.60
(67)	Butch Wynegar	2.00	1.00	.60
(68)	Carl Yastrzemski	10.00	5.00	3.00
(69)	Robin Yount	8.00	4.00	2.50
(70)	Richie Zisk	2.00	1.00	.60

1950s Bill Zuber's Restaurant

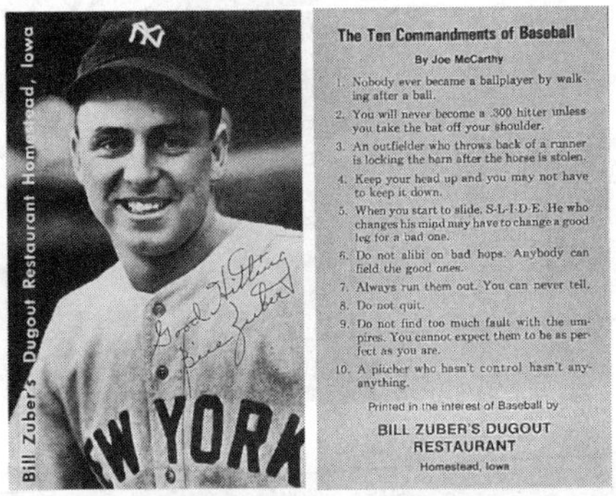

This 3-1/2" x 5-1/2" black-and-white photo card was apparently produced as a promotional item for an Iowa restaurant owned by the former big league pitcher (1936-47). The semi-gloss front has a portrait, a facsimile autograph and an advertising line. On back are printed Joe McCarthy's "Ten Commandments of Baseball".

	NM	EX	VG
Bill Zuber	8.00	4.00	2.50

MODERN MAJOR LEAGUE (1981-2000)

The vast majority of cards and collectibles listed in this section were issued between 1981 and mid-2000 and feature major league players only. The term "card" is used rather loosely as in this context it is construed to include virtually any series of cardboard or paper product, of whatever size and/or shape, depicting baseball players. Further, "cards" printed on wood, metal, plastic and other materials are either by their association with other issues or by their compatibility in size with the current 2-1/2" x 3-1/2" card standard also listed here.

Because modern cards are generally not popularly collected in lower grades, cards in this section carry only a Mint (MT) value quote. In general, post-1980 cards which grade Near Mint (NM) will retail at about 75% of the Mint price, while Excellent (EX) condition cards bring 40%.

A

1990 Ace Novelty MVP Pins

This series of collector pins features a blister pack containing a color player pin and the player's card from the 1990 Score set. The pin comes attached to a 2-1/2" x 3-1/2" card with a baseball diamond, bats, ball and the player's team logo. A checklist appears on the back of the 6-7/8" x 8-5/8" blister pack. Player pins measure about 1" x 1-1/2". The set is checklisted here alphabetically. Prices quoted are for unopened pin/card packs.

		MT
Complete Set (108):		225.00
Common Player:		2.00
(1)	Jim Abbott	2.00
(2)	Harold Baines	2.00
(3)	George Bell	2.00
(4)	Craig Biggio	2.00
(5)	Bert Blyleven	2.00
(6)	Barry Bonds	6.00
(7)	Bobby Bonilla	2.00
(8)	Wade Boggs	5.00
(9)	George Brett	6.00
(10)	Tom Brunansky	2.00
(11)	Brett Butler	2.00
(12)	Jose Canseco	3.50
(13)	Jack Clark	2.00
(14)	Will Clark	3.00
(15)	Roger Clemens	4.00
(16)	Alvin Davis	2.00
(17)	Eric Davis	2.00
(18)	Glenn Davis	2.00
(19)	Andre Dawson	2.00
(20)	Bill Doran	2.00
(21)	Brian Downing	2.00
(22)	Doug Drabek	2.00
(23)	Shawon Dunston	2.00
(24)	Lenny Dykstra	2.00
(25)	Dennis Eckersley	2.00
(26)	Sid Fernandez	2.00
(27)	Tony Fernandez	2.00
(28)	Carlton Fisk	3.00
(29)	Julio Franco	2.00
(30)	Gary Gaetti	2.00
(31)	Andres Galarraga	
(32)	Kirk Gibson	2.00
(33)	Dan Gladden	2.00
(34)	Tom Glavine	2.00
(35)	Doc Gooden	2.50
(36)	Tom Gordon	2.00
(37)	Mark Grace	3.00
(38)	Mike Greenwell	2.00
(39)	Ken Griffey Jr.	10.00
(40)	Ken Griffey Sr.	2.00
(41)	Pedro Guerrero	2.00
(42)	Ozzie Guillen	2.00
(43)	Tony Gwynn	5.00
(44)	Von Hayes	2.00
(45)	Rickey Henderson	2.00
(46)	Tom Herr	2.00
(47)	Orel Hershiser	2.00
(48)	Teddy Higuera	2.00
(49)	Kent Hrbek	2.00
(50)	Bo Jackson	2.50
(51)	Danny Jackson	2.00
(52)	Brook Jacoby	2.00
(53)	Howard Johnson	2.00
(54)	Doug Jones	2.00
(55)	Wally Joyner	2.00
(56)	Chet Lemon	2.00
(57)	Jeffrey Leonard	2.00
(58)	Dennis Martinez	2.00
(59)	Don Mattingly	7.50
(60)	Roger McDowell	2.00
(61)	Fred McGriff	2.00
(62)	Mark McGwire	10.00
(63)	Kevin Mitchell	2.00
(64)	Paul Molitor	3.00
(65)	Jack Morris	2.00
(66)	Dale Murphy	3.00
(67)	Gregg Olson	2.00
(68)	Kirby Puckett	6.00
(69)	Tim Raines	2.00
(70)	Dennis Rasmussen	2.00
(71)	Harold Reynolds	2.00
(72)	Dave Righetti	2.00
(73)	Billy Ripken	2.00
(74)	Cal Ripken Jr.	9.00
(75)	Nolan Ryan	9.00
(76)	Bret Saberhagen	2.00
(77)	Chris Sabo	2.00
(78)	Ryne Sandberg	3.50
(79)	Benito Santiago	2.00
(80)	Steve Sax	2.00
(81)	Mike Scioscia	2.00
(82)	Mike Scott	2.00
(83)	Ruben Sierra	2.00
(84)	Lee Smith	2.00
(85)	Lonnie Smith	2.00
(86)	Ozzie Smith	3.50
(87)	John Smoltz	2.50
(88)	Cory Snyder	2.00
(89)	Dave Stewart	2.00
(90)	Dave Stieb	2.00
(91)	Darryl Strawberry	2.50
(92)	B.J. Surhoff	2.00
(93)	Greg Swindell	2.00
(94)	Mickey Tettleton	2.00
(95)	Bobby Thigpen	2.00
(96)	Alan Trammell	2.00
(97)	Fernando Valenzuela	2.00
(98)	Andy Van Slyke	2.00
(99)	Frank Viola	2.00
(100)	Greg Walker	2.00
(101)	Tim Wallach	2.00
(102)	Jerome Walton	2.00
(103)	Lou Whitaker	2.00
(104)	Matt Williams	2.00
(105)	Mitch Williams	2.00
(106)	Dave Winfield	3.00
(107)	Todd Worrell	2.00
(108)	Robin Yount	4.00

1991 Ace Novelty MVP Pins

In its second and final year of producing collector pins matched with contemporary Score cards in a blister pack, Ace Novelty changed the pins from die-cut silhouettes to a standard 1-1/8" x 1-3/8" format with a color photo at center, surrounded by a gold border with team and player name at bottom. Backs have previous season stats printed in black. The unnumbered pins are checklisted here alphabetically. Prices shown are for unopened pin/card blister packs.

		MT
Complete Set (48):		150.00
Common Player:		2.00
(1)	Sandy Alomar Jr.	2.50
(2)	Eric Anthony	2.00
(3)	Wade Boggs	3.50
(4)	Barry Bonds	5.00
(5)	George Brett	5.00
(6)	Jose Canseco	3.00
(7)	Will Clark	2.50
(8)	Roger Clemens	3.50
(9)	Eric Davis	2.00
(10)	Andre Dawson	2.00
(11)	Delino DeShields	2.00
(12)	Cecil Fielder	2.00
(13)	Carlton Fisk	3.00
(14)	Travis Fryman	2.00
(15)	Ron Gant	2.00
(16)	Dwight Gooden	2.50
(17)	Mark Grace	2.50
(18)	Ken Griffey Jr.	7.50
(19)	Tony Gwynn	4.00
(20)	Rickey Henderson	2.50
(21)	Bo Jackson	2.50
(22)	Gregg Jefferies	2.00
(23)	David Justice	2.00
(24)	Ben McDonald	2.00
(25)	Mark McGwire	5.00
(26)	Kevin Maas	2.00
(27)	Ramon Martinez	2.00
(28)	Tino Martinez	2.00
(29)	Don Mattingly	5.00
(30)	Kevin Mitchell	2.00
(31)	Paul Molitor	3.00
(32)	Hal Morris	2.00
(33)	Dale Murphy	2.50
(34)	Eddie Murray	2.50
(35)	John Olerud	2.00
(36)	Kirby Puckett	5.00
(37)	Cal Ripken Jr.	6.00
(38)	Nolan Ryan	6.00
(39)	Ryne Sandberg	3.00
(40)	David Segui	2.00
(41)	Ozzie Smith	4.00
(42)	Sammy Sosa	4.00
(43)	Kevin Tapani	2.00
(44)	Frank Thomas	5.00
(45)	Mo Vaughn	2.50
(46)	Matt Williams	2.00
(47)	Robin Yount	3.00
(48)	Todd Zeile	2.00

1991 Acme Reproductions Ryan-Seaver

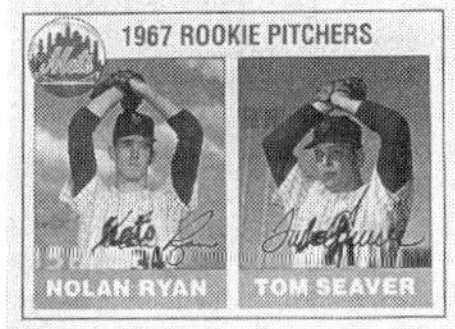

This collectors issue was produced in an edition of 10,000. In a style approximating a 1967 Topps card, the future Hall of Famers are pictured in their early days with the Mets. Facsimile autographs appear at the bottom of each photo. A total of 420 of the cards were authentically autographed by both players. Backs have a cartoon and biographical data on each player, plus a career summary up to 1967. Original issue price was $29, or $109 for the autographed card. Each came in a lucite holder with numbered certificate of authenticity.

	MT
Nolan Ryan, Tom Seaver	24.00
Nolan Ryan, Tom Seaver (autographed)	225.00

1988 Action Packed

Action Packed released this test set in an effort to receive a license from Major League Baseball. The cards are styled like the Action Packed football issues on the card fronts. The flip sides are styled like Score baseball cards. The Ozzie Smith card is considered scarcer than the other five cards in the test set, while a hoard of Mattingly cards revealed in 1998 drove down the price of his card. Action Packed did not receive a license to produce baseball cards.

		MT
Complete Set (6):		250.00
Common Player:		40.00
(1)	Wade Boggs	75.00
(2)	Andre Dawson	45.00
(3)	Dwight Gooden	45.00
(4)	Carney Lansford	30.00
(5)	Don Mattingly	25.00
(6)	Ozzie Smith	75.00

1992 Action Packed Promos

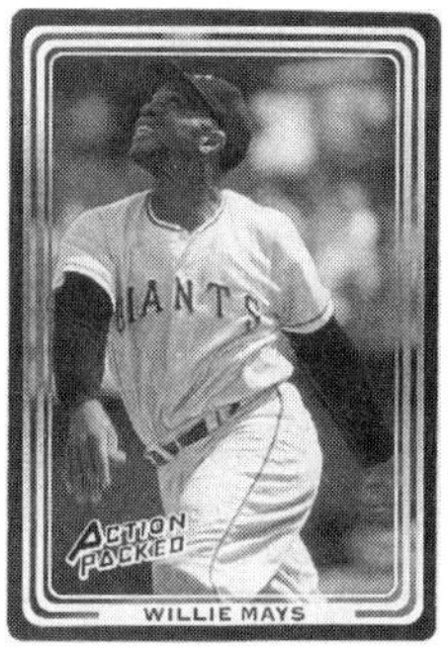

This set was produced to preview Action Packed's All-Star Gallery card issue. The promo cards are identical in format to the regularly issued cards and use the same player photos. The only differences in the promos are found on the back, where the card number is missing from the lower-left corner and where a white "1992 Prototype" is overprinted on the gray background beneath the black career highlights. The promos were widely distributed at trade shows and to Action Packed's dealer network. The unnumbered promo cards are checklisted here alphabetically.

		MT
Complete Set (5):		15.00
Common Player:		2.00
(1)	Yogi Berra	4.00
(2)	Bob Gibson	3.00
(3)	Willie Mays	7.50
(4)	Warren Spahn	3.00
(5)	Willie Stargell	3.00

1992 Action Packed All-Star Gallery Series I

Action Packed, makers of a high quality, embossed style

football card for several years, entered the baseball card field in 1992 with its 84-card All-Star Gallery, Series One. The cards feature former baseball greats, with 72 of the 84 cards in color and the remaining in sepia tone. Each foil pack of seven cards reportedly contained at least one Hall of Famer, and the company also made special 24K, gold leaf stamped cards of all of the HOFers that were randomly inserted in the packs.

		MT
Complete Set (84):		15.00
Common Player:		.15
1	Yogi Berra	.35
2	Lou Brock	.20
3	Bob Gibson	.25
4	Ferguson Jenkins	.20
5	Ralph Kiner	.20
6	Al Kaline	.25
7	Lou Boudreau	.20
8	Bobby Doerr	.20
9	Billy Herman	.20
10	Monte Irvin	.20
11	George Kell	.20
12	Robin Roberts	.20
13	Johnny Mize	.20
14	Willie Mays	.75
15	Enos Slaughter	.20
16	Warren Spahn	.25
17	Willie Stargell	.20
18	Billy Williams	.20
19	Vernon Law	.15
20	Virgil Trucks	.15
21	Mel Parnell	.15
22	Wally Moon	.15
23	Gene Woodling	.15
24	Richie Ashburn	.25
25	Mark Fidrych	.15
26	Elroy Face	.15
27	Larry Doby	.20
28	Dick Groat	.15
29	Cesar Cedeno	.15
30	Bob Horner	.15
31	Bobby Richardson	.15
32	Bobby Murcer	.15
33	Gil McDougald	.15
34	Roy White	.15
35	Bill Skowron	.20
36	Mickey Lolich	.15
37	Minnie Minoso	.15
38	Billy Pierce	.15
39	Ron Santo	.20
40	Sal Bando	.15
41	Ralph Branca	.15
42	Bert Campaneris	.15
43	Joe Garagiola	.25
44	Vida Blue	.15
45	Frank Crosetti	.15
46	Luis Tiant	.15
47	Maury Wills	.15
48	Sam McDowell	.15
49	Jimmy Piersall	.20
50	Jim Lonborg	.15
51	Don Newcombe	.20
52	Bobby Thomson	.20
53	Wilbur Wood	.15
54	Carl Erskine	.15
55	Chris Chambliss	.15
56	Dave Kingman	.15
57	Ken Holtzman	.15
58	Bud Harrelson	.15
59	Clem Labine	.15
60	Tony Oliva	.20
61	George Foster	.15
62	Bobby Bonds	.20
63	Harvey Haddix	.15
64	Steve Garvey	.20
65	Rocky Colavito	.25
66	Orlando Cepeda	.25
67	Ed Lopat	.15
68	Al Oliver	.15
69	Bill Mazeroski	.20
70	Al Rosen	.15
71	Bob Grich	.15
72	Curt Flood	.15
73	Willie Horton	.15
74	Rico Carty	.15
75	Davey Johnson	.15
76	Don Kessinger	.15
77	Frank Thomas	.15
78	Bobby Shantz	.15
79	Herb Score	.20
80	Boog Powell	.20
81	Rusty Staub	.20
82	Bill Madlock	.15
83	Manny Mota	.15
84	Bill White	.15

1993 Action Packed All-Star Gallery Series II

The Second Series of Action Packed All-Star Gallery was released in 1993, with cards numbered from 85 to 168. In a similar fashion to the First Series, Series Two features 52 cards in color, 31 in sepia tone and one as a colorized black and white. The series also includes two tongue-in-cheek cards - "Who's on First?" duo Bud Abbot and Lou Costello, and a card highlighting the TV and radio career of Bob Uecker.

		MT
Complete Set (84):		20.00
Common Player:		.15
85	Cy Young	.25
86	Honus Wagner	.25
87	Christy Mathewson	.25
88	Ty Cobb	.75
89	Eddie Collins	.20
90	Walter Johnson	.25
91	Tris Speaker	.25
92	Grover Alexander	.20
93	Edd Roush	.20
94	Babe Ruth	1.00
95	Rogers Hornsby	.25
96	Pie Traynor	.20
97	Lou Gehrig	.75
98	Mickey Cochrane	.20
99	Lefty Grove	.20
100	Jimmie Foxx	.25
101	Tony Lazzeri	.20
102	Mel Ott	.20
103	Carl Hubbell	.20
104	Al Lopez	.20
105	Lefty Gomez	.20
106	Dizzy Dean	.25
107	Hank Greenberg	.20
108	Joe Medwick	.20
109	Arky Vaughan	.20
110	Bob Feller	.25
111	Hal Newhouser	.20
112	Early Wynn	.20
113	Bob Lemon	.20
114	Red Schoendienst	.20
115	Satchel Paige	.45
116	Whitey Ford	.25
117	Eddie Mathews	.25
118	Harmon Killebrew	.25
119	Roberto Clemente	1.00
120	Brooks Robinson	.30
121	Don Drysdale	.25
122	Luis Aparicio	.20
123	Willie McCovey	.20
124	Juan Marichal	.20
125	Gaylord Perry	.20
126	Catfish Hunter	.20
127	Jim Palmer	.25
128	Rod Carew	.25
129	Tom Seaver	.30
130	Rollie Fingers	.20
131	Joe Jackson	1.00
132	Pepper Martin	.15
133	Joe Gordon	.15
134	Marty Marion	.15
135	Allie Reynolds	.15
136	Johnny Sain	.20
137	Gil Hodges	.25
138	Ted Kluszewski	.25
139	Nellie Fox	.30
140	Billy Martin	.20
141	Smoky Burgess	.15
142	Lew Burdette	.15
143	Joe Black	.15
144	Don Larsen	.20
145	Ken Boyer	.15
146	Johnny Callison	.15
147	Norm Cash	.20
148	Keith Hernandez	.15
149	Jim Kaat	.15
150	Bill Freehan	.15
151	Joe Torre	.20
152	Bob Uecker	.20
153	Dave McNally	.15
154	Denny McLain	.20
155	Dick Allen	.20
156	Jimmy Wynn	.15
157	Tommy John	.15
158	Paul Blair	.15
159	Reggie Smith	.15
160	Jerry Koosman	.15
161	Thurman Munson	.25
162	Graig Nettles	.15
163	Ron Cey	.15
164	Cecil Cooper	.15
165	Dave Parker	.20
166	Jim Rice	.20
167	Kent Tekulve	.15
168	Who's on First? (Bud Abbott, Lou Costello)	.50

1992-93 Action Packed Gold

Essentially identical to the regular-issue Action Packed All-Star Gallery cards, these premium inserts are specially numbered with a "G" prefix and highlighted with 24-karat gold detailing.

		MT
Complete Set (65):		700.00
Common Player:		10.00
Series I		
1	Yogi Berra	15.00
2	Lou Brock	12.50
3	Bob Gibson	12.50
4	Ferguson Jenkins	10.00
5	Ralph Kiner	10.00
6	Al Kaline	12.50
7	Lou Boudreau	10.00
8	Bobby Doerr	10.00
9	Billy Herman	10.00
10	Monte Irvin	10.00
11	George Kell	10.00
12	Robin Roberts	10.00
13	Johnny Mize	10.00
14	Willie Mays	30.00
15	Enos Slaughter	10.00
16	Warren Spahn	12.50
17	Willie Stargell	10.00
18	Billy Williams	10.00
Series II		
19	Cy Young	12.50
20	Honus Wagner	17.50
21	Christy Mathewson	12.50
22	Ty Cobb	22.00
23	Eddie Collins	10.00
24	Walter Johnson	12.50
25	Tris Speaker	12.50
26	Grover Alexander	12.50
27	Edd Roush	10.00
28	Babe Ruth	45.00
29	Rogers Hornsby	12.50
30	Pie Traynor	10.00
31	Lou Gehrig	30.00
32	Mickey Cochrane	12.50
33	Lefty Grove	12.50
34	Jimmie Foxx	12.50
35	Tony Lazzeri	10.00
36	Mel Ott	10.00
37	Carl Hubbell	10.00
38	Al Lopez	10.00
39	Lefty Gomez	10.00
40	Dizzy Dean	15.00
41	Hank Greenberg	15.00
42	Joe Medwick	10.00
43	Arky Vaughan	10.00
44	Bob Feller	12.50
45	Hal Newhouser	10.00
46	Early Wynn	10.00
47	Bob Lemon	10.00
48	Red Schoendienst	10.00
49	Satchel Paige	22.00
50	Whitey Ford	12.50
51	Eddie Mathews	12.50
52	Harmon Killebrew	12.50
53	Roberto Clemente	25.00
54	Brooks Robinson	12.50
55	Don Drysdale	12.50
56	Luis Aparicio	10.00
57	Willie McCovey	12.50
58	Juan Marichal	10.00
59	Gaylord Perry	10.00
60	Catfish Hunter	10.00
61	Jim Palmer	12.50
62	Rod Carew	12.50
63	Tom Seaver	12.50
64	Rollie Fingers	10.00
65	Who's on First? (Bud Abbott, Lou Costello)	12.50

1993 Action Packed Amoco/Coke

A special version of 18 of its All-Star Gallery cards was created by Action Packed for use as a premium by Amoco gas stations and Coca-Cola. Card fronts feature the same embossed color or sepia player photos with a heavily lacquered finish and gold-foil and black borders. Gray backs have biographical and career data, a few stats and sponsors' logos. Complete sets were available via a mail-in offer from Coke products. Most of these cards share card numbers and photos with AP's Series I ASG cards.

		MT
Complete Set (18):		6.00
Common Player:		.50
1	Yogi Berra	1.00
2	Lou Brock	.50
3	Bob Gibson	.50
4	Red Schoendienst	.50
5	Ralph Kiner	.50
6	Al Kaline	.90
7	Lou Boudreau	.50
8	Bobby Doerr	.50
9	Gaylord Perry	.50
10	Monte Irvin	.50
11	George Kell	.50
12	Robin Roberts	.80
13	Johnny Mize	.50
14	Willie Mays	2.00
15	Enos Slaughter	.50
16	Warren Spahn	.50
17	Willie Stargell	.50
18	Billy Williams	.50

1993 Action Packed Tom Seaver Prototypes

Tom Seaver's career was highlighted in this five-card promo set. Each card has an embossed front color photo surrounded by three gold pinstripes and a red border. Seaver's name is in red in a gold bar at bottom. Backs are printed in black and gold with a white undertype reading "1993 Prototype." Backs have biographical and career data, lifetime stats and a few sentences of career highlights. Cards have a "TS" prefix to the card number.

		MT
Complete Set:		24.00
Common Card:		5.00
1	The Franchise	5.00
2	Amazin' Mets	8.00
3	A Tearful Goodbye	5.00
4	Tom Terrific	8.00
5	Dazzling the Windy City	5.00

1993 Adohr Farms California Angels

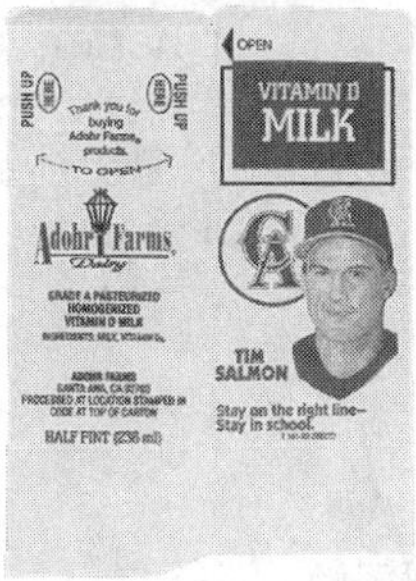

Four California Angels rookies were featured on the side panels of these half-pint milk cartons distributed only in schools and hospitals in L.A. and Orange Counties. The player picture portion of the carton is approximately 2-1/4" x 2-7/8" and printed in red on white. Values shown are for cut panels; complete cartons would command a premium.

		MT
Complete Set (4):		10.00
Common Player:		2.00
(1)	Chad Curtis	2.00
(2)	Damion Easley	2.00
(3)	Tim Salmon	5.00
(4)	J.T. Snow	3.00

1996 Advance Auto Parts Pittsburgh Pirates

For 1996 the Pirates' annual issue of player cards in the large format (3-1/2" x 5-3/4") was sponsored by an auto parts retailer. On front color player photos are vignetted in shades of red, gold and yellow. A box at bottom has uniform number, player name and position and the team's '96 logo. Backs are in black-and-white and offer minimal player biographical data and a sponsor's logo. It is possible other cards of late-season additions to the Pirates' roster were also issued.

		MT
Complete Set (46):		20.00
Common Player:		.50
(1)	Jermaine Allensworth	1.00
(2)	Jay Bell	1.00
(3)	Steve Blass (announcer)	.50
(4)	Cam Bonifay	.50

(5)	Greg Brown (announcer)	.50
(6)	Jacob Brumfield	.50
(7)	Jason Christiansen	.50
(8)	Dave Clark	.50
(9)	Steve Cooke	.50
(10)	Francisco Cordova	.75
(11)	Danny Darwin	.50
(12)	Elmer Dessens	.50
(13)	Rich Donnelly	.50
(14)	Angelo Encarnacion	.50
(15)	John Ericks	.50
(16)	Lanny Frattare (announcer)	.50
(17)	Carlos Garcia	.50
(18)	Charlie Hayes	.50
(19)	Mark Johnson	.50
(20)	Jason Kendall	1.50
(21)	Jeff King	.75
(22)	Mike Kingery	.50
(23a)	Gene Lamont (coach)	.50
(23b)	Gene Lamont (manager)	.50
(24)	Jim Leyland	.50
(25)	Jon Lieber	.50
(26)	Nelson Liriano	.50
(27)	Al Martin	.50
(28)	Milt May	.50
(29)	Kevin McClatchy	.50
(30)	Orlando Merced	.50
(31)	Dan Miceli	.50
(32)	Ray Miller	.50
(33)	Ramon Morel	.50
(34)	Denny Neagle	.60
(35)	Keith Osik	.50
(36)	Steve Parris	.50
(37a)	Chris Peters (black jersey)	.50
(37b)	Chris Peters (white jersey)	.50
(38)	Dan Plesac	.50
(39)	Tommy Sandt	.50
(40)	Zane Smith	.50
(41)	Paul Wagner	.50
(42)	Bob Walk (announcer)	.50
(43)	John Wehner	.50
(44)	Marc Wilkins	.50
(45)	Spin Williams	.50
(46)	Pirate Parrot (mascot)	.50

1997 Advance Auto Parts Pittsburgh Pirates

For a second consecutive year, the Pirates' annual player photocard issue was sponsored by a local chain of auto parts stores. The 3-1/2" x 5-3/4" cards have posed player portraits on front, bordered by, successively, a black-and-white barred strip, a brown border made to appear like aged parchment, and black. Player name and uniform number appear on the parchment portion. Backs repeat the border motif in black-and-white horizontal format with large team and sponsor logos and a few tidbits of player data. This checklist may be incomplete as in previous years the team has issued update cards as players are added to the roster.

		MT
Complete Set (46):		16.00
Common Player:		.50
2	Kevin Polcovich	.50
5	Tony Womack	1.00
6	Lou Collier	.50
10	Kevin Elster	.50
11	Jose Guillen	1.00
12	Turner Ward	.50
13	Adrian Brown	.50
15	Keith Osik	.50
16	Joe Randa	.60
17	Dale Sveum	.50
18	Jason Kendall	.75
19	Emil Brown	.50
23	Lloyd McClendon	.50
25	Mark Smith	.60
26	Steve Cooke	.50
28	Al Martin	.60
29	Kevin Young	.60
30	Midre Cummings	.60
32	Gene Lamont	.50
34	Esteban Loaiza	.75
35	Mark Wilkins	.50
36	Mark Johnson	.50
37	Joe Jones	.50
38	Chris Peters	.50
39	Jeff Granger	.50
41	Jason Christiansen	.50
42	Jason Schmidt	.50
44	Rick Renick	.50
45	Jack Lind	.50
46	Jermaine Allensworth	.75
47	Jon Lieber	.50
49	Matt Ruebel	.50
50	Pete Vuckovich	.50
51	Rich Loiselle	.60
53	Dave Wainhouse	.50
54	Spin Williams	.50
56	Jose Silva	.50
57	John Ericks	.50
63	Clint Sodowsky	.50
67	Francisco Cordova	.65
73	Ricardo Rincon	.50
	ANNOUNCERS	
---	Steve Blass	.50
---	Greg Brown	.50
---	Lanny Frattare	.50
---	Bob Walk	.50

1998 Advance Auto Parts Pittsburgh Pirates

Made for personal use of the players and staff, and not available from the team, these photocards recycled the 1997 design, but on a smaller 3-1/2" x 4-3/4" format. Fronts retain the color photo off-centered on a parchment background. Backs repeat the background and have player personal data, a uniform number and logos of the team and sponsor. Some photos were reused in the 1998 set, and other players continued to use the larger 3-1/2" x 5-3/4" cards of 1997 to answer autograph requests.

		MT
Complete Set (24):		13.00
Common Player:		.50
(1)	Jermaine Allensworth	.75
(2)	Steve Blass (broadcaster)	.50
(3)	Greg Brown (broadcaster)	.50
(4)	Lou Collier	.50
(5)	Elmer Dessens	.50
(6)	Lanny Frattare (broadcaster)	.50
(7)	Jose Guillen	1.00
(8)	Jason Kendall	.65
(9)	Gene Lamont	.50
(10)	Jon Lieber	.50
(11)	Scott Little	.50
(12)	Esteban Loiaza	.50
(13)	Rich Loiselle	.50
(14)	Javier Martinez	.50
(15)	Manny Martinez	.50
(16)	Keith Osik	.50
(17)	Chris Peters	.50
(18)	Kevin Polcovich	.50
(19)	Aramis Ramirez	2.00
(20)	Ricardo Rincon	.50
(21)	Chance Sanford	.50
(22)	Jason Schmidt	.50
(23)	Doug Strange	.50
(24)	Jeff Tabaka	.50

1983 Affiliated Food Rangers

This 28-card set, featuring the Texas Rangers, was issued as a promotion by the Affiliated Food Stores chain of Arlington, Texas, late during the 1983 baseball season. Complete sets were given out free to youngsters 13 and under at the Sept. 3, 1983, Rangers game. The cards measure 2-3/8" x 3-1/2" and feature a full-color photo on the front. Also on the front, located inside a blue box, is the player's name, uniform number, and the words "1983 Rangers." The card backs contain a small player photo plus biographical and statistical information, along with the Affiliated logo and a brief promotional message. A total of 10,000 sets was reportedly printed. Cards are numbered by the players' uniform numbers in the checklist that follows.

		MT
Complete Set (28):		8.00
Common Player:		.35
1	Bill Stein	.35
2	Mike Richardt	.35
3	Wayne Tolleson	.35
5	Billy Sample	.35
6	Bobby Jones	.35
7	Bucky Dent	.45
8	Bobby Johnson	.35
9	Pete O'Brien	.35
10	Jim Sundberg	.35
11	Doug Rader	.35
12	Dave Hostetler	.35
14	Larry Biittner	.35
15	Larry Parrish	.35
17	Mickey Rivers	.45
21	Odell Jones	.35
24	Dave Schmidt	.35
25	Buddy Bell	.50
26	George Wright	.35
28	Frank Tanana	.35
29	John Butcher	.35
32	Jon Matlack	.35
40	Rick Honeycutt	.35
41	Dave Tobik	.35
44	Danny Darwin	.35
46	Jim Anderson	.35
48	Mike Smithson	.35
49	Charlie Hough	.50
----	Coaching Staff (Rich Donnelly, Glenn Ezell, Merv Rettenmund, Dick Such, Wayne Terwilliger)	.35

1990 Agfa Film

This "old-timers" set was distributed in three-card packs with the purchase of Agfa film. Produced by Michael Schechter Associates, whose logo appears on the back, the cards were not licensed by Major League Baseball, so team logos had to be eliminated from the photos. Cards have a white background with the film company's logos in the upper corners. Backs are in black-and-white and have full major league regular season and post-season stats.

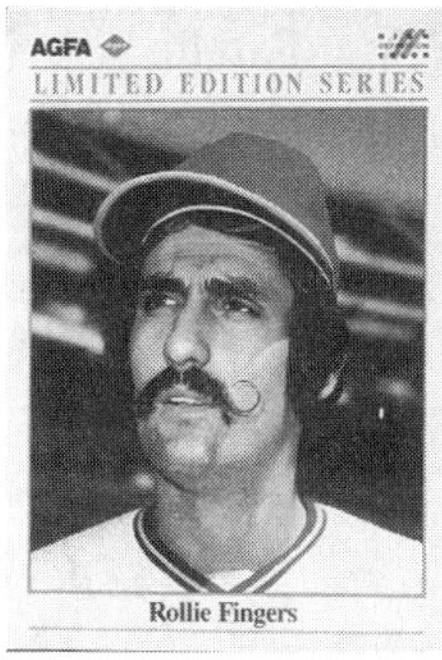

		MT
Complete Set (22):		17.50
Common Player:		.50
1	Willie Mays	2.00
2	Carl Yastrzemski	1.00
3	Harmon Killebrew	1.00
4	Joe Torre	.75
5	Al Kaline	1.00
6	Hank Aaron	2.00
7	Rod Carew	1.00
8	Roberto Clemente	4.00
9	Luis Aparicio	.75
10	Roger Maris	1.50
11	Joe Morgan	.75
12	Maury Wills	.50
13	Brooks Robinson	1.00
14	Tom Seaver	1.00
15	Steve Carlton	1.00
16	Whitey Ford	1.25
17	Jim Palmer	.75
18	Rollie Fingers	.75
19	Bruce Sutter	.50
20	Willie McCovey	1.00
21	Mike Schmidt	1.50
22	Yogi Berra	1.50

1983 Ajax Dog Food

Hardly worth the title of "collectors issue," this piece of junk was marketed in early 1984 by persons attempting to pass it off as an issue of "Ajax Dog Food." On some cards the words "Ajax Dog Products" can be found in small white type in the lower-left border, though on most the poor print quality has obscured most or all of the type. The 2-1/2" x 3-1/2" cards have player action photos that were stolen from elsewhere and printed on a white background surrounded by a black border. The name is in outline type at the bottom. An even lower-quality photocopied reprint of the Ripken card has been seen.

		MT
Complete Set (6):		3.00
Common Card:		.50
(1)	Chili Davis	.50
(2)	Pedro Guerrero	.50
(3)	Rickey Henderson	.75
(4)	Kent Hrbeck (Hrbek)	.50
(5)	Willie McGee	.50
(6)	Cal Ripken	2.50

1984 Ajax Dog Food

A second series of this collectors issue was released in 1984, this time adding a picture of a beagle named Ajax to player photos stolen from other sources. The cards feature young stars of the time, most of whom have faded. Cards are printed in 2-1/2" x 3-1/2" black-and-white, on semi-gloss stock. Backs are blank. The unnumbered cards are checklisted here in alphabetical order.

		MT
Complete Set (9):		4.50
Common Player:		.50
(1)	George Bell	.50
(2)	Wade Boggs	1.00
(3)	Jody Davis	.50
(4)	Len Faedo	.50
(5)	Julio Franco	.50
(6)	Gary Gaetti	.50
(7)	Mel Hall	.50
(8)	Ron Kittle	.50
(9)	Darryl Strawberry	.65

1990 All American Baseball Team

Produced by Mike Schechter Associates, this 24-card set includes many of the top players in the game. Team logos are airbrushed from the color photo on front, which is surrounded by a red, white and blue border and the MLB Players' Association logo. The backs are printed in blue on white stock, with a facsimile autograph appearing above the statistics.

		MT
Complete Set:		25.00
Common Player:		.15
1	George Brett	1.25
2	Mark McGwire	4.00
3	Wade Boggs	1.00
4	Cal Ripken, Jr.	3.50
5	Rickey Henderson	.60
6	Dwight Gooden	.45
7	Bo Jackson	.45
8	Roger Clemens	1.00
9	Orel Hershiser	.45
10	Ozzie Smith	1.00
11	Don Mattingly	2.00
12	Kirby Puckett	1.00
13	Robin Yount	1.25
14	Tony Gwynn	1.25
15	Jose Canseco	.75
16	Nolan Ryan	3.50

17	Ken Griffey, Jr.	4.00
18	Will Clark	.60
19	Ryne Sandberg	1.25
20	Kent Hrbek	.45
21	Carlton Fisk	.75
22	Paul Molitor	1.00
23	Dave Winfield	.60
24	Andre Dawson	.50

1989 All-Star Time Nolan Ryan

This card was produced as part of a packaged set with a high-quality wrist watch honoring Nolan Ryan's 5,000th strikeout on Aug. 22, 1989. The 2-1/4" x 3-1/4" card is printed on thin, blank-backed cardboard. The photo of Ryan is in color, the graphics are black-and-white. The watch set originally sold for nearly $300, but the value of the card alone is undetermined.

		MT
Complete Set (1):		
(1)	Nolan Ryan	

1987 Allstate Insurance

This 6-card set was the second promotional series of baseball cards created by Allstate Insurance graphic artist Ray Lending for internal use by the company. Modeled after the famous "Diamond Stars" from the 1930s, this set features full-color player portraits of legendary sluggers. "Life Grand Slam" (the promotion theme) is printed beneath the player portrait and the player's name appears in an upper corner. Black and white backs provide personal information, player profiles and career highlights. 15,000 sets of the cards were distributed, although only a few filtered into the collecting hobby. Cards measure 2-3/4" x 3-5/8" in size. Full-color 22" x 28" reproductions of the cards in this set were produced in poster format.

		MT
Complete Set (6):		45.00
Common Player:		4.50
(1)	Hank Aaron	7.50
(2)	Joe DiMaggio	15.00
(3)	Jimmie Foxx	4.50
(4)	Lou Gehrig	9.00
(5)	Babe Ruth	15.00
(6)	Ted Williams	7.50

1991 Alrak Griffey Gazette

Ken Griffey, Jr. was featured in a 1991 set of four cards entitled "Griffey Gazette" that was released by Alrak Enterprises. The card sets were limited to 100,000, and major league logos were airbrushed out from caps and uniforms.

		MT
Complete Set (4):		4.00
(1)	Crowd Pleaser (Ken Griffey, Jr.)	1.00
(2)	Holdin On! (Ken Griffey, Jr.)	1.00
(3)	24ct Gold Moment (Ken Griffey, Jr.)	1.00
(4)	Next of Ken (Ken Griffey, Jr. with Ken Griffey, Sr.)	1.00

1992 Alrak Griffey's Golden Moments

Printed on plastic in format similar to a credit card, these 2-1/8" x 3-3/8" cards depict Ken Griffey Sr. and Jr. in various poses. Seattle Mariners uniform logos have been removed from the photos. A "Griffey's Golden Moments" logo appears on each side of the cards. Backs are in black-and-white and contain player information and/or stats. While the cards are numbered, "X of 20" on back, only 10 were issued, reportedly in an edition of 10,000 sets.

		MT
Complete Set (10):		20.00
Common Card:		2.50
1	Ken Griffey Jr. (batting, horizontal format)	2.50
2	Ken Griffey Jr. (fielding)	2.50
3	Ken Griffey Jr. (sliding)	2.50
4	Ken Griffey Jr. (holding bat)	2.50
5	Ken Griffey Jr., Ken Griffey Sr.	2.50
6	Ken Griffey Jr. (batting)	2.50
7	Ken Griffey Jr. (holding All-Star trophy)	2.50
8	Ken Griffey Jr. (portrait)	2.50
9	Ken Griffey Jr. (on base)	2.50
10	Ken Griffey Jr., Ken Griffey Sr. (in dugout)	2.50

1993 Alrak Ken Griffey, Jr.

Ken Griffey, Jr. was the subject of a four-card set released in 1993 by Alrak Enterprises. The set features Griffey in various poses and is highlighted with a 1992 All-Star MVP commemorative card. The cards are UV coated and gold foil stamped and limited to 24,000 sets. Additionally, the company also issued a Griffey Jr. Triple Play card in an oversized format (3-1/2" x 7-1/2") limited to 15,000.

		MT
Complete Set (4):		6.00
Common Card:		1.50
(1)	Ken Griffey, Jr. (portrait)	1.50
(2)	Ken Griffey, Jr. (batting)	1.50
(3)	Ken Griffey, Jr. (throwing)	1.50
(4)	Ken Griffey, Jr. (All-Star MVP)	1.50

1993 Alrak Ken Griffey Jr., Triple Play

This triple-size (3-1/2" x 7-1/2") card features on one side a large batting photo of Griffey, Jr., with 1992 and career stats beneath and a "TRIPLE PLAY" header in the white border above. The back has a central title card area flanked by portrait and game-action photos. A total of 15,000 of these cards was reportedly produced.

		MT
Complete Set:		3.00
(1)	Ken Griffey Jr.	3.00

1994 AMC Theaters S.F. Giants

This series of large-format (about 4-1/4" x 11"), blank-back photocards was sponsored by a Bay Area movie house chain. Cards have black-and-white action photos at center with player identification below. At top is a team logo, at bottom is a sponsor's logo. The unnumbered cards are checklisted here in alphabetical order.

		MT
Complete Set (33)		30.00
Common Player:		1.00
(1)	Dusty Baker	1.25
(2)	Rod Beck (ready to pitch)	1.25
(3)	Rod Beck (piching follow through)	1.25
(4)	Mike Benjamin	1.00
(5)	Todd Benzinger	1.00
(6)	Barry Bonds ('93 jersey)	5.00
(7)	Barry Bonds ('94 jersey)	5.00
(8)	Dave Burba	1.00
(9)	John Burkett	1.25
(10)	Mark Carreon	1.00
(11)	Royce Clayton	1.00
(12)	Steve Frey	1.00
(13)	Bryan Hickerson	1.00
(14)	Mike Jackson	1.00
(15)	Darren Lewis	1.00
(16)	Kirt Manwaring	1.00
(17)	Dave Martinez ('93 jersey)	1.00
(18)	Dave Martinez ('94 jersey)	1.00
(19)	Willie McGee	1.00
(20)	Rich Monteleone	1.00
(21)	John Patterson	1.00
(22)	Mark Portugal (negative reversed, pitching lefty)	1.00
(23)	Mark Portugal (correct, pitching righty)	1.00
(24)	Jeff Reed	1.00
(25)	Kevin Rogers (standing)	1.00
(26)	Kevin Rogers (pitching)	1.00
(27)	Steve Scarsone	1.00
(28)	Bill Swift	1.00
(29)	Robby Thompson ('93 jersey)	1.00
(30)	Robby Thompson ('94 jersey)	1.00
(31)	Salomon Torres	1.00
(32)	Matt Williams (batting)	2.00
(33)	Matt Williams (fielding)	2.00

1994 American Archives Origins of Baseball

This collectors' issue presents the history of baseball in America from 1744-1899. Sold in box-set form only, the cards are in standard 2-1/2" x 3-1/2" format. Fronts feature sepia-toned photos and line-art on a black background. Backs have a lengthy narrative, also printed in sepia on black. Both sides are UV coated. Individual cards feature early players, team photos, game action scenes or other historical vignettes. The set was produced by American Archives.

		MT
Complete Set:		22.00
Common Card:		.25
1	Abner Doubleday	.25
2	Doubleday Field	.25
3	Rounders 1744	.25
4	Early Baseball 700 A.D.	.25
5	The Knickerbockers	.25
6	Alex Cartwright	.25
7	Baseball in the 1850s	.25
8	Social Clubs	.25
9	Brooklyn Eckfords	.25
10	New England Baseball	.25
11	Henry Chadwick	.25
12	Brooklyn Excelsiors	.25
13	Abraham Lincoln	.25
14	Andrew Johnson	.25
15	First Enclosed Park	.25
16	Brooklyn Atlantics	.25
17	James Creighton	.25
18	Baseball in the 1860s	.25
19	1869 Red Stockings	.25
20	Cincinnati Celebration	.25
21	Harry Wright	.25
22	Boston Ball Club 1872	.25
23	Arthur Cummings	.25
24	William Hulbert	.25
25	George Wright	.25
26	Albert Spalding	.25
27	Albert Bushong	.25
28	Bid McPhee	.25
29	James O'Rourke	.25
30	Pud Galvin	.25
31	Edwin Bligh	.25
32	William Purcell	.25
33	Roger Connor	.25
34	Cincinnati Ball Club 1882	.25
35	Peter Browning	.25
36	William Gleason	.25
37	Paul Hines	.25
38	Baseball in the 1880s	.25
39	Robert Carruthers	.25
40	New York Metropolitans	.25
41	St. George's Field	.25
42	Charles Radbourne	.25
43	George Andrews	.25
44	William Hoy	.25
45	Chicago Ball Club 1886	.25
46	Cap Anson	.25
47	John Clarkson	.25
48	Mike Kelly	.25
49	Buffalo Bisons 1887	.25
50	Moses Walker	.25
51	Detroit Ball Club 1887	.25
52	Little League	.25
53	Louisville Ball Club 1888	.25
54	John Farrell	.25
55	Walter Latham	.25
56	Fred Dunlap	.25
57	Tim Keefe	.25
58	Cincinnati Ball Club 1888	.25
59	1889 World Tour	.25
60	Dan Brouthers	.25
61	John M. Ward	.25
62	Albert Spalding	.25
63	The Baseball Cap	.25
64	Tom Esterbrook	.25
65	Mark Baldwin	.25
66	Tony Mullane	.25
67	John Glasscock	.25
68	Amos Rusie	.25
69	Jake Beckley	.25
70	Jimmy Collins	.25
71	Charles Comiskey	.25
72	Tom Connolly	.25
73	Mickey Welch	.25
74	Ed Delahanty	.25
75	Hugh Duffy	.25
76	Buck Ewing	.25
77	Clark Griffith	.25
78	Kid Nichols	.25
79	Billy Hamilton	.25
80	Ban Johnson	.25
81	Willie Keeler	.25
82	Bobby Wallace	.25
83	Napoleon Lajoie	.25
84	Connie Mack	.25
85	Fred Clarke	.25
86	Tommy McCarthy	.25
87	John McGraw	.25
88	Jesse Burkett	.25
89	Frank Chance	.25
90	Mordecai Brown	.25
91	New York Nationals	.25
92	Jack Chesbro	.25
93	Sam Thompson	.25
94	Boston v. New York 1891	.25
95	Rube Waddell	.25
96	Joel Kelley	.25
97	Addie Joss	.25
98	The Boston Beaneaters	.25
99	Baltimore Baseball Club	.25
100	The Game in 1899	.25
----	Bibliography	.25

Player names in *Italic* type indicate a rookie card.

1994 Ameritech Robin Yount Phone Cards

On the occasion of retirement ceremonies for Robin Yount in Milwaukee at the end of May, 1994, Ameritech issued this series of "Coin$aver" phone cards. Fans attending the game were given the 50-cent card and information about how to acquire the others. Announced production was 14,000 sets. Fronts of the standard 2-1/8" x 3-3/8" rounded-corner plastic cards have color action photos of Yount at various stages of his career. Backs have information on the use of the card for making long distance phone calls.

		MT
Complete Set (4):		20.00
Common Card:		3.00
$.50	Robin Yount (uniform number retired)	3.00
$2	Robin Yount (1980 All-Star)	4.00
$5	Robin Yount (1989 MVP)	5.00
$10	Robin Yount (3,000 hit)	8.00

1995 AmeriVox Legends of Baseball Phone Cards

Sold only as a complete set in a cardboard fold-out collector's album, these $10 phone cards feature a quartet of Hall of Famers. Player photos on the 2-1/8" x 3-3/8" plastic cards have had uniform logos airbrushed away. The AmeriVox logo appears at top and there is a red facsimile autograph at bottom. The denomination appears in the lower-right corner. Backs are printed in black-and-white and contain information for use of the cards, the player's name and their serial number from within an announced production of 5,000 sets. Marked sample cards of each player also exist.

		MT
Complete Set (4):		20.00
Common Player:		5.00
(1)	Yogi Berra	5.00
(2)	Harmon Killebrew	5.00
(3)	Brooks Robinson	5.00
(4)	Duke Snider	5.00

1989 Ames 20/20 Club

This 33-card set was produced by Topps for the Ames toy store chain. As its name implies, the special boxed set highlights players who have recorded 20 home runs and 20 stolen bases in the same season. The glossy cards feature action or posed photos on the front with the player's name at the top and "Ames 20/20 Club" along the bottom. The Topps logo appears in the upper-right corner. Backs have lifetime stats, biographical data and career highlights.

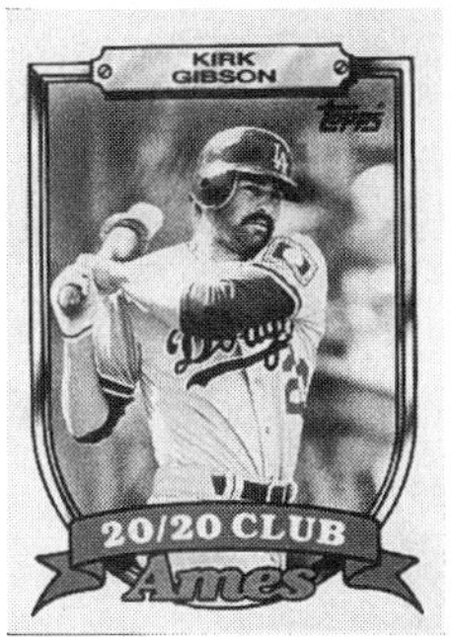

		MT
Complete Set (33):		4.00
Common Player:		.10
1	Jesse Barfield	.10
2	Kevin Bass	.10
3	Don Baylor	.10
4	George Bell	.10
5	Barry Bonds	1.00
6	Phil Bradley	.10
7	Ellis Burks	.10
8	Jose Canseco	.50
9	Joe Carter	.10
10	Kal Daniels	.10
11	Eric Davis	.10
12	Mike Davis	.10
13	Andre Dawson	.10
14	Kirk Gibson	.10
15	Pedro Guerrero	.10
16	Rickey Henderson	.25
17	Bo Jackson	.25
18	Howard Johnson	.10
19	Jeffrey Leonard	.10
20	Kevin McReynolds	.10
21	Dale Murphy	.20
22	Dwayne Murphy	.10
23	Dave Parker	.10
24	Kirby Puckett	.50
25	Juan Samuel	.10
26	Ryne Sandberg	.45
27	Mike Schmidt	.60
28	Darryl Strawberry	.15
29	Alan Trammell	.10
30	Andy Van Slyke	.10
31	Devon White	.10
32	Dave Winfield	.15
33	Robin Yount	.60

1990 Ames All-Stars

This 33-card set was the second consecutive issue produced by Topps for the Ames toy store chain. The cards measure 2-1/2" x 3-1/2" in size and feature baseball's top active hitters. Both the Ames and Topps logos appear on the cards.

		MT
Complete Set (33):		4.00
Common Player:		.10
1	Dave Winfield	.15
2	George Brett	.75
3	Jim Rice	.10
4	Dwight Evans	.10
5	Robin Yount	.50
6	Dave Parker	.10
7	Eddie Murray	.40
8	Keith Hernandez	.10
9	Andre Dawson	.10
10	Fred Lynn	.10
11	Dale Murphy	.15
12	Jack Clark	.10
13	Rickey Henderson	.25
14	Paul Molitor	.50
15	Cal Ripken	1.00
16	Wade Boggs	.45
17	Tim Raines	.10
18	Don Mattingly	.80
19	Kent Hrbek	.10
20	Kirk Gibson	.10
21	Julio Franco	.10
22	George Bell	.10
23	Darryl Strawberry	.15
24	Kirby Puckett	.75
25	Juan Samuel	.10
26	Alvin Davis	.10
27	Joe Carter	.10
28	Eric Davis	.10
29	Jose Canseco	.50
30	Wally Joyner	.10
31	Will Clark	.25
32	Ruben Sierra	.10
33	Danny Tartabull	.10

1984 Arby's Detroit Tigers Poster

This poster was issued by Arby's restaurants to honor the World's Champion 1984 Detroit Tigers. The 16-3/4" x 22-1/4" poster features a woodgrain-look frame with variously sized artwork of key players and their facsimile signatures. The players on the poster are listed here alphabetically.

	MT
Complete Poster:	
Sparky Anderson, Darrell Evans, Kirk Gibson, Willie Hernandez, Larry Herndon, Chet Lemon, Jack Morris, Lance , Lou Whitaker	15.00

1991 Arena Holograms

Superstars from four sports are featured in this hologram set. The cards were distributed through hobby dealers and are numbered on the back. The front of the card features the hologram, while the back features player information and a photo of the athlete in formal wear. The first five holograms were produced in an edition of 250,000 each, the Pat Falloon hologram was in an edition of 198,000. Suggested retail price was $7.95 per card at time of issue.

		MT
Complete Set (6):		12.00
Common Player:		2.00
1	Joe Montana	3.00
2	Ken Griffey, Jr.	3.00
3	Frank Thomas	3.00
4	Barry Sanders	3.00
5	David Robinson	2.00
6	Pat Falloon	2.00

1991 Arena Holograms Signature Series

Five of the six players who appeared in the multi-sport hologram set signed 2,500 cards in a Signature Series. Fronts of the autographed cards are identical to the unsigned versions and backs are nearly so. The Signature Series cards have a line of type beneath the photo on back indicating the special status. Each card also carries a hand-penned serial number from within the edition of 2,500 in the yellow stripe at bottom-back. Retail price at time of issue was about $40 ($300 for Robinson).

		MT
Complete Set (6):		250.00
Common Player:		15.00
1	Joe Montana	45.00
2	Ken Griffey, Jr.	75.00
3	Frank Thomas	45.00
4	Barry Sanders	45.00
5	David Robinson (only 250 signed)	300.00
6	Pat Falloon	15.00

1992 Arena Kid Griff Holograms

Ken Griffey Jr. went to the dogs in this hologram issue. Each of the five cards in the set pictures a comic book-style holographic picture of Griffey on front. Backs are conventionally printed and chronicle a fantasy ball game between "Kid Griff" and Downr Dawg. Cards were sold in one-card foil packs, with a plastic protector for the card. According to advertised production figures, enough cards were printed for nearly 100,000 sets. Gold edition parallel versions of the cards were random pack inserts and are valued at 2x-3x the standard silver hologram version. Suggested retal price at issue was $1.99 per pack.

		MT
Complete Set:		7.50
Common Card:		1.50
1	The "Kid" (Ken Griffey Jr.)	1.50
2	Speed (Ken Griffey Jr.)	1.50
3	Power (Ken Griffey Jr.)	1.50
4	Defense (Ken Griffey Jr.)	1.50
5	Superstar (Ken Griffey Jr.)	1.50

1996 Arizona Lottery

To promote its Diamond Bucks scratch-off lottery game, the Arizona Lottery issued this three-card set of Hall of Fame players' cards. Fronts have black-and-white photos which have had uniform logos airbrushed away. Borders are black. Backs are also in black-and-white, with player data and career highlights, along with the sponsors logos. Sets were given with the purchase of $5 in lottery tickets.

		MT
Complete Set:		12.00
Common Player:		3.00
(1)	Ernie Banks	5.00
(2)	Gaylord Perry	3.00
(3)	Brooks Robinson	5.00

1985 Armstrong's Pro Ceramic Cards

Five potential Hall of Famers are featured in two related series of ceramic baseball cards. Identical color action photos were fired onto 40mm thick ceramic cards in 2-1/2" x 3-1/2" and 3-1/4" x 5" sizes. While a facsimile autograph appears on the red and black back of the smaller version, each piece in the larger version is hand-autographed in gold ink by the player. The autographed version was limited to 1,000 serially numbered pieces of each player. Issue price was about $50 for the small version set of five; $150 for the signed larger version. Each piece was delivered in a red, white and blue cardboard display folder.

		MT
Complete Small Set:		60.00
Common Small Player:		10.00
Complete Large Set:		175.00
Complete Large Player:		25.00
	Small (2-1/2" x 3-1/2") series:	
1	Reggie Jackson	15.00
2	Steve Garvey	10.00
3	Pete Rose	20.00
4	George Brett	20.00
5	Tom Seaver	12.50
	Large (3-1/4" x 5") autographed series:	
1	Reggie Jackson	35.00
2	Steve Garvey	25.00
3	Pete Rose	50.00
4	George Brett	50.00
5	Tom Seaver	25.00

1981 Atlanta Braves Police

The first Atlanta Braves police set was a cooperative effort of the team, Hostess, Coca-Cola and the Atlanta Police Department. Card fronts feature full-color photos of 27 different Braves and manager Bobby Cox. Police and team logos are on the card backs. Card backs offer capsule biographies of the players, along with a tip for youngsters. The 2-5/8" x 4-1/8" cards are numbered by uniform number. Terry Harper (#19) appears to be somewhat scarcer than the other cards in the set. Reportedly, 33,000 sets were printed.

		MT
Complete Set (27):		12.50
Common Player:		.30
1	Jerry Royster	.30
3	Dale Murphy	6.00
4	Biff Pocoroba	.30
5	Bob Horner	.75
6	Bob Cox	.50
9	Luis Gomez	.30
10	Chris Chambliss	.30
15	Bill Nahorodny	.30
16	Rafael Ramirez	.30
17	Glenn Hubbard	.30
18	Claudell Washington	.30
19	Terry Harper (SP)	.75
20	Bruce Benedict	.30
24	John Montefusco	.30
25	Rufino Linares	.30
26	Gene Garber	.30
30	Brian Asselstine	.30
34	Larry Bradford	.30
35	Phil Niekro	2.00
37	Rick Camp	.30
39	Al Hrabosky	.30
40	Tommy Boggs	.30
42	Rick Mahler	.30
45	Ed Miller	.30
46	Gaylord Perry	2.00
49	Preston Hanna	.30
---	Hank Aaron	10.00

1982 Atlanta Braves Police

After their successful debut in 1981, the Atlanta Braves, the Atlanta Police Department, Coca-Cola and Hostess issued another card set in '82. This 30-card set is extremely close in format to the 1981 set and again measures 2-5/8" x 4-1/8". The full-color player photos are outstanding, and each card front also bears a statement marking the 1982 Braves' record-breaking 13-game win streak at the season's beginning. Card backs offer short biographies and "Tips from the Braves." Sponsors logos are also included. Reportedly, only 8,000 of these sets were printed.

		MT
Complete Set (30):		15.00
Common Player:		.30
1	Jerry Royster	.30
3	Dale Murphy	4.00
4	Biff Pocoroba	.30
5	Bob Horner	.50
6	Randy Johnson	.30
8	Bob Watson	.35
9	Joe Torre	.75
10	Chris Chambliss	.30
15	Claudell Washington	.30
16	Rafael Ramirez	.30
17	Glenn Hubbard	.30
20	Bruce Benedict	.30
22	Brett Butler	.75
23	Tommie Aaron	.50
25	Rufino Linares	.30
26	Gene Garber	.30
27	Larry McWilliams	.30
28	Larry Whisenton	.30
32	Steve Bedrosian	.35
35	Phil Niekro	2.00
37	Rick Camp	.30
38	Joe Cowley	.30
39	Al Hrabosky	.30
42	Rick Mahler	.30
43	Bob Walk	.30
45	Bob Gibson	3.00
49	Preston Hanna	.30
52	Joe Pignatano	.30
53	Dal Maxvill	.30
54	Rube Walker	.30

1983 Atlanta Braves Police

An almost exact replica of their 1982 set, the 1983 Atlanta Braves police set includes 30 cards numbered by uniform. Sponsors Hostess, Coca-Cola and the Atlanta Police Department returned for the third year. The cards are again 2-5/8" x 4-1/8", with full-color photos and police and team logos on the card fronts. A statement noting the team's 1982 National League Western Division title in the upper right corner is the key difference on the card fronts. As in 1982, 8,000 sets were reportedly printed.

		MT
Complete Set (30):		6.00
Common Player:		.15
1	Jerry Royster	.15
3	Dale Murphy	2.00
4	Biff Pocoroba	.15
5	Bob Horner	.25
6	Randy G. Johnson	.15
8	Bob Watson	.20
9	Joe Torre	.45
10	Chris Chambliss	.15
11	Ken Smith	.15
15	Claudell Washington	.15
16	Rafael Ramirez	.15
17	Glenn Hubbard	.15
19	Terry Harper	.15
20	Bruce Benedict	.15
22	Brett Butler	.40
24	Larry Owen	.15
26	Gene Garber	.15
27	Pascual Perez	.15
29	Craig McMurtry	.15
32	Steve Bedrosian	.15
33	Pete Falcone	.15
35	Phil Niekro	1.00
36	Sonny Jackson	.15
37	Rick Camp	.15
45	Bob Gibson	1.50
49	Rick Behenna	.15
51	Terry Forster	.15
52	Joe Pignatano	.15
53	Dal Maxvill	.15
54	Rube Walker	.15

1984 Atlanta Braves Police

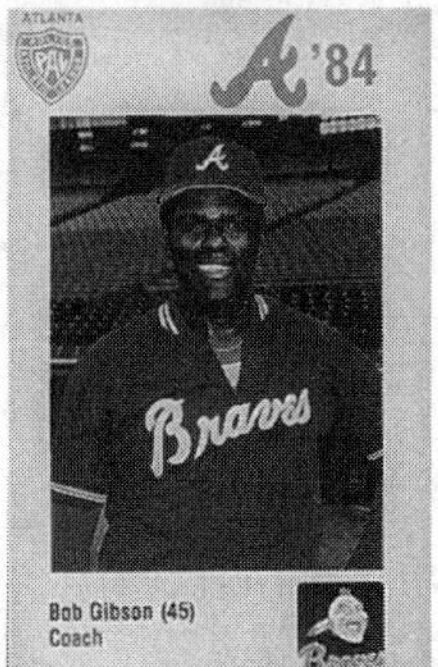

A fourth annual effort by the Braves, the Atlanta Police Department, Coca-Cola and Hostess, this 30-card set continued to be printed in a 2-5/8" x 4-1/8" format, with full-color photos plus team and police logos on the card fronts. For the first time, the cards also have a large logo and date in the upper right corner. Hostess and Coke logos again are on the card backs, with brief player information and a safety tip. Two cards in the set (Pascual Perez and Rafael Ramirez) were issued in Spanish. Cards were distributed two per week by Atlanta police officers. As in 1982 and 1983, a reported 8,000 sets were printed.

		MT
Complete Set (30):		8.00
Common Player:		.25
1	Jerry Royster	.25
3	Dale Murphy	3.50
5	Bob Horner	.50
6	Randy Johnson	.25
8	Bob Watson	.25
9	Joe Torre	.50
10	Chris Chambliss	.25
11	Mike Jorgensen	.25
15	Claudell Washington	.25
16	Rafael Ramirez	.25
17	Glenn Hubbard	.25
19	Terry Harper	.25
20	Bruce Benedict	.25
25	Alex Trevino	.25
26	Gene Garber	.25
27	Pascual Perez	.25
28	Gerald Perry	.25
29	Craig McMurtry	.25
31	Donnie Moore	.25
32	Steve Bedrosian	.25
33	Pete Falcone	.25
37	Rick Camp	.25
39	Len Barker	.25
42	Rick Mahler	.25
45	Bob Gibson	2.00
51	Terry Forster	.25
52	Joe Pignatano	.25
53	Dal Maxvill	.25
54	Rube Walker	.25
55	Luke Appling	2.00

1985 Atlanta Braves Police

There are again 30 full-color cards in this fifth annual set. Hostess, Coca-Cola and the Atlanta Police Department joined the team as sponsors again for the 2-5/8" x 4-1/8" set. Card backs are similar to previous years, with the only difference on the fronts being a swap in position for the year and team logo. The cards are checklisted by uniform number.

		MT
Complete Set (30):		6.00
Common Player:		.25
2	Albert Hall	.25
3	Dale Murphy	2.50
5	Rick Cerone	.25
7	Bobby Wine	.25
10	Chris Chambliss	.25
11	Bob Horner	.45
12	Paul Runge	.25
15	Claudell Washington	.25
16	Rafael Ramirez	.25
17	Glenn Hubbard	.25
18	Paul Zuvella	.25
19	Terry Harper	.25
20	Bruce Benedict	.25
22	Eddie Haas	.25
24	Ken Oberkfell	.25
26	Gene Garber	.25
27	Pascual Perez	.25
28	Gerald Perry	.25
29	Craig McMurtry	.25
32	Steve Bedrosian	.30
33	Johnny Sain	.30
34	Zane Smith	.25
36	Brad Komminsk	.25
37	Rick Camp	.25
39	Len Barker	.25
40	Bruce Sutter	.30
42	Rick Mahler	.25
51	Terry Forster	.25
52	Leo Mazzone	.30
53	Bobby Dews	.25

1985 Atlanta Braves team issue

Some of the '85 Braves' most popular players were featured in a set of 4-1/8" x 5-3/8" black-and-white photo cards. The blank-backed photos feature player poses on front with the name in all-capital letters in the bottom border. Photos are unnumbered and the checklist here is presented alphabetically. Sets were originally sold for $4 by the team.

		MT
Complete Set (8):		6.00
Common Player:		.50
(1)	Len Barker	.50
(2)	Steve Bedrosian	.50
(3)	Bruce Benedict	.50
(4)	Terry Forster	.50
(5)	Bob Horner	.75
(6)	Dale Murphy	3.00
(7)	Rafael Ramirez	.50
(8)	Claudell Washington	.50

1986 Atlanta Braves Police

The Police Athletic League of Atlanta issued a 30-card full-color set featuring Braves players and personnel. Cards measure 2-5/8" x 4-1/8". Fronts include player photos with name, uniform number and position below the photo. Backs offer the 100th Anniversary Coca-Cola logo, player information, statistics and a safety related tip. This was the sixth consecutive year that the Braves issued a safety set available from police officers in Atlanta.

		MT
Complete Set (30):		4.00
Common Player:		.15
2	Russ Nixon	.15
3	Dale Murphy	1.50
4	Bob Skinner	.15
5	Billy Sample	.15
7	Chuck Tanner	.15
8	Willie Stargell	1.00
9	Ozzie Virgil	.15
10	Chris Chambliss	.15
11	Bob Horner	.25
14	Andres Thomas	.15
15	Claudell Washington	.15
16	Rafael Ramirez	.15
17	Glenn Hubbard	.15
18	Omar Moreno	.15
19	Terry Harper	.15
20	Bruce Benedict	.15
23	Ted Simmons	.15
24	Ken Oberkfell	.15
26	Gene Garber	.15
29	Craig McMurtry	.15
30	Paul Assenmacher	.15
33	Johnny Sain	.25
34	Zane Smith	.15
38	Joe Johnson	.15
40	Bruce Sutter	.15
42	Rick Mahler	.15
46	David Palmer	.15
48	Duane Ward	.15
49	Jeff Dedmon	.15
52	Al Monchak	.15

1987 Atlanta Braves Fire Safety

These fire safety cards were given out at several different Atlanta games, with about 25,000 sets in all being distributed. The 4" x 6" cards feature Braves players in an oval frame, bordered in red, white and blue. Only the player's last name is shown on front. Backs contain the player's name, position and personal data plus a Smokey the Bear cartoon fire safety message.

		MT
Complete Set (27):		6.00
Common Player:		.25
1	Zane Smith	.25
2	Charlie Puleo	.25
3	Randy O'Neal	.25
4	David Palmer	.25
5	Rick Mahler	.25
6	Ed Olwine	.25
7	Jeff Dedmon	.25
8	Paul Assenmacher	.25
9	Gene Garber	.25
10	Jim Acker	.25

11	Bruce Benedict	.25
12	Ozzie Virgil	.25
13	Ted Simmons	.25
14	Dale Murphy	1.50
15	Graig Nettles	.40
16	Ken Oberkfell	.25
17	Gerald Perry	.25
18	Rafael Ramirez	.25
19	Ken Griffey	.30
20	Andres Thomas	.25
21	Glenn Hubbard	.25
22	Damaso Garcia	.25
23	Gary Roenicke	.25
24	Dion James	.25
25	Albert Hall	.25
26	Chuck Tanner	.25
---	Smokey Bear Logo Card/Checklist	.10

1988 Atlanta Braves team issue

These large-format (3" x 5") black-and-white player cards were provided to players for use in answering fan requests for pictures and autographs. The cards have portrait photos with white borders. In the wide white bottom border are the player's name and team. Backs are blank. The unnumbered cards are listed alphabetically. Complete sets were not available from the team.

		MT
Complete Set (19):		25.00
Common Player:		1.00
(1)	Jim Acker	1.00
(2)	Jose Alvarez	1.00
(3)	Paul Assenmacher	1.00
(4)	Bruce Benedict	1.00
(5)	Jeff Blauser	1.00
(6)	Terry Blocker	1.00
(7)	Ron Gant	1.50
(8)	Tommy Greene	1.00
(9)	Tom Glavine	3.00
(10)	Derek Lilliquist	1.00
(11)	Dale Murphy	4.00
(12)	Russ Nixon	1.00
(13)	Gerald Perry	1.00
(14)	Charlie Puleo	1.00
(15)	Paul Runge	1.00
(16)	Pete Smith	1.00
(17)	John Smoltz	3.00
(18)	Bruce Sutter	1.00
(19)	Andre Thomas	1.00

1986 Ault Foods Blue Jays stickers

The Ault Foods Blue Jays set is comprised of 24 full-color stickers. Designed to be placed in a special album, the stickers measure 2" x 3" in size. The attractive album measures 9" x 12" and is printed on glossy stock. While the stickers carry no information except for the player's last name and uniform number, the 20-page album contains extensive personal and statistical information about each of the 24 players.

		MT
Complete Set (24):		35.00
Common Player:		1.00
Album:		8.00
1	Tony Fernandez	1.50
5	Rance Mulliniks	1.00
7	Damaso Garcia	1.00
11	George Bell	2.50
12	Ernie Whitt	1.00
13	Buck Martinez	1.00
15	Lloyd Moseby	1.25
16	Garth Iorg	1.00
17	Kelly Gruber	1.25
18	Jim Clancy	1.00
22	Jimmy Key	2.50
23	Cecil Fielder	8.00
25	Steve Davis	1.00
26	Willie Upshaw	1.00
29	Jesse Barfield	1.50
31	Jim Acker	1.00
33	Doyle Alexander	1.00
36	Bill Caudill	1.00
37	Dave Stieb	1.50
39	Don Gordon	1.00
44	Cliff Johnson	1.00
46	Gary Lavelle	1.00
50	Tom Henke	1.50
53	Dennis Lamp	1.00

1996 Authentic Images Cal Ripken

Highlights of Cal Ripken's career are commemorated in this collectors' edition of high-tech cards. Each card is produced in a 2-1/2" x 3-1/2" 24K Gold Metal format using AI's "PhotoGold" method to emboss a gold image onto a metal base. Each piece is serially numbered and encased in a lucite block. The cards were produced in editions of 600 (#1-3) or 1,008 (#4) each. Suggested retail price at issue was about $100.

		MT
Complete Set (4):		400.00
Single Card:		100.00
(1)	Cal Ripken Jr. (2,131 Consecutive Games)	100.00
(2)	Cal Ripken Jr. (Two Time MVP)	100.00
(3)	Cal Ripken Jr. (13 Consecutive All-Star Games)	100.00
(4)	Cal Ripken Jr. (Golden Edge Collectible)	100.00

1996 Authentic Images Nolan Ryan

Highlights of Nolan Ryan's career are commemorated in this collectors' edition of high-tech cards. Each card is produced in a 2-1/2" x 3-1/2" "Double Metal" format using AI's patented method to emboss a metallic image onto a metal base. Each piece is serially numbered and encased in a lucite block. The cards were produced in editions of 807 each. Suggested retail price at issue was about $100.

		MT
Complete Set (3):		300.00
Single Card:		100.00
(1)	Nolan Ryan (5,714 Career Strikeouts)	100.00
(2)	Nolan Ryan (324 Career Wins)	100.00
(3)	Nolan Ryan (7 Career No-Hitters)	100.00

1997 Authentic Images Gold Metal Series

Using a "PhotoGold" imaging technology to create a player action photo, this set was one of the high-end card/memorabilia issues of 1997. The issue is limited to 750 serially numbered cards of each player. Cards are sold in a heavy lucite holder and custom gift box. Original retail price was about $100 each.

		MT
Complete Set (6):		600.00
Common Player:		100.00
(1)	Ken Griffey Jr.	100.00
(2)	Derek Jeter	100.00
(3)	Greg Maddux	100.00
(4)	Mike Piazza	100.00
(5)	Alex Rodriguez	100.00
(6)	Frank Thomas	100.00

1997 Authentic Images Gold Signature Series

Combining a four-color cel card with 24-karat gold facsimile signature, this set was one of the high-end card/memorabilia issues of 1997. The issue is limited to 750 serially numbered cards of each player. Cards are sold in a heavy lucite holder and custom gift box. Original retail price was about $30 each.

		MT
Complete Set (6):		180.00
Common Player:		30.00
(1)	Ken Griffey Jr.	30.00
(2)	Derek Jeter	30.00
(3)	Greg Maddux	30.00
(4)	Mike Piazza	30.00
(5)	Alex Rodriguez	30.00
(6)	Frank Thomas	30.00

1998 Authentic Images Gold Prospects

Six top stars were selected by AI for this issue of limited edition high-tech collectors items. Two types of cards were produced for each player. A 24-karat Gold Metal card has an action image created by the company's "PhotoGold" technology. The same photo is used on a matching 24K Gold Signature Die-Cut card. Each version has a gold facsimile signature on front, is individually numbered and sold in a heavy lucite holder and leatherette jewel case. Suggested retail price at issue was about $100 for the Metal version, $30 for the Signature Die-Cut. Production numbers were announced at 600 each for the Metal cards; 1,999 each for the Signature Die-Cuts, except for Clemens, produced in an edition of 3,000.

		MT
Complete Set Gold Metal (6):		600.00
Complete Set Signature-Cel (6):		210.00
Common Player Gold Metal:		100.00
Common Player Signature-Cel:		35.00
(1)	Tony Clark (Gold Metal)	100.00
(1)	Tony Clark (Signature-Cel)	35.00
(2)	Jose Cruz Jr. (Gold Metal)	100.00
(2)	Jose Cruz Jr. (Signature-Cel)	35.00
(3)	Nomar Garciaparra (Gold Metal)	100.00
(3)	Nomar Garciaparra (Signature-Cel)	35.00
(4)	Derek Jeter (Gold Metal)	100.00
(5)	Derek Jeter (Signature-Cel)	35.00
(5)	Chipper Jones (Gold Metal)	100.00
(5)	Chipper Jones (Signature-Cel)	35.00
(6)	Travis Lee (Gold Metal)	100.00
(6)	Travis Lee (Signature-Cel)	35.00

1998 Authentic Images Home Run Record Breakers

The home run record race of 1998 was commemorated in this series of limited edition collectors' cards. Each card was produced in two versions. A 24K Gold Metal card utilizes AI's "PhotoGold" technology to create an embossed gold image on a 3-1/2" x 2-1/2" metal base. Each card is individually serial numbered and includes a gold facsimile autograph. Cards are sold in a lucite holder and leatherette jewel case. The matching Gold Signature card is printed in full color on a 5-1/8" x 3" horizontal format, also featuring a serial number and gold facsimile signature. The Signature cards are sold in a protective holder and plastic stand. Suggested retail price at issue was about $100 for the Gold Metal cards, $30 for the Gold Signature.

		MT
Complete Set Gold Metal (3):		300.00
Complete Set Gold Signature (3):		90.00
Single Gold Metal:		100.00
Single Gold Signature:		30.00
(1)	Roger Maris - 61 HR (Gold Metal edition of 610)	100.00
(1)	Roger Maris - 61 HR (Gold Signature edition of 10,000)	30.00
(2)	Mark McGwire - 62 HR (Gold Metal edition of 6,200)	100.00
(2)	Mark McGwire - 62 HR (Gold Signature edition of 62,000)	30.00
(3)	Sammy Sosa - 62 HR (Gold Metal edition of 2,500)	100.00
(3)	Sammy Sosa - 62 HR (Gold Signature edition of 25,000)	30.00

1998 Authentic Images Mickey Mantle

Three of The Mick's career highlights are commemorated in this collectors' edition of high-tech cards. Each card is produced in two versions. A 2-1/2" x 3-1/2" 24K Gold Metal card uses AI's "PhotoGold" method to emboss a 24-karat gold image and facsimile autograph onto a metal base. Each piece is serially numbered and encased in a lucite block. The same image is used on the 24K Gold Signature Cel cards which are printed in full color on a 3" x 5" plastic stock which also features the gold facsimile autograph. Both types were produced in editions of 536 each. Suggested retail price at issue was $125 for the Gold Metal, $35 for the Signature Cel.

		MT
Complete Set Gold Metal (3):		375.00
Complete Set Signature Cel (3):		105.00
Single Gold Metal:		125.00
Single Signature Cel:		35.00
(1)	1951 Rookie Season (Mickey Mantle) (Gold Metal)	125.00
(1)	1951 Rookie Season (Mickey Mantle) (Signature Cel)	35.00
(2)	1956 Triple Crown (Mickey Mantle) (Gold Metal)	125.00
(2)	1956 Triple Crown (Mickey Mantle) (Signature Cel)	35.00
(3)	536 Career HR (Mickey Mantle) (Gold Metal)	125.00
(3)	536 Career HR (Mickey Mantle) (Signature Cel)	35.00

1998-1999 Authentic Images Mickey Mantle Career Collection

Ten of The Mick's career highlights are scheduled to be commemorated in this collectors' edition of high-tech cards. Each card is produced in two versions. A 2-1/2" x 3-1/2" 24K Gold Metal card uses AI's "PhotoGold" method to emboss a 24-karat gold image onto a metal base. Each piece is serially numbered and encased in a lucite block. The same image is used on the 24K Gold Signature card which is printed in full color on a 3" x 5" format which also features a gold facsimile autograph. Both types were produced in editions of 536 each. Suggested retail price at issue was $130-135 for each pair.

	MT
Complete Set (2):	270.00
Gold Metal/Signature Pair:	135.00
1998 Mickey Mantle (Rookie Season 1951)	135.00
1999 Mickey Mantle (Triple Crown 1956)	135.00

1998 Authentic Images Mickey Mantle Gallery

Mickey Mantle's first major league hit is captured in 24-karat gold embossed onto a metal base in this limited edition (1,951) collectors' item. Three sequential images are featured on the 4-1/2" x 8-3/4" piece which is sold in a heavy lucite holder which features a gold facsimile autograph and serial number. Original issue price was about $450.

	MT
Mickey Mantle (First Major League Hit)	450.00

1998 Authentic Images Special Issues

During the course of the year Authentic Images produced several special issues of limited edition collectibles in either or both of their high-tech formats. Gold Metal cards feature images in 24-karat gold which have been embossed onto a metal base. Gold Signature cards are in full color and feature gold facsimile signatures. Cards are usually individually serial numbered and sold in a lucite block or other protective holder.

		MT
(1)	Juan Gonzalez (Signature edition of 1,000)	35.00
(2)	Ben Grieve (Signature edition of 1,998)	30.00
(3)	Mark McGwire - Wheaties #70 (Metal edition of 7,000)	100.00
(4)	Mark McGwire - Wheaties #70 (Signature edition of 70,000)	30.00
(5)	Mark McGwire - 60, 61, 62 (Signature edition of 25,000)	30.00
(6)	Mark McGwire - 62 HR Mini (Metal edition of 6,200)	55.00
(7)	Mark McGwire - 62 HR Standee (Signature edition of 62,000)	60.00
(8)	Mark McGwire - 70 HR (Signature edition of 70,000)	30.00
(9)	Mark McGwire - 70 HR Standee (Signature edition of 70,000)	60.00
(10)	Cal Ripken Jr. - 2,632 Games (Metal edition of 2,632)	100.00
(11)	Cal Ripken Jr. - 2,632 Games (Signature edition of 26,320)	30.00
(12)	Ivan "Pudge" Rodriguez (Signature edition of 1,000)	35.00
(13)	Sammy Sosa - 60, 61, 62 (Signature edition of 10,000)	30.00
(14)	Sammy Sosa - 62 HR Mini (Metal edition of 2,500)	55.00
(15)	Sammy Sosa - 66 HR (Signature edition of 66,000)	30.00
(16)	Kerry Wood (Signature edition of 1,998)	30.00

1999 Authentic Images Gold Stars

Six sensational young players were selected by AI for this issue of limited edition (250) high-tech collectors items. Two types of cards were produced for each player. A 24-karat Gold Metal card has an action image created by the company's "PhotoGold" technology. The same photo is used on a matching 24K Gold Signature-Cel card which is printed on transparent plastic with a gold facsimile signature. Each card is individually numbered and sold in a heavy lucite holder and leatherette jewel case. Suggested retail price at issue was about $100 for the Metal version, $35 for the Signature-Cel.

		MT
Complete Set Gold Metal (6):		600.00
Complete Set Signature Die-Cut (6):		180.00
Common Player Gold Metal:		100.00
Common Player Signature Die-Cut		30.00
(1)	Roger Clemens (Gold Metal)	100.00
(1)	Roger Clemens (Signature Die-Cut)	30.00
(2)	Ken Griffey Jr. (Gold Metal)	100.00
(2)	Ken Griffey Jr. (Signature Die-Cut)	30.00
(3)	Derek Jeter (Gold Metal)	100.00
(3)	Derek Jeter (Signature Die-Cut)	30.00
(4)	Mark McGwire (Gold Metal)	100.00
(4)	Mark McGwire (Signature Die-Cut)	30.00
(5)	Alex Rodriguez (Gold Metal)	100.00
(5)	Alex Rodriguez (Signature Die-Cut)	30.00
(6)	Sammy Sosa (Gold Metal)	100.00
(6)	Sammy Sosa (Signature Die-Cut)	30.00

1998 Authentic Images Team Gold

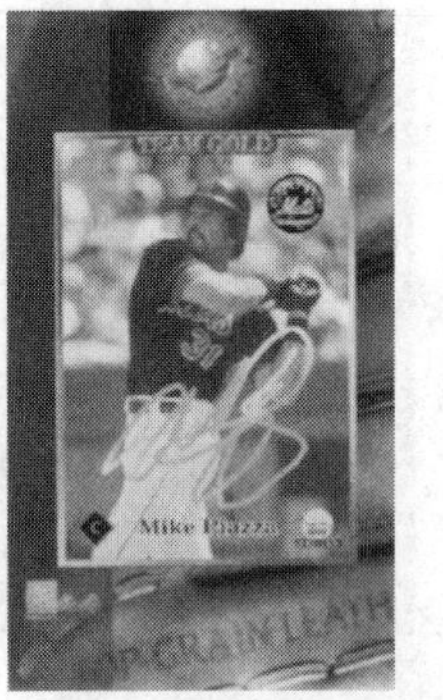

The best player at each position was selected by AI for this issue of limited edition (700) high-tech collectors items. Two types of cards were produced for each player. A 24-karat Gold Metal card has an action image created by the company's "PhotoGold" technology. The same photo is used on a matching 24K Gold Signature-Cel card which is printed on transparent plastic with a gold facsimile signature. Each card is individually numbered and sold in a heavy lucite holder and leatherette jewel case. Suggested retail price at issue was about $100 for the Metal version, $35 for the Signature-Cel.

		MT
Complete Set Gold Metal (11):		1100.
Complete Set Signature-Cel (11):		385.00
Common Player Gold Metal:		100.00
Common Player Signature-Cel:		35.00
(1)	Roberto Alomar (Gold Metal)	100.00
(1)	Roberto Alomar (Signature-Cel)	35.00
(2)	Barry Bonds (Gold Metal)	100.00
(2)	Barry Bonds (Signature-Cel)	35.00
(3)	Roger Clemens (Gold Metal)	100.00
(3)	Roger Clemens (Signature-Cel)	35.00
(4)	Ken Griffey Jr. (Gold Metal)	100.00
(4)	Ken Griffey Jr. (Signature-Cel)	35.00
(5)	Tony Gwynn (Gold Metal)	100.00
(5)	Tony Gwynn (Signature-Cel)	35.00
(6)	Greg Maddux (Gold Metal)	100.00
(6)	Greg Maddux (Signature-Cel)	35.00
(7)	Mark McGwire (Gold Metal)	100.00
(7)	Mark McGwire (Signature-Cel)	35.00
(8)	Mike Piazza (Gold Metal)	100.00
(8)	Mike Piazza (Signature-Cel)	35.00
(9)	Cal Ripken Jr. (Gold Metal)	100.00
(9)	Cal Ripken Jr. (Signature-Cel)	35.00
(10)	Alex Rodriguez (Gold Metal)	100.00
(10)	Alex Rodriguez (Signature-Cel)	35.00
(11)	Frank Thomas (Gold Metal)	100.00
(11)	Frank Thomas (Signature-Cel)	35.00

1982 Authentic Sports Autographs Mickey Mantle Story

This 72-card set chronicles the life of Mickey Mantle in contemporary photos, many from Mantle's own collection and many picturing him with such stars of the era as Maris, DiMaggio, Ted Williams, Mays, etc. A total of 20,000 sets was produced; 5,000 of them feature a genuine Mantle autograph on card #1 and 15,000 sets have no autograph. Backs of cards from the autographed sets are printed in blue while the unautographed sets have backs printed in red.

		MT
Comp. Set, #1 Autographed (72):		125.00
Comp. Set, Unautographed (72):		90.00
Common Card:		1.00
1	Header card	1.00
2	Mickey & Merlyn 12/23/51	1.00
3	Spring Training 1951	2.50
4	Spring Training 1951	2.50
5	Mickey's Mom, Mickey & Merlyn	1.00
6	4/15/51 1st Homer in NY	2.00
7	1951 - DiMaggio, Mantle, Williams	2.50
8	1951- Mickey signs for 1952	2.00
9	Martin & Mickey Jr. 4/12/52	1.00
10	Brothers Roy and Ray	1.00
11	Spring Training 1952	2.00
12	1952- Bauer, Hopp, Mantle	1.50
13	1952 Season	2.00
14	Mantle & Martin 1952 Series	1.50
15	Billy & Mickey 1953	1.50
16	Knee Injury 1953	1.00
17	1953 - Before knee surgery	1.00
18	New business 1953	1.00
19	1953 World Series Power	2.00
20	1953 The long Home Run	2.50
21	1955 Hall of Fame Game	1.50
22	1955	2.00
23	1955 - Skowron, Rizzuto, Mantle	1.50
24	1954 - Jackie Robinson at 1st	2.00
25	1956 - Mickey with Ted Williams	2.50
26	1955 - Skowron, Berra, Mantle	1.50
27	1956 - Mickey safe at first	2.00
28	1956 World Series	2.00
29	1957 - Yogi, Whitey, Mickey	2.00
30	1957 - Roy Sievers with Mickey	1.00
31	1957 World Series	2.00
32	1957 Hitchcock Award	1.50
33	1957 - Mickey with Cardinal Spellman	1.00
34	1957 - Singing with Teresa Brewer	1.00
35	1957 - Brooks Robinson & Mickey	1.50
36	1958 World Series	2.00
37	1958 All Star Game with Banks	1.50
38	With Stengel 1959	1.50
39	1960 - With Roger Maris	2.50
40	1960 World Series	2.00
41	1961 All Star Game with Maris & Mays	2.00
42	Maris, Berra, Mantle, Howard, Skowron, Blanchard	1.50
43	1961 - with Maris & Mrs. Babe Ruth	1.50
44	1961 - Mickey Congratulates Maris	2.00
45	1961 - Maris & Mantle	2.00
46	400th Career HR 9/11/62	2.00
47	1962 World Series	1.50
48	1963 season	1.50
49	1963 World Series	1.50
50	1964 World Series	1.50
51	1964 - Pepitone, Ford, Mantle	1.00
52	1964 season	1.50
53	1965 Mickey's Day	1.50
54	1965 season	1.50
55	1966 - with Joe DiMaggio	2.50
56	Mantle family	1.00
57	1967 season	1.50
58	1968 - hits HR No. 529	2.00
59	1968 - Retirement	2.00
60	1968 - His farewell	1.50
61	Mickey's trophy room	1.00
62	1970 - Welcome back Coach	1.00
63	1973 - TV commercial	1.00
64	1974 visit	1.00
65	1974 visit	1.00
66	1974 Hall of Fame inductees	1.00
67	1979 Old Timers Game	1.00
68	1981 Old Timers Game	1.00
69	Family Day	1.00
70	The Mantle Swing	1.00
71	The Mantle Swing	1.00
72	The Mantle Swing	1.00

Player names in *Italic* type indicate a rookie card.

1983 Authentic Sports Autographs Hank Aaron Story

This collectors issue was part of a series featuring past greats of the game. The Hank Aaron Story is a 12-card set. Fronts feature black-and-white or color photos of the Brave great at various stages of his career. Green graphics in the white border frame the pictures, each of which is titled at bottom. Backs have a green border and present a narrative of the player's career. Some of the backs have a small portrait photo. Sets were sold both with and without card No. 1 bearing an autograph.

		MT
Complete Set, #1 Autographed (12):		25.00
Complete Set, Unautographed (12):		12.00
Common Card:		1.50
1	Title card	2.00
2	1953 Jacksonville	2.00
3	1954 Welcome to Milwaukee	1.50
4	1957 Slugging Outfield	1.50
5	1958 Ready for the World Series	1.50
6	1958 World Series (w/Mantle)	5.00
7	1965 Last Day in Milwaukee (w/Mathews)	1.50
8	1969	1.50
9	1970 Atlanta All Stars (w/Rico Carty)	1.50
10	1973 Home Run #700	1.50
11	1973 Home Run #712	1.50
12	1973 Home Run Trio	1.50

1983 Authentic Sports Autographs Yogi Berra Story

This collectors issue was part of a series featuring past greats of the game. The Yogi Berra Story is a 12-card set. Fronts feature black-and-white or color photos of the Yankee great at various stages of his career. Green graphics in the white border frame the pictures, each of which is titled at bottom. Backs have a green border and present a narrative of the player's career. Some of the backs have a small portrait photo. Sets were sold both with and without card No. 1 bearing an autograph.

		MT
Complete Set, #1 Autographed (12):		20.00
Complete Set, Unautographed (12):		10.00
Common Card:		1.00
1	Title card	2.00
2	Youthful Yogi	1.50
3	1953 Sluggers (w/ Mantle, others)	2.00
4	1958 (w/Maglie, Larsen)	1.00
5	1950 World Series Line Up	2.00
6	1961 Sluggers (w/ Mantle, Maris, etc.)	2.00
7	1964 Yankees Manager (w/ Stengel)	1.00
8	Old Timers Day 1967	1.00
9	Yankee Catching Tradition (w/Dickey, Howard, Munson)	1.50
10	Mets Coach (w/ Hodges, others)	1.00
11	1973 Mets Manager (w/Walter Alston)	1.00
12	1978 Yankees Coach	1.00

1983 Authentic Sports Autographs Joe DiMaggio Story

This collectors issue was part of a series featuring past greats of the game. The Joe DiMaggio Story is a 12-card set. Fronts feature black-and-white or color photos of the Yankee great at various stages of his career. Green graphics in the white border frame the pictures, each of which is titled at bottom. Backs have a green border and present a narrative of the player's career. Some of the backs have a small portrait photo. Sets were sold both with and without card No. 1 bearing an autograph.

		MT
Complete Set, #1 Autographed (12):		200.00
Complete Set, Unautographed (12):		30.00
Common Card:		2.00
1	Title card	2.50
2	1935, S.F. Seals (w/ brother Dom)	2.50
3	1936 World Champions (w/ Gehrig, others)	2.00
4	1936 Murderers Row (w/Gehrig, Dickey, Selkirk)	2.00
5	1941 - Classic Stance	2.00
6	1942 - Joe and Ted Williams	6.00
7	1946 Outfield (w/ Keller and Henrich)	2.00
8	1950 Spring Training	3.00
9	1951 - Joe with rookie Mickey Mantle	8.00
10	1951 - Joe's Farewell (w/Mel Allen)	2.00
11	1968-69 Oakland A's Coach	2.00
12	1978 Old-Timers Day (w/Martin, Mantle, Ford)	2.50

1983 Authentic Sports Autographs Bob Feller Story

This collectors issue was part of a series featuring past greats of the game. The Bob Feller Story is a 12-card set. Fronts feature black-and-white or color photos of the Indians great at various stages of his career. Red graphics in the white border frame the pictures, each of which is titled at bottom. Backs have a red border and present a narrative of the player's career. Some of the backs have a small portrait photo. Sets were sold both with and without card No. 1 bearing an autograph.

		MT
Complete Set, #1 Autographed (12):		15.00
Complete Set, Unautographed (12):		8.00
Common Card:		1.00
1	Title card	1.00
2	1937	1.00
3	1942 Navy Induction	1.00
4	1946 Baseball School	1.00
5	1946 (w/Satchel Paige)	1.00
6	1947 (w/Bill Veeck)	1.00
7	1947 (w/Hal Newhouser)	1.00
8	1947 (w/Keltner, Gordon)	1.00
9	1950 (w/Bob Lemon)	1.00
10	1951, 200th Win	1.00
11	1954 Pitching Staff	1.00
12	The Feller Style	1.00

1983 Authentic Sports Autographs Juan Marichal Story

This collectors issue was part of a series featuring past greats of the game. The Juan Marichal Story is a 12-card set. Fronts feature black-and-white or color photos of the Giant great at various stages of his career. Green graphics in the white border frame the pictures, each of which is titled at bottom. Backs have a green border and present a narrative of the player's career. Some of the backs have a small portrait photo. Sets were sold both with and without card No. 1 bearing an autograph.

		MT
Complete Set, #1 Autographed (12):		20.00
Complete Set, Unautographed (12):		7.50
Common Card:		.50
1	Title card	.75
2	1960 Giants Rookie	1.00
3	1962 at the Polo Grounds	.50
4	1966	.50
5	1971 with Willie Mays	1.00
6	1972	.50
7	1973 with Willie McCovey	.75
8	1973	.50
9	1975 with Walt Alston	.50
10	Last Day in the Big Leagues	.50
11	1983 Hall of Fame	.50
12	1983 Cracker Jack All-Star Game	.50

1983 Authentic Sports Autographs Willie Mays Story

This collectors issue was part of a series featuring past greats of the game. The Willie Mays Story is a 12-card set. Fronts feature black-and-white or color photos of the Giant great at various stages of his career. Green graphics in the white border frame the pictures, each of which is titled at bottom. Backs have a green border and present a narrative of the player's career. Some of the backs have a small portrait photo. Sets were sold both with and without card No. 1 bearing an autograph.

		MT
Complete Set, #1 Autographed (12):		25.00
Complete Set, Unautographed (12):		12.00
Common Card:		1.50
1	Title cards	2.00
2	1951 with the Minneapolis Millers	1.50
3	1951 Rookies at the World Series (w/ Mantle)	5.00
4	1953 Army Induction	1.50
5	1954 "Say Hey" Day at the Polo Grounds	1.50
6	1956 All Star Game (w/Musial)	2.00
7	1957 Spring Training	1.50
8	1969 All Star Game (w/Clemente, Aaron)	2.50
9	1972 Traded to the Mets	1.50
10	1972 Clemente Joins 3000 hit club (w/ Clemente)	2.00
11	1972 Welcome Back to S.F.	1.50
12	Old Timers Day 1982 (w/Kiner)	1.50

1983 Authentic Sports Autographs Johnny Mize Story

This collectors issue was part of a series featuring past greats of the game. The Johnny Mize Story is a 12-card set. Fronts feature black-and-white or color photos of the HoF great at various stages of his career. Green graphics in the white border frame the pictures, each of which is titled at bottom. Backs have a green border and present a narrative of the player's career. Some of the backs have a small portrait photo. Sets were sold both with and without card No. 1 bearing an autograph.

		MT
Complete Set, #1 Autographed (12):		20.00
Complete Set, Unautographed (12):		7.50
Common Card:		.50
1	Title card	.75
2	1933-35 with Rochester	.50
3	1936 Home Run in Chicago	.50
4	1939 (w/teammates)	.50
5	1943 - Traded to the Giants	1.00
6	1948 - New York Giants (w/ teammates)	.50
7	1949 Traded to the Yankees	1.00
8	1949 World Series Hero	.50
9	1951 World Series (w/DiMaggio, others)	1.00
10	1953 - Meeting Royalty	.50
11	What Pressure?	.50
12	1973 - Recreation Director	.50

1983 Authentic Sports Autographs Brooks Robinson Story

This collectors issue was part of a series featuring past greats of the game. The Brooks Robinson Story is a 12-card set. Fronts feature black-and-white or color photos of the Oriole great at various stages of his career. Green graphics in the white border frame the pictures, each of which is titled at bottom. Backs have a green border and present a narrative of the player's career. Some of the backs have a small portrait photo. Sets were sold both with and without card No. 1 bearing an autograph.

		MT
Complete Set, #1 Autographed (12):		15.00
Complete Set, Unautographed (12):		8.00
Common Card:		1.00
1	Title card	1.50
2	1956 Spring Training	1.00
3	Best Fielding 3rd Baseman Ever	1.00
4	1966	1.00
5	1969 World Series	1.00
6	1971 All Star Game	1.00
7	Spring Training	1.00
8	1971 Stockton Award (w/Bench)	1.00
9	Spring Training	1.00
10	1972 All Star	1.00
11	Spring Training	1.00
12	1974	1.00

1983 Authentic Sports Autographs Frank Robinson Story

This collectors issue was part of a series featuring past greats of the game. The Frank Robinson Story is a 12-card set. Fronts feature black-and-white or color photos of the HoF great at various stages of his career. Green graphics in the white border frame the pictures, each of which is titled at bottom. Backs have a green border and present a narrative of the player's career. Some of the backs have a small portrait photo. Sets were sold both with and without card No. 1 bearing an autograph.

		MT
Complete Set, #1 Autographed (12):		20.00
Complete Set, Unautographed (12):		8.00
Common Card:		1.00
1	Title card	1.50
2	1962 with the Reds	1.00
3	1959 with the Reds	1.00
4	1961 with the Reds	1.00
5	Traded to the Orioles 1966	1.00
6	A great year in 1966	1.00
7	1969 World Series	1.00
8	1969 with Baltimore	1.00
9	1972 Home Run #521	1.50
10	1972 Santurce Manager	1.00
11	1978 Rochester Manager	1.00
12	1982 Giants Manager	1.50

1983 Authentic Sports Autographs Duke Snider Story

This collectors issue was part of a series featuring past greats of the game. The Duke Snider Story is a 12-card set. Fronts feature black-and-white or color photos of the Dodger great at various stages of his career. Green graphics in the white border frame the pictures, each of which is titled at bottom. Backs have a green border and present a narrative of the player's career. Some of the backs have a small portrait photo. Sets were sold both with and without card No. 1 bearing an autograph.

		MT
Complete Set, #1 Autographed (12):		20.00
Complete Set, Unautographed (12):		9.00
Common Card:		1.00
1	Title card	1.50
2	1948	1.00
3	1952 Boys of Summer	1.00
4	1950 - Sliding Home	1.00
5	1953 All Stars	1.00
6	1955 Taking Aim (w/ Hodges, Reese, Hoak)	1.00
7	1953 (w/Black, Dressen)	1.00
8	1952 World Series	1.00
9	1955 Dodgers Win World Series	1.00
10	1958 Dodgers Move to L.A.	2.00
11	1963 Traded to the Mets	2.00
12	1964 with the Giants	2.00

1983 Authentic Sports Autographs Warren Spahn Story

This collectors issue was part of a series featuring past greats of the game. The Warren Spahn Story is a 12-card set. Fronts feature black-and-white or color photos of the Brave great at various stages of his career. Green graphics in the white border frame the pictures, each of which is titled at bottom. Backs have a green border and present a narrative of the player's career. Some of the backs have a small portrait photo. Sets were sold both with and without card No. 1 bearing an autograph.

		MT
Complete Set, #1 Autographed (12):		15.00
Complete Set, Unautographed (12):		8.00
Common Card:		.50
1	Title card	1.00
2	1947 - High Kick	.50
3	1948 World Series	.50
4	1950 (w/Sain, Bickford)	.50
5	1951 Spring Training	.50
6	1956 Haney's First Day	.50
7	1957	.50
8	1958 On to the World Series	.50
9	1961 40th Birthday	.50
10	1959 - Strikeout #2,382	.50
11	1965 - With the Mets	.75
12	1973 Indians Coach-Hall of Fame	.75

B

1987 R.F. Ball Old Judge Color Lithographs

An artistic success but commercial failure, this set of color lithos reproduced eight Old Judge cabinet cards of 1887 in a colorized 9-1/8" x 14" format. Two series of four pieces each were produced; the first in an edition of 1,200, the second in an edition of 2,000.

		MT
Complete Set (8):		50.00
Common Player:		6.50
	FIRST SERIES	
1	Cap Anson	7.50
2	King Kelly	7.50
3	Ed Delahanty	7.50
4	Jim O'Rourke	7.50
	SECOND SERIES	
1	Buck Ewing	6.50
2	Tim Keefe	6.50
3	Harry Stovey	6.50
4	Dan Brouthers	6.50

1998 Ball Park Detroit Tigers

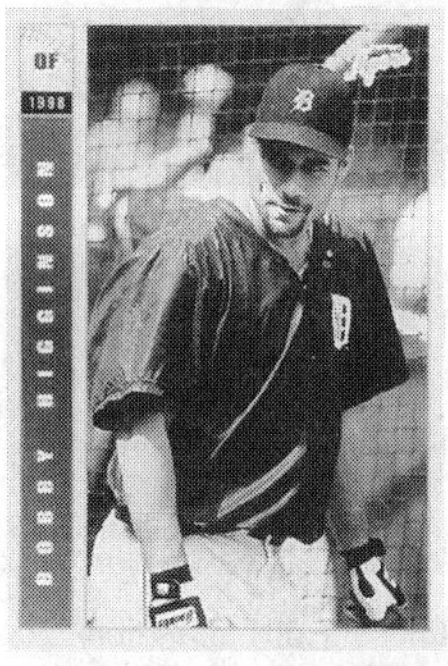

Fans in attendance at the Aug. 9 game at Tiger Stadium received this team set sponsored by Ball Park franks, the stadium hot dog concessionairre. Cards are standard 2-1/2" x 3-1/2" format printed on light cardboard. Fronts have color posed or action photos with white borders. Player identification is in a strip at left. Backs have a light blue background, overprinted in dark blue with the player's personal data, stats and a 1997 season highlight, along with the sponsor's logo and a picture of a moving baseball.

		MT
Complete Set (26):		9.00
Common Player:		.50
01	Gabe Alvarez	1.00
02	Matt Anderson	2.00
03	Paul Bako	.75
04	Trey Beamon	.50
05	Buddy Bell	.50
06	Geronimo Berroa	.50
07	Doug Bochtler	.50
08	Doug Brocail	.50
09	Raul Casanova	.50
10	Frank Castillo	.50
11	Frank Catalanotto	.50
12	Tony Clark	1.00
13	Dean Crow	.50
14	Deivi Cruz	.50
15	Damion Easley	.50
16	Bryce Florie	.50
17	Luis Gonzalez	.65
18	Seth Greisinger	.50
19	Bobby Higginson	1.00
20	Brian Hunter	.50
21	Todd Jones	.50
22	Brian Moehler	.50
23	Brian Powell	.50
24	Joe Randa	.50
25	Sean Runyan	.50
26	Justin Thompson	.50

1991 Ballstreet Journal Insert Cards

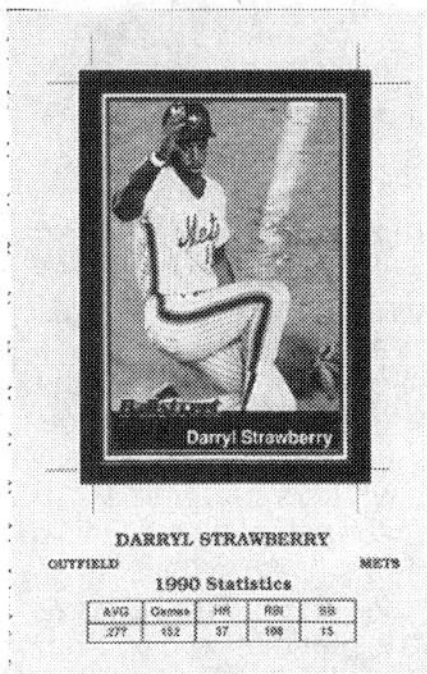

Ostensibly a compilation of price guide data from other hobby periodicals, this bimonthly magazine was little more than a wrapper for unauthorized collector issue cards bound inside. In the premiere edition of the $5 "magazine," the collector cards were printed on 4" x 6" glossy stock. The 2-1/2" x 3-1/2" cards are centered on the page with cutting guidelines. In the bottom border are 1990 stats. Backs are printed in black and green and offer an investment recommendation about the player on front. Trimmed in gold foil, the Ballstreet cards were among the first to be so highlighted. Production was advertised as 25,000 of each issue. By early 1992, complete magazines were selling as high as $40, with single cards priced as high as $12.

		MT
Complete Set (60):		36.00
Common Player:		
	Issue #1 (Nolan Ryan cover)	
1	Darryl Strawberry	.50
2	Ken Griffey Jr.	2.50
3	Nolan Ryan	2.00
4	Cecil Fielder	.50
5	Don Mattingly	1.50
6	Jose Canseco	.60
7	Bo Jackson	.50
8	Ryne Sandberg	.75
9	Will Clark	.50
10	George Brett	.75
	Issue #2 (Bo Jackson)	
11	Bo Jackson	.50
12	Cal Ripken Jr.	2.00
13	Roger Clemens	.75
14	Todd Van Poppel	.50
15	Eric Davis	.50
16	David Justice	.50
17	Kevin Maas	.50
18	Rickey Henderson	.50
19	Michael Jordan	2.00
20	Ken Griffey Jr.	2.50
	Pete Rose (postcard)	1.00
	Issue #3 (Ken Griffey, Jr.)	
21	Rickey Henderson	.50
22	Bo Jackson (crutches)	.50
23	Frank Thomas	1.00
24	Ken Griffey Jr.	2.50
25	Darryl Strawberry (Dodgers)	.50
26	Nolan Ryan	2.00
27	Mark McGwire	2.50
28	Wade Boggs	.60
29	Gregg Jefferies	.50
30	Jose Canseco	.60
	Issue #4 (Rickey Henderson)	
31	Kirby Puckett	.60
32	Reid Ryan	.50
33	Rickey Henderson (holding base)	.50
34	Nolan Ryan (7th No-hitter)	2.00
35	Mark Grace	.50
36	Matt Williams	.50
37	Barry Bonds	.65
38	Bo Jackson (White Sox)	.50
39	Tony Gwynn	.75
40	Ramon Martinez	.50
	Issue #5 (Cal Ripken, Jr.)	
41	Eric Lindros	.75
42	Mo Vaughn	.50
43	Bobby Bonilla	.50
44	Andre Dawson	.50
45	Juan Gonzalez	.65
46	Vince Coleman	.50
47	Carlton Fisk	.75
48	Scott Erickson	.50
49	Cal Ripken Jr.	2.00
50	Don Mattingly	1.50
	Issue #6 (Frank Thomas)	
51	Frank Thomas	1.00
52	Jose Canseco	.60
53	Roger Clemens	.75
54	Robin Ventura	.50
55	David Justice	.50
56	Ryne Sandberg	.75
57	Will Clark	.50
58	Robin Yount	.75
59	Danny Tartabull	.50
60	Ken Griffey Jr.	2.50

1992 Ballstreet Journal Chicago Cubs

Inserted within the pages of the August, 1992, issue of Cubs Quarterly magazine was a sheet of nine Cubs player cards produced by Ballstreet Journal, "The Consolidated Baseball Card Pocket Price Guide" which existed for the sole purpose of selling unlicensed sportscards. Individual cards on the 7-1/2" x 10-1/2" sheet measure the standard 2-1/2" x 3-1/2". Fronts have borderless color action photos. A white stripe diagonally at top-left has "BALLSTREET" printed in gold. A Cubs logo is at bottom-left, with the player name in a black strip. An All-Star logo graces the cards of Ryne Sandberg and Greg Maddux. Backs are printed in black, red and yellow with minimal player data and advertising for Ballstreet.

		MT
Complete Set, Singles (9):		18.00
Complete Magazine:		24.00
Common Player:		.25
1	Ryne Sandberg (base running)	3.00
2	Ryne Sandberg (running w/bat)	3.00
3	Ryne Sandberg (portrait)	3.00
4	Frank Castillo	.25
5	Kal Daniels	.25
6	Joe Girardi	.25
7	Steve Buechele	.25
8	Greg Maddux	4.50
9	Sammy Sosa	6.00

1982 Baseball Card News "History of Baseball Cards"

A concise history of card collecting is featured on the backs of these cards issued to promote the then-new monthly collectors newspaper. Cards are in 2-1/2" x 3-1/2" format with rounded corners printed in black-and-white on semi-gloss cardboard.

		MT
Complete Set (20):		15.00
Common Player:		.45
1	Mickey Mantle	2.50
2	Ted Williams	1.50
3	Stan Musial	1.00
4	Yogi Berra	.75
5	Roger Maris	1.00
6	Hank Aaron	1.25
7	Willie Mays	1.25
8	Hall of Famers (Joe DiMaggio, Bob Feller)	1.00
9	Lou Brock	.60
10	Roberto Clemente	2.00
11	Ernie Banks	.60
12	Lou Brock	.60
13	Dodger All Time Greats (Roy Campanella, Jackie Robinson)	1.00
14	Maury Wills	.45
15	Bob Feller	.60
16	Roy Campanella	.75
17	Sandy Koufax	1.25
18	Joe DiMaggio	1.50
19	Satchel Paige	.75
20	Babe Ruth	1.50

1984-88 Baseball Cards Magazine Repli-cards

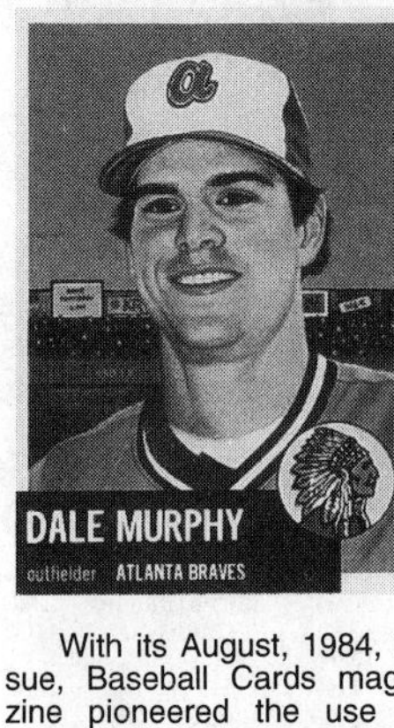

With its August, 1984, issue, Baseball Cards magazine pioneered the use of "repli-cards" to enhance feature articles and increase sales. The cards were printed on cardboard stock and stapled into the magazines. Most of the cards were done in the style of earlier popular card issues. though some featured original designs and others were reproductions of actual cards. Some of baseball's best artists and photographers work appears on the cards. The inclusion of repli-cards ceased after 1993 when abuses by other "publishers" caused baseball's licensors to threaten legal action. Values quoted are for single cards cut from the panel; complete panels or magazines command a premium. Cards are grouped by year of magazine issue and numbered with a month designation.

		MT
Common Player:		.50
	1984 Baseball Cards Magazine	
Aug.	Ted Williams (1953 Topps style)	6.00
Aug.	Dale Murphy (1953 Topps style)	4.00
Oct.	Mickey Mantle (1949 Bowman style)	7.50
	1985 Baseball Cards Magazine	
April	Chuck Connors (original design)	2.00
April	Chuck Connors (1952 Topps style)	2.00
June	Pete Rose (reproduction 1965 Topps)	3.00
June	Fritz Ackley, Steve Carlton (reproduction 1965 Topps)	1.50
Oct.	Mickey Mantle (reproduction 1955 Bowman #202)	4.00
Oct.	Ernie Banks (reproduction 1955 Bowman #242)	2.00
	1986 Baseball Cards Magazine	
April	Vince Coleman (Kondritz Trading Cards sample)	.50
April	Vince Coleman (Kondritz Trading Cards sample)	.50
June	Stan Musial (reproduction 1953 Bowman)	2.00
June	Roy Campanella (reproduction 1953 Bowman)	2.00
June	Yogi Berra (reproduction 1953 Bowman)	2.00
Dec.	Don Mattingly (1951 Topps Red Back style)	4.00
Dec.	Wally Joyner (1951 Topps Red Back style)	1.50
Dec.	Wade Boggs (1951 Topps All-Stars style)	2.50
Dec.	Dwight Gooden (1951 Topps All-Stars style)	1.00
Dec.	George Brett (reproduction 1981 Donruss proof)	1.50
Dec.	Reggie Jackson (reproduction 1981 Donruss proof)	1.50
Dec.	Lou Piniella (reproduction 1982 Fleer proof)	.50
	1987 Baseball Cards Magazine	
April	Don Mattingly (1983 Donruss style)	7.50
April	Don Mattingly (1983 Topps style)	7.50
Sept.	Ozzie Canseco (original "Future Stars" design)	.50
Sept.	Patrick Lennon (original "Future Stars" design)	.50
Oct.	Eric Davis (1951 Bowman style)	1.00
Oct.	Bo Jackson (1951 Bowman style)	1.00
Oct.	Stan Musial (1951 Bowman style)	2.00
Dec.	Dale Murphy (1981 Fleer style)	.75
Dec.	Tim Raines (1981 Fleer style)	.50
Dec.	Double Trouble (Eric Davis, Mark McGwire) (1981 Fleer style)	3.00
	1988 Baseball Cards Magazine	
Feb.	Babe Ruth (1936 Diamond Stars style)	2.00
Feb.	Wade Boggs (1936 Diamond Stars style)	1.25
Feb.	Mark McGwire (1936 Diamond Stars style; available only via mail-in offer)	12.00
April	Ted Williams (1952 Topps style)	2.00
April	Ted Williams (reproduction 1954 Bowman #66)	3.00
June	Joey Meyer (original design)	.50
June	Sam Horn (original design)	.50
Aug.	Roger "Rocket" Clemens (1941 Play Ball style)	3.00
Aug.	Kirk Gibson (1941 Play Ball style)	1.50
Aug.	Jack Clark (1941 Play Ball style)	.50
Oct.	Mickey Mantle (1956 Bowman proof style)	5.00
Oct.	Jackie Robinson (1952 Bowman style)	2.50
Oct.	Dave Winfield (1974 Topps "Washington" style)	.75
Dec.	Mickey Mantle (reproduction 1952 Bowman)	3.00
Dec.	Mickey Mantle (reproduction 1951 Bowman)	4.00
Dec.	Mickey Mantle (reproduction 1952 Topps)	5.00

1989 Baseball Cards Magazine Repli-cards

Beginning with its January, 1989, issue, Baseball Cards magazine began issuing its repli-cards in panels of six cards per month, creating an annual set of 72 insert cards. Contemporary players were presented in the designs of classic Topps sets of the 1950s-1970s. In 1989 the magazine's cards were in the style of 1959 Topps. Besides the individual player's cards, specialty cards included "Rookie Stars of 1989" and multi-player feature cards.

		MT
Complete Set (45):		60.00
Common Player:		.50
1	Keith Hernandez	.50
2	Will Clark	1.50
3	Andres Galarraga	.75
4	Mark McGwire	5.00
5	Don Mattingly	3.00
6	Ricky Jordan (Rookie Stars)	.50
7	Juan Samuel	.50
8	Julio Franco	.50
9	Harold Reynolds	.50
10	Gregg Jefferies (Rookie Stars)	1.00
11	Ryne Sandberg	2.00
12	Lou Whitaker	.50
13	Ozzie Smith	1.50
14	Gary Sheffield (Rookie Stars)	.75
15	Alan Trammell	.50
16	Cal Ripken Jr.	4.00
17	Barry Larkin	.50
18	Tony Fernandez	.50
19	Mike Schmidt	2.00
20	Wade Boggs	2.00
21	Gary Gaetti	.50
22	Chris Sabo (Rookie Stars)	.50
23	Paul Molitor	1.00
24	Carney Lansford	.50
25	Dave Winfield	1.00
26	Darryl Strawberry	.75
27	Tony Gwynn	1.50
28	Darryl Hamilton	.50
29	Jose Canseco	1.00
30	Andre Dawson	.65
31	Kirby Puckett	2.00
32	Cameron Drew (Rookie Stars)	.50
33	Robin Yount	1.50
34	Ellis Burks	.50
35	Eric Davis	.50
36	Joe Carter	.50
37	George Bell	.50
38	Kevin McReynolds	.50
39	Tim Raines	.50
40	Luis Medina (Rookie Stars)	.50
41	Mike Greenwell	.50
42	Kal Daniels	.50
43	Dwight Gooden	.75
44	Roger Clemens	1.50
45	Nolan Ryan	4.00
46	Erik Hanson	.50
47	Orel Hershiser	.50
48	Bret Saberhagen	.50
49	Jimmy Key	.50
50	Frank Viola	.50
51	Bruce Hurst	.50
52	Norm Charlton (Rookie Stars)	.50
53	Ted Higuera	.50
54	Mark Langston	.50
55	Damon Berryhill	.50
56	Carlton Fisk	1.00
57	Terry Steinbach	.50
58	Sandy Alomar (Rookie Stars)	.75
59	Benito Santiago	.50
60	Bob Boone	.50
61	Jerome Walton (Rookie Stars)	.50
62	Jaime Navarro (Rookie Stars)	.50
63	Ken Griffey Jr. (Rookie Stars)	6.00
64	Jim Abbott (Rookie Stars)	.65
65	Junior Felix (Rookie Stars)	.50
66	Tom Gordon	.50
67	Power Plus (Kirby Puckett, Don Mattingly)	2.00
68	Fence Busters (Julio Franco, Eric Davis, Ruben Sierra)	.50
69	N.L. Hitting Kings (Will Clark, Tony Gwynn)	1.00
70	Keystone Combo (Ozzie Smith, Ryne Sandberg)	1.00
71	Dinger Duo (Howard Johnson, Kevin Mitchell)	.50
72	Texas Heat (Nolan Ryan, Mike Scott)	2.50

1990 Baseball Cards Magazine Repli-cards

Beginning with its January, 1989, issue, Baseball Cards magazine began issuing its repli-cards in panels of six cards per month, creating an annual set of 72 insert cards. Contemporary players were presented in the designs of classic Topps sets of the 1950s-1970s. In 1990 the magazine's cards were in the style of 1969 Topps. Besides the individual player's cards, there were a number of multi-player "Rookie Stars" cards.

		MT
Complete Set (72):		50.00
Common Player:		.50
1	Craig Biggio	.50
2	Kevin Mitchell	.50
3	Orel Hershiser	.50
4	Will Clark	1.00
5	Eric Davis	.50
6	Tony Gwynn	1.50
7	Mike Scott	.50
8	Barry Larkin	.50
9	John Smoltz	.50
10	Glenn Davis	.50
11	Roberto Alomar	.75
12	Rick Reuschel	.50
13	N.L. West Rookie Stars (Eric Anthony, Ed Whited)	.50
14	N.L. West Rookie Stars (Andy Benes, Steve Avery)	1.00
15	N.L. West Rookie Stars (John Wetteland, Joe Oliver)	.65
16	Giants Rookie Stars (Randy McCament, Greg Litton)	.50
17	Dodgers Rookie Stars (Jose Offerman, Jose Vizcaino)	.50
18	Reds Rookie Stars (Scott Scudder, Rosario Rodriguez)	.50
19	Darryl Strawberry	.75
20	Von Hayes	.50
21	Dwight Smith	.50
22	Howard Johnson	.50
23	Pedro Guerrero	.50
24	Tim Raines	.50
25	Ozzie Smith	1.50
26	Barry Bonds	1.50
27	Jerome Walton	.50
28	Ryne Sandberg	1.50
29	Bobby Bonilla	.50
30	Mark Grace	.75
31	Cards Rookie Stars (Todd Zeile, Alex Cole)	.65
32	N.L. East Rookie Stars (Pat Combs, Dean Wilkins)	.50
33	N.L. East Rookie Stars (Steve Carter, Jeff Huson)	.50
34	Cubs Rookie Stars (Greg Smith, Derrick May)	.50
35	Expos Rookie Stars (Marquis Grissom, Larry Walker)	1.50
36	Mets Rookie Stars (Wally Whitehurst, Blaine Beatty)	.50
37	Ken Griffey Jr.	4.00
38	Kirby Puckett	2.00
39	Julio Franco	.50
40	Ruben Sierra	.50
41	Bo Jackson	.75
42	Jose Canseco	1.00
43	Dennis Eckersley	.50
44	Bret Saberhagen	.50
45	Wally Joyner	.50
46	Rickey Henderson	.65
47	Carlton Fisk	.75
48	Nolan Ryan	3.00
49	White Sox Rookie Stars (Robin Ventura, Sammy Sosa)	3.00
50	A.L. West Rookie Stars (John Orton, Scott Radinsky)	.50
51	A.L. West Rookie Stars (Bobby Rose, Bob Hamelin)	.50
52	Rangers Rookie Stars (Monty Fariss, Juan Gonzalez)	2.00
53	Mariners Rookie Stars (Tino Martinez, Roger Salkeld)	.75
54	Twins Rookie Stars (Terry Jorgensen, Paul Sorrento)	.50
55	Don Mattingly	2.00
56	Roger Clemens	1.50
57	Cal Ripken	3.00
58	Robin Yount	1.50
59	Wade Boggs	1.50
60	Fred McGriff	.75
61	Cecil Fielder	.50
62	Ellis Burks	.50
63	Sandy Alomar	.60
64	Alan Trammell	.50
65	Steve Sax	.50
66	Paul Molitor	1.00
67	Brewers Rookie Stars (Bert Hefferman, Matias Carillo)	.50
68	A.L. East Rookie Stars (Ben McDonald, John Olerud)	.65
69	A.L. East Rookie Stars (Mark Whiten, Phil Clark)	.50
70	Yankees Rookie Stars (Jim Leyritz, Kevin Maas)	.50
71	Indians Rookie Stars (Mark Lewis, Carlos Baerga)	.50
72	Orioles Rookie Stars (David Segui, Chris Hoiles)	.50

1991 Baseball Cards Magazine Repli-cards

For the third year in 1991, Baseball Cards magazine issued its repli-cards in panels of six cards per month, creating an annual set of 72 insert cards. Contemporary players were presented in the classic Topps design of 1966. Besides the individual players' cards, there are a number of multi-player feature cards and "Rookie Stars of 1991" multi-player cards, plus a 1952 Topps-style card of Don Mattingly.

		MT
Complete Set (72):		45.00
Common Player:		.50
1	Eric Davis	.50
2	Cubs Rookie Stars (Lance Dickson, Hector Villanueva)	.50
3	Bobby Bonilla	.50
4	Len Dykstra	.50
5	John Franco	.50
6	Matt Williams	.50
7	Barry Bonds	1.50
8	Cards Rookie Stars (Geronimo Pena, Ray Lankford, Bernard Gilkey)	.75
9	Andre Dawson	.50
10	Dave Justice	.50
11	Triple Expos-ure (Larry Walker, Marquis Grissom, Delino DeShields)	.50
12	Howard Johnson	.50
13	Darryl Strawberry	.50
14	Astros Rookie Stars (Karl Rhodes, Andujar Cedeno, Mike Simms)	.50
15	Will Clark	.75
16	Barry Larkin	.50
17	Ramon Martinez	.50
18	Ron Gant	.50
19	Gregg Jefferies	.50
20	Giants Rookie Stars (Steve Decker, Steve Hosey, Mark Leonard)	.50
21	Todd Zeile	.50
22	Benito Santiago	.50
23	Eddie Murray	.75
24	Randy Myers	.50
25	Greg Maddux	2.50
26	Phillies Rookie Stars (Mickey Morandini, Wes Chamberlain)	.50
27	Tim Wallach	.50
28	Dale Murphy	.50
29	Doug Drabek	.50
30	Kevin Mitchell	.50
31	Frank Viola	.50
32	Padres Rookie Stars (Rafael Valdez, Paul Faries)	.50
33	Hal Morris	.50
34	Pedro Guerrero	.50

35 Dwight Gooden .50
36 Shawon Dunston .50
37 Ken Griffey Jr. 4.00
38 Royals Rookie Stars (Sean Berry, Brian McRae) .50
39 Roger Clemens 1.50
40 Ellis Burks .50
41 Robin Yount .75
42 Frank Thomas 2.50
43 Ruben Sierra .50
44 Red Sox Rookie Stars (Mo Vaughn, Phil Plantier, Tim Naehring) .65
45 Tim Raines .50
46 Dave Parker .50
47 Jose Canseco .65
48 Glenn Davis .50
49 Dave Winfield .60
50 Chuck Knoblauch, Scott Leius, Willie Banks (Twins Rookie Stars) .50
51 Joe Carter .50
52 Cal Ripken 3.00
53 Carlton Fisk .75
54 Julio Franco .50
55 Don Mattingly 2.00
56 Blue Jays Rookie Stars (Eddie Zosky, William Suero, Derek Bell) .50
57 Sandy Alomar .60
58 Juan Gonzalez 1.50
59 Don Mattingly (1952 Topps style) 2.00
60 Mike Greenwell .50
61 Chuck Finley .50
62 Rangers Rookie Stars (Dean Palmer, Ivan Rodriguez, Gerald Alexander) 1.25
63 Scott Erickson .50
64 Paul Molitor .75
65 Triple Terrors (Cecil Fielder, Jose Canseco, Mark McGwire) 1.50
66 Dennis Eckersley .50
67 Brian Harper .50
68 A.L. Rookie Stars (Bernie Williams, Wilson Alvarez) (no designation on front banner) .50
69 Robin Ventura .50
70 Kirby Puckett 1.00
71 Rafael Palmeiro .50
72 Roberto Alomar .65

1992 Baseball Cards Magazine Repli-cards

The annual repli-card series inserted in Baseball Cards magazine began in January with six-card panels each month. In May, panels were increased to eight cards and a UV coating was added to the front. Contemporary players were presented in the designs of classic Topps sets of the 1950s-1970s. In 1992 the magazine's cards were in the style of 1970 Topps. Besides the individual player's cards, specialty cards included "1992 Rookie Stars" multi-player and Team USA cards.

MT
Complete Set (88): 55.00
Common Player: .50
1 Eddie Murray .65
2 Braves Rookie Stars (Ryan Klesko, Mark Wohlers) .65
3 Barry Bonds 1.25
4 Will Clark .65
5 Jose Canseco .65
6 Ron Gant .50
7 Ruben Sierra .50
8 Reds Rookie Stars (Reggie Sanders, Mo Sanford) .50
9 Terry Pendleton .50
10 Hal Morris .50
11 Kirby Puckett 1.00
12 Paul Molitor 1.00
13 Jack McDowell .50
14 Dodgers Rookie Stars (Eric Karros, Tom Goodwin) .50
15 Ramon Martinez .50
16 Steve Avery .50
17 Roger Clemens 1.25
18 Jim Abbott .50
19 Phil Plantier .50
20 Giants Rookie Stars (Royce Clayton, Ted Wood) .50
21 Frank Thomas 2.00
22 Juan Gonzalez 1.25
23 Felix Jose .50
24 Chuck Knoblauch .50
25 Tony Gwynn 1.25
26 Julio Franco .50
27 Greg Blosser, Frankie Rodriguez .50
28 Wade Boggs .75
29 Robin Ventura .50
30 Shane Mack .50
31 Roberto Alomar .60
32 Don Mattingly 2.00
33 Astros Rookie Stars (Ryan Bowen, Jeff Juden) .50
34 Cal Ripken Jr. 2.50
35 Ozzie Smith .75
36 Ken Griffey Jr. 3.00
37 Ivan Rodriguez .65
38 Matt Williams .50
39 Craig Biggio .50
40 John Kruk .50
41 George Brett 1.00
42 Carlton Fisk .75
43 Indians Rookie Stars (Kenny Lofton, Jim Thome) .75
44 Andre Dawson .50
45 Nolan Ryan 2.50
46 Robin Yount .75
47 Ryne Sandberg .75
48 Rickey Henderson .60
49 Bobby Thigpen .50
50 Dennis Eckersley .50
51 Cards Rookie Stars (Brian Jordan, Dmitri Young) .50
52 Jeff Reardon .50
53 Bryan Harvey .50
54 Tom Henke .50
55 Lee Smith .50
56 John Franco .50
57 Cecil Fielder .50
58 Darryl Strawberry .50
59 Twins Rookie Stars (David McCarty, Scott Stahoviak) .50
60 Mark McGwire 3.00
61 George Bell .50
62 Fred McGriff .50
63 Danny Tartabull .50
64 Joe Carter .50
65 Deion Sanders .65
66 Roberto Alomar .65
67 A.L. Rookie Stars (Eduardo Perez, Joe Vitiello, Bret Boone) .50
68 Bip Roberts .50
69 Ray Lankford .50
70 Brady Anderson .50
71 Tim Raines .50
72 Marquis Grissom .50
73 Dave Fleming .50
74 Andy Benes .50
75 Yankees Rookie Stars (Bob Wickman, Mark Hutton) .50
76 Bill Swift .50
77 Mike Mussina .50
78 Donovan Osborne .50
79 Juan Guzman .50
80 Kevin Brown .65
81 Charles Johnson (USA) .75
82 Jeffrey Hammonds (USA) .50
83 Rick Helling (USA) .50
84 Chris Wimmer (USA) .50
85 Darren Dreifort (USA) .50
86 Calvin Murray (USA) .50
87 Phil Nevin (USA) .50
88 B.J. Wallace (USA) .50

1992 BB Card/Sports Card Price Guide Repli-cards

(See SCD Baseball Card Price Guide)

1993 Baseball Cards/Sports Cards Magazine Repli-cards

The annual repli-card series began in Baseball Cards magazine in 1989 continued in 1993 with eight-card panels of UV-coated repli-cards stapled into each monthly issue. (Only seven cards were included in July; there are two #32 and no #40.) Contemporary players were presented in the design of the classic 1968 Topps set. Backs are printed in black, white and yellow and include an investment advisory about the player's cards. Besides the individual player's repli-cards, there is a group of "1993 Rookie Stars" multi-player cards. Effective with its May issue, the magazine's title was changed to Sports Cards, the copyright line on back reflecting that change.

MT
Complete Set (96): 65.00
Common Player: .50
1 Andy Van Slyke .50
2 Ruben Sierra .50
3 Carlos Baerga .50
4 Gary Sheffield .50
5 Chuck Knoblauch .50
6 Danny Tartabull .50
7 Angels Rookie Stars (Chad Curtis, Tim Salmon) .65
8 Darren Daulton .50
9 Deion Sanders .50
10 Pat Listach .50
11 Albert Belle 1.00
12 Frank Thomas 2.00
13 Dave Hollins .50
14 Braves Rookie Stars (Javy Lopez, Mike Kelly) .65
15 Travis Fryman .50
16 Edgar Martinez .50
17 Barry Bonds 1.00
18 Dennis Eckersley .50
19 Brady Anderson .50
20 Fred McGriff .50
21 Paul Molitor 1.00
22 Juan Gonzalez 1.50
23 Dodgers Rookie Stars (Bill Ashley, Mike Piazza) 1.50
24 Larry Walker .50
25 Dave Winfield .75
26 Robin Yount 1.00
27 George Brett 1.25
28 Jack Morris .50
29 Eddie Murray .60
30 Nolan Ryan 3.00
31 Carlton Fisk .75
32a Dale Murphy .65
32b Jeff Bagwell 1.00
33 Eric Karros .50
34 Roberto Alomar .65
35 Robin Ventura .50
36 Delino DeShields .50
37 Ken Griffey Jr. 3.50
38 Eric Anthony .50
39 Marquis Grissom .50
40 not issued
41 Cecil Fielder .50
42 Mark McGwire 3.50
43 Ryne Sandberg 1.00
44 Kirby Puckett 1.00
45 Cal Ripken Jr. 3.00
46 David McCarty .50
47 Joe Carter .50
48 Dean Palmer .50
49 Jack McDowell .50
50 Roger Clemens 1.00
51 Cal Eldred .50
52 Tom Glavine .50
53 Steve Avery .50
54 Mike Mussina .50
55 Brien Taylor .50
56 Mark Grace .65
57 Ray Lankford .50
58 Shane Mack .50
59 Terry Pendleton .50
60 Tony Gwynn 1.00
61 Rafael Palmeiro .50
62 Will Clark .65
63 Wil Cordero .50
64 Cliff Floyd .50
65 Aaron Sele .50
66 Chipper Jones 2.50
67 Frank Rodriguez .50
68 Ryan Klesko .50
69 Manny Ramirez .75
70 Carlos Delgado .50
71 Paul Shuey .50
72 Barry Bonds 1.00
73 Andre Dawson .50
74 Paul Molitor 1.00
75 Greg Maddux 1.50
76 Wade Boggs .80
77 Bryan Harvey .50
78 Andres Galarraga .50
79 Gregg Jefferies .50
80 Mike Piazza 2.00
81 J.T. Snow .50
82 Ivan Rodriguez .75
83 Derrick May .50
84 Tim Salmon .50
85 Greg Vaughn .50
86 Kenny Lofton .50
87 John Olerud .50
88 Sammy Sosa 2.00
89 Lee Smith .50
90 Matt Williams .50
91 Don Mattingly 2.00
92 Willie Greene .50
93 Jim Abbott .50
94 Mo Vaughn .55
95 Randy Johnson .60

1990-92 Baseball Cards Presents Repli-cards

Taking advantage of the boom in sports card collecting, Baseball Cards magazine began a series of special newsstand magazine titles. Beginning with "Baseball Card Boom," dated Feb. 1990, the series, officially known as "Baseball Cards Presents . . ." included baseball (and other sports) repli-cards in most of its issues through Aug. 1992. Cards are listed here by issue in which they were inserted.

MT
Complete Set (61): 65.00
Common Player: .50

Baseball Card Boom 2/90 (1980 Topps style)
1 Don Mattingly 2.00
2 Dwight Gooden .50
3 Jose Canseco .75
4 Bo Jackson .50
5 Ken Griffey Jr. 4.00

Beginner's Guide to Baseball Cards 6/90 (1952 Topps style)
1 John Olerud .50
2 Eric Anthony .50
3 Greg Vaughn .50
4 Todd Zeile .50
5 Ben McDonald .50
6 Deion Sanders (mail-in offer only) 2.00

Fantasy Baseball 8/90 (original design)
1 Mark Davis .50
2 Bret Saberhagen .50
3 Kirby Puckett 1.00
4 Rickey Henderson .50
5 Kevin Mitchell .50

Baseball Card Boom 2/91 (1933 Goudey style)
1 Cecil Fielder .50
2 Rickey Henderson .50
3 Barry Bonds 1.50
4 Ryne Sandberg 1.00
5 Roger Clemens 1.50

Superstar and Rookie Special 4/91 (1975 Topps style. Either panel #1-5 or #6-10 found in each issue.)
1 Nolan Ryan 3.00
2 Eric Davis .50
3 Ryne Sandberg 1.00
4 Rickey Henderson .50
5 Kevin Maas .50
6 Dave Justice .65
7 Jose Canseco .75
8 Bo Jackson .75
9 Roger Clemens 1.50
10 Ken Griffey Jr. 4.00

Investor's Guide to Baseball Cards
1 Babe Ruth (1936 Diamond Stars style) 1.50
1 Ted Williams (1952 Topps style) 1.00
2 Rickey Henderson (1933 Goudey style) .50
5 Roger Clemens (1941 Play Ball style) 1.00
325 Stan Musial (1951 Bowman style) .50

Superstar and Rookie Special 8/91 (1975 Topps style)
11 Frank Thomas 2.00
12 Dwight Gooden .50
13 David Robinson (basketball) .50
14 Will Clark .50
15 Darryl Strawberry .50

Superstar and Rookie Special 12/91 (1975 Topps style)
16 Kevin Mitchell .50
17 Tony Gwynn 1.50
18 Cal Ripken Jr. 3.00
19 Michael Jordan 3.00
20 Don Mattingly 2.00

Sports Card Boom 2/92 (1933 DeLong style)
1 Frank Thomas 2.00
2 Scott Erickson .50
3 Terry Pendleton .50
4 Cal Ripken 3.00
5 Barry Bonds 1.50

Investor's Guide to Baseball Cards 6/92 (1955 Bowman style)
1 Frank Thomas 2.00
2 Jeff Bagwell 1.00
3 Cecil Fielder .50
4 Ken Griffey Jr. 4.00
5 Juan Gonzalez 2.00

Beginner's Guide to Card Collecting 8/92 (1972 Topps style)
1 Ryne Sandberg 1.00
2 Phil Plantier .50
3 Barry Larkin .50
4 Cecil Fielder .50
5 Dave Justice .65

1992 The Baseball Enquirer

This set of "Mystery Interview" cards parodies baseball players and baseball cards. The 2-1/2" x 3-1/2" cards have caricatures of well-known players on front, surrounded by a gray border and a blank white name box. A blue "Fun Stuff" trademark is at bottom right. Backs are printed in blue and black on white with a card number, another blank name box, issuer's trademarks and a mock interview with the player. Actual player names are not seen anywhere on the cards. Issued in 10-card polypacks at 49 cents, complete sets - 184,000 of them - were also issued at $5.

		MT
Complete Set (64):		10.00
Common Player:		.50
1	Bo Jackson	.75
2	Jose Canseco	.75
3	Mark Langston	.50
4	Billy Ripken	.60
5	David Justice	.75
6	Rob Deer	.50
7	Jack McDowell	.50
8	Cecil Fielder	.50
9	John Smoltz	.75
10	Will Clark	1.00
11	Ken Caminiti	.65
12	Kent Hrbek	.50
13	Gregg Jefferies	.50
14	Bob Uecker	.75
15	Mike Greenwell	.50
16	No player	.06
17	Ken Griffey Jr.	3.50
18	Robin Yount	1.50
19	Joe DiMaggio	2.00
20	Mackey Sasser	.50
21	Dave Stewart	.50
22	Barry Bonds	1.25
23	Don Zimmer	.50
24	Jack Morris	.50
25	George Brett	1.50
26	Tommy Lasorda	.60
27	Whitey Ford	.60
28	Bill Buckner	.50
29	Ozzie Smith	1.25
30	Stump Merrill	.50
31	Randy Johnson	1.00
32	George Bell	.50
33	Johnny Bench	1.00
34	Rickey Henderson	.60
35	Unidentified Player	.50
36	Jim Palmer	.75
37	Lenny Dykstra	.50
38	George Steinbrenner	.60
39	Dave Stieb	.50
40	Nolan Ryan	3.00
41	Chris Sabo	.50
42	Unidentified player	.50
43	Kirby Puckett	1.25
44	Lou Piniella	.50
45	Wade Boggs	.75
46	Andre Dawson	.60
47	Roger Clemens	1.00
48	Pete Rose	1.75
49	David Cone	.60
50	Warren Cromartie	.50
51	Unidentified Umpire	.50
52	Phil Rizzuto	.60
53	Dan Gladden	.50
54	Mark Lemke	.50
55	Buck Rodgers	.50
56	Darryl Strawberry	.60
57	Rob Dibble	.50
58	Deion Sanders	.75
59	Tony Gwynn	1.25
60	Dale Murphy	.75
61	Albert Belle	.75
62	Don Mattingly	1.75
63	Andres Galarraga	.60
64	Babe Ruth	2.50

1985 Baseball Greats Caricatures

One of the more innovative collectors issues of the mid-1980s, these cards feature excellent color caricatures of the players. Backs of the 2-1/2" x 3-1/2" cards are printed in black and offer a career summary. Cards are checklisted here in alphabetical order.

		MT
Complete Set (10):		5.00
Common Player:		.50
1	Ted Williams	1.00
2	Joe DiMaggio	1.00
3	Stan Musial	.50
4	Bob Feller	.50
5	Reggie Jackson	.75
6	Warren Spahn	.50
7	Mickey Mantle	3.00
8	Willie Mays	1.00
9	Bob Gibson	.50
10	George Brett	.75

1980-88 Baseball Immortals

One of the most popular of the "collectors' issues," this set is produced with the permission of Major League Baseball by Renata Galasso Inc. and TCMA. The set features players in the Baseball Hall of Fame and was first issued in 1980. For several years thereafter the set was updated to include new inductees. The cards measure 2-1/2" x 3-1/2" and have colorful borders. The card fronts include the player's name, position and year of induction. The backs feature a short biography and a trivia question. The photos used are color; most players who were active before 1950 have colored black-and-white photos. The designation "first printing" appears on all cards issued in 1981 and after.

		MT
Complete Set (199):		35.00
Common Player:		.10
1	Babe Ruth	1.50
2	Ty Cobb	.60
3	Walter Johnson	.20
4	Christy Mathewson	.20
5	Honus Wagner	.20
6	Morgan Bulkeley	.10
7	Ban Johnson	.10
8	Larry Lajoie	.10
9	Connie Mack	.10
10	John McGraw	.10
11	Tris Speaker	.15
12	George Wright	.10
13	Cy Young	.15
14	Grover Alexander	.15
15	Alexander Cartwright	.10
16	Henry Chadwick	.10
17	Cap Anson	.15
18	Eddie Collins	.10
19	Charles Comiskey	.10
20	Candy Cummings	.10
21	Buck Ewing	.10
22	Lou Gehrig	1.00
23	Willie Keeler	.10
24	Hoss Radbourne	.10
25	George Sisler	.10
26	Albert Spalding	.10
27	Rogers Hornsby	.15
28	Judge Landis	.10
29	Roger Bresnahan	.10
30	Dan Brouthers	.10
31	Fred Clarke	.10
32	James Collins	.10
33	Ed Delahanty	.10
34	Hugh Duffy	.10
35	Hughie Jennings	.10
36	Mike "King" Kelly	.10
37	James O'Rourke	.10
38	Wilbert Robinson	.10
39	Jesse Burkett	.10
40	Frank Chance	.10
41	Jack Chesbro	.10
42	John Evers	.10
43	Clark Griffith	.10
44	Thomas McCarthy	.10
45	Joe McGinnity	.10
46	Eddie Plank	.10
47	Joe Tinker	.10
48	Rube Waddell	.10
49	Ed Walsh	.10
50	Mickey Cochrane	.10
51	Frankie Frisch	.10
52	Lefty Grove	.10
53	Carl Hubbell	.10
54	Herb Pennock	.10
55	Pie Traynor	.10
56	Three Finger Brown	.10
57	Charlie Gehringer	.10
58	Kid Nichols	.10
59	Jimmie Foxx	.15
60	Mel Ott	.10
61	Harry Heilmann	.10
62	Paul Waner	.10
63	Ed Barrow	.10
64	Chief Bender	.10
65	Tom Connolly	.10
66	Dizzy Dean	.15
67	Bill Klem	.10
68	Al Simmons	.10
69	Bobby Wallace	.10
70	Harry Wright	.10
71	Bill Dickey	.15
72	Rabbit Maranville	.10
73	Bill Terry	.10
74	Home Run Baker	.10
75	Joe DiMaggio	1.50
76	Gabby Hartnett	.10
77	Ted Lyons	.10
78	Ray Schalk	.10
79	Dazzy Vance	.10
80	Joe Cronin	.10
81	Hank Greenberg	.15
82	Sam Crawford	.10
83	Joe McCarthy	.10
84	Zack Wheat	.10
85	Max Carey	.10
86	Billy Hamilton	.10
87	Bob Feller	.20
88	Bill McKechnie	.10
89	Jackie Robinson	1.00
90	Edd Roush	.10
91	John Clarkson	.10
92	Elmer Flick	.10
93	Sam Rice	.10
94	Eppa Rixey	.10
95	Luke Appling	.10
96	Red Faber	.10
97	Burleigh Grimes	.10
98	Miller Huggins	.10
99	Tim Keefe	.10
100	Heinie Manush	.10
101	John Ward	.10
102	Pud Galvin	.10
103	Casey Stengel	.10
104	Ted Williams	.75
105	Branch Rickey	.10
106	Red Ruffing	.10
107	Lloyd Waner	.10
108	Kiki Cuyler	.10
109	Goose Goslin	.10
110	Joe (Ducky) Medwick	.10
111	Roy Campanella	.20
112	Stan Coveleski	.10
113	Waite Hoyt	.10
114	Stan Musial	.30
115	Lou Boudreau	.10
116	Earle Combs	.10
117	Ford Frick	.10
118	Jesse Haines	.10
119	Dave Bancroft	.10
120	Jake Beckley	.10
121	Chick Hafey	.10
122	Harry Hooper	.10
123	Joe Kelley	.10
124	Rube Marquard	.10
125	Satchel Paige	.45
126	George Weiss	.10
127	Yogi Berra	.20
128	Josh Gibson	.10
129	Lefty Gomez	.10
130	Will Harridge	.10
131	Sandy Koufax	.50
132	Buck Leonard	.10
133	Early Wynn	.10
134	Ross Youngs	.10
135	Roberto Clemente	1.50
136	Billy Evans	.10
137	Monte Irvin	.10
138	George Kelly	.10
139	Warren Spahn	.10
140	Mickey Welch	.10
141	Cool Papa Bell	.10
142	Jim Bottomley	.10
143	Jocko Conlan	.10
144	Whitey Ford	.15
145	Mickey Mantle	2.00
146	Sam Thompson	.10
147	Earl Averill	.10
148	Bucky Harris	.10
149	Billy Herman	.10
150	Judy Johnson	.10
151	Ralph Kiner	.10
152	Oscar Charleston	.10
153	Roger Connor	.10
154	Cal Hubbard	.10
155	Bob Lemon	.10
156	Fred Lindstrom	.10
157	Robin Roberts	.10
158	Ernie Banks	.25
159	Martin Dihigo	.10
160	Pop Lloyd	.10
161	Al Lopez	.10
162	Amos Rusie	.10
163	Joe Sewell	.10
164	Addie Joss	.10
165	Larry MacPhail	.10
166	Eddie Mathews	.10
167	Warren Giles	.10
168	Willie Mays	.50
169	Hack Wilson	.10
170	Duke Snider	.20
171	Al Kaline	.15
172	Chuck Klein	.10
173	Tom Yawkey	.10
174	Bob Gibson	.15
175	Rube Foster	.10
176	Johnny Mize	.10
177	Hank Aaron	.50
178	Frank Robinson	.15
179	Happy Chandler	.10
180	Travis Jackson	.10
181	Brooks Robinson	.15
182	Juan Marichal	.10
183	George Kell	.10
184	Walter Alston	.10
185	Harmon Killebrew	.15
186	Luis Aparicio	.10
187	Don Drysdale	.15
188	Pee Wee Reese	.15
189	Rick Ferrell	.10
190	Willie McCovey	.15
191	Ernie Lombardi	.10
192	Bobby Doerr	.10
193	Arky Vaughan	.10
194	Enos Slaughter	.10
195	Lou Brock	.10
196	Hoyt Wilhelm	.10
197	Billy Williams	.10
198	"Catfish" Hunter	.10
199	Ray Dandridge	.10

1987 Baseball's All-Time Greats

Though the producer is not identified anywhere on the cards, this collectors issue was created primarily for insertion in beginner's baseball card kits. One series of 50 cards was produced about 1987, a second series some years later. All cards have a bright green border with a rather small "window" at center in which players are pictured in either color or black-and-white photos, or artwork. The player's major league career span is in a tan oval towards bottom. Horizontal backs have a red strip at top with personal data and also include a career summary. The unnumbered cards are checklisted here in alphabetical order.

		MT
Complete Set (100):		20.00
Common Player:		.15
(1)	Henry Aaron	.40
(2)	Joe Adcock	.15
(3)	Richie Allen	.25
(4)	Grover C. Alexander	.15
(5)	Luis Aparicio	.15
(6)	Luke Appling	.15
(7)	Ernie Banks	.15
(8)	Hank Bauer	.15
(9)	Johnny Bench	.15
(10)	"Yogi" Berra	.25
(11)	Lou Boudreau	.15
(12)	Lou Brock	.15
(13)	"Three Finger" Brown	.15
(14)	Jim Bunning	.15
(15)	Roy Campanella	.30
(16)	Rod Carew	.15
(17)	Orlando Cepeda	.15
(18)	Roberto Clemente	1.00
(19)	Ty Cobb	.30
(20)	Mickey Cochrane	.15
(21)	Rocky Colavito	.15
(22)	Eddie Collins	.15
(23)	Sam Crawford	.15
(24)	Joe Cronin	.15
(25)	Alvin Dark	.15
(26)	Dizzy Dean	.15
(27)	Bill Dickey	.15
(28)	Joe DiMaggio	.75
(29)	Larry Doby	.15
(30)	Don Drysdale	.15
(31)	Leo Durocher	.15
(32)	Carl Erskine	.15
(33)	Bob Feller	.15
(34)	Curt Flood	.15
(35)	Whitey Ford	.25
(36)	Jimmie Foxx	.15
(37)	Frankie Frisch	.15
(38)	Carl Furillo	.15
(39)	Lou Gehrig	.60
(40)	Charlie Gehringer	.15
(41)	Hank Greenberg	.25
(42)	"Lefty" Grove	.15
(43)	"Gabby" Hartnett	.15
(44)	Gil Hodges	.15
(45)	Rogers Hornsby	.15
(46)	Carl Hubbell	.15
(47)	Jim Hunter	.15
(48)	Monte Irvin	.15
(49)	Ferguson Jenkins	.15
(50)	Walter Johnson	.15
(51)	Jim Kaat	.15
(52)	George Kell	.15
(53)	Ralph Kiner	.15
(54)	Ted Kluszewski	.15
(55)	Don Larsen	.15
(56)	Bob Lemon	.15
(57)	Ernie Lombardi	.15
(58)	Eddie Lopat	.15
(59)	Mickey Mantle	1.50
(60)	Juan Marichal	.15
(61)	Roger Maris	.75
(62)	Billy Martin	.15
(63)	Eddie Mathews	.15
(64)	Christy Mathewson	.15
(65)	Willie Mays	.40
(66)	Bill Mazeroski	.15
(67)	Joe Morgan	.15
(68)	Thurman Munson	.25
(69)	Stan Musial	.30
(70)	Tony Oliva	.15
(71)	Mel Ott	.15
(72)	Jim Palmer	.15
(73)	Gaylord Perry	.15
(74)	Boog Powell	.15
(75)	Pee Wee Reese	.15
(76)	Robin Roberts	.15
(77)	Brooks Robinson	.15
(78)	Jackie Robinson	.50
(79)	Babe Ruth	.75
(80)	Tom Seaver	.15
(81)	Bobby Shantz	.15
(82)	Al Simmons	.15
(83)	George Sisler	.15
(84)	Enos Slaughter	.15
(85)	Duke Snider	.15
(86)	Tris Speaker	.15
(87)	Willie Stargell	.15
(88)	Bill Terry	.15
(89)	Bobby Thomson	.15
(90)	Pie Traynor	.15
(91)	Honus Wagner	.25
(92)	Ed Walsh	.15
(93)	Paul Waner	.15
(94)	Hoyt Wilhelm	.15
(95)	Billy Williams	.15
(96)	Ted Williams	.50
(97)	Maury Wills	.15
(98)	Early Wynn	.15
(99)	Carl Yastrzemski	.15
(100)	Robin Yount	.15

1990 Baseball Wit

This 108-card set was released in two printings. The first printing featured unnumbered cards and several errors. The second printing featured corrections and numbered cards. The set was available at several retail chains and feature trivia questions on the card backs. The set was dedicated to Little League baseball.

		MT
Complete Set (108):		15.00
Common Player:		.10
1	Orel Hershiser	.15
2	Tony Gwynn	1.00
3	Mickey Mantle	2.50
4	Willie Stargell	.20
5	Don Baylor	.15
6	Hank Aaron	.75
7	Don Larsen	.15
8	Lee Mazzilli	.10
9	Boog Powell	.15
10	Little League World Series	.10
11	Jose Canseco	.40
12	Mike Scott	.10
13	Bob Feller	.20
14	Ron Santo	.15
15	Mel Stottlemyre	.10
16	Shea Stadium	.10
17	Brooks Robinson	.25
18	Willie Mays	.75
19	Ernie Banks	.30
20	Keith Hernandez	.10
21	Bret Saberhagen	.15
22	Hall of Fame	.10
23	Luis Aparicio	.15
24	Yogi Berra	.30
25	Manny Mota	.10
26	Steve Garvey	.10
27	Bill Shea	.10
28	Fred Lynn	.10
29	Todd Worrell	.10
30	Roy Campanella	.30
31	Bob Gibson	.20
32	Gary Carter	.15
33	Jim Palmer	.20
34	Carl Yastrzemski	.25
35	Dwight Gooden	.15
36	Stan Musial	.50
37	Rickey Henderson	.20
38	Dale Murphy	.15
39	Mike Schmidt	.50
40	Gaylord Perry	.20
41	Ozzie Smith	.40
42	Reggie Jackson	.50
43	Steve Carlton	.20
44	Jim Perry	.10
45	Vince Coleman	.10
46	Tom Seaver	.25
47	Marty Marion	.10
48	Frank Robinson	.25
49	Joe DiMaggio	1.00
50	Ted Williams	.85
51	Rollie Fingers	.10
52	Jackie Robinson	1.00
53	Victor Raschi	.10
54	Johnny Bench	.25
55	Nolan Ryan	1.50
56	Ty Cobb	.85
57	Harry Steinfeldt	.10
58	James O'Rourke	.10
59	John McGraw	.10
60	Candy Cummings	.10
61	Jimmie Foxx	.15
62	Walter Johnson	.20
63	1903 World Series	.10
64	Satchel Paige	.35
65	Bobby Wallace	.10
66	Cap Anson	.10
67	Hugh Duffy	.10
68	Buck Ewing	.10
69	Bobo Holloman	.10
70	Ed Delehanty (Delahanty)	.10
71	Dizzy Dean	.15
72	Tris Speaker	.15
73	Lou Gehrig	1.00
74	Wee Willie Keeler	.10
75	Cal Hubbard	.10
76	Eddie Collins	.10
77	Chris Von Der Ahe	.10
78	Sam Crawford	.10
79	Cy Young	.15
80	Johnny Vander Meer	.10
81	Joey Jay	.10
82	Zack Wheat	.10
83	Jim Bottomley	.10
84	Honus Wagner	.30
85	Casey Stengel	.20
86	Babe Ruth	2.00
87	John Lindemuth	.10
88	Max Carey	.10
89	Mordecai Brown	.10
90	1869 Red Stockings	.10
91	Rube Marquard	.10
92	Horse Radbourne	.10
93	Hack Wilson	.10
94	Lefty Grove	.10
95	Carl Hubbell	.10
96	A.J. Cartwright	.10
97	Rogers Hornsby	.15
98	Ernest Thayer	.10
99	Connie Mack	.10
100	1939 Centennial Celebration	.10
101	Branch Rickey	.10
102	Dan Brouthers	.10
103	First Baseball Uniform	.10
104	Christy Mathewson	.25
105	Joe Nuxhall	.15
106	1939 Centennial Celebration	.10
107	President Taft	.10
108	Abner Doubleday	.10

1984 Baltimore Orioles Postcards

WAYNE GROSS

Only the slightly wider borders around the color portrait photos distinguish this issue from the previous year's effort. The player name is printed beneath the photo on front of the 3-1/2" x 5-1/4" cards. Backs have a stamp box and address lines. The unnumbered cards are checklisted here in alphabetical order.

		MT
Complete Set (35):		45.00
Common Player:		2.00
(1)	Joe Altobelli	2.00
(2)	Benny Ayala	2.00
(3)	Mike Boddicker	2.00
(4)	Al Bumbry	2.00
(5)	Todd Cruz	2.00
(6)	Rich Dauer	2.00
(7)	Storm Davis	2.00
(8)	Rick Dempsey	2.00
(9)	Jim Dwyer	2.00
(10)	Mike Flanagan	2.00
(11)	Dan Ford	2.00
(12)	Wayne Gross	2.00
(13)	Ellie Hendricks	2.00
(14)	John Lowenstein	2.00
(15)	Dennis Martinez	3.00
(16)	Tippy Martinez	2.00
(17)	Scott McGregor	2.00
(18)	Ray Miller	2.00
(19)	Eddie Murray	5.00
(20)	Joe Nolan	2.00
(21)	Jim Palmer	5.00
(22)	Floyd Rayford	2.00
(23)	Cal Ripken Jr.	8.00
(24)	Cal Ripken Sr.	2.50
(25)	Gary Roenicke	2.00
(26)	Ralph Rowe	2.00
(27)	Lenn Sakata	2.00
(28)	John Shelby	2.00
(29)	Ken Singleton	2.00
(30)	Sammy Stewart	2.00
(31)	Bill Swaggerty	2.00
(32)	Tom Underwood	2.00
(33)	Jimy Williams	2.00
(34)	Mike Young	2.00
(35)	The Bird (mascot)	2.00

1986 Baltimore Orioles team issue

Tips for physical and mental health attributed to Orioles players are featured on the backs of these 3-1/2" x 5-1/4" cards. Fronts have color studio portraits with player name in the white border below. A number of the players' cards can be found with two or more health messages on back. The unnumbered cards are checklisted here alphabetically. One of Mike Flanagan's cards can be found with a headline on back which reads "Orioles Safety Message" instead of "Orioles Health Message."

CAL RIPKEN, JR.

		MT
Complete Set (33):		40.00
Common Player:		.50
(1)	Don Aase (message begins "When the team...")	.50
(2a)	Mike Boddicker (message begins "I always...")	.50
(2b)	Mike Boddicker (message begins "They call...")	.50
(3)	Storm Davis (message begins "To make it...")	.50
(4a)	Rick Dempsey (message begins "I always...")	.50
(4b)	Rick Dempsey (message begins "In baseball...")	.50
(5)	Ken Dixon (message begins "Good winners...")	.50
(6)	Jim Dwyer (message begins "Bumps and...")	.50
(7a)	Mike Flanagan (message begins "I know...")	.50
(7b)	Mike Flanagan ("Health" message begins "It's a special...")	.50
(7c)	Mike Flanagan ("Safety" message begins "It's a special...")	.50
(8)	Lee Lacy (message begins "I only steal...")	.50
(9a)	Fred Lynn (message begins "I need...")	.60
(9b)	Fred Lynn (message begins "There are...")	.60
(10)	Dennis Martinez (message begins "I know...")	.75
(11)	Tippy Martinez (message begins "Never answer...")	.50
(12)	Scott McGregor (message begins "When my...")	.50
(13a)	Eddie Murray (message begins "Do you...")	3.00
(13b)	Eddie Murray (message begins "During my...")	3.00
(13c)	Eddie Murray (message begins "You can't...")	3.00
(14a)	Floyd Rayford (message begins "I always...")	.50
(14b)	Floyd Rayford (message begins "I had...")	.50
(15)	Cal Ripken, Jr. (message begins "A good...")	8.00
(15b)	Cal Ripken, Jr. (message begins "Drinking ...")	8.00
(15c)	Cal Ripken, Jr. (message begins "To hit...")	8.00
(16a)	Larry Sheets (message begins "As a...")	.50
(16b)	Larry Sheets (message begins "There is...")	.50
(17)	John Shelby (message begins "You can't...")	.50
(18)	Nate Snell (message begins "Bumps and...")	.50
(19)	Earl Weaver (message begins "My team...")	.75
(20)	Alan Wiggins (message begins "An athlete's...")	.50
(21a)	Mike Young (message begins "A good...")	.50
(21b)	Mike Young (message begins "I like...")	.50

1987 Baltimore Orioles Postcards

TERRY KENNEDY

This was the O's fifth consecutive annual issue of post-card-back team issues. The basic 3-1/2" x 5-1/4" format was carried over as was the design of player portrait photos surrounded by a white border with the name at bottom. Backs have a stamp box and lines printed for the mailing address. The unnumbered cards are checklisted here in alphabetical order. Some of the player pictures are repeats from earlier issues or may have slight cropping differences.

		MT
Complete Set (38):		32.00
Common Player:		1.00
(1)	Don Aase	1.00
(2)	Tony Arnold	1.00
(3)	Jeff Ballard	1.00
(4)	Eric Bell	1.00
(5)	Mike Boddicker	1.00
(6)	Rick Burleson	1.00
(7)	Terry Crowley	1.00
(8)	Luis DeLeon	1.00
(9)	Ken Dixon	1.00
(10)	Jim Dwyer	1.00
(11)	Mike Flanagan	1.00
(12)	Ken Gerhart	1.00
(13)	Rene Gonzalez	1.00
(14)	John Habyan	1.00
(15)	Elrod Hendricks	1.00
(16)	Terry Kennedy	1.00
(17)	Ray Knight	1.00
(18)	Lee Lacy	1.00
(19)	Fred Lynn	1.00
(20)	Scott McGregor	1.00
(21)	Eddie Murray	3.00
(22)	Tom Niedenfuer	1.00
(23)	Jack O'Connor	1.00
(24)	Floyd Rayford	1.00
(25)	Cal Ripken Jr.	6.00
(26)	Cal Ripken Sr.	1.50
(27)	Frank Robinson	3.00
(28)	Dave Schmidt	1.00
(29)	Larry Sheets	1.00
(30)	John Shelby	1.00
(31)	Dave Van Gorder	1.00
(32)	Mark Wiley	1.00
(33)	Alan Wiggins	1.00
(34)	Jimy Williams	1.00
(35)	Mark Williamson	1.00
(36)	Mike Young	1.00
(37)	Memorial Stadium	1.50
(38)	The Bird (mascot)	1.00

Player names in *Italic* type indicate a rookie card.

1988 Baltimore Orioles Postcards

JOE ORSULAK

There is really nothing to distinguish this issue from previous years' although some of the repeated player photos exhibit slight cropping differences. Once again the 3-1/2" x 5-1/4" cards have color player portraits surrounded by white borders with the player name at bottom. Backs have a stamp box and address lines. The cards are not numbered and are checklisted here in alphabetical order.

		MT
Complete Set (41):		35.00
Common Player:		1.00
(1)	Don Aase	1.00
(2)	Jeff Ballard	1.00
(3)	Jose Bautista	1.00
(4)	Eric Bell	1.00
(5)	Mike Boddicker	1.00
(6)	Don Buford	1.00
(7)	Terry Crowley	1.00
(8)	Jim Dwyer	1.00
(9)	Ken Gerhart	1.00
(10)	Rene Gonzalez	1.00
(11)	John Habyan	1.00
(12)	John Hart	1.00
(13)	Elrod Hendricks	1.00
(14)	Keith Hughes	1.00
(15)	Terry Kennedy	1.00
(16)	Fred Lynn	1.00
(17)	Scott McGregor	1.00
(18)	Minnie Mendoza	1.00
(19)	Mike Morgan	1.00
(20)	Eddie Murray	3.00
(21)	Tom Niedenfuer	1.00
(22)	Joe Orsulak	1.00
(23)	Ozzie Peraza	1.00
(24)	Bill Ripken	1.00
(25)	Cal Ripken Jr.	6.00
(26)	Cal Ripken Sr.	1.50
(27)	Frank Robinson	3.00
(28)	Wade Rowdon	1.00
(29)	Dave Schmidt	1.00
(30)	Rick Schu	1.00
(31)	Larry Sheets	1.00
(32)	Doug Sisk	1.00
(33)	Pete Stanicek	1.00
(34)	Herm Starrette	1.00
(35)	Mickey Tettleton	1.00
(36)	Mark Thurmond	1.00
(37)	Jay Tibbs	1.00
(38)	Jim Traber	1.00
(39)	Mark Williamson	1.00
(40)	Municipal Stadium	1.50
(41)	The Bird (mascot)	1.00

1989-91 Baltimore Orioles Postcards

SAM HORN

While the eagle-eyed collector may spot a few subtle variations in cropping, etc., the team-issued postcards from 1989-91 share a basic format. The 3-1/2" x 5-1/4" cards have player portrait photos on a light blue background. Players are shown in white jerseys with orange script "Orioles" on chest and black caps with the newly adopted bird logo. Backs are in black-and-white with the team address at upper-left, a stamp box and address lines at right and a vertical dividing line at center. The unnumbered cards are checklisted here alphabetically.

		MT
Complete Set (54)		24.00
Common Player:		.50
(1)	Brady Anderson	.75
(2)	Jeff Ballard	.50
(3)	Jose Bautista	.50
(4)	Juan Bell	.50
(5)	Phil Bradley	.50
(6)	Glenn Davis	.50
(7)	Mike Devereaux	.50
(8)	Joe Durham	.50
(9)	Dwight Evans	.65
(10)	Steve Finley	.50
(11)	Mike Flanagan	.50
(12)	Todd Frohwirth	.50
(13)	Leo Gomez	.50
(14)	Rene Gonzalez	.50
(15)	John Habyan	.50
(16)	Pete Harnisch	.50
(17)	Elrod Hendricks	.50
(18)	Kevin Hickey	.50
(19)	Chris Hoiles	.50
(20)	Brian Holton	.50
(21)	Sam Horn	.50
(22)	Tim Hulett	.50
(23)	Al Jackson	.50
(24)	Dave Johnson	.50
(25)	Paul Kilgus	.50
(26)	Brad Komminsk	.50
(27)	Tom McCraw	.50
(28)	Ben McDonald	.60
(29)	Jeff McKnight	.50
(30)	Bob Melvin	.50
(31)	Jose Mesa	.60
(32)	Bob Milacki	.50
(33)	Randy Milligan	.50
(34)	Curt Motton	.50
(35)	John Oates	.50
(36)	Gregg Olson	.50
(37)	Joe Orsulak	.50
(38)	Joe Price	.50
(39)	Bill Ripken	.50
(40)	Cal Ripken Jr.	3.00
(41)	Cal Ripken Sr.	.50
(42)	Frank Robinson	1.00
(43)	Jeff Robinson	.50
(44)	Dave Schmidt	.50
(45)	Dave Segui	.50
(46)	Larry Sheets	.50
(47)	Roy Smith	.50
(48)	Pete Stanicek	.50
(49)	Mickey Tettleton	.50
(50)	Mark Thurmond	.50
(51)	Jay Tibbs	.50
(52)	Jim Traber	.50
(53)	Mark Williamson	.50
(54)	Craig Worthington	.50

1994 Baltimore Orioles Program Cards

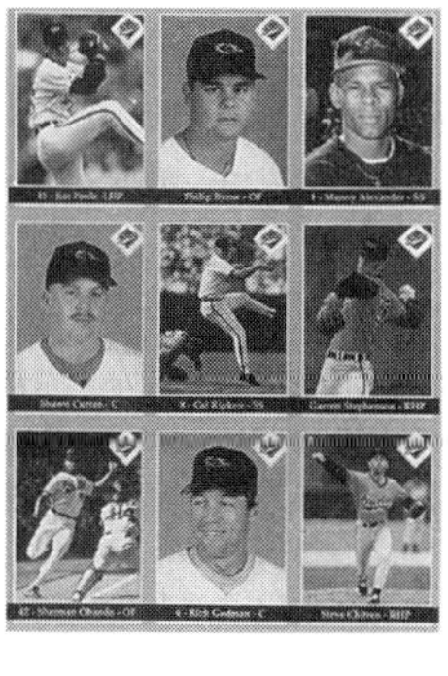

Virtually the entire O's organization, major and minor leaguers, was included in this season-long promotion. One of 12 nine-card sheets was inserted into the team's programs, which sold for $3. A reported 17,000 sets were produced. The sheets are unperforated and measure 7-1/2" x 10-1/2". Fronts have color game-action or posed photos within an orange border. A team logo is at top-right. At bottom is a black strip with the player's number (if a major leaguer), name and position in white. Backs are printed in black and orange on white with biographical details and complete major and minor league stats. The unnumbered cards are checklisted here alphabetically.

		MT
Complete Set, Sheets (12):		25.00
Complete Set, Singles (108):		20.00
Common Player:		.25
(1)	Manny Alexander	.35
(2)	Brady Anderson	.75
(3)	Matt Anderson	.25
(4)	Harold Baines	.35
(5)	Myles Barnden	.25
(6)	Kimera Bartee	.30
(7)	Juan Bautista	.25
(8)	Armando Benitez	.30
(9)	Joe Borowski	.25
(10)	Brian Brewer	.25
(11)	Brandon Bridgers	.25
(12)	Cory Brown	.25
(13)	Damon Buford	.25
(14)	Philip Byrne	.25
(15)	Rocco Cafaro	.25
(16)	Paul Carey	.30
(17)	Carlos Chavez	.25
(18)	Eric Chavez	.25
(19)	Steve Chitren	.25
(20)	Mike Cook	.25
(21)	Shawn Curran	.25
(22)	Kevin Curtis	.25
(23)	Joey Dawley	.25
(24)	Jim Dedrick	.25
(25)	Cesar Devarez	.25
(26)	Mike Devereaux	.25
(27)	Brian DuBois	.25
(28)	Keith Eaddy	.25
(29)	Mark Eichhorn	.25
(30)	Scott Emerson	.25
(31)	Vaughn Eshelman	.35
(32)	Craig Faulkner	.25
(33)	Sid Fernandez	.25
(34)	Rick Forney	.25
(35)	Jim Foster	.25
(36)	Jesse Garcia	.25
(37)	Mike Garguilo	.25
(38)	Rich Gedman	.25
(39)	Leo Gomez	.35
(40)	Rene Gonzalez	.25
(41)	Curtis Goodwin	.35
(42)	Kris Gresham	.25
(43)	Shane Hale	.25
(44)	Jeffrey Hammonds	.90
(45)	Jimmy Haynes	.25
(46)	Chris Hoiles	.35
(47)	Tim Hullett	.25
(48)	Matt Jarvis	.25
(49)	Scott Klingenbeck	.25
(50)	Rick Krivda	.25
(51)	David Lamb	.25
(52)	Chris Lemp	.25
(53)	T.R. Lewis	.35
(54)	Brian Link	.25
(55)	John Lombardi	.25
(56)	Rob Lukachyk	.25
(57)	Calvin Maduro	.25
(58)	Barry Manuel	.25
(59)	Lincoln Martin	.25
(60)	Scott McClain	.25
(61)	Ben McDonald	.25
(62)	Kevin McGehee	.25
(63)	Mark McLemore	.25
(64)	Miguel Mejia	.25
(65)	Feliciano Mercedes	.25
(66)	Jose Millares	.25
(67)	Brent Miller	.25
(68)	Alan Mills	.25
(69)	Jamie Moyer	.25
(70)	Mike Mussina	1.50
(71)	Sherman Obando	.40
(72)	Alex Ochoa	.50
(73)	John O'Donoghue	.25
(74)	Mike Oquist	.25
(75)	Bo Ortiz	.25
(76)	Billy Owens	.25
(77)	Rafael Palmeiro	2.50
(78)	Dave Paveloff	.25
(79)	Brad Pennington	.45
(80)	Bill Percibel	.25
(81)	Jim Poole	.25
(82)	Jay Powell	.25
(83)	Arthur Rhodes	.30
(84)	Matt Riemer	.25
(85)	Cal Ripken Jr.	5.00
(86)	Kevin Ryan	.25
(87)	Chris Sabo	.25
(88)	Brian Sackinsky	.25
(89)	Francisco Saneaux	.25
(90)	Jason Satre	.25
(91)	David Segui	.50
(92)	Jose Serra	.25
(93)	Larry Shenk	.25
(94)	Lee Smith	.50
(95)	Lonnie Smith	.25
(96)	Mark Smith	.45
(97)	Garrett Stephenson	.25
(98)	Jeff Tackett	.25
(99)	Brad Tyler	.25
(100)	Pedro Ulises	.25
(101)	Jack Voight	.25
(102)	Jim Walker	.25
(103)	B.J. Waszgis	.25
(104)	Jim Wawruck	.25
(105)	Mel Wearing	.25
(106)	Mark Williamson	.25
(107)	Brian Wood	.25
(108)	Greg Zaun	.45

1999 Baltimore Orioles Photo Cards

Placement of the union printers' label can differentiate the 1999 team-issued photocards from those of nearly identical design of the previous year. Cards are 3-1/2" x 5" with borderless color photos (mostly game-action on front). Backs have orange stripes at top and bottom with a "Player Profile," facsimile autograph and team logo between. The union logo on the 1999 cards is just above the bottom orange stripe; on the '98 cards it was in the bottom stripe. It is possible this checklist may be incomplete due to late-season issues.

		MT
Complete Set (29):		20.00
Common Player:		1.00
(1)	Rich Amaral	1.00
(2)	Harold Baines	1.50
(3)	Albert Belle	2.50
(4)	Ricky Bones	1.00
(5)	Mike Bordick	1.00
(6)	Will Clark	2.00
(7)	Jeff Conine	1.00
(8)	Rocky Coppinger	1.00
(9)	Terry Crowley	1.00
(10)	Delino DeShields	1.00
(11)	Scott Erickson	1.50
(12)	Mike Fetters	1.00
(13)	Mike Figga	1.00
(14)	Marv Foley	1.00
(15)	Juan Guzman	1.00
(16)	Doug Johns	1.00
(17)	Charles Johnson	1.50
(18)	Jason Johnson	1.00
(19)	Bruce Kison	1.00
(20)	Ray Miller	1.00
(21)	Eddie Murray	2.50
(22)	Sam Perlozzo	1.00
(23)	Sidney Ponson	1.00
(24)	Cal Ripken Jr.	5.00
(25)	B.J. Surhoff	1.50
(26)	Mike Timlin	1.00
(27)	Lenny Webster	1.00
(28)	Frank Wren (gm)	1.00
(29)	Camden Yards	1.50

1999 Baltimore Orioles Winter Carnival Postcards

In conjunction with the team winter fanfest a set of nine color portrait postcards was issued. The 3-1/2" x 5" cards are borderless and have no graphics on front. Player identification is on the post-card-style backs. The cards are unnumbered and checklisted here alphabetically.

		MT
Complete Set (9):		24.00
Common Player:		3.00
(1)	Chip Alley	3.00
(2)	Albert Belle	5.00
(3)	Will Clark	5.00
(4)	Terry Crowley	3.00
(5)	Delino DeShields	3.00
(6)	Charles Johnson	3.00
(7)	Ryan Minor	5.00
(8)	Calvin Pickering	5.00
(9)	Alvie Shepherd	3.00

1999 Bank One Arizona Diamondbacks

This series of four "magic motion" cards was produced for distribution at four different home D'backs home games. Ten thousand of each card were distributed. Cards measure 4" x 3" and have borderless action shots on front with team and sponsor logos. Backs are in black-and-white with a blue Bank One logo and have player data and stats.

		MT
Complete Set (4):		8.00
Common Player:		2.00
(1)	Randy Johnson	3.00
(2)	Travis Lee	2.00
(3)	Matt Williams	2.50
(4)	Bank One Ballpark	2.00

1988 Bazooka

This 22-card set from Topps marks the first Bazooka issue since 1971. Full-color player photos are bordered in white, with the player name printed on a red, white and blue bubble gum box in the lower right corner. Flip sides are also red, white and blue, printed vertically. A large, but faint, Bazooka logo backs the Topps baseball logo team name, card number, player's name and position, followed by batting records, personal information and brief career highlights. Cards were sold inside specially marked 59¢ and 79¢ Bazooka gum and candy boxes, one card per box.

		MT
Complete Set (22):		6.00
Common Player:		.20
1	George Bell	.20
2	Wade Boggs	.60
3	Jose Canseco	.60
4	Roger Clemens	.60
5	Vince Coleman	.20
6	Eric Davis	.25
7	Tony Fernandez	.20
8	Dwight Gooden	.25
9	Tony Gwynn	.60
10	Wally Joyner	.25
11	Don Mattingly	.75
12	Willie McGee	.20
13	Mark McGwire	2.00
14	Kirby Puckett	.75
15	Tim Raines	.20
16	Dave Righetti	.20
17	Cal Ripken, Jr.	2.00
18	Juan Samuel	.20
19	Ryne Sandberg	.50
20	Benny Santiago	.20
21	Darryl Strawberry	.25
22	Todd Worrell	.20

1989 Bazooka

Topps produced this 22-card set in 1989 to be included (one card per box) in specially-marked boxes of its Bazooka brand bubble gum. The player photos have the words "Shining Star" along the top, while the player's name appears along the bottom of the card, along with the Topps Bazooka logo in the lower right corner. The cards are numbered alphabetically.

		MT
Complete Set (22):		5.00
Common Player:		.15
1	Tim Belcher	.15
2	Damon Berryhill	.15
3	Wade Boggs	.60
4	Jay Buhner	.20
5	Jose Canseco	.60
6	Vince Coleman	.15
7	Cecil Espy	.15
8	Dave Gallagher	.15
9	Ron Gant	.20
10	Kirk Gibson	.15
11	Paul Gibson	.15
12	Mark Grace	.50
13	Tony Gwynn	.75
14	Rickey Henderson	.35
15	Orel Hershiser	.20
16	Gregg Jefferies	.20
17	Ricky Jordan	.15
18	Chris Sabo	.15
19	Gary Sheffield	.30
20	Darryl Strawberry	.20
21	Frank Viola	.15
22	Walt Weiss	.15

1990 Bazooka

For the second consecutive year, Bazooka entitled its set "Shining Stars." Full color action and posed player shots are featured on the card fronts. The flip sides feature player statistics in a style much like the cards from the previous two Bazooka issues. Unlike the past two releases, the cards are not numbered alphabetically. The cards measure 2-1/2" x 3-1/2" in size and 22 cards complete the set.

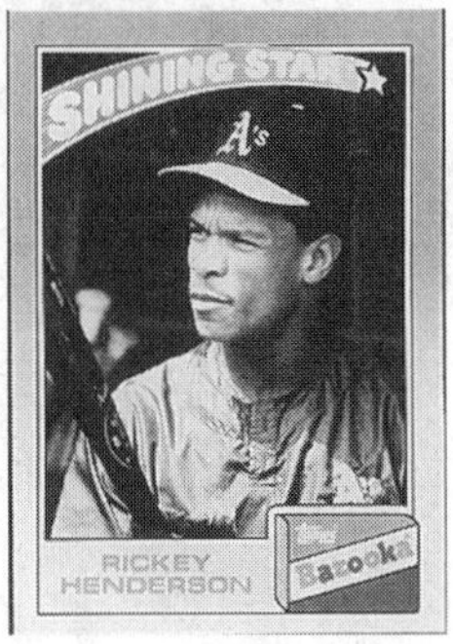

		MT
Complete Set (22):		5.00
Common Player:		.15
1	Kevin Mitchell	.15
2	Robin Yount	.35
3	Mark Davis	.15
4	Bret Saberhagen	.20
5	Fred McGriff	.25
6	Tony Gwynn	.50
7	Kirby Puckett	.50
8	Vince Coleman	.15
9	Rickey Henderson	.30
10	Ben McDonald	.15
11	Gregg Olson	.15
12	Todd Zeile	.15
13	Carlos Martinez	.15
14	Gregg Jefferies	.20
15	Craig Worthington	.15
16	Gary Sheffield	.25
17	Greg Briley	.15
18	Ken Griffey, Jr.	2.50
19	Jerome Walton	.15
20	Bob Geren	.15
21	Tom Gordon	.15
22	Jim Abbott	.20

1991 Bazooka

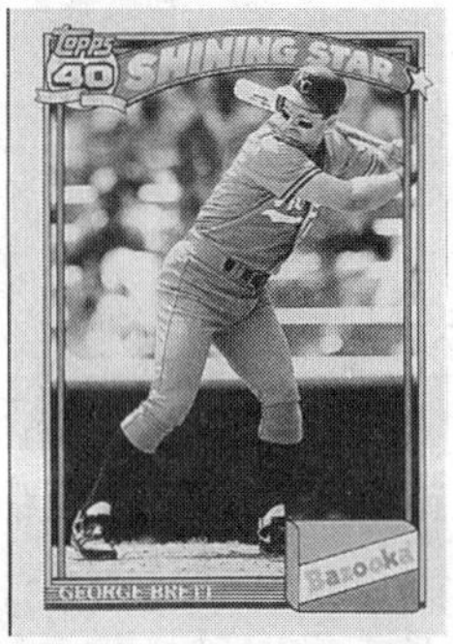

For the third consecutive year Bazooka entitled its set "Shining Stars." The cards are styled like the 1990 issue, but include the Topps "40th Anniversary" logo. The 1991 issue is considered much scarcer than the previous releases. The cards measure 2-1/2" x 3-1/2" in size and 22 cards complete the set.

		MT
Complete Set (22):		10.00
Common Player:		.30
1	Barry Bonds	1.50
2	Rickey Henderson	.35
3	Bob Welch	.30
4	Doug Drabek	.30
5	Alex Fernandez	.30
6	Jose Offerman	.30
7	Frank Thomas	1.50
8	Cecil Fielder	.30
9	Ryne Sandberg	.75
10	George Brett	.90
11	Willie McGee	.30
12	Vince Coleman	.30
13	Hal Morris	.30
14	Delino DeShields	.30
15	Robin Ventura	.35
16	Jeff Huson	.30
17	Felix Jose	.30
18	Dave Justice	.35
19	Larry Walker	.50
20	Sandy Alomar, Jr.	.35
21	Kevin Appier	.30
22	Scott Radinsky	.30

1992 Bazooka

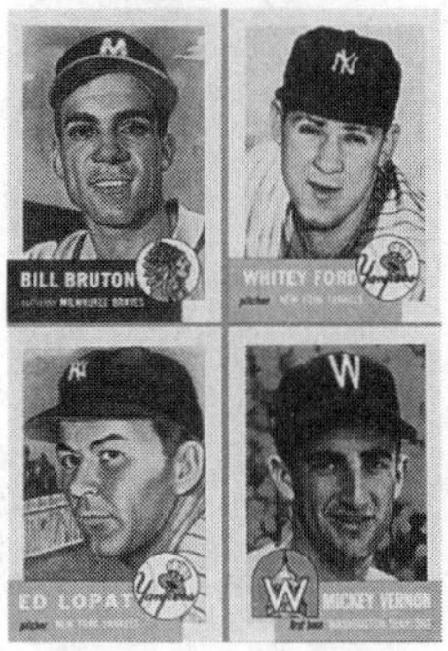

This set of 22 cards features miniature versions of the 1953 Topps Archives issue. The mini-cards are set against a blue background on front and back. Besides reproductions of issued 1953 Topps cards, these "Quadracards" include miniature versions of many of the special cards created for the Archives set. Cards feature the Bazooka logo on back, and were distributed in boxes of that bubble gum. They are readily available in complete set form.

		MT
Complete Set (22):		10.00
Common Player:		.50
1	Joe Adcock, Bob Lemon, Willie Mays, Vic Wertz	2.00
2	Carl Furillo, Don Newcombe, Phil Rizzuto, Hank Sauer	.50
3	Ferris Fain, John Logan, Ed Mathews, Bobby Shantz	.50
4	Yogi Berra, Del Crandall, Howie Pollett, Gene Woodling	.50
5	Richie Ashburn, Leo Durocher, Allie Reynolds, Early Wynn	.50
6	Hank Aaron, Ray Boone, Luke Easter, Dick Williams	2.00
7	Ralph Branca, Bob Feller, Rogers Hornsby, Bobby Thomson	.50
8	Jim Gilliam, Billy Martin, Orestes Minoso, Hal Newhouser	.50
9	Smoky Burgess, John Mize, Preacher Roe, Warren Spahn	.50
10	Monte Irvin, Bobo Newsom, Duke Snider, Wes Westrum	.50
11	Carl Erskine, Jackie Jensen, George Kell, Al Schoendienst	.50
12	Bill Bruton, Whitey Ford, Ed Lopat, Mickey Vernon	.50
13	Joe Black, Lew Burdette, Johnny Pesky, Enos Slaughter	.50
14	Gus Bell, Mike Garcia, Mel Parnell, Jackie Robinson	1.50
15	Alvin Dark, Dick Groat, Pee Wee Reese, John Sain	.50
16	Gil Hodges, Sal Maglie, Wilmer Mizell, Billy Pierce	.50
17	Nellie Fox, Ralph Kiner, Ted Kluszewski, Eddie Stanky	.50
18	Ewell Blackwell, Vern Law, Satchell Paige, Jim Wilson	.75
19	Lou Boudreau, Roy Face, Harvey Haddix, Bill Rigney	.50
20	Roy Campanella, Walt Dropo, Harvey Kuenn, Al Rosen	.50
21	Joe Garagiola, Robin Roberts, Casey Stengel, Hoyt Wilhelm	.50
22	John Antonelli, Bob Friend, Dixie Walker, Ted Williams	1.50

1993 Bazooka Team USA

The members of Team USA are featured on this boxed set. The 2-1/2" x 3-1/2" cards feature the same basic design as 1993 Topps baseball, except for a Bazooka gum logo in one of the upper corners. Both front and back feature posed player photos. Backs have a design simulating the U.S. flag and include amateur stats, biographical details and career highlights. The cards are virtually identical to the same players' cards in the 1993 Topps Traded set, with the addition of the Bazooka logo on front and the differences in card numbers.

		MT
Complete Set (22):		12.00
Common Player:		.25
1	Terry Harvey	.25
2	Dante Powell	.90
3	Andy Barkett	.25
4	Steve Reich	.25
5	Charlie Nelson	.25
6	Todd Walker	1.50
7	Dustin Hermanson	1.00
8	Pat Clougherty	.25
9	Danny Graves	.25
10	Paul Wilson	.75
11	Todd Helton	2.00
12	Russ Johnson	.75
13	Darren Grass	.25
14	A.J. Hinch	.35
15	Mark Merila	.25
16	John Powell	.25
17	Bob Scafa	.25
18	Matt Beaumont	.40
19	Todd Dunn	.35
20	Mike Martin	.25
21	Carlton Loewer	.25
22	Bret Wagner	.25

1995 Bazooka

Topps returned to the beginner's level baseball card niche in 1995 by resurrecting its Bazooka brand name. The set was unabashedly aimed at the younger collector, offering five cards and a Bazooka Joe cartoon-wrapped chunk of bubble gum for 50 cents. Cards feature on their backs a "roulette" wheel design based on the player's 1994 stats, to be used to play a game of spinner baseball. A game instruction card and cardboard spinner was included in each pack. Limiting the set to 132 cards allowed for a concentration of established stars and hot rookies. A 22-card Red Hot insert set is found at the rate of one card per six packs, on average.

		MT
Complete Set (132):		10.00
Common Player:		.05
Wax Box:		15.00
1	Greg Maddux	.75
2	Cal Ripken Jr.	1.50
3	Lee Smith	.05
4	Sammy Sosa	1.00
5	Jason Bere	.05
6	Dave Justice	.10
7	Kevin Mitchell	.05
8	Ozzie Guillen	.05
9	Roger Clemens	.50
10	Mike Mussina	.30
11	Sandy Alomar	.10
12	Cecil Fielder	.10
13	Dennis Martinez	.05
14	Randy Myers	.05
15	Jay Buhner	.05
16	Ivan Rodriguez	.35
17	Mo Vaughn	.35
18	Ryan Klesko	.15
19	Chuck Finley	.05
20	Barry Bonds	.60
21	Dennis Eckersley	.05
22	Kenny Lofton	.30
23	Rafael Palmeiro	.15
24	Mike Stanley	.05
25	Gregg Jefferies	.05
26	Robin Ventura	.10
27	Mark McGwire	1.50
28	Ozzie Smith	.40
29	Troy Neel	.05
30	Tony Gwynn	.75
31	Ken Griffey Jr.	2.00
32	Will Clark	.25
33	Craig Biggio	.10
34	Shawon Dunston	.05
35	Wilson Alvarez	.05
36	Bobby Bonilla	.05
37	Marquis Grissom	.05
38	Ben McDonald	.05
39	Delino DeShields	.05
40	Barry Larkin	.15
41	John Olerud	.10
42	Jose Canseco	.35
43	Greg Vaughn	.10
44	Gary Sheffield	.20
45	Paul O'Neill	.10
46	Bob Hamelin	.05
47	Don Mattingly	.60
48	John Franco	.05
49	Bret Boone	.05
50	Rick Aguilera	.05
51	Tim Wallach	.05
52	Roberto Kelly	.05
53	Danny Tartabull	.05
54	Randy Johnson	.25
55	Greg McMichael	.05
56	Bip Roberts	.05
57	David Cone	.10
58	Raul Mondesi	.25
59	Travis Fryman	.05
60	Jeff Conine	.05
61	Jeff Bagwell	.50
62	Rickey Henderson	.20
63	Fred McGriff	.25
64	Matt Williams	.25
65	Rick Wilkins	.05
66	Eric Karros	.05
67	Mel Rojas	.05
68	Juan Gonzalez	.75
69	Chuck Carr	.05
70	Moises Alou	.10
71	Mark Grace	.20
72	Alex Fernandez	.05
73	Rod Beck	.05
74	Ray Lankford	.05
75	Dean Palmer	.05
76	Joe Carter	.08
77	Mike Piazza	.75
78	Eddie Murray	.40
79	Dave Nilsson	.05
80	Brett Butler	.05
81	Roberto Alomar	.35
82	Jeff Kent	.05
83	Andres Galarraga	.15
84	Brady Anderson	.05
85	Jimmy Key	.05
86	Bret Saberhagen	.08
87	Chili Davis	.05
88	Jose Rijo	.05
89	Wade Boggs	.35
90	Len Dykstra	.05
91	Steve Howe	.05
92	Hal Morris	.05
93	Larry Walker	.35
94	Jeff Montgomery	.05
95	Wil Cordero	.05
96	Jay Bell	.05
97	Tom Glavine	.15
98	Chris Hoiles	.05
99	Steve Avery	.05
100	Ruben Sierra	.05
101	Mickey Tettleton	.05
102	Paul Molitor	.40
103	Carlos Baerga	.05
104	Walt Weiss	.05
105	Darren Daulton	.05
106	Jack McDowell	.05
107	Doug Drabek	.05
108	Mark Langston	.05
109	Manny Ramirez	.40
110	Kevin Appier	.05
111	Andy Benes	.05
112	Chuck Knoblauch	.10
113	Kirby Puckett	.60
114	Dante Bichette	.15
115	Deion Sanders	.20
116	Albert Belle	.40
117	Todd Zeile	.05
118	Devon White	.05
119	Tim Salmon	.15
120	Frank Thomas	.75
121	John Wetteland	.05
122	James Mouton	.05
123	Javy Lopez	.10
124	Carlos Delgado	.25
125	Cliff Floyd	.05
126	Alex Gonzalez	.05
127	Billy Ashley	.05
128	Rondell White	.05
129	Rico Brogna	.05
130	Melvin Nieves	.05
131	Jose Oliva	.05
132	J.R. Phillips	.05

1995 Bazooka Red Hot Inserts

Twenty-two of the game's biggest stars were chosen for inclusion in 1995 Bazooka's only insert set - Red Hots. The chase cards are found at an average rate of one per six packs. Red Hots are identical to the players' cards in the regular set except that the background has been rendered in shades of red, and the player name printed in gold foil. Card numbers have an "RH" prefix.

		MT
Complete Set (22):		16.00
Common Player:		.25
1	Greg Maddux	2.00
2	Cal Ripken Jr.	3.00
3	Barry Bonds	1.50
4	Kenny Lofton	.60
5	Mike Stanley	.25
6	Tony Gwynn	1.50
7	Ken Griffey Jr.	4.00
8	Barry Larkin	.30
9	Jose Canseco	.75
10	Paul O'Neill	.25
11	Randy Johnson	.75
12	David Cone	.35
13	Jeff Bagwell	1.50
14	Matt Williams	.75
15	Mike Piazza	2.00
16	Roberto Alomar	1.00
17	Jimmy Key	.25
18	Wade Boggs	.75
19	Paul Molitor	.75
20	Carlos Baerga	.25
21	Albert Belle	1.00
22	Frank Thomas	1.00

1996 Bazooka

Using a simple, yet nostalgic design, Topps' 1996 Bazooka set offers collectors a source of fun with its cards geared for a flipping game. Each front has a full-color action photo of the player. The back contains one of five different Bazooka Joe characters, along with the Bazooka Ball game, the player's biographical data, and 1995 and career stats. Each card also contains a Funny Fortune, which predicts the fate of a player on a particular date. Cards were available five per pack for 50 cents. The complete set of all 132 cards is also offered in a factory set, packaged in an attractive gift box. All the top veterans, rookies and rising stars are included, as well as a Bazooka Ball info card containing all the rules to play the flipping game. As an exclusive bonus, one 1959 Bazooka Mickey Mantle reprint card can be found in every factory set. This card was originally found on boxes of Bazooka gum sold that year. Ten pieces of Mega Bazooka Gum are also included with the set.

		MT
Complete Set (132):		12.00
Common Player:		.05
Wax Box:		15.00
1	Ken Griffey Jr.	2.00
2	J.T. Snow	.05
3	Rondell White	.10
4	Reggie Sanders	.05
5	Jeff Montgomery	.05
6	Mike Stanley	.05
7	Bernie Williams	.25
8	Mike Piazza	1.00
9	Brian Hunter	.05
10	Len Dykstra	.05
11	Ray Lankford	.05
12	Kenny Lofton	.45
13	Robin Ventura	.10
14	Devon White	.05
15	Cal Ripken Jr.	1.50
16	Heathcliff Slocumb	.05
17	Ryan Klesko	.20
18	Terry Steinbach	.05
19	Travis Fryman	.05
20	Sammy Sosa	1.00
21	Jim Thome	.10
22	Kenny Rogers	.05
23	Don Mattingly	.75
24	Kirby Puckett	.75
25	Matt Williams	.25
26	Larry Walker	.25
27	Tim Wakefield	.05
28	Greg Vaughn	.10
29	Denny Neagle	.05
30	Ken Caminiti	.10
31	Garret Anderson	.10
32	Brady Anderson	.05
33	Carlos Baerga	.05
34	Wade Boggs	.35
35	Roberto Alomar	.50
36	Eric Karros	.05
37	Jay Buhner	.05
38	Dante Bichette	.15
39	Darren Daulton	.05
40	Jeff Bagwell	.75
41	Jay Bell	.05
42	Dennis Eckersley	.05
43	Will Clark	.25
44	Tom Glavine	.15
45	Rick Aguilera	.05
46	Kevin Seitzer	.05
47	Bret Boone	.05
48	Mark Grace	.35
49	Ray Durham	.05
50	Rico Brogna	.05
51	Kevin Appier	.05
52	Moises Alou	.10
53	Jeff Conine	.05
54	Marty Cordova	.05
55	Jose Mesa	.05
56	Rod Beck	.05
57	Marquis Grissom	.05
58	David Cone	.10
59	Albert Belle	.50
60	Lee Smith	.05
61	Frank Thomas	.75
62	Roger Clemens	.65
63	Bobby Bonilla	.05
64	Paul Molitor	.35
65	Chuck Knoblauch	.10
66	Steve Finley	.05
67	Craig Biggio	.10
68	Ramon Martinez	.05
69	Jason Isringhausen	.05
70	Mark Wohlers	.05
71	Vinny Castilla	.05
72	Ron Gant	.10
73	Juan Gonzalez	.75
74	Mark McGwire	1.50
75	Jeff King	.05
76	Pedro Martinez	.35
77	Chad Curtis	.05
78	John Olerud	.15
79	Greg Maddux	1.00
80	Derek Jeter	1.00
81	Mike Mussina	.30
82	Gregg Jefferies	.05
83	Jim Edmonds	.05
84	Carlos Perez	.05
85	Mo Vaughn	.35
86	Todd Hundley	.05
87	Roberto Hernandez	.05
88	Derek Bell	.05
89	Andres Galarraga	.10
90	Brian McRae	.05
91	Joe Carter	.10
92	Orlando Merced	.05
93	Cecil Fielder	.10
94	Dean Palmer	.05
95	Randy Johnson	.35
96	Chipper Jones	1.00
97	Barry Larkin	.20
98	Hideo Nomo	.35
99	Gary Gaetti	.05
100	Edgar Martinez	.05
101	John Wetteland	.05
102	Rafael Palmeiro	.15
103	Chuck Finley	.05
104	Ivan Rodriguez	.15
105	Shawn Green	.25
106	Manny Ramirez	.75
107	Lance Johnson	.05
108	Jose Canseco	.25
109	Fred McGriff	.30
110	David Segui	.05
111	Tim Salmon	.25
112	Hal Morris	.05
113	Tino Martinez	.15
114	Bret Saberhagen	.08
115	Brian Jordan	.05
116	David Justice	.25
117	Jack McDowell	.05
118	Barry Bonds	.65
119	Mark Langston	.05
120	John Valentin	.05
121	Raul Mondesi	.20
122	Quilvio Veras	.05
123	Randy Myers	.05
124	Tony Gwynn	.75
125	Johnny Damon	.15
126	Doug Drabek	.05
127	Bill Pulsipher	.05
128	Paul O'Neill	.10
129	Rickey Henderson	.25
130	Deion Sanders	.15
131	Orel Hershiser	.05
132	Gary Sheffield	.15

1996 Bazooka Mickey Mantle 1959 Reprint

Continuing its tribute to the late Mickey Mantle across all of its product lines, Topps produced a special reprint of the 1959 Bazooka Mantle card exclusively for inclusion in factory sets of its 1996 Bazooka cards. While the original '59 Mantle was printed in nearly 3" x 5" size on the bottom of gum boxes, the reprint is in the current 2-1/2" x 3-1/2" size.

	MT
Mickey Mantle	6.00

1992 Ben's Bakery Super Hitters Discs

Ben's Bakery, a small, eastern Canadian bakery, inserted promotional discs in its hot dog and hamburger buns in 1992. As in the case of 1991, which was the company's first year in the promotion, the 1992 set contained 20 different players, including many of the top stars in the country. Twenty of the game's top hitters, with a special emphasis on Blue Jays players, are featured in this regional issue by a small Eastern Canada bakery. The 2-3/4" diameter discs were packaged in the company's hot dog and hamburger buns. Fronts feature a color photo on which team logos have been airbrushed away. The bakery logo is flanked by a red "Super Hitters" in the white border at top. The player's name appears in white in an orange banner beneath the photo, with his team and position in blue at bottom. Backs are printed in black and include a few biographical details and 1991 stats, along with a card number and appropriate logos and copyright notices.

		MT
Complete Set (20):		20.00
Common Player:		1.00
1	Cecil Fielder	1.00
2	Joe Carter	1.00
3	Roberto Alomar	1.50
4	Devon White	1.00
5	Kelly Gruber	1.00
6	Cal Ripken, Jr.	4.00
7	Kirby Puckett	2.50
8	Paul Molitor	2.00
9	Julio Franco	1.00
10	Ken Griffey, Jr.	5.00
11	Frank Thomas	2.00
12	Jose Canseco	2.00
13	Danny Tartabull	1.00
14	Terry Pendleton	1.00
15	Tony Gwynn	2.50
16	Howard Johnson	1.00
17	Will Clark	1.50
18	Barry Bonds	2.50
19	Ryne Sandberg	2.50
20	Bobby Bonilla	1.00

1993 Ben's Bakery Super Pitchers Discs

An emphasis on Toronto's pitchers is noted in the checklist for this regional bakery issue. The 2-3/4" diameter discs were packed with hot dog and hamburger buns and follow a 1991 issue by the company featuring super hitters. A color player portrait at center has had the uniform logos airbrushed away. "Super Pitchers" in red flanks the bakery logo in the white border above the photo. The player's name appears in white in an orange banner beneath the photo, with his team and position in blue at bottom. Backs are printed in black and include minimal biographical data, a card number, 1992 stats and copyright information.

		MT
Complete Set (20):		14.00
Common Player:		.60
1	Dennis Eckersley	.75
2	Chris Bosio	.60
3	Jack Morris	.60
4	Greg Maddux	4.00
5	Dennis Martinez	.75
6	Tom Glavine	1.00
7	Doug Drabek	.60
8	John Smoltz	.75
9	Randy Myers	.60
10	Jack McDowell	.60
11	John Wetteland	.60
12	Roger Clemens	3.00
13	Mike Mussina	1.50
14	Juan Guzman	.60
15	Jose Rijo	.60
16	Tom Henke	.60
17	Gregg Olson	.60
18	Jim Abbott	.75
19	Jimmy Key	.60
20	Rheal Cormier	.60

1987 David Berg Hot Dogs Cubs

Changing sponsors from Gatorade to David Berg Pure Beef Hot Dogs, the Chicago Cubs handed out a 26-card set of baseball cards to fans attending the July 29th game at Wrigley Field. The cards are printed in full-color on white stock and measure 2-7/8" x 4-1/4" in size. The set is numbered by the players' uniform numbers. The card backs contain player personal and statistical information, plus a full-color picture of a David Berg hot dog in a bun with all the garnishings. The set marked the sixth consecutive year the Cubs held a baseball card giveaway promotion.

		MT
Complete Set (26):		15.00
Common Player:		.20
1	Dave Martinez	.40
4	Gene Michael	.40
6	Keith Moreland	.40
7	Jody Davis	.40
8	Andre Dawson	2.00
10	Leon Durham	.40
11	Jim Sundberg	.40
12	Shawon Dunston	.50
19	Manny Trillo	.40
20	Bob Dernier	.40
21	Scott Sanderson	.40
22	Jerry Mumphrey	.40
23	Ryne Sandberg	6.00
24	Brian Dayett	.40
29	Chico Walker	.40
31	Greg Maddux	6.00
33	Frank DiPino	.40
34	Steve Trout	.40
36	Gary Matthews	.40
37	Ed Lynch	.40
39	Ron Davis	.40
40	Rick Sutcliffe	.40
46	Lee Smith	.50
47	Dickie Noles	.40
49	Jamie Moyer	.40
----	The Coaching Staff (Johnny Oates, Jim Snyder, Herm Starrette, John Vukovich, Billy Williams)	.40

1988 David Berg Hot Dogs Cubs

This oversized (2-7/8" x 4-1/2") set of 26 cards was distributed to fans at Wrigley Field on August 24th. The set includes cards for the manager and coaching staff, as well as players. Full-color action photos are framed in red and blue on a white background. The backs feature small black and white player close-ups, colorful team logos, statistics and sponsor logos (David Berg Hot Dogs and Venture Store Restaurants). The numbers in the following checklist refer to players' uniforms.

		MT
Complete Set (27):		15.00
Common Player:		.35
2	Vance Law	.40
4	Don Zimmer	.40
7	Jody Davis	.40
8	Andre Dawson	1.50
9	Damon Berryhill	.40
12	Shawon Dunston	.50
17	Mark Grace	3.00
18	Angel Salazar	.40
19	Manny Trillo	.40
21	Scott Sanderson	.40
22	Jerry Mumphrey	.40
23	Ryne Sandberg	6.00
24	Gary Varsho	.40
25	Rafael Palmeiro	3.00
28	Mitch Webster	.40
30	Darrin Jackson	.40
31	Greg Maddux	6.00
32	Calvin Schiraldi	.40
33	Frank DiPino	.40
37	Pat Perry	.40
40	Rick Sutcliffe	.40
41	Jeff Pico	.40
45	Al Nipper	.40
49	Jamie Moyer	.40
50	Les Lancaster	.40
54	Rich Gossage	.50
----	The Coaching Staff (Joe Altobelli, Chuck Cottier, Larry Cox, Jose Martinez, Dick Pole)	.40

1985 Big Apple Art Cards

This collectors' issue features rather crude black-and-white line drawings of New York Yankees and Mets on a 3-1/2" x 5-1/2" glossy format. Backs are blank. The unnumbered cards are checklisted here in alphabetical order. The set was sold in a polybag with an advertising sheet for $5.

		MT
Complete Set (8):		4.00
Common Player:		.25
(1)	Gary Carter	.35
(2)	Dwight Gooden	.40
(3)	Rickey Henderson	.50
(4)	Keith Hernandez	.25
(5)	Don Mattingly	2.00
(6)	Dave Righetti	.25
(7)	Darryl Strawberry	.50
(8)	Dave Winfield	.60
--	Ad card	.10

1986 Big Apple California All Stars

Young stars and veteran players from California's major league teams are featured in this collectors' set. The 2-1/2" x 3-1/2" cards have black-and-white line drawings on front, with a pair of yellow stripes at bottom. Backs have minimal identification.

		MT
Complete Set (11):		3.00
Common Player:		.25
(1)	Wally Joyner	.35
(2)	Reggie Jackson	.50
(3)	Jose Canseco	.60
(4)	Jose Rijo	.25
(5)	Will Clark	.40
(6)	Chili Davis	.25
(7)	Orel Hershiser	.35
(8)	Pedro Guerrero	.25
(9)	Steve Garvey	.35
(10)	Tony Gwynn	.75
(11)	Checklist	.25

1986 Big Apple Pete Incaviglia

The first card of Rangers phenom Pete Incaviglia came not from Topps or Fleer, but from Big Apple Card Co., Baldwin, N.Y. The card was advertised as "approved" by the player and team and proclaimed as his "rookie card." The 2-1/2" x 3-1/2" card has a color photo with a wide blue border on front. The back has his college stats and records and details of his acquisition by the Rangers.

	MT
Pete Incaviglia	1.00

1986 Big Apple Super Rookies

This was one of several collectors' issues by this New York card dealer. The 3-1/2" x 5-1/2" blank-back cards have crude line art portraits of the players on front, surrounded by a black border.

		MT
Complete Set (13):		3.00
Common Player:		.25
(1)	Vince Coleman	.25
(2)	Bret Saberhagen	.50
(3)	Orel Hershiser	.25
(4)	Oddibe McDowell	.25
(5)	Tom Browning	.25
(6)	Phil Bradley	.25
(7)	Ozzie Guillen	.25
(8)	John Franco	.25
(9)	Dan Pasqua	.25
(10)	Brian Fisher	.25
(11)	Mariano Duncan	.25
(12)	Shawon Dunston	.25
(13)	Checklist	.25

1986 Big Apple Superstars

This collectors' issue by Big Apple Card Co., Baldwin, N.Y., features Yankees and Mets players on a glossy 3-1/2" x 5-1/2" blank-back stock. The line art drawings are in black-and-white and there is a bright blue border at left and bottom.

		MT
Complete Set (13):		5.00
Common Player:		.25
1	Dwight Gooden, Don Mattingly	.50
2	Dwight Gooden	.50
3	Don Mattingly	2.00
4	Rickey Henderson	.50
5	Ron Darling	.25
6	Keith Hernandez	.25
7	Gary Carter	.35
8	Darryl Strawberry	.35
9	Kevin Mitchell	.25
10	Mike Easler	.25
11	Dave Winfield	.50
12	Ron Guidry	.25
13	Checklist	.25

1987 Big Apple Pete Incaviglia

Capitalizing on its early marketing relationship with the Rangers' rookie, Big Apple Card Co. issued a 10-card set recapping his debut season. Like the early "rookie card," the set features color photos in a bright blue border with the player's name in white at top. Black-and-white backs are unnumbered and have a few words about some aspect of the 1986 season, or stats, along with copyright notice. Cards are in the standard 2-1/2" x 3-1/2" format. Production was reported to be 8,000 sets.

	MT
Complete Set (10):	5.00
Single Card:	.50
1-10 Pete Incaviglia	.50

1994 Big Apple 1969 Mets Discs

Big Apple Collector, Inc. released the "1969 World Champion Miracle Mets Commemorative Cap Sheet," which has likenesses of each of the 31 members of the squad captured in oil paintings by sports artist Ron Lewis. The player's likeness is centered in a 1-5/8" diameter round commemorative cap which is die cut but remains in place on the sheet. Each cap is gold foil accented, and each 11" x 14" sheet is produced in full color on 48-point card stock. The sheet has a suggested retail price of $39.95.

		MT
Complete Set (31):		25.00
Common Player:		.50
(1)	Gil Hodges	3.00
(2)	Rube Walker	.50
(3)	Yogi Berra	3.00
(4)	Joe Pignatano	.50
(5)	Ed Yost	.50
(6)	Tommie Agee	.50
(7)	Ken Boswell	.50
(8)	Don Cardwell	.50
(9)	Ed Charles	.50
(10)	Donn Clendenon	.50
(11)	Jack DiLauro	.50
(12)	Duffy Dyer	.50
(13)	Wayne Garrett	.50
(14)	Rod Gaspar	.50
(15)	Gary Gentry	.50
(16)	Jerry Grote	.50
(17)	Bud Harrelson	.75
(18)	Cleon Jones	.75
(19)	Cal Koonce	.50
(20)	Jerry Koosman	.75
(21)	Ed Kranepool	.65
(22)	J.C. Martin	.50
(23)	Jim McAndrew	.50
(24)	Tug McGraw	.75
(25)	Bob Pfeil	.50
(26)	Nolan Ryan	8.00
(27)	Tom Seaver	4.00
(28)	Art Shamsky	.50
(29)	Ron Swoboda	.65
(30)	Ron Taylor	.50
(31)	Al Weis	.50

1986 Big League Chew

The 1986 Big League Chew set consists of 12 cards featuring the players who have hit 500 or more career home runs. The cards, which measure 2-1/2" x 3-1/2", were inserted in specially marked packages of Big League Chew, the shredded bubble gum developed by former major leaguer Jim Bouton. The set is entitled "Home Run Legends" and was available through a write-in offer on the package. Recent-day players in the set are shown in color photos, while the older sluggers are pictured in black and white.

		MT
Complete Set (12):		5.00
Common Player:		.40
1	Hank Aaron	.60
2	Babe Ruth	1.00
3	Willie Mays	.60
4	Frank Robinson	.40
5	Harmon Killebrew	.40
6	Mickey Mantle	2.00
7	Jimmie Foxx	.40
8	Ted Williams	.60
9	Ernie Banks	.40
10	Eddie Mathews	.40
11	Mel Ott	.40
12	500-HR Group Card	.50

1997 Big League Chew Alumni

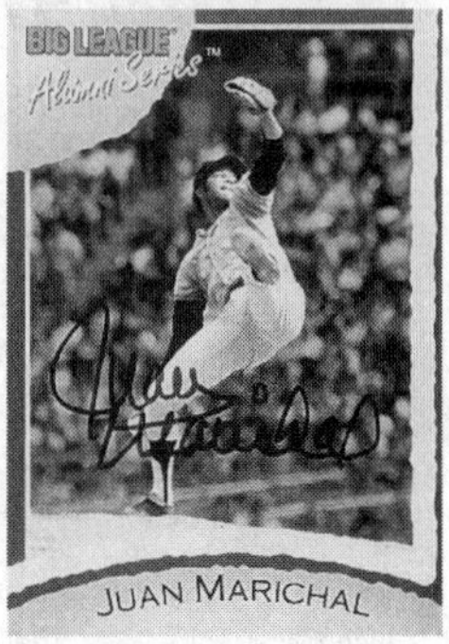

Autographed cards of three Hall of Famers were available through a mail-in offer by Big League Chew shredded bubble gum. Cards could be obtained by sending in proofs of purchase from pouches with the players' photos on them. Each card comes with a certificate of authenticity from Major League Baseball Players Alumni, which licensed the issue. Because the cards are not licensed by Major League Baseball, uniform logos have been removed from the color photos. Cards have a green, orange and white color scheme on front and back and are standard 2-1/2" x 3-1/2". Backs include career highlights and lifetime stats.

		MT
Complete Set (3):		25.00
Common Player:		7.50
(1)	Juan Marichal	7.50
(2)	Brooks Robinson	10.00
(3)	Billy Williams	7.50

1982 Big League Collectibles Diamond Classics, Series 1

Attempting to recapture the flavor of vintage baseball cards this collectors' set presents former stars in a 2-1/2" x 3-3/4" format on thick white cardboard stock. Fronts have a painted player portrait in color with no other graphic elements. Backs are in black and blue and include in-depth biographical sketches and career stats. The edition was limited to 10,000 sets.

		MT
Complete Set:		24.00
Common Player:		.50
1	Joe DiMaggio	2.50
2	Enos Slaughter	.50
3	Smokey Joe Wood (Smoky)	.50
4	Roy Campanella	1.00
5	Charlie Gehringer	.50
6	Carl Hubbell	.50

7	Rogers Hornsby	.50
8	Arky Vaughan	.50
9	Al Simmons	.50
10	Wally Berger	.50
11	Sam Rice	.50
12	Dizzy Dean	.50
13	Babe Ruth	3.00
14	Frankie Frisch	.50
15	George Kell	.50
16	Pee Wee Reese	.50
17	Earl Averill	.50
18	Willie Mays	2.00
19	Frank Baker	.50
20	Hack Wilson	.50
21	Ted Williams	2.00
22	Chuck Klein	.50
23	Bill Dickey	.50
24	Johnny Mize	.50
25	Luke Appling	.50
26	Duke Snider	.50
27	Wahoo Sam Crawford	.50
28	Waite Hoyt	.50
29	Eddie Collins	.50
30	Warren Spahn	.50
31	Satchel Paige	1.00
32	Ernie Lombardi	.50
33	Dom DiMaggio	.50
34	Joe Garagiola	.50
35	Lou Gehrig	2.50
36	Burleigh Grimes	.50
37	Walter Johnson	.50
38	Bill Terry	.50
39	Ty Cobb	2.50
40	Pie Traynor	.50
41	Ted Lyons	.50
42	Richie Ashburn	.50
43	Lefty Grove	.50
44	Edd Roush	.50
45	Phil Rizzuto	.50
46	Stan Musial	2.00
47	Bob Feller	.50
48	Jackie Robinson	2.00
49	Hank Greenberg	1.00
50	Mel Ott	.50
51	Joe Cronin	.50
52	Lefty O'Doul	.50
53	Indian Bob Johnson	.50
54	Kiki Cuyler	.50
55	Mickey Mantle	6.00
---	Checklist	.50

1983 Big League Collectibles Diamond Classics, Series 2

A second series of cards featuring past greats was issued by Big League Collectibles in 1983. Again at 55 cards, the set featured painted portraits of the players on front, devoid of any other graphics. Backs are in red and black and include a lengthy career summary along with innovative stats and a few biographical bits. The 2-1/2" x 3-3/4" cards are printed on a heavy white cardboard stock. The series was produced in an edition of 10,000 sets.

		MT
Complete Set (56):		45.00
Common Player:		1.00
56	Ernie Banks	2.00
57	Stan Coveleski	1.00
58	Vince DiMaggio	1.00
59	Sunny Jim Bottomley	1.00
60	Sandy Koufax	4.00
61	Doc Cramer	1.00
62	Ted Kluszewski	1.00
63	Zeke Bonura	1.00
64	Spud Davis	1.00
65	Jackie Jensen	1.00
66	Honus Wagner	1.00
67	Brooks Robinson	2.00
68	Dazzy Vance	1.00
69	George Uhle	1.00
70	Juan Marichal	1.00
71	Bobo Newsom	1.00
72	Billy Herman	1.00
73	Al Rosen	1.00
74	Roberto Clemente	6.00
75	George Case	1.00
76	Bill Nicholson	1.00
77	Tommy Bridges	1.00
78	Rabbit Maranville	1.00
79	Bob Lemon	1.00
80	Heinie Groh	1.00
81	Tris Speaker	1.00
82	Hank Aaron	4.00
83	Whitey Ford	2.00
84	Guy Bush	1.00
85	Jimmie Foxx	1.00
86	Marty Marion	1.00
87	Hal Newhouser	1.00
88	George Kelley (Kelly)	1.00
89	Harmon Killebrew	1.00
90	Willie McCovey	1.00
91	Mel Harder	1.00
92	Vada Pinson	1.00
93	Luis Aparicio	1.00
94	Grover Alexander	1.00
95	Joe Kuhel	1.00
96	Casey Stengel	1.00
97	Joe Sewell	1.00
98	Red Lucas	1.00
99	Luke Sewell	1.00
100	Charlie Grimm	1.00
101	Cecil Travis	1.00
102	Travis Jackson	1.00
103	Lou Boudreau	1.00
104	Nap Rucker	1.00
105	Chief Bender	1.00
106	Riggs Stephenson	1.00
107	Red Ruffing	1.00
108	Robin Roberts	1.00
109	Harland Clift (Harlond)	1.00
110	Ralph Kiner	1.00
---	Checklist	.15

1983 Big League Collectibles Promo Card

This promo was distributed at card shows to advertise the Diamond Classics and Original All-Stars collectors issues. Front has a color portrait painting of Al Simmons. Back of the 2-1/2" x 3-3/4" card is printed in black and blue.

	MT
Al Simmons	8.00

1983 Big League Collectibles Original All-Stars

Players in the first modern All-Star Game, staged in conjunction with the Chicago World's Fair in 1933, are featured in this collectors' issue. The 2-1/2" x 3-3/4" cards feature pastel paintings of the players on front. A circled baseball at lower-left has player and set identification. Backs are printed in blue and black and include All-Star Game and overall 1933 season performance.

		MT
Complete Set (40):		60.00
Common Player:		1.50
1	American League	1.50
2	Connie Mack	1.50
3	Alvin Crowder	1.50
4	Lefty Gomez	1.50
5	Jimmy Dykes	1.50
6	Earl Averill	1.50
7	Charlie Gehringer	1.50
8	Lefty Grove	1.50
9	Lou Gehrig	4.00
10	Al Simmons	1.50
11	Ben Chapman	1.50
12	Jimmie Foxx	1.50
13	Oral Hildebrand	1.50
14	Joe Cronin	1.50
15	Bill Dickey	1.50
16	Sam West	1.50
17	Rick Ferrell	1.50
18	Tony Lazzeri	1.50
19	Wes Ferrell	1.50
20	Babe Ruth	8.00
21	National League	1.50
22	John McGraw	1.50
23	Pepper Martin	1.50
24	Woody English	1.50
25	Paul Waner	1.50
26	Lefty O'Doul	1.50
27	Chuck Klein	1.50
28	Tony Cuccinello	1.50
29	Frankie Frisch	1.50
30	Gabby Hartnett	1.50
31	Carl Hubbell	1.50
32	Chick Hafey	1.50
33	Dick Bartell	1.50
34	Bill Hallahan	1.50
35	Hal Schumacher	1.50
36	Lon Warneke	1.50
37	Wally Berger	1.50
38	Bill Terry	1.50
39	Jimmy Wilson	1.50
40	Pie Traynor	1.50

1985 Big League Collectibles National Pastime 1930-1939

Major league baseball in the 1930s is chronicled in this boxed collectors' set. In 2-1/8" x 3-1/8" format (the same size as the 1951-52 Bowmans), the cards feature painted player portraits on front with identification in the white border at bottom. Backs are in black and red on thick white cardboard stock and feature in-depth career summaries and unique stats. The edition was limited to 5,000 sets, with a serially numbered header card.

		MT
Complete Set (90):		50.00
Common Player:		.50
1	Header card	.50
2	William H. Walters	.50
3	Montgomery M. Pearson	.50
4	Stanley C. Hack	.50
5	Joseph E. Cronin	.50
6	Leo E. Durocher	.50
7	Max F. Bishop	.50
8	Frank O'Donnell Hurst	.50
9	W. Barney McCosky	.50
10	Remy P. Kremer	.50
11	Julius J. Solters	.50
12	Daniel K. MacFayden	.50
13	Gordon S. Cochrane	.50
14	Ethan N. Allen	.50
15	Luzerne A. Blue	.50
16	John R. Mize	.50
17	Joseph P. DiMaggio	3.00
18	George F. Grantham	.50
19	William E. Kamm	.50
20	Charles A. Root	.50
21	Morris Berg	1.50
22	Floyd C. Herman	.50
23	Henry E. Manush	.50
24	Adolf L. Camilli	.50
25	Rudolph P. York	.50
26	Truett B. Sewell	.50
27	Richard B. Ferrell	.50
28	Arthur C. Whitney	.50
29	Edmund J. Miller	.50
30	August R. Mancuso	.50
31	John B. Conlan	.50
32	Joseph M. Medwick	.50
33	John T. Allen	.50
34	John S. Vander Meer	.50
35	H. Earl Averill	.50
36	Taylor L. Douthit	.50
37	Charles S. Myer	.50
38	Van Lingle Mungo	.50
39	Smead P. Jolley	.50
40	C. Flint Rhem	.50
41	Leon A. Goslin	.50
42	Adam A. Comorosky	.50
43	Jack I. Burns	.50
44	Edward A. Brandt	.50
45	Robert L. Johnson	.50
46	Melvin T. Ott	.50
47	Monty F.P. Stratton	.50
48	Paul D. Dean	.50
49	H. Louis Gehrig	2.50
50	Frank A. McCormick	.50
51	J. Geoffrey Heath	.50
52	Charles L. Hartnett	.50
53	Oswald L. Bluege	.50
54	George H. Ruth	5.00
55	Robert P. Doerr	.50
56	Virgil L. Davis	.50
57	D. Dale Alexander	.50
58	James A. Tobin	.50
59	Joseph F. Vosmik	.50
60	Alfonso R. Lopez	.50
61	James E. Foxx	.50
62	Frederick L. Fitzsimmons	.50
63	Robert R. Fothergill	.50
64	Morton C. Cooper	.50
65	George A. Selkirk	.50
66	Burton E. Shotton	.50
67	Robert W.A. Feller	.50
68	Lawrence H. French	.50
69	Joseph I. Judge	.50
70	Clyde L. Sukeforth	.50
71	James R. Tabor	.50
72	Silas K. Johnson	.50
73	W. Earl Webb	.50
74	Charles F. Lucas	.50
75	Ralph Kress	.50
76	Charles D. Stengel	.50
77	George W. Haas	.50
78	Joe G. Moore	.50
79	Carl N. Reynolds	.50
80	James O. Carleton	.50
81	John J. Murphy	.50
82	Paul Derringer	.50
83	Harold A. Trosky, Sr.	.50
84	Fred C. Lindstrom	.50
85	Jack E. Russell	.50
86	Stanley G. Bordagaray	.50
87	Roy C. Johnson	.50
88	Sylvester W. Johnson	.50
89	Michael F. Higgins	.50
90	J. Floyd Vaughan	.50

1989 Bimbo Cookies Super Stars Discs

A dozen Hispanic players are featured in this set of 2-3/4" diameter discs distributed in Puerto Rico in boxes of cookies. Color portrait photos at center have cap logos removed because the discs are licensed only by the players' union, not MLB; typical for issues from Michael Schechter Associates. The Bimbo bear logo is at top-center, with the player name in a yellow strip at bottom; team and position are in blue in the white border beneath that. Yellow stars, blue baseballs and red words "SUPER STARS" flank the player photo. Backs are printed in blue and have a few biographical details, 1988 and career stats, card number and appropriate logos.

		MT
Complete Set (12):		25.00
Common Player:		2.00
1	Carmelo Martinez	2.00
2	Candy Maldonado	2.00
3	Benito Santiago	2.00
4	Rey Quinones	2.00
5	Jose Oquendo	2.00
6	Ruben Sierra	2.00
7	Jose Lind	2.00
8	Juan Beniquez	2.00
9	Willie Hernandez	2.00
10	Juan Nieves	2.00
11	Jose Guzman	2.00
12	Roberto Alomar (photo actually Sandy Alomar Jr.)	5.00

1991-1992 Bleacher Promos

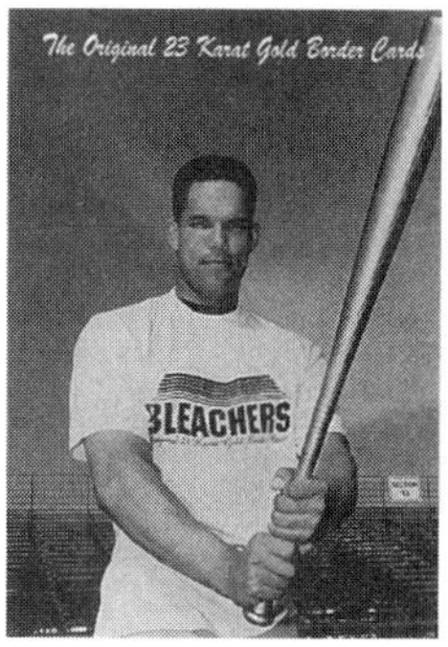

To introduce its 1992 lineup of single-player 23-karat gold trimmed card sets, Bleachers produced a series of promo cards. Fronts have color portraits of the players. Backs have another picture of the player and information about ordering and coming releases. The Nolan Ryan card, showing him winding up in a tuxedo, is known in several variations with different card show names stamped on front in gold, representing venues at which sample cards were given away.

		MT
Complete Set (3):		5.00
(1)	Ken Griffey Jr.	3.00
(2)	David Justice	1.00
(3)	Nolan Ryan	2.00

1991 Bleachers Frank Thomas

This limited edition three-card set features 23-karat gold cards. The photos feature Frank Thomas at different stages of his baseball career before the big leagues. Production was limited to 10,000 sets and 1,500 uncut strips. All are numbered and feature a gold facsimile autograph on the back.

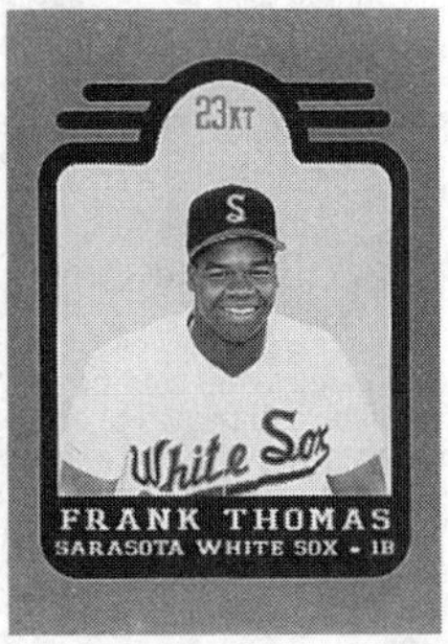

		MT
Complete Set (3):		11.00
Common Card:		4.50
1	Frank Thomas (Auburn Tigers)	4.50
2	Frank Thomas (Sarasota White Sox)	4.50
3	Frank Thomas (Birmingham Barons)	4.50

1992 Bleachers Ken Griffey, Jr.

Young superstar Ken Griffey, Jr. is honored in this three-card set featuring him at different stages of his baseball career. The 23-karat gold cards feature full-color photos and a facsimile autograph on the back. Production was limited to 10,000 cut sets and 1,500 uncut strips.

		MT
Complete Set (3):		15.00
Common Card:		6.00
1	Ken Griffey, Jr. (Moeller High School)	6.00
2	Ken Griffey, Jr. (Bellingham Mariners)	6.00
3	Ken Griffey, Jr. (San Bernadino Spirit)	6.00

1992 Bleachers David Justice

Atlanta Brave slugger David Justice is the subject of this three card 23-karat gold set. The cards depict Justice at different stages of his baseball career. Like the other Bleachers issues, production was limited to 10,000 cut card sets and 1,500 uncut strips.

		MT
Complete Set (3):		10.00
Common Card:		4.00
1	David Justice (Durham Bulls)	4.00
2	David Justice (Greenville Braves)	4.00
3	David Justice (Richmond Braves)	4.00

1992 Bleachers Nolan Ryan

Three stops along Ryan's minor league trail are recalled in this collectors' issue. The 2-1/2" x 3-1/2" cards have photos of Ryan at center with different colored borders and trim on each card. "23KT," his name and team are gold-foil stamped on front. Backs have career information and highlights, along with a serial number from within an edition of 10,000. Cards with silver prismatic foil on front rather than gold were random inserts in sets. Three-card uncut strips were made available in an edition of 1,500.

		MT
Complete Set (3):		12.00
Common Card:		4.00
Silver-foil: 2x		
1	Nolan Ryan (Marion Mets)	4.00
2	Nolan Ryan (Greenville Mets)	4.00
3	Nolan Ryan (Jacksonville Suns)	4.00

1993 Bleachers Promos

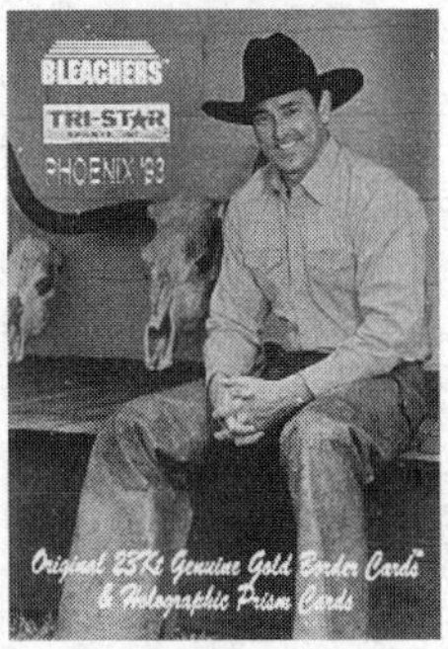

To introduce its 1993 issues, Bleachers distributed large quantities of promo cards within the hobby to dealers and to the public at several large card shows. Most of the '93 promos can be found with several different show logos overprinted in gold foil on the front. All cards carry a 1993 copyright date on back, except the plain Ryan/tuxedo card, which has a 1992 date on back, but 1993 cards show indicia on front.

		MT
Common Card:		1.00
(1)	Barry Bonds (throwing)	1.00
(2)	Ken Griffey Jr. (Moeller High School uniform)	3.00
(3)	Nolan Ryan (triple-exposure pitching)	2.00
(4)	Nolan Ryan (tuxedo, '92 copyright)	2.00
(5)	Nolan Ryan (tuxedo, gold background)	3.00
(6)	Nolan Ryan (tuxedo, silver speckled background)	3.00
(7)	Nolan Ryan (tuxedo, wavy silver background)	3.00
(8)	Nolan Ryan (Western clothing)	2.00
(9)	Nolan Ryan (w/glove and ball in Bleachers cap)	2.00
(10)	Nolan Ryan (with Yellow Lab puppy)	3.00
(11)	Ryne Sandberg (3-sport high school photos)	1.00

1993 Bleachers Barry Bonds

The pre-major league career of Barry Bonds is featured on this trio of collectors' cards. Fronts have color photos of Bonds within a gold border. His name, team and the notation "23KT" are printed in gold foil. Backs have career data and highlights, along with a serial number. It was reported that 10,000 sets and 1,500 three-card strips were issued. Cards found with silver prismatic borders on front are random inserts in sets.

		MT
Complete Set (3):		9.00
Common Card:		3.00
Silver: 2x		
1	Barry Bonds (Arizona State University)	3.00
2	Barry Bonds (Price Williams Pirates)	3.00
3	Barry Bonds (Hawaii Islanders)	3.00

1993 Bleachers Nolan Ryan

Nolan Ryan's career is recapped in this set of collectors issues. Fronts have prismatic foil borders around color or colorized photos. Information on front is stamped in gold foil. Backs have a photo of a young Ryan along with career data and stats, and a serial number from within an announced edition of 10,000 sets and 1,500 three-card uncut strips.

		MT
Complete Set (6):		30.00
Common Card:		5.00
1	Nolan Ryan (Little League)	5.00
2	Nolan Ryan (high school)	5.00
3	Nolan Ryan (minor league highlights)	5.00
4	Nolan Ryan (minor league stats)	5.00
5	Nolan Ryan (strikeout record)	5.00
6	Nolan Ryan (career highlights)	5.00

1993 Bleachers Nolan Ryan 23KT

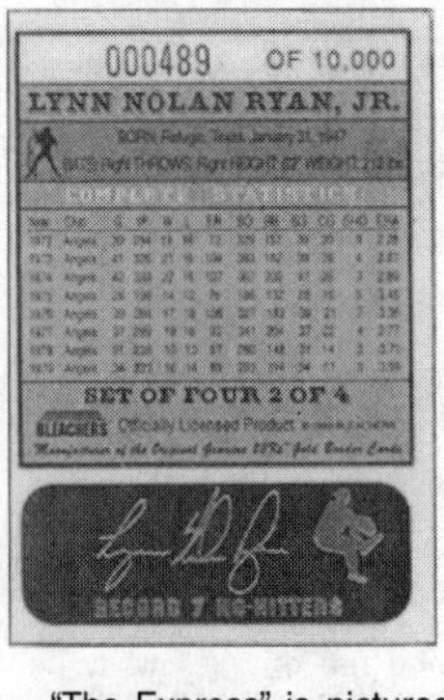

"The Express" is pictured with each of his four major league teams in this collectors issue. Each 2-1/2" x 3-1/2" card has a color photo of Ryan at center with variously colored borders and gold-foil graphic highlights. Backs have his stats with that team, a facsimile autograph and a serial number from within an edition of 10,000 sets. Uncut strips were also issued, numbered to 1,500.

		MT
Complete Set (4):		20.00
Uncut Strip:		30.00
Common Card:		5.00
1	Nolan Ryan (Mets)	5.00
2	Nolan Ryan (Angels)	5.00
3	Nolan Ryan (Astros)	5.00
4	Nolan Ryan (Rangers)	5.00

1993 Bleachers Ryne Sandberg

Ryno's pre-major league career is featured on this trio of collectors' cards. Fronts have color photos of Sandberg within a gold border. His name, team and the notation "23KT" are printed in gold foil. Backs have career data and highlights, along with a serial number. It was reported that 10,000 sets and 1,500 three-card strips were issued. Cards found with silver prismatic borders on front are random inserts in sets.

		MT
Complete Set (3):		11.00
Common Card:		4.00
Silver: 3X		
1	Ryne Sandberg (North Central H.S.)	4.00
2	Ryne Sandberg (Helena Phillies)	4.00
3	Ryne Sandberg (Reading Phillies)	4.00

1995 Bleachers 23-Karat Gold

During 1995, Bleachers issued a series of what it called "Original 23 Karat Gold Foil Sculptured Trading Cards". The 2-1/2" x 3-1/2" cards feature player images and graphics embossed from gold foil. The cards were sold individually and were packaged in a hard plastic case and cardboard box which included a certificate of authenticity. Each card carries on its back an individual serial number from within a specific edition limit.

	MT
Iron Men (Lou Gehrig, Cal Ripken Jr.) (20,000)	15.00
The "Kid" (Ken Griffey Jr.) (gold/silver edition of 10,000)	20.00

1996 Bleachers 23-Karat Gold

During 1996, Bleachers issued a series of what it called "Original 23 Karat Gold Foil Sculptured Trading Cards". The 2-1/2" x 3-1/2" cards feature player images and graphics embossed from gold foil. The cards were sold individually and were packaged in a hard plastic case and cardboard box which included a certificate of authenticity. Each card carries on its back an individual serial number from within a specific edition limit. "Diamond Stars" series cards have color photos on front.

	MT
Ken Griffey Junior (Junior)	15.00
Mickey Mantle (Triple Crown - Diamond Stars)	20.00
Mickey Mantle (Greatest Switch Hitter)	20.00
Cal Ripken Jr. (2,131 games - Diamond Stars)	15.00
Nolan Ryan (All-Time Strikeout King)	15.00
Ted Williams (Baseball's Greatest Hitter)	10.00

1997 Bleachers 23-Karat Gold

During 1997, Bleachers issued a series of what it called "Original 23 Karat Gold Foil Sculptured Trading Card". The 2-1/2" x 3-1/2" cards feature player images and graphics embossed from gold foil. The cards were sold individually and were packaged in a hard plastic case and cardboard box which included a certificate of authenticity. Each card carries on its back an individual serial number from within a specific edition limit.

		MT
(1)	Whitey Ford	7.50

1998 Bleachers 23-Karat Gold

During 1998, Bleachers issued a series of what it called "Original 23 Karat Gold Foil Sculptured Trading Card". The 2-1/2" x 3-1/2" cards feature player images and graphics embossed from gold foil. The cards were sold individually and were packaged in a hard plastic case and cardboard box which included a certificate of authenticity. Each card is individually serial numbered from within a stated edition limit.

		MT
(1)	Mark McGwire (62nd Home Run Die-Cut)	15.00

1999 Bleachers Home Run Derby Ken Griffey, Jr.

To honor Junior's victory in the 1999 All-Star Game Home Run Derby, this oversize (2-1/2" x 4-3/4" gold-foil card was created in a serially-numbered edition of 100 which was sold exclusively on eBay. The card has dimensional action (front) and portrait (back) pictures of Griffey in 23-karat gold, with facsimile autographs front and back. Backs have complete major league stats through July 11, 1999. On front is a stamped black foil HR Derby Winner logo, with his name and borders in teal foil.

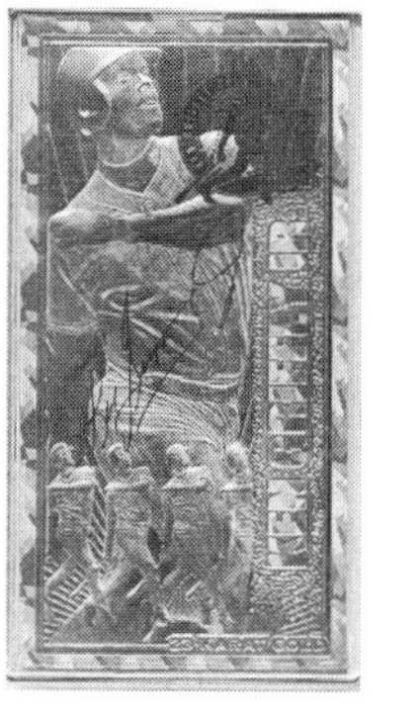

		MT
	Ken Griffey Jr.	25.00

2000 Bleachers Ken Griffey Traded to Cincinnati

Junior's trade to the Reds was commemorated with this 23-karat gold embossed card. The 2-1/2" x 3-1/2" card has on front portrait and action embossments of Griffey, along with a facsimile autograph and his new "30" uniform number. At top, the large "GRIFFEY" is highlighted in red. At bottom in black is a simulated newspaper with the date Feb. 10 and a headline about the trade. Backs have another pair of Griffey pictures, some personal data and a serial number. Cards were issued in a plastic case and decorative box.

		MT
	Ken Griffey Jr.	24.00

1988 Blue Cross/Blue Shield Bob Uecker Reprint

Issued as a fund-raiser and sold for $3 to benefit Bob Uecker's Ride for the Arts bicycling event in 1988, this 2-1/2" x 3-1/2" card features on its front a reprint of Uecker's card from the 1963 Topps set. Back has history and details of the fund-raiser and the logos of Blue Cross and Blue Shield.

		MT
(1)	Bob Uecker	5.00

1987 Boardwalk and Baseball

Created by Topps for distribution at the Boardwalk and Baseball theme park near Orlando, Fla., the cards are standard size with a thin, pink border around a color action photo. The backs are printed in black and light red, with the Topps and B/B logos at the bottom. There are 33-cards in the "Top Run Makers" boxed set, all hitters. A checklist appears on the back panel of the box. A much scarcer version of each card can be found with no slash between the "B"s on front.

		MT
Complete Set (33):		5.00
Common Player:		.10
1	Mike Schmidt	.50
2	Eddie Murray	.35
3	Dale Murphy	.20
4	Dave Winfield	.25
5	Jim Rice	.15
6	Cecil Cooper	.10
7	Dwight Evans	.10
8	Rickey Henderson	.30
9	Robin Yount	.50
10	Andre Dawson	.20
11	Gary Carter	.20
12	Keith Hernandez	.10
13	George Brett	.75
14	Bill Buckner	.10
15	Tony Armas	.10
16	Harold Baines	.15
17	Don Baylor	.15
18	Steve Garvey	.20
19	Lance Parrish	.10
20	Dave Parker	.10
21	Buddy Bell	.10
22	Cal Ripken, Jr.	2.00
23	Bob Horner	.10
24	Tim Raines	.15
25	Jack Clark	.10
26	Leon Durham	.10
27	Pedro Guerrero	.10
28	Kent Hrbek	.10
29	Kirk Gibson	.10
30	Ryne Sandberg	.60
31	Wade Boggs	.60
32	Don Mattingly	1.00
33	Darryl Strawberry	.15

1987 Bohemian Hearth Bread Padres

Bohemian Hearth Bread of San Diego issued this Padres team set. Produced in conjunction with Mike Schechter Associates, the cards are 2-1/2" x 3-1/2". Fronts have a color portrait photo encompassed by a yellow border. The Bohemian Hearth logo is located in the upper-left corner. Card backs are printed in light brown on a cream stock and carry player personal and statistical information, along with a facsimile autograph.

		MT
Complete Set (22):		45.00
Common Player:		1.00
1	Garry Templeton	1.00
4	Jose Cora	1.00
5	Randy Ready	1.00
6	Steve Garvey	5.00
7	Kevin Mitchell	1.50
8	John Kruk	1.50
9	Benito Santiago	2.50
10	Larry Bowa	1.00
11	Tim Flannery	1.00
14	Carmelo Martinez	1.00
16	Marvell Wynne	1.00
19	Tony Gwynn	25.00
21	James Steels	1.00
22	Stan Jefferson	1.00
30	Eric Show	1.00
31	Ed Whitson	1.00
34	Storm Davis	1.00
37	Craig Lefferts	1.00
40	Andy Hawkins	1.00
41	Lance McCullers	1.00
43	Dave Dravecky	1.50
54	Rich Gossage	1.50

1984 Borden's Reds Stickers

This regional set of eight Reds stickers was issued by Borden Dairy in the Cincinnati area in 1984. Originally issued in two perforated sheets of four stickers each, the individual stickers measure 2-1/2" x 3-7/8", while a full sheet measures 5-1/2" x 8". The colorful stickers feature a player photo surrounded by a bright red border with the Reds logo and the Borden logo in the corners. The backs display coupons for Borden dairy products. The set is numbered according to the players' uniform numbers.

		MT
Complete Panel Set (2):		11.00
Complete Singles Set (8):		6.00
Common Player:		.50
	PANEL (1)	4.00
2	Gary Redus	.50
20	Eddie Milner	.50
24	Tony Perez	3.00
46	Jeff Russell	.50
	PANEL (2)	8.00
16	Ron Oester	.50
36	Mario Soto	.50
39	Dave Parker	1.00
44	Eric Davis	2.00
2	Gary Redus	.50
20	Eddie Milner	.50
24	Tony Perez	1.00
46	Jeff Russell	.50
16	Ron Oester	.50
36	Mario Soto	.50
39	Dave Parker	1.50
44	Eric Davis	2.00

1982 Boston Red Sox Favorites

No issuer is identified on this collectors' set, though some attribute it to the Boston Globe newspaper. The 2-1/2" x 3-1/2" cards are black-and-white with rather wide white borders on front. There is no player identification on front. Backs are roughly in the style of 1955 Bowmans and have player identification, personal data, stats, career highlights and a trivia question.

		MT
Complete Set (128):		35.00
Common Player:		.25
1	Harry Agganis	2.50
2	Ken Aspromonte	.25
3	Bobby Avila	.45
4	Frank Baumann	.25
5	Lou Berberet	.25
6	Milt Bolling	.25
7	Lou Boudreau	.50
8	Ted Bowsfield	.25
9	Tom Brewer	.25
10	Don Buddin	.25
11	Jerry Casale	.25
12	Billy Consolo	.25
13	Pete Daley	.25
14	Ike Delock	.25
15	Dom DiMaggio	1.00
16	Bobby Doerr	.50
17	Walt Dropo	.50
18	Arnold Earley	.25
19	Hoot Evers	.40
20	Mike Fornieles	.25
21	Gary Geiger	.25
22	Don Gile	.25
23	Joe Ginsberg	.25
24	Billy Goodman	.25
25	Pumpsie Green	.35
26	Grady Hatten	.25
27	Mike Higgins	.25
28	Jackie Jensen	.50
29	George Kell	.50
30	Marty Keough	.25
31	Leo Kiely	.25
32	Ellis Kinder	.25
33	Billy Klaus	.25
34	Don Lenhardt	.25
35	Ted Lepcio	.25
36	Frank Malzone	.35
37	Gene Mauch	.35
38	Maury McDermott	.25
39	Bill Monbouquette	.25
40	Chet Nichols	.25
41	Willard Nixon	.25
42	Jim Pagliaroni	.25
43	Mel Parnell	.25
44	Johnny Pesky	.25
45	Jimmy Piersall	.50
46	Bob Porterfield	.25
47	Pete Runnels	.35
48	Dave Sisler	.25
49	Riverboat Smith	.25
50	Gene Stephens	.25
51	Vern Stephens	.25
52	Chuck Stobbs	.25
53	Dean Stone	.25
54	Frank Sullivan	.25
55	Haywood Sullivan	.25
56	Birdie Tebbetts	.25
57	Mickey Vernon	.40
58	Vic Wertz	.25
59	Sammy White	.25
60	Ted Williams	6.00
61	Ted Wills	.25
62	Earl Wilson	.35
63	Al Zarilla	.25
64	Norm Zauchin	.25
65	Ted Williams, Carl Yastrzemski	4.00
66	Jim Lonborg, George Scott, Dick Williams, Carl Yastrzemski	2.00
67	Billy Conigliaro, Tony Conigliaro	1.00
68	Jerry Adair	.25
69	Mike Andrews	.25
70	Gary Bell	.25
71	Dennis Bennett	.25
72	Ed Bressoud	.25
73	Ken Brett	.25
74	Lu Clinton	.25
75	Tony Conigliaro	.75
76	Billy Conigliaro	.25
77	Gene Conley	.25
78	Ray Culp	.25
79	Dick Ellsworth	.25
80	Joe Foy	.25
81	Russ Gibson	.25
82	Jim Gosger	.25
83	Lennie Green	.25
84	Ken Harrelson	.35
85	Tony Horton	.35
86	Elston Howard	.35
87	Dalton Jones	.25
88	Eddie Kasko	.25
89	Joe Lahoud	.25
90	Jack Lamabe	.25
91	Jim Lonborg	.50
92	Sparky Lyle	.50
93	Felix Mantilla	.25
94	Roman Mejias	.25
95	Don McMahon	.25
96	Dave Morehead	.25
97	Gerry Moses	.25
98	Mike Nagy	.25
99	Russ Nixon	.30
100	Gene Oliver	.25
101	Dan Osinski	.25
102	Rico Petrocelli	.50
103	Juan Pizzaro	.25
104	Dick Radatz	.35
105	Vicente Romo	.25
106	Mike Ryan	.25
107	Jose Santiago	.25
108	Chuck Schilling	.25
109	Dick Schofield	.25
110	Don Schwall	.25
111	George Scott	.40
112	Norm Siebern	.25
113	Sonny Seibert	.25
114	Reggie Smith	.35
115	Bill Spanswick	.25
116	Tracy Stallard	.25
117	Lee Stange	.25
118	Jerry Stephenson	.25
119	Dick Stuart	.25
120	Tom Sturdivant	.25
121	Jose Tartabull	.25
122	George Thomas	.25
123	Lee Thomas	.25
124	Bob Tillman	.25
125	Gary Waslewski	.25
126	Dick Williams	.35
127	John Wyatt	.25
128	Carl Yastrzemski	4.00

1983 Boston Herald Sox Stamps

Current and former Red Sox stars are featured in this set of stamps issued by one of Boston's daily newspapers. Coupons in the paper could be redeemed for packets of stamps which could be mounted on a large (34" x 22") colorful wallchart. Persons completing the set could enter a contest for various prizes. Stamps #1-26 and 39-42 are in color and feature portrait photos of the '83 team. They measure 1" x 1-3/4". Stamps #27-38 and 43-50 are 1" x 1-1/8" and may have either color or black-and-white photos of current and former players. Values shown are for unused stamps.

		MT
Complete Set (50):		30.00
Common Player:		.50
Wallchart:		15.00
1	Jerry Remy	.50
2	Glenn Hoffman	.50
3	Luis Aponte	.50
4	Jim Rice	1.00
5	Mark Clear	.50
6	Reid Nichols	.50
7	Wade Boggs	5.00
8	Dennis Eckersley	2.00
9	Jeff Newman	.50
10	Bob Ojeda	.50
11	Ed Jurak	.50
12	Rick Miller	.50
13	Carl Yastrzemski	7.50
14	Mike Brown	.50
15	Bob Stanley	.50
16	John Tudor	.50
17	Gary Allenson	.50
18	Rich Gedman	.50
19	Tony Armas	.75
20	Doug Bird	.50
21	Bruce Hurst	.50
22	Dave Stapleton	.50
23	Dwight Evans	1.00
24	Julio Valdez	.50
25	John Henry Johnson	.50
26	Ralph Houk	.60
27	George Scott	.75
28	Bobby Doerr	.60
29	Frank Malzone	.50
30	Rico Petrocelli	.75
31	Carl Yastrzemski	5.00
32	Ted Williams	6.00
33	Dwight Evans	.75
34	Carlton Fisk	3.00
35	Dick Radatz	.50
36	Luis Tiant	.75
37	Mel Parnell	.50
38	Jim Rice	.75
39	Dennis Boyd	.60
40	Marty Barrett	.50
41	Brian Denman	.50
42	Steve Crawford	.50
43	Cy Young	.75
44	Jimmy Collins	.50
45	Tris Speaker	.75
46	Harry Hooper	.50
47	Lefty Grove	.60
48	Joe Cronin	.50
49	Jimmie Foxx	.75
50	Ted Williams	6.00

1989 Boston Red Sox team issue

These large-format (3-1/2" x 6") black-and-white cards were provided to players and coaches for use in answering fan requests for pictures and autographs. The cards have borderless portrait photos with the player's name overprinted at bottom center. Backs are blank. The unnumbered cards are listed alphabetically. Complete sets were not available from the team.

		MT
Complete Set (30):		45.00
Common Player:		1.00
(1)	Marty Barrett	1.00
(2)	Dick Berardino	1.00
(3)	Mike Boddicker	1.00
(4)	Wade Boggs	4.00
(5)	Oil Can Boyd	1.25
(6)	Al Bumbry	1.00
(7)	Ellis Burks	1.25
(8)	Rick Cerone	1.00
(9)	Roger Clemens	5.00
(10)	John Dopson	1.00
(11)	Nick Esasky	1.00
(12)	Dwight Evans	2.00
(13)	Bill Fischer	1.00
(14)	Wes Gardner	1.00
(15)	Rich Gedman	1.00
(16)	Mike Greenwell	1.50
(17)	Richie Hebner	1.00
(18)	Danny Heep	1.00
(19)	Randy Kutcher	1.00
(20)	Dennis Lamp	1.00
(21)	Joe Morgan	1.00
(22)	Rob Murphy	1.00
(23)	Jody Reed	1.00
(24)	Jim Rice	2.50
(25)	Kevin Romine	1.00
(26)	Lee Smith	1.50
(27)	Mike Smithson	1.00
(28)	Bob Stanley	1.00
(29)	Ted Williams	7.50
(30)	Carl Yastrzemski	5.00

1993 Boston Red Sox Police

This police set was issued by the police department and local sponsors around the Red Sox spring training base in Florida. Card fronts have studio poses of the players. The Winter Haven P.D. and Police Athletic League logos are at top, while the Red Sox logo, player ID and uniform number are beneath the portrait. Backs have a little personal data, some stats, a safety message and the names of sponsoring businesses.

		MT
Complete Set (24):		12.00
Common Player:		.50
1	Checklist	.50
2	Scott Bankhead	.50
3	Danny Darwin	.50
4	Andre Dawson	1.00
5	Scott Fletcher	.50
6	Billy Hatcher	.50
7	Jack Clark	.50
8	Roger Clemens	4.00
9	Scott Cooper	.50
10	John Dopson	.50
11	Paul Quantrill	.50
12	Mike Greenwell	.50
13	Greg A. Harris	.50
14	Joe Hesketh	.50
15	Peter Hoy	.50
16	Daryl Irvine	.50
17	John Marzano	.50
18	Jeff McNeeley	.50
19	Tim Naehring	.50
20	Matt Young	.50
21	Jeff Plympton	.50
22	Bob Melvin	.50
23	Tony Pena	.50
24	Luis Rivera	.50

1989 Bowman

Topps, which purchased Bowman in 1955, revived the brand name in 1989, issuing a 484-card set. The 2-1/2" x 3-3/4" cards are slightly taller than current standard. Fronts contain a full-color player photo, with facsimile autograph and the Bowman logo in an upper corner. Backs include a breakdown of the player's stats against each team in his league. A series of "Hot Rookie Stars" highlights the set. The cards were distributed in both wax packs and rack packs. Each pack included a special reproduction of a classic Bowman card with a sweepstakes on the back.

		MT
Complete Set (484):		25.00
Common Player:		.05
Wax Box:		50.00
1	Oswald Peraza	.05
2	Brian Holton	.05
3	Jose Bautista	.05
4	*Pete Harnisch*	.20
5	Dave Schmidt	.05
6	Gregg Olson	.05
7	Jeff Ballard	.05
8	Bob Melvin	.05
9	Cal Ripken, Jr.	.75
10	Randy Milligan	.05
11	*Juan Bell*	.05
12	Billy Ripken	.05
13	Jim Trabor	.05
14	Pete Stanicek	.05
15	*Steve Finley*	.25
16	Larry Sheets	.05
17	Phil Bradley	.05
18	Brady Anderson	.40
19	Lee Smith	.08
20	Tom Fischer	.05
21	Mike Boddicker	.05
22	Rob Murphy	.05
23	Wes Gardner	.05
24	John Dopson	.05
25	Bob Stanley	.05
26	Roger Clemens	.50
27	Rich Gedman	.05
28	Marty Barrett	.05
29	Luis Rivera	.05
30	Jody Reed	.05
31	Nick Esasky	.05
32	Wade Boggs	.40
33	Jim Rice	.10
34	Mike Greenwell	.05
35	Dwight Evans	.08
36	Ellis Burks	.12
37	Chuck Finley	.05
38	Kirk McCaskill	.05
39	Jim Abbott	.10
40	*Bryan Harvey*	.05
41	Bert Blyleven	.08
42	Mike Witt	.05
43	Bob McClure	.05
44	Bill Schroeder	.05
45	Lance Parrish	.08
46	Dick Schofield	.05
47	Wally Joyner	.10
48	Jack Howell	.05
49	Johnny Ray	.05
50	Chili Davis	.08
51	Tony Armas	.05
52	Claudell Washington	.05
53	Brian Downing	.05
54	Devon White	.08
55	Bobby Thigpen	.05
56	Bill Long	.05
57	Jerry Reuss	.05
58	Shawn Hillegas	.05
59	Melido Perez	.05
60	Jeff Bittiger	.05
61	Jack McDowell	.08
62	Carlton Fisk	.15
63	Steve Lyons	.05
64	Ozzie Guillen	.05
65	Robin Ventura	.20
66	Fred Manrique	.05
67	Dan Pasqua	.05
68	Ivan Calderon	.05
69	Ron Kittle	.05
70	Daryl Boston	.05
71	Dave Gallagher	.05
72	Harold Baines	.08
73	*Charles Nagy*	.25
74	John Farrell	.05
75	Kevin Wickander	.05
76	Greg Swindell	.05
77	Mike Walker	.05
78	Doug Jones	.05
79	Rich Yett	.05
80	Tom Candiotti	.05
81	Jesse Orosco	.05
82	Bud Black	.05
83	Andy Allanson	.05
84	Pete O'Brien	.05
85	Jerry Browne	.05
86	Brook Jacoby	.05
87	*Mark Lewis*	.10
88	Luis Aguayo	.05
89	Cory Snyder	.05
90	Oddibe McDowell	.05
91	Joe Carter	.08
92	Frank Tanana	.05
93	Jack Morris	.08
94	Doyle Alexander	.05
95	Steve Searcy	.05
96	Randy Bockus	.05
97	Jeff Robinson	.05
98	Mike Henneman	.05
99	Paul Gibson	.05
100	Frank Williams	.05
101	Matt Nokes	.05
102	Rico Brogna	.05
103	Lou Whitaker	.08
104	Al Pedrique	.05
105	Alan Trammell	.10
106	Chris Brown	.05
107	Pat Sheridan	.05
108	Gary Pettis	.05
109	Keith Moreland	.05
110	Mel Stottlemyre, Jr.	.05
111	Bret Saberhagen	.08
112	Floyd Bannister	.05
113	Jeff Montgomery	.05
114	Steve Farr	.05
115	Tom Gordon	.05
116	Charlie Leibrandt	.05
117	Mark Gubicza	.05
118	Mike MacFarlane	.05
119	Bob Boone	.05
120	Kurt Stillwell	.05
121	George Brett	.40
122	Frank White	.05
123	Kevin Seitzer	.05
124	Willie Wilson	.08
125	Pat Tabler	.05
126	Bo Jackson	.20
127	Hugh Walker	.05
128	Danny Tartabull	.05
129	Teddy Higuera	.05
130	Don August	.05
131	Juan Nieves	.05
132	Mike Birkbeck	.05
133	Dan Plesac	.05
134	Chris Bosio	.05
135	Bill Wegman	.05
136	Chuck Crim	.05
137	B.J. Surhoff	.08
138	Joey Meyer	.05
139	Dale Sveum	.05
140	Paul Molitor	.40
141	Jim Gantner	.05
142	Gary Sheffield	.30
143	Greg Brock	.05
144	Robin Yount	.40
145	Glenn Braggs	.05
146	Rob Deer	.05
147	Fred Toliver	.05
148	Jeff Reardon	.05
149	Allan Anderson	.05
150	Frank Viola	.05
151	Shane Rawley	.05
152	Juan Berenguer	.05
153	Johnny Ard	.05
154	Tim Laudner	.05
155	Brian Harper	.05
156	Al Newman	.05
157	Kent Hrbek	.08
158	Gary Gaetti	.08
159	Wally Backman	.05
160	Gene Larkin	.05
161	Greg Gagne	.05
162	Kirby Puckett	.50
163	Danny Gladden	.05
164	Randy Bush	.05
165	Dave LaPoint	.05
166	Andy Hawkins	.05
167	Dave Righetti	.05
168	Lance McCullers	.05
169	Jimmy Jones	.05
170	Al Leiter	.08
171	John Candelaria	.05
172	Don Slaught	.05
173	Jamie Quirk	.05
174	Rafael Santana	.05
175	Mike Pagliarulo	.05
176	Don Mattingly	.40
177	Ken Phelps	.05
178	Steve Sax	.05
179	Dave Winfield	.20
180	Stan Jefferson	.05
181	Rickey Henderson	.20
182	Bob Brower	.05
183	Roberto Kelly	.05
184	Curt Young	.05
185	Gene Nelson	.05
186	Bob Welch	.05
187	Rick Honeycutt	.05
188	Dave Stewart	.05
189	Mike Moore	.05
190	Dennis Eckersley	.08
191	Eric Plunk	.05
192	Storm Davis	.05
193	Terry Steinbach	.05
194	Ron Hassey	.05
195	Stan Royer	.05
196	Walt Weiss	.05
197	Mark McGwire	1.50
198	Carney Lansford	.05
199	Glenn Hubbard	.05
200	Dave Henderson	.05
201	Jose Canseco	.30
202	Dave Parker	.08
203	Scott Bankhead	.05
204	Tom Niedenfuer	.05
205	Mark Langston	.08
206	*Erik Hanson*	.08
207	Mike Jackson	.05
208	Dave Valle	.05
209	Scott Bradley	.05
210	Harold Reynolds	.08
211	Tino Martinez	.25
212	Rich Renteria	.05
213	Rey Quinones	.05
214	Jim Presley	.05
215	Alvin Davis	.05
216	Edgar Martinez	.05
217	Darnell Coles	.05
218	Jeffrey Leonard	.05
219	Jay Buhner	.08
220	*Ken Griffey, Jr.*	18.00
221	Drew Hall	.05
222	Bobby Witt	.05
223	Jamie Moyer	.05
224	Charlie Hough	.05
225	Nolan Ryan	.75
226	Jeff Russell	.05
227	Jim Sundberg	.05
228	Julio Franco	.08
229	Buddy Bell	.05
230	Scott Fletcher	.05
231	Jeff Kunkel	.05
232	Steve Buechele	.05
233	Monty Fariss	.05
234	Rick Leach	.05
235	Ruben Sierra	.05
236	Cecil Espy	.05
237	Rafael Palmeiro	.15
238	Pete Incaviglia	.05
239	Dave Steib	.05
240	Jeff Musselman	.05
241	Mike Flanagan	.05
242	Todd Stottlemyre	.08
243	Jimmy Key	.05
244	Tony Castillo	.05
245	Alex Sanchez	.05
246	Tom Henke	.05
247	John Cerutti	.05
248	Ernie Whitt	.05
249	Bob Brenly	.05
250	Rance Mulliniks	.05
251	Kelly Gruber	.05
252	Ed Sprague	.10
253	Fred McGriff	.15
254	Tony Fernandez	.08
255	Tom Lawless	.05
256	George Bell	.08
257	Jesse Barfield	.05
258	Sandy Alomar, Sr.	.05
259	Ken Griffey (with Ken Griffey, Jr.)	1.00
260	Cal Ripken, Sr.	.15
261	Mel Stottlemyre, Sr.	.05
262	Zane Smith	.05
263	Charlie Puleo	.05
264	Derek Lilliquist	.05
265	Paul Assenmacher	.05
266	John Smoltz	.25
267	Tom Glavine	.15
268	*Steve Avery*	.10
269	*Pete Smith*	.05
270	Jody Davis	.05
271	Bruce Benedict	.05
272	Andres Thomas	.05
273	Gerald Perry	.05
274	Ron Gant	.15
275	Darrell Evans	.08
276	Dale Murphy	.20
277	Dion James	.05
278	Lonnie Smith	.05
279	Geronimo Berroa	.05
280	Steve Wilson	.05
281	Rick Suctcliffe	.05
282	Kevin Coffman	.05
283	Mitch Williams	.05
284	Greg Maddux	.60
285	Paul Kilgus	.05
286	Mike Harkey	.05
287	Lloyd McClendon	.05
288	Damon Berryhill	.05
289	Ty Griffin	.05
290	Ryne Sandberg	.50
291	Mark Grace	.35
292	Curt Wilkerson	.05
293	Vance Law	.05
294	Shawon Dunston	.12
295	Jerome Walton	.05
296	Mitch Webster	.05
297	Dwight Smith	.05
298	Andre Dawson	.15
299	Jeff Sellers	.05
300	Jose Rijo	.05
301	John Franco	.05
302	Rick Mahler	.05
303	Ron Robinson	.05
304	Danny Jackson	.05
305	Rob Dibble	.05
306	Tom Browning	.05
307	Bo Diaz	.05
308	Manny Trillo	.05
309	Chris Sabo	.05
310	Ron Oester	.05
311	Barry Larkin	.15
312	Todd Benzinger	.05
313	Paul O'Neill	.10
314	Kal Daniels	.05
315	Joel Youngblood	.05
316	Eric Davis	.10
317	Dave Smith	.05
318	Mark Portugal	.05
319	Brian Meyer	.05
320	Jim Deshaies	.05
321	Juan Agosto	.05
322	Mike Scott	.05
323	Rick Rhoden	.05
324	Jim Clancy	.05

325	Larry Andersen	.05
326	Alex Trevino	.05
327	Alan Ashby	.05
328	Craig Reynolds	.05
329	Bill Doran	.05
330	Rafael Ramirez	.05
331	Glenn Davis	.05
332	*Willie Ansley*	.05
333	Gerald Young	.05
334	Cameron Drew	.05
335	Jay Howell	.05
336	Tim Belcher	.05
337	Fernando Valenzuela	.08
338	Ricky Horton	.05
339	Tim Leary	.05
340	Bill Bene	.05
341	Orel Hershiser	.08
342	Mike Scioscia	.05
343	Rick Dempsey	.05
344	Willie Randolph	.05
345	Alfredo Griffin	.05
346	Eddie Murray	.35
347	Mickey Hatcher	.05
348	Mike Sharperson	.05
349	John Shelby	.05
350	Mike Marshall	.05
351	Kirk Gibson	.05
352	Mike Davis	.05
353	Bryn Smith	.05
354	Pascual Perez	.05
355	Kevin Gross	.05
356	Andy McGaffigan	.05
357	Brian Holman	.05
358	Dave Wainhouse	.05
359	Denny Martinez	.08
360	Tim Burke	.05
361	Nelson Santovenia	.05
362	Tim Wallach	.05
363	Spike Owen	.05
364	Rex Hudler	.05
365	Andres Galarraga	.15
366	Otis Nixon	.05
367	Hubie Brooks	.05
368	Mike Aldrete	.05
369	Rock Raines	.08
370	Dave Martinez	.05
371	Bob Ojeda	.05
372	Ron Darling	.05
373	Wally Whitehurst	.05
374	Randy Myers	.05
375	David Cone	.15
376	Dwight Gooden	.10
377	Sid Fernandez	.05
378	Dave Proctor	.05
379	Gary Carter	.10
380	Keith Miller	.05
381	Gregg Jefferies	.10
382	Tim Teufel	.05
383	Kevin Elster	.05
384	Dave Magadan	.05
385	Keith Hernandez	.08
386	Mookie Wilson	.05
387	Darryl Strawberry	.10
388	Kevin McReynolds	.05
389	Mark Carreon	.05
390	Jeff Parrett	.05
391	Mike Maddux	.05
392	Don Carman	.05
393	Bruce Ruffin	.05
394	Ken Howell	.05
395	Steve Bedrosian	.05
396	Floyd Youmans	.05
397	Larry McWilliams	.05
398	Pat Combs	.05
399	Steve Lake	.05
400	Dickie Thon	.05
401	Ricky Jordan	.05
402	Mike Schmidt	.40
403	Tom Herr	.05
404	Chris James	.05
405	Juan Samuel	.05
406	Von Hayes	.05
407	Ron Jones	.05
408	Curt Ford	.05
409	Bob Walk	.05
410	Jeff Robinson	.05
411	Jim Gott	.05
412	Scott Medvin	.05
413	John Smiley	.05
414	Bob Kipper	.05
415	Brian Fisher	.05
416	Doug Drabek	.05
417	Mike Lavalliere	.05
418	Ken Oberkfell	.05
419	Sid Bream	.05
420	Austin Manahan	.05
421	Jose Lind	.05
422	Bobby Bonilla	.10
423	Glenn Wilson	.05
424	Andy Van Slyke	.05
425	Gary Redus	.05
426	Barry Bonds	.50
427	Don Heinkel	.05
428	Ken Dayley	.05
429	Todd Worrell	.05
430	Brad DuVall	.05
431	Jose DeLeon	.05
432	Joe Magrane	.05
433	John Ericks	.05
434	Frank DiPino	.05
435	Tony Pena	.05
436	Ozzie Smith	.40
437	Terry Pendleton	.05
438	Jose Oquendo	.05
439	Tim Jones	.05
440	Pedro Guerrero	.05
441	Milt Thompson	.05
442	Willie McGee	.08
443	Vince Coleman	.05
444	Tom Brunansky	.05
445	Walt Terrell	.05
446	Eric Show	.05
447	Mark Davis	.05
448	*Andy Benes*	.25
449	Eddie Whitson	.05
450	Dennis Rasmussen	.05
451	Bruce Hurst	.05
452	Pat Clements	.05
453	Benito Santiago	.08
454	Sandy Alomar, Jr.	.15
455	Garry Templeton	.05
456	Jack Clark	.05
457	Tim Flannery	.05
458	Roberto Alomar	.30
459	Camelo Martinez	.05
460	John Kruk	.05
461	Tony Gwynn	.50
462	Jerald Clark	.05
463	Don Robinson	.05
464	Craig Lefferts	.05
465	Kelly Downs	.05
466	Rick Rueschel	.05
467	Scott Garrelts	.05
468	Wil Tejada	.05
469	Kirt Manwaring	.05
470	Terry Kennedy	.05
471	Jose Uribe	.05
472	*Royce Clayton*	.10
473	Robby Thompson	.05
474	Kevin Mitchell	.05
475	Ernie Riles	.05
476	Will Clark	.20
477	Donnell Nixon	.05
478	Candy Maldonado	.05
479	Tracy Jones	.05
480	Brett Butler	.08
481	Checklist 1-121	.05
482	Checklist 122-242	.05
483	Checklist 243-363	.05
484	Checklist 364-484	.05

1989 Bowman Tiffany

A special collectors' version of the revitalized Bowman cards was produced in 1989, differing from the regular-issue cards in the application of a high-gloss finish to the front and the use of a white cardboard stock. The "Tiffany" version (as the glossies are known to collectors), was sold only in complete boxed sets, with an estimated production of 6,000 sets.

	MT
Complete (Sealed) Set (495):	800.00
Complete (Opened) Set (495):	150.00
Common Player:	.25
(Star/rookie cards valued at 4-5X regular-issue 1989 Bowman.)	

1989 Bowman Inserts

Bowman inserted sweepstakes cards in its 1989 packs. Each sweepstakes card reproduces a classic Bowman card on the front, with a prominent "REPRINT" notice. With one card in each pack, they are by no means scarce. A "Tiffany" version of the reprints was produced for inclusion in the factory set of 1989 Bowman cards. The glossy-front inserts are valued at 10X the standard version.

		MT
	Complete Set (11):	5.00
	Common Player:	.10
(1)	Richie Ashburn	.10
(2)	Yogi Berra	.15
(3)	Whitey Ford	.10
(4)	Gil Hodges	.10
(5)	Mickey Mantle (1951)	2.00
(6)	Mickey Mantle (1953)	1.00
(7)	Willie Mays	.50
(8)	Satchel Paige	.25
(9)	Jackie Robinson	.75
(10)	Duke Snider	.15
(11)	Ted Williams	.75

1990 Bowman

Bowman followed its 1989 rebirth with a 528-card set in 1990. The 1990 cards follow the classic Bowman style featuring a full-color photo bordered in white. The Bowman logo appears in the upper-left corner. The player's team nickname and name appear on the bottom border of the card photo. Unlike the 1989 set, the 1990 cards are standard 2-1/2" x 3-1/2". Backs are horizontal and display the player's statistics against the teams in his league. Included in the set are special insert cards featuring a painted image of a modern-day superstar done in the style of the 1951 Bowman cards. The paintings were produced for Bowman by artist Craig Pursley. Insert backs contain a sweepstakes offer with a chance to win a complete set of 11 lithographs made from these paintings.

		MT
	Complete Set (528):	20.00
	Common Player:	.05
	Wax Box:	20.00
1	*Tommy Greene*	.20
2	Tom Glavine	.15
3	Andy Nezelek	.05
4	Mike Stanton	.05
5	Rick Lueken	.05
6	Kent Mercker	.05
7	Derek Lilliquist	.05
8	Charlie Liebrandt	.05
9	Steve Avery	.10
10	John Smoltz	.15
11	Mark Lemke	.05
12	Lonnie Smith	.05
13	Oddibe McDowell	.05
14	*Tyler Houston*	.10
15	Jeff Blauser	.05
16	Ernie Whitt	.05
17	Alexis Infante	.05
18	Jim Presley	.05
19	Dale Murphy	.15
20	Nick Esasky	.05
21	Rick Sutcliffe	.05
22	Mike Bielecki	.05
23	Steve Wilson	.05
24	Kevin Blankenship	.05
25	Mitch Williams	.05
26	Dean Wilkins	.05
27	Greg Maddux	.75
28	Mike Harkey	.05
29	Mark Grace	.30
30	Ryne Sandberg	.40
31	Greg Smith	.05
32	Dwight Smith	.05
33	Damon Berryhill	.05
34	Earl Cunningham	.05
35	Jerome Walton	.05
36	Lloyd McClendon	.05
37	Ty Griffin	.05
38	Shawon Dunston	.10
39	Andre Dawson	.15
40	Luis Salazar	.05
41	Tim Layana	.05
42	Rob Dibble	.05
43	Tom Browning	.05
44	Danny Jackson	.05
45	Jose Rijo	.05
46	Scott Scudder	.05
47	Randy Myers	.08
48	Brian Lane	.05
49	Paul O'Neill	.08
50	Barry Larkin	.10
51	Reggie Jefferson	.10
52	Jeff Branson	.05
53	Chris Sabo	.05
54	Joe Oliver	.05
55	Todd Benzinger	.05
56	Rolando Roomes	.05
57	Hal Morris	.05
58	Eric Davis	.12
59	Scott Bryant	.05
60	Ken Griffey	.08
61	*Darryl Kile*	.30
62	Dave Smith	.05
63	Mark Portugal	.05
64	*Jeff Juden*	.20
65	Bill Gullickson	.05
66	Danny Darwin	.05
67	Larry Andersen	.05
68	Jose Cano	.05
69	Dan Schatzeder	.05
70	Jim Deshaies	.05
71	Mike Scott	.05
72	Gerald Young	.05
73	Ken Caminiti	.10
74	Ken Oberkfell	.05
75	Dave Rhode	.05
76	Bill Doran	.05
77	Andujar Cedeno	.05
78	Craig Biggio	.08
79	Karl Rhodes	.05
80	Glenn Davis	.05
81	*Eric Anthony*	.15
82	John Wetteland	.15
83	Jay Howell	.05
84	Orel Hershiser	.10
85	Tim Belcher	.05
86	Kiki Jones	.05
87	Mike Hartley	.05
88	Ramon Martinez	.08
89	Mike Scioscia	.05
90	Willie Randolph	.05
91	Juan Samuel	.05
92	*Jose Offerman*	.15
93	Dave Hansen	.05
94	Jeff Hamilton	.05
95	Alfredo Griffin	.05
96	Tom Goodwin	.05
97	Kirk Gibson	.05
98	Jose Vizcaino	.05
99	Kal Daniels	.05
100	Hubie Brooks	.05
101	Eddie Murray	.30
102	Dennis Boyd	.05
103	Tim Burke	.05
104	Bill Sampen	.05
105	Brett Gideon	.05
106	Mark Gardner	.05
107	Howard Farmer	.05
108	Mel Rojas	.05
109	Kevin Gross	.05
110	Dave Schmidt	.05
111	Denny Martinez	.08
112	Jerry Goff	.05
113	Andres Galarraga	.10
114	Tim Welch	.05
115	*Marquis Grissom*	.50
116	Spike Owen	.05
117	*Larry Walker*	1.50
118	Rock Raines	.08
119	*Delino DeShields*	.20
120	Tom Foley	.05
121	Dave Martinez	.05
122	Frank Viola	.05
123	Julio Valera	.05
124	Alejandro Pena	.05
125	David Cone	.08
126	Dwight Gooden	.10
127	Kevin Brown	.20
128	John Franco	.05
129	Terry Bross	.05
130	Blaine Beatty	.05
131	Sid Fernandez	.05
132	Mike Marshall	.05
133	Howard Johnson	.05
134	Jaime Roseboro	.05
135	Alan Zinter	.05
136	Keith Miller	.05
137	Kevin Elster	.05
138	Kevin McReynolds	.05
139	Barry Lyons	.05
140	Gregg Jefferies	.15
141	Darryl Strawberry	.12
142	*Todd Hundley*	.25
143	Scott Service	.05
144	Chuck Malone	.05
145	Steve Ontiveros	.05
146	Roger McDowell	.05
147	Ken Howell	.05
148	Pat Combs	.10
149	Jeff Parrett	.05
150	Chuck McElroy	.05
151	Jason Grimsley	.10
152	Len Dykstra	.05
153	Mickey Morandini	.05
154	John Kruk	.05
155	Dickie Thon	.05
156	Ricky Jordan	.05
157	Jeff Jackson	.05
158	Darren Daulton	.05
159	Tom Herr	.05
160	Von Hayes	.05
161	*Dave Hollins*	.20
162	Carmelo Martinez	.05
163	Bob Walk	.05
164	Doug Drabek	.05
165	Walt Terrell	.05
166	Bill Landrum	.05
167	Scott Ruskin	.05
168	Bob Patterson	.05
169	Bobby Bonilla	.10
170	Jose Lind	.05
171	Andy Van Slyke	.05
172	Mike LaValliere	.05
173	*Willie Greene*	.15
174	Jay Bell	.08
175	Sid Bream	.05
176	Tom Prince	.05
177	Wally Backman	.05
178	*Moises Alou*	.25
179	Steve Carter	.05
180	Gary Redus	.05
181	Barry Bonds	.50
182	Don Slaught	.05
183	Joe Magrane	.05
184	Bryn Smith	.05
185	Todd Worrell	.05
186	Jose Deleon	.05
187	Frank DiPino	.05
188	John Tudor	.05
189	Howard Hilton	.05
190	John Ericks	.05
191	Ken Dayley	.05
192	*Ray Lankford*	.40
193	Todd Zeile	.10
194	Willie McGee	.08
195	Ozzie Smith	.40
196	Milt Thompson	.05
197	Terry Pendleton	.05
198	Vince Coleman	.05
199	Paul Coleman	.05
200	Jose Oquendo	.05
201	Pedro Guerrero	.05
202	Tom Brunansky	.05
203	Roger Smithberg	.05
204	Eddie Whitson	.05
205	Dennis Rasmussen	.05
206	Craig Lefferts	.05
207	Andy Benes	.10
208	Bruce Hurst	.05
209	Eric Show	.05
210	Rafael Valdez	.05
211	Joey Cora	.05
212	Thomas Howard	.10
213	Rob Nelson	.05
214	Jack Clark	.05
215	Garry Templeton	.05
216	Fred Lynn	.08
217	Tony Gwynn	.50
218	Benny Santiago	.05
219	Mike Pagliarulo	.05
220	Joe Carter	.15
221	Roberto Alomar	.30
222	Bip Roberts	.05
223	Rick Reuschel	.05
224	Russ Swan	.05
225	Eric Gunderson	.05
226	Steve Bedrosian	.05
227	Mike Remlinger	.05
228	Scott Garrelts	.05
229	Ernie Camacho	.05
230	Andres Santana	.05
231	Will Clark	.20
232	Kevin Mitchell	.05
233	Robby Thompson	.05
234	Bill Bathe	.05
235	Tony Perezchica	.05
236	Gary Carter	.10
237	Brett Butler	.10
238	Matt Williams	.20
239	Ernie Riles	.05
240	Kevin Bass	.05
241	Terry Kennedy	.05
242	*Steve Hosey*	.10
243	*Ben McDonald*	.15
244	Jeff Ballard	.05
245	Joe Price	.05
246	Curt Schilling	.08
247	Pete Harnisch	.05
248	Mark Williamson	.05
249	Gregg Olson	.05
250	Chris Myers	.05
251	David Segui	.08
252	Joe Orsulak	.05
253	Craig Worthington	.05
254	Mickey Tettleton	.05
255	Cal Ripken, Jr.	.90
256	Billy Ripken	.05
257	Randy Milligan	.05
258	Brady Anderson	.10
259	*Chris Hoiles*	.20
260	Mike Devereaux	.05
261	Phil Bradley	.05
262	*Leo Gomez*	.10
263	Lee Smith	.08
264	Mike Rochford	.05
265	Jeff Reardon	.05
266	Wes Gardner	.05
267	Mike Boddicker	.05
268	Roger Clemens	.75
269	Rob Murphy	.05
270	Mickey Pina	.05
271	Tony Pena	.05

272	Jody Reed	.05
273	Kevin Romine	.05
274	Mike Greenwell	.05
275	*Mo Vaughn*	2.50
276	Danny Heep	.05
277	Scott Cooper	.05
278	*Greg Blosser*	.10
279	Dwight Evans	.05
280	Ellis Burks	.10
281	Wade Boggs	.40
282	Marty Barrett	.05
283	Kirk McCaskill	.05
284	Mark Langston	.05
285	Bert Blyleven	.08
286	Mike Fetters	.05
287	Kyle Abbott	.05
288	Jim Abbott	.12
289	Chuck Finley	.05
290	Gary DiSarcina	.05
291	Dick Schofield	.05
292	Devon White	.08
293	Bobby Rose	.05
294	Brian Downing	.05
295	Lance Parrish	.08
296	Jack Howell	.05
297	Claudell Washington	.05
298	John Orton	.05
299	Wally Joyner	.08
300	Lee Stevens	.05
301	Chili Davis	.08
302	Johnny Ray	.05
303	Greg Hibbard	.05
304	Eric King	.05
305	Jack McDowell	.10
306	Bobby Thigpen	.05
307	Adam Peterson	.05
308	*Scott Radinsky*	.10
309	Wayne Edwards	.05
310	Melido Perez	.05
311	Robin Ventura	.25
312	*Sammy Sosa*	5.00
313	Dan Pasqua	.05
314	Carlton Fisk	.25
315	Ozzie Guillen	.05
316	Ivan Calderon	.05
317	Daryl Boston	.05
318	Craig Grebeck	.05
319	Scott Fletcher	.05
320	*Frank Thomas*	3.00
321	Steve Lyons	.05
322	Carlos Martinez	.05
323	Joe Skalski	.05
324	Tom Candiotti	.05
325	Greg Swindell	.05
326	Steve Olin	.05
327	Kevin Wickander	.05
328	Doug Jones	.05
329	Jeff Shaw	.05
330	Kevin Bearse	.05
331	Dion James	.05
332	Jerry Browne	.05
333	Albert Belle	.75
334	Felix Fermin	.05
335	Candy Maldonado	.05
336	Cory Snyder	.05
337	Sandy Alomar	.12
338	Mark Lewis	.05
339	*Carlos Baerga*	.15
340	Chris James	.05
341	Brook Jacoby	.05
342	Keith Hernandez	.08
343	Frank Tanana	.05
344	Scott Aldred	.05
345	Mike Henneman	.05
346	Steve Wapnick	.05
347	Greg Gohr	.05
348	Eric Stone	.05
349	Brian DuBois	.05
350	Kevin Ritz	.05
351	Rico Brogna	.05
352	Mike Heath	.05
353	Alan Trammell	.10
354	Chet Lemon	.05
355	Dave Bergman	.05
356	Lou Whitaker	.08
357	Cecil Fielder	.10
358	Milt Cuyler	.05
359	Tony Phillips	.05
360	*Travis Fryman*	.35
361	Ed Romero	.05
362	Lloyd Moseby	.05
363	Mark Gubicza	.05
364	Bret Saberhagen	.08
365	Tom Gordon	.05
366	Steve Farr	.05
367	Kevin Appier	.08
368	Storm Davis	.05
369	Mark Davis	.05
370	Jeff Montgomery	.05
371	Frank White	.05
372	Brent Mayne	.05
373	Bob Boone	.05
374	Jim Eisenreich	.05
375	Danny Tartabull	.05
376	Kurt Stillwell	.05
377	Bill Pecota	.05
378	Bo Jackson	.15
379	*Bob Hamelin*	.15
380	Kevin Seitzer	.05
381	Rey Palacios	.05
382	George Brett	.50
383	Gerald Perry	.05
384	Teddy Higuera	.05
385	Tom Filer	.05
386	Dan Plesac	.05
387	*Cal Eldred*	.15
388	Jaime Navarro	.05
389	Chris Bosio	.05
390	Randy Veres	.05
391	Gary Sheffield	.12
392	George Canale	.05
393	B.J. Surhoff	.08
394	Tim McIntosh	.05
395	Greg Brock	.05
396	Greg Vaughn	.12
397	Darryl Hamilton	.05
398	Dave Parker	.10
399	Paul Molitor	.40
400	Jim Gantner	.05
401	Rob Deer	.05
402	Billy Spiers	.05
403	Glenn Braggs	.05
404	Robin Yount	.40
405	Rick Aguilera	.05
406	Johnny Ard	.05
407	*Kevin Tapani*	.15
408	Park Pittman	.05
409	Allan Anderson	.05
410	Juan Berenguer	.05
411	Willie Banks	.05
412	Rich Yett	.05
413	Dave West	.05
414	Greg Gagne	.05
415	*Chuck Knoblauch*	.75
416	Randy Bush	.05
417	Gary Gaetti	.08
418	Kent Hrbek	.08
419	Al Newman	.05
420	Danny Gladden	.05
421	Paul Sorrento	.05
422	Derek Parks	.05
423	Scott Leius	.08
424	Kirby Puckett	.60
425	Willie Smith	.05
426	Dave Righetti	.05
427	Jeff Robinson	.05
428	Alan Mills	.05
429	Tim Leary	.05
430	Pascual Perez	.05
431	Alvaro Espinoza	.05
432	Dave Winfield	.20
433	Jesse Barfield	.05
434	Randy Velarde	.05
435	Rick Cerone	.05
436	Steve Balboni	.05
437	Mel Hall	.05
438	Bob Geren	.05
439	*Bernie Williams*	1.50
440	Kevin Maas	.05
441	Mike Blowers	.05
442	Steve Sax	.05
443	Don Mattingly	.60
444	Roberto Kelly	.05
445	Mike Moore	.05
446	Reggie Harris	.05
447	Scott Sanderson	.05
448	Dave Otto	.05
449	Dave Stewart	.08
450	Rick Honeycutt	.05
451	Dennis Eckersley	.10
452	Carney Lansford	.05
453	Scott Hemond	.05
454	Mark McGwire	1.50
455	Felix Jose	.05
456	Terry Steinbach	.05
457	Rickey Henderson	.20
458	Dave Henderson	.05
459	Mike Gallego	.05
460	Jose Canseco	.30
461	Walt Weiss	.05
462	Ken Phelps	.05
463	*Darren Lewis*	.20
464	Ron Hassey	.05
465	*Roger Salkeld*	.10
466	Scott Bankhead	.05
467	Keith Comstock	.05
468	Randy Johnson	.35
469	Erik Hanson	.05
470	Mike Schooler	.05
471	Gary Eave	.05
472	Jeffrey Leonard	.05
473	Dave Valle	.05
474	Omar Vizquel	.08
475	Pete O'Brien	.05
476	Henry Cotto	.05
477	Jay Buhner	.10
478	Harold Reynolds	.08
479	Alvin Davis	.05
480	Darnell Coles	.05
481	Ken Griffey, Jr.	2.00
482	Greg Briley	.05
483	Scott Bradley	.05
484	Tino Martinez	.20
485	Jeff Russell	.05
486	Nolan Ryan	.75
487	Robb Nen	.05
488	Kevin Brown	.08
489	Brian Bohanon	.05
490	Ruben Sierra	.05
491	Pete Incaviglia	.05
492	*Juan Gonzalez*	4.00
493	Steve Buechele	.05
494	Scott Coolbaugh	.05
495	Geno Petralli	.05
496	Rafael Palmeiro	.12
497	Julio Franco	.08
498	Gary Pettis	.05
499	Donald Harris	.05
500	Monty Fariss	.05
501	Harold Baines	.08
502	Cecil Espy	.05
503	Jack Daugherty	.05
504	Willie Blair	.05
505	Dave Steib	.05
506	Tom Henke	.05
507	John Cerutti	.05
508	Paul Kilgus	.05
509	Jimmy Key	.08
510	*John Olerud*	.50
511	Ed Sprague	.05
512	Manny Lee	.05
513	Fred McGriff	.15
514	Glenallen Hill	.08
515	George Bell	.05
516	Mookie Wilson	.05
517	Luis Sojo	.05
518	Nelson Liriano	.05
519	Kelly Gruber	.05
520	Greg Myers	.05
521	Pat Borders	.05
522	Junior Felix	.05
523	Eddie Zosky	.12
524	Tony Fernandez	.08
525	Checklist	.05
526	Checklist	.05
527	Checklist	.05
528	Checklist	.05

1990 Bowman Tiffany

Reported production of fewer than 10,000 sets has created a significant premium for these glossy "Tiffany" versions of Bowman's 1990 baseball card set. The use of white cardboard stock and high-gloss front finish distinguishes these cards from regular-issue Bowmans.

	MT
Complete (Sealed) Set (539):	600.00
Complete (Opened) Set (539):	150.00
Common Player:	.25

(Star/rookie cards valued about 4-5X regular-issue 1990 Bowman.)

1990 Bowman Inserts

Bowman inserted sweepstakes cards in its 1990 packs, much like in 1989. This 11-card set features current players displayed in drawings by Craig Pursley.

		MT
Complete Set (11):		1.25
Common Player:		.05
(1)	Will Clark	.10
(2)	Mark Davis	.05
(3)	Dwight Gooden	.10
(4)	Bo Jackson	.10
(5)	Don Mattingly	.25
(6)	Kevin Mitchell	.05
(7)	Gregg Olson	.05
(8)	Nolan Ryan	.50
(9)	Bret Saberhagen	.05
(10)	Jerome Walton	.05
(11)	Robin Yount	.15

1990 Bowman Lithographs

The paintings which were the basis for the sweepstakes insert cards in 1990 Bowman were also used in the creation of a set of 11" x 14" lithographs. The lithographs were offered as a prize in the sweepstakes or could be purchased from hobby dealers for a retail price in the $400-450 rang

		MT
Complete Set (11):		250.00
Common Player:		10.00
(1)	Will Clark	20.00
(2)	Mark Davis	10.00
(3)	Dwight Gooden	20.00
(4)	Bo Jackson	20.00
(5)	Don Mattingly	50.00
(6)	Kevin Mitchell	10.00
(7)	Gregg Olson	10.00
(8)	Nolan Ryan	100.00
(9)	Bret Saberhagen	10.00
(10)	Jerome Walton	10.00
(11)	Robin Yount	25.00

1991 Bowman

The 1991 Bowman set features 704 cards compared to 528 cards in the 1990 issue. The cards imitate the 1953 Bowman style. Special Rod Carew cards and gold foil-stamped cards are included. The set is numbered by teams. Like the 1989 and 1990 issues, the card backs feature a breakdown of performance against each other team in the league.

		MT
Complete Set (704):		40.00
Common Player:		.05
Wax Box:		75.00
1	Rod Carew-I	.10
2	Rod Carew-II	.10
3	Rod Carew-III	.10
4	Rod Carew-IV	.10
5	Rod Carew-V	.10
6	Willie Fraser	.05
7	John Olerud	.15
8	William Suero	.05
9	Roberto Alomar	.30
10	Todd Stottlemyre	.08
11	Joe Carter	.10
12	*Steve Karsay*	.15
13	Mark Whiten	.05
14	Pat Borders	.05
15	Mike Timlin	.05
16	Tom Henke	.05
17	Eddie Zosky	.05
18	Kelly Gruber	.05
19	Jimmy Key	.08
20	Jerry Schunk	.05
21	Manny Lee	.05
22	Dave Steib	.05
23	Pat Hentgen	.08
24	Glenallen Hill	.05
25	Rene Gonzales	.05
26	Ed Sprague	.05
27	Ken Dayley	.05
28	Pat Tabler	.05
29	*Denis Boucher*	.08
30	Devon White	.08
31	Dante Bichette	.15
32	Paul Molitor	.35
33	Greg Vaughn	.08
34	Dan Plesac	.05
35	Chris George	.05
36	Tim McIntosh	.05
37	Franklin Stubbs	.05
38	Bo Dodson	.05
39	Ron Robinson	.05
40	Ed Nunez	.05
41	Greg Brock	.05
42	Jaime Navarro	.05
43	Chris Bosio	.05
44	B.J. Surhoff	.08
45	Chris Johnson	.05
46	Willie Randolph	.05
47	Narciso Elvira	.05
48	Jim Gantner	.05
49	Kevin Brown	.05
50	Julio Machado	.05
51	Chuck Crim	.05
52	Gary Sheffield	.20
53	Angel Miranda	.05
54	Teddy Higuera	.05
55	Robin Yount	.35
56	Cal Eldred	.05
57	Sandy Alomar	.15
58	Greg Swindell	.05
59	Brook Jacoby	.05
60	Efrain Valdez	.05
61	Ever Magallanes	.05
62	Tom Candiotti	.05
63	Eric King	.05
64	Alex Cole	.05
65	Charles Nagy	.08
66	Mitch Webster	.05
67	Chris James	.05
68	*Jim Thome*	2.50
69	Carlos Baerga	.08
70	Mark Lewis	.05
71	Jerry Browne	.05
72	Jesse Orosco	.05
73	Mike Huff	.05
74	Jose Escobar	.05
75	Jeff Manto	.05
76	*Turner Ward*	.10
77	Doug Jones	.05
78	*Bruce Egloff*	.05
79	Tim Costo	.05
80	Beau Allred	.05
81	Albert Belle	.40
82	John Farrell	.05
83	Glenn Davis	.05
84	Joe Orsulak	.05
85	Mark Williamson	.05
86	Ben McDonald	.08
87	Billy Ripken	.05
88	Leo Gomez	.05
89	Bob Melvin	.05
90	Jeff Robinson	.05
91	Jose Mesa	.05
92	Gregg Olson	.05
93	Mike Devereaux	.05
94	Luis Mercedes	.05
95	*Arthur Rhodes*	.20
96	Juan Bell	.05
97	*Mike Mussina*	3.00
98	Jeff Ballard	.05
99	Chris Hoiles	.05
100	Brady Anderson	.10
101	Bob Milacki	.05
102	David Segui	.05
103	Dwight Evans	.08
104	Cal Ripken, Jr.	1.25
105	Mike Linskey	.05
106	*Jeff Tackett*	.05
107	Jeff Reardon	.05
108	Dana Kiecker	.05
109	Ellis Burks	.08
110	Dave Owen	.05
111	Danny Darwin	.05
112	Mo Vaughn	.35
113	Jeff McNeely	.05
114	Tom Bolton	.05
115	Greg Blosser	.05
116	Mike Greenwell	.05
117	*Phil Plantier*	.15
118	Roger Clemens	.50
119	John Marzano	.05
120	Jody Reed	.05
121	Scott Taylor	.05
122	Jack Clark	.05
123	Derek Livernois	.05
124	Tony Pena	.05
125	Tom Brunansky	.05
126	Carlos Quintana	.05
127	Tim Naehring	.05
128	Matt Young	.05
129	Wade Boggs	.35
130	Kevin Morton	.05
131	Pete Incaviglia	.05
132	Rob Deer	.05
133	Bill Gullickson	.05
134	Rico Brogna	.05
135	Lloyd Moseby	.05
136	Cecil Fielder	.10
137	Tony Phillips	.05
138	Mark Leiter	.05
139	John Cerutti	.05
140	Mickey Tettleton	.05
141	Milt Cuyler	.05
142	Greg Gohr	.05
143	Tony Bernazard	.05
144	Dan Gakeler	.05
145	Travis Fryman	.10

146	Dan Petry	.05
147	Scott Aldred	.05
148	John DeSilva	.05
149	Rusty Meacham	.05
150	Lou Whitaker	.08
151	Dave Haas	.05
152	Luis de los Santos	.05
153	Ivan Cruz	.05
154	Alan Trammell	.12
155	Pat Kelly	.05
156	*Carl Everett*	2.50
157	Greg Cadaret	.05
158	Kevin Maas	.05
159	Jeff Johnson	.05
160	Willie Smith	.05
161	Gerald Williams	.08
162	Mike Humphreys	.05
163	Alvaro Espinoza	.05
164	Matt Nokes	.05
165	Wade Taylor	.05
166	Roberto Kelly	.05
167	John Habyan	.05
168	Steve Farr	.05
169	Jesse Barfield	.05
170	Steve Sax	.05
171	Jim Leyritz	.08
172	Robert Eenhoorn	.05
173	Bernie Williams	.30
174	Scott Lusader	.05
175	Torey Lovullo	.05
176	Chuck Cary	.05
177	Scott Sanderson	.05
178	Don Mattingly	.50
179	Mel Hall	.05
180	Juan Gonzalez	.60
181	Hensley Meulens	.05
182	Jose Offerman	.05
183	*Jeff Bagwell*	10.00
184	*Jeff Conine*	.25
185	*Henry Rodriguez*	.40
186	Jimmie Reese	.10
187	Kyle Abbott	.05
188	Lance Parrish	.08
189	Rafael Montalvo	.05
190	Floyd Bannister	.05
191	Dick Schofield	.05
192	Scott Lewis	.05
193	Jeff Robinson	.05
194	Kent Anderson	.05
195	Wally Joyner	.08
196	Chuck Finley	.05
197	Luis Sojo	.05
198	Jeff Richardson	.05
199	Dave Parker	.10
200	Jim Abbott	.12
201	Junior Felix	.05
202	Mark Langston	.08
203	*Tim Salmon*	3.00
204	Cliff Young	.05
205	Scott Bailes	.05
206	Bobby Rose	.05
207	Gary Gaetti	.08
208	Ruben Amaro	.05
209	Luis Polonia	.05
210	Dave Winfield	.25
211	Bryan Harvey	.05
212	Mike Moore	.05
213	Rickey Henderson	.20
214	Steve Chitren	.05
215	Bob Welch	.05
216	Terry Steinbach	.05
217	Ernie Riles	.05
218	*Todd Van Poppel*	.10
219	Mike Gallego	.05
220	Curt Young	.05
221	Todd Burns	.05
222	Vance Law	.05
223	Eric Show	.05
224	*Don Peters*	.05
225	Dave Stewart	.08
226	Dave Henderson	.05
227	Jose Canseco	.35
228	Walt Weiss	.05
229	Dann Howitt	.05
230	Willie Wilson	.05
231	Harold Baines	.08
232	Scott Hemond	.05
233	Joe Slusarski	.05
234	Mark McGwire	1.50
235	*Kirk Dressendorfer*	.12
236	*Craig Paquette*	.08
237	Dennis Eckersley	.10
238	Dana Allison	.05
239	Scott Bradley	.05
240	Brian Holman	.05
241	Mike Schooler	.05
242	Rich DeLucia	.05
243	Edgar Martinez	.05
244	Henry Cotto	.05
245	Omar Vizquel	.08
246a	Ken Griffey, Jr.	2.00
246b	Ken Griffey Sr. (should be #255)	.10
247	Jay Buhner	.08
248	Bill Krueger	.05
249	*Dave Fleming*	.15
250	*Patrick Lennon*	.10
251	Dave Valle	.05
252	Harold Reynolds	.08
253	Randy Johnson	.20
254	Scott Bankhead	.05
255	(Not issued, see #246b)	
256	Greg Briley	.05
257	Tino Martinez	.10
258	Alvin Davis	.05
259	Pete O'Brien	.05
260	Erik Hanson	.05
261	*Bret Boone*	.50
262	Roger Salkeld	.05
263	Dave Burba	.05
264	*Kerry Woodson*	.10
265	Julio Franco	.05
266	Dan Peltier	.05
267	Jeff Russell	.05
268	Steve Buechele	.05
269	Donald Harris	.05
270	Robb Nen	.08
271	Rich Gossage	.08
272	*Ivan Rodriguez*	6.00
273	Jeff Huson	.05
274	Kevin Brown	.10
275	*Dan Smith*	.10
276	Gary Pettis	.05
277	Jack Daugherty	.05
278	Mike Jeffcoat	.05
279	Brad Arnsberg	.05
280	Nolan Ryan	.75
281	Eric McCray	.05
282	Scott Chiamparino	.05
283	Ruben Sierra	.05
284	Geno Petralli	.05
285	Monty Fariss	.05
286	Rafael Palmeiro	.20
287	Bobby Witt	.05
288	Dean Palmer	.10
289	Tony Scruggs	.05
290	Kenny Rogers	.08
291	Bret Saberhagen	.08
292	*Brian McRae*	.20
293	Storm Davis	.05
294	Danny Tartabull	.05
295	David Howard	.05
296	Mike Boddicker	.05
297	Joel Johnston	.05
298	Tim Spehr	.05
299	Hector Wagner	.05
300	George Brett	.40
301	Mike Macfarlane	.05
302	Kirk Gibson	.05
303	Harvey Pulliam	.05
304	Jim Eisenreich	.05
305	Kevin Seitzer	.05
306	Mark Davis	.05
307	Kurt Stillwell	.05
308	Jeff Montgomery	.05
309	Kevin Appier	.05
310	Bob Hamelin	.08
311	Tom Gordon	.05
312	*Kerwin Moore*	.05
313	Hugh Walker	.05
314	Terry Shumpert	.05
315	Warren Cromartie	.05
316	Gary Thurman	.05
317	Steve Bedrosian	.05
318	Danny Gladden	.05
319	Jack Morris	.08
320	Kirby Puckett	.45
321	Kent Hrbek	.08
322	Kevin Tapani	.08
323	Denny Neagle	.05
324	Rich Garces	.05
325	Larry Casian	.05
326	Shane Mack	.05
327	Allan Anderson	.05
328	Junior Ortiz	.05
329	*Paul Abbott*	.08
330	Chuck Knoblauch	.20
331	Chili Davis	.08
332	*Todd Ritchie*	.05
333	Brian Harper	.05
334	Rick Aguilera	.05
335	Scott Erickson	.08
336	Pedro Munoz	.05
337	Scott Leuis	.05
338	Greg Gagne	.05
339	Mike Pagliarulo	.05
340	Terry Leach	.05
341	Willie Banks	.05
342	Bobby Thigpen	.05
343	*Roberto Hernandez*	.20
344	Melido Perez	.05
345	Carlton Fisk	.20
346	*Norberto Martin*	.08
347	*Johnny Ruffin*	.05
348	*Jeff Carter*	.05
349	Lance Johnson	.05
350	Sammy Sosa	1.00
351	Alex Fernandez	.15
352	Jack McDowell	.08
353	Bob Wickman	.05
354	Wilson Alvarez	.05
355	Charlie Hough	.05
356	Ozzie Guillen	.05
357	Cory Snyder	.05
358	Robin Ventura	.15
359	Scott Fletcher	.05
360	Cesar Bernhardt	.05
361	Dan Pasqua	.05
362	Tim Raines	.08
363	Brian Drahman	.05
364	Wayne Edwards	.05
365	Scott Radinsky	.05
366	Frank Thomas	1.50
367	Cecil Fielder	.10
368	Julio Franco	.08
369	Kelly Gruber	.05
370	Alan Trammell	.12
371	Rickey Henderson	.25
372	Jose Canseco	.25
373	Ellis Burks	.10
374	Lance Parrish	.08
375	Dave Parker	.08
376	Eddie Murray	.25
377	Ryne Sandberg	.25
378	Matt Williams	.15
379	Barry Larkin	.08
380	Barry Bonds	.40
381	Bobby Bonilla	.08
382	Darryl Strawberry	.08
383	Benny Santiago	.05
384	Don Robinson	.05
385	Paul Coleman	.05
386	Milt Thompson	.05
387	Lee Smith	.08
388	Ray Lankford	.15
389	Tom Pagnozzi	.05
390	Ken Hill	.05
391	Jamie Moyer	.05
392	*Greg Carmona*	.05
393	John Ericks	.05
394	Bob Tewksbury	.05
395	Jose Oquendo	.05
396	Rheal Cormier	.05
397	*Mike Milchin*	.05
398	Ozzie Smith	.40
399	*Aaron Holbert*	.08
400	Jose DeLeon	.05
401	Felix Jose	.05
402	Juan Agosto	.05
403	Pedro Guerrero	.08
404	Todd Zeile	.08
405	Gerald Perry	.05
406	Not issued	
407	Bryn Smith	.05
408	Bernard Gilkey	.08
409	Rex Hudler	.05
410a	Ralph Branca, Bobby Thomson	.10
410b	Donovan Osborne	.08
411	Lance Dickson	.05
412	Danny Jackson	.05
413	Jerome Walton	.05
414	Sean Cheetham	.05
415	Joe Girardi	.05
416	Ryne Sandberg	.25
417	Mike Harkey	.05
418	George Bell	.05
419	*Rick Wilkins*	.25
420	Earl Cunningham	.05
421	Heathcliff Slocumb	.05
422	Mike Bielecki	.05
423	*Jessie Hollins*	.08
424	Shawon Dunston	.08
425	Dave Smith	.05
426	Greg Maddux	.60
427	Jose Vizcaino	.05
428	Luis Salazar	.05
429	Andre Dawson	.10
430	Rick Sutcliffe	.05
431	Paul Assenmacher	.05
432	Erik Pappas	.05
433	Mark Grace	.25
434	Denny Martinez	.08
435	Marquis Grissom	.12
436	*Wil Cordero*	.20
437	Tim Wallach	.05
438	*Brian Barnes*	.05
439	Barry Jones	.05
440	Ivan Calderon	.05
441	*Stan Spencer*	.05
442	Larry Walker	.35
443	*Chris Haney*	.08
444	Hector Rivera	.05
445	Delino DeShields	.08
446	Andres Galarraga	.10
447	Gilberto Reyes	.05
448	Willie Greene	.05
449	Greg Colbrunn	.05
450	*Rondell White*	.60
451	Steve Frey	.05
452	*Shane Andrews*	.12
453	Mike Fitzgerald	.05
454	Spike Owen	.05
455	Dave Martinez	.05
456	Dennis Boyd	.05
457	Eric Bullock	.05
458	*Reid Cornelius*	.10
459	Chris Nabholz	.05
460	David Cone	.08
461	Hubie Brooks	.05
462	Sid Fernandez	.05
463	*Doug Simons*	.08
464	Howard Johnson	.05
465	Chris Donnels	.05
466	Anthony Young	.10
467	Todd Hundley	.10
468	Rick Cerone	.05
469	Kevin Elster	.05
470	Wally Whitehurst	.05
471	Vince Coleman	.05
472	Dwight Gooden	.10
473	Charlie O'Brien	.05
474	*Jeromy Burnitz*	1.50
475	John Franco	.05
476	Daryl Boston	.05
477	Frank Viola	.05
478	D.J. Dozier	.05
479	Kevin McReynolds	.05
480	Tom Herr	.05
481	Gregg Jefferies	.08
482	Pete Schourek	.05
483	Ron Darling	.05
484	Dave Magadan	.05
485	*Andy Ashby*	.10
486	Dale Murphy	.12
487	Von Hayes	.05
488	*Kim Batiste*	.08
489	*Tony Longmire*	.10
490	Wally Backman	.05
491	Jeff Jackson	.05
492	Mickey Morandini	.05
493	Darrel Akerfelds	.05
494	Ricky Jordan	.05
495	Randy Ready	.05
496	Darrin Fletcher	.05
497	Chuck Malone	.05
498	Pat Combs	.05
499	Dickie Thon	.05
500	Roger McDowell	.05
501	Len Dykstra	.05
502	Joe Boever	.05
503	John Kruk	.05
504	Terry Mulholland	.08
505	Wes Chamberlain	.05
506	*Mike Lieberthal*	.25
507	Darren Daulton	.05
508	Charlie Hayes	.05
509	John Smiley	.05
510	Gary Varsho	.05
511	Curt Wilkerson	.05
512	*Orlando Merced*	.20
513	Barry Bonds	.40
514	Mike Lavalliere	.05
515	Doug Drabek	.05
516	Gary Redus	.05
517	*William Pennyfeather*	.05
518	Randy Tomlin	.05
519	*Mike Zimmerman*	.05
520	Jeff King	.05
521	*Kurt Miller*	.10
522	Jay Bell	.08
523	Bill Landrum	.05
524	Zane Smith	.05
525	Bobby Bonilla	.10
526	Bob Walk	.05
527	Austin Manahan	.05
528	*Joe Ausanio*	.05
529	Andy Van Slyke	.05
530	Jose Lind	.05
531	*Carlos Garcia*	.15
532	Don Slaught	.05
533	Colin Powell	.25
534	*Frank Bolick*	.05
535	*Gary Scott*	.05
536	Nikco Riesgo	.05
537	*Reggie Sanders*	.40
538	*Tim Howard*	.05
539	*Ryan Bowen*	.10
540	Eric Anthony	.05
541	Jim Deshaies	.05
542	Tom Nevers	.05
543	Ken Caminiti	.10
544	Karl Rhodes	.05
545	Xavier Hernandez	.05
546	Mike Scott	.05
547	Jeff Juden	.08
548	Darryl Kile	.05
549	Willie Ansley	.05
550	*Luis Gonzalez*	.35
551	*Mike Simms*	.08
552	Mark Portugal	.05
553	Jimmy Jones	.05
554	Jim Clancy	.05
555	Pete Harnisch	.05
556	Craig Biggio	.10
557	Eric Yelding	.05
558	Dave Rohde	.05
559	Casey Candaele	.05
560	Curt Schilling	.08
561	Steve Finley	.05
562	Javier Ortiz	.05
563	Andujar Cedeno	.05
564	Rafael Ramirez	.05
565	*Kenny Lofton*	2.00
566	Steve Avery	.05
567	Lonnie Smith	.05
568	Kent Mercker	.05
569	*Chipper Jones*	15.00
570	Terry Pendleton	.05
571	Otis Nixon	.05
572	Juan Berenguer	.05
573	Charlie Leibrandt	.05
574	Dave Justice	.20
575	Keith Mitchell	.05
576	Tom Glavine	.15
577	Greg Olson	.05
578	Rafael Belliard	.05
579	Ben Rivera	.05
580	John Smoltz	.10
581	Tyler Houston	.05
582	*Mark Wohlers*	.15
583	Ron Gant	.10
584	Ramon Caraballo	.05
585	Sid Bream	.05
586	Jeff Treadway	.05
587	*Javier Lopez*	2.00
588	Deion Sanders	.15
589	Mike Heath	.05
590	*Ryan Klesko*	1.50
591	Bob Ojeda	.05
592	Alfredo Griffin	.05
593	*Raul Mondesi*	5.00
594	Greg Smith	.05
595	Orel Hershiser	.08
596	Juan Samuel	.05
597	Brett Butler	.08
598	Gary Carter	.10
599	Stan Javier	.05
600	Kal Daniels	.05
601	*Jamie McAndrew*	.10
602	Mike Sharperson	.05
603	Jay Howell	.05
604	*Eric Karros*	.40
605	Tim Belcher	.05
606	Dan Opperman	.05
607	Lenny Harris	.05
608	Tom Goodwin	.08
609	Darryl Strawberry	.10
610	Ramon Martinez	.08
611	Kevin Gross	.05
612	Zakary Shinall	.05
613	Mike Scioscia	.05
614	Eddie Murray	.35
615	Ronnie Walden	.05
616	Will Clark	.25
617	Adam Hyzdu	.05
618	Matt Williams	.20
619	Don Robinson	.05
620	Jeff Brantley	.05
621	Greg Litton	.05
622	Steve Decker	.05
623	Robby Thompson	.05
624	*Mark Leonard*	.08
625	Kevin Bass	.05
626	Scott Garrelts	.05
627	Jose Uribe	.05
628	Eric Gunderson	.05
629	Steve Hosey	.05
630	Trevor Wilson	.05
631	Terry Kennedy	.05
632	Dave Righetti	.05
633	Kelly Downs	.05
634	Johnny Ard	.05
635	*Eric Christopherson*	.10
636	Kevin Mitchell	.05
637	John Burkett	.05
638	*Kevin Rogers*	.10
639	Bud Black	.05
640	Willie McGee	.08
641	Royce Clayton	.08
642	Tony Fernandez	.08
643	Ricky Bones	.05
644	Thomas Howard	.05
645	Dave Staton	.05
646	Jim Presley	.05
647	Tony Gwynn	.50
648	Marty Barrett	.05
649	Scott Coolbaugh	.05
650	Craig Lefferts	.05
651	Eddie Whitson	.05
652	Oscar Azocar	.05
653	Wes Gardner	.05
654	Bip Roberts	.05
655	*Robbie Beckett*	.08
656	Benny Santiago	.05
657	Greg W. Harris	.05
658	Jerald Clark	.05
659	Fred McGriff	.20
660	Larry Andersen	.05
661	Bruce Hurst	.05
662	Steve Martin	.05
663	Rafael Valdez	.05
664	*Paul Faries*	.05
665	Andy Benes	.08
666	Randy Myers	.08
667	Rob Dibble	.05
668	Glenn Sutko	.05
669	Glenn Braggs	.05
670	Billy Hatcher	.05
671	Joe Oliver	.05
672	Freddie Benavides	.05
673	Barry Larkin	.10
674	Chris Sabo	.05
675	Mariano Duncan	.05
676	*Chris Jones*	.10
677	*Gino Minutelli*	.05
678	Reggie Jefferson	.05
679	Jack Armstrong	.05
680	Chris Hammond	.05
681	Jose Rijo	.05
682	Bill Doran	.05
683	Terry Lee	.05
684	Tom Browning	.05
685	Paul O'Neill	.10
686	Eric Davis	.12
687	*Dan Wilson*	.15
688	Ted Power	.05
689	Tim Layana	.05
690	Norm Charlton	.05
691	Hal Morris	.05
692	Rickey Henderson	.20
693	*Sam Militello*	.08
694	*Matt Mieske*	.10
695	*Paul Russo*	.05
696	*Domingo Mota*	.05
697	*Todd Guggiana*	.05
698	Marc Newfield	.05
699	Checklist	.05
700	Checklist	.05
701	Checklist	.05
702	Checklist	.05
703	Checklist	.05
704	Checklist	.05

The election of former players to the Hall of Fame does not always have an immediate upward effect on card prices. The hobby market generally has done a good job of predicting those inductions and adjusting values over the course of several years.

1992 Bowman

Topps introduced several changes with the release of its 1992 Bowman set. The 705-card set features 45 special insert cards stamped with gold foil. The cards are printed with a premium UV coated glossy card stock. Several players without major league experience are featured in the set. Included in this group are 1991 MVP's of the minor leagues and first round draft choices. Eighteen of the gold-foil enchanced cards have been identified as short-prints (designated SP in the listings), printed in quantities one-half the other foils.

		MT
Complete Set (705):		325.00
Common Player:		.20
Wax Box:		240.00
1	Ivan Rodriguez	3.00
2	Kirk McCaskill	.20
3	Scott Livingstone	.25
4	*Salomon Torres*	.20
5	Carlos Hernandez	.20
6	Dave Hollins	.30
7	Scott Fletcher	.20
8	Jorge Fabregas	.25
9	Andujar Cedeno	.20
10	Howard Johnson	.25
11	*Trevor Hoffman*	2.50
12	Roberto Kelly	.20
13	Gregg Jefferies	.35
14	Marquis Grissom	.40
15	Mike Ignasiak	.20
16	Jack Morris	.25
17	William Pennyfeather	.20
18	Todd Stottlemyre	.25
19	Chito Martinez	.20
20	Roberto Alomar	2.50
21	Sam Militello	.20
22	Hector Fajardo	.20
23	*Paul Quantrill*	.40
24	Chuck Knoblauch	.40
25	Reggie Jefferson	.25
26	Jeremy McGarity	.20
27	Jerome Walton	.20
28	Chipper Jones	50.00
29	*Brian Barber*	.45
30	Ron Darling	.20
31	*Roberto Petagine*	.20
32	Chuck Finley	.20
33	Edgar Martinez	.30
34	Napolean Robinson	.20
35	Andy Van Slyke	.20
36	Bobby Thigpen	.20
37	Travis Fryman	.30
38	Eric Christopherson	.20
39	Terry Mulholland	.25
40	Darryl Strawberry	.35
41	*Manny Alexander*	.60
42	*Tracey Sanders*	.25
43	Pete Incaviglia	.20
44	Kim Batiste	.20
45	Frank Rodriguez	.25
46	Greg Swindell	.20
47	Delino DeShields	.20
48	John Ericks	.20
49	Franklin Stubbs	.20
50	Tony Gwynn	4.00
51	*Clifton Garrett*	.25
52	Mike Gardella	.20
53	Scott Erickson	.25
54	Gary Caballo	.20
55	*Jose Oliva*	.30
56	Brook Fordyce	.20
57	Mark Whiten	.20
58	Joe Slusarski	.20
59	*J.R. Phillips*	.50
60	Barry Bonds	3.00
61	Bob Milacki	.20
62	Keith Mitchell	.20
63	Angel Miranda	.20
64	Raul Mondesi	12.00
65	Brian Koelling	.20
66	Brian McRae	.30
67	John Patterson	.20
68	John Wetteland	.25
69	Wilson Alvarez	.25
70	Wade Boggs	1.00
71	Darryl Ratliff	.20
72	Jeff Jackson	.20
73	Jeremy Hernandez	.25
74	Darryl Hamilton	.25
75	Rafael Belliard	.20
76	Ricky Trlicek	.20
77	*Felipe Crespo*	.45
78	Carney Lansford	.20
79	Ryan Long	.20
80	Kirby Puckett	3.00
81	Earl Cunningham	.20
82	Pedro Martinez	30.00
83	Scott Hatteberg	.25
84	Juan Gonzalez	5.00
85	Robert Nutting	.20
86	*Calvin Reese*	2.00
87	Dave Silvestri	.20
88	*Scott Ruffcorn*	1.00
89	Rick Aguilera	.20
90	Cecil Fielder	.30
91	Kirk Dressendorfer	.20
92	Jerry DiPoto	.20
93	Mike Felder	.20
94	Craig Paquette	.25
95	Elvin Paulino	.20
96	Donovan Osborne	.20
97	Hubie Brooks	.20
98	*Derek Lowe*	.25
99	David Zancanaro	.20
100	Ken Griffey, Jr.	12.00
101	Todd Hundley	1.50
102	Mike Trombley	.25
103	*Ricky Gutierrez*	.50
104	Braulio Castillo	.20
105	Craig Lefferts	.20
106	Rick Sutcliffe	.20
107	Dean Palmer	.40
108	Henry Rodriguez	.75
109	*Mark Clark*	2.00
110	Kenny Lofton	6.00
111	Mark Carreon	.20
112	*J.T. Bruett*	.20
113	Gerald Williams	.25
114	Frank Thomas	5.00
115	Kevin Reimer	.20
116	Sammy Sosa	5.00
117	Mickey Tettleton	.20
118	Reggie Sanders	.30
119	Trevor Wilson	.20
120	Cliff Brantley	.20
121	Spike Owen	.20
122	Jeff Montgomery	.20
123	Alex Sutherland	.20
124	*Brien Taylor*	.35
125	Brian Williams	.25
126	Kevin Seitzer	.20
127	*Carlos Delgado*	20.00
128	Gary Scott	.20
129	Scott Cooper	.20
130	*Domingo Jean*	.20
131	*Pat Mahomes*	.50
132	Mike Boddicker	.20
133	Roberto Hernandez	.35
134	Dave Valle	.20
135	Kurt Stillwell	.20
136	*Brad Pennington*	.50
137	Jermaine Swifton	.20
138	Ryan Hawblitzel	.20
139	Tito Navarro	.20
140	Sandy Alomar	.35
141	Todd Benzinger	.20
142	Danny Jackson	.20
143	*Melvin Nieves*	1.00
144	Jim Campanis	.20
145	Luis Gonzalez	.25
146	Dave Doorneweerd	.20
147	Charlie Hayes	.20
148	Greg Maddux	7.00
149	Brian Harper	.20
150	Brent Miller	.20
151	*Shawn Estes*	2.00
152	Mike Williams	.20
153	Charlie Hough	.20
154	Randy Myers	.25
155	*Kevin Young*	3.00
156	Rick Wilkins	.20
157	Terry Schumpert	.20
158	Steve Karsay	.30
159	Gary DiSarcina	.20
160	Deion Sanders	1.50
161	Tom Browning	.20
162	Dickie Thon	.20
163	Luis Mercedes	.20
164	Ricardo Ingram	.20
165	*Tavo Alavarez*	.50
166	Rickey Henderson	.50
167	Jaime Navarro	.20
168	*Billy Ashley*	1.00
169	Phil Dauphin	.20
170	Ivan Cruz	.20
171	Harold Baines	.25
172	Bryan Harvey	.20
173	Alex Cole	.20
174	Curtis Shaw	.20
175	Matt Williams	1.50
176	Felix Jose	.20
177	Sam Horn	.20
178	Randy Johnson	1.50
179	Ivan Calderon	.20
180	Steve Avery	.25
181	William Suero	.20
182	Bill Swift	.20
183	*Howard Battle*	.80
184	Ruben Amaro	.20
185	Jim Abbott	.35
186	Mike Fitzgerald	.20
187	Bruce Hurst	.20
188	Jeff Juden	.50
189	Jeromy Burnitz	6.00
190	Dave Burba	.20
191	Kevin Brown	.20
192	Patrick Lennon	.20
193	Jeffrey McNeely	.20
194	Wil Cordero	.25
195	Chili Davis	.25
196	Milt Cuyler	.20
197	Von Hayes	.20
198	Todd Revening	.20
199	Joel Johnson	.20
200	Jeff Bagwell	5.00
201	Alex Fernandez	.50
202	Todd Jones	.20
203	Charles Nagy	.30
204	Tim Raines	.30
205	Kevin Maas	.20
206	Julio Franco	.25
207	Randy Velarde	.20
208	Lance Johnson	.20
209	Scott Leius	.20
210	Derek Lee	.30
211	Joe Sondrini	.20
212	Royce Clayton	.25
213	Chris George	.20
214	Gary Sheffield	1.00
215	Mark Gubicza	.20
216	Mike Moore	.20
217	Rick Huisman	.20
218	Jeff Russell	.20
219	D.J. Dozier	.20
220	Dave Martinez	.20
221	Al Newman	.20
222	Nolan Ryan	8.00
223	Teddy Higuera	.20
224	*Damon Buford*	.45
225	Ruben Sierra	.20
226	Tom Nevers	.20
227	Tommy Greene	.30
228	*Nigel Wilson*	.40
229	John DeSilva	.20
230	Bobby Witt	.20
231	Greg Cadaret	.20
232	John VanderWal	.20
233	Jack Clark	.20
234	Bill Doran	.20
235	Bobby Bonilla	.35
236	Steve Olin	.20
237	Derek Bell	.35
238	David Cone	.45
239	Victor Cole	.20
240	Rod Bolton	.20
241	Tom Pagnozzi	.20
242	Rob Dibble	.20
243	Michael Carter	.20
244	Don Peters	.20
245	Mike LaValliere	.20
246	Joe Perona	.20
247	Mitch Williams	.20
248	Jay Buhner	.35
249	Andy Benes	.30
250	*Alex Ochoa*	1.00
251	Greg Blosser	.20
252	Jack Armstrong	.20
253	Juan Samuel	.20
254	Terry Pendleton	.20
255	Ramon Martinez	.25
256	Rico Brogna	.25
257	John Smiley	.20
258	Carl Everett	.30
259	Tim Salmon	7.00
260	Will Clark	.75
261	*Ugueth Urbina*	1.50
262	Jason Wood	.20
263	Dave Magadan	.20
264	Dante Bichette	.90
265	Jose DeLeon	.20
266	*Mike Neill*	.30
267	Paul O'Neill	.35
268	Anthony Young	.25
269	Greg Harris	.20
270	Todd Van Poppel	.25
271	Pete Castellano	.20
272	Tony Phillips	.25
273	Mike Gallego	.20
274	*Steve Cooke*	.25
275	Robin Ventura	.35
276	Kevin Mitchell	.20
277	Doug Linton	.20
278	Robert Eenhorn	.20
279	*Gabe White*	.50
280	Dave Stewart	.30
281	Mo Sanford	.20
282	Greg Perschke	.20
283	Kevin Flora	.20
284	Jeff Williams	.20
285	Keith Miller	.20
286	Andy Ashby	.20
287	Doug Dascenzo	.20
288	Eric Karros	.50
289	*Glenn Murray*	.25
290	*Troy Percival*	1.00
291	Orlando Merced	.20
292	Peter Hoy	.20
293	Tony Fernandez	.25
294	Juan Guzman	.20
295	Jesse Barfield	.20
296	Sid Fernandez	.20
297	Scott Cepicky	.20
298	*Garret Anderson*	4.00
299	Cal Eldred	.20
300	Ryne Sandberg	1.25
301	Jim Gantner	.20
302	*Mariano Rivera*	10.00
303	Ron Lockett	.20
304	Jose Offerman	.20
305	Denny Martinez	.25
306	*Luis Ortiz*	.25
307	David Howard	.20
308	Russ Springer	.40
309	Chris Howard	.20
310	Kyle Abbott	.25
311	*Aaron Sele*	4.00
312	Dave Justice	.60
313	Pete O'Brien	.20
314	Greg Hansell	.20
315	Dave Winfield	.60
316	Lance Dickson	.20
317	Eric King	.20
318	Vaughn Eshelman	.20
319	Tim Belcher	.20
320	Andres Galarraga	.45
321	Scott Bullett	.20
322	Doug Strange	.20
323	Jerald Clark	.20
324	Dave Righetti	.20
325	Greg Hibbard	.20
326	Eric Dillman	.20
327	*Shane Reynolds*	5.00
328	Chris Hammond	.20
329	Albert Belle	3.00
330	*Rich Becker*	.50
331	Eddie Williams	.20
332	Donald Harris	.20
333	Dave Smith	.20
334	Steve Fireovid	.20
335	Steve Buechele	.20
336	Mike Schooler	.20
337	Kevin McReynolds	.20
338	Hensley Meulens	.20
339	*Benji Gil*	.90
340	Don Mattingly	2.50
341	Alvin Davis	.20
342	Alan Mills	.20
343	Kelly Downs	.20
344	Leo Gomez	.20
345	*Tarrik Brock*	.20
346	Ryan Turner	.50
347	John Smoltz	.50
348	Bill Sampen	.20
349	Paul Byrd	.20
350	Mike Bordick	.20
351	Jose Lind	.20
352	David Wells	.35
353	Barry Larkin	.40
354	Bruce Ruffin	.20
355	Luis Rivera	.20
356	Sid Bream	.20
357	Julian Vasquez	.20
358	*Jason Bere*	.75
359	Ben McDonald	.25
360	Scott Stahoviak	.20
361	Kirt Manwaring	.20
362	Jeff Johnson	.20
363	Rob Deer	.20
364	Tony Pena	.20
365	Melido Perez	.20
366	Clay Parker	.20
367	Dale Sveum	.20
368	Mike Scioscia	.20
369	Roger Salkeld	.25
370	Mike Stanley	.20
371	Jack McDowell	.25
372	Tim Wallach	.20
373	Billy Ripken	.20
374	Mike Christopher	.20
375	Paul Molitor	1.00
376	Dave Stieb	.20
377	Pedro Guerrero	.20
378	Russ Swan	.20
379	Bob Ojeda	.20
380	Donn Pall	.20
381	Eddie Zosky	.30
382	Darnell Coles	.20
383	Tom Smith	.20
384	Mark McGwire	8.00
385	Gary Carter	.35
386	Rich Amaral	.20
387	Alan Embree	.20
388	Jonathan Hurst	.20
389	*Bobby Jones*	1.00
390	Rico Rossy	.20
391	Dan Smith	.35
392	Terry Steinbach	.20
393	Jon Farrell	.20
394	Dave Anderson	.20
395	Benito Santiago	.30
396	Mark Wohlers	.20
397	Mo Vaughn	3.50
398	Randy Kramer	.20
399	*John Jaha*	3.00
400	Cal Ripken, Jr.	7.50
401	Ryan Bowen	.40
402	Tim McIntosh	.20
403	Bernard Gilkey	.30
404	Junior Felix	.20
405	Cris Colon	.20
406	Marc Newfield	.50
407	Bernie Williams	3.00
408	Jay Howell	.20
409	Zane Smith	.20
410	Jeff Shaw	.20
411	Kerry Woodson	.20
412	Wes Chamberlain	.20
413	Dave Mlicki	.20
414	Benny Distefano	.20
415	Kevin Rogers	.20
416	Tim Naehring	.20
417	Clemente Nunez	.30
418	Luis Sojo	.20
419	Kevin Ritz	.20
420	Omar Oliveras	.20
421	Manuel Lee	.20
422	Julio Valera	.20
423	Omar Vizquel	.30
424	Darren Burton	.20
425	Mel Hall	.20
426	Dennis Powell	.20
427	Lee Stevens	.20
428	Glenn Davis	.20
429	Willie Greene	.30
430	Kevin Wickander	.20
431	Dennis Eckersley	.30
432	Joe Orsulak	.20
433	Eddie Murray	.75
434	*Matt Stairs*	4.00
435	Wally Joyner	.30
436	Rondell White	6.00
437	Rob Mauer	.20
438	Joe Redfield	.20
439	Mark Lewis	.20
440	Darren Daulton	.20
441	Mike Henneman	.20
442	John Cangelosi	.20
443	*Vince Moore*	.25
444	John Wehner	.20
445	Kent Hrbek	.30
446	Mark McLemore	.20
447	Bill Wegman	.20
448	Robby Thompson	.20
449	Mark Anthony	.20
450	Archi Cianfrocco	.20
451	Johnny Ruffin	.20
452	Javier Lopez	8.00
453	Greg Gohr	.20
454	Tim Scott	.20
455	Stan Belinda	.20
456	Darrin Jackson	.20
457	Chris Gardner	.20
458	Esteban Beltre	.20
459	Phil Plantier	.20
460	Jim Thome	15.00
461	*Mike Piazza*	50.00
462	Matt Sinatro	.20
463	Scott Servais	.30
464	*Brian Jordan*	4.00
465	Doug Drabek	.20
466	Carl Willis	.20
467	Bret Barbarie	.20
468	Hal Morris	.25
469	Steve Sax	.20
470	Jerry Willard	.20
471	Dan Wilson	.25
472	Chris Hoiles	.20
473	Rheal Cormier	.20
474	John Morris	.20
475	Jeff Reardon	.20
476	Mark Leiter	.20
477	Tom Gordon	.20
478	*Kent Bottenfield*	2.00
479	Gene Larkin	.20
480	Dwight Gooden	.45
481	B.J. Surhoff	.25
482	Andy Stankiewicz	.20
483	Tino Martinez	1.00
484	Craig Biggio	.50
485	Denny Neagle	.25
486	Rusty Meacham	.20
487	Kal Daniels	.20
488	Dave Henderson	.20
489	Tim Costo	.20
490	Doug Davis	.20
491	Frank Viola	.20
492	Cory Snyder	.20
493	Chris Martin	.20
494	Dion James	.20
495	Randy Tomlin	.20
496	Greg Vaughn	.25
497	Dennis Cook	.20
498	Rosario Rodriguez	.20
499	Dave Staton	.20
500	George Brett	3.00
501	Brian Barnes	.20
502	Butch Henry	.20
503	Harold Reynolds	.25
504	*David Nied*	.25
505	Lee Smith	.30
506	Steve Chitren	.20
507	Ken Hill	.20
508	Robbie Beckett	.20
509	Troy Afenir	.20
510	Kelly Gruber	.20
511	Bret Boone	.30
512	Jeff Branson	.25
513	Mike Jackson	.20
514	Pete Harnisch	.20
515	Chad Kreuter	.20
516	Joe Vitko	.20
517	Orel Hershiser	.25
518	*John Doherty*	.30
519	Jay Bell	.30
520	Mark Langston	.25
521	Dann Howitt	.20
522	Bobby Reed	.20
523	Roberto Munoz	.20
524	Todd Ritchie	.20
525	Bip Roberts	.20
526	*Pat Listach*	.40
527	*Scott Brosius*	4.00
528	*John Roper*	.35
529	*Phil Hiatt*	.40
530	Denny Walling	.20
531	Carlos Baerga	.25
532	*Manny Ramirez*	50.00
533	Pat Clements	.20
534	Ron Gant	.30
535	Pat Kelly	.20
536	Billy Spiers	.20
537	Darren Reed	.30
538	Ken Caminiti	.40

539	*Butch Huskey*	2.50
540	Matt Nokes	.20
541	John Kruk	.20
542	John Jaha (Foil, SP)	1.00
543	*Justin Thompson*	2.00
544	Steve Hosey	.35
545	Joe Kmak	.20
546	John Franco	.20
547	Devon White	.30
548	Elston Hansen (Foil, SP)	.25
549	Ryan Klesko	4.00
550	Danny Tartabull	.20
551	Frank Thomas (Foil, SP)	5.00
552	Kevin Tapani	.20
553a	Willie Banks	.20
553b	Pat Clements	.20
554	*B.J. Wallace* (Foil, SP)	.50
555	*Orlando Miller*	.35
556	*Mark Smith*	.25
557	Tim Wallach (Foil)	.30
558	Bill Gullickson	.20
559	Derek Bell (Foil)	1.50
560	Joe Randa (Foil)	.50
561	Frank Seminara	.20
562	Mark Gardner	.20
563	Rick Greene (Foil)	.60
564	Gary Gaetti	.25
565	Ozzie Guillen	.20
566	Charles Nagy (Foil)	.40
567	Mike Milchin	.20
568	Ben Shelton (Foil)	.40
569	Chris Roberts (Foil)	.50
570	Ellis Burks	.25
571	Scott Scudder	.20
572	Jim Abbott (Foil)	.45
573	Joe Carter	.30
574	Steve Finley	.20
575	Jim Olander (Foil)	.25
576	Carlos Garcia	.20
577	Greg Olson	.20
578	Greg Swindell (Foil)	.25
579	Matt Williams (Foil)	1.00
580	Mark Grace	.40
581	Howard House (Foil)	.20
582	Luis Polonia	.20
583	Erik Hanson	.20
584	Salomon Torres (Foil)	.25
585	Carlton Fisk	.40
586	Bret Saberhagen	.25
587	*Chad McDonnell* (Foil)	.30
588	Jimmy Key	.25
589	Mike MacFarlane	.20
590	Barry Bonds (Foil)	3.00
591	Jamie McAndrew	.40
592	Shane Mack	.20
593	Kerwin Moore	.20
594	Joe Oliver	.20
595	Chris Sabo	.20
596	*Alex Gonzalez*	2.00
597	Brett Butler	.30
598	Mark Hutton	.20
599	Andy Benes (Foil)	.80
600	Jose Canseco	.75
601	Darryl Kile	.50
602	Matt Stairs (Foil, SP)	.30
603	Rob Butler (Foil)	.25
604	Willie McGee	.25
605	Jack McDowell	.25
606	Tom Candiotti	.20
607	Ed Martel	.20
608	Matt Mieske (Foil)	.50
609	Darrin Fletcher	.20
610	Rafael Palmeiro	.40
611	Bill Swift (Foil)	.30
612	Mike Mussina	4.00
613	Vince Coleman	.20
614	Scott Cepicky (Foil)	.30
615	Mike Greenwell	.20
616	Kevin McGehee	.20
617	Jeffrey Hammonds (Foil)	2.00
618	Scott Taylor	.30
619	Dave Otto	.20
620	Mark McGwire (Foil)	8.00
621	Kevin Tatar	.20
622	Steve Farr	.20
623	Ryan Klesko (Foil)	1.50
625	Andre Dawson	.60
626	Tino Martinez (Foil, SP)	1.00
627	*Chad Curtis*	.75
628	Mickey Morandini	.20
629	Gregg Olson (Foil, SP)	.50
630	Lou Whitaker	.25
631	Arthur Rhodes	.25
632	Brandon Wilson	.20
633	*Lance Jennings*	.30
634	*Allen Watson*	.05
635	Len Dykstra	.25
636	Joe Girardi	.20
637	Kiki Hernandez (Foil, SP)	.30
638	*Mike Hampton*	6.00
639	Al Osuna	.20
640	Kevin Appier	.25
641	Rick Helling (Foil, SP)	.30
642	Jody Reed	.20
643	Ray Lankford	.35
644	John Olerud	.50
645	Paul Molitor (Foil, SP)	1.50
646	Pat Borders	.20
647	Mike Morgan	.20
648	Larry Walker	2.00
649	Pete Castellano (Foil, SP)	.30
650	Fred McGriff	.60
651	Walt Weiss	.20
652	*Calvin Murray* (Foil, SP)	1.00
653	Dave Nilsson	.20
654	Greg Pirkl	.20
655	Robin Ventura (Foil, SP)	.50
656	Mark Portugal	.20
657	Roger McDowell	.20
658	Rick Hirtensteiner (Foil, SP)	.30
659	Glenallen Hill	.20
660	Greg Gagne	.20
661	Charles Johnson (Foil, SP)	4.00
662	Brian Hunter	.40
663	Mark Lemke	.20
664	Tim Belcher (Foil, SP)	.40
665	Rich DeLucia	.20
666	Bob Walk	.20
667	Joe Carter (Foil, SP)	1.00
668	Jose Guzman	.20
669	Otis Nixon	.20
670	Phil Nevin (Foil)	.40
671	Eric Davis	.30
672	*Damion Easley*	1.00
673	Will Clark (Foil)	.75
674	Mark Kiefer	.20
675	Ozzie Smith	1.25
676	Manny Ramirez (Foil)	10.00
677	Gregg Olson	.20
678	*Cliff Floyd*	3.00
679	Duane Singleton	.25
680	Jose Rijo	.20
681	Willie Randolph	.20
682	*Michael Tucker* (Foil)	4.00
683	Darren Lewis	.20
684	Dale Murphy	.35
685	Mike Pagliarulo	.20
686	Paul Miller	.20
687	Mike Robertson	.20
688	Mike Devereaux	.20
689	Pedro Astacio	.60
690	Alan Trammell	.40
691	Roger Clemens	4.00
692	Bud Black	.20
693	Turk Wendell	.30
694	Barry Larkin (Foil, SP)	1.50
695	Todd Zeile	.20
696	Pat Hentgen	.25
697	*Eddie Taubensee*	.40
698	Guillermo Vasquez	.20
699	Tom Glavine	.35
700	Robin Yount	1.00
701	Checklist	.20
702	Checklist	.20
703	Checklist	.20
704	Checklist	.20
705	Checklist	.20

1993 Bowman

Bowman's 708-card 1993 set once again features a premium UV-coated glossy stock. There are also 48 special insert cards, with gold foil stamping, randomly inserted one per pack or two per jumbo pack. The foil cards, numbered 339-374 and 693-704, feature top prospects and rookie-of-the-year candidates, as do several regular cards in the set. Cards are standard size.

		MT
Complete Set (708):		95.00
Common Player:		.10
Wax Box:		60.00
1	Glenn Davis	.10
2	*Hector Roa*	.15
3	*Ken Ryan*	.25
4	*Derek Wallace*	.20
5	Jorge Fabregas	.10
6	Joe Oliver	.10
7	Brandon Wilson	.15
8	*Mark Thompson*	.40
9	Tracy Sanders	.10
10	Rich Renteria	.10
11	Lou Whitaker	.15
12	*Brian Hunter*	1.00
13	Joe Vitiello	.20
14	Eric Karros	.25
15	Joe Kmak	.10
16	Tavo Alvarez	.10
17	*Steve Dunn*	.30
18	Tony Fernandez	.12
19	Melido Perez	.10
20	Mike Lieberthal	.20
21	Terry Steinbach	.10
22	Stan Belinda	.10
23	Jay Buhner	.15
24	Allen Watson	.10
25	*Daryl Henderson*	.25
26	*Ray McDavid*	.25
27	Shawn Green	2.00
28	Bud Black	.10
29	*Sherman Obando*	.25
30	*Mike Hostetler*	.10
31	*Nate Hinchey*	.20
32	Randy Myers	.10
33	*Brian Grebeck*	.20
34	John Roper	.10
35	Larry Thomas	.10
36	Alex Cole	.10
37	*Tom Kramer*	.15
38	*Matt Whisenant*	.25
39	*Chris Gomez*	.40
40	Luis Gonzalez	.12
41	Kevin Appier	.12
42	*Omar Daal*	3.00
43	Duane Singleton	.10
44	Bill Risley	.10
45	*Pat Meares*	.25
46	Butch Huskey	.15
47	Bobby Munoz	.10
48	Juan Bell	.10
49	*Scott Lydy*	.25
50	Dennis Moeller	.10
51	Marc Newfield	.10
52	*Tripp Cromer*	.20
53	Kurt Miller	.10
54	Jim Pena	.10
55	Juan Guzman	.10
56	Matt Williams	.45
57	Harold Reynolds	.12
58	*Donnie Elliott*	.15
59	*Jon Shave*	.25
60	*Kevin Roberson*	.20
61	*Hilly Hathaway*	.15
62	Jose Rijo	.10
63	*Kerry Taylor*	.20
64	Ryan Hawblitzel	.10
65	Glenallen Hill	.10
66	*Ramon D. Martinez*	.20
67	Travis Fryman	.15
68	Tom Nevers	.10
69	Phil Hiatt	.12
70	Tim Wallach	.10
71	B.J. Surhoff	.12
72	Rondell White	.65
73	*Denny Hocking*	.20
74	*Mike Oquist*	.25
75	Paul O'Neill	.20
76	Willie Banks	.10
77	Bob Welch	.10
78	*Jose Sandoval*	.20
79	Bill Haselman	.10
80	Rheal Cormier	.10
81	Dean Palmer	.15
82	*Pat Gomez*	.25
83	Steve Karsay	.15
84	*Carl Hanselman*	.20
85	*T.R. Lewis*	.25
86	Chipper Jones	5.00
87	Scott Hatteberg	.20
88	Greg Hibbard	.10
89	*Lance Painter*	.20
90	*Chad Mottola*	.40
91	Jason Bere	.25
92	Dante Bichette	.35
93	Sandy Alomar	.15
94	Carl Everett	.15
95	*Danny Bautista*	.25
96	Steve Finley	.10
97	David Cone	.20
98	Todd Hollandsworth	.50
99	Matt Mieske	.10
100	Larry Walker	.75
101	Shane Mack	.10
102	*Aaron Ledesma*	.20
103	*Andy Pettitte*	4.00
104	Kevin Stocker	.10
105	Mike Mobler	.10
106	Tony Menedez	.10
107	Derek Lowe	.10
108	Basil Shabazz	.10
109	Dan Smith	.10
110	*Scott Sanders*	.25
111	Todd Stottlemyre	.10
112	*Benji Sikonton*	.25
113	Rick Sutcliffe	.10
114	*Lee Heath*	.15
115	Jeff Russell	.10
116	*Dave Stevens*	.20
117	*Mark Holzemer*	.20
118	Tim Belcher	.10
119	Bobby Thigpen	.10
120	*Roger Bailey*	.20
121	*Tony Mitchell*	.25
122	Junior Felix	.10
123	*Rich Robertson*	.20
124	*Andy Cook*	.20
125	*Brian Bevil*	.25
126	Darryl Strawberry	.25
127	Cal Eldred	.10
128	Cliff Floyd	.20
129	Alan Newman	.10
130	Howard Johnson	.10
131	Jim Abbott	.15
132	Chad McConnell	.10
133	*Miguel Jimenez*	.20
134	*Brett Backlund*	.20
135	*John Cummings*	.30
136	Brian Barber	.10
137	Rafael Palmeiro	.20
138	*Tim Worrell*	.20
139	*Jose Pett*	.20
140	Barry Bonds	1.00
141	Damon Buford	.10
142	Jeff Blauser	.10
143	Frankie Rodriguez	.15
144	Mike Morgan	.10
145	Gary DeSarcina	.10
146	Calvin Reese	.10
147	Johnny Ruffin	.10
148	David Nied	.10
149	Charles Nagy	.12
150	*Mike Myers*	.20
151	*Kenny Carlyle*	.20
152	Eric Anthony	.10
153	Jose Lind	.10
154	Pedro Martinez	3.00
155	Mark Kiefer	.10
156	*Tim Laker*	.20
157	Pat Mahomes	.10
158	Bobby Bonilla	.15
159	Domingo Jean	.10
160	Darren Daulton	.10
161	Mark McGwire	6.00
162	*Jason Kendall*	5.00
163	Desi Relaford	.25
164	Ozzie Canseco	.10
165	Rick Helling	.10
166	*Steve Pegues*	.20
167	Paul Molitor	.40
168	*Larry Carter*	.20
169	Arthur Rhodes	.10
170	*Damon Hollins*	.40
171	Frank Viola	.10
172	*Steve Trachsel*	1.50
173	*J.T. Snow*	1.50
174	*Keith Gordon*	.20
175	Carlton Fisk	.15
176	*Jason Bates*	.20
177	*Mike Crosby*	.20
178	Benny Santiago	.10
179	Mike Moore	.10
180	Jeff Juden	.20
181	Darren Burton	.10
182	*Todd Williams*	.20
183	John Jaha	.10
184	*Mike Lansing*	.75
185	*Pedro Grifol*	.20
186	Vince Coleman	.10
187	Pat Kelly	.10
188	*Clemente Alvarez*	.20
189	Ron Darling	.10
190	Orlando Merced	.10
191	Chris Bosio	.10
192	*Steve Dixon*	.20
193	Doug Dascenzo	.10
194	*Ray Holbert*	.25
195	Howard Battle	.10
196	Willie McGee	.12
197	*John O'Donoghue*	.20
198	Steve Avery	.10
199	Greg Blosser	.10
200	Ryne Sandberg	.75
201	Joe Grahe	.10
202	Dan Wilson	.10
203	*Domingo Martinez*	.20
204	Andres Galarraga	.20
205	*Jamie Taylor*	.20
206	*Darrell Whitmore*	.25
207	*Ben Blomdahl*	.20
208	Doug Drabek	.10
209	Keith Miller	.10
210	Billy Ashley	.20
211	*Mike Farrell*	.20
212	John Wetteland	.10
213	Randy Tomlin	.10
214	Sid Fernandez	.10
215	*Quilvio Veras*	.25
216	Dave Hollins	.15
217	Mike Neill	.10
218	Andy Van Slyke	.10
219	Bret Boone	.20
220	Tom Pagnozzi	.10
221	*Mike Welch*	.20
222	Frank Seminara	.10
223	Ron Villone	.10
224	*D.J. Thielen*	.25
225	Cal Ripken, Jr.	4.00
226	*Pedro Borbon*	.20
227	Carlos Quintana	.10
228	*Tommy Shields*	.20
229	Tim Salmon	.60
230	John Smiley	.10
231	Ellis Burks	.15
232	Pedro Castellano	.10
233	Paul Byrd	.10
234	Bryan Harvey	.10
235	Scott Livingstone	.10
236	*James Mouton*	.35
237	Joe Randa	.15
238	Pedro Astacio	.15
239	Darryl Hamilton	.10
240	*Joey Eischen*	.40
241	*Edgar Herrera*	.20
242	Dwight Gooden	.15
243	Sam Militello	.10
244	*Ron Blazier*	.20
245	Ruben Sierra	.10
246	Al Martin	.10
247	Mike Felder	.10
248	Bob Tewksbury	.10
249	Craig Lefferts	.10
250	Luis Lopez	.10
251	Devon White	.12
252	Will Clark	.35
253	Mark Smith	.15
254	Terry Pendleton	.10
255	Aaron Sele	.25
256	*Jose Viera*	.15
257	Damion Easley	.15
258	*Rod Lofton*	.20
259	*Chris Snopek*	.40
260	*Quinton McCracken*	1.00
261	*Mike Matthews*	.25
262	*Hector Carrasco*	.40
263	Rick Greene	.10
264	*Chris Bolt*	.25
265	George Brett	1.00
266	*Rick Gorecki*	.25
267	*Francisco Gamez*	.15
268	Marquis Grissom	.15
269	Kevin Tapani	.10
270	Ryan Thompson	.15
271	Gerald Williams	.12
272	*Paul Fletcher*	.20
273	Lance Blankenship	.10
274	*Marty Neff*	.20
275	Shawn Estes	.50
276	*Rene Arocha*	.25
277	*Scott Eyre*	.25
278	Phil Plantier	.10
279	*Paul Spoljaric*	.30
280	Chris Gahbs	.10
281	Harold Baines	.12
282	*Jose Oliva*	.15
283	Matt Whiteside	.15
284	*Brant Brown*	2.00
285	Russ Springer	.10
286	Chris Sabo	.10
287	Ozzie Guillen	.10
288	*Marcus Moore*	.20
289	Chad Ogea	.25
290	Walt Weiss	.10
291	Brian Edmondson	.10
292	Jimmy Gonzalez	.10
293	*Danny Miceli*	.30
294	Jose Offerman	.10
295	Greg Vaughn	.15
296	Frank Bolick	.10
297	*Mike Maksudian*	.25
298	John Franco	.10
299	Danny Tartabull	.10
300	Len Dykstra	.10
301	Bobby Witt	.10
302	*Trey Beamon*	.90
303	Tino Martinez	.25
304	Aaron Holbert	.10
305	Juan Gonzalez	1.50
306	*Billy Hall*	.25
307	Duane Ward	.10
308	Rod Beck	.10
309	*Jose Mercedes*	.25
310	Otis Nixon	.10
311	*Gettys Glaze*	.25
312	Candy Maldonado	.10
313	Chad Curtis	.15
314	Tim Costo	.10
315	Mike Robertson	.10
316	Nigel Wilson	.10
317	*Greg McMichael*	.25
318	*Scott Pose*	.20
319	Ivan Cruz	.10
320	Greg Swindell	.10
321	Kevin McReynolds	.10
322	Tom Candiotti	.10
323	*Bob Wishnevski*	.20
324	Ken Hill	.10
325	Kirby Puckett	1.00
326	*Tim Bogar*	.20
327	Mariano Rivera	.45
328	Mitch Williams	.10
329	Craig Paquette	.10
330	Jay Bell	.15
331	*Jose Martinez*	.35
332	Rob Deer	.10
333	Brook Fordyce	.10
334	Matt Nokes	.10
335	Derek Lee	.15
336	*Paul Ellis*	.20
337	*Desi Wilson*	.15
338	Roberto Alomar	.75
339	Jim Tatum (Foil)	.20
340	J.T. Snow (Foil)	.30
341	Tim Salmon (Foil)	.75
342	*Russ Davis* (Foil)	1.00
343	Javier Lopez (Foil)	.60
344	*Troy O'Leary* (Foil)	.75
345	*Marty Cordova* (Foil)	2.50
346	*Bubba Smith* (Foil)	.25
347	Chipper Jones (Foil)	5.00
348	Jessie Hollins (Foil)	.20
349	Willie Greene (Foil)	.25
350	Mark Thompson (Foil)	.30
351	Nigel Wilson (Foil)	.25
352	Todd Jones (Foil)	.20
353	Raul Mondesi (Foil)	.90
354	Cliff Floyd (Foil)	.40
355	Bobby Jones (Foil)	.30
356	Kevin Stocker (Foil)	.20
357	Midre Cummings (Foil)	.35
358	Allen Watson (Foil)	.20
359	Ray McDavid (Foil)	.30
360	Steve Hosey (Foil)	.25

361	Brad Pennington (Foil)	.25
362	Frankie Rodriguez (Foil)	.25
363	Troy Percival (Foil)	.25
364	Jason Bere (Foil)	.25
365	Manny Ramirez (Foil)	4.00
366	Justin Thompson (Foil)	.50
367	Joe Vitello (Foil)	.25
368	Tyrone Hill (Foil)	.20
369	David McCarty (Foil)	.15
370	Brien Taylor (Foil)	.20
371	Todd Van Poppel (Foil)	.15
372	Marc Newfield (Foil)	.25
373	*Terrell Lowery* (Foil)	.50
374	Alex Gonzalez (Foil)	.40
375	Ken Griffey, Jr.	5.00
376	Donovan Osborne	.10
377	*Ritchie Moody*	.15
378	Shane Andrews	.30
379	Carlos Delgado	1.00
380	Bill Swift	.10
381	Leo Gomez	.10
382	Ron Gant	.15
383	Scott Fletcher	.10
384	*Matt Walbeck*	.15
385	Chuck Finley	.10
386	Kevin Mitchell	.10
387	Wilson Alvarez	.10
388	*John Burke*	.25
389	Alan Embree	.10
390	Trevor Hoffman	.20
391	Alan Trammell	.15
392	Todd Jones	.10
393	Felix Jose	.10
394	Orel Hershiser	.15
395	Pat Listach	.10
396	Gabe White	.10
397	*Dan Serafini*	.30
398	Todd Hundley	.15
399	Wade Boggs	.50
400	Tyler Green	.10
401	Mike Bordick	.10
402	Scott Bullett	.10
403	*Lagrande Russell*	.20
404	Ray Lankford	.15
405	Nolan Ryan	3.00
406	Robbie Beckett	.10
407	*Brent Bowers*	.20
408	*Adell Davenport*	.20
409	Brady Anderson	.25
410	Tom Glavine	.15
411	*Doug Hecker*	.25
412	Jose Guzman	.10
413	Luis Polonia	.10
414	Brian Williams	.10
415	Bo Jackson	.20
416	Eric Young	.15
417	Kenny Lofton	.90
418	Orestes Destrade	.10
419	Tony Phillips	.10
420	Jeff Bagwell	1.00
421	Hark Gardner	.10
422	Brett Butler	.15
423	*Graeme Lloyd*	.15
424	Delino DeShields	.10
425	Scott Erickson	.10
426	Jeff Kent	.10
427	Jimmy Key	.10
428	Mickey Morandini	.10
429	*Marcos Arkas*	.25
430	Don Slaught	.10
431	Randy Johnson	.45
432	Omar Olivares	.10
433	Charlie Leibrandt	.10
434	Kurt Stillwell	.10
435	*Scott Brow*	.15
436	Robby Thompson	.10
437	Ben McDonald	.15
438	Deion Sanders	.50
439	Tony Pena	.10
440	Mark Grace	.35
441	Eduardo Perez	.10
442	*Tim Pugh*	.30
443	Scott Ruffcorn	.10
444	*Jay Gainer*	.20
445	Albert Belle	1.00
446	Bret Barberie	.10
447	Justin Mashore	.10
448	Pete Harnisch	.10
449	Greg Gagne	.10
450	Eric Davis	.15
451	Dave Mlicki	.10
452	Moises Alou	.15
453	Rick Aguilera	.10
454	Eddie Murray	.50
455	Bob Wickman	.10
456	Wes Chamberlain	.10
457	Brent Gates	.10
458	Paul Weber	.10
459	Mike Hampton	.10
460	Ozzie Smith	.50
461	Tom Henke	.10
462	Ricky Gutuerrez	.10
463	Jack Morris	.12
464	*Joel Chimelis*	.20
465	Gregg Olson	.10
466	Javier Lopez	.40
467	Scott Cooper	.10
468	Willie Wilson	.12
469	Mark Langston	.10
470	Barry Larkin	.20
471	Rod Bolton	.10
472	Freddie Benavides	.10
473	*Ken Ramos*	.20
474	Chuck Carr	.10
475	Cecil Fielder	.25
476	Eddie Taubensee	.10
477	*Chris Eddy*	.25
478	Greg Hansell	.10
479	Kevin Reimer	.10
480	Denny Martinez	.12
481	Chuck Knoblauch	.25
482	Mike Draper	.10
483	Spike Owen	.10
484	Terry Mulholland	.10
485	Dennis Eckersley	.12
486	Blas Minor	.10
487	Dave Fleming	.10
488	Dan Cholonsky	.10
489	Ivan Rodriguez	.75
490	Gary Sheffield	.25
491	Ed Sprague	.10
492	Steve Hosey	.10
493	*Jimmy Haynes*	.50
494	John Smoltz	.25
495	Andre Dawson	.25
496	Rey Sanchez	.10
497	*Ty Van Burkleo*	.20
498	*Bobby Ayala*	.40
499	Tim Raines	.15
500	Charlie Hayes	.10
501	Paul Sorrento	.10
502	*Richie Lewis*	.30
503	*Jason Pfaff*	.15
504	Ken Caminiti	.25
505	Mike Macfarlane	.10
506	Jody Reed	.10
507	*Bobby Hughes*	.75
508	Wil Cordero	.10
509	*George Tsanis*	.20
510	Bret Saberhagen	.12
511	*Derek Jeter*	30.00
512	Gene Schall	.30
513	Curtis Shaw	.10
514	Steve Cooke	.10
515	Edgar Martinez	.15
516	Mike Milchin	.10
517	Billy Ripken	.10
518	Andy Benes	.12
519	*Juan de la Rosa*	.20
520	John Burkett	.10
521	Alex Ochoa	.20
522	*Tony Tarasco*	.25
523	Luis Ortiz	.10
524	Rick Williams	.10
525	*Chris Turner*	.20
526	Rob Dibble	.10
527	Jack McDowell	.12
528	Daryl Boston	.10
529	*Bill Wertz*	.20
530	Charlie Hough	.10
531	Sean Bergman	.15
532	Doug Jones	.10
533	Jeff Montgomery	.10
534	*Roger Cedeno*	1.00
535	Robin Yount	.50
536	Mo Vaughn	.75
537	Brian Harper	.10
538	Juan Castillo	.10
539	Steve Farr	.10
540	John Kruk	.10
541	Troy Neel	.15
542	*Danny Clyburn*	.30
543	*Jim Converse*	.25
544	Gregg Jefferies	.15
545	Jose Canseco	.40
546	*Julio Bruno*	.25
547	Rob Butler	.10
548	Royce Clayton	.10
549	Chris Hoiles	.10
550	Greg Maddux	2.50
551	*Joe Ciccarella*	.25
552	Ozzie Timmons	.10
553	Chili Davis	.12
554	Brian Koelling	.10
555	Frank Thomas	2.00
556	Vinny Castilla	1.00
557	Reggie Jefferson	.10
558	Rob Natal	.10
559	Mike Henneman	.10
560	Craig Biggio	.20
561	*Billy Brewer*	.20
562	Dan Melendez	.10
563	*Kenny Felder*	.40
564	*Miguel Batista*	.25
565	Dave Winfield	.30
566	Al Shirley	.10
567	Robert Eenhoorn	.10
568	Mike Williams	.10
569	*Tanyon Sturtze*	.25
570	Tim Wakefield	.10
571	Greg Pirkl	.10
572	*Sean Lowe*	.40
573	*Terry Burows*	.15
574	*Kevin Higgins*	.25
575	Joe Carter	.20
576	Kevin Rogers	.10
577	Manny Alexander	.10
578	Dave Justice	.35
579	*Brian Conroy*	.15
580	*Jessie Hollins*	.20
581	*Ron Watson*	.20
582	Bip Roberts	.10
583	*Tom Urbani*	.15
584	*Jason Hutchins*	.25
585	Carlos Baerga	.20
586	Jeff Mutis	.10
587	Justin Thompson	.30
588	Orlando Miller	.15
589	Brian McRae	.15
590	Ramon Martinez	.12
591	Dave Nilsson	.10
592	*Jose Vidro*	.35
593	Rich Becker	.10
594	*Preston Wilson*	2.50
595	Don Mattingly	1.25
596	Tony Longmire	.10
597	Kevin Seitzer	.10
598	*Midre Cummings*	.45
599	Omar Vizquel	.15
600	Lee Smith	.12
601	*David Hulse*	.15
602	*Darrell Sherman*	.20
603	Alex Gonzalez	.25
604	Geronimo Pena	.10
605	Mike Devereaux	.10
606	*Sterling Hitchcock*	.40
607	Mike Greenwell	.10
608	Steve Buechele	.10
609	Troy Percival	.10
610	Bobby Kelly	.10
611	*James Baldwin*	.75
612	Jerald Clark	.10
613	*Albie Lopez*	.25
614	Dave Magadan	.10
615	Mickey Tettleton	.10
616	*Sean Runyan*	.25
617	Bob Hamelin	.10
618	Raul Mondesi	1.00
619	Tyrone Hill	.20
620	Darrin Fletcher	.10
621	Mike Trombley	.10
622	Jeromy Burnitz	.15
623	Bernie Williams	.60
624	*Mike Farmer*	.20
625	Rickey Henderson	.45
626	Carlos Garcia	.10
627	*Jeff Darwin*	.25
628	Todd Zeile	.15
629	Benji Gil	.10
630	Tony Gwynn	2.00
631	*Aaron Small*	.25
632	*Joe Rosselli*	.25
633	Mike Mussina	.50
634	Ryan Klesko	.50
635	Roger Clemens	2.00
636	Sammy Sosa	3.00
637	*Orlando Palmeiro*	.20
638	Willie Greene	.10
639	George Bell	.10
640	*Garvin Alston*	.30
641	*Pete Janicki*	.25
642	*Chris Sheff*	.25
643	*Felipe Lira*	.40
644	Roberto Petagine	.10
645	Wally Joyner	.12
646	Mike Piazza	3.00
647	Jaime Navarro	.10
648	*Jeff Hartsock*	.25
649	David McCarty	.15
650	Bobby Jones	.20
651	Mark Hutton	.10
652	Kyle Abbott	.10
653	*Steve Cox*	.50
654	Jeff King	.10
655	Norm Charlton	.10
656	*Mike Gulan*	.25
657	Julio Franco	.10
658	*Cameron Cairncross*	.25
659	John Olerud	.35
660	Salomon Torres	.10
661	Brad Pennington	.10
662	Melvin Nieves	.10
663	Ivan Calderon	.10
664	Turk Wendell	.10
665	Chris Pritchett	.10
666	Reggie Sanders	.15
667	Robin Ventura	.25
668	Joe Girardi	.10
669	Manny Ramirez	3.00
670	Jeff Conine	.15
671	Greg Gohr	.10
672	Andujar Cedeno	.10
673	*Les Norman*	.15
674	*Mike James*	.20
675	*Marshall Boze*	.30
676	B.J. Wallace	.15
677	Kent Hrbek	.12
678	Jack Voight	.10
679	Brien Taylor	.15
680	Curt Schilling	.15
681	Todd Van Poppel	.12
682	Kevin Young	.15
683	Tommy Adams	.10
684	Bernard Gilkey	.12
685	Kevin Brown	.10
686	Fred McGriff	.30
687	Pat Borders	.10
688	Kirt Manwaring	.10
689	Sid Bream	.10
690	John Valentin	.15
691	*Steve Olsen*	.20
692	*Roberto Mejia*	.25
693	Carlos Delgado (Foil)	1.00
694	*Steve Gibralter* (Foil)	.40
695	Gary Mota (Foil)	.25
696	*Jose Malave* (Foil)	.75
697	*Larry Sutton* (Foil)	.75
698	*Dan Frye* (Foil)	.25
699	*Tim Clark* (Foil)	.30
700	*Brian Rupp* (Foil)	.25
701	Felipe Alou, Moises Alou (Foil)	.25
702	Bobby Bonds, Barry Bonds (Foil)	.75
703	Ken Griffey Sr., Ken Griffey Jr. (Foil)	1.50
704	Hal McRae, Brian McRae (Foil)	.25
705	Checklist 1	.10
706	Checklist 2	.10
707	Checklist 3	.10
708	Checklist 4	.10

1994 Bowman Previews

Bowman Preview cards were randomly inserted into Stadium Club 1994 Baseball Series II at a rate of one every 24 packs. This 10-card set featured several proven major league stars, as well as minor league players. Card number 10, James Mouton, is designed as a special MVP foil card.

		MT
Complete Set (10):		35.00
Common Player:		2.00
1	Frank Thomas	10.00
2	Mike Piazza	7.50
3	Albert Belle	5.00
4	Javier Lopez	4.00
5	Cliff Floyd	2.50
6	Alex Gonzalez	2.00
7	Ricky Bottalico	2.00
8	Tony Clark	4.00
9	Mac Suzuki	2.00
10	James Mouton (Foil)	2.50

1994 Bowman

Bowman baseball for 1994 was a 682-card set issued all in one series, including a 52-card foil subset. There were 11 regular cards plus one foil card in each pack, with a suggested retail price of $2. The cards have a full-bleed design, with gold-foil stamping on every card. As in the past, the set includes numerous rookies and prospects, along with the game's biggest stars. The 52-card foil subset features 28 Top Prospects, with the player's team logo in the background; 17 Minor League MVPs, with a stadium in the background; and seven Diamonds in the Rough, with, you guessed it, a diamond as a backdrop.

		MT
Complete Set (682):		120.00
Common Player:		.10
Wax Box:		50.00
1	Joe Carter	.25
2	Marcus Moore	.10
3	*Doug Creek*	.15
4	Pedro Martinez	1.00
5	Ken Griffey, Jr.	5.00
6	Greg Swindell	.10
7	J.J. Johnson	.10
8	*Homer Bush*	.25
9	*Arquimedez Pozo*	.30
10	Bryan Harvey	.10
11	J.T. Snow	.20
12	*Alan Benes*	2.00
13	Chad Kreuter	.10
14	Eric Karros	.15
15	Frank Thomas	1.50
16	Bret Saberhagen	.15
17	Terrell Lowery	.10
18	Rod Bolton	.10
19	Harold Baines	.15
20	Matt Walbeck	.10
21	Tom Glavine	.15
22	Todd Jones	.10
23	Alberto Castillo	.10
24	Ruben Sierra	.10
25	Don Mattingly	1.00
26	Mike Morgan	.10
27	*Jim Musselwhite*	.20
28	*Matt Brunson*	.25
29	*Adam Meinershagen*	.20
30	Joe Girardi	.10
31	Shane Halter	.10
32	*Jose Paniagua*	.20
33	Paul Perkins	.10
34	*John Hudek*	.40
35	Frank Viola	.10
36	*David Lamb*	.15
37	Marshall Boze	.10
38	*Jorge Posada*	4.00
39	*Brian Anderson*	1.00
40	Mark Whiten	.10
41	Sean Bergman	.10
42	*Jose Parra*	.20
43	Mike Robertson	.10
44	*Pete Walker*	.15
45	Juan Gonzalez	1.50
46	*Cleveland Ladell*	.20
47	Mark Smith	.10
48	*Kevin Jarvis*	.20
49	*Amaury Telemaco*	.25
50	Andy Van Slyke	.10
51	*Rikkert Faneyte*	.20
52	Curtis Shaw	.10
53	*Matt Drews*	.40
54	Wilson Alvarez	.10
55	Manny Ramirez	2.00
56	Bobby Munoz	.10
57	Ed Sprague	.10
58	*Jamey Wright*	1.50
59	Jeff Montgomery	.10
60	Kirk Rueter	.10
61	Edgar Martinez	.15
62	Luis Gonzalez	.15
63	*Tim Vanegmond*	.15
64	Bip Roberts	.10
65	John Jaha	.10
66	Chuck Carr	.10
67	Chuck Finley	.10
68	Aaron Holbert	.10
69	Cecil Fielder	.25
70	*Tom Engle*	.15
71	Ron Karkovice	.10
72	Joe Orsulak	.10
73	*Duff Brumley*	.25
74	*Craig Clayton*	.15
75	Cal Ripken, Jr.	3.00
76	*Brad Fullmer*	4.00
77	Tony Tarasco	.10
78	*Terry Farrar*	.15
79	Matt Williams	.25
80	Rickey Henderson	.35
81	Terry Mulholland	.10
82	Sammy Sosa	3.00
83	Paul Sorrento	.10
84	Pete Incaviglia	.10
85	*Darren Hall*	.40
86	Scott Klingenbeck	.10
87	*Dario Perez*	.15
88	Ugueth Urbina	.15
89	*Dave Vanhof*	.15
90	Domingo Jean	.10
91	Otis Nixon	.10
92	Andres Berumen	.10
93	Jose Valentin	.10
94	*Edgar Renteria*	4.00
95	Chris Turner	.10
96	Ray Lankford	.15
97	Danny Bautista	.10
98	*Chan Ho Park*	5.00
99	*Glenn DiSarcina*	.15
100	Butch Huskey	.15
101	Ivan Rodriguez	.75
102	Johnny Ruffin	.10
103	Alex Ochoa	.20
104	*Torii Hunter*	.35
105	Ryan Klesko	.40
106	Jay Bell	.15
107	*Kurt Peltzer*	.15
108	Miguel Jimenez	.10
109	Russ Davis	.15
110	Derek Wallace	.10
111	*Keith Lockhart*	.25
112	Mike Lieberthal	.15
113	Dave Stewart	.10
114	Tom Schmidt	.10
115	Brian McRae	.15
116	Moises Alou	.15
117	Dave Fleming	.10
118	Jeff Bagwell	1.00
119	Luis Ortiz	.10
120	Tony Gwynn	1.50
121	Jaime Navarro	.10

122	Benny Santiago	.10
123	Darrel Whitmore	.10
124	*John Mabry*	.25
125	Mickey Tettleton	.10
126	Tom Candiotti	.10
127	Tim Raines	.15
128	Bobby Bonilla	.15
129	John Dettmer	.10
130	Hector Carrasco	.10
131	Chris Hoiles	.10
132	Rick Aguilera	.10
133	Dave Justice	.40
134	*Esteban Loaiza*	.25
135	Barry Bonds	.75
136	Bob Welch	.10
137	Mike Stanley	.10
138	Roberto Hernandez	.10
139	Sandy Alomar	.20
140	Darren Daulton	.10
141	*Angel Martinez*	.25
142	Howard Johnson	.10
143	Bob Hamelin	.10
144	*J.J. Thobe*	.20
145	Roger Salkeld	.10
146	Orlando Miller	.10
147	Dmitri Young	.10
148	*Tim Hyers*	.25
149	*Mark Loretta*	.25
150	Chris Hammond	.10
151	*Joel Moore*	.20
152	Todd Zeile	.15
153	Wil Cordero	.10
154	Chris Smith	.10
155	James Baldwin	.15
156	*Edgardo Alfonzo*	8.00
157	*Kym Ashworth*	.50
158	*Paul Bako*	.20
159	*Rick Krivda*	.20
160	Pat Mahomes	.10
161	Damon Hollins	.15
162	*Felix Martinez*	.15
163	*Jason Myers*	.20
164	*Izzy Molina*	.25
165	Brien Taylor	.10
166	*Kevin Orie*	1.50
167	*Casey Whitten*	.20
168	Tony Longmire	.10
169	John Olerud	.35
170	Mark Thompson	.10
171	Jorge Fabregas	.10
172	John Wetteland	.10
173	Dan Wilson	.10
174	Doug Drabek	.10
175	Jeffrey McNeely	.10
176	Melvin Nieves	.10
177	*Doug Glanville*	.75
178	*Javier De La Hoya*	.20
179	Chad Curtis	.10
180	Brian Barber	.10
181	Mike Henneman	.10
182	Jose Offerman	.10
183	*Robert Ellis*	.20
184	John Franco	.10
185	Benji Gil	.10
186	Hal Morris	.10
187	Chris Sabo	.10
188	*Blaise Ilsley*	.15
189	Steve Avery	.15
190	*Rick White*	.25
191	Rod Beck	.10
(192)	Mark McGwire (no card number)	6.00
193	Jim Abbott	.15
194	Randy Myers	.10
195	Kenny Lofton	.75
196	Mariano Duncan	.10
197	*Lee Daniels*	.15
198	Armando Reynoso	.10
199	Joe Randa	.10
200	Cliff Floyd	.30
201	*Tim Harkrider*	.20
202	*Kevin Gallaher*	.15
203	Scott Cooper	.10
204	*Phil Stidham*	.20
205	*Jeff D'Amico*	.75
206	Matt Whisenant	.10
207	De Shawn Warren	.10
208	Rene Arocha	.10
209	*Tony Clark*	8.00
210	*Jason Jacome*	.50
211	*Scott Christman*	.20
212	Bill Pulsipher	.15
213	Dean Palmer	.15
214	Chad Mottola	.15
215	Manny Alexander	.10
216	Rich Becker	.15
217	*Andre King*	.30
218	Carlos Garcia	.10
219	*Ron Pezzoni*	.15
220	Steve Karsay	.10
221	*Jose Musset*	.20
222	Karl Rhodes	.10
223	*Frank Cimorelli*	.15
224	*Kevin Jordan*	.25
225	Duane Ward	.10
226	John Burke	.10
227	Mike MacFarlane	.10
228	Mike Lansing	.15
229	Chuck Knoblauch	.35
230	Ken Caminiti	.25
231	*Gar Finnvold*	.15
232	*Derrek Lee*	3.00
233	Brady Anderson	.25
234	*Vic Darensbourg*	.15
235	Mark Langston	.10
236	*T.J. Mathews*	.25
237	Lou Whitaker	.15
238	Roger Cedeno	.15
239	Alex Fernandez	.15
240	Ryan Thompson	.10
241	*Kerry Lacy*	.15
242	Reggie Sanders	.15
243	Brad Pennington	.10
244	*Bryan Eversgerd*	.15
245	Greg Maddux	2.00
246	Jason Kendall	.75
247	J.R. Phillips	.15
248	Bobby Witt	.10
249	Paul O'Neill	.25
250	Ryne Sandberg	.75
251	Charles Nagy	.15
252	Kevin Stocker	.10
253	Shawn Green	.65
254	Charlie Hayes	.10
255	Donnie Elliott	.10
256	*Rob Fitzpatrick*	.15
257	Tim Davis	.10
258	James Mouton	.15
259	Mike Greenwell	.10
260	Ray McDavid	.10
261	Mike Kelly	.10
262	*Andy Larkin*	.25
(263)	Marquis Riley (no card number)	.10
264	Bob Tewksbury	.10
265	Brian Edmondson	.10
266	*Eduardo Lantigua*	.15
267	Brandon Wilson	.10
268	Mike Welch	.10
269	Tom Henke	.10
270	Calvin Reese	.10
271	*Greg Zaun*	.25
272	Todd Ritchie	.10
273	Javier Lopez	.30
274	Kevin Young	.10
275	Kirt Manwaring	.10
276	*Bill Taylor*	.15
277	Robert Eenhoorn	.10
278	Jessie Hollins	.10
279	*Julian Tavarez*	.35
280	Gene Schall	.10
281	Paul Molitor	.90
282	*Neifi Perez*	3.00
283	Greg Gagne	.10
284	Marquis Grissom	.15
285	Randy Johnson	.50
286	Pete Harnisch	.10
287	*Joel Bennett*	.25
288	Derek Bell	.15
289	Darryl Hamilton	.10
290	Gary Sheffield	.25
291	Eduardo Perez	.10
292	Basil Shabazz	.10
293	Eric Davis	.15
294	Pedro Astacio	.10
295	Robin Ventura	.25
296	Jeff Kent	.15
297	Rick Helling	.10
298	Joe Oliver	.10
299	Lee Smith	.15
300	Dave Winfield	.25
301	Deion Sanders	.30
302	*Ravelo Manzanillo*	.15
303	Mark Portugal	.10
304	Brent Gates	.10
305	Wade Boggs	.50
306	Rick Wilkins	.10
307	Carlos Baerga	.15
308	Curt Schilling	.15
309	Shannon Stewart	.50
310	Darren Holmes	.10
311	*Robert Toth*	.20
312	Gabe White	.15
313	*Mac Suzuki*	.40
314	*Alvin Morman*	.15
315	Mo Vaughn	.75
316	*Bryce Florie*	.15
317	*Gabby Martinez*	.25
318	Carl Everett	.15
319	Kerwin Moore	.10
320	Tom Pagnozzi	.10
321	Chris Gomez	.15
322	Todd Williams	.10
323	Pat Hentgen	.10
324	*Kirk Presley*	.50
325	Kevin Brown	.10
326	*Jason Isringhausen*	1.50
327	*Rick Forney*	.25
328	*Carlos Pulido*	.20
329	*Terrell Wade*	.20
330	Al Martin	.10
331	*Dan Carlson*	.20
332	*Mark Acre*	.15
333	Sterling Hitchcock	.10
334	*Jon Ratliff*	.25
335	*Alex Ramirez*	1.00
336	*Phil Geisler*	.20
337	*Eddie Zambrano* (Foil)	.25
338	Jim Thome (Foil)	1.00
339	James Mouton (Foil)	.25
340	Cliff Floyd (Foil)	.40
341	Carlos Delgado (Foil)	.60
342	Roberto Petagine (Foil)	.10
343	Tim Clark (Foil)	.10
344	Bubba Smith (Foil)	.15
345	*Randy Curtis* (Foil)	.20
346	*Joe Biasucci* (Foil)	.20
347	*D.J. Boston* (Foil)	.10
348	*Ruben Rivera* (Foil)	4.00
349	*Bryan Link* (Foil)	.20
350	*Mike Bell* (Foil)	.50
351	*Marty Watson* (Foil)	.20
352	Jason Myers (Foil)	.20
353	Chipper Jones (Foil)	2.50
354	Brooks Kieschnick (Foil)	.65
355	Calvin Reese (Foil)	.10
356	John Burke (Foil)	.10
357	Kurt Miller (Foil)	.10
358	Orlando Miller (Foil)	.10
359	Todd Hollandsworth (Foil)	.75
360	Rondell White (Foil)	.40
361	Bill Pulsipher (Foil)	.25
362	Tyler Green (Foil)	.15
363	Midre Cummings (Foil)	.25
364	Brian Barber (Foil)	.10
365	Melvin Nieves (Foil)	.10
366	Salomon Torres (Foil)	.10
367	Alex Ochoa (Foil)	.20
368	Frank Rodriguez (Foil)	.15
369	Brian Anderson (Foil)	.25
370	James Baldwin (Foil)	.35
371	Manny Ramirez (Foil)	2.00
372	Justin Thompson (Foil)	.15
373	Johnny Damon (Foil)	.85
374	Jeff D'Amico (Foil)	.50
375	Rich Becker (Foil)	.15
376	Derek Jeter (Foil)	4.00
377	Steve Karsay (Foil)	.20
378	Mac Suzuki (Foil)	.30
379	Benji Gil (Foil)	.10
380	Alex Gonzalez (Foil)	.25
381	Jason Bere (Foil)	.25
382	Brett Butler (Foil)	.25
383	Jeff Conine (Foil)	.15
384	Darren Daulton (Foil)	.15
385	Jeff Kent (Foil)	.15
386	Don Mattingly (Foil)	1.00
387	Mike Piazza (Foil)	2.00
388	Ryne Sandberg (Foil)	.75
389	Rich Amaral	.10
390	Craig Biggio	.35
391	*Jeff Suppan*	1.50
392	Andy Benes	.10
393	Cal Eldred	.10
394	Jeff Conine	.15
395	Tim Salmon	.35
396	*Ray Suplee*	.20
397	Tony Phillips	.10
398	Ramon Martinez	.15
399	Julio Franco	.10
400	Dwight Gooden	.15
401	*Kevin Lomon*	.15
402	Jose Rijo	.10
403	Mike Devereaux	.10
404	*Mike Zolecki*	.20
405	Fred McGriff	.25
406	Danny Clyburn	.10
407	Robby Thompson	.10
408	Terry Steinbach	.10
409	Luis Polonia	.10
410	Mark Grace	.35
411	Albert Belle	1.25
412	John Kruk	.10
413	*Scott Spiezio*	1.00
414	Ellis Burks	.15
415	Joe Vitiello	.15
416	Tim Costo	.10
417	Marc Newfield	.10
418	*Oscar Henriquez*	.20
419	*Matt Perisho*	.25
420	Julio Bruno	.10
421	Kenny Felder	.10
422	Tyler Green	.10
423	Jim Edmonds	.35
424	Ozzie Smith	.50
425	Rick Greene	.10
426	Todd Hollandsworth	.25
427	*Eddie Pearson*	.20
428	Quilvio Veras	.10
429	Kenny Rogers	.10
430	Willie Greene	.10
431	Vaughn Eshelman	.20
432	Pat Meares	.10
433	*Jermaine Dye*	2.00
434	Steve Cooke	.10
435	Bill Swift	.10
436	*Fausto Cruz*	.25
437	Mark Hutton	.10
438	*Brooks Kieschnick*	1.50
439	Yorkis Perez	.10
440	Len Dykstra	.10
441	Pat Borders	.10
442	*Doug Walls*	.20
443	Wally Joyner	.15
444	Ken Hill	.10
445	Eric Anthony	.10
446	Mitch Williams	.10
447	*Cory Bailey*	.25
448	Dave Staton	.10
449	Greg Vaughn	.15
450	Dave Magadan	.10
451	Chili Davis	.10
452	*Gerald Santos*	.20
453	Joe Perona	.10
454	Delino DeShields	.10
455	Jack McDowell	.10
456	Todd Hundley	.15
457	Ritchie Moody	.10
458	Bret Boone	.10
459	Ben McDonald	.10
460	Kirby Puckett	.75
461	Gregg Olson	.10
462	*Rich Aude*	.30
463	John Burkett	.10
464	Troy Neel	.10
465	Jimmy Key	.10
466	Ozzie Timmons	.10
467	Eddie Murray	.40
468	*Mark Tranberg*	.15
469	Alex Gonzalez	.25
470	David Nied	.10
471	Barry Larkin	.20
472	*Brian Looney*	.25
473	Shawn Estes	.30
474	*A.J. Sager*	.15
475	Roger Clemens	2.00
476	Vince Moore	.10
477	*Scott Karl*	.15
478	Kurt Miller	.10
479	Garret Anderson	.60
480	Allen Watson	.10
481	*Jose Lima*	6.00
482	Rick Gorecki	.10
483	*Jimmy Hurst*	.50
484	Preston Wilson	.50
485	Will Clark	.35
486	*Mike Ferry*	.15
487	*Curtis Goodwin*	.40
488	Mike Myers	.10
489	Chipper Jones	2.50
490	Jeff King	.10
491	*Bill Van Landingham*	.60
492	*Carlos Reyes*	.20
493	Andy Pettitte	1.50
494	Brant Brown	.15
495	Daron Kirkreit	.15
496	*Ricky Bottalico*	.40
497	Devon White	.15
498	*Jason Johnson*	.20
499	Vince Coleman	.10
500	Larry Walker	.50
501	Bobby Ayala	.10
502	Steve Finley	.10
503	Scott Fletcher	.10
504	Brad Ausmus	.10
505	*Scott Talanoa*	.20
506	Orestes Destrade	.10
507	Gary DiSarcina	.10
508	*Willie Smith*	.20
509	Alan Trammell	.15
510	Mike Piazza	2.00
511	Ozzie Guillen	.10
512	Jeromy Burnitz	.15
513	Darren Oliver	.10
514	Kevin Mitchell	.10
515	Rafael Palmeiro	.25
516	David McCarty	.10
517	Jeff Blauser	.10
518	Trey Beamon	.15
519	Royce Clayton	.10
520	Dennis Eckersley	.15
521	Bernie Williams	.60
522	Steve Buechele	.10
523	Denny Martinez	.15
524	Dave Hollins	.10
525	Joey Hamilton	.30
526	Andres Galarraga	.25
527	Jeff Granger	.10
528	Joey Eischen	.10
529	Desi Relaford	.10
530	Roberto Petagine	.10
531	Andre Dawson	.15
532	Ray Holbert	.10
533	Duane Singleton	.10
534	*Kurt Abbott*	.30
535	Bo Jackson	.15
536	Gregg Jefferies	.15
537	David Mysel	.10
538	Raul Mondesi	.75
539	Chris Snopek	.15
540	Brook Fordyce	.10
541	*Ron Frazier*	.25
542	Brian Koelling	.10
543	Jimmy Haynes	.15
544	Marty Cordova	.75
545	*Jason Green*	.30
546	Orlando Merced	.10
547	*Lou Pote*	.20
548	Todd Van Poppel	.15
549	Pat Kelly	.10
550	Turk Wendell	.10
551	*Herb Perry*	.15
552	*Ryan Karp*	.25
553	Juan Guzman	.10
554	*Bryan Rekar*	.25
555	Kevin Appier	.10
556	*Chris Schwab*	.20
557	Jay Buhner	.20
558	Andujar Cedeno	.10
559	*Ryan McGuire*	.60
560	Ricky Gutierrez	.10
561	*Keith Kimsey*	.20
562	Tim Clark	.10
563	Damion Easley	.10
564	*Clint Davis*	.15
565	Mike Moore	.10
566	Orel Hershiser	.15
567	Jason Bere	.15
568	Kevin McReynolds	.10
569	*Leland Macon*	.20
570	*John Courtright*	.20
571	Sid Fernandez	.10
572	Chad Roper	.10
573	Terry Pendleton	.10
574	Danny Miceli	.10
575	Joe Rosselli	.10
576	Mike Bordick	.10
577	Danny Tartabull	.10
578	Jose Guzman	.10
579	Omar Vizquel	.15
580	Tommy Greene	.10
581	Paul Spoljaric	.10
582	Walt Weiss	.10
583	*Oscar Jimenez*	.20
584	Rod Henderson	.10
585	Derek Lowe	.10
586	*Richard Hidalgo*	3.00
587	*Shayne Bennett*	.15
588	*Tim Belk*	.20
589	Matt Mieske	.10
590	Nigel Wilson	.15
591	*Jeff Knox*	.15
592	Bernard Gilkey	.15
593	David Cone	.30
594	*Paul LoDuca*	.25
595	Scott Ruffcorn	.10
596	Chris Roberts	.10
597	*Oscar Munoz*	.25
598	*Scott Sullivan*	.20
599	*Matt Jarvis*	.15
600	Jose Canseco	.50
601	*Tony Graffanino*	.20
602	Don Slaught	.10
603	*Brett King*	.20
604	*Jose Herrera*	.40
605	Melido Perez	.10
606	*Mike Hubbard*	.15
607	Chad Ogea	.15
608	*Wayne Gomes*	.35
609	Roberto Alomar	.50
610	*Angel Echevarria*	.20
611	Jose Lind	.10
612	Darrin Fletcher	.10
613	Chris Bosio	.10
614	Darryl Kile	.10
615	Frank Rodriguez	.15
616	Phil Plantier	.10
617	Pat Listach	.10
618	Charlie Hough	.10
619	*Ryan Hancock*	.30
620	*Darrel Deak*	.20
621	Travis Fryman	.15
622	Brett Butler	.15
623	Lance Johnson	.10
624	Pete Smith	.10
625	James Hurst	.10
626	Roberto Kelly	.10
627	Mike Mussina	.50
628	Kevin Tapani	.10
629	John Smoltz	.15
630	Midro Cummings	.15
631	Salomon Torres	.10
632	Willie Adams	.10
633	Derek Jeter	4.00
634	Steve Trachsel	.25
635	Albie Lopez	.15
636	Jason Moler	.10
637	Carlos Delgado	.40
638	Roberto Mejia	.10
639	Darren Burton	.10
640	B.J. Wallace	.10
641	*Brad Clontz*	.15
642	*Billy Wagner*	1.00
643	Aaron Sele	.25
644	Cameron Cairncross	.10
645	Brian Harper	.10
(646)	Marc Valdes (no card number)	.15
647	Mark Ratekin	.10
648	*Terry Bradshaw*	.35
649	Justin Thompson	.15
650	*Mike Busch*	.25
651	*Joe Hall*	.15
652	Bobby Jones	.15
653	*Kelly Stinnett*	.25
654	*Rod Steph*	.20
655	*Jay Powell*	.35
(656)	*Keith Garagozzo* (no card number)	.15
657	Todd Dunn	.15
658	*Charles Peterson*	.20
659	Darren Lewis	.10
660	*John Wasdin*	.50
661	*Tate Seefried*	.60
662	*Hector Trinidad*	.40
663	*John Carter*	.20
664	Larry Mitchell	.10
665	*David Catlett*	.20
666	Dante Bichette	.30
667	Felix Jose	.10
668	Rondell White	.30
669	Tino Martinez	.40
670	Brian Hunter	.35
671	Jose Malave	.15
672	Archi Cianfrocco	.10
673	*Mike Matheny*	.15
674	Bret Barberie	.10
675	*Andrew Lorraine*	.60
676	Brian Jordan	.15
677	Tim Belcher	.10
678	*Antonio Osuna*	.20
679	Checklist I	.10
680	Checklist II	.10
681	Checklist III	.10
682	Checklist IV	.10

1994 Bowman Superstar Sampler

As an insert in 1994 Topps retail factory sets, three-card cello packs of "Superstar Sampler" cards were included. The packs contained special versions of the same player's 1994 Bowman, Finest and Stadium Club cards. Forty-five of the game's top stars are represented in the issue. The Bowman cards in this issue are identical to the cards in the regular set except for the appearance of a round "Topps Superstar Sampler" logo on back.

		MT
Complete Set (45):		200.00
Common Player:		2.50
1	Joe Carter	2.50
5	Ken Griffey Jr.	35.00
15	Frank Thomas	25.00
21	Tom Glavine	3.00
25	Don Mattingly	15.00
45	Juan Gonzalez	11.00
50	Andy Van Slyke	2.50
55	Manny Ramirez	5.00
69	Cecil Fielder	3.00
75	Cal Ripken Jr.	30.00
79	Matt Williams	4.00
118	Jeff Bagwell	7.50
120	Tony Gwynn	9.00
128	Bobby Bonilla	2.50
133	Dave Justice	3.00
135	Barry Bonds	12.00
140	Darren Daulton	2.50
169	John Olerud	3.00
200	Cliff Floyd	2.50
245	Greg Maddux	12.00
250	Ryne Sandberg	9.00
281	Paul Molitor	6.00
284	Marquis Grissom	2.50
285	Randy Johnson	4.00
290	Gary Sheffield	3.00
307	Carlos Baerga	2.50
315	Mo Vaughn	6.00
395	Tim Salmon	3.00
405	Fred McGriff	3.00
410	Mark Grace	4.00
411	Albert Belle	6.00
440	Len Dykstra	2.50
455	Jack McDowell	2.50
460	Kirby Puckett	9.00
471	Barry Larkin	2.50
475	Roger Clemens	7.50
485	Will Clark	4.00
500	Larry Walker	4.00
510	Mike Piazza	15.00
515	Rafael Palmeiro	3.00
526	Andres Galarraga	2.50
536	Gregg Jefferies	2.50
538	Raul Mondesi	3.00
600	Jose Canseco	6.00
609	Roberto Alomar	5.00

1994 Bowman's Best

The first ever set of Bowman's Best consisted of 90 Blue cards, 90 Red cards and 20 Mirror Images, featuring a Red veteran and a Blue prospect player matched by position on each card. This 200-card set utilized Topps Finest technology and includes full-color photos front and back with a high-gloss finish. Bowman's Best was available in eight-card wax packs, with each pack containing seven cards and a Mirror Image card. There is also a 200-card parallel set officially titled "Special Effects," which uses Topps' refractor technology. Both the Red and Blue set are numbered 1-90, with the Mirror Image cards numbered 91-110.

		MT
Complete Set (200):		95.00
Common Player:		.50
Wax Box:		100.00
Red Set		
1	Paul Molitor	1.50
2	Eddie Murray	1.50
3	Ozzie Smith	2.00
4	Rickey Henderson	1.00
5	Lee Smith	.50
6	Dave Winfield	1.00
7	Roberto Alomar	2.50
8	Matt Williams	1.25
9	Mark Grace	1.00
10	Lance Johnson	.50
11	Darren Daulton	.50
12	Tom Glavine	.75
13	Gary Sheffield	.75
14	Rod Beck	.50
15	Fred McGriff	1.00
16	Joe Carter	.50
17	Dante Bichette	1.00
18	Danny Tartabull	.50
19	Juan Gonzalez	5.00
20	Steve Avery	.50
21	John Wetteland	.50
22	Ben McDonald	.50
23	Jack McDowell	.50
24	Jose Canseco	2.00
25	Tim Salmon	1.00
26	Wilson Alvarez	.50
27	Gregg Jefferies	.60
28	John Burkett	.50
29	Greg Vaughn	.50
30	Robin Ventura	.65
31	Paul O'Neill	.65
32	Cecil Fielder	.60
33	Kevin Mitchell	.50
34	Jeff Conine	.50
35	Carlos Baerga	.50
36	Greg Maddux	5.00
37	Roger Clemens	3.50
38	Deion Sanders	1.00
39	Delino DeShields	.50
40	Ken Griffey, Jr.	10.00
41	Albert Belle	3.00
42	Wade Boggs	2.00
43	Andres Galarraga	.60
44	Aaron Sele	.50
45	Don Mattingly	4.00
46	David Cone	.60
47	Len Dykstra	.50
48	Brett Butler	.50
49	Bill Swift	.50
50	Bobby Bonilla	.60
51	Rafael Palmeiro	1.25
52	Moises Alou	.50
53	Jeff Bagwell	3.50
54	Mike Mussina	2.00
55	Frank Thomas	5.00
56	Jose Rijo	.50
57	Ruben Sierra	.50
58	Randy Myers	.50
59	Barry Bonds	3.00
60	Jimmy Key	.50
61	Travis Fryman	.50
62	John Olerud	.75
63	Dave Justice	.75
64	Ray Lankford	.50
65	Bob Tewksbury	.50
66	Chuck Carr	.50
67	Jay Buhner	.50
68	Kenny Lofton	2.50
69	Marquis Grissom	.60
70	Sammy Sosa	6.00
71	Cal Ripken, Jr.	8.00
72	Ellis Burks	.50
73	Jeff Montgomery	.50
74	Julio Franco	.50
75	Kirby Puckett	4.00
76	Larry Walker	1.50
77	Andy Van Slyke	.50
78	Tony Gwynn	4.00
79	Will Clark	1.50
80	Mo Vaughn	2.00
81	Mike Piazza	6.00
82	James Mouton	.50
83	Carlos Delgado	1.00
84	Ryan Klesko	.40
85	Javier Lopez	.75
86	Raul Mondesi	1.50
87	Cliff Floyd	.90
88	Manny Ramirez	3.00
89	Hector Carrasco	.50
90	Jeff Granger	.50
Blue Set		
1	Chipper Jones	6.00
2	Derek Jeter	6.00
3	Bill Pulsipher	1.00
4	James Baldwin	1.00
5	*Brooks Kieschnick*	1.00
6	Justin Thompson	1.50
7	Midre Cummings	.50
8	Joey Hamilton	1.50
9	Calvin Reese	1.00
10	Brian Barber	.50
11	John Burke	.50
12	De Shawn Warren	.50
13	*Edgardo Alfonzo*	12.00
14	*Eddie Pearson*	.50
15	Jimmy Haynes	.50
16	Danny Bautista	.50
17	Roger Cedeno	1.00
18	Jon Lieber	.50
19	*Billy Wagner*	1.00
20	*Tate Seefried*	.75
21	Chad Mottola	1.00
22	Jose Malave	.50
23	*Terrell Wade*	.50
24	Shane Andrews	1.50
25	*Chan Ho Park*	4.00
26	*Kirk Presley*	1.50
27	Robbie Beckett	.50
28	Orlando Miller	.65
29	*Jorge Posada*	5.00
30	Frank Rodriguez	1.00
31	Brian Hunter	2.00
32	Billy Ashley	1.00
33	Rondell White	2.00
34	John Roper	.50
35	Marc Valdes	.50
36	Scott Ruffcorn	1.00
37	Rod Henderson	.50
38	Curt Goodwin	.50
39	Russ Davis	1.50
40	Rick Gorecki	.50
41	Johnny Damon	2.50
42	Roberto Petagine	.50
43	Chris Snopek	.65
44	Mark Acre	.50
45	Todd Hollandsworth	1.50
46	Shawn Green	5.00
47	John Carter	.50
48	Jim Pittsley	.75
49	*John Wasdin*	.75
50	D.J. Boston	.50
51	Tim Clark	.75
52	Alex Ochoa	1.50
53	Chad Roper	.75
54	Mike Kelly	.50
55	*Brad Fullmer*	5.00
56	Carl Everett	1.00
57	*Tim Belk*	.50
58	*Jimmy Hurst*	.50
59	*Mac Suzuki*	1.00
60	Michael Moore	.50
61	*Alan Benes*	2.00
62	*Tony Clark*	8.00
63	*Edgar Renteria*	4.00
64	Trey Beamon	.50
65	*LaTroy Hawkins*	1.00
66	*Wayne Gomes*	1.50
67	Ray McDavid	.50
68	John Dettmer	.50
69	Willie Greene	.75
70	Dave Stevens	.50
71	*Kevin Orie*	1.00
72	Chad Ogea	1.00
73	Ben Van Ryn	.50
74	Kym Ashworth	.75
75	Dmitri Young	.75
76	Herb Perry	.50
77	Joey Eischen	1.00
78	*Arquimedez Pozo*	1.00
79	Ugueth Urbina	1.00
80	Keith Williams	.50
81	*John Frascatore*	.50
82	Garey Ingram	.75
83	Aaron Small	.50
84	*Olmedo Saenz*	.50
85	Jesus Tavarez	.50
86	*Jose Silva*	1.00
87	*Gerald Witasick, Jr.*	.50
88	Jay Maldonado	.50
89	Keith Heberling	.50
90	*Rusty Greer*	5.00
Mirror Images		
91	Frank Thomas, Kevin Young	4.00
92	Fred McGriff, Brooks Kieschnick	1.50
93	Matt Williams, Shane Andrews	1.50
94	Cal Ripken, Jr., Kevin Orie	5.00
95	Barry Larkin, Derek Jeter	3.00
96	Ken Griffey, Jr., Johnny Damon	7.50
97	Barry Bonds, Rondell White	2.50
98	Albert Belle, Jimmy Hurst	1.50
99	Raul Mondesi, *Ruben Rivera*	3.00
100	Roger Clemens, Scott Ruffcorn	2.00
101	Greg Maddux, John Wasdin	2.50
102	Tim Salmon, Chad Mottola	1.00
103	Carlos Baerga, Arquimedez Pozo	1.00
104	Mike Piazza, Buddy Hughes	3.00
105	Carlos Delgado, Melvin Nieves	1.50
106	Javier Lopez, Jorge Posada	2.00
107	Manny Ramirez, Jose Malave	2.50
108	Travis Fryman, Chipper Jones	3.00
109	Steve Avery, Bill Pulsipher	1.00
110	John Olerud, Shawn Green	2.50

1994 Bowman's Best Refractors

This 200-card parallel set, officially titled "Special Effects," uses Topps' refractor technology. The refractors were packed at the rate of three per wax box of Bowman's Best, but are very difficult to differentiate from the regular high-tech cards.

	MT
Complete Set (200):	750.00
Common Player:	1.00
Superstars: 8-10X	
Stars: 4-8X	

(See 1994 Bowman's Best for checklist and base card values.)

1995 Bowman

Large numbers of rookie cards and a lengthy run of etched-foil cards distinguishes the 1995 Bowman set. The set's basic cards share a design with a large color photo flanked at left by a severely horizontally compressed mirror image in green, and at bottom by a similar version in brown. Most of the bottom image is covered by the player's last name printed in silver (cards #1-220, rookies) or gold (cards #275-439, veterans) foil. A color team logo is in the lower-left corner of all cards, and the Bowman logo is in red foil at top. In between are the foil-etched subsets of "Minor League MVPs," "1st Impressions," and "Prime Prospects." Each of these cards, seeded one per regular pack and two per jumbo, has the player photo set against a background of textured color foil, with a prismatic silver border. Each of the foil cards can also be found in a gold-toned version, in a ratio of six silver to one gold. Backs of the rookies' cards have a portrait photo at right and a scouting report at left. Veterans' cards have either a scouting report for younger players, or a chart of stats versus each team played in 1994. Backs of all the foil cards have a scouting report.

		MT
Complete Set (439):		240.00
Common Player:		.10
Wax Box:		220.00
1	Billy Wagner	.50
2	Chris Widger	.10
3	Brent Bowers	.10
4	*Bob Abreu*	6.00
5	*Lou Collier*	.30
6	*Juan Acevedo*	.50
7	*Jason Kelley*	.20
8	Brian Sackinsky	.10
9	Scott Christman	.10
10	Damon Hollins	.15
11	*Willis Otanez*	.25
12	*Jason Ryan*	.20
13	Jason Giambi	.75
14	*Andy Taulbee*	.25
15	Mark Thompson	.10
16	*Hugo Pivaral*	.25
17	Brien Taylor	.10
18	Antonio Osuna	.10
19	Edgardo Alfonzo	.25
20	Carl Everett	.15
21	Matt Drews	.15
22	*Bartolo Colon*	8.00
23	*Andruw Jones*	30.00
24	*Robert Person*	.25
25	Derrek Lee	1.50
26	*John Ambrose*	.20
27	*Eric Knowles*	.25
28	Chris Roberts	.10
29	Don Wengert	.10
30	*Marcus Jensen*	.30
31	Brian Barber	.10
32	Kevin Brown	.10
33	Benji Gil	.10
34	Mike Hubbard	.10
35	*Bart Evans*	.35
36	*Enrique Wilson*	2.00
37	*Brian Buchanan*	.20
38	*Ken Ray*	.25
39	*Micah Franklin*	.40
40	*Ricky Otero*	.30
41	Jason Kendall	.15
42	Jimmy Hurst	.10
43	*Jerry Wolak*	.20
44	*Jayson Peterson*	.30
45	*Allen Battle*	.20
46	Scott Stahoviak	.10
47	*Steve Schrenk*	.30
48	*Travis Miller*	.20
49	*Eddie Rios*	.25
50	Mike Hampton	.10
51	*Chad Frontera*	.25
52	*Tom Evans*	.30
53	C.J. Nitkowski	.10
54	*Clay Caruthers*	.25
55	Shannon Stewart	.10
56	Jorge Posada	.15
57	Aaron Holbert	.10
58	*Harry Berrios*	.20
59	Steve Rodriguez	.10
60	Shane Andrews	.15
61	*Will Cunnane*	.25
62	Richard Hidalgo	1.50
63	*Bill Selby*	.20
64	*Jay Cranford*	.20
65	Jeff Suppan	.15
66	Curtis Goodwin	.10
67	*John Thomson*	.30
68	Justin Thompson	.10
69	Troy Percival	.10
70	*Matt Wagner*	.25
71	Terry Bradshaw	.10
72	Greg Hansell	.10
73	John Burke	.10
74	Jeff D'Amico	.10
75	Ernie Young	.10
76	Jason Bates	.10
77	Chris Stynes	.10
78	*Cade Gaspar*	.25
79	Melvin Nieves	.10
80	Rick Gorecki	.10
81	*Felix Rodriguez*	.20
82	Ryan Hancock	.10
83	*Chris Carpenter*	3.00
84	Ray McDavid	.10
85	Chris Wimmer	.10
86	Doug Glanville	.15
87	DeShawn Warren	.10
88	*Damian Moss*	1.00
89	*Rafael Orellano*	.20
90	*Vladimir Guerrero*	60.00
91	*Raul Casanova*	.75
92	*Karim Garcia*	1.50
93	Bryce Florie	.10
94	Kevin Orie	.75
95	*Ryan Nye*	.25
96	*Matt Sachse*	.25
97	*Ivan Arteaga*	.25
98	Glenn Murray	.10
99	*Stacy Hollins*	.20
100	Jim Pittsley	.10
101	*Craig Mattson*	.30
102	Neifi Perez	.40
103	Keith Williams	.10
104	Roger Cedeno	.10
105	*Tony Terry*	.25
106	Jose Malave	.10
107	Joe Rosselli	.10
108	Kevin Jordan	.10
109	*Sid Roberson*	.20
110	Alan Embree	.10
111	Terrell Wade	.10
112	Bob Wolcott	.10
113	*Carlos Perez*	.25
114	*Mike Bovee*	.30
115	*Tommy Davis*	.30
116	*Jeremey Kendall*	.25
117	Rich Aude	.10
118	Rick Huisman	.10
119	Tim Belk	.10
120	Edgar Renteria	.75
121	*Calvin Maduro*	.25
122	*Jerry Martin*	.25
123	*Ramon Fermin*	.20
124	*Kimera Bartee*	.35
125	Mark Farris	.10
126	Frank Rodriguez	.10
127	*Bobby Higginson*	4.00
128	Bret Wagner	.10
129	*Edwin Diaz*	.30
130	Jimmy Haynes	.10
131	*Chris Weinke*	.75
132	*Damian Jackson*	1.00

133	Felix Martinez	.10
134	*Edwin Hurtado*	.40
135	*Matt Raleigh*	.30
136	Paul Wilson	.40
137	Ron Villone	.10
138	*Eric Stuckenschneider*	.20
139	Tate Seefried	.10
140	*Rey Ordonez*	3.50
141	Eddie Pearson	.10
142	Kevin Gallaher	.10
143	Torii Hunter	.20
144	Daron Kirkreit	.10
145	Craig Wilson	.10
146	Ugueth Urbina	.15
147	Chris Snopek	.10
148	Kym Ashworth	.10
149	Wayne Gomes	.10
150	Mark Loretta	.10
151	*Ramon Morel*	.25
152	Trot Nixon	.50
153	Desi Relaford	.10
154	Scott Sullivan	.10
155	Marc Barcelo	.10
156	Willie Adams	.10
157	*Derrick Gibson*	5.00
158	*Brian Meadows*	.20
159	Julian Tavarez	.10
160	Bryan Rekar	.10
161	Steve Gibralter	.10
162	Esteban Loaiza	.10
163	John Wasdin	.10
164	Kirk Presley	.10
165	Mariano Rivera	.65
166	Andy Larkin	.10
167	*Sean Whiteside*	.20
168	*Matt Apana*	.25
169	*Shawn Senior*	.15
170	Scott Gentile	.10
171	Quilvio Veras	.10
172	*Elieser Marrero*	2.00
173	*Mendy Lopez*	.20
174	Homer Bush	.10
175	*Brian Stephenson*	.25
176	Jon Nunnally	.10
177	Jose Herrera	.10
178	*Corey Avrard*	.25
179	David Bell	.10
180	Jason Isringhausen	.75
181	Jamey Wright	.10
182	*Lonell Roberts*	.15
183	Marty Cordova	.15
185	Amaury Telemaco	.10
185	John Mabry	.10
186	*Andrew Vessel*	.20
187	*Jim Cole*	.15
188	Marquis Riley	.10
189	Todd Dunn	.10
190	John Carter	.10
191	*Donnie Sadler*	1.00
192	Mike Bell	.10
193	*Chris Cumberland*	.20
194	Jason Schmidt	.10
195	Matt Brunson	.15
196	James Baldwin	.10
197	*Bill Simas*	.20
198	Gus Gandarillas	.10
199	Mac Suzuki	.15
200	*Rick Holifield*	.25
201	*Fernando Lunar*	.20
202	Kevin Jarvis	.10
203	*Everett Stull*	.10
204	Steve Wojciechowski	.10
205	Shawn Estes	.15
206	Jermaine Dye	.20
207	Marc Kroon	.10
208	*Peter Munro*	.30
209	Pat Watkins	.10
210	Matt Smith	.10
211	Joe Vitiello	.10
212	Gerald Witasick, Jr.	.10
213	*Freddy Garcia*	1.00
214	*Glenn Dishman*	.20
215	*Jay Canizaro*	.20
216	Angel Martinez	.10
217	*Yamil Benitez*	.25
218	*Fausto Macey*	.20
219	Eric Owens	.10
220	Checklist	.10
221	*Dwayne Hosey* (Minor League MVPs)	.20
222	*Brad Woodall* (Minor League MVPs)	.25
223	Billy Ashley (Minor League MVPs)	.10
224	*Mark Grudzielanek* (Minor League MVPs)	1.00
225	*Mark Johnson* (Minor League MVPs)	.40
226	*Tim Unroe* (Minor League MVPs)	.30
227	Todd Greene (Minor League MVPs)	3.00
228	Larry Sutton (Minor League MVPs)	.10
229	Derek Jeter (Minor League MVPs)	4.00
230	*Sal Fasano* (Minor League MVPs)	.10
231	Ruben Rivera (Minor League MVPs)	2.00
232	*Chris Truby* (Minor League MVPs)	.15
233	John Donati (Minor League MVPs)	.10
234	*Decomba Conner* (Minor League MVPs)	.25
235	*Sergio Nunez* (Minor League MVPs)	.20
236	*Ray Brown* (Minor League MVPs)	.50
237	*Juan Melo* (Minor League MVPs)	1.00
238	*Hideo Nomo* (First Impressions)	4.00
239	*Jaime Bluma* (First Impressions)	.20
240	*Jay Payton* (First Impressions)	.75
241	Paul Konerko (First Impressions)	6.00
242	*Scott Elarton* (First Impressions)	1.00
243	*Jeff Abbott* (First Impressions)	1.00
244	*Jim Brower* (First Impressions)	.30
245	*Geoff Blum* (First Impressions)	.30
246	*Aaron Boone* (First Impressions)	1.00
247	J.R. Phillips (Top Prospects)	.15
248	Alex Ochoa (Top Prospects)	.40
249	Nomar Garciaparra (Top Prospects)	30.00
250	Garret Anderson (Top Prospects)	.40
251	Ray Durham (Top Prospects)	.30
252	Paul Shuey (Top Prospects)	.10
253	Tony Clark (Top Prospects)	2.00
254	Johnny Damon (Top Prospects)	.65
255	Duane Singleton (Top Prospects)	.10
256	LaTroy Hawkins (Top Prospects)	.10
257	Andy Pettitte (Top Prospects)	1.50
258	Ben Grieve (Top Prospects)	12.00
259	Marc Newfield (Top Prospects)	.10
260	Terrell Lowery (Top Prospects)	.10
261	Shawn Green (Top Prospects)	.75
262	Chipper Jones (Top Prospects)	2.00
263	Brooks Kieschnick (Top Prospects)	.30
264	Calvin Reese (Top Prospects)	.10
265	Doug Million (Top Prospects)	.10
266	Marc Valdes (Top Prospects)	.10
267	Brian Hunter (Top Prospects)	.35
268	Todd Hollandsworth (Top Prospects)	.75
269	Rod Henderson (Top Prospects)	.20
270	Bill Pulsipher (Top Prospects)	.20
271	*Scott Rolen* (Top Prospects)	35.00
272	Trey Beamon (Top Prospects)	.10
273	Alan Benes (Top Prospects)	.40
274	Dustin Hermanson (Top Prospects)	.25
275	Ricky Bottalico	.10
276	Albert Belle	1.00
277	Deion Sanders	.30
278	Matt Williams	.50
279	Jeff Bagwell	1.50
280	Kirby Puckett	1.50
281	Dave Hollins	.10
282	Don Mattingly	1.50
283	Joey Hamilton	.25
284	Bobby Bonilla	.15
285	Moises Alou	.15
286	Tom Glavine	.15
287	Brett Butler	.15
288	Chris Hoiles	.10
289	Kenny Rogers	.10
290	Larry Walker	.65
291	Tim Raines	.15
292	Kevin Appier	.10
293	Roger Clemens	2.00
294a	Chuck Carr	.10
294b	Cliff Floyd (Should be #394)	.20
295	Randy Myers	.10
296	Dave Nilsson	.10
297	Joe Carter	.15
298	Chuck Finley	.10
299	Ray Lankford	.15
300	Roberto Kelly	.10
301	Jon Lieber	.10
302	Travis Fryman	.10
303	Mark McGwire	5.00
304	Tony Gwynn	2.50
305	Kenny Lofton	.75
306	Mark Whiten	.10
307	Doug Drabek	.10
308	Terry Steinbach	.10
309	Ryan Klesko	.40
310	Mike Piazza	3.00
311	Ben McDonald	.10
312	Reggie Sanders	.15
313	Alex Fernandez	.10
314	Aaron Sele	.10
315	Gregg Jefferies	.15
316	Rickey Henderson	.25
317	Brian Anderson	.10
318	Jose Valentin	.10
319	Rod Beck	.10
320	Marquis Grissom	.15
321	Ken Griffey Jr.	4.00
322	Bret Saberhagen	.15
323	Juan Gonzalez	2.00
324	Paul Molitor	.50
325	Gary Sheffield	.60
326	Darren Daulton	.10
327	Bill Swift	.10
328	Brian McRae	.10
329	Robin Ventura	.20
330	Lee Smith	.10
331	Fred McGriff	.50
332	Delino DeShields	.10
333	Edgar Martinez	.15
334	Mike Mussina	1.00
335	Orlando Merced	.10
336	Carlos Baerga	.15
337	Wil Cordero	.10
338	Tom Pagnozzi	.10
339	Pat Hentgen	.10
340	Chad Curtis	.10
341	Darren Lewis	.10
342	Jeff Kent	.10
343	Bip Roberts	.10
344	Ivan Rodriguez	1.50
345	Jeff Montgomery	.10
346	Hal Morris	.10
347	Danny Tartabull	.10
348	Raul Mondesi	.60
349	Ken Hill	.10
350	Pedro Martinez	1.50
351	Frank Thomas	1.50
352	Manny Ramirez	1.50
353	Tim Salmon	.30
354	William Van Landingham	.10
355	Andres Galarraga	.20
356	Paul O'Neill	.20
357	Brady Anderson	.15
358	Ramon Martinez	.15
359	John Olerud	.25
360	Ruben Sierra	.10
361	Cal Eldred	.10
362	Jay Buhner	.15
363	Jay Bell	.15
364	Wally Joyner	.15
365	Chuck Knoblauch	.20
366	Len Dykstra	.10
367	John Wetteland	.10
368	Roberto Alomar	.75
369	Craig Biggio	.25
370	Ozzie Smith	.75
371	Terry Pendleton	.10
372	Sammy Sosa	3.00
373	Carlos Garcia	.10
374	Jose Rijo	.10
375	Chris Gomez	.10
376	Barry Bonds	1.00
377	Steve Avery	.10
378	Rick Wilkins	.10
379	Pete Harnisch	.10
380	Dean Palmer	.10
381	Bob Hamelin	.10
382	Jason Bere	.10
383	Jimmy Key	.10
384	Dante Bichette	.35
385	Rafael Palmeiro	.25
386	David Justice	.25
387	Chili Davis	.10
388	Mike Greenwell	.10
389	Todd Zeile	.10
390	Jeff Conine	.10
391	Rick Aguilera	.10
392	Eddie Murray	.40
393	Mike Stanley	.10
394	(Not issued - see #294)	
395	Randy Johnson	.75
396	David Nied	.10
397	Devon White	.10
398	Royce Clayton	.10
399	Andy Benes	.10
400	John Hudek	.10
401	Bobby Jones	.10
402	Eric Karros	.15
403	Will Clark	.35
404	Mark Langston	.10
405	Kevin Brown	.10
406	Greg Maddux	2.50
407	David Cone	.10
408	Wade Boggs	.05
409	Steve Trachsel	.10
410	Greg Vaughn	.10
411	Mo Vaughn	1.00
412	Wilson Alvarez	.10
413	Cal Ripken Jr.	4.00
414	Rico Brogna	.10
415	Barry Larkin	.30
416	Cecil Fielder	.15
417	Jose Canseco	.40
418	Jack McDowell	.10
419	Mike Lieberthal	.10
420	Andrew Lorraine	.10
421	Rich Becker	.10
422	Tony Phillips	.10
423	Scott Ruffcorn	.10
424	Jeff Granger	.10
425	Greg Pirkl	.10
426	Dennis Eckersley	.10
427	Jose Lima	.10
428	Russ Davis	.10
429	Armando Benitez	.10
430	Alex Gonzalez	.10
431	Carlos Delgado	.50
432	Chan Ho Park	.15
433	Mickey Tettleton	.10
434	Dave Winfield	.20
435	John Burkett	.10
436	Orlando Miller	.10
437	Rondell White	.25
438	Jose Oliva	.10
439	Checklist	.10

1995 Bowman Gold

The only chase cards in the '95 Bowman set are gold versions of the foil-etched "Minor League MVPs," "1st Impressions" and "Prime Prospects." The gold cards are found in every 6th (regular) or 12th (jumbo) pack, on average, in place of the silver versions.

	MT
Complete Set (54):	100.00
Common Player:	.50
Superstars: 1-1.5X	
Stars: 1.5-2X	
(See 1995 Bowman #221-274 for checklist and base card values.)	

1995 Bowman's Best

Actually made up of three subsets, all cards feature a player photo set against a silver foil background. The 90 veterans' cards have a broad red-foil stripe in the background beneath the team logo; the 90 rookies' cards have a similar stripe in tones of blue. All of those cards are printed in Topps' Finest technology. The 15 Mirror Image cards are in horizontal format, printed more conventionally on metallic foil, and have a rookie and veteran sharing the card. Backs of each card continue the color theme, have '94 and career stats and a highlight or two. Standard packaging was seven-card foil packs with inserts consisting of higher-tech parallel sets of the regular issue.

		MT
Complete Set (195):		250.00
Common Player:		.25
Wax Box:		250.00
Complete Set Red (90):		60.00
1	Randy Johnson	1.00
2	Joe Carter	.30
3	Chili Davis	.25
4	Moises Alou	.25
5	Gary Sheffield	.50
6	Kevin Appier	.25
7	Denny Neagle	.25
8	Ruben Sierra	.25
9	Darren Daulton	.25
10	Cal Ripken Jr.	6.00
11	Bobby Bonilla	.25
12	Manny Ramirez	2.00
13	Barry Bonds	2.00
14	Eric Karros	.25
15	Greg Maddux	4.50
16	Jeff Bagwell	2.50
17	Paul Molitor	.75
18	Ray Lankford	.25
19	Mark Grace	.65
20	Kenny Lofton	1.50
21	Tony Gwynn	2.50
22	Will Clark	.50
23	Roger Clemens	3.00
24	Dante Bichette	.40
25	Barry Larkin	.35
26	Wade Boggs	.75
27	Kirby Puckett	2.50
28	Cecil Fielder	.30
29	Jose Canseco	.75
30	Juan Gonzalez	3.00
31	David Cone	.50
32	Craig Biggio	.35
33	Tim Salmon	.75
34	David Justice	.50
35	Sammy Sosa	4.00
36	Mike Piazza	4.00
37	Carlos Baerga	.25
38	Jeff Conine	.25
39	Rafael Palmeiro	.60
40	Bret Saberhagen	.25
41	Len Dykstra	.25
42	Mo Vaughn	1.50
43	Wally Joyner	.25
44	Chuck Knoblauch	.30
45	Robin Ventura	.35
46	Don Mattingly	3.00
47	Dave Hollins	.25
48	Andy Benes	.25
49	Ken Griffey Jr.	8.00
50	Albert Belle	2.00
51	Matt Williams	.50
52	Rondell White	.40
53	Raul Mondesi	.50
54	Brian Jordan	.25
55	Greg Vaughn	.25
56	Fred McGriff	.50
57	Roberto Alomar	1.50
58	Dennis Eckersley	.25
59	Lee Smith	.25
60	Eddie Murray	.75
61	Kenny Rogers	.25
62	Ron Gant	.35
63	Larry Walker	1.00
64	Chad Curtis	.25
65	Frank Thomas	3.00
66	Paul O'Neill	.30
67	Kevin Seitzer	.25
68	Marquis Grissom	.25
69	Mark McGwire	7.00
70	Travis Fryman	.25
71	Andres Galarraga	.35
72	*Carlos Perez*	.40
73	Tyler Green	.25
74	Marty Cordova	.25
75	Shawn Green	.50
76	Vaughn Eshelman	.25
77	John Mabry	.25
78	Jason Bates	.25
79	Jon Nunnally	.25
80	Ray Durham	.40
81	Edgardo Alfonzo	.35
82	Esteban Loaiza	.25
83	*Hideo Nomo*	5.00
84	Orlando Miller	.25
85	Alex Gonzalez	.25
86	*Mark Grudzielanek*	1.00
87	Julian Tavarez	.25
88	Benji Gil	.25
89	Quilvio Veras	.25
90	Ricky Bottalico	.25
Complete Set Blue (90):		150.00
1	Derek Jeter	5.00
2	*Vladimir Guerrero*	80.00
3	*Bob Abreu*	6.00
4	Chan Ho Park	.75
5	Paul Wilson	.50
6	Chad Ogea	.40
7	*Andruw Jones*	30.00
8	Brian Barber	.25
9	Andy Larkin	.25
10	*Richie Sexson*	15.00
11	*Everett Stull*	.25
12	Brooks Kieschnick	.60
13	Matt Murray	.25
14	John Wasdin	.25
15	Shannon Stewart	.75
16	Luis Ortiz	.25
17	Marc Kroon	.25
18	Todd Greene	2.00
19	Juan Acevedo	.25
20	Tony Clark	4.00
21	Jermaine Dye	.75

22 Derrek Lee 2.00
23 Pat Watkins .25
24 Calvin Reese .25
25 Ben Grieve 15.00
26 *Julio Santana* .25
27 *Felix Rodriguez* .35
28 Paul Konerko 8.00
29 Nomar Garciaparra 30.00
30 Pat Ahearne .25
31 Jason Schmidt .50
32 Billy Wagner 1.50
33 *Rey Ordonez* 3.00
34 Curtis Goodwin .25
35 *Sergio Nunez* .50
36 Tim Belk .25
37 *Scott Elarton* 1.00
38 Jason Isringhausen .75
39 Trot Nixon 1.00
40 Sid Roberson .25
41 Ron Villone .60
42 Ruben Rivera 1.00
43 Rick Huisman .25
44 Todd Hollandsworth .75
45 Johnny Damon .50
46 Garret Anderson .50
47 Jeff D'Amico .25
48 Dustin Hermanson .25
49 *Juan Encarnacion* 15.00
50 Andy Pettitte 2.50
51 Chris Stynes .25
52 Troy Percival .25
53 LaTroy Hawkins .50
54 Roger Cedeno .50
55 Alan Benes .75
56 *Karim Garcia* 4.00
57 Andrew Lorraine .25
58 *Gary Rath* .50
59 Bret Wagner .25
60 Jeff Suppan .25
61 Bill Pulsipher .40
62 *Jay Payton* .75
63 Alex Ochoa .50
64 Ugueth Urbina .50
65 Armando Benitez .25
66 George Arias .25
67 *Raul Casanova* 1.00
68 Matt Drews .50
69 Jimmy Haynes .25
70 Jimmy Hurst .25
71 C.J. Nitkowski .25
72 *Tommy Davis* .50
73 *Bartolo Colon* 10.00
74 *Chris Carpenter* 3.00
75 Trey Beamon .25
76 Bryan Rekar .50
77 James Baldwin .25
78 Marc Valdes .25
79 *Tom Fordham* .35
80 Marc Newfield .25
81 Angel Martinez .25
82 Brian Hunter .25
83 Jose Herrera .25
84 *Glenn Dishman* .35
85 *Jacob Cruz* 5.00
86 Paul Shuey .25
87 *Scott Rolen* 40.00
88 Doug Million .25
89 Desi Relaford .25
90 Michael Tucker .35
Mirror Image: .50
1 *Ben Davis*, Ivan Rodriguez 5.00
2 *Mark Redman*, Manny Ramirez 2.00
3 *Reggie Taylor*, Deion Sanders 1.50
4 Ryan Jaroncyk, Shawn Green 1.00
5 Juan LeBron, Juan Gonzalez 1.00
6 Toby McKnight, Craig Biggio .50
7 *Michael Barrett*, Travis Fryman 10.00
8 Corey Jenkins, Mo Vaughn 1.00
9 Ruben Rivera, Frank Thomas 2.00
10 Curtis Goodwin, Kenny Lofton 1.50
11 Brian Hunter, Tony Gwynn 1.00
12 Todd Greene, Ken Griffey Jr. 5.00
13 Karim Garcia, Matt Williams 1.50
14 Billy Wagner, Randy Johnson 1.00
15 Pat Watkins, Jeff Bagwell 1.50

1995 Bowman's Best Refractors

The large volume of silver foil in the background of the red and blue subsets in '95 Best make the Refractor technology much easier to see than in Best issues. The chase cards, found one per six packs on average, also have a small "REFRACTOR" printed near the lower-left corner on back. The 15-card Mirror Image subset was not paralleled in Refractor technology, but in a process Topps calls "diffraction-foil" which creates a strong vertical-stripe rainbow effect in the background. Cards #72 (Carlos Perez) and #84 (Orlando Miller) can be found both with and without the "REFRACTOR" notice on back; neither version commands a premium.

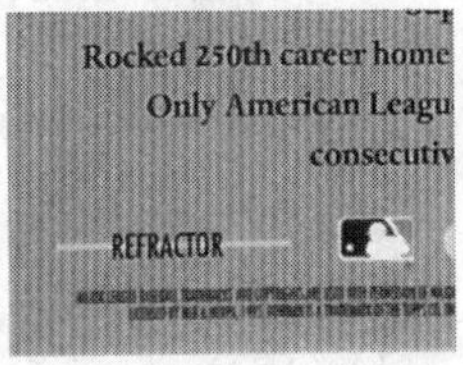

	MT
Complete Set (195):	1900.
Common Player:	1.00
Superstars: 1.5-3X	
Stars: 2-4X	
(See 1995 Bowman's Best for checklist and base card values.)	

1995 Bowman's Best Refractors - Jumbo

These super-size versions of Bowman's Best Refractors were produced exclusively for inclusion as a one-per-box insert in retail boxes of the product distributed by ANCO to large retail chains. The 4-1/4" x 5-3/4" cards are identical in all ways except size to the regular refractors. The jumbo inserts were not produced in equal quantities, with the most popular players being printed in greater numbers.

	MT
Complete Set (10):	150.00
Common Player:	6.00
10 Cal Ripken Jr.	25.00
15 Greg Maddux	15.00
21 Tony Gwynn	15.00
35 Sammy Sosa	15.00
36 Mike Piazza	20.00
42 Mo Vaughn	7.50
49 Ken Griffey Jr.	30.00
50 Albert Belle	10.00
65 Frank Thomas	15.00
83 Hideo Nomo	6.00

1996 Bowman

In a "Guaranteed Value Program," Topps stated it would pay $100 for this set in 1999, if collectors mail in a request form (one per three packs), a $5 fee and the complete set in numerical order (only one per person). Every set redeemed was destroyed. The 385-card set has 110 veteran stars and 275 prospects. Backs of the prospects' cards provide a detailed scouting report. A "1st Bowman Card" gold-foil stamped logo was included on the card front for 156 players making their first appearance in a Bowman set. Insert sets include Bowman's Best Previews (along with Refractor and Atomic Refractor versions), a 1952 Mickey Mantle Bowman reprint (1 in 48 packs) and Minor League Player of the Year candidates. A 385-card parallel version of the entire base set was also produced on 18-point foilboard; seeded one per pack.

	MT
Complete Set (385):	125.00
Common Player:	.15
Foils: 1x to 2x	
Wax Box:	110.00

1 Cal Ripken Jr. 3.00
2 Ray Durham .15
3 Ivan Rodriguez 1.50
4 Fred McGriff .25
5 Hideo Nomo .75
6 Troy Percival .15
7 Moises Alou .15
8 Mike Stanley .15
9 Jay Buhner .25
10 Shawn Green .35
11 Ryan Klesko .40
12 Andres Galarraga .25
13 Dean Palmer .15
14 Jeff Conine .15
15 Brian Hunter .15
16 J.T. Snow .15
17 Larry Walker .60
18 Barry Larkin .25
19 Alex Gonzalez .15
20 Edgar Martinez .15
21 Mo Vaughn 1.25
22 Mark McGwire 5.00
23 Jose Canseco .50
24 Jack McDowell .15
25 Dante Bichette .25
26 Wade Boggs .50
27 Mike Piazza 3.00
28 Ray Lankford .15
29 Craig Biggio .20
30 Rafael Palmeiro .35
31 Ron Gant .25
32 Javy Lopez .25
33 Brian Jordan .25
34 Paul O'Neill .20
35 Mark Grace .35
36 Matt Williams .40
37 Pedro Martinez .50
38 Rickey Henderson .25
39 Bobby Bonilla .20
40 Todd Hollandsworth .25
41 Jim Thome .60
42 Gary Sheffield .75
43 Tim Salmon .30
44 Gregg Jefferies .15
45 Roberto Alomar 1.25
45p Roberto Alomar (unmarked promo card, fielding photo on front) 20.00
46 Carlos Baerga .15
47 Mark Grudzielanek .15
48 Randy Johnson .50
49 Tino Martinez .20
50 Robin Ventura .20
51 Ryne Sandberg 1.00
52 Jay Bell .20
53 Jason Schmidt .15
54 Frank Thomas 1.50
55 Kenny Lofton 1.00
56 Ariel Prieto .15
57 David Cone .25
58 Reggie Sanders .15
59 Michael Tucker .15
60 Vinny Castilla .15
61 Lenny Dykstra .15
62 Todd Hundley .25
63 Brian McRae .15
64 Dennis Eckersley .15
65 Rondell White .15
66 Eric Karros .15
67 Greg Maddux 2.50
68 Kevin Appier .15
69 Eddie Murray .50
70 John Olerud .20
71 Tony Gwynn 2.00
72 David Justice .25
73 Ken Caminiti .40
74 Terry Steinbach .15
75 Alan Benes .15
76 Chipper Jones 3.00
77 Jeff Bagwell 1.50
77p Jeff Bagwell (unmarked promo card, name in gold) 15.00
78 Barry Bonds 1.00
79 Ken Griffey Jr. 4.00
80 Roger Cedeno .15
81 Joe Carter .15
82 Henry Rodriguez .15
83 Jason Isringhausen .15
84 Chuck Knoblauch .25
85 Manny Ramirez 1.50
86 Tom Glavine .25
87 Jeffrey Hammonds .15
88 Paul Molitor .50
89 Roger Clemens 1.50
90 Greg Vaughn .15
91 Marty Cordova .20
92 Albert Belle 1.00
93 Mike Mussina .75
94 Garret Anderson .15
95 Juan Gonzalez 2.00
96 John Valentin .15
97 Jason Giambi .25
98 Kirby Puckett 1.50
99 Jim Edmonds .25
100 Cecil Fielder .20
101 Mike Aldrete .15
102 Marquis Grissom .15
103 Derek Bell .15
104 Raul Mondesi .40
105 Sammy Sosa 2.50
106 Travis Fryman .15
107 Rico Brogna .15
108 Will Clark .30
109 Bernie Williams .75
110 Brady Anderson .20
111 Torii Hunter .15
112 Derek Jeter 2.50
113 *Mike Kusiewicz* .15
114 Scott Rolen 4.00
115 Ramon Castro .15
116 *Jose Guillen* 4.00
117 *Wade Walker* .40
118 Shawn Senior .15
119 *Onan Masaoka* .40
120 *Marlon Anderson* 5.00
121 *Katsuhiro Maeda* 1.00
122 *Garrett Stephenson* .15
123 Butch Huskey .15
124 *D'Angelo Jimenez* 1.00
125 *Tony Mounce* .15
126 Jay Canizaro .15
127 Juan Melo .20
128 Steve Gibralter .15
129 Freddy Garcia .15
130 Julio Santana .15
131 Richard Hidalgo .25
132 Jermaine Dye .20
133 Willie Adams .15
134 Everett Stull .15
135 Ramon Morel .15
136 Chan Ho Park .20
137 Jamey Wright .15
138 *Luis Garcia* .15
139 Dan Serafini .15
140 *Ryan Dempster* 1.00
141 Tate Seefried .15
142 Jimmy Hurst .15
143 Travis Miller .15
144 Curtis Goodwin .15
145 *Rocky Coppinger* .50
146 Enrique Wilson .40
147 Jaime Bluma .15
148 Andrew Vessel .15
149 Damian Moss .50
150 *Shawn Gallagher* 2.00
151 Pat Watkins .15
152 Jose Paniagua .15
153 Danny Graves .15
154 *Bryon Gainey* .15
155 Steve Soderstrom .15
156 *Cliff Brumbaugh* .15
157 *Eugene Kingsale* .50
158 Lou Collier .15
159 Todd Walker 4.00
160 *Kris Detmers* 1.00
161 *Josh Booty* .35
162 *Greg Whiteman* .15
163 Damian Jackson .15
164 Tony Clark 1.00
165 Jeff D'Amico .15
166 Johnny Damon .40
167 Rafael Orellano .15
168 Ruben Rivera .20
169 Alex Ochoa .20
170 Jay Powell .15
171 Tom Evans .15
172 Ron Villone .15
173 Shawn Estes .15
174 John Wasdin .15
175 Bill Simas .15
176 Kevin Brown .15
177 Shannon Stewart .15
178 Todd Greene .15
179 Bob Wolcott .15
180 Chris Snopek .15
181 Nomar Garciaparra 4.00
182 *Cameron Smith* .15
183 Matt Drews .15
184 Jimmy Haynes .15
185 Chris Carpenter .25
186 Desi Relaford .15
187 Ben Grieve 3.00
188 Mike Bell .15
189 *Luis Castillo* 1.50
190 Ugueth Urbina .15
191 Paul Wilson .15
191p Paul Wilson (unmarked promo card, name in gold) 5.00
192 Andruw Jones 4.00
193 Wayne Gomes .15
194 *Craig Counsell* .75
195 Jim Cole .15
196 Brooks Kieshnick .15
197 Trey Beamon .15
198 *Marino Santana* .30
199 Bob Abreu .40
200 Calvin Reese .15
201 Dante Powell 1.50
202 George Arias .15
202p George Arias (unmarked promo card, name in gold) 5.00
203 *Jorge Velandia* .15
204 *George Lombard* 3.00
205 *Byron Browne* .30
206 John Frascatore .15
207 Terry Adams .15
208 *Wilson Delgado* .40
209 Billy McMillon .15
210 Jeff Abbott .20
211 Trot Nixon .25
212 Amaury Telemaco .15
213 Scott Sullivan .15
214 Justin Thompson .15
215 Decomba Conner .15
216 Ryan McGuire .15
217 *Matt Luke* .40
218 Doug Million .15
219 *Jason Dickson* 1.50
220 *Ramon Hernandez* 4.00
221 *Mark Bellhorn* 1.00
222 *Eric Ludwick* .15
223 *Luke Wilcox* .30
224 *Marty Malloy* .30
225 *Gary Coffee* .30
226 *Wendell Magee* .75
227 *Brett Tomko* 1.50
228 Derek Lowe .15
229 *Jose Rosado* 1.00
230 *Steve Bourgeois* .30
231 *Neil Weber* .30
232 Jeff Ware .15
233 Edwin Diaz .20
234 Greg Norton .15
235 Aaron Boone .25
236 Jeff Suppan .15
237 Bret Wagner .15
238 Elieser Marrero .15
239 Will Cunnane .15
240 *Brian Barkley* .40
241 Jay Payton .75
242 Marcus Jensen .15
243 Ryan Nye .15
244 Chad Mottola .15
245 *Scott McClain* .40
246 *Jesse Ibarra* .40
247 *Mike Darr* 1.00
248 *Bobby Estalella* 3.00
249 Michael Barrett 2.50
250 *Jamie Lopiccolo* .25
251 *Shane Spencer* 3.00
252 *Ben Petrick* 5.00
253 *Jason Bell* .40
254 *Arnold Gooch* .40
255 T.J. Mathews .15
256 Jason Ryan .15
257 *Pat Cline* .40
258 *Rafael Carmona* .40
259 *Carl Pavano* 6.00
260 Ben Davis 1.00
261 *Matt Lawton* .75
262 *Kevin Sefcik* .30
263 *Chris Fussell* .50
264 *Mike Cameron* 3.00
265 *Marty Janzen* .30
266 *Livan Hernandez* 3.00
267 *Raul Ibanez* .65
268 Juan Encarnacion 2.00
269 *David Yocum* .40
270 *Jonathan Johnson* .40
271 Reggie Taylor .15
272 *Danny Buxbaum* .30
273 Jacob Cruz .20
274 *Bobby Morris* .40
275 *Andy Fox* .40
276 Greg Keagle .15
277 Charles Peterson .15
278 Derrek Lee .35
279 *Bryant Nelson* .40
280 Antone Williamson .15
281 Scott Elarton .15
282 *Shad Williams* .40
283 *Rich Hunter* .40
284 Chris Sheff .15
285 Derrick Gibson 2.00
286 Felix Rodriguez .15
287 *Brian Banks* .40
288 Jason McDonald .15
289 *Glendon Rusch* 1.50
290 Gary Rath .15
291 Peter Munro .15
292 Tom Fordham .15
293 Jason Kendall .25
294 Russ Johnson .15
295 *Joe Long* .25
296 *Robert Smith* 1.50
297 *Jarrod Washburn* 1.00
298 *Dave Coggin* .30
299 *Jeff Yoder* .30
300 *Jed Hansen* .40
301 *Matt Morris* 3.00
302 *Josh Bishop* .30
303 Dustin Hermanson .15
304 Mike Gulan .15
305 Felipe Crespo .15
306 Quinton McCracken .15
307 *Jim Bonnici* .30
308 Sal Fasano .15
309 *Gabe Alvarez* 2.00
310 *Heath Murray* .30
311 *Jose Valentin* 1.50
312 Bartolo Colon .75
313 Olmedo Saenz .15
314 *Norm Hutchins* 1.50

315	*Chris Holt*	.30
316	*David Doster*	.40
317	Robert Person	.15
318	*Donne Wall*	.40
319	*Adam Riggs*	.40
320	Homer Bush	.15
321	*Brad Rigby*	.40
322	*Lou Merloni*	.40
323	Neifi Perez	.15
324	Chris Cumberland	.15
325	*Alvie Shepherd*	.40
326	*Jarrod Patterson*	.40
327	*Ray Ricken*	.40
328	*Danny Klassen*	.60
329	*David Miller*	.30
330	*Chad Alexander*	.60
331	Matt Beaumont	.15
332	Damon Hollins	.15
333	Todd Dunn	.15
334	*Mike Sweeney*	3.00
335	Richie Sexson	1.00
336	Billy Wagner	.40
337	*Ron Wright*	4.00
338	Paul Konerko	1.00
339	*Tommy Phelps*	.30
340	Karim Garcia	1.00
341	*Mike Grace*	.25
342	*Russell Branyan*	6.00
343	*Randy Winn*	.30
344	*A.J. Pierzynski*	.40
345	*Mike Busby*	.40
346	*Matt Beech*	.40
347	*Jose Cepeda*	.40
348	Brian Stephenson	.15
349	Rey Ordonez	.75
350	*Rich Aurilia*	.30
351	*Edgard Velazquez*	2.50
352	Raul Casanova	.15
353	*Carlos Guillen*	3.00
354	*Bruce Aven*	.40
355	*Ryan Jones*	1.50
356	*Derek Aucoin*	.40
357	*Brian Rose*	1.50
358	*Richard Almanzar*	.40
359	*Fletcher Bates*	.40
360	*Russ Ortiz*	.40
361	*Wilton Guerrero*	1.00
362	*Geoff Jenkins*	6.00
363	Pete Janicki	.15
364	Yamil Benitez	.15
365	Aaron Holbert	.15
366	Tim Belk	.15
367	Terrell Wade	.15
368	Terrence Long	.15
369	Brad Fullmer	.25
370	Matt Wagner	.15
371	Craig Wilson	.15
372	Mark Loretta	.15
373	Eric Owens	.15
374	Vladimir Guerrero	3.00
375	Tommy Davis	.15
376	Donnie Sadler	.15
377	Edgar Renteria	.60
378	Todd Helton	8.00
379	*Ralph Milliard*	.40
380	*Darin Blood*	1.50
381	Shayne Bennett	.15
382	Mark Redman	.15
383	Felix Martinez	.15
384	*Sean Watkins*	.40
385	Oscar Henriquez	.15

1996 Bowman 1952 Mickey Mantle Reprints

Reprints of Mickey Mantle's 1952 Bowman baseball card were created for insertion in Bowman and Bowman's Best products for 1996. The 2-1/2" x 3-1/2" card can be found in regular (gold seal on front), Finest, Finest Refractor and Atomic Refractor versions.

		MT
Complete Set (4):		60.00
Common Player:		10.00
20	Mickey Mantle (reprint)	10.00
20	Mickey Mantle (Finest)	10.00
20	Mickey Mantle (Refractor)	20.00
20	Mickey Mantle (Atomic Refractor)	30.00

1996 Bowman Minor League Player of the Year

Fifteen prospects who were candidates for Minor League Player of the Year are featured in this 1996 Bowman baseball insert set. Cards were seeded one per every 12 packs.

		MT
Complete Set (15):		40.00
Common Player:		1.00
1	Andruw Jones	10.00
2	Derrick Gibson	3.00
3	Bob Abreu	1.00
4	Todd Walker	4.00
5	Jamey Wright	1.50
6	Wes Helms	4.00
7	Karim Garcia	4.00
8	Bartolo Colon	1.00
9	Alex Ochoa	1.00
10	Mike Sweeney	1.00
11	Ruben Rivera	1.50
12	Gabe Alvarez	1.50
13	Billy Wagner	3.00
14	Vladimir Guerrero	8.00
15	Edgard Velazquez	5.00

1996 Bowman's Best Preview

These cards use Topps' Finest technology. The cards were seeded one per every 12 packs of 1996 Bowman baseball cards. Fifteen veterans and 15 prospects are featured in the set.

		MT
Complete Set (30):		100.00
Common Player:		1.50
1	Chipper Jones	10.00
2	Alan Benes	1.00
3	Brooks Kieshnick	1.00
4	Barry Bonds	5.00
5	Rey Ordonez	2.00
6	Tim Salmon	1.50
7	Mike Piazza	10.00
8	Billy Wagner	2.00
9	Andruw Jones	6.00
10	Tony Gwynn	8.00
11	Paul Wilson	1.00
12	Calvin Reese	1.00
13	Frank Thomas	6.00
14	Greg Maddux	9.00
15	Derek Jeter	10.00
16	Jeff Bagwell	8.00
17	Barry Larkin	1.50
18	Todd Greene	1.50
19	Ruben Rivera	1.00
20	Richard Hidalgo	1.50
21	Larry Walker	3.00
22	Carlos Baerga	1.00
23	Derrick Gibson	1.50
24	Richie Sexson	1.50
25	Mo Vaughn	4.00
26	Hideo Nomo	2.00
27	Nomar Garciaparra	12.00
28	Cal Ripken Jr.	12.00
29	Karim Garcia	1.50
30	Ken Griffey Jr.	18.00

1996 Bowman's Best Preview Refractors

Bowman took its hot Refractor technology to a higher level by adding an Atomic Refractor version with a "foil-patterned, starburst-like effect" to the Best Preview cards featured as a Bowman insert. Refractor cards are seeded one per 24 packs of 1996 Bowman baseball; Atomic Refractors are seeded one per 48 packs. Fifteen veterans and 15 prospects are featured.

		MT
Complete Set (30):		300.00
Common Player:		5.00
Atomic Refractors: 1.5-2X		
1	Chipper Jones	20.00
2	Alan Benes	5.00
3	Brooks Kieshnick	5.00
4	Barry Bonds	10.00
5	Rey Ordonez	5.00
6	Tim Salmon	8.00
7	Mike Piazza	20.00
8	Billy Wagner	5.00
9	Andruw Jones	15.00
10	Tony Gwynn	18.00
11	Paul Wilson	5.00
12	Calvin Reese	5.00
13	Frank Thomas	15.00
14	Greg Maddux	20.00
15	Derek Jeter	20.00
16	Jeff Bagwell	15.00
17	Barry Larkin	8.00
18	Todd Greene	5.00
19	Ruben Rivera	5.00
20	Richard Hidalgo	5.00
21	Larry Walker	8.00
22	Carlos Baerga	5.00
23	Derrick Gibson	5.00
24	Richie Sexson	6.00
25	Mo Vaughn	10.00
26	Hideo Nomo	6.00
27	Nomar Garciaparra	20.00
28	Cal Ripken Jr.	25.00
29	Karim Garcia	5.00
30	Ken Griffey Jr.	35.00

1996 Bowman's Best

Bowman's Best returns in its traditional format of 180 cards: 90 established stars and 90 up-and-coming prospects and rookies. Three types of insert sets are found in Bowman's Best - Mirror Image, Bowman's Best Cuts and the 1952 Bowman Mickey Mantle reprints. There are also parallel sets of Refractors and Atomic Refractors randomly seeded in packs. Refractors are found on average of one per 12 packs; Atomic Refractors are seeded one per 48 packs. Mirror Image Refractors are found one per 96 packs, while Mirror Image Atomic Refractors are seeded one per 192 packs. Refractors are seeded in every 48th pack, while Bowman's Best Cuts Atomic Refractors are in every 96th pack. Refractor versions of the Mantle reprint are seeded one per every 96 packs; Atomic Refractor Mantle reprints are seeded in every 192nd pack.

		MT
Complete Set (180):		100.00
Common Player:		.25
Wax Box:		160.00
1	Hideo Nomo	.75
2	Edgar Martinez	.25
3	Cal Ripken Jr.	5.00
4	Wade Boggs	.75
5	Cecil Fielder	.25
6	Albert Belle	1.50
7	Chipper Jones	4.00
8	Ryne Sandberg	1.50
9	Tim Salmon	.50
10	Barry Bonds	1.50
11	Ken Caminiti	.75
12	Ron Gant	.25
13	Frank Thomas	2.00
14	Dante Bichette	.75
15	Jason Kendall	.35
16	Mo Vaughn	1.50
17	Rey Ordonez	.45
18	Henry Rodriguez	.25
19	Ryan Klesko	.40
20	Jeff Bagwell	2.00
21	Randy Johnson	1.00
22	Jim Edmonds	.40
23	Kenny Lofton	1.00
24	Andy Pettitte	1.00
25	Brady Anderson	.25
26	Mike Piazza	4.00
27	Greg Vaughn	.25
28	Joe Carter	.25
29	Jason Giambi	.25
30	Ivan Rodriguez	1.25
31	Jeff Conine	.25
32	Rafael Palmeiro	.40
33	Roger Clemens	2.00
34	Chuck Knoblauch	.50
35	Reggie Sanders	.25
36	Andres Galarraga	.40
37	Paul O'Neill	.50
38	Tony Gwynn	3.00
39	Paul Wilson	.25
40	Garret Anderson	.25
41	David Justice	.40
42	Eddie Murray	.75
43	*Mike Grace*	.25
44	Marty Cordova	.25
45	Kevin Appier	.25
46	Raul Mondesi	.50
47	Jim Thome	.75
48	Sammy Sosa	4.00
49	Craig Biggio	.35
50	Marquis Grissom	.25
51	Alan Benes	.25
52	Manny Ramirez	2.00
53	Gary Sheffield	.75
54	Mike Mussina	1.00
55	Robin Ventura	.35
56	Johnny Damon	.25
57	Jose Canseco	.75
58	Juan Gonzalez	3.00
59	Tino Martinez	.50
60	Brian Hunter	.25
61	Fred McGriff	.45
62	Jay Buhner	.25
63	Carlos Delgado	.50
64	Moises Alou	.25
65	Roberto Alomar	1.00
66	Barry Larkin	.40
67	Vinny Castilla	.25
68	Ray Durham	.25
69	Travis Fryman	.25
70	Jason Isringhausen	.25
71	Ken Griffey Jr.	7.00
72	John Smoltz	.40
73	Matt Williams	.50
74	Chan Ho Park	.25
75	Mark McGwire	7.00
76	Jeffrey Hammonds	.25
77	Will Clark	.50
78	Kirby Puckett	2.00
79	Derek Jeter	4.00
80	Derek Bell	.25
81	Eric Karros	.25
82	Lenny Dykstra	.25
83	Larry Walker	.75
84	Mark Grudzielanek	.25
85	Greg Maddux	3.00
86	Carlos Baerga	.25
87	Paul Molitor	.50
88	John Valentin	.25
89	Mark Grace	.40
90	Ray Lankford	.25
91	Andruw Jones	4.00
92	Nomar Garciaparra	5.00
93	Alex Ochoa	.25
94	Derrick Gibson	1.50
95	Jeff D'Amico	.25
96	Ruben Rivera	.25
97	Vladimir Guerrero	3.00
98	Calvin Reese	.25
99	Richard Hidalgo	.25
100	Bartolo Colon	1.00
101	Karim Garcia	1.00
102	Ben Davis	1.00
103	Jay Powell	.25
104	Chris Snopek	.25
105	*Glendon Rusch*	.25
106	Enrique Wilson	.50
107	*Antonio Alfonseca*	.25
108	*Wilton Guerrero*	1.00
109	*Jose Guillen*	3.00
110	*Miguel Mejia*	.25
111	Jay Payton	.50
112	Scott Elarton	.50
113	Brooks Kieschnick	.25
114	Dustin Hermanson	.25
115	Roger Cedeno	.25
116	Matt Wagner	.25
117	Lee Daniels	.25
118	Ben Grieve	3.00
119	Ugueth Urbina	.25
120	Danny Graves	.25
121	*Dan Donato*	.25
122	*Matt Ruebel*	.25
123	*Mark Sievert*	.25
124	Chris Stynes	.25
125	Jeff Abbott	.25
126	*Rocky Coppinger*	.50
127	Jermaine Dye	.25
128	Todd Greene	.25
129	Chris Carpenter	.25
130	Edgar Renteria	.75
131	Matt Drews	.25
132	*Edgard Velazquez*	2.00
133	Casey Whitten	.25
134	*Ryan Jones*	.75
135	Todd Walker	4.00
136	*Geoff Jenkins*	4.00
137	*Matt Morris*	4.00
138	Richie Sexson	1.50
139	*Todd Dunwoody*	4.00
140	*Gabe Alvarez*	2.00
141	J.J. Johnson	.25
142	Shannon Stewart	.25
143	Brad Fullmer	.50
144	Julio Santana	.25
145	Scott Rolen	4.00
146	Amaury Telemaco	.25
147	Trey Beamon	.25
148	Billy Wagner	.40
149	Todd Hollandsworth	.25
150	Doug Million	.25
151	*Jose Valentin*	1.00
152	*Wes Helms*	4.00
153	Jeff Suppan	.25
154	*Luis Castillo*	1.00
155	Bob Abreu	.25
156	Paul Konerko	1.00
157	Jamey Wright	.25
158	Eddie Pearson	.25
159	Jimmy Haynes	.25
160	Derrek Lee	.50
161	Damian Moss	.50
162	*Carlos Guillen*	4.00
163	*Chris Fussell*	.50
164	*Mike Sweeney*	.50
165	Donnie Sadler	.25
166	Desi Relaford	.25
167	Steve Gibralter	.25
168	Neifi Perez	.25
169	Antone Williamson	.25
170	*Marty Janzen*	.25
171	Todd Helton	6.00
172	*Raul Ibanez*	.75
173	Bill Selby	.25
174	*Shane Monahan*	1.00
175	*Robin Jennings*	.25
176	*Bobby Chouinard*	.25
177	Einar Diaz	.25
178	Jason Thompson	.25
179	*Rafael Medina*	.65
180	Kevin Orie	.25

1996 Bowman's Best Refractors

Parallel sets of 180 Refractors and Atomic Refractors were randomly seeded in Bowman's Best packs at the average rate of one per 12 packs for Refractors, with Atomic Refractors seeded one per 48 packs. Mirror Image Refractors are found one per 96 packs, while Mirror Image Atomic Refractors are seeded one per 192 packs.

	MT
Complete Refractor Set (180):	1500.
Common Refractor:	2.00
Refractors: 4-8X	
Common Atomic Refractor:	6.00
Atomics: 6-12X	

(See 1996 Bowman's Best for checklist and base card values.)

1996 Bowman's Best Cuts

Bowman's Best Cuts gave collectors the first die-cut chromium cards in a 15-card set of top stars. The cards were seeded one per 24 packs. Refractor versions are inserted on average of one per 48 packs; Atomic Refractor versions are found one per 96 packs.

		MT
Complete Set (15):		100.00
Common Player:		2.00
1	Ken Griffey Jr.	25.00
2	Jason Isringhausen	2.00
3	Derek Jeter	15.00
4	Andruw Jones	12.00
5	Chipper Jones	15.00
6	Ryan Klesko	2.50
7	Raul Mondesi	3.00
8	Hideo Nomo	4.00
9	Mike Piazza	15.00
10	Manny Ramirez	9.00
11	Cal Ripken Jr.	20.00
12	Ruben Rivera	2.00
13	Tim Salmon	3.00
14	Frank Thomas	10.00
15	Jim Thome	5.00

1996 Bowman's Best Cuts Refractors

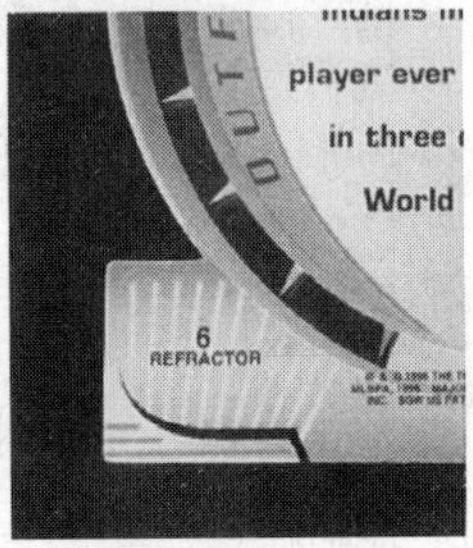

Two Refractor versions are made of these die-cut chromium cards - regular Refractors and Atomic Refractors. The regular versions are seeded one per every 48 packs; Atomic Refractors appear in every 96th pack.

		MT
Complete Set (15):		325.00
Common Player:		8.00
Atomics: 2x		
1	Ken Griffey Jr.	60.00
2	Jason Isringhausen	8.00
3	Derek Jeter	40.00
4	Andruw Jones	30.00
5	Chipper Jones	40.00
6	Ryan Klesko	8.00
7	Raul Mondesi	10.00
8	Hideo Nomo	10.00
9	Mike Piazza	40.00
10	Manny Ramirez	15.00
11	Cal Ripken Jr.	50.00
12	Ruben Rivera	10.00
13	Tim Salmon	10.00
14	Frank Thomas	20.00
15	Jim Thome	12.00

1996 Bowman's Best Mirror Image

Mirror Image inserts feature four top players at 10 different positions, pairing an American League veteran and a prospect on one side and a National League veteran and prospect on the other. These cards are seeded one per every 48 packs. Mirror Image Refractors (one in every 96 packs) and Mirror Image Atomic Refractors (one in every 192 packs) were also produced.

		MT
Complete Set (10):		90.00
Common Player:		5.00
Refractors: 1.5x to 2x		
Atomics: 2x to 4x		
1	Jeff Bagwell, Todd Helton, Frank Thomas, Richie Sexson	15.00
2	Craig Biggio, Luis Castillo, Roberto Alomar, Desi Relaford	5.00
3	Chipper Jones, Scott Rolen, Wade Boggs, George Arias	12.50
4	Barry Larkin, Neifi Perez, Cal Ripken Jr., Mark Bellhorn	12.50
5	Larry Walker, Karim Garcia, Albert Belle, Ruben Rivera	5.00
6	Barry Bonds, Andruw Jones, Kenny Lofton, Donnie Sadler	9.00
7	Tony Gwynn, Vladimir Guerrero, Ken Griffey Jr., Ben Grieve	25.00
8	Mike Piazza, Ben Davis, Ivan Rodriguez, Jose Valentin	12.00
9	Greg Maddux, Jamey Wright, Mike Mussina, Bartolo Colon	10.00
10	Tom Glavine, Billy Wagner, Randy Johnson, Jarrod Washburn	5.00

1997 Bowman Pre-production

The format for 1997 Bowman's base set was previewed in this sample issue distributed to card dealers and the hobby press. The samples are virtually identical to the issued versions of the same players' cards, except they carry a "PP" prefix to the number on back.

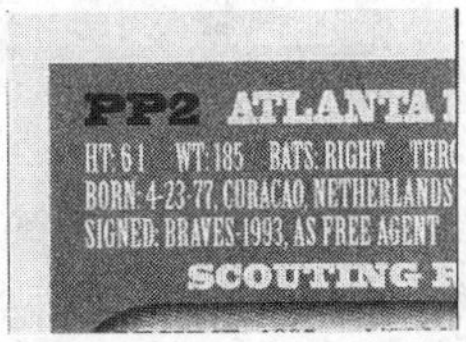

		MT
Complete Set (4):		16.00
Common Player:		3.00
PP1	Jose Cruz, Jr.	3.00
PP2	Andruw Jones	5.00
PP3	Derek Jeter	7.50
PP4	Sammy Sosa	8.00

1997 Bowman

The 1997 Bowman set consists of 440 base cards, an increase of 55 cards from the '96 set. Fronts have a player photo within a red or blue frame with black borders. Backs feature another color photo, along with 1996 statistics broken down by opponent. Players making their first appearance in a Bowman set have a "1st Bowman Card" designation on the card. Prospects' cards have red foil on front; veterans have blue. Inserts include International parallels, Certified Autographs, Scout's Honor Roll and Bowman's Best Previews. Cards were sold in 10-card packs with a suggested retail price of $2.50. Topps offered collectors a $125 guarantee on the value of the set through the year 2000.

		MT
Complete Set (440):		150.00
Complete Series 1 Set (221):		80.00
Complete Series 2 Set (219):		70.00
Common Player:		.15
Series 1 Box:		110.00
Series 2 Box:		90.00
1	Derek Jeter	2.50
2	Edgar Renteria	.15
3	Chipper Jones	2.50
4	Hideo Nomo	.75
5	Tim Salmon	.25
6	Jason Giambi	.15
7	Robin Ventura	.20
8	Tony Clark	.75
9	Barry Larkin	.25
10	Paul Molitor	.50
11	Bernard Gilkey	.15
12	Jack McDowell	.15
13	Andy Benes	.15
14	Ryan Klesko	.40
15	Mark McGwire	5.00
16	Ken Griffey Jr.	4.00
17	Robb Nen	.15
18	Cal Ripken Jr.	3.00
19	John Valentin	.15
20	Ricky Bottalico	.15
21	Mike Lansing	.15
22	Ryne Sandberg	1.00
23	Carlos Delgado	.40
24	Craig Biggio	.20
25	Eric Karros	.15
26	Kevin Appier	.15
27	Mariano Rivera	.20
28	Vinny Castilla	.15
29	Juan Gonzalez	1.75
30	Al Martin	.15
31	Jeff Cirillo	.15
32	Eddie Murray	.50
33	Ray Lankford	.15
34	Manny Ramirez	1.50
35	Roberto Alomar	.75
36	Will Clark	.25
37	Chuck Knoblauch	.20
38	Harold Baines	.15
39	Trevor Hoffman	.15
40	Edgar Martinez	.15
41	Geronimo Berroa	.15
42	Rey Ordonez	.25
43	Mike Stanley	.15
44	Mike Mussina	.75
45	Kevin Brown	.15
46	Dennis Eckersley	.15
47	Henry Rodriguez	.15
48	Tino Martinez	.25
49	Eric Young	.15
50	Bret Boone	.15
51	Raul Mondesi	.25
52	Sammy Sosa	2.50
53	John Smoltz	.25
54	Billy Wagner	.15
55	Jeff D'Amico	.15
56	Ken Caminiti	.25
57	Jason Kendall	.15
58	Wade Boggs	.50
59	Andres Galarraga	.25
60	Jeff Brantley	.15
61	Mel Rojas	.15
62	Brian Hunter	.15
63	Bobby Bonilla	.15
64	Roger Clemens	2.00
65	Jeff Kent	.15
66	Matt Williams	.40
67	Albert Belle	1.00
68	Jeff King	.15
69	John Wetteland	.15
70	Deion Sanders	.40
71	*Bubba Trammell*	2.00
72	*Felix Heredia*	.60
73	*Billy Koch*	1.50
74	*Sidney Ponson*	.40
75	*Ricky Ledee*	6.00
76	Brett Tomko	.15
77	*Braden Looper*	.50
78	Damian Jackson	.15
79	Jason Dickson	.40
80	*Chad Green*	1.00
81	*R.A. Dickey*	.40
82	Jeff Liefer	.40
83	Matt Wagner	.15
84	Richard Hidalgo	.15
85	Adam Riggs	.15
86	Robert Smith	.15
87	*Chad Hermansen*	4.00
88	Felix Martinez	.15
89	J.J. Johnson	.15
90	Todd Dunwoody	1.00
91	Katsuhiro Maeda	.15
92	Darin Erstad	2.00
93	Elieser Marrero	.15
94	Bartolo Colon	.15
95	Chris Fussell	.25
96	Ugueth Urbina	.15
97	*Josh Paul*	.50
98	Jaime Bluma	.15
99	*Seth Greisinger*	.40
100	*Jose Cruz*	2.00
101	Todd Dunn	.15
102	*Joe Young*	.40
103	Jonathan Johnson	.15
104	*Justin Towle*	2.00
105	Brian Rose	1.00
106	Jose Guillen	1.00
107	Andruw Jones	2.00
108	*Mark Kotsay*	3.00
109	Wilton Guerrero	.15
110	Jacob Cruz	.15
111	Mike Sweeney	.25
112	Julio Mosquera	.15
113	Matt Morris	.40
114	Wendell Magee	.15
115	John Thomson	.15
116	*Javier Valentin*	.30
117	Tom Fordham	.15
118	Ruben Rivera	.15
119	*Mike Drumright*	.50
120	Chris Holt	.15
121	*Sean Maloney*	.40
122	Michael Barrett	.50
123	*Tony Saunders*	1.50
124	Kevin Brown	.15
125	Richard Almanzar	.15
126	Mark Redman	.15
127	*Anthony Sanders*	1.50
128	Jeff Abbott	.15
129	Eugene Kingsale	.15
130	Paul Konerko	1.00
131	*Randall Simon*	1.00
132	Andy Larkin	.15
133	Rafael Medina	.25
134	Mendy Lopez	.15
135	Freddy Garcia	.15
136	Karim Garcia	.40
137	*Larry Rodriguez*	.50
138	Carlos Guillen	.15
139	Aaron Boone	.15
140	Donnie Sadler	.15
141	Brooks Kieschnick	.15
142	Scott Spiezio	.15
143	Everett Stull	.15
144	Enrique Wilson	.15
145	*Milton Bradley*	3.00
146	Kevin Orie	.20
147	Derek Wallace	.15
148	Russ Johnson	.15
149	*Joe Lagarde*	.40
150	Luis Castillo	.40
151	Jay Payton	.25
152	Joe Long	.15
153	Livan Hernandez	.60
154	*Vladimir Nunez*	1.00
155	Not issued	.15
156a	George Arias	.15
156b	Calvin Reese (Should be #155)	.15
157	Homer Bush	.15
158	Not issued	.15
159a	*Eric Milton*	2.00
159b	Chris Carpenter (Should be #158)	.15
160	Richie Sexson	.25
161	Carl Pavano	1.00
162	*Chris Gissell*	.40
163	Mac Suzuki	.15
164	Pat Cline	.15
165	Ron Wright	1.00
166	Dante Powell	.40
167	Mark Bellhorn	.25
168	George Lombard	.50
169	*Pee Wee Lopez*	.40
170	*Paul Wilder*	2.00
171	Brad Fullmer	.15
172	*Willie Martinez*	.75
173	*Dario Veras*	.40
174	Dave Coggin	.15
175	*Kris Benson*	4.00
176	Torii Hunter	.15
177	*D.T. Cromer*	.40
178	*Nelson Figueroa*	1.25
179	*Hiram Bocachica*	1.50
180	Shane Monahan	.25
181	*Jimmy Anderson*	.75
182	Juan Melo	.15
183	*Pablo Ortega*	1.00
184	*Calvin Pickering*	2.50
185	Reggie Taylor	.15
186	*Jeff Farnsworth*	.40
187	Terrence Long	.15
188	Geoff Jenkins	.40
189	*Steve Rain*	.40
190	*Nerio Rodriguez*	1.00
191	Derrick Gibson	.50
192	Darin Blood	.40
193	Ben Davis	.15
194	*Adrian Beltre*	5.00
195	*Damian Sapp*	2.00
196	*Kerry Wood*	5.00
197	*Nate Rolison*	1.50
198	*Fernando Tatis*	8.00
199	*Brad Penny*	4.00
200	*Jake Westbrook*	.75
201	Edwin Diaz	.15
202	*Joe Fontenot*	.60
203	*Matt Halloran*	.75
204	*Blake Stein*	.40
205	Onan Masaoka	.15
206	Ben Petrick	.15
207	*Matt Clement*	3.00
208	Todd Greene	.15
209	Ray Ricken	.15
210	*Eric Chavez*	5.00
211	Edgard Velazquez	.40
212	*Bruce Chen*	4.00
213	*Danny Patterson*	.40
214	Jeff Yoder	.15
215	*Luis Ordaz*	.40
216	Chris Widger	.15
217	Jason Brester	.15
218	Carlton Loewer	.15
219	*Chris Reitsma*	1.50
220	Neifi Perez	.15
221	*Hideki Irabu*	3.00
222	Ellis Burks	.15
223	Pedro Martinez	.45
224	Kenny Lofton	1.00
225	Randy Johnson	.75
226	Terry Steinbach	.15
227	Bernie Williams	.75
228	Dean Palmer	.15
229	Alan Benes	.15
230	Marquis Grissom	.15
231	Gary Sheffield	.40
232	Curt Schilling	.15
233	Reggie Sanders	.15
234	Bobby Higginson	.15
235	Moises Alou	.25
236	Tom Glavine	.30
237	Mark Grace	.30
238	Ramon Martinez	.15
239	Rafael Palmeiro	.30
240	John Olerud	.15
241	Dante Bichette	.25
242	Greg Vaughn	.15
243	Jeff Bagwell	1.50
244	Barry Bonds	1.00
245	Pat Hentgen	.15
246	Jim Thome	.75
247	Jermaine Allensworth	.15
248	Andy Pettitte	1.00
249	Jay Bell	.15
250	John Jaha	.15
251	Jim Edmonds	.15
252	Ron Gant	.15
253	David Cone	.30
254	Jose Canseco	.50
255	Jay Buhner	.20
256	Greg Maddux	2.50
257	Brian McRae	.15
258	Lance Johnson	.15
259	Travis Fryman	.15

260	Paul O'Neill	.30
261	Ivan Rodriguez	.85
262	Gregg Jefferies	.15
263	Fred McGriff	.25
264	Derek Bell	.15
265	Jeff Conine	.15
266	Mike Piazza	2.50
267	Mark Grudzielanek	.15
268	Brady Anderson	.15
269	Marty Cordova	.15
270	Ray Durham	.15
271	Joe Carter	.15
272	Brian Jordan	.15
273	David Justice	.40
274	Tony Gwynn	2.00
275	Larry Walker	.40
276	Cecil Fielder	.20
277	Mo Vaughn	1.00
278	Alex Fernandez	.15
279	Michael Tucker	.15
280	Jose Valentin	.15
281	Sandy Alomar	.15
282	Todd Hollandsworth	.15
283	Rico Brogna	.15
284	Rusty Greer	.15
285	Roberto Hernandez	.15
286	Hal Morris	.15
287	Johnny Damon	.15
288	Todd Hundley	.30
289	Rondell White	.30
290	Frank Thomas	1.50
291	*Don Denbow*	.15
292	Derrek Lee	.15
293	Todd Walker	.50
294	Scott Rolen	1.50
295	Wes Helms	1.50
296	Bob Abreu	.15
297	*John Patterson*	2.00
298	*Alex Gonzalez*	2.00
299	*Grant Roberts*	3.00
300	Jeff Suppan	.15
301	Luke Wilcox	.15
302	Marlon Anderson	.15
303	Ray Brown	.15
304	*Mike Caruso*	1.50
305	*Sam Marsonek*	.40
306	*Brady Raggio*	.40
307	*Kevin McGlinchy*	.75
308	*Roy Halladay*	4.00
309	*Jeremi Gonzalez*	1.50
310	*Aramis Ramirez*	3.00
311	*Dermal Brown*	3.00
312	Justin Thompson	.15
313	*Jay Tessmer*	.20
314	Mike Johnson	.15
315	Danny Clyburn	.15
316	Bruce Aven	.15
317	*Keith Foulke*	.40
318	*Jimmy Osting*	.40
319	*Valerio DeLosSantos*	.40
320	Shannon Stewart	.15
321	Willie Adams	.15
322	Larry Barnes	.15
323	Mark Johnson	.15
324	*Chris Stowers*	.40
325	Brandon Reed	.15
326	Randy Winn	.15
327	Steven Chavez	.15
328	Nomar Garciaparra	2.00
329	*Jacque Jones*	3.00
330	Chris Clemons	.15
331	Todd Helton	1.50
332	*Ryan Brannan*	.40
333	*Alex Sanchez*	1.00
334	Arnold Gooch	.15
335	Russell Branyan	1.00
336	Daryle Ward	1.50
337	*John LeRoy*	.40
338	Steve Cox	.15
339	Kevin Witt	1.50
340	Norm Hutchins	.15
341	Gabby Martinez	.15
342	Kris Detmers	.15
343	*Mike Villano*	.50
344	Preston Wilson	.15
345	*Jim Manias*	.40
346	*Deivi Cruz*	1.00
347	*Donzell McDonald*	.50
348	*Rod Myers*	.40
349	*Shawn Chacon*	.75
350	*Elvin Hernandez*	.40
351	*Orlando Cabrera*	1.00
352	Brian Banks	.15
353	Robbie Bell	.75
354	Brad Rigby	.15
355	Scott Elarton	.15
356	*Kevin Sweeney*	.75
357	Steve Soderstrom	.15
358	Ryan Nye	.15
359	*Marlon Allen*	.40
360	*Donny Leon*	.40
361	*Garrett Neubart*	.40
362	*Abraham Nunez*	1.50
363	*Adam Eaton*	.40
364	*Octavio Dotel*	2.00
365	*Dean Crow*	.40
366	*Jason Baker*	.40
367	Sean Casey	10.00
368	*Joe Lawrence*	.40
369	*Adam Johnson*	1.00
370	*Scott Schoeneweis*	.40
371	Gerald Witasick, Jr.	.15
372	*Ronnie Belliard*	2.00
373	Russ Ortiz	.15
374	*Robert Stratton*	.40
375	Bobby Estalella	.40
376	*Corey Lee*	.75
377	Carlos Beltran	3.00
378	Mike Cameron	.50
379	*Scott Randall*	.40
380	*Corey Erickson*	1.50
381	Jay Canizaro	.15
382	*Kerry Robinson*	.40
383	*Todd Noel*	.50
384	*A.J. Zapp*	2.50
385	Jarrod Washburn	.15
386	Ben Grieve	1.00
387	*Javier Vazquez*	1.00
388	Tony Graffanino	.15
389	*Travis Lee*	5.00
390	DaRond Stovall	.15
391	*Dennis Reyes*	1.00
392	Danny Buxbaum	.15
393	*Marc Lewis*	1.50
394	*Kelvim Escobar*	1.00
395	Danny Klassen	.25
396	*Ken Cloude*	2.00
397	Gabe Alvarez	.15
398	*Jaret Wright*	3.00
399	Raul Casanova	.15
400	*Clayton Brunner*	.75
401	*Jason Marquis*	1.00
402	Marc Kroon	.15
403	Jamey Wright	.15
404	*Matt Snyder*	.40
405	*Josh Garrett*	1.00
406	Juan Encarnacion	.75
407	Heath Murray	.15
408	*Brett Herbison*	.50
409	*Brent Butler*	2.50
410	*Danny Peoples*	1.50
411	*Miguel Tejada*	4.00
412	Damian Moss	.15
413	Jim Pittsley	.15
414	Dmitri Young	.15
415	Glendon Rusch	.15
416	Vladimir Guerrero	1.50
417	*Cole Liniak*	1.50
418	Ramon Hernandez	.50
419	*Cliff Politte*	.75
420	*Mel Rosario*	.50
421	*Jorge Carrion*	.50
422	*John Barnes*	.40
423	*Chris Stowe*	.40
424	*Vernon Wells*	5.00
425	*Brett Caradonna*	2.00
426	*Scott Hodges*	1.00
427	*Jon Garland*	2.00
428	*Nathan Haynes*	.60
429	*Geoff Goetz*	.75
430	*Adam Kennedy*	1.00
431	*T.J. Tucker*	.50
432	*Aaron Akin*	.75
433	*Jayson Werth*	4.00
434	*Glenn Davis*	1.00
435	*Mark Mangum*	.50
436	*Troy Cameron*	2.00
437	*J.J. Davis*	2.50
438	*Lance Berkman*	6.00
439	*Jason Standridge*	.75
440	*Jason Dellaero*	1.00
441	Hideki Irabu	1.00

1997 Bowman Certified Autographs

Ninety players signed autographs for inclusion in Series 1 and 2 packs. Each autograph card features a gold-foil Certified Autograph stamp on front and can be found in one of three versions: Blue, 1:96 packs; black, 1:503 packs and gold, 1:1,509 packs. Derek Jeter's card can also be found in a green-ink autographed version, inserted one per 1,928 packs. Card numbers have a "CA" prefix.

	MT
Complete Set (90):	1000.
Complete Series 1 Set (46):	450.00
Complete Series 2 Set (44):	600.00
Common Blue:	5.00
Black: 1.5-2.5X	
Gold: 4-6X	
Derek Jeter Green: 1.5X	

1	Jeff Abbott	5.00
2	Bob Abreu	20.00
3	Willie Adams	5.00
4	Brian Banks	5.00
5	Kris Benson	20.00
6	Darin Blood	5.00
7	Jaime Bluma	5.00
8	Kevin Brown	20.00
9	Ray Brown	5.00
10	Homer Bush	10.00
11	Mike Cameron	20.00
12	Jay Canizaro	10.00
13	Luis Castillo	10.00
14	Dave Coggin	10.00
15	Bartolo Colon	20.00
16	Rocky Coppinger	10.00
17	Jacob Cruz	15.00
18	Jose Cruz	15.00
19	Jeff D'Amico	10.00
20	Ben Davis	15.00
21	Mike Drumbright	5.00
22	Scott Elarton	15.00
23	Darin Erstad	30.00
24	Bobby Estalella	15.00
25	Joe Fontenot	5.00
26	Tom Fordham	5.00
27	Brad Fullmer	25.00
28	Chris Fussell	5.00
29	Karim Garcia	25.00
30	Kris Detmers	5.00
31	Todd Greene	15.00
32	Ben Grieve	50.00
33	Vladimir Guerrero	60.00
34	Jose Guillen	25.00
35	Roy Halladay	30.00
36	Wes Helms	25.00
37	Chad Hermansen	45.00
38	Richard Hidalgo	25.00
39	Todd Hollandsworth	20.00
40	Damian Jackson	10.00
41	Derek Jeter	80.00
42	Andruw Jones	50.00
43	Brooks Kieschnick	10.00
44	Eugene Kingsale	5.00
45	Paul Konerko	25.00
46	Marc Kroon	5.00
47	Derrek Lee	25.00
48	Travis Lee	35.00
49	Terrence Long	5.00
50	Curt Lyons	5.00
51	Elieser Marrero	10.00
52	Rafael Medina	5.00
53	Juan Melo	20.00
54	Shane Monahan	20.00
55	Julio Mosquera	5.00
56	Heath Murray	5.00
57	Ryan Nye	10.00
58	Kevin Orie	10.00
59	Russ Ortiz	5.00
60	Carl Pavano	20.00
61	Jay Payton	15.00
62	Neifi Perez	20.00
63	Sidney Ponson	10.00
64	Calvin Reese	10.00
65	Ray Ricken	5.00
66	Brad Rigby	10.00
67	Adam Riggs	10.00
68	Ruben Rivera	20.00
69	J.J. Johnson	5.00
70	Scott Rolen	60.00
71	Tony Saunders	10.00
72	Donnie Sadler	15.00
73	Richie Sexson	20.00
74	Scott Spiezio	10.00
75	Everett Stull	5.00
76	Mike Sweeney	10.00
77	Fernando Tatis	40.00
78	Miguel Tejada	25.00
79	Justin Thompson	10.00
80	Justin Towle	10.00
81	Billy Wagner	30.00
82	Todd Walker	15.00
83	Luke Wilcox	5.00
84	Paul Wilder	10.00
85	Enrique Wilson	10.00
86	Kerry Wood	40.00
87	Jamey Wright	10.00
88	Ron Wright	10.00
89	Dmitri Young	10.00
90	Nelson Figueroa	5.00

1997 Bowman International

Inserted at the rate of one per pack, the International parallel set replaces the regular photo background on front and back with the flag of the player's native land. Card #441 from the regular-issue version does not exist as an International parallel.

	MT
Complete Set (440):	125.00
Complete Series 1 (221):	60.00
Complete Series 2 (219):	60.00
Common Player:	.25
Stars and Rookies: 1-2X	
(See 1997 Bowman for checklist and base card values.)	

1997 Bowman International Best

This Series 2 insert set features a flag design in the background of each card front depicting the player's country of origin. On back is another color photo, player personal data, a record of his best season and colored flags representing 14 nations which have sent players to the major leagues. One International Best card was inserted in every second series pack. Card numbers carry a "BBI" prefix. Refractor versions are a 1:48 parallel with Atomic Refractors found 1:96.

	MT
Complete Set (20):	75.00
Common Player:	1.50
Refractors: 1.5x to 2x	
Atomic Refractors: 2x to 3x	

1	Frank Thomas	5.00
2	Ken Griffey Jr.	15.00
3	Juan Gonzalez	7.00
4	Bernie Williams	4.00
5	Hideo Nomo	3.00
6	Sammy Sosa	10.00
7	Larry Walker	2.00
8	Vinny Castilla	1.50
9	Mariano Rivera	1.50
10	Rafael Palmeiro	2.00
11	Nomar Garciaparra	10.00
12	Todd Walker	3.00
13	Andruw Jones	6.00
14	Vladimir Guerrero	5.00
15	Ruben Rivera	1.50
16	Bob Abreu	1.50
17	Karim Garcia	2.00
18	Katsuhiro Maeda	1.50
19	Jose Cruz Jr.	2.00
20	Damian Moss	1.50

1997 Bowman Rookie of the Year Candidates

This 15-card insert was inserted in one per 12 packs of Bowman Series 2. Fronts feature a color shot of the player over a textured foil background, with the player's name across the bottom and the words "Rookie of the Year Favorites" across the top with the word "Rookie" in large script letters. Card numbers have a "ROY" prefix.

	MT
Complete Set (15):	30.00
Common Player:	1.50

1	Jeff Abbott	1.50
2	Karim Garcia	2.50
3	Todd Helton	4.00
4	Richard Hidalgo	1.50
5	Geoff Jenkins	2.00
6	Russ Johnson	1.50
7	Paul Konerko	4.00
8	Mark Kotsay	5.00
9	Ricky Ledee	6.00
10	Travis Lee	4.00
11	Derrek Lee	2.00
12	Elieser Marrero	1.50
13	Juan Melo	1.50
14	Brian Rose	2.00
15	Fernando Tatis	4.00

1997 Bowman Scout's Honor Roll

This insert features 15 prospects deemed to have the most potential by Topps' scouts. Each card features a double-etched foil design and is inserted 1:12 packs.

	MT
Complete Set (15):	60.00
Common Player:	1.50

1	Dmitri Young	1.50
2	Bob Abreu	1.50
3	Vladimir Guerrero	6.00
4	Paul Konerko	5.00
5	Kevin Orie	2.00
6	Todd Walker	2.50
7	Ben Grieve	3.00
8	Darin Erstad	6.00
9	Derrek Lee	1.50
10	Jose Cruz	2.00
11	Scott Rolen	8.00
12	Travis Lee	6.00
13	Andruw Jones	6.00
14	Wilton Guerrero	1.50
15	Nomar Garciaparra	8.00

1997 Bowman Chrome

Bowman Chrome was released in one 300-card series following the conclusion of the 1997 season. Four-card foil packs carried an SRP of $3. Each card reprints one of the regular Bowman set, utilizing chromium technology on front. Inserts include: International parallels, Rookie of the Year Favorites and Scout's Honor Roll.

	MT
Complete Set (300):	300.00
Common Player:	.25
Wax Box:	220.00

1 Derek Jeter 5.00
2 Chipper Jones 4.00
3 Hideo Nomo 1.00
4 Tim Salmon .60
5 Robin Ventura .40
6 Tony Clark 1.00
7 Barry Larkin .75
8 Paul Molitor 1.00
9 Andy Benes .25
10 Ryan Klesko .50
11 Mark McGwire 8.00
12 Ken Griffey Jr. 7.00
13 Robb Nen .25
14 Cal Ripken Jr. 5.00
15 John Valentin .25
16 Ricky Bottalico .25
17 Mike Lansing .25
18 Ryne Sandberg 2.00
19 Carlos Delgado .75
20 Craig Biggio .50
21 Eric Karros .40
22 Kevin Appier .25
23 Mariano Rivera .50
24 Vinny Castilla .40
25 Juan Gonzalez 3.00
26 Al Martin .25
27 Jeff Cirillo .25
28 Ray Lankford .25
29 Manny Ramirez 2.00
30 Roberto Alomar 1.25
31 Will Clark .75
32 Chuck Knoblauch .75
33 Harold Baines .25
34 Edgar Martinez .40
35 Mike Mussina 1.25
36 Kevin Brown .40
37 Dennis Eckersley .40
38 Tino Martinez .75
39 Raul Mondesi .50
40 Sammy Sosa 5.00
41 John Smoltz .50
42 Billy Wagner .25
43 Ken Caminiti .50
44 Wade Boggs .50
45 Andres Galarraga .75
46 Roger Clemens 3.00
47 Matt Williams .75
48 Albert Belle 1.50
49 Jeff King .25
50 John Wetteland .25
51 Deion Sanders .75
52 Ellis Burks .25
53 Pedro Martinez .75
54 Kenny Lofton 1.50
55 Randy Johnson 1.00
56 Bernie Williams 1.00
57 Marquis Grissom .40
58 Gary Sheffield .75
59 Curt Schilling .50
60 Reggie Sanders .25
61 Bobby Higginson .25
62 Moises Alou .40
63 Tom Glavine .50
64 Mark Grace .75
65 Rafael Palmeiro .60
66 John Olerud .50
67 Dante Bichette .50
68 Jeff Bagwell 2.50
69 Barry Bonds 1.50
70 Pat Hentgen .25
71 Jim Thome 1.00
72 Andy Pettitte 1.00
73 Jay Bell .25
74 Jim Edmonds .40
75 Ron Gant .40
76 David Cone .40
77 Jose Canseco .75
78 Jay Buhner .50
79 Greg Maddux 4.00
80 Lance Johnson .25
81 Travis Fryman .40
82 Paul O'Neill .50
83 Ivan Rodriguez 1.50
84 Fred McGriff .50
85 Mike Piazza 4.00
86 Brady Anderson .40
87 Marty Cordova .25
88 Joe Carter .40
89 Brian Jordan .25
90 David Justice .75
91 Tony Gwynn 3.50
92 Larry Walker .75
93 Mo Vaughn 1.50
94 Sandy Alomar .40
95 Rusty Greer .40
96 Roberto Hernandez .25
97 Hal Morris .25
98 Todd Hundley .25
99 Rondell White .50
100 Frank Thomas 2.00
101 *Bubba Trammell* 2.50
102 *Sidney Ponson* 4.00
103 *Ricky Ledee* 12.00
104 Brett Tomko .25
105 *Braden Looper* 1.00
106 Jason Dickson .40
107 *Chad Green* 3.00
108 *R.A. Dickey* .75
109 Jeff Liefer .40
110 Richard Hidalgo .25
111 *Chad Hermansen* 10.00
112 Felix Martinez .25
113 J.J. Johnson .25
114 Todd Dunwoody 1.50
115 Katsuhiro Maeda .25
116 Darin Erstad 2.50
117 Elieser Marrero .25
118 Bartolo Colon .25
119 Ugueth Urbina .25
120 Jaime Bluma .25
121 *Seth Greisinger* 3.00
122 *Jose Cruz Jr.* 4.00
123 Todd Dunn .25
124 *Justin Towle* 4.00
125 Brian Rose 1.50
126 Jose Guillen 1.50
127 Andruw Jones 3.50
128 *Mark Kotsay* 8.00
129 Wilton Guerrero .25
130 Jacob Cruz .25
131 Mike Sweeney .25
132 Matt Morris .50
133 John Thomson .25
134 *Javier Valentin* .40
135 *Mike Drumright* 1.50
136 Michael Barrett .75
137 *Tony Saunders* 3.00
138 Kevin Brown .25
139 *Anthony Sanders* 4.00
140 Jeff Abbott .25
141 Eugene Kingsale .25
142 Paul Konerko 2.00
143 *Randall Simon* 3.00
144 Freddy Garcia .25
145 Karim Garcia .40
146 Carlos Guillen .25
147 Aaron Boone .25
148 Donnie Sadler .25
149 Brooks Kieschnick .25
150 Scott Spiezio .25
151 Kevin Orie .25
152 Russ Johnson .25
153 Livan Hernandez .40
154 *Vladimir Nunez* 3.00
155 Calvin Reese .25
156 Chris Carpenter .25
157 *Eric Milton* 8.00
158 Richie Sexson .40
159 Carl Pavano 1.50
160 Pat Cline .25
161 Ron Wright .25
162 Dante Powell .25
163 Mark Bellhorn .25
164 George Lombard 1.50
165 *Paul Wilder* 4.00
166 Brad Fullmer .50
167 *Kris Benson* 8.00
168 Torii Hunter .25
169 D.T. Cromer .25
170 *Nelson Figueroa* 2.00
171 *Hiram Bocachica* 2.50
172 Shane Monahan .25
173 Juan Melo .25
174 *Calvin Pickering* 10.00
175 Reggie Taylor .25
176 Geoff Jenkins .50
177 Steve Rain 1.00
178 Nerio Rodriguez 1.00
179 Derrick Gibson 1.00
180 Darin Blood .25
181 Ben Davis .25
182 *Adrian Beltre* 15.00
183 *Kerry Wood* 15.00
184 Nate Rolison 3.00
185 *Fernando Tatis* 15.00
186 Jake Westbrook 2.00
187 Edwin Diaz .25
188 Joe Fontenot 2.00
189 Matt Halloran 1.00
190 *Matt Clement* 6.00
191 Todd Greene .25
192 *Eric Chavez* 15.00
193 Edgard Velazquez .25
194 *Bruce Chen* 8.00
195 Jason Brester .25
196 *Chris Reitsma* 1.50
197 Neifi Perez .25
198 *Hideki Irabu* 4.00
199 *Don Denbow* .25
200 Derrek Lee .25
201 Todd Walker .75
202 Scott Rolen 4.00
203 Wes Helms 2.00
204 Bob Abreu .25
205 *John Patterson* 4.00
206 *Alex Gonzalez* 6.00
207 *Grant Roberts* 4.00
208 Jeff Suppan .25
209 Luke Wilcox .25
210 Marlon Anderson .25
211 *Mike Caruso* 5.00
212 *Roy Halladay* 12.00
213 *Jeremi Gonzalez* 3.00
214 *Aramis Ramirez* 8.00
215 *Dermal Brown* 8.00
216 Justin Thompson .25
217 Danny Clyburn .25
218 Bruce Aven .25
219 Keith Foulke .25
220 Shannon Stewart .25
221 Larry Barnes .25
222 Mark Johnson .75
223 Randy Winn .25
224 Nomar Garciaparra 5.00
225 *Jacque Jones* 8.00
226 Chris Clemons .25
227 Todd Helton 3.00
228 *Ryan Brannan* 1.50
229 *Alex Sanchez* 2.00
230 Russell Branyan 2.00
231 Daryle Ward 3.00
232 Kevin Witt 5.00
233 Gabby Martinez .25
234 Preston Wilson .25
235 *Donzell McDonald* 2.00
236 *Orlando Cabrera* 2.00
237 Brian Banks .25
238 Robbie Bell 2.00
239 Brad Rigby .25
240 Scott Elarton .25
241 *Donny Leon* .75
242 *Abraham Nunez* 3.00
243 *Adam Eaton* .75
244 *Octavio Dotel* 4.00
245 Sean Casey 25.00
246 *Joe Lawrence* .75
247 *Adam Johnson* 3.00
248 *Ronnie Belliard* 4.00
249 Bobby Estalella .25
250 *Corey Lee* 1.50
251 Mike Cameron .75
252 *Kerry Robinson* 1.50
253 *A.J. Zapp* 6.00
254 Jarrod Washburn .25
255 Ben Grieve 3.00
256 *Javier Vazquez* 2.00
257 *Travis Lee* 12.00
258 *Dennis Reyes* 3.00
259 Danny Buxbaum .25
260 *Kelvim Escobar* 2.00
261 Danny Klassen .35
262 *Ken Cloude* 5.00
263 Gabe Alvarez .25
264 *Clayton Brunner* 1.50
265 *Jason Marquis* 5.00
266 Jamey Wright .25
267 *Matt Snyder* .75
268 *Josh Garrett* 3.00
269 Juan Encarnacion 1.00
270 Heath Murray .25
271 *Brent Butler* 8.00
272 *Danny Peoples* 3.00
273 *Miguel Tejada* 10.00
274 Jim Pittsley .25
275 Dmitri Young .25
276 Vladimir Guerrero 2.50
277 *Cole Liniak* 8.00
278 Ramon Hernandez .75
279 *Cliff Politte* 2.00
280 *Mel Rosario* .75
281 *Jorge Carrion* 1.00
282 *John Barnes* 3.00
283 *Chris Stowe* 1.50
284 *Vernon Wells* 12.00
285 *Brett Caradonna* 5.00
286 *Scott Hodges* 2.00
287 *Jon Garland* 6.00
288 *Nathan Haynes* 2.00
289 *Geoff Goetz* 3.00
290 *Adam Kennedy* 3.00
291 *T.J. Tucker* .75
292 *Aaron Akin* 1.50
293 *Jayson Werth* 8.00
294 *Glenn Davis* 3.00
295 *Mark Mangum* 1.50
296 *Troy Cameron* 5.00
297 *J.J. Davis* 7.00
298 *Lance Berkman* 12.00
299 *Jason Standridge* 3.00
300 *Jason Dellaero* 3.00

1997 Bowman Chrome Refractors

All 300 cards in Bowman Chrome were reprinted in Refractor versions and inserted one per 12 packs. The cards are very similar to the base cards, but feature a refractive foil finish on front.

	MT
Complete Set (300):	2000.
Common Player:	1.50
Stars: 3-6X	
Rookies: 2-4X	

(See 1997 Bowman Chrome for checklist and base card values.)

1997 Bowman Chrome International

Internationals paralleled all 300 cards in the base set with a flag from the player's native country in the background. These inserts were seeded one per four packs.

Complete Set (300):
Common Player:
Stars: 2X
Inserted 1:4
(See 1997 Bowman Chrome for checklist and base card values.)

1997 Bowman Chrome International Refractors

Each International parallel card was also reprinted in a Refractor version. International Refractors were seeded one per 24 packs.

	MT
Complete Set (300):	2000.
Common Player:	2.50
Veteran Stars: 6-12X	
Young Stars/RCs: 3-6X	

(See 1997 Bowman Chrome for checklist and base card values.)

1997 Bowman Chrome ROY Candidates

This 15-card insert set features color action photos of 1998 Rookie of the Year candidates printed on chromium finish cards. Card backs are numbered with a "ROY" prefix and were inserted one per 24 packs of Bowman Chrome. Refractor versions are seeded one per 72 packs.

		MT
Complete Set (15):		70.00
Common Player:		2.00
Refractors: 1.5x to 2.5x		
1	Jeff Abbott	2.00
2	Karim Garcia	2.50
3	Todd Helton	7.00
4	Richard Hidalgo	2.00
5	Geoff Jenkins	2.00
6	Russ Johnson	2.00
7	Paul Konerko	7.00
8	Mark Kotsay	10.00
9	Ricky Ledee	8.00
10	Travis Lee	10.00
11	Derrek Lee	2.00
12	Elieser Marrero	2.00
13	Juan Melo	2.00
14	Brian Rose	3.00
15	Fernando Tatis	8.00

1997 Bowman Chrome Scout's Honor Roll

This 15-card set features top prospects and rookies as selected by the Topps' scouts. These chromium cards are numbered with a "SHR" prefix and are inserted one per 12 packs, while Refractor versions are seeded one per 36 packs.

		MT
Complete Set (15):		70.00
Common Player:		1.50
Refractors: 1.5x to 2.5x		
1	Dmitri Young	1.50
2	Bob Abreu	1.50
3	Vladimir Guerrero	5.00
4	Paul Konerko	4.00
5	Kevin Orie	1.50
6	Todd Walker	2.00
7	Ben Grieve	5.00
8	Darin Erstad	4.00
9	Derrek Lee	1.50
10	Jose Cruz, Jr.	2.00
11	Scott Rolen	10.00
12	Travis Lee	6.00
13	Andruw Jones	6.00
14	Wilton Guerrero	1.50
15	Nomar Garciaparra	12.00

1997 Bowman's Best Preview

This 20-card set, featuring 10 veterans and 10 prospects, is a preview of the format used in the Bowman's Best product. Three different versions of the Preview cards were available: Regular (1:12 packs), Refractors (1:48) and Atomic Refractors (1:96).

		MT
Complete Set (20):		100.00
Common Player:		1.50
Refractors: 2X		
Atomic Refractors: 3-4X		
1	Frank Thomas	5.00
2	Ken Griffey Jr.	15.00
3	Barry Bonds	4.00
4	Derek Jeter	10.00
5	Chipper Jones	10.00
6	Mark McGwire	15.00
7	Cal Ripken Jr.	12.00
8	Kenny Lofton	3.00
9	Gary Sheffield	2.00
10	Jeff Bagwell	7.00
11	Wilton Guerrero	1.50
12	Scott Rolen	6.00
13	Todd Walker	2.50
14	Ruben Rivera	1.50
15	Andruw Jones	8.00
16	Nomar Garciaparra	10.00
17	Vladimir Guerrero	5.00
18	Miguel Tejada	4.00
19	Bartolo Colon	1.50
20	Katsuhiro Maeda	1.50

1997 Bowman's Best

The 200-card base set is divided into a 100-card subset featuring current stars on a gold-chromium stock, and 100 cards of top prospects in silver chromium. Packs contain six cards and were issued with a suggested retail price of $5. Autographed cards of 10 different players were randomly inserted into packs, with each player signing regular, Refractor and Atomic Refractor versions of their cards. Bowman's

Best Laser Cuts and Mirror Image are the two other inserts, each with Refractor and Atomic Refractor editions.

	MT
Complete Set (200):	100.00
Common Player:	.25
Star Refractors: 6-10X	
Young Star & RC Refractors: 4-8X	
Star Atomics: 12-20X	
Young Star & RC Atomics: 8-15X	
Wax Box:	150.00

1	Ken Griffey Jr.	5.00
2	Cecil Fielder	.40
3	Albert Belle	1.50
4	Todd Hundley	.40
5	Mike Piazza	3.00
6	Matt Williams	.75
7	Mo Vaughn	1.00
8	Ryne Sandberg	1.50
9	Chipper Jones	3.00
10	Edgar Martinez	.25
11	Kenny Lofton	1.00
12	Ron Gant	.25
13	Moises Alou	.35
14	Pat Hentgen	.25
15	Steve Finley	.25
16	Mark Grace	.50
17	Jay Buhner	.50
18	Jeff Conine	.25
19	Jim Edmonds	.25
20	Todd Hollandsworth	.25
21	Andy Petitte	1.25
22	Jim Thome	.75
23	Eric Young	.25
24	Ray Lankford	.25
25	Marquis Grissom	.25
26	Tony Clark	1.00
27	Jermaine Allensworth	.25
28	Ellis Burks	.25
29	Tony Gwynn	2.50
30	Barry Larkin	.50
31	John Olerud	.25
32	Mariano Rivera	.40
33	Paul Molitor	1.00
34	Ken Caminiti	.50
35	Gary Sheffield	.75
36	Al Martin	.25
37	John Valentin	.25
38	Frank Thomas	1.50
39	John Jaha	.25
40	Greg Maddux	3.00
41	Alex Fernandez	.25
42	Dean Palmer	.25
43	Bernie Williams	1.25
44	Deion Sanders	.50
45	Mark McGwire	6.00
46	Brian Jordan	.25
47	Bernard Gilkey	.25
48	Will Clark	.50
49	Kevin Appier	.25
50	Tom Glavine	.40
51	Chuck Knoblauch	.50
52	Rondell White	.25
53	Greg Vaughn	.25
54	Mike Mussina	1.25
55	Brian McRae	.25
56	Chili Davis	.25
57	Wade Boggs	.50
58	Jeff Bagwell	2.00
59	Roberto Alomar	1.25
60	Dennis Eckersley	.25
61	Ryan Klesko	.40
62	Manny Ramirez	1.50
63	John Wetteland	.25
64	Cal Ripken Jr.	4.00
65	Edgar Renteria	.25
66	Tino Martinez	.75
67	Larry Walker	.75
68	Gregg Jefferies	.25
69	Lance Johnson	.25
70	Carlos Delgado	.75
71	Craig Biggio	.40
72	Jose Canseco	.40
73	Barry Bonds	1.50
74	Juan Gonzalez	2.50
75	Eric Karros	.25
76	Reggie Sanders	.25
77	Robin Ventura	.25
78	Hideo Nomo	1.00
79	David Justice	.40
80	Vinny Castilla	.25
81	Travis Fryman	.25
82	Derek Jeter	2.50
83	Sammy Sosa	3.00
84	Ivan Rodriguez	1.50
85	Rafael Palmeiro	.40
86	Roger Clemens	2.00
87	Jason Giambi	[illegible]
88	Andres Galarraga	.50
89	Jermaine Dye	.25
90	Joe Carter	.25
91	Brady Anderson	.25
92	Derek Bell	.25
93	Randy Johnson	1.00
94	Fred McGriff	.40
95	John Smoltz	.40
96	Harold Baines	.25
97	Raul Mondesi	.50
98	Tim Salmon	.50
99	Carlos Baerga	.25
100	Dante Bichette	.50
101	Vladimir Guerrero	2.00
102	Richard Hidalgo	.25
103	Paul Konerko	1.00
104	*Alex Gonzalez*	3.00
105	Jason Dickson	.40
106	Jose Rosado	.25
107	Todd Walker	.75
108	*Seth Greisinger*	.50
109	Todd Helton	2.00
110	Ben Davis	.25
111	Bartolo Colon	.25
112	Elieser Marrero	.25
113	Jeff D'Amico	.25
114	*Miguel Tejada*	4.00
115	Darin Erstad	1.50
116	*Kris Benson*	5.00
117	*Adrian Beltre*	6.00
118	Neifi Perez	.25
119	Calvin Reese	.25
120	Carl Pavano	1.25
121	Juan Melo	.25
122	*Kevin McGlinchy*	.25
123	Pat Cline	.25
124	*Felix Heredia*	.60
125	Aaron Boone	.25
126	Glendon Rusch	.25
127	Mike Cameron	.75
128	Justin Thompson	.25
129	*Chad Hermansen*	6.00
130	*Sidney Ponson*	.50
131	*Willie Martinez*	1.00
132	*Paul Wilder*	2.00
133	Geoff Jenkins	.30
134	*Roy Halladay*	6.00
135	Carlos Guillen	.25
136	Tony Batista	.25
137	Todd Greene	.25
138	Luis Castillo	.25
139	*Jimmy Anderson*	.75
140	Edgard Velazquez	.40
141	Chris Snopek	.25
142	Ruben Rivera	.25
143	*Javier Valentin*	.40
144	Brian Rose	1.50
145	*Fernando Tatis*	8.00
146	*Dean Crow*	.25
147	Karim Garcia	.40
148	Dante Powell	.25
149	*Hideki Irabu*	3.00
150	Matt Morris	.50
151	Wes Helms	1.00
152	Russ Johnson	.25
153	Jarrod Washburn	.25
154	*Kerry Wood*	6.00
155	*Joe Fontenot*	.60
156	Eugene Kingsale	.25
157	Terrence Long	.25
158	Calvin Maduro	.25
159	Jeff Suppan	.25
160	DaRond Stovall	.25
161	Mark Redman	.25
162	*Ken Cloude*	2.50
163	Bobby Estalella	.25
164	*Abraham Nunez*	2.00
165	Derrick Gibson	.50
166	*Mike Drumright*	.75
167	Katsuhiro Maeda	.25
168	Jeff Liefer	.40
169	Ben Grieve	1.00
170	Bob Abreu	.25
171	Shannon Stewart	.25
172	*Braden Looper*	.50
173	Brant Brown	.25
174	Marlon Anderson	.25
175	Brad Fullmer	.75
176	Carlos Beltran	3.00
177	Nomar Garciaparra	3.00
178	Derrek Lee	.25
179	*Valerio DeLosSantos*	.25
180	Dmitri Young	.25
181	Jamey Wright	.25
182	*Hiram Bocachica*	1.50
183	Wilton Guerrero	.25
184	Chris Carpenter	.25
185	Scott Spiezio	.25
186	Andruw Jones	2.00
187	*Travis Lee*	6.00
188	*Jose Cruz Jr.*	2.00
189	Jose Guillen	1.00
190	Jeff Abbott	.25
191	*Ricky Ledee*	7.00
192	Mike Sweeney	.25
193	Donnie Sadler	.25
194	Scott Rolen	2.50
195	Kevin Orie	.25
196	*Jason Conti*	.75
197	*Mark Kotsay*	5.00
198	*Eric Milton*	2.50
199	Russell Branyan	1.50
200	*Alex Sanchez*	1.00

1997 Bowman's Best Autographs

Ten different players each signed 10 regular versions of their respective Bowman's Best cards (1:170 packs), 10 of their Bowman's Best Refractors (1:2,036 packs) and 10 of their Bowman's Best Atomic Refractors (1:6,107 packs). Each autograph card features a special Certified Autograph stamp on the front.

		MT
Complete Set (10):		600.00
Common Player:		25.00
Refractors: 1.5-2X		
Atomics: 4-6X		
29	Tony Gwynn	125.00
33	Paul Molitor	40.00
82	Derek Jeter	140.00
91	Brady Anderson	30.00
98	Tim Salmon	35.00
107	Todd Walker	30.00
183	Wilton Guerrero	25.00
185	Scott Spiezio	25.00
188	Jose Cruz Jr.	30.00
194	Scott Rolen	65.00

1997 Bowman's Best Cuts

Each of these 20-card inserts features a laser-cut pattern in the chromium stock. Backs have another color photo and list several of the player's career "Bests". Three different versions of each card are available: Regular (1:24 packs), Refractor (1:48) and Atomic Refractor (1:96). Cards are numbered with a "BC" prefix.

		MT
Complete Set (20):		75.00
Common Player:		1.50
Refractors: 1.5-2X		
Atomic Refractors: 2-3X		
1	Derek Jeter	6.00
2	Chipper Jones	6.00
3	Frank Thomas	6.00
4	Cal Ripken Jr.	7.50
5	Mark McGwire	12.50
6	Ken Griffey Jr.	12.50
7	Jeff Bagwell	4.00
8	Mike Piazza	6.00
9	Ken Caminiti	1.50
10	Albert Belle	3.00
11	Jose Cruz Jr.	3.00
12	Wilton Guerrero	1.50
13	Darin Erstad	3.50
14	Andruw Jones	5.00
15	Scott Rolen	5.00
16	Jose Guillen	2.50
17	Bob Abreu	1.50
18	Vladimir Guerrero	4.00
19	Todd Walker	2.00
20	Nomar Garciaparra	6.00

1997 Bowman's Best Mirror Image

This 10-card insert features four players on each double-sided card - two veterans and two rookies - utilizing Finest technology. Regular Mirror Image cards are found 1:48 packs, while Refractor versions are seeded 1:96 packs and Atomic Refractors are found 1:192 packs. Cards are numbered with an "MI" prefix.

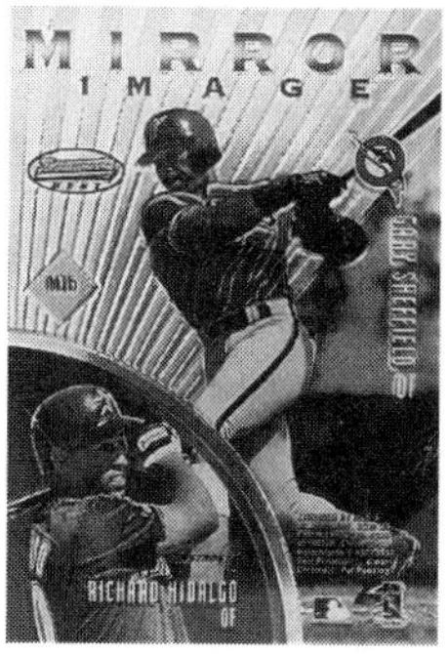

		MT
Complete Set (10):		90.00
Common Card:		5.00
Refractors: 1.5X		
Atomic Refractors: 2-3X		
1	Nomar Garciaparra, Derek Jeter, Hiram Bocachica, Barry Larkin	12.00
2	Travis Lee, Frank Thomas, Derrek Lee, Jeff Bagwell	10.00
3	Kerry Wood, Greg Maddux, Kris Benson, John Smoltz	9.00
4	Kevin Brown, Ivan Rodriguez, Elieser Marrero, Mike Piazza	12.00
5	Jose Cruz Jr., Ken Griffey Jr., Andruw Jones, Barry Bonds	15.00
6	Jose Guillen, Juan Gonzalez, Richard Hidalgo, Gary Sheffield	9.00
7	Paul Konerko, Mark McGwire, Todd Helton, Rafael Palmeiro	15.00
8	Wilton Guerrero, Craig Biggio, Donnie Sadler, Chuck Knoblauch	5.00
9	Russell Branyan, Matt Williams, Adrian Beltre, Chipper Jones	10.00
10	Bob Abreu, Kenny Lofton, Vladimir Guerrero, Albert Belle	6.00

1997 Bowman's Best Jumbos

This large-format (4" x 5-5/8") version of 1997 Bowman's Best features 16 of the season's top stars and hottest rookies. Utilizing chromium, Refractor and Atomic Refractor technologies, the cards are identical in every way except size to the regular-issue Bowman's Best. The jumbos were sold only through Topps Stadium Club. Each of the sets consists of 12 chromium cards, plus three randomly packaged Refractors and one Atomic Refractor. About 900 sets were produced according to Topps sales literature, which breaks down to 700 regular cards, 170 Refractors and 60 Atomic Refractors of each player.

		MT
Complete Set (16):		125.00
Common Player:		6.00
Refractor: 3-5X		
Atomic Refractor: 6-9X		
1	Ken Griffey Jr.	12.00
5	Mike Piazza	9.00
9	Chipper Jones	9.00
11	Kenny Lofton	6.00
29	Tony Gwynn	7.50
33	Paul Molitor	6.00
38	Frank Thomas	9.00
45	Mark McGwire	12.00
64	Cal Ripken Jr.	10.00
73	Barry Bonds	6.00
74	Juan Gonzalez	6.00
82	Derek Jeter	8.00
101	Vladimir Guerrero	7.50
177	Nomar Garciaparra	7.50
186	Andruw Jones	6.00
188	Jose Cruz, Jr.	5.00

1998 Bowman

Bowman was a 441-card set released in a pair of 220-card series in 1998 (Orlando Hernandez, #221, was late Series 1 addition.) Within each series were 150 prospects printed in a silver and blue design and 70 veterans printed in silver and red. Cards feature a Bowman seal, and in cases where it's the player's first Bowman card a "Bowman Rookie Card" stamp is applied. The player's facsimile signature from their first contract runs down the side. The entire set was paralleled twice in Bowman International (one per pack) and Golden Anniversary (serially numbered to 50). Inserts in Series 1 include Autographs, Scout's Choice, and Japanese Rookies. Inserts in Series 2 include Autographs, 1999 Rookie of the Year Favorites, Minor League MVPs and Japanese Rookies.

		MT
Complete Set (441):		160.00
Complete Series 1 set (221):		90.00
Complete Series 2 set (220):		75.00
Common Player:		.20
Unlisted Stars: .50 to .75		
Internationals: 1.5-3X		
Inserted 1:1		
Ser I Wax Box:		85.00
Ser II Wax Box:		70.00
1	Nomar Garciaparra	2.50
2	Scott Rolen	1.50
3	Andy Pettitte	.75
4	Ivan Rodriguez	1.00
5	Mark McGwire	5.00
6	Jason Dickson	.20
7	Jose Cruz Jr.	.75
8	Jeff Kent	.20
9	Mike Mussina	.75
10	Jason Kendall	.20
11	Brett Tomko	.20
12	Jeff King	.20
13	Brad Radke	.20
14	Robin Ventura	.35
15	Jeff Bagwell	1.50
16	Greg Maddux	2.00
17	John Jaha	.20
18	Mike Piazza	2.50
19	Edgar Martinez	.20
20	David Justice	.40
21	Todd Hundley	.20
22	Tony Gwynn	2.00
23	Larry Walker	.60
24	Bernie Williams	.75
25	Edgar Renteria	.20
26	Rafael Palmeiro	.40
27	Tim Salmon	.50
28	Matt Morris	.40
29	Shawn Estes	.20
30	Vladimir Guerrero	1.50
31	Fernando Tatis	.75
32	Justin Thompson	.20
33	Ken Griffey Jr.	4.00
34	Edgardo Alfonzo	.30
35	Mo Vaughn	1.00
36	Marty Cordova	.20

37 Craig Biggio .40
38 Roger Clemens 1.50
39 Mark Grace .50
40 Ken Caminiti .40
41 Tony Womack .20
42 Albert Belle 1.00
43 Tino Martinez .75
44 Sandy Alomar .40
45 Jeff Cirillo .20
46 Jason Giambi .20
47 Darin Erstad 1.00
48 Livan Hernandez .20
49 Mark Grudzielanek .20
50 Sammy Sosa 3.00
51 Curt Schilling .40
52 Brian Hunter .20
53 Neifi Perez .20
54 Todd Walker .40
55 Jose Guillen .40
56 Jim Thome .75
57 Tom Glavine .40
58 Todd Greene .20
59 Rondell White .40
60 Roberto Alomar .75
61 Tony Clark .60
62 Vinny Castilla .40
63 Barry Larkin .40
64 Hideki Irabu .50
65 Johnny Damon .20
66 Juan Gonzalez 2.00
67 John Olerud .40
68 Gary Sheffield .50
69 Raul Mondesi .40
70 Chipper Jones 2.50
71 David Ortiz .75
72 *Warren Morris* 1.50
73 Alex Gonzalez .35
74 Nick Bierbrodt .20
75 Roy Halladay .50
76 Danny Buxbaum .20
77 Adam Kennedy .40
78 *Jared Sandberg* 1.50
79 Michael Barrett .50
80 Gil Meche .40
81 Jayson Werth .50
82 Abraham Nunez .50
83 Ben Petrick .20
84 Brett Caradonna .40
85 *Mike Lowell* 3.00
86 *Clay Bruner* 1.00
87 *John Curtice* 1.00
88 Bobby Estalella .20
89 Juan Melo .20
90 Arnold Gooch .20
91 *Kevin Millwood* 8.00
92 Richie Sexson .20
93 Orlando Cabrera .40
94 Pat Cline .20
95 Anthony Sanders .50
96 Russ Johnson .20
97 Ben Grieve 1.00
98 Kevin McGlinchy .20
99 Paul Wilder .20
100 Russ Ortiz .20
101 *Ryan Jackson* 2.00
102 Heath Murray .20
103 Brian Rose .40
104 *Ryan Radmanovich* 1.00
105 Ricky Ledee 1.50
106 *Jeff Wallace* .50
107 *Ryan Minor* 5.00
108 Dennis Reyes .25
109 *James Manias* 1.00
110 Chris Carpenter .20
111 Daryle Ward .20
112 Vernon Wells .75
113 Chad Green .40
114 *Mike Stoner* 4.00
115 Brad Fullmer .20
116 Adam Eaton .20
117 Jeff Liefer .20
118 *Corey Koskie* 2.00
119 Todd Helton .75
120 *Jaime Jones* 1.00
121 Mel Rosario .20
122 Geoff Goetz .20
123 Adrian Beltre 3.00
124 Jason Dellaero .50
125 *Gabe Kapler* 10.00
126 Scott Schoeneweis .20
127 Ryan Brannan .20
128 Aaron Akin .20
129 *Ryan Anderson* 6.00
130 Brad Penny .20
131 Bruce Chen .50
132 Eli Marrero .20
133 Eric Chavez 2.00
134 *Troy Glaus* 10.00
135 Troy Cameron .50
136 *Brian Sikorski* .75
137 *Mike Kinkade* 2.00
138 Braden Looper .20
139 Mark Mangum .20
140 Danny Peoples .50
141 J.J. Davis .75
142 Ben Davis .20
143 Jacque Jones .50
144 Derrick Gibson .20
145 Bronson Arroyo .50
146 *Cristian Guzman* .50
147 Jeff Abbott .20
148 *Mike Cuddyer* 6.00
149 Jason Romano .75
150 Shane Monahan .20
151 *Ntema Ndungidi* 1.00
152 Alex Sanchez .40
153 *Jack Cust* 4.00
154 Brent Butler 1.00
155 Ramon Hernandez .20
156 Norm Hutchins .20
157 Jason Marquis .20
158 Jacob Cruz .20
159 *Rob Burger* 1.50
160 Eric Milton .75
161 Preston Wilson .20
162 *Jason Fitzgerald* 1.00
163 Dan Serafini .20
164 Peter Munro .20
165 Trot Nixon .20
166 Homer Bush .20
167 Dermal Brown 1.00
168 Chad Hermansen 1.50
169 *Julio Moreno* .75
170 *John Roskos* 1.00
171 Grant Roberts 1.00
172 Ken Cloude .50
173 Jason Brester .20
174 Jason Conti .20
175 Jon Garland .50
176 Robbie Bell .20
177 Nathan Haynes .20
178 *Ramon Ortiz* 5.00
179 Shannon Stewart .20
180 Pablo Ortega .20
181 *Jimmy Rollins* 1.00
182 Sean Casey .50
183 *Ted Lilly* .50
184 *Chris Enochs* 3.00
185 *Magglio Ordonez* 8.00
186 Mike Drumright .20
187 Aaron Boone .20
188 Matt Clement .40
189 Todd Dunwoody .40
190 Larry Rodriguez .20
191 Todd Noel .20
192 Geoff Jenkins .20
193 George Lombard .20
194 Lance Berkman 2.00
195 *Marcus McCain* .50
196 Ryan McGuire .20
197 *Jhensy Sandoval* 2.00
198 Corey Lee .20
199 Mario Valdez .20
200 *Robert Fick* 2.50
201 Donnie Sadler .20
202 Marc Kroon .20
203 David Miller .20
204 Jarrod Washburn .20
205 Miguel Tejada 1.50
206 Raul Ibanez .20
207 John Patterson .50
208 Calvin Pickering .75
209 Felix Martinez .20
210 Mark Redman .20
211 Scott Elarton .20
212 *Jose Amado* .75
213 Kerry Wood 2.00
214 Dante Powell .20
215 Aramis Ramirez 1.00
216 A.J. Hinch 1.50
217 *Dustin Carr* .50
218 Mark Kotsay 1.50
219 Jason Standridge .20
220 Luis Ordaz .20
221 *Orlando Hernandez* 8.00
222 Cal Ripken Jr. 3.00
223 Paul Molitor .75
224 Derek Jeter 2.50
225 Barry Bonds 1.00
226 Jim Edmonds .20
227 John Smoltz .40
228 Eric Karros .30
229 Ray Lankford .30
230 Rey Ordonez .30
231 Kenny Lofton .75
232 Alex Rodriguez 2.50
233 Dante Bichette .35
234 Pedro Martinez .75
235 Carlos Delgado .50
236 Rod Beck .20
237 Matt Williams .50
238 Charles Johnson .20
239 Rico Brogna .20
240 Frank Thomas 1.50
241 Paul O'Neill .50
242 Jaret Wright 1.00
243 Brant Brown .20
244 Ryan Klesko .30
245 Chuck Finley .20
246 Derek Bell .20
247 Delino DeShields .20
248 Chan Ho Park .40
249 Wade Boggs .60
250 Jay Buhner .35
251 Butch Huskey .20
252 Steve Finley .20
253 Will Clark .50
254 John Valentin .20
255 Bobby Higginson .20
256 Darryl Strawberry .40
257 Randy Johnson .75
258 Al Martin .20
259 Travis Fryman .20
260 Fred McGriff .40
261 Jose Valentin .20
262 Andruw Jones 1.00
263 Kenny Rogers .20
264 Moises Alou .40
265 Denny Neagle .20
266 Ugueth Urbina .20
267 Derrek Lee .20
268 Ellis Burks .20
269 Mariano Rivera .40
270 Dean Palmer .20
271 Eddie Taubensee .20
272 Brady Anderson .20
273 Brian Giles .20
274 Quinton McCracken .20
275 Henry Rodriguez .20
276 Andres Galarraga .35
277 Jose Canseco .60
278 David Segui .20
279 Bret Saberhagen .20
280 Kevin Brown .40
281 Chuck Knoblauch .60
282 Jeromy Burnitz .30
283 Jay Bell .20
284 Manny Ramirez 1.50
285 Rick Helling .20
286 Francisco Cordova .20
287 Bob Abreu .20
288 J.T. Snow Jr. .20
289 Hideo Nomo .50
290 Brian Jordan .20
291 Javy Lopez .20
292 Travis Lee 1.00
293 Russell Branyan .20
294 Paul Konerko .40
295 *Masato Yoshii* 1.50
296 Kris Benson .40
297 Juan Encarnacion .20
298 Eric Milton .20
299 Mike Caruso .20
300 *Ricardo Aramboles* 2.00
301 Bobby Smith .20
302 Billy Koch .20
303 Richard Hidalgo .20
304 *Justin Baughman* 1.00
305 Chris Gissell .20
306 *Donnie Bridges* 1.50
307 *Nelson Lara* 1.00
308 *Randy Wolf* 4.00
309 *Jason LaRue* 1.50
310 *Jason Gooding* .50
311 *Edgar Clemente* .50
312 Andrew Vessel .20
313 Chris Reitsma .20
314 *Jesus Sanchez* 1.00
315 *Buddy Carlyle* .75
316 Randy Winn .20
317 Luis Rivera 2.00
318 *Marcus Thames* 1.50
319 A.J. Pierzynski .20
320 Scott Randall .20
321 Damian Sapp .20
322 *Eddie Yarnell* 3.00
323 *Luke Allen* 1.50
324 J.D. Smart .20
325 Willie Martinez .20
326 Alex Ramirez .20
327 *Eric DuBose* 1.50
328 Kevin Witt .20
329 *Dan McKinley* .75
330 Cliff Politte .20
331 Vladimir Nunez .20
332 *John Halama* .50
333 Nerio Rodriguez .20
334 Desi Relaford .20
335 Robinson Checo .20
336 *John Nicholson* 1.00
337 *Tom LaRosa* .75
338 *Kevin Nicholson* 2.00
339 Javier Vazquez .20
340 A.J. Zapp .20
341 Tom Evans .20
342 Kerry Robinson .20
343 *Gabe Gonzalez* .75
344 Ralph Milliard .20
345 Enrique Wilson .20
346 Elvin Hernandez .20
347 *Mike Lincoln* 1.50
348 *Cesar King* 2.00
349 *Cristian Guzman* 1.00
350 Donzell McDonald .20
351 *Jim Parque* 2.00
352 *Mike Saipe* 1.00
353 *Carlos Febles* 3.00
354 *Dernell Stenson* 5.00
355 *Mark Osborne* 1.50
356 *Odalis Perez* 2.00
357 *Jason Dewey* 1.00
358 Joe Fontenot .20
359 *Jason Grilli* 1.50
360 *Kevin Haverbusch* 1.50
361 *Jay Yennaco* .50
362 Brian Buchanan .20
363 John Barnes .20
364 Chris Fussell .20
365 *Kevin Gibbs* .75
366 Joe Lawrence .20
367 DaRond Stovall .20
368 *Brian Fuentes* 2.00
369 Jimmy Anderson .20
370 *Laril Gonzalez* 2.00
371 *Scott Williamson* 2.00
372 Milton Bradley .20
373 *Jason Halper* .75
374 *Brent Billingsley* .75
375 *Joe DePastino* .20
376 Jake Westbrook .20
377 Octavio Dotel .20
378 *Jason Williams* .50
379 *Julio Ramirez* 3.00
380 Seth Greisinger .20
381 *Mike Judd* 1.00
382 *Ben Ford* .50
383 Tom Bennett .20
384 *Adam Butler* .50
385 *Wade Miller* .75
386 *Kyle Peterson* .75
387 *Tommy Peterman* 1.00
388 Onan Masaoka .20
389 *Jason Rakers* .75
390 Rafael Medina .20
391 Luis Lopez .20
392 Jeff Yoder .20
393 *Vance Wilson* .75
394 *Fernando Seguignol* 5.00
395 Ron Wright .20
396 *Ruben Mateo* 8.00
397 *Steve Lomasney* .75
398 Damian Jackson .20
399 *Mike Jerzembeck* .75
400 *Luis Rivas* 1.50
401 *Kevin Burford* 1.50
402 Glenn Davis .20
403 *Robert Luce* .75
404 Cole Liniak .20
405 *Matthew LeCroy* 1.00
406 *Jeremy Giambi* 6.00
407 Shawn Chacon .20
408 *Dewayne Wise* 2.00
409 *Steve Woodard* .75
410 *Francisco Cordero* .50
411 *Damon Minor* .75
412 Lou Collier .20
413 Justin Towle .20
414 Juan LeBron .20
415 Michael Coleman .20
416 Felix Rodriguez .20
417 *Paul Ah Yat* .75
418 *Kevin Barker* 1.50
419 Brian Meadows .20
420 *Darnell McDonald* 4.00
421 *Matt Kinney* .75
422 *Mike Vavrek* .75
423 *Courtney Duncan* .75
424 *Kevin Millar* 3.00
425 Ruben Rivera .20
426 *Steve Shoemaker* .50
427 *Dan Reichert* .75
428 *Carlos Lee* 5.00
429 *Rod Barajas* .75
430 *Pablo Ozuna* 4.00
431 *Todd Belitz* .50
432 Sidney Ponson .20
433 *Steve Carver* 1.00
434 Esteban Yan 1.50
435 *Cedrick Bowers* .75
436 Marlon Anderson .20
437 Carl Pavano .20
438 *Jae Weong Seo* 1.50
439 *Jose Taveras* 1.50
440 *Matt Anderson* 3.00
441 *Darron Ingram* 2.00

1998 Bowman Golden Anniversary

This 441-card parallel set celebrates Bowman's 50th anniversary with a gold, rather than black, facsimile autograph on each card. Golden Anniversary cards were inserted in both Series 1 (1:237) and Series 2 (1:194) packs and are sequentially numbered to 50.

	MT
Common Player:	7.50
Veteran Stars: 40-80X	
Young Stars: 20-40X	
Rookie Cards: 6-12X	

(See 1998 Bowman for checklist and base card values.)

1998 Bowman International

All 441 cards in Bowman Series 1 and 2 are paralleled in an International version, with the player's native country highlighted. Background map designs and vital information were translated into the player's native language on these one per pack parallel cards.

	MT
Complete Set (441):	200.00
Common Player:	.25
Stars: 1.5-3X	
Inserted 1:1	

(See 1998 Bowman for checklist and base card values.)

1998 Bowman Autographs

Rookies and prospects are featured on the certified autograph cards found as '98 Bowman inserts. Each player signed cards in blue, silver and gold ink. The front of each autographed card bears a certification seal. The base-level blue signatures are found at the rate of one per 149 packs Series 1, and 1:122 in second series. Silver-signed cards are seeded at 1:902 and 1:815, respectively. The rare gold inked versions are found 1:2976 in Series 1 and 1:2445 in Series 2. Relative values in the current market come nowhere near reflecting those scarcities.

		MT
Complete Set, Blue (70):		750.00
Common Player:		7.50
Inserted 1:149		
Silvers: 1.5-2.5X		
Inserted 1:992		
Golds: 2-4X		
Inserted 1:2,976		
1	Adrian Beltre	20.00
2	Brad Fullmer	17.50
3	Ricky Ledee	20.00
4	David Ortiz	12.50
5	Fernando Tatis	20.00
6	Kerry Wood	20.00
7	Mel Rosario	7.50
8	Cole Liniak	10.00
9	A.J. Hinch	12.50
10	Jhensy Sandoval	7.50
11	Jose Cruz Jr.	12.50
12	Richard Hidalgo	10.00
13	Geoff Jenkins	7.50
14	Carl Pavano	12.50
15	Richie Sexson	15.00
16	Tony Womack	10.00
17	Scott Rolen	30.00
18	Ryan Minor	20.00
19	Elieser Marrero	7.50
20	Jason Marquis	7.50
21	Mike Lowell	15.00
22	Todd Helton	20.00
23	Chad Green	7.50
24	Scott Elarton	7.50
25	Russell Branyan	10.00
26	Mike Drumright	7.50
27	Ben Grieve	25.00
28	Jacque Jones	15.00
29	Jared Sandberg	10.00
30	Grant Roberts	12.50
31	Mike Stoner	15.00
32	Brian Rose	7.50
33	Randy Winn	7.50
34	Justin Towle	12.50
35	Anthony Sanders	7.50
36	Rafael Medina	7.50
37	Corey Lee	7.50
38	Mike Kinkade	7.50
39	Norm Hutchins	7.50
40	Jason Brester	7.50
41	Ben Davis	7.50
42	Nomar Garciaparra	60.00
43	Jeff Liefer	7.50
44	Eric Milton	10.00
45	Preston Wilson	20.00
46	Miguel Tejada	20.00
47	Luis Ordaz	7.50
48	Travis Lee	40.00
49	Kris Benson	12.50
50	Jacob Cruz	10.00
51	Dermal Brown	12.50
52	Marc Kroon	7.50
53	Chad Hermansen	20.00
54	Roy Halladay	25.00
55	Eric Chavez	35.00
56	Jason Conti	7.50
57	Juan Encarnacion	15.00
58	Paul Wilder	12.50
59	Aramis Ramirez	25.00
60	Cliff Politte	7.50
61	Todd Dunwoody	10.00
62	Paul Konerko	12.50
63	Shane Monahan	9.00
64	Alex Sanchez	7.50
65	Jeff Abbott	12.50
66	John Patterson	7.50
67	Peter Munro	7.50
68	Jarrod Washburn	15.00
69	Derrek Lee	7.50
70	Ramon Hernandez	10.00

1998 Bowman Japanese Rookies

Bowman offered collectors a chance to receive original 1991 BBM-brand Japanese rookie cards of three players. Series 1 had rookie cards of Hideo Nomo and Shigetoshi Hasegawa inserted in one per 2,685 packs, while Series 2 offered Hideki Irabu seeded one per 4,411 packs. Card numbers have a "BBM" prefix.

		MT
Complete Set (3):		40.00
Common Player:		10.00
11	Hideo Nomo	20.00
17	Shigetosi Hasegawa	10.00
	Hideki Irabu	15.00

1998 Bowman Minor League MVP

This 11-card insert set features players who are former Minor League MVPs who had graduated to the majors. Minor League MVPs are seeded one per 12 packs of Series 2 and are numbered with a "MVP" prefix.

		MT
Complete Set (11):		18.00
Common Player:		1.00
1	Jeff Bagwell	3.00
2	Andres Galarraga	1.00
3	Juan Gonzalez	4.00
4	Tony Gwynn	4.00
5	Vladimir Guerrero	2.00
6	Derek Jeter	4.00
7	Andruw Jones	2.00
8	Tino Martinez	1.00
9	Manny Ramirez	2.50
10	Gary Sheffield	1.00
11	Jim Thome	1.00

1998 Bowman Scout's Choice

This 21-card insert has players with potential for Major League stardom. Scout's Choice inserts were seeded one per 12 packs of Series 1. Fronts have action photos with gold-foil highlights. Backs have a portrait photo and an assessment of the player's skills in the traditional five areas of raw talent. Cards are numbered with an "SC" prefix.

		MT
Complete Set (21):		35.00
Common Player:		.75
Inserted 1:12		
1	Paul Konerko	2.00
2	Richard Hidalgo	1.00
3	Mark Kotsay	1.50
4	Ben Grieve	2.50
5	Chad Hermansen	2.00
6	Matt Clement	1.00
7	Brad Fullmer	1.50
8	Eli Marrero	.75
9	Kerry Wood	2.50
10	Adrian Beltre	2.50
11	Ricky Ledee	1.50
12	Travis Lee	3.00
13	Abraham Nunez	.75
14	Ryan Anderson	5.00
15	Dermal Brown	1.00
16	Juan Encarnacion	1.00
17	Aramis Ramirez	3.00
18	Todd Helton	2.00
19	Kris Benson	2.50
20	Russell Branyan	.75
21	Mike Stoner	2.50

1998 Bowman Rookie of the Year Favorites

Rookie of the Year Favorites displays 10 players who had a legitimate shot at the 1999 ROY award in the opinion of the Bowman Scouts. The insert was seeded one per 12 packs of Series 2 and numbered with an "ROY" prefix.

		MT
Complete Set (10):		20.00
Common Player:		.75
1	Adrian Beltre	2.50
2	Troy Glaus	7.50
3	Chad Hermansen	1.00
4	Matt Clement	2.00
5	Eric Chavez	6.00
6	Kris Benson	.75
7	Richie Sexson	1.50
8	Randy Wolf	1.50
9	Ryan Minor	4.00
10	Alex Gonzalez	.75

1998 Bowman Chrome

All 441 cards in Bowman 1 and 2 were reprinted with a chromium finish for Bowman Chrome. Issued in two Series, Chrome contains International and Golden Anniversary parallels, like Bowman. Internationals are seeded one per four packs, with Refractor versions every 24 packs. Golden Anniversary parallels are exclusive to hobby packs and inserted one per 164 packs and sequentially numbered to 50 sets. Refractor versions are seeded one per 1,279 packs and numbered to just five sets. In addition, 50 Bowman Chrome Reprints were inserted with 25 in each series.

		MT
Complete Set (441):		300.00
Complete Series 1 Set (221):		180.00
Complete Series 2 Set (220):		120.00
Common Player:		.20
1	Nomar Garciaparra	5.00
2	Scott Rolen	3.00
3	Andy Pettitte	1.50
4	Ivan Rodriguez	2.00
5	Mark McGwire	10.00
6	Jason Dickson	.40
7	Jose Cruz Jr.	1.00
8	Jeff Kent	.40
9	Mike Mussina	1.50
10	Jason Kendall	.40
11	Brett Tomko	.40
12	Jeff King	.40
13	Brad Radke	.40
14	Robin Ventura	.50
15	Jeff Bagwell	3.00
16	Greg Maddux	5.00
17	John Jaha	.40
18	Mike Piazza	5.00
19	Edgar Martinez	.40
20	David Justice	.75
21	Todd Hundley	.40
22	Tony Gwynn	4.00
23	Larry Walker	1.00
24	Bernie Williams	1.50
25	Edgar Renteria	.40
26	Rafael Palmeiro	.75
27	Tim Salmon	1.00
28	Matt Morris	.50
29	Shawn Estes	.40
30	Vladimir Guerrero	3.00
31	Fernando Tatis	.60
32	Justin Thompson	.40
33	Ken Griffey Jr.	8.00
34	Edgardo Alfonzo	.40
35	Mo Vaughn	2.00
36	Marty Cordova	.40
37	Craig Biggio	.75
38	Roger Clemens	3.00
39	Mark Grace	.75
40	Ken Caminiti	.60
41	Tony Womack	.40
42	Albert Belle	2.00
43	Tino Martinez	1.00
44	Sandy Alomar	.60
45	Jeff Cirillo	.40
46	Jason Giambi	.40
47	Darin Erstad	2.00
48	Livan Hernandez	.40
49	Mark Grudzielanek	.40
50	Sammy Sosa	6.00
51	Curt Schilling	.60
52	Brian Hunter	.40
53	Neifi Perez	.40
54	Todd Walker	.60
55	Jose Guillen	.60
56	Jim Thome	1.00
57	Tom Glavine	.60
58	Todd Greene	.40
59	Rondell White	.50
60	Roberto Alomar	1.50
61	Tony Clark	1.25
62	Vinny Castilla	.50
63	Barry Larkin	.75
64	Hideki Irabu	.75
65	Johnny Damon	.40
66	Juan Gonzalez	4.00
67	John Olerud	.60
68	Gary Sheffield	.75
69	Raul Mondesi	.60
70	Chipper Jones	5.00
71	David Ortiz	1.50
72	*Warren Morris*	4.00
73	Alex Gonzalez	.50
74	Nick Bierbrodt	.40
75	Roy Halladay	.50
76	Danny [illegible]	[illegible]
77	Adam Kennedy	.40
78	*Jared Sandberg*	5.00
79	Michael Barrett	.75
80	Gil Meche	.40
81	Jayson Werth	2.50
82	Abraham Nunez	.75
83	Ben Petrick	.40
84	Brett Caradonna	.40
85	*Mike Lowell*	6.00
86	*Clay Bruner*	2.00
87	*John Curtice*	5.00
88	Bobby Estalella	.40
89	Juan Melo	.40
90	Arnold Gooch	.40
91	*Kevin Millwood*	20.00
92	Richie Sexson	.40
93	Orlando Cabrera	.40
94	Pat Cline	.40
95	Anthony Sanders	.50
96	Russ Johnson	.40
97	Ben Grieve	2.50
98	Kevin McGlinchy	.40
99	Paul Wilder	.40
100	Russ Ortiz	.40
101	*Ryan Jackson*	4.00
102	Heath Murray	.40
103	Brian Rose	.40
104	*Ryan Radmanovich*	2.00
105	Ricky Ledee	1.50
106	*Jeff Wallace*	2.00
107	*Ryan Minor*	10.00
108	Dennis Reyes	.50
109	*James Manias*	2.00
110	Chris Carpenter	.40
111	Daryle Ward	.50
112	Vernon Wells	2.50
113	Chad Green	.40
114	*Mike Stoner*	10.00
115	Brad Fullmer	.60
116	Adam Eaton	.40
117	Jeff Liefer	.40
118	*Corey Koskie*	5.00
119	Todd Helton	2.00
120	*Jaime Jones*	2.00
121	Mel Rosario	.40
122	Geoff Goetz	.40
123	Adrian Beltre	3.00
124	Jason Dellaero	.50
125	*Gabe Kapler*	20.00
126	Scott Schoeneweis	.40
127	Ryan Brannan	.40
128	Aaron Akin	.40
129	*Ryan Anderson*	12.00
130	Brad Penny	.40
131	Bruce Chen	.50
132	Eli Marrero	.40
133	Eric Chavez	3.00
134	*Troy Glaus*	20.00
135	Troy Cameron	.50
136	*Brian Sikorski*	2.00
137	*Mike Kinkade*	4.00
138	Braden Looper	.40
139	Mark Mangum	.40
140	Danny Peoples	.50
141	J.J. Davis	1.50
142	Ben Davis	.40
143	Jacque Jones	.50
144	Derrick Gibson	.40
145	Bronson Arroyo	.50
146	*Luis DeLosSantos*	3.00
147	Jeff Abbott	.40
148	*Mike Cuddyer*	8.00
149	Jason Romano	1.50
150	Shane Monahan	.40
151	*Ntema Ndungidi*	4.00
152	Alex Sanchez	.40
153	*Jack Cust*	10.00
154	Brent Butler	2.00
155	Ramon Hernandez	.40
156	Norm Hutchins	.40
157	Jason Marquis	.40
158	Jacob Cruz	.40
159	*Rob Burger*	2.50
160	Eric Milton	1.50
161	Preston Wilson	.40
162	*Jason Fitzgerald*	2.50
163	Dan Serafini	.40
164	Peter Munro	.40
165	Trot Nixon	.50
166	Homer Bush	.40
167	Dermal Brown	2.00
168	Chad Hermansen	3.00
169	*Julio Moreno*	2.00
170	*John Roskos*	4.00
171	Grant Roberts	1.50
172	Ken Cloude	.50
173	Jason Brester	.40
174	Jason Conti	.40
175	Jon Garland	.50
176	Robbie Bell	.40
177	Nathan Haynes	.40
178	*Ramon Ortiz*	10.00
179	Shannon Stewart	.40
180	Pablo Ortega	.40
181	*Jimmy Rollins*	4.00
182	Sean Casey	1.00
183	*Ted Lilly*	3.00
184	*Chris Enochs*	6.00
185	*Magglio Ordonez*	15.00
186	Mike Drumright	.40
187	Aaron Boone	.40
188	Matt Clement	.50
189	Todd Dunwoody	.40
190	Larry Rodriguez	.40
191	Todd Noel	.40
192	Geoff Jenkins	.40
193	George Lombard	.50
194	Lance Berkman	[illegible]
195	*Marcus McCain*	.75
196	Ryan McGuire	.40
197	*Jhensy Sandoval*	7.00
198	Corey Lee	.40
199	Mario Valdez	.40
200	*Robert Fick*	4.00
201	Donnie Sadler	.40
202	Marc Kroon	.40
203	David Miller	.40
204	Jarrod Washburn	.40
205	Miguel Tejada	3.00
206	Raul Ibanez	.40
207	John Patterson	.60
208	Calvin Pickering	2.00
209	Felix Martinez	.40
210	Mark Redman	.40
211	Scott Elarton	.40
212	*Jose Amado*	1.50
213	Kerry Wood	4.00
214	Dante Powell	.40
215	Aramis Ramirez	4.00
216	A.J. Hinch	3.00
217	*Dustin Carr*	2.00
218	Mark Kotsay	3.00
219	Jason Standridge	.40
220	Luis Ordaz	.40
221	*Orlando Hernandez*	15.00
222	Cal Ripken Jr.	6.00
223	Paul Molitor	1.50
224	Derek Jeter	5.00
225	Barry Bonds	2.00
226	Jim Edmonds	.40
227	John Smoltz	.40
228	Eric Karros	.40
229	Ray Lankford	.20
230	Rey Ordonez	.20
231	Kenny Lofton	2.00
232	Alex Rodriguez	5.00
233	Dante Bichette	.50
234	Pedro Martinez	1.50
235	Carlos Delgado	.75
236	Rod Beck	.20
237	Matt Williams	.50
238	Charles Johnson	.20
239	Rico Brogna	.20
240	Frank Thomas	3.00
241	Paul O'Neill	.75
242	Jaret Wright	2.00
243	Brant Brown	.20
244	Ryan Klesko	.40
245	Chuck Finley	.20
246	Derek Bell	.20
247	Delino DeShields	.20
248	Chan Ho Park	.50
249	Wade Boggs	.50
250	Jay Buhner	.75
251	Butch Huskey	.20
252	Steve Finley	.20
253	Will Clark	.75
254	John Valentin	.20
255	Bobby Higginson	.20
256	Darryl Strawberry	.50
257	Randy Johnson	1.50
258	Al Martin	.20
259	Travis Fryman	.20
260	Fred McGriff	.50
261	Jose Valentin	.20
262	Andruw Jones	2.00
263	Kenny Rogers	.20
264	Moises Alou	.50
265	Denny Neagle	.20
266	Ugueth Urbina	.20
267	Derrek Lee	.20
268	Ellis Burks	.20
269	Mariano Rivera	.50
270	Dean Palmer	.20
271	Eddie Taubensee	.20
272	Brady Anderson	.20
273	Brian Giles	.20
274	Quinton McCracken	.20
275	Henry Rodriguez	.20
276	Andres Galarraga	.75
277	Jose Canseco	1.00
278	David Segui	.20
279	Bret Saberhagen	.20
280	Kevin Brown	.50
281	Chuck Knoblauch	.75
282	Jeromy Burnitz	.20
283	Jay Bell	.20
284	Manny Ramirez	2.50
285	Rick Helling	.20
286	Francisco Cordova	.20
287	Bob Abreu	.20
288	J.T. Snow Jr.	.20
289	Hideo Nomo	1.00
290	Brian Jordan	.20
291	Javy Lopez	.20
292	Travis Lee	2.00
293	Russell Branyan	.20
294	Paul Konerko	.50
295	*Masato Yoshii*	3.00
296	Kris Benson	.75
297	Juan Encarnacion	.20
298	Eric Milton	.20
299	Mike Caruso	.20
300	*Ricardo Aramboles*	8.00
301	Bobby Smith	.20
302	Billy Koch	.20
303	Richard Hidalgo	.20
304	*Justin Baughman*	2.00
305	Chris Gissell	.20
306	*Donnie Bridges*	3.00
307	*Nelson Lara*	3.00
308	*Randy Wolf*	10.00
309	*Jason LaRue*	4.00
310	*Jason Gooding*	2.00
311	*Edgar Clemente*	1.00
312	Andrew Vessel	[illegible]
313	Chris Reitsma	.20
314	*Jesus Sanchez*	2.00
315	*Buddy Carlyle*	3.00
316	Randy Winn	.20
317	Luis Rivera	6.00
318	*Marcus Thames*	4.00
319	A.J. Pierzynski	.20
320	Scott Randall	.20
321	Damian Sapp	.20
322	*Eddie Yarnell*	8.00
323	*Luke Allen*	4.00
324	J.D. Smart	.20
325	Willie Martinez	.20
326	Alex Ramirez	.20
327	*Eric DuBose*	3.00
328	Kevin Witt	.20
329	*Dan McKinley*	1.50

330	Cliff Politte	.20
331	Vladimir Nunez	.20
332	*John Halama*	1.00
333	Nerio Rodriguez	.20
334	Desi Relaford	.20
335	Robinson Checo	.20
336	*John Nicholson*	3.00
337	*Tom LaRosa*	2.00
338	*Kevin Nicholson*	4.00
339	Javier Vazquez	.20
340	A.J. Zapp	.20
341	Tom Evans	.20
342	Kerry Robinson	.20
343	*Gabe Gonzalez*	1.50
344	Ralph Milliard	.20
345	Enrique Wilson	.20
346	Elvin Hernandez	.20
347	*Mike Lincoln*	3.00
348	*Cesar King*	5.00
349	Cristian Guzman	2.00
350	Donzell McDonald	.20
351	*Jim Parque*	4.00
352	*Mike Saipe*	2.00
353	*Carlos Febles*	8.00
354	*Dernell Stenson*	10.00
355	*Mark Osborne*	4.00
356	*Odalis Perez*	6.00
357	*Jason Dewey*	2.00
358	Joe Fontenot	.20
359	*Jason Grilli*	4.00
360	*Kevin Haverbusch*	4.00
361	*Jay Yennaco*	2.00
362	Brian Buchanan	.20
363	John Barnes	.20
364	Chris Fussell	.20
365	*Kevin Gibbs*	1.50
366	Joe Lawrence	.20
367	DaRond Stovall	.20
368	*Brian Fuentes*	2.00
369	Jimmy Anderson	.20
370	*Laril Gonzalez*	4.00
371	*Scott Williamson*	5.00
372	Milton Bradley	.20
373	*Jason Halper*	2.00
374	*Brent Billingsley*	2.00
375	*Joe DePastino*	.20
376	Jake Westbrook	.20
377	Octavio Dotel	.20
378	*Jason Williams*	1.00
379	*Julio Ramirez*	4.00
380	Seth Greisinger	.20
381	*Mike Judd*	3.00
382	*Ben Ford*	2.00
383	*Tom Bennett*	2.00
384	*Adam Butler*	2.00
385	*Wade Miller*	2.00
386	*Kyle Peterson*	2.00
387	*Tommy Peterman*	2.00
388	Onan Masaoka	.20
389	*Jason Rakers*	1.50
390	Rafael Medina	.20
391	Luis Lopez	.20
392	Jeff Yoder	.20
393	*Vance Wilson*	1.50
394	*Fernando Seguignol*	6.00
395	Ron Wright	.20
396	*Ruben Mateo*	20.00
397	*Steve Lomasney*	2.00
398	Damian Jackson	.20
399	*Mike Jerzembeck*	1.50
400	*Luis Rivas*	4.00
401	*Kevin Burford*	4.00
402	Glenn Davis	.20
403	*Robert Luce*	1.50
404	Cole Liniak	.20
405	*Matthew LeCroy*	4.00
406	*Jeremy Giambi*	10.00
407	Shawn Chacon	.20
408	*Dewayne Wise*	5.00
409	*Steve Woodard*	1.50
410	*Francisco Cordero*	1.00
411	*Damon Minor*	2.00
412	Lou Collier	.20
413	Justin Towle	.20
414	Juan LeBron	.20
415	Michael Coleman	.20
416	Felix Rodriguez	.20
417	*Paul Ah Yat*	2.00
418	*Kevin Barker*	2.00
419	Brian Meadows	.20
420	*Darnell McDonald*	8.00
421	*Matt Kinney*	2.00
422	*Mike Vavrek*	2.00
423	*Courtney Duncan*	1.50
424	*Kevin Millar*	4.00
425	Ruben Rivera	.20
426	*Steve Shoemaker*	1.00
427	*Dan Reichert*	1.50
428	*Carlos Lee*	10.00
429	Rod Barajas	2.00
430	*Pablo Ozuna*	10.00
431	*Todd Belitz*	1.00
432	Sidney Ponson	.20
433	*Steve Carver*	2.00
434	Esteban Yan	3.00
435	*Cedrick Bowers*	2.00
436	Marlon Anderson	.20
437	Carl Pavano	.20
438	*Jae Weong Seo*	3.00
439	*Jose Taveras*	3.00
440	*Matt Anderson*	5.00
441	*Darron Ingram*	4.00

Player names in *Italic* type indicate a rookie card.

1998 Bowman's Best Mirror Image Fusion

This 20-card die-cut insert features a veteran star on one side and a young player at the same position on the other. Regular versions are seeded one per 12 packs, while Refractors are found 1:809 packs and numbered within an edition of 100, and Atomic Refractors are a 1:3237 find numbered to 25. All have a "MI" prefix to the card number.

		MT
Complete Set (20):		120.00
Common Player (1:12):		1.50
1	Frank Thomas, David Ortiz	10.00
2	Chuck Knoblauch, Enrique Wilson	1.50
3	Nomar Garciaparra, Miguel Tejada	10.00
4	Alex Rodriguez, Mike Caruso	10.00
5	Cal Ripken Jr., Ryan Minor	15.00
6	Ken Griffey Jr., Ben Grieve	20.00
7	Juan Gonzalez, Juan Encarnacion	8.00
8	Jose Cruz Jr., Ruben Mateo	4.00
9	Randy Johnson, Ryan Anderson	3.00
10	Ivan Rodriguez, A.J. Hinch	5.00
11	Jeff Bagwell, Paul Konerko	5.00
12	Mark McGwire, Travis Lee	25.00
13	Craig Biggio, Chad Hermanson	1.50
14	Mark Grudzielanek, Alex Gonzalez	2.00
15	Chipper Jones, Adrian Beltre	10.00
16	Larry Walker, Mark Kotsay	2.00
17	Tony Gwynn, Preston Wilson	8.00
18	Barry Bonds, Richard Hidalgo	5.00
19	Greg Maddux, Kerry Wood	10.00
20	Mike Piazza, Ben Petrick	12.00

1998 Bowman's Best Mirror Image Refractors

All 20 cards in the Mirror Image insert were reprinted in both Refractor and Atomic Refractor versions. Refractors were seeded one per 809 packs and numbered to 100 sets, while Atomic Refractors were seeded one per 3,237 packs and numbered with a "MI" prefix to 25 sets.

		MT
Complete Set (20):		2200.
Common Player:		25.00
Production 100 sets		
Atomic Refractors: 1.5x to 2.5x		
Production 25 sets		
1	Frank Thomas, David Ortiz	100.00
2	Chuck Knoblauch, Enrique Wilson	40.00
3	Nomar Garciaparra, Miguel Tejada	200.00
4	Alex Rodriguez, Mike Caruso	200.00
5	Cal Ripken Jr., Ryan Minor	225.00
6	Ken Griffey Jr., Ben Grieve	300.00
7	Juan Gonzalez, Juan Encarnacion	150.00
8	Jose Cruz Jr., Ruben Mateo	75.00
9	Randy Johnson, Ryan Anderson	60.00
10	Ivan Rodriguez, A.J. Hinch	80.00
11	Jeff Bagwell, Paul Konerko	100.00
12	Mark McGwire, Travis Lee	300.00
13	Craig Biggio, Chad Hermanson	50.00
14	Mark Grudzielanek, Alex Gonzalez	25.00
15	Chipper Jones, Adrian Beltre	150.00
16	Larry Walker, Mark Kotsay	40.00
17	Tony Gwynn, Preston Wilson	150.00
18	Barry Bonds, Richard Hidalgo	75.00
19	Greg Maddux, Kerry Wood	175.00
20	Mike Piazza, Ben Petrick	200.00

1998 Bowman's Best Performers

Performers are 10 players who had the best Minor League seasons in 1997. Regular versions were inserted one per six packs, while Refractors are seeded 1:809 and serially numbered to 200, and Atomic Refractors are 1:3237 and numbered to 50 sets. All versions have card numbers with a "BP" prefix.

		MT
Complete Set (10):		15.00
Common Player:		1.00
1	Ben Grieve	2.00
2	Travis Lee	3.00
3	Ryan Minor	2.00
4	Todd Helton	1.50
5	Brad Fullmer	1.50
6	Paul Konerko	1.00
7	Adrian Beltre	2.00
8	Richie Sexson	1.00
9	Aramis Ramirez	1.00
10	Russell Branyan	1.00

1998 Bowman's Best Performers Refractors

All 10 cards in the Performers insert also arrived in Refractor and Atomic Refractor versions. Refractors were seeded one per 809 packs and numbered to 200 sets, while Atomic Refractors are seeded one per 3,237 packs and numbered to 50 on the back.

		MT
Complete Set (10):		500.00
Common Player:		10.00
Production 200 sets		
Atomic Refractors: 1.5x to 2.5x		
Production 50 sets		
BP1	Ben Grieve	75.00
BP2	Travis Lee	75.00
BP3	Ryan Minor	100.00
BP4	Todd Helton	60.00
BP5	Brad Fullmer	15.00
BP6	Paul Konerko	25.00
BP7	Adrian Beltre	90.00
BP8	Richie Sexson	10.00
BP9	Aramis Ramirez	40.00
BP10	Russell Branyan	10.00

1999 Bowman Pre-Production

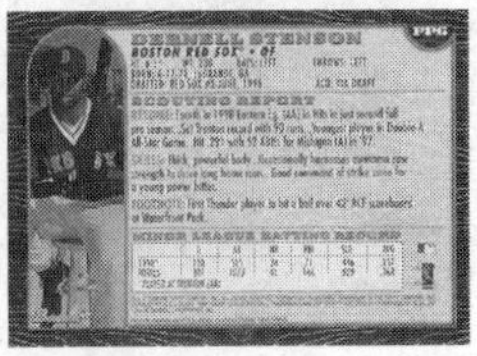

Bowman's 1999 issue was introduced with this group of sample cards. Format is nearly identical to the issued cards, except for the use of a "PP" prefix to the card number on back.

		MT
Complete Set (6):		12.00
Common Player:		2.00
1	Andres Galarraga	2.00
2	Raul Mondesi	2.50
3	Vinny Castilla	2.00
4	Corey Koskie	3.00
5	Octavio Dotel	3.00
6	Dernell Stenson	4.00

1999 Bowman

The set was issued in two 220-card series, each comprised of 70 veterans and 150 rookies and prospects. Rookie/prospect cards have blue metallic foil highlights; veteran cards are highlighted with red foil. On each card is the player's facsimile autograph, reproduced from their initial Topps contract.

		MT
Complete Set (440):		130.00
Complete Series 1 (220):		60.00
Complete Series 2 (220):		70.00
Common Player:		.15
Series 1 Wax Box:		60.00
Series 2 Wax Box:		80.00
1	Ben Grieve	.75
2	Kerry Wood	1.00
3	Ruben Rivera	.15
4	Sandy Alomar	.25
5	Cal Ripken Jr.	3.00
6	Mark McGwire	5.00
7	Vladimir Guerrero	1.50
8	Moises Alou	.25
9	Jim Edmonds	.15
10	Greg Maddux	2.50
11	Gary Sheffield	.25
12	John Valentin	.15
13	Chuck Knoblauch	.40
14	Tony Clark	.40
15	Rusty Greer	.15
16	Al Leiter	.15
17	Travis Lee	.75
18	Jose Cruz Jr.	.50
19	Pedro Martinez	.75
20	Paul O'Neill	.40
21	Todd Walker	.25
22	Vinny Castilla	.25
23	Barry Larkin	.40
24	Curt Schilling	.40
25	Jason Kendall	.25
26	Scott Erickson	.15
27	Andres Galarraga	.40
28	Jeff Shaw	.15
29	John Olerud	.25
30	Orlando Hernandez	1.00
31	Larry Walker	.75
32	Andruw Jones	1.00
33	Jeff Cirillo	.15
34	Barry Bonds	1.00
35	Manny Ramirez	2.00
36	Mark Kotsay	.15
37	Ivan Rodriguez	1.00
38	Jeff King	.15
39	Brian Hunter	.15
40	Ray Durham	.15
41	Bernie Williams	.75
42	Darin Erstad	1.00
43	Chipper Jones	2.50
44	Pat Hentgen	.15
45	Eric Young	.15
46	Jaret Wright	.50
47	Juan Guzman	.15
48	Jorge Posada	.25
49	Bobby Higginson	.15
50	Jose Guillen	.15
51	Trevor Hoffman	.15
52	Ken Griffey Jr.	4.00
53	David Justice	.40
54	Matt Williams	.40
55	Eric Karros	.25
56	Derek Bell	.15
57	Ray Lankford	.15
58	Mariano Rivera	.25
59	Brett Tomko	.15
60	Mike Mussina	.60
61	Kenny Lofton	1.00
62	Chuck Finley	.15
63	Alex Gonzalez	.15
64	Mark Grace	.30
65	Raul Mondesi	.30
66	David Cone	.25
67	Brad Fullmer	.25
68	Andy Benes	.15
69	John Smoltz	.25
70	Shane Reynolds	.25
71	Bruce Chen	.40
72	Adam Kennedy	.15
73	Jack Cust	.15
74	Matt Clement	.15
75	Derrick Gibson	.15
76	Darnell McDonald	.15
77	*Adam Everett*	2.00
78	Ricardo Aramboles	.15
79	*Mark Quinn*	2.50
80	Jason Rakers	.15
81	*Seth Etherton*	2.00
82	*Jeff Urban*	1.00
83	Manny Aybar	.15
84	*Mike Nannini*	1.50
85	Onan Masaoka	.15
86	Rod Barajas	.15
87	Mike Frank	.15
88	Scott Randall	.15
89	*Justin Bowles*	.50
90	Chris Haas	.15
91	*Arturo McDowell*	1.00
92	*Matt Belisle*	1.00
93	Scott Elarton	.15
94	Vernon Wells	.15
95	Pat Cline	.15
96	Ryan Anderson	1.00
97	Kevin Barker	.15
98	Ruben Mateo	2.00
99	Robert Fick	.15
100	Corey Koskie	.15
101	Ricky Ledee	.25
102	*Rick Elder*	3.00
103	*Jack Cressend*	.75
104	Joe Lawrence	.15
105	Mike Lincoln	.15
106	*Kit Pellow*	1.00
107	*Matt Burch*	2.00
108	Brent Butler	.15
109	Jason Dewey	.15
110	Cesar King	.15
111	Julio Ramirez	.15
112	Jake Westbrook	.15
113	*Eric Valent*	5.00
114	*Roosevelt Brown*	.75
115	*Choo Freeman*	1.50
116	Juan Melo	.15
117	Jason Grilli	.15
118	Jared Sandberg	.15
119	Glenn Davis	.15
120	*David Riske*	.75
121	Jacque Jones	.15
122	Corey Lee	.15
123	Michael Barrett	.40
124	Lariel Gonzalez	.15
125	Mitch Meluskey	.30
126	Freddy Garcia	.40
127	*Tony Torcato*	1.00
128	Jeff Liefer	.15
129	Ntema Ndungidi	.15
130	*Andy Brown*	1.50
131	*Ryan Mills*	2.00
132	*Andy Abad*	.50
133	Carlos Febles	.15
134	*Jason Tyner*	1.00
135	Mark Osborne	.15
136	*Phil Norton*	1.00
137	Nathan Haynes	.15
138	Roy Halladay	.15
139	Juan Encarnacion	.15
140	Brad Penny	.15
141	Grant Roberts	.15
142	Aramis Ramirez	.15
143	Cristian Guzman	.15
144	*Mamon Tucker*	1.50
145	Ryan Bradley	.15
146	Brian Simmons	.15
147	Dan Reichert	.15
148	Russ Branyon	.15
149	*Victor Valencia*	2.00
150	Scott Schoeneweis	.15

151	*Sean Spencer*	.75
152	Odalis Perez	.15
153	Joe Fontenot	.15
154	Milton Bradley	.15
155	*Josh McKinley*	1.50
156	Terrence Long	.15
157	Danny Klassen	.15
158	*Paul Hoover*	1.00
159	Ron Belliard	.15
160	Armando Rios	.15
161	Ramon Hernandez	.15
162	Jason Conti	.15
163	Chad Hermansen	.15
164	Jason Standridge	.15
165	Jason Dellaero	.15
166	John Curtice	.15
167	*Clayton Andrews*	2.00
168	Jeremy Giambi	.25
169	Alex Ramirez	.15
170	*Gabe Molina*	.15
171	*Mario Encarnacion*	1.50
172	*Mike Zywica*	1.50
173	*Chip Ambres*	1.50
174	Trot Nixon	.15
175	*Pat Burrell*	10.00
176	Jeff Yoder	.15
177	*Chris Jones*	1.00
178	Kevin Witt	.15
179	*Keith Luuloa*	.50
180	Billy Koch	.15
181	*Damaso Marte*	1.00
182	*Ryan Glynn*	1.50
183	Calvin Pickering	.40
184	Michael Cuddyer	.15
185	*Nick Johnson*	5.00
186	*Doug Mientkiewicz*	1.00
187	*Nate Cornejo*	1.00
188	Octavio Dotel	.15
189	Wes Helms	.15
190	Nelson Lara	.15
191	*Chuck Abbott*	1.50
192	Tony Armas, Jr.	.15
193	Gil Meche	.15
194	Ben Petrick	.15
195	*Chris George*	1.50
196	*Scott Hunter*	.75
197	Ryan Brannan	.15
198	*Amaury Garcia*	.75
199	Chris Gissell	.15
200	*Austin Kearns*	3.00
201	Alex Gonzalez	.15
202	Wade Miller	.15
203	Scott Williamson	.15
204	Chris Enochs	.15
205	Fernando Seguignol	.50
206	Marlon Anderson	.15
207	Todd Sears	.75
208	*Nate Bump*	1.50
209	*J.M. Gold*	3.00
210	Matt LeCroy	.15
211	Alex Hernandez	.15
212	Luis Rivera	.15
213	Troy Cameron	.15
214	*Alex Escobar*	5.00
215	Jason LaRue	.15
216	Kyle Peterson	.15
217	Brent Butler	.15
218	Dernell Stenson	.40
219	Adrian Beltre	.75
220	Daryle Ward	.15
----	Series 1 Checklist Folder	.15
221	Jim Thome	.50
222	Cliff Floyd	.15
223	Rickey Henderson	.25
224	Garret Anderson	.15
225	Ken Caminiti	.25
226	Bret Boone	.15
227	Jeromy Burnitz	.15
228	Steve Finley	.15
229	Miguel Tejada	.15
230	Greg Vaughn	.25
231	Jose Offerman	.15
232	Andy Ashby	.15
233	Albert Belle	1.00
234	Fernando Tatis	.40
235	Todd Helton	.50
236	Sean Casey	.75
237	Brian Giles	.15
238	Andy Pettitte	.25
239	Fred McGriff	.25
240	Roberto Alomar	.75
241	Edgar Martinez	.15
242	Lee Stevens	.15
243	Shawn Green	.40
244	Ryan Klesko	.25
245	Sammy Sosa	2.50
246	Todd Hundley	.15
247	Shannon Stewart	.15
248	Randy Johnson	.75
249	Rondell White	.25
250	Mike Piazza	2.50
251	Craig Biggio	.50
252	David Wells	.15
253	Brian Jordan	.15
254	Edgar Renteria	.15
255	Bartolo Colon	.15
256	Frank Thomas	1.50
257	Will Clark	.50
258	Dean Palmer	.15
259	Dmitri Young	.15
260	Scott Rolen	1.00
261	Jeff Kent	.15
262	Dante Bichette	.40
263	Nomar Garciaparra	2.50
264	Tony Gwynn	2.00
265	Alex Rodriguez	2.50
266	Jose Canseco	.75
267	Jason Giambi	.15
268	Jeff Bagwell	1.50
269	Carlos Delgado	.50
270	Tom Glavine	.25
271	Eric Davis	.15
272	Edgardo Alfonzo	.25
273	Tim Salmon	.25
274	Johnny Damon	.15
275	Rafael Palmeiro	.75
276	Denny Neagle	.15
277	Neifi Perez	.15
278	Roger Clemens	1.50
279	Brant Brown	.15
280	Kevin Brown	.25
281	Jay Bell	.15
282	Jay Buhner	.25
283	Matt Lawton	.15
284	Robin Ventura	.25
285	Juan Gonzalez	1.50
286	Mo Vaughn	1.00
287	Kevin Millwood	.50
288	Tino Martinez	.50
289	Justin Thompson	.15
290	Derek Jeter	2.50
291	Ben Davis	.15
292	Mike Lowell	.15
293	*Joe Crede*	.40
294	*Micah Bowie*	1.00
295	Lance Berkman	.25
296	Jason Marquis	.15
297	Chad Green	.15
298	Dee Brown	.15
299	Jerry Hairston	.15
300	Gabe Kapler	.50
301	*Brent Stentz*	.50
302	*Scott Mullen*	.50
303	Brandon Reed	.15
304	*Shea Hillenbrand*	1.50
305	*J.D. Closser*	1.00
306	Gary Matthews Jr.	.15
307	*Toby Hall*	.75
308	*Jason Phillips*	.50
309	*Jose Macias*	.40
310	*Jung Bong*	2.00
311	*Ramon Soler*	.75
312	*Kelly Dransfeldt*	1.00
313	*Carlos Hernandez*	.50
314	Kevin Haverbusch	.15
315	*Aaron Myette*	1.50
316	*Chad Harville*	.50
317	*Kyle Farnsworth*	1.50
318	*Travis Dawkins*	1.50
319	Willie Martinez	.15
320	Carlos Lee	.15
321	*Carlos Pena*	3.00
322	*Peter Bergeron*	1.50
323	*A.J. Burnett*	3.00
324	*Bucky Jacobsen*	1.00
325	*Mo Bruce*	1.00
326	Reggie Taylor	.15
327	Jackie Rexrode	.15
328	*Alvin Morrow*	.50
329	Carlos Beltran	.50
330	Eric Chavez	.40
331	John Patterson	.15
332	Jayson Werth	.15
333	Richie Sexson	.15
334	Randy Wolf	.15
335	Eli Marrero	.15
336	Paul LoDuca	.15
337	J.D. Smart	.15
338	Ryan Minor	.15
339	Kris Benson	.15
340	George Lombard	.15
341	Troy Glaus	.75
342	Eddie Yarnell	.15
343	*Kip Wells*	2.50
344	*C.C. Sabathia*	3.00
345	*Sean Burroughs*	5.00
346	*Felipe Lopez*	2.00
347	*Ryan Rupe*	1.00
348	*Orber Moreno*	.75
349	*Rafael Roque*	.75
350	*Alfonso Soriano*	6.00
351	Pablo Ozuna	.15
352	*Corey Patterson*	8.00
353	Braden Looper	.15
354	Robbie Bell	.15
355	*Mark Mulder*	2.50
356	Angel Pena	.15
357	Kevin McGlinchy	.15
358	*Michael Restovich*	4.00
359	Eric DuBose	.15
360	Geoff Jenkins	.15
361	*Mark Harriger*	1.00
362	*Junior Herndon*	.50
363	*Tim Raines, Jr.*	.75
364	*Rafael Furcal*	3.00
365	*Marcus Giles*	3.00
366	Ted Lilly	.15
367	*Jorge Toca*	2.00
368	*David Kelton*	.75
369	*Adam Dunn*	[illegible]
370	*Guillermo Mota*	1.00
371	*Brett Laxton*	.50
372	*Travis Harper*	.50
373	*Tom Davey*	.50
374	*Darren Blakely*	.75
375	*Tim Hudson*	5.00
376	Jason Romano	.15
377	Dan Reichert	.15
378	*Julio Lugo*	.50
379	*Jose Garcia*	.50
380	*Erubiel Durazo*	10.00
381	Jose Jimenez	.15
382	Chris Fussell	.15
383	Steve Lomasney	.15
384	*Juan Pena*	1.00
385	*Allen Levrault*	.50
386	*Juan Rivera*	1.00
387	*Steve Colyer*	.50
388	*Joe Nathan*	1.50
389	*Ron Walker*	.75
390	Nick Bierbrodt	.15
391	*Luke Prokopec*	1.00
392	*Dave Roberts*	.75
393	Mike Darr	.15
394	*Abraham Nunez*	2.50
395	*Giuseppe Chiaramonte*	1.00
396	*Jermaine Van Buren*	.50
397	Mike Kusiewicz	.15
398	*Matt Wise*	.50
399	*Joe McEwing*	3.00
400	*Matt Holliday*	1.00
401	*Willi Mo Pena*	4.00
402	*Ruben Quevedo*	.75
403	*Rob Ryan*	.50
404	*Freddy Garcia*	6.00
405	*Kevin Eberwein*	.50
406	*Jesus Colome*	.75
407	*Chris Singleton*	1.50
408	*Bubba Crosby*	.50
409	*Jesus Cordero*	.50
410	Donny Leon	.15
411	*Goefrey Tomlinson*	.50
412	*Jeff Winchester*	.50
413	*Adam Piatt*	4.00
414	Robert Stratton	.15
415	T.J. Tucker	.15
416	*Ryan Langerhans*	.50
417	*Anthony Shumaker*	.50
418	*Matt Miller*	.50
419	*Doug Clark*	.75
420	*Kory DeHaan*	1.00
421	*David Eckstein*	.50
422	*Brian Cooper*	.50
423	*Brady Clark*	.50
424	*Chris Magruder*	.50
425	*Bobby Seay*	1.50
426	*Aubrey Huff*	.15
427	Mike Jerzembeck	.15
428	*Matt Blank*	.50
429	*Benny Agbayani*	3.00
430	*Kevin Beirne*	.50
431	*Josh Hamilton*	6.00
432	*Josh Girdley*	.75
433	*Kyle Snyder*	1.50
434	*Mike Paradis*	1.00
435	*Jason Jennings*	.75
436	*David Walling*	2.00
437	*Omar Ortiz*	.50
438	*Jay Gehrke*	1.00
439	*Casey Burns*	.50
440	*Carl Crawford*	2.00

1999 Bowman Gold

Gold, rather than black, ink for the facsimile autograph, Bowman logo and player name on front, and a serial number on back from within an edition of 99, designate these parallels. Stated odds of finding the Gold cards were one per 111 packs of Series 1, and 1:59 in Series 2.

	MT
Common Player:	5.00
Veteran Stars: 20-40X	
Young Stars/RCs: 4-10X	

(See 1999 Bowman for checklist and base card values.)

1999 Bowman International

International parallels are a one-per-pack insert. Fronts are printed in metallic silver on which the photo's background has been replaced with a scenic picture supposed to be indicative of the player's native land. That location is spelled out at the lower-left corner of the photo, Backs of the Internationals are printed in the player's native language.

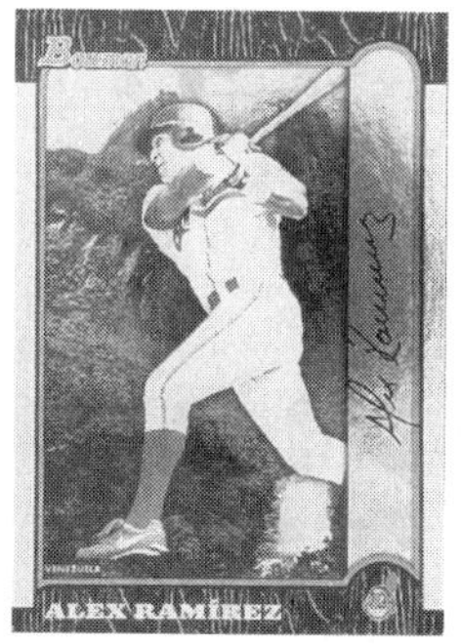

	MT
Complete Set (220):	150.00
Common Player:	.25
Veteran Stars: 1.5-2X	
Young Stars/RCs: 1-1.5X	

(See 1999 Bowman for checklist and base card values.)

1999 Bowman Autographs

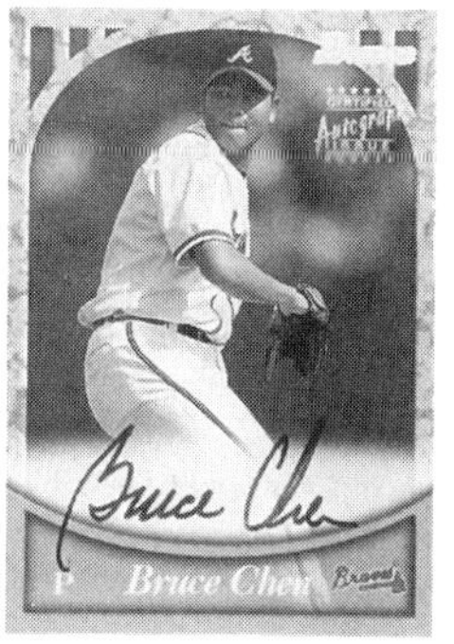

Autographs were randomly seeded in Series 1 and 2 packs, with each card bearing a Topps Certified Autograph seal on the front and numbered with a "BA" prefix on back. Levels of scarcity are color coded by the metallic-foil highlights on front: Golds are the most difficult to find at 1:1941 Series 1 packs and 1:1024 Series 2. Silvers are seeded 1:485 in Series 1, 1:256 Series 2. Blues are found at an average rate of 1:162 in first series and 1:85 in second series.

		MT
Common Player:		6.00
Blues inserted 1:162 or 1:85		
Silvers inserted 1:485 or 1:256		
Golds inserted 1:1954 or 1:1024		
1	Ruben Mateo B	50.00
2	Troy Glaus G	40.00
3	Ben Davis G	25.00
4	Jayson Werth B	10.00
5	Jerry Hairston Jr. S	20.00
6	Darnell McDonald B	10.00
7	Calvin Pickering S	25.00
8	Ryan Minor S	20.00
9	Alex Escobar B	25.00
10	Grant Roberts B	10.00
11	Carlos Guillen B	10.00
12	Ryan Anderson S	25.00
13	Gil Meche S	15.00
14	Russell Branyan S	20.00
15	Alex Ramirez S	25.00
16	Jason Rakers S	20.00
17	Eddie Yarnall B	10.00
18	Freddy Garcia B	50.00
19	Jason Conti B	6.00
20	Corey Koskie B	8.00
21	Roosevelt Brown B	8.00
22	Willie Martinez B	6.00
23	Mike Jerzembeck B	6.00
24	Lariel Gonzalez B	6.00
25	Fernando Seguignol B	20.00
26	Robert Fick S	20.00
27	J.D. Smart B	6.00
28	Ryan Mills B	6.00
29	Chad Hermansen G	50.00
30	Jason Grilli B	8.00
31	Michael Cuddyer B	10.00
32	Jacque Jones S	20.00
33	Reggie Taylor B	8.00
34	Richie Sexson G	50.00
35	Michael Barrett B	20.00
36	Paul LoDuca B	10.00
37	Adrian Beltre G	40.00
38	Peter Bergeron B	10.00
39	Joe Fontenot B	8.00
40	Randy Wolf B	10.00
41	Nick Johnson B	40.00
42	Ryan Bradley B	20.00
43	Mike Lowell S	15.00
44	Ricky Ledee B	15.00
45	Mike Lincoln S	15.00
46	Jeremy Giambi B	15.00
47	Dermal Brown S	20.00
48	Derrick Gibson B	12.00
49	Scott Randall B	6.00
50	Ben Petrick S	10.00
51	Jason LaRue B	6.00
52	Cole Liniak B	10.00
53	John Curtice B	6.00
54	Jackie Rexrode B	6.00
55	John Patterson B	10.00
56	Brad Penny S	20.00
57	Jared Sandberg B	8.00
58	Kerry Wood G	40.00
59	Eli Marrero B	7.00
60	Jason Marquis B	15.00
61	George Lombard S	15.00
62	Bruce Chen S	25.00
63	Kevin Witt S	8.00
64	Vernon Wells B	25.00
65	Billy Koch B	6.00
66	Roy Halladay B	50.00
67	Nathan Haynes B	6.00
68	Ben Grieve G	60.00
69	Eric Chavez G	30.00
70	Lance Berkman S	25.00

1999 Bowman Early Risers

This insert set features 11 current baseball superstars who have already won a Rookie of the Year award and who continue to excel. The insertion rate is 1:12. Cards have an "ER" prefix to the number on back.

		MT
Complete Set (11):		20.00
Common Player:		.75
Inserted 1:12		
1	Mike Piazza	3.50
2	Cal Ripken Jr.	4.00
3	Jeff Bagwell	2.00
4	Ben Grieve	1.00
5	Kerry Wood	.75
6	Mark McGwire	7.00
7	Nomar Garciaparra	3.50
8	Derek Jeter	3.50
9	Scott Rolen	1.25
10	Jose Canseco	1.00
11	Raul Mondesi	.75

1999 Bowman Late Bloomers

This 10-card set features late-round picks from previous drafts who have emerged as bona fide stars. These inserts are numbered with an "LB" prefix and seeded 1:12 packs.

	MT
Complete Set (10):	12.00
Common Player:	.50
Inserted 1:12	
LB1 Mike Piazza	6.00
LB2 Jim Thome	2.00
LB3 Larry Walker	1.50
LB4 Vinny Castilla	.50
LB5 Andy Pettitte	.75
LB6 Jim Edmonds	.50
LB7 Kenny Lofton	2.50
LB8 John Smoltz	.50
LB9 Mark Grace	.75
LB10 Trevor Hoffman	.50

1999 Bowman Scout's Choice

Scout's Choice inserts were randomly inserted in Series 1 packs and feature a borderless, double-etched design. The 21-card set focuses on prospects who have potential to win a future Rookie of the Year award. These are seeded 1:12 packs.

	MT
Complete Set (21):	45.00
Common Player:	1.00
Inserted 1:12	
SC1 Ruben Mateo	6.00
SC2 Ryan Anderson	4.00
SC3 Pat Burrell	15.00
SC4 Troy Glaus	7.00
SC5 Eric Chavez	5.00
SC6 Adrian Beltre	2.50
SC7 Bruce Chen	1.50
SC8 Carlos Beltran	2.00
SC9 Alex Gonzalez	1.00
SC10 Carlos Lee	2.00
SC11 George Lombard	2.00
SC12 Matt Clement	1.00
SC13 Calvin Pickering	1.00
SC14 Marlon Anderson	1.00
SC15 Chad Hermansen	1.00
SC16 Russell Branyan	1.00
SC17 Jeremy Giambi	2.00
SC18 Ricky Ledee	1.00
SC19 John Patterson	1.00
SC20 Roy Halladay	2.00
SC21 Michael Barrett	1.50

1998 Bowman Chrome International

All 441 cards throughout Bowman Chrome Series 1 and 2 were paralleled in International versions. Card fronts have the regular background replaced by a map denoting the player's birthplace. Backs are written in the player's native language. Regular versions were inserted one per four packs while Refractor versions arrived every 24 packs.

	MT
Complete Set (441):	450.00
Common Player:	.50
Stars and rookies: 1.5-2.5X	
Inserted: 1:4	

(See 1998 Bowman Chrome for checklist and base card values.)

1998 Bowman Chrome Golden Anniversary

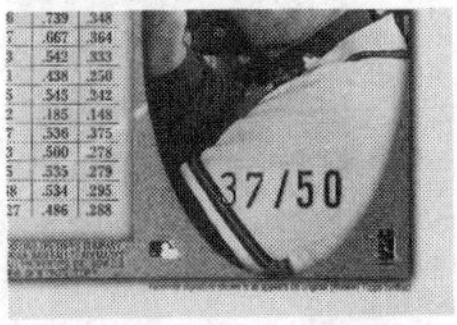

Golden Anniversary parallels were printed for all 441 cards in Bowman Chrome. They are exclusive to hobby packs, seeded one per 164 packs and sequentially numbered to 50 sets. Refractor versions were also available, numbered to just five sets and inserted one per 1,279 packs.

	MT
Common Player:	7.50
Veteran Stars: 20-40X	
Young Stars: 15-25X	

(See 1998 Bowman Chrome for checklist and base card values. Golden Anniversary Refractors cannot be accurately priced due to their rarity (five each).)

1998 Bowman Chrome Refractors

Refractor versions for all 441 cards in Bowman Chrome Series I and II were inserted one per 12 packs. The cards contained the word "Refractor" on the back in black letters directly under the card number.

	MT
Complete Set (441):	1500.
Common Player:	2.00
Stars: 5-10X	
Young Stars/RCs: 3-6X	
Inserted 1:12	
Int'l Refractors: 8-15X	
Young Stars/RCs: 4-10X	
Inserted 1:24	

(See 1998 Bowman Chrome for checklist and base card values.)

1998 Bowman Chrome Reprints

Bowman Chrome Reprints showcase 50 of the most popular rookie cards to appear in the brand since 1948. Regular versions were seeded one per 12 packs, while Refractor versions were seeded 1:36. The 25 odd-numbered cards are found in Series 1; the evens in Series 2. The Reprints are numbered with a "BC" prefix.

		MT
Complete Set (50):		65.00
Common Player:		.50
Inserted 1:12		
Refractors: 1.5-2.5X		
Inserted 1:36		
1	Yogi Berra	3.00
2	Jackie Robinson	6.00
3	Don Newcombe	.50
4	Satchel Paige	2.50
5	Willie Mays	4.00
6	Gil McDougald	.50
7	Don Larsen	1.00
8	Elston Howard	.50
9	Robin Ventura	.50
10	Brady Anderson	.50
11	Gary Sheffield	.50
12	Tino Martinez	.50
13	Ken Griffey Jr.	7.50
14	John Smoltz	.50
15	Sandy Alomar Jr.	.50
16	Larry Walker	.50
17	Todd Hundley	.50
18	Mo Vaughn	.50
19	Sammy Sosa	5.00
20	Frank Thomas	3.00
21	Chuck Knoblauch	.50
22	Bernie Williams	.50
23	Juan Gonzalez	2.00
24	Mike Mussina	.50
25	Jeff Bagwell	1.00
26	Tim Salmon	.50
27	Ivan Rodriguez	1.00
28	Kenny Lofton	.50
29	Chipper Jones	5.00
30	Javier Lopez	.50
31	Ryan Klesko	.50
32	Raul Mondesi	.50
33	Jim Thome	.50
34	Carlos Delgado	.75
35	Mike Piazza	5.00
36	Manny Ramirez	1.00
37	Andy Pettitte	.50
38	Derek Jeter	5.00
39	Brad Fullmer	.50
40	Richard Hidalgo	.50
41	Tony Clark	.50
42	Andruw Jones	1.50
43	Vladimir Guerrero	1.50
44	Nomar Garciaparra	5.00
45	Paul Konerko	.50
46	Ben Grieve	.50
47	Hideo Nomo	.50
48	Scott Rolen	1.00
49	Jose Guillen	.50
50	Livan Hernandez	.50

1998 Bowman's Best

Bowman's Best was issued in a single 200-card series comprised of 100 prospects and 100 veterans. Prospects are shown on a silver background, while the veterans are showcased on gold. The set was paralleled twice: A Refractor version is seeded one per 20 packs and sequentially numbered to 400, while an Atomic Refractor version is a 1:82 find and numbered to 100 sets. Inserts include regular, Refractor and Atomic Refractor versions of: Autographs, Mirror Image and Performers.

		MT
Complete Set (200):		60.00
Common Player:		.25
Wax Box:		110.00
1	Mark McGwire	6.00
2	Hideo Nomo	.50
3	Barry Bonds	1.25
4	Dante Bichette	.50
5	Chipper Jones	3.00
6	Frank Thomas	2.00
7	Kevin Brown	.40
8	Juan Gonzalez	2.50
9	Jay Buhner	.50
10	Chuck Knoblauch	.50
11	Cal Ripken Jr.	4.00
12	Matt Williams	.50
13	Jim Edmonds	.25
14	Manny Ramirez	1.50
15	Tony Clark	.75
16	Mo Vaughn	1.25
17	Bernie Williams	1.00
18	Scott Rolen	1.50
19	Gary Sheffield	.60
20	Albert Belle	1.25
21	Mike Piazza	3.00
22	John Olerud	.50
23	Tony Gwynn	2.50
24	Jay Bell	.25
25	Jose Cruz Jr.	.75
26	Justin Thompson	.25
27	Ken Griffey Jr.	5.00
28	Sandy Alomar	.40
29	Mark Grudzielanek	.25
30	Mark Grace	.50
31	Ron Gant	.40
32	Javy Lopez	.25
33	Jeff Bagwell	2.00
34	Fred McGriff	.50
35	Rafael Palmeiro	.50
36	Vinny Castilla	.40
37	Andy Benes	.25
38	Pedro Martinez	1.00
39	Andy Pettitte	.75
40	Marty Cordova	.25
41	Rusty Greer	.25
42	Kevin Orie	.25
43	Chan Ho Park	.75
44	Ryan Klesko	.50
45	Alex Rodriguez	3.00
46	Travis Fryman	.25
47	Jeff King	.25
48	Roger Clemens	2.00
49	Darin Erstad	1.25
50	Brady Anderson	.25
51	Jason Kendall	.25
52	John Valentin	.25
53	Ellis Burks	.25
54	Brian Hunter	.25
55	Paul O'Neill	.50
56	Ken Caminiti	.50
57	David Justice	.60
58	Eric Karros	.40
59	Pat Hentgen	.25
60	Greg Maddux	3.00
61	Craig Biggio	.50
62	Edgar Martinez	.25
63	Mike Mussina	1.00
64	Larry Walker	.75
65	Tino Martinez	.75
66	Jim Thome	1.00
67	Tom Glavine	.50
68	Raul Mondesi	.50
69	Marquis Grissom	.25
70	Randy Johnson	1.00
71	Steve Finley	.25
72	Jose Guillen	.50
73	Nomar Garciaparra	3.00
74	Wade Boggs	.75
75	Bobby Higginson	.25
76	Robin Ventura	.40
77	Derek Jeter	2.50
78	Andruw Jones	1.25
79	Ray Lankford	.25
80	Vladimir Guerrero	1.25
81	Kenny Lofton	1.25
82	Ivan Rodriguez	1.25
83	Neifi Perez	.25
84	John Smoltz	.40
85	Tim Salmon	.50
86	Carlos Delgado	.50
87	Sammy Sosa	4.00
88	Jaret Wright	1.25
89	Roberto Alomar	.75
90	Paul Molitor	.75
91	Dean Palmer	.25
92	Barry Larkin	.50
93	Jason Giambi	.25
94	Curt Schilling	.40
95	Eric Young	.25
96	Denny Neagle	.25
97	Moises Alou	.40
98	Livan Hernandez	.25
99	Todd Hundley	.25
100	Andres Galarraga	.50
101	Travis Lee	1.50
102	Lance Berkman	2.00
103	Orlando Cabrera	.40
104	*Mike Lowell*	3.00
105	Ben Grieve	1.50
106	*Jae Weong Seo*	.75
107	Richie Sexson	.25
108	Eli Marrero	.25
109	Aramis Ramirez	2.50
110	Paul Konerko	.50
111	Carl Pavano	.25
112	Brad Fullmer	.50
113	Matt Clement	.50
114	Donzell McDonald	.25
115	Todd Helton	1.25
116	Mike Caruso	.25
117	Donnie Sadler	.25
118	Bruce Chen	.50
119	Jarrod Washburn	.25
120	Adrian Beltre	3.00
121	*Ryan Jackson*	2.50
122	*Kevin Millar*	1.50
123	*Corey Koskie*	2.50
124	Dermal Brown	1.00
125	Kerry Wood	3.00
126	Juan Melo	.25
127	Ramon Hernandez	.25
128	Roy Halladay	.40
129	Ron Wright	.25
130	*Darnell McDonald*	4.00
131	*Odalis Perez*	4.00
132	*Alex Cora*	1.00
133	Justin Towle	.50
134	Juan Encarnacion	.25
135	Brian Rose	.40
136	Russell Branyan	.25
137	*Cesar King*	3.00
138	Ruben Rivera	.25
139	Ricky Ledee	.50
140	Vernon Wells	1.00
141	*Luis Rivas*	2.00
142	Brent Butler	1.00
143	Karim Garcia	.25
144	George Lombard	.40
145	*Masato Yoshii*	1.50
146	Braden Looper	.25
147	Alex Sanchez	.40
148	Kris Benson	1.00
149	Mark Kotsay	1.50
150	Richard Hidalgo	.25
151	Scott Elarton	.25
152	*Ryan Minor*	6.00
153	*Troy Glaus*	10.00
154	*Carlos Lee*	6.00
155	Michael Coleman	.25
156	*Jason Grilli*	2.00
157	*Julio Ramirez*	2.00
158	*Randy Wolf*	5.00
159	Ryan Brannan	.25
160	*Edgar Clemente*	.50
161	Miguel Tejada	1.50
162	Chad Hermansen	1.50
163	*Ryan Anderson*	6.00
164	Ben Petrick	.25
165	Alex Gonzalez	.50
166	Ben Davis	.25
167	John Patterson	.50
168	Cliff Politte	.25
169	Randall Simon	1.50
170	Javier Vazquez	.25
171	Kevin Witt	.50
172	Geoff Jenkins	.25
173	David Ortiz	1.00
174	Derrick Gibson	.25
175	Abraham Nunez	.50
176	A.J. Hinch	1.50
177	*Ruben Mateo*	10.00
178	*Magglio Ordonez*	8.00
179	Todd Dunwoody	.25
180	Daryle Ward	.50
181	*Mike Kinkade*	2.50
182	Willie Martinez	.25
183	*Orlando Hernandez*	8.00
184	Eric Milton	.75
185	Eric Chavez	2.00
186	Damian Jackson	.25
187	*Jim Parque*	2.50
188	*Dan Reichert*	1.00
189	Mike Drumright	.25
190	Todd Walker	.50
191	Shane Monahan	.25
192	Derrek Lee	.25
193	*Jeremy Giambi*	5.00
194	*Dan McKinley*	.75
195	*Tony Armas*	4.00
196	*Matt Anderson*	3.00
197	*Jim Chamblee*	.75
198	*Francisco Cordero*	.75
199	Calvin Pickering	1.00
200	Reggie Taylor	.25

1998 Bowman's Best Refractors

Refractor versions for all 200 cards in Bowman's Best were available. Fronts featured a reflective finish, while backs were numbered to 400 and inserted one per 20 packs.

	MT
Complete Set (200):	2500.
Common Player:	5.00
Stars: 10x to 15x	
Young Stars/RC's: 5x to 10x	
Production 400 sets	

(See 1998 Bowman's Best for checklist and base card values.)

1998 Bowman's Best Atomic Refractors

Atomic Refractor versions were available for all 200 cards in Bowman's Best. The cards were printed in a prismatic foil on the front, sequentially numbered to 100 sets on the back and inserted one per 82 packs.

	MT
Common Player:	15.00
Stars: 25x to 40x	
Young Stars/RCs: 15x to 30x	

Production 100 sets
(See 1998 Bowman's Best for checklist and base card values.)

1998 Bowman's Best Autographs

This 10-card set offers autographs from five prospects and five veteran stars. Each card has on front the Topps "Certified Autograph Issue" logo for authentication. Regular versions are seeded one per 180 packs, Refractor versions, 1:2158 and Atomic Refractor versions, 1:6437.

		MT
Complete Set (10):		250.00
Common Player:		15.00
Inserted 1:180		
Refractors: 1.5-2.5X		
Inserted 1:2,158		
Atomics: 2-4X		
Inserted 1:6,437		
5	Chipper Jones	75.00
10	Chuck Knoblauch	25.00
15	Tony Clark	20.00
20	Albert Belle	40.00
25	Jose Cruz Jr.	15.00
105	Ben Grieve	25.00
110	Paul Konerko	15.00
115	Todd Helton	25.00
120	Adrian Beltre	20.00
125	Kerry Wood	25.00

1999 Bowman 2000 Rookie of the Year

Randomly inserted in Series 2 packs at a rate of 1:12, these cards have a borderless, double-etched foil design. The 10-card set focuses on players that have potential to win the 2000 Rookie of the Year award.

		MT
Complete Set (10):		15.00
Common Player:		.75
Inserted 1:12		
1	Ryan Anderson	.75
2	Pat Burrell	5.00
3	A.J. Burnett	1.50
4	Ruben Mateo	1.00
5	Alex Escobar	2.00
6	Pablo Ozuna	.75
7	Mark Mulder	1.00
8	Corey Patterson	2.50
9	George Lombard	.75
10	Nick Johnson	4.00

1999 Bowman Chrome

Bowman Chrome was released in two 220-card series as an upscale chromium parallel version of Bowman Baseball. Like Bowman, each series has 150 prospect cards with blue foil, while 70 veteran cards have red foil. Packs contain four cards with an original SRP of $3.

	MT
Complete Set (440):	400.00
Complete Series 1 (220):	150.00
Complete Series 2 (220):	250.00
Common Player:	.40
Series 1 Wax Box:	90.00
Series 2 Wax Box:	135.00

1	Ben Grieve	1.50
2	Kerry Wood	1.50
3	Ruben Rivera	.40
4	Sandy Alomar	.50
5	Cal Ripken Jr.	6.00
6	Mark McGwire	10.00
7	Vladimir Guerrero	3.00
8	Moises Alou	.75
9	Jim Edmonds	.50
10	Greg Maddux	5.00
11	Gary Sheffield	.75
12	John Valentin	.40
13	Chuck Knoblauch	.75
14	Tony Clark	.75
15	Rusty Greer	.40
16	Al Leiter	.60
17	Travis Lee	1.50
18	Jose Cruz Jr.	1.00
19	Pedro Martinez	2.00
20	Paul O'Neill	.75
21	Todd Walker	.50
22	Vinny Castilla	.50
23	Barry Larkin	.75
24	Curt Schilling	.75
25	Jason Kendall	.50
26	Scott Erickson	.40
27	Andres Galarraga	.75
28	Jeff Shaw	.40
29	John Olerud	.50
30	Orlando Hernandez	2.00
31	Larry Walker	1.50
32	Andruw Jones	2.00
33	Jeff Cirillo	.40
34	Barry Bonds	2.00
35	Manny Ramirez	4.00
36	Mark Kotsay	.40
37	Ivan Rodriguez	2.00
38	Jeff King	.40
39	Brian Hunter	.40
40	Ray Durham	.40
41	Bernie Williams	1.50
42	Darin Erstad	1.50
43	Chipper Jones	5.00
44	Pat Hentgen	.40
45	Eric Young	.40
46	Jaret Wright	.75
47	Juan Guzman	.40
48	Jorge Posada	.50
49	Bobby Higginson	.40
50	Jose Guillen	.40
51	Trevor Hoffman	.40
52	Ken Griffey Jr.	8.00
53	David Justice	.75
54	Matt Williams	.75
55	Eric Karros	.50
56	Derek Bell	.40
57	Ray Lankford	.40
58	Mariano Rivera	.50
59	Brett Tomko	.40
60	Mike Mussina	1.50
61	Kenny Lofton	2.00
62	Chuck Finley	.40
63	Alex Gonzalez	.40
64	Mark Grace	.75
65	Raul Mondesi	.60
66	David Cone	.75
67	Brad Fullmer	.50
68	Andy Benes	.40
69	John Smoltz	.50
70	Shane Reynolds	.50
71	Bruce Chen	.75
72	Adam Kennedy	.40
73	Jack Cust	.40
74	Matt Clement	.40
75	Derrick Gibson	.40
76	Darnell McDonald	.40
77	*Adam Everett*	4.00
78	Ricardo Aramboles	.40
79	*Mark Quinn*	6.00
80	Jason Rakers	.40
81	*Seth Etherton*	4.00
82	*Jeff Urban*	2.50
83	Manny Aybar	.40
84	*Mike Nannini*	3.00
85	Onan Masaoka	.40
86	Rod Barajas	.40
87	Mike Frank	.40
88	Scott Randall	.40
89	*Justin Bowles*	1.00
90	Chris Haas	.40
91	*Arturo McDowell*	2.50
92	*Matt Belisle*	3.00
93	Scott Elarton	.40
94	Vernon Wells	.40
95	Pat Cline	.40
96	Ryan Anderson	2.00
97	Kevin Barker	.40
98	Ruben Mateo	2.00
99	Robert Fick	.40
100	Corey Koskie	.10
101	Ricky Ledee	.50
102	*Rick Elder*	8.00
103	*Jack Cressend*	2.00
104	Joe Lawrence	.40
105	Mike Lincoln	.40
106	*Kit Pellow*	2.50
107	*Matt Burch*	5.00
108	Brent Butler	.40
109	Jason Dewey	.40
110	Cesar King	.40
111	Julio Ramirez	.40
112	Jake Westbrook	.40
113	*Eric Valent*	7.00
114	*Roosevelt Brown*	2.00
115	*Choo Freeman*	4.00
116	Juan Melo	.40
117	Jason Grilli	.40
118	Jared Sandberg	.40
119	Glenn Davis	.40
120	*David Riske*	2.00
121	Jacque Jones	.40
122	Corey Lee	.40
123	Michael Barrett	.40
124	Lariel Gonzalez	.40
125	Mitch Meluskey	.75
126	*Freddy Garcia*	5.00
127	*Tony Torcato*	2.50
128	Jeff Liefer	.40
129	Ntema Ndungidi	.40
130	*Andy Brown*	5.00
131	*Ryan Mills*	5.00
132	*Andy Abad*	1.50
133	Carlos Febles	.40
134	*Jason Tyner*	2.50
135	Mark Osborne	.40
136	*Phil Norton*	2.50
137	Nathan Haynes	.40
138	Roy Halladay	.40
139	Juan Encarnacion	.75
140	Brad Penny	.40
141	Grant Roberts	.40
142	Aramis Ramirez	.40
143	Cristian Guzman	.40
144	*Mamon Tucker*	4.00
145	Ryan Bradley	.40
146	Brian Simmons	.40
147	Dan Reichert	.40
148	Russ Branyon	.40
149	*Victor Valencia*	5.00
150	Scott Schoeneweis	.40
151	*Sean Spencer*	2.00
152	Odalis Perez	.75
153	Joe Fontenot	.40
154	Milton Bradley	.40
155	*Josh McKinley*	4.00
156	Terrence Long	.40
157	Danny Klassen	.40
158	*Paul Hoover*	2.50
159	Ron Belliard	.40
160	Armando Rios	.40
161	Ramon Hernandez	.40
162	Jason Conti	.40
163	Chad Hermansen	.40
164	Jason Standridge	.40
165	Jason Dellaero	.40
166	John Curtice	.40
167	*Clayton Andrews*	5.00
168	Jeremy Giambi	.75
169	Alex Ramirez	.40
170	*Gabe Molina*	.40
171	*Mario Encarnacion*	4.00
172	*Mike Zywica*	4.00
173	*Chip Ambres*	4.00
174	Trot Nixon	.40
175	*Pat Burrell*	20.00
176	Jeff Yoder	.40
177	*Chris Jones*	2.50
178	Kevin Witt	.40
179	*Keith Luuloa*	1.50
180	Billy Koch	.40
181	*Damaso Marte*	2.50
182	*Ryan Glynn*	4.00
183	Calvin Pickering	.40
184	Michael Cuddyer	.40
185	*Nick Johnson*	15.00
186	*Doug Mientkiewicz*	2.50
187	*Nate Cornejo*	2.50
188	Octavio Dotel	.40
189	Wes Helms	.40
190	Nelson Lara	.40
191	*Chuck Abbott*	3.00
192	Tony Armas, Jr.	.40
193	Gil Meche	.40
194	Ben Petrick	.40
195	*Chris George*	4.00
196	*Scott Hunter*	2.00
197	Ryan Brannan	.40
198	*Amaury Garcia*	2.00
199	Chris Gissell	.40
200	*Austin Kearns*	6.00
201	Alex Gonzalez	.40
202	Wade Miller	.40
203	Scott Williamson	.40
204	Chris Enochs	.40
205	Fernando Seguignol	1.00
206	Marlon Anderson	.40
207	Todd Sears	1.50
208	*Nate Bump*	4.00
209	*J.M. Gold*	6.00
210	Matt LeCroy	.40
211	Alex Hernandez	.40
212	Luis Rivera	.40
213	Troy Cameron	.40
214	*Alex Escobar*	10.00
215	Jason LaRue	.40
216	Kyle Peterson	.40
217	Brent Butler	.40
218	Dernell Stenson	.40
219	Adrian Beltre	1.50
220	Daryle Ward	.40
221	Jim Thome	1.00
222	Cliff Floyd	.40
223	Rickey Henderson	1.00
224	Garret Anderson	.40
225	Ken Caminiti	.75
226	Bret Boone	.40
227	Jeromy Burnitz	.40
228	Steve Finley	.40
229	Miguel Tejada	.40
230	Greg Vaughn	.75
231	Jose Offerman	.40
232	Andy Ashby	.40
233	Albert Belle	1.50
234	Fernando Tatis	1.00
235	Todd Helton	1.50
236	Sean Casey	1.00
237	Brian Giles	.40
238	Andy Pettitte	.75
239	Fred McGriff	.75
240	Roberto Alomar	1.50
241	Edgar Martinez	.40
242	Lee Stevens	.40
243	Shawn Green	1.50
244	Ryan Klesko	.50
245	Sammy Sosa	5.00
246	Todd Hundley	.40
247	Shannon Stewart	.40
248	Randy Johnson	1.00
249	Rondell White	.75
250	Mike Piazza	5.00
251	Craig Biggio	1.00
252	David Wells	.40
253	Brian Jordan	.40
254	Edgar Renteria	.40
255	Bartolo Colon	.40
256	Frank Thomas	2.50
257	Will Clark	1.00
258	Dean Palmer	.40
259	Dmitri Young	.40
260	Scott Rolen	2.00
261	Jeff Kent	.40
262	Dante Bichette	.75
263	Nomar Garciaparra	5.00
264	Tony Gwynn	4.00
265	Alex Rodriguez	5.00
266	Jose Canseco	2.00
267	Jason Giambi	.40
268	Jeff Bagwell	2.00
269	Carlos Delgado	1.50
270	Tom Glavine	.75
271	Eric Davis	.40
272	Edgardo Alfonzo	.75
273	Tim Salmon	.75
274	Johnny Damon	.40
275	Rafael Palmeiro	1.00
276	Denny Neagle	.40
277	Neifi Perez	.40
278	Roger Clemens	3.00
279	Brant Brown	.40
280	Kevin Brown	.75
281	Jay Bell	.40
282	Jay Buhner	.75
283	Matt Lawton	.40
284	Robin Ventura	.75
285	Juan Gonzalez	4.00
286	Mo Vaughn	1.50
287	Kevin Millwood	1.00
288	Tino Martinez	1.00
289	Justin Thompson	.40
290	Derek Jeter	5.00
291	Ben Davis	.40
292	Mike Lowell	.40
293	*Joe Crede*	.75
294	*Micah Bowie*	2.00
295	Lance Berkman	.40
296	Jason Marquis	.40
297	Chad Green	.40
298	Dee Brown	.40
299	Jerry Hairston	.40
300	Gabe Kapler	1.50
301	*Brent Stentz*	1.50
302	*Scott Mullen*	2.00
303	Brandon Reed	.40
304	*Shea Hillenbrand*	3.00
305	*J.D. Closser*	3.00
306	Gary Matthews Jr.	2.00
307	*Toby Hall*	2.00
308	*Jason Phillips*	2.00
309	*Jose Macias*	1.00
310	*Jung Bong*	4.00
311	*Ramon Soler*	1.50
312	*Kelly Dransfeldt*	3.00
313	*Carlos Hernandez*	1.50
314	Kevin Haverbusch	.40
315	*Aaron Myette*	3.00
316	*Chad Harville*	1.50
317	*Kyle Farnsworth*	3.00
318	*Travis Dawkins*	4.00
319	Willie Martinez	.40
320	Carlos Lee	.60
321	*Carlos Pena*	6.00
322	*Peter Bergeron*	4.00
323	*A.J. Burnett*	5.00
324	*Bucky Jacobsen*	2.00
325	*Mo Bruce*	2.00
326	Reggie Taylor	.40
327	Jackie Rexrode	.40
328	*Alvin Morrow*	1.50
329	Carlos Beltran	2.00
330	Eric Chavez	.75
331	John Patterson	.75
332	Jayson Werth	.40
333	Richie Sexson	.75
334	Randy Wolf	.40
335	Eli Marrero	.40
336	Paul LoDuca	.40
337	J.D. Smart	.40
338	Ryan Minor	.75
339	Kris Benson	.40
340	George Lombard	.40
341	Troy Glaus	1.00
342	Eddie Yarnell	.40
343	*Kip Wells*	5.00
344	*C.C. Sabathia*	4.00
345	*Sean Burroughs*	15.00
346	*Felipe Lopez*	10.00
347	*Ryan Rupe*	2.00
348	*Orber Moreno*	1.50
349	*Rafael Roque*	1.50
350	*Alfonso Soriano*	15.00
351	Pablo Ozuna	.40
352	*Corey Patterson*	30.00
353	Braden Looper	.40
354	Robbie Bell	.40
355	*Mark Mulder*	4.00
356	Angel Pena	.40
357	Kevin McGlinchy	.40
358	*Michael Restovich*	8.00
359	Eric DuBose	.40
360	Geoff Jenkins	.40
361	*Mark Harriger*	2.00
362	*Junior Herndon*	1.50
363	*Tim Raines, Jr.*	3.00
364	*Rafael Furcal*	6.00
365	*Marcus Giles*	6.00
366	Ted Lilly	.40
367	*Jorge Toca*	4.00
368	*David Kelton*	1.00
369	*Adam Dunn*	8.00
370	*Guillermo Mota*	2.00
371	*Brett Laxton*	1.00
372	*Travis Harper*	1.00
373	*Tom Davey*	1.00
374	*Darren Blakely*	1.00
375	*Tim Hudson*	10.00
376	Jason Romano	.40
377	Dan Reichert	.40
378	*Julio Lugo*	1.50
379	*Jose Garcia*	1.50
380	*Erubiel Durazo*	10.00
381	Jose Jimenez	.40
382	Chris Fussell	.40
383	Steve Lomasney	.40
384	*Juan Pena*	2.00
385	*Allen Levrault*	1.50
386	*Juan Rivera*	2.00
387	*Steve Colyer*	1.50
388	*Joe Nathan*	3.00
389	*Ron Walker*	1.00
390	Nick Bierbrodt	.40
391	*Luke Prokopec*	2.00
392	*Dave Roberts*	1.50
393	Mike Darr	.40
394	*Abraham Nunez*	10.00
395	*Giuseppe Chiaramonte*	2.00
396	*Jermaine Van Buren*	1.00
397	Mike Kusiewicz	.40
398	*Matt Wise*	1.50
399	*Joe McEwing*	6.00
400	*Matt Holliday*	3.00
401	*Willi Mo Pena*	15.00
402	*Ruben Quevedo*	2.00
403	*Rob Ryan*	1.50
404	*Freddy Garcia*	12.00
405	*Kevin Eberwein*	1.00
406	*Jesus Colome*	2.00
407	*Chris Singleton*	3.00
408	*Bubba Crosby*	2.00
409	*Jesus Cordero*	1.00
410	Donny Leon	.40
411	*Goefrey Tomlinson*	1.00
412	*Jeff Winchester*	2.00
413	*Adam Piatt*	10.00
414	Robert Stratton	.40
415	T.J. Tucker	.40
416	*Ryan Langerhans*	1.00
417	*Chris Wakeland*	1.00
418	*Matt Miller*	1.00
419	*Doug Clark*	2.00
420	*Kory DeHaan*	2.00
421	*David Eckstein*	1.00
422	*Brian Cooper*	1.00
423	*Brady Clark*	1.50
424	*Chris Magruder*	1.00
425	*Bobby Seay*	3.00
426	*Aubrey Huff*	1.00
427	Mike Jerzembeck	.40
428	*Matt Blank*	2.00
429	*Benny Agbayani*	5.00
430	*Kevin Beirne*	1.00
431	*Josh Hamilton*	20.00
432	*Josh Girdley*	2.00
433	*Kyle Snyder*	3.00
434	*Mike Paradis*	2.00
435	*Jason Jennings*	2.00
436	*David Walling*	4.00
437	*Omar Ortiz*	1.00
438	*Jay Gehrke*	8.00
439	*Casey Burns*	1.50
440	*Carl Crawford*	5.00

1999 Bowman Chrome Gold

A gold, rather than black, facsimile signature differentiates this parallel from the base-card issue. At an average insertion rate of 1:12, the Series 1 Golds are twice as easy as the Series 2 (1:24). Conversely, a Refractor version which is limited to 25 serially numbered sets, is an easier pull in Series 2 (1:200) than in Series 1 (1:305).

	MT
Complete Set (440):	1200.
Complete Series 1 (220):	450.00
Complete Series 2 (220):	750.00
Common Player, Series 1:	1.50
Common Player, Series 2:	2.00
Series 1 Stars: 3X	
Series 2 Stars: 4X	
Common Refractor:	20.00
Refractor Stars: 25X	

(See 1999 Bowman Chrome for checklist and base card values.)

1999 Bowman Chrome International

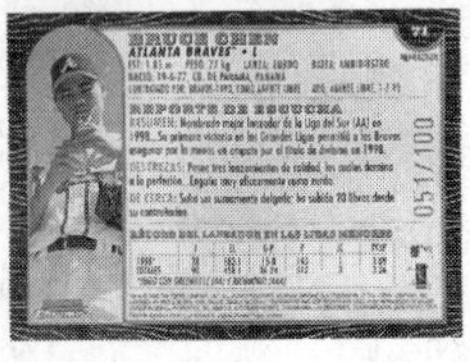

Replacing the regular-card background with a scene from the player's native land gives this parallel issue an international flavor. For the geographically challenged, the place of birth is spelled out in the lower-left corner of the photo. In addition, the card backs are printed in the player's native language. Series 1 Internationals are found on the average of one per four packs, while the scarcer Series 2 Internationals are a 1:12 pick. Conversely, the Refractor version, individually numbered within an edition of 100 each is scarcer in Series 1 (1:76) than in Series 2 (1:50).

	MT
Complete Set (440):	800.00
Complete Series 1 (220):	250.00
Complete Series 2 (220):	550.00
Common Player, Series 1:	.50
Common Player, Series 2:	1.00
Series 1 Stars: 1.5X	
Series 2 Stars: 2X	
Common Refractor:	5.00
Refractor Stars: 8X	

(See 1999 Bowman Chrome for checklist and base card values.)

1999 Bowman Chrome Refractors

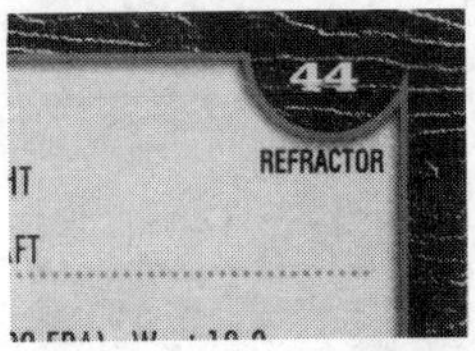

Refractor versions of all Bowman Chrome base cards and inserts were also created. Base card Refractors are found at the average rate of one per 12 packs. Scout's Choice Refractors are a 1:48 find; International Refractors (serially numbered within an edition of 100 each) are 1:76 and Diamond Aces Refractors are 1:84.

	MT
Common Player:	2.00
Refractor Stars: 4X	

(See 1999 Bowman Chrome for checklist and base card values.)

1999 Bowman Chrome Diamond Aces

This 18-card set features nine emerging stars along with nine proven veterans. The cards have a prismatic look with "Diamond Aces" across the top. They are inserted in Series 1 packs at an average rate of 1:21. A parallel Refractor version is also randomly inserted and found 1:84 packs.

		MT
Complete Set (18):		150.00
Common Player:		3.00
Inserted 1:21		
Refractors: 1.5-2X		
Inserted 1:84		
DA1	Troy Glaus	5.00
DA2	Eric Chavez	4.00
DA3	Fernando Seguignol	3.00
DA4	Ryan Anderson	3.00
DA5	Ruben Mateo	6.00
DA6	Carlos Beltran	4.00
DA7	Adrian Beltre	4.00
DA8	Bruce Chen	3.00
DA9	Pat Burrell	25.00
DA10	Mike Piazza	12.00
DA11	Ken Griffey Jr.	20.00
DA12	Chipper Jones	10.00
DA13	Derek Jeter	12.00
DA14	Mark McGwire	25.00
DA15	Nomar Garciaparra	12.00
DA16	Sammy Sosa	12.00
DA17	Juan Gonzalez	10.00
DA18	Alex Rodriguez	12.00

1999 Bowman Chrome Impact

The checklist of this Series 2 insert (one per 15 packs, on average) mixes a dozen youngsters - labeled "Early Impact" on front - who are already making a mark in the majors with eight veteran stars, whose cards are labeled "Lasting Impact". A Refractor version - a 1:75 pack insert - is a parallel.

		MT
Complete Set (20):		75.00
Common Player:		1.50
Inserted 1:15		
Refractor: 1.5-3X		
Inserted 1:75		
1	Alfonso Soriano	5.00
2	Pat Burrell	6.00
3	Ruben Mateo	2.00
4	A.J. Burnett	2.50
5	Corey Patterson	4.00
6	Daryle Ward	1.50
7	Eric Chavez	1.50
8	Troy Glaus	2.00
9	Sean Casey	2.00
10	Joe McEwing	2.00
11	Gabe Kapler	2.00
12	Michael Barrett	1.50
13	Sammy Sosa	6.00
14	Alex Rodriguez	6.00
15	Mark McGwire	12.00
16	Derek Jeter	6.00
17	Nomar Garciaparra	6.00
18	Mike Piazza	6.00
19	Chipper Jones	6.00
20	Ken Griffey Jr.	10.00

1999 Bowman Chrome Scout's Choice

This is a chromium parallel of the inserts found in Series 1 Bowman. The 21-card set is inserted in Series 1 Chrome packs at a rate of 1:12 and showcases prospects that have potential to win a future Rookie of the Year award. Refractor parallels are also randomly inserted 1:48 packs.

		MT
Complete Set (21):		75.00
Common Player:		2.00
Inserted 1:12		
Refractors: 1.5x to 2x		
Inserted 1:48		
SC1	Ruben Mateo	8.00
SC2	Ryan Anderson	6.00
SC3	Pat Burrell	20.00
SC4	Troy Glaus	10.00
SC5	Eric Chavez	8.00
SC6	Adrian Beltre	4.00
SC7	Bruce Chen	3.00
SC8	Carlos Beltran	3.00
SC9	Alex Gonzalez	2.00
SC10	Carlos Lee	3.00
SC11	George Lombard	3.00
SC12	Matt Clement	2.00
SC13	Calvin Pickering	2.00
SC14	Marlon Anderson	2.00
SC15	Chad Hermansen	2.00
SC16	Russell Branyan	2.00
SC17	Jeremy Giambi	2.00
SC18	Ricky Ledee	2.00
SC19	John Patterson	2.00
SC20	Roy Halladay	2.00
SC21	Michael Barrett	3.00

1999 Bowman Chrome 2000 Rookie of the Year

This is a chromium parallel of the inserts found in Series 2 Bowman. The 10-card set is inserted in Series 2 Chrome packs at a rate of 1:20 and showcases prospects that have potential to win the 2000 Rookie of the Year award. Refractor parallels are also randomly inserted 1:100 packs.

		MT
Complete Set (10):		25.00
Common Player:		1.50
Inserted 1:20		
Refractors: 1.5-3X		
Inserted 1:100		
1	Ryan Anderson	2.00
2	Pat Burrell	8.00
3	A.J. Burnett	2.50
4	Ruben Mateo	2.00
5	Alex Escobar	3.00
6	Pablo Ozuna	1.50
7	Mark Mulder	2.00
8	Corey Patterson	5.00
9	George Lombard	1.50
10	Nick Johnson	6.00

1999 Bowman's Best Pre-production

These cards were issued to draw interest to the '99 Bowman's Best issue. The promos are virtually identical to the issued version of each player's card except for the card number which is preceeded by a "PP" prefix.

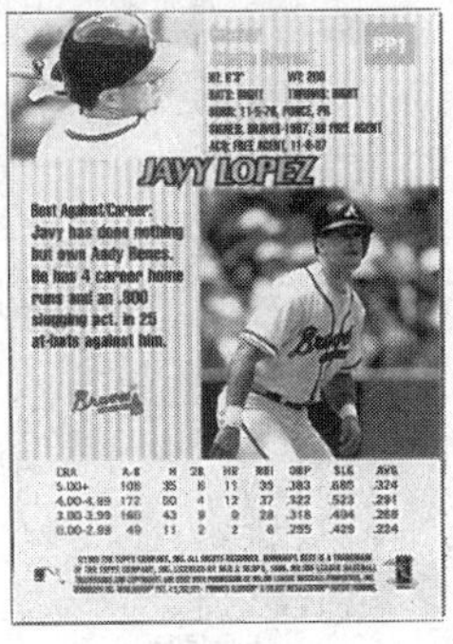

		MT
Complete Set (3):		5.00
Common Player:		2.00
PP1	Javy Lopez	2.00
PP2	Marlon Anderson	2.00
PP3	J.M. Gold	2.00

1999 Bowman's Best

Bowman's Best consists of 200 cards printed on thick 27-point stock. Within the base set are 85 veteran stars printed on gold foil, 15 Best Performers on bronze foil, 50 Prospects on silver foil and 50 rookies on blue foil. The rookies are seeded one per pack. There are also two parallel versions: Refractors and Atomic Refractors. Refractors are inserted 1:15 packs and are sequentially numbered to 400, while Atomic Refractors are found 1:62 packs and are sequentially numbered to 100.

		MT
Complete Set (200):		150.00
Common Player:		.25
Common SP (151-200):		1.50
Inserted 1:1		
Wax Box:		100.00
1	Chipper Jones	2.50
2	Brian Jordan	.25
3	David Justice	.50
4	Jason Kendall	.40
5	Mo Vaughn	1.25
6	Jim Edmonds	.25
7	Wade Boggs	.50
8	Jeromy Burnitz	.25
9	Todd Hundley	.25
10	Rondell White	.40
11	Cliff Floyd	.25
12	Sean Casey	.50
13	Bernie Williams	1.00
14	Dante Bichette	.50
15	Greg Vaughn	.40
16	Andres Galarraga	.75
17	Ray Durham	.25
18	Jim Thome	.75
19	Gary Sheffield	.40
20	Frank Thomas	2.00
21	Orlando Hernandez	1.00
22	Ivan Rodriguez	1.25
23	Jose Cruz Jr.	.50
24	Jason Giambi	.25
25	Craig Biggio	.75
26	Kerry Wood	1.00
27	Manny Ramirez	1.50
28	Curt Schilling	.40
29	Mike Mussina	1.00
30	Tim Salmon	.50
31	Mike Piazza	3.00
32	Roberto Alomar	1.00
33	Larry Walker	1.00
34	Barry Larkin	.75
35	Nomar Garciaparra	3.00
36	Paul O'Neill	.50
37	Todd Walker	.25
38	Eric Karros	.40
39	Brad Fullmer	.25
40	John Olerud	.40
41	Todd Helton	1.00
42	Raul Mondesi	.40
43	Jose Canseco	1.00
44	Matt Williams	.75
45	Ray Lankford	.25
46	Carlos Delgado	.50
47	Darin Erstad	1.00
48	Vladimir Guerrero	1.50
49	Robin Ventura	.40
50	Alex Rodriguez	3.00
51	Vinny Castilla	.25
52	Tony Clark	.50
53	Pedro Martinez	1.25
54	Rafael Palmeiro	.75
55	Scott Rolen	1.50
56	Tino Martinez	.75
57	Tony Gwynn	2.50
58	Barry Bonds	1.25
59	Kenny Lofton	1.25
60	Javy Lopez	.25
61	Mark Grace	.50
62	Travis Lee	1.00
63	Kevin Brown	.50
64	Al Leiter	.25
65	Albert Belle	1.25
66	Sammy Sosa	3.00
67	Greg Maddux	3.00
68	Mark Kotsay	.25
69	Dmitri Young	.25
70	Mark McGwire	6.00
71	Juan Gonzalez	2.50
72	Andruw Jones	1.25
73	Derek Jeter	3.00
74	Randy Johnson	1.00
75	Cal Ripken Jr.	4.00
76	Shawn Green	.50
77	Moises Alou	.40
78	Tom Glavine	.40
79	Sandy Alomar	.25
80	Ken Griffey Jr.	5.00
81	Ryan Klesko	.40
82	Jeff Bagwell	1.25
83	Ben Grieve	1.00
84	John Smoltz	.25
85	Roger Clemens	1.50
86	Ken Griffey Jr.	2.50
87	Roger Clemens	.75
88	Derek Jeter	1.50
89	Nomar Garciaparra	1.50
90	Mark McGwire	3.00
91	Sammy Sosa	1.50
92	Alex Rodriguez	1.50
93	Greg Maddux	1.50
94	Vladimir Guerrero	.75
95	Chipper Jones	1.25
96	Kerry Wood	.50
97	Ben Grieve	.50
98	Tony Gwynn	1.25
99	Juan Gonzalez	1.25
100	Mike Piazza	1.50
101	Eric Chavez	.75
102	Billy Koch	.25
103	Dernell Stenson	.25
104	Marlon Anderson	.25
105	Ron Belliard	.25
106	Bruce Chen	.25
107	Carlos Beltran	.75
108	Chad Hermansen	.25
109	Ryan Anderson	.75
110	Michael Barrett	1.00
111	Matt Clement	.25
112	Ben Davis	.25
113	Calvin Pickering	.25
114	Brad Penny	.25
115	Paul Konerko	.25
116	Alex Gonzalez	.25
117	George Lombard	.25
118	John Patterson	.25
119	Rob Bell	.25
120	Ruben Mateo	1.50
121	*Peter Bergeron*	2.00
122	Ryan Bradley	.25
123	Carlos Lee	.25
124	Gabe Kapler	1.50
125	Ramon Hernandez	.25
126	Carlos Febles	.75
127	Mitch Meluskey	.50
128	Michael Cuddyer	.25
129	Pablo Ozuna	.25
130	Jayson Werth	.25
131	Ricky Ledee	.25
132	Jeremy Giambi	.75
133	Danny Klassen	.25
134	Mark DeRosa	.25
135	Randy Wolf	.25
136	Roy Halladay	.50
137	Derrick Gibson	.25
138	Ben Petrick	.25
139	Warren Morris	.25
140	Lance Berkman	.25
141	Russell Branyan	.25
142	Adrian Beltre	.75
143	Juan Encarnacion	.50
144	Fernando Seguignol	.25
145	Corey Koskie	.25
146	Preston Wilson	.25
147	Homer Bush	.25
148	Daryle Ward	.25
149	*Joe McEwing*	4.00
150	*Peter Bergeron*	2.50

151	*Pat Burrell*	15.00
152	*Choo Freeman*	3.00
153	*Matt Belisle*	2.50
154	*Carlos Pena*	5.00
155	*A.J. Burnett*	4.00
156	*Doug Mientkiewicz*	2.00
157	*Sean Burroughs*	6.00
158	*Mike Zywica*	3.00
159	*Corey Patterson*	15.00
160	*Austin Kearns*	5.00
161	*Chip Ambres*	3.00
162	*Kelly Dransfeldt*	1.50
163	*Mike Nannini*	3.00
164	*Mark Mulder*	4.00
165	*Jason Tyner*	2.50
166	*Bobby Seay*	2.50
167	*Alex Escobar*	5.00
168	*Nick Johnson*	10.00
169	*Alfonso Soriano*	15.00
170	*Clayton Andrews*	4.00
171	*C.C. Sabathia*	2.00
172	*Matt Holliday*	3.00
173	*Brad Lidge*	3.00
174	*Kit Pellow*	2.00
175	*J.M. Gold*	4.00
176	*Roosevelt Brown*	2.00
177	*Eric Valent*	4.00
178	*Adam Everett*	4.00
179	*Jorge Toca*	3.00
180	*Matt Roney*	3.00
181	*Andy Brown*	3.00
182	*Phil Norton*	2.00
183	*Mickey Lopez*	1.50
184	*Chris George*	3.00
185	*Arturo McDowell*	2.00
186	*Jose Fernandez*	1.50
187	*Seth Etherton*	4.00
188	*Josh McKinley*	3.00
189	*Nate Cornejo*	2.00
190	*Giuseppe Chiaramonte*	2.50
191	*Mamon Tucker*	3.00
192	*Ryan Mills*	5.00
193	*Chad Moeller*	3.00
194	*Tony Torcato*	2.00
195	*Jeff Winchester*	3.00
196	*Rick Elder*	6.00
197	*Matt Burch*	4.00
198	*Jeff Urban*	2.00
199	*Chris Jones*	2.00
200	*Masao Kida*	1.50

1999 Bowman's Best Refractors

Inserted at an average rate of about one per 15 packs, Best Refractor's are so marked on the back in the card-number box at upper right. Also found on back is a serial number stamped in gold-foil from within an edition of 400.

	MT
Complete Set (200):	1250.
Common Player:	2.00
(Stars valued at 8-15X base card; short-prints valued about 3-5X base.)	

1999 Bowman's Best Atomic Refractors

The vibrant refractive background on front announces these parallels which are found on average of about once per 62 packs. Backs identify the variation in the card-number box at upper right and with a serial number from within an edition of 100 per card.

	MT
Common Player:	4.00
(Stars valued 25-40X base cards; short-prints valued about 6-12X base.)	

1999 Bowman's Best Franchise Best

Ten league leaders are featured in this insert set on three different technologies: Mach I, Mach II and Mach III. Mach I feature die-cut Serillusion stock and is numbered to 3,000. Mach II features die-cut refractive styrene stock, numbered to 1,000; and Mach III features die-cut polycarbonate stock and is limited to 500 numbered sets. All cards numbers have an "FB" prefix.

		MT
Complete Set (10):		100.00
Common Player:		5.00
Production 3,000 sets		
Mach II: 1.5-2X		
Production 1,000 sets		
Mach III: 2-3X		
Production 500 sets		
1	Mark McGwire	25.00
2	Ken Griffey Jr.	20.00
3	Sammy Sosa	12.00
4	Nomar Garciaparra	12.00
5	Alex Rodriguez	12.00
6	Derek Jeter	12.00
7	Mike Piazza	12.00
8	Frank Thomas	8.00
9	Chipper Jones	10.00
10	Juan Gonzalez	10.00

1999 Bowman's Best Franchise Favorites

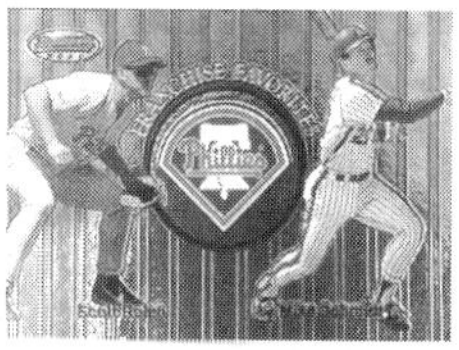

This six-card set features retired legends and current stars in three versions. Version A features a current star, Version B features a retired player and Version C pairs the current star with the retired player. The insert rate is 1:40 packs. Cards have an "FR" prefix to the number on back.

		MT
Complete Set (6):		40.00
Common Player:		5.00
1A	Derek Jeter	15.00
1B	Don Mattingly	5.00
1C	Derek Jeter, Don Mattingly	10.00
2A	Scott Rolen	8.00
2B	Mike Schmidt	5.00
2C	Scott Rolen, Mike Schmidt	6.00

1999 Bowman's Best Franchise Favorites Autographs

This is a parallel autographed version of the regular Franchise Favorites inserts. The insert rate is 1:1,548 for Versions A and B, and 1:6,191 packs for Version C.

		MT
Common Player:		100.00
Version A & B 1:1548		
Version C 1:6191		
1A	Derek Jeter	200.00
1B	Don Mattingly	175.00
1C	Derek Jeter, Don Mattingly	400.00
2A	Scott Rolen	100.00
2B	Mike Schmidt	120.00
2C	Scott Rolen, Mike Schmidt	325.00

1999 Bowman's Best Future Foundations

Ten up-and-coming players are featured in this set that has the same technologies as the Franchise Best inserts and broken down the same way. The insert rates are 1:41 packs for Mach I, 1:124 for Mach II and 1:248 for Mach III.

		MT
Complete Set (10):		75.00
Common Player:		3.00
Production 3,000 sets		
Mach II: 1.5-2X		
Production 1,000 sets		
Mach III: 2-3X		
Production 500 sets		
1	Ruben Mateo	6.00
2	Troy Glaus	8.00
3	Eric Chavez	6.00
4	Pat Burrell	30.00
5	Adrian Beltre	5.00
6	Ryan Anderson	5.00
7	Alfonso Soriano	30.00
8	Brad Penny	3.00
9	Derrick Gibson	3.00
10	Bruce Chen	3.00

1999 Bowman's Best Mirror Image

These inserts feature a veteran player on one side and a prospect on the other side for a total of 10 double-sided cards featuring 20 players. The insert rate is 1:24 packs. There are also parallel Refractor and Atomic Refractor versions. Refractors are inserted 1:96 packs while Atomic Refractors are seeded 1:192 packs.

		MT
Complete Set (10):		100.00
Common Player:		4.00
Inserted 1:24		
Refractors: 1.5-2X		
Inserted 1:96		
Atomic Refractors: 2-4X		
Inserted 1:192		
1	Alex Rodriguez, Alex Gonzalez	10.00
2	Ken Griffey Jr., Ruben Mateo	18.00
3	Derek Jeter, Alfonso Soriano	18.00
4	Sammy Sosa, Corey Patterson	10.00
5	Greg Maddux, Bruce Chen	10.00
6	Chipper Jones, Eric Chavez	8.00
7	Vladimir Guerrero, Carlos Beltran	6.00
8	Frank Thomas, Nick Johnson	6.00
9	Nomar Garciaparra, Pablo Ozuna	10.00
10	Mark McGwire, Pat Burrell	25.00

1999 Bowman's Best Rookie Locker Room Autographs

This five-card set features autographs of baseball's current hot prospects. Each card is branded with a "Topps Certified Autograph Issue" stamp and the issue is inserted 1:248 packs.

		MT
Complete Set (5):		180.00
Common Player:		25.00
Inserted 1:248		
1	Pat Burrell	75.00
2	Michael Barrett	25.00
3	Troy Glaus	50.00
4	Gabe Kapler	40.00
5	Eric Chavez	30.00

1999 Bowman's Best Rookie Locker Room Game-Used Lumber

This six-card set features actual pieces of each player's game-used bat embedded into the cards. The insertion rate is about one card per 258 packs.

		MT
Complete Set (6):		400.00
Common Player:		50.00
Inserted 1:258		
1	Pat Burrell	150.00
2	Michael Barrett	50.00
3	Troy Glaus	90.00
4	Gabe Kapler	75.00
5	Eric Chavez	60.00
6	Richie Sexson	50.00

1999 Bowman's Best Rookie Locker Room Game-Worn Jerseys

This four-card set spotlights hot prospects and has a swatch of game-used jersey from the featured player embedded into the card. These are inserted one card per 270 packs.

		MT
Complete Set (4):		200.00
Common Player:		50.00
Inserted 1:270		
1	Richie Sexson	50.00
2	Michael Barrett	50.00
3	Troy Glaus	90.00
4	Eric Chavez	60.00

1999 Bowman's Best Rookie of the Year

This set salutes 1998 AL and NL Rookie of Year award winners Kerry Wood and Ben Grieve. They are inserted 1:95 packs and are numbered with a ROY prefix. Ben Grieve also autographed some of the inserts which feature a "Topps Certified Autograph Issue" stamp. Autographs are seeded 1:1,241 packs.

	MT
Complete Set (2):	12.00
ROY1Ben Grieve	8.00
ROY2Kerry Wood	6.00
ROYA1Ben Grieve (Auto.)	50.00

1982 Builders Emporium Los Angeles Dodgers

Shoppers at this chain of building supply stores in Southern California were able to receive one of this seven-card set with each visit. Cards are printed in black-and-white in 11" x 8-1/2" format with blank backs. Fronts of the player cards have both portrait and action photos, the manager's card has only a portrait. Team and sponsors' logos are at bottom-right. The unnumbered cards are checklisted here in alphabetical order.

		MT
Complete Set (7):		55.00
Common Player:		8.00
(1)	Dusty Baker	8.00
(2)	Ron Cey	8.00
(3)	Steve Garvey	9.00
(4)	Pedro Guerrero	8.00
(5)	Tommy Lasorda	9.00
(6)	Jerry Reuss	8.00
(7)	Steve Sax	8.00

1982 Burger King Braves

A set consisting of 27 "Collector Lids" featuring the Atlanta Braves was issued by Burger King restaurants in 1982. The plastic lids, 3-5/8"

in diameter, were placed on a special Coca-Cola cup which listed the scores of the Braves' season-opening 13-game win streak. A black-and-white photo plus the player's name, position, height, weight, and 1981 statistics are found on the lid front. The unnumbered, blank-backed lids also contain logos for Burger King, Coca-Cola, and the Major League Baseball Players Association.

		MT
Complete Set (27):		40.00
Common Player:		1.00
(1)	Steve Bedrosian	1.25
(2)	Bruce Benedict	1.00
(3)	Tommy Boggs	1.00
(4)	Brett Butler	2.50
(5)	Rick Camp	1.00
(6)	Chris Chambliss	1.00
(7)	Ken Dayley	1.00
(8)	Gene Garber	1.00
(9)	Preston Hanna	1.00
(10)	Terry Harper	1.00
(11)	Bob Horner	2.00
(12)	Al Hrabosky	1.00
(13)	Glenn Hubbard	1.00
(14)	Randy Johnson	1.00
(15)	Rufino Linares	1.00
(16)	Rick Mahler	1.00
(17)	Larry McWilliams	1.00
(18)	Dale Murphy	10.00
(19)	Phil Niekro	4.00
(20)	Biff Pocoroba	1.00
(21)	Rafael Ramirez	1.00
(22)	Jerry Royster	1.00
(23)	Ken Smith	1.00
(24)	Bob Walk	1.00
(25)	Claudell Washington	1.00
(26)	Bob Watson	1.25
(27)	Larry Whisenton	1.00

1982 Burger King Indians

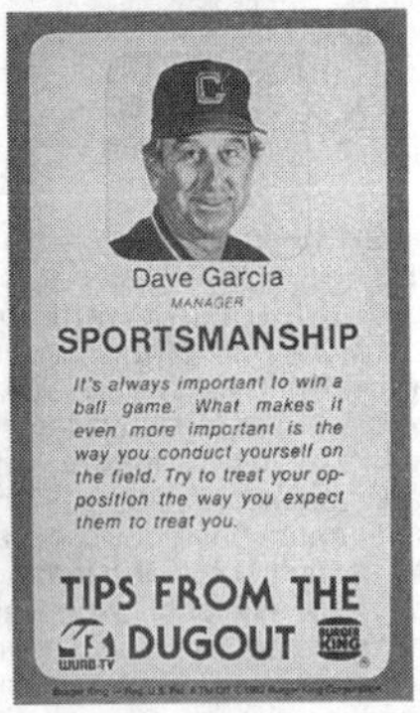
Dave Garcia
MANAGER
SPORTSMANSHIP
It's always important to win a ball game. What makes it even more important is the way you conduct yourself on the field. Try to treat your opposition the way you expect them to treat you.
TIPS FROM THE DUGOUT

This set was sponsored by WUAB-TV and Burger Kings in the Cleveland vicinity. The cards' green borders encompass a large yellow area which contains a black-and-white photo plus a baseball tip. Manager Dave Garcia and his coaches provide the baseball hints. The cards, which measure 3" x 5", are unnumbered and blank-backed.

		MT
Complete Set (12):		7.00
Common Player:		.75
(1)	Dave Garcia (Be In The Game)	.75
(2)	Dave Garcia (Sportsmanship)	.75
(3)	Johnny Goryl (Rounding The Bases)	.75
(4)	Johnny Goryl (3rd Base Running)	.75
(5)	Tom McCraw (Follow Thru)	.75
(6)	Tom McCraw (Selecting A Bat)	.75
(7)	Tom McCraw (Watch The Ball)	.75
(8)	Mel Queen (Master One Pitch)	.75
(9)	Mel Queen (Warm Up)	.75
(10)	Dennis Sommers (Get Down On A Ground Ball)	.75
(11)	Dennis Sommers (Protect Your Fingers)	.75
(12)	Dennis Sommers (Tagging First Base)	.75

1986 Burger King

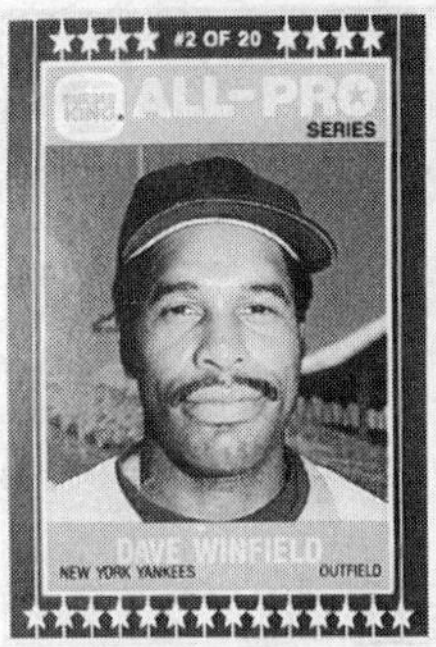

Burger King restaurants in the Pennsylvania and New Jersey areas issued a set entitled "All-Pro Series". Cards were issued with the purchase of a Whopper sandwich and came in folded panels of two cards each, along with a coupon card. Fronts feature a color photo and identification plus the Burger King logo. Due to a lack of MLB licensing, team insignias on the players' uniforms were airbrushed away. Backs are in black-and-white and contain brief biographical and statistical information.

		MT
Complete Panel Set (10):		12.00
Complete Singles Set (20):		6.00
Common Panel:		.50
Common Single Player:		.10
	PANEL (1)	.75
1	Tony Pena	.10
2	Dave Winfield	.25
	PANEL (2)	2.00
3	Fernando Valenzuela	.10
4	Pete Rose	1.00
	PANEL (3)	2.00
5	Mike Schmidt	.60
6	Steve Carlton	.40
	PANEL (4)	.50
7	Glenn Wilson	.10
8	Jim Rice	.15
	PANEL (5)	1.00
9	Wade Boggs	.50
10	Juan Samuel	.10
	PANEL (6)	1.00
11	Dale Murphy	.20
12	Reggie Jackson	.25
	PANEL (7)	.75
13	Kirk Gibson	.15
14	Eddie Murray	.20
	PANEL (8)	2.00
15	Cal Ripken Jr.	1.00
16	Willie McGee	.10
	PANEL (9)	.75
17	Dwight Gooden	.15
18	Steve Garvey	.20
	PANEL (10)	2.00
19	Don Mattingly	.50
20	George Brett	.50

1987 Burger King

The 1987 "All-Pro 2nd Edition Series" set was part of a giveaway promotion at participating Burger King restaurants. The set is comprised of 20 players on ten different panels. Cards measure 2-1/2" x 3-1/2" each with a three-card panel (includes a coupon card) measuring 7-5/8" x 3-1/2". Fronts feature a full-color photo and Burger King logo surrounded by a blue stars-and-stripes border. Backs are black-and-white with a brief biography and 1986/Career statistics. The set was produced by Mike Schecter Associates and, as with many MSA issues, all team insignias were airbrushed away.

		MT
Complete Panel Set (10):		3.00
Complete Singles Set (20):		1.50
Common Panel:		.15
Common Single Player:		.05
	PANEL (1)	.25
1	Wade Boggs	.15
2	Gary Carter	.05
	PANEL (2)	.40
3	Will Clark	.10
4	Roger Clemens	.25
	PANEL (3)	.20
5	Steve Garvey	.10
6	Ron Darling	.05
	PANEL (4)	.15
7	Pedro Guerrero	.05
8	Von Hayes	.05
	PANEL (5)	.15
9	Rickey Henderson	.10
10	Keith Hernandez	.05
	PANEL (6)	.15
11	Wally Joyner	.05
12	Mike Krukow	.05
	PANEL (7)	.75
13	Don Mattingly	.25
14	Ozzie Smith	.20
	PANEL (8)	.15
15	Tony Pena	.05
16	Jim Rice	.10
	PANEL (9)	.75
17	Ryne Sandberg	.15
18	Mike Schmidt	.25
	PANEL (10)	.20
19	Darryl Strawberry	.10
20	Fernando Valenzuela	.05

1994 Burger King Cal Ripken Jr.

Although the cards themselves do not indicate it, this issue was co-sponsored by Burger King and Coke, and distributed in BK restaurants in the Baltimore-Washington area. Cards were available in three-card packs for 25 cents with the purchase of a Coke product. Each pack contains two regular cards and a gold card. Each of the nine cards could be found in a regular and gold version. Cards feature color photos with a semi-circular black border at top or left. "Score '94" appears in orange in one of the upper corners, along with an Orioles logo. Cal Ripken, Jr.'s name appears at the bottom. On the gold premium version, there is a gold-foil circle around the Orioles logo and Ripken's name appears in gold, rather than white. Backs have a smaller color photo, again meeting at a semi-circular edge with the black border at left and bottom. In the black are another Score logo, a card number, an Orioles logo, a headline and a few career details and/or stats. Cards are UV coated on each side. Several hundred of the cards were personally autographed by Ripken and distributed in a drawing.

		MT
Complete Set (9):		3.00
Complete Set, Gold (9):		7.50
Common Card:		.50
Common Card, Gold:		1.00
Autographed Card:		300.00
1	Double Honors	.50
1a	Double Honors (gold)	1.00
2	Perennial All-Star	.50
2a	Perennial All-Star (gold)	1.00
3	Peerless Power	.50
3a	Peerless Power (gold)	1.00
4	Fitness Fan	.50
4a	Fitness Fan (gold)	1.00
5	Prime Concerns	.50
5a	Prime Concerns (gold)	1.00
6	Home Run Club	.50
6a	Home Run Club (gold)	1.00
7	The Iron Man	.50
7a	The Iron Man (gold)	1.00
8	Heavy Hitter	.50
8a	Heavy Hitter (gold)	1.00
9	Gold Glover	.50
9a	Gold Glover (gold)	1.00

1997 Burger King Cal Ripken Jr.

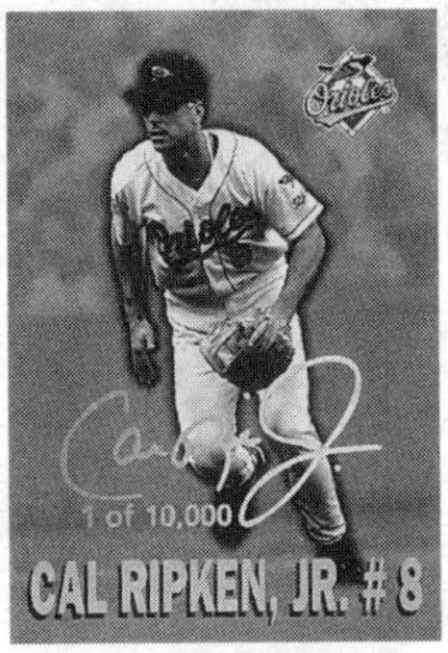

Three years after its 1994 tribute, Burger King in 1997 created an eight-card set honoring the future Hall of Famer. Participating BK outlets in Maryland, the District of Columbia, Delaware, Pennsylvania, Virginia and West Virginia offered the cards for 99Û with a meal purchase or $1.15 without. Each card was produced in two forms: with and without a gold holographic foil facsimile autograph and "1 of 10,000" notation. The 2-1/2" x 3-1/2" cards have action photos of Ripken on front with muted backgrounds. His name, uniform number and team logo also appear. Backs, numbered "X/8" have another color photo with ghosted background and a paragraph of a career highlight. Autographed cards were part of a prize structure explained on information cards accompanying the Ripken card in each pack.

		MT
Complete Set (8):		5.00
Complete Gold Set (8):		20.00
Common Card:		1.00
Common Gold Card:		3.00
Autographed Card:		300.00
1-8	Cal Ripken Jr.	1.00
--	Autograph information card	.25

Player names in *Italic* type indicate a rookie card.

1999 Burger King N.Y. Yankees

Members of the World Champion 1998 N.Y. Yankees are featured on this three-sheet set of cards sold by metropolitan New York Burger King restaurants in April-May, 1999. The 12-1/2" x 10-1/2" perforated sheets each include nine standard-size cards. Fronts feature action photos with the Yankees and Fleer logos. Backs have the same photo along with season and career stats and highlights, printed on a ghosted background of a Yankees pinstriped jersey. The Fleer and team logos appear on back, as do those of the players' union and the restaurant chain. On the sheet along with the player cards are a checklist, team schedule, mention of the BK Cancer Foundation of New York and a kids' club offer.

		MT
Complete Sheet Set (3):		24.00
Complete Singles Set (27):		16.00
Common Player:		.50
	SHEET 1	12.00
1	Derek Jeter	3.00
2	Paul O'Neill	.75
3	Scott Brosius	.50
4	Mariano Rivera	.50
5	Chuck Knoblauch	.75
6	Graeme Lloyd	.50
7	Joe Girardi	.50
8	Orlando Hernandez	1.50
9	Tim Raines	.75
	SHEET 2	7.50
10	Bernie Williams	.75
11	Tino Martinez	.65
12	Andy Pettitte	.75
13	Hideki Irabu	.65
14	Ramiro Mendoza	.50
15	Jeff Nelson	.50
16	Homer Bush	.50
17	Darren Holmes	.50
18	Yankees Championship History	.50
	SHEET 3	7.50
19	David Cone	.75
20	David Wells	.75
21	Chili Davis	.65
22	Darryl Strawberry	.75
23	Ricky Ledee	.75
24	Jorge Posada	.50
25	Luis Sojo	.50
26	Chad Curtis	.50
27	Mike Stanton	.50

1989 Butter Krust Bread Super Stars Discs

(See 1989 Holsum Bakeries for checklist and price guide. Distributed in Penn.)

1988-89 BYN Puerto Rican League

For the 1988-89 Puerto Rican League season, BYN (Blanco y Negro) Cards of San Juan produced team sets featuring many current, former and future major leaguers. The cards are numbered contiguously from 1-192. The team sets share a common design in a 2-1/2" x 3-1/2" format. Color player photos are framed in one color and bordered with another. Team logos are in the upper-left corner. Backs utilize one of the front colors for a border and have stats and biographical data, all in Spanish. Both team set and overall set numbers appear on the cards' backs. Each team set also includes an advertising card from the producer.

		MT
	Complete Set (192):	200.00
	Common Player:	.25
	Arecibo Lobos team set	35.00
1	(Marv Foley)	.25
2	(Edwin Alicea)	.25
3	(Saul Barreto)	.25
4	(Jorgo Candelaria)	.25
5	(Luis Cruz)	.25
6	(Fernando Figuerda)	.25
7	(Willie Lozado)	.25
8	(Juan Marina)	.25
9	(Francisco Melendez)	.25
10	(Angel Miranda)	1.00
11	(Adalberto Pena)	.25
12	(Benny Puig)	.25
13	(German Rivera)	.25
14	(Jesus Rivera)	.25
15	(Jose Rivera)	.25
16	(Angel Rodriguez)	.25
17	(Edwin Rodriguez)	.25
18	(Ferdinand Rodriguez)	.25
19	(Aristarco Tirado)	.25
20	(Miguel Torres)	.25
21	(Hector Vargas)	.25
22	(Jay Buhner)	20.00
23	(Mark Davis)	2.00
24	(Wayne Edwards)	.25
25	(Bob Geren)	.25
26	(Greg Hibbard)	1.00
27	(Don Pall)	.50
28	(Rick Raether)	.25
29	(James Randall)	.25
30	(Steve Rosenberg)	.50
31	Arecibo Lobos checklist	.25
32	Arecibo Lobos logo	.25
	Caguas Criollos team set	40.00
33	Santos Alomar	15.00
34	Roberto Alomar	25.00
35	Henry Cotto	.25
36	Angelo Cuevas	.25
37	Jose DeJesus	.25
38	Edgar Diaz	.25
39	Mario Diaz	.25
40	Otto Gonzalez	.25
41	Orestes Marrero	.25
42	Vilato Marrero	.25
43	Agustin Meizoso	.25
44	Jose Melendez	.25
45	Orlando Mercado	.25
46	Jose Munoz	.25
47	Omar Olivares	.25
48	Francisco Javier Oliveras	.25
49	Melvin Rosario	.25
50	Ricky Torres	.25
51	Hediberto Vargas	.25
52	Chuck Cary	.25
53	Danny Clay	.25
54	Kevin Coffman	.25
55	Rob Dibble	.50
56	Cecil Espy	.25
57	Ron Gant	7.50
58	Sam Horn	.75
59	Bill Landrum	.25
60	Mick Kinnunen	.25
61	Van Snider	.25
62	Ed Vosberg	.25
63	Criollos checklist	.25
64	Criollos logo	.25
	Mayaguez Indians team set	35.00
65	(Tom Gamboa)	.25
66	(Jose Birriel)	.25
67	(Luis de Leon)	.25
68	(Alex Diaz)	.25
69	(Carlos Escalera)	.25
70	(Roberto Hernandez)	4.00
71	(Luis Lopez)	.25
72	(Luis Martinez)	.25
73	(Charlie Montoya)	.25
74	(Luis Rivera)	.25
75	(Javier Ocasio)	.25
76	(Luis Raul Quinones)	.25
77	(Luis Rivera)	.25
78	(Julio Valera)	.25
79	(Jeff Brantley)	1.00
80	(Ken Caminiti)	20.00
81	(Steve Davis)	.25
82	(Jeff Facero) (Fassero)	3.00
83	(Steve Finley)	3.00
84	(Ken Gerhart) (Gerhardt)	.25
85	(Don Heinkel)	.25
86	(Chris Hoiles)	3.00
87	(Shawn Holman)	.25
88	(Tom Howard)	1.00
89	(Ron Jones)	.25
90	(Ricky Jordan)	1.00
91	(Alex Madrid)	.25
92	(Kirt Manwaring)	1.50
93	(Tom McCarthy)	.25
94	(Al Newman)	.25
95	Indians checklist	.25
96	Indians logo	.25
	Ponce Leones team set	45.00
97	Jim Essian	.25
98	Luis Aguayo	.25
99	Ricky Bones	1.00
100	Francisco Burgos	.25
101	Edgar Castro	.25
102	Rafael Chavez	.25
103	David Colon	.25
104	Joey Cora	2.00
105	Juan Gonzalez	35.00
106	Ken Juarbe	.25
107	Pedro Lopez	.25
108	Johnny Monell	.25
109	Armando Moreno	.25
110	Pedro Munoz	1.50
111	Adalberto Ortiz	.25
112	Julian Perez	.25
113	David Rivera	.25
114	Gabriel Rodriguez	.25
115	Victor Rodriguez	.25
116	Hector Villanueva	.25
117	Mike Felder	.25
118	Marvin Freeman	.25
119	Stan Jefferson	.25
120	Ray Krawczyk	.25
121	David Meads	.25
122	Randy Milligan	1.00
123	John Pawlowski	.25
124	Ernest Riles	.25
125	Roger Samuels	.25
126	Trevor Wilson	1.00
127	Leones checklist	.25
128	Ponce Leones logo	.25
	San Juan Metros team set	45.00
129	Mako Oliveras	.25
130	Miguel Alicea	.25
131	Carlos Baerga	5.00
132	Hector Berrios	.25
133	Mike Diaz	.25
134	Ruben Escalera	.25
135	Orlando Lind	.25
136	Javier Lopez	22.00
137	Rafael Montalvo	.25
138	Rafael Muratti	.25
139	Carlos Rios	.25
140	David Rosario	.25
141	Elam "Rico" Rossy	.25
142	Hector Stewart	.25
143	Jose Velez	.25
144	Carlos Zayas	.25
145	Tom Barrett	.25
146	Joe Boever	.25
147	Sherman Corbett	.25
148	Doug Dascenzo	.25
149	Joel Davis	.25
150	Benny Distefano	.25
151	Charlie Hayes	3.00
152	Rex Hudler	2.00
153	Morris Madden	.25
154	Lonnie Smith	1.00
155	John Trautwein	.25
156	Jeff Wetherby	.25
157	Rick Wrona	.35
158	Floyd Youmans	.25
159	Metros checklist	.25
160	San Juan Metros logo	.25
	Santurce Sandcrabs team set	27.50
161	Kevin Kennedy	1.00
162	Juan Jose Beniquez	.50
163	John Burgos	.25
164	Jose Calderon	.25
165	Ivan DeJesus	1.00
166	Carlos Laboy	.25
167	Sixto Lezcano	.25
168	Jose Lind	1.50
169	Luis Lopez	.25
170	Angel Morris	.25
171	Jaime Navarro	1.50
172	Jorge Ojeda	.25
173	Mike Perez	1.50
174	Edgardo Romero	.25
175	Geraldo Sanchez	.25
176	Orlando Sanchez	.25
177	Amilcar Valdez	.25
178	John Valentin	9.00
179	Mike Basso	.25
180	Dennis Burtt	.25
181	Mike Devereaux	1.00
182	Mike Hartley	.50
183	Dwayne Henry	.25
184	Mike Jones	.25
185	Jeff Manto	1.00
186	Mike Munoz	.25
187	Javier Ortiz	.25
188	Dwight Smith	.50
189	John Wetteland	6.00
190	Rich Yett	.25
191	Santurce Sandcrabs checklist	.25
192	Santurce Sandcrabs logo	.25

1989 BYN Puerto Rican League Update

Each of the team sets in the regular BYN league issue is updated with this set, designed in similar format. Like the regular issue, the updates have both a team-set card number and a number within the overall set; the latter are used here. Cards #53-64 feature only stats, no player photos.

		MT
	Complete Set (64):	48.00
	Common Player:	.50
1	Darryl Boston	.50
2	Mike Campbell	.50
3	Reggie Dobie	.50
4	Jeff Hull	.50
5	Carlos Lezcano	.75
6	Candido Maldonado	1.00
7	Roger Mason	.50
8	Orlando Merced	3.00
9	Wally Ritchie	.50
10	Tom Romano	.50
11	Ricky Torres	.50
12	Gene Walter	.50
13	Bernie Williams	12.00
14	Shawn Abner	1.00
15	Wilfredo Cordero	5.00
16	Jack Daugherty	.75
17	Mike Jeffcoat	.50
18	Sixto Lezcano	.50
19	Otis Nixon	4.00
20	Luis Ojeda	.50
21	Rey Sanchez	.75
22	Luis Aquino	.60
23	Juan Belbru	.50
24	John Cangelosi	.75
25	Jeff Gray	.50
26	Keith Hughes	.50
27	Tom Pagnozzi	2.00
28	Rey Palacios	.50
29	Keith Smith	.50
30	Jay Aldrich	.50
31	Duffy Dyer	.50
32	Greg Harris	.50
33	Ron Karkovice	1.00
34	Luis Martinez	.50
35	Angel Ortiz	.50
36	Rolando Roomes	.50
37	Luis Alicea	.50
38	Jose Anglero	.50
39	Randy Kramer	.50
40	Billy Moore	.50
41	Ed Olwine	.50
42	Stu Pederson	.50
43	Mike Ramsey	.50
44	Russ Swan	.50
45	Dorn Taylor	.50
46	Marcos Vazquez	.50
47	Dave Clark	.50
48	Tony Colon	.50
49	Steve Davis	.50
50	Jose Marzan	.50
51	Dave Oliveras	.50
52	Ruben Sierra	4.00
53	Season/Semi-Final Standings	.10
54	Final Series/ Caribbean Series Standings	.10
55	.300 Hitters/RBI Leaders	.10
56	Home Runs/Runs Leaders	.10
57	Hits/Doubles Leaders	.10
58	Triples/Stolen Base Leaders	.10
59	Wins/ERA Leaders	.10
60	Complete Games/ Shutout Leaders	.10
61	Strikeouts/Saves Leaders	.10
62	Innings Pitched/ Games Started Leaders	.10
63	Checklist	.10
64	Checklist	.10

1989-90 BYN Puerto Rican League

Action photos with a white border are featured in the second annual edition by the San Juan card issuer covering the 1989-90 Puerto Rican winter league. Team and manufacturer logos are superimposed on the bottom corners on the front photos. Backs offer PR League stats and personal data, all in Spanish. Sold in team sets the cards feature both a team-set number and a number within the overall issue of 201 cards. Each team set includes an advertising card from BYN.

		MT
	Complete Set (201):	175.00
	Common Player:	.25
	San Juan Metros team set	45.00
1	Metros logo	.25
2	Mako Oliveras	.25
3	Miguel Alicea	.25
4	Carlos Baerga	4.00
5	Hector Berrios	.25
6	Ruben Escalera	.25
7	Orlando Lind	.25
8	Javier Lopez	15.00
9	Edgar Martinez	12.00
10	Rafael Montalvo	.25
11	Adalberto "Junior" Ortiz	1.50
12	Carlos Rios	.25
13	Pablo Rivera	.25
14	David Rosario	.25
15	Elam "Rico" Rossy	.25
16	Rey Sanchez	1.50
17	Ricardo Ufret	.25
18	Ramon Valdez	.25
19	Marcos Vazquez	.25
20	Hector Villanueva	.25
21	Carlos Zayas	.25
22	Dennis Burtt	.25
23	Joaquin Contreras	.25
24	Mike Hartley	.25
25	Barry Jones	.25
26	Paul McClellan	.25
27	Mike Schwabe	.25
28	Greg Tubbs	.25
29	Don Vesling	.25
30	Ramon L. Conde	.25
31	Jesus Hernaiz	.25
32	Luis Isaac	.25
33	Jerry Morales	.25
34	Metros checklist	.25
	Caguas Criollos team set	45.00
35	Criollos logo	.25
36	Ramon Aviles	.25
37	Henry Cotto	1.00
38	Angelo Cuevas	.25
39	Jose DeJesus	.25
40	Edgar Diaz	.25
41	Mario Diaz	.25
42	Juan Gonzalez	32.50
43	Gilberto Martinez	.25
44	Agustin Meizoso	.25
45	Jose Melendez	.25
46	Orlando Mercado	.25
47	Jose Munoz	.25
48	Omar Oliveras	.25
49	Francisco J. Oliveras	.25
50	Jorge Robles	.25
51	Ivan Rodriguez	24.00
52	Victor Rodriguez	.25
53	Melvin Rosario	.25
54	Geraldo Sanchez	.25
55	Hector Stewart	.25
56	Beau Allred	.25
57	Tom Barrett	.25
58	Randy Bockus	.25
59	George Canale	.25
60	Pat Gomez	.25
61	Brad Moore	.25
62	Andy Nezelek	.25
63	Doug Strange	.25
64	Luis Arroyo	.25
65	Juan Lopez	.25
66	Jaime Marrero	.25
67	Criollos checklist	.25
	Mayaguez Indios team set	22.00
68	Indios logo	.25
69	Jim Riggleman	.75
70	Juan Agosto	1.00
71	Luis Aquino	.25
72	Jose Birriel	.25
73	Luis DeLeon	.25
74	Alex Diaz	.75
75	Luis Faccio	.25
76	Leo Gomez	1.50
77	Roberto Hernandez	4.00
78	Juan Lopez	.25
79	Luis Lopez	.25
80	Charlie Montoya	.25
81	Melvin Nieves	1.00
82	Javier Ocasio	.25
83	Rey Palacios	.25
84	Luis R. Quinones	.25
85	Lino Rivera	.25
86	Luis Rivera	.25
87	Roy Silver	.25
88	Julio Valera	.25
89	Billy Bates	.25
90	Stan Clarke	.25
91	Jeff Gray	.25
92	Matt Kinzer	.25
93	Ray Lankford	8.00
94	Jim Lindeman	.25
95	Tim Meeks	.25
96	Tom Pagnozzi	1.50
97	Dan Radison	.25
98	Mark Riggins	.25
99	Hector Valle	.25
100	Indios checklist	.25
	Ponce Leones team set	60.00
101	Leones logo	.25
102	Santos Alomar	7.50
103	Luis Aguayo	.25
104	Roberto Alomar	22.00
105	Sandy Alomar Jr.	15.00
106	Ricky Bones	1.50
107	Francisco Burgos	.25
108	Ivan Calderon	.25
109	Edgar Castro	.25
110	Rafael Chavez	.25
111	David Colon	.25
112	Joey Cora	2.00
113	Felix Dedos	.25
114	Luis Galindez	.25
115	Otto Gonzalez	.25
116	Jose Hernandez	.25
117	Ken Juarbe	.25
118	Pedro Lopez	.25
119	Luis Martinez	.25
120	Armando Moreno	.25
121	Edwin Nunez	.25
122	Julian Perez	.25
123	Gabriel Rodriguez	.25
124	Edwin Rosado	.25
125	Terry Francona	.60
126	Tom Howard	1.50
127	Ray Krawczyk	.25
128	Dan Murphy	.25
129	Greg Vaughn	12.00
130	Gary Lance	.25
131	Efrain Maldonado	.25
132	Abraham Martinez	.25
133	Luis Melendez	.25
134	Leones checklist	.25
	Santurce Sandcrabs team set	23.00
135	Santurce Sandcrabs logo	.25
136	Ray Miller	.50
137	Jose Anglero	.25
138	Juan Belbru	.25
139	Jose Calderon	.25
140	Ivan DeJesus	1.00
141	Carlos Laboy	.25
142	Jose Lebron	.25
143	Jose Lind	1.50
144	Luis Lopez	.25
145	Jose Marzan	.25
146	Angel Morris	.25
147	Jaime Navarro	1.50
148	Jorge Ojeda	.25
149	Mike Perez	1.00
150	Rey Quinones	.25
151	Jose Rivera	.25
152	Tomas Rodriguez	.25
153	Osvaldo Sanchez	.25
154	Ulises Sierra	.25
155	Jose Valentin	.25
156	Albert Hall	.25
157	Charlie Hayes	3.00
158	Randy Kramer	.25
159	Terry McGriff	.25
160	Rick Reed	.25
161	Mike Roesler	.25
162	Mark Ryal	1.00
163	Bob Sebra	2.00
164	Guillermo Montanez	1.00
165	Juan Pizzaro	1.00
166	Eliseo Rodriguez	1.00
167	Santurce Sandcrabs checklist	.25
	Arecibo Lobos team set	22.00
168	Arecibo Lobos logo	.25
169	Fernando Gonzalez	.25
170	Edwin Alicea	.25
171	Jorge Candelaria	.25
172	Hernan Cortes	.25
173	Luis Cruz	.25
174	Fernando Figueroa	.25
175	Victor Garcia	.25
176	Javier Gonzalez	.25
177	Wallace Gonzalez	.25
178	Francisco Melendez	.25
179	Orlando Merced	2.50
180	Angel Miranda	1.00
181	Roberto Munoz	.25
182	Adalberto Pena	.25

183	Benny Puig	.25
184	David Rivera	.25
185	Aristarco Tirado	.25
186	Ricky Torres	.25
187	Hector Vargas	.25
188	Hediberto Vargas	.25
189	Bernie Williams	20.00
190	Brian Giles	.25
191	Erik Hanson	1.00
192	Gene Harris	.25
193	Kelly Mann	.25
194	Terry Taylor	.25
195	Jim Wilson	.25
196	Clint Zavaras	.25
197	Carlos Arroyo	.25
198	Jose Laboy	.25
199	Carlos Lezcano	.25
200	Dan Warthen	.25
201	Arecibo Lobos checklist	.25

1990 BYN Puerto Rican League Update

All-Stars, league leaders and roster changes during the 1990 Puerto Rican League season are reflected in this update issue. Like the regular issue, the update cards have both a team-set number and a number from within the overall set; the latter is used for this checklist. Cards #56-71 feature original paintings of the leaders or co-leaders in the particular stats.

		MT
Complete Set (75):		55.00
Common player:		.50
1	Tony Brown	.50
2	Lenny Harris	1.00
3	Johnny Maldonado	.50
4	Reggie Ritter	.50
5	Frank DiMichele	.50
6	Mike Kinnunen	.50
7	Rafael Muratti	.50
8	Rafael Novoa	.75
9	Terry Shumpert	.75
10	Nelson Simmons	.65
11	Andy Stankiewicz	2.00
12	John Barfield	.50
13	Danny Clay	.50
14	Bill Fulton	.50
15	Randy McCament	.60
16	Armando Moreno	.50
17	Carlos Rivera	.75
18	Lou Thornton	.90
19	Lee Tunnell	.50
20	Gene Walter	.50
21	Greg Harris	.50
22	Alan Sadler	.50
23	Roger Smithberg	.50
24	Jeff Yurtin	.50
25	Jose Birriel	.50
26	Shawn Holman	.50
27	Jim Hvizda	.50
28	Luis Lopez Santos	.75
29	Morris Madden	.50
30	Bob Patterson	2.00
31	Scott Ruskin	.50
32	Delvy Santiago	.50
33	Osvaldo Virgil	1.00
34	Carlos Escalera	.50
35	Jimmy Kremers	.50
36	Chito Martinez	1.00
37	Ferdinand "Boi" Rodriguez	2.00
38	Matt Sinatro	.60
39	Mike Walker	.50
40	(Carlos Baerga, Edgar Martinez) (MVPs)	2.00
41	Alex Diaz (Rookie of the Year)	1.00
42	Ricky Bones (Pitcher of the Year)	1.00
43	Ramon Aviles (Manager of the Year)	.50
44	Luis Aguayo (Comeback of the Year)	.75
45	Santos Alomar, Hijo (All-Star)	2.00
46	Terry Francona (All-Star)	1.00
47	Carlos Baerga (All-Star)	2.00
48	Edgar Martinez (All-Star)	3.00
49	Joey Cora (All-Star)	1.50
50	Greg Vaughn (All-Star)	5.00
51	Henry Cotto (All-Star)	1.00
52	Juan Gonzalez (All-Star)	12.00
53	Roy Silver (All-Star)	.50
54	Ricky Bones (All-Star)	1.00
55	David Rosario (All-Star)	.50
56	Hitting Leaders	.50
57	RBI Leaders	.50
58	Home Run Leaders	.50
59	Runs Leaders	.50
60	Hits Leaders	.50
61	Doubles Leaders	.50
62	Triples Leaders	.50
63	Stolen Base Leaders	.50
64	Wins Leaders	.50
65	ERA Leaders	.50
66	Complete Games Leaders	.50
67	Shutout Leaders	.50
68	Strikeout Leaders	.50
69	Saves Leaders	.50
70	Innings Pitched Leaders	.50
71	Games Started Leaders	.50
72	Season/Semi-Final Standings	.50
73	Final Series/ Caribbean Series Standings	.50
74	Checklist	.10
75	Checklist	.10

C

1989 Cadaco All-Star Baseball Discs

This set of player discs was sold with and intended for use in a board game. Fronts of the 3-1/2" diameter position players' discs have a yellow border sectioned with numbers from 1 to 14, indicating that player's likelihood of performing a specific baseball result based on career stats. At center is a color player photo from which the uniform details have been airbrushed. Logos of the game's producer and the Major League Players' Association flank the portrait. The player's name, team and position are below the photo. Backs have up to five years of recent stats and lifetime totals, along with a few biographical data. Several of the discs have player names misspelled. Four error discs from the initial print run were corrected. The unnumbered discs are checklisted alphabetically.

		MT
Complete Set (63):		12.00
Common Player:		.25
(1)	Harold Baines	.25
(2)	Wade Boggs	.60
(3)	Bobby Bonilla	.25
(4)	George Brett	1.00
(5)	Jose Canseco	.50
(6)	Gary Carter	.30
(7)	Joe Carter	.30
(8)	Will Clark	.40
(9a)	Rodger Clemens (first name misspelled)	2.00
(9b)	Roger Clemens (corrected)	.45
(10)	Vince Coleman	.25
(11)	David Cone	.25
(12)	Alvin Davis	.25
(13)	Eric Davis	.25
(14)	Glenn Davis	.25
(15)	Andre Dawson	.35
(16)	Shawon Dunston	.25
(17)	Dennis Eckersley	.30
(18)	Carlton Fisk	.35
(19)	Scott Fletcher	.25
(20a)	John Frannko (last name misspelled)	.50
(20b)	John Franco (corrected)	.25
(21)	Julio Franko (Franco)	.25
(22)	Gary Gaetti	.25
(23)	Andres Galarraga	.30
(24)	Kirk Gibson	.25
(25)	Mike Greenwell	.25
(26)	Mark Gubicza	.25
(27)	Pedro Guerrero	.25
(28)	Tony Gwynn	.50
(29)	Rickey Henderson	.35
(30)	Orel Hershiser	.25
(31)	Kent Hrbek	.25
(32)	Danny Jackson	.25
(33a)	Barry Larkin (wrong photo)	.90
(33b)	Barry Larkin (corrected)	.25
(34)	Greg Maddux	1.00
(35)	Don Mattingly	1.00
(36a)	Mark McGuire (last name misspelled)	2.00
(36b)	Mark McGwire (corrected)	1.50
(37)	Fred McGriff	.40
(38)	Paul Molitor	.50
(39)	Tony Pena	.25
(40)	Gerald Perry	.25
(41)	Dan Plesac	.25
(42)	Kirby Puckett	.75
(43)	Johnny Ray	.25
(44)	Jeff Reardon	.25
(45)	Cal Ripken, Jr.	1.50
(46)	Babe Ruth	1.00
(47)	Nolan Ryan	1.00
(48)	Juan Samuel	.25
(49)	Ryne Sandberg	.65
(50)	Benito Santiago	.25
(51)	Steve Sax	.25
(52)	Mike Schmidt	.75
(53)	Kevin Seitzer	.25
(54)	Ozzie Smith	.50
(55)	Terry Steinbach	.25
(56)	Dave Stewart	.25
(57)	Darryl Strawberry	.30
(58)	Andres Thomas	.25
(59)	Alan Trammell (Trammell)	.30
(60)	Andy Van Slyke	.25
(61)	Frank Viola	.25
(62)	Dave Winfield	.40
(63)	Todd Worrell	.25

1991 Cadaco All-Star Baseball Discs

This set of player discs was sold with and intended for use in a board game. Fronts of the 3-1/2" diameter discs have a yellow border sectioned with numbers from 1 to 14, indicating that player's likelihood of performing a specific baseball result based on career stats. At center is a color player photo from which the uniform details have been airbrushed. Logos of the game's producer and the Major League Players' Association flank the portrait. The player's name, team and position are below the photo. Backs have up to five years of recent stats and lifetime totals, along with a few biographical data. The unnumbered discs are checklisted alphabetically.

		MT
Complete Set (62):		15.00
Common Player:		.25
(1)	Roberto Alomar	.25
(2)	Harold Baines	.25
(3)	Craig Biggio	.25
(4)	Wade Boggs	.50
(5)	Barry Bonds	1.00
(6)	Bobby Bonilla	.25
(7)	Jose Canseco	.75
(8)	Will Clark	.45
(9)	Roger Clemens	.75
(10)	Roberto Clemente	2.50
(11)	Ty Cobb	1.00
(12)	Vince Coleman	.25
(13)	Eric Davis	.25
(14)	Glenn Davis	.25
(15)	Andre Dawson	.25
(16)	Delino DeShields	.25
(17)	Shawon Dunston	.25
(18)	Tony Fernandez	.25
(19)	Cecil Fielder	.25
(20)	Carlton Fisk	.35
(21)	Julio Franco	.25
(22)	Gary Gaetti	.25
(23)	Lou Gehrig	2.00
(24)	Kirk Gibson	.25
(25)	Mark Grace	.50
(26)	Ken Griffey Jr.	3.00
(27)	Kelly Gruber	.25
(28)	Tony Gwynn	1.50
(29)	Rickey Henderson	.50
(30)	Orel Hershiser	.25
(31)	David Justice	.25
(32)	Bo Jackson	.35
(33)	Howard Johnson	.25
(34)	Barry Larkin	.25
(35)	Ramon Martinez	.25
(36)	Don Mattingly	.75
(37)	Fred McGriff	.25
(38)	Mark McGwire	3.00
(39)	Kevin Mitchell	.25
(40)	Lance Parrish	.25
(41)	Tony Pena	.25
(42)	Kirby Puckett	.75
(43)	Cal Ripken Jr.	2.00
(44)	Babe Ruth	2.50
(45)	Nolan Ryan	2.00
(46)	Bret Saberhagen	.45
(47)	Chris Sabo	.25
(48)	Ryne Sandberg	.50
(49)	Benito Santiago	.25
(50)	Steve Sax	.25
(51)	Gary Sheffield	.25
(52)	Ruben Sierra	.25
(53)	Ozzie Smith	.50
(54)	Terry Steinbach	.25
(55)	Dave Stewart	.25
(56)	Mickey Tettleton	.25
(57)	Alan Trammell	.25
(58)	Jose Uribe	.25
(59)	Honus Wagner	.50
(60)	Lou Whitaker	.25
(61)	Matt Williams	.25
(62)	Robin Yount	.75

1993 Cadaco All-Star Baseball Discs

This set of player discs was sold with and intended for use in a board game. Fronts of the 3-1/2" diameter discs have a yellow border sectioned with numbers from 1 to 14, indicating that player's likelihood of performing a specific baseball result based on career stats. At center is a color player photo from which the uniform details have been airbrushed. Logos of the game's producer and the Major League Players' Association flank the portrait. The player's name, team and position are below the photo. Backs have up to five years of recent stats and lifetime totals, along with a few biographical data. The unnumbered discs are checklisted alphabetically.

		MT
Complete Set (62):		15.00
Common Player:		.25
(1)	Kevin Appier	.25
(2)	Carlos Baerga	.25
(3)	Harold Baines	.25
(4)	Derek Bell	.25
(5)	George Bell	.25
(6)	Jay Bell	.25
(7)	Mike Boddicker	.25
(8)	Wade Boggs	.50
(9)	Hubie Brooks	.25
(10)	Jose Canseco	.45
(11)	Roger Clemens	.50
(12)	Roberto Clemente	2.00
(13)	Ty Cobb	.50
(14)	Alex Cole	.25
(15)	Jeff Conine	.25
(16)	Andre Dawson	.35
(17)	Shawon Dunston	.25
(18)	Lenny Dykstra	.25
(19)	Carlton Fisk	.45
(20)	Darrin Fletcher	.25
(21)	Gary Gaetti	.25
(22)	Greg Gagne	.25
(23)	Mike Gallego	.25
(24)	Lou Gehrig	1.00
(25)	Kirk Gibson	.25
(26)	Tom Glavine	.35
(27)	Mark Grace	.40
(28)	Ken Griffey Jr.	2.50
(29)	Tony Gwynn	.75
(30)	Charlie Hayes	.25
(31)	Rickey Henderson	.35
(32)	Orel Hershiser	.25
(33)	Bo Jackson	.35
(34)	Howard Johnson	.25
(35)	Randy Johnson	.35
(36)	Ricky Jordan	.25
(37)	David Justice	.35
(38)	Ray Lankford	.25
(39)	Ramon Martinez	.35
(40)	Don Mattingly	.75
(41)	Mark McGwire	2.50
(42)	Brian McRae	.25
(43)	Joe Oliver	.25
(44)	Tony Pena	.25
(45)	Kirby Puckett	.75
(46)	Cal Ripken Jr.	2.00
(47)	Babe Ruth	1.00
(48)	Nolan Ryan	2.00
(49)	Bret Saberhagen	.35
(50)	Chris Sabo	.25
(51)	Ryne Sandberg	.60
(52)	Benito Santiago	.25
(53)	Steve Sax	.25
(54)	Gary Sheffield	.40
(55)	Ozzie Smith	.65
(56)	Dave Stewart	.25
(57)	Darryl Strawberry	.25
(58)	Frank Thomas	1.50
(59)	Robin Ventura	.35
(60)	Hector Villanueva	.25
(61)	Honus Wagner	.50
(62)	Lou Whitaker	.25

1985 Cain's Potato Chips Tigers

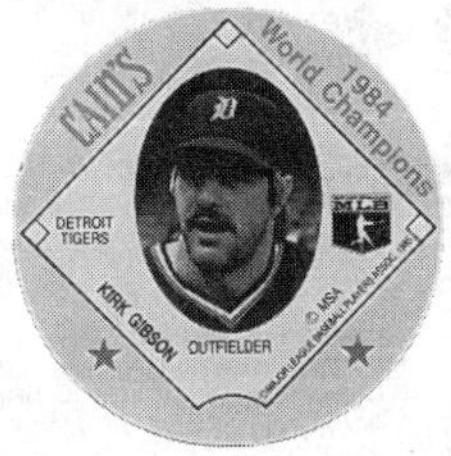

This set commemorating the 1984 World Champion Tigers were issued in bags of Cain's Potato Chips in the Michigan area in 1985. The yellow-bordered, unnumbered cards measure 2-3/4" in diameter and feature full-color oval photos inside a diamond. The word "Cain's" appears in the upper left corner, while the player's name appears in the lower left with his position directly below the photo. The words "1984 World Champions" are printed in the upper right corner. Backs include 1984 statistics.

		MT
Complete Set (20):		12.50
Common Player:		.50
(1)	Doug Bair	.50
(2)	Juan Berenguer	.50
(3)	Dave Bergman	.50
(4)	Tom Brookens	.50
(5)	Marty Castillo	.50
(6)	Darrell Evans	.75
(7)	Barbaro Garbey	.50
(8)	Kirk Gibson	.75
(9)	John Grubb	.50
(10)	Willie Hernandez	.50
(11)	Larry Herndon	.50
(12)	Chet Lemon	.50
(13)	Aurelio Lopez	.50
(14)	Jack Morris	.75
(15)	Lance Parrish	.75
(16)	Dan Petry	.50
(17)	Bill Scherrer	.50
(18)	Alan Trammell	2.00
(19)	Lou Whitaker	1.25
(20)	Milt Wilcox	.50

1986 Cain's Potato Chips Tigers

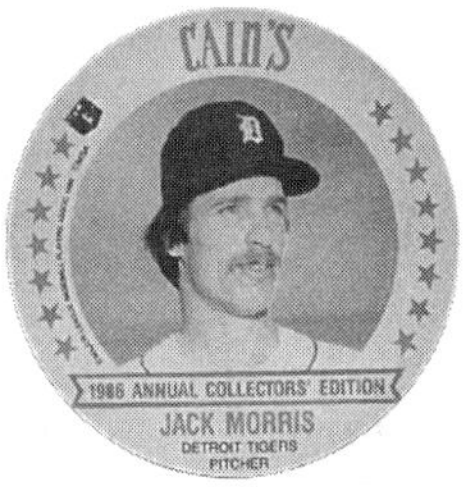

For the second year in a row, player discs of the Detroit Tigers were found in boxes of Cain's Potato Chips sold in the Detroit area. Twenty discs make up the set which is branded as a "1986 Annual Collectors' Edition." Discs, measuring 2-3/4" in diameter, have fronts which contain a color photo plus the player's name, team and position. The Cain's logo and the Major League Baseball Players Association's logo also appear. The backs, which display black print on white stock, contain player information plus the card number.

		MT
Complete Set (20):		25.00
Common Player:		1.00
1	Tom Brookens	1.00
2	Willie Hernandez	1.00
3	Dave Bergman	1.00
4	Lou Whitaker	2.50
5	Dave LaPoint	1.00
6	Lance Parrish	1.50
7	Randy O'Neal	1.00
8	Nelson Simmons	1.00
9	Larry Herndon	1.00
10	Doug Flynn	1.00
11	Jack Morris	1.50
12	Dan Petry	1.00
13	Walt Terrell	1.00
14	Chet Lemon	1.00
15	Frank Tanana	1.00
16	Kirk Gibson	1.50
17	Darrell Evans	1.50
18	Dave Collins	1.00
19	John Grubb	1.00
20	Alan Trammell	4.00

1987 Cain's Potato Chips Tigers

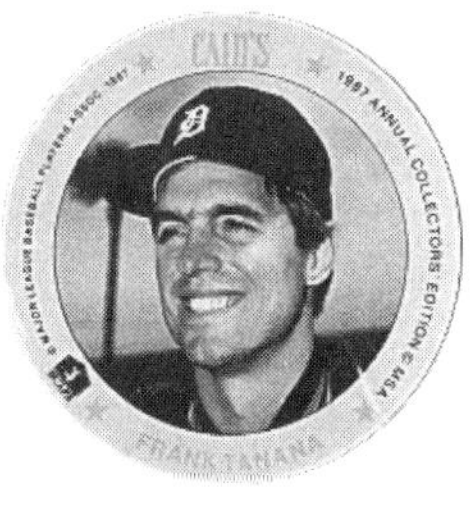

Player discs of the Detroit Tigers were inserted in boxes of Cain's Potato Chips for the third consecutive year. The 1987 edition is made up of cards each measuring 2-3/4" in diameter. The discs, which were packaged in a cellophane wrapper, feature a full-color photo surrounded by an orange border. Backs are printed in red on white stock. The set was produced by Mike Schechter and Associates.

		MT
Complete Set (20):		30.00
Common Player:		1.25
1	Tom Brookens	1.25
2	Darnell Coles	1.25
3	Mike Heath	1.25
4	Dave Bergman	1.25
5	Dwight Lowry	1.25
6	Darrell Evans	2.00
7	Alan Trammell	5.00
8	Lou Whitaker	3.50
9	Kirk Gibson	2.00
10	Chet Lemon	1.25
11	Larry Herndon	1.25
12	John Grubb	1.25
13	Willie Hernandez	1.25
14	Jack Morris	2.00
15	Dan Petry	1.25
16	Walt Terrell	1.25
17	Mark Thurmond	1.25
18	Pat Sheridan	1.25
19	Eric King	1.25
20	Frank Tanana	1.25

1984 California Angels Fire Safety

This 32-card set was distributed at a June home game to fans 14 and under. Cards measure 2-1/2" x 3-1/2". Fronts have full-color action photos along a portrait of Smokey the Bear and U.S. and California Forest Service logos commemorating Smokey's 40th birthday. Black-and-white backs have minimal player data and stats and a tip for preventing forest fires.

		MT
Complete Set (32):		7.50
Common Player:		.25
(1)	Don Aase	.25
(2)	Juan Beniquez	.25
(3)	Bob Boone	.45
(4)	Rick Burleson	.25
(5)	Rod Carew	1.50
(6)	John Curtis	.25
(7)	Doug DeCinces	.25
(8)	Brian Downing	.25
(9)	Ken Forsch	.25
(10)	Bobby Grich	.25
(11)	Reggie Jackson	2.00
(12)	Ron Jackson	.25
(13)	Tommy John	.50
(14)	Curt Kaufman	.25
(15)	Bruce Kison	.25
(16)	Frank LaCorte	.25
(17)	Fred Lynn	.40
(18)	John McNamara	.25
(19)	Jerry Narron	.25
(20)	Gary Pettis	.25
(21)	Robert Picciolo	.25
(22)	Ron Romanick	.25
(23)	Luis Sanchez	.25
(24)	Dick Schofield	.25
(25)	Daryl Sconiers	.25
(26)	Jim Slaton	.25
(27)	Ellis Valentine	.25
(28)	Robert Wilfong	.25
(29)	Mike Witt	.25
(30)	Geoff Zahn	.25
---	Forestry Dept. Logo Card	.10
---	Smokey Logo Card	.10

1985 California Angels Fire Safety

This full-color set of large-format cards was given to fans attending the July 14 game at Anaheim Stadium. Fronts feature player photos with their last name at the top above the picture. In the bottom border are a portrait of Smokey the Bear, and logos of the Angels, California Forestry Service and U.S. Forestry Service. Cards measure 4-1/4" x 6". On back, printed in black-and-white, are personal data, a few stats and a wildfire safety tip.

		MT
Complete Set (24):		6.00
Common Player:		.25
1	Mike Witt	.25
2	Reggie Jackson	1.50
3	Bob Boone	.45
4	Mike Brown	.25
5	Rod Carew	1.00
6	Doug DeCinces	.25
7	Brian Downing	.25
8	Ken Forsch	.25
9	Gary Pettis	.25
10	Jerry Narron	.25
11	Ron Romanick	.25
12	Bobby Grich	.25
13	Dick Schofield	.25
14	Juan Beniquez	.25
15	Geoff Zahn	.25
16	Luis Sanchez	.25
17	Jim Slaton	.25
18	Doug Corbett	.25
19	Ruppert Jones	.25
20	Rob Wilfong	.25
21	Donnie Moore	.25
22	Pat Clements	.25
23	Tommy John	.50
24	Gene Mauch	.25

1986 California Angels Fire Safety

The Angels, in conjuction with the U.S. and California Forestry Services, issued this set promoting Wildfire Prevention. Cards measure 4-1/4" x 6" and offer a full-color front with the player's picture in an oval frame. Backs have player stats with a drawing and fire safety tip. The sets were given out Aug. 9 at the game in Anaheim Stadium.

		MT
Complete Set (24):		6.50
Common Player:		.25
1	Mike Witt	.25
2	Reggie Jackson	1.50
3	Bob Boone	.40
4	Don Sutton	1.00
5	Kirk McCaskill	.25
6	Doug DeCinces	.25
7	Brian Downing	.25
8	Doug Corbett	.25
9	Gary Pettis	.25
10	Jerry Narron	.25
11	Ron Romanick	.25
12	Bobby Grich	.25
13	Dick Schofield	.25
14	George Hendrick	.25
15	Rick Burleson	.25
16	John Candelaria	.25
17	Jim Slaton	.25
18	Darrell Miller	.25
19	Ruppert Jones	.25
20	Rob Wilfong	.25
21	Donnie Moore	.25
22	Wally Joyner	1.00
23	Terry Forster	.25
24	Gene Mauch	.25

1987 California Angels Fire Safety

The U.S. Forestry Service distributed this set to 25,000 fans in attendance at Anaheim Stadium on Aug. 1. The full-color cards measure 4" x 6". Fronts carry a design of baseballs and bats framing the player photo. Only the player's last name is given. At bottom is a Smokey the Bear portrait and team logo. Backs contain the player's name, position and personal data along with a Smokey Bear cartoon fire prevention tip and sponsors' logos.

		MT
Complete Set (24):		6.00
Common Player:		.25
1	John Candelaria	.25
2	Don Sutton	1.00
3	Mike Witt	.25
4	Gary Lucas	.25
5	Kirk McCaskill	.25
6	Chuck Finley	.25
7	Willie Fraser	.25
8	Donnie Moore	.25
9	Urbano Lugo	.25
10	Butch Wynegar	.25
11	Darrell Miller	.25
12	Wally Joyner	.75
13	Mark McLemore	.35
14	Mark Ryal	.25
15	Dick Schofield	.25
16	Jack Howell	.25
17	Doug DeCinces	.25
18	Gus Polidor	.25
19	Brian Downing	.25
20	Gary Pettis	.25
21	Ruppert Jones	.25
22	George Hendrick	.25
23	Devon White	.75
---	Smokey Bear Logo Card/Checklist	.10

1988 California Angels Fire Safety

These borderless full-color cards (2-1/2" x 3-1/2") are highlighted by a thin white outline on front. The player name, team logo and a Smokey the Bear picture logo appear in the photo's lower-right corner. Backs are black-and-white and include personal information and a large cartoon fire prevention tip. Part of the U.S. Forest Service fire prevention campaign, the cards were distributed in three separate in-stadium giveaways during August and September games.

		MT
Complete Set (25):		7.00
Common Player:		.30
1	Cookie Rojas	.30
2	Johnny Ray	.30
3	Jack Howell	.30
4	Mike Witt	.30
5	Tony Armas	.30
6	Gus Polidor	.30
7	DeWayne Buice	.30
8	Dan Petry	.30
9	Bob Boone	.50
10	Chili Davis	.30
11	Greg Minton	.30
12	Kirk McCaskill	.30
13	Devon White	.50
14	Willie Fraser	.30
15	Chuck Finley	.30
16	Dick Schofield	.30
17	Wally Joyner	.50
18	Brian Downing	.30
19	Stewart Cliburn	.30
20	Donnie Moore	.30
21	Bryan Harvey	.30
22	Mark McLemore	.30
23	Butch Wynegar	.30
24	George Hendrick	.30
---	Team Logo/Checklist	.10

1989 California Angels All-Stars Fire Safety

The U.S. Forest Service, in conjunction with the California Angels, issued this all-time team set. The 2-1/2" x 3-1/2" cards have a silver border with the player photo outlined in red. Beneath the photo a banner across homeplate reads "Angels All-Stars," along with the player's name and position, which are flanked by Smokey the Bear on the left and the Angels 1989 All-Star Game logo on the right. Card backs highlight the player's career with the Angels and include an illustrated fire prevention tip.

		MT
Complete Set (20):		11.00
Common Player:		.30
1	Bill Rigney	.30
2	Dean Chance	.40
3	Jim Fregosi	.30
4	Bobby Knoop	.30
5	Don Mincher	.30
6	Clyde Wright	.30
7	Nolan Ryan	3.50
8	Frank Robinson	1.50
9	Frank Tanana	.30
10	Rod Carew	1.00
11	Bobby Grich	.30
12	Brian Downing	.30
13	Don Baylor	.35
14	Fred Lynn	.35
15	Reggie Jackson	1.50
16	Doug DeCinces	.30
17	Bob Boone	.35
18	Wally Joyner	.50
19	Mike Witt	.30
20	Johnny Ray	.30

1990 California Angels Fire Safety

This set was released by the U.S. Forestry Service in conjunction with the California Angels. The sets were distributed at the May 27 home game. The 2-1/2" x 3-1/2" cards feature full-color action photos surrounded by metallic silver borders. Team and Smokey the Bear logos appear on front. Backs contain player data and a cartoon Smokey Bear message urging the prevention of forest fires.

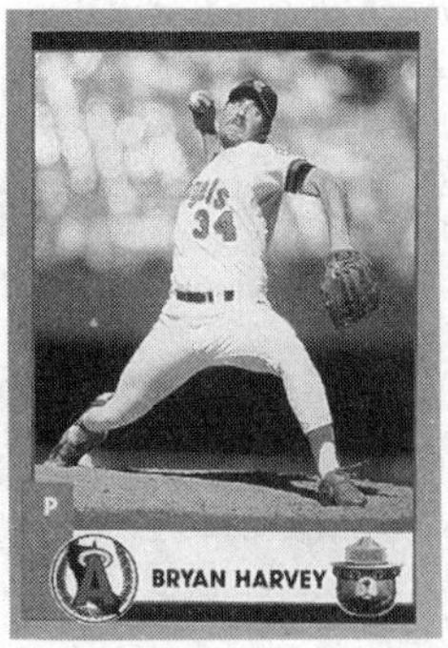

		MT
Complete Set (20):		5.00
Common Player:		.25
1	Jim Abbott	.50
2	Bert Blyleven	.30
3	Chili Davis	.30
4	Brian Downing	.25
5	Chuck Finley	.25
6	Willie Fraser	.25
7	Bryan Harvey	.25
8	Jack Howell	.25
9	Wally Joyner	.40
10	Mark Langston	.30
11	Kirk McCaskill	.25
12	Mark McLemore	.25
13	Lance Parrish	.30
14	Johnny Ray	.25
15	Dick Schofield	.25
16	Mike Witt	.25
17	Claudell Washington	.25
18	Devon White	.35
19	Scott Bailes	.25
20	Bob McClure	.25

1991 California Angels Fire Safety

This set was sponsored by the California Department of Forestry. Front of the 2-1/2" x 3-1/2" cards features gray borders surrounding full-color action photos. The flip sides feature a fire safety cartoon and biographical information, along with sponsor logos.

		MT
Complete Set (20):		8.00
Common Player:		.25
1	Luis Polonia	.25
2	Junior Felix	.25
3	Dave Winfield	1.00
4	Dave Parker	.45
5	Lance Parrish	.35
6	Wally Joyner	.45
7	Jim Abbott	.45
8	Mark Langston	.35
9	Chuck Finley	.25
10	Kirk McCaskill	.25
11	Jack Howell	.25
12	Donnie Hill	.25
13	Gary Gaetti	.35
14	Dick Schofield	.25
15	Luis Sojo	.25
16	Mark Eichhorn	.25
17	Bryan Harvey	.25
18	Jeff Robinson	.25
19	Scott Lewis	.25
20	John Orton	.25

Player names in *Italic* type indicate a rookie card.

1992 California Angels Police

This safety set was sponsored by Carl's Jr. fast food restaurants and distributed by the Orange County Sheriff's Dept. Single cards were distributed to children over the course of the season and complete sets were handed out at the Angels' Sept. 19 game. Fronts have color player action photos on a star-studded red, white and blue border. Backs have a small black-and-white portrait photo, stats, career highlights, an anti-drug message and sponsors' logos.

		MT
Complete Set (18):		8.00
Common Player:		.50
1	Jim Abbott	.75
2	Gene Autry	1.00
3	Bert Blyleven	.60
4	Hubie Brooks	.50
5	Chad Curtis	.60
6	Alvin Davis	.50
7	Gary DiSarcina	.50
8	Junior Felix	.50
9	Chuck Finley	.60
10	Gary Gaetti	.75
11	Rene Gonzalez	.50
12	Von Hayes	.50
13	Carl Karcher	.50
14	Mark Langston	.75
15	Luis Polonia	.50
16	Bobby Rose	.50
17	Lee Stevens	.50
18	Happy Star (mascot)	.50

1993 California Angels Police

Sponsored by the Carl's Jr. hamburger restaurant chain and distributed through the California Chiefs & Sheriffs Assn., it was reported that 20,000-25,000 sets were produced. The 2-1/2" x 3-1/2" cards have a player action photo on front. Backs are printed in blue and black and include a portrait photo, career highlights, stats and an anti-drug message.

		MT
Complete Set (21):		20.00
Common Player:		.50
1	Gene Autry	2.00
2	Carl Karcher	.50
3	Buck Rodgers	.50
4	Rod Carew	2.00
5	Kelly Gruber	.50
6	Chili Davis	.50
7	Chad Curtis	.60
8	Mark Langston	.75
9	Scott Sanderson	.50
10	J.T. Snow	4.00
11	Rene Gonzalez	.50
12	Jimmie Reese	.50
13	Damion Easley	.60
14	Julio Valera	.50
15	Luis Polonia	.50
16	John Orton	.50
17	Gary DiSarcina	.50
18	Greg Myers	.50
19	Chuck Finley	.60
20	Tim Salmon	6.00
21	Happy Star (mascot)	.50

1997 California Lottery Baseball Legends

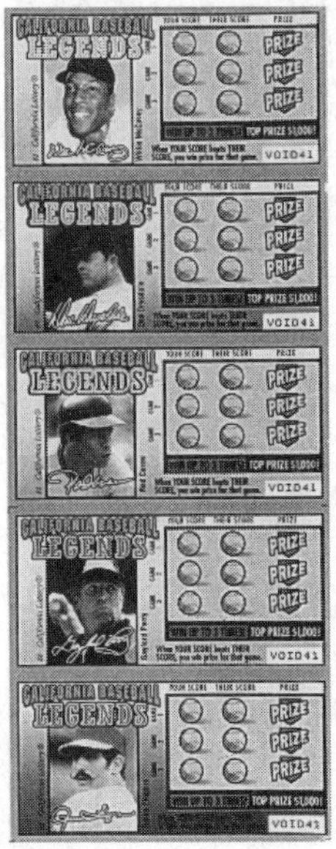

Five Hall of Famers who played some or all of their careers with California teams are pictured on this series of scratch-off $1 lottery tickets. Because they are licensed by the players, but not Major League Baseball, the color photos on the tickets are devoid of uniform logos. Each ticket features a facsimile autograph on the front. Backs are printed in black-and-white with redemption notices and security bar codes. Tickets measure 4" x 2" and are perforated at top and bottom. Values quoted are for unscratched tickets.

		MT
Complete Set (5):		10.00
Common Player:		2.00
(1)	Rod Carew	2.00
(2)	Don Drysdale	2.00
(3)	Rollie Fingers	2.00
(4)	Willie McCovey	2.00
(5)	Gaylord Perry	2.00

The election of former players to the Hall of Fame does not always have an immediate upward effect on card prices. The hobby market generally has done a good job of predicting those inductions and adjusting values over the course of several years.

1992-93 Canadian Card News Repli-cards

Krause Publications short-lived attempt to service the Canadian card collecting market with a newsstand magazine included the use of repli-card panels of five in each of the magazine's five issues. The cards feature a mix of hockey players, CFL stars and Blue Jays and Expos. Only the baseball players are listed here.

		MT
Complete (Baseball) Set (12):		6.50
Common Player:		.50
	1992 Canadian Card News (Parkhurst style)	
2	Kelly Gruber	.50
3	Roberto Alomar	.75
5	Larry Walker, Marquis Grissom, Delino DeShields	.50
8	Dave Winfield	.75
14	Ken Hill	.50
	1993 Canadian Card News (original design)	
16	Jimmy Key	.50
17	Pat Borders	.50
21	Joe Carter	.50
22	Larry Walker	.75
23	Delino DeShields	.50
24	Derek Bell	.50
25	Wil Cordero	.50

1996 Canadian Club Classic Stars of the Game

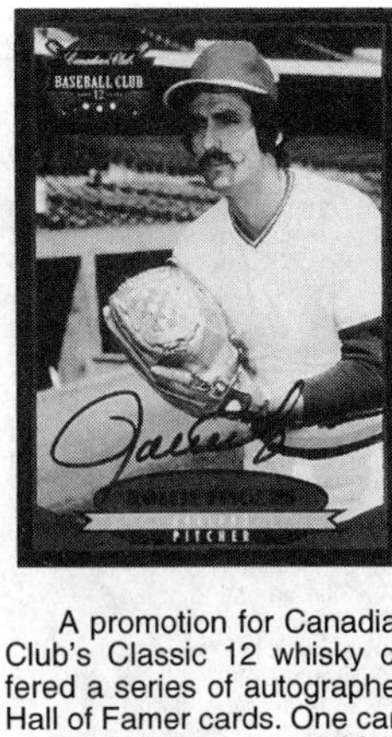

A promotion for Canadian Club's Classic 12 whisky offered a series of autographed Hall of Famer cards. One card was included in a special folder attached to bottles. An offer sheet inside gave details for ordering other cards for $5 each plus proof of purchase. Also in the bottle-hanger was a certificate of authenticity for the enclosed signed card. In standard 2-1/2" x 3-1/2" format, cards feature vintage color player photos on which uniform logos have been deleted. Cards have a black border, are highlighted in gold foil and have an authentic autograph on front. Backs have career stats and summary. Cards #1-4 were labeled as Series I, cards #5-6 are Series II.

		MT
Complete Set (6):		40.00
Common Player:		6.00
1	Brooks Robinson	8.00
2	Billy Williams	6.00
3	Willie Stargell	6.00
4	Ernie Banks	10.00
5	Frank Robinson	6.00
6	Rollie Fingers	6.00

1987 Canon Chicago Cubs Photocards

The team's "official" camera took over sponsorship of the Cubs player photocards in 1987. Given to players for use in answering fan mail for autographs or pictures, the 3-1/2" x 5-1/2" cards have black-and-white player portrait photos with a white border. The player name is in all-caps beneath the photo, with sponsor and team logos in the bottom corners. Backs are blank. The unnumbered cards are checklisted here in alphabetical order. Complete sets were not available from the team.

		MT
Complete Set (38):		70.00
Common Player:		2.00
(1)	Glenn Brummer	2.00
(2)	Phil Claussen	2.00
(3)	Jody Davis	2.00
(4)	Ron Davis	2.00
(5)	Andre Dawson	4.00
(6)	Brian Dayett	2.00
(7)	Bob Dernier	2.00
(8)	Frank DiPino	2.00
(9)	Shawon Dunston	2.50
(10)	Leon Durham	2.00
(11)	John Fierro	2.00
(12)	Dallas Green	2.00
(13)	Lester Lancaster	2.00
(14)	Frank Lucchesi	2.00
(15)	Ed Lynch	2.00
(16)	Greg Maddux	15.00
(17)	David Martinez	2.00
(18)	Gary Mathews	2.00
(19)	Gene Michael	2.00
(20)	Keith Moreland	2.00
(21)	Jamie Moyer	2.00
(22)	Jerry Mumphrey	2.00
(23)	Dickie Noles	2.00
(24)	Johnny Oates	2.00
(25)	Jimmy Piersall	3.00
(26)	Ryne Sandberg	8.00
(27)	Scott Sanderson	2.00
(28)	Bob Searles	2.00
(29)	Lee Smith	2.50
(30)	Jim Snyder	2.00
(31)	Herm Starrette	2.00
(32)	Jim Sundberg	2.00
(33)	Rick Sutcliffe	2.00
(34)	Manny Trillo	2.00
(35)	Steve Trout	2.00
(36)	John Vukovich	2.00
(37)	Chico Walker	2.00
(38)	Billy Williams	4.00

1988 Canon Chicago Cubs Photocards

The team's "official" camera again sponsored the Cubs player photocards in 1988. Given to players for use in answering fan mail for autographs or pictures, the 3-1/2" x 5-1/2" cards have black-and-white player portrait photos with a white border. The player name is in all-caps beneath the photo, with sponsor and team logos in the bottom corners. Backs are blank. The unnumbered cards are checklisted here in alphabetical order. Complete sets were not available from the team.

		MT
Complete Set (27):		50.00
Common Player:		2.00
(1)	Joe Altobelli	2.00
(2)	Chuck Cottier	2.00
(3)	Larry Cox	2.00
(4)	Jody Davis	2.00
(5)	Andre Dawson	4.00
(6)	Frank DiPino	2.00
(7)	Shawon Dunston	2.00
(8)	Leon Durham	2.00
(9)	Goose Gossage	2.50
(10)	Drew Hall	2.00
(11)	Darrin Jackson	2.00
(12)	Lester Lancaster	2.00
(13)	Vance Law	2.00
(14)	Greg Maddux	9.00
(15)	David Martinez	2.00
(16)	Jose Martinez	2.00
(17)	Jamie Moyer	2.00
(18)	Jerry Mumphrey	2.00
(19)	Al Nipper	2.00
(20)	Rafael Palmeiro	5.00
(21)	Dick Pole	2.00
(22)	Ryne Sandberg	6.00
(23)	Calvin Schiraldi	2.00
(24)	Jim Sundberg	2.00
(25)	Rick Sutcliffe	2.50
(26)	Manny Trillo	2.00
(27)	Don Zimmer	2.00

1989 Cap'n Crunch

This 22-card set was produced by Topps for Cap'n Crunch cereal boxes. Two cards and a stick of gum were included in each cereal box while the offer was active. The fronts of these 2-1/2" x 3-1/2" cards feature red, white and blue borders. The card backs are horizontal and feature lifetime statistics. The set was not offered in any complete set deal.

		MT
Complete Set (22):		11.00
Common Player:		.50
1	Jose Canseco	.75
2	Kirk Gibson	.50
3	Orel Hershiser	.50
4	Frank Viola	.50
5	Tony Gwynn	1.00
6	Cal Ripken	2.00
7	Darryl Strawberry	.50
8	Don Mattingly	1.50
9	George Brett	1.00
10	Andre Dawson	.50
11	Dale Murphy	.60
12	Alan Trammell	.50
13	Eric Davis	.50
14	Jack Clark	.50
15	Eddie Murray	.75
16	Mike Schmidt	.85
17	Dwight Gooden	.50
18	Roger Clemens	1.00
19	Will Clark	.60
20	Kirby Puckett	1.00
21	Robin Yount	1.00
22	Mark McGwire	2.50

1994 Capital Cards 1969 Mets Postcards

Capital Cards, produced a 32-card postcard set of members of the 1969 World Champion New York Mets from Ron Lewis paintings, limited to 25,000 sets. Capital Cards also produced 5,000 uncut sheets that are individually numbered and carried a suggested retail price of $99.95. The boxed postcard set retailed for $39.95. The cards could also be purchased with autographs.

		MT
Complete Set (32):		20.00
Common Player:		.50
1	Logo Card	.50
2	Gil Hodges	3.00
3	Rube Walker	.50
4	Yogi Berra	3.00
5	Joe Pignatano	.50
6	Ed Yost	.50
7	Tommie Agee	.50
8	Ken Boswell	.50
9	Don Cardwell	.50
10	Ed Charles	.50
11	Donn Clendenon	.50
12	Jack DiLauro	.50
13	Duffy Dyer	.50
14	Wayne Garrett	.50
15	Rod Gaspar	.50
16	Gary Gentry	.50
17	Jerry Grote	.50
18	Bud Harrelson	.75
19	Cleon Jones	.75
20	Cal Koonce	.50
21	Jerry Koosman	.90
22	Ed Kranepool	.75
23	J.C. Martin	.50
24	Jim McAndrew	.50
25	Tug McGraw	.75
26	Bob Pfeil	.50
27	Nolan Ryan	7.00
28	Tom Seaver	3.00
29	Art Shamsky	.50
30	Ron Swoboda	.75
31	Ron Taylor	.50
32	Al Weis	.50

1986 Card Collectors 1951 Bowman Reprint

One of several high-quality reprints of popular vintage card sets was this 324-piece re-issue of the 1951 Bowman gum cards, complete with Mantle and Mays rookies. Reproduced slightly larger than the originals, in 2-3/16" x 3-1/4" size, the CCC version has a glossy "Diamond Vue" coating on front. Backs have a reprint line printed at the bottom. The set was sold in a colorful box with an original retail price of $29.95. Because licensing restrictions prohibit further re-printing, values of this re-issue has risen with demand in recent years.

	MT
Complete Boxed Set (324):	65.00
(See 1951 Bowman for checklist.)	

1986 Card Collectors Company Mickey Mantle Ad Cards

This issue of collectors cards was made available as a premium by CCC; one card was given away with each $10 worth of other merchandise purchased. The 2-1/2" x 3-1/2" cards are miniature versions of 10 different 8" x 10" pictures of the star which could be purchased in autographed form from CCC. Fronts have full color photos, black-and-white backs advertise the signed photos for sale at $15 each.

		MT
Complete Set (10):		24.00
Common Card:		3.00
1	Mickey Mantle ('49 Bowman-style card)	3.00
2	Mickey Mantle ('51 Bowman reprint)	3.00
3	Mickey Mantle ('53 Bowman reprint)	3.00
4	Mickey Mantle (seated pose)	3.00
5	Mickey Mantle (in long-sleeve jersey)	3.00
6	Mickey Mantle (batting pose - lefty)	3.00
7	Mickey Mantle (batting pose - righty)	3.00
8	Mickey Mantle (leaning on bat)	3.00
9	Mickey Mantle (waist-up portrait)	3.00
10	Mickey Mantle (portrait - coach)	3.00

1987 Card Collectors Company Mark McGwire Ad Cards

This issue of collectors cards was made available as a premium by CCC; one card was given away with each $10 worth of other merchandise purchased. The 2-1/2" x 3-1/2" cards are miniature versions of 10 different 8" x 10" pictures of the star which could be purchased in autographed form from CCC. Fronts have full color photos, black-and-white backs advertise the signed photos for sale at $15 each.

		MT
Complete Set (10):		18.00
Common Card:		2.50
1	Mark McGwire (portrait by Eisenstein)	2.50
2	Mark McGwire (fist in glove)	2.50
3	Mark McGwire (on deck)	2.50
4	Mark McGwire (kneeling)	2.50
5	Mark McGwire (batting, arms extended)	2.50
6	Mark McGwire (batting follow-through)	2.50
7	Mark McGwire (throwing)	2.50
8	Mark McGwire (fielding)	2.50
9	Mark McGwire (at bat rack)	2.50
10	Mark McGwire (bats on shoulder)	2.50

1987 Card Collectors 1952 Bowman Reprint

One of several high-quality reprints of popular vintage card sets was this 252-piece re-issue of the 1952 Bowman gum cards. Reproduced slightly larger than the originals, in 2-3/16" x 3-1/4" size, the CCC version has a glossy "Diamond Vue" coating on front. Backs have a reprint line printed at the bottom. The set was sold in a colorful box with an original retail price of $24.95. Because licensing restrictions prohibit further re-printing, the value has risen on this re-issue in recent years.

	MT
Complete Boxed Set (252):	175.00
(See 1952 Bowman for checklist.)	

1989 Card Collectors Gregg Jefferies

"The Wonder Kid" is pictured in this collectors' issue in 16 color photos from boyhood into 1989. Cards are 2-1/2" x 3-1/2" and have a glossy front surface. The borderless photos on front have no extraneous graphics. Black-and-white backs identify the front photo and have an ad for the sponsor. The Jefferies set was issued as a premium by Card Collectors' Co., which also retailed the issue at $10 per set.

		MT
Complete Set (16):		3.00
Common Player:		.25
1	Gregg Jefferies (Age 3)	.25
2	Gregg Jefferies (Youth baseball)	.25
3	Gregg Jefferies (3B George's Place)	.25
4	Gregg Jefferies (Age 8)	.25
5	Gregg Jefferies (Age 9)	.25
6	Gregg Jefferies (Age 10)	.25
7	Gregg Jefferies (High school)	.25
8	Gregg Jefferies (Age 6)	.25
9	Gregg Jefferies (Age 5)	.25
10	Gregg Jefferies (1985 draft pick)	.25
11	Gregg Jefferies (Age 15)	.25
12	Gregg Jefferies (Batting cage)	.25
13	Gregg Jefferies (Swing sequence)	.25
14	Gregg Jefferies (Swing sequence)	.25
15	Gregg Jefferies (Swing sequence)	.25
16	Gregg Jefferies (Swing sequence)	.25

1990 Card Collectors Dave Justice

The star outfielder is pictured in this collectors' issue in 16 color and black-and-white photos from boyhood up. Cards are 2-1/2" x 3-1/2" and have a glossy front surface. The red-bordered photos on front have no extraneous graphics. Black-and-white backs identify the front photo and have an ad for the Card Collectors' Co., which retailed the issue at $10 per set.

		MT
Complete Set (16):		3.00
Common Card:		.25
1	Dave Justice (Age 4)	.25
2	Dave Justice (Sunday best)	.25
3	Dave Justice (Kindergarten)	.25
4	Dave Justice (Party time)	.25
5	Dave Justice (1st Grade)	.25
6	Dave Justice (First Communion)	.25
7	Dave Justice (4th Grade)	.25
8	Dave Justice (Age 10)	.25
9	Dave Justice (Ohio champs)	.25
10	Dave Justice (Football)	.25
11	Dave Justice (3rd Grade)	.25
12	Dave Justice (Senior picture)	.25
13	Dave Justice (Age 16)	.25
14	Dave Justice (Legion ball)	.25
15	Dave Justice (Basketball)	.25
16	Dave Justice (Thomas Moore College)	.25

1990 Card Collectors Darryl Strawberry

"The Straw Man" is pictured in this collectors' issue in 16 color and black-and-white photos from boyhood into 1990. Cards are 2-1/2" x 3-1/2" and have a glossy front surface. The borderless photos on front have no extraneous graphics. Black-and-white backs identify the front photo and have an ad for the sponsor. The Strawberry set was issued as a premium by Card Collectors' Co., which also retailed the issue at $10 per set.

		MT
Complete Set (16):		3.00
Common Card:		.25
1	Darryl Strawberry (Age 7)	.25
2	Darryl Strawberry (Junior high football jersey)	.25
3	Darryl Strawberry (High school outfielder)	.25
4	Darryl Strawberry (1980)	.25
5	Darryl Strawberry (Regent t-shirt)	.25

6	Darryl Strawberry (Coat and tie)	.25
7	Darryl Strawberry (HS basketball, dribbling)	.25
8	Darryl Strawberry (HS basketball, shooting)	.25
9	Darryl Strawberry (Crenshaw Cougars HS)	.25
10	Darryl Strawberry (Cap and gown)	.25
11	Darryl Strawberry (Suit and tie)	.25
12	Darryl Strawberry (Holding bat)	.25
13	Darryl Strawberry (TV interview)	.25
14	Darryl Strawberry (N.Y. Mets)	.25
15	Darryl Strawberry (Family portrait)	.25
16	Darryl Strawberry ("Straw" haircut)	.25

1991 Card Collectors Dwight Gooden

"The Doc" is pictured in this collectors' issue in 16 photos from boyhood into 1991. Cards are 2-1/2" x 3-1/2" and have a glossy front surface. The borderless photos on front have no extraneous graphics. Black-and-white backs identify the front photo and have an ad for the sponsor. The Gooden set was issued as a premium for Card Collectors' Co., which also retailed the issue at $10 per set.

		MT
Complete Set (16):		3.00
Common Player:		.25
		.25
1	Dwight Gooden (Age 2)	.25
2	Dwight Gooden (Age 2)	.25
3	Dwight Gooden (5th grade)	.25
4	Dwight Gooden (1971 w/niece)	.25
5	Dwight Gooden (2nd grade)	.25
6	Dwight Gooden (6th grade)	.25
7	Dwight Gooden (team jacket)	.25
8	Dwight Gooden (Little League)	.25
9	Dwight Gooden (13 years old)	.25
10	Dwight Gooden (Belmont Heights team photo)	.25
11	Dwight Gooden (Belmont Heights Cubs team photo)	.25
12	Dwight Gooden (Belmont Heights Reds team photo)	.25
13	Dwight Gooden (High school team photo)	.25
14	Dwight Gooden (All-Star Game jacket)	.25
15	Dwight Gooden (Tuxedo)	.25
16	Dwight Gooden (Family portrait)	.25

1991 Card Collectors T205 Reprint

One of several high-quality reprints of popular vintage card sets was this 208-piece re-issue of the 1911 T205 Gold Borders, complete with most variations. Reproduced in the original 1-7/16" x 2-5/8" size, the CCC version has a glossy "Diamond Vue" coating on front. Backs have the word "REPRINT" printed toward the bottom. The set was sold in a colorful box with an original retail price of $29.95. A subset of 18 Hall of Famer reprints was available for $5.95. Because licensing restrictions prohibit further reprints, value has risen with demand in recent years.

	MT
Complete Boxed Set (208):	95.00
Hall of Famer Subset:	6.00
(See 1911 T205 Gold Border for checklist.)	

1991 Card Guard Griffey Promo

This card was issued to promote the sale of plastic card holders endorsed by Ken Griffey Jr. Front of the 2-1/2" x 3-1/2" card has a photo of Junior in a tuxedo holding his 1989 Upper Deck rookie card in a Card Guard plastic. His facsimile autograph is printed in gold. Black-and-white backs have information about the product.

	MT
Ken Griffey Jr.	1.00

1991 Cardboard Dreams

This collectors' issue was ostensibly issued to promote the sports art of Harry Woolery. The 3-1/2" x 2-1/2" horizontal format cards feature a mix of color portrait and action paintings on the front. Backs are printed in blue and contain a cartoon and career highlights. Most of the players included are baseball stars, but several other sports were also represented.

		MT
Complete Set (16):		5.00
Common Players:		.25
1	Willie Mays	.25
2	Nolan Ryan	.50
3	Tony Gwynn	.25
4	Wayne Gretzky	.25
5	Jose Canseco (w/ Madonna)	.40
6	Ken Griffey Jr.	1.00
7	Bo Jackson	.25
8	Michael Jordan	1.00
9	Mickey Mantle	1.00
10	Sandy Koufax, Nolan Ryan	.25
11	Frank Thomas, David Justice	.25
12	Brett Hull	.25
13	Ted Williams, Joe DiMaggio	.35
14	Barry Sanders	.25
15	Larry Bird, Magic Johnson	.25
16	Dan Marino	.25

1995 Cardtoons

Just about everything related to baseball comes in for the jab in this set of parody cards. Players, team, attitudes, owners, mascots, Hall of Famers, announcers and the business of baseball are all panned. Besides a base set of 95 cards, there are several insert issues and send-away prizes. Cards are standard 2-1/2" x 3-1/2" with easily identifiable caricatures on front and sophomoric humor on the back. The cards make a point of stating they are parodies and not licensed either by the players or Major League Baseball. While they carry a 1993 copyright date, the cards were not issued until 1995.

		MT
Complete Set (95):		15.00
Common Card:		.25
1	Hey Abbott	.25
2	Robin Adventura	.25
3	Roberto Alamode	.40
4	Don Battingly	1.00
5	Cow Belle	.90
6	Jay Bellhop	.25
7	Fowl Boggs	.40
8	Treasury Bonds	.60
9	True Brett	1.25
10	Wild Pitch Mitch	.25
11	Balou's Brothers (Felipe Balou, Moises Balou)	.25
12	Charlie Bustle	2.00
13	Brett Butter	.25
14	Rambo Canseco	.50
15	Roberto Cementie	4.00
16	Roger Clemency	.60
17	Will Clock	.40
18	David Clone	.25
19	Tom Clowning	.25
20	Mr. Club	.50
21	Joe Crater	.25
22	Doolin' Daulton	.25
23	Chili Dog Davis	.25
24	Doug Drawback	.25
25	Dennis Excellency	.25
26	Silly Fanatic	.25
27	Wand Gonzalez	.50
28	Amazing Grace	.40
29	Tom Grapevine	.25
30	Marquis Gruesome	.25
31	Homerin' Hank	2.00
32	Kevin Happier	.25
33	Pete Harness	.25
34	Charlie Haze	.25
35	Egotisticky Henderson	.40
36	Sayanora Infielder	.25
37	Snoozin' Ted & Tarzan Jane	.25
38	Cloud Johnson	.35
39	Sandy K-Fax	1.50
40	The Say What Kid	2.00
41	Tommy Lasagna	.25
42	Greg Maddogs	1.25
43	Stamp the Man	1.00
44	Mark McBash	5.00
45	Fred McGruff	.40
46	Mount Mick	5.00
47	Pat Moustache	.25
48	Ozzie Myth	1.25
49	Bob Nukesbury	.25
50	Reggie October	.60
51	Doctor OK	.25
52	Rafael Palmist	.40
53	Lose Piniella	.25
54	Vince Poleman	.25
55	Charlie Puff	.25
56	Rob Quibble	.25
57	Darryl Razzberry	.30
58	Cal Ripkenwinkle	4.00
59	Budge Rodriguez	.50
60	Ryne Sandbox	1.00
61	Steve Saxophone	.25
62	Harry Scary	.25
63	Scary Sheffield	.35
64	Ruben Siesta	.25
65	Dennis Smartinez	.25
66	Lee Smite	.25
67	Ken Spiffey Jr.	5.00
68	Nails Spikestra	.25
69	The Splendid Spinner	2.00
70	Toad Stottlemyre	.25
71	Raging Tartabull	.25
72	Robbery Thompson	.25
73	Alan Trampoline	.25
74	Monster Truk	.25
75	Shawon Tungsten	.25
76	Tony Twynn	.75
77	Andy Van Tyke	.25
78	Derrick Ventriloquist	.25
79	Frank Violin	.25
80	Rap Winfielder	.60
81	Robinhood Yount	.60
82	Swift Justice	.35
83	Brat Saberhagen	.25
84	Mike Pizazz	1.50
85	Andres Colorado	.25
86	Money Bagswell	.60
87	Video Nomo	1.50
88	Out of the Park	.35
89	Tim Wallet	.25
90	Checklist	.13
91	Greenback Jack	.25
92	Mighty Matt Power Hitter	.30
93	Frankenthomas	3.00
94	Neon Peon Slanders	.50
95	Just Air Jordan	4.00
---	Replacement Card No. 1 (Redeemable for "Cardtoons Annual Awards" set with payment of $26.95)	.13
---	Replacement Card No. 2 (Redeemable for Cardtoons binder and plastic sheets with payment of $18.95.)	.13
---	Replacement card No. 3 (Redeemable for Cardtoons phone card set of four with payment of $39.95.)	.13

> The election of former players to the Hall of Fame does not always have an immediate upward effect on card prices. The hobby market generally has done a good job of predicting those inductions and adjusting values over the course of several years.

1995 Cardtoons Awards Replacement Set

This set was available via a mail-in offer for $26.95.

		MT
Complete Set (8):		12.50
Common Card:		2.00
R1	No Ball Peace Prize	2.00
R2	Forrest Grump	2.00
R3	Most Virtous Player	2.00
R4	Golden Glove Award	2.00
R5	Comdown Player of the Year	2.00
R6	Corkville Slugger	2.00
R7	Can't Get No Relief	2.00
R8	1994 World Series Champ	2.00

> Player names in *Italic* type indicate a rookie card.

1995 Cardtoons Big Bang Bucks

This insert set lampoons baseball's top 20 salaried players. Fronts resemble U.S. currency overprinted with gold foil in denominations of five, six and seven million. A player caricature portrait is in color at center of the 3-1/2" x 2-1/2" card. Backs give the player's salary history and rationale for his being overpaid. A statement on back says the cards are intended to be a parody and that they are not licensed by MLB or the players' union. The cards are numbered with the "BB" prefix.

		MT
Complete Set (20):		48.00
Common Card:		2.00
1	Treasury Bonds	3.00
2	Sayanora Infielder	2.00
3	Cal Ripkenwinkle	4.00
4	Bobby Bonus	2.00
5	Joe Crater	2.00
6	Kirby Plunkit	3.00
7	David Clone	2.00
8	Ken Spiffey, Jr.	5.00
9	Ruben Siesta	2.00
10	Greg Maddogs	4.00
11	Mark McBash	5.00
12	Rafael Palmist	2.00
13	Roberto Alamode	2.00
14	Greenback Jack	2.00
15	Raging Tartabull	2.00
16	Jimmy Kiwi	2.00
17	Roger Clemency	2.50
18	Rambo Canseco	2.00
19	Tom Grapevine	2.00
20	John Smileyface	2.00

1995 Cardtoons Field of Greed Puzzle Set

These nine-cards are inserts which form a "Field of Greed" picture when the individual cards are aligned. Fronts have 1/9th of the cartoon puzzle, backs have a history of baseball's recent labor problems. Cards have an "FOG" prefix to their number.

		MT
Complete Set (9):		1.50
Common Card:		.20
1	1972 Strike	.25
2	1973 Lockout	.25
3	1976 Lockout	.25
4	1980 Strike	.25
5	1981 Strike	.25
6	1985 Strike	.25
7	1990 Lockout	.25
8	1994 Strike	.25
9	Future Problems	.25

1995 Cardtoons Grand Slam Foils

This insert set utilizes foil printing technology to give a high-tech look to the caricatures of major leaguers. Fronts have cartoon parodies of the players, backs attempt to be humorous. A note on back says the cards are not licensed by either the players or Major League Baseball. Cards are numbered with an "F" prefix.

		MT
Complete Set (10):		28.00
Common Player:		2.00
1	Bo Action	2.50
2	Andre Awesome	2.00
3	Bobby Bonus	2.00
4	Steve Bravery	2.00
5	Carlton Fist	2.50
6	E.T. McGee	2.00
7	Kirby Plunkit	3.00
8	Jose Rheostat	2.00
9	Sir Noble Ryan	8.00
10	Day-Glo Sabo	2.00

1995 Cardtoons Politics in Baseball

This insert sets takes a poke at the perceived problems of baseball during the 1994-95 strike. Fronts have cartoons, backs have pointed commentary. Cards are numbered with the "S" prefix.

		MT
Complete Set (11):		3.00
Common Card:		.15
1	Pledge of Allegiance	.15
2	The Wave	.15
3	Slick Willie	1.50
4	Umpires Convention	.15
5	The Slide	.15
6	SH-H-H-H-H-H-H	.15
7	Throwing Out the First Contract	.15
8	Babe Rush	1.00
9	Hot Prospect	.15
10	Let's Play Ball	.15
11	Role Model	.15

1992 Carl's Jr. Padres

For the fifth consecutive year the San Diego Padres issued a card set in conjunction with the Jr. Padres program. Carl's Jr., a fast food chain, began sponsoring the set in 1991. The set contains 25 cards and was available in either nine-card perforated sheets or precut. At 2-9/16" x 3-9/16" the cards are slightly larger than current standard. Player photos feature an All-Star Game logo in the lower-right corner. On the white border, the player's name and position are printed in dark blue beneath the photo. The team name is in light brown above the photo. On back, the player's stats, career highlights and biographical data are printed in dark blue. The unnumbered cards are checklisted here in alphabetical order.

		MT
Complete Set (25):		9.00
Common Player:		.25
(1)	Larry Anderson	.25
(2)	Oscar Azocar	.25
(3)	Andy Benes	.80
(4)	Dann Bilardello	.25
(5)	Jerald Clark	.25
(6)	Tony Fernandez	.25
(7)	Tony Gwynn	3.00
(8)	Greg Harris	.25
(9)	Bruce Hurst	.25
(10)	Darrin Jackson	.25
(11)	Craig Lefferts	.25
(12)	Mike Maddux	.25
(13)	Fred McGriff	.90
(14)	Jose Melendez	.25
(15)	Randy Myers	.35
(16)	Greg Riddoch	.25
(17)	Rich Rodriguez	.25
(18)	Benito Santiago	.25
(19)	Gary Sheffield	.90
(20)	Craig Shipley	.30
(21)	Kurt Stillwell	.25
(22)	Tim Teufel	.25
(23)	Kevin Ward	.25
(24)	Ed Whitson	.25
(25)	All-Star logo	.25

1992 Carlson Travel 1982 Brewers

The team's American League Championship season of 1982 was commemorated a decade later with this card set given away at a Brewers promotional date. The cards were sponsored by Carlson Travel and United Airlines, whose logos appear on the front of the cards, along with Channel 6 television, whose logo is on the back. Fronts feature game-action photos of the '82 Brewers, borderless at top and sides. Beneath the photo is a thin gold stripe, then a blue stripe with the player's name and position in white. A red, white and blue 1982 World Series logo appears in the lower-left corner. Backs are printed in blue, and include 1982 stats and a summary of the player's season. Player cards are numbered by uniform number in the upper-left.

		MT
Complete Set (31):		9.00
Common Player:		.25
4	Paul Molitor	2.00
5	Ned Yost	.25
7	Don Money	.25
10	Bob McClure	.25
11	Ed Romero	.25
13	Roy Howell	.25
15	Cecil Cooper	.25
16	Marshall Edwards	.25
17	Jim Gantner	.25
19	Robin Yount	3.00
20	Gorman Thomas	.25
21	Don Sutton	.75
22	Charlie Moore	.25
23	Ted Simmons	.25
24	Ben Oglivie	.25
27	Pete Ladd	.25
29	Mark Brouhard	.25
30	Moose Haas	.25
32	Harvey Kuenn	.25
33	Doc Medich	.25
34	Rollie Fingers	.75
41	Jim Slaton	.25
46	Jerry Augustine	.25
47	Dwight Bernard	.25
48	Mike Caldwell	.25
50	Pete Vuckovich	.25
---	Coaches (Pat Dobson, Larry Haney, Ron Hansen, Cal McLish, Harry Warner)	.25
---	Team card	.25
---	Bernie Brewer (mascot)	.25
---	Post-season Rally	.25
---	$50 travel coupon	.25

1992 Cartwright's Aces

Top players of 1992 are featured on these sheets issued in conjunction with Cartwright's hobby magazine. Each 8-3/4" x 12" sheet has a large Aces logo and four 2-1/2" x 3-1/2" cards featuring the paintings of Thomas Chung. Backs repeat the color Aces logo and have a few words about the player.

		MT
Complete Set (8):		8.00
Common Player:		.50
1	Darryl Strawberry	.50
2	Nolan Ryan	1.50
3	Frank Thomas	1.00
4	Ken Griffey Jr.	2.00
5	Tom Glavine	.50
6	Cal Ripken Jr.	1.50
7	Roger Clemens	.80
8	Ryne Sandberg Mark McGwire	.80

1992 Cartwright's Players' Choice

This set was issued as an insert in the pages of Cartwright's sports collectors magazine, which was one of many to spring up in the early 1990s to circumvent licensing restrictions by wrapping a magazine around popular players' cards. Cards were printed nine per 8-3/4" x 12" sheet. Individual cards measure the standard 2-1/2" x 3-1/2" when cut from the sheets. Fronts have color photos with gold-foil borders for established stars and silver borders for young players. Backs are in color with a few biographical details and career highlights.

		MT
Complete Set (72):		15.00
Common Player:		.25
	GOLD SERIES	
1	Jose Canseco	.35
2	Darryl Strawberry	.25
3	Dave Justice	[illegible]
4	Will Clark	.30
5	Ken Griffey Jr.	2.00
6	Kirby Puckett	.50
7	Barry Bonds	.50
8	Nolan Ryan	1.50
9	Benito Santiago	.25
10	Dwight Gooden	.25
11	Lenny Dykstra	.25
12	Steve Avery	.25
13	Eric Davis	.25
14	Lonnie Smith	.25
15	Chris Sabo	.25
16	Frank Thomas	1.00
17	Robin Ventura	.30
18	Scott Erickson	.25
19	Tom Glavine	.25
20	Cal Ripken Jr.	1.50
21	Roger Clemens	.50
22	Cecil Fielder	.25
23	Rickey Henderson	.35
24	Tom Seaver	.30
25	Bobby Bonilla	.25
26	Bo Jackson	.30
27	Ryne Sandberg	.50
28	Tony Gwynn	.50
29	Fred McGriff	.25
30	Deion Sanders	.25
31	Ben McDonald	.25
32	Ron Gant	.25
33	Ozzie Smith	.50
34	Roberto Alomar	.35
35	Mark McGwire	2.00
36	Mickey Mantle	2.00
37		
38		
39		
40		
41		
42		
43	Nolan Ryan	1.50
44	Jose Canseco	.35
45	Babe Ruth	1.50
	SILVER SERIES	
1	Mike Kelly	.25
2	Brien Taylor	.25
3	Rico Brogna	.25
4	Jeff Juden	.25
5	Frankie Rodriguez	.25
6	Bret Boone	.25
7	Ryan Klesko	.25
8	Wil Cordero	.25
9	Chipper Jones	1.00
10	Todd Hundley	.25
11	Pedro Martinez	.40
12	Mark Wohlers	.25
13	Derek Bell	.25
14	Kenny Lofton	.25
15	Reggie Sanders	.25
16	Eric Lindros	.25
17	Todd Van Poppel	.25
18	Jim Thome	.25
19	Phil Nevin	.25
20	Brian Jordan	.25
21	Joey Hamilton	.25
22	Mike Mussina	.40
23	Royce Clayton	.25
24	Dave Fleming	.25
25	Andy Stankiewicz	.25
26	Mike Piazza	1.00
27	David McCarty	.25

1992 Cartwright's Rookie Series

This set was issued as an insert in the pages of Cartwright's sports collectors magazine, which was one of many to spring up in the early 1990s to circumvent licensing restrictions by wrapping a magazine around popular players' cards. Cards were printed nine per 8-3/4" x 12" sheet. Individual cards measure the standard 2-1/2" x 3-1/2" when cut from the sheets. Fronts have color photos with black frames and silver-foil borders. Backs are in color with a few biographical details, stats and career highlights.

		MT
Complete Set (9):		2.50
Common Player:		.25
1	Jeff Bagwell	.65
2	Phil Plantier	.25
3	Chuck Knoblauch	.35
4	Juan Guzman	.25
5	Ray Lankford	.25
6	Ivan Rodriguez	.45
7	Mike Timlin	.25
8	Mike Stanton	.25
9	Chuck McElroy	.25

1992 Cartwright's Tobacco Series

This series was one of several produced by Cartwright's in conjunction with its sports collectors magazine in the early 1990s. The 2" x 3-1/4" cards have pastel player art and earth-tone borders. A facsimile signature is in black to identify the player. Backs have player name, nickname, career summary and copyright. The cards were printed on a sheet inserted in the Winter, 1992, premiere issue.

		MT
Complete Set (6):		5.00
Common Player:		.50
1	Lou Gehrig	1.00
2	Ty Cobb	1.00
3	Joe Jackson	2.00
4	Ed Plank	.50
5	Christy Mathewson	.75
6	Joe Kelley	.50

1985 CBS Radio Game of the Week

To promote its Game of the Week radio broadcasts, CBS issued a six-card set picturing network announcers, including Hall of Famer Johnny Bench. The cards, standard 2-1/2" x 3-1/2" format, were sent to CBS affiliate stations only. Fronts of the full-color cards picture the announcers in CBS Radio Sports baseball-style uniforms.

		MT
Complete Set (6):		30.00
Common Player:		2.00
(1)	Johnny Bench	15.00
(2)	Brent Musburger	9.00
(3)	Lindsey Nelson	5.00
(4)	John Rooney	2.00
(5)	Dick Stockton	3.00
(6)	Bill White	5.00

1986 CBS Radio Game of the Week

For the second consecutive year, CBS Radio Sports issued a five-card set featuring announcers used by the network for the Game of the Week and post-season broadcasts. The cards, packaged in a custom-designed wax wrapper, were sent to CBS radio affiliates as a promotion. The color cards measure 2-1/2" x 3-1/2".

		MT
Complete Set (5):		25.00
Common Player:		2.00
(1)	Sparky Anderson	10.00
(2)	Jack Buck	6.00
(3)	Howard David	2.00
(4)	Ernie Harwell	7.00
(5)	Ted Robinson	2.00

1987 Champion Phillies

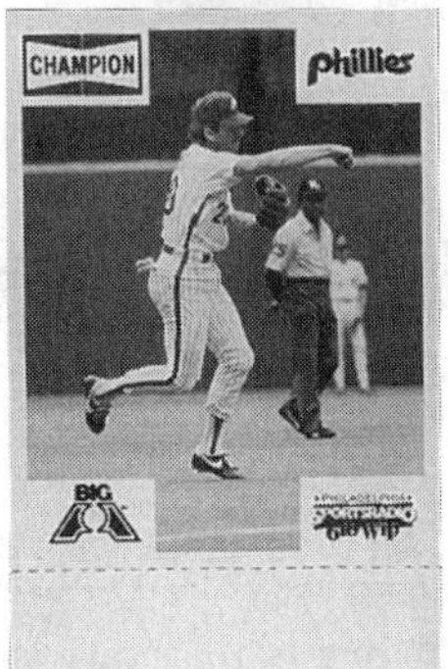

This four card set is interesting in that the players are not identified on the card fronts or backs. The full-color cards, which measure 2-3/4" x 4-5/16", were produced by the Champion Spark Plug Co. as part of a contest held at participating Big A, Car Quest and Pep Boys auto parts stores. Entrants were advised to return the scratch-off coupon portion of the card for a chance to win a Blackbird Racer. Each card contains a scratch-off portion which may have contained an instant prize. Each card can be found with either a Big A, Car Quest or Pep Boys logo in the lower left corner on the card front. The contest was also sponsored in part by the Philadelphia Phillies and radio station WIP.

		MT
Complete Set (4):		15.00
Common Player:		1.00
(1)	Von Hayes (glove on knee)	1.00
(2)	Steve Jeltz (#30 on uniform)	1.00
(3)	Juan Samuel (laying on base)	1.00
(4)	Mike Schmidt (making throw)	12.00

1981 Champions of American Sport

From June, 1981, through June, 1982, Phillip Morris and Miller Beer sponsored a traveling exhibition of sporting art and artifacts from The National Portrait Gallery and the Smithsonian Institution. In conjunction with the exhibitions in Washington, D.C., Chicago, Los Angeles and New York, an 18-card souvenir set was issued featuring many of the top athletes featured in the exhibits. The set was released in the form of an 8" x 11" eight-page booklet. Inside were two sheets of nine cards each. The perforated cards could be separated into individual cards of 2-1/2" x 3-3/4" dimensions. Fronts featured colored photos or artwork, backs had quotes about the athlete and stats. The unnumbered cards are checklisted here alphabetically.

		MT
Complete Set, Booklet:		60.00
Complete Set, Singles (18):		40.00
Common Player:		2.00
(1)	Muhammad Ali	6.00
(2)	Arthur Ashe	2.00
(3)	Peggy Fleming	2.00
(4)	A.J. Foyt	2.00
(5)	Eric Heiden	2.00
(6)	Bobby Hull	4.00
(7)	Sandy Koufax	6.00
(8)	Joe Louis	3.00
(9)	Bob Mathias	2.00
(10)	Willie Mays	6.00
(11)	Joe Namath	4.00
(12)	Jack Nicklaus	3.00
(13)	Knute Rockne	2.00
(14)	Bill Russell	4.00
(15)	Jim Ryun	2.00
(16)	Willie Shoemaker	2.00
(17)	Casey Stengel	2.00
(18)	Johnny Unitas	2.00

1988 Chef Boyardee

This uncut sheet features 12 each American and National League players. Color player portraits are printed beneath a red, white and blue "1988 1st Annual Collector's Edition" header. The player name, team and position appear beneath his photo. Card backs are printed in blue on red and include biographical information, stats and career highlights. The set was produced by American Home Food Products for distribution via a mail-in offer involving proofs of purchase from the company's Chef Boyardee products. Photos, licensed only by the players' union, have had uniform logos airbrushed off.

		MT
Complete Set, Sheet:		22.00
Complete Set, Singles (24):		15.00
Common Player:		.50
1	Mark McGwire	2.50
2	Eric Davis	.50
3	Jack Morris	.50
4	George Bell	.50
5	Ozzie Smith	.90
6	Tony Gwynn	1.00
7	Cal Ripken, Jr.	2.00
8	Todd Worrell	.50
9	Larry Parrish	.50
10	Gary Carter	.50
11	Ryne Sandberg	.90
12	Keith Hernandez	.50
13	Kirby Puckett	1.00
14	Mike Schmidt	1.00
15	Frank Viola	.50
16	Don Mattingly	1.50
17	Dale Murphy	.65
18a	Andre Dawson (1987 team is Expos)	.75
18b	Andre Dawson (1987 team is Cubs)	.75
19	Mike Scott	.50
20	Rickey Henderson	.75
21	Jim Rice	.65
22	Wade Boggs	.75
23	Roger Clemens	1.00
24	Fernando Valenzuela	.50

1996 Chevrolet/Geo Pirates Team Sheet

Western Pennsylvania Chevy/Geo dealers sponsored this issue of a team card set given away at the May 12 game vs. the Giants. The individual 2-1/4" x 3-1/4" cards are perforated for removal from the sheet. Individual cards have a color player photo at center with team name and '96 logo at top in a red stripe and the player name and Chevy logo at bottom in an orange stripe. Backs are in black-and-white. The cards are checklisted here in alphabetical order.

		MT
Complete Set, Uncut Sheet:		9.00
Complete Set, Singles:		7.00
Common Player:		.25
(1)	Jay Bell	.35
(2)	Cam Bonifay	.25
(3)	Jacob Brumfield	.25
(4)	Jason Christiansen	.25
(5)	Dave Clark	.25
(6)	Steve Cooke	.25
(7)	Francisco Cordova	.40
(8)	Danny Darwin	.25
(9)	John Ericks	.25
(10)	Carlos Garcia	.35
(11)	Lee Hancock	.25
(12)	Charlie Hayes	.35
(13)	Mark Johnson	.25
(14)	Jason Kendall	.45
(15)	Jim Leyland	.25
(16)	Jeff King	.35
(17)	Mike Kingery	.25
(18)	Nelson Liriano	.25
(19)	Jon Lieber	.25
(20)	Al Martin	.35
(21)	Orlando Merced	.35
(22)	Dan Miceli	.25
(23)	Denny Neagle	.40
(24)	Keith Osik	.25
(25)	Steve Parris	.25
(26)	Dan Plesac	.25
(27)	Zane Smith	.25
(28)	Paul Wagner	.25
(29)	John Wehner	.25
(30)	Pirate Parrot (mascot)	.25

1992 Chevron Giants Hall of Fame Pins

This series of card/pin combinations was distributed by Chevron gas stations honoring San Francisco Giants enshrined in baseball's Hall of Fame. Fronts of the 2-1/2" x 5" cards have a color player photo in an oval frame with an orange border. The player name and team logo are in a large white strip at bottom. Black-and-white backs have a small player portrait photo, some personal data, career highlights and pictures of the pins in the set. An enameled pin, about 1-1/8" x 1-1/4", with a representation of the player in action, is attached at the bottom of the card.

		MT
Complete Set (3):		15.00
Common Player:		4.00
24	Willie Mays	8.00
36	Gaylord Perry	4.00
44	Willie McCovey	4.00

1998 Chex All-Star Fotoballs

More than two dozen top players were available on Fotoballs issued in conjunction with a mail-in redemption offer on Chex cereals. Coupons on specially marked boxes could be sent in with two proofs of purchase and $1 for each ball ordered. The offer was limited to three balls per family or address. The balls feature a color player portrait with his name and team identification on one panel. The opposite panel has a sponsor's logo. The unnumbered balls are listed here in alphabetical order. The checklist is remarkably similar to that of the 1997 Wheaties Fotoball issue.

		MT
Complete Set (26):		
Common Player:		
(1)	Jeff Bagwell	6.00
(2)	Andy Benes	3.00
(3)	Barry Bonds	5.00
(4)	Ellis Burks	3.00
(5)	Ken Caminiti	3.00
(6)	David Cone	3.00
(7)	Alex Fernandez	3.00
(8)	Andres Galarraga	3.00
(9)	Juan Gonzalez	6.50
(10)	Ken Griffey Jr.	12.00
(11)	Tony Gwynn	7.50
(12)	Chipper Jones	8.00
(13)	David Justice	4.00
(14)	Greg Maddux	8.00
(15)	Mark McGwire	12.00
(16)	Mike Mussina	3.00
(17)	Hideo Nomo	5.00
(18)	Mike Piazza	8.00
(19)	Cal Ripken Jr.	10.00
(20)	Mariano Rivera	3.00
(21)	Alex Rodriguez	10.00
(22)	Ivan Rodriguez	5.00
(23)	John Smoltz	3.00
(24)	Frank Thomas	7.50
(25)	Mo Vaughn	3.00
(26)	Bernie Williams	3.00

1985 Chicago Cubs Playing Cards

A regular 52-card deck plus two jokers comprise this set produced by long-time

Cubs broadcaster Jack Brickhouse, whose photo and trademark phrase "Hey Hey!" are featured on the back of each card. Card fronts have a black-and-white photo with player (s) names and a date beneath. Traditional suit and value marking of a playing card deck are included in the corners of the 2-1/2" x 3-1/2" round-cornered cards. The cards are arranged in roughly chronological order.

		MT
Complete Set (54):		8.00
Common Player:		.10
AH	Jack Brickhouse	.10
2H	1876 Champions (Team composite photo)	.10
3H	Cap Anson	.10
4H	Joe Tinker, Johnny Evers, Frank Chance, Harry Steinfeldt	.25
5H	Ed Reulbach	.10
6H	Mordecai Brown	.10
7H	Jim Vaughn	.10
8H	Joe McCarthy	.10
9H	Jimmy Cooney	.10
10H	Rogers Hornsby	.25
JH	Hack Wilson	.10
QH	"Homers Row" (Hack Wilson, Babe Ruth, Lou Gehrig)	.25
KH	Babe Ruth ("Called the Shot")	1.00
AC	Lon Warneke	.10
2C	Augie Galan	.10
3C	1935 Pennant Winning Cubs (Team photo)	.10
4C	Dizzy Dean	.25
5C	Gabby Hartnett	.10
6C	Billy Herman	.10
7C	Charlie Root	.10
8C	Charlie Grimm	.10
9C	Andy Pafko	.10
10C	Stan Hack	.10
JC	Phil Cavarretta	.10
QC	National League Champs 1945 (Team photo)	.10
KC	Bill Nicholson	.10
KD	Hank Sauer	.10
QD	Ernie Banks	1.00
JD	Sam Jones	.10
10D	Dale Long	.10
9D	Lou Boudreau	.15
8D	Don Cardwell	.10
7D	Ken Hubbs	.25
6D	Billy Williams	.15
5D	1969 Cubs - The Team That Almost Made It (Composite photo)	.10
4D	Ken Holtzman	.10
3D	Ron Santo	.15
2D	Fergie Jenkins	.20
AD	Burt Hooten (Hooton)	.10
KS	Milt Pappas	.10
QS	Rick Reuschel	.10
JS	Bill Madlock	.10
10S	Dallas Green	.10
9S	Jody Davis	.10
8S	Rick Sutcliffe	.10
7S	Jim Frey	.10
6S	Ryne Sandberg	1.00
5S	Eastern Division Champs 1984 (Team photo)	.10
4S	Bob Dernier	.10
3S	Gary Matthews	.10
2S	Keith Moreland	.10
AS	Leon Durham	.10
Joker	Ron Cey	.10
Joker	Hey Hey! and Holy Cow! (Jack Brickhouse, Harry Caray)	.10

1988 Chicago Cubs Fire Safety

This set of four oversize (approximately 3-7/8" x 5-1/2") cards was produced on a single perforated sheet for distribution to fans as part of a U.S. Forest Service fire prevention campaign. Card fronts feature color player photos framed with vertical blue and pink borders and the player's name in light blue at bottom. Team and Smokey logos flank the name while the team name is printed in red above the photo. Backs have a bit of player biography and a large cartoon fire safety message.

		MT
Complete Set (4):		7.00
Common Card:		1.00
1	Vance Law (with Smokey)	2.00
2	Vance Law (fielding)	2.00
3	Vance Law (batting)	2.00
4	Smokey the Bear	1.00

1992 1919 Chicago White Sox team issue reprints

Card dealer Greg Manning, who purchased the unique original set of 1919 White Sox team-issue cards in 1991 issued a collectors' reprint set a year later. The reprints are in 2" x 3" format, slightly larger than the originals. The cards of the banned "Black Sox" have had a black frame added around the picture and have career information and 1919 stats on back. The other cards have blank backs. A second, colorized, card of Joe Jackson was added to the reprint set. The unnumbered cards are checklisted here in alphabetical order.

		MT
Complete Set (26):		15.00
Common Player:		.50
(1)	Joe Benz	.50
(2)	Eddie Cicotte	2.00
(3)	Eddie Collins	.75
(4)	Shano Collins	.50
(5)	Charles Comiskey	.75
(6)	Dave Danforth	.50
(7)	Red Faber	.75
(8)	Happy Felsch	1.00
(9)	Chick Gandil	2.00
(10)	Kid Gleason	.50
(11)	Joe Jackson (black-and-white)	3.50
(12)	Joe Jackson (colorized)	3.00
(12)	Joe Jenkins	.50
(13)	Ted Jourdan	.50
(14)	Nemo Leibold	.50
(15)	Byrd Lynn	.50
(16)	Fred McMullin	1.00
(17)	Eddie Murphy	.50
(18)	Swede Risberg	1.00
(19)	Pants Rowland	.50
(20)	Reb Russell	.50
(21)	Ray Schalk	.75
(22)	James Scott	.50
(23)	Buck Weaver	1.50
(24)	Lefty Williams	1.00
(25)	Mellie Wolfgang	.50

1988 Chiquita Brands Billy Martin

The year of issue given is speculative and because the card can be found with different numbers on back, it was likely reissued at least once. The card was used as a promotion by Billy Martin in his role as "Sports Marketing Consultant" for the famed banana company. It was produced by Jim Bouton's Big League Cards company. The front has a color photo of Martin in a pinstriped jersey, along with the Chiquita logo. On back is personal data and a career summary.

	MT
24A447 Billy Martin	5.00

1995 Choice Marketing Ted Williams Tunnel Opening Set

These cards were produced for distribution at a luncheon in conjunction with the Dec. 15, 1995, opening of the Ted Williams Tunnel, connecting South Boston with the city's airport and running beneath Boston Harbor. The set consists of a Topps header card and a 12-card run produced by Choice Marketing. A reported 3,000 sets were produced. The Topps #9 card is in the style of the company's regular 1996 baseball card set. The other 12 cards depict work on the tunnel and Williams with various political figures connected with the construction project. Those cards are on thinner cardboard with color photos on front bordered in blue with a red pinstripe. Backs are in black-and-white.

		MT
Complete Set (13):		110.00
Common Player:		2.00
1	Ted Williams/tunnel entrance (Ted Williams)	9.00
2	Governor William F. Weld (Ted Williams)	9.00
3	The Super Scoop	2.00
4	Lt. Governor Paul Cellucci (Ted Williams)	9.00
5	(The tunnel's tubes)	2.00
6	(Federal and stats officials tour tunnel)	2.00
7	(Coffer dam)	2.00
8	(Construction crew)	2.00
9	James J. Kerasiotes, State Secretary of Transportation (Ted Williams)	9.00
9	Ted Williams (Topps header card)	50.00
10	The Tile Signing (Ted Williams)	9.00
11	(Aerial view of tunnel ramps)	2.00
12	The Ted Williams Tunnel Plaque	9.00

1990s Christian Testimonial Cards

This series of related issues is not a set in the usual hobby sense. Rather, the cards are issued individually by players in an attempt to share their Christian beliefs. In standard 2-1/2" x 3-1/2" size, the cards can be found in either a bordered or borderless format. The bordered cards appear to be the earlier issues. Fronts have color action photos or poses with the player name. Backs have player identification, personal information, a testimonial and, usually, a favorite Bible verse. Most cards have a line at bottom, "This card was printed by (player name) and is not for sale". Since the series is ongoing, this list is not complete. Cards are often found autographed.

	MT
Common Player:	2.00
Andy Benes (blue jersey - English)	2.50
Andy Benes (pinstripes - Spanish)	2.50
Shawn Boskie (Orioles)	2.00
Doug Henry (Astros)	2.00
Brian Hommel (Brewers)	2.00
Matt Mieske (Brewers)	2.00
John Olerud (Mets)	2.50
Kevin Seitzer (Brewers)	2.00
Andy Stankiewicz (Expos)	2.00
Bill Wegman (Brewers)	2.00

1994 Churchs Chicken Hometown Stars

Produced by Pinnacle Brands for distribution in the fried chicken restaurant chain, the cards were distributed in packs of four with the purchase of a nine-piece family meal or were sold separately for 69 cents. Each foil pack contained three regular cards and one card with gold foil instead of regular printing on the player's name and "Hometown Stars." Every fourth pack contains one of 10 "Show Stoppers" Dufex-process chase cards. In standard 2-1/2" x 3-1/2", the cards featured full-bleed front action photos with the Churchs logo at lower-left and the player's name at lower-right. "Hometown Stars" is printed vertically at top-left. Backs have a portrait photo at left, a career summary and 1993 and career stats. Because the cards were licensed by the Major League Baseball Players Association, but not Major League Baseball, both the front and the back photos on each card have had the uniform logos airbrushed away.

		MT
Complete Set (28):		8.00
Complete Set (Gold) (28):		15.00
Common Player:		.25
Common Player (Gold):		.35
1	Brian McRae	.25
1a	Brian McRae (gold)	.35
2	Dwight Gooden	.30
2a	Dwight Gooden (gold)	.35
3	Ruben Sierra	.25
3a	Ruben Sierra (gold)	.35
4	Greg Maddux	1.00
4a	Greg Maddux (gold)	1.50
5	Kirby Puckett	.75
5a	Kirby Puckett (gold)	1.00
6	Jeff Bagwell	.60
6a	Jeff Bagwell (gold)	.90
7	Cal Ripken, Jr.	1.50
7a	Cal Ripken, Jr. (gold)	2.50
8	Lenny Dykstra	.25
8a	Lenny Dykstra (gold)	.35
9	Tim Salmon	.50
9a	Tim Salmon (gold)	.75
10	Matt Williams	.40
10a	Matt Williams (gold)	.75
11	Roberto Alomar	.50
11a	Roberto Alomar (gold)	.75
12	Barry Larkin	.35
12a	Barry Larkin (gold)	.45
13	Roger Clemens	.50
13a	Roger Clemens (gold)	1.00
14	Mike Piazza	1.25
14a	Mike Piazza (gold)	2.00
15	Travis Fryman	.25
15a	Travis Fryman (gold)	.45
16	Ryne Sandberg	.75
16a	Ryne Sandberg (gold)	1.00
17	Robin Ventura	.35
17a	Robin Ventura (gold)	.50
18	Gary Sheffield	.50
18a	Gary Sheffield (gold)	.75
19	Carlos Baerga	.35
19a	Carlos Baerga (gold)	.65
20	Jay Bell	.25
20a	Jay Bell (gold)	.35
21	Edgar Martinez	.25
21a	Edgar Martinez (gold)	[illegible]
22	Phil Plantier	.25
22a	Phil Plantier (gold)	.35
23	Danny Tartabull	.25
23a	Danny Tartabull (gold)	.35
24	Marquis Grissom	.25
24a	Marquis Grissom (gold)	.35
25	Robin Yount	.75
25a	Robin Yount (gold)	1.25
26	Ozzie Smith	.60
26a	Ozzie Smith (gold)	.90
27	Ivan Rodriguez	.35
27a	Ivan Rodriguez (gold)	.60
28	Dante Bichette	.35
28a	Dante Bichette (gold)	.45

1994 Churchs Chicken Show Stoppers

Ten of baseball's top home run hitters are featured in this insert set. Found approximately once every four packs in the four-card packs distributed by the fried chicken chain, the cards were produced by Pinnacle Brands using its foil-printing Dufex process. A player action photo is depicted inside a home-plate shaped frame at right. "Show Stoppers" is printed vertically at left in red and yellow tones. The background merges from green at left to purple at right, with the player's name in black in a yellow-to-red rainbow effect box beneath the photo. The Churchs logo is at bottom-left. On back is a portrait photo in a light blue box. There is a description of the player's home run prowess along with gold boxes showing his 1993 homers, slugging percentage and at bat/home run ratio. The border mirrors the front's green-to-purple effect. Because the cards are not licensed by Major League Baseball, the uniform logos have been removed from both the front and back photos.

		MT
Complete Set (10):		40.00
Common Player:		1.50
1	Juan Gonzalez	5.00
2	Barry Bonds	5.00
3	Ken Griffey, Jr.	7.00
4	David Justice	4.00
5	Frank Thomas	5.00
6	Fred McGriff	3.00
7	Albert Belle	4.00
8	Joe Carter	1.50
9	Cecil Fielder	1.50
10	Mickey Tettleton	1.50

1982 Cincinnati Reds Yearbook Cards

In 1982 the Reds began a series of yearbook inserts consisting of two nine-card sheets. The 16-3/4" x 10-7/8" sheet contains 18 perforated 2-5/8" x 3-3/4" cards. Fronts have color photos wth red graphics and a white border. Backs are in black-and-white and include complete major and minor league stats. The cards are checklisted here by uniform number.

		MT
Complete Set, Sheet:		7.50
Complete Set, Singles (18):		6.00
Common Player:		.25
3	John McNamara	.25
5	Johnny Bench	3.00
13	Dave Concepcion	.40
16	Ron Oester	.25
21	Paul Householder	.25
22	Dan Driessen	.25
28	Cesar Cedeno	.25
29	Alex Trevino	.25
30	Clint Hurdle	.25
35	Frank Pastore	.25
36	Mario Soto	.25
38	Bruce Berenyi	.25
41	Tom Seaver	2.00
47	Tom Hume	.25
49	Joe Price	.25
51	Mike LaCoss	.25
---	Best in Baseball	.25
---	Riverfront Stadium	.25

1983 Cincinnati Reds Yearbook Cards

This 16-3/4" x 10-7/8" cardboard sheet was stapled into the Reds 1983 yearbook. The sheet contains 18 2-5/8" x 3-3/4" cards perforated for removal. Fronts have color game-action photos with red graphics. Backs are in black-and-white and include complete career stats. Cards are checklisted here by uniform number.

		MT
Complete Set, Sheet:		6.00
Complete Set, Singles (18):		5.00
Common Player:		.25
2	Gary Redus	.25
5	Johnny Bench	3.00
7	Russ Nixon	.25
13	Dave Concepcion	.35
16	Ron Oester	.25
20	Eddie Milner	.25
21	Paul Householder	.25
22	Dan Driessen	.25
25	Charlie Puleo	.25
28	Cesar Cedeno	.25
29	Alex Trevino	.25
32	Rich Gale	.25
35	Frank Pastore	.25
36	Mario Soto	.25
38	Bruce Berenyi	.25
47	Tom Hume	.25
49	Joe Price	.25
---	Riverfront Stadium	.25

1984 Cincinnati Reds Yearbook Cards

Once again in 1984 the Reds inserted a 16-3/4" x 11" cardboard panel into their yearbook. The sheet contains 18 cards, 2-5/8" x 3-3/4", perforated for removal. Fronts have color phots with a large red frame and white borders. Backs are in black-and-white with complete major and minor league stats. Cards are checklisted here by uniform number.

		MT
Complete Set, Sheet:		6.00
Complete Set, Singles (18):		5.00
Common Player:		.25
2	Gary Redus	.25
9	Vern Rapp	.25
11	Dann Bilardello	.25
12	Nick Esasky	.25
13	Dave Concepcion	.35
16	Ron Oester	.25
20	Eddie Milner	.25
22	Dan Driessen	.25
24	Tony Perez	1.00
26	Duane Walker	.25
34	Bill Scherrer	.25
35	Frank Pastore	.25
36	Mario Soto	.25
38	Bruce Berenyi	.25
39	Dave Parker	.45
47	Tom Hume	.25
49	Joe Price	.25
---	Bob Howsam (president)	.25

1996 Circa

This hobby-exclusive product was limited to 2,000 sequentially numbered cases. The regular-issue set has 196 player cards, including 18 top prospects and four prospects. Circa also has a 200-card parallel set called Rave which is limited to 150 sets. Each Rave card is sequentially numbered from 1-150. Two other insert sets were also produced - Access and Boss.

		MT
Complete Set (200):		25.00
Common Player:		.10
Wax Box:		40.00
1	Roberto Alomar	.75
2	Brady Anderson	.20
3	*Rocky Coppinger*	.10
4	Eddie Murray	.50
5	Mike Mussina	.75
6	Randy Myers	.10
7	Rafael Palmeiro	.25
8	Cal Ripken Jr.	2.50
9	Jose Canseco	.45
10	Roger Clemens	1.00
11	Mike Greenwell	.10
12	Tim Naehring	.10
13	John Valentin	.15
14	Mo Vaughn	.90
15	Tim Wakefield	.10
16	Jim Abbott	.10
17	Garret Anderson	.10
18	Jim Edmonds	.25
19	*Darin Erstad*	2.50
20	Chuck Finley	.10
21	Troy Percival	.10
22	Tim Salmon	.20
23	J.T. Snow	.15
24	Wilson Alvarez	.10
25	Harold Baines	.12
26	Ray Durham	.10
27	Alex Fernandez	.20
28	Tony Phillips	.15
29	Frank Thomas	1.00
30	Robin Ventura	.20
31	Sandy Alomar Jr.	.20
32	Albert Belle	.75
33	Kenny Lofton	.90
34	Dennis Martinez	.10
35	Jose Mesa	.10
36	Charles Nagy	.10
37	Manny Ramirez	1.00
37p	Manny Ramirez (overprinted "PROMOTIONAL SAMPLE")	3.00
38	Jim Thome	.50
39	Travis Fryman	.10
40	Bob Higginson	.20
41	Melvin Nieves	.10
42	Alan Trammell	.10
43	Kevin Appier	.10
44	Johnny Damon	.10
45	Keith Lockhart	.10
46	Jeff Montgomery	.10
47	Joe Randa	.10
48	Bip Roberts	.10
49	Ricky Bones	.10
50	Jeff Cirillo	.10
51	Marc Newfield	.10
52	Dave Nilsson	.10
53	Kevin Seitzer	.10
54	Ron Coomer	.10
55	Marty Cordova	.15
56	Roberto Kelly	.10
57	Chuck Knoblauch	.30
58	Paul Molitor	.65
59	Kirby Puckett	1.00
60	Scott Stahoviak	.10
61	Wade Boggs	.40
62	David Cone	.20
63	Cecil Fielder	.15
64	Dwight Gooden	.15
65	Derek Jeter	2.00
66	Tino Martinez	.30
67	Paul O'Neill	.20
68	Andy Pettitte	.90
69	Ruben Rivera	.15
70	Bernie Williams	.50
71	Geronimo Berroa	.10
72	Jason Giambi	.20
73	Mark McGwire	4.00
74	Terry Steinbach	.10
75	Todd Van Poppel	.10
76	Jay Buhner	.15
77	Norm Charlton	.10
78	Ken Griffey Jr.	4.00
79	Randy Johnson	.50
80	Edgar Martinez	.10
81	Alex Rodriguez	3.00
82	Paul Sorrento	.10
83	Dan Wilson	.10
84	Will Clark	.30
85	Kevin Elster	.10
86	Juan Gonzalez	1.50
87	Rusty Greer	.10
88	Ken Hill	.10
89	Mark McLemore	.10
90	Dean Palmer	.10
91	Roger Pavlik	.10
92	Ivan Rodriguez	.75
93	Joe Carter	.15
94	Carlos Delgado	.40
95	Juan Guzman	.10
96	John Olerud	.20
97	Ed Sprague	.10
98	Jermaine Dye	.15
99	Tom Glavine	.20
100	Marquis Grissom	.10
101	Andruw Jones	1.50
102	Chipper Jones	2.00
103	David Justice	.25
104	Ryan Klesko	.25
105	Greg Maddux	2.00
106	Fred McGriff	.40
107	John Smoltz	.25
108	Brant Brown	.10
109	Mark Grace	.25
110	Brian McRae	.10
111	Ryne Sandberg	.75
112	Sammy Sosa	1.50
113	Steve Trachsel	.10
114	Bret Boone	.10
115	Eric Davis	.12
116	Steve Gibralter	.10
117	Barry Larkin	.20
118	Reggie Sanders	.15
119	John Smiley	.10
120	Dante Bichette	.15
121	Ellis Burks	.15
122	Vinny Castilla	.10
123	Andres Galarraga	.20
124	Larry Walker	.40
125	Eric Young	.10
126	Kevin Brown	.15
127	Greg Colbrunn	.10
128	Jeff Conine	.15
129	Charles Johnson	.15
130	Al Leiter	.12
131	Gary Sheffield	.40
132	Devon White	.12
133	Jeff Bagwell	1.25
134	Derek Bell	.15
135	Craig Biggio	.20
136	Doug Drabek	.10
137	Brian Hunter	.10
138	Darryl Kile	.10
139	Shane Reynolds	.10
140	Brett Butler	.10
141	Eric Karros	.15
142	Ramon Martinez	.10
143	Raul Mondesi	.25
144	Hideo Nomo	.50
145	Chan Ho Park	.15
146	Mike Piazza	2.00
147	Moises Alou	.20
148	Yamil Benitez	.10
149	Mark Grudzielanek	.10
150	Pedro Martinez	.35
151	Henry Rodriguez	.10
152	David Segui	.10
153	Rondell White	.20
154	Carlos Baerga	.10
155	John Franco	.10
156	Bernard Gilkey	.10
157	Todd Hundley	.20
158	Jason Isringhausen	.15
159	Lance Johnson	.10
160	Alex Ochoa	.10
161	Rey Ordonez	.25
162	Paul Wilson	.20
163	Ron Blazier	.10
164	Ricky Bottalico	.10
165	Jim Eisenreich	.10
166	Pete Incaviglia	.10
167	Mickey Morandini	.10
168	Ricky Otero	.10
169	Curt Schilling	.10
170	Jay Bell	.10
171	Charlie Hayes	.10
172	Jason Kendall	.15
173	Jeff King	.10
174	Al Martin	.10
175	Alan Benes	.15
176	Royce Clayton	.10
177	Brian Jordan	.10
178	Ray Lankford	.10
179	John Mabry	.10
180	Willie McGee	.10
181	Ozzie Smith	.65
182	Todd Stottlemyre	.10
183	Andy Ashby	.10
184	Ken Caminiti	.25
185	Steve Finley	.10
186	Tony Gwynn	1.50
187	Rickey Henderson	.20
188	Wally Joyner	.15
189	Fernando Valenzuela	.10
190	Greg Vaughn	.10
191	Rod Beck	.10
192	Barry Bonds	1.00
193	Shawon Dunston	.10
194	Chris Singleton	.10
195	Robby Thompson	.10
196	Matt Williams	.25
197	Checklist (Barry Bonds)	.30
198	Checklist (Ken Griffey Jr.)	1.00
199	Checklist (Cal Ripken Jr.)	.75
200	Checklist (Frank Thomas)	.50

1996 Circa Rave

Rainbow metallic foil highlights on front and a serial number on back from within an edition of 150 of each card differentiate this parallel issue from the Circa base cards. Announced insertion rate for Raves was one per 60 packs.

	MT
Complete Set (200):	550.00
Common Player:	4.00
Veteran Stars: 25-50X	
Young Stars: 25-50X	

(See 1996 Circa for checklist and base card values.)

1996 Circa Access

This 1996 Fleer Circa insert set highlights 30 players

on a three-panel foldout design that includes multiple photographs, personal information and statistics. The cards were seeded about one every 12 packs.

		MT
Complete Set (30):		75.00
Common Player:		1.00
1	Cal Ripken Jr.	7.50
2	Mo Vaughn	2.50
3	Tim Salmon	1.25
4	Frank Thomas	4.00
5	Albert Belle	2.50
6	Kenny Lofton	2.50
7	Manny Ramirez	3.00
8	Paul Molitor	1.50
9	Kirby Puckett	4.00
10	Paul O'Neill	1.00
11	Mark McGwire	12.50
12	Ken Griffey Jr.	10.00
13	Randy Johnson	2.00
14	Greg Maddux	5.00
15	John Smoltz	1.50
16	Sammy Sosa	6.00
17	Barry Larkin	1.50
18	Gary Sheffield	2.00
19	Jeff Bagwell	4.00
20	Hideo Nomo	1.50
21	Mike Piazza	6.00
22	Moises Alou	1.00
23	Henry Rodriguez	1.00
24	Rey Ordonez	1.50
25	Jay Bell	1.00
26	Ozzie Smith	2.00
27	Tony Gwynn	4.00
28	Rickey Henderson	1.50
29	Barry Bonds	2.50
30	Matt Williams	1.50
30p	Matt Williams (overprinted "PROMOTIONAL SAMPLE")	1.50

1996 Circa Boss

This insert set showcases the game's top stars on an embossed design. Cards were seeded one per six packs.

		MT
Complete Set (50):		65.00
Common Player:		.50
1	Roberto Alomar	1.50
2	Cal Ripken Jr.	6.00
2p	Cal Ripken Jr. (overprinted "PROMOTIONAL SAMPLE")	4.00
3	Jose Canseco	.80
4	Mo Vaughn	2.00
5	Tim Salmon	.75
6	Frank Thomas	3.00
7	Robin Ventura	.60
8	Albert Belle	2.00
9	Kenny Lofton	2.00
10	Manny Ramirez	2.50
11	Dave Nilsson	.50
12	Chuck Knoblauch	.75
13	Paul Molitor	1.50
14	Kirby Puckett	3.00
15	Wade Boggs	.80
16	Dwight Gooden	.50
17	Paul O'Neill	.50
18	Mark McGwire	10.00
19	Jay Buhner	.75
20	Ken Griffey Jr.	7.50
21	Randy Johnson	1.25
22	Will Clark	.75
23	Juan Gonzalez	4.00
24	Joe Carter	.50
25	Tom Glavine	.50
26	Ryan Klesko	.75
27	Greg Maddux	5.00
28	John Smoltz	.75
29	Ryne Sandberg	2.50
30	Sammy Sosa	4.00
31	Barry Larkin	.80
32	Reggie Sanders	.50
33	Dante Bichette	.75
34	Andres Galarraga	.75
35	Charles Johnson	.50
36	Gary Sheffield	1.00
37	Jeff Bagwell	4.00
38	Hideo Nomo	1.00
39	Mike Piazza	5.00
40	Moises Alou	.50
41	Henry Rodriguez	.50
42	Rey Ordonez	.65
43	Ricky Otero	.50
44	Jay Bell	.50
45	Royce Clayton	.50
46	Ozzie Smith	1.50
47	Tony Gwynn	3.00
48	Rickey Henderson	.80
49	Barry Bonds	2.00
50	Matt Williams	1.00

1997 Circa

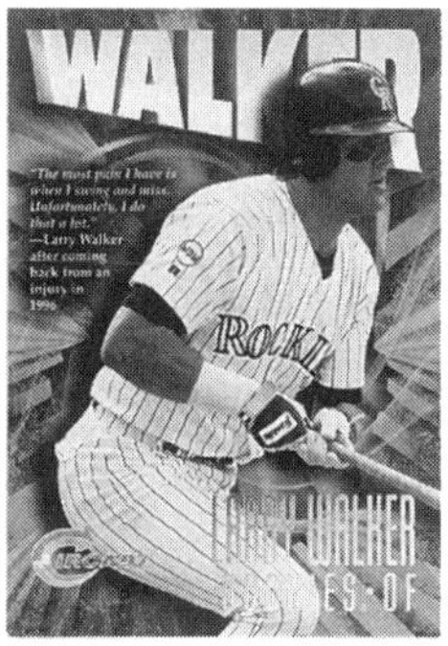

Circa baseball returned for the second year in 1997, with a 400-card set, including 393 player cards and seven checklists. Cards feature action photos on a dynamic graphic arts background, and arrived in eight-card packs. The set was paralelled in a Rave insert and was accompanied by five inserts: Boss, Fast Track, Icons, Limited Access and Rave Reviews.

		MT
Complete Set (400):		40.00
Common Player:		.10
Hobby Box:		55.00
1	Kenny Lofton	.75
2	Ray Durham	.10
3	Mariano Rivera	.20
4	Jon Lieber	.10
5	Tim Salmon	.20
6	Mark Grudzielanek	.10
7	Neifi Perez	.10
8	Cal Ripken Jr.	2.50
9	John Olerud	.10
10	Edgar Renteria	.10
11	Jose Rosado	.10
12	Mickey Morandini	.10
13	Orlando Miller	.10
14	Ben McDonald	.10
15	Hideo Nomo	.50
16	Fred McGriff	.25
17	Sean Berry	.10
18	Roger Pavlik	.10
19	Aaron Sele	.10
20	Joey Hamilton	.10
21	Roger Clemens	1.00
22	Jose Herrera	.10
23	Ryne Sandberg	.75
24	Ken Griffey Jr.	3.00
25	Barry Bonds	.75
26	Dan Naulty	.10
27	Wade Boggs	.20
28	Ray Lankford	.10
29	Rico Brogna	.10
30	Wally Joyner	.10
31	F.P. Santangelo	.10
32	Vinny Castilla	.10
33	Eddie Murray	.40
34	Kevin Elster	.10
35	Mike Macfarlane	.10
36	Jeff Kent	.10
37	Orlando Merced	.10
38	Jason Isringhausen	.10
39	Chad Ogea	.10
40	Greg Gagne	.10
41	Curt Lyons	.25
42	Mo Vaughn	.75
43	Rusty Greer	.10
44	Shane Reynolds	.10
45	Frank Thomas	1.00
46	Chris Hoiles	.10
47	Scott Sanders	.10
48	Mark Lemke	.10
49	Fernando Vina	.10
50	Mark McGwire	3.00
51	Bernie Williams	.50
52	Bobby Higginson	.10
53	Kevin Tapani	.10
54	Rich Becker	.10
55	*Felix Heredia*	.40
56	Delino DeShields	.10
57	Rick Wilkins	.10
58	Edgardo Alfonzo	.10
59	Brett Butler	.10
60	Ed Sprague	.10
61	Joe Randa	.10
62	Ugueth Urbina	.10
63	Todd Greene	.10
64	Devon White	.10
65	Bruce Ruffin	.10
66	Mark Gardner	.10
67	Omar Vizquel	.10
68	Luis Gonzalez	.10
69	Tom Glavine	.20
70	Cal Eldred	.10
71	William VanLandingham	.10
72	Jay Buhner	.20
73	James Baldwin	.10
74	Robin Jennings	.10
75	Terry Steinbach	.10
76	Billy Taylor	.10
77	Armando Benitez	.10
78	Joe Girardi	.10
79	Jay Bell	.10
80	Damon Buford	.10
81	Deion Sanders	.40
82	Bill Haselman	.10
83	John Flaherty	.10
84	Todd Stottlemyre	.10
85	J.T. Snow	.10
86	Felipe Lira	.10
87	Steve Avery	.10
88	Trey Beamon	.10
89	Alex Gonzalez	.10
90	Mark Clark	.10
91	Shane Andrews	.10
92	Randy Myers	.10
93	Gary Gaetti	.10
94	Jeff Blauser	.10
95	Tony Batista	.10
96	Todd Worrell	.10
97	Jim Edmonds	.10
98	Eric Young	.10
99	Roberto Kelly	.10
100	Alex Rodriguez	3.00
100p	Alex Rodriguez (overprinted "PROMOTIONAL SAMPLE")	5.00
101	Julio Franco	.10
102	Jeff Bagwell	1.25
103	Bobby Witt	.10
104	Tino Martinez	.25
105	Shannon Stewart	.10
106	Brian Banks	.10
107	Eddie Taubensee	.10
108	Terry Mulholland	.10
109	Lyle Mouton	.10
110	Jeff Conine	.10
111	Johnny Damon	.10
112	Quilvio Veras	.10
113	Wilton Guerrero	.20
114	Dmitri Young	.10
115	Garret Anderson	.10
116	Bill Pulsipher	.10
117	Jacob Brumfield	.10
118	Mike Lansing	.10
119	Jose Canseco	.30
120	Mike Bordick	.10
121	Kevin Stocker	.10
122	Frank Rodriguez	.10
123	Mike Cameron	.10
124	*Tony Womack*	.40
125	Bret Boone	.10
126	Moises Alou	.10
127	Tim Naehring	.10
128	Brant Brown	.20
129	Todd Zeile	.10
130	Dave Nilsson	.10
131	Donne Wall	.10
132	Jose Mesa	.10
133	Mark McLemore	.10
134	Mike Stanton	.10
135	Dan Wilson	.10
136	Jose Offerman	.10
137	David Justice	.30
138	Kirt Manwaring	.10
139	Raul Casanova	.10
140	Ron Coomer	.10
141	Dave Hollins	.10
142	Shawn Estes	.10
143	Darren Daulton	.10
144	Turk Wendell	.10
145	Darrin Fletcher	.10
146	Marquis Grissom	.10
147	Andy Benes	.10
148	Nomar Garciaparra	2.00
149	Andy Pettitte	.75
150	Tony Gwynn	1.50
151	Robb Nen	.10
152	Kevin Seitzer	.10
153	Ariel Prieto	.10
154	Scott Karl	.10
155	Carlos Baerga	.10
156	Wilson Alvarez	.10
157	Thomas Howard	.10
158	Kevin Appier	.10
159	Russ Davis	.10
160	Justin Thompson	.10
161	Pete Schourek	.10
162	John Burkett	.10
163	Roberto Alomar	.75
164	Darren Holmes	.10
165	Travis Miller	.10
166	Mark Langston	.10
167	Juan Guzman	.10
168	Pedro Astacio	.10
169	Mark Johnson	.10
170	Mark Leiter	.10
171	Heathcliff Slocumb	.10
172	Dante Bichette	.20
173	*Brian Giles*	1.00
174	Paul Wilson	.10
175	Eric Davis	.10
176	Charles Johnson	.10
177	Willie Greene	.10
178	Geronimo Berroa	.10
179	Mariano Duncan	.10
180	Robert Person	.10
181	David Segui	.10
182	Ozzie Guillen	.10
183	Osvaldo Fernandez	.10
184	Dean Palmer	.10
185	Bob Wickman	.10
186	Eric Karros	.10
187	Travis Fryman	.10
188	Andy Ashby	.10
189	Scott Stahoviak	.10
190	Norm Charlton	.10
191	Craig Paquette	.10
192	John Smoltz	.25
193	Orel Hershiser	.10
194	Glenallen Hill	.10
195	George Arias	.10
196	Brian Jordan	.10
197	Greg Vaughn	.10
198	Rafael Palmeiro	.20
199	Darryl Kile	.10
200	Derek Jeter	2.00
201	Jose Vizcaino	.10
202	Rick Aguilera	.10
203	Jason Schmidt	.10
204	Trot Nixon	.10
205	Tom Pagnozzi	.10
206	Mark Wohlers	.10
207	Lance Johnson	.10
208	Carlos Delgado	.25
209	Cliff Floyd	.10
210	Kent Mercker	.10
211	Matt Mieske	.10
212	Ismael Valdes	.10
213	Shawon Dunston	.10
214	Melvin Nieves	.10
215	Tony Phillips	.10
216	Scott Spiezio	.10
217	Michael Tucker	.10
218	Matt Williams	.25
219	Ricky Otero	.10
220	Kevin Ritz	.10
221	Darryl Strawberry	.10
222	Troy Percival	.10
223	Eugene Kingsale	.10
224	Julian Tavarez	.10
225	Jermaine Dye	.10
226	Jason Kendall	.10
227	Sterling Hitchcock	.10
228	Jeff Cirillo	.10
229	Roberto Hernandez	.10
230	Ricky Bottalico	.10
231	Bobby Bonilla	.10
232	Edgar Martinez	.10
233	John Valentin	.10
234	Ellis Burks	.10
235	Benito Santiago	.10
236	Terrell Wade	.10
237	Armando Reynoso	.10
238	Danny Graves	.10
239	Ken Hill	.10
240	Dennis Eckersley	.10
241	Darin Erstad	1.00
242	Lee Smith	.10
243	Cecil Fielder	.20
244	Tony Clark	.50
245	Scott Erickson	.10
246	Bob Abreu	.10
247	Ruben Sierra	.10
248	Chili Davis	.10
249	Darryl Hamilton	.10
250	Albert Belle	.75
251	Todd Hollandsworth	.10
252	Terry Adams	.10
253	Rey Ordonez	.10
254	Steve Finley	.10
255	Jose Valentin	.10
256	Royce Clayton	.10
257	Sandy Alomar	.10
258	Mike Lieberthal	.10
259	Ivan Rodriguez	.50
260	Rod Beck	.10
261	Ron Karkovice	.10
262	Mark Gubicza	.10
263	Chris Holt	.10
264	Jaime Bluma	.10
265	Francisco Cordova	.15
266	Javy Lopez	.20
267	Reggie Jefferson	.10
268	Kevin Brown	.10
269	Scott Brosius	.10
270	Dwight Gooden	.10
271	Marty Cordova	.10
272	Jeff Brantley	.10
273	Joe Carter	.10
274	Todd Jones	.10
275	Sammy Sosa	1.50
276	Randy Johnson	.50
277	B.J. Surhoff	.10
278	Chan Ho Park	.10
279	Jamey Wright	.10
280	Manny Ramirez	1.00
281	John Franco	.10
282	Tim Worrell	.10
283	Scott Rolen	1.25
284	Reggie Sanders	.10
285	Mike Fetters	.10
286	Tim Wakefield	.10
287	Trevor Hoffman	.10
288	Donovan Osborne	.10
289	Phil Nevin	.10
290	Jermaine Allensworth	.10
291	Rocky Coppinger	.10
292	Tim Raines	.10
293	Henry Rodriguez	.10
294	Paul Sorrento	.10
295	Tom Goodwin	.10
296	Raul Mondesi	.25
297	Allen Watson	.10
298	Derek Bell	.10
299	Gary Sheffield	.40
300	Paul Molitor	.40
301	Shawn Green	.10
302	Darren Oliver	.10
303	Jack McDowell	.10
304	Denny Neagle	.10
305	Doug Drabek	.10
306	Mel Rojas	.10
307	Andres Galarraga	.20
308	Alex Ochoa	.10
309	Gary DiSarcina	.10
310	Ron Gant	.10
311	Gregg Jefferies	.10
312	Ruben Rivera	.10
313	Vladimir Guerrero	1.00
314	Willie Adams	.10
315	Bip Roberts	.10
316	Mark Grace	.20
317	Bernard Gilkey	.10
318	Marc Newfield	.10
319	Al Leiter	.10
320	Otis Nixon	.10
321	Tom Candiotti	.10
322	Mike Stanley	.10
323	Jeff Fassero	.10
324	Billy Wagner	.10
325	Todd Walker	.75
326	Chad Curtis	.10
327	Quinton McCracken	.10
328	Will Clark	.25
329	Andruw Jones	1.50
330	Robin Ventura	.10
331	Curtis Pride	.10
332	Barry Larkin	.30
333	Jimmy Key	.10
334	David Wells	.10
335	Mike Holtz	.10
336	Paul Wagner	.10
337	Greg Maddux	2.00
338	Curt Schilling	.10
339	Steve Trachsel	.10
340	John Wetteland	.10
341	Rickey Henderson	.10
342	Ernie Young	.10
343	Harold Baines	.10
344	Bobby Jones	.10
345	Jeff D'Amico	.10
346	John Mabry	.10
347	Pedro Martinez	.10
348	Mark Lewis	.10
349	Dan Miceli	.10
350	Chuck Knoblauch	.10
351	John Smiley	.10
352	Brady Anderson	.10
353	Jim Leyritz	.10
354	Al Martin	.10
355	Pat Hentgen	.10
356	Mike Piazza	2.00
357	Charles Nagy	.10
358	Luis Castillo	.15
359	Paul O'Neill	.10
360	Steve Reed	.10
361	Tom Gordon	.10
362	Craig Biggio	.10
363	Jeff Montgomery	.10
364	Jamie Moyer	.10
365	Ryan Klesko	.25
366	Todd Hundley	.20
367	Bobby Estalella	.10
368	Jason Giambi	.10
369	Brian Hunter	.10
370	Ramon Martinez	.10
371	Carlos Garcia	.10
372	Hal Morris	.10
373	Juan Gonzalez	1.25
374	Brian McRae	.10
375	Mike Mussina	.60
376	John Ericks	.10
377	Larry Walker	.35
378	Chris Gomez	.10
379	John Jaha	.10
380	Rondell White	.20

381	Chipper Jones	2.00
382	David Cone	.20
383	Alan Benes	.20
384	Troy O'Leary	.10
385	Ken Caminiti	.30
386	Jeff King	.10
387	Mike Hampton	.10
388	Jaime Navarro	.10
389	Brad Radke	.10
390	Joey Cora	.10
391	Jim Thome	.40
392	Alex Fernandez	.20
393	Chuck Finley	.10
394	Andruw Jones CL	.75
395	Ken Griffey Jr. CL	1.50
396	Frank Thomas CL	.50
397	Alex Rodriguez CL	1.50
398	Cal Ripken Jr. CL	1.25
399	Mike Piazza CL	1.00
400	Greg Maddux CL	1.00

1997 Circa Rave

In its second year, Circa Rave parallel inserts were limited to inclusion only in hobby packs at the stated. rate of one card per "30 to 40" packs. Raves are distinguished from regular-edition Circa cards by the use of purple metallic foil for the brand name and player identification on front. Rave backs carry a silver-foil serial number detailing its position within a production of 150 for each card.

	MT
Complete Set (400):	600.00
Common Player:	5.00
Veteran Stars: 25-40X	
Young Stars: 15-30X	

(See 1997 Circa for checklist and base card values.)

1997 Circa Boss

Boss was Circa's most common insert series. Twenty embossed cards were seeded one per six packs, displaying some of baseball's best players. A Super Boss parallel insert features metallic-foil background and graphics on front, and is inserted at a rate of one per 36 packs.

		MT
Complete Set (20):		40.00
Common Player:		.50
Super Boss: 2-3X		
1	Jeff Bagwell	3.00
2	Albert Belle	2.00
3	Barry Bonds	2.00
4	Ken Caminiti	1.00
5	Juan Gonzalez	3.00
6	Ken Griffey Jr.	8.00
7	Tony Gwynn	3.00
8	Derek Jeter	5.00
9	Andruw Jones	4.00
10	Chipper Jones	5.00
11	Greg Maddux	5.00
12	Mark McGwire	10.00
13	Mike Piazza	5.00
14	Manny Ramirez	2.50
15	Cal Ripken Jr.	6.00
16	Alex Rodriguez	8.00
17	John Smoltz	1.00
18	Frank Thomas	3.00
19	Mo Vaughn	2.00
20	Bernie Williams	1.50

1997 Circa Emerald Autograph Redemption Cards

These box-topper cards were a hobby exclusive redeemable until May 31, 1998, for autographed special cards of six young stars. Fronts have a green-foil enhanced player action photo. Backs provide details of the redemption program.

		MT
Complete Set (6):		20.00
Common Player:		1.50
(1)	Darin Erstad	3.50
(2)	Todd Hollandsworth	1.50
(3)	Alex Ochoa	1.50
(4)	Alex Rodriguez	12.50
(5)	Scott Rolen	5.00
(6)	Todd Walker	2.00

1997 Circa Emerald Autographs

Special green-foil enhanced cards of six top young stars were available via a mail-in redemption. The cards feature authentic player signatures on front and an embossed authentication seal. Backs are identical to the regular card of each featured player.

		MT
Complete Set (6):		200.00
Common Player:		15.00
100	Alex Rodriguez	90.00
241	Darin Erstad	35.00
251	Todd Hollandsworth	15.00
283	Scott Rolen	45.00
308	Alex Ochoa	15.00
325	Todd Walker	20.00

1997 Circa Fast Track

Fast Track highlights 10 top rookies and young stars on a flocked background simulating grass. Cards were inserted every 24 packs.

		MT
Complete Set (10):		30.00
Common Player:		1.00
1	Vladimir Guerrero	3.00
2	Todd Hollandsworth	1.00
3	Derek Jeter	6.00
4	Andruw Jones	3.00
5	Chipper Jones	4.00
6	Andy Pettitte	2.00
7	Mariano Rivera	3.00
8	Alex Rodriguez	7.50
9	Scott Rolen	3.00
10	Todd Walker	2.00

Checklists with card numbers in parentheses ( ) indicates the numbers do not appear on the card.

1997 Circa Icons

Twelve of baseball's top sluggers were displayed on 100-percent holofoil cards in Icons. Icons were found at a rate of one per 36 packs.

		MT
Complete Set (12):		55.00
Common Player:		2.00
1	Juan Gonzalez	5.00
2	Ken Griffey Jr.	15.00
3	Tony Gwynn	5.00
4	Derek Jeter	6.00
5	Chipper Jones	6.00
6	Greg Maddux	5.00
7	Mark McGwire	15.00
8	Mike Piazza	6.00
9	Cal Ripken Jr.	7.50
10	Alex Rodriguez	6.00
11	Frank Thomas	4.00
12	Matt Williams	2.00

1997 Circa Limited Access

Limited Access was a retail-only insert found every 18 packs. Cards feature an in-depth, statistical analysis including the player's favorite pitcher to hit and each pitcher's least favorite hitter to face. Limited Access is formatted as a die-cut, bi-fold design resembling a book.

		MT
Complete Set (15):		110.00
Common Player:		2.00
1	Jeff Bagwell	8.00
2	Albert Belle	5.00
3	Barry Bonds	5.00
4	Juan Gonzalez	8.00
5	Ken Griffey Jr.	20.00
6	Tony Gwynn	10.00
7	Derek Jeter	12.00
8	Chipper Jones	12.00
9	Greg Maddux	12.00
10	Mark McGwire	25.00
11	Mike Piazza	12.00
12	Cal Ripken Jr.	15.00
13	Alex Rodriguez	12.00
14	Frank Thomas	8.00
15	Mo Vaughn	5.00

1997 Circa Rave Reviews

Hitters that continually put up great numbers were selected for Rave Reviews. The insert was found in every 288 packs and was printed on 100-percent holofoil.

		MT
Complete Set (12):		275.00
Common Player:		10.00
1	Albert Belle	15.00
2	Barry Bonds	15.00
3	Juan Gonzalez	25.00
4	Ken Griffey Jr.	50.00
5	Tony Gwynn	25.00
6	Greg Maddux	25.00
7	Mark McGwire	50.00
8	Eddie Murray	10.00
9	Mike Piazza	30.00
10	Cal Ripken Jr.	40.00
11	Alex Rodriguez	30.00
12	Frank Thomas	20.00

1998 Circa Thunder

Circa Thunder was issued as one series of 300 cards, sold in packs of eight for $1.59. The set marked SkyBox's brand transition from Circa to Thunder so the cards are labeled with both names. Inserts include: Rave and Super Rave parallels, Boss, Fast Track, Quick Strike, Limited Access, Rave Review and Thunder Boomers.

		MT
Complete Set (300):		25.00
Common Player:		.15
Wax Box:		50.00
1	Ben Grieve	1.25
2	Derek Jeter	2.00
3	Alex Rodriguez	2.00
4	Paul Molitor	.50
5	Nomar Garciaparra	2.00
6	Fred McGriff	.25
7	Kenny Lofton	.75
8a	Cal Ripken Jr.	2.50
8b	Marquis Grissom (should be #280)	.15
8s	Cal Ripken Jr. ("PROMOTIONAL SAMPLE" on back)	3.00
9	Matt Williams	.30
10	Chipper Jones	2.00
11	Barry Larkin	.25
12	Steve Finley	.15
13	Billy Wagner	.15
14	Rico Brogna	.15
15	Tim Salmon	.30
16	Hideo Nomo	.50
17	Tony Clark	.50
18	Jason Kendall	.15
19	Juan Gonzalez	1.50
20	Jeromy Burnitz	.15
21	Roger Clemens	1.00
22	Mark Grace	.30
23	Robin Ventura	.25
24	Manny Ramirez	1.00
25	Mark McGwire	4.00
26	Gary Sheffield	.30
27	Vladimir Guerrero	.75
28	Butch Huskey	.15
29	Cecil Fielder	.25
30	Roderick Myers	.15
31	Greg Maddux	2.00
32	Bill Mueller	.15
33	Larry Walker	.30
34	Henry Rodriguez	.15
35	Mike Mussina	.60
36	Ricky Ledee	.25
37	Bobby Bonilla	.25
38	Curt Schilling	.30
39	Luis Gonzalez	.15
40	Troy Percival	.15
41	Eric Milton	.40
42	Mo Vaughn	.75
43	Raul Mondesi	.30
44	Kenny Rogers	.15
45	Frank Thomas	1.50
46	Jose Canseco	.30
47	Tom Glavine	.25
48	*Rich Butler*	.40
49	Jay Buhner	.25
50	Jose Cruz Jr.	.20
51	Bernie Williams	.50
52	Doug Glanville	.15
53	Travis Fryman	.15
54	Rey Ordonez	.15
55	Jeff Conine	.15
56	Trevor Hoffman	.15
57	Kirk Rueter	.15
58	Ron Gant	.25
59	Carl Everett	.15
60	Joe Carter	.25
61	Livan Hernandez	.25
62	John Jaha	.15
63	Ivan Rodriguez	.75
64	Willie Blair	.15
65	Todd Helton	.75
66	Kevin Young	.15
67	Mike Caruso	.15
68	Steve Trachsel	.15
69	Marty Cordova	.15
70	Alex Fernandez	.15
71	Eric Karros	.25
72	Reggie Sanders	.15
73	Russ Davis	.15
74	Roberto Hernandez	.15
75	Barry Bonds	.75
76	Alex Gonzalez	.15
77	Roberto Alomar	.50
78	Troy O'Leary	.15
79	Bernard Gilkey	.15
80	Ismael Valdes	.15
81	Travis Lee	.75
82	Brant Brown	.15
83	Gary DiSarcina	.15
84	Joe Randa	.15
85	Jaret Wright	1.50

86	Quilvio Veras	.15
87	Rickey Henderson	.15
88	Randall Simon	.25
89	Mariano Rivera	.25
90	Ugueth Urbina	.15
91	Fernando Vina	.15
92	Alan Benes	.25
93	Dante Bichette	.25
94	Karim Garcia	.15
95	A.J. Hinch	.75
96	Shane Reynolds	.15
97	Kevin Stocker	.15
98	John Wetteland	.15
99	Terry Steinbach	.15
100	Ken Griffey Jr.	3.00
101	Mike Cameron	.25
102	Damion Easley	.15
103	Randy Myers	.15
104	Jason Schmidt	.15
105	Jeff King	.15
106	Gregg Jefferies	.15
107	Sean Casey	.40
108	Mark Kotsay	.40
109	Brad Fullmer	.15
110	Wilson Alvarez	.15
111	Sandy Alomar Jr.	.25
112	Walt Weiss	.15
113	Doug Jones	.15
114	Andy Benes	.25
115	Paul O'Neill	.25
116	Dennis Eckersley	.15
117	Todd Greene	.15
118	Bobby Jones	.15
119	Darrin Fletcher	.15
120	Eric Young	.15
121	Jeffrey Hammonds	.15
122	Mickey Morandini	.15
123	Chuck Knoblauch	.40
124	Moises Alou	.25
125	Miguel Tejada	.50
126	Brian Anderson	.15
127	Edgar Renteria	.15
128	Mike Lansing	.15
129	Quinton McCracken	.15
130	Ray Lankford	.15
131	Andy Ashby	.15
132	Kelvim Escobar	.15
133	*Mike Lowell*	.25
134	Randy Johnson	.50
135	Andres Galarraga	.35
136	Armando Benitez	.15
137	Rusty Greer	.15
138	Jose Guillen	.25
139	Paul Konerko	.75
140	Edgardo Alfonzo	.15
141	Jim Leyritz	.15
142	Mark Clark	.15
143	Brian Johnson	.15
144	Scott Rolen	1.00
145	David Cone	.25
146	Jeff Shaw	.15
147	Shannon Stewart	.15
148	Brian Hunter	.15
149	Garret Anderson	.15
150	Jeff Bagwell	1.00
151	James Baldwin	.15
152	Devon White	.15
153	Jim Thome	.40
154	Wally Joyner	.15
155	Mark Wohlers	.15
156	Jeff Cirillo	.15
157	Jason Giambi	.15
158	Royce Clayton	.15
159	Dennis Reyes	.15
160	Raul Casanova	.15
161	Pedro Astacio	.15
162	Todd Dunwoody	.15
163	Sammy Sosa	2.00
164	Todd Hundley	.15
165	Wade Boggs	.25
166	Robb Nen	.15
167	Dan Wilson	.15
168	Hideki Irabu	.50
169	B.J. Surhoff	.15
170	Carlos Delgado	.25
171	Fernando Tatis	.15
172	Bob Abreu	.15
173	David Ortiz	.25
174	Tony Womack	.15
175	*Magglio Ordonez*	1.00
176	Aaron Boone	.15
177	Brian Giles	.15
178	Kevin Appier	.15
179	Chuck Finley	.15
180	Brian Rose	.25
181	Ryan Klesko	.20
182	Mike Stanley	.15
183	Dave Nilsson	.15
184	Carlos Perez	.15
185	Jeff Blauser	.15
186	Richard Hidalgo	.15
187	Charles Johnson	.25
188	Vinny Castilla	.25
189	Joey Hamilton	.15
190	Bubba Trammell	.15
191	Eli Marrero	.15
192	Scott Erickson	.15
193	Pat Hentgen	.15
194	Jorge Fabregas	.15
195	Tino Martinez	.30
196	Bobby Higginson	.15
197	Dave Hollins	.15
198	*Rolando Arrojo*	.40
199	Joey Cora	.15
200	Mike Piazza	2.00
201	Reggie Jefferson	.15
202	John Smoltz	.25
203	Bobby Smith	.15
204	Tom Goodwin	.15
205	Omar Vizquel	.15
206	John Olerud	.25
207	Matt Stairs	.15
208	Bobby Estalella	.15
209	Miguel Cairo	.15
210	Shawn Green	.15
211	Jon Nunnally	.15
212	Al Leiter	.15
213	Matt Lawton	.15
214	Brady Anderson	.15
215	Jeff Kent	.15
216	Ray Durham	.15
217	Al Martin	.15
218	Jeff D'Amico	.15
219	Kevin Tapani	.15
220	Jim Edmonds	.25
221	Jose Vizcaino	.15
222	Jay Bell	.15
223	Ken Caminiti	.25
224	Craig Biggio	.30
225	Bartolo Colon	.25
226	Neifi Perez	.15
227	Delino DeShields	.15
228	Javier Lopez	.15
229	David Wells	.15
230	Brad Rigby	.15
231	John Franco	.15
232	Michael Coleman	.15
233	Edgar Martinez	.25
234	Francisco Cordova	.15
235	Johnny Damon	.15
236	Deivi Cruz	.15
237	J.T. Snow	.15
238	Enrique Wilson	.15
239	Rondell White	.25
240	Aaron Sele	.25
241	Tony Saunders	.15
242	Ricky Bottalico	.15
243	Cliff Floyd	.15
244	Chili Davis	.15
245	Brian McRae	.15
246	Brad Radke	.15
247	Chan Ho Park	.25
248	Lance Johnson	.15
249	Rafael Palmeiro	.25
250	Tony Gwynn	1.50
251	Denny Neagle	.15
252	Dean Palmer	.15
253	Jose Valentin	.15
254	Matt Morris	.15
255	Ellis Burks	.15
256	Jeff Suppan	.15
257	Jimmy Key	.15
258	Justin Thompson	.15
259	Brett Tomko	.15
260	Mark Grudzielanek	.15
261	Mike Hampton	.15
262	Jeff Fassero	.15
263	Charles Nagy	.15
264	Pedro Martinez	.40
265	Todd Zeile	.15
266	Will Clark	.30
267	Abraham Nunez	.15
268	Dave Martinez	.15
269	Jason Dickson	.15
270	Eric Davis	.15
271	Kevin Orie	.15
272	Derrek Lee	.25
273	Andruw Jones	.75
274	Juan Encarnacion	.15
275	Carlos Baerga	.15
276	Andy Pettitte	.50
277	Brent Brede	.15
278	Paul Sorrento	.15
279	Mike Lieberthal	.15
280	(Not issued, see #8)	
281	Darin Erstad	.75
282	Willie Greene	.15
283	Derek Bell	.15
284	Scott Spiezio	.15
285	David Segui	.15
286	Albert Belle	.75
287	Ramon Martinez	.15
288	Jeremi Gonzalez	.15
289	Shawn Estes	.15
290	Ron Coomer	.15
291	John Valentin	.15
292	Kevin Brown	.15
293	Michael Tucker	.15
294	Brian Jordan	.15
295	Darryl Kile	.15
296	David Justice	.30
297	Jose Cruz Jr. CL	.20
298	Ken Griffey Jr. CL	1.50
299	Alex Rodriguez CL	1.00
300	Frank Thomas CL	.75

1998 Circa Thunder Rave

Rave parallels each card in Circa Thunder except for the four checklist cards. A special silver sparkling foil is used on the player's name and the Thunder logo on front. This 296-card set was inserted approximately one per 36 packs and sequentially numbered to 150 sets on the back.

	MT
Complete Set (296):	1650.
Common Player:	5.00
Veteran Stars: 25-50X	
Young Stars: 25-50X	

(See 1998 Circa Thunder for checklist and base card values.)

1998 Circa Thunder Super Rave

Only 25 Super Rave parallel sets were printed and they were inserted approximately one per 216 packs. The set contains 296 player cards (no checklist cards). Fronts are identified by sparkling gold foil on the player's name and the Thunder logo, with sequential numbering on the back to 25.

	MT
Common Player:	15.00
Veteran Stars: 150-250X	
Young Stars: 75-150X	

(See 1998 Circa Thunder for checklist and base card values.)

1998 Circa Thunder Boss

This 20-card insert, seeded one per six packs, has cards embossed with the player's last name in large letters across the top.

		MT
Complete Set (20):		25.00
Common Player:		.50
1B	Jeff Bagwell	1.25
2B	Barry Bonds	.75
3B	Roger Clemens	1.25
4B	Jose Cruz Jr.	.75
5B	Nomar Garciaparra	2.00
6B	Juan Gonzalez	1.50
7B	Ken Griffey Jr.	3.00
8B	Tony Gwynn	1.50
9B	Derek Jeter	2.00
10B	Chipper Jones	2.00
11B	Travis Lee	.75
12B	Greg Maddux	1.50
13B	Pedro Martinez	.75
14B	Mark McGwire	4.00
15B	Mike Piazza	2.00
16B	Cal Ripken Jr.	2.50
17B	Alex Rodriguez	2.00
18B	Scott Rolen	1.00
19B	Frank Thomas	1.25
20B	Larry Walker	.50

1998 Circa Thunder Fast Track

This 10-card insert showcases some of the top young stars in baseball and was seeded one per 24 packs. Fronts picture the player over a closeup of a gold foil baseball on the left. The right side has smaller head shots of all 10 players with the featured player's head in gold foil.

		MT
Complete Set (10):		35.00
Common Player:		1.50
1FT	Jose Cruz Jr.	1.50
2FT	Juan Encarnacion	1.50
3FT	Brad Fullmer	3.00
4FT	Nomar Garciaparra	7.50
5FT	Todd Helton	3.00
6FT	Livan Hernandez	1.50
7FT	Travis Lee	5.00
8FT	Neifi Perez	1.50
9FT	Scott Rolen	5.00
10FT	Jaret Wright	5.00

1998 Circa Thunder Limited Access

This retail exclusive insert was seeded one per 18 packs. Cards are bi-fold and die-cut with foil stamping on front. The theme of the insert was to provide an in-depth statistical scouting analysis of each player.

		MT
Complete Set (15):		90.00
Common Player:		2.00
1LA	Jeff Bagwell	6.00
2LA	Roger Clemens	6.00
3LA	Jose Cruz Jr.	2.00
4LA	Nomar Garciaparra	10.00
5LA	Juan Gonzalez	8.00
6LA	Ken Griffey Jr.	15.00
7LA	Tony Gwynn	8.00
8LA	Derek Jeter	10.00
9LA	Greg Maddux	10.00
10LA	Pedro Martinez	2.00
11LA	Mark McGwire	20.00
12LA	Mike Piazza	10.00
13LA	Alex Rodriguez	10.00
14LA	Frank Thomas	6.00
15LA	Larry Walker	2.00

1998 Circa Thunder Quick Strike

This insert pictures players over a colorful die-cut foilboard front. Quick Strikes were seeded one per 36 packs of Circa Thunder.

		MT
Complete Set (12):		90.00
Common Player:		3.00
1QS	Jeff Bagwell	8.00
2QS	Roger Clemens	8.00
3QS	Jose Cruz Jr.	3.00
4QS	Nomar Garciaparra	12.00
5QS	Ken Griffey Jr.	20.00
6QS	Greg Maddux	12.00
7QS	Pedro Martinez	3.00
8QS	Mark McGwire	25.00
9QS	Mike Piazza	12.00
10QS	Alex Rodriguez	12.00
11QS	Frank Thomas	8.00
12QS	Larry Walker	3.00

1998 Circa Thunder Rave Reviews

Rave Reviews were inserted at one per 288 packs of Circa Thunder. The cards are die-cut in a horizontal design with bronze foil etching and the image of a ballfield in the background.

		MT
Complete Set (15):		500.00
Common Player:		10.00
1RR	Jeff Bagwell	25.00
2RR	Barry Bonds	20.00
3RR	Roger Clemens	35.00
4RR	Jose Cruz Jr.	10.00
5RR	Nomar Garciaparra	50.00
6RR	Juan Gonzalez	40.00
7RR	Ken Griffey Jr.	80.00
8RR	Tony Gwynn	40.00
9RR	Derek Jeter	50.00
10RR	Greg Maddux	40.00
11RR	Mark McGwire	100.00
12RR	Mike Piazza	50.00
13RR	Alex Rodriguez	50.00
14RR	Frank Thomas	25.00
15RR	Larry Walker	10.00

1998 Circa Thunder Thunder Boomers

Thunder Boomers feature top power hitters imposed over a see-through cloud-like plastic center with the imagery of a wooden fence with a large hole blasted through the middle of it. This 12-card set was inserted one per 96 packs of Circa Thunder.

	MT
Complete Set (12):	125.00
Common Player:	5.00
1TB Jeff Bagwell	15.00
2TB Barry Bonds	10.00
3TB Jay Buhner	5.00
4TB Andres Galarraga	5.00
5TB Juan Gonzalez	20.00
6TB Ken Griffey Jr.	40.00
7TB Tino Martinez	5.00
8TB Mark McGwire	45.00
9TB Mike Piazza	25.00
10TB Frank Thomas	15.00
11TB Jim Thome	6.00
12TB Larry Walker	5.00

1985 Circle K

Produced by Topps for Circle K stores, this set is titled "Baseball All Time Home Run Kings". The 2-1/2" x 3-1/2" cards are numbered on the back according to the player's position on the all-time career home run list. Joe DiMaggio, who ranked 31st, was not included in the set. Glossy card fronts generally feature a color photo, although black-and-whites were utilized for a few of the homer kings who played before 1960. Backs have blue and red print on white stock and contain the player's career batting statistics. The set was issued in a specially designed box.

	MT
Complete Set (33):	5.00
Common Player:	.15
1 Hank Aaron	.75
2 Babe Ruth	1.00
3 Willie Mays	.75
4 Frank Robinson	.25
5 Harmon Killebrew	.25
6 Mickey Mantle	2.00
7 Jimmie Foxx	.25
8 Willie McCovey	.25
9 Ted Williams	.75
10 Ernie Banks	.35
11 Eddie Mathews	.25
12 Mel Ott	.20
13 Reggie Jackson	.35
14 Lou Gehrig	1.00
15 Stan Musial	.60
16 Willie Stargell	.20
17 Carl Yastrzemski	.35
18 Billy Williams	.20
19 Mike Schmidt	.50
20 Duke Snider	.35
21 Al Kaline	.35
22 Johnny Bench	.35
23 Frank Howard	.15
24 Orlando Cepeda	.20
25 Norm Cash	.20
26 Dave Kingman	.15
27 Rocky Colavito	.25
28 Tony Perez	.15
29 Gil Hodges	.25
30 Ralph Kiner	.20
31 Not issued	
32 Johnny Mize	.20
33 Yogi Berra	.35
34 Lee May	.15

1993 City Pride Roberto Clemente

To assist in the building of the statue of Roberto Clemente which was unveiled at Three Rivers Stadium during All-Star festivities in 1994, Pittsburgh's City Pride bakery contributed a portion of sales proceeds from a special run of bread loaves featuring Roberto Clemente cards. The cards came in a special plastic pouch within the bread wrapper to protect them from stains. The wrapper itself included a portrait of Clemente and details of the statue project. The 2-1/2" x 3-1/2" cards featured sepia-toned or color photos of Clemente inside black and gold borders. A color team logo appears in the lower-right corner with his name in an orange stripe at the bottom of the photo. Backs are in black-and-white and contain a narrative of Clemente's career, with one card containing his lifetime stats. The unnumbered cards are checklisted here in chronological order.

	MT
Complete Set (6):	5.00
Common Card:	1.00
(1) Roberto Clemente (1934-1958, batting, sepia photo)	1.00
(2) Roberto Clemente (1960-1966, batting, color photo)	1.00
(3) Roberto Clemente (1971-1972, running to first base)	1.00
(4) Roberto Clemente (1972-1973, portrait)	1.00
(5) Roberto Clemente (Fielding records, kneeling with one bat)	1.00
(6) Roberto Clemente (Batting record, kneeling with five bats)	1.00

1993 Clark Candy Reggie Jackson

The reintroduction of the "Reggie" candy bar by the Clark company was accompanied by a three-card set highlighting his career produced by Upper Deck. One card was found in each candy bar. Cards have a color photo of Jackson on front, on which uniform logos have been removed. Backs have an equipment montage and a paragraph about the slugger. Clark and UD logos appear on front, with an UD hologram on back. A limited number (200) of autographed cards were randomly inserted.

	MT
Complete Set (3):	3.00
Common Player:	1.00
Autographed Card:	90.00
C1 Reggie Jackson (Hall of Fame, 1993)	1.00
C2 Reggie Jackson (Mr. October, 1977)	1.00
C3 Reggie Jackson (A.L. MVP, 1973)	1.00

1987 Classic Major League Baseball Game

The "Classic Major League Baseball Board Game" set consists of 100 full-color cards used to play the game in which participants answer trivia questions found on the card backs. Cards measure 2-1/2" x 3-1/2" and are printed on semi-gloss stock. Backs carry the player's career stats besides the trivia questions. The game was produced by Game Time, Ltd. of Marietta, Ga., and sold for $19.95 in most retail outlets. In 1991-92 the set was selling for $200 or more, with the Bo Jackson card advertised as high as $80.

	MT
Complete Set (100):	35.00
Common Player:	.10
1 Pete Rose	2.50
2 Len Dykstra	.10
3 Darryl Strawberry	.15
4 Keith Hernandez	.10
5 Gary Carter	.25
6 Wally Joyner	.15
7 Andres Thomas	.10
8 Pat Dodson	.10
9 Kirk Gibson	.10
10 Don Mattingly	3.00
11 Dave Winfield	.50
12 Rickey Henderson	.50
13 Dan Pasqua	.10
14 Don Baylor	.10
15 Bo Jackson	4.00
16 Pete Incaviglia	.10
17 Kevin Bass	.10
18 Barry Larkin	.35
19 Dave Magadan	.10
20 Steve Sax	.10
21 Eric Davis	.12
22 Mike Pagliarulo	.10
23 Fred Lynn	.10
24 Reggie Jackson	.50
25 Larry Parrish	.10
26 Tony Gwynn	1.00
27 Steve Garvey	.20
28 Glenn Davis	.10
29 Tim Raines	.12
30 Vince Coleman	.10
31 Willie McGee	.12
32 Ozzie Smith	.75
33 Dave Parker	.10
34 Tony Pena	.10
35 Ryne Sandberg	2.50
36 Brett Butler	.12
37 Dale Murphy	.35
38 Bob Horner	.10
39 Pedro Guerrero	.10
40 Brook Jacoby	.10
41 Carlton Fisk	.25
42 Harold Baines	.12
43 Rob Deer	.10
44 Robin Yount	.75
45 Paul Molitor	.75
46 Jose Canseco	3.00
47 George Brett	3.00
48 Jim Presley	.10
49 Rich Gedman	.10
50 Lance Parrish	.10
51 Eddie Murray	.75
52 Cal Ripken, Jr.	10.00
53 Kent Hrbek	.12
54 Gary Gaetti	.12
55 Kirby Puckett	2.50
56 George Bell	.10
57 Tony Fernandez	.12
58 Jesse Barfield	.10
59 Jim Rice	.12
60 Wade Boggs	.75
61 Marty Barrett	.10
62 Mike Schmidt	1.00
63 Von Hayes	.10
64 Jeff Leonard	.10
65 Chris Brown	.10
66 Dave Smith	.10
67 Mike Krukow	.10
68 Ron Guidry	.12
69 Rob Woodward (photo actually Pat Dodson)	.10
70 Rob Murphy	.10
71 Andres Galarraga	.20
72 Dwight Gooden	.15
73 Bob Ojeda	.10
74 Sid Fernandez	.10
75 Jesse Orosco	.10
76 Roger McDowell	.10
77 John Tutor (Tudor)	.10
78 Tom Browning	.10
79 Rick Aguilera	.10
80 Lance McCullers	.10
81 Mike Scott	.10
82 Nolan Ryan	7.00
83 Bruce Hurst	.10
84 Roger Clemens	1.00
85 Oil Can Boyd	.10
86 Dave Righetti	.10
87 Dennis Rasmussen	.10
88 Bret Saberhagan (Saberhagen)	.15
89 Mark Langston	.10
90 Jack Morris	.10
91 Fernando Valenzuela	.12
92 Orel Hershiser	.12
93 Rick Honeycutt	.10
94 Jeff Reardon	.10
95 John Habyan	.10
96 Goose Gossage	.12
97 Todd Worrell	.10
98 Floyd Youmans	.10
99 Don Aase	.10
100 John Franco	.10

1987 Classic Travel Update (Yellow)

Game Time, Ltd. of Marietta, Ga., issued as an update to its Classic Baseball Board Game a 50-card set entitled "Travel Edition." Cards measure 2-1/2" x 3-1/2" in the same format as the first release, though with yellow, rather than green, borders. Numbered from 101 to 150, the "Travel Edition," besides updating player trades and showcasing rookies, offers several highlights from the 1987 season. All new trivia questions are found on the card backs.

	MT
Complete Set (50):	10.00
Common Player:	.10
101 Mike Schmidt	.75
102 Eric Davis	.12
103 Pete Rose	1.00
104 Don Mattingly	.75
105 Wade Boggs	.50
106 Dale Murphy	.15
107 Glenn Davis	.10
108 Wally Joyner	.12
109 Bo Jackson	.35
110 Cory Snyder	.10
111 Jim Lindeman	.10
112 Kirby Puckett	.75
113 Barry Bonds	1.50
114 Roger Clemens	.75
115 Oddibe McDowell	.10
116 Bret Saberhagen	.12
117 Joe Magrane	.10
118 Scott Fletcher	.10
119 Mark McLemore	.10
120 Who Me? (Joe Niekro)	.25
121 Mark McGwire	2.00
122 Darryl Strawberry	.15
123 Mike Scott	.10
124 Andre Dawson	.12
125 Jose Canseco	.40
126 Kevin McReynolds	.10
127 Joe Carter	.10
128 Casey Candaele	.10
129 Matt Nokes	.10
130 Kal Daniels	.10
131 Pete Incaviglia	.10
132 Benito Santiago	.10
133 Barry Larkin	.20
134 Gary Pettis	.10
135 B.J. Surhoff	.12
136 Juan Nieves	.10
137 Jim Deshaies	.10
138 Pete O'Brien	.10
139 Kevin Seitzer	.10
140 Devon White	.12
141 Rob Deer	.10
142 Kurt Stillwell	.10
143 Edwin Correa	.10
144 Dion James	.10
145 Danny Tartabull	.10
146 Jerry Browne	.10
147 Ted Higuera	.10
148 Jack Clark	.10
149 Ruben Sierra	.10
150 Mark McGwire, Eric Davis	1.50

1988 Classic Travel Update I (Red)

This set was produced for use with the travel edition of Game Time's Classic Baseball Board Game. Special cards in the set include a McGwire/Mattingly, an instruction card with McGwire/Canseco and three different cards featuring Phil Niekro (in different uniforms). Update I card fronts have red borders, a yellow Classic logo in the upper-left corner and a black and beige name banner beneath the photo. Backs are printed in red and pink on white and include the player name, personal info, major league records, a baseball question and space for the player autograph. Classic card series sold via hobby dealers and retail toy stores nationwide. Game Time Ltd., the set's producer, was purchased by Scoreboard of Cherry Hill, N.J. in 1988.

	MT
Complete Set (50):	10.00
Common Player:	.10
151 Don Mattingly, Mark McGwire	2.00
152 Don Mattingly	.80
153 Mark McGwire	3.00

154	Eric Davis	.10
155	Wade Boggs	.50
156	Dale Murphy	.15
157	Andre Dawson	.12
158	Roger Clemens	.75
159	Kevin Seitzer	.10
160	Benito Santiago	.10
161	Kal Daniels	.10
162	John Kruk	.10
163	Bill Ripken	.10
164	Kirby Puckett	.75
165	Jose Canseco	.50
166	Matt Nokes	.10
167	Mike Schmidt	.75
168	Tim Raines	.12
169	Ryne Sandberg	.60
170	Dave Winfield	.25
171	Dwight Gooden	.12
172	Bret Saberhagen	.12
173	Willie McGee	.10
174	Jack Morris	.10
175	Jeff Leonard	.10
176	Cal Ripken, Jr.	3.00
177	Pete Incaviglia	.10
178	Devon White	.10
179	Nolan Ryan	3.00
180	Ruben Sierra	.10
181	Todd Worrell	.10
182	Glenn Davis	.10
183	Frank Viola	.10
184	Cory Snyder	.10
185	Tracy Jones	.10
186	Terry Steinbach	.10
187	Julio Franco	.10
188	Larry Sheets	.10
189	John Marzano	.10
190	Kevin Elster	.10
191	Vincente Palacios	.10
192	Kent Hrbek	.12
193	Eric Bell	.10
194	Kelly Downs	.10
195	Jose Lind	.10
196	Dave Stewart	.10
197	Jose Canseco, Mark McGwire	2.00
198	Phil Niekro	.20
199	Phil Niekro	.20
200	Phil Niekro	.20

1988 Classic Travel Update II (Blue)

This set was produced for use with the travel edition of Game Time's Classic Baseball Board Game. Fronts have blue borders, a yellow Classic logo in the upper-left corner and a black and beige name banner beneath the photo. Backs are printed in blue on white and include the player name, personal info, major league records, a baseball question and space for the player autograph. Classic card series are sold via hobby dealers and retail toy stores nationwide. Game Time Ltd., the set's producer, was purchased by Scoreboard of Cherry Hill, N.J. in 1988.

		MT
Complete Set (50):		9.00
Common Player:		.10
201	Dale Murphy, Eric Davis	.20
202	B.J. Surhoff	.12
203	John Kruk	.10
204	Sam Horn	.10
205	Jack Clark	.10
206	Wally Joyner	.12
207	Matt Nokes	.10
208	Bo Jackson	.30
209	Darryl Strawberry	.15
210	Ozzie Smith	.40
211	Don Mattingly	.75
212	Mark McGwire	2.00
213	Eric Davis	.12
214	Wade Boggs	.50
215	Dale Murphy	.25
216	Andre Dawson	.15
217	Roger Clemens	.65
218	Kevin Seitzer	.10
219	Benito Santiago	.10
220	Tony Gwynn	.75
221	Mike Scott	.10
222	Steve Bedrosian	.10
223	Vince Coleman	.10
224	Rick Sutcliffe	.10
225	Will Clark	.35
226	Pete Rose	1.25
227	Mike Greenwell	.10
228	Ken Caminiti	.15
229	Ellis Burks	.10
230	Dave Magadan	.10
231	Alan Trammell	.12
232	Paul Molitor	.40
233	Gary Gaetti	.10
234	Rickey Henderson	.20
235	Danny Tartabull	.10
236	Bobby Bonilla	.15
237	Mike Dunne	.10
238	Al Leiter	.12
239	John Farrell	.10
240	Joe Magrane	.10
241	Mike Henneman	.10
242	George Bell	.10
243	Gregg Jefferies	.25
244	Jay Buhner	.20
245	Todd Benzinger	.10
246	Matt Williams	.25
(247)	Don Mattingly, Mark McGwire (No card number on back)	2.00
248	George Brett	1.00
249	Jimmy Key	.10
250	Mark Langston	.10

1989 Classic

This 100-card set was released by The Score Board to accompany trivia board games. Fronts have a wide border which graduates from pink at the top to blue at the bottom. Card backs are printed in blue. The flip side includes personal information, and major league record in a boxed area. Another boxed area below the record presents five trivia questions. The lower border on back provides an autograph space. The Classic card series was sold by retail stores and hobby dealers nationwide.

		MT
Complete Set (100):		10.00
Common Player:		.10
1	Orel Hershiser	.12
2	Wade Boggs	.60
3	Jose Canseco	.60
4	Mark McGwire	2.00
5	Don Mattingly	.90
6	Gregg Jefferies	.20
7	Dwight Gooden	.15
8	Darryl Strawberry	.15
9	Eric Davis	.12
10	Joey Meyer	.10
11	Joe Carter	.10
12	Paul Molitor	.50
13	Mark Grace	.35
14	Kurt Stillwell	.10
15	Kirby Puckett	.90
16	Keith Miller	.10
17	Glenn Davis	.10
18	Will Clark	.50
19	Cory Snyder	.10
20	Jose Lind	.10
21	Andres Thomas	.10
22	Dave Smith	.10
23	Mike Scott	.10
24	Kevin McReynolds	.10
25	B.J. Surhoff	.10
26	Mackey Sasser	.10
27	Chad Kreuter	.10
28	Hal Morris	.10
29	Wally Joyner	.12
30	Tony Gwynn	.75
31	Kevin Mitchell	.10
32	Dave Winfield	.25
33	Billy Bean	.10
34	Steve Bedrosian	.10
35	Ron Gant	.10
36	Len Dykstra	.10
37	Andre Dawson	.12
38	Brett Butler	.12
39	Rob Deer	.10
40	Tommy John	.15
41	Gary Gaetti	.10
42	Tim Raines	.12
43	George Bell	.10
44	Dwight Evans	.10
45	Denny Martinez	.12
46	Andres Galarraga	.20
47	George Brett	.90
48	Mike Schmidt	.90
49	Dave Steib	.10
50	Rickey Henderson	.30
51	Craig Biggio	.15
52	Mark Lemke	.10
53	Chris Sabo	.10
54	Jeff Treadway	.10
55	Kent Hrbek	.12
56	Cal Ripken, Jr.	2.00
57	Tim Belcher	.10
58	Ozzie Smith	.50
59	Keith Hernandez	.10
60	Pedro Guerrero	.10
61	Greg Swindell	.10
62	Bret Saberhagen	.12
63	John Tudor	.10
64	Gary Carter	.15
65	Kevin Seitzer	.10
66	Jesse Barfield	.10
67	Luis Medina	.10
68	Walt Weiss	.12
69	Terry Steinbach	.10
70	Barry Larkin	.20
71	Pete Rose	1.50
72	Luis Salazar	.10
73	Benito Santiago	.10
74	Kal Daniels	.10
75	Kevin Elster	.10
76	Rob Dibble	.10
77	Bobby Witt	.10
78	Steve Searcy	.10
79	Sandy Alomar	.15
80	Chili Davis	.12
81	Alvin Davis	.10
82	Charlie Leibrandt	.10
83	Robin Yount	.50
84	Mark Carreon	.10
85	Pascual Perez	.10
86	Dennis Rasmussen	.10
87	Ernie Riles	.10
88	Melido Perez	.10
89	Doug Jones	.10
90	Dennis Eckersley	.12
91	Bob Welch	.10
92	Bob Milacki	.10
93	Jeff Robinson	.10
94	Mike Henneman	.10
95	Randy Johnson	.50
96	Ron Jones	.10
97	Jack Armstrong	.10
98	Willie McGee	.12
99	Ryne Sandberg	.65
100	David Cone, Danny Jackson	.10

1989 Classic Travel Update I (Orange)

Sold only as a 50-card complete set under the official name of "Travel Update I," these cards are identical in format to the 1989 Classic 100-card set with the exception that the borders are orange at the top, graduating to maroon at the bottom. Backs are maroon.

		MT
Complete Set (50):		15.00
Common Player:		.10
101	Gary Sheffield	.35
102	Wade Boggs	.55
103	Jose Canseco	.55
104	Mark McGwire	1.00
105	Orel Hershiser	.12
106	Don Mattingly	.90
107	Dwight Gooden	.15
108	Darryl Strawberry	.15
109	Eric Davis	.15
110	Bam Bam Meulens	.10
111	Andy Van Slyke	.10
112	Al Leiter	.12
113	Matt Nokes	.10
114	Mike Krukow	.10
115	Tony Fernandez	.10
116	Fred McGriff	.15
117	Barry Bonds	.75
118	Gerald Perry	.10
119	Roger Clemens	.50
120	Kirk Gibson	.10
121	Greg Maddux	.55
122	Bo Jackson	.25
123	Danny Jackson	.10
124	Dale Murphy	.15
125	David Cone	.10
126	Tom Browning	.10
127	Roberto Alomar	.50
128	Alan Trammell	.12
129	Ricky Jordan	.10
130	Ramon Martinez	.15
131	Ken Griffey, Jr.	9.00
132	Gregg Olson	.10
133	Carlos Quintana	.10
134	Dave West	.10
135	Cameron Drew	.10
136	Ted Higuera	.10
137	Sil Campusano	.10
138	Mark Gubicza	.10
139	Mike Boddicker	.10
140	Paul Gibson	.10
141	Jose Rijo	.10
142	John Costello	.10
143	Cecil Espy	.10
144	Frank Viola	.10
145	Erik Hanson	.10
146	Juan Samuel	.10
147	Harold Reynolds	.10
148	Joe Magrane	.10
149	Mike Greenwell	.10
150	Darryl Strawberry, Will Clark	.25

1989 Classic Travel Update II (Purple)

Numbered from 151-200, this set features rookies and traded players with their new teams. The cards are purple and gray and were sold as part of a board game with baseball trivia questions.

		MT
Complete Set (50):		12.00
Common Player:		.05
151	Jim Abbott	.20
152	Ellis Burks	.10
153	Mike Schmidt	.75
154	Gregg Jefferies	.20
155	Mark Grace	.25
156	Jerome Walton	.05
157	Bo Jackson	.25
158	Jack Clark	.05
159	Tom Glavine	.10
160	Eddie Murray	.25
161	John Dopson	.05
162	Ruben Sierra	.05
163	Rafael Palmeiro	.20
164	Nolan Ryan	1.50
165	Barry Larkin	.12
166	Tommy Herr	.05
167	Roberto Kelly	.05
168	Glenn Davis	.05
169	Glenn Braggs	.05
170	Juan Bell	.05
171	Todd Burns	.05
172	Derek Lilliquist	.05
173	Orel Hershiser	.10
174	John Smoltz	.15
175	Ozzie Guillen, Ellis Burks	.10
176	Kirby Puckett	.75
177	Robin Ventura	.20
178	Allan Anderson	.05
179	Steve Sax	.05
180	Will Clark	.25
181	Mike Devereaux	.05
182	Tom Gordon	.05
183	Rob Murphy	.05
184	Pete O'Brien	.05
185	Cris Carpenter	.05
186	Tom Brunansky	.05
187	Bob Boone	.05
188	Lou Whitaker	.05
189	Dwight Gooden	.10
190	Mark McGwire	1.50
191	John Smiley	.05
192	Tommy Gregg	.05
193	Ken Griffey, Jr.	7.50
194	Bruce Hurst	.05
195	Greg Swindell	.05
196	Nelson Liriano	.05
197	Randy Myers	.05
198	Kevin Mitchell	.05
199	Dante Bichette	.15
200	Deion Sanders	.75

1990 Classic

Classic baseball returned in 1990 with a 150-card set. Cards have a blue border on front, with splashes of pink. The cards were again sold as part of a baseball trivia game.

		MT
Complete Set (150):		5.50
Common Player:		.05
1	Nolan Ryan	.95
2	Bo Jackson	.15
3	Gregg Olson	.05
4	Tom Gordon	.05
5	Robin Ventura	.15
6	Will Clark	.30
7	Ruben Sierra	.05
8	Mark Grace	.25
9	Luis de los Santos	.05
10	Bernie Williams	.30
11	Eric Davis	.10
12	Carney Lansford	.05
13	John Smoltz	.10
14	Gary Sheffield	.25
15	Kent Merker	.05
16	Don Mattingly	.60
17	Tony Gwynn	.45
18	Ozzie Smith	.35
19	Fred McGriff	.15
20	Ken Griffey, Jr.	1.50
21a	Deion Sanders ("Prime Time")	.75
21b	Deion Sanders (Deion "Prime Time" Sanders)	.50
22	Jose Canseco	.35
23	Mitch Williams	.05
24	Cal Ripken, Jr.	.95
25	Bob Geren	.05
26	Wade Boggs	.30
27	Ryne Sandberg	.50
28	Kirby Puckett	.60
29	Mike Scott	.05
30	Dwight Smith	.05
31	Craig Worthington	.05
32	Ricky Jordan	.05
33	Darryl Strawberry	.15
34	Jerome Walton	.05
35	John Olerud	.20
36	Tom Glavine	.10
37	Rickey Henderson	.15
38	Rolando Roomes	.05
39	Mickey Tettleton	.05
40	Jim Abbott	.10
41	Dave Righetti	.05
42	Mike LaValliere	.05
43	Rob Dibble	.05
44	Pete Harnisch	.05
45	Jose Offerman	.05
46	Walt Weiss	.05
47	Mike Greenwell	.05
48	Barry Larkin	.15
49	Dave Gallagher	.05
50	Junior Felix	.05
51	Roger Clemens	.50

52	Lonnie Smith	.05
53	Jerry Browne	.05
54	Greg Briley	.05
55	Delino DeShields	.05
56	Carmelo Martinez	.05
57	Craig Biggio	.10
58	Dwight Gooden	.12
59a	Bo, Ruben, Mark (Bo Jackson, Ruben Sierra, Mark McGwire)	1.00
59b	A.L. Fence Busters (Bo Jackson, Ruben Sierra, Mark McGwire)	1.00
60	Greg Vaughn	.15
61	Roberto Alomar	.15
62	Steve Bedrosian	.05
63	Devon White	.05
64	Kevin Mitchell	.05
65	Marquis Grissom	.08
66	Brian Holman	.05
67	Julio Franco	.05
68	Dave West	.05
69	Harold Baines	.08
70	Eric Anthony	.05
71	Glenn Davis	.05
72	Mark Langston	.05
73	Matt Williams	.20
74	Rafael Palmeiro	.20
75	Pete Rose, Jr.	.25
76	Ramon Martinez	.10
77	Dwight Evans	.05
78	Mackey Sasser	.05
79	Mike Schooler	.05
80	Dennis Cook	.05
81	Orel Hershiser	.10
82	Barry Bonds	.60
83	Geronimo Berroa	.05
84	George Bell	.05
85	Andre Dawson	.12
86	John Franco	.05
87a	Clark/Gwynn (Will Clark, Tony Gwynn)	.50
87b	N.L. Hit Kings (Will Clark, Tony Gwynn)	.40
88	Glenallen Hill	.05
89	Jeff Ballard	.05
90	Todd Zeile	.10
91	Frank Viola	.05
92	Ozzie Guillen	.05
93	Jeff Leonard	.05
94	Dave Smith	.05
95	Dave Parker	.08
96	Jose Gonzalez	.05
97	Dave Steib	.05
98	Charlie Hayes	.05
99	Jesse Barfield	.05
100	Joey Belle	.75
101	Jeff Reardon	.05
102	Bruce Hurst	.05
103	Luis Medina	.05
104	Mike Moore	.05
105	Vince Coleman	.05
106	Alan Trammell	.10
107	Randy Myers	.05
108	Frank Tanana	.05
109	Craig Lefferts	.05
110	John Wetteland	.08
111	Chris Gwynn	.05
112	Mark Carreon	.05
113	Von Hayes	.05
114	Doug Jones	.05
115	Andres Galarraga	.10
116	Carlton Fisk	.15
117	Paul O'Neill	.08
118	Tim Raines	.10
119	Tom Brunansky	.05
120	Andy Benes	.12
121	Mark Portugal	.05
122	Willie Randolph	.05
123	Jeff Blauser	.05
124	Don August	.05
125	Chuck Cary	.05
126	John Smiley	.05
127	Terry Mullholland	.05
128	Harold Reynolds	.05
129	Hubie Brooks	.05
130	Ben McDonald	.05
131	Kevin Ritz	.05
132	Luis Quinones	.05
133a	Bam Bam Muelens (last name incorrect)	.50
133b	Bam Bam Meulens (last name correct)	.05
134	Bill Spiers	.05
135	Andy Hawkins	.05
136	Alvin Davis	.05
137	Lee Smith	.05
138	Joe Carter	.08
139	Bret Saberhagen	.08
140	Sammy Sosa	1.00
141	Matt Nokes	.05
142	Bert Blyleven	.05
143	Bobby Bonilla	.10
144	Howard Johnson	.05
145	Joe Magrane	.05
146	Pedro Guerrero	.05
147	Robin Yount	.45
148	Dan Gladden	.05
149	Steve Sax	.05
150a	Clark/Mitchell (Will Clark, Kevin Mitchell)	.50
150b	Bay Bombers (Will Clark, Kevin Mitchell)	.25

1990 Classic Series II

As in previous years, Classic released a 50-card second series set for use with its trivia board game. Unlike earlier update sets, the 1990 Series II set is numbered 1-50 with a "T" designation accompanying the card number. Cards measure 2-1/2" x 3-1/2" and share the format of the original 1990 Classic cards; Series II cards have pink borders with blue highlights. The cards were issued only in complete set form.

		MT
	Complete Set (50):	3.50
	Common Player:	.05
1	Gregg Jefferies	.10
2	Steve Adkins	.05
3	Sandy Alomar, Jr.	.10
4	Steve Avery	.05
5	Mike Blowers	.05
6	George Brett	.50
7	Tom Browning	.05
8	Ellis Burks	.05
9	Joe Carter	.05
10	Jerald Clark	.05
11	"Hot Corners" (Matt Williams, Will Clark)	.25
12	Pat Combs	.05
13	Scott Cooper	.05
14	Mark Davis	.05
15	Storm Davis	.05
16	Larry Walker	.10
17	Brian DuBois	.05
18	Len Dykstra	.05
19	John Franco	.05
20	Kirk Gibson	.05
21	Juan Gonzalez	1.50
22	Tommy Greene	.05
23	Kent Hrbek	.08
24	Mike Huff	.05
25	Bo Jackson	.15
26	Nolan Knows Bo (Bo Jackson, Nolan Ryan)	2.00
27	Roberto Kelly	.05
28	Mark Langston	.05
29	Ray Lankford	.10
30	Kevin Maas	.05
31	Julio Machado	.05
32	Greg Maddux	.50
33	Mark McGwire	1.50
34	Paul Molitor	.30
35	Hal Morris	.05
36	Dale Murphy	.15
37	Eddie Murray	.30
38	Jaime Navarro	.05
39	Dean Palmer	.08
40	Derek Parks	.05
41	Bobby Rose	.05
42	Wally Joyner	.08
43	Chris Sabo	.05
44	Benito Santiago	.05
45	Mike Stanton	.05
46	Terry Steinbach	.05
47	Dave Stewart	.05
48	Greg Swindell	.05
49	Jose Vizcaino	.05
---	"Royal Flush" (Bret Saberhagen, Mark Davis)	.08

1990 Classic Series III

Classic's third series of 1990 features the same format as the previous two releases. Series III borders are yellow with blue accents. The cards have trivia questions on back and are numbered 1T-100T. No card 51T or 57T exists. Two cards in the set are unnumbered. Like other Classic issues, the cards are designed for use with the trivia board game and were sold only as complete sets.

		MT
	Complete Set (100):	5.50
	Common Player:	.05
1	Ken Griffey, Jr.	2.00
2	John Tudor	.05
3	John Kruk	.05
4	Mark Gardner	.05
5	Scott Radinsky	.05
6	John Burkett	.05
7	Will Clark	.15
8	Gary Carter	.08
9	Ted Higuera	.05
10	Dave Parker	.05
11	Dante Bichette	.08
12	Don Mattingly	.65
13	Greg Harris	.05
14	David Hollins	.05
15	Matt Nokes	.05
16	Kevin Tapani	.05
17	Shane Mack	.05
18	Randy Myers	.05
19	Greg Olson	.05
20	Shawn Abner	.05
21	Jim Presley	.05
22	Randy Johnson	.12
23	Edgar Martinez	.05
24	Scott Coolbaugh	.05
25	Jeff Treadway	.05
26	Joe Klink	.05
27	Rickey Henderson	.10
28	Sam Horn	.05
29	Kurt Stillwell	.05
30	Andy Van Slyke	.05
31	Willie Banks	.05
32	Jose Canseco	.30
33	Felix Jose	.05
34	Candy Maldonado	.05
35	Carlos Baerga	.05
36	Keith Hernandez	.05
37	Frank Viola	.05
38	Pete O'Brien	.05
39	Pat Borders	.05
40	Mike Heath	.05
41	Kevin Brown	.05
42	Chris Bosio	.05
43	Shawn Boskie	.05
44	Carlos Quintana	.05
45	Juan Samuel	.05
46	Tim Layana	.05
47	Mike Harkey	.05
48	Gerald Perry	.05
49	Mike Witt	.05
50	Joe Orsulak	.05
51	(Not issued)	
52	Willie Blair	.05
53	Gene Larkin	.05
54	Jody Reed	.05
55	Jeff Reardon	.05
56	Kevin McReynolds	.05
57	(Not issued)	
58	Eric Yelding	.05
59	Fred Lynn	.05
60	Jim Leyritz	.05
61	John Orton	.05
62	Mike Lieberthal	.10
63	Mike Hartley	.05
64	Kal Daniels	.05
65	Terry Shumpert	.05
66	Sil Campusano	.05
67	Tony Pena	.05
68	Barry Bonds	.50
69	Oddibe McDowell	.05
70	Kelly Gruber	.05
71	Willie Randolph	.05
72	Rick Parker	.05
73	Bobby Bonilla	.08
74	Jack Armstrong	.05
75	Hubie Brooks	.05
76	Sandy Alomar, Jr.	.10
77	Ruben Sierra	.05
78	Erik Hanson	.05
79	Tony Phillips	.05
80	Rondell White	.35
81	Bobby Thigpen	.05
82	Ron Walden	.05
83	Don Peters	.05
84	#6 (Nolan Ryan)	.75
85	Lance Dickson	.05
86	Ryne Sandberg	.40
87	Eric Christopherson	.05
88	Shane Andrews	.10
89	Marc Newfield	.05
90	Adam Hyzdu	.05
91	"Texas Heat" (Nolan Ryan, Reid Ryan)	1.00
92	Chipper Jones	2.00
93	Frank Thomas	2.00
94	Cecil Fielder	.05
95	Delino DeShields	.05
96	John Olerud	.15
97	Dave Justice	.50
98	Joe Oliver	.05
99	Alex Fernandez	.08
100	Todd Hundley	.10
---	Mike Marshall (Game instructions on back)	.05
---	4 in 1 (Frank Viola, Nolan/Reid Ryan, Chipper Jones, Don Mattingly)	.50

1991 Classic

Top rookies and draft picks highlight this set from Classic. The cards come with a trivia board game and accessories. Fronts have fading blue borders with a touch of red. A blank-back "4-in-1" micro-player card is included with each game set.

		MT
	Complete Set (99):	5.50
	Common Player:	.05
1	John Olerud	.10
2	Tino Martinez	.20
3	Ken Griffey, Jr.	1.50
4	Jeromy Burnitz	.08
5	Ron Gant	.05
6	Mike Benjamin	.05
7	Steve Decker	.05
8	Matt Williams	.20
9	Rafael Novoa	.05
10	Kevin Mitchell	.05
11	Dave Justice	.20
12	Leo Gomez	.05
13	Chris Hoiles	.05
14	Ben McDonald	.05
15	David Segui	.05
16	Anthony Telford	.05
17	Mike Mussina	.10
18	Roger Clemens	.50
19	Wade Boggs	.45
20	Tim Naehring	.05
21	Joe Carter	.08
22	Phil Plantier	.05
23	Rob Dibble	.05
24	Mo Vaughn	.60
25	Lee Stevens	.05
26	Chris Sabo	.05
27	Mark Grace	.20
28	Derrick May	.05
29	Ryne Sandberg	.30
30	Matt Stark	.05
31	Bobby Thigpen	.05
32	Frank Thomas	.75
33	Don Mattingly	.75
34	Eric Davis	.08
35	Reggie Jefferson	.05
36	Alex Cole	.05
37	Mark Lewis	.05
38	Tim Costo	.05
39	Sandy Alomar, Jr.	.10
40	Travis Fryman	.08
41	Cecil Fielder	.08
42	Milt Cuyler	.05
43	Andujar Cedeno	.05
44	Danny Darwin	.05
45	Randy Henis	.05
46	George Brett	.65
47	Jeff Conine	.08
48	Bo Jackson	.15
49	Brian McRae	.08
50	Brent Mayne	.05
51	Eddie Murray	.25
52	Ramon Martinez	.05
53	Jim Neidlinger	.05
54	Jim Poole	.05
55	Tim McIntosh	.05
56	Randy Veres	.05
57	Kirby Puckett	.75
58	Todd Ritchie	.05
59	Rich Garces	.05
60	Moises Alou	.15
61	Delino DeShields	.05
62	Oscar Azocar	.05
63	Kevin Maas	.05
64	Alan Mills	.05
65	John Franco	.05
66	Chris Jelic	.05
67	Dave Magadan	.05
68	Darryl Strawberry	.10
69	Hensley Meulens	.05
70	Juan Gonzalez	.75
71	Reggie Harris	.05
72	Rickey Henderson	.15
73	Mark McGwire	.75
74	Willie McGee	.05
75	Todd Van Poppel	.10
76	Bob Welch	.05
77	"Future Aces" (Todd Van Poppel, Don Peters, David Zancanaro, Kirk Dressendorfer)	.10
78	Lenny Dykstra	.05
79	Mickey Morandini	.05
80	Wes Chamberlain	.05
81	Barry Bonds	.60
82	Doug Drabek	.05
83	Randy Tomlin	.05
84	Scott Chiamparino	.05
85	Rafael Palmeiro	.12
86	Nolan Ryan	1.00
87	Bobby Witt	.05
88	Fred McGriff	.15
89	Dave Steib	.05
90	Ed Sprague	.05
91	Vince Coleman	.05
92	Rod Brewer	.05
93	Bernard Gilkey	.08
94	Roberto Alomar	.15
95	Chuck Finley	.05
96	Dale Murphy	.15
97	Jose Rijo	.05
98	Hal Morris	.05
99	"Friendly Foes" (Dwight Gooden, Darryl Strawberry)	.15
---	John Olerud, Dwight Gooden, Jose Canseco, Darryl Strawberry	.25

1991 Classic Series II

Classic released a 100-card second series in 1991. Cards feature the same format as the first series, with the exception of border color; Series II features maroon borders. The cards are designed for trivia game use. Series II includes several players with new teams and top rookies. Special Four-In-One, 300 Game Winner and Strikout Kings cards are included with each set.

		MT
	Complete Set (100):	4.50
	Common Player:	.05
1	Ken Griffey, Jr.	1.00
2	Wilfredo Cordero	.08
3	Cal Ripken, Jr.	.90
4	D.J. Dozier	.05
5	Darrin Fletcher	.05
6	Glenn Davis	.05
7	Alex Fernandez	.08
8	Cory Snyder	.05
9	Tim Raines	.08
10	Greg Swindell	.05
11	Mark Lewis	.05
12	Rico Brogna	.05
13	Gary Sheffield	.20
14	Paul Molitor	.45
15	Kent Hrbek	.08
16	Scott Erickson	.08
17	Steve Sax	.05
18	Dennis Eckersley	.08

19	Jose Canseco	.25
20	Kirk Dressendorfer	.05
21	Ken Griffey, Sr.	.05
22	Erik Hanson	.05
23	Dan Peltier	.05
24	John Olerud	.10
25	Eddie Zosky	.05
26	Steve Avery	.05
27	John Smoltz	.10
28	Frank Thomas	.75
29	Jerome Walton	.05
30	George Bell	.05
31	Jose Rijo	.05
32	Randy Myers	.05
33	Barry Larkin	.10
34	Eric Anthony	.05
35	Dave Hansen	.05
36	Eric Karros	.08
37	Jose Offerman	.05
38	Marquis Grissom	.08
39	Dwight Gooden	.10
40	Gregg Jefferies	.10
41	Pat Combs	.05
42	Todd Zeile	.08
43	Benito Santiago	.08
44	Dave Staton	.05
45	Tony Fernandez	.05
46	Fred McGriff	.15
47	Jeff Brantley	.05
48	Junior Felix	.05
49	Jack Morris	.05
50	Chris George	.05
51	Henry Rodriguez	.10
52	Paul Marak	.05
53	Ryan Klesko	.10
54	Darren Lewis	.05
55	Lance Dickson	.05
56	Anthony Young	.05
57	Willie Banks	.05
58	Mike Bordick	.05
59	Roger Salkeld	.05
60	Steve Karsay	.05
61	Bernie Williams	.20
62	Mickey Tettleton	.05
63	Dave Justice	.25
64	Steve Decker	.05
65	Roger Clemens	.45
66	Phil Plantier	.05
67	Ryne Sandberg	.50
68	Sandy Alomar,Jr.	.10
69	Cecil Fielder	.08
70	George Brett	.50
71	Delino DeShields	.05
72	Dave Magadan	.05
73	Darryl Strawberry	.08
74	Juan Gonzalez	.50
75	Rickey Henderson	.15
76	Willie McGee	.05
77	Todd Van Poppel	.08
78	Barry Bonds	.45
79	Doug Drabek	.05
80	Nolan Ryan (300 games)	.75
81	Roberto Alomar	.10
82	Ivan Rodriguez	.25
83	Dan Opperman	.05
84	Jeff Bagwell	.60
85	Braulio Castillo	.05
86	Doug Simons	.05
87	Wade Taylor	.05
88	Gary Scott	.05
89	Dave Stewart	.05
90	Mike Simms	.05
91	Luis Gonzalez	.05
92	Bobby Bonilla	.10
93	Tony Gwynn	.45
94	Will Clark	.20
95	Rich Rowland	.05
96	Alan Trammell	.10
97	"Strikeout Kings" (Nolan Ryan, Roger Clemens)	.75
98	Joe Carter	.05
99	Jack Clark	.05
100	Four-In-One	.25

1991 Classic Series III

Green borders highlight Classic's third series of cards for 1991. The set includes a gameboard and player cards featuring trivia questions on the back. Statistics and biographical information are also found on back.

		MT
Complete Set (100):		5.00
Common Player:		.05
1	Jim Abbott	.10
2	Craig Biggio	.10
3	Wade Boggs	.35
4	Bobby Bonilla	.10
5	Ivan Calderon	.05
6	Jose Canseco	.35
7	Andy Benes	.10
8	Wes Chamberlain	.05
9	Will Clark	.30
10	Royce Clayton	.05
11	Gerald Alexander	.05
12	Chili Davis	.05
13	Eric Davis	.08
14	Andre Dawson	.10
15	Rob Dibble	.05
16	Chris Donnels	.05
17	Scott Erickson	.08
18	Monty Fariss	.05
19	Ruben Amaro, Jr.	.05
20	Chuck Finley	.05
21	Carlton Fisk	.12
22	Carlos Baerga	.10
23	Ron Gant	.10
24	Dave Justice, Ron Gant	.25
25	Mike Gardiner	.05
26	Tom Glavine	.08
27	Joe Grahe	.05
28	Derek Bell	.10
29	Mike Greenwell	.05
30	Ken Griffey, Jr.	1.00
31	Leo Gomez	.05
32	Tom Goodwin	.05
33	Tony Gwynn	.25
34	Mel Hall	.05
35	Brian Harper	.05
36	Dave Henderson	.05
37	Albert Belle	.50
38	Orel Hershiser	.08
39	Brian Hunter	.05
40	Howard Johnson	.05
41	Felix Jose	.05
42	Wally Joyner	.08
43	Jeff Juden	.08
44	Pat Kelly	.05
45	Jimmy Key	.05
46	Chuck Knoblauch	.15
47	John Kruk	.05
48	Ray Lankford	.10
49	Ced Landrum	.05
50	Scott Livingstone	.05
51	Kevin Maas	.05
52	Greg Maddux	.50
53	Dennis Martinez	.10
54	Edgar Martinez	.05
55	Pedro Martinez	.45
56	Don Mattingly	.75
57	Orlando Merced	.05
58	Keith Mitchell	.05
59	Kevin Mitchell	.05
60	Paul Molitor	.25
61	Jack Morris	.05
62	Hal Morris	.05
63	Kevin Morton	.05
64	Pedro Munoz	.05
65	Eddie Murray	.25
66	Jack McDowell	.05
67	Jeff McNeely	.05
68	Brian McRae	.08
69	Kevin McReynolds	.05
70	Gregg Olson	.05
71	Rafael Palmeiro	.15
72	Dean Palmer	.08
73	Tony Phillips	.05
74	Kirby Puckett	.60
75	Carlos Quintana	.05
76	Pat Rice	.05
77	Cal Ripken, Jr.	.90
78	Ivan Rodriguez	.20
79	Nolan Ryan	1.00
80	Bret Saberhagen	.08
81	Tim Salmon	.35
82	Juan Samuel	.05
83	Ruben Sierra	.05
84	Heathcliff Slocumb	.05
85	Joe Slusarski	.05
86	John Smiley	.05
87	Dave Smith	.05
88	Ed Sprague	.05
89	Todd Stottlemyre	.05
90	Mike Timlin	.05
91	Greg Vaughn	.10
92	Frank Viola	.05
93	John Wehner	.05
94	Devon White	.05
95	Matt Williams	.20
96	Rick Wilkins	.05
97	Bernie Williams	.25
98	Starter & Stopper (Goose Gossage, Nolan Ryan)	.20
99	Gerald Williams	.05
----	4-in-1 (Bobby Bonilla, Will Clark, Cal Ripken Jr., Scott Erickson)	.25

Player names in *Italic* type indicate a rookie card.

1991 Classic Collector's Edition

The Classic Collector's edition made its debut in 1991. This package includes a board game, trivia baseball player cards, a baseball tips booklet and a certificate of authenticity, all packaged in a collector's edition box. Each box is individually and sequentially numbered on the outside, with a reported 100,000 available.

		MT
Complete Set (200):		15.00
Common Player:		.05
1	Frank Viola	.05
2	Tim Wallach	.05
3	Lou Whitaker	.05
4	Brett Butler	.08
5	Jim Abbott	.08
6	Jack Armstrong	.05
7	Craig Biggio	.10
8	Brian Barnes	.05
9	Dennis "Oil Can" Boyd	.05
10	Tom Browning	.05
11	Tom Brunansky	.05
12	Ellis Burks	.08
13	Harold Baines	.05
14	Kal Daniels	.05
15	Mark Davis	.05
16	Storm Davis	.05
17	Tom Glavine	.10
18	Mike Greenwell	.05
19	Kelly Gruber	.05
20	Mark Gubicza	.05
21	Pedro Guerrero	.05
22	Mike Harkey	.05
23	Orel Hershiser	.08
24	Ted Higuera	.05
25	Von Hayes	.05
26	Andre Dawson	.12
27	Shawon Dunston	.05
28	Roberto Kelly	.05
29	Joe Magrane	.05
30	Dennis Martinez	.08
31	Kevin McReynolds	.05
32	Matt Nokes	.05
33	Dan Plesac	.05
34	Dave Parker	.08
35	Randy Johnson	.20
36	Bret Saberhagen	.08
37	Mackey Sasser	.05
38	Mike Scott	.05
39	Ozzie Smith	.35
40	Kevin Seitzer	.05
41	Ruben Sierra	.05
42	Kevin Tapani	.05
43	Danny Tartabull	.05
44	Robby Thompson	.05
45	Andy Van Slyke	.05
46	Greg Vaughn	.10
47	Harold Reynolds	.05
48	Will Clark	.35
49	Gary Gaetti	.05
50	Joe Grahe	.05
51	Carlton Fisk	.12
52	Robin Ventura	.08
53	Ozzie Guillen	.05
54	Tom Candiotti	.05
55	Doug Jones	.05
56	Eric King	.05
57	Kirk Gibson	.05
58	Tim Costo	.05
59	Robin Yount	.40
60	Sammy Sosa	.75
61	Jesse Barfield	.05
62	Marc Newfield	.05
63	Jimmy Key	.05
64	Felix Jose	.05
65	Mark Whiten	.05
66	Tommy Greene	.05
67	Kent Mercker	.05
68	Greg Maddux	.40
69	Danny Jackson	.05
70	Reggie Sanders	.08
71	Eric Yelding	.05
72	Karl Rhodes	.05
73	Fernando Valenzuela	.08
74	Chris Nabholz	.05
75	Andres Galarraga	.08
76	Howard Johnson	.05
77	Hubie Brooks	.05
78	Terry Mulholland	.05
79	Paul Molitor	.40
80	Roger McDowell	.05
81	Darren Daulton	.05
82	Zane Smith	.05
83	Ray Lankford	.10
84	Bruce Hurst	.05
85	Andy Benes	.10
86	John Burkett	.05
87	Dave Righetti	.05
88	Steve Karsay	.05
89	D.J. Dozier	.05
90	Jeff Bagwell	.60
91	Joe Carter	.05
92	Wes Chamberlain	.05
93	Vince Coleman	.05
94	Pat Combs	.05
95	Jerome Walton	.05
96	Jeff Conine	.05
97	Alan Trammell	.10
98	Don Mattingly	.75
99	Ramon Martinez	.10
100	Dave Magadan	.05
101	Greg Swindell	.05
102	Dave Stewart	.08
103	Gary Sheffield	.25
104	George Bell	.05
105	Mark Grace	.20
106	Steve Sax	.05
107	Ryne Sandberg	.50
108	Chris Sabo	.05
109	Jose Rijo	.05
110	Cal Ripken, Jr.	.90
111	Kirby Puckett	.75
112	Eddie Murray	.30
113	Roberto Alomar	.10
114	Randy Myers	.05
115	Rafael Palmeiro	.15
116	John Olerud	.10
117	Gregg Jefferies	.10
118	Kent Hrbek	.08
119	Marquis Grissom	.08
120	Ken Griffey, Jr.	1.00
121	Dwight Gooden	.08
122	Juan Gonzalez	.75
123	Ron Gant	.08
124	Travis Fryman	.08
125	John Franco	.05
126	Dennis Eckersley	.10
127	Cecil Fielder	.08
128	Phil Plantier	.05
129	Kevin Mitchell	.05
130	Kevin Maas	.05
131	Mark McGwire	1.00
132	Ben McDonald	.05
133	Lenny Dykstra	.05
134	Delino DeShields	.05
135	Jose Canseco	.35
136	Eric Davis	.08
137	George Brett	.50
138	Steve Avery	.05
139	Eric Anthony	.05
140	Bobby Thigpen	.05
141	Ken Griffey, Sr.	.05
142	Barry Larkin	.10
143	Jeff Brantley	.05
144	Bobby Bonilla	.10
145	Jose Offerman	.05
146	Mike Mussina	.10
147	Erik Hanson	.05
148	Dale Murphy	.15
149	Roger Clemens	.50
150	Tino Martinez	.10
151	Todd Van Poppel	.08
152	Mo Vaughn	.50
153	Derrick May	.05
154	Jack Clark	.05
155	Dave Hansen	.05
156	Tony Gwynn	.35
157	Brian McRae	.08
158	Matt Williams	.10
159	Kirk Dressendorfer	.05
160	Scott Erickson	.05
161	Tony Fernandez	.05
162	Willie McGee	.05
163	Fred McGriff	.15
164	Leo Gomez	.05
165	Bernard Gilkey	.08
166	Bobby Witt	.05
167	Doug Drabek	.05
168	Rob Dibble	.05
169	Glenn Davis	.05
170	Danny Darwin	.05
171	Eric Karros	.25
172	Eddie Zosky	.05
173	Todd Zeile	.08
174	Tim Raines	.08
175	Benito Santiago	.05
176	Dan Peltier	.05
177	Darryl Strawberry	.10
178	Hal Morris	.05
179	Hensley Meulens	.05
180	John Smoltz	.10
181	Frank Thomas	.75
182	Dave Staton	.05
183	Scott Chiamparino	.05
184	Alex Fernandez	.08
185	Mark Lewis	.05
186	Bo Jackson	.25
187	Mickey Morandini (photo actually Darren Daulton)	.15
188	Cory Snyder	.05
189	Rickey Henderson	.25
190	Junior Felix	.05
191	Milt Cuyler	.05
192	Wade Boggs	.35
193	"Justice Prevails" (David Justice)	.30
194	Sandy Alomar, Jr.	.10
195	Barry Bonds	.60
196	Nolan Ryan	.90
197	Rico Brogna	.05
198	Steve Decker	.05
199	Bob Welch	.05
200	Andujar Cedeno	.05

1991 Classic/ American Collectables Nolan Ryan

This set of Nolan Ryan highlights was produced by Classic for American Collectables and sold as a limited-edition issue. The cards feature color photos of Ryan bordered in a garish green and yellow design. Backs have personal data and stats printed in black on green, along with a color MLB logo.

		MT
Complete Set:		10.00
Common Card:		1.00
1	Nolan Ryan (Mets '66-'71)	1.00
2	Nolan Ryan (Angels '72-'79)	1.00
3	Nolan Ryan (Astros '80-'88)	1.00
4	Nolan Ryan (Rangers '89-'90)	1.00
5	Nolan Ryan (5000 K's)	1.00
6	Nolan Ryan (6th No-No)	1.00
7	Nolan Ryan (Angels '72-'79)	1.00
8	Nolan Ryan (Astros '80-'88)	1.00
9	Nolan Ryan (Rangers '89-'90)	1.00
10	Nolan Ryan (300 Wins)	1.00

1992 Classic Series I

Classic introduced an innovative design with the release of its 1992 set. Fronts feature full-color photos bordered in white, while backs feature statistics, biographical information and trivia questions accented by a fading stadium shot. The cards were released with a gameboard and are numbered on back with a "T" prefix.

		MT
Complete Set (100):		5.00
Common Player:		.05
1	Jim Abbott	.10
2	Kyle Abbott	.05
3	Scott Aldred	.05
4	Roberto Alomar	.15
5	Wilson Alvarez	.08
6	Andy Ashby	.05
7	Steve Avery	.05
8	Jeff Bagwell	.40
9	Bret Barberie	.05
10	Kim Batiste	.05
11	Derek Bell	.10
12	Jay Bell	.05
13	Albert Belle	.35
14	Andy Benes	.10
15	Sean Berry	.05
16	Barry Bonds	.40
17	Ryan Bowen	.05
18	Trifecta (Alejandro Pena, Mark Wohlers, Kent Mercker)	.05
19	Scott Brosius	.05
20	Jay Buhner	.10
21	David Burba	.05
22	Jose Canseco	.25
23	Andujar Cedeno	.05
24	Will Clark	.20
25	Royce Clayton	.05
26	Roger Clemens	.35
27	David Cone	.10
28	Scott Cooper	.05
29	Chris Cron	.05
30	Len Dykstra	.05
31	Cal Eldred	.05
32	Hector Fajardo	.05
33	Cecil Fielder	.10
34	Dave Fleming	.05
35	Steve Foster	.05
36	Julio Franco	.05
37	Carlos Garcia	.05
38	Tom Glavine	.08
39	Tom Goodwin	.05
40	Ken Griffey, Jr.	1.00
41	Chris Haney	.05
42	Bryan Harvey	.05
43	Rickey Henderson	.10
44	Carlos Hernandez	.05
45	Roberto Hernandez	.05
46	Brook Jacoby	.05
47	Howard Johnson	.05
48	Pat Kelly	.05
49	Darryl Kile	.05
50	Chuck Knoblauch	.10
51	Ray Lankford	.08
52	Mark Leiter	.05
53	Darren Lewis	.05
54	Scott Livingstone	.05
55	Shane Mack	.05
56	Chito Martinez	.05
57	Dennis Martinez	.08
58	Don Mattingly	.50
59	Paul McClellan	.05
60	Chuck McElroy	.05
61	Fred McGriff	.15
62	Orlando Merced	.05
63	Luis Mercedes	.05
64	Kevin Mitchell	.05
65	Hal Morris	.05
66	Jack Morris	.05
67	Mike Mussina	.10
68	Denny Neagle	.10
69	Tom Pagnozzi	.05
70	Terry Pendleton	.05
71	Phil Plantier	.05
72	Kirby Puckett	.50
73	Carlos Quintana	.05
74	Willie Randolph	.05
75	Arthur Rhodes	.05
76	Cal Ripken	.75
77	Ivan Rodriguez	.25
78	Nolan Ryan	.75
79	Ryne Sandberg	.25
80	Deion Sanders	.20
81	Reggie Sanders	.10
82	Mo Sanford	.05
83	Terry Shumpert	.05
84	Tim Spehr	.05
85	Lee Stevens	.05
86	Darryl Strawberry	.12
87	Kevin Tapani	.05
88	Danny Tartabull	.05
89	Frank Thomas	.65
90	Jim Thome	.15
91	Todd Van Poppel	.08
92	Andy Van Slyke	.05
93	John Wehner	.05
94	John Wetteland	.05
95	Devon White	.05
96	Brian Williams	.05
97	Mark Wohlers	.08
98	Robin Yount	.25
99	Eddie Zosky	.05
---	4-in-1 (Barry Bonds, Roger Clemens, Steve Avery, Nolan Ryan)	.50

1992 Classic Series II

The 100-cards in Classic's 1992 Series II came packaged with a gameboard and spinner. In a completely different format from Classic's other '92 issues, Series II features player photos bordered at left and right with red or blue color bars which fade toward top and bottom. Backs have biographical data, previous-year and career statistics and five trivia questions, along with a color representation of the team's uniform. Cards, except the 4-In-1, are numbered with a "T" prefix.

		MT
Complete Set (100):		5.00
Common Player:		.05
1	Jim Abbott	.08
2	Jeff Bagwell	.35
3	Jose Canseco	.25
4	Julio Valera	.05
5	Scott Brosius	.05
6	Mark Langston	.05
7	Andy Stankiewicz	.05
8	Gary DiSarcina	.05
9	Pete Harnisch	.05
10	Mark McGwire	.75
11	Ricky Bones	.05
12	Steve Avery	.05
13	Deion Sanders	.20
14	Mike Mussina	.10
15	Dave Justice	.20
16	Pat Hentgen	.05
17	Tom Glavine	.08
18	Juan Guzman	.05
19	Ron Gant	.10
20	Kelly Gruber	.05
21	Eric Karros	.12
22	Derrick May	.05
23	Dave Hansen	.05
24	Andre Dawson	.12
25	Eric Davis	.10
26	Ozzie Smith	.25
27	Sammy Sosa	.50
28	Lee Smith	.10
29	Ryne Sandberg	.25
30	Robin Yount	.20
31	Matt Williams	.15
32	John Vander Wal	.05
33	Bill Swift	.05
34	Delino DeShields	.05
35	Royce Clayton	.05
36	Moises Alou	.08
37	Will Clark	.20
38	Darryl Strawberry	.10
39	Larry Walker	.15
40	Ramon Martinez	.08
41	Howard Johnson	.05
42	Tino Martinez	.10
43	Dwight Gooden	.08
44	Ken Griffey, Jr.	.75
45	David Cone	.05
46	Kenny Lofton	.10
47	Bobby Bonilla	.10
48	Carlos Baerga	.08
49	Don Mattingly	.40
50	Sandy Alomar, Jr.	.08
51	Lenny Dykstra	.05
52	Tony Gwynn	.25
53	Felix Jose	.05
54	Rick Sutcliffe	.05
55	Wes Chamberlain	.05
56	Cal Ripken, Jr.	.50
57	Kyle Abbott	.05
58	Leo Gomez	.05
59	Gary Sheffield	.12
60	Anthony Young	.05
61	Roger Clemens	.25
62	Rafael Palmeiro	.15
63	Wade Boggs	.25
64	Andy Van Slyke	.05
65	Ruben Sierra	.05
66	Denny Neagle	.08
67	Nolan Ryan	.50
68	Doug Drabek	.05
69	Ivan Rodriguez	.15
70	Barry Bonds	.35
71	Chuck Knoblauch	.10
72	Reggie Sanders	.05
73	Cecil Fielder	.10
74	Barry Larkin	.12
75	Scott Aldred	.05
76	Rob Dibble	.05
77	Brian McRae	.08
78	Tim Belcher	.05
79	George Brett	.40
80	Frank Viola	.05
81	Roberto Kelly	.05
82	Jack McDowell	.05
83	Mel Hall	.05
84	Esteban Beltre	.05
85	Robin Ventura	.10
86	George Bell	.05
87	Frank Thomas	.45
88	John Smiley	.05
89	Bobby Thigpen	.05
90	Kirby Puckett	.40
91	Kevin Mitchell	.05
92	Peter Hoy	.05
93	Russ Springer	.08
94	Donovan Osborne	.05
95	Dave Silvestri	.05
96	Chad Curtis	.08
97	Pat Mahomes	.05
98	Danny Tartabull	.05
99	John Doherty	.05
---	4-in-1 (Ryne Sandberg, Mike Mussina, Reggie Sanders, Jose Canseco)	.25

1992 Classic Collector's Edition

The second annual 200-card "Collector's Edition" set was packaged with a gameboard, spinner, generic player pieces, a mechanical scoreboard and a book of tips from star players. The UV-coated card fronts feature color player photos against a deep purple border. Backs have a few biographical details, previous season and career stats, plus five trivia questions in case anyone actually wanted to play the game.

		MT
Complete Set (200):		11.00
Common Player:		.05
1	Chuck Finley	.05
2	Craig Biggio	.10
3	Luis Gonzalez	.05
4	Pete Harnisch	.08
5	Jeff Juden	.08
6	Harold Baines	.08
7	Kirk Dressendorfer	.05
8	Dennis Eckersley	.10
9	Dave Henderson	.05
10	Dave Stewart	.08
11	Joe Carter	.15
12	Juan Guzman	.05
13	Dave Stieb	.05
14	Todd Stottlemyre	.05
15	Ron Gant	.12
16	Brian Hunter	.05
17	Dave Justice	.20
18	John Smoltz	.10
19	Mike Stanton	.05
20	Chris George	.05
21	Paul Molitor	.40
22	Omar Olivares	.05
23	Lee Smith	.08
24	Ozzie Smith	.35
25	Todd Zeile	.08
26	George Bell	.05
27	Andre Dawson	.15
28	Shawon Dunston	.15
29	Mark Grace	.35
30	Greg Maddux	.50
31	Dave Smith	.05
32	Brett Butler	.10
33	Orel Hershiser	.10
34	Eric Karros	.08
35	Ramon Martinez	.08
36	Jose Offerman	.05
37	Juan Samuel	.05
38	Delino DeShields	.05
39	Marquis Grissom	.10
40	Tim Wallach	.05
41	Eric Gunderson	.05
42	Willie McGee	.05
43	Dave Righetti	.05
44	Robby Thompson	.05
45	Matt Williams	.20
46	Sandy Alomar, Jr.	.12
47	Reggie Jefferson	.05
48	Mark Lewis	.05
49	Robin Ventura	.10
50	Tino Martinez	.10
51	Roberto Kelly	.05
52	Vince Coleman	.05
53	Dwight Gooden	.10
54	Todd Hundley	.10
55	Kevin Maas	.05
56	Wade Taylor	.05
57	Bryan Harvey	.05
58	Leo Gomez	.05
59	Ben McDonald	.05
60	Ricky Bones	.05
61	Tony Gwynn	.40
62	Benito Santiago	.10
63	Wes Chamberlain	.05
64	Tommy Greene	.05
65	Dale Murphy	.15
66	Steve Buechele	.05
67	Doug Drabek	.05
68	Joe Grahe	.05
69	Rafael Palmeiro	.15
70	Wade Boggs	.35
71	Ellis Burks	.10
72	Mike Greenwell	.05
73	Mo Vaughn	.40
74	Derek Bell	.08
75	Rob Dibble	.05
76	Barry Larkin	.12
77	Jose Rijo	.05
78	Doug Henry	.05
79	Chris Sabo	.05
80	Pedro Guerrero	.05
81	George Brett	.50
82	Tom Gordon	.05
83	Mark Gubicza	.05
84	Mark Whiten	.05
85	Brian McRae	.08
86	Danny Jackson	.05
87	Milt Cuyler	.05
88	Travis Fryman	.08
89	Mickey Tettleton	.05
90	Alan Trammell	.12
91	Lou Whitaker	.05
92	Chili Davis	.05
93	Scott Erickson	.05
94	Kent Hrbek	.08
95	Alex Fernandez	.08
96	Carlton Fisk	.15
97	Ramon Garcia	.05
98	Ozzie Guillen	.05
99	Tim Raines	.10
100	Bobby Thigpen	.05
101	Kirby Puckett	.65
102	Bernie Williams	.25
103	Dave Hansen	.05
104	Kevin Tapani	.05
105	Don Mattingly	.75
106	Frank Thomas	.75
107	Monty Fariss	.05
108	Bo Jackson	.12
109	Jim Abbott	.12
110	Jose Canseco	.30
111	Phil Plantier	.05
112	Brian Williams	.05
113	Mark Langston	.05
114	Wilson Alvarez	.05
115	Roberto Hernandez	.05
116	Darryl Kile	.05
117	Ryan Bowen	.05
118	Rickey Henderson	.20
119	Mark McGwire	1.50
120	Devon White	.05
121	Roberto Alomar	.20
122	Kelly Gruber	.05
123	Eddie Zosky	.05
124	Tom Glavine	.08
125	Kal Daniels	.05
126	Cal Eldred	.05
127	Deion Sanders	.25
128	Robin Yount	.40
129	Cecil Fielder	.10
130	Ray Lankford	.10
131	Ryne Sandberg	.35
132	Darryl Strawberry	.12
133	Chris Haney	.05
134	Dennis Martinez	.08
135	Bryan Hickerson	.05
136	Will Clark	.25
137	Hal Morris	.05
138	Charles Nagy	.05
139	Jim Thome	.10
140	Albert Belle	.45
141	Reggie Sanders	.12
142	Scott Cooper	.05
143	David Cone	.08
144	Anthony Young	.05
145	Howard Johnson	.05
146	Arthur Rhodes	.05
147	Scott Aldred	.05
148	Mike Mussina	.10
149	Fred McGriff	.15
150	Andy Benes	.10
151	Ruben Sierra	.05
152	Len Dykstra	.05
153	Andy Van Slyke	.05
154	Orlando Merced	.05
155	Barry Bonds	.40
156	John Smiley	.05
157	Julio Franco	.05
158	Juan Gonzalez	.45
159	Ivan Rodriguez	.25
160	Willie Banks	.05
161	Eric Davis	.10
162	Eddie Murray	.25
163	Dave Fleming	.05
164	Wally Joyner	.08
165	Kevin Mitchell	.05
166	Ed Taubensee	.05
167	Danny Tartabull	.05
168	Ken Hill	.05
169	Willie Randolph	.05
170	Kevin McReynolds	.05
171	Gregg Jefferies	.10
172	Patrick Lennon	.05
173	Luis Mercedes	.05
174	Glenn Davis	.05
175	Bret Saberhagen	.10
176	Bobby Bonilla	.10
177	Kenny Lofton	.20
178	Jose Lind	.05
179	Royce Clayton	.05
180	Scott Scudder	.05
181	Chuck Knoblauch	.15
182	Terry Pendleton	.05
183	Nolan Ryan	1.00
184	Rob Maurer	.05
185	Brian Bohanon	.05
186	Ken Griffey, Jr.	1.50
187	Jeff Bagwell	.50
188	Steve Avery	.05
189	Roger Clemens	.40
190	Cal Ripken, Jr.	1.00
191	Kim Batiste	.05
192	Bip Roberts	.05
193	Greg Swindell	.05
194	Dave Winfield	.20
195	Steve Sax	.05
196	Frank Viola	.05
197	Mo Sanford	.05
198	Kyle Abbott	.05
199	Jack Morris	.05
200	Andy Ashby	.05

1993 Classic

A 100-card travel edition of Classic's baseball trivia cards was produced for 1993. Cards feature game-action player photos with dark blue borders. Backs have previous season and career stats along with five trivia questions. Card numbers have a "T" prefix.

		MT
Complete Set (100):		6.00
Common Player:		.05
1	Jim Abbott	.10
2	Roberto Alomar	.15
3	Moises Alou	.08
4	Brady Anderson	.08
5	Eric Anthony	.05
6	Alex Arias	.05
7	Pedro Astacio	.05
8	Steve Avery	.05
9	Carlos Baerga	.08
10	Jeff Bagwell	.35
11	George Bell	.05
12	Albert Belle	.30
13	Craig Biggio	.10
14	Barry Bonds	.30
15	Bobby Bonilla	.10
16	Mike Bordick	.05
17	George Brett	.60
18	Jose Canseco	.30
19	Joe Carter	.08
20	Royce Clayton	.05
21	Roger Clemens	.50
22	Greg Colbrunn	.05
23	David Cone	.08
24	Darren Daulton	.05
25	Delino DeShields	.05
26	Rob Dibble	.05
27	Dennis Eckersley	.08
28	Cal Eldred	.05
29	Scott Erickson	.05
30	Junior Felix	.05
31	Tony Fernandez	.05
32	Cecil Fielder	.08
33	Steve Finley	.05
34	Dave Fleming	.05
35	Travis Fryman	.10

36	Tom Glavine	.08
37	Juan Gonzalez	.50
38	Ken Griffey, Jr.	1.00
39	Marquis Grissom	.10
40	Juan Guzman	.05
41	Tony Gwynn	.40
42	Rickey Henderson	.15
43	Felix Jose	.05
44	Wally Joyner	.08
45	David Justice	.25
46	Eric Karros	.10
47	Roberto Kelly	.05
48	Ryan Klesko	.10
49	Chuck Knoblauch	.15
50	John Kruk	.05
51	Ray Lankford	.10
52	Barry Larkin	.08
53	Pat Listach	.05
54	Kenny Lofton	.15
55	Shane Mack	.05
56	Greg Maddux	.40
57	Dave Magadan	.05
58	Edgar Martinez	.05
59	Don Mattingly	.65
60	Ben McDonald	.05
61	Jack McDowell	.05
62	Fred McGriff	.15
63	Mark McGwire	1.00
64	Kevin McReynolds	.05
65	Sam Militello	.05
66	Paul Molitor	.35
67	Jeff Montgomery	.05
68	Jack Morris	.05
69	Eddie Murray	.25
70	Mike Mussina	.12
71	Otis Nixon	.05
72	Donovan Osborne	.05
73	Terry Pendleton	.05
74	Mike Piazza	.75
75	Kirby Puckett	.50
76	Cal Ripken, Jr.	.80
77	Bip Roberts	.05
78	Ivan Rodriguez	.25
79	Nolan Ryan	.80
80	Ryne Sandberg	.35
81	Deion Sanders	.25
82	Reggie Sanders	.05
83	Frank Seminara	.05
84	Gary Sheffield	.15
85	Ruben Sierra	.05
86	John Smiley	.05
87	Lee Smith	.08
88	Ozzie Smith	.35
89	John Smoltz	.08
90	Danny Tartabull	.05
91	Bob Tewksbury	.05
92	Frank Thomas	.65
93	Andy Van Slyke	.05
94	Mo Vaughn	.35
95	Robin Ventura	.10
96	Tim Wakefield	.05
97	Larry Walker	.15
98	Dave Winfield	.25
99	Robin Yount	.40
---	4-in-1 (Mark McGwire, Sam Militello, Ryan Klesko, Greg Maddux)	.75

1995 Classic Phone Card Promos

Issued in mid-1995 to promote its forthcoming series of licensed baseball player phone cards, these 2-1/8" x 3-3/8" cards are printed on plastic and feature borderless color action photos on front. Backs are printed in black and carry a sales message for the issue. Each $10-denominated promo card is overprinted on front and back: "For Promotional Use Only". The unnumbered cards are checklisted here alphabetically.

		MT
Complete Set (8):		20.00
Common Player:		1.50
(1)	Barry Bonds	2.00
(2)	Will Clark	1.50
(3)	Juan Gonzalez	2.00
(4)	Ken Griffey Jr.	6.00
(5)	Mike Piazza	4.00
(6)	Cal Ripken Jr.	5.00
(7)	Ozzie Smith	2.00
(8)	Frank Thomas	2.50

1995 Classic Phone Cards

Five special cards honoring Cal Ripken, and bi-lingual cards of Manny Ramirez and Hideo Nomo are featured in Classic's Major League Baseball phone card set. At the time of its issue in late 1995, it was the largest ever to feature individual players. Each of the 2-1/8" x 3-3/8" plastic cards was sold in an individual blister pack and carried $10 worth of long distance phone time. Fronts feature borderless color action photos and team logos while backs are in black-and-white and have instructions for the card's use. The unnumbered cards are checklisted here alphabetically.

		MT
Complete Set (61):		150.00
Common Player:		2.00
(1)	Roberto Alomar	2.50
(2)	Kevin Appier	2.00
(3)	Jeff Bagwell	3.00
(4)	Carlos Baerga	2.00
(5)	Albert Belle	3.00
(6)	Dante Bichette	2.00
(7)	Craig Biggio	2.00
(8)	Wade Boggs	2.50
(9)	Barry Bonds	3.00
(10)	Jose Canseco	2.50
(11)	Joe Carter	2.00
(12)	Will Clark	2.00
(13)	Roger Clemens	3.00
(14)	Jeff Conine	2.00
(15)	Len Dykstra	2.00
(16)	Darren Daulton	2.00
(17)	Cecil Fielder	2.00
(18)	Travis Fryman	2.00
(19)	Andres Galarraga	2.00
(20)	Ron Gant	2.00
(21)	Juan Gonzalez	3.00
(22)	Mark Grace	2.50
(23)	Ken Griffey Jr.	6.00
(24)	Tony Gwynn	3.00
(25)	Rickey Henderson	2.50
(26)	Randy Johnson	2.00
(27)	Chipper Jones	4.50
(28)	Dave Justice	2.50
(29)	Jeff Kent	2.00
(30)	Barry Larkin	2.00
(31)	Kenny Lofton	2.00
(32)	Greg Maddux	3.00
(33)	Fred McGriff	2.00
(34)	Mark McGwire	6.00
(35)	Don Mattingly	3.00
(36)	Raul Mondesi	2.00
(37)	Eddie Murray	2.50
(38)	Mike Mussina	2.50
(39)	Denny Neagle	2.00
(40)	Hideo Nomo (English/Japanese)	4.00
(41)	Paul O'Neill	2.00
(42)	Mike Piazza	4.50
(43)	Carlos Perez	2.00
(44)	Kirby Puckett	3.00
(45)	Manny Ramirez (English/Spanish)	3.00
(46)	Cal Ripken Jr.	5.00
(47)	Cal Ripken Jr.	5.00
(48)	Cal Ripken Jr.	5.00
(49)	Cal Ripken Jr.	5.00
(50)	Cal Ripken Jr.	5.00
(51)	Ivan Rodriguez	3.00
(52)	Tim Salmon	2.00
(53)	Deion Sanders	2.00
(54)	Reggie Sanders	2.00
(55)	Ozzie Smith	2.50
(56)	Sammy Sosa	3.00
(57)	Frank Thomas	4.00
(58)	Mo Vaughn	2.00
(59)	Robin Ventura	2.50
(60)	Larry Walker	2.50
(61)	Matt Williams	2.00

1996 Classic Phone Card Promo

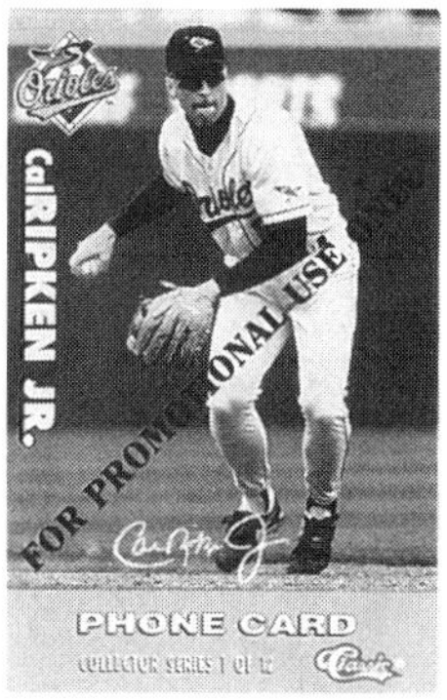

In conjunction with its participation at the 1994 National Sports Collectors Convention, Classic handed out a sample phone card similar to the cards issued the same summer at 7-Eleven convenience stores. The National Convention promo card does not have the 7-Eleven log on front and is overprinted "FOR PROMOTIONAL USE ONLY". Backs have a serial number which could be matched with numbers on a prize board at the Classic booth at the show.

		MT
1	Cal Ripken Jr.	6.00

1996 Classic/ Metallic Impressions Nolan Ryan

Nolan Ryan's career is traced in this set of 2-5/8" x 3-5/8" embossed metal cards produced for Classic by Metallic Impressions. The center of each card's front is a raised color photo which continues in muted tones of yellow and orange to the edges. The Classic and The Metal Edge logos are embossed, as well. Horizontal backs are identical in design with a color portrait of Ryan at left and a paragraph describing a highlight or milestone at right. Classic and Cooperstown Collection logos are in opposite corners. Each of 14,950 sets was sold with a numbered certificate of authenticity in an embossed lithographed metal box.

		MT
Complete Boxed Set:		24.00
Single Card:		2.00
1	Nolan Ryan (Career ends with Rangers)	2.00
2	Nolan Ryan (1970s, California Angels)	2.00
3	Nolan Ryan (Major League debut)	2.00
4	Nolan Ryan (Over-40 no-hitters)	2.00
5	Nolan Ryan (Rangers no-hitters)	2.00
6	Nolan Ryan (Mets trade Ryan)	2.00
7	Nolan Ryan (Joins Astros)	2.00
8	Nolan Ryan (Career records)	2.00
9	Nolan Ryan (Lean years in Houston)	2.00
10	Nolan Ryan ("Ryan Express" returns to A.L.)	2.00

1996 Classic/Sports Cards Phone Card

This card, commemorating Cal Ripken's 2,131st game, was available exclusively by subscribing to Sports Card magazine in the spring of 1995. The card is the standard 3-3/8" x 2-1/8" plastic format.

	MT
Cal Ripken Jr.	5.00

1981 Cleveland Indians Photocards

This 1981 team issue is almost identical in format to the previous year's cards. Again featuring black-and-white player portraits on a 3-1/2" x 5-1/2" format, the cards have player and team name at bottom in all-capital letters. The principal difference between the two years' cards is that on the '82s, the players are depicted in dark jerseys. The unnumbered cards are checklisted here alphabetically.

		MT
Complete Set (29):		24.00
Common Player:		.50
(1)	Alan Bannister	.50
(2)	Len Barker	.50
(3)	Bert Blyleven	.75
(4)	Joe Charboneau	1.50
(5)	John Denny	.50
(6)	Bo Diaz	.50
(7)	Miguel Dilone	.50
(8)	Dave Duncan	.50
(9)	Jerry Dybzinski	.50
(10)	Wayne Garland	.50
(11)	Mike Hargrove	.65
(12)	Toby Harrah	.65
(13)	Pat Kelly	.50
(14)	Duane Kuiper	.50
(15)	Bob Lacey	.50
(16)	Larry Littleton	.50
(17)	Rick Manning	.50
(18)	Tom McCraw	.50
(19)	Sid Monge	.50
(20)	Joe Nossek	.50
(21)	Jorge Orta	.50
(22)	Ron Pruitt	.50
(23)	Dave Rosello	.50
(24)	Dennis Sommers	.50
(25)	Dan Spillner	.50
(26)	Mike Stanton	.50
(27)	Andre Thornton	.65
(28)	Tom Veryzer	.50
(29)	Rick Waits	.50

1982 Cleveland Indians Photocards

The addition of the player's position between his name and team name in the bottom border helps identify the Indians' 1982 photocard issue. The cards retain the same format of a black-and-white portrait photo on 3-1/2" x 5-1/2" blank-back stock. The unnumbered cards are checklisted here in alphabetical order. Sets were originally sold by mail for $5.25 from the team gift shop.

		MT
Complete Set (37):		10.00
Common Player:		.25
(1)	Bud Anderson	.25
(2)	Chris Bando	.25
(3)	Alan Bannister	.25
(4)	Len Barker	.25
(5)	Bert Blyleven	.50
(6)	John Bohnet	.25
(7)	Tom Brennan	.25
(8)	Carmelo Castillo	.25
(9)	Joe Charboneau	.75
(10)	Rodney Craig	.25
(11)	John Denny	.25
(12)	Miguel Dilone	.25
(13)	Jerry Dybzinski	.25
(14)	Mike Fischlin	.25
(15)	Dave Garcia	.25
(16)	Gordy Glaser	.25
(17)	Ed Glynn	.25
(18)	John Goryl	.25
(19)	Mike Hargrove	.35
(20)	Toby Harrah	.35
(21)	Ron Hassey	.25
(22)	Von Hayes	.25
(23)	Neal Heaton	.25
(24)	Dennis Lewallyn	.25
(25)	Rick Manning	.25
(26)	Bake McBride	.25
(27)	Tom McCraw	.25
(28)	Bill Nahorodny	.25
(29)	Jack Perconte	.25
(30)	Mel Queen	.25
(31)	Dennis Sommers	.25
(32)	Lary Sorenson	.25
(33)	Dan Spillner	.25
(34)	Rick Sutcliffe	.40
(35)	Andre Thornton	.45
(36)	Rick Waits	.25
(37)	Ed Whitson	.25

1983 Cleveland Indians Photocards

A switch of the team name to a horizontally compressed block letter style is the major difference between the 1983 Indians photocards and the previous year's issue. Most players in the '83 set are shown in dark jerseys with "INDIANS" across the chest, and dark caps with the "C" logo. As in the past, players are shown on the black-and-white, blank-backed 3-1/2" x 5-1/2" in portrait photos. The unnumbered cards are listed here in alphabetical order.

	MT
Complete Set (43):	12.00
Common Player:	.25
(1) Bud Anderson	.25
(2) Jay Baller	.25
(3) Chris Bando	.25
(4) Alan Bannister	.25
(5) Len Barker	.25
(6) Bert Blyleven	.50
(7) Carmen Castillo	.25
(8) Wil Culmer	.25
(9) Miguel Dilone	.25
(10) Jerry Dybzinski	.25
(11) Jamie Easterley	.25
(12) Juan Eichelberger	.25
(13) Jim Essian	.25
(14) Mike Ferraro	.25
(15) Mike Fischlin	.25
(16) Julio Franco	1.00
(17) Ed Glynn	.25
(18) Johnny Goryl	.25
(19) Mike Hargrove	.45
(20) Toby Harrah	.45
(21) Ron Hassey	.25
(22) Neal Heaton	.25
(23) Rick Manning	.25
(24) Bake McBride	.25
(25) Don McMahon	.25
(26) Ed Napoleon	.25
(27) Karl Pagel	.25
(28) Jack Perconte	.25
(29) Broderick Perkins	.25
(30) Jerry Reed	.25
(31) Kevin Rhomberg	.25
(32) Ramon Romero	.25
(33) Dennis Sommers	.25
(34) Lary Sorenson	.25
(35) Dan Spillner	.25
(36) Rick Sutcliffe	.40
(37) Pat Tabler	.25
(38) Gorman Thomas	.25
(39) Andre Thornton	.40
(40) Manny Trillo	.25
(41) Otto Velez	.25
(42) George Vukovich	.25
(43) Rick Waits	.25

1984 Cleveland Indians Photocards

Sharing a format with annual sets issued before and since, these are 3-1/2" x 5-1/2", blank-back, black-and-white cards. As before, player name, position and team are in capital letters in the bottom white border. It can be helpful to distinguish individual cards from the 1984 issue by virtue of the fact that most (but not all) of the player portraits show the dark jersey with Chief Wahoo patch, and all players are wearing the dark cap with "C" on front. The unnumbered cards are checklisted here alphabetically.

	MT
Complete Set (30):	8.00
Common Player:	.25
(1) Luis Aponte	.25
(2) Chris Bando	.25
(3) Rick Behenna	.25
(4) Tony Bernazard	.25
(5) Bert Blyleven	.40
(6) Bobby Bonds	.35
(7) Brett Butler	.60
(8) Carmen Castillo	.25
(9) Pat Corrales	.25
(10) Jamie Easterley	.25
(11) Mike Fischlin	.25
(12) Julio Franco	.40
(13) George Frazier	.25
(14) Johnny Goryl	.25
(15) Mike Hargrove	.25
(16) Ron Hassey	.25
(17) Neal Heaton	.25
(18) Brook Jacoby	.25
(19) Mike Jeffcoat	.25
(20) Don McMahon	.25
(21) Ed Napoleon	.25
(22) Otis Nixon	.25
(23) Broderick Perkins	.25
(24) Kevin Rhomberg	.25
(25) Dennis Sommers	.25
(26) Dan Spillner	.25
(27) Rick Sutcliffe	.40
(28) Pat Tabler	.25
(29) Andre Thornton	.40
(30) George Vukovich	.25

1985 Cleveland Indians Photocards

This set of blank-backed black-and-white cards was available by mail order or at the team's gift shop. Cards feature portrait photos of the manager, coaches and players on a 3-1/2" x 5-1/2" format with a semi-gloss front surface. Because the cards share a format with those of the surrounding years, distinguishing the year of issue for individual cards can be difficult. All of the portraits in the 1985 set picture the player in white jerseys with "INDIANS" across chest and in dark caps with "C". The unnumbered cards are checklisted here alphabetically.

	MT
Complete Set (36):	8.00
Common Player:	.25
(1) Chris Bando	.25
(2) Rick Behenna	.25
(3) Butch Benton	.25
(4) Tony Bernazard	.25
(5) Bert Blyleven	.40
(6) Bobby Bonds	.40
(7) Brett Butler	.60
(8) Ernie Camacho	.25
(9) Joe Carter	2.00
(10) Carmen Castillo	.25
(11) Pat Corrales	.25
(12) Jamie Easterly	.25
(13) Mike Fischlin	.25
(14) Julio Franco	.40
(15) John Goryl	.25
(16) Mel Hall	.25
(17) Mike Hargrove	.25
(18) Neal Heaton	.25
(19) Brook Jacoby	.25
(20) Mike Jeffcoat	.25
(21) Don McMahon	.25
(22) Ed Napoleon	.25
(23) Otis Nixon	.25
(24) Geno Petralli	.25
(25) Ramon Romero	.25
(26) Vern Ruhle	.25
(27) Don Schulze	.25
(28) Jim Siwy	.25
(29) Roy Smith	.25
(30) Dennis Sommers	.25
(31) Pat Tabler	.25
(32) Andre Thornton	.40
(33) Dave Von Ohlen	.25
(34) George Vukovich	.25
(35) Tom Waddell	.25
(36) Jerry Willard	.25

1986 Cleveland Indians Photocards

The same basic format of previous years is used on this 3-1/2" x 5-1/2" black-and-white blank-back set of player portrait photos.

	MT
Complete Set (51):	12.00
Common Player:	.25
(1) Jack Aker	.25
(2) Andy Allanson	.25
(3) Scott Bailes	.25
(4) Chris Bando	.25
(5) Jay Bell	.75
(6) Tony Bernazard	.25
(7) Bobby Bonds	.35
(8) Bernardo Brito	.25
(9) Kevin Buckley	.25
(10) John Butcher	.25
(11) Ernie Camacho	.25
(12) Tom Candiotti	.25
(13) Joe Carter	1.00
(14) Carmen Castillo	.25
(15) Dave Clark	.25
(16) Pat Corrales	.25
(17) Keith Creel	.25
(18) Jamie Easterly	.25
(19) Doc Edwards	.25
(20) Julio Franco	.35
(21) Vic Garcia	.25
(22) John Goryl	.25
(23) Mel Hall	.25
(24) Neal Heaton	.25
(25) Brook Jacoby	.25
(26) Jim Kern	.25
(27) Fran Mullins	.25
(28) Phil Niekro	1.00
(29) Otis Nixon	.35
(30) Junior Noboa	.25
(31) Dickie Noles	.25
(32) Bryan Oelkers	.25
(33) Craig Pippin	.25
(34) Reggie Ritter	.25
(35) Scott Roberts	.25
(36) Dan Rohn	.25
(37) Jose Roman	.25
(38) Miguel Roman	.25
(39) Ken Schrom	.25
(40) Don Schulze	.25
(41) Cory Snyder	.25
(42) Dain Syverson	.25
(43) Pat Tabler	.25
(44) Andre Thornton	.35
(45) Tom Waddell	.25
(46) Curt Wardle	.25
(47) Randy Washington	.25
(48) Jim Weaver	.25
(49) Ed Williams	.25
(50) Jim Wilson	.25
(51) Rich Yett	.25

1987 Cleveland Indians Photocards

Because they are identical in format to the photo cards issued prior to 1987, individual cards can be difficult to attribute to a specific year of issue. Black-and-white player portrait photos are once again featured on the blank-back, 3-1/2" x 5-1/2" cards, with player name, team and position in black in the bottom border. Players in the 1987 set are all pictured in the dark cap with Chief Wahoo logo, and white uniform jerseys with no neck stripes or piping. Unnumbered cards are checklisted here in alphabetical order.

	MT
Complete Set (39):	11.00
Common Player:	.25
(1) Jack Aker	.25
(2) Andy Allanson	.25
(3) Scott Bailes	.25
(4) Chris Bando	.25
(5) Tony Bernazard	.25
(6) Bobby Bonds	.35
(7) Bernardo Brito	.25
(8) Brett Butler	.50
(9) Ernie Camacho	.25
(10) Tom Candiotti	.25
(11) Joe Carter	1.00
(12) Carmen Castillo	.25
(13) Dave Clark	.25
(14) Pat Corrales	.25
(15) Rick Dempsey	.25
(16) Doc Edwards	.25
(17) John Farrell	.25
(18) Julio Franco	.40
(19) Johnny Goryl	.25
(20) Mel Hall	.25
(21) Brook Jacoby	.25
(22) Doug Jones	.25
(23) Kent Murphy	.25
(24) Mike Murphy	.25
(25) Phil Niekro	1.00
(26) Otis Nixon	.25
(27) Junior Noboa	.25
(28) Bryan Oelkers	.25
(29) Scott Roberts	.25
(30) Miguel Roman	.25
(31) Ken Schrom	.25
(32) Cory Snyder	.25
(33) Greg Swindell	.35
(34) Pat Tabler	.25
(35) Andre Thornton	.40
(36) Ed Vande Berg	.25
(37) Tom Waddell	.25
(38) Frank Wills	.25
(39) Rich Yett	.25

1988 Cleveland Indians Photocards

Another series of black-and-white player photocards was issued by the Tribe in 1988. The 3-1/2" x 5-1/2" cards are blank-backed and unnumbered. They are checklisted here in alphabetical order.

	MT
Complete Set (40):	9.00
Common Player:	.25
(1) Darrel Akerfelds	.25
(2) Andy Allanson	.25
(3) Scott Bailes	.25
(4) Chris Bando	.25
(5) Jay Bell	.50
(6) Bud Black	.25
(7) Tom Candiotti	.25
(8) Joe Carter	1.00
(9) Carmen Castillo	.25
(10) Dave Clark	.25
(11) Doc Edwards	.25
(12) John Farrell	.25
(13) Julio Franco	.35
(14) Terry Francona	.25
(15) Don Gordon	.25
(16) Johnny Goryl	.25
(17) Mel Hall	.25
(18) Brad Havens	.25
(19) Tommy Hinzo	.25
(20) Luis Isaac	.25
(21) Brook Jacoby	.25
(22) Doug Jones	.25
(23) Ron Kittle	.25
(24) Bill Laskey	.25
(25) Don Lovell	.25
(26) Charlie Manuel	.25
(27) Jon Perlman	.25
(28) Domingo Ramos	.25
(29) Rick Rodriguez	.25
(30) Dan Schatzeder	.25
(31) Charlie Scott	.25
(32) Cory Snyder	.25
(33) Tom Spencer	.25
(34) Greg Swindell	.25
(35) Pat Tabler	.25
(36) Willie Upshaw	.25
(37) Ron Washington	.25
(38) Mark Wiley	.25
(39) Eddie Williams	.25
(40) Rich Yett	.25

1988 Cleveland Indians 1948 Picture Pack Reprints

The actual source of these collector-issue cards is unverified. It has been claimed that they were sold at Municipal Stadium in 1988 as a 40th anniversary tribute to the World Champion Cleveland Indians. The cards are 2-1/2" x 3-1/2", blank-back, black-and-white reprints of the team-issued photo-pack pictures of 1948. Each card features a facsimile autograph on front.

	MT
Complete Set (30):	5.00
Common Player:	.10
(1) Gene Bearden	.10
(2) Johnny Berardino	.20
(3) Don Black	.10
(4) Lou Boudreau	.15
(5) Russ Christopher	.10
(6) Allie Clark	.10
(7) Larry Doby	.50
(8) Hank Edwards	.10
(9) Bob Feller	.25
(10) Joe Gordon	.10
(11) Hank Greenberg	.50
(12) Steve Gromek	.10
(13) Mel Harder	.10
(14) Jim Hegan	.10
(15) Walt Judnich	.10
(16) Ken Keltner	.10
(17) Bob Kennedy	.10
(18) Ed Klieman	.10
(19) Bob Lemon	.15
(20) Bill McKechnie	.15
(21) Dale Mitchell	.10
(22) Bob Muncrief	.10
(23) Satchel Paige	.50
(24) Hal Peck	.10
(25) Eddie Robinson	.10
(26) Muddy Ruel	.10
(27) Joe Tipton	.10
(28) Thurman Tucker	.10
(29) Bill Veeck (owner)	.25
(30) Sam Zoldak	.10
(31) Cleveland Stadium	.25

1989 Cleveland Indians team issue

The Cleveland Indians released this oversized (2-3/4" x 4-1/2") set in 1989. Cards feature a full-color player photo on front with the "Tribe" logo in the upper left corner. Card backs include major and minor league statistics and a facsimile autograph.

		MT
Complete Set (28):		6.00
Common Player:		.25
(1)	Doc Edwards	.25
(2)	Joel Skinner	.25
(3)	Andy Allanson	.25
(4)	Tom Candiotti	.25
(5)	Doug Jones	.25
(6)	Keith Atherton	.25
(7)	Rich Yett	.25
(8)	John Farrell	.25
(9)	Rod Nichols	.25
(10)	Joe Skalski	.25
(11)	Pete O'Brien	.25
(12)	Jerry Browne	.25
(13)	Brook Jacoby	.25
(14)	Felix Fermin	.25
(15)	Bud Black	.25
(16)	Brad Havens	.25
(17)	Greg Swindell	.25
(18)	Scott Bailes	.25
(19)	Jesse Orosco	.25
(20)	Oddibe McDowell	.25
(21)	Joe Carter	.90
(22)	Cory Snyder	.25
(23)	Louie Medina	.25
(24)	Dave Clark	.25
(25)	Brad Komminsk	.25
(26)	Luis Aguayo	.25
(27)	Pat Keedy	.25
(28)	Tribe Coaches	.25

1992 McDonald's/ WUAB Cleveland Indians

These larger-than-standard (2-7/8" x 4-1/4") cards were given to members of the Tribe Kids Fan Club, sponsored by McDonald's and television station WUAB, whose logos appear on front and back, respectively. Cards have poses or game photos with red frames, white borders and a row of vertical blue diamonds on front. Horizontally formatted backs are in black-and-white with complete career stats. Cards are listed here in order of the uniform numbers which appear on front.

		MT
Complete Set (30):		8.00
Common Player:		.25
0	Junior Ortiz	.25
1	Glenallen Hill	.35
2	Alex Cole	.25
4	Bob Skinner	.25
7	Kenny Lofton	1.50
8	Albert Belle	3.00
9	Carlos Baerga	.35
10	Mark Lewis	.35
11	Paul Sorrento	.25
15	Sandy Alomar Jr.	.65
16	Felix Fermin	.25
20	Tony Perezchica	.25
21	Mike Hargrove	.35
23	Mark Whiten	.25
25	Jim Thome	1.00
26	Brook Jacoby	.25
27	Dave Otto	.25
28	Derek Lilliquist	.25
31	Steve Olin	.25
33	Thomas Howard	.25
36	Brad Arnsberg	.25
39	Dennis Cook	.25
41	Charles Nagy	.45
44	Reggie Jefferson	.25
47	Scott Scudder	.25
48	Ted Power	.25
54	Rod Nichols	.25
63	Eric Bell	.25
77	Jack Armstrong	.25
	The Coaches (Rick Adair, Ken Bolek, Dom Chiti, Ron Clark, Jose Morales, Dave Nelson, Jeff Newman)	.25

1993 WUAB Cleveland Indians

Only the mascot's card carries the logo of the television station which sponsored this team set. In 2-1/2" x 3-1/2" format printed on thin cardboard, the fronts feature color game-action photos with borders of red, white and blue. The player's uniform number appears in the lower-left corner. Backs are in black-and-white with major league career stats and a log commemorating the team's 61 years at Municipal Stadium. The set is checklisted here alphabetically.

		MT
Complete Set (34):		12.00
Common Player:		.25
(1)	Sandy Alomar Jr.	.75
(2)	Carlos Baerga	.25
(3)	Albert Belle	3.00
(4)	Mike Bielecki	.25
(5)	Mike Christopher	.25
(6)	Mark Clark	.25
(7)	Dennis Cook	.25
(8)	Alvaro Espinoza	.25
(9)	Felix Fermin	.25
(10)	Mike Hargrove	.25
(11)	Glenallen Hill	.25
(12)	Thomas Howard	.25
(13)	Reggie Jefferson	.25
(14)	Wayne Kirby	.25
(15)	Tom Kramer	.25
(16)	Mark Lewis	.25
(17)	Derek Lilliquist	.25
(18)	Kenny Lofton	.75
(19)	Carlos Martinez	.25
(20)	Jose Mesa	.25
(21)	Jeff Mutis	.25
(22)	Charles Nagy	.40
(23)	Bob Ojeda	.25
(24)	Junior Ortiz	.25
(25)	Eric Plunk	.25
(26)	Ted Power	.25
(27)	Scott Scudder	.25
(28)	Joel Skinner	.25
(29)	Paul Sorrento	.25
(30)	Jim Thome	1.00
(31)	Jeff Treadway	.25
(32)	Kevin Wickander	.25
(33)	Indians coaches (Rick Adair, Ken Bolke, Dom Chiti, Ron Clark, Jose Morales, Dave Nelson, Jeff Newman)	.25
(34)	Slider (mascot)	.25

1989 CMC Jose Canseco

This collecting kit from Collector's Marketing Corporation includes a talking baseball card, a 20-card Jose Canseco set, an embossed collectors album with plastic sheets and "The Jose Canseco Story" booklet. Each kit is numbered on the back of the box.

	MT
Complete Set:	4.00
Single Card:	.50

1989 CMC Mickey Mantle

A 20-card set honoring Mickey Mantle is among the items found in this collecting kit produced by Collectors Marketing Corporation. The cards were released along with a special album, a talking baseball card and a story about Mantle. The Yankee logo appears on the front and backs of the cards.

	MT
Complete Set:	18.00
Single Card:	.60

1988 CMC Don Mattingly

This collecting kit released by Collector's Marketing Corporation features a talking baseball card, a 20-card Don Mattingly set, an embossed collectors album and the Don Mattingly story. Each kit is numbered on the box.

	MT
Complete Set:	6.00
Single Card:	.50

1989 CMC Babe Ruth

Produced by Collectors Marketing Corporation, this collecting kit features a 20-card set, an embossed collectors album, a talking baseball card and a story about Ruth. Each kit is numbered on the back of the collectors box and on the front display.

	MT
Complete Set:	7.50
Single Card:	.50

Player names in *Italic* type indicate a rookie card.

1990 CMC Collect-A-Books

Capsule histories of three dozen contemporary and past stars are presented in these 8-page, 2-1/2" x 3-1/2" booklets. Heavy cardstock covers have a color or black-and-white photo on front and a caricature of the player on back. Inside pages have more photos, personal data, career highlights, stats, quotes, etc. The books were sold in 12 packs featuring nine current and three former players. (See Line Drive for 1991 Collect A Books.)

		MT
Complete Set (36):		8.00
Common Player:		.10
1	Bo Jackson	.15
2	Dwight Gooden	.15
3	Ken Griffey Jr.	2.00
4	Will Clark	.25
5	Ozzie Smith	.25
6	Orel Hershiser	.10
7	Ruben Sierra	.10
8	Rickey Henderson	.15
9	Robin Yount	.25
10	Babe Ruth	1.00
11	Ernie Banks	.25
12	Carl Yastrzemski	.15
13	Don Mattingly	.75
14	Nolan Ryan	2.00
15	Jerome Walton	.10
16	Kevin Mitchell	.10
17	Tony Gwynn	.75
18	Dave Stewart	.10
19	Roger Clemens	.50
20	Darryl Strawberry	.10
21	George Brett	.75
22	Hank Aaron	1.00
23	Ted Williams	1.00
24	Warren Spahn	.10
25	Jose Canseco	.45
26	Wade Boggs	.35
27	Jim Abbott	.10
28	Eric Davis	.10
29	Ryne Sandberg	.75
30	Bret Saberhagen	.10
31	Mark Grace	.35
32	Gregg Olson	.10
33	Kirby Puckett	.75
34	Lou Gehrig	1.00
35	Roberto Clemente	2.00
36	Bob Feller	.10

1981 Coca-Cola

In 1981 Topps produced for Coca-Cola 12-card sets for 11 various American and National League teams. The sets include 11 player cards and one unnumbered header card. The 2-1/2" x 3-1/2" cards are identical in format to the 1981 Topps regular issue save for the Coca-Cola logo. Backs differ from the '81 Topps regular set in that they are numbered 1-11 and carry the Coca-Cola trademark and copyright line. The header cards contain an offer for 132-card uncut sheets of 1981 Topps baseball cards. Some cards were prepared, but never issued, of N.Y. Yankees; to date, only three of the supposed 11 player cards are known.

		MT
Complete Set (no Yankees) (132):		35.00
Common Player:		.10
Boston Red Sox Team Set		2.50
1	Tom Burgmeier	.10
2	Dennis Eckersley	.50
3	Dwight Evans	.15
4	Bob Stanley	.10
5	Glenn Hoffman	.10
6	Carney Lansford	.10
7	Frank Tanana	.10
8	Tony Perez	.50
9	Jim Rice	.25
10	Dave Stapleton	.10
11	Carl Yastrzemski	2.25
----	Red Sox header card	.03
Chicago Cubs Team Set		1.00
1	Tim Blackwell	.10
2	Bill Buckner	.25
3	Ivan DeJesus	.10
4	Leon Durham	.10
5	Steve Henderson	.10
6	Mike Krukow	.10
7	Ken Reitz	.10
8	Rick Reuschel	.10
9	Scot Thompson	.10
10	Dick Tidrow	.10
11	Mike Tyson	.10
----	Cubs header card	.03
Chicago White Sox Team Set		1.00
1	Britt Burns	.10
2	Todd Cruz	.10
3	Rich Dotson	.10
4	Jim Essian	.10
5	Ed Farmer	.10
6	Lamar Johnson	.10
7	Ron LeFlore	.10
8	Chet Lemon	.10
9	Bob Molinaro	.10
10	Jim Morrison	.10
11	Wayne Nordhagen	.10
----	White Sox header card	.03
Cincinnati Reds Team Set		6.00
1	Johnny Bench	3.00
2	Dave Collins	.10
3	Dave Concepcion	.15
4	Dan Driessen	.10
5	George Foster	.25
6	Ken Griffey	.15
7	Tom Hume	.10
8	Ray Knight	.15
9	Ron Oester	.10
10	Tom Seaver	2.50
11	Mario Soto	.10
----	Reds header card	.03
Detroit Tigers Team Set		2.00
1	Champ Summers	.10
2	Al Cowens	.10
3	Rich Hebner	.10
4	Steve Kemp	.10
5	Aurelio Lopez	.10
6	Jack Morris	.15
7	Lance Parrish	.15
8	Johnny Wockenfuss	.10
9	Alan Trammell	1.00
10	Lou Whitaker	.35
11	Kirk Gibson	.35
----	Tigers header card	.03
Houston Astros Team Set		12.00
1	Alan Ashby	.10
2	Cesar Cedeno	.10
3	Jose Cruz	.10
4	Art Howe	.10
5	Rafael Landestoy	.10
6	Joe Niekro	.15
7	Terry Puhl	.10
8	J.R. Richard	.15
9	Nolan Ryan	12.00
10	Joe Sambito	.10
11	Don Sutton	.50
----	Astros Header Card	.03
Kansas City Royals Team Set		4.00
1	Willie Aikens	.10
2	George Brett	4.00
3	Larry Gura	.10
4	Dennis Leonard	.10
5	Hal McRae	.15
6	Amos Otis	.10
7	Dan Quisenberry	.10
8	U.L. Washington	.10
9	John Wathan	.10
10	Frank White	.10
11	Willie Wilson	.15
----	Royals header card	.03
New York Mets Team Set		1.00

1	Neil Allen	.10
2	Doug Flynn	.10
3	Dave Kingman	.25
4	Randy Jones	.10
5	Pat Zachry	.10
6	Lee Mazzilli	.10
7	Rusty Staub	.15
8	Craig Swan	.10
9	Frank Taveras	.10
10	Alex Trevino	.10
11	Joel Youngblood	.10
----	Mets Header Card	.03
New York Yankees Team Set		75.00
1	Rich Gossage	15.00
2	Reggie Jackson	60.00
3	Rick Cerone	12.50
----	Yankees Header Card	4.00
Philadelphia Phillies Team Set		6.00
1	Bob Boone	.30
2	Larry Bowa	.15
3	Steve Carlton	2.50
4	Greg Luzinski	.15
5	Garry Maddox	.10
6	Bake McBride	.10
7	Tug McGraw	.15
8	Pete Rose	3.00
9	Mike Schmidt	3.00
10	Lonnie Smith	.10
11	Manny Trillo	.10
----	Phillies header card	.03
Pittsburgh Pirates Team Set		2.50
1	Jim Bibby	.10
2	John Candelaria	.10
3	Mike Easler	.10
4	Tim Foli	.10
5	Phil Garner	.10
6	Bill Madlock	.15
7	Omar Moreno	.10
8	Ed Ott	.10
9	Dave Parker	.40
10	Willie Stargell	2.50
11	Kent Tekulve	.10
----	Pirates header card	.03
St. Louis Cardinals Team Set		1.00
1	Bob Forsch	.10
2	George Hendrick	.10
3	Keith Hernandez	.15
4	Tom Herr	.10
5	Sixto Lezcano	.10
6	Ken Oberkfell	.10
7	Darrell Porter	.10
8	Tony Scott	.10
9	Lary Sorensen	.10
10	Bruce Sutter	.15
11	Garry Templeton	.10
----	Cardinals Header Card	.03

1982 Coca-Cola Brigham's Red Sox

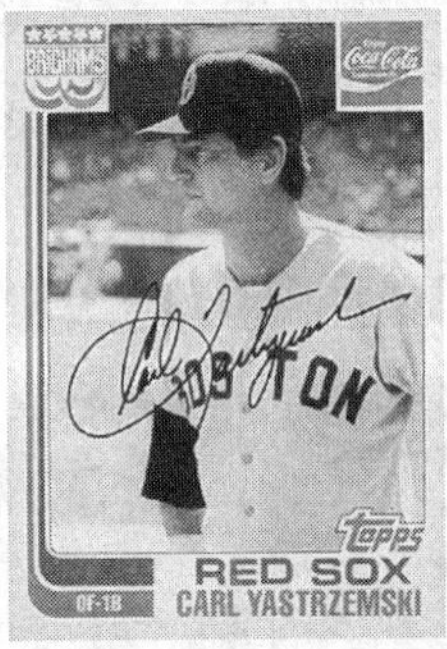

Coca-Cola, in conjunction with Brigham's Ice Cream stores, issued a 23-card set in the Boston area featuring Red Sox players. The Topps-produced cards, 2-1/2" x 3-1/2", are identical in format to the regular 1982 Topps set but contain the Coca-Cola and Brigham's logos in the corners. The cards were distributed in three-card cello packs, including an unnumbered header card.

		MT
Complete Set (23):		10.00
Common Player:		.50
1	Gary Allenson	.50
2	Tom Burgmeier	.50
3	Mark Clear	.50
4	Steve Crawford	.50
5	Dennis Eckersley	1.00
6	Dwight Evans	.65
7	Rich Gedman	.50
8	Garry Hancock	.50
9	Glen Hoffman (Glenn)	.50
10	Carney Lansford	.50
11	Rick Miller	.50
12	Reid Nichols	.50
13	Bob Ojeda	.50
14	Tony Perez	1.50
15	Chuck Rainey	.50
16	Jerry Remy	.50
17	Jim Rice	1.50
18	Bob Stanley	.50
19	Dave Stapleton	.50
20	Mike Torrez	.50
21	John Tudor	.50
22	Carl Yastrzemski	6.00
---	Header card	.10

1982 Coca-Cola Reds

Produced by Topps for Coca-Cola, the set consists of 23 cards featuring the Cincinnati Reds and was distributed in the Cincinnati area. The cards, which are 2-1/2" x 3-1/2" in size, are identical in design to the regular 1982 Topps set but have a Coca-Cola logo on the front and red backs. An unnumbered header card is included in the set.

		MT
Complete Set (23):		7.00
Common Player:		.25
1	Johnny Bench	3.00
2	Bruce Berenyi	.25
3	Larry Biittner	.25
4	Cesar Cedeno	.35
5	Dave Concepcion	.35
6	Dan Driessen	.25
7	Greg Harris	.25
8	Paul Householder	.25
9	Tom Hume	.25
10	Clint Hurdle	.25
11	Jim Kern	.25
12	Wayne Krenchicki	.25
13	Rafael Landestoy	.25
14	Charlie Leibrandt	.25
15	Mike O'Berry	.25
16	Ron Oester	.25
17	Frank Pastore	.25
18	Joe Price	.25
19	Tom Seaver	2.50
20	Mario Soto	.25
21	Alex Trevino	.25
22	Mike Vail	.25
----	Header card	.05

1985 Coca-Cola Dodgers Photocards

The first of two annual player photocard sets sponsored by Coke, these 3-1/2" x 5-1/2" cards feature color player action photos on front, surrounded by a white border. Below the photo is a 1985 copyright notice; the player's name is at bottom. Backs have a Coca-Cola logo in the lower-right corner, and may be found both with and without a printed message. The unnumbered cards are checklisted here in alphabetical order.

		MT
Complete Set (34):		15.00
Common Player:		.50
(1)	Joe Amalfitano	.50
(2)	Dave Anderson	.50
(3)	Bob Bailor	.50
(4)	Monty Basgall	.50
(5)	Tom Brennan	.50
(6)	Greg Brock	.50
(7)	Bobby Castillo	.50
(8)	Mark Cresse	.50
(9)	Carlos Diaz	.50
(10)	Mariano Duncan	.75
(11)	Pedro Guerrero	.50
(12)	Orel Hershiser	2.00
(13)	Rick Honeycutt	.50
(14)	Steve Howe	.60
(15)	Ken Howell	.50
(16)	Jay Johnstone	.50
(17)	Ken Landreaux	.50
(18)	Tommy Lasorda	.75
(19)	Candy Maldonado	.50
(20)	Mike Marshall	.50
(21)	Manny Mota	.50
(22)	Tom Niedenfuer	.50
(23)	Al Oliver	.60
(24)	Alejandro Pena	.50
(25)	Ron Perranoski	.50
(26)	Jerry Reuss	.50
(27)	R.J. Reynolds	.50
(28)	Bill Russell	.50
(29)	Steve Sax	.50
(30)	Mike Scioscia	.50
(31)	Fernando Valenzuela	.75
(32)	Bob Welch	.50
(33)	Terry Whitfield	.50
(34)	Steve Yeager	.50

1985 Coca-Cola White Sox

Featuring past and present White Sox players, the cards in this set were given out on Tuesday night home games. The 2-5/8" x 4-1/8" cards contain a color photo of a current Sox member. A red box at the bottom of the card carries the team logo, player name, uniform number and position, plus a small oval portrait of a past Sox player. Backs contain the Coca-Cola logo and lifetime stats for the current and past player. The set is listed here by the player's uniform number with the last three cards being unnumbered. Complete sets were available through a fan club offer found in White Sox programs.

		MT
Complete Set (30):		10.00
Common Player:		.25
0	Oscar Gamble, Zeke Bonura	.25
1	Scott Fletcher, Luke Appling	.40
3	Harold Baines, Bill Melton	.50
5	Luis Salazar, Chico Carrasquel	.25
7	Marc Hill, Sherman Lollar	.25
8	Daryl Boston, Jim Landis	.25
10	Tony LaRussa, Al Lopez	.50
12	Julio Cruz, Nellie Fox	.90
13	Ozzie Guillen, Luis Aparicio	.90
17	Jerry Hairston, Smoky Burgess	.40
20	Joe DeSa, Carlos May	.25
22	Joel Skinner, J.C. Martin	.25
23	Rudy Law, Bill Skowron	.40
24	Floyd Bannister, Red Faber	.35
29	Greg Walker, Dick Allen	.50
30	Gene Nelson, Early Wynn	.35
32	Tim Hulett, Pete Ward	.25
34	Richard Dotson, Ed Walsh	.35
37	Dan Spillner, Thornton Lee	.25
40	Britt Burns, Gary Peters	.25
41	Tom Seaver, Ted Lyons	2.00
42	Ron Kittle, Minnie Minoso	.50
43	Bob James, Hoyt Wilhelm	.35
44	Tom Paciorek, Eddie Collins	.35
46	Tim Lollar, Billy Pierce	.25
50	Juan Agosto, Wilbur Wood	.25
72	Carlton Fisk, Ray Schalk	1.00
--	Comiskey Park	.50
--	Ribbie and Roobarb (mascots)	.25
--	Nancy Faust (organist)	.25

1985 Coca-Cola Pirates

A companion set to the cards issued in the 1985 Pirates yearbook, this set was given away to the first 10,000 youngsters attending May 18 and July 13 home games. The card of Kent Tekulve was withdrawn after his trade to the Phillies, making it quite scarce. The 2-1/2" x 3-1/2" cards have a color photo at center, surrounded by black and gold borders. A white panel at bottom has the player's name, position and uniform number. Backs are in black-and-white and feature complete major and minor league stats, plus the Cameron/Coca-Cola sponsors' logos.

		MT
Complete Set (29) (no Tekulve):		12.00
Complete Set (30) (w/ Tekulve):		20.00
Common Player:		.50
2	Jim Morrison	.50
3	Johnny Ray	.50
5	Bill Madlock	1.00
6	Tony Pena	.60
7	Chuck Tanner	.50
10	Tim Foli	.50
11	Joe Orsulak	.50
12	Bill Almon	.50
13	Steve Kemp	.50
15	George Hendrick	.50
16	Lee Mazzilli	.50
17	Jerry Dybzinski	.50
19	Rod Scurry	.50
22	Lee Tunnell	.50
25	Jose DeLeon	.50
27	Kent Tekulve	7.50
28	Sixto Lezcano	.50
29	Rick Rhoden	.50
30	Jason Thompson	.50
34	Mike Bielecki	.50
35	Al Holland	.50
36	Marvell Wynne	.50
37	Rafael Belliard	.50
43	Don Robinson	.50
45	John Candelaria	.50
47	Cecilio Guante	.50
49	Larry McWilliams	.50
51	Doug Frobel	.50
--	Pirates coaches	.50

1986 Coca-Cola Dodgers Photocards

For a second year Coke sponsored this set of 3-1/2" x 5-1/2" color postcards. Fronts feature player action photo with white borders. Beneath the photo is a 1986 copyright line; the player's name is at bottom. Backs have a red Coca-Cola logo in the lower-right corner, and can be found either otherwise blank or with a message to fans from the pictured player, along with a facsimile autograph. The unnumbered cards are checklisted here alphabetically.

		MT
Complete Set (34):		14.00
Common Player:		.50
(1)	Joe Amalfitano	.50
(2)	Dave Anderson	.50
(3)	Monty Basgall	.50
(4)	Greg Brock	.50
(5)	Enos Cabell	.50
(6)	Cesar Cedeno	.50
(7)	Mark Cresse	.50
(8)	Carlos Diaz	.50
(9)	Mariano Duncan	.50
(10)	Pedro Guerrero	.50
(11)	Orel Hershiser	1.00
(12)	Ben Hines	.50
(13)	Rick Honeycutt	.50
(14)	Ken Howell	.50
(15)	Ken Landreaux	.50
(16)	Tom Lasorda	.75
(17)	Bill Madlock	.60
(18)	Mike Marshall	.50
(19)	Len Matuszek	.50
(20)	Manny Mota	.50
(21)	Tom Niedenfuer	.50
(22)	Alejandro Pena	.50
(23)	Ron Perranoski	.50
(24)	Dennis Powell	.50
(25)	Jerry Reuss	.50
(26)	Bill Russell	.50
(27)	Steve Sax	.50
(28)	Mike Scioscia	.50
(29)	Franklin Stubbs	.50
(30)	Alex Trevino	.50
(31)	Fernando Valenzuela	.75
(32)	Ed Vande Berg	.50
(33)	Bob Welch	.50
(34)	Terry Whitfield	.50

1986 Coca-Cola White Sox

For the second year in a row, Coca-Cola, in conjunction with the Chicago White Sox, issued a 30-card set. As in 1985, cards were given out at the park on Tuesday night games. Full sets were available through a fan club offer found in the White Sox program. The 2-5/8" x 4-1/8" cards feature 25 players plus other team personnel. Fronts have a color photo (a game-action shot in most instances) and a white bar at the bottom. A black and white bat with "SOX" shown on the barrel is located within the white bar, along with the player's name, position and uniform number. The white and gray backs with black print include the Coca-Cola trademark. Lifetime statistics are shown on all player cards, but there is no personal information such as height, weight or age. The non-player cards are blank-backed save for the name and logo at the top. The cards in the checklist that follows are numbered by the players' uniform numbers, with the last five cards of the set being unnumbered.

		MT
Complete Set (30):		11.00
Common Player:		.25
1	Wayne Tolleson	.25
3	Harold Baines	.45
7	Marc Hill	.25
8	Daryl Boston	.25
12	Julio Cruz	.25
13	Ozzie Guillen	.35
17	Jerry Hairston	.25
19	Floyd Bannister	.25
20	Reid Nichols	.25
22	Joel Skinner	.25
24	Dave Schmidt	.25
26	Bobby Bonilla	1.50
29	Greg Walker	.25
30	Gene Nelson	.25
32	Tim Hulett	.25
33	Neil Allen	.25
34	Richard Dotson	.25
40	Joe Cowley	.25
41	Tom Seaver	2.00
42	Ron Kittle	.25
43	Bob James	.25
44	John Cangelosi	.25
50	Juan Agosto	.25
52	Joel Davis	.25
72	Carlton Fisk	2.00
----	Ribbie & Roobarb (mascots)	.25
----	Nancy Faust (organist)	.25
----	Ken "Hawk" Harrelson	.25
----	Tony LaRussa	.40
----	Minnie Minoso	.75

1987 Coca-Cola Tigers

Coca-Cola and S. Abraham & Sons, Inc. issued a set of 18 baseball cards featuring members of the Detroit Tigers. The set is comprised of six four-part folding panels. Each panel includes three player cards (each 2-1/2" x 3-1/2") and one team logo card. A bright yellow border surrounds the full-color photo. The backs are designed on a vertical format and contain personal data and career statistics. The set was produced by Mike Schecter and Associates.

		MT
Complete Panel Set (6):		5.50
Complete Singles Set (18):		2.00
Common Panel:		.50
Common Player:		.05
Panel		.85
1	Kirk Gibson	.30
2	Larry Herndon	.05
3	Walt Terrell	.05
Panel		1.50
4	Alan Trammell	.60
5	Frank Tanana	.05
6	Pat Sheridan	.05
Panel		.85
7	Jack Morris	.30
8	Mike Heath	.05
9	Dave Bergman	.05
Panel		.50
10	Chet Lemon	.10
11	Dwight Lowry	.05
12	Dan Petry	.05
Panel		.85
13	Darrell Evans	.25
14	Darnell Coles	.05
15	Willie Hernandez	.10
Panel		1.00
16	Lou Whitaker	.35
17	Tom Brookens	.05
18	John Grubb	.05

1987 Coca-Cola White Sox

The Chicago White Sox Fan Club, in conjunction with Coca-Cola, offered members a set of 30 trading cards. For the $10 membership fee, fans received the set plus additional fan club gifts and privileges. The cards, 2-5/8" x 4", feature full-color photos inside a blue and red border. Backs include the player's name, position, uniform number and statistics, plus the Coca-Cola logo. Cards are checklisted here by uniform number.

		MT
Complete Set (30):		8.00
Common Player:		.25
1	Jerry Royster	.25
3	Harold Baines	.45
5	Ron Karkovice	.25
8	Daryl Boston	.25
10	Fred Manrique	.25
12	Steve Lyons	.25
13	Ozzie Guillen	.40
14	Russ Morman	.25
15	Donnie Hill	.25
16	Jim Fregosi	.30
17	Jerry Hairston	.25
19	Floyd Bannister	.25
21	Gary Redus	.25
22	Ivan Calderon	.25
25	Ron Hassey	.25
26	Jose DeLeon	.25
29	Greg Walker	.25
32	Tim Hulett	.25
33	Neil Allen	.25
34	Rich Dotson	.25
36	Ray Searage	.25
37	Bobby Thigpen	.25
40	Jim Winn	.25
43	Bob James	.25
50	Joel McKeon	.25
52	Joel Davis	.25
72	Carlton Fisk	1.00
----	Ribbie & Roobarb (mascots)	.25
----	Nancy Faust (organist)	.25
----	Minnie Minoso	.50

1988 Coca-Cola Padres

A 20-card set sponsored by Coca-Cola was designed as part of the San Diego Padres Junior Fan Club promotion for 1988. This set was distributed as a nine-card starter sheet, with 11 additional single cards handed out during various home games. The standard-size cards feature full-color player photos framed by a black and orange border. The player's name is printed above the photo; uniform number and position appear at lower-right. A large Padres logo curves upward from the lower-left corner. Backs are brown on white and include the Padres logo at upper-left opposite the player's name and personal information. Career highlights and 1987 stats appear in the center of the card back above the Coca-Cola and Junior Padres Fan Club logos.

		MT
Complete Set (21):		30.00
Common Player:		.50
Panel		
1	Garry Templeton	.60
5	Randy Ready	.50
10	Larry Bowa	.60
11	Tim Flannery	.50
35	Chris Brown	.50
45	Jimmy Jones	.50
48	Mark Davis	.50
55	Mark Grant	.50
----	20th Anniversary Logo Card	.10
Singles		
7	Keith Moreland	1.00
8	John Kruk	3.00
9	Benito Santiago	3.00
14	Carmelo Martinez	1.00
15	Jack McKeon	1.00
19	Tony Gwynn	8.00
22	Stan Jefferson	1.00
27	Mark Parent	1.00
30	Eric Show	1.00
31	Ed Whitson	1.00
41	Lance McCullers	1.00
51	Greg Booker	1.00

1988 Coca-Cola White Sox

Part of a fan club membership package, this unnumbered 30-card set features full-color photos of 27 players, the team mascot, team organist and Comiskey Park. Cards have a bright red border, with team logo in the photo's lower-left corner. The player name fills the bottom border. Backs are printed in black on gray and white and include player name, personal info and career summary. The set was included in the $10 membership package, with a portion of the cost going to the ChiSox Kids Charity.

		MT
Complete Set (30):		7.00
Common Player:		.25
(1)	Harold Baines	.50
(2)	Daryl Boston	.25
(3)	Ivan Calderon	.25
(4)	John Davis	.25
(5)	Jim Fregosi	.25
(6)	Carlton Fisk	1.00
(7)	Ozzie Guillen	.35
(8)	Donnie Hill	.25
(9)	Rick Horton	.25
(10)	Lance Johnson	.40
(11)	Dave LaPoint	.25
(12)	Bill Long	.25
(13)	Steve Lyons	.25
(14)	Jack McDowell	.30
(15)	Fred Manrique	.25
(16)	Minnie Minoso	.75
(17)	Dan Pasqua	.25
(18)	John Pawlowski	.25
(19)	Melido Perez	.25
(20)	Billy Pierce	.25
(21)	Gary Redus	.25
(22)	Jerry Reuss	.25
(23)	Mark Salas	.25
(24)	Jose Segura	.25
(25)	Bobby Thigpen	.25
(26)	Greg Walker	.25
(27)	Kenny Williams	.25
(28)	Nancy Faust (organist)	.25
(29)	Ribbie & Roobarb (mascots)	.25
(30)	Comiskey Park	.40

1989 Coca-Cola Padres

This 20-card set is part of the Junior Padres Fan Club membership package. Members receive a nine-card starter set printed on one large perforated sheet. Additional cards are distributed to kids at specially designated games (free admission for kids). Fronts feature an orange-and-brown double border, with a bright orange Padres logo printed at lower-left. Uniform number and position are printed diagonally across the upper-right corner, with the player's name in large block letters along the bottom border.

		MT
Complete Set (21):		26.00
Common Player:		.50
Panel		
1	Garry Templeton	.60
5	Randy Ready	.50
12	Roberto Alomar	4.50
14	Carmelo Martinez	.50
15	Jack McKeon	.50
30	Eric Show	.50
31	Ed Whitson	.50
43	Dennis Rasmussen	.50
----	Logo card	.10
Singles		
6	Luis Salazar	1.00
9	Benito Santiago	1.50
10	Leon Roberts	1.00
11	Tim Flannery	1.00
18	Chris James	1.00
19	Tony Gwynn	8.00
25	Jack Clark	1.00
27	Mark Parent	1.00
35	Walt Terrell	1.00
47	Bruce Hurst	1.00
48	Mark Davis	1.00
55	Mark Grant	1.00

1989 Coca-Cola White Sox

For the fifth straight year, Coca-Cola sponsored a set of cards featuring the Chicago White Sox. The 30-card set was distributed to fans attending a special promotional day at Comiskey Park and was also available by mail to members of the ChiSox fan club. Card fronts feature a red, white and blue color scheme and include a pair of crossed bats. "White Sox" appears along the top, while player name and position are in the lower-right, and a pennant proclaiming "Chicago's American Pastime" is just below the photo. Horizontal backs include player biographies, other data, special facts about Comiskey Park and the Coca-Cola logo.

		MT
Complete Set (30):		6.00
Common Player:		.20
1	New Comiskey Park, 1991	.40
2	Comiskey Park	.40
3	Jeff Torborg	.20
4	Coaching staff	.20
5	Harold Baines	.45
6	Daryl Boston	.20
7	Ivan Calderon	.20
8	Carlton Fisk	1.00
9	Dave Gallagher	.20
10	Ozzie Guillen	.25
11	Shawn Hillegas	.20
12	Barry Jones	.20
13	Ron Karkovice	.20
14	Eric King	.20
15	Ron Kittle	.20
16	Bill Long	.20
17	Steve Lyons	.20
18	Donn Pall	.20
19	Dan Pasqua	.20
20	Ken Patterson	.20
21	Melido Perez	.20
22	Jerry Reuss	.20
23	Billy Jo Robidoux	.20
24	Steve Rosenberg	.20
25	Jeff Schaefer	.20
26	Bobby Thigpen	.20
27	Greg Walker	.20
28	Eddie Williams	.20
29	Nancy Faust (organist)	.20
30	Minnie Minoso	.50

1990 Coca-Cola Garry Templeton

Coca-Cola, Vons stores and the Padres joined forces to release this special pin/baseball card collectible in honor of Garry Templeton becoming the club's all-time leader in games played. The card front features a full-color photo of Templeton and displays "Most Games Played" and "The Captain" in orange at the top of the photo. "Templeton" appears vertically in white along the left border. The Coca-Cola and Padre logos also appear on the card front. The bottom of the card features a perforated edge where the pin is attached as an extension of the card. The card back is printed in black and white and displays biographical information, career highlights and career statistics.

		MT
Complete Set (1/1):		1.50
(1)	Most Games Played card (Garry Templeton)	.50
(2)	Most Games Played pin (Garry Templeton)	1.00

The election of former players to the Hall of Fame does not always have an immediate upward effect on card prices. The hobby market generally has done a good job of predicting those inductions and adjusting values over the course of several years.

1990 Coca-Cola Padres

This set was designed for members of the Junior Padres Club sponsored by Coca-Cola. Each member received an eight-card panel and then received two different single cards at every Junior Padres Club game attended. Card fronts feature full-color photos with the Padres logo in the upper-right corner of the card. Backs feature statistics, career highlights and a red Coca-Cola logo. The cards are numbered by the player's uniform number.

		MT
Complete Set (21):		18.00
Common Player:		.35
Panel		
10	Bip Roberts	.50
15	Jack McKeon	.35
30	Eric Show	.35
31	Ed Whitson	.35
40	Andy Benes	.90
43	Dennis Rasmussen	.35
55	Mark Grant	.35
----	Logo card	.35
Singles		
1	Garry Templeton	1.00
8	Fred Lynn	1.00
9	Benito Santiago	1.50
11	Craig Lefferts	.80
12	Roberto Alomar	4.00
13	Mike Pagliarulo	1.00
17	Joe Carter	1.50
19	Tony Gwynn	6.00
25	Jack Clark	.80
27	Mark Parent	.80
38	Calvin Schiraldi	.80
46	Greg Harris	.80
47	Bruce Hurst	.80

1990 Coca-Cola Tigers

Once again utilizing the larger 2-7/8" x 4-1/4" format, this set was jointly sponsored by Coke and Kroger grocery stores and distributed at the July 14 game. Cards feature color action photos on front, surrounded by green borders. Backs have a black-and-white portrait photo, the appropriate logos and complete minor and major league stats. The player's uniform number appears in the upper-left corner.

		MT
Complete Set (28):		6.00
Common Player:		.15
(1)	Sparky Anderson	.50
(2)	Dave Bergman	.15
(3)	Brian DuBois	.15
(4)	Cecil Fielder	.25
(5)	Paul Gibson	.15
(6)	Jerry Don Gleaton	.15
(7)	Mike Heath	.15
(8)	Mike Henneman	.25
(9)	Tracy Jones	.15
(10)	Chet Lemon	.15
(11)	Urbano Lugo	.15
(12)	Jack Morris	.20
(13)	Lloyd Moseby	.15
(14)	Matt Nokes	.15
(15)	Edwin Nunez	.15
(16)	Dan Petry	.15
(17)	Tony Phillips	.25
(18)	Kevin Ritz	.15
(19)	Jeff Robinson	.15
(20)	Ed Romero	.15
(21)	Mark Salas	.15
(22)	Larry Sheets	.15
(23)	Frank Tanana	.15
(24)	Alan Trammell	.75
(25)	Gary Ward	.15
(26)	Lou Whitaker	.40
(27)	Ken Williams	.15
(28)	Coaches (Billy Consolo, Alex Grammas, Billy Muffett, Vada Pinson, Dick Tracewski)	.15

1990 Coca-Cola White Sox

An attractive "Comiskey Park 1910-1990" logo is featured on the front of each card in this set. Fronts also feature full-color photos with a thin white inner border. The cards are numbered according to uniform number, with the exception of four special cards including Top Prospect Frank Thomas. Horizontal card backs feature black print on white and gray stock; 1989 statistics and career highlights are provided. The 1990 set marks the sixth straight year that Coca-Cola sponsored a White Sox set.

		MT
Complete Set (30):		15.00
Common Player:		.15
1	Lance Johnson	.25
7	Scott Fletcher	.15
10	Jeff Torborg	.15
12	Steve Lyons	.15
13	Ozzie Guillen	.15
14	Craig Grebeck	.15
17	Dave Gallagher	.15
20	Ron Karkovice	.15
22	Ivan Calderon	.15
23	Robin Ventura	3.00
24	Carlos Martinez	.15
25	Sammy Sosa	10.00
27	Greg Hibbard	.15
29	Jack McDowell	.20
30	Donn Pall	.15
31	Scott Radinsky	.15
33	Melido Perez	.15
34	Ken Patterson	.15
36	Eric King	.15
37	Bobby Thigpen	.15
42	Ron Kittle	.15
44	Dan Pasqua	.15
45	Wayne Edwards	.15
50	Barry Jones	.15
52	Jerry Kutzler	.15
72	Carlton Fisk	3.00
--	Top Prospect (Frank Thomas)	7.50
--	White Sox manager, coaches (Jeff Torborg)	.15
--	Captains (Ozzie Guillen, Carlton Fisk)	.50
----	Rookies (Wayne Edwards, Craig Greback, Jerry Kutzler, Scott Radinsky, Robin Ventura)	.25

1991 Coca-Cola Don Mattingly

Though sponsored by Coca-Cola, the manner of distribution of this issue is unclear. The "Mattingly's 23" logo on each side of the card suggests a connection to his Evansville, Ind., restaurant. Fronts of the 2-1/2" x 3-1/2" cards have photos in black-and-white or color, or artwork. The border is white with blue pinstripes. The year of the picture is at top of the photo and there is a Coca-Cola logo at bottom. Backs are printed in red and blue and contain career highlights and stats, along with a card number and logos.

		MT
Complete Set (15):		10.00
Common Card:		1.00
1	Don Mattingly (1978)	1.00
2	Don Mattingly (1979)	1.00
3	Don Mattingly (1980)	1.00
4	Don Mattingly (1981)	1.00
5	Don Mattingly (1982)	1.00
6	Don Mattingly (1983)	1.00
7	Don Mattingly (1983-84)	1.00
8	Don Mattingly (1984)	1.00
9	Don Mattingly (1985)	1.00
10	Don Mattingly (1986)	1.00
11	Don Mattingly (1987)	1.00
12	Don Mattingly (1990)	1.00
13	Don Mattingly (1991)	1.00
14	Don Mattingly (1991)	1.00
15	Don Mattingly (1991)	1.00

1991 Coca-Cola Tigers

This set was sponsored by Coca-Cola and Kroger. The oversized cards feature color photos on front along with the player's name vertically printed on the right border and the Tigers logo in the lower-right corner. Backs are printed horizontally and feature statistics. The set is numbered according to uniform number.

		MT
Complete Set (27):		6.00
Common Player:		.20
1	Lou Whitaker	.40
3	Alan Trammell	.75
4	Tony Phillips	.25
10	Andy Allanson	.20
11	Sparky Anderson	.50
14	Dave Bergman	.20
15	Lloyd Moseby	.20
19	Jerry Don Gleaton	.20
20	Mickey Tettleton	.30
22	Milt Cuyler	.25
23	Mark Leiter	.20
24	Travis Fryman	.75
25	John Shelby	.20
26	Frank Tanana	.20
27	Mark Salas	.20
29	Pete Incaviglia	.25
31	Kevin Ritz	.20
35	Walt Terrell	.20
36	Bill Gullickson	.20
39	Mike Henneman	.25
44	Rob Deer	.20
45	Cecil Fielder	.50
46	Dan Petry	.20
48	Paul Gibson	.20
49	Steve Searcy	.20
55	John Cerutti	.20
--	Tigers Coaches (Billy Consolo, Jim Davenport, Alex Grammas, Billy Muffett, Vada Pinson, Dick	.20

1992 Coca-Cola Nolan Ryan Career Series

This 26-card set was produced by Donruss in conjunction with Coca-Cola to honor Nolan Ryan's 26 major league seasons. One Nolan Ryan card was packaged with three regular 1992 Donruss cards in special 12-packs of Coca-Cola. Complete sets, in a black, red and gold box, were available through a mail-in offer. The 2-1/2" x 3-1/2" cards have a full-color photo on front, framed by a gold border. Ryan's name is printed in gold toward the bottom, above a blue bar which presents a team and year. The Coke logo is at upper right. On back there are details of Ryan's performance in the indicated year, the card number, and team and Coke logos. An 18" x 12" color poster picturing the cards and a photo of a Ryan-autographed ball was issued as a point-of-purchase display.

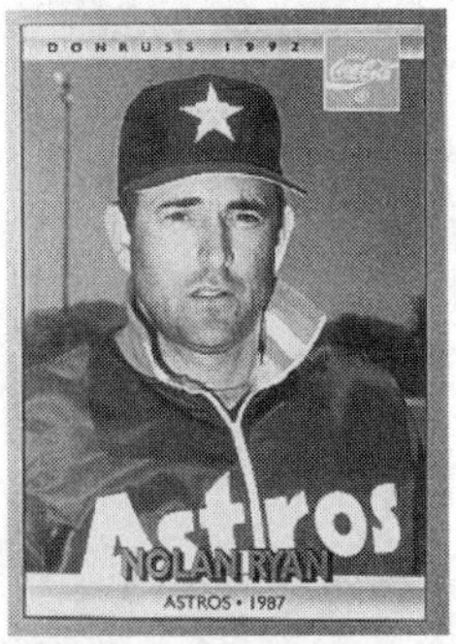

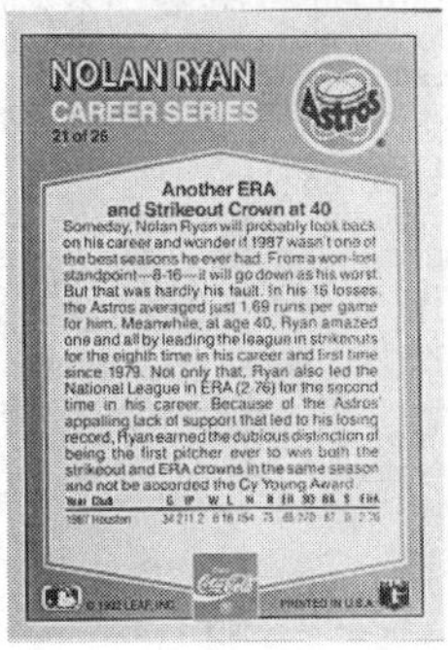

		MT
Complete Set (26):		20.00
Common Card:		1.25
Display Poster:		5.00
	NEW YORK METS	
1	1966 Breaking In	1.25
2	1968 Record-Setting Rookie	1.25
3	1969 World Champions	1.25
4	1970 Growing Pains	1.25
5	1971 Traded	1.25
	CALIFORNIA ANGELS	
6	1972 Fitted for a Halo	1.25
7	1973 First Two No-Nos and a Record	1.25
8	1974 No-Hitter No. 3/ Another K Record	1.25
9	1975 Tying Koufax	1.25
10	1976 Back on Track	1.25
11	1977 Carrying the Load	1.25
12	1978 A Year of Injuries	1.25
13	1979 California Farewell	1.25
	HOUSTON ASTROS	
14	1980 Coming Home	1.25
15	1981 A Gusher in Houston	1.25
16	1982 Mounting 'Em Up	1.25
17	1983 Passing the Big Train	1.25
18	1984 Misleading Signs of Age	1.25
19	1985 Another Milestone/A New Contract	1.25
20	1986 The Elbow Flares Up Again	1.25
21	1987 Another ERA/ Strikeout Crown at 40	1.25
22	1988 Leaving Home Again	1.25
	TEXAS RANGERS	
23	1989 5,000 Strikeouts	1.25
24	1990 Win No. 300, No-Hitter No. 6	1.25
25	1991 No-Hitter No. 7	1.25
26	1992 Man of Records	1.25

Player names in *Italic* type indicate a rookie card.

1992 Coca-Cola Tigers

This set of large-format (2-7/8" x 4-1/4") cards features central photos of the Bengals in action. Dark blue stripes at top and bottom have the team name in white, while the player name, uniform number and position are printed in black on an orange stripe directly beneath the photo. A color team logo in the upper-right completes the front design. Backs have complete major and minor league stats, a few personal data and color logos of Coke and the Kroger grocery chain.

		MT
Complete Set (28):		6.00
Common Player:		.15
1	Lou Whitaker	.35
3	Alan Trammell	.60
4	Tony Phillips	.25
7	Scott Livingstone	.15
9	"Skeeter" Barnes	.15
11	Sparky Anderson	.50
14	Dave Bergman	.15
15	Mark Carreon	.15
18	Gary Pettis	.15
19	Chad Kreuter	.15
20	Mickey Tettleton	.20
22	Milt Cuyler	.15
23	Mark Leiter	.15
24	Travis Fryman	.25
26	Frank Tanana	.15
27	Kurt Knudsen	.15
28	Rob Deer	.15
31	Kevin Ritz	.15
32	Dan Gladden	.15
35	Walt Terrell	.15
36	Bill Gullickson	.15
39	Mike Henneman	.20
43	Mike Munoz	.15
44	John Doherty	.15
45	Cecil Fielder	.35
46	John Kiely	.15
48	Les Lancaster	.15
---	Tigers coaches (Billy Consolo, Gene Roof, Larry Herndon, Dick Tracewksi, Billy Muffett, Dan	.15

1992 Coca-Cola/ Hardees Major League Line-Up Discs

This set of 3" diameter "Major League Line-Up" cardboard discs was a regional give-away sponsored by Coca-Cola and distributed by Hardee's restaurants. The glossy discs have player photos at center with position and uniform numbers at the sides. Backs are in black-and-white with a few stats and career highlights and various logos. A checklist disc was also distributed.

		MT
Complete Set (24):		16.00
Common Player:		.50
1	Roger Clemens	2.00
2	Sandy Alomar Jr.	.50
3	Rafael Palmeiro	.75
4	Roberto Alomar	1.25
5	Kelly Gruber	.50
6	Ozzie Guillen	.50
7	Devon White	.50
8	David Henderson	.50
9	Robin Yount	2.00
10	Chili Davis	.50
11	Chuck Knoblauch	.75
12	Paul Molitor	1.50
13	Tom Glavine	.60
14	Benito Santiago	.50
15	Hal Morris	.50
16	Delino DeShields	.50
17	Matt Williams	.75
18	Ozzie Smith	1.50
19	Andy Van Slyke	.50
20	Andre Dawson	.50
21	Ron Gant	.50
22	Jeff Bagwell	2.00
23	Terry Pendleton	.50
24	Brett Butler	.50

1993 Coca-Cola Commanders of the Hill

Coca-Cola and Topps teamed up to print a 30-card Commanders of the Hill set in 1993. The cards were available in five-card packages with soft-drink purchases on military bases at base exchange food court concessions. The set was divided into three areas: Cy Young Winners, Strikeout Leaders and Team ERA Leaders, with the National League player's names in yellow on a red background and the American League in red on yellow.

		MT
Complete Set (30):		7.50
Common Player:		.25
1	Dennis Eckersley	.35
2	Mike Mussina	.40
3	Roger Clemens	1.00
4	Jim Abbott	.25
5	Jack McDowell	.25
6	Charles Nagy	.25
7	Bill Gullickson	.25
8	Kevin Appier	.25
9	Bill Wegman	.25
10	John Smiley	.25
11	Melido Perez	.25
12	Dave Stewart	.25
13	Dave Fleming	.25
14	Kevin Brown	.35
15	Juan Guzman	.25
16	Randy Johnson	.50
17	Greg Maddux	1.00
18	Tom Glavine	.35
19	Greg Maddux	1.00
20	Jose Rijo	.25
21	Pete Harnisch	.25
22	Tom Candiotti	.25
23	Denny Martinez	.25
24	Sid Fernandez	.25
25	Curt Schilling	.25
26	Doug Drabek	.25
27	Bob Tewksbury	.25
28	Andy Benes	.25
29	Bill Swift	.25
30	John Smoltz	.40

1995 Coca-Cola Minnesota Twins POGs

Coca-Cola and the Twins teamed to offer fans a set of 33 POGs during the 1995 season. Sets of 11 were given to fans at the July 1, July 17 and July 28 games at the Metrodome. A reported 15,000 sets were produced. The unnumbered POGs are checklisted here within series.

		MT
Complete Set (33):		12.00
Common Player:		.50
	SERIES 1	
(1)	Rick Aguilera	.50
(2)	Rich Becker	.75
(3)	Marty Cordova	.75
(4)	Terry Crowley	.50
(5)	Eddie Guardado	.50
(6)	Jeff Reboulet	.50
(7)	Rich Robertson	.50
(8)	Scott Stahoviak	.50
(9)	Dick Such	.50
(10)	Kevin Tapani	.65
(11)	Matt Walbeck	.50
	SERIES 2	
(12)	Alex Cole	.50
(13)	Scott Erickson	.75
(14)	Ron Gardenhire	.50
(15)	Chip Hale	.50
(16)	Chuck Knoblauch	1.00
(17)	Scott Leius	.50
(18)	Pat Mahomes	.50
(19)	Pedro Munoz	.50
(20)	Erik Schullstrom	.50
(21)	Dave Stevens	.50
(22)	Scott Ullger	.50
	SERIES 3	
(23)	Jerald Clark	.50
(24)	Mark Guthrie	.50
(25)	Tom Kelly	.50
(26)	Kevin Maas	.50
(27)	Pat Meares	.50
(28)	Matt Merullo	.50
(29)	Kirby Puckett	4.00
(30)	Brad Radke	.50
(31)	Rick Stelmaszek	.50
(32)	Mike Trombley	.50
(33)	Jerry White	.50

1995 Coca-Cola Pittsburgh Pirates POGs

To celebrate the 25th anniversary of Three Rivers Stadium, Coca-Cola and the Pirates issued a set of POGs marking the 25 greatest baseball moments at the stadium. The POGs were issued nine apiece on heavy 6" x 8" cardboard panels. Individual POGs measure about 1-3/4" diameter and are perforated at the edge so they can be removed from the panel. Most fronts have a border of team-color orange and black, with central photos in black-and-white or color. Backs of #1-8 have a green Fruitopia ad; backs of #10-18 have an ad for Sprite in green, while #9, 19-25 have a red Coca-Cola ad on back.

		MT
Complete Set Panels (3):		15.00
Complete Set Singles (27):		9.00
Common POG:		.25
1	1994 All-Star Game (All-Star logo)	.25
2	Roberto Clemente (3,000th Hit)	2.00
3	Roberto Clemente (uniform #21 retired)	2.00
4	Pirates Win 1979 N.L. Pennant (We Are Family logo)	.25
5	John Candelaria (No-Hits Dodgers)	.25
6	Willie Stargell (uniform #8 retired)	.50
7	Mike Schmidt (500th Home Run)	.75
8	Kent Tekulve (First Game, 7/16/70)	.25
--	Coke/Fruitopia logos	.05
9	First World Series Night Game	.25
10	Nellie Briles (1971 World Series 2-Hitter)	.25
11	Pirates Win 1971 N.L. Pennant	.25
12	Pirates Clinch N.L. East, 1979	.25
13	Pirates Clinch N.L. East, 1992 (Jim Leyland)	.25
14	Bob Gibson (No-Hits Pirates 8/14/71)	.40
15	1979 World Series Game 5 (Jim Rooker)	.25
16	Pirates Clinch N.L. East, 1971	.25
17	Beat Braves in NLCS Game 5, 1992	.25
18	John Milner (Grand Slam Beats Phillis 8/5/79)	.25
19	Barry Bonds (11th Inning HR Beats St. Louis 8/12/91)	.75
20	Jeff King (5 Runs in 9th to Beat Dodgers, 5/28/90)	.25
21	Danny Murtaugh (Murtaugh, Joe L. Brown Retire)	.25
22	"Gunner" Returns to Broadcast Booth	.25
23	Sweep Phillies in 9/29/78 Doubleheader	.25
24	Jim Leyland (Makes Pittsburgh Debut)	.25
25	1974 All-Star Game (program)	.25
---	Coke logos	.05

1995 Coca-Cola/Publix Florida Marlins

Coca-Cola and the Publix grocery store chain sponsored this team set issue. Fronts of the standard-size (2-1/2" x 3-1/2") cards have color player action photos on a large background of the team logo. Backs have a color portrait photo and stats. Cards are checklisted here by uniform number.

		MT
Complete Set (27):		15.00
Common Player:		.50
3	Quilvio Veras	.75
4	Greg Colbrunn	.75
6	Tommy Gregg	.50
7	Kurt Abbott	.75
8	Andre Dawson	2.00
9	Terry Pendleton	.75
10	Gary Sheffield	2.50
11	Chris Hammond	.50
14	Jerry Browne	.50
15	Marcel Lacheman	.50
17	Darrell Whitmore	.50
21	Chuck Carr	.50
23	Charles Johnson	2.50
26	Alex Arias	.50
28	Mark Gardner	.50
29	Mario Diaz	.50
31	Robb Nen	.50
33	John Burkett	.50
34	Bryan Harvey	.50
35	David Weathers	.50
42	Jeremy Hernandez	.50
48	Pat Rapp	.50
51	Terry Mathews	.50
52	Randy Veres	.50
58	Yorkis Perez	.50
---	Coaches	.50
---	Billy the Marlin (mascot)	.50

1996 Coca-Cola/ Kroger Nolan Ryan Card/Pin

Culminating activities during Nolan Ryan Appreciation Week at Arlington, Sept. 12-15, fans attending the Sept. 15 game, during which Ryan's uniform number was retired by the Rangers, received a baseball card/pin combination sponsored by Coca-Cola and Kroger grocers. The giveaway is a 2-1/2" x 5-1/2" cardboard panel. At top is a 2-1/2" x 3-7/8" card separated by perforations from the bottom panel on which the 1-1/8" x 1-1/2" enameled jersey pin is affixed. The front has a spring-training game-action color photo of Ryan. The back is in black-and-white with a career summary, sponsor' logos and a picture of the pin.

	MT
Card/Pin Combination:	7.00
Nolan Ryan	

1986 Barry Colla Jose Canseco Advertising Cards

This set of 2-1/2" x 3-1/2" cards of then-rookie phenom Jose Canseco was issued to advertise the availability of 8" x 10" autographed photos. Each card is a miniature reproduction of the available photo, borderless and printed on glossy stock. Black-and-white backs have details on ordering the photos.

	MT
Complete Set (10):	8.00
Single Card:	1.00
Jose Canseco	

1987 Barry Colla Mark McGwire Advertising Cards

These cards were issued to advertise the availability of autographed color photos of then-rookie phenom Mark McGwire. Each of the 2-1/2" x 3-1/2" cards is a miniature reproduction of one of the photos, borderless, printed on glossy stock. Backs are in black-and-white and have ordering information.

	MT
Complete Set (10):	15.00
Single Card:	2.00
Mark McGwire	

1987 Barry Colla N.Y. Mets Photocards

A comprehensive set of New York Mets player postcards was produced by one of the hobby's top photographers for team and player distribution. Complete sets were not available. Cards measure 3-1/2" x 5-1/2" with borderless color photos on front; most photos are full-length, or nearly so. Backs have a "Dear Mets Fan" message and facsimile autograph. While the cards are numbered in the lower-right with an "87" suffix, they are checklisted here in alphabetical order.

		MT
Complete Set (54):		65.00
Common Player:		2.00
(1)	Rick Anderson	2.00
(2)	Wally Backman	2.00
(3)	Jose Bautista	2.00
(4)	Terry Blocker	2.00
(5)	Bob Buchanan	2.00
(6)	Tom Burns	2.00
(7)	Mark Carreon	2.00
(8)	Gary Carter	4.00
(9)	Charlie Corbell	2.00
(10)	Reggie Dobie	2.00

(11)	Lenny Dykstra	2.50
(12)	Kevin Elster	2.00
(13)	Sid Fernandez	2.00
(14)	John Gibbons	2.00
(15)	Brian Givens	2.00
(16)	Dwight Gooden	3.00
(17)	Bud Harrelson	2.00
(18)	Keith Hernandez	3.00
(19)	Vern Hoscheit	2.00
(20)	Clint Hurdle	2.00
(21)	Davey Johnson	2.00
(22)	Howard Johnson	2.50
(23)	Arthur Jones	2.00
(24)	Ralph Kiner	2.00
(25)	Marcus Lawton	2.00
(26)	Terry Leach	2.00
(27)	Barry Lyons	2.00
(28)	Dave Magadan	2.00
(29)	Lee Mazzilli	2.00
(30)	Tom McCarthy	2.00
(31)	Roger McDowell	2.00
(32)	Kevin McReynolds	2.00
(33)	Keith Miller	2.00
(34)	John Mitchell	2.00
(35)	Bob Murphy	2.00
(36)	Randy Myers	2.00
(37)	Bob Ojeda	2.00
(38)	Greg Olson	2.00
(39)	Jesse Orosco	2.00
(40)	Al Pedrique	2.00
(41)	Sam Perlozzo	2.00
(42)	Bill Robinson	2.00
(43)	Zoilo Sanchez	2.00
(44)	Rafael Santana	2.00
(45)	Doug Sisk	2.00
(46)	Arthur Smith	2.00
(47)	Mel Stottlemyre	2.00
(48)	Darryl Strawberry	3.00
(49)	Gary Thorne	2.00
(50)	Tim Teufel	2.00
(51)	Gene Walter	2.00
(52)	Dave West	2.00
(53)	Mookie Wilson	2.00
(54)	Team photo (4" x 6")	3.00

1988 Barry Colla Photoprints

High quality posed and action photos and high resolution printing on glossy cardstock make this issue of large format (8" x 10") photocards stand out from similar issues. The only graphics on the borderless front is the Major League Baseball licensee logo at lower-right. Backs are printed in black-and-white With player ID at top-left, a card number at top-right and logos and copyright data across the bottom.

		MT
Complete Set (12):		18.00
Common Player:		1.00
188	Mark McGwire (batting pose)	3.00
288	Mark McGwire (game-action swing)	3.00
388	Mark McGwire (holding bat horizontally)	3.00
488	Joe DiMaggio	3.00
588	Kal Daniels	1.00
688	Pete Rose	2.00
788	Terry Steinbach	1.00
888	Will Clark	1.50
988	Cory Snyder	1.00
1088	Jose Canseco	2.00
1188	Mike Aldrete	1.00
1288	Don Mattingly	2.00

1989 Barry Colla Postcards

In 1989 California baseball photographer Barry Colla began a series of player postcard sets. Each set contains eight postcards of the player and is sold in a white paper envelope with the team logo. The postcards are identical in format, measuring 3-1/2" x 5-1/2". Fronts feature borderless color photos on a high-gloss stock. Backs are printed in black-and-white and feature a team logo at center. The player's name, uniform number, team and position are printed in the upper-left. A card number appears at top-center.

		MT
1-8	Jose Canseco	6.00
1-8	Andre Dawson	4.00
1-8	Mike Greenwell	4.00
1-8	Don Mattingly	6.00
1-8	Mark McGwire	12.00
1-8	Kevin Mitchell	4.00
1-8	Ozzie Smith	6.00

1990 Colla Collection Promos

Each of the 12-card single-player sets produced by photographer Barry Colla in 1990 was preceded by a promo card. The promos feature the same borderless color photography as the issued cards. Backs have information on date and size of the limited-edition issues and ordering information printed in black and white. Checklist of the unnumbered cards is presented here in alphabetical order.

		MT
Complete Set (4):		8.00
Common Player:		1.00
(1)	Jose Canseco	3.00
(2)	Will Clark	2.00
(3)	Kevin Maas	1.00
(4)	Don Mattingly	3.00

1990 Barry Colla

In 1990 baseball photographer Barry Colla began production of a series of single-player card sets. In standard 2-1/2" x 3-1/2" size, the cards featured high-gloss borderless photos on front, with no extraneous graphics. Backs feature stats, career notes, personal data and team logos. The 12-card sets were sold in small decorative cardboard boxes. Production figures are noted in parentheses.

		MT
1-12	Jose Canseco (20,000)	6.00
1-12	Will Clark (15,000)	5.00
1-12	Kevin Maas (7,500)	3.00
1-12	Don Mattingly (15,000)	9.00

1990 Barry Colla Postcards

Barry Colla continued his series of single-player postcard sets with two additions in 1990. The basic format continued unchanged. The 3-1/2" x 5-1/2" card feature borderless color game-action and posed photos on a high-gloss stock. Black-and-white backs feature a team logo at center, a card number at top and, in the upper-left, the player's name, uniform number, team and position. Sets were sold in white paper envelopes with color team logos on the front.

		MT
1-8	Will Clark	5.00
1-8	Mark Grace	5.00

1991 Colla Collection Promos

Each of the eight 12-card single-player sets produced by California photographer Barry Colla in 1991 was preceded by the issue of a promo card. Identical in format, the promos feature high quality borderless photos on glossy stock. Backs are printed in black-and-white and include information on the size and release date of the limited-edition set, along with ordering information and appropriate logos. The checklist of the unnumbered promo cards is presented here alphabetically.

		MT
Complete Set (10):		16.00
Common Player:		1.00
(1a)	Roberto Alomar	2.00
(1b)	Roberto Alomar (French)	2.00
(2)	Barry Bonds	3.00
(3a)	Joe Carter	1.00
(3b)	Joe Carter (French)	1.00
(4)	Dwight Gooden	1.00
(5)	Ken Griffey, Jr.	5.00
(6)	Dave Justice	2.00
(7)	Ryne Sandberg	3.00
(8)	Darryl Strawberry	1.00

1991 Barry Colla

In 1991 baseball photographer Barry Colla continued production of a series of single-player card sets. In standard 2-1/2" x 3-1/2" size, the cards featured high-gloss borderless photos on front, with no extraneous graphics. Backs feature stats, career notes, personal data and team logos. The 12-card sets were sold in small decorative cardboard boxes. Production figures are noted in parentheses.

		MT
1-12	Roberto Alomar (7,500)	5.00
1-12	Barry Bonds (7,500)	7.50
1-12	Joe Carter (7,500)	3.00
1-12	Dwight Gooden (15,000)	3.00
1-12	Ken Griffey Jr. (15,000)	30.00
1-12	David Justice (15,000)	5.00
1-12	Ryne Sandberg (15,000)	6.00
1-12	Darryl Strawberry (15,000)	3.00

1991 Barry Colla Postcards

Only one single-player postcard set was produced by Barry Colla in 1991: Ryne Sandberg. The eight-card set, like the 1989-90 issues, features full-color game-action and posed photos presented on a borderless, high-gloss 3-1/2" x 5-1/2" format. Back design was changed for the 1991 issue. The team logo now appears in the upper-left corner with the player's name at top and his uniform number, team and position beneath. Sets were sold in a white paper envelope featuring a color Cubs logo.

		MT
1-8	Ryne Sandberg	5.00

1992 Colla Collection Promos

Each of the seven card sets produced by California photographer Barry Colla in 1992 was preceded by a promo card. In standard 2-1/2" x 3-1/2" size, the promos follow the format of the regular-issue cards with a borderless color photo on high-gloss stock. All of the card backs are printed in black-and-white and feature ordering information about the sets, expected release date and issue size and appropriate logos. Some promo cards feature checklists of all existing Colla Collection card sets. The unnumbered promo cards are checklisted here alphabetically.

		MT
Complete Set (7):		16.00
Common Player:		3.00
(1)	All-Star Set (Juan Guzman)	2.00
(2)	Steve Avery	2.00
(3)	Jeff Bagwell	3.00
(4)	Tony Gwynn	2.00
(5)	Mark McGwire	5.00
(6)	Frank Thomas	3.00
(7)	Nolan Ryan	4.00

1992 Barry Colla

In 1992 photographer Barry Colla continued production of a series of single-player card sets. In standard 2-1/2" x 3-1/2" size, the cards featured high-gloss borderless photos on front, with no extraneous graphics. Backs feature stats, career notes, personal data, team logos and/or a cartoon. Card #1 in each set was serially numbered on the back. The 12-card sets were sold in small decorative cardboard boxes. Production figures are noted in parentheses.

		MT
1-12	Steve Avery (7,500)	4.00
1-12	Jeff Bagwell (25,000)	6.00
1-12	Barry Bonds (7,500)	6.00
1-12	Tony Gwynn (7,500)	6.00
1-12	Mark McGwire (15,000)	20.00
1-12	Nolan Ryan (25,000)	20.00
1-12	Frank Thomas (25,000)	15.00

1992 Colla All-Stars

The 1992 Colla All-Star set consists of 24 players from the All-Star game in San Diego that year, packaged in a collector's box. Limited to 25,000 sets, the first card in each set is numbered and collectors had the opportunity to win numbered and autographed Roberto Alomar cards. Two hundred autographed Frank Thomas cards were also created for use as a premium, but he did not play in the 1992 All-Star Game due to injury.

		MT
Complete Set (24):		11.00
Common Player:		.30
1	Mark McGwire	4.00
2	Will Clark	.60
3	Roberto Alomar	.35
3a	Roberto Alomar (autographed)	65.00
4	Ryne Sandberg	1.25
5	Cal Ripken, Jr.	3.50
6	Ozzie Smith	.50
7	Wade Boggs	.35
8	Terry Pendleton	.30
9	Kirby Puckett	.50
10	Chuck Knoblauch	.40
11	Ken Griffey, Jr.	4.00
12	Joe Carter	.30
13	Sandy Alomar, Jr.	.35
14	Benito Santiago	.30
15	Mike Mussina	.40
16	Fred McGriff	.40
17	Dennis Eckersley	.30
18	Tony Gwynn	.50
19	Roger Clemens	.50
20	Gary Sheffield	.35
21	Jose Canseco	.35
22	Barry Bonds	.50
23	Ivan Rodriguez	.50
24	Tony Fernandez	.30
---	Frank Thomas (autographed)	125.00

1992 Barry Colla Postcards

Only one single-player postcard set was produced by Barry Colla in 1992: Ivan Rodriguez. The four-card set, like the 1989-91 issues, features full-color game-action and posed photos presented on a borderless, high-gloss 3-1/2" x 5-1/2" format.

		MT
Complete Set (4):		4.00
1-4	Ivan Rodriguez	1.00

1993 Colla All-Stars

For the second year in 1993 California photographer Barry Colla produced a 24-card All-Star set commemorating the game played in Baltimore on July 13. The specially boxed collector's edition includes an unnumbered All-Star logo/checklist card. Cards feature black borders on the UV-coated front, featuring game-action or posed photos. Team logos are centered beneath the photo, with the player's name and position in white at bottom. Backs are also bordered in black and include another player color photo, league and All-Star logos and information and stats on prior All-Star Game appearances.

		MT
Complete Set (25):		12.00
Common Player:		.25
1	Roberto Alomar	.35
2	Barry Bonds	.75
3	Ken Griffey, Jr.	1.50
4	John Kruk	.25
5	Kirby Puckett	.65
6	Darren Daulton	.25
7	Wade Boggs	.45
8	Matt Williams	.35
9	Cal Ripken, Jr.	1.00
10	Ryne Sandberg	.65
11	Ivan Rodriguez	.40
12	Andy Van Slyke	.25
13	John Olerud	.30
14	Tom Glavine	.25
15	Juan Gonzalez	.75
16	David Justice	.35
17	Mike Mussina	.30
18	Tony Gwynn	.65
19	Joe Carter	.25
20	Barry Larkin	.25
21	Brian Harper	.25
22	Ozzie Smith	.50
23	Mark McGwire	1.50
24	Mike Piazza	.90
----	Checklist	.05

1993 Barry Colla Postcards

Following a one-year layoff, Barry Colla continued his single-player, eight-card postcard series in 1993 with a pair of sets. Like the earlier issues, the cards are 3-1/2" x 5-1/2" and feature high-gloss fronts with borderless game-action and posed photos. Black-and-white backs have a more traditional postcard format than earlier issues. The sets were sold in white paper envelopes with color team logos on front. A version of each set was made with an embossed gold-foil team logo on front; they are valued about 5X the regular issue.

		MT
1-8	Mike Piazza	6.00
1-8	Cal Ripken Jr.	8.00

1994 Collector's Choice Promos

Upper Deck used a pair of promo cards to preview its new 1994 Collector's Choice brand. Ken Griffey, Jr. was featured on the promos, though the photos differ from those which appear on his regular-issue card, as does the card number. "For Promotional Use Only" is printed diagonally in black on both the front and back of the regular-size card. The 5" x 7-3/8" promo card uses the same front photo as the smaller promo and has advertising on the back describing the Collector's Choice issue.

		MT
Complete Set (2):		10.00
50	Ken Griffey, Jr.	6.00
---	Ken Griffey, Jr. (jumbo)	6.00

1994 Collector's Choice

This base-brand set, released in two series, was more widely available than the regular 1994 Upper Deck issue. Cards feature UD production staples such as UV coating and hologram and have large photos with a narrow pinstripe border. Backs have stats and a color photo. Series 1 has 320 cards and subsets titled Rookie Class, Draft Picks and Top Performers. Series 2 subsets are Up Close and Personal, Future Foundation and Rookie Class. Each of the set's player cards can also be found with either a gold- (1 in 36 packs) or silver-foil replica-autograph card; one silver-signature card appears in every pack.

		MT
Complete Set (670):		30.00
Complete Series 1 (320):		12.00
Complete Series 2 (350):		18.00
Common Player:		.05
Series 1 or 2 Wax Box:		25.00
1	*Rich Becker*	.05
2	Greg Blosser	.05
3	Midre Cummings	.05
4	Carlos Delgado	.25
5	*Steve Dreyer*	.05
6	*Carl Everett*	.15
7	Cliff Floyd	.10
8	Alex Gonzalez	.15
9	Shawn Green	.25
10	Butch Huskey	.10
11	Mark Hutton	.05
12	Miguel Jimenez	.05
13	Steve Karsay	.10
14	Marc Newfield	.05
15	Luis Ortiz	.05
16	Manny Ramirez	.75
17	Johnny Ruffin	.05
18	*Scott Stahoviak*	.10
19	Salomon Torres	.05
20	*Gabe White*	.10
21	*Brian Anderson*	.10
22	*Wayne Gomes*	.10
23	Jeff Granger	.10
24	*Steve Soderstrom*	.10
25	*Trot Nixon*	.25
26	*Kirk Presley*	.05
27	*Matt Brunson*	.05
28	*Brooks Kieschnick*	.20
29	*Billy Wagner*	.40
30	*Matt Drews*	.10
31	*Kurt Abbott*	.20
32	Luis Alicea	.05
33	Roberto Alomar	.40
34	Sandy Alomar Jr.	.10
35	Moises Alou	.10
36	Wilson Alvarez	.05
37	Rich Amaral	.05
38	Eric Anthony	.05
39	Luis Aquino	.05
40	Jack Armstrong	.05
41	Rene Arocha	.05
42	*Rich Aude*	.05
43	Brad Ausmus	.05
44	Steve Avery	.05
45	Bob Ayrault	.05
46	Willie Banks	.05
47	Bret Barberie	.05
48	Kim Batiste	.05
49	Rod Beck	.05
50	Jason Bere	.05
51	Sean Berry	.05
52	Dante Bichette	.15
53	Jeff Blauser	.05
54	Mike Blowers	.05
55	Tim Bogar	.05
56	Tom Bolton	.05
57	Ricky Bones	.05
58	Bobby Bonilla	.05
59	Bret Boone	.05
60	Pat Borders	.05
61	Mike Bordick	.05
62	Daryl Boston	.05
63	Ryan Bowen	.05
64	Jeff Branson	.05
65	George Brett	.35
66	Steve Buechele	.05
67	Dave Burba	.05
68	John Burkett	.05
69	Jeromy Burnitz	.10
70	Brett Butler	.05
71	Rob Butler	.05
72	Ken Caminiti	.20
73	Cris Carpenter	.05
74	Vinny Castilla	.10
75	Andujar Cedeno	.05
76	Wes Chamberlain	.05
77	Archi Cianfrocco	.05
78	Dave Clark	.05
79	Jerald Clark	.05
80	Royce Clayton	.05
81	David Cone	.10
82	Jeff Conine	.05
83	Steve Cooke	.05
84	Scott Cooper	.05
85	Joey Cora	.05
86	Tim Costa	.05
87	Chad Curtis	.05
88	Ron Darling	.05
89	Danny Darwin	.05
90	Rob Deer	.05
91	Jim Deshaies	.05
92	Delino DeShields	.05
93	Rob Dibble	.05
94	Gary DiSarcina	.05
95	Doug Drabek	.05
96	Scott Erickson	.05
97	*Rikkert Faneyte*	.05
98	Jeff Fassero	.05
99	Alex Fernandez	.10
100	Cecil Fielder	.05
101	Dave Fleming	.05
102	Darrin Fletcher	.05
103	Scott Fletcher	.05
104	Mike Gallego	.05
105	Carlos Garcia	.05
106	Jeff Gardner	.05
107	Brent Gates	.10
108	Benji Gil	.05
109	Bernard Gilkey	.05
110	Chris Gomez	.05
111	Luis Gonzalez	.05
112	Tom Gordon	.05
113	Jim Gott	.05
114	Mark Grace	.10
115	Tommy Greene	.05
116	Willie Greene	.05
117	Ken Griffey, Jr.	1.50
118	Bill Gullickson	.05
119	Ricky Gutierrez	.05
120	Juan Guzman	.05
121	Chris Gwynn	.05
122	Tony Gwynn	.50
123	Jeffrey Hammonds	.10
124	Erik Hanson	.05
125	Gene Harris	.05
126	Greg Harris	.05
127	Bryan Harvey	.05
128	Billy Hatcher	.05
129	Hilly Hathaway	.05
130	Charlie Hayes	.05
131	Rickey Henderson	.15
132	Mike Henneman	.05
133	Pat Hentgen	.10
134	Roberto Hernandez	.05
135	Orel Hershiser	.05
136	Phil Hiatt	.10
137	Glenallen Hill	.05
138	Ken Hill	.05
139	Eric Hillman	.05
140	Chris Hoiles	.05
141	Dave Hollins	.05
142	David Hulse	.05
143	Todd Hundley	.15
144	Pete Incaviglia	.05
145	Danny Jackson	.05
146	John Jaha	.05
147	Domingo Jean	.05
148	Gregg Jefferies	.05
149	Reggie Jefferson	.05
150	Lance Johnson	.05
151	Bobby Jones	.10
152	Chipper Jones	.75
153	Todd Jones	.05
154	Brian Jordan	.10
155	Wally Joyner	.05
156	Dave Justice	.15
157	Ron Karkovice	.05
158	Eric Karros	.10
159	Jeff Kent	.05
160	Jimmy Key	.10
161	Mark Kiefer	.05
162	Darryl Kile	.05
163	Jeff King	.05
164	Wayne Kirby	.05
165	Ryan Klesko	.15
166	Chuck Knoblauch	.15
167	Chad Kreuter	.05
168	John Kruk	.05
169	Mark Langston	.05
170	Mike Lansing	.05
171	Barry Larkin	.15
172	Manuel Lee	.05
173	*Phil Leftwich*	.05
174	Darren Lewis	.05
175	Derek Lilliquist	.05
176	Jose Lind	.05
177	Albie Lopez	.05
178	Javier Lopez	.20
179	Torey Lovullo	.05
180	Scott Lydy	.05
181	Mike Macfarlane	.05
182	Shane Mack	.05
183	Greg Maddux	1.00
184	Dave Magadan	.05
185	Joe Magrane	.05
186	Kirt Manwaring	.05
187	Al Martin	.05
188	*Pedro A. Martinez*	.10
189	Pedro J. Martinez	.15
190	Ramon Martinez	.10
191	Tino Martinez	.20
192	Don Mattingly	.50
193	Derrick May	.05
194	David McCarty	.05
195	Ben McDonald	.05
196	Roger McDowell	.05
197	Fred McGriff	.20
198	Mark McLemore	.05
199	Greg McMichael	.05
200	Jeff McNeely	.05
201	Brian McRae	.05
202	Pat Meares	.05
203	Roberto Mejia	.05
204	Orlando Merced	.05
205	Jose Mesa	.05
206	Blas Minor	.05
207	Angel Miranda	.05
208	Paul Molitor	.35
209	Raul Mondesi	.50
210	Jeff Montgomery	.05
211	Mickey Morandini	.05
212	Mike Morgan	.05
213	Jamie Moyer	.05
214	Bobby Munoz	.05
215	Troy Neel	.05
216	Dave Nilsson	.05
217	John O'Donoghue	.05
218	Paul O'Neill	.10
219	Jose Offerman	.05
220	Joe Oliver	.05
221	Greg Olson	.05
222	Donovan Osborne	.05
223	Jayhawk Owens	.05
224	Mike Pagliarulo	.05
225	Craig Paquette	.05

226 Roger Pavlik .05
227 Brad Pennington .05
228 Eduardo Perez .05
229 Mike Perez .05
230 Tony Phillips .05
231 Hipolito Pichardo .05
232 Phil Plantier .05
233 *Curtis Pride* .15
234 Tim Pugh .05
235 Scott Radinsky .05
236 Pat Rapp .05
237 Kevin Reimer .05
238 Armando Reynoso .05
239 Jose Rijo .05
240 Cal Ripken, Jr. 1.50
241 Kevin Roberson .05
242 Kenny Rogers .05
243 Kevin Rogers .05
244 Mel Rojas .05
245 John Roper .05
246 Kirk Rueter .05
247 Scott Ruffcorn .05
248 Ken Ryan .05
249 Nolan Ryan .75
250 Bret Saberhagen .10
251 Tim Salmon .25
252 Reggie Sanders .05
253 Curt Schilling .10
254 David Segui .05
255 Aaron Sele .10
256 Scott Servais .05
257 Gary Sheffield .25
258 Ruben Sierra .05
259 Don Slaught .05
260 Lee Smith .05
261 Cory Snyder .05
262 Paul Sorrento .05
263 Sammy Sosa .75
264 Bill Spiers .05
265 Mike Stanley .05
266 Dave Staton .05
267 Terry Steinbach .05
268 Kevin Stocker .05
269 Todd Stottlemyre .10
270 Doug Strange .05
271 Bill Swift .05
272 Kevin Tapani .05
273 Tony Tarasco .05
274 *Julian Tavarez* .05
275 Mickey Tettleton .05
276 Ryan Thompson .05
277 Chris Turner .05
278 John Valentin .05
279 Todd Van Poppel .05
280 Andy Van Slyke .05
281 Mo Vaughn .30
282 Robin Ventura .10
283 Frank Viola .05
284 Jose Vizcaino .05
285 Omar Vizquel .05
286 Larry Walker .20
287 Duane Ware .05
288 Allen Watson .05
289 Bill Wegman .05
290 Turk Wendell .05
291 Lou Whitaker .05
292 Devon White .05
293 Rondell White .15
294 Mark Whiten .05
295 Darrell Whitmore .05
296 Bob Wickman .05
297 Rick Wilkins .05
298 Bernie Williams .25
299 Matt Williams .30
300 Woody Williams .05
301 Nigel Wilson .05
302 Dave Winfield .15
303 Anthony Young .05
304 Eric Young .05
305 Todd Zeile .05
306 Jack McDowell, John Burkett, Tom Glavine (Top Performers) .10
307 Randy Johnson (Top Performers) .15
308 Randy Myers (Top Performers) .05
309 Jack McDowell (Top Performers) .05
310 Mike Piazza (Top Performers) .40
311 Barry Bonds (Top Performers) .25
312 Andres Galarraga (Top Performers) .10
313 Juan Gonzalez, Barry Bonds (Top Performers) .35
314 Albert Belle (Top Performers) .30
315 Kenny Lofton (Top Performers) .10
316 Checklist 1-64 (Barry Bonds) .10
317 Checklist 65-128 (Ken Griffey, Jr.) .30
318 Checklist 129-192 (Mike Piazza) .15
319 Checklist 193-256 (Kirby Puckett) .10
320 Checklist 257-320 (Nolan Ryan) .25
321 Checklist 321-370 (Roberto Alomar) .15
322 Checklist 371-420 (Roger Clemens) .15
323 Checklist 421-470 (Juan Gonzalez) .15
324 Checklist 471-520 (Ken Griffey, Jr.) .30
325 Checklist 521-570 (David Justice) .10
326 Checklist 571-620 (John Kruk) .05
327 Checklist 621-670 (Frank Thomas) .25
328 Angels Checklist (Tim Salmon) .10
329 Astros Checklist (Jeff Bagwell) .15
330 Athletics Checklist (Mark McGwire) .75
331 Blue Jays Checklist (Roberto Alomar) .15
332 Braves Checklist (David Justice) .10
333 Brewers Checklist (Pat Listach) .05
334 Cardinals Checklist (Ozzie Smith) .10
335 Cubs Checklist (Ryne Sandberg) .10
336 Dodgers Checklist (Mike Piazza) .25
337 Expos Checklist (Cliff Floyd) .05
338 Giants Checklist (Barry Bonds) .15
339 Indians Checklist (Albert Belle) .20
340 Mariners Checklist (Ken Griffey, Jr.) .50
341 Marlins Checklist (Gary Sheffield) .20
342 Mets Checklist (Dwight Gooden) .05
343 Orioles Checklist (Cal Ripken, Jr.) .50
344 Padres Checklist (Tony Gwynn) .20
345 Phillies Checklist (Lenny Dykstra) .05
346 Pirates Checklists (Andy Van Slyke) .05
347 Rangers Checklist (Juan Gonzalez) .20
348 Red Sox Checklist (Roger Clemens) .15
349 Reds Checklist (Barry Larkin) .10
350 Rockies Checklist (Andres Galarraga) .10
351 Royals Checklist (Kevin Appier) .05
352 Tigers Checklist (Cecil Fielder) .10
353 Twins Checklist (Kirby Puckett) .20
354 White Sox Checklist (Frank Thomas) .40
355 Yankees Checklist (Don Mattingly) .30
356 Bo Jackson .10
357 Randy Johnson .30
358 Darren Daulton .05
359 Charlie Hough .05
360 Andres Galarraga .10
361 Mike Felder .05
362 Chris Hammond .05
363 Shawon Dunston .05
364 Junior Felix .05
365 Ray Lankford .05
366 Darryl Strawberry .10
367 Dave Magadan .05
368 Gregg Olson .05
369 Len Dykstra .05
370 Darrin Jackson .05
371 Dave Stewart .05
372 Terry Pendleton .05
373 Arthur Rhodes .05
374 Benito Santiago .05
375 Travis Fryman .10
376 Scott Brosius .05
377 Stan Belinda .05
378 Derek Parks .05
379 Kevin Seitzer .05
380 Wade Boggs .20
381 Wally Whitehurst .05
382 Scott Leius .05
383 Danny Tartabull .05
384 Harold Reynolds .05
385 Tim Raines .05
386 Darryl Hamilton .05
387 Felix Fermin .05
388 Jim Eisenreich .05
389 Kurt Abbott .05
390 Kevin Appier .05
391 Chris Bosio .05
392 Randy Tomlin .05
393 Bob Hamelin .05
394 Kevin Gross .05
395 Wil Cordero .05
396 Joe Girardi .05
397 Orestes Destrade .05
398 Chris Haney .05
399 Xavier Hernandez .05
400 Mike Piazza .75
401 Alex Arias .05
402 Tom Candiotti .05
403 Kirk Gibson .05
404 Chuck Carr .05
405 Brady Anderson .10
406 Greg Gagne .05
407 Bruce Ruffin .05
408 Scott Hemond .05
409 Keith Miller .05
410 John Wetteland .05
411 Eric Anthony .05
412 Andre Dawson .05
413 Doug Henry .05
414 John Franco .05
415 Julio Franco .05
416 Dave Hansen .05
417 Mike Harkey .05
418 Jack Armstrong .05
419 Joe Orsulak .05
420 John Smoltz .15
421 Scott Livingstone .05
422 Darren Holmes .05
423 Ed Sprague .05
424 Jay Buhner .10
425 Kirby Puckett .60
426 Phil Clark .05
427 Anthony Young .05
428 Reggie Jefferson .05
429 Mariano Duncan .05
430 Tom Glavine .15
431 Dave Henderson .05
432 Melido Perez .05
433 Paul Wagner .05
434 Tim Worrell .05
435 Ozzie Guillen .05
436 Mike Butcher .05
437 Jim Deshaies .05
438 Kevin Young .05
439 Tom Browning .05
440 Mike Greenwell .05
441 Mike Stanton .05
442 John Doherty .05
443 John Dopson .05
444 Carlos Baerga .05
445 Jack McDowell .05
446 Kent Mercker .05
447 Ricky Jordan .05
448 Jerry Browne .05
449 Fernando Vina .05
450 Jim Abbott .05
451 Teddy Higuera .05
452 Tim Naehring .05
453 Jim Leyritz .05
454 Frank Castillo .05
455 Joe Carter .10
456 Craig Biggio .10
457 Geronimo Pena .05
458 Alejandro Pena .05
459 Mike Moore .05
460 Randy Myers .05
461 Greg Myers .05
462 Greg Hibbard .05
463 Jose Guzman .05
464 Tom Pagnozzi .05
465 Marquis Grissom .05
466 Tim Wallach .05
467 Joe Grahe .05
468 Bob Tewksbury .05
469 B.J. Surhoff .05
470 Kevin Mitchell .05
471 Bobby Witt .05
472 Milt Thompson .05
473 John Smiley .05
474 Alan Trammell .05
475 Mike Mussina .20
476 Rick Aguilera .05
477 Jose Valentin .05
478 Harold Baines .05
479 Bip Roberts .05
480 Edgar Martinez .05
481 Rheal Cormier .05
482 Hal Morris .05
483 Pat Kelly .05
484 Roberto Kelly .05
485 Chris Sabo .05
486 Kent Hrbek .05
487 Scott Kamieniecki .05
488 Walt Weiss .05
489 Karl Rhodes .05
490 Derek Bell .05
491 Chili Davis .05
492 Brian Harper .05
493 Felix Jose .05
494 Trevor Hoffman .05
495 Dennis Eckersley .05
496 Pedro Astacio .05
497 Jay Bell .05
498 Randy Velarde .05
499 David Wells .10
500 Frank Thomas 1.00
501 Mark Lemke .05
502 Mike Devereaux .05
503 Chuck McElroy .05
504 Luis Polonia .05
505 Damion Easley .05
506 Greg A. Harris .05
507 Chris James .05
508 Terry Mulholland .05
509 Pete Smith .05
510 Rickey Henderson .15
511 Sid Fernandez .05
512 Al Leiter .10
513 Doug Jones .05
514 Steve Farr .05
515 Chuck Finley .05
516 Bobby Thigpen .05
517 Jim Edmonds .15
518 Graeme Lloyd .05
519 Dwight Gooden .10
520 Pat Listach .05
521 Kevin Bass .05
522 Willie Banks .05
523 Steve Finley .05
524 Delino DeShields .05
525 Mark McGwire 2.00
526 Greg Swindell .05
527 Chris Nabholz .05
528 Scott Sanders .05
529 David Segui .05
530 Howard Johnson .05
531 Jaime Navarro .05
532 Jose Vizcaino .05
533 Mark Lewis .05
534 Pete Harnisch .05
535 Robby Thompson .05
536 Marcus Moore .05
537 Kevin Brown .10
538 Mark Clark .05
539 Sterling Hitchcock .05
540 Will Clark .20
541 Denis Boucher .05
542 Jack Morris .05
543 Pedro Munoz .05
544 Bret Boone .05
545 Ozzie Smith .25
546 Dennis Martinez .05
547 Dan Wilson .05
548 Rick Sutcliffe .05
549 Kevin McReynolds .05
550 Roger Clemens .35
551 Todd Benzinger .05
552 Bill Haselman .05
553 Bobby Munoz .05
554 Ellis Burks .05
555 Ryne Sandberg .25
556 Lee Smith .05
557 Danny Bautista .05
558 Rey Sanchez .05
559 Norm Charlton .05
560 Jose Canseco .25
561 Tim Belcher .05
562 Denny Neagle .05
563 Eric Davis .05
564 Jody Reed .05
565 Kenny Lofton .15
566 Gary Gaetti .05
567 Todd Worrell .05
568 Mark Portugal .05
569 Dick Schofield .05
570 Andy Benes .10
571 Zane Smith .05
572 Bobby Ayala .05
573 Chip Hale .05
574 Bob Welch .05
575 Deion Sanders .20
576 Dave Nied .05
577 Pat Mahomes .05
578 Charles Nagy .05
579 Otis Nixon .05
580 Dean Palmer .05
581 Roberto Petagine .05
582 Dwight Smith .05
583 Jeff Russell .05
584 Mark Dewey .05
585 Greg Vaughn .10
586 Brian Hunter .05
587 Willie McGee .05
588 Pedro J. Martinez .20
589 Roger Salkeld .05
590 Jeff Bagwell .50
591 Spike Owen .05
592 Jeff Reardon .05
593 Erik Pappas .05
594 Brian Williams .05
595 Eddie Murray .25
596 Henry Rodriguez .05
597 Erik Hanson .05
598 Stan Javier .05
599 Mitch Williams .05
600 John Olerud .10
601 Vince Coleman .05
602 Damon Berryhill .05
603 Tom Brunansky .05
604 Robb Nen .05
605 Rafael Palmeiro .15
606 Cal Eldred .05
607 Jeff Brantley .05
608 Alan Mills .05
609 Jeff Nelson .05
610 Barry Bonds .40
611 *Carlos Pulido* .10
612 *Tim Hyers* .15
613 Steve Howe .05
614 *Brian Turang* .05
615 Leo Gomez .05
616 Jesse Orosco .05
617 Dan Pasqua .05
618 Marvin Freeman .05
619 Tony Fernandez .05
620 Albert Belle .50
621 Eddie Taubensee .05
622 Mike Jackson .05
623 Jose Bautista .05
624 Jim Thome .20
625 Ivan Rodriguez .30
626 Ben Rivera .05
627 Dave Valle .05
628 Tom Henke .05
629 Omar Vizquel .05
630 Juan Gonzalez .40
631 Roberto Alomar (Up Close) .15
632 Barry Bonds (Up Close) .20
633 Juan Gonzalez (Up Close) .25
634 Ken Griffey, Jr. (Up Close) .75
635 Michael Jordan (Up Close) 3.00
636 Dave Justice (Up Close) .10
637 Mike Piazza (Up Close) .40
638 Kirby Puckett (Up Close) .25
639 Tim Salmon (Up Close) .15
640 Frank Thomas (Up Close) .50
641 *Alan Benes* (Future Foundation) .60
642 Johnny Damon (Future Foundation) .10
643 *Brad Fullmer* (Future Foundation) 1.00
644 Derek Jeter (Future Foundation) 2.00
645 *Derrek Lee* (Future Foundation) .50
646 Alex Ochoa (Future Foundation) .10
647 *Alex Rodriguez* (Future Foundation) 5.00
648 *Jose Silva* (Future Foundation) .10
649 *Terrell Wade* (Future Foundation) .05
650 Preston Wilson (Future Foundation) .25
651 Shane Andrews (Rookie Class) .05
652 James Baldwin (Rookie Class) .05
653 *Ricky Bottalico* (Rookie Class) .10
654 Tavo Alvarez (Rookie Class) .05
655 Donnie Elliott (Rookie Class) .10
656 Joey Eischen (Rookie Class) .05
657 Jason Giambi (Rookie Class) .35
658 Todd Hollandsworth (Rookie Class) .20
659 Brian Hunter (Rookie Class) .10
660 Charles Johnson (Rookie Class) .20
661 *Michael Jordan* (Rookie Class) 7.50
662 Jeff Juden (Rookie Class) .05
663 Mike Kelly (Rookie Class) .05
664 James Mouton (Rookie Class) .05
665 Ray Holbert (Rookie Class) .10
666 Pokey Reese (Rookie Class) .05
667 *Ruben Santana* (Rookie Class) .10
668 Paul Spoljaric (Rookie Class) .05
669 Luis Lopez (Rookie Class) .05
670 Matt Walbeck (Rookie Class) .10

1994 Collector's Choice Silver Signature

Each of the cards in the debut edition of Upper Deck's Collector's Choice brand was also issued in a parallel edition bearing a facsimile silver-foil signature on front. The silver-signature cards were inserted at a one-per-pack rate in the set's foil packs, and proportionately in other types of packaging.

	MT
Complete Set (670):	200.00
Complete Series 1 (1-320):	120.00
Complete Series 2 (321-670):	80.00
Common Player:	.25

Stars: 1.5-3X
(See 1994 Collector's Choice for checklist and base card values.)

1994 Collector's Choice Gold Signature

A super-scarce parallel set of the premiere-issue Collector's Choice in 1994 was the gold-signature version found on average of only once per 36 foil packs. In addition to a gold-foil facsimile signature on the card front, this edition features gold-colored borders on the regular player cards.

	MT
Complete Set (670):	2000.
Complete Series 1 (1-320):	1200.
Complete Series 2 (321-670):	1100.
Common Player:	1.50

Stars: 20-40X
(See 1994 Collector's Choice for checklist and base card values.)

1994 Collector's Choice Home Run All-Stars

Among the most attractive of the 1994 chase cards, the perceived high production (over a million sets according to stated odds of winning) of this set keeps it affordable. Sets were available by a mail-in offer to persons who found a winner card in Series 1 foil packs (about one per box). Cards feature a combination of brick-bordered hologram and color player photo on front, along with a gold-foil facsimile autograph. On back the brick border is repeated, as is the photo on the hologram, though this time in full color. There is a stadium photo in the background, over which is printed a description of the player's home run prowess. A numbering error resulted in two cards numbered HA4 and no card with the HA5 number.

		MT
Complete Set (8):		4.00
Common Player:		.25
1HA	Juan Gonzalez	1.00
2HA	Ken Griffey, Jr.	3.00
3HA	Barry Bonds	.75
4HAa	Bobby Bonilla	.25
4HAb	Cecil Fielder	.25
6HA	Albert Belle	.60
7HA	David Justice	.40
8HA	Mike Piazza	1.50

1995 Collector's Choice

Issued in a single series, Upper Deck's base-brand baseball series features a number of subsets within the main body of the issue, as well as several insert sets. Basic cards feature large photos on front and back, with the back having full major league stats. The set opens with a 27-card Rookie Class subset featuring front photos on which the background has been rendered in hot pink tones. Backs have a lime-green box with a scouting report on the player and a box featuring 1994 minor and major league stats. The next 18 cards are Future Foundation cards which have the prospects pictured with a posterized background on front, with backs similar to the Rookie Class cards. Career finale cards of five retired superstars follow, then a run of Best of the '90s cards honoring record-setting achievements, followed by cards depicting major award winners of the previous season. Each of the last three named subsets features borderless color photos on front, with backs similar to the regular cards. Immediately preceding the regular cards, which are arranged in team-set order, is a five-card "What's the Call?" subset featuring cartoon representations of the players. A set of five checklist cards marking career highlights ends the set.

		MT
Complete Set (530):		20.00
Common Player:		.05
Wax Box:		30.00
1	Charles Johnson (Rookie Class)	.15
2	Scott Ruffcorn (Rookie Class)	.05
3	Ray Durham (Rookie Class)	.15
4	Armando Benitez (Rookie Class)	.05
5	Alex Rodriguez (Rookie Class)	2.00
6	Julian Tavarez (Rookie Class)	.08
7	Chad Ogea (Rookie Class)	.05
8	Quilvio Veras (Rookie Class)	.10
9	Phil Nevin (Rookie Class)	.05
10	Michael Tucker (Rookie Class)	.10
11	Mark Thompson (Rookie Class)	.05
12	Rod Henderson (Rookie Class)	.05
13	Andrew Lorraine (Rookie Class)	.05
14	Joe Randa (Rookie Class)	.05
15	Derek Jeter (Rookie Class)	1.00
16	Tony Clark (Rookie Class)	.60
17	Juan Castillo (Rookie Class)	.05
18	Mark Acre (Rookie Class)	.05
19	Orlando Miller (Rookie Class)	.05
20	Paul Wilson (Rookie Class)	.15
21	John Mabry (Rookie Class)	.05
22	Garey Ingram (Rookie Class)	.05
23	*Garret Anderson* (Rookie Class)	.15
24	Dave Stevens (Rookie Class)	.05
25	Dustin Hermanson (Rookie Class)	.05
26	Paul Shuey (Rookie Class)	.05
27	J.R. Phillips (Rookie Class)	.05
28	Ruben Rivera (Future Foundation)	.40
29	Nomar Garciaparra (Future Foundation)	1.50
30	John Wasdin (Future Foundation)	.05
31	Jim Pittsley (Future Foundation)	.05
32	*Scott Elarton* (Future Foundation)	.20
33	*Raul Casanova* (Future Foundation)	.40
34	Todd Greene (Future Foundation)	.05
35	Bill Pulsipher (Future Foundation)	.15
36	Trey Beamon (Future Foundation)	.10
37	Curtis Goodwin (Future Foundation)	.05
38	Doug Million (Future Foundation)	.05
39	*Karim Garcia* (Future Foundation)	1.00
40	Ben Grieve (Future Foundation)	1.50
41	Mark Farris (Future Foundation)	.05
42	*Juan Acevedo* (Future Foundation)	.15
43	C.J. Nitkowski (Future Foundation)	.05
44	*Travis Miller* (Future Foundation)	.15
45	Reid Ryan (Future Foundation)	.10
46	Nolan Ryan	1.00
47	Robin Yount	.25
48	Ryne Sandberg	.40
49	George Brett	.60
50	Mike Schmidt	.40
51	Cecil Fielder (Best of the 90's)	.10
52	Nolan Ryan (Best of the 90's)	.60
53	Rickey Henderson (Best of the 90's)	.05
54	George Brett, Robin Yount, Dave Winfield (Best of the 90's)	.25
55	Sid Bream (Best of the 90's)	.05
56	Carlos Baerga (Best of the 90's)	.05
57	Lee Smith (Best of the 90's)	.05
58	Mark Whiten (Best of the 90's)	.05
59	Joe Carter (Best of the 90's)	.10
60	Barry Bonds (Best of the 90's)	.25
61	Tony Gwynn (Best of the 90's)	.35
62	Ken Griffey Jr. (Best of the 90's)	1.00
63	Greg Maddux (Best of the 90's)	.75
64	Frank Thomas (Best of the 90's)	.50
65	Dennis Martinez, Kenny Rogers (Best of the 90's)	.05
66	David Cone (Cy Young)	.10
67	Greg Maddux (Cy Young)	1.00
68	Jimmy Key (Most Victories)	.05
69	Fred McGriff (All-Star MVP)	.25
70	Ken Griffey Jr. (HR Champ)	2.00
71	Matt Williams (HR Champ)	.25
72	Paul O'Neill (Batting Title)	.05
73	Tony Gwynn (Batting Title)	.50
74	Randy Johnson (Ks Leader)	.35
75	Frank Thomas (MVP)	1.00
76	Jeff Bagwell (MVP)	.60
77	Kirby Puckett (RBI leader)	.60
78	Bob Hamelin (ROY)	.05
79	Raul Mondesi (ROY)	.25
80	Mike Piazza (All-Star)	.75
81	Kenny Lofton (SB Leader)	.40
82	Barry Bonds (Gold Glove)	.40
83	Albert Belle (All-Star)	.50
84	Juan Gonzalez (HR Champ)	.50
85	Cal Ripken Jr. (2,000 Straight Games)	2.00
86	Barry Bonds (What's the Call?)	.20
87	Mike Piazza (What's the Call?)	.40
88	Ken Griffey Jr. (What's the Call?)	1.00
89	Frank Thomas (What's the Call?)	.50
90	Juan Gonzalez (What's the Call?)	.30
91	Jorge Fabregas	.05
92	J.T. Snow	.10
93	Spike Owen	.05
94	Eduardo Perez	.05
95	Bo Jackson	.10
96	Damion Easley	.05
97	Gary DiSarcina	.05
98	Jim Edmonds	.15
99	Chad Curtis	.05
100	Tim Salmon	.15
101	Chili Davis	.05
102	Chuck Finley	.05
103	Mark Langston	.05
104	Brian Anderson	.05
105	Lee Smith	.05
106	Phil Leftwich	.05
107	Chris Donnels	.05
108	John Hudek	.05
109	Craig Biggio	.10
110	Luis Gonzalez	.05
111	Brian L. Hunter	.10
112	James Mouton	.05
113	Scott Servais	.05
114	Tony Eusebio	.05
115	Derek Bell	.05
116	Doug Drabek	.05
117	Shane Reynolds	.05
118	Darryl Kile	.05
119	Greg Swindell	.05
120	Phil Plantier	.05
121	Todd Jones	.05
122	Steve Ontiveros	.05
123	Bobby Witt	.05
124	Brent Gates	.05
125	Rickey Henderson	.05
126	Scott Brosius	.05
127	Mike Bordick	.05
128	Fausto Cruz	.05
129	Stan Javier	.05
130	Mark McGwire	2.00
131	Geronimo Berroa	.05
132	Terry Steinbach	.05
133	Steve Karsay	.05
134	Dennis Eckersley	.05
135	Ruben Sierra	.05
136	Ron Darling	.05
137	Todd Van Poppel	.05
138	Alex Gonzalez	.10
139	John Olerud	.10
140	Roberto Alomar	.50
141	Darren Hall	.05
142	Ed Sprague	.05
143	Devon White	.05
144	Shawn Green	.10
145	Paul Molitor	.25
146	Pat Borders	.05
147	Carlos Delgado	.25
148	Juan Guzman	.05
149	Pat Hentgen	.05
150	Joe Carter	.10
151	Dave Stewart	.05
152	Todd Stottlemyre	.05
153	Dick Schofield	.05
154	Chipper Jones	1.00
155	Ryan Klesko	.20
156	Dave Justice	.25
157	Mike Kelly	.05
158	Roberto Kelly	.05
159	Tony Tarasco	.05
160	Javier Lopez	.10
161	Steve Avery	.05
162	Greg McMichael	.05
163	Kent Mercker	.05
164	Mark Lemke	.05
165	Tom Glavine	.15
166	Jose Oliva	.05
167	John Smoltz	.15
168	Jeff Blauser	.05
169	Troy O'Leary	.05
170	Greg Vaughn	.05
171	Jody Reed	.05
172	Kevin Seitzer	.05
173	Jeff Cirillo	.05
174	B.J. Surhoff	.05
175	Cal Eldred	.05
176	Jose Valentin	.05
177	Turner Ward	.05
178	Darryl Hamilton	.05
179	Pat Listach	.05
180	Matt Mieske	.05
181	Brian Harper	.05
182	Dave Nilsson	.05
183	Mike Fetters	.05
184	John Jaha	.05
185	Ricky Bones	.05
186	Geronimo Pena	.05
187	Bob Tewksbury	.05
188	Todd Zeile	.05
189	Danny Jackson	.05
190	Ray Lankford	.05
191	Bernard Gilkey	.05
192	Brian Jordan	.05
193	Tom Pagnozzi	.05
194	Rick Sutcliffe	.05
195	Mark Whiten	.05
196	Tom Henke	.05
197	Rene Arocha	.05
198	Allen Watson	.05
199	Mike Perez	.05
200	Ozzie Smith	.25
201	Anthony Young	.05
202	Rey Sanchez	.05
203	Steve Buechele	.05
204	Shawon Dunston	.05
205	Mark Grace	.10
206	Glenallen Hill	.05
207	Eddie Zambrano	.05
208	Rick Wilkins	.05
209	Derrick May	.05
210	Sammy Sosa	.75
211	Kevin Roberson	.05
212	Steve Trachsel	.05
213	Willie Banks	.05
214	Kevin Foster	.05
215	Randy Myers	.05
216	Mike Morgan	.05
217	Rafael Bournigal	.05
218	Delino DeShields	.05
219	Tim Wallach	.05
220	Eric Karros	.10
221	Jose Offerman	.05
222	Tom Candiotti	.05
223	Ismael Valdes	.10
224	Henry Rodriguez	.05
225	Billy Ashley	.10
226	Darren Dreifort	.05
227	Ramon Martinez	.10
228	Pedro Astacio	.05
229	Orel Hershiser	.05
230	Brett Butler	.05
231	Todd Hollandsworth	.10
232	Chan Ho Park	.10
233	Mike Lansing	.05
234	Sean Berry	.05
235	Rondell White	.15
236	Ken Hill	.05
237	Marquis Grissom	.05
238	Larry Walker	.20
239	John Wetteland	.05
240	Cliff Floyd	.10
241	Joey Eischen	.05
242	Lou Frazier	.05
243	Darrin Fletcher	.05
244	Pedro J. Martinez	.15
245	Wil Cordero	.05
246	Jeff Fassero	.05
247	Butch Henry	.05
248	Mel Rojas	.05
249	Kirk Rueter	.05
250	Moises Alou	.10
251	Rod Beck	.05
252	John Patterson	.05
253	Robby Thompson	.05
254	Royce Clayton	.05
255	William Van Landingham	.08
256	Darren Lewis	.05
257	Kirt Manwaring	.05
258	Mark Portugal	.05
259	Bill Swift	.05
260	Rikkert Faneyte	.05
261	Mike Jackson	.05
262	Todd Benzinger	.05
263	Bud Black	.05
264	Salomon Torres	.05
265	Eddie Murray	.25
266	Mark Clark	.05
267	Paul Sorrento	.05
268	Jim Thome	.30
269	Omar Vizquel	.05
270	Carlos Baerga	.05
271	Jeff Russell	.05
272	Herbert Perry	.05
273	Sandy Alomar Jr.	.05
274	Dennis Martinez	.05
275	Manny Ramirez	.50
276	Wayne Kirby	.05
277	Charles Nagy	.05
278	Albie Lopez	.05
279	Jeromy Burnitz	.05
280	Dave Winfield	.08
281	Tim Davis	.05
282	Marc Newfield	.08
283	Tino Martinez	.10
284	Mike Blowers	.05
285	Goose Gossage	.05
286	Luis Sojo	.05
287	Edgar Martinez	.05
288	Rich Amaral	.05
289	Felix Fermin	.05
290	Jay Buhner	.10
291	Dan Wilson	.05
292	Bobby Ayala	.05
293	Dave Fleming	.05
294	Greg Pirkl	.05
295	Reggie Jefferson	.05
296	Greg Hibbard	.05
297	Yorkis Perez	.05
298	Kurt Miller	.05
299	Chuck Carr	.05
300	Gary Sheffield	.20
301	Jerry Browne	.05
302	Dave Magadan	.05
303	Kurt Abbott	.05
304	Pat Rapp	.05
305	Jeff Conine	.05

306	Benito Santiago	.05
307	Dave Weathers	.05
308	Robb Nen	.05
309	Chris Hammond	.05
310	Bryan Harvey	.05
311	Charlie Hough	.05
312	Greg Colbrunn	.05
313	David Segui	.05
314	Rico Brogna	.05
315	Jeff Kent	.05
316	Jose Vizcaino	.05
317	Jim Lindeman	.05
318	Carl Everett	.05
319	Ryan Thompson	.05
320	Bobby Bonilla	.10
321	Joe Orsulak	.05
322	Pete Harnisch	.05
323	Doug Linton	.05
324	Todd Hundley	.15
325	Bret Saberhagen	.05
326	Kelly Stinnett	.05
327	Jason Jacome	.08
328	Bobby Jones	.05
329	John Franco	.05
330	Rafael Palmeiro	.10
331	Chris Hoiles	.05
332	Leo Gomez	.05
333	Chris Sabo	.05
334	Brady Anderson	.10
335	Jeffrey Hammonds	.10
336	Dwight Smith	.05
337	Jack Voigt	.05
338	Harold Baines	.05
339	Ben McDonald	.05
340	Mike Mussina	.30
341	Bret Barberie	.05
342	Jamie Moyer	.05
343	Mike Oquist	.05
344	Sid Fernandez	.05
345	Eddie Williams	.05
346	Joey Hamilton	.05
347	Brian Williams	.05
348	Luis Lopez	.05
349	Steve Finley	.05
350	Andy Benes	.10
351	Andujar Cedeno	.05
352	Bip Roberts	.05
353	Ray McDavid	.05
354	Ken Caminiti	.15
355	Trevor Hoffman	.05
356	Mel Nieves	.05
357	Brad Ausmus	.05
358	Andy Ashby	.05
359	Scott Sanders	.05
360	Gregg Jefferies	.05
361	Mariano Duncan	.05
362	Dave Hollins	.05
363	Kevin Stocker	.05
364	Fernando Valenzuela	.05
365	Lenny Dykstra	.05
366	Jim Eisenreich	.05
367	Ricky Bottalico	.05
368	Doug Jones	.05
369	Ricky Jordan	.05
370	Darren Daulton	.05
371	Mike Lieberthal	.05
372	Bobby Munoz	.05
373	John Kruk	.05
374	Curt Schilling	.05
375	Orlando Merced	.05
376	Carlos Garcia	.05
377	Lance Parrish	.05
378	Steve Cooke	.05
379	Jeff King	.05
380	Jay Bell	.05
381	Al Martin	.05
382	Paul Wagner	.05
383	Rick White	.05
384	Midre Cummings	.05
385	Jon Lieber	.05
386	Dave Clark	.05
387	Don Slaught	.05
388	Denny Neagle	.05
389	Zane Smith	.05
390	Andy Van Slyke	.05
391	Ivan Rodriguez	.40
392	David Hulse	.05
393	John Burkett	.05
394	Kevin Brown	.05
395	Dean Palmer	.05
396	Otis Nixon	.05
397	Rick Helling	.05
398	Kenny Rogers	.05
399	Darren Oliver	.05
400	Will Clark	.25
401	Jeff Frye	.05
402	Kevin Gross	.05
403	John Dettmer	.05
404	Manny Lee	.05
405	Rusty Greer	.05
406	Aaron Sele	.10
407	Carlos Rodriguez	.05
408	Scott Cooper	.05
409	John Valentin	.05
410	Roger Clemens	.50
411	Mike Greenwell	.05
412	Tim Vanegmond	.05
413	Tom Brunansky	.05
414	Steve Farr	.05
415	Jose Canseco	.30
416	Joe Hesketh	.05
417	Ken Ryan	.05
418	Tim Naehring	.05
419	Frank Viola	.05
420	Andre Dawson	.08
421	Mo Vaughn	.40
422	Jeff Brantley	.05
423	Pete Schourek	.05
424	Hal Morris	.05
425	Deion Sanders	.30
426	Brian L. Hunter	.15
427	Bret Boone	.05
428	Willie Greene	.05
429	Ron Gant	.10
430	Barry Larkin	.10
431	Reggie Sanders	.05
432	Eddie Taubensee	.05
433	Jack Morris	.05
434	Jose Rijo	.05
435	Johnny Ruffin	.05
436	John Smiley	.05
437	John Roper	.05
438	David Nied	.05
439	Roberto Mejia	.05
440	Andres Galarraga	.10
441	Mike Kingery	.05
442	Curt Leskanic	.05
443	Walt Weiss	.05
444	Marvin Freeman	.05
445	Charlie Hayes	.05
446	Eric Young	.05
447	Ellis Burks	.05
448	Joe Girardi	.05
449	Lance Painter	.05
450	Dante Bichette	.10
451	Bruce Ruffin	.05
452	Jeff Granger	.05
453	Wally Joyner	.05
454	Jose Lind	.05
455	Jeff Montgomery	.05
456	Gary Gaetti	.05
457	Greg Gagne	.05
458	Vince Coleman	.05
459	Mike Macfarlane	.05
460	Brian McRae	.05
461	Tom Gordon	.05
462	Kevin Appier	.05
463	Billy Brewer	.05
464	Mark Gubicza	.05
465	Travis Fryman	.10
466	Danny Bautista	.05
467	Sean Bergman	.05
468	Mike Henneman	.05
469	Mike Moore	.05
470	Cecil Fielder	.10
471	Alan Trammell	.05
472	Kirk Gibson	.05
473	Tony Phillips	.05
474	Mickey Tettleton	.05
475	Lou Whitaker	.05
476	Chris Gomez	.05
477	John Doherty	.05
478	Greg Gohr	.05
479	Bill Gullickson	.05
480	Rick Aguilera	.05
481	Matt Walbeck	.05
482	Kevin Tapani	.05
483	Scott Erickson	.05
484	Steve Dunn	.05
485	David McCarty	.05
486	Scott Leius	.05
487	Pat Meares	.05
488	Jeff Reboulet	.05
489	Pedro Munoz	.05
490	Chuck Knoblauch	.10
491	Rich Becker	.05
492	Alex Cole	.05
493	Pat Mahomes	.05
494	Ozzie Guillen	.05
495	Tim Raines	.05
496	Kirk McCaskill	.05
497	Olmedo Saenz	.05
498	Scott Sanderson	.05
499	Lance Johnson	.05
500	Michael Jordan	2.50
501	Warren Newson	.05
502	Ron Karkovice	.05
503	Wilson Alvarez	.05
504	Jason Bere	.05
505	Robin Ventura	.05
506	Alex Fernandez	.05
507	Roberto Hernandez	.05
508	Norberto Martin	.05
509	Bob Wickman	.05
510	Don Mattingly	.75
511	Melido Perez	.05
512	Pat Kelly	.05
513	Randy Velarde	.05
514	Tony Fernandez	.05
515	Jack McDowell	.10
516	Luis Polonia	.05
517	Bernie Williams	.35
518	Danny Tartabull	.05
519	Mike Stanley	.05
520	Wade Boggs	.25
521	Jim Leyritz	.05
522	Steve Howe	.05
523	Scott Kamieniecki	.05
524	Russ Davis	.05
525	Jim Abbott	.05
526	Checklist 1-106 (Eddie Murray)	.10
527	Checklist 107-212 (Alex Rodriguez)	.40
528	Checklist 213-318 (Jeff Bagwell)	.15
529	Checklist 319-424 (Joe Carter)	.05
530	Checklist 425-530 (Fred McGriff)	.10
---	National Packtime offer card	.05

1995 Collector's Choice Silver Signature

A silver-foil facsimile autograph added to the card front is the only difference between these chase cards and regular-issue Collector's Choice cards. The silver-signature inserts are found one per pack in regular foil packs, and two per pack in retail jumbo packs.

	MT
Complete Set (530):	50.00
Common Player:	.10
Veteran Stars: 1.5-3X	
Young Stars/RCs: 1-2X	
(See 1995 Collector's Choice for checklist and base card values.)	

1995 Collector's Choice Gold Signature

The top-of-the-line chase card in 1995 Collector's Choice is the Gold Signature parallel set. Each of the 530 cards in the set was created in a special gold version that was found on average only one per box of foil packs. Other than the addition of a gold-foil facsimile autograph on front, the cards are identical to regular-issue Collector's Choice.

	MT
Complete Set (530):	800.00
Common Player:	2.00
Veteran Stars: 8-15X	
Young Stars/RCs: 4-8X	
(See 1995 Collector's Choice for checklist and base card values.)	

1995 Collector's Choice "You Crash the Game"

These insert cards gave collectors a reason to follow box scores around the major leagues between June 18-Oct. 1. Each of 20 noted home run hitters can be found with three different dates foil-stamped on the card front. If the player hit a home run on that day, the card could be redeemed for a set of 20 special prize cards. Stated odds of finding a You Crash the Game card were one in five packs. Most of the inserts are silver-foil enhanced, with about one in eight being found with gold foil. Winning cards are much scarcer than the others since they had to be mailed in for redemption.

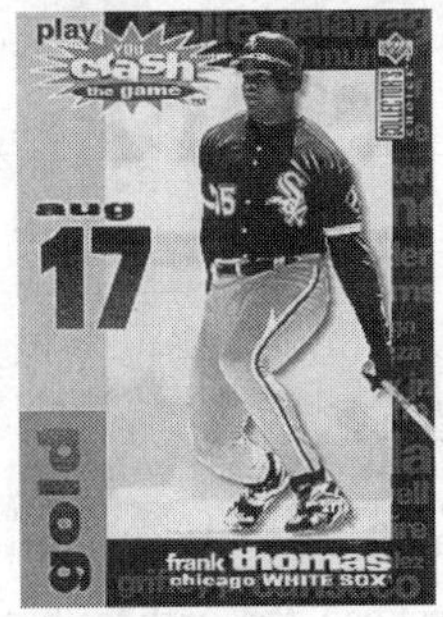

	MT
Complete Set, Silver (20):	7.00
Common Player, Silver:	.25
Complete Set, Gold (20):	18.00
Common Player, Gold:	.50
Silver Set	7.00
CG1 Jeff Bagwell (July 30)	.25
CG1 Jeff Bagwell (Aug. 13)	.25
CG1 Jeff Bagwell (Sept. 28)	.25
CG2 Albert Belle (June 18)	.40
CG2 Albert Belle (Aug. 26)	.40
CG2 Albert Belle (Sept. 20)	.40
CG3 Barry Bonds (June 28)	.50
CG3 Barry Bonds (July 9)	.50
CG3 Barry Bonds (Sept. 6)	.50
CG4 Jose Canseco (June 30) (winner)	2.00
CG4 Jose Canseco (July 30) (winner)	2.00
CG4 Jose Canseco (Sept. 3)	.50
CG5 Joe Carter (July 14)	.25
CG5 Joe Carter (Aug. 9)	.25
CG5 Joe Carter (Sept. 23)	.25
CG6 Cecil Fielder (July 4)	.25
CG6 Cecil Fielder (Aug. 2)	.25
CG6 Cecil Fielder (Oct. 1)	.25
CG7 Juan Gonzalez (June 29)	.60
CG7 Juan Gonzalez (Aug. 13)	.60
CG7 Juan Gonzalez (Sept. 3) (winner)	3.00
CG8 Ken Griffey Jr. (July 2)	1.00
CG8 Ken Griffey Jr. (Aug. 24) (winner)	5.00
CG8 Ken Griffey Jr. (Sept. 15)	1.00
CG9 Bob Hamelin (July 23)	.25
CG9 Bob Hamelin (Aug. 1)	.25
CG9 Bob Hamelin (Sept. 29)	.25
CG10David Justice (June 24)	.25
CG10David Justice (July 25)	.25
CG10David Justice (Sept. 17)	.25
CG11Ryan Klesko (July 13)	.25
CG11Ryan Klesko (Aug. 20)	.25
CG11Ryan Klesko (Sept. 10)	.25
CG12Fred McGriff (Aug. 25)	.25
CG12Fred McGriff (Sept. 8)	.25
CG12Fred McGriff (Sept. 24)	.25
CG13Mark McGwire (July 23)	1.00
CG13Mark McGwire (Aug. 3) (winner)	3.50
CG13Mark McGwire (Sept. 27)	1.00
CG14Raul Mondesi (July 27) (winner)	2.00
CG14Raul Mondesi (Aug. 13)	.40
CG14Raul Mondesi (Sept. 15) (winner)	2.00
CG15Mike Piazza (July 23) (winner)	3.00
CG15Mike Piazza (Aug. 27) (winner)	3.00
CG15Mike Piazza (Sept. 19)	.65
CG16Manny Ramirez (June 21)	.25
CG16Manny Ramirez (Aug. 13)	.25
CG16Manny Ramirez (Sept. 26)	.25
CG17Alex Rodriguez (Sept. 10)	.50
CG17Alex Rodriguez (Sept. 18)	.50
CG17Alex Rodriguez (Sept. 24)	.50
CG18Gary Sheffield (July 5)	.25
CG18Gary Sheffield (Aug. 13)	.25
CG18Gary Sheffield (Sept. 4) (winner)	2.00
CG19Frank Thomas (July 26)	.75
CG19Frank Thomas (Aug. 17)	.75
CG19Frank Thomas (Sept. 23)	.75
CG20Matt Williams (July 29)	.25
CG20Matt Williams (Aug. 12)	.25
CG20Matt Williams (Sept. 19)	.25
Gold Set	18.00
CG1 Jeff Bagwell (July 30)	1.00
CG1 Jeff Bagwell (Aug. 13)	1.00
CG1 Jeff Bagwell (Sept. 28)	1.00
CG2 Albert Belle (June 18)	1.25
CG2 Albert Belle (Aug. 26)	1.25
CG2 Albert Belle (Sept. 20)	1.25
CG3 Barry Bonds (June 28)	1.50
CG3 Barry Bonds (July 9)	1.50
CG3 Barry Bonds (Sept. 6)	1.50
CG4 Jose Canseco (June 30) (winner)	3.00
CG4 Jose Canseco (July 30) (winner)	3.00
CG4 Jose Canseco (Sept. 3)	1.25
CG5 Joe Carter (July 14)	.75
CG5 Joe Carter (Aug. 9)	.75
CG5 Joe Carter (Sept. 23)	.75
CG6 Cecil Fielder (July 4)	.75
CG6 Cecil Fielder (Aug. 2)	.75
CG6 Cecil Fielder (Oct. 1)	.75
CG7 Juan Gonzalez (June 29)	1.50
CG7 Juan Gonzalez (Aug. 13)	1.50
CG7 Juan Gonzalez (Sept. 3) (winner)	4.00
CG8 Ken Griffey Jr. (July 2)	3.00
CG8 Ken Griffey Jr. (Aug. 24) (winner)	6.00
CG8 Ken Griffey Jr. (Sept. 15)	3.00
CG9 Bob Hamelin (July 23)	.50
CG9 Bob Hamelin (Aug. 1)	.50
CG9 Bob Hamelin (Sept. 29)	.50
CG10David Justice (June 24)	.75
CG10David Justice (July 25)	.75
CG10David Justice (Sept. 17)	.75
CG11Ryan Klesko (July 13)	.75
CG11Ryan Klesko (Aug. 20)	.75
CG11Ryan Klesko (Sept. 10)	.75
CG12Fred McGriff (Aug. 25)	.75
CG12Fred McGriff (Sept. 8)	.75
CG12Fred McGriff (Sept. 24)	.75
CG13Mark McGwire (July 23)	2.00
CG13Mark McGwire (Aug. 3) (winner)	6.00
CG13Mark McGwire (Sept. 27)	2.00
CG14Raul Mondesi (July 27) (winner)	2.50
CG14Raul Mondesi (Aug. 13)	.90
CG14Raul Mondesi (Sept. 15) (winner)	2.50
CG15Mike Piazza (July 23) (winner)	4.00
CG15Mike Piazza (Aug. 27) (winner)	4.00
CG15Mike Piazza (Sept. 19)	1.25
CG16Manny Ramirez (June 21)	.75
CG16Manny Ramirez (Aug. 13)	.75
CG16Manny Ramirez (Sept. 26)	.75

CG17	Alex Rodriguez (Sept. 10)	1.25
CG17	Alex Rodriguez (Sept. 18)	1.25
CG17	Alex Rodriguez (Sept. 24)	1.25
CG18	Gary Sheffield (July 5)	.75
CG18	Gary Sheffield (Aug. 13)	.75
CG18	Gary Sheffield (Sept. 4) (winner)	2.50
CG19	Frank Thomas (July 26)	1.50
CG19	Frank Thomas (Aug. 17)	1.50
CG19	Frank Thomas (Sept. 23)	1.50
CG20	Matt Williams (July 29)	1.00
CG20	Matt Williams (Aug. 12)	1.00
CG20	Matt Williams (Sept. 19)	1.00

1995 Collector's Choice "Crash" Winners

These 20-card sets were awarded to collectors who redeemed "You Crash the Game" winners cards. A silver-foil enhanced set was sent to winners with silver redemption cards, a gold version was sent to gold winners. A $3 redemption fee was required. Fronts are similar to the game cards, except for the foil printing down the left side in the place of the game date. Instead of redemption rules on the back of award cards there are career highlights at left and a panel at right with the names of the players in the set.

		MT
Complete Set, Silver (20):		12.00
Complete Set, Gold (20):		45.00
Common Player, Silver:		.50
Common Player, Gold:		2.00
	SILVER SET	
CR1	Jeff Bagwell	1.50
CR2	Albert Belle	1.50
CR3	Barry Bonds	1.50
CR4	Jose Canseco	1.50
CR5	Joe Carter	.75
CR6	Cecil Fielder	.75
CR7	Juan Gonzalez	2.00
CR8	Ken Griffey Jr.	6.00
CR9	Bob Hamelin	.50
CR10	Dave Justice	1.00
CR11	Ryan Klesko	.75
CR12	Fred McGriff	1.00
CR13	Mark McGwire	5.00
CR14	Raul Mondesi	1.00
CR15	Mike Piazza	3.00
CR16	Manny Ramirez	1.00
CR17	Alex Rodriguez	1.50
CR18	Gary Sheffield	.75
CR19	Frank Thomas	3.00
CR20	Matt Williams	1.00
	GOLD SET	
CR1	Jeff Bagwell	5.00
CR2	Albert Belle	5.00
CR3	Barry Bonds	5.00
CR4	Jose Canseco	4.00
CR5	Joe Carter	2.00
CR6	Cecil Fielder	2.00
CR7	Juan Gonzalez	7.50
CR8	Ken Griffey Jr.	15.00
CR9	Bob Hamelin	2.00
CR10	Dave Justice	3.50
CR11	Ryan Klesko	3.50
CR12	Fred McGriff	3.50
CR13	Mark McGwire	12.50
CR14	Raul Mondesi	3.50
CR15	Mike Piazza	7.50
CR16	Manny Ramirez	3.50
CR17	Alex Rodriguez	5.00
CR18	Gary Sheffield	3.00
CR19	Frank Thomas	5.00
CR20	Matt Williams	4.00

1995 Collector's Choice Trade Cards

A series of five mail-in redemption cards was included as inserts into UD Collector's Choice, at the rate of approximately one per 11 packs. The cards could be sent in with $2 to receive 11 Collector's Choice Update cards, as specified on the front of the card. The trade offer expired on Feb. 1, 1996. Cards are numbered with the "TC" prefix.

		MT
Complete Set (5):		2.50
Common Player:		.50
1	Larry Walker (#531-541)	.75
2	David Cone (#542-552)	.75
3	Marquis Grissom (#553-563)	.50
4	Terry Pendleton (#564-574)	.50
5	Fernando Valenzuela (#575-585)	.50

1995 Collector's Choice Redemption Cards

These update cards were available only via a mail-in offer involving trade cards found in foil packs. Each trade card was redeemable for a specific 11-card set of players shown in their new uniforms as a result of rookie call-ups, trades and free agent signings. The cards are in the same format as the regular 1995 Collector's Choice issue. The update redemption cards are numbered by team nickname from Angels through Yankees, the numbers running contiguously from the body of the CC set.

		MT
Complete Set (55):		6.00
Common Player:		.25
531	Tony Phillips	.25
532	Dave Magadan	.25
533	Mike Gallego	.25
534	Dave Stewart	.25
535	Todd Stottlemyre	.30
536	David Cone	1.00
537	Marquis Grissom	.75
538	Derrick May	.25
539	Joe Oliver	.25
540	Scott Cooper	.25
541	Ken Hill	.25
542	Howard Johnson	.25
543	Brian McRae	.35
544	Jaime Navarro	.25
545	Ozzie Timmons	.25
546	Roberto Kelly	.25
547	Hideo Nomo	2.00
548	Shane Andrews	.60
549	Mark Grudzielanek	.30
550	Carlos Perez	.25
551	Henry Rodriguez	.25
552	Tony Tarasco	.25
553	Glenallen Hill	.25
554	Terry Mulholland	.25
555	Orel Hershiser	.75
556	Darren Bragg	.25
557	John Burkett	.25
558	Bobby Witt	.25
559	Terry Pendleton	.25
560	Andre Dawson	.50
561	Brett Butler	.35
562	Kevin Brown	.75
563	Doug Jones	.25
564	Andy Van Slyke	.25
565	Jody Reed	.25
566	Fernando Valenzuela	.35
567	Charlie Hayes	.25
568	Benji Gil	.25
569	Mark McLemore	.25
570	Mickey Tettleton	.25
571	Bob Tewksbury	.25
572	Rheal Cormier	.25
573	Vaughn Eshelman	.25
574	Mike Macfarlane	.25
575	Mark Whiten	.25
576	Benito Santiago	.25
577	Jason Bates	.25
578	Bill Swift	.25
579	Larry Walker	.60
580	Chad Curtis	.35
581	Bobby Higginson	.35
582	Marty Cordova	.75
583	Mike Devereaux	.25
584	John Kruk	.25
585	John Wetteland	.25

1995 Collector's Choice Michael Jordan Jumbo

A limited edition of 10,000 of these 3" x 5" cards was produced for direct sales to consumers. The card is in the format of the 1995 Collector's Choice Rookie Class subset and includes a silver foil facsimile of Jordan's autograph on front. Back includes a serial number in the lower-right corner.

		MT
661	Michael Jordan	25.00

1995 Collector's Choice/SE

The first Upper Deck baseball card issue for 1995 was this 265-card issue which uses blue borders and a blue foil "Special Edition" trapezoidal logo to impart a premium look. The set opens with a Rookie Class subset of 25 cards on which the background has been rendered in orange hues. A series of six Record Pace cards, horizontal with blue and yellow backgrounds, immediately precedes the regular cards. Base cards in the set are arranged in team-alpha order. Front and back have large color photos, while backs offer complete major league stats. Interspersed within the teams are special cards with borderless front designs honoring players who won significant awards in the 1994 season. Another subset, Stat Leaders, pictures various players in a silver dollar-sized circle at the center of the card and lists the 1994 leaders in that category on the back. A dozen-card Fantasy Team subset near the end of the set lists on back the top-rated players at each position, picturing one of them on front, with a giant blue baseball. The set closes with five checklists honoring career highlights from the '94 season.

		MT
Complete Set (265):		20.00
Common Player:		.05
Wax Box:		35.00
1	Alex Rodriguez	3.00
2	Derek Jeter	1.50
3	Dustin Hermanson	.15
4	Bill Pulsipher	.15
5	Terrell Wade	.05
6	Darren Dreifort	.05
7	LaTroy Hawkins	.15
8	Alex Ochoa	.08
9	Paul Wilson	.15
10	Ernie Young	.08
11	Alan Benes	.15
12	Garret Anderson	.15
13	Armando Benitez	.15
14	Robert Perez	.05
15	Herbert Perry	.05
16	Jose Silva	.05
17	Orlando Miller	.10
18	Russ Davis	.10
19	Jason Isringhausen	.15
20	Ray McDavid	.05
21	Duane Singleton	.05
22	Paul Shuey	.05
23	Steve Dunn	.05
24	Mike Lieberthal	.10
25	Chan Ho Park	.10
26	Ken Griffey Jr. (Record Pace)	1.00
27	Tony Gwynn (Record Pace)	.35
28	Chuck Knoblauch (Record Pace)	.10
29	Frank Thomas (Record Pace)	.75
30	Matt Williams (Record Pace)	.10
31	Chili Davis	.05
32	Chad Curtis	.05
33	Brian Anderson	.05
34	Chuck Finley	.05
35	Tim Salmon	.25
36	Bo Jackson	.10
37	Doug Drabek	.05
38	Craig Biggio	.10
39	Ken Caminiti	.20
40	Jeff Bagwell	1.00
41	Darryl Kile	.05
42	John Hudek	.05
43	Brian L. Hunter	.08
44	Dennis Eckersley	.08
45	Mark McGwire	3.00
46	Brent Gates	.05
47	Steve Karsay	.05
48	Rickey Henderson	.12
49	Terry Steinbach	.05
50	Ruben Sierra	.05
51	Roberto Alomar	.60
52	Carlos Delgado	.25
53	Alex Gonzalez	.10
54	Joe Carter	.08
55	Paul Molitor	.40
56	Juan Guzman	.05
57	John Olerud	.15
58	Shawn Green	.15
59	Tom Glavine	.15
60	Greg Maddux	15.00
61	Roberto Kelly	.05
62	Ryan Klesko	.20
63	Javier Lopez	.15
64	Jose Oliva	.05
65	Fred McGriff	.20
66	Steve Avery	.05
67	Dave Justice	.15
68	Ricky Bones	.05
69	Cal Eldred	.05
70	Greg Vaughn	.10
71	Dave Nilsson	.05
72	Jose Valentin	.05
73	Matt Mieske	.05
74	Todd Zeile	.05
75	Ozzie Smith	.40
76	Bernard Gilkey	.05
77	Ray Lankford	.08
78	Bob Tewksbury	.05
79	Mark Whiten	.05
80	Gregg Jefferies	.05
81	Randy Myers	.05
82	Shawon Dunston	.05
83	Mark Grace	.15
84	Derrick May	.05
85	Sammy Sosa	.75
86	Steve Trachsel	.05
87	Brett Butler	.08
88	Delino DeShields	.05
89	Orel Hershiser	.10
90	Mike Piazza	1.50
91	Todd Hollandsworth	.15
92	Eric Karros	.08
93	Ramon Martinez	.10
94	Tim Wallach	.05
95	Raul Mondesi	.25
96	Larry Walker	.25
97	Wil Cordero	.05
98	Marquis Grissom	.05
99	Ken Hill	.05
100	Cliff Floyd	.10
101	Pedro J. Martinez	.25
102	John Wetteland	.05
103	Rondell White	.15
104	Moises Alou	.10
105	Barry Bonds	.75
106	Darren Lewis	.05
107	Mark Portugal	.05
108	Matt Williams	.25
109	William VanLandingham	.05
110	Bill Swift	.05
111	Robby Thompson	.05
112	Rod Beck	.05
113	Darryl Strawberry	.10
114	Jim Thome	.30
115	Dave Winfield	.10
116	Eddie Murray	.35
117	Manny Ramirez	.75
118	Carlos Baerga	.05
119	Kenny Lofton	.45
120	Albert Belle	.60
121	Mark Clark	.05
122	Dennis Martinez	.05
123	Randy Johnson	.40
124	Jay Buhner	.10
125	Ken Griffey Jr.	3.00
125a	Ken Griffey Jr. (overprinted "For Promotional Use Only")	3.00
126	Rich Gossage	.05
127	Tino Martinez	.10
128	Reggie Jefferson	.05
129	Edgar Martinez	.05
130	Gary Sheffield	.20
131	Pat Rapp	.05
132	Bret Barberie	.05
133	Chuck Carr	.05
134	Jeff Conine	.05
135	Charles Johnson	.15
136	Benito Santiago	.05
137	Matt Williams (Stat Leaders)	.15
138	Jeff Bagwell (Stat Leaders)	.35
139	Kenny Lofton (Stat Leaders)	.15
140	Tony Gwynn (Stat Leaders)	.35
141	Jimmy Key (Stat Leaders)	.05
142	Greg Maddux (Stat Leaders)	.60
143	Randy Johnson (Stat Leaders)	.20
144	Lee Smith (Stat Leaders)	.05
145	Bobby Bonilla	.05
146	Jason Jacome	.05
147	Jeff Kent	.05
148	Ryan Thompson	.05
149	Bobby Jones	.05
150	Bret Saberhagen	.05
151	John Franco	.05
152	Lee Smith	.05
153	Rafael Palmeiro	.15
154	Brady Anderson	.10
155	Cal Ripken Jr.	2.50
156	Jeffrey Hammonds	.10
157	Mike Mussina	.30

158 Chris Hoiles .05
159 Ben McDonald .05
160 Tony Gwynn 1.00
161 Joey Hamilton .10
162 Andy Benes .05
163 Trevor Hoffman .08
164 Phil Plantier .05
165 Derek Bell .05
166 Bip Roberts .05
167 Eddie Williams .05
168 Fernando Valenzuela .05
169 Mariano Duncan .05
170 Lenny Dykstra .05
171 Darren Daulton .05
172 Danny Jackson .05
173 Bobby Munoz .05
174 Doug Jones .05
175 Jay Bell .05
176 Zane Smith .05
177 Jon Lieber .05
178 Carlos Garcia .05
179 Orlando Merced .05
180 Andy Van Slyke .05
181 Rick Helling .05
182 Rusty Greer .05
183 Kenny Rogers .05
184 Will Clark .25
185 Jose Canseco .40
186 Juan Gonzalez 1.00
187 Dean Palmer .05
188 Ivan Rodriguez .50
189 John Valentin .10
190 Roger Clemens 1.00
191 Aaron Sele .05
192 Scott Cooper .05
193 Mike Greenwell .05
194 Mo Vaughn .60
195 Andre Dawson .10
196 Ron Gant .08
197 Jose Rijo .05
198 Bret Boone .05
199 Deion Sanders .15
200 Barry Larkin .15
201 Hal Morris .05
202 Reggie Sanders .05
203 Kevin Mitchell .05
204 Marvin Freeman .05
205 Andres Galarraga .15
206 Walt Weiss .05
207 Charlie Hayes .05
208 David Nied .05
209 Dante Bichette .15
210 David Cone .10
211 Jeff Montgomery .05
212 Felix Jose .05
213 Mike Macfarlane .05
214 Wally Joyner .05
215 Bob Hamelin .05
216 Brian McRae .05
217 Kirk Gibson .05
218 Lou Whitaker .05
219 Chris Gomez .05
220 Cecil Fielder .10
221 Mickey Tettleton .05
222 Travis Fryman .08
223 Tony Phillips .05
224 Rick Aguilera .05
225 Scott Erickson .05
226 Chuck Knoblauch .15
227 Kent Hrbek .05
228 Shane Mack .05
229 Kevin Tapani .05
230 Kirby Puckett 1.00
231 Julio Franco .05
232 Jack McDowell .05
233 Jason Bere .05
234 Alex Fernandez .08
235 Frank Thomas 1.50
236 Ozzie Guillen .05
237 Robin Ventura .08
238 Michael Jordan 3.50
239 Wilson Alvarez .05
240 Don Mattingly .75
241 Jim Abbott .05
242 Jim Leyritz .05
243 Paul O'Neill .08
244 Melido Perez .05
245 Wade Boggs .35
246 Mike Stanley .05
247 Danny Tartabull .05
248 Jimmy Key .05
249 Greg Maddux (Fantasy Team) .60
250 Randy Johnson (Fantasy Team) .20
251 Bret Saberhagen (Fantasy Team) .05
252 John Wetteland (Fantasy Team) .05
253 Mike Piazza (Fantasy Team) .50
254 Jeff Bagwell (Fantasy Team) .30
255 Craig Biggio (Fantasy Team) .05
256 Matt Williams (Fantasy Team) .10
257 Wil Cordero (Fantasy Team) .05
258 Kenny Lofton (Fantasy Team) .15
259 Barry Bonds (Fantasy Team) .30
260 Dante Bichette (Fantasy Team) .10
261 Checklist 1-53 .05
262 Checklist 54-106 .05
263 Checklist 107-159 .05
264 Checklist 160-212 .05
265 Checklist 213-265 .05

1995 Collector's Choice/SE Silver

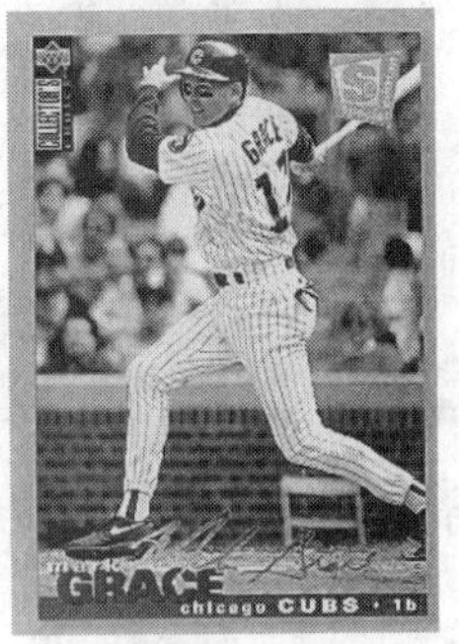

The cards in this parallel edition feature the addition of a silver-foil facsimile autograph on the card front. Also, the blue SE logo and card borders have been replaced with silver on the chase cards, which are found on average of one per pack.

	MT
Complete Set (265):	50.00
Common Player:	.15

Stars: 1.5-3X
Young Stars/RCs: 1-2X
(For checklist and base card values, see 1995 Collector's Choice SE.)

1995 Collector's Choice/SE Gold

Each of the cards in the SE issue can be found in a premium chase card version which replaces the blue border and SE logo with gold, and adds a gold-foil facsimile autograph to the front of the card. The gold-version SE inserts are found on average of one per 36 packs.

	MT
Complete Set (265):	1200.
Common Player:	2.00

Stars: 10-20X
Young Stars/RCs: 8-12X
(For checklist and base card values, see 1995 Collector's Choice SE.)

1996 Collector's Choice Promo

To introduce its base-brand set, Upper Deck issued a promotional sample card of Ken Griffey, Jr. Numbered 100 (he's #310 in the issued set), the back is overprinted "For Promotional Use Only".

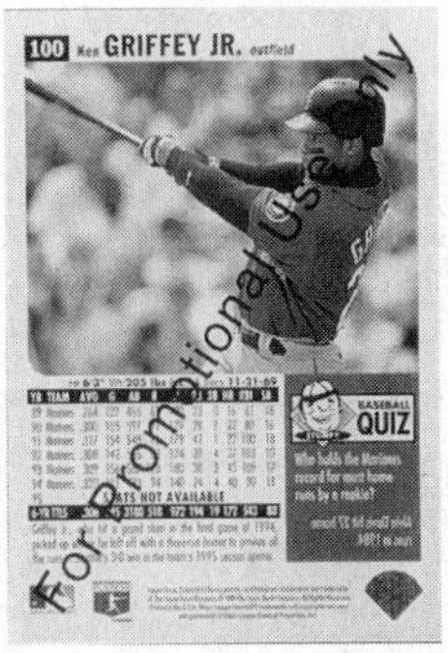

		MT
100	Ken Griffey Jr.	6.00

1996 Collector's Choice

The third year for Collector's Choice includes 730 cards in two series with packs formatted in retail and hobby versions. The 280 regular player cards are joined by subsets of Rookie Class, International Flavor, Traditional Threads, Fantasy Team, Stat Leaders, Season Highlights, First Class, Arizona Fall League, Awards and Checklists. Packs feature a number of different insert sets including silver and gold signature parallel sets, interactive "You Make the Play" cards, four cards from the cross-brand Cal Ripken Collection and three postseason trade cards redeemable for 10-card sets recalling the League Championships and World Series. An additional 30 cards (#761-790) featuring traded players in their new uniforms was issued only in factory sets.

	MT
Complete Series 1-2 Set: (760):	20.00
Complete Factory Set (790):	30.00
Complete Series 1 (1-365):	10.00
Complete Series 2 (396-760):	10.00
Traded Set (366T-395T):	6.00
Common Player:	.05
Wax Box:	28.00

1 Cal Ripken Jr. 1.75
2 Edgar Martinez, Tony Gwynn (1995 Stat Leaders) .35
3 Albert Belle, Dante Bichette (1995 Stat Leaders) .30
4 Albert Belle, Mo Vaughn, Dante Bichette (1995 Stat Leaders) .30
5 Kenny Lofton, Quilvio Veras (1995 Stat Leaders) .30
6 Mike Mussina, Greg Maddux (1995 Stat Leaders) 1.00
7 Randy Johnson, Hideo Nomo (1995 Stat Leaders) .25
8 Randy Johnson, Greg Maddux (1995 Stat Leaders) 1.00
9 Jose Mesa, Randy Myers (1995 Stat Leaders) .05
10 Johnny Damon (Rookie Class) .25
11 Rick Krivda (Rookie Class) .05
12 Roger Cedeno (Rookie Class) .05
13 Angel Martinez (Rookie Class) .05
14 Ariel Prieto (Rookie Class) .05
15 John Wasdin (Rookie Class) .05
16 Edwin Hurtado (Rookie Class) .05
17 Lyle Mouton (Rookie Class) .05
18 Chris Snopek (Rookie Class) .10
19 Mariano Rivera (Rookie Class) .15
20 Ruben Rivera (Rookie Class) .40
21 *Juan Castro* (Rookie Class) .15
22 Jimmy Haynes (Rookie Class) .05
23 Bob Wolcott (Rookie Class) .05
24 Brian Barber (Rookie Class) .05
25 Frank Rodriguez (Rookie Class) .05
26 Jesus Tavarez (Rookie Class) .05
27 Glenn Dishman (Rookie Class) .05
28 Jose Herrera (Rookie Class) .05
29 Chan Ho Park (Rookie Class) .05
30 Jason Isringhausen (Rookie Class) .15
31 Doug Johns (Rookie Class) .05
32 Gene Schall (Rookie Class) .05
33 Kevin Jordan (Rookie Class) .05
34 *Matt Lawton* (Rookie Class) .20
35 Karim Garcia (Rookie Class) .30
36 George Williams (Rookie Class) .05
37 Orlando Palmeiro (Rookie Class) .05
38 Jamie Brewington (Rookie Class) .05
39 Robert Person (Rookie Class) .05
40 Greg Maddux 1.00
41 Marquis Grissom .10
42 Chipper Jones 1.25
43 David Justice .15
44 Mark Lemke .05
45 Fred McGriff .25
46 Javy Lopez .15
47 Mark Wohlers .05
48 Jason Schmidt .10
49 John Smoltz .15
50 Curtis Goodwin .05
51 Greg Zaun .05
52 Armando Benitez .05
53 Manny Alexander .05
54 Chris Hoiles .05
55 Harold Baines .05
56 Ben McDonald .05
57 Scott Erickson .05
58 Jeff Manto .05
59 Luis Alicea .05
60 Roger Clemens .35
61 Rheal Cormier .05
62 Vaughn Eshelman .05
63 Zane Smith .05
64 Mike Macfarlane .05
65 Erik Hanson .05
66 Tim Naehring .05
67 Lee Tinsley .05
68 Troy O'Leary .05
69 Garret Anderson .05
70 Chili Davis .05
71 Jim Edmonds .15
72 Troy Percival .05
73 Mark Langston .05
74 Spike Owen .05
75 Tim Salmon .25
76 Brian Anderson .05
77 Lee Smith .05
78 Jim Abbott .05
79 Jim Bullinger .05
80 Mark Grace .10
81 Todd Zeile .05
82 Kevin Foster .05
83 Howard Johnson .05
84 Brian McRae .05
85 Randy Myers .05
86 Jaime Navarro .05
87 Luis Gonzalez .05
88 Ozzie Timmons .05
89 Wilson Alvarez .05
90 Frank Thomas 1.00
91 James Baldwin .05
92 Ray Durham .05
93 Alex Fernandez .05
94 Ozzie Guillen .05
95 Tim Raines .05
96 Roberto Hernandez .05
97 Lance Johnson .05
98 John Kruk .05
99 Mark Portugal .05
100 Don Mattingly (Traditional Threads) .50
101 Jose Canseco (Traditional Threads) .20
102 Raul Mondesi (Traditional Threads) .20
103 Cecil Fielder (Traditional Threads) .05
104 Ozzie Smith (Traditional Threads) .15
105 Frank Thomas (Traditional Threads) .50
106 Sammy Sosa (Traditional Threads) .50
107 Fred McGriff (Traditional Threads) .20
108 Barry Bonds (Traditional Threads) .25
109 Thomas Howard .05
110 Ron Gant .05
111 Eddie Taubensee .05
112 Hal Morris .05
113 Jose Rijo .05
114 Pete Schourek .05
115 Reggie Sanders .05
116 Benito Santiago .05
117 Jeff Brantley .05
118 Julian Tavarez .05
119 Carlos Baerga .15
120 Jim Thome .30
121 Jose Mesa .05
122 Dennis Martinez .05
123 Dave Winfield .05
124 Eddie Murray .25
125 Manny Ramirez .75
126 Paul Sorrento .05
127 Kenny Lofton .50
128 Eric Young .05
129 Jason Bates .05
130 Bret Saberhagen .05
131 Andres Galarraga .10
132 Joe Girardi .05
133 John Vander Wal .05
134 David Nied .05
135 Dante Bichette .20
136 Vinny Castilla .05
137 Kevin Ritz .05
138 Felipe Lira .05
139 Joe Boever .05
140 Cecil Fielder .15
141 John Flaherty .05
142 Kirk Gibson .05
143 Brian Maxcy .05
144 Lou Whitaker .05
145 Alan Trammell .05
146 Bobby Higginson .05
147 Chad Curtis .05
148 Quilvio Veras .05
149 Jerry Browne .05
150 Andre Dawson .05
151 Robb Nen .05
152 Greg Colbrunn .05
153 Chris Hammond .05
154 Kurt Abbott .05
155 Charles Johnson .05
156 Terry Pendleton .05
157 Dave Weathers .05
158 Mike Hampton .05
159 Craig Biggio .05
160 Jeff Bagwell .75
161 Brian L. Hunter .10
162 Mike Henneman .05
163 Dave Magadan .05
164 Shane Reynolds .05
165 Derek Bell .05
166 Orlando Miller .05
167 James Mouton .05
168 Melvin Bunch .05
169 Tom Gordon .05
170 Kevin Appier .05
171 Tom Goodwin .05
172 Greg Gagne .05
173 Gary Gaetti .05
174 Jeff Montgomery .05
175 Jon Nunnally .05
176 Michael Tucker .05
177 Joe Vitiello .05
178 Billy Ashley .05
179 Tom Candiotti .05
180 Hideo Nomo .25
181 Chad Fonville .05
182 Todd Hollandsworth .10
183 Eric Karros .05
184 Roberto Kelly .05
185 Mike Piazza 1.00
186 Ramon Martinez .05
187 Tim Wallach .05
188 Jeff Cirillo .05
189 Sid Roberson .05
190 Kevin Seitzer .05
191 Mike Fetters .05

192	Steve Sparks	.05
193	Matt Mieske	.05
194	Joe Oliver	.05
195	B.J. Surhoff	.05
196	Alberto Reyes	.05
197	Fernando Vina	.05
198	LaTroy Hawkins	.05
199	Marty Cordova	.10
200	Kirby Puckett	.75
201	Brad Radke	.05
202	(Pedro Munoz)	.05
203	Scott Klingenbeck	.05
204	Pat Meares	.05
205	Chuck Knoblauch	.05
206	Scott Stahoviak	.05
207	Dave Stevens	.05
208	Shane Andrews	.05
209	Moises Alou	.05
210	David Segui	.05
211	Cliff Floyd	.05
212	Carlos Perez	.05
213	Mark Grudzielanek	.05
214	Butch Henry	.05
215	Rondell White	.10
216	Mel Rojas	.05
217	Ugueth Urbina	.05
218	Edgardo Alfonzo	.05
219	Carl Everett	.05
220	John Franco	.05
221	Todd Hundley	.05
222	Bobby Jones	.05
223	Bill Pulsipher	.15
224	Rico Brogna	.05
225	Jeff Kent	.05
226	Chris Jones	.05
227	Butch Huskey	.05
228	Robert Eenhoorn	.05
229	Sterling Hitchcock	.05
230	Wade Boggs	.15
231	Derek Jeter	1.00
232	Tony Fernandez	.05
233	Jack McDowell	.10
234	Andy Pettitte	.50
235	David Cone	.10
236	Mike Stanley	.05
237	Don Mattingly	.75
238	Geronimo Berroa	.05
239	Scott Brosius	.05
240	Rickey Henderson	.10
241	Terry Steinbach	.05
242	Mike Gallego	.05
243	Jason Giambi	.05
244	Steve Ontiveros	.05
245	Dennis Eckersley	.05
246	Dave Stewart	.05
247	Don Wengert	.05
248	Paul Quantrill	.05
249	Ricky Bottalico	.05
250	Kevin Stocker	.05
251	Lenny Dykstra	.05
252	Tony Longmire	.05
253	Tyler Green	.05
254	Mike Mimbs	.05
255	Charlie Hayes	.05
256	Mickey Morandini	.05
257	Heathcliff Slocumb	.05
258	Jeff King	.05
259	Midre Cummings	.05
260	Mark Johnson	.05
261	Freddy Garcia	.05
262	Jon Lieber	.05
263	Esteban Loaiza	.10
264	Danny Miceli	.05
265	Orlando Merced	.05
266	Denny Neagle	.05
267	Steve Parris	.05
268	Fantasy Team '95 (Greg Maddux)	.60
269	Fantasy Team '95 (Randy Johnson)	.10
270	Fantasy Team '95 (Hideo Nomo)	.25
271	Fantasy Team '95 (Jose Mesa)	.05
272	Fantasy Team '95 (Mike Piazza)	.50
273	Fantasy Team '95 (Mo Vaughn)	.30
274	Fantasy Team '95 (Craig Biggio)	.05
275	Fantasy Team '95 (Edgar Martinez)	.05
276	Fantasy Team '95 (Barry Larkin)	.15
277	Fantasy Team '95 (Sammy Sosa)	.50
278	Fantasy Team '95 (Dante Bichette)	.05
279	Fantasy Team '95 (Albert Belle)	.40
280	Ozzie Smith	.30
281	Mark Sweeney	.05
282	Terry Bradshaw	.05
283	Allen Battle	.05
284	Danny Jackson	.05
285	Tom Henke	.05
286	Scott Cooper	.05
287	Tripp Cromer	.05
288	Bernard Gilkey	.05
289	Brian Jordan	.05
290	Tony Gwynn	.75
291	Brad Ausmus	.05
292	Bryce Florie	.05
293	Andres Berumen	.05
294	Ken Caminiti	.10
295	Bip Roberts	.05
296	Trevor Hoffman	.05
297	Roberto Petagine	.05
298	Jody Reed	.05
299	Fernando Valenzuela	.05
300	Barry Bonds	.50
301	Mark Leiter	.05
302	Mark Carreon	.05
303	Royce Clayton	.05
304	Kirt Manwaring	.05
305	Glenallen Hill	.05
306	Deion Sanders	.20
307	Joe Rosselli	.05
308	Robby Thompson	.05
309	William VanLandingham	.05
310	Ken Griffey Jr.	2.00
311	Bobby Ayala	.05
312	Joey Cora	.05
313	Mike Blowers	.05
314	Darren Bragg	.05
315	Randy Johnson	.25
316	Alex Rodriguez	2.00
317	Andy Benes	.05
318	Tino Martinez	.05
319	Dan Wilson	.05
320	Will Clark	.30
321	Jeff Frye	.05
322	Benji Gil	.05
323	Rick Helling	.05
324	Mark McLemore	.05
325	Dave Nilsson (International Flavor)	.05
326	Larry Walker (International Flavor)	.20
327	Jose Canseco (International Flavor)	.20
328	Raul Mondesi (International Flavor)	.25
329	Manny Ramirez (International Flavor)	.40
330	Robert Eenhoorn (International Flavor)	.05
331	Chili Davis (International Flavor)	.05
332	Hideo Nomo (International Flavor)	.25
333	Benji Gil (International Flavor)	.05
334	Fernando Valenzuela (International Flavor)	.05
335	Dennis Martinez (International Flavor)	.05
336	Roberto Kelly (International Flavor)	.05
337	Carlos Baerga (International Flavor)	.10
338	Juan Gonzalez (International Flavor)	.40
339	Roberto Alomar (International Flavor)	.25
340	Chan Ho Park (International Flavor)	.05
341	Andres Galarraga (International Flavor)	.10
342	Midre Cummings (International Flavor)	.05
343	Otis Nixon	.05
344	Jeff Russell	.05
345	Ivan Rodriguez	.25
346	Mickey Tettleton	.05
347	Bob Tewksbury	.05
348	Domingo Cedeno	.05
349	Lance Parrish	.05
350	Joe Carter	.15
351	Devon White	.05
352	Carlos Delgado	.25
353	Alex Gonzalez	.05
354	Darren Hall	.05
355	Paul Molitor	.25
356	Al Leiter	.05
357	Randy Knorr	.05
358	Checklist 1-46 (12-player Astros-Padres trade)	.05
359	Checklist 47-92 (Hideo Nomo)	.10
360	Checklist 93-138 (Ramon Martinez)	.05
361	Checklist 139-184 (Robin Ventura)	.05
362	Checklist 185-230 (Cal Ripken Jr.)	.30
363	Checklist 231-275 (Ken Caminiti)	.05
364	Checklist 276-320 (Eddie Murray)	.10
365	Checklist 321-365 (Randy Johnson)	.10
366	A.L. Divisional Series (Tony Pena)	.10
367	A.L. Divisional Series (Jim Thome)	.10
368	A.L. Divisional Series (Don Mattingly)	.40
369	A.L. Divisional Series (Jim Leyritz)	.10
370	A.L. Divisional Series (Ken Griffey Jr.)	1.25
371	A.L. Divisional Series (Edgar Martinez)	.10
372	N.L. Divisional Series (Pete Schourek)	.10
373	N.L. Divisional Series (Mark Lewis)	.10
374	N.L. Divisional Series (Chipper Jones)	1.00
375	N.L. Divisonal Series (Fred McGriff)	.25
376	N.L. Championship Series (Javy Lopez)	.15
377	N.L. Championship Series (Fred McGriff)	.25
378	N.L. Championship Series (Charlie O'Brien)	.10
379	N.L. Championship Series (Mike Devereaux)	.10
380	N.L. Championship Series (Mark Wohlers)	.10
381	A.L. Championship Series (Bob Wolcott)	.10
382	A.L. Championship Series (Manny Ramirez)	.25
383	A.L. Championship Series (Jay Buhner)	.15
384	A.L. Championship Series (Orel Hershiser)	.10
385	A.L. Championship Series (Kenny Lofton)	.25
386	World Series (Greg Maddux)	1.00
387	World Series (Javy Lopez)	.15
388	World Series (Kenny Lofton)	.25
389	World Series (Eddie Murray)	.30
390	World Series (Luis Polonia)	.10
391	World Series (Pedro Borbon)	.10
392	World Series (Jim Thome)	.20
393	World Series (Orel Hershiser)	.15
394	World Series (David Justice)	.20
395	World Series (Tom Glavine)	.20
396	Braves Team Checklist (Greg Maddux)	.25
397	Mets Team Checklist (Brett Butler)	.05
398	Phillies Team Checklist (Darren Daulton)	.05
399	Marlins Team Checklist (Gary Sheffield)	.10
400	Expos Team Checklist (Moises Alou)	.05
401	Reds Team Checklist (Barry Larkin)	.10
402	Astros Team Checklist (Jeff Bagwell)	.20
403	Cubs Team Checklist (Sammy Sosa)	.40
404	Cardinals Team Checklist (Ozzie Smith)	.10
405	Pirates Team Checklist (Jeff King)	.05
406	Dodgers Team Checklist (Mike Piazza)	.25
407	Rockies Team Checklist (Dante Bichette)	.10
408	Padres Team Checklist (Tony Gwynn)	.15
409	Giants Team Checklist (Barry Bonds)	.15
410	Indians Team Checklist (Kenny Lofton)	.15
411	Royals Team Checklist (Jon Nunnally)	.05
412	White Sox Team Checklist (Frank Thomas)	.25
413	Brewers Team Checklist (Greg Vaughn)	.05
414	Twins Team Checklist (Paul Molitor)	.10
415	Mariners Team Checklist (Ken Griffey Jr.)	.50
416	Angels Team Checklist (Jim Edmonds)	.05
417	Rangers Team Checklist (Juan Gonzalez)	.25
418	Athletics Team Checklist (Mark McGwire)	.75
419	Red Sox Team Checklist (Roger Clemens)	.15
420	Yankees Team Checklist (Wade Boggs)	.05
421	Orioles Team Checklist (Cal Ripken Jr.)	.40
422	Tigers Team Checklist (Cecil Fielder)	.05
423	Blue Jays Team Checklist (Joe Carter)	.05
424	*Osvaldo Fernandez* (Rookie Class)	.20
425	Billy Wagner (Rookie Class)	.10
426	George Arias (Rookie Class)	.05
427	Mendy Lopez (Rookie Class)	.05
428	Jeff Suppan (Rookie Class)	.05
429	Rey Ordonez (Rookie Class)	.25
430	Brooks Kieschnick (Rookie Class)	.10
431	*Raul Ibanez* (Rookie Class)	.10
432	*Livan Hernandez* (Rookie Class)	.75
433	Shannon Stewart (Rookie Class)	.05
434	Steve Cox (Rookie Class)	.05
435	Trey Beamon (Rookie Class)	.05
436	Sergio Nunez (Rookie Class)	.05
437	Jermaine Dye (Rookie Class)	.15
438	*Mike Sweeney* (Rookie Class)	.15
439	Richard Hidalgo (Rookie Class)	.05
440	Todd Greene (Rookie Class)	.15
441	*Robert Smith* (Rookie Class)	.25
442	Rafael Orellano (Rookie Class)	.15
443	*Wilton Guerrero* (Rookie Class)	.35
444	*David Doster* (Rookie Class)	.05
445	Jason Kendall (Rookie Class)	.10
446	Edgar Renteria (Rookie Class)	.15
447	Scott Spiezio (Rookie Class)	.10
448	Jay Canizaro (Rookie Class)	.10
449	Enrique Wilson (Rookie Class)	.05
450	Bob Abreu (Rookie Class)	.05
451	Dwight Smith	.05
452	Jeff Blauser	.05
453	Steve Avery	.05
454	Brad Clontz	.05
455	Tom Glavine	.10
456	Mike Mordecai	.05
457	Rafael Belliard	.05
458	Greg McMichael	.05
459	Pedro Borbon	.05
460	Ryan Klesko	.20
461	Terrell Wade	.05
462	Brady Anderson	.10
463	Roberto Alomar	.40
464	Bobby Bonilla	.05
465	Mike Mussina	.35
466	*Cesar Devarez*	.05
467	Jeffrey Hammonds	.05
468	Mike Devereaux	.05
469	B.J. Surhoff	.05
470	Rafael Palmeiro	.15
471	John Valentin	.05
472	Mike Greenwell	.05
473	Dwayne Hosey	.05
474	Tim Wakefield	.05
475	Jose Canseco	.25
476	Aaron Sele	.05
477	Stan Belinda	.05
478	Mike Stanley	.05
479	Jamie Moyer	.05
480	Mo Vaughn	.50
481	Randy Velarde	.05
482	Gary DiSarcina	.05
483	Jorge Fabregas	.05
484	Rex Hudler	.05
485	Chuck Finley	.05
486	Tim Wallach	.05
487	Eduardo Perez	.05
488	Scott Sanderson	.05
489	J.T. Snow	.05
490	Sammy Sosa	.75
491	Terry Adams	.05
492	Matt Franco	.05
493	Scott Servais	.05
494	Frank Castillo	.05
495	Ryne Sandberg	.35
496	Rey Sanchez	.05
497	Steve Trachsel	.05
498	Jose Hernandez	.05
499	Dave Martinez	.05
500	Babe Ruth (First Class)	1.00
501	Ty Cobb (First Class)	.50
502	Walter Johnson (First Class)	.15
503	Christy Mathewson (First Class)	.05
504	Honus Wagner (First Class)	.25
505	Robin Ventura	.05
506	Jason Bere	.05
507	*Mike Cameron*	.50
508	Ron Karkovice	.05
509	Matt Karchner	.05
510	Harold Baines	.05
511	Kirk McCaskill	.05
512	Larry Thomas	.05
513	Danny Tartabull	.05
514	Steve Gibralter	.05
515	Bret Boone	.05
516	Jeff Branson	.05
517	Kevin Jarvis	.05
518	Xavier Hernandez	.05
519	Eric Owens	.05
520	Barry Larkin	.15
521	Dave Burba	.05
522	John Smiley	.05
523	Paul Assenmacher	.05
524	Chad Ogea	.05
525	Orel Hershiser	.05
526	Alan Embree	.05
527	Tony Pena	.05
528	Omar Vizquel	.05
529	Mark Clark	.05
530	Albert Belle	.60
531	Charles Nagy	.05
532	Herbert Perry	.05
533	Darren Holmes	.05
534	Ellis Burks	.05
535	Bill Swift	.05
536	Armando Reynoso	.05
537	Curtis Leskanic	.05
538	Quinton McCracken	.05
539	Steve Reed	.05
540	Larry Walker	.15
541	Walt Weiss	.05
542	Bryan Rekar	.05
543	Tony Clark	.50
544	Steve Rodriguez	.05
545	C.J. Nitkowski	.05
546	Todd Steverson	.05
547	Jose Lima	.05
548	Phil Nevin	.05
549	Chris Gomez	.05
550	Travis Fryman	.05
551	Mark Lewis	.05
552	Alex Arias	.05
553	Marc Valdes	.05
554	Kevin Brown	.05
555	Jeff Conine	.05
556	John Burkett	.05
557	Devon White	.05
558	Pat Rapp	.05
559	Jay Powell	.05
560	Gary Sheffield	.20
561	Jim Dougherty	.05
562	Todd Jones	.05
563	Tony Eusebio	.05
564	Darryl Kile	.05
565	Doug Drabek	.05
566	Mike Simms	.05
567	Derrick May	.05
568	*Donne Wall*	.05
569	Greg Swindell	.05
570	Jim Pittsley	.05
571	Bob Hamelin	.05
572	Mark Gubicza	.05
573	Chris Haney	.05
574	Keith Lockhart	.05
575	Mike Macfarlane	.05
576	Les Norman	.05
577	Joe Randa	.05
578	Chris Stynes	.05
579	Greg Gagne	.05
580	Raul Mondesi	.25
581	Delino DeShields	.05
582	Pedro Astacio	.05
583	Antonio Osuna	.05
584	Brett Butler	.05
585	Todd Worrell	.05
586	Mike Blowers	.05
587	Felix Rodriguez	.05
588	Ismael Valdes	.05
589	Ricky Bones	.05
590	Greg Vaughn	.05
591	Mark Loretta	.05
592	Cal Eldred	.05
593	Chuck Carr	.05
594	Dave Nilsson	.05
595	John Jaha	.05
596	Scott Karl	.05
597	Pat Listach	.05
598	*Jose Valentin*	.15
599	Mike Trombley	.05
600	Paul Molitor	.20
601	Dave Hollins	.05

602	Ron Coomer	.05
603	Matt Walbeck	.05
604	Roberto Kelly	.05
605	Rick Aguilera	.05
606	Pat Mahomes	.05
607	Jeff Reboulet	.05
608	Rich Becker	.05
609	Tim Scott	.05
610	Pedro J. Martinez	.05
611	Kirk Rueter	.05
612	Tavo Alvarez	.05
613	Yamil Benitez	.05
614	Darrin Fletcher	.05
615	Mike Lansing	.05
616	Henry Rodriguez	.05
617	Tony Tarasco	.05
618	Alex Ochoa	.05
619	Tim Bogar	.05
620	Bernard Gilkey	.05
621	Dave Mlicki	.05
622	Brent Mayne	.05
623	Ryan Thompson	.05
624	Pete Harnisch	.05
625	Lance Johnson	.05
626	Jose Vizcaino	.05
627	Doug Henry	.05
628	Scott Kamieniecki	.05
629	Jim Leyritz	.05
630	Ruben Sierra	.05
631	Pat Kelly	.05
632	Joe Girardi	.05
633	John Wetteland	.05
634	Melido Perez	.05
635	Paul O'Neill	.05
636	Jorge Posada	.10
637	Bernie Williams	.20
638	Mark Acre	.25
639	Mike Bordick	.05
640	Mark McGwire	2.50
641	Fausto Cruz	.05
642	Ernie Young	.05
643	Todd Van Poppel	.05
644	Craig Paquette	.05
645	Brent Gates	.05
646	Pedro Munoz	.05
647	Andrew Lorraine	.05
648	Sid Fernandez	.05
649	Jim Eisenreich	.05
650	Johnny Damon (Arizona Fall League)	.15
651	Dustin Hermanson (Arizona Fall League)	.05
652	Joe Randa (Arizona Fall League)	.05
653	Michael Tucker (Arizona Fall League)	.10
654	Alan Benes (Arizona Fall League)	.20
655	Chad Fonville (Arizona Fall League)	.05
656	David Bell (Arizona Fall League)	.05
657	Jon Nunnally (Arizona Fall League)	.05
658	Chan Ho Park (Arizona Fall League)	.05
659	LaTroy Hawkins (Arizona Fall League)	.05
660	Jamie Brewington (Arizona Fall League)	.05
661	Quinton McCracken (Arizona Fall League)	.05
662	Tim Unroe (Arizona Fall League)	.05
663	Jeff Ware (Arizona Fall League)	.05
664	Todd Greene (Arizona Fall League)	.15
665	Andrew Lorraine (Arizona Fall League)	.05
666	Ernie Young (Arizona Fall League)	.05
667	Toby Borland	.05
668	Lenny Webster	.05
669	Benito Santiago	.05
670	Gregg Jefferies	.05
671	Darren Daulton	.05
672	Curt Schilling	.05
673	Mark Whiten	.05
674	Todd Zeile	.05
675	Jay Bell	.05
676	Paul Wagner	.05
677	Dave Clark	.05
678	Nelson Liriano	.05
679	Ramon Morel	.10
680	Charlie Hayes	.05
681	Angelo Encaracion	.05
682	Al Martin	.05
683	Jacob Brumfield	.05
684	Mike Kingery	.05
685	Carlos Garcia	.05
686	Tom Pagnozzi	.05
687	David Bell	.05
688	Todd Stottlemyre	.05
689	Jose Oliva	.05
690	Ray Lankford	.05
691	Mike Morgan	.05
692	John Frascatore	.05
693	John Mabry	.05
694	Mark Petkovsek	.05
695	Alan Benes	.25
696	Steve Finley	.05
697	Marc Newfield	.05
698	Andy Ashby	.05
699	Marc Kroon	.05
700	Wally Joyner	.05
701	Joey Hamilton	.05
702	Dustin Hermanson	.05
703	Scott Sanders	.05
704	Marty Cordova (Award Win.-ROY)	.05
705	Hideo Nomo (Award Win.-ROY)	.20
706	Mo Vaughn (Award Win.-MVP)	.25
707	Barry Larkin (Award Win.-MVP)	.15
708	Randy Johnson (Award Win.-CY)	.15
709	Greg Maddux (Award Win.-CY)	.60
710	Mark McGwire (Award-Comeback)	.75
711	Ron Gant (Award-Comeback)	.05
712	Andujar Cedeno	.05
713	Brian Johnson	.05
714	J.R. Phillips	.05
715	Rod Beck	.05
716	Sergio Valdez	.05
717	*Marvin Benard*	.05
718	Steve Scarsone	.05
719	*Rich Aurilia*	.10
720	Matt Williams	.30
721	John Patterson	.05
722	Shawn Estes	.05
723	Russ Davis	.05
724	Rich Amaral	.05
725	Edgar Martinez	.05
726	Norm Charlton	.05
727	Paul Sorrento	.05
728	Luis Sojo	.05
729	Arquimedez Pozo	.05
730	Jay Buhner	.15
731	Chris Bosio	.05
732	Chris Widger	.05
733	Kevin Gross	.05
734	Darren Oliver	.05
735	Dean Palmer	.05
736	Matt Whiteside	.05
737	Luis Ortiz	.05
738	Roger Pavlik	.05
739	Damon Buford	.05
740	Juan Gonzalez	.75
741	Rusty Greer	.05
742	Lou Frazier	.05
743	Pat Hentgen	.05
744	Tomas Perez	.05
745	Juan Guzman	.05
746	Otis Nixon	.05
747	Robert Perez	.05
748	Ed Sprague	.05
749	Tony Castillo	.05
750	John Olerud	.05
751	Shawn Green	.05
752	Jeff Ware	.05
753	Checklist 396-441/ Blake St. Bombers (Dante Bichette, Larry Walker, Andres Galarraga, Vinny Castilla)	.10
754	Checklist 442-487 (Greg Maddux)	.35
755	Checklist 488-533 (Marty Cordova)	.05
756	Checklist 534-579 (Ozzie Smith)	.15
757	Checklist 580-625 (John Vander Wal)	.05
758	Checklist 626-670 (Andres Galarraga)	.10
759	Checklist 671-715 (Frank Thomas)	.25
760	Checklist 716-760 (Tony Gwynn)	.30
761	Randy Myers	.10
762	Kent Mercker	.10
763	David Wells	.10
764	Tom Gordon	.10
765	Wil Cordero	.10
766	Dave Magadan	.10
767	Doug Jones	.10
768	Kevin Tapani	.10
769	Curtis Goodwin	.10
770	Julio Franco	.10
771	Jack McDowell	.15
772	Al Leiter	.10
773	Sean Berry	.10
774	Bip Roberts	.10
775	Jose Offerman	.10
776	Ben McDonald	.15
777	Dan Serafini	.25
778	Ryan McGuire	.25
779	Tim Raines	.10
780	Tino Martinez	.15
781	Kenny Rogers	.10
782	Bob Tewksbury	.10
783	Rickey Henderson	.15
784	Ron Gant	.20
785	Gary Gaetti	.10
786	Andy Benes	.15
787	Royce Clayton	.10
788	Darryl Hamilton	.10
789	Ken Hill	.10
790	Erik Hanson	.10

1996 Collector's Choice Silver Signature

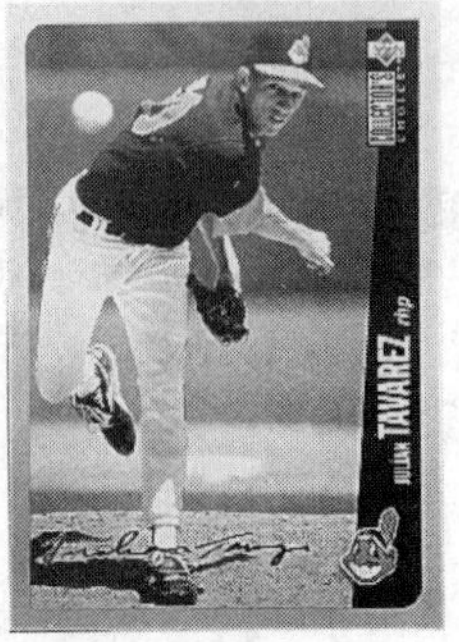

A silver border instead of white, and a facsimile autograph in silver ink on the card front differentiate these parallel insert cards from the regular-issue Collector's Choice. The inserts are seeded at the rate of one per pack.

	MT
Complete Set (730):	75.00
Common Player:	.10
Stars: 1-2.5X	
(See 1996 Collector's Choice for checklist and base card values.)	

1996 Collector's Choice Gold Signature

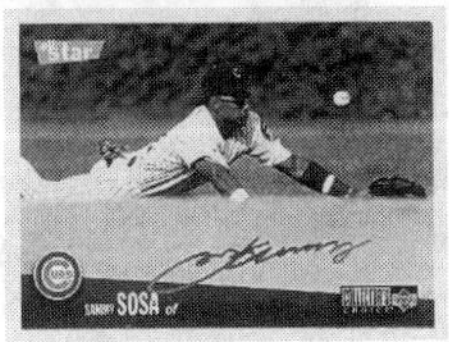

This insert set parallels each card in the regular Collector's Choice set. Found on average of one per 35 packs, the cards are nearly identical to the regular version except for the presence of a facsimile autograph in gold ink on the front and gold, instead of white borders.

	MT
Complete Set (730):	1200.
Common Player:	1.00
Veteran Stars: 10-20X	
Young Stars: 8-15X	
(See 1996 Collector's Choice for checklist and base card values.)	

1996 Collector's Choice A Cut Above

This 10-card set highlights the career of Ken Griffey Jr. The front had a color photo with "The Griffey Years" printed in the left border and the year of his accomplishment in the right border. The backs have a headshot and description of his achievement. This set was inserted one per six-card retail pack.

	MT
Complete Set (10):	8.00
Common Card:	1.00
1-10 Ken Griffey Jr.	1.00

Player names in *Italic* type indicate a rookie card.

1996 Collector's Choice Crash the Game

For a second season, UD continued its interactive chase card series, "You Crash the Game." At a ratio of about one per five packs for a silver version and one per 49 packs for a gold version, cards of the game's top sluggers can be found bearing one of three date ranges representing a three- or four-game series in which that player was scheduled to play during the 1996 season. If the player hit a home run during the series shown on the card, the card could be redeemed (for $1.75) by mail for a "Super Premium" wood-and-plastic card of the player. Both silver and gold Crash cards feature silver and red prismatic foil behind the player action photo. Silver versions have the Crash logo, series dates and player ID in silver foil on front; those details are in gold foil on the gold cards. Backs have contest rules printed on a gray (silver) or yellow (gold) background. Card numbers are preceded by a "CG" prefix. Cards were redeemable only until Nov. 25, 1996. Winning cards are indicated with an asterisk; they would be in shorter supply than those which could not be redeemed.

		MT
Complete Silver Set (90):		40.00
Common Silver Player:		.50
Gold Version: 5-6X		
1a	Chipper Jones (July 11-14*)	3.00
1b	Chipper Jones (Aug. 27-29*)	3.00
1c	Chipper Jones (Sept. 19-23)	2.00
2a	Fred McGriff (July 1-3)	.50
2b	Fred McGriff (Aug. 30-Sept. 1)	.50
2c	Fred McGriff (Sept. 10-12*)	.90
3a	Rafael Palmeiro (July 4-7*)	.90
3b	Rafael Palmeiro (Aug. 29-Sept. 1)	.50
3c	Rafael Palmeiro (Sept. 26-29)	.50
4a	Cal Ripken Jr. (June 27-30)	3.00
4b	Cal Ripken Jr. (July 25-28*)	6.00
4c	Cal Ripken Jr. (Sept. 2-4)	3.00
5a	Jose Canseco (June 27-30)	.50
5b	Jose Canseco (July 11-14*)	.90
5c	Jose Canseco (Aug. 23-25)	.50
6a	Mo Vaughn (June 21-23*)	.90
6b	Mo Vaughn (July 18-21*)	.90
6c	Mo Vaughn (Sept. 20-22)	.50
7a	Jim Edmonds (July 18-21*)	.90
7b	Jim Edmonds (Aug. 16-18*)	.90
7c	Jim Edmonds (Sept. 20-22)	.50
8a	Tim Salmon (June 20-23)	.50
8b	Tim Salmon (July 30-Aug. 1)	.50
8c	Tim Salmon (Sept. 9-12)	.50
9a	Sammy Sosa (July 4-7*)	3.00
9b	Sammy Sosa (Aug. 1-4*)	3.00
9c	Sammy Sosa (Sept. 2-4)	1.50
10a	Frank Thomas (June 27-30)	1.00
10b	Frank Thomas (July 4-7)	1.00
10c	Frank Thomas (Sept. 2-4*)	2.00
11a	Albert Belle (June 25-26)	.75
11b	Albert Belle (Aug. 2-5*)	1.50
11c	Albert Belle (Sept. 6-8)	.75
12a	Manny Ramirez (July 18-21*)	.90
12b	Manny Ramirez (Aug. 26-28)	.50
12c	Manny Ramirez (Sept. 9-12*)	.90
13a	Jim Thome (June 27-30)	.50
13b	Jim Thome (July 4-7*)	.90
13c	Jim Thome (Sept. 23-25)	.50
14a	Dante Bichette (July 11-14*)	.90
14b	Dante Bichette (Aug. 9-11)	.50
14c	Dante Bichette (Sept. 9-12)	.50
15a	Vinny Castilla (July 1-3)	.50
15b	Vinny Castilla (Aug. 23-25*)	.90
15c	Vinny Castilla (Sept. 13-15*)	.90
16a	Larry Walker (June 24-26)	.65
16b	Larry Walker (July 18-21)	.65
16c	Larry Walker (Sept. 27-29)	.65
17a	Cecil Fielder (June 27-30)	.50
17b	Cecil Fielder (July 30-Aug. 1*)	.90
17c	Cecil Fielder (Sept. 17-19*)	.50
18a	Gary Sheffield (July 4-7)	.50
18b	Gary Sheffield (Aug. 2-4)	.50
18c	Gary Sheffield (Sept. 5-8*)	.90
19a	Jeff Bagwell (July 4-7*)	1.50
19b	Jeff Bagwell (Aug. 16-18)	.90
19c	Jeff Bagwell (Sept. 13-15)	.90
20a	Eric Karros (July 4-7*)	.90
20b	Eric Karros (Aug. 13-15*)	.90
20c	Eric Karros (Sept. 16-18)	.50
21a	Mike Piazza (June 27-30*)	4.00
21b	Mike Piazza (July 26-28)	2.50
21c	Mike Piazza (Sept. 12-15*)	4.00
22a	Ken Caminiti (July 11-14*)	.90
22b	Ken Caminiti (Aug. 16-18*)	.90
22c	Ken Caminiti (Sept. 19-22*)	.90
23a	Barry Bonds (June 27-30*)	3.00
23b	Barry Bonds (July 22-24)	1.50
23c	Barry Bonds (Sept. 24-26)	1.50
24a	Matt Williams (July 11-14*)	1.00
24b	Matt Williams (Aug. 19-21)	.55
24c	Matt Williams (Sept. 27-29)	.55
25a	Jay Buhner (June 20-23)	.50
25b	Jay Buhner (July 25-28)	.50
25c	Jay Buhner (Aug. 29-Sept. 1*)	.90
26a	Ken Griffey Jr. (July 18-21*)	6.00
26b	Ken Griffey Jr. (Aug. 16-18*)	6.00
26c	Ken Griffey Jr. (Sept. 20-22*)	6.00
27a	Ron Gant (June 24-27*)	.90

27b Ron Gant (July 11-14*) .90
27c Ron Gant (Sept. 27-29*) .90
28a Juan Gonzalez (June 28-30*) 3.00
28b Juan Gonzalez (July 15-17*) 3.00
28c Juan Gonzalez (Aug. 6-8) 1.50
29a Mickey Tettleton (July 4-7*) .90
29b Mickey Tettleton (Aug. 6-8) .50
29c Mickey Tettleton (Sept. 6-8*) .90
30a Joe Carter (June 25-27) .50
30b Joe Carter (Aug. 5-8) .50
30c Joe Carter (Sept. 23-25) .50

1996 Collector's Choice Crash Winners

Collectors who held "You Crash The Game" insert cards with date ranges on which the pictured player hit a home run could redeem them (for $1.75 per card) for a premium card of that player. The redemption cards have a layer of clear plastic bonded to a wood-laminate front. Within a starburst cutout at center is the player photo with a red background. Cards have a Crash/Game logo in the lower-right corner, in either silver or gold, depending on which winning card was submitted for exchange. Backs have 1995 and career stats along with licensing and copyright data. There were no winning cards of Tim Salmon, Larry Walker or Joe Carter.

	MT
Complete Set (27):	140.00
Common Player:	3.00
Gold Version: 4-5X	
CR1 Chipper Jones	12.00
CR2 Fred McGriff	3.00
CR3 Rafael Palmeiro	4.00
CR4 Cal Ripken Jr.	12.50
CR5 Jose Canseco	4.00
CR6 Mo Vaughn	5.00
CR7 Jim Edmonds	3.00
CR9 Sammy Sosa	9.00
CR10 Frank Thomas	6.00
CR11 Albert Belle	6.00
CR12 Manny Ramirez	4.00
CR13 Jim Thome	3.00
CR14 Dante Bichette	3.00
CR15 Vinny Castilla	3.00
CR17 Cecil Fielder	3.00
CR18 Gary Sheffield	3.00
CR19 Jeff Bagwell	7.50
CR20 Eric Karros	3.00
CR21 Mike Piazza	10.00
CR22 Ken Caminiti	3.00
CR23 Barry Bonds	7.50
CR24 Matt Williams	4.00
CR25 Jay Buhner	3.00
CR26 Ken Griffey Jr.	15.00
CR27 Ron Gant	3.00
CR28 Juan Gonzalez	7.50
CR29 Mickey Tettleton	3.00

1996 Collector's Choice Nomo Scrapbook

The five-card, regular-sized set was randomly inserted in 1996 Collector's Choice baseball. Fronts depict the Dodgers pitcher in action with his name in atypical lower-case type up the right border. Backs feature in-depth text below Nomo's name.

	MT
Complete Set (5):	5.00
Common Player:	1.00
1-5 Hideo Nomo	1.00

1996 Collector's Choice Ripken Collection

The 23-card, regular-sized Cal Ripken Collection was randomly inserted in various Upper Deck baseball releases in 1996. Cards #1-4 were found in Series 1 Collector's Choice; cards 5-8 were found in Upper Deck Series 1; cards 9-12 in Collector's Choice Series 2; cards 13-17 in Upper Deck Series 2; cards 18-22 in SP baseball and the header card in Collector's Choice.

	MT
Complete Set (1-4, 9-12)	40.00
Common Card:	4.00
Header Card:	4.00

(See also Upper Deck Series 1 and 2, and Upper Deck/SP)

1996 Collector's Choice Cal Ripken Jr. Jumbo

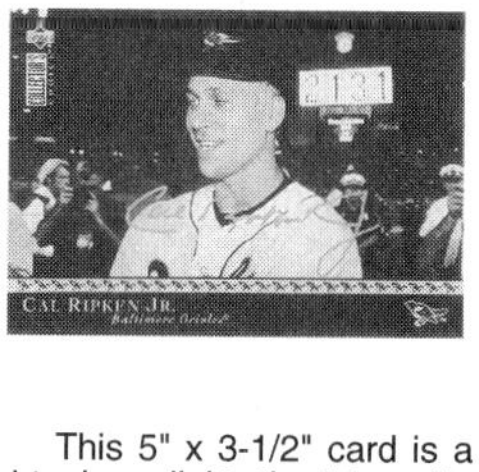

This 5" x 3-1/2" card is a virtual parallel to the #1 card in the multi-brand Ripken set which was issued to mark his career to the point of his 2,131st consecutive game. This version, however, was sold only through a television shopping program. The front has a silver facsimile autograph. On back is a "Limited Edition" seal and a serial number within an edition of 21,310.

	MT
1 Cal Ripken Jr.	7.00

1996 Collector's Choice "You Make the Play"

This insert series of interactive game cards was packaged with Series 1 Collector's Choice. Each player's card can be found with one of two play outcomes printed thereon, which are then used to play a baseball card game utilizing a playing field and scorecard found on box bottoms. Regular versions of the cards are seeded one per pack, while gold-signature versions are found one per 36 packs.

	MT
Complete Set (45):	11.00
Common Player:	.25
Gold version: 8-12X	
1a Kevin Appier (Strike out)	.25
1b Kevin Appier (Pick off)	.25
2a Carlos Baerga (Home run)	.25
2b Carlos Baerga (Ground out)	.25
3a Jeff Bagwell (Walk)	.40
3b Jeff Bagwell (Strike out)	.40
4a Jay Bell (Sacrifice)	.25
4b Jay Bell (Walk)	.25
5a Albert Belle (Fly out)	.75
5b Albert Belle (Home run)	.75
6a Craig Biggio (Single)	.35
6b Craig Biggio (Strike out)	.35
7a Wade Boggs (Single)	.45
7b Wade Boggs (Ground out)	.45
8a Barry Bonds (Strike out)	.60
8b Barry Bonds (Reach on error)	.60
9a Bobby Bonilla (Walk)	.25
9b Bobby Bonilla (Strike out)	.25
10a Jose Canseco (Strike out)	.35
10b Jose Canseco (Double)	.35
11a Joe Carter (Double)	.25
11b Joe Carter (Fly out)	.25
12a Darren Daulton (Ground out)	.25
12b Darren Daulton (Catcher's interference)	.25
13a Cecil Fielder (Stolen base)	.25
13b Cecil Fielder (Home run)	.25
14a Ron Gant (Home run)	.25
14b Ron Gant (Fly out)	.25
15a Juan Gonzalez (Double)	.60
15b Juan Gonzalez (Fly out)	.60
16a Ken Griffey Jr. (Home run)	2.00
16b Ken Griffey Jr. (Hit by pitch)	2.00
17a Tony Gwynn (Single)	.60
17b Tony Gwynn (Ground out)	.60
18a Randy Johnson (Strike out)	.45
18b Randy Johnson (K - reach on wild pitch)	.45
19a Chipper Jones (Walk)	.75
19b Chipper Jones (Strike out)	.75
20a Barry Larkin (Ground out)	.25
20b Barry Larkin (Stolen base)	.25
21a Kenny Lofton (Triple)	.30
21b Kenny Lofton (Stolen base)	.30
22a Greg Maddux (Single)	.50
22b Greg Maddux (Strike out)	.50
23a Don Mattingly (Fly out)	.50
23b Don Mattingly (Double)	.50
24a Fred McGriff (Double)	.30
24b Fred McGriff (Home run)	.30
25a Mark McGwire (Strike out)	1.75
25b Mark McGwire (Home run)	1.75
26a Paul Molitor (Ground out)	.45
26b Paul Molitor (Single)	.45
27a Raul Mondesi (Single)	.35
27b Raul Mondesi (Fly out)	.35
28a Eddie Murray (Sacrifice fly)	.45
28b Eddie Murray (Ground out)	.45
29a Hideo Nomo (Strike out)	.40
29b Hideo Nomo (Balk)	.40
30a Jon Nunnally (Single)	.25
30b Jon Nunnally (Error)	.25
31a Mike Piazza (Strike out)	.75
31b Mike Piazza (Single)	.75
32a Kirby Puckett (Walk)	.45
32b Kirby Puckett (Ground out)	.45
33a Cal Ripken Jr. (Home run)	1.75
33b Cal Ripken Jr. (Double)	1.75
34a Alex Rodriguez (Strike out)	.75
34b Alex Rodriguez (Triple)	.75
35a Tim Salmon (Sacrifice fly)	.35
35b Tim Salmon (Strike out)	.35
36a Gary Sheffield (Fly out)	.25
36b Gary Sheffield (Single)	.25
37a Lee Smith (Strike out)	.25
37b Lee Smith (Pick off of lead runner)	.25
38a Ozzie Smith (Ground out)	.45
38b Ozzie Smith (Single)	.45
39a Sammy Sosa (Stolen base)	1.00
39b Sammy Sosa (Single)	1.00
40a Frank Thomas (Walk)	1.00
40b Frank Thomas (Home run)	1.00
41a Greg Vaughn (Sacrifice fly)	.25
41b Greg Vaughn (Strike out)	.25
42a Mo Vaughn (Hit by Pitch)	.35
42b Mo Vaughn (Stolen base)	.35
43a Larry Walker (Strike out)	.35
43b Larry Walker (Walk)	.35
44a Rondell White (Triple)	.25
44b Rondell White (Fly out)	.25
45a Matt Williams (Home run)	.35
45b Matt Williams (Single)	.35

1997 Collector's Choice

The 246-card, standard-size set contains four subsets: Rookie Class (1-27), Leaders (56-63), Postseason (218-224) and Ken Griffey Jr. Checklists (244-246). Insert sets are: Stick'Ums, Premier Power, Clearly Dominant and The Big Show. Basic card fronts feature a color action shot with the player's name appearing on the bottom edge. The team logo is located in the lower-left corner and each card features a white border. Backs contain another action shot on the upper half with biography, and career/season stats. The cards were issued in 12-card packs retailing for 99 cents.

	MT
Complete Set (506):	30.00
Complete Series 1 Set (246):	15.00
Complete Series 2 Set (260):	18.00
Common Player:	.05
Series 1 Wax Box:	28.00
Series 2 Wax Box:	35.00
1 Andruw Jones (Rookie Class)	1.00
2 Rocky Coppinger (Rookie Class)	.05
3 Jeff D'Amico (Rookie Class)	.05
4 Dmitri Young (Rookie Class)	.05
5 Darin Erstad (Rookie Class)	.75
6 Jermaine Allensworth (Rookie Class)	.05
7 Damian Jackson (Rookie Class)	.05
8 Bill Mueller (Rookie Class)	.10
9 Jacob Cruz (Rookie Class)	.30
10 Vladimir Guerrero (Rookie Class)	.60
11 Marty Janzen (Rookie Class)	.05
12 Kevin L. Brown (Rookie Class)	.05
13 Willie Adams (Rookie Class)	.05
14 Wendell Magee (Rookie Class)	.05
15 Scott Rolen (Rookie Class)	1.00
16 Matt Beech (Rookie Class)	.05
17 Neifi Perez (Rookie Class)	.05
18 Jamey Wright (Rookie Class)	.05
19 Jose Paniagua (Rookie Class)	.05
20 Todd Walker (Rookie Class)	.40
21 Justin Thompson (Rookie Class)	.05
22 Robin Jennings (Rookie Class)	.05
23 *Dario Veras* (Rookie Class)	.05
24 Brian Lesher (Rookie Class)	.05
25 Nomar Garciaparra (Rookie Class)	1.25
26 Luis Castillo (Rookie Class)	.10
27 *Brian Giles* (Rookie Class)	.75
28 Jermaine Dye	.10
29 Terrell Wade	.05
30 Fred McGriff	.25
31 Marquis Grissom	.05
32 Ryan Klesko	.20
33 Javier Lopez	.10
34 Mark Wohlers	.05
35 Tom Glavine	.15
36 Denny Neagle	.05
37 Scott Erickson	.05
38 Chris Hoiles	.05
39 Roberto Alomar	.50
40 Eddie Murray	.30
41 Cal Ripken Jr.	1.75
42 Randy Myers	.05
43 B.J. Surhoff	.05
44 Rick Krivda	.05

45	Jose Canseco	.25
46	Heathcliff Slocumb	.05
47	Jeff Suppan	.05
48	Tom Gordon	.05
49	Aaron Sele	.05
50	Mo Vaughn	.40
51	Darren Bragg	.05
52	Wil Cordero	.05
53	Scott Bullett	.05
54	Terry Adams	.05
55	Jackie Robinson	.05
56	Tony Gwynn, Alex Rodriguez (Batting Leaders)	.50
57	Andres Galarraga, Mark McGwire (Homer Leaders)	.75
58	Andres Galarraga, Albert Belle (RBI Leaders)	.25
59	Eric Young, Kenny Lofton (SB Leaders)	.10
60	John Smoltz, Andy Pettitte (Victory Leaders)	.25
61	John Smoltz, Roger Clemens (Strikout Leaders)	.30
62	Kevin Brown, Juan Guzman (ERA Leaders)	.05
63	John Wetteland, Todd Worrell, Jeff Brantley (Save Leaders)	.05
64	Scott Servais	.05
65	Sammy Sosa	.85
66	Ryne Sandberg	.60
67	Frank Castillo	.05
68	Rey Sanchez	.05
69	Steve Trachsel	.05
70	Robin Ventura	.05
71	Wilson Alvarez	.05
72	Tony Phillips	.05
73	Lyle Mouton	.05
74	Mike Cameron	.05
75	Harold Baines	.05
76	Albert Belle	.50
77	Chris Snopek	.05
78	Reggie Sanders	.05
79	Jeff Brantley	.05
80	Barry Larkin	.15
81	Kevin Jarvis	.05
82	John Smiley	.05
83	Pete Schourek	.05
84	Thomas Howard	.05
85	Lee Smith	.05
86	Omar Vizquel	.05
87	Julio Franco	.05
88	Orel Hershiser	.05
89	Charles Nagy	.05
90	Matt Williams	.20
91	Dennis Martinez	.05
92	Jose Mesa	.05
93	Sandy Alomar Jr.	.05
94	Jim Thome	.20
95	Vinny Castilla	.05
96	Armando Reynoso	.05
97	Kevin Ritz	.05
98	Larry Walker	.20
99	Eric Young	.05
100	Dante Bichette	.15
101	Quinton McCracken	.05
102	John Vander Wal	.05
103	Phil Nevin	.05
104	Tony Clark	.40
105	Alan Trammell	.05
106	Felipe Lira	.05
107	Curtis Pride	.05
108	Bobby Higginson	.05
109	Mark Lewis	.05
110	Travis Fryman	.05
111	Al Leiter	.05
112	Devon White	.05
113	Jeff Conine	.05
114	Charles Johnson	.05
115	Andre Dawson	.05
116	Edgar Renteria	.20
117	Robb Nen	.05
118	Kevin Brown	.05
119	Derek Bell	.05
120	Bob Abreu	.05
121	Mike Hampton	.05
122	Todd Jones	.05
123	Billy Wagner	.15
124	Shane Reynolds	.05
125	Jeff Bagwell	1.00
126	Brian L. Hunter	.05
127	Jeff Montgomery	.05
128	*Rod Myers*	.05
129	Tim Belcher	.05
130	Kevin Appier	.05
131	Mike Sweeney	.05
132	Craig Paquette	.05
133	Joe Randa	.05
134	Michael Tucker	.05
135	Raul Mondesi	.20
136	Tim Wallach	.05
137	Brett Butler	.05
138	Karim Garcia	.35
139	Todd Hollandsworth	.10
140	Eric Karros	.05
141	Hideo Nomo	.25
142	Ismael Valdes	.05
143	Cal Eldred	.05
144	Scott Karl	.05
145	Matt Mieske	.05
146	Mike Fetters	.05
147	Mark Loretta	.05
148	Fernando Vina	.05
149	Jeff Cirillo	.05
150	Dave Nilsson	.05
151	Kirby Puckett	1.00
152	Rich Becker	.05
153	Chuck Knoblauch	.15
154	Marty Cordova	.05
155	Paul Molitor	.35
156	Rick Aguilera	.05
157	Pat Meares	.05
158	Frank Rodriguez	.05
159	David Segui	.05
160	Henry Rodriguez	.05
161	Shane Andrews	.05
162	Pedro J. Martinez	.05
163	Mark Grudzielanek	.05
164	Mike Lansing	.05
165	Rondell White	.05
166	Ugueth Urbina	.05
167	Rey Ordonez	.20
168	Robert Person	.05
169	Carlos Baerga	.05
170	Bernard Gilkey	.05
171	John Franco	.05
172	Pete Harnisch	.05
173	Butch Huskey	.05
174	Paul Wilson	.10
175	Bernie Williams	.25
176	Dwight Gooden	.05
177	Wade Boggs	.25
178	Ruben Rivera	.10
179	Jim Leyritz	.05
180	Derek Jeter	1.00
181	Tino Martinez	.15
182	Tim Raines	.05
183	Scott Brosius	.05
184	Jason Giambi	.15
185	Geronimo Berroa	.05
186	Ariel Prieto	.05
187	Scott Spiezio	.05
188	John Wasdin	.05
189	Ernie Young	.05
190	Mark McGwire	2.50
191	Jim Eisenreich	.05
192	Ricky Bottalico	.05
193	Darren Daulton	.05
194	David Doster	.05
195	Gregg Jefferies	.05
196	Lenny Dykstra	.05
197	Curt Schilling	.05
198	Todd Stottlemyre	.05
199	Willie McGee	.05
200	Ozzie Smith	.35
201	Dennis Eckersley	.05
202	Ray Lankford	.05
203	John Mabry	.05
204	Alan Benes	.05
205	Ron Gant	.10
206	Archi Cianfrocco	.05
207	Fernando Valenzuela	.05
208	Greg Vaughn	.05
209	Steve Finley	.05
210	Tony Gwynn	.75
211	Rickey Henderson	.05
212	Trevor Hoffman	.05
213	Jason Thompson	.05
214	Osvaldo Fernandez	.05
215	Glenallen Hill	.05
216	William VanLandingham	.05
217	Marvin Benard	.05
218	Juan Gonzalez (Postseason)	.40
219	Roberto Alomar (Postseason)	.25
220	Brian Jordan (Postseason)	.05
221	John Smoltz (Postseason)	.15
222	Javy Lopez (Postseason)	.05
223	Bernie Williams (Postseason)	.15
224	Jim Leyritz, John Wetteland (Postseason)	.05
225	Barry Bonds	.60
226	Rich Aurilia	.05
227	Jay Canizaro	.05
228	Dan Wilson	.05
229	Bob Wolcott	.05
230	Ken Griffey Jr.	2.00
231	Sterling Hitchcock	.05
232	Edgar Martinez	.05
233	Joey Cora	.05
234	Norm Charlton	.05
235	Alex Rodriguez	1.50
236	Bobby Witt	.05
237	Darren Oliver	.05
238	Kevin Elster	.05
239	Rusty Greer	.05
240	Juan Gonzalez	1.00
241	Will Clark	.20
242	Dean Palmer	.05
243	Ivan Rodriguez	.30
244	Checklist (Ken Griffey Jr.)	.50
245	Checklist (Ken Griffey Jr.)	.50
246	Checklist (Ken Griffey Jr.)	.50
247	Checklist (Ken Griffey Jr.)	.50
248	Checklist (Ken Griffey Jr.)	.50
249	Checklist (Ken Griffey Jr.)	.50
250	Eddie Murray	.25
251	Troy Percival	.05
252	Garret Anderson	.05
253	Allen Watson	.05
254	Jason Dickson	.15
255	Jim Edmonds	.10
256	Chuck Finley	.05
257	Randy Velarde	.05
258	Shigetosi Hasegawa	.05
259	Todd Greene	.05
260	Tim Salmon	.20
261	Mark Langston	.05
262	Dave Hollins	.05
263	Gary DiSarcina	.05
264	Kenny Lofton	.40
265	John Smoltz	.15
266	Greg Maddux	1.00
267	Jeff Blauser	.05
268	Alan Embree	.05
269	Mark Lemke	.05
270	Chipper Jones	1.25
271	Mike Mussina	.35
272	Rafael Palmeiro	.15
273	Jimmy Key	.05
274	Mike Bordick	.05
275	Brady Anderson	.10
276	Eric Davis	.05
277	Jeffrey Hammonds	.05
278	Reggie Jefferson	.05
279	Tim Naehring	.05
280	John Valentin	.05
281	Troy O'Leary	.05
282	Shane Mack	.05
283	Mike Stanley	.05
284	Tim Wakefield	.05
285	Brian McRae	.05
286	Brooks Kieschnick	.05
287	Shawon Dunston	.05
288	Kevin Foster	.05
289	Mel Rojas	.05
290	Mark Grace	.15
291	Brant Brown	.05
292	Amaury Telemaco	.05
293	Dave Martinez	.05
294	Jaime Navarro	.05
295	Ray Durham	.05
296	Ozzie Guillen	.05
297	Roberto Hernandez	.05
298	Ron Karkovice	.05
299	James Baldwin	.05
300	Frank Thomas	1.00
301	Eddie Taubensee	.05
302	Bret Boone	.05
303	Willie Greene	.05
304	Dave Burba	.05
305	Deion Sanders	.15
306	Reggie Sanders	.05
307	Hal Morris	.05
308	Pokey Reese	.05
309	Tony Fernandez	.05
310	Manny Ramirez	.65
311	Chad Ogea	.05
312	Jack McDowell	.05
313	Kevin Mitchell	.05
314	Chad Curtis	.05
315	Steve Kline	.05
316	Kevin Seitzer	.05
317	Kirt Manwaring	.05
318	Bill Swift	.05
319	Ellis Burks	.05
320	Andres Galarraga	.10
321	Bruce Ruffin	.05
322	Mark Thompson	.05
323	Walt Weiss	.05
324	Todd Jones	.05
325	Andruw Jones (Griffey Hot List)	.50
326	Chipper Jones (Griffey Hot List)	.60
327	Mo Vaughn (Griffey Hot List)	.15
328	Frank Thomas (Griffey Hot List)	.50
329	Albert Belle (Griffey Hot List)	.30
330	Mark McGwire (Griffey Hot List)	1.00
331	Derek Jeter (Griffey Hot List)	.65
332	Alex Rodriguez (Griffey Hot List)	1.00
333	Juan Gonzalez (Griffey Hot List)	.50
334	Ken Griffey Jr. (Griffey Hot List)	1.00
335	Brian L. Hunter	.05
336	Brian Johnson	.05
337	Omar Olivares	.05
338	*Deivi Cruz*	.05
339	Damion Easley	.05
340	Melvin Nieves	.05
341	Moises Alou	.05
342	Jim Eisenreich	.05
343	Mark Hutton	.05
344	Alex Fernandez	.05
345	Gary Sheffield	.15
346	Pat Rapp	.05
347	Brad Ausmus	.05
348	Sean Berry	.05
349	Darryl Kile	.05
350	Craig Biggio	.10
351	Chris Holt	.05
352	Luis Gonzalez	.05
353	Pat Listach	.05
354	Jose Rosado	.05
355	Mike Macfarlane	.05
356	Tom Goodwin	.05
357	Chris Haney	.05
358	Chili Davis	.05
359	Jose Offerman	.05
360	Johnny Damon	.05
361	Bip Roberts	.05
362	Ramon Martinez	.05
363	Pedro Astacio	.05
364	Todd Zeile	.05
365	Mike Piazza	1.25
366	Greg Gagne	.05
367	Chan Ho Park	.05
368	Wilton Guerrero	.10
369	Todd Worrell	.05
370	John Jaha	.05
371	Steve Sparks	.05
372	Mike Matheny	.05
373	Marc Newfield	.05
374	Jeromy Burnitz	.05
375	Jose Valentin	.05
376	Ben McDonald	.05
377	Roberto Kelly	.05
378	Bob Tewksbury	.05
379	Ron Coomer	.05
380	Brad Radke	.05
381	Matt Lawton	.05
382	Dan Naulty	.05
383	Scott Stahoviak	.05
384	Matt Wagner	.05
385	Jim Bullinger	.05
386	Carlos Perez	.05
387	Darrin Fletcher	.05
388	Chris Widger	.05
389	F.P. Santangelo	.05
390	Lee Smith	.05
391	Bobby Jones	.05
392	John Olerud	.05
393	Mark Clark	.05
394	Jason Isringhausen	.05
395	Todd Hundley	.15
396	Lance Johnson	.05
397	Edgardo Alfonzo	.10
398	Alex Ochoa	.05
399	Darryl Strawberry	.10
400	David Cone	.15
401	Paul O'Neill	.10
402	Joe Girardi	.05
403	Charlie Hayes	.05
404	Andy Pettitte	.40
405	Mariano Rivera	.15
406	Mariano Duncan	.05
407	Kenny Rogers	.05
408	Cecil Fielder	.05
409	George Williams	.05
410	Jose Canseco	.25
411	Tony Batista	.05
412	Steve Karsay	.05
413	Dave Telgheder	.05
414	Billy Taylor	.05
415	Mickey Morandini	.05
416	Calvin Maduro	.05
417	Mark Leiter	.05
418	Kevin Stocker	.05
419	Mike Lieberthal	.05
420	Rico Brogna	.05
421	Mark Portugal	.05
422	Rex Hudler	.05
423	Mark Johnson	.05
424	Esteban Loiaza	.05
425	Lou Collier	.05
426	Kevin Elster	.05
427	Francisco Cordova	.05
428	Marc Wilkins	.05
429	Joe Randa	.05
430	Jason Kendall	.05
431	Jon Lieber	.05
432	Steve Cooke	.05
433	*Emil Brown*	.10
434	*Tony Womack*	.25
435	Al Martin	.05
436	Jason Schmidt	.05
437	Andy Benes	.05
438	Delino DeShields	.05
439	Royce Clayton	.05
440	Brian Jordan	.05
441	Donovan Osborne	.05
442	Gary Gaetti	.05
443	Tom Pagnozzi	.05
444	Joey Hamilton	.05
445	Wally Joyner	.05
446	John Flaherty	.05
447	Chris Gomez	.05
448	Sterling Hitchcock	.05
449	Andy Ashby	.05
450	Ken Caminiti	.15
451	Tim Worrell	.05
452	Jose Vizcaino	.05
453	Rod Beck	.05
454	Wilson Delgado	.05
455	Darryl Hamilton	.05
456	Mark Lewis	.05
457	Mark Gardner	.05
458	Rick Wilkins	.05
459	Scott Sanders	.05
460	Kevin Orie	.05
461	Glendon Rusch	.05
462	Juan Melo	.05
463	Richie Sexson	.10
464	Bartolo Colon	.05
465	Jose Guillen	.50
466	Heath Murray	.05
467	Aaron Boone	.05
468	*Bubba Trammell*	.40
469	Jeff Abbott	.05
470	Derrick Gibson	.15
471	Matt Morris	.15
472	Ryan Jones	.05
473	Pat Cline	.05
474	Adam Riggs	.05
475	Jay Payton	.05
476	Derrek Lee	.15
477	Elieser Marrero	.05
478	Lee Tinsley	.05
479	Jamie Moyer	.05
480	Jay Buhner	.10
481	Bob Wells	.05
482	Jeff Fassero	.05
483	Paul Sorrento	.05
484	Russ Davis	.05
485	Randy Johnson	.40
486	Roger Pavlik	.05
487	Damon Buford	.05
488	Julio Santana	.05
489	Mark McLemore	.05
490	Mickey Tettleton	.05
491	Ken Hill	.05
492	Benji Gil	.05
493	Ed Sprague	.05
494	Mike Timlin	.05
495	Pat Hentgen	.05
496	Orlando Merced	.05
497	Carlos Garcia	.05
498	Carlos Delgado	.25
499	Juan Guzman	.05
500	Roger Clemens	.75
501	Erik Hanson	.05
502	Otis Nixon	.05
503	Shawn Green	.05
504	Charlie O'Brien	.05
505	Joe Carter	.10
506	Alex Gonzalez	.05

1997 Collector's Choice All-Star Connection

This 45-card insert from Series 2 highlights All-Star caliber players. Cards feature a large starburst pattern on a metallic-foil background behind the player's photo. They were inserted one per pack.

		MT
Complete Set (45):		9.00
Common Player:		.10
1	Mark McGwire	1.50
2	Chuck Knoblauch	.10
3	Jim Thome	.20
4	Alex Rodriguez	1.25
5	Ken Griffey Jr.	1.50
6	Brady Anderson	.10
7	Albert Belle	.40
8	Ivan Rodriguez	.25
9	Pat Hentgen	.10
10	Frank Thomas	.65
11	Roberto Alomar	.20
12	Robin Ventura	.15
13	Cal Ripken Jr.	1.20
14	Juan Gonzalez	.50
15	Manny Ramirez	.40
16	Bernie Williams	.20
17	Terry Steinbach	.10
18	Andy Pettitte	.25
19	Jeff Bagwell	.50
20	Craig Biggio	.10
21	Ken Caminiti	.10
22	Barry Larkin	.10
23	Tony Gwynn	.45
24	Barry Bonds	.30
25	Kenny Lofton	.25
26	Mike Piazza	.75
27	John Smoltz	.15
28	Andres Galarraga	.10
29	Ryne Sandberg	.25
30	Chipper Jones	.75
31	Mark Grudzielanek	.10
32	Sammy Sosa	.75
.3	Steve Finley	.10
34	Gary Sheffield	.15
35	Todd Hundley	.10
36	Greg Maddux	.65
37	Mo Vaughn	.25
38	Eric Young	.10
39	Vinny Castilla	.10
40	Derek Jeter	.75
41	Lance Johnson	.10
42	Ellis Burks	.10
43	Dante Bichette	.10
44	Javy Lopez	.10
45	Hideo Nomo	.20

1997 Collector's Choice Big Shots

This 20-card insert depicts the game's top stars in unique photos. Cards were inserted 1:12 packs. Gold Signature Editions, featuring a gold foil-stamped facsimile autograph, were inserted 1:144 packs. Fronts are highlighted in silver foil. Backs repeat a portion of the front photo, have a picture of the photographer and his comments about the picture.

		MT
Complete Set (19):		45.00
Common Player:		.50
Gold Signature Edition: 2-3X		
1	Ken Griffey Jr.	8.00
2	Nomar Garciaparra	4.50
3	Brian Jordan	.50
4	Scott Rolen	3.00
5	Alex Rodriguez	6.00
6	Larry Walker	.75
7	Mariano Rivera	.50
8	Cal Ripken Jr.	6.00
9	Deion Sanders	.50
10	Frank Thomas	2.50
11	Dean Palmer	.50
12	Ken Caminiti	.50
13	Derek Jeter	4.50
14	Barry Bonds	2.50
15	Chipper Jones	4.50
16	Mo Vaughn	.50
17	Jay Buhner	.50
18	Mike Piazza	6.00
19	Tony Gwynn	3.00

1997 Collector's Choice Big Show

The 45-card, regular-sized set was inserted one per pack of Series 1. Backs feature player comments written by ESPN SportsCenter hosts Keith Olbermann and Dan Patrick, whose portraits appear both front and back. On front, printed on metallic foil, is an action shot of the player, with his name printed along the left border of the horizontal cards. The cards are numbered "X/45." A parallel set to this chase card series carries a gold-foil "World Headquarters Edition" seal at lower-right and was a 1:35 insert.

		MT
Complete Set (45):		10.00
Common Player:		.25
World Headquarters: 8-15X		
1	Greg Maddux	1.00
2	Chipper Jones	1.00
3	Andruw Jones	.50
4	John Smoltz	.35
5	Cal Ripken Jr.	2.00
6	Roberto Alomar	.50
7	Rafael Palmeiro	.35
8	Eddie Murray	.50
9	Jose Canseco	.35
10	Roger Clemens	.60
11	Mo Vaughn	.50
12	Jim Edmonds	.25
13	Tim Salmon	.25
14	Sammy Sosa	1.50
15	Albert Belle	.50
16	Frank Thomas	1.50
17	Barry Larkin	.25
18	Kenny Lofton	.35
19	Manny Ramirez	.50
20	Matt Williams	.40
21	Dante Bichette	.25
22	Gary Sheffield	.25
23	Craig Biggio	.25
24	Jeff Bagwell	1.00
25	Todd Hollandsworth	.25
26	Raul Mondesi	.25
27	Hideo Nomo	.25
28	Mike Piazza	1.00
29	Paul Molitor	.75
30	Kirby Puckett	1.00
31	Rondell White	.25
32	Rey Ordonez	.25
33	Paul Wilson	.25
34	Derek Jeter	2.00
35	Andy Pettitte	.35
36	Mark McGwire	3.00
37	Jason Kendall	.25
38	Ozzie Smith	.75
39	Tony Gwynn	1.00
40	Barry Bonds	.75
41	Alex Rodriguez	2.00
42	Jay Buhner	.25
43	Ken Griffey Jr.	3.00
44	Randy Johnson	.40
45	Juan Gonzalez	1.00

1997 Collector's Choice Big Show World HQ parallel

The 45-card chase set in Series 2 is also found in a special parallel version which carries a "World Headquarters Edition" gold-foil seal on front at the lower-right.

	MT
Complete Set (45):	150.00
Common Player:	1.00
(Star cards valued at 4X-8X regular Big Show version)	

1997 Collector's Choice Clearly Dominant

The five-card, regular-sized set features Seattle outfielder Ken Griffey Jr. on each card and was inserted every 144 packs of 1997 Collector's Choice baseball.

		MT
Complete Set (5):		40.00
Common Card:		10.00
CD1	Ken Griffey Jr.	12.00
CD2	Ken Griffey Jr.	12.00
CD3	Ken Griffey Jr.	12.00
CD4	Ken Griffey Jr.	12.00
CD5	Ken Griffey Jr.	12.00

Checklists with card numbers in parentheses ( ) indicates the numbers do not appear on the card.

1997 Collector's Choice Clearly Dominant Jumbos

Each of the five Ken Griffey Jr. cards from the Collector's Choice insert set was also produced in a special retail-only 5" x 3-1/2" jumbo version. The supersize Clearly Dominant cards were packaged in a special collectors' kit which also included a Griffey stand-up figure and eight packs of CC cards, retailing for about $15. The cards could also be purchased as a complete set for $10. Cards are numbered with a "CD" prefix.

		MT
Complete Set (5):		10.00
Common Card:		2.00
1	Ken Griffey Jr.	2.00
2	Ken Griffey Jr.	2.00
3	Ken Griffey Jr.	2.00
4	Ken Griffey Jr.	2.00
5	Ken Griffey Jr.	2.00

1997 Collector's Choice Hot List Jumbos

These 5" x 7" versions of the "Ken Griffey Jr.'s Hot List" subset from Series 1 are an exclusive box-topper in certain retail packaging of Series 2 Collector's Choice. Other than size, the jumbos are identical to the regular Hot List cards, including foil background printing on front.

		MT
Complete Set (10):		30.00
Common Player:		2.00
325	Andruw Jones	2.50
326	Chipper Jones	4.00
327	Mo Vaughn	2.00
328	Frank Thomas	2.50
329	Albert Belle	2.00
330	Mark McGwire	6.00
331	Derek Jeter	4.00
332	Alex Rodriguez	4.50
333	Juan Gonzalez	3.00
334	Ken Griffey Jr.	6.00

1997 Collector's Choice New Frontier

This is a 40-card Series 2 insert highlighting anticipated interleague matchups. Cards were designed with each player's action photo superimposed on a metallic-foil background depicting half of a ball field. Pairs could then be displayed side-by-side. Cards were inserted 1:69 packs. They are numbered and carry an "NF" prefix.

		MT
Complete Set (40):		250.00
Common Player:		2.50
1	Alex Rodriguez	20.00
2	Tony Gwynn	9.00
3	Jose Canseco	5.00
4	Hideo Nomo	2.50
5	Mark McGwire	30.00
6	Barry Bonds	5.00
7	Juan Gonzalez	12.50
8	Ken Caminiti	2.50
9	Tim Salmon	4.00
10	Mike Piazza	12.50
11	Ken Griffey Jr.	30.00
12	Andres Galarraga	2.50
13	Jay Buhner	2.50
14	Dante Bichette	2.50
15	Frank Thomas	10.00
16	Ryne Sandberg	5.00
17	Roger Clemens	7.50
18	Andruw Jones	4.00
19	Jim Thome	2.50
20	Sammy Sosa	10.00
21	David Justice	2.50
22	Deion Sanders	2.50
23	Todd Walker	2.50
24	Kevin Orie	2.50
25	Albert Belle	5.00
26	Jeff Bagwell	7.50
27	Manny Ramirez	6.00
28	Brian Jordan	2.50
29	Derek Jeter	20.00
30	Chipper Jones	15.00
31	Mo Vaughn	5.00
32	Gary Sheffield	2.50
33	Carlos Delgado	2.50
34	Vladimir Guerrero	4.00
35	Cal Ripken Jr.	20.00
36	Greg Maddux	10.00
37	Cecil Fielder	2.50
38	Todd Hundley	2.50
39	Mike Mussina	4.00
40	Scott Rolen	5.00

1997 Collector's Choice Premier Power

The 20-card, regular-sized set was included one per 15 packs of Series 1. Fronts feature an action photo with the "Premier Power" logo in silver foil in the lower half and "spotlights" aiming out toward the sides. The bottom portion of the card is transparent red. Backs are bordered in red with the same card front shot appearing in black-and-white above a brief description and "Power Facts." The cards are numbered with a "PP" prefix. A parallel gold-foil version was available every 69 packs.

		MT
Complete Set (20):		35.00
Common Player:		.50
Gold: 3-4X		
1	Mark McGwire	9.00
2	Brady Anderson	.50
3	Ken Griffey Jr.	9.00
4	Albert Belle	2.00
5	Juan Gonzalez	3.50
6	Andres Galarraga	.50
7	Jay Buhner	.50
8	Mo Vaughn	2.00
9	Barry Bonds	2.00
10	Gary Sheffield	.50
11	Todd Hundley	.50
12	Frank Thomas	3.00
13	Sammy Sosa	5.00
14	Ken Caminiti	.50
15	Vinny Castilla	.50
16	Ellis Burks	.50
17	Rafael Palmeiro	.50
18	Alex Rodriguez	6.00
19	Mike Piazza	5.00
20	Eddie Murray	1.00

1997 Collector's Choice Premier Power Jumbo

Each factory set of 1997 Collector's Choice included 10 super-size (3" x 5") versions of the Premier Power inserts. Besides the size, the jumbos differ from the insert version in the addition of a metallic facsimile autograph on front.

		MT
Complete Set (20):		20.00
Common Player:		.50
1	Mark McGwire	5.00
2	Brady Anderson	.50
3	Ken Griffey Jr.	5.00
4	Albert Belle	.50
5	Juan Gonzalez	2.00
6	Andres Galarraga	.50
7	Jay Buhner	.50
8	Mo Vaughn	1.00
9	Barry Bonds	1.00
10	Gary Sheffield	.50
11	Todd Hundley	.50
12	Frank Thomas	1.50
13	Sammy Sosa	2.50
14	Ken Caminiti	.50
15	Vinny Castilla	.50
16	Ellis Burks	.50
17	Rafael Palmeiro	.50
18	Alex Rodriguez	3.00
19	Mike Piazza	2.50
20	Eddie Murray	.50

1997 Collector's Choice Stick'Ums

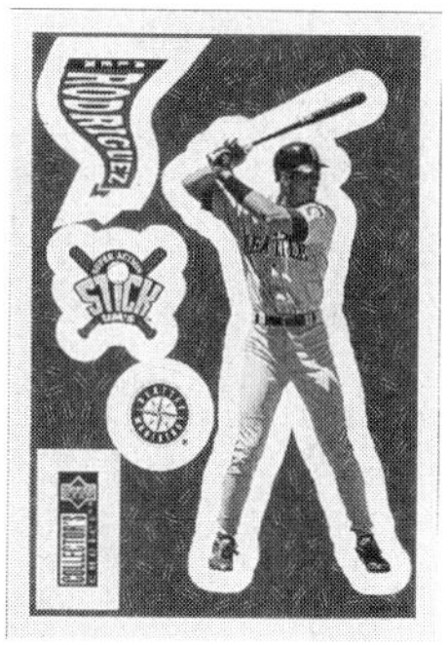

The 30-piece 2-1/2" x 3-1/2" sticker set was inserted one per three packs of Series 1 Collector's Choice. Fronts feature a bright background color and include five different peel-off stickers: An action shot of the player, a pennant in team colors featuring the player's name, a team logo, an Upper Deck Collector's Choice logo and a "Super Action Stick'Ums" decal. Backs feature the player checklist in black ink over a gray background. An unnumbered version of the stickers (without Smith and Puckett) was sold in a special retail-only package.

		MT
Complete Set (30):		20.00
Common Player:		.25
1	Ozzie Smith	.75
2	Andruw Jones	1.00
3	Alex Rodriguez	2.00
4	Paul Molitor	.50
5	Jeff Bagwell	1.25
6	Manny Ramirez	1.00
7	Kenny Lofton	.50
8	Albert Belle	.75

9	Jay Buhner	.25
10	Chipper Jones	1.50
11	Barry Larkin	.25
12	Dante Bichette	.25
13	Mike Piazza	1.50
14	Andres Galarraga	.25
15	Barry Bonds	.75
16	Brady Anderson	.25
17	Gary Sheffield	.25
18	Jim Thome	.25
19	Tony Gwynn	1.25
20	Cal Ripken Jr.	2.50
21	Sammy Sosa	1.50
22	Juan Gonzalez	1.00
23	Greg Maddux	1.00
24	Ken Griffey Jr.	3.00
25	Mark McGwire	3.00
26	Kirby Puckett	1.00
27	Mo Vaughn	.40
28	Vladimir Guerrero	.60
29	Ken Caminiti	.25
30	Frank Thomas	1.50

1997 Collector's Choice Team Sets

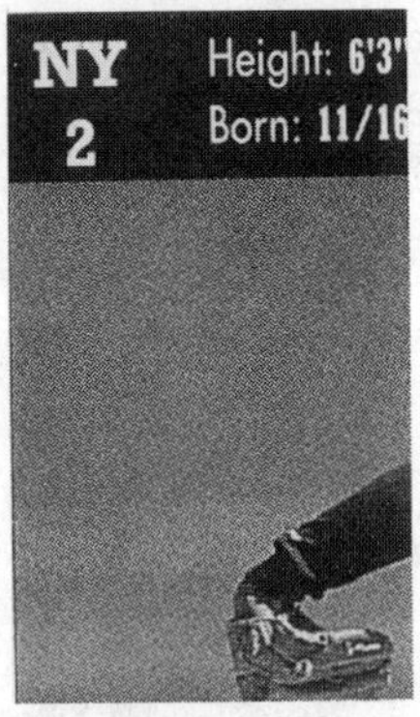

A special version of Collector's Choice cards for several popular major league teams was produced in two retail packages by Upper Deck. In one version, blister packs containing 13 player cards and a metallic-foil team logo/checklist card was sold for a suggested retail price of $1.99. The second version, exclusive to Wal-Mart, is a hard plastic blister pack containing two cello-wrapped packages. One holds a random assortment of 15 Series 1 Collector's Choice cards. The other has 13 player cards and a foil logo/checklist card for a specific team. The team-set cards are identical to the regular-issue cards, from either Series 1 or Series 2, except each of the team-set cards has a number on back which differs from the regular edition. Packaged with the Wal-Mart version is a 3-1/2" x 5" "Home Team Heroes" card, listed seperately.

		MT
	Common Player:	.10
	Atlanta Braves team set:	4.00
AB	Team logo/checklist	.10
AB1	Andruw Jones	1.00
AB2	Kenny Lofton	.30
AB3	Fred McGriff	.20
AB4	Michael Tucker	.10
AB5	Ryan Klesko	.20
AB6	Javy Lopez	.15
AB7	Mark Wohlers	.10
AB8	Tom Glavine	.20
AB9	Denny Neagle	.10
AB10	Chipper Jones	1.25
AB11	Jeff Blauser	.10
AB12	Greg Maddux	1.00
AB13	John Smoltz	.20
	Baltimore Orioles team set:	2.00
BO	Team logo/checklist	.10
BO1	Rocky Coppinger	.10
BO2	Scott Erickson	.10
BO3	Chris Hoiles	.10
BO4	Roberto Alomar	.40
BO5	Cal Ripken Jr.	1.50
BO6	Randy Myers	.10
BO7	B.J. Surhoff	.10
BO8	Mike Mussina	.35
BO9	Rafael Palmeiro	.30
BO10	Jimmy Key	.10
BO11	Mike Bordick	.10
BO12	Brady Anderson	.20
BO13	Eric Davis	.10
	Chicago White Sox team set:	2.50
CW	Team logo/checklist	.10
CW1	Robin Ventura	.10
CW2	Wilson Alvarez	.10
CW3	Tony Phillips	.10
CW4	Lyle Mouton	.10
CW5	James Baldwin	.10
CW6	Harold Baines	.10
CW7	Albert Belle	.75
CW8	Chris Snopek	.10
CW9	Ray Durham	.10
CW10	Frank Thomas	1.00
CW11	Ozzie Guillen	.10
CW12	Roberto Hernandez	.10
CW13	Jaime Navarro	.10
	Cleveland Indians team set:	1.50
CI	Team logo/checklist	.10
CI1	Brian Giles	.10
CI2	Omar Vizquel	.10
CI3	Julio Franco	.10
CI4	Orel Hershiser	.10
CI5	Charles Nagy	.10
CI6	Matt Williams	.20
CI7	Jose Mesa	.10
CI8	Sandy Alomar	.20
CI9	Jim Thome	.35
CI10	David Justice	.25
CI11	Marquis Grissom	.15
CI12	Chad Ogea	.10
CI13	Manny Ramirez	.65
	Colorado Rockies team set:	1.25
CR	Team logo/checklist	.10
CR1	Dante Bichette	.20
CR2	Vinny Castilla	.10
CR3	Kevin Ritz	.10
CR4	Larry Walker	.30
CR5	Eric Young	.10
CR6	Quinton McCracken	.10
CR7	John Vander Wal	.10
CR8	Jamey Wright	.10
CR9	Mark Thompson	.10
CR10	Andres Galarraga	.25
CR11	Ellis Burks	.10
CR12	Kirt Manwaring	.10
CR13	Walt Weiss	.10
	Florida Marlins team set:	2.00
FM	Team logo/checklist	.10
FM1	(Luis Castillo)	.10
FM2	(Al Leiter)	.15
FM3	(Devon White)	.15
FM4	(Jeff Conine)	.10
FM5	(Charles Johnson)	.15
FM6	(Edgar Renteria)	.20
FM7	(Robb Nen)	.10
FM8	(Kevin Brown)	.50
FM9	(Gary Sheffield)	.25
FM10	(Alex Fernandez)	.15
FM11	(Pat Rapp)	.10
FM12	(Moises Alou)	.25
FM13	(Bobby Bonilla)	.10
	L.A. Dodgers team set:	3.00
LA	Team logo/checklist	.10
LA1	(Raul Mondesi)	.35
LA2	(Brett Butler)	.10
LA3	(Todd Hollandsworth)	.10
LA4	(Eric Karros)	.10
LA5	(Hideo Nomo)	.50
LA6	(Ismael Valdes)	.15
LA7	(Wilton Guerrero)	.10
LA8	(Ramon Martinez)	.15
LA9	(Greg Gagne)	.10
LA10	(Mike Piazza)	1.00
LA11	(Chan Ho Park)	.35
LA12	(Todd Worrell)	.10
LA13	(Todd Zeile)	.10
	New York Yankees team set:	3.00
NY	Team logo/checklist	.10
NY1	Bernie Williams	.35
NY2	Dwight Gooden	.15
NY3	Wade Boggs	.35
NY4	Ruben Rivera	.15
NY5	Derek Jeter	1.25
NY6	Tino Martinez	.15
NY7	Tim Raines	.10
NY8	Joe Girardi	.10
NY9	Charlie Hayes	.10
NY10	Andy Pettitte	.35
NY11	Cecil Fielder	.15
NY12	Paul O'Neill	.20
NY13	David Cone	.20
	Seattle Mariners team set:	3.00
SM	Team logo/checklist	.10
SM1	Dan Wilson	.10
SM2	Ken Griffey Jr.	2.00
SM3	Edgar Martinez	.10
SM4	Joey Cora	.10
SM5	Norm Charlton	.10
SM6	Alex Rodriguez	1.50
SM7	Randy Johnson	.40
SM8	Paul Sorrento	.10
SM9	Jamie Moyer	.10
SM10	Jay Buhner	.10
SM11	Russ Davis	.10
SM12	Jeff Fassero	.10
SM13	Bob Wells	.10
	Texas Rangers team set:	3.00
TR	Team logo/checklist	.10
TR1	Bobby Witt	.10
TR2	Darren Oliver	.10
TR3	Rusty Greer	.10
TR4	Juan Gonzalez	1.00
TR5	Will Clark	.40
TR6	Dean Palmer	.10
TR7	Ivan Rodriguez	.60
TR8	John Wetteland	.10
TR9	Mark McLemore	.10
TR10	John Burkett	.10
TR11	Benji Gil	.10
TR12	Ken Hill	.10
TR13	Mickey Tettleton	.10

1997 Collector's Choice Toast of the Town

This 30-card Series 2 insert features top stars on foil-enhanced cards. Odds of finding one are 1:35 packs. Cards are numbered with a "T" prefix.

		MT
	Complete Set (30):	120.00
	Common Player:	1.00
1	Andruw Jones	4.00
2	Chipper Jones	7.50
3	Greg Maddux	6.00
4	John Smoltz	1.00
5	Kenny Lofton	2.00
6	Brady Anderson	1.00
7	Cal Ripken Jr.	12.00
8	Mo Vaughn	2.00
9	Sammy Sosa	7.50
10	Albert Belle	2.00
11	Frank Thomas	4.00
12	Barry Larkin	1.00
13	Manny Ramirez	4.00
14	Jeff Bagwell	5.00
15	Mike Piazza	7.50
16	Paul Molitor	2.00
17	Vladimir Guerrero	3.00
18	Todd Hundley	1.00
19	Derek Jeter	7.50
20	Andy Pettitte	1.00
21	Bernie Williams	1.00
22	Mark McGwire	15.00
23	Scott Rolen	5.00
24	Ken Caminiti	1.00
25	Tony Gwynn	5.00
26	Barry Bonds	3.00
27	Ken Griffey Jr.	15.00
28	Alex Rodriguez	12.50
29	Juan Gonzalez	5.00
30	Roger Clemens	3.00

1997 Collector's Choice Update

This update set was offered via a mail-in redemption offer. Traded players in their new uniforms and 1997 rookies are the focus of the set. Fronts are color photos which are borderless at top and sides. Beneath each photo the player's name and team logo appear in a red (A.L.) or blue (N.L.) baseball design. Backs have another photo, major and minor league career stats and a trivia question. Cards are numbered with a "U" prefix.

		MT
	Complete Set (30):	5.00
	Common Player:	.15
1	Jim Leyritz	.15
2	Matt Perisho	.15
3	Michael Tucker	.15
4	Mike Johnson	.15
5	Jaime Navarro	.15
6	Doug Drabek	.15
7	Terry Mulholland	.35
8	Brett Tomko	.15
9	Marquis Grissom	.40
10	David Justice	.40
11	Brian Moehler	.15
12	Bobby Bonilla	.30
13	Todd Dunwoody	.40
14	Tony Saunders	.15
15	Jay Bell	.15
16	Jeff King	.15
17	Terry Steinbach	.15
18	Steve Bieser	.15
19	*Takashi Kashiwada*	.40
20	Hideki Irabu	1.00
21	Damon Mashore	.15
22	Quilvio Veras	.15
23	Will Cunnane	.15
24	Jeff Kent	.35
25	J.T. Snow	.40
26	Dante Powell	.15
27	Jose Cruz Jr.	.50
28	John Burkett	.15
29	John Wetteland	.15
30	Benito Santiago	.15

1997 Collector's Choice You Crash the Game

A 30-card interactive set found in Series 2 packs features the game's top home run hitters. Cards were inserted 1:5 packs. Fronts feature a red-foil Crash logo and a range of game dates. Those holding cards of players who homered in that span could (for $2 per card handling fee) redeem them for high-tech versions. Instant winner cards (seeded 1:721) were redeemable for complete 30-card upgrade sets. Winning cards are marked with an asterisk; theoretically they would be scarcer than losing cards because many were redeemed. The contest cards expired on Sept. 8, 1997. Cards are numbered with a "CG" prefix.

		MT
	Complete Set (30):	40.00
	Common Player:	.50
1	Ryan Klesko	
	July 28-30	.50
	August 8-11	.50
	Sept. 19-21	.50
2	Chipper Jones	
	August 15-17	3.00
	August 29-31	3.00
	Sept. 12-14	3.00
3	Andruw Jones	
	August 22-24*	3.00
	Sept. 1-3	1.50
	Sept. 19-22	1.50
4	Brady Anderson	
	July 31-Aug. 3*	1.00
	Sept. 4-7	.50
	Sept. 19-22	.50
5	Rafael Palmeiro	
	July 29-30	.50
	Aug. 29-31	.50
	Sept. 26-28	.50
6	Cal Ripken Jr.	
	August 8-10*	6.00
	Sept. 1-3*	6.00
	Sept. 11-14	4.00
7	Mo Vaughn	
	August 14-17	.75
	August 29-31*	1.50
	Sept. 23-25*	1.50
8	Sammy Sosa	
	August 1-3*	4.50
	August 29-31	3.00
	Sept. 19-21*	4.50
9	Albert Belle	
	August 7-10	.65
	Sept. 11-14	.65
	Sept. 19-21*	1.25
10	Frank Thomas	
	August 29-31	2.50
	Sept. 1-3	2.50
	Sept. 23-25*	5.00
11	Manny Ramirez	
	August 12-14*	1.00
	August 29-31	.50
	Sept. 11-14*	1.00
12	Jim Thome	
	July 28-30	.50
	August 15-18*	1.00
	Sept. 19-22	.50
13	Matt Williams	
	August 4-5	.50
	Sept. 1-3*	1.00
	Sept. 23-25	.50
14	Dante Bichette	
	July 24-27*	1.00
	August 28-29	.50
	Sept. 26-28*	1.00
15	Vinny Castilla	
	August 12-13	.50
	Sept. 4-7*	1.00
	Sept. 19-21	.50
16	Andres Galarraga	
	August 8-10*	1.00
	August 30-31	.50
	Sept. 12-14	.50
17	Gary Sheffield	
	August 1-3*	1.00
	Sept. 1-3*	1.00
	Sept. 12-14*	1.00
18	Jeff Bagwell	
	Sept. 9-10	.75
	Sept. 19-22*	1.50
	Sept. 23-25*	1.50
19	Eric Karros	
	August 1-3	.50
	August 15-17	.50
	Sept. 25-28*	1.00
20	Mike Piazza	
	August 11-12	2.00
	Sept. 5-8*	4.00
	Sept. 19-21*	4.00
21	Vladimir Guerrero	
	August 22-24	1.00
	August 29-31	1.00
	Sept. 19-22	1.00
22	Cecil Fielder	
	August 29-31	.50
	Sept. 4-7	.50
	Sept. 26-28*	1.00
23	Jose Canseco	
	August 22-24	.65
	Sept. 12-14	.65
	Sept. 26-28	.65
24	Mark McGwire	
	July 31-Aug. 3	2.50
	August 30-31	2.50
	Sept. 19-22*	5.00
25	Ken Caminiti	
	August 8-10	.50
	Sept. 4-7	.50
	Sept. 17-18*	1.00
26	Barry Bonds	
	August 5-7	.90
	Sept. 4-7*	2.00
	Sept. 23-24*	2.00
27	Jay Buhner	
	August 7-10	.50
	August 28-29	.50
	Sept. 1-3	.50
28	Ken Griffey Jr.	
	August 22-24*	5.00
	August 28-29	3.00
	Sept. 19-22*	5.00
29	Alex Rodriguez	
	July 29-31	1.50
	August 30-31	1.50

	Sept. 12-15	1.50
30	Juan Gonzalez	
	August 11-13*	2.00
	August 30-31	1.00
	Sept. 19-21*	2.00

1997 Collector's Choice You Crash the Game Winners

These are the prize cards from CC's interactive "You Crash the Game" cards in Series 2. Persons who redeemed a Crash card with the correct date(s) on which the pictured player homered received (for a $2 handling fee) this high-end version of the Crash card. The redemption cards have the same basic design as the contest cards, but use different player photos with fronts printed on metallic-foil stock, and a team logo in place of the Crash foil logo. Where the contest cards have game rules on back, the redemption cards have another photo of the player and career highlights. Complete redemption sets were available upon redeeming an instant winner card, found on average of one per 721 packs. Because some cards were only available in complete redemption sets (marked with an "SP" here), and others might have been available for more than one date range, some cards will be scarcer than others.

	MT
Complete Set (30):	40.00
Common Player:	1.00
CG1 Ryan Klesko (SP)	1.50
CG2 Chipper Jones (SP)	10.00
CG3 Andruw Jones	1.00
CG4 Brady Anderson	1.00
CG5 Rafael Palmeiro (SP)	4.00
CG6 Cal Ripken Jr.	6.00
CG7 Mo Vaughn	1.00
CG8 Sammy Sosa	3.00
CG9 Albert Belle	1.50
CG10Frank Thomas	2.00
CG11Manny Ramirez	1.50
CG12Jim Thome	1.00
CG13Matt Williams	1.00
CG14Dante Bichette	1.00
CG15Vinny Castilla	1.00
CG16Andres Galarraga	1.00
CG17Gary Sheffield	1.00
CG18Jeff Bagwell	1.50
CG19Eric Karros	1.00
CG20Mike Piazza	4.00
CG21Vladimir Guerrero (SP)	6.00
CG22Cecil Fielder (SP)	1.50
CG23Jose Canseco (SP)	4.00
CG24Mark McGwire	6.00
CG25Ken Caminiti	1.00
CG26Barry Bonds	1.50
CG27Jay Buhner (SP)	1.50
CG28Ken Griffey Jr.	6.00
CG29Alex Rodriguez (SP)	15.00
CG30Juan Gonzalez	2.00

1997 Collector's Choice You Crash/ Game Instant Winner

Found on average of one per 721 packs, these Instant Winner cards could be redeemed (with a $2 handling fee) for a complete set of You Crash the Game exchange cards - the only way eight of the Crash winner cards could be obtained. These special cards have a red foil "instant winner!" logo on front and a congratulatory message on back, along with instructions for redemption prior to the Dec. 8, 1997, deadline.

	MT
Complete Set (30):	200.00
Common Player:	2.00
(High-demand players' cards valued at 8X regular You Crash the Game cards.)	

1998 Collector's Choice

The 530-card Collectors Choice set was issued in two 265-card series. Series 1 features 197-regular cards, five checklists and four subsets: Cover Story features 18 of the leagues' top stars, Rookie Class has 27 young players, the nine-card Top of the Charts subset honors 1997's statistical leaders and Masked Marauders is a nine-card subset. Inserts in Series One are Super Action Stick-Ums, Evolution Revolution and StarQuest. Series 2 has 233 regular cards, five checklist cards, an 18-card Rookie Class subset and the nine-card Golden Jubilee subset. Inserts in Series 2 include Mini Bobbing Head Cards, You Crash the Game and StarQuest.

		MT
Complete Set (530):		30.00
Complete Series I Set (265):		15.00
Complete Series II Set (265):		15.00
Common Player:		.05
Unlisted Stars: .25 to .50		
Wax Box:		40.00
1	Nomar Garciaparra (Cover Glory)	.60
2	Roger Clemens (Cover Glory)	.30
3	Larry Walker (Cover Glory)	.10
4	Mike Piazza (Cover Glory)	.60
5	Mark McGwire (Cover Glory)	1.00
6	Tony Gwynn (Cover Glory)	.50
7	Jose Cruz Jr. (Cover Glory)	.15
8	Frank Thomas (Cover Glory)	.50
9	Tino Martinez (Cover Glory)	.10
10	Ken Griffey Jr. (Cover Glory)	1.00
11	Barry Bonds (Cover Glory)	.25
12	Scott Rolen (Cover Glory)	.50
13	Randy Johnson (Cover Glory)	.15
14	Ryne Sandberg (Cover Glory)	.25
15	Eddie Murray (Cover Glory)	.10
16	Kevin Brown (Cover Glory)	.05
17	Greg Maddux (Cover Glory)	.60
18	Sandy Alomar Jr. (Cover Glory)	.05
19	Checklist (Ken Griffey Jr., Adam Riggs)	.50
20	Checklist (Nomar Garciaparra, Charlie O'Brien)	.30
21	Checklist (Ben Grieve, Ken Griffey Jr., Larry Walker, Mark McGwire)	1.00
22	Checklist (Mark McGwire, Cal Ripken Jr.)	1.00
23	Checklist (Tino Martinez)	.05
24	Jason Dickson	.05
25	Darin Erstad	.60
26	Todd Greene	.15
27	Chuck Finley	.05
28	Garret Anderson	.05
29	Dave Hollins	.05
30	Rickey Henderson	.05
31	John Smoltz	.15
32	Michael Tucker	.05
33	Jeff Blauser	.05
34	Javier Lopez	.10
35	Andruw Jones	1.00
36	Denny Neagle	.05
37	Randall Simon	.15
38	Mark Wohlers	.05
39	Harold Baines	.05
40	Cal Ripken Jr.	1.50
41	Mike Bordick	.05
42	Jimmy Key	.05
43	Armando Benitez	.05
44	Scott Erickson	.05
45	Eric Davis	.05
46	Bret Saberhagen	.05
47	Darren Bragg	.05
48	Steve Avery	.05
49	Jeff Frye	.05
50	Aaron Sele	.05
51	Scott Hatteberg	.05
52	Tom Gordon	.05
53	Kevin Orie	.05
54	Kevin Foster	.05
55	Ryne Sandberg	.50
56	Doug Glanville	.05
57	Tyler Houston	.05
58	Steve Trachsel	.05
59	Mark Grace	.15
60	Frank Thomas	1.00
61	*Scott Eyre*	.15
62	Jeff Abbott	.05
63	Chris Clemons	.05
64	Jorge Fabregas	.05
65	Robin Ventura	.10
66	Matt Karchner	.05
67	Jon Nunnally	.05
68	Aaron Boone	.05
69	Pokey Reese	.05
70	Deion Sanders	.15
71	Jeff Shaw	.05
72	Eduardo Perez	.05
73	Brett Tomko	.05
74	Bartolo Colon	.05
75	Manny Ramirez	.50
76	Jose Mesa	.05
77	Brian Giles	.05
78	Richie Sexson	.05
79	Orel Hershiser	.05
80	Matt Williams	.20
81	Walt Weiss	.05
82	Jerry DiPoto	.05
83	Quinton McCracken	.05
84	Neifi Perez	.05
85	Vinny Castilla	.10
86	Ellis Burks	.05
87	John Thomson	.05
88	Willie Blair	.05
89	Bob Hamelin	.05
90	Tony Clark	.35
91	Todd Jones	.05
92	Deivi Cruz	.05
93	*Frank Catalanotto*	.15
94	Justin Thompson	.05
95	Gary Sheffield	.25
96	Kevin Brown	.15
97	Charles Johnson	.10
98	Bobby Bonilla	.10
99	Livan Hernandez	.05
100	Paul Konerko (Rookie Class)	.60
101	Craig Counsell (Rookie Class)	.05
102	*Magglio Ordonez* (Rookie Class)	.50
103	Garrett Stephenson (Rookie Class)	.05
104	Ken Cloude (Rookie Class)	.15
105	Miguel Tejada (Rookie Class)	.40
106	Juan Encarnacion (Rookie Class)	.20
107	Dennis Reyes (Rookie Class)	.15
108	Orlando Cabrera (Rookie Class)	.05
109	Kelvim Escobar (Rookie Class)	.05
110	Ben Grieve (Rookie Class)	.75
111	Brian Rose (Rookie Class)	.05
112	Fernando Tatis (Rookie Class)	.20
113	Tom Evans (Rookie Class)	.05
114	Tom Fordham (Rookie Class)	.05
115	Mark Kotsay (Rookie Class)	.40
116	Mario Valdez (Rookie Class)	.05
117	Jeremi Gonzalez (Rookie Class)	.05
118	Todd Dunwoody (Rookie Class)	.05
119	Javier Valentin (Rookie Class)	.05
120	Todd Helton (Rookie Class)	.50
121	Jason Varitek (Rookie Class)	.05
122	Chris Carpenter (Rookie Class)	.05
123	*Kevin Millwood* (Rookie Class)	1.00
124	Brad Fullmer (Rookie Class)	.05
125	Jaret Wright (Rookie Class)	1.00
126	Brad Rigby (Rookie Class)	.05
127	Edgar Renteria	.05
128	Robb Nen	.05
129	Tony Pena	.05
130	Craig Biggio	.15
131	Brad Ausmus	.05
132	Shane Reynolds	.05
133	Mike Hampton	.05
134	Billy Wagner	.05
135	Richard Hidalgo	.05
136	Jose Rosado	.05
137	Yamil Benitez	.05
138	Felix Martinez	.05
139	Jeff King	.05
140	Jose Offerman	.05
141	Joe Vitiello	.05
142	Tim Belcher	.05
143	Brett Butler	.05
144	Greg Gagne	.05
145	Mike Piazza	1.25
146	Ramon Martinez	.10
147	Raul Mondesi	.20
148	Adam Riggs	.05
149	Eddie Murray	.20
150	Jeff Cirillo	.05
151	Scott Karl	.05
152	Mike Fetters	.05
153	Dave Nilsson	.05
154	Antone Williamson	.05
155	Jeff D'Amico	.05
156	Jose Valentin	.05
157	Brad Radke	.05
158	Torii Hunter	.05
159	Chuck Knoblauch	.15
160	Paul Molitor	.35
161	Travis Miller	.05
162	Rich Robertson	.05
163	Ron Coomer	.05
164	Mark Grudzielanek	.05
165	Lee Smith	.05
166	Vladimir Guerrero	.60
167	Dustin Hermanson	.05
168	Ugueth Urbina	.05
169	F.P. Santangelo	.05
170	Rondell White	.15
171	Bobby Jones	.05
172	Edgardo Alfonzo	.15
173	John Franco	.05
174	Carlos Baerga	.05
175	Butch Huskey	.05
176	Rey Ordonez	.10
177	Matt Franco	.05
178	Dwight Gooden	.15
179	Chad Curtis	.05
180	Tino Martinez	.15
181	Charlie O'Brien (Masked Marauders)	.05
182	Sandy Alomar Jr. (Masked Marauders)	.05
183	Raul Casanova (Masked Marauders)	.05
184	Jim Leyritz (Masked Marauders)	.05
185	Mike Piazza (Masked Marauders)	.60
186	Ivan Rodriguez (Masked Marauders)	.25
187	Charles Johnson (Masked Marauders)	.10
188	Brad Ausmus (Masked Marauders)	.05
189	Brian Johnson (Masked Marauders)	.05
190	Wade Boggs	.20
191	David Wells	.05
192	Tim Raines	.05
193	Ramiro Mendoza	.05
194	Willie Adams	.05
195	Matt Stairs	.05
196	Jason McDonald	.05
197	Dave Magadan	.05
198	Mark Bellhorn	.05
199	Ariel Prieto	.05
200	Jose Canseco	.20
201	Bobby Estalella	.05
202	*Tony Barron*	.05
203	Midre Cummings	.05
204	Ricky Bottalico	.05
205	Mike Grace	.05
206	Rico Brogna	.05
207	Mickey Morandini	.05
208	Lou Collier	.05
209	*Kevin Polcovich*	.05
210	Kevin Young	.05
211	Jose Guillen	.25
212	Esteban Loaiza	.05
213	Marc Wilkins	.05
214	Jason Schmidt	.05
215	Gary Gaetti	.05
216	Fernando Valenzuela	.05
217	Willie McGee	.05
218	Alan Benes	.15
219	Eli Marrero	.05
220	Mark McGwire	2.50
221	Matt Morris	.05
222	Trevor Hoffman	.05
223	Will Cunnane	.05
224	Joey Hamilton	.05
225	Ken Caminiti	.15
226	Derrek Lee	.15
227	Mark Sweeney	.05
228	Carlos Hernandez	.05
229	Brian Johnson	.05
230	Jeff Kent	.05
231	Kirk Rueter	.05
232	Bill Mueller	.05
233	Dante Powell	.05
234	J.T. Snow	.15
235	Shawn Estes	.05
236	Dennis Martinez	.05
237	Jamie Moyer	.05
238	Dan Wilson	.05
239	Joey Cora	.05
240	Ken Griffey Jr.	2.00
241	Paul Sorrento	.05
242	Jay Buhner	.20
243	*Hanley Frias*	.05
244	John Burkett	.05
245	Juan Gonzalez	1.00
246	Rick Helling	.05
247	Darren Oliver	.05
248	Mickey Tettleton	.05
249	Ivan Rodriguez	.50
250	Joe Carter	.15
251	Pat Hentgen	.05
252	Marty Janzen	.05
253	Frank Thomas, Tony Gwynn (Top of the Charts)	.25
254	Mark McGwire, Ken Griffey Jr., Larry Walker (Top of the Charts)	1.00
255	Ken Griffey Jr., Andres Galarraga (Top of the Charts)	.50
256	Brian Hunter, Tony Womack (Top of the Charts)	.05
257	Roger Clemens, Denny Neagle (Top of the Charts)	.20
258	Roger Clemens, Curt Schilling (Top of the Charts)	.20
259	Roger Clemens, Pedro J. Martinez (Top of the Charts)	.20
260	Randy Myers, Jeff Shaw (Top of the Charts)	.05
261	Nomar Garciaparra, Scott Rolen (Top of the Charts)	.30
262	Charlie O'Brien	.05
263	Shannon Stewart	.05
264	Robert Person	.05
265	Carlos Delgado	.25
266	Checklist (Matt Williams, Travis Lee)	.25
267	Checklist (Nomar Garciaparra, Cal Ripken Jr.)	.40
268	Checklist (Mark McGwire, Mike Piazza)	.75
269	Checklist (Tony Gwynn, Ken Griffey Jr.)	.50
270	Checklist (Fred McGriff, Jose Cruz Jr.)	.10
271	Andruw Jones (Golden Jubilee)	.25
272	Alex Rodriguez (Golden Jubilee)	.60

273	Juan Gonzalez (Golden Jubilee)	.50
274	Nomar Garciaparra (Golden Jubilee)	.60
275	Ken Griffey Jr. (Golden Jubilee)	1.00
276	Tino Martinez (Golden Jubilee)	.15
277	Roger Clemens (Golden Jubilee)	.40
278	Barry Bonds (Golden Jubilee)	.25
279	Mike Piazza (Golden Jubilee)	.60
280	Tim Salmon (Golden Jubilee)	.15
281	Gary DiSarcina	.05
282	Cecil Fielder	.15
283	Ken Hill	.05
284	Troy Percival	.05
285	Jim Edmonds	.05
286	Allen Watson	.05
287	Brian Anderson	.05
288	Jay Bell	.05
289	Jorge Fabregas	.05
290	Devon White	.05
291	Yamil Benitez	.05
292	Jeff Suppan	.05
293	Tony Batista	.05
294	Brent Brede	.05
295	Andy Benes	.15
296	Felix Rodriguez	.05
297	Karim Garcia	.05
298	Omar Daal	.05
299	Andy Stankiewicz	.05
300	Matt Williams	.25
301	Willie Blair	.05
302	Ryan Klesko	.20
303	Tom Glavine	.15
304	Walt Weiss	.05
305	Greg Maddux	1.25
306	Chipper Jones	1.25
307	Keith Lockhart	.05
308	Andres Galarraga	.20
309	Chris Hoiles	.05
310	Roberto Alomar	.40
311	Joe Carter	.15
312	Doug Drabek	.05
313	Jeffrey Hammonds	.05
314	Rafael Palmeiro	.20
315	Mike Mussina	.40
316	Brady Anderson	.05
317	B.J. Surhoff	.05
318	Dennis Eckersley	.05
319	Jim Leyritz	.05
320	Mo Vaughn	.50
321	Nomar Garciaparra	1.25
322	Reggie Jefferson	.05
323	Tim Naehring	.05
324	Troy O'Leary	.05
325	Pedro J. Martinez	.25
326	John Valentin	.05
327	Mark Clark	.05
328	Rod Beck	.05
329	Mickey Morandini	.05
330	Sammy Sosa	1.50
331	Jeff Blauser	.05
332	Lance Johnson	.05
333	Scott Servais	.05
334	Kevin Tapani	.05
335	Henry Rodriguez	.05
336	Jaime Navarro	.05
337	Benji Gil	.05
338	James Baldwin	.05
339	Mike Cameron	.05
340	Ray Durham	.05
341	Chris Snopek	.05
342	Eddie Taubensee	.05
343	Bret Boone	.05
344	Willie Greene	.05
345	Barry Larkin	.15
346	Chris Stynes	.05
347	Pete Harnisch	.05
348	Dave Burba	.05
349	Sandy Alomar Jr.	.15
350	Kenny Lofton	.50
351	Geronimo Berroa	.05
352	Omar Vizquel	.05
353	Travis Fryman	.05
354	Dwight Gooden	.05
355	Jim Thome	.40
356	David Justice	.25
357	Charles Nagy	.05
358	Chad Ogea	.05
359	Pedro Astacio	.05
360	Larry Walker	.25
361	Mike Lansing	.05
362	Kirt Manwaring	.05
363	Dante Bichette	.15
364	Jamey Wright	.05
365	Darryl Kile	.05
366	Luis Gonzalez	.05
367	Joe Randa	.05
368	Raul Casanova	.05
369	Damion Easley	.05
370	Brian L. Hunter	.05
371	Bobby Higginson	.05
372	Brian Moehler	.05
373	Scott Sanders	.05
374	Jim Eisenreich	.05
375	Derrek Lee	.05
376	Jay Powell	.05
377	Cliff Floyd	.05
378	Alex Fernandez	.05
379	Felix Heredia	.05
380	Jeff Bagwell	.75
381	Bill Spiers	.05
382	Chris Holt	.05
383	Carl Everett	.05
384	Derek Bell	.05
385	Moises Alou	.15
386	Ramon Garcia	.05
387	Mike Sweeney	.05
388	Glendon Rusch	.05
389	Kevin Appier	.05
390	Dean Palmer	.05
391	Jeff Conine	.05
392	Johnny Damon	.05
393	Jose Vizcaino	.05
394	Todd Hollandsworth	.05
395	Eric Karros	.05
396	Todd Zeile	.05
397	Chan Ho Park	.15
398	Ismael Valdes	.05
399	Eric Young	.05
400	Hideo Nomo	.40
401	Mark Loretta	.05
402	Doug Jones	.05
403	Jeromy Burnitz	.05
404	John Jaha	.05
405	Marquis Grissom	.05
406	Mike Matheny	.05
407	Todd Walker	.05
408	Marty Cordova	.05
409	Matt Lawton	.05
410	Terry Steinbach	.05
411	Pat Meares	.05
412	Rick Aguilera	.05
413	Otis Nixon	.05
414	Derrick May	.05
415	Carl Pavano (Rookie Class)	.05
416	A.J. Hinch (Rookie Class)	.15
417	*David Dellucci* (Rookie Class)	.25
418	Bruce Chen (Rookie Class)	.15
419	*Darron Ingram* (Rookie Class)	.05
420	Sean Casey (Rookie Class)	.05
421	Mark L. Johnson (Rookie Class)	.05
422	Gabe Alvarez (Rookie Class)	.05
423	Alex Gonzalez (Rookie Class)	.05
424	Daryle Ward (Rookie Class)	.15
425	Russell Branyan (Rookie Class)	.05
426	Mike Caruso (Rookie Class)	.05
427	*Mike Kinkade* (Rookie Class)	.25
428	Ramon Hernandez (Rookie Class)	.05
429	Matt Clement (Rookie Class)	.10
430	Travis Lee (Rookie Class)	.60
431	Shane Monahan (Rookie Class)	.05
432	*Rich Butler* (Rookie Class)	.25
433	Chris Widger	.05
434	Jose Vidro	.05
435	Carlos Perez	.05
436	Ryan McGuire	.05
437	Brian McRae	.05
438	Al Leiter	.05
439	Rich Becker	.05
440	Todd Hundley	.05
441	Dave Mlicki	.05
442	Bernard Gilkey	.05
443	John Olerud	.15
444	Paul O'Neill	.15
445	Andy Pettitte	.40
446	David Cone	.15
447	Chili Davis	.05
448	Bernie Williams	.40
449	Joe Girardi	.05
450	Derek Jeter	1.25
451	Mariano Rivera	.15
452	George Williams	.05
453	Kenny Rogers	.05
454	Tom Candiotti	.05
455	Rickey Henderson	.05
456	Jason Giambi	.05
457	Scott Spiezio	.05
458	Doug Glanville	.05
459	Desi Relaford	.05
460	Curt Schilling	.15
461	Bob Abreu	.05
462	Gregg Jefferies	.05
463	Scott Rolen	.75
464	Mike Lieberthal	.05
465	Tony Womack	.05
466	Jermaine Allensworth	.05
467	Francisco Cordova	.05
468	Jon Lieber	.05
469	Al Martin	.05
470	Jason Kendall	.05
471	Todd Stottlemyre	.05
472	Royce Clayton	.05
473	Brian Jordan	.05
474	John Mabry	.05
475	Ray Lankford	.05
476	Delino DeShields	.05
477	Ron Gant	.05
478	Mark Langston	.05
479	Steve Finley	.05
480	Tony Gwynn	1.00
481	Andy Ashby	.05
482	Wally Joyner	.05
483	Greg Vaughn	.05
484	Sterling Hitchcock	.05
485	J. Kevin Brown	.05
486	Orel Hershiser	.05
487	Charlie Hayes	.05
488	Darryl Hamilton	.05
489	Mark Gardner	.05
490	Barry Bonds	.50
491	Robb Nen	.05
492	Kirk Rueter	.05
493	Randy Johnson	.40
494	Jeff Fassero	.05
495	Alex Rodriguez	1.25
496	David Segui	.05
497	Rich Amaral	.05
498	Russ Davis	.05
499	Bubba Trammell	.05
500	Wade Boggs	.20
501	Roberto Hernandez	.05
502	Dave Martinez	.05
503	Dennis Springer	.05
504	Paul Sorrento	.05
505	Wilson Alvarez	.05
506	Mike Kelly	.05
507	Albie Lopez	.05
508	Tony Saunders	.05
509	John Flaherty	.05
510	Fred McGriff	.15
511	Quinton McCracken	.05
512	Terrell Wade	.05
513	Kevin Stocker	.05
514	Kevin Elster	.05
515	Will Clark	.20
516	Bobby Witt	.05
517	Tom Goodwin	.05
518	Aaron Sele	.05
519	Lee Stevens	.05
520	Rusty Greer	.05
521	John Wetteland	.05
522	Darrin Fletcher	.05
523	Jose Canseco	.25
524	Randy Myers	.05
525	Jose Cruz Jr.	.15
526	Shawn Green	.05
527	Tony Fernandez	.05
528	Alex Gonzalez	.05
529	Ed Sprague	.05
530	Roger Clemens	.75

Misspellings of names are not uncommon on modern minor league cards. Unless a corrected version was issued, such errors have no effect on value.

1998 Collector's Choice Cover Glory 5x7

		MT
Complete Set (10):		10.00
Common Player:		1.00
1	Nomar Garciaparra	2.00
2	Roger Clemens	1.50
3	Larry Walker	1.00
4	Mike Piazza	2.00
5	Mark McGwire	3.00
6	Tony Gwynn	1.50
7	Jose Cruz Jr.	1.00
8	Frank Thomas	1.50
9	Tino Martinez	1.00
10	Ken Griffey Jr.	3.00

1998 Collector's Choice Evolution Revolution

This 28-card insert features one player from each Major League team. The fronts picture the team jersey and open to reveal the player's top 1997 accomplishment. Evolution Revolution was inserted one per 13 Series 1 packs. Cards are numbered with an "ER" prefix.

		MT
Complete Set (28):		60.00
Common Player:		.75
Inserted 1:13		
1	Tim Salmon	1.25
2	Greg Maddux	5.00
3	Cal Ripken Jr.	8.00
4	Mo Vaughn	2.50
5	Sammy Sosa	6.00
6	Frank Thomas	4.00
7	Barry Larkin	1.00
8	Jim Thome	1.50
9	Larry Walker	1.25
10	Travis Fryman	.75
11	Gary Sheffield	1.50
12	Jeff Bagwell	4.00
13	Johnny Damon	.75
14	Mike Piazza	6.00
15	Jeff Cirillo	.75
16	Paul Molitor	2.00
17	Vladimir Guerrero	3.00
18	Todd Hundley	.75
19	Tino Martinez	.75
20	Jose Canseco	1.00
21	Scott Rolen	5.00
22	Al Martin	.75
23	Mark McGwire	12.00
24	Tony Gwynn	5.00
25	Barry Bonds	2.50
26	Ken Griffey Jr.	10.00
27	Juan Gonzalez	5.00
28	Roger Clemens	4.00

1998 Collector's Choice Mini Bobbing Heads

The cards in this 30-card insert series can be punched out and assembled into a stand-up figure with a removable bobbing head. They were inserted 1:3 in Series 2 packs.

		MT
Complete Set (30):		20.00
Common Player:		.25
Inserted 1:3		
1	Tim Salmon	.40
2	Travis Lee	.75
3	Matt Williams	.25
4	Chipper Jones	1.50
5	Greg Maddux	1.00
6	Cal Ripken Jr.	2.00
7	Nomar Garciaparra	1.50
8	Mo Vaughn	.75
9	Sammy Sosa	1.50
10	Frank Thomas	1.20
11	Kenny Lofton	.75
12	Jaret Wright	.75
13	Larry Walker	.50
14	Tony Clark	.50
15	Edgar Renteria	.25
16	Jeff Bagwell	1.00
17	Mike Piazza	1.50
18	Vladimir Guerrero	.90
19	Derek Jeter	1.50
20	Ben Grieve	.85
21	Scott Rolen	.80
22	Mark McGwire	3.00
23	Tony Gwynn	1.25
24	Barry Bonds	.90
25	Ken Griffey Jr.	3.00
26	Alex Rodriguez	1.50
27	Fred McGriff	.40
28	Juan Gonzalez	1.25
29	Roger Clemens	1.00
30	Jose Cruz Jr.	.25

1998 Collector's Choice Rookie Class: Prime Choice

This 18-card set is a parallel of the Rookie Class subset. Each card is foil-stamped with the words "Prime Choice Reserve." This hobby-only set is sequentially numbered to 500 and was inserted in Series 2 packs.

		MT
Complete Set (18):		100.00
Common Player:		5.00
415	Carl Pavano	7.50
416	A.J. Hinch	7.50
417	David Dellucci	9.00
418	Bruce Chen	10.00
419	Darron Ingram	5.00
420	Sean Casey	15.00
421	Mark L. Johnson	5.00
422	Gabe Alvarez	5.00
423	Alex Gonzalez	7.50
424	Daryle Ward	5.00
425	Russell Branyan	5.00
426	Mike Caruso	7.50
427	Mike Kinkade	5.00
428	Ramon Hernandez	5.00
429	Matt Clement	5.00
430	Travis Lee	15.00
431	Shane Monahan	5.00
432	Rich Butler	10.00

1998 Collector's Choice StarQuest - Series 1

The StarQuest insert in Series 1 consists of 90 cards within four tiers. The tiers are designated by the number of stars found on front, the more the better. Special Delivery (#1-45, one star) was inserted 1:1, Students of the Game (two stars, #46-65) 1:21, Super Powers (three stars, #66-80) 1:71 and Super Star Domain (four stars, #81-90) 1:145. All cards are numbered with an "SQ" prefix.

	MT
Complete Set (90):	500.00
Common Special Delivery (1-45)	.20
Inserted 1:1	
Common Student of the Game	

	(46-65):	1.50
	Inserted 1:21	
	Common Super Power (66-80):	5.00
	Inserted 1:71	
	Common Superstar Domain (81-90):	10.00
	Inserted 1:145	
1	Nomar Garciaparra	2.00
2	Scott Rolen	1.50
3	Jason Dickson	.20
4	Jaret Wright	1.50
5	Kevin Orie	.20
6	Jose Guillen	.50
7	Matt Morris	.20
8	Mike Cameron	.30
9	Kevin Polcovich	.20
10	Jose Cruz Jr.	.25
11	Miguel Tejada	.50
12	Fernando Tatis	.40
13	Todd Helton	.75
14	Ken Cloude	.20
15	Ben Grieve	1.00
16	Dante Powell	.20
17	Bubba Trammell	.30
18	Juan Encarnacion	.40
19	Derrek Lee	.20
20	Paul Konerko	1.00
21	Richard Hidalgo	.20
22	Denny Neagle	.20
23	David Justice	.40
24	Pedro J. Martinez	.40
25	Greg Maddux	2.00
26	Edgar Martinez	.20
27	Cal Ripken Jr.	2.50
28	Tim Salmon	.40
29	Shawn Estes	.20
30	Ken Griffey Jr.	3.00
31	Brad Radke	.20
32	Andy Pettitte	.50
33	Curt Schilling	.20
34	Raul Mondesi	.40
35	Alex Rodriguez	2.00
36	Jeff Kent	.20
37	Jeff Bagwell	1.25
38	Juan Gonzalez	1.50
39	Barry Bonds	.75
40	Mark McGwire	4.00
41	Frank Thomas	1.50
42	Ray Lankford	.20
43	Tony Gwynn	1.50
44	Mike Piazza	2.00
45	Tino Martinez	.20
46	Nomar Garciaparra	10.00
47	Paul Molitor	3.00
48	Chuck Knoblauch	2.00
49	Rusty Greer	1.50
50	Cal Ripken Jr.	12.00
51	Roberto Alomar	3.00
52	Scott Rolen	7.00
53	Derek Jeter	10.00
54	Mark Grace	2.00
55	Randy Johnson	2.50
56	Craig Biggio	1.50
57	Kenny Lofton	4.00
58	Eddie Murray	2.00
59	Ryne Sandberg	4.00
60	Rickey Henderson	1.50
61	Darin Erstad	4.00
62	Jim Edmonds	1.50
63	Ken Caminiti	2.00
64	Ivan Rodriguez	3.00
65	Tony Gwynn	8.00
66	Tony Clark	8.00
67	Andres Galarraga	6.00
68	Rafael Palmeiro	6.00
69	Manny Ramirez	8.00
70	Albert Belle	10.00
71	Jay Buhner	5.00
72	Mo Vaughn	10.00
73	Barry Bonds	10.00
74	Chipper Jones	25.00
75	Jeff Bagwell	18.00
76	Jim Thome	8.00
77	Sammy Sosa	12.00
78	Todd Hundley	5.00
79	Matt Williams	6.00
80	Vinny Castilla	5.00
81	Jose Cruz Jr.	10.00
82	Frank Thomas	25.00
83	Juan Gonzalez	30.00
84	Mike Piazza	40.00
85	Alex Rodriguez	40.00
86	Larry Walker	12.00
87	Tino Martinez	10.00
88	Greg Maddux	35.00
89	Mark McGwire	70.00
90	Ken Griffey Jr.	65.00

1998 Collector's Choice StarQuest - Series 2

The 30-card StarQuest insert was included in Series 2 packs. The insert has four parallel tiers - Single, Double, Triple and Home Run - designated by the number of baseball diamond icons on the card front. Single cards were inserted 1:1, Doubles 1:21, Triples 1:71 and Home Runs are sequentially numbered to 100. The second series SQ cards feature a front design with the letters "QSUTEASRT" in color block vertically at left.

		MT
	Complete Set (30):	18.00
	Common Player:	.25
	Singles 1:1	
	Doubles 1:21 4-8X	
	Triples 1:71 12-20X	
1	Ken Griffey Jr.	2.00
2	Jose Cruz Jr.	.25
3	Cal Ripken Jr.	1.50
4	Roger Clemens	.75
5	Frank Thomas	1.00
6	Derek Jeter	1.00
7	Alex Rodriguez	1.25
8	Andruw Jones	.50
9	Vladimir Guerrero	.50
10	Mark McGwire	3.00
11	Kenny Lofton	.50
12	Pedro J. Martinez	.25
13	Greg Maddux	1.00
14	Larry Walker	.25
15	Barry Bonds	.50
16	Chipper Jones	1.25
17	Jeff Bagwell	.75
18	Juan Gonzalez	1.00
19	Tony Gwynn	1.00
20	Mike Piazza	1.25
21	Tino Martinez	.25
22	Mo Vaughn	.50
23	Ben Grieve	.60
24	Scott Rolen	.60
25	Nomar Garciaparra	1.25
26	Paul Konerko	.25
27	Jaret Wright	.50
28	Gary Sheffield	.25
29	Travis Lee	.60
30	Todd Helton	.50

1998 Collector's Choice StarQuest Home Run

StarQuest Home Run cards are the fourth tier of the insert in Series Two. The cards have four baseball diamond icons to designate their level. Home Run cards are sequentially numbered to 100.

		MT
	Common Player:	10.00
	Semistars:	25.00
	Production 100 sets	
1	Ken Griffey Jr.	150.00
2	Jose Cruz Jr.	20.00
3	Cal Ripken Jr.	120.00
4	Roger Clemens	60.00
5	Frank Thomas	75.00
6	Derek Jeter	80.00
7	Alex Rodriguez	100.00
8	Andruw Jones	40.00
9	Vladimir Guerrero	40.00
10	Mark McGwire	150.00
11	Kenny Lofton	40.00
12	Pedro J. Martinez	20.00
13	Greg Maddux	100.00
14	Larry Walker	25.00
15	Barry Bonds	40.00
16	Chipper Jones	90.00
17	Jeff Bagwell	60.00
18	Juan Gonzalez	75.00
19	Tony Gwynn	75.00
20	Mike Piazza	100.00
21	Tino Martinez	20.00
22	Mo Vaughn	40.00
23	Ben Grieve	50.00
24	Scott Rolen	50.00
25	Nomar Garciaparra	90.00
26	Paul Konerko	10.00
27	Jaret Wright	40.00
28	Gary Sheffield	20.00
29	Travis Lee	30.00
30	Todd Helton	40.00

1998 Collector's Choice Stickums

This 30-card insert was seeded 1:3 Series 1 packs. The stickers can be peeled off the card and reused.

		MT
	Complete Set (30):	20.00
	Common Player:	.25
	Inserted 1:3	
1	Andruw Jones	.60
2	Chipper Jones	1.50
3	Cal Ripken Jr.	2.00
4	Nomar Garciaparra	1.50
5	Mo Vaughn	.60
6	Ryne Sandberg	.60
7	Sammy Sosa	1.25
8	Frank Thomas	1.00
9	Albert Belle	.60
10	Jim Thome	.40
11	Manny Ramirez	.75
12	Larry Walker	.40
13	Gary Sheffield	.40
14	Jeff Bagwell	.75
15	Mike Piazza	1.50
16	Paul Molitor	.50
17	Pedro J. Martinez	.50
18	Todd Hundley	.25
19	Derek Jeter	1.50
20	Tino Martinez	.50
21	Curt Schilling	.25
22	Mark McGwire	3.00
23	Tony Gwynn	1.25
24	Barry Bonds	.60
25	Ken Griffey Jr.	2.50
26	Alex Rodriguez	1.50
27	Juan Gonzalez	1.25
28	Ivan Rodriguez	.60
29	Roger Clemens	1.25
30	Jose Cruz Jr.	.25

1998 Collector's Choice You Crash the Game

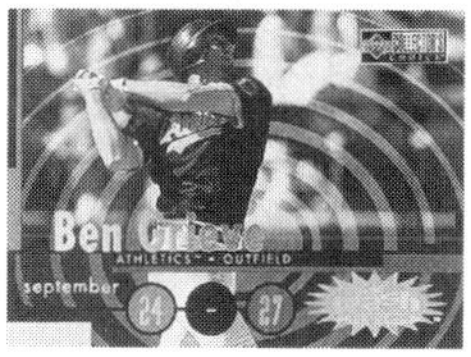

These 90 game cards were inserted one per five Series 2 packs. Each card features a player and a list of dates. If the pictured player hit a home run on one of those days, collectors with the card could mail it in for a graphically enhanced prize version. Instant Winner cards of each player were also inserted at the rate of 1:721 and could be exchanged for the complete 30-card prize set. Deadline for exchange of all winning cards was Dec. 1, 1998. Winning cards are designated here with an asterisk and can be expected to be somewhat scarcer than non-winning dates.

	MT
Complete Set (90):	90.00
Common Player:	.50
Instant Winner: 25X	
Inserted 1:5	
CG1 Ken Griffey Jr. (June 26-28*)	6.00
CG1 Ken Griffey Jr. (July 7)	4.00
CG1 Ken Griffey Jr. (Sept. 21-24*)	6.00
CG2 Travis Lee (July 27-30)	.50
CG2 Travis Lee (Aug. 27-30)	.50
CG2 Travis Lee (Sept. 17-20)	.50
CG3 Larry Walker (July 17-19)	.75
CG3 Larry Walker (Aug. 27-30*)	1.50
CG3 Larry Walker (Sept. 25-27*)	1.50
CG4 Tony Clark (July 9-12*)	.75
CG4 Tony Clark (June 30-July 2)	.50
CG4 Tony Clark (Sept. 4-6)	.50
CG5 Cal Ripken Jr. (June 22-25*)	4.00
CG5 Cal Ripken Jr. (July 7)	3.00
CG5 Cal Ripken Jr. (Sept. 4-6)	4.00
CG6 Tim Salmon (June 22-25)	.50
CG6 Tim Salmon (Aug. 28-30)	.50
CG6 Tim Salmon (Sept. 14-15)	.50
CG7 Vinny Castilla (June 30-July 2*)	.75
CG7 Vinny Castilla (Aug. 27-30*)	.75
CG7 Vinny Castilla (Sept. 7-10*)	.75
CG8 Fred McGriff (June 22-25)	.50
CG8 Fred McGriff (July 3-5)	.50
CG8 Fred McGriff (Sept. 18-20*)	.75
CG9 Matt Williams (July 17-29)	.50
CG9 Matt Williams (Sept. 14-16*)	.75
CG9 Matt Williams (Sept. 18-20)	.50
CG10Mark McGwire (July 7)	4.00
CG10Mark McGwire (July 24-26*)	6.00
CG10Mark McGwire (Aug. 18-19*)	6.00
CG11Albert Belle (July 3-5)	.75
CG11Albert Belle (Aug. 21-23*)	1.50
CG11Albert Belle (Sept. 11-13)	.75
CG12Jay Buhner (July 9-12*)	.75
CG12Jay Buhner (Aug. 6-9)	.50
CG12Jay Buhner (Sept. 25-27)	.50
CG13Vladimir Guerrero (June 22-25)	1.00
CG13Vladimir Guerrero (Aug. 10-12*)	1.50
CG13Vladimir Guerrero (Sept. 14-16*)	1.50
CG14Andruw Jones (July 16-19*)	1.50
CG14Andruw Jones (Aug. 27-30*)	1.50
CG14Andruw Jones (Sept. 17-20)	1.00
CG15Nomar Garciaparra (July 9-12)	2.00
CG15Nomar Garciaparra (Aug. 13-16*)	3.00
CG15Nomar Garciaparra (Sept. 24-27)	2.00
CG16Ken Caminiti (June 26-28*)	.75
CG16Ken Caminiti (July 13-15*)	.75
CG16Ken Caminiti (Sept. 10-13)	.50
CG17Sammy Sosa (July 9-12*)	4.00
CG17Sammy Sosa (Aug. 27-30*)	4.00
CG17Sammy Sosa (Sept. 10-20)	3.00
CG18Ben Grieve (June 30-July 2*)	1.50
CG18Ben Grieve (Aug. 14-16)	1.00
CG18Ben Grieve (Sept. 24-27)	1.00
CG19Mo Vaughn (July 7)	.50
CG19Mo Vaughn (Sept. 7-9)	.50
CG19Mo Vaughn (Sept. 24-27*)	.75
CG20Frank Thomas (July 7)	1.50
CG20Frank Thomas (July 17-19*)	2.50
CG20Frank Thomas (Sept. 4-6)	1.50
CG21Manny Ramirez (July 9-12)	1.00
CG21Manny Ramirez (Aug. 13-16*)	1.50
CG21Manny Ramirez (Sept. 18-20*)	1.50
CG22Jeff Bagwell (July 7)	1.25
CG22Jeff Bagwell (Aug. 28-30*)	2.00
CG22Jeff Bagwell (Sept. 4-6*)	2.00
CG23Jose Cruz Jr. (July 9-12)	.50
CG23Jose Cruz Jr. (Aug. 13-16)	.50
CG23Jose Cruz Jr. (Sept. 18-20)	.50
CG24Alex Rodriguez (July 7*)	3.00
CG24Alex Rodriguez (Aug. 6-9*)	3.00
CG24Alex Rodriguez (Sept. 21-23*)	3.00
CG25Mike Piazza (June 22-25*)	2.50
CG25Mike Piazza (July 7)	2.00
CG25Mike Piazza (Sept. 10-13*)	2.50
CG26Tino Martinez (June 26-28*)	.75
CG26Tino Martinez (July 9-12)	.50
CG26Tino Martinez (Aug. 13-16)	.50
CG27Chipper Jones (July 3-5)	2.00
CG27Chipper Jones (Aug. 27-30)	2.00
CG27Chipper Jones (Sept. 17-20)	2.00
CG28Juan Gonzalez (July 7)	1.50
CG28Juan Gonzalez (Aug. 6-9*)	2.50
CG28Juan Gonzalez (Sept. 11-13*)	2.50
CG29Jim Thome (June 22-23)	.50
CG29Jim Thome (July 23-26*)	.75
CG29Jim Thome (Sept. 24-27)	.50
CG30Barry Bonds (July 7*)	2.00
CG30Barry Bonds (Sept. 4-6)	1.50
CG30Barry Bonds (Sept. 18-20*)	2.00

1998 Collector's Choice You Crash the Game Winners

Collectors who redeemed winning "Crash" cards prior to the Dec. 1, 1998, deadline received an upgraded version of that player's card. Similar in format, the winners' cards have an action photo on front (different than the game card), with a metallic foil background. Instead of dates in the three circles at bottom are the letters "W I N". Backs have a career summary and stats, instead of the redemption instructions found on the game cards. The cards are numbered with a "CG" prefix. Cards of players who didn't homer during their designated dates were available only by redeeming a scarce (1:721 packs) Instant Win card. They are indicated here by "SP".

		MT
	Complete Set (30):	110.00
	Common Player:	1.50
CG1	Ken Griffey Jr.	12.00
CG2	Travis Lee (SP)	15.00
CG3	Larry Walker	2.25
CG4	Tony Clark	2.25
CG5	Cal Ripken Jr.	9.00
CG6	Tim Salmon (SP)	6.00
CG7	Vinny Castilla	1.50
CG8	Fred McGriff	1.50

CG9	Matt Williams	2.25
CG10	Mark McGwire	8.00
CG11	Albert Belle	3.00
CG12	Jay Buhner	1.50
CG13	Vladimir Guerrero	3.00
CG14	Andruw Jones	3.00
CG15	Nomar Garciaparra	7.50
CG16	Ken Caminiti	1.50
CG17	Sammy Sosa	3.00
CG18	Ben Grieve	3.00
CG19	Mo Vaughn	3.00
CG20	Frank Thomas	4.00
CG21	Manny Ramirez	3.00
CG22	Jeff Bagwell	4.50
CG23	Jose Cruz Jr. (SP)	6.00
CG24	Alex Rodriguez	7.50
CG25	Mike Piazza	7.50
CG26	Tino Martinez	2.25
CG27	Chipper Jones (SP)	24.00
CG28	Juan Gonzalez	6.00
CG29	Jim Thome	2.25
CG30	Barry Bonds	3.00

1998 Collector's Choice You Crash/ Game Instant Winner

Found on average of one per 721 packs, these Instant Winner cards could be redeemed (with a $2 handling fee) for a complete set of You Crash the Game exchange cards - the only way Crash winner cards of Travis Lee, Jose Cruz Jr. and Chipper Jones could be obtained. These special cards have an instant winner logo on front in place of game dates, and a congratulatory message on back along with instructions for redemption prior to the Dec. 1, 1998, deadline.

	MT
Complete Set (30):	250.00
Common Player:	5.00
(High-demand players' cards valued at 8X regular Crash game cards.)	

1998 Collector's Choice 5x7

These super-size (5" x 7") cards were one-per-box inserts in Series 2 retail packaging. Besides being four times the size of a normal card, the 5x7s are identical to the regular versions.

		MT
Complete Set (10):		15.00
Common Player:		1.00
306	Chipper Jones	3.00
321	Nomar Garciaparra	3.00
360	Larry Walker	1.00
450	Derek Jeter	3.00
463	Scott Rolen	2.00
480	Tony Gwynn	2.00
490	Barry Bonds	2.00
495	Alex Rodriguez	3.00
525	Jose Cruz Jr.	1.00
530	Roger Clemens	2.50

1983 Colonial Bread

The MVP of the 1982 World Series appears on this one-card set promoting a local bakery. The 3-1/2" x 2-1/2" card is printed in blue-and-white and has a picture of the player holding a loaf of bread on front. Backs have an ad for the baker and details of a sweepstakes.

		MT
(1)	Darrell Porter	3.00

1994 Colorado Rockies Police

The Rockies' premiere police set is an oversized (2-5/8" x 4") effort with posed and action player photos on a yellow and purple background on front. Team logo and name are above the photo, while ID and uniform number are beneath the photo. Backs are in black-and-white with a few bits of personal data and stats, a safety message and sponsors' logos. The cards are checklisted here in alphabetical order.

		MT
Complete Set (27):		11.00
Common Player:		.40
(1)	Don Baylor	.50
(2)	Dante Bichette	1.50
(3)	Willie Blair	.40
(4)	Kent Bottenfield	.40
(5)	Ellis Burks	.50
(6)	Vinny Castilla	.75
(7)	Marvin Freeman	.40
(8)	Andres Galarraga	2.00
(9)	Andres Galarraga (batting champion)	1.50
(10)	Joe Girardi	.40
(11)	Mike Harkey	.40
(12)	Greg Harris	.40
(13)	Charlie Hayes	.50
(14)	Darren Holmes	.50
(15)	Howard Johnson	.40
(16)	Nelson Liriano	.40
(17)	Roberto Mejia	.40
(18)	Mike Munoz	.40
(19)	David Nied	.40
(20)	Steve Reed	.40
(21)	Armando Reynoso	.40
(22)	Bruce Ruffin	.40
(23)	Danny Sheaffer	.40
(24)	Darrell Sherman	.40
(25)	Walt Weiss	.50
(26)	Eric Young	1.00
(27)	Rockies coaches (Larry Bearnarth, Dwight Evans, Gene Glynn, Ron Hassey, Bill Plummer, Don Zimmer)	.40

1995 Colorado Rockies Police

With only a dozen players included, this is one of the smallest safety sets of the genre. The 2-5/8" x 4" cards have color player action photos on front, bordered in black with the team logo in the lower-right corner. The player's last name and year appear in orange in the upper-right. Backs are in black-and-white and include a safety message or cartoon, and a few biographical data and stats. Cards are checklisted by uniform number.

		MT
Complete Set (12):		9.00
Common Player:		.50
6	Jason Bates	.50
7	Joe Girardi	.50
9	Vinny Castilla	1.00
10	Dante Bichette	1.00
12	Mike Kingery	.50
14	Andres Galarraga	1.50
20	Bill Swift	.50
21	Eric Young	.75
22	Walt Weiss	.50
25	Don Baylor	.60
26	Ellis Burks	.60
33	Larry Walker	2.50

1996 Colorado Rockies Police

The Rockies third annual police/fire safety set is the team's largest, at 27 cards. The set is identical in format (2-5/8" x 4") and design to the 1996 Royals police set, and has the same sponsor, Kansas City Life Insurance. Fronts have game-action photos, with the team logo, player last name and uniform number at bottom. Backs are printed in purple and feature a safety-message cartoon. The set was initially distributed to fans attending an April game. The set is checklisted here by uniform number.

		MT
Complete Set (27):		8.00
Common Player:		.25
1	Trenidad Hubbard	.25
3	Quinton McCracken	.25
6	Jason Bates	.25
9	Vinny Castilla	.45
10	Dante Bichette	.75
14	Andres Galarraga	.75
16	Curtis Leskanic	.25
18	Bruce Ruffin	.25
20	Bill Swift	.25
21	Eric Young	.35
22	Walt Weiss	.25
23	Bryan Rekar	.25
25	Don Baylor	.35
26	Ellis Burks	.35
28	Lance Painter	.25
30	Kevin Ritz	.25
31	Bret Saberhagen	.35
32	Mark Thompson	.25
33	Larry Walker	1.00
34	Jayhawk Owens	.25
35	John Vander Wal	.25
38	Roger Bailey	.25
39	Steve Reed	.25
40	Darren Holmes	.25
42	Armando Reynoso	.25
43	Mike Munoz	.25
44	Marvin Freeman	.25

1997 Colorado Rockies Police

In conjunction with the Colorado Association of Chiefs of Police, the Rockies handed out this safety set at a designated home game early in the season. It is the team's fourth annual safety set. The 2-1/2" x 3-1/2" cards feature game-action photos on front surrounded by a white border. The team logo is at upper-left; player identification is in purple and gray stripes diagonally at bottom. Backs are in black-and-white and have some player personal data, a career-best stat lines and a safety message. Cards are numbered by uniform number in a baseball at upper-right.

		MT
Complete Set (12):		10.00
Common Player:		.60
3	Quinton McCracken	.60
8	Kirt Manwaring	.60
9	Vinny Castilla	.90
10	Dante Bichette	1.50
14	Andres Galarraga	1.50
20	Bill Swift	.60
21	Eric Young	1.00
22	Walt Weiss	.60
25	Don Baylor	.75
26	Ellis Burks	.60
33	Larry Walker	2.00
00	Dinger (mascot)	.60

1998 Colorado Rockies Police

Children attending a May 31 promotional game at Coors Field received this set of Rockies cards. Game-action color photos are featured on front, borderless at top, bottom and left. At right is a vertical gray stripe with the player's name and position; team logo and name are at bottom. On back is a player portrait photo, identification, biographical details, an inspirational message and logos of the sponsoring organizations.

		MT
Complete Set (12):		12.00
Common Player:		.35
3	Mike Lansing	.75
5	Neifi Perez	.75
8	Kirt Manwaring	.50
9	Vinny Castilla	1.50
10	Dante Bichette	1.00
17	Todd Helton	3.00
25	Don Baylor	.75
26	Ellis Burks	.50
33	Larry Walker	2.00
34	Pedro Astacio	.50
57	Darryl Kile	.50
00	Dinger (mascot)	.50

1998 ComEd Sammy Sosa

This single-card promotional giveaway was distributed to fans at the Sept. 20 Cubs game. The 2-1/2" x 3-1/2" card has a color action photo of Sosa on front, within blue borders. "SLAMMIN' SAMMY!" is printed at top; the Cubs logo and year are printed at bottom. Back has a photo of Sosa in the field, biographical details and highlights of the 1998 season. The sponsor's logo is at bottom.

	MT
Sammy Sosa	8.00

1995 Comic Images National Pastime Promo

This unnumbered card was issued to promote Comic Images' set of baseball history cards. The 2-1/2" x 3-1/2" card has a familiar color photo of company spokesman Phil Rizzuto on front, done up in chromium technology and with the Yankees team logos removed from the uniform. The back advertises the forthcoming card set.

	MT
Phil Rizzuto	3.00

1995 Comic Images The National Pastime

This set is principally made up of 19th Century baseball images done up in 20th Century chromium card technology to detail the history of baseball from the 1860s through the 1950s. As might be expected, there was little positive reaction from collectors. Photos of old baseball collectibles, including a few vintage baseball cards are scattered throughout the set as are a few actual player photos. Hall of Famer Phil Rizzuto was tapped to promote the issue, but his name was misspelled on the cards' box.

		MT
Complete Set (90):		8.00
Common Card:		.10
1	Sportsman's Park	.10
2	Harper's Weekly, August, 1913	.10
3	Shibe Park	.10
4	Polo Grounds Print	.10
5	Forbes Field	.10
6	Hall of Fame (Phil Rizzuto)	.25
7	League Park	.10
8	Highlander Park	.10
9	South Side Park	.10
10	Catchers' Mitt	.10
11	Baseball Trophy	.10
12	Baseball Plate	.10
13	Bisque Figure	.10
14	Beanbag	.10
15	Tobacco Carved Figure	.10
16	Sunday Magazine	.10
17	Street & Smith Sport	.10
18	Collier's	.10
19	Bluebook	.10
20	Chadwick's	.10
21	Harper's Weekly	.10
22	American Magazine	.10
23	Crazy Baseball Stories	.10
24	New York Giants, 1892	.10
25	Cincinnati American Association, 1882	.10
26	Chicago White Stockings, 1885	.10
27	Baltimore Blues, 1890	.10
28	Chicago & All-Americans, 1889	.10
29	Philadelphia Baseball Team, 1910	.10
30	1887 Goodwin & Co. Champions	.25
31	John McGraw	.15
32	Home Run (1885 trade card)	.10
33	Lorillard Chicago BBC	.10
34	Boston BBC	.10
35	Out at First (trade card)	.10
36	"Coffee Cards"	.10
37	Uncut Sheet - Detail	.10
38	Tobin Lithographers	.10
39	Uncut Sheet - Die Cut	.10
40	Patsy Dougherty (T207)	.10
41	A Regular Corker (1885 trade card)	.10
42	Barker's Advertising Book	.10
43	Toledo BBC Tobacco Poster	.10
44	Shredded Wheat Advertisement	.10
45	BVD Advertisement	.10
46	[illegible]	[illegible]
47	Japanese Poster	.10
48	Safe Hit Vegetable Crate Label	.10
49	Slide, Kelly, Slide Poster	.10
50	Peck & Snyder Hat Advertisement	.10
51	Reach Gloves Catalog	.10
52	New York Giants Scorecard	.10
53	Game Card	.10
54	Wright & Ditson Guide	.10
55	1933 All-Star Game Program	.10
56	Stadium Scene	.10
57	Currier & Ives Print	.10
58	Scorecard Artwork	.10
59	Folk Art	.10
60	Batter (wrong front, belongs to #73)	.10
61	Cartoon	.10
62	Teddy Roosevelt Cartoon	.10
63	Uncle Sam Cartoon	.10
64	Casey at the Bat	.15
65	Seymour Church Print	.10
66	Valentine Card	.10
67	Pinup Book	.10
68	Uncle Sam WWI Sheet Music	.10
69	Baseball Sheet Music	.10
70	Saturday Globe	.10
71	Ft. Wayne Woman Player	.15
72	Spalding Baseball Guide	.10
73	Rally Day Postcard (wrong front, belongs to #60)	.10
74	Spalding Advertisement Die Cut	.10
75	Our Baseball Club Cover	.10
76	Jake Beckley	.15
77	Cap Anson (Allen & Ginter album page)	.25
78	St. Louis Player	.10
79	Sam Thompson (Scrap's Die Cut)	.15
80	Bobby Wallace (Turkey Red cabinet)	.15
81	Fogarty & McGuire (Jim Fogarty, Deacon McGuire) (1887 Kalamazoo Bats detail)	.15
82	Yank Robinson (1887 die-cut game card)	.15
83	Charles Comiskey (1887 Scrap's tobacco die-cut)	.15
84	Picked Off! (action photo)	.10
85	Error (action photo)	.10
86	Third Base (action photo)	.10
87	Safe at Home (action photo)	.10
88	Baseball Action (action photo)	.10
89	Great Fielding (action photo)	.10
90	Checklist	.10

1991 Conlon Collection Prototypes

The cards which previewed the debut set of Conlon Collection cards in the 1990s can generally be identified by the lack of Major League Baseball logo and Curtis Management copyright information on back. Except for the colorized Babe Ruth card, they are not otherwise marked as prototypes. While most of the 1991 Conlon prototypes were distributed in relatively small quantities, reportedly 2,940, the colorized Ty Cobbs was an edition of 60,000 and the colorized Babe Ruth card was produced for the 12th National Sports Collectors Convention in Anaheim, Calif., to the tune of 225,000 cards.

		MT
Complete Set (6):		30.00
Common Player:		5.00
13	Ty Cobb (colorized edition of 60,000)	3.00
34	Dizzy Dean	4.00
111	Lou Gehrig	6.00
145	Babe Ruth	7.50
145	Babe Ruth (colorized, edition of 225,000)	6.00
250	Ty Cobb	6.00

1991 Conlon Collection

This 330-card set features the photography of Charles Martin Conlon, who was active from before 1910 through the early 1940s. Black-and-white photos are set against black borders on the UV-coated card fronts. Megacards worked with The Sporting News (owners of the Conlon photos) to release the set. Several subsets are featured such as Hall of Famers, 1927 New York Yankees, MVPs and more. The backs feature statistics and career highlights and can be found either with or without the MLB logo.

		MT
Complete Set (330):		24.00
Common Player:		.10
1	Rogers Hornsby	.15
2	James E. Foxx	.15
3	Jay H. Dean	.15
4	Walter J.V. Maranville	.15
5	Paul G. Waner	.15
6	Lloyd J. Waner	.15
7	Melvin T. Ott	.15
8	John P. Wagner	.15
9	Walter P. Johnson	.15
10	Carl O. Hubbell	.15
11	Frank F. Frisch	.15
12	Hazen S. Cuyler	.15
13	Charles H. Ruffing	.15
14	Henry B. Greenberg	.15
15	John J. Evers	.15
16	Hugh A. Jennings	.15
17	David J. Bancroft	.15
18	Joseph M. Medwick	.15
19	Theodore A. Lyons	.15
20	Charles A. Bender	.15
21	Edward T. Collins	.15
22	James L. Bottomley	.15
23	Robert M. Grove	.15
24	Max Carey	.15
25	Burleigh A. Grimes	.15
26	Ross M. Youngs	.15
27	Ernest N. Lombardi	.15
28	Joseph V. McCarthy	.15
29	Lewis R. Wilson	.15
30	Charles H. Klein	.15
31	Howard E. Averill Sr.	.15
32	Grover C. Alexander	.15
33	Charles J. Hafey	.15
34	William B. McKechnie	.15
35	Robert W.A. Feller	.15
36	Harold J. Traynor	.15
37	Charles D. Stengel	.15
38	Joseph F. Vaughan	.15
39	Eppa Rixey	[illegible]
40	Joseph W. Sewell	.15
41	Urban C. Faber	.15
42	Travis C. Jackson	.15
43	Jesse J. Haines	.15
44	Tristram E. Speaker	.15
45	Cornelius Mack	.15
46	Cornelius Mack	.15
47	Cornelius Mack	.15
48	Raymond W. Schalk	.15
49	Aloysius H. Simmons	.15
50	Joseph E. Cronin	.15
51	Gordon S. Cochrane	.15
52	Harry E. Hellmann	.15
53	John R. Mize	.15
54	Edgar C. Rice	.15
55	Edd J. Roush	.15
56	Enos B. Slaughter	.15
57	Christopher Mathewson	.15
58	Fred C. Lindstrom	.15
59	Charles L. Hartnett	.15
60	George L. Kelly	.15
61	Stanley R. Harris	.15
62	Leon A. Goslin	.15
63	Henry E. Manush	.15
64	William H. Terry	.15
65	John J. McGraw	.15
66	George H. Sisler	.15
67	Vernon L. Gomez	.10
68	Joseph I. Judge	.10
69	Thomas J. Thevenow	.10
70	Charles M. Gelbert	.10
71	Minter C. Hayes	.10
72	Robert R. Fothergill	.10
73	Adam A. Comorosky	.10
74	Earl S. Smith	.10
75	Samuel D. Gray	.10
76	Peter W. Appleton	.10
77	Eugene Moore Jr.	.10
78	Arndt L. Jorgens	.10
79	William H. Knickerbocker	.10
80	Carl N. Reynolds	.10
81	Oscar D. Melillo	.10
82	John H. Burnett	.10
83	Alvin J. Powell	.10
84	John J. Murphy	.10
85	Leroy E. Parmelee	.10
86	James A. Ripple	.10
87	Gerald H. Walker	.10
88	George L. Earnshaw	.10
89	William H. Southworth	.10
90	Wallace Moses	.10
91	George E. Walberg	.10
92	James J. Dykes	.10
93	Charles H. Root	.10
94	John W. Cooney	.10
95	Charles J. Grimm	.10
96	Robert L. Johnson	.10
97	John W. Scott	.10
98	Raymond A. Radcliff	.10
99	Frederick R. Ostermueller	.10
100	Julian V. Wera	.10
101	Miller J. Huggins	.15
102	Raymond A. Morehart	.10
103	Bernard O. Bengough	.10
104	Walter H. Ruether	.10
105	Earle B. Combs	.15
106	Myles L. Thomas	.10
107	Benjamin E. Paschal	.10
108	Cedric M. Durst	.10
109	William W. Moore	.10
110	George H. Ruth	.50
111	Louis H. Gehrig	.50
112	Joseph A. Dugan	.10
113	Anthony M. Lazzeri	.15
114	Urban J. Shocker	.10
115	Waite C. Hoyt	.15
116	Charles T. O'Leary	.10
117	Arthur Fletcher	.10
118	Tharon L. Collins	.10
119	Joseph O. Giard	.10
120	Herbert J. Pennock	.15
121	Michael Gazella	.10
122	Robert W. Meusel	.10
123	George W. Pipgras	.10
124	John P. Grabowski	.10
125	Mark A. Koenig	.10
126	Stanley C. Hack	.10
127	Earl O. Whitehill	.10
128	William C. Lee	.10
129	Frank O. Mancuso	.10
130	Francis R. Blades	.10
131	John I. Burns	.10
132	Clinton H. Brown	.10
133	William J. Dietrich	.10
134	Darrell E. Blanton	.10
135	Harry B. Hooper	.15
136	Charles H. Shorten	.10
137	Clarence W. Walker	.10
138	George Foster	.10
139	John J. Barry	.10
140	Samuel P. Jones	.10
141	Ernest G. Shore	.10
142	Hubert B. Leonard	.10
143	Herbert J. Pennock	.15
144	Harold C. Janvrin	.10
145	George H. Ruth	.40
146	George E. Lewis	.10
147	William L. Gardner	.10
148	Richard C. Hoblitzel	.10
149	Lewis E. Scott	.10
150	Carl W. Mays	.10
151	John A. Niehoff	.10
152	[illegible]	.10
153	Leon K. Ames	.10
154	Fred Williams	.10
155	William W. Hinchman	.10
156	James R. Shawkey	.10
157	Walter C. Pipp	.10
158	George J. Burns	.10
159	Robert H. Veach	.10
160	Harold H. Chase	.10
161	Thomas L. Hughes	.10
162	Derrill B. Pratt	.10
163	Henry K. Groh	.10
164	Zachariah D. Wheat	.15
165	Francis J. O'Doul	.10
166	William E. Kamm	.10
167	Paul G. Waner	.15
168	Fred C. Snodgrass	.10
169	Floyd C. Herman	.10
170	Albert H. Bridwell	.10
171	John T. Meyers	.10
172	John B. Lobert	.10
173	Raymond B. Bressler	.10
174	Samuel P. Jones	.10
175	Robert A. O'Farrell	.10
176	George Toporcer	.10
177	George E. McNeely	.10
178	John H. Knott	.10
179	Clarence F. Mueller	.10
180	Thomas J.D. Bridges	.10
181	Lloyd A. Brown	.10
182	Lawrence J. Benton	.10
183	Max F. Bishop	.10
184	Morris Berg	.30
185	Ralph F. Perkins	.10
186	Stephen F. O'Neill	.10
187	Glenn C. Myatt	.10
188	Joseph A. Kuhel	.10
189	Martin J. McManus	.10
190	Charles F. Lucas	.10
191	John P. McInnis	.10
192	Edmund J. Miller	.10
193	James L. Sewell	.10
194	William H. Sherdel	.10
195	Harold J. Rhyne	.10
196	Guy T. Bush	.10
197	Ervin Fox	.10
198	Wesley C. Ferrell	.10
199	Roy C. Johnson	.10
200	William Wambsganss	.10
201	George H. Burns	.10
202	Clarence E. Mitchell	.10
203	Cornelius Ball	.10
204	John H. Neun	.10
205	Homer W. Summa	.10
206	Ernest K. Padgett	.10
207	Walter H. Holke	.10
208	Forrest G. Wright	.10
209	Henry M. Gowdy	.10
210	James W. Taylor	.10
211	Benjamin C. Cantwell	.10
212	Joseph F. Demaree	.10
213	Samuel P. Derringer	.10
214	William A. Hallahan	.10
215	Daniel K. MacFayden	.10
216	Harry F. Rice	.10
217	Robert Eldridge Smith	.10
218	Jackson R. Stephenson	.10
219	Perce L. Malone	.10
220	Henry B. Tate	.10
221	Joseph F. Vosmik	.10
222	George A. Watkins	.10
223	James Wilson	.10
224	George E. Uhle	.10
225	Melvin T. Ott	.15
226	Nicholas Altrock	.10
227	Charles H. Ruffing	.15
228	Joseph V.L. Krakauskas	.10
229	Walter A. Berger	.10
230	Norman L. Newsom	.10
231	Lonnie Warneke	.10
232	Frank E. Snyder	.10
233	Myril O. Hoag	.10
234	Baldomero M. Almada	.10
235	Ivy B. Wingo	.10
236	James P. Austin	.10
237	Henry J. Bonura	.10
238	Russell G. Wrightstone	.10
239	Alfred C. Todd	.10
240	Harold B. Warstler	.10
241	Samuel F. West	.10
242	Arthur C. Reinhart	.10
243	Walter C. Stewart	.10
244	John B. Gooch	.10
245	Eugene F. Hargrave	.10
246	George W. Harper	.10
247	George W. Connally	.10
248	Edgar G. Braxton	.10
249	Walter H. Schang	.10
250	Tyrus R. Cobb	.50
251	Rogers Hornsby	.15
252	Richard W. Marquard	.15
253	Carl O. Hubbell	.15
254	Joe Wood	.10
255	Robert M. Grove	.15
256	Lynwood T. Rowe	.10
257	Alvin F. Crowder	.10
258	Walter P. Johnson	.15
259	Charles J. Hafey	.15
260	Frederick L. Fitzsimmons	.10
261	William E. Webb	.10
262	Earle B. Combs	.15
263	Edward J. Konetchy	.10
264	Taylor L. Douthit	.10
265	Lloyd J. Waner	.15
266	Gordon S. Cochrane	.15
267	John O. Wilson	.10
268	Harold J. Traynor	.10
269	Virgil L. Davis	.10
270	Henry E. Manush	.15
271	Michael F. Higgins	.10
272	Adrian Joss	.15
273	Edward Augustine Walsh	.15
274	Johnny L.R. Martin	.10
275	Joseph W. Sewell	.15
276	Hubert B. Leonard	.10
277	Clifford C. Cravath	.10
278	Oral C. Hildebrand	.10
279	Remy P. Kremer	.10
280	Frank A. Pytlak	.10
281	Samuel D. Byrd	.10

282 Curtis B. Davis .10
283 Lewis A. Fonseca .10
284 Herold D. Ruel .10
285 Julius J. Solters .10
286 Fred W. Schulte .10
287 John P. Quinn .10
288 Arthur C. Whitney .10
289 Jonathon T. Stone .10
290 Hugh M. Critz .10
291 Ira J. Flagstead .10
292 George F. Grantham .10
293 Samuel D. Hale .10
294 James F. Hogan .10
295 Oswald L. Bluege .10
296 Debs Garms .10
297 Augistaf B. Friberg .10
298 Edward A. Brandt .10
299 Ralston B. Hemsley .10
300 Charles H. Klein .15
301 Morton C. Cooper .10
302 James L. Bottomley .10
303 James E. Foxx .15
304 Frank Schulte .10
305 Frank F. Frisch .15
306 Frank A. McCormick .10
307 Jacob E. Daubert .10
308 Roger T. Peckinpaugh .10
309 George H. Burns .10
310 Louis H. Gehrig .40
311 Aloysius H. Simmons .15
312 Edward T. Collins .15
313 Charles L. Hartnett .15
314 Joseph E. Cronin .15
315 Paul G. Waner .15
316 Robert A. O'Farrell .10
317 Lawrence J. Doyle .10
318 Lynford H. Lary .10
319 Frank S. May .10
320 Roy H. Spencer .10
321 Samuel R. Coffman .10
322 Peter J. Donohue .10
323 George W. Haas .10
324 Edward S. Farrell .10
325 Charles F. Rhem .10
326 Frederick Marberry .10
327 Charles Martin Conlon .10
328 Checklist 1-110 .10
329 Checklist 111-220 .10
330 Checklist 221-330 .10

1992 Conlon Collection Prototypes

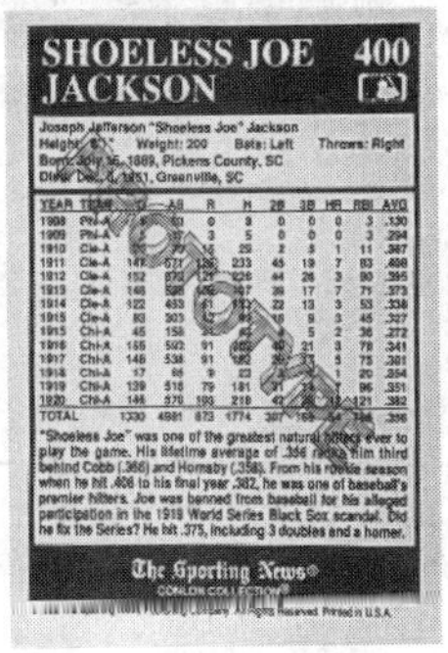

Along with the 1991 Babe Ruth prototype card, these five cards were distributed at the Anaheim National Sports Collectors Convention in 1991. The announced distribution was 20,000 of each card except the Joe Jackson, which had a press run of 67,000. Except for card 331, all the prototypes have different numbers than the same card in the regular-issue Conlon set. Each of the 1992 cards has a gray "PROTOTYPE" overprinted diagonally on the back.

		MT
Complete Set (6):		12.00
Common Player:		1.00
14	Joe Jackson (colorized, edition of 60,000)	4.00
331	Christy Mathewson	2.00
400	Joe Jackson	3.00
450	Hughie Jennings	1.00
500	Ty Cobb	2.50
520	Goose Goslin	1.00

1992 Conlon Collection

In their second season, the 330 cards of the Conlon Collection were numbered consecutively where the 1991 premiere issue ended. Cards 331-660 also maintained the high-gloss black-and-white format of the previous year. Many subsets within the issue carry special designations on the card fronts. Subsets included no-hitters, Triple Crown winners, "Great Stories," nicknames and more.

		MT
Complete Set (330):		12.00
Common Player:		.10

331 Christopher Mathewson .15
332 George L. Wiltse .10
333 George N. Rucker .10
334 Leon K. Ames .10
335 Charles A. Bender .15
336 Joe Wood .10
337 Edward Augustine Walsh .15
338 George J. Mullin .10
339 Earl A. Hamilton .10
340 Charles M Tesreau .10
341 James Scott .10
342 Richard W. Marquard .10
343 Claude R. Hendrix .15
344 James S. Lavender .10
345 Leslie A. Bush .10
346 Hubert B. Leonard .10
347 Fred A. Toney .10
348 James L. Vaughn .10
349 Ernest G. Koob .10
350 Robert Groom .10
351 Ernest G. Shore .10
352 Horace O. Eller .10
353 Walter P. Johnson .15
354 Charles C. Robertson .10
355 Jesse L. Barnes .10
356 Samuel P. Jones .10
357 Howard J. Ehmke .10
358 Jesse J. Haines .15
359 Theodore A. Lyons .15
360 Carl O. Hubbell .15
361 Wesley C. Ferrell .10
362 Robert J. Burke .10
363 Paul D. Dean .10
364 Norman L. Newsom .10
365 Lloyd V. Kennedy .10
366 William J. Dietrich .10
367 John S. Vander Meer .10
368 John S. Vander Meer .10
369 Montgomery M. Pearson .10
370 Robert W.A. Feller .15
371 Lonnie Warneke .10
372 James A. Tobin .10
373 Earl A. Moore .10
374 William H. Dineen .10
375 Malcolm W. Eason .10
376 George A. Mogridge .10
377 Clarence A. Vance .15
378 James O. Carleton .10
379 Clyde M. Shoun .10
380 Franklin W. Hayes .10
381 Benjamin R. Frey .10
382 Henry W. Johnson .10
383 Ralph Kress .10
384 John T. Allen .10
385 Harold A. Trosky Sr. .10
386 Eugene E. Robertson .10
387 Lemuel F. Young .10
388 George A. Selkirk .10
389 Edwin L. Wells .10
390 James D. Weaver .10
391 George H. McQuinn .10
392 John B. Lobert .10
393 Ernest E. Swanson .10
394 Ernest A. Nevers .10
395 James J. Levey .10
396 Hugo F. Bezdek .10
397 Walter E. French .10
398 Charles F. Berry .10
399 Franklin T. Grube .10
400 Charles W. Dressen .10
401 Alfred E. Neale .10
402 Henry A. Vick .10
403 James F. Thorpe .50
404 Walter J. Gilbert .10
405 John L. Urban .10
406 Everett V. Purdy .10
407 Albert O. Wright .10
408 William M. Urbanski .10
409 Charles W. Fischer .10
410 John R. Warner .10
411 Chalmer W. Cissell .10
412 Mervin D.J. Shea .10
413 Adolfo Luque .10
414 John L. Bassler .10
415 Arvel O. Hale .10
416 Lawrence R. French .10
417 William C. Walker .10
418 Allen L. Cooke .10
419 Philip J. Todt .10
420 Ivy P. Andrews .10
421 William J. Herman .15
422 Tristram E. Speaker .15
423 Aloysius H. Simmons .15
424 Lewis R. Wilson .15
425 Tyrus R. Cobb .40
426 George H. Ruth .50
427 Ernest N. Lombardi .15
428 Jay H. Dean .15
429 Lloyd J. Waner .15
430 Henry B. Greenberg .15
431 Robert M. Grove .15
432 Gordon S. Cochrane .15
433 Burleigh A. Grimes .15
434 Harold J. Traynor .15
435 John R. Mize .15
436 Edgar C. Rice .15
437 Leon A. Goslin .15
438 Charles H. Klein .15
439 Cornelius Mack .15
440 James L. Bottomley .15
441 Jackson R. Stephenson .10
442 Kenneth Williams .10
443 Charles B. Adams .10
444 Joseph J. Jackson .50
445 Harold Newhouser .15
446 Wesley C. Ferrell .10
447 Francis J. O'Doul .10
448 Walter H. Schang .10
449 Sherwood R. Magee .10
450 Michael J. Donlin .10
451 Roger M. Cramer .10
452 Richard W. Bartell .10
453 Earle T. Mack .10
454 Walter G. Brown .10
455 John A. Heving .10
456 Percy L. Jones .10
457 Theodore Blankenship .10
458 Absalom H. Wingo .10
459 Roger P. Bresnahan .15
460 William J. Klem .15
461 Charles L. Gehringer .15
462 Stanley A. Coveleski .15
463 Edward S. Plank .15
464 Clark C.F. Griffith .15
465 Herbert J. Pennock .15
466 Earle B. Combs .15
467 Robert P. Doerr .15
468 Waite C. Hoyt .15
469 Thomas H. Connolly .15
470 Harry B. Hooper .15
471 Richard B. Ferrell .15
472 William G. Evans .15
473 William J. Herman .15
474 William M. Dickey .15
475 Lucius B. Appling .15
476 Ralph A. Pinelli .10
477 Donald E. McNair .10
478 John F. Blake .10
479 Valentine J. Picinich .10
480 Fred A. Heimach .10
481 John G. Graney .10
482 Ewell A. Russell .10
483 Urban C. Faber .15
484 Benjamin M. Kauff .10
485 Clarence L. Rowland .10
486 Robert H. Veach .10
487 James C. Bagby .10
488 William D. Perritt .10
489 Charles L. Herzog .10
490 Arthur Fletcher .10
491 Walter H. Holke .10
492 Arthur N. Nehf .10
493 Lafayette F. Thompson .10
494 James D. Welsh .10
495 Oscar J. Vitt .10
496 Owen T. Carroll .10
497 James K. O'Dea .10
498 Fredrick M. Frankhouse .10
499 Jewel W. Ens .10
500 Morris Arnovich .10
501 Walter Gerber .10
502 George W. Davis .10
503 Charles S. Myer .10
504 Samuel A. Leslie .10
505 William C. Bolton .10
506 Fred Walker .10
507 John W. Smith .10
508 Irving D. Hadley .10
509 Clyde E. Crouse .10
510 Joseph C. Glenn .10
511 Clyde E. Kimsey .10
512 Louis K. Finney .10
513 Alfred V. Lawson .10
514 Charles P. Fullis .10
515 Earl H. Sheely .10
516 George Gibson .10
517 John J. Broaca .10
518 Bibb A. Falk .10
519 Frank O. Hurst .10
520 Grover A. Hartley .10
521 Donald H. Heffner .10
522 Harvey L. Hendrick .10
523 Allen S. Sothoron .10
524 Anthony F. Piet .10
525 Tyrus R. Cobb .40
526 James E. Foxx .15
527 Rogers Hornsby .15
528 Napoleon LaJoie .15
529 Louis H. Gehrig .40
530 Henry Zimmerman .10
531 Charles H. Klein .15
532 Hugh Duffy .15
533 Robert M. Grove .15
534 Grover C. Alexander .15
535 Amos W. Rusie .15
536 Vernon L. Gomez .15
537 William H. Walters .10
538 Urban J. Hodapp .10
539 Bruce D. Campbell .10
540 Horace M. Lisenbee .10
541 John F. Fournier .10
542 James R. Tabor .10
543 John H. Burnett .10
544 Roy A. Hartzell .10
545 Walter P. Gautreau .10
546 Emil O. Yde .10
547 Robert L. Johnson .10
548 Joseph J. Hauser .10
549 Edward M. Reulbach .10
550 Baldomero M. Almada .10
551 Gordon S. Cochrane .15
552 Carl O. Hubbell .15
553 Charles L. Gehringer .15
554 Aloysius H. Simmons .15
555 Mordecai P.C. Brown .15
556 Hugh A. Jennings .15
557 Norman A. Elberfeld .10
558 Charles D. Stengel .10
559 Alexander Schacht .10
560 James E. Foxx .15
561 George L. Kelly .15
562 Lloyd J. Waner .15
563 Paul G. Waner .15
564 Walter P. Johnson .15
565 John Franklin Baker .15
566 Roy J. Hughes .10
567 Lewis S. Riggs .10
568 John H. Whitehead .10
569 Elam R. Vangilder .10
570 William A. Zitzmann .10
571 Walter J. Schmidt .10
572 John A. Tavener .10
573 Joseph E. Genewich .10
574 John A. Marcum .10
575 Fred Hofmann .10
576 Robert A. Rolfe .10
577 Victor G. Sorrell .10
578 Floyd J. Scott .10
579 Alphonse Thomas .10
580 Alfred J. Smith .10
581 Walter J. Henline .10
582 Edward T. Collins .15
583 Earle B. Combs .15
584 John J. McGraw .15
585 Lewis R. Wilson .15
586 Charles L. Hartnett .15
587 Hazen S. Cuyler .15
588 William H. Terry .15
589 Joseph V. McCarthy .15
590 Henry B. Greenberg .15
591 Tristram E. Speaker .15
592 William B. McKechnie .15
593 Stanley R. Harris .15
594 Herbert J. Pennock .15
595 George H. Sisler .15
596 Fred C. Lindstrom .15
597 Howard E. Averill Sr. .15
598 David J. Bancroft .15
599 Cornelius Mack .15
600 Joseph E. Cronin .15
601 Kenneth L. Ash .10
602 Alfred R. Spohrer .10
603 Lee R. Mahaffey .10
604 James F. O'Rourke .10
605 Ulysses S.G. Stoner .10
606 Frank H. Gabler .10
607 Thomas F. Padden .10
608 Charles A. Shires .10
609 Sherrod M. Smith .10
610 Philip Weintraub .10
611 Russell Van Atta .10
612 Joyner C. White .10
613 Clifford G. Melton .10
614 James J. Ring .10
615 John H. Sand .10
616 David D. Alexander .10
617 Kent Greenfield .10
618 Edwin H. Dyer .10
619 William H. Sherdel .10
620 Hubert M. Lanier .10
621 Robert A. O'Farrell .10
622 Rogers Hornsby .15
623 William A. Beckman .10
624 Morton C. Cooper .10
625 William P. Delancey .10
626 Martin W. Marion .10
627 William H. Southworth .10
628 John R. Mize .15
629 Joseph M. Medwick .15
630 Grover C. Alexander .15
631 Paul D. Dean .10
632 Herman S. Bell .10
633 William W. Cooper .10
634 Frank F. Frisch .15
635 Jay H. Dean .15
636 Donald J. Gutteridge .10
637 Johnny L.R. Martin .10
638 Edward J. Konetchy .10
639 William A. Hallahan .10
640 Lonnie Warneke .10
641 Terry B. Moore .10
642 Enos B. Slaughter .15
643 Clarence F. Mueller .10
644 George Toporcer .10
645 James L. Bottomely .15
646 Francis R. Blades .10
647 Jesse J. Haines .10
648 Andrew A. High .10
649 Miller J. Huggins .10
650 Ernesto R. Orsatti .10
651 Lester R. Bell .10
652 Charles E. Street .10
653 Walter H. Roettger .10
654 Sylvester W. Johnson .10
655 Miguel A. Gonzalez .10
656 James A. Collins .15
657 Charles J. Hafey .15
658 Checklist 331-440 .10
659 Checklist 441-550 .10
660 Checklist 551-660 .10

1992-94 Conlon Collection Gold

Four of the heroes of the inaugural All-Star Game of 1933 were featured in a pop-up ad in the program for the 1992 Game in San Diego. One card was inserted into each of the programs printed for distribution at the game and by mail order. Each card was reported printed in an edition of 34,000. Cards are similar in format to the regular Conlon Collection issues except for the gold-foil border around the player photo on front and the use of a "G" suffix to the card number. A banner at top front reads, "Game of the Century." On back is a summary of the player's 1933 All-Star performance and his stats. Gold editions of other Conlon cards were also issued in several different venues in 1993-94. Six cards (#665-880) were included in 1992 Conlon factory sets in editions of up to 90,000. The Johnson-Ryan gold card was available only in packaging sold in Eckerd stores, while the 1994 Cobb gold card was only available at Toys R Us. Cards are numbered with a "G" suffix.

		MT
Complete Set (12):		30.00
Common Player:		2.00
661	Bill Terry	2.00
662	Lefty Gomez	2.00
663	Babe Ruth	7.50
664	Frankie Frisch	2.00
665	Carl Hubbell	2.00
667	Charlie Gehringer (edition of 20,000)	2.00
730	Luke Appling (edition of 20,000)	2.00
770	Tommy Henrich	2.00
820	John McGraw	2.00
880	Gabby Hartnett	2.00
934	Walter Johnson, Nolan Ryan (edition of 100,000)	6.00
1000	Ty Cobb (edition of 100,000)	3.00

1992 Conlon Collection 13th National

These samples of the 1993 Conlon Collection series were distributed at the National Sports Collectors Convention in Atlanta in 1992. Other than the Joe Jackson card, they carry the same numbers as the regularly issued versions. Designs are also identical except for the overprint on back in outline letters, "13TH NATIONAL".

		MT
Complete Set (4):		4.00
Common Player:		.50
14	Joe Jackson	1.00
663	George H. Ruth	2.00
775	John T. Meyers	.50
800	James L. Vaughn	.50

1993 Conlon Collection Prototypes

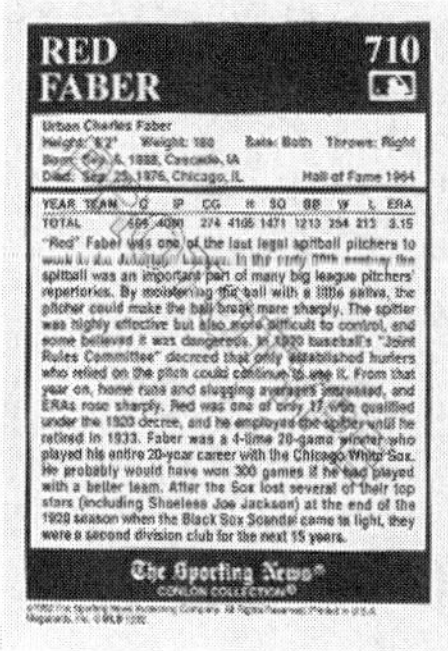

The cards in this issue were produced to preview the basic set and various subsets of the 1993 Conlon Collection issue. Cards are similar to the regular-issue set with the exception that the word "PROTOTYPE" is printed in gray diagonally on back. Production of most of the black-and-white cards was 60,000, though Gomez and Frisch were limited to 10,000 apiece.

		MT
Complete Set (8):		3.00
Common Player:		1.00
661	Bill Terry	1.00
662	Lefty Gomez	1.00
663	Babe Ruth	6.00
664	Frankie Frisch	1.00
710	Red Faber	1.00
775	Chief Meyers	1.00
800	Hippo Vaughn	1.00
888	Babe Ruth (colorized, edition of 52,000)	5.00
905	Lena Blackburne	1.00
934	Walter Johnson, Nolan Ryan (colorized edition of 52,000)	4.00

1993 Conlon Collection

The third annual Conlon Collection issue of 330 cards is numbered 661-990, a continuation of the series produced in 1991-92. The format of black-and-white photos produced 50-90 years ago by Charles Martin Conlon and surrounded by a wide black border and UV coating was continued. As with earlier issues, card backs contain brief biographical data, a few stats and well-written career highlights. The 1993 set also featured many subsets arranged by topic, such as spitballers, native Americans, players who overcame handicaps, etc. One subset compared Nolan Ryan with star pitchers in baseball history and included a fantasy photo of Ryan shaking hands in the dugout with Walter Johnson (card #934).

		MT
Complete Set (330):		15.00
Common Player:		.10
661	William H. Terry	.15
662	Vernon L. Gomez	.15
663	George H. Ruth	.50
664	Frank F. Frisch	.15
665	Carl O. Hubbell	.15
666	Aloysius H. Simmons	.15
667	Charles L. Gehringer	.15
668	Howard E. Averill Sr.	.15
669	Robert M. Grove	.15
670	Harold J. Traynor	.15
671	Charles H. Klein	.15
672	Paul G. Waner	.15
673	Louis H. Gehrig	.40
674	Richard B. Ferrell	.15
675	Charles L. Hartnett	.15
676	Joseph E. Cronin	.15
677	Charles J. Hafey	.15
678	James J. Dykes	.10
679	Samuel F. West	.10
680	Johnny L.R. Martin	.10
681	Francis J. O'Doul	.10
682	Alvin F. Crowder	.10
683	James Wilson	.10
684	Richard W. Bartell	.10
685	William A. Hallahan	.10
686	Walter A. Berger	.10
687	Lonnie Warneke	.10
688	William B. Chapman	.10
689	Elwood G. English	.10
690	James H. Reese	.10
691	Roscoe A. Holm	.10
692	Charles D. Jamieson	.10
693	Jonathan T.W. Zachary	.10
694	John C. Ryan	.10
695	Earl J. Adams	.10
696	William E. Hunnefield	.10
697	Henry L. Meadows	.10
698	Thomas F. Carey	.10
699	John W. Rawlings	.10
700	Kenneth E. Holloway	.10
701	Lance C. Richbourg	.10
702	Raymond L. Fisher	.10
703	Edward Augustine Walsh	.15
704	Richard Rudolph	.10
705	Raymond B. Caldwell	.10
706	Burleigh A. Grimes	.15
707	Stanley A. Coveleski	.15
708	George A. Hildebrand	.10
709	John P. Quinn	.10
710	Urban C. Faber	.15
711	Urban J. Shocker	.10
712	Hubert B. Leonard	.10
713	Louis L. Koupal	.10
714	James C. Wasdell	.10
715	John H. Lindell	.10
716	Don W. Padgett	.10
717	Nelson T. Potter	.10
718	Lynwood T. Rowe	.10
719	David C. Danforth	.10
720	Claude W. Passeau	.10
721	Harry L. Kelley	.10
722	John T. Allen	.10
723	Thomas J.D. Bridges	.10
724	William O. Lee	.10
725	Fredrick M. Frankhouse	.10
726	John J. McCarthy	.10
727	Glen D. Russell	.10
728	Emory E. Rigney	.10
729	Howard S. Shanks	.10
730	Lucius B. Appling	.10
731	William J. Byron	.10
732	Earle B. Combs	.15
733	Henry B. Greenberg	.15
734	Walter W. Beck	.10
735	Hollis J. Thurston	.10
736	Lewis R. Wilson	.15
737	William A. McGowan	.10
738	Henry J. Bonura	.10
739	Thomas C. Baker	.10
740	William C. Jacobson	.10
741	Hazen S. Cuyler	.15
742	George F. Blaeholder	.10
743	Wilson D. Miles	.10
744	Lee E. Handley	.10
745	John F. Collins	.10
746	Wilfred P. Ryan	.10
747	Aaron L. Ward	.10
748	Montgomery M. Pearson	.10
749	Jacob W. Early	.10
750	William F. Atwood	.10
751	Mark A. Koenig	.10
752	John A. Hassett	.10
753	David J. Jones	.10
754	John P. Wagner	.15
755	William M. Dickey	.15
756	Albert M. Butcher	.10
757	Waite C. Hoyt	.15
758	Walter P. Johnson	.15
759	Howard J. Ehmke	.10
760	Norman L. Newsom	.10
761	Anthony M. Lazzeri	.15
762	Anthony M. Lazzeri	.15
763	Spurgeon F. Chandler	.15
764	Walter K. Higbe	.10
765	Paul R. Richards	.10
766	Rogers Hornsby	.15
767	Joseph F. Vosmik	.10
768	Jesse J. Haines	.15
769	William H. Walters	.10
770	Thomas D. Henrich	.10
771	James F. Thorpe	.40
772	Euel W. Moore	.10
773	Rudolph P. York	.10
774	Charles A. Bender	.15
775	John T. Meyers	.10
776	Robert L. Johnson	.10
777	Roy C. Johnson	.10
778	Richard T. Porter	.10
779	Ethan N. Allen	.10
780	Harry F. Sallee	.10
781	Roy C. Bell	.10
782	Arnold J. Statz	.10
783	Frank J. Henry	.10
784	Charles L. Woodall	.10
785	Philip E. Collins	.10
786	Joseph W. Sewell	.15
787	William J. Herman	.15
788	Rueben H. Oldring	.10
789	William H. Walker	.10
790	Joseph C. Schultz	.10
791	Fred E. Maguire	.10
792	Claude W. Willoughby	.10
793	James A. Ferguson	.10
794	John D. Morrison	.10
795	Tristram E. Speaker	.15
796	Tyrus R. Cobb	.40
797	Max Carey	.15
798	George H. Sisler	.15
799	Charles J. Hollocher	.10
800	James L. Vaughn	.10
801	Samuel P. Jones	.10
802	Harry B. Hooper	.15
803	Clifford C. Cravath	.10
804	Walter P. Johnson	.15
805	Jacob E. Daubert	.10
806	Jesse C. Milan	.10
807	Hugh A. McQuillan	.10
808	George F. Brickell	.10
809	Joseph V. Stripp	.10
810	Urban J. Hodapp	.10
811	John L. Vergez	.10
812	Linus R. Frey	.10
813	William W. Regan	.10
814	Norman R. Young	.10
815	Charles C. Robertson	.10
816	Walter F. Judnich	.10
817	Joseph B. Tinker	.15
818	John Evers	.15
819	Frank L. Chance	.15
820	John J. McGraw	.15
821	Charles J. Grimm	.10
822	Ted Lyons	.15
823	Joe McCarthy	.15
824	Connie Mack	.15
825	George Gibson	.10
826	Steve O'Neill	.10
827	Tristram E. Speaker	.15
828	William F. Carrigan	.10
829	Charles D. Stengel	.15
830	Miller J. Huggins	.15
831	William B. McKechnie	.15
832	Charles W. Dressen	.10
833	Charles E. Street	.10
834	Melvin T. Ott	.15
835	Frank F. Frisch	.15
836	George H. Sisler	.15
837	Napoleon LaJoie	.15
838	Tyrus R. Cobb	.40
839	William H. Southworth	.10
840	Clark C.F. Griffith	.15
841	William H. Terry	.15
842	Rogers Hornsby	.15
843	Joseph E. Cronin	.15
844	Alfonso R. Lopez	.15
845	Stanley R. Harris	.15
846	Wilbert Robinson	.15
847	Hugh A. Jennings	.15
848	James J. Dykes	.10
849	Roy J. Cullenbine	.10
850	Graham E. Moore	.10
851	John H. Rothrock	.10
852	William H. Lamar	.10
853	Monte Weaver	.10
854	Ival R. Goodman	.10
855	Henry L. Severeid	.10
856	Fred G. Haney	.10
857	Joseph B. Shaute	.10
858	Smead P. Jolley	.10
859	Edwin D. Williams	.10
860	Bernard O. Bengough	.10
861	Richard B. Ferrell	.15
862	Robert A. O'Farrell	.10
863	Virgil L. Davis	.10
864	Franklin W. Hayes	.10
865	Herold D. Ruel	.10
866	Gordon S. Cochrane	.15
867	John Kling	.10
868	Ivy B. Wingo	.10
869	William M. Dickey	.15
870	Frank E. Snyder	.10
871	Roger P. Bresnahan	.15
872	Walter H. Schang	.10
873	Alfonso R. Lopez	.15
874	James Wilson	.10
875	Valentine J. Picinich	.10
876	Stephen F. O'Neill	.10
877	Ernest N. Lombardi	.15
878	John L. Bassler	.10
879	Raymond W. Schalk	.15
880	Charles L. Hartnett	.15
881	Bruce D. Campbell	.10
882	Charles H. Ruffing	.15
883	Mordecai P.C. Brown	.15
884	Peter J. Archer	.10
885	David E. Keefe	.10
886	Nathan H. Andrews	.10
887	Edgar C. Rice	.15
888	George H. Ruth	.50
889	Charles J. Hafey	.15
890	Oscar D. Melillo	.10
891	Joe Wood	.10
892	John J. Evers	.15
893	George Toporcer	.10
894	Myril O. Hoag	.10
895	Robert G. Weiland	.10
896	Joseph A. Marty	.10
897	Sherwood R. Magee	.10
898	Daniel T. Taylor	.10
899	William E. Kamm	.10
900	Samuel J.T. Sheckard	.10
901	Sylvester W. Johnson	.10
902	Stephen R. Sundra	.10
903	Roger M. Cramer	.10
904	Hubert S. Pruett	.10
905	Russell A. Blackburne	.10
906	Eppa Rixey	.15
907	Leon A. Goslin	.15
908	George L. Kelly	.15
909	James L. Bottomley	.15
910	Christopher Mathewson	.15
911	Anthony M. Lazzeri	.15
912	John A. Mostil	.10
913	Robert P. Doerr	.15
914	Walter J.V. Maranville	.15
915	Harry E. Heilmann	.15
916	Rodrick J. Wallace	.15
917	James E. Foxx	.15
918	John R. Mize	.10
919	John N. Bentley	.10
920	Alexander Schacht	.10
921	Parke E. Coleman	.10
922	George H. Paskert	.10
923	Horace H. Ford	.10
924	Randolph E. Moore	.10
925	Milburn J. Shoffner	.10
926	Richard W. Siebert	.10
927	Anthony C. Kaufmann	.10
928	Jay H. Dean, Nolan Ryan	.25
929	Clarence A. Vance, Nolan Ryan	.25
930	Robert M. Grove, Nolan Ryan	.25
931	George E. Waddell, Nolan Ryan	.25
932	Grover C. Alexander, Nolan Ryan	.25
933	Robert W.A. Feller, Nolan Ryan	.25
934	Walter P. Johnson, Nolan Ryan	.50
935	Theodore A. Lyons, Nolan Ryan	.25
936	James C. Bagby	.10
937	Joseph Sugden	.10
938	Robert E. Grace	.10
939	John G. Heath	.10
940	Kenneth Williams	.10
941	Marvin J. Owen	.10
942	Cyril R. Weatherly	.10
943	Edward C. Morgan	.10
944	John C. Rizzo	.10
945	Archie R. McKain	.10
946	Robert M. Garbark	.10
947	John B. Osborn	.10
948	John S. Podgajny	.10
949	Joseph P. Evans	.10
950	George A. Rensa	.10
951	John H. Humphries	.10
952	Merritt P. Cain	.10
953	Roy E. Hansen	.10
954	John A. Niggeling	.10
955	Harold J. Wiltse	.10
956	Alejandro A.A.E. Carrasquel	.10
957	George A. Grant	.10
958	Philip W. Weinert	.10
959	Ervin B. Brame	.10
960	Raymond J. Harrell	.10
961	Edward K. Linke	.10
962	Samuel B. Gibson	.10
963	John C. Watwood	.10
964	James T. Prothro	.10
965	Julio G. Bonetti	.10
966	Howard R. Mills	.10
967	Clarence E. Galloway	.10
968	Harold J. Kelleher	.10
969	Elon C. Hogsett	.10
970	Edward B. Heusser	.10
971	Edward J. Baecht	.10
972	Otto H. Saltzgaver	.10
973	Leroy G. Herrmann	.10
974	Beveric B. Bean	.10
975	Harry Seibold	.10
976	Howard V. Keen	.10
977	William J. Barrett	.10
978	Patrick H. McNulty	.10
979	George E. Turbeville	.10
980	Edward D. Phillips	.10
981	Garland M. Buckeye	.10
982	Victor P. Frasier	.10
983	John G. Rhodes	.10
984	Emile D. Barnes	.10
985	James C. Edwards	.10
986	Herschel E. Bennett	.10
987	Carmen P. Hill	.10
988	Checklist 661-770	.10
989	Checklist 771-880	.10
990	Checklist 881-990	.10

1993-95 Conlon Collection Color

The cards in this set were previously released in black-and-white in regular 1991-94 Conlon sets. Cards 1-12 were issued as bonus cards in Megacards accessory items; 250,000 of each were produced. Cards 13-20 were randomly inserted in 1993 Conlon counter and blister packs; 100,000 of those were produced. Cards 21-22, in an edition of 75,000, were only available through a send-away offer. Card 23 was available exclusively as an insert in the 7th Edition SCD Baseball Card Price Guide, in an edition of 60,000. Cards 24-39 were issued in 1994. Numbers 24-28 were random inserts printed to the number of 84,000 apiece. Cards 29-30 were a send-away premium; #31-33 were hobby foil inserts. All were issued in quantities of 12,000. Cards 34-37 - 48,000 of each - were a Toys R Us exclusive insert. Cards 38-39 were special-offer premiums. A special printing of 24,000 of #28 were issued with a "Conlon Collection Day" overprint on back and were distributed at the Sept. 11, 1994, St. Louis Cardinals game.

		MT
Complete Set (47):		50.00
Common Player:		1.00
1	Sunny Jim Bottomley	1.00
2	Lefty Grove	1.00
3	Lou Gehrig	3.50
4	Babe Ruth	4.00
5	Casey Stengel	1.50
6	Rube Marquard	1.00
7	Walter Johnson	1.50
8	Lou Gehrig	2.50
9	Christy Mathewson	1.50
10	Ty Cobb	2.50
11	Mel Ott	1.00
12	Carl Hubbell	1.00
13	Al Simmons	1.00

14	Connie Mack	1.00
15	Grover C. Alexander	1.00
16	Jimmie Foxx	1.50
17	Lloyd Waner	1.00
18	Tris Speaker	2.00
19	Dizzy Dean	2.50
20	Rogers Hornsby	1.50
21	Shoeless Joe Jackson	4.00
22	Jim Thorpe	3.50
23	Bob Feller	4.00
24	Hal Newhouser	1.00
25	Hughie Jennings	1.00
26	Red Faber	1.00
27	Enos Slaughter	1.00
28	Johnny Mize	1.00
28CCD	Johnny Mize	2.00
29	Pie Traynor	1.00
30	Walter Johnson, Nolan Ryan	1.00
31	Lou Gehrig	1.00
32	Benny Bengough	1.00
33	Babe Ruth	1.00
34	Charlie Gehringer	1.00
35	Babe Ruth	1.00
36	Bill Dickey	1.00
37	Mordecai Brown	1.00
38	Ray Schalk	2.00
39	Home Run Baker	2.50
40	Frank Frisch	1.00
41	Hack Wilson	1.00
42	Ty Cobb	3.00
43	Honus Wagner	2.00
44	John McGraw	1.00
45	Indians vs. Yanks	1.00
46	Reds vs. Giants	1.00
47	Babe Ruth	6.00

1993 Conlon Collection Master Series

"The Best There Was" was the subtitle on this portfolio of oversized (10" x 8") cards produced from the photos of Charles Martin Conlon. On the high-gloss card fronts, a wide black border surrounds the black-and-white photo, with a gold-foil pinstripe border between the two. The player's name appears in gold at the bottom. Backs are printed in black-and-white and feature a large player portrait, complete major league stats and a career summary. A serial numbered certificate placing the set within an edition of 25,000 was included with the set; a deluxe portfolio album to house the collection was available for $10.

		MT
Complete Set (9):		17.50
Common Card:		1.50
1	Title card	.50
2	Babe Ruth	4.50
3	Lou Gehrig, Walter Johnson	3.00
4	Honus Wagner	2.00
5	Mickey Cochrane	1.50
6	Tris Speaker	1.50
7	Ty Cobb	3.00
8	Rogers Hornsby	1.50
9	Pie Traynor	1.50

1993 Conlon Collection Color Masters

Some of the premier photography of Charles Martin Conlon was computer color-enhanced and placed on these oversized (10" x 8") cards in a special edition of 25,000. High-gloss fronts feature the colorized photos separated by a thin white pinstripe from the dark blue background. Backs are printed in black and blue on white and feature a career summary or other historical data, along with a description of the front photo. A serially numbered certificate of authenticity accompanied the set and could be redeemed, along with $10, for a deluxe portfolio to house the collection.

		MT
Complete Set (9):		17.50
Common Player:		1.50
1	Title card	.50
2	Napoleon Lajoie	1.50
3	Walter Johnson, Nolan Ryan (fantasy photo)	4.50
4	Action at Hilltop Park	.50
5	Babe Ruth	4.50
6	Frank Baker	1.50
7	John McGraw	1.50
8	John McGraw, Wilbert Robinson, Christy Mathewson	1.50
9	Hughie Jennings	1.50

1994 Conlon Collection Prototypes

A large gray "PROTOTYPE" overprint on back identifies these cards as samples of the fourth annual edition of Conlon Collection cards by Megacards. Cards carry the same number as issued versions. It was reported that 26,000 prototypes were issued of Martin, Traynor, Hubbell, Klem and Koenig; while 52,000 each were issued of Jackson and the Deans.

		MT
Complete Set (8)		8.00
Common Player		1.00
991	Pepper Martin	1.00
1030	Joe Jackson	3.00
1050	Pie Traynor	1.00
1105	Carl Hubbell	1.00
1140	Lefty Grove	1.00
1170	Dizzy Dean, Paul Dean	1.50
1190	Bill Klem	1.00
1230	Mark Koenig	1.00

1994 Conlon Collection

The production of "old-timers" cards based on the baseball photography of Charles M. Conlon from the 1910s through the 1930s continued into a fourth year in 1994 with another 330-card series, numbered 991-1320. Once again the format of previous years was continued. Subsets included the 1919 Chicago White Sox, major league brothers and action photos.

		MT
Complete Set (330):		16.00
Common Player:		.10
991	Johnny L.R. Martin	.10
992	Joseph W. Sewell	.15
993	Edd J. Roush	.15
994	Richard B. Ferrell	.15
995	John J. Broaca	.10
996	James L. Sewell	.10
997	Burleigh A. Grimes	.15
998	Lewis R. Wilson	.15
999	Robert M. Grove	.15
1000	Tyrus R. Cobb	.30
1001	John J. McGraw	.15
1002	Edward S. Plank	.15
1003	Samuel P. Jones	.10
1004	James L. Bottomley	.15
1005	Henry B. Greenberg	.15
1006	Lloyd J. Waner	.15
1007	William W. Moore	.10
1008	Lucius B. Appling	.15
1009	Harold Newhouser	.15
1010	Alfonso R. Lopez	.15
1011	Tyrus R. Cobb	.40
1012	Charles A. Nichols	.10
1013	Edward Augustine Walsh	.15
1014	Hugh Duffy	.15
1015	Richard W. Marquard	.15
1016	Adrian Joss	.15
1017	Rodrick J. Wallace	.15
1018	William H. Keeler	.15
1019	Jacob E. Daubert	.10
1020	Harry F. Sallee	.10
1021	Adolfo Luque	.10
1022	Ivy B. Wingo	.10
1023	Edd J. Roush	.15
1024	William A. Rariden	.10
1025	Sherwood R. Magee	.10
1026	Louis B. Duncan	.10
1027	Horace O. Eller	.10
1028	Alfred E. Neale	.10
1029	George D. Weaver	.10
1030	Joseph J. Jackson	.50
1031	Arnold Gandil	.10
1032	Charles A. Risberg	.10
1033	Raymond W. Schalk	.15
1034	Edward V. Cicotte	.10
1035	William H. James	.10
1036	Harry L. Leibold	.10
1037	Richard H. Kerr	.10
1038	William J. Gleason	.10
1039	Frederick W. McMullin	.10
1040	Edward T. Collins	.15
1041	Sox Pitchers (Lefty Williams, Bill James, Ed Cicotte, Dicky Kerr)	.10
1042	Sox Outfielders (Nemo Leibold, Happy Felsch, Shano Collins)	.10
1043	Kenneth F. Keltner	.10
1044	Charles F. Berry	.10
1045	Walter J. Lutzke	.10
1046	John C. Schulte	.10
1047	John V. Welch	.10
1048	Jack E. Russell	.10
1049	John J. Murray	.10
1050	Harold J. Traynor	.15
1051	Michael J. Donlin	.10
1052	Charles L. Hartnett	.15
1053	Anthony M. Lazzeri	.15
1054	Lawrence H. Miller	.10
1055	Clarence A. Vance	.15
1056	Williams F. Carrigan	.10
1057	John J. Murphy	.10
1058	Clifton E Heathcote	.10
1059	Joseph A. Dugan	.10
1060	Walter J.V. Maranville	.15
1061	Thomas D. Henrich	.10
1062	Leroy E. Parmelee	.10
1063	Vernon L. Gomez	.15
1064	Ernest N. Lombardi	.15
1065	David J. Bancroft	.15
1066	William B. McKechnie	.15
1067	John A. Hassett	.10
1068	Spurgeon F. Chandler	.10
1069	Roy J. Hughes	.10
1070	George A. Dauss	.10
1071	Joseph J. Hauser	.10
1072	Virgil L. Davis	.10
1073	Albert M. Butcher	.10
1074	Louis P. Chiozza	.10
1075	Center Field Bleachers	.10
1076	Charles L. Gehringer	.15
1077	Henry E. Manush	.15
1078	Charles H. Ruffing	.15
1079	Melvin L. Harder	.10
1080	George H. Ruth	.50
1081	William B. Chapman	.10
1082	Louis H. Gehrig	.40
1083	James E. Foxx	.15
1084	Aloysius H. Simmons	.15
1085	Joseph E. Cronin	.15
1086	William M. Dickey	.15
1087	Gordon S. Cochrane	.15
1088	Vernon L. Gomez	.15
1089	Howard E. Averill Sr.	.15
1090	Samuel F. West	.10
1091	Frank F. Frisch	.15
1092	William J. Herman	.15
1093	Harold J. Traynor	.15
1094	Joseph M. Medwick	.15
1095	Charles H. Klein	.15
1096	Hazen S. Cuyler	.15
1097	Melvin T. Ott	.15
1098	Walter T. Berger	.10
1099	Paul G. Waner	.15
1100	William H. Terry	.15
1101	Travis C. Jackson	.15
1102	Joseph F. Vaughan	.15
1103	Charles L. Hartnett	.15
1104	Alfonso R. Lopez	.15
1105	Carl O. Hubbell	.15
1106	Lonnie Warneke	.10
1107	Van L. Mungo	.10
1108	Johnny J.R. Martin	.15
1109	Jay H. Dean	.15
1110	Fredrick M. Frankhouse	.10
1111	Giullaedeau Spink Heydler	.10
1112	JG Taylor Spink/ Mrs. Spink	.10
1113	Hirchman, Keller	.10
1114	Victor E. Aldridge	.10
1115	Michael F. Higgins	.10
1116	Harold G. Carlson	.10
1117	Frederick L. Fitzsimmons	.10
1118	William H. Walters	.10
1119	Nicholas Altrock	.10
1120	Charles W. Dressen	.10
1121	Mark A. Koenig	.10
1122	Charles L. Gehringer	.15
1123	Lloyd V. Kennedy	.10
1124	Harlond B. Clift	.10
1125	Ernest G. Phelps	.10
1126	John R. Mize	.15
1127	Harold H. Schumacher	.10
1128	Ethan N. Allen	.10
1129	William A. Wambsganss	.10
1130	Frederick Leach	.10
1131	John W. Clancy	.10
1132	John F. Stewart	.10
1133	Wilbur L. Brubaker	.10
1134	Leslie Mann	.10
1135	Howard J. Ehmke	.10
1136	Aloysius H. Simmons	.15
1137	George L. Earnshaw	.10
1138	George W. Haas	.10
1139	Edmund J. Miller	.10
1140	Robert M. Grove	.15
1141	John P. Boley	.10
1142	Edward T. Collins Sr.	.15
1143	Walter E. French	.10
1144	Donald E. McNair	.10
1145	William D. Shores	.10
1146	Gordon S. Cochrane	.15
1147	Homer W. Summa	.10
1148	John P. Quinn	.10
1149	Max F. Bishop	.10
1150	James J. Dykes	.10
1151	George E. Walberg	.10
1152	James E. Foxx	.15
1153	George H. Burns	.10
1154	Roger M. Cramer	.10
1155	Samuel D. Hale	.10
1156	Edwin A. Rommel	.10
1157	Ralph F. Perkins	.10
1158	James J. Cronin	.15
1159	Cornelios Mack	.15
1160	Raymond C. Kolp	.10
1161	Clyde J. Manion	.10
1162	Franklin T. Grube	.10
1163	Stephen A. Swetonic	.10
1164	Joseph B. Tinker	.15
1165	John J. Evers	.15
1166	Frank L. Chance	.15
1167	Emerson Dickman	.10
1168	John T. Tobin	.10
1169	Wesley C. Ferrell	.10
1170	Jay H. Dean	.15
1171	Tony & Al Cuccinello (Tony Cuccinello, Al Cuccinello)	.10
1172	Harry Coveleski, Stan Coveleski	.10
1173	Bob Johnson, Roy Johnson	.10
1174	Andy & Hugh High	.10
1175	Joe Sewell, Luke Sewell	.10
1176	Joe Heving, John Heving	.10
1177	Ab & Ivy Wingo	.10
1178	Wade Killefer, Bill Killefer	.10
1179	Bubbles Hargrave, Pinky Hargrave	.10
1180	Paul Waner, Lloyd Waner	.10
1181	John S. Vander Meer	.10
1182	Joe G. Moore	.10
1183	Robert J. Burke	.10
1184	John F. Moore	.10
1185	John J. Egan	.10
1186	Thomas H. Connolly	.15
1187	Frank H. O'Loughlin	.10
1188	John E. Reardon	.10
1189	Charles B. Moran	.10
1190	William J. Klem	.15
1191	Albert D. Stark	.10
1192	Albert L. Orth	.10
1193	William E. Bransfield	.10
1194	Roy Van Graflan	.10
1195	Eugene F. Hart	.10
1196	John B. Conlan	.15
1197	Ralph A. Pinelli	.10
1198	John F. Sheridan	.10
1199	Richard F. Nallin	.10
1200	William H. Dineen	.10
1201	Henry F. O'Day	.10
1202	Charles Rigler	.10
1203	Robert D. Emslie	.10
1204	Charles H. Pfirman	.10
1205	Harry C. Geisel	.10
1206	Ernest C. Quigley	.10
1207	Emmett T. Ormsby	.10
1208	George A. Hildebrand	.10
1209	George J. Moriarty	.10
1210	William G. Evans	.10
1211	Clarence B. Owens	.10
1212	William A. McGowan	.15
1213	Walter K. Higbe	.10
1214	Taylor L. Douthit	.10
1215	Delmar D. Baker	.10
1216	Albert W. Demaree	.10
1217	Cornelius Mack	.15
1218	Napoleon Lajoie	.15
1219	John P. Wagner	.15
1220	Christopher Mathewson	.15
1221	Samuel E. Crawford	.15
1222	Tristram E. Speaker	.15
1223	Grover C. Alexander	.15
1224	Joseph E. Bowman	.10
1225	John D. Rigney	.10
1226	William E. Webb	.10
1227	Lloyd A. Moore	.10
1228	Bruce D. Campbell	.10
1229	Luzerne A. Blue	.10
1230	Mark A. Koenig	.10
1231	Walter H. Schang	.10
1232	Max Carey	.15
1233	Frank F. Frisch	.15
1234	Owen J. Bush	.10
1235	Goerge S. Davis	.10
1236	William G. Rogell	.10
1237	James A. Collins	.15
1238	Mauricel L. Burrus	.10
1239	Ernest E. Swanson	.10
1240	Elwood G. English	.10
1241	Joseph Harris	.10
1242	Harry H. McCurdy	.10
1243	Richard W. Bartell	.10
1244	Rupert L. Thompson	.10
1245	Charles B. Adams	.10
1246	Arthur N. Nehf	.10
1247	John G. Graney	.10
1248	Theodore A. Lyons	.15
1249	Louis H. Gehrig	.40
1250	Michael F. Welch	.15
1251	Urban C. Faber	.15
1252	Joseph J. McGinnity	.15
1253	Rogers Hornsby	.15
1254	Melvin T. Ott	.15
1255	Walter P. Johnson	.15
1256	Edgar C. Rice	.15
1257	James A. Tobin	.10
1258	Roger T. Peckinpaugh	.10
1259	George T. Stovall	.10
1260	Fredrick C. Merkle	.10
1261	Harry W. Collins	.10
1262	Henry C. Lind	.10
1263	George N. Rucker	.10
1264	Hollis J. Thurston	.10
1265	Alexander Metzler	.10
1266	Charles Martin Conlon	.10
1267	McCarty Gets Magee (Lew McCarty, Lee Magee)	.10
1268	Sliding Home	.10
1269	Kauff Safe at 3rd (Benny Kauff)	.10
1270	Groh Out at 3rd (Heine Groh)	.10
1271	Mollwitz Out at the Plate (Fred Mollwitz)	.10
1272	Burns Safe at Home	.10
1273	Lee Magee Out Stealing 3rd (Lee Magee)	.10
1274	Killefer Out at Plate (Bill Killefer)	.10
1275	John M. Warhop	.10
1276	Emil J. Leonard	.10
1277	Alvin F. Crowder	.10
1278	Chester P. Laabs	.10
1279	Leslie A. Bush	.10
1280	Raymond B. Bressler	.10
1281	Robret M. Brown	.10
1282	Bernard Deviveiros	.10
1283	Leslie W. Tietje	.10
1284	Charles Devens	.10
1285	Elliott A. Bigelow	.10
1286	John O. Dickshot	.10
1287	Charles L. Chatham	.10
1288	Walter E. Beall	.10
1289	Richard D. Attreau	.10
1290	Anthony V. Brief	.10
1291	James J. Gleason	.10
1292	Walter D. Shaner	.10
1293	Clifford R. Crawford	.10
1294	Manuel Salvo	.10
1295	Calvin L. Dorsett	.10
1296	Russell D. Peters	.10
1297	John D. Couch	.10
1298	Frank W. Ulrich	.10

1299	James M. Bivin	.10
1300	Paul E. Strand	.10
1301	John Y. Lanning	.10
1302	William R. Brenzel	.10
1303	Don Songer	.10
1304	Emil H. Levsen	.10
1305	Otto A. Bluege	.10
1306	Fabian S. Gaffke	.10
1307	Maurice J. Archdeacon	.10
1308	James B. Chaplin	.10
1309	Lawrence J. Rosenthal	.10
1310	William M. Bagwell	.10
1311	Ralph F. Dawson	.10
1312	John P.J. Sturm	.10
1313	Haskell C. Billings	.10
1314	Vernon S. Wilshere	.10
1315	Robert A. Asbjornson	.10
1316	Henry J. Steinbacher	.10
1317	Stanwood F. Baumgartner	.10
1318	Checklist 991-1100	.10
1319	Checklist 1101-1210	.10
1320	Checklist 1211-1320	.10

1994 Conlon Collection Burgundy

A parallel version of the 1994 Conlon series with burgundy, rather than black, borders was issued as a one-per-pack insert.

	MT
Complete Set (330):	50.00
Common Player:	.15
(Major stars valued at 2-4X regular version. See 1994 Conlon Collection for checklist and base values.)	

1995 Conlon Collection Prototypes

Megacards issued this 10-card series of prototypes to introduce its basic series for 1995. Cards are similar to the issued versions except that they lack the gold-foil enhancements on front and have different card numbers on some of the card backs. Cards have "PROMOTIONAL" printed diagonally on the back. Prototypes are listed here alphabetically.

		MT
Complete Set (10):		12.00
Common Player:		2.00
(1)	Lou Boudreau	2.00
(2)	Ray Chapman	3.00
(3)	Charles Comiskey	2.00
(4)	Bill Dickey	2.00
(5)	Bob Feller	3.00
(6)	Lou Gehrig	[illegible]
(7)	Charles L. Hartnett	2.00
(8)	Walter J.V. Maranville	2.00
(9)	Babe Ruth	4.00
(10)	Tris Speaker	2.00

1995 Conlon Collection

Gold-foil enhanced printing and issue in two series were firsts for the Conlon Collection in 1995. For the first time, each regular card in the issue featured gold borders around the black-and-white photos, and a gold Conlon Collection seal at lower-right. Background for the 1995 cards is in dark green, with typography in white. Backs are black-and-white and feature an in-depth historical vignette. In its fifth year, numbers for Conlon Collection cards continued from previous years, beginning at #1321. The first series, cards 1321-1430, were issued in February, a second series, #1431-1540, was issued in August. A special Babe Ruth 100th birthday anniversary card was included with the issue, bearing a combined Topps/Conlon Collection logo and paralleling card #3 in the 1995 Topps issue. Conlon cards for 1995 were issued in plastic clam-shell packaging of 22, 55 or 110 cards. Once again, many of the cards in the set were grouped into themes such as "Baseball Goes to War," "Nicknames" and "Beating the Odds."

		MT
Complete Set (111):		18.00
Common Player:		.05
	Series 1 (1321-1430)	
1321	Grover Alexander	.10
1322	Christy Mathewson	.15
1323	Eddie Grant	.05
1324	Gabby Street	.05
1325	Hank Gowdy	.05
1326	Jack Bentley	.05
1327	Eppa Rixey	.05
1328	Bob Shawkey	.05
1329	Rabbit Maranville	.05
1330	Casey Stengel	.10
1331	Herb Pennock	.05
1332	Eddie Collins	.05
1333	Buddy Hassett	.05
1334	Andy Cohen	.05
1335	Hank Greenberg	.10
1336	Andy High	.05
1337	Bob Feller	.15
1338	George Earnshaw	.05
1339	Jack Knott	.05
1340	Larry French	.05
1341	Skippy Roberge	.05
1342	Boze Berger	.05
1343	Bill Posedel	.05
1344	Kirby Higbe	.05
1345	Bob Neighbors	.05
1346	Hugh Mulcahy	.05
1347	Harry Walker	.05
1348	Buddy Lewis	.05
1349	Cecil Travis	.05
1350	Moe Berg	.45
1351	Nixey Callahan	.05
1352	Heinie Peitz	.05
1353	Doc White	.05
1354	Smoky Joe Wood	.05
1355	Larry Gardner	.05
1356	Steve O'Neill	.05
1357	Tris Speaker	.10
1358	Bill Wambsganss	.05
1359	Geo. H. Burns	.05
1360	Charlie Jamieson	.05
1361	Les Nunamaker	.05
1362	Stan Coveleski	.05
1363	Joe Sewell	.10
1364	Jim Bagby	.05
1365	Duster Mails	.05
1366	Jack Graney	.05
1367	Elmer Smith	.05
1368	Tommy Leach	.05
1369	Russ Ford	.05
1370	Harry Wolter	.05
1371	Dazzy Vance	.05
1372	Germany Schaefer	.05
1373	Elbie Fletcher	.05
1374	Clark Griffith	.10
1375	Al Simmons	.05
1376	Billy Jurges	.05
1377	Earl Averill	.05
1378	Bill Klem	.05
1379	Armando Marsans	.10
1380	Mike Gonzalez	.10
1381	Jacques Fournier	.05
1382	Ol' Stubblebeard (Burleigh Grimes)	.05
1383	Freshest Man on Earth (Arlie Latham)	.05
1384	Cracker (Ray Schalk)	.05
1385	Goose (Goose Goslin)	.05
1386	Unser Choe (Joe Hauser)	.05
1387	The People's Cherce (Dixie Walker)	.05
1388	The Crab (Jesse Burkett)	.05
1389	Mountain Music (Cliff Melton)	.05
1390	Gee (Gee Walker)	.05
1391	Tony Cuccinello	.05
1392	Vern Kennedy	.05
1393	Tuck Stainback	.05
1394	Ed Barrow	.05
1395	Ford Frick	.05
1396	Ban Johnson	.05
1397	Charles Comiskey	.05
1398	Jacob Ruppert	.05
1399	Branch Rickey	.05
1400	Jack Kieran	.05
1401	Mike Ryba	.05
1402	Stan Spence	.05
1403	Red Barrett	.05
1404	Gabby Hartnett	.05
1405	Babe Ruth	.50
1406	Fred Merkle	.05
1407	Claude Passeau	.05
1408	Smoky Joe Wood	.05
1409	Cliff Heathcote	.05
1110	Walt Cruise	.05
1411	Cookie Lavagetto	.05
1412	Tony Lazzari	.05
1413	Atley Donald	.05
1414	Ken Raffensberger	.05
1415	Dizzy Trout	.05
1416	Augie Galan	.05
1417	Monty Stratton	.10
1418	Claude Passeau	.05
1419	Oscar Grimes Jr.	.05
1420	Rollie Hemsley	.05
1421	Lou Gehrig	.20
1422	Tom Sunkel	.05
1423	Tris Speaker	.10
1424	Chick Fewster	.05
1425	Lou Boudreau	.05
1426	Hank Leiber	.05
1427	Eddie Mayo	.05
1428	Charley Gelbert	.05
1429	Jackie Hayes	.05
1430	Checklist 1321-1430	.05
3C	Babe Ruth (100th Birthday)	4.00

1995 Conlon Collection In the Zone

An eight-card set comparing Ken Griffey Jr. with superstars of the game's past was randomly inserted into the plastic clam-shell packaging of the 1995 Conlon Collection cards. Fronts feature a colorized background photo of the player with whom Griffey is being compared. A smaller color photo of Griffey is in the foreground. An "In the Zone" logo is at lower-left. Backs share a background photo of Griffey and have a black-and-white portrait of the comparison player in the upper-left. Narrative describes how the two players compare. A card number is at upper-right in the Zone logo. Megacard and Cooperstown Collection logos are at bottom. The first six cards of the series could be found in Conlon Collection packs, cards 7 and 8 were available only through a mail-in offer for $2 plus five proofs-of-purchase. The print run was announced as no more than 50,000 sets.

		MT
Complete Set (8):		15.00
Common Card:		2.00
1	Ken Griffey Jr., Babe Ruth	3.50
2	Ken Griffey Jr., Lou Gehrig	3.00
3	Ken Griffey Jr., Ty Cobb	3.00
4	Ken Griffey Jr., Jimmie Foxx	2.00
5	Ken Griffey Jr., Mel Ott	2.00
6	Ken Griffey Jr., Joe Jackson	3.00
7	Ken Griffey Jr., Tris Speaker	2.00
8	Ken Griffey Jr., Jim Bottomley	2.00

1998 Coors Big Bat Cans

Six memorable major league at-bats are commemorated on a series of beer cans by Coors. The 12-oz. cans are printed in the brewery's familiar blue and pale yellow colors and picture players (without uniform logos) on the fronts. Also on front are a title and a few words about the historical moment. A biography is printed on the side. The players in the series are listed here alphabetically. Values are for cans opened at the bottom.

		MT
Complete Set (6):		8.00
Common Player:		2.00
(1)	Ernie Banks (Down, Not Out)	2.00
(2)	Roberto Clemente (The Last Hit)	4.00
(3)	Carlton Fisk ("Go Fair!")	2.00
(4)	Kirk Gibson (The Injured Hero)	2.00
(5)	Willie McCovey 4-for-4 Debut)	2.00
(6)	Babe Ruth (The Called Shot)	4.00

1997 Corinthian Headliners Baseball

Some of the game's most popular players are featured in this series of 3" to 3-1/2" tall plastic statues. The figures have extra-large heads which allow for more realistic modeling. Each figure was sold in a blister pack and includes a removeable cap. Uniform details are painted on and there is a green base with the player's last name. Suggested retail price was about $4 apiece at retail stores, though the inventory was quickly picked over by collectors and dealers stocking up on the most popular players. The issue is checklisted here alphabetically. Values shown are for unopened blister packs.

	MT
Complete Set (33):	160.00
Common Player:	5.00
Roberto Alomar	5.00
Albert Belle	5.00
Wade Boggs	6.00
Barry Bonds	7.50
Ken Caminiti	5.00
Jose Canseco A's	5.00
Jose Canseco Red Sox	5.00
Lenny Dykstra	5.00
Andres Galarraga	5.00
Ken Griffey Jr.	12.00
Tony Gwynn	7.50
Orel Hershiser	5.00
Randy Johnson	5.00
Chipper Jones	9.00
David Justice	5.00
Eric Karros	5.00
Barry Larkin	5.00
Kenny Lofton Braves	5.00
Kenny Lofton Indians	5.00
Fred McGriff	5.00
Mark McGwire	12.00
Paul Molitor	5.00
Raul Mondesi	5.00
Hideo Nomo	5.00
Paul O'Neill	5.00
Mike Piazza	9.00
Cal Ripken Jr.	10.00
Ivan Rodriguez	6.00
Ryne Sandberg	6.00
Gary Sheffield	5.00
Frank Thomas	9.00
Mo Vaughn	5.00
Matt Williams	5.00

1998 Corinthian Headliners Baseball

	MT
Complete Set (41):	200.00
Common Player:	6.00
Roberto Alomar	6.00
Wade Boggs	7.50
Barry Bonds	7.50
Jay Buhner	6.00
Ken Caminiti	6.00
Roger Clemens	8.00
Dennis Eckersley	6.00
Jim Edmonds	6.00
Juan Gonzalez	8.00
Ken Griffey Jr.	10.00
Tony Gwynn	8.00
Orel Hershiser Giants	6.00
Orel Hershiser Indians	6.00
Derek Jeter	8.00
Charles Johnson	6.00
Randy Johnson	6.00
Chipper Jones	8.00
David Justice	6.00
Eric Karros	6.00
Barry Larkin	6.00

Kenny Lofton Braves	6.00
Kenny Lofton Indians	6.00
Fred McGriff	6.00
Raul Mondesi	6.00
Hideo Nomo	6.00
Paul O'Neill	6.00
Rey Ordonez	6.00
Chan Ho Park	6.00
Mike Piazza	8.00
Cal Ripken Jr.	9.00
Alex Rodriguez	9.00
Ivan Rodriguez	7.50
Tim Salmon	6.00
Deion Sanders	6.00
Gary Sheffield	6.00
Sammy Sosa	9.00
Jim Thome	6.00
Frank Thomas	8.00
Bernie Williams	6.00
Matt Williams D'backs	6.00
Matt Williams Indians	6.00

1998 Corinthian Headliners Baseball XL

	MT
Complete Set (12):	200.00
Common Player:	20.00

Set price doesn't include blue versions

Barry Bonds	20.00
Andres Galarraga	20.00
Ken Griffey Jr. Blue	25.00
Ken Griffey Jr. White	25.00
Derek Jeter	20.00
Chipper Jones	20.00
David Justice	20.00
Mark McGwire Blue	50.00
Mark McGwire White	85.00
Hideo Nomo	20.00
Mike Piazza	20.00
Cal Ripken Jr.	20.00
Alex Rodriguez	20.00
Frank Thomas	20.00

1991 Country Hearth Mariners

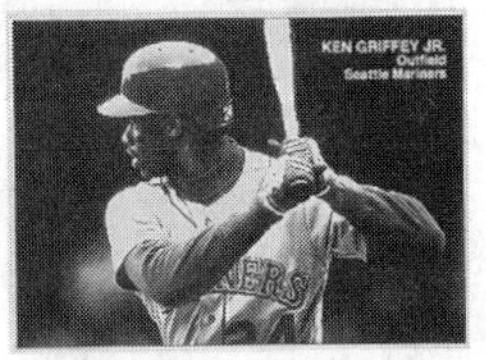

This 29-card set was inserted in loaves of bread and also given away at a Mariner home game. The card fronts feature full-color glossy photos, while the flip sides feature statistics.

		MT
Complete Set (29):		20.00
Common Player:		.25
1	Jim Lefebvre	.25
2	Jeff Schaefer	.25
3	Harold Reynolds	.40
4	Greg Briley	.25
5	Scott Bradley	.25
6	Dave Valle	.25
7	Edgar Martinez	.70
8	Pete O'Brien	.25
9	Omar Vizquel	.50
10	Tino Martinez	.75
11	Scott Bankhead	.25
12	Bill Swift	.25
13	Jay Buhner	1.00
14	Alvin Davis	.25
15	Ken Griffey, Jr.	10.00
16	Tracy Jones	.25
17	Brent Knackert	.25
18	Henry Cotto	.25
19	Ken Griffey, Sr.	.40
20	Keith Comstock	.25
21	Brian Holman	.25
22	Russ Swan	.25
23	Mike Jackson	.25
24	Erik Hanson	.25
25	Mike Schooler	.25
26	Randy Johnson	1.50
27	Rich DeLucia	.25
28	The Griffeys (Ken Griffey Jr., Ken Griffey Sr.)	1.50
29	Mascot	.25

1982 Cracker Jack

The Topps-produced 1982 Cracker Jack set was issued to promote the first "Old Timers Baseball Classic," held in Washington, D.C. The set was issued in two sheets of eight player cards, plus an advertising card located in the center. Individual cards are 2-1/2" x 3-1/2," with the complete sheets measuring 7-1/2" x 10-1/2". Cards #1-8 feature American League players with #9-16 being former National League stars. Fronts feature a full-color photo inside a Cracker Jack border. Backs contain the sponsor's logo plus a short player biography and his lifetime pitching or batting record. Complete sheets were available through a write-in offer.

		MT
Complete Panel Set (2):		12.00
Complete Singles Set (17):		8.00
Common Single Player:		.25
A.L. Panel		7.00
1	Larry Doby	.50
2	Bob Feller	.50
3	Whitey Ford	.50
4	Al Kaline	.40
5	Harmon Killebrew	.25
6	Mickey Mantle	5.00
7	Tony Oliva	.25
8	Brooks Robinson	.35
N.L. Panel		6.00
9	Hank Aaron	2.00
10	Ernie Banks	.35
11	Ralph Kiner	.25
12	Eddie Mathews	.25
13	Willie Mays	2.00
14	Robin Roberts	.25
15	Duke Snider	.35
16	Warren Spahn	.25

1991 Cracker Jack Topps 1st Series

In their first issue in almost 10 years, Cracker Jack inserted miniature cards (1-1/4" x 1-3/4") as the toy surprise in packages of the famous snack. The company produced two 36-card series, portraying many of the top stars in the game. Card fronts are identical to the corresponding regular-issue Topps cards, but the backs are significantly different because of the small amount of space available for statistics. The Cracker Jack sailor logo appears on the bright red backs, along with copyright information listing Borden, Cracker Jack's parent company. These are sometimes found on 2-1/2" x 3-1/2" cards bearing four different of the mini-cards; these were cut from sheets stolen from the printer and have no legitimate collector value.

		MT
Complete Set (36):		9.00
Common Player:		.25
1	Nolan Ryan	2.00
2	Paul Molitor	.75
3	Tim Raines	.25
4	Frank Viola	.25
5	Sandy Alomar Jr.	.25
6	Ryne Sandberg	1.00
7	Don Mattingly	1.00
8	Pedro Guerrero	.25
9	Jose Rijo	.25
10	Jose Canseco	.50
11	Dave Parker	.25
12	Doug Drabek	.25
13	Cal Ripken	2.00
14	Dave Justice	.40
15	George Brett	1.00
16	Eric Davis	.30
17	Mark Langston	.25
18	Rickey Henderson	.35
19	Barry Bonds	1.25
20	Kevin Maas	.25
21	Len Dykstra	.25
22	Roger Clemens	.65
23	Robin Yount	.75
24	Mark Grace	.40
25	Bo Jackson	.30
26	Tony Gwynn	1.00
27	Mark McGwire	2.50
28	Dwight Gooden	.25
29	Wade Boggs	.65
30	Kevin Mitchell	.25
31	Cecil Fielder	.25
32	Bobby Thigpen	.25
33	Benito Santiago	.25
34	Kirby Puckett	.75
35	Will Clark	.40
36	Ken Griffey Jr.	2.50

1991 Cracker Jack Topps 2nd Series

A second series of 36 micro cards was found in Cracker Jack boxes later in the 1991 season. Again numbered from 1-18, the 1-1/4" x 1-3/4" cards carry a "2nd Series" designation on the back above the card number. Like the first series, these cards replicate the front of the 1991 Topps issue and have modified back design which includes the "Sailor Jack" logo of the candy company. Four-card panels, believed to have been cut from sheets illegally removed from the printer, are known.

		MT
Complete Set (36):		4.00
Common Player:		.25
1	Eddie Murray	.45
2	Carlton Fisk	.50
3	Eric Anthony	.30
4	Kelly Gruber	.25
5	Von Hayes	.25
6	Ben McDonald	.25
7	Andre Dawson	.30
8	Ellis Burks	.25
9	Matt Williams	.35
10	Dave Stewart	.25
11	Barry Larkin	.30
12	Chuck Finley	.25
13	Shane Andrews	.25
14	Bret Saberhagen	.30
15	Bobby Bonilla	.30
16	Roberto Kelly	.25
17	Orel Hershiser	.25
18	Ruben Sierra	.25
19	Ron Gant	.30
20	Frank Thomas	1.50
21	Tim Wallach	.25
22	Gregg Olson	.25
23	Shawon Dunston	.25
24	Kent Hrbek	.25
25	Ramon Martinez	.30
26	Alan Trammell	.25
27	Ozzie Smith	.75
28	Bob Welch	.25
29	Chris Sabo	.25
30	Steve Sax	.25
31	Bip Roberts	.25
32	Dave Steib	.25
33	Howard Johnson	.25
34	Mike Greenwell	.25
35	Delino DeShields	.25
36	Alex Fernandez	.30

1992 Cracker Jack Donruss Series 1

In 1992, Cracker Jack turned to Donruss to produce the cards for the surprise in their packages. The first series of micro cards (1-1/4" x 1-3/4") was numbered 1-36 and features many top players. Card fronts are identical to the regular-issue '92 Donruss, but the backs have a different format and much less information because of the tiny space available. The backs have a blue border, with some spot red printing and the Cracker Jack sailor logo in the lower-left corner.

		MT
Complete Set (36):		24.00
Common Player:		.50
1	Dennis Eckersley	.50
2	Jeff Bagwell	1.25
3	Jim Abbott	.50
4	Steve Avery	.50
5	Kelly Gruber	.50
6	Ozzie Smith	1.00
7	Lance Dickson	.50
8	Robin Yount	1.00
9	Brett Butler	.50
10	Sandy Alomar Jr.	.50
11	Travis Fryman	.50
12	Ken Griffey, Jr.	4.00
13	Cal Ripken, Jr.	3.00
14	Will Clark	.80
15	Nolan Ryan	3.00
16	Tony Gwynn	1.00
17	Roger Clemens	.90
18	Wes Chamberlain	.50
19	Barry Larkin	.50
20	Brian McRae	.50
21	Marquis Grissom	.50
22	Cecil Fielder	.50
23	Dwight Gooden	.50
24	Chuck Knoblauch	.50
25	Jose Canseco	1.00
26	Terry Pendleton	.50
27	Ivan Rodriguez	.90
28	Ryne Sandberg	1.00
29	Kent Hrbek	.50
30	Ramon Martinez	.50
31	Todd Zeile	.50
32	Hal Morris	.50
33	Robin Ventura	.50
34	Doug Drabek	.50
35	Frank Thomas	2.00
36	Don Mattingly	2.00

1992 Cracker Jack Donruss Series 2

The Second Series of the 1992 Cracker Jack Donruss set is almost identical to the first series, with the only change being different players and red border on the back instead of blue. The micro cards are numbered 1-36, just as in the first series.

		MT
Complete Set (36):		16.00
Common Player:		.50
1	Craig Biggio	.50
2	Tom Glavine	.50
3	David Justice	.60
4	Lee Smith	.50
5	Mark Grace	.60
6	George Bell	.50
7	Darryl Strawberry	.50
8	Eric Davis	.50
9	Ivan Calderon	.50
10	Royce Clayton	.50
11	Matt Williams	.50
12	Fred McGriff	.60
13	Len Dykstra	.50
14	Barry Bonds	1.50
15	Reggie Sanders	.50
16	Chris Sabo	.50
17	Howard Johnson	.50
18	Bobby Bonilla	.50
19	Rickey Henderson	.65
20	Mark Langston	.50
21	Joe Carter	.50
22	Paul Molitor	.90
23	Glenallen Hill	.50
24	Edgar Martinez	.50
25	Gregg Olson	.50
26	Ruben Sierra	.50
27	Julio Franco	.50
28	Phil Plantier	.50
29	Wade Boggs	.80
30	George Brett	1.00
31	Alan Trammell	.50
32	Kirby Puckett	1.00
33	Scott Erickson	.50
34	Matt Nokes	.50
35	Danny Tartabull	.50
36	Jack McDowell	.50

1993 Cracker Jack Anniversary

In 1993, as part of the company's 100th anniversary celebration, Cracker Jack issued a 24-card set of mini replicas of its famous 1915 cards. The cards, 1-1/4" x 1-3/4", were included in specially-marked packages of the famous snack. The set features Hall of Famers such as Cobb, Mathewson, Walter Johnson and others, plus the Joe Jackson card. A red plastic album, with color pictures of the replicas inside, was also available.

		MT
Complete Set (24):		10.00
Common Player:		.50
Album:		10.00
(1)	Ty Cobb	1.00
(2)	Nap Lajoie	.50
(3)	Connie Mack	.50
(4)	Leslie Bush	.50
(5)	Tris Speaker	.50
(6)	Harry Hooper	.50
(7)	Eddie Collins	.50
(8)	Ed Walsh	.50
(9)	Joe Jackson	2.00
(10)	Branch Rickey	.50
(11)	Walter Johnson	.75
(12)	Honus Wagner	.75
(13)	Fred Clarke	.50
(14)	Christy Mathewson	.60
(15)	John McGraw	.50
(16)	Johnny Evers	.50
(17)	Walter Maranville	.50
(18)	Zack Wheat	.50
(19)	Miller Huggins	.50
(20)	Grover Alexander	.50
(21)	Joe Tinker	.50
(22)	Mordecai Brown	.50
(23)	Eddie Plank	.50
(24)	Rube Marquard	.50

1997 Cracker Jack All Stars

After a hiatus of three years, Cracker Jack resumed the use of baseball cards as premiums in 1997 with a 20-card All Stars set. Like the other CJ issues of the 1990s, this set features miniature (1-5/16" x 1-3/4") cards. Cards feature player action photos on front along with a Cracker Jack All

Stars logo. Photos have uniform logos removed as the set is licensed only by the Players Association and not Major League Baseball. Backs are printed in red and blue with Cracker Jack and MLBPA logos, a few stats and personal data.

		MT
Complete Set (20):		20.00
Common Player:		1.00
1	Jeff Bagwell	1.50
2	Chuck Knoblauch	1.00
3	Cal Ripken Jr.	3.00
4	Chipper Jones	2.00
5	Derek Jeter	2.00
6	Barry Larkin	1.00
7	Bernie Williams	1.00
8	Barry Bonds	1.50
9	Kenny Lofton	1.00
10	Gary Sheffield	1.00
11	Sammy Sosa	2.00
12	Paul Molitor	1.50
13	Andres Galarraga	1.00
14	Ivan Rodriguez	1.25
15	Mike Piazza	2.00
16	Andy Pettitte	1.00
17	Tom Glavine	1.00
18	Albert Belle	1.50
19	Mark McGwire	5.00
20	Mo Vaughn	1.00

1999 Cracker Jack Mac Stickers

In conjunction with its season-long promotion with Rawlings in which various Big Mac equipment items were given away, individual boxes of the snack could be found bearing one of 10 different McGwire stickers. The 1-1/2" x 2-1/8" stickers each include some type of interactive play element. Values shown are for opened, but complete, prize booklets. The color photos of McGwire on the stickers have had uniform logos removed.

	MT
Complete Set (10):	5.00
Common Sticker:	.50
1-10 Mark McGwire	.50

1980-83 Cramer Baseball Legends

Consecutively numbered, this set was issued over a period of four years by Cramer Sports Promotions, the forerunner of today's Pacific card company. Sold in wax packs and measuring the standard 2-1/2" x 3-1/2", the cards have a sepia-toned photo on front with a black frame. In the background is a weathered wooden slat design with the player's name on a hanging board beneath. The borders are dull yellow. Backs are printed in brown and include a few personal data, career stats and a career summary. Cards 1-30 were issued in 1980; #31-60 in 1981; #61-90 in 1982 and #90-124 in 1983. Cards #121-124 were issued on the 1983 wax box.

		NM
Complete Set (124):		45.00
Common Player:		.25
1980		
1	Babe Ruth	4.00
2	Heinie Manush	.25
3	Rabbit Maranville	.25
4	Earl Averill	.25
5	Joe DiMaggio	3.00
6	Mickey Mantle	4.00
7	Hank Aaron	2.50
8	Stan Musial	2.00
9	Bill Terry	.25
10	Sandy Koufax	1.50
11	Ernie Lombardi	.25
12	Dizzy Dean	.35
13	Lou Gehrig	3.00
14	Walter Alston	.25
15	Jackie Robinson	2.00
16	Jimmie Foxx	.25
17	Billy Southworth	.25
18	Honus Wagner	.35
19	Duke Snider	.35
20	Rogers Hornsby	.25
21	Paul Waner	.25
22	Luke Appling	.25
23	Billy Herman	.25
24	Lloyd Waner	.25
25	Fred Hutchinson	.25
26	Eddie Collins	.25
27	Lefty Grove	.25
28	Chuck Connors	.45
29	Lefty O'Doul	.25
30	Hank Greenberg	.25
1981		
31	Ty Cobb	3.00
32	Enos Slaughter	.25
33	Ernie Banks	.45
34	Christy Mathewson	.35
35	Mel Ott	.25
36	Pie Traynor	.25
37	Clark Griffith	.25
38	Mickey Cochrane	.25
39	Joe Cronin	.25
40	Leo Durocher	.25
41	Frank Baker	.25
42	Joe Tinker	.25
43	John McGraw	.25
44	Bill Dickey	.25
45	Walter Johnson	.35
46	Frankie Frisch	.25
47	Casey Stengel	.25
48	Willie Mays	2.00
49	Johnny Mize	.25
50	Roberto Clemente	3.00
51	Burleigh Grimes	.25
52	Pee Wee Reese	.35
53	Bob Feller	.35
54	Brooks Robinson	.35
55	Sam Crawford	.25
56	Robin Roberts	.25
57	Warren Spahn	.25
58	Joe McCarthy	.25
59	Jocko Conlan	.25
60	Satchel Paige	.75
1982		
61	Ted Williams	2.00
62	George Kelly	.25
63	Gil Hodges	.45
64	Jim Bottomley	.25
65	Al Kaline	.35
66	Harvey Kuenn	.25
67	Yogi Berra	.35
68	Nellie Fox	.35
69	Harmon Killebrew	.35
70	Edd Roush	.25
71	Mordecai Brown	.25
72	Gabby Hartnett	.25
73	Early Wynn	.25
74	Nap Lajoie	.25
75	Charlie Grimm	.25
76	Joe Garagiola	.35
77	Ted Lyons	.25
78	Mickey Vernon	.25
79	Lou Boudreau	.25
80	Al Dark	.25
81	Ralph Kiner	.25
82	Phil Rizzuto	.35
83	Stan Hack	.25
84	Frank Chance	.25
85	Ray Schalk	.25
86	Bill McKechnie	.25
87	Travis Jackson	.25
88	Pete Reiser	.25
89	Carl Hubbell	.25
90	Roy Campanella	.35
1983		
91	Cy Young	.35
92	Kiki Cuyler	.25
93	Chief Bender	.25
94	Richie Ashburn	.25
95	Riggs Stephenson	.25
96	Minnie Minoso	.25
97	Hack Wilson	.25
98	Al Lopez	.25
99	Willie Keeler	.25
100	Fred Lindstrom	.25
101	Roger Maris	.75
102	Roger Bresnahan	.25
103	Monty Stratton	.25
104	Goose Goslin	.25
105	Earle Combs	.25
106	Pepper Martin	.25
107	Joe Jackson	3.00
108	George Sisler	.25
109	Red Ruffing	.25
110	Johnny Vander Meer	.25
111	Herb Pennock	.25
112	Chuck Klein	.25
113	Paul Derringer	.25
114	Addie Joss	.25
115	Bobby Thomson	.25
116	Chick Hafey	.25
117	Lefty Gomez	.25
118	George Kell	.25
119	Al Simmons	.25
120	Bob Lemon	.25
121	Hoyt Wilhelm	.25
122	Arky Vaughan	.25
123	Frank Robinson	.35
124	Grover Alexander	.25

1995 Crayola Texas Rangers

Crayola, the Crayon people, sponsored this 36-card set of the Texas Rangers. Blank-back cards in 3" x 5" format feature color player portraits. In a blue box at bottom are the team and sponsor logos and the player's name and position. The set was sold by the Rangers souvenir department for $6.50. The unnumbered cards are checklisted here alphabetically.

		MT
Complete Set (36):		11.00
Common Player:		.25
(1)	Jose Alberro	.25
(2)	Esteban Beltre	.25
(3)	Dick Bosman	.25
(4)	Terry Burrows	.25
(5)	Will Clark	1.50
(6)	Bucky Dent	.25
(7)	Hector Fajardo	.25
(8)	Jeff Frye	.25
(9)	Benji Gil	.25
(10)	Juan Gonzalez	3.00
(11)	Rusty Greer	.50
(12)	Kevin Gross	.25
(13)	Larry Hardy	.25
(14)	Shawn Hare	.25
(15)	Rudy Jaramillo	.25
(16)	Roger McDowell	.25
(17)	Mark McLemore	.25
(18)	Ed Napoleon	.25
(19)	Jerry Narron	.25
(20)	Chris Nichting	.25
(21)	Otis Nixon	.25
(22)	Johnny Oates	.25
(23)	Darren Oliver	.25
(24)	Mike Pagliarulo	.25
(25)	Dean Palmer	.40
(26)	Roger Pavlik	.25
(27)	Kenny Rogers	.25
(28)	Ivan Rodriguez	1.50
(29)	Jeff Russell	.25
(30)	Mickey Tettleton	.40
(31)	Bob Tewksbury	.40
(32)	David Valle	.25
(33)	Jack Voigt	.25
(34)	Ed Vosberg	.25
(35)	Matt Whiteside	.25
(36)	Stadium photo	.25

1991 Crown/Coke Orioles

Claiming to include every player for the modern (1954-1991) Baltimore Orioles, this 501-card set was issued in four series. The first three series contain 120 cards each in a format of a dozen perforated cards on each of 10 sheets. Those series were given away at May 17, June 28 and Aug. 11 home games. The fourth series, 12 sheets of 12 cards each, including three blank cards, was available only at participating Crown gas stations, which also sold the first three series following the give-away days at the ballpark. Cards measure 2-1/2" x 3-3/16" and are perforated on two, three or four sides, depending on their position on the sheet. All players are featured in sepia-toned head shots, virtually all in Orioles' uniforms. Around the photos are borders of, successively, green, orange, black and white. The player's name and position appear in a black banner above the photo. In the lower-left corner is a 1954-1991 Memorial Stadium "Season to Remember" logo. That logo is repeated at bottom-center of the black-and-white backs, flanked by the logos of Coca-Cola and Crown. A card number appears in the lower-right. Most cards were numbered alphabetically. Backs include stats for the player's major league career and time with the Orioles.

		MT
Complete Set (501):		50.00
Common Player:		.10
1	Don Aase	.10
2	Cal Abrams	.10
3	Jerry Adair	.10
4	Bobby Adams	.10
5	Mike Adamson	.10
6	Jay Aldrich	.10
7	Bob Alexander	.10
8	Doyle Alexander	.10
9	Brady Anderson	.25
10	John Anderson	.10
11	Mike Anderson	.10
12	Luis Aparicio	.75
13	Tony Arnold	.10
14	Bobby Avila	.15
15	Benny Ayala	.10
16	Bob Bailor	.10
17	Frank Baker	.10
18	Jeff Ballard	.10
19	George Bamberger	.10
20	Steve Barber	.10
21	Ray "Buddy" Barker	.10
22	Ed Barnowski	.10
23	Jose Bautista	.10
24	Don Baylor	.25
25	Charlie Beamon	.10
26	Fred Beene	.10
27	Mark Belanger	.15
28	Eric Bell	.10
29	Juan Bell	.10
30	Juan Beniquez	.10
31	Neil Berry	.10
32	Frank Bertaina	.10
33	Fred Besana	.10
34	Vern Bickford	.10
35	Babe Birrer	.10
36	Paul Blair	.10
37	Curt Blefary	.10
38	Mike Blyzka	.10
39	Mike Boddicker	.10
40	Juan Bonilla	.10
41	Bob Bonner	.10
42	Dan Boone	.10
43	Rich Bordi	.10
44	Dave Boswell	.10
45	Sam Bowens	.10
46	Bob Boyd	.10
47	Gene Brabender	.10
48	Phil Bradley	.10
49	Jackie Brandt	.10
50	Marv Breeding	.10
51	Jim Brideweser	.10
52	Nellie Briles	.10
53	Dick Brown	.10
54	Hal Brown	.10
55	Larry Brown	.10
56	Mark Brown	.10
57	Marty Brown	.10
58	George Brunet	.10
59	Don Buford	.15
60	Al Bumbry	.10
61	Wally Bunker	.10
62	Leo Burke	.10
63	Rick Burleson	.10
64	Pete Burnside	.10
65	Jim Busby	.10
66	John Buzhardt	.10
67	Harry Byrd	.10
68	Enos Cabell	.10
69	Chico Carrasquel	.10
70	Camilo Carreon	.10
71	Foster Castleman	.10
72	Wayne Causey	.10
73	Art Ceccarelli	.10
74	Bob Chakales	.10
75	Tony Chevez	.10
76	Tom Chism	.10
77	Gino Cimoli	.10
78	Gil Coan	.10
79	Rich Coggins	.10
80	Joe Coleman	.10
81	Rip Coleman	.10
82	Fritz Connally	.10
83	Sandy Consuegra	.10
84	Doug Corbett	.10
85	Mark Corey	.10
86	Clint Courtney	.10
87	Billy Cox	.10
88	Dave Criscione	.10
89	Terry Crowley	.10
90	Todd Cruz	.10
91	Mike Cuellar	.20
92	Angie Dagres	.10
93	Clay Dalrymple	.10
94	Rich Dauer	.10
95	Jerry DaVanon	.10
96	Butch Davis	.10
97	Storm Davis	.10
98	Tommy Davis	.15
99	Doug DeCinces	.15
100	Luis DeLeon	.10
101	Ike Delock	.10
102	Rick Dempsey	.15
103	Mike Devereaux	.10
104	Chuck Diering	.10
105	Gordon Dillard	.10
106	Bill Dillman	.10
107	Mike Dimmel	.10
108	Ken Dixon	.10
109	Pat Dobson	.10
110	Tom Dodd	.10
111	Harry Dorish	.10
112	Moe Drabowsky	.10
113	Dick Drago	.10
114	Walt Dropo	.15
115	Tom Dukes	.10
116	Dave Duncan	.10
117	Ryne Duren	.15
118	Joe Durham	.10
119	Jim Dwyer	.10
120	Jim Dyck	.10
121	Mike Epstein	.10
122	Chuck Essegian	.10
123	Chuck Estrada	.10
124	Andy Etchebarren	.10
125	Hoot Evers	.10
126	Ed Farmer	.10
127	Chico Fernandez	.10
128	Don Ferrarese	.10
129	Jim Finigan	.10

130	Steve Finley	.15
131	Mike Fiore	.10
132	Eddie Fisher	.10
133	Jack Fisher	.10
134	Tom Fisher	.10
135	Mike Flanagan	.10
136	John Flinn	.10
137	Bobby Floyd	.10
138	Hank Foiles	.10
139	Dan Ford	.10
140	Dave Ford	.10
141	Mike Fornieles	.10
142	Howie Fox	.10
143	Tito Francona	.10
144	Joe Frazier	.10
145	Roger Freed	.10
146	Jim Fridley	.10
147	Jim Fuller	.10
148	Joe Gaines	.10
149	Vinicio "Chico" Garcia	.10
150	Kiko Garcia	.10
151	Billy Gardner	.10
152	Wayne Garland	.10
153	Tommy Gastall	.10
154	Jim Gentile	.15
155	Ken Gerhart	.10
156	Paul Gilliford	.10
157	Joe Ginsberg	.10
158	Leo Gomez	.10
159	Rene Gonzales	.10
160	Billy Goodman	.10
161	Dan Graham	.10
162	Ted Gray	.10
163	Gene Green	.10
164	Lenny Green	.10
165	Bobby Grich	.20
166	Mike Griffin	.10
167	Ross Grimsley	.10
168	Wayne Gross	.10
169	Glenn Gulliver	.10
170	Jackie Gutierrez	.10
171	John Habyan	.10
172	Harvey Haddix	.10
173	Bob Hale	.10
174	Dick Hall	.10
175	Bert Hamric	.10
176	Larry Haney	.10
177	Ron Hansen	.10
178	Jim Hardin	.10
179	Larry Harlow	.10
180	Pete Harnisch	.20
181	Tommy Harper	.15
182	Bob Harrison	.10
183	Roric Harrison	.10
184	Jack Harshman	.10
185	Mike Hart	.10
186	Paul Hartzell	.10
187	Grady Hatton	.10
188	Brad Havens	.10
189	Drungo Hazewood	.10
190	Jehosie Heard	.10
191	Mel Held	.10
192	Woodie Held	.10
193	Ellie Hendricks	.15
194	Leo Hernandez	.10
195	Whitey Herzog	.20
196	Kevin Hickey	.10
197	Billy Hoeft	.10
198	Chris Hoiles	.20
199	Fred Holdsworth	.10
200	Brian Holton	.10
201	Ken Holtzman	.10
202	Don Hood	.10
203	Sam Horn	.10
204	Art Houtteman	.10
205	Bruce Howard	.10
206	Rex Hudler	.10
207	Phil Huffman	.10
208	Keith Hughes	.10
209	Mark Huismann	.10
210	Tim Hulett	.10
211	Billy Hunter	.10
212	Dave Huppert	.10
213	Jim Hutto	.10
214	Dick Hyde	.10
215	Grant Jackson	.10
216	Lou Jackson	.10
217	Reggie Jackson	2.50
218	Ron Jackson	.10
219	Jesse Jefferson	.10
220	Stan Jefferson	.10
221	Bob Johnson	.10
222	Connie Johnson	.10
223	Darrell Johnson	.10
224	Dave Johnson	.10
225	Davey Johnson	.15
226	David Johnson	.10
227	Don Johnson	.10
228	Ernie Johnson	.10
229	Gordon Jones	.10
230	Ricky Jones	.10
231	O'Dell Jones	.10
232	Sam Jones	.10
233	George Kell	.50
234	Frank Kellert	.10
235	Pat Kelly	.10
236	Bob Kennedy	.10
237	Terry Kennedy	.10
238	Joe Kerrigan	.10
239	Mike Kinnunen	.10
240	Willie Kirkland	.10
241	Ron Kittle	.10
242	Billy Klaus	.10
243	Ray Knight	.15
244	Darold Knowles	.10
245	Dick Kokos	.10
246	Brad Komminsk	.10
247	Dave Koslo	.10
248	Wayne Krenchicki	.10
249	Lou Kretlow	.10
250	Dick Kryhoski	.10
251	Bob Kuzava	.10
252	Lee Lacy	.10
253	Hobie Landrith	.10
254	Tito Landrum	.10
255	Don Larsen	.15
256	Charlie Lau	.15
257	Jim Lehew	.10
258	Ken Lehman	.10
259	Don Lenhardt	.10
260	Dave Leonhard	.10
261	Don Leppert	.10
262	Dick Littlefield	.10
263	Charlie Locke	.10
264	Whitey Lockman	.10
265	Billy Loes	.10
266	Ed Lopat	.10
267	Carlos Lopez	.10
268	Marcelino Lopez	.10
269	John Lowenstein	.10
270	Steve Luebber	.10
271	Dick Luebke	.10
272	Fred Lynn	.30
273	Bobby Mabe	.10
274	Elliott Maddox	.10
275	Hank Majeski	.10
276	Roger Marquis	.10
277	Freddie Marsh	.10
278	Jim Marshall	.10
279	Morrie Martin	.10
280	Dennis Martinez	.20
281	Tippy Martinez	.15
282	Tom Matchick	.10
283	Charlie Maxwell	.10
284	Dave May	.10
285	Lee May	.10
286	Rudy May	.10
287	Mike McCormick	.10
288	Ben McDonald	.10
289	Jim McDonald	.10
290	Scott McGregor	.15
291	Mickey McGuire	.10
292	Jeff McKnight	.10
293	Dave McNally	.15
294	Sam Mele	.10
295	Francisco Melendez	.10
296	Bob Melvin	.10
297	Jose Mesa	.10
298	Eddie Miksis	.10
299	Bob Milacki	.10
300	Bill Miller	.10
301	Dyar Miller	.10
302	John Miller	.10
303	Randy Miller	.10
304	Stu Miller	.10
305	Randy Milligan	.10
306	Paul Mirabella	.10
307	Willy Miranda	.10
308	John Mitchell	.10
309	Paul Mitchell	.10
310	Ron Moeller	.10
311	Bob Molinaro	.10
312	Ray Moore	.10
313	Andres Mora	.10
314	Jose Morales	.10
315	Keith Moreland	.10
316	Mike Morgan	.10
317	Dan Morogiello	.10
318	John Morris	.10
319	Les Moss	.10
320	Curt Motton	.10
321	Eddie Murray	.90
322	Ray Murray	.10
323	Tony Muser	.10
324	Buster Narum	.10
325	Bob Nelson	.10
326	Roger Nelson	.10
327	Carl Nichols	.10
328	Dave Nicholson	.10
329	Tom Niedenfuer	.10
330	Bob Nieman	.10
331	Donell Nixon	.10
332	Joe Nolan	.10
333	Dickie Noles	.10
334	Tim Nordbrook	.10
335	Jim Northrup	.10
336	Jack O'Connor	.10
337	Billy O'Dell	.10
338	John O'Donoghue	.10
339	Tom O'Malley	.10
340	Johnny Oates	.10
341	Chuck Oertel	.10
342	Bob Oliver	.10
343	Gregg Olson	.10
344	John Orsino	.10
345	Joe Orsulak	.10
346	John Pacella	.10
347	Dave Pagan	.10
348	Erv Palica	.10
349	Jim Palmer	.90
350	John Papa	.10
351	Milt Pappas	.10
352	Al Pardo	.10
353	Kelly Paris	.10
354	Mike Parrott	.10
355	Tom Patton	.10
356	Albie Pearson	.10
357	Orlando Pena	.10
358	Oswaldo Peraza	.10
359	Buddy Peterson	.10
360	Dave Philley	.10
361	Tom Phoebus	.10
362	Al Pilarcik	.10
363	Duane Pillette	.10
364	Lou Piniella	.15
365	Dave Pope	.10
366	Arnie Portocarrero	.10
367	Boog Powell	.60
368	Johnny Powers	.10
369	Carl Powis	.10
370	Joe Price	.10
371	Jim Pyburn	.10
372	Art Quirk	.10
373	Jamie Quirk	.10
374	Allan Ramirez	.10
375	Floyd Rayford	.10
376	Mike Reinbach	.10
377	Merv Rettenmund	.10
378	Bob Reynolds	.10
379	Del Rice	.10
380	Pete Richert	.10
381	Jeff Rineer	.10
382	Bill Ripken	.10
383	Cal Ripken	6.00
384	Robin Roberts	.75
385	Brooks Robinson	2.50
386	Earl Robinson	.10
387	Eddie Robinson	.10
388	Frank Robinson	2.00
389	Sergio Robles	.10
390	Aurelio Rodriguez	.10
391	Vic Rodriguez	.10
392	Gary Roenicke	.10
393	Saul Rogovin	.10
394	Wade Rowdon	.10
395	Ken Rowe	.10
396	Willie Royster	.10
397	Vic Roznovsky	.10
398	Ken Rudolph	.10
399	Lenn Sakata	.10
400	Chico Salmon	.10
401	Orlando Sanchez	.10
402	Bob Saverine	.10
403	Art Schallock	.10
404	Bill Scherrer	.10
405	Curt Schilling	.20
406	Dave Schmidt	.10
407	Johnny Schmitz	.10
408	Jeff Schneider	.10
409	Rick Schu	.10
410	Mickey Scott	.10
411	Kal Segrist	.10
412	David Segui	.10
413	Al Severinsen	.10
414	Larry Sheets	.10
415	John Shelby	.10
416	Barry Shetrone	.10
417	Tom Shopay	.10
418	Bill Short	.10
419	Norm Siebern	.10
420	Nelson Simmons	.10
421	Ken Singleton	.15
422	Doug Sisk	.10
423	Dave Skaggs	.10
424	Lou Sleater	.10
425	Al Smith	.10
426	Billy Smith	.10
427	Hal Smith	.10
428	"Texas" Mike Smith	.10
429	Nate Smith	.10
430	Nate Snell	.10
431	Russ Snyder	.10
432	Don Stanhouse	.10
433	Pete Stanicek	.10
434	Herm Starrette	.10
435	John Stefero	.10
436	Gene Stephens	.10
437	Vern Stephens	.10
438	Earl Stephenson	.10
439	Sammy Stewart	.10
440	Royle Stillman	.10
441	Wes Stock	.10
442	Tim Stoddard	.10
443	Dean Stone	.10
444	Jeff Stone	.10
445	Steve Stone	.15
446	Marlin Stuart	.10
447	Gordie Sundin	.10
448	Bill Swaggerty	.10
449	Willie Tasby	.10
450	Joe Taylor	.10
451	Dorn Taylor	.10
452	Anthony Telford	.10
453	Johnny Temple	.10
454	Mickey Tettleton	.10
455	Valmy Thomas	.10
456	Bobby Thomson	.15
457	Marv Thorneberry	.10
458	Mark Thurmond	.10
459	Jay Tibbs	.10
460	Mike Torrez	.10
461	Jim Traber	.10
462	Gus Triandos	.10
463	Paul "Dizzy" Trout	.10
464	Bob Turley	.10
465	Tom Underwood	.10
466	Fred Valentine	.10
467	Dave Van Gorder	.10
468	Dave Vineyard	.10
469	Ozzie Virgil	.10
470	Eddie Waitkus	.10
471	Greg Walker	.10
472	Jerry Walker	.10
473	Pete Ward	.10
474	Carl Warwick	.10
475	Ron Washington	.10
476	Eddie Watt	.10
477	Don Welchel	.10
478	George Werley	.10
479	Vic Wertz	.10
480	Wally Westlake	.10
481	Mickey Weston	.10
482	Alan Wiggins	.10
483	Bill Wight	.10
484	Hoyt Wilhelm	.35
485	Dallas Williams	.10
486	Dick Williams	.10
487	Earl Williams	.10
488	Mark Williamson	.10
489	Jim Wilson	.10
490	Gene Woodling	.10
491	Craig Worthington	.10
492	Bobby Young	.10
493	Mike Young	.10
494	Frank Zupo	.10
495	George Zuverink	.10
496	Glenn Davis	.10
497	Dwight Evans	.15
498	Dave Gallagher	.10
499	Paul Kilgus	.10
500	Jeff Robinson	.10
501	Ernie Whitt	.10

1992 Crown Orioles Action Standups

Crown Petroleum released a set of standup cards in 1992 of 12 Oriole greats, most retired, that was sold at service stations in three series. The 4-1/4" x 9" cards have color photos on a white background on front; backs have black-and-white stats, logos, and career highlights. Cal Ripken, Jr. and Tippy Martinez were the only active players portrayed in the set. Suggested retail price at issue was $4 per series; about $2 with a gasoline purchase. A collector's album could also be purchased.

		MT
Complete Set (12):		20.00
Common Player:		.90
	SET 1	9.00
(1)	Frank Robinson	3.00
(2)	Brooks Robinson	4.00
(3)	Jim Palmer	3.00
(4)	Rick Dempsey	.90
	SET 2	10.00
(5)	Cal Ripken Jr.	8.00
(6)	Tippy Martinez	.90
(7)	Bobby Grich	.90
(8)	Earl Weaver	1.00
	SET 3	3.00
(9)	Boog Powell	1.00
(10)	Paul Blair	.90
(11)	Terry Crowley	.90
(12)	Ken Singleton	.90

1996 Crown Pro Magnets

		MT
Complete Set (94):		50.00
Common Player:		.50
1	Fred McGriff	.75
2	Ryan Klesko	.75
3	David Justice	1.00
4	Greg Maddux	3.00
5	Jaime Navarro	.50
6	Shawon Dunston	.50
7	Brian McRae	.50
8	Barry Larkin	.50
9	Reggie Sanders	.50
10	Benito Santiago	.50
11	Dante Bichette	.75
12	Vinny Castilla	.50
13	Andres Galarraga	.75
14	Larry Walker	.60
15	Gary Sheffield	.75
16	Jeff Conine	.50
17	Terry Pendleton	.50
18	Jeff Bagwell	2.50
19	Doug Drabek	.50
20	Shane Reynolds	.50
21	Mike Piazza	3.00
22	Delino DeShields	.50
23	Hideo Nomo	1.00
24	Wil Cordero	.50
25	Pedro Martinez	.75
26	Todd Hundley	.50
27	Jose Vizcaino	.50
28	Jim Eisenreich	.50
29	Gregg Jefferies	.50
30	Darren Daulton	.50
31	Orlando Merced	.50
32	Carlos Garcia	.50
33	Jay Bell	.50
34	Brian Jordan	.50
35	Ray Lankford	.50
36	Tom Pagnozzi	.50
37	Ozzie Smith	1.50
38	Tony Gwynn	2.50
39	Andujar Cedeno	.50
40	Andy Ashby	.50
41	Matt Williams	.75
42	Barry Bonds	1.50
43	Deion Sanders	.75
44	Cal Ripken Jr.	4.00
45	Bobby Bonilla	.50
46	Mike Mussina	.75
47	Rafael Palmeiro	.75
48	Mo Vaughn	1.00
49	Jose Canseco	.75
50	Mike Greenwell	.50
51	Tim Salmon	.75
52	J.T. Snow	.50
53	Brady Anderson	.50
54	Frank Thomas	2.50
55	Ozzie Guillen	.50
56	Robin Ventura	.50
57	Ron Karkovice	.50
58	Kenny Lofton	1.00
59	Albert Belle	2.00
60	Eddie Murray	1.00
61	Manny Ramirez	1.50
62	Charles Nagy	.50
63	Travis Fryman	.50
64	Alan Trammell	.50
65	Cecil Fielder	.50
66	Jon Nunnally	.50
67	Kevin Appier	.50
68	Kevin Seitzer	.50
69	Pat Listach	.50
70	John Jaha	.50
71	Chuck Knoblauch	.60
72	Kirby Puckett	2.00
73	Marty Cordova	.50
74	Wade Boggs	.75
75	Jimmy Key	.50
76	Paul O'Neill	.50
77	David Cone	.50
78	Mark McGwire	5.00
79	Terry Steinbach	.50
80	Danny Tartabull	.50
81	Randy Johnson	.75
82	Ken Griffey Jr.	5.00
83	Jay Buhner	.50
84	Edgar Martinez	.50
85	Alex Rodriguez	4.00
86	Will Clark	.75
87	Juan Gonzalez	2.00
88	Ivan Rodriguez	.75
89	Benji Gil	.50
90	Roberto Alomar	1.00
91	Pat Hentgen	.50
92	Joe Carter	.50
93	John Olerud	.60
94	Carlos Delgado	.60

1997 Crown Pro Heroes of the Locker Room

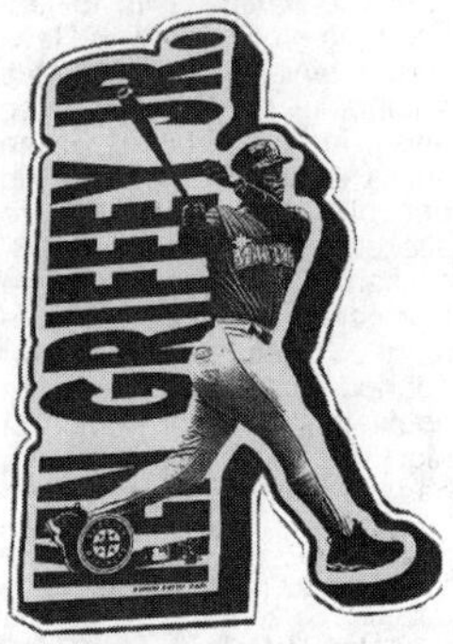

Two baseball players are included in the multi-sport set of large (about 2-1/2" x 4-1/4") format diecut magnets. The blank-back magnets have player action photos superimposed on a large team logo against a white background. The 5/8" thick magnets were sold in a locker-look box with a suggested retail price of $4.59 when issued.

	MT
Complete Set (2):	10.00
(1) Ken Griffey Jr.	5.00
(2) Cal Ripken Jr.	5.00

1997 Crown Pro Magnets

Four baseball players are featured along with 10 football and basketball players in this set of 2-1/2" x 3-1/2" blank-back magnets. The pieces feature player action photos set against a large team logo on a white background. Individual magnets carried a suggested retail price of $1.49 at issue.

	MT
Complete Set (4):	12.00
S1 Frank Thomas	3.00
S2 Ken Griffey Jr.	3.00
S3 Cal Ripken Jr.	3.00
S4 Alex Rodriguez	3.00

1997 Crown Pro Pro-Files

Sixteen football, basketball and baseball stars are featured in this collection of magnets (only the baseball players are listed here). Blank-back magnets measure about 3-3/4" square and combine player portrait and action photos with team logos on a white background. These magnets were originally sold singly at a suggested retail price of $1.99. Cards are numbered with the "PF" prefix.

	MT
Complete Set (4):	12.00
1 Ken Griffey Jr.	3.00
2 Frank Thomas	3.00
3 Cal Ripken Jr.	3.00
4 Chipper Jones	3.00

1997 Crown Pro Pro Stamps

Packaged either as an assortment of Major League stars or in team packs of the Yankees, Braves, Cubs and White Sox, these 1-1/2" x 1-7/8" blank-back stickers were originally sold in packs of 12 for $1.49. The assortment pack contains 12 different player stamps while the team packs have a duplicated group of five players and a team logo. All stickers have a white background for the player's action photo. A team logo is in one of the lower corners. Player names are carried vertically down one side, opposite a large "1997 USA" logo in orange.

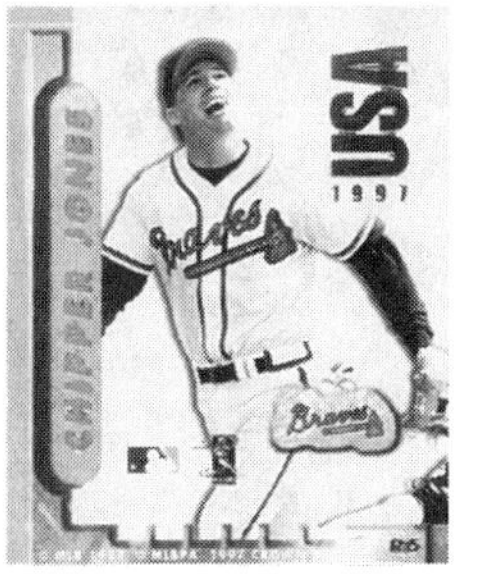

	MT
Complete Set (36):	8.00
Common Player:	.25
Assortment pack	
R1 Andruw Jones	.75
R2 Alex Rodriguez	1.00
R3 Johnny Damon	.35
R4 Derek Jeter	1.00
R5 Cal Ripken Jr.	1.25
R6 Chipper Jones	1.00
R7 Ken Griffey Jr.	1.50
R8 Andres Galarraga	.75
R9 Barry Bonds	.90
R10 Frank Thomas	1.00
R11 Juan Gonzalez	1.00
R12 Mike Piazza	1.00
Braves team pack	
(1) Andruw Jones	.75
(2) Chipper Jones	1.00
(3) Ryan Klesko	.35
(4) Greg Maddux	.75
(5) John Smoltz	.25
(6) Braves logo	.25
Cubs team pack	
(1) Shawon Dunston	.25
(2) Mark Grace	.60
(3) Brian McRae	.25
(4) Ryne Sandberg	1.00
(5) Sammy Sosa	1.50
(6) Cubs logo	.25
White Sox team pack	
(1) Harold Baines	.25
(2) Albert Belle	.90
(3) Ozzie Guillen	.25
(4) Frank Thomas	1.00
(5) Robin Ventura	.35
(6) White Sox logo	.25
Yankees team pack	
(1) Derek Jeter	1.00
(2) Paul O'Neill	.25
(3) Andy Pettitte	.40
(4) Darryl Strawberry	.40
(5) Bernie Williams	.40
(6) Yankees logo	.25

1997 Crown Pro 3D Diecut Magnets

Crown's line-up of extra-large (about 4-1/2" x 6-1/2" and 5/8" thick) magnets included two baseball players as well as half a dozen football and basketball stars. The magnets have a player action photo on a white background with the player name in large team-color letters vertically at left. The 3D Diecut magnets were sold individually with a suggested retail price at issue of $4.99.

	MT
Complete Set (2):	9.00
(1) Ken Griffey Jr.	5.00
(2) Cal Ripken Jr.	4.50

1986 Scott Cunningham

These collectors issues were ostensibly produced as samples for 5" x 7" or 8" x 10" photos which could be purchased from various sources. The sample cards are in the standard 2-1/2" x 3-1/2" format with rounded corners and glossy finish. Borderless color front photos have only the player's name in black or white. Backs are in black-and-white with player ID, photographer's credit and the offer of photos. Some cards have a checklist back. Four cards were produced earlier and in smaller quantities than the others, they are noted with an "*" in the alphabetical checklist here.

	MT
Complete Set (20):	24.00
Common Player:	1.00
(1) Wade Boggs	1.50
(2) Gary Carter	1.00
(3) Vince Coleman	1.00
(4) Steve Garvey	1.00
(5) Dwight Gooden (*) (walking)	2.00
(6) Dwight Gooden (pitching)	1.00
(7) Rickey Henderson	1.00
(8) Orel Hershiser	1.00
(9) Don Mattingly (*)	3.00
(10) Dale Murphy (*)	2.00
(11) Dale Murphy (flaming bat)	1.00
(12) Eddie Murray	1.00
(13) Lance Parrish	1.00
(14) Cal Ripken Jr.	3.00
(15) Pete Rose (*)	3.00
(16) Ryne Sandberg	1.50
(17) Mike Schmidt	2.00
(18) Ozzie Smith	1.50
(19) Darryl Strawberry	1.00
(20) Lou Whitaker	1.00

1998 CyberAction

During the 1998 National Sports Collectors Convention in Chicago, CyberAction gave away samples of its product. The cards are printed on flimsy cardboard in standard 2-1/2" x 3-1/2" format. Fronts have a blue-bordered action photo at center. In the background is a large team logo. The firm's web site address is at top; its logo at bottom. Backs have details on winning a World Series trip.

	MT
Complete Set (6):	12.00
Common Player:	2.00
1 Ken Griffey Jr.	4.00
2 Mark McGwire	3.00
3 Barry Bonds	2.00
4 Derek Jeter	2.50
5 Greg Maddux	2.00
6 Larry Walker	2.00

D

1992 Dairy Queen Team USA

In 1992, in conjunction with the Dairy Queen Team USA Sundae-in-a-Helmet promotion, customers received a four-card pack of Team USA cards, part of a 33-card set manufactured by Topps for the company. Included in the set are Team USA players from the 1984 and 1988 Olympics, many of whom have gone on to major league stardom. The set also has 15 Team USA Prospects, a 1988 Gold Medal team celebration card and a card of 1992 coach Ron Fraser. Fronts feature each player in their Team USA uniform and the backs include statistics from amateur, Team USA and professional competition.

	MT
Complete Set (33):	25.00
Common Player:	.45
1 Mark McGwire (1984)	15.00
2 Will Clark (1984)	4.50
3 John Marzano (1984)	.45
4 Barry Larkin (1984)	2.50
5 Bobby Witt (1984)	.45
6 Scott Bankhead (1984)	.45
7 B.J. Surhoff (1984)	1.00
8 Shane Mack (1984)	.60
9 Jim Abbott (1988)	1.50
10 Ben McDonald (1988)	.50
11 Robin Ventura (1988)	2.50
12 Charles Nagy (1988)	1.00
13 Andy Benes (1988)	1.50
14 Joe Slusarski (1988)	.45
15 Ed Sprague (1988)	.45
16 Bret Barberie (1988)	.45
17 Gold Medal - 1988 (1988)	.45
18 Jeff Granger (1992)	.45
19 John Dettmer (1992)	.45
20 Todd Greene (1992)	.45
21 Jeffrey Hammonds (1992)	1.25
22 Dan Melendez (1992)	.45
23 Kennie Steenstra (1992)	.45
24 Todd Johnson (1992)	.45
25 Chris Roberts (1992)	.45
26 Steve Rodriguez (1992)	.45
27 Charles Johnson (1992)	2.50
28 Chris Wimmer (1992)	.45
29 Tony Phillips (1992)	.45
30 Craig Wilson (1992)	.45
31 Jason Giambi (1992)	1.25
32 Paul Shuey (1992)	.50
33 Ron Fraser (1992 coach)	.45

1994 Dairy Queen Ken Griffey, Jr.

Distributed by Dairy Queen stores in the Pacific Northwest, this set was issued in two different versions, with green borders and with gold borders. All cards feature a "Ken Griffey Jr. Golden Moments" logo in the upper-left corner. His name and the DQ logo appear at the bottom. Backs have another photo of Griffey along with a description of the career highlight depicted on front, sponsors' logos and a card number. Values shown here are for green-bordered cards; gold-bordered cards sell for about twice those figures.

	MT
Complete Set (10):	12.00
Common Player:	1.50
Gold: 2X	
1 Ken Griffey, Jr. ("The Spider Man Catch")	1.50
2 Ken Griffey, Jr. ("Back to Back Homeruns")	1.50
3 Ken Griffey, Jr. (Hit .327 in 1991)	1.50
4 Ken Griffey, Jr. (1992 All-Star MVP)	1.50
5 Ken Griffey, Jr. ("Dialing Long Distance")	1.50
6 Ken Griffey, Jr. ("8 Straight Homeruns")	1.50
7 Ken Griffey, Jr. (4-Time Golden Glove Winner)	1.50
8 Ken Griffey, Jr. (45 Homeruns in 1993)	1.50
9 Ken Griffey, Jr. (Major League Career Hitting Record)	1.50
10 Ken Griffey, Jr. ("Looking to 1994")	1.50

1998 Danbury Mint McGwire/Sosa

MLB's homerun heroes of 1998 were featured on this pair of collectors' issue cards from one of the nation's largest creators of collectibles. The players are pictured in action poses on 2-1/2" x 3-1/2" embossed gold-foil cards. Backs have complete career stats and biographical details. Unlike many similar issues, these cards are licensed by MLB and thus team logos are used in both the design and player pictures. Issue price was about $21 each, which included plastic cases for the cards and a hardcover folio for storage.

		MT
Complete Set (2):		42.00
	Mark McGwire	21.00
	Sammy Sosa	21.00

1982 Davco Publishers Hall of Fame Baseball Stars

Most of baseball's top players in the Hall of Fame prior to 1982 are included in this collectors issue. The 7-1/4" x 4-1/4" horizontal-format cards feature color player portraits and action paintings on front along with a few career highlights. Backs are blank. Cards are checklisted here in alphabetical order.

		MT
Complete Set (25):		40.00
Common Player:		2.50
(1)	Hank Aaron	5.00
(2)	Grover C. Alexander	2.50
(3)	Roy Campanella	4.00
(4)	Ty Cobb	5.00
(5)	Joe DiMaggio	7.50
(6)	Bob Feller	2.50
(7)	Jimmy Foxx (Jimmie)	2.50
(8)	Frank Frisch	2.50
(9)	Lou Gehrig	7.50
(10)	Bob Gibson	2.50
(11)	Hank Greenberg	4.00
(12)	Rogers Hornsby	2.50
(13)	Walter Johnson	2.50
(14)	Sandy Koufax	4.00
(15)	Mickey Mantle	15.00
(16)	Christy Mathewson	2.50
(17)	Willie Mays	5.00
(18)	Stan Musial	4.00
(19)	Jackie Robinson	4.00
(20)	Babe Ruth	12.50
(21)	Tris Speaker	2.50
(22)	Pie Traynor	2.50
(23)	Honus Wagner	2.50
(24)	Ted Williams	5.00
(25)	Cy Young	2.50

1991 Jimmy Dean

Baseball cards were inserted into packages of Jimmy Dean sausages in 1991. The complete set consists of 25 star players' cards. Red and yellow borders surround color player photos on the card fronts. No team logos appear on the cards. The card backs feature statistics, biographical information and a facsimile autograph. The set is entitled the "Signature Edition."

		MT
Complete Set (25):		9.00
Common Player:		.30
1	Will Clark	.50
2	Ken Griffey, Jr.	2.00
3	Dale Murphy	.40
4	Barry Bonds	.90
5	Darryl Strawberry	.30
6	Ryne Sandberg	.65
7	Gary Sheffield	.45
8	Sandy Alomar, Jr.	.35
9	Frank Thomas	1.25
10	Barry Larkin	.30
11	Kirby Puckett	.65
12	George Brett	.75
13	Kevin Mitchell	.30
14	Dave Justice	.45
15	Cal Ripken, Jr.	1.50
16	Craig Biggio	.35
17	Rickey Henderson	.45
18	Roger Clemens	.65
19	Jose Canseco	.45
20	Ozzie Smith	.65
21	Cecil Fielder	.30
22	Dave Winfield	.40
23	Kevin Maas	.30
24	Nolan Ryan	1.50
25	Dwight Gooden	.30

1992 Jimmy Dean

For the second year in a row, baseball cards were inserted into packages of Jimmy Dean sausage in 1992. Featuring 18 star players, the set portrays the player's name on a vertical panel at the left of the card, along with his team name and position. The Jimmy Dean logo appears in the lower-right corner. Major League team logos have been eliminated from the photos.

		MT
Complete Set (18):		15.00
Common Player:		.35
1	Jim Abbott	.35
2	Barry Bonds	1.50
3	Jeff Bagwell	.90
4	Frank Thomas	2.50
5	Steve Avery	.35
6	Chris Sabo	.35
7	Will Clark	.75
8	Don Mattingly	1.50
9	Darryl Strawberry	.35
10	Roger Clemens	.90
11	Ken Griffey, Jr.	5.00
12	Chuck Knoblauch	.50
13	Tony Gwynn	.90
14	Juan Gonzalez	1.50
15	Cecil Fielder	.35
16	Bobby Bonilla	.35
17	Wes Chamberlain	.35
18	Ryne Sandberg	.75

1992 Jimmy Dean Living Legends

Approximately 100,000 of these six-card sets were made available via a mail-in offer for $1 and proofs of purchase from the company's breakfast meats. Color photos on front have had uniform logos removed and are overprinted with a gold-foil facsimile autograph. Other gold foil highlights the player, team and sponsor names on front. Backs are printed in black and yellow and include a few biographical details, career highlights and summary statistics.

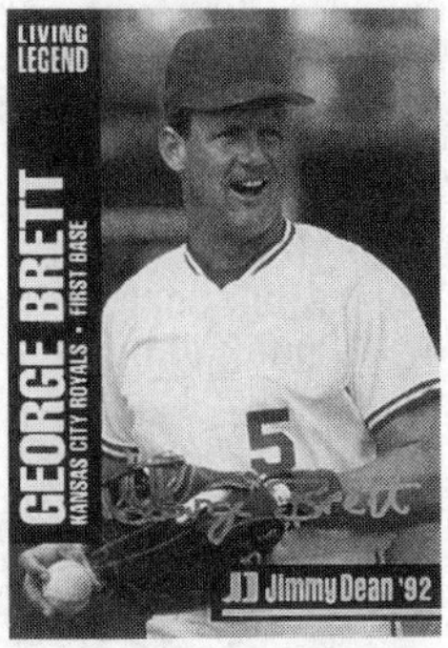

		MT
Complete Set (6):		15.00
Common Player:		1.50
1	George Brett	3.00
2	Carlton Fisk	2.50
3	Ozzie Smith	3.00
4	Robin Yount	3.00
5	Cal Ripken, Jr.	4.50
6	Nolan Ryan	4.50

1992 Jimmy Dean Rookie Stars

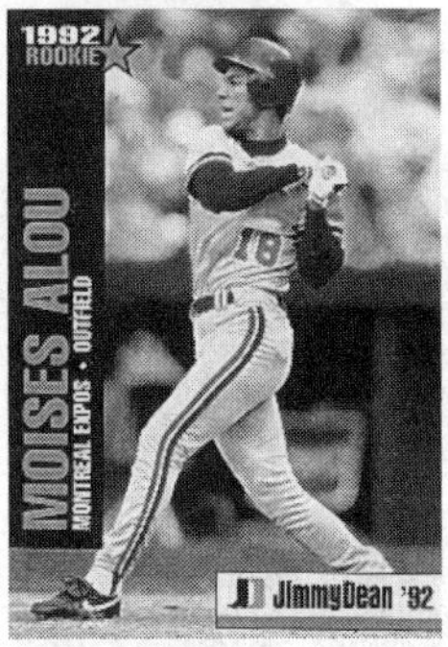

Nine of 1992's hottest rookies were featured in this set issued as inserts into various Jimmy Dean meat products. Cards feature full-bleed photos on which uniform logos have been airbrushed away. A 1992 Rookie Star logo appears at upper-left, atop a black vertical strip containing the player's name, team and position. A white strip at bottom has the Jimmy Dean logo. On back, personal data and minor and major league stats are featured in a center panel, surrounded by a light blue border.

		MT
Complete Set (9):		7.00
Common Player:		.35
1	Andy Stankiewicz	.35
2	Pat Listach	.35
3	Brian Jordan	1.50
4	Eric Karros	2.00
5	Reggie Sanders	1.00
6	Dave Fleming	.35
7	Donovan Osborne	.35
8	Kenny Lofton	2.50
9	Moises Alou	2.00

1993 Jimmy Dean

Issued in the company's meat products and via a mail-in offer, this set once again features player photos on which the uniform logos have been airbrushed away, due to lack of a license from Major League Baseball. A pair of horizontal color bars in one of the lower corners contains a Jimmy Dean logo and the player's name. Backs have a line drawing portrait of the player, along with stats, personal data and logos.

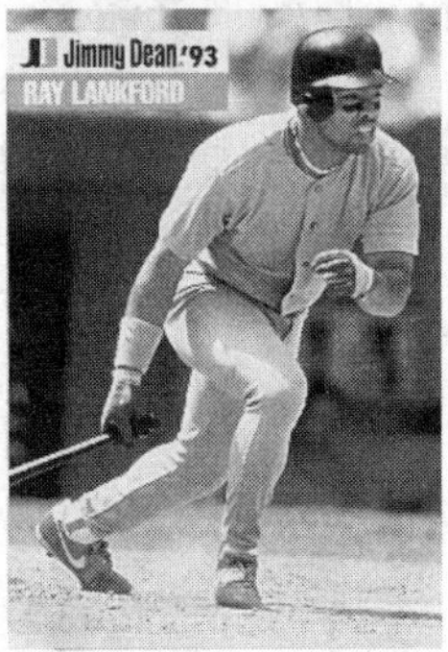

		MT
Complete Set (28):		7.50
Common Player:		.25
1	Frank Thomas	1.50
2	Barry Larkin	.35
3	Cal Ripken, Jr.	1.50
4	Andy Van Slyke	.25
5	Darren Daulton	.25
6	Don Mattingly	.90
7	Roger Clemens	.75
8	Juan Gonzalez	.85
9	Mark Langston	.25
10	Barry Bonds	.90
11	Ken Griffey, Jr.	2.00
12	Cecil Fielder	.25
13	Kirby Puckett	.75
14	Tom Glavine	.30
15	George Brett	1.00
16	Nolan Ryan	1.50
17	Eddie Murray	.40
18	Gary Sheffield	.35
19	Doug Drabek	.25
20	Ray Lankford	.25
21	Benito Santiago	.25
22	Mark McGwire	2.00
23	Kenny Lofton	.50
24	Eric Karros	.25
25	Ryne Sandberg	.65
26	Charlie Hayes	.25
27	Mike Mussina	.30
28	Pat Listach	.25

1993 Jimmy Dean Rookie Cards

Jimmy Dean Foods issued a Rookie Stars baseball card set in 1993. The nine-card set features promising rookies, with players highlighted against a marblized background with color photos on both sides of the cards. The cards were distributed randomly in three-card sets in specially-marked packages of Jimmy Dean products.

		MT
Complete Set (9):		6.00
Common Player:		.25
(1)	Rich Amaral	.25
(2)	Vinny Castilla	1.00
(3)	Jeff Conine	.50
(4)	Brent Gates	.35
(5)	Wayne Kirby	.25
(6)	Mike Lansing	.50
(7)	David Nied	.25
(8)	Mike Piazza	3.00
(9)	Tim Salmon	1.50

Player names in *Italic* type indicate a rookie card.

1995 Jimmy Dean All Time Greats

Six Hall of Famers are featured in this promotion for the country singer's breakfast meats. Besides inclusion of regular cards in food packages, a send-away deal offered autographed cards of three of the players for proofs of purchase and $7 apiece. Cards feature action photos on which team uniform logos have been removed; while the cards are licensed by the Major League Baseball Players Alumni, they are not sanctioned by MLB. A large "1995 All Time Greats Collectors Set" logo appears in the upper-right corner on front, while the Jimmy Dean logo and player name are in the lower-left. Full color backs offer a career summary and lifetime stats, along with a ghost image of the front photo.

		MT
Complete Set (6):		10.00
Common Player:		2.00
1	Rod Carew	2.00
2	Jim "Catfish" Hunter	1.00
2a	Jim "Catfish" Hunter (autographed)	9.00
3	Al Kaline	3.00
3a	Al Kaline (autographed)	10.00
4	Mike Schmidt	3.00
5	Billy Williams	1.00
5a	Billy Williams (autographed)	9.00
6	Carl Yastrzemski	3.00

1997 Jimmy Dean Great Moments

These two-card sets were available via a mail-in offer for $12.95 apiece plus proofs of purchase. Each set consists of an autographed "Great Moments in Baseball" card with an action photo and a "Great Baseball Stadiums" card featuring a player photo set against the stadium background. All pictures are sepia toned with uniform logos removed. Cards have player or stadium information on the backs and came with a certificate of authenticity.

		MT
Complete Set (4):		40.00
(1)	Yogi Berra (autograph)	15.00
(2)	Yogi Berra (Yankee Stadium)	5.00
(3)	Brooks Robinson (autograph)	15.00

(4)	Brooks Robinson (Memorial Stadium)	5.00

1984 Decathalon Negro League Baseball Stars

According to contemporary advertising, this set was produced in conjunction with the Negro Baseball Hall of History in Kentucky, to a total of 2,000 sets and 300 uncut sheets. The cards and checklist are identical to the 1986 issue by Larry Fritsch Cards, which purchased rights to the set, except for the copyright line at bottom on back.

	MT
Complete Set:	12.50
Common Player:	.10

(See Larry Fritsch Cards for checklist and single card values)

1992 Delphi Plate Promo Card

Certainly the greatest quantity ever produced of a Babe Ruth baseball card would be that of the promo card done by a collectible plate manufacturer to introduce its "Babe Ruth: The Called Shot" plate. The first in an intended "Legends of Baseball" series. The fully licensed, 2-1/2" x 3-1/2" card has a color painting of Ruth on front with multi-colored baseball graphics around and a red border. The black-and-white back has information about the plate and Ruth's career, along with copyright and licensor data. The promo card was included in direct-mail solicitations for the plate numbering into the millions over several years.

	MT
Babe Ruth	.50

Checklists with card numbers in parentheses ( ) indicates the numbers do not appear on the card.

1993 Dempster's Blue Jays

One of several Canadian baseball card issues marking the 1992 World Series victory of the Toronto Blue Jays, the Dempster's stores set is a 25-card issue in standard 2-1/2" x 3-1/2", UV-coatd on both sides. Fronts have a large dark blue border with white horizontal pinstripes. An action photo is at center, with the player's name and position below. The Jays World Championship logo and Players Association logo are at top; the sponsor's logo at lower-right. A baseball at bottom center has the card number. Backs feature a large portrait photo at top, against a dark blue background. Color bars carry the player's '92 and career stats. A facsimile autograph appears beneath the team logo at right.

		MT
Complete Set (25):		16.00
Common Player:		.50
1	Juan Guzman	.50
2	Roberto Alomar	2.00
3	Danny Cox	.50
4	Paul Molitor	4.00
5	Todd Stottlemyre	.50
6	Joe Carter	.50
7	Jack Morris	.50
8	Ed Sprague	.50
9	Turner Ward	.50
10	John Olerud	1.50
11	Duane Ward	.50
12	Alfredo Griffin	.50
13	Cito Gaston	.50
14	Dave Stewart	.50
15	Mark Eichhorn	.50
16	Darnell Coles	.50
17	Randy Knorr	.50
18	Al Leiter	.75
19	Pat Hentgen	.50
20	Devon White	.75
21	Pat Borders	.50
22	Darrin Jackson	.50
23	Dick Schofield	.50
24	Luis Sojo	.50
25	Mike Timlin	.50

1991 Denny's Grand Slam

This 26-card set was produced by Upper Deck and features one player from each Major League team. One hologram card was distributed with the purchase of a Grand Slam meal. The cards are numbered on the front and are 3-D. The card backs describe grand slams hit by the featured player.

		MT
Complete Set (26):		30.00
Common Player:		.75
1	Ellis Burks	.75
2	Cecil Fielder	.75
3	Will Clark	1.50
4	Eric Davis	.75
5	Dave Parker	.75
6	Kelly Gruber	.75
7	Kent Hrbek	.75
8	Don Mattingly	2.00
9	Brook Jacoby	.75
10	Mark McGwire	4.00
11	Howard Johnson	.75
12	Tim Wallach	.75
13	Ricky Jordan	.75
14	Andre Dawson	1.00
15	Eddie Murray	1.00
16	Danny Tartabull	.75
17	Bobby Bonilla	.75
18	Benito Santiago	.75
19	Alvin Davis	.75
20	Cal Ripken	3.00
21	Ruben Sierra	.75
22	Pedro Guerrero	.75
23	Wally Joyner	.75
24	Craig Biggio	.75
25	Dave Justice	1.50
26	Tim Raines	.75

1992 Denny's Grand Slam

The second year of the Denny's Gland Slam promotion featured one power hitter from each major league team, portrayed on a hologram in front of a scene from his team's city. As in the first year, the cards were produced by Upper Deck and given away, one at a time, with a Denny's purchase during the middle of the summer. An album with plastic pages holding four cards each was also available.

		MT
Complete Set (26):		25.00
Common Player:		.75
Album:		10.00
1	Marquis Grissom	.75
2	Ken Caminiti	.75
3	Fred McGriff	1.00
4	Felix Jose	.75
5	Jack Clark	.75
6	Albert Belle	1.50
7	Sid Bream	.75
8	Robin Ventura	.75
9	Cal Ripken, Jr.	3.00
10	Ryne Sandberg	1.50
11	Paul O'Neill	.75
12	Luis Polonia	.75
13	Cecil Fielder	.75
14	Kal Daniels	.75
15	Brian McRae	.75
16	Howard Johnson	.75
17	Greg Vaughn	.75
18	Dale Murphy	1.00
19	Kent Hrbek	.75
20	Barry Bonds	2.00
21	Matt Nokes	.75
22	Jose Canseco	1.50
23	Jay Buhner	.75
24	Will Clark	1.00
25	Ruben Sierra	.75
26	Joe Carter	.75

1993 Denny's Grand Slam

The 1993 Denny's Grand Slam set expanded to 28 cards with the addition of the Florida and Colorado expansion teams. The featured color photos of one grand slam slugger for each team superimposed over a hologram background. The reverse of each card gives anecdotes about the player's grand slams along with his career total. The cards were distributed at participating Denny's restaurants during mid-summer.

		MT
Complete Set (28):		25.00
Common Player:		.75
1	Chili Davis	.75
2	Eric Anthony	.75
3	Rickey Henderson	1.00
4	Joe Carter	.75
5	Terry Pendleton	.75
6	Robin Yount	2.00
7	Ray Lankford	.75
8	Ryne Sandberg	1.50
9	Darryl Strawberry	.75
10	Marquis Grissom	.75
11	Will Clark	1.00
12	Albert Belle	1.00
13	Edgar Martinez	.75
14	Benito Santiago	.75
15	Eddie Murray	1.00
16	Cal Ripken, Jr.	3.00
17	Gary Sheffield	.90
18	Dave Hollins	.75
19	Andy Van Slyke	.75
20	Juan Gonzalez	2.00
21	John Valentin	.75
22	Joe Oliver	.75
23	Dante Bichette	.75
24	Wally Joyner	.75
25	Cecil Fielder	.75
26	Kirby Puckett	2.00
27	Robin Ventura	.90
28	Danny Tartabull	.75

1994 Denny's Grand Slam

For its fourth annual hologram card promotion, Denny's chose a horizontal format with portrait and action photos of one player from each major league team. Designated the "Anniversary Edition," the set features the 125th year logo at bottom center, with the player's name at left; Upper Deck and Denny's logos are at top. On back the same two photos are conventionally printed along with a brief player biography, appropriate logos and copyright notices. The cards are numbered alphabetically. Cards were available with certain menu items from July 1 through Aug. 31. Each restaurant received one special boxed set for use as a contest prize. These sets include a special Reggie Jackson "Route to Cooperstown" hologram card; the edition was limited to about 1,500.

		MT
Complete Set (28/no Jackson):		25.00
Complete Set (29/w Jackson):		125.00
Common Player:		.50
1	Jim Abbott	.50
2	Roberto Alomar	.60
3	Kevin Appier	.50
4	Jeff Bagwell	1.50
5	Albert Belle	1.00
6	Barry Bonds	2.00
7	Bobby Bonilla	.50
8	Lenny Dykstra	.50
9	Cal Eldred	.50
10	Cecil Fielder	.50
11	Andres Galarraga	.60
12	Juan Gonzalez	1.50
13	Ken Griffey, Jr.	3.00
14	Tony Gwynn	1.50
15	Rickey Henderson	.60
16	Kent Hrbek	.50
17	David Justice	.85
18	Mike Piazza	2.00
19	Jose Rijo	.50
20	Cal Ripken, Jr.	2.50
21	Tim Salmon	.85
22	Ryne Sandberg	1.00
23	Gary Sheffield	.75
24	Ozzie Smith	1.00
25	Frank Thomas	2.50
26	Andy Van Slyke	.50
27	Mo Vaughn	.75
28	Larry Walker	.75
---	Reggie Jackson	100.00

1995 Denny's Classic Hits

For the fifth consecutive year, this Aug. 1-Sept. 30 promotion offered a hologram baseball card with the purchase of selected items from the restaurant's "Classic Hits" menu. The cards were produced for Denny's by Upper Deck and combine photographic and holographic images of the player on the horizontal-format front. Backs have another color photo, career highlights, and past-season/lifetime stats. Each Major League team is represented in the set by one player card. According to advertisements for the promotion, a total of 8,000,000 cards was produced - about 286,000 of each player.

		MT
Complete Set (28):		30.00
Common Player:		.75
1	Roberto Alomar	.75
2	Moises Alou	.75
3	Jeff Bagwell	1.50
4	Albert Belle	1.00
5	Jason Bere	.75
6	Roger Clemens	1.50
7	Darren Daulton	.75
8	Cecil Fielder	.75
9	Andres Galarraga	.75
10	Juan Gonzalez	1.50
11	Ken Griffey Jr.	3.00
12	Tony Gwynn	1.50
13	Barry Larkin	.75
14	Greg Maddux	1.50
15	Don Mattingly	1.50
16	Mark McGwire	3.00
17	Orlando Merced	.75
18	Jeff Montgomery	.75
19	Rafael Palmeiro	.90
20	Mike Piazza	2.00
21	Kirby Puckett	1.50
22	Bret Saberhagen	.75
23	Tim Salmon	1.25

24	Gary Sheffield	1.00
25	Ozzie Smith	1.25
26	Sammy Sosa	2.00
27	Greg Vaughn	.75
28	Matt Williams	.75

1996 Denny's Grand Slam

Exploding fireworks in the background are an allegory for the firepower brought to the plate by the sluggers featured in this chase set from Denny's annual baseball card promotion. A Grand Slam card is randomly substituted for the standard hologram card about once every 56 packs.

		MT
Complete Set (10):		45.00
Common Player:		2.50
1	Cal Ripken Jr.	7.00
2	Frank Thomas	5.00
3	Mike Piazza	5.00
4	Tony Gwynn	5.00
5	Sammy Sosa	5.00
6	Barry Bonds	2.50
7	Jeff Bagwell	3.50
8	Albert Belle	4.00
9	Mo Vaughn	2.50
10	Kirby Puckett	5.00

1996 Denny's Grand Slam Artist's Proofs

A specially marked Artist's Proof version of the Grand Slam chase cards are substituted for the standard hologram card in about every 360 packs, according to stated odds.

		MT
Complete Set (10):		175.00
Common Player:		5.00
1	Cal Ripken Jr.	50.00
2	Frank Thomas	30.00
3	Mike Piazza	30.00
4	Tony Gwynn	20.00
5	Sammy Sosa	25.00
6	Barry Bonds	15.00
7	Jeff Bagwell	15.00
8	Albert Belle	15.00
9	Mo Vaughn	5.00
10	Kirby Puckett	15.00

1996 Denny's Instant Replay Holograms

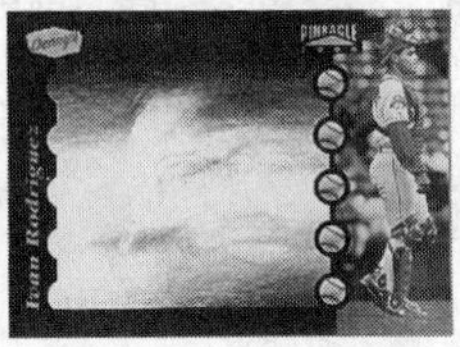

Pinnacle, in its first year as supplier for Denny's annual baseball card promotion, attempted breakthrough technology that didn't quite hit the mark. The hologram portion of the card front was supposed to show as much as four seconds of on-field action, but unless viewed at exactly the right distance and angle, and under exacting light requirements, the action is little more than a silver-foil streak. Card fronts also included a color player photo. Another color photo appears on the back, along with a description of the action on front for those who couldn't master the "Full Motion" hologram. Cards were sold in single-card foil packs for 49 cents (limit two) with a qualifying purchase. Besides the hologram card, each pack includes a card explaining "How To View a Full Motion Hologram". Besides the regular cards, two "Grand Slam" chase sets were issued along with instant winner cards for complete card sets or trips to the World Series. Stated odds on the chase cards would indicate about 750,000 of each regular card were produced. One player from each team is represented in the checklist.

		MT
Complete Set (28):		6.00
Common Player:		.25
1	Greg Maddux	1.25
2	Cal Ripken Jr.	2.00
3	Frank Thomas	1.50
4	Albert Belle	.75
5	Mo Vaughn	.50
6	Jeff Bagwell	.75
7	Jay Buhner	.25
8	Barry Bonds	1.00
9	Ryne Sandberg	.50
10	Hideo Nomo	.65
11	Kirby Puckett	.75
12	Gary Sheffield	.50
13	Barry Larkin	.25
14	Wade Boggs	.50
15	Tony Gwynn	.75
16	Tim Salmon	.35
17	Jason Isringhausen	.25
18	Cecil Fielder	.25
19	Dante Bichette	.25
20	Ozzie Smith	.75
21	Ivan Rodriguez	.50
22	Kevin Appier	.25
23	Joe Carter	.25
24	Moises Alou	.25
25	Mark McGwire	3.00
26	Kevin Seitzer	.25
27	Darren Daulton	.25
28	Jay Bell	.25

1997 Denny's 3-D Holograms

Denny's seventh annual baseball card issue was produced by Pinnacle and showcases two popular card technologies. Fronts of the 3-1/2" x 2-1/2" horizontal cards feature a deep 3D look. Backs have a player portrait hologram at the right. A partial baseball at left is the background for player data and stats along with sponsor and licensor logos. Cards were distributed one per pack for 59 cents from June 26-Sept. 3, with 10 cents from the sale of each card being donated to children's charities. The set features one player from each major league team, plus a Jackie Robinson tribute card.

		MT
Complete Set (29):		18.00
Common Player:		.50
1	Tim Salmon	.75
2	Rafael Palmeiro	.65
3	Mo Vaughn	.75
4	Frank Thomas	2.50
5	David Justice	.75
6	Travis Fryman	.50
7	Johnny Damon	.50
8	John Jaha	.50
9	Chuck Knoblauch	.50
10	Mark McGwire	4.00
11	Alex Rodriguez	3.00
12	Juan Gonzalez	1.50
13	Roger Clemens	1.00
14	Derek Jeter	2.50
15	Andruw Jones	1.00
16	Sammy Sosa	2.50
17	Barry Larkin	.50
18	Dante Bichette	.50
19	Jeff Bagwell	1.00
20	Mike Piazza	2.50
21	Gary Sheffield	.50
22	Vladimir Guerrero	2.00
23	Todd Hundley	.50
24	Jason Kendall	.50
25	Ray Lankford	.50
26	Ken Caminiti	.50
27	Barry Bonds	1.50
28	Scott Rolen	1.00
29	Jackie Robinson (50th Anniversary Commemorative)	2.50

1997 Denny's Larry Doby

In the same format as the restaurant chain's regular set of 1997, this card honors the first black player to appear in the American League. The card was available only at the All-Star FanFest and All-Star Game in Cleveland in early July. Fronts have a black-and-white 3-D image; backs have a color hologram at right and a 50th anniversary logo at upper-left. Personal data, career highlights and stats are included, as well as appropriate logos.

		MT
1	Larry Doby	9.00

1981 Detroit News Tigers Centennial

The 100th anniversary of professional baseball in Detroit was marked by "The Detroit News" with the issue of this set honoring "The Boys of Summer." The 2-1/2" x 3-1/2" cards have black-and-white photos on front, over a mock sports page. Cards can be found either with or without a red border on front, though the relative scarcity of each version is not known. Black-and-white backs have player data, career summary and stats, or a description of the front photo/highlight.

		MT
Complete Set (135):		24.00
Common Player:		.25
1	Detroit Boys of Summer 100th Anniversary	.25
2	Charles W. Bennett	.25
3	Mickey Cochrane	.25
4	Harry Heilmann	.25
5	Walter O. Briggs	.25
6	Mark Fidrych	.40
7	1887 Tigers	.25
8	Tiger Stadium	.25
9	Rudy York	.25
10	George Kell	.25
11	Steve O'Neill	.25
12	John Hiller	.25
13	1934 Tigers	.25
14	Charlie Gehringer	.35
15	Denny McLain	.50
16	Billy Rogell	.25
17	Ty Cobb	2.00
18	Sparky Anderson	.40
19	Davy Jones	.25
20	Kirk Gibson	.35
21	Pat Mullin	.25
22	1972 Tigers	.25
23	What a Night	.25
24	"Doc" Cramer	.25
25	Mickey Stanley	.25
26	Johnny Lipon	.25
27	Jo Jo White	.25
28	Recreation Park	.25
29	Wild Bill Donovan	.25
30	Ray Oyler	.25
31	Earl Whitehill	.25
32	Billy Hoeft	.25
33	Johnny Groth	.25
34	Hughie Jennings	.25
35	Mayo Smith	.25
36	Bennett Park	.25
37	Tigers Win	.25
38	Donie Bush	.25
39	Harry Coveleski	.25
40	Paul Richards	.25
41	Jonathan Stone	.25
42	Bill Swift	.25
43	Roy Cullenbine	.25
44	Hoot Evers	.25
45	Tigers Win Series	.25
46	Art Houtteman	.25
47	Aurelio Rodriguez	.25
48	Fred Hutchinson	.25
49	Don Mossi	.25
50	Gehrig's Streak Ends in Detroit (Lou Gehrig)	1.00
51	Earl Wilson	.25
52	Jim Northrup	.25
53	1907 Tigers	.25
54	Greenberg's Two Homers Ties Ruth (Hank Greenberg)	.35
55	Mickey Lolich	.35
56	Tommy Bridges	.25
57	Al Benton	.25
58	Del Baker	.25
59	Lou Whitaker	.35
60	Navin Field	.25
61	1945 Tigers	.25
62	Ernie Harwell	.25
63	League Champs	.25
64	Bobo Newsom	.25
65	Don Wert	.25
66	Ed Summers	.25
67	Billy Martin	.35
68	Alan Trammell	.45
69	Dale Alexander	.25
70	Ed Brinkman	.25
71	Right Man in Right Place Wins	.25
72	Bill Freehan	.25
73	Norm Cash	.40
74	George Dauss	.25
75	Aurelio Lopez	.25
76	Charlie Maxwell	.25
77	Ed Barrow	.25
78	Willie Horton	.25
79	Denny Sets Record (Denny McLain)	.35
80	Dan Brouthers	.25
81	John E. Fetzer	.25
82	Heinie Manush	.25
83	1935 Tigers	.25
84	Ray Boone	.25
85	Bob Fothergill	.25
86	Steve Kemp	.25
87	Ed Killian	.25
88	Giebell is Ineligible (Floyd Giebell)	.25
89	Pinky Higgins	.25
90	Lance Parrish	.25
91	Eldon Auker	.25
92	Birdie Tebbetts	.25
93	Schoolboy Rowe	.25
94	McLain Wins 30th (Denny McLain)	.30
95	1909 Tigers	.25
96	Harvey Kuenn	.30
97	Jim Bunning	.45
98	1940 Tigers	.25
99	Rocky Colavito	1.00
100	Kaline Enters Hall of Fame (Al Kaline)	.75
101	Billy Bruton	.25
102	Germany Schaefer	.25
103	Frank Bolling	.25
104	Briggs Stadium	.25
105	Bucky Harris	.25
106	Gates Brown	.25
107	Martin Made the Difference (Billy Martin)	.25
108	1908 Tigers	.25
109	"Gee" Walker	.25
110	Pete Fox	.25
111	Virgil Trucks	.25
112	1968 Tigers	.40
113	Dizzy Trout	.25
114	Barney McCosky	.25
115	Lu Blue	.25
116	Hal Newhouser	.25
117	Tigers are Home for Series	.25
118	Bobby Veach	.25
119	George Mullins (Mullin)	.25
120	Reggie's Super Homer (Reggie Jackson)	.45
121	Sam Crawford	.25
122	Hank Aguirre	.25
123	Vic Wertz	.25
124	Goose Goslin	.25
125	Frank Lary	.25
126	Joe Coleman	.25
127	Ed Katalinas	.25
128	Jack Morris	.25
129	3 Time AL Leaders	.25
130	James A. Campbell	.25
131	Ted Gray	.25
132	Al Kaline	2.00
133	Hank Greenberg	1.00
134	Dick McAuliffe	.25
135	Ozzie Virgil	.25

1983 Detroit Tigers Photocards

These black-and-white blank-back photocards feature a facsimile autograph on front and are approximately postcard size.

		MT
Complete Set (35):		17.50
Common Player:		.50
(1)	Sparky Anderson	1.00
(2)	Sal Butera	.50
(3)	Howard Bailey	.50
(4)	Juan Berenguer	.50
(5)	Tom Brookens	.50
(6)	Gates Brown	.50
(7)	Enos Cabell	.50
(8)	Bill Consolo	.50
(9)	Roger Craig	.50
(10)	Bill Fahey	.50
(11)	Kirk Gibson	.75
(12)	Alex Grammas	.50
(13)	John Grubb	.50
(14)	Larry Herndon	.50
(15)	Mike Ivie	.50
(16)	Howard Johnson	.60
(17)	Lynn Jones	.50
(18)	Rick Leach	.50
(19)	Chet Lemon	.60
(20)	Aurelio Lopez	.50
(21)	Jack Morris	.75
(22)	Lance Parrish	.75
(23)	Larry Pashnick	.50
(24)	Dan Petry	.50
(25)	Dave Rozema	.50
(26)	Dave Rucker	.50
(27)	Dick Tracewski	.50
(28)	Alan Trammell	2.00
(29)	Jerry Ujdur	.50
(30)	Pat Underwood	.50
(31)	Lou Whitaker	.75
(32)	Milt Wilcox	.50
(33)	Glenn Wilson	.50
(34)	John Wockenfuss	.50
(35)	Tiger Stadium	.75

1985 Detroit Tigers Placemats

These 17" x 11" paper placemats feature members of the World Champion Tigers. Sponsored by a local restaurant chain and a radio station, the mats have colorful portrait and action artwork of two players each. A large team logo is at center. The unnumbered items are checklisted here alphabetically.

		MT
Complete Set (4):		20.00
Common Placemat:		4.00
(1)	Chet Lemon, Willie Hernandez	4.00
(2)	Jack Morris, Lance Parrish	5.00
(3)	Dan Petry, Kirk Gibson	5.00
(4)	Alan Trammell, Lou Whitaker	7.50

1988 Detroit Tigers Police

This unnumbered issue, sponsored by the Michigan State Police features 13 players and manager Sparky Anderson in full-color standard-size (2-1/2" x 3-1/2") cards. Player photos are framed by a blue border, with the Detroit logo upper left and a large name block that lists the player's name, position batting/throwing preference, height, weight and birthday beneath the photo. The backs carry an anti-drug or anti-crime message.

	MT
Complete Set (14):	9.00
Common Player:	.50
(1) Doyle Alexander	.50
(2) Sparky Anderson	1.00
(3) Dave Bergman	.50
(4) Tom Brookens	.50
(5) Darrell Evans	.60
(6) Larry Herndon	.50
(7) Chet Lemon	.50
(8) Jack Morris	.60
(9) Matt Nokes	.50
(10) Jeff Robinson	.50
(11) Frank Tanana	.50
(12) Walt Terrell	.50
(13) Alan Trammell	1.50
(14) Lou Whitaker	.90

1989 Detroit Tigers Police

(21) GUILLERMO HERNANDEZ—P
B-L, T-L, HT: 6'2", WT: 185, BORN: 11-14-54

This unnumbered issue, distributed and sponsored by the Michigan State Police Department features 14 full-color 2-1/2" x 3-1/2" cards. Player photos are framed by a blue and orange border, with the team logo in the upper left and biographical information below the photo. The card backs featue anti-drug or anti-crime messages.

	MT
Complete Set (14):	5.00
Common Player:	.25
(1) Doyle Alexander	.25
(2) Sparky Anderson	.75
(3) Dave Bergman	.25
(4) Mike Henneman	.35
(5) Guillermo Hernandez	.25
(6) Chet Lemon	.25
(7) Fred Lynn	.25
(8) Jack Morris	.35
(9) Matt Nokes	.25
(10) Jeff Robinson	.25
(11) Pat Sheridan	.25
(12) Frank Tanana	.25
(13) Alan Trammell	.90
(14) Lou Whitaker	.60

1989 Detroit Tigers team issue

These large-format (4" x 5") black-and-white cards were provided to players and coaches for use in answering fan requests for pictures and autographs. The cards have portrait photos with white borders and the player's facsimile autograph overprinted in blue at bottom center. Backs are blank. The unnumbered cards are listed alphabetically. Complete sets were not available from the team.

	MT
Complete Set (25):	25.00
Common Player:	1.00
(1) Doyle Alexander	1.00
(2) Sparky Anderson	2.00
(3) Dave Bergman	1.00
(4) Mike Brumley	1.00
(5) Billy Consolo	1.00
(6) Paul Gibson	1.00
(7) Alex Grammas	1.00
(8) Mike Heath	1.00
(9) Mike Henneman	1.25
(10) Willie Hernandez	1.25
(11) Charles Hudson	1.00
(12) Chet Lemon	1.25
(13) Fred Lynn	1.50
(14) Jack Morris	2.00
(15) Billy Muffett	1.00
(16) Matt Nokes	1.50
(17) Gary Pettis	1.00
(18) Vada Pinson	1.25
(19) Jeff Robinson	1.00
(20) Frank Tanana	1.00
(21) Dick Tracewski	1.00
(22) Alan Trammell	3.00
(23) Louis Whitaker	2.00
(24) Frank Williams	1.00
(25) Lee Williams	1.00

1991 Detroit Tigers Police

One of the scarcer safety issues is this Tigers team issue. Cards have a color player action photo on front with orange and blue team-color graphics. Backs have a safety message and the logos of sponsors HSP and Team Michigan, along with the Michigan State Police. The unnumbered cards are checklisted here alphabetically.

	MT
Complete Set (14):	18.00
Common Player:	1.00
(1) Sparky Anderson	1.50
(2) Dave Bergman	1.00
(3) Cecil Fielder	1.50
(4) Travis Fryman	1.50
(5) Paul Gibson	1.00
(6) Jerry Don Gleaton	1.00
(7) Lloyd Moseby	1.00
(8) Dan Petry	1.00
(9) Tony Phillips	1.50
(10) Mark Salas	1.00
(11) John Shelby	1.00
(12) Frank Tanana	1.00
(13) Alan Trammell	3.00
(14) Lou Whitaker	1.50

1994 Dial Soap

Collector's Edge produced this special FX technology see-through plastic card of David Justice for use in a mail-away offer by Dial Soap. Background printing is in blue, green and purple, with the sponsor and team logos in red and yellow. Back has career highlights and a Dial ad. The card was offered only in the Mid-Atlantic states.

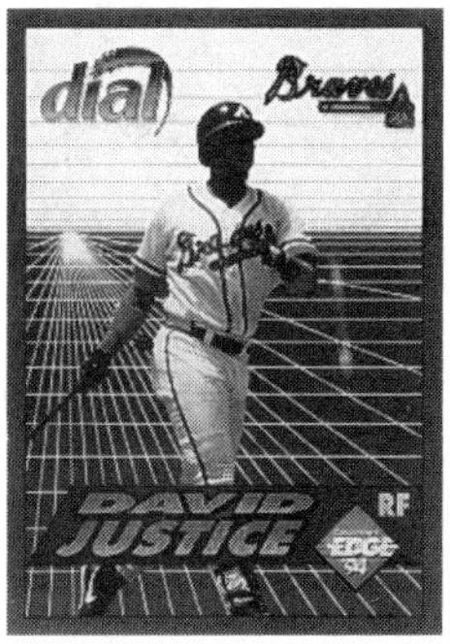

	MT
Complete Set:	
(1) Dave Justice	5.00

1994 Diamond Connection Ken Griffey Jr. Phone Card

In conjunction with MCI, Diamond Connection produced a five-card phone card issue of Ken Griffey Jr., and introduced the set with a promo card give-away at the 1994 National Sports Collectors Convention in Houston. Printed in color on plastic in a 2-1/8" x 3-3/8" format, the cards picture Griffey in a variety of batting poses and portraits. Back are in black-and-white and have details for the cards' phone use. The issue was limited to 5,000 numbered sets.

	MT
Complete Set (6):	20.00
Common Card:	5.00
(1) Ken Griffey Jr. (promo - 2 Units)	20.00
(2) Ken Griffey Jr. (10 Units - batting)	5.00
(3) Ken Griffey Jr. (10 Units - batting)	5.00
(4) Ken Griffey Jr. (10 Units - batting)	5.00
(5) Ken Griffey Jr. (10 Units - portrait)	5.00
(6) Ken Griffey Jr. (10 Units - portrait)	5.00

1993 DiamondMarks Promos

In the same format as the regular-issue DiamondMark cards, these promos were produced to preview the concept for dealers and collectors. The promo cards feature different photos than those used on the issued version. The unnumbered cards are listed here alphabetically.

	MT
Complete Set (8):	125.00
Common Player:	15.00
(1) Roberto Alomar	20.00
(2) Will Clark	25.00
(3) Dennis Eckersley	15.00
(4) Ken Griffey, Jr.	40.00
(5) Juan Gonzalez	25.00
(6) Ryne Sandberg	20.00
(7) Frank Thomas	35.00
(8) Kirby Puckett	30.00

1993 DiamondMarks

While they look like baseball cards and were sold in foil packs like baseball cards, DiamondMarks were licensed as book marks. Issued by Barry Colla Productions, the 2-1/2" x 5" cards feature Barry Colla's trademark high-quality player photos on front and back. The UV-coated fronts feature black borders with the player's name in white above the photo and a color team logo beneath. Backs, also bordered in black, feature two color player photos in an open book design. There is a portrait photo on the left and a head-and-shoulders reproduction of the front photo at right. A bookmark with team logo is incorporated in the design. The 120-card set is unnumbered and is arranged in the checklist below alphabetically within league and team.

	MT
Complete Set (120):	20.00
Common Player:	.25
Atlanta Braves	
(1) Steve Avery	.25
(2) Ron Gant	.40
(3) Tom Glavine	.35
(4) David Justice	.75
(5) Terry Pendleton	.25
(6) Deion Sanders	.75
(7) John Smoltz	.40
Chicago Cubs	
(8) Mark Grace	.55
(9) Randy Myers	.25
(10) Ryne Sandberg	.75
(11) Jose Vizcaino	.25
Cincinnati Reds	
(12) Bobby Kelly	.25
(13) Barry Larkin	.40
(14) Kevin Mitchell	.25
(15) Jose Rijo	.25
(16) Reggie Sanders	.35
Colorado Rockies	
(17) Dante Bichette	.75
(18) Daryl Boston	.25
(19) Andres Galarraga	.50
(20) Charlie Hayes	.30
Florida Marlins	
(21) Orestes Destrade	.25
(22) Dave Magadan	.25
(23) Benito Santiago	.35
(24) Walt Weiss	.25
Houston Astros	
(25) Jeff Bagwell	1.00
(26) Craig Biggio	.50
(27) Ken Caminiti	.50
(28) Luis Gonzalez	.25
Los Angeles Dodgers	
(29) Brett Butler	.35
(30) Eric Davis	.30
(31) Orel Hershiser	.30
(32) Eric Karros	.30
(33) Ramon Martinez	.30
(34) Mike Piazza	2.50
(35) Darryl Strawberry	.30
Montreal Expos	
(36) Moises Alou	.30
(37) Delino DeShields	.25
(38) Marquis Grissom	.40
(39) Dennis Martinez	.35
(40) Larry Walker	.75
New York Mets	
(41) Bobby Bonilla	.30
(42) Dwight Gooden	.30
(43) Howard Johnson	.25
(44) Eddie Murray	.75
Philadelphia Phillies	
(45) Darren Daulton	.25
(46) Lenny Dykstra	.25
(47) Dave Hollins	.25
(48) John Kruk	.25
Pittsburgh Pirates	
(49) Jay Bell	.25
(50) Al Martin	.25
(51) Orlando Merced	.25
(52) Andy Van Slyke	.25
St. Louis Cardinals	
(53) Gregg Jefferies	.25
(54) Tom Pagnozzi	.25
(55) Ozzie Smith	1.00
(56) Todd Zeile	.25
San Diego Padres	
(57) Derek Bell	.30
(58) Tony Gwynn	1.00
(59) Fred McGriff	.50
(60) Gary Sheffield	.50
San Francisco Giants	
(61) Barry Bonds	1.50
(62) John Burkett	.25
(63) Will Clark	.75
(64) Matt Williams	.50
Baltimore Orioles	
(65) Brady Anderson	.40
(66) Mike Mussina	.40
(67) Cal Ripken, Jr.	2.50
Boston Red Sox	
(68) Roger Clemens	1.50
(69) Andre Dawson	.35
(70) Mike Greenwell	.25
(71) Mo Vaughn	.75
Detroit Tigers	
(72) Cecil Fielder	.35
(73) Tony Phillips	.25
(74) Mickey Tettleton	.25
(75) Alan Trammell	.50
Cleveland Indians	
(76) Sandy Alomar Jr.	.50
(77) Carlos Baerga	.25
(78) Albert Belle	1.50
(79) Kenny Lofton	.75
Chicago White Sox	
(80) Bo Jackson	.35
(81) Frank Thomas	3.00
(82) Robin Ventura	.35
California Angels	
(83) Chad Curtis	.25
(84) Gary DiSarcina	.25
(85) Tim Salmon	.75
(86) J.T. Snow	.35
Kansas City Royals	
(87) George Brett	2.00
(88) Wally Joyner	.30
(89) Mike MacFarlane	.25
(90) Brian McRae	.25
Milwaukee Brewers	
(91) Darryl Hamilton	.25
(92) Pat Listach	.25
(93) B.J. Surhoff	.25
(94) Robin Yount	1.00
Minnesota Twins	
(95) Kent Hrbek	.35
(96) Chuck Knoblauch	.60
(97) Kirby Puckett	1.50
(98) Dave Winfield	.75
New York Yankees	
(99) Wade Boggs	.75
(100) Don Mattingly	1.50
(101) Danny Tartabull	.25
Oakland Athletics	
(102) Dennis Eckersley	.30
(103) Rickey Henderson	.50
(104) Mark McGwire	3.00
(105) Ruben Sierra	.25
(106) Terry Steinbach	.25
Seattle Mariners	
(107) Ken Griffey, Jr.	4.00
(108) Edgar Martinez	.25
(109) Pete O'Brien	.25
(110) David Valle	.25
Texas Rangers	
(111) Jose Canseco	.75
(112) Juan Gonzalez	1.50
(113) Ivan Rodriguez	.65
(114) Nolan Ryan	2.50
Toronto Blue Jays	
(115) Roberto Alomar	.45
(116) Pat Borders	.25
(117) Joe Carter	.30
(118) Juan Guzman	.25
(119) Paul Molitor	1.00
(120) Dave Stewart	.25

1993 DiamondMarks Inserts

Randomly inserted into packs of DiamondMarks cards at the rate of one per 48-pack carton was a series of eight cards featuring the baseball artwork of Terry Smith. The inserts are the same 2-1/2" x 5" size as the regular issue and carry on with the basic black bordered design, though the inserts are UV-coated both front and back. Beneath the fantasy-design player art on the front is the player's name. On back the open book design is seen again, with a short player profile on the left and a Barry Colla photo portrait on the right, along with the appropriate team logo.

		MT
Complete Set (8):		100.00
Common Player:		10.00
(1)	Roberto Alomar	15.00
(2)	Barry Bonds	20.00
(3)	Ken Griffey, Jr.	35.00
(4)	David Justice	20.00
(5)	John Olerud	10.00
(6)	Nolan Ryan	30.00
(7)	Frank Thomas	25.00
(8)	Robin Yount	20.00

1992 Diet Pepsi Collector Series

This Canadian issue includes 30 top stars, with a slight emphasis on the two Canadian teams. Because the set is licensed only by the players' association, and not Major League Baseball, all photos have had team logos eliminated. Fronts feature action photo with Diet Pepsi logos in a strip below. Backs have a portrait photo, recent stats and a facsimile autograph. Card number 5 of Tom Glavine can be found showing him pitching right-handed (error) or left-handed (right). Cards are UV coated on both sides. A poster picturing all 30 cards was also issued.

		MT
Complete Set (30):		12.00
Poster:		35.00
Common Player:		.25
1	Roger Clemens	.75
2	Dwight Gooden	.35
3	Tom Henke	.25
4	Dennis Martinez	.25
5a	Tom Glavine (pitching right-handed)	.30
5b	Tom Glavine (pitching left-handed)	.90
6	Jack Morris	.25
7	Dennis Eckersley	.30
8	Jeff Reardon	.25
9	Bryan Harvey	.25
10	Sandy Alomar Jr.	.30
11	Carlton Fisk	.65
12	Gary Carter	.30
13	Cecil Fielder	.25
14	Will Clark	.60
15	Roberto Alomar	.60
16	Ryne Sandberg	.90
17	Cal Ripken Jr.	2.00
18	Barry Larkin	.30
19	Ozzie Smith	.75
20	Kelly Gruber	.25
21	Wade Boggs	.65
22	Tim Wallach	.25
23	Howard Johnson	.25
24	Jose Canseco	.75
25	Joe Carter	.25
26	Ken Griffey Jr.	2.50
27	Kirby Puckett	.85
28	Rickey Henderson	.50
29	Barry Bonds	.90
30	Dave Winfield	.50

1987 Phil Dixon Negro Leagues

Negro Leagues' players from the Hall of Famers to virtual unknowns are included in this collectors set. In 3" x 5" format, the cards have black-and-white photos on front with a white border. Backs have a short career summary, a few biographical bits and copyright notice. Sets were originally sold for around $20.

		MT
Complete Set (45):		20.00
Common Player:		.50
1	Samuel Hairston	.75
2	Elander Harris	.50
3	Theodore Trent	.50
4	Edward Dwight	.50
5	Jessie Williams	.50
6	Joshua Gibson	2.00
7	Jose Mendez	.75
8	Joe Green	.50
9	Robert Boyd	.50
10	William P. Drake	.50
11	Alfred Cooper	.50
12	Charles Taylor	.50
13	R. Whitworth	.50
14	Tobe Smith	.50
15	William Dismukes	.50
16	Richard Byas	.50
17	Hurley McNair	.50
18	Roy Partlow	.50
19	Carroll Mothell	.50
20	John O'Neil	1.50
21	Leroy Paige	3.00
22	Moses Walker	2.00
23	Quincy Gilmore	.50
24	James Bell	1.50
25	Andrew Foster	1.50
26	George Sweatt	.50
27	Hilton Lee Smith	.50
28	Thomas Young	.50
29	Chester Brewer	.50
30	Walter Leonard	1.50
31	Walter Lee Joseph	.50
32	Eugene Baker	.50
33	Jack Robinson	3.00
34	Wilbur Rogan	1.00
35	Norman Stearns	1.50
36	Albert Haywood	.50
37	Lorenzo Davis	.50
38	Francisco Coimbre	.50
39	Robert Thurman	.50
40	Booker McDaniel (McDaniels)	.50
41	Newt Allen	.50
42	Willie Wells	.65
43	Clifford Johnson	.50
44	George Giles	.50
45	Frank Duncan	.50

1984-85 Dominican League stamps

Many American players - current, former and future - are included in this sticker set chronicling the winter baseball season in the Dominican Republic, 1984-85. An album issued to house the set indicates the issuer was Postalitas Dominicanas of Santo Domingo. The color stickers are printed on thin paper, 1-15/16" x 2-1/2". On most stickers, a player name and sticker number are printed in black at the bottom, though some stickers lack this identification, resulting in gaps in the checklist presented here. A nine-piece composite photo of Juan Marichal throwing batting practice comprises stickers #1-9. Collector input is sought to fill the gaps in the checklist.

		MT
Common Player:		2.00
1	Puzzle piece (Juan Marichal)	2.00
2	Puzzle piece (Juan Marichal)	2.00
3	Puzzle piece (Juan Marichal)	2.00
4	Puzzle piece (Juan Marichal)	2.00
5	Puzzle piece (Juan Marichal)	2.00
6a	Puzzle piece (Juan Marichal)	2.00
6b	Miguel de la Cruz	1.00
7	Puzzle piece (Juan Marichal)	2.00
8	Puzzle piece (Juan Marichal)	2.00
9	Puzzle piece (Juan Marichal)	2.00
10		
11	Rafael Landestoy	1.00
12	Tim Conroy	1.00
13		
14	Mike Torres	1.00
15	Victor Mata	1.00
16	Victor Cruz	1.00
17	Ken Howell	1.25
18	Ramon Lora	1.00
19	Jorge Bell	1.75
20	Tom Brennan	1.00
21	Cesarin Geronimo	1.50
22	Luis Pujols	1.00
23	Ed Amelung	1.00
24	R.J. Reinolds (Reynolds)	1.25
25	Franklin Stubbs	1.25
26	Darnell Coles	1.25
27	Steve Howe	6.00
28	Anazario Araujo	1.00
29		
30	Balbino Galvez	1.00
31	Pintacora de los Santos	1.00
32		
33		
34		
35	Jose Rijo	6.00
36	Mariano Duncan	3.00
37		
38	Teodoro Martinez	1.00
39	Hipolito Pena	1.00
40	Julian Gonzalez	1.00
41	Silvano Quezada	1.00
42	Elvio Jiminez	1.00
43	Terry Collins	1.25
44		
45	Stanley Javier	3.00
46		
47		
48		
49	Nino Espinosa	1.00
50	Dan Morogiello	1.00
51	Leopoldo Sanchez	1.00
52	Jim Winn	1.00
53	Luis Silverio	1.00
54	Ernesto Borbon	1.00
55		
56	Luis Polonia	1.50
57	Ruben Rodriguez	1.00
58	Pedro Guzman	1.00
59	Stu Cliburn	1.25
60	Ray Krawczyk	1.00
61	Luis Lara	1.00
62	Miguel Dilone	1.00
63		
64		
65		
66		
67		
68		
69	Arturo Pena	1.00
70		
71		
72		
73		
74	Juan Jiminez	1.00
75	Victor Ramirez	1.00
76		
77	Chilote Llenas	1.00
78	Pedro Hernandez	1.00
79	Jose Cesar Pena	1.00
80	Bonny Castillo (Bobby)	1.00
81	Randt Gomez (Randy)	1.00
82	Ruben Robles	1.00
83		
84	Manuel Hernandez	1.00
85	Inocencio Guerrero	1.00
86	Juan Delgado	1.00
87	Julio Solano	1.00
88	Pablo Peguero	1.00
89	Mark Grant	1.25
90	Leonel Vargas	1.00
91	Casey Parsons	1.25
92	Tim Krauss	1.00
93	Porfirio Paris	1.00
94	Randy Kutcher	1.25
95		
96	Rafael Matos	1.00
97	John Rabb	1.00
98		
99		
100		
101		
102	Miguel Pokmil	1.00
103	Ubaldo Regaldo	1.00
104	Pedro Sanchez	1.00
105		
106	Jaime Wildams (Williams)	1.00
107	Luis Roman	1.00
108		
109	Ramon Linares	1.00
110		
111	Bob Miller	1.00
112		
113	Luis Lora	1.00
114		
115		
116		
117		
118		
119		
120		
121		
122		
123		
124		
125	Sergio Perez	1.00
126	Erasmo DeLeon	1.00
127	Jim Dorsey	1.00
128	Glen Cook	1.00
129	Carmen Castillo	1.00
130	Mickey Mahler	1.25
131		
132	Rafael Belliard	2.00
133	Dwight Lowry	1.00
134	Wilfredo Tejada	2.00
135	Jose Segura	1.00
136	John Morris	1.25
137	Tomas Giron	1.00
138	Nelson Simmons	1.25
139		
140		
141		
142	Pepe Lucas	1.00
143	Jesus Rojas Alou	4.00
144	Mateo Rojas Alou	3.00
145	Felipe Rojas Alou	5.00
146	Domingo Ramos	1.25
147	Mitch Webster	1.50
148	Rafael Santana	1.25
149	Fred McGriff	15.00
150	Jim Presley	1.50
151	Mario Guerrero	1.00
152	Tom Filer	1.00
153		
154	Bernardo Tatis	1.00
155	Arturo DeFreites	1.00
156	Hilario Soriano	1.00
157	Radhames Mills (Rhadames)	1.00
158	Carlos Julio Perez	1.00
159	Rene Rivas	1.00
160	Martin Rivas	1.00
161	Juan Espino	1.00
162	Gibson Alba	1.00
163	Adriano Pena	1.00
164		
165		
166		
167		
168	Eugenio Cotes	1.00
169	Freddy Tiburcio	1.00
170	Ignacio Javier	1.00
171	Lee Gutterman (Guetterman)	1.25
172		
173		
174	Alexis Marte	1.00
175	Andres Thomas	1.25
176		
177	Phil Regan	1.50
178	Victor Horacio Nazario	1.00
179	Cuqui Rojas (Cookie)	3.00
180	Rufino Linares	1.00
181	Adriano Rodriguez	1.00
182	Julio Cipaula	1.00
183	Ralph Bryant	1.00
184	Mike Pagliarulo	1.50
185	Brian Dayett	1.25
186	Junior Noboa	1.25
187	Nelson Norman	1.25
188	Leo Ortiz	1.00
189	Jose Reyes	1.00
190	Rafael Pimentel	1.00
191	Tim Birtsas	1.25
192		
193	Melanio Pozo	1.00
194		
195		
196	Jose Gomez	1.00
197		
198		
199		
200	Mark Silva	1.00
201	Simon Rosario	1.00
202	Julio Valdez	1.00
203	Rickey Keeton	1.00
204	Mark Huismann	1.25
205	Fransisco Jabalera	1.00
206	Miguel de la Cruz	1.00
207	Alfonso Rosario	1.00
208	Edmundo Borrome	1.00
209	Manuel Abreu	1.00
210	Jesus Figueroa	1.00
211	Lazaro Del Orbe	1.00
212	Federico Velazquez	1.00
213	Manuel Mota	2.00
214	Joaquin Andujar (three-piece composite)	1.00
215	Joaquin Andujar (three-piece composite)	1.00
216	Joaquin Andujar (three-piece composite)	1.00
---	(American player posing in Escogido Leones jacket)	
---	(#31 swinging bat in front of crowd)	
---	(American with hands on hips in Licey Tigres white jersey) (Terry Collins?)	
---	(Bearded Licey player kneeling, leaning on bat)	

1988 Domino's Pizza Tigers

Domino's Pizza produced a 28-card set commemorating the 20th anniversary of the 1968 World Champion Detroit Tigers. The cards were given away at an Old Timers Game at Tiger Stadium in 1988. The cards, which measure 2-1/2" x 3-1/2", feature black and white photos semi-surrounded by a two-stripe band. The stripes on the card's left side are the same color (red and light blue) as the Domino's Pizza logo in the upper corner. The stripes on the card's right side match the colors of the Tigers logo (red and dark blue). The backs of all the cards (except for Ernie Harwell) contain a brief summary of the Tigers' 1968 season. Located at the bottom on the card backs are the players' major league records through 1968 plus their 1968 World Series statistics.

		MT
Complete Set (29):		7.00
Common Player:		.20
(1)	Gates Brown	.30
(2)	Norm Cash	.90
(3)	Wayne Comer	.20
(4)	Pat Dobson	.20
(5)	Bill Freehan	.60
(6)	John Hiller	.20
(7)	Ernie Harwell (announcer)	.30
(8)	Willie Horton	.40
(9a)	Al Kaline (batting)	3.00
(9b)	Al Kaline (in outfield)	3.00
(10)	Fred Lasher	.20
(11)	Mickey Lolich	.75
(12)	Tom Matchick	.20
(13)	Ed Mathews	1.25
(14)	Dick McAuliff (McAuliffe)	.40
(15)	Denny McLain	.90
(16)	Don McMahon	.20
(17)	Jim Northrup	.20
(18)	Ray Oyler	.20
(19)	Daryl Patterson	.20
(20)	Jim Price	.20
(21)	Joe Sparma	.20
(22)	Mickey Stanley	.20
(23)	Dick Tracewski	.20
(24)	Jon Warden	.20
(25)	Don Wert	.20
(26)	Earl Wilson	.20
(27)	Header Card	.05
(28)	Coupon Card	.05

1981 Donruss Promo Sheet

Rookie sensation Joe Charbonneau was the featured attraction when this sample sheet was issued to introduce Donruss' debut baseball card issue. The 10" x 7" sheet is comprised of eight of the cards which appeared in the set.

		MT
Complete Sheet:		50.00
82	Joe Charboneau	
83	Cecil Cooper	
93	Tommy Hutton	
94	Carl Yastrzemski	
104	Amos Otis	
105	Graig Nettles	
115	Ken Singleton	
116	Gary Roenicke	

1981 Donruss

The Donruss Co. of Memphis, Tenn., produced its premiere baseball card issue in 1981 with a set that consisted of 600 numbered cards and five unnumbered checklists. The cards, which measure 2-1/2" x 3-1/2", are printed on thin stock. The card fronts contain the Donruss logo plus the year of issue. The card backs are designed on a vertical format and have black print on red and white. The set, entitled "First Edition Collector Series," contains nearly 40 variations, those being first-printing errors that were corrected in a subsequent print run. The cards were sold in wax packs with bubble gum. The complete set price does not include the higher priced variations.

		MT
Complete Set (605):		45.00
Complete Set, Uncut Sheets (5):		75.00
Common Player:		.08
Wax Box:		70.00
Eight-card promo sheet:		20.00
1	Ozzie Smith	4.00
2	Rollie Fingers	.75
3	Rick Wise	.08
4	Gene Richards	.08
5	Alan Trammell	.60
6	Tom Brookens	.08
7a	Duffy Dyer (1980 Avg. .185)	.50
7b	Duffy Dyer (1980 Avg. 185)	.10
8	Mark Fidrych	.10
9	Dave Rozema	.08
10	Ricky Peters	.08
11	Mike Schmidt	3.00
12	Willie Stargell	.80
13	Tim Foli	.08
14	Manny Sanguillen	.08
15	Grant Jackson	.08
16	Eddie Solomon	.08
17	Omar Moreno	.08
18	Joe Morgan	.60
19	Rafael Landestoy	.08
20	Bruce Bochy	.08
21	Joe Sambito	.08
22	Manny Trillo	.08
23a	*Dave Smith* (incomplete box around stats)	.50
23b	*Dave Smith* (complete box around stats)	.50
24	Terry Puhl	.08
25	Bump Wills	.08
26a	John Ellis (Danny Walton photo - with bat)	.60
26b	John Ellis (John Ellis photo - with glove)	.10
27	Jim Kern	.08
28	Richie Zisk	.08
29	John Mayberry	.08
30	Bob Davis	.08
31	Jackson Todd	.08
32	Al Woods	.08
33	Steve Carlton	1.50
34	Lee Mazzilli	.08
35	John Stearns	.08
36	Roy Jackson	.08
37	Mike Scott	.15
38	Lamar Johnson	.08
39	Kevin Bell	.08
40	Ed Farmer	.08
41	Ross Baumgarten	.08
42	Leo Sutherland	.08
43	Dan Meyer	.08
44	Ron Reed	.08
45	Mario Mendoza	.08
46	Rick Honeycutt	.08
47	Glenn Abbott	.08
48	Leon Roberts	.08
49	Rod Carew	1.50
50	Bert Campaneris	.10
51a	Tom Donahue (incorrect spelling)	.50
51b	Tom Donohue (Donohue on front)	.10
52	Dave Frost	.08
53	Ed Halicki	.08
54	Dan Ford	.08
55	Garry Maddox	.10
56a	Steve Garvey (Surpassed 25 HR..)	1.25
56b	Steve Garvey (Surpassed 21 HR..)	.60
57	Bill Russell	.10
58	Don Sutton	.65
59	Reggie Smith	.10
60	Rick Monday	.10
61	Ray Knight	.10
62	Johnny Bench	1.25
63	Mario Soto	.08
64	Doug Bair	.08
65	George Foster	.20

66	Jeff Burroughs	.08
67	Keith Hernandez	.20
68	Tom Herr	.08
69	Bob Forsch	.08
70	John Fulgham	.08
71a	Bobby Bonds (lifetime HR 986)	.50
71b	Bobby Bonds (lifetime HR 326)	.15
72a	Rennie Stennett ("...breaking broke leg..." on back)	.50
72b	Rennie Stennett ("...breaking leg..." on back)	.10
73	Joe Strain	.08
74	Ed Whitson	.08
75	Tom Griffin	.08
76	Bill North	.08
77	Gene Garber	.08
78	Mike Hargrove	.08
79	Dave Rosello	.08
80	Ron Hassey	.08
81	Sid Monge	.08
82a	*Joe Charboneau* ("For some reason, Phillies..." on back)	1.00
82b	*Joe Charboneau* ("Phillies..." on back)	.25
83	Cecil Cooper	.15
84	Sal Bando	.08
85	Moose Haas	.08
86	Mike Caldwell	.08
87a	Larry Hisle ("...Twins with 28 RBI." on back)	.50
87b	Larry Hisle ("...Twins with 28 HR" on back)	.10
88	Luis Gomez	.08
89	Larry Parrish	.08
90	Gary Carter	.60
91	*Bill Gullickson*	.15
92	Fred Norman	.08
93	Tommy Hutton	.08
94	Carl Yastrzemski	1.25
95	Glenn Hoffman	.08
96	Dennis Eckersley	1.00
97a	Tom Burgmeier (Throws: Right)	.50
97b	Tom Burgmeier (Throws: Left)	.10
98	Win Remmerswaal	.08
99	Bob Horner	.15
100	George Brett	6.00
101	Dave Chalk	.08
102	Dennis Leonard	.08
103	Renie Martin	.08
104	Amos Otis	.08
105	Graig Nettles	.15
106	Eric Soderholm	.08
107	Tommy John	.20
108	Tom Underwood	.08
109	Lou Piniella	.12
110	Mickey Klutts	.08
111	Bobby Murcer	.10
112	Eddie Murray	4.00
113	Rick Dempsey	.08
114	Scott McGregor	.08
115	Ken Singleton	.10
116	Gary Roenicke	.08
117	Dave Revering	.08
118	Mike Norris	.08
119	Rickey Henderson	4.00
120	Mike Heath	.08
121	Dave Cash	.08
122	Randy Jones	.08
123	Eric Rasmussen	.08
124	Jerry Mumphrey	.08
125	Richie Hebner	.08
126	Mark Wagner	.08
127	Jack Morris	.45
128	Dan Petry	.08
129	Bruce Robbins	.08
130	Champ Summers	.08
131a	Pete Rose ("see card 251" on back)	2.50
131b	Pete Rose ("see card 371" on back)	2.00
132	Willie Stargell	.80
133	Ed Ott	.08
134	Jim Bibby	.08
135	Bert Blyleven	.12
136	Dave Parker	.45
137	Bill Robinson	.08
138	Enos Cabell	.08
139	Dave Bergman	.08
140	J.R. Richard	.10
141	Ken Forsch	.08
142	Larry Bowa	.15
143	Frank LaCorte (photo actually Randy Niemann)	.08
144	Dennis Walling	.08
145	Buddy Bell	.12
146	Fergie Jenkins	.75
147	Danny Darwin	.08
148	John Grubb	.08
149	Alfredo Griffin	.08
150	Jerry Garvin	.08
151	*Paul Mirabella*	.08
152	Rick Bosetti	.08
153	Dick Ruthven	.08
154	Frank Taveras	.08
155	Craig Swan	.08
156	*Jeff Reardon*	1.50
157	Steve Henderson	.08
158	Jim Morrison	.08

159	Glenn Borgmann	.08
160	*Lamarr Hoyt (LaMarr)*	.10
161	Rich Wortham	.08
162	Thad Bosley	.08
163	Julio Cruz	.08
164a	Del Unser (no 3B in stat heads)	.50
164b	Del Unser (3B in stat heads)	.10
165	Jim Anderson	.08
166	Jim Beattie	.08
167	Shane Rawley	.08
168	Joe Simpson	.08
169	Rod Carew	1.50
170	Fred Patek	.08
171	Frank Tanana	.08
172	Alfredo Martinez	.08
173	Chris Knapp	.08
174	Joe Rudi	.10
175	Greg Luzinski	.15
176	Steve Garvey	.65
177	Joe Ferguson	.08
178	Bob Welch	.10
179	Dusty Baker	.10
180	Rudy Law	.08
181	Dave Concepcion	.15
182	Johnny Bench	1.25
183	Mike LaCoss	.08
184	Ken Griffey	.12
185	Dave Collins	.08
186	Brian Asselstine	.08
187	Garry Templeton	.10
188	Mike Phillips	.08
189	Pete Vukovich	.08
190	John Urrea	.08
191	Tony Scott	.08
192	Darrell Evans	.12
193	Milt May	.08
194	Bob Knepper	.08
195	Randy Moffitt	.08
196	Larry Herndon	.08
197	Rick Camp	.08
198	Andre Thornton	.10
199	Tom Veryzer	.08
200	Gary Alexander	.08
201	Rick Waits	.08
202	Rick Manning	.08
203	Paul Molitor	3.00
204	Jim Gantner	.08
205	Paul Mitchell	.08
206	Reggie Cleveland	.08
207	Sixto Lezcano	.08
208	Bruce Benedict	.08
209	Rodney Scott	.08
210	John Tamargo	.08
211	Bill Lee	.08
212	Andre Dawson	1.00
213	Rowland Office	.08
214	Carl Yastrzemski	1.25
215	Jerry Remy	.08
216	Mike Torrez	.08
217	Skip Lockwood	.08
218	Fred Lynn	.20
219	Chris Chambliss	.08
220	Willie Aikens	.08
221	John Wathan	.08
222	Dan Quisenberry	.15
223	Willie Wilson	.15
224	Clint Hurdle	.08
225	Bob Watson	.08
226	Jim Spencer	.08
227	Ron Guidry	.25
228	Reggie Jackson	2.50
229	Oscar Gamble	.08
230	Jeff Cox	.08
231	Luis Tiant	.12
232	Rich Dauer	.08
233	Dan Graham	.08
234	Mike Flanagan	.10
235	John Lowenstein	.08
236	Benny Ayala	.08
237	Wayne Gross	.08
238	Rick Langford	.08
239	Tony Armas	.10
240a	Bob Lacy (incorrect spelling)	.50
240b	Bob Lacey (correct spelling)	.10
241	Gene Tenace	.08
242	Bob Shirley	.08
243	Gary Lucas	.08
244	Jerry Turner	.08
245	John Wockenfuss	.08
246	Stan Papi	.08
247	Milt Wilcox	.08
248	Dan Schatzeder	.08
249	Steve Kemp	.08
250	Jim Lentine	.08
251	Pete Rose	2.50
252	Bill Madlock	.12
253	Dale Berra	.08
254	Kent Tekulve	.08
255	Enrique Romo	.08
256	Mike Easler	.08
257	Chuck Tanner	.08
258	Art Howe	.12
259	Alan Ashby	.08
260	Nolan Ryan	8.00
261a	Vern Ruhle (Ken Forsch photo - head shot)	.50
261b	Vern Ruhle (Vern Ruhle photo - waist to head shot)	.10
262	Bob Boone	.10
263	Cesar Cedeno	.12
264	Jeff Leonard	.08
265	Pat Putnam	.08

266	Jon Matlack	.08
267	Dave Rajsich	.08
268	Billy Sample	.08
269	*Damaso Garcia*	.10
270	Tom Buskey	.08
271	Joey McLaughlin	.08
272	Barry Bonnell	.08
273	Tug McGraw	.10
274	Mike Jorgensen	.08
275	Pat Zachry	.08
276	Neil Allen	.08
277	Joel Youngblood	.08
278	Greg Pryor	.08
279	*Britt Burns*	.10
280	*Rich Dotson*	.25
281	Chet Lemon	.08
282	Rusty Kuntz	.08
283	Ted Cox	.08
284	Sparky Lyle	.10
285	Larry Cox	.08
286	Floyd Bannister	.08
287	Byron McLaughlin	.08
288	Rodney Craig	.08
289	Bobby Grich	.10
290	Dickie Thon	.08
291	Mark Clear	.08
292	Dave Lemanczyk	.08
293	Jason Thompson	.08
294	Rick Miller	.08
295	Lonnie Smith	.08
296	Ron Cey	.12
297	Steve Yeager	.08
298	Bobby Castillo	.08
299	Manny Mota	.08
300	Jay Johnstone	.08
301	Dan Driessen	.08
302	Joe Nolan	.08
303	Paul Householder	.08
304	Harry Spilman	.08
305	Cesar Geronimo	.08
306a	Gary Mathews (Mathews on front)	.65
306b	Gary Matthews (Matthews on front)	.10
307	Ken Reitz	.08
308	Ted Simmons	.10
309	John Littlefield	.08
310	George Frazier	.08
311	Dane Iorg	.08
312	Mike Ivie	.08
313	Dennis Littlejohn	.08
314	Gary LaVelle (Lavelle)	.08
315	Jack Clark	.25
316	Jim Wohlford	.08
317	Rick Matula	.08
318	Toby Harrah	.08
319a	Dwane Kuiper (Dwane on front)	.50
319b	Duane Kuiper (Duane on front)	.10
320	Len Barker	.08
321	Victor Cruz	.08
322	Dell Alston	.08
323	Robin Yount	4.00
324	Charlie Moore	.08
325	Lary Sorensen	.08
326a	Gorman Thomas ("...30-HR mark 4th..." on back)	.65
326b	Gorman Thomas ("...30-HR mark 3rd..." on back)	.10
327	Bob Rodgers	.08
328	Phil Niekro	.75
329	Chris Speier	.08
330a	Steve Rodgers (Rodgers on front)	.50
330b	Steve Rogers (Rogers on front)	.10
331	Woodie Fryman	.08
332	Warren Cromartie	.08
333	Jerry White	.08
334	Tony Perez	.25
335	Carlton Fisk	1.50
336	Dick Drago	.08
337	Steve Renko	.08
338	Jim Rice	.30
339	Jerry Royster	.08
340	Frank White	.10
341	Jamie Quirk	.08
342a	Paul Spittorff (Spittorff on front)	.50
342b	Paul Splittorff (Splittorff on front)	.10
343	Marty Pattin	.08
344	Pete LaCock	.08
345	Willie Handolph	.10
346	Rick Cerone	.08
347	Rich Gossage	.20
348	Reggie Jackson	2.50
349	Ruppert Jones	.08
350	Dave McKay	.08
351	Yogi Berra	.45
352	Doug Decinces (DeCinces)	.10
353	Jim Palmer	1.00
354	Tippy Martinez	.08
355	Al Bumbry	.08
356	Earl Weaver	.50
357a	Bob Picciolo (Bob on front)	.50
357b	Rob Picciolo (Rob on front)	.10
358	Matt Keough	.08
359	Dwayne Murphy	.08
360	Brian Kingman	.08
361	Bill Fahey	.08

362 Steve Mura .08
363 Dennis Kinney .08
364 Dave Winfield 2.00
365 Lou Whitaker .45
366 Lance Parrish .20
367 Tim Corcoran .08
368 Pat Underwood .08
369 Al Cowens .08
370 Sparky Anderson .15
371 Pete Rose 2.50
372 Phil Garner .08
373 Steve Nicosia .08
374 John Candelaria .10
375 Don Robinson .08
376 Lee Lacy .08
377 John Milner .08
378 Craig Reynolds .08
379a Luis Pujois (Pujois on front) .50
379b Luis Pujols (Pujols on front) .10
380 Joe Niekro .12
381 Joaquin Andujar .08
382 *Keith Moreland* .20
383 Jose Cruz .12
384 Bill Virdon .08
385 Jim Sundberg .08
386 Doc Medich .08
387 Al Oliver .15
388 Jim Norris .08
389 Bob Bailor .08
390 Ernie Whitt .08
391 Otto Velez .08
392 Roy Howell .08
393 *Bob Walk* .10
394 Doug Flynn .08
395 Pete Falcone .08
396 Tom Hausman .08
397 Elliott Maddox .08
398 Mike Squires .08
399 Marvis Foley .08
400 Steve Trout .08
401 Wayne Nordhagen .08
402 Tony Larussa (LaRussa) .12
403 Bruce Bochte .08
404 Bake McBride .08
405 Jerry Narron .08
406 Rob Dressler .08
407 Dave Heaverlo .08
408 Tom Paciorek .08
409 Carney Lansford .08
410 Brian Downing .10
411 Don Aase .08
412 Jim Barr .08
413 Don Baylor .15
414 Jim Fregosi .08
415 Dallas Green .08
416 Dave Lopes .10
417 Jerry Reuss .10
418 Rick Sutcliffe .20
419 Derrel Thomas .08
420 Tommy LaSorda (Lasorda) .50
421 *Charlie Leibrandt* .50
422 Tom Seaver 2.00
423 Ron Oester .08
424 Junior Kennedy .08
425 Tom Seaver 2.00
426 Bobby Cox .10
427 *Leon Durham* .20
428 Terry Kennedy .08
429 Silvio Martinez .08
430 George Hendrick .08
431 Red Schoendienst .25
432 John LeMaster .08
433 Vida Blue .12
434 John Montefusco .08
435 Terry Whitfield .08
436 Dave Bristol .08
437 Dale Murphy .75
438 Jerry Dybzinski .08
439 Jorge Orta .08
440 Wayne Garland .08
441 Miguel Dilone .08
442 Dave Garcia .08
443 Don Money .08
444a Buck Martinez (photo reversed) .50
444b Buck Martinez (photo correct) .10
445 Jerry Augustine .08
446 Ben Oglivie .08
447 Jim Slaton .08
448 Doyle Alexander .08
449 Tony Bernazard .08
450 Scott Sanderson .08
451 Dave Palmer .08
452 Stan Bahnsen .08
453 Dick Williams .08
454 Rick Burleson .08
455 Gary Allenson .08
456 Bob Stanley .08
457a *John Tudor* (lifetime W/L 9.7) .75
457b *John Tudor* (lifetime W/L 9-7) .50
458 Dwight Evans .15
459 Glenn Hubbard .08
460 U L Washington .08
461 Larry Gura .08
462 Rich Gale .08
463 Hal McRae .10
464 Jim Frey .08
465 Bucky Dent .10
466 Dennis Werth .08
467 Ron Davis .08
468 Reggie Jackson 2.50
469 Bobby Brown .08
470 *Mike Davis* .10
471 Gaylord Perry .75
472 Mark Belanger .08
473 Jim Palmer 1.00
474 Sammy Stewart .08
475 Tim Stoddard .08
476 Steve Stone .10
477 Jeff Newman .08
478 Steve McCatty .08
479 Billy Martin .12
480 Mitchell Page .08
481 Steve Carlton (CY) .40
482 Bill Buckner .12
483a Ivan DeJesus (lifetime hits 702) .50
483b Ivan DeJesus (lifetime hits 642) .10
484 Cliff Johnson .08
485 Lenny Randle .08
486 Larry Milbourne .08
487 Roy Smalley .08
488 John Castino .08
489 Ron Jackson .08
490a Dave Roberts (1980 highlights begins "Showed pop...") .50
490b Dave Roberts (1980 highlights begins "Declared himself...") .10
491 George Brett (MVP) 3.00
492 Mike Cubbage .08
493 Rob Wilfong .08
494 Danny Goodwin .08
495 Jose Morales .08
496 Mickey Rivers .08
497 Mike Edwards .08
498 Mike Sadek .08
499 Lenn Sakata .08
500 Gene Michael .08
501 Dave Roberts .08
502 Steve Dillard .08
503 Jim Essian .08
504 Rance Mulliniks .08
505 Darrell Porter .08
506 Joe Torre .25
507 Terry Crowley .08
508 Bill Travers .08
509 Nelson Norman .08
510 Bob McClure .08
511 *Steve Howe* .15
512 Dave Rader .08
513 Mick Kelleher .08
514 Kiko Garcia .08
515 Larry Biittner .08
516a Willie Norwood (1980 highlights begins "Spent most...") .50
516b Willie Norwood (1980 highlights begins "Traded to...") .10
517 Bo Diaz .08
518 Juan Beniquez .08
519 Scot Thompson .08
520 Jim Tracy .08
521 Carlos Lezcano .08
522 Joe Amalfitano .08
523 Preston Hanna .08
524a Ray Burris (1980 highlights begins "Went on...") .50
524b Ray Burris (1980 highlights begins "Drafted by...") .10
525 Broderick Perkins .08
526 Mickey Hatcher .08
527 John Goryl .08
528 Dick Davis .08
529 Butch Wynegar .08
530 Sal Butera .08
531 Jerry Koosman .10
532a Jeff (Geoff) Zahn (1980 highlights begins "Was 2nd in...") .50
532b Jeff (Geoff) Zahn (1980 highlights begins "Signed a 3 year ...") .10
533 Dennis Martinez .12
534 Gary Thomasson .08
535 Steve Macko .08
536 Jim Kaat .20
537 Best Hitters (George Brett, Rod Carew) 1.50
538 *Tim Raines* 6.00
539 Keith Smith .08
540 Ken Macha .08
541 Burt Hooton .08
542 Butch Hobson .08
543 Bill Stein .08
544 Dave Stapleton .08
545 Bob Pate .08
546 Doug Corbett .08
547 Darrell Jackson .08
548 Pete Redfern .08
549 Roger Erickson .08
550 Al Hrabosky .08
551 Dick Tidrow .08
552 Dave Ford .08
553 Dave Kingman .12
554a Mike Vail (1980 highlights begins "After...") .50
554b Mike Vail (1980 highlights begins "Traded...") .10
555a Jerry Martin (1980 highlights begins "Overcame...") .50
555b Jerry Martin (1980 highlights begins "Traded...") .10
556a Jesus Figueroa (1980 highlights begins "Had...") .50
556b Jesus Figueroa (1980 highlights begins "Traded...") .10
557 Don Stanhouse .08
558 Barry Foote .08
559 Tim Blackwell .08
560 Bruce Sutter .15
561 Rick Reuschel .10
562 Lynn McGlothen .08
563a Bob Owchinko (1980 highlights begins "Traded...") .50
563b Bob Owchinko (1980 highlights begins "Involved...") .10
564 John Verhoeven .08
565 Ken Landreaux .08
566a Glen Adams (Glen on front) .50
566b Glenn Adams (Glenn on front) .10
567 Hosken Powell .08
568 Dick Noles .08
569 *Danny Ainge* 4.00
570 Bobby Mattick .08
571 Joe LeFebvre (Lefebvre) .08
572 Bobby Clark .08
573 Dennis Lamp .08
574 Randy Lerch .08
575 *Mookie Wilson* .30
576 Ron LeFlore .08
577 Jim Dwyer .08
578 Bill Castro .08
579 Greg Minton .08
580 Mark Littell .08
581 Andy Hassler .08
582 Dave Stieb .15
583 Ken Oberkfell .08
584 Larry Bradford .08
585 Fred Stanley .08
586 Bill Caudill .08
587 Doug Capilla .08
588 George Riley .08
589 Willie Hernandez .10
590 Mike Schmidt (MVP) 1.00
591 Steve Stone (Cy Young 1980) .10
592 Rick Sofield .08
593 Bombo Rivera .08
594 Gary Ward .08
595a Dave Edwards (1980 highlights begins "Sidelined...") .50
595b Dave Edwards (1980 highlights begins "Traded...") .10
596 Mike Proly .08
597 Tommy Boggs .08
598 Greg Gross .08
599 Elias Sosa .08
600 Pat Kelly .08
---- Checklist 1-120 (51 Tom Donohue) .50
---- Checklist 1-120 (51 Tom Donahue) .10
---- Checklist 121-240 .10
---- Checklist 241-360 (306 Gary Mathews) .50
---- Checklist 241-360 (306 Gary Matthews) .10
---- Checklist 361-480 (379 Luis Pujois) .50
---- Checklist 361-480 (379 Luis Pujols) .10
---- Checklist 481-600 (566 Glen Adams) .50
---- Checklist 481-600 (566 Glenn Adams) .10

1982 Donruss

Using card stock thicker than the previous year, Donruss issued a 660-card set which includes 653 numbered cards and seven unnumbered checklists. The cards were sold with puzzle pieces rather than gum as a result of a lawsuit by Topps. The puzzle pieces (three pieces on one card per pack) feature Babe Ruth. The first 26 cards of the set, entitled Diamond Kings, showcase the artwork of Dick Perez. Card fronts display the Donruss logo and the year of issue. Backs have black and blue ink on white stock and include the player's career highlights. The complete set price does not include the higher priced variations.

	MT
Complete Set (660):	85.00
Common Player:	.08
Babe Ruth Puzzle:	3.00
Wax Box:	120.00

1 Pete Rose (Diamond King) 3.00
2 Gary Carter (DK) .50
3 Steve Garvey (DK) .30
4 Vida Blue (DK) .12
5a Alan Trammel (DK) (last name incorrect) 1.50
5b Alan Trammell (DK) (corrected) .40
6 Len Barker (DK) .08
7 Dwight Evans (DK) .15
8 Rod Carew (DK) .60
9 George Hendrick (DK) .08
10 Phil Niekro (DK) .60
11 Richie Zisk (DK) .08
12 Dave Parker (DK) .30
13 Nolan Ryan (DK) 4.00
14 Ivan DeJesus (DK) .08
15 George Brett (DK) 1.50
16 Tom Seaver (DK) .90
17 Dave Kingman (DK) .15
18 Dave Winfield (DK) 1.00
19 Mike Norris (DK) .08
20 Carlton Fisk (DK) .80
21 Ozzie Smith (DK) 1.50
22 Roy Smalley (DK) .08
23 Buddy Bell (DK) .12
24 Ken Singleton (DK) .10
25 John Mayberry (DK) .08
26 Gorman Thomas (DK) .10
27 Earl Weaver .45
28 Rollie Fingers .60
29 Sparky Anderson .10
30 Dennis Eckersley .75
31 Dave Winfield 2.00
32 Burt Hooton .08
33 Rick Waits .08
34 George Brett 3.00
35 Steve McCatty .08
36 Steve Rogers .08
37 Bill Stein .08
38 Steve Renko .08
39 Mike Squires .08
40 George Hendrick .08
41 Bob Knepper .08
42 Steve Carlton 1.00
43 Larry Biittner .08
44 Chris Welsh .08
45 Steve Nicosia .08
46 Jack Clark .25
47 Chris Chambliss .08
48 Ivan DeJesus .08
49 Lee Mazzilli .08
50 Julio Cruz .08
51 Pete Redfern .08
52 Dave Stieb .12
53 Doug Corbett .08
54 *George Bell* 1.00
55 Joe Simpson .08
56 Rusty Staub .10
57 Hector Cruz .08
58 Claudell Washington .10
59 Enrique Romo .08
60 Gary Lavelle .08
61 Tim Flannery .08
62 Joe Nolan .08
63 Larry Bowa .15
64 Sixto Lezcano .08
65 Joe Sambito .08
66 Bruce Kison .08
67 Wayne Nordhagen .08
68 Woodie Fryman .08
69 Billy Sample .08
70 Amos Otis .08
71 Matt Keough .08
72 Toby Harrah .08
73 *Dave Righetti* .30
74 Carl Yastrzemski 1.00
75 Bob Welch .12
76a Alan Trammel (last name misspelled) 2.00
76b Alan Trammell (corrected) .60
77 Rick Dempsey .08
78 Paul Molitor 2.50
79 Dennis Martinez .10
80 Jim Slaton .08
81 Champ Summers .08
82 Carney Lansford .08
83 Barry Foote .08
84 Steve Garvey .45
85 Rick Manning .08
86 John Wathan .08
87 Brian Kingman .08
88 Andre Dawson .75
89 Jim Kern .08
90 Bobby Grich .10
91 Bob Forsch .08
92 Art Howe .10
93 Marty Bystrom .08
94 Ozzie Smith 2.50
95 Dave Parker .30
96 Doyle Alexander .08
97 Al Hrabosky .08
98 Frank Taveras .08
99 Tim Blackwell .08
100 Floyd Bannister .08
101 Alfredo Griffin .08
102 Dave Engle .08
103 Mario Soto .08
104 Ross Baumgarten .08
105 Ken Singleton .10
106 Ted Simmons .10
107 Jack Morris .30
108 Bob Watson .08
109 Dwight Evans .15
110 Tom Lasorda .40
111 Bert Blyleven .12
112 Dan Quisenberry .15
113 Rickey Henderson 2.00
114 Gary Carter .50
115 Brian Downing .10
116 Al Oliver .15
117 LaMarr Hoyt .08
118 Cesar Cedeno .10
119 Keith Moreland .10
120 Bob Shirley .08
121 Terry Kennedy .08
122 Frank Pastore .08
123 Gene Garber .08
124 Tony Pena .25
125 Allen Ripley .08
126 Randy Martz .08
127 Richie Zisk .08
128 Mike Scott .15
129 Lloyd Moseby .10
130 Rob Wilfong .08
131 Tim Stoddard .08
132 Gorman Thomas .08
133 Dan Petry .08
134 Bob Stanley .08
135 Lou Piniella .15
136 Pedro Guerrero .25
137 Len Barker .08
138 Richard Gale .08
139 Wayne Gross .08
140 *Tim Wallach* 1.00
141 Gene Mauch .08
142 Doc Medich .08
143 Tony Bernazard .08
144 Bill Virdon .08
145 John Littlefield .08
146 Dave Bergman .08
147 Dick Davis .08
148 Tom Seaver 1.00
149 Matt Sinatro .08
150 Chuck Tanner .08
151 Leon Durham .08
152 Gene Tenace .08
153 Al Bumbry .08
154 Mark Brouhard .08
155 Rick Peters .08
156 Jerry Remy .08
157 Rick Reuschel .10
158 Steve Howe .08
159 Alan Bannister .08
160 U L Washington .08
161 Rick Langford .08
162 Bill Gullickson .08
163 Mark Wagner .08
164 Geoff Zahn .08
165 Ron LeFlore .08
166 Dane Iorg .08
167 Joe Niekro .12
168 Pete Rose 2.50
169 Dave Collins .08
170 Rick Wise .08
171 Jim Bibby .08
172 Larry Herndon .08
173 Bob Horner .12
174 Steve Dillard .08
175 Mookie Wilson .12
176 Dan Meyer .08
177 Fernando Arroyo .08
178 Jackson Todd .08
179 Darrell Jackson .08
180 Al Woods .08
181 Jim Anderson .08
182 Dave Kingman .12
183 Steve Henderson .08
184 Brian Asselstine .08
185 Rod Scurry .08
186 Fred Breining .08
187 Danny Boone .08
188 Junior Kennedy .08
189 Sparky Lyle .10
190 Whitey Herzog .08
191 Dave Smith .08
192 Ed Ott .08
193 Greg Luzinski .15
194 Bill Lee .08
195 Don Zimmer .08

196	Hal McRae	.15
197	Mike Norris	.08
198	Duane Kuiper	.08
199	Rick Cerone	.08
200	Jim Rice	.30
201	Steve Yeager	.08
202	Tom Brookens	.08
203	Jose Morales	.08
204	Roy Howell	.08
205	Tippy Martinez	.08
206	Moose Haas	.08
207	Al Cowens	.08
208	Dave Stapleton	.08
209	Bucky Dent	.10
210	Ron Cey	.12
211	Jorge Orta	.08
212	Jamie Quirk	.08
213	Jeff Jones	.08
214	Tim Raines	1.00
215	Jon Matlack	.08
216	Rod Carew	1.00
217	Jim Kaat	.20
218	Joe Pittman	.08
219	Larry Christenson	.08
220	Juan Bonilla	.08
221	Mike Easler	.08
222	Vida Blue	.12
223	Rick Camp	.08
224	Mike Jorgensen	.08
225	*Jody Davis*	.15
226	Mike Parrott	.08
227	Jim Clancy	.08
228	Hosken Powell	.08
229	Tom Hume	.08
230	Britt Burns	.08
231	Jim Palmer	1.00
232	Bob Rodgers	.08
233	Milt Wilcox	.08
234	Dave Revering	.08
235	Mike Torrez	.08
236	Robert Castillo	.08
237	*Von Hayes*	.25
238	Renie Martin	.08
239	Dwayne Murphy	.08
240	Rodney Scott	.08
241	Fred Patek	.08
242	Mickey Rivers	.08
243	Steve Trout	.08
244	Jose Cruz	.12
245	Manny Trillo	.08
246	Lary Sorensen	.08
247	Dave Edwards	.08
248	Dan Driessen	.08
249	Tommy Boggs	.08
250	Dale Berra	.08
251	Ed Whitson	.08
252	*Lee Smith*	8.00
253	Tom Paciorek	.08
254	Pat Zachry	.08
255	Luis Leal	.08
256	John Castino	.08
257	Rich Dauer	.08
258	Cecil Cooper	.15
259	Dave Rozema	.08
260	John Tudor	.08
261	Jerry Mumphrey	.08
262	Jay Johnstone	.08
263	Bo Diaz	.08
264	Dennis Leonard	.08
265	Jim Spencer	.08
266	John Milner	.08
267	Don Aase	.08
268	Jim Sundberg	.08
269	Lamar Johnson	.08
270	Frank LaCorte	.08
271	Barry Evans	.08
272	Enos Cabell	.08
273	Del Unser	.08
274	George Foster	.20
275	*Brett Butler*	2.00
276	Lee Lacy	.08
277	Ken Reitz	.08
278	Keith Hernandez	.20
279	Doug DeCinces	.10
280	Charlie Moore	.08
281	Lance Parrish	.20
282	Ralph Houk	.08
283	Rich Gossage	.20
284	Jerry Reuss	.10
285	Mike Stanton	.08
286	Frank White	.10
287	Bob Owchinko	.08
288	Scott Sanderson	.08
289	Bump Wills	.08
290	Dave Frost	.08
291	Chet Lemon	.08
292	Tito Landrum	.08
293	Vern Ruhle	.08
294	Mike Schmidt	2.25
295	Sam Mejias	.08
296	Gary Lucas	.08
297	John Candelaria	.08
298	Jerry Martin	.08
299	Dale Murphy	.75
300	Mike Lum	.08
301	Tom Hausman	.08
302	Glenn Abbott	.08
303	Roger Erickson	.08
304	Otto Velez	.08
305	Danny Goodwin	.08
306	John Mayberry	.08
307	Lenny Randle	.08
308	Bob Bailor	.08
309	Jerry Morales	.08
310	Rufino Linares	.08
311	Kent Tekulve	.08
312	Joe Morgan	.75
313	John Urrea	.08
314	Paul Householder	.08
315	Garry Maddox	.08
316	Mike Ramsey	.08
317	Alan Ashby	.08
318	Bob Clark	.08
319	Tony LaRussa	.15
320	Charlie Lea	.08
321	Danny Darwin	.08
322	Cesar Geronimo	.08
323	Tom Underwood	.08
324	Andre Thornton	.10
325	Rudy May	.08
326	Frank Tanana	.08
327	Davey Lopes	.10
328	Richie Hebner	.08
329	Mike Flanagan	.10
330	Mike Caldwell	.08
331	Scott McGregor	.08
332	Jerry Augustine	.08
333	Stan Papi	.08
334	Rick Miller	.08
335	Graig Nettles	.15
336	Dusty Baker	.10
337	Dave Garcia	.08
338	Larry Gura	.08
339	Cliff Johnson	.08
340	Warren Cromartie	.08
341	Steve Comer	.08
342	Rick Burleson	.08
343	John Martin	.08
344	Craig Reynolds	.08
345	Mike Proly	.08
346	Ruppert Jones	.08
347	Omar Moreno	.08
348	Greg Minton	.08
349	*Rick Mahler*	.10
350	Alex Trevino	.08
351	Mike Krukow	.08
352a	Shane Rawley (Jim Anderson photo - shaking hands)	.75
352b	Shane Rawley (correct photo - kneeling)	.15
353	Garth Iorg	.08
354	Pete Mackanin	.08
355	Paul Moskau	.08
356	Richard Dotson	.10
357	Steve Stone	.10
358	Larry Hisle	.08
359	Aurelio Lopez	.08
360	Oscar Gamble	.08
361	Tom Burgmeier	.08
362	Terry Forster	.08
363	Joe Charboneau	.15
364	Ken Brett	.08
365	Tony Armas	.10
366	Chris Speier	.08
367	Fred Lynn	.20
368	Buddy Bell	.12
369	Jim Essian	.08
370	Terry Puhl	.08
371	Greg Gross	.08
372	Bruce Sutter	.15
373	Joe Lefebvre	.08
374	Ray Knight	.10
375	Bruce Benedict	.08
376	Tim Foli	.08
377	Al Holland	.08
378	Ken Kravec	.08
379	Jeff Burroughs	.08
380	Pete Falcone	.08
381	Ernie Whitt	.08
382	Brad Havens	.08
383	Terry Crowley	.08
384	Don Money	.08
385	Dan Schatzeder	.08
386	Gary Allenson	.08
387	Yogi Berra	.35
388	Ken Landreaux	.08
389	Mike Hargrove	.10
390	Darryl Motley	.08
391	Dave McKay	.08
392	Stan Bahnsen	.08
393	Ken Forsch	.08
394	Mario Mendoza	.08
395	Jim Morrison	.08
396	Mike Ivie	.08
397	Broderick Perkins	.08
398	Darrell Evans	.15
399	Ron Reed	.08
400	Johnny Bench	1.50
401	*Steve Bedrosian*	.20
402	Bill Robinson	.08
403	Bill Buckner	.12
404	Ken Oberkfell	.08
405	*Cal Ripken, Jr.*	50.00
406	Jim Gantner	.08
407	Kirk Gibson	.50
408	Tony Perez	.30
409	Tommy John	.20
410	*Dave Stewart*	2.50
411	Dan Spillner	.08
412	Willie Aikens	.08
413	Mike Heath	.08
414	Ray Burris	.08
415	Leon Roberts	.08
416	*Mike Witt*	.20
417	Bobby Molinaro	.08
418	Steve Braun	.08
419	Nolan Ryan	9.00
420	Tug McGraw	.12
421	Dave Concepcion	.12
422a	Juan Eichelberger (Gary Lucas photo - white player)	.75
422b	Juan Eichelberger (correct photo - black player)	.08
423	Rick Rhoden	.08
424	Frank Robinson	.30
425	Eddie Miller	.08
426	Bill Caudill	.08
427	Doug Flynn	.08
428	Larry Anderson (Andersen)	.08
429	Al Williams	.08
430	Jerry Garvin	.08
431	Glenn Adams	.08
432	Barry Bonnell	.08
433	Jerry Narron	.08
434	John Stearns	.08
435	Mike Tyson	.08
436	Glenn Hubbard	.08
437	Eddie Solomon	.08
438	Jeff Leonard	.08
439	Randy Bass	.08
440	Mike LaCoss	.08
441	Gary Matthews	.08
442	Mark Littell	.08
443	Don Sutton	.45
444	John Harris	.08
445	Vada Pinson	.10
446	Elias Sosa	.08
447	Charlie Hough	.10
448	Willie Wilson	.15
449	Fred Stanley	.08
450	Tom Veryzer	.08
451	Ron Davis	.08
452	Mark Clear	.08
453	Bill Russell	.10
454	Lou Whitaker	.40
455	Dan Graham	.08
456	Reggie Cleveland	.08
457	Sammy Stewart	.08
458	Pete Vuckovich	.08
459	John Wockenfuss	.08
460	Glenn Hoffman	.08
461	Willie Randolph	.10
462	Fernando Valenzuela	.25
463	Ron Hassey	.08
464	Paul Splittorff	.08
465	Rob Picciolo	.08
466	Larry Parrish	.08
467	Johnny Grubb	.08
468	Dan Ford	.08
469	Silvio Martinez	.08
470	Kiko Garcia	.08
471	Bob Boone	.10
472	Luis Salazar	.08
473	Randy Niemann	.08
474	Tom Griffin	.08
475	Phil Niekro	.60
476	Hubie Brooks	.25
477	Dick Tidrow	.08
478	Jim Beattie	.08
479	Damaso Garcia	.08
480	Mickey Hatcher	.08
481	Joe Price	.08
482	Ed Farmer	.08
483	Eddie Murray	2.00
484	Ben Oglivie	.08
485	Kevin Saucier	.08
486	Bobby Murcer	.10
487	Bill Campbell	.08
488	Reggie Smith	.10
489	Wayne Garland	.08
490	Jim Wright	.08
491	Billy Martin	.12
492	Jim Fanning	.08
493	Don Baylor	.12
494	Rick Honeycutt	.08
495	Carlton Fisk	1.00
496	Denny Walling	.08
497	Bake McBride	.08
498	Darrell Porter	.08
499	Gene Richards	.08
500	Ron Oester	.08
501	*Ken Dayley*	.12
502	Jason Thompson	.08
503	Milt May	.08
504	Doug Bird	.08
505	Bruce Bochte	.08
506	Neil Allen	.08
507	Joey McLaughlin	.08
508	Butch Wynegar	.08
509	Gary Roenicke	.08
510	Robin Yount	2.50
511	Dave Tobik	.08
512	*Rich Gedman*	.15
513	*Gene Nelson*	.08
514	Rick Monday	.10
515	Miguel Dilone	.08
516	Clint Hurdle	.08
517	Jeff Newman	.08
518	Grant Jackson	.08
519	Andy Hassler	.08
520	Pat Putnam	.08
521	Greg Pryor	.08
522	Tony Scott	.08
523	Steve Mura	.08
524	Johnnie LeMaster	.08
525	Dick Ruthven	.08
526	John McNamara	.08
527	Larry McWilliams	.08
528	*Johnny Ray*	.10
529	*Pat Tabler*	.10
530	Tom Herr	.10
531a	San Diego Chicken (w/trademark symbol)	.75
531b	San Diego Chicken (no trademark symbol)	.80
532	Sal Butera	.08
533	Mike Griffin	.08
534	Kelvin Moore	.08
535	Reggie Jackson	2.00
536	Ed Romero	.08
537	Derrel Thomas	.08
538	Mike O'Berry	.08
539	Jack O'Connor	.08
540	*Bob Ojeda*	.50
541	Roy Lee Jackson	.08
542	Lynn Jones	.08
543	Gaylord Perry	.60
544a	Phil Garner (photo reversed)	.75
544b	Phil Garner (photo correct)	.10
545	Garry Templeton	.10
546	Rafael Ramirez	.08
547	Jeff Reardon	.40
548	Ron Guidry	.25
549	*Tim Laudner*	.12
550	John Henry Johnson	.08
551	Chris Bando	.08
552	Bobby Brown	.08
553	Larry Bradford	.08
554	*Scott Fletcher*	.40
555	Jerry Royster	.08
556	Shooty Babbitt	.08
557	*Kent Hrbek*	2.00
558	Yankee Winners (Ron Guidry, Tommy John)	.15
559	Mark Bomback	.08
560	Julio Valdez	.08
561	Buck Martinez	.08
562	*Mike Marshall*	.15
563	Rennie Stennett	.08
564	Steve Crawford	.08
565	Bob Babcock	.08
566	Johnny Podres	.10
567	Paul Serna	.08
568	Harold Baines	.65
569	Dave LaRoche	.08
570	Lee May	.08
571	Gary Ward	.10
572	John Denny	.08
573	Roy Smalley	.08
574	*Bob Brenly*	.20
575	Bronx Bombers (Reggie Jackson, Dave Winfield)	2.00
576	Luis Pujols	.08
577	Butch Hobson	.08
578	Harvey Kuenn	.10
579	Cal Ripken, Sr.	.08
580	Juan Berenguer	.08
581	Benny Ayala	.08
582	Vance Law	.08
583	*Rick Leach*	.12
584	George Frazier	.08
585	Phillies Finest (Pete Rose, Mike Schmidt)	1.00
586	Joe Rudi	.10
587	Juan Beniquez	.08
588	*Luis DeLeon*	.08
589	Craig Swan	.08
590	Dave Chalk	.08
591	Billy Gardner	.08
592	Sal Bando	.08
593	Bert Campaneris	.10
594	Steve Kemp	.08
595a	Randy Lerch (Braves)	.75
595b	Randy Lerch (Brewers)	.08
596	Bryan Clark	.08
597	Dave Ford	.08
598	Mike Scioscia	.20
599	John Lowenstein	.08
600	Rene Lachmann (Lachemann)	.08
601	Mick Kelleher	.08
602	Ron Jackson	.08
603	Jerry Koosman	.10
604	Dave Goltz	.08
605	Ellis Valentine	.08
606	Lonnie Smith	.08
607	Joaquin Andujar	.08
608	Garry Hancock	.08
609	Jerry Turner	.08
610	Bob Bonner	.08
611	Jim Dwyer	.08
612	Terry Bulling	.08
613	Joel Youngblood	.08
614	Larry Milbourne	.08
615	Phil Roof (photo actually Gene Roof)	.08
616	Keith Drumright	.08
617	Dave Rosello	.08
618	Rickey Keeton	.08
619	Dennis Lamp	.08
620	Sid Monge	.08
621	Jerry White	.08
622	*Luis Aguayo*	.08
623	Jamie Easterly	.08
624	*Steve Sax*	.75
625	Dave Roberts	.08
626	Rick Bosetti	.08
627	*Terry Francona*	.12
628	Pride of the Reds (Johnny Bench, Tom Seaver)	.80
629	Paul Mirabella	.08
630	Rance Mulliniks	.08
631	Kevin Hickey	.08
632	Reid Nichols	.08
633	Dave Geisel	.08
634	Ken Griffey	.12
635	Bob Lemon	.25
636	Orlando Sanchez	.08
637	Bill Almon	.08
638	Danny Ainge	1.25
639	Willie Stargell	.75
640	Bob Sykes	.08
641	Ed Lynch	.08
642	John Ellis	.08
643	Fergie Jenkins	.50
644	Lenn Sakata	.08
645	Julio Gonzales	.08
646	Jesse Orosco	.10
647	Jerry Dybzinski	.08
648	Tommy Davis	.08
649	Ron Gardenhire	.08
650	Felipe Alou	.12
651	Harvey Haddix	.08
652	Willie Upshaw	.15
653	Bill Madlock	.12
----	Checklist 1-26 DK (5 Trammel)	.50
----	Checklist 1-26 DK (5 Trammell)	.08
----	Checklist 27-130	.08
----	Checklist 131-234	.08
----	Checklist 235-338	.08
----	Checklist 339-442	.08
----	Checklist 443-544	.08
----	Checklist 545-653	.08

1982-89 Donruss Puzzle Promo Sheets

Part of the advertising materials which Donruss issued each year was a series of approximately 8" x 10-7/8" color glossy sheets picturing the Dick Perez art which appear on the Diamond Kings puzzle pieces inserted into card packs.

		MT
Complete Set (9):		75.00
Common Player:		10.00
(1)	Babe Ruth (1982)	10.00
(2)	Ty Cobb (1983)	10.00
(3)	Duke Snider (1984)	10.00
(4)	Ted Williams (1984)	10.00
(5)	Lou Gehrig (1985)	10.00
(6)	Hank Aaron (1986)	10.00
(7)	Roberto Clemente (1987)	10.00
(8)	Stan Musial (1988)	10.00
(9)	Warren Spahn (1989)	20.00

Player names in *Italic* type indicate a rookie card.

1983 Donruss Promo Sheet

To debut its 1983 card design for dealers, Donruss prepared this eight-card sheet, including one Diamond Stars card. Card fronts are identical to the issued versions. Backs of most cards differ in the Career Highlights write-up. The sheet measures 10" x 7".

		MT
Uncut Sheet:		10.00
1	Fernando Valenzuela (Diamond King)	
27	Gary Roenicke	
28	Dwight Bernard	
29	Pat Underwood	
37	John Butcher	
38	Don Aase	
39	Jerry Koosman	
40	Bruce Sutter	

1983 Donruss

The 1983 Donruss set consists of 653 numbered cards plus seven unnumbered checklists. The 2-1/2" x 3-1/2" cards were issued with puzzle pieces (three pieces on one card per pack) that feature Ty Cobb. The first 26 cards in the set were once again the Diamond Kings series. The card fronts display the Donruss logo and the year of issue. The card backs have black print on yellow and white and include statistics, career highlights, and the player's contract status. (DK) in the checklist below indicates cards which belong to the Diamond Kings series.

		MT
Complete Set (660):		90.00
Common Player:		.08
Ty Cobb Puzzle:		3.00
Wax Box:		180.00
1	Fernando Valenzuela (DK)	.25
2	Rollie Fingers (DK)	.50
3	Reggie Jackson (DK)	.75
4	Jim Palmer (DK)	.50
5	Jack Morris (DK)	.25
6	George Foster (DK)	.25
7	Jim Sundberg (DK)	.08
8	Willie Stargell (DK)	.50
9	Dave Stieb (DK)	.12
10	Joe Niekro (DK)	.12
11	Rickey Henderson (DK)	2.00
12	Dale Murphy (DK)	.50
13	Toby Harrah (DK)	.08
14	Bill Buckner (DK)	.15
15	Willie Wilson (DK)	.20
16	Steve Carlton (DK)	.50
17	Ron Guidry (DK)	.20
18	Steve Rogers (DK)	.08
19	Kent Hrbek (DK)	.20
20	Keith Hernandez (DK)	.20
21	Floyd Bannister (DK)	.08
22	Johnny Bench (DK)	.75
23	Britt Burns (DK)	.08
24	Joe Morgan (DK)	.50
25	Carl Yastrzemski (DK)	.80
26	Terry Kennedy (DK)	.08
27	Gary Roenicke	.08
28	Dwight Bernard	.08
29	Pat Underwood	.08
30	Gary Allenson	.08
31	Ron Guidry	.25
32	Burt Hooton	.08
33	Chris Bando	.08
34	Vida Blue	.12
35	Rickey Henderson	2.50
36	Ray Burris	.08
37	John Butcher	.08
38	Don Aase	.08
39	Jerry Koosman	.10
40	Bruce Sutter	.15
41	Jose Cruz	.12
42	Pete Rose	2.50
43	Cesar Cedeno	.12
44	Floyd Chiffer	.08
45	Larry McWilliams	.08
46	Alan Fowlkes	.08
47	Dale Murphy	.75
48	Doug Bird	.08
49	Hubie Brooks	.12
50	Floyd Bannister	.08
51	Jack O'Connor	.08
52	Steve Senteney	.08
53	*Gary Gaetti*	.75
54	Damaso Garcia	.08
55	Gene Nelson	.08
56	Mookie Wilson	.10
57	Allen Ripley	.08
58	Bob Horner	.12
59	Tony Pena	.10
60	Gary Lavelle	.08
61	Tim Lollar	.08
62	Frank Pastore	.08
63	Garry Maddox	.08
64	Bob Forsch	.08
65	Harry Spilman	.08
66	Geoff Zahn	.08
67	Salome Barojas	.08
68	David Palmer	.08
69	Charlie Hough	.08
70	Dan Quisenberry	.15
71	Tony Armas	.10
72	Rick Sutcliffe	.12
73	Steve Balboni	.08
74	Jerry Remy	.08
75	Mike Scioscia	.08
76	John Wockenfuss	.08
77	Jim Palmer	.80
78	Rollie Fingers	.60
79	Joe Nolan	.08
80	Pete Vuckovich	.08
81	Rick Leach	.08
82	Rick Miller	.08
83	Graig Nettles	.15
84	Ron Cey	.12
85	Miguel Dilone	.08
86	John Wathan	.08
87	Kelvin Moore	.08
88a	Byrn Smith (first name incorrect)	.70
88b	Bryn Smith (first name correct)	.08
89	Dave Hostetler	.08
90	Rod Carew	1.00
91	Lonnie Smith	.08
92	Bob Knepper	.08
93	Marty Bystrom	.08
94	Chris Welsh	.08
95	Jason Thompson	.08
96	Tom O'Malley	.08
97	Phil Niekro	.65
98	Neil Allen	.08
99	Bill Buckner	.12
100	*Ed Vande Berg*	.08
101	Jim Clancy	.08
102	Robert Castillo	.08
103	Bruce Berenyi	.08
104	Carlton Fisk	.75
105	Mike Flanagan	.08
106	Cecil Cooper	.10
107	Jack Morris	.45
108	Mike Morgan	.12
109	Luis Aponte	.08
110	Pedro Guerrero	.15
111	Len Barker	.08
112	Willie Wilson	.15
113	Dave Beard	.08
114	Mike Gates	.08
115	Reggie Jackson	1.50
116	George Wright	.08
117	Vance Law	.08
118	Nolan Ryan	8.50
119	Mike Krukow	.08
120	Ozzie Smith	2.00
121	Broderick Perkins	.08
122	Tom Seaver	1.50
123	Chris Chambliss	.08
124	Chuck Tanner	.08
125	Johnnie LeMaster	.08
126	*Mel Hall*	.15
127	Bruce Bochte	.08
128	*Charlie Puleo*	.08
129	Luis Leal	.08
130	John Pacella	.08
131	Glenn Gulliver	.08
132	Don Money	.08
133	Dave Rozema	.08
134	Bruce Hurst	.15
135	Rudy May	.08
136	Tom LaSorda (Lasorda)	.45
137	Dan Spillner (photo actually Ed Whitson)	.08
138	Jerry Martin	.08
139	Mike Norris	.08
140	Al Oliver	.15
141	Daryl Sconiers	.08
142	Lamar Johnson	.08
143	Harold Baines	.20
144	Alan Ashby	.08
145	Garry Templeton	.08
146	Al Holland	.08
147	Bo Diaz	.08
148	Dave Concepcion	.12
149	Rick Camp	.08
150	Jim Morrison	.08
151	Randy Martz	.08
152	Keith Hernandez	.20
153	John Lowenstein	.08
154	Mike Caldwell	.08
155	Milt Wilcox	.08
156	Rich Gedman	.08
157	Rich Gossage	.20
158	Jerry Reuss	.10
159	Ron Hassey	.08
160	Larry Gura	.08
161	Dwayne Murphy	.08
162	Woodie Fryman	.08
163	Steve Comer	.08
164	Ken Forsch	.08
165	Dennis Lamp	.08
166	David Green	.08
167	Terry Puhl	.08
168	Mike Schmidt	2.50
169	*Eddie Milner*	.08
170	John Curtis	.08
171	Don Robinson	.08
172	Richard Gale	.08
173	Steve Bedrosian	.08
174	Willie Hernandez	.08
175	Ron Gardenhire	.08
176	Jim Beattie	.08
177	Tim Laudner	.08
178	Buck Martinez	.08
179	Kent Hrbek	.50
180	Alfredo Griffin	.08
181	Larry Andersen	.08
182	Pete Falcone	.08
183	Jody Davis	.08
184	Glenn Hubbard	.08
185	Dale Berra	.08
186	Greg Minton	.08
187	Gary Lucas	.08
188	Dave Van Gorder	.08
189	Bob Dernier	.08
190	*Willie McGee*	1.50
191	Dickie Thon	.08
192	Bob Boone	.10
193	Britt Burns	.08
194	Jeff Reardon	.50
195	Jon Matlack	.08
196	*Don Slaught*	.20
197	Fred Stanley	.08
198	Rick Manning	.08
199	Dave Righetti	.20
200	Dave Stapleton	.08
201	Steve Yeager	.08
202	Enos Cabell	.08
203	Sammy Stewart	.08
204	Moose Haas	.08
205	Lenn Sakata	.08
206	Charlie Moore	.08
207	Alan Trammell	.40
208	Jim Rice	.25
209	Roy Smalley	.08
210	Bill Russell	.08
211	Andre Thornton	.10
212	Willie Aikens	.08
213	Dave McKay	.08
214	Tim Blackwell	.08
215	Buddy Bell	.12
216	Doug DeCinces	.10
217	Tom Herr	.10
218	Frank LaCorte	.08
219	Steve Carlton	1.00
220	Terry Kennedy	.08
221	Mike Easler	.08
222	Jack Clark	.25
223	Gene Garber	.08
224	Scott Holman	.08
225	Mike Proly	.08
226	Terry Bulling	.08
227	Jerry Garvin	.08
228	Ron Davis	.08
229	Tom Hume	.08
230	Marc Hill	.08
231	Dennis Martinez	.10
232	Jim Gantner	.08
233	Larry Pashnick	.08
234	Dave Collins	.08
235	Tom Burgmeier	.08
236	Ken Landreaux	.08
237	John Denny	.08
238	Hal McRae	.12
239	Matt Keough	.08
240	Doug Flynn	.08
241	Fred Lynn	.15
242	Billy Sample	.08
243	Tom Paciorek	.08
244	Joe Sambito	.08
245	Sid Monge	.08
246	Ken Oberkfell	.08
247	Joe Pittman (photo actually Juan Eichelberger)	.08
248	Mario Soto	.08
249	Claudell Washington	.08
250	Rick Rhoden	.10
251	Darrell Evans	.15
252	Steve Henderson	.08
253	Manny Castillo	.08
254	Craig Swan	.08
255	Joey McLaughlin	.08
256	Pete Redfern	.08
257	Ken Singleton	.10
258	Robin Yount	2.50
259	Elias Sosa	.08
260	Bob Ojeda	.08
261	Bobby Murcer	.10
262	*Candy Maldonado*	.20
263	Rick Waits	.08
264	Greg Pryor	.08
265	Bob Owchinko	.08
266	Chris Speier	.08
267	Bruce Kison	.08
268	Mark Wagner	.08
269	Steve Kemp	.08
270	Phil Garner	.08
271	Gene Richards	.08
272	Renie Martin	.08
273	Dave Roberts	.08
274	Dan Driessen	.08
275	Rufino Linares	.08
276	Lee Lacy	.08
277	*Ryne Sandberg*	14.00
278	Darrell Porter	.08
279	Cal Ripken, Jr.	16.00
280	Jamie Easterly	.08
281	Bill Fahey	.08
282	Glenn Hoffman	.08
283	Willie Randolph	.10
284	Fernando Valenzuela	.25
285	Alan Bannister	.08
286	Paul Splittorff	.08
287	Joe Rudi	.10
288	Bill Gullickson	.08
289	Danny Darwin	.08
290	Andy Hassler	.08
291	Ernesto Escarrega	.08
292	Steve Mura	.08
293	Tony Scott	.08
294	Manny Trillo	.08
295	Greg Harris	.08
296	Luis DeLeon	.08
297	Kent Tekulve	.08
298	Atlee Hammaker	.08
299	Bruce Benedict	.08
300	Fergie Jenkins	.45
301	Dave Kingman	.15
302	Bill Caudill	.08
303	John Castino	.08
304	Ernie Whitt	.08
305	Randy S. Johnson	.08
306	Garth Iorg	.08
307	Gaylord Perry	.60
308	Ed Lynch	.08
309	Keith Moreland	.08
310	Rafael Ramirez	.08
311	Bill Madlock	.12
312	Milt May	.08
313	John Montefusco	.08
314	Wayne Krenchicki	.08
315	George Vukovich	.08
316	Joaquin Andujar	.08
317	Craig Reynolds	.08
318	Rick Burleson	.08
319	Richard Dotson	.08
320	Steve Rogers	.08
321	Dave Schmidt	.08
322	*Bud Black*	.20
323	Jeff Burroughs	.08
324	Von Hayes	.08
325	Butch Wynegar	.08
326	Carl Yastrzemski	.80
327	Ron Roenicke	.08
328	*Howard Johnson*	1.00
329	Rick Dempsey	.08
330a	Jim Slaton (one yellow box on back)	.70
330b	Jim Slaton (two yellow boxes on back)	.08
331	Benny Ayala	.08
332	Ted Simmons	.12
333	Lou Whitaker	.25
334	Chuck Rainey	.08
335	Lou Piniella	.12
336	Steve Sax	.15
337	Toby Harrah	.08
338	George Brett	3.00
339	Davey Lopes	.10
340	Gary Carter	.40
341	John Grubb	.08
342	Tim Foli	.08
343	Jim Kaat	.15
344	Mike LaCoss	.08
345	Larry Christenson	.08
346	Juan Bonilla	.08
347	Omar Moreno	.08
348	Chili Davis	.50
349	Tommy Boggs	.08
350	Rusty Staub	.10
351	Bump Wills	.08
352	Rick Sweet	.08
353	*Jim Gott*	.20
354	Terry Felton	.08
355	Jim Kern	.08
356	Bill Almon	.08
357	Tippy Martinez	.08
358	Roy Howell	.08
359	Dan Petry	.08
360	Jerry Mumphrey	.08
361	Mark Clear	.08
362	Mike Marshall	.10
363	Lary Sorensen	.08
364	Amos Otis	.08
365	Rick Langford	.08
366	Brad Mills	.08
367	Brian Downing	.10
368	Mike Richardt	.08
369	Aurelio Rodriguez	.08
370	Dave Smith	.08
371	Tug McGraw	.12
372	Doug Bair	.08
373	Ruppert Jones	.08
374	Alex Trevino	.08
375	Ken Dayley	.08
376	Rod Scurry	.08
377	Bob Brenly	.08
378	Scot Thompson	.08
379	Julio Cruz	.08
380	John Stearns	.08
381	Dale Murray	.08
382	*Frank Viola*	1.50
383	Al Bumbry	.08
384	Ben Oglivie	.08
385	Dave Tobik	.08
386	Bob Stanley	.08
387	Andre Robertson	.08
388	Jorge Orta	.08
389	Ed Whitson	.08
390	Don Hood	.08
391	Tom Underwood	.08
392	Tim Wallach	.20
393	Steve Renko	.08
394	Mickey Rivers	.08
395	Greg Luzinski	.15
396	Art Howe	.08
397	Alan Wiggins	.08
398	Jim Barr	.08
399	Ivan DeJesus	.08
400	*Tom Lawless*	.08
401	Bob Walk	.08
402	Jimmy Smith	.08
403	Lee Smith	1.50
404	George Hendrick	.08
405	Eddie Murray	2.50
406	Marshall Edwards	.08
407	Lance Parrish	.35
408	Carney Lansford	.08
409	Dave Winfield	1.50
410	Bob Welch	.10
411	Larry Milbourne	.08
412	Dennis Leonard	.08
413	Dan Meyer	.08
414	Charlie Lea	.08
415	Rick Honeycutt	.08
416	Mike Witt	.10
417	Steve Trout	.08
418	Glenn Brummer	.08
419	Denny Walling	.08
420	Gary Matthews	.10
421	Charlie Liebrandt (Leibrandt)	.08
422	Juan Eichelberger	.08
423	*Matt Guante (Cecilio)*	.08
424	Bill Laskey	.08
425	Jerry Royster	.08
426	Dickie Noles	.08
427	George Foster	.15
428	*Mike Moore*	.50
429	Gary Ward	.08
430	Barry Bonnell	.08
431	Ron Washington	.08
432	Rance Mulliniks	.08
433	Mike Stanton	.08
434	Jesse Orosco	.10
435	Larry Bowa	.10
436	Biff Pocoroba	.08
437	Johnny Ray	.08
438	Joe Morgan	.60
439	*Eric Show*	.25
440	Larry Biittner	.08
441	Greg Gross	.08
442	Gene Tenace	.08
443	Danny Heep	.08
444	Bobby Clark	.08
445	Kevin Hickey	.08
446	Scott Sanderson	.08
447	Frank Tanana	.08
448	Cesar Geronimo	.08
449	Jimmy Sexton	.08
450	Mike Hargrove	.08
451	Doyle Alexander	.08
452	Dwight Evans	.15
453	Terry Forster	.08
454	Tom Brookens	.08
455	Rich Dauer	.08
456	Rob Picciolo	.08
457	Terry Crowley	.08
458	Ned Yost	.08
459	Kirk Gibson	.20
460	Reid Nichols	.08
461	Oscar Gamble	.08
462	Dusty Baker	.12
463	Jack Perconte	.08
464	Frank White	.10
465	Mickey Klutts	.08
466	Warren Cromartie	.08
467	Larry Parrish	.08
468	Bobby Grich	.10
469	Dane Iorg	.08
470	Joe Niekro	.12
471	Ed Farmer	.08
472	Tim Flannery	.08
473	Dave Parker	.35
474	Jeff Leonard	.08
475	Al Hrabosky	.08
476	Ron Hodges	.08
477	Leon Durham	.08
478	Jim Essian	.08
479	Roy Lee Jackson	.08
480	Brad Havens	.08
481	Joe Price	.08
482	Tony Bernazard	.08
483	Scott McGregor	.08
484	Paul Molitor	1.75
485	Mike Ivie	.08
486	Ken Griffey	.12
487	Dennis Eckersley	.65
488	Steve Garvey	.45
489	Mike Fischlin	.08
490	U.L. Washington	.08
491	Steve McCatty	.08
492	Roy Johnson	.08
493	Don Baylor	.12
494	Bobby Johnson	.08
495	Mike Squires	.08
496	Bert Roberge	.08
497	Dick Ruthven	.08
498	Tito Landrum	.08
499	Sixto Lezcano	.08
500	Johnny Bench	1.00
501	Larry Whisenton	.08
502	Manny Sarmiento	.08
503	Fred Breining	.08
504	Bill Campbell	.08
505	Todd Cruz	.08
506	Bob Bailor	.08
507	Dave Stieb	.12

508	Al Williams	.08
509	Dan Ford	.08
510	Gorman Thomas	.08
511	Chet Lemon	.08
512	Mike Torrez	.08
513	Shane Rawley	.08
514	Mark Belanger	.08
515	Rodney Craig	.08
516	Onix Concepcion	.08
517	Mike Heath	.08
518	Andre Dawson	1.25
519	Luis Sanchez	.08
520	Terry Bogener	.08
521	Rudy Law	.08
522	Ray Knight	.10
523	Joe Lefebvre	.08
524	Jim Wohlford	.08
525	*Julio Franco*	4.00
526	Ron Oester	.08
527	Rick Mahler	.08
528	Steve Nicosia	.08
529	Junior Kennedy	.08
530a	Whitey Herzog (one yellow box on back)	.70
530b	Whitey Herzog (two yellow boxes on back)	.10
531a	Don Sutton (blue frame)	.45
531b	Don Sutton (green frame)	.45
532	Mark Brouhard	.08
533a	Sparky Anderson (one yellow box on back)	.70
533b	Sparky Anderson (two yellow boxes on back)	.10
534	Roger LaFrancois	.08
535	George Frazier	.08
536	Tom Niedenfuer	.08
537	Ed Glynn	.08
538	Lee May	.00
539	Bob Kearney	.08
540	Tim Raines	.35
541	Paul Mirabella	.08
542	Luis Tiant	.12
543	Ron LeFlore	.08
544	*Dave LaPoint*	.12
545	Randy Moffitt	.08
546	Luis Aguayo	.08
547	Brad Lesley	.08
548	Luis Salazar	.08
549	John Candelaria	.08
550	Dave Bergman	.08
551	Bob Watson	.08
552	Pat Tabler	.08
553	Brent Gaff	.08
554	Al Cowens	.08
555	Tom Brunansky	.10
556	Lloyd Moseby	.08
557a	Pascual Perez (Twins)	.90
557b	Pascual Perez (Braves)	.15
558	Willie Upshaw	.08
559	Richie Zisk	.08
560	Pat Zachry	.08
561	Jay Johnstone	.08
562	Carlos Diaz	.08
563	John Tudor	.10
564	Frank Robinson	.25
565	Dave Edwards	.08
566	Paul Householder	.08
567	Ron Reed	.08
568	Mike Ramsey	.08
569	Kiko Garcia	.08
570	Tommy John	.20
571	Tony LaRussa	.12
572	Joel Youngblood	.08
573	*Wayne Tolleson*	.08
574	Keith Creel	.08
575	Billy Martin	.12
576	Jerry Dybzinski	.08
577	Rick Cerone	.08
578	Tony Perez	.25
579	*Greg Brock*	.15
580	Glen Wilson (Glenn)	.20
581	Tim Stoddard	.08
582	Bob McClure	.08
583	Jim Dwyer	.08
584	Ed Romero	.08
585	Larry Herndon	.08
586	*Wade Boggs*	15.00
587	Jay Howell	.10
588	Dave Stewart	.50
589	Bert Blyleven	.12
590	Dick Howser	.08
591	Wayne Gross	.08
592	Terry Francona	.08
593	Don Werner	.08
594	Bill Stein	.08
595	Jesse Barfield	.40
596	Bobby Molinaro	.08
597	Mike Vail	.08
598	*Tony Gwynn*	30.00
599	Gary Rajsich	.08
600	Jerry Ujdur	.08
601	Cliff Johnson	.08
602	Jerry White	.08
603	Bryan Clark	.08
604	Joe Ferguson	.08
605	Guy Sularz	.08
606a	Ozzie Virgil (green frame around photo)	.90
606b	Ozzie Virgil (orange frame around photo)	.08
607	Terry Harper	.08
608	Harvey Kuenn	.08
609	Jim Sundberg	.08
610	Willie Stargell	.75
611	Reggie Smith	.10
612	Rob Wilfong	.08
613	Niekro Brothers (Joe Niekro, Phil Niekro)	.25
614	Lee Elia	.08
615	Mickey Hatcher	.08
616	Jerry Hairston	.08
617	John Martin	.08
618	Wally Backman	.08
619	*Storm Davis*	.10
620	Alan Knicely	.08
621	John Stuper	.08
622	Matt Sinatro	.08
623	*Gene Petralli*	.08
624	Duane Walker	.08
625	Dick Williams	.08
626	Pat Corrales	.08
627	Vern Ruhle	.08
628	Joe Torre	.08
629	Anthony Johnson	.08
630	Steve Howe	.08
631	Gary Woods	.08
632	Lamarr Hoyt (LaMarr)	.08
633	Steve Swisher	.08
634	Terry Leach	.08
635	Jeff Newman	.08
636	Brett Butler	.10
637	Gary Gray	.08
638	Lee Mazzilli	.08
639a	Ron Jackson (A's)	6.00
639b	Ron Jackson (Angels - green frame around photo)	.90
639c	Ron Jackson (Angels - red frame around photo)	.20
640	Juan Beniquez	.08
641	Dave Rucker	.08
642	Luis Pujols	.08
643	Rick Monday	.10
644	Hosken Powell	.08
645	San Diego Chicken	.20
646	Dave Engle	.08
647	Dick Davis	.08
648	MVP's (Vida Blue, Joe Morgan, Frank Robinson)	.15
649	Al Chambers	.08
650	Jesus Vega	.08
651	Jeff Jones	.08
652	Marvis Foley	.08
653	Ty Cobb (puzzle)	.08
----	DK checklist (Dick Perez) (no word "Checklist" on back)	.70
----	DK Checklist (Dick Perez) (word "Checklist" on back)	.08
----	Checklist 27-130	.08
----	Checklist 131-234	.08
----	Checklist 235-338	.08
----	Checklist 339-442	.08
----	Checklist 443-546	.08
----	Checklist 547-653	.08

1983 Donruss Action All-Stars Promo Sheet

To introduce its series of large-format star cards, Donruss issued this sample sheet with four players on a 10" x 7" format.

		MT
Complete Sheet:		15.00
31	Pete Rose	
32	Mookie Wilson	
36	Dave Winfield	
37	Tim Lollar	

1983 Donruss Action All-Stars

The cards in this 60-card set are designed on a horizontal format and contain a large close-up photo of the player on the left and a smaller action photo on the right. The 5" x 3-1/2" cards have deep red borders and contain the Donruss logo and the year of issue. Backs are printed in black on red and white and contain statistical and biographical information. The cards were sold with puzzle pieces (three pieces on one card per pack) that feature Mickey Mantle.

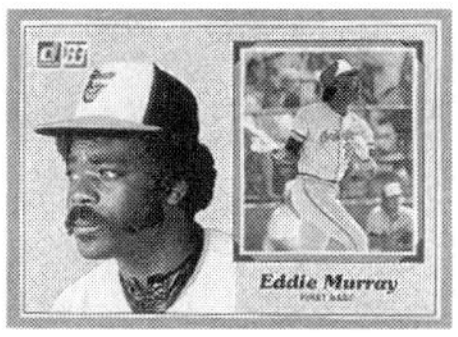

		MT
Complete Set (60):		7.00
Common Player:		.05
Mickey Mantle puzzle:		12.50
1	Eddie Murray	.30
2	Dwight Evans	.05
3a	Reggie Jackson (red covers part of statistics on back)	.30
3b	Reggie Jackson (red does not cover any statistics on back)	.30
4	Greg Luzinski	.08
5	Larry Herndon	.05
6	Al Oliver	.05
7	Bill Buckner	.05
8	Jason Thompson	.05
9	Andre Dawson	.15
10	Greg Minton	.05
11	Terry Kennedy	.05
12	Phil Niekro	.20
13	Willie Wilson	.05
14	Johnny Bench	.30
15	Ron Guidry	.05
16	Hal McRae	.05
17	Damaso Garcia	.05
18	Gary Ward	.05
19	Cecil Cooper	.05
20	Keith Hernandez	.05
21	Ron Cey	.05
22	Rickey Henderson	.30
23	Nolan Ryan	2.50
24	Steve Carlton	.30
25	John Stearns	.05
26	Jim Sundberg	.05
27	Joaquin Andujar	.05
28	Gaylord Perry	.20
29	Jack Clark	.05
30	Bill Madlock	.05
31	Pete Rose	1.00
32	Mookie Wilson	.05
33	Rollie Fingers	.20
34	Lonnie Smith	.05
35	Tony Pena	.05
36	Dave Winfield	.30
37	Tim Lollar	.05
38	Rod Carew	.30
39	Toby Harrah	.05
40	Buddy Bell	.05
41	Bruce Sutter	.05
42	George Brett	.75
43	Carlton Fisk	.30
44	Carl Yastrzemski	.50
45	Dale Murphy	.20
46	Bob Horner	.05
47	Dave Concepcion	.05
48	Dave Stieb	.05
49	Kent Hrbek	.08
50	Lance Parrish	.05
51	Joe Niekro	.05
52	Cal Ripken, Jr.	2.50
53	Fernando Valenzuela	.08
54	Rickie Zisk	.05
55	Leon Durham	.05
56	Robin Yount	.30
57	Mike Schmidt	.75
58	Gary Carter	.08
59	Fred Lynn	.05
60	Checklist	.03

Player names in *Italic* type indicate a rookie card.

1983 Donruss Hall of Fame Heroes Promo Sheet

To introduce its series of former star Perez-Steele art cards, Donruss issued this sample sheet which reproduces four of the cards in a 5" x 7" format.

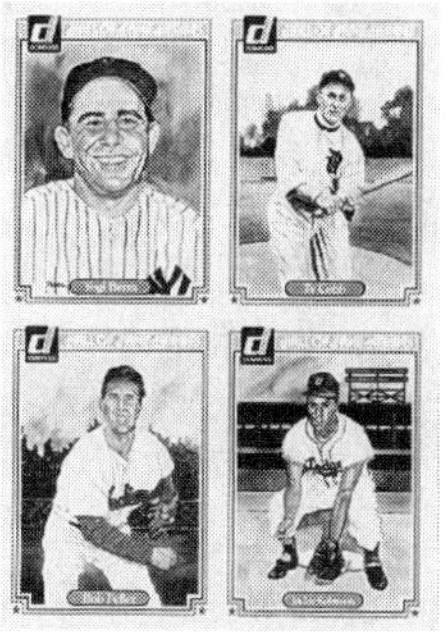

		MT
Complete Sheet:		10.00
1	Ty Cobb	
6	Jackie Robinson	
24	Yogi Berra	
36	Bob Feller	

1983 Donruss Hall of Fame Heroes

The artwork of Dick Perez is featured in the 44-card Hall of Fame Heroes set issued in 1983. The 2-1/2" x 3-1/2" cards were available in wax packs that contained eight cards plus a Mickey Mantle puzzle piece card (three pieces on one card). Backs display red and blue print on white stock and contain a short biograpical sketch.

		MT
Complete Set (44):		8.00
Common Player:		.10
Mickey Mantle Puzzle:		12.50
1	Ty Cobb	.75
2	Walter Johnson	.15
3	Christy Mathewson	.15
4	Josh Gibson	.15
5	Honus Wagner	.25
6	Jackie Robinson	.75
7	Mickey Mantle	2.00
8	Luke Appling	.10
9	Ted Williams	.75
10	Johnny Mize	.10
11	Satchel Paige	.25
12	Lou Boudreau	.10
13	Jimmie Foxx	.10
14	Duke Snider	.35
15	Monte Irvin	.10
16	Hank Greenberg	.25
17	Roberto Clemente	1.00
18	Al Kaline	.25
19	Frank Robinson	.25
20	Joe Cronin	.10
21	Burleigh Grimes	.10
22	The Waner Brothers (Lloyd Waner, Paul Waner)	.10
23	Grover Alexander	.10
24	Yogi Berra	.35
25	James Bell	.10
26	Bill Dickey	.10
27	Cy Young	.15
28	Charlie Gehringer	.10
29	Dizzy Dean	.15
30	Bob Lemon	.10
31	Red Ruffing	.10
32	Stan Musial	.75
33	Carl Hubbell	.15
34	Hank Aaron	.75
35	John McGraw	.10
36	Bob Feller	.20
37	Casey Stengel	.10
38	Ralph Kiner	.10
39	Roy Campanella	.35
40	Mel Ott	.10
41	Robin Roberts	.10
42	Early Wynn	.10
43	Mickey Mantle Puzzle Card	.10
---	Checklist	.05

1984 Donruss Promo Sheet

The front designs of nine 1984 Donruss baseball cards were printed on this glossy paper sheet to introduce the company's design for 1994. The 7-1/2" x 10-1/2" sheets are blank-backed. Players are listed here alphabetically.

	MT
Complete Sheet: Harold Baines, Buddy Bell, Leon Durham, Reggie Jackson, Eddie Murray, Darryl Strawberry, Robin Yount, Robin Yount (Diamond King), Richie Zisk	35.00

1984 Donruss

The 1984 Donruss set consists of 651 numbered cards, seven unnumbered checklists and two "Living Legends" cards (designated A and B). The A and B cards were issued only in wax packs and were not available to hobby dealers purchasing factory sets. The card fronts differ in style from the previous years, however the Donruss logo and year of issue are still included. Backs have black print on green and white and are identical in format to the preceding year. The 2-1/2" x 3-1/2" cards were issued in packs with three pieces of a 63-piece puzzle of Duke Snider. The complete set price in the checklist that follows does not include the higher priced variations. Cards marked with (DK) or (RR) in the checklist refer to the Diamond Kings and Rated Rookies subsets. Each of the Diamond Kings cards and the DK checklist can be found in two varieties. The more common has Frank Steele's name misspelled

"Steel" in the credit line at the bottom-right corner on the back. The error was later corrected.

		MT
	Complete Set (660):	180.00
	Common Player:	.15
	Duke Snider Puzzle:	3.50
	Wax Box:	300.00
A	Living Legends (Rollie Fingers, Gaylord Perry)	5.00
B	Living Legends (Johnny Bench, Carl Yastrzemski)	8.00
1a	Robin Yount (DK) (Steel)	3.00
1b	Robin Yount (DK) (Steele)	5.00
2a	Dave Concepcion (DK) (Steel)	.30
2b	Dave Concepcion (DK) (Steele)	.60
3a	Dwayne Murphy (DK) (Steel)	.25
3b	Dwayne Murphy (DK) (Steele)	.60
4a	John Castino (DK) (Steel)	.20
4b	John Castino (DK) (Steele)	.60
5a	Leon Durham (DK) (Steel)	.25
5b	Leon Durham (DK) (Steele)	.60
6a	Rusty Staub (DK) (Steel)	.30
6b	Rusty Staub (DK) (Steele)	.60
7a	Jack Clark (DK) (Steel)	.25
7b	Jack Clark (DK) (Steele)	.60
8a	Dave Dravecky (DK) (Steel)	.25
8b	Dave Dravecky (DK) (Steele)	.60
9a	Al Oliver (DK) (Steel)	.35
9b	Al Oliver (DK) (Steele)	.70
10a	Dave Righetti (DK) (Steel)	.25
10b	Dave Righetti (DK) (Steele)	.60
11a	Hal McRae (DK) (Steel)	.30
11b	Hal McRae (DK) (Steele)	.60
12a	Ray Knight (DK) (Steel)	.25
12b	Ray Knight (DK) (Steele)	.60
13a	Bruce Sutter (DK) (Steel)	.25
13b	Bruce Sutter (DK) (Steele)	.60
14a	Bob Horner (DK) (Steel)	.25
14b	Bob Horner (DK) (Steele)	.60
15a	Lance Parrish (DK) (Steel)	.25
15b	Lance Parrish (DK) (Steele)	.60
16a	Matt Young (DK) (Steel)	.25
16b	Matt Young (DK) (Steele)	.60
17a	Fred Lynn (DK) (Steel)	.35
17b	Fred Lynn (DK) (Steele)	.70
18a	Ron Kittle (DK) (Steel)	.25
18b	Ron Kittle (DK) (Steele)	.60
19a	Jim Clancy (DK) (Steel)	.25
19b	Jim Clancy (DK) (Steele)	.60
20a	Bill Madlock (DK) (Steel)	.30
20b	Bill Madlock (DK) (Steele)	.60
21a	Larry Parrish (DK) (Steel)	.25
21b	Larry Parrish (DK) (Steele)	.60
22a	Eddie Murray (DK) (Steel)	2.00
22b	Eddie Murray (DK) (Steele)	4.00
23a	Mike Schmidt (DK) (Steel)	4.00
23b	Mike Schmidt (DK) (Steele)	5.00
24a	Pedro Guerrero (DK) (Steel)	.25
24b	Pedro Guerrero (DK) (Steele)	.60
25a	Andre Thornton (DK) (Steel)	.25
25b	Andre Thornton (DK) (Steele)	.60
26a	Wade Boggs (DK) (Steel)	3.00
26b	Wade Boggs (DK) (Steele)	4.00
27	*Joel Skinner* (RR)	.15
28	Tom Dunbar (RR)	.15
29a	Mike Stenhouse (RR) (no number on back)	.15
29b	Mike Stenhouse (RR) (29 on back)	3.00
30a	*Ron Darling* (RR) (no number on back)	2.00
30b	*Ron Darling* (RR) (30 on back)	3.00
31	*Dion James* (RR)	.15
32	*Tony Fernandez* (RR)	3.00
33	Angel Salazar (RR)	.15
34	*Kevin McReynolds* (RR)	1.50
35	*Dick Schofield* (RR)	.20
36	*Brad Komminsk* (RR)	.15
37	*Tim Teufel* (RR)	.30
38	Doug Frobel (RR)	.15
39	*Greg Gagne* (RR)	.80
40	Mike Fuentes (RR)	.15
41	*Joe Carter* (RR)	40.00
42	Mike Brown (RR)	.15
43	Mike Jeffcoat (RR)	.15
44	*Sid Fernandez* (RR)	4.00
45	Brian Dayett (RR)	.15
46	Chris Smith (RR)	.15
47	Eddie Murray	8.00
48	Robin Yount	6.00
49	Lance Parrish	.40
50	Jim Rice	.50
51	Dave Winfield	6.00
52	Fernando Valenzuela	.40
53	George Brett	12.00
54	Rickey Henderson	5.00
55	Gary Carter	.65
56	Buddy Bell	.20
57	Reggie Jackson	6.00
58	Harold Baines	.30
59	Ozzie Smith	6.00
60	Nolan Ryan	30.00
61	Pete Rose	8.00
62	Ron Oester	.15
63	Steve Garvey	.75
64	Jason Thompson	.15
65	Jack Clark	.25
66	Dale Murphy	1.50
67	Leon Durham	.15
68	Darryl Strawberry	10.00
69	Richie Zisk	.15
70	Kent Hrbek	.40
71	Dave Stieb	.25
72	Ken Schrom	.15
73	George Bell	.40
74	John Moses	.15
75	Ed Lynch	.15
76	Chuck Rainey	.15
77	Biff Pocoroba	.15
78	Cecilio Guante	.15
79	Jim Barr	.15
80	Kurt Bevacqua	.15
81	Tom Foley	.15
82	Joe Lefebvre	.15
83	*Andy Van Slyke*	2.00
84	Bob Lillis	.15
85	Rick Adams	.15
86	Jerry Hairston	.15
87	Bob James	.15
88	Joe Altobelli	.15
89	Ed Romero	.15
90	John Grubb	.15
91	John Henry Johnson	.15
92	Juan Espino	.15
93	Candy Maldonado	.15
94	Andre Thornton	.20
95	Onix Concepcion	.15
96	*Don Hill*	.15
97	Andre Dawson	2.00
98	Frank Tanana	.15
99	*Curt Wilkerson*	.15
100	Larry Gura	.15
101	Dwayne Murphy	.15
102	Tom Brennan	.15
103	Dave Righetti	.40
104	Steve Sax	.30
105	Dan Petry	.15
106	Cal Ripken, Jr.	30.00
107	Paul Molitor	8.00
108	Fred Lynn	.35
109	Neil Allen	.15
110	Joe Niekro	.20
111	Steve Carlton	5.00
112	Terry Kennedy	.15
113	Bill Madlock	.20
114	Chili Davis	.20
115	Jim Gantner	.15
116	Tom Seaver	5.00
117	Bill Buckner	.20
118	Bill Caudill	.15
119	Jim Clancy	.15
120	John Castino	.15
121	Dave Concepcion	.20
122	Greg Luzinski	.20
123	Mike Boddicker	.20
124	Pete Ladd	.15
125	Juan Berenguer	.15
126	John Montefusco	.15
127	Ed Jurak	.15
128	Tom Niedenfuer	.15
129	Bert Blyleven	.30
130	Bud Black	.15
131	Gorman Heimueller	.15
132	Dan Schatzeder	.15
133	Ron Jackson	.15
134	*Tom Henke*	1.50
135	Kevin Hickey	.15
136	Mike Scott	.15
137	Bo Diaz	.15
138	Glenn Brummer	.15
139	Sid Monge	.15
140	Rich Gale	.15
141	Brett Butler	.20
142	Brian Harper	.25
143	John Rabb	.15
144	Gary Woods	.15
145	Pat Putnam	.15
146	*Jim Acker*	.15
147	Mickey Hatcher	.15
148	Todd Cruz	.15
149	Tom Tellmann	.15
150	John Wockenfuss	.15
151	Wade Boggs	12.00
152	Don Baylor	.20
153	Bob Welch	.20
154	Alan Bannister	.15
155	Willie Aikens	.15
156	Jeff Burroughs	.15
157	Bryan Little	.15
158	Bob Boone	.20
159	Dave Hostetler	.15
160	Jerry Dybzinski	.15
161	Mike Madden	.15
162	Luis DeLeon	.15
163	Willie Hernandez	.15
164	Frank Pastore	.15
165	Rick Camp	.15
166	Lee Mazzilli	.15
167	Scot Thompson	.15
168	Bob Forsch	.15
169	Mike Flanagan	.15
170	Rick Manning	.15
171	Chet Lemon	.15
172	Jerry Remy	.15
173	Ron Guidry	.20
174	Pedro Guerrero	.25
175	Willie Wilson	.25
176	Carney Lansford	.15
177	Al Oliver	.30
178	Jim Sundberg	.15
179	Bobby Grich	.20
180	Richard Dotson	.15
181	Joaquin Andujar	.15
182	Jose Cruz	.20
183	Mike Schmidt	12.00
184	*Gary Redus*	.25
185	Garry Templeton	.15
186	Tony Pena	.20
187	Greg Minton	.15
188	Phil Niekro	1.00
189	Fergie Jenkins	1.00
190	Mookie Wilson	.20
191	Jim Beattie	.15
192	Gary Ward	.15
193	Jesse Barfield	.20
194	Pete Filson	.15
195	Roy Lee Jackson	.15
196	Rick Sweet	.15
197	Jesse Orosco	.15
198	*Steve Lake*	.15
199	Ken Dayley	.15
200	Manny Sarmiento	.15
201	Mark Davis	.15
202	Tim Flannery	.15
203	Bill Scherrer	.15
204	Al Holland	.15
205	David Von Ohlen	.15
206	Mike LaCoss	.15
207	Juan Beniquez	.15
208	*Juan Agosto*	.15
209	Bobby Ramos	.15
210	Al Bumbry	.15
211	Mark Brouhard	.15
212	Howard Bailey	.15
213	Bruce Hurst	.15
214	Bob Shirley	.15
215	Pat Zachry	.15
216	Julio Franco	1.00
217	Mike Armstrong	.15
218	Dave Beard	.15
219	Steve Rogers	.15
220	John Butcher	.15
221	*Mike Smithson*	.15
222	Frank White	.20
223	Mike Heath	.15
224	Chris Bando	.15
225	Roy Smalley	.15
226	Dusty Baker	.20
227	Lou Whitaker	.40
228	John Lowenstein	.15
229	Ben Oglivie	.15
230	Doug DeCinces	.15
231	Lonnie Smith	.15
232	Ray Knight	.15
233	Gary Matthews	.15
234	Juan Bonilla	.15
235	Rod Scurry	.15
236	Atlee Hammaker	.15
237	Mike Caldwell	.15
238	Keith Hernandez	.25
239	Larry Bowa	.20
240	Tony Bernazard	.15
241	Damaso Garcia	.15
242	Tom Brunansky	.15
243	Dan Driessen	.15
244	Ron Kittle	.15
245	Tim Stoddard	.15
246	Bob L. Gibson	.15
247	Marty Castillo	.15
248	*Don Mattingly*	55.00
249	Jeff Newman	.15
250	*Alejandro Pena*	.25
251	Toby Harrah	.15
252	Cesar Geronimo	.15
253	Tom Underwood	.15
254	Doug Flynn	.15
255	Andy Hassler	.15
256	Odell Jones	.15
257	Rudy Law	.15
258	Harry Spilman	.15
259	Marty Bystrom	.15
260	Dave Rucker	.15
261	Ruppert Jones	.15
262	Jeff Jones	.15
263	*Gerald Perry*	.25
264	Gene Tenace	.15
265	Brad Wellman	.15
266	Dickie Noles	.15
267	Jamie Allen	.15
268	Jim Gott	.15
269	Ron Davis	.15
270	Benny Ayala	.15
271	Ned Yost	.15
272	Dave Rozema	.15
273	Dave Stapleton	.15
274	Lou Piniella	.20
275	Jose Morales	.15
276	Brod Perkins	.15
277	Butch Davis	.15
278	Tony Phillips	1.00
279	Jeff Reardon	.25
280	Ken Forsch	.15
281	*Pete O'Brien*	.50
282	Tom Paciorek	.15
283	Frank LaCorte	.15
284	Tim Lollar	.15
285	Greg Gross	.15
286	Alex Trevino	.15
287	Gene Garber	.15
288	Dave Parker	.50
289	Lee Smith	2.00
290	Dave LaPoint	.15
291	*John Shelby*	.15
292	Charlie Moore	.15
293	Alan Trammell	1.50
294	Tony Armas	.20
295	Shane Rawley	.15
296	Greg Brock	.15
297	Hal McRae	.20
298	Mike Davis	.15
299	Tim Raines	1.00
300	Bucky Dent	.15
301	Tommy John	.35
302	Carlton Fisk	4.00
303	Darrell Porter	.15
304	Dickie Thon	.15
305	Garry Maddox	.15
306	Cesar Cedeno	.20
307	Gary Lucas	.15
308	Johnny Ray	.15
309	Andy McGaffigan	.15
310	Claudell Washington	.15
311	Ryne Sandberg	18.00
312	George Foster	.30
313	*Spike Owen*	.50
314	Gary Gaetti	.35
315	Willie Upshaw	.15
316	Al Williams	.15
317	Jorge Orta	.15
318	Orlando Mercado	.15
319	*Junior Ortiz*	.15
320	Mike Proly	.15
321	Randy S. Johnson	.15
322	Jim Morrison	.15
323	Max Venable	.15
324	Tony Gwynn	20.00
325	Duane Walker	.15
326	Ozzie Virgil	.15
327	Jeff Lahti	.15
328	*Bill Dawley*	.15
329	Rob Wilfong	.15
330	Marc Hill	.15
331	Ray Burris	.15
332	Allan Ramirez	.15
333	Chuck Porter	.15
334	Wayne Krenchicki	.15
335	Gary Allenson	.15
336	*Bob Meacham*	.15
337	Joe Beckwith	.15
338	Rick Sutcliffe	.25
339	*Mark Huismann*	.15
340	*Tim Conroy*	.15
341	Scott Sanderson	.15
342	Larry Biittner	.15
343	Dave Stewart	.50
344	Darryl Motley	.15
345	*Chris Codiroli*	.15
346	Rick Behenna	.15
347	Andre Robertson	.15
348	Mike Marshall	.25
349	Larry Herndon	.15
350	Rich Dauer	.15
351	Cecil Cooper	.15
352	Rod Carew	4.00
353	Willie McGee	.40
354	Phil Garner	.20
355	Joe Morgan	1.00
356	Luis Salazar	.15
357	John Candelaria	.15
358	Bill Laskey	.15
359	Bob McClure	.15
360	Dave Kingman	.20
361	Ron Cey	.20
362	*Matt Young*	.15
363	Lloyd Moseby	.20
364	Frank Viola	.45
365	Eddie Milner	.15
366	Floyd Bannister	.15
367	Dan Ford	.15
368	Moose Haas	.15
369	Doug Bair	.15
370	*Ray Fontenot*	.15
371	Luis Aponte	.15
372	Jack Fimple	.15
373	*Neal Heaton*	.20
374	Greg Pryor	.15
375	Wayne Gross	.15
376	Charlie Lea	.15
377	Steve Lubratich	.15
378	Jon Matlack	.15
379	Julio Cruz	.15
380	John Mizerock	.15
381	*Kevin Gross*	.50
382	Mike Ramsey	.15
383	Doug Gwosdz	.15
384	Kelly Paris	.15
385	Pete Falcone	.15
386	Milt May	.15
387	Fred Breining	.15
388	*Craig Lefferts*	.25
389	Steve Henderson	.15
390	Randy Moffitt	.15
391	Ron Washington	.15
392	Gary Roenicke	.15
393	*Tom Candiotti*	.75
394	Larry Pashnick	.15
395	Dwight Evans	.30
396	Goose Gossage	.25
397	Derrel Thomas	.15
398	Juan Eichelberger	.15
399	Leon Roberts	.15
400	Davey Lopes	.15
401	Bill Gullickson	.15
402	Geoff Zahn	.15
403	Billy Sample	.15
404	Mike Squires	.15
405	Craig Reynolds	.15
406	Eric Show	.15
407	John Denny	.15
408	Dann Bilardello	.15
409	Bruce Benedict	.15
410	Kent Tekulve	.15
411	Mel Hall	.15
412	John Stuper	.15
413	Rick Dempsey	.15
414	Don Sutton	.90
415	Jack Morris	.50
416	John Tudor	.15
417	Willie Randolph	.20
418	Jerry Reuss	.15
419	Don Slaught	.15
420	Steve McCatty	.15
421	Tim Wallach	.25
422	Larry Parrish	.15
423	Brian Downing	.15
424	Britt Burns	.15
425	David Green	.15
426	Jerry Mumphrey	.15
427	Ivan DeJesus	.15
428	Mario Soto	.15
429	Gene Richards	.15
430	Dale Berra	.15
431	Darrell Evans	.25
432	Glenn Hubbard	.15
433	Jody Davis	.15
434	Danny Heep	.15
435	*Ed Nunez*	.15
436	Bobby Castillo	.15
437	Ernie Whitt	.15
438	Scott Ullger	.15
439	Doyle Alexander	.15
440	Domingo Ramos	.15
441	Craig Swan	.15
442	Warren Brusstar	.15
443	Len Barker	.15
444	Mike Easler	.15
445	Renie Martin	.15
446	*Dennis Rasmussen*	.30
447	Ted Power	.15
448	*Charlie Hudson*	.15
449	*Danny Cox*	.50
450	Kevin Bass	.15
451	Daryl Sconiers	.15
452	Scott Fletcher	.15
453	Bryn Smith	.15
454	Jim Dwyer	.15
455	Rob Picciolo	.15
456	Enos Cabell	.15
457	*Dennis Boyd*	.20
458	Butch Wynegar	.15
459	Burt Hooton	.15
460	Ron Hassey	.15
461	*Danny Jackson*	.50
462	Bob Kearney	.15
463	Terry Francona	.15
464	Wayne Tolleson	.15
465	Mickey Rivers	.15
466	John Wathan	.15
467	Bill Almon	.15
468	George Vukovich	.15
469	Steve Kemp	.15
470	Ken Landreaux	.15
471	Milt Wilcox	.15
472	Tippy Martinez	.15
473	Ted Simmons	.15
474	Tim Foli	.15
475	George Hendrick	.15
476	Terry Puhl	.15
477	Von Hayes	.15
478	Bobby Brown	.15
479	Lee Lacy	.15
480	Joel Youngblood	.15
481	Jim Slaton	.15
482	*Mike Fitzgerald*	.15
483	Keith Moreland	.15
484	Ron Roenicke	.15
485	Luis Leal	.15
486	Bryan Oelkers	.15
487	Bruce Berenyi	.15
488	LaMarr Hoyt	.15

489 Joe Nolan .15
490 Marshall Edwards .15
491 *Mike Laga* .15
492 Rick Cerone .15
493 Mike Miller (Rick) .15
494 Rick Honeycutt .15
495 Mike Hargrove .15
496 Joe Simpson .15
497 *Keith Atherton* .15
498 Chris Welsh .15
499 Bruce Kison .15
500 Bob Johnson .15
501 Jerry Koosman .15
502 Frank DiPino .15
503 Tony Perez .75
504 Ken Oberkfell .15
505 *Mark Thurmond* .15
506 Joe Price .15
507 Pascual Perez .15
508 *Marvell Wynne* .15
509 Mike Krukow .15
510 Dick Ruthven .15
511 Al Cowens .15
512 Cliff Johnson .15
513 *Randy Bush* .15
514 Sammy Stewart .15
515 *Bill Schroeder* .15
516 Aurelio Lopez .15
517 Mike Brown .15
518 Graig Nettles .35
519 Dave Sax .15
520 Gerry Willard .15
521 Paul Splittorff .15
522 Tom Burgmeier .15
523 Chris Speier .15
524 Bobby Clark .15
525 George Wright .15
526 Dennis Lamp .15
527 Tony Scott .15
528 Ed Whitson .15
529 Ron Reed .15
530 Charlie Puleo .15
531 Jerry Royster .15
532 Don Robinson .15
533 Steve Trout .15
534 Bruce Sutter .30
535 Bob Horner .20
536 Pat Tabler .15
537 Chris Chambliss .15
538 Bob Ojeda .15
539 Alan Ashby .15
540 Jay Johnstone .15
541 Bob Dernier .15
542 *Brook Jacoby* .25
543 U.L. Washington .15
544 Danny Darwin .15
545 Kiko Garcia .15
546 Vance Law .15
547 Tug McGraw .20
548 Dave Smith .15
549 Len Matuszek .15
550 Tom Hume .15
551 Dave Dravecky .15
552 Rick Rhoden .15
553 Duane Kuiper .15
554 Rusty Staub .20
555 Bill Campbell .15
556 Mike Torrez .15
557 Dave Henderson .15
558 Len Whitehouse .15
559 Barry Bonnell .15
560 Rick Lysander .15
561 Garth Iorg .15
562 Bryan Clark .15
563 Brian Giles .15
564 Vern Ruhle .15
565 Steve Bedrosian .20
566 Larry McWilliams .15
567 Jeff Leonard .15
568 Alan Wiggins .15
569 *Jeff Russell* .50
570 Salome Barojas .15
571 Dane Iorg .15
572 Bob Knepper .15
573 Gary Lavelle .15
574 Gorman Thomas .15
575 Manny Trillo .15
576 Jim Palmer 3.00
577 Dale Murray .15
578 Tom Brookens .15
579 Rich Gedman .15
580 *Bill Doran* .50
581 Steve Yeager .15
582 Dan Spillner .15
583 Dan Quisenberry .15
584 Rance Mulliniks .15
585 Storm Davis .15
586 Dave Schmidt .15
587 Bill Russell .15
588 *Pat Sheridan* .15
589 Rafael Ramirez .15
590 Bud Anderson .15
591 George Frazier .15
592 *Lee Tunnell* .15
593 Kirk Gibson .50
594 Scott McGregor .15
595 Bob Bailor .15
596 Tom Herr .15
597 Luis Sanchez .15
598 Dave Engle .15
599 *Craig McMurtry* .15
600 Carlos Diaz .15
601 Tom O'Malley .15
602 *Nick Esasky* .15
603 Ron Hodges .15
604 Ed Vande Berg .15
605 Alfredo Griffin .15
606 Glenn Hoffman .15
607 Hubie Brooks .20
608 Richard Barnes (photo actually Neal Heaton) .15
609 *Greg Walker* .20
610 Ken Singleton .20
611 Mark Clear .15
612 Buck Martinez .15
613 Ken Griffey .20
614 Reid Nichols .15
615 *Doug Sisk* .15
616 Bob Brenly .15
617 Joey McLaughlin .15
618 Glenn Wilson .15
619 Bob Stoddard .15
620 Len Sakata (Lenn) .15
621 *Mike Young* .15
622 John Stefero .15
623 *Carmelo Martinez* .15
624 Dave Bergman .15
625 Runnin' Reds (David Green, Willie McGee, Lonnie Smith, Ozzie Smith) .75
626 Rudy May .15
627 Matt Keough .15
628 *Jose DeLeon* .15
629 Jim Essian .15
630 *Darnell Coles* .15
631 Mike Warren .15
632 Del Crandall .15
633 Dennis Martinez .20
634 Mike Moore .15
635 Lary Sorensen .15
636 Ricky Nelson .15
637 Omar Moreno .15
638 Charlie Hough .15
639 Dennis Eckersley 2.00
640 *Walt Terrell* .20
641 Denny Walling .15
642 *Dave Anderson* .15
643 *Jose Oquendo* .25
644 Bob Stanley .15
645 Dave Geisel .15
646 *Scott Garrelts* .25
647 *Gary Pettis* .25
648 Duke Snider Puzzle Card .15
649 Johnnie LeMaster .15
650 Dave Collins .15
651 San Diego Chicken .25
---- Checklist 1-26 DK (Perez-Steel on back) .15
---- Checklist 1-26 DK (Perez-Steele on back) .40
---- Checklist 27-130 .15
---- Checklist 131-234 .15
---- Checklist 235-338 .15
---- Checklist 339-442 .15
---- Checklist 443-546 .15
---- Checklist 547-651 .15

1984 Donruss Action All-Stars

Full-color photos on the card fronts and backs make the 1984 Donruss Action All-Stars set somewhat unusual. Fronts contain a large action photo plus the Donruss logo and year of issue inside a deep red border. The top half of the backs feature a close-up photo with the bottom portion containing biographical and statistical information. The 3-1/2" x 5" cards were sold with Ted Williams puzzle pieces.

	MT
Complete Set (60):	7.50
Common Player:	.10
Ted Williams Puzzle:	10.00

1 Gary Lavelle .10
2 Willie McGee .10
3 Tony Pena .10
4 Lou Whitaker .10
5 Robin Yount .65
6 Doug DeCinces .10
7 John Castino .10
8 Terry Kennedy .10
9 Rickey Henderson .65
10 Bob Horner .10
11 Harold Baines .10
12 Buddy Bell .10
13 Fernando Valenzuela .15
14 Nolan Ryan 2.50
15 Andre Thornton .10
16 Gary Redus .10
17 Pedro Guerrero .10
18 Andre Dawson .20
19 Dave Stieb .10
20 Cal Ripken, Jr. 3.00
21 Ken Griffey .10
22 Wade Boggs .70
23 Keith Hernandez .10
24 Steve Carlton .40
25 Hal McRae .10
26 John Lowenstein .10
27 Fred Lynn .10
28 Bill Buckner .10
29 Chris Chambliss .10
30 Richie Zisk .10
31 Jack Clark .10
32 George Hendrick .10
33 Bill Madlock .10
34 Lance Parrish .10
35 Paul Molitor .60
36 Reggie Jackson .65
37 Kent Hrbek .10
38 Steve Garvey .25
39 Carney Lansford .10
40 Dale Murphy .25
41 Greg Luzinski .10
42 Larry Parrish .10
43 Ryne Sandberg .65
44 Dickie Thon .10
45 Bert Blyleven .10
46 Ron Oester .10
47 Dusty Baker .10
48 Steve Rogers .10
49 Jim Clancy .10
50 Eddie Murray .60
51 Ron Guidry .10
52 Jim Rice .10
53 Tom Seaver .50
54 Pete Rose 1.00
55 George Brett .75
56 Dan Quisenberry .10
57 Mike Schmidt .75
58 Ted Simmons .10
59 Dave Righetti .10
60 Checklist .05

1984 Donruss Champions

The 60-card Donruss Champions set includes ten Hall of Famers, forty-nine current players and a numbered checklist. The Hall of Famers' cards (called Grand Champions) feature the artwork of Dick Perez, while cards of the current players (called Champions) are color photos. All cards measure 3-1/2" x 5". The Grand Champions represent hallmarks of excellence in various statistical categories, while the Champions are the leaders among then-active players in each category. The cards were issued with Duke Snider puzzle pieces.

	MT
Complete Set (60):	7.00
Common Player:	.10
Duke Snider Puzzle:	3.50

1 Babe Ruth 1.00
2 George Foster .10
3 Dave Kingman .10
4 Jim Rice .10
5 Gorman Thomas .10
6 Ben Oglivie .10
7 Jeff Burroughs .10
8 Hank Aaron .75
9 Reggie Jackson .30
10 Carl Yastrzemski .35
11 Mike Schmidt .50
12 Graig Nettles .10
13 Greg Luzinski .15
14 Ted Williams .75
15 George Brett .60
16 Wade Boggs .50
17 Hal McRae .10
18 Bill Buckner .10
19 Eddie Murray .40
20 Rogers Hornsby .15
21 Rod Carew .25
22 Bill Madlock .10
23 Lonnie Smith .10
24 Cecil Cooper .10
25 Ken Griffey .10
26 Ty Cobb .60
27 Pete Rose .60
28 Rusty Staub .10
29 Tony Perez .12
30 Al Oliver .10
31 Cy Young .15
32 Gaylord Perry .15
33 Ferguson Jenkins .15
34 Phil Niekro .15
35 Jim Palmer .20
36 Tommy John .10
37 Walter Johnson .20
38 Steve Carlton .20
39 Nolan Ryan .75
40 Tom Seaver .25
41 Don Sutton .10
42 Bert Blyleven .10
43 Frank Robinson .25
44 Joe Morgan .15
45 Rollie Fingers .15
46 Keith Hernandez .10
47 Robin Yount .35
48 Cal Ripken, Jr. 1.50
49 Dale Murphy .25
50 Mickey Mantle 2.00
51 Johnny Bench .40
52 Carlton Fisk .20
53 Tug McGraw .10
54 Paul Molitor .35
55 Carl Hubbell .10
56 Steve Garvey .15
57 Dave Parker .10
58 Gary Carter .15
59 Fred Lynn .10
60 Checklist .05

1985 Donruss Promo Sheet

To introduce its design for 1985, Donruss distributed this 8-1/2" x 11" paper sample sheet to dealers. The blank-back sheet has examples of nine Donruss cards from the '85 set. Players are listed here in alphabetical order.

	MT
Complete Sheet: Harold Baines, Buddy Bell, Alvin Davis, Keith Hernandez, Reggie Jackson, Eddie Murray, Ryno Sandberg, Lou Whitaker (Diamond King), Robin Yount	10.00

1985 Donruss

The black-bordered 1985 Donruss set includes 653 numbered cards and seven unnumbered checklists. Displaying the artwork of Dick Perez for the fourth consecutive year, cards #1-26 feature the Diamond Kings series. Donruss, reacting to the hobby craze over rookie cards, included a Rated Rookies subset (cards #27-46). The cards, in standard 2-1/2" x 3-1/2", were issued with a Lou Gehrig puzzle. Backs repeat the format of previous years with black print on yellow and white. The complete set price does not include the higher priced variations. (DK) and (RR) refer to the Diamond Kings and Rated Rookies subsets.

	MT
Complete Set (660):	110.00
Common Player:	.10
Lou Gehrig Puzzle:	3.00
Wax Box:	215.00

1 Ryno Sandberg (DK) 2.50
2 Doug DeCinces (DK) .10
3 Rich Dotson (DK) .10
4 Bert Blyleven (DK) .15
5 Lou Whitaker (DK) .15
6 Dan Quisenberry (DK) .10
7 Don Mattingly (DK) 3.50
8 Carney Lansford (DK) .10
9 Frank Tanana (DK) .10
10 Willie Upshaw (DK) .10
11 Claudell Washington (DK) .10
12 Mike Marshall (DK) .10
13 Joaquin Andujar (DK) .10
14 Cal Ripken, Jr. (DK) 8.00
15 Jim Rice (DK) .25
16 Don Sutton (DK) .30
17 Frank Viola (DK) .15
18 Alvin Davis (DK) .10
19 Mario Soto (DK) .10
20 Jose Cruz (DK) .10
21 Charlie Lea (DK) .10
22 Jesse Orosco (DK) .10
23 Juan Samuel (DK) .10
24 Tony Pena (DK) .10
25 Tony Gwynn (DK) 3.00
26 Bob Brenly (DK) .10
27 *Danny Tartabull* (RR) 1.50
28 *Mike Bielecki* (RR) .15
29 *Steve Lyons* (RR) .20
30 *Jeff Reed* (RR) .15
31 Tony Brewer (RR) .10
32 *John Morris* (RR) .10
33 *Daryl Boston* (RR) .15
34 Alfonso Pulido (RR) .10
35 *Steve Kiefer* (RR) .10
36 *Larry Sheets* (RR) .10
37 *Scott Bradley* (RR) .10
38 *Calvin Schiraldi* (RR) .10
39 *Shawon Dunston* (RR) 1.50
40 Charlie Mitchell (RR) .10
41 *Billy Hatcher* (RR) .50
42 Russ Stephans (RR) .10
43 Alejandro Sanchez (RR) .10
44 *Steve Jeltz* (RR) .10
45 *Jim Traber* (RR) .10
46 Doug Loman (RR) .10
47 Eddie Murray 2.50
48 Robin Yount 2.50
49 Lance Parrish .15
50 Jim Rice .15
51 Dave Winfield 1.00
52 Fernando Valenzuela .15
53 George Brett 4.00
54 Dave Kingman .15
55 Gary Carter .40
56 Buddy Bell .12
57 Reggie Jackson 1.50
58 Harold Baines .25
59 Ozzie Smith 2.50
60 Nolan Ryan 10.00
61 Mike Schmidt 4.00
62 Dave Parker .35
63 Tony Gwynn 7.50
64 Tony Pena .12
65 Jack Clark .15
66 Dale Murphy .60
67 Ryne Sandberg 6.00
68 Keith Hernandez .20
69 *Alvin Davis* .25
70 Kent Hrbek .20
71 Willie Upshaw .10

72	Dave Engle	.10
73	Alfredo Griffin	.10
74a	Jack Perconte (last line of highlights begins "Batted .346...")	.10
74b	Jack Perconte (last line of highlights begins "Led the ...")	.75
75	Jesse Orosco	.10
76	Jody Davis	.10
77	Bob Horner	.12
78	Larry McWilliams	.10
79	Joel Youngblood	.10
80	Alan Wiggins	.10
81	Ron Oester	.10
82	Ozzie Virgil	.10
83	*Ricky Horton*	.10
84	Bill Doran	.12
85	Rod Carew	1.00
86	LaMarr Hoyt	.10
87	Tim Wallach	.12
88	Mike Flanagan	.10
89	Jim Sundberg	.10
90	Chet Lemon	.10
91	Bob Stanley	.10
92	Willie Randolph	.12
93	Bill Russell	.10
94	Julio Franco	.50
95	Dan Quisenberry	.12
96	Bill Caudill	.10
97	Bill Gullickson	.10
98	Danny Darwin	.10
99	Curtis Wilkerson	.10
100	Bud Black	.10
101	Tony Phillips	.20
102	Tony Bernazard	.10
103	Jay Howell	.10
104	Burt Hooton	.10
105	Milt Wilcox	.10
106	Rich Dauer	.10
107	Don Sutton	.45
108	Mike Witt	.12
109	Bruce Sutter	.15
110	Enos Cabell	.10
111	John Denny	.10
112	Dave Dravecky	.10
113	Marvell Wynne	.10
114	Johnnie LeMaster	.10
115	Chuck Porter	.10
116	John Gibbons	.10
117	Keith Moreland	.10
118	Darnell Coles	.10
119	Dennis Lamp	.10
120	Ron Davis	.10
121	Nick Esasky	.10
122	Vance Law	.10
123	Gary Roenicke	.10
124	Bill Schroeder	.10
125	Dave Rozema	.10
126	Bobby Meacham	.10
127	Marty Barrett	.15
128	*R.J. Reynolds*	.15
129	Ernie Camacho	.10
130	Jorge Orta	.10
131	Lary Sorensen	.10
132	Terry Francona	.10
133	Fred Lynn	.20
134	Bobby Jones	.10
135	Jerry Hairston	.10
136	Kevin Bass	.10
137	Garry Maddox	.10
138	Dave LaPoint	.10
139	Kevin McReynolds	.20
140	Wayne Krenchicki	.10
141	Rafael Ramirez	.10
142	Rod Scurry	.10
143	Greg Minton	.10
144	Tim Stoddard	.10
145	Steve Henderson	.10
146	George Bell	.20
147	Dave Meier	.10
148	Sammy Stewart	.10
149	Mark Brouhard	.10
150	Larry Herndon	.10
151	Oil Can Boyd	.10
152	Brian Dayett	.10
153	Tom Niedenfuer	.10
154	Brook Jacoby	.10
155	Onix Concepcion	.10
156	Tim Conroy	.10
157	*Joe Hesketh*	.12
158	Brian Downing	.10
159	Tommy Dunbar	.10
160	Marc Hill	.10
161	Phil Garner	.12
162	Jerry Davis	.10
163	Bill Campbell	.10
164	*John Franco*	1.00
165	Len Barker	.10
166	*Benny Distefano*	.10
167	George Frazier	.10
168	Tito Landrum	.10
169	Cal Ripken, Jr.	10.00
170	Cecil Cooper	.10
171	Alan Trammell	.40
172	Wade Boggs	3.00
173	Don Baylor	.15
174	Pedro Guerrero	.12
175	Frank White	.12
176	Rickey Henderson	2.00
177	Charlie Lea	.10
178	Pete O'Brien	.10
179	Doug DeCinces	.12
180	Ron Kittle	.10
181	George Hendrick	.10
182	Joe Niekro	.12
183	Juan Samuel	.10
184	Mario Soto	.10
185	Goose Gossage	.25
186	Johnny Ray	.10
187	Bob Brenly	.10
188	Craig McMurtry	.10
189	Leon Durham	.10
190	Dwight Gooden	1.50
191	Barry Bonnell	.10
192	Tim Teufel	.10
193	Dave Stieb	.15
194	Mickey Hatcher	.10
195	Jesse Barfield	.10
196	Al Cowens	.10
197	Hubie Brooks	.10
198	Steve Trout	.10
199	Glenn Hubbard	.10
200	Bill Madlock	.15
201	*Jeff Robinson*	.10
202	Eric Show	.10
203	Dave Concepcion	.15
204	Ivan DeJesus	.10
205	Neil Allen	.10
206	Jerry Mumphrey	.10
207	Mike Brown	.10
208	Carlton Fisk	.75
209	Bryn Smith	.10
210	Tippy Martinez	.10
211	Dion James	.10
212	Willie Hernandez	.10
213	Mike Easler	.10
214	Ron Guidry	.10
215	Rick Honeycutt	.10
216	Brett Butler	.15
217	Larry Gura	.10
218	Ray Burris	.10
219	Steve Rogers	.10
220	Frank Tanana	.10
221	Ned Yost	.10
222	Bret Saberhagen	1.50
223	Mike Davis	.10
224	Bert Blyleven	.15
225	Steve Kemp	.10
226	Jerry Reuss	.10
227	Darrell Evans	.15
228	Wayne Gross	.10
229	Jim Gantner	.10
230	Bob Boone	.12
231	Lonnie Smith	.10
232	Frank DiPino	.10
233	Jerry Koosman	.10
234	Graig Nettles	.12
235	John Tudor	.10
236	John Rabb	.10
237	Rick Manning	.10
238	Mike Fitzgerald	.10
239	Gary Matthews	.10
240	*Jim Presley*	.10
241	Dave Collins	.10
242	Gary Gaetti	.15
243	Dann Bilardello	.10
244	Rudy Law	.10
245	John Lowenstein	.10
246	Tom Tellmann	.10
247	Howard Johnson	.20
248	Ray Fontenot	.10
249	Tony Armas	.12
250	Candy Maldonado	.10
251	*Mike Jeffcoat*	.10
252	Dane Iorg	.10
253	Bruce Bochte	.10
254	Pete Rose	2.50
255	Don Aase	.10
256	George Wright	.10
257	Britt Burns	.10
258	Mike Scott	.15
259	Len Matuszek	.10
260	Dave Rucker	.10
261	Craig Lefferts	.10
262	*Jay Tibbs*	.10
263	Bruce Benedict	.10
264	Don Robinson	.10
265	Gary Lavelle	.10
266	Scott Sanderson	.10
267	Matt Young	.10
268	Ernie Whitt	.10
269	Houston Jimenez	.10
270	*Ken Dixon*	.10
271	Peter Ladd	.10
272	Juan Berenguer	.10
273	Roger Clemens	50.00
274	Rick Cerone	.10
275	Dave Anderson	.10
276	George Vukovich	.10
277	Greg Pryor	.10
278	Mike Warren	.10
279	Bob James	.10
280	Bobby Grich	.12
281	*Mike Mason*	.10
282	Ron Reed	.10
283	Alan Ashby	.10
284	Mark Thurmond	.10
285	Joe Lefebvre	.10
286	Ted Power	.10
287	Chris Chambliss	.10
288	Lee Tunnell	.10
289	Rich Bordi	.10
290	Glenn Brummer	.10
291	Mike Boddicker	.10
292	Rollie Fingers	.40
293	Lou Whitaker	.20
294	Dwight Evans	.15
295	Don Mattingly	6.00
296	Mike Marshall	.15
297	Willie Wilson	.12
298	Mike Heath	.10
299	Tim Raines	.45
300	Larry Parrish	.12
301	Geoff Zahn	.10
302	Rich Dotson	.10
303	David Green	.10
304	Jose Cruz	.12
305	Steve Carlton	1.25
306	Gary Redus	.10
307	Steve Garvey	.40
308	Jose DeLeon	.10
309	Randy Lerch	.10
310	Claudell Washington	.10
311	Lee Smith	.75
312	Darryl Strawberry	.75
313	Jim Beattie	.10
314	John Butcher	.10
315	Damaso Garcia	.10
316	Mike Smithson	.10
317	Luis Leal	.10
318	Ken Phelps	.10
319	Wally Backman	.10
320	Ron Cey	.12
321	Brad Komminsk	.10
322	Jason Thompson	.10
323	*Frank Williams*	.10
324	Tim Lollar	.10
325	*Eric Davis*	1.50
326	Von Hayes	.10
327	Andy Van Slyke	.30
328	Craig Reynolds	.10
329	Dick Schofield	.10
330	Scott Fletcher	.10
331	Jeff Reardon	.12
332	Rick Dempsey	.10
333	Ben Oglivie	.10
334	Dan Petry	.10
335	Jackie Gutierrez	.10
336	Dave Righetti	.10
337	Alejandro Pena	.10
338	Mel Hall	.10
339	Pat Sheridan	.10
340	Keith Atherton	.10
341	David Palmer	.10
342	Gary Ward	.10
343	Dave Stewart	.15
344	*Mark Gubicza*	.50
345	Carney Lansford	.10
346	Jerry Willard	.10
347	Ken Griffey	.12
348	*Franklin Stubbs*	.10
349	Aurelio Lopez	.10
350	Al Bumbry	.10
351	Charlie Moore	.10
352	Luis Sanchez	.10
353	Darrell Porter	.10
354	Bill Dawley	.10
355	Charlie Hudson	.10
356	Garry Templeton	.10
357	Cecilio Guante	.10
358	Jeff Leonard	.10
359	Paul Molitor	3.00
360	Ron Gardenhire	.10
361	Larry Bowa	.12
362	Bob Kearney	.10
363	Garth Iorg	.10
364	Tom Brunansky	.15
365	Brad Gulden	.10
366	Greg Walker	.10
367	Mike Young	.10
368	Rick Waits	.10
369	Doug Bair	.10
370	Bob Shirley	.10
371	Bob Ojeda	.10
372	Bob Welch	.10
373	Neal Heaton	.10
374	Danny Jackson (photo actually Steve Farr)	.80
375	Donnie Hill	.10
376	Mike Stenhouse	.10
377	Bruce Kison	.10
378	Wayne Tolleson	.10
379	Floyd Bannister	.10
380	Vern Ruhle	.10
381	Tim Corcoran	.10
382	Kurt Kepshire	.10
383	Bobby Brown	.10
384	Dave Van Gorder	.10
385	Rick Mahler	.10
386	Lee Mazzilli	.10
387	Bill Laskey	.10
388	Thad Bosley	.10
389	Al Chambers	.10
390	Tony Fernandez	.50
391	Ron Washington	.10
392	Bill Swaggerty	.10
393	Bob L. Gibson	.10
394	Marty Castillo	.10
395	Steve Crawford	.10
396	Clay Christiansen	.10
397	Bob Bailor	.10
398	Mike Hargrove	.10
399	Charlie Leibrandt	.10
400	Tom Burgmeier	.10
401	Razor Shines	.10
402	Rob Wilfong	.10
403	Tom Henke	.12
404	Al Jones	.10
405	Mike LaCoss	.10
406	Luis DeLeon	.10
407	Greg Gross	.10
408	Tom Hume	.10
409	Rick Camp	.10
410	Milt May	.10
411	*Henry Cotto*	.10
412	Dave Von Ohlen	.10
413	Scott McGregor	.10
414	Ted Simmons	.10
415	Jack Morris	.20
416	Bill Buckner	.15
417	Butch Wynegar	.10
418	Steve Sax	.15
419	Steve Balboni	.10
420	Dwayne Murphy	.10
421	Andre Dawson	.50
422	Charlie Hough	.10
423	Tommy John	.25
424a	Tom Seaver (Floyd Bannister photo, left-hander)	2.00
424b	Tom Seaver (correct photo)	30.00
425	Tom Herr	.10
426	Terry Puhl	.10
427	Al Holland	.10
428	Eddie Milner	.10
429	Terry Kennedy	.10
430	John Candelaria	.10
431	Manny Trillo	.10
432	Ken Oberkfell	.10
433	Rick Sutcliffe	.15
434	Ron Darling	.15
435	Spike Owen	.10
436	Frank Viola	.25
437	Lloyd Moseby	.10
438	Kirby Puckett	30.00
439	Jim Clancy	.10
440	Mike Moore	.10
441	Doug Sisk	.10
442	Dennis Eckersley	.75
443	Gerald Perry	.10
444	Dale Berra	.10
445	Dusty Baker	.12
446	Ed Whitson	.10
447	Cesar Cedeno	.12
448	*Rick Schu*	.10
449	Joaquin Andujar	.10
450	*Mark Bailey*	.10
451	*Ron Romanick*	.10
452	Julio Cruz	.10
453	Miguel Dilone	.10
454	Storm Davis	.10
455	Jaime Cocanower	.10
456	Barbaro Garbey	.10
457	Rich Gedman	.10
458	Phil Niekro	.40
459	Mike Scioscia	.10
460	Pat Tabler	.10
461	Darryl Motley	.10
462	Chris Codoroli (Codiroli)	.10
463	Doug Flynn	.10
464	Billy Sample	.10
465	Mickey Rivers	.10
466	John Wathan	.10
467	Bill Krueger	.10
468	Andre Thornton	.12
469	Rex Hudler	.12
470	*Sid Bream*	.60
471	Kirk Gibson	.20
472	John Shelby	.10
473	Moose Haas	.10
474	Doug Corbett	.10
475	Willie McGee	.15
476	Bob Knepper	.10
477	Kevin Gross	.10
478	Carmelo Martinez	.10
479	Kent Tekulve	.10
480	Chili Davis	.12
481	Bobby Clark	.10
482	Mookie Wilson	.12
483	Dave Owen	.10
484	Ed Nunez	.10
485	Rance Mulliniks	.10
486	Ken Schrom	.10
487	Jeff Russell	.10
488	Tom Paciorek	.10
489	Dan Ford	.10
490	Mike Caldwell	.10
491	Scottie Earl	.10
492	Jose Rijo	.25
493	Bruce Hurst	.10
494	Ken Landreaux	.10
495	Mike Fischlin	.10
496	Don Slaught	.10
497	Steve McCatty	.10
498	Gary Lucas	.10
499	Gary Pettis	.10
500	Marvis Foley	.10
501	Mike Squires	.10
502	*Jim Pankovitz*	.10
503	Luis Aguayo	.10
504	Ralph Citarella	.10
505	Bruce Bochy	.10
506	Bob Owchinko	.10
507	Pascual Perez	.10
508	Lee Lacy	.10
509	Atlee Hammaker	.10
510	Bob Dernier	.10
511	Ed Vande Berg	.10
512	Cliff Johnson	.10
513	Len Whitehouse	.10
514	Dennis Martinez	.12
515	Ed Romero	.10
516	Rusty Kuntz	.10
517	Rick Miller	.10
518	Dennis Rasmussen	.10
519	Steve Yeager	.10
520	Chris Bando	.10
521	U.L. Washington	.10
522	*Curt Young*	.10
523	Angel Salazar	.10
524	Curt Kaufman	.10
525	Odell Jones	.10
526	Juan Agosto	.10
527	Denny Walling	.10
528	Andy Hawkins	.15
529	Sixto Lezcano	.10
530	Skeeter Barnes	.10
531	Randy S. Johnson	.10
532	Jim Morrison	.10
533	Warren Brusstar	.10
534a	*Jeff Pendleton* (error)	3.00
534b	*Terry Pendleton* (correct)	12.00
535	Vic Rodriguez	.10
536	Bob McClure	.10
537	Dave Bergman	.10
538	Mark Clear	.10
539	*Mike Pagliarulo*	.35
540	Terry Whitfield	.10
541	Joe Beckwith	.10
542	Jeff Burroughs	.10
543	Dan Schatzeder	.10
544	Donnie Scott	.10
545	Jim Slaton	.10
546	Greg Luzinski	.12
547	*Mark Salas*	.10
548	Dave Smith	.10
549	John Wockenfuss	.10
550	Frank Pastore	.10
551	Tim Flannery	.10
552	Rick Rhoden	.10
553	Mark Davis	.10
554	*Jeff Dedmon*	.12
555	Gary Woods	.10
556	Danny Heep	.10
557	Mark Langston	1.00
558	Darrell Brown	.10
559	Jimmy Key	1.00
560	Rick Lysander	.10
561	Doyle Alexander	.10
562	Mike Stanton	.10
563	Sid Fernandez	.20
564	Richie Hebner	.10
565	Alex Trevino	.10
566	Brian Harper	.10
567	*Dan Gladden*	.30
568	Luis Salazar	.10
569	Tom Foley	.10
570	Larry Andersen	.10
571	Danny Cox	.10
572	Joe Sambito	.10
573	Juan Beniquez	.10
574	Joel Skinner	.10
575	*Randy St. Claire*	.10
576	Floyd Rayford	.10
577	Roy Howell	.10
578	John Grubb	.10
579	Ed Jurak	.10
580	John Montefusco	.10
581	*Orel Hershiser*	3.50
582	*Tom Waddell*	.10
583	Mark Huismann	.10
584	Joe Morgan	.40
585	Jim Wohlford	.10
586	Dave Schmidt	.10
587	*Jeff Kunkel*	.10
588	Hal McRae	.12
589	Bill Almon	.10
590	Carmen Castillo	.10
591	Omar Moreno	.10
592	*Ken Howell*	.10
593	Tom Brookens	.10
594	Joe Nolan	.10
595	Willie Lozado	.10
596	*Tom Nieto*	.10
597	Walt Terrell	.10
598	Al Oliver	.15
599	Shane Rawley	.10
600	*Denny Gonzalez*	.10
601	*Mark Grant*	.10
602	Mike Armstrong	.10
603	George Foster	.15
604	Davey Lopes	.10
605	Salome Barojas	.10
606	Roy Lee Jackson	.10
607	Pete Filson	.10
608	Duane Walker	.10
609	Glenn Wilson	.10
610	*Rafael Santana*	.10
611	Hoy Smith	.10
612	Ruppert Jones	.10
613	Joe Cowley	.10
614	*Al Nipper* (photo actually Mike Brown)	.15
615	Gene Nelson	.10
616	Joe Carter	4.00
617	Ray Knight	.12
618	Chuck Rainey	.10
619	Dan Driessen	.10
620	Daryl Sconiers	.10
621	Bill Stein	.10
622	Roy Smalley	.10
623	Ed Lynch	.10
624	*Jeff Stone*	.10
625	Bruce Berenyi	.10
626	Kelvin Chapman	.10
627	Joe Price	.10
628	Steve Bedrosian	.12
629	Vic Mata	.10
630	Mike Krukow	.10
631	*Phil Bradley*	.15
632	Jim Gott	.10
633	Randy Bush	.10
634	*Tom Browning*	.60
635	Lou Gehrig Puzzle Card	.10
636	Reid Nichols	.10
637	*Dan Pasqua*	.60
638	German Rivera	.10
639	*Don Schulze*	.10
640a	Mike Jones (last line of highlights begins "Was 11- 7...")	.10

640b	Mike Jones (last line of highlights begins "Spent some ...")	.75
641	Pete Rose	2.00
642	*Wade Rowdon*	.10
643	Jerry Narron	.10
644	*Darrell Miller*	.10
645	*Tim Hulett*	.10
646	Andy McGaffigan	.10
647	Kurt Bevacqua	.10
648	*John Russell*	.10
649	*Ron Robinson*	.10
650	Donnie Moore	.10
651a	Two for the Title (Don Mattingly, Dave Winfield) (yellow letters)	4.00
651b	Two for the Title (Don Mattingly, Dave Winfield) (white letters)	6.00
652	Tim Laudner	.10
653	*Steve Farr*	.15
----	Checklist 1-26 DK	.10
----	Checklist 27-130	.10
----	Checklist 131-234	.10
----	Checklist 235-338	.10
----	Checklist 339-442	.10
----	Checklist 443-546	.10
----	Checklist 547-653	.10

1985 Donruss Box Panels

In 1985, Donruss placed on the bottoms of its wax pack boxes a four-card panel which included three player cards and a Lou Gehrig puzzle card. The player cards, numbered PC1 through PC3, have backs identical to the regular 1985 Donruss issue. The card fronts are identical in design to the regular issue, but carry different photos.

		MT
Complete Panel:		5.00
Complete Singles Set (4):		3.50
Common Player:		.10
PC1	Dwight Gooden	1.00
PC2	Ryne Sandberg	3.00
PC3	Ron Kittle	.10
---	Lou Gehrig (puzzle card)	.10

1985 Donruss Action All-Stars

In 1985, Donruss issued an Action All-Stars set for the third consecutive year. Card fronts feature an action photo with an inset portrait of the player inside a black border with grey boxes through it. The card backs have black print on blue and white and include statistical and biographical information. The cards were issued with a Lou Gehrig puzzle.

		MT
Complete Set (60):		8.00
Common Player:		.15
Lou Gehrig Puzzle:		3.00
1	Tim Raines	.25
2	Jim Gantner	.15
3	Mario Soto	.15
4	Spike Owen	.15
5	Lloyd Moseby	.15
6	Damaso Garcia	.15
7	Cal Ripken, Jr.	3.50
8	Dan Quisenberry	.15
9	Eddie Murray	.75
10	Tony Pena	.15
11	Buddy Bell	.15
12	Dave Winfield	.50
13	Ron Kittle	.15
14	Rich Gossage	.15
15	Dwight Evans	.15
16	Al Davis	.15
17	Mike Schmidt	.90
18	Pascual Perez	.15
19	Tony Gwynn	1.50
20	Nolan Ryan	3.00
21	Robin Yount	.75
22	Mike Marshall	.15
23	Brett Butler	.20
24	Ryne Sandberg	1.00
25	Dale Murphy	.35
26	George Brett	.90
27	Jim Rice	.20
28	Ozzie Smith	.75
29	Larry Parrish	.15
30	Jack Clark	.15
31	Manny Trillo	.15
32	Dave Kingman	.15
33	Geoff Zahn	.15
34	Pedro Guerrero	.15
35	Dave Parker	.15
36	Rollie Fingers	.25
37	Fernando Valenzuela	.20
38	Wade Boggs	.75
39	Reggie Jackson	.50
40	Kent Hrbek	.20
41	Keith Hernandez	.15
42	Lou Whitaker	.15
43	Tom Herr	.15
44	Alan Trammell	.20
45	Butch Wynegar	.15
46	Leon Durham	.15
47	Dwight Gooden	.30
48	Don Mattingly	1.00
49	Phil Niekro	.25
50	Johnny Ray	.15
51	Doug DeCinces	.15
52	Willie Upshaw	.15
53	Lance Parrish	.15
54	Jody Davis	.15
55	Steve Carlton	.40
56	Juan Samuel	.15
57	Gary Carter	.20
58	Harold Baines	.15
59	Eric Show	.15
60	Checklist	.05

1985 Donruss Diamond Kings Supers

The 1985 Donruss Diamond Kings Supers are enlarged versions of the Diamond Kings cards in the regular 1985 Donruss set. The cards measure 4-15/16" x 6-3/4". The Diamond Kings series features the artwork of Dick Perez. Twenty-eight cards make up the Super set - 26 DK cards, an unnumbered checklist, and an unnumbered Dick Perez card. The back of the Perez card contains a brief history of Dick Perez and the Perez-Steele Galleries. The set could be obtained through a mail-in offer found on wax pack wrappers.

		MT
Complete Set (28):		15.00
Common Player:		.50
1	Ryne Sandberg	4.00
2	Doug DeCinces	.50
3	Richard Dotson	.50
4	Bert Blyleven	.50
5	Lou Whitaker	.50
6	Dan Quisenberry	.50
7	Don Mattingly	5.00
8	Carney Lansford	.50
9	Frank Tanana	.50
10	Willie Upshaw	.50
11	Claudell Washington	.50
12	Mike Marshall	.50
13	Joaquin Andujar	.50
14	Cal Ripken, Jr.	8.00
15	Jim Rice	.75
16	Don Sutton	.75
17	Frank Viola	.50
18	Alvin Davis	.50
19	Mario Soto	.50
20	Jose Cruz	.50
21	Charlie Lea	.50
22	Jesse Orosco	.50
23	Juan Samuel	.50
24	Tony Pena	.50
25	Tony Gwynn	5.00
26	Bob Brenly	.50
---	Checklist	.05
---	Dick Perez (DK artist)	.50

1985 Donruss Highlights

Designed in the style of the regular 1985 Donruss set, this issue features the Player of the Month in the major leagues plus highlight cards of special baseball events and milestones of the 1985 season. Fifty-six cards, including an unnumbered checklist, comprise the set which was available only through hobby dealers. The cards measure 2-1/2" x 3-1/2" and have glossy fronts. The last two cards in the set feature Donruss' picks for the A.L. and N.L. Rookies of the Year. The set was issued in a specially designed box.

		MT
Complete Set (56):		7.50
Common Player:		.05
1	Sets Opening Day Record (Tom Seaver)	.20
2	Establishes A.L. Save Mark (Rollie Fingers)	.08
3	A.L. Player of the Month - April (Mike Davis)	.05
4	A.L. Pitcher of the Month - April (Charlie Leibrandt)	.05
5	N.L. Player of the Month - April (Dale Murphy)	.15
6	N.L. Pitcher of the Month - April (Fernando Valenzuela)	.08
7	N.L. Shortstop Record (Larry Bowa)	.05
8	Joins Reds 2000 Hit Club (Dave Concepcion)	.05
9	Eldest Grand Slammer (Tony Perez)	.08
10	N.L. Career Run Leader (Pete Rose)	.60
11	A.L. Player of the Month - May (George Brett)	.45
12	A.L. Pitcher of the Month - May (Dave Stieb)	.05
13	N.L. Player of the Month - May (Dave Parker)	.05
14	N.L. Pitcher of the Month - May (Andy Hawkins)	.05
15	Records 11th Straight Win (Andy Hawkins)	.05
16	Two Homers In First Inning (Von Hayes)	.05
17	A.L. Player of the Month - June (Rickey Henderson)	.30
18	A.L. Pitcher of the Month - June (Jay Howell)	.05
19	N.L. Player of the Month - June (Pedro Guerrero)	.05
20	N.L. Pitcher of the Month - June (John Tudor)	.05
21	Marathon Game Iron Men (Gary Carter, Keith Hernandez)	.05
22	Records 4000th K (Nolan Ryan)	1.00
23	All-Star Game MVP (LaMarr Hoyt)	.05
24	1st Ranger To Hit For Cycle (Oddibe McDowell)	.05
25	A.L. Player of the Month - July (George Brett)	.45
26	A.L. Pitcher of the Month - July (Bret Saberhagen)	.08
27	N.L. Player of the Month - July (Keith Hernandez)	.05
28	N.L. Pitcher of the Month - July (Fernando Valenzuela)	.08
29	Record Setting Base Stealers (Vince Coleman, Willie McGee)	.10
30	Notches 300th Career Win (Tom Seaver)	.20
31	Strokes 3000th Hit (Rod Carew)	.20
32	Establishes Met Record (Dwight Gooden)	.13
33	Achieves Strikeout Milestone (Dwight Gooden)	.13
34	Explodes For 9 RBI (Eddie Murray)	.20
35	A.L. Career Hbp Leader (Don Baylor)	.05
36	A.L. Player of the Month - August (Don Mattingly)	.75
37	A.L. Pitcher of the Month - August (Dave Righetti)	.05
38	N.L. Player of the Month (Willie McGee)	.05
39	N.L. Pitcher of the Month - August (Shane Rawley)	.05
40	Ty-Breaking Hit (Pete Rose)	1.00
41	Hits 3 HRs, Drives In 8 Runs (Andre Dawson)	.05
42	Sets Yankee Theft Mark (Rickey Henderson)	.30
43	20 Wins In Rookie Season (Tom Browning)	.05
44	Yankee Milestone For Hits (Don Mattingly)	.75
45	A.L. Player of the Month - September (Don Mattingly)	.75
46	A.L. Pitcher of the Month - September (Charlie Leibrandt)	.05
47	N.L. Player of the Month - September (Gary Carter)	.05
48	N.L. Pitcher of the Month - September (Dwight Gooden)	.13
49	Major League Record Setter (Wade Boggs)	.60
50	Hurls Shutout For 300th Win (Phil Niekro)	.13
51	Venerable HR King (Darrell Evans)	.05
52	N.L. Switch-hitting Record (Willie McGee)	.05
53	Equals DiMaggio Feat (Dave Winfield)	.15
54	Donruss N.L. Rookie of the Year (Vince Coleman)	.25
55	Donruss A.L. Rookie of the Year (Ozzie Guillen)	.20
----	Checklist	.03

1985 Donruss Sluggers of The Hall of Fame

In much the same manner as the 1959-71 Bazooka cards were issued, this eight-player set consists of cards printed on the bottom panel of a box of bubble gum. When cut off the box, cards measure 3-1/2" x 6-1/2", with blank backs. Players are pictured on the cards in paintings done by Dick Perez.

		MT
Complete Set (8):		12.00
Common Player:		.60
1	Babe Ruth	2.50
2	Ted Williams	1.50
3	Lou Gehrig	2.00
4	Johnny Mize	.60
5	Stan Musial	1.50
6	Mickey Mantle	3.00
7	Hank Aaron	1.50
8	Frank Robinson	.90

1986 Donruss

In 1986, Donruss issued a 660-card set which included 653 numbered cards and seven unnumbered checklists. The 2-1/2" x 3-1/2" cards have fronts that feature blue borders and backs that have black print on blue and white. For the fifth year in a row, the first 26 cards in the set are Diamond Kings. The Rated Rookies subset (#27-46) appears once again. The cards were distributed with a Hank Aaron puzzle. The complete set price does not include the higher priced variations. In the checklist that follows, (DK)

and (RR) refer to the Diamond Kings and Rated Rookies series.

No.	Player	MT
	Complete Set (660):	60.00
	Complete Factory Set (660):	80.00
	Common Player:	.08
	Hank Aaron Puzzle:	5.00
	Wax Box:	120.00
1	Kirk Gibson (DK)	.15
2	Goose Gossage (DK)	.15
3	Willie McGee (DK)	.15
4	George Bell (DK)	.15
5	Tony Armas (DK)	.10
6	Chili Davis (DK)	.10
7	Cecil Cooper (DK)	.12
8	Mike Boddicker (DK)	.10
9	Davey Lopes (DK)	.10
10	Bill Doran (DK)	.10
11	Bret Saberhagen (DK)	.25
12	Brett Butler (DK)	.15
13	Harold Baines (DK)	.25
14	Mike Davis (DK)	.10
15	Tony Perez (DK)	.25
16	Willie Randolph (DK)	.12
17	Bob Boone (DK)	.10
18	Orel Hershiser (DK)	.20
19	Johnny Ray (DK)	.10
20	Gary Ward (DK)	.10
21	Rick Mahler (DK)	.08
22	Phil Bradley (DK)	.10
23	Jerry Koosman (DK)	.12
24	Tom Brunansky (DK)	.15
25	Andre Dawson (DK)	.50
26	Dwight Gooden (DK)	.35
27	*Kal Daniels* (RR)	.10
28	*Fred McGriff* (RR)	6.00
29	*Cory Snyder* (RR)	.20
30	*Jose Guzman* (RR)	.10
31	*Ty Gainey* (RR)	.08
32	*Johnny Abrego* (RR)	.08
33a	*Andres Galarraga* (RR) accent mark over e of Andres on back)	6.00
33b	*Andres Galarraga* (RR) no accent mark)	6.00
34	*Dave Shipanoff* (RR)	.08
35	*Mark McLemore* (RR)	.30
36	*Marty Clary* (RR)	.08
37	*Paul O'Neill* (RR)	5.00
38	Danny Tartabull (RR)	.25
39	*Jose Canseco* (RR)	50.00
40	*Juan Nieves* (RR)	.10
41	*Lance McCullers* (RR)	.20
42	*Rick Surhoff* (RR)	.08
43	*Todd Worrell* (RR)	.40
44	Bob Kipper (RR)	.08
45	*John Habyan* (RR)	.15
46	*Mike Woodard* (RR)	.08
47	Mike Boddicker	.10
48	Robin Yount	1.75
49	Lou Whitaker	.20
50	Dennis Boyd	.08
51	Rickey Henderson	1.00
52	Mike Marshall	.10
53	George Brett	2.00
54	Dave Kingman	.15
55	Hubie Brooks	.10
56	*Oddibe McDowell*	.10
57	Doug DeCinces	.10
58	Britt Burns	.08
59	Ozzie Smith	2.00
60	Jose Cruz	.10
61	Mike Schmidt	2.00
62	Pete Rose	2.00
63	Steve Garvey	.30
64	Tony Pena	.10
65	Chili Davis	.10
66	Dale Murphy	.35
67	Ryne Sandberg	2.00
68	Gary Carter	.35
69	Alvin Davis	.08
70	Kent Hrbek	.20
71	George Bell	.15
72	Kirby Puckett	6.00
73	Lloyd Moseby	.10
74	Bob Kearney	.08
75	Dwight Gooden	.50
76	Gary Matthews	.08
77	Rick Mahler	.08
78	Benny Distefano	.08
79	Jeff Leonard	.08
80	Kevin McReynolds	.20
81	Ron Oester	.08
82	John Russell	.08
83	Tommy Herr	.08
84	Jerry Mumphrey	.08
85	Ron Romanick	.08
86	Daryl Boston	.08
87	Andre Dawson	.75
88	Eddie Murray	1.50
89	Dion James	.08
90	Chet Lemon	.08
91	Bob Stanley	.08
92	Willie Randolph	.10
93	Mike Scioscia	.08
94	Tom Waddell	.08
95	Danny Jackson	.08
96	Mike Davis	.08
97	Mike Fitzgerald	.08
98	Gary Ward	.08
99	Pete O'Brien	.08
100	Bret Saberhagen	.45
101	Alfredo Griffin	.08
102	Brett Butler	.12
103	Ron Guidry	.12
104	Jerry Reuss	.08
105	Jack Morris	.20
106	Rick Dempsey	.08
107	Ray Burris	.08
108	Brian Downing	.08
109	Willie McGee	.15
110	Bill Doran	.10
111	Kent Tekulve	.08
112	Tony Gwynn	3.50
113	Marvell Wynne	.08
114	David Green	.08
115	Jim Gantner	.08
116	George Foster	.15
117	Steve Trout	.08
118	Mark Langston	.30
119	Tony Fernandez	.20
120	John Butcher	.08
121	Ron Robinson	.08
122	Dan Spillner	.08
123	Mike Young	.08
124	Paul Molitor	2.00
125	Kirk Gibson	.20
126	Ken Griffey	.12
127	Tony Armas	.10
128	*Mariano Duncan*	.15
129	Pat Tabler (Mr. Clutch)	.08
130	Frank White	.10
131	Carney Lansford	.08
132	Vance Law	.08
133	Dick Schofield	.08
134	Wayne Tolleson	.08
135	Greg Walker	.08
136	Denny Walling	.08
137	Ozzie Virgil	.08
138	Ricky Horton	.08
139	LaMarr Hoyt	.08
140	Wayne Krenchicki	.08
141	Glenn Hubbard	.08
142	Cecilio Guante	.08
143	Mike Krukow	.08
144	Lee Smith	.12
145	Edwin Nunez	.08
146	Dave Stieb	.12
147	Mike Smithson	.08
148	Ken Dixon	.08
149	Danny Darwin	.08
150	Chris Pittaro	.08
151	Bill Buckner	.12
152	Mike Pagliarulo	.08
153	Bill Russell	.08
154	Brook Jacoby	.08
155	Pat Sheridan	.08
156	*Mike Gallego*	.15
157	Jim Wohlford	.08
158	Gary Pettis	.08
159	Toby Harrah	.08
160	Richard Dotson	.08
161	Bob Knepper	.08
162	Dave Dravecky	.08
163	Greg Gross	.08
164	Eric Davis	.40
165	Gerald Perry	.08
166	Rick Rhoden	.08
167	Keith Moreland	.08
168	Jack Clark	.10
169	Storm Davis	.08
170	Cecil Cooper	.10
171	Alan Trammell	.35
172	Roger Clemens	5.00
173	Don Mattingly	4.00
174	Pedro Guerrero	.20
175	Willie Wilson	.12
176	Dwayne Murphy	.08
177	Tim Raines	.40
178	Larry Parrish	.08
179	Mike Witt	.08
180	Harold Baines	.20
181	*Vince Coleman*	.35
182	*Jeff Heathcock*	.08
183	Steve Carlton	.75
184	Mario Soto	.08
185	Goose Gossage	.20
186	Johnny Ray	.08
187	Dan Gladden	.08
188	Bob Horner	.12
189	Rick Sutcliffe	.12
190	Keith Hernandez	.10
191	Phil Bradley	.10
192	Tom Brunansky	.10
193	Jesse Barfield	.10
194	Frank Viola	.10
195	Willie Upshaw	.08
196	Jim Beattie	.08
197	Darryl Strawberry	.35
198	Ron Cey	.10
199	Steve Bedrosian	.12
200	Steve Kemp	.08
201	Manny Trillo	.08
202	Garry Templeton	.08
203	Dave Parker	.15
204	John Denny	.08
205	Terry Pendleton	.08
206	Terry Puhl	.08
207	Bobby Grich	.08
208	*Ozzie Guillen*	.90
209	Jeff Reardon	.12
210	Cal Ripken, Jr.	6.00
211	Bill Schroeder	.08
212	Dan Petry	.08
213	Jim Rice	.20
214	Dave Righetti	.08
215	Fernando Valenzuela	.20
216	Julio Franco	.10
217	Darryl Motley	.08
218	Dave Collins	.08
219	Tim Wallach	.12
220	George Wright	.08
221	Tommy Dunbar	.08
222	Steve Balboni	.08
223	Jay Howell	.08
224	Joe Carter	.75
225	Ed Whitson	.08
226	Orel Hershiser	.25
227	Willie Hernandez	.08
228	Lee Lacy	.08
229	Rollie Fingers	.35
230	Bob Boone	.10
231	Joaquin Andujar	.08
232	Craig Reynolds	.08
233	Shane Rawley	.08
234	Eric Show	.08
235	Jose DeLeon	.08
236	*Jose Uribe*	.08
237	Moose Haas	.08
238	Wally Backman	.08
239	Dennis Eckersley	.15
240	Mike Moore	.08
241	Damaso Garcia	.08
242	Tim Teufel	.08
243	Dave Concepcion	.12
244	Floyd Bannister	.08
245	Fred Lynn	.20
246	Charlie Moore	.08
247	Walt Terrell	.08
248	Dave Winfield	1.00
249	Dwight Evans	.12
250	*Dennis Powell*	.08
251	Andre Thornton	.10
252	Onix Concepcion	.08
253	Mike Heath	.08
254a	David Palmer (2B on front)	.08
254b	David Palmer (P on front)	.50
255	Donnie Moore	.08
256	Curtis Wilkerson	.08
257	Julio Cruz	.08
258	Nolan Ryan	6.00
259	Jeff Stone	.08
260a	John Tudor (1981 Games is .18)	.10
260b	John Tudor (1981 Games is 18)	.50
261	Mark Thurmond	.08
262	Jay Tibbs	.08
263	Rafael Ramirez	.08
264	Larry McWilliams	.08
265	Mark Davis	.08
266	Bob Dernier	.08
267	Matt Young	.08
268	Jim Clancy	.08
269	Mickey Hatcher	.08
270	Sammy Stewart	.08
271	Bob L. Gibson	.08
272	Nelson Simmons	.08
273	Rich Gedman	.08
274	Butch Wynegar	.08
275	Ken Howell	.08
276	Mel Hall	.08
277	Jim Sundberg	.08
278	Chris Codiroli	.08
279	*Herman Winningham*	.10
280	Rod Carew	1.00
281	Don Slaught	.08
282	Scott Fletcher	.08
283	Bill Dawley	.08
284	Andy Hawkins	.08
285	Glenn Wilson	.08
286	Nick Esasky	.08
287	Claudell Washington	.08
288	Lee Mazzilli	.08
289	Jody Davis	.08
290	Darrell Porter	.08
291	Scott McGregor	.08
292	Ted Simmons	.08
293	Aurelio Lopez	.08
294	Marty Barrett	.08
295	Dale Berra	.08
296	Greg Brock	.08
297	Charlie Leibrandt	.08
298	Bill Krueger	.08
299	Bryn Smith	.08
300	Burt Hooton	.08
301	*Stu Cliburn*	.08
302	Luis Salazar	.08
303	Ken Dayley	.08
304	Frank DiPino	.08
305	Von Hayes	.08
306a	Gary Redus (1983 2B is .20)	.08
306b	Gary Redus (1983 2B is 20)	1.00
307	Craig Lefferts	.08
308	Sam Khalifa	.08
309	Scott Garrelts	.08
310	Rick Cerone	.08
311	Shawon Dunston	.20
312	Howard Johnson	.12
313	Jim Presley	.08
314	Gary Gaetti	.15
315	Luis Leal	.08
316	Mark Salas	.08
317	Bill Caudill	.08
318	Dave Henderson	.08
319	Rafael Santana	.08
320	Leon Durham	.08
321	Bruce Sutter	.12
322	Jason Thompson	.08
323	Bob Brenly	.08
324	Carmelo Martinez	.08
325	Eddie Milner	.08
326	Juan Samuel	.08
327	Tom Nieto	.08
328	Dave Smith	.08
329	*Urbano Lugo*	.08
330	Joel Skinner	.08
331	Bill Gullickson	.08
332	Floyd Rayford	.08
333	Ben Oglivie	.08
334	Lance Parrish	.20
335	Jackie Gutierrez	.08
336	Dennis Rasmussen	.12
337	Terry Whitfield	.08
338	Neal Heaton	.08
339	Jorge Orta	.08
340	Donnie Hill	.08
341	Joe Hesketh	.08
342	Charlie Hough	.10
343	Dave Rozema	.08
344	Greg Pryor	.08
345	Mickey Tettleton	.50
346	George Vukovich	.08
347	Don Baylor	.15
348	Carlos Diaz	.08
349	Barbaro Garbey	.08
350	Larry Sheets	.08
351	*Ted Higuera*	.15
352	Juan Beniquez	.08
353	Bob Forsch	.08
354	Mark Bailey	.08
355	Larry Andersen	.08
356	Terry Kennedy	.08
357	Don Robinson	.08
358	Jim Gott	.08
359	*Earnest Riles*	.08
360	*John Christensen*	.08
361	Ray Fontenot	.08
362	Spike Owen	.08
363	Jim Acker	.08
364a	Ron Davis (last line in highlights ends with "...in May.")	.08
364b	Ron Davis (last line in highlights ends with "...relievers (9).")	.50
365	Tom Hume	.08
366	Carlton Fisk	.60
367	Nate Snell	.08
368	Rick Manning	.08
369	Darrell Evans	.15
370	Ron Hassey	.08
371	Wade Boggs	1.50
372	Rick Honeycutt	.08
373	Chris Bando	.08
374	Bud Black	.08
375	Steve Henderson	.08
376	Charlie Lea	.08
377	Reggie Jackson	1.25
378	Dave Schmidt	.08
379	Bob James	.08
380	Glenn Davis	.15
381	Tim Corcoran	.08
382	Danny Cox	.08
383	Tim Flannery	.08
384	Tom Browning	.08
385	Rick Camp	.08
386	Jim Morrison	.08
387	Dave LaPoint	.08
388	Davey Lopes	.08
389	Al Cowens	.08
390	Doyle Alexander	.08
391	Tim Laudner	.08
392	Don Aase	.08
393	Jaime Cocanower	.08
394	Randy O'Neal	.08
395	Mike Easler	.08
396	Scott Bradley	.08
397	Tom Niedenfuer	.08
398	Jerry Willard	.08
399	Lonnie Smith	.08
400	Bruce Bochte	.08
401	Terry Francona	.08
402	Jim Slaton	.08
403	Bill Stein	.08
404	Tim Hulett	.08
405	Alan Ashby	.08
406	Tim Stoddard	.08
407	Garry Maddox	.08
408	Ted Power	.08
409	Len Barker	.08
410	Denny Gonzalez	.08
411	George Frazier	.08
412	Andy Van Slyke	.15
413	Jim Dwyer	.08
414	Paul Householder	.08
415	Alejandro Sanchez	.08
416	Steve Crawford	.08
417	Dan Pasqua	.08
418	Enos Cabell	.08
419	Mike Jones	.08
420	Steve Kiefer	.08
421	*Tim Burke*	.10
422	Mike Mason	.08
423	Ruppert Jones	.08
424	Jerry Hairston	.08
425	Tito Landrum	.08
426	Jeff Calhoun	.08
427	*Don Carman*	.08
428	Tony Perez	.20
429	Jerry Davis	.08
430	Bob Walk	.08
431	Brad Wellman	.08
432	Terry Forster	.08
433	Billy Hatcher	.08
434	Clint Hurdle	.08
435	*Ivan Calderon*	.15
436	Pete Filson	.08
437	Tom Henke	.08
438	Dave Engle	.08
439	Tom Filer	.08
440	Gorman Thomas	.08
441	*Rick Aguilera*	.50
442	Scott Sanderson	.08
443	Jeff Dedmon	.08
444	*Joe Orsulak*	.15
445	Atlee Hammaker	.08
446	Jerry Royster	.08
447	Buddy Bell	.10
448	Dave Rucker	.08
449	Ivan DeJesus	.08
450	Jim Pankovits	.08
451	Jerry Narron	.08
452	Bryan Little	.08
453	Gary Lucas	.08
454	Dennis Martinez	.12
455	Ed Romero	.08
456	*Bob Melvin*	.08
457	Glenn Hoffman	.08
458	Bob Shirley	.08
459	Bob Welch	.10
460	Carmen Castillo	.08
461	Dave Leeper	.08
462	*Tim Birtsas*	.08
463	Randy St. Claire	.08
464	Chris Welsh	.08
465	Greg Harris	.08
466	Lynn Jones	.08
467	Dusty Baker	.12
468	Roy Smith	.08
469	Andre Robertson	.08
470	Ken Landreaux	.08
471	Dave Bergman	.08
472	Gary Roenicke	.08
473	Pete Vuckovich	.08
474	*Kirk McCaskill*	.40
475	Jeff Lahti	.08
476	Mike Scott	.10
477	*Darren Daulton*	2.00
478	Graig Nettles	.15
479	Bill Almon	.08
480	Greg Minton	.08
481	Randy Ready	.08
482	*Len Dykstra*	2.00
483	Thad Bosley	.08
484	*Harold Reynolds*	.40
485	Al Oliver	.12
486	Roy Smalley	.08
487	John Franco	.10
488	Juan Agosto	.08
489	Al Pardo	.08
490	*Bill Wegman*	.15
491	Frank Tanana	.08
492	*Brian Fisher*	.08
493	Mark Clear	.08
494	Len Matuszek	.08
495	Ramon Romero	.08
496	John Wathan	.08
497	Rob Picciolo	.08
498	U.L. Washington	.08
499	John Candelaria	.08
500	Duane Walker	.08
501	Gene Nelson	.08
502	John Mizerock	.08
503	Luis Aguayo	.08
504	Kurt Kepshire	.08
505	Ed Wojna	.08
506	Joe Price	.08
507	*Milt Thompson*	.20
508	Junior Ortiz	.08
509	Vida Blue	.10
510	Steve Engel	.08
511	Karl Best	.08
512	*Cecil Fielder*	3.00
513	Frank Eufemia	.08
514	Tippy Martinez	.08
515	*Billy Robidoux*	.08
516	Bill Scherrer	.08
517	Bruce Hurst	.08
518	Rich Bordi	.08
519	Steve Yeager	.08
520	Tony Bernazard	.08
521	Hal McRae	.10
522	Jose Rijo	.08
523	*Mitch Webster*	.08
524	*Jack Howell*	.08
525	Alan Bannister	.08
526	Ron Kittle	.08
527	Phil Garner	.10
528	Kurt Bevacqua	.08
529	Kevin Gross	.08
530	Bo Diaz	.08
531	Ken Oberkfell	.08
532	Rick Reuschel	.08
533	Ron Meridith	.08
534	Steve Braun	.08
535	Wayne Gross	.08
536	Ray Searage	.08
537	Tom Brookens	.08
538	Al Nipper	.08
539	Billy Sample	.08
540	Steve Sax	.12
541	Dan Quisenberry	.10
542	Tony Phillips	.12
543	*Floyd Youmans*	.08
544	*Steve Buechele*	.35
545	Craig Gerber	.08
546	Joe DeSa	.08
547	Brian Harper	.08
548	Kevin Bass	.08
549	Tom Foley	.08
550	Dave Van Gorder	.08
551	Bruce Bochy	.08
552	R.J. Reynolds	.08
553	*Chris Brown*	.12
554	Bruce Benedict	.08
555	Warren Brusstar	.08
556	Danny Heep	.08
557	Darnell Coles	.08
558	Greg Gagne	.08
559	Ernie Whitt	.08

560	Ron Washington	.08
561	Jimmy Key	.15
562	Billy Swift	.08
563	Ron Darling	.08
564	Dick Ruthven	.08
565	Zane Smith	.10
566	Sid Bream	.10
567a	Joel Youngblood (P on front)	.08
567b	Joel Youngblood (IF on front)	.50
568	Mario Ramirez	.08
569	Tom Runnells	.08
570	Rick Schu	.08
571	Bill Campbell	.08
572	Dickie Thon	.08
573	Al Holland	.08
574	Reid Nichols	.08
575	Bert Roberge	.08
576	Mike Flanagan	.08
577	Tim Leary	.10
578	Mike Laga	.08
579	Steve Lyons	.10
580	Phil Niekro	.45
581	Gilberto Reyes	.08
582	Jamie Easterly	.08
583	Mark Gubicza	.12
584	*Stan Javier*	.10
585	Bill Laskey	.08
586	Jeff Russell	.08
587	Dickie Noles	.08
588	Steve Farr	.08
589	*Steve Ontiveros*	.10
590	Mike Hargrove	.10
591	Marty Bystrom	.08
592	Franklin Stubbs	.08
593	Larry Herndon	.08
594	Bill Swaggerty	.08
595	Carlos Ponce	.08
596	*Pat Perry*	.08
597	Ray Knight	.08
598	*Steve Lombardozzi*	.10
599	Brad Havens	.08
600	*Pat Clements*	.08
601	Joe Niekro	.12
602	Hank Aaron Puzzle Card	.08
603	*Dwayne Henry*	.08
604	Mookie Wilson	.10
605	Buddy Biancalana	.08
606	Rance Mulliniks	.08
607	Alan Wiggins	.08
608	Joe Cowley	.08
609a	Tom Seaver (green stripes around name)	1.00
609b	Tom Seaver (yellow stripes around name)	3.00
610	Neil Allen	.08
611	Don Sutton	.35
612	*Fred Toliver*	.08
613	Jay Baller	.08
614	Marc Sullivan	.08
615	John Grubb	.08
616	Bruce Kison	.08
617	Bill Madlock	.12
618	Chris Chambliss	.08
619	Dave Stewart	.15
620	Tim Lollar	.08
621	Gary Lavelle	.08
622	Charles Hudson	.08
623	*Joel Davis*	.08
624	*Joe Johnson*	.08
625	Sid Fernandez	.12
626	Dennis Lamp	.08
627	Terry Harper	.08
628	Jack Lazorko	.08
629	*Roger McDowell*	.25
630	Mark Funderburk	.08
631	Ed Lynch	.08
632	Rudy Law	.08
633	*Roger Mason*	.08
634	*Mike Felder*	.08
635	Ken Schrom	.08
636	Bob Ojeda	.08
637	Ed Vande Berg	.08
638	Bobby Meacham	.08
639	Cliff Johnson	.08
640	Garth Iorg	.08
641	Dan Driessen	.08
642	Mike Brown	.08
643	John Shelby	.08
644	Pete Rose (RB)	.50
645	Knuckle Brothers (Joe Niekro, Phil Niekro)	.25
646	Jesse Orosco	.08
647	*Billy Beane*	.08
648	Cesar Cedeno	.10
649	Bert Blyleven	.15
650	Max Venable	.08
651	Fleet Feet (Vince Coleman, Willie McGee)	.35
652	Calvin Schiraldi	.08
653	King of Kings (Pete Rose)	2.50
----	Checklist 1-26 DK	.08
----	Checklist 27-130 (45 is Beane)	.08
----	Checklist 27-130 (45 is Habyan)	.30
----	Checklist 131-234	.08
----	Checklist 235-338	.08
----	Checklist 339-442	.08
----	Checklist 443-546	.08
----	Checklist 547-653	.08

1986 Donruss Box Panels

For the second year in a row, Donruss placed baseball cards on the bottom of its wax and cello pack boxes. The cards, printed four to a panel, are standard 2-1/2" x 3-1/2". With numbering that begins where Donruss left off in 1985, cards PC4 through PC6 were found on boxes of regular Donruss issue wax packs. Cards PC7 through PC9 were found on boxes of the 1986 All- Star/Pop-up packs. An unnumbered Hank Aaron puzzle card was included on each box.

		MT
Complete Panel Set (2):		3.00
Complete Singles Set (8):		2.00
Common Single Player:		.15
Panel		1.00
PC4	Kirk Gibson	.25
PC5	Willie Hernandez	.15
PC6	Doug DeCinces	.15
---	Aaron Puzzle Card	.04
Panel		2.00
PC7	Wade Boggs	.75
PC8	Lee Smith	.25
PC9	Cecil Cooper	.15
---	Aaron Puzzle Card	.04

1986 Donruss All-Stars

Issued in conjunction with the 1986 Donruss Pop-Ups set, the All-Stars consist of 60 cards in 3-1/2" x 5" format. Fifty-nine players involved in the 1985 All-Star game plus an unnumbered checklist comprise the set. Card fronts have the same blue border found on the regular 1986 Donruss issue. Retail packs included one Pop-up card, three All-Star cards and one Hank Aaron puzzle-piece card.

		MT
Complete Set (60):		8.00
Common Player:		.10
Hank Aaron puzzle:		5.00
1	Tony Gwynn	1.00
2	Tommy Herr	.10
3	Steve Garvey	.30
4	Dale Murphy	.30
5	Darryl Strawberry	.30
6	Graig Nettles	.10
7	Terry Kennedy	.10
8	Ozzie Smith	.75
9	LaMarr Hoyt	.10
10	Rickey Henderson	.50
11	Lou Whitaker	.10
12	George Brett	.75
13	Eddie Murray	.50
14	Cal Ripken, Jr.	2.50
15	Dave Winfield	.50
16	Jim Rice	.15
17	Carlton Fisk	.35
18	Jack Morris	.10
19	Jose Cruz	.10
20	Tim Raines	.15
21	Nolan Ryan	2.00
22	Tony Pena	.10
23	Jack Clark	.10
24	Dave Parker	.10
25	Tim Wallach	.10
26	Ozzie Virgil	.10
27	Fernando Valenzuela	.15
28	Dwight Gooden	.20
29	Glenn Wilson	.10
30	Garry Templeton	.10
31	Goose Gossage	.10
32	Ryne Sandberg	.75
33	Jeff Reardon	.10
34	Pete Rose	1.50
35	Scott Garrelts	.10
36	Willie McGee	.10
37	Ron Darling	.10
38	Dick Williams	.10
39	Paul Molitor	.50
40	Damaso Garcia	.10
41	Phil Bradley	.10
42	Dan Petry	.10
43	Willie Hernandez	.10
44	Tom Brunansky	.10
45	Alan Trammell	.20
46	Donnie Moore	.10
47	Wade Boggs	.60
48	Ernie Whitt	.10
49	Harold Baines	.10
50	Don Mattingly	1.00
51	Gary Ward	.10
52	Bert Blyleven	.10
53	Jimmy Key	.10
54	Cecil Cooper	.10
55	Dave Stieb	.10
56	Rich Gedman	.10
57	Jay Howell	.10
58	Sparky Anderson	.10
59	Minneapolis Metrodome	.10
---	Checklist	.05

1986 Donruss Diamond Kings Supers

Donruss produced a set of large-format Diamond Kings in 1986 for the second year in a row. The 4-11/16" x 6-3/4" cards are enlarged versions of the 26 Diamond Kings cards found in the regular 1986 Donruss set, plus an unnumbered checklist and an unnumbered Pete Rose "King of Kings" card.

		MT
Complete Set (28):		12.00
Common Player:		.50
1	Kirk Gibson	.75
2	Goose Gossage	.60
3	Willie McGee	.75
4	George Bell	.50
5	Tony Armas	.50
6	Chili Davis	.60
7	Cecil Cooper	.50
8	Mike Boddicker	.50
9	Davey Lopes	.50
10	Bill Doran	.50
11	Bret Saberhagen	.75
12	Brett Butler	.75
13	Harold Baines	.60
14	Mike Davis	.50
15	Tony Perez	.75
16	Willie Randolph	.50
18	Orel Hershiser	.75
19	Johnny Ray	.50
20	Gary Ward	.50
21	Rick Mahler	.50
22	Phil Bradley	.50
23	Jerry Koosman	.50
24	Tom Brunansky	.50
25	Andre Dawson	.75
26	Dwight Gooden	.75
---	Checklist	.05
---	King of Kings (Pete Rose)	1.50

1986 Donruss Highlights

Donruss, for the second year in a row, issued a 56-card highlights set featuring cards of each league's Player of the Month plus significant events of the 1986 season. The cards, 2-1/2" x 3-1/2," are similar in design to the regular 1986 Donruss set but have a gold border instead of blue. A "Highlights" logo appears in the lower-left corner of each card front. Backs are designed on a vertical format and feature black print on a yellow background. As in 1985, the set includes Donruss' picks for the Rookies of the Year. A new feature was three cards honoring the 1986 Hall of Fame inductees. The set, available only through hobby dealers, was issued in a specially designed box.

		MT
Complete Set (56):		4.50
Common Player:		.08
1	Homers In First At-Bat (Will Clark)	.75
2	Oakland Milestone For Strikeouts (Jose Rijo)	.08
3	Royals' All-Time Hit Man (George Brett)	.35
4	Phillies RBI Leader (Mike Schmidt)	.35
5	KKKKKKKKKKKK KKKKKKKK (Roger Clemens)	.75
6	A.L. Pitcher of the Month-April (Roger Clemens)	.25
7	A.L. Player of the Month-April (Kirby Puckett)	.45
8	N.L. Pitcher of the Month-April (Dwight Gooden)	.15
9	N.L. Player of the Month-April (Johnny Ray)	.08
10	Eclipses Mantle HR Record (Reggie Jackson)	.20
11	First Five Hit Game of Career (Wade Boggs)	.20
12	A.L. Pitcher of the Month-May (Don Aase)	.08
13	A.L. Player of the Month-May (Wade Boggs)	.20
14	N.L. Pitcher of the Month-May (Jeff Reardon)	.08
15	N.L. Player of the Month-May (Hubie Brooks)	.08
16	Notches 300th Career Win (Don Sutton)	.10
17	Starts Season 14-0 (Roger Clemens)	.20
18	A.L. Pitcher of the Month-June (Roger Clemens)	.20
19	A.L. Player of the Month-June (Kent Hrbek)	.08
20	N.L. Pitcher of the Month-June (Rick Rhoden)	.08
21	N.L. Player of the Month-June (Kevin Bass)	.08
22	Blasts 4 HRS in 1 Game (Bob Horner)	.10
23	Starting All Star Rookie (Wally Joyner)	.08
24	Starts 3rd Straight All Star Game (Darryl Strawberry)	.10
25	Ties All Star Game Record (Fernando Valenzuela)	.08
26	All Star Game MVP (Roger Clemens)	.20
27	A.L. Pitcher of the Month-July (Jack Morris)	.08
28	A.L. Player of the Month-July (Scott Fletcher)	.08
29	N.L. Pitcher of the Month-July (Todd Worrell)	.08
30	N.L. PLayer of the Month-July (Eric Davis)	.08
31	Records 3000th Strikeout (Bert Blyleven)	.08
32	1986 Hall of Fame Inductee (Bobby Doerr)	.08
33	1986 Hall of Fame Inductee (Ernie Lombardi)	.08
34	1986 Hall of Fame Inductee (Willie McCovey)	.20
35	Notches 4000th K (Steve Carlton)	.20
36	Surpasses DiMaggio Record (Mike Schmidt)	.35
37	Records 3rd "Quadruple Double" (Juan Samuel)	.08
38	A.L. Pitcher of the Month-August (Mike Witt)	.08
39	A.L. Player of the Month-August (Doug DeCinces)	.08
40	N.L. Pitcher of the Month-August (Bill Gullickson)	.08
41	N.L. Player of the Month-August (Dale Murphy)	.10
42	Sets Tribe Offensive Record (Joe Carter)	.08
43	Longest HR In Royals Stadium (Bo Jackson)	.25
44	Majors 1st No-Hitter In 2 Years (Joe Cowley)	.08
45	Sets M.L. Strikeout Record (Jim Deshaies)	.08
46	No Hitter Clinches Division (Mike Scott)	.08
47	A.L. Pitcher of the Month-September (Bruce Hurst)	.08
48	A.L. Player of the Month-September (Don Mattingly)	.40
49	N.L. Pitcher of the Month-September (Mike Krukow)	.08
50	N.L. Player of the Month-September (Steve Sax)	.08
51	A.L. Record For Steals By A Rookie (John Cangelosi)	.08
52	Shatters M.L. Save Mark (Dave Righetti)	.08
53	Yankee Record For Hits & Doubles (Don Mattingly)	.40
54	Donruss N.L. Rookie of the Year (Todd Worrell)	.08
55	Donruss A.L. Rookie of the Year (Jose Canseco)	1.00
56	Highlight Checklist	.04

1986 Donruss Pop-Ups

Issued in conjunction with the 1986 Donruss All-Stars set, the Pop-Ups (18 unnumbered cards) feature the 1985 All-Star Game starting line-ups. The cards, 2-1/2" x 5", are die-cut and fold out to form a three-dimensional stand-up card. The background for the cards is the Minneapolis Metrodome, site of the 1985 All-Star Game. Retail packs included one Pop-Up card, three All-Star cards and one Hank Aaron puzzle card.

		MT
Complete Set (18):		3.00
Common Player:		.10
Hank Aaron Puzzle:		5.00
(1)	George Brett	.50
(2)	Carlton Fisk	.30
(3)	Steve Garvey	.20
(4)	Tony Gwynn	.75
(5)	Rickey Henderson	.40
(6)	Tommy Herr	.10
(7)	LaMarr Hoyt	.10
(8)	Terry Kennedy	.10
(9)	Jack Morris	.10
(10)	Dale Murphy	.20
(11)	Eddie Murray	.40
(12)	Graig Nettles	.10
(13)	Jim Rice	.10
(14)	Cal Ripken, Jr.	.90
(15)	Ozzie Smith	.40
(16)	Darryl Strawberry	.30
(17)	Lou Whitaker	.10
(18)	Dave Winfield	.30

1986 Donruss Rookies

Entitled "The Rookies," this 56-card set includes the top 55 rookies of 1986 plus an unnumbered checklist. The cards are similar in format to the 1986 Donruss regular issue, except that the borders are green rather than blue. Several of the rookies who had cards in the regular 1986 Donruss set appear again in "The Rookies" set. The sets, which were only available through hobby dealers, came in a specially designed box.

		MT
Complete Unopened Set (56):		27.50
Complete Opened Set (56):		20.00
Common Player:		.10
1	*Wally Joyner*	.75
2	Tracy Jones	.10
3	Allan Anderson	.10
4	Ed Correa	.10
5	Reggie Williams	.10
6	Charlie Kerfeld	.10
7	Andres Galarraga	2.50
8	Bob Tewksbury	.60
9	Al Newman	.10
10	Andres Thomas	.10
11	*Barry Bonds*	10.00
12	Juan Nieves	.10
13	Mark Eichhorn	.10
14	Dan Plesac	.15
15	Cory Snyder	.10
16	Kelly Gruber	.10
17	*Kevin Mitchell*	.30
18	Steve Lombardozzi	.10
19	Mitch Williams	.15
20	John Cerutti	.10
21	Todd Worrell	.15
22	Jose Canseco	8.00
23	*Pete Incaviglia*	.30
24	Jose Guzman	.10
25	Scott Bailes	.10
26	Greg Mathews	.10
27	Eric King	.10
28	Paul Assenmacher	.10
29	Jeff Sellers	.10
30	*Bobby Bonilla*	.90
31	*Doug Drabek*	.75
32	*Will Clark*	4.00
33	Bip Roberts	.15
34	Jim Deshaies	.10
35	Mike LaValliere	.10
36	Scott Bankhead	.10
37	Dale Sveum	.10
38	*Bo Jackson*	1.50
39	Rob Thompson	.15
40	Eric Plunk	.10
41	Bill Bathe	.10
42	*John Kruk*	.45
43	Andy Allanson	.10
44	Mark Portugal	.10
45	Danny Tartabull	.25
46	Bob Kipper	.10
47	Gene Walter	.10
48	Rey Quinonez	.10
49	Bobby Witt	.25
50	Bill Mooneyham	.10
51	John Cangelosi	.10
52	*Ruben Sierra*	.35
53	Rob Woodward	.10
54	Ed Hearn	.10
55	Joel McKeon	.10
56	Checklist 1-56	.05

1987 Donruss

The 1987 Donruss set consists of 660 numbered cards, each measuring 2-1/2" x 3-1/2". Color photos are surrounded by a bold black border separated by two narrow bands of yellow which enclose a brown area filled with baseballs. The player's name, team and team logo appear on the card fronts along with the words "Donruss '87". The card backs are designed on a horizontal format and contain black print on a yellow and white background. The backs are very similar to those in previous years' sets. Backs of cards issued in wax and rack packs face to the left when turned over, while those issued in factory sets face to the right. Cards were sold with Roberto Clemente puzzle pieces in each pack. Cards checklisted with a (DK) suffix are Diamond Kings; cards with an (RR) suffix are Rated Rookies.

		MT
Complete Set (660):		60.00
Common Player:		.05
Roberto Clemente Puzzle:		9.00
Wax Box:		55.00
1	Wally Joyner (DK)	.25
2	Roger Clemens (DK)	1.00
3	Dale Murphy (DK)	.15
4	Darryl Strawberry (DK)	.15
5	Ozzie Smith (DK)	.45
6	Jose Canseco (DK)	.65
7	Charlie Hough (DK)	.08
8	Brook Jacoby (DK)	.10
9	Fred Lynn (DK)	.12
10	Rick Rhoden (DK)	.10
11	Chris Brown (DK)	.10
12	Von Hayes (DK)	.10
13	Jack Morris (DK)	.10
14a	Kevin McReynolds (DK) (no yellow stripe on back)	.75
14b	Kevin McReynolds (DK) (yellow stripe on back)	.20
15	George Brett (DK)	.75
16	Ted Higuera (DK)	.05
17	Hubie Brooks (DK)	.10
18	Mike Scott (DK)	.08
19	Kirby Puckett (DK)	.75
20	Dave Winfield (DK)	.45
21	Lloyd Moseby (DK)	.10
22a	Eric Davis (DK) (no yellow stripe on back)	1.00
22b	Eric Davis (DK) (yellow stripe on back)	.15
23	Jim Presley (DK)	.08
24	Keith Moreland (DK)	.08
25a	Greg Walker (DK) (no yellow stripe on back)	.50
25b	Greg Walker (DK) (yellow stripe on back)	.10
26	Steve Sax (DK)	.12
27	Checklist 1-27	.05
28	*B.J. Surhoff* (RR)	.30
29	*Randy Myers* (RR)	.65
30	*Ken Gerhart* (RR)	.08
31	Benito Santiago (RR)	.40
32	*Greg Swindell* (RR)	.15
33	*Mike Birkbeck* (RR)	.10
34	*Terry Steinbach* (RR)	.50
35	Bo Jackson (RR)	2.00
36	*Greg Maddux* (RR)	25.00
37	*Jim Lindeman* (RR)	.05
38	*Devon White* (RR)	.75
39	*Eric Bell* (RR)	.08
40	*Will Fraser* (RR)	.10
41	*Jerry Browne* (RR)	.15
42	*Chris James* (RR)	.10
43	*Rafael Palmeiro* (RR)	8.00
44	*Pat Dodson* (RR)	.05
45	*Duane Ward* (RR)	.25
46	Mark McGwire (RR)	25.00
47	*Bruce Fields* (RR) (Photo actually Darnell Coles)	.10
48	Eddie Murray	.60
49	Ted Higuera	.05
50	Kirk Gibson	.10
51	Oil Can Boyd	.05
52	Don Mattingly	1.00
53	Pedro Guerrero	.10
54	George Brett	1.00
55	Jose Rijo	.05
56	Tim Raines	.30
57	*Ed Correa*	.05
58	Mike Witt	.05
59	Greg Walker	.05
60	Ozzie Smith	.60
61	Glenn Davis	.05
62	Glenn Wilson	.05
63	Tom Browning	.05
64	Tony Gwynn	1.00
65	R.J. Reynolds	.05
66	Will Clark	2.50
67	Ozzie Virgil	.05
68	Rick Sutcliffe	.12
69	Gary Carter	.12
70	Mike Moore	.05
71	Bert Blyleven	.12
72	Tony Fernandez	.15
73	Kent Hrbek	.10
74	Lloyd Moseby	.08
75	Alvin Davis	.05
76	Keith Hernandez	.15
77	Ryne Sandberg	.90
78	Dale Murphy	.30
79	Sid Bream	.05
80	Chris Brown	.05
81	Steve Garvey	.25
82	Mario Soto	.05
83	Shane Rawley	.05
84	Willie McGee	.12
85	Jose Cruz	.08
86	Brian Downing	.08
87	Ozzie Guillen	.05
88	Hubie Brooks	.05
89	Cal Ripken, Jr.	2.50
90	Juan Nieves	.05
91	Lance Parrish	.08
92	Jim Rice	.12
93	Ron Guidry	.15
94	Fernando Valenzuela	.08
95	*Andy Allanson*	.05
96	Willie Wilson	.12
97	Jose Canseco	2.00
98	Jeff Reardon	.10
99	*Bobby Witt*	.20
100	Checklist 28-133	.05
101	Jose Guzman	.05
102	Steve Balboni	.05
103	Tony Phillips	.05
104	Brook Jacoby	.05
105	Dave Winfield	.30
106	Orel Hershiser	.15
107	Lou Whitaker	.10
108	Fred Lynn	.10
109	Bill Wegman	.05
110	Donnie Moore	.05
111	Jack Clark	.10
112	Bob Knepper	.05
113	Von Hayes	.05
114	*Bip Roberts*	.40
115	Tony Pena	.08
116	Scott Garrelts	.05
117	Paul Molitor	.75
118	Darryl Strawberry	.25
119	Shawon Dunston	.05
120	Jim Presley	.05
121	Jesse Barfield	.05
122	Gary Gaetti	.10
123	*Kurt Stillwell*	.10
124	Joel Davis	.05
125	Mike Boddicker	.05
126	Robin Yount	.75
127	Alan Trammell	.25
128	Dave Righetti	.08
129	Dwight Evans	.12
130	Mike Scioscia	.05
131	Julio Franco	.05
132	Bret Saberhagen	.12
133	Mike Davis	.05
134	Joe Hesketh	.05
135	Wally Joyner	.25
136	Don Slaught	.05
137	Daryl Boston	.05
138	Nolan Ryan	2.50
139	Mike Schmidt	1.00
140	Tommy Herr	.10
141	Garry Templeton	.05
142	Kal Daniels	.05
143	Billy Sample	.05
144	Johnny Ray	.05
145	*Rob Thompson*	.25
146	Bob Dernier	.05
147	Danny Tartabull	.05
148	Ernie Whitt	.05
149	Kirby Puckett	1.00
150	Mike Young	.05
151	Ernest Riles	.05
152	Frank Tanana	.05
153	Rich Gedman	.05
154	Willie Randolph	.10
155a	Bill Madlock (name in brown band)	.12
155b	Bill Madlock (name in red band)	.50
156a	Joe Carter (name in brown band)	.10
156b	Joe Carter (name in red band)	.40
157	Danny Jackson	.05
158	Carney Lansford	.05
159	Bryn Smith	.05
160	Gary Pettis	.05
161	Oddibe McDowell	.05
162	*John Cangelosi*	.12
163	Mike Scott	.10
164	Eric Show	.05
165	Juan Samuel	.05
166	Nick Esasky	.05
167	Zane Smith	.05
168	Mike Brown	.05
169	Keith Moreland	.05
170	John Tudor	.05
171	Ken Dixon	.05
172	Jim Gantner	.05
173	Jack Morris	.15
174	Bruce Hurst	.05
175	Dennis Rasmussen	.05
176	Mike Marshall	.05
177	Dan Quisenberry	.08
178	Eric Plunk	.08
179	Tim Wallach	.10
180	Steve Buechele	.05
181	Don Sutton	.40
182	Dave Schmidt	.05
183	Terry Pendleton	.08
184	*Jim Deshaies*	.15
185	Steve Bedrosian	.12
186	Pete Rose	1.25
187	Dave Dravecky	.08
188	Rick Reuschel	.05
189	Dan Gladden	.05
190	Rick Mahler	.05
191	Thad Bosley	.05
192	Ron Darling	.10
193	Matt Young	.05
194	Tom Brunansky	.10
195	Dave Stieb	.12
196	Frank Viola	.10
197	Tom Henke	.08
198	Karl Best	.05
199	Dwight Gooden	.25
200	Checklist 134-239	.05
201	Steve Trout	.05
202	Rafael Ramirez	.05
203	Bob Walk	.05
204	Roger Mason	.05
205	Terry Kennedy	.05
206	Ron Oester	.05
207	John Russell	.05
208	*Greg Mathews*	.05
209	Charlie Kerfeld	.05
210	Reggie Jackson	.35
211	Floyd Bannister	.05
212	Vance Law	.05
213	Rich Bordi	.05
214	*Dan Plesac*	.10
215	Dave Collins	.05
216	Bob Stanley	.05
217	Joe Niekro	.10
218	Tom Niedenfuer	.05
219	Brett Butler	.12
220	Charlie Leibrandt	.05
221	Steve Ontiveros	.05
222	Tim Burke	.05
223	Curtis Wilkerson	.05
224	*Pete Incaviglia*	.25
225	Lonnie Smith	.05
226	Chris Codiroli	.05
227	*Scott Bailes*	.05
228	Rickey Henderson	.65
229	Ken Howell	.05
230	Darnell Coles	.05
231	Don Aase	.05
232	Tim Leary	.05
233	Bob Boone	.08
234	Ricky Horton	.05
235	Mark Bailey	.05
236	Kevin Gross	.05
237	Lance McCullers	.05
238	Cecilio Guante	.05
239	Bob Melvin	.05
240	Billy Jo Robidoux	.05
241	Roger McDowell	.12
242	Leon Durham	.05
243	Ed Nunez	.05
244	Jimmy Key	.12
245	Mike Smithson	.05
246	Bo Diaz	.05
247	Carlton Fisk	.30
248	Larry Sheets	.05
249	*Juan Castillo*	.05
250	*Eric King*	.05
251	Doug Drabek	.10
252	Wade Boggs	1.00
253	Mariano Duncan	.05
254	Pat Tabler	.05
255	Frank White	.10
256	Alfredo Griffin	.05
257	Floyd Youmans	.05
258	Rob Wilfong	.05
259	Pete O'Brien	.05
260	Tim Hulett	.05
261	Dickie Thon	.05
262	Darren Daulton	.10
263	Vince Coleman	.10
264	Andy Hawkins	.05
265	Eric Davis	.20
266	*Andres Thomas*	.05
267	*Mike Diaz*	.05
268	Chili Davis	.08
269	Jody Davis	.05
270	Phil Bradley	.05
271	George Bell	.08
272	Keith Atherton	.05
273	Storm Davis	.10
274	Rob Deer	.10
275	Walt Terrell	.05
276	Roger Clemens	1.00
277	Mike Easler	.05
278	Steve Sax	.10
279	Andre Thornton	.05
280	Jim Sundberg	.05
281	Bill Bathe	.05
282	Jay Tibbs	.05
283	Dick Schofield	.05
284	Mike Mason	.05
285	Jerry Hairston	.05
286	Bill Doran	.05
287	Tim Flannery	.05
288	Gary Redus	.05
289	John Franco	.10
290	*Paul Assenmacher*	.15
291	Joe Orsulak	.05
292	Lee Smith	.20
293	Mike Laga	.05
294	Rick Dempsey	.05
295	Mike Felder	.05
296	Tom Brookens	.05
297	Al Nipper	.05
298	Mike Pagliarulo	.10
299	Franklin Stubbs	.05
300	Checklist 240-345	.05
301	Steve Farr	.05
302	*Bill Mooneyham*	.05
303	Andres Galarraga	.50
304	Scott Fletcher	.05
305	Jack Howell	.05
306	*Russ Morman*	.10
307	Todd Worrell	.10
308	Dave Smith	.05
309	Jeff Stone	.05
310	Ron Robinson	.05
311	Bruce Bochy	.05
312	Jim Winn	.05
313	Mark Davis	.05
314	Jeff Dedmon	.05
315	*Jamie Moyer*	.08
316	Wally Backman	.05
317	Ken Phelps	.05
318	Steve Lombardozzi	.05
319	Rance Mulliniks	.05
320	Tim Laudner	.05
321	*Mark Eichhorn*	.08
322	*Lee Guetterman*	.05
323	Sid Fernandez	.05
324	Jerry Mumphrey	.05
325	David Palmer	.05
326	Bill Almon	.05
327	Candy Maldonado	.05

328	John Kruk	.10
329	John Denny	.05
330	Milt Thompson	.05
331	*Mike LaValliere*	.15
332	Alan Ashby	.05
333	Doug Corbett	.05
334	*Ron Karkovice*	.10
335	Mitch Webster	.05
336	Lee Lacy	.05
337	*Glenn Braggs*	.15
338	Dwight Lowry	.05
339	Don Baylor	.15
340	Brian Fisher	.05
341	*Reggie Williams*	.05
342	Tom Candiotti	.05
343	Rudy Law	.05
344	Curt Young	.05
345	Mike Fitzgerald	.05
346	Ruben Sierra	.10
347	*Mitch Williams*	.25
348	Jorge Orta	.05
349	Mickey Tettleton	.10
350	Ernie Camacho	.05
351	Ron Kittle	.05
352	Ken Landreaux	.05
353	Chet Lemon	.05
354	John Shelby	.05
355	Mark Clear	.05
356	Doug DeCinces	.05
357	Ken Dayley	.05
358	Phil Garner	.08
359	Steve Jeltz	.05
360	Ed Whitson	.05
361	Barry Bonds	4.00
362	Vida Blue	.10
363	Cecil Cooper	.05
364	Bob Ojeda	.05
365	Dennis Eckersley	.25
366	Mike Morgan	.05
367	Willie Upshaw	.05
368	*Allan Anderson*	.05
369	Bill Gullickson	.05
370	*Bobby Thigpen*	.10
371	Juan Beniquez	.05
372	Charlie Moore	.05
373	Dan Petry	.05
374	Rod Scurry	.05
375	Tom Seaver	.50
376	Ed Vande Berg	.05
377	Tony Bernazard	.05
378	Greg Pryor	.05
379	Dwayne Murphy	.05
380	Andy McGaffigan	.05
381	Kirk McCaskill	.05
382	Greg Harris	.05
383	Rich Dotson	.05
384	Craig Reynolds	.05
385	Greg Gross	.05
386	Tito Landrum	.05
387	Craig Lefferts	.05
388	Dave Parker	.25
389	Bob Horner	.10
390	Pat Clements	.05
391	Jeff Leonard	.05
392	Chris Speier	.05
393	John Moses	.05
394	Garth Iorg	.05
395	Greg Gagne	.05
396	Nate Snell	.05
397	*Bryan Clutterbuck*	.05
398	Darrell Evans	.12
399	Steve Crawford	.05
400	Checklist 346-451	.05
401	*Phil Lombardi*	.05
402	Rick Honeycutt	.05
403	Ken Schrom	.05
404	Bud Black	.05
405	Donnie Hill	.05
406	Wayne Krenchicki	.05
407	*Chuck Finley*	.35
408	Toby Harrah	.08
409	Steve Lyons	.08
410	Kevin Bass	.05
411	Marvell Wynne	.05
412	Ron Roenicke	.05
413	*Tracy Jones*	.08
414	Gene Garber	.05
415	Mike Bielecki	.05
416	Frank DiPino	.05
417	Andy Van Slyke	.10
418	Jim Dwyer	.05
419	Ben Oglivie	.05
420	Dave Bergman	.05
421	Joe Sambito	.05
422	*Bob Tewksbury*	.30
423	Len Matuszek	.05
424	*Mike Kingery*	.05
425	Dave Kingman	.10
426	*Al Newman*	.05
427	Gary Ward	.05
428	Ruppert Jones	.05
429	Harold Baines	.15
430	Pat Perry	.05
431	Terry Puhl	.05
432	Don Carman	.05
433	Eddie Milner	.05
434	LaMarr Hoyt	.05
435	Rick Rhoden	.10
436	Jose Uribe	.05
437	Ken Oberkfell	.05
438	Ron Davis	.05
439	Jesse Orosco	.08
440	Scott Bradley	.05
441	Randy Bush	.05
442	*John Cerutti*	.10
443	Roy Smalley	.05
444	Kelly Gruber	.05
445	Bob Kearney	.05
446	*Ed Hearn*	.05
447	Scott Sanderson	.05
448	Bruce Benedict	.05
449	Junior Ortiz	.05
450	*Mike Aldrete*	.05
451	Kevin McReynolds	.10
452	*Rob Murphy*	.08
453	Kent Tekulve	.05
454	Curt Ford	.05
455	Davey Lopes	.08
456	Bobby Grich	.10
457	Jose DeLeon	.05
458	Andre Dawson	.30
459	Mike Flanagan	.05
460	*Joey Meyer*	.08
461	*Chuck Cary*	.05
462	Bill Buckner	.10
463	Bob Shirley	.05
464	*Jeff Hamilton*	.08
465	Phil Niekro	.30
466	Mark Gubicza	.12
467	Jerry Willard	.05
468	*Bob Sebra*	.05
469	Larry Parrish	.05
470	Charlie Hough	.08
471	Hal McRae	.10
472	*Dave Leiper*	.05
473	Mel Hall	.05
474	Dan Pasqua	.10
475	Bob Welch	.10
476	Johnny Grubb	.05
477	Jim Traber	.05
478	*Chris Bosio*	.25
479	Mark McLemore	.08
480	John Morris	.05
481	Billy Hatcher	.05
482	Dan Schatzeder	.05
483	Rich Gossage	.15
484	Jim Morrison	.05
485	Bob Brenly	.05
486	Bill Schroeder	.05
487	Mookie Wilson	.10
488	*Dave Martinez*	.15
489	Harold Reynolds	.10
490	Jeff Hearron	.05
491	Mickey Hatcher	.05
492	*Barry Larkin*	2.00
493	Bob James	.05
494	John Habyan	.05
495	*Jim Adduci*	.05
496	Mike Heath	.05
497	Tim Stoddard	.05
498	Tony Armas	.08
499	Dennis Powell	.05
500	Checklist 452-557	.05
501	Chris Bando	.05
502	*David Cone*	2.50
503	Jay Howell	.05
504	Tom Foley	.05
505	*Ray Chadwick*	.05
506	*Mike Loynd*	.05
507	Neil Allen	.05
508	Danny Darwin	.05
509	Rick Schu	.05
510	Jose Oquendo	.05
511	Gene Walter	.05
512	*Terry McGriff*	.05
513	Ken Griffey	.10
514	Benny Distefano	.05
515	*Terry Mulholland*	.40
516	Ed Lynch	.05
517	Bill Swift	.05
518	Manny Lee	.05
519	Andre David	.05
520	Scott McGregor	.05
521	Rick Manning	.05
522	Willie Hernandez	.05
523	Marty Barrett	.05
524	Wayne Tolleson	.05
525	*Jose Gonzalez*	.05
526	Cory Snyder	.05
527	Buddy Biancalana	.05
528	Moose Haas	.05
529	*Wilfredo Tejada*	.05
530	Stu Cliburn	.05
531	*Dale Mohorcic*	.05
532	Ron Hassey	.05
533	Ty Gainey	.05
534	Jerry Royster	.05
535	*Mike Maddux*	.05
536	Ted Power	.05
537	Ted Simmons	.05
538	*Rafael Belliard*	.12
539	Chico Walker	.05
540	Bob Forsch	.05
541	John Stefero	.05
542	*Dale Sveum*	.08
543	Mark Thurmond	.05
544	*Jeff Sellers*	.05
545	Joel Skinner	.05
546	Alex Trevino	.05
547	*Randy Kutcher*	.05
548	Joaquin Andujar	.05
549	*Casey Candaele*	.10
550	Jeff Russell	.05
551	John Candelaria	.10
552	Joe Cowley	.05
553	Danny Cox	.05
554	Denny Walling	.05
555	*Bruce Ruffin*	.20
556	Buddy Bell	.10
557	*Jimmy Jones*	.10
558	Bobby Bonilla	.40
559	Jeff Robinson	.05
560	Ed Olwine	.05
561	*Glenallen Hill*	.75
562	Lee Mazzilli	.05
563	Mike Brown	.05
564	George Frazier	.05
565	*Mike Sharperson*	.10
566	*Mark Portugal*	.10
567	Rick Leach	.05
568	Mark Langston	.12
569	Rafael Santana	.05
570	Manny Trillo	.05
571	Cliff Speck	.05
572	Bob Kipper	.05
573	*Kelly Downs*	.10
574	*Randy Asadoor*	.05
575	*Dave Magadan*	.25
576	*Marvin Freeman*	.05
577	Jeff Lahti	.05
578	Jeff Calhoun	.05
579	Gus Polidor	.05
580	Gene Nelson	.05
581	Tim Teufel	.05
582	Odell Jones	.05
583	Mark Ryal	.05
584	Randy O'Neal	.05
585	*Mike Greenwell*	.50
586	Ray Knight	.05
587	*Ralph Bryant*	.05
588	Carmen Castillo	.05
589	Ed Wojna	.05
590	Stan Javier	.05
591	*Jeff Musselman*	.10
592	*Mike Stanley*	.20
593	Darrell Porter	.05
594	*Drew Hall*	.05
595	*Rob Nelson*	.05
596	Bryan Oelkers	.05
597	*Scott Nielsen*	.05
598	*Brian Holton*	.10
599	Kevin Mitchell	.10
600	Checklist 558-660	.05
601	Jackie Gutierrez	.05
602	*Barry Jones*	.10
603	Jerry Narron	.05
604	Steve Lake	.05
605	Jim Pankovits	.05
606	Ed Romero	.05
607	Dave LaPoint	.05
608	Don Robinson	.05
609	Mike Krukow	.05
610	*Dave Valle*	.10
611	Len Dykstra	.10
612	Roberto Clemente Puzzle Card	.25
613	Mike Trujillo	.05
614	Damaso Garcia	.05
615	Neal Heaton	.05
616	Juan Berenguer	.05
617	Steve Carlton	.35
618	Gary Lucas	.05
619	Geno Petralli	.05
620	Rick Aguilera	.05
621	Fred McGriff	.75
622	Dave Henderson	.05
623	*Dave Clark*	.05
624	Angel Salazar	.05
625	Randy Hunt	.05
626	John Gibbons	.05
627	*Kevin Brown*	5.00
628	Bill Dawley	.05
629	Aurelio Lopez	.05
630	Charlie Hudson	.05
631	Ray Soff	.05
632	*Ray Hayward*	.05
633	Spike Owen	.05
634	Glenn Hubbard	.05
635	*Kevin Elster*	.12
636	Mike LaCoss	.05
637	Dwayne Henry	.05
638	*Rey Quinones*	.05
639	Jim Clancy	.05
640	Larry Andersen	.05
641	Calvin Schiraldi	.05
642	*Stan Jefferson*	.05
643	Marc Sullivan	.05
644	Mark Grant	.05
645	Cliff Johnson	.05
646	Howard Johnson	.10
647	Dave Sax	.05
648	Dave Stewart	.10
649	Danny Heep	.05
650	Joe Johnson	.05
651	*Bob Brower*	.05
652	Rob Woodward	.05
653	John Mizerock	.05
654	*Tim Pyznarski*	.05
655	*Luis Aquino*	.05
656	Mickey Brantley	.10
657	Doyle Alexander	.05
658	Sammy Stewart	.05
659	Jim Acker	.05
660	Pete Ladd	.05

1987 Donruss Box Panels

Continuing with an idea they initiated in 1985, Donruss once again placed baseball cards on the bottoms of their retail boxes. The cards, which are 2-1/2" x 3-1/2" in size, come four to a panel with each panel containing an unnumbered Roberto Clemente puzzle card. With numbering that begins where Donruss left off in 1986, cards PC 10 through PC 12 were found on boxes of Donruss regular issue wax packs. Cards PC 13 through PC 15 were located on boxes of the 1987 All-Star/Pop-Up packs.

		MT
Complete Panel Set (2):		3.00
Complete Singles Set (8):		3.00
Common Single Player:		.15
Panel		2.00
10	Dale Murphy	.35
11	Jeff Reardon	.15
12	Jose Canseco	1.50
----	Roberto Clemente Puzzle Card	.15
Panel		2.00
13	Mike Scott	.15
14	Roger Clemens	1.50
15	Mike Krukow	.15
----	Roberto Clemente Puzzle Card	.15

1987 Donruss All-Stars

Issued in conjunction with the Donruss Pop-Ups set for the second consecutive year, the 1987 Donruss All-Stars consist of 59 players (plus a checklist) who were selected to the 1986 All-Star Game. Measuring 3-1/2" x 5" in size, the card fronts feature black borders and American or National League logos. Included on back are the player's career highlights and All-Star Game statistics. Retail packs included one Pop-Up card, three All-Star cards and one Roberto Clemente puzzle card.

		MT
Complete Set (60):		5.00
Common Player:		.10
Roberto Clemente Puzzle:		9.00
1	Wally Joyner	.15
2	Dave Winfield	.40
3	Lou Whitaker	.10
4	Kirby Puckett	.75
5	Cal Ripken, Jr.	2.00
6	Rickey Henderson	.25
7	Wade Boggs	.65
8	Roger Clemens	.75
9	Lance Parrish	.10
10	Dick Howser	.10
11	Keith Hernandez	.10
12	Darryl Strawberry	.15
13	Ryne Sandberg	.75
14	Dale Murphy	.25
15	Ozzie Smith	.45
16	Tony Gwynn	.85
17	Mike Schmidt	.75
18	Dwight Gooden	.15
19	Gary Carter	.15
20	Whitey Herzog	.10
21	Jose Canseco	.60
22	John Franco	.10
23	Jesse Barfield	.10
24	Rick Rhoden	.10
25	Harold Baines	.15
26	Sid Fernandez	.10
27	George Brett	.75
28	Steve Sax	.10
29	Jim Presley	.10
30	Dave Smith	.10
31	Eddie Murray	.40
32	Mike Scott	.10
33	Don Mattingly	.90
34	Dave Parker	.10
35	Tony Fernandez	.10
36	Tim Raines	.12
37	Brook Jacoby	.10
38	Chili Davis	.15
39	Rich Gedman	.10
40	Kevin Bass	.10
41	Frank White	.10
42	Glenn Davis	.10
43	Willie Hernandez	.10
44	Chris Brown	.10
45	Jim Rice	.10
46	Tony Pena	.10
47	Don Aase	.10
48	Hubie Brooks	.10
49	Charlie Hough	.10
50	Jody Davis	.10
51	Mike Witt	.10
52	Jeff Reardon	.10
53	Ken Schrom	.10
54	Fernando Valenzuela	.12
55	Dave Righetti	.10
56	Shane Rawley	.10
57	Ted Higuera	.10
58	Mike Krukow	.10
59	Lloyd Moseby	.10
60	Checklist	.05

1987 Donruss Diamond Kings Supers

For a third season, Donruss produced a set of enlarged Diamond Kings, measuring 4-11/16" x 6-3/4". The 28-cards feature the artwork of Dick Perez, and contain 26 player cards, a checklist and a Roberto Clemente puzzle card. The set was available through a mail-in offer for $9.50 plus three wrappers.

		MT
Complete Set (28):		7.50
Common Player:		.25
1	Wally Joyner	.25
2	Roger Clemens	1.50
3	Dale Murphy	.30
4	Darryl Strawberry	.25
5	Ozzie Smith	.50
6	Jose Canseco	.75
7	Charlie Hough	.15
8	Brook Jacoby	.15
9	Fred Lynn	.15
10	Rick Rhoden	.15
11	Chris Brown	.15
12	Von Hayes	.15
13	Jack Morris	.15
14	Kevin McReynolds	.15
15	George Brett	1.00
16	Ted Higuera	.15
17	Hubie Brooks	.15
18	Mike Scott	.15
19	Kirby Puckett	.75
20	Dave Winfield	.40
21	Lloyd Moseby	.15
22	Eric Davis	.25
23	Jim Presley	.15
24	Keith Moreland	.15
25	Greg Walker	.15
26	Steve Sax	.15
27	Checklist	.04
---	Roberto Clemente Puzzle Card	.20

1987 Donruss Highlights

For a third consecutive year, Donruss produced a 56-card set which highlighted the special events of the 1987 baseball season. The 2-1/2" x 3-1/2" cards have a front design similar to the regular 1987 Donruss set. A blue border and the "Highlights" logo are the significant differences. The backs feature black print on a white background and include the date the event took place plus the particulars. As in the past, the set includes Donruss' picks for the A.L. and N.L. Rookies of the Year. The set was issued in a specially designed box and was available only through hobby dealers.

		MT
Complete Unopended Set (56):		9.00
Complete Set (56):		5.00
Common Player:		.10
1	First No-Hitter For Brewers (Juan Nieves)	.10
2	Hits 500th Homer (Mike Schmidt)	.75
3	N.L. Player of the Month - April (Eric Davis)	.15
4	N.L. Pitcher of the Month - April (Sid Fernandez)	.10
5	A.L. Player of the Month - April (Brian Downing)	.10
6	A.L. Pitcher of the Month - April (Bret Saberhagen)	.10
7	Free Agent Holdout Returns (Tim Raines)	.10
8	N.L. Player of the Month - May (Eric Davis)	.15
9	N.L. Pitcher of the Month - May (Steve Bedrosian)	.10
10	A.L. Player of the Month - May (Larry Parrish)	.10
11	A.L. Pitcher of the Month - May (Jim Clancy)	.10
12	N.L. Player of the Month - June (Tony Gwynn)	.35
13	N.L. Pitcher of the Month - June (Orel Hershiser)	.10
14	A.L. Player of the Month - June (Wade Boggs)	.35
15	A.L. Pitcher of the Month - June (Steve Ontiveros)	.10
16	All Star Game Hero (Tim Raines)	.10
17	Consecutive Game Homer Streak (Don Mattingly)	.75
18	1987 Hall of Fame Inductee (Jim "Catfish" Hunter)	.25
19	1987 Hall of Fame Inductee (Ray Dandridge)	.25
20	1987 Hall of Fame Inductee (Billy Williams)	.25
21	N.L. Player of the Month - July (Bo Diaz)	.10
22	N.L. Pitcher of the Month - July (Floyd Youmans)	.10
23	A.L. Player of the Month - July (Don Mattingly)	.35
24	A.L. Pitcher of the Month - July (Frank Viola)	.10
25	Strikes Out 4 Batters In 1 Inning (Bobby Witt)	.10
26	Ties A.L. 9-Inning Game Hit Mark (Kevin Seitzer)	.10
27	Sets Rookie Home Run Record (Mark McGwire)	1.50
28	Sets Cubs' 1st Year Homer Mark (Andre Dawson)	.10
29	Hits In 39 Straight Games (Paul Molitor)	.20
30	Record Weekend (Kirby Puckett)	.35
31	N.L. Player of the Month - August (Andre Dawson)	.10
32	N.L. Pitcher of the Month - August (Doug Drabek)	.10
33	A.L. Player of the Month - August (Dwight Evans)	.10
34	A.L. Pitcher of the Month - August (Mark Langston)	.10
35	100 RBI In 1st 2 Major League Seasons (Wally Joyner)	.10
36	100 SB In 1st 3 Major League Seasons (Vince Coleman)	.10
37	Orioles' All Time Homer King (Eddie Murray)	.25
38	Ends Consecutive Innings Streak (Cal Ripken)	1.50
39	Blue Jays Hit Record 10 Homers In 1 Game (Rob Ducey, Fred McGriff, Ernie Whitt)	.10
40	Equal A's RBI Marks (Jose Canseco, Mark McGwire)	1.50
41	Sets All-Time Catching Record (Bob Boone)	.10
42	Sets Mets' One-Season HR Mark (Darryl Strawberry)	.15
43	N.L.'s All-Time Switch Hit HR King (Howard Johnson)	.10
44	Five Straight 200-Hit Seasons (Wade Boggs)	.35
45	Eclipses Rookie Game Hitting Streak (Benito Santiago)	.10
46	Eclipses Jackson's A's HR Record (Mark McGwire)	2.00
47	13th Rookie To Collect 200 Hits (Kevin Seitzer)	.10
48	Sets Slam Record (Don Mattingly)	2.00
49	N.L. Player of the Month - September (Darryl Strawberry)	.15
50	N.L. Pitcher of the Month - September (Pascual Perez)	.10
51	A.L. Player of the Month - September (Alan Trammell)	.10
52	A.L. Pitcher of the Month - September (Doyle Alexander)	.10
53	Strikeout King - Again (Nolan Ryan)	1.50
54	Donruss A.L. Rookie of the Year (Mark McGwire)	2.00
55	Donruss N.L. Rookie of the Year (Benito Santiago)	.25
56	Highlight Checklist	.10

1987 Donruss Opening Day

The Donruss Opening Day set includes all players in major league baseball's starting lineups on the opening day of the 1987 baseball season. Cards in the 272-piece set measure 2-1/2" x 3-1/2" and have a glossy coating. The fronts are identical in design to the regular Donruss set, but new photos were utilized along with maroon borders as opposed to black. The backs carry black printing on white and yellow and offer a brief player biography plus the player's career statistics. The set was packaged in a sturdy 15" by 5" by 2" box with a clear acetate lid.

		MT
Complete Set (272):		12.00
Common Player:		.10
1	Doug DeCinces	.10
2	Mike Witt	.10
3	George Hendrick	.10
4	Dick Schofield	.10
5	Devon White	.15
6	Butch Wynegar	.10
7	Wally Joyner	.25
8	Mark McLemore	.10
9	Brian Downing	.10
10	Gary Pettis	.10
11	Bill Doran	.10
12	Phil Garner	.10
13	Jose Cruz	.10
14	Kevin Bass	.10
15	Mike Scott	.10
16	Glenn Davis	.10
17	Alan Ashby	.10
18	Billy Hatcher	.10
19	Craig Reynolds	.10
20	Carney Lansford	.10
21	Mike Davis	.10
22	Reggie Jackson	.30
23	Mickey Tettleton	.15
24	Jose Canseco	1.75
25	Rob Nelson	.10
26	Tony Phillips	.15
27	Dwayne Murphy	.10
28	Alfredo Griffin	.10
29	Curt Young	.10
30	Willie Upshaw	.10
31	Mike Sharperson	.10
32	Rance Mulliniks	.10
33	Ernie Whitt	.10
34	Jesse Barfield	.10
35	Tony Fernandez	.10
36	Lloyd Moseby	.10
37	Jimmy Key	.15
38	Fred McGriff	.40
39	George Bell	.12
40	Dale Murphy	.40
41	Rick Mahler	.10
42	Ken Griffey	.10
43	Andres Thomas	.10
44	Dion James	.10
45	Ozzie Virgil	.10
46	Ken Oberkfell	.10
47	Gary Roenicke	.10
48	Glenn Hubbard	.10
49	Bill Schroeder	.10
50	Greg Brock	.10
51	Billy Jo Robidoux	.10
52	Glenn Braggs	.10
53	Jim Gantner	.10
54	Paul Molitor	.35
55	Dale Sveum	.10
56	Ted Higuera	.10
57	Rob Deer	.10
58	Robin Yount	.65
59	Jim Lindeman	.10
60	Vince Coleman	.10
61	Tommy Herr	.10
62	Terry Pendleton	.10
63	John Tudor	.10
64	Tony Pena	.10
65	Ozzie Smith	.55
66	Tito Landrum	.10
67	Jack Clark	.10
68	Bob Dernier	.10
69	Rick Sutcliffe	.10
70	Andre Dawson	.25
71	Keith Moreland	.10
72	Jody Davis	.10
73	Brian Dayett	.10
74	Leon Durham	.10
75	Ryne Sandberg	.75
76	Shawon Dunston	.15
77	Mike Marshall	.10
78	Bill Madlock	.10
79	Orel Hershiser	.15
80	Mike Ramsey	.10
81	Ken Landreaux	.10
82	Mike Scioscia	.10
83	Franklin Stubbs	.10
84	Mariano Duncan	.10
85	Steve Sax	.10
86	Mitch Webster	.10
87	Reid Nichols	.10
88	Tim Wallach	.10
89	Floyd Youmans	.10
90	Andres Galarraga	.25
91	Hubie Brooks	.10
92	Jeff Reed	.10
93	Alonzo Powell	.10
94	Vance Law	.10
95	Bob Brenly	.10
96	Will Clark	1.00
97	Chili Davis	.10
98	Mike Krukow	.10
99	Jose Uribe	.10
100	Chris Brown	.10
101	Rob Thompson	.10
102	Candy Maldonado	.10
103	Jeff Leonard	.10
104	Tom Candiotti	.10
105	Chris Bando	.10
106	Cory Snyder	.10
107	Pat Tabler	.10
108	Andre Thornton	.10
109	Joe Carter	.25
110	Tony Bernazard	.10
111	Julio Franco	.12
112	Brook Jacoby	.10
113	Brett Butler	.15
114	Donnell Nixon	.10
115	Alvin Davis	.10
116	Mark Langston	.12
117	Harold Reynolds	.10
118	Ken Phelps	.10
119	Mike Kingery	.10
120	Dave Valle	.10
121	Rey Quinones	.10
122	Phil Bradley	.10
123	Jim Presley	.10
124	Keith Hernandez	.10
125	Kevin McReynolds	.10
126	Rafael Santana	.10
127	Bob Ojeda	.10
128	Darryl Strawberry	.25
129	Mookie Wilson	.10
130	Gary Carter	.15
131	Tim Teufel	.10
132	Howard Johnson	.10
133	Cal Ripken, Jr.	2.50
134	Rick Burleson	.10
135	Fred Lynn	.10
136	Eddie Murray	.40
137	Ray Knight	.10
138	Alan Wiggins	.10
139	John Shelby	.10
140	Mike Boddicker	.10
141	Ken Gerhart	.10
142	Terry Kennedy	.10
143	Steve Garvey	.25
144	Marvell Wynne	.10
145	Kevin Mitchell	.15
146	Tony Gwynn	.75
147	Joey Cora	.10
148	Benito Santiago	.15
149	Eric Show	.10
150	Garry Templeton	.10
151	Carmelo Martinez	.10
152	Von Hayes	.10
153	Lance Parrish	.12
154	Milt Thompson	.10
155	Mike Easler	.10
156	Juan Samuel	.10
157	Steve Jeltz	.10
158	Glenn Wilson	.10
159	Shane Rawley	.10
160	Mike Schmidt	.75
161	Andy Van Slyke	.10
162	Johnny Ray	.10
163a	Barry Bonds (dark jersey, photo actually Johnny Ray)	175.00
163b	Barry Bonds (white jersey, correct photo)	2.50
164	Junior Ortiz	.10
165	Rafael Belliard	.10
166	Bob Patterson	.10
167	Bobby Bonilla	.25
168	Sid Bream	.10
169	Jim Morrison	.10
170	Jerry Browne	.10
171	Scott Fletcher	.10
172	Ruben Sierra	.12
173	Larry Parrish	.10
174	Pete O'Brien	.10
175	Pete Incaviglia	.12
176	Don Slaught	.10
177	Oddibe McDowell	.10
178	Charlie Hough	.10
179	Steve Buechele	.10
180	Bob Stanley	.10
181	Wade Boggs	.75
182	Jim Rice	.10
183	Bill Buckner	.10
184	Dwight Evans	.10
185	Spike Owen	.10
186	Don Baylor	.12
187	Marc Sullivan	.10
188	Marty Barrett	.10
189	Dave Henderson	.10
190	Bo Diaz	.10
191	Barry Larkin	.35
192	Kal Daniels	.10
193	Terry Francona	.10
194	Tom Browning	.10
195	Ron Oester	.10
196	Buddy Bell	.10
197	Eric Davis	.15
198	Dave Parker	.12
199	Steve Balboni	.10
200	Danny Tartabull	.10
201	Ed Hearn	.10
202	Buddy Biancalana	.10
203	Danny Jackson	.10
204	Frank White	.10
205	Bo Jackson	.50
206	George Brett	.75
207	Kevin Seitzer	.10
208	Willie Wilson	.10
209	Orlando Mercado	.10
210	Darrell Evans	.10
211	Larry Herndon	.10
212	Jack Morris	.10
213	Chet Lemon	.10
214	Mike Heath	.10
215	Darnell Coles	.10
216	Alan Trammell	.15
217	Terry Harper	.10
218	Lou Whitaker	.10
219	Gary Gaetti	.15
220	Tom Nieto	.10
221	Kirby Puckett	.75
222	Tom Brunansky	.10
223	Greg Gagne	.10
224	Dan Gladden	.10
225	Mark Davidson	.10
226	Bert Blyleven	.10
227	Steve Lombardozzi	.10
228	Kent Hrbek	.12
229	Gary Redus	.10
230	Ivan Calderon	.10
231	Tim Hulett	.10
232	Carlton Fisk	.15
233	Greg Walker	.10
234	Ron Karkovice	.10
235	Ozzie Guillen	.10
236	Harold Baines	.10
237	Donnie Hill	.10
238	Rich Dotson	.10
239	Mike Pagliarulo	.10
240	Joel Skinner	.10
241	Don Mattingly	1.50
242	Gary Ward	.10
243	Dave Winfield	.40
244	Dan Pasqua	.10
245	Wayne Tolleson	.10
246	Willie Randolph	.10
247	Dennis Rasmussen	.10
248	Rickey Henderson	.40
249	Angels Checklist	.05
250	Astros Checklist	.05
251	Athletics Checklist	.05
252	Blue Jays Checklist	.05
253	Braves Checklist	.05
254	Brewers Checklist	.05
255	Cardinals Checklist	.05
256	Dodgers Checklist	.05
257	Expos Checklist	.05
258	Giants Checklist	.05
259	Indians Checklist	.05
260	Mariners Checklist	.05
261	Orioles Checklist	.05
262	Padres Checklist	.05
263	Phillies Checklist	.05
264	Pirates Checklist	.05
265	Rangers Checklist	.05
266	Red Sox Checklist	.05
267	Reds Checklist	.05
268	Royals Checklist	.05
269	Tigers Checklist	.05
270	Twins Checklist	.05
271	White Sox/Cubs Checklist	.05
272	Yankees/Mets Checklist	.05

1987 Donruss Pop-Ups

For the second straight year, Donruss released in conjunction with its All-Stars issue a set of cards designed to fold out to form a three-dimensional stand-up card. Consisting of 20 cards, as opposed to the previous year's 18, the 1987 Donruss Pop-Ups set contains players selected to the 1986 All-Star Game. Background for the 2-1/2" x 5" cards is the Houston Astrodome, site of the 1986 mid-summer classic. Retail packs included one Pop-Up card, three All-Star cards and one Roberto Clemente puzzle card.

		MT
Complete Set (20):		3.00
Common Player:		.20
Roberto Clemente Puzzle:		9.00
(1)	Wade Boggs	.50
(2)	Gary Carter	.25
(3)	Roger Clemens	.90
(4)	Dwight Gooden	.25
(5)	Tony Gwynn	.80
(6)	Rickey Henderson	.40
(7)	Keith Hernandez	.20
(8)	Whitey Herzog	.20
(9)	Dick Howser	.20
(10)	Wally Joyner	.25
(11)	Dale Murphy	.30
(12)	Lance Parrish	.20
(13)	Kirby Puckett	.75
(14)	Cal Ripken, Jr.	1.50
(15)	Ryne Sandberg	.75
(16)	Mike Schmidt	.75
(17)	Ozzie Smith	.40
(18)	Darryl Strawberry	.25
(19)	Lou Whitaker	.20
(20)	Dave Winfield	.35

1987 Donruss Rookies

As they did in 1986, Donruss issued a 56-card set highlighting the major leagues' most promising rookies. The cards are standard 2-1/2" x 3-1/2" and are identical in design to the regular Donruss issue. The card fronts have green borders as opposed to the black found in the regular issue and carry the words "The Rookies" in the lower-left portion of the card. The set came housed in a specially designed box and was available only through hobby dealers.

		MT
Complete Unopened Set (56):		20.00
Complete Set (56):		15.00
Common Player:		.05
1	Mark McGwire	10.00
2	Eric Bell	.05
3	Mark Williamson	.05
4	Mike Greenwell	.08
5	Ellis Burks	.10
6	DeWayne Buice	.05
7	Mark Mclemore (McLemore)	.08
8	Devon White	.10
9	Willie Fraser	.05
10	Lester Lancaster	.05
11	Ken Williams	.05
12	Matt Nokes	.05
13	Jeff Robinson	.05
14	Bo Jackson	.30
15	Kevin Seitzer	.05
16	Billy Ripken	.05
17	B.J. Surhoff	.10
18	Chuck Crim	.05
19	Mike Birbeck	.05
20	Chris Bosio	.05
21	Les Straker	.05
22	Mark Davidson	.05
23	Gene Larkin	.05
24	Ken Gerhart	.05
25	Luis Polonia	.05
26	Terry Steinbach	.08
27	Mickey Brantley	.05
28	Mike Stanley	.05
29	Jerry Browne	.05
30	Todd Benzinger	.05
31	Fred McGriff	.50
32	Mike Henneman	.08
33	Casey Candaele	.05
34	Dave Magadan	.05
35	David Cone	.75
36	Mike Jackson	.05
37	John Mitchell	.05
38	Mike Dunne	.05
39	John Smiley	.05
40	Joe Magrane	.05
41	Jim Lindeman	.05
42	Shane Mack	.05
43	Stan Jefferson	.05
44	Benito Santiago	.08
45	Matt Williams	1.25
46	Dave Meads	.05
47	Rafael Palmeiro	.50
48	Bill Long	.05
49	Bob Brower	.05
50	James Steels	.05
51	Paul Noce	.05
52	Greg Maddux	9.00
53	Jeff Musselman	.05
54	Brian Holton	.05
55	Chuck Jackson	.05
56	Checklist 1-56	.03

1988 Donruss Promo Sheet

The full effect of the 1988 Donruss border design of black, blue and red geometric patterns was previewed on this promo sheet. Printed on glossy paper with blank-back, eight regular cards (all pitchers!) and a Diamond King are showcased on the 7-1/2" x 10-1/2" sheet.

		MT
Uncut Sheet:		10.00
(1)	Scott Bankhead	
(2)	Mike Birkbeck	
(3)	DeWayne Buice	
(4)	Ed Correa	
(5)	Jose DeLeon	
(6)	Ken Dixon	
(7)	Dwight Gooden	
(8)	Tim Raines (Diamond King)	
(9)	Rick Sutcliffe	

1988 Donruss

The 1988 Donruss set consists of 660 cards, each measuring 2-1/2" x 3-1/2". Fronts feature a full-color photo surrounded by a colorful border - alternating stripes of black, red, black, blue, black, blue, black, red and black (in that order) - separated by soft-focus edges and airbrushed fades. The player's name and position appear in a red band at the bottom of the card. The Donruss logo is situated in the upper-left corner, while the team logo is located in the lower-right. For the seventh consecutive season, Donruss included a subset of "Diamond Kings" cards (#1-27) in the issue. And for the fifth straight year, Donruss incorporated the popular "Rated Rookies" (card #28-47) with the set. Twenty-six of the cards between #603-660 were short-printed to accommodate the printing of the 26 MVP insert cards.

		MT
Complete Factory Set, Sealed (660):		15.00
Complete Set (660):		12.00
Common Player:		.05
Stan Musial Puzzle:		1.00
Wax Box:		9.00
1	Mark McGwire (DK)	.75
2	Tim Raines (DK)	.08
3	Benito Santiago (DK)	.08
4	Alan Trammell (DK)	.08
5	Danny Tartabull (DK)	.05
6	Ron Darling (DK)	.08
7	Paul Molitor (DK)	.15
8	Devon White (DK)	.10
9	Andre Dawson (DK)	.10
10	Julio Franco (DK)	.10
11	Scott Fletcher (DK)	.08
12	Tony Fernandez (DK)	.10
13	Shane Rawley (DK)	.05
14	Kal Daniels (DK)	.05
15	Jack Clark (DK)	.08
16	Dwight Evans (DK)	.08
17	Tommy John (DK)	.08
18	Andy Van Slyke (DK)	.10
19	Gary Gaetti (DK)	.08
20	Mark Langston (DK)	.08
21	Will Clark (DK)	.25
22	Glenn Hubbard (DK)	.05
23	Billy Hatcher (DK)	.05
24	Bob Welch (DK)	.05
25	Ivan Calderon (DK)	.05
26	Cal Ripken, Jr. (DK)	.35
27	Checklist 1-27	.05
28	*Mackey Sasser* (RR)	.10
29	*Jeff Treadway* (RR)	.05
30	*Mike Campbell* (RR)	.05
31	*Lance Johnson* (RR)	.15
32	*Nelson Liriano* (RR)	.08
33	Shawn Abner (RR)	.05
34	*Roberto Alomar* (RR)	1.50
35	*Shawn Hillegas* (RR)	.05
36	Joey Meyer (RR)	.05
37	Kevin Elster (RR)	.10
38	*Jose Lind* (RR)	.12
39	*Kirt Manwaring* (RR)	.15
40	*Mark Grace* (RR)	.50
41	*Jody Reed* (RR)	.15
42	*John Farrell* (RR)	.05
43	*Al Leiter* (RR)	.20
44	*Gary Thurman* (RR)	.08
45	*Vicente Palacios* (RR)	.05
46	*Eddie Williams* (RR)	.10
47	*Jack McDowell* (RR)	.25
48	Ken Dixon	.05
49	Mike Birkbeck	.05
50	Eric King	.05
51	Roger Clemens	.40
52	Pat Clements	.05
53	Fernando Valenzuela	.08
54	Mark Gubicza	.08
55	Jay Howell	.05
56	Floyd Youmans	.05
57	Ed Correa	.05
58	*DeWayne Buice*	.10
59	Jose DeLeon	.05
60	Danny Cox	.05
61	Nolan Ryan	.60
62	Steve Bedrosian	.05
63	Tom Browning	.05
64	Mark Davis	.05
65	R.J. Reynolds	.05
66	Kevin Mitchell	.05
67	Ken Oberkfell	.05
68	Rick Sutcliffe	.08
69	Dwight Gooden	.12
70	Scott Bankhead	.05
71	Bert Blyleven	.10
72	Jimmy Key	.10
73	*Les Straker*	.05
74	Jim Clancy	.05
75	Mike Moore	.05
76	Ron Darling	.08
77	Ed Lynch	.05
78	Dale Murphy	.15
79	Doug Drabek	.08
80	Scott Garrelts	.05
81	Ed Whitson	.05
82	Rob Murphy	.05
83	Shane Rawley	.05
84	Greg Mathews	.05
85	Jim Deshaies	.08
86	Mike Witt	.08
87	Donnie Hill	.05
88	Jeff Reed	.05
89	Mike Boddicker	.05
90	Ted Higuera	.05
91	Walt Terrell	.05
92	Bob Stanley	.05
93	Dave Righetti	.08
94	Orel Hershiser	.10
95	Chris Bando	.05
96	Bret Saberhagen	.10
97	Curt Young	.05
98	Tim Burke	.05
99	Charlie Hough	.08
100a	Checklist 28-137	.05
100b	Checklist 28-133	.10
101	Bobby Witt	.10
102	George Brett	.40
103	Mickey Tettleton	.08
104	Scott Bailes	.05
105	Mike Pagliarulo	.08
106	Mike Scioscia	.05
107	Tom Brookens	.05
108	Ray Knight	.08
109	Dan Plesac	.05
110	Wally Joyner	.12
111	Bob Forsch	.05
112	Mike Scott	.08
113	Kevin Gross	.05
114	Benito Santiago	.10
115	Bob Kipper	.05
116	Mike Krukow	.05
117	Chris Bosio	.05
118	Sid Fernandez	.05
119	Jody Davis	.05
120	Mike Morgan	.05
121	Mark Eichhorn	.05
122	Jeff Reardon	.05
123	John Franco	.00
124	Richard Dotson	.05
125	Eric Bell	.05
126	Juan Nieves	.05
127	Jack Morris	.08
128	Rick Rhoden	.05
129	Rich Gedman	.05
130	Ken Howell	.05
131	Brook Jacoby	.05
132	Danny Jackson	.05
133	Gene Nelson	.05
134	Neal Heaton	.05
135	Willie Fraser	.05
136	Jose Guzman	.05
137	Ozzie Guillen	.08
138	Bob Knepper	.05
139	*Mike Jackson*	.10
140	*Joe Magrane*	.08
141	Jimmy Jones	.05
142	Ted Power	.05
143	Ozzie Virgil	.05
144	*Felix Fermin*	.08
145	Kelly Downs	.05
146	Shawon Dunston	.08
147	Scott Bradley	.05
148	Dave Stieb	.10
149	Frank Viola	.10
150	Terry Kennedy	.05
151	Bill Wegman	.05
152	*Matt Nokes*	.10
153	Wade Boggs	.35
154	Wayne Tolleson	.05
155	Mariano Duncan	.05
156	Julio Franco	.08
157	Charlie Leibrandt	.05
158	Terry Steinbach	.10
159	Mike Fitzgerald	.05
160	Jack Lazorko	.05
161	Mitch Williams	.08
162	Greg Walker	.05
163	Alan Ashby	.05
164	Tony Gwynn	.40
165	Bruce Ruffin	.05
166	Ron Robinson	.05
167	Zane Smith	.05
168	Junior Ortiz	.05
169	Jamie Moyer	.05
170	Tony Pena	.05
171	Cal Ripken, Jr.	.50
172	B.J. Surhoff	.10
173	Lou Whitaker	.10
174	*Ellis Burks*	.25
175	Ron Guidry	.10
176	Steve Sax	.05
177	Danny Tartabull	.05
178	Carney Lansford	.05
179	Casey Candaele	.05
180	Scott Fletcher	.05
181	Mark McLemore	.05
182	Ivan Calderon	.05
183	Jack Clark	.08
184	Glenn Davis	.05
185	Luis Aguayo	.05
186	Bo Diaz	.05
187	Stan Jefferson	.05
188	Sid Bream	.05
189	Bob Brenly	.05
190	Dion James	.05
191	Leon Durham	.05
192	Jesse Orosco	.05
193	Alvin Davis	.05
194	Gary Gaetti	.08
195	Fred McGriff	.25
196	Steve Lombardozzi	.05
197	Rance Mulliniks	.05
198	Rey Quinones	.05
199	Gary Carter	.10
200a	Checklist 138-247	.05
200b	Checklist 134-239	.10
201	Keith Moreland	.05
202	Ken Griffey	.08
203	*Tommy Gregg*	.05
204	Will Clark	.25
205	John Kruk	.08
206	Buddy Bell	.08
207	Von Hayes	.05
208	Tommy Herr	.05
209	Craig Reynolds	.05
210	Gary Pettis	.05
211	Harold Baines	.10
212	Vance Law	.05
213	Ken Gerhart	.05
214	Jim Gantner	.05
215	Chet Lemon	.05
216	Dwight Evans	.10
217	Don Mattingly	.35
218	Franklin Stubbs	.05
219	Pat Tabler	.05
220	Bo Jackson	.25
221	Tony Phillips	.08
222	Tim Wallach	.08
223	Ruben Sierra	.05
224	Steve Buechele	.05
225	Frank White	.05
226	Alfredo Griffin	.05
227	Greg Swindell	.05
228	Willie Randolph	.08
229	Mike Marshall	.05
230	Alan Trammell	.15
231	Eddie Murray	.20
232	Dale Sveum	.05
233	Dick Schofield	.05
234	Jose Oquendo	.05
235	Bill Doran	.05
236	Milt Thompson	.05
237	Marvell Wynne	.05
238	Bobby Bonilla	.15
239	Chris Speier	.05
240	Glenn Braggs	.05
241	Wally Backman	.05
242	Ryne Sandberg	.30
243	Phil Bradley	.05
244	Kelly Gruber	.05
245	Tom Brunansky	.05
246	Ron Oester	.05
247	Bobby Thigpen	.05
248	Fred Lynn	.08
249	Paul Molitor	.30
250	Darrell Evans	.10
251	Gary Ward	.05
252	Bruce Hurst	.05
253	Bob Welch	.08
254	Joe Carter	.10
255	Willie Wilson	.10
256	Mark McGwire	1.50
257	Mitch Webster	.05
258	Brian Downing	.05
259	Mike Stanley	.05
260	Carlton Fisk	.15
261	Billy Hatcher	.05
262	Glenn Wilson	.05
263	Ozzie Smith	.25
264	Randy Ready	.05
265	Kurt Stillwell	.05
266	David Palmer	.05
267	Mike Diaz	.05
268	Rob Thompson	.05
269	Andre Dawson	.15
270	Lee Guetterman	.05
271	Willie Upshaw	.05
272	Randy Bush	.05
273	Larry Sheets	.05
274	Rob Deer	.05
275	Kirk Gibson	.08
276	Marty Barrett	.05
277	Rickey Henderson	.20
278	Pedro Guerrero	.05
279	Brett Butler	.08
280	Kevin Seitzer	.08
281	Mike Davis	.05
282	Andres Galarraga	.20
283	Devon White	.12
284	Pete O'Brien	.05
285	Jerry Hairston	.05
286	Kevin Bass	.05
287	Carmelo Martinez	.05
288	Juan Samuel	.08
289	Kal Daniels	.05
290	Albert Hall	.05
291	Andy Van Slyke	.08
292	Lee Smith	.10
293	Vince Coleman	.08
294	Tom Niedenfuer	.05
295	Robin Yount	.25
296	*Jeff Robinson*	.05
297	*Todd Benzinger*	.10
298	Dave Winfield	.15
299	Mickey Hatcher	.05
300a	Checklist 248-357	.05
300b	Checklist 240-345	.10
301	Bud Black	.05
302	Jose Canseco	.25
303	Tom Foley	.05
304	Pete Incaviglia	.05
305	Bob Boone	.08
306	*Bill Long*	.05
307	Willie McGee	.10
308	*Ken Caminiti*	.50
309	Darren Daulton	.08
310	Tracy Jones	.05
311	Greg Booker	.05
312	Mike LaValliere	.08
313	Chili Davis	.10

314	Glenn Hubbard	.05
315	*Paul Noce*	.05
316	Keith Hernandez	.08
317	Mark Langston	.12
318	Keith Atherton	.05
319	Tony Fernandez	.10
320	Kent Hrbek	.08
321	John Cerutti	.05
322	Mike Kingery	.05
323	Dave Magadan	.08
324	Rafael Palmeiro	.20
325	Jeff Dedmon	.05
326	Barry Bonds	.50
327	Jeffrey Leonard	.05
328	Tim Flannery	.05
329	Dave Concepcion	.05
330	Mike Schmidt	.30
331	Bill Dawley	.05
332	Larry Andersen	.05
333	Jack Howell	.05
334	*Ken Williams*	.05
335	Bryn Smith	.05
336	*Billy Ripken*	.08
337	Greg Brock	.05
338	Mike Heath	.05
339	Mike Greenwell	.08
340	Claudell Washington	.05
341	Jose Gonzalez	.05
342	Mel Hall	.05
343	Jim Eisenreich	.05
344	Tony Bernazard	.05
345	Tim Raines	.08
346	Bob Brower	.05
347	Larry Parrish	.05
348	Thad Bosley	.05
349	Dennis Eckersley	.12
350	Cory Snyder	.05
351	Rick Cerone	.05
352	John Shelby	.05
353	Larry Herndon	.05
354	John Habyan	.05
355	*Chuck Crim*	.05
356	Gus Polidor	.05
357	Ken Dayley	.05
358	Danny Darwin	.05
359	Lance Parrish	.10
360	*James Steels*	.05
361	*Al Pedrique*	.05
362	Mike Aldrete	.05
363	Juan Castillo	.05
364	Len Dykstra	.10
365	Luis Quinones	.05
366	Jim Presley	.05
367	Lloyd Moseby	.05
368	Kirby Puckett	.50
369	Eric Davis	.12
370	Gary Redus	.05
371	Dave Schmidt	.05
372	Mark Clear	.05
373	Dave Bergman	.05
374	Charles Hudson	.05
375	Calvin Schiraldi	.05
376	Alex Trevino	.05
377	Tom Candiotti	.05
378	Steve Farr	.05
379	Mike Gallego	.05
380	Andy McGaffigan	.05
381	Kirk McCaskill	.08
382	Oddibe McDowell	.05
383	Floyd Bannister	.05
384	Denny Walling	.05
385	Don Carman	.05
386	Todd Worrell	.08
387	Eric Show	.05
388	Dave Parker	.08
389	Rick Mahler	.05
390	*Mike Dunne*	.08
391	Candy Maldonado	.05
392	Bob Dernier	.05
393	Dave Valle	.05
394	Ernie Whitt	.05
395	Juan Berenguer	.05
396	Mike Young	.05
397	Mike Felder	.05
398	Willie Hernandez	.05
399	Jim Rice	.10
400a	Checklist 358-467	.05
400b	Checklist 346-451	.10
401	Tommy John	.15
402	Brian Holton	.05
403	Carmen Castillo	.05
404	Jamie Quirk	.05
405	Dwayne Murphy	.05
406	*Jeff Parrett*	.05
407	Don Sutton	.15
408	Jerry Browne	.05
409	Jim Winn	.05
410	Dave Smith	.05
411	*Shane Mack*	.15
412	Greg Gross	.05
413	Nick Esasky	.05
414	Damaso Garcia	.05
415	Brian Fisher	.05
416	Brian Dayett	.05
417	Curt Ford	.05
418	*Mark Williamson*	.05
419	Bill Schroeder	.05
420	*Mike Henneman*	.15
421	*John Marzano*	.05
422	Ron Kittle	.05
423	Matt Young	.05
424	Steve Balboni	.05
425	*Luis Polonia*	.10
426	Randy St. Claire	.05
427	Greg Harris	.05
428	Johnny Ray	.05
429	Ray Searage	.05
430	Ricky Horton	.05
431	*Gerald Young*	.05
432	Rick Schu	.05
433	Paul O'Neill	.25
434	Rich Gossage	.12
435	John Cangelosi	.05
436	Mike LaCoss	.05
437	Gerald Perry	.05
438	Dave Martinez	.05
439	Darryl Strawberry	.15
440	John Moses	.05
441	Greg Gagne	.05
442	Jesse Barfield	.05
443	George Frazier	.05
444	Garth Iorg	.05
445	Ed Nunez	.05
446	Rick Aguilera	.05
447	Jerry Mumphrey	.05
448	Rafael Ramirez	.05
449	*John Smiley*	.10
450	Atlee Hammaker	.05
451	Lance McCullers	.05
452	Guy Hoffman	.05
453	Chris James	.05
454	Terry Pendleton	.05
455	*Dave Meads*	.05
456	Bill Buckner	.08
457	*John Pawlowski*	.05
458	Bob Sebra	.05
459	Jim Dwyer	.05
460	*Jay Aldrich*	.05
461	Frank Tanana	.05
462	Oil Can Boyd	.05
463	Dan Pasqua	.08
464	*Tim Crews*	.10
465	Andy Allanson	.05
466	*Bill Pecota*	.05
467	Steve Ontiveros	.05
468	Hubie Brooks	.05
469	*Paul Kilgus*	.05
470	Dale Mohorcic	.05
471	Dan Quisenberry	.08
472	Dave Stewart	.10
473	Dave Clark	.05
474	Joel Skinner	.05
475	Dave Anderson	.05
476	Dan Petry	.05
477	*Carl Nichols*	.05
478	Ernest Riles	.05
479	George Hendrick	.05
480	John Morris	.05
481	*Manny Hernandez*	.05
482	Jeff Stone	.05
483	Chris Brown	.05
484	Mike Bielecki	.05
485	Dave Dravecky	.08
486	Rick Manning	.05
487	Bill Almon	.05
488	Jim Sundberg	.05
489	Ken Phelps	.05
490	Tom Henke	.08
491	Dan Gladden	.05
492	Barry Larkin	.15
493	*Fred Manrique*	.05
494	Mike Griffin	.05
495	*Mark Knudson*	.05
496	Bill Madlock	.10
497	Tim Stoddard	.05
498	*Sam Horn*	.05
499	*Tracy Woodson*	.05
500a	Checklist 468-577	.05
500b	Checklist 452-557	.10
501	Ken Schrom	.05
502	Angel Salazar	.05
503	Eric Plunk	.05
504	Joe Hesketh	.05
505	Greg Minton	.05
506	Geno Petralli	.05
507	Bob James	.05
508	*Robbie Wine*	.05
509	Jeff Calhoun	.05
510	Steve Lake	.05
511	Mark Grant	.05
512	Frank Williams	.05
513	*Jeff Blauser*	.15
514	Bob Walk	.05
515	Craig Lefferts	.05
516	Manny Trillo	.05
517	Jerry Reed	.05
518	Rick Leach	.05
519	*Mark Davidson*	.05
520	*Jeff Ballard*	.05
521	*Dave Stapleton*	.05
522	Pat Sheridan	.05
523	Al Nipper	.05
524	Steve Trout	.05
525	Jeff Hamilton	.05
526	*Tommy Hinzo*	.05
527	Lonnie Smith	.05
528	*Greg Cadaret*	.05
529	Rob McClure (Bob)	.05
530	Chuck Finley	.10
531	Jeff Russell	.05
532	Steve Lyons	.05
533	Terry Puhl	.05
534	*Eric Nolte*	.05
535	Kent Tekulve	.05
536	*Pat Pacillo*	.05
537	Charlie Puleo	.05
538	*Tom Prince*	.05
539	Greg Maddux	1.00
540	Jim Lindeman	.05
541	*Pete Stanicek*	.05
542	Steve Kiefer	.05
543	Jim Morrison	.05
544	Spike Owen	.05
545	*Jay Buhner*	.75
546	*Mike Devereaux*	.15
547	Jerry Don Gleaton	.05
548	Jose Rijo	.05
549	Dennis Martinez	.10
550	Mike Loynd	.05
551	Darrell Miller	.05
552	Dave LaPoint	.05
553	John Tudor	.05
554	*Rocky Childress*	.05
555	*Wally Ritchie*	.05
556	Terry McGriff	.05
557	Dave Leiper	.05
558	Jeff Robinson	.05
559	Jose Uribe	.05
560	Ted Simmons	.05
561	*Lester Lancaster*	.10
562	*Keith Miller*	.05
563	Harold Reynolds	.08
564	*Gene Larkin*	.05
565	Cecil Fielder	.10
566	Roy Smalley	.05
567	Duane Ward	.08
568	*Bill Wilkinson*	.05
569	Howard Johnson	.08
570	Frank DiPino	.05
571	*Pete Smith*	.05
572	Darnell Coles	.05
573	Don Robinson	.05
574	Rob Nelson	.05
575	Dennis Rasmussen	.05
576	Steve Jeltz (photo actually Juan Samuel)	.05
577	*Tom Pagnozzi*	.08
578	Ty Gainey	.05
579	Gary Lucas	.05
580	Ron Hassey	.05
581	Herm Winningham	.05
582	*Rene Gonzales*	.05
583	Brad Komminsk	.05
584	Doyle Alexander	.05
585	Jeff Sellers	.05
586	Bill Gullickson	.05
587	Tim Belcher	.08
588	*Doug Jones*	.10
589	*Melido Perez*	.10
590	Rick Honeycutt	.05
591	Pascual Perez	.05
592	Curt Wilkerson	.05
593	Steve Howe	.05
594	*John Davis*	.05
595	Storm Davis	.05
596	Sammy Stewart	.05
597	Neil Allen	.05
598	Alejandro Pena	.05
599	Mark Thurmond	.05
600a	Checklist 578-BC26	.05
600b	Checklist 558-660	.10
601	*Jose Mesa*	.10
602	*Don August*	.05
603	Terry Leach (SP)	.10
604	*Tom Newell*	.05
605	*Randall Byers* (SP)	.10
606	Jim Gott	.05
607	Harry Spilman	.05
608	John Candelaria	.05
609	*Mike Brumley*	.05
610	Mickey Brantley	.05
611	*Jose Nunez* (SP)	.10
612	Tom Nieto	.05
613	Rick Reuschel	.05
614	Lee Mazzilli (SP)	.10
615	*Scott Lusader*	.05
616	Bobby Meacham	.05
617	Kevin McReynolds (SP)	.15
618	Gene Garber	.05
619	*Barry Lyons* (SP)	.10
620	Randy Myers	.10
621	Donnie Moore	.05
622	Domingo Ramos	.05
623	Ed Romero	.05
624	*Greg Myers*	.08
625	Ripken Baseball Family (Billy Ripken, Cal Ripken, Jr., Cal Ripken, Sr.)	.30
626	Pat Perry	.05
627	Andres Thomas (SP)	.10
628	Matt Williams (SP)	.75
629	*Dave Hengel*	.05
630	Jeff Musselman (SP)	.10
631	Tim Laudner	.05
632	Bob Ojeda (SP)	.12
633	Rafael Santana	.05
634	*Wes Gardner*	.05
635	*Roberto Kelly* (SP)	.15
636	Mike Flanagan (SP)	.10
637	*Jay Bell*	.35
638	Bob Melvin	.05
639	*Damon Berryhill*	.10
640	*David Wells* (SP)	.40
641	Stan Musial Puzzle Card	.05
642	Doug Sisk	.05
643	*Keith Hughes*	.05
644	*Tom Glavine*	.50
645	Al Newman	.05
646	Scott Sanderson	.05
647	Scott Terry	.05
648	Tim Teufel (SP)	.12
649	Garry Templeton (SP)	.10
650	Manny Lee (SP)	.10
651	Roger McDowell (SP)	.15
652	Mookie Wilson (SP)	.15
653	David Cone (SP)	.25
654	*Ron Gant* (SP)	.25
655	Joe Price (SP)	.10
656	George Bell (SP)	.15
657	*Gregg Jefferies* (SP)	.25
658	*Todd Stottlemyre* (SP)	.15
659	*Geronimo Berroa* (SP)	.30
660	Jerry Royster (SP)	.10

1988 Donruss MVP

This 26-card set of standard-size player cards replaced the Donruss box-bottom cards in 1988. The bonus cards (numbered BC1 - BC26) were randomly inserted in Donruss wax or rack packs. Cards feature the company's choice of Most Valuable Player for each major league team and are titled "Donruss MVP." The MVP cards were not included in the factory-collated sets. Fronts carry the same basic red-blue-black border design as the 1988 Donruss basic issue. Backs are the same as the regular issue, except for the numbering system.

		MT
Complete Set (26):		5.00
Common Player:		.15
1	Cal Ripken, Jr.	1.00
2	Eric Davis	.15
3	Paul Molitor	.40
4	Mike Schmidt	.45
5	Ivan Calderon	.15
6	Tony Gwynn	.50
7	Wade Boggs	.40
8	Andy Van Slyke	.15
9	Joe Carter	.15
10	Andre Dawson	.20
11	Alan Trammell	.20
12	Mike Scott	.15
13	Wally Joyner	.20
14	Dale Murphy	.20
15	Kirby Puckett	.60
16	Pedro Guerrero	.15
17	Kevin Seitzer	.15
18	Tim Raines	.20
19	George Bell	.15
20	Darryl Strawberry	.25
21	Don Mattingly	.60
22	Ozzie Smith	.40
23	Mark McGwire	1.00
24	Will Clark	.25
25	Alvin Davis	.15
26	Ruben Sierra	.15

1988 Donruss All-Stars

For the third consecutive year, this set of 64 cards was marketed in conjunction with Donruss Pop-Ups. The 1988 issue included a major change - the cards were reduced in size from 3-1/2" x 5" to a standard 2-1/2" x 3-1/2". The set features players from the 1987 All-Star Game starting lineup. Card fronts feature full-color photos, framed in blue, black and white, with a Donruss logo at upper-left. Player name and position appear in a red banner below the photo, along with the appropriate National or American League logo. Backs include player stats and All-Star Game record. In 1988, All-Stars cards were distributed in individual packages containing three All-Stars, one Pop-Up and three Stan Musial puzzle pieces.

		MT
Complete Set (64):		3.00
Common Player:		.10
Stan Musial Puzzle:		1.00
1	Don Mattingly	.90
2	Dave Winfield	.25
3	Willie Randolph	.10
4	Rickey Henderson	.40
5	Cal Ripken, Jr.	1.25
6	George Bell	.10
7	Wade Boggs	.75
8	Bret Saberhagen	.10
9	Terry Kennedy	.10
10	John McNamara	.10
11	Jay Howell	.10
12	Harold Baines	.10
13	Harold Reynolds	.10
14	Bruce Hurst	.10
15	Kirby Puckett	.75
16	Matt Nokes	.10
17	Pat Tabler	.10
18	Dan Plesac	.10
19	Mark McGwire	1.50
20	Mike Witt	.10
21	Larry Parrish	.10
22	Alan Trammell	.15
23	Dwight Evans	.10
24	Jack Morris	.10
25	Tony Fernandez	.10
26	Mark Langston	.10
27	Kevin Seitzer	.10
28	Tom Henke	.10
29	Dave Righetti	.10
30	Oakland Coliseum	.10
31	Wade Boggs (Top Vote Getter)	.35
32	Checklist 1-32	.05
33	Jack Clark	.10
34	Darryl Strawberry	.15
35	Ryne Sandberg	.75
36	Andre Dawson	.15
37	Ozzie Smith	.40
38	Eric Davis	.15
39	Mike Schmidt	.75
40	Mike Scott	.10
41	Gary Carter	.12
42	Davey Johnson	.10
43	Rick Sutcliffe	.10
44	Willie McGee	.10
45	Hubie Brooks	.10
46	Dale Murphy	.30
47	Bo Diaz	.10
48	Pedro Guerrero	.10
49	Keith Hernandez	.10
50	Ozzie Virgil	.10
51	Tony Gwynn	.60
52	Rick Reuschel	.10
53	John Franco	.10
54	Jeffrey Leonard	.10
55	Juan Samuel	.10
56	Orel Hershiser	.10
57	Tim Raines	.10
58	Sid Fernandez	.10
59	Tim Wallach	.10
60	Lee Smith	.10
61	Steve Bedrosian	.10
62	(Tim Raines) (MVP)	.15
63	(Ozzie Smith) (Top Vote Getter)	.15
64	Checklist 33-64	.05

1988 Donruss Baseball's Best

The design of this 336-card set is similar to the regular 1988 Donruss issue with the exception of the borders which are orange, instead of blue. Player photos on the glossy front are framed by the Donruss logo upper-left, team logo lower-right and a bright red and white player name that spans the bottom margin. Backs are black and white, framed by a yellow border, and include personal information, year-by-year stats and major league totals. This set was packaged in a bright red cardboard box containing six individually shrink-wrapped packs of 56 cards. Donruss marketed the set via retail chain outlets.

		MT
Complete Set (336):		9.00
Common Player:		.05
1	Don Mattingly	.75
2	Ron Gant	.10
3	Bob Boone	.08
4	Mark Grace	.45
5	Andy Allanson	.05
6	Kal Daniels	.05
7	Floyd Bannister	.05
8	Alan Ashby	.05
9	Marty Barrett	.05
10	Tim Belcher	.05
11	Harold Baines	.08
12	Hubie Brooks	.05
13	Doyle Alexander	.05
14	Gary Carter	.10
15	Glenn Braggs	.05
16	Steve Bedrosian	.05
17	Barry Bonds	.75
18	Bert Blyleven	.08
19	Tom Brunansky	.05
20	John Candelaria	.05
21	Shawn Abner	.05
22	Jose Canseco	.45
23	Brett Butler	.08
24	Scott Bradley	.05
25	Ivan Calderon	.05
26	Rich Gossage	.08
27	Brian Downing	.05
28	Jim Rice	.08
29	Dion James	.05
30	Terry Kennedy	.05
31	George Bell	.05
32	Scott Fletcher	.05
33	Bobby Bonilla	.15
34	Tim Burke	.05
35	Darrell Evans	.08
36	Mike Davis	.05
37	Shawon Dunston	.05
38	Kevin Bass	.05
39	George Brett	.45
40	David Cone	.15
41	Ron Darling	.05
42	Roberto Alomar	.30
43	Dennis Eckersley	.10
44	Vince Coleman	.05
45	Sid Bream	.05
46	Gary Gaetti	.08
47	Phil Bradley	.05
48	Jim Clancy	.05
49	Jack Clark	.05
50	Mike Krukow	.05
51	Henry Cotto	.05
52	Rich Dotson	.05
53	Jim Gantner	.05
54	John Franco	.05
55	Pete Incaviglia	.05
56	Joe Carter	.08
57	Roger Clemens	.75
58	Gerald Perry	.05
59	Jack Howell	.05
60	Vance Law	.05
61	Jay Bell	.08
62	Eric Davis	.10
63	Gene Garber	.05
64	Glenn Davis	.05
65	Wade Boggs	.45
66	Kirk Gibson	.08
67	Carlton Fisk	.10
68	Casey Candaele	.05
69	Mike Heath	.05
70	Kevin Elster	.05
71	Greg Brock	.05
72	Don Carman	.05
73	Doug Drabek	.08
74	Greg Gagne	.05
75	Danny Cox	.05
76	Rickey Henderson	.30
77	Chris Brown	.05
78	Terry Steinbach	.05
79	Will Clark	.35
80	Mickey Brantley	.05
81	Ozzie Guillen	.05
82	Greg Maddux	.75
83	Kirk McCaskill	.05
84	Dwight Evans	.08
85	Ozzie Virgil	.05
86	Mike Morgan	.05
87	Tony Fernandez	.08
88	Jose Guzman	.05
89	Mike Dunne	.05
90	Andres Galarraga	.10
91	Mike Henneman	.05
92	Alfredo Griffin	.05
93	Rafael Palmeiro	.20
94	Jim Deshaies	.05
95	Mark Gubicza	.05
96	Dwight Gooden	.10
97	Howard Johnson	.05
98	Mark Davis	.05
99	Dave Stewart	.08
100	Joe Magrane	.05
101	Brian Fisher	.05
102	Kent Hrbek	.08
103	Kevin Gross	.05
104	Tom Henke	.05
105	Mike Pagliarulo	.05
106	Kelly Downs	.05
107	Alvin Davis	.05
108	Willie Randolph	.05
109	Rob Deer	.05
110	Bo Diaz	.05
111	Paul Kilgus	.05
112	Tom Candiotti	.05
113	Dale Murphy	.15
114	Rick Mahler	.05
115	Wally Joyner	.08
116	Ryne Sandberg	.50
117	John Farrell	.05
118	Nick Esasky	.05
119	Bo Jackson	.25
120	Bill Doran	.05
121	Ellis Burks	.08
122	Pedro Guerrero	.05
123	Dave LaPoint	.05
124	Neal Heaton	.05
125	Willie Hernandez	.05
126	Roger McDowell	.05
127	Ted Higuera	.05
128	Von Hayes	.05
129	Mike LaValliere	.05
130	Dan Gladden	.05
131	Willie McGee	.05
132	Al Lieter	.08
133	Mark Grant	.05
134	Bob Welch	.05
135	Dave Dravecky	.05
136	Mark Langston	.08
137	Dan Pasqua	.05
138	Rick Sutcliffe	.05
139	Dan Petry	.05
140	Rich Gedman	.05
141	Ken Griffey	.05
142	Eddie Murray	.30
143	Jimmy Key	.08
144	Dale Mohorcic	.05
145	Jose Lind	.05
146	Dennis Martinez	.08
147	Chet Lemon	.05
148	Orel Hershiser	.10
149	Dave Martinez	.05
150	Billy Hatcher	.05
151	Charlie Leibrandt	.05
152	Keith Hernandez	.08
153	Kevin McReynolds	.05
154	Tony Gwynn	.75
155	Stan Javier	.05
156	Tony Pena	.05
157	Andy Van Slyke	.05
158	Gene Larkin	.05
159	Chris James	.05
160	Fred McGriff	.10
161	Rick Rhoden	.05
162	Scott Garrelts	.05
163	Mike Campbell	.05
164	Dave Righetti	.05
165	Paul Molitor	.20
166	Danny Jackson	.05
167	Pete O'Brien	.05
168	Julio Franco	.05
169	Mark McGwire	1.00
170	Zane Smith	.05
171	Johnny Ray	.05
172	Lester Lancaster	.05
173	Mel Hall	.05
174	Tracy Jones	.05
175	Kevin Seitzer	.05
176	Bob Knepper	.05
177	Mike Greenwell	.08
178	Mike Marshall	.05
179	Melido Perez	.05
180	Tim Raines	.10
181	Jack Morris	.05
182	Darryl Strawberry	.10
183	Robin Yount	.30
184	Lance Parrish	.05
185	Darnell Coles	.05
186	Kirby Puckett	.45
187	Terry Pendleton	.05
188	Don Slaught	.05
189	Jimmy Jones	.05
190	Dave Parker	.08
191	Mike Aldrete	.05
192	Mike Moore	.05
193	Greg Walker	.05
194	Calvin Schiraldi	.05
195	Dick Schofield	.05
196	Jody Reed	.05
197	Pete Smith	.05
198	Cal Ripken, Jr.	1.00
199	Lloyd Moseby	.05
200	Ruben Sierra	.10
201	R.J. Reynolds	.05
202	Bryn Smith	.05
203	Gary Pettis	.05
204	Steve Sax	.05
205	Frank DiPino	.05
206	Mike Scott	.05
207	Kurt Stillwell	.05
208	Mookie Wilson	.05
209	Lee Mazzilli	.05
210	Lance McCullers	.05
211	Rick Honeycutt	.05
212	John Tudor	.05
213	Jim Gott	.05
214	Frank Viola	.05
215	Juan Samuel	.05
216	Jesse Barfield	.05
217	Claudell Washington	.05
218	Rick Reuschel	.05
219	Jim Presley	.05
220	Tommy John	.05
221	Dan Plesac	.05
222	Barry Larkin	.10
223	Mike Stanley	.05
224	Cory Snyder	.05
225	Andre Dawson	.10
226	Ken Oberkfell	.05
227	Devon White	.08
228	Jamie Moyer	.05
229	Brook Jacoby	.05
230	Rob Murphy	.05
231	Bret Saberhagen	.08
232	Nolan Ryan	.90
233	Bruce Hurst	.05
234	Jesse Orosco	.05
235	Bobby Thigpen	.05
236	Pascual Perez	.05
237	Matt Nokes	.05
238	Bob Ojeda	.05
239	Joey Meyer	.05
240	Shane Rawley	.05
241	Jeff Robinson	.05
242	Jeff Reardon	.05
243	Ozzie Smith	.15
244	Dave Winfield	.30
245	John Kruk	.05
246	Carney Lansford	.05
247	Candy Maldonado	.05
248	Ken Phelps	.05
249	Ken Williams	.05
250	Al Nipper	.05
251	Mark McLemore	.05
252	Lee Smith	.08
253	Albert Hall	.05
254	Billy Ripken	.05
255	Kelly Gruber	.05
256	Charlie Hough	.05
257	John Smiley	.05
258	Tim Wallach	.05
259	Frank Tanana	.05
260	Mike Scioscia	.05
261	Damon Berryhill	.05
262	Dave Smith	.05
263	Willie Wilson	.05
264	Len Dykstra	.05
265	Randy Myers	.05
266	Keith Moreland	.05
267	Eric Plunk	.05
268	Todd Worrell	.05
269	Bob Walk	.05
270	Keith Atherton	.05
271	Mike Schmidt	.50
272	Mike Flanagan	.05
273	Rafael Santana	.05
274	Rob Thompson	.05
275	Rey Quinones	.05
276	Cecilio Guante	.05
277	B.J. Surhoff	.08
278	Chris Sabo	.05
279	Mitch Williams	.05
280	Greg Swindell	.05
281	Alan Trammell	.10
282	Storm Davis	.05
283	Chuck Finley	.05
284	Dave Stieb	.05
285	Scott Bailes	.05
286	Larry Sheets	.05
287	Danny Tartabull	.05
288	Checklist	.05
289	Todd Benzinger	.05
290	John Shelby	.05
291	Steve Lyons	.05
292	Mitch Webster	.05
293	Walt Terrell	.05
294	Pete Stanicek	.05
295	Chris Bosio	.05
296	Milt Thompson	.05
297	Fred Lynn	.08
298	Juan Berenguer	.05
299	Ken Dayley	.05
300	Joel Skinner	.05
301	Benito Santiago	.08
302	Ron Hassey	.05
303	Jose Uribe	.05
304	Harold Reynolds	.05
305	Dale Sveum	.05
306	Glenn Wilson	.05
307	Mike Witt	.05
308	Ron Robinson	.05
309	Denny Walling	.05
310	Joe Orsulak	.05
311	David Wells	.05
312	Steve Buechele	.05
313	Jose Oquendo	.05
314	Floyd Youmans	.05
315	Lou Whitaker	.05
316	Fernando Valenzuela	.08
317	Mike Boddicker	.05
318	Gerald Young	.05
319	Frank White	.05
320	Bill Wegman	.05
321	Tom Niedenfuer	.05
322	Ed Whitson	.05
323	Curt Young	.05
324	Greg Mathews	.05
325	Doug Jones	.05
326	Tommy Herr	.05
327	Kent Tekulve	.05
328	Rance Mulliniks	.05
329	Checklist	.05
330	Craig Lefferts	.05
331	Franklin Stubbs	.05
332	Rick Cerone	.05
333	Dave Schmidt	.05
334	Larry Parrish	.05
335	Tom Browning	.05
336	Checklist	.05

1988 Donruss Diamond Kings Supers

This 28-card set (including the checklist) marks the fourth edition of Donruss' super-size (5" x 7") set. These cards are exact duplicates of the 1988 Diamond Kings that feature player portraits by Dick Perez. A 12-piece Stan Musial puzzle was also included with the purchase of the super-size set which was marketed via a mail-in offer printed on Donruss wrappers.

		MT
Complete Set (28):		10.00
Common Player:		.25
1	Mark McGwire	4.00
2	Tim Raines	.30
3	Benito Santiago	.25
4	Alan Trammell	.30
5	Danny Tartabull	.25
6	Ron Darling	.25
7	Paul Molitor	.50
8	Devon White	.30
9	Andre Dawson	.30
10	Julio Franco	.25
11	Scott Fletcher	.25
12	Tony Fernandez	.25
13	Shane Rawley	.25
14	Kal Daniels	.25
15	Jack Clark	.25
16	Dwight Evans	.25
17	Tommy John	.25
18	Andy Van Slyke	.25
19	Gary Gaetti	.30
20	Mark Langston	.25
21	Will Clark	1.00
22	Glenn Hubbard	.25
23	Billy Hatcher	.25
24	Bob Welch	.25
25	Ivan Calderon	.25
26	Cal Ripken, Jr.	4.00
27	Checklist	.10
641	Stan Musial Puzzle Card	.25

1988 Donruss Pop-Ups

Donruss' 1988 Pop-Up cards were reduced to the standard 2-1/2" x 3-1/2". The set includes 20 cards that fold out so that the upper portion of the player stands upright, giving a three-dimensional effect. Pop-Ups feature players from the All-Star Game starting lineup. Card fronts feature full-color photos, with the player's name, team and position printed in black on a yellow banner near the bottom. As in previous issues, the backs contain only the player's name, league and position. Pop-Ups were distributed in individual packages containing one Pop-Up, three Stan Musial puzzle pieces and three All-Star cards.

		MT
Complete Set (20):		2.00
Common Player:		.10
Stan Musial Puzzle:		1.00
(1)	George Bell	.10
(2)	Wade Boggs	.50
(3)	Gary Carter	.12
(4)	Jack Clark	.10
(5)	Eric Davis	.15
(6)	Andre Dawson	.15
(7)	Rickey Henderson	.35
(8)	Davey Johnson	.10
(9)	Don Mattingly	.75
(10)	Terry Kennedy	.10
(11)	John McNamara	.10
(12)	Willie Randolph	.10
(13)	Cal Ripken, Jr.	1.00
(14)	Bret Saberhagen	.15
(15)	Ryne Sandberg	.65
(16)	Mike Schmidt	.70
(17)	Mike Scott	.10
(18)	Ozzie Smith	.35
(19)	Darryl Strawberry	.15
(20)	Dave Winfield	.30

1988 Donruss Rookies

For the third consecutive year, Donruss issued a 56-card boxed set highlighting current rookies. The complete set includes a checklist and a 15-piece Stan Musial Diamond Kings puzzle. As in previous years, the set is similar to the company's basic issue, with the exception of the logo and border color. Card fronts feature red, green and black-striped borders, with a red-and-white player name printed in the lower-left corner beneath the photo. "The Rookies" logo is printed in red, white and black in the lower-right corner. Backs are printed in black on bright aqua and include personal data, recent performance stats and major league totals, as well as 1984-88 minor league stats. The cards are the standard 2-1/2" x 3-1/2".

		MT
Complete Set (56):		9.00
Common Player:		.10
1	Mark Grace	2.50
2	Mike Campbell	.10
3	Todd Frowirth	.10
4	Dave Stapleton	.10
5	Shawn Abner	.10

6	Jose Cecena	.10
7	Dave Gallagher	.10
8	Mark Parent	.10
9	Cecil Espy	.10
10	Pete Smith	.10
11	Jay Buhner	1.50
12	Pat Borders	.20
13	Doug Jennings	.10
14	*Brady Anderson*	1.00
15	Pete Stanicek	.10
16	Roberto Kelly	.15
17	Jeff Treadway	.10
18	Walt Weiss	.25
19	Paul Gibson	.10
20	Tim Crews	.10
21	Melido Perez	.10
22	Steve Peters	.10
23	Craig Worthington	.10
24	John Trautwein	.10
25	DeWayne Vaughn	.10
26	David Wells	1.50
27	Al Leiter	.15
28	Tim Belcher	.15
29	Johnny Paredes	.10
30	Chris Sabo	.20
31	Damon Berryhill	.10
32	Randy Milligan	.10
33	Gary Thurman	.10
34	Kevin Elster	.15
35	Roberto Alomar	3.00
36	*Edgar Martinez* (photo actually Edwin Nunez)	1.25
37	Todd Stottlemyre	.15
38	Joey Meyer	.10
39	Carl Nichols	.10
40	Jack McDowell	.20
41	Jose Bautista	.10
42	Sil Campusano	.10
43	John Dopson	.10
44	Jody Reed	.15
45	Darrin Jackson	.20
46	Mike Capel	.10
47	Ron Gant	.40
48	John Davis	.10
49	Kevin Coffman	.10
50	Cris Carpenter	.10
51	Mackey Sasser	.10
52	Luis Alicea	.10
53	Bryan Harvey	.10
54	Steve Ellsworth	.10
55	Mike Macfarlane	.10
56	Checklist 1-56	.05

1988 Donruss Team Books

Three pages of nine cards each and a Stan Musial puzzle highlight these special team collection books. The cards feature the same design as the regular 1988 Donruss cards, but contain a 1988 copyright date instead of 1987 like the regular set. The cards are numbered like the regular issue with the exception of new cards of traded players and rookies produced especially for the team collection books. Books are commonly found complete with the cards and puzzle. The puzzle pieces are perforated for removal, but the card sheets are not.

		MT
Complete Set, Books (5):		20.00
Common Player:		.08
	Boston Red Sox team book	6.00
NEW	Brady Anderson	1.50
NEW	Rick Cerone	.08
NEW	Steve Ellsworth	.08
NEW	Dennis Lamp	.08
NEW	Kevin Romine	.08
NEW	Lee Smith	.35
NEW	Mike Smithson	.08
NEW	John Trautwein	.08
41	Jody Reed	.10
51	Roger Clemens	.90
92	Bob Stanley	.08
129	Rich Gedman	.08
153	Wade Boggs	.75
174	Ellis Burks	.20
216	Dwight Evans	.08
252	Bruce Hurst	.08
276	Marty Barrett	.08
297	Todd Benzinger	.10
339	Mike Greenwell	.08
399	Jim Rice	.10
421	John Marzano	.08
462	Oil Can Boyd	.08
498	Sam Horn	.08
544	Spike Owen	.08
585	Jeff Sellers	.08
623	Ed Romero	.08
634	Wes Gardner	.08
	Chicago Cubs team book:	5.00
NEW	Mike Bielecki	.08
NEW	Rich Gossage	.15
NEW	Drew Hall	.08
NEW	Darrin Jackson	.15
NEW	Vance Law	.08
NEW	Al Nipper	.08
NEW	Angel Salazar	.08
NEW	Calvin Schiraldi	.08
40	Mark Grace	2.00
68	Rick Sutcliffe	.10
119	Jody Davis	.08
146	Shawon Dunston	.10
169	Jamie Moyer	.08
191	Leon Durham	.08
242	Ryne Sandberg	.90
269	Andre Dawson	.25
315	Paul Noce	.08
324	Rafael Palmeiro	.70
438	Dave Martinez	.08
447	Jerry Mumphrey	.08
488	Jim Sundberg	.08
516	Manny Trillo	.08
539	Greg Maddux	1.50
561	Les Lancaster	.08
570	Frank DiPino	.08
639	Damon Berryhill	.08
646	Scott Sanderson	.08
	N.Y. Mets team book:	4.00
NEW	Jeff Innis	.08
NEW	Mackey Sasser	.08
NEW	Gene Walter	.08
37	Kevin Elster	.10
69	Dwight Gooden	.25
76	Ron Darling	.08
118	Sid Fernandez	.08
199	Gary Carter	.30
241	Wally Backman	.08
316	Keith Hernandez	.10
323	Dave Magadan	.10
364	Len Dykstra	.15
439	Darryl Strawberry	.15
446	Rick Aguilera	.10
562	Keith Miller	.08
569	Howard Johnson	.08
603	Terry Leach	.08
614	Lee Mazzilli	.08
617	Kevin McReynolds	.08
619	Barry Lyons	.08
620	Randy Myers	.15
632	Bob Ojeda	.08
648	Tim Teufel	.08
651	Roger McDowell	.10
652	Mookie Wilson	.08
653	David Cone	.25
657	Gregg Jefferies	1.75
	N.Y. Yankees team book:	6.00
NEW	John Candelaria	.08
NEW	Jack Clark	.15
NEW	Jose Cruz	.15
NEW	Richard Dotson	.08
NEW	Cecilio Guante	.08
NEW	Lee Guetterman	.08
NEW	Rafael Santana	.08
NEW	Steve Shields	.08
NEW	Don Slaught	.25
43	Al Leiter	.25
93	Dave Righetti	.10
105	Mike Pagliarulo	.10
128	Rick Rhoden	.08
175	Ron Guidry	.10
217	Don Mattingly	1.50
228	Willie Randolph	.08
251	Gary Ward	.08
277	Rickey Henderson	.60
278	Dave Winfield	.50
340	Claudell Washington	.08
374	Charles Hudson	.08
401	Tommy John	.15
474	Joel Skinner	.08
497	Tim Stoddard	.08
545	Jay Buhner	.60
616	Bobby Meacham	.08
635	Roberto Kelly	.10
	Oakland A's team book:	6.00
NEW	Don Baylor	.20
NEW	Ron Hassey	.08
NEW	Dave Henderson	.08
NEW	Glenn Hubbard	.08
NEW	Stan Javier	.08
NEW	Doug Jennings	.08
NEW	Ed Jurak	.08
NEW	Dave Parker	.10
NEW	Walt Weiss	.15
NEW	Bob Welch	.08
NEW	Matt Young	.08
97	Curt Young	.08
133	Gene Nelson	.08
158	Terry Steinbach	.10
178	Carney Lansford	.08
221	Tony Phillips	.08
256	Mark McGwire	3.00
302	Jose Canseco	1.00
349	Dennis Eckersley	.15
379	Mike Gallego	.08
425	Luis Polonia	.08
467	Steve Ontiveros	.08
472	Dave Stewart	.10
503	Eric Plunk	.08
528	Greg Cadaret	.08
590	Rick Honeycutt	.08
595	Storm Davis	.08

1989 Donruss Promo Sheet

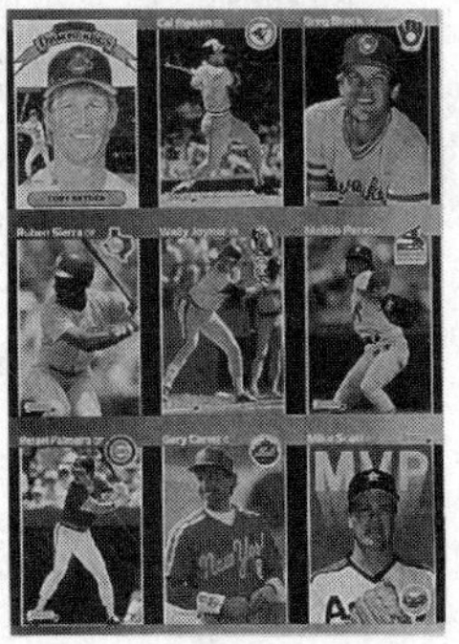

To introduce its card design for 1989, Donruss produced this sheet. Printed on semi-gloss paper, the 7-1/2" x 10-1/2" blank-back sheet has images of seven regular cards, a Diamond King and an MVP.

		MT
Complete Sheet:		15.00
(1)	Greg Brock	
(2)	Gary Carter	
(3)	Wally Joyner	
(4)	Rafael Palmeiro	
(5)	Melido Perez	
(6)	Cal Ripken Jr.	
(7)	Mike Scott (MVP)	
(8)	Ruben Sierra	
(9)	Cory Snyder (DK)	

1989 Donruss

This basic annual issue consists of 660 2-1/2" x 3-1/2" cards, including 26 Diamond Kings (DK) portrait cards and 20 Rated Rookies (RR) cards. Top and bottom borders of the cards are printed in a variety of colors that fade from dark to light. A white-lettered player name is printed across the top margin. The team logo appears upper-right and the Donruss logo lower-left. A black outer stripe varnish gives faintly visible filmstrip texture to the border. Backs are in orange and black, similar to the 1988 design, with personal info, recent stats and major league totals. Team logo sticker cards (22 total) and Warren Spahn puzzle cards (63 total) are included in individual wax packs of cards. Each regular player card can be found with a back variation in the header line above the stats: i.e., "*Denotes" or "*Denotes*". Neither version carries a premium.

		MT
Complete Factory Set, Unopened (660):		40.00
Complete Set (660):		25.00
Common Player:		.05
Warren Spahn Puzzle:		1.00
Wax Box:		25.00
1	Mike Greenwell (DK)	.05
2	Bobby Bonilla (DK)	.08
3	Pete Incaviglia (DK)	.05
4	Chris Sabo (DK)	.08
5	Robin Yount (DK)	.15
6	Tony Gwynn (DK)	.25
7	Carlton Fisk (DK)	.12
8	Cory Snyder (DK)	.05
9	David Cone (DK)	.08
10	Kevin Seitzer (DK)	.08
11	Rick Reuschel (DK)	.05
12	Johnny Ray (DK)	.05
13	Dave Schmidt (DK)	.05
14	Andres Galarraga (DK)	.15
15	Kirk Gibson (DK)	.08
16	Fred McGriff (DK)	.15
17	Mark Grace (DK)	.20
18	Jeff Robinson (DK)	.05
19	Vince Coleman (DK)	.05
20	Dave Henderson (DK)	.08
21	Harold Reynolds (DK)	.08
22	Gerald Perry (DK)	.05
23	Frank Viola (DK)	.08
24	Steve Bedrosian (DK)	.08
25	Glenn Davis (DK)	.08
26	Don Mattingly (DK)	.30
27	Checklist 1-27	.05
28	*Sandy Alomar, Jr.* (RR)	.45
29	*Steve Searcy* (RR)	.08
30	*Cameron Drew* (RR)	.05
31	*Gary Sheffield* (RR)	.75
32	*Erik Hanson* (RR)	.25
33	*Ken Griffey, Jr.* (RR)	20.00
34	*Greg Harris* (RR)	.05
35	Gregg Jefferies (RR)	.35
36	*Luis Medina* (RR)	.05
37	*Carlos Quintana* (RR)	.05
38	*Felix Jose* (RR)	.15
39	*Cris Carpenter* (RR)	.05
40	*Ron Jones* (RR)	.05
41	*Dave West* (RR)	.08
42	*Randy Johnson* (RR)	1.00
43	*Mike Harkey* (RR)	.10
44	*Pete Harnisch* (RR)	.15
45	*Tom Gordon* (RR)	.12
46	*Gregg Olson* (RR)	.10
47	*Alex Sanchez* (RR)	.05
48	Ruben Sierra	.08
49	Rafael Palmeiro	.25
50	Ron Gant	.15
51	Cal Ripken, Jr.	.75
52	Wally Joyner	.10
53	Gary Carter	.10
54	Andy Van Slyke	.08
55	Robin Yount	.25
56	Pete Incaviglia	.08
57	Greg Brock	.05
58	Melido Perez	.05
59	Craig Lefferts	.05
60	Gary Pettis	.05
61	Danny Tartabull	.05
62	Guillermo Hernandez	.05
63	Ozzie Smith	.25
64	Gary Gaetti	.12
65	Mark Davis	.05
66	Lee Smith	.08
67	Dennis Eckersley	.10
68	Wade Boggs	.30
69	Mike Scott	.05
70	Fred McGriff	.30
71	Tom Browning	.08
72	Claudell Washington	.05
73	Mel Hall	.05
74	Don Mattingly	.45
75	Steve Bedrosian	.05
76	Juan Samuel	.05
77	Mike Scioscia	.05
78	Dave Righetti	.05
79	Alfredo Griffin	.05
80	Eric Davis	.10
81	Juan Berenguer	.05
82	Todd Worrell	.08
83	Joe Carter	.25
84	Steve Sax	.05
85	Frank White	.05
86	John Kruk	.08
87	Rance Mulliniks	.05
88	Alan Ashby	.05
89	Charlie Leibrandt	.05
90	Frank Tanana	.05
91	Jose Canseco	.35
92	Barry Bonds	.50
93	Harold Reynolds	.08
94	Mark McLemore	.05
95	Mark McGwire	1.00
96	Eddie Murray	.20
97	Tim Raines	.08
98	Rob Thompson	.05
99	Kevin McReynolds	.08
100	Checklist 28-137	.05
101	Carlton Fisk	.12
102	Dave Martinez	.05
103	Glenn Braggs	.05
104	Dale Murphy	.12
105	Ryne Sandberg	.40
106	Dennis Martinez	.10
107	Pete O'Brien	.05
108	Dick Schofield	.05
109	Henry Cotto	.05
110	Mike Marshall	.05
111	Keith Moreland	.05
112	Tom Brunansky	.05
113	Kelly Gruber	.05
114	Brook Jacoby	.05
115	*Keith Brown*	.05
116	Matt Nokes	.08
117	Keith Hernandez	.05
118	Bob Forsch	.05
119	Bert Blyleven	.10
120	Willie Wilson	.08
121	Tommy Gregg	.05
122	Jim Rice	.08
123	Bob Knepper	.05
124	Danny Jackson	.08
125	Eric Plunk	.05
126	Brian Fisher	.05
127	Mike Pagliarulo	.05
128	Tony Gwynn	.45
129	Lance McCullers	.05
130	Andres Galarraga	.20
131	Jose Uribe	.05
132	Kirk Gibson	.08
133	David Palmer	.05
134	R.J. Reynolds	.05
135	Greg Walker	.05
136	Kirk McCaskill	.05
137	Shawon Dunston	.08
138	Andy Allanson	.05
139	Rob Murphy	.05
140	Mike Aldrete	.05
141	Terry Kennedy	.05
142	Scott Fletcher	.05
143	Steve Balboni	.05
144	Bret Saberhagen	.12
145	Ozzie Virgil	.05
146	Dale Sveum	.05
147	Darryl Strawberry	.12
148	Harold Baines	.10
149	George Bell	.08
150	Dave Parker	.12
151	Bobby Bonilla	.10
152	Mookie Wilson	.05
153	Ted Power	.05
154	Nolan Ryan	.75
155	Jeff Reardon	.05
156	Tim Wallach	.08
157	Jamie Moyer	.05
158	Rich Gossage	.08
159	Dave Winfield	.25
160	Von Hayes	.05
161	Willie McGee	.10
162	Rich Gedman	.05
163	Tony Pena	.05
164	Mike Morgan	.05
165	Charlie Hough	.05
166	Mike Stanley	.05
167	Andre Dawson	.20
168	Joe Boever	.05
169	Pete Stanicek	.05
170	Bob Boone	.08
171	Ron Darling	.08
172	Bob Walk	.05
173	Rob Deer	.05
174	Steve Buechele	.05
175	Ted Higuera	.05
176	Ozzie Guillen	.05
177	Candy Maldonado	.05
178	Doyle Alexander	.05
179	Mark Gubicza	.10
180	Alan Trammell	.15
181	Vince Coleman	.08
182	Kirby Puckett	.45
183	Chris Brown	.05
184	Marty Barrett	.05
185	Stan Javier	.05
186	Mike Greenwell	.08
187	Billy Hatcher	.05
188	Jimmy Key	.08
189	Nick Esasky	.05
190	Don Slaught	.05
191	Cory Snyder	.05
192	John Candelaria	.05
193	Mike Schmidt	.35
194	Kevin Gross	.05
195	John Tudor	.05
196	Neil Allen	.05
197	Orel Hershiser	.08
198	Kal Daniels	.05
199	Kent Hrbek	.15
200	Checklist 138-247	.05
201	Joe Magrane	.05
202	Scott Bailes	.05
203	Tim Belcher	.10
204	George Brett	.40
205	Benito Santiago	.12
206	Tony Fernandez	.10
207	Gerald Young	.05
208	Bo Jackson	.25
209	Chet Lemon	.05
210	Storm Davis	.05
211	Doug Drabek	.05
212	Mickey Brantley (photo actually Nelson Simmons)	.05
213	Devon White	.08
214	Dave Stewart	.08

215	Dave Schmidt	.05
216	Bryn Smith	.05
217	Brett Butler	.08
218	Bob Ojeda	.05
219	*Steve Rosenberg*	.05
220	Hubie Brooks	.05
221	B.J. Surhoff	.05
222	Rick Mahler	.05
223	Rick Sutcliffe	.05
224	Neal Heaton	.05
225	Mitch Williams	.08
226	Chuck Finley	.08
227	Mark Langston	.10
228	Jesse Orosco	.05
229	Ed Whitson	.05
230	Terry Pendleton	.08
231	Lloyd Moseby	.05
232	Greg Swindell	.05
233	John Franco	.05
234	Jack Morris	.10
235	Howard Johnson	.08
236	Glenn Davis	.05
237	Frank Viola	.08
238	Kevin Seitzer	.05
239	Gerald Perry	.05
240	Dwight Evans	.10
241	Jim Deshaies	.05
242	Bo Diaz	.05
243	Carney Lansford	.05
244	Mike LaValliere	.05
245	Rickey Henderson	.20
246	Roberto Alomar	.60
247	Jimmy Jones	.05
248	Pascual Perez	.05
249	Will Clark	.35
250	Fernando Valenzuela	.10
251	Shane Rawley	.05
252	Sid Bream	.05
253	Steve Lyons	.05
254	Brian Downing	.05
255	Mark Grace	.30
256	Tom Candiotti	.05
257	Barry Larkin	.12
258	Mike Krukow	.05
259	Billy Ripken	.05
260	Cecilio Guante	.05
261	Scott Bradley	.05
262	Floyd Bannister	.05
263	Pete Smith	.05
264	Jim Gantner	.05
265	Roger McDowell	.05
266	Bobby Thigpen	.05
267	Jim Clancy	.05
268	Terry Steinbach	.08
269	Mike Dunne	.05
270	Dwight Gooden	.10
271	Mike Heath	.05
272	Dave Smith	.05
273	Keith Atherton	.05
274	Tim Burke	.05
275	Damon Berryhill	.05
276	Vance Law	.05
277	Rich Dotson	.05
278	Lance Parrish	.08
279	Geronimo Berroa	.08
280	Roger Clemens	.40
281	Greg Mathews	.05
282	Tom Niedenfuer	.05
283	Paul Kilgus	.05
284	Jose Guzman	.05
285	Calvin Schiraldi	.05
286	Charlie Puleo	.05
287	Joe Orsulak	.05
288	Jack Howell	.05
289	Kevin Elster	.05
290	Jose Lind	.08
291	Paul Molitor	.25
292	Cecil Espy	.05
293	Bill Wegman	.05
294	Dan Pasqua	.05
295	Scott Garrelts	.05
296	Walt Terrell	.05
297	Ed Hearn	.05
298	Lou Whitaker	.08
299	Ken Dayley	.05
300	Checklist 248-357	.05
301	Tommy Herr	.05
302	Mike Brumley	.05
303	Ellis Burks	.10
304	Curt Young	.05
305	Jody Reed	.10
306	Bill Doran	.05
307	David Wells	.08
308	Ron Robinson	.05
309	Rafael Santana	.05
310	Julio Franco	.10
311	Jack Clark	.05
312	Chris James	.05
313	Milt Thompson	.05
314	John Shelby	.05
315	Al Leiter	.05
316	Mike Davis	.05
317	*Chris Sabo*	.15
318	Greg Gagne	.05
319	Jose Oquendo	.05
320	John Farrell	.05
321	Franklin Stubbs	.05
322	Kurt Stillwell	.05
323	Shawn Abner	.05
324	Mike Flanagan	.05
325	Kevin Bass	.05
326	Pat Tabler	.05
327	Mike Henneman	.08
328	Rick Honeycutt	.05
329	John Smiley	.10
330	Rey Quinones	.05
331	Johnny Ray	.05
332	Bob Welch	.08
333	Larry Sheets	.05
334	Jeff Parrett	.05
335	Rick Reuschel	.05
336	Randy Myers	.10
337	Ken Williams	.05
338	Andy McGaffigan	.05
339	Joey Meyer	.05
340	Dion James	.05
341	Les Lancaster	.05
342	Tom Foley	.05
343	Geno Petralli	.05
344	Dan Petry	.05
345	Alvin Davis	.05
346	Mickey Hatcher	.05
347	Marvell Wynne	.05
348	Danny Cox	.05
349	Dave Stieb	.08
350	Jay Bell	.08
351	Jeff Treadway	.05
352	Luis Salazar	.05
353	Len Dykstra	.15
354	Juan Agosto	.05
355	Gene Larkin	.05
356	Steve Farr	.05
357	Paul Assenmacher	.05
358	Todd Benzinger	.05
359	Larry Andersen	.05
360	Paul O'Neill	.12
361	Ron Hassey	.05
362	Jim Gott	.05
363	Ken Phelps	.05
364	Tim Flannery	.05
365	Randy Ready	.05
366	*Nelson Santovenia*	.05
367	Kelly Downs	.05
368	Danny Heep	.05
369	Phil Bradley	.05
370	Jeff Robinson	.05
371	Ivan Calderon	.05
372	Mike Witt	.05
373	Greg Maddux	.75
374	Carmen Castillo	.05
375	Jose Rijo	.05
376	Joe Price	.05
377	R.C. Gonzalez	.05
378	Oddibe McDowell	.05
379	Jim Presley	.05
380	Brad Wellman	.05
381	Tom Glavine	.25
382	Dan Plesac	.05
383	Wally Backman	.05
384	*Dave Gallagher*	.05
385	Tom Henke	.05
386	Luis Polonia	.05
387	Junior Ortiz	.05
388	David Cone	.12
389	Dave Bergman	.05
390	Danny Darwin	.05
391	Dan Gladden	.05
392	*John Dopson*	.05
393	Frank DiPino	.05
394	Al Nipper	.05
395	Willie Randolph	.05
396	Don Carman	.05
397	Scott Terry	.05
398	Rick Cerone	.05
399	Tom Pagnozzi	.05
400	Checklist 358-467	.05
401	Mickey Tettleton	.08
402	Curtis Wilkerson	.05
403	Jeff Russell	.05
404	Pat Perry	.05
405	*Jose Alvarez*	.05
406	Rick Schu	.05
407	*Sherman Corbett*	.05
408	Dave Magadan	.08
409	Bob Kipper	.05
410	Don August	.05
411	Bob Brower	.05
412	Chris Bosio	.05
413	Jerry Reuss	.05
414	Atlee Hammaker	.05
415	Jim Walewander	.05
416	*Mike Macfarlane*	.08
417	Pat Sheridan	.05
418	Pedro Guerrero	.05
419	Allan Anderson	.05
420	*Mark Parent*	.08
421	Bob Stanley	.05
422	Mike Gallego	.05
423	Bruce Hurst	.05
424	Dave Meads	.05
425	Jesse Barfield	.05
426	*Rob Dibble*	.15
427	Joel Skinner	.05
428	Ron Kittle	.05
429	Rick Rhoden	.05
430	Bob Dernier	.05
431	Steve Jeltz	.05
432	Rick Dempsey	.05
433	Roberto Kelly	.10
434	Dave Anderson	.05
435	Herm Winningham	.05
436	Al Newman	.05
437	Jose DeLeon	.05
438	Doug Jones	.08
439	Brian Holton	.05
440	Jeff Montgomery	.10
441	Dickie Thon	.05
442	Cecil Fielder	.20
443	*John Fishel*	.05
444	Jerry Don Gleaton	.05
445	*Paul Gibson*	.05
446	Walt Weiss	.08
447	Glenn Wilson	.05
448	Mike Moore	.05
449	Chili Davis	.10
450	Dave Henderson	.05
451	*Jose Bautista*	.05
452	Rex Hudler	.05
453	Bob Brenly	.05
454	Mackey Sasser	.05
455	Daryl Boston	.05
456	Mike Fitzgerald	.05
457	Jeffery Leonard	.05
458	Bruce Sutter	.05
459	Mitch Webster	.05
460	Joe Hesketh	.05
461	Bobby Witt	.05
462	Stew Cliburn	.05
463	Scott Bankhead	.05
464	*Ramon Martinez*	.40
465	Dave Leiper	.05
466	*Luis Alicea*	.08
467	John Cerutti	.05
468	Ron Washington	.05
469	Jeff Reed	.05
470	Jeff Robinson	.05
471	Sid Fernandez	.05
472	Terry Puhl	.05
473	Charlie Lea	.05
474	*Israel Sanchez*	.05
475	Bruce Benedict	.05
476	Oil Can Boyd	.05
477	Craig Reynolds	.05
478	Frank Williams	.05
479	Greg Cadaret	.05
480	*Randy Kramer*	.05
481	*Dave Eiland*	.05
482	Eric Show	.05
483	Garry Templeton	.05
484	Wallace Johnson	.05
485	Kevin Mitchell	.08
486	Tim Crews	.05
487	Mike Maddux	.05
488	Dave LaPoint	.05
489	Fred Manrique	.05
490	Greg Minton	.05
491	*Doug Dascenzo*	.08
492	Willie Upshaw	.05
493	*Jack Armstrong*	.10
494	Kirt Manwaring	.10
495	Jeff Ballard	.05
496	Jeff Kunkel	.05
497	Mike Campbell	.05
498	Gary Thurman	.05
499	Zane Smith	.05
500	Checklist 468-577	.05
501	Mike Birkbeck	.05
502	Terry Leach	.05
503	Shawn Hillegas	.05
504	Manny Lee	.05
505	*Doug Jennings*	.08
506	Ken Oberkfell	.05
507	Tim Teufel	.05
508	Tom Brookens	.05
509	Rafael Ramirez	.05
510	Fred Toliver	.05
511	*Brian Holman*	.05
512	Mike Bielecki	.05
513	*Jeff Pico*	.05
514	Charles Hudson	.05
515	Bruce Ruffin	.05
516	Larry McWilliams	.05
517	Jeff Sellers	.05
518	*John Costello*	.05
519	Brady Anderson	.25
520	Craig McMurtry	.05
521	Ray Hayward	.05
522	Drew Hall	.05
523	*Mark Lemke*	.05
524	*Oswald Peraza*	.05
525	*Bryan Harvey*	.10
526	Rick Aguilera	.05
527	Tom Prince	.05
528	Mark Clear	.05
529	Jerry Browne	.05
530	Juan Castillo	.05
531	Jack McDowell	.15
532	Chris Speier	.05
533	Darrell Evans	.08
534	Luis Aquino	.05
535	Eric King	.05
536	*Ken Hill*	.40
537	Randy Bush	.05
538	Shane Mack	.05
539	Tom Bolton	.05
540	Gene Nelson	.05
541	Wes Gardner	.05
542	Ken Caminiti	.10
543	Duane Ward	.05
544	*Norm Charlton*	.12
545	*Hal Morris*	.40
546	Rich Yett	.05
547	*Hensley Meulens*	.10
548	Greg Harris	.05
549	Darren Daulton	.08
550	Jeff Hamilton	.05
551	Luis Aguayo	.05
552	Tim Leary	.05
553	Ron Oester	.05
554	Steve Lombardozzi	.05
555	*Tim Jones*	.05
556	Bud Black	.05
557	Alejandro Pena	.05
558	*Jose DeJesus*	.05
559	Dennis Rasmussen	.05
560	*Pat Borders*	.08
561	*Craig Biggio*	.50
562	*Luis de los Santos*	.05
563	Fred Lynn	.10
564	*Todd Burns*	.05
565	Felix Fermin	.05
566	Darnell Coles	.05
567	Willie Fraser	.05
568	Glenn Hubbard	.05
569	*Craig Worthington*	.05
570	*Johnny Paredes*	.05
571	Don Robinson	.05
572	Barry Lyons	.05
573	Bill Long	.05
574	Tracy Jones	.05
575	Juan Nieves	.05
576	Andres Thomas	.05
577	*Rolando Roomes*	.05
578	Luis Rivera	.05
579	*Chad Kreuter*	.15
580	Tony Armas	.08
581	Jay Buhner	.15
582	Ricky Horton	.05
583	Andy Hawkins	.05
584	*Sil Campusano*	.05
585	Dave Clark	.05
586	*Van Snider*	.05
587	Todd Frohwirth	.05
588	Warren Spahn Puzzle Card	.05
589	*William Brennan*	.05
590	*German Gonzalez*	.05
591	Ernie Whitt	.05
592	Jeff Blauser	.05
593	Spike Owen	.05
594	Matt Williams	.35
595	Lloyd McClendon	.05
596	Steve Ontiveros	.05
597	*Scott Medvin*	.05
598	*Hipolito Pena*	.05
599	*Jerald Clark*	.05
600a	Checklist 578-BC26 (#635 is Kurt Schilling)	.15
600b	Checklist 578-BC26 (#635 is Curt Schilling)	.05
601	Carmelo Martinez	.05
602	Mike LaCoss	.05
603	Mike Devereaux	.05
604	*Alex Madrid*	.05
605	Gary Redus	.05
606	Lance Johnson	.08
607	*Terry Clark*	.05
608	Manny Trillo	.05
609	*Scott Jordan*	.05
610	Jay Howell	.05
611	*Francisco Melendez*	.05
612	Mike Boddicker	.05
613	Kevin Brown	.10
614	Dave Valle	.05
615	Tim Laudner	.05
616	*Andy Nezelek*	.05
617	Chuck Crim	.05
618	Jack Savage	.05
619	Adam Peterson	.05
620	Todd Stottlemyre	.05
621	*Lance Blankenship*	.10
622	*Miguel Garcia*	.05
623	Keith Miller	.05
624	*Ricky Jordan*	.08
625	Ernest Riles	.05
626	John Moses	.05
627	Nelson Liriano	.05
628	Mike Smithson	.05
629	Scott Sanderson	.05
630	Dale Mohorcic	.05
631	Marvin Freeman	.05
632	Mike Young	.05
633	Dennis Lamp	.05
634	*Dante Bichette*	.75
635	*Curt Schilling*	.75
636	*Scott May*	.05
637	*Mike Schooler*	.05
638	Rick Leach	.05
639	*Tom Lampkin*	.05
640	*Brian Meyer*	.05
641	Brian Harper	.05
642	John Smoltz	.75
643	Jose Canseco (40/40)	.20
644	Bill Schroeder	.05
645	Edgar Martinez	.15
646	*Dennis Cook*	.08
647	Barry Jones	.05
648	(Orel Hershiser) (59 and Counting)	.15
649	*Rod Nichols*	.05
650	Jody Davis	.05
651	*Bob Milacki*	.05
652	Mike Jackson	.05
653	*Derek Lilliquist*	.10
654	Paul Mirabella	.05
655	Mike Diaz	.05
656	Jeff Musselman	.05
657	Jerry Reed	.05
658	*Kevin Blankenship*	.08
659	Wayne Tolleson	.05
660	*Eric Hetzel*	.05

1989 Donruss Grand Slammers

One card from this 12-card set was included in each Donruss cello pack. The complete insert set was included in factory sets. The featured players all hit grand slams in 1988. The 2-1/2" x 3-1/2" cards feature full color action photos. Backs tell the story of the player's grand slam. Border color variations on the front of the card have been discovered, but the prices are consistent with all forms of the cards.

		MT
Complete Set (12):		2.50
Common Player:		.25
1	Jose Canseco	.40
2	Mike Marshall	.25
3	Walt Weiss	.25
4	Kevin McReynolds	.25
5	Mike Greenwell	.25
6	Dave Winfield	.30
7	Mark McGwire	1.00
8	Keith Hernandez	.25
9	Franklin Stubbs	.25
10	Danny Tartabull	.25
11	Jesse Barfield	.25
12	Ellis Burks	.25

1989 Donruss MVP

This set, numbered BC1-BC26, was randomly inserted in Donruss wax packs, but not included in factory sets or other card packs. Players highlighted were selected by Donruss, one player per team. MVP cards feature a variation of the design in the basic Donruss issue, with multi-color upper and lower borders and black side borders. The "MVP" designation in large, bright letters serves as a backdrop for the full-color player photo. The cards measure 2-1/2" x 3-1/2".

		MT
Complete Set (26):		3.00
Common Player:		.10
1	Kirby Puckett	.50
2	Mike Scott	.10
3	Joe Carter	.10
4	Orel Hershiser	.10
5	Jose Canseco	.40
6	Darryl Strawberry	.15
7	George Brett	.45
8	Andre Dawson	.20
9	Paul Molitor	.45
10	Andy Van Slyke	.10
11	Dave Winfield	.30
12	Kevin Gross	.10
13	Mike Greenwell	.10
14	Ozzie Smith	.40
15	Cal Ripken	1.00
16	Andres Galarraga	.20
17	Alan Trammell	.15
18	Kal Daniels	.10
19	Fred McGriff	.20
20	Tony Gwynn	.45
21	Wally Joyner	.10
22	Will Clark	.35
23	Ozzie Guillen	.10
24	Gerald Perry	.10
25	Alvin Davis	.10
26	Ruben Sierra	.10

1989 Donruss All-Stars

For the fourth consecutive year Donruss featured a 64-card set with players from the 1988 All-Star Game. The card fronts include a red-to-gold fade or gold-to-red fade border and blue vertical side borders. The top border features the player's name and position along with the "Donruss 89" logo. Each full-color player photo is highlighted by a thin white line and includes a league logo in the lower right corner. Card backs reveal an orange-gold border and black and white printing. The player's ID and personal information is displayed with a gold star on both sides. The star in the left corner includes the card number. 1988 All-Star game statistics and run totals follow along with a career highlights feature surrounded by the team, All-Star Game MLB, MLBPA, and Leaf Inc. logos. The All-Stars were distributed in wax packages containing five All-Stars, one Pop-Up, and one three-piece Warren Spahn puzzle card.

		MT
Complete Set (64):		5.00
Common Player:		.10
Warren Spahn Puzzle:		1.00
1	Mark McGwire	1.00
2	Jose Canseco	.60
3	Paul Molitor	.25
4	Rickey Henderson	.25
5	Cal Ripken, Jr.	1.50
6	Dave Winfield	.25
7	Wade Boggs	.50
8	Frank Viola	.10
9	Terry Steinbach	.10
10	Tom Kelly	.10
11	George Brett	.60
12	Doyle Alexander	.10
13	Gary Gaetti	.10
14	Roger Clemens	.75
15	Mike Greenwell	.10
16	Dennis Eckersley	.15
17	Carney Lansford	.10
18	Mark Gubicza	.10
19	Tim Laudner	.10
20	Doug Jones	.10
21	Don Mattingly	.75
22	Dan Plesac	.10
23	Kirby Puckett	.75
24	Jeff Reardon	.10
25	Johnny Ray	.10
26	Jeff Russell	.10
27	Harold Reynolds	.10
28	Dave Stieb	.10
29	Kurt Stillwell	.10
30	Jose Canseco	.60
31	Terry Steinbach	.10
32	A.L. Checklist	.05
33	Will Clark	.40
34	Darryl Strawberry	.20
35	Ryne Sandberg	.65
36	Andre Dawson	.12
37	Ozzie Smith	.25
38	Vince Coleman	.10
39	Bobby Bonilla	.12
40	Dwight Gooden	.10
41	Gary Carter	.12
42	Whitey Herzog	.10
43	Shawon Dunston	.10
44	David Cone	.12
45	Andres Galarraga	.15
46	Mark Davis	.10
47	Barry Larkin	.15
48	Kevin Gross	.10
49	Vance Law	.10
50	Orel Hershiser	.10
51	Willie McGee	.10
52	Danny Jackson	.10
53	Rafael Palmeiro	.25
54	Bob Knepper	.10
55	Lance Parrish	.10
56	Greg Maddux	.75
57	Gerald Perry	.10
58	Bob Walk	.10
59	Chris Sabo	.10
60	Todd Worrell	.10
61	Andy Van Slyke	.10
62	Ozzie Smith	.25
63	Riverfront Stadium	.10
64	N.L. Checklist	.05

1989 Donruss Baseball's Best

For the second consecutive year, Donruss issued a "Baseball's Best" set in 1989 to highlight the game's top players. The special 336-card set was packaged in a special box and was sold at various retail chains nationwide following the conclusion of the 1989 baseball season. The cards are styled after the regular 1989 Donruss set with green borders and a glossy finish. The set included a Warren Spahn puzzle.

		MT
Complete Unopened Set (336):		200.00
Complete Set (336):		20.00
Common Player:		.05
1	Don Mattingly	.90
2	Tom Glavine	.15
3	Bert Blyleven	.05
4	Andre Dawson	.10
5	Pete O'Brien	.05
6	Eric Davis	.10
7	George Brett	.50
8	Glenn Davis	.05
9	Ellis Burks	.10
10	Kirk Gibson	.08
11	Carlton Fisk	.12
12	Andres Galarraga	.15
13	Alan Trammell	.15
14	Dwight Gooden	.15
15	Paul Molitor	.15
16	Roger McDowell	.05
17	Doug Drabek	.05
18	Kent Hrbek	.08
19	Vince Coleman	.05
20	Steve Sax	.05
21	Roberto Alomar	.35
22	Carney Lansford	.05
23	Will Clark	.50
24	Alvin Davis	.05
25	Bobby Thigpen	.05
26	Ryne Sandberg	.75
27	Devon White	.08
28	Mike Greenwell	.05
29	Dale Murphy	.20
30	Jeff Ballard	.05
31	Kelly Gruber	.05
32	Julio Franco	.08
33	Bobby Bonilla	.10
34	Tim Wallach	.05
35	Lou Whitaker	.08
36	Jay Howell	.05
37	Greg Maddux	.75
38	Bill Doran	.05
39	Danny Tartabull	.05
40	Darryl Strawberry	.10
41	Ron Darling	.05
42	Tony Gwynn	.50
43	Mark McGwire	1.50
44	Ozzie Smith	.25
45	Andy Van Slyke	.05
46	Juan Berenguer	.05
47	Von Hayes	.05
48	Tony Fernandez	.08
49	Eric Plunk	.05
50	Ernest Riles	.05
51	Harold Reynolds	.05
52	Andy Hawkins	.05
53	Robin Yount	.30
54	Danny Jackson	.05
55	Nolan Ryan	1.25
56	Joe Carter	.10
57	Jose Canseco	.75
58	Jody Davis	.05
59	Lance Parrish	.05
60	Mitch Williams	.05
61	Brook Jacoby	.05
62	Tom Browning	.05
63	Kurt Stillwell	.05
64	Rafael Ramirez	.05
65	Roger Clemens	.60
66	Mike Scioscia	.05
67	Dave Gallagher	.05
68	Mark Langston	.08
69	Chet Lemon	.05
70	Kevin McReynolds	.05
71	Rob Deer	.05
72	Tommy Herr	.05
73	Barry Bonds	.75
74	Frank Viola	.05
75	Pedro Guerrero	.05
76	Dave Righetti	.05
77	Bruce Hurst	.05
78	Rickey Henderson	.30
79	Robby Thompson	.05
80	Randy Johnson	.35
81	Harold Baines	.08
82	Calvin Schiraldi	.05
83	Kirk McCaskill	.05
84	Lee Smith	.08
85	John Smoltz	.15
86	Mickey Tettleton	.05
87	Jimmy Key	.08
88	Rafael Palmeiro	.15
89	Sid Bream	.05
90	Dennis Martinez	.08
91	Frank Tanana	.05
92	Eddie Murray	.30
93	Shawon Dunston	.10
94	Mike Scott	.05
95	Bret Saberhagen	.10
96	David Cone	.15
97	Kevin Elster	.05
98	Jack Clark	.05
99	Dave Stewart	.05
100	Jose Oquendo	.05
101	Jose Lind	.05
102	Gary Gaetti	.05
103	Ricky Jordan	.05
104	Fred McGriff	.20
105	Don Slaught	.05
106	Jose Uribe	.05
107	Jeffrey Leonard	.05
108	Lee Guetterman	.05
109	Chris Bosio	.05
110	Barry Larkin	.12
111	Ruben Sierra	.05
112	Greg Swindell	.05
113	Gary Sheffield	.35
114	Lonnie Smith	.05
115	Chili Davis	.05
116	Damon Berryhill	.05
117	Tom Candiotti	.05
118	Kal Daniels	.05
119	Mark Gubicza	.05
120	Jim Deshaies	.05
121	Dwight Evans	.05
122	Mike Morgan	.05
123	Dan Pasqua	.05
124	Bryn Smith	.05
125	Doyle Alexander	.05
126	Howard Johnson	.05
127	Chuck Crim	.05
128	Darren Daulton	.05
129	Jeff Robinson	.05
130	Kirby Puckett	.50
131	Joe Magrane	.05
132	Jesse Barfield	.05
133	Mark Davis (Photo actually Dave Leiper)	.05
134	Dennis Eckersley	.10
135	Mike Krukow	.05
136	Jay Buhner	.10
137	Ozzie Guillen	.05
138	Rick Sutcliffe	.05
139	Wally Joyner	.10
140	Wade Boggs	.50
141	Jeff Treadway	.05
142	Cal Ripken	1.50
143	Dave Steib	.05
144	Pete Incaviglia	.05
145	Bob Walk	.05
146	Nelson Santovenia	.05
147	Mike Heath	.05
148	Willie Randolph	.05
149	Paul Kilgus	.05
150	Billy Hatcher	.05
151	Steve Farr	.05
152	Gregg Jefferies	.10
153	Randy Myers	.05
154	Garry Templeton	.05
155	Walt Weiss	.05
156	Terry Pendleton	.05
157	John Smiley	.05
158	Greg Gagne	.05
159	Lenny Dykstra	.05
160	Nelson Liriano	.05
161	Alvaro Espinoza	.05
162	Rick Reuschel	.05
163	Omar Vizquel	.10
164	Clay Parker	.05
165	Dan Plesac	.05
166	John Franco	.05
167	Scott Fletcher	.05
168	Cory Snyder	.05
169	Bo Jackson	.25
170	Tommy Gregg	.05
171	Jim Abbott	.10
172	Jerome Walton	.05
173	Doug Jones	.05
174	Todd Benzinger	.05
175	Frank White	.05
176	Craig Biggio	.10
177	John Dopson	.05
178	Alfredo Griffin	.05
179	Melido Perez	.05
180	Tim Burke	.05
181	Matt Nokes	.05
182	Gary Carter	.12
183	Ted Higuera	.05
184	Ken Howell	.05
185	Rey Quinones	.05
186	Wally Backman	.05
187	Tom Brunansky	.05
188	Steve Balboni	.05
189	Marvell Wynne	.05
190	Dave Henderson	.05
191	Don Robinson	.05
192	Ken Griffey, Jr.	4.00
193	Ivan Calderon	.05
194	Mike Bielecki	.05
195	Johnny Ray	.05
196	Rob Murphy	.05
197	Andres Thomas	.05
198	Phil Bradley	.05
199	Junior Felix	.05
200	Jeff Russell	.05
201	Mike LaValliere	.05
202	Kevin Gross	.05
203	Keith Moreland	.05
204	Mike Marshall	.05
205	Dwight Smith	.05
206	Jim Clancy	.05
207	Kevin Seitzer	.05
208	Keith Hernandez	.05
209	Bob Ojeda	.05
210	Ed Whitson	.05
211	Tony Phillips	.05
212	Milt Thompson	.05
213	Randy Kramer	.05
214	Randy Bush	.05
215	Randy Ready	.05
216	Duane Ward	.05
217	Jimmy Jones	.05
218	Scott Garrelts	.05
219	Scott Bankhead	.05
220	Lance McCullers	.05
221	B.J. Surhoff	.05
222	Chris Sabo	.05
223	Steve Buechele	.05
224	Joel Skinner	.05
225	Orel Hershiser	.08
226	Derek Lilliquist	.05
227	Claudell Washington	.05
228	Lloyd McClendon	.05
229	Felix Fermin	.05
230	Paul O'Neill	.12
231	Charlie Leibrandt	.05
232	Dave Smith	.05
233	Bob Stanley	.05
234	Tim Belcher	.05
235	Eric King	.05
236	Spike Owen	.05
237	Mike Henneman	.05
238	Juan Samuel	.05
239	Greg Brock	.05
240	John Kruk	.05
241	Glenn Wilson	.05
242	Jeff Reardon	.05
243	Todd Worrell	.05
244	Dave LaPoint	.05
245	Walt Terrell	.05
246	Mike Moore	.05
247	Kelly Downs	.05
248	Dave Valle	.05
249	Ron Kittle	.05
250	Steve Wilson	.05
251	Dick Schofield	.05
252	Marty Barrett	.05
253	Dion James	.05
254	Bob Milackl	.05
255	Ernie Whitt	.05
256	Kevin Brown	.05
257	R.J. Reynolds	.05
258	Tim Raines	.10
259	Frank Williams	.05
260	Jose Gonzalez	.05
261	Mitch Webster	.05
262	Ken Caminiti	.15
263	Bob Boone	.05
264	Dave Magadan	.05
265	Rick Aguilera	.05
266	Chris James	.05
267	Bob Welch	.05
268	Ken Dayley	.05
269	Junior Ortiz	.05
270	Allan Anderson	.05
271	Steve Jeltz	.05
272	George Bell	.05
273	Roberto Kelly	.08
274	Brett Butler	.10
275	Mike Schooler	.05
276	Ken Phelps	.05
277	Glenn Braggs	.05
278	Jose Rijo	.05
279	Bobby Witt	.05
280	Jerry Browne	.05
281	Kevin Mitchell	.10
282	Craig Worthington	.05
283	Greg Minton	.05
284	Nick Esasky	.05
285	John Farrell	.05
286	Rick Mahler	.05
287	Tom Gordon	.05
288	Gerald Young	.05
289	Jody Reed	.05
290	Jeff Hamilton	.05
291	Gerald Perry	.05
292	Hubie Brooks	.05
293	Bo Diaz	.05
294	Terry Puhl	.05
295	Jim Gantner	.05
296	Jeff Parrett	.05
297	Mike Boddicker	.05
298	Dan Gladden	.05
299	Tony Pena	.05
300	Checklist	.05
301	Tom Henke	.05
302	Pascual Perez	.05
303	Steve Bedrosian	.05
304	Ken Hill	.05
305	Jerry Reuss	.05
306	Jim Eisenreich	.05
307	Jack Howell	.05
308	Rick Cerone	.05
309	Tim Leary	.05
310	Joe Orsulak	.05
311	Jim Dwyer	.05
312	Geno Petralli	.05
313	Rick Honeycutt	.05
314	Tom Foley	.05
315	Kenny Rogers	.08
316	Mike Flanagan	.05
317	Bryan Harvey	.05
318	Billy Ripken	.05
319	Jeff Montgomery	.05
320	Erik Hanson	.05
321	Brian Downing	.05
322	Gregg Olson	.05
323	Terry Steinbach	.08
324	Sammy Sosa	8.00
325	Gene Harris	.05
326	Mike Devereaux	.05
327	Dennis Cook	.05
328	David Wells	.08
329	Checklist	.05
330	Kirt Manwaring	.05
331	Jim Presley	.05
332	Checklist	.05
333	Chuck Finley	.05
334	Rob Dibble	.05
335	Cecil Espy	.05
336	Dave Parker	.08

1989 Donruss Diamond King Supers

Once again for 1989, collectors could acquire a 4-3/4" x 6-3/4" version of the Diamond King subset via a wrapper mail-in offer. Other than size, cards are identical to the DKs in the regular issue.

		MT
Complete Set (27):		14.00
Common Player:		.25
1	Mike Greenwell	.25
2	Bobby Bonilla	.50
3	Pete Incaviglia	.25
4	Chris Sabo	.25
5	Robin Yount	1.50
6	Tony Gwynn	2.50
7	Carlton Fisk	1.00
8	Cory Snyder	.25
9	David Cone	.75
10	Kevin Seitzer	.25
11	Rick Reuschel	.25
12	Johnny Ray	.25
13	Dave Schmidt	.25
14	Andres Galarraga	.75
15	Kirk Gibson	.30
16	Fred McGriff	1.00
17	Mark Grace	1.50
18	Jeff Robinson	.25
19	Vince Coleman	.25
20	Dave Henderson	.25
21	Harold Reynolds	.25
22	Gerald Perry	.25
23	Frank Viola	.25
24	Steve Bedrosian	.25
25	Glenn Davis	.25
26	Don Mattingly	4.00

27	Checklist	.05

1989 Donruss Pop-Ups

This set features the eighteen starters from the 1988 Major League All-Star game. The cards are designed with a perforated outline so each player can be popped up to stand upright. The flip side features a red, white, and blue "Cincinnati Reds All-Star Game" logo at the top, a league designation, and the player's name and position. The lower portion displays instructions for creating the base of the Pop-Up. The Pop-Ups were marketed in conjunction with All-Star and Warren Spahn Puzzle Cards.

		MT
Complete Set (20):		3.00
Common Player:		.20
Warren Spahn Puzzle:		1.00
(1)	Mark McGwire	1.00
(2)	Jose Canseco	.60
(3)	Paul Molitor	.35
(4)	Rickey Henderson	.35
(5)	Cal Ripken, Jr.	1.00
(6)	Dave Winfield	.25
(7)	Wade Boggs	.50
(8)	Frank Viola	.20
(9)	Terry Steinbach	.20
(10)	Tom Kelly	.20
(11)	Will Clark	.45
(12)	Darryl Strawberry	.20
(13)	Ryne Sandberg	.50
(14)	Andre Dawson	.20
(15)	Ozzie Smith	.35
(16)	Vince Coleman	.20
(17)	Bobby Bonilla	.20
(18)	Dwight Gooden	.20
(19)	Gary Carter	.20
(20)	Whitey Herzog	.20

1989 Donruss Rookies

For the fourth straight year, Donruss issued a 56-card "Rookies" set in 1989. As in previous years, the set is similar in design to the regular Donruss set, except for a new "The Rookies" logo and a green and black border.

		MT
Complete Unopened Set (56):		30.00
Complete Set (56):		24.00
Common Player:		.10
1	Gary Sheffield	.75
2	Gregg Jefferies	.25
3	Ken Griffey, Jr.	20.00
4	Tom Gordon	.10
5	Billy Spiers	.10
6	*Deion Sanders*	1.00
7	Donn Pall	.10
8	Steve Carter	.10
9	Francisco Oliveras	.10
10	Steve Wilson	.10
11	Bob Geren	.10
12	Tony Castillo	.10
13	*Kenny Rogers*	.20
14	Carlos Martinez	.10
15	Edgar Martinez	.20
16	Jim Abbott	.15
17	Torey Lovullo	.10
18	Mark Carreon	.15
19	Geronimo Berroa	.10
20	Luis Medina	.10
21	Sandy Alomar, Jr.	.30
22	Bob Milacki	.10
23	*Joe Girardi*	.15
24	German Gonzalez	.10
25	Craig Worthington	.10
26	Jerome Walton	.10
27	Gary Wayne	.10
28	Tim Jones	.10
29	*Dante Bichette*	1.50
30	Alexis Infante	.10
31	*Ken Hill*	.15
32	Dwight Smith	.10
33	Luis de los Santos	.10
34	Eric Yelding	.10
35	Gregg Olson	.10
36	Phil Stephenson	.10
37	Ken Patterson	.10
38	Rick Wrona	.10
39	Mike Brumley	.10
40	Cris Carpenter	.10
41	Jeff Brantley	.10
42	Ron Jones	.10
43	Randy Johnson	.90
44	Kevin Brown	.10
45	*Ramon Martinez*	.40
46	Greg Harris	.10
47	*Steve Finley*	.20
48	Randy Kramer	.10
49	Erik Hanson	.10
50	Matt Merullo	.10
51	Mike Devereaux	.10
52	Clay Parker	.10
53	Omar Vizquel	.25
54	Derek Lilliquist	.10
55	Junior Felix	.10
56	Checklist	.05

1989 Donruss Traded

Donruss issued its first "Traded" set in 1989, releasing a 56-card boxed set designed in the same style as the regular 1989 Donruss set. The set included a Stan Musial puzzle card and a checklist.

		MT
Complete Set (56):		3.00
Common Player:		.10
1	Jeffrey Leonard	.10
2	Jack Clark	.10
3	Kevin Gross	.10
4	Tommy Herr	.10
5	Bob Boone	.10
6	Rafael Palmeiro	.40
7	John Dopson	.10
8	Willie Randolph	.10
9	Chris Brown	.10
10	Wally Backman	.10
11	Steve Ontiveros	.10
12	Eddie Murray	.30
13	Lance McCullers	.10
14	Spike Owen	.10
15	Rob Murphy	.10
16	Pete O'Brien	.10
17	Ken Williams	.10
18	Nick Esasky	.10
19	Nolan Ryan	1.50
20	Brian Holton	.10
21	Mike Moore	.10
22	Joel Skinner	.10
23	Steve Sax	.10
24	Rick Mahler	.10
25	Mike Aldrete	.10
26	Jesse Orosco	.10
27	Dave LaPoint	.10
28	Walt Terrell	.10
29	Eddie Williams	.10
30	Mike Devereaux	.10
31	Julio Franco	.15
32	Jim Clancy	.10
33	Felix Fermin	.10
34	Curtis Wilkerson	.10
35	Bert Blyleven	.10
36	Mel Hall	.10
37	Eric King	.10
38	Mitch Williams	.10
39	Jamie Moyer	.10
40	Rick Rhoden	.10
41	Phil Bradley	.10
42	Paul Kilgus	.10
43	Milt Thompson	.10
44	Jerry Browne	.10
45	Bruce Hurst	.10
46	Claudell Washington	.10
47	Todd Benzinger	.10
48	Steve Balboni	.10
49	Oddibe McDowell	.10
50	Charles Hudson	.10
51	Ron Kittle	.10
52	Andy Hawkins	.10
53	Tom Brookens	.10
54	Tom Niedenfuer	.10
55	Jeff Parrett	.10
56	Checklist	.10

1990 Donruss Previews

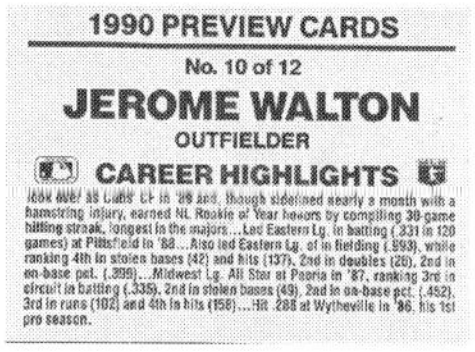

To introduce its 1990 baseball issue, Donruss sent two preview cards from a set of 12 to each member of its dealers' network. Though the photos are different than those used on the issued versions, the front format was the same. Backs are printed in black on white and contain career highlights, but no stats. Issued at the dawn of the "promo card" craze, and succeeding the relatively valueless sample sheets used by most companies in earlier years, little value was attached to these preview cards initially. Today they are among the scarcest of the early-1990s promos.

		MT
Complete Set (12):		225.00
Common Player:		7.50
1	Todd Zeile	7.50
2	Ben McDonald	7.50
3	Bo Jackson	15.00
4	Will Clark	25.00
5	Dave Stewart	7.50
6	Kevin Mitchell	7.50
7	Nolan Ryan	150.00
8	Howard Johnson	7.50
9	Tony Gwynn	50.00
10	Jerome Walton	7.50
11	Wade Boggs	40.00
12	Kirby Puckett	45.00

1990 Donruss

Donruss marked its 10th anniversary in the baseball card hobby with a 715-card set in 1990, up from previous 660-card sets. The standard-size cards feature bright red borders with the player's name in script at the top. The set includes 26 "Diamond Kings" (DK) in the checklist, 20 "Rated Rookies" (RR) and a Carl Yastrzemski puzzle. Each All-Star card back has two variations. The more common has the stats box headed "All-Star Performance". Slightly scarcer versions say "Recent Major League Performance", and are worth about twice the value of the correct version.

		MT
Unopened Factory Set (716):		15.00
Complete Set (716):		10.00
Common Player:		.05
Carl Yastrzemski Puzzle:		1.00
Wax Box:		8.00
1	Bo Jackson (Diamond King)	.15
2	Steve Sax (DK)	.08
3a	Ruben Sierra (DK) (no vertical black line at top-right on back)	.25
3b	Ruben Sierra (DK) (vertical line at top-right on back)	.10
4	Ken Griffey, Jr. (DK)	.50
5	Mickey Tettleton (DK)	.08
6	Dave Stewart (DK)	.10
7	Jim Deshaies (DK)	.05
8	John Smoltz (DK)	.10
9	Mike Bielecki (DK)	.05
10a	Brian Downing (DK) (reversed negative)	.50
10b	Brian Downing (DK) (corrected)	.15
11	Kevin Mitchell (DK)	.08
12	Kelly Gruber (DK)	.05
13	Joe Magrane (DK)	.05
14	John Franco (DK)	.05
15	Ozzie Guillen (DK)	.08
16	Lou Whitaker (DK)	.08
17	John Smiley (DK)	.08
18	Howard Johnson (DK)	.08
19	Willie Randolph (DK)	.08
20	Chris Bosio (DK)	.05
21	Tommy Herr (DK)	.05
22	Dan Gladden (DK)	.05
23	Ellis Burks (DK)	.08
24	Pete O'Brien (DK)	.08
25	Bryn Smith (DK)	.05
26	Ed Whitson (DK)	.05
27	Checklist 1-27	.05
28	Robin Ventura (Rated Rookie)	.25
29	*Todd Zeile* (RR)	.15
30	Sandy Alomar, Jr. (RR)	.15
31	*Kent Mercker* (RR)	.20
32	*Ben McDonald* (RR)	.25
33a	*Juan Gonzalez* (*reversed negative*) (RR)	4.00
33b	*Juan Gonzalez* (RR) (corrected)	2.00
34	*Eric Anthony* (RR)	.15
35	*Mike Fetters* (RR)	.10
36	*Marquis Grissom* (RR)	.50
37	*Greg Vaughn* (RR)	.25
38	*Brian Dubois* (RR)	.08
39	*Steve Avery* (RR)	.20
40	*Mark Gardner* (RR)	.15
41	Andy Benes (RR)	.20
42	*Delino DeShields* (RR)	.15
43	*Scott Coolbaugh* (RR)	.05
44	*Pat Combs* (RR)	.08
45	*Alex Sanchez* (RR)	.05
46	*Kelly Mann* (RR)	.05
47	*Julio Machado* (RR)	.08
48	Pete Incaviglia	.05
49	Shawon Dunston	.08
50	Jeff Treadway	.05
51	Jeff Ballard	.05
52	Claudell Washington	.05
53	Juan Samuel	.05
54	John Smiley	.05
55	Rob Deer	.05
56	Geno Petralli	.05
57	Chris Bosio	.08
58	Carlton Fisk	.12
59	Kirt Manwaring	.05
60	Chet Lemon	.05
61	Bo Jackson	.25
62	Doyle Alexander	.05
63	Pedro Guerrero	.05
64	Allan Anderson	.05
65	Greg Harris	.05
66	Mike Greenwell	.08
67	Walt Weiss	.05
68	Wade Boggs	.25
69	Jim Clancy	.05
70	*Junior Felix*	.08
71	Barry Larkin	.12
72	Dave LaPoint	.05
73	Joel Skinner	.05
74	Jesse Barfield	.05
75	Tommy Herr	.05
76	Ricky Jordan	.05
77	Eddie Murray	.20
78	Steve Sax	.05
79	Tim Belcher	.05
80	Danny Jackson	.05
81	Kent Hrbek	.10
82	Milt Thompson	.05
83	Brook Jacoby	.05
84	Mike Marshall	.05
85	Kevin Seitzer	.05
86	Tony Gwynn	.35
87	Dave Steib	.05
88	Dave Smith	.05
89	Bret Saberhagen	.08
90	Alan Trammell	.10
91	Tony Phillips	.05
92	Doug Drabek	.05
93	Jeffrey Leonard	.05
94	Wally Joyner	.10
95	Carney Lansford	.05
96	Cal Ripken, Jr.	.60
97	Andres Galarraga	.15
98	Kevin Mitchell	.05
99	Howard Johnson	.08
100a	Checklist 28-129	.05
100b	Checklist 28-125	.05
101	Melido Perez	.05
102	Spike Owen	.05
103	Paul Molitor	.25
104	Geronimo Berroa	.05
105	Ryne Sandberg	.25
106	Bryn Smith	.05
107	Steve Buechele	.05
108	Jim Abbott	.10
109	Alvin Davis	.05
110	Lee Smith	.08
111	Roberto Alomar	.25
112	Rick Reuschel	.05
113a	Kelly Gruber (Born 2/22)	.05
113b	Kelly Gruber (Born 2/26)	.25
114	Joe Carter	.10
115	Jose Rijo	.05
116	Greg Minton	.05
117	Bob Ojeda	.05
118	Glenn Davis	.05
119	Jeff Reardon	.05
120	Kurt Stillwell	.05
121	John Smoltz	.15
122	Dwight Evans	.08
123	Eric Yelding	.08
124	John Franco	.05
125	Jose Canseco	.20
126	Barry Bonds	.30
127	Lee Guetterman	.05
128	Jack Clark	.05
129	Dave Valle	.05
130	Hubie Brooks	.05
131	Ernest Riles	.05
132	Mike Morgan	.05
133	Steve Jeltz	.05
134	Jeff Robinson	.05
135	Ozzie Guillen	.05
136	Chili Davis	.08
137	Mitch Webster	.05
138	Jerry Browne	.05
139	Bo Diaz	.05
140	Robby Thompson	.05
141	Craig Worthington	.05
142	Julio Franco	.08
143	Brian Holman	.05
144	George Brett	.25
145	Tom Glavine	.20
146	Robin Yount	.20
147	Gary Carter	.10
148	Ron Kittle	.05
149	Tony Fernandez	.08
150	Dave Stewart	.08
151	Gary Gaetti	.08
152	Kevin Elster	.05
153	Gerald Perry	.05
154	Jesse Orosco	.05
155	Wally Backman	.05
156	Dennis Martinez	.08
157	Rick Sutcliffe	.05
158	Greg Maddux	.60
159	Andy Hawkins	.05
160	John Kruk	.05
161	Jose Oquendo	.05
162	John Dopson	.05
163	Joe Magrane	.05
164	Billy Ripken	.05
165	Fred Manrique	.05
166	Nolan Ryan	.60
167	Damon Berryhill	.05
168	Dale Murphy	.10
169	Mickey Tettleton	.05
170a	Kirk McCaskill (Born 4/19)	.05
170b	Kirk McCaskill (Born 4/9)	.25
171	Dwight Gooden	.10
172	Jose Lind	.05
173	B.J. Surhoff	.05
174	Ruben Sierra	.05
175	Dan Plesac	.05
176	Dan Pasqua	.05
177	Kelly Downs	.05
178	Matt Nokes	.05
179	Luis Aquino	.05
180	Frank Tanana	.05
181	Tony Pena	.05
182	Dan Gladden	.05
183	Bruce Hurst	.05
184	Roger Clemens	.35

185	Mark McGwire	1.00
186	Rob Murphy	.05
187	Jim Deshaies	.05
188	Fred McGriff	.15
189	Rob Dibble	.05
190	Don Mattingly	.35
191	Felix Fermin	.05
192	Roberto Kelly	.05
193	Dennis Cook	.05
194	Darren Daulton	.05
195	Alfredo Griffin	.05
196	Eric Plunk	.05
197	Orel Hershiser	.10
198	Paul O'Neill	.15
199	Randy Bush	.05
200a	Checklist 130-231	.05
200b	Checklist 126-223	.05
201	Ozzie Smith	.20
202	Pete O'Brien	.05
203	Jay Howell	.05
204	Mark Gubicza	.05
205	Ed Whitson	.05
206	George Bell	.05
207	Mike Scott	.05
208	Charlie Leibrandt	.05
209	Mike Heath	.05
210	Dennis Eckersley	.10
211	Mike LaValliere	.05
212	Darnell Coles	.05
213	Lance Parrish	.08
214	Mike Moore	.05
215	*Steve Finley*	.20
216	Tim Raines	.10
217a	Scott Garrelts (Born 10/20)	.05
217b	Scott Garrelts (Born 10/30)	.25
218	Kevin McReynolds	.05
219	Dave Gallagher	.05
220	Tim Wallach	.05
221	Chuck Crim	.05
222	Lonnie Smith	.05
223	Andre Dawson	.12
224	Nelson Santovenia	.05
225	Rafael Palmeiro	.12
226	Devon White	.05
227	Harold Reynolds	.05
228	Ellis Burks	.10
229	Mark Parent	.05
230	Will Clark	.25
231	Jimmy Key	.08
232	John Farrell	.05
233	Eric Davis	.10
234	Johnny Ray	.05
235	Darryl Strawberry	.12
236	Bill Doran	.05
237	Greg Gagne	.05
238	Jim Eisenreich	.05
239	Tommy Gregg	.05
240	Marty Barrett	.05
241	Rafael Ramirez	.05
242	Chris Sabo	.08
243	Dave Henderson	.05
244	Andy Van Slyke	.05
245	Alvaro Espinoza	.05
246	Garry Templeton	.05
247	Gene Harris	.05
248	Kevin Gross	.05
249	Brett Butler	.08
250	Willie Randolph	.05
251	Roger McDowell	.05
252	Rafael Belliard	.05
253	Steve Rosenberg	.05
254	Jack Howell	.05
255	Marvell Wynne	.05
256	Tom Candiotti	.05
257	Todd Benzinger	.05
258	Don Robinson	.05
259	Phil Bradley	.05
260	Cecil Espy	.05
261	Scott Bankhead	.05
262	Frank White	.05
263	Andres Thomas	.05
264	Glenn Braggs	.05
265	David Cone	.10
266	Bobby Thigpen	.05
267	Nelson Liriano	.05
268	Terry Steinbach	.05
269	Kirby Puckett	.35
270	Gregg Jefferies	.15
271	Jeff Blauser	.05
272	Cory Snyder	.05
273	Roy Smith	.05
274	Tom Foley	.05
275	Mitch Williams	.05
276	Paul Kilgus	.05
277	Don Slaught	.05
278	Von Hayes	.05
279	Vince Coleman	.05
280	Mike Boddicker	.05
281	Ken Dayley	.05
282	Mike Devereaux	.05
283	*Kenny Rogers*	.10
284	Jeff Russell	.05
285	*Jerome Walton*	.08
286	Derek Lilliquist	.05
287	Joe Orsulak	.05
288	Dick Schofield	.05
289	Ron Darling	.05
290	Bobby Bonilla	.10
291	Jim Gantner	.05
292	Bobby Witt	.05
293	Greg Brock	.05
294	Ivan Calderon	.05
295	Steve Bedrosian	.05
296	Mike Henneman	.05
297	Tom Gordon	.05
298	Lou Whitaker	.08
299	Terry Pendleton	.05
300a	Checklist 232-333	.05
300b	Checklist 224-321	.05
301	Juan Berenguer	.05
302	Mark Davis	.05
303	Nick Esasky	.05
304	Rickey Henderson	.20
305	Rick Cerone	.05
306	Craig Biggio	.15
307	Duane Ward	.05
308	Tom Browning	.05
309	Walt Terrell	.05
310	Greg Swindell	.05
311	Dave Righetti	.05
312	Mike Maddux	.05
313	Len Dykstra	.08
314	Jose Gonzalez	.05
315	Steve Balboni	.05
316	Mike Scioscia	.05
317	Ron Oester	.05
318	*Gary Wayne*	.05
319	Todd Worrell	.05
320	Doug Jones	.05
321	Jeff Hamilton	.05
322	Danny Tartabull	.05
323	Chris James	.05
324	Mike Flanagan	.05
325	Gerald Young	.05
326	Bob Boone	.08
327	Frank Williams	.05
328	Dave Parker	.08
329	Sid Bream	.05
330	Mike Schooler	.05
331	Bert Blyleven	.08
332	Bob Welch	.05
333	Bob Milacki	.05
334	Tim Burke	.05
335	Jose Uribe	.05
336	Randy Myers	.05
337	Eric King	.05
338	Mark Langston	.10
339	Ted Higuera	.05
340	Oddibe McDowell	.05
341	Lloyd McClendon	.05
342	Pascual Perez	.05
343	Kevin Brown	.05
344	Chuck Finley	.05
345	Erik Hanson	.05
346	Rich Gedman	.05
347	Bip Roberts	.05
348	Matt Williams	.20
349	Tom Henke	.05
350	Brad Komminsk	.05
351	Jeff Reed	.05
352	Brian Downing	.05
353	Frank Viola	.05
354	Terry Puhl	.05
355	Brian Harper	.05
356	Steve Farr	.05
357	Joe Boever	.05
358	Danny Heep	.05
359	Larry Andersen	.05
360	Rolando Roomes	.05
361	Mike Gallego	.05
362	Bob Kipper	.05
363	Clay Parker	.05
364	Mike Pagliarulo	.05
365	Ken Griffey, Jr.	2.00
366	Rex Hudler	.05
367	Pat Sheridan	.05
368	Kirk Gibson	.08
369	Jeff Parrett	.05
370	Bob Walk	.05
371	Ken Patterson	.05
372	Bryan Harvey	.05
373	Mike Bielecki	.05
374	*Tom Magrann*	.05
375	Rick Mahler	.05
376	Craig Lefferts	.05
377	Gregg Olson	.05
378	Jamie Moyer	.05
379	Randy Johnson	.25
380	Jeff Montgomery	.05
381	Marty Clary	.05
382	*Bill Spiers*	.05
383	Dave Magadan	.05
384	*Greg Hibbard*	.05
385	Ernie Whitt	.05
386	Rick Honeycutt	.05
387	Dave West	.05
388	Keith Hernandez	.05
389	Jose Alvarez	.05
390	Albert Belle	.50
391	Rick Aguilera	.05
392	Mike Fitzgerald	.05
393	*Dwight Smith*	.05
394	*Steve Wilson*	.05
395	*Bob Geren*	.05
396	Randy Ready	.05
397	Ken Hill	.05
398	Jody Reed	.05
399	Tom Brunansky	.05
400a	Checklist 334-435	.05
400b	Checklist 322-419	.05
401	Rene Gonzales	.05
402	Harold Baines	.08
403	Cecilio Guante	.05
404	Joe Girardi	.08
405a	*Sergio Valdez* (black line crosses S in Sergio)	.25
405b	Sergio Valdez (corrected)	.05
406	Mark Williamson	.05
407	Glenn Hoffman	.05
408	*Jeff Innis*	.05
409	Randy Kramer	.05
410	Charlie O'Brien	.05
411	Charlie Hough	.05
412	Gus Polidor	.05
413	Ron Karkovice	.05
414	Trevor Wilson	.08
415	*Kevin Ritz*	.10
416	Gary Thurman	.05
417	Jeff Robinson	.05
418	Scott Terry	.05
419	Tim Laudner	.05
420	Dennis Rasmussen	.05
421	Luis Rivera	.05
422	Jim Corsi	.05
423	Dennis Lamp	.05
424	Ken Caminiti	.10
425	David Wells	.08
426	Norm Charlton	.05
427	Deion Sanders	.25
428	Dion James	.05
429	Chuck Cary	.05
430	Ken Howell	.05
431	Steve Lake	.05
432	Kal Daniels	.05
433	Lance McCullers	.05
434	Lenny Harris	.05
435	*Scott Scudder*	.05
436	Gene Larkin	.05
437	Dan Quisenberry	.05
438	*Steve Olin*	.05
439	Mickey Hatcher	.05
440	Willie Wilson	.05
441	Mark Grant	.05
442	Mookie Wilson	.05
443	Alex Trevino	.05
444	Pat Tabler	.05
445	Dave Bergman	.05
446	Todd Burns	.05
447	R.J. Reynolds	.05
448	Jay Buhner	.08
449	*Lee Stevens*	.10
450	Ron Hassey	.05
451	Bob Melvin	.05
452	Dave Martinez	.05
453	*Greg Litton*	.05
454	Mark Carreon	.05
455	Scott Fletcher	.05
456	Otis Nixon	.05
457	*Tony Fossas*	.05
458	John Russell	.05
459	Paul Assenmacher	.05
460	Zane Smith	.05
461	*Jack Daugherty*	.05
462	*Rich Monteleone*	.05
463	Greg Briley	.05
464	Mike Smithson	.05
465	Benito Santiago	.08
466	*Jeff Brantley*	.08
467	Jose Nunez	.05
468	Scott Bailes	.05
469	Ken Griffey	.08
470	Bob McClure	.05
471	Mackey Sasser	.05
472	Glenn Wilson	.05
473	*Kevin Tapani*	.25
474	Bill Buckner	.05
475	Ron Gant	.10
476	Kevin Romine	.05
477	Juan Agosto	.05
478	Herm Winningham	.05
479	Storm Davis	.05
480	Jeff King	.10
481	*Kevin Mmahat*	.05
482	Carmelo Martinez	.05
483	*Omar Vizquel*	.10
484	Jim Dwyer	.05
485	Bob Knepper	.05
486	Dave Anderson	.05
487	Ron Jones	.05
488	Jay Bell	.05
489	*Sammy Sosa*	5.00
490	*Kent Anderson*	.05
491	Domingo Ramos	.05
492	Dave Clark	.05
493	Tim Birtsas	.05
494	Ken Oberkfell	.05
495	Larry Sheets	.05
496	Jeff Kunkel	.05
497	Jim Presley	.05
498	Mike Macfarlane	.05
499	Pete Smith	.05
500a	Checklist 436-537	.05
500b	Checklist 420-517	.05
501	Gary Sheffield	.25
502	*Terry Bross*	.05
503	*Jerry Kutzler*	.05
504	Lloyd Moseby	.05
505	Curt Young	.05
506	Al Newman	.05
507	Keith Miller	.05
508	*Mike Stanton*	.15
509	Rich Yett	.05
510	*Tim Drummond*	.05
511	Joe Hesketh	.05
512	*Rick Wrona*	.10
513	Luis Salazar	.05
514	Hal Morris	.05
515	Terry Mullholland	.08
516	John Morris	.05
517	Carlos Quintana	.05
518	Frank DiPino	.05
519	Randy Milligan	.05
520	Chad Kreuter	.05
521	Mike Jeffcoat	.05
522	Mike Harkey	.05
523a	Andy Nezelek (Born 1985)	.05
523b	Andy Nezelek (Born 1965)	.25
524	Dave Schmidt	.05
525	Tony Armas	.05
526	Barry Lyons	.05
527	*Rick Reed*	.05
528	Jerry Reuss	.05
529	*Dean Palmer*	.15
530	*Jeff Peterek*	.05
531	*Carlos Martinez*	.08
532	Atlee Hammaker	.05
533	Mike Brumley	.05
534	Terry Leach	.05
535	*Doug Strange*	.05
536	Jose DeLeon	.05
537	Shane Rawley	.05
538	Joey Cora	.10
539	Eric Hetzel	.05
540	Gene Nelson	.05
541	Wes Gardner	.05
542	Mark Portugal	.05
543	Al Leiter	.05
544	Jack Armstrong	.05
545	Greg Cadaret	.05
546	Rod Nichols	.05
547	Luis Polonia	.05
548	Charlie Hayes	.05
549	Dickie Thon	.05
550	Tim Crews	.05
551	Dave Winfield	.20
552	Mike Davis	.05
553	Ron Robinson	.05
554	Carmen Castillo	.05
555	John Costello	.05
556	Bud Black	.05
557	Rick Dempsey	.05
558	Jim Acker	.05
559	Eric Show	.05
560	Pat Borders	.05
561	Danny Darwin	.05
562	*Rick Luecken*	.05
563	Edwin Nunez	.05
564	Felix Jose	.05
565	John Cangelosi	.05
566	Billy Swift	.05
567	Bill Schroeder	.05
568	Stan Javier	.05
569	Jim Traber	.05
570	Wallace Johnson	.05
571	Donell Nixon	.05
572	Sid Fernandez	.05
573	Lance Johnson	.08
574	Andy McGaffigan	.05
575	Mark Knudson	.05
576	*Tommy Greene*	.20
577	Mark Grace	.15
578	*Larry Walker*	1.50
579	Mike Stanley	.05
580	Mike Witt	.05
581	Scott Bradley	.05
582	Greg Harris	.05
583a	Kevin Hickey (black stripe over top of "K" vertical stroke)	.05
583b	Kevin Hickey (black stripe under "K")	.05
584	Lee Mazzilli	.05
585	Jeff Pico	.05
586	*Joe Oliver*	.05
587	Willie Fraser	.05
588	Puzzle card (Carl Yastrzemski)	.05
589	Kevin Bass	.05
590	John Moses	.05
591	Tom Pagnozzi	.05
592	*Tony Castillo*	.05
593	Jerald Clark	.05
594	Dan Schatzeder	.05
595	Luis Quinones	.05
596	Pete Harnisch	.08
597	Gary Redus	.05
598	Mel Hall	.05
599	Rick Schu	.05
600a	Checklist 538-639	.05
600b	Checklist 518-617	.05
601	Mike Kingery	.05
602	Terry Kennedy	.05
603	Mike Sharperson	.05
604	Don Carman	.05
605	Jim Gott	.05
606	Donn Pall	.05
607	Rance Mulliniks	.05
608	Curt Wilkerson	.05
609	Mike Felder	.05
610	Guillermo Hernandez	.05
611	Candy Maldonado	.05
612	Mark Thurmond	.05
613	Rick Leach	.05
614	Jerry Reed	.05
615	Franklin Stubbs	.05
616	Billy Hatcher	.05
617	Don August	.05
618	Tim Teufel	.05
619	Shawn Hillegas	.05
620	Manny Lee	.05
621	Gary Ward	.05
622	*Mark Guthrie*	.05
623	Jeff Musselman	.05
624	Mark Lemke	.05
625	Fernando Valenzuela	.08
626	*Paul Sorrento*	.10
627	Glenallen Hill	.05
628	Les Lancaster	.05
629	Vance Law	.05
630	Randy Velarde	.08
631	Todd Frohwirth	.05
632	Willie McGee	.08
633	Oil Can Boyd	.05
634	Cris Carpenter	.05
635	Brian Holton	.05
636	Tracy Jones	.05
637	Terry Steinbach (AS)	.08
638	Brady Anderson	.12
639a	Jack Morris (black line crosses J of Jack)	.25
639b	Jack Morris (corrected)	.08
640	*Jaime Navarro*	.05
641	Darrin Jackson	.05
642	*Mike Dyer*	.05
643	Mike Schmidt	.25
644	Henry Cotto	.05
645	John Cerutti	.05
646	*Francisco Cabrera*	.05
647	Scott Sanderson	.05
648	Brian Meyer	.05
649	Ray Searage	.05
650	Bo Jackson (AS)	.15
651	Steve Lyons	.05
652	Mike LaCoss	.05
653	Ted Power	.05
654	Howard Johnson (AS)	.05
655	*Mauro Gozzo*	.05
656	*Mike Blowers*	.15
657	Paul Gibson	.05
658	Neal Heaton	.05
659a	Nolan Ryan 5,000 K's (King of Kings (#665) back)	2.50
659b	Nolan Ryan 5,000 K's (correct back)	.50
660a	Harold Baines (AS) (black line through star on front, Recent Major League Performance on back)	.50
660b	Harold Baines (AS) (black line through star on front, All-Star Game Performance on back)	1.50
660c	Harold Baines (AS) (black line behind star on front, Recent Major League Performance on back)	.75
660d	Harold Baines (AS) (black line behind star on front, All-Star Game Performance on back)	.10
661	Gary Pettis	.05
662	*Clint Zavaras*	.05
663	Rick Reuschel (AS)	.05
664	Alejandro Pena	.05
665a	Nolan Ryan (King of Kings) 5,000 K's (#659) back)	2.50
665b	Nolan Ryan (King of Kings) (correct back)	.50
665c	Nolan Ryan (King of Kings) (no number on back)	1.00
666	Ricky Horton	.05
667	Curt Schilling	.05
668	Bill Landrum	.05
669	Todd Stottlemyre	.05
670	Tim Leary	.05
671	*John Wetteland*	.25
672	Calvin Schiraldi	.05
673	Ruben Sierra (AS)	.05
674	Pedro Guerrero (AS)	.05
675	Ken Phelps	.05
676	Cal Ripken (AS)	.25
677	Denny Walling	.05
678	Goose Gossage	.05
679	*Gary Mielke*	.05
680	Bill Bathe	.05
681	Tom Lawless	.05
682	*Xavier Hernandez*	.15
683	Kirby Puckett (AS)	.20
684	Mariano Duncan	.05
685	Ramon Martinez	.10
686	Tim Jones	.05
687	Tom Filer	.05
688	Steve Lombardozzi	.05
689	*Bernie Williams*	1.00
690	*Chip Hale*	.05
691	*Beau Allred*	.05
692	Ryne Sandberg (AS)	.25
693	*Jeff Huson*	.10
694	Curt Ford	.05
695	Eric Davis (AS)	.05
696	Scott Lusader	.05
697	Mark McGwire (AS)	.50
698	*Steve Cummings*	.05
699	*George Canale*	.05
700a	Checklist 640-715/ BC1-BC26	.05
700b	Checklist 640-716/ BC1-BC26	.05
700c	Checklist 618-716	.05
701	Julio Franco (AS)	.05
702	*Dave Johnson*	.05
703	Dave Stewart (AS)	.05
704	*Dave Justice*	.40
705	Tony Gwynn (AS)	.15
706	Greg Myers	.05
707	Will Clark (AS)	.10
708	Benito Santiago (AS)	.05
709	Larry McWilliams	.05
710	Ozzie Smith (AS)	.10

711	*John Olerud*	.50
712	Wade Boggs (AS)	.10
713	*Gary Eave*	.05
714	Bob Tewksbury	.05
715	Kevin Mitchell (AS)	.05
716	A. Bartlett Giamatti	.25

1990 Donruss Grand Slammers

For the second consecutive year Donruss produced a set in honor of players who hit grand slams in the previous season. The cards are styled after the 1990 Donruss regular issue. The cards were inserted into 1990 Donruss factory sets, and one card per cello pack.

		MT
Complete Set (12):		2.00
Common Player:		.10
1	Matt Williams	.30
2	Jeffrey Leonard	.10
3	Chris James	.10
4	Mark McGwire	1.00
5	Dwight Evans	.10
6	Will Clark	.25
7	Mike Scioscia	.10
8	Todd Benzinger	.10
9	Fred McGriff	.30
10	Kevin Bass	.10
11	Jack Clark	.10
12	Bo Jackson	.25

1990 Donruss MVP

This special 26-card set includes one player from each Major League team. Numbered BC-1 (the "BC" stands for "Bonus Card") through BC-26, the cards from this set were randomly packed in 1990 Donruss wax packs and were not available in factory sets or other types of packaging. The red-bordered cards are similar in design to the regular 1990 Donruss set, except the player photos are set against a special background made up of the "MVP" logo.

		MT
Complete Set (26):		1.25
Common Player:		.10
1	Bo Jackson	.25
2	Howard Johnson	.10
3	Dave Stewart	.10
4	Tony Gwynn	.35
5	Orel Hershiser	.10
6	Pedro Guerrero	.10
7	Tim Raines	.12
8	Kirby Puckett	.35
9	Alvin Davis	.10
10	Ryne Sandberg	.40
11	Kevin Mitchell	.10
12a	John Smoltz (photo of Tom Glavine)	2.00
12b	John Smoltz (corrected)	.40
13	George Bell	.10
14	Julio Franco	.10
15	Paul Molitor	.25
16	Bobby Bonilla	.15
17	Mike Greenwell	.10
18	Cal Ripken	.60
19	Carlton Fisk	.15
20	Chili Davis	.10
21	Glenn Davis	.10
22	Steve Sax	.10
23	Eric Davis	.15
24	Greg Swindell	.10
25	Von Hayes	.10
26	Alan Trammell	.12

1990 Donruss Best A.L.

This 144-card set features the top players of the American League. The 2-1/2" x 3-1/2" cards feature the same front design as the regular Donruss set, exception with blue borders instead of red. Backs feature a yellow frame with complete statistics and biographical information provided. This marks the first year that Donruss divided its baseball-best issue into two sets designated by league.

		MT
Complete Set (144):		6.00
Common Player:		.05
1	Ken Griffey, Jr.	1.50
2	Bob Milacki	.05
3	Mike Boddicker	.05
4	Bert Blyleven	.05
5	Carlton Fisk	.10
6	Greg Swindell	.05
7	Alan Trammell	.08
8	Mark Davis	.05
9	Chris Bosio	.05
10	Gary Gaetti	.05
11	Matt Nokes	.05
12	Dennis Eckersley	.08
13	Kevin Brown	.05
14	Tom Henke	.05
15	Mickey Tettleton	.05
16	Jody Reed	.05
17	Mark Langston	.08
18	Melido Perez	.05
19	John Farrell	.05
20	Tony Phillips	.05
21	Bret Saberhagen	.08
22	Robin Yount	.10
23	Kirby Puckett	.25
24	Steve Sax	.05
25	Dave Stewart	.05
26	Alvin Davis	.05
27	Geno Petralli	.05
28	Mookie Wilson	.05
29	Jeff Ballard	.05
30	Ellis Burks	.05
31	Wally Joyner	.08
32	Bobby Thigpen	.05
33	Keith Hernandez	.05
34	Jack Morris	.05
35	George Brett	.20
36	Dan Plesac	.05
37	Brian Harper	.05
38	Don Mattingly	.45
39	Dave Henderson	.05
40	Scott Bankhead	.05
41	Rafael Palmeiro	.10
42	Jimmy Key	.05
43	Gregg Olson	.05
44	Tony Pena	.05
45	Jack Howell	.05
46	Eric King	.05
47	Cory Snyder	.05
48	Frank Tanana	.05
49	Nolan Ryan	.60
50	Bob Boone	.05
51	Dave Parker	.08
52	Allan Anderson	.05
53	Tim Leary	.05
54	Mark McGwire	1.50
55	Dave Valle	.05
56	Fred McGriff	.20
57	Cal Ripken	1.50
58	Roger Clemens	.25
59	Lance Parrish	.05
60	Robin Ventura	.10
61	Doug Jones	.05
62	Lloyd Moseby	.05
63	Bo Jackson	.15
64	Paul Molitor	.10
65	Kent Hrbek	.08
66	Mel Hall	.05
67	Bob Welch	.05
68	Erik Hanson	.05
69	Harold Baines	.08
70	Junior Felix	.05
71	Craig Worthington	.05
72	Jeff Reardon	.05
73	Johnny Ray	.05
74	Ozzie Guillen	.05
75	Brook Jacoby	.05
76	Chet Lemon	.05
77	Mark Gubicza	.05
78	B.J. Surhoff	.08
79	Rick Aguilera	.05
80	Pascual Perez	.05
81	Jose Canseco	.35
82	Mike Schooler	.05
83	Jeff Huson	.05
84	Kelly Gruber	.05
85	Randy Milligan	.05
86	Wade Boggs	.35
87	Dave Winfield	.15
88	Scott Fletcher	.05
89	Tom Candiotti	.05
90	Mike Heath	.05
91	Kevin Seitzer	.05
92	Ted Higuera	.05
93	Kevin Tapani	.05
94	Roberto Kelly	.05
95	Walt Weiss	.05
96	Checklist	.05
97	Sandy Alomar	.10
98	Pete O'Brien	.05
99	Jeff Russell	.05
100	John Olerud	.12
101	Pete Harnisch	.05
102	Dwight Evans	.05
103	Chuck Finley	.05
104	Sammy Sosa	1.00
105	Mike Henneman	.05
106	Kurt Stillwell	.05
107	Greg Vaughn	.08
108	Dan Gladden	.05
109	Jesse Barfield	.05
110	Willie Randolph	.05
111	Randy Johnson	.20
112	Julio Franco	.08
113	Tony Fernandez	.05
114	Ben McDonald	.05
115	Mike Greenwell	.05
116	Luis Polonia	.05
117	Carney Lansford	.05
118	Bud Black	.05
119	Lou Whitaker	.05
120	Jim Eisenreich	.05
121	Gary Sheffield	.10
122	Shane Mack	.05
123	Alvaro Espinoza	.05
124	Rickey Henderson	.15
125	Jeffrey Leonard	.05
126	Gary Pettis	.05
127	Dave Steib	.05
128	Danny Tartabull	.05
129	Joe Orsulak	.05
130	Tom Brunansky	.05
131	Dick Schofield	.05
132	Candy Maldonado	.05
133	Cecil Fielder	.05
134	Terry Shumpert	.05
135	Greg Gagne	.05
136	Dave Righetti	.05
137	Terry Steinbach	.05
138	Harold Reynolds	.05
139	George Bell	.05
140	Carlos Quintana	.05
141	Ivan Calderon	.05
142	Greg Brock	.05
143	Ruben Sierra	.05
144	Checklist	.05

1990 Donruss Best N.L.

This 144-card set features the top players in the National League for 1990. The 2-1/2" x 3-1/2" cards feature the same design as the regular 1990 Donruss cards, except they have blue, rather than red borders. Traded players are featured with their new teams. This set, along with the A.L. Best set, was available at select retail stores and within the hobby.

		MT
Complete Set (144):		4.00
Common Player:		.05
1	Eric Davis	.10
2	Tom Glavine	.08
3	Mike Bielecki	.05
4	Jim Deshaies	.05
5	Mike Scioscia	.05
6	Spike Owen	.05
7	Dwight Gooden	.12
8	Ricky Jordan	.05
9	Doug Drabek	.05
10	Bryn Smith	.05
11	Tony Gwynn	.40
12	John Burkett	.05
13	Nick Esasky	.05
14	Greg Maddux	.75
15	Joe Oliver	.05
16	Mike Scott	.05
17	Tim Belcher	.05
18	Kevin Gross	.05
19	Howard Johnson	.05
20	Darren Daulton	.05
21	John Smiley	.05
22	Ken Dayley	.05
23	Craig Lefferts	.05
24	Will Clark	.25
25	Greg Olson	.05
26	Ryne Sandberg	.45
27	Tom Browning	.05
28	Eric Anthony	.08
29	Juan Samuel	.05
30	Dennis Martinez	.08
31	Kevin Elster	.08
32	Tom Herr	.05
33	Sid Bream	.05
34	Terry Pendleton	.05
35	Roberto Alomar	.30
36	Kevin Bass	.05
37	Jim Presley	.05
38	Les Lancaster	.05
39	Paul O'Neill	.10
40	Dave Smith	.05
41	Kirk Gibson	.05
42	Tim Burke	.05
43	David Cone	.08
44	Ken Howell	.05
45	Barry Bonds	.50
46	Joe Magrane	.05
47	Andy Benes	.08
48	Gary Carter	.10
49	Pat Combs	.05
50	John Smoltz	.08
51	Mark Grace	.15
52	Barry Larkin	.15
53	Danny Darwin	.05
54	Orel Hershiser	.08
55	Tim Wallach	.05
56	Dave Magadan	.05
57	Roger McDowell	.05
58	Bill Landrum	.05
59	Jose DeLeon	.05
60	Bip Roberts	.05
61	Matt Williams	.12
62	Dale Murphy	.10
63	Dwight Smith	.05
64	Chris Sabo	.05
65	Glenn Davis	.05
66	Jay Howell	.05
67	Andres Galarraga	.08
68	Frank Viola	.05
69	John Kruk	.05
70	Bobby Bonilla	.08
71	Todd Zeile	.08
72	Joe Carter	.08
73	Robby Thompson	.05
74	Jeff Blauser	.05
75	Mitch Williams	.05
76	Rob Dibble	.05
77	Rafael Ramirez	.05
78	Eddie Murray	.20
79	Dave Martinez	.05
80	Darryl Strawberry	.10
81	Dickie Thon	.05
82	Jose Lind	.05
83	Ozzie Smith	.20
84	Bruce Hurst	.05
85	Kevin Mitchell	.05
86	Lonnie Smith	.05
87	Joe Girardi	.05
88	Randy Myers	.05
89	Craig Biggio	.10
90	Fernando Valenzuela	.08
91	Larry Walker	.15
92	John Franco	.05
93	Dennis Cook	.05
94	Bob Walk	.05
95	Pedro Guerrero	.05
96	Checklist	.05
97	Andre Dawson	.10
98	Ed Whitson	.05
99	Steve Bedrosian	.05
100	Oddibe McDowell	.05
101	Todd Benzinger	.05
102	Bill Doran	.05
103	Alfredo Griffin	.05
104	Tim Raines	.10
105	Sid Fernandez	.05
106	Charlie Hayes	.05
107	Mike LaValliere	.05
108	Jose Oquendo	.05
109	Jack Clark	.05
110	Scott Garrelts	.05
111	Ron Gant	.10
112	Shawon Dunston	.05
113	Mariano Duncan	.05
114	Eric Yelding	.05
115	Hubie Brooks	.05
116	Delino DeShields	.05
117	Gregg Jefferies	.10
118	Len Dykstra	.05
119	Andy Van Slyke	.05
120	Lee Smith	.08
121	Benito Santiago	.05
122	Jose Uribe	.05
123	Jeff Treadway	.05
124	Jerome Walton	.05
125	Billy Hatcher	.05
126	Ken Caminiti	.10
127	Kal Daniels	.05
128	Marquis Grissom	.12
129	Kevin McReynolds	.05
130	Wally Backman	.06
131	Willie McGee	.05
132	Terry Kennedy	.05
133	Garry Templeton	.05
134	Lloyd McClendon	.05
135	Daryl Boston	.05
136	Jay Bell	.05
137	Mike Pagliarulo	.05
138	Vince Coleman	.05
139	Brett Butler	.08
140	Von Hayes	.05
141	Ramon Martinez	.10
142	Jack Armstrong	.05
143	Franklin Stubbs	.05
144	Checklist	.05

1990 Donruss Diamond Kings Supers

Donruss made this set available through a mail-in offer. Three wrappers, $10 and $2 for postage were necessary to obtain this set. The cards are exactly the same design as the regular Donruss Diamond Kings except they measure approximately 5" x 6-3/4" in size. The artwork of Dick Perez is featured.

		MT
Complete Set (26):		6.00
Common Player:		.10
1	Bo Jackson	.50
2	Steve Sax	.10
3	Ruben Sierra	.10
4	Ken Griffey, Jr.	4.00
5	Mickey Tettleton	.10
6	Dave Stewart	.10
7	Jim Deshaies	.10
8	John Smoltz	.35
9	Mike Bielecki	.10
10	Brian Downing	.10
11	Kevin Mitchell	.10
12	Kelly Gruber	.10
13	Joe Magrane	.10
14	John Franco	.10
15	Ozzie Guillen	.10
16	Lou Whitaker	.10
17	John Smiley	.10
18	Howard Johnson	.10
19	Willie Randolph	.10
20	Chris Bosio	.10
21	Tommy Herr	.10
22	Dan Gladden	.10
23	Ellis Burks	.10
24	Pete O'Brien	.10
25	Bryn Smith	.10
26	Ed Whitson	.10

1990 Donruss Learning Series

Cards from this 55-card set were released as part of an educational package available to schools. The cards are styled like the regular-issue 1990 Donruss cards, but feature a special "learning series" logo on the front. The backs feature career highlights, statistics and card numbers. The cards were not released directly to the hobby.

		MT
Complete Set (55):		20.00
Common Player:		.25
1	George Brett (DK)	2.00
2	Kevin Mitchell	.25
3	Andy Van Slyke	.25
4	Benito Santiago	.25
5	Gary Carter	.40
6	Jose Canseco	1.00
7	Rickey Henderson	.85
8	Ken Griffey, Jr.	8.00
9	Ozzie Smith	2.00
10	Dwight Gooden	.35
11	Ryne Sandberg (DK)	2.00
12	Don Mattingly	3.00
13	Ozzie Guillen	.25
14	Dave Righetti	.25
15	Rick Dempsey	.25
16	Tom Herr	.25
17	Julio Franco	.25
18	Von Hayes	.25
19	Cal Ripken	5.00
20	Alan Trammell	.35
21	Wade Boggs	2.00
22	Glenn Davis	.25
23	Will Clark	.75
24	Nolan Ryan	5.00
25	George Bell	.25
26	Cecil Fielder	.25
27	Gregg Olson	.25
28	Tim Wallach	.25
29	Ron Darling	.25
30	Kelly Gruber	.25
31	Shawn Boskie	.25
32	Mike Greenwell	.25
33	Dave Parker	.30
34	Joe Magrane	.25
35	Dave Stewart	.25
36	Kent Hrbek	.25
37	Robin Yount	1.00
38	Bo Jackson	.50
39	Fernando Valenzuela	.25
40	Sandy Alomar, Jr.	.35
41	Lance Parrish	.25
42	Candy Maldonado	.25
43	Mike LaValliere	.25
44	Jim Abbott	.25
45	Edgar Martinez	.25
46	Kirby Puckett	2.50
47	Delino DeShields	.25
48	Tony Gwynn	2.00
49	Carlton Fisk	.40
50	Mike Scott	.25
51	Barry Larkin	.30
52	Andre Dawson	.40
53	Tom Glavine	.35
54	Tom Browning	.25
55	Checklist	.05

1990 Donruss Rookies

For the fifth straight year, Donruss issued a 56-card "Rookies" set in 1990. As in previous years, the set is similar in design to the regular Donruss set, except for a new "The Rookies" logo and green borders instead of red. The set is packaged in a special box and includes a Carl Yastrzemski puzzle card.

		MT
Complete Set (56):		2.00
Common Player:		.10
1	Sandy Alomar	.25
2	John Olerud	.40
3	Pat Combs	.10
4	Brian Dubois	.10
5	Felix Jose	.10
6	Delino DeShields	.10
7	Mike Stanton	.10
8	Mike Munoz	.10
9	Craig Grebeck	.10
10	Joe Kraemer	.10
11	Jeff Huson	.10
12	Bill Sampen	.10
13	Brian Bohanon	.10
14	Dave Justice	.50
15	Robin Ventura	.30
16	Greg Vaughn	.20
17	Wayne Edwards	.10
18	Shawn Boskie	.10
19	*Carlos Baerga*	.20
20	Mark Gardner	.10
21	Kevin Appier	.30
22	Mike Harkey	.10
23	Tim Layana	.10
24	Glenallen Hill	.10
25	Jerry Kutzler	.10
26	Mike Blowers	.10
27	Scott Ruskin	.10
28	Dana Kiecker	.10
29	Willie Blair	.10
30	Ben McDonald	.15
31	Todd Zeile	.15
32	Scott Coolbaugh	.10
33	Xavier Hernandez	.10
34	Mike Hartley	.10
35	Kevin Tapani	.10
36	Kevin Wickander	.10
37	Carlos Hernandez	.10
38	Brian Traxler	.10
39	Marty Brown	.10
40	Scott Radinsky	.10
41	Julio Machado	.10
42	Steve Avery	.10
43	Mark Lemke	.10
44	Alan Mills	.10
45	Marquis Grissom	.50
46	Greg Olson	.10
47	Dave Hollins	.15
48	Jerald Clark	.10
49	Eric Anthony	.10
50	Tim Drummond	.10
51	John Burkett	.15
52	Brent Knackert	.10
53	Jeff Shaw	.10
54	John Orton	.10
55	Terry Shumpert	.10
56	Checklist	.05

1991 Donruss Previews

Once again in late 1990 Donruss distributed individual cards from a 12-card preview issue to its dealer network as an introduction to its 1991 issue. Like the previous year's preview cards, the '91 samples utilized the format which would follow on the regular-issue cards, but the photos were different. This has helped create demand for these cards from superstar collectors. Backs are printed in black-and-white and have little more than a player name, card number and MLB logos.

		MT
Complete Set (12):		750.00
Common Player:		9.00
1	Dave Justice	75.00
2	Doug Drabek	9.00
3	Scott Chiamparino	9.00
4	Ken Griffey, Jr.	250.00
5	Bob Welch	9.00
6	Tino Martinez	45.00
7	Nolan Ryan	250.00
8	Dwight Gooden	15.00
9	Ryne Sandberg	95.00
10	Barry Bonds	100.00
11	Jose Canseco	75.00
12	Eddie Murray	60.00

1991 Donruss

Donruss used a two-series format in 1991. The first series was released in December, 1990, and the second in February, 1991. The 1991 design is somewhat reminiscent of the 1986 set, with blue borders on Series I cards; green on Series II. Limited edition cards including an autographed Ryne Sandberg card (5,000) were randomly inserted in wax packs. Other features of the set include 40 Rated Rookies, (RR) in the checklist, Legends and Elite insert series, and another Diamond King (DK) subset. Cards were distributed in packs with Willie Stargell puzzle pieces.

		MT
Factory Set w/Leaf or Studio Preview:		10.00
Complete Set (792):		8.00
Common Player:		.05
Willie Stargell Puzzle:		1.00
Series 1 or 2 Wax Box:		9.00
1	Dave Steib (Diamond King)	.05
2	Craig Biggio (DK)	.05
3	Cecil Fielder (DK)	.08
4	Barry Bonds (DK)	.20
5	Barry Larkin (DK)	.10
6	Dave Parker (DK)	.05
7	Len Dykstra (DK)	.05
8	Bobby Thigpen (DK)	.05
9	Roger Clemens (DK)	.15
10	Ron Gant (DK)	.08
11	Delino DeShields (DK)	.05
12	Roberto Alomar (DK)	.15
13	Sandy Alomar (DK)	.08
14	Ryne Sandberg (DK)	.15
15	Ramon Martinez (DK)	.05
16	Edgar Martinez (DK)	.05
17	Dave Magadan (DK)	.05
18	Matt Williams (DK)	.12
19	Rafael Palmeiro (DK)	.10
20	Bob Welch (DK)	.05
21	Dave Righetti (DK)	.05
22	Brian Harper (DK)	.05
23	Gregg Olson (DK)	.05
24	Kurt Stillwell (DK)	.05
25	Pedro Guerrero (DK)	.05
26	Chuck Finley (DK)	.05
27	Diamond King checklist	.05
28	Tino Martinez (Rated Rookie)	.15
29	Mark Lewis (RR)	.10
30	*Bernard Gilkey* (RR)	.15
31	Hensley Meulens (RR)	.05
32	*Derek Bell* (RR)	.30
33	Jose Offerman (RR)	.08
34	Terry Bross (RR)	.08
35	*Leo Gomez* (RR)	.08
36	Derrick May (RR)	.08
37	*Kevin Morton* (RR)	.05
38	Moises Alou (RR)	.15
39	*Julio Valera* (RR)	.05
40	Milt Cuyler (RR)	.05
41	*Phil Plantier* (RR)	.10
42	*Scott Chiamparino* (RR)	.05
43	*Ray Lankford* (RR)	.20
44	*Mickey Morandini* (RR)	.10
45	Dave Hansen (RR)	.10
46	*Kevin Belcher* (RR)	.08
47	Darrin Fletcher (RR)	.10
48	Steve Sax (All Star)	.05
49	Ken Griffey, Jr. (AS)	.50
50a	Jose Canseco (AS) (A's in stat line on back)	.12
50b	Jose Canseco (AS) (AL in stat line on back)	.15
51	Sandy Alomar (AS)	.08
52	Cal Ripken, Jr. (AS)	.20
53	Rickey Henderson (AS)	.15
54	Bob Welch (AS)	.05
55	Wade Boggs (AS)	.10
56	Mark McGwire (AS)	.50
57	Jack McDowell	.08
58	Jose Lind	.05
59	Alex Fernandez	.20
60	Pat Combs	.05
61	*Mike Walker*	.05
62	Juan Samuel	.05
63	Mike Blowers	.05
64	Mark Guthrie	.05
65	Mark Salas	.05
66	Tim Jones	.05
67	Tim Leary	.05
68	Andres Galarraga	.10
69	Bob Milacki	.05
70	Tim Belcher	.05
71	Todd Zeile	.08
72	Jerome Walton	.05
73	Kevin Seitzer	.05
74	Jerald Clark	.05
75	John Smoltz	.10
76	Mike Henneman	.05
77	Ken Griffey, Jr.	1.50
78	Jim Abbott	.08
79	Gregg Jefferies	.10
80	Kevin Reimer	.05
81	Roger Clemens	.35
82	Mike Fitzgerald	.05
83	Bruce Hurst	.05
84	Eric Davis	.10
85	Paul Molitor	.25
86	Will Clark	.25
87	Mike Bielecki	.05
88	Bret Saberhagen	.10
89	Nolan Ryan	.50
90	Bobby Thigpen	.05
91	Dickie Thon	.05
92	Duane Ward	.05
93	Luis Polonia	.05
94	Terry Kennedy	.05
95	Kent Hrbek	.08
96	Danny Jackson	.05
97	Sid Fernandez	.05
98	Jimmy Key	.08
99	Franklin Stubbs	.05
100	Checklist 28-103	.05
101	R.J. Reynolds	.05
102	Dave Stewart	.08
103	Dan Pasqua	.05
104	Dan Plesac	.05
105	Mark McGwire	1.00
106	John Farrell	.05
107	Don Mattingly	.35
108	Carlton Fisk	.10
109	Ken Oberkfell	.05
110	Darrel Akerfelds	.05
111	Gregg Olson	.05
112	Mike Scioscia	.05
113	Bryn Smith	.05
114	Bob Geren	.05
115	Tom Candiotti	.05
116	Kevin Tapani	.08
117	Jeff Treadway	.05
118	Alan Trammell	.10
119	Pete O'Brien	.05
120	Joel Skinner	.05
121	Mike LaValliere	.05
122	Dwight Evans	.08
123	Jody Reed	.05
124	Lee Guetterman	.05
125	Tim Burke	.05
126	Dave Johnson	.05
127	Fernando Valenzuela	.10
128	Jose DeLeon	.05
129	Andre Dawson	.10
130	Gerald Perry	.05
131	Greg Harris	.05
132	Tom Glavine	.10
133	Lance McCullers	.05
134	Randy Johnson	.25
135	Lance Parrish	.08
136	Mackey Sasser	.05
137	Geno Petralli	.05
138	Dennis Lamp	.05
139	Dennis Martinez	.08
140	Mike Pagliarulo	.05
141	Hal Morris	.05
142	Dave Parker	.08
143	Brett Butler	.08
144	Paul Assenmacher	.05
145	Mark Gubicza	.05
146	Charlie Hough	.05
147	Sammy Sosa	.75
148	Randy Ready	.05
149	Kelly Gruber	.05
150	Devon White	.10
151	Gary Carter	.12
152	Gene Larkin	.05
153	Chris Sabo	.05
154	David Cone	.10
155	Todd Stottlemyre	.08
156	Glenn Wilson	.05
157	Bob Walk	.05
158	Mike Gallego	.05
159	Greg Hibbard	.05
160	Chris Bosio	.05
161	Mike Moore	.05
162	Jerry Browne	.05
163	Steve Sax	.05
164	Melido Perez	.05
165	Danny Darwin	.05
166	Roger McDowell	.05
167	Bill Ripken	.05
168	Mike Sharperson	.05
169	Lee Smith	.08
170	Matt Nokes	.05
171	Jesse Orosco	.05
172	Rick Aguilera	.05
173	Jim Presley	.05
174	Lou Whitaker	.08
175	Harold Reynolds	.08
176	Brook Jacoby	.05
177	Wally Backman	.05
178	Wade Boggs	.25
179	Chuck Cary	.05
180	Tom Foley	.05
181	Pete Harnisch	.05
182	Mike Morgan	.05
183	Bob Tewksbury	.05
184	Joe Girardi	.05
185	Storm Davis	.05
186	Ed Whitson	.05
187	Steve Avery	.05
188	Lloyd Moseby	.05
189	Scott Bankhead	.05
190	Mark Langston	.08
191	Kevin McReynolds	.05
192	Julio Franco	.08
193	John Dopson	.05
194	Oil Can Boyd	.05
195	Bip Roberts	.05
196	Billy Hatcher	.05
197	Edgar Diaz	.05
198	Greg Litton	.05
199	Mark Grace	.20
200	Checklist 104-179	.05
201	George Brett	.30
202	Jeff Russell	.05
203	Ivan Calderon	.05
204	Ken Howell	.05
205	Tom Henke	.05
206	Bryan Harvey	.05
207	Steve Bedrosian	.05
208	Al Newman	.05
209	Randy Myers	.08
210	Daryl Boston	.05
211	Manny Lee	.05
212	Dave Smith	.05
213	Don Slaught	.05
214	Walt Weiss	.05
215	Donn Pall	.05
216	Jamie Navarro	.05
217	Willie Randolph	.05
218	Rudy Seanez	.05
219	*Jim Leyritz*	.15
220	Ron Karkovice	.05
221	Ken Caminiti	.10
222a	Von Hayes (Traded players' first names included in How Acquired on back)	.05
222b	Von Hayes (No first names)	.05
223	Cal Ripken, Jr.	.75
224	Lenny Harris	.05
225	Milt Thompson	.05
226	Alvaro Espinoza	.05
227	Chris James	.05
228	Dan Gladden	.05
229	Jeff Blauser	.05
230	Mike Heath	.05
231	Omar Vizquel	.08
232	Doug Jones	.05
233	Jeff King	.05
234	Luis Rivera	.05
235	Ellis Burks	.08
236	Greg Cadaret	.05
237	Dave Martinez	.05
238	Mark Williamson	.05
239	Stan Javier	.05
240	Ozzie Smith	.25
241	*Shawn Boskie*	.08
242	Tom Gordon	.05
243	Tony Gwynn	.35
244	Tommy Gregg	.05
245	Jeff Robinson	.05
246	Keith Comstock	.05
247	Jack Howell	.05
248	Keith Miller	.05
249	Bobby Witt	.05
250	Rob Murphy	.05
251	Spike Owen	.05
252	Garry Templeton	.05
253	Glenn Braggs	.05
254	Ron Robinson	.05
255	Kevin Mitchell	.05
256	Les Lancaster	.05
257	*Mel Stottlemyre*	.10
258	Kenny Rogers	.08
259	Lance Johnson	.05
260	John Kruk	.08
261	Fred McGriff	.15
262	Dick Schofield	.05
263	Trevor Wilson	.05

264	David West	.05
265	Scott Scudder	.05
266	Dwight Gooden	.10
267	*Willie Blair*	.08
268	Mark Portugal	.05
269	Doug Drabek	.05
270	Dennis Eckersley	.10
271	Eric King	.05
272	Robin Yount	.25
273	Carney Lansford	.05
274	Carlos Baerga	.08
275	Dave Righetti	.05
276	Scott Fletcher	.05
277	Eric Yelding	.05
278	Charlie Hayes	.05
279	Jeff Ballard	.05
280	Orel Hershiser	.10
281	Jose Oquendo	.05
282	Mike Witt	.05
283	Mitch Webster	.05
284	Greg Gagne	.05
285	*Greg Olson*	.05
286	Tony Phillips	.08
287	Scott Bradley	.05
288	Cory Snyder	.05
289	Jay Bell	.08
290	Kevin Romine	.05
291	Jeff Robinson	.05
292	Steve Frey	.05
293	Craig Worthington	.05
294	Tim Crews	.05
295	Joe Magrane	.05
296	*Hector Villanueva*	.05
297	*Terry Shumpert*	.05
298	Joe Carter	.08
299	Kent Mercker	.05
300	Checklist 180-255	.05
301	Chet Lemon	.05
302	Mike Schooler	.05
303	Dante Bichette	.08
304	Kevin Elster	.05
305	Jeff Huson	.05
306	Greg Harris	.05
307	Marquis Grissom	.12
308	Calvin Schiraldi	.05
309	Mariano Duncan	.05
310	Bill Spiers	.05
311	Scott Garrelts	.05
312	Mitch Williams	.05
313	Mike Macfarlane	.05
314	Kevin Brown	.05
315	Robin Ventura	.15
316	Darren Daulton	.05
317	Pat Borders	.05
318	Mark Eichhorn	.05
319	Jeff Brantley	.05
320	Shane Mack	.05
321	Rob Dibble	.05
322	John Franco	.05
323	Junior Felix	.05
324	Casey Candaele	.05
325	Bobby Bonilla	.08
326	Dave Henderson	.05
327	Wayne Edwards	.05
328	Mark Knudson	.05
329	Terry Steinbach	.08
330	*Colby Ward*	.05
331	*Oscar Azocar*	.05
332	*Scott Radinsky*	.10
333	Eric Anthony	.05
334	Steve Lake	.05
335	Bob Melvin	.05
336	Kal Daniels	.05
337	Tom Pagnozzi	.05
338	*Alan Mills*	.08
339	Steve Olin	.05
340	Juan Berenguer	.05
341	Francisco Cabrera	.05
342	Dave Bergman	.05
343	Henry Cotto	.05
344	Sergio Valdez	.05
345	Bob Patterson	.05
346	John Marzano	.05
347	*Dana Kiecker*	.05
348	Dion James	.05
349	Hubie Brooks	.05
350	Bill Landrum	.05
351	*Bill Sampen*	.05
352	Greg Briley	.05
353	Paul Gibson	.05
354	Dave Eiland	.05
355	Steve Finley	.05
356	Bob Boone	.05
357	Steve Buechele	.05
358	Chris Hoiles	.08
359	Larry Walker	.25
360	Frank DiPino	.05
361	Mark Grant	.05
362	Dave Magadan	.05
363	Robby Thompson	.05
364	Lonnie Smith	.05
365	Steve Farr	.05
366	Dave Valle	.05
367	*Tim Naehring*	.08
368	Jim Acker	.05
369	Jeff Reardon	.05
370	Tim Teufel	.05
371	Juan Gonzalez	.60
372	Luis Salazar	.05
373	Rick Honeycutt	.05
374	Greg Maddux	.75
375	Jose Uribe	.05
376	Donnie Hill	.05
377	Don Carman	.05
378	*Craig Grebeck*	.05
379	Willie Fraser	.05
380	Glenallen Hill	.08
381	Joe Oliver	.05
382	Randy Bush	.05
383	Alex Cole	.05
384	Norm Charlton	.05
385	Gene Nelson	.05
386a	Checklist 256-331 (blue borders)	.05
386b	Checklist 256-331 (green borders)	.05
387	Rickey Henderson (MVP)	.15
388	Lance Parrish (MVP)	.05
389	Fred McGriff (MVP)	.10
390	Dave Parker (MVP)	.05
391	Candy Maldonado (MVP)	.05
392	Ken Griffey, Jr. (MVP)	.40
393	Gregg Olson (MVP)	.05
394	Rafael Palmeiro (MVP)	.10
395	Roger Clemens (MVP)	.20
396	George Brett (MVP)	.15
397	Cecil Fielder (MVP)	.10
398	Brian Harper (MVP)	.05
399	Bobby Thigpen (MVP)	.05
400	Roberto Kelly (MVP)	.05
401	Danny Darwin (MVP)	.05
402	Dave Justice (MVP)	.25
403	Lee Smith (MVP)	.05
404	Ryne Sandberg (MVP)	.15
405	Eddie Murray (MVP)	.15
406	Tim Wallach (MVP)	.05
407	Kevin Mitchell (MVP)	.05
408	Darryl Strawberry (MVP)	.08
409	Joe Carter (MVP)	.05
410	Len Dykstra (MVP)	.05
411	Doug Drabek (MVP)	.05
412	Chris Sabo (MVP)	.05
413	*Paul Marak* (RR)	.05
414	Tim McIntosh (RR)	.05
415	*Brian Barnes* (RR)	.05
416	*Eric Gunderson* (RR)	.05
417	*Mike Gardiner* (RR)	.10
418	Steve Carter (RR)	.08
419	*Gerald Alexander* (RR)	.05
420	*Rich Garces* (RR)	.05
421	*Chuck Knoblauch* (RR)	.45
422	*Scott Aldred* (RR)	.05
423	*Wes Chamberlain* (RR)	.10
424	*Lance Dickson* (RR)	.08
425	*Greg Colbrunn* (RR)	.15
426	*Rich Delucia* (RR)	.08
427	*Jeff Conine* (RR)	.40
428	*Steve Decker* (RR)	.10
429	*Turner Ward* (RR)	.10
430	Mo Vaughn (RR)	.65
431	*Steve Chitren* (RR)	.10
432	Mike Benjamin (RR)	.10
433	Ryne Sandberg (AS)	.10
434	Len Dykstra (AS)	.05
435	Andre Dawson (AS)	.10
436	Mike Scioscia (AS)	.05
437	Ozzie Smith (AS)	.10
438	Kevin Mitchell (AS)	.05
439	Jack Armstrong (AS)	.05
440	Chris Sabo (AS)	.05
441	Will Clark (AS)	.10
442	Mel Hall	.05
443	Mark Gardner	.05
444	Mike Devereaux	.05
445	Kirk Gibson	.05
446	Terry Pendleton	.05
447	Mike Harkey	.05
448	Jim Eisenreich	.05
449	Benito Santiago	.08
450	Oddibe McDowell	.05
451	Cecil Fielder	.08
452	Ken Griffey, Sr.	.08
453	Bert Blyleven	.08
454	Howard Johnson	.05
455	Monty Farris	.05
456	Tony Pena	.05
457	Tim Raines	.08
458	Dennis Rasmussen	.05
459	Luis Quinones	.05
460	B.J. Surhoff	.08
461	Ernest Riles	.05
462	Rick Sutcliffe	.05
463	Danny Tartabull	.05
464	Pete Incaviglia	.05
465	Carlos Martinez	.05
466	Ricky Jordan	.05
467	John Cerutti	.05
468	Dave Winfield	.15
469	Francisco Oliveras	.05
470	Roy Smith	.05
471	Barry Larkin	.12
472	Ron Darling	.05
473	David Wells	.08
474	Glenn Davis	.05
475	Neal Heaton	.05
476	Ron Hassey	.05
477	Frank Thomas	.75
478	Greg Vaughn	.08
479	Todd Burns	.05
480	Candy Maldonado	.05
481	Dave LaPoint	.05
482	Alvin Davis	.05
483	Mike Scott	.05
484	Dale Murphy	.12
485	Ben McDonald	.08
486	Jay Howell	.05
487	Vince Coleman	.05
488	Alfredo Griffin	.05
489	Sandy Alomar	.15
490	Kirby Puckett	.35
491	Andres Thomas	.05
492	Jack Morris	.08
493	Matt Young	.05
494	Greg Myers	.05
495	Barry Bonds	.35
496	Scott Cooper	.05
497	Dan Schatzeder	.05
498	Jesse Barfield	.05
499	Jerry Goff	.05
500	Checklist 332-408	.05
501	*Anthony Telford*	.08
502	Eddie Murray	.20
503	*Omar Olivares*	.12
504	Ryne Sandberg	.25
505	Jeff Montgomery	.05
506	Mark Parent	.05
507	Ron Gant	.10
508	Frank Tanana	.05
509	Jay Buhner	.08
510	Max Venable	.05
511	Wally Whitehurst	.05
512	Gary Pettis	.05
513	Tom Brunansky	.05
514	Tim Wallach	.08
515	Craig Lefferts	.05
516	*Tim Layana*	.05
517	Darryl Hamilton	.05
518	Rick Reuschel	.05
519	Steve Wilson	.05
520	Kurt Stillwell	.05
521	Rafael Palmeiro	.20
522	Ken Patterson	.05
523	Len Dykstra	.08
524	Tony Fernandez	.08
525	Kent Anderson	.05
526	*Mark Leonard*	.08
527	Allan Anderson	.05
528	Tom Browning	.05
529	Frank Viola	.05
530	John Olerud	.20
531	Juan Agosto	.05
532	Zane Smith	.05
533	Scott Sanderson	.05
534	Barry Jones	.05
535	Mike Felder	.05
536	Jose Canseco	.25
537	Felix Fermin	.05
538	Roberto Kelly	.05
539	Brian Holman	.05
540	Mark Davidson	.05
541	Terry Mulholland	.08
542	Randy Milligan	.05
543	Jose Gonzalez	.05
544	*Craig Wilson*	.08
545	Mike Hartley	.05
546	Greg Swindell	.05
547	Gary Gaetti	.08
548	Dave Justice	.30
549	Steve Searcy	.05
550	Erik Hanson	.05
551	Dave Stieb	.08
552	Andy Van Slyke	.05
553	Mike Greenwell	.05
554	Kevin Maas	.05
555	Delino Deshields	.08
556	Curt Schilling	.10
557	Ramon Martinez	.08
558	Pedro Guerrero	.05
559	Dwight Smith	.05
560	Mark Davis	.05
561	Shawn Abner	.05
562	Charlie Leibrandt	.05
563	John Shelby	.05
564	Bill Swift	.05
565	Mike Fetters	.05
566	Alejandro Pena	.05
567	Ruben Sierra	.08
568	Carlos Quintana	.05
569	Kevin Gross	.05
570	Derek Lilliquist	.05
571	Jack Armstrong	.05
572	Greg Brock	.05
573	Mike Kingery	.05
574	Greg Smith	.05
575	*Brian McRae*	.25
576	Jack Daugherty	.05
577	Ozzie Guillen	.05
578	Joe Boever	.05
579	Luis Sojo	.05
580	Chili Davis	.08
581	Don Robinson	.05
582	Brian Harper	.05
583	Paul O'Neill	.12
584	Bob Ojeda	.05
585	Mookie Wilson	.05
586	Rafael Ramirez	.05
587	Gary Redus	.05
588	Jamie Quirk	.05
589	Shawn Hilligas	.05
590	*Tom Edens*	.05
591	Joe Klink	.05
592	Charles Nagy	.08
593	Eric Plunk	.05
594	Tracy Jones	.05
595	Craig Biggio	.15
596	Jose DeJesus	.05
597	Mickey Tettleton	.05
598	Chris Gwynn	.05
599	Rex Hudler	.05
600	Checklist 409-506	.05
601	Jim Gott	.05
602	Jeff Manto	.05
603	Nelson Liriano	.05
604	Mark Lemke	.05
605	Clay Parker	.05
606	Edgar Martinez	.08
607	*Mark Whiten*	.20
608	Ted Power	.05
609	Tom Bolton	.05
610	Tom Herr	.05
611	Andy Hawkins	.05
612	Scott Ruskin	.05
613	Ron Kittle	.05
614	John Wetteland	.08
615	*Mike Perez*	.08
616	Dave Clark	.05
617	Brent Mayne	.08
618	Jack Clark	.05
619	Marvin Freeman	.05
620	Edwin Nunez	.05
621	Russ Swan	.05
622	Johnny Ray	.05
623	Charlie O'Brien	.05
624	*Joe Bitker*	.05
625	Mike Marshall	.05
626	Otis Nixon	.05
627	Andy Benes	.10
628	Ron Oester	.05
629	Ted Higuera	.05
630	Kevin Bass	.05
631	Damon Berryhill	.05
632	Bo Jackson	.15
633	Brad Arnsberg	.05
634	Jerry Willard	.05
635	Tommy Greene	.05
636	*Bob MacDonald*	.05
637	Kirk McCaskill	.05
638	John Burkett	.05
639	*Paul Abbott*	.05
640	Todd Benzinger	.05
641	Todd Hundley	.08
642	George Bell	.05
643	*Javier Ortiz*	.05
644	Sid Bream	.05
645	Bob Welch	.05
646	Phil Bradley	.05
647	Bill Krueger	.05
648	Rickey Henderson	.20
649	Kevin Wickander	.05
650	Steve Balboni	.05
651	Gene Harris	.05
652	Jim Deshaies	.05
653	Jason Grimsley	.05
654	Joe Orsulak	.05
655	*Jimmy Poole*	.05
656	Felix Jose	.05
657	Dennis Cook	.05
658	Tom Brookens	.05
659	Junior Ortiz	.05
660	Jeff Parrett	.05
661	Jerry Don Gleaton	.05
662	Brent Knackert	.05
663	Rance Mulliniks	.05
664	John Smiley	.05
665	Larry Andersen	.05
666	Willie McGee	.08
667	*Chris Nabholz*	.05
668	Brady Anderson	.10
669	*Darren Holmes*	.12
670	Ken Hill	.05
671	Gary Varsho	.05
672	Bill Pecota	.05
673	Fred Lynn	.08
674	Kevin D. Brown	.05
675	Dan Petry	.05
676	Mike Jackson	.05
677	Wally Joyner	.08
678	Danny Jackson	.05
679	*Bill Haselman*	.05
680	Mike Boddicker	.05
681	*Mel Rojas*	.12
682	Roberto Alomar	.25
683	Dave Justice (R.O.Y.)	.25
684	Chuck Crim	.05
685a	Matt Williams (Last line of Career Highlights ends, "most DP's in")	.20
685b	Matt Williams (last line ends "8/24-27/87.")	.25
686	Shawon Dunston	.05
687	*Jeff Schulz*	.05
688	*John Barfield*	.05
689	Gerald Young	.05
690	*Luis Gonzalez*	.15
691	Frank Wills	.05
692	Chuck Finley	.05
693	Sandy Alomar (R.O.Y.)	.10
694	Tim Drummond	.05
695	Herm Winningham	.05
696	Darryl Strawberry	.10
697	Al Leiter	.08
698	*Karl Rhodes*	.08
699	Stan Belinda	[illegible]
700	Checklist 507-604	.05
701	Lance Blankenship	.05
702	Willie Stargell (Puzzle Card)	.05
703	Jim Gantner	.05
704	*Reggie Harris*	.05
705	Rob Ducey	.05
706	Tim Hulett	.05
707	Atlee Hammaker	.05
708	Xavier Hernandez	.05
709	Chuck McElroy	.05
710	John Mitchell	.05
711	Carlos Hernandez	.05
712	Geronimo Pena	.05
713	*Jim Neidlinger*	.05
714	John Orton	.05
715	Terry Leach	.05
716	Mike Stanton	.05
717	Walt Terrell	.05
718	Luis Aquino	.05
719	Bud Black	.05
720	Bob Kipper	.05
721	*Jeff Gray*	.05
722	Jose Rijo	.05
723	Curt Young	.05
724	Jose Vizcaino	.08
725	*Randy Tomlin*	.05
726	Junior Noboa	.05
727	Bob Welch (Award Winner)	.05
728	Gary Ward	.05
729	Rob Deer	.05
730	*David Segui*	.08
731	Mark Carreon	.05
732	Vicente Palacios	.05
733	Sam Horn	.05
734	*Howard Farmer*	.08
735	Ken Dayley	.05
736	Kelly Mann	.05
737	*Joe Grahe*	.05
738	Kelly Downs	.05
739	*Jimmy Kremers*	.05
740	Kevin Appier	.12
741	Jeff Reed	.05
742	Jose Rijo (World Series)	.05
743	*Dave Rohde*	.08
744	Dr. Dirt/Mr. Clean (Len Dykstra, Dale Murphy)	.08
745	Paul Sorrento	.05
746	Thomas Howard	.05
747	*Matt Stark*	.05
748	Harold Baines	.08
749	Doug Dascenzo	.05
750	Doug Drabek (Award Winner)	.05
751	Gary Sheffield	.10
752	*Terry Lee*	.05
753	*Jim Vatcher*	.05
754	Lee Stevens	.05
755	Randy Veres	.05
756	Bill Doran	.05
757	Gary Wayne	.05
758	*Pedro Munoz*	.10
759	Chris Hammond	.05
760	Checklist 605-702	.05
761	Rickey Henderson (MVP)	.15
762	Barry Bonds (MVP)	.25
763	Billy Hatcher (World Series)	.05
764	Julio Machado	.05
765	Jose Mesa	.05
766	Willie Randolph (World Series)	.05
767	*Scott Erickson*	.10
768	Travis Fryman	.10
769	*Rich Rodriguez*	.10
770	Checklist 703-770; BC1-BC22	.05

1991 Donruss Elite

Donruss released a series of special inserts in 1991. Ten thousand of each Elite card was released, while 7,500 Legend cards and 5,000 Signature cards were issued. Cards were inserted in wax packs and feature marble borders. The Legend card features a Dick Perez drawing. Each card is designated with a serial number on the back.

		MT
Complete Set (10):		400.00
Common Player:		10.00
1	Barry Bonds	50.00
2	George Brett	90.00
3	Jose Canseco	40.00
4	Andre Dawson	10.00
5	Doug Drabek	10.00
6	Cecil Fielder	10.00
7	Rickey Henderson	25.00
8	Matt Williams	35.00
---	Nolan Ryan (Legend)	200.00
---	Ryne Sandberg (Signature)	275.00

1991 Donruss Highlights

This insert features highlights from the 1990 season. Cards have a "BC" prefix to the number and are styled after the 1991 regular-issue Donruss cards. Cards 1-10 feature blue borders due to their release with Series I cards. Cards 11-22 feature green borders and were released with Series II cards. A highlight logo appears on the front of the card. Each highlight is explained in depth on the card back.

		MT
	Complete Set (22):	2.00
	Common Player:	.10
1	Mark Langston, Mike Witt (No-Hits Mariners)	.10
2	Randy Johnson (No-Hits Tigers)	.20
3	Nolan Ryan (No-Hits A's)	.40
4	Dave Stewart (No-Hits Blue Jays)	.10
5	Cecil Fielder (50 Homer Club)	.10
6	Carlton Fisk (Record Home Run)	.20
7	Ryne Sandberg (Sets Fielding Records)	.25
8	Gary Carter (Breaks Catching Mark)	.10
9	Mark McGwire (Home Run Milestone)	.50
10	Bo Jackson (4 Consecutive HRs)	.25
11	Fernando Valenzuela (No-Hits Cardinals)	.10
12	Andy Hawkins (No-Hits White Sox)	.10
13	Melido Perez (No-Hits Yankees)	.10
14	Terry Mulholland (No-Hits Giants)	.10
15	Nolan Ryan (300th Win)	.40
16	Delino DeShields (4 Hits In Debut)	.10
17	Cal Ripken (Errorless Games)	.50
18	Eddie Murray (Switch Hit Homers)	.25
19	George Brett (3 Decade Champ)	.25
20	Bobby Thigpen (Shatters Save Mark)	.10
21	Dave Stieb (No-Hits Indians)	.10
22	Willie McGee (NL Batting Champ)	.10

1991 Donruss Grand Slammers

This set features players who hit grand slams in 1990. The cards are styled after the 1991 Donruss regular-issue cards. The featured player is showcased with a star in the background. The set was included in factory sets and randomly in jumbo packs.

		MT
	Complete Set (14):	1.50
	Common Player:	.10
1	Joe Carter	.10
2	Bobby Bonilla	.15
3	Kal Daniels	.10
4	Jose Canseco	.30
5	Barry Bonds	.35
6	Jay Buhner	.15
7	Cecil Fielder	.10
8	Matt Williams	.25
9	Andres Galarraga	.15
10	Luis Polonia	.10
11	Mark McGwire	.75
12	Ron Karkovice	.10
13	Darryl Strawberry	.15
14	Mike Greenwell	.10

1991 Donruss Rookies

Red borders highlight the 1991 Donruss Rookies cards. This set marks the sixth year that Donruss produced such an issue. As in past years, "The Rookies" logo appears on the card fronts. The set is packaged in a special box and includes a Willie Stargell puzzle card.

		MT
	Complete Set (56):	4.00
	Common Player:	.10
1	Pat Kelly	.10
2	Rich DeLucia	.10
3	Wes Chamberlain	.10
4	Scott Leius	.10
5	Darryl Kile	.10
6	Milt Cuyler	.10
7	Todd Van Poppel	.10
8	Ray Lankford	.30
9	Brian Hunter	.10
10	Tony Perezchica	.10
11	Ced Landrum	.10
12	Dave Burba	.10
13	Ramon Garcia	.10
14	Ed Sprague	.10
15	Warren Newson	.10
16	Paul Faries	.10
17	Luis Gonzalez	.15
18	Charles Nagy	.15
19	Chris Hammond	.10
20	Frank Castillo	.10
21	Pedro Munoz	.10
22	Orlando Merced	.10
23	Jose Melendez	.10
24	Kirk Dressendorfer	.10
25	Heathcliff Slocumb	.10
26	Doug Simons	.10
27	Mike Timlin	.15
28	Jeff Fassero	.10
29	Mark Leiter	.10
30	*Jeff Bagwell*	3.00
31	Brian McRae	.25
32	Mark Whiten	.10
33	*Ivan Rodriguez*	2.00
34	Wade Taylor	.10
35	Darren Lewis	.15
36	Mo Vaughn	1.00
37	Mike Remlinger	.10
38	Rick Wilkins	.15
39	Chuck Knoblauch	.60
40	Kevin Morton	.10
41	Carlos Rodriguez	.10
42	Mark Lewis	.15
43	Brent Mayne	.10
44	Chris Haney	.10
45	Denis Boucher	.10
46	Mike Gardiner	.10
47	Jeff Johnson	.10
48	Dean Palmer	.15
49	Chuck McElroy	.10
50	Chris Jones	.10
51	Scott Kamieniecki	.10
52	Al Osuna	.10
53	Rusty Meacham	.10
54	Chito Martinez	.10
55	Reggie Jefferson	.10
56	Checklist	.05

1991 Donruss Diamond Kings Supers

Donruss made this set available through a mail-in offer. Three wrappers, $12 and postage were necessary to obtain this set. The cards are exactly the same design as the regular Donruss Diamond Kings except they measure approximately 5" x 6-3/4" in size. The artwork of Dick Perez is featured.

		MT
	Complete Set (26):	12.00
	Common Player:	.25
1	Dave Steib	.25
2	Craig Biggio	.50
3	Cecil Fielder	.25
4	Barry Bonds	2.00
5	Barry Larkin	.35
6	Dave Parker	.25
7	Len Dykstra	.25
8	Bobby Thigpen	.25
9	Roger Clemens	2.00
10	Ron Gant	.25
11	Delino DeShields	.25
12	Roberto Alomar	1.00
13	Sandy Alomar	.85
14	Ryno Sandberg	2.00
15	Ramon Martinez	.50
16	Edgar Martinez	.25
17	Dave Magadan	.25
18	Matt Williams	.65
19	Rafael Palmeiro	.75
20	Bob Welch	.25
21	Dave Righetti	.25
22	Brian Harper	.25
23	Gregg Olson	.25
24	Kurt Stillwell	.25
25	Pedro Guerrero	.25
26	Chuck Finley	.25

1992 Donruss Previews

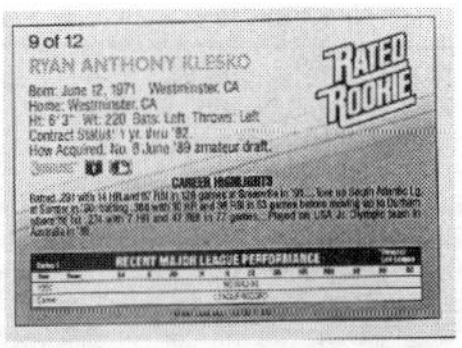

Four-card cello packs distributed to members of the Donruss dealers' network previewed the forthcoming 1992 baseball card issue. The preview cards have the same format, front and back photos as their counterparts in the regular set. Only the card number, the security underprinting, "Donruss Preview Card", and the stats, complete only through 1990, differ.

		MT
	Complete Set (12):	300.00
	Common Player:	5.00
1	Wade Boggs	25.00
2	Barry Bonds	35.00
3	Will Clark	20.00
4	Andre Dawson	9.00
5	Dennis Eckersley	9.00
6	Robin Ventura	15.00
7	Ken Griffey, Jr.	90.00
8	Kelly Gruber	5.00
9	Ryan Klesko (Rated Rookie)	25.00
10	Cal Ripken, Jr.	85.00
11	Nolan Ryan (Highlight)	70.00
12	Todd Van Poppel	5.00

1992 Donruss

For the second consecutive year, Donruss released its card set in two series. The 1992 cards feature improved stock, an anti-counterfeit feature and include both front and back photos. Once again Rated Rookies and All-Stars are included in the set. Special highlight cards also can be found in the 1992 Donruss set. Production was reduced in 1992 compared to 1988-1991.

		MT
	Complete Factory Set, Retail (788):	15.00
	Complete Factory Set, Hobby (784):	12.00
	Complete Set (784):	12.00
	Common Player:	.05
	Series 1 or 2 Wax Box:	15.00
1	*Mark Wohlers* (Rated Rookie)	.30
2	Wil Cordero (Rated Rookie)	.30
3	Kyle Abbott (Rated Rookie)	.08
4	*Dave Nilsson* (Rated Rookie)	.12
5	Kenny Lofton (Rated Rookie)	2.00
6	*Luis Mercedes* (Rated Rookie)	.10
7	*Roger Salkeld* (Rated Rookie)	.15
8	Eddie Zosky (Rated Rookie)	.10
9	*Todd Van Poppel* (Rated Rookie)	.15
10	*Frank Seminara* (Rated Rookie)	.10
11	*Andy Ashby* (Rated Rookie)	.20
12	Reggie Jefferson (Rated Rookie)	.10
13	Ryan Klesko (Rated Rookie)	.75
14	*Carlos Garcia* (Rated Rookie)	.15
15	*John Ramos* (Rated Rookie)	.05
16	Eric Karros (Rated Rookie)	.25
17	*Pat Lennon* (Rated Rookie)	.05
18	*Eddie Taubensee* (Rated Rookie)	.10
19	*Roberto Hernandez* (Rated Rookie)	.10
20	D.J. Dozier (Rated Rookie)	.05
21	Dave Henderson (All-Star)	.05
22	Cal Ripken, Jr. (All-Star)	.30
23	Wade Boggs (All-Star)	.10
24	Ken Griffey, Jr. (All-Star)	.75
25	Jack Morris (All-Star)	.05
26	Danny Tartabull (All-Star)	.05
27	Cecil Fielder (All-Star)	.05
28	Roberto Alomar (All-Star)	.20
29	Sandy Alomar (All-Star)	.08
30	Rickey Henderson (All-Star)	.15
31	Ken Hill	.05
32	John Habyan	.05
33	Otis Nixon (Highlight)	.05
34	Tim Wallach	.08
35	Cal Ripken, Jr.	.75
36	Gary Carter	.10
37	Juan Agosto	.05
38	Doug Dascenzo	.05
39	Kirk Gibson	.05
40	Benito Santiago	.05
41	Otis Nixon	.05
42	Andy Allanson	.05
43	Brian Holman	.05
44	Dick Schofield	.05
45	Dave Magadan	.05
46	Rafael Palmeiro	.20
47	Jody Reed	.05
48	Ivan Calderon	.05
49	Greg Harris	.05
50	Chris Sabo	.05
51	Paul Molitor	.25
52	Robby Thompson	.05
53	Dave Smith	.05
54	Mark Davis	.05
55	Kevin Brown	.05
56	Donn Pall	.05
57	Len Dykstra	.08
58	Roberto Alomar	.30
59	Jeff Robinson	.05
60	Willie McGee	.08
61	Jay Buhner	.10
62	Mike Pagliarulo	.05
63	Paul O'Neill	.15
64	Hubie Brooks	.05
65	Kelly Gruber	.05
66	Ken Caminiti	.12
67	Gary Redus	.05
68	Harold Baines	.08
69	Charlie Hough	.05
70	B.J. Surhoff	.08
71	Walt Weiss	.05
72	Shawn Hillegas	.05
73	Roberto Kelly	.05
74	Jeff Ballard	.05
75	Craig Biggio	.12
76	Pat Combs	.05
77	Jeff Robinson	.05
78	Tim Belcher	.05
79	Cris Carpenter	.05
80	Checklist 1-79	.05
81	Steve Avery	.05
82	Chris James	.05
83	Brian Harper	.05
84	Charlie Leibrandt	.05
85	Mickey Tettleton	.05
86	Pete O'Brien	.05
87	Danny Darwin	.05
88	Bob Walk	.05
89	Jeff Reardon	.05
90	Bobby Rose	.05
91	Danny Jackson	.05
92	John Morris	.05
93	Bud Black	.05
94	Tommy Greene (Highlight)	.05
95	Rick Aguilera	.05
96	Gary Gaetti	.05
97	David Cone	.12
98	John Olerud	.20
99	Joel Skinner	.05
100	Jay Bell	.10
101	Bob Milacki	.05
102	Norm Charlton	.05
103	Chuck Crim	.05
104	Terry Steinbach	.05
105	Juan Samuel	.05
106	Steve Howe	.05
107	Rafael Belliard	.05
108	Joey Cora	.05
109	Tommy Greene	.08
110	Gregg Olson	.05
111	Frank Tanana	.05
112	Lee Smith	.08
113	Greg Harris	.05
114	Dwayne Henry	.05
115	Chili Davis	.08
116	Kent Mercker	.05
117	Brian Barnes	.05
118	Rich DeLucia	.05
119	Andre Dawson	.15
120	Carlos Baerga	.10
121	Mike LaValliere	.05
122	Jeff Gray	.05
123	Bruce Hurst	.05
124	Alvin Davis	.05
125	John Candelaria	.05
126	Matt Nokes	.05
127	George Bell	.05
128	Bret Saberhagen	.10
129	Jeff Russell	.05
130	Jim Abbott	.08
131	Bill Gullickson	.05
132	Todd Zeile	.08
133	Dave Winfield	.15
134	Wally Whitehurst	.05
135	Matt Williams	.20
136	Tom Browning	.05
137	Marquis Grissom	.10
138	Erik Hanson	.05
139	Rob Dibble	.05
140	Don August	.05
141	Tom Henke	.05
142	Dan Pasqua	.05
143	George Brett	.25
144	Jerald Clark	.05
145	Robin Ventura	.15
146	Dale Murphy	.15
147	Dennis Eckersley	.10
148	Eric Yelding	.05
149	Mario Diaz	.05
150	Casey Candaele	.05
151	Steve Olin	.05
152	Luis Salazar	.05

153	Kevin Maas	.05
154	Nolan Ryan (Highlight)	.40
155	Barry Jones	.05
156	Chris Hoiles	.08
157	Bobby Ojeda	.05
158	Pedro Guerrero	.05
159	Paul Assenmacher	.05
160	Checklist 80-157	.05
161	Mike Macfarlane	.05
162	Craig Lefferts	.05
163	*Brian Hunter*	.05
164	Alan Trammell	.12
165	Ken Griffey, Jr.	1.50
166	Lance Parrish	.08
167	Brian Downing	.05
168	John Barfield	.05
169	Jack Clark	.05
170	Chris Nabholz	.05
171	Tim Teufel	.05
172	Chris Hammond	.05
173	Robin Yount	.25
174	Dave Righetti	.05
175	Joe Girardi	.05
176	Mike Boddicker	.05
177	Dean Palmer	.10
178	Greg Hibbard	.05
179	Randy Ready	.05
180	Devon White	.08
181	Mark Eichhorn	.05
182	Mike Felder	.05
183	Joe Klink	.05
184	Steve Bedrosian	.05
185	Barry Larkin	.10
186	John Franco	.05
187	*Ed Sprague*	.15
188	Mark Portugal	.05
189	Jose Lind	.05
190	Bob Welch	.05
191	Alex Fernandez	.15
192	Gary Sheffield	.15
193	Rickey Henderson	.20
194	Rod Nichols	.05
195	*Scott Kamieniecki*	.10
196	Mike Flanagan	.05
197	Steve Finley	.08
198	Darren Daulton	.05
199	Leo Gomez	.05
200	Mike Morgan	.05
201	Bob Tewksbury	.05
202	Sid Bream	.05
203	Sandy Alomar	.12
204	Greg Gagne	.05
205	Juan Berenguer	.05
206	Cecil Fielder	.08
207	Randy Johnson	.25
208	Tony Pena	.05
209	Doug Drabek	.05
210	Wade Boggs	.25
211	Bryan Harvey	.05
212	Jose Vizcaino	.05
213	*Alonzo Powell*	.05
214	Will Clark	.20
215	Rickey Henderson (Highlight)	.10
216	Jack Morris	.08
217	Junior Felix	.05
218	Vince Coleman	.05
219	Jimmy Key	.08
220	Alex Cole	.05
221	Bill Landrum	.05
222	Randy Milligan	.05
223	Jose Rijo	.05
224	Greg Vaughn	.10
225	Dave Stewart	.08
226	Lenny Harris	.05
227	Scott Sanderson	.05
228	Jeff Blauser	.05
229	Ozzie Guillen	.05
230	John Kruk	.05
231	Bob Melvin	.05
232	Milt Cuyler	.05
233	Felix Jose	.05
234	Ellis Burks	.10
235	Pete Harnisch	.05
236	Kevin Tapani	.05
237	Terry Pendleton	.05
238	Mark Gardner	.05
239	Harold Reynolds	.05
240	Checklist 158-237	.05
241	Mike Harkey	.05
242	Felix Fermin	.05
243	Barry Bonds	.35
244	Roger Clemens	.35
245	Dennis Rasmussen	.05
246	Jose DeLeon	.05
247	Orel Hershiser	.10
248	Mel Hall	.05
249	*Rick Wilkins*	.15
250	Tom Gordon	.05
251	Kevin Reimer	[illegible]
252	Luis Polonia	.05
253	Mike Henneman	.05
254	Tom Pagnozzi	.05
255	Chuck Finley	.05
256	Mackey Sasser	.05
257	John Burkett	.05
258	Hal Morris	.05
259	Larry Walker	.20
260	Billy Swift	.05
261	Joe Oliver	.05
262	Julio Machado	.05
263	Todd Stottlemyre	.05
264	Matt Merullo	.05
265	Brent Mayne	.05
266	Thomas Howard	.05
267	Lance Johnson	.05
268	Terry Mulholland	.05
269	Rick Honeycutt	.05
270	Luis Gonzalez	.08
271	Jose Guzman	.05
272	Jimmy Jones	.05
273	Mark Lewis	.05
274	Rene Gonzales	.05
275	*Jeff Johnson*	.05
276	Dennis Martinez (Highlight)	.05
277	Delino DeShields	.05
278	Sam Horn	.05
279	Kevin Gross	.05
280	Jose Oquendo	.05
281	Mark Grace	.20
282	Mark Gubicza	.05
283	Fred McGriff	.15
284	Ron Gant	.10
285	Lou Whitaker	.08
286	Edgar Martinez	.08
287	Ron Tingley	.05
288	Kevin McReynolds	.05
289	Ivan Rodriguez	.25
290	Mike Gardiner	.05
291	*Chris Haney*	.05
292	Darrin Jackson	.05
293	Bill Doran	.05
294	Ted Higuera	.05
295	Jeff Brantley	.05
296	Les Lancaster	.05
297	Jim Eisenreich	.05
298	Ruben Sierra	.05
299	Scott Radinsky	.05
300	Jose DeJesus	.05
301	*Mike Timlin*	.15
302	Luis Sojo	.05
303	Kelly Downs	.05
304	Scott Bankhead	.05
305	Pedro Munoz	.05
306	Scott Scudder	.05
307	Kevin Elster	.05
308	Duane Ward	.05
309	*Darryl Kile*	.15
310	Orlando Merced	.05
311	Dave Henderson	.05
312	Tim Raines	.10
313	Mark Lee	.05
314	Mike Gallego	.05
315	Charles Nagy	.08
316	Jesse Barfield	.05
317	Todd Frohwirth	.05
318	Al Osuna	.05
319	Darrin Fletcher	.05
320	Checklist 238-316	.05
321	David Segui	.05
322	Stan Javier	.05
323	Bryn Smith	.05
324	Jeff Treadway	.05
325	Mark Whiten	.05
326	Kent Hrbek	.08
327	Dave Justice	.25
328	Tony Phillips	.05
329	Rob Murphy	.05
330	Kevin Morton	.05
331	John Smiley	.05
332	Luis Rivera	.05
333	Wally Joyner	.08
334	*Heathcliff Slocumb*	.08
335	Rick Cerone	.05
336	*Mike Remlinger*	.05
337	Mike Moore	.05
338	Lloyd McClendon	.05
339	Al Newman	.05
340	Kirk McCaskill	.05
341	Howard Johnson	.05
342	Greg Myers	.05
343	Kal Daniels	.05
344	Bernie Williams	.25
345	Shane Mack	.05
346	Gary Thurman	.05
347	Dante Bichette	.10
348	Mark McGwire	2.00
349	Travis Fryman	.10
350	Ray Lankford	.08
351	Mike Jeffcoat	.05
352	Jack McDowell	.08
353	Mitch Williams	.05
354	Mike Devereaux	.05
355	Andres Galarraga	.10
356	Henry Cotto	.05
357	Scott Bailes	.05
358	Jeff Bagwell	.75
359	Scott Leius	.05
360	Zane Smith	.05
361	Bill Pecota	.05
362	Tony Fernandez	.08
363	Glenn Braggs	.05
364	Bill Spiers	.05
365	Vicente Palacios	.05
366	Tim Burke	.05
367	Randy Tomlin	.05
368	Kenny Rogers	.08
369	Brett Butler	.08
370	Pat Kelly	.05
371	Bip Roberts	.05
372	Gregg Jefferies	.10
373	Kevin Bass	.05
374	Ron Karkovice	.05
375	Paul Gibson	.05
376	Bernard Gilkey	.08
377	Dave Gallagher	.05
378	Bill Wegman	.05
379	Pat Borders	.05
380	Ed Whitson	.05
381	Gilberto Reyes	.05
382	Russ Swan	.05
383	Andy Van Slyke	.05
384	Wes Chamberlain	.05
385	Steve Chitren	.05
386	Greg Olson	.05
387	Brian McRae	.08
388	Rich Rodriguez	.05
389	Steve Decker	.05
390	Chuck Knoblauch	.12
391	Bobby Witt	.05
392	Eddie Murray	.25
393	Juan Gonzalez	.60
394	Scott Ruskin	.05
395	Jay Howell	.05
396	Checklist 317-396	.05
397	Royce Clayton (Rated Rookie)	.15
398	*John Jaha* (Rated Rookie)	.15
399	Dan Wilson (Rated Rookie)	.10
400	*Archie Corbin* (Rated Rookie)	.08
401	*Barry Manuel* (Rated Rookie)	.05
402	Kim Batiste (Rated Rookie)	.08
403	*Pat Mahomes* (Rated Rookie)	.15
404	Dave Fleming (Rated Rookie)	.05
405	Jeff Juden (Rated Rookie)	.10
406	*Jim Thome* (Rated Rookie)	.45
407	Sam Militello (Rated Rookie)	.10
408	*Jeff Nelson* (Rated Rookie)	.05
409	Anthony Young (Rated Rookie)	.15
410	Tino Martinez (Rated Rookie)	.25
411	*Jeff Mutis* (Rated Rookie)	.08
412	*Rey Sanchez* (Rated Rookie)	.10
413	*Chris Gardner* (Rated Rookie)	.08
414	*John Vander Wal* (Rated Rookie)	.08
415	Reggie Sanders (Rated Rookie)	.15
416	*Brian Williams* (Rated Rookie)	.10
417	Mo Sanford (Rated Rookie)	.15
418	*David Weathers* (Rated Rookie)	.08
419	*Hector Fajardo* (Rated Rookie)	.08
420	*Steve Foster* (Rated Rookie)	.08
421	Lance Dickson (Rated Rookie)	.10
422	Andre Dawson (All-Star)	.08
423	Ozzie Smith (All-Star)	.10
424	Chris Sabo (All-Star)	.05
425	Tony Gwynn (All-Star)	.10
426	Tom Glavine (All-Star)	.05
427	Bobby Bonilla (All-Star)	.08
428	Will Clark (All-Star)	.15
429	Ryne Sandberg (All-Star)	.20
430	Benito Santiago (All-Star)	.08
431	Ivan Calderon (All-Star)	.05
432	Ozzie Smith	.25
433	Tim Leary	.05
434	Bret Saberhagen (Highlight)	.05
435	Mel Rojas	.05
436	Ben McDonald	.08
437	Tim Crews	.05
438	Rex Hudler	.05
439	Chico Walker	.05
440	Kurt Stillwell	.05
441	Tony Gwynn	.20
442	John Smoltz	.10
443	Lloyd Moseby	.05
444	Mike Schooler	.05
445	Joe Grahe	.05
446	Dwight Gooden	.10
447	Oil Can Boyd	.05
448	John Marzano	.05
449	Bret Barberie	.05
450	Mike Maddux	.05
451	Jeff Reed	.05
452	Dale Sveum	.05
453	Jose Uribe	.05
454	Bob Scanlan	.05
455	Kevin Appier	.08
456	Jeff Huson	.05
457	Ken Patterson	.05
458	Ricky Jordan	.05
459	Tom Candiotti	.05
460	Lee Stevens	.05
461	*Rod Beck*	.15
462	Dave Valle	.05
463	Scott Erickson	.10
464	Chris Jones	.05
465	Mark Carreon	.05
466	Rob Ducey	.05
467	Jim Corsi	.05
468	Jeff King	.05
469	Curt Young	.05
470	Bo Jackson	.15
471	Chris Bosio	.05
472	Jamie Quirk	.05
473	Jesse Orosco	.05
474	Alvaro Espinoza	.05
475	Joe Orsulak	.05
476	Checklist 397-477	.05
477	Gerald Young	.05
478	Wally Backman	.05
479	Juan Bell	.05
480	Mike Scioscia	.05
481	Omar Olivares	.05
482	Francisco Cabrera	.05
483	Greg Swindell	.05
484	Terry Leach	.05
485	Tommy Gregg	.05
486	Scott Aldred	.05
487	Greg Briley	.05
488	Phil Plantier	.05
489	Curtis Wilkerson	.05
490	Tom Brunansky	.05
491	Mike Fetters	.05
492	Frank Castillo	.05
493	Joe Boever	.05
494	Kirt Manwaring	.05
495	Wilson Alvarez (Highlight)	.05
496	Gene Larkin	.05
497	Gary DiSarcina	.05
498	Frank Viola	.05
499	Manuel Lee	.05
500	Albert Belle	.35
501	Stan Belinda	.05
502	Dwight Evans	.05
503	Eric Davis	.12
504	Darren Holmes	.05
505	Mike Bordick	.05
506	Dave Hansen	.05
507	Lee Guetterman	.05
508	*Keith Mitchell*	.05
509	Melido Perez	.05
510	Dickie Thon	.05
511	Mark Williamson	.05
512	Mark Salas	.05
513	Milt Thompson	.05
514	Mo Vaughn	.30
515	Jim Deshaies	.05
516	Rich Garces	.05
517	Lonnie Smith	.05
518	Spike Owen	.05
519	Tracy Jones	.05
520	Greg Maddux	.60
521	Carlos Martinez	.05
522	Neal Heaton	.05
523	Mike Greenwell	.05
524	Andy Benes	.08
525	Jeff Schaefer	.05
526	Mike Sharperson	.05
527	Wade Taylor	.05
528	Jerome Walton	.05
529	Storm Davis	.05
530	*Jose Hernandez*	.05
531	Mark Langston	.05
532	Rob Deer	.05
533	Geronimo Pena	.05
534	*Juan Guzman*	.12
535	Pete Schourek	.05
536	Todd Benzinger	.05
537	Billy Hatcher	.05
538	Tom Foley	.05
539	Dave Cochrane	.05
540	Mariano Duncan	.05
541	Edwin Nunez	.05
542	Rance Mulliniks	.05
543	Carlton Fisk	.10
544	Luis Aquino	.05
545	Ricky Bones	.05
546	Craig Grebeck	.05
547	Charlie Hayes	.05
548	Jose Canseco	.25
549	Andujar Cedeno	.05
550	Geno Petralli	.05
551	Javier Ortiz	.05
552	Rudy Seanez	.05
553	Rich Gedman	.05
554	Eric Plunk	.05
555	Nolan Ryan, Rich Gossage (Highlight)	.20
556	Checklist 478-555	.05
557	Greg Colbrunn	.05
558	*Chito Martinez*	.05
559	Darryl Strawberry	.10
560	Luis Alicea	.05
561	Dwight Smith	.05
562	Terry Shumpert	.05
563	Jim Vatcher	.05
564	Deion Sanders	.10
565	Walt Terrell	.05
566	Dave Burba	.05
567	Dave Howard	.05
568	Todd Hundley	[illegible]
569	Jack Daugherty	.05
570	Scott Cooper	.05
571	Bill Sampen	.05
572	Jose Melendez	.05
573	Freddie Benavides	.05
574	Jim Gantner	.05
575	Trevor Wilson	.05
576	Ryne Sandberg	.20
577	Kevin Seitzer	.05
578	Gerald Alexander	.05
579	Mike Huff	.05
580	Von Hayes	.05
581	Derek Bell	.15
582	Mike Stanley	.05
583	Kevin Mitchell	.05
584	Mike Jackson	.05
585	Dan Gladden	.05
586	Ted Power	.05
587	Jeff Innis	.05
588	Bob MacDonald	.05
589	*Jose Tolentino*	.05
590	Bob Patterson	.05
591	*Scott Brosius*	.10
592	Frank Thomas	1.00
593	Darryl Hamilton	.05
594	Kirk Dressendorfer	.05
595	Jeff Shaw	.05
596	Don Mattingly	.35
597	Glenn Davis	.05
598	Andy Mota	.05
599	Jason Grimsley	.05
600	Jimmy Poole	.05
601	Jim Gott	.05
602	Stan Royer	.08
603	Marvin Freeman	.05
604	Denis Boucher	.05
605	Denny Neagle	.05
606	Mark Lemke	.05
607	Jerry Don Gleaton	.05
608	Brent Knackert	.05
609	Carlos Quintana	.05
610	Bobby Bonilla	.12
611	Joe Hesketh	.05
612	Daryl Boston	.05
613	Shawon Dunston	.05
614	Danny Cox	.05
615	Darren Lewis	.10
616	Alejandro Pena, Kent Mercker, Mark Wohlers (Highlight)	.10
617	Kirby Puckett	.35
618	Franklin Stubbs	.05
619	Chris Donnels	.10
620	David Wells	.08
621	Mike Aldrete	.05
622	Bob Kipper	.05
623	Anthony Telford	.05
624	Randy Myers	.05
625	Willie Randolph	.05
626	Joe Slusarski	.06
627	John Wetteland	.05
628	Greg Cadaret	.05
629	Tom Glavine	.10
630	Wilson Alvarez	.10
631	Wally Ritchie	.05
632	Mike Mussina	.30
633	Mark Leiter	.05
634	Gerald Perry	.05
635	Matt Young	.05
636	Checklist 556-635	.05
637	Scott Hemond	.05
638	David West	.05
639	Jim Clancy	.05
640	Doug Piatt	.05
641	Omar Vizquel	.08
642	Rick Sutcliffe	.05
643	Glenallen Hill	.05
644	Gary Varsho	.05
645	Tony Fossas	.05
646	Jack Howell	.05
647	*Jim Campanis*	.10
648	Chris Gwynn	.05
649	Jim Leyritz	.05
650	Chuck McElroy	.05
651	Sean Berry	.08
652	Donald Harris	.05
653	Don Slaught	.05
654	*Rusty Meacham*	.05
655	Scott Terry	.05
656	Ramon Martinez	.10
657	Keith Miller	.05
658	Ramon Garcia	.05
659	*Milt Hill*	.05
660	Steve Frey	.05
661	Bob McClure	.05
662	*Ced Landrum*	.05
663	*Doug Henry*	.05
664	Candy Maldonado	.05
665	Carl Willis	.05
666	Jeff Montgomery	.05
667	*Craig Shipley*	.10
668	*Warren Newson*	.05
669	Mickey Morandini	.05
670	Brook Jacoby	.05
671	*Ryan Bowen*	.10
672	Bill Krueger	.05
673	Rob Mallicoat	.05
674	Doug Jones	.05
675	Scott Livingstone	.05
676	Danny Tartabull	.05
677	Joe Carter (Highlight)	.05
678	Cecil Espy	.05
679	Randy Velarde	.05
680	Bruce Ruffin	.05
681	*Ted Wood*	.05
682	Dan Plesac	.05
683	Eric Bullock	.05
684	Junior Ortiz	.05
685	Dave Hollins	.08
686	Dennis Martinez	.08
687	Larry Andersen	.05
688	Doug Simons	.05
689	*Tim Spehr*	.05
690	*Calvin Jones*	.05
691	Mark Guthrie	.05
692	Alfredo Griffin	.05
693	Joe Carter	.10
694	*Terry Mathews*	.08
695	Pascual Perez	.05
696	Gene Nelson	.05
697	Gerald Williams	.08
698	*Chris Cron*	.08
699	Steve Buechele	.05
700	Paul McClellan	.05
701	Jim Lindeman	.05
702	Francisco Oliveras	.05

703	*Rob Maurer*	.05
704	*Pat Hentgen*	.25
705	Jaime Navarro	.05
706	*Mike Magnante*	.05
707	Nolan Ryan	.75
708	Bobby Thigpen	.05
709	John Cerutti	.05
710	Steve Wilson	.05
711	Hensley Meulens	.05
712	*Rheal Cormier*	.20
713	Scott Bradley	.05
714	Mitch Webster	.05
715	Roger Mason	.05
716	Checklist 636-716	.05
717	*Jeff Fassero*	.10
718	Cal Eldred	.08
719	Sid Fernandez	.05
720	*Bob Zupcic*	.05
721	Jose Offerman	.08
722	*Cliff Brantley*	.10
723	Ron Darling	.05
724	Dave Stieb	.05
725	Hector Villanueva	.05
726	Mike Hartley	.05
727	*Arthur Rhodes*	.15
728	Randy Bush	.05
729	Steve Sax	.05
730	Dave Otto	.05
731	*John Wehner*	.05
732	Dave Martinez	.05
733	*Ruben Amaro*	.05
734	Billy Ripken	.05
735	Steve Farr	.05
736	Shawn Abner	.05
737	*Gil Heredia*	.10
738	Ron Jones	.05
739	Tony Castillo	.05
740	Sammy Sosa	.75
741	Julio Franco	.05
742	Tim Naehring	.05
743	*Steve Wapnick*	.05
744	Craig Wilson	.05
745	*Darrin Chapin*	.08
746	*Chris George*	.08
747	Mike Simms	.05
748	Rosario Rodriguez	.05
749	Skeeter Barnes	.05
750	Roger McDowell	.05
751	Dann Howitt	.05
752	Paul Sorrento	.05
753	*Braulio Castillo*	.08
754	*Yorkis Perez*	.05
755	Willie Fraser	.05
756	*Jeremy Hernandez*	.05
757	Curt Schilling	.10
758	Steve Lyons	.05
759	Dave Anderson	.05
760	Willie Banks	.05
761	Mark Leonard	.05
762	Jack Armstrong	.05
763	Scott Servais	.05
764	Ray Stephens	.05
765	Junior Noboa	.05
766	*Jim Olander*	.05
767	Joe Magrane	.05
768	Lance Blankenship	.05
769	*Mike Humphreys*	.10
770	*Jarvis Brown*	.08
771	Damon Berryhill	.05
772	Alejandro Pena	.05
773	Jose Mesa	.05
774	*Gary Cooper*	.05
775	Carney Lansford	.05
776	Mike Bielecki	.05
777	Charlie O'Brien	.05
778	Carlos Hernandez	.05
779	Howard Farmer	.05
780	Mike Stanton	.05
781	Reggie Harris	.05
782	Xavier Hernandez	.05
783	*Bryan Hickerson*	.05
784	Checklist 717-BC8	.05

1992 Donruss Bonus Cards

The eight bonus cards were randomly inserted in 1992 foil packs and are numbered with a "BC" prefix. Both leagues' MVPs, Cy Young and Rookie of the Year award winners are featured, as are logo cards for the expansion Colorado Rockies and Florida Marlins. Cards are standard size in a format similar to the regular issue.

		MT
Complete Set (8):		3.00
Common Player:		.30
1	Cal Ripken, Jr. (MVP)	1.00
2	Terry Pendleton (MVP)	.30
3	Roger Clemens (Cy Young)	.75
4	Tom Glavine (Cy Young)	.40
5	Chuck Knoblauch (Rookie of the Year)	.60
6	Jeff Bagwell (Rookie of the Year)	1.00
7	Colorado Rockies	.50
8	Florida Marlins	.50

1992 Donruss Diamond Kings

Donruss changed its Diamond Kings style and distribution in 1992. The cards still feature the art of Dick Perez, but quality was improved from past years. The cards were randomly inserted in foil packs. One player from each team is featured. Card numbers have a "DK" prefix.

		MT
Complete Set (27):		25.00
Common Player:		.35
1	Paul Molitor	2.00
2	Will Clark	.50
3	Joe Carter	.35
4	Julio Franco	.25
5	Cal Ripken, Jr.	7.50
6	Dave Justice	.50
7	George Bell	.35
8	Frank Thomas	4.50
9	Wade Boggs	1.50
10	Scott Sanderson	.35
11	Jeff Bagwell	4.00
12	John Kruk	.35
13	Felix Jose	.35
14	Harold Baines	.45
15	Dwight Gooden	.45
16	Brian McRae	.35
17	Jay Bell	.45
18	Brett Butler	.35
19	Hal Morris	.35
20	Mark Langston	.35
21	Scott Erickson	.35
22	Randy Johnson	1.00
23	Greg Swindell	.35
24	Dennis Martinez	.35
25	Tony Phillips	.35
26	Fred McGriff	.75
27	Checklist	.10

1992 Donruss Diamond Kings Supers

Produced in very limited numbers, possibly as a prototype for use in a sales presentation to a major retail chain, these 4-7/8" x 6-3/4" cards are identical in virtually everything but size to the regular 1992 DK inserts. Both front and back feature a high-gloss finish.

		MT
Complete Set (27):		4000.
Common Player:		50.00
1	Paul Molitor	350.00
2	Will Clark	200.00
3	Joe Carter	65.00
4	Julio Franco	50.00
5	Cal Ripken, Jr.	1500.
6	Dave Justice	200.00
7	George Bell	50.00
8	Frank Thomas	1000.
9	Wade Boggs	350.00
10	Scott Sanderson	50.00
11	Jeff Bagwell	400.00
12	John Kruk	50.00
13	Felix Jose	50.00
14	Harold Baines	60.00
15	Dwight Gooden	60.00
16	Brian McRae	50.00
17	Jay Bell	75.00
18	Brett Butler	50.00
19	Hal Morris	50.00
20	Mark Langston	50.00
21	Scott Erickson	50.00
22	Randy Johnson	250.00
23	Greg Swindell	50.00
24	Dennis Martinez	50.00
25	Tony Phillips	50.00
26	Fred McGriff	200.00
27	Checklist (Dick Perez)	25.00

1992 Donruss Elite

Donruss continued its Elite series in 1992 by inserting cards in foil packs. Each card was released in the same quantity as the 1991 inserts - 10,000 Elite, 7,500 Legend and 5,000 Signature. The Elite cards, now featuring a prismatic border, are numbered as a continuation of the 1991 issue.

		MT
Complete Set (12):		800.00
Common Player:		10.00
9	Wade Boggs	30.00
10	Joe Carter	10.00
11	Will Clark	25.00
12	Dwight Gooden	15.00
13	Ken Griffey, Jr.	160.00
14	Tony Gwynn	50.00
15	Howard Johnson	10.00
16	Terry Pendleton	10.00
17	Kirby Puckett	65.00
18	Frank Thomas	40.00
---	Rickey Henderson (Legend)	65.00
---	Cal Ripken, Jr. (Signature)	375.00

1992 Donruss Rookie Phenoms

The first 12 cards in this insert set were available in Donruss Rookies foil packs. Cards 13-20 were found randomly packed in jumbo packs. Predominantly black on both front and back, the borders are highlighted with gold. A gold-foil "Phenoms" appears at top front.

		MT
Complete Set (20):		25.00
Common Player:		.40
1	Moises Alou	2.00
2	Bret Boone	1.50
3	Jeff Conine	.75
4	Dave Fleming	.40
5	Tyler Green	.40
6	Eric Karros	.75
7	Pat Listach	.40
8	Kenny Lofton	9.00
9	Mike Piazza	15.00
10	Tim Salmon	6.00
11	Andy Stankiewicz	.40
12	Dan Walters	.40
13	Ramon Caraballo	.40
14	Brian Jordan	2.00
15	Ryan Klesko	4.00
16	Sam Militello	.40
17	Frank Seminara	.40
18	Salomon Torres	.40
19	John Valentin	1.50
20	Wil Cordero	.40

1992 Donruss Rookies

Donruss increased the size of its Rookies set in 1992 to include 132 cards. In the past the cards were released only in boxed set form, but the 1992 cards were available in packs. Special "Phenoms" cards were randomly inserted into Rookies packs. The Phenoms cards feature black borders, while the Rookies cards are styled after the regular 1992 Donruss issue. The cards are numbered alphabetically.

		MT
Complete Set (132):		8.00
Common Player:		.05
Wax Box:		25.00
1	Kyle Abbott	.05
2	Troy Afenir	.05
3	Rich Amaral	.05
4	Ruben Amaro	.05
5	Billy Ashley	.05
6	Pedro Astacio	.15
7	Jim Austin	.05
8	Robert Ayrault	.05
9	Kevin Baez	.05
10	Estaban Beltre	.05
11	Brian Bohanon	.05
12	Kent Bottenfield	.05
13	Jeff Branson	.05
14	Brad Brink	.05
15	John Briscoe	.05
16	Doug Brocail	.05
17	Rico Brogna	.20
18	J.T. Bruett	.05
19	Jacob Brumfield	.05
20	Jim Bullinger	.05
21	Kevin Campbell	.05
22	Pedro Castellano	.05
23	Mike Christopher	.05
24	Archi Cianfrocco	.05
25	Mark Clark	.05
26	Craig Colbert	.05
27	Victor Cole	.05
28	Steve Cooke	.05
29	Tim Costo	.05
30	Chad Curtis	.30
31	Doug Davis	.05
32	Gary DiSarcina	.05
33	John Doherty	.05
34	Mike Draper	.05
35	Monty Fariss	.05
36	Bien Figueroa	.05
37	John Flaherty	.05
38	Tim Fortugno	.05
39	Eric Fox	.05
40	*Jeff Frye*	.05
41	Ramon Garcia	.05
42	Brent Gates	.20
43	Tom Goodwin	.05
44	Buddy Groom	.05
45	Jeff Grotewold	.05
46	Juan Guerrero	.05
47	Johnny Guzman	.05
48	Shawn Hare	.05
49	Ryan Hawblitzel	.05
50	Bert Heffernan	.05
51	Butch Henry	.05
52	Cesar Hernandez	.05
53	Vince Horsman	.05
54	Steve Hosey	.05
55	Pat Howell	.05
56	Peter Hoy	.05
57	Jon Hurst	.05
58	Mark Hutton	.05
59	Shawn Jeter	.05
60	Joel Johnston	.05
61	Jeff Kent	.40
62	Kurt Knudsen	.05
63	Kevin Koslofski	.05
64	Danny Leon	.05
65	Jesse Levis	.05
66	Tom Marsh	.05
67	Ed Martel	.05
68	Al Martin	.20
69	Pedro Martinez	2.00
70	Derrick May	.05
71	Matt Maysey	.05
72	Russ McGinnis	.05
73	Tim McIntosh	.05
74	Jim McNamara	.05
75	Jeff McNeely	.20
76	Rusty Meacham	.05
77	Tony Melendez	.05
78	Henry Mercedes	.05
79	Paul Miller	.05
80	Joe Millette	.05
81	Blas Minor	.05
82	Dennis Moeller	.05
83	Raul Mondesi	1.50
84	Rob Natal	.05
85	Troy Neel	.15
86	David Nied	.05
87	Jerry Nielsen	.05
88	Donovan Osborne	.05
89	John Patterson	.15
90	Roger Pavlik	.05
91	Dan Peltier	.05
92	Jim Pena	.05
93	William Pennyfeather	.05
94	Mike Perez	.05
95	Hipolito Pichardo	.05
96	Greg Pirkl	.05
97	Harvey Pulliam	.05
98	*Manny Ramirez*	6.00
99	Pat Rapp	.05
100	Jeff Reboulet	.05
101	Darren Reed	.15
102	Shane Reynolds	.05
103	Bill Risley	.05
104	Ben Rivera	.05
105	Henry Rodriguez	.15
106	Rico Rossy	.05
107	Johnny Ruffin	.05
108	Steve Scarsone	.05
109	Tim Scott	.05
110	Steve Shifflett	.05
111	Dave Silvestri	.05
112	Matt Stairs	.10
113	William Suero	.05
114	Jeff Tackett	.05
115	Eddie Taubensee	.25
116	Rick Trlicek	.05
117	Scooter Tucker	.05
118	Shane Turner	.05
119	Julio Valera	.05
120	Paul Wagner	.05
121	Tim Wakefield	.15
122	Mike Walker	.05
123	Bruce Walton	.05
124	Lenny Webster	.05
125	Bob Wickman	.05
126	Mike Williams	.05
127	Kerry Woodson	.05
128	Eric Young	.25
129	Kevin Young	.15
130	Pete Young	.05
131	Checklist	.05
132	Checklist	.05

Player names in *Italic* type indicate a rookie card.

1992 Donruss Update

Each retail factory set of 1992 Donruss cards contained a cello-wrapped four-card selection from this 22-card Update set. The cards feature the same basic format as the regular '92 Donruss, except they carry a "U" prefix to the card number on back. The cards feature rookies, highlights and traded players from the 1992 season.

		MT
Complete Set (22):		40.00
Common Player:		.75
1	Pat Listach (Rated Rookie)	.75
2	Andy Stankiewicz (Rated Rookie)	.75
3	Brian Jordan (Rated Rookie)	2.00
4	Dan Walters (Rated Rookie)	.75
5	Chad Curtis (Rated Rookie)	1.75
6	Kenny Lofton (Rated Rookie)	12.50
7	Mark McGwire (Highlight)	20.00
8	Eddie Murray (Highlight)	2.50
9	Jeff Reardon (Highlight)	.75
10	Frank Viola	.75
11	Gary Sheffield	2.50
12	George Bell	.75
13	Rick Sutcliffe	.75
14	Wally Joyner	1.00
15	Kevin Seitzer	.75
16	Bill Krueger	.75
17	Danny Tartabull	.75
18	Dave Winfield	3.50
19	Gary Carter	1.00
20	Bobby Bonilla	1.00
21	Cory Snyder	.75
22	Bill Swift	.75

1992 Donruss Durivage Montreal Expos

		MT
Complete Set (21):		20.00
Common Player:		.50
Album:		5.00
1	Bret Barberie	.50
2	Chris Haney	.50
3	Bill Sampen	.50
4	Ivan Calderon	.50
5	Gary Carter	3.00
6	Delino DeShields	.75
7	Jeff Fassero	.75
8	Darrin Fletcher	.50
9	Mark Gardner	.50
10	Marquis Grissom	4.00
11	Ken Hill	.75
12	Dennis Martinez	.75
13	Chris Nabholz	.50
14	Spike Owen	.50
15	Tom Runnells	.50
16	John Vander Wal	.50
17	Bill Landrum	.50
18	Larry Walker	10.00
19	Tim Wallach	.50
20	John Wetteland	.75
---	Checklist	.25

1993 Donruss Previews

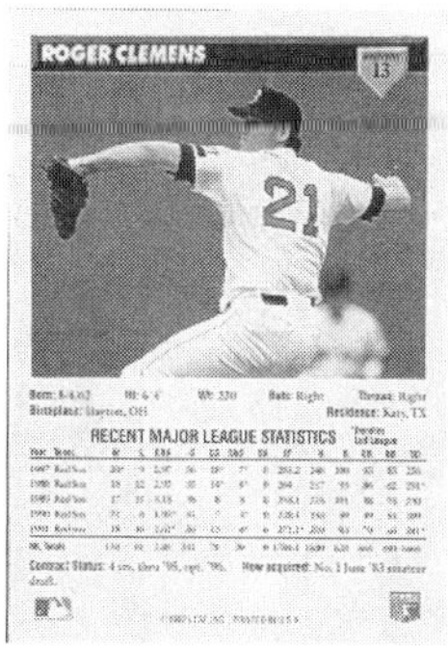

Twenty-two of the game's biggest stars were selected for inclusion in the preview version of Donruss' 1993 baseball card set. The previews follow the same basic format of the regular-issue 1993 except for the addition of the word "PREVIEW" above the card number in the home plate on back. Front photos are different between the preview and issued versions.

		MT
Complete Set (22):		135.00
Common Player:		3.00
1	Tom Glavine	3.00
2	Ryne Sandberg	8.00
3	Barry Larkin	4.00
4	Jeff Bagwell	7.50
5	Eric Karros	3.00
6	Larry Walker	7.00
7	Eddie Murray	7.00
8	Darren Daulton	3.00
9	Andy Van Slyke	3.00
10	Gary Sheffield	5.00
11	Will Clark	7.00
12	Cal Ripken Jr.	15.00
13	Roger Clemens	10.00
14	Frank Thomas	8.00
15	Cecil Fielder	3.00
16	George Brett	8.00
17	Robin Yount	7.50
18	Don Mattingly	12.00
19	Dennis Eckersley	4.00
20	Ken Griffey Jr.	15.00
21	Jose Canseco	7.50
22	Roberto Alomar	5.00

1993 Donruss

Rated Rookies and a randomly inserted Diamond Kings subset once again are featured in the 1993 Donruss set. Series I of the set includes 396 cards. Card fronts feature white borders surrounding a full-color player photo. The flip sides feature an additional photo, biographical information and career statistics. The cards are numbered on the back and the card's series is given with the number. The cards are UV coated. Series II contains a subset of players labeled with an "Expansion Draft" headline over their Marlins or Rockies team logo on front, even though the player photos are in the uniform of their previous team.

		MT
Complete Set (792):		20.00
Common Player:		.05
Series 1 or 2 Wax Box:		24.00
1	Craig Lefferts	.05
2	Kent Mercker	.05
3	Phil Plantier	.05
4	*Alex Arias*	.15
5	Julio Valera	.05
6	Dan Wilson	.12
7	Frank Thomas	1.00
8	Eric Anthony	.05
9	Derek Lilliquist	.05
10	*Rafael Bournigal*	.12
11	*Manny Alexander* (Rated Rookie)	.12
12	Bret Barberie	.05
13	Mickey Tettleton	.05
14	Anthony Young	.08
15	Tim Spehr	.05
16	*Bob Ayrault*	.10
17	Bill Wegman	.05
18	Jay Bell	.08
19	Rick Aguilera	.05
20	Todd Zeile	.08
21	Steve Farr	.05
22	Andy Benes	.08
23	Lance Blankenship	.05
24	Ted Wood	.05
25	Omar Vizquel	.08
26	Steve Avery	.05
27	Brian Bohanon	.05
28	Rick Wilkins	.05
29	Devon White	.08
30	*Bobby Ayala*	.12
31	Leo Gomez	.05
32	Mike Simms	.05
33	Ellis Burks	.08
34	Steve Wilson	.05
35	Jim Abbott	.08
36	Tim Wallach	.05
37	Wilson Alvarez	.05
38	Daryl Boston	.05
39	Sandy Alomar, Jr.	.10
40	Mitch Williams	.05
41	Rico Brogna	.10
42	Gary Varsho	.05
43	Kevin Appier	.08
44	Eric Wedge (Rated Rookie)	.05
45	Dante Bichette	.08
46	Jose Oquendo	.05
47	*Mike Trombley*	.05
48	Dan Walters	.05
49	Gerald Williams	.08
50	Bud Black	.05
51	Bobby Witt	.05
52	Mark Davis	.05
53	*Shawn Barton*	.10
54	Paul Assenmacher	.05
55	Kevin Reimer	.05
56	*Billy Ashley* (Rated Rookie)	.20
57	Eddie Zosky	.05
58	Chris Sabo	.05
59	Billy Ripken	.05
60	*Scooter Tucker*	.10
61	*Tim Wakefield* (Rated Rookie)	.15
62	Mitch Webster	.05
63	Jack Clark	.05
64	Mark Gardner	.05
65	Lee Stevens	.05
66	Todd Hundley	.08
67	Bobby Thigpen	.05
68	Dave Hollins	.10
69	Jack Armstrong	.05
70	Alex Cole	.05
71	Mark Carreon	.05
72	Todd Worrell	.05
73	*Steve Shifflett*	.05
74	Jerald Clark	.05
75	Paul Molitor	.25
76	*Larry Carter*	.05
77	Rich Rowland	.05
78	Damon Berryhill	.05
79	Willie Banks	.05
80	Hector Villanueva	.05
81	Mike Gallego	.05
82	Tim Belcher	.05
83	Mike Bordick	.05
84	Craig Biggio	.10
85	Lance Parrish	.05
86	Brett Butler	.08
87	Mike Timlin	.05
88	Brian Barnes	.05
89	Brady Anderson	.10
90	D.J. Dozier	.05
91	Frank Viola	.05
92	Darren Daulton	.05
93	Chad Curtis	.10
94	Zane Smith	.05
95	George Bell	.05
96	Rex Hudler	.05
97	Mark Whiten	.05
98	Tim Teufel	.05
99	Kevin Ritz	.05
100	Jeff Brantley	.05
101	Jeff Conine	.08
102	Vinny Castilla	.10
103	Greg Vaughn	.08
104	Steve Buechele	.05
105	Darren Reed	.05
106	Bip Roberts	.05
107	John Habyan	.05
108	Scott Servais	.05
109	Walt Weiss	.05
110	*J.T. Snow* (Rated Rookie)	.75
111	Jay Buhner	.08
112	Darryl Strawberry	.08
113	*Roger Pavlik*	.10
114	Chris Nabholz	.05
115	Pat Borders	.05
116	*Pat Howell*	.10
117	Gregg Olson	.05
118	Curt Schilling	.10
119	Roger Clemens	.40
120	*Victor Cole*	.05
121	Gary DiSarcina	.05
122	Checklist 1-80	.05
123	Steve Sax	.05
124	Chuck Carr	.05
125	Mark Lewis	.05
126	Tony Gwynn	.40
127	Travis Fryman	.10
128	Dave Burba	.05
129	Wally Joyner	.08
130	John Smoltz	.08
131	Cal Eldred	.05
132	Checklist 81-159	.05
133	Arthur Rhodes	.05
134	Jeff Blauser	.05
135	Scott Cooper	.05
136	Doug Strange	.05
137	Luis Sojo	.05
138	*Jeff Branson*	.10
139	Alex Fernandez	.08
140	Ken Caminiti	.10
141	Charles Nagy	.08
142	Tom Candiotti	.05
143	Willie Green (Rated Rookie)	.10
144	John Vander Wal	.05
145	*Kurt Knudsen*	.05
146	John Franco	.05
147	*Eddie Pierce*	.05
148	Kim Batiste	.05
149	Darren Holmes	.05
150	*Steve Cooke*	.15
151	Terry Jorgensen	.05
152	*Mark Clark*	.10
153	Randy Velarde	.05
154	Greg Harris	.05
155	*Kevin Campbell*	.10
156	John Burkett	.05
157	Kevin Mitchell	.05
158	Deion Sanders	.20
159	Jose Canseco	.25
160	*Jeff Hartsock*	.05
161	*Tom Quinlan*	.10
162	*Tim Pugh*	.10
163	Glenn Davis	.05
164	*Shane Reynolds*	.12
165	Jody Reed	.05
166	Mike Sharperson	.05
167	Scott Lewis	.05
168	Dennis Martinez	.08
169	Scott Radinsky	.05
170	Dave Gallagher	.05
171	Jim Thome	.25
172	Terry Mulholland	.05
173	Milt Cuyler	.05
174	Bob Patterson	.05
175	Jeff Montgomery	.05
176	Tim Salmon (Rated Rookie)	.50
177	Franklin Stubbs	.05
178	Donovan Osborne	.05
179	*Jeff Reboulet*	.05
180	*Jeremy Hernandez*	.08
181	Charlie Hayes	.05
182	Matt Williams	.20
183	Mike Raczka	.05
184	Francisco Cabrera	.05
185	Rich DeLucia	.05
186	Sammy Sosa	1.00
187	Ivan Rodriguez	.40
188	Bret Boone (Rated Rookie)	.15
189	Juan Guzman	.10
190	Tom Browning	.05
191	Randy Milligan	.05
192	Steve Finley	.08
193	John Patterson (Rated Rookie)	.10
194	Kip Gross	.05
195	Tony Fossas	.05
196	Ivan Calderon	.05
197	Junior Felix	.05
198	Pete Schourek	.05
199	Craig Grebeck	.05
200	Juan Bell	.05
201	Glenallen Hill	.05
202	Danny Jackson	.05
203	John Kiely	.05
204	Bob Tewksbury	.05
205	*Kevin Koslofski*	.10
206	Craig Shipley	.05
207	John Jaha	.10
208	Royce Clayton	.05
209	Mike Piazza (Rated Rookie)	1.50
210	Ron Gant	.08
211	Scott Erickson	.05
212	Doug Dascenzo	.05
213	Andy Stankiewicz	.08
214	Geronimo Berroa	.05
215	Dennis Eckersley	.08
216	Al Osuna	.05
217	Tino Martinez	.10
218	*Henry Rodriguez*	.12
219	Ed Sprague	.05
220	Ken Hill	.05
221	Chito Martinez	.05
222	Bret Saberhagen	.08
223	Mike Greenwell	.05
224	Mickey Morandini	.05
225	Chuck Finley	.05
226	Denny Neagle	.05
227	Kirk McCaskill	.05
228	Rheal Cormier	.05
229	Paul Sorrento	.05
230	Darrin Jackson	.05
231	Rob Deer	.05
232	Bill Swift	.05
233	Kevin McReynolds	.05
234	Terry Pendleton	.05
235	Dave Nilsson	.05
236	Chuck McElroy	.05
237	Derek Parks	.05
238	Norm Charlton	.05
239	Matt Nokes	.05
240	*Juan Guerrero*	.08
241	Jeff Parrett	.05
242	Ryan Thompson (Rated Rookie)	.15
243	Dave Fleming	.05
244	Dave Hansen	.05
245	Monty Fariss	.05
246	*Archi Cianfrocco*	.05
247	*Pat Hentgen*	.15
248	Bill Pecota	.05
249	Ben McDonald	.05
250	Cliff Brantley	.05
251	*John Valentin*	.15
252	Jeff King	.05
253	*Reggie Williams*	.10
254	Checklist 160-238	.05
255	Ozzie Guillen	.05
256	Mike Perez	.05
257	Thomas Howard	.05
258	Kurt Stillwell	.05
259	Mike Henneman	.05
260	Steve Decker	.05
261	Brent Mayne	.05
262	Otis Nixon	.05
263	*Mark Keifer*	.05
264	Checklist 239-317	.05
265	*Richie Lewis*	.05
266	*Pat Gomez*	.10
267	*Scott Taylor*	.10
268	Shawon Dunston	.05
269	Greg Myers	.05
270	Tim Costo	.05
271	Greg Hibbard	.05
272	Pete Harnisch	.05
273	*Dave Mlicki*	.08
274	Orel Hershiser	.08
275	Sean Berry (Rated Rookie)	.08
276	Doug Simons	.05
277	*John Doherty*	.10
278	Eddie Murray	.20
279	Chris Haney	.05
280	Stan Javier	.05
281	Jaime Navarro	.05
282	Orlando Merced	.05
283	Kent Hrbek	.08
284	Bernard Gilkey	.05
285	Russ Springer	.05
286	Mike Maddux	.05
287	*Eric Fox*	.10
288	Mark Leonard	.05
289	Tim Leary	.05
290	Brian Hunter	.05
291	Donald Harris	.05
292	Bob Scanlan	.05
293	Turner Ward	.05
294	Hal Morris	.05
295	Jimmy Poole	.05
296	Doug Jones	.05
297	Tony Pena	.05
298	Ramon Martinez	.08
299	*Tim Fortugno*	.10
300	Marquis Grissom	.10
301	Lance Johnson	.05
302	*Jeff Kent*	.15
303	Reggie Jefferson	.05
304	Wes Chamberlain	.05
305	*Shawn Hare*	.10
306	Mike LaValliere	.05
307	Gregg Jefferies	.08
308	*Troy Neel* (Rated Rookie)	.20
309	Pat Listach	.05
310	Geronimo Pena	.05
311	Pedro Munoz	.05
312	*Guillermo Velasquez*	.10
313	Roberto Kelly	.05
314	Mike Jackson	.05
315	Rickey Henderson	.20
316	Mark Lemke	.05
317	Erik Hanson	.05
318	Derrick May	.05
319	Geno Petralli	.05
320	Melvin Nieves (Rated Rookie)	.10
321	*Doug Linton*	.10
322	Rob Dibble	.05
323	Chris Hoiles	.05
324	Jimmy Jones	.05
325	Dave Staton (Rated Rookie)	.08
326	Pedro Martinez	.05
327	*Paul Quantrill*	.10
328	Greg Colbrunn	.05
329	*Hilly Hathaway*	.10
330	Jeff Innis	.05
331	Ron Karkovice	.05
332	*Keith Shepherd*	.10
333	*Alan Embree*	.12
334	*Paul Wagner*	.10
335	*Dave Haas*	.10
336	Ozzie Canseco	.05
337	Bill Sampen	.05
338	Rich Rodriguez	.05
339	Dean Palmer	.08
340	Greg Litton	.05
341	Jim Tatum (Rated Rookie)	.10
342	*Todd Haney*	.05
343	Larry Casian	.05
344	Ryne Sandberg	.35
345	*Sterling Hitchcock*	.15
346	Chris Hammond	.05
347	*Vince Horsman*	.12
348	*Butch Henry*	.12
349	Dann Howitt	.05
350	Roger McDowell	.05
351	Jack Morris	.05
352	Bill Krueger	.05
353	*Cris Colon*	.08
354	*Joe Vitko*	.10
355	Willie McGee	.08
356	Jay Baller	.05
357	Pat Mahomes	.05

358	Roger Mason	.05
359	*Jerry Nielsen*	.10
360	Tom Pagnozzi	.05
361	*Kevin Baez*	.08
362	*Tim Scott*	.08
363	*Domingo Martinez*	.10
364	Kirt Manwaring	.05
365	Rafael Palmeiro	.20
366	Ray Lankford	.08
367	Tim McIntosh	.05
368	*Jessie Hollins*	.08
369	Scott Leius	.05
370	Bill Doran	.05
371	*Sam Militello*	.10
372	Ryan Bowen	.05
373	Dave Henderson	.05
374	Dan Smith (Rated Rookie)	.10
375	*Steve Reed*	.12
376	Jose Offerman	.05
377	Kevin Brown	.05
378	Darrin Fletcher	.05
379	Duane Ward	.05
380	Wayne Kirby (Rated Rookie)	.12
381	*Steve Scarsone*	.08
382	Mariano Duncan	.05
383	*Ken Ryan*	.15
384	Lloyd McClendon	.05
385	Brian Holman	.05
386	Braulio Castillo	.05
387	*Danny Leon*	.08
388	Omar Olivares	.05
389	Kevin Wickander	.05
390	Fred McGriff	.20
391	Phil Clark	.12
392	Darren Lewis	.08
393	*Phil Hiatt*	.10
394	Mike Morgan	.05
395	Shane Mack	.05
396	Checklist 318-396	.05
397	David Segui	.05
398	Rafael Belliard	.05
399	Tim Naehring	.05
400	Frank Castillo	.05
401	Joe Grahe	.05
402	Reggie Sanders	.08
403	Roberto Hernandez	.05
404	Luis Gonzalez	.08
405	Carlos Baerga	.08
406	Carlos Hernandez	.05
407	Pedro Astacio (Rated Rookie)	.15
408	Mel Rojas	.05
409	Scott Livingstone	.05
410	Chico Walker	.05
411	Brian McRae	.05
412	Ben Rivera	.05
413	Ricky Bones	.05
414	Andy Van Slyke	.05
415	Chuck Knoblauch	.15
416	Luis Alicea	.05
417	Bob Wickman	.05
418	Doug Brocail	.05
419	Scott Brosius	.05
420	Rod Beck	.05
421	Edgar Martinez	.05
422	Ryan Klesko	.25
423	Nolan Ryan	1.00
424	Rey Sanchez	.05
425	Roberto Alomar	.35
426	Barry Larkin	.10
427	Mike Mussina	.25
428	Jeff Bagwell	.75
429	Mo Vaughn	.40
430	Eric Karros	.08
431	John Orton	.05
432	Wil Cordero	.05
433	Jack McDowell	.08
434	Howard Johnson	.05
435	Albert Belle	.50
436	John Kruk	.05
437	Skeeter Barnes	.05
438	Don Slaught	.05
439	Rusty Meacham	.05
440	Tim Laker (Rated Rookie)	.10
441	Robin Yount	.25
442	Brian Jordan	.10
443	Kevin Tapani	.05
444	Gary Sheffield	.15
445	Rich Monteleone	.05
446	Will Clark	.25
447	Jerry Browne	.05
448	Jeff Treadway	.05
449	Mike Schooler	.05
450	Mike Harkey	.05
451	Julio Franco	.05
452	Kevin Young (Rated Rookie)	.20
453	Kelly Gruber	.05
454	Jose Rijo	.05
455	Mike Devereaux	.05
456	Andujar Cedeno	.05
457	Damion Easley (Rated Rookie)	.15
458	Kevin Gross	.05
459	Matt Young	.05
460	Matt Stairs	.05
461	Luis Polonia	.05
462	Dwight Gooden	.08
463	Warren Newson	.05
464	Jose DeLeon	.05
465	Jose Mesa	.05
466	Danny Cox	.05
467	Dan Gladden	.05
468	Gerald Perry	.05
469	Mike Boddicker	.05
470	Jeff Gardner	.05
471	Doug Henry	.05
472	Mike Benajmin	.05
473	Dan Peltier (Rated Rookie)	.05
474	Mike Stanton	.05
475	John Smiley	.05
476	Dwight Smith	.05
477	Jim Leyritz	.05
478	Dwayne Henry	.05
479	Mark McGwire	2.00
480	Pete Incaviglia	.05
481	Dave Cochrane	.05
482	Eric Davis	.08
483	John Olerud	.15
484	Ken Bottenfield	.05
485	Mark McLemore	.05
486	Dave Magadan	.05
487	John Marzano	.05
488	Ruben Amaro	.05
489	Rob Ducey	.05
490	Stan Belinda	.05
491	Dan Pasqua	.05
492	Joe Magrane	.05
493	Brook Jacoby	.05
494	Gene Harris	.05
495	Mark Leiter	.05
496	Bryan Hickerson	.05
497	Tom Gordon	.05
498	Pete Smith	.05
499	Chris Bosio	.05
500	Shawn Boskie	.05
501	Dave West	.05
502	Milt Hill	.05
503	Pat Kelly	.05
504	Joe Boever	.05
505	Terry Steinbach	.05
506	Butch Huskey (Rated Rookie)	.15
507	David Valle	.05
508	Mike Scioscia	.05
509	Kenny Rogers	.08
510	Moises Alou	.10
511	David Wells	.08
512	Mackey Sasser	.05
513	Todd Frohwirth	.05
514	Ricky Jordan	.05
515	Mike Gardiner	.05
516	Gary Redus	.05
517	Gary Gaetti	.05
518	Checklist 397-476	.05
519	Carlton Fisk	.10
520	Ozzie Smith	.25
521	Rod Nichols	.05
522	Benito Santiago	.05
523	Bill Gullickson	.05
524	Robby Thompson	.05
525	Mike Macfarlane	.05
526	Sid Bream	.05
527	Darryl Hamilton	.05
528	Checklist 477-555	.05
529	Jeff Tackett	.05
530	Greg Olson	.05
531	Bob Zupcic	.05
532	Mark Grace	.10
533	Steve Frey	.05
534	Dave Martinez	.05
535	Robin Ventura	.15
536	Casey Candaele	.05
537	Kenny Lofton	.30
538	Jay Howell	.05
539	Fernando Ramsey (Rated Rookie)	.10
540	Larry Walker	.25
541	Cecil Fielder	.08
542	Lee Guetterman	.05
543	Keith Miller	.05
544	Len Dykstra	.05
545	B.J. Surhoff	.08
546	Bob Walk	.05
547	Brian Harper	.05
548	Lee Smith	.05
549	Danny Tartabull	.05
550	Frank Seminara	.05
551	Henry Mercedes	.05
552	Dave Righetti	.05
553	Ken Griffey, Jr.	2.00
554	Tom Glavine	.08
555	Juan Gonzalez	.60
556	Jim Bullinger	.05
557	Derek Bell	.08
558	Cesar Hernandez	.05
559	Cal Ripken, Jr.	2.00
560	Eddie Taubensee	.05
561	John Flaherty	.05
562	Todd Benzinger	.05
563	Hubie Brooks	.05
564	Delino DeShields	.05
565	Tim Raines	.08
566	Sid Fernandez	.05
567	Steve Olin	.05
568	Tommy Greene	.05
569	Buddy Groom	.05
570	Randy Tomlin	.05
571	Hipolito Pichardo	.05
572	Rene Arocha (Rated Rookie)	.08
573	Mike Fetters	.05
574	Felix Jose	.05
575	Gene Larkin	.05
576	Bruce Hurst	.05
577	Bernie Williams	.40
578	Trevor Wilson	.05
579	Bob Welch	.05
580	Dave Justice	.20
581	Randy Johnson	.35
582	Jose Vizcaino	.05
583	Jeff Huson	.05
584	Rob Maurer (Rated Rookie)	.05
585	Todd Stottlemyre	.05
586	Joe Oliver	.05
587	Bob Milacki	.05
588	Rob Murphy	.05
589	Greg Pirkl (Rated Rookie)	.05
590	Lenny Harris	.05
591	Luis Rivera	.05
592	John Wetteland	.05
593	Mark Langston	.05
594	Bobby Bonilla	.08
595	Esteban Beltre	.05
596	Mike Hartley	.05
597	Felix Fermin	.05
598	Carlos Garcia	.05
599	Frank Tanana	.05
600	Pedro Guerrero	.05
601	Terry Shumpert	.05
602	Wally Whitehurst	.05
603	Kevin Seitzer	.05
604	Chris James	.05
605	Greg Gohr (Rated Rookie)	.05
606	Mark Wohlers	.05
607	Kirby Puckett	.40
608	Greg Maddux	1.00
609	Don Mattingly	.60
610	Greg Cadaret	.05
611	Dave Stewart	.08
612	Mark Portugal	.05
613	Pete O'Brien	.05
614	Bobby Ojeda	.05
615	Joe Carter	.08
616	Pete Young	.05
617	Sam Horn	.05
618	Vince Coleman	.05
619	Wade Boggs	.25
620	*Todd Pratt*	.10
621	Ron Tingley	.05
622	Doug Drabek	.05
623	Scott Hemond	.05
624	Tim Jones	.05
625	Dennis Cook	.05
626	Jose Melendez	.05
627	Mike Munoz	.05
628	Jim Pena	.05
629	Gary Thurman	.05
630	Charlie Leibrandt	.05
631	Scott Fletcher	.05
632	Andre Dawson	.10
633	Greg Gagne	.05
634	Greg Swindell	.05
635	Kevin Maas	.05
636	Xavier Hernandez	.05
637	Ruben Sierra	.05
638	Dimitri Young (Rated Rookie)	.12
639	Harold Reynolds	.05
640	Tom Goodwin	.05
641	Todd Burns	.05
642	Jeff Fassero	.05
643	Dave Winfield	.20
644	Willie Randolph	.05
645	Luis Mercedes	.05
646	Dale Murphy	.10
647	Danny Darwin	.05
648	Dennis Moeller	.05
649	Chuck Crim	.05
650	Checklist 556-634	.05
651	Shawn Abner	.05
652	Tracy Woodson	.05
653	Scott Scudder	.05
654	Tom Lampkin	.05
655	Alan Trammell	.10
656	Cory Snyder	.05
657	Chris Gwynn	.05
658	Lonnie Smith	.05
659	Jim Austin	.05
660	Checklist 635-713	.05
661	(Tim Hulett)	.05
662	Marvin Freeman	.05
663	Greg Harris	.05
664	Heathcliff Slocumb	.05
665	Mike Butcher	.05
666	Steve Foster	.05
667	Donn Pall	.05
668	Darryl Kile	.05
669	Jesse Levis	.08
670	Jim Gott	.05
671	*Mark Hutton*	.10
672	Brian Drahman	.05
673	Chad Kreuter	.05
674	Tony Fernandez	.08
675	Jose Lind	.05
676	Kyle Abbott	.05
677	Dan Plesac	.05
678	Barry Bonds	.60
679	Chili Davis	.08
680	Stan Royer	.05
681	Scott Kamieniecki	.05
682	Carlos Martinez	.05
683	Mike Moore	.05
684	Candy Maldanado	.05
685	Jeff Nelson	.05
686	Lou Whitaker	.08
687	Jose Guzman	.05
688	Manuel Lee	.05
689	Bob MacDonald	.05
690	Scott Bankhead	.05
691	Alan Mills	.05
692	Brian Williams	.05
693	Tom Brunansky	.05
694	Lenny Webster	.05
695	Greg Briley	.05
696	Paul O'Neill	.08
697	Joey Cora	.05
698	Charlie O'Brien	.05
699	Junior Ortiz	.05
700	Ron Darling	.05
701	Tony Phillips	.05
702	William Pennyfeather	.05
703	Mark Gubicza	.05
704	Steve Hosey (Rated Rookie)	.12
705	Henry Cotto	.05
706	*David Hulse*	.15
707	Mike Pagliarulo	.05
708	Dave Stieb	.05
709	Melido Perez	.05
710	Jimmy Key	.05
711	Jeff Russell	.05
712	David Cone	.10
713	Russ Swan	.05
714	Mark Guthrie	.05
715	Checklist 714-792	.05
716	Al Martin (Rated Rookie)	.15
717	Randy Knorr	.05
718	Mike Stanley	.05
719	Rick Sutcliffe	.05
720	Terry Leach	.05
721	Chipper Jones (Rated Rookie)	1.50
722	Jim Eisenreich	.05
723	Tom Henke	.05
724	Jeff Frye	.05
725	Harold Baines	.08
726	Scott Sanderson	.05
727	Tom Foley	.05
728	Bryan Harvey (Expansion Draft)	.05
729	Tom Edens	.05
730	Eric Young (Expansion Draft)	.12
731	Dave Weathers (Expansion Draft)	.05
732	Spike Owen	.05
733	Scott Aldred (Expansion Draft)	.05
734	Cris Carpenter (Expansion Draft)	.05
735	Dion James	.05
736	Joe Girardi (Expansion Draft)	.05
737	Nigel Wilson (Expansion Draft)	.08
738	Scott Chiamparino (Expansion Draft)	.05
739	Jeff Reardon	.05
740	Willie Blair (Expansion Draft)	.05
741	Jim Corsi (Expansion Draft)	.05
742	Ken Patterson	.05
743	Andy Ashby (Expansion Draft)	.05
744	Rob Natal (Expansion Draft)	.05
745	Kevin Bass	.05
746	Freddie Benavides (Expansion Draft)	.05
747	Chris Donnels (Expansion Draft)	.05
748	*Kerry Woodson*	.10
749	Calvin Jones (Expansion Draft)	.05
750	Gary Scott	.05
751	Joe Orsulak	.05
752	Armando Reynoso (Expansion Draft)	.05
753	Monty Farriss (Expansion Draft)	.05
754	Billy Hatcher	.05
755	Denis Boucher (Expansion Draft)	.05
756	Walt Weiss	.05
757	Mike Fitzgerald	.05
758	Rudy Seanez	.05
759	Bret Barberie (Expansion Draft)	.05
760	Mo Sanford (Expansion Draft)	.05
761	*Pedro Castellano* (Expansion Draft)	.12
762	Chuck Carr (Expansion Draft)	.05
763	Steve Howe	.05
764	Andres Galarraga	.10
765	Jeff Conine (Expansion Draft)	.08
766	Ted Power	.05
767	Butch Henry (Expansion Draft)	.05
768	Steve Decker (Expansion Draft)	.05
769	Storm Davis	.05
770	Vinny Castilla (Expansion Draft)	.10
771	Junior Felix (Expansion Draft)	.05
772	Walt Terrell	.05
773	Brad Ausmus (Expansion Draft)	.08
774	Jamie McAndrew (Expansion Draft)	.05
775	Milt Thompson	.05
776	Charlie Hayes (Expansion Draft)	.05
777	Jack Armstrong (Expansion Draft)	.05
778	Dennis Rasmussen	.05
779	Darren Holmes (Expansion Draft)	.05
780	*Alex Arias*	.12
781	Randy Bush	.05
782	Javier Lopez (Rated Rookie)	.60
783	Dante Bichette	.10
784	John Johnstone (Expansion Draft)	.05
785	Rene Gonzales	.05
786	Alex Cole (Expansion Draft)	.05
787	Jeromy Burnitz (Rated Rookie)	.15
788	Michael Huff	.05
789	Anthony Telford	.05
790	Jerald Clark (Expansion Draft)	.05
791	Joel Johnston	.05
792	David Nied (Rated Rookie)	.08

1993 Donruss Diamond Kings

The traditional Donruss Diamond Kings cards were again used as an insert in Series I and Series II foil packs in 1993. The first 15 cards were found in Series I packs, while cards 16-31 were available in the second series packs.

		MT
Complete Set (31):		32.50
Common Player:		.75
1	Ken Griffey, Jr.	10.00
2	Ryne Sandberg	4.00
3	Roger Clemens	4.00
4	Kirby Puckett	4.50
5	Bill Swift	.75
6	Larry Walker	1.00
7	Juan Gonzalez	3.00
8	Wally Joyner	.75
9	Andy Van Slyke	.75
10	Robin Ventura	1.00
11	Bip Roberts	.75
12	Roberto Kelly	.75
13	Carlos Baerga	.75
14	Orel Hershiser	.75
15	Cecil Fielder	.75
16	Robin Yount	1.50
17	Darren Daulton	.75
18	Mark McGwire	10.00
19	Tom Glavine	.75
20	Roberto Alomar	2.50
21	Gary Sheffield	.90
22	Bob Tewksbury	.75
23	Brady Anderson	.75
24	Craig Biggio	1.00
25	Eddie Murray	1.50
26	Luis Polonia	.75
27	Nigel Wilson	.75
28	David Nied	.75
29	Pat Listach	.75
30	Eric Karros	.75
31	Checklist	.05

1993 Donruss Elite

Continuing the card numbering from the 1992 Elite set, the Elite '93 inserts utilized a silver-foil prismatic front border with blue back printing. Each card is serial numbered as one of 10,000; this identified production number helping to make the Elites among the more valuable of insert cards.

		MT
	Complete Set (20):	500.00
	Common Player:	10.00
19	Fred McGriff	10.00
20	Ryne Sandberg	30.00
21	Eddie Murray	30.00
22	Paul Molitor	30.00
23	Barry Larkin	15.00
24	Don Mattingly	45.00
25	Dennis Eckersley	10.00
26	Roberto Alomar	30.00
27	Edgar Martinez	10.00
28	Gary Sheffield	15.00
29	Darren Daulton	10.00
30	Larry Walker	25.00
31	Barry Bonds	30.00
32	Andy Van Slyke	10.00
33	Mark McGwire	60.00
34	Cecil Fielder	10.00
35	Dave Winfield	15.00
36	Juan Gonzalez	45.00
---	Robin Yount (Legend)	25.00
---	Will Clark (Signature)	125.00

1993 Donruss Elite Supers

A Wal-Mart exclusive, Donruss produced 3-1/2" x 5" versions of its 1993 Elite inserts, added Nolan Ryan and Frank Thomas and a new card of Barry Bonds in his Giants uniform and packaged them one per shrink-wrapped box with Series I Donruss leftovers. Each super-size card features a color player photo and silver-foil prismatic borders on front. Backs are printed in blue and include a serial number identifying each of the cards from an edition of 5,000.

		MT
	Complete Set (20):	600.00
	Common Player:	12.00
1	Fred McGriff	20.00
2	Ryne Sandberg	60.00
3	Eddie Murray	40.00
4	Paul Molitor	40.00
5	Barry Larkin	20.00
6	Don Mattingly	75.00
7	Dennis Eckersley	12.00
8	Roberto Alomar	35.00
9	Edgar Martinez	12.00
10	Gary Sheffield	20.00
11	Darren Daulton	12.00
12	Larry Walker	25.00
13	Barry Bonds	65.00
14	Andy Van Slyke	12.00
15	Mark McGwire	100.00
16	Cecil Fielder	12.00
17	Dave Winfield	35.00
18	Juan Gonzalez	65.00
19	Frank Thomas	75.00
20	Nolan Ryan	150.00

1993 Donruss Long Ball Leaders

Carrying a prefix of "LL" before the card number, these inserts were released in Series I (LL1-9) and Series II (LL10-18) jumbo packs, detailing mammoth home runs of the previous season.

		MT
	Complete Set (18):	55.00
	Common Player:	.75
1	Rob Deer	.75
2	Fred McGriff	1.50
3	Albert Belle	3.50
4	Mark McGwire	15.00
5	Dave Justice	1.50
6	Jose Canseco	2.50
7	Kent Hrbek	.75
8	Roberto Alomar	2.50
9	Ken Griffey, Jr.	15.00
10	Frank Thomas	6.00
11	Darryl Strawberry	1.25
12	Felix Jose	.75
13	Cecil Fielder	.75
14	Juan Gonzalez	4.00
15	Ryne Sandberg	3.00
16	Gary Sheffield	1.25
17	Jeff Bagwell	5.00
18	Larry Walker	2.00

1993 Donruss MVP's

This set was inserted in jumbo packs of both Series I and Series II. Cards carry a MVP prefix to the card number.

		MT
	Complete Set (26):	30.00
	Common Player:	.50
1	Luis Polonia	.50
2	Frank Thomas	3.00
3	George Brett	2.50
4	Paul Molitor	1.50
5	Don Mattingly	3.50
6	Roberto Alomar	2.00
7	Terry Pendleton	.50
8	Eric Karros	.75
9	Larry Walker	1.00
10	Eddie Murray	1.25
11	Darren Daulton	.50
12	Ray Lankford	.50
13	Will Clark	1.00
14	Cal Ripken, Jr.	5.00
15	Roger Clemens	2.50
16	Carlos Baerga	.50
17	Cecil Fielder	.50
18	Kirby Puckett	3.50
19	Mark McGwire	6.00
20	Ken Griffey, Jr.	6.00
21	Juan Gonzalez	2.50
22	Ryne Sandberg	2.50
23	Bip Roberts	.50
24	Jeff Bagwell	3.00
25	Barry Bonds	2.00
26	Gary Sheffield	1.00

1993 Donruss Spirit of the Game

Series I and Series II foil and jumbo packs could be found with these cards randomly inserted. Several multi-player cards are included in the set. Card numbers bear an SG prefix.

		MT
	Complete Set (20):	25.00
	Common Player:	1.00
1	Turning Two (Dave Winfield, Mike Bordick)	1.00
2	Play at the Plate (David Justice)	2.00
3	In There (Roberto Alomar)	2.00
4	Pumped (Dennis Eckersley)	1.00
5	Dynamic Duo (Juan Gonzalez, Jose Canseco)	2.50
6	Gone (Frank Thomas, George Bell)	1.50
7	Safe or Out? (Wade Boggs)	1.50
8	The Thrill (Will Clark)	1.00
9	Safe at Home (Damon Berryhill, Bip Roberts, Glenn Braggs)	1.00
10	Thirty X 31 (Cecil Fielder, Mickey Tettleton, Rob Deer)	1.00
11	Bag Bandit (Kenny Lofton)	2.00
12	Back to Back (Fred McGriff, Gary Sheffield)	1.00
13	Range Rovers (Greg Gagne, Barry Larkin)	1.00
14	The Ball Stops Here (Ryne Sandberg)	2.00
15	Over the Top (Carlos Baerga, Gary Gaetti)	1.00
16	At the Wall (Danny Tartabull)	1.00
17	Head First (Brady Anderson)	1.00
18	Big Hurt (Frank Thomas)	3.00
19	No-Hitter (Kevin Gross)	1.00
20	3,000 (Robin Yount)	1.50

1993 Donruss Elite Dominators

Created as a premium to move left-over boxes of its 1993 product on a home shopping network at $100 apiece, this special edition was produced in standard 2-1/2" x 3-1/2" size in a format similar to the 1991-93 Donruss Elite chase cards. Cards feature green prismatic borders, liberal use of foil stamping, etc. Only 5,000 of each card were produced, and each card is serially numbered on the back. Half of the cards of Nolan Ryan, Juan Gonzalez, Don Mattingly and Paul Molitor were personally autographed by the player.

		MT
	Complete Set (20):	750.00
	Common Player:	20.00
1	Ryne Sandberg	25.00
2	Fred McGriff	20.00
3	Greg Maddux	50.00
4	Ron Gant	20.00
5	Dave Justice	20.00
6	Don Mattingly	50.00
7	Tim Salmon	20.00
8	Mike Piazza	50.00
9	John Olerud	22.00
10	Nolan Ryan	60.00
11	Juan Gonzalez	40.00
12	Ken Griffey, Jr.	75.00
13	Frank Thomas	30.00
14	Tom Glavine	20.00
15	George Brett	45.00
16	Barry Bonds	35.00
17	Albert Belle	25.00
18	Paul Molitor	25.00
19	Cal Ripken, Jr.	60.00
20	Roberto Alomar	30.00
	Autographed Cards:	
6	Don Mattingly	125.00
10	Nolan Ryan	175.00
11	Juan Gonzalez	100.00
18	Paul Molitor	85.00

1993 Donruss Masters of the Game

Donruss issued a series of "Masters of the Game" art cards that were available only at Wal-Mart stores. The over-sized cards (3-1/2" x 5") feature the artwork of Dick Perez, creator of the Diamond Kings cards for the same company. The cards came issued one to a pack, along with a foil pack of 1993 Donruss cards for a retail price of about $3.

		MT
	Complete Set (16):	45.00
	Common Player:	2.50
1	Frank Thomas	4.00
2	Nolan Ryan	6.00
3	Gary Sheffield	2.50
4	Fred McGriff	2.50
5	Ryne Sandberg	3.00
6	Cal Ripken, Jr.	6.00
7	Jose Canseco	3.00
8	Ken Griffey, Jr.	7.50
9	Will Clark	2.50
10	Roberto Alomar	2.50
11	Juan Gonzalez	4.00
12	David Justice	2.50
13	Kirby Puckett	4.00
14	Barry Bonds	4.00
15	Robin Yount	3.50
16	Deion Sanders	2.50

1993 Donruss 1992 Blue Jays Commemorative Set

Issued only as a special gold-boxed set, this series commemorates the Toronto Blue Jays 1992 World Championship. Each player on the Jays '92 roster has a card. There are also special cards recalling each game of the Series and a SkyDome card. The World Series highlights cards have a bunting design at top and a gold-foil World Series logo on front. Player cards feature borderless photos; a Blue Jays "Commemorative Set" logo is at lower-left. Backs have a player photo at top and a stat box at bottom with season, career and 1992 LCS and World Series numbers.

		MT
	Complete Set (54):	6.00
	Common Card:	.10
1	Checklist/Logo card	.10
2	Roberto Alomar	.75
3	Derek Bell	.25
4	Pat Borders	.15
5	Joe Carter	.35
6	Alfredo Griffin	.10
7	Kelly Gruber	.10
8	Manuel Lee	.10
9	Candy Maldonado	.10
10	John Olerud	.75
11	Ed Sprague	.15
12	Pat Tabler	.10
13	Devon White	.30
14	Dave Winfield	.60
15	David Cone	.25
16	Mark Eichhorn	.10
17	Juan Guzman	.20
18	Tom Henke	.15
19	Jimmy Key	.15
20	Jack Morris	.25
21	Todd Stottlemyre	.15
22	Mike Timlin	.15
23	Duane Ward	.20
24	David Wells	.25
25	Randy Knorr	.10
26	Rance Mulliniks	.10
27	Tom Quinlan	.10
28	Cito Gaston	.25
29	Dave Steib	.20
30	Ken Dayley	.10
31	Turner Ward	.10
32	Eddie Zosky	.20
33	Pat Hentgen	.30
34	Al Leiter	.20
35	Doug Linton	.10
36	Bob MacDonald	.10
37	Rick Trlicek	.10
38	Domingo Martinez	.10
39	Mike Maksudian	.10
40	Rob Ducey	.10
41	Jeff Kent	.15
42	Greg Myers	.10
43	Dave Weathers	.10
44	Skydome	.10
45	Trophy Presentation (Jim Kaat, Cito Gaston, Paul Beeston, Bobby Brown)	.10
	World Series Highlights	.10
1WS	Series Opener (Blue Jays vs. Braves)	.10
2WS	Game 1 - Carter Homers in 4th	.10
3WS	Game 2 - Sprague's Game-Winning Pinch Homer	.10
4WS	Game 3 - Maldonado Drives in Game-Winner	.10
5WS	Game 4 - Key's Win Puts Jays Up 3-1	.10
6WS	Game 5 - Olerud Scores Both Jays Runs	.10
7WS	Game 6 - Winfield's Double in 11th Wins	.10
8WS	Pat Border Series MVP	.10
9WS	World Champs Celebration	.10

1994 Donruss Promos

To introduce both its regular 1994 issue and the "Special Edition" gold cards, Donruss produced this 12-card promo set for distribution to its dealer network. The promos are virtually identical in format to the regular cards except for the large gray diagonal overprint "Promotional Sample" on both front and back. Card numbers also differ on the promos.

		MT
Complete Set (12):		45.00
Common Player:		1.50
1	Barry Bonds	4.00
2	Darren Daulton	1.50
3	John Olerud	2.50
4	Frank Thomas	4.50
5	Mike Piazza	5.00
6	Tim Salmon	3.00
7	Ken Griffey, Jr.	7.50
8	Fred McGriff	2.50
9	Don Mattingly	5.00
10	Gary Sheffield	3.00
Special Edition Gold:		
1G	Barry Bonds (Special Edition Gold)	5.00
4G	Frank Thomas (Special Edition Gold)	7.50

1994 Donruss

Donruss released its 1994 set in two 330-card series. Each series also includes, 50 Special Edition gold cards and several insert sets. Regular cards have full-bleed photos and are UV coated and foil stamped. Special Edition cards are gold-foil stamped on both sides and are included in each pack. Insert sets titled Spirit of the Game and Decade Dominators were produced in regular and super (3-1/2" x 5") formats. Other inserts were MVPs and Long Ball Leaders in regular size and super-size Award Winners. An Elite series of cards, continuing from previous years with #37-48, was also issued as inserts. A 10th Anniversary insert set features 10 popular 1984 Donruss cards in gold-foil enhanced reprint versions.

		MT
Complete Set (660):		35.00
Common Player:		.05
Series 1 Wax Box:		45.00
Series 2 Wax Box:		40.00
1	Nolan Ryan (Career Salute 27 Years)	2.50
2	Mike Piazza	1.50
3	Moises Alou	.10
4	Ken Griffey, Jr.	3.00
5	Gary Sheffield	.15
6	Roberto Alomar	.75
7	John Kruk	.05
8	Gregg Olson	.05
9	Gregg Jefferies	.08
10	Tony Gwynn	1.25
11	Chad Curtis	.08
12	Craig Biggio	.15
13	John Burkett	.05
14	Carlos Baerga	.08
15	Robin Yount	.40
16	Dennis Eckersley	.08
17	Dwight Gooden	.08
18	Ryne Sandberg	.50
19	Rickey Henderson	.20
20	Jack McDowell	.05
21	Jay Bell	.08
22	Kevin Brown	.08
23	Robin Ventura	.12
24	Paul Molitor	.25
25	Dave Justice	.15
26	Rafael Palmeiro	.15
27	Cecil Fielder	.05
28	Chuck Knoblauch	.10
29	Dave Hollins	.08
30	Jimmy Key	.05
31	Mark Langston	.05
32	Darryl Kile	.05
33	Ruben Sierra	.05
34	Ron Gant	.08
35	Ozzie Smith	.25
36	Wade Boggs	.30
37	Marquis Grissom	.10
38	Will Clark	.25
39	Kenny Lofton	.60
40	Cal Ripken, Jr.	3.00
41	Steve Avery	.05
42	Mo Vaughn	.60
43	Brian McRae	.05
44	Mickey Tettleton	.05
45	Barry Larkin	.12
46	Charlie Hayes	.05
47	Kevin Appier	.05
48	Robby Thompson	.05
49	Juan Gonzalez	1.00
50	Paul O'Neill	.10
51	Marcos Armas	.05
52	Mike Butcher	.05
53	Ken Caminiti	.10
54	Pat Borders	.05
55	Pedro Munoz	.05
56	Tim Belcher	.05
57	Paul Assenmacher	.05
58	Damon Berryhill	.05
59	Ricky Bones	.05
60	Rene Arocha	.05
61	Shawn Boskie	.05
62	Pedro Astacio	.05
63	Frank Bolick	.05
64	Bud Black	.05
65	Sandy Alomar, Jr.	.10
66	Rich Amaral	.05
67	Luis Aquino	.05
68	Kevin Baez	.05
69	Mike Devereaux	.05
70	Andy Ashby	.08
71	Larry Andersen	.05
72	Steve Cooke	.05
73	Mario Daiz	.05
74	Rob Deer	.05
75	Bobby Ayala	.05
76	Freddie Benavides	.05
77	Stan Belinda	.05
78	John Doherty	.05
79	Willie Banks	.05
80	Spike Owen	.05
81	Mike Bordick	.05
82	Chili Davis	.08
83	Luis Gonzalez	.08
84	Ed Sprague	.05
85	Jeff Reboulet	.05
86	Jason Bere	.08
87	Mark Hutton	.05
88	Jeff Blauser	.05
89	Cal Eldred	.05
90	Bernard Gilkey	.05
91	Frank Castillo	.05
92	Jim Gott	.05
93	Greg Colbrunn	.05
94	Jeff Brantley	.05
95	Jeremy Hernandez	.05
96	Norm Charlton	.05
97	Alex Arias	.05
98	John Franco	.05
99	Chris Hoiles	.05
100	Brad Ausmus	.05
101	Wes Chamberlain	.05
102	Mark Dewey	.05
103	Benji Gil (Rated Rookie)	.10
104	John Dopson	.05
105	John Smiley	.05
106	David Nied	.05
107	George Brett (Career Salute 21 Years)	1.00
108	Kirk Gibson	.05
109	Larry Casian	.05
110	Checklist (Ryne Sandberg 2,000 Hits)	.15
111	Brent Gates	.08
112	Damion Easley	.08
113	Pete Harnisch	.05
114	Danny Cox	.05
115	Kevin Tapani	.05
116	Roberto Hernandez	.05
117	Domingo Jean	.05
118	Sid Bream	.05
119	Doug Henry	.05
120	Omar Olivares	.05
121	Mike Harkey	.05
122	Carlos Hernandez	.05
123	Jeff Fassero	.08
124	Dave Burba	.05
125	Wayne Kirby	.05
126	John Cummings	.05
127	Bret Barberie	.05
128	Todd Hundley	.10
129	Tim Hulett	.05
130	Phil Clark	.05
131	Danny Jackson	.05
132	Tom Foley	.05
133	Donald Harris	.05
134	Scott Fletcher	.05
135	Johnny Ruffin (Rated Rookie)	.05
136	Jerald Clark	.05
137	Billy Brewer	.05
138	Dan Gladden	.05
139	Eddie Guardado	.05
140	Checklist (Cal Ripken, Jr. 2,000 Hits)	.25
141	Scott Hemond	.05
142	Steve Frey	.05
143	Xavier Hernandez	.05
144	Mark Eichhorn	.05
145	Ellis Burks	.08
146	Jim Leyritz	.05
147	Mark Lemke	.05
148	Pat Listach	.05
149	Donovan Osborne	.05
150	Glenallen Hill	.05
151	Orel Hershiser	.08
152	Darrin Fletcher	.05
153	Royce Clayton	.05
154	Derek Lilliquist	.05
155	Mike Felder	.05
156	Jeff Conine	.08
157	Ryan Thompson	.05
158	Ben McDonald	.05
159	Ricky Gutierrez	.05
160	Terry Mulholland	.05
161	Carlos Garcia	.05
162	Tom Henke	.05
163	Mike Greenwell	.05
164	Thomas Howard	.05
165	Joe Girardi	.05
166	Hubie Brooks	.05
167	Greg Gohr	.05
168	Chip Hale	.05
169	Rick Honeycutt	.05
170	Hilly Hathaway	.05
171	Todd Jones	.05
172	Tony Fernandez	.05
173	Bo Jackson	.15
174	Bobby Munoz	.05
175	Greg McMichael	.05
176	Graeme Lloyd	.05
177	Tom Pagnozzi	.05
178	Derrick May	.05
179	Pedro Martinez	.12
180	Ken Hill	.05
181	Bryan Hickerson	.05
182	Jose Mesa	.05
183	Dave Fleming	.05
184	Henry Cotto	.05
185	Jeff Kent	.05
186	Mark McLemore	.05
187	Trevor Hoffman	.08
188	Todd Pratt	.05
189	Blas Minor	.05
190	Charlie Leibrandt	.05
191	Tony Pena	.05
192	*Larry Luebbers*	.08
193	Greg Harris	.05
194	David Cone	.10
195	Bill Gullickson	.05
196	Brian Harper	.05
197	Steve Karsay (Rated Rookie)	.20
198	Greg Myers	.05
199	Mark Portugal	.05
200	Pat Hentgen	.08
201	Mike La Valliere	.05
202	Mike Stanley	.05
203	Kent Mercker	.05
204	Dave Nilsson	.05
205	Erik Pappas	.05
206	Mike Morgan	.05
207	Roger McDowell	.05
208	Mike Lansing	.08
209	Kirt Manwaring	.05
210	Randy Milligan	.05
211	Erik Hanson	.05
212	Orestes Destrade	.05
213	Mike Maddux	.05
214	Alan Mills	.05
215	Tim Mauser	.05
216	Ben Rivera	.05
217	Don Slaught	.05
218	Bob Patterson	.05
219	Carlos Quintana	.05
220	Checklist (Tim Raines 2,000 Hits)	.05
221	Hal Morris	.05
222	Darren Holmes	.05
223	Chris Gwynn	.05
224	Chad Kreuter	.05
225	Mike Hartley	.05
226	Scott Lydy	.05
227	Eduardo Perez	.05
228	Greg Swindell	.05
229	Al Leiter	.08
230	Scott Radinsky	.05
231	Bob Wickman	.05
232	Otis Nixon	.05
233	Kevin Reimer	.05
234	Geronimo Pena	.05
235	Kevin Roberson (Rated Rookie)	.10
236	Jody Reed	.05
237	Kirk Rueter (Rated Rookie)	.15
238	Willie McGee	.05
239	Charles Nagy	.08
240	Tim Leary	.05
241	Carl Everett	.05
242	Charlie O'Brien	.05
243	Mike Pagliarulo	.05
244	Kerry Taylor	.05
245	Kevin Stocker	.05
246	Joel Johnston	.05
247	Geno Petralli	.05
248	Jeff Russell	.05
249	Joe Oliver	.05
250	Robert Mejia	.05
251	Chris Haney	.05
252	Bill Krueger	.05
253	Shane Mack	.05
254	Terry Steinbach	.05
255	Luis Polonia	.05
256	Eddie Taubensee	.05
257	Dave Stewart	.05
258	Tim Raines	.08
259	Bernie Williams	.40
260	John Smoltz	.10
261	Kevin Seitzer	.05
262	Bob Tewksbury	.05
263	Bob Scanlan	.05
264	Henry Rodriguez	.05
265	Tim Scott	.05
266	Scott Sanderson	.05
267	Eric Plunk	.05
268	Edgar Martinez	.08
269	Charlie Hough	.05
270	Joe Orsulak	.05
271	Harold Reynolds	.05
272	Tim Teufel	.05
273	Bobby Thigpen	.05
274	Randy Tomlin	.05
275	Gary Redus	.05
276	Ken Ryan	.05
277	Tim Pugh	.05
278	Jayhawk Owens	.05
279	Phil Hiatt (Rated Rookie)	.08
280	Alan Trammell	.08
281	Dave McCarty (Rated Rookie)	.08
282	Bob Welch	.05
283	J.T. Snow	.20
284	Brian Williams	.05
285	Devon White	.05
286	Steve Sax	.05
287	Tony Tarasco	.05
288	Bill Spiers	.05
289	Allen Watson	.05
290	Checklist (Rickey Henderson 2,000 Hits)	.05
291	Joe Vizcaino	.05
292	Darryl Strawberry	.08
293	John Wetteland	.05
294	Bill Swift	.05
295	Jeff Treadway	.05
296	Tino Martinez	.10
297	Richie Lewis	.05
298	Bret Saberhagen	.08
299	Arthur Rhodes	.05
300	Guillermo Velasquez	.05
301	Milt Thompson	.05
302	Doug Strange	.05
303	Aaron Sele	.12
304	Bip Roberts	.05
305	Bruce Ruffin	.05
306	Jose Lind	.05
307	David Wells	.08
308	Bobby Witt	.05
309	Mark Wohlers	.05
310	B.J. Surhoff	.08
311	Mark Whiten	.05
312	Turk Wendell	.05
313	Raul Mondesi	.60
314	*Brian Turang*	.08
315	Chris Hammond	.05
316	Tim Bogar	.05
317	Brad Pennington	.05
318	Tim Worrell	.05
319	Mitch Williams	.05
320	Rondell White (Rated Rookie)	.30
321	Frank Viola	.05
322	Manny Ramirez (Rated Rookie)	2.00
323	Gary Wayne	.05
324	Mike Macfarlane	.05
325	Russ Springer	.05
326	Tim Wallach	.05
327	Salomon Torres (Rated Rookie)	.08
328	Omar Vizquel	.08
329	*Andy Tomberlin*	.10
330	Chris Sabo	.05
331	Mike Mussina	.40
332	Andy Benes	.08
333	Darren Daulton	.05
334	Orlando Merced	.05
335	Mark McGwire	4.00
336	Dave Winfield	.25
337	Sammy Sosa	1.50
338	Eric Karros	.10
339	Greg Vaughn	.08
340	Don Mattingly	1.00
341	Frank Thomas	1.00
342	Fred McGriff	.20
343	Kirby Puckett	1.00
344	Roberto Kelly	.05
345	Wally Joyner	.08
346	Andres Galarraga	.12
347	Bobby Bonilla	.08
348	Benito Santiago	.05
349	Barry Bonds	.75
350	Delino DeShields	.08
351	Albert Belle	.75
352	Randy Johnson	.40
353	Tim Salmon	.20
354	John Olerud	.20
355	Dean Palmer	.05
356	Roger Clemens	1.00
357	Jim Abbott	.08
358	Mark Grace	.15
359	Ozzie Guillen	.05
360	Lou Whitaker	.05
361	Jose Rijo	.05
362	Jeff Montgomery	.05
363	Chuck Finley	.05
364	Tom Glavine	.08
365	Jeff Bagwell	1.00
366	Joe Carter	.08
367	Ray Lankford	.05
368	Ramon Martinez	.08
369	Jay Buhner	.08
370	Matt Williams	.25
371	Larry Walker	.25
372	Jose Canseco	.25
373	Len Dykstra	.05
374	Bryan Harvey	.05
375	Andy Van Slyke	.05
376	Ivan Rodriguez	.50
377	Kevin Mitchell	.05
378	Travis Fryman	.10
379	Duane Ward	.05
380	Greg Maddux	1.00
381	Scott Servais	.05
382	Greg Olson	.05
383	Rey Sanchez	.05
384	Tom Kramer	.05
385	David Valle	.05
386	Eddie Murray	.15
387	Kevin Higgins	.05
388	Dan Wilson	.05
389	Todd Frohwirth	.05
390	Gerald Williams	.05
391	Hipolito Pichardo	.05
392	Pat Meares	.05
393	Luis Lopez	.05
394	Ricky Jordan	.05
395	Bob Walk	.05
396	Sid Fernandez	.05
397	Todd Worrell	.05
398	Darryl Hamilton	.05
399	Randy Myers	.05
400	Rod Brewer	.05
401	Lance Blankenship	.05
402	Steve Finley	.05
403	*Phil Leftwich*	.05
404	Juan Guzman	.05
405	Anthony Young	.05
406	Jeff Gardner	.05
407	Ryan Bowen	.05
408	Fernando Valenzuela	.05
409	David West	.05
410	Kenny Rogers	.05
411	Bob Zupcic	.05
412	Eric Young	.08
413	Bret Boone	.08
414	Danny Tartabull	.05
415	Bob MacDonald	.05
416	Ron Karkovice	.05
417	Scott Cooper	.05
418	Dante Bichette	.15
419	Tripp Cromer	.05
420	Billy Ashley	.05
421	Roger Smithberg	.05
422	Dennis Martinez	.08
423	Mike Blowers	.05
424	Darren Lewis	.05
425	Junior Ortiz	.05
426	Butch Huskey	.10
427	Jimmy Poole	.05
428	Walt Weiss	.05
429	Scott Bankhead	.05
430	Deion Sanders	.15
431	Scott Bullett	.05
432	Jeff Huson	.05
433	Tyler Green	.05
434	Billy Hatcher	.05
435	Bob Hamelin	.05
436	Reggie Sanders	.10
437	Scott Erickson	.08
438	Steve Reed	.05
439	Randy Velarde	.05
440	Checklist (Tony Gwynn 2,000 Hits)	.15
441	Terry Leach	.05
442	Danny Bautista	.05
443	Kent Hrbek	.08
444	Rick Wilkins	.05
445	Tony Phillips	.08
446	Dion James	.05

447	Joey Cora	.05
448	Andre Dawson	.10
449	Pedro Castellano	.05
450	Tom Gordon	.05
451	Rob Dibble	.05
452	Ron Darling	.05
453	Chipper Jones	1.00
454	Joe Grahe	.05
455	Domingo Cedeno	.05
456	Tom Edens	.05
457	Mitch Webster	.05
458	Jose Bautista	.05
459	Troy O'Leary	.05
460	Todd Zeile	.08
461	Sean Berry	.05
462	*Brad Holman*	.05
463	Dave Martinez	.05
464	Mark Lewis	.05
465	Paul Carey	.05
466	Jack Armstrong	.05
467	David Telgheder	.05
468	Gene Harris	.05
469	Danny Darwin	.05
470	Kim Batiste	.05
471	Tim Wakefield	.08
472	Craig Lefferts	.05
473	Jacob Brumfield	.05
474	Lance Painter	.05
475	Milt Cuyler	.05
476	Melido Perez	.05
477	Derek Parks	.05
478	Gary DiSarcina	.05
479	Steve Bedrosian	.05
480	Eric Anthony	.05
481	Julio Franco	.08
482	Tommy Greene	.05
483	Pat Kelly	.05
484	Nate Minchey (Rated Rookie)	.05
485	William Pennyfeather	.05
486	Harold Baines	.08
487	Howard Johnson	.05
488	Angel Miranda	.05
489	Scott Sanders	.05
490	Shawon Dunston	.05
491	Mel Rojas	.05
492	Jeff Nelson	.05
493	Archi Cianfrocco	.05
494	Al Martin	.05
495	Mike Gallego	.05
496	Mike Henneman	.05
497	Armando Reynoso	.05
498	Mickey Morandini	.05
499	Rick Renteria	.05
500	Rick Sutcliffe	.05
501	Bobby Jones (Rated Rookie)	.15
502	Gary Gaetti	.05
503	Rick Aguilera	.05
504	Todd Stottlemyre	.05
505	Mike Mohler	.05
506	Mike Stanton	.05
507	Jose Guzman	.05
508	Kevin Rogers	.05
509	Chuck Carr	.05
510	Chris Jones	.05
511	Brent Mayne	.05
512	Greg Harris	.05
513	Dave Henderson	.05
514	Eric Hillman	.05
515	Dan Peltier	.05
516	Craig Shipley	.05
517	John Valentin	.08
518	Wilson Alvarez	.05
519	Andujar Cedeno	.05
520	Troy Neel	.05
521	Tom Candiotti	.05
522	Matt Mieske	.05
523	Jim Thome	.25
524	Lou Frazier	.05
525	Mike Jackson	.05
526	Pedro Martinez	.08
527	Roger Pavlik	.05
528	Kent Bottenfield	.05
529	Felix Jose	.05
530	Mark Guthrie	.05
531	Steve Farr	.05
532	Craig Paquette	.05
533	Doug Jones	.05
534	Luis Alicea	.05
535	Cory Snyder	.05
536	Paul Sorrento	.05
537	Nigel Wilson	.05
538	Jeff King	.05
539	Willie Green	.05
540	Kirk McCaskill	.05
541	Al Osuna	.05
542	Greg Hibbard	.05
543	Brett Butler	.08
544	Jose Valentin	.05
545	Wil Cordero	.05
546	Chris Bosio	.05
547	Jamie Moyer	.05
548	Jim Eisenreich	.05
549	Vinny Castilla	.08
550	Checklist (Dave Winfield 3,000 Hits)	.05
551	John Roper	.05
552	Lance Johnson	.05
553	Scott Kamieniecki	.05
554	Mike Moore	.05
555	Steve Buechele	.05
556	Terry Pendleton	.05
557	Todd Van Poppel	.05
558	Rob Butler	.05
559	Zane Smith	.05
560	David Hulse	.05
561	Tim Costo	.05
562	John Habyan	.05
563	Terry Jorgensen	.05
564	Matt Nokes	.05
565	Kevin McReynolds	.05
566	Phil Plantier	.05
567	Chris Turner	.05
568	Carlos Delgado	.40
569	John Jaha	.08
570	Dwight Smith	.05
571	John Vander Wal	.05
572	Trevor Wilson	.05
573	Felix Fermin	.05
574	Marc Newfield (Rated Rookie)	.10
575	Jeromy Burnitz	.08
576	Leo Gomez	.05
577	Curt Schilling	.10
578	Kevin Young	.08
579	*Jerry Spradlin*	.08
580	Curt Leskanic	.05
581	Carl Willis	.05
582	Alex Fernandez	.08
583	Mark Holzemer	.05
584	Domingo Martinez	.05
585	Pete Smith	.05
586	Brian Jordan	.05
587	Kevin Gross	.05
588	J.R. Phillips (Rated Rookie)	.15
589	Chris Nabholz	.05
590	Bill Wertz	.05
591	Derek Bell	.08
592	Brady Anderson	.08
593	Matt Turner	.05
594	Pete Incaviglia	.05
595	Greg Gagne	.05
596	John Flaherty	.05
597	Scott Livingstone	.05
598	Rod Bolton	.05
599	Mike Perez	.05
600	Checklist (Roger Clemens 2,000 Strikeouts)	.08
601	Tony Castillo	.05
602	Henry Mercedes	.05
603	Mike Fetters	.05
604	Rod Beck	.05
605	Damon Buford	.05
606	Matt Whiteside	.05
607	Shawn Green	.25
608	Midre Cummings (Rated Rookie)	.10
609	Jeff McNeeley	.05
610	Danny Sheaffer	.05
611	Paul Wagner	.05
612	Torey Lovullo	.05
613	Javier Lopez	.25
614	Mariano Duncan	.05
615	Doug Brocail	.05
616	Dave Hansen	.05
617	Ryan Klesko	.25
618	Eric Davis	.08
619	Scott Ruffcorn (Rated Rookie)	.10
620	Mike Trombley	.05
621	Jaime Navarro	.05
622	Rheal Cormier	.05
623	Jose Offerman	.05
624	David Segui	.05
625	Robb Nen (Rated Rookie)	.05
626	Dave Gallagher	.05
627	*Julian Tavarez*	.10
628	Chris Gomez	.05
629	Jeffrey Hammonds (Rated Rookie)	.15
630	Scott Brosius	.05
631	Willie Blair	.05
632	Doug Drabek	.05
633	Bill Wegman	.05
634	Jeff McKnight	.05
635	Rich Rodriguez	.05
636	Steve Trachsel	.10
637	Buddy Groom	.05
638	Sterling Hitchcock	.08
639	Chuck McElroy	.05
640	Rene Gonzales	.05
641	Dan Plesac	.05
642	Jeff Branson	.05
643	Darrell Whitmore	.05
644	Paul Quantrill	.05
645	Rich Rowland	.05
646	*Curtis Pride*	.20
647	Erik Plantenberg	.05
648	Albie Lopez	.05
649	*Rich Batchelor*	.05
650	Lee Smith	.08
651	Cliff Floyd	.10
652	Pete Schourek	.05
653	Reggie Jefferson	.05
654	Bill Haselman	.05
655	Steve Hosey	.05
656	Mark Clark	.05
657	Mark Davis	.05
658	Dave Magadan	.05
659	Candy Maldonado	.05
660	Checklist (Mark Langston 2,0000 Strikeouts)	.05

1994 Donruss Special Edition - Gold

In 1994 Donruss added a Special Edition subset of 100 of the game's top players. Fifty cards each were included one or two per pack in all types of Donruss' Series I and II packaging. The cards use the same photos and format as the regular-issue version, but have special gold-foil stamping on front in the area of the team logo and player name, and on back in a "Special Edition" number box in the upper-left corner.

		MT
	Complete Set (100):	35.00
	Common Player:	.25
1	Nolan Ryan	3.00
2	Mike Piazza	2.50
3	Moises Alou	.25
4	Ken Griffey, Jr.	5.00
5	Gary Sheffield	.50
6	Roberto Alomar	1.00
7	John Kruk	.25
8	Gregg Olson	.25
9	Gregg Jefferies	.30
10	Tony Gwynn	1.25
11	Chad Curtis	.25
12	Craig Biggio	.30
13	John Burkett	.25
14	Carlos Baerga	.25
15	Robin Yount	.75
16	Dennis Eckersley	.25
17	Dwight Gooden	.35
18	Ryne Sandberg	.90
19	Rickey Henderson	.40
20	Jack McDowell	.25
21	Jay Bell	.25
22	Kevin Brown	.30
23	Robin Ventura	.30
24	Paul Molitor	.75
25	David Justice	.50
26	Rafael Palmeiro	.35
27	Cecil Fielder	.25
28	Chuck Knoblauch	.40
29	Dave Hollins	.25
30	Jimmy Key	.25
31	Mark Langston	.25
32	Darryl Kile	.25
33	Ruben Sierra	.25
34	Ron Gant	.30
35	Ozzie Smith	.60
36	Wade Boggs	.60
37	Marquis Grissom	.30
38	Will Clark	.40
39	Kenny Lofton	.40
40	Cal Ripken, Jr.	4.00
41	Steve Avery	.25
42	Mo Vaughn	.85
43	Brian McRae	.25
44	Mickey Tettleton	.25
45	Barry Larkin	.35
46	Charlie Hayes	.25
47	Kevin Appier	.25
48	Robby Thompson	.25
49	Juan Gonzalez	1.25
50	Paul O'Neill	.30
51	Mike Mussina	.40
52	Andy Benes	.25
53	Darren Daulton	.25
54	Orlando Merced	.25
55	Mark McGwire	5.00
56	Dave Winfield	.35
57	Sammy Sosa	2.00
58	Eric Karros	.25
59	Greg Vaughn	.25
60	Don Mattingly	1.50
61	Frank Thomas	1.50
62	Fred McGriff	.40
63	Kirby Puckett	1.50
64	Roberto Kelly	.25
65	Wally Joyner	.25
66	Andres Galarraga	.30
67	Bobby Bonilla	.25
68	Benito Santiago	.25
69	Barry Bonds	1.50
70	Delino DeShields	.25
71	Albert Belle	1.00
72	Randy Johnson	.60
73	Tim Salmon	.40
74	John Olerud	.30
75	Dean Palmer	.25
76	Roger Clemens	1.25
77	Jim Abbott	.25
78	Mark Grace	.35
79	Ozzie Guillen	.25
80	Lou Whitaker	.25
81	Jose Rijo	.25
82	Jeff Montgomery	.25
83	Chuck Finley	.25
84	Tom Glavine	.25
85	Jeff Bagwell	1.50
86	Joe Carter	.25
87	Ray Lankford	.25
88	Ramon Martinez	.25
89	Jay Buhner	.25
90	Matt Williams	.35
91	Larry Walker	.60
92	Jose Canseco	.50
93	Len Dykstra	.25
94	Bryan Harvey	.25
95	Andy Van Slyke	.25
96	Ivan Rodriguez	1.00
97	Kevin Mitchell	.25
98	Travis Fryman	.25
99	Duane Ward	.25
100	Greg Maddux	2.50

1994 Donruss Anniversary-1984

This set commemorates and features 10 of the most popular cards from Donruss' 1984 set. The cards, inserted in Series I hobby foil packs only, are "holographically enhanced" with foil stamping and UV coating.

		MT
	Complete Set (10):	50.00
	Common Player:	2.00
1	Joe Carter	2.00
2	Robin Yount	3.50
3	George Brett	5.00
4	Rickey Henderson	2.00
5	Nolan Ryan	15.00
6	Cal Ripken, Jr.	15.00
7	Wade Boggs	2.00
8	Don Mattingly	7.50
9	Ryne Sandberg	4.00
10	Tony Gwynn	6.00

1994 Donruss Award Winners Supers

Major award winners of the 1993 season are honored in this super-size (3-1/2" x 5") insert set. One card was packaged in each box of U.S. jumbo packs and in each Canadian foil-pack box. On a gold-tone background, the card backs have another player photo, a description of his award winning performance and a white strip with a serial number identifying the card's place in an edition of 10,000.

		MT
	Complete Set (10):	45.00
	Common Player:	3.00
1	Barry Bonds (N.L. MVP)	5.00
2	Greg Maddux (N.L. Cy Young)	6.00
3	Mike Piazza (N.L. ROY)	7.50
4	Barry Bonds (N.L. HR Champ)	5.00
5	Kirby Puckett (All-Star MVP)	6.00
6	Frank Thomas (A.L. MVP)	6.00
7	Jack McDowell (A.L. Cy Young)	3.00
8	Tim Salmon (A.L. ROY)	4.00
9	Juan Gonzalez (A.L. HR Champ)	6.00
10	Paul Molitor (World Series MVP)	5.00

1994 Donruss Decade Dominators

Donruss selected 10 top home run hitters (Series I) and 10 RBI leaders of the 1990s for this insert set. Cards were issued in all types of Series I and II packs. Full-bleed UV-coated cards were gold-foil enhanced on the front. Backs featured another full-color player photo and charted information on his 1990s home run or RBI output and ranking.

		MT
	Complete Set (20):	40.00
	Common Player:	.75
	Series 1	
1	Cecil Fielder	.75
2	Barry Bonds	2.00
3	Fred McGriff	1.00
4	Matt Williams	.75
5	Joe Carter	.75
6	Juan Gonzalez	4.00
7	Jose Canseco	1.50
8	Ron Gant	.75
9	Ken Griffey, Jr.	8.00
10	Mark McGwire	8.00
	Series 2	
1	Tony Gwynn	4.00
2	Frank Thomas	4.00
3	Paul Molitor	2.00
4	Edgar Martinez	.75
5	Kirby Puckett	3.00
6	Ken Griffey, Jr.	8.00
7	Barry Bonds	2.50
8	Willie McGee	.75
9	Len Dykstra	.75
10	John Kruk	.75

The election of former players to the Hall of Fame does not always have an immediate upward effect on card prices. The hobby market generally has done a good job of predicting those inductions and adjusting values over the course of several years.

1994 Donruss Decade Dominators Supers

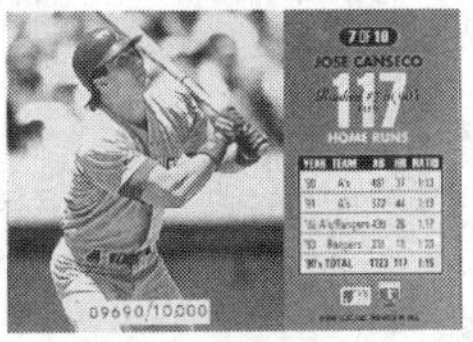

Super-size (3-1/2" x 5") versions of the 1994 Donruss Decade Dominators insert cards were produced as a premium, one card being packaged in a paper checklist envelope in each hobby box of Donruss foil packs. The supers are identical in format to the regular-size cards with the exception of a white serial number strip on the back, identifying each card's position in an edition of 10,000.

		MT
Complete Set (20):		60.00
Common Player:		4.00
Series 1		
1	Cecil Fielder	3.00
2	Barry Bonds	6.00
3	Fred McGriff	3.00
4	Matt Williams	3.00
5	Joe Carter	3.00
6	Juan Gonzalez	7.50
7	Jose Canseco	4.00
8	Ron Gant	3.00
9	Ken Griffey, Jr.	9.00
10	Mark McGwire	9.00
Series 2		
1	Tony Gwynn	5.00
2	Frank Thomas	5.00
3	Paul Molitor	4.00
4	Edgar Martinez	3.00
5	Kirby Puckett	5.00
6	Ken Griffey, Jr.	8.00
7	Barry Bonds	7.50
8	Willie McGee	3.00
9	Lenny Dykstra	3.00
10	John Kruk	3.00

1994 Donruss Diamond Kings

The artwork of Dick Perez is again featured on this insert set included in foil packs. Player art is set against garish color backgrounds with a red-and-silver "Diamond Kings" foil logo above, and the player's name in script at bottom. Backs are printed in red on pale yellow and feature a 1993 season summary. Cards have a DK preface to the number. Cards #1-14 and #29, Dave Winfield, were included in Series I packs; cards #15-28 were found in Series II, along with the checklist card (#30), featuring a Dick Perez self-portrait.

		MT
Complete Set (30):		42.00
Common Player:		.60
1	Barry Bonds	2.50
2	Mo Vaughn	1.00
3	Steve Avery	.60
4	Tim Salmon	1.00
5	Rick Wilkins	.60
6	Brian Harper	.60
7	Andres Galarraga	.75
8	Albert Belle	2.00
9	John Kruk	.60
10	Ivan Rodriguez	1.25
11	Tony Gwynn	3.50
12	Brian McRae	.60
13	Bobby Bonilla	.60
14	Ken Griffey, Jr.	8.00
15	Mike Piazza	5.00
16	Don Mattingly	3.50
17	Barry Larkin	.75
18	Ruben Sierra	.60
19	Orlando Merced	.60
20	Greg Vaughn	.60
21	Gregg Jefferies	.60
22	Cecil Fielder	.60
23	Moises Alou	.60
24	John Olerud	.75
25	Gary Sheffield	.75
26	Mike Mussina	.60
27	Jeff Bagwell	2.50
28	Frank Thomas	3.50
29	Dave Winfield (King of Kings)	1.75
30	Dick Perez (Checklist)	.60

1994 Donruss Diamond Kings Supers

Each retail box of 1994 Donruss foil packs contains one super-size (4-7/8" x 6-13/16") version of the Diamond Kings inserts. Series I boxes offer cards #1-14, while #15-28 are found in Series II boxes. A 29th card, honoring Dave Winfield, was also produced. Super DKs are identical in format to the regular-size inserts, with the exception of a white serial number strip on the back which identifies the card within an edition of 10,000.

		MT
Complete Set (29):		75.00
Common Player:		3.00
1	Barry Bonds	5.00
2	Mo Vaughn	3.00
3	Steve Avery	2.00
4	Tim Salmon	3.00
5	Rick Wilkins	2.00
6	Brian Harper	2.00
7	Andres Galarraga	3.00
8	Albert Belle	4.00
9	John Kruk	2.00
10	Ivan Rodriguez	4.00
11	Tony Gwynn	5.00
12	Brian McRae	3.00
13	Bobby Bonilla	3.00
14	Ken Griffey, Jr.	7.50
15	Mike Piazza	6.00
16	Don Mattingly	5.00
17	Barry Larkin	4.00
18	Ruben Sierra	3.00
19	Orlando Merced	3.00
20	Greg Vaughn	3.00
21	Gregg Jefferies	3.00
22	Cecil Fielder	3.00
23	Moises Alou	3.00
24	John Olerud	3.00
25	Gary Sheffield	3.00
26	Mike Mussina	3.00
27	Jeff Bagwell	5.00
28	Frank Thomas	3.00
29	Dave Winfield	4.00

1994 Donruss Elite

Donruss continued its popular Elite Series with 12 more players in 1994. The cards, numbered #37-48, were inserted in foil packs only. The cards feature the player in a diamond on the front; the back offers an opinion of why the player is considered an elite and is serially numbered to 10,000.

		MT
Complete Set (12):		175.00
Common Player:		6.00
37	Frank Thomas	20.00
38	Tony Gwynn	25.00
39	Tim Salmon	9.00
40	Albert Belle	11.00
41	John Kruk	6.00
42	Juan Gonzalez	20.00
43	John Olerud	9.00
44	Barry Bonds	18.50
45	Ken Griffey, Jr.	45.00
46	Mike Piazza	30.00
47	Jack McDowell	6.00
48	Andres Galarraga	6.00

1994 Donruss Long Ball Leaders

The "Tale of the Tape" for the 1993 season is chronicled in this Series II hobby-only foil-pack insert. Silver prismatic foil highlights the typography on the front of the card which includes the "Long Ball Leaders" logos (complete with embossed baseball), the player's last name and the distance of his blast. Card backs have another player photo superimposed on the venue in which the home run was hit. The distance is repeated in silver over the ballpark photo. In a wide silver box at bottom are data about the home run.

		MT
Complete Set (10):		20.00
Common Player:		.50
1	Cecil Fielder	.50
2	Dean Palmer	.50
3	Andres Galarraga	.50
4	Bo Jackson	.75
5	Ken Griffey, Jr.	6.00
6	Dave Justice	1.00
7	Mike Piazza	4.50
8	Frank Thomas	3.00
9	Barry Bonds	2.50
10	Juan Gonzalez	3.00

1994 Donruss MVPs

These inserts were included in 1994 jumbo packs only. The fronts have a large metallic blue MVP logo, beneath which is a red stripe with the player's name and position in white. Backs have a portrait photo, stats for 1993 and a summary of why the player was selected as team MVP.

		MT
Complete Set (28):		30.00
Common Player:		.25
1	Dave Justice	.40
2	Mark Grace	.65
3	Jose Rijo	.25
4	Andres Galarraga	.30
5	Bryan Harvey	.25
6	Jeff Bagwell	1.50
7	Mike Piazza	6.00
8	Moises Alou	.25
9	Bobby Bonilla	.25
10	Len Dykstra	.25
11	Jeff King	.25
12	Gregg Jefferies	.25
13	Tony Gwynn	2.50
14	Barry Bonds	2.00
15	Cal Ripken, Jr.	7.00
16	Mo Vaughn	.75
17	Tim Salmon	.50
18	Frank Thomas	4.00
19	Albert Belle	1.50
20	Cecil Fielder	.25
21	Wally Joyner	.25
22	Greg Vaughn	.30
23	Kirby Puckett	2.50
24	Don Mattingly	2.00
25	Ruben Sierra	.25
26	Ken Griffey, Jr.	8.00
27	Juan Gonzalez	2.00
28	John Olerud	.35

1994 Donruss Spirit of the Game

Ten players are featured in this insert set, packaged exclusively in retail boxes. Horizontal in format, fronts feature a color player action photo set against a gold-tone background which has the appearance of a multiple-exposure photo. On back a player portrait photo is set against a backdrop of red, white and blue bunting. There is a short previous-season write-up at right. Cards #1-5 were included with Series I, cards 6-10 were in Series II packs.

		MT
Complete Set (10):		30.00
Common Player:		1.50
1	John Olerud	2.00
2	Barry Bonds	5.00
3	Ken Griffey, Jr.	8.00
4	Mike Piazza	6.00
5	Juan Gonzalez	3.00
6	Frank Thomas	3.00
7	Tim Salmon	2.00
8	Dave Justice	2.00
9	Don Mattingly	4.00
10	Len Dykstra	1.50

1994 Donruss Spirit of the Game Supers

Virtually identical in format to the regular-size "Spirit of the Game" cards, these 3-1/2" x 5" versions have gold-foil, rather than holographic printing on the front, and have a serial number on back identifying it from an edition of 10,000. One super card was inserted in each specially designated retail box.

		MT
Complete Set (10):		50.00
Common Player:		3.00
1	John Olerud	5.00
2	Barry Bonds	6.00
3	Ken Griffey, Jr.	9.00
4	Mike Piazza	7.50
5	Juan Gonzalez	6.00
6	Frank Thomas	5.00
7	Tim Salmon	4.00
8	Dave Justice	3.00
9	Don Mattingly	6.00
10	Len Dykstra	3.00

1995 Donruss Samples

The cards in this preview release of Donruss' 1995 baseball issue are virtually identical to the issued versions of the same players' cards except for the overprinted notation of sample status on each side.

		MT
Complete Set (7):		50.00
Common Player:		7.50
5	Mike Piazza	10.00
8	Barry Bonds	7.50
20	Jeff Bagwell	9.00
42	Juan Gonzalez	9.00
55	Don Mattingly	10.00
275	Frank Thomas	8.00
331	Greg Maddux	8.00

1995 Donruss

A pair of player photos on the front of each card and silver-foil highlights are featured on the 1995 Donruss set. Besides the main action photo on front, each card has a second photo in a home plate frame at lower-left. A silver-foil ribbon beneath has the player's team and name embossed. Above the small photo is the player's position, with a half-circle of stars over all; both elements in silver foil. Completing the silver-foil highlights is the Donruss logo at upper-left. Full-bleed backs have yet another action photo at center, with a large team logo at left and five years' worth of stats plus career numbers at bottom. Donruss was issued in retail and hobby 12-card packs, magazine distributor packs of 16 and jumbo packs of 20 cards. New to Donruss in 1995 were Super Packs. These were packs that contained complete insert sets and were seeded every 90 packs.

	MT
Complete Set (550):	35.00
Complete Series 1:	20.00

Complete Series 2:		15.00
Common Player:		.05
Press Proofs: 10-20X		
Series 1 or 2 Wax Box:		40.00
1	Dave Justice	.20
2	Rene Arocha	.08
3	Sandy Alomar Jr.	.15
4	Luis Lopez	.08
5	Mike Piazza	1.50
6	Bobby Jones	.08
7	Damion Easley	.08
8	Barry Bonds	.75
9	Mike Mussina	.35
10	Kevin Seitzer	.05
11	John Smiley	.05
12	W. VanLandingham	.05
13	Ron Darling	.05
14	Walt Weiss	.05
15	Mike Lansing	.08
16	Allen Watson	.08
17	Aaron Sele	.10
18	Randy Johnson	.45
19	Dean Palmer	.05
20	Jeff Bagwell	.75
21	Curt Schilling	.15
22	Darrell Whitmore	.08
23	Steve Trachsel	.10
24	Dan Wilson	.10
25	Steve Finley	.05
26	Bret Boone	.10
27	Charles Johnson	.10
28	Mike Stanton	.05
29	Ismael Valdes	.10
30	Salomon Torres	.05
31	Eric Anthony	.05
32	Spike Owen	.05
33	Joey Cora	.05
34	Robert Eenhoorn	.05
35	Rick White	.05
36	Omar Vizquel	.08
37	Carlos Delgado	.40
38	Eddie Williams	.05
39	Shawon Dunston	.05
40	Darrin Fletcher	.05
41	Leo Gomez	.05
42	Juan Gonzalez	1.50
43	Luis Alicea	.05
44	Ken Ryan	.08
45	Lou Whitaker	.05
46	Mike Blowers	.05
47	Willie Blair	.05
48	Todd Van Poppel	.05
49	Roberto Alomar	.60
50	Ozzie Smith	.40
51	Sterling Hitchcock	.08
52	Mo Vaughn	.60
53	Rick Aguilera	.05
54	Kent Mercker	.05
55	Don Mattingly	1.00
56	Bob Scanlan	.05
57	Wilson Alvarez	.08
58	Jose Mesa	.05
59	Scott Kamieniecki	.08
60	Todd Jones	.05
61	John Kruk	.05
62	Mike Stanley	.08
63	Tino Martinez	.10
64	Eddie Zambrano	.08
65	Todd Hundley	.15
66	Jamie Moyer	.05
67	Rich Amaral	.05
68	Jose Valentin	.05
69	Alex Gonzalez	.15
70	Kurt Abbott	.08
71	Delino DeShields	.08
72	Brian Anderson	.10
73	John Vander Wal	.05
74	Turner Ward	.05
75	Tim Raines	.08
76	Mark Acre	.05
77	Jose Offerman	.08
78	Jimmy Key	.08
79	Mark Whiten	.05
80	Mark Gubicza	.05
81	Darren Hall	.05
82	Travis Fryman	.15
83	Cal Ripken, Jr.	2.50
84	Geronimo Berroa	.05
85	Bret Barberie	.08
86	Andy Ashby	.10
87	Steve Avery	.05
88	Rich Becker	.05
89	John Valentin	.10
90	Glenallen Hill	.05
91	Carlos Garcia	.08
92	Dennis Martinez	.10
93	Pat Kelly	.05
94	Orlando Miller	.08
95	Felix Jose	.05
96	Mike Kingery	.05
97	Jeff Kent	.05
98	Pete Incaviglia	.05
99	Chad Curtis	.10
100	Thomas Howard	.05
101	Hector Carrasco	.05
102	Tom Pagnozzi	.05
103	Danny Tartabull	.05
104	Donnie Elliott	.05
105	Danny Jackson	.05
106	Steve Dunn	.05
107	Roger Salkeld	.05
108	Jeff King	.08
109	Cecil Fielder	.08
110	Checklist	.05
111	Denny Neagle	.05
112	Troy Neel	.08
113	Rod Beck	.05
114	Alex Rodriguez	3.00
115	Joey Eischen	.05
116	Tom Candiotti	.05
117	Ray McDavid	.05
118	Vince Coleman	.05
119	Pete Harnisch	.05
120	David Nied	.05
121	Pat Rapp	.08
122	Sammy Sosa	1.50
123	Steve Reed	.05
124	Jose Oliva	.05
125	Rick Bottalico	.08
126	Jose DeLeon	.05
127	Pat Hentgen	.08
128	Will Clark	.35
129	Mark Dewey	.05
130	Greg Vaughn	.08
131	Darren Dreifort	.05
132	Ed Sprague	.08
133	Lee Smith	.08
134	Charles Nagy	.08
135	Phil Plantier	.05
136	Jason Jacome	.05
137	Jose Lima	.10
138	J.R. Phillips	.05
139	J.T. Snow	.08
140	Mike Huff	.05
141	Billy Brewer	.05
142	Jeromy Burnitz	.08
143	Ricky Bones	.05
144	Carlos Rodriguez	.05
145	Luis Gonzalez	.08
146	Mark Lemke	.05
147	Al Martin	.05
148	Mike Bordick	.08
149	Robb Nen	.05
150	Wil Cordero	.05
151	Edgar Martinez	.08
152	Gerald Williams	.08
153	Esteban Beltre	.05
154	Mike Moore	.05
155	Mark Langston	.05
156	Mark Clark	.05
157	Bobby Ayala	.05
158	Rick Wilkins	.05
159	Bobby Munoz	.05
160	Checklist	.05
161	Scott Erickson	.05
162	Paul Molitor	.35
163	Jon Lieber	.05
164	Jason Grimsley	.05
165	Norberto Martin	.05
166	Javier Lopez	.10
167	Brian McRae	.08
168	Gary Sheffield	.30
169	Marcus Moore	.05
170	John Hudek	.05
171	Kelly Stinett	.05
172	Chris Gomez	.05
173	Rey Sanchez	.05
174	Juan Guzman	.05
175	Chan Ho Park	.15
176	Terry Shumpert	.05
177	Steve Ontiveros	.05
178	Brad Ausmus	.05
179	Tim Davis	.05
180	Billy Ashley	.05
181	Vinny Castilla	.10
182	Bill Spiers	.05
183	Randy Knorr	.05
184	Brian Hunter	.05
185	Pat Meares	.05
186	Steve Buechele	.05
187	Kirt Manwaring	.05
188	Tim Naehring	.05
189	Matt Mieske	.05
190	Josias Manzanillo	.05
191	Greg McMichael	.05
192	Chuck Carr	.05
193	Midre Cummings	.08
194	Darryl Strawberry	.10
195	Greg Gagne	.05
196	Steve Cooke	.08
197	Woody Williams	.05
198	Ron Karkovice	.05
199	Phil Leftwich	.05
200	Jim Thome	.30
201	Brady Anderson	.15
202	Pedro Martinez	.15
203	Steve Karsay	.08
204	Reggie Sanders	.08
205	Bill Risley	.05
206	Jay Bell	.08
207	Kevin Brown	.15
208	Tim Scott	.05
209	Len Dykstra	.05
210	Willie Greene	.05
211	Jim Eisenreich	.05
212	Cliff Floyd	.08
213	Otis Nixon	.05
214	Eduardo Perez	.05
215	Manuel Lee	.05
216	*Armando Benitez*	.15
217	Dave McCarty	.05
218	Scott Livingstone	.05
219	Chad Kreuter	.05
220	Checklist	.05
221	Brian Jordan	.10
222	Matt Whiteside	.05
223	Jim Edmonds	.15
224	Tony Gwynn	.75
225	Jose Lind	.05
226	Marvin Freeman	.05
227	Ken Hill	.05
228	David Hulse	.05
229	Joe Hesketh	.05
230	Roberto Petagine	.05
231	Jeffrey Hammonds	.08
232	John Jaha	.05
233	John Burkett	.08
234	Hal Morris	.05
235	Tony Castillo	.05
236	Ryan Bowen	.08
237	Wayne Kirby	.05
238	Brent Mayne	.05
239	Jim Bullinger	.05
240	Mike Lieberthal	.08
241	Barry Larkin	.20
242	David Segui	.05
243	Jose Bautista	.05
244	Hector Fajardo	.05
245	Orel Hershiser	.08
246	James Mouton	.05
247	Scott Leius	.05
248	Tom Glavine	.20
249	Danny Bautista	.05
250	Jose Mercedes	.05
251	Marquis Grissom	.10
252	Charlie Hayes	.05
253	Ryan Klesko	.25
254	Vicente Palacios	.05
255	Matias Carillo	.05
256	Gary DiSarcina	.05
257	Kirk Gibson	.05
258	Garey Ingram	.05
259	Alex Fernandez	.08
260	John Mabry	.05
261	Chris Howard	.05
262	Miguel Jimenez	.05
263	Heath Slocumb	.05
264	Albert Belle	.75
265	Dave Clark	.05
266	Joe Orsulak	.05
267	Joey Hamilton	.08
268	Mark Portugal	.05
269	Kevin Tapani	.05
270	Sid Fernandez	.05
271	Steve Dreyer	.05
272	Denny Hocking	.05
273	Troy O'Leary	.05
274	Milt Cuyler	.05
275	Frank Thomas	1.50
276	Jorge Fabregas	.08
277	Mike Gallego	.05
278	Mickey Morandini	.05
279	Roberto Hernandez	.08
280	Henry Rodriguez	.08
281	Garret Anderson	.08
282	Bob Wickman	.05
283	Gar Finnvold	.05
284	Paul O'Neill	.10
285	Royce Clayton	.05
286	Chuck Knoblauch	.20
287	Johnny Ruffin	.05
288	Dave Nilsson	.05
289	David Cone	.08
290	Chuck McElroy	.05
291	Kevin Stocker	.05
292	Jose Rijo	.05
293	Sean Berry	.05
294	Ozzie Guillen	.05
295	Chris Hoiles	.05
296	Kevin Foster	.05
297	Jeff Frye	.05
298	Lance Johnson	.05
299	Mike Kelly	.05
300	Ellis Burks	.08
301	Roberto Kelly	.05
302	Dante Bichette	.15
303	Alvaro Espinoza	.05
304	Alex Cole	.05
305	Rickey Henderson	.10
306	Dave Weathers	.05
307	Shane Reynolds	.08
308	Bobby Bonilla	.08
309	Junior Felix	.05
310	Jeff Fassero	.08
311	Darren Lewis	.05
312	John Doherty	.05
313	Scott Servais	.05
314	Rick Helling	.05
315	Pedro Martinez	.15
316	Wes Chamberlain	.05
317	Bryan Eversgerd	.05
318	Trevor Hoffman	.08
319	John Patterson	.05
320	Matt Walbeck	.05
321	Jeff Montgomery	.05
322	Mel Rojas	.05
323	Eddie Taubensee	.05
324	Ray Lankford	.08
325	Jose Vizcaino	.05
326	Carlos Baerga	.08
327	Jack Voigt	.05
328	Julio Franco	.05
329	Brent Gates	.08
330	Checklist	.05
331	Greg Maddux	1.50
332	Jason Bere	.08
333	Bill Wegman	.05
334	Tuffy Rhodes	.05
335	Kevin Young	.08
336	Andy Benes	.08
337	Pedro Astacio	.05
338	Reggie Jefferson	.05
339	Tim Belcher	.05
340	Ken Griffey Jr.	3.00
341	Mariano Duncan	.05
342	Andres Galarraga	.10
343	Rondell White	.10
344	Cory Bailey	.05
345	Bryan Harvey	.05
346	John Franco	.05
347	Greg Swindell	.05
348	David West	.05
349	Fred McGriff	.30
350	Jose Canseco	.30
351	Orlando Merced	.05
352	Rheal Cormier	.05
353	Carlos Pulido	.05
354	Terry Steinbach	.05
355	Wade Boggs	.25
356	B.J. Surhoff	.08
357	Rafael Palmeiro	.20
358	Anthony Young	.08
359	Tom Brunansky	.05
360	Todd Stottlemyre	.08
361	Chris Turner	.05
362	Joe Boever	.05
363	Jeff Blauser	.05
364	Derek Bell	.08
365	Matt Williams	.30
366	Jeremy Hernandez	.05
367	Joe Girardi	.05
368	Mike Devereaux	.05
369	Jim Abbott	.08
370	Manny Ramirez	1.00
371	Kenny Lofton	.60
372	Mark Smith	.05
373	Dave Fleming	.05
374	Dave Stewart	.08
375	Roger Pavlik	.05
376	Hipolito Pichardo	.05
377	Bill Taylor	.05
378	Robin Ventura	.10
379	Bernard Gilkey	.10
380	Kirby Puckett	1.00
381	Steve Howe	.05
382	Devon White	.08
383	Roberto Mejia	.05
384	Darrin Jackson	.05
385	Mike Morgan	.05
386	Rusty Meacham	.05
387	Bill Swift	.05
388	Lou Frazier	.05
389	Andy Van Slyke	.05
390	Brett Butler	.08
391	Bobby Witt	.05
392	Jeff Conine	.08
393	Tim Hyers	.05
394	Terry Pendleton	.05
395	Ricky Jordan	.05
396	Eric Plunk	.05
397	Melido Perez	.05
398	Darryl Kile	.08
399	Mark McLemore	.05
400	Greg Harris	.05
401	Jim Leyritz	.05
402	Doug Strange	.05
403	Tim Salmon	.25
404	Terry Mulholland	.05
405	Robby Thompson	.05
406	Ruben Sierra	.05
407	Tony Phillips	.08
408	Moises Alou	.10
409	Felix Fermin	.05
410	Pat Listach	.05
411	Kevin Bass	.05
412	Ben McDonald	.05
413	Scott Cooper	.05
414	Jody Reed	.05
415	Deion Sanders	.20
416	Ricky Gutierrez	.05
417	Gregg Jefferies	.08
418	Jack McDowell	.08
419	Al Leiter	.08
420	Tony Longmire	.05
421	Paul Wagner	.05
422	Geronimo Pena	.05
423	Ivan Rodriguez	.60
424	Kevin Gross	.05
425	Kirk McCaskill	.05
426	Greg Myers	.05
427	Roger Clemens	1.00
428	Chris Hammond	.05
429	Randy Myers	.05
430	Roger Mason	.05
431	Bret Saberhagen	.08
432	Jeff Reboulet	.05
433	John Olerud	.20
434	Bill Gullickson	.05
435	Eddie Murray	.40
436	Pedro Munoz	.05
437	Charlie O'Brien	.05
438	Jeff Nelson	.05
439	Mike Macfarlane	.05
440	Checklist	.05
441	Derrick May	.05
442	John Roper	.05
443	Darryl Hamilton	.05
444	Dan Miceli	.05
445	Tony Eusebio	.05
446	Jerry Browne	.05
447	Wally Joyner	.08
448	Brian Harper	.05
449	Scott Fletcher	.05
450	Rip Roberts	.05
451	Pete Smith	.05
452	Chili Davis	.08
453	Dave Hollins	.08
454	Tony Pena	.05
455	Butch Henry	.05
456	Craig Biggio	.15
457	Zane Smith	.05
458	Ryan Thompson	.08
459	Mike Jackson	.05
460	Mark McGwire	4.00
461	John Smoltz	.20
462	Steve Scarsone	.05
463	Greg Colbrunn	.05
464	Shawn Green	.25
465	David Wells	.08
466	Jose Hernandez	.05
467	Chip Hale	.05
468	Tony Tarasco	.05
469	Kevin Mitchell	.05
470	Billy Hatcher	.05
471	Jay Buhner	.15
472	Ken Caminiti	.20
473	Tom Henke	.05
474	Todd Worrell	.05
475	Mark Eichhorn	.05
476	Bruce Ruffin	.05
477	Chuck Finley	.05
478	Marc Newfield	.05
479	Paul Shuey	.05
480	Bob Tewksbury	.05
481	Ramon Martinez	.08
482	Melvin Nieves	.05
483	Todd Zeile	.08
484	Benito Santiago	.05
485	Stan Javier	.05
486	Kirk Rueter	.05
487	Andre Dawson	.10
488	Eric Karros	.08
489	Dave Magadan	.05
490	Checklist	.05
491	Randy Velarde	.05
492	Larry Walker	.20
493	Cris Carpenter	.05
494	Tom Gordon	.05
495	Dave Burba	.05
496	Darren Bragg	.05
497	Darren Daulton	.05
498	Don Slaught	.05
499	Pat Borders	.05
500	Lenny Harris	.05
501	Joe Ausanio	.05
502	Alan Trammell	.08
503	Mike Fetters	.05
504	Scott Ruffcorn	.05
505	Rich Rowland	.05
506	Juan Samuel	.05
507	Bo Jackson	.15
508	Jeff Branson	.05
509	Bernie Williams	.40
510	Paul Sorrento	.05
511	Dennis Eckersley	.08
512	Pat Mahomes	.05
513	Rusty Greer	.08
514	Luis Polonia	.05
515	Willie Banks	.05
516	John Wetteland	.05
517	Mike LaValliere	.05
518	Tommy Greene	.05
519	Mark Grace	.20
520	Bob Hamelin	.05
521	Scott Sanderson	.05
522	Joe Carter	.08
523	Jeff Brantley	.05
524	Andrew Lorraine	.05
525	Rico Brogna	.05
526	Shane Mack	.05
527	Mark Wohlers	.05
528	Scott Sanders	.05
529	Chris Bosio	.05
530	Andujar Cedeno	.05
531	Kenny Rogers	.05
532	Doug Drabek	.05
533	Curt Leskanic	.05
534	Craig Shipley	.05
535	Craig Grebeck	.05
536	Cal Eldred	.05
537	Mickey Tettleton	.05
538	Harold Baines	.08
539	Tim Wallach	.05
540	Damon Buford	.05
541	Lenny Webster	.05
542	Kevin Appier	.05
543	Raul Mondesi	.40
544	Eric Young	.08
545	Russ Davis	.08
546	Mike Benjamin	.05
547	Mike Greenwell	.05
548	Scott Brosius	.05
549	Brian Dorsett	.05
550	Checklist	.05

1995 Donruss Press Proofs

Designated as Press Proofs, the first 2,000 cards of each player in the '95 Donruss set were enhanced with gold, rather than silver, foil and inserted into packs at an average rate of one per 20 packs.

	MT
Complete Set (550):	600.00
Complete Series 1 (330):	350.00
Complete Series 2 (220):	250.00
Common Player:	2.00
Stars: 10-20X	
(See 1995 Donruss for checklist and base card values.)	

1995 Donruss All-Stars

Exclusive to Wal-Mart jumbo packs were Donruss All-Stars. Nine cards featuring American Leaguers were inserted into Series 1, while nine National League All-Stars were inserted into Series 2 jumbos.

		MT
Complete Set (18):		70.00
Common Player:		1.00
AL1	Jimmy Key	1.00
AL2	Ivan Rodriguez	3.50
AL3	Frank Thomas	9.00
AL4	Roberto Alomar	3.00
AL5	Wade Boggs	2.50
AL6	Cal Ripken, Jr.	12.50
AL7	Joe Carter	1.00
AL8	Ken Griffey, Jr.	15.00
AL9	Kirby Puckett	6.00
NL1	Greg Maddux	9.00
NL2	Mike Piazza	10.00
NL3	Gregg Jefferies	1.00
NL4	Mariano Duncan	1.00
NL5	Matt Williams	1.50
NL6	Ozzie Smith	3.00
NL7	Barry Bonds	4.00
NL8	Tony Gwynn	8.00
NL9	Dave Justice	2.00

1995 Donruss Bomb Squad

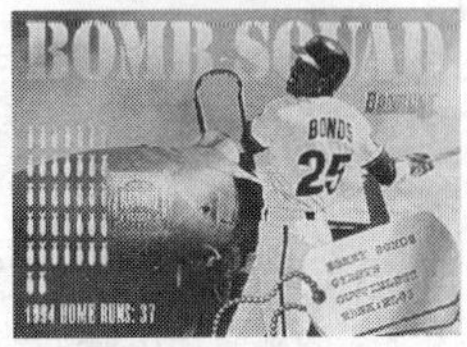

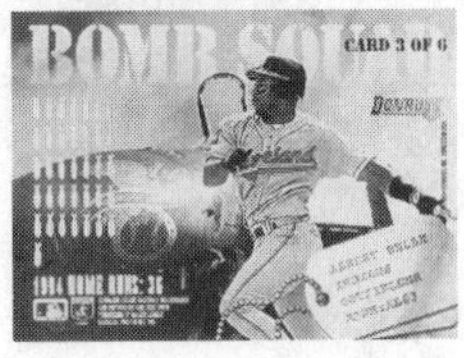

Bomb Squad features the top six home run hitters in each league on double-sided cards. These cards were only inserted into Series I retail and magazine distributor packs at a rate of one per 24 retail packs and one per 16 magazine distributor packs.

		MT
Complete Set (6):		6.00
Common Player:		.50
1	Ken Griffey, Jr., Matt Williams	2.50
2	Frank Thomas, Jeff Bagwell	1.50
3	Albert Belle, Barry Bonds	1.00
4	Jose Canseco, Fred McGriff	.75
5	Cecil Fielder, Andres Galarraga	.50
6	Joe Carter, Kevin Mitchell	.50

1995 Donruss Diamond Kings

Continuing a tradition begun in 1982, artist Dick Perez painted a series of 28 water colors to produce insert cards of the game's best; 14 in each series. A portrait of the player appears on a party-colored background, with Diamond Kings in gold across the top. DKs were inserted in Series 1 and 2 packs at a rate of one per 10.

		MT
Complete Set (29):		22.00
Common Player:		.50
1	Frank Thomas	3.00
2	Jeff Bagwell	2.50
3	Chili Davis	.50
4	Dante Bichette	.50
5	Ruben Sierra	.50
6	Jeff Conine	.50
7	Paul O'Neill	.50
8	Bobby Bonilla	.50
9	Joe Carter	.50
10	Moises Alou	.50
11	Kenny Lofton	1.00
12	Matt Williams	.50
13	Kevin Seitzer	.50
14	Sammy Sosa	3.00
15	Scott Cooper	.50
16	Raul Mondesi	.50
17	Will Clark	.75
18	Lenny Dykstra	.50
19	Kirby Puckett	2.50
20	Hal Morris	.50
21	Travis Fryman	.50
22	Greg Maddux	3.00
23	Rafael Palmeiro	.60
24	Tony Gwynn	2.50
25	David Cone	.75
26	Al Martin	.50
27	Ken Griffey Jr.	5.00
28	Gregg Jefferies	.50
29	Checklist	.15

1995 Donruss Dominators

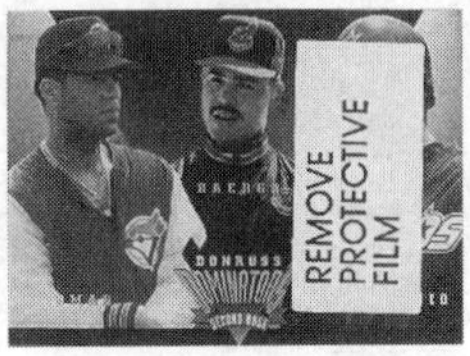

Dominators is a nine-card chase set inserted into hobby packs of Series II Donruss baseball at a rate of one per 24 packs. These acetate cards feature three of the top players at each position on a horizontal format.

		MT
Complete Set (9):		15.00
Common Player:		.50
1	David Cone, Mike Mussina, Greg Maddux	1.50
2	Ivan Rodriguez, Mike Piazza, Darren Daulton	2.50
3	Fred McGriff, Frank Thomas, Jeff Bagwell	2.50
4	Roberto Alomar, Carlos Baerga, Craig Biggio	1.00
5	Robin Ventura, Travis Fryman, Matt Williams	1.00
6	Cal Ripken Jr., Barry Larkin, Wil Cordero	4.00
7	Albert Belle, Barry Bonds, Moises Alou	1.50
8	Ken Griffey Jr., Kenny Lofton, Marquis Grissom	4.00
9	Kirby Puckett, Paul O'Neill, Tony Gwynn	2.50

1995 Donruss Elite

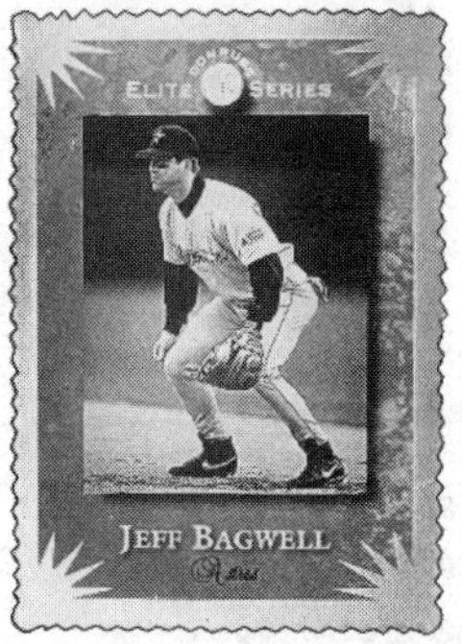

Another Donruss insert tradition continues with the fifth annual presentation of the Elite series. Each of the 12 cards (six each Series 1 and 2) is produced in a numbered edition of 10,000 and inserted into all types of packaging at the rate of one per 210 packs.

		MT
Complete Set (12):		300.00
Common Player:		8.00
49	Jeff Bagwell	30.00
50	Paul O'Neill	8.00
51	Greg Maddux	30.00
52	Mike Piazza	40.00
53	Matt Williams	9.00
54	Ken Griffey, Jr.	75.00
55	Frank Thomas	30.00
56	Barry Bonds	20.00
57	Kirby Puckett	25.00
58	Fred McGriff	9.00
59	Jose Canseco	10.00
60	Albert Belle	15.00

1995 Donruss Long Ball Leaders

Exclusive to Series 1 hobby packs, these cards feature the top long-distance home runs of 1994 in an eye-popping holographic foil presentation. Stated odds of picking one from a hobby pack are one in 24.

		MT
Complete Set (8):		24.00
Common Player:		1.00
1	Frank Thomas	4.00
2	Fred McGriff	1.00
3	Ken Griffey, Jr.	6.00
4	Matt Williams	1.00
5	Mike Piazza	5.00
6	Jose Canseco	1.50
7	Barry Bonds	2.00
8	Jeff Bagwell	3.00

1995 Donruss Mound Marvels

Mound Marvels is an eight-card insert set containing some of the best pitchers in baseball. Cards were inserted into one per 18 retail and magazine packs of Donruss Series II. Each card features a two-way mirror that allows collectors to see the players' face through the mirror.

		MT
Complete Set (8):		15.00
Common Player:		1.00
1	Greg Maddux	6.00
2	David Cone	1.50
3	Mike Mussina	2.00
4	Bret Saberhagen	1.25
5	Jimmy Key	1.00
6	Doug Drabek	1.00
7	Randy Johnson	3.00
8	Jason Bere	1.00

1995 Donruss/Top of the Order Card Game

In one of the earliest efforts to wed the play factor and collectibility that had made various fantasy card games so successful in 1994-95, Donruss created the interactive Top of the Order baseball card game. Printed on playing card stock with rounded corners and semi-gloss surface, the player cards feature color action photos and all manners of game-action indicators. Backs of each card are printed primarily in green with Donruss logos. Cards were sold in several types of packaging, including 80- and 160-card boxed sets, and 12-card foil "booster" packs. Stars' cards were printed in lesser quantities than those of journeyman players, resulting in values higher than would be the case based on player popularity alone if all cards were printed in equal quantities. The unnumbered cards are checklisted here in alphabetical order within team and league.

		MT
Complete Set (360):		175.00
Common Player:		.10
(1)	Brady Anderson	.10
(2)	Harold Baines	.10
(3)	Bret Barberie	.10
(4)	Armando Benitez	.10
(5)	Bobby Bonilla	.20
(6)	Scott Erickson	.15
(7)	Leo Gomez	.10
(8)	Curtis Goodwin	.10
(9)	Jeffrey Hammonds	.10
(10)	Chris Hoiles	.10
(11)	Doug Jones	.10
(12)	Ben McDonald	.10
(13)	Mike Mussina	1.50
(14)	Rafael Palmeiro	2.50
(15)	Cal Ripken Jr.	25.00
(16)	Rick Aguilera	.10
(17)	Luis Alicea	.10
(18)	Jose Canseco	2.50
(19)	Roger Clemens	4.50
(20)	Mike Greenwell	.10
(21)	Erik Hanson	.10
(22)	Mike Macfarlane	.10
(23)	Tim Naehring	.10
(24)	Troy O'Leary	.10
(25)	Ken Ryan	.10
(26)	Aaron Sele	.15
(27)	Lee Tinsley	.10
(28)	John Valentin	.10
(29)	Mo Vaughn	3.50
(30)	Jim Abbott	.25
(31)	Mike Butcher	.10
(32)	Chili Davis	.10
(33)	Gary DiSarcina	.10
(34)	Damion Easley	.10
(35)	Jim Edmonds	1.50
(36)	Chuck Finley	.10
(37)	Mark Langston	.10
(38)	Greg Myers	.10
(39)	Spike Owen	.10
(40)	Troy Percival	.10
(41)	Tony Phillips	.10
(42)	Tim Salmon	2.00
(43)	Lee Smith	.50
(44)	J.T. Snow	.15
(45)	Jason Bere	.10
(46)	Mike Devereaux	.15
(47)	Ray Durham	.15
(48)	Alex Fernandez	.15
(49)	Ozzie Guillen	.10
(50)	Roberto Hernandez	.10
(51)	Lance Johnson	.10
(52)	Ron Karkovice	.10
(53)	Tim Raines	.20
(54)	Frank Thomas	17.50
(55)	Robin Ventura	1.50
(56)	Sandy Alomar Jr.	.20
(57)	Carlos Baerga	.25
(58)	Albert Belle	5.00
(59)	Kenny Lofton	5.00
(60)	Dennis Martinez	.15
(61)	Jose Mesa	.10
(62)	Eddie Murray	3.00
(63)	Charles Nagy	.10
(64)	Tony Pena	.10
(65)	Eric Plunk	.10
(66)	Manny Ramirez	6.00
(67)	Paul Sorrento	.10
(68)	Jim Thome	2.00
(69)	Omar Vizquel	.10
(70)	Danny Bautista	.10
(71)	Joe Boever	.10
(72)	Chad Curtis	.10
(73)	Cecil Fielder	.25
(74)	John Flaherty	.10
(75)	Travis Fryman	.40
(76)	Kirk Gibson	.10
(77)	Chris Gomez	.10
(78)	Mike Henneman	.10
(79)	Bob Higginson	.25
(80)	Alan Trammell	.50
(81)	Lou Whitaker	.25
(82)	Kevin Appier	.10
(83)	Billy Brewer	.10
(84)	Vince Coleman	.10
(85)	Gary Gaetti	.10
(86)	Greg Gagne	.10
(87)	Tom Goodwin	.10
(88)	Tom Gordon	.10
(89)	Mark Gubicza	.10
(90)	Bob Hamelin	.10
(91)	Phil Hiatt	.10
(92)	Wally Joyner	.15
(93)	Brent Mayne	.10
(94)	Jeff Montgomery	.10
(95)	Ricky Bones	.10
(96)	Mike Fetters	.10
(97)	Darryl Hamilton	.10
(98)	Pat Listach	.10
(99)	Matt Mieske	.10
(100)	Dave Nilsson	.10
(101)	Joe Oliver	.10
(102)	Kevin Seitzer	.10
(103)	B.J. Surhoff	.10
(104)	Jose Valentin	.10
(105)	Greg Vaughn	.15
(106)	Bill Wegman	.10
(107)	Alex Cole	.10
(108)	Marty Cordova	.25
(109)	Chuck Knoblauch	1.50
(110)	Scott Leius	.10
(111)	Pat Meares	.10
(112)	Pedro Munoz	.10
(113)	Kirby Puckett	17.50
(114)	Scott Stahoviak	.10
(115)	Mike Trombley	.10
(116)	Matt Walbeck	.10
(117)	Wade Boggs	12.00
(118)	David Cone	.15

(119) Tony Fernandez	.10
(120) Don Mattingly	15.00
(121) Jack McDowell	.10
(122) Paul O'Neill	.15
(123) Melido Perez	.10
(124) Luis Polonia	.10
(125) Ruben Sierra	.10
(126) Mike Stanley	.10
(127) Randy Velarde	.10
(128) John Wetteland	.10
(129) Bob Wickman	.10
(130) Bernie Williams	.35
(131) Gerald Williams	.10
(132) Geronimo Berroa	.10
(133) Mike Bordick	.10
(134) Scott Brosius	.10
(135) Dennis Eckersley	.35
(136) Brent Gates	.10
(137) Rickey Henderson	3.00
(138) Stan Javier	.10
(139) Mark McGwire	25.00
(140) Steve Ontiveros	.10
(141) Terry Steinbach	.10
(142) Todd Stottlemyre	.10
(143) Danny Tartabull	.10
(144) Bobby Ayala	.10
(145) Andy Benes	.15
(146) Mike Blowers	.10
(147) Jay Buhner	.20
(148) Joey Cora	.10
(149) Alex Diaz	.10
(150) Ken Griffey Jr.	25.00
(151) Randy Johnson	4.50
(152) Edgar Martinez	.25
(153) Tino Martinez	.15
(154) Bill Risley	.10
(155) Alex Rodriguez	12.00
(156) Dan Wilson	.10
(157) Will Clark	7.00
(158) Jeff Frye	.10
(159) Benji Gil	.10
(160) Juan Gonzalez	5.00
(161) Rusty Greer	.10
(162) Mark McLemore	.10
(163) Otis Nixon	.10
(164) Dean Palmer	.10
(165) Ivan Rodriguez	3.50
(166) Kenny Rogers	.10
(167) Jeff Russell	.10
(168) Mickey Tettleton	.10
(169) Bob Tewksbury	.10
(170) Bobby Witt	.10
(171) Roberto Alomar	11.00
(172) Joe Carter	1.50
(173) Alex Gonzalez	.25
(174) Candy Maldonado	.10
(175) Paul Molitor	2.50
(176) John Olerud	.25
(177) Lance Parrish	.10
(178) Ed Sprague	.10
(179) Devon White	.10
(180) Woody Williams	.10
(181) Steve Avery	.10
(182) Jeff Blauser	.10
(183) Tom Glavine	1.00
(184) Marquis Grissom	.15
(185) Chipper Jones	12.00
(186) Dave Justice	5.00
(187) Ryan Klesko	.25
(188) Mark Lemke	.10
(189) Javier Lopez	.20
(190) Greg Maddux	17.50
(191) Fred McGriff	2.50
(192) Greg McMichael	.10
(193) John Smoltz	4.00
(194) Mark Wohlers	.10
(195) Jim Bullinger	.10
(196) Shawon Dunston	.10
(197) Kevin Foster	.10
(198) Luis Gonzalez	.10
(199) Mark Grace	3.50
(200) Brian McRae	.10
(201) Randy Myers	.10
(202) Jaime Navarro	.10
(203) Rey Sanchez	.10
(204) Scott Servais	.10
(205) Sammy Sosa	4.00
(206) Steve Trachsel	.10
(207) Todd Zeile	.10
(208) Bret Boone	1.00
(209) Jeff Branson	.10
(210) Jeff Brantley	.10
(211) Hector Carrasco	.10
(212) Ron Gant	.20
(213) Lenny Harris	.10
(214) Barry Larkin	2.50
(215) Darren Lewis	.10
(216) Hal Morris	.10
(217) Mark Portugal	.10
(218) [illegible]	.10
(219) Reggie Sanders	.75
(220) Pete Schourek	.10
(221) John Smiley	.10
(222) Eddie Taubensee	.10
(223) Dave Wells	.15
(224) Jason Bates	.10
(225) Dante Bichette	4.00
(226) Vinny Castilla	.20
(227) Andres Galarraga	4.00
(228) Joe Girardi	.10
(229) Mike Kingery	.10
(230) Steve Reed	.10
(231) Bruce Ruffin	.10
(232) Bret Saberhagen	.15
(233) Bill Swift	.10
(234) Larry Walker	3.50
(235) Walt Weiss	.10
(236) Eric Young	.10

(237) Kurt Abbott	.10
(238) John Burkett	.10
(239) Chuck Carr	.10
(240) Greg Colbrunn	.10
(241) Jeff Conine	1.00
(242) Andre Dawson	.25
(243) Chris Hammond	.10
(244) Charles Johnson	.10
(245) Robb Nen	.10
(246) Terry Pendleton	.10
(247) Gary Sheffield	2.50
(248) Quilvio Veras	.10
(249) Jeff Bagwell	4.50
(250) Derek Bell	.20
(251) Craig Biggio	.25
(252) Doug Drabek	.10
(253) Tony Eusebio	.10
(254) John Hudek	.10
(255) Brian Hunter	.10
(256) Todd Jones	.10
(257) Dave Magadan	.10
(258) Orlando Miller	.10
(259) James Mouton	.10
(260) Shane Reynolds	.10
(261) Greg Swindell	.10
(262) Billy Ashley	.10
(263) Tom Candiotti	.10
(264) Delino DeShields	.10
(265) Eric Karros	2.50
(266) Roberto Kelly	.10
(267) Ramon Martinez	.15
(268) Raul Mondesi	2.50
(269) Hideo Nomo	9.00
(270) Jose Offerman	.10
(271) Mike Piazza	20.00
(272) Kevin Tapani	.10
(273) Ismael Valdes	.15
(274) Tim Wallach	.10
(275) Todd Worrell	.10
(276) Moises Alou	1.00
(277) Sean Berry	.10
(278) Wil Cordero	.10
(279) Jeff Fassero	.10
(280) Darrin Fletcher	.10
(281) Mike Lansing	.10
(282) Pedro J. Martinez	.50
(283) Carlos Perez	.15
(284) Mel Rojas	.10
(285) Tim Scott	.10
(286) David Segui	.10
(287) Tony Tarasco	.10
(288) Rondell White	.20
(289) Rico Brogna	.10
(290) Brett Butler	.10
(291) John Franco	.10
(292) Pete Harnisch	.10
(293) Todd Hundley	.15
(294) Bobby Jones	.10
(295) Jeff Kent	.10
(296) Joe Orsulak	.10
(297) Ryan Thompson	.10
(298) Jose Vizcaino	.10
(299) Ricky Bottalico	.10
(300) Darren Daulton	.10
(301) Mariano Duncan	.10
(302) Lenny Dykstra	.10
(303) Jim Eisenreich	.10
(304) Tyler Green	.10
(305) Charlie Hayes	.10
(306) Dave Hollins	.10
(307) Gregg Jefferies	.25
(308) Mickey Morandini	.10
(309) Curt Schilling	.20
(310) Heathcliff Slocumb	.10
(311) Kevin Stocker	.10
(312) Jay Bell	.10
(313) Jacob Brumfield	.10
(314) Dave Clark	.10
(315) Carlos Garcia	.10
(316) Mark Johnson	.10
(317) Jeff King	.10
(318) Nelson Liriano	.10
(319) Al Martin	.10
(320) Orlando Merced	.10
(321) Dan Miceli	.10
(322) Denny Neagle	.10
(323) Mark Parent	.10
(324) Dan Plesac	.10
(325) Scott Cooper	.10
(326) Bernard Gilkey	.10
(327) Tom Henke	.10
(328) Ken Hill	.10
(329) Danny Jackson	.10
(330) Brian Jordan	.15
(331) Ray Lankford	.10
(332) John Mabry	.10
(333) Jose Oquendo	.10
(334) Tom Pagnozzi	.10
(335) Ozzie Smith	2.50
[illegible]	[illegible]
(337) Brad Ausmus	.10
(338) Ken Caminiti	.20
(339) Andujar Cedeno	.10
(340) Steve Finley	.10
(341) Tony Gwynn	15.00
(342) Joey Hamilton	.10
(343) Trevor Hoffman	.15
(344) Jody Reed	.10
(345) Bip Roberts	.10
(346) Eddie Williams	.10
(347) Rod Beck	.10
(348) Mike Benjamin	.10
(349) Barry Bonds	12.50
(350) Royce Clayton	.10
(351) Glenallen Hill	.10
(352) Kirt Manwaring	.10
(353) Terry Mulholland	.10
(354) John Patterson	.10
(355) J.R. Phillips	.10
(356) Deion Sanders	6.00
(357) Steve Scarsone	.10
(358) Robby Thompson	.10
(359) William VanLandingham	.10
(360) Matt Williams	3.50

1996 Donruss Samples

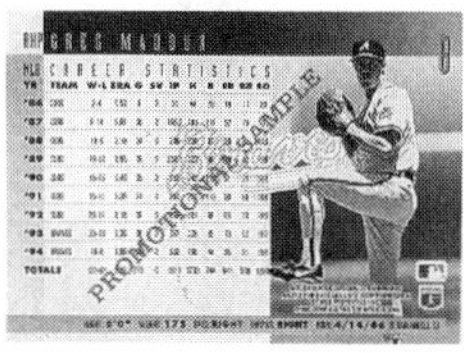

To introduce its 1996 series to dealers and the hobby press, Donruss issued an eight-card sample set. Identical in format to the issued version, the samples are numbered differently from the same players' cards in the regular issue (except #1, Frank Thomas). The samples also differ in that they lack 1995 stats on back, may have slightly different wording in the career highlights, and have printed on front and back a diagonal gray "PROMOTIONAL SAMPLE".

		MT
Complete Set (8):		30.00
Common Player:		3.50
1	Frank Thomas	4.50
2	Barry Bonds	3.50
3	Hideo Nomo	3.00
4	Ken Griffey Jr.	7.00
5	Cal Ripken Jr.	6.50
6	Manny Ramirez	4.50
7	Mike Piazza	6.00
8	Greg Maddux	4.50

1996 Donruss

A clean, borderless look marks the 1996 Donruss regular-issue cards. Besides the player name in white inside a fading team-color stripe at top-right, the only graphic enhancement on front is a 7/8" square foil box at bottom-center with the company and team name, team logo, player position and uniform number. The foil box is enhanced with team colors, which are carried over to the horizontal backs. [illegible] tion photo, a large gray team logo, stats and career highlights. Basic packaging was 12-card foil packs with a suggested retail price of $1.79. Several types of insert cards were offered, each at a virtually unprecedented rate of scarcity. The set was issued in two series; Series 1 with 330 cards, Series 2 with 220 cards.

		MT
Complete Set (550):		45.00
Complete Series 1 (330):		25.00
Complete Series 2 (220):		20.00
Common Player:		.05
Press Proofs: 8-15X		
Series 1 Wax Box:		45.00
Series 2 Wax Box:		30.00
1	Frank Thomas	1.50
2	Jason Bates	.05
3	Steve Sparks	.05
4	Scott Servais	.05
5	Angelo Encarnacion	.05
6	Scott Sanders	.05
7	Billy Ashley	.05
8	Alex Rodriguez	3.00
9	Sean Bergman	.05
10	Brad Radke	.05
11	Andy Van Slyke	.05
12	Joe Girardi	.05
13	Mark Grudzielanek	.10
14	Rick Aguilera	.05
15	Randy Veres	.05
16	Tim Bogar	.05
17	Dave Veres	.05
18	Kevin Stocker	.05
19	Marquis Grissom	.08
20	Will Clark	.30
21	Jay Bell	.08
22	Allen Battle	.05
23	Frank Rodriguez	.05
24	Terry Steinbach	.05
25	Gerald Williams	.08
26	Sid Roberson	.05
27	Greg Zaun	.05
28	Ozzie Timmons	.05
29	Vaughn Eshelman	.05
30	Ed Sprague	.05
31	Gary DiSarcina	.05
32	Joe Boever	.05
33	Steve Avery	.05
34	Brad Ausmus	.05
35	Kirt Manwaring	.05
36	Gary Sheffield	.40
37	Jason Bere	.05
38	Jeff Manto	.05
39	David Cone	.15
40	Manny Ramirez	1.00
41	Sandy Alomar	.08
42	Curtis Goodwin (Rated Rookie)	.05
43	Tino Martinez	.10
44	Woody Williams	.05
45	Dean Palmer	.08
46	Hipolito Pichardo	.05
47	Jason Giambi	.05
48	Lance Johnson	.05
49	Bernard Gilkey	.08
50	Kirby Puckett	1.00
51	Tony Fernandez	.05
52	Alex Gonzalez	.08
53	Bret Saberhagen	.08
54	Lyle Mouton (Rated Rookie)	.05
55	Brian McRae	.05
56	Mark Gubicza	.05
57	Sergio Valdez	.05
58	Darrin Fletcher	.05
59	Steve Parris	.05
60	Johnny Damon (Rated Rookie)	.20
61	Rickey Henderson	.20
62	Darrell Whitmore	.05
63	Roberto Petagine	.05
64	Trenidad Hubbard	.05
65	Heathcliff Slocumb	.05
66	Steve Finley	.05
67	Mariano Rivera	.35
68	Brian Hunter	.05
69	Jamie Moyer	.05
70	Ellis Burks	.05
71	Pat Kelly	.05
72	Mickey Tettleton	.05
73	Garret Anderson	.15
74	Andy Pettitte (Rated Rookie)	1.00
75	Glenallen Hill	.05
76	Brent Gates	.05
77	Lou Whitaker	.05
78	David Segui	.05
79	Dan Wilson	.05
80	Pat Listach	.05
81	Jeff Bagwell	1.00
82	Ben McDonald	.05
83	John Valentin	.08
84	John Jaha	.05
85	Pete Schourek	.05
86	Bryce Florie	.05
87	Brian Jordan	.10
88	Ron Karkovice	.05
89	Al Leiter	.08
90	Tony Longmire	.05
[illegible]	[illegible]	[illegible]
92	David Bell	.05
93	Kevin Gross	.05
94	Tom Candiotti	.05
95	Dave Martinez	.05
96	Greg Myers	.05
97	Rheal Cormier	.05
98	Chris Hammond	.05
99	Randy Myers	.05
100	Bill Pulsipher (Rated Rookie)	.15
101	Jason Isringhausen (Rated Rookie)	.20
102	Dave Stevens	.05
103	Roberto Alomar	.75
104	Bob Higginson (Rated Rookie)	.25
105	Eddie Murray	.35
106	Matt Walbeck	.05
107	Mark Wohlers	.05
108	Jeff Nelson	.05
109	Tom Goodwin	.05
110	Checklist 1-83 (Cal Ripken Jr.) (2,131 Consecutive Games)	1.50
111	Rey Sanchez	.05
112	Hector Carrasco	.05
113	B.J. Surhoff	.08
114	Dan Miceli	.05
115	Dean Hartgraves	.05
116	John Burkett	.05
117	Gary Gaetti	.05
118	Ricky Bones	.05
119	Mike Macfarlane	.05
120	Bip Roberts	.05
121	Dave Mlicki	.05
122	Chili Davis	.08
123	Mark Whiten	.05
124	Herbert Perry	.05
125	Butch Henry	.05
126	Derek Bell	.08
127	Al Martin	.05
128	John Franco	.05
129	William VanLandingham	.05
130	Mike Bordick	.05
131	Mike Mordecai	.05
132	Robby Thompson	.05
133	Greg Colbrunn	.05
134	Domingo Cedeno	.05
135	Chad Curtis	.08
136	Jose Hernandez	.05
137	Scott Klingenbeck	.05
138	Ryan Klesko	.25
139	John Smiley	.05
140	Charlie Hayes	.05
141	Jay Buhner	.15
142	Doug Drabek	.05
143	Roger Pavlik	.05
144	Todd Worrell	.05
145	Cal Ripken Jr.	2.50
146	Steve Reed	.05
147	Chuck Finley	.05
148	Mike Blowers	.05
149	Orel Hershiser	.08
150	Allen Watson	.05
151	Ramon Martinez	.08
152	Melvin Nieves	.05
153	Tripp Cromer	.05
154	Yorkis Perez	.05
155	Stan Javier	.05
156	Mel Rojas	.05
157	Aaron Sele	.05
158	Eric Karros	.10
159	Robb Nen	.05
160	Raul Mondesi	.30
161	John Wetteland	.05
162	Tim Scott	.05
163	Kenny Rogers	.05
164	Melvin Bunch	.05
165	Rod Beck	.05
166	Andy Benes	.05
167	Lenny Dykstra	.05
168	Orlando Merced	.05
169	Tomas Perez	.05
170	Xavier Hernandez	.05
171	Ruben Sierra	.05
172	Alan Trammell	.08
173	Mike Fetters	.05
174	Wilson Alvarez	.05
175	Erik Hanson	.05
176	Travis Fryman	.10
177	Jim Abbott	.08
178	Bret Boone	.08
179	Sterling Hitchcock	.05
180	Pat Mahomes	.05
181	Mark Acre	.05
182	Charles Nagy	.08
183	Rusty Greer	.10
184	Mike Stanley	.05
185	Jim Bullinger	.05
186	Shane Andrews	.05
187	Brian Keyser	.05
188	Tyler Green	.05
189	Mark Grace	.20
190	Bob Hamelin	.05
191	Luis Ortiz	.05
192	Joe Carter	.08
193	Eddie Taubensee	.05
194	Brian Anderson	.08
195	Edgardo Alfonzo	.15
196	Pedro Munoz	.05
197	David Justice	.25
198	Trevor Hoffman	.08
199	Bobby Ayala	.05
200	Tony Eusebio	.05
201	[illegible]	[illegible]
202	Mike Hampton	.05
203	Walt Weiss	.05
204	Joey Hamilton	.05
205	Roberto Hernandez	.05
206	Greg Vaughn	.08
207	Felipe Lira	.05
208	Harold Baines	.08
209	Tim Wallach	.05
210	Manny Alexander	.05
211	Tim Laker	.05
212	Chris Haney	.05
213	Brian Maxcy	.05
214	Eric Young	.08
215	Darryl Strawberry	.08
216	Barry Bonds	.85
217	Tim Naehring	.05
218	Scott Brosius	.05
219	Reggie Sanders	.05

220	Checklist 84-166 (Eddie Murray) (3,000 Career Hits)	.20
221	Luis Alicea	.05
222	Albert Belle	.75
223	Benji Gil	.05
224	Dante Bichette	.25
225	Bobby Bonilla	.10
226	Todd Stottlemyre	.05
227	Jim Edmonds	.10
228	Todd Jones	.05
229	Shawn Green	.15
230	Javy Lopez	.15
231	Ariel Prieto	.05
232	Tony Phillips	.05
233	James Mouton	.05
234	Jose Oquendo	.05
235	Royce Clayton	.05
236	Chuck Carr	.05
237	Doug Jones	.05
238	Mark Mclemore (McLemore)	.05
239	Bill Swift	.05
240	Scott Leius	.05
241	Russ Davis	.05
242	Ray Durham (Rated Rookie)	.08
243	Matt Mieske	.05
244	Brent Mayne	.05
245	Thomas Howard	.05
246	Troy O'Leary	.05
247	Jacob Brumfield	.05
248	Mickey Morandini	.05
249	Todd Hundley	.20
250	Chris Bosio	.05
251	Omar Vizquel	.08
252	Mike Lansing	.08
253	John Mabry	.05
254	Mike Perez	.05
255	Delino DeShields	.05
256	Wil Cordero	.05
257	Mike James	.05
258	Todd Van Poppel	.05
259	Joey Cora	.05
260	Andre Dawson	.08
261	Jerry DiPoto	.05
262	Rick Krivda	.05
263	Glenn Dishman	.05
264	Mike Mimbs	.05
265	John Ericks	.05
266	Jose Canseco	.35
267	Jeff Branson	.05
268	Curt Leskanic	.05
269	Jon Nunnally	.05
270	Scott Stahoviak	.05
271	Jeff Montgomery	.05
272	Hal Morris	.05
273	Esteban Loaiza	.08
274	Rico Brogna	.05
275	Dave Winfield	.20
276	J.R. Phillips	.05
277	Todd Zeile	.08
278	Tom Pagnozzi	.05
279	Mark Lemke	.05
280	Dave Magadan	.05
281	Greg McMichael	.05
282	Mike Morgan	.05
283	Moises Alou	.15
284	Dennis Martinez	.08
285	Jeff Kent	.05
286	Mark Johnson	.05
287	Darren Lewis	.05
288	Brad Clontz	.05
289	Chad Fonville (Rated Rookie)	.15
290	Paul Sorrento	.05
291	Lee Smith	.08
292	Tom Glavine	.20
293	Antonio Osuna	.05
294	Kevin Foster	.05
295	*Sandy Martinez*	.05
296	Mark Leiter	.05
297	Julian Tavarez	.05
298	Mike Kelly	.05
299	Joe Oliver	.05
300	John Flaherty	.05
301	Don Mattingly	.75
302	Pat Meares	.05
303	John Doherty	.05
304	Joe Vitiello	.05
305	Vinny Castilla	.08
306	Jeff Brantley	.05
307	Mike Greenwell	.05
308	Midre Cummings	.05
309	Curt Shilling	.10
310	Ken Caminiti	.25
311	Scott Erickson	.05
312	Carl Everett	.05
313	Charles Johnson	.08
314	Alex Diaz	.05
315	Jose Mesa	.05
316	Mark Carreon	.05
317	Carlos Perez (Rated Rookie)	.15
318	Ismael Valdes	.08
319	Frank Castillo	.05
320	Tom Henke	.05
321	Spike Owen	.05
322	Joe Orsulak	.05
323	Paul Menhart	.05
324	Pedro Borbon	.05
325	Checklist 167-249 (Paul Molitor) (1,000 Career RBI)	.25
326	Jeff Cirillo	.05
327	Edwin Hurtado	.05
328	Orlando Miller	.05
329	Steve Ontiveros	.05
330	Checklist 250-330 (Kirby Puckett) (1,000 Career RBI)	.50
331	Scott Bullett	.05
332	Andres Galarraga	.20
333	Cal Eldred	.05
334	Sammy Sosa	1.50
335	Don Slaught	.05
336	Jody Reed	.05
337	Roger Cedeno	.05
338	Ken Griffey Jr.	3.00
339	Todd Hollandsworth	.08
340	Mike Trombley	.05
341	Gregg Jefferies	.08
342	Larry Walker	.30
343	Pedro Martinez	.08
344	Dwayne Hosey	.05
345	Terry Pendleton	.05
346	Pete Harnisch	.05
347	Tony Castillo	.05
348	Paul Quantrill	.05
349	Fred McGriff	.35
350	Ivan Rodriguez	.65
351	Butch Huskey	.05
352	Ozzie Smith	.50
353	Marty Cordova	.15
354	John Wasdin	.05
355	Wade Boggs	.25
356	Dave Nilsson	.05
357	Rafael Palmeiro	.20
358	Luis Gonzalez	.08
359	Reggie Jefferson	.05
360	Carlos Delgado	.40
361	Orlando Palmeiro	.05
362	Chris Gomez	.05
363	John Smoltz	.20
364	Marc Newfield	.05
365	Matt Williams	.30
366	Jesus Tavarez	.05
367	Bruce Ruffin	.05
368	Sean Berry	.05
369	Randy Velarde	.05
370	Tony Pena	.05
371	Jim Thome	.50
372	Jeffrey Hammonds	.05
373	Bob Wolcott	.05
374	Juan Guzman	.05
375	Juan Gonzalez	1.50
376	Michael Tucker	.05
377	Doug Johns	.05
378	*Mike Cameron*	1.00
379	Ray Lankford	.08
380	Jose Parra	.05
381	Jimmy Key	.08
382	John Olerud	.15
383	Kevin Ritz	.05
384	Tim Raines	.08
385	Rich Amaral	.05
386	Keith Lockhart	.05
387	Steve Scarsone	.05
388	Cliff Floyd	.08
389	Rich Aude	.05
390	Hideo Nomo	.60
391	Geronimo Berroa	.05
392	Pat Rapp	.05
393	Dustin Hermanson	.05
394	Greg Maddux	2.00
395	Darren Daulton	.05
396	Kenny Lofton	.60
397	Ruben Rivera	.30
398	Billy Wagner	.10
399	Kevin Brown	.15
400	Mike Kingery	.05
401	Bernie Williams	.50
402	Otis Nixon	.05
403	Damion Easley	.05
404	Paul O'Neill	.10
405	Deion Sanders	.35
406	Dennis Eckersley	.08
407	Tony Clark	.50
408	Rondell White	.15
409	Luis Sojo	.05
410	David Hulse	.05
411	Shane Reynolds	.05
412	Chris Hoiles	.05
413	Lee Tinsley	.05
414	Scott Karl	.05
415	Ron Gant	.15
416	Brian Johnson	.05
417	Jose Oliva	.05
418	Jack McDowell	.08
419	Paul Molitor	.35
420	Ricky Bottalico	.05
421	Paul Wagner	.05
422	Terry Bradshaw	.05
423	Bob Tewksbury	.05
424	Mike Piazza	2.00
425	*Luis Andujar*	.05
426	Mark Langston	.05
427	Stan Belinda	.05
428	Kurt Abbott	.05
429	Shawon Dunston	.05
430	Bobby Jones	.05
431	Jose Vizcaino	.05
432	*Matt Lawton*	.05
433	Pat Hentgen	.05
434	Cecil Fielder	.08
435	Carlos Baerga	.08
436	Rich Becker	.05
437	Chipper Jones	2.00
438	Bill Risley	.05
439	Kevin Appier	.05
440	Checklist	.05
441	Jaime Navarro	.05
442	Barry Larkin	.20
443	*Jose Valentin*	.10
444	Bryan Rekar	.05
445	Rick Wilkins	.05
446	Quilvio Veras	.05
447	Greg Gagne	.05
448	Mark Kiefer	.05
449	Bobby Witt	.05
450	Andy Ashby	.08
451	Alex Ochoa	.05
452	Jorge Fabregas	.05
453	Gene Schall	.05
454	Ken Hill	.05
455	Tony Tarasco	.05
456	Donnie Wall	.05
457	Carlos Garcia	.05
458	Ryan Thompson	.05
459	*Marvin Benard*	.08
460	Jose Herrera	.05
461	Jeff Blauser	.05
462	Chris Hook	.05
463	Jeff Conine	.08
464	Devon White	.05
465	Danny Bautista	.05
466	Steve Trachsel	.05
467	C.J. Nitkowski	.05
468	Mike Devereaux	.05
469	David Wells	.08
470	Jim Eisenreich	.05
471	Edgar Martinez	.08
472	Craig Biggio	.10
473	Jeff Frye	.05
474	Karim Garcia	.50
475	Jimmy Haynes	.05
476	Darren Holmes	.05
477	Tim Salmon	.25
478	Randy Johnson	.35
479	Eric Plunk	.05
480	Scott Cooper	.05
481	Chan Ho Park	.08
482	Ray McDavid	.05
483	Mark Petkovsek	.05
484	Greg Swindell	.05
485	George Williams	.05
486	Yamil Benitez	.08
487	Tim Wakefield	.05
488	Kevin Tapani	.05
489	Derrick May	.05
490	Checklist (Ken Griffey Jr.)	1.50
491	Derek Jeter	2.00
492	Jeff Fassero	.08
493	Benito Santiago	.05
494	Tom Gordon	.05
495	Jamie Brewington	.05
496	Vince Coleman	.05
497	Kevin Jordan	.05
498	Jeff King	.05
499	Mike Simms	.05
500	Jose Rijo	.05
501	Denny Neagle	.05
502	Jose Lima	.08
503	Kevin Seitzer	.05
504	Alex Fernandez	.15
505	Mo Vaughn	.75
506	Phil Nevin	.08
507	J.T. Snow	.08
508	Andujar Cedeno	.05
509	Ozzie Guillen	.05
510	Mark Clark	.05
511	Mark McGwire	4.00
512	Jeff Reboulet	.05
513	Armando Benitez	.05
514	LaTroy Hawkins	.05
515	Brett Butler	.08
516	Tavo Alvarez	.05
517	Chris Snopek	.08
518	Mike Mussina	.30
519	Darryl Kile	.08
520	Wally Joyner	.08
521	Willie McGee	.08
522	Kent Mercker	.05
523	Mike Jackson	.05
524	Troy Percival	.05
525	Tony Gwynn	1.50
526	Ron Coomer	.05
527	Darryl Hamilton	.05
528	Phil Plantier	.05
529	Norm Charlton	.05
530	Craig Paquette	.05
531	Dave Burba	.05
532	Mike Henneman	.05
533	Terrell Wade	.05
534	Eddie Williams	.05
535	Robin Ventura	.10
536	Chuck Knoblauch	.20
537	Les Norman	.05
538	Brady Anderson	.10
539	Roger Clemens	1.50
540	Mark Portugal	.05
541	Mike Matheny	.05
542	Jeff Parrett	.05
543	Roberto Kelly	.05
544	Damon Buford	.05
545	Chad Ogea	.05
546	Jose Offerman	.05
547	Brian Barber	.05
548	Danny Tartabull	.05
549	Duane Singleton	.05
550	Checklist (Tony Gwynn)	.50

1996 Donruss Press Proofs

The first 2,000 of each regular card issued in the 1996 Donruss set are distinguished by the addition of a gold-foil "PRESS PROOF" stamped along the right side. As opposed to regular-issue cards which have silver-and-black card numbers and personal data strip at bottom, the Press Proof cards have those elements printed in black-on-gold. Stated odds of finding a Press Proof are one per 12 packs in Series 1, one per 10 packs in Series 2, on average.

	MT
Complete Set (550):	1250.
Complete Series 1 (330):	650.00
Complete Series 2 (220):	600.00
Common Player:	1.00
(Star cards valued 8X-15X corresponding regular-issue cards.)	

1996 Donruss Diamond Kings

The most "common" of the '96 Donruss inserts are the popular Diamond Kings, featuring the portraits of Dick Perez on a black background within a mottled gold-foil frame. Once again, the DKs feature one player from each team, with 14 issued in each of Series 1 and 2. Like all '96 Donruss inserts, the DKs are numbered on back, within an edition of 10,000. Also on back are color action photos and career highlights. Diamond Kings are inserted at the rate of one per 60 foil packs (Series 1), and one per 30 packs (Series 2), on average.

		MT
Complete Set (31):		225.00
Complete Series 1 (1-14):		110.00
Complete Series 2 (15-31):		110.00
Common Player Series 1:		4.50
Common Player Series 2:		3.00
1	Frank Thomas	12.50
2	Mo Vaughn	7.50
3	Manny Ramirez	9.00
4	Mark McGwire	30.00
5	Juan Gonzalez	15.00
6	Roberto Alomar	7.50
7	Tim Salmon	5.00
8	Barry Bonds	11.00
9	Tony Gwynn	15.00
10	Reggie Sanders	4.50
11	Larry Walker	7.50
12	Pedro Martinez	7.00
13	Jeff King	3.00
14	Mark Grace	6.00
15	Greg Maddux	15.00
16	Don Mattingly	11.00
17	Gregg Jefferies	3.00
18	Chad Curtis	3.00
19	Jason Isringhausen	4.50
20	B.J. Surhoff	3.00
21	Jeff Conine	3.00
22	Kirby Puckett	11.00
23	Derek Bell	3.00
24	Wally Joyner	3.00
25	Brian Jordan	3.00
26	Edgar Martinez	3.00
27	Hideo Nomo	4.50
28	Mike Mussina	5.00
29	Eddie Murray	4.50
30	Cal Ripken Jr.	24.00
31	Checklist	.50

1996 Donruss Elite

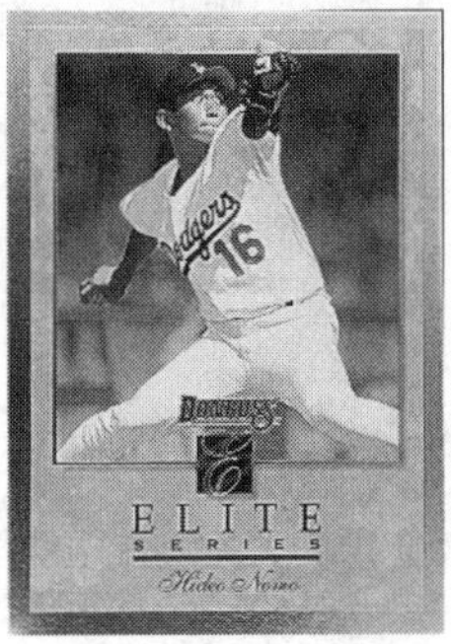

The Elite series continued as a Donruss insert in 1996, and they are the elite of the chase cards, being found on average only once per 140 packs (Series 1) or once per 75 packs (Series 2). The '96 Elite cards have a classic look bespeaking value. Player action photos at top center are framed in mottled silver foil and bordered in bright silver. Backs have another action photo, a few words about the player and a serial number from within an edition of 10,000 cards each. As usual, card numbering continues from the previous year.

		MT
Complete Set (12):		110.00
Complete Series 1 (61-66):		50.00
Complete Series 2 (67-72):		65.00
Common Player Series 1:		7.50
Common Player Series 2:		5.00
61	Cal Ripken Jr.	20.00
62	Hideo Nomo	7.50
63	Reggie Sanders	4.00
64	Mo Vaughn	7.50
65	Tim Salmon	5.00
66	Chipper Jones	15.00
67	Manny Ramirez	7.50
68	Greg Maddux	12.50
69	Frank Thomas	12.50
70	Ken Griffey Jr.	25.00
71	Dante Bichette	4.00
72	Tony Gwynn	12.50

1996 Donruss Freeze Frame

One of two insert sets exclusive to Series 2 Donruss is the Freeze Frame issue. Printed on heavy, round-cornered cardboard stock, the inserts feature multiple photos of the player on both front and back. Fronts combine matte and glossy finish plus a gold-foil Donruss logo. Backs are conventionally printed, include

1995 season highlights and a serial number from within the edition of 5,000. Stated odds of pulling a Freeze Frame insert are one per 60 packs.

		MT
Complete Set (8):		85.00
Common Player:		8.00
1	Frank Thomas	12.00
2	Ken Griffey Jr.	17.50
3	Cal Ripken Jr.	15.00
4	Hideo Nomo	4.00
5	Greg Maddux	12.00
6	Albert Belle	6.00
7	Chipper Jones	12.50
8	Mike Piazza	12.50

1996 Donruss Hit List

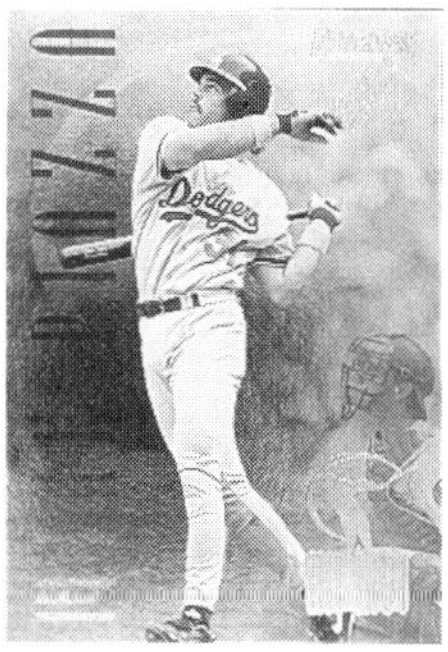

Printed on metallic foil with gold-foil graphic highlights, players who hit for high average with power or who collected milestone hits are featured in this insert set. Eight inserts were included in each of Series 1 and 2. Backs have a color action photo, a description of the player's batting prowess and a serial number from an edition of 10,000 cards each. Hit List inserts are found at an average rate of one per 106 foil packs in Series 1 and once per 60 packs in Series 2.

		MT
Complete Set (16):		60.00
Complete Set Series 1 (8):		35.00
Complete Set Series 2 (9-16):		25.00
Common Player Series 1:		1.25
Common Player Series 2:		1.75
1	Tony Gwynn	7.50
2	Ken Griffey Jr.	18.00
3	Will Clark	1.75
4	Mike Piazza	10.00
5	Carlos Baerga	1.25
6	Mo Vaughn	2.50
7	Mark Grace	1.50
8	Kirby Puckett	4.00
9	Frank Thomas	7.50
10	Barry Bonds	4.00
11	Jeff Bagwell	4.00
12	Edgar Martinez	1.75
13	Tim Salmon	2.00
14	Wade Boggs	2.50
15	Don Mattingly	3.50
16	Eddie Murray	2.50

1996 Donruss Long Ball Leaders

Once again the previous season's longest home runs are recalled in this retail-only insert set, found at an average rate of once per 96 packs in Series 1 only. Fronts are bordered and trimmed in bright silver foil and feature the player in his home run stroke against a black background. The date, location and distance of his tape-measure shot are in an arc across the card front. Backs feature another batting action photo, further details of the home run and a serial number within an edition of 5,000.

		MT
Complete Set (8):		100.00
Common Player:		4.00
1	Barry Bonds	12.00
2	Ryan Klesko	5.00
3	Mark McGwire	45.00
4	Raul Mondesi	4.00
5	Cecil Fielder	4.00
6	Ken Griffey Jr.	45.00
7	Larry Walker	9.00
8	Frank Thomas	15.00

1996 Donruss Power Alley

Among the most visually dazzling of 1996's inserts is this hobby-only chase set featuring baseball's top sluggers. Action batting photos are found within several layers of prismatic foil in geometric patterns on front. Backs are horizontally formatted, feature portrait photos at left and power stats at right and bottom. In the lower-left corner is an individual serial number from within an edition of 5,000 cards each. The first 500 of each player's cards are specially die-cut at left- and right-center. Found only in Series 1 hobby foil packs, Power Alley inserts are a one per 92 pack pick.

		MT
Complete Set (10):		90.00
Common Player		4.00
Die-cuts 2-3X		
1	Frank Thomas	12.00
2	Barry Bonds	10.00
3	Reggie Sanders	4.00
4	Albert Belle	9.00
5	Tim Salmon	6.00
6	Dante Bichette	6.00
7	Mo Vaughn	8.00
8	Jim Edmonds	4.00
9	Manny Ramirez	10.00
10	Ken Griffey Jr.	30.00

1996 Donruss Pure Power

These cards were random inserts found only in Series 2 retail packs. Fronts are printed on foil backgrounds and at bottom have a die-cut hole giving the impression a baseball has been batted through the card. On back the inserts are individually serial numbered within an edition of 5,000.

		MT
Complete Set (8):		45.00
Common Player:		3.00
1	Raul Mondesi	3.00
2	Barry Bonds	6.00
3	Albert Belle	5.00
4	Frank Thomas	9.00
5	Mike Piazza	15.00
6	Dante Bichette	4.00
7	Manny Ramirez	6.00
8	Mo Vaughn	5.00

1996 Donruss Round Trippers

An embossed white home plate design bearing the player's 1995 dinger output is featured on this Series II insert set. The entire background has been rendered in gold-flecked sepia tones. Typography on front is in bronze foil. Backs repeat the sepia background photo and include a month-by-month bar graph of the player's 1995 and career homers. Within the white home plate frame is the card's unique serial number from within an edition of 5,000. Odds of finding a Round Trippers card are stated at one per 55 packs, in hobby packs only.

		MT
Complete Set (10):		75.00
Common Player:		3.00
1	Albert Belle	5.00
2	Barry Bonds	5.00
3	Jeff Bagwell	7.50
4	Tim Salmon	3.00
5	Mo Vaughn	4.00
6	Ken Griffey Jr.	20.00
7	Mike Piazza	12.50
8	Cal Ripken Jr.	[illegible]
9	Frank Thomas	7.50
9p	Frank Thomas (Promo)	3.00
10	Dante Bichette	3.00

1996 Donruss Showdown

Baseball's top hitters and pitchers are matched on a silver and black foil background in this insert set. Gold-foil graphic highlights complete the horizontal front design. Backs are printed on a black and gold background with color action photos and write-ups about each player. At top is a serial number from within an edition of 10,000 cards each. Showdown inserts are found at an average rate of one per Series 1 foil packs.

		MT
Complete Set (8):		65.00
Common Player:		2.00
1	Frank Thomas, Hideo Nomo	9.00
2	Barry Bonds, Randy Johnson	7.50
3	Greg Maddux, Ken Griffey Jr.	20.00
4	Roger Clemens, Tony Gwynn	12.50
5	Mike Piazza, Mike Mussina	12.50
6	Cal Ripken Jr., Pedro Martinez	15.00
7	Tim Wakefield, Matt Williams	2.00
8	Manny Ramirez, Carlos Perez	4.00

1997 Donruss

Donruss' 1997 Series 1 features 270 base cards with a full-bleed color action photo on the front. Horizontal backs have a photo, career statistics, a brief player profile and biographical tidbits. A Press Proofs parallel was made of the base cards in an edition of 2,000 each. Other Series 1 inserts include the annual Diamond Kings, Elites, Armed and Dangerous cards, Longball Leaders and Rocket Launchers. A 180-card Update set was released later as a follow-up to the regular. '97 Donruss series. The Updates are numbered contiguously, #271-450, from the first series. Press Proofs and Gold Press Proof parallel inserts were available; other Update inserts include Dominators, Franchise Futures, Power Alley, Rookie Diamond Kings and a special Cal Ripken Jr. set.

		MT
Complete Set (450):		30.00
Series 1 Set (270):		15.00
Update Set (180):		15.00
Common Player:		.10
Series 1 Wax Box:		40.00
Update Box:		30.00
1	Juan Gonzalez	1.25
2	Jim Edmonds	.15
3	Tony Gwynn	1.25
4	Andres Galarraga	.15
5	Joe Carter	.15
6	Raul Mondesi	.20
7	Greg Maddux	1.50
8	Travis Fryman	.10
9	Brian Jordan	.10
10	Henry Rodriguez	.10
11	Manny Ramirez	1.00
12	Mark McGwire	3.00
13	Marc Newfield	.10
14	Craig Biggio	.10
15	Sammy Sosa	1.50
16	Brady Anderson	.10
17	Wade Boggs	.25
18	Charles Johnson	.10
19	Matt Williams	.20
20	Denny Neagle	.10
21	Ken Griffey Jr.	2.50
22	Robin Ventura	.15
23	Barry Larkin	.20
24	Todd Zeile	.10
25	Chuck Knoblauch	.15
26	Todd Hundley	.10
27	Roger Clemens	.75
28	Michael Tucker	.10
29	Rondell White	.10
30	Osvaldo Fernandez	.10
31	Ivan Rodriguez	.50
32	Alex Fernandez	.10
33	Jason Isringhausen	.10
34	Chipper Jones	1.50
35	Paul O'Neill	.10
36	Hideo Nomo	.40
37	Roberto Alomar	.75
38	Derek Bell	.10
39	Paul Molitor	.30
40	Andy Benes	.10
41	Steve Trachsel	.10
42	J.T. Snow	.10
43	Jason Kendall	.10
44	Alex Rodriguez	2.50
45	Joey Hamilton	.10
46	Carlos Delgado	.40
47	Jason Giambi	.10
48	Larry Walker	.30
49	Derek Jeter	1.50
50	Kenny Lofton	.75
51	Devon White	.10
52	Matt Mieske	.10
53	Melvin Nieves	.10
54	Jose Canseco	.30
55	Tino Martinez	.30
56	Rafael Palmeiro	.15
57	Edgardo Alfonzo	.15
58	Jay Buhner	.15
59	Shane Reynolds	.10
60	Steve Finley	.10
61	Bobby Higginson	.10
62	Dean Palmer	.10
63	Terry Pendleton	.10
64	Marquis Grissom	.10
65	Mike Stanley	.10
66	Moises Alou	.10
67	Ray Lankford	.10
68	Marty Cordova	.15
69	John Olerud	.10
70	David Cone	.10
71	Benito Santiago	.10
72	Ryne Sandberg	.60
73	Rickey Henderson	.15
74	Roger Cedeno	.10
75	Wilson Alvarez	.10
76	Tim Salmon	.20
77	Orlando Merced	.10
78	Vinny Castilla	.10
79	Ismael Valdes	.10
80	Dante Bichette	.15
81	Kevin Brown	.15
82	Andy Pettitte	.60
83	Scott Stahoviak	.10
84	Mickey Tettleton	.10
85	Jack McDowell	.10
86	Tom Glavine	.10
87	Gregg Jefferies	.10
88	Chili Davis	.10
89	Randy Johnson	.35
90	John Mabry	.10
91	Billy Wagner	.10
92	Jeff Cirillo	.10
93	Trevor Hoffman	.10
94	Juan Guzman	.10
95	Geronimo Berroa	.10
96	Bernard Gilkey	.10
97	Danny Tartabull	.10
98	Johnny Damon	.20
99	Charlie Hayes	.10
100	Reggie Sanders	.10
101	Robby Thompson	.10
102	Bobby Bonilla	.10
103	Reggie Jefferson	.10
104	John Smoltz	.20
105	Jim Thome	.35
106	Ruben Rivera	.25
107	Darren Oliver	.10
108	Mo Vaughn	[illegible]
109	Roger Pavlik	.10
110	Terry Steinbach	.10
111	Jermaine Dye	.10
112	Mark Grudzielanek	.10
113	Rick Aguilera	.10
114	Jamey Wright	.10
115	Eddie Murray	.35
116	Brian Hunter	.10
117	Hal Morris	.10
118	Tom Pagnozzi	.10
119	Mike Mussina	.35
120	Mark Grace	.25
121	Cal Ripken Jr.	2.00
122	Tom Goodwin	.10
123	Paul Sorrento	.10
124	Jay Bell	.10
125	Todd Hollandsworth	.10
126	Edgar Martinez	.10

127	George Arias	.10
128	Greg Vaughn	.10
129	Roberto Hernandez	.10
130	Delino DeShields	.10
131	Bill Pulsipher	.10
132	Joey Cora	.10
133	Mariano Rivera	.25
134	Mike Piazza	1.50
135	Carlos Baerga	.10
136	Jose Mesa	.10
137	Will Clark	.25
138	Frank Thomas	1.50
139	John Wetteland	.10
140	Shawn Estes	.10
141	Garret Anderson	.10
142	Andre Dawson	.10
143	Eddie Taubensee	.10
144	Ryan Klesko	.25
145	Rocky Coppinger	.10
146	Jeff Bagwell	1.25
147	Donovan Osborne	.10
148	Greg Myers	.10
149	Brant Brown	.10
150	Kevin Elster	.10
151	Bob Wells	.10
152	Wally Joyner	.10
153	Rico Brogna	.10
154	Dwight Gooden	.10
155	Jermaine Allensworth	.10
156	Ray Durham	.10
157	Cecil Fielder	.10
158	Ryan Hancock	.10
159	Gary Sheffield	.20
160	Albert Belle	.75
161	Tomas Perez	.10
162	David Doster	.10
163	John Valentin	.10
164	Danny Graves	.10
165	Jose Paniagua	.10
166	*Brian Giles*	1.00
167	Barry Bonds	.75
168	Sterling Hitchcock	.10
169	Bernie Williams	.50
170	Fred McGriff	.25
171	George Williams	.10
172	Amaury Telemaco	.10
173	Ken Caminiti	.10
174	Ron Gant	.10
175	David Justice	.15
176	James Baldwin	.10
177	Pat Hentgen	.10
178	Ben McDonald	.10
179	Tim Naehring	.10
180	Jim Eisenreich	.10
181	Ken Hill	.10
182	Paul Wilson	.10
183	Marvin Benard	.10
184	Alan Benes	.10
185	Ellis Burks	.10
186	Scott Servais	.10
187	David Segui	.10
188	Scott Brosius	.10
189	Jose Offerman	.10
190	Eric Davis	.10
191	Brett Butler	.10
192	Curtis Pride	.10
193	Yamil Benitez	.10
194	Chan Ho Park	.10
195	Bret Boone	.10
196	Omar Vizquel	.10
197	Orlando Miller	.10
198	Ramon Martinez	.10
199	Harold Baines	.10
200	Eric Young	.10
201	Fernando Vina	.10
202	Alex Gonzalez	.10
203	Fernando Valenzuela	.10
204	Steve Avery	.10
205	Ernie Young	.10
206	Kevin Appier	.10
207	Randy Myers	.10
208	Jeff Suppan	.10
209	James Mouton	.10
210	Russ Davis	.10
211	Al Martin	.10
212	Troy Percival	.10
213	Al Leiter	.10
214	Dennis Eckersley	.10
215	Mark Johnson	.10
216	Eric Karros	.10
217	Royce Clayton	.10
218	Tony Phillips	.10
219	Tim Wakefield	.10
220	Alan Trammell	.10
221	Eduardo Perez	.10
222	Butch Huskey	.10
223	Tim Belcher	.10
224	Jamie Moyer	.10
225	F.P. Santangelo	.10
226	Rusty Greer	.10
227	Jeff Brantley	.10
228	Mark Langston	.10
229	Ray Montgomery	.10
230	Rich Becker	.10
231	Ozzie Smith	.50
232	Rey Ordonez	.20
233	Ricky Otero	.10
234	Mike Cameron	.10
235	Mike Sweeney	.10
236	Mark Lewis	.10
237	Luis Gonzalez	.10
238	Marcus Jensen	.10
239	Ed Sprague	.10
240	Jose Valentin	.10
241	Jeff Frye	.10
242	Charles Nagy	.10
243	Carlos Garcia	.10
244	Mike Hampton	.10
245	B.J. Surhoff	.10
246	Wilton Guerrero	.10
247	Frank Rodriguez	.10
248	Gary Gaetti	.10
249	Lance Johnson	.10
250	Darren Bragg	.10
251	Darryl Hamilton	.10
252	John Jaha	.10
253	Craig Paquette	.10
254	Jaime Navarro	.10
255	Shawon Dunston	.10
256	Ron Wright	.75
257	Tim Belk	.10
258	Jeff Darwin	.10
259	Ruben Sierra	.10
260	Chuck Finley	.10
261	Darryl Strawberry	.10
262	Shannon Stewart	.10
263	Pedro Martinez	.10
264	Neifi Perez	.10
265	Jeff Conine	.10
266	Orel Hershiser	.10
267	Checklist 1-90 (Eddie Murray) (500 Career HR)	.10
268	Checklist 91-180 (Paul Molitor) (3,000 Career Hits)	.10
269	Checklist 181-270 (Barry Bonds) (300 Career HR)	.30
270	Checklist - inserts (Mark McGwire) (300 Career HR)	.75
271	Matt Williams	.30
272	Todd Zeile	.10
273	Roger Clemens	.75
274	Michael Tucker	.10
275	J.T. Snow	.10
276	Kenny Lofton	.75
277	Jose Canseco	.25
278	Marquis Grissom	.10
279	Moises Alou	.10
280	Benito Santiago	.10
281	Willie McGee	.10
282	Chili Davis	.10
283	Ron Coomer	.10
284	Orlando Merced	.10
285	Delino DeShields	.10
286	John Wetteland	.10
287	Darren Daulton	.10
288	Lee Stevens	.10
289	Albert Belle	.75
290	Sterling Hitchcock	.10
291	David Justice	.20
292	Eric Davis	.10
293	Brian Hunter	.10
294	Darryl Hamilton	.10
295	Steve Avery	.10
296	Joe Vitiello	.10
297	Jaime Navarro	.10
298	Eddie Murray	.30
299	Randy Myers	.10
300	Francisco Cordova	.10
301	Javier Lopez	.15
302	Geronimo Berroa	.10
303	Jeffrey Hammonds	.10
304	Deion Sanders	.25
305	Jeff Fassero	.10
306	Curt Schilling	.10
307	Robb Nen	.10
308	Mark McLemore	.10
309	Jimmy Key	.10
310	Quilvio Veras	.10
311	Bip Roberts	.10
312	Esteban Loaiza	.10
313	Andy Ashby	.10
314	Sandy Alomar Jr.	.10
315	Shawn Green	.10
316	Luis Castillo	.10
317	Benji Gil	.10
318	Otis Nixon	.10
319	Aaron Sele	.10
320	Brad Ausmus	.10
321	Troy O'Leary	.10
322	Terrell Wade	.10
323	Jeff King	.10
324	Kevin Seitzer	.10
325	Mark Wohlers	.10
326	Edgar Renteria	.10
327	Dan Wilson	.10
328	Brian McRae	.10
329	Rod Beck	.10
330	Julio Franco	.10
331	Dave Nilsson	.10
332	Glenallen Hill	.10
333	Kevin Elster	.10
334	Joe Girardi	.10
335	David Wells	.10
336	Jeff Blauser	.10
337	Darryl Kile	.10
338	Jeff Kent	.10
339	Jim Leyritz	.10
340	Todd Stottlemyre	.10
341	Tony Clark	.25
342	Chris Hoiles	.10
343	Mike Lieberthal	.10
344	Matt Lawton	.10
345	Alex Ochoa	.10
346	Chris Snopek	.10
347	Rudy Pemberton	.10
348	Eric Owens	.10
349	Joe Randa	.10
350	John Olerud	.10
351	Steve Karsay	.10
352	Mark Whiten	.10
353	Bob Abreu	.10
354	Bartolo Colon	.10
355	Vladimir Guerrero	1.00
356	Darin Erstad	1.00
357	Scott Rolen	1.25
358	Andruw Jones	1.50
359	Scott Spiezio	.10
360	Karim Garcia	.10
361	*Hideki Irabu*	1.50
362	Nomar Garciaparra	1.25
363	Dmitri Young	.10
364	*Bubba Trammell*	1.00
365	Kevin Orie	.10
366	Jose Rosado	.10
367	Jose Guillen	.75
368	Brooks Kieschnick	.10
369	Pokey Reese	.10
370	Glendon Rusch	.10
371	Jason Dickson	.15
372	Todd Walker	.60
373	Justin Thompson	.10
374	Todd Greene	.10
375	Jeff Suppan	.10
376	Trey Beamon	.10
377	Damon Mashore	.10
378	Wendell Magee	.10
379	Shigetosi Hasegawa	.10
380	Bill Mueller	.10
381	Chris Widger	.10
382	Tony Grafannino	.10
383	Derrek Lee	.10
384	Brian Moehler	.10
385	Quinton McCracken	.10
386	Matt Morris	.10
387	Marvin Benard	.10
388	*Deivi Cruz*	.50
389	*Javier Valentin*	.15
390	Todd Dunwoody	.40
391	Derrick Gibson	.20
392	Raul Casanova	.10
393	George Arias	.10
394	*Tony Womack*	.25
395	Antone Williamson	.10
396	*Jose Cruz Jr.*	.75
397	Desi Relaford	.10
398	Frank Thomas (Hit List)	.75
399	Ken Griffey Jr. (Hit List)	1.50
400	Cal Ripken Jr. (Hit List)	1.25
401	Chipper Jones (Hit List)	1.00
402	Mike Piazza (Hit List)	1.00
403	Gary Sheffield (Hit List)	.15
404	Alex Rodriguez (Hit List)	1.50
405	Wade Boggs (Hit List)	.15
406	Juan Gonzalez (Hit List)	.60
407	Tony Gwynn (Hit List)	.60
408	Edgar Martinez (Hit List)	.10
409	Jeff Bagwell (Hit List)	.60
410	Larry Walker (Hit List)	.15
411	Kenny Lofton (Hit List)	.35
412	Manny Ramirez (Hit List)	.50
413	Mark McGwire (Hit List)	1.50
414	Roberto Alomar (Hit List)	.25
415	Derek Jeter (Hit List)	1.00
416	Brady Anderson (Hit List)	.10
417	Paul Molitor (Hit List)	.20
418	Dante Bichette (Hit List)	.15
419	Jim Edmonds (Hit List)	.10
420	Mo Vaughn (Hit List)	.35
421	Barry Bonds (Hit List)	.35
422	Rusty Greer (Hit List)	.10
423	Greg Maddux (King of the Hill)	1.00
424	Andy Pettitte (King of the Hill)	.35
425	John Smoltz (King of the Hill)	.10
426	Randy Johnson (King of the Hill)	.25
427	Hideo Nomo (King of the Hill)	.25
428	Roger Clemens (King of the Hill)	.35
429	Tom Glavine (King of the Hill)	.15
430	Pat Hentgen (King of the Hill)	.10
431	Kevin Brown (King of the Hill)	.10
432	Mike Mussina (King of the Hill)	.25
433	Alex Fernandez (King of the Hill)	.10
434	Kevin Appier (King of the Hill)	.10
435	David Cone (King of the Hill)	.15
436	Jeff Fassero (King of the Hill)	.10
437	John Wetteland (King of the Hill)	.10
438	Barry Bonds, Ivan Rodriguez (Interleague Showdown)	.25
439	Ken Griffey Jr., Andres Galarraga (Interleague Showdown)	1.00
440	Fred McGriff, Rafael Palmeiro (Interleague Showdown)	.15
441	Barry Larkin, Jim Thome (Interleague Showdown)	.20
442	Sammy Sosa, Albert Belle (Interleague Showdown)	1.50
443	Bernie Williams, Todd Hundley (Interleague Showdown)	.20
444	Chuck Knoblauch, Brian Jordan (Interleague Showdown)	.15
445	Mo Vaughn, Jeff Conine (Interleague Showdown)	.25
446	Ken Caminiti, Jason Giambi (Interleague Showdown)	.15
447	Raul Mondesi, Tim Salmon (Interleague Showdown)	.15
448	Checklist (Cal Ripken Jr.)	.75
449	Checklist (Greg Maddux)	.60
450	Checklist (Ken Griffey Jr.)	1.00

1997 Donruss Press Proofs

Each of the 450 cards in the Donruss base set was also produced in a Press Proof parallel edition of 2,000 cards. Virtually identical in design to the regular cards, the Press Proofs are printed on a metallic background with silver-foil highlights. Most Press Proof backs carry the notation "1 of 2000". Stated odds of finding a press proof are one per eight packs. A special "gold" press proof chase set features cards with gold-foil highlights, diecut at top and bottom and the note "1 of 500" on back. Gold press proofs are found on average of once per 32 packs.

	MT
Complete Set (270):	600.00
Common Player:	1.00
Stars/Rookies: 6-10X	
Complete Gold Set (270):	1800.
Common Gold Player:	4.00
Gold Stars/Rookies: 15-25X	

(See 1997 Donruss for checklist and base card values.)

1997 Donruss Armed and Dangerous

These 15 cards are numbered up to 5,000. They were inserted in 1997 Donruss Series 1 retail packs only.

		MT
	Complete Set (15):	70.00
	Common Player:	1.50
1	Ken Griffey Jr.	15.00
2	Raul Mondesi	2.50
3	Chipper Jones	10.00
4	Ivan Rodriguez	4.00
5	Randy Johnson	3.00
6	Alex Rodriguez	12.50
7	Larry Walker	2.50
8	Cal Ripken Jr.	12.50
9	Kenny Lofton	3.00
10	Barry Bonds	4.00
11	Derek Jeter	10.00
12	Charles Johnson	1.50
13	Greg Maddux	9.00
14	Roberto Alomar	3.00
15	Barry Larkin	1.50

1997 Donruss Diamond Kings

Diamond Kings for 1997 are sequentially numbered from 1 to 10,000. To celebrate 15 years of this popular insert set, Donruss offered collectors a one-of-a-kind piece of artwork if they find one of the 10 cards with the serial number 1,982 (1982 was the first year of the Diamond Kings). Those who find these cards can redeem them for an original artwork provided by artist Dan Gardiner. In addition, Donruss printed the first 500 of each card on canvas stock.

		MT
	Complete Set (10):	60.00
	Common Player:	2.50
	Canvas (1st 500): 2-4X	
1	Ken Griffey Jr.	15.00
2	Cal Ripken Jr.	12.50
3	Mo Vaughn	5.00
4	Chuck Knoblauch	3.50
5	Jeff Bagwell	6.00
6	Henry Rodriguez	2.50
7	Mike Piazza	10.00
8	Ivan Rodriguez	5.00
9	Frank Thomas	7.50
10	Chipper Jones	10.00

1997 Donruss Elite Promos

Each of the 12 cards in Series 1 Donruss Elite inserts can be found in a sample card version. The promos differ from the issued version in the diagonal black overprint "SAMPLE CARD" on front and back, and the "PROMO/2500" at back bottom in place of the issued version's serial number.

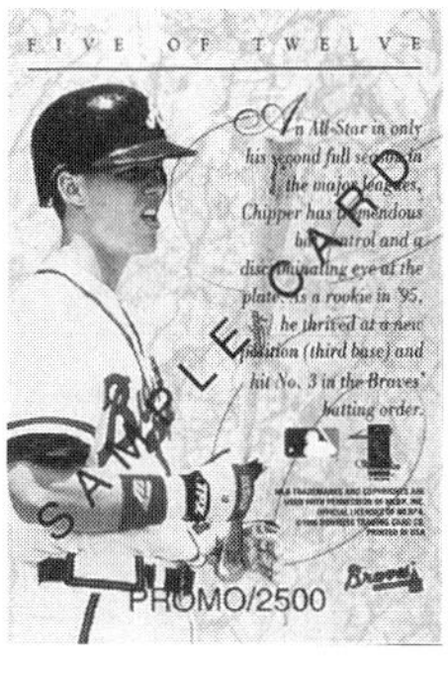

		MT
Complete Set (12):		100.00
Common Player:		3.75
1	Frank Thomas	7.50
2	Paul Molitor	6.00
3	Sammy Sosa	7.50
4	Barry Bonds	9.00
5	Chipper Jones	12.50
6	Alex Rodriguez	15.00
7	Ken Griffey Jr.	17.50
8	Jeff Bagwell	7.50
9	Cal Ripken Jr.	15.00
10	Mo Vaughn	3.50
11	Mike Piazza	12.00
12	Juan Gonzalez	7.50

1997 Donruss Elite Inserts

There were 2,500 sets of these insert cards made. The cards were randomly included in 1997 Donruss Series I packs. Fronts have a white marbled border and are graphically enhanced with silver foil, including a large script "E". On back is another photo, a career summary and a serial number from within the edition limit of 2,500.

		MT
Complete Set (12):		310.00
Common Player:		10.00
1	Frank Thomas	25.00
2	Paul Molitor	12.50
3	Sammy Sosa	27.50
4	Barry Bonds	12.50
5	Chipper Jones	30.00
6	Alex Rodriguez	40.00
7	Ken Griffey Jr.	55.00
8	Jeff Bagwell	15.00
9	Cal Ripken Jr.	45.00
10	Mo Vaughn	10.00
11	Mike Piazza	30.00
12	Juan Gonzalez	25.00

1997 Donruss Jackie Robinson Sweepstakes Scratch-Off

This pack insert features inside a scratch-off contest in which genuine vintage 1948-49 Leaf Jackie Robinson cards were awarded. The 2-3/8" x 2-7/8" folder has a color photo of the Leaf Robinson rookie card on front. On back is information on ordering numbered lithographs of the Robinson card; an edition of 1,000 selling for $199 apiece, an edition of 500 autographed by his widow selling for $299 apiece.

	MT
Jackie Robinson	.50

1997 Donruss Longball Leaders

These 1997 Donruss Series 1 inserts were limited to 5,000 each. They were seeded in retail packs only.

		MT
Complete Set (15):		45.00
Common Player:		1.00
1	Frank Thomas	5.00
2	Albert Belle	3.00
3	Mo Vaughn	3.00
4	Brady Anderson	1.00
5	Greg Vaughn	1.00
6	Ken Griffey Jr.	12.50
7	Jay Buhner	1.00
8	Juan Gonzalez	5.00
9	Mike Piazza	7.50
10	Jeff Bagwell	5.00
11	Sammy Sosa	7.00
12	Mark McGwire	12.50
13	Cecil Fielder	1.00
14	Ryan Klesko	1.50
15	Jose Canseco	2.00

1997 Donruss Rated Rookies

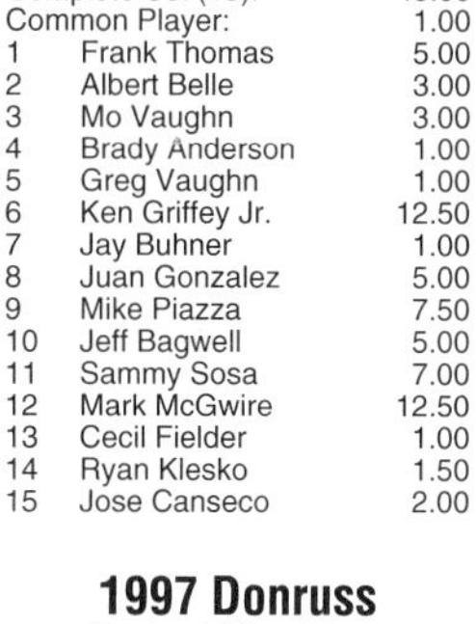

Although numbered more like an insert set, Rated Rookies are part of the regular-issue set. Cards are numbered 1-30, with no ratio given on packs. The cards are differentiated by a large silver-foil strip on the top right side with the words Rated Rookie.

		MT
Complete Set (30):		25.00
Common Player:		.75
1	Jason Thompson	.75
2	LaTroy Hawkins	.75
3	Scott Rolen	5.00
4	Trey Beamon	.75
5	Kimera Bartee	.75
6	Nerio Rodriguez	.75
7	Jeff D'Amico	.75
8	Quinton McCracken	.75
9	John Wasdin	.75
10	Robin Jennings	.75
11	Steve Gibralter	.75
12	Tyler Houston	.75
13	Tony Clark	2.00
14	Ugueth Urbina	.90
15	Billy McMillon	.75
16	Raul Casanova	.75
17	Brooks Kieschnick	.75
18	Luis Castillo	.75
19	Edgar Renteria	1.25
20	Andruw Jones	5.00
21	Chad Mottola	.75
22	Makoto Suzuki	.75
23	Justin Thompson	.75
24	Darin Erstad	4.00
25	Todd Walker	2.50
26	Todd Greene	.75
27	Vladimir Guerrero	4.00
28	Darren Dreifort	.75
29	John Burke	.75
30	Damon Mashore	.75

1997 Donruss Rocket Launchers

These 1997 Donruss Series 1 inserts are limited to 5,000 each. They were only included in magazine packs.

		MT
Complete Set (15):		50.00
Common Player:		1.50
1	Frank Thomas	6.00
2	Albert Belle	3.00
3	Chipper Jones	7.50
4	Mike Piazza	7.50
5	Mo Vaughn	3.00
6	Juan Gonzalez	6.00
7	Fred McGriff	2.00
8	Jeff Bagwell	4.00
9	Matt Williams	2.00
10	Gary Sheffield	1.50
11	Barry Bonds	3.00
12	Manny Ramirez	3.00
13	Henry Rodriguez	1.50
14	Jason Giambi	1.50
15	Cal Ripken Jr.	10.00

> The values of some parallel-card issues will have to be calculated based on figures presented in the heading for the regular-issue card set.

1997 Donruss Update Dominators

This 20-card insert highlights players known for being able to "take over a game." Each card features silver-foil highlights on front and stats on back.

		MT
Complete Set (20):		80.00
Common Player:		2.00
1	Frank Thomas	7.50
2	Ken Griffey Jr.	15.00
3	Greg Maddux	9.00
4	Cal Ripken Jr.	12.00
5	Alex Rodriguez	12.00
6	Albert Belle	4.00
7	Mark McGwire	15.00
8	Juan Gonzalez	7.00
9	Chipper Jones	9.00
10	Hideo Nomo	2.00
11	Roger Clemens	4.00
12	John Smoltz	2.00
13	Mike Piazza	9.00
14	Sammy Sosa	10.00
15	Matt Williams	2.50
16	Kenny Lofton	2.50
17	Barry Larkin	2.00
18	Rafael Palmeiro	2.00
19	Ken Caminiti	2.00
20	Gary Sheffield	2.00

1997 Donruss Update Franchise Features

This hobby-exclusive insert consists of 15 cards designed with a movie poster theme. The double-front design highlights a top veteran player on one side with an up-and-coming rookie on the other. The side featuring the veteran has the designation "Now Playing," while the rookie side carries the banner "Coming Attraction." Each card is printed on an all-foil stock and numbered to 3,000.

		MT
Complete Set (15):		175.00
Common Player:		5.00
1	Ken Griffey Jr., Andruw Jones	25.00
2	Frank Thomas, Darin Erstad	10.00
3	Alex Rodriguez, Nomar Garciaparra	20.00
4	Chuck Knoblauch, Wilton Guerrero	5.00
5	Juan Gonzalez, Bubba Trammell	12.50
6	Chipper Jones, Todd Walker	15.00
7	Barry Bonds, Vladimir Guerrero	7.50
8	Mark McGwire, Dmitri Young	25.00
9	Mike Piazza, Mike Sweeney	15.00
10	Mo Vaughn, Tony Clark	7.50
11	Gary Sheffield, Jose Guillen	2.50
12	Kenny Lofton, Shannon Stewart	7.50
13	Cal Ripken Jr., Scott Rolen	20.00
14	Derek Jeter, Pokey Reese	15.00
15	Tony Gwynn, Bob Abreu	15.00

1997 Donruss Update Power Alley

This 24-card insert is fractured into three different styles: Gold, Blue and Green. Each card is micro-etched and printed on holographic foil board. All cards are sequentially numbered, with the first 250 cards in each level being die-cut. Twelve players' cards feature a green finish and are numbered to 4,000. Eight players are printed on blue cards that are numbered to 2,000. Four players are found on gold cards numbered to 1,000.

		MT
Complete Set (24):		400.00
Common Gold:		20.00
Common Blue:		10.00
Common Green:		5.00
Die-Cuts: 2-4X		
1	Frank Thomas (G)	25.00
2	Ken Griffey Jr. (G)	60.00
3	Cal Ripken Jr. (G)	45.00
4	Jeff Bagwell (B)	20.00
5	Mike Piazza (B)	30.00
6	Andruw Jones (GR)	15.00
7	Alex Rodriguez (G)	40.00
8	Albert Belle (GR)	10.00
9	Mo Vaughn (GR)	9.00
10	Chipper Jones (B)	30.00
11	Juan Gonzalez (B)	20.00
12	Ken Caminiti (GR)	10.00
13	Manny Ramirez (GR)	12.00
14	Mark McGwire (GR)	30.00
15	Kenny Lofton (B)	10.00
16	Barry Bonds (GR)	10.00
17	Gary Sheffield (GR)	7.50
18	Tony Gwynn (GR)	15.00
19	Vladimir Guerrero (B)	15.00
20	Ivan Rodriguez (B)	10.00
21	Paul Molitor (B)	10.00
22	Sammy Sosa (GR)	25.00
23	Matt Williams (GR)	5.00
24	Derek Jeter (GR)	20.00

1997 Donruss Update Press Proofs

This 180-card parallel set is printed on an all-foil stock with bright foil accents. Each card is numbered "1 of 2,000". Special die-cut gold versions are numbered as "1 of 500".

	MT
Complete Set (180):	650.00
Common Player:	2.00
Stars: 15-25X	
Complete Set, Gold (180):	2500.
Common Player, Gold:	6.00
Gold Stars: 45-60X	

(See 1997 Donruss (#271-450) for checklist, base card values.)

1997 Donruss Update Cal Ripken

This 10-card set salutes Cal Ripken Jr. and is printed on an all-foil stock with foil highlights. Photos and text are taken from Ripken's autobiography, "The Only Way I Know." The first nine cards of the set were randomly inserted into packs. The 10th card was only available inside the book. Each card found within packs was numbered to 5,000.

		MT
Complete Set (10):		90.00
Common Card:		10.00
1-9	Cal Ripken Jr.	10.00
10	Cal Ripken Jr. (book insert)	20.00

1997 Donruss Update Rookie Diamond Kings

This popular Donruss Update insert set features a new twist - all 10 cards feature promising rookies. Each card is sequentially numbered to 10,000, with the first 500 cards of each player printed on actual canvas.

		MT
Complete Set (10):		80.00
Common Player:		4.00
Canvas: 2-4X		
1	Andruw Jones	15.00
2	Vladimir Guerrero	12.00
3	Scott Rolen	15.00
4	Todd Walker	6.00
5	Bartolo Colon	5.00
6	Jose Guillen	7.00
7	Nomar Garciaparra	20.00
8	Darin Erstad	12.00
9	Dmitri Young	4.00
10	Wilton Guerrero	4.00

1997 Donruss Team Sets

A total of 165 cards were part of the Donruss Team Set issue. Packs consisted solely of players from one of 11 different teams. In addition, a full 150-card parallel set called Pennant Edition was available, featuring red and gold foil and a special "Pennant Edition" logo. Cards were sold in five-card packs for $1.99 each. The Angels and Indians set were sold only at their teams' souvenir outlets. Cards #131 Bernie Williams and #144, Russ Davis, were never issued. The Team Set cards utilize team-color foil highlights and the numbers on back differ from the regular-issue version.

		MT
Comp. Angels Set (1-15):		2.50
Comp. Braves Set (16-30):		6.00
Comp. Orioles Set (31-45):		3.50
Comp. Red Sox Set (46-60):		3.00
Comp. White Sox Set (61-75):		4.00
Comp. Indians Set (76-90):		3.00
Comp. Rockies Set (91-105):		2.50
Comp. Dodgers Set (106-120):		3.50
Comp. Yankees Set (121-135):		5.00
Comp. Mariners Set (136-150):		10.00
Common Player:		.10
Pennant Edition Stars: 8-12X		
1	Jim Edmonds	.15
2	Tim Salmon	.25
3	Tony Phillips	.10
4	Garret Anderson	.10
5	Troy Percival	.10
6	Mark Langston	.10
7	Chuck Finley	.10
8	Eddie Murray	.50
9	Jim Leyritz	.10
10	Darin Erstad	1.00
11	Jason Dickson	.10
12	Allen Watson	.10
13	Shigetosi Hasegawa	.10
14	Dave Hollins	.10
15	Gary DiSarcina	.10
16	Greg Maddux	2.00
17	Denny Neagle	.15
18	Chipper Jones	2.00
19	Tom Glavine	.20
20	John Smoltz	.20
21	Ryan Klesko	.40
22	Fred McGriff	.30
23	Michael Tucker	.10
24	Kenny Lofton	.75
25	Javier Lopez	.15
26	Mark Wohlers	.10
27	Jeff Blauser	.10
28	Andruw Jones	1.50
29	Tony Graffanino	.10
30	Terrell Wade	.10
31	Brady Anderson	.15
32	Roberto Alomar	.60
33	Rafael Palmeiro	.20
34	Mike Mussina	.60
35	Cal Ripken Jr.	2.50
36	Rocky Coppinger	.10
37	Randy Myers	.10
38	B.J. Surhoff	.10
39	Eric Davis	.10
40	Armando Benitez	.10
41	Jeffrey Hammonds	.10
42	Jimmy Key	.10
43	Chris Hoiles	.10
44	Mike Bordick	.10
45	Pete Incaviglia	.10
46	Mike Stanley	.10
47	Reggie Jefferson	.10
48	Mo Vaughn	.75
49	John Valentin	.10
50	Tim Naehring	.10
51	Jeff Suppan	.10
52	Tim Wakefield	.10
53	Jeff Frye	.10
54	Darren Bragg	.10
55	Steve Avery	.10
56	Shane Mack	.10
57	Aaron Sele	.10
58	Troy O'Leary	.10
59	Rudy Pemberton	.10
60	Nomar Garciaparra	2.00
61	Robin Ventura	.15
62	Wilson Alvarez	.10
63	Roberto Hernandez	.10
64	Frank Thomas	2.00
65	Ray Durham	.10
66	James Baldwin	.10
67	Harold Baines	.10
68	Doug Drabek	.10
69	Mike Cameron	.10
70	Albert Belle	.75
71	Jaime Navarro	.10
72	Chris Snopek	.10
73	Lyle Mouton	.10
74	Dave Martinez	.10
75	Ozzie Guillen	.10
76	Manny Ramirez	1.00
77	Jack McDowell	.10
78	Jim Thome	.50
79	Jose Mesa	.10
80	Brian Giles	.10
81	Omar Vizquel	.10
82	Charles Nagy	.10
83	Orel Hershiser	.10
84	Matt Williams	.25
85	Marquis Grissom	.15
86	David Justice	.20
87	Sandy Alomar	.10
88	Kevin Seitzer	.10
89	Julio Franco	.10
90	Bartolo Colon	.10
91	Andres Galarraga	.20
92	Larry Walker	.30
93	Vinny Castilla	.10
94	Dante Bichette	.15
95	Jamey Wright	.10
96	Ellis Burks	.10
97	Eric Young	.10
98	Neifi Perez	.10
99	Quinton McCracken	.10
100	Bruce Ruffin	.10
101	Walt Weiss	.10
102	Roger Bailey	.10
103	Jeff Reed	.10
104	Bill Swift	.10
105	Kirt Manwaring	.10
106	Raul Mondesi	.20
107	Hideo Nomo	.50
108	Roger Cedeno	.10
109	Ismael Valdes	.10
110	Todd Hollandsworth	.10
111	Mike Piazza	2.00
112	Brett Butler	.10
113	Chan Ho Park	.10
114	Ramon Martinez	.10
115	Eric Karros	.10
116	Wilton Guerrero	.10
117	Todd Zeile	.10
118	Karim Garcia	.20
119	Greg Gagne	.10
120	Darren Dreifort	.10
121	Wade Boggs	.45
122	Paul O'Neill	.20
123	Derek Jeter	2.00
124	Tino Martinez	.25
125	David Cone	.20
126	Andy Pettitte	.60
127	Charlie Hayes	.10
128	Mariano Rivera	.20
129	Dwight Gooden	.15
130	Cecil Fielder	.10
131	Not Issued	
132	Darryl Strawberry	.15
133	Joe Girardi	.10
134	David Wells	.10
135	Hideki Irabu	1.50
136	Ken Griffey Jr.	3.00
137	Alex Rodriguez	2.50
138	Jay Buhner	.10
139	Randy Johnson	.50
140	Paul Sorrento	.10
141	Edgar Martinez	.10
142	Joey Cora	.10
143	Bob Wells	.10
144	Not Issued	
145	Jamie Moyer	.10
146	Jeff Fassero	.10
147	Dan Wilson	.10
148	Jose Cruz, Jr.	.50
149	Scott Sanders	.10
150	Rich Amaral	.10
151	Brian Jordan	.10
152	Andy Benes	.10
153	Ray Lankford	.10
154	John Mabry	.10
155	Tom Pagnozzi	.10
156	Ron Gant	.10
157	Alan Benes	.10
158	Dennis Eckersley	.10
159	Royce Clayton	.10
160	Todd Stottlemyre	.10
161	Gary Gaetti	.10
162	Willie McGee	.10
163	Delino DeShields	.10
164	Dmitri Young	.10
165	Matt Morris	.10

1997 Donruss Team Sets MVP

The top players at each position were available in this 18-card insert set. Each card is sequentially numbered to 1,000. Fronts are printed with a textured foil background and holographic foil highlights. Backs have a portrait photo.

		MT
Complete Set (18):		240.00
Common Player:		2.00
1	Ivan Rodriguez	7.50
2	Mike Piazza	25.00
3	Frank Thomas	25.00
4	Jeff Bagwell	17.50
5	Chuck Knoblauch	3.00
6	Eric Young	2.00
7	Alex Rodriguez	30.00
8	Barry Larkin	2.00
9	Cal Ripken Jr.	30.00
10	Chipper Jones	25.00
11	Albert Belle	7.50
12	Barry Bonds	7.50
13	Ken Griffey Jr.	40.00
14	Kenny Lofton	5.00
15	Juan Gonzalez	20.00
16	Larry Walker	3.00
17	Roger Clemens	12.50
18	Greg Maddux	22.50

1997 Donruss Elite

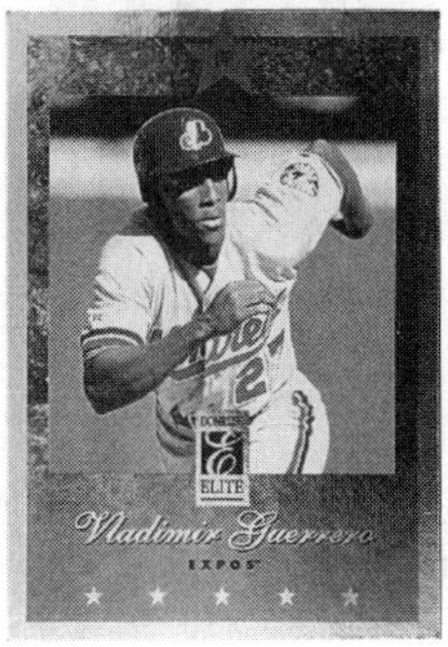

Donruss Elite Baseball is a 150-card, single-series set distributed as a hobby-only product. The regular-issue cards feature a silver border around the entire card, with a marblized frame around a color player photo at center. Backs feature a color player photo and minimal statistics and personal data. Elite was accompanied by an Elite Stars parallel set and three inserts: Leather and Lumber, Passing the Torch and Turn of the Century.

		MT
Complete Set (150):		20.00
Common Player:		.15
Wax Box:		75.00
1	Juan Gonzalez	1.75
2	Alex Rodriguez	4.00
3	Frank Thomas	2.00
4	Greg Maddux	2.50
5	Ken Griffey Jr.	4.00
6	Cal Ripken Jr.	3.00
7	Mike Piazza	2.50
8	Chipper Jones	2.50
9	Albert Belle	1.00
10	Andruw Jones	2.00
11	Vladimir Guerrero	2.00
12	Mo Vaughn	.75
13	Ivan Rodriguez	1.00
14	Andy Pettitte	.75
15	Tony Gwynn	2.00
16	Barry Bonds	1.00
17	Jeff Bagwell	1.75
18	Manny Ramirez	1.25
19	Kenny Lofton	.60
20	Roberto Alomar	.75
21	Mark McGwire	5.00
22	Ryan Klesko	.30
23	Tim Salmon	.30
24	Derek Jeter	2.50
25	Eddie Murray	.50
26	Jermaine Dye	.15
27	Ruben Rivera	.25
28	Jim Edmonds	.15
29	Mike Mussina	.50
30	Randy Johnson	.50
31	Sammy Sosa	2.00
32	Hideo Nomo	.25
33	Chuck Knoblauch	.35
34	Paul Molitor	.50
35	Rafael Palmeiro	.30
36	Brady Anderson	.20
37	Will Clark	.30
38	Craig Biggio	.30
39	Jason Giambi	.15
40	Roger Clemens	1.50
41	Jay Buhner	.20
42	Edgar Martinez	.15
43	Gary Sheffield	.25
44	Fred McGriff	.20
45	Bobby Bonilla	.15
46	Tom Glavine	.25
47	Wade Boggs	.35
48	Jeff Conine	.15
49	John Smoltz	.25
50	Jim Thome	.30
51	Billy Wagner	.20
52	Jose Canseco	.30
53	Javy Lopez	.15
54	Cecil Fielder	.15
55	Garret Anderson	.15
56	Alex Ochoa	.15
57	Scott Rolen	1.50
58	Darin Erstad	1.25
59	Rey Ordonez	.20
60	Dante Bichette	.20
61	Joe Carter	.20
62	Moises Alou	.25
63	Jason Isringhausen	.15
64	Karim Garcia	.35
65	Brian Jordan	.15
66	Ruben Sierra	.15
67	Todd Hollandsworth	.15
68	Paul Wilson	.15
69	Ernie Young	.15
70	Ryne Sandberg	1.25
71	Raul Mondesi	.30
72	George Arias	.15
73	Ray Durham	.15
74	Dean Palmer	.15
75	Shawn Green	.25
76	Eric Young	.15
77	Jason Kendall	.15
78	Greg Vaughn	.15
79	Terrell Wade	.15
80	Bill Pulsipher	.15
81	Bobby Higginson	.15
82	Mark Grudzielanek	.15
83	Ken Caminiti	.40
84	Todd Greene	.15
85	Carlos Delgado	.50
86	Mark Grace	.25
87	Rondell White	.25
88	Barry Larkin	.25
89	J.T. Snow	.15
90	Alex Gonzalez	.15
91	Raul Casanova	.15
92	Marc Newfield	.15
93	Jermaine Allensworth	.15
94	John Mabry	.15
95	Kirby Puckett	1.50
96	Travis Fryman	.15
97	Kevin Brown	.25
98	Andres Galarraga	.20
99	Marty Cordova	.15
100	Henry Rodriguez	.15
101	Sterling Hitchcock	.15
102	Trey Beamon	.15
103	Brett Butler	.15
104	Rickey Henderson	.25
105	Tino Martinez	.30
106	Kevin Appier	.15
107	Brian Hunter	.15
108	Eric Karros	.15
109	Andre Dawson	.15
110	Darryl Strawberry	.15
111	James Baldwin	.15
112	Chad Mottola	.15
113	Dave Nilsson	.15
114	Carlos Baerga	.15
115	Chan Ho Park	.20
116	John Jaha	.15
117	Alan Benes	.20
118	Mariano Rivera	.25
119	Ellis Burks	.15
120	Tony Clark	.30
121	Todd Walker	.50
122	Dwight Gooden	.15
123	Ugueth Urbina	.15
124	David Cone	.25
125	Ozzie Smith	.60
126	Kimera Bartee	.15
127	Rusty Greer	.15
128	Pat Hentgen	.15
129	Charles Johnson	.15
130	Quinton McCracken	.15
131	Troy Percival	.15
132	Shane Reynolds	.15
133	Charles Nagy	.15
134	Tom Goodwin	.15
135	Ron Gant	.15
136	Dan Wilson	.15

137	Matt Williams	.35
138	LaTroy Hawkins	.15
139	Kevin Seitzer	.15
140	Michael Tucker	.15
141	Todd Hundley	.25
142	Alex Fernandez	.15
143	Marquis Grissom	.15
144	Steve Finley	.15
145	Curtis Pride	.15
146	Derek Bell	.15
147	Butch Huskey	.15
148	Dwight Gooden	.15
149	Al Leiter	.15
150	Hideo Nomo	.25

1997 Donruss Elite Stars

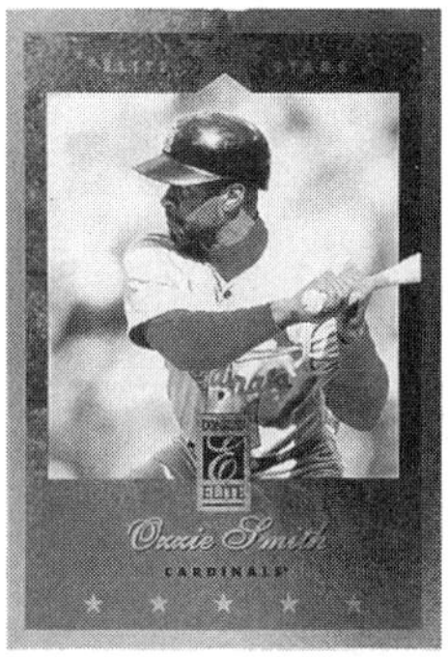

Gold, rather than silver, foil differentiates the parallel set of Elite Stars from the regular-issue versions of each of the base cards in the Elite set. The parallels also have a small "Elite Stars" printed at top, flanking the position. Stated odds of finding a Stars insert are about one per five packs.

		MT
Complete Set (150):		600.00
Common Player:		2.00
	(Star players in the Elite Star parallel issue valued at 15-30X regular Elites.)	

1997 Donruss Elite Leather & Lumber

Leather and Lumber is a 10-card insert set filled with veterans. Genuine leather is featured on one side of the card, while wood card stock is on the other. There were 500 sequentially numbered sets produced.

		MT
Complete Set (10):		400.00
Common Player:		15.00
1	Ken Griffey Jr.	90.00
2	Alex Rodriguez	60.00
3	Frank Thomas	50.00
4	Chipper Jones	60.00
5	Ivan Rodriguez	25.00
6	Cal Ripken Jr.	75.00
7	Barry Bonds	25.00
8	Chuck Knoblauch	15.00
9	Manny Ramirez	20.00
10	Mark McGwire	90.00

Player names in *Italic* type indicate a rookie card.

1997 Donruss Elite Passing the Torch

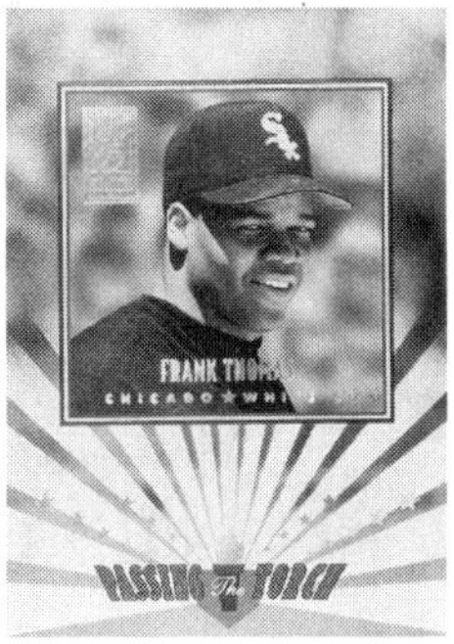

Passing the Torch is a 12-card insert limited to 1,500 individually numbered sets. It features eight different stars, each with their own cards and then featured on a double-sided card with another player from the set.

		MT
Complete Set (12):		300.00
Common Player:		15.00
1	Cal Ripken Jr.	60.00
2	Alex Rodriguez	60.00
3	Cal Ripken Jr., Alex Rodriguez	50.00
4	Kirby Puckett	20.00
5	Andruw Jones	25.00
6	Kirby Puckett, Andruw Jones	25.00
7	Cecil Fielder	15.00
8	Frank Thomas	30.00
9	Cecil Fielder, Frank Thomas	20.00
10	Ozzie Smith	20.00
11	Derek Jeter	40.00
12	Ozzie Smith, Derek Jeter	25.00

1997 Donruss Elite Passing the Torch Autographs

The first 150 individually numbered sets of the Passing the Torch insert were autographed. This means that cards 3, 6, 9 and 12 are dual-autographed on their double-sided format.

		MT
Complete Set (12):		2250.
Common Card:		50.00
1	Cal Ripken Jr.	300.00
2	Alex Rodriguez	250.00
3	Cal Ripken Jr., Alex Rodriguez	1200.
4	Kirby Puckett	150.00
5	Andruw Jones	90.00
6	Kirby Puckett, Andruw Jones	250.00
7	Cecil Fielder	50.00
8	Frank Thomas	150.00
9	Cecil Fielder, Frank Thomas	150.00
10	Ozzie Smith	125.00
11	Derek Jeter	150.00
12	Ozzie Smith, Derek Jeter	225.00

1997 Donruss Elite Turn of the Century

Turn of the Century includes 20 potential year 2000 superstars on an insert set numbered to 3,500. The first 500 of these sets feature an external die-cut design. Cards feature the player over a framed background image on silver foil board, with black strips down each side. Backs have a color photo, a few words about the player and the serial number.

		MT
Complete Set (20):		175.00
Common Player:		4.00
Complete Die-Cut Set (20):		400.00
Die-Cuts: 3-4X		
1	Alex Rodriguez	30.00
2	Andruw Jones	20.00
3	Chipper Jones	25.00
4	Todd Walker	8.00
5	Scott Rolen	15.00
6	Trey Beamon	4.00
7	Derek Jeter	25.00
7s	Derek Jeter ("SAMPLE" overprint)	10.00
8	Darin Erstad	12.00
9	Tony Clark	8.00
10	Todd Greene	5.00
11	Jason Giambi	4.00
12	Justin Thompson	5.00
13	Ernie Young	4.00
14	Jason Kendall	5.00
15	Alex Ochoa	4.00
15s	Alex Ochoa ("SAMPLE" overprint)	3.00
16	Brooks Kieschnick	4.00
17	Bobby Higginson	5.00
17s	Bobby Higginson ("SAMPLE" overprint)	3.00
18	Ruben Rivera	4.00
18s	Ruben Rivera ("SAMPLE" overprint)	3.00
19	Chan Ho Park	5.00
20	Chad Mottola	4.00

1997 Donruss Limited

Each of the 200 base cards in this set features a double-front design showcasing an action photo on each side. The set is divided into four subsets. Counterparts (100 cards) highlights two different players from the same position; Double Team (40 cards) features some of the majors' top teammate duos; Star Factor (40 cards) consists of two photos of some of the hobby's favorite players; and Unlimited Potential/Talent (20 cards) combines a top veteran with a top prospect. The issue also includes a Limited Exposure parallel set and a multi-tiered insert called Fabric of the Game. Odds of finding any insert card were 1:5 packs. Less than 1,100 base sets were available. Cards were sold in five-card packs for $4.99.

		MT
Complete Set (200):		900.00
Common Counterpart:		.25
Common Double Team:		1.00
Common Star Factor:		2.50
Common Unlimited:		2.00
Wax Box:		75.00
1	Ken Griffey Jr., Rondell White (Counterparts)	3.00
2	Greg Maddux, David Cone (Counterparts)	1.75
3	Gary Sheffield, Moises Alou (Double Team)	2.00
4	Frank Thomas (Star Factor)	12.50
5	Cal Ripken Jr., Kevin Orie (Counterparts)	2.00
6	Vladimir Guerrero, Barry Bonds (Unlimited Potential/Talent)	15.00
7	Eddie Murray, Reggie Jefferson (Counterparts)	.40
8	Manny Ramirez, Marquis Grissom (Double Team)	4.00
9	Mike Piazza (Star Factor)	25.00
10	Barry Larkin, Rey Ordonez (Counterparts)	.40
11	Jeff Bagwell, Eric Karros (Counterparts)	1.00
12	Chuck Knoblauch, Ray Durham (Counterparts)	.40
13	Alex Rodriguez, Edgar Renteria (Counterparts)	2.00
14	Matt Williams, Vinny Castilla (Counterparts)	.40
15	Todd Hollandsworth, Bob Abreu (Counterparts)	.25
16	John Smoltz, Pedro Martinez (Counterparts)	.40
17	Jose Canseco, Chili Davis (Counterparts)	.40
18	Jose Cruz, Jr., Ken Griffey Jr. (Unlimited Potential/Talent)	30.00
19	Ken Griffey Jr. (Star Factor)	35.00
20	Paul Molitor, John Olerud (Counterparts)	.75
21	Roberto Alomar, Luis Castillo (Counterparts)	.50
22	Derek Jeter, Lou Collier (Counterparts)	2.00
23	Chipper Jones, Robin Ventura (Counterparts)	2.50
24	Gary Sheffield, Ron Gant (Counterparts)	.40
25	Ramon Martinez, Bobby Jones (Counterparts)	.25
26	Mike Piazza, Raul Mondesi (Double Team)	15.00
27	Darin Erstad, Jeff Bagwell (Unlimited Potential/Talent)	7.50
28	Ivan Rodriguez (Star Factor)	10.00
29	J.T. Snow, Kevin Young (Counterparts)	.25
30	Ryne Sandberg, Julio Franco (Counterparts)	.70
31	Travis Fryman, Chris Snopek (Counterparts)	.25
32	Wade Boggs, Russ Davis (Counterparts)	.40
33	Brooks Kieschnick, Marty Cordova (Counterparts)	.25
34	Andy Pettitte, Denny Neagle (Counterparts)	.70
35	Paul Molitor, Matt Lawton (Double Team)	2.00
36	Scott Rolen, Cal Ripken Jr. (Unlimited Potential/Talent)	30.00
37	Cal Ripken Jr. (Star Factor)	30.00
38	Jim Thome, Dave Nilsson (Counterparts)	.50
39	*Tony Womack*, Carlos Baerga (Counterparts)	.25
40	Nomar Garciaparra, Mark Grudzielanek (Counterparts)	1.75
41	Todd Greene, Chris Widger (Counterparts)	.25
42	Deion Sanders, Bernard Gilkey (Counterparts)	.40
43	Hideo Nomo, Charles Nagy (Counterparts)	.40
44	Ivan Rodriguez, Rusty Greer (Double Team)	3.00
45	Todd Walker, Chipper Jones (Unlimited Potential/Talent)	20.00
46	Greg Maddux (Star Factor)	20.00
47	Mo Vaughn, Cecil Fielder (Counterparts)	.75
48	Craig Biggio, Scott Spiezio (Counterparts)	.25
49	Pokey Reese, Jeff Blauser (Counterparts)	.25
50	Ken Caminiti, Joe Randa (Counterparts)	.40
51	Albert Belle, Shawn Green (Counterparts)	.75
52	Randy Johnson, Jason Dickson (Counterparts)	.60
53	Hideo Nomo, Chan Ho Park (Double Team)	2.50
54	Scott Spiezio, Chuck Knoblauch (Unlimited Potential/Talent)	3.00
55	Chipper Jones (Star Factor)	25.00
56	Tino Martinez, Ryan McGuire (Counterparts)	.40
57	Eric Young, Wilton Guerrero (Counterparts)	.25
58	Ron Coomer, Dave Hollins (Counterparts)	.25
59	Sammy Sosa, Angel Echevarria (Counterparts)	1.75
60	*Dennis Reyes*, Jimmy Key (Counterparts)	.25
61	Barry Larkin, Deion Sanders (Double Team)	1.00
62	Wilton Guerrero, Roberto Alomar (Unlimited Potential/Talent)	3.00
63	Albert Belle (Star Factor)	10.00
64	Mark McGwire, Andres Galarraga (Counterparts)	2.00
65	Edgar Martinez, Todd Walker (Counterparts)	.40
66	Steve Finley, Rich Becker (Counterparts)	.25
67	Tom Glavine, Andy Ashby (Counterparts)	.40
68	Sammy Sosa, Ryne Sandberg (Double Team)	15.00
69	Nomar Garciaparra, Alex Rodriguez (Unlimited Potential/Talent)	35.00
70	Jeff Bagwell (Star Factor)	15.00
71	Darin Erstad, Mark Grace (Counterparts)	1.00
72	Scott Rolen, Edgardo Alfonzo (Counterparts)	1.00
73	Kenny Lofton, Lance Johnson (Counterparts)	.00
74	Joey Hamilton, Brett Tomko (Counterparts)	.25
75	Eddie Murray, Tim Salmon (Double Team)	1.50
76	Dmitri Young, Mo Vaughn (Unlimited Potential/Talent)	3.00
77	Juan Gonzalez (Star Factor)	20.00
78	Frank Thomas, Tony Clark (Counterparts)	1.00
79	Shannon Stewart, Bip Roberts (Counterparts)	.25

80	Shawn Estes, Alex Fernandez (Counterparts)	.25
81	John Smoltz, Javier Lopez (Double Team)	2.00
82	Todd Greene, Mike Piazza (Unlimited Potential/Talent)	25.00
83	Derek Jeter (Star Factor)	25.00
84	Dmitri Young, Antone Williamson (Counterparts)	.25
85	Rickey Henderson, Darryl Hamilton (Counterparts)	.35
86	Billy Wagner, Dennis Eckersley (Counterparts)	.50
87	Larry Walker, Eric Young (Double Team)	1.50
88	Mark Kotsay, Juan Gonzalez (Unlimited Potential/Talent)	6.00
89	Barry Bonds (Star Factor)	10.00
90	Will Clark, Jeff Conine (Counterparts)	.40
91	Tony Gwynn, Brett Butler (Counterparts)	1.25
92	John Wetteland, Rod Beck (Counterparts)	.25
93	Bernie Williams, Tino Martinez (Double Team)	2.00
94	Andruw Jones, Kenny Lofton (Unlimited Potential/Talent)	8.00
95	Mo Vaughn (Star Factor)	5.00
96	Joe Carter, Derrek Lee (Counterparts)	.25
97	John Mabry, F.P. Santangelo (Counterparts)	.25
98	Esteban Loaiza, Wilson Alvarez (Counterparts)	.25
99	Matt Williams, David Justice (Double Team)	1.25
100	Derrek Lee, Frank Thomas (Unlimited Potential/Talent)	7.50
101	Mark McGwire (Star Factor)	35.00
102	Fred McGriff, Paul Sorrento (Counterparts)	.40
103	Jermaine Allensworth, Bernie Williams (Counterparts)	.50
104	Ismael Valdes, Chris Holt (Counterparts)	.25
105	Fred McGriff, Ryan Klesko (Double Team)	1.25
106	Tony Clark, Mark McGwire (Unlimited Potential/Talent)	35.00
107	Tony Gwynn (Star Factor)	20.00
108	Jeffrey Hammonds, Ellis Burks (Counterparts)	.25
109	Shane Reynolds, Andy Benes (Counterparts)	.25
110	Roger Clemens, Carlos Delgado (Double Team)	4.00
111	Karim Garcia, Albert Belle (Unlimited Potential/Talent)	4.00
112	Paul Molitor (Star Factor)	7.50
113	Trey Beamon, Eric Owens (Counterparts)	.25
114	Curt Schilling, Darryl Kile (Counterparts)	.25
115	Tom Glavine, Michael Tucker (Double Team)	1.00
116	Pokey Reese, Derek Jeter (Unlimited Potential/Talent)	20.00
117	Manny Ramirez (Star Factor)	9.00
118	Juan Gonzalez, Brant Brown (Counterparts)	1.25
119	Juan Guzman, Francisco Cordova (Counterparts)	.25
120	Randy Johnson, Edgar Martinez (Double Team)	2.00
121	Hideki Irabu, Greg Maddux (Unlimited Potential/Talent)	6.50
122	Alex Rodriguez (Star Factor)	30.00
123	Barry Bonds, Quinton McCracken (Counterparts)	.75
124	Roger Clemens, Alan Benes (Counterparts)	.75
125	Wade Boggs, Paul O'Neill (Double Team)	2.00
126	Mike Cameron, Larry Walker (Unlimited Potential/Talent)	3.00
127	Gary Sheffield (Star Factor)	2.50
128	Andruw Jones, Raul Mondesi (Counterparts)	1.00
129	Brian Anderson, Terrell Wade (Counterparts)	.25
130	Brady Anderson, Rafael Palmeiro (Double Team)	2.50
131	Neifi Perez, Barry Larkin (Unlimited Potential/Talent)	2.00
132	Ken Caminiti (Star Factor)	4.00
133	Larry Walker, Rusty Greer (Counterparts)	.40
134	Mariano Rivera, Mark Wohlers (Counterparts)	.30
135	Hideki Irabu, Andy Pettitte (Double Team)	3.00
136	Jose Guillen, Tony Gwynn (Unlimited Potential/Talent)	6.00
137	Hideo Nomo (Star Factor)	3.50
138	Vladimir Guerrero, Jim Edmonds (Counterparts)	.60
139	Justin Thompson, Dwight Gooden (Counterparts)	.25
140	Andres Galarraga, Dante Bichette (Double Team)	1.00
141	Kenny Lofton (Star Factor)	5.00
142	Tim Salmon, Manny Ramirez (Counterparts)	1.00
143	Kevin Brown, Matt Morris (Counterparts)	.25
144	Craig Biggio, Bob Abreu (Double Team)	1.00
145	Roberto Alomar (Star Factor)	5.00
146	Jose Guillen, Brian Jordan (Counterparts)	.50
147	Bartolo Colon, Kevin Appier (Counterparts)	.25
148	Ray Lankford, Brian Jordan (Double Team)	1.00
149	Chuck Knoblauch (Star Factor)	5.00
150	Henry Rodriguez, Ray Lankford (Counterparts)	.25
151	*Jaret Wright*, Ben McDonald (Counterparts)	.65
152	Bobby Bonilla, Kevin Brown (Double Team)	2.50
153	Barry Larkin (Star Factor)	2.50
154	David Justice, Reggie Sanders (Counterparts)	.40
155	Mike Mussina, Ken Hill (Counterparts)	.50
156	Mark Grace, Brooks Kieschnick (Double Team)	1.25
157	Jim Thome (Star Factor)	2.50
158	Michael Tucker, Curtis Goodwin (Counterparts)	.25
159	Jeff Suppan, Jeff Fassero (Counterparts)	.25
160	Mike Mussina, Jeffrey Hammonds (Double Team)	2.00
161	John Smoltz (Star Factor)	3.50
162	Moises Alou, Eric Davis (Counterparts)	.25
163	Sandy Alomar Jr., Dan Wilson (Counterparts)	.25
164	Rondell White, Henry Rodriguez (Double Team)	2.50
165	Roger Clemens (Star Factor)	10.00
166	Brady Anderson, Al Martin (Counterparts)	.25
167	Jason Kendall, Charles Johnson (Counterparts)	.25
168	Jason Giambi, Jose Canseco (Double Team)	1.25
169	Larry Walker (Star Factor)	4.00
170	Jay Buhner, Geronimo Berroa (Counterparts)	.40
171	Ivan Rodriguez, Mike Sweeney (Counterparts)	.60
172	Kevin Appier, Jose Rosado (Double Team)	2.50
173	Bernie Williams (Star Factor)	2.50
174	Todd Dunwoody, *Brian Giles* (Counterparts)	.75
175	Javier Lopez, Scott Hatteberg (Counterparts)	.30
176	John Jaha, Jeff Cirillo (Double Team)	2.50
177	Andy Pettitte (Star Factor)	2.50
178	Dante Bichette, Butch Huskey (Counterparts)	.40
179	Raul Casanova, Todd Hundley (Counterparts)	.40
180	Jim Edmonds, Garret Anderson (Double Team)	2.50
181	Deion Sanders (Star Factor)	2.50
182	Ryan Klesko, Paul O'Neill (Counterparts)	.40
183	Joe Carter, Pat Hentgen (Double Team)	2.50
184	Brady Anderson (Star Factor)	2.50
185	Carlos Delgado, Wally Joyner (Counterparts)	.50
186	Jermaine Dye, Johnny Damon (Double Team)	2.50
187	Randy Johnson (Star Factor)	5.00
188	Todd Hundley, Carlos Baerga (Double Team)	2.50
189	Tom Glavine (Star Factor)	2.50
190	Damon Mashore, Jason McDonald (Double Team)	2.50
191	Wade Boggs (Star Factor)	5.00
192	Al Martin, Jason Kendall (Double Team)	2.50
193	Matt Williams (Star Factor)	3.00
194	Will Clark, Dean Palmer (Double Team)	1.25
195	Sammy Sosa (Star Factor)	20.00
196	Jose Cruz, Jr., Jay Buhner (Double Team)	1.00
197	Eddie Murray (Star Factor)	5.00
198	Darin Erstad, Jason Dickson (Double Team)	3.00
199	Fred McGriff (Star Factor)	2.50
200	Bubba Trammell, Bobby Higginson (Double Team)	2.00

1997 Donruss Limited Exposure

A complete 200-card parallel set printed with Holographic Poly-Chromium technology on both sides and featuring a special "Limited Exposure" stamp. Less than 40 sets of the Star Factor Limited Exposures are thought to exist.

	MT
Complete Set (200):	6000.
Common Counterparts:	2.00
Counterparts Stars: 4-8X	
Common Double Team:	6.00
Double Team Stars: 5-7X	
Common Star Factor:	10.00
Star Factor Stars: 3-5X	
Common Unlimited:	8.00
Unlimited Stars: 3-5X	

(See 1997 Donruss Limited for checklist and base card values.)

1997 Donruss Limited Exposure Non-Glossy

In error, half (100 cards) of the Limited Exposure parallels were produced in regular technology (non-chrome) on regular (non-glossy) cardboard stock. These cards do carry the Limited Exposure identification in the card-number box on back, but do not carry the correct cards' higher values. No checklist of which 100 cards were involved in the error is available.

	MT
Common Non-Glossy:	1.00
Stars: 15-25%	

(See 1997 Donruss Limited and Limited Exposure to calculate base card values.)

1997 Donruss Limited Fabric of the Game

This fractured insert set consists of 69 different cards highlighting three different technologies representing three statistical categories: Canvas (stolen bases), Leather (doubles) and Wood (home runs). Each of the 23 cards in each category are found in varying levels of scarcity: Legendary Material (one card per theme; numbered to 100), Hall of Fame Material (four cards numbered to 250), Superstar Material (five cards numbered to 500), Star Material (six cards numbered to 750), and Major League Material (seven cards numbered to 1,000).

	MT
Complete Set: (69):	1650.
Common Player:	5.00
Complete Canvas Set (23):	325.00
Rickey Henderson (100)	45.00
Barry Bonds (250)	30.00
Kenny Lofton (250)	25.00
Roberto Alomar (250)	25.00
Ryne Sandberg (250)	30.00
Tony Gwynn (500)	30.00
Barry Larkin (500)	10.00
Brady Anderson (500)	10.00
Chuck Knoblauch (500)	12.50
Craig Biggio (500)	10.00
Sammy Sosa (750)	30.00
Gary Sheffield (750)	12.50
Eric Young (750)	7.50
Larry Walker (750)	15.00
Ken Griffey Jr. (750)	65.00
Deion Sanders (750)	10.00
Raul Mondesi (1,000)	10.00
Rondell White (1,000)	7.50
Derek Jeter (1,000)	25.00
Nomar Garciaparra (1,000)	20.00
Wilton Guerrero (1,000)	5.00
Pokey Reese (1,000)	5.00
Darin Erstad (1,000)	17.50
Complete Leather Set (23):	350.00
Paul Molitor (100)	60.00
Wade Boggs (250)	25.00
Cal Ripken Jr. (250)	80.00
Tony Gwynn (250)	50.00
Joe Carter (250)	12.50
Rafael Palmeiro (500)	15.00
Mark Grace (500)	15.00
Bobby Bonilla (500)	7.50
Andres Galarraga (500)	7.50
Edgar Martinez (500)	7.50
Ken Caminiti (750)	10.00
Ivan Rodriguez (750)	17.50
Frank Thomas (750)	35.00
Jeff Bagwell (750)	25.00
Albert Belle (750)	15.00
Bernie Williams (750)	15.00
Chipper Jones (1,000)	25.00
Rusty Greer (1,000)	5.00
Todd Walker (1,000)	10.00
Scott Rolen (1,000)	20.00
Bob Abreu (1,000)	5.00
Jose Guillen (1,000)	7.50
Jose Cruz, Jr. (1,000)	5.00
Complete Wood Set (23);	425.00
Eddie Murray (100)	50.00
Cal Ripken Jr. (250)	75.00
Barry Bonds (250)	30.00
Mark McGwire (250)	75.00
Fred McGriff (250)	12.50
Ken Griffey Jr. (500)	70.00
Albert Belle (500)	17.50
Frank Thomas (500)	40.00
Juan Gonzalez (500)	25.00
Matt Williams (500)	12.50
Mike Piazza (750)	30.00
Jeff Bagwell (750)	20.00
Mo Vaughn (750)	15.00
Gary Sheffield (750)	10.00
Tim Salmon (750)	10.00
David Justice (750)	10.00
Manny Ramirez (1,000)	15.00
Jim Thome (1,000)	7.50
Tino Martinez (1,000)	7.50
Andruw Jones (1,000)	10.00
Vladimir Guerrero (1,000)	15.00
Tony Clark (1,000)	7.50
Dmitri Young (1,000)	5.00

1997 Donruss Preferred

Each of the 200 base cards is printed on all-foil microetched stock. Conventional backs have a color player photo and a few stats. The set is fractured into four increasingly scarce levels: 100 Bronze cards, 70 Silver, 20 Gold and 10 Platinum. Instead of traditional packs, cards were sold in five-card collectible tins. Four different inserts were included with the product: Staremaster, X-Ponential Power, Cut To The Chase (a die-cut parallel) and Precious Metals. Odds of finding any insert were 1:4 packs.

		MT
Complete Set (200):		400.00
Common Bronze:		.10
Common Silver:		.75
Common Gold:		2.00
Common Platinum:		5.00
Cut to the Chase Bronze: 3-6X		
Cut to the Chase Silver: 1.5-3X		
Cut to the Chase Gold: 2X		
Cut to the Chase Platinum: 2X		
Wax Box:		60.00
1	Frank Thomas P	17.50
2	Ken Griffey Jr. P	40.00
3	Cecil Fielder B	.10
4	Chuck Knoblauch G	4.00
5	Garret Anderson B	.10
6	Greg Maddux P	20.00
7	Matt Williams S	1.00
8	Marquis Grissom S	.75
9	Jason Isringhausen B	.10
10	Larry Walker S	1.25
11	Charles Nagy B	.10
12	Dan Wilson B	.10
13	Albert Belle G	6.00
14	Javier Lopez B	.10
15	David Cone B	.15
16	Bernard Gilkey B	.10
17	Andres Galarraga S	.75
18	Bill Pulsipher B	.10
19	Alex Fernandez B	.10
20	Andy Pettitte S	2.00
21	Mark Grudzielanek B	.10
22	Juan Gonzalez P	20.00
23	Reggie Sanders B	.10
24	Kenny Lofton G	4.00
25	Andy Ashby B	.10
26	John Wetteland B	.10
27	Bobby Bonilla B	.10
28	Hideo Nomo G	3.00
29	Joe Carter B	.10
30	Jose Canseco B	.25
31	Ellis Burks B	.10
32	Edgar Martinez S	.75
33	Chan Ho Park B	.10
34	David Justice B	.20
35	Carlos Delgado B	.50
36	Jeff Cirillo S	.75
37	Charles Johnson B	.10
38	Manny Ramirez G	6.00
39	Greg Vaughn B	.10
40	Henry Rodriguez B	.10
41	Darryl Strawberry B	.10
42	Jim Thome G	3.00
43	Ryan Klesko S	1.50
44	Jermaine Allensworth B	.10
45	Brian Jordan G	3.00
46	Tony Gwynn P	20.00
47	Rafael Palmeiro G	5.00
48	Dante Bichette S	.75
49	Ivan Rodriguez G	7.50
50	Mark McGwire G	17.50
51	Tim Salmon S	1.00
52	Roger Clemens B	.50
53	Matt Lawton B	.10
54	Wade Boggs S	1.50
55	Travis Fryman B	.10
56	Bobby Higginson S	.75
57	John Jaha S	.75
58	Rondell White S	.75
59	Tom Glavine S	1.00
60	Eddie Murray S	2.50
61	Vinny Castilla B	.10
62	Todd Hundley B	.20
63	Jay Buhner S	.75
64	Paul O'Neill B	.10
65	Steve Finley B	.10
66	Kevin Appier B	.10
67	Ray Durham B	.10
68	Dave Nilsson B	.10
69	Jeff Bagwell G	10.00
70	Al Martin S	.75
71	Paul Molitor G	5.00
72	Kevin Brown S	1.00
73	Ron Gant B	.10
74	Dwight Gooden B	.10
75	Quinton McCracken B	.10
76	Rusty Greer S	.75
77	Juan Guzman B	.10
78	Fred McGriff S	.75
79	Tino Martinez B	.20
80	Ray Lankford B	.10
81	Ken Caminiti G	3.00
82	James Baldwin B	.10
83	Jermaine Dye G	2.00
84	Mark Grace S	1.00
85	Pat Hentgen S	.75
86	Jason Giambi S	.75
87	Brian Hunter B	.10
88	Andy Benes B	.10
89	Jose Rosado B	.10
90	Shawn Green B	.20
91	Jason Kendall B	.10
92	Alex Rodriguez P	30.00
93	Chipper Jones P	25.00
94	Barry Bonds G	5.00
95	Brady Anderson G	2.00
96	Ryne Sandberg S	2.50
97	Lance Johnson B	.10
98	Cal Ripken Jr. P	30.00
99	Craig Biggio S	.75
100	Dean Palmer B	.10
101	Gary Sheffield G	3.00
102	Johnny Damon B	.10
103	Mo Vaughn G	4.00
104	Randy Johnson S	1.50
105	Raul Mondesi S	.75
106	Roberto Alomar G	4.00
107	Mike Piazza P	25.00
108	Rey Ordonez B	.10
109	Barry Larkin G	2.00
110	Tony Clark S	1.50
111	Bernie Williams S	2.00
112	John Smoltz G	3.00
113	Moises Alou B	.10
114	Will Clark B	.15
115	Sammy Sosa G	12.50
116	Jim Edmonds S	.75
117	Jeff Conine B	.10
118	Joey Hamilton B	.10
119	Todd Hollandsworth B	.10
120	Troy Percival B	.10
121	Paul Wilson B	.10
122	Ken Hill B	.10
123	Mariano Rivera S	.75
124	Eric Karros B	.10
125	Derek Jeter G	15.00
126	Eric Young S	.75
127	John Mabry B	.10
128	Gregg Jefferies B	.10
129	Ismael Valdes S	.75
130	Marty Cordova B	.10
131	Omar Vizquel B	.10
132	Mike Mussina S	2.00
133	Darin Erstad B	.50
134	Edgar Renteria S	.75
135	Billy Wagner B	.10
136	Alex Ochoa B	.10
137	Luis Castillo B	.10
138	Rocky Coppinger B	.10
139	Mike Sweeney B	.10
140	Michael Tucker B	.10
141	Chris Snopek B	.10
142	Dmitri Young S	.75
143	Andruw Jones P	15.00
144	Mike Cameron S	.75
145	Brant Brown B	.10
146	Todd Walker G	2.00
147	Nomar Garciaparra G	15.00
148	Glendon Rusch B	.10
149	Karim Garcia S	.75
150	*Bubba Trammell S*	2.00
151	Todd Greene B	.10
152	Wilton Guerrero G	2.00
153	Scott Spiezio B	.10
154	Brooks Kieschnick B	.10
155	Vladimir Guerrero G	9.00
156	Brian Giles S	.75
157	Pokey Reese B	.10
158	Jason Dickson G	2.00
159	Kevin Orie S	.75
160	Scott Rolen G	9.00
161	Bartolo Colon S	.75
162	Shannon Stewart G	2.00
163	Wendell Magee B	.10
164	Jose Guillen S	2.00
165	Bob Abreu S	.75
166	*Deivi Cruz B*	.25
167	Alex Rodriguez B (National Treasures)	2.00
168	Frank Thomas B (National Treasures)	1.00
169	Cal Ripken Jr. B (National Treasures)	2.50
170	Chipper Jones B (National Treasures)	1.50
171	Mike Piazza B (National Treasures)	1.50
172	Tony Gwynn S (National Treasures)	4.00
173	Juan Gonzalez B (National Treasures)	.50
174	Kenny Lofton S (National Treasures)	2.50
175	Ken Griffey Jr. B (National Treasures)	6.00
176	Mark McGwire B (National Treasures)	4.00
177	Jeff Bagwell B (National Treasures)	.50
178	Paul Molitor S (National Treasures)	1.50
179	Andruw Jones B (National Treasures)	1.00
180	Manny Ramirez S (National Treasures)	2.50
181	Ken Caminiti S (National Treasures)	1.00
182	Barry Bonds B (National Treasures)	.40
183	Mo Vaughn B (National Treasures)	.30
184	Derek Jeter B (National Treasures)	1.00
185	Barry Larkin S (National Treasures)	1.00
186	Ivan Rodriguez B (National Treasures)	.25
187	Albert Belle S (National Treasures)	2.00
188	John Smoltz S (National Treasures)	.75
189	Chuck Knoblauch S (National Treasures)	1.00
190	Brian Jordan S (National Treasures)	.75
191	Gary Sheffield S (National Treasures)	1.00
192	Jim Thome S (National Treasures)	2.00
193	Brady Anderson S (National Treasures)	.75
194	Hideo Nomo S (National Treasures)	1.50
195	Sammy Sosa S (National Treasures)	6.00
196	Greg Maddux B (National Treasures)	.60
197	Checklist (Vladimir Guerrero B)	.40
198	Checklist (Scott Rolen B)	.25
199	Checklist (Todd Walker B)	.10
200	Checklist (Nomar Garciaparra B)	.50

1997 Donruss Preferred Cut To The Chase

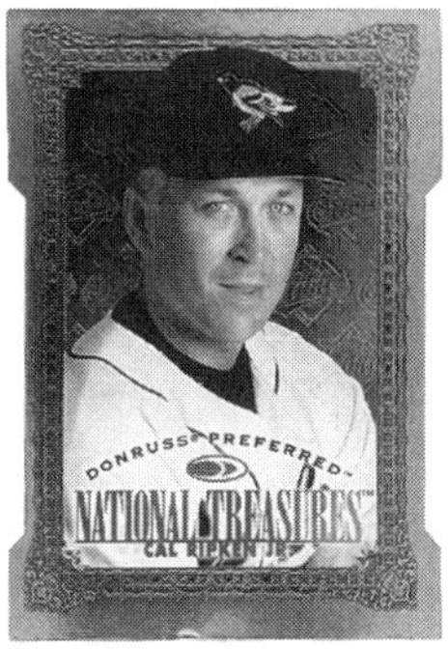

Each of the cards in the Donruss Preferred series can also be found in this parallel set with die-cut borders, in the same bronze, silver, gold and platinum finishes. Multiplier values of the die-cuts are inverse to that usually found, with platinum cards the lowest, followed by gold, silver and bronze. Besides die-cutting, the chase cards feature a "CUT TO THE CHASE" designation at bottom.

	MT
Complete Set (200):	4000.
Common Bronze:	.50
Bronze Stars: 3-6X	
Common Silver:	1.50
Silver Stars: 1.5-3X	
Common Gold:	4.00
Gold Stars: 2X	
Common Platinum:	10.00
Platinum Stars: 2X	
(See 1997 Donruss Preferred for checklist and base card values.)	

1997 Donruss Preferred Precious Metals

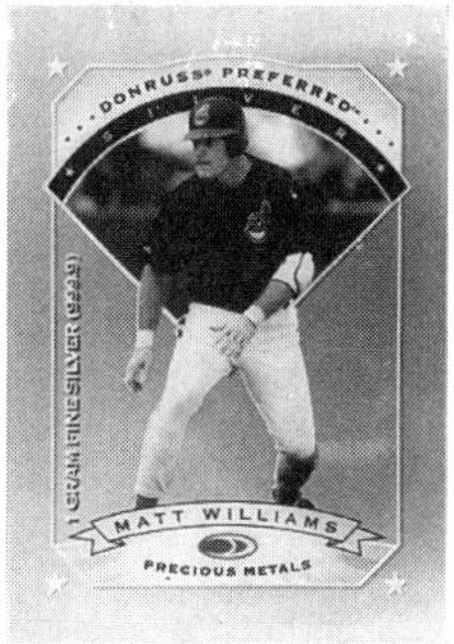

This 25-card partial parallel set features cards printed on actual silver, gold and platinum stock. Only 100 of each card were produced.

		MT
Complete Set (25):		4000.
Common Player:		20.00
1	Frank Thomas (P)	125.00
2	Ken Griffey Jr. (P)	250.00
3	Greg Maddux (P)	125.00
4	Albert Belle (G)	60.00
5	Juan Gonzalez (P)	125.00
6	Kenny Lofton (G)	55.00
7	Tony Gwynn (P)	125.00
8	Ivan Rodriguez (G)	60.00
9	Mark McGwire (G)	200.00
10	Matt Williams (S)	25.00
11	Wade Boggs (S)	35.00
12	Eddie Murray (S)	40.00
13	Jeff Bagwell (G)	75.00
14	Ken Caminiti (G)	55.00
15	Alex Rodriguez (P)	150.00
16	Chipper Jones (P)	125.00
17	Barry Bonds (G)	60.00
18	Cal Ripken Jr. (P)	200.00
19	Mo Vaughn (G)	55.00
20	Mike Piazza (P)	150.00
21	Derek Jeter (G)	125.00
22	Bernie Williams (S)	35.00
23	Andruw Jones (P)	90.00
24	Vladimir Guerrero (G)	60.00
25	Jose Guillen (S)	30.00

1997 Donruss Preferred Staremasters

A 20-card insert printed on foil stock and accented with holographic foil, Staremasters is designed to show up-close "game-face" photography. Each card is sequentially numbered to 1,500. Each of the Staremasters inserts can also be found in a version overprinted with a large diagonal black "SAMPLE" on front and back. These were distributed to dealers and the media. The sample cards have a "PROMO/1500" on back in place of a serial number.

		MT
Complete Set (20):		275.00
Common Player:		6.00
Samples: 20%		
1	Alex Rodriguez	25.00
2	Frank Thomas	20.00
3	Chipper Jones	25.00
4	Cal Ripken Jr.	30.00
5	Mike Piazza	25.00
6	Juan Gonzalez	17.50
7	Derek Jeter	20.00
8	Jeff Bagwell	15.00
9	Ken Griffey Jr.	40.00
10	Tony Gwynn	17.50
11	Barry Bonds	10.00
12	Albert Belle	7.50
13	Greg Maddux	20.00
14	Mark McGwire	40.00
15	Ken Caminiti	6.00
16	Hideo Nomo	6.00
17	Gary Sheffield	6.00
18	Andruw Jones	15.00
19	Mo Vaughn	7.50
20	Ivan Rodriguez	9.00

1997 Donruss Preferred Tins

Twenty-five different players are featured on the lithographed steel tins which were the "packs" of Donruss Preferred baseball. The 3" x 4-1/2" x 5/8" tins are hinged along the left side and were produced in two versions. Predominantly blue tins are the standard package. A premium parallel version is gold-colored and serially numbered within an edition of 1,200. Gold tins were packed one per 24-pack box of Preferred. Values shown are for opened tins. Shrink-wrapped unopened tins are valued about 1.5-3X the figures shown.

		MT
Complete Set, Blue (25):		15.00
Common Tin:		.50
Gold: 7-10X		
1	Frank Thomas	1.00
2	Ken Griffey Jr.	2.00
3	Andruw Jones	1.25
4	Cal Ripken Jr.	1.50
5	Mike Piazza	1.25
6	Chipper Jones	1.25
7	Alex Rodriguez	1.50
8	Derek Jeter	1.00
9	Juan Gonzalez	.75
10	Albert Belle	.60
11	Tony Gwynn	.75
12	Greg Maddux	.75
13	Jeff Bagwell	.60
14	Roger Clemens	.75
15	Mark McGwire	1.50
16	Gary Sheffield	.50
17	Manny Ramirez	.60
18	Hideo Nomo	.50
19	Kenny Lofton	.50
20	Mo Vaughn	.50
21	Ryne Sandberg	.50
22	Barry Bonds	.60
23	Sammy Sosa	1.00
24	John Smoltz	.50
25	Ivan Rodriguez	.60

1997 Donruss Preferred Tin Boxes

Twenty-five different players are featured on the lithographed steel boxes in which the "packs" of Donruss Preferred baseball were sold. Boxes measure about 5-1/4" x

9-1/4" x 5-3/8". Inside the removable lid is a serial number from within an edition of 1,200 (blue) or 299 (gold). The gold versions were a later, hobby-only release.

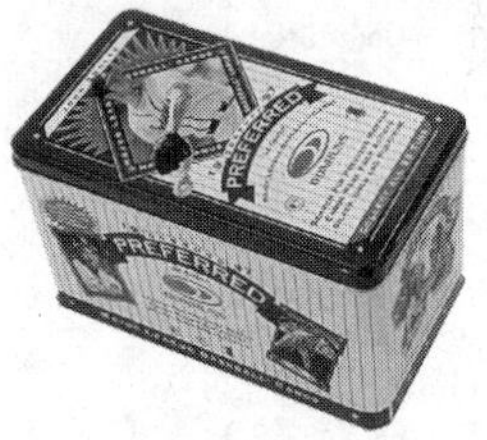

		MT
Complete Set, Blue (25):		115.00
Common Box:		3.00
Gold: 6-8X		
1	Frank Thomas	6.00
2	Ken Griffey Jr.	12.00
3	Andruw Jones	5.00
4	Cal Ripken Jr.	9.00
5	Mike Piazza	7.50
6	Chipper Jones	7.50
7	Alex Rodriguez	7.50
8	Derek Jeter	6.00
9	Juan Gonzalez	4.50
10	Albert Belle	3.50
11	Tony Gwynn	4.50
12	Greg Maddux	4.00
13	Jeff Bagwell	3.50
14	Roger Clemens	4.50
15	Mark McGwire	10.00
16	Gary Sheffield	3.00
17	Manny Ramirez	3.50
18	Hideo Nomo	3.00
19	Kenny Lofton	3.00
20	Mo Vaughn	3.00
21	Ryne Sandberg	3.50
22	Barry Bonds	4.00
23	Sammy Sosa	4.50
24	John Smoltz	3.00
25	Ivan Rodriguez	3.50

1997 Donruss Preferred X-Ponential Power

This 20-card die-cut insert contains two top hitters from 10 different teams. Placing the cards of teammates together forms an "X" shape. Cards are printed on thick plastic stock and gold holographic foil stamping and are sequentially numbered to 3,000.

		MT
Complete Set (20):		200.00
Common Player:		3.50
1A	Manny Ramirez	9.00
1B	Jim Thome	6.00
2A	Paul Molitor	5.50
2B	Chuck Knoblauch	3.50
3A	Ivan Rodriguez	6.50
3B	Juan Gonzalez	15.00
4A	Albert Belle	7.50
4B	Frank Thomas	15.00
5A	Roberto Alomar	6.50
5B	Cal Ripken Jr.	30.00
6A	Tim Salmon	3.50
6B	Jim Edmonds	3.50
7A	Ken Griffey Jr.	35.00
7B	Alex Rodriguez	25.00
8A	Chipper Jones	20.00
8B	Andruw Jones	12.00
9A	Mike Piazza	20.00
9B	Raul Mondesi	3.50
10A	Tony Gwynn	12.00
10B	Ken Caminiti	3.50

1997 Donruss Signature

Donruss ventured in the autograph-per-pack market with this series featuring 100 base cards (unsigned) and various types and versions of authentically autographed cards. The suggested retail price for each five-card pack was $14.99. Base cards have textured silver-foil borders and highlights on front. Backs have a second photo and lengthy stats. A parallel insert edition of each base card was also issued. labeled "Platinum Press Proof", the parallels have blue metallic foil on front and are designated "1 of 150" on the back.

		MT
Complete Set (100):		40.00
Common Player:		.20
1	Mark McGwire	5.00
2	Kenny Lofton	.75
3	Tony Gwynn	2.00
4	Tony Clark	.45
5	Tim Salmon	.40
6	Ken Griffey Jr.	4.00
7	Mike Piazza	2.50
8	Greg Maddux	2.00
9	Roberto Alomar	.75
10	Andres Galarraga	.30
11	Roger Clemens	1.50
12	Bernie Williams	.60
13	Rondell White	.30
14	Kevin Appler	.20
15	Ray Lankford	.20
16	Frank Thomas	2.00
17	Will Clark	.35
18	Chipper Jones	2.50
19	Jeff Bagwell	1.50
20	Manny Ramirez	1.00
21	Ryne Sandberg	1.00
22	Paul Molitor	.65
23	Gary Sheffield	.40
24	Jim Edmonds	.20
25	Barry Larkin	.30
26	Rafael Palmeiro	.30
27	Alan Benes	.20
28	David Justice	.30
29	Randy Johnson	.60
30	Barry Bonds	1.00
31	Mo Vaughn	.75
32	Michael Tucker	.20
33	Larry Walker	.40
34	Tino Martinez	.25
35	Jose Guillen	.60
36	Carlos Delgado	.75
37	Jason Dickson	.20
38	Tom Glavine	.30
39	Raul Mondesi	.30
40	*Jose Cruz Jr.*	.75
41	Johnny Damon	.20
42	Mark Grace	.30
43	Juan Gonzalez	2.00
44	Vladimir Guerrero	1.50
45	Kevin Brown	.25
46	Justin Thompson	.20
47	Eric Young	.20
48	Ron Coomer	.20
49	Mark Kotsay	.40
50	Scott Rolen	1.50
51	Derek Jeter	2.50
52	Jim Thome	.65
53	Fred McGriff	.30
54	Albert Belle	.75
55	Garret Anderson	.20
56	Wilton Guerrero	.20
57	Jose Canseco	.30
58	Cal Ripken Jr.	3.00
59	Sammy Sosa	2.00
60	Dmitri Young	.20
61	Alex Rodriguez	2.50
62	Javier Lopez	.20
63	Sandy Alomar Jr.	.25
64	Joe Carter	.20
65	Dante Bichette	.25
66	Al Martin	.20
67	Darin Erstad	1.25
68	Pokey Reese	.20
69	Brady Anderson	.25
70	Andruw Jones	1.50
71	Ivan Rodriguez	.75
72	Nomar Garciaparra	2.00
73	Moises Alou	.25
74	Andy Pettitte	.60
75	Jay Buhner	.25
76	Craig Biggio	.40
77	Wade Boggs	.50
78	Shawn Estes	.20
79	Neifi Perez	.20
80	Rusty Greer	.20
81	Pedro Martinez	.40
82	Mike Mussina	.60
83	Jason Giambi	.20
84	Hideo Nomo	.45
85	Todd Hundley	.20
86	Deion Sanders	.25
87	Mike Cameron	.20
88	Bobby Bonilla	.25
89	Todd Greene	.20
90	Kevin Orie	.20
91	Ken Caminiti	.30
92	Chuck Knoblauch	.40
93	Matt Morris	.20
94	Matt Williams	.40
95	Pat Hentgen	.20
96	John Smoltz	.30
97	Edgar Martinez	.20
98	Jason Kendall	.20
99	Ken Griffey Jr.	2.00
100	Frank Thomas	.75

1997 Donruss Signature Platinum Press Proofs

This parallel insert set features metallic blue borders and graphics on front and has a "1 of 150" notation on back.

	MT
Complete Set (100):	1500.
Common Player:	4.00
Stars: 15-25X	
(See 1997 Donruss Signature for checklist and base card prices.)	

1997 Donruss Signature Autographs (Red)

The basic level of authentically autographed cards found one per ($15) pack in Donruss Signature is the unnumbered "red" version. Cards have the background of the front photo printed only in red. For most players, 3,900 cards of the red version were autographed for insertion. Some players, however, signed fewer reds. Exchange cards had to be issued for Raul Mondesi and Edgar Renteria, whose signed cards were not ready when the set was first issued. It has been reported that Mondesi never signed any of the red version autograph cards. Cards are checklisted here in alphabetical order, in concordance with the larger Millenium checklist. The reported number of red cards signed appears in parentheses. This list differs significantly from the original list announced by Donruss in Nov. 1997 due to last minute additions and deletions. Players signed in black and/or blue ink. Some players also added personal touches to some or all of their signatures, such as Bible verse citations, uniform numbers, etc.

		MT
Complete Set (116):		1300.
Common Player:		5.00
(1)	Jeff Abbott (3900)	5.00
(2)	Bob Abreu (3900)	6.00
(3)	Edgardo Alfonzo (3900)	15.00
(4)	Roberto Alomar (150)	90.00
(5)	Sandy Alomar Jr. (1400)	15.00
(6)	Moises Alou (900)	20.00
(7)	Garret Anderson (3900)	10.00
(8)	Andy Ashby (3900)	6.00
(10)	Trey Beamon (3900)	5.00
(12)	Alan Benes (3900)	10.00
(13)	Geronimo Berroa (3900)	5.00
(14)	Wade Boggs (150)	100.00
(18)	Kevin L. Brown (3900)	5.00
(20)	Brett Butler (1400)	15.00
(21)	Mike Cameron (3900)	10.00
(22)	Giovanni Carrara (2900)	5.00
(23)	Luis Castillo (3900)	5.00
(24)	Tony Clark (3900)	15.00
(25)	Will Clark (1400)	25.00
(27)	Lou Collier (3900)	5.00
(28)	Bartolo Colon (3900)	9.00
(29)	Ron Coomer (3900)	5.00
(30)	Marty Cordova (3900)	5.00
(31)	Jacob Cruz (3900)	12.00
(32)	Jose Cruz Jr. (900)	35.00
(33)	Russ Davis (3900)	5.00
(34)	Jason Dickson (3900)	6.00
(35)	Todd Dunwoody (3900)	12.00
(36)	Jermaine Dye (3900)	5.00
(37)	Jim Edmonds (3900)	15.00
(38)	Darin Erstad (900)	40.00
(39)	Bobby Estalella (3900)	7.50
(40)	Shawn Estes (3900)	10.00
(41)	Jeff Fassero (3900)	7.50
(42)	Andres Galarraga (900)	20.00
(43)	Karim Garcia (3900)	12.00
(45)	Derrick Gibson (3900)	12.00
(46)	Brian Giles (3900)	7.50
(47)	Tom Glavine (150)	60.00
(49)	Rick Gorecki (900)	5.00
(50)	Shawn Green (1900)	25.00
(51)	Todd Greene (3900)	12.00
(52)	Rusty Greer (3900)	10.00
(53)	Ben Grieve (3900)	20.00
(54)	Mark Grudzielanek (3900)	5.00
(55)	Vladimir Guerrero (1900)	40.00
(56)	Wilton Guerrero (2150)	5.00
(57)	Jose Guillen (2900)	20.00
(59)	Jeffrey Hammonds (2150)	7.50
(60)	Todd Helton (1400)	25.00
(61)	Todd Hollandsworth (2900)	10.00
(62)	Trenidad Hubbard (900)	7.50
(63)	Todd Hundley (1400)	15.00
(66)	Bobby Jones (3900)	5.00
(68)	Brian Jordan (1400)	12.00
(69)	David Justice (900)	35.00
(70)	Eric Karros (650)	20.00
(71)	Jason Kendall (3900)	10.00
(72)	Jimmy Key (3900)	10.00
(73)	Brooks Kieschnick (3900)	5.00
(74)	Ryan Klesko (225)	40.00
(76)	Paul Konerko (3900)	20.00
(77)	Mark Kotsay (2400)	20.00
(78)	Ray Lankford (3900)	7.50
(79)	Barry Larkin (150)	50.00
(80)	Derrek Lee (3900)	12.00
(81)	Esteban Loaiza (3900)	5.00
(82)	Javier Lopez (1400)	20.00
(84)	Edgar Martinez (150)	40.00
(85)	Pedro Martinez (900)	50.00
(87)	Rafael Medina (3900)	5.00
(88)	Raul Mondesi (may not exist)	
(88)	Raul Mondesi (Exchange card)	5.00
(89)	Matt Morris (3900)	5.00
(92)	Paul O'Neill (900)	25.00
(93)	Kevin Orie (3900)	5.00
(94)	David Ortiz (3900)	5.00
(95)	Rafael Palmeiro (900)	25.00
(96)	Jay Payton (3900)	5.00
(97)	Neifi Perez (3900)	6.00
(99)	Manny Ramirez (900)	35.00
(100)	Joe Randa (3900)	5.00
(101)	Calvin Reese (3900)	5.00
(102)	Edgar Renteria (?)	25.00
(102)	Edgar Renteria (Exchange card)	5.00
(103)	Dennis Reyes (3900)	5.00
(106)	Henry Rodriguez (3900)	7.50
(108)	Scott Rolen (1900)	50.00
(109)	Kirk Rueter (2900)	5.00
(110)	Ryne Sandberg (400)	100.00
(112)	Dwight Smith (2900)	5.00
(113)	J.T. Snow (900)	15.00
(114)	Scott Spiezio (3900)	5.00
(115)	Shannon Stewart (2900)	10.00
(116)	Jeff Suppan (1900)	10.00
(117)	Mike Sweeney (3900)	5.00
(118)	Miguel Tejada (3900)	20.00
(121)	Justin Thompson (2400)	10.00
(122)	Brett Tomko (3900)	5.00
(123)	Bubba Trammell (3900)	15.00
(124)	Michael Tucker (3900)	5.00
(125)	Javier Valentin (3900)	5.00
(126)	Mo Vaughn (150)	100.00
(127)	Robin Ventura (1400)	20.00
(128)	Terrell Wade (3900)	5.00
(129)	Billy Wagner (3900)	10.00
(130)	Larry Walker (900)	50.00
(131)	Todd Walker (2400)	12.00
(132)	Rondell White (3900)	15.00
(133)	Kevin Wickander (900)	7.50
(134)	Chris Widger (3900)	5.00
(136)	Matt Williams (150)	50.00
(137)	Antone Williamson (3900)	5.00
(138)	Dan Wilson (3900)	5.00
(139)	Tony Womack (3900)	7.50
(140)	Jaret Wright (3900)	20.00
(141)	Dmitri Young (3900)	5.00
(142)	Eric Young (3900)	6.00
(143)	Kevin Young (3900)	5.00

1997 Donruss Signature Century Marks (Blue)

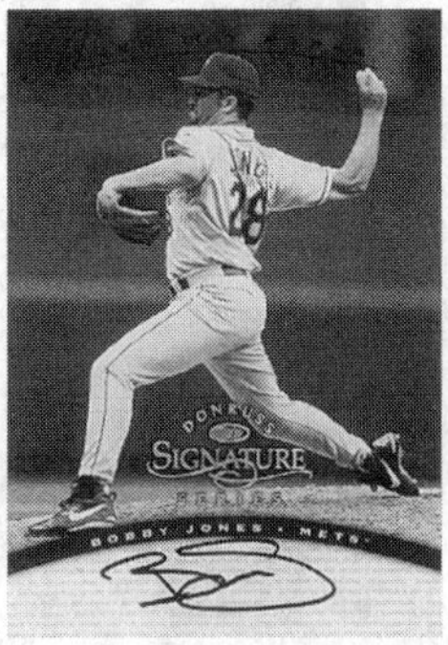

Only the top-name stars and rookies from the Signature series autograph line-up are included in the top level of scarcity. Virtually identical to the more common red and green (Millennium) versions, the Century Marks are identifiable at first glance by the use of blue ink in the background of the front photo and the "Century Marks" designation at top. On back, the cards are numbered from 0001 through

0100 in metallic foil at center. Several players initially had to be represented in the set by exchange cards. The unnumbered cards are checklisted here alphabetically, with the assigned card numbered keyed to the full 143-card issue in green.

		MT
Common Player:		20.00
(4)	Roberto Alomar	50.00
(9)	Jeff Bagwell	75.00
(11)	Albert Belle	60.00
(14)	Wade Boggs	50.00
(15)	Barry Bonds	75.00
(19)	Jay Buhner	20.00
(24)	Tony Clark	25.00
(25)	Will Clark	50.00
(26)	Roger Clemens	150.00
(32)	Jose Cruz Jr.	25.00
(37)	Jim Edmonds	20.00
(38)	Darin Erstad	30.00
(42)	Andres Galarraga	35.00
(44)	Nomar Garciaparra (SP)	200.00
(48)	Juan Gonzalez	125.00
(53)	Ben Grieve	40.00
(55)	Vladimir Guerrero	75.00
(57)	Jose Guillen	25.00
(58)	Tony Gwynn	150.00
(60)	Todd Helton	30.00
(64)	Derek Jeter	150.00
(65)	Andruw Jones	50.00
(67)	Chipper Jones	150.00
(69)	David Justice	30.00
(74)	Ryan Klesko	25.00
(75)	Chuck Knoblauch	30.00
(76)	Paul Konerko	20.00
(77)	Mark Kotsay	20.00
(79)	Barry Larkin	30.00
(83)	Greg Maddux	150.00
(84)	Edgar Martinez	20.00
(85)	Pedro Martinez	60.00
(86)	Tino Martinez	25.00
(88)	Raul Mondesi	35.00
(88)	Raul Mondesi (Exchange card)	5.00
(90)	Eddie Murray	40.00
(90)	Eddie Murray (Exchange card)	5.00
(91)	Mike Mussina	35.00
(95)	Rafael Palmeiro	40.00
(98)	Andy Pettitte	25.00
(99)	Manny Ramirez	60.00
(104)	Cal Ripken Jr.	200.00
(105)	Alex Rodriguez	175.00
(107)	Ivan Rodriguez	75.00
(108)	Scott Rolen	50.00
(110)	Ryne Sandberg	75.00
(111)	Gary Sheffield	35.00
(118)	Miguel Tejada	30.00
(119)	Frank Thomas	75.00
(120)	Jim Thome	35.00
(120)	Jim Thome (Exchange card)	5.00
(126)	Mo Vaughn	40.00
(130)	Larry Walker	40.00
(135)	Bernie Williams	40.00
(136)	Matt Williams	30.00
(140)	Jaret Wright	20.00

1997 Donruss Signature Millennium Marks (Green)

One thousand cards of each of the players who signed Signature Autographs are found in an edition marked on front as "Millennium Marks". These cards are also distinguished by the use of green ink in the background of the front photo. On back, the cards have a silver-foil serial number between (generally) 0101-1,000. Some cards as noted in the alphabetical checklist here were produced in lower numbers. The MM autographs were a random insert among the one-per-pack autographed cards found in $15 packs of Donruss Signature. Packs carried exchange cards redeemable for autographed cards of Raul Mondesi, Edgar Renteria and Jim Thome. This checklist differs significantly from that released in Nov., 1997, by Donruss due to the last-minute addition, deletion and substitution of players. It is possible that cards exist of players not shown here.

		MT
Complete Set (143):		1575.
Common Player:		5.00
(1)	Jeff Abbott	5.00
(2)	Bob Abreu	5.00
(3)	Edgardo Alfonzo	12.50
(4)	Roberto Alomar	15.00
(5)	Sandy Alomar Jr.	10.00
(6)	Moises Alou	7.50
(7)	Garret Anderson	5.00
(8)	Andy Ashby	7.50
(9)	Jeff Bagwell (400)	50.00
(10)	Trey Beamon	5.00
(11)	Albert Belle (400)	35.00
(12)	Alan Benes	5.00
(13)	Geronimo Berroa	5.00
(14)	Wade Boggs	30.00
(15)	Barry Bonds (400)	45.00
(16)	Bobby Bonilla (900)	12.50
(17)	Kevin Brown (000)	6.00
(18)	Kevin L. Brown	10.00
(19)	Jay Buhner (900)	6.00
(20)	Brett Butler	7.50
(21)	Mike Cameron	5.00
(22)	Giovanni Carrara	5.00
(23)	Luis Castillo	5.00
(24)	Tony Clark	10.00
(25)	Will Clark	15.00
(26)	Roger Clemens (400)	65.00
(27)	Lou Collier	5.00
(28)	Bartolo Colon	9.00
(29)	Ron Coomer	5.00
(30)	Marty Cordova	5.00
(31)	Jacob Cruz	5.00
(32)	Jose Cruz Jr.	7.50
(33)	Russ Davis	5.00
(34)	Jason Dickson	7.50
(35)	Todd Dunwoody	7.50
(36)	Jermaine Dye	5.00
(37)	Jim Edmonds	7.50
(38)	Darin Erstad	15.00
(39)	Bobby Estalella	5.00
(40)	Shawn Estes	5.00
(41)	Jeff Fassero	5.00
(42)	Andres Galarraga	9.00
(43)	Karim Garcia	7.50
(44)	Nomar Garciaparra (650)	90.00
(45)	Derrick Gibson	10.00
(46)	Brian Giles	7.50
(47)	Tom Glavine	15.00
(48)	Juan Gonzalez (900)	40.00
(49)	Rick Gorecki	5.00
(50)	Shawn Green	25.00
(51)	Todd Greene	7.50
(52)	Rusty Greer	5.00
(53)	Ben Grieve	15.00
(54)	Mark Grudzielanek	5.00
(55)	Vladimir Guerrero	20.00
(56)	Wilton Guerrero	5.00
(57)	Jose Guillen	10.00
(58)	Tony Gwynn (900)	35.00
(59)	Jeffrey Hammonds	5.00
(60)	Todd Helton	7.50
(61)	Todd Hollandsworth	5.00
(62)	Trenidad Hubbard	5.00
(63)	Todd Hundley	6.00
(64)	Derek Jeter (400)	100.00
(65)	Andruw Jones (900)	25.00
(66)	Bobby Jones	5.00
(67)	Chipper Jones	45.00
(68)	Brian Jordan	7.50
(69)	David Justice	9.00
(70)	Eric Karros	7.50
(71)	Jason Kendall	7.50
(72)	Jimmy Key	5.00
(73)	Brooks Kieschnick	5.00
(74)	Ryan Klesko	5.00
(75)	Chuck Knoblauch (900)	15.00
(76)	Paul Konerko	9.00
(77)	Mark Kotsay	12.50
(78)	Ray Lankford	5.00
(79)	Barry Larkin	9.00
(80)	Derrek Lee	6.00
(81)	Esteban Loaiza	5.00
(82)	Javy Lopez	8.00
(83)	Greg Maddux (400)	75.00
(84)	Edgar Martinez	6.00
(85)	Pedro Martinez	25.00
(86)	Tino Martinez (900)	15.00
(87)	Rafael Medina	5.00
(88)	Raul Mondesi	15.00
(88)	Raul Mondesi (Exchange card)	5.00
(89)	Matt Morris	5.00
(90)	Eddie Murray (900)	25.00
(91)	Mike Mussina (900)	12.50
(92)	Paul O'Neill	10.00
(93)	Kevin Orie	5.00
(94)	David Ortiz	5.00
(95)	Rafael Palmeiro	12.50
(96)	Jay Payton	5.00
(97)	Neifi Perez	5.00
(98)	Andy Petitte (900)	9.00
(99)	Manny Ramirez	15.00
(100)	Joe Randa	5.00
(101)	Calvin Reese	5.00
(102)	Edgar Renteria	12.50
(102)	Edgar Renteria (Exchange card)	5.00
(103)	Dennis Reyes	5.00
(104)	Cal Ripken Jr. (400)	150.00
(105)	Alex Rodriguez (400)	100.00
(106)	Henry Rodriguez	6.00
(107)	Ivan Rodriguez (900)	20.00
(108)	Scott Rolen	25.00
(109)	Kirk Rueter	5.00
(110)	Ryne Sandberg	35.00
(111)	Gary Sheffield (400)	25.00
(112)	Dwight Smith	5.00
(113)	J.T. Snow	7.50
(114)	Scott Spiezio	5.00
(115)	Shannon Stewart	5.00
(116)	Jeff Suppan	5.00
(117)	Mike Sweeney	5.00
(118)	Miguel Tejada	7.50
(119)	Frank Thomas (400)	75.00
(120)	Jim Thome (900)	15.00
(120)	Jim Thome (Exchange card)	5.00
(121)	Justin Thompson	5.00
(122)	Brett Tomko	5.00
(123)	Bubba Trammell	9.00
(124)	Michael Tucker	5.00
(125)	Javier Valentin	5.00
(126)	Mo Vaughn	15.00
(127)	Robin Ventura	12.50
(128)	Terrell Wade	5.00
(129)	Billy Wagner	12.50
(130)	Larry Walker	15.00
(131)	Todd Walker	9.00
(132)	Rondell White	7.50
(133)	Kevin Wickander	5.00
(134)	Chris Widger	5.00
(135)	Bernie Williams (400)	25.00
(136)	Matt Williams	15.00
(137)	Antone Williamson	5.00
(138)	Dan Wilson	5.00
(139)	Tony Womack	5.00
(140)	Jaret Wright	9.00
(141)	Dmitri Young	5.00
(142)	Eric Young	6.00
(143)	Kevin Young	5.00

1997 Donruss Signature Notable Nicknames

Current and former players whose nicknames are instantly recognized are featured in this Signature Series insert. The autographs are generally enhanced by the appearance of those nicknames, though Roger Clemens omitted "The Rocket" from many of his cards. Backs have a serial number from within an edition of 200 of each card.

		MT
Complete Set (13):		950.00
Common Player:		50.00
(1)	Ernie Banks (Mr. Cub)	100.00
(2)	Tony Clark (The Tiger)	50.00
(3)	Roger Clemens (The Rocket)	150.00
(4)	Reggie Jackson (Mr. October)	125.00
(5)	Randy Johnson (Big Unit)	100.00
(6)	Stan Musial (The Man)	150.00
(7)	Ivan Rodriguez (Pudge)	100.00
(8)	Frank Thomas (The Big Hurt)	125.00
(9)	Mo Vaughn (Hit Dog)	100.00
(10)	Billy Wagner (The Kid)	50.00

1997 Donruss Signature Significant Signatures

Retired superstars from the early 1960s through the mid 1990s are featured in this insert series. Cards are horizontal in format with color photos on front and back. Generally autographed on front, each card is serially numbered on back from within an edition of 2,000. The unnumbered cards are listed here in alphabetical order.

		MT
Complete Set (22):		850.00
Common Player:		15.00
(1)	Ernie Banks	50.00
(2)	Johnny Bench	60.00
(3)	Yogi Berra	50.00
(4)	George Brett	75.00
(5)	Lou Brock	30.00
(6)	Rod Carew	30.00
(7)	Steve Carlton	30.00
(8)	Larry Doby	30.00
(9)	Carlton Fisk	35.00
(10)	Bob Gibson	30.00
(11)	Reggie Jackson	60.00
(12)	Al Kaline	30.00
(13)	Harmon Killebrew	30.00
(14)	Don Mattingly	75.00
(15)	Stan Musial	75.00
(16)	Jim Palmer	30.00
(17)	Brooks Robinson	40.00
(18)	Frank Robinson	30.00
(19)	Mike Schmidt	75.00
(20)	Tom Seaver	40.00
(21)	Duke Snider	30.00
(22)	Carl Yastrzemski	50.00

1997 Donruss VXP 1.0

This set was issued to accompany the hobby's first major effort to bring baseball cards into the computer age. The standard-format cards have motion-variable portrait and action photos on front and another photo on back. Cards were sold in packs of 10 with one of six CD ROMs for about $10.

		MT
Complete Set (50):		35.00
Common Player:		.50
1	Darin Erstad	1.50
2	Jim Thome	.50
3	Alex Rodriguez	2.50
4	Greg Maddux	2.00
5	Scott Rolen	1.50
6	Roberto Alomar	.50
7	Tony Clark	.50
8	Randy Johnson	.75
9	Sammy Sosa	2.00
10	Jose Guillen	.50
11	Cal Ripken Jr.	3.00
12	Paul Molitor	1.50
13	Jose Cruz Jr.	.50
14	Barry Larkin	.50
15	Ken Caminiti	.50
16	Rafael Palmeiro	.75
17	Chuck Knoblauch	.50
18	Juan Gonzalez	2.00
19	Larry Walker	.75
20	Tony Gwynn	1.75
21	Brady Anderson	.50
22	Derek Jeter	2.00
23	Rusty Greer	.50
24	Gary Sheffield	.50
25	Barry Bonds	1.50
26	Mo Vaughn	.75
27	Tino Martinez	.50
28	Ivan Rodriguez	.75
29	Jeff Bagwell	.75
30	Tim Salmon	.50
31	Nomar Garciaparra	1.75
32	Bernie Williams	.50
33	Kenny Lofton	.50
34	Mike Piazza	2.00
35	Jim Edmonds	.50
36	Frank Thomas	2.00
37	Andy Pettitte	.50
38	Andruw Jones	1.50
39	Raul Mondesi	.75
40	John Smoltz	.50
41	Albert Belle	.75
42	Mark McGwire	5.00
43	Chipper Jones	2.50
44	Hideo Nomo	.60
45	David Justice	.50
46	Manny Ramirez	.75
47	Ken Griffey Jr.	5.00
48	Roger Clemens	1.50
49	Vladimir Guerrero	1.50
50	Ryne Sandberg	1.00

1997 Donruss VXP 1.0 CDs

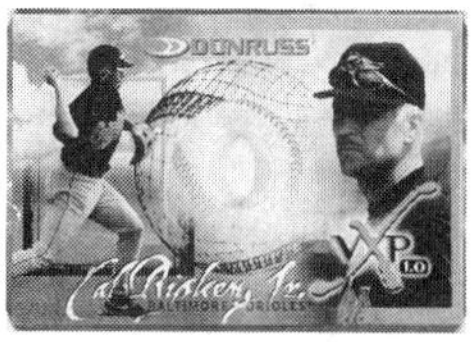

One of the earliest attempts to bring baseball cards into the computer age was Donruss "VXP 1.0 CD ROM" trading cards. Retailed, with 10 special series player cards for about $10, the 4" x 2-3/4" "card" is a CD with player portrait and action photos on front. The CD was sold in a cardboard folder with the player's picture on front and instructions for use inside. CDs feature player stats, action footage and other interactive elements.

		MT
Complete Set (6):		25.00
Common Player:		4.00
(1)	Ken Griffey Jr.	6.00
(2)	Greg Maddux	4.00
(3)	Mike Piazza	4.00
(4)	Cal Ripken Jr.	5.00
(5)	Alex Rodriguez	5.00
(6)	Frank Thomas	4.00

1998 Donruss

This 170-card set includes 155 regular player cards, the 10-card Fan Club subset and five checklists. The cards have color photos and the player's name listed at the bottom. The backs have a horizontal layout with stats and a biography on the left and another photo on the right. The base set is paralleled twice. Silver Press Proofs is a silver foil and die-cut parallel numbered "1 of 1,500." Gold Press Proofs is die-cut, has gold foil and is numbered "1 of 500." The inserts are Crusade, Diamond Kings, Longball Leaders, Production Line and Rated Rookies.

	MT
Complete Set (420):	45.00
Complete Series 1 (170):	20.00

Complete Update 2 (250):		25.00
Common Player:		.10
Wax Box:		45.00
1	Paul Molitor	.50
2	Juan Gonzalez	1.50
3	Darryl Kile	.10
4	Randy Johnson	.40
5	Tom Glavine	.20
6	Pat Hentgen	.10
7	David Justice	.25
8	Kevin Brown	.15
9	Mike Mussina	.60
10	Ken Caminiti	.20
11	Todd Hundley	.20
12	Frank Thomas	1.50
13	Ray Lankford	.10
14	Justin Thompson	.10
15	Jason Dickson	.10
16	Kenny Lofton	.75
17	Ivan Rodriguez	.60
18	Pedro Martinez	.40
19	Brady Anderson	.20
20	Barry Larkin	.20
21	Chipper Jones	2.00
22	Tony Gwynn	1.50
23	Roger Clemens	1.00
24	Sandy Alomar Jr.	.15
25	Tino Martinez	.20
26	Jeff Bagwell	1.25
27	Shawn Estes	.10
28	Ken Griffey Jr.	3.00
29	Javier Lopez	.20
30	Denny Neagle	.10
31	Mike Piazza	2.00
32	Andres Galarraga	.20
33	Larry Walker	.25
34	Alex Rodriguez	2.50
35	Greg Maddux	1.50
36	Albert Belle	.75
37	Barry Bonds	.75
38	Mo Vaughn	.75
39	Kevin Appier	.10
40	Wade Boggs	.30
41	Garret Anderson	.10
42	Jeffrey Hammonds	.10
43	Marquis Grissom	.10
44	Jim Edmonds	.10
45	Brian Jordan	.10
46	Raul Mondesi	.20
47	John Valentin	.10
48	Brad Radke	.10
49	Ismael Valdes	.10
50	Matt Stairs	.10
51	Matt Williams	.20
52	Reggie Jefferson	.10
53	Alan Benes	.10
54	Charles Johnson	.10
55	Chuck Knoblauch	.25
56	Edgar Martinez	.10
57	Nomar Garciaparra	1.75
58	Craig Biggio	.20
59	Bernie Williams	.50
60	David Cone	.20
61	Cal Ripken Jr.	2.50
62	Mark McGwire	4.00
63	Roberto Alomar	.50
64	Fred McGriff	.20
65	Eric Karros	.10
66	Robin Ventura	.15
67	Darin Erstad	.75
68	Michael Tucker	.10
69	Jim Thome	.40
70	Mark Grace	.25
71	Lou Collier	.10
72	Karim Garcia	.20
73	Alex Fernandez	.10
74	J.T. Snow	.10
75	Reggie Sanders	.10
76	John Smoltz	.10
77	Tim Salmon	.25
78	Paul O'Neill	.20
79	Vinny Castilla	.10
80	Rafael Palmeiro	.20
81	Jaret Wright	.75
82	Jay Buhner	.20
83	Brett Butler	.10
84	Todd Greene	.10
85	Scott Rolen	1.50
86	Sammy Sosa	2.00
87	Jason Giambi	.10
88	Carlos Delgado	.40
89	Deion Sanders	.15
90	Wilton Guerrero	.10
91	Andy Pettitte	.50
92	Brian Giles	.10
93	Dmitri Young	.10
94	Ron Coomer	.10
95	Mike Cameron	.10
96	Edgardo Alfonzo	.20
97	Jimmy Key	.10
98	Ryan Klesko	.20
99	Andy Benes	.10
100	Derek Jeter	1.75
101	Jeff Fassero	.10
102	Neifi Perez	.10
103	Hideo Nomo	.35
104	Andruw Jones	1.50
105	Todd Helton	.75
106	Livan Hernandez	.15
107	Brett Tomko	.10
108	Shannon Stewart	.10
109	Bartolo Colon	.10
110	Matt Morris	.10
111	Miguel Tejada	.50
112	Pokey Reese	.10
113	Fernando Tatis	.25
114	Todd Dunwoody	.10
115	Jose Cruz Jr.	.25
116	Chan Ho Park	.10
117	Kevin Young	.10
118	Rickey Henderson	.20
119	Hideki Irabu	.75
120	Francisco Cordova	.10
121	Al Martin	.10
122	Tony Clark	.30
123	Curt Schilling	.15
124	Rusty Greer	.10
125	Jose Canseco	.25
126	Edgar Renteria	.10
127	Todd Walker	.20
128	Wally Joyner	.10
129	Bill Mueller	.10
130	Jose Guillen	.40
131	Manny Ramirez	.75
132	Bobby Higginson	.10
133	Kevin Orie	.10
134	Will Clark	.20
135	Dave Nilsson	.10
136	Jason Kendall	.10
137	Ivan Cruz	.10
138	Gary Sheffield	.25
139	Bubba Trammell	.20
140	Vladimir Guerrero	1.00
141	Dennis Reyes	.10
142	Bobby Bonilla	.15
143	Ruben Rivera	.10
144	Ben Grieve	.75
145	Moises Alou	.20
146	Tony Womack	.10
147	Eric Young	.10
148	Paul Konerko	.75
149	Dante Bichette	.20
150	Joe Carter	.15
151	Rondell White	.20
152	Chris Holt	.10
153	Shawn Green	.25
154	Mark Grudzielanek	.10
155	Jermaine Dye	.10
156	Ken Griffey Jr. (Fan Club)	1.50
157	Frank Thomas (Fan Club)	.75
158	Chipper Jones (Fan Club)	1.00
159	Mike Piazza (Fan Club)	1.00
160	Cal Ripken Jr. (Fan Club)	1.25
161	Greg Maddux (Fan Club)	1.00
162	Juan Gonzalez (Fan Club)	.75
163	Alex Rodriguez (Fan Club)	1.25
164	Mark McGwire (Fan Club)	1.50
165	Derek Jeter Fan Club)	1.00
166	Larry Walker CL	.20
167	Tony Gwynn CL	.75
168	Tino Martinez CL	.15
169	Scott Rolen CL	.75
170	Nomar Garciaparra CL	1.00
171	Mike Sweeney	.10
172	Dustin Hermanson	.10
173	Darren Dreifort	.10
174	Ron Gant	.20
175	Todd Hollandsworth	.10
176	John Jaha	.10
177	Kerry Wood	.50
178	Chris Stynes	.10
179	Kevin Elster	.10
180	Derek Bell	.10
181	Darryl Strawberry	.20
182	Damion Easley	.10
183	Jeff Cirillo	.10
184	John Thomson	.10
185	Dan Wilson	.10
186	Jay Bell	.10
187	Bernard Gilkey	.10
188	Marc Valdes	.10
189	Ramon Martinez	.20
190	Charles Nagy	.10
191	Derek Lowe	.10
192	Andy Benes	.10
193	Delino DeShields	.10
194	*Ryan Jackson*	.40
195	Kenny Lofton	.75
196	Chuck Knoblauch	.25
197	Andres Galarraga	.25
198	Jose Canseco	.25
199	John Olerud	.25
200	Lance Johnson	.10
201	Darryl Kile	.10
202	Luis Castillo	.10
203	Joe Carter	.15
204	Dennis Eckersley	.20
205	Steve Finley	.10
206	Esteban Loaiza	.10
207	*Ryan Christenson*	.25
208	Deivi Cruz	.10
209	Mariano Rivera	.15
210	*Mike Judd*	.25
211	Billy Wagner	.15
212	Scott Spiezio	.10
213	Russ Davis	.10
214	Jeff Suppan	.10
215	Doug Glanville	.10
216	Dmitri Young	.10
217	Rey Ordonez	.10
218	Cecil Fielder	.15
219	*Masato Yoshii*	.50
220	Raul Casanova	.10
221	*Rolando Arrojo*	.40
222	Ellis Burks	.10
223	Butch Huskey	.10
224	Brian Hunter	.10
225	Marquis Grissom	.10
226	Kevin Brown	.15
227	Joe Randa	.10
228	Henry Rodriguez	.10
229	Omar Vizquel	.10
230	Fred McGriff	.25
231	Matt Williams	.25
232	Moises Alou	.20
233	Travis Fryman	.20
234	Wade Boggs	.35
235	Pedro Martinez	.65
236	Rickey Henderson	.25
237	Bubba Trammell	.10
238	Mike Caruso	.20
239	Wilson Alvarez	.10
240	Geronimo Berroa	.10
241	Eric Milton	.10
242	Scott Erickson	.10
243	*Todd Erdos*	.20
244	Bobby Hughes	.10
245	Dave Hollins	.10
246	Dean Palmer	.10
247	Carlos Baerga	.10
248	Jose Silva	.10
249	*Jose Cabrera*	.20
250	Tom Evans	.10
251	Marty Cordova	.10
252	*Hanley Frias*	.20
253	Javier Valentin	.10
254	Mario Valdez	.10
255	Joey Cora	.10
256	Mike Lansing	.10
257	Jeff Kent	.10
258	*David Dellucci*	.50
259	*Curtis King*	.10
260	David Segui	.10
261	Royce Clayton	.10
262	Jeff Blauser	.10
263	*Manny Aybar*	.25
264	*Mike Cather*	.20
265	Todd Zeile	.10
266	Richard Hidalgo	.10
267	Dante Powell	.10
268	*Mike DeJean*	.10
269	Ken Cloude	.10
270	Danny Klassen	.20
271	Sean Casey	.25
272	A.J. Hinch	.50
273	*Rich Butler*	.25
274	*Ben Ford*	.10
275	Billy McMillon	.10
276	Wilson Delgado	.10
277	Orlando Cabrera	.10
278	Geoff Jenkins	.10
279	Enrique Wilson	.10
280	Derrek Lee	.10
281	*Marc Pisciotta*	.10
282	Abraham Nunez	.20
283	Aaron Boone	.10
284	Brad Fullmer	.20
285	*Rob Stanifer*	.25
286	Preston Wilson	.10
287	Greg Norton	.10
288	Bobby Smith	.10
289	Josh Booty	.10
290	Russell Branyan	.10
291	Jeremi Gonzalez	.10
292	Michael Coleman	.10
293	Cliff Politte	.10
294	Eric Ludwick	.10
295	Rafael Medina	.10
296	Jason Varitek	.10
297	Ron Wright	.10
298	Mark Kotsay	.25
299	David Ortiz	.15
300	*Frank Catalanotto*	.20
301	Robinson Checo	.10
302	*Kevin Millwood*	2.50
303	Jacob Cruz	.10
304	Javier Vazquez	.10
305	*Magglio Ordonez*	1.50
306	Kevin Witt	.10
307	Derrick Gibson	.10
308	Shane Monahan	.10
309	Brian Rose	.10
310	Bobby Estalella	.10
311	Felix Heredia	.10
312	Desi Relaford	.10
313	*Esteban Yan*	.20
314	Ricky Ledee	.25
315	*Steve Woodard*	.25
316	Pat Watkins	.10
317	Damian Moss	.10
318	Bob Abreu	.10
319	Jeff Abbott	.10
320	Miguel Cairo	.10
321	*Rigo Beltran*	.10
322	Tony Saunders	.10
323	Randall Simon	.25
324	Hiram Bocachica	.10
325	Richie Sexson	.10
326	Karim Garcia	.10
327	*Mike Lowell*	.40
328	Pat Cline	.10
329	Matt Clement	.10
330	Scott Elarton	.10
331	*Manuel Barrios*	.10
332	Bruce Chen	.40
333	Juan Encarnacion	.10
334	Travis Lee	.75
335	Wes Helms	.10
336	*Chad Fox*	.10
337	Donnie Sadler	.10
338	*Carlos Mendoza*	.35
339	Damian Jackson	.10
340	*Julio Ramirez*	.40
341	*John Halama*	.30
342	Edwin Diaz	.10
343	Felix Martinez	.10
344	Eli Marrero	.10
345	Carl Pavano	.10
346	Vladimir Guerrero (Hit List)	.40
347	Barry Bonds (Hit List)	.40
348	Darin Erstad (Hit List)	.40
349	Albert Belle (Hit List)	.40
350	Kenny Lofton (Hit List)	.40
351	Mo Vaughn (Hit List)	.40
352	Jose Cruz Jr. (Hit List)	.25
353	Tony Clark (Hit List)	.25
354	Roberto Alomar (Hit List)	.25
355	Manny Ramirez (Hit List)	.50
356	Paul Molitor (Hit List)	.25
357	Jim Thome (Hit List)	.25
358	Tino Martinez (Hit List)	.20
359	Tim Salmon (Hit List)	.20
360	David Justice (Hit List)	.20
361	Raul Mondesi (Hit List)	.10
362	Mark Grace (Hit List)	.10
363	Craig Biggio (Hit List)	.10
364	Larry Walker (Hit List)	.10
365	Mark McGwire (Hit List)	1.50
366	Juan Gonzalez (Hit List)	.75
367	Derek Jeter (Hit List)	.75
368	Chipper Jones (Hit List)	1.00
369	Frank Thomas (Hit List)	.50
370	Alex Rodriguez (Hit List)	1.00
371	Mike Piazza (Hit List)	1.00
372	Tony Gwynn (Hit List)	.75
373	Jeff Bagwell (Hit List)	.50
374	Nomar Garciaparra (Hit List)	1.00
375	Ken Griffey Jr. (Hit List)	1.50
376	Livan Hernandez (Untouchables)	.10
377	Chan Ho Park (Untouchables)	.10
378	Mike Mussina (Untouchables)	.25
379	Andy Pettitte (Untouchables)	.25
380	Greg Maddux (Untouchables)	1.00
381	Hideo Nomo (Untouchables)	.25
382	Roger Clemens (Untouchables)	.75
383	Randy Johnson (Untouchables)	.25
384	Pedro Martinez (Untouchables)	.25
385	Jaret Wright (Untouchables)	.40
386	Ken Griffey Jr. (Spirit of the Game)	1.50
387	Todd Helton (Spirit of the Game)	.40
388	Paul Konerko (Spirit of the Game)	.10
389	Cal Ripken Jr. (Spirit of the Game)	1.25
390	Larry Walker (Spirit of the Game)	.10
391	Ken Caminiti (Spirit of the Game)	.10
392	Jose Guillen (Spirit of the Game)	.10
393	Jim Edmonds (Spirit of the Game)	.10
394	Barry Larkin (Spirit of the Game)	.10
395	Bernie Williams (Spirit of the Game)	.25
396	Tony Clark (Spirit of the Game)	.20
397	Jose Cruz Jr. (Spirit of the Game)	.25
398	Ivan Rodriguez (Spirit of the Game)	.40
399	Darin Erstad (Spirit of the Game)	.40
400	Scott Rolen (Spirit of the Game)	.50
401	Mark McGwire (Spirit of the Game)	1.50
402	Andruw Jones (Spirit of the Game)	.40
403	Juan Gonzalez (Spirit of the Game)	.75
404	Derek Jeter (Spirit of the Game)	.75
405	Chipper Jones (Spirit of the Game)	1.00
406	Greg Maddux (Spirit of the Game)	1.00
407	Frank Thomas (Spirit of the Game)	.50
408	Alex Rodriguez (Spirit of the Game)	1.00
409	Mike Piazza (Spirit of the Game)	1.00
410	Tony Gwynn (Spirit of the Game)	.75
411	Jeff Bagwell (Spirit of the Game)	.50
412	Nomar Garciaparra (Spirit of the Game)	1.00
413	Hideo Nomo (Spirit of the Game)	.25
414	Barry Bonds (Spirit of the Game)	.40
415	Ben Grieve (Spirit of the Game)	.50
416	Checklist (Barry Bonds)	.25
417	Checklist (Mark McGwire)	1.00
418	Checklist (Roger Clemens)	.40
419	Checklist (Livan Hernandez)	.10
420	Checklist (Ken Griffey Jr.)	1.00

1998 Donruss Silver Press Proofs

Silver Press Proofs paralleled all 420 cards in the Donruss and Donruss Update Baseball. Cards featured silver foil stamping and a die-cut top right corner. Backs had a silver tint and were numbered "1 of 1500" in the bottom left corner.

	MT
Complete Set (420):	1500.
Common Player:	1.50

Stars: 6x to 12x
Young Stars/RCs: 4x to 8x
Production 1,500 sets
(See 1998 Donruss for checklist and base card values.)

1998 Donruss Gold Press Proofs

All 420 cards in Donruss and Donruss Update were also issued in Gold Press Proofs. These cards were die-cut on the top right corner and contained gold foil stamping. Backs featured a gold tint and "1 of 500" was printed in black in the bottom left corner.

	MT
Complete Set (420):	4000.
Common Player:	4.00

Stars: 20x to 40x
Young Stars/RCs: 12x to 25x
Production 500 sets
(See 1998 Donruss for checklist and base card values.)

1998 Donruss Crusade

This 100-card insert was included in 1998 Donruss (40 cards), Leaf (30) and Donruss Update (30). The cards use refractive technology and the background features heraldic-style lions. The cards are sequentially numbered to 250. Crusade Purple (numbered to 100) and Red (25) parallels were also inserted in the three products.

		MT
Complete Set (40):		600.00
Common Player:		5.00
Production 250 sets		
Purples: 1.5X		
Production 100 sets		
Reds: 4-6X		
Production 25 sets		
5	Jason Dickson	5.00
6	Todd Greene	10.00
7	Roberto Alomar	15.00
8	Cal Ripken Jr.	75.00
12	Mo Vaughn	20.00
13	Nomar Garciaparra	45.00
16	Mike Cameron	7.50
20	Sandy Alomar Jr.	10.00
21	David Justice	12.50
25	Justin Thompson	5.00
27	Kevin Appier	5.00
33	Tino Martinez	10.00
36	Hideki Irabu	7.50
37	Jose Canseco	12.50
39	Ken Griffey Jr.	100.00
42	Edgar Martinez	5.00
45	Will Clark	12.50
47	Rusty Greer	5.00
50	Shawn Green	17.50
51	Jose Cruz Jr.	7.50
52	Kenny Lofton	15.00
53	Chipper Jones	45.00
62	Kevin Orie	5.00
65	Deion Sanders	7.50
67	Larry Walker	15.00
68	Dante Bichette	7.50
71	Todd Helton	20.00
74	Bobby Bonilla	7.50
75	Kevin Brown	10.00
78	Craig Biggio	10.00
82	Wilton Guerrero	5.00
85	Pedro Martinez	20.00
86	Edgardo Alfonzo	7.50
88	Scott Rolen	35.00
89	Francisco Cordova	5.00
90	Jose Guillen	10.00
92	Ray Lankford	5.00
93	Mark McGwire	125.00
94	Matt Morris	7.50
100	Shawn Estes	5.00

1998 Donruss Diamond Kings

Diamond Kings is a 20-card insert featuring a painted portrait by Dan Gardiner of the player on the card front. The backs have a ghosted image of the portrait with a player biography and the card's number overprinted. A total of 10,000 sets were produced with the first 500 of each card printed on canvas. A Frank Thomas sample card was also created.

		MT
Complete Set (20):		150.00
Common Player:		4.00
Production 9,500 sets		
Canvas (1st 500 sets): 2-4X		
1	Cal Ripken Jr.	20.00
2	Greg Maddux	12.50
3	Ivan Rodriguez	7.50
4	Tony Gwynn	10.00
5	Paul Molitor	5.00
6	Kenny Lofton	5.00
7	Andy Pettitte	4.00
8	Darin Erstad	7.50
9	Randy Johnson	5.00
10	Derek Jeter	15.00
11	Hideo Nomo	4.00
12	David Justice	4.00
13	Bernie Williams	4.00
14	Roger Clemens	9.00
15	Barry Larkin	4.00
16	Andruw Jones	7.50
17	Mike Piazza	15.00
18	Frank Thomas	12.50
19	Alex Rodriguez	20.00
20	Ken Griffey Jr.	25.00

1998 Donruss Longball Leaders

Longball Leaders features 24 top home run hitters. The right border features a home run meter with zero at the bottom, 61 at the top and the player's 1997 home run total marked. Each card is sequentially numbered to 5,000.

		MT
Complete Set (24):		125.00
Common Player:		1.00
Production 5,000 sets		
1	Ken Griffey Jr.	20.00
2	Mark McGwire	20.00
3	Tino Martinez	1.00
4	Barry Bonds	3.50
5	Frank Thomas	7.50
6	Albert Belle	2.00
7	Mike Piazza	10.00
8	Chipper Jones	10.00
9	Vladimir Guerrero	3.00
10	Matt Williams	1.50
11	Sammy Sosa	9.00
12	Tim Salmon	1.00
13	Raul Mondesi	1.00
14	Jeff Bagwell	5.00
15	Mo Vaughn	3.00
16	Manny Ramirez	4.00
17	Jim Thome	2.00
18	Jim Edmonds	1.00
19	Tony Clark	2.00
20	Nomar Garciaparra	9.00
21	Juan Gonzalez	5.00
22	Scott Rolen	4.00
23	Larry Walker	4.00
24	Andres Galarraga	1.00

1998 Donruss Production Line-ob

This 20-card insert is printed on holographic foil board. Inserted in magazine packs, this insert features player's with a high on-base percentage in 1997. Each player's card is sequentially numbered to his on-base percentage from that season. The card back has a player photo and a list of the 20 players with their stat.

		MT
Complete Set (20):		500.00
Common Player:		7.50
1	Frank Thomas (456)	40.00
2	Edgar Martinez (456)	7.50
3	Barry Bonds (446)	20.00
4	Barry Larkin (410)	7.50
5	Mike Piazza (431)	70.00
6	Jeff Bagwell (425)	40.00
7	Gary Sheffield (424)	10.00
8	Mo Vaughn (420)	15.00
9	Craig Biggio (415)	10.00
10	Kenny Lofton (409)	15.00
11	Tony Gwynn (409)	50.00
12	Bernie Williams (408)	15.00
13	Rusty Greer (405)	7.50
14	Brady Anderson (393)	7.50
15	Mark McGwire (393)	100.00
16	Chuck Knoblauch (390)	12.50
17	Roberto Alomar (390)	15.00
18	Ken Griffey Jr. (382)	100.00
19	Chipper Jones (371)	70.00
20	Derek Jeter (370)	65.00

1998 Donruss Production Line-pi

This 20-card insert was printed on holographic board. The set features players with a high power index from 1997. Each card is sequentially numbered to that player's power index from that season.

		MT
Complete Set (20):		300.00
Common Player:		5.00
1	Larry Walker (1,172)	9.00
2	Mike Piazza (1,070)	30.00
3	Frank Thomas (1,067)	25.00
4	Mark McGwire (1,039)	50.00
5	Barry Bonds (1,031)	12.50
6	Ken Griffey Jr. (1,028)	50.00
7	Jeff Bagwell (1,017)	20.00
8	David Justice (1,013)	5.00
9	Jim Thome (1,001)	7.50
10	Mo Vaughn (980)	6.00
11	Tony Gwynn (957)	25.00
12	Manny Ramirez (953)	12.50
13	Bernie Williams (952)	7.50
14	Tino Martinez (948)	5.00
15	Brady Anderson (863)	5.00
16	Chipper Jones (850)	30.00
17	Scott Rolen (846)	15.00
18	Alex Rodriguez (846)	35.00
19	Vladimir Guerrero (833)	12.50
20	Albert Belle (823)	12.50

1998 Donruss Production Line-sg

This 20-card insert was printed on holographic board. It featured players with high slugging percentages in 1997. Each card is sequentially numbered to the player's slugging percentage from that season.

		MT
Complete Set (20):		400.00
Common Player:		7.50
1	Larry Walker (720)	10.00
2	Ken Griffey Jr. (646)	75.00
3	Mark McGwire (646)	75.00
4	Mike Piazza (638)	45.00
5	Frank Thomas (611)	35.00
6	Jeff Bagwell (592)	30.00
7	Juan Gonzalez (589)	35.00
8	Andres Galarraga (585)	7.50
9	Barry Bonds (585)	20.00
10	Jim Thome (579)	7.50
11	Tino Martinez (577)	7.50
12	Mo Vaughn (560)	10.00
13	Raul Mondesi (541)	7.50
14	Manny Ramirez (538)	17.50
15	Nomar Garciaparra (601)	40.00
16	Tim Salmon (517)	7.50
17	Tony Clark (500)	7.50
18	Jose Cruz Jr. (499)	7.50
19	Alex Rodriguez (496)	50.00
20	Cal Ripken Jr. (402)	55.00

1998 Donruss Rated Rookies

This 30-card insert features top young players. The fronts have a color player photo in front of a stars and stripes background, with "Rated Rookies" and the player's name printed on the right. The backs have another photo, basic player information and career highlights. A rare (250 each) Medalist version is micro-etched on gold holographic foil.

		MT
Complete Set (30):		35.00
Common Player:		1.00
Medalists (250 sets): 5-10X		
1	Mark Kotsay	2.00
2	Neifi Perez	1.00
3	Paul Konerko	2.00
4	Jose Cruz Jr.	1.50
5	Hideki Irabu	1.25
6	Mike Cameron	1.00
7	Jeff Suppan	1.00
8	Kevin Orie	1.00
9	Pokey Reese	1.00
10	Todd Dunwoody	1.00
11	Miguel Tejada	2.00
12	Jose Guillen	1.50
13	Bartolo Colon	1.00
14	Derrek Lee	1.00
15	Antone Williamson	1.00
16	Wilton Guerrero	1.00
17	Jaret Wright	2.00
18	Todd Helton	2.00
19	Shannon Stewart	1.00
20	Nomar Garciaparra	7.50
21	Brett Tomko	1.00
22	Fernando Tatis	2.00
23	Raul Ibanez	1.00
24	Dennis Reyes	1.00
25	Bobby Estalella	1.00
26	Lou Collier	1.00
27	Bubba Trammell	1.00
28	Ben Grieve	2.50
29	Ivan Cruz	1.00
30	Karim Garcia	1.50

1998 Donruss Update Crusade

This 30-card insert is continued from 1998 Donruss and Leaf baseball sets. Each card features a color action photo in front of a Medieval background. The player's name and background are green and each card is serial numbered to 250. Purple (numbered to 100) and Red (25) parallel versions were also created. Crusade is a 130-card cross-brand insert with 40 cards included in 1998 Donruss and 30 each in 1998 Leaf and Leaf Rookies & Stars.

		MT
Complete Set (30):		400.00
Common Player:		5.00
Production 250 sets		
Purples (100 sets). 1.5X		
Reds (25 sets): 4-6X		
1	Tim Salmon	7.50
8	Garret Anderson	[illegible]
9	Rafael Palmeiro	12.50
10	Brady Anderson	5.00
14	Frank Thomas	45.00
17	Robin Ventura	10.00
22	Matt Williams	10.00
23	Tony Clark	9.00
29	Chuck Knoblauch	10.00
31	Bernie Williams	10.00
32	Derek Jeter	50.00
38	Jason Giambi	5.00
43	Jay Buhner	7.50
44	Juan Gonzalez	50.00
49	Carlos Delgado	10.00
55	Greg Maddux	60.00
57	Tom Glavine	7.50
60	Mark Grace	12.50
61	Sammy Sosa	60.00
63	Barry Larkin	7.50
69	Neifi Perez	5.00
72	Gary Sheffield	9.00
77	Jeff Bagwell	37.50
80	Raul Mondesi	7.50
81	Hideo Nomo	7.50
83	Rondell White	7.50
84	Vladimir Guerrero	25.00
87	Todd Hundley	5.00
96	Brian Jordan	5.00
99	Barry Bonds	25.00

1998 Donruss Update Dominators

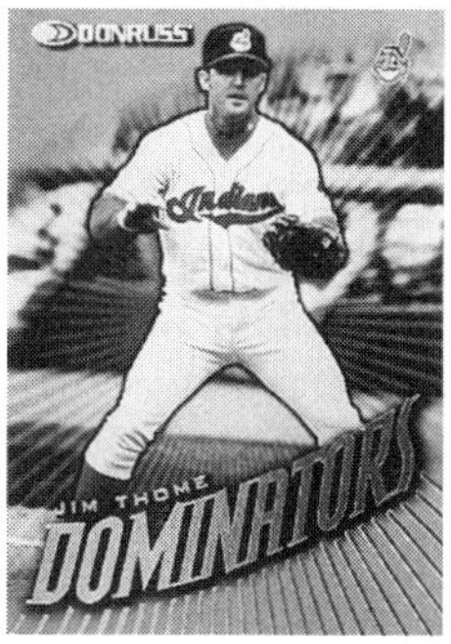

This 30-card insert features color player photos and holographic foil.

		MT
Complete Set (30):		100.00
Common Player:		1.25
Approx: 1:12		
1	Roger Clemens	5.00
2	Tony Clark	1.50
3	Darin Erstad	3.00
4	Jeff Bagwell	5.00
5	Ken Griffey Jr.	12.50
6	Andruw Jones	3.00
7	Juan Gonzalez	6.00
8	Ivan Rodriguez	3.00
9	Randy Johnson	2.00
10	Tino Martinez	1.50
11	Mark McGwire	12.50
12	Chuck Knoblauch	1.50
13	Jim Thome	1.50
14	Alex Rodriguez	9.00
15	Hideo Nomo	1.50
16	Jose Cruz Jr.	1.50
17	Chipper Jones	7.50
18	Tony Gwynn	6.00
19	Barry Bonds	3.00
20	Mo Vaughn	1.50
21	Cal Ripken Jr.	10.00
22	Greg Maddux	6.00
23	Manny Ramirez	2.00
24	Andres Galarraga	1.50
25	Vladimir Guerrero	2.00
26	Albert Belle	2.00
27	Nomar Garciaparra	6.00
28	Kenny Lofton	1.50
29	Mike Piazza	7.50
30	Frank Thomas	5.00

1998 Donruss Update Elite

This 20-card insert features color player photos in a diamond-shaped border at the top with the Elite Series logo and player's name at the bottom. The fronts have a cream-colored border. The cards are sequentially numbered to 2,500.

		MT
Complete Set (20):		200.00
Common Player:		2.50

Production 2,500 sets

1	Jeff Bagwell	10.00
2	Andruw Jones	5.00
3	Ken Griffey Jr.	25.00
4	Derek Jeter	15.00
5	Juan Gonzalez	12.50
6	Mark McGwire	25.00
7	Ivan Rodriguez	7.50
8	Paul Molitor	5.00
9	Hideo Nomo	5.00
10	Mo Vaughn	5.00
11	Chipper Jones	15.00
12	Nomar Garciaparra	12.50
13	Mike Piazza	15.00
14	Frank Thomas	10.00
15	Greg Maddux	12.50
16	Cal Ripken Jr.	20.00
17	Alex Rodriguez	17.50
18	Scott Rolen	7.50
19	Barry Bonds	7.50
20	Tony Gwynn	12.50

1998 Donruss Update FANtasy Team

This 20-card set features the top vote getters from the Donruss online Fan Club ballot box. The top ten make up the 1st Team FANtasy Team and are sequentially numbered to 2,000. The other players are included in the 2nd Team FANtasy Team and are numbered to 4,000. The first 250 cards of each player are die-cut. The front of the cards feature a color photo inside a stars and stripes border.

		MT
Complete Set (20):		250.00
Common Player (1-10) (1,750 sets):		6.00
Common Player (11-20) (3,750 sets):		2.00
Die-Cuts (250 each): 4-6X		
1	Frank Thomas	15.00
2	Ken Griffey Jr.	40.00
3	Cal Ripken Jr.	30.00
4	Jose Cruz Jr.	8.00
5	Travis Lee	10.00
6	Greg Maddux	20.00
7	Alex Rodriguez	25.00
8	Mark McGwire	40.00
9	Chipper Jones	25.00
10	Andruw Jones	10.00
11	Mike Piazza	15.00
12	Tony Gwynn	12.00
13	Larry Walker	4.00
14	Nomar Garciaparra	15.00
15	Jaret Wright	6.00
16	Livan Hernandez	4.00
17	Roger Clemens	10.00
18	Derek Jeter	12.50
19	Scott Rolen	8.00
20	Jeff Bagwell	10.00

Player names in *Italic* type indicate a rookie card.

1998 Donruss Update Rookie Diamond Kings

The Rookie Diamond Kings insert features color portraits by artist Dan Gardiner of young players inside a golden border. Player identification and Rookie Diamond Kings logo are at the bottom. Each card is sequentially numbered to 10,000 with the first 500 printed on canvas.

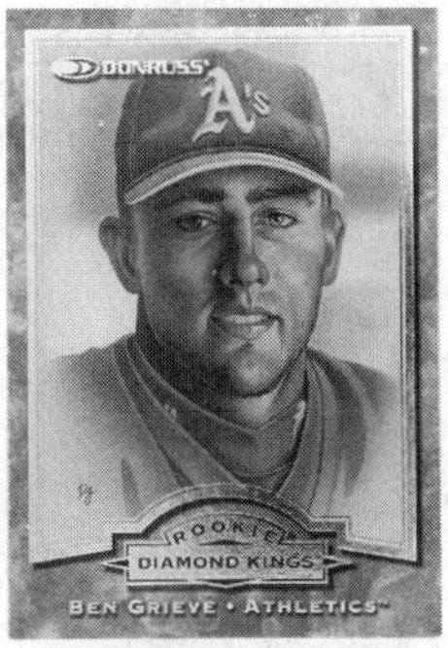

		MT
Complete Set (12):		60.00
Common Player:		2.00
Production 9,500 sets		
Canvas (500 sets): 3-5X		
1	Travis Lee	10.00
2	Fernando Tatis	5.00
3	Livan Hernandez	2.00
4	Todd Helton	10.00
5	Derrek Lee	2.00
6	Jaret Wright	9.00
7	Ben Grieve	10.00
8	Paul Konerko	6.00
9	Jose Cruz Jr.	2.00
10	Mark Kotsay	6.00
11	Todd Greene	2.00
12	Brad Fullmer	6.00

1998 Donruss Update Sony MLB 99

This 20-card set promotes the MLB '99 game for Sony PlayStation systems. The card front has a color player photo with a red border on two sides. The Donruss, PlayStation and MLB '99 logos appear on the front as well. The backs have a MLB '99 Tip and instructions on entering the PlayStation MLB '99 Sweepstakes.

		MT
Complete Set (20):		10.00
Common Player:		.25
1	Cal Ripken Jr.	1.50
2	Nomar Garciaparra	1.20
3	Barry Bonds	.60
4	Mike Mussina	.50
5	Pedro Martinez	.40
6	Derek Jeter	1.25
7	Andruw Jones	.60
8	Kenny Lofton	.50
9	Gary Sheffield	.25
10	Raul Mondesi	.25
11	Jeff Bagwell	.75
12	Tim Salmon	.25
13	Tom Glavine	.25
14	Ben Grieve	.75
15	Matt Williams	.25
16	Juan Gonzalez	1.00
17	Mark McGwire	2.00
18	Bernie Williams	.35
19	Andres Galarraga	.25
20	Jose Cruz Jr.	.25

1998 Donruss Collections

Collections consists of a 750-card base set made up of cards from the Donruss (200 cards), Leaf (200), Donruss Elite (150) and Donruss Preferred (200) sets. The cards were reproduced with a chromium finish and have the scripted word "Collections" vertically at left-front. The Collections logo is repeated on back and each card has a second number within the 750-piece set. The Donruss and Leaf cards were inserted two per pack, Elite was inserted one per pack and Preferred cards had a production run of less than 1,400, averaging one card per two packs.

		MT
Complete Set (750):		650.00
Complete Donruss Set (200):		75.00
Complete Leaf Set (200):		60.00
Complete Elite Set (150):		150.00
Complete Preferred Set (200):		400.00
Prized Collections Parallel: 4-6X		
	DONRUSS	
1	Paul Molitor	.50
2	Juan Gonzalez	1.50
3	Darryl Kile	.10
4	Randy Johnson	.40
5	Tom Glavine	.20
6	Pat Hentgen	.10
7	David Justice	.25
8	Kevin Brown	.25
9	Mike Mussina	.45
10	Ken Caminiti	.20
11	Todd Hundley	.20
12	Frank Thomas	2.00
13	Ray Lankford	.10
14	Justin Thompson	.10
15	Jason Dickson	.10
16	Kenny Lofton	.60
17	Ivan Rodriguez	.75
18	Pedro Martinez	.40
19	Brady Anderson	.15
20	Barry Larkin	.15
21	Chipper Jones	2.00
22	Tony Gwynn	1.50
23	Roger Clemens	1.00
24	Sandy Alomar Jr.	.15
25	Tino Martinez	.15
26	Jeff Bagwell	1.25
27	Shawn Estes	.10
28	Ken Griffey Jr.	3.00
29	Javier Lopez	.15
30	Denny Neagle	.10
31	Mike Piazza	2.00
32	Andres Galarraga	.15
33	Larry Walker	.25
34	Alex Rodriguez	2.50
35	Greg Maddux	1.50
36	Albert Belle	.75
37	Barry Bonds	.75
38	Mo Vaughn	.60
39	Kevin Appier	.10
40	Wade Boggs	.25
41	Garret Anderson	.10
42	Jeffrey Hammonds	.10
43	Marquis Grissom	.10
44	Jim Edmonds	.10
45	Brian Jordan	.10
46	Raul Mondesi	.20
47	John Valentin	.10
48	Brad Radke	.10
49	Ismael Valdes	.10
50	Matt Stairs	.10
51	Matt Williams	.20
52	Reggie Jefferson	.10
53	Alan Benes	.10
54	Charles Johnson	.10
55	Chuck Knoblauch	.15
56	Edgar Martinez	.10
57	Nomar Garciaparra	2.00
58	Craig Biggio	.20
59	Bernie Williams	.45
60	David Cone	.20
61	Cal Ripken Jr.	2.50
62	Mark McGwire	4.00
63	Roberto Alomar	.50
64	Fred McGriff	.15
65	Eric Karros	.10
66	Robin Ventura	.15
67	Darin Erstad	.50
68	Michael Tucker	.10
69	Jim Thome	.30
70	Mark Grace	.25
71	Lou Collier	.10
72	Karim Garcia	.20
73	Alex Fernandez	.10
74	J.T. Snow	.10
75	Reggie Sanders	.10
76	John Smoltz	.15
77	Tim Salmon	.20
78	Paul O'Neill	.20
79	Vinny Castilla	.10
80	Rafael Palmeiro	.20
81	Jaret Wright	.50
82	Jay Buhner	.15
83	Brett Butler	.10
84	Todd Greene	.10
85	Scott Rolen	1.50
86	Sammy Sosa	1.50
87	Jason Giambi	.10
88	Carlos Delgado	.15
89	Deion Sanders	.20
90	Wilton Guerrero	.10
91	Andy Pettitte	.50
92	Brian Giles	.15
93	Dmitri Young	.10
94	Ron Coomer	.10
95	Mike Cameron	.10
96	Edgardo Alfonzo	.20
97	Jimmy Key	.10
98	Ryan Klesko	.20
99	Andy Benes	.10
100	Derek Jeter	2.00
101	Jeff Fassero	.10
102	Neifi Perez	.10
103	Hideo Nomo	.45
104	Andruw Jones	1.50
105	Todd Helton	.60
106	Livan Hernandez	.20
107	Brett Tomko	.10
108	Shannon Stewart	.10
109	Bartolo Colon	.10
110	Matt Morris	.10
111	Miguel Tejada	.50
112	Pokey Reese	.10
113	Fernando Tatis	.25
114	Todd Dunwoody	.10
115	Jose Cruz Jr.	.50
116	Chan Ho Park	.15
117	Kevin Young	.10
118	Rickey Henderson	.25
119	Hideki Irabu	.50
120	Francisco Cordova	.10
121	Al Martin	.10
122	Tony Clark	.30
123	Curt Schilling	.15
124	Rusty Greer	.10
125	Jose Canseco	.35
126	Edgar Renteria	.10
127	Todd Walker	.20
128	Wally Joyner	.10
129	Bill Mueller	.10
130	Jose Guillen	.40
131	Manny Ramirez	.50
132	Bobby Higginson	.10
133	Kevin Orie	.10
134	Will Clark	.20
135	Dave Nilsson	.10
136	Jason Kendall	.10
137	Ivan Cruz	.10
138	Gary Sheffield	.25
139	Bubba Trammell	.20
140	Vladimir Guerrero	1.00
141	Dennis Reyes	.15
142	Bobby Bonilla	.15
143	Ruben Rivera	.10
144	Ben Grieve	1.00
145	Moises Alou	.20
146	Tony Womack	.10
147	Eric Young	.10
148	Paul Konerko	.50
149	Dante Bichette	.20
150	Joe Carter	.15
151	Rondell White	.20
152	Chris Holt	.10
153	Shawn Green	.25
154	Mark Grudzielanek	.10
155	Jermaine Dye	.10
156	Ken Griffey Jr. (Fan Club)	1.50
157	Frank Thomas (Fan Club)	1.00
158	Chipper Jones (Fan Club)	1.00
159	Mike Piazza (Fan Club)	1.25
160	Cal Ripken Jr. (Fan Club)	1.25
161	Greg Maddux (Fan Club)	.90
162	Juan Gonzalez (Fan Club)	.75
163	Alex Rodriguez (Fan Club)	1.25
164	Mark McGwire (Fan Club)	2.50
165	Derek Jeter (Fan Club)	1.50
166	Larry Walker (Checklist)	.20
167	Tony Gwynn (Checklist)	.75
168	Tino Martinez (Checklist)	.10
169	Scott Rolen (Checklist)	.60
170	Nomar Garciaparra (Checklist)	1.00
	DONRUSS RATED ROOKIES	
1	Mark Kotsay	2.00
2	Neifi Perez	1.00
3	Paul Konerko	2.00
4	Jose Cruz Jr.	4.00
5	Hideki Irabu	4.00
6	Mike Cameron	1.00
7	Jeff Suppan	1.00
8	Kevin Orie	1.00
9	Pokey Reese	1.00
10	Todd Dunwoody	1.00
11	Miguel Tejada	2.00
12	Jose Guillen	1.50
13	Bartolo Colon	2.00
14	Derrek Lee	1.00
15	Antone Williamson	1.00
16	Wilton Guerrero	1.00
17	Jaret Wright	2.00
18	Todd Helton	2.00
19	Shannon Stewart	1.00
20	Nomar Garciaparra	5.00
21	Brett Tomko	1.00
22	Fernando Tatis	1.50
23	Raul Ibanez	1.00
24	Dennis Reyes	1.00
25	Bobby Estalella	1.00
26	Lou Collier	1.00
27	Bubba Trammell	1.00
28	Ben Grieve	2.50
29	Ivan Cruz	1.00
30	Karim Garcia	1.50
	LEAF	
1	Rusty Greer	.10
2	Tino Martinez	.20
3	Bobby Bonilla	.15
4	Jason Giambi	.10
5	Matt Morris	.20
6	Craig Counsell	.10
7	Reggie Jefferson	.10
8	Brian Rose	.25
9	Ruben Rivera	.10
10	Shawn Estes	.10
11	Tony Gwynn	1.50
12	Jeff Abbott	.10
13	Jose Cruz Jr.	.75
14	Francisco Cordova	.10
15	Ryan Klesko	.20
16	Tim Salmon	.25
17	Brett Tomko	.10
18	Matt Williams	.25
19	Joe Carter	.15
20	Harold Baines	.15
21	Gary Sheffield	.25
22	Charles Johnson	.15
23	Aaron Boone	.15
24	Eddie Murray	.25
25	Matt Stairs	.10
26	David Cone	.20
27	Jon Nunnally	.10
28	Chris Stynes	.10
29	Enrique Wilson	.10
30	Randy Johnson	.50
31	Garret Anderson	.10
32	Manny Ramirez	.60
33	Jeff Suppan	.10
34	Rickey Henderson	.25
35	Scott Spiezio	.10
36	Rondell White	.20
37	Todd Greene	.20
38	Delino DeShields	.10
39	Kevin Brown	.20
40	Chili Davis	.10
41	Jimmy Key	.10
42	NOT ISSUED	
43	Mike Mussina	.45
44	Joe Randa	.10
45	Chan Ho Park	.20
46	Brad Radke	.10
47	Geronimo Berroa	.10
48	Wade Boggs	.25
49	Kevin Appier	.10
50	Moises Alou	.15
51	David Justice	.25
52	Ivan Rodriguez	.75
53	J.T. Snow	.15
54	Brian Giles	.15
55	Will Clark	.25
56	Justin Thompson	.10
57	Javier Lopez	.15
58	Hideki Irabu	.30
59	Mark Grudzielanek	.10
60	Abraham Nunez	.15
61	Todd Hollandsworth	.10
62	Jay Bell	.10
63	Nomar Garciaparra	2.00
64	Vinny Castilla	.10
65	Lou Collier	.10
66	Kevin Orie	.10
67	John Valentin	.10
68	Robin Ventura	.20
69	Denny Neagle	.10
70	Tony Womack	.10
71	Dennis Reyes	.10
72	Wally Joyner	.10
73	Kevin Brown	.20
74	Ray Durham	.10
75	Mike Cameron	.15
76	Dante Bichette	.20
77	Jose Guillen	.25
78	Carlos Delgado	.20
79	Paul Molitor	.40
80	Jason Kendall	.10
81	Mark Belhorn	.10
82	Damian Jackson	.10
83	Bill Mueller	.10

84	Kevin Young	.10
85	Curt Schilling	.20
86	Jeffrey Hammonds	.10
87	Sandy Alomar Jr.	.15
88	Bartolo Colon	.10
89	Wilton Guerrero	.10
90	Bernie Williams	.50
91	Deion Sanders	.25
92	Mike Piazza	2.00
93	Butch Huskey	.10
94	Edgardo Alfonzo	.25
95	Alan Benes	.10
96	Craig Biggio	.20
97	Mark Grace	.25
98	Shawn Green	.25
99	Derrek Lee	.15
100	Ken Griffey Jr.	3.00
101	Tim Raines	.10
102	Pokey Reese	.10
103	Lee Stevens	.10
104	Shannon Stewart	.10
105	John Smoltz	.15
106	Frank Thomas	1.50
107	Jeff Fassero	.10
108	Jay Buhner	.15
109	Jose Canseco	.25
110	Omar Vizquel	.10
111	Travis Fryman	.10
112	Dave Nilsson	.10
113	John Olerud	.15
114	Larry Walker	.25
115	Jim Edmonds	.15
116	Bobby Higginson	.20
117	Todd Hundley	.10
118	Paul O'Neill	.20
119	Bip Roberts	.10
120	Ismael Valdes	.10
121	Pedro Martinez	.25
122	Jeff Cirillo	.10
123	Andy Benes	.10
124	Bobby Jones	.10
125	Brian Hunter	.10
126	Darryl Kile	.10
127	Pat Hentgen	.10
128	Marquis Grissom	.10
129	Eric Davis	.10
130	Chipper Jones	2.00
131	Edgar Martinez	.10
132	Andy Pettitte	.25
133	Cal Ripken Jr.	2.50
134	Scott Rolen	1.50
135	Ron Coomer	.10
136	Luis Castillo	.10
137	Fred McGriff	.15
138	Neifi Perez	.10
139	Eric Karros	.15
140	Alex Fernandez	.10
141	Jason Dickson	.10
142	Lance Johnson	.10
143	Ray Lankford	.10
144	Sammy Sosa	1.50
145	Eric Young	.10
146	Bubba Trammell	.20
147	Todd Walker	.20
148	Mo Vaughn (Curtain Calls)	1.00
149	Jeff Bagwell (Curtain Calls)	1.00
150	Kenny Lofton (Curtain Calls)	.50
151	Raul Mondesi (Curtain Calls)	.50
152	Mike Piazza (Curtain Calls)	2.00
153	Chipper Jones (Curtain Calls)	2.00
154	Larry Walker (Curtain Calls)	.75
155	Greg Maddux (Curtain Calls)	2.00
156	Ken Griffey Jr. (Curtain Calls)	3.00
157	Frank Thomas (Curtain Calls)	2.00
158	Darin Erstad (Gold Leaf Stars)	1.50
159	Roberto Alomar (Gold Leaf Stars)	1.00
160	Albert Belle (Gold Leaf Stars)	1.50
161	Jim Thome (Gold Leaf Stars)	.75
162	Tony Clark (Gold Leaf Stars)	1.00
163	Chuck Knoblauch (Gold Leaf Stars)	.75
164	Derek Jeter (Gold Leaf Stars)	4.00
165	Alex Rodriguez (Gold Leaf Stars)	5.00
166	Tony Gwynn (Gold Leaf Stars)	4.00
167	Roger Clemens (Gold Leaf Stars)	2.50
168	Barry Larkin (Gold Leaf Stars)	.50
169	Andres Galarraga (Gold Leaf Stars)	.50
170	Vladimir Guerrero (Gold Leaf Stars)	1.50
171	Mark McGwire (Gold Leaf Stars)	5.00
172	Barry Bonds (Gold Leaf Stars)	1.50
173	Juan Gonzalez (Gold Leaf Stars)	3.00
174	Andruw Jones (Gold Leaf Stars)	2.50
175	Paul Molitor (Gold Leaf Stars)	1.50
176	Hideo Nomo (Gold Leaf Stars)	1.50
177	Cal Ripken Jr. (Gold Leaf Stars)	4.00
178	Brad Fullmer (Gold Leaf Rookies)	1.00
179	Jaret Wright (Gold Leaf Rookies)	2.00
180	Bobby Estalella (Gold Leaf Rookies)	.75
181	Ben Grieve (Gold Leaf Rookies)	2.00
182	Paul Konerko (Gold Leaf Rookies)	1.50
183	David Ortiz (Gold Leaf Rookies)	.75
184	Todd Helton (Gold Leaf Rookies)	1.50
185	Juan Encarnacion (Gold Leaf Rookies)	.75
186	Miguel Tejada (Gold Leaf Rookies)	1.50
187	Jacob Cruz (Gold Leaf Rookies)	.50
188	Mark Kotsay (Gold Leaf Rookies)	.75
189	Fernando Tatis (Gold Leaf Rookies)	.50
190	Ricky Ledee (Gold Leaf Rookies)	.65
191	Richard Hidalgo (Gold Leaf Rookies)	.75
192	Richie Sexson (Gold Leaf Rookies)	.75
193	Luis Ordaz (Gold Leaf Rookies)	.75
194	Eli Marrero (Gold Leaf Rookies)	.50
195	Livan Hernandez (Gold Leaf Rookies)	.75
196	Homer Bush (Gold Leaf Rookies)	.75
197	Raul Ibanez (Gold Leaf Rookies)	.75
198	Checklist (Nomar Garciaparra)	.75
199	Checklist (Scott Rolen)	.50
200	Checklist (Jose Cruz Jr.)	.25
201	(Al Martin)	.25

ELITE

1	Ken Griffey Jr.	4.00
2	Frank Thomas	2.00
3	Alex Rodriguez	2.50
4	Mike Piazza	2.50
5	Greg Maddux	2.00
6	Cal Ripken Jr.	3.00
7	Chipper Jones	2.50
8	Derek Jeter	2.50
9	Tony Gwynn	1.50
10	Andruw Jones	1.00
11	Juan Gonzalez	1.50
12	Jeff Bagwell	1.25
13	Mark McGwire	4.00
14	Roger Clemens	1.25
15	Albert Belle	.75
16	Barry Bonds	.75
17	Kenny Lofton	.65
18	Ivan Rodriguez	.75
19	Manny Ramirez	.75
20	Jim Thome	.50
21	Chuck Knoblauch	.40
22	Paul Molitor	.60
23	Barry Larkin	.30
24	Andy Pettitte	.50
25	John Smoltz	.25
26	Randy Johnson	.50
27	Bernie Williams	.75
28	Larry Walker	.30
29	Mo Vaughn	.75
30	Bobby Higginson	.25
31	Edgardo Alfonzo	.45
32	Justin Thompson	.25
33	Jeff Suppan	.25
34	Roberto Alomar	.75
35	Hideo Nomo	.75
36	Rusty Greer	.25
37	Tim Salmon	.30
38	Jim Edmonds	.25
39	Gary Sheffield	.30
40	Ken Caminiti	.45
41	Sammy Sosa	3.00
42	Tony Womack	.25
43	Matt Williams	.30
44	Andres Galarraga	.25
45	Garret Anderson	.25
46	Rafael Palmeiro	.35
47	Mike Mussina	.75
48	Craig Biggio	.35
49	Wade Boggs	.40
50	Tom Glavine	.30
51	Jason Giambi	.25
52	Will Clark	.35
53	David Justice	.35
54	Sandy Alomar Jr.	.25
55	Edgar Martinez	.25
56	Brady Anderson	.25
57	Eric Young	.25
58	Ray Lankford	.25
59	Kevin Brown	.35
60	Raul Mondesi	.30
61	Bobby Bonilla	.25
62	Javier Lopez	.25
63	Fred McGriff	.30
64	Rondell White	.25
65	Todd Hundley	.25
66	Mark Grace	.30
67	Alan Benes	.25
68	Jeff Abbott	.25
69	Bob Abreu	.25
70	Deion Sanders	.30
71	Tino Martinez	.30
72	Shannon Stewart	.25
73	Homer Bush	.25
74	Carlos Delgado	.30
75	Raul Ibanez	.25
76	Hideki Irabu	.75
77	Jose Cruz Jr.	.75
78	Tony Clark	.60
79	Wilton Guerrero	.25
80	Vladimir Guerrero	1.00
81	Scott Rolen	1.50
82	Nomar Garciaparra	2.50
83	Darin Erstad	.75
84	Chan Ho Park	.35
85	Mike Cameron	.25
86	Todd Walker	.25
87	Todd Dunwoody	.25
88	Neifi Perez	.25
89	Brett Tomko	.25
90	Jose Guillen	.40
91	Matt Morris	.25
92	Bartolo Colon	.45
93	Jaret Wright	.75
94	Shawn Estes	.25
95	Livan Hernandez	.25
96	Bobby Estalella	.25
97	Ben Grieve	1.50
98	Paul Konerko	.75
99	David Ortiz	.55
100	Todd Helton	1.00
101	Juan Encarnacion	.30
102	Bubba Trammell	.25
103	Miguel Tejada	.75
104	Jacob Cruz	.25
105	Todd Greene	.25
106	Kevin Orie	.25
107	Mark Kotsay	.60
108	Fernando Tatis	.30
109	Jay Payton	.25
110	Pokey Reese	.25
111	Derrek Lee	.25
112	Richard Hidalgo	.35
113	Ricky Ledee	.75
114	Lou Collier	.25
115	Ruben Rivera	.25
116	Shawn Green	.75
117	Moises Alou	.35
118	Ken Griffey Jr. (Generations)	2.00
119	Frank Thomas (Generations)	1.00
120	Alex Rodriguez (Generations)	1.50
121	Mike Piazza (Generations)	1.25
122	Greg Maddux (Generations)	1.00
123	Cal Ripken Jr. (Generations)	1.50
124	Chipper Jones (Generations)	1.25
125	Derek Jeter (Generations)	1.25
126	Tony Gwynn (Generations)	1.00
127	Andruw Jones (Generations)	.90
128	Juan Gonzalez (Generations)	1.00
129	Jeff Bagwell (Generations)	.75
130	Mark McGwire (Generations)	3.00
131	Roger Clemens (Generations)	.75
132	Albert Belle (Generations)	.50
133	Barry Bonds (Generations)	.50
134	Kenny Lofton (Generations)	.45
135	Ivan Rodriguez (Generations)	.40
136	Manny Ramirez (Generations)	.50
137	Jim Thome (Generations)	.30
138	Chuck Knoblauch (Generations)	.25
139	Paul Molitor (Generations)	.35
140	Barry Larkin (Generations)	.25
141	Mo Vaughn (Generations)	.50
142	Hideki Irabu (Generations)	.50
143	Jose Cruz Jr. (Generations)	.65
144	Tony Clark (Generations)	.40
145	Vladimir Guerrero (Generations)	.90
146	Scott Rolen (Generations)	1.00
147	Nomar Garciaparra (Generations)	1.50
148	Checklist (Garciaparra)	.75
149	Checklist (Walker)	.25
150	Checklist (Martinez)	.25

PREFERRED

1	Ken Griffey Jr. EX	15.00
2	Frank Thomas EX	7.50
3	Cal Ripken Jr. EX	12.50
4	Alex Rodriguez EX	12.50
5	Greg Maddux EX	10.00
6	Mike Piazza EX	15.00
7	Chipper Jones EX	15.00
8	Tony Gwynn FB	10.00
9	Derek Jeter FB	15.00
10	Jeff Bagwell EX	7.50
11	Juan Gonzalez EX	7.50
12	Nomar Garciaparra EX	12.50
13	Andruw Jones FB	7.50
14	Hideo Nomo FB	3.00
15	Roger Clemens FB	6.00
16	Mark McGwire FB	15.00
17	Scott Rolen FB	6.00
18	Vladimir Guerrero FB	6.00
19	Barry Bonds FB	5.00
20	Darin Erstad FB	5.00
21	Albert Belle FB	5.00
22	Kenny Lofton FB	4.00
23	Mo Vaughn FB	4.00
24	Tony Clark FB	3.00
25	Ivan Rodriguez FB	6.00
26	Larry Walker CL	2.00
27	Eddie Murray CL	3.00
28	Andy Pettitte CL	1.50
29	Roberto Alomar CL	3.00
30	Randy Johnson CL	5.00
31	Manny Ramirez CL	7.50
32	Paul Molitor FB	6.00
33	Mike Mussina CL	5.00
34	Jim Thome FB	3.00
35	Tino Martinez CL	3.00
36	Gary Sheffield CL	2.00
37	Chuck Knoblauch CL	2.00
38	Bernie Williams CL	2.00
39	Tim Salmon CL	1.50
40	Sammy Sosa CL	12.50
41	Wade Boggs MZ	4.50
42	Will Clark GS	3.00
43	Andres Galarraga CL	1.50
44	Raul Mondesi CL	1.50
45	Rickey Henderson GS	1.50
46	Jose Canseco GS	1.50
47	Pedro Martinez GS	2.00
48	Jay Buhner GS	1.00
49	Ryan Klesko GS	1.00
50	Barry Larkin CL	1.00
51	Charles Johnson GS	1.00
52	Tom Glavine GS	1.00
53	Edgar Martinez CL	1.00
54	Fred McGriff GS	1.00
55	Moises Alou MZ	1.00
56	Dante Bichette GS	1.00
57	Jim Edmonds CL	1.00
58	Mark Grace MZ	2.00
59	Chan Ho Park MZ	1.50
60	Justin Thompson MZ	1.50
61	John Smoltz MZ	1.00
62	Craig Biggio CL	2.00
63	Ken Caminiti MZ	2.00
64	Deion Sanders MZ	1.50
65	Carlos Delgado GS	1.00
66	David Justice CL	1.50
67	J.T. Snow GS	1.00
68	Jason Giambi CL	1.00
69	Garret Anderson MZ	1.00
70	Rondell White MZ	1.00
71	Matt Williams MZ	1.25
72	Brady Anderson MZ	1.00
73	Eric Karros GS	1.00
74	Javier Lopez GS	1.00
75	Pat Hentgen GS	1.00
76	Todd Hundley GS	1.00
77	Ray Lankford GS	1.00
78	Denny Neagle GS	1.00
79	Henry Rodriguez GS	1.00
80	Sandy Alomar Jr. MZ	1.25
81	Rafael Palmeiro MZ	2.00
82	Robin Ventura GS	2.00
83	John Olerud GS	1.50
84	Omar Vizquel GS	1.00
85	Joe Randa GS	1.00
86	Lance Johnson GS	1.00
87	Kevin Brown GS	1.50
88	Curt Schilling GS	1.25
89	Ismael Valdes GS	1.00
90	Francisco Cordova GS	1.00
91	David Cone GS	1.25
92	Paul O'Neill GS	1.50
93	Jimmy Key GS	1.00
94	Brad Radke GS	1.00
95	Kevin Appier GS	1.00
96	Al Martin GS	1.00
97	Rusty Greer MZ	1.00
98	Reggie Jefferson GS	1.00
99	Ron Coomer GS	1.00
100	Vinny Castilla GS	1.00
101	Bobby Bonilla MZ	1.50
102	Eric Young GS	1.00
103	Tony Womack GS	1.00
104	Jason Kendall GS	1.00
105	Jeff Suppan GS	1.00
106	Shawn Estes MZ	1.00
107	Shawn Green GS	2.00
108	Edgardo Alfonzo MZ	2.00
109	Alan Benes MZ	1.00
110	Bobby Higginson GS	1.50
111	Mark Grudzielanek GS	1.00
112	Wilton Guerrero GS	1.00
113	Todd Greene MZ	1.50
114	Pokey Reese GS	1.00
115	Jose Guillen CL	2.00
116	Neifi Perez MZ	1.00
117	Luis Castillo GS	1.00
118	Edgar Renteria GS	1.50
119	Karim Garcia GS	1.50
120	Butch Huskey GS	1.00
121	Michael Tucker GS	1.00
122	Jason Dickson GS	1.00
123	Todd Walker MZ	2.00
124	Brian Jordan GS	1.00
125	Joe Carter GS	1.00
126	Matt Morris MZ	1.00
127	Brett Tomko MZ	1.00
128	Mike Cameron CL	1.00
129	Russ Davis GS	1.00
130	Shannon Stewart MZ	1.00
131	Kevin Orie GS	1.00
132	Scott Spiezio GS	1.00
133	Brian Giles GS	1.00
134	Raul Casanova GS	1.00
135	Jose Cruz Jr. CL	2.50
136	Hideki Irabu GS	2.50
137	Bubba Trammell GS	1.50
138	Richard Hidalgo CL	2.00
139	Paul Konerko CL	2.00
140	Todd Helton FB	5.00
141	Miguel Tejada CL	2.00
142	Fernando Tatis MZ	1.50
143	Ben Grieve FB	2.00
144	Travis Lee FB	2.00
145	Mark Kotsay CL	1.50
146	Eli Marrero MZ	1.00
147	David Ortiz CL	1.50
148	Juan Encarnacion MZ	1.50
149	Jaret Wright MZ	2.50
150	Livan Hernandez CL	2.00
151	Ruben Rivera GS	1.00
152	Brad Fullmer MZ	2.00
153	Dennis Reyes GS	1.00
154	Enrique Wilson MZ	1.00
155	Todd Dunwoody MZ	1.50
156	Derrick Gibson MZ	1.50
157	Aaron Boone MZ	1.50
158	Ron Wright MZ	1.00
159	Preston Wilson MZ	2.00
160	Abraham Nunez GS	1.25
161	Shane Monahan GS	1.25
162	Carl Pavano GS	1.50
163	Derrek Lee GS	1.50
164	Jeff Abbott GS	1.00
165	Wes Helms MZ	1.00
166	Brian Rose GS	1.00
167	Bobby Estalella GS	1.00
168	Ken Griffey Jr. GS	6.00
169	Frank Thomas GS	4.00
170	Cal Ripken Jr. GS	5.00
171	Alex Rodriguez GS	5.00
172	Greg Maddux GS	4.00
173	Mike Piazza GS	5.00
174	Chipper Jones GS	5.00
175	Tony Gwynn GS	3.00
176	Derek Jeter GS	4.00
177	Jeff Bagwell GS	2.00
178	Juan Gonzalez GS	3.00
179	Nomar Garciaparra GS	4.00
180	Andruw Jones GS	1.50
181	Hideo Nomo GS	1.00
182	Roger Clemens GS	2.50
183	Mark McGwire GS	5.00
184	Scott Rolen GS	2.00
185	Barry Bonds GS	1.50
186	Darin Erstad GS	1.50
187	Mo Vaughn GS	1.50
188	Ivan Rodriguez GS	1.50
189	Larry Walker MZ	2.00
190	Andy Pettitte GS	1.00
191	Randy Johnson MZ	2.50
192	Paul Molitor GS	1.50
193	Jim Thome GS	1.00
194	Tino Martinez MZ	1.00
195	Gary Sheffield GS	1.00
196	Albert Belle GS	1.50
197	Jose Cruz Jr. GS	1.50
198	Todd Helton GS	1.50
199	Ben Grieve GS	2.50
200	Paul Konerko GS	1.50

1998 Donruss Elite

Donruss Elite consists of a 150-card base set with two parallels and five inserts. The base cards feature a foil background with player photo on front. Another photo is on the back with stats and basic player information. The Aspirations parallel is numbered to 750 and the Status parallel is numbered to 100. The base set also includes the 30-card Generations subset and three checklists. The inserts are Back to the Future, Back to the Future Autographs, Craftsmen, Prime Numbers and Prime Numbers Die-Cuts.

		MT
Complete Set (150):		25.00
Common Player:		.15
Wax Box:		65.00
1	Ken Griffey Jr.	4.00
2	Frank Thomas	2.00
3	Alex Rodriguez	2.50
4	Mike Piazza	2.50
5	Greg Maddux	2.00
6	Cal Ripken Jr.	3.00
7	Chipper Jones	2.50
8	Derek Jeter	2.50
9	Tony Gwynn	2.00
10	Andruw Jones	2.00
11	Juan Gonzalez	2.00
12	Jeff Bagwell	1.50
13	Mark McGwire	4.00
14	Roger Clemens	1.50
15	Albert Belle	.75
16	Barry Bonds	1.00
17	Kenny Lofton	.75
18	Ivan Rodriguez	.75
19	Manny Ramirez	.75
20	Jim Thome	.50
21	Chuck Knoblauch	.40
22	Paul Molitor	.60
23	Barry Larkin	.30
24	Andy Pettitte	.60
25	John Smoltz	.25
26	Randy Johnson	.50
27	Bernie Williams	.75
28	Larry Walker	.30
29	Mo Vaughn	.75
30	Bobby Higginson	.15
31	Edgardo Alfonzo	.20
32	Justin Thompson	.15
33	Jeff Suppan	.15
34	Roberto Alomar	.75
35	Hideo Nomo	.50
36	Rusty Greer	.15
37	Tim Salmon	.30
38	Jim Edmonds	.15
39	Gary Sheffield	.30
40	Ken Caminiti	.25
41	Sammy Sosa	2.50
42	Tony Womack	.15
43	Matt Williams	.30
44	Andres Galarraga	.30
45	Garret Anderson	.15
46	Rafael Palmeiro	.25
47	Mike Mussina	.50
48	Craig Biggio	.25
49	Wade Boggs	.35
50	Tom Glavine	.25
51	Jason Giambi	.15
52	Will Clark	.25
53	David Justice	.25
54	Sandy Alomar Jr.	.20
55	Edgar Martinez	.15
56	Brady Anderson	.20
57	Eric Young	.15
58	Ray Lankford	.15
59	Kevin Brown	.25
60	Raul Mondesi	.30
61	Bobby Bonilla	.20
62	Javier Lopez	.15
63	Fred McGriff	.20
64	Rondell White	.25
65	Todd Hundley	.25
66	Mark Grace	.35
67	Alan Benes	.15
68	Jeff Abbott	.15
69	Bob Abreu	.15
70	Deion Sanders	.20
71	Tino Martinez	.20
72	Shannon Stewart	.15
73	Homer Bush	.15
74	Carlos Delgado	.50
75	Raul Ibanez	.15
76	Hideki Irabu	.75
77	Jose Cruz Jr.	.50
78	Tony Clark	.60
79	Wilton Guerrero	.15
80	Vladimir Guerrero	1.25
81	Scott Rolen	2.00
82	Nomar Garciaparra	2.50
83	Darin Erstad	1.00
84	Chan Ho Park	.25
85	Mike Cameron	.15
86	Todd Walker	.25
87	Todd Dunwoody	.15
88	Neifi Perez	.15
89	Brett Tomko	.15
90	Jose Guillen	.40
91	Matt Morris	.15
92	Bartolo Colon	.15
93	Jaret Wright	1.00
94	Shawn Estes	.15
95	Livan Hernandez	.20
96	Bobby Estalella	.15
97	Ben Grieve	1.50
98	Paul Konerko	1.00
99	David Ortiz	.50
100	Todd Helton	1.00
101	Juan Encarnacion	.30
102	Bubba Trammell	.15
103	Miguel Tejada	.75
104	Jacob Cruz	.15
105	Todd Greene	.15
106	Kevin Orie	.15
107	Mark Kotsay	.60
108	Fernando Tatis	.30
109	Jay Payton	.15
110	Pokey Reese	.15
111	Derrek Lee	.20
112	Richard Hidalgo	.15
113	Ricky Ledee	1.00
114	Lou Collier	.15
115	Ruben Rivera	.15
116	Shawn Green	.25
117	Moises Alou	.25
118	Ken Griffey Jr. (Generations)	2.00
119	Frank Thomas (Generations)	1.00
120	Alex Rodriguez (Generations)	1.25
121	Mike Piazza (Generations)	1.25
122	Greg Maddux (Generations)	1.25
123	Cal Ripken Jr. (Generations)	1.50
124	Chipper Jones (Generations)	1.25
125	Derek Jeter (Generations)	1.25
126	Tony Gwynn (Generations)	1.00
127	Andruw Jones (Generations)	1.00
128	Juan Gonzalez (Generations)	1.00
129	Jeff Bagwell (Generations)	.75
130	Mark McGwire (Generations)	2.50
131	Roger Clemens (Generations)	.75
132	Albert Belle (Generations)	.50
133	Barry Bonds (Generations)	.50
134	Kenny Lofton (Generations)	.50
135	Ivan Rodriguez (Generations)	.40
136	Manny Ramirez (Generations)	.40
137	Jim Thome (Generations)	.30
138	Chuck Knoblauch (Generations)	.25
139	Paul Molitor (Generations)	.30
140	Barry Larkin (Generations)	.15
141	Mo Vaughn (Generations)	.50
142	Hideki Irabu (Generations)	.40
143	Jose Cruz Jr. (Generations)	.50
144	Tony Clark (Generations)	.40
145	Vladimir Guerrero (Generations)	.60
146	Scott Rolen (Generations)	1.00
147	Nomar Garciaparra (Generations)	1.25
148	Checklist (Garciaparra) (Hit Streaks)	.75
149	Checklist (Walker) (Long HR-Coors)	.15
150	Checklist (Martinez) (3 HR in game)	.15

1998 Donruss Elite Aspirations

A parallel edition of 750 of each player are found in this die-cut set. Cards have a scalloped treatment cut into the top and sides and red, rather than silver metallic borders. The word "ASPIRATIONS" in printed on front at bottom-right. Backs have the notation "1 of 750".

	MT
Complete Set (150):	550.00
Common Player:	2.00
Stars and rookies: 4-8X	
(See 1998 Donruss Elite for checklist and base card values.)	

1998 Donruss Elite Status

Just 100 serially numbered cards of each player are found in this die-cut parallel set. Cards have a scalloped treatment cut into the top and sides and red, rather than silver metallic borders.

	MT
Common Player:	6.00
Stars and rookies 30-60X	
(See 1998 Donruss Elite for checklist and base card values.)	

1998 Donruss Elite Back to the Future

These double-front cards feature a veteran or retired star on one side and a young player on the other. Each player's name, team and "Back to the Future" are printed in the border. The cards are numbered to 1,500, with the first 100 of each card signed by both players. Exceptions are cards #1 and #6. Ripken and Konerko did not sign the same cards and Frank Thomas did not sign his Back to the Future card. Thomas instead signed 100 copies of his Elite base set card which was specially marked.

		MT
Complete Set (8):		175.00
Common Player:		10.00
Production 1,400 sets		
1	Cal Ripken Jr., Paul Konerko	30.00
2	Jeff Bagwell, Todd Helton	20.00
3	Eddie Mathews, Chipper Jones	25.00
4	Juan Gonzalez, Ben Grieve	25.00
5	Hank Aaron, Jose Cruz Jr.	25.00
6	Frank Thomas, David Ortiz	10.00
7	Nolan Ryan, Greg Maddux	35.00
8	Alex Rodriguez, Nomar Garciaparra	35.00

Player names in *Italic* type indicate a rookie card.

1998 Donruss Elite Back to the Future Autographs

The first 100 of each card in the Back to the Future insert was autographed by both players. Exceptions are cards #1 and #6. Ripken and Konerko did not sign the same cards and Frank Thomas did not sign his Back to the Future card. Thomas instead signed 100 specially marked copies of his Elite base-set card.

		MT
Common Autograph:		125.00
F. Thomas Redemption:		450.00
C. Ripken Redemption:		450.00
Production 100 sets		
1	Paul Konerko	125.00
2	Jeff Bagwell, Todd Helton	350.00
3	Eddie Mathews, Chipper Jones	400.00
4	Juan Gonzalez, Ben Grieve	600.00
5	Hank Aaron, Jose Cruz Jr.	500.00
7	Nolan Ryan, Greg Maddux	1000.
8	Alex Rodriguez, Nomar Garciaparra	600.00

1998 Donruss Elite Craftsmen

This 30-card insert has color player photos on the front and back. The set is sequentially numbered to 3,500. The Master Craftsmen parallel is numbered to 100.

		MT
Complete Set (30):		150.00
Common Player:		2.00
Production 3,500 sets		
Master Craftsman: 3-6X		
Production 100 sets		
1	Ken Griffey Jr.	15.00
2	Frank Thomas	7.50
3	Alex Rodriguez	10.00
4	Cal Ripken Jr.	10.00
5	Greg Maddux	8.00
6	Mike Piazza	9.00
7	Chipper Jones	9.00
8	Derek Jeter	9.00
9	Tony Gwynn	7.50
10	Nomar Garciaparra	9.00
11	Scott Rolen	5.00
12	Jose Cruz Jr.	2.00
13	Tony Clark	2.50
14	Vladimir Guerrero	5.00
15	Todd Helton	3.00
16	Ben Grieve	5.00
17	Andruw Jones	5.00
18	Jeff Bagwell	5.00
19	Mark McGwire	15.00
20	Juan Gonzalez	7.50
21	Roger Clemens	7.50
22	Albert Belle	4.00
23	Barry Bonds	4.00
24	Kenny Lofton	3.00
25	Ivan Rodriguez	4.00
26	Paul Molitor	3.00
27	Barry Larkin	2.00
28	Mo Vaughn	3.00
29	Larry Walker	3.00
30	Tino Martinez	2.00

1998 Donruss Elite Prime Numbers Samples

Each of the 36 Elite Prime Numbers inserts was also created in a promo version. They are virtually identical to the much rarer inserts, but have no serial number on back, and display a large black "SAMPLE" overprint.

		MT
Complete Set (36):		175.00
Common Player:		3.00
1A	Ken Griffey Jr. 2 (94)	10.00
1B	Ken Griffey Jr. 9 (204)	10.00
1C	Ken Griffey Jr. 4 (290)	10.00
2A	Frank Thomas 4 (56)	5.00
2B	Frank Thomas 5 (406)	5.00
2C	Frank Thomas 6 (450)	5.00
3A	Mark McGwire 3 (87)	10.00
3B	Mark McGwire 8 (307)	10.00
3C	Mark McGwire 7 (380)	10.00
4A	Cal Ripken Jr. 5 (17)	9.00
4B	Cal Ripken Jr. 1 (507)	9.00
4C	Cal Ripken Jr. 7 (510)	9.00
5A	Mike Piazza 5 (76)	7.50
5B	Mike Piazza 7 (506)	7.50
5C	Mike Piazza 6 (570)	7.50
6A	Chipper Jones 4 (89)	7.50
6B	Chipper Jones 8 (409)	7.50
6C	Chipper Jones 9 (480)	7.50
7A	Tony Gwynn 3 (72)	6.00
7B	Tony Gwynn 7 (302)	6.00
7C	Tony Gwynn 2 (370)	6.00
8A	Barry Bonds 3 (74)	3.00
8B	Barry Bonds 7 (304)	3.00
8C	Barry Bonds 4 (370)	3.00
9A	Jeff Bagwell 4 (25)	3.00
9B	Jeff Bagwell 2 (405)	3.00
9C	Jeff Bagwell 5 (420)	3.00
10A	Juan Gonzalez 5 (89)	3.00
10B	Juan Gonzalez 8 (509)	3.00
10C	Juan Gonzalez 9 (580)	3.00
11A	Alex Rodriguez 5 (34)	7.50
11B	Alex Rodriguez 3 (504)	7.50
11C	Alex Rodriguez 4 (530)	7.50
12A	Kenny Lofton 3 (54)	3.00
12B	Kenny Lofton 5 (304)	3.00
12C	Kenny Lofton 4 (350)	3.00

1998 Donruss Elite Prime Numbers

This 36-card insert includes three cards for each of 12 players. Each card has a single number in the background. The three numbers for each player represent a key statistic for the player (ex. Mark McGwire's cards are 3-8-7; his career home run total at the time was 387). Each card in the set is sequentially numbered. The total is dependent upon the player's statistic.

		MT
	Common Player:	10.00
1A	Ken Griffey Jr. 2 (94)	140.00
1B	Ken Griffey Jr. 9 (204)	70.00
1C	Ken Griffey Jr. 4 (290)	60.00
2A	Frank Thomas 4 (56)	80.00
2B	Frank Thomas 5 (406)	20.00
2C	Frank Thomas 6 (450)	20.00
3A	Mark McGwire 3 (87)	140.00
3B	Mark McGwire 8 (307)	60.00
3C	Mark McGwire 7 (380)	60.00
4A	Cal Ripken Jr. 5 (17)	400.00
4B	Cal Ripken Jr. 1 (507)	40.00
4C	Cal Ripken Jr. 7 (510)	40.00
5A	Mike Piazza 5 (76)	90.00
5B	Mike Piazza 7 (506)	30.00
5C	Mike Piazza 6 (570)	30.00
6A	Chipper Jones 4 (89)	75.00
6B	Chipper Jones 8 (409)	20.00
6C	Chipper Jones 9 (480)	20.00
7A	Tony Gwynn 3 (72)	80.00
7B	Tony Gwynn 7 (302)	30.00
7C	Tony Gwynn 2 (370)	30.00
8A	Barry Bonds 3 (74)	40.00
8B	Barry Bonds 7 (304)	15.00
8C	Barry Bonds 4 (370)	15.00
9A	Jeff Bagwell 4 (25)	150.00
9B	Jeff Bagwell 2 (405)	20.00
9C	Jeff Bagwell 5 (420)	20.00
10A	Juan Gonzalez 5 (89)	75.00
10B	Juan Gonzalez 8 (509)	24.00
10C	Juan Gonzalez 9 (580)	24.00
11A	Alex Rodriguez 5 (34)	150.00
11B	Alex Rodriguez 3 (504)	30.00
11C	Alex Rodriguez 4 (530)	30.00
12A	Kenny Lofton 3 (54)	45.00
12B	Kenny Lofton 5 (304)	15.00
12C	Kenny Lofton 4 (350)	15.00

1998 Donruss Elite Prime Numbers Die-Cuts

This set is a die-cut parallel of the Prime Numbers insert. Each card is sequentially numbered. The production run for each player is the number featured on his first card times 100, his second card times 10 and his third card is sequentially numbered to the number featured on the card.

		MT
	Common Player:	15.00
1A	Ken Griffey Jr. 2 (200)	90.00
1B	Ken Griffey Jr. 9 (90)	200.00
1C	Ken Griffey Jr. 4 (4)	650.00
2A	Frank Thomas 4 (400)	25.00
2B	Frank Thomas 5 (50)	100.00
2C	Frank Thomas 6 (6)	250.00
3A	Mark McGwire 3 (300)	75.00
3B	Mark McGwire 8 (80)	200.00
3C	Mark McGwire 7 (7)	450.00
4A	Cal Ripken Jr. 5 (500)	50.00
4B	Cal Ripken Jr. 1 (10)	350.00
4C	Cal Ripken Jr. 7 (7)	400.00
5A	Mike Piazza 5 (500)	37.00
5B	Mike Piazza 7 (70)	100.00
5C	Mike Piazza 6 (6)	200.00
6A	Chipper Jones 4 (400)	25.00
6B	Chipper Jones 8 (80)	100.00
6C	Chipper Jones 9 (9)	200.00
7A	Tony Gwynn 3 (300)	35.00
7B	Tony Gwynn 7 (70)	90.00
7C	Tony Gwynn 2 (2)	600.00
8A	Barry Bonds 3 (300)	20.00
8B	Barry Bonds 7 (70)	50.00
8C	Barry Bonds 4 (4)	250.00
9A	Jeff Bagwell 4 (400)	15.00
9B	Jeff Bagwell 2 (20)	100.00
9C	Jeff Bagwell 5 (5)	200.00
10A	Juan Gonzalez 5 (500)	25.00
10B	Juan Gonzalez 8 (80)	75.00
10C	Juan Gonzalez 9 (9)	200.00
11A	Alex Rodriguez 5 (500)	30.00
11B	Alex Rodriguez 3 (30)	225.00
11C	Alex Rodriguez 4 (4)	600.00
12A	Kenny Lofton 3 (300)	15.00
12B	Kenny Lofton 5 (50)	60.00
12C	Kenny Lofton 4 (4)	150.00

1998 Donruss Preferred

The Donruss Preferred 200-card base set is broken down into five subsets: 100 Grand Stand cards (5:1), 40 Mezzanine (1:6), 30 Club Level (1:12), 20 Field Box (1:23) and 10 Executive Suite (1:65). The base set is paralleled in the Preferred Seating set. Each subset has a different die-cut in the parallel. Inserts in this product include Great X-Pectations, Precious Metals and Title Waves.

		MT
	Complete Set (200):	450.00
	Common Grand Stand (5:1):	.10
	Common Mezzanine (1:6):	.75
	Common Club Level (1:12):	1.00
	Common Field Box: (1:23)	1.50
	Common Executive Suite (1:65):	15.00
	Wax Box:	50.00
1	Ken Griffey Jr. EX	45.00
2	Frank Thomas EX	25.00
3	Cal Ripken Jr. EX	30.00
4	Alex Rodriguez EX	25.00
5	Greg Maddux EX	20.00
6	Mike Piazza EX	25.00
7	Chipper Jones EX	25.00
8	Tony Gwynn FB	17.50
9	Derek Jeter FB	15.00
10	Jeff Bagwell EX	17.50
11	Juan Gonzalez EX	20.00
12	Nomar Garciaparra EX	22.50
13	Andruw Jones FB	7.50
14	Hideo Nomo FB	5.00
15	Roger Clemens FB	12.50
16	Mark McGwire FB	30.00
17	Scott Rolen FB	10.00
18	Vladimir Guerrero FB	10.00
19	Barry Bonds FB	7.50
20	Darin Erstad FB	7.50
21	Albert Belle FB	7.50
22	Kenny Lofton FB	7.50
23	Mo Vaughn FB	7.50
24	Tony Clark FB	4.00
25	Ivan Rodriguez FB	7.50
26	Larry Walker CL	2.50
27	Eddie Murray CL	2.00
28	Andy Pettitte CL	4.00
29	Roberto Alomar CL	4.00
30	Randy Johnson CL	4.00
31	Manny Ramirez CL	5.00
32	Paul Molitor FB	6.00
33	Mike Mussina CL	4.00
34	Jim Thome FB	5.00
35	Tino Martinez CL	2.50
36	Gary Sheffield CL	2.50
37	Chuck Knoblauch CL	2.50
38	Bernie Williams CL	4.00
39	Tim Salmon CL	3.00
40	Sammy Sosa CL	10.00
41	Wade Boggs MZ	1.50
42	Will Clark GS	.25
43	Andres Galarraga CL	2.50
44	Raul Mondesi CL	2.50
45	Rickey Henderson GS	.10
46	Jose Canseco GS	.25
47	Pedro Martinez GS	.40
48	Jay Buhner GS	.25
49	Ryan Klesko GS	.25
50	Barry Larkin CL	2.50
51	Charles Johnson GS	.10
52	Tom Glavine GS	.25
53	Edgar Martinez CL	1.00
54	Fred McGriff GS	.25
55	Moises Alou MZ	.70
56	Dante Bichette GS	.25
57	Jim Edmonds CL	1.00
58	Mark Grace MZ	1.25
59	Chan Ho Park MZ	1.25
60	Justin Thompson MZ	.70
61	John Smoltz MZ	1.25
62	Craig Biggio CL	2.00
63	Ken Caminiti MZ	1.25
64	Deion Sanders MZ	1.25
65	Carlos Delgado GS	.50
66	David Justice CL	2.00
67	J.T. Snow GS	.10
68	Jason Giambi CL	1.00
69	Garret Anderson MZ	.10
70	Rondell White MZ	.25
71	Matt Williams MZ	.30
72	Brady Anderson MZ	.20
73	Eric Karros GS	.25
74	Javier Lopez GS	.20
75	Pat Hentgen GS	.20
76	Todd Hundley GS	.10
77	Ray Lankford GS	.10
78	Denny Neagle GS	.10
79	Henry Rodriguez GS	.10
80	Sandy Alomar Jr. MZ	.70
81	Rafael Palmeiro MZ	1.25
82	Robin Ventura GS	.20
83	John Olerud GS	.20
84	Omar Vizquel GS	.10
85	Joe Randa GS	.10
86	Lance Johnson GS	.10
87	Kevin Brown GS	.20
88	Curt Schilling GS	.25
89	Ismael Valdes GS	.10
90	Francisco Cordova GS	.10
91	David Cone GS	.20
92	Paul O'Neill GS	.20
93	Jimmy Key GS	.10
94	Brad Radke GS	.10
95	Kevin Appier GS	.10
96	Al Martin GS	.10
97	Rusty Greer MZ	.70
98	Reggie Jefferson GS	.10
99	Ron Coomer GS	.10
100	Vinny Castilla GS	.20
101	Bobby Bonilla MZ	.70
102	Eric Young GS	.10
103	Tony Womack GS	.10
104	Jason Kendall GS	.10
105	Jeff Suppan GS	.10
106	Shawn Estes MZ	.70
107	Shawn Green GS	.10
108	Edgardo Alfonzo MZ	.70
109	Alan Benes MZ	.70
110	Bobby Higginson GS	.10
111	Mark Grudzielanek GS	.10
112	Wilton Guerrero GS	.10
113	Todd Greene MZ	.70
114	Pokey Reese GS	.10
115	Jose Guillen CL	1.00
116	Neifi Perez MZ	.70
117	Luis Castillo GS	.10
118	Edgar Renteria GS	.10
119	Karim Garcia GS	.10
120	Butch Huskey GS	.10
121	Michael Tucker GS	.10
122	Jason Dickson GS	.10
123	Todd Walker MZ	1.25
124	Brian Jordan GS	.10
125	Joe Carter GS	.10
126	Matt Morris MZ	.70
127	Brett Tomko MZ	.70
128	Mike Cameron CL	1.50
129	Russ Davis GS	.10
130	Shannon Stewart MZ	.70
131	Kevin Orie GS	.10
132	Scott Spiezio GS	.10
133	Brian Giles GS	.10
134	Raul Casanova GS	.10
135	Jose Cruz Jr. CL	4.00
136	Hideki Irabu GS	.40
137	Bubba Trammell GS	.10
138	Richard Hidalgo CL	1.00
139	Paul Konerko CL	3.00
140	Todd Helton FB	7.50
141	Miguel Tejada CL	4.00
142	Fernando Tatis MZ	.70
143	Ben Grieve FB	12.50
144	Travis Lee FB	7.50
145	Mark Kotsay CL	4.00
146	Eli Marrero MZ	.70
147	David Ortiz CL	2.50
148	Juan Encarnacion MZ	.70
149	Jaret Wright MZ	5.00
150	Livan Hernandez CL	2.00
151	Ruben Rivera GS	.10
152	Brad Fullmer MZ	2.00
153	Dennis Reyes GS	.10
154	Enrique Wilson MZ	.70
155	Todd Dunwoody MZ	.70
156	Derrick Gibson MZ	.70
157	Aaron Boone MZ	.70
158	Ron Wright MZ	.70
159	Preston Wilson MZ	.70
160	Abraham Nunez GS	.10
161	Shane Monahan GS	.10
162	Carl Pavano GS	.25
163	Derrek Lee GS	.25
164	Jeff Abbott GS	.10
165	Wes Helms MZ	.10
166	Brian Rose GS	.15
167	Bobby Estalella GS	.10
168	Ken Griffey Jr. GS	1.50
169	Frank Thomas GS	.70
170	Cal Ripken Jr. GS	1.25
171	Alex Rodriguez GS	1.00
172	Greg Maddux GS	1.00
173	Mike Piazza GS	1.00
174	Chipper Jones GS	1.00
175	Tony Gwynn GS	.70
176	Derek Jeter GS	1.00
177	Jeff Bagwell GS	.50
178	Juan Gonzalez GS	.70
179	Nomar Garciaparra GS	1.00
180	Andruw Jones GS	.40
181	Hideo Nomo GS	.25
182	Roger Clemens GS	.60
183	Mark McGwire GS	2.00
184	Scott Rolen GS	.50
185	Barry Bonds GS	.40
186	Darin Erstad GS	.40
187	Mo Vaughn GS	.40
188	Ivan Rodriguez GS	.50
189	Larry Walker MZ	2.00
190	Andy Pettitte GS	.25
191	Randy Johnson MZ	2.00
192	Paul Molitor GS	.30
193	Jim Thome GS	.20
194	Tino Martinez MZ	2.00
195	Gary Sheffield GS	.20
196	Albert Belle GS	.40
197	Jose Cruz Jr. GS	.25
198	Todd Helton GS	.40
199	Ben Grieve GS	.60
200	Paul Konerko GS	.40

1998 Donruss Preferred Seating

Preferred Seating is a die-cut parallel of the base set. Each section of the base set has a different die-cut.

	MT
Common Grand Stand:	.75
Stars and Rookies: 6-8X	
Common Mezzanine:	2.50
Stars and Rookies: 2-2.5X	
Common Club Level:	4.00
Stars and Rookies: 2X	
Common Field Box:	6.00
Stars and Rookies: 1.5-2X	
Common Executive Suite:	20.00
Stars and Rookies: 1-1.5X	

(See 1998 Donruss Preferred for checklist and base card values.)

1998 Donruss Preferred Great X-pectations

This 26-card insert features a veteran player on one side and a young player on the other. A large "GX" appears in the background on each side. The cards are sequentially numbered to 2,700, with the first 300 of each die-cut around the "GX".

		MT
	Complete Set (26):	225.00
	Common Player:	3.00
	Die-Cuts: 2-3X	
1	Jeff Bagwell, Travis Lee	10.00
2	Jose Cruz Jr., Ken Griffey Jr.	5.00
3	Larry Walker, Ben Grieve	10.00
4	Frank Thomas, Todd Helton	10.00
5	Jim Thome, Paul Konerko	4.00
6	Alex Rodriguez, Miguel Tejada	15.00
7	Greg Maddux, Livan Hernandez	12.50
8	Roger Clemens, Jaret Wright	10.00
9	Albert Belle, Juan Encarnacion	6.00
10	Mo Vaughn, David Ortiz	6.00
11	Manny Ramirez, Mark Kotsay	5.00
12	Tim Salmon, Brad Fullmer	3.00
13	Cal Ripken Jr., Fernando Tatis	20.00
14	Hideo Nomo, Hideki Irabu	3.00
15	Mike Piazza, Todd Greene	15.00
16	Gary Sheffield, Richard Hidalgo	4.00
17	Paul Molitor, Darin Erstad	6.00
18	Ivan Rodriguez, Eli Marrero	6.00
19	Ken Caminiti, Todd Walker	4.00
20	Tony Gwynn, Jose Guillen	12.50
21	Derek Jeter, Nomar Garciaparra	15.00
22	Chipper Jones, Scott Rolen	15.00
23	Juan Gonzalez, Andruw Jones	12.50
24	Barry Bonds, Vladimir Guerrero	6.00
25	Mark McGwire, Tony Clark	25.00
26	Bernie Williams, Mike Cameron	5.00

1998 Donruss Preferred Precious Metals

Precious Metals s a 30-card partial parallel of the Preferred base set. Each card was printed on stock using real silver, gold or platinum. Fifty complete sets were produced.

		MT
	Complete Set (30):	3000.
	Common Player:	25.00
1	Ken Griffey Jr.	300.00
2	Frank Thomas	100.00
3	Cal Ripken Jr.	250.00
4	Alex Rodriguez	225.00
5	Greg Maddux	175.00
6	Mike Piazza	200.00
7	Chipper Jones	200.00
8	Tony Gwynn	150.00
9	Derek Jeter	200.00
10	Jeff Bagwell	100.00
11	Juan Gonzalez	150.00
12	Nomar Garciaparra	200.00
13	Andruw Jones	75.00
14	Hideo Nomo	30.00
15	Roger Clemens	125.00
16	Mark McGwire	300.00
17	Scott Rolen	75.00
18	Barry Bonds	75.00
19	Darin Erstad	55.00
20	Kenny Lofton	45.00
21	Mo Vaughn	45.00
22	Ivan Rodriguez	50.00
23	Randy Johnson	50.00
24	Paul Molitor	60.00
25	Jose Cruz Jr.	25.00
26	Paul Konerko	25.00
27	Todd Helton	60.00
28	Ben Grieve	60.00
29	Travis Lee	60.00
30	Mark Kotsay	25.00

1998 Donruss Preferred Tins

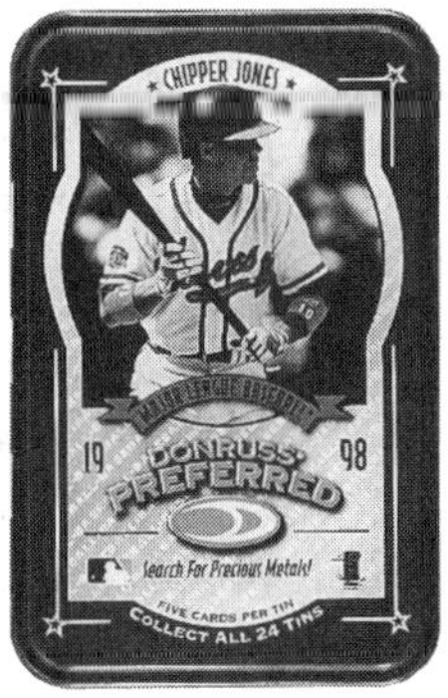

Donruss Preferred was packaged in collectible tins. Each tin contained five cards and featured one of 24 players on the top. Silver (numbered to 999) and gold (199) parallel tins were also produced and included in hobby-only boxes. The values shown are for empty tins.

		MT
Complete Set (24):		20.00
Common Player:		.25
Gold Tins (199): 15X		
Silver Tins (999): 5x		
1	Todd Helton	.75
2	Ben Grieve	1.00
3	Cal Ripken Jr.	2.00
4	Alex Rodriguez	1.75
5	Greg Maddux	1.25
6	Mike Piazza	1.50
7	Chipper Jones	1.50
8	Travis Lee	1.00
9	Derek Jeter	1.50
10	Jeff Bagwell	1.00
11	Juan Gonzalez	1.25
12	Mark McGwire	2.50
13	Hideo Nomo	.50
14	Roger Clemens	1.00
15	Andruw Jones	.75
16	Paul Molitor	.50
17	Vladimir Guerrero	.75
18	Jose Cruz Jr.	.25
19	Nomar Garciaparra	1.50
20	Scott Rolen	1.00
21	Ken Griffey Jr.	2.50
22	Larry Walker	.25
23	Frank Thomas	1.00
24	Tony Gwynn	1.25

1998 Donruss Preferred Double-Wide Tins

Double-wide flip-top tins of Donruss Preferred cards were a real exclusive with a price tag of about $6. The double-wide retail tins use the same player checklist and photo as the green hobby-version single tins, but have predominantly blue color. Values shown are for opened tins.

		MT
Complete Set (12):		25.00
Common Tin:		.75
1	Todd Helton, Ben Grieve	.75
2	Cal Ripken Jr., Alex Rodriguez	5.00
3	Greg Maddux, Mike Piazza	3.00
4	Chipper Jones, Travis Lee	2.50
5	Derek Jeter, Jeff Bagwell	3.00
6	Juan Gonzalez, Mark McGwire	5.00
7	Hideo Nomo, Roger Clemens	2.00
8	Andruw Jones, Paul Molitor	1.50
9	Vladimir Guerrero, Jose Cruz Jr.	.75
10	Nomar Garciaparra, Scott Rolen	2.00
11	Ken Griffey Jr., Larry Walker	3.00
12	Tony Gwynn, Frank Thomas	2.00

1998 Donruss Preferred Tin Boxes

The boxes for 1998 Donruss Preferred consisted of a lithographed steel lidded box which contained 24 tin packs. The basic tin box was green in color and individually serial numbered to 999. A parallel gold box issue was randomly inserted in Preferred cases and had boxes numbered to 199. Values shown are for empty boxes.

		MT
Complete Set (24):		110.00
Common Player:		2.00
Gold: 2.5X		
1	Todd Helton	3.50
2	Ben Grieve	5.00
3	Cal Ripken Jr.	10.00
4	Alex Rodriguez	9.00
5	Greg Maddux	6.50
6	Mike Piazza	7.50
7	Chipper Jones	7.50
8	Travis Lee	5.00
9	Derek Jeter	7.50
10	Jeff Bagwell	5.00
11	Juan Gonzalez	6.00
12	Mark McGwire	12.50
13	Hideo Nomo	2.50
14	Roger Clemens	5.00
15	Andruw Jones	4.00
16	Paul Molitor	2.50
17	Vladimir Guerrero	4.00
18	Jose Cruz Jr.	2.00
19	Nomar Garciaparra	7.50
20	Scott Rolen	5.00
21	Ken Griffey Jr.	12.50
22	Larry Walker	2.00
23	Frank Thomas	5.00
24	Tony Gwynn	6.00

1998 Donruss Preferred Title Waves

This 30-card set features players who won awards or titles between 1993-1997. Printed on plastic stock, each card is sequentially numbered to the year the player won the award. The card fronts feature the Title Waves logo, a color player photo in front of a background of fans and the name of the award the player won.

		MT
Complete Set (30):		350.00
Common Player:		4.00
1	Nomar Garciaparra	20.00
2	Scott Rolen	10.00
3	Roger Clemens	15.00
4	Gary Sheffield	4.00
5	Jeff Bagwell	15.00
6	Cal Ripken Jr.	25.00
7	Frank Thomas	15.00
8	Ken Griffey Jr.	35.00
9	Larry Walker	5.00
10	Derek Jeter	20.00
11	Juan Gonzalez	17.50
12	Bernie Williams	6.00
13	Andruw Jones	12.50
14	Andy Pettitte	5.00
15	Ivan Rodriguez	10.00
16	Alex Rodriguez	22.50
17	Mark McGwire	35.00
18	Andres Galarraga	4.00
19	Hideo Nomo	5.00
20	Mo Vaughn	7.50
21	Randy Johnson	6.00
22	Chipper Jones	20.00
23	Greg Maddux	17.50
24	Manny Ramirez	7.50
25	Tony Gwynn	17.50
26	Albert Belle	6.00
27	Kenny Lofton	5.00
28	Mike Piazza	20.00
29	Paul Molitor	6.00
30	Barry Bonds	7.50

1998 Donruss Signature Series Preview

This 29-card insert was a surprise addition to Donruss Update. The set features autographs from top rookies and stars. The number of cards produced varies for each player. The card fronts have a color player photo in front of a checkered border with the signature in a white area near the bottom.

	MT
Common Player:	15.00
Sandy Alomar Jr. (96)	45.00
Andy Benes (135)	30.00
Russell Branyan (188)	25.00
Tony Clark (188)	40.00
Juan Encarnacion (193)	20.00
Brad Fullmer (396)	15.00
Juan Gonzalez (108)	250.00
Ben Grieve (100)	150.00
Todd Helton (101)	100.00
Richard Hidalgo (380)	15.00
A.J. Hinch (400)	15.00
Damian Jackson (15)	200.00
Chipper Jones (112)	300.00
Chuck Knoblauch (98)	80.00
Travis Lee (101)	75.00
Mike Lowell (450)	15.00
Greg Maddux (92)	250.00
Kevin Millwood (395)	80.00
Magglio Ordonez (420)	20.00
David Ortiz (393)	15.00
Rafael Palmeiro (107)	75.00
Cal Ripken Jr. (22)	1200.
Alex Rodriguez (23)	1000.
Curt Schilling (100)	75.00
Randall Simon (380)	15.00
Fernando Tatis (400)	15.00
Miguel Tejada (375)	20.00
Robin Ventura (95)	50.00
Kerry Wood (373)	30.00

1998 Donruss Signature Series

The 140-card base set has a white border encasing the player photo with the logo stamped with silver foil. Card backs have a small photo and complete year-by-year statistics. Signature Proofs are a parallel to the base set utilizing holo-foil treatment and "Signature Proof" written down the left edge of the card front. Each card is numbered "1 of 150" on the card back.

		MT
Complete Set (140):		75.00
Common Player:		.15
Wax Box:		250.00
1	David Justice	.30
2	Derek Jeter	2.50
3	Nomar Garciaparra	2.50
4	Ryan Klesko	.25
5	Jeff Bagwell	1.00
6	Dante Bichette	.25
7	Ivan Rodriguez	1.00
8	Albert Belle	.75
9	Cal Ripken Jr.	3.00
10	Craig Biggio	.50
11	Barry Larkin	.40
12	Jose Guillen	.20
13	Will Clark	.30
14	J.T. Snow	.15
15	Chuck Knoblauch	.30
16	Todd Walker	.20
17	Scott Rolen	.75
18	Rickey Henderson	.40
19	Juan Gonzalez	1.25
20	Justin Thompson	.15
21	Roger Clemens	1.25
22	Ray Lankford	.15
23	Jose Cruz Jr.	.25
24	Ken Griffey Jr.	4.00
25	Andruw Jones	.60
26	Darin Erstad	.60
27	Jim Thome	.30
28	Wade Boggs	.40
29	Ken Caminiti	.20
30	Todd Hundley	.15
31	Mike Piazza	2.50
32	Sammy Sosa	2.50
33	Larry Walker	.75
34	Matt Williams	.30
35	Frank Thomas	1.00
36	Gary Sheffield	.25
37	Alex Rodriguez	2.50
38	Hideo Nomo	.25
39	Kenny Lofton	.50
40	John Smoltz	.20
41	Mo Vaughn	.50
42	Edgar Martinez	.15
43	Paul Molitor	.50
44	Rafael Palmeiro	.50
45	Barry Bonds	.60
46	Vladimir Guerrero	1.00
47	Carlos Delgado	.75
48	Bobby Higginson	.15
49	Greg Maddux	2.00
50	Jim Edmonds	.15
51	Randy Johnson	.75
52	Mark McGwire	4.00
53	Rondell White	.20
54	Raul Mondesi	.20
55	Manny Ramirez	1.00
56	Pedro Martinez	1.00
57	Tim Salmon	.25
58	Moises Alou	.20
59	Fred McGriff	.20
60	Garret Anderson	.15
61	Sandy Alomar Jr.	.15
62	Chan Ho Park	.20
63	Mark Kotsay	.20
64	Mike Mussina	.50
65	Tom Glavine	.25
66	Tony Clark	.40
67	Mark Grace	.25
68	Tony Gwynn	2.00
69	Tino Martinez	.40
70	Kevin Brown	.25
71	Todd Greene	.15
72	Andy Pettitte	.30
73	Livan Hernandez	.15
74	Curt Shilling	.25
75	Andres Galarraga	.30
76	Rusty Greer	.15
77	Jay Buhner	.15
78	Bobby Bonilla	.20
79	Chipper Jones	2.00
80	Eric Young	.15
81	Jason Giambi	.15
82	Javy Lopez	.20
83	Roberto Alomar	.40
84	Bernie Williams	.40
85	A.J. Hinch	.15
86	Kerry Wood	1.00
87	Juan Encarnacion	.25
88	Brad Fullmer	.15
89	Ben Grieve	.60
90	*Magglio Ordonez*	6.00
91	Todd Helton	.50
92	Richard Hidalgo	.15
93	Paul Konerko	.25
94	Aramis Ramirez	.25
95	Ricky Ledee	.40
96	Derrek Lee	.15
97	Travis Lee	.50
98	*Matt Anderson*	1.00
99	Jaret Wright	.50
100	David Ortiz	.20
101	Carl Pavano	.20
102	*Orlando Hernandez*	5.00
103	Fernando Tatis	.40
104	Miguel Tejada	.20
105	*Rolando Arrojo*	2.00
106	*Kevin Millwood*	6.00
107	Ken Griffey Jr. (Checklist)	1.25
108	Frank Thomas (Checklist)	.75
109	Cal Ripken Jr. (Checklist)	1.00
110	Greg Maddux (Checklist)	.75
111	John Olerud	.40
112	David Cone	.30
113	Vinny Castilla	.20
114	Jason Kendall	.20
115	Brian Jordan	.15
116	Hideki Irabu	.25
117	Bartolo Colon	.15
118	Greg Vaughn	.25
119	David Segui	.15
120	Bruce Chen	.25
121	*Julio Ramirez*	1.00
122	*Troy Glaus*	8.00
123	*Jeremy Giambi*	2.00
124	*Ryan Minor*	3.00
125	Richie Sexson	.15
126	Dermal Brown	.25
127	Adrian Beltre	.50
128	Eric Chavez	.50
129	*J.D. Drew*	20.00
130	*Gabe Kapler*	6.00
131	*Masato Yoshii*	.50
132	*Mike Lowell*	1.00
133	*Jim Parque*	1.00
134	Roy Halladay	.40
135	*Carlos Lee*	4.00
136	*Jin Ho Cho*	.40
137	Michael Barrett	.50
138	*Fernando Seguignol*	2.00
139	*Odalis Perez*	1.50
140	Mark McGwire (Checklist)	1.50

1998 Donruss Signature Series Proofs

This parallel set differs from the regular issue Signature Series base cards in the presence at left-front of a vertical stack of gold refractive foil strips on which SIGNATURE PROOF is spelled out. Also, backs of the proofs have a gold, rather than white, background.

	MT
Complete Set (140):	1200.
Common Player:	2.00
Veteran Stars: 15-20X	
Young Stars/Rookies: 8-15X	
(See 1998 Donruss Signature Series for checklist and base card values.)	

1998 Donruss Signature Series Autographs (Red)

Autographs were inserted one per pack and feature the player photo over a silver and red foil background. The featured player's autograph appears on the bottom portion on front with the Donruss logo stamped in gold foil. Autographs are un-numbered. The first 100 cards signed by each player are blue, sequentially numbered and designated as "Century Marks". The next 1,000 signed are green, sequentially numbered and designated as "Millennium

Marks." Greg Maddux signed only 12 regular Donruss Signature Autographs.

	MT
Common Player:	2.50
Roberto Alomar (150)	50.00
Sandy Alomar Jr. (700)	12.50
Moises Alou (900)	12.50
Gabe Alvarez (2,900)	2.50
Wilson Alvarez (1,600)	4.00
Jay Bell (1,500)	4.00
Adrian Beltre (1,900)	12.50
Andy Benes (2,600)	5.00
Aaron Boone (3,400)	2.50
Russell Branyan (1,650)	4.00
Orlando Cabrera (3,100)	2.50
Mike Cameron (1,150)	7.50
Joe Carter (400)	15.00
Sean Casey (2,275)	15.00
Bruce Chen (150)	25.00
Tony Clark (2,275)	7.50
Will Clark (1,400)	15.00
Matt Clement (1,400)	7.50
Pat Cline (400)	10.00
Ken Cloude (3,400)	4.00
Michael Coleman (2,800)	2.50
David Cone (25)	125.00
Jeff Conine (1,400)	5.00
Jacob Cruz (3,200)	2.50
Russ Davis (3,500)	2.50
Jason Dickson (1,400)	4.00
Todd Dunwoody (3,500)	2.50
Juan Encarnacion (3,400)	7.50
Darin Erstad (700)	25.00
Bobby Estalella (3,400)	2.50
Jeff Fassero (3,400)	2.50
John Franco (1,800)	2.50
Brad Fullmer (3,100)	5.00
Jason Giambi (3,100)	5.00
Derrick Gibson (1,200)	5.00
Todd Greene (1,400)	5.00
Ben Grieve (1,400)	20.00
Mark Grudzielanek (3,200)	4.00
Vladimir Guerrero (2,100)	15.00
Wilton Guerrero (1,900)	4.00
Jose Guillen (2,400)	6.00
Todd Helton (1,300)	15.00
Richard Hidalgo (3,400)	4.00
A.J. Hinch (2,900)	4.00
Butch Huskey (1,900)	4.00
Raul Ibanez (3,300)	2.50
Damian Jackson (900)	2.50
Geoff Jenkins (3,100)	4.00
Eric Karros (650)	9.00
Ryan Klesko (400)	12.00
Mark Kotsay (3,600)	5.00
Ricky Ledee (2,200)	12.50
Derrek Lee (3,400)	4.00
Travis Lee (150)	35.00
Travis Lee (facsimile autograph, "SAMPLE" on back)	3.00
Javier Lopez (650)	10.00
Mike Lowell (3,500)	7.50
Greg Maddux (12)	450.00
Eli Marrero (3,400)	2.50
Al Martin (1,300)	4.00
Rafael Medina (1,400)	2.50
Scott Morgan (900)	7.50
Abraham Nunez (3,500)	2.50
Paul O'Neill (1,000)	12.50
Luis Ordaz (2,700)	4.00
Magglio Ordonez (3,200)	6.00
Kevin Orie (1,350)	5.00
David Ortiz (3,400)	5.00
Rafael Palmeiro (1,000)	15.00
Carl Pavano (2,600)	4.00
Neifi Perez (3,300)	2.50
Dante Powell (3,050)	2.50
Aramis Ramirez (2,800)	7.50
Mariano Rivera (900)	10.00
Felix Rodriguez (1,400)	5.00
Henry Rodriguez (3,400)	4.00
Scott Rolen (1,900)	30.00
Brian Rose (1,400)	5.00
Curt Schilling (900)	12.50
Richie Sexson (3,500)	7.50
Randall Simon (3,500)	5.00
J.T. Snow (400)	10.00
Jeff Suppan (1,400)	5.00
Fernando Tatis (3,900)	5.00
Miguel Tejada (3,800)	5.00
Brett Tomko (3,400)	2.50
Bubba Trammell (3,900)	2.50
Ismael Valdez (1,900)	5.00
Robin Ventura (1,400)	10.00
Billy Wagner (3,900)	4.00
Todd Walker (1,900)	7.50
Daryle Ward (400)	7.50
Rondell White (3,400)	7.50
Antone Williamson (3,350)	2.50
Dan Wilson (2,400)	2.50
Enrique Wilson (3,400)	2.50
Preston Wilson (2,100)	5.00
Tony Womack (3,500)	2.50
Kerry Wood (3,400)	10.00

1998 Donruss Signature Series Century Marks (Blue)

This 121-card set is a serially numbered, blue-foil parallel of the Autographs insert set and limited to 100 cards signed by each featured player (unless otherwise shown in the checklist).

	MT
Common Player:	15.00
Roberto Alomar	60.00
Sandy Alomar Jr.	20.00
Moises Alou	20.00
Gabe Alvarez	15.00
Wilson Alvarez	15.00
Brady Anderson	20.00
Jay Bell	15.00
Albert Belle	60.00
Adrian Beltre	50.00
Andy Benes	20.00
Wade Boggs	65.00
Barry Bonds	90.00
Aaron Boone	15.00
Russell Branyan	15.00
Jay Buhner	20.00
Ellis Burks	15.00
Orlando Cabrera	15.00
Mike Cameron	20.00
Ken Caminiti	30.00
Joe Carter	15.00
Sean Casey	20.00
Bruce Chen	20.00
Tony Clark	25.00
Will Clark	35.00
Roger Clemens	125.00
Matt Clement	20.00
Pat Cline	15.00
Ken Cloude	15.00
Michael Coleman	15.00
David Cone	25.00
Jeff Conine	15.00
Jacob Cruz	15.00
Jose Cruz Jr.	20.00
Russ Davis	15.00
Jason Dickson	15.00
Todd Dunwoody	15.00
Scott Elarton	15.00
Darin Erstad	35.00
Bobby Estalella	15.00
Jeff Fassero	15.00
John Franco	15.00
Brad Fullmer	20.00
Andres Galarraga	35.00
Nomar Garciaparra	175.00
Jason Giambi	20.00
Derrick Gibson	20.00
Tom Glavine	25.00
Juan Gonzalez	150.00
Todd Greene	15.00
Ben Grieve	60.00
Mark Grudzielanek	15.00
Vladimir Guerrero	60.00
Wilton Guerrero	15.00
Jose Guillen	20.00
Tony Gwynn	150.00
Todd Helton	45.00
Richard Hidalgo	20.00
A.J. Hinch	20.00
Butch Huskey	20.00
Raul Ibanez	15.00
Damian Jackson	15.00
Geoff Jenkins	20.00
Derek Jeter	150.00
Randy Johnson	50.00
Chipper Jones	150.00
Eric Karros (50)	25.00
Ryan Klesko	25.00
Chuck Knoblauch	45.00
Mark Kotsay	20.00
Ricky Ledee	20.00
Derrek Lee	15.00
Travis Lee	35.00
Javier Lopez	20.00
Mike Lowell	25.00
Greg Maddux	200.00
Eli Marrero	15.00
Al Martin	15.00
Rafael Medina	15.00
Paul Molitor	65.00
Scott Morgan	20.00
Mike Mussina	50.00
Abraham Nunez	15.00
Paul O'Neill	30.00
Luis Ordaz	15.00
Magglio Ordonez	20.00
Kevin Orie	15.00
David Ortiz	20.00
Rafael Palmeiro	40.00
Carl Pavano	20.00
Neifi Perez	15.00
Andy Pettitte	40.00
Aramis Ramirez	20.00
Cal Ripken Jr.	250.00
Mariano Rivera	30.00
Alex Rodriguez	200.00
Felix Rodriguez	15.00
Henry Rodriguez	20.00
Scott Rolen	80.00
Brian Rose	15.00
Curt Schilling	30.00
Richie Sexson	30.00
Randall Simon	20.00
J.T. Snow	15.00
Darryl Strawberry	30.00
Jeff Suppan	20.00
Fernando Tatis	20.00
Brett Tomko	15.00
Bubba Trammell	15.00
Ismael Valdez	20.00
Robin Ventura	30.00
Billy Wagner	20.00
Todd Walker	20.00
Daryle Ward	15.00
Rondell White	25.00
Matt Williams (80)	45.00
Antone Williamson	15.00
Dan Wilson	15.00
Enrique Wilson	15.00
Preston Wilson	20.00
Tony Womack	15.00
Kerry Wood	35.00

1998 Donruss Signature Series Millennium Marks (Green)

This is a green-foil parallel version of the Autographs insert set and features 1,000 cards signed by the featured player (unless otherwise shown in the checklist. Cards are not numbered.

	MT
Complete Set (125):	
Common Player:	6.00
Roberto Alomar	25.00
Sandy Alomar Jr.	10.00
Moises Alou	12.50
Gabe Alvarez	6.00
Wilson Alvarez	6.00
Brady Anderson (800)	10.00
Jay Bell	6.00
Albert Belle (400)	50.00
Adrian Beltre	20.00
Andy Benes	7.50
Wade Boggs (900)	30.00
Barry Bonds (400)	65.00
Aaron Boone	6.00
Russell Branyan	7.50
Jay Buhner (400)	17.50
Ellis Burks (900)	7.50
Orlando Cabrera	6.00
Mike Cameron	7.50
Ken Caminiti (900)	15.00
Joe Carter	10.00
Sean Casey	20.00
Bruce Chen	10.00
Tony Clark	12.50
Will Clark	20.00
Roger Clemens (400)	85.00
Matt Clement (900)	6.00
Pat Cline	6.00
Ken Cloude	6.00
Michael Coleman	6.00
David Cone	17.50
Jeff Conine	6.00
Jacob Cruz	6.00
Jose Cruz Jr. (850)	10.00
Russ Davis (950)	6.00
Jason Dickson (950)	6.00
Todd Dunwoody	6.00
Scott Elarton (900)	6.00
Juan Encarnacion	10.00
Darin Erstad	20.00
Bobby Estalella	6.00
Jeff Fassero	6.00
John Franco (950)	6.00
Brad Fullmer	10.00
Andres Galarraga (900)	12.50
Nomar Garciaparra (400)	100.00
Jason Giambi	7.50
Derrick Gibson	6.00
Tom Glavine (700)	20.00
Juan Gonzalez	60.00
Todd Greene	6.00
Ben Grieve	25.00
Mark Grudzielanek	6.00
Vladimir Guerrero	25.00
Wilton Guerrero	6.00
Jose Guillen	7.50
Tony Gwynn (900)	60.00
Todd Helton	20.00
Richard Hidalgo	7.50
A.J. Hinch	7.50
Butch Huskey	7.50
Raul Ibanez	6.00
Damian Jackson	6.00
Geoff Jenkins	7.50
Derek Jeter (400)	90.00
Randy Johnson (800)	25.00
Chipper Jones (900)	65.00
Eric Karros	7.50
Ryan Klesko	7.50
Chuck Knoblauch (900)	20.00
Mark Kotsay	10.00
Ricky Ledee	15.00
Derrek Lee	7.50
Travis Lee	20.00
Javier Lopez (800)	10.00
Mike Lowell	10.00
Greg Maddux (400)	125.00
Eli Marrero	6.00
Al Martin (950)	6.00
Rafael Medina (850)	6.00
Paul Molitor (900)	30.00
Scott Morgan	7.50
Mike Mussina (900)	15.00
Abraham Nunez	6.00
Paul O'Neill (900)	12.50
Luis Ordaz	6.00
Magglio Ordonez	10.00
Kevin Orie	6.00
David Ortiz	10.00
Rafael Palmeiro (900)	20.00
Carl Pavano	7.50
Neifi Perez	6.00
Andy Pettitte (900)	15.00
Dante Powell (950)	6.00
Aramis Ramirez	12.50
Cal Ripken Jr. (375)	150.00
Mariano Rivera	15.00
Alex Rodriguez (350)	125.00
Felix Rodriguez	7.50
Henry Rodriguez	7.50
Scott Rolen	40.00
Brian Rose	7.50
Curt Schilling	12.50
Richie Sexson	12.50
Randall Simon	10.00
J.T. Snow	6.00
Darryl Strawberry (900)	17.50
Jeff Suppan	7.50
Fernando Tatis	12.50
Miguel Tejada	10.00
Brett Tomko	6.00
Bubba Trammell	6.00
Ismael Valdes	7.50
Robin Ventura	15.00
Billy Wagner (900)	7.50
Todd Walker	12.50
Daryle Ward	6.00
Rondell White	12.50
Matt Williams (820)	20.00
Antone Williamson	6.00
Dan Wilson	6.00
Enrique Wilson	6.00
Preston Wilson (400)	12.50
Tony Womack	6.00
Kerry Wood	25.00

1998 Donruss Signature Series Significant Signatures

This 18-card autographed set features some of baseball's all-time great players. Each card is sequentially numbered to 2,000. The Sandy Koufax autographs weren't received in time prior to release and were redeemable by sending in the Billy Williams autograph, the collector would then receive both the Williams and Koufax back. Exchange cards were also initially released for Nolan Ryan and Ozzie Smith.

	MT
Complete Set (18):	1200.
Common Player:	25.00
Ernie Banks	50.00
Yogi Berra	60.00
George Brett	80.00
Catfish Hunter	25.00
Al Kaline	40.00
Harmon Killebrew	40.00
Ralph Kiner	30.00
Sandy Koufax	150.00
Eddie Mathews	50.00
Don Mattingly	80.00
Willie McCovey	25.00
Stan Musial	75.00
Phil Rizzuto (edition of 1,000)	45.00
Nolan Ryan	150.00
Nolan Ryan (Exchange card)	30.00
Ozzie Smith	60.00
Ozzie Smith (Exchange card)	15.00
Duke Snider	50.00
Don Sutton	25.00
Billy Williams	50.00

1998 Donruss Signature Series Redemption Baseballs

Redemption cards authentically autographed baseballs were randomly inserted in Donruss Signature Series packs. Baseballs are laser burned with a Donruss seal to ensure authenticity. Every ball, except Ben Grieve's, is serial numbered within the edition limit shown. Redemption cards, no longer valid, are valued about 10% of the corresponding ball.

	MT
Common Autographed Ball:	35.00
Signing Bonus Redemption Card: 10%	
Roberto Alomar (60)	90.00
Sandy Alomar Jr. (60)	45.00
Ernie Banks (12)	175.00
Ken Caminiti (60)	60.00
Tony Clark (60)	45.00
Jacob Cruz (12)	100.00
Russ Davis (60)	35.00
Juan Encarnacion (60)	60.00
Bobby Estalella (60)	35.00
Jeff Fassero (60)	35.00

Mark Grudzielanek (60)	35.00
Ben Grieve (30)	75.00
Jose Guillen (120)	35.00
Tony Gwynn (60)	200.00
Al Kaline (12)	175.00
Paul Konerko (100)	35.00
Travis Lee (100)	60.00
Mike Lowell (60)	35.00
Eli Marrero (60)	35.00
Eddie Mathews (12)	160.00
Paul Molitor (60)	125.00
Stan Musial (12)	225.00
Abraham Nunez (12)	100.00
Luis Ordaz (12)	75.00
Magglio Ordonez (12)	75.00
Scott Rolen (60)	100.00
Bubba Trammell (24)	60.00
Robin Ventura (60)	75.00
Billy Wagner (60)	50.00
Rondell White (60)	45.00
Antone Williamson (12)	35.00
Tony Womack (60)	35.00

1986 Dorman's Cheese

Found in specially-marked packages of Dorman's American Cheese Singles, this set consists of 10 two-card panels of baseball superstars. Labeled "Super Star Limited Edition," the panels measure 2" x 1-1/2" and have a perforation line in the center. Fronts have a color photo along with the Dorman's logo and the player's name, team and position. Due to a lack of MLB licensing, all team insignias have been airbrushed from the players' caps. Backs contain brief player statistics. The unnumbered panels and cards are listed here alphabetically by the player on the left.

		MT
	Complete Panel Set (10):	15.00
	Complete Singles Set (20):	5.00
	Common Panel:	.50
	Common Player:	.10
	Panel (1)	2.00
(1)	George Brett	.50
(2)	Jack Morris	.10
	Panel (2)	4.00
(3)	Gary Carter	.10
(4)	Cal Ripken Jr.	1.00
	Panel (3)	.50
(5)	Dwight Gooden	.10
(6)	Kent Hrbek	.10
	Panel (4)	2.00
(7)	Rickey Henderson	.30
(8)	Mike Schmidt	.50
	Panel (5)	1.00
(9)	Keith Hernandez	.10
(10)	Dale Murphy	.25
	Panel (6)	2.00
(11)	Reggie Jackson	.40
(12)	Eddie Murray	.25
	Panel (7)	2.50
(13)	Don Mattingly	.50
(14)	Ryne Sandberg	.35
	Panel (8)	1.00
(15)	Willie McGee	.10
(16)	Robin Yount	.40
	Panel (9)	1.00
(17)	Rick Sutcliff (Sutcliffe)	.10
(18)	Wade Boggs	.50
	Panel (10)	1.00
(19)	Dave Winfield	.35
(20)	Jim Rice	.10

1981 Drake's

Producing its first baseball card set since 1950, Drake Bakeries, in conjunction with Topps, issued a 33-card set entitled "Big Hitters." The cards, in standard 2-1/2" x 3-1/2" size, feature 19 American League and 14 National League sluggers. Full-color action photos, containing a facsimile autograph, are positioned in red frames for A.L. players and blue frames for N.L. hitters. The player's name, team, position, and Drake's logo are also on front. Backs, which are similar to the regular 1981 Topps issue, contain the card number, statistical and biographical information, and the Drake's logo.

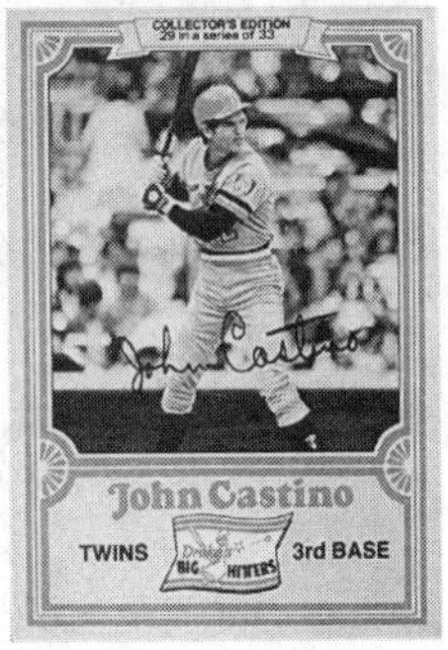

		MT
	Complete Set (33):	7.50
	Common Player:	.20
1	Carl Yastrzemski	1.00
2	Rod Carew	.75
3	Pete Rose	1.50
4	Dave Parker	.25
5	George Brett	1.00
6	Eddie Murray	.70
7	Mike Schmidt	1.00
8	Jim Rice	.35
9	Fred Lynn	.25
10	Reggie Jackson	.90
11	Steve Garvey	.50
12	Ken Singleton	.25
13	Bill Buckner	.25
14	Dave Winfield	.70
15	Jack Clark	.25
16	Cecil Cooper	.25
17	Bob Horner	.25
18	George Foster	.25
19	Dave Kingman	.30
20	Cesar Cedeno	.25
21	Joe Charboneau	.35
22	George Hendrick	.25
23	Gary Carter	.30
24	Al Oliver	.25
25	Bruce Bochte	.25
26	Jerry Mumphrey	.25
27	Steve Kemp	.25
28	Bob Watson	.25
29	John Castino	.25
30	Tony Armas	.25
31	John Mayberry	.25
32	Carlton Fisk	.75
33	Lee Mazzilli	.25

1982 Drake's

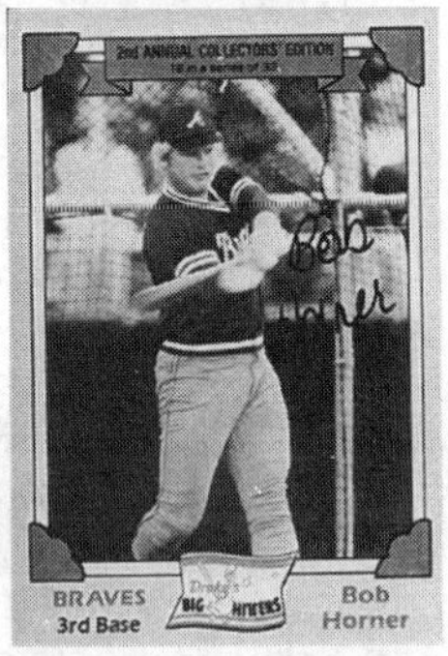

Drake Bakeries produced, in conjunction with Topps, a "2nd Annual Collectors' Edition" in 1982. Thirty-three standard-size cards (2-1/2" x 3-1/2") make up the set. Like the previous year, the set is entitled "Big Hitters" and is comprised of 19 American League players and 14 from the National League. Fronts have a mounted photo appearance and contain a facsimile autograph. The player's name, team, position, and the Drake's logo also are on front. Backs, other than being numbered 1-33 and containing a Drake's copyright line, are identical to the regular 1982 Topps.

		MT
	Complete Set (33):	4.00
	Common Player:	.15
1	Tony Armas	.15
2	Buddy Bell	.15
3	Johnny Bench	.60
4	George Brett	.75
5	Bill Buckner	.15
6	Rod Carew	.50
7	Gary Carter	.25
8	Jack Clark	.15
9	Cecil Cooper	.15
10	Jose Cruz	.15
11	Dwight Evans	.15
12	Carlton Fisk	.45
13	George Foster	.15
14	Steve Garvey	.25
15	Kirk Gibson	.15
16	Mike Hargrove	.15
17	George Hendrick	.15
18	Bob Horner	.15
19	Reggie Jackson	.55
20	Terry Kennedy	.15
21	Dave Kingman	.15
22	Greg Luzinski	.15
23	Bill Madlock	.15
24	John Mayberry	.15
25	Eddie Murray	.35
26	Graig Nettles	.15
27	Jim Rice	.15
28	Pete Rose	1.00
29	Mike Schmidt	.70
30	Ken Singleton	.15
31	Dave Winfield	.45
32	Butch Wynegar	.15
33	Richie Zisk	.15

1983 Drake's

Seventeen American League and 16 National League "Big Hitters" make up the 33-card "3rd Annual Collectors' Edition" set issued by Drake Bakeries in 1983. The Topps-produced cards measure 2-1/2" x 3-1/2". Fronts are somewhat similar in design to the previous year's set. Backs are identical to the 1983 Topps regular issue except for being numbered 1-33 and containing a Drake's logo and copyright line.

		MT
	Complete Set (33):	5.00
	Common Player:	.15
1	Don Baylor	.15
2	Bill Buckner	.15
3	Rod Carew	.40
4	Gary Carter	.25
5	Jack Clark	.15
6	Cecil Cooper	.15
7	Dwight Evans	.15
8	George Foster	.15
9	Pedro Guerrero	.15
10	George Hendrick	.15
11	Bob Horner	.15
12	Reggie Jackson	.40
13	Steve Kemp	.15
14	Dave Kingman	.15
15	Bill Madlock	.15
16	Gary Matthews	.15
17	Hal McRae	.15
18	Dale Murphy	.25
19	Eddie Murray	.40
20	Ben Oglivie	.15
21	Al Oliver	.15
22	Jim Rice	.20
23	Cal Ripken, Jr.	2.00
24	Pete Rose	1.00
25	Mike Schmidt	.75
26	Ken Singleton	.15
27	Gorman Thomas	.15
28	Jason Thompson	.15
29	Mookie Wilson	.15
30	Willie Wilson	.15
31	Dave Winfield	.40
32	Carl Yastrzemski	.50
33	Robin Yount	.50

1984 Drake's

For the fourth year in a row, Drake Bakeries issued a 33-card "Big Hitters" set. The 1984 edition, produced again by Topps, includes 17 National League players and 16 from the American League. As in all previous years, card fronts feature the player in a batting pose. Backs are identical to the 1984 Topps regular issue except for being numbered 1-33 and carrying the Drake's logo and copyright line. The cards are the standard 2-1/2" x 3-1/2".

		MT
	Complete Set (33):	5.00
	Common Player:	.15
1	Don Baylor	.15
2	Wade Boggs	.65
3	George Brett	.75
4	Bill Buckner	.15
5	Rod Carew	.50
6	Gary Carter	.25
7	Ron Cey	.15
8	Cecil Cooper	.15
9	Andre Dawson	.20
10	Steve Garvey	.25
11	Pedro Guerrero	.15
12	George Hendrick	.15
13	Keith Hernandez	.15
14	Bob Horner	.15
15	Reggie Jackson	.50
16	Steve Kemp	.15
17	Ron Kittle	.15
18	Greg Luzinski	.15
19	Fred Lynn	.15
20	Bill Madlock	.15
21	Gary Matthews	.15
22	Dale Murphy	.25
23	Eddie Murray	.40
24	Al Oliver	.15
25	Jim Rice	.20
26	Cal Ripken, Jr.	1.50
27	Pete Rose	1.00
28	Mike Schmidt	.75
29	Darryl Strawberry	.20
30	Alan Trammell	.15
31	Mookie Wilson	.15
32	Dave Winfield	.40
33	Robin Yount	.50

1985 Drake's

The "5th Annual Collectors' Edition" set produced by Topps for Drake Bakeries consists of 33 "Big Hitters" and 11 "Super Pitchers." The new "Super Pitchers" feature increased the set's size from the usual 33 cards to 44. The 2-1/2" x 3-1/2" cards show the player in a game-action photo. Backs differ from the regular 1985 Topps issue only in that they are numbered 1-44 and carry the Drake's logo.

		MT
	Complete Set (44):	7.00
	Common Player:	.15
1	Tony Armas	.15
2	Harold Baines	.15
3	Don Baylor	.15
4	George Brett	.75
5	Gary Carter	.25
6	Ron Cey	.15
7	Jose Cruz	.15
8	Alvin Davis	.15
9	Chili Davis	.15
10	Dwight Evans	.15
11	Steve Garvey	.25
12	Kirk Gibson	.15
13	Pedro Guerrero	.15
14	Tony Gwynn	.75
15	Keith Hernandez	.15
16	Kent Hrbek	.15
17	Reggie Jackson	.50
18	Gary Matthews	.15
19	Don Mattingly	.90
20	Dale Murphy	.25
21	Eddie Murray	.40
22	Dave Parker	.15
23	Lance Parrish	.15
24	Tim Raines	.20
25	Jim Rice	.20
26	Cal Ripken, Jr.	1.50
27	Juan Samuel	.15
28	Ryne Sandberg	.60
29	Mike Schmidt	.75
30	Darryl Strawberry	.20
31	Alan Trammell	.15
32	Dave Winfield	.40
33	Robin Yount	.50
34	Mike Boddicker	.15
35	Steve Carlton	.50
36	Dwight Gooden	.15
37	Willie Hernandez	.15
38	Mark Langston	.15
39	Dan Quisenberry	.15
40	Dave Righetti	.15
41	Tom Seaver	.50
42	Bob Stanley	.15
43	Rick Sutcliffe	.15
44	Bruce Sutter	.15

1986 Drake's

For the sixth consecutive year, Drake Bakeries issued a baseball card set. The 1986 set was the first in that sequence not produced by Topps. Cards were available only by buying the snack products on whose boxes the cards were printed. Cards, measuring 2-1/2" x 3-1/2", were issued in either two-, three-, or four-card panels. Fourteen panels, consisting of 37 different players, comprise the set. The players who make up the set are tabbed as either "Big Hitters" or "Super Pitchers." Logos of various Drake's products can be found on the panel backs. The value of the set is higher when collected in either panel or complete box form.

		MT
	Complete Panel Set (14):	45.00
	Complete Singles Set (37):	15.00
	Common Panel:	1.00
	Common Player:	.25
	Panel (1)	1.50
1	Gary Carter	.35
2	Dwight Evans	.25
	Panel (2)	2.00
3	Reggie Jackson	.45
4	Dave Parker	.25
	Panel (3)	1.50
5	Rickey Henderson	.35
6	Pedro Guerrero	.25

	Panel (4)	2.50
7	Don Mattingly	.75
8	Mike Marshall	.25
9	Keith Moreland	.25
	Panel (5)	7.50
10	Keith Hernandez	.25
11	Cal Ripken Jr.	2.00
	Panel (6)	2.00
12	Dale Murphy	.45
13	Jim Rice	.25
	Panel (7)	3.00
14	George Brett	.75
15	Tim Raines	.25
	Panel (8)	1.50
16	Darryl Strawberry	.25
17	Bill Buckner	.25
	Panel (9)	5.00
18	Dave Winfield	.40
19	Ryne Sandberg	.60
20	Steve Balboni	.25
21	Tommy Herr	.25
	Panel (10)	6.50
22	Pete Rose	1.00
23	Willie McGee	.25
24	Harold Baines	.25
25	Eddie Murray	.45
	Panel (11)	5.00
26	Mike Schmidt	.75
27	Wade Boggs	.50
28	Kirk Gibson	.25
	Panel (12)	2.00
29	Bret Saberhagen	.25
30	John Tudor	.25
31	Orel Hershiser	.25
	Panel (13)	7.50
32	Ron Guidry	.25
33	Nolan Ryan	2.00
34	Dave Steib	.25
	Panel (12)	2.00
35	Dwight Gooden	.25
36	Fernando Valenzuela	.25
37	Tom Browning	.25

1987 Drake's

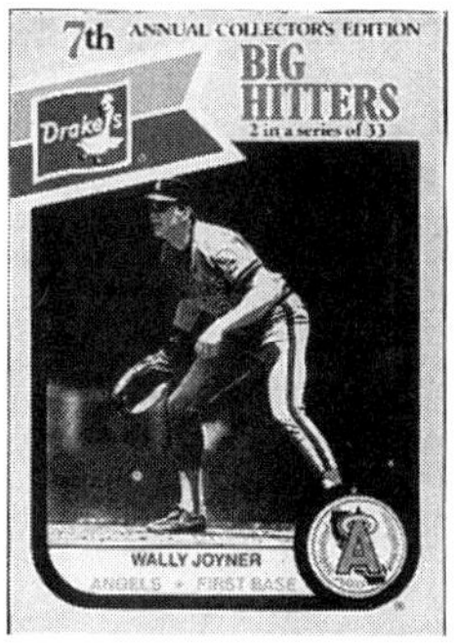

For the seventh consecutive season, Drake Bakeries produced a baseball card set. The 2-1/2" x 3-1/2" cards were printed in either two-, three-, or four-card panels on boxes of various snack products distributed in the eastern U.S. The set is comprised of 33 cards, with 25 players branded as "Big Hitters" and eight as "Super Pitchers". Fronts carry a game-action photo and the Drake's logo surrounded by a brown and yellow border. Backs have the player's complete major league record.

		MT
Complete Panel Set (12):		35.00
Complete Singles Set (33):		15.00
Common Panel:		1.50
Common Single Player:		.25
	Panel (1)	1.75
1	Darryl Strawberry	.25
2	Wally Joyner	.35
	Panel (2)	2.00
3	Von Hayes	.25
4	Jose Canseco	.45
	Panel (3)	7.50
5	Dave Winfield	.40
6	Cal Ripken Jr.	2.00
7	Keith Moreland	.25
	Panel (4)	3.00
8	Don Mattingly	1.00
9	Willie McGee	.25
	Panel (5)	2.00
10	Keith Hernandez	.25
11	Tony Gwynn	.65
	Panel (6)	4.00
12	Rickey Henderson	.35
13	Dale Murphy	.35
14	George Brett	.50
15	Jim Rice	.25
	Panel (7)	6.00
16	Wade Boggs	.45
17	Kevin Bass	.25
18	Dave Parker	.25
19	Kirby Puckett	.75
	Panel (8)	3.00
20	Gary Carter	.25
21	Ryne Sandberg	.45
22	Harold Baines	.25
	Panel (9)	4.00
23	Mike Schmidt	.75
24	Eddie Murray	.40
25	Steve Sax	.25
	Panel (10)	1.50
26	Dwight Gooden	.25
27	Jack Morris	.25
	Panel (11)	2.00
28	Ron Darling	.25
29	Fernando Valenzuela	.25
30	John Tudor	.25
	Panel (12)	8.00
31	Roger Clemens	.60
32	Nolan Ryan	2.00
33	Mike Scott	.25

1988 Drake's

The 8th annual edition of this set includes 33 glossy full-color cards printed on cut-out panels of two, three or four cards on Drake's dessert snack boxes. Card fronts have white borders with a large red and blue "Super Pitchers" (6 cards) or "Big Hitters" (27 cards) caption upper-left, beside the "8th Annual Collector's Edition" label. Backs are printed in black and include the card number, personal data, batting/pitching record and sponsor logos.

		MT
Complete Panel Set (12):		35.00
Complete Singles Set (33):		12.00
Common Panel:		1.50
Common Player:		.25
	Panel (1)	2.00
1	Don Mattingly	.50
2	Tim Raines	.25
	Panel (2)	2.00
3	Darryl Strawberry	.25
4	Wade Boggs	.45
	Panel (3)	2.00
5	Keith Hernandez	.25
6	Mark McGwire	2.00
	Panel (4)	3.00
7	Rickey Henderson	.35
8	Mike Schmidt	.50
9	Dwight Evans	.25
	Panel (5)	2.00
10	Gary Carter	.25
11	Paul Molitor	.40
	Panel (6)	4.00
12	Dave Winfield	.40
13	Alan Trammell	.25
14	Tony Gwynn	.50
	Panel (7)	4.00
15	Dale Murphy	.35
16	Andre Dawson	.35
17	Von Hayes	.25
18	Willie Randolph	.25
	Panel (8)	4.00
19	Kirby Puckett	.75
20	Juan Samuel	.25
21	Eddie Murray	.40
	Panel (9)	2.00
22	George Bell	.25
23	Larry Sheets	.25
24	Eric Davis	.25
	Panel (10)	7.50
25	Cal Ripken Jr.	2.00
26	Pedro Guerrero	.25
27	Will Clark	.40
	Panel (11)	1.50
28	Dwight Gooden	.25
29	Frank Viola	.25
	Panel (12)	5.00
30	Roger Clemens	.50
31	Rick Sutcliffe	.25
32	Jack Morris	.25
33	John Tudor	.25

1989 Dubuque Braves

Given away at Sunday home games to correspond with player appearances at a stadium autograph booth, these 2-3/8" x 3-1/2" cards were sponsored by the Braves' hot dog concessionaire, Dubuque Meats. Cards have player photos centered within a dark blue border. A Braves cap is at upper-left, the hot dog company's logo at lower-left. The player's name, team and position are in white. Backs, printed in black on white, have the Braves logo, a few personal facts and figures and previous year/career stats. Because only 15,000 of each card were distributed over the course of the season, compilation of complete sets is extremely challenging. The checklist here is arranged in alphabetical order. Dion James' card was never officially released, but several specimens have been found on uncut sheets.

		MT
Complete Set (29):		45.00
Common Player:		1.00
(1)	Paul Assenmacher	1.00
(2)	Jim Acker	1.00
(3)	Jose Alvarez	1.00
(4)	Bruce Benedict	1.00
(5)	Jeff Blauser	1.50
(6)	Joe Boever	1.00
(7)	Marty Clary	1.00
(8)	Bruce dal Canton	1.00
(9)	Jody Davis	1.00
(10)	Mark Eichhorn	1.00
(11)	Ron Gant	4.00
(12)	Tom Glavine	6.00
(13)	Tommy Gregg	1.00
(14)	Dion James	8.00
(15)	Clarence Jones	1.00
(16)	Derek Lilliquist	1.00
(17)	Roy Majtyka	1.00
(18)	Oddibe McDowell	1.00
(19)	Dale Murphy	6.00
(20)	Russ Nixon	1.00
(21)	Gerald Perry	1.00
(22)	John Russell	1.00
(23)	Lonnie Smith	1.00
(24)	Pete Smith	1.00
(25)	Zane Smith	1.00
(26)	John Smoltz	4.00
(27)	Brian Snitker	1.00
(28)	Andres Thomas	1.00
(29)	Jeff Treadway	1.00
(30)	Jeff Wetherby	1.00
(31)	Ed Whited	1.00
(32)	Bobby Wine	1.00

1990 Dubuque Braves

For a second season, the Braves' hot dog vendor, Dubuque Meats, sponsored this season-long promotion. Up to four different player cards were given out at Sunday home games, corresponding with player appearances at an autograph booth. Some player cards were distributed more than once, while others, such as Dale Murphy, who was traded, were only given out one day. Players were added to the set right up through the final Sunday home game of the season. Complete sets are extremely difficult to assemble. The player photo on these 2-3/8" x 3-1/2" cards have a white border. A red banner beneath the photo has the player's name, uniform number and position printed in black. Backs are printed in dark blue and feature full minor and major league stats. The checklist here is arranged alphabetically.

		MT
Complete Set (35):		60.00
Common Player:		1.00
(1)	Steve Avery	1.00
(2)	Jeff Blauser	1.00
(3)	Joe Boever	1.00
(4)	Francisco Cabrera	1.00
(5)	Pat Corrales	1.00
(6)	Bobby Cox	1.00
(7)	Nick Esasky	1.00
(8)	Ron Gant	2.50
(9)	Tom Glavine	3.00
(10)	Mark Grant	1.00
(11)	Tommy Gregg	1.00
(12)	Dwayne Henry	1.00
(13)	Alexis Infante	1.00
(14)	Clarence Jones	1.00
(15)	Dave Justice	7.50
(16)	Jimmy Kremers	1.00
(17)	Charlie Leibrandt	1.00
(18)	Mark Lemke	1.00
(19)	Roy Majtyka	1.00
(20)	Leo Mazzone	1.00
(21)	Oddibe McDowell	1.00
(22)	Dale Murphy	5.00
(23)	Phil Niekro	4.00
(24)	Greg Olson	1.00
(25)	Jim Presley	1.00
(26)	Lonnie Smith	1.00
(27)	Pete Smith	1.00
(28)	John Smoltz	3.00
(29)	Brian Snitker	1.00
(30)	Andres Thomas	1.00
(31)	Jeff Treadway	1.00
(32)	Ernie Whitt	1.00
(33)	Jimy Williams	1.00
(34)	Homer the Brave (mascot)	1.00
(35)	Rally (mascot)	1.00

1990 Dubuque Braves Team Photo Set

This three-panel team set was given away at an early-season game, commemorating the Braves' 25th season in Atlanta. The sheet measures 11" x 28-1/2". The top panel is a team photo. The two lower panels contain 30 individual cards, 2-1/2" x 3-1/4", perforated to allow them to be separated. Backs are printed in red and blue. The perforated team set is much more common than the Dubuque cards given out a few at a time during Sunday home games. The checklist below is arranged according to uniform numbers which appear on the front of each card.

		MT
Complete Panel:		12.50
Common Player:		.25
1	Oddibe McDowell	.25
2	Russ Nixon	.25
3	Dale Murphy	2.00
4	Jeff Blauser	.25
5	Ron Gant	1.00
10	Greg Olson	.25
12	Ernie Whitt	.25
14	Andres Thomas	.25
15	Jeff Treadway	.25
16	Tommy Gregg	.25
17	Nick Esasky	.25
18	Jim Presley	.25
19	Francisco Cabrera	.25
20	Mark Lemke	.25
23	Dave Justice	2.50
24	Derek Lilliquist	.25
25	Pete Smith	.25
27	Lonnie Smith	.25
29	John Smoltz	1.50
30	Mike Stanton	.25
36	Tony Castillo	.25
37	Joe Boever	.25
40	Charlie Kerfeld	.25
45	Charlie Leibrandt	.25
46	Dwayne Henry	.25
47	Tom Glavine	1.50
48	Marty Clary	.25
49	Rick Luecken	.25
58a	Joe Hesketh	.25
58b	Alexis Infante	.25

1991 Dubuque Braves

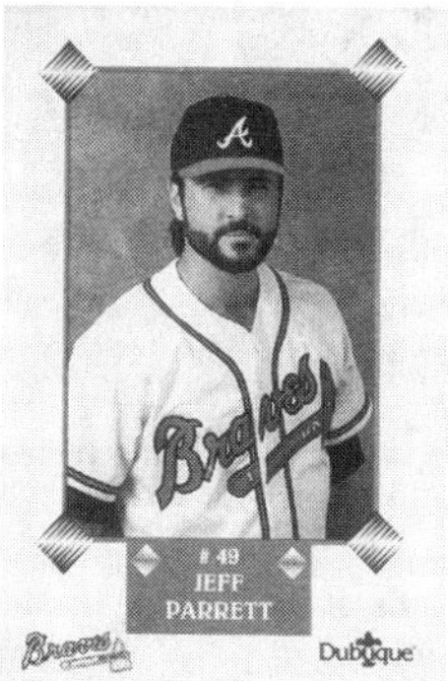

At each Sunday home game the Braves distributed some 15,000 of each of three to six player cards to kids under 14. The cards corresponded to appearances by those players at an autograph session. That method of distribution makes accumulation of complete sets very difficult. Sponsor of the set for the third straight year was the stadium's hot dog concessionaire, Dubuque Meats. Their logo appears in the upper-left corner of the player photo. At lower-right on the 2-1/4" x 3-1/2" cards is a baseball diamond figure with the team and player name and the year of issue. There is a white outer border on the card, with the photo framed in white-pinstriped dark blue. Backs are printed in dark blue, with logos, complete stats, biographical information and the player's uniform number. Cards are checklisted here in alphabetical order.

		MT
Complete Set (41):		60.00
Common Player:		1.00
(1)	Steve Avery	1.00
(2)	Jim Beauchamp	1.00
(3)	Mike Bell	1.00
(4)	Rafael Belliard	1.00
(5)	Juan Berenguer	1.00
(6)	Jeff Blauser	1.00
(7)	Sid Bream	1.00
(8)	Francisco Cabrera	1.00
(9)	Jim Clancy	1.00
(10)	Pat Corrales	1.00

(11)	Bobby Cox	1.00
(12)	Nick Esasky	1.00
(13)	Marvin Freeman	1.00
(14)	Ron Gant	4.00
(15)	Tom Glavine	3.00
(16)	Mark Grant	1.00
(17)	Tommy Gregg	1.00
(18)	Mike Heath	1.00
(19)	Brian Hunter	1.00
(20)	Clarence Jones	1.00
(21)	David Justice	5.00
(22)	Charlie Leibrandt	1.00
(23)	Mark Lemke	1.00
(24)	Leo Mazzone	1.00
(25)	Kent Mercker	1.00
(26)	Keith Mitchell	1.00
(27)	Otis Nixon	1.00
(28)	Greg Olson	1.00
(29)	Jeff Parrett	1.00
(30)	Terry Pendleton	1.00
(31)	Armando Reynoso	1.00
(32)	Deion Sanders	5.00
(33)	Lonnie Smith	1.00
(34)	Pete Smith	1.00
(35)	John Smoltz	3.00
(36)	Mike Stanton	1.00
(37)	Jeff Treadway	1.00
(38)	Jimy Williams	1.00
(39)	Ned Yost	1.00
(40)	Homer the Brave (mascot)	1.00
(41)	Rally (mascot)	1.00

1991 Dubuque Braves Team Photo Set

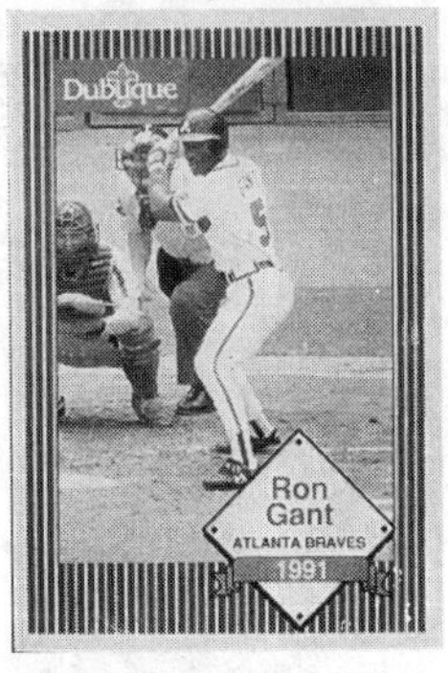

This team photo/player card triptych was an early season give-away. Each of the three fold-out panels measures about 9-1/2" x 10-1/2". The 30 individual player cards have perforated edges for easy removal from the sheet. The 2-1/8" x 3-1/8" cards have a player portrait photo at center, with blue diamond designs at the corners. A red box below the photo has the player's name and uniform number. Blue Braves and Dubuque logos appear at the lower corners of the white border. Backs are printed in red and blue and include full stats and a facsimile autograph, plus a few biographical details. The team sheet cards are considered much more common than the other Braves baseball card promotional giveaways, especially in complete sets. Cards are checklisted here alphabetically.

		MT
Complete Panel:		12.00
Common Player:		.25
(1)	Steve Avery	.25
(2)	Rafael Belliard	.25
(3)	Juan Berenguer	.25
(4)	Jeff Blauser	.25
(5)	Sid Bream	.25
(6)	Francisco Cabrera	.25
(7)	Bobby Cox	.25
(8)	Nick Esasky	.25
(9)	Marvin Freeman	.25
(10)	Ron Gant	.75
(11)	Tom Glavine	.75
(12)	Mark Grant	.25
(13)	Tommy Gregg	.25
(14)	Mike Heath	.25
(15)	Danny Heep	.25
(16)	David Justice	2.00
(17)	Charlie Leibrandt	.25
(18)	Mark Lemke	.25
(19)	Kent Mercker	.25
(20)	Otis Nixon	.25
(21)	Greg Olson	.25
(22)	Jeff Parrett	.25
(23)	Terry Pendleton	.35
(24)	Deion Sanders	.75
(25)	Doug Sisk	.25
(26)	Lonnie Smith	.25
(27)	Pete Smith	.25
(28)	John Smoltz	.75
(29)	Mike Stanton	.25
(30)	Jeff Treadway	.25

1992 Dunkin' Donuts Red Sox

The 1992 Boston Red Sox were the subject of a set of 30 cards, including the manager and coaches. Co-sponsored by Dunkin' Donuts and WVIT-TV and released in May in Connecticut, the set was sold as an uncut, perforated sheet of 30 cards, measuring about 9-1/2" x 10-3/4". Individual perforated cards could be removed from the sheet; they measure 2-1/8" x 3-1/8". Fronts have a player photo framed in black on a white background. In the border beneath the photo are the player's name, position, uniform number and sponsors' logos. Backs have complete major and minor league stats. The cards are checklisted here by uniform number, which appears on the card front.

		MT
Complete Panel:		6.00
Common Player:		.20
2	Luis Rivera	.20
3	Jody Reed	.20
6	Tony Pena	.20
7	Rick Burleson	.20
11	Tim Naehring	.20
12	Ellis Burks	.50
16	Frank Viola	.25
17	Butch Hobson	.20
18	Carlos Quintana	.20
20	John Marzano	.20
21	Roger Clemens	2.00
23	Tom Brunansky	.20
25	Jack Clark	.20
26	Wade Boggs	2.00
27	Greg Harris	.20
29	Phil Plantier	.20
30	Matt Young	.20
32	Gary Allenson	.20
34	Don Zimmer	.20
35	Rich Gale	.20
37	Al Bumbry	.20
39	Mike Greenwell	.25
41	Jeff Reardon	.20
42	Mo Vaughn	1.50
43	Kevin Morton	.20
44	Danny Darwin	.20
47	Mike Gardiner	.20
48	Tony Fossas	.20
50	Tom Bolton	.20
55	Joe Hesketh	.20

1993 Duracell Power Players

The Duracell battery company issued a 48-card set in 1993 that was presented in two 24-card series. The cards were available through the mail with proofs of purchase from selected Duracell products. Cards feature a Duracell logo at top, with a black and orange border surrounding a color photo of the player. The player's name is printed in yellow with team and position in white on top of a green background. Because the set was not licensed to use major league uniform logos, they were airbrushed off the photos. Backs have a player portrait photo, a facsimile autograph, recent stats and a few biographical and career details printed over a ballpark scene. Series I cards are numbered "X of 24", Series II cards are so indicated beneath the card number.

		MT
Complete Set (48):		8.00
Common Player:		.10
Series 1		5.00
1	Roger Clemens	.50
2	Frank Thomas	.75
3	Andre Dawson	.15
4	Orel Hershiser	.10
5	Kirby Puckett	.45
6	Edgar Martinez	.10
7	Craig Biggio	.10
8	Terry Pendleton	.10
9	Mark McGwire	2.00
10	Dave Stewart	.10
11	Ozzie Smith	.35
12	Doug Drabek	.10
13	Dwight Gooden	.10
14	Tony Gwynn	.50
15	Carlos Baerga	.10
16	Robin Yount	.35
17	Barry Bonds	.45
18	Bip Roberts	.10
19	Don Mattingly	.60
20	Nolan Ryan	1.00
21	Tom Glavine	.15
22	Will Clark	.30
23	Cecil Fielder	.10
24	Dave Winfield	.30
Series 2		3.00
1	Cal Ripken, Jr.	1.00
2	Melido Perez	.10
3	John Kruk	.10
4	Charlie Hayes	.10
5	George Brett	.45
6	Ruben Sierra	.10
7	Deion Sanders	.20
8	Andy Van Slyke	.10
9	Fred McGriff	.20
10	Benito Santiago	.10
11	Charles Nagy	.10
12	Greg Maddux	.50
13	Ryne Sandberg	.40
14	Dennis Martinez	.10
15	Ken Griffey, Jr.	2.00
16	Jim Abbott	.10
17	Barry Larkin	.15
18	Gary Sheffield	.15
19	Jose Canseco	.40
20	Jack McDowell	.10
21	Darryl Strawberry	.15
22	Delino DeShields	.10
23	Dennis Eckersley	.10
24	Paul Molitor	.40

1992 Dynasty

This unauthorized collectors' issue features original artwork of top players in standard 2-1/2" x 3-1/2" format. Fronts have the player paintings against a colored background with the player's first, last and nickname in white vertically at upper left. Backs have a few biographic notes, a line of 1991 stats and a Dynasty logo.

		MT
Complete Set (8):		5.00
Common Player:		.50
		.50
1	Dave Justice	.50
2	Ken Griffey, Jr.	2.00
3	Rickey Henderson	.50
4	Bo Jackson	.50
5	Will Clark	.50
6	Sandy Alomar	.50
7	Eric Davis	.50
8	Nolan Ryan	1.50

E

1990 Eclipse Stars of the Negro Leagues

Better known in the field of comic books than baseball cards, Eclipse of California produced this set of cards honoring stars of the defunct Negro Leagues. The 2-1/2" x 3-1/2" cards have water color paintings (by Mark Chiarello) of the players on front. Well-written (by Jack Morelli) career summaries on back give a real flavor for this brand of pro ball and its era. Copyright lines for all parties are at bottom back. The issue was sold only as a boxed set.

		MT
Complete Set (36):		15.00
Common Player:		.25
1	Header card	.25
2a	Josh Gibson (wrong picture, "H" on cap)	2.00
2b	Josh Gibson (correct picture, "G" on cap)	2.00
3	Cannonball Redding	.25
4	Biz Mackey	.50
5	Pop Lloyd	.50
6	Bingo DeMoss	.50
7	Willard Brown	.25
8	John Donaldson	.25
9	Monte Irvin	.75
10	Ben Taylor	.25
11	Willie Wells	.65
12	Dave Brown	.25
13	Leon Day	.50
14	Ray Dandridge	.50
15	Turkey Stearnes	.50
16	Rube Foster	.50
17	Oliver Marcelle	.25
18	Judy Johnson	.50
19	Christobel Torrienti	.25
20	Satchel Paige	2.00
21	Mule Suttles	.35
22	John Beckwith	.25
23	Martin Dihigo	.50
24	Willie Foster	.25
25	Dick Lundy	.25
26	Buck Leonard	.50
27	Smokey Joe Williams	.50
28	Cool Papa Bell	.50
29	Bullet Rogan	.50
30	Newt Allen	.35
31	Bruce Petway	.25
32	Jose Mendez	.25
33	Louis Santop	.25
34	Jud Wilson	.25
35	Sammy Hughes	.25
36a	Oscar Charleston (wrong picture, "G" on cap)	.50
36b	Oscar Charleston (correct picture, "H" on cap)	.50

1992 Eclipse Negro League

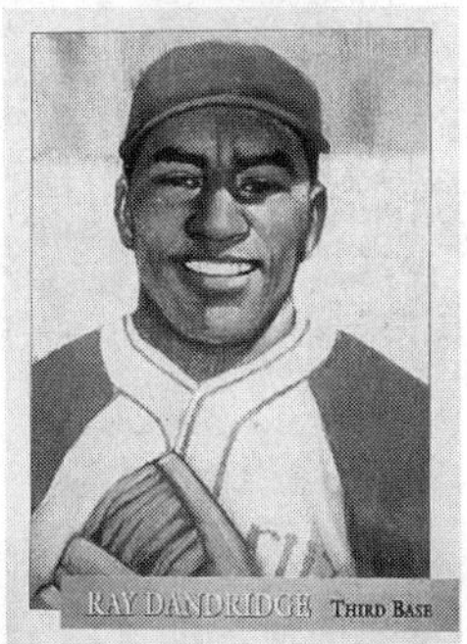

Four Negro League baseball cards were handed out to the first 50,000 fans attending Negro League Baseball Players Association night at Shea Stadium on June 2. Cards feature the artwork of Paul Lee on front. Backs have a career summary and biographical details, along with the Mets and Eclipse logos.

		MT
Complete Set (4):		5.00
Common Player:		1.00
1	Monte Irvin	1.50
2	"Buck" Leonard	1.00
3	Josh Gibson	2.00
4	Ray Dandridge	1.00

1992 Eclipse Negro League BPA

Sponsored by Kraft, and produced by Eclipse, 15,000 sets of these cards were made for distribution at The Negro League Baseball Players Association night, Aug. 9 at Lackawanna County Stadium, home of the Scranton Wilkes-Barre Red Barons. The 2-1/2" x 3-1/2" cards have watercolor player pictures on front, by artist John Clapp. Backs have career summaries, sponsor and issuer logos and copyright information.

		MT
Complete Set (18):		6.00
Common Player:		.25
1	Leon Day	.50
2	Clinton (Casey) Jones	.25
3	Lester Lockett	.25
4	Monte Irvin	.75
5	Armando Vazquez	.25
6	Jimmie Crutchfield	.25
7	Ted Radcliffe	.25
8	Albert Haywood	.25
9	Artie Wilson	.45
10	Sam Jethroe	.45
11	Edsall Walker	.25
12	Bill Wright	.25
13	Jim Cohen	.25
14	Andy Porter	.25
15	Tommy Sampson	.25
16	Buck Leonard	.50
17	Josh Gibson	.75
18	Martinez Jackson	.50

1990 Elite Senior League

This 126-card set features the players of the first Senior League season. Cards are printed on high quality stock and feature full-color photos. The card backs feature statistics. Earl Weaver and Mike Easler cards were distributed as promo cards.

		MT
Complete Set:		6.00
Common Player:		.05
1	Curt Flood	.10
2	Bob Tolan	.05
3	Dick Bosman	.05
4	Ivan DeJesus	.05
5	Dock Ellis	.05
6	Roy Howell	.05
7	Lamar Johnson	.05
8	Steve Kemp	.05
9	Ken Landreaux	.05
10	Randy Lerch	.05
11	Jon Matlack	.05
12	Gary Rajsich	.05
13	Lenny Randle	.05
14	Elias Sosa	.05
15	Ozzie Virgil	.05
16	Milt Wilcox	.05
17	Steve Henderson	.05
18	Ray Burris	.05
19	Mike Easler	.05
20	Juan Eichelberger	.05
21	Rollie Fingers	.50
22	Toby Harrah	.05
23	Randy Johnson	.05
24	Dave Kingman	.10
25	Lee Lacy	.05
26	Tito Landrum	.05
27	Paul Mirabella	.05
28	Mickey Rivers	.10
29	Rodney Scott	.05
30	Tim Stoddard	.05
31	Ron Washington	.05
32	Jerry White	.05
33	Dick Williams	.05
34	Clete Boyer	.10
35	Steve Dillard	.05
36	Garth Iorg	.05
37	Bruce Kison	.05
38	Wayne Krenchicki	.05
39	Ron LeFlore	.10
40	Tippy Martinez	.05
41	Omar Moreno	.05
42	Jim Morrison	.05
43	Graig Nettles	.10
44	Jim Nettles	.05
45	Wayne Nordhagen	.05
46	Al Oliver	.10
47	Jerry Royster	.05
48	Sammy Stewart	.05
49	Randy Bass	.05
50	Vida Blue	.10
51	Bruce Bochy	.05
52	Doug Corbett	.05
53	Jose Cruz	.05
54	Jamie Easterly	.05
55	Pete Falcone	.05
56	Bob Galasso	.05
57	Johnny Grubb	.05
58	Bake McBride	.05
59	Dyar Miller	.05
60	Tom Paciorek	.05
61	Ken Reitz	.05
62	U.L. Washington	.05
63	Alan Ashby	.05
64	Pat Dobson	.05
65	Doug Bird	.05
66	Marty Castillo	.05
67	Dan Driessen	.05
68	Wayne Garland	.05
69	Tim Ireland	.05
70	Ron Jackson	.05
71	Bobby Jones	.05
72	Dennis Leonard	.05
73	Rick Manning	.05
74	Amos Otis	.05
75	Pat Putnam	.05
76	Eric Rasmussen	.05
77	Paul Blair	.05
78	Bert Campaneris	.05
79	Cesar Cedeno	.10
80	Ed Figueroa	.05
81	Ross Grimsley	.05
82	George Hendrick	.05
83	Cliff Johnson	.05
84	Mike Kekich	.05
85	Rafael Landestoy	.05
86	Larry Milbourne	.05
87	Bobby Molinaro	.05
88	Sid Monge	.05
89	Rennie Stennett	.05
90	Derrell Thomas	.05
91	Earl Weaver	.25
92	Gary Allenson	.05
93	Pedro Borbon	.05
94	Al Bumbry	.05
95	Bill Campbell	.05
96	Bernie Carbo	.05
97	Ferguson Jenkins	.50
98	Pete LaCock	.05
99	Bill Lee	.05
100	Tommy McMillan	.05
101	Joe Pittman	.05
102	Gene Richards	.05
103	Leon Roberts	.05
104	Tony Scott	.05
105	Doug Simunic	.05
106	Rick Wise	.05
107	Willie Aikens	.05
108	Juan Beniquez	.05
109	Bobby Bonds	.10
110	Sergio Ferrer	.05
111	Chuck Ficks	.05
112	George Foster	.10
113	Dave Hilton	.05
114	Al Holland	.05
115	Clint Hurdle	.05
116	Bill Madlock	.10
117	Steve Ontiveros	.05
118	Roy Thomas	.05
119	Luis Tiant	.10
120	Walt Williams	.05
121	Vida Blue	.10
122	Bobby Bonds	.10
123	Rollie Fingers	.50
124	George Foster	.10
125	Fergie Jenkins	.50
126	Dave Kingman	.10

1983 English's Chicken Baltimore Orioles Lids

The World Champion O's were featured on this set of fried chicken bucket lids. Printed on thick cardboard discs with the blank backs heavily waxed, the lids come in two sizes, 8-3/8" diameter and 7-1/4". The design is the same on each, with a black, white and orange player portrait at center, flanked by some personal data and '83 stats. His name is in orange below, with his position and team in black beneath that. In the wide orange border is "English's Salutes / 1983 Champions". The player's union logo is at right of the portrait, but cap logos are missing because the issue was not licensed through MLB. The lids are not numbered.

		MT
Complete Set (13):		25.00
Common Player:		1.00
	SMALL LIDS (7-1/4")	
(1)	Mike Boddicker	1.00
(2)	Rich Dauer	1.00
(3)	Storm Davis	1.00
(4)	Mike Flanagan	1.00
(5)	John Lowenstein	1.00
(6)	Tippy Martinez	1.00
(7)	Gary Roenicke	1.00
(8)	Ken Singleton	1.00
	LARGE LIDS (8-3/8")	
(9)	Rick Dempsey	1.00
(10)	Scott McGregor	1.00
(11)	Eddie Murray	4.00
(12)	Jim Palmer	4.00
(13)	Cal Ripken, Jr.	12.00

1991 Enor Kevin Maas Story

This 20-card set was produced by one of the hobby's leading manufacturers of plastic supplies. Not surprisingly, the set was housed in a 6" by 8-1/4" plastic album with eight four-card plastic sheets inside. Besides the cards and album, the set came with a biographical brochure on the 1990 A.L. Rookie of the Year runner-up. Each of the 2-1/2" x 3-1/2" cards features one or more color photos of the player on front. A series of red stripes at the top of the card features the player's name in the uppermost stripe. Backs have the same stripe motif at top and include career information or stats at center. The logos of MLB, the Yankees and Enor appear at the bottom.

	MT
Complete Set w/Album (20):	4.00
Single Card:	.10

F

1988 Fantastic Sam's

This set of color player discs (2-1/2" diameter) was distributed during a Superstar Sweepstakes sponsored by Fantastic Sam's Family Haircutters' 1,800 stores nationwide. Each card consists of two connected discs (bright orange fronts, white backs) perforated for easy separation. One disc features the baseball player photo, the other carries the sweepstakes logo and a list of prizes. Player discs carry a Fantastic Sam's Baseball Superstars header curved above the photo, with player name, team and position printed in black. Backs are black-and-white and include personal info, card number and 1987 stats. Sweepstakes discs list contest prizes (Grand Prize was 4 tickets to a 1988 Championship game) on the front and an entry form on the flipside. Below the prize list is a silver scratch-off rectangle which may reveal an instant prize.

		MT
Complete Set (20):		5.00
Uncut Sheet:		25.00
Common Player:		.20
1	Kirby Puckett	.75
2	George Brett	.90
3	Mark McGwire	3.00
4	Wally Joyner	.30
5	Paul Molitor	.65
6	Alan Trammell	.25
7	George Bell	.20
8	Wade Boggs	.65
9	Don Mattingly	.90
10	Julio Franco	.20
11	Ozzie Smith	.65
12	Will Clark	.40
13	Dale Murphy	.30
14	Eric Davis	.25
15	Andre Dawson	.25
16	Tim Raines	.30
17	Darryl Strawberry	.25
18	Tony Gwynn	.75
19	Mike Schmidt	.75
20	Pedro Guerrero	.20

1994 FanFest Roberto Clemente Commemorative

In an unpricedented show of co-operation, the five Major League Baseball trading card licensees created this set of Roberto Clemente commemorative cards for distribution at the All-Star FanFest. Cards were available at participating manufacturers' booths, making complete sets somewhat difficult to assemble. Topps anf Fleer based their commemorative cards on their companies' respective 1955 and 1963 Clemente cards. Donruss had artist Dick Perez create a Diamond King card of Clemente, while Upper Deck and Score Select created new designs. It is believed fewer than 10,000 of each card exist.

		MT
Complete Set (5):		100.00
Common Card:		15.00
1	Roberto Clemente (Donruss Diamond King)	20.00
2	Roberto Clemente (Fleer 1963 reprint)	20.00
3	Roberto Clemente (Score Select)	20.00
4	Roberto Clemente (Topps 1955 reprint)	30.00
5	Roberto Clemente (Upper Deck)	20.00

1995 FanFest Nolan Ryan Commemorative

At the July 7-11, 1995, FanFest, held in Dallas, Tex., site of the All-Star Game, five of Major League Baseball's principal licensees combined on a wrapper redemption program which offered Nolan Ryan Tribute cards. With 3,000 of the cards pegged as each day's maximum giveaway, only 15,000 total sets were available. Most of the companies opted for gold-leaf and/or foil-print extravaganzas, while Topps chose to recreate a single-player 1968-style Nolan Ryan rookie card with full career stats on the back.

		MT
Complete Set (5):		45.00
Common Card:		10.00
1	Nolan Ryan (Upper Deck)	10.00
2	Nolan Ryan (Topps)	12.00
3	Nolan Ryan (Pinnacle)	10.00
4	Nolan Ryan (Fleer Ultra)	10.00
5	Nolan Ryan (Donruss)	10.00

1996 FanFest Steve Carlton Commemorative

Philadelphia's most famous Lefty (before Rocky Balboa) was chosen as the subject of the '96 All-Star FanFest multi-company card tribute. Each of the five largest baseball card licensees produced a Carlton card for use in a wrapper redemption promotion at the annual show. Each of the cards featured the Liberty Bell All-Star Game logo along with such bells and whistles as embossing, metallic-foil highlights, etc.

		MT
Complete Set (5):		20.00
Common Card:		5.00
1	Steve Carlton (Donruss)	5.00
2	Steve Carlton (Fleer Ultra)	5.00
3	Steve Carlton (Pinnacle)	5.00
4	Steve Carlton (Topps)	7.50
5	Steve Carlton (Upper Deck)	5.00

1997 FanFest Jackie Robinson Commemorative

In conjunction with FanFest in Cleveland, July 4-8, preceding the All-Star Game, five of the major card companies combined to create a card set honoring Jackie Robinson. Each company made its card available at the show in a wrapper redemption exchange. In most cases the tribute cards showcased the respective companies' technical expertise. Production of each card was limited to 15,000.

		MT
Complete Set (5):		35.00
Common Card:		7.00
1	Jackie Robinson (Pinnacle Dufex)	7.00
2	Jackie Robinson (Topps Finest '52 reprint)	9.00
3	Jackie Robinson (Upper Deck)	7.00
4	Jackie Robinson (Donruss - 1948 Leaf reprint)	7.00
5	Jackie Robinson (Fleer)	7.00

1998 FanFest Lou Brock Commemorative

In the years before the Rockies joined the National League, Denver's "home team" was the St. Louis Cardinals. One of that team's greatest players of the 1960s and 1970s, Hall of Famer Lou Brock, was selected to be honored in the annual All-Star FanFest commemorative series used by the card companies as a wrapper redemption premium (five wrappers for each card). Card fronts include the All-Star Game logo, backs have the Cooperstown Collection logo. Topps' card is a chromium version reproduction of Brock's 1962 rookie card, which depicts him as a Cub.

		MT
Complete Set (5):		18.00
Common Card:		3.00
1	Lou Brock (Topps)	6.00
2	Lou Brock (Pinnacle)	4.50
3	Lou Brock (Fleer)	3.00
4	Lou Brock (Donruss DK)	4.50
5	Lou Brock (Upper Deck)	3.00

1984 Farmer Jack Detroit Tigers

Though there is no indication on the pictures themselves, this issue was a promotion by the Farmer Jack grocery store chain. Printed on semi-gloss paper, the color photos are bordered in white and measure 6" x 9". A facsimile autograph is printed on front. The unnumbered pictures are blank-backed and are checklisted here in alphabetical order.

		MT
Complete Set (16):		15.00
Common Player:		.50
(1)	Dave Bergman	.50
(2)	Darrell Evans	1.25
(3)	Barbaro Garbey	.50
(4)	Kirk Gibson	1.00
(5)	John Grubb	.50
(6)	Willie Hernandez	.50
(7)	Larry Herndon	.50
(8)	Howard Johnson	.90
(9)	Chet Lemon	.75
(10)	Jack Morris	.90
(11)	Lance Parrish	1.00
(12)	Dan Petry	.50
(13)	Dave Rozema	.50
(14)	Alan Trammell	4.00
(15)	Lou Whitaker	2.50
(16)	Milt Wilcox	.50

1987 Farmland Dairies Mets

The New York Mets and Farmland Dairies produced a nine-card panel of baseball cards for members of the Junior Mets Club. Members of the club, kids 14 years of age and younger, received the perforated panel as part of a package featuring gifts and special privileges. The cards are the standard 2-1/2" x 3-1/2" with fronts containing a full-color photo encompassed by a blue border. The backs are designed on a vertical format and have player statistics and career highlights. The Farmland Dairies and Junior Mets Club logos are also carried on the card backs.

		MT
Complete Panel Set:		5.00
Complete Singles Set (9):		3.50
Common Single Player:		.25
1	Mookie Wilson	.25
4	Lenny Dykstra	.50
8	Gary Carter	1.00
12	Ron Darling	.25
18	Darryl Strawberry	1.00
19	Bob Ojeda	.25
22	Kevin McReynolds	.25
42	Roger McDowell	.25
---	Team card	.25

1988 Farmland Dairies Mets

Part of the Junior Mets Fan Club membership package, this set of nine standard size cards was printed on a single panel. Card fronts feature full-color action shots framed in orange and blue. A white player name runs across the top border, with a large team logo, uniform number and position printed below the photo. Card backs are blue on brown and include personal data, stats and 1987 season highlights. The set was offered to fans 14 years and younger for a $6 fan club membership fee, with a $1 discount for those who sent in two proofs of purchase from Farmland Dairies milk cartons.

		MT
Complete Panel Set:		5.00
Complete Singles Set (9):		3.00
Common Single Player:		.25
8	Gary Carter	1.00
16	Dwight Gooden	1.00
17	Keith Hernandez	.50
18	Darryl Strawberry	1.00
20	Howard Johnson	.25
21	Kevin Elster	.25
42	Roger McDowell	.25
48	Randy Myers	.25
50	Sid Fernandez	.25

1989 Farmland Dairies Mets

For the third consecutive year in 1989, Farmland Dairies sponsored the Junior Mets fan club. One of the club's membership benefits was a nine-card set issued on a 7-1/2" x 10-1/2" perforated sheet. Individual cards measure the standard 2-1/2" x 3-1/2" with team-color borders of blue and gold. Backs have the Junior Mets and Farmland logos along with 1988 highlights and stats, career stats and some biographical data. The checklist is by uniform number as shown on the card fronts.

		MT
Complete Set, Sheet		4.00
Complete Set, Singles (9):		3.50
Common Player:		.50
8	Gary Carter	.75
9	Gregg Jefferies	.75
16	Dwight Gooden	.50
18	Darryl Strawberry	.50
22	Kevin McReynolds	.25
25	Keith Miller	.25
42	Roger McDowell	.25
44	David Cone	1.00
---	1988 Eastern Division Champs (team photo)	.25

1993 Fax Pax

Titled "Fax Pax World of Sports," this 40-card set was issued in Great Britain and features top athletes from many sports around the world. The 2-1/2" x 3-1/2" cards have borderless color action photos on front. A white strip near the bottom carries the player's name and the flag of his nation. Black, white and red backs have biographical data, stats and a career summary. Only the baseball players are listed here.

		MT
Common Player:		1.00
1	Roger Clemens	1.00
2	Ken Griffey Jr.	3.00
3	John Olerud	1.00
4	Nolan Ryan	3.00

1982 FBI Foods Discs

This set was issued in the form of a pair of 2-7/8" diameter discs printed on the bottoms of six-pack cartons of Canadian soft drinks. The discs have black-and-white player portrait photos at center, with cap logos airbrushed off. At top is a green and orange FBI logo. Player identification flanks the photo. The copyright and logo of the players' association appear at right, while the initials of the set's producer, Mike Schechter Associates, appears at lower-left. The unnumbered discs are checklisted here in alphabetical order. Because of their appearance on the bottom of a cardboard box, many cards suffer scuffing on the front. A premium of 25-50% attaches to intact boxes or panels.

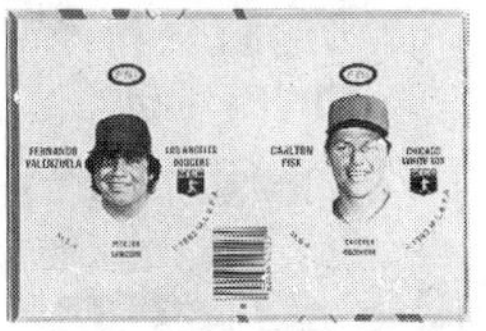

		MT
Complete Set, Singles (30):		400.00
Common Player:		8.00
(1)	Vida Blue	8.00
(2)	George Brett	35.00
(3)	Rod Carew	12.00
(4)	Steve Carlton	12.00
(5)	Gary Carter	9.00
(6)	Warren Cromartie	8.00
(7)	Andre Dawson	9.00
(8)	Rollie Fingers	12.00
(9)	Carlton Fisk	12.00
(10)	Steve Garvey	12.00
(11)	Goose Gossage	9.00
(12)	Bill Gullickson	8.00
(13)	Steve Henderson	8.00
(14)	Keith Hernandez	9.00
(15)	John Mayberry	8.00
(16)	Al Oliver	9.00
(17)	Dave Parker	9.00
(18)	Tim Raines	9.00
(19)	Jim Rice	9.00
(20)	Steve Rogers	8.00
(21)	Pete Rose	55.00
(22)	Nolan Ryan	150.00
(23)	Mike Schmidt	30.00
(24)	Tom Seaver	18.00
(25)	Ken Singleton	8.00
(26)	Dave Steib	8.00
(27)	Bruce Sutter	8.00
(28)	Ellis Valentine	8.00
(29)	Fernando Valenzuela	8.00
(30)	Dave Winfield	12.00

1984 Fina Atlanta Braves Posters

This oil company promotional issue is in the format of 11" x 16" posters featuring color action photos. A facsimile autograph appears on each poster and at bottom are sponsor and team logos. The unnumbered posters are checklisted here in alphabetical order.

		MT
Complete Set (8):		40.00
Common Player:		4.00
(1)	Bruce Benedict	4.00
(2)	Rick Camp	4.00
(3)	Chris Chambliss	4.00
(4)	Bob Horner	5.00
(5)	Glenn Hubbard	4.00
(6)	Craig McMurtry	4.00
(7)	Donnie Moore	4.00
(8)	Dale Murphy	12.00

The election of former players to the Hall of Fame does not always have an immediate upward effect on card prices. The hobby market generally has done a good job of predicting those inductions and adjusting values over the course of several years.

1993 Finest Promos

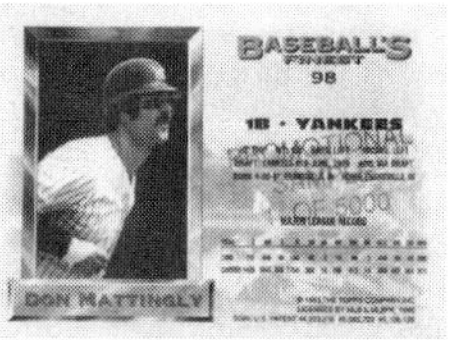

Debuting at the 1993 National Convention in Chicago, this three-card set introduced the hobby to the Topps Finest baseball issue. While the promos are identical in high-tech format to the regular Finest cards issued later, including the same card numbers, there are differences in the promos; some subtle, some glaring. For instance, the Ryan and Alomar cards were issued in promo form in the "gray" style of the basic set. In the regularly issued set, those cards were in the green All-Star format. Each of the promos is overprinted in red on the back, "Promotional Sample 1 of 5000". Of considerably greater rarity are refractor versions of these promo cards, with production numbers unknown.

		MT
Complete Set (3):		35.00
Complete Set, Refractors (3):		4500.
88	Roberto Alomar	10.00
88r	Roberto Alomar (refractor)	1500.
98	Don Mattingly	15.00
98r	Don Mattingly (refractor)	1500.
107	Nolan Ryan	20.00
107r	Nolan Ryan (refractor)	2500.

1993 Finest

This 199-card set uses a process of multi-color metallization; this chromium technology adds depth and dimension to the card. The set has a 33-card subset of All-Stars; a parallel version of these cards (Refractors) were also created with refracting foil using the metallization enhancement process. There is one refracting foil card in every nine packs. Packs have five cards. Each 18-count box contains a 5" x 7" version of one of the 33 All-Star players in the set.

		MT
Complete Set (199):		200.00
Common Player:		1.00
Wax Box:		600.00
1	Dave Justice	2.00
2	Lou Whitaker	1.00
3	Bryan Harvey	1.00
4	Carlos Garcia	1.00
5	Sid Fernandez	1.00
6	Brett Butler	1.00
7	Scott Cooper	1.00
8	B.J. Surhoff	1.00
9	Steve Finley	1.50
10	Curt Schilling	2.00
11	Jeff Bagwell	8.00
12	Alex Cole	1.00
13	John Olerud	1.50
14	John Smiley	1.00
15	Bip Roberts	1.00
16	Albert Belle	5.00
17	Duane Ward	1.00
18	Alan Trammell	1.00
19	Andy Benes	1.50
20	Reggie Sanders	1.00
21	Todd Zeile	1.00
22	Rick Aguilera	1.00
23	Dave Hollins	1.00
24	Jose Rijo	1.00
25	Matt Williams	3.00
26	Sandy Alomar	1.50
27	Alex Fernandez	1.00
28	Ozzie Smith	6.00
29	Ramon Martinez	2.00
30	Bernie Williams	6.00
31	Gary Sheffield	3.00
32	Eric Karros	1.50
33	Frank Viola	1.00
34	Kevin Young	1.00
35	Ken Hill	1.00
36	Tony Fernandez	1.00
37	Tim Wakefield	1.00
38	John Kruk	1.00
39	Chris Sabo	1.00
40	Marquis Grissom	1.50
41	Glenn Davis	1.00
42	Jeff Montgomery	1.00
43	Kenny Lofton	5.00
44	John Burkett	1.00
45	Darryl Hamilton	1.00
46	Jim Abbott	1.00
47	Ivan Rodriguez	7.50
48	Eric Young	1.00
49	Mitch Williams	1.00
50	Harold Reynolds	1.00
51	Brian Harper	1.00
52	Rafael Palmeiro	4.00
53	Bret Saberhagen	1.25
54	Jeff Conine	1.50
55	Ivan Calderon	1.00
56	Juan Guzman	1.00
57	Carlos Baerga	1.00
58	Charles Nagy	1.00
59	Wally Joyner	1.00
60	Charlie Hayes	1.00
61	Shane Mack	1.00
62	Pete Harnisch	1.00
63	George Brett	10.00
64	Lance Johnson	1.00
65	Ben McDonald	1.00
66	Bobby Bonilla	1.50
67	Terry Steinbach	1.00
68	Ron Gant	1.50
69	Doug Jones	1.00
70	Paul Molitor	4.00
71	Brady Anderson	1.50
72	Chuck Finley	1.00
73	Mark Grace	2.00
74	Mike Devereaux	1.00
75	Tony Phillips	1.00
76	Chuck Knoblauch	2.50
77	Tony Gwynn	12.50
78	Kevin Appier	1.00
79	Sammy Sosa	12.50
80	Mickey Tettleton	1.00
81	Felix Jose	1.00
82	Mark Langston	1.00
83	Gregg Jefferies	1.50
84	Andre Dawson (AS)	1.50
85	Greg Maddux (AS)	12.50
86	Rickey Henderson (AS)	2.50
87	Tom Glavine (AS)	2.50
88	Roberto Alomar (AS)	5.00
89	Darryl Strawberry (AS)	1.50
90	Wade Boggs (AS)	3.00
91	Bo Jackson (AS)	2.00
92	Mark McGwire (AS)	25.00
93	Robin Ventura (AS)	1.50
94	Joe Carter (AS)	1.00
95	Lee Smith (AS)	1.00
96	Cal Ripken, Jr. (AS)	17.50
97	Larry Walker (AS)	4.00
98	Don Mattingly (AS)	10.00
99	Jose Canseco (AS)	2.50
100	Dennis Eckersley (AS)	1.00
101	Terry Pendleton (AS)	1.00
102	Frank Thomas (AS)	12.50
103	Barry Bonds (AS)	6.00
104	Roger Clemens	12.00
105	Ryne Sandberg (AS)	6.00
106	[illegible]	[illegible]
107	Nolan Ryan (AS)	20.00
108	Will Clark (AS)	3.00
109	Pat Listach (AS)	1.00
110	Ken Griffey, Jr. (AS)	25.00
111	Cecil Fielder (AS)	1.00
112	Kirby Puckett (AS)	10.00
113	Dwight Gooden (AS)	1.25
114	Barry Larkin (AS)	3.00
115	David Cone (AS)	1.50
116	Juan Gonzalez (AS)	12.00
117	Kent Hrbek	1.00
118	Tim Wallach	1.00
119	Craig Biggio	2.00
120	Bobby Kelly	1.00
121	Greg Olson	1.00
122	Eddie Murray	4.00
123	Wil Cordero	1.00
124	Jay Buhner	2.00
125	Carlton Fisk	1.50
126	Eric Davis	1.00
127	Doug Drabek	1.00
128	Ozzie Guillen	1.00
129	John Wetteland	1.00
130	Andres Galarraga	2.00
131	Ken Caminiti	1.50
132	Tom Candiotti	1.00
133	Pat Borders	1.00
134	Kevin Brown	1.50
135	Travis Fryman	2.00
136	Kevin Mitchell	1.00
137	Greg Swindell	1.00
138	Benny Santiago	1.00
139	Reggie Jefferson	1.00
140	Chris Bosio	1.00
141	Deion Sanders	2.00
142	Scott Erickson	1.00
143	Howard Johnson	1.00
144	Orestes Destrade	1.00
145	Jose Guzman	1.00
146	Chad Curtis	1.00
147	Cal Eldred	1.00
148	Willie Greene	1.00
149	Tommy Greene	1.00
150	Erik Hanson	1.00
151	Bob Welch	1.00
152	John Jaha	1.00
153	Harold Baines	1.00
154	Randy Johnson	5.00
155	Al Martin	1.00
156	*J.T. Snow*	3.00
157	Mike Mussina	5.00
158	Ruben Sierra	1.00
159	Dean Palmer	1.00
160	Steve Avery	1.00
161	Julio Franco	1.00
162	Dave Winfield	2.00
163	Tim Salmon	4.00
164	Tom Henke	1.00
165	Mo Vaughn	6.00
166	John Smoltz	2.00
167	Danny Tartabull	1.00
168	Delino DeShields	1.00
169	Charlie Hough	1.00
170	Paul O'Neill	1.50
171	Darren Daulton	1.00
172	Jack McDowell	1.00
173	Junior Felix	1.00
174	Jimmy Key	1.00
175	George Bell	1.00
176	Mike Stanton	1.00
177	Len Dykstra	1.00
178	Norm Charlton	1.00
179	Eric Anthony	1.00
180	Bob Dibble	1.00
181	Otis Nixon	1.00
182	Randy Myers	1.00
183	Tim Raines	1.00
184	Orel Hershiser	1.25
185	Andy Van Slyke	1.00
186	*Mike Lansing*	2.00
187	Ray Lankford	1.00
188	Mike Morgan	1.00
189	Moises Alou	2.00
190	Edgar Martinez	1.00
191	John Franco	1.00
192	Robin Yount	4.00
193	Bob Tewksbury	1.00
194	Jay Bell	1.00
195	Luis Gonzalez	1.00
196	Dave Fleming	1.00
197	Mike Greenwell	1.00
198	David Nied	1.00
199	Mike Piazza	30.00

1993 Finest Refractors

This parallel insert set comprises each of the 199 cards from the regular Topps Finest set recreated with refracting foil using the metallization enhancement process. One refracting foil card was inserted in every nine packs, on average. Estimated production is about 250 of each card.

		MT
Complete Set (199):		8500.
Common Player:		20.00
1	Dave Justice	65.00
2	Lou Whitaker	25.00
3	Bryan Harvey	25.00
4	Carlos Garcia	20.00
[illegible]	[illegible]	20.00
6	Brett Butler	25.00
7	Scott Cooper	20.00
8	B.J. Surhoff	25.00
9	Steve Finley	25.00
10	Curt Schilling	40.00
11	Jeff Bagwell	150.00
12	Alex Cole	20.00
13	John Olerud	45.00
14	John Smiley	20.00
15	Bip Roberts	20.00
16	Albert Belle	100.00
17	Duane Ward	20.00
18	Alan Trammell	25.00
19	Andy Benes	20.00
20	Reggie Sanders	20.00
21	Todd Zeile	20.00
22	Rick Aguilera	20.00
23	Dave Hollins	20.00
24	Jose Rijo	20.00
25	Matt Williams	45.00
26	Sandy Alomar	35.00
27	Alex Fernandez	25.00
28	Ozzie Smith	125.00
29	Ramon Martinez	20.00
30	Bernie Williams	60.00
31	Gary Sheffield	50.00
32	Eric Karros	20.00
33	Frank Viola	20.00
34	Kevin Young	20.00
35	Ken Hill	20.00
36	Tony Fernandez	20.00
37	Tim Wakefield	20.00
38	John Kruk	20.00
39	Chris Sabo	20.00
40	Marquis Grissom	20.00
41	Glenn Davis	20.00
42	Jeff Montgomery	20.00
43	Kenny Lofton	60.00
44	John Burkett	20.00
45	Darryl Hamilton	20.00
46	Jim Abbott	20.00
47	Ivan Rodriguez	200.00
48	Eric Young	20.00
49	Mitch Williams	20.00
50	Harold Reynolds	20.00
51	Brian Harper	20.00
52	Rafael Palmeiro	75.00
53	Bret Saberhagen	25.00
54	Jeff Conine	20.00
55	Ivan Calderon	20.00
56	Juan Guzman	20.00
57	Carlos Baerga	20.00
58	Charles Nagy	30.00
59	Wally Joyner	30.00
60	Charlie Hayes	20.00
61	Shane Mack	20.00
62	Pete Harnisch	20.00
63	George Brett	200.00
64	Lance Johnson	20.00
65	Ben McDonald	20.00
66	Bobby Bonilla	30.00
67	Terry Steinbach	20.00
68	Ron Gant	25.00
69	Doug Jones	20.00
70	Paul Molitor	125.00
71	Brady Anderson	25.00
72	Chuck Finley	20.00
73	Mark Grace	60.00
74	Mike Devereaux	20.00
75	Tony Phillips	20.00
76	Chuck Knoblauch	45.00
77	Tony Gwynn	200.00
78	Kevin Appier	20.00
79	Sammy Sosa	250.00
80	Mickey Tettleton	20.00
81	Felix Jose	20.00
82	Mark Langston	20.00
83	Gregg Jefferies	20.00
84	Andre Dawson (AS)	30.00
85	Greg Maddux (AS)	200.00
86	Rickey Henderson (AS)	50.00
87	Tom Glavine (AS)	45.00
88	Roberto Alomar (AS)	75.00
89	Darryl Strawberry (AS)	30.00
90	Wade Boggs (AS)	45.00
91	Bo Jackson (AS)	35.00
92	Mark McGwire (AS)	750.00
93	Robin Ventura (AS)	40.00
94	Joe Carter (AS)	25.00
95	Lee Smith (AS)	20.00
96	Cal Ripken, Jr. (AS)	700.00
97	Larry Walker (AS)	100.00
98	Don Mattingly (AS)	175.00
99	Jose Canseco (AS)	75.00
100	Dennis Eckersley (AS)	30.00
101	Terry Pendleton (AS)	20.00
102	Frank Thomas (AS)	200.00
103	Barry Bonds (AS)	150.00
104	Roger Clemens	200.00
105	Ryne Sandberg (AS)	150.00
106	Fred McGriff (AS)	50.00
107	Nolan Ryan (AS)	650.00
108	Will Clark (AS)	60.00
109	Pat Listach (AS)	20.00
110	Ken Griffey, Jr. (AS)	800.00
111	Cecil Fielder (AS)	25.00
112	Kirby Puckett (AS)	175.00
113	Dwight Gooden (AS)	30.00
114	Barry Larkin (AS)	35.00
115	David Cone (AS)	25.00
116	Juan Gonzalez (AS)	350.00
117	Kent Hrbek	20.00
118	Tim Wallach	20.00
119	Craig Biggio	45.00
120	Bobby Kelly	20.00
121	Greg Olson	20.00
122	Eddie Murray	90.00
123	Wil Cordero	20.00
124	Jay Buhner	30.00
125	Carlton Fisk	60.00
126	Eric Davis	25.00
127	Doug Drabek	20.00
128	Ozzie Guillen	20.00
129	John Wetteland	20.00
130	Andres Galarraga	40.00
131	Ken Caminiti	40.00
132	Tom Candiotti	20.00
133	Pat Borders	20.00
134	Kevin Brown	45.00
135	Travis Fryman	30.00
136	Kevin Mitchell	20.00
137	Greg Swindell	20.00
138	Benny Santiago	20.00
139	Reggie Jefferson	20.00
140	Chris Bosio	20.00
141	Deion Sanders	30.00
142	Scott Erickson	20.00
143	Howard Johnson	20.00
144	Orestes Destrade	20.00
145	Jose Guzman	20.00
146	Chad Curtis	20.00
147	Cal Eldred	20.00
148	Willie Greene	20.00
149	Tommy Greene	20.00
150	Erik Hanson	20.00
151	Bob Welch	20.00
152	John Jaha	20.00
153	Harold Baines	20.00
154	Randy Johnson	75.00
155	Al Martin	20.00
156	J.T. Snow	25.00
157	Mike Mussina	60.00
158	Ruben Sierra	20.00
159	Dean Palmer	20.00
160	Steve Avery	20.00
161	Julio Franco	20.00
162	Dave Winfield	45.00
163	Tim Salmon	50.00
164	Tom Henke	20.00
165	Mo Vaughn	75.00
166	John Smoltz	45.00
167	Danny Tartabull	20.00
168	Delino DeShields	20.00
169	Charlie Hough	20.00
170	Paul O'Neill	60.00
171	Darren Daulton	20.00
172	Jack McDowell	20.00
173	Junior Felix	20.00
174	Jimmy Key	20.00
175	George Bell	20.00
176	Mike Stanton	20.00
177	Len Dykstra	20.00
178	Norm Charlton	20.00
179	Eric Anthony	20.00
180	Bob Dibble	20.00
181	Otis Nixon	20.00
182	Randy Myers	20.00
183	Tim Raines	30.00
184	Orel Hershiser	30.00
185	Andy Van Slyke	20.00
186	*Mike Lansing*	25.00
187	Ray Lankford	20.00
188	Mike Morgan	20.00
189	Moises Alou	30.00
190	Edgar Martinez	25.00
191	John Franco	20.00
192	Robin Yount	90.00
193	Bob Tewksbury	20.00
194	Jay Bell	20.00
195	Luis Gonzalez	20.00
196	Dave Fleming	20.00
197	Mike Greenwell	20.00
198	David Nied	20.00
199	Mike Piazza	300.00

1993 Finest Jumbo All-Stars

These 4-1/2" x 6" cards were produced using the chromium metallization process. Each 18-pack Finest box contains one of the All-Star jumbo cards. Based on '93 Finest production, it is estimated fewer than 1,500 of each were issued.

		MT
Complete Set (33):		225.00
Common Player:		2.00
84	Andre Dawson	2.00
85	Greg Maddux	15.00
86	Rickey Henderson	4.00
87	Tom Glavine	4.00
88	Roberto Alomar	6.00
89	Darryl Strawberry	4.00
90	Wade Boggs	5.00
91	Bo Jackson	2.00
92	Mark McGwire	25.00
93	Robin Ventura	3.00
94	Joe Carter	2.00
95	Lee Smith	2.00
96	Cal Ripken, Jr.	25.00
97	Larry Walker	4.00

98	Don Mattingly	10.00
99	Jose Canseco	4.00
100	Dennis Eckersley	2.00
101	Terry Pendleton	2.00
102	Frank Thomas	15.00
103	Barry Bonds	7.50
104	Roger Clemens	10.00
105	Ryne Sandberg	7.50
106	Fred McGriff	3.00
107	Nolan Ryan	25.00
108	Will Clark	4.00
109	Pat Listach	2.00
110	Ken Griffey, Jr.	30.00
111	Cecil Fielder	2.00
112	Kirby Puckett	10.00
113	Dwight Gooden	2.00
114	Barry Larkin	2.50
115	David Cone	2.50
116	Juan Gonzalez	12.50

1994 Finest Pre-Production

Forty cards premiering the upcoming 1994 Topps Finest set were issued as a random insert in packs of Topps Series 2 regular-issue cards. The promos are in the same format as the regular-issue Finest cards and share the same card numbers. On back there is a red "Pre-Production" notice printed diagonally over the statistics.

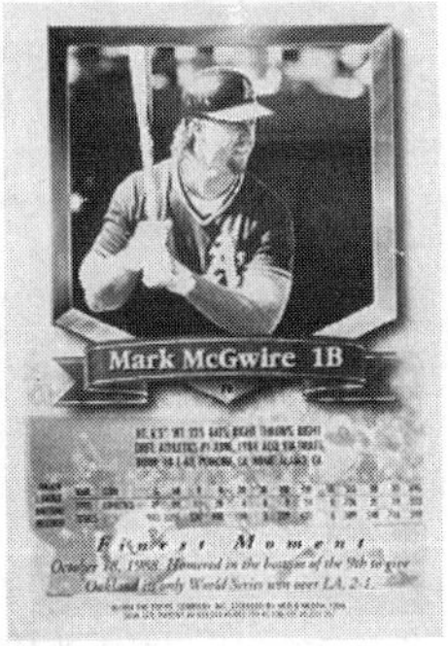

		MT
Complete Set (40):		100.00
Common Player:		2.50
22	Deion Sanders	4.00
23	Jose Offerman	2.50
26	Alex Fernandez	2.50
31	Steve Finley	2.50
35	Andres Galarraga	3.00
43	Reggie Sanders	2.50
47	Dave Hollins	2.50
52	David Cone	3.50
59	Dante Bichette	3.00
61	Orlando Merced	2.50
62	Brian McRae	2.50
66	Mike Mussina	4.00
76	Mike Stanley	2.50
78	Mark McGwire	20.00
79	Pat Listach	2.50
82	Dwight Gooden	3.00
84	Phil Plantier	2.50
90	Jeff Russell	2.50
92	Gregg Jefferies	2.50
93	Jose Guzman	2.50
100	John Smoltz	3.00
102	Jim Thome	4.00
121	Moises Alou	3.00
125	Devon White	2.50
126	Ivan Rodriguez	6.00
130	Dave Magadan	2.50
136	Ozzie Smith	9.00
141	Chris Hoiles	2.50
149	Jim Abbott	2.50
151	Bill Swift	2.50
154	Edgar Martinez	2.50
157	J.T. Snow	3.00
159	Alan Trammell	3.00
163	Roberto Kelly	2.50
166	Scott Erickson	2.50
168	Scott Cooper	2.50
169	Rod Beck	2.50
177	Dean Palmer	2.50
182	Todd Van Poppel	2.50
185	Paul Sorrento	2.50

1994 Finest

The 1994 Finest set comprises two series of 220 cards each; subsets of 20 superstars and 20 top rookies are featured in each series. Each card has a metallic look to it, using Topps Finest technology. Backs picture the player on the top half and statistics on the bottom. Baseball's Finest was limited to 4,000 cases and available to dealers through an allocation process, based on their sales the previous year. Along with the regular-issue set, there was a parallel set, called Refractors, of 440 cards and a 4 x 6-inch version of the 80 subset cards.

		MT
Complete Set (440):		150.00
Common Player:		.50
Series 1 or 2 Wax Box:		60.00
1	Mike Piazza	7.50
2	Kevin Stocker	.50
3	Greg McMichael	.50
4	Jeff Conine	.50
5	Rene Arocha	.50
6	Aaron Sele	.50
7	Brent Gates	.50
8	Chuck Carr	.50
9	Kirk Rueter	.50
10	Mike Lansing	.50
11	Al Martin	.50
12	Jason Bere	.50
13	Troy Neel	.50
14	Armando Reynoso	.50
15	Jeromy Burnitz	.60
16	Rich Amaral	.50
17	David McCarty	.50
18	Tim Salmon	1.50
19	Steve Cooke	.50
20	Wil Cordero	.50
21	Kevin Tapani	.50
22	Deion Sanders	1.00
23	Jose Offerman	.50
24	Mark Langston	.50
25	Ken Hill	.50
26	Alex Fernandez	.75
27	Jeff Blauser	.50
28	Royce Clayton	.50
29	Brad Ausmus	.50
30	Ryan Bowen	.50
31	Steve Finley	.50
32	Charlie Hayes	.50
33	Jeff Kent	.50
34	Mike Henneman	.50
35	Andres Galarraga	1.00
36	Wayne Kirby	.50
37	Joe Oliver	.50
38	Terry Steinbach	.50
39	Ryan Thompson	.50
40	Luis Alicea	.50
41	Randy Velarde	.50
42	Bob Tewksbury	.50
43	Reggie Sanders	.75
44	Brian Williams	.50
45	Joe Orsulak	.50
46	Jose Lind	.50
47	Dave Hollins	.50
48	Graeme Lloyd	.50
49	Jim Gott	.50
50	Andre Dawson	.60
51	Steve Buechele	.50
52	David Cone	1.00
53	Ricky Gutierrez	.50
54	Lance Johnson	.50
55	Tino Martinez	.60
56	Phil Hiatt	.50
57	Carlos Garcia	.50
58	Danny Darwin	.50
59	Dante Bichette	1.00
60	Scott Kamieniecki	.50
61	Orlando Merced	.50
62	Brian McRae	.50
63	Pat Kelly	.50
64	Tom Henke	.50
65	Jeff King	.50
66	Mike Mussina	2.00
67	Tim Pugh	.50
68	Robby Thompson	.50
69	Paul O'Neill	.75
70	Hal Morris	.50
71	Ron Karkovice	.50
72	Joe Girardi	.50
73	Eduardo Perez	.50
74	Raul Mondesi	2.00
75	Mike Gallego	.50
76	Mike Stanley	.50
77	Kevin Roberson	.50
78	Mark McGwire	12.00
79	Pat Listach	.50
80	Eric Davis	.50
81	Mike Bordick	.50
82	Dwight Gooden	.60
83	Mike Moore	.50
84	Phil Plantier	.50
85	Darren Lewis	.50
86	Rick Wilkins	.50
87	Darryl Strawberry	.60
88	Rob Dibble	.50
89	Greg Vaughn	.65
90	Jeff Russell	.50
91	Mark Lewis	.50
92	Gregg Jefferies	.50
93	Jose Guzman	.50
94	Kenny Rogers	.50
95	Mark Lemke	.50
96	Mike Morgan	.50
97	Andujar Cedeno	.50
98	Orel Hershiser	.65
99	Greg Swindell	.50
100	John Smoltz	1.00
101	Pedro Martinez	1.50
102	Jim Thome	1.50
103	David Segui	.50
104	Charles Nagy	.60
105	Shane Mack	.50
106	John Jaha	.50
107	Tom Candiotti	.50
108	David Wells	.60
109	Bobby Jones	.50
110	Bob Hamelin	.50
111	Bernard Gilkey	.50
112	Chili Davis	.50
113	Todd Stottlemyre	.50
114	Derek Bell	.50
115	Mark McLemore	.50
116	Mark Whiten	.50
117	Mike Devereaux	.50
118	Terry Pendleton	.50
119	Pat Meares	.50
120	Pete Harnisch	.50
121	Moises Alou	.60
122	Jay Buhner	.75
123	Wes Chamberlain	.50
124	Mike Perez	.50
125	Devon White	.50
126	Ivan Rodriguez	3.00
127	Don Slaught	.50
128	John Valentin	.50
129	Jaime Navarro	.50
130	Dave Magadan	.50
131	Brady Anderson	.75
132	Juan Guzman	.50
133	John Wetteland	.50
134	Dave Stewart	.50
135	Scott Servais	.50
136	Ozzie Smith	2.50
137	Darrin Fletcher	.50
138	Jose Mesa	.50
139	Wilson Alvarez	.50
140	Pete Incaviglia	.50
141	Chris Hoiles	.50
142	Darryl Hamilton	.50
143	Chuck Finley	.50
144	Archi Cianfrocco	.50
145	Bill Wegman	.50
146	Joey Cora	.50
147	Darrell Whitmore	.50
148	David Hulse	.50
149	Jim Abbott	.50
150	Curt Schilling	.75
151	Bill Swift	.50
152	Tommy Greene	.50
153	Roberto Mejia	.50
154	Edgar Martinez	.75
155	Roger Pavlik	.50
156	Randy Tomlin	.50
157	J.T. Snow	.75
158	Bob Welch	.50
159	Alan Trammell	.50
160	Ed Sprague	.50
161	Ben McDonald	.50
162	Derrick May	.50
163	Roberto Kelly	.50
164	Bryan Harvey	.50
165	Ron Gant	.60
166	Scott Erickson	.50
167	Anthony Young	.50
168	Scott Cooper	.50
169	Rod Beck	.50
170	John Franco	.50
171	Gary DiSarcina	.50
172	Dave Fleming	.50
173	Wade Boggs	1.50
174	Kevin Appier	.50
175	Jose Bautista	.50
176	Wally Joyner	.50
177	Dean Palmer	.50
178	Tony Phillips	.50
179	John Smiley	.50
180	Charlie Hough	.50
181	Scott Fletcher	.50
182	Todd Van Poppel	.50
183	Mike Blowers	.50
184	Willie McGee	.50
185	Paul Sorrento	.50
186	Eric Young	.50
187	Bret Barberie	.50
188	Manuel Lee	.50
189	Jeff Branson	.50
190	Jim Deshaies	.50
191	Ken Caminiti	1.00
192	Tim Raines	.50
193	Joe Grahe	.50
194	Hipolito Pichardo	.50
195	Denny Neagle	.50
196	Jeff Gardner	.50
197	Mike Benjamin	.50
198	Milt Thompson	.50
199	Bruce Ruffin	.50
200	Chris Hammond	.50
201	Tony Gwynn	5.00
202	Robin Ventura	1.00
203	Frank Thomas	5.00
204	Kirby Puckett	5.00
205	Roberto Alomar	3.00
206	Dennis Eckersley	.50
207	Joe Carter	.75
208	Albert Belle	4.00
209	Greg Maddux	7.50
210	Ryne Sandberg	3.00
211	Juan Gonzalez	5.00
212	Jeff Bagwell	5.00
213	Randy Johnson	1.50
214	Matt Williams	1.00
215	Dave Winfield	.75
216	Larry Walker	1.00
217	Roger Clemens	4.00
218	Kenny Lofton	3.00
219	Cecil Fielder	.75
220	Darren Daulton	.50
221	John Olerud	.75
222	Jose Canseco	1.50
223	Rickey Henderson	1.00
224	Fred McGriff	1.50
225	Gary Sheffield	1.50
226	Jack McDowell	.50
227	Rafael Palmeiro	1.00
228	Travis Fryman	.60
229	Marquis Grissom	.60
230	Barry Bonds	3.00
231	Carlos Baerga	.50
232	Ken Griffey, Jr.	12.00
233	Dave Justice	.75
234	Bobby Bonilla	.60
235	Cal Ripken	10.00
236	Sammy Sosa	5.00
237	Len Dykstra	.50
238	Will Clark	1.00
239	Paul Molitor	2.50
240	Barry Larkin	.75
241	Bo Jackson	.75
242	Mitch Williams	.50
243	Ron Darling	.50
244	Darryl Kile	.50
245	Geronimo Berroa	.50
246	Gregg Olson	.50
247	Brian Harper	.50
248	Rheal Cormier	.50
249	Rey Sanchez	.50
250	Jeff Fassero	.50
251	Sandy Alomar	.65
252	Chris Bosio	.50
253	Andy Stankiewicz	.50
254	Harold Baines	.50
255	Andy Ashby	.50
256	Tyler Green	.50
257	Kevin Brown	.65
258	Mo Vaughn	3.00
259	Mike Harkey	.50
260	Dave Henderson	.50
261	Kent Hrbek	.50
262	Darrin Jackson	.50
263	Bob Wickman	.50
264	Spike Owen	.50
265	Todd Jones	.50
266	Pat Borders	.50
267	Tom Glavine	1.25
268	Dave Nilsson	.50
269	Rich Batchelor	.50
270	Delino DeShields	.50
271	Felix Fermin	.50
272	Orestes Destrade	.50
273	Mickey Morandini	.50
274	Otis Nixon	.50
275	Ellis Burks	.50
276	Greg Gagne	.50
277	John Doherty	.50
278	Julio Franco	.50
279	Bernie Williams	1.50
280	Rick Aguilera	.50
281	Mickey Tettleton	.50
282	David Nied	.50
283	Johnny Ruffin	.50
284	Dan Wilson	.50
285	Omar Vizquel	.50
286	Willie Banks	.50
287	Erik Pappas	.50
288	Cal Eldred	.50
289	Bobby Witt	.50
290	Luis Gonzalez	.50
291	Greg Pirkl	.50
292	Alex Cole	.50
293	Ricky Bones	.50
294	Denis Boucher	.50
295	John Burkett	.50
296	Steve Trachsel	.50
297	Ricky Jordan	.50
298	Mark Dewey	.50
299	Jimmy Key	.50
300	Mike MacFarlane	.50
301	Tim Belcher	.50
302	Carlos Reyes	.50
303	Greg Harris	.50
304	*Brian Anderson*	1.00
305	Terry Mulholland	.50
306	Felix Jose	.50
307	Darren Holmes	.50
308	Jose Rijo	.50
309	Paul Wagner	.50
310	Bob Scanlan	.50
311	Mike Jackson	.50
312	Jose Vizcaino	.50
313	Rob Butler	.50
314	Kevin Seitzer	.50
315	Geronimo Pena	.50
316	Hector Carrasco	.50
317	Eddie Murray	2.00
318	Roger Salkeld	.50
319	Todd Hundley	1.00
320	Danny Jackson	.50
321	Kevin Young	.50
322	Mike Greenwell	.50
323	Kevin Mitchell	.50
324	Chuck Knoblauch	.75
325	Danny Tartabull	.50
326	Vince Coleman	.50
327	Marvin Freeman	.50
328	Andy Benes	.50
329	Mike Kelly	.50
330	Karl Rhodes	.50
331	Allen Watson	.50
332	Damion Easley	.50
333	Reggie Jefferson	.50
334	Kevin McReynolds	.50
335	Arthur Rhodes	.50
336	Brian Hunter	.50
337	Tom Browning	.50
338	Pedro Munoz	.50
339	Billy Ripken	.50
340	Gene Harris	.50
341	Fernando Vina	.50
342	Sean Berry	.50
343	Pedro Astacio	.50
344	B.J. Surhoff	.50
345	Doug Drabek	.50
346	Jody Reed	.50
347	Ray Lankford	.50
348	Steve Farr	.50
349	Eric Anthony	.50
350	Pete Smith	.50
351	Lee Smith	.50
352	Mariano Duncan	.50
353	Doug Strange	.50
354	Tim Bogar	.50
355	Dave Weathers	.50
356	Eric Karros	.50
357	Randy Myers	.50
358	Chad Curtis	.50
359	Steve Avery	.50
360	Brian Jordan	.50
361	Tim Wallach	.50
362	Pedro Martinez	.75
363	Bip Roberts	.50
364	Lou Whitaker	.50
365	Luis Polonia	.50
366	Benny Santiago	.50
367	Brett Butler	.50
368	Shawon Dunston	.50
369	Kelly Stinnett	.50
370	Chris Turner	.50
371	Ruben Sierra	.50
372	Greg Harris	.50
373	Xavier Hernandez	.50
374	Howard Johnson	.50
375	Duane Ward	.50
376	Roberto Hernandez	.50
377	Scott Leius	.50
378	Dave Valle	.50
379	Sid Fernandez	.50
380	Doug Jones	.50
381	Zane Smith	.50
382	Craig Biggio	.75
383	Rick White	.50
384	Tom Pagnozzi	.50
385	Chris James	.50
386	Bret Boone	.50
387	Jeff Montgomery	.50
388	Chad Kreuter	.50
389	Greg Hibbard	.50
390	Mark Grace	1.00
391	Phil Leftwich	.50
392	Don Mattingly	5.00
393	Ozzie Guillen	.50
394	Gary Gaetti	.50
395	Erik Hanson	.50
396	Scott Brosius	.50
397	Tom Gordon	.50
398	Bill Gullickson	.50
399	Matt Mieske	.50
400	Pat Hentgen	.50
401	Walt Weiss	.50
402	Greg Blosser	.50
403	Stan Javier	.50
404	Doug Henry	.50
405	Ramon Martinez	.50
406	Frank Viola	.50
407	Mike Hampton	.50
408	Andy Van Slyke	.50
409	Bobby Ayala	.50
410	Todd Zeile	.50
411	Jay Bell	.50
412	Denny Martinez	.50
413	Mark Portugal	.50
414	Bobby Munoz	.50
415	Kirt Manwaring	.50
416	John Kruk	.50
417	Trevor Hoffman	.50
418	Chris Sabo	.50
419	Bret Saberhagen	.50
420	Chris Nabholz	.50
421	James Mouton	.50
422	Tony Tarasco	.50
423	Carlos Delgado	1.00
424	Rondell White	1.50
425	Javier Lopez	.75
426	*Chan Ho Park*	1.50
427	Cliff Floyd	.50
428	Dave Staton	.50
429	J.R. Phillips	.50
430	Manny Ramirez	4.00
431	Kurt Abbott	.65

432	Melvin Nieves	.50
433	Alex Gonzalez	.75
434	Rick Helling	.50
435	Danny Bautista	.50
436	Matt Walbeck	.50
437	Ryan Klesko	1.50
438	Steve Karsay	.60
439	Salomon Torres	.50
440	Scott Ruffcorn	.50

1994 Finest Refractors

It takes an experienced eye and good light to detect a Refractor parallel card from a regular-issue Topps Finest. The Refractor utilizes a variation of the Finest metallic printing process to produce rainbow-effect highlights on the card front. The Refractors share the checklist with the regular-issue Finest and were inserted at a rate of about one per 10 packs.

	MT
Complete Set (440):	1750.
Common Player:	1.50
Veteran Stars: 6X	
Young Stars: 3X	
(See 1994 Finest for checklist and base card prices.)	

1994 Finest Superstar Jumbos

Identical in format to the Superstars subset in the Finest issue, these cards measure about 4" x 5-1/2" and were distributed one per box in Finest foil packs. Backs carry a card number under the banner with the player's name and position. Since there were 20 rookies and 20 superstars from both Series 1 and Series 2, this is an 80-card set.

		MT
Complete Set (80):		250.00
Common Player:		1.00
1	Mike Piazza	22.50
2	Kevin Stocker	1.00
3	Greg McMichael	1.00
4	Jeff Conine	1.00
5	Rene Arocha	1.00
6	Aaron Sele	1.00
7	Brent Gates	1.00
8	Chuck Carr	1.00
9	Kirk Rueter	1.00
10	Mike Lansing	1.00
11	Al Martin	1.00
12	Jason Bere	1.00
13	Troy Neel	1.00
14	Armando Reynoso	1.00
15	Jeromy Burnitz	1.50
16	Rich Amaral	1.00
17	David McCarty	1.00
18	Tim Salmon	4.00
19	Steve Cooke	1.00
20	Wil Cordero	1.00
201	Tony Gwynn	9.00
202	Robin Ventura	3.00
203	Frank Thomas	20.00
204	Kirby Puckett	15.00
205	Roberto Alomar	9.00
206	Dennis Eckersley	1.25
207	Joe Carter	1.50
208	Albert Belle	10.00
209	Greg Maddux	20.00
210	Ryne Sandberg	7.50
211	Juan Gonzalez	9.00
212	Jeff Bagwell	12.00
213	Randy Johnson	5.00
214	Matt Williams	4.00
215	Dave Winfield	4.00
216	Larry Walker	3.00
217	Roger Clemens	7.50
218	Kenny Lofton	7.50
219	Cecil Fielder	1.00
220	Darren Daulton	1.00
221	John Olerud	2.00
222	Jose Canseco	6.00
223	Rickey Henderson	4.00
224	Fred McGriff	4.00
225	Gary Sheffield	4.00
226	Jack McDowell	1.00
227	Rafael Palmeiro	3.00
228	Travis Fryman	1.50
229	Marquis Grissom	1.00
230	Barry Bonds	10.00
231	Carlos Baerga	1.00
232	Ken Griffey Jr.	35.00
233	Dave Justice	4.00
234	Bobby Bonilla	1.00
235	Cal Ripken	25.00
236	Sammy Sosa	15.00
237	Len Dykstra	1.00
238	Will Clark	4.50
239	Paul Molitor	4.50
240	Barry Larkin	2.00
421	James Mouton	1.00
422	Tony Tarasco	1.00
423	Carlos Delgado	1.50
424	Rondell White	1.50
425	Javier Lopez	2.00
426	Chan Ho Park	2.00
427	Cliff Floyd	1.50
428	Dave Staton	1.00
429	J.R. Phillips	1.00
430	Manny Ramirez	10.00
431	Kurt Abbott	1.00
432	Melvin Nieves	1.00
433	Alex Gonzalez	1.00
434	Rick Helling	1.00
435	Danny Bautista	1.00
436	Matt Walbeck	1.00
437	Ryan Klesko	2.50
438	Steve Karsay	1.00
439	Salomon Torres	1.00
440	Scott Ruffcorn	1.00

1994 Finest Superstar Sampler

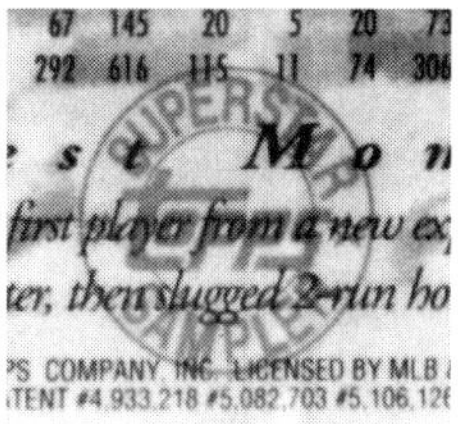

This special version of 45 of the biggest-name stars from the 1994 Topps Finest set was issued in a three-card cello pack with the same player's '94 Bowman and Stadium Club cards. The packs were available only in 1994 Topps retail factory sets. Cards are identical to the regular-issue Finest cards except for a round, red "Topps Superstar Sampler" logo printed at bottom center on back.

		MT
Complete Set (45):		275.00
Common Player:		3.00
1	Mike Piazza	15.00
18	Tim Salmon	4.50
35	Andres Galarraga	4.00
74	Raul Mondesi	4.00
92	Gregg Jefferies	4.00
201	Tony Gwynn	7.50
203	Frank Thomas	20.00
204	Kirby Puckett	10.00
205	Roberto Alomar	6.00
207	Joe Carter	3.00
208	Albert Belle	7.50
209	Greg Maddux	20.00
210	Ryne Sandberg	12.50
211	Juan Gonzalez	10.00
212	Jeff Bagwell	10.00
213	Randy Johnson	5.00
214	Matt Williams	4.50
216	Larry Walker	5.00
217	Roger Clemens	7.50
219	Cecil Fielder	3.00
220	Darren Daulton	3.00
221	John Olerud	4.50
222	Jose Canseco	6.00
224	Fred McGriff	4.00
225	Gary Sheffield	4.50
226	Jack McDowell	3.00
227	Rafael Palmeiro	5.00
229	Marquis Grissom	4.00
230	Barry Bonds	10.00
231	Carlos Baerga	3.00
232	Ken Griffey Jr.	35.00
233	Dave Justice	4.50
234	Bobby Bonilla	3.50
235	Cal Ripken Jr.	30.00
237	Len Dykstra	3.00
238	Will Clark	5.00
239	Paul Molitor	4.50
240	Barry Larkin	4.00
258	Mo Vaughn	6.00
267	Tom Glavine	4.00
390	Mark Grace	5.00
392	Don Mattingly	17.50
408	Andy Van Slyke	3.00
427	Cliff Floyd	3.00
430	Manny Ramirez	7.50

1994 Finest Bronze

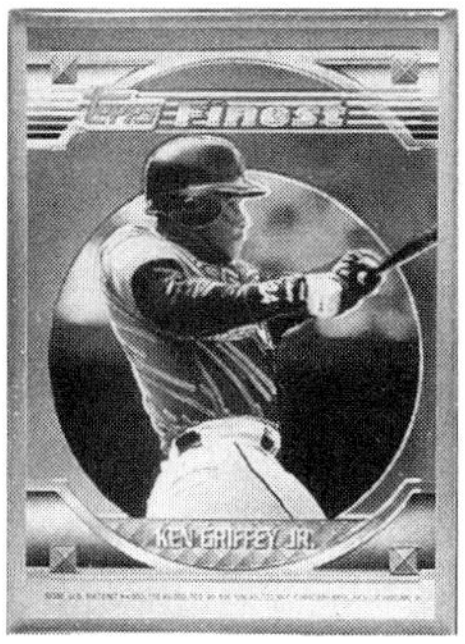

This three-card set was included as part of the purchase of a 1994 Topps Stadium Club Members Only set, but was also made available on a limited basis via newspaper ads. The cards feature a version of Topps' Finest technology with the multi-colored front design laminated to a bronze base by a heavy lucite overlay. Backs are engraved in black on bronze and contain complete major and minor league stats and a few personal data. The Finest bronze cards are slightly larger than current standard size, measuring 2-3/4" x 3-3/4".

		MT
Complete Set (3):		75.00
Common Player:		25.00
1	Barry Bonds	25.00
2	Ken Griffey, Jr.	50.00
3	Frank Thomas	20.00

1995 Finest

In its third year Finest baseball was reduced to a 220-card base set. All cards feature the chrome-printing technology associated with the Finest logo and include a peel-off plastic protector on the card front. Backgrounds are green with gold pinstripes. Behind the action photo at center is a large diamond with each corner intersected by a silver semi-circle. On the Finest Rookies subset which makes up the first 30 cards of the issue, the diamond has a graduated pink to orange center, with flecks of red throughout. Veterans cards have a graduated blue to purple center of the diamond. On the rookies cards there is a teal brand name at top, while the vets show a gold "FINEST". Backs repeat the front background motif in shades of green. There is a player photo at right, with biographical data, 1994 and career stats, and a "Finest Moment" career highlight at left. Finest was sold in seven-card packs with a suggested retail price of $4.99.

		MT
Complete Set (220):		80.00
Common Player:		.25
Series 1 or 2 Wax Box:		80.00
1	Raul Mondesi (Rookie Theme)	.75
2	Kurt Abbott (Rookie Theme)	.30
3	Chris Gomez (Rookie Theme)	.25
4	Manny Ramirez (Rookie Theme)	2.50
5	Rondell White (Rookie Theme)	.50
6	William Van Landingham (Rookie Theme)	.25
7	Jon Lieber (Rookie Theme)	.25
8	Ryan Klesko (Rookie Theme)	.75
9	John Hudek (Rookie Theme)	.25
10	Joey Hamilton (Rookie Theme)	.75
11	Bob Hamelin (Rookie Theme)	.25
12	Brian Anderson (Rookie Theme)	.25
13	Mike Lieberthal (Rookie Theme)	.35
14	Rico Brogna (Rookie Theme)	.25
15	Rusty Greer (Rookie Theme)	.30
16	Carlos Delgado (Rookie Theme)	.75
17	Jim Edmonds (Rookie Theme)	.75
18	Steve Trachsel (Rookie Theme)	.25
19	Matt Walbeck (Rookie Theme)	.25
20	Armando Benitez (Rookie Theme)	.30
21	Steve Karsay (Rookie Theme)	.25
22	Jose Oliva (Rookie Theme)	.25
23	Cliff Floyd (Rookie Theme)	.30
24	Kevin Foster (Rookie Theme)	.25
25	Javier Lopez (Rookie Theme)	.75
26	Jose Valentin (Rookie Theme)	.25
27	James Mouton (Rookie Theme)	.25
28	Hector Carrasco (Rookie Theme)	.25
29	Orlando Miller (Rookie Theme)	.25
30	Garret Anderson (Rookie Theme)	.25
31	Marvin Freeman	.25
32	Brett Butler	.25
33	Roberto Kelly	.25
34	Rod Beck	.25
35	Jose Rijo	.25
36	Edgar Martinez	.25
37	Jim Thome	1.50
38	Rick Wilkins	.25
39	Wally Joyner	.30
40	Wil Cordero	.25
41	Tommy Greene	.25
42	Travis Fryman	.30
43	Don Slaught	.25
44	Brady Anderson	.30
45	Matt Williams	.75
46	Rene Arocha	.25
47	Rickey Henderson	.50
48	Mike Mussina	1.00
49	Greg McMichael	.25
50	Jody Reed	.25
51	Tino Martinez	.35
52	Dave Clark	.25
53	John Valentin	.25
54	Bret Boone	.25
55	Walt Weiss	.25
56	Kenny Lofton	2.00
57	Scott Leius	.25
58	Eric Karros	.30
59	John Olerud	.40
60	Chris Hoiles	.25
61	Sandy Alomar	.30
62	Tim Wallach	.25
63	Cal Eldred	.25
64	Tom Glavine	.35
65	Mark Grace	.50
66	Rey Sanchez	.25
67	Bobby Ayala	.25
68	Dante Bichette	.75
69	Andres Galarraga	.35
70	Chuck Carr	.25
71	Bobby Witt	.25
72	Steve Avery	.25
73	Bobby Jones	.25
74	Delino DeShields	.25
75	Kevin Tapani	.25
76	Randy Johnson	1.50
77	David Nied	.25
78	Pat Hentgen	.25
79	Tim Salmon	.75
80	Todd Zeile	.25
81	John Wetteland	.25
82	Albert Belle	2.50
83	Ben McDonald	.25
84	Bobby Munoz	.25
85	Bip Roberts	.25
86	Mo Vaughn	2.00
87	Chuck Finley	.25
88	Chuck Knoblauch	.50
89	Frank Thomas	4.00
90	Danny Tartabull	.25
91	Dean Palmer	.25
92	Len Dykstra	.25
93	J.R. Phillips	.25
94	Tom Candiotti	.25
95	Marquis Grissom	.25
96	Barry Larkin	.50
97	Bryan Harvey	.25
98	Dave Justice	.50
99	David Cone	.40
100	Wade Boggs	.50
101	Jason Bere	.25
102	Hal Morris	.25
103	Fred McGriff	.50
104	Bobby Bonilla	.30
105	Jay Buhner	.30
106	Allen Watson	.25
107	Mickey Tettleton	.25
108	Kevin Appier	.25
109	Ivan Rodriguez	2.50
110	Carlos Garcia	.25
111	Andy Benes	.25
112	Eddie Murray	1.50
113	Mike Piazza	7.00
114	Greg Vaughn	.35
115	Paul Molitor	1.50
116	Terry Steinbach	.25
117	Jeff Bagwell	4.00
118	Ken Griffey Jr.	10.00
119	Gary Sheffield	2.00
120	Cal Ripken Jr.	8.00
121	Jeff Kent	.25
122	Jay Bell	.25
123	Will Clark	.75
124	Cecil Fielder	.25
125	Alex Fernandez	.30
126	Don Mattingly	4.00
127	Reggie Sanders	.25
128	Moises Alou	.30
129	Craig Biggio	.40
130	Eddie Williams	.25
131	John Franco	.25
132	John Kruk	.25
133	Jeff King	.25
134	Royce Clayton	.25
135	Doug Drabek	.25
136	Ray Lankford	.25
137	Roberto Alomar	2.00
138	Todd Hundley	.50
139	Alex Cole	.25
140	Shawon Dunston	.25
141	John Roper	.25
142	Mark Langston	.25
143	Tom Pagnozzi	.25
144	Wilson Alvarez	.25
145	Scott Cooper	.25
146	Kevin Mitchell	.25
147	Mark Whiten	.25
148	Jeff Conine	.25
149	Chili Davis	.25
150	Luis Gonzalez	.25
151	Juan Guzman	.25
152	Mike Greenwell	.25
153	Mike Henneman	.25
154	Rick Aguilera	.25
155	Dennis Eckersley	.30
156	Darrin Fletcher	.25
157	Darren Lewis	.25
158	Juan Gonzalez	5.00
159	Dave Hollins	.25
160	Jimmy Key	.25
161	Roberto Hernandez	.25
162	Randy Myers	.25
163	Joe Carter	.30
164	Darren Daulton	.25
165	Mike MacFarlane	.25
166	Bret Saberhagen	.25
167	Kirby Puckett	4.00
168	Lance Johnson	.25
169	Mark McGwire	10.00
170	Jose Canseco	1.00
171	Mike Stanley	.25
172	Lee Smith	.25
173	Robin Ventura	.45
174	Greg Gagne	.25
175	Brian McRae	.25
176	Mike Bordick	.25
177	Rafael Palmeiro	.50
178	Kenny Rogers	.25
179	Chad Curtis	.25
180	Devon White	.30
181	Paul O'Neill	.35

182	Ken Caminiti	.75
183	Dave Nilsson	.25
184	Tim Naehring	.25
185	Roger Clemens	3.00
186	Otis Nixon	.25
187	Tim Raines	.25
188	Dennis Martinez	.25
189	Pedro Martinez	.40
190	Jim Abbott	.25
191	Ryan Thompson	.25
192	Barry Bonds	2.50
193	Joe Girardi	.25
194	Steve Finley	.25
195	John Jaha	.25
196	Tony Gwynn	4.00
197	Sammy Sosa	5.00
198	John Burkett	.25
199	Carlos Baerga	.25
200	Ramon Martinez	.25
201	Aaron Sele	.25
202	Eduardo Perez	.25
203	Alan Trammell	.25
204	Orlando Merced	.25
205	Deion Sanders	.40
206	Robb Nen	.25
207	Jack McDowell	.25
208	Ruben Sierra	.25
209	Bernie Williams	2.00
210	Kevin Seitzer	.25
211	Charles Nagy	.25
212	Tony Phillips	.25
213	Greg Maddux	6.00
214	Jeff Montgomery	.25
215	Larry Walker	.75
216	Andy Van Slyke	.25
217	Ozzie Smith	1.50
218	Geronimo Pena	.25
219	Gregg Jefferies	.25
220	Lou Whitaker	.25

1995 Finest Refractors

A parallel set with a counterpart to each of the 220 cards in the regular Finest emission, the Refractors are printed in a version of the Finest chrome technology that produces a rainbow effect when viewed at the proper angle. The relatively open spaces of the 1995 Finest design make the Refractors easier to spot than the previous years' versions, but just to assist the identification process, Topps placed a small black "REFRACTOR" in the dark green background on the cards' backs, as well. Advertised rate of insertion for the Refractors was about one per 12 packs.

	MT
Complete Set (220):	2250.
Common Player:	4.00
Stars: 7-12X	

(See 1995 Finest for checklist and base card values.)

1995 Finest Flame Throwers

The scarcest of the Finest inserts is the nine-card set of baseball's hardest throwing pitchers. Flame Throwers cards are found at an average rate of one per 48 packs. Fronts have a central photo of a pitcher bringing his best heat. Behind the photo is the Flame Throwers typographic logo in tones of red, yellow and orange. Backs have another photo and a bar graph rating the pitcher's skill levels.

		MT
Complete Set (9):		35.00
Common Player:		2.50
1	Jason Bere	2.50
2	Roger Clemens	15.00
3	Juan Guzman	2.50
4	John Hudek	2.50
5	Randy Johnson	7.50
6	Pedro Martinez	7.50
7	Jose Rijo	2.50
8	Bret Saberhagen	3.00
9	John Wetteland	2.50

1995 Finest Power Kings

The emphasis is on youth in this chase set of baseball's top distance threats. Found at a rate of one per 24 packs, on average, the Power Kings inserts have a central photo of the player in batting action. The background, in shades of blue, features lightning strokes. Backs feature another pair of player photos and a bar graph charting the hitter's power skills.

		MT
Complete Set (18):		90.00
Common Player:		1.50
1	Bob Hamelin	1.50
2	Raul Mondesi	2.50
3	Ryan Klesko	2.00
4	Carlos Delgado	3.00
5	Manny Ramirez	7.50
6	Mike Piazza	15.00
7	Jeff Bagwell	10.00
8	Mo Vaughn	7.50
9	Frank Thomas	10.00
10	Ken Griffey Jr.	25.00
11	Albert Belle	5.00
12	Sammy Sosa	12.50
13	Dante Bichette	2.00
14	Gary Sheffield	2.00
15	Matt Williams	2.50
16	Fred McGriff	2.00
17	Barry Bonds	7.50
18	Cecil Fielder	1.50

1995 Finest Update

Players who changed teams through trades or free agent signings and more of the season's rookie player crop are included in the Finest Update series of 110 cards. The cards are numbered contiguously with the base Finest set and share the same design. Once again, Refractor cards were found on an average of once per 12 packs. Finest Update was sold in seven-card packs with a suggested retail price of $4.99.

		MT
Complete Set (110):		25.00
Common Player:		.25
221	Chipper Jones	8.00
222	Benji Gil	.25
223	Tony Phillips	.25
224	Trevor Wilson	.25
225	Tony Tarasco	.25
226	Roberto Petagine	.25
227	Mike MacFarlane	.25
228	*Hideo Nomo*	8.00
229	Mark McLemore	.25
230	Ron Gant	.50
231	Andujar Cedeno	.25
232	*Mike Mimbs*	.40
233	Jim Abbott	.25
234	Ricky Bones	.25
235	Marty Cordova	1.00
236	Mark Johnson	.50
237	Marquis Grissom	.25
238	Tom Henke	.25
239	Terry Pendleton	.25
240	John Wetteland	.25
241	Lee Smith	.25
242	Jaime Navarro	.25
243	Luis Alicea	.25
244	Scott Cooper	.25
245	Gary Gaetti	.25
246	Edgardo Alfonzo	.50
247	Brad Clontz	.25
248	Dave Mlicki	.25
249	Dave Winfield	.75
250	*Mark Grudzielanek*	3.00
251	Alex Gonzalez	.25
252	Kevin Brown	.50
253	Esteban Loaiza	.40
254	Vaughn Eshelman	.25
255	Bill Swift	.25
256	Brian McRae	.25
257	*Bobby Higginson*	5.00
258	Jack McDowell	.25
259	Scott Stahoviak	.25
260	Jon Nunnally	.25
261	Charlie Hayes	.25
262	Jacob Brumfield	.25
263	Chad Curtis	.25
264	Heathcliff Slocumb	.25
265	Mark Whiten	.25
266	Mickey Tettleton	.25
267	Jose Mesa	.25
268	Doug Jones	.25
269	Trevor Hoffman	.50
270	Paul Sorrento	.25
271	Shane Andrews	.25
272	Brett Butler	.25
273	Curtis Goodwin	.25
274	Larry Walker	.75
275	Phil Plantier	.25
276	Ken Hill	.25
277	Vinny Castilla	.35
278	Billy Ashley	.25
279	Derek Jeter	8.00
280	Bob Tewksbury	.25
281	Jose Offerman	.25
282	Glenallen Hill	.25
283	Tony Fernandez	.25
284	Mike Devereaux	.25
285	John Burkett	.25
286	Geronimo Berroa	.25
287	Quilvio Veras	.25
288	Jason Bates	.25
289	Lee Tinsley	.25
290	Derek Bell	.25
291	Jeff Fassero	.25
292	Ray Durham	.50
293	Chad Ogea	.25
294	Bill Pulsipher	.35
295	Phil Nevin	.25
296	*Carlos Perez*	1.00
297	Roberto Kelly	.25
298	Tim Wakefield	.25
299	Jeff Manto	.25
300	Brian Hunter	.25
301	C.J. Nitkowski	.25
302	Dustin Hermanson	.25
303	John Mabry	.25
304	Orel Hershiser	.25
305	Ron Villone	.25
306	Sean Bergman	.25
307	Tom Goodwin	.25
308	Al Reyes	.25
309	Todd Stottlemyre	.25
310	Rich Becker	.25
311	Joey Cora	.25
312	Ed Sprague	.25
313	John Smoltz	.75
314	Frank Castillo	.25
315	Chris Hammond	.25
316	Ismael Valdes	.25
317	Pete Harnisch	.25
318	Bernard Gilkey	.25
319	John Kruk	.25
320	Marc Newfield	.25
321	Brian Johnson	.25
322	Mark Portugal	.25
323	David Hulse	.25
324	Luis Ortiz	.25
325	Mike Benjamin	.25
326	Brian Jordan	.25
327	Shawn Green	1.00
328	Joe Oliver	.25
329	Felipe Lira	.25
330	Andre Dawson	.35

1995 Finest Update Refractors

The special version of Topps' chromium printing process which creates a rainbow effect was applied to a limited number of each card in the Finest Update set to create a parallel Refractor edition. To assist in identification, a small black "REFRACTOR" is printed on the cards' backs as well. Refractors are found on average once every 12 packs of Finest Update.

	MT
Complete Set (110):	450.00
Common Player:	4.00
Stars: 7-12X	

(See 1995 Finest Update for checklist and base card values.)

1995 Finest Bronze League Leaders

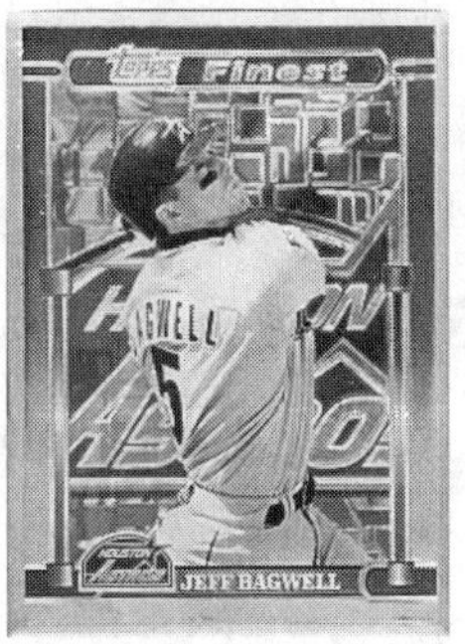

Available only by mail directly from Topps, this set features N.L. and A.L. leaders in various batting categories for the 1994 season. Fronts employ Topps' Finest technology with a stained-glass effect in the background, overlaid with a heavy layer of resin. Backs are bronze and feature 1994 stats and highlights embossed in blue. The cards are oversized, measuring 2-3/4" x 3-3/4".

		MT
Complete Set (6):		125.00
Common Player:		10.00
1	Matt Williams	10.00
2	Tony Gwynn	25.00
3	Jeff Bagwell	25.00
4	Ken Griffey Jr.	50.00
5	Paul O'Neill	10.00
6	Frank Thomas	15.00

1996 Finest

Utilizing three levels of base-card scarcity, the 359-card Finest set comprises 220 Commons (Bronze), 91 Uncommons (Silver) and 49 Rares (Gold). Cards were somewhat randomly assigned a status. Uncommon cards are found one in four packs; Rare cards are seeded one per 24 packs. The set has eight themes. Series 1 themes are Phenoms, Intimidators, Gamers and Sterling, the latter of which consists of star players already included within the first three themes. Series 2 themes are Franchise, Additions, Prodigies and Sterling. Regular-issue cards are not only numbered from 1-359 in the set as a whole, but also numbered within each subset. Finest Refractor parallel cards were also made. Rare Refractor cards are found one every 288 packs (fewer than 150 of each produced), while Uncommon Refractors are found one per 48 packs. Common Refractors are seeded 1:12.

		MT
Complete Set (359):		750.00
Bronze Set (220):		40.00
Common Bronze:		.15
Silver Set (91):		200.00
Typical Silver:		1.00
Gold Set (47):		600.00
Typical Gold:		5.00
Series 1 Wax Box:		100.00
Series 2 Wax Box:		75.00
1	Greg Maddux S (Intimidators)	7.50
2	Bernie Williams S (Gamers)	2.50
3	Ivan Rodriguez S (Intimidators)	5.00
4	Marty Cordova G (Phenoms)	5.00
5	Roberto Hernandez (Intimidators)	.15
6	Tony Gwynn G (Gamers)	17.50
7	Barry Larkin S (Sterling)	1.00
8	Terry Pendleton (Gamers)	.15
9	Albert Belle G (Sterling)	12.50
10	Ray Lankford S (Gamers)	1.00
11	Mike Piazza S (Sterling)	7.50
12	Ken Caminiti (Gamers)	.25
13	Larry Walker S (Intimidators)	2.00
14	Matt Williams S (Intimidators)	1.50
15	Dan Miceli (Phenoms)	.15
16	Chipper Jones (Sterling)	2.50
17	John Wetteland (Intimidators)	.15
18	Kirby Puckett G (Sterling)	15.00
19	Tim Naehring (Gamers)	.15
20	Karim Garcia G (Phenoms)	7.50
21	Eddie Murray (Gamers)	.40
22	Tim Salmon S (Intimidators)	1.50
23	Kevin Appier (Intimidators)	.15
24	Ken Griffey Jr. (Sterling)	12.00
25	Cal Ripken Jr. G (Gamers)	30.00
26	Brian McRae (Gamers)	.15
27	Pedro Martinez (Intimidators)	.40
28	Brian Jordan (Gamers)	.15
29	Mike Fetters (Intimidators)	.15
30	Carlos Delgado (Phenoms)	.50
31	Shane Reynolds (Intimidators)	.15
32	Terry Steinbach (Gamers)	.15
33	Hideo Nomo G (Sterling)	7.50
34	Mark Leiter (Gamers)	.15
35	Edgar Martinez S (Intimidators)	1.00

36 David Segui (Gamers) .15
37 Gregg Jefferies S (Gamers) 1.00
38 Bill Pulsipher S (Phenoms) 1.00
39 Ryne Sandberg G (Gamers) 10.00
40 Fred McGriff (Intimidators) .40
41 Shawn Green S (Phenoms) 2.50
42 Jeff Bagwell G (Sterling) 17.50
43 Jim Abbott S (Gamers) 1.00
44 Glenallen Hill (Intimidators) .15
45 Brady Anderson (Gamers) .15
46 Roger Clemens S (Intimidators) 3.00
47 Jim Thome (Gamers) .40
48 Frank Thomas (Sterling) 2.00
49 Chuck Knoblauch (Gamers) .20
50 Lenny Dykstra (Gamers) .15
51 Jason Isringhausen G (Phenoms) 5.00
52 Rondell White S (Phenoms) 1.00
53 Tom Pagnozzi (Gamers) .15
54 Dennis Eckersley S (Intimidators) 1.00
55 Ricky Bones (Gamers) .15
56 David Justice (Intimidators) .35
57 Steve Avery (Gamers) .15
58 Robby Thompson (Gamers) .15
59 Hideo Nomo S (Phenoms) 3.00
60 Gary Sheffield S (Intimidators) 1.50
61 Tony Gwynn (Sterling) 1.25
62 Will Clark S (Gamers) 1.50
63 Denny Neagle (Gamers) .15
64 Mo Vaughn G (Intimidators) 10.00
65 Bret Boone S (Gamers) 1.00
66 Dante Bichette G (Sterling) 6.00
67 Robin Ventura (Gamers) .25
68 Rafael Palmeiro S (Intimidators) 1.25
69 Carlos Baerga S (Gamers) 1.00
70 Kevin Seitzer (Gamers) .15
71 Ramon Martinez (Intimidators) .20
72 Tom Glavine S (Gamers) 1.25
73 Garret Anderson S (Phenoms) 1.00
74 Mark McGwire G (Intimidators) 40.00
75 Brian Hunter (Phenoms) .25
76 Alan Benes (Phenoms) .25
77 Randy Johnson S (Intimidators) 3.00
78 Jeff King S (Gamers) 1.00
79 Kirby Puckett S (Intimidators) 5.00
80 Ozzie Guillen (Gamers) .15
81 Kenny Lofton G (Intimidators) 10.00
82 Benji Gil (Phenoms) .15
83 Jim Edmonds G (Gamers) 5.00
84 Cecil Fielder S (Intimidators) 1.00
85 Todd Hundley (Gamers) .35
86 Reggie Sanders S (Intimidators) 1.00
87 Pat Hentgen (Gamers) .15
88 Ryan Klesko S (Intimidators) 2.00
89 Chuck Finley (Gamers) .15
90 Mike Mussina G (Intimidators) 9.00
91 John Valentin S (Intimidators) 1.00
92 Derek Jeter (Phenoms) 5.00
93 Paul O'Neill (Intimidators) .25
94 Darrin Fletcher (Gamers) .15
95 Manny Ramirez S (Phenoms) 5.00
96 Delino DeShields (Gamers) .15
97 Tim Salmon (Sterling) .40
98 John Olerud (Gamers) .25
99 Vinny Castilla S (Intimidators) 1.25
100 Jeff Conine G (Gamers) 5.00
101 Tim Wakefield (Gamers) .15
102 Johnny Damon G (Phenoms) 5.00
103 Dave Stevens (Gamers) .15
104 Orlando Merced (Gamers) .15
105 Barry Bonds G (Sterling) 12.50
106 Jay Bell (Gamers) .15
107 John Burkett (Gamers) .15
108 Chris Hoiles (Gamers) .15
109 Carlos Perez S (Phenoms) 1.00
110 Dave Nilsson (Gamers) .15
111 Rod Beck (Intimidators) .15
112 Craig Biggio S (Gamers) 2.00
113 Mike Piazza (Intimidators) 4.00
114 Mark Langston (Gamers) .15
115 Juan Gonzalez S (Intimidators) 6.00
116 Rico Brogna (Gamers) .15
117 Jose Canseco G (Intimidators) 9.00
118 Tom Goodwin (Gamers) .15
119 Bryan Rekar (Phenoms) .15
120 David Cone (Intimidators) .20
121 Ray Durham S (Phenoms) 1.00
122 Andy Pettitte (Phenoms) .70
123 Chili Davis (Intimidators) .15
124 John Smoltz (Gamers) .25
125 Heathcliff Slocumb (Intimidators) .15
126 Dante Bichette (Intimidators) .25
127 C.J. Nitkowski S (Phenoms) 1.00
128 Alex Gonzalez (Phenoms) .15
129 Jeff Montgomery (Intimidators) .15
130 Raul Mondesi S (Intimidators) 1.25
131 Denny Martinez (Gamers) .15
132 Mel Rojas (Intimidators) .15
133 Derek Bell (Gamers) .15
134 Trevor Hoffman (Intimidators) .20
135 Ken Griffey Jr. G (Intimidators) 45.00
136 Darren Daulton (Gamers) .15
137 Pete Schourek (Gamers) .15
138 Phil Nevin (Phenoms) .15
139 Andres Galarraga (Intimidators) .20
140 Chad Fonville (Phenoms) .15
141 Chipper Jones G (Phenoms) 25.00
142 Lee Smith S (Intimidators) 1.00
143 Joe Carter S (Gamers) 1.00
144 J.T. Snow (Gamers) .15
145 Greg Maddux G (Sterling) 25.00
146 Barry Bonds (Intimidators) .70
147 Orel Hershiser (Gamers) .15
148 Quilvio Veras (Phenoms) .15
149 Will Clark (Sterling) [illegible]
150 Jose Rijo (Gamers) .15
151 Mo Vaughn S (Sterling) 4.00
152 Travis Fryman (Gamers) .20
153 Frank Rodriguez S (Phenoms) 1.00
154 Alex Fernandez (Gamers) .15
155 Wade Boggs (Gamers) .35
156 Troy Percival (Phenoms) .15
157 Moises Alou (Gamers) .25
158 Javy Lopez (Gamers) .25
159 Jason Giambi (Phenoms) .15
160 Steve Finley S (Gamers) 1.00
161 Jeff Bagwell S (Intimidators) 6.00
162 Mark McGwire (Sterling) 5.00
163 Eric Karros (Gamers) .15
164 Jay Buhner G (Intimidators) 6.00
165 Cal Ripken Jr. S (Sterling) 15.00
166 Mickey Tettleton (Intimidators) .15
167 Barry Larkin (Intimidators) .40
168 Lyle Mouton S (Phenoms) 1.00
169 Ruben Sierra (Intimidators) .15
170 Bill Swift (Gamers) .15
171 Sammy Sosa S (Intimidators) 10.00
172 Chad Curtis (Gamers) .15
173 Dean Palmer (Gamers) .15
174 John Franco S (Gamers) 1.00
175 Bobby Bonilla (Intimidators) .15
176 Greg Colbrunn (Gamers) .15
177 Jose Mesa (Intimidators) .15
178 Mike Greenwell (Gamers) .15
179 Greg Vaughn S (Intimidators) 1.25
180 Mark Wohlers S (Intimidators) 1.00
181 Doug Drabek (Gamers) .15
182 Paul O'Neill S (Sterling) 1.50
183 Wilson Alvarez (Gamers) .15
184 Marty Cordova (Sterling) .20
185 Hal Morris (Gamers) .15
186 Frank Thomas G (Intimidators) 15.00
187 Carlos Garcia (Gamers) .15
188 Albert Belle S (Intimidators) 4.00
189 Mark Grace S (Gamers) 2.50
190 Marquis Grissom (Gamers) .15
191 Checklist .15
192 Chipper Jones G 25.00
193 Will Clark .35
194 Paul Molitor .40
195 Kenny Rogers .15
196 Reggie Sanders .15
197 Roberto Alomar G 10.00
198 Dennis Eckersley G 5.00
199 Raul Mondesi .40
200 Lance Johnson .15
201 Alvin Morman .15
202 George Arias G 5.00
203 Jack McDowell .15
204 Randy Myers .15
205 Harold Baines .15
206 Marty Cordova .20
207 *Rich Hunter* .15
208 Al Leiter .20
209 Greg Gagne .15
210 Ben McDonald .15
211 Ernie Young S 1.00
212 Terry Adams .15
213 Paul Sorrento .15
214 Albert Belle .70
215 Mike Blowers .15
216 Jim Edmonds .40
217 Felipe Crespo .15
218 Fred McGriff S 1.25
219 Shawon Dunston .15
220 Jimmy Haynes .15
221 Jose Canseco .40
222 Eric Davis .15
223 Kimera Bartee S 1.00
224 Tim Raines .15
225 Tony Phillips .15
226 Charlie Hayes .15
227 Eric Owens .15
228 Roberto Alomar .60
229 Rickey Henderson S 2.00
230 Sterling Hitchcock S 1.00
231 Bernard Gilkey S 1.00
232 Hideo Nomo G 7.50
233 Kenny Lofton .70
234 Ryne Sandberg S 3.00
235 Greg Maddux S 7.50
236 Mark McGwire 5.00
237 Jay Buhner .20
238 Craig Biggio .25
239 Todd Stottlemyre S 1.00
240 Barry Bonds .70
241 Jason Kendall S 1.50
242 Paul O'Neill S 1.50
243 Chris Snopek G 5.00
244 Ron Gant .20
245 Paul Wilson .20
246 Todd Hollandsworth .15
247 Todd Zeile .15
248 David Justice .25
249 Tim Salmon G 6.00
250 Moises Alou .20
251 Bob Wolcott .15
252 David Wells .15
253 Juan Gonzalez 1.25
254 Andres Galarraga .25
255 Dave Hollins .15
256 Devon White S 1.00
257 Sammy Sosa 1.25
258 Ivan Rodriguez .50
259 Bip Roberts .15
260 Tino Martinez .25
261 Chuck Knoblauch S 1.25
262 Mike Stanley .15
263 Wally Joyner S 1.00
264 Butch Huskey .15
265 Jeff Conine .15
266 Matt Williams G 6.00
267 Mark Grace .25
268 Jason Schmidt .15
269 Otis Nixon .15
270 Randy Johnson G 10.00
271 Kirby Puckett 2.00
272 *Andy Fox S* 1.00
273 Andy Benes .15
274 Sean Berry S 1.00
275 Mike Piazza 4.00
276 Rey Ordonez .40
277 Benito Santiago S 1.00
278 Gary Gaetti .15
279 Paul Molitor G 7.50
280 Robin Ventura .25
281 Cal Ripken Jr. 5.00
282 Carlos Baerga .15
283 Roger Cedeno .25
284 Chad Mottola S 1.00
285 Terrell Wade .15
286 Kevin Brown .25
287 Rafael Palmeiro .25
288 Mo Vaughn .70
289 Dante Bichette S 1.25
290 Cecil Fielder G 5.00
291 Doc Gooden S 1.50
292 Bob Tewksbury .15
293 Kevin Mitchell S 1.00
294 *Livan Hernandez G* 9.00
295 Russ Davis S 1.00
296 Chan Ho Park S 2.00
297 T.J. Mathews .15
298 Manny Ramirez 2.00
299 Jeff Bagwell 1.50
300 *Marty Janzen G* 5.00
301 Wade Boggs .35
302 Larry Walker S 2.00
303 Steve Gibralter .15
304 B.J. Surhoff .15
305 Ken Griffey Jr. S 25.00
306 Royce Clayton .15
307 Sal Fasano .15
308 Ron Gant G 5.00
309 Gary Sheffield .40
310 Ken Hill .15
311 Joe Girardi .15
312 *Matt Lawton* .15
313 Billy Wagner S 2.00
314 Julio Franco .15
315 Joe Carter .20
316 Brooks Kieschnick .15
317 *Mike Grace S* 1.50
318 Heathcliff Slocumb .15
319 Barry Larkin .40
320 Tony Gwynn 1.25
321 Ryan Klesko G 8.00
322 Frank Thomas 1.50
323 Edgar Martinez .15
324 Jermaine Dye G 5.00
325 Henry Rodriguez .15
326 *Marvin Benard* .25
327 Kenny Lofton S 4.00
328 Derek Bell S 1.00
329 Ugueth Urbina .15
330 Jason Giambi G 5.00
331 Roger Salkeld .15
332 Edgar Renteria .25
333 Ryan Klesko .50
334 Ray Lankford .15
335 Edgar Martinez G 5.00
336 Justin Thompson .15
337 Gary Sheffield S 2.00
338 Rey Ordonez G 7.50
339 Mark Clark .15
340 Ruben Rivera .40
341 Mark Grace S 1.50
342 Matt Williams .25
343 *Francisco Cordova* .20
344 Cecil Fielder .20
345 Andres Galarraga S 1.25
346 Brady Anderson S 1.25
347 Sammy Sosa G 20.00
348 Mark Grudzielanek .15
349 Ron Coomer .15
350 Derek Jeter S 9.00
351 Rich Aurilla .15
352 Jose Herrera .15
353 Jay Buhner S 1.50
354 Juan Gonzalez G 20.00
355 Craig Biggio G 7.50
356 Tony Clark .50
357 Tino Martinez S 1.25
358 *Dan Naulty* .15
359 Checklist .15

1996 Finest Refractors

Finest Refractor cards were created as a parallel set to Topps' 1996 Finest set. Rare Refractor cards are found one per every 288 packs (less than 150 of these sets were produced), while uncommon Refractors are found one per every 48 packs. Common Refractors are seeded one per every 12 packs.

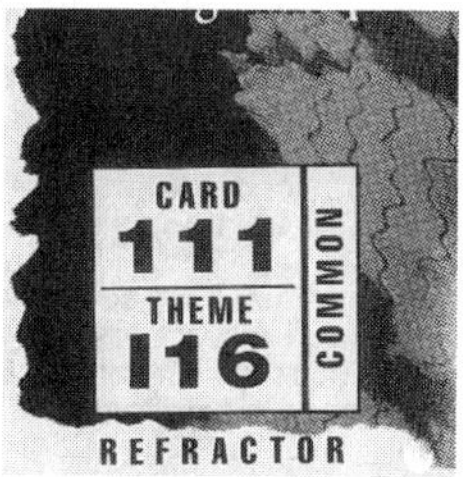

	MT
Complete Set (359):	2500.
Bronze Set (220):	600.00
Common Bronze:	2.00
Bronze Stars: 8X	
Silver Set (91):	600.00
Typical Silver:	3.50
Silver Stars: 3X	
Gold Set (48):	1500.
Typical Gold:	12.50
Gold Stars: 2.5X	

(See 1996 Finest for checklist and base card values.)

1997 Finest Samples

Many of the subsets included in the 1997 Finest issue were previewed with a cello-wrapped pack of five cards distributed to hobby dealers. Cards are virtually identical to the issued versions and are designated a Refractor on back. Overprinted on back is a red notice, "PROMOTIONAL SAMPLE / NOT FOR RESALE"

		MT
Complete Set (5):		15.00
Common Player:		2.00
1	Barry Bonds	3.00
15	Derek Jeter	4.00
30	Mark McGwire	4.00
143	Hideo Nomo	2.00
159	Jeff Bagwell	3.00

1997 Finest

Finest returned for 1997 in its three-tiered format from 1996, but added several new twists. Issued in two series of 175 cards each, cards numbered 1-100 and 176-275 are bronze; 101-150 and 276-325 are silver and 151-175 and

326-350 are gold. All cards are designated among one of five different subsets per series. In Series 1 they are: Warriors, Blue Chips, Power, Hurlers and Masters. Series 2 subsets are: Power, Masters, Blue Chips, Competitors and Acquisitions. The bronze cards are the "common" card, while silvers are found every four packs and golds every 24 packs. Each card has a parallel Refractor version: bronze (1:12), silver (1:48) and gold (1:288). In addition, silver and gold cards have an additional parallel set. Silvers are found in an embossed version (1:16) and embossed Refractor version (1:192), while golds are found in a die-cut embossed version (1:96) and a die-cut embossed Refractor (1:1152).

		MT
Complete Set (350):		600.00
Bronze Set (200):		35.00
Common Bronze:		.15
Silver Set (100):		200.00
Typical Silver:		1.00
Complete Gold Set (50):		400.00
Typical Gold:		4.00
Series 1 Box		60.00
Series 2 Box:		50.00
1	Barry Bonds B	.75
2	Ryne Sandberg B	.75
3	Brian Jordan B	.15
4	Rocky Coppinger B	.15
5	Dante Bichette B	.25
6	Al Martin B	.15
7	Charles Nagy B	.15
8	Otis Nixon B	.15
9	Mark Johnson B	.15
10	Jeff Bagwell B	1.25
11	Ken Hill B	.15
12	Willie Adams B	.15
13	Raul Mondesi B	.25
14	Reggie Sanders B	.15
15	Derek Jeter B	3.00
16	Jermaine Dye B	.15
17	Edgar Renteria B	.35
18	Travis Fryman B	.15
19	Roberto Hernandez B	.15
20	Sammy Sosa B	3.00
21	Garret Anderson B	.15
22	Rey Ordonez B	.35
23	Glenallen Hill B	.15
24	Dave Nilsson B	.15
25	Kevin Brown B	.25
26	Brian McRae B	.15
27	Joey Hamilton B	.15
28	Jamey Wright B	.15
29	Frank Thomas B	2.00
30	Mark McGwire B	6.00
31	Ramon Martinez B	.15
32	Jaime Bluma B	.15
33	Frank Rodriguez B	.15
34	Andy Benes B	.15
35	Jay Buhner B	.20
36	Justin Thompson B	.15
37	Darin Erstad B	1.25
38	Gregg Jefferies B	.15
39	Jeff D'Amico B	.15
40	Pedro Martinez B	.25
41	Nomar Garciaparra B	1.25
42	Jose Valentin B	.15
43	Pat Hentgen B	.15
44	Will Clark B	.25
45	Bernie Williams B	.50
46	Luis Castillo B	.15
47	B.J. Surhoff B	.15
48	Greg Gagne B	.15
49	Pete Schourek B	.15
50	Mike Piazza B	3.00
51	Dwight Gooden B	.15
52	Javy Lopez B	.20
53	Chuck Finley B	.15
54	James Baldwin B	.15
55	Jack McDowell B	.15
56	Royce Clayton B	.15
57	Carlos Delgado B	.50
58	Neifi Perez B	.15
59	Eddie Taubensee B	.15
60	Rafael Palmeiro B	.25
61	Marty Cordova B	.15
62	Wade Boggs B	.25
63	Rickey Henderson B	.25
64	Mike Hampton B	.15
65	Troy Percival B	.15
66	Barry Larkin B	.20
67	Jermaine Allensworth B	.15
68	Mark Clark B	.15
69	Mike Lansing B	.15
70	Mark Grudzielanek B	.15
71	Todd Stottlemyre B	.15
72	Juan Guzman B	.15
73	John Burkett B	.15
74	Wilson Alvarez B	.15
75	Ellis Burks B	.20
76	Bobby Higginson B	.25
77	Ricky Bottalico B	.15
78	Omar Vizquel B	.15
79	Paul Sorrento B	.15
80	Denny Neagle B	.15
81	Roger Pavlik B	.15
82	Mike Lieberthal B	.15
83	Devon White B	.15
84	John Olerud B	.25
85	Kevin Appier B	.15
86	Joe Girardi B	.15
87	Paul O'Neill B	.20
88	Mike Sweeney B	.15
89	John Smiley B	.15
90	Ivan Rodriguez B	.50
91	Randy Myers B	.15
92	Bip Roberts B	.15
93	Jose Mesa B	.15
94	Paul Wilson B	.20
95	Mike Mussina B	.50
96	Ben McDonald B	.15
97	John Mabry B	.15
98	Tom Goodwin B	.15
99	Edgar Martinez B	.20
100	Andruw Jones B	1.25
101	Jose Canseco S	1.50
102	Billy Wagner S	1.50
103	Dante Bichette S	1.50
104	Curt Schilling S	1.50
105	Dean Palmer S	1.00
106	Larry Walker S	2.50
107	Bernie Williams S	3.00
108	Chipper Jones S	7.50
109	Gary Sheffield S	2.00
110	Randy Johnson S	2.50
111	Roberto Alomar S	3.00
112	Todd Walker S	2.50
113	Sandy Alomar S	1.00
114	John Jaha S	1.00
115	Ken Caminiti S	2.00
116	Ryan Klesko S	2.50
117	Mariano Rivera S	1.50
118	Jason Giambi S	1.00
119	Lance Johnson S	1.00
120	Robin Ventura S	1.50
121	Todd Hollandsworth S	1.00
122	Johnny Damon S	1.00
123	William VanLandingham S	1.00
124	Jason Kendall S	1.25
125	Vinny Castilla S	1.25
126	Harold Baines S	1.00
127	Joe Carter S	1.00
128	Craig Biggio S	1.25
129	Tony Clark S	3.00
130	Ron Gant S	1.00
131	David Segui S	1.00
132	Steve Trachsel S	1.00
133	Scott Rolen S	7.50
134	Mike Stanley S	1.00
135	Cal Ripken Jr. S	10.00
136	John Smoltz S	2.00
137	Bobby Jones S	1.00
138	Manny Ramirez S	4.00
139	Ken Griffey Jr. S	15.00
140	Chuck Knoblauch S	1.50
141	Mark Grace S	1.50
142	Chris Snopek S	1.00
143	Hideo Nomo S	2.00
144	Tim Salmon S	1.50
145	David Cone S	1.50
146	Eric Young S	1.00
147	Jeff Brantley S	1.00
148	Jim Thome S	2.50
149	Trevor Hoffman S	1.25
150	Juan Gonzalez S	6.00
151	Mike Piazza G	20.00
152	Ivan Rodriguez G	7.50
153	Mo Vaughn G	6.00
154	Brady Anderson G	4.00
155	Mark McGwire G	35.00
156	Rafael Palmeiro G	6.00
157	Barry Larkin G	4.00
158	Greg Maddux G	17.50
159	Jeff Bagwell G	15.00
160	Frank Thomas G	10.00
161	Ken Caminiti G	7.50
162	Andruw Jones G	10.00
163	Dennis Eckersley G	4.00
164	Jeff Conine G	4.00
165	Jim Edmonds G	4.00
166	Derek Jeter G	17.50
167	Vladimir Guerrero G	10.00
168	Sammy Sosa G	20.00
169	Tony Gwynn G	15.00
170	Andres Galarraga G	4.00
171	Todd Hundley G	6.00
172	Jay Buhner G	4.00
173	Paul Molitor G	6.00
174	Kenny Lofton G	6.00
175	Barry Bonds G	7.50
176	Gary Sheffield B	.25
177	Dmitri Young B	.15
178	Jay Bell B	.15
179	David Wells B	.15
180	Walt Weiss B	.15
181	Paul Molitor B	.50
182	Jose Guillen B	.75
183	Al Leiter B	.15
184	Mike Fetters B	.15
185	Mark Langston B	.15
186	Fred McGriff B	.20
187	Darrin Fletcher B	.15
188	Brant Brown B	.15
189	Geronimo Berroa B	.15
190	Jim Thome B	.50
191	Jose Vizcaino B	.15
192	Andy Ashby B	.15
193	Rusty Greer B	.15
194	Brian Hunter B	.15
195	Chris Hoiles B	.15
196	Orlando Merced B	.15
197	Brett Butler B	.15
198	Derek Bell B	.15
199	Bobby Bonilla B	.15
200	Alex Ochoa B	.15
201	Wally Joyner B	.15
202	Mo Vaughn B	.60
203	Doug Drabek B	.15
204	Tino Martinez B	.25
205	Roberto Alomar B	.50
206	*Brian Giles B*	1.50
207	Todd Worrell B	.15
208	Alan Benes B	.15
209	Jim Leyritz B	.15
210	Darryl Hamilton B	.15
211	Jimmy Key B	.15
212	Juan Gonzalez B	1.25
213	Vinny Castilla B	.15
214	Chuck Knoblauch B	.20
215	Tony Phillips B	.15
216	Jeff Cirillo B	.15
217	Carlos Garcia B	.15
218	Brooks Kieschnick B	.15
219	Marquis Grissom B	.15
220	Dan Wilson B	.15
221	Greg Vaughn B	.20
222	John Wetteland B	.15
223	Andres Galarraga B	.20
224	Ozzie Guillen B	.15
225	Kevin Elster B	.15
226	Bernard Gilkey B	.15
227	Mike MacFarlane B	.15
228	Heathcliff Slocumb B	.15
229	Wendell Magee Jr. B	.15
230	Carlos Baerga B	.15
231	Kevin Seitzer B	.15
232	Henry Rodriguez B	.15
233	Roger Clemens B	.75
234	Mark Wohlers B	.15
235	Eddie Murray B	.40
236	Todd Zeile B	.15
237	J.T. Snow B	.15
238	Ken Griffey Jr. B	2.50
239	Sterling Hitchcock B	.15
240	Albert Belle B	.60
241	Terry Steinbach B	.15
242	Robb Nen B	.15
243	Mark McLemore B	.15
244	Jeff King B	.15
245	Tony Clark B	.60
246	Tim Salmon B	.20
247	Benito Santiago B	.15
248	Robin Ventura B	.25
249	*Bubba Trammell B*	.75
250	Chili Davis B	.15
251	John Valentin B	.15
252	Cal Ripken Jr. B	4.00
253	Matt Williams B	.25
254	Jeff Kent B	.15
255	Eric Karros B	.15
256	Ray Lankford B	.15
257	Ed Sprague B	.15
258	Shane Reynolds B	.15
259	Jaime Navarro B	.15
260	Eric Davis B	.15
261	Orel Hershiser B	.15
262	Mark Grace B	.25
263	Rod Beck B	.15
264	Ismael Valdes B	.15
265	Manny Ramirez B	.75
266	Ken Caminiti B	.20
267	Tim Naehring B	.15
268	Jose Rosado B	.15
269	Greg Colbrunn B	.15
270	Dean Palmer B	.15
271	David Justice B	.25
272	Scott Spiezio B	.15
273	Chipper Jones B	3.00
274	Mel Rojas B	.15
275	Bartolo Colon B	.15
276	Darin Erstad S	6.00
277	Sammy Sosa S	9.00
278	Rafael Palmeiro S	1.50
279	Frank Thomas S	5.00
280	Ruben Rivera S	1.00
281	Hal Morris S	1.00
282	Jay Buhner S	1.25
283	Kenny Lofton S	4.00
284	Jose Canseco S	1.50
285	Alex Fernandez S	1.00
286	Todd Helton S	4.00
287	Andy Pettitte S	3.00
288	John Franco S	1.00
289	Ivan Rodriguez S	5.00
290	Ellis Burks S	1.00
291	Julio Franco S	1.00
292	Mike Piazza S	9.00
293	Brian Jordan S	1.00
294	Greg Maddux S	7.50
295	Bob Abreu S	1.25
296	Rondell White S	1.25
297	Moises Alou S	1.25
298	Tony Gwynn S	6.00
299	Deion Sanders S	1.25
300	Jeff Montgomery S	1.00
301	Ray Durham S	1.00
302	John Wasdin S	1.00
303	Ryne Sandberg S	5.00
304	Delino DeShields S	1.00
305	Mark McGwire S	15.00
306	Andruw Jones S	6.00
307	Kevin Orie S	1.00
308	Matt Williams S	1.25
309	Karim Garcia S	1.50
310	Derek Jeter S	7.50
311	Mo Vaughn S	4.00
312	Brady Anderson S	1.00
313	Barry Bonds S	4.00
314	Steve Finley S	1.00
315	Vladimir Guerrero S	4.00
316	Matt Morris S	1.00
317	Tom Glavine S	1.50
318	Jeff Bagwell S	6.00
319	Albert Belle S	4.00
320	*Hideki Irabu S*	4.00
321	Andres Galarraga S	1.50
322	Cecil Fielder S	1.00
323	Barry Larkin S	1.00
324	Todd Hundley S	1.50
325	Fred McGriff S	1.50
326	Gary Sheffield G	6.00
327	Craig Biggio G	7.50
328	Raul Mondesi G	6.00
329	Edgar Martinez G	4.00
330	Chipper Jones G	20.00
331	Bernie Williams G	6.00
332	Juan Gonzalez G	15.00
333	Ron Gant G	4.00
334	Cal Ripken Jr. G	25.00
335	Larry Walker G	6.00
336	Matt Williams G	7.50
337	Jose Cruz Jr. G	4.00
338	Joe Carter G	4.00
339	Wilton Guerrero G	4.00
340	Cecil Fielder G	4.00
341	Todd Walker G	5.00
342	Ken Griffey Jr. G	35.00
343	Ryan Klesko G	5.00
344	Roger Clemens G	10.00
345	Hideo Nomo G	5.00
346	Dante Bichette G	4.00
347	Albert Belle G	7.50
348	Randy Johnson G	7.50
349	Manny Ramirez G	9.00
350	John Smoltz G	5.00

1997 Finest Embossed

Each Uncommon (silver) and Rare (gold) card in both Series 1 and 2 Finest was also issued in a parallel Embossed version. The Embossed Silver were a 1:16 find, while the die-cut Embossed Gold were found on average of just one per 96 packs.

	MT
Common Embossed Silver:	1.00
Embossed Silver Stars: 3X	
Common Embossed Gold:	5.00
Embossed/Die-Cut Gold Stars: 2X	

(See 1997 Finest for checklist and base card values.)

1997 Finest Refractors

Every card in '97 Finest - both regular and embossed parallel - has a Refractor version. The Uncommon parallel set of Refractors features a mosaic pattern in the background while the Rare embossed die-cut parallel set of Refractors are produced with a hyper-plaid foil design. The number of cards and the insertion ratios for each level of Refractors is as follows: Common (200 cards, 1:12 packs), Uncommon (100, 1:48), Rare (50, 1:288), Embossed Uncommon (100, 1:192), Embossed Die-cut Rare (50, 1:1152).

	MT
Common Bronze:	2.00
Bronze Stars: 6X	
Typical Silver:	3.00
Silver Stars: 3X	
Typical Gold:	8.00
Gold Stars: 2X	
Typical Embossed Silver:	7.50
Embossed Silver Stars: 8X	
Typical Embossed Gold:	20.00
Embossed Gold Stars: 2X	

(See 1997 Finest for cheklist and base card values.)

1998 Finest Pre-Production

Five-card cello packs of '98 Finest were distributed in the hobby market to preview the always-popular issue. The cards are virtually identical to the issued versions except for the card number, which bears a "PP" prefix.

		MT
Complete Set (5):		10.00
Common Player:		1.50
1	Nomar Garciaparra	3.00
2	Mark McGwire	4.00
3	Ivan Rodriguez	3.00
4	Ken Griffey Jr.	4.50
5	Roger Clemens	3.00

1998 Finest

Finest dropped its three-tiered format in 1998 and produced a 275-card set on a thicker 26-point stock, with 150 cards in Series 1 and 125 in Series 2. The catch in 1998 was that each card arrived in Protector, No-Protector, Protector Refractor and No-Protector Refractor versions. Six-card packs sold for a suggested retail price of $5. Finest also included insert sets for the first time since 1995. Included in Series 1 packs were Centurions, Mystery Finest and Power Zone inserts. Series 2 had Mystery Finest, Stadium Stars and The Man. Throughout both series, Finest Protector cards are considered base cards, while No-Protector are inserted one per two packs (HTA odds 1:1), No-Protector Refractors are seeded 1:24 packs (HTA odds 1:10) and Finest Refractors are seeded 1:12 packs (HTA odds 1:5).

		MT
Complete Set (275):		75.00
Complete Series 1 Set (150):		40.00
Complete Series 2 Set (125):		35.00
Common Player:		.15
Ser I Wax Box:		50.00
Ser II Wax Box:		70.00
1	Larry Walker	.50
2	Andruw Jones	.90
3	Ramon Martinez	.15
4	Geronimo Berroa	.15
5	David Justice	.30
6	Rusty Greer	.15
7	Chad Ogea	.15
8	Tom Goodwin	.15
9	Tino Martinez	.35
10	Jose Guillen	.25
11	Jeffrey Hammonds	.15
12	Brian McRae	.15
13	Jeremi Gonzalez	.15
14	Craig Counsell	.15
15	Mike Piazza	2.00
16	Greg Maddux	1.75
17	Todd Greene	.15
18	Rondell White	.25
19	Kirk Rueter	.15
20	Tony Clark	.50
21	Brad Radke	.15
22	Jaret Wright	1.00
23	Carlos Delgado	.50
24	Dustin Hermanson	.25
25	Gary Sheffield	.40
26	Jose Canseco	.25
27	Kevin Young	.15
28	David Wells	.15
29	Mariano Rivera	.25
30	Reggie Sanders	.15
31	Mike Cameron	.25
32	Bobby Witt	.15
33	Kevin Orie	.15
34	Royce Clayton	.15
35	Edgar Martinez	.20
36	Neifi Perez	.15
37	Kevin Appier	.15
38	Darryl Hamilton	.15
39	Michael Tucker	.15

40	Roger Clemens	1.25
41	Carl Everett	.15
42	Mike Sweeney	.15
43	Pat Meares	.15
44	Brian Giles	.15
45	Matt Morris	.15
46	Jason Dickson	.15
47	Rich Loiselle	.15
48	Joe Girardi	.15
49	Steve Trachsel	.15
50	Ben Grieve	1.00
51	Jose Vizcaino	.15
52	Hideki Irabu	.50
53	J.T. Snow	.15
54	Mike Hampton	.15
55	Dave Nilsson	.15
56	Alex Fernandez	.15
57	Brett Tomko	.15
58	Wally Joyner	.15
59	Kelvim Escobar	.15
60	Roberto Alomar	.60
61	Todd Jones	.15
62	Paul O'Neill	.25
63	Jamie Moyer	.15
64	Mark Wohlers	.15
65	Jose Cruz Jr.	.25
66	Troy Percival	.15
67	Rick Reed	.15
68	Will Clark	.25
69	Jamey Wright	.15
70	Mike Mussina	.60
71	David Cone	.25
72	Ryan Klesko	.30
73	Scott Hatteberg	.15
74	James Baldwin	.15
75	Tony Womack	.15
76	Carlos Perez	.15
77	Charles Nagy	.15
78	Jeromy Burnitz	.15
79	Shane Reynolds	.15
80	Cliff Floyd	.15
81	Jason Kendall	.15
82	Chad Curtis	.15
83	Matt Karchner	.15
84	Ricky Bottalico	.15
85	Sammy Sosa	2.00
86	Javy Lopez	.20
87	Jeff Kent	.15
88	Shawn Green	.25
89	Devon White	.15
90	Tony Gwynn	1.50
91	Bob Tewksbury	.15
92	Derek Jeter	2.50
93	Eric Davis	.15
94	Jeff Fassero	.15
95	Denny Neagle	.15
96	Ismael Valdes	.15
97	Tim Salmon	.50
98	Mark Grudzielanek	.15
99	Curt Schilling	.40
100	Ken Griffey Jr.	4.00
101	Edgardo Alfonzo	.25
102	Vinny Castilla	.15
103	Jose Rosado	.15
104	Scott Erickson	.15
105	Alan Benes	.15
106	Shannon Stewart	.15
107	Delino DeShields	.15
108	Mark Loretta	.15
109	Todd Hundley	.25
110	Chuck Knoblauch	.40
111	Quinton McCracken	.15
112	F.P. Santangelo	.15
113	Gerald Williams	.15
114	Omar Vizquel	.15
115	John Valentin	.15
116	Damion Easley	.15
117	Matt Lawton	.15
118	Jim Thome	.50
119	Sandy Alomar	.25
120	Albert Belle	.75
121	Chris Stynes	.15
122	Butch Huskey	.15
123	Shawn Estes	.15
124	Terry Adams	.15
125	Ivan Rodriguez	.80
126	Ron Gant	.20
127	John Mabry	.15
128	Jeff Shaw	.15
129	Jeff Montgomery	.15
130	Justin Thompson	.20
131	Livan Hernandez	.20
132	Ugueth Urbina	.15
133	Doug Glanville	.15
134	Troy O'Leary	.15
135	Cal Ripken Jr.	2.50
136	Quilvio Veras	.15
137	Pedro Astacio	.15
138	Willie Greene	.15
139	Lance Johnson	.15
140	Nomar Garciaparra	2.00
141	Jose Offerman	.15
142	Scott Rolen	1.25
143	Derek Bell	.15
144	Johnny Damon	.15
145	Mark McGwire	4.00
146	Chan Ho Park	.25
147	Edgar Renteria	.15
148	Eric Young	.15
149	Craig Biggio	.25
150	Checklist 1-150	.15
151	Frank Thomas	1.25
152	John Wetteland	.15
153	Mike Lansing	.15
154	Pedro Martinez	.50
155	Rico Brogna	.15
156	Kevin Brown	.20
157	Alex Rodriguez	2.50
158	Wade Boggs	.25
159	Richard Hidalgo	.15
160	Mark Grace	.25
161	Jose Mesa	.15
162	John Olerud	.25
163	Tim Belcher	.15
164	Chuck Finley	.15
165	Brian Hunter	.15
166	Joe Carter	.20
167	Stan Javier	.15
168	Jay Bell	.15
169	Ray Lankford	.15
170	John Smoltz	.20
171	Ed Sprague	.15
172	Jason Giambi	.15
173	Todd Walker	.25
174	Paul Konerko	.40
175	Rey Ordonez	.15
176	Dante Bichette	.20
177	Bernie Williams	.50
178	Jon Nunnally	.15
179	Rafael Palmeiro	.40
180	Jay Buhner	.20
181	Devon White	.15
182	Jeff D'Amico	.15
183	Walt Weiss	.15
184	Scott Spiezio	.15
185	Moises Alou	.25
186	Carlos Baerga	.15
187	Todd Zeile	.15
188	Gregg Jefferies	.15
189	Mo Vaughn	.65
190	Terry Steinbach	.15
191	Ray Durham	.15
192	Robin Ventura	.20
193	Jeff Reed	.15
194	Ken Caminiti	.25
195	Eric Karros	.20
196	Wilson Alvarez	.15
197	Gary Gaetti	.15
198	Andres Galarraga	.25
199	Alex Gonzalez	.15
200	Garret Anderson	.15
201	Andy Benes	.15
202	Harold Baines	.15
203	Ron Coomer	.15
204	Dean Palmer	.15
205	Reggie Jefferson	.15
206	John Burkett	.15
207	Jermaine Allensworth	.15
208	Bernard Gilkey	.15
209	Jeff Bagwell	1.00
210	Kenny Lofton	.60
211	Bobby Jones	.15
212	Bartolo Colon	.25
213	Jim Edmonds	.20
214	Pat Hentgen	.15
215	Matt Williams	.40
216	Bob Abreu	.15
217	Jorge Posada	.15
218	Marty Cordova	.15
219	Ken Hill	.15
220	Steve Finley	.15
221	Jeff King	.15
222	Quinton McCracken	.15
223	Matt Stairs	.15
224	Darin Erstad	.75
225	Fred McGriff	.25
226	Marquis Grissom	.15
227	Doug Glanville	.15
228	Tom Glavine	.20
229	John Franco	.15
230	Darren Bragg	.15
231	Barry Larkin	.25
232	Trevor Hoffman	.15
233	Brady Anderson	.15
234	Al Martin	.15
235	B.J. Surhoff	.15
236	Ellis Burks	.15
237	Randy Johnson	.50
238	Mark Clark	.15
239	Tony Saunders	.15
240	Hideo Nomo	.25
241	Brad Fullmer	.25
242	Chipper Jones	2.00
243	Jose Valentin	.15
244	Manny Ramirez	1.00
245	Derrek Lee	.15
246	Jimmy Key	.15
247	Tim Naehring	.15
248	Bobby Higginson	.15
249	Charles Johnson	.15
250	Chili Davis	.15
251	Tom Gordon	.15
252	Mike Lieberthal	.15
253	Billy Wagner	.15
254	Juan Guzman	.15
255	Todd Stottlemyre	.15
256	Brian Jordan	.15
257	Barry Bonds	.75
258	Dan Wilson	.15
259	Paul Molitor	.50
260	Juan Gonzalez	1.50
261	Francisco Cordova	.15
262	Cecil Fielder	.15
263	Travis Lee	.60
264	Kevin Tapani	.15
265	Raul Mondesi	.25
266	Travis Fryman	.15
267	Armando Benitez	.15
268	Pokey Reese	.15
269	Rick Aguilera	.15
270	Andy Pettitte	.50
271	Jose Vizcaino	.15
272	Kerry Wood	.65
273	Vladimir Guerrero	.90
274	John Smiley	.15
275	Checklist 151-275	.15

1998 Finest Refractors

All 275 cards from Finest Series 1 and 2 are available in both Protector and No-Protector Refractor versions. Protector versions are seeded one per 12 packs, while No-Protector versions are every 24 packs.

	MT
Complete Set, Protector (275):	750.00
Complete Set, No-Protector (275):	1600.
Common Protector:	2.00
Common No-Protector:	4.00
Stars Protector: 8X	
Stars No-Protector: 15X	

(See 1998 Finest for checklist and base card values.)

1998 Finest No-Protector

This parallel to the 275-card base set foregoes the peel-off front protector and adds Finest technology to the back of the card. Stated insertion rates were one per two packs or one per pack in Home Team Advantage (HTA) boxes.

	MT
Complete Set (275):	250.00
Common Player:	.50
Stars: 2.5X	
Refractors: 15X	

(See 1998 Finest for checklist and base card values.)

1998 Finest Centurions

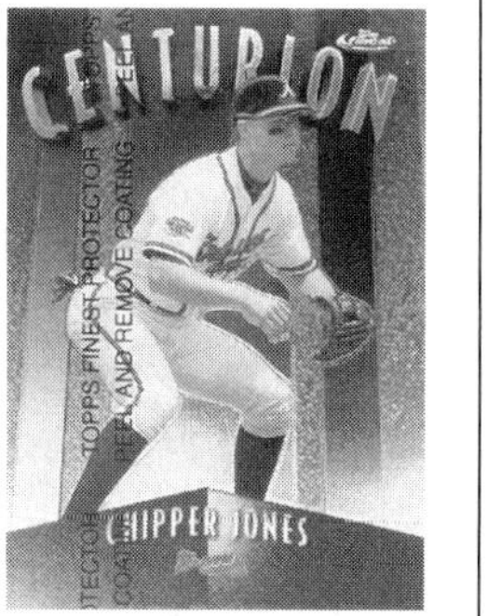

Centurions is a 20-card insert found only Series 1 hobby (1:153) and Home Team Advantage packs (1:71). The theme of the insert to top players who will lead the game into the next century. Each card is sequentially numbered on the back to 500, while Refractor versions are numbered to 75.

		MT
Complete Set (20):		150.00
Common Player:		2.50
Production 500 sets		
Refractors: 3X		
Production 75 sets		
C1	Andruw Jones	6.00
C2	Vladimir Guerrero	12.00
C3	Nomar Garciaparra	20.00
C4	Scott Rolen	8.00
C5	Ken Griffey Jr.	35.00
C6	Jose Cruz Jr.	2.50
C7	Barry Bonds	8.00
C8	Mark McGwire	35.00
C9	Juan Gonzalez	10.00
C10	Jeff Bagwell	8.00
C11	Frank Thomas	10.00
C12	Paul Konerko	2.50
C13	Alex Rodriguez	20.00
C14	Mike Piazza	20.00
C15	Travis Lee	4.00
C16	Chipper Jones	15.00
C17	Larry Walker	5.00
C18	Mo Vaughn	6.00
C19	Livan Hernandez	2.50
C20	Jaret Wright	4.00

1998 Finest Mystery Finest

This 50-card insert was seeded one per 36 Series 1 packs and one per 15 HTA packs. The set includes 20 top players, each matched on a double-sided card with three other players and once with himself. Each side of the card is printed on a chromium finish and arrives with a black opaque protector. Mystery Finest inserts are numbered with an "M" prefix. Refractor versions were seeded one per 64 packs (HTA odds 1:15).

		MT
Complete Set (50):		500.00
Common Player:		5.00
Refractors: 2X		
M1	Frank Thomas, Ken Griffey Jr.	25.00
M2	Frank Thomas, Mike Piazza	17.50
M3	Frank Thomas, Mark McGwire	25.00
M4	Frank Thomas, Frank Thomas	20.00
M5	Ken Griffey Jr., Mike Piazza	25.00
M6	Ken Griffey Jr., Mark McGwire	30.00
M7	Ken Griffey Jr., Ken Griffey Jr.	35.00
M8	Mike Piazza, Mark McGwire	25.00
M9	Mike Piazza, Mike Piazza	20.00
M10	Mark McGwire, Mark McGwire	35.00
M11	Nomar Garciaparra, Jose Cruz Jr.	9.00
M12	Nomar Garciaparra, Derek Jeter	17.50
M13	Nomar Garciaparra, Andruw Jones	12.50
M14	Nomar Garciaparra, Nomar Garciaparra	20.00
M15	Jose Cruz Jr., Derek Jeter	12.50
M16	Jose Cruz Jr., Andruw Jones	5.00
M17	Jose Cruz Jr., Jose Cruz Jr.	7.50
M18	Derek Jeter, Andruw Jones	12.50
M19	Derek Jeter, Derek Jeter	20.00
M20	Andruw Jones, Andruw Jones	10.00
M21	Cal Ripken Jr., Tony Gwynn	17.50
M22	Cal Ripken Jr., Barry Bonds	15.00
M23	Cal Ripken Jr., Greg Maddux	17.50
M24	Cal Ripken Jr., Cal Ripken Jr.	25.00
M25	Tony Gwynn, Barry Bonds	12.50
M26	Tony Gwynn, Greg Maddux	12.50
M27	Tony Gwynn, Tony Gwynn	15.00
M28	Barry Bonds, Greg Maddux	10.00
M29	Barry Bonds, Barry Bonds	12.50
M30	Greg Maddux, Greg Maddux	15.00
M31	Juan Gonzalez, Larry Walker	10.00
M32	Juan Gonzalez, Andres Galarraga	10.00
M33	Juan Gonzalez, Chipper Jones	12.50
M34	Juan Gonzalez, Juan Gonzalez	15.00
M35	Larry Walker, Andres Galarraga	7.50
M36	Larry Walker, Chipper Jones	10.00
M37	Larry Walker, Larry Walker	7.50
M38	Andres Galarraga, Chipper Jones	10.00
M39	Andres Galarraga, Andres Galarraga	5.00
M40	Chipper Jones, Chipper Jones	20.00
M41	Gary Sheffield, Sammy Sosa	12.50
M42	Gary Sheffield, Jeff Bagwell	10.00
M43	Gary Sheffield, Tino Martinez	5.00
M44	Gary Sheffield, Gary Sheffield	7.50
M45	Sammy Sosa, Jeff Bagwell	10.00
M46	Sammy Sosa, Tino Martinez	7.50
M47	Sammy Sosa, Sammy Sosa	12.50
M48	Jeff Bagwell, Tino Martinez	5.00
M49	Jeff Bagwell, Jeff Bagwell	12.50
M50	Tino Martinez, Tino Martinez	5.00

1998 Finest Mystery Finest 2

Forty more Mystery Finest inserts were seeded in Series 2 packs at a rate of one per 36 packs (HTA odds 1:15), with Refrators every 1:144 packs (HTA odds 1:64). As with Series 1, 20 players are in the checklist; some players are found with another player on the back or by himself on each side. Each side was issued with the opaque protector.

		MT
Complete Set (40):		650.00
Common Player:		6.00
Refractors: 2X		
M1	Nomar Garciaparra, Frank Thomas	30.00
M2	Nomar Garciaparra, Albert Belle	25.00
M3	Nomar Garciaparra, Scott Rolen	25.00
M4	Frank Thomas, Albert Belle	20.00
M5	Frank Thomas, Scott Rolen	15.00
M6	Albert Belle, Scott Rolen	9.00
M7	Ken Griffey Jr., Jose Cruz	35.00
M8	Ken Griffey Jr., Alex Rodriguez	45.00
M9	Ken Griffey Jr., Roger Clemens	40.00
M10	Jose Cruz, Alex Rodriguez	25.00
M11	Jose Cruz, Roger Clemens	15.00
M12	Alex Rodriguez, Roger Clemens	30.00
M13	Mike Piazza, Barry Bonds	25.00
M14	Mike Piazza, Derek Jeter	30.00
M15	Mike Piazza, Bernie Williams	25.00
M16	Barry Bonds, Derek Jeter	24.00
M17	Barry Bonds, Bernie Williams	10.00
M18	Derek Jeter, Bernie Williams	20.00
M19	Mark McGwire, Jeff Bagwell	40.00
M20	Mark McGwire, Mo Vaughn	35.00
M21	Mark McGwire, Jim Thome	35.00
M22	Jeff Bagwell, Mo Vaughn	12.50
M23	Jeff Bagwell, Jim Thome	12.50
M24	Mo Vaughn, Jim Thome	4.00
M25	Juan Gonzalez, Travis Lee	15.00
M26	Juan Gonzalez, Ben Grieve	15.00
M27	Juan Gonzalez, Fred McGriff	10.00
M28	Travis Lee, Ben Grieve	10.00
M29	Travis Lee, Fred McGriff	8.00
M30	Ben Grieve, Fred McGriff	8.00

M31	Albert Belle, Albert Belle	8.00
M32	Scott Rolen, Scott Rolen	8.00
M33	Alex Rodriguez, Alex Rodriguez	20.00
M34	Roger Clemens, Roger Clemens	12.00
M35	Bernie Williams, Bernie Williams	6.00
M36	Mo Vaughn, Mo Vaughn	6.00
M37	Jim Thome, Jim Thome	6.00
M38	Travis Lee, Travis Lee	12.00
M39	Fred McGriff, Fred McGriff	6.00
M40	Ben Grieve, Ben Grieve	10.00

1998 Finest Mystery Finest Jumbo

Series 2 Home Team Advantage (HTA) boxes were the exclusive venue for these large-format (3" x 5") versions of Mystery Finest. Regular cards were found one per six boxes of HTA, while Refractor versions were a 1:12 seed.

		MT
Complete Set (3):		25.00
Common Card:		5.00
Refractor: 1.5X		
1	Ken Griffey Jr., Alex Rodriguez	12.00
2	Derek Jeter, Bernie Williams	5.00
3	Mark McGwire, Jeff Bagwell	10.00

1998 Finest Power Zone

This Series 1 insert features Topps' new "Flop Inks" technology which changes the color of the card depending at what angle it is viewed. They are inserted one per 72 hobby packs (HTA odds 1:32). Cards are numbered with a "P" prefix.

		MT
Complete Set (20):		150.00
Common Player:		3.00
1	Ken Griffey Jr.	25.00
2	Jeff Bagwell	10.00
3	Jose Cruz Jr.	3.00
4	Barry Bonds	6.00
5	Mark McGwire	25.00
6	Jim Thome	4.50
7	Mo Vaughn	6.00
8	Gary Sheffield	3.50
9	Andres Galarraga	3.00
10	Nomar Garciaparra	12.50
11	Rafael Palmeiro	3.00
12	Sammy Sosa	12.50
13	Jay Buhner	3.00
14	Tony Clark	4.50
15	Mike Piazza	15.00
16	Larry Walker	3.50
17	Albert Belle	6.00
18	Tino Martinez	3.50
19	Juan Gonzalez	12.00
20	Frank Thomas	12.00

1998 Finest Stadium Stars

Stadium Stars is a 24-card insert that features Topps' new lenticular holographic chromium technology. These are exclusive to Series 2 packs and carried an insertion rate of one per 72 packs (HTA odds 1:32).

		MT
Complete Set (24):		300.00
Common Player:		4.00
SS1	Ken Griffey Jr.	35.00
SS2	Alex Rodriguez	22.00
SS3	Mo Vaughn	7.50
SS4	Nomar Garciaparra	20.00
SS5	Frank Thomas	20.00
SS6	Albert Belle	9.00
SS7	Derek Jeter	17.50
SS8	Chipper Jones	20.00
SS9	Cal Ripken Jr.	25.00
SS10	Jim Thome	5.00
SS11	Mike Piazza	20.00
SS12	Juan Gonzalez	17.50
SS13	Jeff Bagwell	12.50
SS14	Sammy Sosa	20.00
SS15	Jose Cruz Jr.	5.00
SS16	Gary Sheffield	4.00
SS17	Larry Walker	6.00
SS18	Tony Gwynn	17.50
SS19	Mark McGwire	35.00
SS20	Barry Bonds	7.50
SS21	Tino Martinez	4.00
SS22	Manny Ramirez	10.00
SS23	Ken Caminiti	4.00
SS24	Andres Galarraga	4.00

1998 Finest The Man

This 20-card insert features the top players in baseball and was exlusive found in Series 2 packs. Regular versions are sequentially numbered to 500 and inserted one per 119 packs, while Refractor versions are numbered to 75 and inserted one per 793 packs.

		MT
Complete Set (20):		500.00
Common Player:		7.50
Refractors: 2X		
TM1	Ken Griffey Jr.	65.00
TM2	Barry Bonds	15.00
TM3	Frank Thomas	30.00
TM4	Chipper Jones	40.00
TM5	Cal Ripken Jr.	45.00
TM6	Nomar Garciaparra	35.00
TM7	Mark McGwire	65.00
TM8	Mike Piazza	40.00
TM9	Derek Jeter	30.00
TM10	Alex Rodriguez	45.00
TM11	Jose Cruz Jr.	7.50
TM12	Larry Walker	7.50
TM13	Jeff Bagwell	20.00
TM14	Tony Gwynn	30.00
TM15	Travis Lee	7.50
TM16	Juan Gonzalez	30.00
TM17	Scott Rolen	20.00
TM18	Randy Johnson	10.00
TM19	Roger Clemens	20.00
TM20	Greg Maddux	35.00

1998 Finest Jumbo

Eight oversized cards were inserted into both Series 1 and Series 2 boxes as box toppers. The cards measure 3" x 5" and are inserted one per three boxes, with Refractor versions every six boxes. The oversized cards are similar to the regular-issued cards except for the numbering which designates each "X of 8".

		MT
Complete Set (16):		90.00
Complete Series 1 (8):		60.00
Complete Series 2 (8):		35.00
Common Player:		2.50
Refractors: 1.5X		
	FIRST SERIES	
1	Mark McGwire	15.00
2	Cal Ripken Jr.	12.50
3	Nomar Garciaparra	10.00
4	Mike Piazza	10.00
5	Greg Maddux	8.00
6	Jose Cruz Jr.	2.50
7	Roger Clemens	6.00
8	Ken Griffey Jr.	15.00
	SECOND SERIES	
1	Frank Thomas	10.00
2	Bernie Williams	3.00
3	Randy Johnson	3.00
4	Chipper Jones	10.00
5	Manny Ramirez	4.00
6	Barry Bonds	4.00
7	Juan Gonzalez	7.50
8	Jeff Bagwell	5.00

1999 Finest

Released in two series, with each consisting of 100 regular and 50 subset cards divided into three categories: Gems, Sensations and Rookies in Series 1, and Sterling, Gamers and Rookies in the second series. The subset cards are short-printed, seeded one per pack. Cards are printed on 27 pt. stock utilizing chromium technology. There are two parallels: Refractors and die-cut Gold Refractors. Refractors are seeded 1:12 packs, while Gold Refractors are numbered to 100 sets. Six-cards packs carried an SRP of $4.99.

		MT
Complete Set (300):		250.00
Complete Series 1 (150):		125.00
Complete Series 2 (150):		125.00
Common Player:		.15
Common SP (101-150, 251-300):		.50
Wax Box, Series 1:		95.00
Wax Box, Series 2:		85.00
1	Darin Erstad	1.25
2	Javy Lopez	.40
3	Vinny Castilla	.15
4	Jim Thome	.75
5	Tino Martinez	.75
6	Mark Grace	.40
7	Shawn Green	.15
8	Dustin Hermanson	.15
9	Kevin Young	.15
10	Tony Clark	.75
11	Scott Brosius	.15
12	Craig Biggio	.75
13	Brian McRae	.15
14	Chan Ho Park	.50
15	Manny Ramirez	1.50
16	Chipper Jones	2.50
17	Rico Brogna	.15
18	Quinton McCracken	.15
19	J.T. Snow Jr.	.15
20	Tony Gwynn	2.50
21	Juan Guzman	.15
22	John Valentin	.15
23	Rick Helling	.15
24	Sandy Alomar	.15
25	Frank Thomas	2.00
26	Jorge Posada	.15
27	Dmitri Young	.15
28	Rick Reed	.15
29	Kevin Tapani	.15
30	Troy Glaus	1.50
31	Kenny Rogers	.15
32	Jeromy Burnitz	.15
33	Mark Grudzielanek	.15
34	Mike Mussina	1.00
35	Scott Rolen	1.25
36	Neifi Perez	.15
37	Brad Radke	.15
38	Darryl Strawberry	.50
39	Robb Nen	.15
40	Moises Alou	.50
41	Eric Young	.15
42	Livan Hernandez	.15
43	John Wetteland	.15
44	Matt Lawton	.15
45	Ben Grieve	1.25
46	Fernando Tatis	.15
47	Travis Fryman	.15
48	David Segui	.15
49	Bob Abreu	.15
50	Nomar Garciaparra	3.00
51	Paul O'Neill	.50
52	Jeff King	.15
53	Francisco Cordova	.15
54	John Olerud	.50
55	Vladimir Guerrero	1.50
56	Fernando Vina	.15
57	Shane Reynolds	.15
58	Chuck Finley	.15
59	Rondell White	.50
60	Greg Vaughn	.50
61	Ryan Minor	.75
62	Tom Gordon	.15
63	Damion Easley	.15
64	Ray Durham	.15
65	Orlando Hernandez	1.50
66	Bartolo Colon	.15
67	Jaret Wright	.50
68	Royce Clayton	.15
69	Tim Salmon	.75
70	Mark McGwire	6.00
71	Alex Gonzalez	.15
72	Tom Glavine	.50
73	David Justice	.50
74	Omar Vizquel	.15
75	Juan Gonzalez	2.50
76	Bobby Higginson	.15
77	Todd Walker	.15
78	Dante Bichette	.50
79	Kevin Millwood	.50
80	Roger Clemens	2.00
81	Kerry Wood	1.00
82	Cal Ripken Jr.	4.00
83	Jay Bell	.15
84	Barry Bonds	1.25
85	Alex Rodriguez	3.00
86	Doug Glanville	.15
87	Jason Kendall	.15
88	Sean Casey	.15
89	Aaron Sele	.15
90	Derek Jeter	3.00
91	Andy Ashby	.15
92	Rusty Greer	.15
93	Rod Beck	.15
94	Matt Williams	.75
95	Mike Piazza	3.00
96	Wally Joyner	.15
97	Barry Larkin	.75
98	Eric Milton	.15
99	Gary Sheffield	.50
100	Greg Maddux	3.00
101	Ken Griffey Jr. (Gem)	6.00
102	Frank Thomas (Gem)	3.00
103	Nomar Garciaparra (Gem)	4.00
104	Mark McGwire (Gem)	8.00
105	Alex Rodriguez (Gem)	4.00
106	Tony Gwynn (Gem)	3.00
107	Juan Gonzalez (Gem)	3.00
108	Jeff Bagwell (Gem)	1.50
109	Sammy Sosa (Gem)	4.00
110	Vladimir Guerrero (Gem)	2.00
111	Roger Clemens (Gem)	2.50
112	Barry Bonds (Gem)	1.50
113	Darin Erstad (Gem)	1.50
114	Mike Piazza (Gem)	4.00
115	Derek Jeter (Gem)	4.00
116	Chipper Jones (Gem)	3.00
117	Larry Walker (Gem)	1.00
118	Scott Rolen (Gem)	1.50
119	Cal Ripken Jr. (Gem)	5.00
120	Greg Maddux (Gem)	4.00
121	Troy Glaus (Sensations)	2.50
122	Ben Grieve (Sensations)	2.00
123	Ryan Minor (Sensations)	1.00
124	Kerry Wood (Sensations)	1.50
125	Travis Lee (Sensations)	1.00
126	Adrian Beltre (Sensations)	1.00
127	Brad Fullmer (Sensations)	.75
128	Aramis Ramirez (Sensations)	.75
129	Eric Chavez (Sensations)	2.00
130	Todd Helton (Sensations)	1.50
131	*Pat Burrell* (Finest Rookies)	20.00
132	*Ryan Mills* (Finest Rookies)	6.00
133	*Austin Kearns* (Finest Rookies)	6.00
134	*Josh McKinley* (Finest Rookies)	4.00
135	*Adam Everett* (Finest Rookies)	5.00
136	Marlon Anderson	2.00
137	Bruce Chen	1.50
138	Matt Clement	1.00
139	Alex Gonzalez	.75
140	Roy Halladay	2.00
141	Calvin Pickering	.75
142	Randy Wolf	2.50
143	Ryan Anderson	2.00
144	Ruben Mateo	3.00
145	*Alex Escobar*	12.00
146	Jeremy Giambi	2.00
147	Lance Berkman	3.00
148	Michael Barrett	2.00
149	Preston Wilson	.75
150	Gabe Kapler	5.00
151	Roger Clemens	2.00
152	Jay Buhner	.40
153	Brad Fullmer	.15
154	Ray Lankford	.15
155	Jim Edmonds	.15
156	Jason Giambi	.15
157	Bret Boone	.15
158	Jeff Cirillo	.15
159	Rickey Henderson	.40
160	Edgar Martinez	.15
161	Ron Gant	.40
162	Mark Kotsay	.15
163	Trevor Hoffman	.15
164	Jason Schmidt	.15
165	Brett Tomko	.15
166	David Ortiz	.15
167	Dean Palmer	.15
168	Hideki Irabu	.40
169	Mike Cameron	.15
170	Pedro Martinez	1.25
171	Tom Goodwin	.15
172	Brian Hunter	.15
173	Al Leiter	.15
174	Charles Johnson	.15
175	Curt Schilling	.40
176	Robin Ventura	.40
177	Travis Lee	1.00
178	Jeff Shaw	.15
179	Ugueth Urbina	.15
180	Roberto Alomar	1.00
181	Cliff Floyd	.15
182	Adrian Beltre	.75
183	Tony Womack	.15
184	Brian Jordan	.15
185	Randy Johnson	1.00
186	Mickey Morandini	.15
187	Todd Hundley	.15
188	Jose Valentin	.15
189	Eric Davis	.15
190	Ken Caminiti	.40
191	David Wells	.15
192	Ryan Klesko	.40
193	Garret Anderson	.15
194	Eric Karros	.15
195	Ivan Rodriguez	1.25
196	Aramis Ramirez	.15
197	Mike Lieberthal	.15
198	Will Clark	.75
199	Rey Ordonez	.15
200	Ken Griffey Jr.	5.00
201	Jose Guillen	.15
202	Scott Erickson	.15
203	Paul Konerko	.50
204	Johnny Damon	.15
205	Larry Walker	.75
206	Denny Neagle	.15
207	Jose Offerman	.15
208	Andy Pettitte	.50
209	Bobby Jones	.15
210	Kevin Brown	.40
211	John Smoltz	.40
212	Henry Rodriguez	.15
213	Tim Belcher	.15
214	Carlos Delgado	.75
215	Andruw Jones	1.00
216	Andy Benes	.15
217	Fred McGriff	.50
218	Edgar Renteria	.15
219	Miguel Tejada	.40
220	Bernie Williams	.75
221	Justin Thompson	.15
222	Marty Cordova	.15
223	Delino DeShields	.15
224	Ellis Burks	.15
225	Kenny Lofton	1.25
226	Steve Finley	.15
227	Eric Chavez	.75

228	Jose Cruz Jr.	.15
229	Marquis Grissom	.15
230	Jeff Bagwell	1.50
231	Jose Canseco	.75
232	Edgardo Alfonzo	.15
233	Richie Sexson	.50
234	Jeff Kent	.15
235	Rafael Palmeiro	.50
236	David Cone	.50
237	Gregg Jefferies	.15
238	Mike Lansing	.15
239	Mariano Rivera	.40
240	Albert Belle	1.25
241	Chuck Knoblauch	.50
242	Derek Bell	.15
243	Pat Hentgen	.15
244	Andres Galarraga	.75
245	Mo Vaughn	1.25
246	Wade Boggs	.50
247	Devon White	.15
248	Todd Helton	.75
249	Raul Mondesi	.40
250	Sammy Sosa	3.00
251	Nomar Garciaparra (Sterling)	4.00
252	Mark McGwire (Sterling)	8.00
253	Alex Rodriguez (Sterling)	4.00
254	Juan Gonzalez (Sterling)	3.00
255	Vladimir Guerrero (Sterling)	2.00
256	Ken Griffey Jr. (Sterling)	6.00
257	Mike Piazza (Sterling)	4.00
258	Derek Jeter (Sterling)	4.00
259	Albert Belle (Sterling)	1.50
260	Greg Vaughn (Sterling)	.75
261	Sammy Sosa (Sterling)	4.00
262	Greg Maddux (Sterling)	3.00
263	Frank Thomas (Sterling)	2.00
264	Mark Grace (Sterling)	.75
265	Ivan Rodriguez (Sterling)	1.50
266	Roger Clemens (Gamers)	2.00
267	Mo Vaughn (Gamers)	1.50
268	Jim Thome (Gamers)	1.00
269	Darin Erstad (Gamers)	1.00
270	Chipper Jones (Gamers)	3.00
271	Larry Walker (Gamers)	1.00
272	Cal Ripken Jr. (Gamers)	5.00
273	Scott Rolen (Gamers)	1.50
274	Randy Johnson (Gamers)	1.00
275	Tony Gwynn (Gamers)	3.00
276	Barry Bonds (Gamers)	1.50
277	*Sean Burroughs*	10.00
278	*J.M. Gold*	6.00
279	Carlos Lee	.75
280	George Lombard	.75
281	Carlos Beltran	1.00
282	Fernando Seguignol	.75
283	Eric Chavez	1.00
284	*Carlos Pena*	6.00
285	*Corey Patterson*	20.00
286	*Alfonso Soriano*	15.00
287	*Nick Johnson*	10.00
288	*Jorge Toca*	4.00
289	*A.J. Burnett*	5.00
290	*Andy Brown*	3.00
291	*Doug Mientkiewicz*	2.00
292	*Bobby Seay*	2.50
293	*Chip Ambres*	3.00
294	*C.C. Sabathia*	2.00
295	*Choo Freeman*	3.00
296	*Eric Valent*	8.00
297	*Matt Belisle*	2.50
298	*Jason Tyner*	2.50
299	*Masao Kida*	2.00
300	Hank Aaron, Mark McGwire (Homerun Kings)	5.00

1999 Finest Refractors

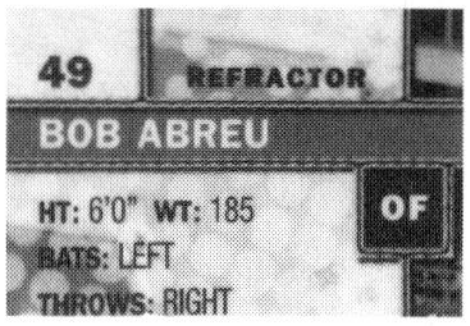

Inserted at the rate of one card per 12 packs, Refractors use special technology to impart a more colorful sheen to the card fronts. To eliminate doubt, the backs have the word "REFRACTOR" printed to the right of the card number at top.

	MT
Complete Set (300):	2250.
Common Player:	2.00
Stars: 6-10X	
SPs: 3-5X	
(See 1999 Finest for checklist and base card values.)	

1999 Finest Gold Refractors

At the top of Finest's chaco-card line-up for 1999 are the Gold Refractors. Fronts have an overall gold tone in the background. Backs are individually serial numbered in gold foil with an edition of 100 each, and have the words "GOLD REFRACTOR" printed at top, to the right of the card number. The Gold Refractors are die-cut along the edges to create a deckled effect. Stated pack insertion rates were between 1:26 and 1:82 depending on series and type.

	MT
Common Player:	7.50
Stars: 30-50X	
SPs: 15-25X	
(See 1999 Finest for checklist and base card values.)	

1999 Finest Hank Aaron Award Contenders

This insert set focuses on nine players who had the best chance to win baseball's newest award. Production varies from card to card, with nine times as many of card #9 as of card #1, and so on. Insertion odds thus vary greatly, from 1:12 to 1:216. Refractor versions are found at odds which vary from 1:96 to 1:1728. Card numbers have an "HA" prefix.

		MT
Complete Set (9):		40.00
Common Player:		3.00
Refractors: 3X		
1	Juan Gonzalez	10.00
2	Vladimir Guerrero	5.00
3	Nomar Garciaparra	7.50
4	Albert Belle	4.00
5	Frank Thomas	[illegible]
6	Sammy Sosa	4.00
7	Alex Rodriguez	4.00
8	Ken Griffey Jr.	5.00
9	Mark McGwire	6.00

1999 Finest Aaron Award Contenders Refractors Parallel

This is a nine-card parallel version of the base inserts. Insertion odds are as follows: card #1 (1:1,944), #2 (1:972), #3 (1:648), #4 (1:486), #5 (1:387), #6 (1:324), #7 (1:279), #8 (1:243), #9 (1:216).

		MT
Complete Set (9):		180.00
Common Player:		8.00
varying odds for each #		
1	Juan Gonzalez	40.00
2	Vladimir Guerrero	20.00
3	Nomar Garciaparra	25.00
4	Albert Belle	12.00
5	Frank Thomas	15.00
6	Sammy Sosa	20.00
7	Alex Rodriguez	20.00
8	Ken Griffey Jr.	30.00
9	Mark McGwire	30.00

1999 Finest Complements

This Series 2 insert set pairs two players on a "split-screen" card front. There are three different versions for each card, Non-Refractor/Refractor (1:56), Refractor/Non-Refractor (1:56) and Refractor/Refractor (1:168). Each card is numbered with a "C" prefix. Values shown are for cards with either the left- or right-side player as Refractor; dual-refractor cards valued at 2X.

		MT
Complete Set (7):		35.00
Common Player:		2.50
Inserted 1:56		
Dual-Refractors: 2X		
Inserted 1:168		
1	Mike Piazza, Ivan Rodriguez	6.00
2	Tony Gwynn, Wade Boggs	5.00
3	Kerry Wood, Roger Clemens	3.00
4	Juan Gonzalez, Sammy Sosa	6.00
5	Derek Jeter, Nomar Garciaparra	6.00
6	Mark McGwire, Frank Thomas	7.50
7	Vladimir Guerrero, Andruw Jones	3.00

1999 Finest Double Feature

Similar to Finest Complements, this Series 2 set utilizes split-screen fronts to accomodate two players on a horizontal format. Each card has three versions: Non-Refractor/Refractor (1:56), Refractor/Non-Refractor (1:56) and Refractor/Refractor (1:168). Card numbers have a "DF" prefix. Values shown are for cards with either left- or right-side Refractor; Dual-Refractor cards are valued at 2X.

		MT
Complete Set (7):		30.00
Common Player:		2.00
Dual-Refractors: 2X		
1	Ken Griffey Jr., Alex Rodriguez	12.50
2	Chipper Jones, Andruw Jones	5.00
3	Darin Erstad, Mo Vaughn	2.50
4	Craig Biggio, Jeff Bagwell	3.00
5	Ben Grieve, Eric Chavez	2.00
6	Albert Belle, Cal Ripken Jr.	7.50
7	Scott Rolen, Pat Burrell	6.00

1999 Finest Franchise Records

This Series 2 insert set focuses on players who led their teams in various statistical categories. They are randomly seeded in 1:129 packs, while a parallel Refractor version is inserted 1:378. Card numbers have a "FR" prefix.

		MT
Complete Set (10):		165.00
Common Player:		7.50
Refractors: 1.5X		
1	Frank Thomas	15.00
2	Ken Griffey Jr.	30.00
3	Mark McGwire	35.00
4	Juan Gonzalez	15.00
5	Nomar Garciaparra	20.00
6	Mike Piazza	20.00
7	Cal Ripken Jr.	25.00
8	Sammy Sosa	20.00
9	Barry Bonds	7.50
10	Tony Gwynn	15.00

1999 Finest Future's Finest

This Series 2 insert focuses on up-and-coming players who are primed to emerge as superstars. These are seeded 1:171 packs and limited to 500 numbered sets. Card numbers have a "FF" prefix.

		MT
Complete Set (10):		75.00
Common Player:		4.00
1	Pat Burrell	25.00
2	Troy Glaus	12.50
3	Eric Chavez	10.00
4	Ryan Anderson	7.50
5	Ruben Mateo	12.50
6	Gabe Kapler	12.50
7	Alex Gonzalez	4.00
8	Michael Barrett	4.00
9	Lance Berkman	4.00
10	Fernando Seguignol	4.00

1999 Finest Leading Indicators

Utilizing a heat-sensitive, thermal ink technology, these cards highlight the 1998 home run totals of 10 players. Touching the left, right or center field portion of the card behind each player's image reveals his 1998 season home run total in that specific direction. These are seeded 1:24 in Series 1 packs.

		MT
Complete Set (10):		45.00
Common Player:		1.00
Inserted 1:24		
L1	Mark McGwire	12.50
L2	Sammy Sosa	9.00
L3	Ken Griffey Jr.	12.50
L4	Greg Vaughn	1.00
L5	Albert Belle	3.00
L6	Juan Gonzalez	5.00
L7	Andres Galarraga	1.00
L8	Alex Rodriguez	10.00
L9	Barry Bonds	3.00
L10	Jeff Bagwell	3.00

1999 Finest Milestones

This Series 2 insert set is fractured into four subsets, each focusing on a statistical category: Hits, Home Runs, RBIs and Doubles. The Hits category is limited to 3,000 numbered sets. Home Runs are limited to 500 numbered sets. RBIs are limited to 1,400 numbered sets and Doubles is limited to 500 numbered sets. Each card number carries an "M" prefix.

		MT
Complete Set (40):		300.00
Common Hits (1-10):		2.00
Common Homeruns (11-20):		5.00
Common RBI (21-30):		2.00
Common Doubles (31-40):		4.00
1	Tony Gwynn (Hits)	5.00
2	Cal Ripken Jr. (Hits)	7.50
3	Wade Boggs (Hits)	2.00
4	Ken Griffey Jr. (Hits)	10.00
5	Frank Thomas (Hits)	4.00
6	Barry Bonds (Hits)	2.50
7	Travis Lee (Hits)	2.00
8	Alex Rodriguez (Hits)	6.50
9	Derek Jeter (Hits)	6.00
10	Vladimir Guerrero (Hits)	2.50
11	Mark McGwire (Home Runs)	35.00
12	Ken Griffey Jr. (Home Runs)	30.00
13	Vladimir Guerrero (Home Runs)	7.50
14	Alex Rodriguez (Home Runs)	20.00
15	Barry Bonds (Home Runs)	7.50
16	Sammy Sosa (Home Runs)	20.00
17	Albert Belle (Home Runs)	5.00
18	Frank Thomas (Home Runs)	10.00
19	Jose Canseco (Home Runs)	5.00
20	Mike Piazza (Home Runs)	20.00
21	Jeff Bagwell (RBI)	5.00
22	Barry Bonds (RBI)	4.00
23	Ken Griffey Jr. (RBI)	15.00
24	Albert Belle (RBI)	4.00
25	Juan Gonzalez (RBI)	7.50
26	Vinny Castilla (RBI)	2.00
27	Mark McGwire (RBI)	15.00
28	Alex Rodriguez (RBI)	10.00
29	Nomar Garciaparra (RBI)	10.00
30	Frank Thomas (RBI)	6.00
31	Barry Bonds (Doubles)	7.50
32	Albert Belle (Doubles)	7.50
33	Ben Grieve (Doubles)	5.00
34	Craig Biggio (Doubles)	5.00
35	Vladimir Guerrero (Doubles)	7.50
36	Nomar Garciaparra (Doubles)	20.00
37	Alex Rodriguez (Doubles)	20.00
38	Derek Jeter (Doubles)	20.00
39	Ken Griffey Jr. (Doubles)	30.00
40	Brad Fullmer (Doubles)	4.00

1999 Finest Peel & Reveal

This Series 1 insert offers 20 players produced in varying levels of scarcity designated by background design: Sparkle is common, Hyperplaid is uncommon and Stadium Stars is rare. Each card has a peel-off opaque protective coating on both front and back. Stated insertion odds are: Sparkle 1:30; Hyperplaid 1:60, and Stadium Stars 1:120. Home Team Advantage (HTA) boxes have odds which are twice as good.

		MT
Complete Set (20):		80.00
Common Player:		2.00
Hyperplaid: 1.5X		
Stadium Stars: 2.5X		
1	Kerry Wood	2.50
2	Mark McGwire	15.00
3	Sammy Sosa	8.00
4	Ken Griffey Jr.	12.00
5	Nomar Garciaparra	7.50
6	Greg Maddux	6.00
7	Derek Jeter	7.50
8	Andres Galarraga	2.00
9	Alex Rodriguez	9.00
10	Frank Thomas	4.50
11	Roger Clemens	3.50
12	Juan Gonzalez	4.50
13	Ben Grieve	2.50
14	Jeff Bagwell	2.50
15	Todd Helton	2.50
16	Chipper Jones	4.50
17	Barry Bonds	2.50
18	Travis Lee	2.50
19	Vladimir Guerrero	3.00
20	Pat Burrell	7.50

1999 Finest Prominent Figures

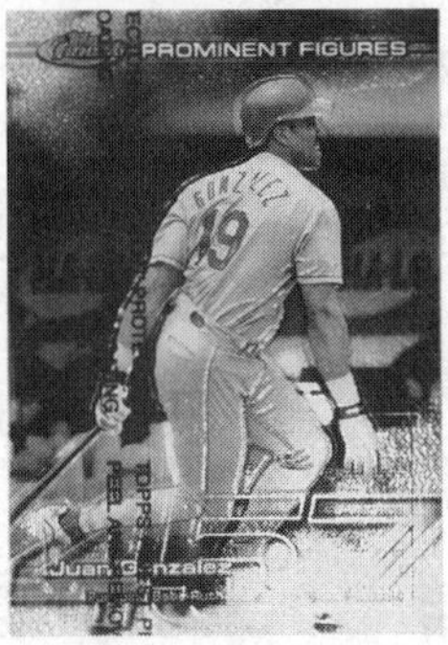

Fifty cards on Refractor technology highlight superstars chasing the all-time records in five different statistical categories: Home Runs, Slugging Percentage, Batting Average, RBIs and Total Bases. Ten players are featured in each category, each sequentially numbered to the all-time single season record statistic for that category. Home Run category is numbered to 70, Slugging Percentage to 847, Batting Average to 424, RBIs to 190 and Total Bases to 457.

		MT
Complete Set (50):		1000.
Common Home Runs (1-10); #d to 70:		12.50
Common Slugging % (11-20); #d to 847:		4.00
Common Batting Ave. (21-30); #d to 424:		6.00
Common RBIs (31-40); #d to 190:		7.50
Common Total Bases (41-50); #d to 457:		7.50
1	Mark McGwire (HR)	150.00
2	Sammy Sosa (HR)	75.00
3	Ken Griffey Jr. (HR)	125.00
4	Mike Piazza (HR)	75.00
5	Juan Gonzalez (HR)	60.00
6	Greg Vaughn (HR)	12.50
7	Alex Rodriguez (HR)	75.00
8	Manny Ramirez (HR)	30.00
9	Jeff Bagwell (HR)	30.00
10	Andres Galarraga (HR)	12.50
11	Mark McGwire (S%)	30.00
12	Sammy Sosa (S%)	20.00
13	Juan Gonzalez (S%)	12.50
14	Ken Griffey Jr. (S%)	25.00
15	Barry Bonds (S%)	7.50
16	Greg Vaughn (S%)	4.00
17	Larry Walker (S%)	5.00
18	Andres Galarraga (S%)	4.00
19	Jeff Bagwell (S%)	7.50
20	Albert Belle (S%)	7.50
21	Tony Gwynn (BA)	20.00
22	Mike Piazza (BA)	25.00
23	Larry Walker (BA)	7.50
24	Alex Rodriguez (BA)	25.00
25	John Olerud (BA)	6.00
26	Frank Thomas (BA)	15.00
27	Bernie Williams (BA)	6.00
28	Chipper Jones (BA)	15.00
29	Jim Thome (BA)	6.00
30	Barry Bonds (BA)	7.50
31	Juan Gonzalez (RBI)	35.00
32	Sammy Sosa (RBI)	45.00
33	Mark McGwire (RBI)	80.00
34	Albert Belle (RBI)	15.00
35	Ken Griffey Jr. (RBI)	75.00
36	Jeff Bagwell (RBI)	17.50
37	Chipper Jones (RBI)	35.00
38	Vinny Castilla (RBI)	7.50
39	Alex Rodriguez (RBI)	45.00
40	Andres Galarraga (RBI)	10.00
41	Sammy Sosa (TB)	25.00
42	Mark McGwire (TB)	45.00
43	Albert Belle (TB)	10.00
44	Ken Griffey Jr. (TB)	40.00
45	Jeff Bagwell (TB)	10.00
46	Juan Gonzalez (TB)	20.00
47	Barry Bonds (TB)	10.00
48	Vladimir Guerrero (TB)	12.50
49	Larry Walker (TB)	7.50
50	Alex Rodriguez (TB)	25.00

1999 Finest Split Screen

Players who share a common bond are highlighted in this Series 1 insert set which includes 14 paired players. Each card is available in three variations: Non-Refractor/Refractor (1:28), Refractor/Non-Refractor (1:28) and Refractor/Refractor (1:84). Values shown are for a card with either left- or right-side Refractor; dual-Refractor cards are worth 2X.

		MT
Complete Set (14):		80.00
Common Card:		3.00
Dual-Refractor: 2X		
1	Mark McGwire, Sammy Sosa	15.00
2	Ken Griffey Jr., Alex Rodriguez	12.50
3	Nomar Garciaparra, Derek Jeter	7.50
4	Barry Bonds, Albert Belle	4.00
5	Cal Ripken Jr., Tony Gwynn	10.00
6	Manny Ramirez, Juan Gonzalez	6.00
7	Frank Thomas, Andres Galarraga	6.00
8	Scott Rolen, Chipper Jones	5.00
9	Ivan Rodriguez, Mike Piazza	7.50
10	Kerry Wood, Roger Clemens	6.00
11	Greg Maddux, Tom Glavine	6.00
12	Troy Glaus, Eric Chavez	4.00
13	Ben Grieve, Todd Helton	3.00
14	Travis Lee, Pat Burrell	10.00

1999 Finest Team Finest

The first 10 cards are showcased in Series 1 while the last 10 cards showcased in Series 2. Team Finest are available in three colors: Blue, Red and Gold (Red and Gold are only available in Home Team Advantage packs). All Team Finest are serially numbered as follows: Blue, numbered to 1,500; Blue Refractors to 150; Red to 500; Red Refractors to 50; Gold to 250 and Gold Refractors to 25. Cards have a TF prefix to the card number.

		MT
Complete Set (20):		135.00
Common Blue:		3.00
Production 1,500 sets		
Blue Refractors: 3X		
Production 150 sets		
Reds: 1.5X		
Production 500 sets		
Red Refractors: 7X		
Production 50 sets		
Golds: 2X		
Production 250 sets		
Gold Refractors: 10X		
Production 25 sets		
1	Greg Maddux	9.00
2	Mark McGwire	20.00
3	Sammy Sosa	10.00
4	Juan Gonzalez	7.50
5	Alex Rodriguez	12.50
6	Travis Lee	3.00
7	Roger Clemens	7.50
8	Darin Erstad	3.00
9	Todd Helton	3.00
10	Mike Piazza	10.00
11	Kerry Wood	4.00
12	Ken Griffey Jr.	15.00
13	Frank Thomas	5.00
14	Jeff Bagwell	4.00
15	Nomar Garciaparra	10.00
16	Derek Jeter	10.00
17	Chipper Jones	7.50
18	Barry Bonds	4.00
19	Tony Gwynn	7.50
20	Ben Grieve	3.00

1993 Flair Promos

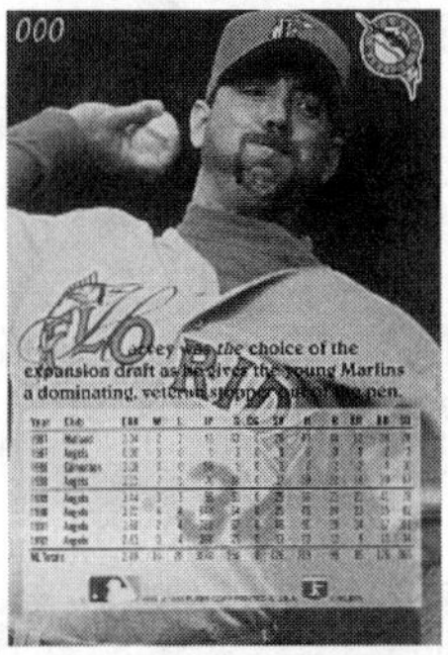

Among the scarcest modern baseball promo cards are those produced to introduce Fleer's new premium product for 1993, Flair. Basically similar to the issued versions, the promo cards have "000" in place of the card number on back. The promos are checklisted here in alphabetical order.

		MT
Complete Set (8):		800.00
Common Player:		50.00
(1)	Will Clark	150.00
(2)	Darren Daulton	50.00
(3)	Andres Galarraga	150.00
(4)	Bryan Harvey	50.00
(5)	David Justice	150.00
(6)	Jody Reed	50.00
(7)	Nolan Ryan	300.00
(8)	Sammy Sosa	250.00

1993 Flair

Designed as Fleer's super-premium card brand, this 300-card set contains extra-thick cards which feature gold-foil highlights and UV coating front and back. Portrait and action photos are combined in a high-tech front picture and there is a muted photo on the back, as well.

		MT
Complete Set (300):		30.00
Common Player:		.25
Wax Box:		50.00
1	Steve Avery	.25
2	Jeff Blauser	.25
3	Ron Gant	.30
4	Tom Glavine	.50
5	Dave Justice	.40
6	Mark Lemke	.25
7	Greg Maddux	4.50
8	Fred McGriff	.75
9	Terry Pendleton	.25
10	Deion Sanders	.45
11	John Smoltz	.50
12	Mike Stanton	.25
13	Steve Buechele	.25
14	Mark Grace	.50
15	Greg Hibbard	.25
16	Derrick May	.25
17	Chuck McElroy	.25
18	Mike Morgan	.25
19	Randy Myers	.25
20	Ryne Sandberg	2.00
21	Dwight Smith	.25
22	Sammy Sosa	6.00
23	Jose Vizcaino	.25
24	Tim Belcher	.25
25	Rob Dibble	.25
26	Roberto Kelly	.25
27	Barry Larkin	.40
28	Kevin Mitchell	.25
29	Hal Morris	.25
30	Joe Oliver	.25
31	Jose Rijo	.25
32	Bip Roberts	.25
33	Chris Sabo	.25
34	Reggie Sanders	.30
35	Dante Bichette	.50
36	Willie Blair	.25
37	Jerald Clark	.25
38	Alex Cole	.25
39	Andres Galarraga	.40
40	Joe Girardi	.25
41	Charlie Hayes	.25
42	Chris Jones	.25
43	David Nied	.25
44	Eric Young	.25
45	Alex Arias	.25
46	Jack Armstrong	.25
47	Bret Barberie	.25
48	Chuck Carr	.25
49	Jeff Conine	.30
50	Orestes Destrade	.25
51	Chris Hammond	.25
52	Bryan Harvey	.25
53	Benito Santiago	.25
54	Gary Sheffield	.75
55	Walt Weiss	.25
56	Eric Anthony	.25
57	Jeff Bagwell	2.50
58	Craig Biggio	.45
59	Ken Caminiti	.50
60	Andujar Cedeno	.25
61	Doug Drabek	.25
62	Steve Finley	.25
63	Luis Gonzalez	.30
64	Pete Harnisch	.25
65	Doug Jones	.25
66	Darryl Kile	.25
67	Greg Swindell	.25
68	Brett Butler	.25
69	Jim Gott	.25
70	Orel Hershiser	.30
71	Eric Karros	.40
72	Pedro Martinez	.60
73	Ramon Martinez	.35
74	Roger McDowell	.25
75	Mike Piazza	5.00
76	Jody Reed	.25
77	Tim Wallach	.25
78	Moises Alou	.40
79	Greg Colbrunn	.25
80	Wil Cordero	.25
81	Delino DeShields	.25
82	Jeff Fassero	.25
83	Marquis Grissom	.35
84	Ken Hill	.25
85	*Mike Lansing*	.60
86	Dennis Martinez	.25
87	Larry Walker	.75
88	John Wetteland	.25
89	Bobby Bonilla	.35
90	Vince Coleman	.25
91	Dwight Gooden	.35
92	Todd Hundley	.50
93	Howard Johnson	.25
94	Eddie Murray	.60
95	Joe Orsulak	.25
96	Bret Saberhagen	.25
97	Darren Daulton	.25
98	Mariano Duncan	.25
99	Len Dykstra	.25
100	Jim Eisenreich	.25
101	Tommy Greene	.25
102	Dave Hollins	.25
103	Pete Incaviglia	.25
104	Danny Jackson	.25
105	John Kruk	.25
106	Terry Mulholland	.25
107	Curt Schilling	.35
108	Mitch Williams	.25
109	Stan Belinda	.25
110	Jay Bell	.25
111	Steve Cooke	.25
112	Carlos Garcia	.25
113	Jeff King	.25
114	Al Martin	.30
115	Orlando Merced	.25
116	Don Slaught	.25
117	Andy Van Slyke	.25
118	Tim Wakefield	.25
119	*Rene Arocha*	.40
120	Bernard Gilkey	.30
121	Gregg Jefferies	.25
122	Ray Lankford	.30
123	Donovan Osborne	.25
124	Tom Pagnozzi	.25
125	Erik Pappas	.25
126	Geronimo Pena	.25
127	Lee Smith	.30
128	Ozzie Smith	1.50
129	Bob Tewksbury	.25
130	Mark Whiten	.25
131	Derek Bell	.25
132	Andy Benes	.30
133	Tony Gwynn	3.00
134	Gene Harris	.25
135	Trevor Hoffman	.30
136	Phil Plantier	.25
137	Rod Beck	.25
138	Barry Bonds	2.00
139	John Burkett	.25
140	Will Clark	.75
141	Royce Clayton	.25
142	Mike Jackson	.25
143	Darren Lewis	.25
144	Kirt Manwaring	.25
145	Willie McGee	.30
146	Bill Swift	.25
147	Robby Thompson	.25
148	Matt Williams	.75
149	Brady Anderson	.40
150	Mike Devereaux	.25
151	Chris Hoiles	.25
152	Ben McDonald	.25
153	Mark McLemore	.25
154	Mike Mussina	1.50
155	Gregg Olson	.25
156	Harold Reynolds	.25
157	Cal Ripken, Jr.	6.00
158	Rick Sutcliffe	.25
159	Fernando Valenzuela	.30
160	Roger Clemens	3.00
161	Scott Cooper	.25
162	Andre Dawson	.35
163	Scott Fletcher	.25
164	Mike Greenwell	.25
165	Greg Harris	.25
166	Billy Hatcher	.25
167	Jeff Russell	.25
168	Mo Vaughn	1.50
169	Frank Viola	.25
170	Chad Curtis	.30
171	Chili Davis	.25
172	Gary DiSarcina	.25
173	Damion Easley	.25
174	Chuck Finley	.25
175	Mark Langston	.25
176	Luis Polonia	.25
177	Tim Salmon	1.50
178	Scott Sanderson	.25
179	*J.T. Snow*	2.00
180	Wilson Alvarez	.25
181	Ellis Burks	.25
182	Joey Cora	.25
183	Alex Fernandez	.30
184	Ozzie Guillen	.25
185	Roberto Hernandez	.25
186	Bo Jackson	.75
187	Lance Johnson	.25
188	Jack McDowell	.25
189	Frank Thomas	5.00
190	Robin Ventura	.50
191	Carlos Baerga	.30
192	Albert Belle	2.00
193	Wayne Kirby	.25
194	Derek Lilliquist	.25
195	Kenny Lofton	1.50
196	Carlos Martinez	.25
197	Jose Mesa	.25
198	Eric Plunk	.25
199	Paul Sorrento	.25
200	John Doherty	.25
201	Cecil Fielder	.25
202	Travis Fryman	.40
203	Kirk Gibson	.25
204	Mike Henneman	.25
205	Chad Kreuter	.25

206	Scott Livingstone	.25
207	Tony Phillips	.25
208	Mickey Tettleton	.25
209	Alan Trammell	.40
210	David Wells	.30
211	Lou Whitaker	.25
212	Kevin Appier	.25
213	George Brett	2.00
214	David Cone	.30
215	Tom Gordon	.25
216	Phil Hiatt	.25
217	Felix Jose	.25
218	Wally Joyner	.30
219	Jose Lind	.25
220	Mike Macfarlane	.25
221	Brian McRae	.25
222	Jeff Montgomery	.25
223	Cal Eldred	.25
224	Darryl Hamilton	.25
225	John Jaha	.30
226	Pat Listach	.25
227	*Graeme Lloyd*	.35
228	Kevin Reimer	.25
229	Bill Spiers	.25
230	B.J. Surhoff	.30
231	Greg Vaughn	.30
232	Robin Yount	2.00
233	Rick Aguilera	.25
234	Jim Deshaies	.25
235	Brian Harper	.25
236	Kent Hrbek	.30
237	Chuck Knoblauch	.50
238	Shane Mack	.25
239	David McCarty	.25
240	Pedro Munoz	.25
241	Mike Pagliarulo	.25
242	Kirby Puckett	3.00
243	Dave Winfield	.50
244	Jim Abbott	.30
245	Wade Boggs	.75
246	Pat Kelly	.25
247	Jimmy Key	.25
248	Jim Leyritz	.25
249	Don Mattingly	2.50
250	Matt Nokes	.25
251	Paul O'Neill	.35
252	Mike Stanley	.25
253	Danny Tartabull	.25
254	Bob Wickman	.25
255	Bernie Williams	1.50
256	Mike Bordick	.25
257	Dennis Eckersley	.30
258	Brent Gates	.30
259	Goose Gossage	.25
260	Rickey Henderson	.50
261	Mark McGwire	8.00
262	Ruben Sierra	.25
263	Terry Steinbach	.25
264	Bob Welch	.25
265	Bobby Witt	.25
266	Rich Amaral	.25
267	Chris Bosio	.25
268	Jay Buhner	.35
269	Norm Charlton	.25
270	Ken Griffey, Jr.	8.00
271	Erik Hanson	.25
272	Randy Johnson	1.00
273	Edgar Martinez	.25
274	Tino Martinez	.40
275	Dave Valle	.25
276	Omar Vizquel	.30
277	Kevin Brown	.35
278	Jose Canseco	.50
279	Julio Franco	.25
280	Juan Gonzalez	3.00
281	Tom Henke	.25
282	David Hulse	.25
283	Rafael Palmeiro	.50
284	Dean Palmer	.25
285	Ivan Rodriguez	2.00
286	Nolan Ryan	5.00
287	Roberto Alomar	1.50
288	Pat Borders	.25
289	Joe Carter	.30
290	Juan Guzman	.25
291	Pat Hentgen	.35
292	Paul Molitor	1.50
293	John Olerud	.40
294	Ed Sprague	.25
295	Dave Stewart	.30
296	Duane Ward	.25
297	Devon White	.30
298	Checklist	.10
299	Checklist	.10
300	Checklist	.10

Player names in *Italic* type indicate a rookie card.

1993 Flair Wave of the Future

The game's top prospects are featured in this insert issue randomly packaged in Flair packs. Cards #19-20, Darrell Whitmore and Nigel Wilson, were printed with each other's back; no corrected version was made.

		MT
Complete Set (20):		30.00
Common Player:		.75
1	Jason Bere	.75
2	Jeremy Burnitz	3.00
3	Russ Davis	.75
4	Jim Edmonds	3.00
5	Cliff Floyd	1.50
6	Jeffrey Hammonds	1.00
7	Trevor Hoffman	2.00
8	Domingo Jean	.75
9	David McCarty	.75
10	Bobby Munoz	.75
11	Brad Pennington	.75
12	Mike Piazza	12.00
13	Manny Ramirez	7.50
14	John Roper	.75
15	Tim Salmon	5.00
16	Aaron Sele	1.50
17	Allen Watson	.75
18	Rondell White	3.00
19	Darell Whitmore	.75
20	Nigel Wilson	.75

1994 Flair

One of the success stories of 1993 returned with the release of Fleer Flair for 1994. At $4 per pack this was pricey stuff, but collectors apparently liked the look that includes an extremely thick card stock, full-bleed photos and gold-foil graphics on both sides with a protective polyester laminate described as "far beyond mere UV coating." In addition to the 250 regular-issue cards, there are three 10-card insert sets; Wave of the Future, Outfield Power and Hot Numbers in Series 1, the last with players' images printed on 100% etched foil. Series 2 has 200 base cards and Hot Glove, Infield Power and 10 more Wave of the Future insert cards.

		MT
Complete Set (450):		85.00
Common Player:		.15
Series 1 Wax Box:		55.00
Series 2 Wax Box:		100.00
1	Harold Baines	.25
2	Jeffrey Hammonds	.20
3	Chris Hoiles	.15
4	Ben McDonald	.15
5	Mark McLemore	.15
6	Jamie Moyer	.15
7	Jim Poole	.15
8	Cal Ripken, Jr.	5.00
9	Chris Sabo	.15
10	Scott Bankhead	.15
11	Scott Cooper	.15
12	Danny Darwin	.15
13	Andre Dawson	.35
14	Billy Hatcher	.15
15	Aaron Sele	.40
15a	Aaron Sele (overprinted "PROMOTIONAL SAMPLE")	3.00
16	John Valentin	.20
17	Dave Valle	.15
18	Mo Vaughn	1.25
19	*Brian Anderson*	.30
20	Gary DiSarcina	.15
21	Jim Edmonds	.60
22	Chuck Finley	.15
23	Bo Jackson	.35
24	Mark Leiter	.15
25	Greg Myers	.15
26	Eduardo Perez	.15
27	Tim Salmon	.75
28	Wilson Alvarez	.15
29	Jason Bere	.15
30	Alex Fernandez	.20
31	Ozzie Guillen	.15
32	Joe Hall	.15
33	Darrin Jackson	.15
34	Kirk McCaskill	.15
35	Tim Raines	.25
36	Frank Thomas	4.00
37	Carlos Baerga	.15
38	Albert Belle	1.25
39	Mark Clark	.30
40	Wayne Kirby	.15
41	Dennis Martinez	.25
42	Charles Nagy	.15
43	Manny Ramirez	2.00
44	Paul Sorrento	.15
45	Jim Thome	.50
46	Eric Davis	.15
47	John Doherty	.15
48	Junior Felix	.15
49	Cecil Fielder	.25
50	Kirk Gibson	.15
51	Mike Moore	.15
52	Tony Phillips	.15
53	Alan Trammell	.30
54	Kevin Appier	.15
55	Stan Belinda	.15
56	Vince Coleman	.15
57	Greg Gagne	.15
58	Bob Hamelin	.15
59	Dave Henderson	.15
60	Wally Joyner	.25
61	Mike Macfarlane	.15
62	Jeff Montgomery	.15
63	Ricky Bones	.15
64	Jeff Bronkey	.15
65	Alex Diaz	.15
66	Cal Eldred	.15
67	Darryl Hamilton	.15
68	John Jaha	.15
69	Mark Kiefer	.15
70	Kevin Seitzer	.15
71	Turner Ward	.15
72	Rich Becker	.15
73	Scott Erickson	.15
74	Keith Garagozzo	.15
75	Kent Hrbek	.25
76	Scott Leius	.15
77	Kirby Puckett	2.00
78	Matt Walkbeck	.15
79	Dave Winfield	.45
80	Mike Gallego	.15
81	Xavier Hernandez	.15
82	Jimmy Key	.15
83	Jim Leyritz	.15
84	Don Mattingly	2.00
85	Matt Nokes	.15
86	Paul O'Neill	.25
87	Melido Perez	.15
88	Danny Tartabull	.15
89	Mike Bordick	.15
90	Ron Darling	.15
91	Dennis Eckersley	.25
92	Stan Javier	.15
93	Steve Karsay	.15
94	Mark McGwire	6.00
95	Troy Neel	.15
96	Terry Steinbach	.15
97	Bill Taylor	.15
98	Eric Anthony	.15
99	Chris Bosio	.15
100	Tim Davis	.15
101	Felix Fermin	.15
102	Dave Fleming	.15
103	Ken Griffey, Jr.	5.00
104	Greg Hibbard	.15
105	Reggie Jefferson	.15
106	Tino Martinez	.30
107	Jack Armstrong	.15
108	Will Clark	.75
109	Juan Gonzalez	1.50
110	Rick Helling	.15
111	Tom Henke	.15
112	David Hulse	.15
113	Manuel Lee	.15
114	Doug Strange	.15
115	Roberto Alomar	1.25
116	Joe Carter	.20
117	Carlos Delgado	.75
118	Pat Hentgen	.15
119	Paul Molitor	.75
120	John Olerud	.35
121	Dave Stewart	.25
122	Todd Stottlemyre	.15
123	Mike Timlin	.15
124	Jeff Blauser	.15
125	Tom Glavine	.35
126	Dave Justice	.35
127	Mike Kelly	.15
128	Ryan Klesko	.50
129	Javier Lopez	.40
130	Greg Maddux	2.00
131	Fred McGriff	.60
132	Kent Mercker	.15
133	Mark Wohlers	.15
134	Willie Banks	.15
135	Steve Buechele	.15
136	Shawon Dunston	.15
137	Jose Guzman	.15
138	Glenallen Hill	.15
139	Randy Myers	.15
140	Karl Rhodes	.15
141	Ryne Sandberg	1.25
142	Steve Trachsel	.25
143	Bret Boone	.15
144	Tom Browning	.15
145	Hector Carrasco	.15
146	Barry Larkin	.30
147	Hal Morris	.15
148	Jose Rijo	.15
149	Reggie Sanders	.25
150	John Smiley	.15
151	Dante Bichette	.50
152	Ellis Burks	.25
153	Joe Girardi	.15
154	Mike Harkey	.15
155	Roberto Mejia	.15
156	Marcus Moore	.15
157	Armando Reynoso	.15
158	Bruce Ruffin	.15
159	Eric Young	.15
160	*Kurt Abbott*	.40
161	Jeff Conine	.25
162	Orestes Destrade	.15
163	Chris Hammond	.15
164	Bryan Harvey	.15
165	Dave Magadan	.15
166	Gary Sheffield	.35
167	David Weathers	.15
168	Andujar Cedeno	.15
169	Tom Edens	.15
170	Luis Gonzalez	.15
171	Pete Harnisch	.15
172	Todd Jones	.15
173	Darryl Kile	.15
174	James Mouton	.15
175	Scott Servais	.15
176	Mitch Williams	.15
177	Pedro Astacio	.15
178	Orel Hershiser	.25
179	Raul Mondesi	1.00
180	Jose Offerman	.15
181	*Chan Ho Park*	1.50
182	Mike Piazza	2.50
183	Cory Snyder	.15
184	Tim Wallach	.15
185	Todd Worrell	.15
186	Sean Berry	.15
187	Wil Cordero	.15
188	Darrin Fletcher	.15
189	Cliff Floyd	.25
190	Marquis Grissom	.25
191	Rod Henderson	.15
192	Ken Hill	.15
193	Pedro Martinez	.30
194	Kirk Rueter	.15
195	Jeromy Burnitz	.20
196	John Franco	.15
197	Dwight Gooden	.25
198	Todd Hundley	.25
199	Bobby Jones	.15
200	Jeff Kent	.25
201	Mike Maddux	.15
202	Ryan Thompson	.15
203	Jose Vizcaino	.15
204	Darren Daulton	.15
205	Len Dykstra	.15
206	Jim Eisenreich	.15
207	Dave Hollins	.15
208	Danny Jackson	.15
209	Doug Jones	.15
210	Jeff Juden	.15
211	Ben Rivera	.15
212	Kevin Stocker	.15
213	Milt Thompson	.15
214	Jay Bell	.15
215	Steve Cooke	.15
216	Mark Dewey	.15
217	Al Martin	.15
218	Orlando Merced	.15
219	Don Slaught	.15
220	Zane Smith	.15
221	Rick White	.15
222	Kevin Young	.15
223	Rene Arocha	.15
224	Rheal Cormier	.15
225	Brian Jordan	.25
226	Ray Lankford	.25
227	Mike Perez	.15
228	Ozzie Smith	1.00
229	Mark Whiten	.15
230	Todd Zeile	.25
231	Derek Bell	.25
232	Archi Cianfrocco	.15
233	Ricky Gutierrez	.15
234	Trevor Hoffman	.20
235	Phil Plantier	.15
236	Dave Staton	.15
237	Wally Whitehurst	.15
238	Todd Benzinger	.15
239	Barry Bonds	1.25
240	John Burkett	.15
241	Royce Clayton	.15
242	Bryan Hickerson	.15
243	Mike Jackson	.15
244	Darren Lewis	.15
245	Kirt Manwaring	.15
246	Mark Portugal	.15
247	Salomon Torres	.15
248	Checklist	.15
249	Checklist	.15
250	Checklist	.15
251	Brady Anderson	.30
252	Mike Devereaux	.15
253	Sid Fernandez	.15
254	Leo Gomez	.15
255	Mike Mussina	.75
256	Mike Oquist	.15
257	Rafael Palmeiro	.40
258	Lee Smith	.25
259	Damon Berryhill	.15
260	Wes Chamberlain	.15
261	Roger Clemens	2.00
262	Gar Finnvold	.15
263	Mike Greenwell	.15
264	Tim Naehring	.15
265	Otis Nixon	.15
266	Ken Ryan	.15
267	Chad Curtis	.15
268	Chili Davis	.25
269	Damion Easley	.15
270	Jorge Fabregas	.15
271	Mark Langston	.15
272	Phil Leftwich	.15
273	Harold Reynolds	.15
274	J.T. Snow	.40
275	Joey Cora	.15
276	Julio Franco	.15
277	Roberto Hernandez	.15
278	Lance Johnson	.15
279	Ron Karkovice	.15
280	Jack McDowell	.15
281	Robin Ventura	.40
282	Sandy Alomar Jr.	.30
283	Kenny Lofton	1.00
284	Jose Mesa	.15
285	Jack Morris	.15
286	Eddie Murray	.35
287	Chad Ogea	.15
288	Eric Plunk	.15
289	Paul Shuey	.15
290	Omar Vizquel	.20
291	Danny Bautista	.15
292	Travis Fryman	.30
293	Greg Gohr	.15
294	Chris Gomez	.15
295	Mickey Tettleton	.15
296	Lou Whitaker	.15
297	David Cone	.20
298	Gary Gaetti	.15
299	Tom Gordon	.15
300	Felix Jose	.15
301	Jose Lind	.15
302	Brian McRae	.15
303	Mike Fetters	.15
304	Brian Harper	.15
305	Pat Listach	.15
306	Matt Mieske	.20
307	Dave Nilsson	.15
308	Jody Reed	.15
309	Greg Vaughn	.25
310	Bill Wegman	.15
311	Rick Aguilera	.15
312	Alex Cole	.15
313	Denny Hocking	.15
314	Chuck Knoblauch	.30
315	Shane Mack	.15
316	Pat Meares	.25
317	Kevin Tapani	.15
318	Jim Abbott	.25
319	Wade Boggs	.40
320	Sterling Hitchcock	.15
321	Pat Kelly	.15
322	Terry Mulholland	.15
323	Luis Polonia	.15
324	Mike Stanley	.15
325	Bob Wickman	.15
326	Bernie Williams	1.50
327	Mark Acre	.15
328	Geronimo Berroa	.15
329	Scott Brosius	.15
330	Brent Gates	.15
331	Rickey Henderson	.40
332	Carlos Reyes	.15
333	Ruben Sierra	.15
334	Bobby Witt	.15
335	Bobby Ayala	.15
336	Jay Buhner	.25
337	Randy Johnson	.75
338	Edgar Martinez	.25
339	Bill Risley	.15
340	*Alex Rodriguez*	60.00
341	Roger Salkeld	.25
342	Dan Wilson	.15
343	Kevin Brown	.25
344	Jose Canseco	.75
345	Dean Palmer	.15
346	Ivan Rodriguez	1.50
347	Kenny Rogers	.15
348	Pat Borders	.15
349	Juan Guzman	.15
350	Ed Sprague	.15
351	Devon White	.15
352	Steve Avery	.15
353	Roberto Kelly	.15
354	Mark Lemke	.15
355	Greg McMichael	.15
356	Terry Pendleton	.15
357	John Smoltz	.30
358	Mike Stanton	.15
359	Tony Tarasco	.15
360	Mark Grace	.30
361	Derrick May	.15

362	Rey Sanchez	.15
363	Sammy Sosa	3.00
364	Rick Wilkins	.15
365	Jeff Brantley	.15
366	Tony Fernandez	.15
367	Chuck McElroy	.15
368	Kevin Mitchell	.15
369	John Roper	.15
370	Johnny Ruffin	.15
371	Deion Sanders	.50
372	Marvin Freeman	.15
373	Andres Galarraga	.25
374	Charlie Hayes	.15
375	Nelson Liriano	.15
376	David Nied	.15
377	Walt Weiss	.15
378	Bret Barberie	.15
379	Jerry Browne	.15
380	Chuck Carr	.15
381	Greg Colbrunn	.15
382	Charlie Hough	.15
383	Kurt Miller	.25
384	Benito Santiago	.20
385	Jeff Bagwell	1.50
386	Craig Biggio	.40
387	Ken Caminiti	.40
388	Doug Drabek	.15
389	Steve Finley	.15
390	John Hudek	.15
391	Orlando Miller	.15
392	Shane Reynolds	.15
393	Brett Butler	.20
394	Tom Candiotti	.15
395	Delino DeShields	.15
396	Kevin Gross	.15
397	Eric Karros	.30
398	Ramon Martinez	.25
399	Henry Rodriguez	.25
400	Moises Alou	.25
401	Jeff Fassero	.15
402	Mike Lansing	.15
403	Mel Rojas	.15
404	Larry Walker	.75
405	John Wetteland	.15
406	Gabe White	.30
407	Bobby Bonilla	.30
408	Josias Manzanillo	.15
409	Bret Saberhagen	.15
410	David Segui	.15
411	Mariano Duncan	.15
412	Tommy Greene	.15
413	Billy Hatcher	.15
414	Ricky Jordan	.15
415	John Kruk	.15
416	Bobby Munoz	.15
417	Curt Schilling	.25
418	Fernando Valenzuela	.25
419	David West	.15
420	Carlos Garcia	.15
421	Brian Hunter	.15
422	Jeff King	.15
423	Jon Lieber	.15
424	Ravelo Manzanillo	.15
425	Denny Neagle	.15
426	Andy Van Slyke	.15
427	Bryan Eversgerd	.15
428	Bernard Gilkey	.25
429	Gregg Jefferies	.25
430	Tom Pagnozzi	.15
431	Bob Tewksbury	.15
432	Allen Watson	.15
433	Andy Ashby	.15
434	Andy Benes	.25
435	Donnie Elliott	.15
436	Tony Gwynn	1.50
437	Joey Hamilton	.75
438	Tim Hyers	.15
439	Luis Lopez	.15
440	Bip Roberts	.15
441	Scott Sanders	.15
442	Rod Beck	.15
443	Dave Burba	.15
444	Darryl Strawberry	.25
445	Bill Swift	.15
446	Robby Thompson	.15
447	*William VanLandingham*	.50
448	Matt Williams	1.00
449	Checklist	.15
450	Checklist	.15

1994 Flair Hot Gloves

Hot Gloves is a 10-card Series 2 insert set. It focuses on players with outstanding defensive ability. Cards feature a die-cut design, with the player photo in front of a baseball glove. Player identification and a "Hot Glove" logo are in gold foil in the lower-left corner.

		MT
Complete Set (10):		100.00
Common Player:		4.00
1	Barry Bonds	7.50
2	Will Clark	4.00
3	Ken Griffey, Jr.	30.00
4	Kenny Lofton	6.00
5	Greg Maddux	15.00
6	Don Mattingly	9.00
7	Kirby Puckett	10.00
8	Cal Ripken, Jr.	25.00
9	Tim Salmon	5.00
10	Matt Williams	4.00

1994 Flair Hot Numbers

Hot Numbers is an insert set found in Series 1 packs at an average rate of 1:24. Each card is printed on 100% etched foil and displays the player in the forefront with a background made up of floating numbers. The player's name is in gold foil across the bottom-right side and a large foil "Hot Numbers" and that player's uniform number are in a square at bottom-left.

		MT
Complete Set (10):		40.00
Common Player:		1.00
1	Roberto Alomar	2.50
2	Carlos Baerga	1.00
3	Will Clark	1.50
4	Fred McGriff	1.25
5	Paul Molitor	2.00
6	John Olerud	1.25
7	Mike Piazza	12.50
8	Cal Ripken, Jr.	16.00
9	Ryne Sandberg	5.00
10	Frank Thomas	7.50

1994 Flair Infield Power

Infield Power is a horizontally formatted insert set. Cards show the player batting on one half and in the field on the other half of the card, divided by a black, diagonal strip that reads "Infield Power" and the player's name. The set spotlights infielders that often hit the longball. Infield Power was inserted into Series 2 packs at an average rate of 1:5.

		MT
Complete Set (10):		12.50
Common Player:		.50
1	Jeff Bagwell	1.25
2	Will Clark	.60
3	Darren Daulton	.50
4	Don Mattingly	1.25
5	Fred McGriff	.50
6	Rafael Palmeiro	.60
7	Mike Piazza	3.00
8	Cal Ripken, Jr.	5.00
9	Frank Thomas	2.50
10	Matt Williams	.60

1994 Flair Outfield Power

Flair's Outfield Power was randomly inserted in Series 1 packs at a 1:5 rate. This vertically formatted card shows the player in the field on top, while the bottom half shows the player at the plate. The photos divided by a black strip with "Outfield Power" and the player's name on it.

		MT
Complete Set (10):		20.00
Common Player:		.75
1	Albert Belle	2.50
2	Barry Bonds	2.50
3	Joe Carter	.75
4	Len Dykstra	.75
5	Juan Gonzalez	3.50
6	Ken Griffey, Jr.	9.00
7	Dave Justice	1.25
8	Kirby Puckett	3.50
9	Tim Salmon	1.25
10	Dave Winfield	1.25

1994 Flair Wave of the Future

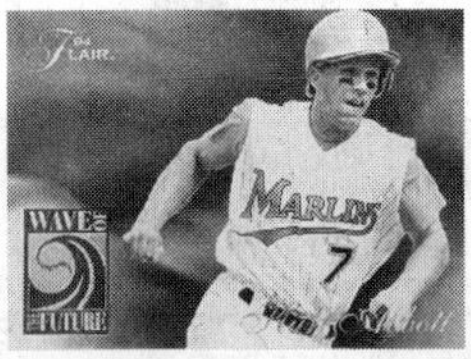

Series 1 Wave of the Future is horizontally formatted and depicts 10 outstanding 1994 rookies who have the potential to become superstars. Each player is featured on a colorful wavelike background. A Wave of the Future gold-foil stamp is placed in the bottom-right corner with the player name in gold foil starting in the opposite bottom corner and running across the bottom. Advertised insertion rate was 1:5.

		MT
Complete Set (10):		12.00
Common Player:		.50
1	Kurt Abbott	.50
2	Carlos Delgado	3.00
3	Steve Karsay	.50
4	Ryan Klesko	3.00
5	Javier Lopez	2.00
6	Raul Mondesi	5.00
7	James Mouton	.50
8	Chan Ho Park	2.00
9	Dave Staton	.50
10	Rick White	.50

1994 Flair Wave of the Future 2

Series 2 Flair also has a Wave of the Future insert set. Unlike the earlier series, this 10-card set is vertically formated. The Wave of the Future logo appears in the bottom-left with the player's name stretching across the rest of the bottom. The background has a swirling water effect, on which the player is superimposed. Insertion rate is one per five packs.

		MT
Complete Set (10):		45.00
Common Player:		.75
1	Mark Acre	.75
2	Chris Gomez	.75
3	Joey Hamilton	3.00
4	John Hudek	.75
5	Jon Lieber	.75
6	Matt Mieske	1.00
7	Orlando Miller	1.00
8	Alex Rodriguez	40.00
9	Tony Tarasco	.75
10	Bill VanLandingham	.75

1995 Flair

There's no mistaking that 1995 Flair is Fleer's super-premium brand. Cards are printed on double-thick cardboard with a background of etched metallic foil: Gold for National Leaguers, silver for American. A portrait and an action photo are featured on the horizontal front design. Backs are vertically formatted with a borderless action photo, several years worth of stats and foil trim. The basic set was issued in two series of 216 basic cards each, along with several insert sets exclusive to each series. Cards were sold in a hard pack of nine with a suggested retail price of $5.

		MT
Complete Set (432):		55.00
Common Player:		.20
Series 1 or 2 Wax Box:		50.00
1	Brady Anderson	.30
2	Harold Baines	.25
3	Leo Gomez	.20
4	Alan Mills	.20
5	Jamie Moyer	.20
6	Mike Mussina	.75
7	Mike Oquist	.20
8	Arthur Rhodes	.20
9	Cal Ripken Jr.	5.00
10	Roger Clemens	1.50
11	Scott Cooper	.20
12	Mike Greenwell	.20
13	Aaron Sele	.20
14	John Valentin	.25
15	Mo Vaughn	1.25
16	Chad Curtis	.20
17	Gary DiSarcina	.20
18	Chuck Finley	.20
19	Andrew Lorraine	.20
20	Spike Owen	.20
21	Tim Salmon	.40
22	J.T. Snow	.30
23	Wilson Alvarez	.20
24	Jason Bere	.20
25	Ozzie Guillen	.20
26	Mike LaValliere	.20
27	Frank Thomas	2.00
28	Robin Ventura	.30
29	Carlos Baerga	.20
30	Albert Belle	1.25
31	Jason Grimsley	.20
32	Dennis Martinez	.25
33	Eddie Murray	.75
34	Charles Nagy	.25
35	Manny Ramirez	1.50
36	Paul Sorrento	.20
37	John Doherty	.20
38	Cecil Fielder	.20
39	Travis Fryman	.25
40	Chris Gomez	.20
41	Tony Phillips	.20
42	Lou Whitaker	.20
43	David Cone	.25
44	Gary Gaetti	.20
45	Mark Gubicza	.20
46	Bob Hamelin	.20
47	Wally Joyner	.25
48	Rusty Meacham	.20
49	Jeff Montgomery	.20
50	Ricky Bones	.20
51	Cal Eldred	.20
52	Pat Listach	.20
53	Matt Mieske	.20
54	Dave Nilsson	.20
55	Greg Vaughn	.25
56	Bill Wegman	.20
57	Chuck Knoblauch	.35
58	Scott Leius	.20
59	Pat Mahomes	.20
60	Pat Meares	.20
61	Pedro Munoz	.20
62	Kirby Puckett	2.00
63	Wade Boggs	.50
64	Jimmy Key	.20
65	Jim Leyritz	.20
66	Don Mattingly	2.00
67	Paul O'Neill	.30
68	Melido Perez	.20
69	Danny Tartabull	.20
70	John Briscoe	.20
71	Scott Brosius	.20
72	Ron Darling	.20
73	Brent Gates	.20
74	Rickey Henderson	.40
75	Stan Javier	.20
76	Mark McGwire	6.00
77	Todd Van Poppel	.20
78	Bobby Ayala	.20
79	Mike Blowers	.20
80	Jay Buhner	.25
81	Ken Griffey Jr.	6.00
82	Randy Johnson	.75
83	Tino Martinez	.30
84	Jeff Nelson	.20
85	Alex Rodriguez	5.00
86	Will Clark	.50
87	Jeff Frye	.20
88	Juan Gonzalez	2.50
89	Rusty Greer	.25
90	Darren Oliver	.20
91	Dean Palmer	.20
92	Ivan Rodriguez	1.25
93	Matt Whiteside	.20
94	Roberto Alomar	1.00
95	Joe Carter	.20
96	Tony Castillo	.20
97	Juan Guzman	.20
98	Pat Hentgen	.20
99	Mike Huff	.20
100	John Olerud	.30
101	Woody Williams	.20
102	Roberto Kelly	.20
103	Ryan Klesko	.50
104	Javier Lopez	.35
105	Greg Maddux	3.00
106	Fred McGriff	.40
107	Jose Oliva	.20
108	John Smoltz	.35
109	Tony Tarasco	.20
110	Mark Wohlers	.20
111	Jim Bullinger	.20
112	Shawon Dunston	.20
113	Derrick May	.20
114	Randy Myers	.20
115	Karl Rhodes	.20
116	Rey Sanchez	.20
117	Steve Trachsel	.20
118	Eddie Zambrano	.20
119	Bret Boone	.20
120	Brian Dorsett	.20
121	Hal Morris	.20
122	Jose Rijo	.20
123	John Roper	.20
124	Reggie Sanders	.25
125	Pete Schourek	.20
126	John Smiley	.20
127	Ellis Burks	.25
128	Vinny Castilla	.25
129	Marvin Freeman	.20
130	Andres Galarraga	.30
131	Mike Munoz	.20
132	David Nied	.20
133	Bruce Ruffin	.20

134	Walt Weiss	.20
135	Eric Young	.20
136	Greg Colbrunn	.20
137	Jeff Conine	.25
138	Jeremy Hernandez	.20
139	Charles Johnson	.25
140	Robb Nen	.20
141	Gary Sheffield	.60
142	Dave Weathers	.20
143	Jeff Bagwell	1.50
144	Craig Biggio	.30
145	Tony Eusebio	.20
146	Luis Gonzalez	.20
147	John Hudek	.20
148	Darryl Kile	.20
149	Dave Veres	.20
150	Billy Ashley	.20
151	Pedro Astacio	.20
152	Rafael Bournigal	.20
153	Delino DeShields	.20
154	Raul Mondesi	.60
155	Mike Piazza	4.00
156	Rudy Seanez	.20
157	Ismael Valdes	.20
158	Tim Wallach	.20
159	Todd Worrell	.20
160	Moises Alou	.25
161	Cliff Floyd	.20
162	Gil Heredia	.20
163	Mike Lansing	.20
164	Pedro Martinez	.35
165	Kirk Rueter	.20
166	Tim Scott	.20
167	Jeff Shaw	.20
168	Rondell White	.30
169	Bobby Bonilla	.25
170	Rico Brogna	.20
171	Todd Hundley	.30
172	Jeff Kent	.20
173	Jim Lindeman	.20
174	Joe Orsulak	.20
175	Bret Saberhagen	.20
176	Toby Borland	.20
177	Darren Daulton	.20
178	Lenny Dykstra	.20
179	Jim Eisenreich	.20
180	Tommy Greene	.20
181	Tony Longmire	.20
182	Bobby Munoz	.20
183	Kevin Stocker	.20
184	Jay Bell	.20
185	Steve Cooke	.20
186	Ravelo Manzanillo	.20
187	Al Martin	.20
188	Denny Neagle	.20
189	Don Slaught	.20
190	Paul Wagner	.20
191	Rene Arocha	.20
192	Bernard Gilkey	.20
193	Jose Oquendo	.20
194	Tom Pagnozzi	.20
195	Ozzie Smith	.75
196	Allen Watson	.20
197	Mark Whiten	.20
198	Andy Ashby	.25
199	Donnie Elliott	.20
200	Bryce Florie	.20
201	Tony Gwynn	2.00
202	Trevor Hoffman	.25
203	Brian Johnson	.20
204	Tim Mauser	.20
205	Bip Roberts	.20
206	Rod Beck	.20
207	Barry Bonds	1.25
208	Royce Clayton	.20
209	Darren Lewis	.20
210	Mark Portugal	.20
211	Kevin Rogers	.20
212	William Van Landingham	.20
213	Matt Williams	.50
214	Checklist	.20
215	Checklist	.20
216	Checklist	.20
217	Bret Barberie	.20
218	Armando Benitez	.20
219	Kevin Brown	.25
220	Sid Fernandez	.20
221	Chris Hoiles	.20
222	Doug Jones	.20
223	Ben McDonald	.20
224	Rafael Palmeiro	.30
225	Andy Van Slyke	.20
226	Jose Canseco	.50
227	Vaughn Eshelman	.20
228	Mike Macfarlane	.20
229	Tim Naehring	.20
230	Frank Rodriguez	.20
231	Lee Tinsley	.20
232	Mark Whiten	.20
233	Garret Anderson	.20
234	Chili Davis	.25
235	Jim Edmonds	.30
236	Mark Langston	.20
237	Troy Percival	.20
238	Tony Phillips	.20
239	Lee Smith	.20
240	Jim Abbott	.25
241	James Baldwin	.20
242	Mike Devereaux	.20
243	Ray Durham	.25
244	Alex Fernandez	.25
245	Roberto Hernandez	.20
246	Lance Johnson	.20
247	Ron Karkovice	.20
248	Tim Raines	.25
249	Sandy Alomar Jr.	.25
250	Orel Hershiser	.25
251	Julian Tavarez	.20
252	Jim Thome	.35
253	Omar Vizquel	.25
254	Dave Winfield	.40
255	Chad Curtis	.20
256	Kirk Gibson	.20
257	Mike Henneman	.20
258	*Bob Higginson*	1.50
259	Felipe Lira	.20
260	Rudy Pemberton	.20
261	Alan Trammell	.25
262	Kevin Appier	.20
263	Pat Borders	.20
264	Tom Gordon	.20
265	Jose Lind	.20
266	Jon Nunnally	.20
267	Dilson Torres	.20
268	Michael Tucker	.20
269	Jeff Cirillo	.20
270	Darryl Hamilton	.20
271	David Hulse	.20
272	Mark Kiefer	.20
273	Graeme Lloyd	.20
274	Joe Oliver	.20
275	Al Reyes	.20
276	Kevin Seitzer	.20
277	Rick Aguilera	.20
278	Marty Cordova	.20
279	Scott Erickson	.20
280	LaTroy Hawkins	.20
281	Brad Radke	.20
282	Kevin Tapani	.20
283	Tony Fernandez	.20
284	Sterling Hitchcock	.20
285	Pat Kelly	.20
286	Jack McDowell	.20
287	Andy Pettitte	1.00
288	Mike Stanley	.20
289	John Wetteland	.25
290	Bernie Williams	1.50
291	Mark Acre	.20
292	Geronimo Berroa	.20
293	Dennis Eckersley	.25
294	Steve Ontiveros	.20
295	Ruben Sierra	.20
296	Terry Steinbach	.20
297	Dave Stewart	.25
298	Todd Stottlemyre	.20
299	Darren Bragg	.20
300	Joey Cora	.20
301	Edgar Martinez	.25
302	Bill Risley	.20
303	Ron Villone	.20
304	Dan Wilson	.20
305	Benji Gil	.20
306	Wilson Heredia	.20
307	Mark McLemore	.20
308	Otis Nixon	.20
309	Kenny Rogers	.20
310	Jeff Russell	.20
311	Mickey Tettleton	.20
312	Bob Tewksbury	.20
313	David Cone	.25
314	Carlos Delgado	.75
315	Alex Gonzalez	.20
316	Shawn Green	.35
317	Paul Molitor	.40
318	Ed Sprague	.20
319	Devon White	.25
320	Steve Avery	.20
321	Jeff Blauser	.20
322	Brad Clontz	.20
323	Tom Glavine	.35
324	Marquis Grissom	.25
325	Chipper Jones	3.00
326	Dave Justice	.40
327	Mark Lemke	.20
328	Kent Mercker	.20
329	Jason Schmidt	.20
330	Steve Buechele	.20
331	Kevin Foster	.20
332	Mark Grace	.35
333	Brian McRae	.20
334	Sammy Sosa	3.00
335	Ozzie Timmons	.20
336	Rick Wilkins	.20
337	Hector Carrasco	.20
338	Ron Gant	.25
339	Barry Larkin	.35
340	Deion Sanders	.30
341	Benito Santiago	.20
342	Roger Bailey	.20
343	Jason Bates	.20
344	Dante Bichette	.40
345	Joe Girardi	.20
346	Bill Swift	.20
347	Mark Thompson	.20
348	Larry Walker	.40
349	Kurt Abbott	.20
350	John Burkett	.20
351	Chuck Carr	.20
352	Andre Dawson	.25
353	Chris Hammond	.20
354	Charles Johnson	.25
355	Terry Pendleton	.20
356	Quilvio Veras	.20
357	Derek Bell	.25
358	Jim Dougherty	.20
359	Doug Drabek	.20
360	Todd Jones	.20
361	Orlando Miller	.20
362	James Mouton	.20
363	Phil Plantier	.20
364	Shane Reynolds	.20
365	Todd Hollandsworth	.25
366	Eric Karros	.25
367	Ramon Martinez	.20
368	*Hideo Nomo*	3.00
369	Jose Offerman	.20
370	Antonio Osuna	.20
371	Todd Williams	.20
372	Shane Andrews	.20
373	Wil Cordero	.20
374	Jeff Fassero	.20
375	Darrin Fletcher	.20
376	*Mark Grudzielanek*	.60
377	*Carlos Perez*	.25
378	Mel Rojas	.20
379	Tony Tarasco	.20
380	Edgardo Alfonzo	.30
381	Brett Butler	.20
382	Carl Everett	.25
383	John Franco	.20
384	Pete Harnisch	.20
385	Bobby Jones	.20
386	Dave Mlicki	.20
387	Jose Vizcaino	.20
388	Ricky Bottalico	.20
389	Tyler Green	.20
390	Charlie Hayes	.20
391	Dave Hollins	.20
392	Gregg Jefferies	.25
393	*Michael Mimbs*	.20
394	Mickey Morandini	.20
395	Curt Schilling	.30
396	Heathcliff Slocumb	.20
397	Jason Christiansen	.20
398	Midre Cummings	.20
399	Carlos Garcia	.20
400	Mark Johnson	.25
401	Jeff King	.20
402	Jon Lieber	.20
403	Esteban Loaiza	.30
404	Orlando Merced	.20
405	*Gary Wilson*	.20
406	Scott Cooper	.20
407	Tom Henke	.20
408	Ken Hill	.20
409	Danny Jackson	.20
410	Brian Jordan	.30
411	Ray Lankford	.25
412	John Mabry	.20
413	Todd Zeile	.25
414	Andy Benes	.25
415	Andres Berumen	.20
416	Ken Caminiti	.30
417	Andujar Cedeno	.20
418	Steve Finley	.20
419	Joey Hamilton	.30
420	Dustin Hermanson	.25
421	Melvin Nieves	.20
422	Roberto Petagine	.20
423	Eddie Williams	.20
424	Glenallen Hill	.20
425	Kirt Manwaring	.20
426	Terry Mulholland	.20
427	J.R. Phillips	.20
428	Joe Rosselli	.20
429	Robby Thompson	.20
430	Checklist	.20
431	Checklist	.20
432	Checklist	.20

1995 Flair Cal Ripken, Jr. Enduring Flair

The career of Cal Ripken, Jr., is traced in this insert set found in Series 2 Flair at the average rate of once per dozen packs. Each card has a vintage photo on front, with a large silver-foil "ENDURING" logo toward bottom. Backs have another color photo, a quote and other information about the milestone. The series was extended by a special mail-in offer for five additional cards which chronicled Ripken's record-breaking 1995 season.

		MT
Complete Set (15):		50.00
Common Card:		3.50
1	Rookie Of The Year	3.50
2	1st MVP Season	3.50
3	World Series Highlight	3.50
4	Family Tradition	3.50
5	8,243 Consecutive Innings	3.50
6	95 Consecutive Errorless Games	3.50
7	All-Star MVP	3.50
8	1,000th RBI	3.50
9	287th Home Run	3.50
10	2,000th Consecutive Game	3.50
11	Record-tying Game	4.00
12	Record-breaking Game	4.00
13	Defensive Prowess	4.00
14	Literacy Work	4.00
15	2,153 and Counting	4.00

1995 Flair Hot Gloves

The cream of the crop among Series 2 Flair inserts is this set featuring fine fielders. Cards have a background of an embossed gold-foil glove, with a color player photo centered in front. Silver foil comprises the card title and player name at bottom and the Flair logo at top. Backs have a white background, a photo of a glove with a career summary overprinted and a player portrait photo in a lower corner. These inserts are found at the average rate of once per 25 packs.

		MT
Complete Set (12):		100.00
Common Player:		4.00
1	Roberto Alomar	7.50
2	Barry Bonds	9.00
3	Ken Griffey Jr.	30.00
4	Marquis Grissom	4.00
5	Barry Larkin	5.00
6	Darren Lewis	4.00
7	Kenny Lofton	7.50
8	Don Mattingly	12.50
9	Cal Ripken Jr.	25.00
10	Ivan Rodriguez	7.50
11	Devon White	4.00
12	Matt Williams	4.00

1995 Flair Hot Numbers

These Series 1 inserts are a 1:9 find. Gold metallic-foil background with 1994 seasonal stat numbers are the background for a color action photo on front. Horizontal backs have a ghosted portrait photo at right and career highlights at left.

		MT
Complete Set (10):		45.00
Common Player:		2.50
1	Jeff Bagwell	4.00
2	Albert Belle	3.00
3	Barry Bonds	3.00
4	Ken Griffey Jr.	12.00
5	Kenny Lofton	2.50
6	Greg Maddux	6.00
7	Mike Piazza	7.50
8	Cal Ripken Jr.	9.00
9	Frank Thomas	6.00
10	Matt Williams	2.50

1995 Flair Infield Power

Power rays and waves eminating from the player's bat in an action photo are the front design of this Series 2 chase set. The card title, name and team at bottom, and the Flair logo at top are in silver foil. Backs repeat the wave theme with a player photo on one end and a career summary at the other. These inserts are seeded at the average rate of one per five packs.

		MT
Complete Set (10):		8.00
Common Player:		.50
1	Jeff Bagwell	1.50
2	Darren Daulton	.50
3	Cecil Fielder	.50
4	Andres Galarraga	.50
5	Fred McGriff	.75
6	Rafael Palmeiro	.75
7	Mike Piazza	2.00
8	Frank Thomas	2.00
9	Mo Vaughn	1.00
10	Matt Williams	.50

1995 Flair Outfield Power

Laser-like colored rays are the background to the action photo on front and portrait on back of this series. The card title, player identification and Flair logo on front are in silver foil. Backs are horizontal, silver-foil enhanced and include a career summary. This chase set is seeded at the average rate of one card per six packs of Series 1 Flair.

		MT
Complete Set (10):		12.00
Common Player:		.50
1	Albert Belle	1.25
2	Dante Bichette	.75
3	Barry Bonds	1.25
4	Jose Canseco	1.25
5	Joe Carter	.50
6	Juan Gonzalez	2.50
7	Ken Griffey Jr.	6.00
8	Kirby Puckett	1.50
9	Gary Sheffield	.75
10	Ruben Sierra	.50

1995 Flair Today's Spotlight

The premier insert set in Flair Series I, found once every 30 packs or so, this die-cut issue has the player action photo spotlighted in a 2-3/8" bright spot, with the rest of the photo muted in gray and dark gray. The card title, Flair logo, player name and team are in silver foil. The horizontal backs have a portrait photo in the spotlight and career summary on the side.

		MT
Complete Set (12):		60.00
Common Player:		3.00
1	Jeff Bagwell	12.50
2	Jason Bere	3.00
3	Cliff Floyd	3.00
4	Chuck Knoblauch	6.00
5	Kenny Lofton	7.50
6	Javier Lopez	4.00
7	Raul Mondesi	5.00
8	Mike Mussina	6.00
9	Mike Piazza	20.00
10	Manny Ramirez	7.50
11	Tim Salmon	4.50
12	Frank Thomas	15.00

1995 Flair Wave Of The Future

The cream of baseball's rookie crop is featured in this Series 2 insert set, found once per eight packs on average. Fronts have a graduated color background with a baseball/wave morph, which is repeated at the bottom in silver foil, along with the player name. A color action photo is at center. The player's name, team and "Wave of the Future" are repeated in horizontal rows behind the photo. Horizontal backs repeat the wave logo, have another player photo and a career summary.

		MT
Complete Set (10):		20.00
Common Player:		.50
1	Jason Bates	.50
2	Armando Benitez	.75
3	Marty Cordova	.50
4	Ray Durham	1.50
5	Vaughn Eshelman	.50
6	Carl Everett	1.50
7	Shawn Green	5.00
8	Dustin Hermanson	1.50
9	Chipper Jones	12.00
10	Hideo Nomo	5.00

1996 Flair Promotional Sheet

Three samples of Flair's 1996 issue and an information card are included on this 5" x 7" promotional sheet.

	MT
Complete Sheet:	7.50
Manny Ramirez, Cal Ripken Jr., Matt Williams, Information card	

1996 Flair

Fleer's 1996 Flair baseball set has 400 cards, a parallel set and four insert types. Regular card fronts have two photos of the featured player; backs have a photo and career statistics. All cards have a silver-foil version and a gold-foil version, with each version appearing in equal numbers. Seven-card packs carried an issue price of $4.99.

		MT
Complete Set (400):		125.00
Common Player:		.25
Wax Box:		55.00
1	Roberto Alomar	2.00
2	Brady Anderson	.30
3	Bobby Bonilla	.30
4	Scott Erickson	.25
5	Jeffrey Hammonds	.25
6	Jimmy Haynes	.25
7	Chris Hoiles	.25
8	Kent Mercker	.25
9	Mike Mussina	1.50
10	Randy Myers	.25
11	Rafael Palmeiro	.50
12	Cal Ripken Jr.	8.00
(12p)	Cal Ripken Jr. (no card #, overprinted "PROMOTIONAL SAMPLE")	5.00
13	B.J. Surhoff	.30
14	David Wells	.30
15	Jose Canseco	.75
16	Roger Clemens	3.00
17	Wil Cordero	.25
18	Tom Gordon	.25
19	Mike Greenwell	.25
20	Dwayne Hosey	.25
21	Jose Malave	.25
22	Tim Naehring	.25
23	Troy O'Leary	.25
24	Aaron Sele	.25
25	Heathcliff Slocumb	.25
26	Mike Stanley	.25
27	Jeff Suppan	.25
28	John Valentin	.25
29	Mo Vaughn	2.00
30	Tim Wakefield	.25
31	Jim Abbott	.25
32	Garret Anderson	.25
33	George Arias	.25
34	Chili Davis	.25
35	Gary DiSarcina	.25
36	Jim Edmonds	.25
37	Chuck Finley	.25
38	Todd Greene	.25
39	Mark Langston	.25
40	Troy Percival	.25
41	Tim Salmon	.50
42	Lee Smith	.25
43	J.T. Snow	.30
44	Randy Velarde	.25
45	Tim Wallach	.25
46	Wilson Alvarez	.25
47	Harold Baines	.30
48	Jason Bere	.25
49	Ray Durham	.25
50	Alex Fernandez	.40
51	Ozzie Guillen	.25
52	Roberto Hernandez	.25
53	Ron Karkovice	.25
54	Darren Lewis	.25
55	Lyle Mouton	.25
56	Tony Phillips	.25
57	Chris Snopek	.25
58	Kevin Tapani	.25
59	Danny Tartabull	.25
60	Frank Thomas	5.00
61	Robin Ventura	.35
62	Sandy Alomar	.30
63	Carlos Baerga	.25
64	Albert Belle	2.50
65	Julio Franco	.25
66	Orel Hershiser	.25
67	Kenny Lofton	2.00
68	Dennis Martinez	.25
69	Jack McDowell	.25
70	Jose Mesa	.25
71	Eddie Murray	1.00
72	Charles Nagy	.25
73	Tony Pena	.25
74	Manny Ramirez	2.50
75	Julian Tavarez	.25
76	Jim Thome	1.00
77	Omar Vizquel	.25
78	Chad Curtis	.25
79	Cecil Fielder	.25
80	Travis Fryman	.25
81	Chris Gomez	.25
82	Bob Higginson	.40
83	Mark Lewis	.25
84	Felipe Lira	.25
85	Alan Trammell	.25
86	Kevin Appier	.25
87	Johnny Damon	.40
88	Tom Goodwin	.25
89	Mark Gubicza	.25
90	Bob Hamelin	.25
91	Keith Lockhart	.25
92	Jeff Montgomery	.25
93	Jon Nunnally	.25
94	Bip Roberts	.25
95	Michael Tucker	.25
96	Joe Vitiello	.25
97	Ricky Bones	.25
98	Chuck Carr	.25
99	Jeff Cirillo	.25
100	Mike Fetters	.25
101	John Jaha	.25
102	Mike Matheny	.25
103	Ben McDonald	.25
104	Matt Mieske	.25
105	Dave Nilsson	.25
106	Kevin Seitzer	.25
107	Steve Sparks	.25
108	Jose Valentin	.25
109	Greg Vaughn	.30
110	Rick Aguilera	.25
111	Rich Becker	.25
112	Marty Cordova	.25
113	LaTroy Hawkins	.25
114	Dave Hollins	.25
115	Roberto Kelly	.25
116	Chuck Knoblauch	.50
117	*Matt Lawton*	.25
118	Pat Meares	.25
119	Paul Molitor	1.50
120	Kirby Puckett	4.00
121	Brad Radke	.25
122	Frank Rodriguez	.25
123	Scott Stahoviak	.25
124	Matt Walbeck	.25
125	Wade Boggs	.55
126	David Cone	.40
127	Joe Girardi	.25
128	Dwight Gooden	.35
129	Derek Jeter	6.00
130	Jimmy Key	.25
131	Jim Leyritz	.25
132	Tino Martinez	.30
133	Paul O'Neill	.35
134	Andy Pettitte	2.00
135	Tim Raines	.25
136	Ruben Rivera	.75
137	Kenny Rogers	.25
138	Ruben Sierra	.25
139	John Wetteland	.25
140	Bernie Williams	2.00
141	Tony Batista	.25
142	Allen Battle	.25
143	Geronimo Berroa	.25
144	Mike Bordick	.25
145	Scott Brosius	.25
146	Steve Cox	.25
147	Brent Gates	.25
148	Jason Giambi	.40
149	Doug Johns	.25
150	Mark McGwire	10.00
151	Pedro Munoz	.25
152	Ariel Prieto	.25
153	Terry Steinbach	.25
154	Todd Van Poppel	.25
155	Bobby Ayala	.25
156	Chris Bosio	.25
157	Jay Buhner	.30
158	Joey Cora	.25
159	Russ Davis	.25
160	Ken Griffey Jr.	10.00
161	Sterling Hitchcock	.25
162	Randy Johnson	2.00
163	Edgar Martinez	.25
164	Alex Rodriguez	8.00
165	Paul Sorrento	.25
166	Dan Wilson	.25
167	Will Clark	.50
168	Benji Gil	.25
169	Juan Gonzalez	4.00
170	Rusty Greer	.25
171	Kevin Gross	.25
172	Darryl Hamilton	.25
173	Mike Henneman	.25
174	Ken Hill	.25
175	Mark McLemore	.25
176	Dean Palmer	.25
177	Roger Pavlik	.25
178	Ivan Rodriguez	2.00
179	Mickey Tettleton	.25
180	Bobby Witt	.25
181	Joe Carter	.30
182	Felipe Crespo	.25
183	Alex Gonzalez	.25
184	Shawn Green	.40
185	Juan Guzman	.25
186	Erik Hanson	.25
187	Pat Hentgen	.25
188	*Sandy Martinez*	.25
189	Otis Nixon	.25
190	John Olerud	.30
191	Paul Quantrill	.25
192	Bill Risley	.25
193	Ed Sprague	.25
194	Steve Avery	.25
195	Jeff Blauser	.25
196	Brad Clontz	.25
197	Jermaine Dye	.25
198	Tom Glavine	.40
199	Marquis Grissom	.25
200	Chipper Jones	6.00
201	David Justice	.50
202	Ryan Klesko	.50
203	Mark Lemke	.25
204	Javier Lopez	.40
205	Greg Maddux	6.00
206	Fred McGriff	1.00
207	Greg McMichael	.25
208	Wonderful Monds	.25
209	Jason Schmidt	.25
210	John Smoltz	.75
211	Mark Wohlers	.25
212	Jim Bullinger	.25
213	Frank Castillo	.25
214	Kevin Foster	.25
215	Luis Gonzalez	.25
216	Mark Grace	.40
217	*Robin Jennings*	.25
218	Doug Jones	.25
219	Dave Magadan	.25
220	Brian McRae	.25
221	Jaime Navarro	.25
222	Rey Sanchez	.25
223	Ryne Sandberg	2.00
224	Scott Servais	.25
225	Sammy Sosa	6.00
226	Ozzie Timmons	.25
227	Bret Boone	.25
228	Jeff Branson	.25
229	Jeff Brantley	.25
230	Dave Burba	.25
231	Vince Coleman	.25
232	Steve Gibralter	.25
233	Mike Kelly	.25
234	Barry Larkin	1.00
235	Hal Morris	.25
236	Mark Portugal	.25
237	Jose Rijo	.25
238	Reggie Sanders	.25
239	Pete Schourek	.25
240	John Smiley	.25
241	Eddie Taubensee	.25
242	Jason Bates	.25
243	Dante Bichette	1.00
244	Ellis Burks	.25
245	Vinny Castilla	.25
246	Andres Galarraga	.50
247	Darren Holmes	.25
248	Curt Leskanic	.25
249	Steve Reed	.25
250	Kevin Ritz	.25
251	Bret Saberhagen	.25
252	Bill Swift	.25
253	Larry Walker	.75
254	Walt Weiss	.25
255	Eric Young	.25
256	Kurt Abbott	.25
257	Kevin Brown	.25
258	John Burkett	.25
259	Greg Colbrunn	.25
260	Jeff Conine	.25
261	Andre Dawson	.30
262	Chris Hammond	.25
263	Charles Johnson	.25
264	Al Leiter	.25
265	Robb Nen	.25
266	Terry Pendleton	.25
267	Pat Rapp	.25
268	Gary Sheffield	1.50
269	Quilvio Veras	.25
270	Devon White	.25
271	Bob Abreu	.50
272	Jeff Bagwell	4.00
273	Derek Bell	.25
274	Sean Berry	.25
275	Craig Biggio	.35
276	Doug Drabek	.25
277	Tony Eusebio	.25
278	Richard Hidalgo	.25
279	Brian Hunter	.25
280	Todd Jones	.25
281	Derrick May	.25
282	Orlando Miller	.25
283	James Mouton	.25
284	Shane Reynolds	.25
285	Greg Swindell	.25
286	Mike Blowers	.25
287	Brett Butler	.25
288	Tom Candiotti	.25
289	Roger Cedeno	.25
290	Delino DeShields	.25
291	Greg Gagne	.25
292	Karim Garcia	1.00
293	Todd Hollandsworth	.25
294	Eric Karros	.25
295	Ramon Martinez	.25
296	Raul Mondesi	.75
297	Hideo Nomo	1.00
298	Mike Piazza	6.00
299	Ismael Valdes	.25
300	Todd Worrell	.25
301	Moises Alou	.25
302	Shane Andrews	.25
303	Yamil Benitez	.25
304	Jeff Fassero	.25
305	Darrin Fletcher	.25
306	Cliff Floyd	.25
307	Mark Grudzielanek	.25
308	Mike Lansing	.25
309	Pedro Martinez	.35
310	Ryan McGuire	.25
311	Carlos Perez	.25
312	Mel Rojas	.25
313	David Segui	.25
314	Rondell White	.25
315	Edgardo Alfonzo	.25
316	Rico Brogna	.25
317	Carl Everett	.25
318	John Franco	.25
319	Bernard Gilkey	.25
320	Todd Hundley	.40
321	Jason Isringhausen	.25
322	Lance Johnson	.25
323	Bobby Jones	.25
324	Jeff Kent	.25
325	Rey Ordonez	.75
326	Bill Pulsipher	.25
327	Jose Vizcaino	.25
328	Paul Wilson	.25
329	Ricky Bottalico	.25
330	Darren Daulton	.25
331	*David Doster*	.25
332	Lenny Dykstra	.25
333	Jim Eisenreich	.25
334	Sid Fernandez	.25
335	Gregg Jefferies	.25
336	Mickey Morandini	.25
337	Benito Santiago	.25
338	Curt Schilling	.30
339	Kevin Stocker	.25
340	David West	.25
341	Mark Whiten	.25
342	Todd Zeile	.25
343	Jay Bell	.25
344	John Ericks	.25
345	Carlos Garcia	.25
346	Charlie Hayes	.25
347	Jason Kendall	.25
348	Jeff King	.25
349	Mike Kingery	.25
350	Al Martin	.25
351	Orlando Merced	.25
352	Dan Miceli	.25
353	Denny Neagle	.25
354	Alan Benes	.25
355	Andy Benes	.25
356	Royce Clayton	.25
357	Dennis Eckersley	.25
358	Gary Gaetti	.25
359	Ron Gant	.30
360	Brian Jordan	.30
361	Ray Lankford	.25
362	John Mabry	.25
363	T.J. Mathews	.25
364	Mike Morgan	.25
365	Donovan Osborne	.25
366	Tom Pagnozzi	.25

367	Ozzie Smith	1.50
368	Todd Stottlemyre	.25
369	Andy Ashby	.25
370	Brad Ausmus	.25
371	Ken Caminiti	.75
372	Andujar Cedeno	.25
373	Steve Finley	.25
374	Tony Gwynn	4.00
375	Joey Hamilton	.25
376	Rickey Henderson	.35
377	Trevor Hoffman	.25
378	Wally Joyner	.25
379	Marc Newfield	.25
380	Jody Reed	.25
381	Bob Tewksbury	.25
382	Fernando Valenzuela	.25
383	Rod Beck	.25
384	Barry Bonds	2.50
385	Mark Carreon	.25
386	Shawon Dunston	.25
387	*Osvaldo Fernandez*	.40
388	Glenallen Hill	.25
389	Stan Javier	.25
390	Mark Leiter	.25
391	Kirt Manwaring	.25
392	Robby Thompson	.25
393	William VanLandingham	.25
394	Allen Watson	.25
395	Matt Williams	.75
396	Checklist	.25
397	Checklist	.25
398	Checklist	.25
399	Checklist	.25
400	Checklist	.25

1996 Flair Diamond Cuts

Ten of the game's top stars are showcased on these 1996 Flair inserts. They are seeded one per 20 packs. Fronts have a textured background rainbow metallic foil and silver glitter.

		MT
Complete Set (12):		90.00
Common Player:		2.50
1	Jeff Bagwell	7.50
2	Albert Belle	4.50
3	Barry Bonds	5.00
4	Juan Gonzalez	9.00
5	Ken Griffey Jr.	20.00
6	Greg Maddux	10.00
7	Eddie Murray	4.00
8	Mike Piazza	12.50
9	Cal Ripken Jr.	15.00
10	Frank Thomas	10.00
11	Mo Vaughn	4.00
12	Matt Williams	2.50

1996 Flair Hot Gloves

Ten top defensive players are highlighted on these die-cut insert cards, a design first made popular in 1994. Hot Gloves can only be found in hobby packs, at a rate of one per every 90 packs.

		MT
Complete Set (10):		225.00
Common Player:		10.00
1	Roberto Alomar	17.50
2	Barry Bonds	25.00
3	Will Clark	10.00
4	Ken Griffey Jr.	60.00
5	Kenny Lofton	20.00
6	Greg Maddux	40.00
7	Mike Piazza	45.00
8	Cal Ripken Jr.	50.00
9	Ivan Rodriguez	25.00
10	Matt Williams	10.00

1996 Flair Powerline

Ten of baseball's top sluggers are featured on these Flair inserts. They are the easiest of the Flair inserts to obtain; seeded one per six packs. Fronts combine yellow-green artwork with the player photo. Backs have a vertical color photo and career information.

		MT
Complete Set (10):		20.00
Common Player:		1.00
1	Albert Belle	1.50
2	Barry Bonds	1.75
3	Juan Gonzalez	2.00
4	Ken Griffey Jr.	7.50
5	Mark McGwire	7.50
6	Mike Piazza	4.00
7	Manny Ramirez	2.00
8	Sammy Sosa	3.50
9	Frank Thomas	3.50
10	Matt Williams	1.00

1996 Flair Wave of the Future

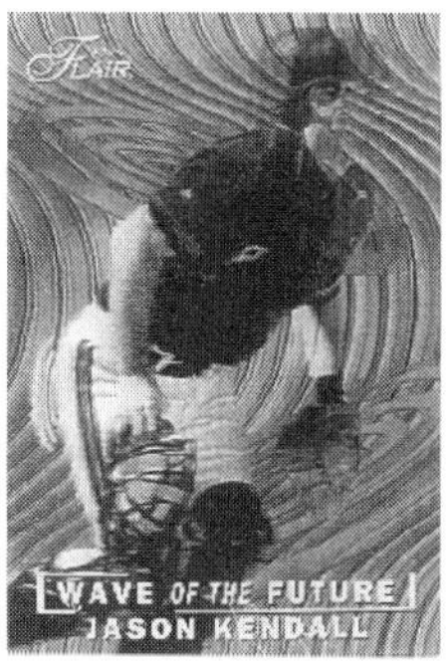

These inserts feature up-and-coming young talent in baseball. Twenty 1996 rookies and prospects are printed on lenticular cards. They are seeded one per every 72 packs.

		MT
Complete Set (20):		125.00
Common Player:		7.50
1	Bob Abreu	10.00
2	George Arias	7.50
3	Tony Batista	7.50
4	Alan Benes	12.50
5	Yamil Benitez	7.50
6	Steve Cox	7.50
7	David Doster	7.50
8	Jermaine Dye	7.50
9	Osvaldo Fernandez	7.50
10	Karim Garcia	10.00
11	Steve Gibralter	7.50
12	Todd Greene	12.50
13	Richard Hidalgo	9.00
14	Robin Jennings	7.50
15	Jason Kendall	17.50
16	Jose Malave	7.50
17	Wonderful Monds	7.50
18	Rey Ordonez	17.50
19	Ruben Rivera	9.00
20	Paul Wilson	7.50

1997 Flair Showcase Promo Strip

The concept of Flair Showcase's Style-Grace-Showcase set composition is debuted on this 7-1/2" x 3-1/2" strip featuring three cards of Alex Rodriguez. The cards are overprinted in gold on front and black on back with "PROMOTIONAL SAMPLE".

		MT
Complete Strip (3):		10.00
ROW0	Alex Rodriguez (Showcase)	
ROW1	Alex Rodriguez (Grace)	
ROW2	Alex Rodriguez (Style)	

1997 Flair Showcase Row 2 (Style)

The 540-card 1997 Flair issue is actually a 180-player set printed in three different versions, all on a super-glossy thick stock. The most common version, Style, is designated Row 2 on back. Fronts have a color action photo with a black-and-white portrait image in the background, all printed on silver foil. Cards #1-60 are designated "Showtime" on back; #61-120 are "Showpiece" and #121-180 are labeled "Showstopper" and were inserted in varying ratios: Showtime - 1.5:1; Showpiece 1:1.5 and Showstopper 1:1. Cards were sold exclusively at hobby shops in five-card packs for $4.99.

		MT
Complete Set (180):		40.00
Common Style/Showtime (1-60):		.20
Common Style/Showpiece (61-120):		.35
Common Style/Showstopper (121-180):		.25
A-Rod Glove Exchange:		250.00
Wax Box:		170.00
1	Andruw Jones	1.50
2	Derek Jeter	3.00
3	Alex Rodriguez	4.00
4	Paul Molitor	1.00
5	Jeff Bagwell	1.50
6	Scott Rolen	1.50
7	Kenny Lofton	1.00
8	Cal Ripken Jr.	4.00
9	Brady Anderson	.20
10	Chipper Jones	3.00
11	Todd Greene	.20
12	Todd Walker	.50
13	Billy Wagner	.30
14	Craig Biggio	.75
15	Kevin Orie	.20
16	Hideo Nomo	.50
17	Kevin Appier	.20
18	*Bubba Trammell*	1.00
19	Juan Gonzalez	1.50
20	Randy Johnson	1.00
21	Roger Clemens	1.50
22	Johnny Damon	.25
23	Ryne Sandberg	1.00
24	Ken Griffey Jr.	5.00
25	Barry Bonds	1.50
26	Nomar Garciaparra	3.00
27	Vladimir Guerrero	2.00
28	Ron Gant	.20
29	Joe Carter	.20
30	Tim Salmon	.75
31	Mike Piazza	3.00
32	Barry Larkin	.75
33	Manny Ramirez	1.50
34	Sammy Sosa	3.00
35	Frank Thomas	1.50
36	Melvin Nieves	.20
37	Tony Gwynn	2.50
38	Gary Sheffield	.50
39	Darin Erstad	1.50
40	Ken Caminiti	.50
41	Jermaine Dye	.20
42	Mo Vaughn	1.25
43	Raul Mondesi	.50
44	Greg Maddux	3.00
45	Chuck Knoblauch	.75
46	Andy Pettitte	.75
47	Deion Sanders	.50
48	Albert Belle	1.00
49	Jamey Wright	.20
50	Rey Ordonez	.35
51	Bernie Williams	1.00
52	Mark McGwire	6.00
53	Mike Mussina	1.00
54	Bob Abreu	.25
55	Reggie Sanders	.20
56	Brian Jordan	.20
57	Ivan Rodriguez	1.50
58	Roberto Alomar	1.00
59	Tim Naehring	.20
60	Edgar Renteria	.25
61	Dean Palmer	.35
62	Benito Santiago	.35
63	David Cone	.50
64	Carlos Delgado	1.00
65	*Brian Giles*	2.00
66	Alex Ochoa	.35
67	Rondell White	.35
68	Robin Ventura	.50
69	Eric Karros	.35
70	Jose Valentin	.35
71	Rafael Palmeiro	.75
72	Chris Snopek	.35
73	David Justice	.75
74	Tom Glavine	.50
75	Rudy Pemberton	.35
76	Larry Walker	1.00
77	Jim Thome	1.00
78	Charles Johnson	.35
79	Dante Powell	.35
80	Derrek Lee	.35
81	Jason Kendall	.35
82	Todd Hollandsworth	.35
83	Bernard Gilkey	.35
84	Mel Rojas	.35
85	Dmitri Young	.35
86	Bret Boone	.35
87	Pat Hentgen	.35
88	Bobby Bonilla	.35
89	John Wetteland	.35
90	Todd Hundley	.25
91	Wilton Guerrero	.25
92	Geronimo Berroa	.35
93	Al Martin	.35
94	Danny Tartabull	.35
95	Brian McRae	.35
96	Steve Finley	.35
97	Todd Stottlemyre	.35
98	John Smoltz	.40
99	Matt Williams	1.00
100	Eddie Murray	1.00
101	Henry Rodriguez	.35
102	Marty Cordova	.35
103	Juan Guzman	.35
104	Ohili Davis	.05
105	Eric Young	.35
106	Jeff Abbott	.35
107	Shannon Stewart	.35
108	Rocky Coppinger	.35
109	Jose Canseco	1.00
110	Dante Bichette	.75
111	Dwight Gooden	.35
112	Scott Brosius	.35
113	Steve Avery	.35
114	Andres Galarraga	.75
115	Sandy Alomar Jr.	.40
116	Ray Lankford	.35
117	Jorge Posada	.35
118	Ryan Klesko	.40
119	Jay Buhner	.50
120	Jose Guillen	.40
121	Paul O'Neill	.50
122	Jimmy Key	.25
123	Hal Morris	.25
124	Travis Fryman	.25
125	Jim Edmonds	.25
126	Jeff Cirillo	.25
127	Fred McGriff	.50
128	Alan Benes	.35
129	Derek Bell	.25
130	Tony Graffanino	.25
131	Shawn Green	.75
132	Denny Neagle	.25
133	Alex Fernandez	.25
134	Mickey Morandini	.25
135	Royce Clayton	.25
136	Jose Mesa	.25
137	Edgar Martinez	.25
138	Curt Schilling	.50
139	Lance Johnson	.25
140	Andy Benes	.25
141	Charles Nagy	.25
142	Mariano Rivera	.50
143	Mark Wohlers	.25
144	Ken Hill	.25
145	Jay Bell	.25
146	Bob Higginson	.40
147	Mark Grudzielanek	.25
148	Ray Durham	.25
149	John Olerud	.50
150	Joey Hamilton	.25
151	Trevor Hoffman	.30
152	Dan Wilson	.25
153	J.T. Snow	.25
154	Marquis Grissom	.40
155	Yamil Benitez	.25
156	Rusty Greer	.25
157	Darryl Kile	.25
158	Ismael Valdes	.25
159	Jeff Conine	.25
160	Darren Daulton	.25
161	Chan Ho Park	.25
162	Troy Percival	.25
163	Wade Boggs	.75
164	Dave Nilsson	.25
165	Vinny Castilla	.25
166	Kevin Brown	.40
167	Dennis Eckersley	.25
168	Wendell Magee Jr.	.25
169	John Jaha	.25
170	Garret Anderson	.25
171	Jason Giambi	.25
172	Mark Grace	.50
173	Tony Clark	.75
174	Moises Alou	.40
175	Brett Butler	.25
176	Cecil Fielder	.25
177	Chris Widger	.25
178	Doug Drabek	.25
179	Ellis Burks	.25
180	Shigetosi Hasegawa	.25

1997 Flair Showcase Row 1 (Grace)

The second level of '97 Flair scarcity is represented by the Row 1/Grace cards (so designated on back). These are visually differentiated on front by the use of a full background to the action photo, and the addition of a color portrait. Row 1/Grace cards are further broken down by their designation on back as: "Showstopper" (#1-60; seeded 1:2.5 packs), "Showtime" (#61-120; 1:2) and "Showpiece" (#121-180; 1:3) with varying insertion rates as shown.

	MT
Complete Set (180):	150.00
Common Showstopper (1-60):	.50
Stars: 2X	
Common Showtime (#61-120):	.35
Stars: 1X	
Common Showpiece (#121-180):	.75
Stars: 2X	

(See 1997 Flair Showcase Row 2 for checklist and base card values.)

1997 Flair Showcase Row 0 (Showcase)

The scarcest level of '97 Flair is the Row 0/Showcase cards (so designated on front and back). These are identifiable on front by the use of a color portrait in the foreground, with a large action photo behind, printed on a gold-flecked metallic background. Row 0/Showcase cards are further broken down by their designation on back as: "Showpiece" (#1-60; seeded 1:24 packs), "Showstopper" (#61-120; 1:12) and "Showtime" (#121-180; 1:5) with varying insertion rates as shown.

	MT
Complete Set (180):	950.00
Common Showpiece (1-60):	3.00
Stars: 10X	
Common Showstopper (61-120):	1.50
Stars: 4X	
Common Showtime (121-180):	.50
Stars: 3X	

(See 1997 Flair Showcase Row 2 for checklist and base card values.)

1997 Flair Showcase Legacy Collection

This 540-card parallel set is printed on matte-finish stock rather than the high-gloss of the regular cards. Front graphic highlights are in blue foil, as is the serial number on back from within each card's edition of just 100. Stated odds of insertion are one per 30 packs. Because all Legacies are printed in identical numbers, there is no premium for cards of different rows.

	MT
Common Player:	10.00
Stars: 25-50X	

(See 1997 Flair Showcase Row 2 for checkist and base card values.)

1997 Flair Showcase Legacy Masterpiece

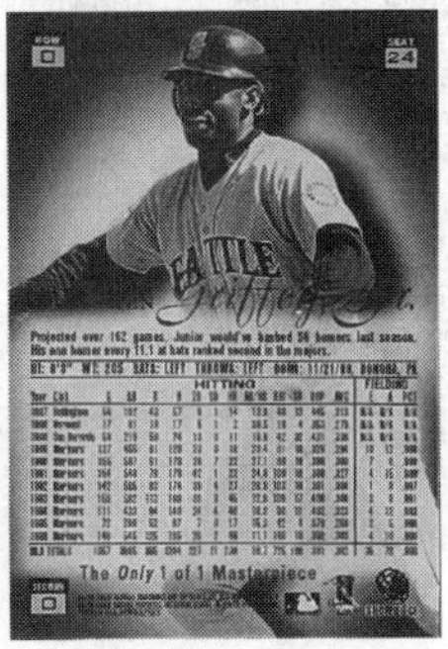

The insert card chase reached its inevitable zenith with the creation of this series of one-of-a-kind inserts. Each of the 180 players' three cards (Row 2/Style, Row 1/Grace, Row 0/Showcase) in the '97 Flair Legacy Collection was also produced in an edition of one card and inserted at a rate of about one per 3,000 packs. Instead of the blue metallic foil on front and highlights on back of the regular Legacy cards, the one-of-a-kind cards are highlighted in purple and carry a notation on back that they are "The Only 1 of 1 Masterpiece". Because of the unique nature of each card, value depends solely on demand, thus presentation of meaningful "catalog" values is not possible.

	MT
Common Player:	100.00
Stars: 15x to 25x (Values undetermined)	

1997 Flair Showcase Diamond Cuts

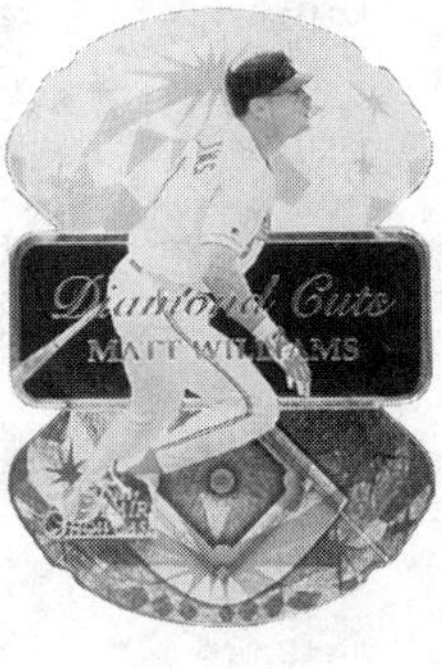

This 20-card insert, found 1:20 packs, features a die-cut design with an action photo of the player appearing above a baseball diamond in the lower background.

		MT
Complete Set (20):		130.00
Common Player:		2.50
1	Jeff Bagwell	7.50
2	Albert Belle	5.00
3	Ken Caminiti	2.50
4	Juan Gonzalez	9.00
5	Ken Griffey Jr.	15.00
6	Tony Gwynn	9.00
7	Todd Hundley	2.50
8	Andruw Jones	5.00
9	Chipper Jones	12.00
10	Greg Maddux	10.00
11	Mark McGwire	15.00
12	Mike Piazza	12.00
13	Derek Jeter	12.00
14	Manny Ramirez	5.00
15	Cal Ripken Jr.	12.50
16	Alex Rodriguez	12.50
17	Frank Thomas	7.50
18	Mo Vaughn	4.00
19	Bernie Williams	4.00
20	Matt Williams	2.50

1997 Flair Showcase Hot Gloves

Inserted 1:90 packs, Hot Gloves features 15 cards with a die-cut "flaming glove" design printed in thermally active inks and saluting some of baseball's best defensive players.

		MT
Complete Set (15):		275.00
Common Player:		5.00
1	Roberto Alomar	10.00
2	Barry Bonds	12.50
3	Juan Gonzalez	25.00
4	Ken Griffey Jr.	50.00
5	Marquis Grissom	5.00
6	Derek Jeter	30.00
7	Chipper Jones	30.00
8	Barry Larkin	5.00
9	Kenny Lofton	10.00
10	Greg Maddux	25.00
11	Mike Piazza	30.00
12	Cal Ripken Jr.	40.00
13	Alex Rodriguez	35.00
14	Ivan Rodriguez	12.50
15	Frank Thomas	25.00

1997 Flair Showcase Wave of the Future

This insert focuses on some of the up-and-coming young stars in the game. Cards were seeded 1:4 packs. A large ocean wave makes up the background of each card front.

		MT
Complete Set (27):		45.00
Common Player:		1.00
1	Todd Greene	1.25
2	Andruw Jones	5.00
3	Randall Simon	1.00
4	Wady Almonte	1.00
5	Pat Cline	1.50
6	Jeff Abbott	1.00
7	Justin Towle	1.00
8	Richie Sexson	1.50
9	Bubba Trammell	2.50
10	Bob Abreu	1.50
11	David Arias (last name actually Ortiz)	2.00
12	Todd Walker	3.00
13	Orlando Cabrera	1.00
14	Vladimir Guerrero	5.00
15	Ricky Ledee	3.00
16	Jorge Posada	2.00
17	Ruben Rivera	1.25
18	Scott Spiezio	1.00
19	Scott Rolen	5.00
20	Emil Brown	1.00
21	Jose Guillen	2.50
22	T.J. Staton	1.00
23	Elieser Marrero	1.00
24	Fernando Tatis	2.50
25	Ryan Jones	1.00
WF1	Hideki Irabu	3.00
WF2	Jose Cruz Jr.	2.50

1998 Flair Showcase Promo Strip

Each of the Row 0, 1, 2 and 3 variations of Cal Ripken's cards are featured on this 10" x 3-1/2" promo strip. The front of each card has "PROMOTIONAL SAMPLE" printed diagonally in gold; on the back the notice is printed in black-and-white.

	MT
Complete Promo Strip: Cal Ripken Jr.	10.00

1998 Flair Showcase Row 3

Row 3, or Flair, cards are considered the base cards of '98 Showcase. They feature a close-up black-and-white portrait photo in the background and an action shot in front, overprinted on a silver-foil background. Flair/Showtime (#1-30) cards are inserted 1:.9 packs, Flair/Showstopper (#31-60) are found 1:1.1 packs, Flair/Showdown (#61-90) cards are inserted 1:1.5 packs and Flair/Showdown (#91-120) cards are inserted 1:2 packs.

		MT
Complete Set (120):		30.00
Common Player (1-30):		.25
Common Player (31-60):		.25
Common Player (61-90):		.35
Common Player (91-120):		.45
1	Ken Griffey Jr.	6.00
2	Travis Lee	1.25
3	Frank Thomas	3.00
4	Ben Grieve	2.00
5	Nomar Garciaparra	4.00
6	Jose Cruz Jr.	.40
7	Alex Rodriguez	4.00
8	Cal Ripken Jr.	5.00
9	Mark McGwire	8.00
10	Chipper Jones	3.00
11	Paul Konerko	1.00
12	Todd Helton	1.50
13	Greg Maddux	4.00
14	Derek Jeter	4.00
15	Jaret Wright	1.00
16	Livan Hernandez	.25
17	Mike Piazza	4.00
18	Juan Encarnacion	.25
19	Tony Gwynn	3.00
20	Scott Rolen	2.00
21	Roger Clemens	3.00
22	Tony Clark	1.00
23	Albert Belle	1.50
24	Mo Vaughn	1.50
25	Andruw Jones	1.50
26	Jason Dickson	.25
27	Fernando Tatis	.50
28	Ivan Rodriguez	1.50
29	Ricky Ledee	.50
30	Darin Erstad	1.50
31	Brian Rose	.25
32	*Magglio Ordonez*	5.00
33	Larry Walker	1.00
34	Bobby Higginson	.25
35	Chili Davis	.25
36	Barry Bonds	1.50
37	Vladimir Guerrero	2.00
38	Jeff Bagwell	1.50
39	Kenny Lofton	1.50
40	Ryan Klesko	.50
41	Mike Cameron	.25
42	Charles Johnson	.25
43	Andy Pettitte	1.00
44	Juan Gonzalez	3.00
45	Tim Salmon	1.00
46	Hideki Irabu	.75
47	Paul Molitor	1.00
48	Edgar Renteria	.25
49	Manny Ramirez	2.00
50	Jim Edmonds	.50
51	Bernie Williams	1.00
52	Roberto Alomar	1.00
53	David Justice	.50
54	Rey Ordonez	.25
55	Ken Caminiti	.50
56	Jose Guillen	.50
57	Randy Johnson	1.00
58	Brady Anderson	.25
59	Hideo Nomo	.50
60	Tino Martinez	1.00
61	John Smoltz	.50
62	Joe Carter	.50
63	Matt Williams	.50
64	Robin Ventura	.50
65	Barry Larkin	.50
66	Dante Bichette	.75
67	Travis Fryman	.35
68	Gary Sheffield	.75
69	Eric Karros	.40
70	Matt Stairs	.35
71	Al Martin	.35
72	Jay Buhner	.60
73	Ray Lankford	.35
74	Carlos Delgado	.50
75	Edgardo Alfonzo	.50
76	Rondell White	.50
77	Chuck Knoblauch	.75
78	Raul Mondesi	.50
79	Johnny Damon	.35
80	Matt Morris	.35
81	Tom Glavine	.50
82	Kevin Brown	.50
83	Garret Anderson	.35
84	Mike Mussina	1.00
85	Pedro Martinez	1.00
86	Craig Biggio	.50
87	Darryl Kile	.35
88	Rafael Palmeiro	.75
89	Jim Thome	1.00
90	Andres Galarraga	1.00
91	Sammy Sosa	4.00
92	Willie Greene	.45
93	Vinny Castilla	.60
94	Justin Thompson	.45
95	Jeff King	.45
96	Jeff Cirillo	.45
97	Mark Grudzielanek	.45
98	Brad Radke	.45
99	John Olerud	.75
100	Curt Schilling	.60
101	Steve Finley	.45
102	J.T. Snow	.45
103	Edgar Martinez	.45
104	Wilson Alvarez	.45
105	Rusty Greer	.45
106	Pat Hentgen	.45
107	David Cone	.50
108	Fred McGriff	.50
109	Jason Giambi	.45
110	Tony Womack	.45
111	Bernard Gilkey	.45
112	Alan Benes	.45
113	Mark Grace	.50
114	Reggie Sanders	.45
115	Moises Alou	.50
116	John Jaha	.45
117	Henry Rodriguez	.45
118	Dean Palmer	.45
119	Mike Lieberthal	.50
120	Shawn Estes	.45

1998 Flair Showcase Row 2

Row 2, or Style (as they are designated on front) cards in Flair Showcase are the second easiest type of card to pull from packs. Fronts are similar to Row 3 base cards, but include the entire background of the action photo and have a color portrait photo. Cards #1-30 are inserted one per three packs, #31-60 are found 1:2.5 packs, #61-90 cards are 1:4 and #91-120 are inserted one per three packs.

	MT
Complete Set (120):	75.00
Common Player (1-30):	.50
Stars: 2X	
Common Player (31-60):	.50
Stars: 1.5X	
Common Player (61-90):	.75
Stars: 2X	
Common Player (91-120):	.75
Stars: 1.5X	

(See 1998 Flair Showcase Row 3 for checklist and base card values.)

1998 Flair Showcase Row 1

Row 1, also referred to as Grace, was the second most difficult type of card to pull from Flair Showcase. The front design has an action photo overprinted on a large portrait which is printed on a rainbow metallic-foil background. Cards #1-30 are seeded one per 16 packs, #31-60 are 1:24, #61-90 are 1:6 and #91-120 are 1:10.

	MT
Complete Set (1-120):	400.00
Commons (1-30):	2.00
Stars: 4X	
Commons (31-60):	2.50
Stars: 6X	
Commons (61-90):	.75
Stars: 2X	
Commons (91-120):	1.50
Stars: 3X	

(See 1998 Flair Showcase Row 3 for checklist and base cards values.)

1998 Flair Showcase Row 0

Row 0 is the most difficult of the four tiers to obtain from packs. Two action photos are combined on a horizontal format with one in a prismatic foil background. The first 30 cards are serially numbered to 250, cards #30-60 are numbered to 500, #61-90 are numbered to 1,000 and #91-120 are numbered within an edition of 2,000.

	MT
Complete Set (120):	1500.
Common Player (1-30):	5.00
Stars: 20X	
Common Player (31-60):	3.00
Stars: 15X	
Common Player (61-90):	2.00
Stars: 9X	
Common Player (91-120):	1.00
Stars: 5X	

(See 1998 Flair Showcase Row 3 for checklist and base card values.)

1998 Flair Showcase Legacy Collection

Legacy Collection parallels all 480 cards in the Flair Showcase set. Each Legacy Collection card displays the player's name in black plate laminated on the back, with the card's sequential numbering to 100 in gold foil.

	MT
Common Player:	6.00
Stars: 15-25X	

(See 1998 Flair Showcase Row 3 for checklist and base card values.)

1998 Flair Showcase Legacy Masterpiece

Each of the 120 players' four cards (Rows 3, 2, 1 and 0) in the '98 Flair Legacy Collection was also produced in an edition of one card and inserted at a rate of about one per 3,000 packs. The one-of-a-kind cards carry a notation on back: "The Only 1 of 1 Masterpiece". With supply a fixed quantity, value depends on demand at any particular time, thus it is not possible to present meaningful "catalog" values.

	MT
Common Player:	100.00
(Values undetermined)	

1998 Flair Showcase Perfect 10

Perfect 10 features the game's most popular players on a silk-screen technology design. The cards were serial numbered to 10 on the back and were inserted into packs of Flair Showcase.

		MT
Complete Set (10):		6000.
Common Player:		150.00
1	Ken Griffey Jr.	1250.
2	Cal Ripken Jr.	1000.
3	Frank Thomas	450.00
4	Mike Piazza	750.00
5	Greg Maddux	600.00
6	Nomar Garciaparra	750.00
7	Mark McGwire	1200.
8	Scott Rolen	150.00
9	Alex Rodriguez	1000.
10	Roger Clemens	300.00

1998 Flair Showcase Wave of the Future

Twelve up-and-coming players with hot minor league stats and Major League potential are displayed in Wave of the Future. The cards contain a clear acetate card inside a plastic covering that is filled with vegetable oil and glitter. These were inserted one per 20 packs and are numbered with a "WF" prefix.

	MT
Complete Set (12):	25.00
Common Player:	1.00
WF1 Travis Lee	10.00
WF2 Todd Helton	0.00
WF3 Ben Grieve	7.50
WF4 Juan Encarnacion	1.00
WF5 Brad Fullmer	3.00
WF6 Ruben Rivera	1.00
WF7 Paul Konerko	2.50
WF8 Derrek Lee	1.00
WF9 Mike Lowell	1.00
WF10 Magglio Ordonez	2.00
WF11 Rich Butler	2.00
WF12 Eli Marrero	1.00

1999 Flair Showcase Row 3 (Power)

Power is one of three tiers in 1999 in Showcase. The card front on this base-level version is rainbow holofoil including the large portrait photo in the background. In the foreground is a color action photo. Matte textured silver spot embossing is printed over the player's name and team at lower-right. All three Rows of Showcase can be found with three different back designs. Showtime presents traditional annual and career stats; horizontally formatted Showpiece cards have a black-and-white player photo as a "Classic Matchup" of the player's stats to those of a past star. Showdown card backs have a color action photo on a brightly-colored wave-pattern background. A stat box at center offers career numbers broken-down into four unique categories like day-night, grass-turf, etc. Each of these three back-design levels of scarcity has a different advertised insertion rate. Within Row 3/Power, these vary only between one card in .9 packs, and one card in 1.2 packs, thus there is no practical value differential. Five-card packs of Flair Showcase had a $4.99 SRP.

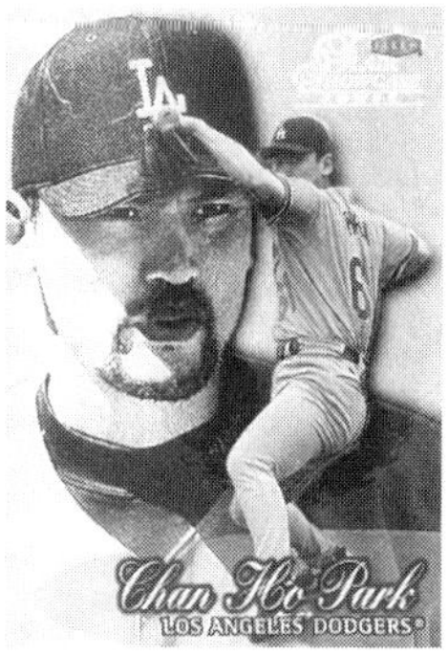

		MT
Complete Set (144):		35.00
Common Player:		.25
Wax box:		80.00
1	Mark McGwire	6.00
2	Sammy Sosa	3.00
3	Ken Griffey Jr.	5.00
4	Chipper Jones	2.50
5	Ben Grieve	1.00
6	J.D. Drew	1.50
7	Jeff Bagwell	1.25
8	Cal Ripken Jr.	4.00
9	Tony Gwynn	2.50
10	Nomar Garciaparra	3.00
11	Travis Lee	1.00
12	Troy Glaus	2.00
13	Mike Piazza	3.00
14	Alex Rodriguez	3.00
15	Kevin Brown	.50
16	Darin Erstad	1.00
17	Scott Rolen	1.50
18	*Micah Bowie*	.75
19	Juan Gonzalez	2.50
20	Kerry Wood	1.00
21	Roger Clemens	2.00
22	Derek Jeter	3.00
23	*Pat Burrell*	10.00
24	Tim Salmon	.75
25	Barry Bonds	1.25
26	*Roosevelt Brown*	1.00
27	Vladimir Guerrero	2.00
28	Randy Johnson	1.00
29	Mo Vaughn	1.00
30	Fernando Seguignol	.25
31	Greg Maddux	3.00
32	Tony Clark	.75
33	Eric Chavez	.50
34	Kris Benson	.25
35	Frank Thomas	2.00
36	Mario Encarnacion	.25
37	Gabe Kapler	1.25
38	Jeremy Giambi	.40
39	*Peter Tucci*	.75
40	Manny Ramirez	2.00
41	Albert Belle	1.25
42	Warren Morris	.25
43	Michael Barrett	1.00
44	Andruw Jones	1.25
45	Carlos Delgado	.75
46	Jaret Wright	.50
47	Juan Encarnacion	.40
48	Scott Hunter	.75
49	Tino Martinez	.75
50	Craig Biggio	.75
51	Jim Thome	.75
52	Vinny Castilla	.40
53	Tom Glavine	.40
54	Bob Higginson	.25
55	Moises Alou	.40
56	Robin Ventura	.25
57	Bernie Williams	1.00
58	Pedro J. Martinez	1.25
59	Greg Vaughn	.40
60	Ray Lankford	.25
61	Jose Canseco	1.00
62	Ivan Rodriguez	1.25
63	Shawn Green	.75
64	Rafael Palmeiro	.75
65	Ellis Burks	.25
66	Jason Kendall	.50
67	David Wells	.25
68	Rondell White	.40
69	Gary Sheffield	.40
70	Ken Caminiti	.25
71	Cliff Floyd	.25
72	Larry Walker	1.00
73	Bartolo Colon	.25
74	Barry Larkin	.75
75	Calvin Pickering	.25
76	Jim Edmonds	.25
77	Henry Rodriguez	.25
78	Roberto Alomar	1.00
79	Andres Galarraga	.75
80	Richie Sexson	.50
81	Todd Helton	.75
82	Damion Easley	.25
83	Livan Hernandez	.25
84	Carlos Beltran	3.00
85	Todd Hundley	.25
86	Todd Walker	.25
87	Scott Brosius	.25
88	Bob Abreu	.25
89	Corey Koskie	.25
90	Ruben Rivera	.25
91	Edgar Renteria	.25
92	Quinton McCracken	.25
93	Bernard Gilkey	.25
94	Shannon Stewart	.25
95	Dustin Hermanson	.25
96	Mike Caruso	.25
97	Alex Gonzalez	.25
98	Raul Mondesi	.40
99	David Cone	.50
100	Curt Schilling	.40
101	Brian Giles	.25
102	Edgar Martinez	.25
103	Rolando Arrojo	.25
104	Derek Bell	.25
105	Denny Neagle	.25
106	Marquis Grissom	.25
107	Bret Boone	.25
108	Mike Mussina	1.00
109	John Smoltz	.25
110	Brett Tomko	.25
111	David Justice	.50
112	Andy Pettitte	.40
113	Eric Karros	.25
114	Dante Bichette	.75
115	Jeromy Burnitz	.25
116	Paul Konerko	.25
117	Steve Finley	.25
118	Ricky Ledee	.50
119	Edgardo Alfonzo	.25
120	Dean Palmer	.25
121	Rusty Greer	.25
122	Luis Gonzalez	.25
123	Randy Winn	.25
124	Jeff Kent	.25
125	Doug Glanville	.25
126	Justin Thompson	.25
127	Bret Saberhagen	.25
128	Wade Boggs	.75
129	Al Leiter	.25
130	Paul O'Neill	.75
131	Chan Ho Park	.50
132	Johnny Damon	.25
133	Darryl Kile	.25
134	Reggie Sanders	.25
135	Kevin Millwood	.75
136	Charles Johnson	.25
137	Ray Durham	.25
138	Rico Brogna	.25
139	Matt Williams	.75
140	Sandy Alomar	.25
141	Jeff Cirillo	.25
142	Devon White	.25
143	Andy Benes	.25
144	Mike Stanley	.25
	Checklist card	.05

1999 Flair Showcase Row 1 (Showcase)

Showcase level - Row 1 - presents two portraits and an action photo and the player's uniform number on a plastic laminate in a horizontal format. A gold-foil serial number is stamped into the upper-left corner in one of three levels of scarcity: Showpiece (#1-48) is limited to 1,500 numbered sets, Showtime (#49-96) is limited to 3,000 sets and Showdown (#97-144) is numbered to 6,000 sets.

	MT
Complete Set (144):	800.00
Common Showpiece (1-48):	2.00
Showpiece Stars: 7X	
Common Showtime (49-96):	1.00
Showtime Stars: 5X	
Common Showdown (97-144):	.75
Showdown Stars: 2X	

(See 1999 Flair Showcase Row 1 for checklist and base card values.)

1999 Flair Showcase Row 2 (Passion)

The metallic-foil background in the second level of Flair Showcase - Row 2/Passion - has an action photo printed in front of large textured numerals representing the player's uniform number. In the foreground is another action shot. Backs have the same three designs as Row 3, but only vary in insertion rate from one card per 1.3 packs to one card per three packs.

	MT
Complete Set:	100.00
Common Player:	.25
Showdown (1-48): 2X	
Showpiece (49-96): 1X	
Showtime (97-144): 1X	

(See 1999 Flair Showcase Row 3 for checklist and base card values.)

1999 Flair Showcase Legacy / Masterpiece

Each of the 402 total cards in Flair Showcase was also produced in a pair of extremely limited parallels. The blue-foil enhanced Legacy Collection cards are serially numbered within an edition of just 99. The presence of purple foil on front signifies a Legacy Masterpiece card, which is identified on back by the notation, "The Only 1 of 1 Masterpiece". Because of their unique nature, determination of a "book value" for Masterpiece cards is not possible.

	MT
Common Legacy:	4.00
Legacy Stars: 15x to 20x	
Common Masterpiece:	75.00
(See 1999 Flair Showcase for checklist.)	

1999 Flair Showcase Measure of Greatness

This 15-card set captures baseball's top superstars who were closing in on milestones during the 1999 season. Each card is sequentially numbered to 500.

		MT
Complete Set (15):		350.00
Common Player:		10.00
Production 500 sets		
1	Roger Clemens	15.00
2	Nomar Garciaparra	20.00
3	Juan Gonzalez	15.00
4	Ken Griffey Jr.	50.00
5	Vladimir Guerrero	10.00
6	Tony Gwynn	15.00
7	Derek Jeter	25.00
8	Chipper Jones	25.00
9	Mark McGwire	50.00
10	Mike Piazza	25.00
11	Manny Ramirez	10.00
12	Cal Ripken Jr.	35.00
13	Alex Rodriguez	30.00
14	Sammy Sosa	25.00
15	Frank Thomas	10.00

1999 Flair Showcase Wave of the Future

This insert set spotlights young stars on the rise and is limited to 1,000 serial numbered sets.

		MT
Complete Set (15):		85.00
Common Player:		3.00
Production 1,000 sets		
1	Kerry Wood	5.00
2	Ben Grieve	5.00
3	J.D. Drew	10.00
4	Juan Encarnacion	4.00
5	Travis Lee	5.00
6	Todd Helton	5.00
7	Troy Glaus	10.00
8	Ricky Ledee	3.00
9	Eric Chavez	7.50
10	Ben Davis	3.00
11	George Lombard	4.00
12	Jeremy Giambi	4.00
13	Roosevelt Brown	4.00
14	Pat Burrell	25.00
15	Preston Wilson	3.00

1981 Fleer

For the first time in 18 years, Fleer issued a baseball card set featuring current players. The 660-card effort included numerous errors in the first print run which were subsequently corrected. The 2-1/2" x 3-1/2" cards are numbered by team in order of the previous season's finish. Card fronts feature a full-color photo inside a border which is color-coded by team. Backs are printed in black, grey and yellow on white stock and carry full player statistical information. The player's batting average or earned run average is located in a circle in the upper-right corner of the back. The complete set price in the checklist that follows does not include the higher priced variations.

		MT
Complete Set (660):		50.00
Common Player:		.08
Wax Box:		60.00
1	Pete Rose	2.50
2	Larry Bowa	.10
3	Manny Trillo	.08
4	Bob Boone	.10
5a	Mike Schmidt (portrait)	2.00
5b	Mike Schmidt (batting)	2.00
6a	Steve Carlton ("Lefty" on front)	1.00
6b	Steve Carlton (Pitcher of the Year on front, date 1066 on back)	2.00
6c	Steve Carlton (Pitcher of the Year on front, date 1966 on back)	3.00
7a	Tug McGraw (Game Saver on front)	.50
7b	Tug McGraw (Pitcher on front)	.12
8	Larry Christenson	.08
9	Bake McBride	.08
10	Greg Luzinski	.15
11	Ron Reed	.08
12	Dickie Noles	.08
13	*Keith Moreland*	.08
14	*Bob Walk*	.10
15	Lonnie Smith	.08
16	Dick Ruthven	.08
17	Sparky Lyle	.10
18	Greg Gross	.08
19	Garry Maddox	.10
20	Nino Espinosa	.08
21	George Vukovich	.08
22	John Vukovich	.08
23	Ramon Aviles	.08
24a	Kevin Saucier (Ken Saucier on back)	.15
24b	Kevin Saucier (Kevin Saucier on back)	.50
25	Randy Lerch	.08
26	Del Unser	.08
27	Tim McCarver	.15
28a	George Brett (batting)	4.00
28b	George Brett (portrait)	1.00
29a	Willie Wilson (portrait)	.50
29b	Willie Wilson (batting)	.15
30	Paul Splittorff	.08
31	Dan Quisenberry	.15
32a	Amos Otis (batting)	.50
32b	Amos Otis (portrait)	.10
33	Steve Busby	.08
34	U.L. Washington	.08
35	Dave Chalk	.08
36	Darrell Porter	.08
37	Marty Pattin	.08
38	Larry Gura	.08
39	Renie Martin	.08
40	Rich Gale	.08
41a	Hal McRae (dark blue "Royals" on front)	.40
41b	Hal McRae (light blue "Royals" on front)	.10
42	Dennis Leonard	.08
43	Willie Aikens	.08
44	Frank White	.08
45	Clint Hurdle	.08
46	John Wathan	.08
47	Pete LaCock	.08
48	Rance Mulliniks	.08
49	Jeff Twitty	.08
50	Jamie Quirk	.08
51	Art Howe	.08
52	Ken Forsch	.08
53	Vern Ruhle	.08
54	Joe Niekro	.12
55	Frank LaCorte	.08
56	J.R. Richard	.10
57	Nolan Ryan	8.00
58	Enos Cabell	.08
59	Cesar Cedeno	.12
60	Jose Cruz	.12
61	Bill Virdon	.08
62	Terry Puhl	.08
63	Joaquin Andujar	.08
64	Alan Ashby	.08
65	Joe Sambito	.08
66	Denny Walling	.08
67	Jeff Leonard	.08
68	Luis Pujols	.08
69	Bruce Bochy	.08
70	Rafael Landestoy	.08
71	*Dave Smith*	.08
72	*Danny Heep*	.08
73	Julio Gonzalez	.08
74	Craig Reynolds	.08
75	Gary Woods	.08
76	Dave Bergman	.08
77	Randy Niemann	.08
78	Joe Morgan	.75
79a	Reggie Jackson (portrait)	4.00
79b	Reggie Jackson (batting)	2.00
80	Bucky Dent	.10
81	Tommy John	.20
82	Luis Tiant	.12
83	Rick Cerone	.08
84	Dick Howser	.08
85	Lou Piniella	.12
86	Ron Davis	.08
87a	Graig Nettles (Craig on back)	10.00
87b	Graig Nettles (Graig on back)	.15
88	Ron Guidry	.15
89	Rich Gossage	.10
90	Rudy May	.08
91	Gaylord Perry	.75
92	Eric Soderholm	.08
93	Bob Watson	.08
94	Bobby Murcer	.10
95	Bobby Brown	.08
96	Jim Spencer	.08
97	Tom Underwood	.08
98	Oscar Gamble	.08
99	Johnny Oates	.08
100	Fred Stanley	.08
101	Ruppert Jones	.08
102	Dennis Werth	.08
103	Joe Lefebvre	.08
104	Brian Doyle	.08
105	Aurelio Rodriguez	.08
106	Doug Bird	.08
107	Mike Griffin	.08
108	Tim Lollar	.08
109	Willie Randolph	.08
110	Steve Garvey	.40
111	Reggie Smith	.10
112	Don Sutton	.45
113	Burt Hooton	.08
114a	Davy Lopes (Davey) (no finger on back)	.08
114b	Davy Lopes (Davey) (small finger on back)	1.00
115	Dusty Baker	.10
116	Tom Lasorda	.45
117	Bill Russell	.12
118	Jerry Reuss	.08
119	Terry Forster	.08
120a	Bob Welch (Bob on back)	.10
120b	Bob Welch (Robert)	.50
121	Don Stanhouse	.08
122	Rick Monday	.08
123	Derrel Thomas	.08
124	Joe Ferguson	.08
125	Rick Sutcliffe	.10
126a	Ron Cey (no finger on back)	.10
126b	Ron Cey (small finger on back)	1.00
127	Dave Goltz	.08
128	Jay Johnstone	.08
129	Steve Yeager	.08
130	Gary Weiss	.08
131	*Mike Scioscia*	.25
132	Vic Davalillo	.08
133	Doug Rau	.08
134	Pepe Frias	.08
135	Mickey Hatcher	.08
136	*Steve Howe*	.10
137	Robert Castillo	.08
138	Gary Thomasson	.08
139	Rudy Law	.08
140	*Fernando Valenzuela*	1.50
141	Manny Mota	.08
142	Gary Carter	.65
143	Steve Rogers	.08
144	Warren Cromartie	.08
145	Andre Dawson	1.00
146	Larry Parrish	.08
147	Rowland Office	.08
148	Ellis Valentine	.08
149	Dick Williams	.08
150	*Bill Gullickson*	.15
151	Elias Sosa	.08
152	John Tamargo	.08
153	Chris Speier	.08
154	Ron LeFlore	.08
155	Rodney Scott	.08
156	Stan Bahnsen	.08
157	Bill Lee	.08
158	Fred Norman	.08
159	Woodie Fryman	.08
160	Dave Palmer	.08
161	Jerry White	.08
162	Roberto Ramos	.08
163	John D'Acquisto	.08
164	Tommy Hutton	.08
165	*Charlie Lea*	.12
166	Scott Sanderson	.08
167	Ken Macha	.08
168	Tony Bernazard	.08
169	Jim Palmer	1.00
170	Steve Stone	.08
171	Mike Flanagan	.08
172	Al Bumbry	.08
173	Doug DeCinces	.08
174	Scott McGregor	.08
175	Mark Belanger	.08
176	Tim Stoddard	.08
177a	Rick Dempsey (no finger on front)	.08
177b	Rick Dempsey (small finger on front)	1.00
178	Earl Weaver	.40
179	Tippy Martinez	.08
180	Dennis Martinez	.10
181	Sammy Stewart	.08
182	Rich Dauer	.08
183	Lee May	.08
184	Eddie Murray	3.00
185	Benny Ayala	.08
186	John Lowenstein	.08
187	Gary Roenicke	.08
188	Ken Singleton	.10
189	Dan Graham	.08
190	Terry Crowley	.08
191	Kiko Garcia	.08
192	Dave Ford	.08
193	Mark Corey	.08
194	Lenn Sakata	.08
195	Doug DeCinces	.08
196	Johnny Bench	1.50
197	Dave Concepcion	.15
198	Ray Knight	.10
199	Ken Griffey	.12
200	Tom Seaver	1.50
201	Dave Collins	.08
202	George Foster	.12
203	Junior Kennedy	.08
204	Frank Pastore	.08
205	Dan Driessen	.08
206	Hector Cruz	.08
207	Paul Moskau	.08
208	*Charlie Leibrandt*	.25
209	Harry Spilman	.08
210	*Joe Price*	.08
211	Tom Hume	.08
212	Joe Nolan	.08
213	Doug Bair	.08
214	Mario Soto	.08
215a	Bill Bonham (no finger on back)	.08
215b	Bill Bonham (small finger on back)	1.00
216a	George Foster (Slugger on front)	.25
216b	George Foster (Outfield on front)	.20
217	Paul Householder	.08
218	Ron Oester	.08
219	Sam Mejias	.08
220	Sheldon Burnside	.08
221	Carl Yastrzemski	1.50
222	Jim Rice	.15
223	Fred Lynn	.15
224	Carlton Fisk	1.00
225	Rick Burleson	.08
226	Dennis Eckersley	.75
227	Butch Hobson	.08
228	Tom Burgmeier	.08
229	Garry Hancock	.08
230	Don Zimmer	.08
231	Steve Renko	.08
232	Dwight Evans	.15
233	Mike Torrez	.08
234	Bob Stanley	.08
235	Jim Dwyer	.08
236	Dave Stapleton	.08
237	Glenn Hoffman	.08
238	Jerry Remy	.08
239	Dick Drago	.08
240	Bill Campbell	.08
241	Tony Perez	.20
242	Phil Niekro	.75
243	Dale Murphy	.75
244	Bob Horner	.12
245	Jeff Burroughs	.08
246	Rick Camp	.08
247	Bob Cox	.10
248	Bruce Benedict	.08
249	Gene Garber	.08
250	Jerry Royster	.08
251a	Gary Matthews (no finger on back)	.08
251b	Gary Matthews (small finger on back)	1.00
252	Chris Chambliss	.08
253	Luis Gomez	.08
254	Bill Nahorodny	.08
255	Doyle Alexander	.08
256	Brian Asselstine	.08
257	Biff Pocoroba	.08
258	Mike Lum	.08
259	Charlie Spikes	.08
260	Glenn Hubbard	.08
261	Tommy Boggs	.08
262	Al Hrabosky	.08
263	Rick Matula	.08
264	Preston Hanna	.08
265	Larry Bradford	.08
266	*Rafael Ramirez*	.08
267	Larry McWilliams	.08
268	Rod Carew	1.50
269	Bobby Grich	.10
270	Carney Lansford	.08
271	Don Baylor	.15
272	Joe Rudi	.08
273	Dan Ford	.08
274	Jim Fregosi	.08
275	Dave Frost	.08
276	Frank Tanana	.08
277	Dickie Thon	.08
278	Jason Thompson	.08
279	Rick Miller	.08
280	Bert Campaneris	.08
281	Tom Donohue	.08
282	Brian Downing	.08
283	Fred Patek	.08
284	Bruce Kison	.08
285	Dave LaRoche	.08
286	Don Aase	.08
287	Jim Barr	.08
288	Alfredo Martinez	.08
289	Larry Harlow	.08
290	Andy Hassler	.08
291	Dave Kingman	.12
292	Bill Buckner	.12
293	Rick Reuschel	.08
294	Bruce Sutter	.08
295	Jerry Martin	.08
296	Scot Thompson	.08
297	Ivan DeJesus	.08
298	Steve Dillard	.08
299	Dick Tidrow	.08
300	Randy Martz	.08
301	Lenny Randle	.08
302	Lynn McGlothen	.08
303	Cliff Johnson	.08
304	Tim Blackwell	.08
305	Dennis Lamp	.08
306	Bill Caudill	.08
307	Carlos Lezcano	.08
308	Jim Tracy	.08
309	Doug Capilla	.08
310	Willie Hernandez	.08
311	Mike Vail	.08
312	Mike Krukow	.08
313	Barry Foote	.08
314	Larry Biittner	.08
315	Mike Tyson	.08
316	Lee Mazzilli	.08
317	John Stearns	.08
318	Alex Trevino	.08
319	Craig Swan	.08
320	Frank Taveras	.08
321	Steve Henderson	.08
322	Neil Allen	.08
323	Mark Bomback	.08
324	Mike Jorgensen	.08
325	Joe Torre	.15
326	Elliott Maddox	.08
327	Pete Falcone	.08
328	Ray Burris	.08
329	Claudell Washington	.08
330	Doug Flynn	.08
331	Joel Youngblood	.08
332	Bill Almon	.08
333	Tom Hausman	.08
334	Pat Zachry	.08
335	*Jeff Reardon*	2.00
336	*Wally Backman*	.15
337	Dan Norman	.08
338	Jerry Morales	.08
339	Ed Farmer	.08
340	Bob Molinaro	.08
341	Todd Cruz	.08
342a	*Britt Burns* (no finger on front)	.10
342b	*Britt Burns* (small finger on front)	1.00
343	Kevin Bell	.08
344	Tony LaRussa	.12
345	Steve Trout	.08
346	*Harold Baines*	4.00
347	Richard Wortham	.08
348	Wayne Nordhagen	.08
349	Mike Squires	.08
350	Lamar Johnson	.08
351	Rickey Henderson	6.00
352	Francisco Barrios	.08
353	Thad Bosley	.08
354	Chet Lemon	.08
355	Bruce Kimm	.08
356	*Richard Dotson*	.08
357	Jim Morrison	.08
358	Mike Proly	.08
359	Greg Pryor	.08
360	Dave Parker	.15
361	Omar Moreno	.08
362a	Kent Tekulve (1071 Waterbury on back)	.15
362b	Kent Tekulve (1971 Waterbury on back)	.50
363	Willie Stargell	.75
364	Phil Garner	.08
365	Ed Ott	.08
366	Don Robinson	.08
367	Chuck Tanner	.08
368	Jim Rooker	.08
369	Dale Berra	.08
370	Jim Bibby	.08
371	Steve Nicosia	.08
372	Mike Easler	.08
373	Bill Robinson	.08
374	Lee Lacy	.08
375	John Candelaria	.08
376	Manny Sanguillen	.08
377	Rick Rhoden	.08
378	Grant Jackson	.08
379	Tim Foli	.08
380	*Rod Scurry*	.08
381	Bill Madlock	.10
382a	Kurt Bevacqua (photo reversed, backwards "P" on cap)	.15
382b	Kurt Bevacqua (correct photo)	.50
383	Bert Blyleven	.08
384	Eddie Solomon	.08
385	Enrique Romo	.08
386	John Milner	.08
387	Mike Hargrove	.08
388	Jorge Orta	.08
389	Toby Harrah	.08
390	Tom Veryzer	.08
391	Miguel Dilone	.08
392	Dan Spillner	.08
393	Jack Brohamer	.08
394	Wayne Garland	.08
395	Sid Monge	.08
396	Rick Waits	.08
397	*Joe Charboneau*	.25

398	Gary Alexander	.08
399	Jerry Dybzinski	.08
400	Mike Stanton	.08
401	Mike Paxton	.08
402	Gary Gray	.08
403	Rick Manning	.08
404	Bo Diaz	.08
405	Ron Hassey	.08
406	Ross Grimsley	.08
407	Victor Cruz	.08
408	Len Barker	.08
409	Bob Bailor	.08
410	Otto Velez	.08
411	Ernie Whitt	.08
412	Jim Clancy	.08
413	Barry Bonnell	.08
414	Dave Stieb	.25
415	*Damaso Garcia*	.10
416	John Mayberry	.08
417	Roy Howell	.08
418	*Dan Ainge*	5.00
419a	Jesse Jefferson (Pirates on back)	.10
419b	Jesse Jefferson (Blue Jays on back)	.50
420	Joey McLaughlin	.08
421	*Lloyd Moseby*	.10
422	Al Woods	.08
423	Garth Iorg	.08
424	Doug Ault	.08
425	*Ken Schrom*	.08
426	Mike Willis	.08
427	Steve Braun	.08
428	Bob Davis	.08
429	Jerry Garvin	.08
430	Alfredo Griffin	.08
431	Bob Mattick	.08
432	Vida Blue	.12
433	Jack Clark	.12
434	Willie McCovey	1.00
435	Mike Ivie	.08
436a	Darrel Evans (Darrel on front)	.15
436b	Darrell Evans (Darrell on front)	.50
437	Terry Whitfield	.08
438	Rennie Stennett	.08
439	John Montefusco	.08
440	Jim Wohlford	.08
441	Bill North	.08
442	Milt May	.08
443	Max Venable	.08
444	Ed Whitson	.08
445	*Al Holland*	.08
446	Randy Moffitt	.08
447	Bob Knepper	.08
448	Gary Lavelle	.08
449	Greg Minton	.08
450	Johnnie LeMaster	.08
451	Larry Herndon	.08
452	Rich Murray	.08
453	Joe Pettini	.08
454	Allen Ripley	.08
455	Dennis Littlejohn	.08
456	Tom Griffin	.08
457	Alan Hargesheimer	.08
458	Joe Strain	.08
459	Steve Kemp	.08
460	Sparky Anderson	.12
461	Alan Trammell	1.00
462	Mark Fidrych	.12
463	Lou Whitaker	.45
464	Dave Rozema	.08
465	Milt Wilcox	.08
466	Champ Summers	.08
467	Lance Parrish	.20
468	Dan Petry	.08
469	Pat Underwood	.08
470	Rick Peters	.08
471	Al Cowens	.08
472	John Wockenfuss	.08
473	Tom Brookens	.08
474	Richie Hebner	.08
475	Jack Morris	.15
476	Jim Lentine	.08
477	Bruce Robbins	.08
478	Mark Wagner	.08
479	Tim Corcoran	.08
480a	Stan Papi (Pitcher on front)	.15
480b	Stan Papi (Shortstop on front)	.50
481	*Kirk Gibson*	3.00
482	Dan Schatzeder	.08
483	Amos Otis	.15
484	Dave Winfield	2.50
485	Rollie Fingers	1.00
486	Gene Richards	.08
487	Randy Jones	.08
488	Ozzie Smith	3.00
489	Gene Tenace	.08
490	Bill Fahey	.08
491	John Curtis	.08
492	Dave Cash	.08
493a	Tim Flannery (photo reversed, batting righty)	.15
493b	Tim Flannery (photo correct, batting lefty)	.50
494	Jerry Mumphrey	.08
495	Bob Shirley	.08
496	Steve Mura	.08
497	Eric Rasmussen	.08
498	Broderick Perkins	.08
499	Barry Evans	.08
500	Chuck Baker	.08
501	*Luis Salazar*	.08
502	Gary Lucas	.08
503	Mike Armstrong	.08
504	Jerry Turner	.08
505	Dennis Kinney	.08
506	Willy Montanez (Willie)	.08
507	Gorman Thomas	.08
508	Ben Oglivie	.08
509	Larry Hisle	.08
510	Sal Bando	.08
511	Robin Yount	3.00
512	Mike Caldwell	.08
513	Sixto Lezcano	.08
514a	Jerry Augustine (Billy Travers photo)	.15
514b	Billy Travers (correct name with photo)	.50
515	Paul Molitor	3.00
516	Moose Haas	.08
517	Bill Castro	.08
518	Jim Slaton	.08
519	Lary Sorensen	.08
520	Bob McClure	.08
521	Charlie Moore	.08
522	Jim Gantner	.08
523	Reggie Cleveland	.08
524	Don Money	.08
525	Billy Travers	.08
526	Buck Martinez	.08
527	Dick Davis	.08
528	Ted Simmons	.08
529	Garry Templeton	.08
530	Ken Reitz	.08
531	Tony Scott	.08
532	Ken Oberkfell	.08
533	Bob Sykes	.08
534	Keith Smith	.08
535	John Littlefield	.08
536	Jim Kaat	.20
537	Bob Forsch	.08
538	Mike Phillips	.08
539	*Terry Landrum*	.08
540	*Leon Durham*	.10
541	Terry Kennedy	.08
542	George Hendrick	.08
543	Dane Iorg	.08
544	Mark Littell (photo actually Jeff Little)	.08
545	Keith Hernandez	.12
546	Silvio Martinez	.08
547a	Pete Vuckovich (photo actually Don Hood)	.15
547b	Don Hood (correct name with photo)	.50
548	Bobby Bonds	.10
549	Mike Ramsey	.08
550	Tom Herr	.08
551	Roy Smalley	.08
552	Jerry Koosman	.08
553	Ken Landreaux	.08
554	John Castino	.08
555	Doug Corbett	.08
556	Bombo Rivera	.08
557	Ron Jackson	.08
558	Butch Wynegar	.08
559	Hosken Powell	.08
560	Pete Redfern	.08
561	Roger Erickson	.08
562	Glenn Adams	.08
563	Rick Sofield	.08
564	Geoff Zahn	.08
565	Pete Mackanin	.08
566	Mike Cubbage	.08
567	Darrell Jackson	.08
568	Dave Edwards	.08
569	Rob Wilfong	.08
570	Sal Butera	.08
571	Jose Morales	.08
572	Rick Langford	.08
573	Mike Norris	.08
574	Rickey Henderson	7.00
575	Tony Armas	.08
576	Dave Revering	.08
577	Jeff Newman	.08
578	Bob Lacey	.08
579	Brian Kingman (photo actually Alan Wirth)	.08
580	Mitchell Page	.08
581	Billy Martin	.12
582	Rob Picciolo	.08
583	Mike Heath	.08
584	Mickey Klutts	.08
585	Orlando Gonzalez	.08
586	*Mike Davis*	.08
587	Wayne Gross	.08
588	Matt Keough	.08
589	Steve McCatty	.08
590	Dwayne Murphy	.08
591	Mario Guerrero	.08
592	Dave McKay	.08
593	Jim Essian	.08
594	Dave Heaverlo	.08
595	Maury Wills	.10
596	Juan Beniquez	.08
597	Rodney Craig	.08
598	Jim Anderson	.08
599	Floyd Bannister	.08
600	Bruce Bochte	.08
601	Julio Cruz	.08
602	Ted Cox	.08
603	Dan Meyer	.08
604	Larry Cox	.08
605	Bill Stein	.08
606	Steve Garvey	.45
607	Dave Roberts	.08
608	Leon Roberts	.08
609	Reggie Walton	.08
610	Dave Edler	.08
611	Larry Milbourne	.08
612	Kim Allen	.08
613	Mario Mendoza	.08
614	Tom Paciorek	.08
615	Glenn Abbott	.08
616	Joe Simpson	.08
617	Mickey Rivers	.08
618	Jim Kern	.08
619	Jim Sundberg	.08
620	Richie Zisk	.08
621	Jon Matlack	.08
622	Fergie Jenkins	.75
623	Pat Corrales	.08
624	Ed Figueroa	.08
625	Buddy Bell	.12
626	Al Oliver	.15
627	Doc Medich	.08
628	Bump Wills	.08
629	Rusty Staub	.10
630	Pat Putnam	.08
631	John Grubb	.08
632	Danny Darwin	.08
633	Ken Clay	.08
634	Jim Norris	.08
635	John Butcher	.08
636	Dave Roberts	.08
637	Billy Sample	.08
638	Carl Yastrzemski	1.25
639	Cecil Cooper	.08
640	Mike Schmidt	2.00
641a	Checklist 1-50 (41 Hal McRae)	.10
641b	Checklist 1-50 (41 Hal McRae Double Threat)	.25
642	Checklist 51-109	.08
643	Checklist 110-168	.08
644a	Checklist 169-220 (202 George Foster)	.10
644b	Checklist 169-220 (202 George Foster "Slugger")	.25
(645a)	Triple Threat (Larry Bowa, Pete Rose, Mike Schmidt) (no number on back)	2.00
645b	Triple Threat (Pete Rose, Larry Bowa, Mike Schmidt) (number on back)	2.00
646	Checklist 221-267	.08
647	Checklist 268-315	.08
648	Checklist 316-359	.08
649	Checklist 360-408	.08
650	Reggie Jackson	2.50
651	Checklist 409-458	.08
652a	Checklist 459-509 (483 Aurelio Lopez)	.10
652b	Checklist 459-506 (no 483)	.25
653	Willie Wilson	.25
654a	Checklist 507-550 (514 Jerry Augustine)	.10
654b	Checklist 507-550 (514 Billy Travers)	.25
655	George Brett	4.00
656	Checklist 551-593	.08
657	Tug McGraw	.15
658	Checklist 594-637	.08
659a	Checklist 640-660 (last number on front is 551)	.10
659b	Checklist 640-660 (last number on front is 483)	.25
660a	Steve Carlton (date 1066 on back)	1.00
660b	Steve Carlton (date 1966 on back)	2.00

1981 Fleer Star Stickers

The 128-card 1981 Fleer Star Sticker set was designed to allow the card fronts to be peeled away from the cardboard backs. Fronts feature color photos with blue and yellow trim. Backs are identical in design to the regular 1981 Fleer set except for color and numbering. The set contains three unnumbered checklist cards whose fronts depict Reggie Jackson, George Brett and Mike Schmidt. The sticker-cards, which are the standard 2-1/2" x 3-1/2", were issued in gum wax packs.

		MT
Complete Set (128):		40.00
Common Player:		.15
Wax Box:		35.00
1	Steve Garvey	.50
2	Ron LeFlore	.13
3	Ron Cey	.13
4	Dave Revering	.13
5	Tony Armas	.13
6	Mike Norris	.13
7	Steve Kemp	.13
8	Bruce Bochte	.13
9	Mike Schmidt	5.00
10	Scott McGregor	.13
11	Buddy Bell	.13
12	Carney Lansford	.13
13	Carl Yastrzemski	4.50
14	Ben Oglivie	.13
15	Willie Stargell	3.75
16	Cecil Cooper	.13
17	Gene Richards	.13
18	Jim Kern	.13
19	Jerry Koosman	.13
20	Larry Bowa	.13
21	Kent Tekulve	.13
22	Dan Driessen	.13
23	Phil Niekro	2.00
24	Dan Quisenberry	.13
25	Dave Winfield	3.75
26	Dave Parker	.40
27	Rick Langford	.13
28	Amos Otis	.13
29	Bill Buckner	.15
30	Al Bumbry	.13
31	Bake McBride	.13
32	Mickey Rivers	.13
33	Rick Burleson	.13
34	Dennis Eckersley	1.00
35	Cesar Cedeno	.13
36	Enos Cabell	.13
37	Johnny Bench	4.50
38	Robin Yount	3.75
39	Mark Belanger	.13
40	Rod Carew	3.75
41	George Foster	.13
42	Lee Mazzilli	.13
43	Triple Threat (Larry Bowa, Pete Rose, Mike Schmidt)	3.00
44	J.R. Richard	.15
45	Lou Piniella	.15
46	Ken Landreaux	.13
47	Rollie Fingers	2.00
48	Joaquin Andujar	.13
49	Tom Seaver	4.50
50	Bobby Grich	.13
51	Jon Matlack	.13
52	Jack Clark	.13
53	Jim Rice	.15
54	Rickey Henderson	4.00
55	Roy Smalley	.13
56	Mike Flanagan	.13
57	Steve Rogers	.13
58	Carlton Fisk	.60
59	Don Sutton	.75
60	Ken Griffey	.20
61	Burt Hooton	.13
62	Dusty Baker	.20
63	Vida Blue	.13
64	Al Oliver	.13
65	Jim Bibby	.13
66	Tony Perez	.25
67	Davy Lopes (Davey)	.13
68	Bill Russell	.15
69	Larry Parrish	.13
70	Garry Maddox	.13
71	Phil Garner	.13
72	Graig Nettles	.13
73	Gary Carter	.60
74	Pete Rose	6.00
75	Greg Luzinski	.20
76	Ron Guidry	.15
77	Gorman Thomas	.13
78	Jose Cruz	.13
79	Bob Boone	.20
80	Bruce Sutter	.13
81	Chris Chambliss	.13
82	Paul Molitor	3.75
83	Tug McGraw	.13
84	Ferguson Jenkins	1.50
85	Steve Carlton	3.75
86	Miguel Dilone	.13
87	Reggie Smith	.13
88	Rick Cerone	.13
89	Alan Trammell	.75
90	Doug DeCinces	.13
91	Sparky Lyle	.13
92	Warren Cromartie	.13
93	Rick Reuschel	.13
94	Larry Hisle	.13
95	Paul Splittorff	.13
96	Manny Trillo	.13
97	Frank White	.13
98	Fred Lynn	.20
99	Bob Horner	.13
100	Omar Moreno	.13
101	Dave Concepcion	.13
102	Larry Gura	.13
103	Ken Singleton	.13
104	Steve Stone	.13
105	Richie Zisk	.13
106	Willie Wilson	.13
107	Willie Randolph	.13
108	Nolan Ryan	9.00
109	Joe Morgan	2.00
110	Bucky Dent	.13
111	Dave Kingman	.20
112	John Castino	.13
113	Joe Rudi	.13
114	Ed Farmer	.13
115	Reggie Jackson	5.00
116	George Brett	5.00
117	Eddie Murray	2.00
118	Rich Gossage	.20
119	Dale Murphy	1.00
120	Ted Simmons	.13
121	Tommy John	.25
122	Don Baylor	.25
123	Andre Dawson	1.00
124	Jim Palmer	3.75
125	Garry Templeton	.13
----	Checklist 1-42 (Reggie Jackson)	1.00
----	Checklist 43-83 (George Brett)	1.00
----	Checklist 84-125 (Mike Schmidt)	1.00

1981 Fleer Superstar Stickers

While these small (about 1-1/2" x 2") stickers carry the Fleer name and were, indeed, produced by Fleer, they are more akin to collectors' issues than legitimate product. Wrappers of 1981 Fleer Star Stickers offered the opportunity to put one's own photo, or the photo of someone else, on 24 stickers for a couple of dollars and proofs of purchase. Some enterprising hobbyist sent in several different pictures of Mickey Mantle and had them made into these collectors stickers. Because they are unauthorized by Mantle, or the other players seen (Boggs, Mattingly, Yaz, etc., there is little collector interest.

	MT
Wade Boggs	2.00
Mickey Mantle	3.00
Don Mattingly	2.00
Carl Yastrzemski	2.00

1982 Fleer

Fleer's 1982 set did not match the quality of the previous year's effort. Many of the card photos are blurred and have muddied backgrounds. The 2-1/2" x 3-1/2" cards feature color photos bordered by a frame which is color-coded by team. Backs are blue, white, and yellow and contain the player's team logo plus the logos of Major League Baseball and the Major League Baseball Players Association. Due to a lawsuit by Topps, Fleer was forced to issue the set with team logo stickers rather than gum. The complete set price does not include the higher priced variations.

		MT
Complete Set (660):		60.00
Common Player:		.08
Wax Box:		110.00
1	Dusty Baker	.10
2	Robert Castillo	.08
3	Ron Cey	.08
4	Terry Forster	.08
5	Steve Garvey	.20
6	Dave Goltz	.08
7	Pedro Guerrero	.08
8	Burt Hooton	.08
9	Steve Howe	.08
10	Jay Johnstone	.08
11	Ken Landreaux	.08
12	Davey Lopes	.08
13	*Mike Marshall*	.12
14	Bobby Mitchell	.08
15	Rick Monday	.08
16	*Tom Niedenfuer*	.08
17	*Ted Power*	.08
18	Jerry Reuss	.08
19	Ron Roenicke	.08
20	Bill Russell	.08
21	*Steve Sax*	.45
22	Mike Scioscia	.08
23	Reggie Smith	.08
24	*Dave Stewart*	2.00
25	Rick Sutcliffe	.08
26	Derrel Thomas	.08
27	Fernando Valenzuela	.15
28	Bob Welch	.08
29	Steve Yeager	.08
30	Bobby Brown	.08
31	Rick Cerone	.08
32	Ron Davis	.08
33	Bucky Dent	.10
34	Barry Foote	.08
35	George Frazier	.08
36	Oscar Gamble	.08
37	Rich Gossage	.10
38	Ron Guidry	.15
39	Reggie Jackson	1.50
40	Tommy John	.15
41	Rudy May	.08
42	Larry Milbourne	.08
43	Jerry Mumphrey	.08
44	Bobby Murcer	.10
45	*Gene Nelson*	.08
46	Graig Nettles	.10
47	Johnny Oates	.08
48	Lou Piniella	.12
49	Willie Randolph	.08
50	Rick Reuschel	.08
51	Dave Revering	.08
52	*Dave Righetti*	.45
53	Aurelio Rodriguez	.08
54	Bob Watson	.08
55	Dennis Werth	.08
56	Dave Winfield	2.00
57	Johnny Bench	1.00
58	Bruce Berenyi	.08
59	Larry Biittner	.08
60	Scott Brown	.08
61	Dave Collins	.08
62	Geoff Combe	.08
63	Dave Concepcion	.08
64	Dan Driessen	.08
65	Joe Edelen	.08
66	George Foster	.10
67	Ken Griffey	.12
68	Paul Householder	.08
69	Tom Hume	.08
70	Junior Kennedy	.08
71	Ray Knight	.10
72	Mike LaCoss	.08
73	Rafael Landestoy	.08
74	Charlie Leibrandt	.08
75	Sam Mejias	.08
76	Paul Moskau	.08
77	Joe Nolan	.08
78	Mike O'Berry	.08
79	Ron Oester	.08
80	Frank Pastore	.08
81	Joe Price	.08
82	Tom Seaver	1.00
83	Mario Soto	.08
84	Mike Vail	.08
85	Tony Armas	.08
86	Shooty Babitt	.08
87	Dave Beard	.08
88	Rick Bosetti	.08
89	Keith Drumright	.08
90	Wayne Gross	.08
91	Mike Heath	.08
92	Rickey Henderson	2.50
93	Cliff Johnson	.08
94	Jeff Jones	.08
95	Matt Keough	.08
96	Brian Kingman	.08
97	Mickey Klutts	.08
98	Rick Langford	.08
99	Steve McCatty	.08
100	Dave McKay	.08
101	Dwayne Murphy	.08
102	Jeff Newman	.08
103	Mike Norris	.08
104	Bob Owchinko	.08
105	Mitchell Page	.08
106	Rob Picciolo	.08
107	Jim Spencer	.08
108	Fred Stanley	.08
109	Tom Underwood	.08
110	Joaquin Andujar	.08
111	Steve Braun	.08
112	Bob Forsch	.08
113	George Hendrick	.08
114	Keith Hernandez	.08
115	Tom Herr	.08
116	Dane Iorg	.08
117	Jim Kaat	.10
118	Tito Landrum	.08
119	Sixto Lezcano	.08
120	Mark Littell	.08
121	John Martin	.08
122	Silvio Martinez	.08
123	Ken Oberkfell	.08
124	Darrell Porter	.08
125	Mike Ramsey	.08
126	Orlando Sanchez	.08
127	Bob Shirley	.08
128	Lary Sorensen	.08
129	Bruce Sutter	.08
130	Bob Sykes	.08
131	Garry Templeton	.08
132	Gene Tenace	.08
133	Jerry Augustine	.08
134	Sal Bando	.08
135	Mark Brouhard	.08
136	Mike Caldwell	.08
137	Reggie Cleveland	.08
138	Cecil Cooper	.08
139	Jamie Easterly	.08
140	Marshall Edwards	.08
141	Rollie Fingers	.65
142	Jim Gantner	.08
143	Moose Haas	.08
144	Larry Hisle	.08
145	Roy Howell	.08
146	Rickey Keeton	.08
147	Randy Lerch	.08
148	Paul Molitor	3.00
149	Don Money	.08
150	Charlie Moore	.08
151	Ben Oglivie	.08
152	Ted Simmons	.08
153	Jim Slaton	.08
154	Gorman Thomas	.08
155	Robin Yount	3.00
156	Pete Vukovich	.08
157	Benny Ayala	.08
158	Mark Belanger	.08
159	Al Bumbry	.08
160	Terry Crowley	.08
161	Rich Dauer	.08
162	Doug DeCinces	.08
163	Rick Dempsey	.08
164	Jim Dwyer	.08
165	Mike Flanagan	.08
166	Dave Ford	.08
167	Dan Graham	.08
168	Wayne Krenchicki	.08
169	John Lowenstein	.08
170	Dennis Martinez	.10
171	Tippy Martinez	.08
172	Scott McGregor	.08
173	Jose Morales	.08
174	Eddie Murray	3.00
175	Jim Palmer	.75
176	*Cal Ripken, Jr.*	50.00
177	Gary Roenicke	.08
178	Lenn Sakata	.08
179	Ken Singleton	.08
180	Sammy Stewart	.08
181	Tim Stoddard	.08
182	Steve Stone	.08
183	Stan Bahnsen	.08
184	Ray Burris	.08
185	Gary Carter	.25
186	Warren Cromartie	.08
187	Andre Dawson	.75
188	*Terry Francona*	.08
189	Woodie Fryman	.08
190	Bill Gullickson	.08
191	Grant Jackson	.08
192	Wallace Johnson	.08
193	Charlie Lea	.08
194	Bill Lee	.08
195	Jerry Manuel	.08
196	Brad Mills	.08
197	John Milner	.08
198	Rowland Office	.08
199	David Palmer	.08
200	Larry Parrish	.08
201	Mike Phillips	.08
202	Tim Raines	.75
203	Bobby Ramos	.08
204	Jeff Reardon	.12
205	Steve Rogers	.08
206	Scott Sanderson	.08
207	Rodney Scott (photo actually Tim Raines)	.10
208	Elias Sosa	.08
209	Chris Speier	.08
210	*Tim Wallach*	1.00
211	Jerry White	.08
212	Alan Ashby	.08
213	Cesar Cedeno	.12
214	Jose Cruz	.12
215	Kiko Garcia	.08
216	Phil Garner	.08
217	Danny Heep	.08
218	Art Howe	.08
219	Bob Knepper	.08
220	Frank LaCorte	.08
221	Joe Niekro	.12
222	Joe Pittman	.08
223	Terry Puhl	.08
224	Luis Pujols	.08
225	Craig Reynolds	.08
226	J.R. Richard	.10
227	Dave Roberts	.08
228	Vern Ruhle	.08
229	Nolan Ryan	9.00
230	Joe Sambito	.08
231	Tony Scott	.08
232	Dave Smith	.08
233	Harry Spilman	.08
234	Don Sutton	.50
235	Dickie Thon	.08
236	Denny Walling	.08
237	Gary Woods	.08
238	*Luis Aguayo*	.08
239	Ramon Aviles	.08
240	Bob Boone	.10
241	Larry Bowa	.08
242	Warren Brusstar	.08
243	Steve Carlton	1.00
244	Larry Christenson	.08
245	Dick Davis	.08
246	Greg Gross	.08
247	Sparky Lyle	.08
248	Garry Maddox	.08
249	Gary Matthews	.08
250	Bake McBride	.08
251	Tug McGraw	.10
252	Keith Moreland	.08
253	Dickie Noles	.08
254	Mike Proly	.08
255	Ron Reed	.08
256	Pete Rose	2.50
257	Dick Ruthven	.08
258	Mike Schmidt	3.00
259	Lonnie Smith	.08
260	Manny Trillo	.08
261	Del Unser	.08
262	George Vukovich	.08
263	Tom Brookens	.08
264	George Cappuzzello	.08
265	Marty Castillo	.08
266	Al Cowens	.08
267	Kirk Gibson	.12
268	Richie Hebner	.08
269	Ron Jackson	.08
270	Lynn Jones	.08
271	Steve Kemp	.08
272	*Rick Leach*	.12
273	Aurelio Lopez	.08
274	Jack Morris	.10
275	Kevin Saucier	.08
276	Lance Parrish	.10
277	Rick Peters	.08
278	Dan Petry	.08
279	David Rozema	.08
280	Stan Papi	.08
281	Dan Schatzeder	.08
282	Champ Summers	.08
283	Alan Trammell	.60
284	Lou Whitaker	.15
285	Milt Wilcox	.08
286	John Wockenfuss	.08
287	Gary Allenson	.08
288	Tom Burgmeier	.08
289	Bill Campbell	.08
290	Mark Clear	.08
291	Steve Crawford	.08
292	Dennis Eckersley	.75
293	Dwight Evans	.15
294	*Rich Gedman*	.20
295	Garry Hancock	.08
296	Glenn Hoffman	.08
297	Bruce Hurst	.08
298	Carney Lansford	.08
299	Rick Miller	.08
300	Reid Nichols	.08
301	*Bob Ojeda*	.25
302	Tony Perez	.20
303	Chuck Rainey	.08
304	Jerry Remy	.08
305	Jim Rice	.15
306	Joe Rudi	.08
307	Bob Stanley	.08
308	Dave Stapleton	.08
309	Frank Tanana	.08
310	Mike Torrez	.08
311	John Tudor	.08
312	Carl Yastrzemski	1.00
313	Buddy Bell	.10
314	Steve Comer	.08
315	Danny Darwin	.08
316	John Ellis	.08
317	John Grubb	.08
318	Rick Honeycutt	.08
319	Charlie Hough	.08
320	Fergie Jenkins	.65
321	John Henry Johnson	.08
322	Jim Kern	.08
323	Jon Matlack	.08
324	Doc Medich	.08
325	Mario Mendoza	.08
326	Al Oliver	.10
327	Pat Putnam	.08
328	Mickey Rivers	.08
329	Leon Roberts	.08
330	Billy Sample	.08
331	Bill Stein	.08
332	Jim Sundberg	.08
333	Mark Wagner	.08
334	Bump Wills	.08
335	Bill Almon	.08
336	Harold Baines	.25
337	Ross Baumgarten	.08
338	Tony Bernazard	.08
339	Britt Burns	.08
340	Richard Dotson	.08
341	Jim Essian	.08
342	Ed Farmer	.08
343	Carlton Fisk	.90
344	Kevin Hickey	.08
345	Lamarr Hoyt (LaMarr)	.08
346	Lamar Johnson	.08
347	Jerry Koosman	.08
348	Rusty Kuntz	.08
349	Dennis Lamp	.08
350	Ron LeFlore	.08
351	Chet Lemon	.08
352	Greg Luzinski	.10
353	Bob Molinaro	.08
354	Jim Morrison	.08
355	Wayne Nordhagen	.08
356	Greg Pryor	.08
357	Mike Squires	.08
358	Steve Trout	.08
359	Alan Bannister	.08
360	Len Barker	.08
361	Bert Blyleven	.08
362	Joe Charboneau	.10
363	John Denny	.08
364	Bo Diaz	.08
365	Miguel Dilone	.08
366	Jerry Dybzinski	.08
367	Wayne Garland	.08
368	Mike Hargrove	.08
369	Toby Harrah	.08
370	Ron Hassey	.08
371	*Von Hayes*	.25
372	Pat Kelly	.08
373	Duane Kuiper	.08
374	Rick Manning	.08
375	Sid Monge	.08
376	Jorge Orta	.08
377	Dave Rosello	.08
378	Dan Spillner	.08
379	Mike Stanton	.08
380	Andre Thornton	.08
381	Tom Veryzer	.08
382	Rick Waits	.08
383	Doyle Alexander	.08
384	Vida Blue	.10
385	Fred Breining	.08
386	Enos Cabell	.08
387	Jack Clark	.08
388	Darrell Evans	.10
389	Tom Griffin	.08
390	Larry Herndon	.08
391	Al Holland	.08
392	Gary Lavelle	.08
393	Johnnie LeMaster	.08
394	Jerry Martin	.08
395	Milt May	.08
396	Greg Minton	.08
397	Joe Morgan	.75
398	Joe Pettini	.08
399	Alan Ripley	.08
400	Billy Smith	.08
401	Rennie Stennett	.08
402	Ed Whitson	.08
403	Jim Wohlford	.08
404	Willie Aikens	.08
405	George Brett	4.00
406	Ken Brett	.08
407	Dave Chalk	.08
408	Rich Gale	.08
409	Cesar Geronimo	.08
410	Larry Gura	.08
411	Clint Hurdle	.08
412	Mike Jones	.08
413	Dennis Leonard	.08
414	Renie Martin	.08
415	Lee May	.08
416	Hal McRae	.12
417	Darryl Motley	.08
418	Rance Mulliniks	.08
419	Amos Otis	.08
420	*Ken Phelps*	.10
421	Jamie Quirk	.08
422	Dan Quisenberry	.10
423	Paul Splittorff	.08
424	U.L. Washington	.08
425	John Wathan	.08
426	Frank White	.08
427	Willie Wilson	.10
428	Brian Asselstine	.08
429	Bruce Benedict	.08
430	Tom Boggs	.08
431	Larry Bradford	.08
432	Rick Camp	.08
433	Chris Chambliss	.08
434	Gene Garber	.08
435	Preston Hanna	.08
436	Bob Horner	.08
437	Glenn Hubbard	.08
438a	Al Hrabosky (All Hrabosky, 5'1" on back)	16.00
438b	Al Hrabosky (Al Hrabosky, 5'1" on back)	1.25
438c	Al Hrabosky (Al Hrabosky, 5'10" on back)	.35
439	Rufino Linares	.08
440	*Rick Mahler*	.12
441	Ed Miller	.08
442	John Montefusco	.08
443	Dale Murphy	.60
444	Phil Niekro	.90
445	Gaylord Perry	.65
446	Biff Pocoroba	.08
447	Rafael Ramirez	.08
448	Jerry Royster	.08
449	Claudell Washington	.08
450	Don Aase	.08
451	Don Baylor	.15
452	Juan Beniquez	.08
453	Rick Burleson	.08
454	Bert Campaneris	.08
455	Rod Carew	1.00
456	Bob Clark	.08
457	Brian Downing	.08
458	Dan Ford	.08
459	Ken Forsch	.08
460	Dave Frost	.08
461	Bobby Grich	.08
462	Larry Harlow	.08
463	John Harris	.08
464	Andy Hassler	.08
465	Butch Hobson	.08
466	Jesse Jefferson	.08
467	Bruce Kison	.08
468	Fred Lynn	.12
469	Angel Moreno	.08
470	Ed Ott	.08
471	Fred Patek	.08
472	Steve Renko	.08
473	*Mike Witt*	.25
474	Geoff Zahn	.08
475	Gary Alexander	.08
476	Dale Berra	.08
477	Kurt Bevacqua	.08
478	Jim Bibby	.08
479	John Candelaria	.08
480	Victor Cruz	.08
481	Mike Easler	.08
482	Tim Foli	.08
483	Lee Lacy	.08
484	Vance Law	.08
485	Bill Madlock	.08
486	Willie Montanez	.08
487	Omar Moreno	.08
488	Steve Nicosia	.08
489	Dave Parker	.20
490	Tony Pena	.10
491	Pascual Perez	.10
492	*Johnny Ray*	.08
493	Rick Rhoden	.08
494	Bill Robinson	.08
495	Don Robinson	.08
496	Enrique Romo	.08
497	Rod Scurry	.08
498	Eddie Solomon	.08
499	Willie Stargell	.75
500	Kent Tekulve	.08
501	Jason Thompson	.08
502	Glenn Abbott	.08
503	Jim Anderson	.08
504	Floyd Bannister	.08
505	Bruce Bochte	.08
506	Jeff Burroughs	.08
507	Bryan Clark	.08
508	Ken Clay	.08
509	Julio Cruz	.08
510	Dick Drago	.08
511	Gary Gray	.08
512	Dan Meyer	.08
513	Jerry Narron	.08
514	Tom Paciorek	.08
515	Casey Parsons	.08
516	Lenny Randle	.08
517	Shane Rawley	.08
518	Joe Simpson	.08
519	Richie Zisk	.08
520	Neil Allen	.08
521	Bob Bailor	.08
522	Hubie Brooks	.10
523	Mike Cubbage	.08
524	Pete Falcone	.08
525	Doug Flynn	.08
526	Tom Hausman	.08
527	Ron Hodges	.08
528	Randy Jones	.08
529	Mike Jorgensen	.08
530	Dave Kingman	.12
531	Ed Lynch	.08
532	Mike Marshall	.08
533	Lee Mazzilli	.08
534	Dyar Miller	.08
535	Mike Scott	.10
536	Rusty Staub	.10
537	John Stearns	.08
538	Craig Swan	.08
539	Frank Taveras	.08
540	Alex Trevino	.08
541	Ellis Valentine	.08
542	Mookie Wilson	.15
543	Joel Youngblood	.08
544	Pat Zachry	.08
545	Glenn Adams	.08
546	Fernando Arroyo	.08
547	John Verhoeven	.08
548	Sal Butera	.08
549	John Castino	.08
550	Don Cooper	.08
551	Doug Corbett	.08
552	Dave Engle	.08
553	Roger Erickson	.08
554	Danny Goodwin	.08
555a	Darrell Jackson (black cap)	1.00
555b	Darrell Jackson (red cap with emblem)	.10
555c	Darrell Jackson (red cap, no emblem)	.25

556	Pete Mackanin	.08
557	Jack O'Connor	.08
558	Hosken Powell	.08
559	Pete Redfern	.08
560	Roy Smalley	.08
561	Chuck Baker	.08
562	Gary Ward	.08
563	Rob Wilfong	.08
564	Al Williams	.08
565	Butch Wynegar	.08
566	Randy Bass	.08
567	Juan Bonilla	.08
568	Danny Boone	.08
569	John Curtis	.08
570	Juan Eichelberger	.08
571	Barry Evans	.08
572	Tim Flannery	.08
573	Ruppert Jones	.08
574	Terry Kennedy	.08
575	Joe Lefebvre	.08
576a	John Littlefield (pitching lefty)	200.00
576b	John Littlefield (pitching righty)	.08
577	Gary Lucas	.08
578	Steve Mura	.08
579	Broderick Perkins	.08
580	Gene Richards	.08
581	Luis Salazar	.08
582	Ozzie Smith	3.00
583	John Urrea	.08
584	Chris Welsh	.08
585	Rick Wise	.08
586	Doug Bird	.08
587	Tim Blackwell	.08
588	Bobby Bonds	.10
589	Bill Buckner	.08
590	Bill Caudill	.08
591	Hector Cruz	.08
592	*Jody Davis*	.10
593	Ivan DeJesus	.08
594	Steve Dillard	.08
595	Leon Durham	.08
596	Rawly Eastwick	.08
597	Steve Henderson	.08
598	Mike Krukow	.08
599	Mike Lum	.08
600	Randy Martz	.08
601	Jerry Morales	.08
602	Ken Reitz	.08
603a	*Lee Smith* (Cubs logo reversed on back)	8.00
603b	*Lee Smith* (corrected)	8.00
604	Dick Tidrow	.08
605	Jim Tracy	.08
606	Mike Tyson	.08
607	Ty Waller	.08
608	Danny Ainge	1.25
609	*Jorge Bell*	1.00
610	Mark Bomback	.08
611	Barry Bonnell	.08
612	Jim Clancy	.08
613	Damaso Garcia	.08
614	Jerry Garvin	.08
615	Alfredo Griffin	.08
616	Garth Iorg	.08
617	Luis Leal	.08
618	Ken Macha	.08
619	John Mayberry	.08
620	Joey McLaughlin	.08
621	Lloyd Moseby	.08
622	Dave Stieb	.08
623	Jackson Todd	.08
624	Willie Upshaw	.08
625	Otto Velez	.08
626	Ernie Whitt	.08
627	Al Woods	.08
628	1981 All-Star Game	.08
629	All-Star Infielders (Bucky Dent, Frank White)	.08
630	Big Red Machine (Dave Concepcion, Dan Driessen, George Foster)	.10
631	Top N.L. Relief Pitcher (Bruce Sutter)	.08
632	Steve & Carlton (Steve Carlton, Carlton Fisk)	.25
633	3000th Game, May 25, 1981 (Carl Yastrzemski)	.35
634	Dynamic Duo (Johnny Bench, Tom Seaver)	.30
635	West Meets East (Gary Carter, Fernando Valenzuela)	.20
636a	N.L. Strikeout King (Fernando Valenzuela) ("...led the National League...")	1.00
636b	N.L. Strikeout King (Fernando Valenzuela) ("... led the National League)	.35
637	Home Run King (Mike Schmidt)	.50
638	N.L. All-Stars (Gary Carter, Dave Parker)	.20
639	Perfect Game! (Len Barker, Bo Diaz)	.08
640	Pete Rose, Pete Rose, Jr. (Re-Pete)	2.00
641	Phillies' Finest (Steve Carlton, Mike Schmidt, Lonnie Smith)	.50
642	Red Sox Reunion (Dwight Evans, Fred Lynn)	.15
643	Most Hits and Runs (Rickey Henderson)	1.50
644	Most Saves 1981 A.L. (Rollie Fingers)	.15
645	Most 1981 Wins (Tom Seaver)	.25
646a	Yankee Powerhouse (Reggie Jackson, Dave Winfield) (comma after "outfielder" on back)	2.00
646b	Yankee Powerhouse (Reggie Jackson, Dave Winfield) (no comma)	2.00
647	Checklist 1-56	.08
648	Checklist 57-109	.08
649	Checklist 110-156	.08
650	Checklist 157-211	.08
651	Checklist 212-262	.08
652	Checklist 263-312	.08
653	Checklist 313-358	.08
654	Checklist 359-403	.08
655	Checklist 404-449	.08
656	Checklist 450-501	.08
657	Checklist 502-544	.08
658	Checklist 545-585	.08
659	Checklist 586-627	.08
660	Checklist 628-646	.08

1982 Fleer Stamps

Issued by Fleer in 1982, this set consists of 242 player stamps, each measuring 1-13/16" x 2-1/2". Originally issued in perforated strips of 10, the full-color stamps are numbered in the lower-left corner and were designed to be placed in an album. Six stamps feature two players each.

		MT
	Complete Set (242):	12.00
	Common Player:	.05
	Stamp Album:	1.50
1	Fernando Valenzuela	.10
2	Rick Monday	.05
3	Ron Cey	.05
4	Dusty Baker	.08
5	Burt Hooton	.05
6	Pedro Guerrero	.05
7	Jerry Reuss	.05
8	Bill Russell	.05
9	Steve Garvey	.20
10	Davey Lopes	.05
11	Tom Seaver	.25
12	George Foster	.05
13	Frank Pastore	.05
14	Dave Collins	.05
15	Dave Concepcion	.05
16	Ken Griffey	.08
17	Johnny Bench	.25
18	Ray Knight	.05
19	Mario Soto	.05
20	Ron Oester	.05
21	Ken Oberkfell	.05
22	Bob Forsch	.05
23	Keith Hernandez	.05
24	Dane Iorg	.05
25	George Hendrick	.05
26	Gene Tenace	.05
27	Garry Templeton	.05
28	Bruce Sutter	.05
29	Darrell Porter	.05
30	Tom Herr	.05
31	Tim Raines	.10
32	Chris Speier	.05
33	Warren Cromartie	.05
34	Larry Parrish	.05
35	Andre Dawson	.15
36	Steve Rogers	.05
37	Jeff Reardon	.05
38	Rodney Scott	.05
39	Gary Carter	.15
40	Scott Sanderson	.05
41	Cesar Cedeno	.05
42	Nolan Ryan	1.00
43	Don Sutton	.20
44	Terry Puhl	.05
45	Joe Niekro	.05
46	Tony Scott	.05
47	Joe Sambito	.05
48	Art Howe	.05
49	Bob Knepper	.05
50	Jose Cruz	.05
51	Pete Rose	.35
52	Dick Ruthven	.05
53	Mike Schmidt	.30
54	Steve Carlton	.25
55	Tug McGraw	.05
56	Larry Bowa	.05
57	Garry Maddox	.05
58	Gary Matthews	.05
59	Manny Trillo	.05
60	Lonnie Smith	.05
61	Vida Blue	.05
62	Milt May	.05
63	Joe Morgan	.25
64	Enos Cabell	.05
65	Jack Clark	.05
66	Claudell Washington	.05
67	Gaylord Perry	.20
68	Phil Niekro	.20
69	Bob Horner	.05
70	Chris Chambliss	.05
71	Dave Parker	.10
72	Tony Pena	.05
73	Kent Tekulve	.05
74	Mike Easler	.05
75	Tim Foli	.05
76	Willie Stargell	.25
77	Bill Madlock	.05
78	Jim Bibby	.05
79	Omar Moreno	.05
80	Lee Lacy	.05
81	Hubie Brooks	.05
82	Rusty Staub	.08
83	Ellis Valentine	.05
84	Neil Allen	.05
85	Dave Kingman	.08
86	Mookie Wilson	.05
87	Doug Flynn	.05
88	Pat Zachry	.05
89	John Stearns	.05
90	Lee Mazzilli	.05
91	Ken Reitz	.05
92	Mike Krukow	.05
93	Jerry Morales	.05
94	Leon Durham	.05
95	Ivan DeJesus	.05
96	Bill Buckner	.05
97	Jim Tracy	.05
98	Steve Henderson	.05
99	Dick Tidrow	.05
100	Mike Tyson	.05
101	Ozzie Smith	.25
102	Ruppert Jones	.05
103	Broderick Perkins	.05
104	Gene Richrds	.05
105	Terry Kennedy	.05
106	Jim Bibby, Willie Stargell	.08
107	Larry Bowa, Pete Rose	.10
108	Warren Spahn, Fernando Valenzuela	.15
109	Dave Concepcion, Pete Rose	.15
110	Reggie Jackson, Dave Winfield	.20
111	Tom Lasorda, Fernando Valenzuela	.20
112	Reggie Jackson	.25
113	Dave Winfield	.20
114	Lou Piniella	.08
115	Tommy John	.08
116	Rich Gossage	.08
117	Ron Davis	.05
118	Rick Cerone	.05
119	Graig Nettles	.05
120	Ron Guidry	.05
121	Willie Randolph	.05
122	Dwayne Murphy	.05
123	Rickey Henderson	.25
124	Wayne Gross	.05
125	Mike Norris	.05
126	Rick Langford	.05
127	Jim Spencer	.05
128	Tony Armas	.05
129	Matt Keough	.05
130	Jeff Jones	.05
131	Steve McCatty	.05
132	Rollie Fingers	.20
133	Jim Gantner	.05
134	Gorman Thomas	.05
135	Robin Yount	.35
136	Paul Molitor	.30
137	Ted Simmons	.05
138	Ben Oglivie	.05
139	Moose Haas	.05
140	Cecil Cooper	.05
141	Pete Vuckovich	.05
142	Doug DeCinces	.05
143	Jim Palmer	.25
144	Steve Stone	.05
145	Mike Flanagan	.05
146	Rick Dempsey	.05
147	Al Bumbry	.05
148	Mark Belanger	.05
149	Scott McGregor	.05
150	Ken Singleton	.05
151	Eddie Murray	.25
152	Lance Parrish	.08
153	David Rozema	.05
154	Champ Summers	.05
155	Alan Trammell	.10
156	Lou Whitaker	.08
157	Milt Wilcox	.05
158	Kevin Saucier	.05
159	Jack Morris	.05
160	Steve Kemp	.05
161	Kirk Gibson	.05
162	Carl Yastrzemski	.25
163	Jim Rice	.08
164	Carney Lansford	.05
165	Dennis Eckersley	.08
166	Mike Torrez	.05
167	Dwight Evans	.05
168	Glenn Hoffman	.05
169	Bob Stanley	.05
170	Tony Perez	.08
171	Jerry Remy	.05
172	Buddy Bell	.05
173	Ferguson Jenkins	.20
174	Mickey Rivers	.05
175	Bump Wills	.05
176	Jon Matlack	.05
177	Steve Comer	.05
178	Al Oliver	.05
179	Bill Stein	.05
180	Pat Putnam	.05
181	Jim Sundberg	.05
182	Ron LeFlore	.05
183	Carlton Fisk	.15
184	Harold Baines	.08
185	Bill Almon	.05
186	Richard Dotson	.05
187	Greg Luzinski	.05
188	Mike Squires	.05
189	Britt Burns	.05
190	Lamarr Hoyt	.05
191	Chet Lemon	.05
192	Joe Charboneau	.05
193	Toby Harrah	.05
194	John Denny	.05
195	Rick Manning	.05
196	Miguel Dilone	.05
197	Bo Diaz	.05
198	Mike Hargrove	.05
199	Bert Blyleven	.05
200	Len Barker	.05
201	Andre Thornton	.05
202	George Brett	.25
203	U.L. Washington	.05
204	Dan Quisenberry	.05
205	Larry Gura	.05
206	Willie Aikens	.05
207	Willie Wilson	.05
208	Dennis Leonard	.05
209	Frank White	.05
210	Hal McRae	.05
211	Amos Otis	.05
212	Don Aase	.05
213	Butch Hobson	.05
214	Fred Lynn	.08
215	Brian Downing	.05
216	Dan Ford	.05
217	Rod Carew	.25
218	Bobby Grich	.05
219	Rick Burleson	.05
220	Don Baylor	.08
221	Ken Forsch	.05
222	Bruce Bochte	.05
223	Richie Zisk	.05
224	Tom Paciorek	.05
225	Julio Cruz	.05
226	Jeff Burroughs	.05
227	Doug Corbett	.05
228	Roy Smalley	.05
229	Gary Ward	.05
230	John Castino	.05
231	Rob Wilfong	.05
232	Dave Stieb	.05
233	Otto Velez	.05
234	Damaso Garcia	.05
235	John Mayberry	.05
236	Alfredo Griffin	.05
237	Ted Williams, Carl Yastrzemski	.35
238	Rick Cerone, Graig Nettles	.05
239	Buddy Bell, George Brett	.15
240	Steve Carlton, Jim Kaat	.10
241	Steve Carlton, Dave Parker	.10
242	Ron Davis, Nolan Ryan	.40

1982 Fleer Test Cards

To test a proposed cardboard stock from International Paper Co., a run of 100 sheets of test cards was printed and delivered to Fleer officials. The cards on the sheet include various combinations of correct picture/name combinations, incorrect picture/name combinations and cards with no player identification. All cards have the words "TEST CARD" overprinted in black in the player identification area at bottom center, along with the letters "o", "n" or both vertically at the left end of the oblong area. Backs are blank. At least half of the 132-card test sheets have made their way into the hobby where they are offered both as complete sheets and as hand-cut single cards or panels. A number of the photos seen on the test cards did not appear in Fleer's 1982 card set and are of un-identified players. The checklist here is arranged by row and card number on the sheets. Player names are as printed, if the photo is not that player it is identified in parentheses. Each of the 66 cards is double-printed on the sheet.

		MT
	Complete Sheet (132):	1500.
	Complete Set (66):	900.00
	Common Card:	15.00
1-1	Jon Matlack (Reds #6)	15.00
1-2	Wayne Gross (Reds #54)	15.00
1-3	Mario Mendoza (Red Sox catcher)	15.00
1-4	Mike Heath (Angels #31)	15.00
1-5	Bump Wills (Mets #16)	15.00
1-6	Steve McCatty (Pirates #57)	15.00
1-7	Steve Stone	40.00
1-8	No identification (Pirates #12)	15.00
1-9	Dennis Martinez (Cubs player)	25.00
1-10	No identification (Red Sox player)	15.00
1-11	Jim Palmer (Del Unser)	40.00
2-1	Billy Sample (Astros player)	15.00
2-2	Tony Armas (Mets #8)	15.00
2-3	Rick Honeycutt (Reds #17)	15.00
2-4	Cliff Jackson (Royals player)	15.00
2-5	John Ellis (Orioles player)	15.00
2-6	Dave McKay (Royals #35)	15.00
2-7	Ken Singleton (Yankees player)	15.00
2-8	No identification (Yankees player)	15.00
2-9	John Lowenstein (Angels #22)	15.00
2-10	No identification (Cubs player)	15.00
2-11	Doug DeCinces (Yankees player)	15.00
3-1	Mickey Rivers (Rangers pitcher)	15.00
3-2	Rickey Henderson (Mike Norris)	40.00
3-3	Jim Sundberg (Jim Kern)	15.00
3-4	Bob Owchinko (Fred Stanley)	15.00
3-5	Buddy Bell (Danny Darwin)	15.00
3-6	Shooty Babbitt (Rick Langford)	15.00
3-7	Sammy Stewart (Tippy Martinez)	15.00
3-8	No identification (Juan Eichelberger)	15.00
3-9	Lenn Sakata (Eddie Murray)	40.00
3-10	No identification (Juan Bonilla)	15.00
3-11	Benny Ayala (Terry Crowley)	15.00
4-1	Al Oliver (Bill Stein)	15.00
4-2	Dwayne Murphy (Matt Keough)	15.00
4-3	Leon Roberts (John Grubb)	15.00
4-4	Rob Picciolo (Brian Kingman)	15.00
4-5	Mark Wagner (Steve Comer)	15.00

4-6 Jeff Jones (Jeff Neumann) 15.00
4-7 Tim Stoddard (Mike Flanagan) 15.00
4-8 No identification (John Urrea) 15.00
4-9 Rick Dempsey (Mark Belanger) 15.00
4-10 No identification (Luis Salazar) 15.00
4-11 Dave Ford (Cal Ripken Jr.) 250.00
5-1 Pat Putnam 25.00
5-2 Mike Norris 25.00
5-3 Jim Kern 25.00
5-4 Fred Stanley 25.00
5-5 Danny Darwin 25.00
5-6 Rick Langford 25.00
5-7 Tippy Martinez 25.00
5-8 No identification (Juan Eichelberger) 15.00
5-9 Eddie Murray 50.00
5-10 No identification (Juan Bonilla) 15.00
5-11 Terry Crowley 25.00
6-1 Bill Stein 25.00
6-2 Matt Keough 25.00
6-3 John Grubb 25.00
6-4 Brian Kingman 25.00
6-5 Steve Comer 25.00
6-6 Jeff Neumann 25.00
6-7 Mike Flanagan 25.00
6-8 No identification (John Urrea) 15.00
6-9 Mark Belanger 25.00
6-10 No identification (Luis Salazar) 15.00
6-11 Cal Ripken, Jr. 400.00

1983 Fleer Promo Sheet

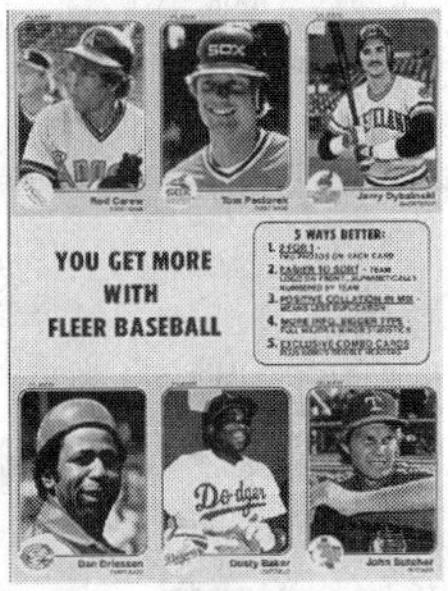

The consumer, rather than dealer, was the target audience for this sheet premiering '83 Fleer. Six player cards, identical to the issued versions, appear on the 9-5/8" x 7-1/2" sheet, along with advertising messages on front and back. Versions of the sheet can be found with the name of hobby publications which inserted the sample into their issues.

	MT
Uncut Sheet:	20.00
81 Rod Carew	
201 Dusty Baker	
248 Tom Paciorek	
406 Jerry Dybzinski	
563 John Butcher	
589 Dan Driessen	

1983 Fleer

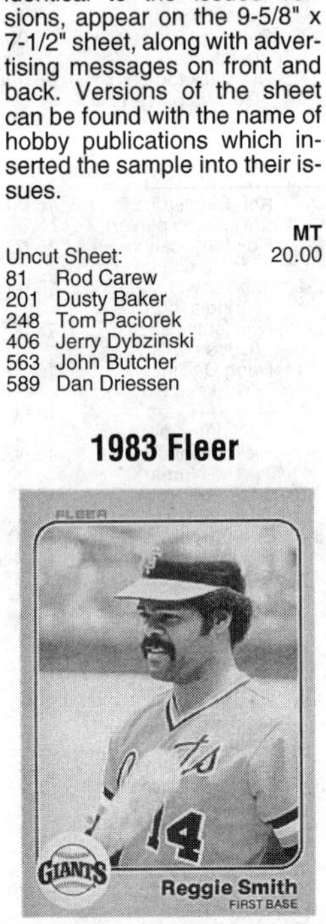

The 1983 Fleer set features color photos set inside a light brown border. The cards are standard 2-1/2" x 3-1/2". A team logo is located at the card bottom and the word "Fleer" is found at the top. The card backs are designed on a vertical format and include a small black and white photo of the player along with biographical and statistical information. The reverses are done in two shades of brown on white stock. The set was issued with team logo stickers.

	MT
Complete Set (660):	100.00
Common Player:	.08
Wax Box:	180.00

1 Joaquin Andujar .08
2 Doug Bair .08
3 Steve Braun .08
4 Glenn Brummer .08
5 Bob Forsch .08
6 David Green .08
7 George Hendrick .08
8 Keith Hernandez .10
9 Tom Herr .08
10 Dane Iorg .08
11 Jim Kaat .12
12 Jeff Lahti .08
13 Tito Landrum .08
14 *Dave LaPoint* .08
15 *Willie McGee* 1.50
16 Steve Mura .08
17 Ken Oberkfell .08
18 Darrell Porter .08
19 Mike Ramsey .08
20 Gene Roof .08
21 Lonnie Smith .08
22 Ozzie Smith 2.50
23 John Stuper .08
24 Bruce Sutter .08
25 Gene Tenace .08
26 Jerry Augustine .08
27 Dwight Bernard .08
28 Mark Brouhard .08
29 Mike Caldwell .08
30 Cecil Cooper .08
31 Jamie Easterly .08
32 Marshall Edwards .08
33 Rollie Fingers .60
34 Jim Gantner .08
35 Moose Haas .08
36 Roy Howell .08
37 Peter Ladd .08
38 Bob McClure .08
39 Doc Medich .08
40 Paul Molitor 2.50
41 Don Money .08
42 Charlie Moore .08
43 Ben Oglivie .08
44 Ed Romero .08
45 Ted Simmons .08
46 Jim Slaton .08
47 Don Sutton .40
48 Gorman Thomas .08
49 Pete Vuckovich .08
50 Ned Yost .08
51 Robin Yount 2.50
52 Benny Ayala .08
53 Bob Bonner .08
54 Al Bumbry .08
55 Terry Crowley .08
56 *Storm Davis* .10
57 Rich Dauer .08
58 Rick Dempsey .08
59 Jim Dwyer .08
60 Mike Flanagan .08
61 Dan Ford .08
62 Glenn Gulliver .08
63 John Lowenstein .08
64 Dennis Martinez .10
65 Tippy Martinez .08
66 Scott McGregor .08
67 Eddie Murray 2.50
68 Joe Nolan .08
69 Jim Palmer .90
70 Cal Ripken, Jr. 15.00
71 Gary Roenicke .08
72 Lenn Sakata .08
73 Ken Singleton .08
74 Sammy Stewart .08
75 Tim Stoddard .08
76 Don Aase .08
77 Don Baylor .10
78 Juan Beniquez .08
79 Bob Boone .08
80 Rick Burleson .08
81 Rod Carew 1.00
82 Bobby Clark .08
83 Doug Corbett .08
84 John Curtis .08
85 Doug DeCinces .08
86 Brian Downing .08
87 Joe Ferguson .08
88 Tim Foli .08
89 Ken Forsch .08
90 Dave Goltz .08
91 Bobby Grich .08
92 Andy Hassler .08
93 Reggie Jackson 1.00
94 Ron Jackson .08
95 Tommy John .10
96 Bruce Kison .08
97 Fred Lynn .10
98 Ed Ott .08
99 Steve Renko .08
100 Luis Sanchez .08
101 Rob Wilfong .08
102 Mike Witt .08
103 Geoff Zahn .08
104 Willie Aikens .08
105 Mike Armstrong .08
106 Vida Blue .08
107 *Bud Black* .50
108 George Brett 3.50
109 Bill Castro .08
110 Onix Concepcion .08
111 Dave Frost .08
112 Cesar Geronimo .08
113 Larry Gura .08
114 Steve Hammond .08
115 Don Hood .08
116 Dennis Leonard .08
117 Jerry Martin .08
118 Lee May .08
119 Hal McRae .08
120 Amos Otis .08
121 Greg Pryor .08
122 Dan Quisenberry .08
123 *Don Slaught* .20
124 Paul Splittorff .08
125 U.L. Washington .08
126 John Wathan .08
127 Frank White .08
128 Willie Wilson .08
129 Steve Bedrosian .08
130 Bruce Benedict .08
131 Tommy Boggs .08
132 Brett Butler .15
133 Rick Camp .08
134 Chris Chambliss .08
135 Ken Dayley .08
136 Gene Garber .08
137 Terry Harper .08
138 Bob Horner .08
139 Glenn Hubbard .08
140 Rufino Linares .08
141 Rick Mahler .08
142 Dale Murphy .45
143 Phil Niekro .60
144 Pascual Perez .08
145 Biff Pocoroba .08
146 Rafael Ramirez .08
147 Jerry Royster .08
148 Ken Smith .08
149 Bob Walk .08
150 Claudell Washington .08
151 Bob Watson .08
152 Larry Whisenton .08
153 Porfirio Altamirano .08
154 Marty Bystrom .08
155 Steve Carlton 1.00
156 Larry Christenson .08
157 Ivan DeJesus .08
158 John Denny .08
159 Bob Dernier .08
160 Bo Diaz .08
161 Ed Farmer .08
162 Greg Gross .08
163 Mike Krukow .08
164 Garry Maddox .08
165 Gary Matthews .08
166 Tug McGraw .08
167 Bob Molinaro .08
168 Sid Monge .08
169 Ron Reed .08
170 Bill Robinson .08
171 Pete Rose 3.00
172 Dick Ruthven .08
173 Mike Schmidt 2.50
174 Manny Trillo .08
175 Ozzie Virgil .08
176 George Vukovich .08
177 Gary Allenson .08
178 Luis Aponte .08
179 *Wade Boggs* 17.50
180 Tom Burgmeier .08
181 Mark Clear .08
182 Dennis Eckersley .30
183 Dwight Evans .10
184 Rich Gedman .08
185 Glenn Hoffman .08
186 Bruce Hurst .08
187 Carney Lansford .08
188 Rick Miller .08
189 Reid Nichols .08
190 Bob Ojeda .08
191 Tony Perez .10
192 Chuck Rainey .08
193 Jerry Remy .08
194 Jim Rice .12
195 Bob Stanley .08
196 Dave Stapleton .08
197 Mike Torrez .08
198 John Tudor .08
199 Julio Valdez .08
200 Carl Yastrzemski 1.00
201 Dusty Baker .08
202 Joe Beckwith .08
203 *Greg Brock* .08
204 Ron Cey .08
205 Terry Forster .08
206 Steve Garvey .30
207 Pedro Guerrero .08
208 Burt Hooton .08
209 Steve Howe .08
210 Ken Landreaux .08
211 Mike Marshall .08
212 *Candy Maldonado* .10
213 Rick Monday .08
214 Tom Niedenfuer .08
215 Jorge Orta .08
216 Jerry Reuss .08
217 Ron Roenicke .08
218 Vicente Romo .08
219 Bill Russell .10
220 Steve Sax .08
221 Mike Scioscia .08
222 Dave Stewart .25
223 Derrel Thomas .08
224 Fernando Valenzuela .10
225 Bob Welch .08
226 Ricky Wright .08
227 Steve Yeager .08
228 Bill Almon .08
229 Harold Baines .15
230 Salome Barojas .08
231 Tony Bernazard .08
232 Britt Burns .08
233 Richard Dotson .08
234 Ernesto Escarrega .08
235 Carlton Fisk .45
236 Jerry Hairston .08
237 Kevin Hickey .08
238 LaMarr Hoyt .08
239 Steve Kemp .08
240 Jim Kern .08
241 *Ron Kittle* .15
242 Jerry Koosman .08
243 Dennis Lamp .08
244 Rudy Law .08
245 Vance Law .08
246 Ron LeFlore .08
247 Greg Luzinski .10
248 Tom Paciorek .08
249 Aurelio Rodriguez .08
250 Mike Squires .08
251 Steve Trout .08
252 Jim Barr .08
253 Dave Bergman .08
254 Fred Breining .08
255 Bob Brenly .08
256 Jack Clark .08
257 Chili Davis .20
258 Darrell Evans .10
259 Alan Fowlkes .08
260 Rich Gale .08
261 Atlee Hammaker .08
262 Al Holland .08
263 Duane Kuiper .08
264 Bill Laskey .08
265 Gary Lavelle .08
266 Johnnie LeMaster .08
267 Renie Martin .08
268 Milt May .08
269 Greg Minton .08
270 Joe Morgan .60
271 Tom O'Malley .08
272 Reggie Smith .08
273 Guy Sularz .08
274 Champ Summers .08
275 Max Venable .08
276 Jim Wohlford .08
277 Ray Burris .08
278 Gary Carter .20
279 Warren Cromartie .08
280 Andre Dawson .50
281 Terry Francona .08
282 Doug Flynn .08
283 Woody Fryman .08
284 Bill Gullickson .08
285 Wallace Johnson .08
286 Charlie Lea .08
287 Randy Lerch .08
288 Brad Mills .08
289 Dan Norman .08
290 Al Oliver .08
291 David Palmer .08
292 Tim Raines .25
293 Jeff Reardon .10
294 Steve Rogers .08
295 Scott Sanderson .08
296 Dan Schatzeder .08
297 Bryn Smith .08
298 Chris Speier .08
299 Tim Wallach .10
300 Jerry White .08
301 Joel Youngblood .08
302 Ross Baumgarten .08
303 Dale Berra .08
304 John Candelaria .08
305 Dick Davis .08
306 Mike Easler .08
307 Richie Hebner .08
308 Lee Lacy .08
309 Bill Madlock .08
310 Larry McWilliams .08
311 John Milner .08
312 Omar Moreno .08
313 Jim Morrison .08
314 Steve Nicosia .08
315 Dave Parker .12
316 Tony Pena .08
317 Johnny Ray .08
318 Rick Rhoden .08
319 Don Robinson .08
320 Enrique Romo .08
321 Manny Sarmiento .08
322 Rod Scurry .08
323 Jim Smith .08
324 Willie Stargell .60
325 Jason Thompson .08
326 Kent Tekulve .08
327a Tom Brookens (narrow (1/4") brown box at bottom on back) .45
327b Tom Brookens (wide (1-1/4") brown box at bottom on back) .08
328 Enos Cabell .08
329 Kirk Gibson .08
330 Larry Herndon .08
331 Mike Ivie .08
332 *Howard Johnson* 1.00
333 Lynn Jones .08
334 Rick Leach .08
335 Chet Lemon .08
336 Jack Morris .10
337 Lance Parrish .10
338 Larry Pashnick .08
339 Dan Petry .08
340 Dave Rozema .08
341 Dave Rucker .08
342 Elias Sosa .08
343 Dave Tobik .08
344 Alan Trammell .45
345 Jerry Turner .08
346 Jerry Ujdur .08
347 Pat Underwood .08
348 Lou Whitaker .10
349 Milt Wilcox .08
350 *Glenn Wilson* .08
351 John Wockenfuss .08
352 Kurt Bevacqua .08
353 Juan Bonilla .08
354 Floyd Chiffer .08
355 Luis DeLeon .08
356 *Dave Dravecky* .30
357 Dave Edwards .08
358 Juan Eichelberger .08
359 Tim Flannery .08
360 *Tony Gwynn* 25.00
361 Ruppert Jones .08
362 Terry Kennedy .08
363 Joe Lefebvre .08
364 Sixto Lezcano .08
365 Tim Lollar .08
366 Gary Lucas .08
367 John Montefusco .08
368 Broderick Perkins .08
369 Joe Pittman .08
370 Gene Richards .08
371 Luis Salazar .08
372 *Eric Show* .08
373 Garry Templeton .08
374 Chris Welsh .08
375 Alan Wiggins .08
376 Rick Cerone .08
377 Dave Collins .08
378 Roger Erickson .08
379 George Frazier .08
380 Oscar Gamble .08
381 Goose Gossage .08
382 Ken Griffey .10
383 Ron Guidry .10
384 Dave LaRoche .08
385 Rudy May .08
386 John Mayberry .08
387 Lee Mazzilli .08
388 Mike Morgan .08
389 Jerry Mumphrey .08
390 Bobby Murcer .08
391 Graig Nettles .08
392 Lou Piniella .10
393 Willie Randolph .08
394 Shane Rawley .08
395 Dave Righetti .08
396 Andre Robertson .08
397 Roy Smalley .08
398 Dave Winfield 2.00
399 Butch Wynegar .08
400 Chris Bando .08
401 Alan Bannister .08
402 Len Barker .08
403 Tom Brennan .08
404 *Carmelo Castillo* .08
405 Miguel Dilone .08
406 Jerry Dybzinski .08
407 Mike Fischlin .08
408 Ed Glynn (photo actually Bud Anderson) .08
409 Mike Hargrove .08
410 Toby Harrah .08
411 Ron Hassey .08
412 Von Hayes .08
413 Rick Manning .08
414 Bake McBride .08
415 Larry Milbourne .08
416 Bill Nahorodny .08
417 Jack Perconte .08
418 Larry Sorensen .08
419 Dan Spillner .08
420 Rick Sutcliffe .08
421 Andre Thornton .08
422 Rick Waits .08
423 Eddie Whitson .08
424 Jesse Barfield .08
425 Barry Bonnell .08
426 Jim Clancy .08
427 Damaso Garcia .08
428 Jerry Garvin .08
429 Alfredo Griffin .08
430 Garth Iorg .08
431 Roy Lee Jackson .08
432 Luis Leal .08
433 Buck Martinez .08
434 Joey McLaughlin .08
435 Lloyd Moseby .08
436 Rance Mulliniks .08
437 Dale Murray .08
438 Wayne Nordhagen .08
439 *Gene Petralli* .08
440 Hosken Powell .08
441 Dave Stieb .08
442 Willie Upshaw .08
443 Ernie Whitt .08
444 Al Woods .08
445 Alan Ashby .08
446 Jose Cruz .08
447 Kiko Garcia .08
448 Phil Garner .08
449 Danny Heep .08

450	Art Howe	.08
451	Bob Knepper	.08
452	Alan Knicely	.08
453	Ray Knight	.08
454	Frank LaCorte	.08
455	Mike LaCoss	.08
456	Randy Moffitt	.08
457	Joe Niekro	.08
458	Terry Puhl	.08
459	Luis Pujols	.08
460	Craig Reynolds	.08
461	Bert Roberge	.08
462	Vern Ruhle	.08
463	Nolan Ryan	8.00
464	Joe Sambito	.08
465	Tony Scott	.08
466	Dave Smith	.08
467	Harry Spilman	.08
468	Dickie Thon	.08
469	Denny Walling	.08
470	Larry Andersen	.08
471	Floyd Bannister	.08
472	Jim Beattie	.08
473	Bruce Bochte	.08
474	Manny Castillo	.08
475	Bill Caudill	.08
476	Bryan Clark	.08
477	Al Cowens	.08
478	Julio Cruz	.08
479	Todd Cruz	.08
480	Gary Gray	.08
481	Dave Henderson	.10
482	*Mike Moore*	.25
483	Gaylord Perry	.50
484	Dave Revering	.08
485	Joe Simpson	.08
486	Mike Stanton	.08
487	Rick Sweet	.08
488	*Ed Vande Berg*	.08
489	Richie Zisk	.08
490	Doug Bird	.08
491	Larry Bowa	.08
492	Bill Buckner	.10
493	Bill Campbell	.08
494	Jody Davis	.08
495	Leon Durham	.08
496	Steve Henderson	.08
497	Willie Hernandez	.08
498	Fergie Jenkins	.50
499	Jay Johnstone	.08
500	Junior Kennedy	.08
501	Randy Martz	.08
502	Jerry Morales	.08
503	Keith Moreland	.08
504	Dickie Noles	.08
505	Mike Proly	.08
506	Allen Ripley	.08
507	*Ryne Sandberg*	15.00
508	Lee Smith	1.25
509	Pat Tabler	.08
510	Dick Tidrow	.08
511	Bump Wills	.08
512	Gary Woods	.08
513	Tony Armas	.08
514	Dave Beard	.08
515	Jeff Burroughs	.08
516	John D'Acquisto	.08
517	Wayne Gross	.08
518	Mike Heath	.08
519	Rickey Henderson	2.50
520	Cliff Johnson	.08
521	Matt Keough	.08
522	Brian Kingman	.08
523	Rick Langford	.08
524	Davey Lopes	.08
525	Steve McCatty	.08
526	Dave McKay	.08
527	Dan Meyer	.08
528	Dwayne Murphy	.08
529	Jeff Newman	.08
530	Mike Norris	.08
531	Bob Owchinko	.08
532	Joe Rudi	.08
533	Jimmy Sexton	.08
534	Fred Stanley	.08
535	Tom Underwood	.08
536	Neil Allen	.08
537	Wally Backman	.08
538	Bob Bailor	.08
539	Hubie Brooks	.08
540	Carlos Diaz	.08
541	Pete Falcone	.08
542	George Foster	.08
543	Ron Gardenhire	.08
544	Brian Giles	.08
545	Ron Hodges	.08
546	Randy Jones	.08
547	Mike Jorgensen	.08
548	Dave Kingman	.10
549	Ed Lynch	.08
550	Jesse Orosco	.08
551	Rick Ownbey	.08
552	*Charlie Puleo*	.08
553	Gary Rajsich	.08
554	Mike Scott	.08
555	Rusty Staub	.10
556	John Stearns	.08
557	Craig Swan	.08
558	Ellis Valentine	.08
559	Tom Veryzer	.08
560	Mookie Wilson	.08
561	Pat Zachry	.08
562	Buddy Bell	.08
563	John Butcher	.08
564	Steve Comer	.08
565	Danny Darwin	.08
566	Bucky Dent	.08
567	John Grubb	.08
568	Rick Honeycutt	.08
569	Dave Hostetler	.08
570	Charlie Hough	.08
571	Lamar Johnson	.08
572	Jon Matlack	.08
573	Paul Mirabella	.08
574	Larry Parrish	.08
575	Mike Richardt	.08
576	Mickey Rivers	.08
577	Billy Sample	.08
578	*Dave Schmidt*	.08
579	Bill Stein	.08
580	Jim Sundberg	.08
581	Frank Tanana	.08
582	Mark Wagner	.08
583	George Wright	.08
584	Johnny Bench	1.00
585	Bruce Berenyi	.08
586	Larry Biittner	.08
587	Cesar Cedeno	.08
588	Dave Concepcion	.08
589	Dan Driessen	.08
590	Greg Harris	.08
591	Ben Hayes	.08
592	Paul Householder	.08
593	Tom Hume	.08
594	Wayne Krenchicki	.08
595	Rafael Landestoy	.08
596	Charlie Leibrandt	.08
597	*Eddie Milner*	.08
598	Ron Oester	.08
599	Frank Pastore	.08
600	Joe Price	.08
601	Tom Seaver	1.00
602	Bob Shirley	.08
603	Mario Soto	.08
604	Alex Trevino	.08
605	Mike Vail	.08
606	Duane Walker	.08
607	Tom Brunansky	.08
608	Bobby Castillo	.08
609	John Castino	.08
610	Ron Davis	.08
611	Lenny Faedo	.08
612	Terry Felton	.08
613	*Gary Gaetti*	.35
614	Mickey Hatcher	.08
615	Brad Havens	.08
616	Kent Hrbek	.25
617	Randy S. Johnson	.08
618	Tim Laudner	.08
619	Jeff Little	.08
620	Bob Mitchell	.08
621	Jack O'Connor	.08
622	John Pacella	.08
623	Pete Redfern	.08
624	Jesus Vega	.08
625	*Frank Viola*	.90
626	Ron Washington	.08
627	Gary Ward	.08
628	Al Williams	.08
629	Red Sox All-Stars (Mark Clear, Dennis Eckersley, Carl Yastrzemski)	.25
630	300 Career Wins (Terry Bulling, Gaylord Perry)	.15
631	Pride of Venezuela (Dave Concepcion, Manny Trillo)	.10
632	All-Star Infielders (Buddy Bell, Robin Yount)	.20
633	Mr. Vet & Mr. Rookie (Kent Hrbek, Dave Winfield)	.25
634	Fountain of Youth (Pete Rose, Willie Stargell)	.40
635	Big Chiefs (Toby Harrah, Andre Thornton)	.08
636	"Smith Bros." (Lonnie Smith, Ozzie Smith)	.10
637	Base Stealers' Threat (Gary Carter, Bo Diaz)	.10
638	All-Star Catchers (Gary Carter, Carlton Fisk)	.20
639	Rickey Henderson (In Action)	.50
640	Home Run Threats (Reggie Jackson, Ben Oglivie)	.25
641	Two Teams - Same Day (Joel Youngblood)	.08
642	Last Perfect Game (Len Barker, Ron Hassey)	.08
643	Blue (Vida Blue)	.08
644	Black & (Bud Black)	.08
645	Power (Reggie Jackson)	.30
646	Speed & (Rickey Henderson)	.30
647	Checklist 1-51	.08
648	Checklist 52-103	.08
649	Checklist 104-152	.08
650	Checklist 153-200	.08
651	Checklist 201-251	.08
652	Checklist 252-301	.08
653	Checklist 302-351	.08
654	Checklist 352-399	.08
655	Checklist 400-444	.08
656	Checklist 445-489	.08
657	Checklist 490-535	.08
658	Checklist 536-583	.08
659	Checklist 584-628	.08
660	Checklist 629-646	.08

1983 Fleer Stickers

This 270-sticker set consists of both player stickers and team logo stickers, all measuring 1-13/16" x 2-1/2". The player stickers are numbered on the back. The front features a full-color photo surrounded by a blue border with two stars at the top. The stickers were issued in strips of ten player stickers plus two team logo stickers. The 26 logo stickers have been assigned numbers 271 through 296.

		MT
	Complete Set (296):	13.00
	Common Player:	.05
1	Bruce Sutter	.05
2	Willie McGee	.08
3	Darrell Porter	.05
4	Lonnie Smith	.05
5	Dane Iorg	.05
6	Keith Hernandez	.05
7	Joaquin Andujar	.05
8	Ken Oberkfell	.05
9	John Stuper	.05
10	Ozzie Smith	.20
11	Bob Forsch	.05
12	Jim Gantner	.05
13	Rollie Fingers	.15
14	Pete Vuckovich	.05
15	Ben Oglivie	.05
16	Don Sutton	.12
17	Bob McClure	.05
18	Robin Yount	.20
19	Paul Molitor	.20
20	Gorman Thomas	.05
21	Mike Caldwell	.05
22	Ted Simmons	.05
23	Cecil Cooper	.05
24	Steve Renko	.05
25	Tommy John	.08
26	Rod Carew	.25
27	Bruce Kison	.05
28	Ken Forsch	.05
29	Geoff Zahn	.05
30	Doug DiCinces	.05
31	Fred Lynn	.08
32	Reggie Jackson	.25
33	Don Baylor	.08
34	Bob Boone	.05
35	Brian Downing	.05
36	Goose Gossage	.05
37	Roy Smalley	.05
38	Graig Nettles	.05
39	Dave Winfield	.20
40	Lee Mazzilli	.05
41	Jerry Mumphrey	.05
42	Dave Collins	.05
43	Rick Cerone	.05
44	Willie Randolph	.05
45	Lou Piniella	.08
46	Ken Griffey	.08
47	Ron Guidry	.05
48	Jack Clark	.05
49	Reggie Smith	.05
50	Atlee Hammaker	.05
51	Fred Breining	.05
52	Gary Lavelle	.05
53	Chili Davis	.08
54	Greg Minton	.05
55	Joe Morgan	.15
56	Al Holland	.05
57	Bill Laskey	.05
58	Duane Kuiper	.05
59	Tom Burgmeier	.05
60	Carl Yastrzemski	.25
61	Mark Clear	.05
62	Mike Torrez	.05
63	Dennis Eckersley	.08
64	Wade Boggs	.40
65	Bob Stanley	.05
66	Jim Rice	.10
67	Carney Lansford	.05
68	Jerry Remy	.05
69	Dwight Evans	.08
70	John Candelaria	.05
71	Bill Madlock	.05
72	Dave Parker	.08
73	Kent Tekulve	.05
74	Tony Pena	.05
75	Manny Sarmiento	.05
76	Johnny Ray	.05
77	Dale Berra	.05
78	Lee Lacy	.05
79	Jason Thompson	.05
80	Mike Easler	.05
81	Willie Stargell	.20
82	Rick Camp	.05
83	Bob Watson	.05
84	Bob Horner	.05
85	Rafael Ramirez	.05
86	Chris Chambliss	.05
87	Gene Garber	.05
88	Claudell Washington	.05
89	Steve Bedrosian	.05
90	Dale Murphy	.15
91	Phil Niekro	.15
92	Jerry Royster	.05
93	Bob Walk	.05
94	Frank White	.05
95	Dennis Leonard	.05
96	Vida Blue	.05
97	U.L. Washington	.05
98	George Brett	.45
99	Amos Otis	.05
100	Dan Quisenberry	.05
101	Willie Aikens	.05
102	Hal McRae	.05
103	Larry Gura	.05
104	Willie Wilson	.05
105	Damaso Garcia	.05
106	Hosken Powell	.05
107	Joey McLaughlin	.05
108	Jim Clancy	.05
109	Barry Bonnell	.05
110	Garth Iorg	.05
111	Dave Stieb	.05
112	Fernando Valenzuela	.08
113	Steve Garvey	.12
114	Rick Monday	.05
115	Burt Hooton	.05
116	Bill Russell	.08
117	Pedro Guerrero	.05
118	Steve Sax	.05
119	Steve Howe	.05
120	Ken Landreaux	.05
121	Dusty Baker	.08
122	Ron Cey	.05
123	Jerry Reuss	.05
124	Bump Wills	.05
125	Keith Moreland	.05
126	Dick Tidrow	.05
127	Bill Campbell	.05
128	Larry Bowa	.05
129	Randy Martz	.05
130	Ferguson Jenkins	.15
131	Leon Durham	.05
132	Bill Buckner	.05
133	Ron Davis	.05
134	Jack O'Connor	.05
135	Kent Hrbek	.08
136	Gary Ward	.05
137	Al Williams	.05
138	Tom Brunansky	.05
139	Bobby Castillo	.05
140	Dusty Baker, Dale Murphy	.08
141	Nolan Ryan	.50
142	Lee Lacey (Lacy), Omar Moreno	.05
143	Al Oliver, Pete Rose	.25
144	Rickey Henderson	.25
145	Ray Knight, Pete Rose, Mike Schmidt	.30
146	Hal McRae, Ben Oglivie	.05
147	Tom Hume, Ray Knight	.05
148	Buddy Bell, Carlton Fisk	.05
149	Steve Kemp	.05
150	Rudy Law	.05
151	Ron LeFlore	.05
152	Jerry Koosman	.05
153	Carlton Fisk	.10
154	Salome Barojas	.05
155	Harold Baines	.08
156	Britt Burns	.05
157	Tom Paciorek	.05
158	Greg Luzinski	.05
159	LaMarr Hoyt	.05
160	George Wright	.05
161	Danny Darwin	.05
162	Lamar Johnson	.05
163	Charlie Hough	.05
164	Buddy Bell	.05
165	John Matlack (Jon)	.05
166	Billy Sample	.05
167	John Grubb	.05
168	Larry Parrish	.05
169	Ivan DeJesus	.05
170	Mike Schmidt	.40
171	Tug McGraw	.05
172	Ron Reed	.05
173	Garry Maddox	.05
174	Pete Rose	.45
175	Manny Trillo	.05
176	Steve Carlton	.20
177	Bo Diaz	.05
178	Gary Matthews	.05
179	Bill Caudill	.05
180	Ed Vande Berg	.05
181	Gaylord Perry	.15
182	Floyd Bannister	.05
183	Richie Zisk	.05
184	Al Cowens	.05
185	Bruce Bochte	.05
186	Jeff Burroughs	.05
187	Dave Beard	.05
188	Davey Lopes	.05
189	Dwayne Murphy	.05
190	Rick Langford	.05
191	Tom Underwood	.05
192	Rickey Henderson	.25
193	Mike Flanagan	.05
194	Scott McGregor	.05
195	Ken Singleton	.05
196	Rich Dauer	.05
197	John Lowenstein	.05
198	Cal Ripken, Jr.	1.00
199	Dennis Martinez	.08
200	Jim Palmer	.20
201	Tippy Martinez	.05
202	Eddie Murray	.20
203	Al Bumbry	.05
204	Dickie Thon	.05
205	Phil Garner	.05
206	Jose Cruz	.05
207	Nolan Ryan	.50
208	Ray Knight	.05
209	Terry Puhl	.05
210	Joe Niekro	.05
211	Art Howe	.05
212	Alan Ashby	.05
213	Tom Hume	.05
214	Johnny Bench	.25
215	Larry Bittner	.05
216	Mario Soto	.05
217	Dan Driessen	.05
218	Tom Seaver	.25
219	Dave Concepcion	.05
220	Wayne Krenchicki	.05
221	Cesar Cedeno	.05
222	Ruppert Jones	.05
223	Terry Kennedy	.05
224	Luis DeLeon	.05
225	Eric Show	.05
226	Tim Flannery	.05
227	Garry Templeton	.05
228	Tim Lollar	.05
229	Sixto Lezcano	.05
230	Bob Bailor	.05
231	Craig Swan	.05
232	Dave Kingman	.08
233	Mookie Wilson	.05
234	John Stearns	.05
235	Ellis Valentine	.05
236	Neil Allen	.05
237	Pat Zachry	.05
238	Rusty Staub	.08
239	George Foster	.08
240	Rick Sutcliffe	.05
241	Andre Thornton	.05
242	Mike Hargrove	.05
243	Dan Spillner	.05
244	Lary Sorensen	.05
245	Len Barker	.05
246	Rick Manning	.05
247	Toby Harrah	.05
248	Milt Wilcox	.05
249	Lou Whitaker	.05
250	Tom Brookens	.05
251	Chet Lemon	.05
252	Jack Morris	.05
253	Alan Trammell	.10
254	John Wockenfuss	.05
255	Lance Parrish	.05
256	Larry Herndon	.05
257	Chris Speier	.05
258	Woody Fryman	.05
259	Scott Sanderson	.05
260	Steve Rogers	.05
261	Warren Cromartie	.05
262	Gary Carter	.12
263	Bill Gullickson	.05
264	Andre Dawson	.12
265	Tim Raines	.08
266	Charlie Lea	.05
267	Jeff Reardon	.05
268	Al Oliver	.05
269	George Hendrick	.05
270	John Montefusco	.05
(271)	A's Logo	.05
(272)	Angels Logo	.05
(273)	Astros Logo	.05
(274)	Blue Jays Logo	.05
(275)	Braves Logo	.05
(276)	Brewers Logo	.05
(277)	Cardinals Logo	.05
(278)	Cubs Logo	.05
(279)	Dodgers Logo	[illegible]
(280)	Expos Logo	.05
(281)	Giants Logo	.05
(282)	Indians Logo	.05
(283)	Mariners Logo	.05
(284)	Mets Logo	.05
(285)	Orioles Logo	.05
(286)	Padres Logo	.05
(287)	Phillies Logo	.05
(288)	Pirates Logo	.05
(289)	Rangers Logo	.05
(290)	Red Sox Logo	.05
(291)	Reds Logo	.05
(292)	Royals Logo	.05
(293)	Tigers Logo	.05
(294)	Twins Logo	.05
(295)	Yankees Logo	.05
(296)	White Sox Logo	.05

1983 Fleer Star Stamps

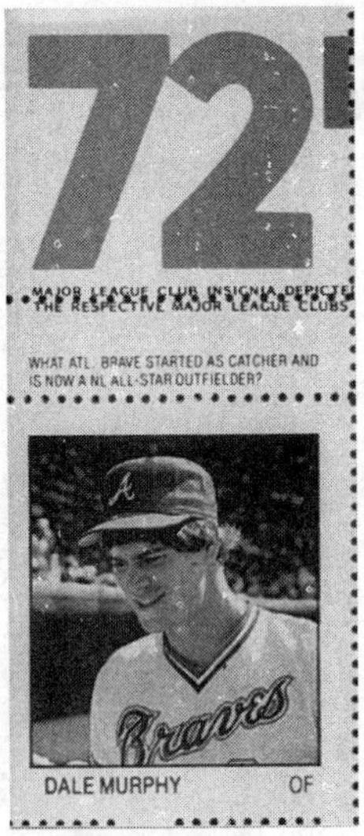

The 1983 Fleer Stamp set consists of 288 stamps, including 224 player stamps and 64 team logo stamps. They were originally issued on four different sheets of 72 stamps each (checklisted below) and in "Vend-A-Stamp" dispensers of 18 stamps each. Sixteen different dispenser strips were needed to complete the set (strips 1-4 comprise Sheet 1; strips 5-8 comprise Sheet 2; strips 9-12 comprise Sheet 3; and strips 13-16 comprise Sheet 4.) Stamps measure 1-1/4" x 1-13/16".

		MT
	Complete Sheet Set (4):	9.00
	Complete Vend-A-Stamp Set (288):	9.00
	Common Sheet:	3.50
	Common Stamp Dispenser:	.50
	Common Single Stamp:	.02
1	Sheet 1 (A's Logo, Angels Logo, Astros Logo, Cardinals Logo, Cubs Logo, Dodgers Logo, Expos Logo), Giants Logo, Indians Logo, (Mets Logo, Orioles Logo, Phillies Logo, Pirates Logo, Red Sox Logo, Twins Logo, White Sox Logo, Neil Allen), Harold Baines Buddy Bell, Dale Berra, Wade Boggs, George Brett, Bill Buckner), Jack Clark, Dave Concepcion, Warren Cromartie, Doug DeCinces, Luis DeLeon, Brian Downing, Dan Driessen, Mike Flanagan, Bob Forsch, Ken Forsch, Toby Harrah, Keith Hernandez, Steve Howe, Reggie Jackson, Ruppert Jones), Ray Knight, Gary Lavelle, Ron LeFlore, Davey Lopes, Lee Mazzilli, Bob McClure, Tug McGraw, Paul Molitor, Rick Monday, John Montefusco, Gaylord Perry, Dan Quisenberry, Ron Reed, Rick Rhoden, Ron Roenicke, Jerry Royster, Mike Schmidt, Roy Smalley, Reggie Smith, Mario Soto, Chris Speier, Willie Stargell, Rick Sutcliffe, Don Sutton, Craig Swan, Kent Tekulve, Dick Tidrow, Willie Upshaw, Fernando Valenzuela, U.L. Washington, Bump Wills, Dave Winfield, Robin Yount, Pat Zachry)	3.50
2	Sheet 2 (Angels Logo, Astros Logo, Braves Logo, Cardinals Logo, Dodgers Logo, Expos Logo, Indians Logo, Mariners Logo, Mets Logo, Phillies Logo, Pirates Logo, Rangers Logo, Reds Logo, Royals Logo, Tigers Logo, Yankees Logo, Willie Aikens, Bob Bailor, Dusty Baker, Floyd Bannister, Len Barker, Hubie Brooks, Tom Brunansky, Chris Chambliss, Mark Clear, Andre Dawson, Bo Diaz, Dennis Eckersley, Rollie Fingers, George Foster, Goose Gossage, Ken Griffey, Ron Guidry, Rickey Henderson, Bob Horner, Lamarr Hoyt (LaMarr) Tom Hume, Garth Iorg, Tommy John, Sixto Lezcano, Fred Lynn, John Matlack (Jon), Scott McGregor, Eddie Milner, Greg Minton, Joe Morgan, Steve Mura, Dwayne Murphy, Ken Oberkfell, Ben Oglivie, Al Oliver, Jim Palmer, Lance Parrish, Larry Parrish, Lou Pinella, Tim Raines, Rafael Ramirez, Jeff Reardon, Jerry Reuss, Jim Rice, Pete Rose, Tom Seaver, Eric Show, Jim Sundberg, Bruce Sutter, Gorman Thomas, Jason Thompson, Tom Underwood, Mookie Wilson, Willie Wilson, John Wockenfuss, Carl Yastrzemski)	3.50
3	Sheet 3 (A's Logo, Angels Logo, Blue Jays Logo, Braves Logo, Brewers Logo, Dodgers Logo, Giants Logo), Indians Logo, Mariners Logo, Orioles Logo, Padres Logo, Reds Logo, Royals Logo, Tigers Logo, Twins Logo, White Sox Logo, Alan Ashby, Dave Beard, Jim Beattie, Johnny Bench, Larry Biittner, Bob Boone, Rod Carew, Gary Carter, Bobby Castillo, Bill Caudill, Cecil Cooper, Mike Easler, Dwight Evans, Carlton Fisk, Gene Garber, Damaso Garcia, Larry Herndon, Al Holland, Burt Hooton, Art Howe, Kent Hrbek), Jerry Koosman, Duane Kulper), Bill Laskey, Dennis Leonard, Garry Maddox, Bill Madlock, Rick Manning, Hal McRae, Keith Moreland, Jerry Mumphrey, Eddie Murray, Joe Niekro, Phil Niekro, Amos Otis, Darrell Porter, Johnny Ray, Mike Richardt, Cal Ripken, Jr., Steve Rogers, Nolan Ryan, Manny Sarmiento, Steve Sax, Ted Simmons, Ken Singleton, Bob Stanley, Rusty Staub, Dave Stieb, Dickie Thon, Andre Thornton), Manny Trillo, John Tudor, Ed Vande Berg, Bob Watson, Frank White, Milt Wilcox)	3.50
4	Sheet 4 (Blue Jays Logo, Braves Logo, Brewers Logo, Cubs Logo, Expos Logo, Giants Logo, Padres Logo), Phillies Logo, Pirates Logo, Rangers Logo, Red Sox Logo, Reds Logo, Royals Logo, Twins Logo, White Sox Logo, Yankees Logo, Joaquin Andujar, Don Baylor, Vida Blue, Bruce Bochte, Larry Bowa, Al Bumbry, Jeff Burroughs, Enos Cabell, Steve Carlton, Cesar Cedeno, Rick Cerone), Ron Cey, Larry Christenson, Jim Clancy, Jose Cruz, Danny Darwin, Rich Dauer, Ron Davis, Ivan DeJesus, Leon Durham, Phil Garner, Steve Garvey, John Grubb, Atlee Hammaker, Mike Hargrove, Tom Herr, Ferguson Jenkins, Steve Kemp, Bruce Kison, Ken Landreaux, Carney Lansford), Charlie Lea, John Lowenstein, Greg Luzinski, Dennis Martinez, Tippy Martinez, Randy Martz, Gary Matthews, Milt May, Dale Murphy, Graig Nettles, Tom Paciorek, Dave Parker, Tony Pena, Hosken Powell, Willie Randolph, Lonnie Smith, Ozzie Smith, Dan Spillner, Ellis Valentine, Pete Vuckovich, Gary Ward, Claudell Washington, Lou Whitaker, Al Williams, Richie Zisk)	3.50

1983 Fleer Star Stamps Poster

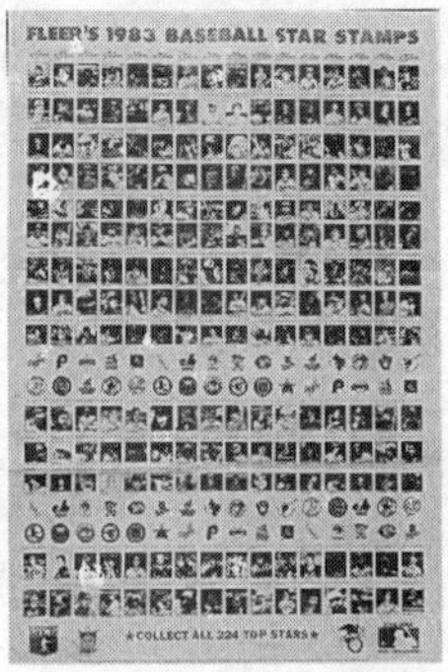

Available via a wrapper redemption offer, this huge (31-3/4" x 21-3/4") poster is printed in red and blue on glossy white paper stock. Besides blue-tone photos of each stamp, the poster has trivia questions and the logos of each team, league, MLB and the players' association. Sheets were folded to 9-1/2" x 12-1/2" for mailing.

	MT
Star Stamp Poster	10.00

1984 Fleer Sample Sheet

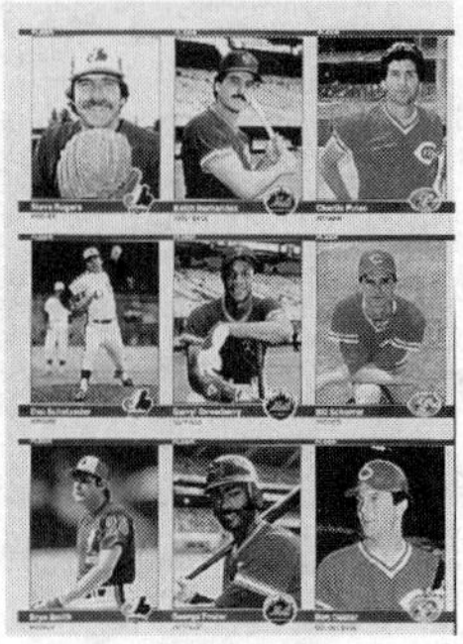

Reportedly available only as an insert in a trade magazine for the grocery industry, this full-color 7-7/8" x 10-7/8" sheet is printed on glossy paper rather than cardboard. The full-color front reproduces nine cards from the forthcoming '84 Fleer issue. The black and red back has details of the cards and ordering informartion.

	MT
Sample Sheet: George Foster, Keith Hernandez, Ron Oester, Charlie Puleo, Steve Rogers, Dan Schatzeder, Bill Scherrer, Bryn Smith, Darryl Strawberry	24.00

1984 Fleer

The 1984 Fleer set contained 660 cards for the fourth consecutive year. The 2-1/2" x 3-1/2" cards feature a color photo surrounded by white borders and horizontal dark blue stripes. The top stripe contains the word "Fleer" with the lower carrying the player's name. Backs have a small black-and-white player photo and are done in blue ink on white stock. The set was issued with team logo stickers.

		MT
	Complete Set (660):	75.00
	Common Player:	.08
	Wax Box:	150.00
1	Mike Boddicker	.08
2	Al Bumbry	.08
3	Todd Cruz	.08
4	Rich Dauer	.08
5	Storm Davis	.08
6	Rick Dempsey	.08
7	Jim Dwyer	.08
8	Mike Flanagan	.08
9	Dan Ford	.08
10	John Lowenstein	.08
11	Dennis Martinez	.12
12	Tippy Martinez	.08
13	Scott McGregor	.08
14	Eddie Murray	4.00
15	Joe Nolan	.08
16	Jim Palmer	1.00
17	Cal Ripken, Jr.	12.50
18	Gary Roenicke	.08
19	Lenn Sakata	.08
20	*John Shelby*	.08
21	Ken Singleton	.08
22	Sammy Stewart	.08
23	Tim Stoddard	.08
24	Marty Bystrom	.08
25	Steve Carlton	3.50
26	Ivan DeJesus	.08
27	John Denny	.08
28	Bob Dernier	.08
29	Bo Diaz	.08
30	Kiko Garcia	.08
31	Greg Gross	.08
32	*Kevin Gross*	.08
33	Von Hayes	.08
34	Willie Hernandez	.08
35	Al Holland	.08
36	*Charles Hudson*	.08
37	Joe Lefebvre	.08
38	Sixto Lezcano	.08
39	Garry Maddox	.08
40	Gary Matthews	.08
41	Len Matuszek	.08
42	Tug McGraw	.08
43	Joe Morgan	.75
44	Tony Perez	.15
45	Ron Reed	.08
46	Pete Rose	7.50
47	*Juan Samuel*	.75
48	Mike Schmidt	8.00
49	Ozzie Virgil	.08
50	*Juan Agosto*	.08
51	Harold Baines	.12
52	Floyd Bannister	.08
53	Salome Barojas	.08
54	Britt Burns	.08
55	Julio Cruz	.08
56	Richard Dotson	.08
57	Jerry Dybzinski	.08
58	Carlton Fisk	1.00
59	Scott Fletcher	.08
60	Jerry Hairston	.08
61	Kevin Hickey	.08
62	Marc Hill	.08
63	LaMarr Hoyt	.08
64	Ron Kittle	.08
65	Jerry Koosman	.08
66	Dennis Lamp	.08
67	Rudy Law	.08
68	Vance Law	.08
69	Greg Luzinski	.12
70	Tom Paciorek	.08
71	Mike Squires	.08
72	Dick Tidrow	.08
73	*Greg Walker*	.08
74	Glenn Abbott	.08
75	Howard Bailey	.08
76	Doug Bair	.08
77	Juan Berenguer	.08
78	Tom Brookens	.08
79	Enos Cabell	.08
80	Kirk Gibson	.08
81	John Grubb	.08
82	Larry Herndon	.08
83	Wayne Krenchicki	.08
84	Rick Leach	.08
85	Chet Lemon	.08
86	Aurelio Lopez	.08
87	Jack Morris	.08
88	Lance Parrish	.12
89	Dan Petry	.08
90	Dave Rozema	.08
91	Alan Trammell	.30
92	Lou Whitaker	.12
93	Milt Wilcox	.08
94	Glenn Wilson	.08
95	John Wockenfuss	.08
96	Dusty Baker	.12
97	Joe Beckwith	.08
98	Greg Brock	.08
99	Jack Fimple	.08
100	Pedro Guerrero	.08
101	Rick Honeycutt	.08
102	Burt Hooton	.08
103	Steve Howe	.08
104	Ken Landreaux	.08
105	Mike Marshall	.08
106	Rick Monday	.08
107	Jose Morales	.08
108	Tom Niedenfuer	.08
109	*Alejandro Pena*	.08
110	Jerry Reuss	.08
111	Bill Russell	.12
112	Steve Sax	.08
113	Mike Scioscia	.08
114	Derrel Thomas	.08
115	Fernando Valenzuela	.12
116	Bob Welch	.08
117	Steve Yeager	.08
118	Pat Zachry	.08
119	Don Baylor	.15
120	Bert Campaneris	.08
121	Rick Cerone	.08
122	*Ray Fontenot*	.08
123	George Frazier	.08
124	Oscar Gamble	.08
125	Goose Gossage	.10
126	Ken Griffey	.12
127	Ron Guidry	.10
128	Jay Howell	.08
129	Steve Kemp	.08
130	Matt Keough	.08
131	*Don Mattingly*	30.00
132	John Montefusco	.08
133	Omar Moreno	.08
134	Dale Murray	.08
135	Graig Nettles	.10
136	Lou Piniella	.10

137	Willie Randolph	.08
138	Shane Rawley	.08
139	Dave Righetti	.08
140	Andre Robertson	.08
141	Bob Shirley	.08
142	Roy Smalley	.08
143	Dave Winfield	3.00
144	Butch Wynegar	.08
145	*Jim Acker*	.08
146	Doyle Alexander	.08
147	Jesse Barfield	.08
148	George Bell	.08
149	Barry Bonnell	.08
150	Jim Clancy	.08
151	Dave Collins	.08
152	*Tony Fernandez*	1.00
153	Damaso Garcia	.08
154	Dave Geisel	.08
155	Jim Gott	.08
156	Alfredo Griffin	.08
157	Garth Iorg	.08
158	Roy Lee Jackson	.08
159	Cliff Johnson	.08
160	Luis Leal	.08
161	Buck Martinez	.08
162	Joey McLaughlin	.08
163	Randy Moffitt	.08
164	Lloyd Moseby	.08
165	Rance Mulliniks	.08
166	Jorge Orta	.08
167	Dave Stieb	.10
168	Willie Upshaw	.08
169	Ernie Whitt	.08
170	Len Barker	.08
171	Steve Bedrosian	.08
172	Bruce Benedict	.08
173	Brett Butler	.10
174	Rick Camp	.08
175	Chris Chambliss	.08
176	Ken Dayley	.08
177	Pete Falcone	.08
178	Torry Forster	.08
179	Gene Garber	.08
180	Terry Harper	.08
181	Bob Horner	.08
182	Glenn Hubbard	.08
183	Randy S. Johnson	.08
184	*Craig McMurtry*	.08
185	Donnie Moore	.08
186	Dale Murphy	.75
187	Phil Niekro	.75
188	Pascual Perez	.08
189	Biff Pocoroba	.08
190	Rafael Ramirez	.08
191	Jerry Royster	.08
192	Claudell Washington	.08
193	Bob Watson	.08
194	Jerry Augustine	.08
195	Mark Brouhard	.08
196	Mike Caldwell	.08
197	*Tom Candiotti*	.60
198	Cecil Cooper	.08
199	Rollie Fingers	.50
200	Jim Gantner	.08
201	Bob L. Gibson	.08
202	Moose Haas	.08
203	Roy Howell	.08
204	Pete Ladd	.08
205	Rick Manning	.08
206	Bob McClure	.08
207	Paul Molitor	4.00
208	Don Money	.08
209	Charlie Moore	.08
210	Ben Oglivie	.08
211	Chuck Porter	.08
212	Ed Romero	.08
213	Ted Simmons	.08
214	Jim Slaton	.08
215	Don Sutton	.45
216	Tom Tellmann	.08
217	Pete Vuckovich	.08
218	Ned Yost	.08
219	Robin Yount	4.00
220	Alan Ashby	.08
221	Kevin Bass	.08
222	Jose Cruz	.08
223	*Bill Dawley*	.08
224	Frank DiPino	.08
225	*Bill Doran*	.08
226	Phil Garner	.08
227	Art Howe	.08
228	Bob Knepper	.08
229	Ray Knight	.08
230	Frank LaCorte	.08
231	Mike LaCoss	.08
232	Mike Madden	.08
233	Jerry Mumphrey	.08
235	Terry Puhl	.08
236	Luis Pujols	.08
237	Craig Reynolds	.08
238	Vern Ruhle	.08
239	Nolan Ryan	17.50
240	Mike Scott	.08
241	Tony Scott	.08
242	Dave Smith	.08
243	Dickie Thon	.08
244	Denny Walling	.08
245	Dale Berra	.08
246	Jim Bibby	.08
247	John Candelaria	.08
248	*Jose DeLeon*	.08
249	Mike Easler	.08
250	Cecilio Guante	.08
251	Richie Hebner	.08
252	Lee Lacy	.08
253	Bill Madlock	.08
254	Milt May	.08
255	Lee Mazzilli	.08
256	Larry McWilliams	.08
257	Jim Morrison	.08
258	Dave Parker	.12
259	Tony Pena	.08
260	Johnny Ray	.08
261	Rick Rhoden	.08
262	Don Robinson	.08
263	Manny Sarmiento	.08
264	Rod Scurry	.08
265	Kent Tekulve	.08
266	Gene Tenace	.08
267	Jason Thompson	.08
268	*Lee Tunnell*	.08
269	*Marvell Wynne*	.08
270	Ray Burris	.08
271	Gary Carter	.45
272	Warren Cromartie	.08
273	Andre Dawson	1.00
274	Doug Flynn	.08
275	Terry Francona	.08
276	Bill Gullickson	.08
277	Bob James	.08
278	Charlie Lea	.08
279	Bryan Little	.08
280	Al Oliver	.10
281	Tim Raines	.45
282	Bobby Ramos	.08
283	Jeff Reardon	.08
284	Steve Rogers	.08
285	Scott Sanderson	.08
286	Dan Schatzeder	.08
287	Bryn Smith	.08
288	Chris Speier	.08
289	Manny Trillo	.08
290	Mike Vail	.08
291	Tim Wallach	.12
292	Chris Welsh	.08
293	Jim Wohlford	.08
294	Kurt Bevacqua	.08
295	Juan Bonilla	.08
296	Bobby Brown	.08
297	Luis DeLeon	.08
298	Dave Dravecky	.08
299	Tim Flannery	.08
300	Steve Garvey	.45
301	Tony Gwynn	12.00
302	*Andy Hawkins*	.20
303	Ruppert Jones	.08
304	Terry Kennedy	.08
305	Tim Lollar	.08
306	Gary Lucas	.08
307	*Kevin McReynolds*	.60
308	Sid Monge	.08
309	Mario Ramirez	.08
310	Gene Richards	.08
311	Luis Salazar	.08
312	Eric Show	.08
313	Elias Sosa	.08
314	Garry Templeton	.08
315	*Mark Thurmond*	.08
316	Ed Whitson	.08
317	Alan Wiggins	.08
318	Neil Allen	.08
319	Joaquin Andujar	.08
320	Steve Braun	.08
321	Glenn Brummer	.08
322	Bob Forsch	.08
323	David Green	.08
324	George Hendrick	.08
325	Tom Herr	.08
326	Dane Iorg	.08
327	Jeff Lahti	.08
328	Dave LaPoint	.08
329	Willie McGee	.12
330	Ken Oberkfell	.08
331	Darrell Porter	.08
332	Jamie Quirk	.08
333	Mike Ramsey	.08
334	Floyd Rayford	.08
335	Lonnie Smith	.08
336	Ozzie Smith	4.00
337	John Stuper	.08
338	Bruce Sutter	.08
339	*Andy Van Slyke*	2.00
340	Dave Von Ohlen	.08
341	Willie Aikens	.08
342	Mike Armstrong	.08
343	Bud Black	.08
344	George Brett	7.50
345	Onix Concepcion	.08
346	Keith Creel	.08
347	Larry Gura	.08
348	Don Hood	.08
349	Dennis Leonard	.08
350	Hal McRae	.12
351	Amos Otis	.08
352	Gaylord Perry	.60
353	Greg Pryor	.08
354	Dan Quisenberry	.08
355	Steve Renko	.08
356	Leon Roberts	.08
357	*Pat Sheridan*	.08
358	Joe Simpson	.08
359	Don Slaught	.08
360	Paul Splittorff	.08
361	U.L. Washington	.08
362	John Wathan	.08
363	Frank White	.08
364	Willie Wilson	.12
365	Jim Barr	.08
366	Dave Bergman	.08
367	Fred Breining	.08
368	Bob Brenly	.08
369	Jack Clark	.08
370	Chili Davis	.12
371	Mark Davis	.08
372	Darrell Evans	.08
373	Atlee Hammaker	.08
374	Mike Krukow	.08
375	Duane Kuiper	.08
376	Bill Laskey	.08
377	Gary Lavelle	.08
378	Johnnie LeMaster	.08
379	Jeff Leonard	.08
380	Randy Lerch	.08
381	Renie Martin	.08
382	Andy McGaffigan	.08
383	Greg Minton	.08
384	Tom O'Malley	.08
385	Max Venable	.08
386	Brad Wellman	.08
387	Joel Youngblood	.08
388	Gary Allenson	.08
389	Luis Aponte	.08
390	Tony Armas	.08
391	Doug Bird	.08
392	Wade Boggs	4.00
393	*Dennis Boyd*	.08
394	Mike Brown	.08
395	Mark Clear	.08
396	Dennis Eckersley	.15
397	Dwight Evans	.10
398	Rich Gedman	.08
399	Glenn Hoffman	.08
400	Bruce Hurst	.08
401	John Henry Johnson	.08
402	Ed Jurak	.08
403	Rick Miller	.08
404	Jeff Newman	.08
405	Reid Nichols	.08
406	Bob Ojeda	.08
407	Jerry Remy	.08
408	Jim Rice	.15
409	Bob Stanley	.08
410	Dave Stapleton	.08
411	John Tudor	.08
412	Carl Yastrzemski	1.00
413	Buddy Bell	.08
414	Larry Biittner	.08
415	John Butcher	.08
416	Danny Darwin	.08
417	Bucky Dent	.08
418	Dave Hostetler	.08
419	Charlie Hough	.08
420	Bobby Johnson	.08
421	Odell Jones	.08
422	Jon Matlack	.08
423	*Pete O'Brien*	.30
424	Larry Parrish	.08
425	Mickey Rivers	.08
426	Billy Sample	.08
427	Dave Schmidt	.08
428	*Mike Smithson*	.08
429	Bill Stein	.08
430	Dave Stewart	.15
431	Jim Sundberg	.08
432	Frank Tanana	.08
433	Dave Tobik	.08
434	Wayne Tolleson	.08
435	George Wright	.08
436	Bill Almon	.08
437	*Keith Atherton*	.08
438	Dave Beard	.08
439	Tom Burgmeier	.08
440	Jeff Burroughs	.08
441	*Chris Codiroli*	.08
442	*Tim Conroy*	.08
443	Mike Davis	.08
444	Wayne Gross	.08
445	Garry Hancock	.08
446	Mike Heath	.08
447	Rickey Henderson	3.00
448	*Don Hill*	.08
449	Bob Kearney	.08
450	Bill Krueger	.08
451	Rick Langford	.08
452	Carney Lansford	.08
453	Davey Lopes	.08
454	Steve McCatty	.08
455	Dan Meyer	.08
456	Dwayne Murphy	.08
457	Mike Norris	.08
458	Ricky Peters	.08
459	Tony Phillips	.25
460	Tom Underwood	.08
461	Mike Warren	.08
462	Johnny Bench	1.00
463	Bruce Berenyi	.08
464	Dann Bilardello	.08
465	Cesar Cedeno	.08
466	Dave Concepcion	.08
467	Dan Driessen	.08
468	*Nick Esasky*	.08
469	Rich Gale	.08
470	Ben Hayes	.08
471	Paul Householder	.08
472	Tom Hume	.08
473	Alan Knicely	.08
474	Eddie Milner	.08
475	Ron Oester	.08
476	Kelly Paris	.08
477	Frank Pastore	.08
478	Ted Power	.08
479	Joe Price	.08
480	Charlie Puleo	.08
481	*Gary Redus*	.25
482	Bill Scherrer	.08
483	Mario Soto	.08
484	Alex Trevino	.08
485	Duane Walker	.08
486	Larry Bowa	.08
487	Warren Brusstar	.08
488	Bill Buckner	.08
489	Bill Campbell	.08
490	Ron Cey	.08
491	Jody Davis	.08
492	Leon Durham	.08
493	Mel Hall	.08
494	Fergie Jenkins	.60
495	Jay Johnstone	.08
496	*Craig Lefferts*	.20
497	*Carmelo Martinez*	.08
498	Jerry Morales	.08
499	Keith Moreland	.08
500	Dickie Noles	.08
501	Mike Proly	.08
502	Chuck Rainey	.08
503	Dick Ruthven	.08
504	Ryne Sandberg	8.00
505	Lee Smith	.15
506	Steve Trout	.08
507	Gary Woods	.08
508	Juan Beniquez	.08
509	Bob Boone	.08
510	Rick Burleson	.08
511	Rod Carew	1.00
512	Bobby Clark	.08
513	John Curtis	.08
514	Doug DeCinces	.08
515	Brian Downing	.08
516	Tim Foli	.08
517	Ken Forsch	.08
518	Bobby Grich	.08
519	Andy Hassler	.08
520	Reggie Jackson	1.50
521	Ron Jackson	.08
522	Tommy John	.12
523	Bruce Kison	.08
524	Steve Lubratich	.08
525	Fred Lynn	.12
526	*Gary Pettis*	.08
527	Luis Sanchez	.08
528	Daryl Sconiers	.08
529	Ellis Valentine	.08
530	Rob Wilfong	.08
531	Mike Witt	.08
532	Geoff Zahn	.08
533	Bud Anderson	.08
534	Chris Bando	.08
535	Alan Bannister	.08
536	Bert Blyleven	.08
537	Tom Brennan	.08
538	Jamie Easterly	.08
539	Juan Eichelberger	.08
540	Jim Essian	.08
541	Mike Fischlin	.08
542	Julio Franco	.25
543	Mike Hargrove	.08
544	Toby Harrah	.08
545	Ron Hassey	.08
546	*Neal Heaton*	.08
547	Bake McBride	.08
548	Broderick Perkins	.08
549	Lary Sorensen	.08
550	Dan Spillner	.08
551	Rick Sutcliffe	.08
552	Pat Tabler	.08
553	Gorman Thomas	.08
554	Andre Thornton	.08
555	George Vukovich	.08
556	Darrell Brown	.08
557	Tom Brunansky	.08
558	*Randy Bush*	.08
559	Bobby Castillo	.08
560	John Castino	.08
561	Ron Davis	.08
562	Dave Engle	.08
563	Lenny Faedo	.08
564	Pete Filson	.08
565	Gary Gaetti	.12
566	Mickey Hatcher	.08
567	Kent Hrbek	.20
568	Rusty Kuntz	.08
569	Tim Laudner	.08
570	Rick Lysander	.08
571	Bobby Mitchell	.08
572	Ken Schrom	.08
573	Ray Smith	.08
574	*Tim Teufel*	.30
575	Frank Viola	.08
576	Gary Ward	.08
577	Ron Washington	.08
578	Len Whitehouse	.08
579	Al Williams	.08
580	Bob Bailor	.08
581	Mark Bradley	.08
582	Hubie Brooks	.08
583	Carlos Diaz	.08
584	George Foster	.08
585	Brian Giles	.08
586	Danny Heep	.08
587	Keith Hernandez	.08
588	Ron Hodges	.08
589	Scott Holman	.08
590	Dave Kingman	.15
591	[illegible]	[illegible]
592	*Jose Oquendo*	.15
593	Jesse Orosco	.08
594	*Junior Ortiz*	.08
595	Tom Seaver	1.50
596	*Doug Sisk*	.08
597	Rusty Staub	.12
598	John Stearns	.08
599	Darryl Strawberry	7.50
600	Craig Swan	.08
601	*Walt Terrell*	.12
602	Mike Torrez	.08
603	Mookie Wilson	.08
604	Jamie Allen	.08
605	Jim Beattie	.08
606	Tony Bernazard	.08
607	Manny Castillo	.08
608	Bill Caudill	.08
609	Bryan Clark	.08
610	Al Cowens	.08
611	Dave Henderson	.08
612	Steve Henderson	.08
613	Orlando Mercado	.08
614	Mike Moore	.08
615	Ricky Nelson	.08
616	*Spike Owen*	.20
617	Pat Putnam	.08
618	Ron Roenicke	.08
619	Mike Stanton	.08
620	Bob Stoddard	.08
621	Rick Sweet	.08
622	Roy Thomas	.08
623	Ed Vande Berg	.08
624	*Matt Young*	.08
625	Richie Zisk	.08
626	'83 All-Star Game Record Breaker (Fred Lynn)	.08
627	'83 All-Star Game Record Breaker (Manny Trillo)	.08
628	N.L. Iron Man (Steve Garvey)	.20
629	A.L. Batting Runner-Up (Rod Carew)	.25
630	A.L. Batting Champion (Wade Boggs)	1.00
631	Letting Go Of The Raines (Tim Raines)	.20
632	Double Trouble (Al Oliver)	.08
633	All-Star Second Base (Steve Sax)	.08
634	All-Star Shortstop (Dickie Thon)	.08
635	Ace Firemen (Tippy Martinez, Dan Quisenberry)	.08
636	Reds Reunited (Joe Morgan, Tony Perez, Pete Rose)	.75
637	Backstop Stars (Bob Boone, Lance Parrish)	.12
638	The Pine Tar Incident, 7/24/83 (George Brett, Gaylord Perry)	.45
639	1983 No-Hitters (Bob Forsch, Dave Righetti, Mike Warren)	.08
640	Retiring Superstars (Johnny Bench, Carl Yastrzemski)	1.00
641	Going Out In Style (Gaylord Perry)	.15
642	300 Club & Strikeout Record (Steve Carlton)	.20
643	The Managers (Joe Altobelli, Paul Owens)	.08
644	The MVP (Rick Dempsey)	.08
645	The Rookie Winner (Mike Boddicker)	.08
646	The Clincher (Scott McGregor)	.08
647	Checklist: Orioles/Royals (Joe Altobelli)	.08
648	Checklist: Phillies/Giants (Paul Owens)	.08
649	Checklist: White Sox/Red Sox (Tony LaRussa)	.08
650	Checklist: Tigers/Rangers (Sparky Anderson)	.08
651	Checklist: Dodgers/A's (Tommy Lasorda)	.10
652	Checklist: Yankees/ Reds (Billy Martin)	.08
653	Checklist: Blue Jays/ Cubs (Bobby Cox)	.08
654	Checklist: Braves/ Angels (Joe Torre)	.08
655	Checklist: Brewers/Indians (Rene Lacheman)	.08
656	Checklist: Astros/ Twins (Bob Lillis)	.08
657	Checklist: Pirates/Mets (Chuck Tanner)	.08
658	Checklist: Expos/Mariners (Bill Virdon)	.08
659	Checklist: Padres/Specials (Dick Williams)	.08
660	Checklist: Cardinals/Specials (Whitey Herzog)	.08

1984 Fleer Update

Following the lead of Topps, Fleer issued near the end of the baseball season a 132-card set to update player trades and include rookies not depicted in the regular issue. The cards are identical in design to the regular issue but are numbered U-1 through U-132. Available only as a boxed set through hobby dealers, the set was printed in limited quantities.

		MT
Complete Set (132):		400.00
Common Player:		.25
1	Willie Aikens	.25
2	Luis Aponte	.25
3	Mark Bailey	.25
4	Bob Bailor	.25
5	Dusty Baker	.35
6	Steve Balboni	.25
7	Alan Bannister	.25
8	Marty Barrett	.25
9	Dave Beard	.25
10	Joe Beckwith	.25
11	Dave Bergman	.25
12	Tony Bernazard	.25
13	Bruce Bochte	.25
14	Barry Bonnell	.25
15	Phil Bradley	.25
16	Fred Breining	.25
17	Mike Brown	.25
18	Bill Buckner	.35
19	Ray Burris	.25
20	John Butcher	.25
21	Brett Butler	.50
22	Enos Cabell	.25
23	Bill Campbell	.25
24	Bill Caudill	.25
25	Bobby Clark	.25
26	Bryan Clark	.25
27	*Roger Clemens*	240.00
28	Jaime Cocanower	.25
29	*Ron Darling*	2.50
30	Alvin Davis	.25
31	Bob Dernier	.25
32	Carlos Diaz	.25
33	Mike Easler	.25
34	Dennis Eckersley	10.00
35	Jim Essian	.25
36	Darrell Evans	.35
37	Mike Fitzgerald	.25
38	Tim Foli	.25
39	John Franco	6.00
40	George Frazier	.25
41	Rich Gale	.25
42	Barbaro Garbey	.25
43	*Dwight Gooden*	10.00
44	Goose Gossage	.40
45	Wayne Gross	.25
46	Mark Gubicza	2.00
47	Jackie Gutierrez	.25
48	Toby Harrah	.25
49	Ron Hassey	.25
50	Richie Hebner	.25
51	Willie Hernandez	.25
52	Ed Hodge	.25
53	Ricky Horton	.25
54	Art Howe	.25
55	Dane Iorg	.25
56	Brook Jacoby	.40
57	Dion James	.25
58	Mike Jeffcoat	.25
59	Ruppert Jones	.25
60	Bob Kearney	.25
61	*Jimmy Key*	8.00
62	Dave Kingman	.50
63	Brad Komminsk	.25
64	Jerry Koosman	.25
65	Wayne Krenchicki	.25
66	Rusty Kuntz	.25
67	Frank LaCorte	.25
68	Dennis Lamp	.25
69	Tito Landrum	.25
70	*Mark Langston*	8.00
71	Rick Leach	.25
72	Craig Lefferts	.25
73	Gary Lucas	.25
74	Jerry Martin	.25
75	Carmelo Martinez	.25
76	Mike Mason	.25
77	Gary Matthews	.25
78	Andy McGaffigan	.25
79	Joey McLaughlin	.25
80	Joe Morgan	6.00
81	Darryl Motley	.25
82	Graig Nettles	.50
83	Phil Niekro	4.00
84	Ken Oberkfell	.25
85	Al Oliver	.35
86	Jorge Orta	.25
87	Amos Otis	.25
88	Bob Owchinko	.25
89	Dave Parker	2.00
90	Jack Perconte	.25
91	Tony Perez	4.00
92	Gerald Perry	.25
93	*Kirby Puckett*	150.00
94	Shane Rawley	.25
95	Floyd Rayford	.25
96	Ron Reed	.25
97	R.J. Reynolds	.25
98	Gene Richards	.25
99	*Jose Rijo*	10.00
100	Jeff Robinson	.25
101	Ron Romanick	.25
102	Pete Rose	15.00
103	*Bret Saberhagen*	15.00
104	Scott Sanderson	.25
105	Dick Schofield	.25
106	Tom Seaver	15.00
107	Jim Slaton	.25
108	Mike Smithson	.25
109	Lary Sorensen	.25
110	Tim Stoddard	.25
111	Jeff Stone	.25
112	Champ Summers	.25
113	Jim Sundberg	.25
114	Rick Sutcliffe	.35
115	Craig Swan	.25
116	Derrel Thomas	.25
117	Gorman Thomas	.25
118	Alex Trevino	.25
119	Manny Trillo	.25
120	John Tudor	.25
121	Tom Underwood	.25
122	Mike Vail	.25
123	Tom Waddell	.25
124	Gary Ward	.25
125	Terry Whitfield	.25
126	Curtis Wilkerson	.25
127	Frank Williams	.25
128	Glenn Wilson	.25
129	John Wockenfuss	.25
130	Ned Yost	.25
131	Mike Young	.25
132	Checklist 1-132	.10

1984 Fleer Stickers

This set was designed to be housed in a special collector's album that was organized according to various league leader categories, resulting in some players being pictured on more than one sticker. Each full-color sticker measures 1-15/16" x 2-1/2" and is framed with a beige border. The stickers, which were sold in packs of six, are numbered on the back.

		MT
Complete Set (126):		10.00
Common Player:		.05
Sticker Album:		1.00
1	Dickie Thon	.05
2	Ken Landreaux	.05
3	Darrell Evans	.05
4	Harold Baines	.08
5	Dave Winfield	.20
6	Bill Madlock	.05
7	Lonnie Smith	.05
8	Jose Cruz	.05
9	George Hendrick	.05
10	Ray Knight	.05
11	Wade Boggs	.40
12	Rod Carew	.25
13	Lou Whitaker	.10
14	Alan Trammell	.10
15	Cal Ripken, Jr.	.50
16	Mike Schmidt	.40
17	Dale Murphy	.20
18	Andre Dawson	.15
19	Pedro Guerrero	.05
20	Jim Rice	.08
21	Tony Armas	.05
22	Ron Kittle	.05
23	Eddie Murray	.25
24	Jose Cruz	.05
25	Andre Dawson	.15
26	Rafael Ramirez	.05
27	Al Oliver	.05
28	Wade Boggs	.40
29	Cal Ripken, Jr.	.50
30	Lou Whitaker	.10
31	Cecil Cooper	.05
32	Dale Murphy	.20
33	Andre Dawson	.15
34	Pedro Guerrero	.05
35	Mike Schmidt	.40
36	George Brett	.40
37	Jim Rice	.08
38	Eddie Murray	.25
39	Carlton Fisk	.10
40	Rusty Staub	.05
41	Duane Walker	.05
42	Steve Braun	.05
43	Kurt Bevacqua	.05
44	Hal McRae	.05
45	Don Baylor	.08
46	Ken Singleton	.05
47	Greg Luzinski	.08
48	Mike Schmidt	.40
49	Keith Hernandez	.05
50	Dale Murphy	.20
51	Tim Raines	.10
52	Wade Boggs	.40
53	Rickey Henderson	.25
54	Rod Carew	.25
55	Ken Singleton	.05
56	John Denny	.05
57	John Candelaria	.05
58	Larry McWilliams	.05
59	Pascual Perez	.05
60	Jesse Orosco	.05
61	Moose Haas	.05
62	Richard Dotson	.05
63	Mike Flanagan	.05
64	Scott McGregor	.05
65	Atlee Hammaker	.05
66	Rick Honeycutt	.05
67	Lee Smith	.08
68	Al Holland	.05
69	Greg Minton	.05
70	Bruce Sutter	.05
71	Jeff Reardon	.05
72	Frank DiPino	.05
73	Dan Quisenberry	.05
74	Bob Stanley	.05
75	Ron Davis	.05
76	Bill Caudill	.05
77	Peter Ladd	.05
78	Steve Carlton	.20
79	Mario Soto	.05
80	Larry McWilliams	.05
81	Fernando Valenzuela	.08
82	Nolan Ryan	.75
83	Jack Morris	.05
84	Floyd Bannister	.05
85	Dave Stieb	.05
86	Dave Righetti	.05
87	Rick Sutcliffe	.05
88	Tim Raines	.10
89	Alan Wiggins	.05
90	Steve Sax	.05
91	Mookie Wilson	.05
92	Rickey Henderson	.25
93	Rudy Law	.05
94	Willie Wilson	.05
95	Julio Cruz	.05
96	Johnny Bench	.30
97	Carl Yastrzemski	.25
98	Gaylord Perry	.15
99	Pete Rose	.45
100	Joe Morgan	.20
101	Steve Carlton	.20
102	Jim Palmer	.20
103	Rod Carew	.25
104	Darryl Strawberry	.20
105	Craig McMurtry	.05
106	Mel Hall	.05
107	Lee Tunnell	.05
108	Bill Dawley	.05
109	Ron Kittle	.05
110	Mike Boddicker	.05
111	Julio Franco	.05
112	Daryl Sconiers	.05
113	Neal Heaton	.05
114	John Shelby	.05
115	Rick Dempsey	.05
116	John Lowenstein	.05
117	Jim Dwyer	.05
118	Bo Diaz	.05
119	Pete Rose	.45
120	Joe Morgan	.20
121	Gary Matthews	.05
122	Garry Maddox	.05
123	Paul Owens	.05
124	Tom Lasorda	.10
125	Joe Altobelli	.05
126	Tony LaRussa	.05

1985 Fleer

The 1985 Fleer set consists of 660 cards, each measuring 2-1/2" x 3-1/2". Card fronts feature a color photo plus the player's team logo and the word "Fleer." The photos have a color-coded frame which corresponds to the player's team. A grey border surrounds the frame. Backs are similar in design to previous years, but have two shades of red and black ink on white stock. For the fourth consecutive year, Fleer included special cards and team checklists in the set. Also incorporated in a set for the first time were ten "Major League Prospect" cards, each featuring two rookie hopefuls. The set was issued with team logo stickers.

		MT
Complete Set (660):		110.00
Common Player:		.06
Wax Box:		275.00
1	Doug Bair	.06
2	Juan Berenguer	.06
3	Dave Bergman	.06
4	Tom Brookens	.06
5	Marty Castillo	.06
6	Darrell Evans	.10
7	Barbaro Garbey	.06
8	Kirk Gibson	.06
9	John Grubb	.06
10	Willie Hernandez	.06
11	Larry Herndon	.06
12	Howard Johnson	.06
13	Ruppert Jones	.06
14	Rusty Kuntz	.06
15	Chet Lemon	.06
16	Aurelio Lopez	.06
17	Sid Monge	.06
18	Jack Morris	.10
19	Lance Parrish	.10
20	Dan Petry	.06
21	Dave Rozema	.06
22	Bill Scherrer	.06
23	Alan Trammell	.25
24	Lou Whitaker	.10
25	Milt Wilcox	.06
26	Kurt Bevacqua	.06
27	*Greg Booker*	.06
28	Bobby Brown	.06
29	Luis DeLeon	.06
30	Dave Dravecky	.06
31	Tim Flannery	.06
32	Steve Garvey	.35
33	Goose Gossage	.12
34	Tony Gwynn	6.00
35	Greg Harris	.06
36	Andy Hawkins	.06
37	Terry Kennedy	.06
38	Craig Lefferts	.06
39	Tim Lollar	.06
40	Carmelo Martinez	.06
41	Kevin McReynolds	.06
42	Graig Nettles	.10
43	Luis Salazar	.06
44	Eric Show	.06
45	Garry Templeton	.06
46	Mark Thurmond	.06
47	Ed Whitson	.06
48	Alan Wiggins	.06
49	Rich Bordi	.06
50	Larry Bowa	.06
51	Warren Brusstar	.06
52	Ron Cey	.06
53	*Henry Cotto*	.06
54	Jody Davis	.06
55	Bob Dernier	.06
56	Leon Durham	.06
57	Dennis Eckersley	.30
58	George Frazier	.06
59	Richie Hebner	.06
60	Dave Lopes	.06
61	Gary Matthews	.06
62	Keith Moreland	.06
63	Rick Reuschel	.06
64	Dick Ruthven	.06
65	Ryne Sandberg	5.00
66	Scott Sanderson	.06
67	Lee Smith	.10
68	Tim Stoddard	.06
69	Rick Sutcliffe	.06
70	Steve Trout	.06
71	Gary Woods	.06
72	Wally Backman	.06
73	Bruce Berenyi	.06
74	Hubie Brooks	.06
75	Kelvin Chapman	.06
76	Ron Darling	.06
77	Sid Fernandez	.06
78	Mike Fitzgerald	.06
79	George Foster	.06
80	Brent Gaff	.06
81	Ron Gardenhire	.06
82	Dwight Gooden	1.00
83	Tom Gorman	.06
84	Danny Heep	.06
85	Keith Hernandez	.06
86	Ray Knight	.06
87	Ed Lynch	.06
88	Jose Oquendo	.06
89	Jesse Orosco	.06
90	*Rafael Santana*	.06
91	Doug Sisk	.06
92	Rusty Staub	.10
93	Darryl Strawberry	1.00
94	Walt Terrell	.06
95	Mookie Wilson	.06
96	Jim Acker	.06
97	Willie Aikens	.06
98	Doyle Alexander	.06
99	Jesse Barfield	.06
100	George Bell	.06
101	Jim Clancy	.06
102	Dave Collins	.06
103	Tony Fernandez	.06
104	Damaso Garcia	.06
105	Jim Gott	.06
106	Alfredo Griffin	.06
107	Garth Iorg	.06
108	Roy Lee Jackson	.06
109	Cliff Johnson	.06
110	Jimmy Key	2.00
111	Dennis Lamp	.06
112	Rick Leach	.06
113	Luis Leal	.06
114	Buck Martinez	.06
115	Lloyd Moseby	.06
116	Rance Mulliniks	.06
117	Dave Stieb	.06
118	Willie Upshaw	.06
119	Ernie Whitt	.06
120	Mike Armstrong	.06
121	Don Baylor	.12
122	Marty Bystrom	.06
123	Rick Cerone	.06
124	Joe Cowley	.06
125	Brian Dayett	.06
126	Tim Foli	.06
127	Ray Fontenot	.06
128	Ken Griffey	.10
129	Ron Guidry	.10
130	Toby Harrah	.06
131	Jay Howell	.06
132	Steve Kemp	.06
133	Don Mattingly	9.00
134	Bobby Meacham	.06
135	John Montefusco	.06
136	Omar Moreno	.06
137	Dale Murray	.06
138	Phil Niekro	.50
139	*Mike Pagliarulo*	.20
140	Willie Randolph	.06
141	Dennis Rasmussen	.06
142	Dave Righetti	.06
143	Jose Rijo	.10
144	Andre Robertson	.06
145	Bob Shirley	.06
146	Dave Winfield	3.00
147	Butch Wynegar	.06
148	Gary Allenson	.06
149	Tony Armas	.06
150	Marty Barrett	.06
151	Wade Boggs	4.50
152	Dennis Boyd	.06
153	Bill Buckner	.06
154	Mark Clear	.06
155	Roger Clemens	50.00
156	Steve Crawford	.06
157	Mike Easler	.06
158	Dwight Evans	.06
159	Rich Gedman	.06
160	Jackie Gutierrez	.06
161	Bruce Hurst	.06
162	John Henry Johnson	.06
163	Rick Miller	.06
164	Reid Nichols	.06
165	*Al Nipper*	.06
166	Bob Ojeda	.06
167	Jerry Remy	.06
168	Jim Rice	.06
169	Bob Stanley	.06
170	Mike Boddicker	.06
171	Al Bumbry	.06
172	Todd Cruz	.06
173	Rich Dauer	.06
174	Storm Davis	.06
175	Rick Dempsey	.06
176	Jim Dwyer	.06
177	Mike Flanagan	.06
178	Dan Ford	.06
179	Wayne Gross	.06
180	John Lowenstein	.06
181	Dennis Martinez	.10
182	Tippy Martinez	.06
183	Scott McGregor	.06
184	Eddie Murray	2.50
185	Joe Nolan	.06
186	Floyd Rayford	.06
187	Cal Ripken, Jr.	10.00
188	Gary Roenicke	.06
189	Lenn Sakata	.06
190	John Shelby	.06
191	Ken Singleton	.06

192	Sammy Stewart	.06
193	Bill Swaggerty	.06
194	Tom Underwood	.06
195	Mike Young	.06
196	Steve Balboni	.06
197	Joe Beckwith	.06
198	Bud Black	.06
199	George Brett	4.50
200	Onix Concepcion	.06
201	*Mark Gubicza*	.80
202	Larry Gura	.06
203	Mark Huismann	.06
204	Dane Iorg	.06
205	Danny Jackson	.06
206	Charlie Leibrandt	.06
207	Hal McRae	.10
208	Darryl Motley	.06
209	Jorge Orta	.06
210	Greg Pryor	.06
211	Dan Quisenberry	.06
212	Bret Saberhagen	2.00
213	Pat Sheridan	.06
214	Don Slaught	.06
215	U.L. Washington	.06
216	John Wathan	.06
217	Frank White	.06
218	Willie Wilson	.06
219	Neil Allen	.06
220	Joaquin Andujar	.06
221	Steve Braun	.06
222	Danny Cox	.06
223	Bob Forsch	.06
224	David Green	.06
225	George Hendrick	.06
226	Tom Herr	.06
227	*Ricky Horton*	.06
228	Art Howe	.06
229	Mike Jorgensen	.06
230	Kurt Kepshire	.06
231	Jeff Lahti	.06
232	Tito Landrum	.06
233	Dave LaPoint	.06
234	Willie McGee	.15
235	*Tom Nieto*	.06
236	*Terry Pendleton*	2.00
237	Darrell Porter	.06
238	Dave Rucker	.06
239	Lonnie Smith	.06
240	Ozzie Smith	3.00
241	Bruce Sutter	.06
242	Andy Van Slyke	.06
243	Dave Von Ohlen	.06
244	Larry Andersen	.06
245	Bill Campbell	.06
246	Steve Carlton	1.50
247	Tim Corcoran	.06
248	Ivan DeJesus	.06
249	John Denny	.06
250	Bo Diaz	.06
251	Greg Gross	.06
252	Kevin Gross	.06
253	Von Hayes	.06
254	Al Holland	.06
255	Charles Hudson	.06
256	Jerry Koosman	.06
257	Joe Lefebvre	.06
258	Sixto Lezcano	.06
259	Garry Maddox	.06
260	Len Matuszek	.06
261	Tug McGraw	.06
262	Al Oliver	.06
263	Shane Rawley	.06
264	Juan Samuel	.06
265	Mike Schmidt	5.00
266	*Jeff Stone*	.06
267	Ozzie Virgil	.06
268	Glenn Wilson	.06
269	John Wockenfuss	.06
270	Darrell Brown	.06
271	Tom Brunansky	.06
272	Randy Bush	.06
273	John Butcher	.06
274	Bobby Castillo	.06
275	Ron Davis	.06
276	Dave Engle	.06
277	Pete Filson	.06
278	Gary Gaetti	.10
279	Mickey Hatcher	.06
280	Ed Hodge	.06
281	Kent Hrbek	.20
282	Houston Jimenez	.06
283	Tim Laudner	.06
284	Rick Lysander	.06
285	Dave Meier	.06
286	Kirby Puckett	30.00
287	Pat Putnam	.06
288	Ken Schrom	.06
289	Mike Smithson	.06
290	Tim Teufel	.06
291	Frank Viola	.06
292	Ron Washington	.06
293	Don Aase	.06
294	Juan Beniquez	.06
295	Bob Boone	.06
296	Mike Brown	.06
297	Rod Carew	1.50
298	Doug Corbett	.06
299	Doug DeCinces	.06
300	Brian Downing	.06
301	Ken Forsch	.06
302	Bobby Grich	.06
303	Reggie Jackson	2.00
304	Tommy John	.10
305	Curt Kaufman	.06
306	Bruce Kison	.06
307	Fred Lynn	.10
308	Gary Pettis	.06
309	*Ron Romanick*	.06
310	Luis Sanchez	.06
311	Dick Schofield	.06
312	Daryl Sconiers	.06
313	Jim Slaton	.06
314	Derrel Thomas	.06
315	Rob Wilfong	.06
316	Mike Witt	.06
317	Geoff Zahn	.06
318	Len Barker	.06
319	Steve Bedrosian	.06
320	Bruce Benedict	.06
321	Rick Camp	.06
322	Chris Chambliss	.06
323	*Jeff Dedmon*	.06
324	Terry Forster	.06
325	Gene Garber	.06
326	*Albert Hall*	.06
327	Terry Harper	.06
328	Bob Horner	.06
329	Glenn Hubbard	.06
330	Randy S. Johnson	.06
331	Brad Komminsk	.06
332	Rick Mahler	.06
333	Craig McMurtry	.06
334	Donnie Moore	.06
335	Dale Murphy	.50
336	Ken Oberkfell	.06
337	Pascual Perez	.06
338	Gerald Perry	.06
339	Rafael Ramirez	.06
340	Jerry Royster	.06
341	Alex Trevino	.06
342	Claudell Washington	.06
343	Alan Ashby	.06
344	*Mark Bailey*	.06
345	Kevin Bass	.06
346	Enos Cabell	.06
347	Jose Cruz	.06
348	Bill Dawley	.06
349	Frank DiPino	.06
350	Bill Doran	.06
351	Phil Garner	.06
352	Bob Knepper	.06
353	Mike LaCoss	.06
354	Jerry Mumphrey	.06
355	Joe Niekro	.06
356	Terry Puhl	.06
357	Craig Reynolds	.06
358	Vern Ruhle	.06
359	Nolan Ryan	10.00
360	Joe Sambito	.06
361	Mike Scott	.06
362	Dave Smith	.06
363	*Julio Solano*	.06
364	Dickie Thon	.06
365	Denny Walling	.06
366	Dave Anderson	.06
367	Bob Bailor	.06
368	Greg Brock	.06
369	Carlos Diaz	.06
370	Pedro Guerrero	.06
371	*Orel Hershiser*	3.50
372	Rick Honeycutt	.06
373	Burt Hooton	.06
374	*Ken Howell*	.15
375	Ken Landreaux	.06
376	Candy Maldonado	.06
377	Mike Marshall	.06
378	Tom Niedenfuer	.06
379	Alejandro Pena	.06
380	Jerry Reuss	.06
381	*R.J. Reynolds*	.06
382	German Rivera	.06
383	Bill Russell	.06
384	Steve Sax	.06
385	Mike Scioscia	.06
386	*Franklin Stubbs*	.06
387	Fernando Valenzuela	.10
388	Bob Welch	.06
389	Terry Whitfield	.06
390	Steve Yeager	.06
391	Pat Zachry	.06
392	Fred Breining	.06
393	Gary Carter	.40
394	Andre Dawson	.90
395	Miguel Dilone	.06
396	Dan Driessen	.06
397	Doug Flynn	.06
398	Terry Francona	.06
399	Bill Gullickson	.06
400	Bob James	.06
401	Charlie Lea	.06
402	Bryan Little	.06
403	Gary Lucas	.06
404	David Palmer	.06
405	Tim Raines	.20
406	Mike Ramsey	.06
407	Jeff Reardon	.06
408	Steve Rogers	.06
409	Dan Schatzeder	.06
410	Bryn Smith	.06
411	Mike Stenhouse	.06
412	Tim Wallach	.10
413	Jim Wohlford	.06
414	Bill Almon	.06
415	Keith Atherton	.06
416	Bruce Bochte	.06
417	Tom Burgmeier	.06
418	Ray Burris	.06
419	Bill Caudill	.06
420	Chris Codiroli	.06
421	Tim Conroy	.06
422	Mike Davis	.06
423	Jim Essian	.06
424	Mike Heath	.06
425	Rickey Henderson	3.00
426	Donnie Hill	.06
427	Dave Kingman	.10
428	Bill Krueger	.06
429	Carney Lansford	.06
430	Steve McCatty	.06
431	Joe Morgan	.40
432	Dwayne Murphy	.06
433	Tony Phillips	.10
434	Lary Sorensen	.06
435	Mike Warren	.06
436	*Curt Young*	.06
437	Luis Aponte	.06
438	Chris Bando	.06
439	Tony Bernazard	.06
440	Bert Blyleven	.06
441	Brett Butler	.10
442	Ernie Camacho	.06
443	Joe Carter	4.00
444	Carmelo Castillo	.06
445	Jamie Easterly	.06
446	*Steve Farr*	.10
447	Mike Fischlin	.06
448	Julio Franco	.06
449	Mel Hall	.06
450	Mike Hargrove	.06
451	Neal Heaton	.06
452	Brook Jacoby	.06
453	*Mike Jeffcoat*	.06
454	*Don Schulze*	.06
455	Roy Smith	.06
456	Pat Tabler	.06
457	Andre Thornton	.06
458	George Vukovich	.06
459	Tom Waddell	.06
460	Jerry Willard	.06
461	Dale Berra	.06
462	John Candelaria	.06
463	Jose DeLeon	.06
464	Doug Frobel	.06
465	Cecilio Guante	.06
466	Brian Harper	.06
467	Lee Lacy	.06
468	Bill Madlock	.06
469	Lee Mazzilli	.06
470	Larry McWilliams	.06
471	Jim Morrison	.06
472	Tony Pena	.06
473	Johnny Ray	.06
474	Rick Rhoden	.06
475	Don Robinson	.06
476	Rod Scurry	.06
477	Kent Tekulve	.06
478	Jason Thompson	.06
479	John Tudor	.06
480	Lee Tunnell	.06
481	Marvell Wynne	.06
482	Salome Barojas	.06
483	Dave Beard	.06
484	Jim Beattie	.06
485	Barry Bonnell	.06
486	*Phil Bradley*	.06
487	Al Cowens	.06
488	*Alvin Davis*	.06
489	Dave Henderson	.06
490	Steve Henderson	.06
491	Bob Kearney	.06
492	Mark Langston	1.50
493	Larry Milbourne	.06
494	Paul Mirabella	.06
495	Mike Moore	.06
496	Edwin Nunez	.06
497	Spike Owen	.06
498	Jack Perconte	.06
499	Ken Phelps	.06
500	*Jim Presley*	.06
501	Mike Stanton	.06
502	Bob Stoddard	.06
503	Gorman Thomas	.06
504	Ed Vande Berg	.06
505	Matt Young	.06
506	Juan Agosto	.06
507	Harold Baines	.15
508	Floyd Bannister	.06
509	Britt Burns	.06
510	Julio Cruz	.06
511	Richard Dotson	.06
512	Jerry Dybzinski	.06
513	Carlton Fisk	.75
514	Scott Fletcher	.06
515	Jerry Hairston	.06
516	Marc Hill	.06
517	LaMarr Hoyt	.06
518	Ron Kittle	.06
519	Rudy Law	.06
520	Vance Law	.06
521	Greg Luzinski	.10
522	Gene Nelson	.06
523	Tom Paciorek	.06
524	Ron Reed	.06
525	Bert Roberge	.06
526	Tom Seaver	1.25
527	Roy Smalley	.06
528	Dan Spillner	.06
529	Mike Squires	.06
530	Greg Walker	.06
531	Cesar Cedeno	.06
532	Dave Concepcion	.06
533	*Eric Davis*	2.50
534	Nick Esasky	.06
535	Tom Foley	.06
536	*John Franco*	.75
537	Brad Gulden	.06
538	Tom Hume	.06
539	Wayne Krenchicki	.06
540	Andy McGaffigan	.06
541	Eddie Milner	.06
542	Ron Oester	.06
543	Bob Owchinko	.06
544	Dave Parker	.25
545	Frank Pastore	.06
546	Tony Perez	.15
547	Ted Power	.06
548	Joe Price	.06
549	Gary Redus	.06
550	Pete Rose	3.00
551	Jeff Russell	.06
552	Mario Soto	.06
553	*Jay Tibbs*	.06
554	Duane Walker	.06
555	Alan Bannister	.06
556	Buddy Bell	.06
557	Danny Darwin	.06
558	Charlie Hough	.06
559	Bobby Jones	.06
560	Odell Jones	.06
561	*Jeff Kunkel*	.06
562	*Mike Mason*	.06
563	Pete O'Brien	.06
564	Larry Parrish	.06
565	Mickey Rivers	.06
566	Billy Sample	.06
567	Dave Schmidt	.06
568	Donnie Scott	.06
569	Dave Stewart	.12
570	Frank Tanana	.06
571	Wayne Tolleson	.06
572	Gary Ward	.06
573	Curtis Wilkerson	.06
574	George Wright	.06
575	Ned Yost	.06
576	Mark Brouhard	.06
577	Mike Caldwell	.06
578	Bobby Clark	.06
579	Jaime Cocanower	.06
580	Cecil Cooper	.06
581	Rollie Fingers	.40
582	Jim Gantner	.06
583	Moose Haas	.06
584	Dion James	.06
585	Pete Ladd	.06
586	Rick Manning	.06
587	Bob McClure	.06
588	Paul Molitor	3.00
589	Charlie Moore	.06
590	Ben Oglivie	.06
591	Chuck Porter	.06
592	*Randy Ready*	.06
593	Ed Romero	.06
594	Bill Schroeder	.06
595	Ray Searage	.06
596	Ted Simmons	.06
597	Jim Sundberg	.06
598	Don Sutton	.35
599	Tom Tellmann	.06
600	Rick Waits	.06
601	Robin Yount	3.00
602	Dusty Baker	.10
603	Bob Brenly	.06
604	Jack Clark	.06
605	Chili Davis	.15
606	Mark Davis	.06
607	*Dan Gladden*	.45
608	Atlee Hammaker	.06
609	Mike Krukow	.06
610	Duane Kuiper	.06
611	Bob Lacey	.06
612	Bill Laskey	.06
613	Gary Lavelle	.06
614	Johnnie LeMaster	.06
615	Jeff Leonard	.06
616	Randy Lerch	.06
617	Greg Minton	.06
618	Steve Nicosia	.06
619	Gene Richards	.06
620	*Jeff Robinson*	.06
621	Scot Thompson	.06
622	Manny Trillo	.06
623	Brad Wellman	.06
624	*Frank Williams*	.06
625	Joel Youngblood	.06
626	Cal Ripken, Jr. (In Action)	4.00
627	Mike Schmidt (In Action)	1.50
628	Giving the Signs (Sparky Anderson)	.10
629	A.L. Pitcher's Nightmare (Rickey Henderson, Dave Winfield)	1.00
630	N.L. Pitcher's Nightmare (Ryne Sandberg, Mike Schmidt)	2.00
631	N.L. All-Stars (Gary Carter, Steve Garvey, Ozzie Smith, Darryl Strawberry)	.25
632	All-Star Game Winning Battery (Gary Carter, Charlie Lea)	.10
633	N.L. Pennant Clinchers (Steve Garvey, Goose Gossage)	.20
634	N.L. Rookie Phenoms (Dwight Gooden, Juan Samuel)	.25
635	Toronto's Big Guns (Willie Upshaw)	.06
636	Toronto's Big Guns (Lloyd Moseby)	.06
637	Holland (Al Holland)	.06
638	Tunnell (Lee Tunnell)	.06
639	Reggie Jackson (In Action)	.50
640	Pete Rose (In Action)	.75
641	Father & Son (Cal Ripken, Jr., Cal Ripken, Sr.)	4.00
642	Cubs team	.10
643	1984's Two Perfect Games & One No-Hitter (Jack Morris, David Palmer, Mike Witt)	.06
644	Major League Prospect (Willie Lozado, Vic Mata)	.06
645	Major League Prospect *(Kelly Gruber)*, *(Randy O'Neal)*	.15
646	Major League Prospect *(Jose Roman)*, *(Joel Skinner)*	.06
647	Major League Prospect *(Steve Kiefer)*, *(Danny Tartabull)*	1.00
648	Major League Prospect *(Rob Deer)*, *(Alejandro Sanchez)*	.15
649	Major League Prospect *(Shawon Dunston)*, *(Bill Hatcher)*	2.00
650	Major League Prospect *(Mike Bielecki)*, *(Ron Robinson)*	.10
651	Major League Prospect *(Zane Smith)*, *(Paul Zuvella)*	.15
652	Major League Prospect *(Glenn Davis)*, *(Joe Hesketh)*	.20
653	Major League Prospect *(Steve Jeltz)*, *(John Russell)*	.10
654	Checklist 1-95	.06
655	Checklist 96-195	.06
656	Checklist 196-292	.06
657	Checklist 293-391	.06
658	Checklist 392-481	.06
659	Checklist 482-575	.06
660	Checklist 576-660	.06

1985 Fleer Update

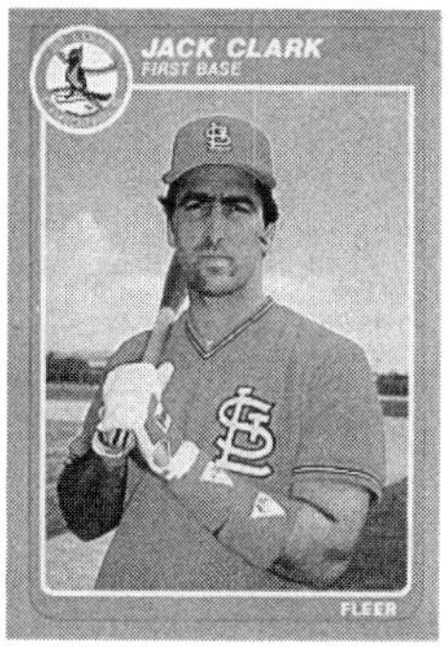

For the second straight year, Fleer issued a 132-card update set. Cards portray traded players on their new teams and also include rookies not depicted in the regular issue. The cards are identical in design to the 1985 Fleer set but are numbered U-1 through U-132. The set was issued with team logo stickers in a specially designed box and was available only through hobby dealers.

		MT
Complete Set (132):		12.00
Common Player:		.10
1	Don Aase	.10
2	Bill Almon	.10
3	Dusty Baker	.20
4	Dale Berra	.10
5	Karl Best	.10
6	Tim Birtsas	.10
7	Vida Blue	.10
8	Rich Bordi	.10
9	Daryl Boston	.15
10	Hubie Brooks	.10
11	Chris Brown	.10
12	Tom Browning	.35
13	Al Bumbry	.10
14	Tim Burke	.10
15	Ray Burris	.10
16	Jeff Burroughs	.10

17	Ivan Calderon	.10
18	Jeff Calhoun	.10
19	Bill Campbell	.10
20	Don Carman	.10
21	Gary Carter	.75
22	Bobby Castillo	.10
23	Bill Caudill	.10
24	Rick Cerone	.10
25	Jack Clark	.15
26	Pat Clements	.10
27	Stewart Cliburn	.10
28	Vince Coleman	.60
29	Dave Collins	.10
30	Fritz Connally	.10
31	Henry Cotto	.10
32	Danny Darwin	.10
33	*Darren Daulton*	3.00
34	Jerry Davis	.10
35	Brian Dayett	.10
36	Ken Dixon	.10
37	Tommy Dunbar	.10
38	Mariano Duncan	.40
39	Bob Fallon	.10
40	Brian Fisher	.10
41	Mike Fitzgerald	.10
42	Ray Fontenot	.10
43	Greg Gagne	.50
44	Oscar Gamble	.10
45	Jim Gott	.10
46	David Green	.10
47	Alfredo Griffin	.10
48	*Ozzie Guillen*	1.50
49	Toby Harrah	.10
50	Ron Hassey	.10
51	Rickey Henderson	3.00
52	Steve Henderson	.10
53	George Hendrick	.10
54	Teddy Higuera	.10
55	Al Holland	.10
56	Burt Hooton	.10
57	Jay Howell	.10
58	LaMarr Hoyt	.10
59	Tim Hulett	.10
60	Bob James	.10
61	Cliff Johnson	.10
62	Howard Johnson	.15
63	Ruppert Jones	.10
64	Steve Kemp	.10
65	Bruce Kison	.10
66	Mike LaCoss	.10
67	Lee Lacy	.10
68	Dave LaPoint	.10
69	Gary Lavelle	.10
70	Vance Law	.10
71	Manny Lee	.10
72	Sixto Lezcano	.10
73	Tim Lollar	.10
74	Urbano Lugo	.10
75	Fred Lynn	.25
76	Steve Lyons	.15
77	Mickey Mahler	.10
78	Ron Mathis	.10
79	Len Matuszek	.10
80	Oddibe McDowell	.10
81	Roger McDowell	.40
82	Donnie Moore	.10
83	Ron Musselman	.10
84	Al Oliver	.15
85	Joe Orsulak	.15
86	Dan Pasqua	.40
87	Chris Pittaro	.10
88	Rick Reuschel	.10
89	Earnie Riles	.10
90	Jerry Royster	.10
91	[illegible]	[illegible]
92	Dave Rucker	.10
93	Vern Ruhle	.10
94	Mark Salas	.10
95	Luis Salazar	.10
96	Joe Sambito	.10
97	Billy Sample	.10
98	Alex Sanchez	.10
99	Calvin Schiraldi	.10
100	Rick Schu	.10
101	Larry Sheets	.10
102	Ron Shepherd	.10
103	Nelson Simmons	.10
104	Don Slaught	.10
105	Roy Smalley	.10
106	Lonnie Smith	.10
107	Nate Snell	.10
108	Lary Sorensen	.10
109	Chris Speier	.10
110	Mike Stenhouse	.10
111	Tim Stoddard	.10
112	John Stuper	.10
113	Jim Sundberg	.10
114	Bruce Sutter	.10
115	Don Sutton	.75
116	Bruce Tanner	.10
117	Kent Tekulve	.10
118	Walt Terrell	.10
119	*Mickey Tettleton*	2.00
120	Rich Thompson	.10
121	Louis Thornton	.10
122	Alex Trevino	.10
123	John Tudor	.10
124	Jose Uribe	.10
125	Dave Valle	.15
126	Dave Von Ohlen	.10
127	Curt Wardle	.10
128	U.L. Washington	.10
129	Ed Whitson	.10
130	Herm Winningham	.10
131	Rich Yett	.10
132	Checklist	.10

1985 Fleer Star Stickers

The 1985 Fleer sticker set consists of 126 player stickers, each measuring 1-15/16" x 2-1/2". Numbered on the back, the stickers were designed to be put in a special album. Distributed in packs of six, the 1985 stickers are the scarcest of all Fleer baseball sticker issues.

		MT
Complete Set (126):		50.00
Common Player:		.15
Sticker Album:		2.50
1	Pete Rose	1.00
2	Pete Rose	1.00
3	Pete Rose	1.00
4	Don Mattingly	3.00
5	Dave Winfield	.75
6	Wade Boggs	2.25
7	Buddy Bell	.15
8	Tony Gwynn	2.50
9	Lee Lacy	.15
10	Chili Davis	.15
11	Ryne Sandberg	3.00
12	Tony Armas	.15
13	Jim Rice	.25
14	Dave Kingman	.15
15	Alvin Davis	.15
16	Gary Carter	.25
17	Mike Schmidt	2.00
18	Dale Murphy	.40
19	Ron Cey	.15
20	Eddie Murray	.75
21	Harold Baines	.20
22	Kirk Gibson	.15
23	Jim Rice	.25
24	Gary Matthews	.15
25	Keith Hernandez	.15
26	Gary Carter	.25
27	George Hendrick	.15
28	Tony Armas	.15
29	Dave Kingman	.20
30	Dwayne Murphy	.15
31	Lance Parrish	.15
32	Andre Thornton	.15
33	Dale Murphy	.40
34	Mike Schmidt	2.00
35	Gary Carter	.25
36	Darryl Strawberry	.40
37	Don Mattingly	3.00
38	Larry Parrish	.15
39	George Bell	.15
40	Dwight Evans	.15
41	Cal Ripken, Jr.	5.00
42	Tim Raines	.25
43	Johnny Ray	.15
44	Juan Samuel	.15
45	Ryne Sandberg	3.00
46	Mike Easler	.15
47	Andre Thornton	.15
48	Dave Kingman	.20
49	Don Baylor	.20
50	Rusty Staub	.15
51	Steve Braun	.15
52	Kevin Bass	.15
53	Greg Gross	.15
54	Rickey Henderson	.75
55	Dave Collins	.15
56	Brett Butler	.20
57	Gary Pettis	.15
58	Tim Raines	.25
59	Juan Samuel	.15
60	Alan Wiggins	.15
61	Lonnie Smith	.15
62	Eddie Murray	.25
63	Eddie Murray	.25
64	Eddie Murray	.25
65	Eddie Murray	.25
66	Eddie Murray	.25
67	Eddie Murray	.25
68	Tom Seaver	.25
69	Tom Seaver	.25
70	Tom Seaver	.25
71	Tom Seaver	.25
72	Tom Seaver	.25
73	Tom Seaver	.25
74	Mike Schmidt	.50
75	Mike Schmidt	.50
76	Mike Schmidt	.50
77	Mike Schmidt	.50
78	Mike Schmidt	.50
79	Mike Schmidt	.50
80	Mike Boddicker	.15
81	Bert Blyleven	.15
82	Jack Morris	.15
83	Dan Petry	.15
84	Frank Viola	.15
85	Joaquin Andujar	.15
86	Mario Soto	.15
87	Dwight Gooden	.25
88	Joe Niekro	.15
89	Rick Sutcliffe	.15
90	Mike Boddicker	.15
91	Dave Stieb	.15
92	Bert Blyleven	.15
93	Phil Niekro	.50
94	Alejandro Pena	.15
95	Dwight Gooden	.25
96	Orel Hershiser	.25
97	Rick Rhoden	.15
98	John Candelaria	.15
99	Dan Quisenberry	.15
100	Bill Caudill	.15
101	Willie Hernandez	.15
102	Dave Righetti	.15
103	Ron Davis	.15
104	Bruce Sutter	.15
105	Lee Smith	.25
106	Jesse Orosco	.15
107	Al Holland	.15
108	Goose Gossage	.15
109	Mark Langston	.20
110	Dave Stieb	.15
111	Mike Witt	.15
112	Bert Blyleven	.15
113	Dwight Gooden	.25
114	Fernando Valenzuela	.20
115	Nolan Ryan	4.50
116	Mario Soto	.15
117	Ron Darling	.15
118	Dan Gladden	.15
119	Jeff Stone	.15
120	John Franco	.15
121	Barbaro Garbey	.15
122	Kirby Puckett	5.00
123	Roger Clemens	5.00
124	Bret Saberhagen	.15
125	Sparky Anderson	.20
126	Dick Williams	.15

1985 Fleer Limited Edition

The 1985 Fleer Limited Edition boxed set was distributed through several chains of retail stores. The cards, which are the standard 2-1/2" x 3-1/2", have full-color photos inside a red and yellow frame. The backs are set in black type against two different shades of yellow and contain the player's personal and statistical information. The set was issued in a specially designed box which carried the complete checklist for the set on the back. Six team logo stickers were also included with the set.

		MT
Complete Set (44):		6.00
Common Player:		.05
1	Buddy Bell	.05
2	Bert Blyleven	.05
3	Wade Boggs	.65
4	George Brett	.75
5	Rod Carew	.30
6	Steve Carlton	.25
7	Alvin Davis	.05
8	Andre Dawson	.15
9	Steve Garvey	.15
10	Goose Gossage	.05
11	Tony Gwynn	.75
12	Keith Hernandez	.05
13	Kent Hrbek	.10
14	Reggie Jackson	.30
15	Dave Kingman	.05
16	Ron Kittle	.05
17	Mark Langston	.05
18	Jeff Leonard	.05
19	Bill Madlock	.05
20	Don Mattingly	.90
21	Jack Morris	.05
22	Dale Murphy	.15
23	Eddie Murray	.30
24	Tony Pena	.05
25	Dan Quisenberry	.05
26	Tim Raines	.05
27	Jim Rice	.10
28	Cal Ripken, Jr.	2.00
29	Pete Rose	.90
30	Nolan Ryan	1.50
31	Ryne Sandberg	.65
32	Steve Sax	.05
33	Mike Schmidt	.75
34	Tom Seaver	.35
35	Ozzie Smith	.30
36	Mario Soto	.05
37	Dave Stieb	.05
38	Darryl Strawberry	.10
39	Rick Sutcliffe	.05
40	Alan Trammell	.10
41	Willie Upshaw	.05
42	Fernando Valenzuela	.05
43	Dave Winfield	.25
44	Robin Yount	.40

1986 Fleer

The 1986 Fleer set contains 660 color cards measuring 2-1/2" x 3-1/2". The card fronts feature a player photo enclosed by a dark blue border. The card backs are minus the black-and-white photo that was included in past Fleer efforts. Player biographical and statistical information appear in black and yellow on white stock. As in 1985, Fleer devoted ten cards, entitled "Major League Prospects," to twenty promising rookie players. The 1986 set, as in the previous four years was issued with team logo stickers.

		MT
Complete Set (660):		50.00
Common Player:		.08
Wax Box:		100.00
1	Steve Balboni	.08
2	Joe Beckwith	.08
3	Buddy Biancalana	.08
4	Bud Black	.08
5	George Brett	2.25
6	Onix Concepcion	.08
7	Steve Farr	.08
8	Mark Gubicza	.08
9	Dane Iorg	.08
10	Danny Jackson	.08
11	Lynn Jones	.08
12	Mike Jones	.08
13	Charlie Leibrandt	.08
14	Hal McRae	.10
15	Omar Moreno	.08
16	Darryl Motley	.08
17	Jorge Orta	.08
18	Dan Quisenberry	.08
19	Bret Saberhagen	.15
20	Pat Sheridan	.08
21	Lonnie Smith	.08
22	Jim Sundberg	.08
23	John Wathan	.08
24	Frank White	.08
25	Willie Wilson	.08
26	Joaquin Andujar	.08
27	Steve Braun	.08
28	Bill Campbell	.08
29	Cesar Cedeno	.08
30	Jack Clark	.08
31	*Vince Coleman*	.40
32	Danny Cox	.08
33	Ken Dayley	.08
34	Ivan DeJesus	.08
35	Bob Forsch	.08
36	Brian Harper	.08
37	Tom Herr	.08
38	Ricky Horton	.08
39	Kurt Kepshire	.08
40	Jeff Lahti	.08
41	Tito Landrum	.08
42	Willie McGee	.10
43	Tom Nieto	.08
44	Terry Pendleton	.08
45	Darrell Porter	.08
46	Ozzie Smith	2.00
47	John Tudor	.08
48	Andy Van Slyke	.08
49	*Todd Worrell*	.40
50	Jim Acker	.08
51	Doyle Alexander	.08
52	Jesse Barfield	.08
53	George Bell	.08
54	Jeff Burroughs	.08
55	Bill Caudill	.08
56	Jim Clancy	.08
57	Tony Fernandez	.10
58	Tom Filer	.08
59	Damaso Garcia	.08
60	Tom Henke	.08
61	Garth Iorg	.08
62	Cliff Johnson	.08
63	Jimmy Key	.10
64	Dennis Lamp	.08
65	Gary Lavelle	.08
66	Buck Martinez	.08
67	Lloyd Moseby	.08
68	Rance Mulliniks	.08
69	Al Oliver	.08
70	Dave Stieb	.08
71	Louis Thornton	.08
72	Willie Upshaw	.08
73	Ernie Whitt	.08
74	*Rick Aguilera*	1.00
75	Wally Backman	.08
76	Gary Carter	.35
77	Ron Darling	.08
78	*Len Dykstra*	2.00
79	Sid Fernandez	.08
80	George Foster	.08
81	Dwight Gooden	.45
82	Tom Gorman	.08
83	Danny Heep	.08
84	Keith Hernandez	.08
85	Howard Johnson	.08
86	Ray Knight	.08
87	Terry Leach	.08
88	Ed Lynch	.08
89	*Roger McDowell*	.40
90	Jesse Orosco	.08
91	Tom Paciorek	.08
92	Ronn Reynolds	.08
93	Rafael Santana	.08
94	Doug Sisk	.08
95	Rusty Staub	.10
96	Darryl Strawberry	.75
97	Mookie Wilson	.08
98	Neil Allen	.08
99	Don Baylor	.12
100	Dale Berra	.08
101	Rich Bordi	.08
102	Marty Bystrom	.08
103	Joe Cowley	.08
104	*Brian Fisher*	.08
105	Ken Griffey	.10
106	Ron Guidry	.12
107	Ron Hassey	.08
108	Rickey Henderson	1.00
109	Don Mattingly	3.00
110	Bobby Meacham	.08
111	John Montefusco	.08
112	Phil Niekro	.50
113	Mike Pagliarulo	.08
114	Dan Pasqua	.08
115	Willie Randolph	.08
116	Dave Righetti	.08
117	Andre Robertson	.08
118	Billy Sample	.08
119	Bob Shirley	.08
120	Ed Whitson	.08
121	Dave Winfield	1.25
122	Butch Wynegar	.08
123	Dave Anderson	.08
124	Bob Bailor	.08
125	Greg Brock	.08
126	Enos Cabell	.08
127	Bobby Castillo	.08
128	Carlos Diaz	.08
129	*Mariano Duncan*	.15
130	Pedro Guerrero	.08
131	Orel Hershiser	.15
132	Rick Honeycutt	.08
133	Ken Howell	.08
134	Ken Landreaux	.08
135	Bill Madlock	.08
136	Candy Maldonado	.08
137	Mike Marshall	.08
138	Len Matuszek	.08
139	Tom Niedenfuer	.08
140	Alejandro Pena	.08
141	Jerry Reuss	.08
142	Bill Russell	.08
143	Steve Sax	.08
144	Mike Scioscia	.08
145	Fernando Valenzuela	.10
146	Bob Welch	.08
147	Terry Whitfield	.08
148	Juan Beniquez	.08
149	Bob Boone	.08
150	John Candelaria	.08
151	Rod Carew	.75
152	*Stewart Cliburn*	.08
153	Doug DeCinces	.08
154	Brian Downing	.08
155	Ken Forsch	.08

156	Craig Gerber	.08
157	Bobby Grich	.08
158	George Hendrick	.08
159	Al Holland	.08
160	Reggie Jackson	1.00
161	Ruppert Jones	.08
162	*Urbano Lugo*	.08
163	*Kirk McCaskill*	.25
164	Donnie Moore	.08
165	Gary Pettis	.08
166	Ron Romanick	.08
167	Dick Schofield	.08
168	Daryl Sconiers	.08
169	Jim Slaton	.08
170	Don Sutton	.35
171	Mike Witt	.08
172	Buddy Bell	.08
173	Tom Browning	.08
174	Dave Concepcion	.08
175	Eric Davis	.45
176	Bo Diaz	.08
177	Nick Esasky	.08
178	John Franco	.08
179	Tom Hume	.08
180	Wayne Krenchicki	.08
181	Andy McGaffigan	.08
182	Eddie Milner	.08
183	Ron Oester	.08
184	Dave Parker	.10
185	Frank Pastore	.08
186	Tony Perez	.15
187	Ted Power	.08
188	Joe Price	.08
189	Gary Redus	.08
190	Ron Robinson	.08
191	Pete Rose	1.00
192	Mario Soto	.08
193	John Stuper	.08
194	Jay Tibbs	.08
195	Dave Van Gorder	.08
196	Max Venable	.08
197	Juan Agosto	.08
198	Harold Baines	.10
199	Floyd Bannister	.08
200	Britt Burns	.08
201	Julio Cruz	.08
202	*Joel Davis*	.08
203	Richard Dotson	.08
204	Carlton Fisk	.50
205	Scott Fletcher	.08
206	*Ozzie Guillen*	.80
207	Jerry Hairston	.08
208	Tim Hulett	.08
209	Bob James	.08
210	Ron Kittle	.08
211	Rudy Law	.08
212	Bryan Little	.08
213	Gene Nelson	.08
214	Reid Nichols	.08
215	Luis Salazar	.08
216	Tom Seaver	1.00
217	Dan Spillner	.08
218	Bruce Tanner	.08
219	Greg Walker	.08
220	Dave Wehrmeister	.08
221	Juan Berenguer	.08
222	Dave Bergman	.08
223	Tom Brookens	.08
224	Darrell Evans	.10
225	Barbaro Garbey	.08
226	Kirk Gibson	.08
227	John Grubb	.08
228	Willie Hernandez	.08
229	Larry Herndon	.08
230	Chet Lemon	.08
231	Aurelio Lopez	.08
232	Jack Morris	.08
233	Randy O'Neal	.08
234	Lance Parrish	.08
235	Dan Petry	.08
236	Alex Sanchez	.08
237	Bill Scherrer	.08
238	Nelson Simmons	.08
239	Frank Tanana	.08
240	Walt Terrell	.08
241	Alan Trammell	.25
242	Lou Whitaker	.10
243	Milt Wilcox	.08
244	Hubie Brooks	.08
245	*Tim Burke*	.10
246	Andre Dawson	.30
247	Mike Fitzgerald	.08
248	Terry Francona	.08
249	Bill Gullickson	.08
250	Joe Hesketh	.08
251	Bill Laskey	.08
252	Vance Law	.08
253	Charlie Lea	.08
254	Gary Lucas	.08
255	David Palmer	.08
256	Tim Raines	.30
257	Jeff Reardon	.08
258	Bert Roberge	.08
259	Dan Schatzeder	.08
260	Bryn Smith	.08
261	Randy St. Claire	.08
262	Scot Thompson	.08
263	Tim Wallach	.08
264	U.L. Washington	.08
265	*Mitch Webster*	.08
266	*Herm Winningham*	.08
267	*Floyd Youmans*	.08
268	Don Aase	.08
269	Mike Boddicker	.08
270	Rich Dauer	.08
271	Storm Davis	.08
272	Rick Dempsey	.08
273	Ken Dixon	.08
274	Jim Dwyer	.08
275	Mike Flanagan	.08
276	Wayne Gross	.08
277	Lee Lacy	.08
278	Fred Lynn	.10
279	Tippy Martinez	.08
280	Dennis Martinez	.10
281	Scott McGregor	.08
282	Eddie Murray	1.50
283	Floyd Rayford	.08
284	Cal Ripken, Jr.	8.00
285	Gary Roenicke	.08
286	Larry Sheets	.08
287	John Shelby	.08
288	Nate Snell	.08
289	Sammy Stewart	.08
290	Alan Wiggins	.08
291	Mike Young	.08
292	Alan Ashby	.08
293	Mark Bailey	.08
294	Kevin Bass	.08
295	Jeff Calhoun	.08
296	Jose Cruz	.08
297	Glenn Davis	.08
298	Bill Dawley	.08
299	Frank DiPino	.08
300	Bill Doran	.08
301	Phil Garner	.08
302	*Jeff Heathcock*	.08
303	*Charlie Kerfeld*	.08
304	Bob Knepper	.08
305	Ron Mathis	.08
306	Jerry Mumphrey	.08
307	Jim Pankovits	.08
308	Terry Puhl	.08
309	Craig Reynolds	.08
310	Nolan Ryan	8.00
311	Mike Scott	.08
312	Dave Smith	.08
313	Dickie Thon	.08
314	Denny Walling	.08
315	Kurt Bevacqua	.08
316	Al Bumbry	.08
317	Jerry Davis	.08
318	Luis DeLeon	.08
319	Dave Dravecky	.08
320	Tim Flannery	.08
321	Steve Garvey	.30
322	Goose Gossage	.08
323	Tony Gwynn	4.00
324	Andy Hawkins	.08
325	LaMarr Hoyt	.08
326	Roy Lee Jackson	.08
327	Terry Kennedy	.08
328	Craig Lefferts	.08
329	Carmelo Martinez	.08
330	*Lance McCullers*	.08
331	Kevin McReynolds	.08
332	Graig Nettles	.08
333	Jerry Royster	.08
334	Eric Show	.08
335	Tim Stoddard	.08
336	Garry Templeton	.08
337	Mark Thurmond	.08
338	Ed Wojna	.08
339	Tony Armas	.08
340	Marty Barrett	.08
341	Wade Boggs	2.00
342	Dennis Boyd	.08
343	Bill Buckner	.10
344	Mark Clear	.08
345	Roger Clemens	7.00
346	Steve Crawford	.08
347	Mike Easler	.08
348	Dwight Evans	.08
349	Rich Gedman	.08
350	Jackie Gutierrez	.08
351	Glenn Hoffman	.08
352	Bruce Hurst	.08
353	Bruce Kison	.08
354	Tim Lollar	.08
355	Steve Lyons	.08
356	Al Nipper	.08
357	Bob Ojeda	.08
358	Jim Rice	.12
359	Bob Stanley	.08
360	Mike Trujillo	.08
361	Thad Bosley	.08
362	Warren Brusstar	.08
363	Ron Cey	.08
364	Jody Davis	.08
365	Bob Dernier	.08
366	Shawon Dunston	.10
367	Leon Durham	.08
368	Dennis Eckersley	.12
369	Ray Fontenot	.08
370	George Frazier	.08
371	Bill Hatcher	.08
372	Dave Lopes	.08
373	Gary Matthews	.08
374	Ron Meredith	.08
375	Keith Moreland	.08
376	Reggie Patterson	.08
377	Dick Ruthven	.08
378	Ryne Sandberg	3.00
379	Scott Sanderson	.08
380	Lee Smith	.12
381	Lary Sorensen	.08
382	Chris Speier	.08
383	Rick Sutcliffe	.08
384	Steve Trout	.08
385	Gary Woods	.08
386	Bert Blyleven	.08
387	Tom Brunansky	.08
388	Randy Bush	.08
389	John Butcher	.08
390	Ron Davis	.08
391	Dave Engle	.08
392	Frank Eufemia	.08
393	Pete Filson	.08
394	Gary Gaetti	.10
395	Greg Gagne	.08
396	Mickey Hatcher	.08
397	Kent Hrbek	.20
398	Tim Laudner	.08
399	Rick Lysander	.08
400	Dave Meier	.08
401	Kirby Puckett	6.00
402	Mark Salas	.08
403	Ken Schrom	.08
404	Roy Smalley	.08
405	Mike Smithson	.08
406	Mike Stenhouse	.08
407	Tim Teufel	.08
408	Frank Viola	.08
409	Ron Washington	.08
410	Keith Atherton	.08
411	Dusty Baker	.10
412	*Tim Birtsas*	.08
413	Bruce Bochte	.08
414	Chris Codiroli	.08
415	Dave Collins	.08
416	Mike Davis	.08
417	Alfredo Griffin	.08
418	Mike Heath	.08
419	Steve Henderson	.08
420	Donnie Hill	.08
421	Jay Howell	.08
422	Tommy John	.10
423	Dave Kingman	.10
424	Bill Krueger	.08
425	Rick Langford	.08
426	Carney Lansford	.08
427	Steve McCatty	.08
428	Dwayne Murphy	.08
429	*Steve Ontiveros*	.08
430	Tony Phillips	.10
431	Jose Rijo	.08
432	Mickey Tettleton	.25
433	Luis Aguayo	.08
434	Larry Andersen	.08
435	Steve Carlton	.60
436	*Don Carman*	.08
437	Tim Corcoran	.08
438	*Darren Daulton*	2.50
439	John Denny	.08
440	Tom Foley	.08
441	Greg Gross	.08
442	Kevin Gross	.08
443	Von Hayes	.08
444	Charles Hudson	.08
445	Garry Maddox	.08
446	Shane Rawley	.08
447	Dave Rucker	.08
448	John Russell	.08
449	Juan Samuel	.08
450	Mike Schmidt	1.50
451	Rick Schu	.08
452	Dave Shipanoff	.08
453	Dave Stewart	.10
454	Jeff Stone	.08
455	Kent Tekulve	.08
456	Ozzie Virgil	.08
457	Glenn Wilson	.08
458	Jim Beattie	.08
459	Karl Best	.08
460	Barry Bonnell	.08
461	Phil Bradley	.08
462	*Ivan Calderon*	.08
463	Al Cowens	.08
464	Alvin Davis	.08
465	Dave Henderson	.08
466	Bob Kearney	.08
467	Mark Langston	.10
468	Bob Long	.08
469	Mike Moore	.08
470	Edwin Nunez	.08
471	Spike Owen	.08
472	Jack Perconte	.08
473	Jim Presley	.08
474	Donnie Scott	.08
475	Bill Swift	.08
476	Danny Tartabull	.10
477	Gorman Thomas	.08
478	Roy Thomas	.08
479	Ed Vande Berg	.08
480	Frank Wills	.08
481	Matt Young	.08
482	Ray Burris	.08
483	Jaime Cocanower	.08
484	Cecil Cooper	.08
485	Danny Darwin	.08
486	Rollie Fingers	.25
487	Jim Gantner	.08
488	Bob Gibson	.08
489	Moose Haas	.08
490	*Teddy Higuera*	.08
491	Paul Householder	.08
492	Pete Ladd	.08
493	Rick Manning	.08
494	Bob McClure	.08
495	Paul Molitor	2.00
496	Charlie Moore	.08
497	Ben Oglivie	.08
498	Randy Ready	.08
499	*Earnie Riles*	.08
500	Ed Romero	.08
501	Bill Schroeder	.08
502	Ray Searage	.08
503	Ted Simmons	.08
504	Pete Vuckovich	.08
505	Rick Waits	.08
506	Robin Yount	2.00
507	Len Barker	.08
508	Steve Bedrosian	.08
509	Bruce Benedict	.08
510	Rick Camp	.08
511	Rick Cerone	.08
512	Chris Chambliss	.08
513	Jeff Dedmon	.08
514	Terry Forster	.08
515	Gene Garber	.08
516	Terry Harper	.08
517	Bob Horner	.08
518	Glenn Hubbard	.08
519	*Joe Johnson*	.08
520	Brad Komminsk	.08
521	Rick Mahler	.08
522	Dale Murphy	.35
523	Ken Oberkfell	.08
524	Pascual Perez	.08
525	Gerald Perry	.08
526	Rafael Ramirez	.08
527	*Steve Shields*	.08
528	Zane Smith	.08
529	Bruce Sutter	.08
530	*Milt Thompson*	.10
531	Claudell Washington	.08
532	Paul Zuvella	.08
533	Vida Blue	.08
534	Bob Brenly	.08
535	*Chris Brown*	.08
536	Chili Davis	.10
537	Mark Davis	.08
538	Rob Deer	.08
539	Dan Driessen	.08
540	Scott Garrelts	.08
541	Dan Gladden	.08
542	Jim Gott	.08
543	David Green	.08
544	Atlee Hammaker	.08
545	Mike Jeffcoat	.08
546	Mike Krukow	.08
547	Dave LaPoint	.08
548	Jeff Leonard	.08
549	Greg Minton	.08
550	Alex Trevino	.08
551	Manny Trillo	.08
552	*Jose Uribe*	.08
553	Brad Wellman	.08
554	Frank Williams	.08
555	Joel Youngblood	.08
556	Alan Bannister	.08
557	Glenn Brummer	.08
558	*Steve Buechele*	.10
559	*Jose Guzman*	.08
560	Toby Harrah	.08
561	Greg Harris	.08
562	*Dwayne Henry*	.08
563	Burt Hooton	.08
564	Charlie Hough	.08
565	Mike Mason	.08
566	*Oddibe McDowell*	.08
567	Dickie Noles	.08
568	Pete O'Brien	.08
569	Larry Parrish	.08
570	Dave Rozema	.08
571	Dave Schmidt	.08
572	Don Slaught	.08
573	Wayne Tolleson	.08
574	Duane Walker	.08
575	Gary Ward	.08
576	Chris Welsh	.08
577	Curtis Wilkerson	.08
578	George Wright	.08
579	Chris Bando	.08
580	Tony Bernazard	.08
581	Brett Butler	.10
582	Ernie Camacho	.08
583	Joe Carter	.50
584	Carmello Castillo (Carmelo)	.08
585	Jamie Easterly	.08
586	Julio Franco	.10
587	Mel Hall	.08
588	Mike Hargrove	.08
589	Neal Heaton	.08
590	Brook Jacoby	.08
591	*Otis Nixon*	.30
592	Jerry Reed	.08
593	Vern Ruhle	.08
594	Pat Tabler	.08
595	Rich Thompson	.08
596	Andre Thornton	.08
597	Dave Von Ohlen	.08
598	George Vukovich	.08
599	Tom Waddell	.08
600	Curt Wardle	.08
601	Jerry Willard	.08
602	Bill Almon	.08
603	Mike Bielecki	.08
604	Sid Bream	.08
605	Mike Brown	.08
606	*Pat Clements*	.08
607	Jose DeLeon	.08
608	Denny Gonzalez	.08
609	Cecilio Guante	.08
610	Steve Kemp	.08
611	Sam Khalifa	.08
612	Lee Mazzilli	.08
613	Larry McWilliams	.08
614	Jim Morrison	.08
615	*Joe Orsulak*	.25
616	Tony Pena	.08
617	Johnny Ray	.08
618	Rick Reuschel	.08
619	R.J. Reynolds	.08
620	Rick Rhoden	.08
621	Don Robinson	.08
622	Jason Thompson	.08
623	Lee Tunnell	.08
624	Jim Winn	.08
625	Marvell Wynne	.08
626	Dwight Gooden (In Action)	.25
627	Don Mattingly (In Action)	1.25
628	Pete Rose (4,192 hits)	.75
629	Rod Carew (3,000 Hits)	.50
630	Phil Niekro, Tom Seaver (300 Wins)	.25
631	Ouch! (Don Baylor)	.10
632	Instant Offense (Tim Raines, Darryl Strawberry)	.25
633	Shortstops Supreme (Cal Ripken, Jr., Alan Trammell)	1.00
634	Boggs & "Hero" (Wade Boggs, George Brett)	1.00
635	Braves Dynamic Duo (Bob Horner, Dale Murphy)	.30
636	Cardinal Ignitors (Vince Coleman, Willie McGee)	.25
637	Terror on the Basepaths (Vince Coleman)	.10
638	Charlie Hustle & Dr. K (Dwight Gooden, Pete Rose)	.50
639	1984 and 1985 A.L. Batting Champs (Wade Boggs, Don Mattingly)	1.00
640	N.L. West Sluggers (Steve Garvey, Dale Murphy, Dave Parker)	.30
641	Staff Aces (Dwight Gooden, Fernando Valenzuela)	.20
642	Blue Jay Stoppers (Jimmy Key, Dave Stieb)	.10
643	A.L. All-Star Backstops (Carlton Fisk, Rich Gedman)	.10
644	Major League Prospect *(Benito Santiago)*, *(Gene Walter)*	.90
645	Major League Prospect *(Colin Ward)*, *(Mike Woodard)*	.10
646	Major League Prospect *(Kal Daniels)*, *(Paul O'Neill)*	4.00
647	Major League Prospect *(Andres Galarraga)*, *(Fred Toliver)*	5.00
648	Major League Prospect *(Curt Ford)*, *(Bob Kipper)*	.10
649	Major League Prospect *(Jose Canseco)*, *(Eric Plunk)*	20.00
650	Major League Prospect *(Mark McLemore)*, *(Gus Polidor)*	.45
651	Major League Prospect *(Mickey Brantley)*, *(Rob Woodward)*	.10
652	Major League Prospect *(Mark Funderburk)*, *(Billy Joe Robidoux)*	.10
653	Major League Prospect *(Cecil Fielder)*, *(Cory Snyder)*	2.50
654	Checklist 1-97	.08
655	Checklist 98-196	.08
656	Checklist 197-291	.08
657	Checklist 292-385	.08
658	Checklist 386-482	.08
659	Checklist 483-578	.08
660	Checklist 579-660	.08

1986 Fleer All Stars

Fleer's choices for a major league All-Star team make up this 12-card set. The cards were randomly inserted in 35¢ wax packs and 59¢ cello packs. The card fronts have a color photo set against a bright red background for A.L. players or a bright blue background for N.L. players. Backs feature the player's career highlights on a red and blue background.

		MT
Complete Set (12):		19.00
Common Player:		.25
1	Don Mattingly	5.00
2	Tom Herr	.25
3	George Brett	5.00
4	Gary Carter	.75
5	Cal Ripken, Jr.	12.00
6	Dave Parker	.35
7	Rickey Henderson	2.00
8	Pedro Guerrero	.25
9	Dan Quisenberry	.25
10	Dwight Gooden	.50
11	Gorman Thomas	.25
12	John Tudor	.25

1986 Fleer Future Hall Of Famers

The 1986 Future Hall of Famers set is comprised of six players Fleer felt would gain eventual entrance into the Baseball Hall of Fame. The cards are the standard 2-1/2" x 3-1/2" and were randomly inserted in three-pack rack packs. Card fronts feature a player photo set against a blue background with horizontal light blue stripes. Backs are printed in black on blue and feature career highlights in narrative form.

		MT
Complete Set (6):		15.00
Common Player:		1.75
1	Pete Rose	2.50
2	Steve Carlton	2.00
3	Tom Seaver	2.00
4	Rod Carew	2.00
5	Nolan Ryan	9.00
6	Reggie Jackson	2.00

1986 Fleer Box Panels

Picking up on a Donruss idea, Fleer issued eight cards in panels of four on the bottoms of the wax and cello pack boxes. The cards are numbered C-1 through C-8 and are 2-1/2" x 3-1/2", with a complete panel measuring 5" x 7-1/8". Included in the eight cards are six players and two team logo/checklist cards.

		MT
Complete Panel Set (2):		3.50
Complete Singles Set (8):		1.75
Common Single Player:		.20
Panel		2.50
1	Royals Logo/ Checklist	.05
2	George Brett	.90
3	Ozzie Guillen	.20
4	Dale Murphy	.40
Panel		1.50
5	Cardinals Logo/ Checklist	.05
6	Tom Browning	.20
7	Gary Carter	.35
8	Carlton Fisk	.35

1986 Fleer Update

Issued near the end of the baseball season, the 1986 Fleer Update set consists of cards numbered U-1 through U-132. The 2-1/2" x 3-1/2" cards are identical in design to the regular 1986 Fleer set. The purpose of the set is to update player trades and include rookies not depicted in the regular issue. The set was issued with team logo stickers in a specially designed box and was available only through hobby dealers.

		MT
Complete Set (132):		25.00
Common Player:		.08
1	Mike Aldrete	.08
2	Andy Allanson	.08
3	Neil Allen	.08
4	Joaquin Andujar	.08
5	Paul Assenmacher	.08
6	Scott Bailes	.08
7	Jay Baller	.08
8	Scott Bankhead	.08
9	Bill Bathe	.08
10	Don Baylor	.25
11	Billy Beane	.08
12	Steve Bedrosian	.08
13	Juan Beniquez	.08
14	*Barry Bonds*	10.00
15	*Bobby Bonilla*	1.50
16	Rich Bordi	.08
17	Bill Campbell	.08
18	Tom Candiotti	.08
19	John Cangelosi	.08
20	*Jose Canseco*	6.00
21	Chuck Cary	.08
22	Juan Castillo	.08
23	Rick Cerone	.08
24	John Cerutti	.10
25	*Will Clark*	4.50
26	Mark Clear	.08
27	Darnell Coles	.08
28	Dave Collins	.08
29	Tim Conroy	.08
30	Ed Correa	.08
31	Joe Cowley	.08
32	Bill Dawley	.08
33	Rob Deer	.08
34	John Denny	.08
35	Jim DeShaies	.10
36	*Doug Drabek*	1.00
37	Mike Easler	.08
38	Mark Eichhorn	.12
39	Dave Engle	.08
40	Mike Fischlin	.08
41	Scott Fletcher	.08
42	Terry Forster	.08
43	Terry Francona	.08
44	Andres Galarraga	2.00
45	Lee Guetterman	.08
46	Bill Gullickson	.08
47	Jackie Gutierrez	.08
48	Moose Haas	.08
49	Billy Hatcher	.08
50	Mike Heath	.08
51	Guy Hoffman	.08
52	Tom Hume	.08
53	*Pete Incaviglia*	.40
54	Dane Iorg	.08
55	Chris James	.08
56	Stan Javier	.10
57	Tommy John	.15
58	Tracy Jones	.08
59	*Wally Joyner*	1.50
60	Wayne Krenchicki	.08
61	*John Kruk*	.50
62	Mike LaCoss	.08
63	Pete Ladd	.08
64	Dave LaPoint	.08
65	Mike LaValliere	.20
66	Rudy Law	.08
67	Dennis Leonard	.08
68	Steve Lombardozzi	.08
69	Aurelio Lopez	.08
70	Mickey Mahler	.08
71	Candy Maldonado	.08
72	Roger Mason	.08
73	Greg Mathews	.08
74	Andy McGaffigan	.08
75	Joel McKeon	.08
76	*Kevin Mitchell*	.50
77	Bill Mooneyham	.08
78	Omar Moreno	.08
79	Jerry Mumphrey	.08
80	Al Newman	.08
81	Phil Niekro	.50
82	Randy Niemann	.08
83	Juan Nieves	.08
84	Bob Ojeda	.08
85	Rick Ownbey	.08
86	Tom Paciorek	.08
87	David Palmer	.08
88	Jeff Parrett	.25
89	Pat Perry	.08
90	Dan Plesac	.08
91	Darrell Porter	.08
92	Luis Quinones	.08
93	Rey Quinonez	.08
94	Gary Redus	.08
95	Jeff Reed	.08
96	Bip Roberts	.60
97	Billy Joe Robidoux	.08
98	Gary Roenicke	.08
99	Ron Roenicke	.08
100	Angel Salazar	.08
101	Joe Sambito	.08
102	Billy Sample	.08
103	Dave Schmidt	.08
104	Ken Schrom	.08
105	*Ruben Sierra*	.75
106	Ted Simmons	.08
107	Sammy Stewart	.08
108	Kurt Stillwell	.08
109	Dale Sveum	.08
110	Tim Teufel	.08
111	Bob Tewksbury	.75
112	Andres Thomas	.08
113	Jason Thompson	.08
114	Milt Thompson	.08
115	Rob Thompson	.20
116	Jay Tibbs	.08
117	Fred Toliver	.08
118	Wayne Tolleson	.08
119	Alex Trevino	.08
120	Manny Trillo	.08
121	Ed Vande Berg	.08
122	Ozzie Virgil	.08
123	Tony Walker	.08
124	Gene Walter	.08
125	Duane Ward	.25
126	Jerry Willard	.08
127	Mitch Williams	.30
128	Reggie Williams	.08
129	Bobby Witt	.30
130	Marvell Wynne	.08
131	Steve Yeager	.08
132	Checklist	.05

1986 Fleer Baseball's Best

The 1986 Fleer Baseball's Best set was produced for the McCrory's retail chain and its affiliated stores. Subtitled "Sluggers vs. Pitchers," the set contains 22 each of the game's best hitters and pitchers. The 2-1/2" x 3-1/2" cards have color action photos on front. Backs are done in blue and red and carry players' personal and statistical data. The sets were issued in a specially designed box with six team logo stickers.

		MT
Complete Set (44):		5.00
Common Player:		.05
1	Bert Blyleven	.05
2	Wade Boggs	.75
3	George Brett	.75
4	Tom Browning	.05
5	Jose Canseco	1.00
6	Will Clark	.65
7	Roger Clemens	1.00
8	Alvin Davis	.05
9	Julio Franco	.05
10	Kirk Gibson	.05
11	Dwight Gooden	.15
12	Goose Gossage	.05
13	Pedro Guerrero	.05
14	Ron Guidry	.05
15	Tony Gwynn	1.00
16	Orel Hershiser	.10
17	Kent Hrbek	.10
18	Reggie Jackson	.50
19	Wally Joyner	.25
20	Charlie Leibrandt	.05
21	Don Mattingly	1.00
22	Willie McGee	.10
23	Jack Morris	.08
24	Dale Murphy	.25
25	Eddie Murray	.35
26	Jeff Reardon	.05
27	Rick Reuschel	.05
28	Cal Ripken, Jr.	2.00
29	Pete Rose	.75
30	Nolan Ryan	2.00
31	Bret Saberhagen	.08
32	Ryne Sandberg	.80
33	Mike Schmidt	.80
34	Tom Seaver	.25
35	Bryn Smith	.05
36	Mario Soto	.05
37	Dave Stieb	.05
38	Darryl Strawberry	.15
39	Rick Sutcliffe	.05
40	John Tudor	.05
41	Fernando Valenzuela	.10
42	Bobby Witt	.05
43	Mike Witt	.05
44	Robin Yount	.35

1986 Fleer League Leaders

Fleer's 1986 "League Leaders" set features 44 of the game's top players and was issued through the Walgreens drug store chain. Fronts contain a color photo and feature player name, team and position in a blue band near the bottom of the card. The words "League Leaders" appear in a red band at the top of the card. The background for the card fronts is alternating blue and white stripes. The card backs are printed in blue, red and white and carry statistical information and team logo. Cards are the standard 2-1/2" x 3-1/2". The set was issued in a special cardboard box, along with six team logo stickers.

		MT
Complete Set (44):		4.00
Common Player:		.05
1	Wade Boggs	.60
2	George Brett	.60
3	Jose Canseco	1.00
4	Rod Carew	.30
5	Gary Carter	.25
6	Jack Clark	.05
7	Vince Coleman	.08
8	Jose Cruz	.05
9	Alvin Davis	.05
10	Mariano Duncan	.05
11	Leon Durham	.05
12	Carlton Fisk	.15
13	Julio Franco	.08
14	Scott Garrelts	.05
15	Steve Garvey	.15
16	Dwight Gooden	.20
17	Ozzie Guillen	.05
18	Willie Hernandez	.05
19	Bob Horner	.05
20	Kent Hrbek	.08
21	Charlie Leibrandt	.05
22	Don Mattingly	1.00
23	Oddibe McDowell	.05
24	Willie McGee	.08
25	Keith Moreland	.05
26	Lloyd Moseby	.05
27	Dale Murphy	.25
28	Phil Niekro	.25
29	Joe Orsulak	.05
30	Dave Parker	.10
31	Lance Parrish	.08
32	Kirby Puckett	1.00
33	Tim Raines	.10
34	Earnie Riles	.05
35	Cal Ripken, Jr.	2.00
36	Pete Rose	.75
37	Bret Saberhagen	.05
38	Juan Samuel	.05
39	Ryne Sandberg	.90
40	Tom Seaver	.30
41	Lee Smith	.08
42	Ozzie Smith	.35
43	Dave Stieb	.05
44	Robin Yount	.35

1986 Fleer Limited Edition

Produced for the McCrory's store chain and its affiliates for the second year in a row, the Limited Edition set contains 44 cards. In standard 2-1/2" x 3-1/2" size, cards have color photos enclosed by green, red and yellow trim. Backs carry black print on two shades of red. The set was issued in a special cardboard box, along with six team logo stickers.

		MT
Complete Set (44):		5.00
Common Player:		.05
1	Doyle Alexander	.05
2	Joaquin Andujar	.05
3	Harold Baines	.08
4	Wade Boggs	.70
5	Phil Bradley	.05
6	George Brett	.70
7	Hubie Brooks	.05
8	Chris Brown	.05

9	Tom Brunansky	.05
10	Gary Carter	.20
11	Vince Coleman	.10
12	Cecil Cooper	.05
13	Jose Cruz	.05
14	Mike Davis	.05
15	Carlton Fisk	.10
16	Julio Franco	.05
17	Damaso Garcia	.05
18	Rich Gedman	.05
19	Kirk Gibson	.05
20	Dwight Gooden	.20
21	Pedro Guerrero	.05
22	Tony Gwynn	.35
23	Rickey Henderson	.40
24	Orel Hershiser	.10
25	LaMarr Hoyt	.05
26	Reggie Jackson	.30
27	Don Mattingly	1.00
28	Oddibe McDowell	.05
29	Willie McGee	.10
30	Paul Molitor	.25
31	Dale Murphy	.15
32	Eddie Murray	.25
33	Dave Parker	.10
34	Tony Pena	.05
35	Jeff Reardon	.05
36	Cal Ripken, Jr.	2.00
37	Pete Rose	.75
38	Bret Saberhagen	.05
39	Juan Samuel	.05
40	Ryne Sandberg	.60
41	Mike Schmidt	.75
42	Lee Smith	.08
43	Don Sutton	.10
44	Lou Whitaker	.05

1986 Fleer Mini

Fleer's 1986 "Classic Miniatures" set contains 120 cards that measure 1-13/16" x 2-9/16". The design of the high-gloss cards is identical to the regular 1986 Fleer set but the player photos are entirely different. The set, which was issued in a specially designed box along with 18 team logo stickers, was available only through hobby dealers.

		MT
Complete Set (120):		6.00
Common Player:		.05
1	George Brett	.80
2	Dan Quisenberry	.05
3	Bret Saberhagen	.08
4	Lonnie Smith	.05
5	Willie Wilson	.05
6	Jack Clark	.05
7	Vince Coleman	.05
8	Tom Herr	.05
9	Willie McGee	.08
10	Ozzie Smith	.50
11	John Tudor	.05
12	Jesse Barfield	.05
13	George Bell	.05
14	Tony Fernandez	.08
15	Damaso Garcia	.05
16	Dave Stieb	.05
17	Gary Carter	.12
18	Ron Darling	.05
19	Dwight Gooden	.15
20	Keith Hernandez	.05
21	Darryl Strawberry	.10
22	Ron Guidry	.10
23	Rickey Henderson	.45
24	Don Mattingly	1.00
25	Dave Righetti	.05
26	Dave Winfield	.45
27	Mariano Duncan	.05
28	Pedro Guerrero	.05
29	Bill Madlock	.05
30	Mike Marshall	.05
31	Fernando Valenzuela	.10
32	Reggie Jackson	.30
33	Gary Pettis	.05
34	Ron Romanick	.05
35	Don Sutton	.15
36	Mike Witt	.05
37	Buddy Bell	.05
38	Tom Browning	.05
39	Dave Parker	.08
40	Pete Rose	.85
41	Mario Soto	.05
42	Harold Baines	.08
43	Carlton Fisk	.12
44	Ozzie Guillen	.05
45	Ron Kittle	.05
46	Tom Seaver	.20
47	Kirk Gibson	.05
48	Jack Morris	.05
49	Lance Parrish	.05
50	Alan Trammell	.15
51	Lou Whitaker	.08
52	Hubie Brooks	.05
53	Andre Dawson	.12
54	Tim Raines	.10
55	Bryn Smith	.05
56	Tim Wallach	.05
57	Mike Boddicker	.05
58	Eddie Murray	.40
59	Cal Ripken, Jr.	2.50
60	John Shelby	.05
61	Mike Young	.05
62	Jose Cruz	.05
63	Glenn Davis	.05
64	Phil Garner	.05
65	Nolan Ryan	2.00
66	Mike Scott	.05
67	Steve Garvey	.12
68	Goose Gossage	.05
69	Tony Gwynn	.60
70	Andy Hawkins	.05
71	Garry Templeton	.05
72	Wade Boggs	.80
73	Roger Clemens	.90
74	Dwight Evans	.05
75	Rich Gedman	.05
76	Jim Rice	.10
77	Shawon Dunston	.15
78	Leon Durham	.05
79	Keith Moreland	.05
80	Ryne Sandberg	.75
81	Rick Sutcliffe	.05
82	Bert Blyleven	.05
83	Tom Brunansky	.05
84	Kent Hrbek	.08
85	Kirby Puckett	.95
86	Bruce Bochte	.05
87	Jose Canseco	1.00
88	Mike Davis	.05
89	Jay Howell	.05
90	Dwayne Murphy	.05
91	Steve Carlton	.20
92	Von Hayes	.05
93	Juan Samuel	.05
94	Mike Schmidt	.50
95	Glenn Wilson	.05
96	Phil Bradley	.05
97	Alvin Davis	.05
98	Jim Presley	.05
99	Danny Tartabull	.05
100	Cecil Cooper	.05
101	Paul Molitor	.50
102	Earnie Riles	.05
103	Robin Yount	.50
104	Bob Horner	.05
105	Dale Murphy	.20
106	Bruce Sutter	.05
107	Claudell Washington	.05
108	Chris Brown	.05
109	Chili Davis	.08
110	Scott Garrelts	.05
111	Oddibe McDowell	.05
112	Pete O'Brien	.05
113	Gary Ward	.05
114	Brett Butler	.10
115	Julio Franco	.08
116	Brook Jacoby	.05
117	Mike Brown	.05
118	Joe Orsulak	.05
119	Tony Pena	.05
120	R.J. Reynolds	.05

1986 Fleer Star Stickers

Fleer's 1986 sticker-card set again measures 2-1/2" x 3-1/2" and features color photos inside dark maroon borders. Backs are identical to the 1986 baseball card issue except for the 1-132 numbering system and blue ink instead of yellow. Card #132 is a multi-player card featuring Dwight Gooden and Dale Murphy on the front and a complete checklist for the set on the reverse. The cards were sold in wax packs with team logo stickers.

		MT
Complete Set (132):		22.00
Common Player:		.10
1	Harold Baines	.15
2	Jesse Barfield	.10
3	Don Baylor	.15
4	Juan Beniquez	.10
5	Tim Birtsas	.10
6	Bert Blyleven	.10
7	Bruce Bochte	.10
8	Wade Boggs	1.75
9	Dennis Boyd	.10
10	Phil Bradley	.10
11	George Brett	2.00
12	Hubie Brooks	.10
13	Chris Brown	.10
14	Tom Browning	.10
15	Tom Brunansky	.10
16	Bill Buckner	.12
17	Britt Burns	.10
18	Brett Butler	.12
19	Jose Canseco	2.00
20	Rod Carew	.80
21	Steve Carlton	.80
22	Don Carman	.10
23	Gary Carter	.30
24	Jack Clark	.10
25	Vince Coleman	.10
26	Cecil Cooper	.10
27	Jose Cruz	.10
28	Ron Darling	.10
29	Alvin Davis	.10
30	Jody Davis	.10
31	Mike Davis	.10
32	Andre Dawson	.30
33	Mariano Duncan	.10
34	Shawon Dunston	.10
35	Leon Durham	.10
36	Darrell Evans	.10
37	Tony Fernandez	.10
38	Carlton Fisk	.25
39	John Franco	.10
40	Julio Franco	.10
41	Damaso Garcia	.10
42	Scott Garrelts	.10
43	Steve Garvey	.30
44	Rich Gedman	.10
45	Kirk Gibson	.10
46	Dwight Gooden	.25
47	Pedro Guerrero	.10
48	Ron Guidry	.10
49	Ozzie Guillen	.10
50	Tony Gwynn	1.00
51	Andy Hawkins	.10
52	Von Hayes	.10
53	Rickey Henderson	.80
54	Tom Henke	.10
55	Keith Hernandez	.10
56	Willie Hernandez	.10
57	Tom Herr	.10
58	Orel Hershiser	.15
59	Teddy Higuera	.10
60	Bob Horner	.10
61	Charlie Hough	.10
62	Jay Howell	.10
63	LaMarr Hoyt	.10
64	Kent Hrbek	.15
65	Reggie Jackson	1.00
66	Bob James	.10
67	Dave Kingman	.12
68	Ron Kittle	.10
69	Charlie Leibrandt	.10
70	Fred Lynn	.12
71	Mike Marshall	.10
72	Don Mattingly	2.00
73	Oddibe McDowell	.10
74	Willie McGee	.12
75	Scott McGregor	.10
76	Paul Molitor	.75
77	Donnie Moore	.10
78	Keith Moreland	.10
79	Jack Morris	.10
80	Dale Murphy	.30
81	Eddie Murray	.75
82	Phil Niekro	.75
83	Joe Orsulak	.10
84	Dave Parker	.05
85	Lance Parrish	.12
86	Larry Parrish	.10
87	Tony Pena	.10
88	Gary Pettis	.10
89	Jim Presley	.10
90	Kirby Puckett	2.00
91	Dan Quisenberry	.10
92	Tim Raines	.15
93	Johnny Ray	.10
94	Jeff Reardon	.10
95	Rick Reuschel	.10
96	Jim Rice	.15
97	Dave Righetti	.10
98	Earnie Riles	.10
99	Cal Ripken, Jr.	3.00
100	Ron Romanick	.10
101	Pete Rose	1.50
102	Nolan Ryan	3.00
103	Bret Saberhagen	.12
104	Mark Salas	.10
105	Juan Samuel	.10
106	Ryne Sandberg	1.00
107	Mike Schmidt	1.75
108	Mike Scott	.10
109	Tom Seaver	.60
110	Bryn Smith	.10
111	Dave Smith	.10
112	Lee Smith	.15
113	Ozzie Smith	.75
114	Mario Soto	.10
115	Dave Stieb	.10
116	Darryl Strawberry	.40
117	Bruce Sutter	.10
118	Garry Templeton	.10
119	Gorman Thomas	.10
120	Andre Thornton	.10
121	Alan Trammell	.15
122	John Tudor	.10
123	Fernando Valenzuela	.15
124	Frank Viola	.10
125	Gary Ward	.10
126	Lou Whitaker	.12
127	Frank White	.10
128	Glenn Wilson	.10
129	Willie Wilson	.10
130	Dave Winfield	.80
131	Robin Yount	.75
132	Dwight Gooden, Dale Murphy	.50

1986 Fleer Star Stickers Box Panels

Four cards, numbered S-1 through S-4, were placed on the bottoms of 1986 Fleer Star Stickers wax pack boxes. The cards are nearly identical in format to the regular issue sticker cards. Individual cards measure 2-1/2" x 3-1/2" in size, while a complete panel of four measures 5" x 7-1/8".

		MT
Complete Panel Set:		2.00
Complete Singles Set (4):		1.00
Common Single Player:		.30
1	Dodgers logo	.05
2	Wade Boggs	1.00
3	Steve Garvey	.30
4	Dave Winfield	.50

1987 Fleer

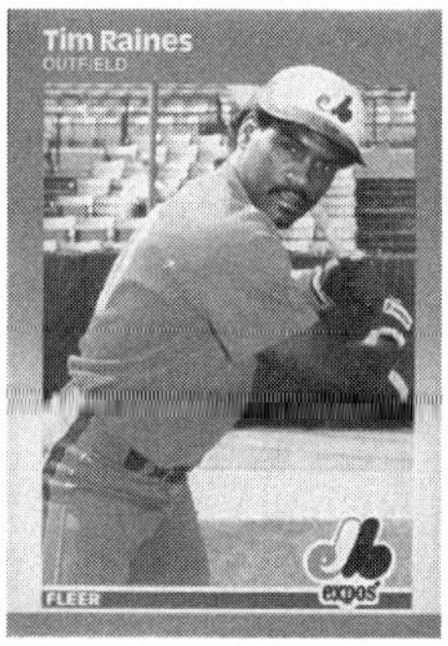

The 1987 Fleer set consists of 660 cards. Fronts feature a graduated blue-to-white border design. The player's name and position appear in the upper-left corner of the card; his team logo is located in the lower-right. Backs are done in blue, red and white and contain an innovative "Pro Scouts Report" feature which rates the player's batting or pitching skills. For the third year in a row, Fleer included its "Major League Prospects" subset. Fleer produced a glossy-finish Collectors Edition set which came housed in a specially-designed tin box. After experiencing a dramatic hike in price during 1987, the glossy set now sells for only a few dollars more than the regular issue.

		MT
Complete Set (660):		70.00
Common Player:		.06
Wax Box:		110.00
1	Rick Aguilera	.06
2	Richard Anderson	.06
3	Wally Backman	.06
4	Gary Carter	.20
5	Ron Darling	.06
6	Len Dykstra	.15
7	*Kevin Elster*	.15
8	Sid Fernandez	.06
9	Dwight Gooden	.25
10	*Ed Hearn*	.06
11	Danny Heep	.06
12	Keith Hernandez	.08
13	Howard Johnson	.08
14	Ray Knight	.06
15	Lee Mazzilli	.06
16	Roger McDowell	.06
17	Kevin Mitchell	.10
18	Randy Niemann	.06
19	Bob Ojeda	.06
20	Jesse Orosco	.06
21	Rafael Santana	.06
22	Doug Sisk	.06
23	Darryl Strawberry	.20
24	Tim Teufel	.06
25	Mookie Wilson	.06
26	Tony Armas	.06
27	Marty Barrett	.06
28	Don Baylor	.12
29	Wade Boggs	1.50
30	Oil Can Boyd	.06
31	Bill Buckner	.08
32	Roger Clemens	3.50
33	Steve Crawford	.06
34	Dwight Evans	.08
35	Rich Gedman	.06
36	Dave Henderson	.06
37	Bruce Hurst	.06
38	Tim Lollar	.06
39	Al Nipper	.06
40	Spike Owen	.06
41	Jim Rice	.08
42	Ed Romero	.06
43	Joe Sambito	.06
44	Calvin Schiraldi	.06
45	Tom Seaver	.75
46	*Jeff Sellers*	.06
47	Bob Stanley	.06
48	Sammy Stewart	.06
49	Larry Andersen	.06
50	Alan Ashby	.06
51	Kevin Bass	.06
52	Jeff Calhoun	.06
53	Jose Cruz	.06
54	Danny Darwin	.06
55	Glenn Davis	.06
56	*Jim Deshaies*	.15
57	Bill Doran	.06
58	Phil Garner	.06
59	Billy Hatcher	.06
60	Charlie Kerfeld	.06
61	Bob Knepper	.06
62	Dave Lopes	.06
63	Aurelio Lopez	.06
64	Jim Pankovits	.06
65	Terry Puhl	.06
66	Craig Reynolds	.06
67	Nolan Ryan	4.00
68	Mike Scott	.06
69	Dave Smith	.06
70	Dickie Thon	.06
71	Tony Walker	.06
72	Denny Walling	.06
73	Bob Boone	.06
74	Rick Burleson	.06
75	John Candelaria	.06
76	Doug Corbett	.06
77	Doug DeCinces	.06
78	Brian Downing	.06
79	*Chuck Finley*	1.00
80	Terry Forster	.06
81	Bobby Grich	.06
82	George Hendrick	.06
83	Jack Howell	.06
84	Reggie Jackson	1.00
85	Ruppert Jones	.06
86	Wally Joyner	.75
87	Gary Lucas	.06
88	Kirk McCaskill	.06
89	Donnie Moore	.06
90	Gary Pettis	.06
91	Vern Ruhle	.06
92	Dick Schofield	.06
93	Don Sutton	.30
94	Rob Wilfong	.06

95	Mike Witt	.06
96	Doug Drabek	.10
97	Mike Easler	.06
98	Mike Fischlin	.06
99	Brian Fisher	.06
100	Ron Guidry	.10
101	Rickey Henderson	.45
102	Tommy John	.10
103	Ron Kittle	.06
104	Don Mattingly	2.25
105	Bobby Meacham	.06
106	Joe Niekro	.06
107	Mike Pagliarulo	.06
108	Dan Pasqua	.06
109	Willie Randolph	.06
110	Dennis Rasmussen	.06
111	Dave Righetti	.06
112	Gary Roenicke	.06
113	Rod Scurry	.06
114	Bob Shirley	.06
115	Joel Skinner	.06
116	Tim Stoddard	.06
117	*Bob Tewksbury*	.50
118	Wayne Tolleson	.06
119	Claudell Washington	.06
120	Dave Winfield	.35
121	Steve Buechele	.06
122	*Ed Correa*	.06
123	Scott Fletcher	.06
124	Jose Guzman	.06
125	Toby Harrah	.06
126	Greg Harris	.06
127	Charlie Hough	.06
128	Pete Incaviglia	.08
129	Mike Mason	.06
130	Oddibe McDowell	.06
131	*Dale Mohorcic*	.06
132	Pete O'Brien	.06
133	Tom Paciorek	.06
134	Larry Parrish	.06
135	Geno Petralli	.06
136	Darrell Porter	.06
137	Jeff Russell	.06
138	Ruben Sierra	.10
139	Don Slaught	.06
140	Gary Ward	.06
141	Curtis Wilkerson	.06
142	*Mitch Williams*	.40
143	*Bobby Witt*	.40
144	Dave Bergman	.06
145	Tom Brookens	.06
146	Bill Campbell	.06
147	*Chuck Cary*	.06
148	Darnell Coles	.06
149	Dave Collins	.06
150	Darrell Evans	.06
151	Kirk Gibson	.06
152	John Grubb	.06
153	Willie Hernandez	.06
154	Larry Herndon	.06
155	*Eric King*	.06
156	Chet Lemon	.06
157	Dwight Lowry	.06
158	Jack Morris	.06
159	Randy O'Neal	.06
160	Lance Parrish	.10
161	Dan Petry	.06
162	Pat Sheridan	.06
163	Jim Slaton	.06
164	Frank Tanana	.06
165	Walt Terrell	.06
166	Mark Thurmond	.06
167	Alan Trammell	.25
168	Lou Whitaker	.12
169	Luis Aguayo	.06
170	Steve Bedrosian	.06
171	Don Carman	.06
172	Darren Daulton	.15
173	Greg Gross	.06
174	Kevin Gross	.06
175	Von Hayes	.06
176	Charles Hudson	.06
177	Tom Hume	.06
178	Steve Jeltz	.06
179	*Mike Maddux*	.06
180	Shane Rawley	.06
181	Gary Redus	.06
182	Ron Roenicke	.06
183	*Bruce Ruffin*	.10
184	John Russell	.06
185	Juan Samuel	.06
186	Dan Schatzeder	.06
187	Mike Schmidt	1.00
188	Rick Schu	.06
189	Jeff Stone	.06
190	Kent Tekulve	.06
191	Milt Thompson	.06
192	Glenn Wilson	.06
193	Buddy Bell	.06
194	Tom Browning	.06
195	Sal Butera	.06
196	Dave Concepcion	.06
197	Kal Daniels	.06
198	Eric Davis	.15
199	John Denny	.06
200	Bo Diaz	.06
201	Nick Esasky	.06
202	John Franco	.06
203	Bill Gullickson	.06
204	*Barry Larkin*	5.00
205	Eddie Milner	.06
206	*Rob Murphy*	.06
207	Ron Oester	.06
208	Dave Parker	.12
209	Tony Perez	.15
210	Ted Power	.06
211	Joe Price	.06
212	Ron Robinson	.06

213	Pete Rose	1.00
214	Mario Soto	.06
215	*Kurt Stillwell*	.06
216	Max Venable	.06
217	Chris Welsh	.06
218	*Carl Willis*	.06
219	Jesse Barfield	.06
220	George Bell	.06
221	Bill Caudill	.06
222	*John Cerutti*	.06
223	Jim Clancy	.06
224	*Mark Eichhorn*	.10
225	Tony Fernandez	.08
226	Damaso Garcia	.06
227	Kelly Gruber	.06
228	Tom Henke	.06
229	Garth Iorg	.06
230	Cliff Johnson	.06
231	Joe Johnson	.06
232	Jimmy Key	.10
233	Dennis Lamp	.06
234	Rick Leach	.06
235	Buck Martinez	.06
236	Lloyd Moseby	.06
237	Rance Mulliniks	.06
238	Dave Stieb	.06
239	Willie Upshaw	.06
240	Ernie Whitt	.06
241	*Andy Allanson*	.06
242	*Scott Bailes*	.06
243	Chris Bando	.06
244	Tony Bernazard	.06
245	John Butcher	.06
246	Brett Butler	.10
247	Ernie Camacho	.06
248	Tom Candiotti	.06
249	Joe Carter	.50
250	Carmen Castillo	.06
251	Julio Franco	.08
252	Mel Hall	.06
253	Brook Jacoby	.06
254	Phil Niekro	.25
255	Otis Nixon	.06
256	Dickie Noles	.06
257	Bryan Oelkers	.06
258	Ken Schrom	.06
259	Don Schulze	.06
260	Cory Snyder	.06
261	Pat Tabler	.06
262	Andre Thornton	.06
263	*Rich Yett*	.06
264	*Mike Aldrete*	.06
265	Juan Berenguer	.06
266	Vida Blue	.06
267	Bob Brenly	.06
268	Chris Brown	.06
269	Will Clark	3.00
270	Chili Davis	.08
271	Mark Davis	.06
272	*Kelly Downs*	.06
273	Scott Garrelts	.06
274	Dan Gladden	.06
275	Mike Krukow	.06
276	*Randy Kutcher*	.06
277	Mike LaCoss	.06
278	Jeff Leonard	.06
279	Candy Maldonado	.06
280	Roger Mason	.06
281	Bob Melvin	.06
282	Greg Minton	.06
283	Jeff Robinson	.06
284	Harry Spilman	.06
285	*Rob Thompson*	.25
286	Jose Uribe	.06
287	Frank Williams	.06
288	Joel Youngblood	.06
289	Jack Clark	.06
290	Vince Coleman	.08
291	Tim Conroy	.06
292	Danny Cox	.06
293	Ken Dayley	.06
294	Curt Ford	.06
295	Bob Forsch	.06
296	Tom Herr	.06
297	Ricky Horton	.06
298	Clint Hurdle	.06
299	Jeff Lahti	.06
300	Steve Lake	.06
301	Tito Landrum	.06
302	*Mike LaValliere*	.20
303	*Greg Mathews*	.06
304	Willie McGee	.08
305	Jose Oquendo	.06
306	Terry Pendleton	.06
307	Pat Perry	.06
308	Ozzie Smith	1.00
309	Ray Soff	.06
310	John Tudor	.06
311	Andy Van Slyke	.06
312	Todd Worrell	.06
313	Dann Bilardello	.06
314	Hubie Brooks	.06
315	Tim Burke	.06
316	Andre Dawson	.25
317	Mike Fitzgerald	.06
318	Tom Foley	.06
319	Andres Galarraga	.60
320	Joe Hesketh	.06
321	Wallace Johnson	.06
322	Wayne Krenchicki	.06
323	Vance Law	.06
324	Dennis Martinez	.10
325	Bob McClure	.06
326	Andy McGaffigan	.06
327	*Al Newman*	.06
328	Tim Raines	.25
329	Jeff Reardon	.06
330	*Luis Rivera*	.06

331	*Bob Sebra*	.06
332	Bryn Smith	.06
333	Jay Tibbs	.06
334	Tim Wallach	.06
335	Mitch Webster	.06
336	Jim Wohlford	.06
337	Floyd Youmans	.06
338	*Chris Bosio*	.25
339	*Glenn Braggs*	.06
340	Rick Cerone	.06
341	Mark Clear	.06
342	*Bryan Clutterbuck*	.06
343	Cecil Cooper	.06
344	Rob Deer	.06
345	Jim Gantner	.06
346	Ted Higuera	.06
347	John Henry Johnson	.06
348	Tim Leary	.06
349	Rick Manning	.06
350	Paul Molitor	1.00
351	Charlie Moore	.06
352	Juan Nieves	.06
353	Ben Oglivie	.06
354	*Dan Plesac*	.12
355	Ernest Riles	.06
356	Billy Joe Robidoux	.06
357	Bill Schroeder	.06
358	*Dale Sveum*	.06
359	Gorman Thomas	.06
360	Bill Wegman	.10
361	Robin Yount	1.00
362	Steve Balboni	.06
363	*Scott Bankhead*	.06
364	Buddy Biancalana	.06
365	Bud Black	.06
366	George Brett	2.00
367	Steve Farr	.06
368	Mark Gubicza	.06
369	Bo Jackson	3.00
370	Danny Jackson	.06
371	*Mike Kingery*	.06
372	Rudy Law	.06
373	Charlie Leibrandt	.06
374	Dennis Leonard	.06
375	Hal McRae	.08
376	Jorge Orta	.06
377	Jamie Quirk	.06
378	Dan Quisenberry	.06
379	Bret Saberhagen	.08
380	Angel Salazar	.06
381	Lonnie Smith	.06
382	Jim Sundberg	.06
383	Frank White	.06
384	Willie Wilson	.08
385	Joaquin Andujar	.06
386	Doug Bair	.06
387	Dusty Baker	.10
388	Bruce Bochte	.06
389	Jose Canseco	3.00
390	Chris Codiroli	.06
391	Mike Davis	.06
392	Alfredo Griffin	.06
393	Moose Haas	.06
394	Donnie Hill	.06
395	Jay Howell	.06
396	Dave Kingman	.10
397	Carney Lansford	.06
398	*David Leiper*	.06
399	*Bill Mooneyham*	.06
400	Dwayne Murphy	.06
401	Steve Ontiveros	.06
402	Tony Phillips	.12
403	Eric Plunk	.06
404	Jose Rijo	.06
405	*Terry Steinbach*	.60
406	[illegible]	[illegible]
407	Mickey Tettleton	.08
408	Dave Von Ohlen	.06
409	Jerry Willard	.06
410	Curt Young	.06
411	Bruce Bochy	.06
412	Dave Dravecky	.06
413	Tim Flannery	.06
414	Steve Garvey	.25
415	Goose Gossage	.12
416	Tony Gwynn	2.50
417	Andy Hawkins	.06
418	LaMarr Hoyt	.06
419	Terry Kennedy	.06
420	John Kruk	.10
421	Dave LaPoint	.06
422	Craig Lefferts	.06
423	Carmelo Martinez	.06
424	Lance McCullers	.06
425	Kevin McReynolds	.06
426	Graig Nettles	.06
427	*Bip Roberts*	.75
428	Jerry Royster	.06
429	Benito Santiago	.15
430	Eric Show	.06
431	Bob Stoddard	.06
432	Garry Templeton	.06
433	Gene Walter	.06
434	Ed Whitson	.06
435	Marvell Wynne	.06
436	Dave Anderson	.06
437	Greg Brock	.06
438	Enos Cabell	.06
439	Mariano Duncan	.06
440	Pedro Guerrero	.06
441	Orel Hershiser	.10
442	Rick Honeycutt	.06
443	Ken Howell	.06
444	Ken Landreaux	.06
445	Bill Madlock	.06
446	Mike Marshall	.06
447	Len Matuszek	.06
448	Tom Niedenfuer	.06

449	Alejandro Pena	.06
450	Dennis Powell	.06
451	Jerry Reuss	.06
452	Bill Russell	.08
453	Steve Sax	.06
454	Mike Scioscia	.06
455	Franklin Stubbs	.06
456	Alex Trevino	.06
457	Fernando Valenzuela	.10
458	Ed Vande Berg	.06
459	Bob Welch	.06
460	*Reggie Williams*	.06
461	Don Aase	.06
462	Juan Beniquez	.06
463	Mike Boddicker	.06
464	Juan Bonilla	.06
465	Rich Bordi	.06
466	Storm Davis	.06
467	Rick Dempsey	.06
468	Ken Dixon	.06
469	Jim Dwyer	.06
470	Mike Flanagan	.06
471	Jackie Gutierrez	.06
472	Brad Havens	.06
473	Lee Lacy	.06
474	Fred Lynn	.12
475	Scott McGregor	.06
476	Eddie Murray	1.00
477	Tom O'Malley	.06
478	Cal Ripken, Jr.	4.00
479	Larry Sheets	.06
480	John Shelby	.06
481	Nate Snell	.06
482	Jim Traber	.06
483	Mike Young	.06
484	Neil Allen	.06
485	Harold Baines	.10
486	Floyd Bannister	.06
487	Daryl Boston	.06
488	Ivan Calderon	.06
489	*John Cangelosi*	.06
490	Steve Carlton	.50
491	Joe Cowley	.06
492	Julio Cruz	.06
493	Bill Dawley	.06
494	Jose DeLeon	.06
495	Richard Dotson	.06
496	Carlton Fisk	.75
497	Ozzie Guillen	.06
498	Jerry Hairston	.06
499	Ron Hassey	.06
500	Tim Hulett	.06
501	Bob James	.06
502	Steve Lyons	.06
503	*Joel McKeon*	.06
504	Gene Nelson	.06
505	Dave Schmidt	.06
506	Ray Searage	.06
507	*Bobby Thigpen*	.15
508	Greg Walker	.06
509	Jim Acker	.06
510	Doyle Alexander	.06
511	*Paul Assenmacher*	.06
512	Bruce Benedict	.06
513	Chris Chambliss	.06
514	Jeff Dedmon	.06
515	Gene Garber	.06
516	Ken Griffey	.10
517	Terry Harper	.06
518	Bob Horner	.06
519	Glenn Hubbard	.06
520	Rick Mahler	.06
521	Omar Moreno	.06
522	Dale Murphy	.25
523	Ken Oberkfell	.06
524	Ed Olwine	.06
525	David Palmer	.06
526	Rafael Ramirez	.06
527	Billy Sample	.06
528	Ted Simmons	.06
529	Zane Smith	.06
530	Bruce Sutter	.06
531	*Andres Thomas*	.06
532	Ozzie Virgil	.06
533	*Allan Anderson*	.06
534	Keith Atherton	.06
535	Billy Beane	.06
536	Bert Blyleven	.06
537	Tom Brunansky	.06
538	Randy Bush	.06
539	George Frazier	.06
540	Gary Gaetti	.10
541	Greg Gagne	.06
542	Mickey Hatcher	.06
543	Neal Heaton	.06
544	Kent Hrbek	.15
545	Roy Lee Jackson	.06
546	Tim Laudner	.06
547	Steve Lombardozzi	.06
548	*Mark Portugal*	.35
549	Kirby Puckett	2.50
550	Jeff Reed	.06
551	Mark Salas	.06
552	Roy Smalley	.06
553	Mike Smithson	.06
554	Frank Viola	.06
555	Thad Bosley	.06
556	Ron Cey	.06
557	Jody Davis	.06
558	Ron Davis	.06
559	Bob Dernier	.06
560	Frank DiPino	.06
561	Shawon Dunston	.10
562	Leon Durham	.06
563	Dennis Eckersley	.20
564	Terry Francona	.06
565	Dave Gumpert	.06

566	Guy Hoffman	.06
567	Ed Lynch	.06
568	Gary Matthews	.06
569	Keith Moreland	.06
570	*Jamie Moyer*	.06
571	Jerry Mumphrey	.06
572	Ryne Sandberg	1.00
573	Scott Sanderson	.06
574	Lee Smith	.10
575	Chris Speier	.06
576	Rick Sutcliffe	.06
577	Manny Trillo	.06
578	Steve Trout	.06
579	Karl Best	.06
580	Scott Bradley	.06
581	Phil Bradley	.06
582	Mickey Brantley	.06
583	Mike Brown	.06
584	Alvin Davis	.06
585	*Lee Guetterman*	.06
586	Mark Huismann	.06
587	Bob Kearney	.06
588	Pete Ladd	.06
589	Mark Langston	.06
590	Mike Moore	.06
591	Mike Morgan	.06
592	John Moses	.06
593	Ken Phelps	.06
594	Jim Presley	.06
595	*Rey Quinonez (Quinones)*	.06
596	Harold Reynolds	.06
597	Billy Swift	.06
598	Danny Tartabull	.05
599	Steve Yeager	.06
600	Matt Young	.06
601	Bill Almon	.06
602	*Rafael Belliard*	.06
603	Mike Bielecki	.06
604	Barry Bonds	25.00
605	Bobby Bonilla	1.00
606	Sid Bream	.06
607	Mike Brown	.06
608	Pat Clements	.06
609	*Mike Diaz*	.06
610	Cecillo Guante	.06
611	*Barry Jones*	.06
612	Bob Kipper	.06
613	Larry McWilliams	.06
614	Jim Morrison	.06
615	Joe Orsulak	.06
616	Junior Ortiz	.06
617	Tony Pena	.06
618	Johnny Ray	.06
619	Rick Reuschel	.06
620	R.J. Reynolds	.06
621	Rick Rhoden	.06
622	Don Robinson	.06
623	Bob Walk	.06
624	Jim Winn	.06
625	Youthful Power (Jose Canseco, Pete Incaviglia)	.40
626	300 Game Winners (Phil Niekro, Don Sutton)	.25
627	A.L. Firemen (Don Aase, Dave Righetti)	.06
628	Rookie All-Stars (Jose Canseco, Wally Joyner)	.40
629	Magic Mets (Gary Carter, Dwight Gooden, Keith Hernandez, Darryl Strawberry)	.15
630	N.L. Best Righties (Mike Krukow, Mike Scott)	.06
631	Sensational Southpaws (John Franco, Fernando Valenzuela)	.06
632	Count 'Em (Bob Horner)	.08
633	A.L. Pitcher's Nightmare (Jose Canseco, Kirby Puckett, Jim Rice)	.40
634	All Star Battery (Gary Carter, Roger Clemens)	.25
635	4,000 Strikeouts (Steve Carlton)	.12
636	Big Bats At First Sack (Glenn Davis, Eddie Murray)	.25
637	On Base (Wade Boggs, Keith Hernandez)	.20
638	Sluggers From Left Side (Don Mattingly, Darryl Strawberry)	.40
639	Former MVP's (Dave Parker, Ryne Sandberg)	.12
640	Dr. K. & Super K (Roger Clemens, Dwight Gooden)	.50
641	A.L. West Stoppers (Charlie Hough, Mike Witt)	.06
642	Doubles & Triples (Tim Raines, Juan Samuel)	.06

643	Outfielders With Punch (Harold Baines, Jesse Barfield)	.06
644	Major League Prospects *(Dave Clark)*, *(Greg Swindell)*	.30
645	Major League Prospects *(Ron Karkovice)*, *(Russ Morman)*	.25
646	Major League Prospects *(Willie Fraser)*, *(Devon White)*	1.00
647	Major League Prospects *(Jerry Browne)*, *(Mike Stanley)*	.25
648	Major League Prospects *(Phil Lombardi)*, *(Dave Magadan)*	.20
649	Major League Prospects *(Ralph Bryant)*, *(Jose Gonzalez)*	.10
650	Major League Prospects *(Randy Asadoor)*, *(Jimmy Jones)*	.10
651	Major League Prospects *(Marvin Freeman)*, *(Tracy Jones)*	.10
652	Major League Prospects *(Kevin Seitzer*, John Stefero)	.25
653	Major League Prospects *(Steve Fireovid)*, *(Rob Nelson)*	.10
654	Checklist 1-95	.06
655	Checklist 96-192	.06
656	Checklist 193-288	.06
657	Checklist 289-384	.06
658	Checklist 385-483	.06
659	Checklist 484-578	.06
660	Checklist 579-660	.06

1987 Fleer All Stars

As in 1986, Fleer All Star Team cards were randomly inserted in wax and cello packs. Twelve cards, measuring the standard 2-1/2" x 3-1/2", comprise the set. Fronts feature a full-color player photo set against a gray background for American League players and a black background for National Leaguers. Backs are printed in black, red and white and feature a lengthy player biography. Fleer's choices for a major league All-Star team is once again the theme for the set.

		MT
Complete Set (12):		15.00
Common Player:		.30
1	Don Mattingly	4.00
2	Gary Carter	.50
3	Tony Fernandez	.30
4	Steve Sax	.30
5	Kirby Puckett	5.00
6	Mike Schmidt	3.50
7	Mike Easler	.30
8	Todd Worrell	.30
9	George Bell	.30
10	Fernando Valenzuela	.45
11	Roger Clemens	5.00
12	Tim Raines	.50

Player names in *Italic* type indicate a rookie card.

1987 Fleer Headliners

A continuation of the 1986 Future Hall of Famers idea, Fleer encountered legal problems with using the Hall of Fame name and abated them by entitling the set "Headliners." The cards were randomly inserted in three-pack rack packs. Fronts feature a player photo set against a beige background with bright red stripes. Backs are printed in black, red and gray and offer a brief biography with an emphasis on the player's performance during the 1986 season.

		MT
Complete Set (6):		6.00
Common Player:		.45
1	Wade Boggs	2.25
2	Jose Canseco	2.00
3	Dwight Gooden	.60
4	Rickey Henderson	1.50
5	Keith Hernandez	.45
6	Jim Rice	.65

1987 Fleer '86 World Series

Fleer issued a set of 12 cards highlighting the 1986 World Series between the Boston Red Sox and New York Mets. The sets were available only with Fleer factory sets, both regular and glossy. The cards, 2-1/2" x 3-1/2", have either horizontal or vertical formats. The fronts are bordered in red, white and blue stars and stripes with a thin gold frame around the photo. Backs are printed in red and blue on white stock and include information regarding the photo on the card fronts.

		MT
Complete Set, Regular (12):		2.00
Complete Set, Glossy (12):		3.00
Common Card:		.25
1	Left-Hand Finesse Beats Mets (Bruce Hurst)	.25
2	Wade Boggs, Keith Hernandez	.50
3	Roger Clemens	.75
4	Gary Carter	.35
5	Ron Darling	.25
6	.433 Series Batting Average (Marty Barrett)	.25
7	Dwight Gooden	.35
8	Strategy At Work	.25
9	Dewey! (Dwight Evans)	.25
10	One Strike From Boston Victory (Dave Henderson, Spike Owen)	.25
11	Ray Knight, Darryl Strawberry	.25
12	Series M.V.P. (Ray Knight)	.25

1987 Fleer Box Panels

For the second straight year, Fleer produced a special set of cards designed to stimulate sales of their wax and cello pack boxes. In 1987, Fleer issued 16 cards in panels of four on the bottoms of retail boxes. The cards are numbered C-1 through C-16 and are 2-1/2" x 3-1/2" in size. The cards have the same design as the regular issue set with the player photos and card numbers being different.

		MT
Complete Panel Set (4):		8.00
Complete Singles Set (16):		3.50
Common Panel:		2.25
Common Single Player:		.15
Panel		2.50
1	Mets Logo	.05
6	Keith Hernandez	.15
8	Dale Murphy	.30
14	Ryne Sandberg	.80
Panel		2.25
2	Jesse Barfield	.15
3	George Brett	.80
5	Red Sox Logo	.05
11	Kirby Puckett	.90
Panel		2.75
4	Dwight Gooden	.30
9	Astros Logo	.05
10	Dave Parker	.15
15	Mike Schmidt	.80
Panel		2.50
7	Wally Joyner	.25
12	Dave Righetti	.15
13	Angels Logo	.05
16	Robin Yount	.50

1987 Fleer Glossy Tin

The three-year run of limited edition, glossy collectors' issues by Fleer from 1987-89 has become known to the hobby as "tins" for the colorful lithographed metal boxes in which complete sets were sold. In their debut year a reported 100,000 sets were made, each serial numbered on a sticker attached to the shrink-wrapped tin box. While the glossy version of the 1987 Fleer set once enjoyed a significant premium over regular cards, today that premium has evaporated and, indeed, it can be harder to find a buyer for the glossy version.

	MT
Complete Set (672):	60.00
Common Player:	.10
(Single star cards valued at .75-1X regular-issue 1987 Fleer.)	

1987 Fleer Update

The 1987 update edition brings the regular Fleer set up to date by including traded players and hot rookies. The cards measure 2-1/2" x 3-1/2" and are housed in a specially designed box with 25 team logo stickers. A glossy-coated Fleer Collectors Edition set was also produced.

		MT
Complete Set (132):		30.00
Common Player:		.08
1	Scott Bankhead	.08
2	Eric Bell	.08
3	Juan Beniquez	.08
4	Juan Berenguer	.08
5	Mike Birkbeck	.08
6	Randy Bockus	.08
7	Rod Booker	.08
8	Thad Bosley	.08
9	Greg Brock	.08
10	Bob Brower	.08
11	Chris Brown	.08
12	Jerry Browne	.08
13	Ralph Bryant	.08
14	DeWayne Buice	.08
15	Ellis Burks	.60
16	Casey Candaele	.08
17	Steve Carlton	.40
18	Juan Castillo	.08
19	Chuck Crim	.08
20	Mark Davidson	.08
21	Mark Davis	.08
22	Storm Davis	.08
23	Bill Dawley	.08
24	Andre Dawson	.35
25	Brian Dayett	.08
26	Rick Dempsey	.08
27	Ken Dowell	.08
28	Dave Dravecky	.08
29	Mike Dunne	.08
30	Dennis Eckersley	.25
31	Cecil Fielder	.50
32	Brian Fisher	.08
33	Willie Fraser	.08
34	Ken Gerhart	.08
35	Jim Gott	.08
36	Dan Gladden	.08
37	Mike Greenwell	.15
38	Cecilio Guante	.08
39	Albert Hall	.08
40	Atlee Hammaker	.08
41	Mickey Hatcher	.08
42	Mike Heath	.08
43	Neal Heaton	.08
44	Mike Henneman	.20
45	Guy Hoffman	.08
46	Charles Hudson	.08
47	Chuck Jackson	.08
48	Mike Jackson	.08
49	Reggie Jackson	.60
50	Chris James	.08
51	Dion James	.08
52	Stan Javier	.08
53	Stan Jefferson	.08
54	Jimmy Jones	.08
55	Tracy Jones	.08
56	Terry Kennedy	.08
57	Mike Kingery	.08
58	Ray Knight	.10
59	Gene Larkin	.08
60	Mike LaValliere	.08
61	Jack Lazorko	.08
62	Terry Leach	.08
63	Rick Leach	.08
64	Craig Lefferts	.08
65	Jim Lindeman	.08
66	Bill Long	.08
67	Mike Loynd	.08
68	*Greg Maddux*	10.00
69	Bill Madlock	.08
70	Dave Magadan	.10
71	Joe Magrane	.10
72	Fred Manrique	.08
73	Mike Mason	.08
74	Lloyd McClendon	.08
75	Fred McGriff	3.00
76	Mark McGwire	20.00
77	Mark McLemore	.08
78	Kevin McReynolds	.08
79	Dave Meads	.08
80	Greg Minton	.08
81	John Mitchell	.08
82	Kevin Mitchell	.10
83	John Morris	.08
84	Jeff Musselman	.10
85	Randy Myers	.35
86	Gene Nelson	.08
87	Joe Niekro	.08
88	Tom Nieto	.08
89	Reid Nichols	.08
90	Matt Nokes	.08
91	Dickie Noles	.08
92	Edwin Nunez	.08
93	Jose Nunez	.08
94	Paul O'Neill	.75
95	Jim Paciorek	.08
96	Lance Parrish	.08
97	Bill Pecota	.08
98	Tony Pena	.08
99	Luis Polonia	.10
100	Randy Ready	.08
101	Jeff Reardon	.08
102	Gary Redus	.08
103	Rick Rhoden	.08
104	Wally Ritchie	.08
105	Jeff Robinson	.08
106	Mark Salas	.08
107	Dave Schmidt	.08
108	Kevin Seitzer	.08
109	John Shelby	.08
110	John Smiley	.10
111	Lary Sorenson	.08
112	Chris Speier	.08
113	Randy St. Claire	.08
114	Jim Sundberg	.08
115	B.J. Surhoff	.25
116	Greg Swindell	.10
117	Danny Tartabull	.08
118	Dorn Taylor	.08
119	Lee Tunnell	.08
120	Ed Vande Berg	.08
121	Andy Van Slyke	.08
122	Gary Ward	.08
123	Devon White	.35
124	Alan Wiggins	.08
125	Bill Wilkinson	.08
126	Jim Winn	.08
127	Frank Williams	.08
128	Ken Williams	.08
129	*Matt Williams*	3.00
130	Herm Winningham	.08
131	Matt Young	.08
132	Checklist 1-132	.08

1987 Fleer Update Glossy Tin

The 1987 Fleer glossy tin update set is identical to the regular-issue updates, except for the high-gloss coating on the cards' fronts and the lithographed metal box in which the sets were sold. Production was estimated at 100,000. Because of perceived overproduction, the glossy tin update set and singles currently carry little, if any, premium over the regular-issue updates.

	MT
Complete Set (132):	35.00
Common Player:	.10
(Star cards valued at .75-1X regular version 1987 Fleer updates.)	

1987 Fleer Award Winners

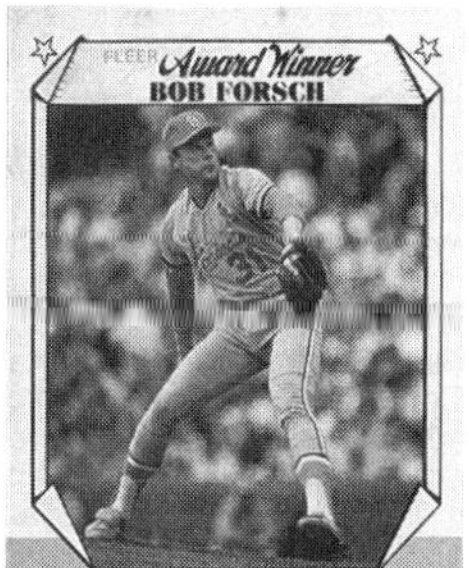

The 1987 Fleer Award Winners boxed set was prepared for distribution by 7-Eleven stores. The 2-1/2" x 3-1/2" cards feature players who have won various major league awards during their careers. Fronts contain full-color photos surrounded by a yellow border. The name of the award the player won is printed at the bottom of the card in an oval-shaped band designed to resemble a metal nameplate on a trophy. Backs are printed in black, yellow and white, and include lifetime major and minor league statistics along with typical personal information. Each boxed set contained six team logo stickers.

		MT
Complete Set (44):		3.00
Common Player:		.05
1	Marty Barrett	.05
2	George Bell	.05
3	Bert Blyleven	.05
4	Bob Boone	.05
5	John Candelaria	.05
6	Jose Canseco	.80
7	Gary Carter	.20
8	Joe Carter	.20
9	Roger Clemens	1.00
10	Cecil Cooper	.05
11	Eric Davis	.15
12	Tony Fernandez	.05
13	Scott Fletcher	.05
14	Bob Forsch	.05
15	Dwight Gooden	.15
16	Ron Guidry	.05
17	Ozzie Guillen	.05
18	Bill Gullickson	.05
19	Tony Gwynn	.75
20	Bob Knepper	.05
21	Ray Knight	.05
22	Mark Langston	.05
23	Candy Maldonado	.05
24	Don Mattingly	.90
25	Roger McDowell	.05
26	Dale Murphy	.15
27	Dave Parker	.05
28	Lance Parrish	.08
29	Gary Pettis	.05
30	Kirby Puckett	.90
31	Johnny Ray	.05
32	Dave Righetti	.05
33	Cal Ripken, Jr.	2.00
34	Bret Saberhagen	.08
35	Ryne Sandberg	.75
36	Mike Schmidt	.75
37	Mike Scott	.05
38	Ozzie Smith	.25
39	Robbie Thompson	.05
40	Fernando Valenzuela	.08
41	Mitch Webster	.05
42	Frank White	.05
43	Mike Witt	.05
44	Todd Worrell	.05

1987 Fleer Baseball All Stars

Produced by Fleer for exclusive distribution through Ben Franklin stores, the "Baseball All Stars" set is comprised of 44 cards in the standard 2-1/2" x 3-1/2" format. Cards have full-color photos surrounded by a bright red border with white pinstripes at the top and bottom. Backs are printed in blue, white and dark red and include complete major and minor league statistics. The set was issued in a special cardboard box with a handful of team logo stickers.

		MT
Complete Set (44):		3.00
Common Player:		.05
1	Harold Baines	.08
2	Jesse Barfield	.05
3	Wade Boggs	.75
4	Dennis "Oil Can" Boyd	.05
5	Scott Bradley	.05
6	Jose Canseco	.80
7	Gary Carter	.15
8	Joe Carter	.15
9	Mark Clear	.05
10	Roger Clemens	1.00
11	Jose Cruz	.05
12	Chili Davis	.08
13	Jody Davis	.05
14	Rob Deer	.05
15	Brian Downing	.05
16	Sid Fernandez	.05
17	John Franco	.05
18	Andres Galarraga	.15
19	Dwight Gooden	.15
20	Tony Gwynn	.75
21	Charlie Hough	.05
22	Bruce Hurst	.05
23	Wally Joyner	.10
24	Carney Lansford	.05
25	Fred Lynn	.05
26	Don Mattingly	.90
27	Willie McGee	.05
28	Jack Morris	.05
29	Dale Murphy	.15
30	Bob Ojeda	.05
31	Tony Pena	.05
32	Kirby Puckett	.90
33	Dan Quisenberry	.05
34	Tim Raines	.10
35	Willie Randolph	.05
36	Cal Ripken, Jr.	2.00
37	Pete Rose	.75
38	Nolan Ryan	1.50
39	Juan Samuel	.05
40	Mike Schmidt	.60
41	Ozzie Smith	.25
42	Andres Thomas	.05
43	Fernando Valenzuela	.08
44	Mike Witt	.05

1987 Fleer Baseball's Best

For a second straight baseball card season, Fleer produced for McCrory's stores and their affiliates a 44-card "Baseball's Best" set. Subtitled "Sluggers vs. Pitchers," 28 everyday players and 16 pitchers are featured. The card design is nearly identical to the previous year's effort. The cards were sold in a specially designed box along with six team logo stickers.

		MT
Complete Set (44):		7.00
Common Player:		.05
1	Kevin Bass	.05
2	Jesse Barfield	.05
3	George Bell	.05
4	Wade Boggs	.75
5	Sid Bream	.05
6	George Brett	.60
7	Ivan Calderon	.05
8	Jose Canseco	.90
9	Jack Clark	.05
10	Roger Clemens	.90
11	Eric Davis	.10
12	Andre Dawson	.15
13	Sid Fernandez	.05
14	John Franco	.05
15	Dwight Gooden	.10
16	Pedro Guerrero	.05
17	Tony Gwynn	.75
18	Rickey Henderson	.50
19	Tom Henke	.05
20	Ted Higuera	.05
21	Pete Incaviglia	.05
22	Wally Joyner	.10
23	Jeff Leonard	.05
24	Joe Magrane	.05
25	Don Mattingly	.90
26	Mark McGwire	2.50
27	Jack Morris	.05
28	Dale Murphy	.15
29	Dave Parker	.08
30	Ken Phelps	.05
31	Kirby Puckett	.75
32	Tim Raines	.10
33	Jeff Reardon	.05
34	Dave Righetti	.05
35	Cal Ripken, Jr.	2.00
36	Bret Saberhagen	.05
37	Mike Schmidt	.75
38	Mike Scott	.05
39	Kevin Seitzer	.05
40	Darryl Strawberry	.15
41	Rick Sutcliffe	.05
42	Pat Tabler	.05
43	Fernando Valenzuela	.10
44	Mike Witt	.05

1987 Fleer Baseball's Best Box Bottom

These special cards were printed on the bottom of retail boxes of Fleer's "Baseball's Best" boxed sets. The box-bottom cards are in the same format as the boxed cards, with red, white and blue borders and a yellow title strip at top. Backs are also similar in design to the regular-issue cards, carrying player data and stats. Cards are numbered with an "M" prefix.

		MT
Complete Panel:		10.00
Complete Set (6):		8.00
Common Player:		.50
1	Steve Bedrosian	.50
2	Will Clark	6.00
3	Vince Coleman	.75
4	Bo Jackson	2.00
5	Cory Snyder	.50
---	K.C. Royals logo	.25

1987 Fleer Exciting Stars

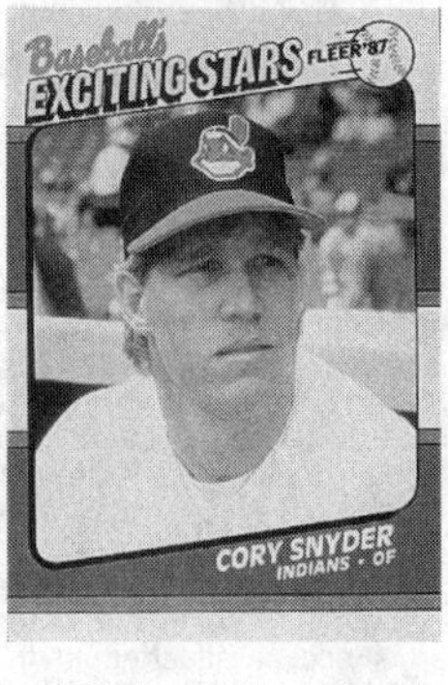

Another entry into the Fleer lineup of individual boxed sets, the "Baseball's Exciting Stars" set was produced for Cumberland Farms stores. The card fronts feature a red, white and blue border with the words "Exciting Stars" printed in yellow at the top. The backs are printed in red and blue and carry complete major and minor league statistics. Included with the boxed set of 44 cards were six team logo stickers.

		MT
Complete Set (44):		5.00
Common Player:		.05
1	Don Aase	.05
2	Rick Aguilera	.05
3	Jesse Barfield	.05
4	Wade Boggs	.60
5	Dennis "Oil Can" Boyd	.05
6	Sid Bream	.05
7	Jose Canseco	.80
8	Steve Carlton	.25
9	Gary Carter	.15
10	Will Clark	.50
11	Roger Clemens	1.00
12	Danny Cox	.05
13	Alvin Davis	.05
14	Eric Davis	.12
15	Rob Deer	.05
16	Brian Downing	.05
17	Gene Garber	.05
18	Steve Garvey	.15
19	Dwight Gooden	.10
20	Mark Gubicza	.05
21	Mel Hall	.05
22	Terry Harper	.05
23	Von Hayes	.05
24	Rickey Henderson	.45
25	Tom Henke	.05
26	Willie Hernandez	.05
27	Ted Higuera	.05
28	Rick Honeycutt	.05
29	Kent Hrbek	.08
30	Wally Joyner	.10
31	Charlie Kerfeld	.05
32	Fred Lynn	.05
33	Don Mattingly	.90
34	Tim Raines	.10
35	Dennis Rasmussen	.05
36	Johnny Ray	.05
37	Jim Rice	.10
38	Pete Rose	.75
39	Lee Smith	.08
40	Cory Snyder	.05
41	Darryl Strawberry	.12
42	Kent Tekulve	.05
43	Willie Wilson	.05
44	Bobby Witt	.05

1987 Fleer Game Winners

The 1987 Fleer "Baseball's Game Winners" boxed set was produced for distribution through Bi-Mart Discount Drug, Pay'n-Save, Mott's 5 & 10, M.E. Moses, and Winn's stores. Cards have a light blue border with the player's name and game winning RBI or games-won statistics in a yellow oval band at the top. Backs are similar to the regular-issue 1987 Fleer, with full professional stats. Included with the boxed set were six team logo stickers.

		MT
Complete Set (44):		5.00
Common Player:		.05
1	Harold Baines	.08
2	Don Baylor	.08
3	George Bell	.05
4	Tony Bernazard	.05
5	Wade Boggs	.65
6	George Brett	.60
7	Hubie Brooks	.05
8	Jose Canseco	.80
9	Gary Carter	.25
10	Roger Clemens	1.00
11	Eric Davis	.12
12	Glenn Davis	.05
13	Shawon Dunston	.05
14	Mark Eichhorn	.05
15	Gary Gaetti	.05
16	Steve Garvey	.15
17	Kirk Gibson	.05
18	Dwight Gooden	.10
19	Von Hayes	.05
20	Willie Hernandez	.05
21	Ted Higuera	.05
22	Wally Joyner	.10
23	Bob Knepper	.05
24	Mike Krukow	.05
25	Jeff Leonard	.05
26	Don Mattingly	.90
27	Kirk McCaskill	.05
28	Kevin McReynolds	.05
29	Jim Morrison	.05
30	Dale Murphy	.15
31	Pete O'Brien	.05
32	Bob Ojeda	.05
33	Larry Parrish	.05
34	Ken Phelps	.05
35	Dennis Rasmussen	.05
36	Ernest Riles	.05
37	Cal Ripken, Jr.	2.00
38	Ron Robinson	.05
39	Steve Sax	.05
40	Mike Schmidt	.75
41	John Tudor	.05
42	Fernando Valenzuela	.08
43	Mike Witt	.05
44	Curt Young	.05

1987 Fleer Hottest Stars

The "Baseball's Hottest Stars" set was produced by Fleer for the Revco Drug Store chain. Measuring the standard 2-1/2" x 3-1/2", the cards feature full-color photos surrounded by a red, white and blue border. Card backs are printed in red, white and black and contain the player's lifetime professional statistics. The set was sold in a special cardboard box with six team logo stickers.

		MT
Complete Set (44):		4.00
Common Player:		.05
1	Joaquin Andujar	.05
2	Harold Baines	.08
3	Kevin Bass	.05
4	Don Baylor	.08
5	Barry Bonds	1.50
6	George Brett	.75
7	Tom Brunansky	.05
8	Brett Butler	.08
9	Jose Canseco	.90
10	Roger Clemens	1.00
11	Ron Darling	.05
12	Eric Davis	.10
13	Andre Dawson	.15
14	Doug DeCinces	.05
15	Leon Durham	.05
16	Mark Eichhorn	.05
17	Scott Garrelts	.05
18	Dwight Gooden	.10
19	Dave Henderson	.05
20	Rickey Henderson	.35
21	Keith Hernandez	.05
22	Ted Higuera	.05
23	Bob Horner	.05
24	Pete Incaviglia	.05
25	Wally Joyner	.10
26	Mark Langston	.05
27	Don Mattingly	1.00
28	Dale Murphy	.15
29	Kirk McCaskill	.05
30	Willie McGee	.05
31	Dave Righetti	.05
32	Pete Rose	.75
33	Bruce Ruffin	.05
34	Steve Sax	.05
35	Mike Schmidt	.50
36	Larry Sheets	.05
37	Eric Show	.05
38	Dave Smith	.05
39	Cory Snyder	.05
40	Frank Tanana	.05
41	Alan Trammell	.10
42	Reggie Williams	.05
43	Mookie Wilson	.05
44	Todd Worrell	.05

1987 Fleer League Leaders

For a second year, Fleer produced a 44-card "League Leaders" set for Walgreens. The card fronts feature a border style which is identical to that used in 1986. However, a trapezoidal shaped full-color player photo is placed diagonally on the front. "1987 Fleer League Leaders" appears in the upper left corner of the front although nowhere on the card does it state in which pitching, hitting or fielding department was the player a league leader. Backs are printed in red and blue on white stock. The cards in the boxed set are the standard 2-1/2" x 3-1/2" size.

		MT
Complete Set (44):		3.00
Common Player:		.05
1	Jesse Barfield	.05
2	Mike Boddicker	.05
3	Wade Boggs	.65
4	Phil Bradley	.05
5	George Brett	.75
6	Hubie Brooks	.05
7	Chris Brown	.05
8	Jose Canseco	.80
9	Joe Carter	.10
10	Roger Clemens	.90
11	Vince Coleman	.05
12	Joe Cowley	.05
13	Kal Daniels	.05
14	Glenn Davis	.05
15	Jody Davis	.05
16	Darrell Evans	.08
17	Dwight Evans	.05
18	John Franco	.05
19	Julio Franco	.05
20	Dwight Gooden	.10
21	Goose Gossage	.05
22	Tom Herr	.05
23	Ted Higuera	.05
24	Bob Horner	.05
25	Pete Incaviglia	.05
26	Wally Joyner	.10
27	Dave Kingman	.05
28	Don Mattingly	1.00
29	Willie McGee	.05
30	Donnie Moore	.05
31	Keith Moreland	.05
32	Eddie Murray	.45
33	Mike Pagliarulo	.05
34	Larry Parrish	.05
35	Tony Pena	.05
36	Kirby Puckett	.80
37	Pete Rose	.75
38	Juan Samuel	.05
39	Ryne Sandberg	.65
40	Mike Schmidt	.75
41	Darryl Strawberry	.10
42	Greg Walker	.05
43	Bob Welch	.05
44	Todd Worrell	.05

1987 Fleer Limited Edition

For the third straight year, Fleer produced a Limited Edition set for the McCrory's store chain and its affiliates. The cards are the standard 2-1/2" x 3-1/2" and feature light blue borders at the top and bottom and a diagonal red and white border running along both sides. The set was issued in a specially prepared cardboard box, along with six team logo stickers.

		MT
Complete Set (44):		4.00
Common Player:		.05
1	Floyd Bannister	.05
2	Marty Barrett	.05
3	Steve Bedrosian	.05
4	George Bell	.05
5	George Brett	.75
6	Jose Canseco	.80
7	Joe Carter	.08
8	Will Clark	.40
9	Roger Clemens	1.00
10	Vince Coleman	.05
11	Glenn Davis	.05
12	Mike Davis	.05
13	Len Dykstra	.05
14	John Franco	.05
15	Julio Franco	.05
16	Steve Garvey	.15
17	Kirk Gibson	.05
18	Dwight Gooden	.10
19	Tony Gwynn	.75
20	Keith Hernandez	.05
21	Teddy Higuera	.05
22	Kent Hrbek	.08
23	Wally Joyner	.08
24	Mike Krukow	.05
25	Mike Marshall	.05
26	Don Mattingly	1.00
27	Oddibe McDowell	.05
28	Jack Morris	.05
29	Lloyd Moseby	.05
30	Dale Murphy	.15
31	Eddie Murray	.40
32	Tony Pena	.05
33	Jim Presley	.05
34	Jeff Reardon	.05
35	Jim Rice	.10
36	Pete Rose	.75
37	Mike Schmidt	.50
38	Mike Scott	.05
39	Lee Smith	.08
40	Lonnie Smith	.05
41	Gary Ward	.05
42	Dave Winfield	.40
43	Todd Worrell	.05
44	Robin Yount	.40

1987 Fleer Limited Edition Box Bottom

These special cards were printed on the bottom of retail boxes of Fleer's "Limited Edition" boxed sets. The box-bottom cards are in the same format as the boxed cards, with red, white and blue borders. Backs are also similar in design to the regular-issue cards, carrying player data and stats.

		MT
Complete Panel:		4.00
Complete Set (6):		2.50
Common Player:		.50
C1	Ron Darling	.50
C2	Bill Buckner	.75
C3	John Candelaria	.50
C4	Jack Clark	.75
C5	Bret Saberhagen	1.00
C6	Houston Astros logo	.50

1987 Fleer Mini

Continuing with an idea originated the previous year, the Fleer "Classic Miniatures" set consists of 120 cards that measure 1-13/16" x 2-9/16". The cards are identical in design to the regular-issue set, but use completely different photos. The set was issued in a specially prepared collectors box along with 18 team logo stickers. The mini set was available only through hobby dealers.

		MT
Complete Set (120):		4.00
Common Player:		.05
1	Don Aase	.05
2	Joaquin Andujar	.05
3	Harold Baines	.08
4	Jesse Barfield	.05
5	Kevin Bass	.05
6	Don Baylor	.08
7	George Bell	.05
8	Tony Bernazard	.05
9	Bert Blyleven	.05
10	Wade Boggs	.75
11	Phil Bradley	.05
12	Sid Bream	.05
13	George Brett	.60
14	Hubie Brooks	.05
15	Chris Brown	.05
16	Tom Candiotti	.05
17	Jose Canseco	.90
18	Gary Carter	.15
19	Joe Carter	.08
20	Roger Clemens	.85
21	Vince Coleman	.05
22	Cecil Cooper	.05
23	Ron Darling	.05
24	Alvin Davis	.05
25	Chili Davis	.08
26	Eric Davis	.15
27	Glenn Davis	.05
28	Mike Davis	.05
29	Doug DeCinces	.05
30	Rob Deer	.05
31	Jim Deshaies	.05
32	Bo Diaz	.05
33	Richard Dotson	.05
34	Brian Downing	.05
35	Shawon Dunston	.05
36	Mark Eichhorn	.05
37	Dwight Evans	.05
38	Tony Fernandez	.05
39	Julio Franco	.05
40	Gary Gaetti	.05
41	Andres Galarraga	.15
42	Scott Garrelts	.05
43	Steve Garvey	.15
44	Kirk Gibson	.05
45	Dwight Gooden	.10
46	Ken Griffey	.08
47	Mark Gubicza	.05
48	Ozzie Guillen	.05
49	Bill Gullickson	.05
50	Tony Gwynn	.75
51	Von Hayes	.05
52	Rickey Henderson	.50
53	Keith Hernandez	.05
54	Willie Hernandez	.05
55	Ted Higuera	.05
56	Charlie Hough	.05
57	Kent Hrbek	.08
58	Pete Incaviglia	.05
59	Wally Joyner	.08
60	Bob Knepper	.05
61	Mike Krukow	.05
62	Mark Langston	.05
63	Carney Lansford	.05
64	Jim Lindeman	.05
65	Bill Madlock	.05
66	Don Mattingly	1.00
67	Kirk McCaskill	.05
68	Lance McCullers	.05
69	Keith Moreland	.05
70	Jack Morris	.05
71	Jim Morrison	.05
72	Lloyd Moseby	.05
73	Jerry Mumphrey	.05
74	Dale Murphy	.15
75	Eddie Murray	.40
76	Pete O'Brien	.05
77	Bob Ojeda	.05
78	Jesse Orosco	.05
79	Dan Pasqua	.05
80	Dave Parker	.05
81	Larry Parrish	.05
82	Jim Presley	.05
83	Kirby Puckett	.90
84	Dan Quisenberry	.05
85	Tim Raines	.10
86	Dennis Rasmussen	.05
87	Johnny Ray	.05
88	Jeff Reardon	.05
89	Jim Rice	.10
90	Dave Righetti	.05
91	Earnest Riles	.05
92	Cal Ripken, Jr.	2.00
93	Ron Robinson	.05
94	Juan Samuel	.05
95	Ryne Sandberg	.75
96	Steve Sax	.05
97	Mike Schmidt	.50
98	Ken Schrom	.05
99	Mike Scott	.05
100	Ruben Sierra	.05
101	Lee Smith	.08
102	Ozzie Smith	.30
103	Cory Snyder	.05
104	Kent Tekulve	.05
105	Andres Thomas	.05
106	Rob Thompson	.05
107	Alan Trammell	.10
108	John Tudor	.05
109	Fernando Valenzuela	.10
110	Greg Walker	.05
111	Mitch Webster	.05
112	Lou Whitaker	.08
113	Frank White	.05
114	Reggie Williams	.05
115	Glenn Wilson	.05
116	Willie Wilson	.05
117	Dave Winfield	.30
118	Mike Witt	.05
119	Todd Worrell	.05
120	Floyd Youmans	.05

1987 Fleer Record Setters

Produced by Fleer for the Eckerd Drug chain, the Record Setters set contains 44 cards in standard 2-1/2" x 3-1/2" size. Although the set is titled "Record Setters," the actual records the players have set is not specified anywhere on the cards. Given that several players included in the set were young prospects, a better title for those cards might have been "Possible Record Setters". The set came housed in a special cardboard box with six team logo stickers.

		MT
Complete Set (44):		3.00
Common Player:		.05
1	George Brett	.75
2	Chris Brown	.05
3	Jose Canseco	.90
4	Roger Clemens	1.00
5	Alvin Davis	.05
6	Shawon Dunston	.05
7	Tony Fernandez	.05
8	Carlton Fisk	.15
9	Gary Gaetti	.05
10	Gene Garber	.05
11	Rich Gedman	.05
12	Dwight Gooden	.10
13	Ozzie Guillen	.05
14	Bill Gullickson	.05
15	Billy Hatcher	.05
16	Orel Hershiser	.10
17	Wally Joyner	.10
18	Ray Knight	.05
19	Craig Lefferts	.05
20	Don Mattingly	1.00
21	Kevin Mitchell	.05
22	Lloyd Moseby	.05
23	Dale Murphy	.15
24	Eddie Murray	.35
25	Phil Niekro	.10
26	Ben Oglivie	.05
27	Jesse Orosco	.05
28	Joe Orsulak	.05
29	Larry Parrish	.05
30	Tim Raines	.08
31	Shane Rawley	.05
32	Dave Righetti	.05
33	Pete Rose	.75
34	Steve Sax	.05
35	Mike Schmidt	.50
36	Mike Scott	.05
37	Don Sutton	.10
38	Alan Trammell	.10
39	John Tudor	.05
40	Gary Ward	.05
41	Lou Whitaker	.05
42	Willie Wilson	.05
43	Todd Worrell	.05
44	Floyd Youmans	.05

1987 Fleer Star Stickers

The 1987 Fleer Star Stickers set contains 132 cards which become stickers if the back is bent and peeled off. As in the previous year, the card backs are identical, save the numbering system, to the regular-issue cards. The cards measure 2-1/2" x 3-1/2" and were sold in wax packs with team logo stickers. The fronts have a green border with a red and white banner wrapped across the upper left corner and the sides. The backs are printed in green and yellow.

		MT
Complete Set (132):		15.00
Common Player:		.05
1	Don Aase	.05
2	Harold Baines	.08
3	Floyd Bannister	.05
4	Jesse Barfield	.05
5	Marty Barrett	.05
6	Kevin Bass	.05
7	Don Baylor	.08
8	Steve Bedrosian	.05
9	George Bell	.05
10	Bert Blyleven	.05
11	Mike Boddicker	.05
12	Wade Boggs	.75
13	Phil Bradley	.05
14	Sid Bream	.05
15	George Brett	.75
16	Hubie Brooks	.05
17	Tom Brunansky	.05
18	Tom Candiotti	.05
19	Jose Canseco	.90
20	Gary Carter	.20
21	Joe Carter	.08
22	Will Clark	.50
23	Mark Clear	.05
24	Roger Clemens	.90
25	Vince Coleman	.05
26	Jose Cruz	.05
27	Ron Darling	.05
28	Alvin Davis	.05
29	Chili Davis	.08
30	Eric Davis	.12
31	Glenn Davis	.05
32	Mike Davis	.05
33	Andre Dawson	.20
34	Doug DeCinces	.05
35	Brian Downing	.05
36	Shawon Dunston	.05
37	Mark Eichhorn	.05
38	Dwight Evans	.05
39	Tony Fernandez	.05
40	Bob Forsch	.05
41	John Franco	.05
42	Julio Franco	.05
43	Gary Gaetti	.05
44	Gene Garber	.05
45	Scott Garrelts	.05
46	Steve Garvey	.20
47	Kirk Gibson	.05
48	Dwight Gooden	.15
49	Ken Griffey	.08
50	Ozzie Guillen	.05
51	Bill Gullickson	.05
52	Tony Gwynn	.75

53	Mel Hall	.05
54	Greg Harris	.05
55	Von Hayes	.05
56	Rickey Henderson	.50
57	Tom Henke	.05
58	Keith Hernandez	.05
59	Willie Hernandez	.05
60	Ted Higuera	.05
61	Bob Horner	.05
62	Charlie Hough	.05
63	Jay Howell	.05
64	Kent Hrbek	.05
65	Bruce Hurst	.05
66	Pete Incaviglia	.05
67	Bob James	.05
68	Wally Joyner	.10
69	Mike Krukow	.05
70	Mark Langston	.05
71	Carney Lansford	.05
72	Fred Lynn	.05
73	Bill Madlock	.05
74	Don Mattingly	1.00
75	Kirk McCaskill	.05
76	Lance McCullers	.05
77	Oddibe McDowell	.05
78	Paul Molitor	.50
79	Keith Moreland	.05
80	Jack Morris	.05
81	Jim Morrison	.05
82	Jerry Mumphrey	.05
83	Dale Murphy	.20
84	Eddie Murray	.50
85	Ben Oglivie	.05
86	Bob Ojeda	.05
87	Jesse Orosco	.05
88	Dave Parker	.05
89	Larry Parrish	.05
90	Tony Pena	.05
91	Jim Presley	.05
92	Kirby Puckett	.75
93	Dan Quisenberry	.05
94	Tim Raines	.10
95	Dennis Rasmussen	.05
96	Shane Rawley	.05
97	Johnny Ray	.05
98	Jeff Reardon	.05
99	Jim Rice	.10
100	Dave Righetti	.05
101	Cal Ripken, Jr.	2.50
102	Pete Rose	.75
103	Nolan Ryan	2.00
104	Juan Samuel	.05
105	Ryne Sandberg	.75
106	Steve Sax	.05
107	Mike Schmidt	.80
108	Mike Scott	.05
109	Dave Smith	.05
110	Lee Smith	.05
111	Lonnie Smith	.05
112	Ozzie Smith	.50
113	Cory Snyder	.05
114	Darryl Strawberry	.15
115	Don Sutton	.20
116	Kent Tekulve	.05
117	Gorman Thomas	.05
118	Alan Trammell	.10
119	John Tudor	.05
120	Fernando Valenzuela	.08
121	Bob Welch	.05
122	Lou Whitaker	.05
123	Frank White	.05
124	Reggie Williams	.05
125	Willie Wilson	.05
126	Dave Winfield	.40
127	Mike Witt	.05
128	Todd Worrell	.05
129	Curt Young	.05
130	Robin Yount	.50
131	Checklist (Jose Canseco, Don Mattingly)	.50
132	Checklist (Bo Jackson, Eric Davis)	.20

1987 Fleer Star Stickers Box Panels

Fleer issued on the bottoms of its Fleer Star Stickers wax pack boxes six player cards plus two team logo/checklist cards. The cards, which measure 2-1/2" x 3-1/2", are numbered S-1 through S-8, and are identical in design to the Star Stickers.

		MT
Complete Panel Set (2):		4.00
Complete Singles Set (8):		2.50
Common Single Player:		.10
Panel		3.50
2	Wade Boggs	1.00
3	Bert Blyleven	.10
6	Phillies Logo	.05
8	Don Mattingly	1.00
Panel		1.00
1	Tigers Logo	.05
4	Jose Cruz	.10
5	Glenn Davis	.10
7	Bob Horner	.10

1988 Fleer

A clean, uncluttered look was the trademark of the 660-card 1988 Fleer set. The cards, which are the standard 2-1/2" x 3-1/2" format, feature blue and red diagonal lines set inside a white border. The player name and position are located on a slant in the upper left corner of the card. The player's team logo appears in the upper right corner. Below the player photo, a blue and red band with the word "Fleer" appears. Card backs include the card number, player personal information and career statistics, plus a new feature called "At Their Best." This feature graphically shows a player's pitching or hitting statistics for home and road games and how he fared during day games as opposed to night contests. The set includes 19 special cards (#622-640) and 12 "Major League Prospects" cards.

		MT
Complete Set (660):		15.00
Common Player:		.06
Wax Box:		25.00
1	Keith Atherton	.06
2	Don Baylor	.10
3	Juan Berenguer	.06
4	Bert Blyleven	.06
5	Tom Brunansky	.06
6	Randy Bush	.06
7	Steve Carlton	.25
8	*Mark Davidson*	.06
9	George Frazier	.06
10	Gary Gaetti	.08
11	Greg Gagne	.06
12	Dan Gladden	.06
13	Kent Hrbek	.15
14	*Gene Larkin*	.06
15	Tim Laudner	.06
16	Steve Lombardozzi	.06
17	Al Newman	.06
18	Joe Niekro	.06
19	Kirby Puckett	.75
20	Jeff Reardon	.06
21a	Dan Schatzader (incorrect spelling)	.20
21b	Dan Schatzeder (correct spelling)	.06
22	Roy Smalley	.06
23	Mike Smithson	.06
24	*Les Straker*	.06
25	Frank Viola	.06
26	Jack Clark	.06
27	Vince Coleman	.06
28	Danny Cox	.06
29	Bill Dawley	.06
30	Ken Dayley	.06
31	Doug DeCinces	.06
32	Curt Ford	.06
33	Bob Forsch	.06
34	David Green	.06
35	Tom Herr	.06
36	Ricky Horton	.06
37	*Lance Johnson*	.50
38	Steve Lake	.06
39	Jim Lindeman	.06
40	*Joe Magrane*	.10
41	Greg Mathews	.06
42	Willie McGee	.08
43	John Morris	.06
44	Jose Oquendo	.06
45	Tony Pena	.06
46	Terry Pendleton	.06
47	Ozzie Smith	.65
48	John Tudor	.06
49	Lee Tunnell	.06
50	Todd Worrell	.06
51	Doyle Alexander	.06
52	Dave Bergman	.06
53	Tom Brookens	.06
54	Darrell Evans	.08
55	Kirk Gibson	.06
56	Mike Heath	.06
57	*Mike Henneman*	.20
58	Willie Hernandez	.06
59	Larry Herndon	.06
60	Eric King	.06
61	Chet Lemon	.06
62	*Scott Lusader*	.06
63	Bill Madlock	.06
64	Jack Morris	.06
65	Jim Morrison	.06
66	*Matt Nokes*	.15
67	Dan Petry	.06
68a	*Jeff Robinson* (Born 12-13-60 on back)	.25
68b	*Jeff Robinson* (Born 12/14/61 on back)	.10
69	Pat Sheridan	.06
70	Nate Snell	.06
71	Frank Tanana	.06
72	Walt Terrell	.06
73	Mark Thurmond	.06
74	Alan Trammell	.10
75	Lou Whitaker	.06
76	Mike Aldrete	.06
77	Bob Brenly	.06
78	Will Clark	.50
79	Chili Davis	.10
80	Kelly Downs	.06
81	Dave Dravecky	.06
82	Scott Garrelts	.06
83	Atlee Hammaker	.06
84	Dave Henderson	.06
85	Mike Krukow	.06
86	Mike LaCoss	.06
87	Craig Lefferts	.06
88	Jeff Leonard	.06
89	Candy Maldonado	.06
90	Ed Milner	.06
91	Bob Melvin	.06
92	Kevin Mitchell	.06
93	*Jon Perlman*	.06
94	Rick Reuschel	.06
95	Don Robinson	.06
96	Chris Speier	.06
97	Harry Spilman	.06
98	Robbie Thompson	.06
99	Jose Uribe	.06
100	*Mark Wasinger*	.06
101	Matt Williams	1.50
102	Jesse Barfield	.06
103	George Bell	.06
104	Juan Beniquez	.06
105	John Cerutti	.06
106	Jim Clancy	.06
107	*Rob Ducey*	.06
108	Mark Eichhorn	.06
109	Tony Fernandez	.06
110	Cecil Fielder	.15
111	Kelly Gruber	.06
112	Tom Henke	.06
113	Garth Iorq (Iorg)	.06
114	Jimmy Key	.08
115	Rick Leach	.06
116	Manny Lee	.06
117	*Nelson Liriano*	.06
118	Fred McGriff	.50
119	Lloyd Moseby	.06
120	Rance Mulliniks	.06
121	Jeff Musselman	.06
122	*Jose Nunez*	.06
123	Dave Stieb	.06
124	Willie Upshaw	.06
125	Duane Ward	.06
126	Ernie Whitt	.06
127	Rick Aguilera	.06
128	Wally Backman	.06
129	*Mark Carreon*	.12
130	Gary Carter	.10
131	David Cone	.50
132	Ron Darling	.06
133	Len Dykstra	.08
134	Sid Fernandez	.06
135	Dwight Gooden	.10
136	Keith Hernandez	.06
137	*Gregg Jefferies*	.75
138	Howard Johnson	.06
139	Terry Leach	.06
140	*Barry Lyons*	.06
141	Dave Magadan	.06
142	Roger McDowell	.06
143	Kevin McReynolds	.06
144	*Keith Miller*	.06
145	*John Mitchell*	.06
146	Randy Myers	.06
147	Bob Ojeda	.06
148	Jesse Orosco	.06
149	Rafael Santana	.06
150	Doug Sisk	.06
151	Darryl Strawberry	.15
152	Tim Teufel	.06
153	Gene Walter	.06
154	Mookie Wilson	.06
155	*Jay Aldrich*	.06
156	Chris Bosio	.06
157	Glenn Braggs	.06
158	Greg Brock	.06
159	Juan Castillo	.06
160	Mark Clear	.06
161	Cecil Cooper	.06
162	*Chuck Crim*	.06
163	Rob Deer	.06
164	Mike Felder	.06
165	Jim Gantner	.06
166	Ted Higuera	.06
167	Steve Kiefer	.06
168	Rick Manning	.06
169	Paul Molitor	.65
170	Juan Nieves	.06
171	Dan Plesac	.06
172	Earnest Riles	.06
173	Bill Schroeder	.06
174	*Steve Stanicek*	.06
175	B.J. Surhoff	.08
176	Dale Sveum	.06
177	Bill Wegman	.06
178	Robin Yount	.75
179	Hubie Brooks	.06
180	Tim Burke	.06
181	Casey Candaele	.06
182	Mike Fitzgerald	.06
183	Tom Foley	.06
184	Andres Galarraga	.25
185	Neal Heaton	.06
186	Wallace Johnson	.06
187	Vance Law	.06
188	Dennis Martinez	.08
189	Bob McClure	.06
190	Andy McGaffigan	.06
191	Reid Nichols	.06
192	Pascual Perez	.06
193	Tim Raines	.10
194	Jeff Reed	.06
195	Bob Sebra	.06
196	Bryn Smith	.06
197	Randy St. Claire	.06
198	Tim Wallach	.06
199	Mitch Webster	.06
200	Herm Winningham	.06
201	Floyd Youmans	.06
202	*Brad Arnsberg*	.06
203	Rick Cerone	.06
204	Pat Clements	.06
205	Henry Cotto	.06
206	Mike Easler	.06
207	Ron Guidry	.10
208	Bill Gullickson	.06
209	Rickey Henderson	.40
210	Charles Hudson	.06
211	Tommy John	.10
212	*Roberto Kelly*	.40
213	Ron Kittle	.06
214	Don Mattingly	.75
215	Bobby Meacham	.06
216	Mike Pagliarulo	.06
217	Dan Pasqua	.06
218	Willie Randolph	.06
219	Rick Rhoden	.06
220	Dave Righetti	.06
221	Jerry Royster	.06
222	Tim Stoddard	.06
223	Wayne Tolleson	.06
224	Gary Ward	.06
225	Claudell Washington	.06
226	Dave Winfield	.50
227	Buddy Bell	.06
228	Tom Browning	.06
229	Dave Concepcion	.06
230	Kal Daniels	.06
231	Eric Davis	.10
232	Bo Diaz	.06
233	Nick Esasky	.06
234	John Franco	.06
235	Guy Hoffman	.06
236	Tom Hume	.06
237	Tracy Jones	.06
238	*Bill Landrum*	.06
239	Barry Larkin	.20
240	Terry McGriff	.06
241	Rob Murphy	.06
242	Ron Oester	.06
243	Dave Parker	.10
244	Pat Perry	.06
245	Ted Power	.06
246	Dennis Rasmussen	.06
247	Ron Robinson	.06
248	Kurt Stillwell	.06
249	*Jeff Treadway*	.06
250	Frank Williams	.06
251	Steve Balboni	.06
252	Bud Black	.06
253	Thad Bosley	.06
254	George Brett	.75
255	*John Davis*	.06
256	Steve Farr	.06
257	Gene Garber	.06
258	Jerry Gleaton	.06
259	Mark Gubicza	.06
260	Bo Jackson	.25
261	Danny Jackson	.06
262	*Ross Jones*	.06
263	Charlie Leibrandt	.06
264	*Bill Pecota*	.06
265	*Melido Perez*	.15
266	Jamie Quirk	.06
267	Dan Quisenberry	.06
268	Bret Saberhagen	.10
269	Angel Salazar	.06
270	Kevin Seitzer	.06
271	Danny Tartabull	.06
272	*Gary Thurman*	.06
273	Frank White	.06
274	Willie Wilson	.06
275	Tony Bernazard	.06
276	Jose Canseco	.65
277	Mike Davis	.06
278	Storm Davis	.06
279	Dennis Eckersley	.10
280	Alfredo Griffin	.06
281	Rick Honeycutt	.06
282	Jay Howell	.06
283	Reggie Jackson	.30
284	Dennis Lamp	.06
285	Carney Lansford	.06
286	Mark McGwire	4.00
287	Dwayne Murphy	.06
288	Gene Nelson	.06
289	Steve Ontiveros	.06
290	Tony Phillips	.12
291	Eric Plunk	.06
292	*Luis Polonia*	.15
293	*Rick Rodriguez*	.06
294	Terry Steinbach	.06
295	Dave Stewart	.10
296	Curt Young	.06
297	Luis Aguayo	.06
298	Steve Bedrosian	.06
299	Jeff Calhoun	.06
300	Don Carman	.06
301	*Todd Frohwirth*	.06
302	Greg Gross	.06
303	Kevin Gross	.06
304	Von Hayes	.06
305	*Keith Hughes*	.06
306	*Mike Jackson*	.06
307	Chris James	.06
308	Steve Jeltz	.06
309	Mike Maddux	.06
310	Lance Parrish	.08
311	Shane Rawley	.06
312	*Wally Ritchie*	.06
313	Bruce Ruffin	.06
314	Juan Samuel	.06
315	Mike Schmidt	.75
316	Rick Schu	.06
317	Jeff Stone	.06
318	Kent Tekulve	.06
319	Milt Thompson	.06
320	Glenn Wilson	.06
321	Rafael Belliard	.06
322	Barry Bonds	1.00
323	Bobby Bonilla	.15
324	Sid Bream	.06
325	John Cangelosi	.06
326	Mike Diaz	.06
327	Doug Drabek	.06
328	*Mike Dunne*	.06
329	Brian Fisher	.06
330	*Brett Gideon*	.06
331	Terry Harper	.06
332	Bob Kipper	.06
333	Mike LaValliere	.06
334	*Jose Lind*	.15
335	Junior Ortiz	.06
336	*Vicente Palacios*	.06
337	*Bob Patterson*	.12
338	*Al Pedrique*	.06
339	R.J. Reynolds	.06
340	*John Smiley*	.20
341	Andy Van Slyke	.06
342	Bob Walk	.06
343	Marty Barrett	.06
344	*Todd Benzinger*	.06
345	Wade Boggs	.65
346	*Tom Bolton*	.06
347	Oil Can Boyd	.06
348	Ellis Burks	.50
349	Roger Clemens	1.00
350	Steve Crawford	.06
351	Dwight Evans	.06
352	*Wes Gardner*	.06
353	Rich Gedman	.06
354	Mike Greenwell	.15
355	*Sam Horn*	.06
356	Bruce Hurst	.06
357	*John Marzano*	.06
358	Al Nipper	.06
359	Spike Owen	.06
360	*Jody Reed*	.30
361	Jim Rice	.08
362	Ed Romero	.06
363	Kevin Romine	.06
364	Joe Sambito	.06
365	Calvin Schiraldi	.06
366	Jeff Sellers	.06
367	Bob Stanley	.06
368	Scott Bankhead	.06
369	Phil Bradley	.06
370	Scott Bradley	.06
371	Mickey Brantley	.06
372	*Mike Campbell*	.06
373	Alvin Davis	.06
374	Lee Guetterman	.06
375	*Dave Hengel*	.06
376	Mike Kingery	.06
377	Mark Langston	.06
378	*Edgar Martinez*	1.50
379	Mike Moore	.06
380	Mike Morgan	.06
381	John Moses	.06

382 *Donnell Nixon* .06
383 Edwin Nunez .06
384 Ken Phelps .06
385 Jim Presley .06
386 Rey Quinones .06
387 Jerry Reed .06
388 Harold Reynolds .06
389 Dave Valle .06
390 *Bill Wilkinson* .06
391 Harold Baines .08
392 Floyd Bannister .06
393 Daryl Boston .06
394 Ivan Calderon .06
395 Jose DeLeon .06
396 Richard Dotson .06
397 Carlton Fisk .20
398 Ozzie Guillen .06
399 Ron Hassey .06
400 Donnie Hill .06
401 Bob James .06
402 Dave LaPoint .06
403 *Bill Lindsey* .06
404 *Bill Long* .06
405 Steve Lyons .06
406 *Fred Manrique* .06
407 *Jack McDowell* .75
408 Gary Redus .06
409 Ray Searage .06
410 Bobby Thigpen .06
411 Greg Walker .06
412 *Kenny Williams* .06
413 Jim Winn .06
414 Jody Davis .06
415 Andre Dawson .20
416 Brian Dayett .06
417 Bob Dernier .06
418 Frank DiPino .06
419 Shawon Dunston .06
420 Leon Durham .06
421 *Les Lancaster* .10
422 Ed Lynch .06
423 Greg Maddux 2.00
424 Dave Martinez .06
425a Keith Moreland (bunting, photo actually Jody Davis) 3.00
425b Keith Moreland (standing upright, correct photo) .06
426 Jamie Moyer .06
427 Jerry Mumphrey .06
428 *Paul Noce* .06
429 Rafael Palmeiro .75
430 Wade Rowdon .06
431 Ryne Sandberg .75
432 Scott Sanderson .06
433 Lee Smith .10
434 Jim Sundberg .06
435 Rick Sutcliffe .06
436 Manny Trillo .06
437 Juan Agosto .06
438 Larry Andersen .06
439 Alan Ashby .06
440 Kevin Bass .06
441 *Ken Caminiti* 2.50
442 *Rocky Childress* .06
443 Jose Cruz .06
444 Danny Darwin .06
445 Glenn Davis .06
446 Jim Deshaies .06
447 Bill Doran .06
448 Ty Gainey .06
449 Billy Hatcher .06
450 Jeff Heathcock .06
451 Bob Knepper .06
452 *Rob Mallicoat* .06
453 *Dave Meads* .06
454 Craig Reynolds .06
455 Nolan Ryan 1.50
456 Mike Scott .06
457 Dave Smith .06
458 Denny Walling .06
459 *Robbie Wine* .06
460 *Gerald Young* .06
461 Bob Brower .06
462a Jerry Browne (white player, photo actually Bob Brower) 2.50
462b Jerry Browne (black player, correct photo) .06
463 Steve Buechele .06
464 Edwin Correa .06
465 *Cecil Espy* .06
466 Scott Fletcher .06
467 Jose Guzman .06
468 Greg Harris .06
469 Charlie Hough .06
470 Pete Incaviglia .06
471 *Paul Kilgus* .06
472 Mike Loynd .06
473 Oddibe McDowell .06
474 Dale Mohorcic .06
475 Pete O'Brien .06
476 Larry Parrish .06
477 Geno Petralli .06
478 Jeff Russell .06
479 Ruben Sierra .06
480 Mike Stanley .06
481 Curtis Wilkerson .06
482 Mitch Williams .06
483 Bobby Witt .06
484 Tony Armas .06
485 Bob Boone .06
486 Bill Buckner .06
487 *DeWayne Buice* .06
488 Brian Downing .06
489 Chuck Finley .06
490 Willie Fraser .06
491 Jack Howell .06
492 Ruppert Jones .06
493 Wally Joyner .10
494 Jack Lazorko .06
495 Gary Lucas .06
496 Kirk McCaskill .06
497 Mark McLemore .06
498 Darrell Miller .06
499 Greg Minton .06
500 Donnie Moore .06
501 Gus Polidor .06
502 Johnny Ray .06
503 Mark Ryal .06
504 Dick Schofield .06
505 Don Sutton .20
506 Devon White .10
507 Mike Witt .06
508 Dave Anderson .06
509 Tim Belcher .06
510 Ralph Bryant .06
511 *Tim Crews* .15
512 *Mike Devereaux* .10
513 Mariano Duncan .06
514 Pedro Guerrero .06
515 Jeff Hamilton .06
516 Mickey Hatcher .06
517 Brad Havens .06
518 Orel Hershiser .10
519 *Shawn Hillegas* .06
520 Ken Howell .06
521 Tim Leary .06
522 Mike Marshall .06
523 Steve Sax .06
524 Mike Scioscia .06
525 Mike Sharperson .06
526 John Shelby .06
527 Franklin Stubbs .06
528 Fernando Valenzuela .08
529 Bob Welch .06
530 Matt Young .06
531 Jim Acker .06
532 Paul Assenmacher .06
533 *Jeff Blauser* .40
534 *Joe Boever* .06
535 Martin Clary .06
536 *Kevin Coffman* .06
537 Jeff Dedmon .06
538 *Ron Gant* 2.50
539 *Tom Glavine* 3.00
540 Ken Griffey .08
541 Al Hall .06
542 Glenn Hubbard .06
543 Dion James .06
544 Dale Murphy .20
545 Ken Oberkfell .06
546 David Palmer .06
547 Gerald Perry .06
548 Charlie Puleo .06
549 Ted Simmons .06
550 Zane Smith .06
551 Andres Thomas .06
552 Ozzie Virgil .06
553 Don Aase .06
554 *Jeff Ballard* .06
555 Eric Bell .06
556 Mike Boddicker .06
557 Ken Dixon .06
558 Jim Dwyer .06
559 Ken Gerhart .06
560 *Rene Gonzales* .06
561 Mike Griffin .06
562 John Hayban (Habyan) .06
563 Terry Kennedy .06
564 Ray Knight .06
565 Lee Lacy .06
566 Fred Lynn .08
567 Eddie Murray .55
568 Tom Niedenfuer .06
569 *Bill Ripken* .06
570 Cal Ripken, Jr. 1.50
571 Dave Schmidt .06
572 Larry Sheets .06
573 *Pete Stanicek* .06
574 *Mark Williamson* .06
575 Mike Young .06
576 Shawn Abner .06
577 Greg Booker .06
578 Chris Brown .06
579 *Keith Comstock* .06
580 *Joey Cora* .06
581 Mark Davis .06
582 Tim Flannery .06
583 Goose Gossage .08
584 Mark Grant .06
585 Tony Gwynn .75
586 Andy Hawkins .06
587 Stan Jefferson .06
588 Jimmy Jones .06
589 John Kruk .06
590 *Shane Mack* .25
591 Carmelo Martinez .06
592 Lance McCullers .06
593 *Eric Nolte* .06
594 Randy Ready .06
595 Luis Salazar .06
596 Benito Santiago .08
597 Eric Show .06
598 Garry Templeton .06
599 Ed Whitson .06
600 Scott Bailes .06
601 Chris Bando .06
602 *Jay Bell* .75
603 Brett Butler .08
604 Tom Candiotti .06
605 Joe Carter .10
606 Carmen Castillo .06
607 *Brian Dorsett* .06
608 *John Farrell* .06
609 Julio Franco .06
610 Mel Hall .06
611 *Tommy Hinzo* .06
612 Brook Jacoby .06
613 *Doug Jones* .30
614 Ken Schrom .06
615 Cory Snyder .06
616 Sammy Stewart .06
617 Greg Swindell .06
618 Pat Tabler .06
619 Ed Vande Berg .06
620 *Eddie Williams* .06
621 Rich Yett .06
622 Slugging Sophomores (Wally Joyner, Cory Snyder) .25
623 Dominican Dynamite (George Bell, Pedro Guerrero) .06
624 Oakland's Power Team (Jose Canseco, Mark McGwire) 2.00
625 Classic Relief (Dan Plesac, Dave Righetti) .06
626 All Star Righties (Jack Morris, Bret Saberhagen, Mike Witt) .06
627 Game Closers (Steve Bedrosian, John Franco) .06
628 Masters of the Double Play (Ryne Sandberg, Ozzie Smith) .35
629 Rookie Record Setter (Mark McGwire) 2.00
630 Changing the Guard in Boston (Todd Benzinger, Ellis Burks, Mike Greenwell) .25
631 N.L. Batting Champs (Tony Gwynn, Tim Raines) .20
632 Pitching Magic (Orel Hershiser, Mike Scott) .06
633 Big Bats At First (Mark McGwire, Pat Tabler) 1.00
634 Hitting King and the Thief (Tony Gwynn, Vince Coleman) .12
635 A.L. Slugging Shortstops (Tony Fernandez, Cal Ripken, Jr., Alan Trammell) .30
636 Tried and True Sluggers (Gary Carter, Mike Schmidt) .25
637 Crunch Time (Eric Davis) .10
638 A.L. All Stars (Matt Nokes, Kirby Puckett) .25
639 N.L. All Stars (Keith Hernandez, Dale Murphy) .10
640 The "O's" Brothers (Bill Ripken, Cal Ripken, Jr.) .50
641 Major League Prospects *(Mark Grace)*, *(Darrin Jackson)* 3.00
642 Major League Prospects *(Damon Berryhill)*, *(Jeff Montgomery)* .20
643 Major League Prospects *(Felix Fermin)*, *(Jessie Reid)* .10
644 Major League Prospects *(Greg Myers)*, *(Greg Tabor)* .10
645 Major League Prospects *(Jim Eppard)*, Joey Meyer) .06
646 Major League Prospects *(Adam Peterson)*, *(Randy Velarde)* .15
647 Major League Prospects *(Chris Gwynn)*, *(Peter Smith)* .15
648 Major League Prospects *(Greg Jelks)*, *(Tom Newell)* .06
649 Major League Prospects *(Mario Diaz)*, *(Clay Parker)* .06
650 Major League Prospects *(Jack Savage)*, *(Todd Simmons)* .06
651 Major League Prospects *(John Burkett)*, *(Kirt Manwaring)* .25
652 Major League Prospects *(Dave Otto)*, *(Walt Weiss)* .40
653 Major League Prospects *(Randell Byers (Randall))*, *(Jeff King)* .75
654a Checklist 1-101 (21 is Schatzader) .08
654b Checklist 1-101 (21 is Schatzeder) .06
655 Checklist 102-201 .06
656 Checklist 202-296 .06
657 Checklist 297-390 .06
658 Checklist 391-483 .06
659 Checklist 484-575 .06
660 Checklist 576-660 .06

1988 Fleer All Stars

For the third consecutive year, Fleer randomly inserted All Star Team cards in its wax and cello packs. Twelve cards make up the set, with players chosen for the set being Fleer's idea of a major league All-Star team.

		MT
Complete Set (12):		6.00
Common Player:		.25
1	Matt Nokes	.25
2	Tom Henke	.25
3	Ted Higuera	.25
4	Roger Clemens	3.00
5	George Bell	.25
6	Andre Dawson	.45
7	Eric Davis	.35
8	Wade Boggs	1.00
9	Alan Trammell	.35
10	Juan Samuel	.25
11	Jack Clark	.25
12	Paul Molitor	2.00

1988 Fleer Headliners

This six-card set was inserted in Fleer three-packs, sold by retail outlets and hobby dealers nationwide. The card fronts feature crisp full-color player cut-outs printed on a grey and white facsimile sports page. "Fleer Headliners 1988" is printed in black and red on a white banner across the top of the card, both front and back. A similar white banner across the card bottom bears the black and white National or American League logo and a red player/team name. Card backs are black on grey with red accents and include the card number and a narrative career summary.

		MT
Complete Set (6):		6.00
Common Player:		.50
1	Don Mattingly	2.00
2	Mark McGwire	4.00
3	Jack Morris	.50
4	Darryl Strawberry	.50
5	Dwight Gooden	.75
6	Tim Raines	.50

1988 Fleer '87 World Series

Highlights of the 1987 Series are captured in this full-color insert set found only in Fleer's regular 660-card factory sets. This second World Series edition by Fleer features cards framed in red, with a blue and white starred bunting draped over the upper edges of the photo and a brief photo caption printed on a yellow band across the lower border. Numbered card backs are red, white and blue and include a description of the action pictured on the front, with stats for the Series.

		MT
Complete Set (12):		2.50
Common Player:		.20
1	"Grand" Hero In Game 1 (Dan Gladden)	.20
2	The Cardinals "Bush" Whacked (Randy Bush, Tony Pena)	.20
3	Masterful Performance Turns Momentum (John Tudor)	.20
4	Ozzie Smith	.75
5	Throw Smoke! (Tony Pena, Todd Worrell)	.20
6	Cardinal Attack - Disruptive Speed (Vince Coleman)	.20
7	Herr's Wallop (Dan Driessen, Tom Herr)	.20
8	Kirby Puckett	1.00
9	Kent Hrbek	.30
10	Rich Hacker (coach), Tom Herr, Lee Weyer (umpire)	.20
11	Game 7's Play At The Plate (Don Baylor, Dave Phillips) (umpire))	.20
12	Frank Viola	.20

1988 Fleer Box Panels

Fleer's third annual box-bottom issue once again included 16 full-color trading cards printed on the bottoms of four different wax and cello pack retail display boxes. Each box contains three player cards and one team logo card. Player cards follow the same design as the basic 1988 Fleer issue. Standard size, the cards are numbered C-1 through C-16.

	MT
Complete Panel Set (4):	8.00
Complete Singles Set (16):	3.00
Common Panel:	2.00
Common Single Player:	.15
Panel	2.00
1 Cardinals Logo	.05
11 Mike Schmidt	.75
14 Dave Stewart	.20
15 Tim Wallach	.15
Panel	2.75
2 Dwight Evans	.15
8 Shane Rawley	.15
10 Ryne Sandberg	.75
13 Tigers Logo	.05
Panel	2.00
3 Andres Galarraga	.30
6 Dale Murphy	.30
9 Giants Logo	.05
12 Kevin Seitzer	.15
Panel	2.75
4 Wally Joyner	.20
5 Twins Logo	.05
7 Kirby Puckett	1.00
16 Todd Worrell	.15

1988 Fleer Glossy Tin

In its second year of production, Fleer radically reduced production numbers on its glossy version of the 1988 baseball card set. With production estimates in the 60,000 set range, values of the '88 tin glossies are about double those of the regular issue cards. Once again the issue was sold only as complete sets in colorful lithographed metal boxes.

	MT
Complete Set (672):	50.00
Common Player:	.15
(Star cards valued at 3-5X regular-issue 1988 Fleer version.)	

1988 Fleer Update

This update set (numbered U-1 through U-132 are 2-1/2" x 3-1/2") features traded veterans and rookies in a mixture of full-color action shots and close-ups, framed by white borders with red and blue stripes. The backs are red, white and blue-grey and include personal info, along with yearly and "At Their Best" (day, night, home, road) stats charts. The set was packaged in white cardboard boxes with red and blue stripes. A glossy-coated edition of the update set was issued in its own box and is valued at two times the regular issue.

		MT
Complete Set (132):		13.00
Common Player:		.06
1	Jose Bautista	.06
2	Joe Orsulak	.06
3	Doug Sisk	.06
4	Craig Worthington	.06
5	Mike Boddicker	.06
6	Rick Cerone	.06
7	Larry Parrish	.06
8	Lee Smith	.10
9	Mike Smithson	.06
10	John Trautwein	.06
11	Sherman Corbett	.06
12	Chili Davis	.10
13	Jim Eppard	.06
14	Bryan Harvey	.25
15	John Davis	.06
16	Dave Gallagher	.06
17	Ricky Horton	.06
18	Dan Pasqua	.06
19	Melido Perez	.06
20	Jose Segura	.06
21	Andy Allanson	.06
22	Jon Perlman	.06
23	Domingo Ramos	.06
24	Rick Rodriguez	.06
25	Willie Upshaw	.06
26	Paul Gibson	.06
27	Don Heinkel	.06
28	Ray Knight	.06
29	Gary Pettis	.06
30	Luis Salazar	.06
31	Mike MacFarlane	.06
32	Jeff Montgomery	.25
33	Ted Power	.06
34	Israel Sanchez	.06
35	Kurt Stillwell	.06
36	Pat Tabler	.06
37	Don August	.06
38	Darryl Hamilton	.30
39	Jeff Leonard	.06
40	Joey Meyer	.06
41	Allan Anderson	.06
42	Brian Harper	.06
43	Tom Herr	.06
44	Charlie Lea	.06
45	John Moses	.06
46	John Candelaria	.06
47	Jack Clark	.06
48	Richard Dotson	.06
49	Al Leiter	.10
50	Rafael Santana	.06
51	Don Slaught	.06
52	Todd Burns	.06
53	Dave Henderson	.06
54	Doug Jennings	.06
55	Dave Parker	.08
56	Walt Weiss	.10
57	Bob Welch	.06
58	Henry Cotto	.06
59	Marion Diaz (Mario)	.06
60	Mike Jackson	.06
61	Bill Swift	.06
62	Jose Cecena	.06
63	Ray Hayward	.06
64	Jim Steels	.06
65	Pat Borders	.10
66	Sil Campusano	.06
67	Mike Flanagan	.06
68	Todd Stottlemyre	.15
69	David Wells	1.50
70	Jose Alvarez	.06
71	Paul Runge	.06
72	Cesar Jimenez (German)	.06
73	Pete Smith	.08
74	*John Smoltz*	3.00
75	Damon Berryhill	.08
76	Goose Gossage	.08
77	Mark Grace	2.00
78	Darrin Jackson	.10
79	Vance Law	.06
80	Jeff Pico	.06
81	Gary Varsho	.06
82	Tim Birtsas	.06
83	Rob Dibble	.06
84	Danny Jackson	.06
85	Paul O'Neill	.35
86	Jose Rijo	.06
87	*Chris Sabo*	.20
88	John Fishel	.06
89	*Craig Biggio*	2.50
90	Terry Puhl	.06
91	Rafael Ramirez	.06
92	Louie Meadows	.06
93	Kirk Gibson	.06
94	Alfredo Griffin	.06
95	Jay Howell	.06
96	Jesse Orosco	.06
97	Alejandro Pena	.06
98	Tracy Woodson	.06
99	John Dopson	.06
100	Brian Holman	.06
101	Rex Hudler	.06
102	Jeff Parrett	.06
103	Nelson Santovenia	.06
104	Kevin Elster	.08
105	Jeff Innis	.06
106	Mackey Sasser	.06
107	Phil Bradley	.06
108	Danny Clay	.06
109	Greg Harris	.06
110	Ricky Jordan	.06
111	David Palmer	.06
112	Jim Gott	.06
113	Tommy Gregg (photo actually Randy Milligan)	.06
114	Barry Jones	.06
115	Randy Milligan	.10
116	Luis Alicea	.10
117	Tom Brunansky	.06
118	John Costello	.06
119	Jose DeLeon	.06
120	Bob Horner	.06
121	Scott Terry	.06
122	*Roberto Alomar*	4.00
123	Dave Leiper	.06
124	Keith Moreland	.06
125	Mark Parent	.06
126	Dennis Rasmussen	.06
127	Randy Bockus	.06
128	Brett Butler	.08
129	Donell Nixon	.06
130	Earnest Riles	.06
131	Roger Samuels	.06
132	Checklist	.06

1988 Fleer Update Glossy Tin

The glossy version of the 1988 Fleer Update set differs from the regular-issue Update set only in the high-gloss finish applied to the cards' fronts and the lithographed metal box in which sets were sold.

	MT
Complete Set (132):	25.00
Common Player:	.15
(Star cards valued about 2X regular-issue 1988 Fleer Updates)	

1988 Fleer Award Winners

This limited edition boxed set of 1987 award-winning player cards also includes six team logo sticker cards. Red, white, blue and yellow bands border the sharp, full-color player photos printed below a "Fleer Award Winners 1988" banner. The player's name and award are printed beneath the photo. Flip sides are red, white and blue and list personal information, career data, team logo and card number. This set was sold exclusively at 7-Eleven stores nationwide.

		MT
Complete Set (44):		4.00
Common Player:		.05
1	Steve Bedrosian	.05
2	George Bell	.05
3	Wade Boggs	.75
4	Jose Canseco	.50
5	Will Clark	.40
6	Roger Clemens	1.00
7	Kal Daniels	.05
8	Eric Davis	.10
9	Andre Dawson	.15
10	Mike Dunne	.05
11	Dwight Evans	.05
12	Carlton Fisk	.12
13	Julio Franco	.05
14	Dwight Gooden	.10
15	Pedro Guerrero	.05
16	Tony Gwynn	.75
17	Orel Hershiser	.10
18	Tom Henke	.05
19	Ted Higuera	.05
20	Charlie Hough	.05
21	Wally Joyner	.10
22	Jimmy Key	.05
23	Don Mattingly	.90
24	Mark McGwire	2.00
25	Paul Molitor	.45
26	Jack Morris	.05
27	Dale Murphy	.15
28	Terry Pendleton	.05
29	Kirby Puckett	.90
30	Tim Raines	.10
31	Jeff Reardon	.05
32	Harold Reynolds	.05
33	Dave Righetti	.05
34	Benito Santiago	.05
35	Mike Schmidt	.50
36	Mike Scott	.05
37	Kevin Seitzer	.05
38	Larry Sheets	.05
39	Ozzie Smith	.45
40	Darryl Strawberry	.10
41	Rick Sutcliffe	.05
42	Danny Tartabull	.05
43	Alan Trammell	.08
44	Tim Wallach	.05

1988 Fleer Baseball All Stars

This limited edition boxed set features major league All-Stars. The standard-size cards feature a sporty bright blue and yellow striped background. Card backs feature a blue and white striped design with a yellow highlighted section at the top that contains the player name, card number, team, position and personal data, followed by lifetime career stats. Fleer All Stars are cello-wrapped in blue and yellow striped boxes with checklist backs. The set includes six team logo sticker cards that feature black-and-white aerial shots of major league ballparks. The set was marketed exclusively by Ben Franklin stores.

		MT
Complete Set (44):		4.00
Common Player:		.05
1	George Bell	.05
2	Wade Boggs	.60
3	Bobby Bonilla	.08
4	George Brett	.75
5	Jose Canseco	.60
6	Jack Clark	.05
7	Will Clark	.50
8	Roger Clemens	1.00
9	Eric Davis	.10
10	Andre Dawson	.12
11	Julio Franco	.05
12	Dwight Gooden	.10
13	Tony Gwynn	.75
14	Orel Hershiser	.08
15	Teddy Higuera	.05
16	Charlie Hough	.05
17	Kent Hrbek	.08
18	Bruce Hurst	.05
19	Wally Joyner	.10
20	Mark Langston	.05
21	Dave LaPoint	.05
22	Candy Maldonado	.05
23	Don Mattingly	.90
24	Roger McDowell	.05
25	Mark McGwire	2.00
26	Jack Morris	.05
27	Dale Murphy	.15
28	Eddie Murray	.35
29	Matt Nokes	.05
30	Kirby Puckett	.75
31	Tim Raines	.10
32	Willie Randolph	.05
33	Jeff Reardon	.05
34	Nolan Ryan	1.50
35	Juan Samuel	.05
36	Mike Schmidt	.75
37	Mike Scott	.05
38	Kevin Seitzer	.05
39	Ozzie Smith	.50
40	Darryl Strawberry	.12
41	Rick Sutcliffe	.05
42	Alan Trammell	.08
43	Tim Wallach	.05
44	Dave Winfield	.35

1988 Fleer Baseball's Best

This boxed set of 44 standard-size cards (2-1/2" x 3-1/2") and six team logo stickers is the third annual issue from Fleer highlighting the best major league sluggers and pitchers. Five additional player cards were printed on retail display box bottoms, along with a checklist logo card (numbered C-1 through C-6). Full-color player photos are framed by a green border that fades to yellow. A red (slugger) or blue (pitcher) player name is printed beneath the photo. Backs are printed in green on a white background with yellow highlights. Card number, player name and personal info appear in a green vertical box on the left-hand side of the card back with a yellow cartoon-style team logo overprinted across a stats chart on the right. This set was produced by Fleer for exclusive distribution by McCrory's stores (McCrory, McClellan, J.J. Newberry, H.L. Green, TG&Y).

		MT
Complete Set (44):		4.00
Common Player:		.05
1	George Bell	.05
2	Wade Boggs	.60
3	Bobby Bonilla	.08
4	Tom Brunansky	.05
5	Ellis Burks	.08
6	Jose Canseco	.60
7	Joe Carter	.08
8	Will Clark	.50
9	Roger Clemens	1.00
10	Eric Davis	.08
11	Glenn Davis	.05
12	Andre Dawson	.15
13	Dennis Eckersley	.08
14	Andres Galarraga	.10
15	Dwight Gooden	.10
16	Pedro Guerrero	.05
17	Tony Gwynn	.75
18	Orel Hershiser	.08
19	Ted Higuera	.05
20	Pete Incaviglia	.05
21	Danny Jackson	.05
22	Doug Jennings	.05
23	Mark Langston	.05
24	Dave LaPoint	.05
25	Mike LaValliere	.05
26	Don Mattingly	.90
27	Mark McGwire	2.00
28	Dale Murphy	.20
29	Ken Phelps	.05
30	Kirby Puckett	.75
31	Johnny Ray	.05
32	Jeff Reardon	.05
33	Dave Righetti	.05
34	Cal Ripkin, Jr. (Ripken)	2.00
35	Chris Sabo	.05
36	Mike Schmidt	.75

37	Mike Scott	.05
38	Kevin Seitzer	.05
39	Dave Stewart	.05
40	Darryl Strawberry	.10
41	Greg Swindell	.05
42	Frank Tanana	.05
43	Dave Winfield	.15
44	Todd Worrell	.05

1988 Fleer Baseball's Best Box Panel

Six cards were placed on the bottoms of retail boxes of the Fleer Baseball's Best boxed sets in 1988. The cards, 2-1/2" x 3-1/2", are identical in design to cards found in the 44-card set. The cards are numbered C-1 through C-6 and were produced for distribution by McCrory stores and its affiliates.

		MT
Complete Panel Set:		1.50
Complete Singles Set (6):		.90
Common Single Player:		.15
1	Ron Darling	.15
2	Rickey Henderson	.60
3	Carney Lansford	.15
4	Rafael Palmeiro	.50
5	Frank Viola	.15
6	Minnesota Twins logo	.05

1988 Fleer Exciting Stars

This boxed set showcases star major leaguers. Player photos are slanted upwards to the right, framed by a blue border with a red and white stripe across the middle. Card backs are numbered and printed in red, white and blue. The set was packaged in a checklist box, with six team logo sticker cards featuring black-and-white stadium photos on the flip sides. Exciting Stars was distributed via Cumberland Farm stores throughout the northeastern U.S. and Florida.

		MT
Complete Set (44):		4.00
Common Player:		.05
1	Harold Baines	.08
2	Kevin Bass	.05
3	George Bell	.05
4	Wade Boggs	.65
5	Mickey Brantley	.05
6	Sid Bream	.05
7	Jose Canseco	.50
8	Jack Clark	.05
9	Will Clark	.45
10	Roger Clemens	1.00
11	Vince Coleman	.05
12	Eric Davis	.10
13	Andre Dawson	.15
14	Julio Franco	.05
15	Dwight Gooden	.10
16	Mike Greenwell	.05
17	Tony Gwynn	.75
18	Von Hayes	.02
19	Tom Henke	.05
20	Orel Hershiser	.08
21	Teddy Higuera	.05
22	Brook Jacoby	.05
23	Wally Joyner	.10
24	Jimmy Key	.05
25	Don Mattingly	.90
26	Mark McGwire	2.00
27	Jack Morris	.05
28	Dale Murphy	.15
29	Matt Nokes	.05
30	Kirby Puckett	.75
31	Tim Raines	.10
32	Ryne Sandberg	.65
33	Benito Santiago	.05
34	Mike Schmidt	.75
35	Mike Scott	.05
36	Kevin Seitzer	.05
37	Larry Sheets	.05
38	Ruben Sierra	.05
39	Darryl Strawberry	.10
40	Rick Sutcliffe	.05
41	Danny Tartabull	.05
42	Alan Trammell	.08
43	Fernando Valenzuela	.05
44	Devon White	.05

1988 Fleer Hottest Stars

This boxed set of standard-size player cards and six team logo stickers was produced by Fleer for exclusive distribution at Revco drug stores nationwide. Card fronts feature full-color photos of players representing every major league team. Photos are framed in red, orange and yellow, with a blue and white player name printed across the bottom of the card front. A flaming baseball logo bearing the words "Hottest Stars" appears in the lower-left corner of the photo. Card backs are red, white and blue. The player's name, position, card number and team logo are printed across the top section, followed by a stats box, personal data, batting and throwing preferences. The set also includes six team logo sticker cards with flipside stadium photos in black-and-white.

		MT
Complete Set (44):		4.00
Common Player:		.05
1	George Bell	.05
2	Wade Boggs	.60
3	Bobby Bonilla	.08
4	George Brett	.80
5	Jose Canseco	.50
6	Will Clark	.50
7	Roger Clemens	1.00
8	Eric Davis	.10
9	Andre Dawson	.15
10	Tony Fernandez	.05
11	Julio Franco	.05
12	Gary Gaetti	.05
13	Dwight Gooden	.10
14	Mike Greenwell	.05
15	Tony Gwynn	.75
16	Rickey Henderson	.45
17	Keith Hernandez	.05
18	Tom Herr	.05
19	Orel Hershiser	.08
20	Ted Higuera	.05
21	Wally Joyner	.10
22	Jimmy Key	.05
23	Mark Langston	.05
24	Don Mattingly	.90
25	Jack McDowell	.05
26	Mark McGwire	2.00
27	Kevin Mitchell	.05
28	Jack Morris	.05
29	Dale Murphy	.15
30	Kirby Puckett	.75
31	Tim Raines	.08
32	Shane Rawley	.05
33	Benito Santiago	.05
34	Mike Schmidt	.75
35	Mike Scott	.05
36	Kevin Seitzer	.05
37	Larry Sheets	.05
38	Ruben Sierra	.05
39	Dave Smith	.05
40	Ozzie Smith	.50
41	Darryl Strawberry	.08
42	Rick Sutcliffe	.05
43	Pat Tabler	.05
44	Alan Trammell	.08

1988 Fleer League Leaders

This boxed set is the third annual limited edition set from Fleer highlighting leading players. The 1988 edition contains the same type of information, front and back, as the previous sets, with a new color scheme and design. Card fronts have bright blue borders, solid on the lower portion, striped on the upper, with a gold bar separating the two sections. The full-color player photo is centered above a yellow name banner. The numbered card backs are blue, pink and white, and contain player stats and personal notes. Six team logo sticker cards, with flipside black-and-white photos of ballparks, accompany this set which was marketed exclusively by Walgreen drug stores.

		MT
Complete Set (44):		4.00
Common Player:		.05
1	George Bell	.05
2	Wade Boggs	.60
3	Ivan Calderon	.05
4	Jose Canseco	.50
5	Will Clark	.45
6	Roger Clemens	1.00
7	Vince Coleman	.05
8	Eric Davis	.10
9	Andre Dawson	.15
10	Bill Doran	.05
11	Dwight Evans	.05
12	Julio Franco	.05
13	Gary Gaetti	.08
14	Andres Galarraga	.10
15	Dwight Gooden	.10
16	Tony Gwynn	.75
17	Tom Henke	.05
18	Keith Hernandez	.05
19	Orel Hershiser	.08
20	Ted Higuera	.05
21	Kent Hrbek	.08
22	Wally Joyner	.08
23	Jimmy Key	.05
24	Mark Langston	.05
25	Don Mattingly	.90
26	Mark McGwire	2.00
27	Paul Molitor	.50
28	Jack Morris	.05
29	Dale Murphy	.15
30	Kirby Puckett	.75
31	Tim Raines	.10
32	Rick Rueschel	.05
33	Bret Saberhagen	.05
34	Benito Santiago	.05
35	Mike Schmidt	.75
36	Mike Scott	.05
37	Kevin Seitzer	.05
38	Larry Sheets	.05
39	Ruben Sierra	.05
40	Darryl Strawberry	.10
41	Rick Sutcliffe	.05
42	Alan Trammell	.08
43	Andy Van Slyke	.05
44	Todd Worrell	.05

1988 Fleer Mini

This third annual issue of miniatures (1-7/8" x 2-5/8") includes 120 high-gloss cards featuring new photos, not copies from the regular issue, although the card designs are identical. Card backs are red, white and blue and include personal data, yearly career stats and a stats breakdown of batting average, slugging percentage and on-base average, listed for day, night, home and road games. Card backs are numbered in alphabetical order by teams which are also listed alphabetically. The set includes 18 team logo stickers with black-and-white aerial stadium photos on the flip sides.

		MT
Complete Set (120):		8.00
Common Player:		.05
1	Eddie Murray	.40
2	Dave Schmidt	.05
3	Larry Sheets	.05
4	Wade Boggs	.65
5	Roger Clemens	.75
6	Dwight Evans	.05
7	Mike Greenwell	.05
8	Sam Horn	.05
9	Lee Smith	.08
10	Brian Downing	.05
11	Wally Joyner	.08
12	Devon White	.08
13	Mike Witt	.05
14	Ivan Calderon	.05
15	Ozzie Guillen	.05
16	Jack McDowell	.05
17	Kenny Williams	.05
18	Joe Carter	.08
19	Julio Franco	.05
20	Pat Tabler	.05
21	Doyle Alexander	.05
22	Jack Morris	.05
23	Matt Nokes	.05
24	Walt Terrell	.05
25	Alan Trammell	.10
26	Bret Saberhagen	.05
27	Kevin Seitzer	.05
28	Danny Tartabull	.05
29	Gary Thurman	.05
30	Ted Higuera	.05
31	Paul Molitor	.50
32	Dan Plesac	.05
33	Robin Yount	.50
34	Gary Gaetti	.05
35	Kent Hrbek	.05
36	Kirby Puckett	.75
37	Jeff Reardon	.05
38	Frank Viola	.05
39	Jack Clark	.05
40	Rickey Henderson	.50
41	Don Mattingly	1.00
42	Willie Randolph	.05
43	Dave Righetti	.05
44	Dave Winfield	.50
45	Jose Canseco	.65
46	Mark McGwire	2.00
47	Dave Parker	.05
48	Dave Stewart	.05
49	Walt Weiss	.05
50	Bob Welch	.05
51	Mickey Brantley	.05
52	Mark Langston	.05
53	Harold Reynolds	.05
54	Scott Fletcher	.05
55	Charlie Hough	.05
56	Pete Incaviglia	.05
57	Larry Parrish	.05
58	Ruben Sierra	.05
59	George Bell	.05
60	Mark Eichhorn	.05
61	Tony Fernandez	.05
62	Tom Henke	.05
63	Jimmy Key	.05
64	Dion James	.05
65	Dale Murphy	.15
66	Zane Smith	.05
67	Andre Dawson	.15
68	Mark Grace	.75
69	Jerry Mumphrey	.05
70	Ryne Sandberg	.65
71	Rick Sutcliffe	.05
72	Kal Daniels	.05
73	Eric Davis	.10
74	John Franco	.05
75	Ron Robinson	.05
76	Jeff Treadway	.05
77	Kevin Bass	.05
78	Glenn Davis	.05
79	Nolan Ryan	1.00
80	Mike Scott	.05
81	Dave Smith	.05
82	Kirk Gibson	.05
83	Pedro Guerrero	.05
84	Orel Hershiser	.08
85	Steve Sax	.05
86	Fernando Valenzuela	.08
87	Tim Burke	.05
88	Andres Galarraga	.15
89	Neal Heaton	.05
90	Tim Raines	.10
91	Tim Wallach	.05
92	Dwight Gooden	.10
93	Keith Hernandez	.05
94	Gregg Jefferies	.25
95	Howard Johnson	.05
96	Roger McDowell	.05
97	Darryl Strawberry	.15
98	Steve Bedrosian	.05
99	Von Hayes	.05
100	Shane Rawley	.05
101	Juan Samuel	.05
102	Mike Schmidt	.60
103	Bobby Bonilla	.08
104	Mike Dunne	.05
105	Andy Van Slyke	.05
106	Vince Coleman	.05
107	Bob Horner	.05
108	Willie McGee	.08
109	Ozzie Smith	.50
110	John Tudor	.05
111	Todd Worrell	.05
112	Tony Gwynn	.75
113	John Kruk	.05
114	Lance McCullers	.05
115	Benito Santiago	.08
116	Will Clark	.40
117	Jeff Leonard	.05
118	Candy Maldonado	.05
119	Kirt Manwaring	.05
120	Don Robinson	.05

1988 Fleer MVP

This boxed set of 44 standard-size cards and six team logo stickers was produced by Fleer for exclusive distribution at Toys "R" Us stores. This premiere edition features full-color player photos framed by a yellow and blue border. Card backs are yellow and blue on a white background. The player's team, position and personal data are followed by stats, logo and a blue banner bearing the player's name, team logo and card number. The six sticker cards feature black-and-white stadium photos on the backs.

		MT
Complete Set (44):		4.00
Common Player:		.05
1	George Bell	.05
2	Wade Boggs	.60
3	Jose Canseco	.50
4	Ivan Calderon	.05
5	Will Clark	.45
6	Roger Clemens	1.00
7	Vince Coleman	.05
8	Eric Davis	.10
9	Andre Dawson	.15
10	Dave Dravecky	.05
11	Mike Dunne	.05
12	Dwight Evans	.05
13	Sid Fernandez	.05
14	Tony Fernandez	.05
15	Julio Franco	.05

16	Dwight Gooden	.10
17	Tony Gwynn	.75
18	Ted Higuera	.05
19	Charlie Hough	.05
20	Wally Joyner	.10
21	Mark Langston	.05
22	Don Mattingly	.90
23	Mark McGwire	2.00
24	Jack Morris	.05
25	Dale Murphy	.15
26	Kirby Puckett	.75
27	Tim Raines	.10
28	Willie Randolph	.05
29	Ryne Sandberg	.65
30	Benito Santiago	.05
31	Mike Schmidt	.75
32	Mike Scott	.05
33	Kevin Seitzer	.05
34	Larry Sheets	.05
35	Ozzie Smith	.50
36	Dave Stewart	.05
37	Darryl Strawberry	.10
38	Rick Sutcliffe	.05
39	Alan Trammell	.08
40	Fernando Valenzuela	.05
41	Frank Viola	.05
42	Tim Wallach	.05
43	Dave Winfield	.45
44	Robin Yount	.50

1988 Fleer Record Setters

For the second consecutive year, Fleer issued this set for exclusive distribution by Eckerd Drug stores. Cards are standard size with red and blue borders framing the full-color player photos. Card backs list personal information and career stats in red and blue on a white background. Each 44-card set comes cello-wrapped in a checklist box that contains six additional cards with peel-off team logo stickers. The sticker cards feature black-and-white aerial photos of major league ballparks, along with stadium statistics such as field size, seating capacity and date of the first game played.

		MT
Complete Set (44):		4.00
Common Player:		.05
1	Jesse Barfield	.05
2	George Bell	.05
3	Wade Boggs	.60
4	Jose Canseco	.50
5	Jack Clark	.05
6	Will Clark	.45
7	Roger Clemens	.75
8	Alvin Davis	.05
9	Eric Davis	.10
10	Andre Dawson	.15
11	Mike Dunne	.05
12	John Franco	.05
13	Julio Franco	.05
14	Dwight Gooden	.10
15	Mark Gubicza	.05
16	Ozzie Guillen	.05
17	Tony Gwynn	.75
18	Orel Hershiser	.08
19	Teddy Higuera	.05
20	Howard Johnson	.05
21	Wally Joyner	.10
22	Jimmy Key	.05
23	Jeff Leonard	.05
24	Don Mattingly	.90
25	Mark McGwire	2.00
26	Jack Morris	.05
27	Dale Murphy	.15
28	Larry Parrish	.05
29	Kirby Puckett	.75
30	Tim Raines	.10
31	Harold Reynolds	.05
32	Dave Righetti	.05
33	Cal Ripken, Jr.	2.00
34	Benito Santiago	.05
35	Mike Schmidt	.75
36	Mike Scott	.05
37	Kevin Seitzer	.05
38	Ozzie Smith	.45
39	Darryl Strawberry	.10
40	Rick Sutcliffe	.05
41	Alan Trammell	.08
42	Frank Viola	.05
43	Mitch Williams	.05
44	Todd Worrell	.05

1988 Fleer Star Stickers

This set of 132 standard-size sticker cards (including a checklist card) features exclusive player photos, different from those in the Fleer regular issue. Card fronts have light gray borders sprinkled with multi-colored stars. Card backs are printed in red, gray and black on white and include personal data and a breakdown of pitching and batting stats into day, night, home and road categories. Cards were marketed in two different display boxes that feature six players and two team logos on the bottoms.

		MT
Complete Set (132):		20.00
Common Player:		.05
1	Mike Boddicker	.05
2	Eddie Murray	.60
3	Cal Ripken, Jr.	2.50
4	Larry Sheets	.05
5	Wade Boggs	.60
6	Ellis Burks	.05
7	Roger Clemens	.75
8	Dwight Evans	.05
9	Mike Greenwell	.05
10	Bruce Hurst	.05
11	Brian Downing	.05
12	Wally Joyner	.10
13	Mike Witt	.05
14	Ivan Calderon	.05
15	Jose DeLeon	.05
16	Ozzie Guillen	.05
17	Bobby Thigpen	.05
18	Joe Carter	.08
19	Julio Franco	.05
20	Brook Jacoby	.05
21	Cory Snyder	.05
22	Pat Tabler	.05
23	Doyle Alexander	.05
24	Kirk Gibson	.05
25	Mike Henneman	.05
26	Jack Morris	.05
27	Matt Nokes	.05
28	Walt Terrell	.05
29	Alan Trammell	.08
30	George Brett	.75
31	Charlie Leibrandt	.05
32	Bret Saberhagen	.08
33	Kevin Seitzer	.05
34	Danny Tartabull	.05
35	Frank White	.05
36	Rob Deer	.05
37	Ted Higuera	.05
38	Paul Molitor	.75
39	Dan Plesac	.05
40	Robin Yount	.60
41	Bert Blyleven	.05
42	Tom Brunansky	.05
43	Gary Gaetti	.05
44	Kent Hrbek	.05
45	Kirby Puckett	.90
46	Jeff Reardon	.05
47	Frank Viola	.05
48	Don Mattingly	1.00
49	Mike Pagliarulo	.05
50	Willie Randolph	.05
51	Rick Rhoden	.05
52	Dave Righetti	.05
53	Dave Winfield	.50
54	Jose Canseco	.60
55	Carney Lansford	.05
56	Mark McGwire	3.00
57	Dave Stewart	.05
58	Curt Young	.05
59	Alvin Davis	.05
60	Mark Langston	.05
61	Ken Phelps	.05
62	Harold Reynolds	.05
63	Scott Fletcher	.05
64	Charlie Hough	.05
65	Pete Incaviglia	.05
66	Oddibe McDowell	.05
67	Pete O'Brien	.05
68	Larry Parrish	.05
69	Ruben Sierra	.05
70	Jesse Barfield	.05
71	George Bell	.05
72	Tony Fernandez	.05
73	Tom Henke	.05
74	Jimmy Key	.05
75	Lloyd Moseby	.05
76	Dion James	.05
77	Dale Murphy	.15
78	Zane Smith	.05
79	Andre Dawson	.15
80	Ryne Sandberg	.65
81	Rick Sutcliffe	.05
82	Kal Daniels	.05
83	Eric Davis	.10
84	John Franco	.05
85	Kevin Bass	.05
86	Glenn Davis	.05
87	Bill Doran	.05
88	Nolan Ryan	2.50
89	Mike Scott	.05
90	Dave Smith	.05
91	Pedro Guerrero	.05
92	Orel Hershiser	.08
93	Steve Sax	.05
94	Fernando Valenzuela	.10
95	Tim Burke	.05
96	Andres Galarraga	.12
97	Tim Raines	.10
98	Tim Wallach	.05
99	Mitch Webster	.05
100	Ron Darling	.05
101	Sid Fernandez	.05
102	Dwight Gooden	.10
103	Keith Hernandez	.05
104	Howard Johnson	.05
105	Roger McDowell	.05
106	Darryl Strawberry	.10
107	Steve Bedrosian	.05
108	Von Hayes	.05
109	Shane Rawley	.05
110	Juan Samuel	.05
111	Mike Schmidt	.75
112	Milt Thompson	.05
113	Sid Bream	.05
114	Bobby Bonilla	.08
115	Mike Dunne	.05
116	Andy Van Slyke	.05
117	Vince Coleman	.05
118	Willie McGee	.05
119	Terry Pendleton	.05
120	Ozzie Smith	.60
121	John Tudor	.05
122	Todd Worrell	.05
123	Tony Gwynn	.75
124	John Kruk	.05
125	Benito Santiago	.08
126	Will Clark	.60
127	Dave Dravecky	.05
128	Jeff Leonard	.05
129	Candy Maldonado	.05
130	Rick Rueschel	.05
131	Don Robinson	.05
132	Checklist	.05

1988 Fleer Star Stickers Box Panels

This set of eight box-bottom cards was printed on two different retail display boxes. Six players and two team logo sticker cards are included in the set, three player photos and one team photo per box. The full-color player photos are exclusive to the Fleer Star Sticker set. The cards, which measure 2-1/2" x 3-1/2", have a light gray border sprinkled with multi-color stars. The backs are printed in navy blue and red.

		MT
Complete Panel Set (2):		2.00
Complete Singles Set (8):		1.00
Common Singles Player:		.15
Panel		1.00
1	Eric Davis	.25
3	Kevin Mitchell	.10
5	Rickey Henderson	.50
7	Tigers Logo	.05
Panel		1.00
2	Gary Carter	.15
4	Ron Guidry	.10
6	Don Baylor	.10
8	Giants Logo	.05

1988 Fleer Superstars

This is the fourth edition of Fleer boxed sets produced for distribution by McCrory's (1985-87 issues were titled "Fleer Limited Edition"). The Superstars standard-size card set features full-color player photos framed by red, white and blue striped top and bottom borders. Card fronts have a semi-glossy slightly textured finish. Card backs are red and blue on white and include card numbers, personal data and statistics. Six team logo sticker cards are also included in this set which was marketed in red, white and blue boxes with checklist backs. Boxed sets were sold exclusively at McCrory's stores and its affiliates.

		MT
Complete Set (44):		4.00
Common Player:		.05
1	Steve Bedrosian	.05
2	George Bell	.05
3	Wade Boggs	.60
4	Barry Bonds	.90
5	Jose Canseco	.60
6	Joe Carter	.08
7	Jack Clark	.05
8	Will Clark	.45
9	Roger Clemens	.90
10	Alvin Davis	.05
11	Eric Davis	.10
12	Glenn Davis	.05
13	Andre Dawson	.15
14	Dwight Gooden	.10
15	Orel Hershiser	.08
16	Teddy Higuera	.05
17	Kent Hrbek	.05
18	Wally Joyner	.08
19	Jimmy Key	.05
20	John Kruk	.05
21	Jeff Leonard	.05
22	Don Mattingly	.90
23	Mark McGwire	2.00
24	Kevin McReynolds	.05
25	Dale Murphy	.15
26	Matt Nokes	.05
27	Terry Pendleton	.05
28	Kirby Puckett	.75
29	Tim Raines	.10
30	Rick Rhoden	.05
31	Cal Ripken, Jr.	2.00
32	Benito Santiago	.05
33	Mike Schmidt	.75
34	Mike Scott	.05
35	Kevin Seitzer	.05
36	Ruben Sierra	.05
37	Cory Snyder	.05
38	Darryl Strawberry	.10
39	Rick Sutcliffe	.05
40	Danny Tartabull	.05
41	Alan Trammell	.08
42	Ken Williams	.05
43	Mike Witt	.05
44	Robin Yount	.50

1989 Fleer

This set includes 660 standard-size cards and was issued with 45 team logo stickers. Individual card fronts feature a grey and white striped background with full-color player photos framed by a bright line of color that slants upward to the right. The set also includes two subsets: 15 Major League Prospects and 12 SuperStar Specials. A special bonus set of 12 All-Star Team cards was randomly inserted in individual wax packs of 15 cards. The last seven cards in the set are checklists, with players listed alphabetically by teams.

		MT
Factory Set, Unopened (660):		30.00
Complete Set (660):		25.00
Common Player:		.05
Wax Box:		30.00
1	Don Baylor	.12
2	*Lance Blankenship*	.10
3	*Todd Burns*	.08
4	Greg Cadaret	.05
5	Jose Canseco	.35
6	Storm Davis	.05
7	Dennis Eckersley	.08
8	Mike Gallego	.05
9	Ron Hassey	.05
10	Dave Henderson	.05
11	Rick Honeycutt	.05
12	Glenn Hubbard	.05
13	Stan Javier	.05
14	*Doug Jennings*	.05
15	*Felix Jose*	.08
16	Carney Lansford	.05
17	Mark McGwire	1.00
18	Gene Nelson	.05
19	Dave Parker	.10
20	Eric Plunk	.05
21	Luis Polonia	.05
22	Terry Steinbach	.05
23	Dave Stewart	.08
24	Walt Weiss	.05
25	Bob Welch	.05
26	Curt Young	.05
27	Rick Aguilera	.05
28	Wally Backman	.05
29	Mark Carreon	.05
30	Gary Carter	.15
31	David Cone	.12
32	Ron Darling	.05
33	Len Dykstra	.10
34	Kevin Elster	.05
35	Sid Fernandez	.05
36	Dwight Gooden	.10
37	Keith Hernandez	.05
38	Gregg Jefferies	.20
39	Howard Johnson	.05
40	Terry Leach	.05
41	Dave Magadan	.05
42	Bob McClure	.05
43	Roger McDowell	.05
44	Kevin McReynolds	.05
45	Keith Miller	.05
46	Randy Myers	.05
47	Bob Ojeda	.05
48	Mackey Sasser	.05
49	Darryl Strawberry	.15
50	Tim Teufel	.05
51	*Dave West*	.12
52	Mookie Wilson	.05
53	Dave Anderson	.05
54	Tim Belcher	.05
55	Mike Davis	.05
56	Mike Devereaux	.05
57	Kirk Gibson	.05

58	Alfredo Griffin	.05
59	Chris Gwynn	.05
60	Jeff Hamilton	.05
61a	Danny Heep (Home: San Antonio, TX)	.50
61b	Danny Heep (Home: Lake Hills, TX)	.05
62	Orel Hershiser	.08
63	Brian Holton	.05
64	Jay Howell	.05
65	Tim Leary	.05
66	Mike Marshall	.05
67	*Ramon Martinez*	.40
68	Jesse Orosco	.05
69	Alejandro Pena	.05
70	Steve Sax	.05
71	Mike Scioscia	.05
72	Mike Sharperson	.05
73	John Shelby	.05
74	Franklin Stubbs	.05
75	John Tudor	.05
76	Fernando Valenzuela	.08
77	Tracy Woodson	.05
78	Marty Barrett	.05
79	Todd Benzinger	.05
80	Mike Boddicker	.05
81	Wade Boggs	.25
82	"Oil Can" Boyd	.05
83	Ellis Burks	.08
84	Rick Cerone	.05
85	Roger Clemens	.50
86	*Steve Curry*	.05
87	Dwight Evans	.05
88	Wes Gardner	.05
89	Rich Gedman	.05
90	Mike Greenwell	.08
91	Bruce Hurst	.05
92	Dennis Lamp	.05
93	Spike Owen	.05
94	Larry Parrish	.05
95	*Carlos Quintana*	.08
96	Jody Reed	.05
97	Jim Rice	.10
98a	Kevin Romine (batting follow-thru, photo actually Randy Kutcher)	.40
98b	Kevin Romine (arms crossed on chest, correct photo)	.40
99	Lee Smith	.10
100	Mike Smithson	.05
101	Bob Stanley	.05
102	Allan Anderson	.05
103	Keith Atherton	.05
104	Juan Berenguer	.05
105	Bert Blyleven	.05
106	*Eric Bullock*	.05
107	Randy Bush	.05
108	John Christensen	.05
109	Mark Davidson	.05
110	Gary Gaetti	.08
111	Greg Gagne	.05
112	Dan Gladden	.05
113	*German Gonzalez*	.05
114	Brian Harper	.05
115	Tom Herr	.05
116	Kent Hrbek	.08
117	Gene Larkin	.05
118	Tim Laudner	.05
119	Charlie Lea	.05
120	Steve Lombardozzi	.05
121a	John Moses (Home: Phoenix, AZ)	.25
121b	John Moses (Home: Tempe, AZ)	.05
122	Al Newman	.05
123	Mark Portugal	.05
124	Kirby Puckett	.40
125	Jeff Reardon	.05
126	Fred Toliver	.05
127	Frank Viola	.05
128	Doyle Alexander	.05
129	Dave Bergman	.05
130a	Tom Brookens (Mike Heath stats on back)	2.00
130b	Tom Brookens (correct stats on back)	.20
131	*Paul Gibson*	.05
132a	Mike Heath (Tom Brookens stats on back)	2.00
132b	Mike Heath (correct stats on back)	.20
133	*Don Heinkel*	.05
134	Mike Henneman	.05
135	Guillermo Hernandez	.05
136	Eric King	.05
137	Chet Lemon	.05
138	Fred Lynn	.08
139	Jack Morris	.05
140	Matt Nokes	.05
141	Gary Pettis	.05
142	Ted Power	.05
143	Jeff Robinson	.05
144	Luis Salazar	.05
145	*Steve Searcy*	.10
146	Pat Sheridan	.05
147	Frank Tanana	.05
148	Alan Trammell	.10
149	Walt Terrell	.05
150	Jim Walewander	.05
151	Lou Whitaker	.05
152	Tim Birtsas	.05
153	Tom Browning	.05
154	*Keith Brown*	.05
155	*Norm Charlton*	.15
156	Dave Concepcion	.05
157	Kal Daniels	.05
158	Eric Davis	.10
159	Bo Diaz	.05
160	*Rob Dibble*	.20
161	Nick Esasky	.05
162	John Franco	.05
163	Danny Jackson	.05
164	Barry Larkin	.15
165	Rob Murphy	.05
166	Paul O'Neill	.15
167	Jeff Reed	.05
168	Jose Rijo	.05
169	Ron Robinson	.05
170	*Chris Sabo*	.15
171	*Candy Sierra*	.05
172	*Van Snider*	.05
173a	Jeff Treadway (blue "target" above head)	15.00
173b	Jeff Treadway (no "target")	.05
174	Frank Williams	.05
175	Herm Winningham	.05
176	Jim Adduci	.05
177	Don August	.05
178	Mike Birkbeck	.05
179	Chris Bosio	.05
180	Glenn Braggs	.05
181	Greg Brock	.05
182	Mark Clear	.05
183	Chuck Crim	.05
184	Rob Deer	.05
185	Tom Filer	.05
186	Jim Gantner	.05
187	*Darryl Hamilton*	.25
188	Ted Higuera	.05
189	Odell Jones	.05
190	Jeffrey Leonard	.05
191	Joey Meyer	.05
192	Paul Mirabella	.05
193	Paul Molitor	.30
194	Charlie O'Brien	.05
195	Dan Plesac	.05
196	*Gary Sheffield*	.75
197	B.J. Surhoff	.08
198	Dale Sveum	.05
199	Bill Wegman	.05
200	Robin Yount	.30
201	Rafael Belliard	.05
202	Barry Bonds	.50
203	Bobby Bonilla	.10
204	Sid Bream	.05
205	Benny Distefano	.05
206	Doug Drabek	.05
207	Mike Dunne	.05
208	Felix Fermin	.05
209	Brian Fisher	.05
210	Jim Gott	.05
211	Bob Kipper	.05
212	Dave LaPoint	.05
213	Mike LaValliere	.05
214	Jose Lind	.05
215	Junior Ortiz	.05
216	Vicente Palacios	.05
217	Tom Prince	.05
218	Gary Redus	.05
219	R.J. Reynolds	.05
220	Jeff Robinson	.05
221	John Smiley	.05
222	Andy Van Slyke	.05
223	Bob Walk	.05
224	Glenn Wilson	.05
225	Jesse Barfield	.05
226	George Bell	.05
227	*Pat Borders*	.15
228	John Cerutti	.05
229	Jim Clancy	.05
230	Mark Eichhorn	.05
231	Tony Fernandez	.05
232	Cecil Fielder	.15
233	Mike Flanagan	.05
234	Kelly Gruber	.05
235	Tom Henke	.05
236	Jimmy Key	.05
237	Rick Leach	.05
238	Manny Lee	.05
239	Nelson Liriano	.05
240	Fred McGriff	.20
241	Lloyd Moseby	.05
242	Rance Mulliniks	.05
243	Jeff Musselman	.05
244	Dave Stieb	.05
245	Todd Stottlemyre	.05
246	Duane Ward	.05
247	David Wells	.08
248	Ernie Whitt	.05
249	Luis Aguayo	.05
250a	Neil Allen (Home: Sarasota, FL)	.25
250b	Neil Allen (Home: Syosset, NY)	.05
251	John Candelaria	.05
252	Jack Clark	.05
253	Richard Dotson	.05
254	Rickey Henderson	.30
255	Tommy John	.10
256	Roberto Kelly	.05
257	Al Leiter	.08
258	Don Mattingly	.50
259	Dale Mohorcic	.05
260	*Hal Morris*	.25
261	Scott Nielsen	.05
262	Mike Pagliarulo	.05
263	*Hipolito Pena*	.05
264	Ken Phelps	.05
265	Willie Randolph	.05
266	Rick Rhoden	.05
267	Dave Righetti	.05
268	Rafael Santana	.05
269	Steve Shields	.05
270	Joel Skinner	.05
271	Don Slaught	.05
272	Claudell Washington	.05
273	Gary Ward	.05
274	Dave Winfield	.25
275	Luis Aquino	.05
276	Floyd Bannister	.05
277	George Brett	.35
278	Bill Buckner	.05
279	*Nick Capra*	.05
280	*Jose DeJesus*	.05
281	Steve Farr	.05
282	Jerry Gleaton	.05
283	Mark Gubicza	.05
284	*Tom Gordon*	.20
285	Bo Jackson	.20
286	Charlie Leibrandt	.05
287	*Mike Macfarlane*	.15
288	Jeff Montgomery	.08
289	Bill Pecota	.05
290	Jamie Quirk	.05
291	Bret Saberhagen	.08
292	Kevin Seitzer	.05
293	Kurt Stillwell	.05
294	Pat Tabler	.05
295	Danny Tartabull	.05
296	Gary Thurman	.05
297	Frank White	.05
298	Willie Wilson	.05
299	Roberto Alomar	.40
300	*Sandy Alomar, Jr.*	.40
301	Chris Brown	.05
302	Mike Brumley	.05
303	Mark Davis	.05
304	Mark Grant	.05
305	Tony Gwynn	.40
306	*Greg Harris*	.05
307	Andy Hawkins	.05
308	Jimmy Jones	.05
309	John Kruk	.05
310	Dave Leiper	.05
311	Carmelo Martinez	.05
312	Lance McCullers	.05
313	Keith Moreland	.05
314	Dennis Rasmussen	.05
315	Randy Ready	.05
316	Benito Santiago	.05
317	Eric Show	.05
318	Todd Simmons	.05
319	Garry Templeton	.05
320	Dickie Thon	.05
321	Ed Whitson	.05
322	Marvell Wynne	.05
323	Mike Aldrete	.05
324	Brett Butler	.08
325	Will Clark	.25
326	Kelly Downs	.05
327	Dave Dravecky	.05
328	Scott Garrelts	.05
329	Atlee Hammaker	.05
330	*Charlie Hayes*	.25
331	Mike Krukow	.05
332	Craig Lefferts	.05
333	Candy Maldonado	.05
334	Kirt Manwaring	.05
335	Bob Melvin	.05
336	Kevin Mitchell	.05
337	Donell Nixon	.05
338	*Tony Perezchica*	.05
339	Joe Price	.05
340	Rick Reuschel	.05
341	Earnest Riles	.05
342	Don Robinson	.05
343	Chris Speier	.05
344	Robby Thompson	.05
345	Jose Uribe	.05
346	Matt Williams	.25
347	*Trevor Wilson*	.15
348	Juan Agosto	.05
349	Larry Andersen	.05
350a	Alan Ashby ("Throws Rig")	.50
350b	Alan Ashby ("Throws Right")	.05
351	Kevin Bass	.05
352	Buddy Bell	.05
353	Craig Biggio	.30
354	Danny Darwin	.05
355	Glenn Davis	.05
356	Jim Deshaies	.05
357	Bill Doran	.05
358	*John Fishel*	.05
359	Billy Hatcher	.05
360	Bob Knepper	.05
361	*Louie Meadows*	.05
362	Dave Meads	.05
363	Jim Pankovits	.05
364	Terry Puhl	.05
365	Rafael Ramirez	.05
366	Craig Reynolds	.05
367	Mike Scott	.05
368	Nolan Ryan	.75
369	Dave Smith	.05
370	Gerald Young	.05
371	Hubie Brooks	.05
372	Tim Burke	.05
373	*John Dopson*	.10
374	Mike Fitzgerald	.05
375	Tom Foley	.05
376	Andres Galarraga	.15
377	Neal Heaton	.05
378	Joe Hesketh	.05
379	*Brian Holman*	.10
380	Rex Hudler	.05
381	*Randy Johnson*	1.50
382	Wallace Johnson	.05
383	Tracy Jones	.05
384	Dave Martinez	.05
385	Dennis Martinez	.08
386	Andy McGaffigan	.05
387	Otis Nixon	.05
388	*Johnny Paredes*	.05
389	Jeff Parrett	.05
390	Pascual Perez	.05
391	Tim Raines	.08
392	Luis Rivera	.05
393	*Nelson Santovenia*	.05
394	Bryn Smith	.05
395	Tim Wallach	.05
396	Andy Allanson	.05
397	*Rod Allen*	.05
398	Scott Bailes	.05
399	Tom Candiotti	.05
400	Joe Carter	.10
401	Carmen Castillo	.05
402	Dave Clark	.05
403	John Farrell	.05
404	Julio Franco	.08
405	Don Gordon	.05
406	Mel Hall	.05
407	Brad Havens	.05
408	Brook Jacoby	.05
409	Doug Jones	.05
410	*Jeff Kaiser*	.05
411	*Luis Medina*	.05
412	Cory Snyder	.05
413	Greg Swindell	.05
414	*Ron Tingley*	.05
415	Willie Upshaw	.05
416	Ron Washington	.05
417	Rich Yett	.05
418	Damon Berryhill	.05
419	Mike Bielecki	.05
420	*Doug Dascenzo*	.05
421	Jody Davis	.05
422	Andre Dawson	.15
423	Frank DiPino	.05
424	Shawon Dunston	.15
425	"Goose" Gossage	.08
426	Mark Grace	.30
427	*Mike Harkey*	.05
428	Darrin Jackson	.05
429	Les Lancaster	.05
430	Vance Law	.05
431	Greg Maddux	.65
432	Jamie Moyer	.05
433	Al Nipper	.05
434	Rafael Palmeiro	.25
435	Pat Perry	.05
436	*Jeff Pico*	.05
437	Ryne Sandberg	.40
438	Calvin Schiraldi	.05
439	Rick Sutcliffe	.05
440a	Manny Trillo ("Throws Rig")	1.50
440b	Manny Trillo ("Throws Right")	.05
441	*Gary Varsho*	.05
442	Mitch Webster	.05
443	*Luis Alicea*	.15
444	Tom Brunansky	.05
445	Vince Coleman	.05
446	*John Costello*	.05
447	Danny Cox	.05
448	Ken Dayley	.05
449	Jose DeLeon	.05
450	Curt Ford	.05
451	Pedro Guerrero	.05
452	Bob Horner	.05
453	*Tim Jones*	.05
454	Steve Lake	.05
455	Joe Magrane	.05
456	Greg Mathews	.05
457	Willie McGee	.08
458	Larry McWilliams	.05
459	Jose Oquendo	.05
460	Tony Pena	.05
461	Terry Pendleton	.05
462	*Steve Peters*	.05
463	Ozzie Smith	.35
464	Scott Terry	.05
465	Denny Walling	.05
466	Todd Worrell	.05
467	Tony Armas	.05
468	*Dante Bichette*	.50
469	Bob Boone	.05
470	*Terry Clark*	.05
471	Stew Cliburn	.05
472	*Mike Cook*	.05
473	*Sherman Corbett*	.05
474	Chili Davis	.08
475	Brian Downing	.05
476	Jim Eppard	.05
477	Chuck Finley	.05
478	Willie Fraser	.05
479	*Bryan Harvey*	.25
480	Jack Howell	.05
481	Wally Joyner	.08
482	Jack Lazorko	.05
483	Kirk McCaskill	.05
484	Mark McLemore	.05
485	Greg Minton	.05
486	Dan Petry	.05
487	Johnny Ray	.05
488	Dick Schofield	.05
489	Devon White	.08
490	Mike Witt	.05
491	Harold Baines	.08
492	Daryl Boston	.05
493	Ivan Calderon	.05
494	Mike Diaz	.05
495	Carlton Fisk	.15
496	*Dave Gallagher*	.05
497	Ozzie Guillen	.05
498	Shawn Hillegas	.05
499	Lance Johnson	.05
500	Barry Jones	.05
501	Bill Long	.05
502	Steve Lyons	.05
503	Fred Manrique	.05
504	Jack McDowell	.05
505	*Donn Pall*	.12
506	Kelly Paris	.05
507	Dan Pasqua	.05
508	*Ken Patterson*	.10
509	Melido Perez	.05
510	Jerry Reuss	.05
511	Mark Salas	.05
512	Bobby Thigpen	.05
513	Mike Woodard	.05
514	Bob Brower	.05
515	Steve Buechele	.05
516	*Jose Cecena*	.05
517	Cecil Espy	.05
518	Scott Fletcher	.05
519	Cecilio Guante	.05
520	Jose Guzman	.05
521	Ray Hayward	.05
522	Charlie Hough	.05
523	Pete Incaviglia	.05
524	Mike Jeffcoat	.05
525	Paul Kilgus	.05
526	*Chad Kreuter*	.15
527	Jeff Kunkel	.05
528	Oddibe McDowell	.05
529	Pete O'Brien	.05
530	Geno Petralli	.05
531	Jeff Russell	.05
532	Ruben Sierra	.05
533	Mike Stanley	.05
534	Ed Vande Berg	.05
535	Curtis Wilkerson	.05
536	Mitch Williams	.05
537	Bobby Witt	.05
538	Steve Balboni	.05
539	Scott Bankhead	.05
540	Scott Bradley	.05
541	Mickey Brantley	.05
542	Jay Buhner	.15
543	Mike Campbell	.05
544	Darnell Coles	.05
545	Henry Cotto	.05
546	Alvin Davis	.05
547	Mario Diaz	.05
548	*Ken Griffey, Jr.*	20.00
549	*Erik Hanson*	.15
550	Mike Jackson	.05
551	Mark Langston	.05
552	Edgar Martinez	.10
553	*Bill McGuire*	.05
554	Mike Moore	.05
555	Jim Presley	.05
556	Rey Quinones	.05
557	Jerry Reed	.05
558	Harold Reynolds	.05
559	*Mike Schooler*	.05
560	Bill Swift	.05
561	Dave Valle	.05
562	Steve Bedrosian	.05
563	Phil Bradley	.05
564	Don Carman	.05
565	Bob Dernier	.05
566	Marvin Freeman	.05
567	Todd Frohwirth	.05
568	Greg Gross	.05
569	Kevin Gross	.05
570	Greg Harris	.05
571	Von Hayes	.05
572	Chris James	.05
573	Steve Jeltz	.05
574	*Ron Jones*	.05
575	*Ricky Jordan*	.05
576	Mike Maddux	.05
577	David Palmer	.05
578	Lance Parrish	.08
579	Shane Rawley	.05
580	Bruce Ruffin	.05
581	Juan Samuel	.05
582	Mike Schmidt	.30
583	Kent Tekulve	.05
584	Milt Thompson	.05
585	*Jose Alvarez*	.05
586	Paul Assenmacher	.05
587	Bruce Benedict	.05
588	Jeff Blauser	.05
589	*Terry Blocker*	.05
590	Ron Gant	.15
591	Tom Glavine	.20
592	Tommy Gregg	.05
593	Albert Hall	.05
594	Dion James	.05
595	Rick Mahler	.05
596	Dale Murphy	.15
597	Gerald Perry	.05
598	Charlie Puleo	.05
599	Ted Simmons	.05
600	Pete Smith	.05
601	Zane Smith	.05
602	John Smoltz	.20
603	Bruce Sutter	.05
604	Andres Thomas	.05
605	Ozzie Virgil	.05
606	Brady Anderson	.30
607	Jeff Ballard	.05
608	*Jose Bautista*	.05
609	Ken Gerhart	.05
610	Terry Kennedy	.05
611	Eddie Murray	.30
612	Carl Nichols	.05

613 Tom Niedenfuer .05
614 Joe Orsulak .05
615 *Oswaldo Peraza* (Oswald)) .05
616a Bill Ripken (vulgarity on bat knob) 8.00
616b Bill Ripken (scribble over vulgarity) 8.00
616c Bill Ripken (black box over vulgarity) .10
616d Bill Ripken (vulgarity whited out) 30.00
617 Cal Ripken, Jr. .75
618 Dave Schmidt .05
619 Rick Schu .05
620 Larry Sheets .05
621 Doug Sisk .05
622 Pete Stanicek .05
623 Mickey Tettleton .05
624 Jay Tibbs .05
625 Jim Traber .05
626 Mark Williamson .05
627 *Craig Worthington* .10
628 Speed and Power (Jose Canseco) .25
629 Pitcher Perfect (Tom Browning) .05
630 Like Father Like Sons (Roberto Alomar, Sandy Alomar, Jr.) .25
631 N.L. All-Stars (Will Clark, Rafael Palmeiro) .20
632 Homeruns Coast to Coast (Will Clark, Darryl Strawberry) .25
633 Hot Corner's Hot Hitters (Wade Boggs, Carney Lansford) .10
634 Triple A's (Jose Canseco, Mark McGwire, Terry Steinbach) .75
635 Dual Heat (Mark Davis, Dwight Gooden) .10
636 N.L. Pitching Power (David Cone, Danny Jackson) .05
637 Cannon Arms (Bobby Bonilla, Chris Sabo) .10
638 Double Trouble (Andres Galarraga, Gerald Perry) .10
639 Power Center (Eric Davis) .10
640 Major League Prospects (*Cameron Drew*), (*Steve Wilson*) .05
641 Major League Prospects (Kevin Brown), (*Kevin Reimer*) .30
642 Major League Prospects (*Jerald Clark*), (*Brad Pounders*) .08
643 Major League Prospects (*Mike Capel*), (*Drew Hall*) .05
644 Major League Prospects (*Joe Girardi*), (*Rolando Roomes*) .20
645 Major League Prospects (*Marty Brown*), (*Lenny Harris*) .12
646 Major League Prospects (*Luis de los Santos*), (*Jim Campbell*) .05
647 Major League Prospects (*Miguel Garcia*), (*Randy Kramer*) .05
648 Major League Prospects (*Torey Lovullo*), (*Robert Palacios*) .08
649 Major League Prospects (*Jim Corsi*), (*Bob Milacki*) .12
650 Major League Prospects (*Grady Hall*), (*Mike Rochford*) .05
651 Major League Prospects (*Vance Lovelace*), (*Terry Taylor*) .05
652 Major League Prospects (*Dennis Cook*), (*Ken Hill*) .25
653 Major League Prospects (*Scott Service*), (*Shane Turner*) .08
654 Checklist 1-101 .05
655 Checklist 102-200 .05
656 Checklist 201-298 .05
657 Checklist 299-395 .05
658 Checklist 396-490 .05
659 Checklist 491-584 .05
660 Checklist 585-660 .05

1989 Fleer All-Stars

This special 12-card set represents Fleer's choices for its 1989 Major League All-Star Team. For the fourth consecutive year, Fleer inserted the special cards randomly inside its regular 1989 wax and cello packs. The cards feature two player photos set against a green background with the "1989 Fleer All Star Team" logo bannered across the top, and the player's name, position and team in the lower left corner. The backs contain a narrative player profile.

		MT
Complete Set (12):		8.00
Common Player:		.50
1	Bobby Bonilla	.60
2	Jose Canseco	1.50
3	Will Clark	1.00
4	Dennis Eckersley	.50
5	Julio Franco	.50
6	Mike Greenwell	.50
7	Orel Hershiser	.50
8	Paul Molitor	2.00
9	Mike Scioscia	.50
10	Darryl Strawberry	.60
11	Alan Trammell	.50
12	Frank Viola	.50

1989 Fleer For The Record

Fleer's "For the Record" set features six players and their achievements from 1988. Fronts of the standard 2-1/2" x 3-1/2" cards feature a photo of the player set against a red scoreboard background. Card backs are grey and describe individual accomplishments. The cards were distributed randomly in rack packs.

		MT
Complete Set (6):		5.00
Common Player:		.50
1	Wade Boggs	1.00
2	Roger Clemens	1.50
3	Andres Galarraga	.75
4	Kirk Gibson	.50
5	Greg Maddux	2.00
6	Don Mattingly	1.50

1989 Fleer World Series

This 12-card set, which depicts highlights of the 1988 World Series, was included as a special sub-set with the regular and glossy factory-collated Fleer set. It was not available as individual cards in wax packs, cello packs or any other form.

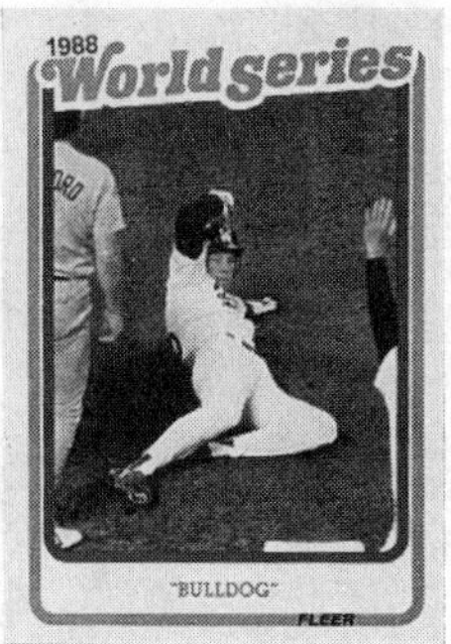

		MT
Complete Set, Regular (12):		1.50
Complete Set, Glossy (12):		1.00
Common Card:		.15
1	Dodgers Secret Weapon (Mickey Hatcher)	.15
2	Rookie Starts Series (Tim Belcher)	.15
3	Jose Canseco	.40
4	Dramatic Comeback (Mike Scioscia)	.15
5	Kirk Gibson	.30
6	Orel Hershiser	.30
7	One Swings, Three RBIs (Mike Marshall)	.15
8	Mark McGwire	.75
9	Sax's Speed Wins Game 4 (Steve Sax)	.15
10	Series Caps Award Winning Year (Walt Weiss)	.15
11	Orel Hershiser	.25
12	Dodger Blue, World Champs	.25

1989 Fleer Box Panels

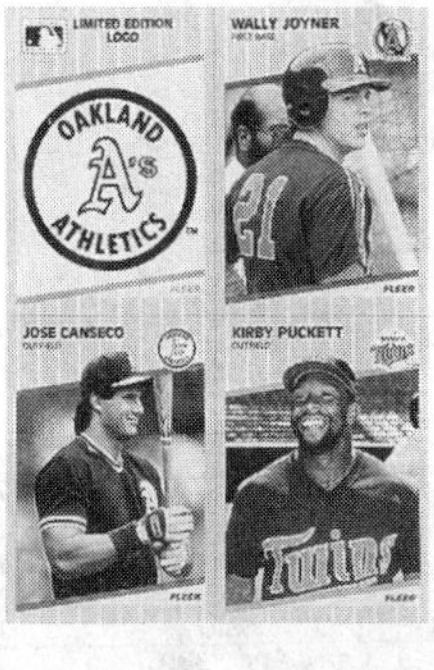

For the fourth consecutive year, Fleer issued a series of cards on the bottom panels of its regular 1989 wax pack boxes. The 28-card set includes 20 players and eight team logo cards, all designed in the identical style of the regular 1989 Fleer set. The box-bottom cards were randomly printed, four cards (three player cards and one team logo) on each bottom panel. The cards are numbered from C-1 to C-28.

		MT
Complete Panel Set (7):		6.00
Complete Singles Set (28):		3.00
Common Single Player:		.15
1	Mets Logo	.05
2	Wade Boggs	.45
3	George Brett	.50
4	Jose Canseco	.50
5	A's Logo	.05
6	Will Clark	.35
7	David Cone	.15
8	Andres Galarraga	.20
9	Dodgers Logo	.05
10	Kirk Gibson	.15
11	Mike Greenwell	.10
12	Tony Gwynn	.75
13	Tigers Logo	.05
14	Orel Hershiser	.15
15	Danny Jackson	.10
16	Wally Joyner	.15
17	Red Sox Logo	.05
18	Yankees Logo	.05
19	Fred McGriff	.25
20	Kirby Puckett	.50
21	Chris Sabo	.15
22	Kevin Seitzer	.10
23	Pirates logo	.05
24	Astros logo	.05
25	Darryl Strawberry	.20
26	Alan Trammell	.20
27	Andy Van Slyke	.10
28	Frank Viola	.10

1989 Fleer Glossy Tin

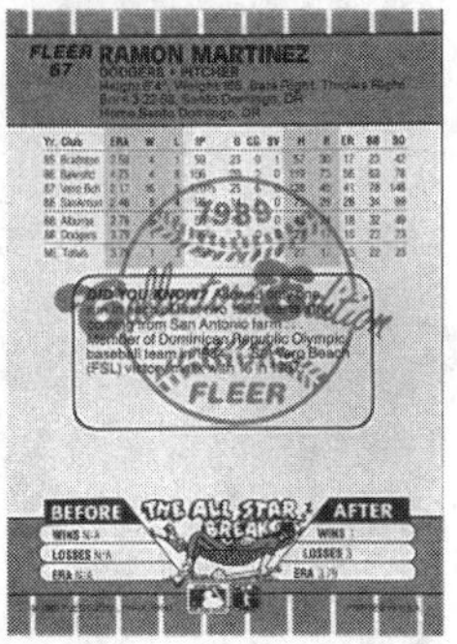

The last of the limited-edition, collector-version glossy tin sets is estimated to have been produced in an edition of 30,000-60,000, creating a significant premium over their counterparts in the regular Fleer set. The issue was sold only in complete-set form in a lithographed metal box. The 1989 glossies differ from the regular cards on back in the use of blue, rather than yellow ink, and the appearance at center of a large baseball logo with 1989 / Collector's Edition / Fleer at center. No glossy version of the '89 Update set was made. Fleer glossy sets were originally wholesaled at $40 each.

	MT
Complete Set, Unopened (672):	250.00
Complete Set (672):	80.00
Common Player:	.25
(Star cards valued at 3X-5X regular 1989 Fleer cards.)	

1989 Fleer Update

Fleer produced its sixth consecutive "Update" set in 1989 to supplement the company's regular set. As in the past, the set consisted of 132 cards (numbered U-1 through U-132) that were sold by hobby dealers in special collector's boxes.

		MT
Complete Set (132):		8.00
Common Player:		.06
1	Phil Bradley	.06
2	Mike Devereaux	.06
3	Steve Finley	.30
4	Kevin Hickey	.06
5	Brian Holton	.06
6	Bob Milacki	.06
7	Randy Milligan	.06
8	John Dopson	.06
9	Nick Esasky	.06
10	Rob Murphy	.06
11	Jim Abbott	.20
12	Bert Blyleven	.06
13	Jeff Manto	.06
14	Bob McClure	.06
15	Lance Parrish	.08
16	Lee Stevens	.06
17	Claudell Washington	.06
18	Mark Davis	.06
19	Eric King	.06
20	Ron Kittle	.06
21	Matt Merullo	.06
22	Steve Rosenberg	.06
23	Robin Ventura	.40
24	Keith Atherton	.06
25	*Joey (Albert) Belle*	4.00
26	Jerry Browne	.06
27	Felix Fermin	.06
28	Brad Komminsk	.06
29	Pete O'Brien	.06
30	Mike Brumley	.06
31	Tracy Jones	.06
32	Mike Schwabe	.06
33	Gary Ward	.06
34	Frank Williams	.06
35	*Kevin Appier*	.40
36	Bob Boone	.06
37	Luis de los Santos	.06
38	Jim Eisenreich	.06
39	*Jaime Navarro*	.20
40	Bill Spiers	.06
41	*Greg Vaughn*	1.50
42	Randy Veres	.06
43	Wally Backman	.06
44	Shane Rawley	.06
45	Steve Balboni	.06
46	Jesse Barfield	.06
47	Alvaro Espinoza	.06
48	Bob Geren	.06
49	Mel Hall	.06
50	Andy Hawkins	.06
51	Hensley Meulens	.06
52	Steve Sax	.06
53	*Deion Sanders*	.75
54	Rickey Henderson	.25
55	Mike Moore	.06
56	Tony Phillips	.10
57	Greg Briley	.06
58	Gene Harris	.06
59	Randy Johnson	.75
60	Jeffrey Leonard	.06
61	Dennis Powell	.06
62	Omar Vizquel	.30
63	Kevin Brown	.10
64	Julio Franco	.08
65	Jamie Moyer	.06
66	Rafael Palmeiro	.25
67	Nolan Ryan	1.00
68	Francisco Cabrera	.06
69	Junior Felix	.06
70	Al Leiter	.08
71	Alex Sanchez	.06
72	Geronimo Berroa	.10
73	Derek Lilliquist	.06
74	Lonnie Smith	.06
75	Jeff Treadway	.06
76	Paul Kilgus	.06
77	Lloyd McClendon	.06
78	Scott Sanderson	.06
79	Dwight Smith	.06
80	Jerome Walton	.06
81	Mitch Williams	.06
82	Steve Wilson	.06
83	Todd Benzinger	.06
84	Ken Griffey	.08
85	Rick Mahler	.06
86	Rolando Roomes	.06
87	Scott Scudder	.06
88	Jim Clancy	.06
89	Rick Rhoden	.06
90	Dan Schatzeder	.06
91	Mike Morgan	.06
92	Eddie Murray	.25
93	Willie Randolph	.06
94	Ray Searage	.06
95	Mike Aldrete	.06
96	Kevin Gross	.06
97	Mark Langston	.06
98	Spike Owen	.06
99	Zane Smith	.06
100	Don Aase	.06
101	Barry Lyons	.06
102	Juan Samuel	.06
103	Wally Whitehurst	.06
104	Dennis Cook	.06
105	Len Dykstra	.08
106	Charlie Hayes	.15
107	Tommy Herr	.06
108	Ken Howell	.06
109	John Kruk	.06
110	Roger McDowell	.06
111	Terry Mulholland	.10
112	Jeff Parrett	.06
113	Neal Heaton	.06
114	Jeff King	.10
115	Randy Kramer	.06
116	Bill Landrum	.06
117	Cris Carpenter	.06
118	Frank DiPino	.06
119	Ken Hill	.15

120	Dan Quisenberry	.06
121	Milt Thompson	.06
122	*Todd Zeile*	.25
123	Jack Clark	.06
124	Bruce Hurst	.06
125	Mark Parent	.06
126	Bip Roberts	.06
127	Jeff Brantley	.15
128	Terry Kennedy	.06
129	Mike LaCoss	.06
130	Greg Litton	.06
131	Mike Schmidt	.50
132	Checklist	.06

1989 Fleer Baseball All Stars

This specially-boxed set was produced by Fleer for the Ben Franklin store chain. The full-color player photos are surrounded by a border of pink and yellow vertical bands. "Fleer Baseball All-Stars" appears along the top in red, white and blue. The set was sold in a box with a checklist on the back.

		MT
Complete Set (44):		3.00
Common Player:		.05
1	Doyle Alexander	.05
2	George Bell	.05
3	Wade Boggs	.60
4	Bobby Bonilla	.10
5	Jose Canseco	.50
6	Will Clark	.40
7	Roger Clemens	1.00
8	Vince Coleman	.05
9	David Cone	.08
10	Mark Davis	.05
11	Andre Dawson	.15
12	Dennis Eckersley	.08
13	Andres Galarraga	.15
14	Kirk Gibson	.05
15	Dwight Gooden	.10
16	Mike Greenwell	.05
17	Mark Gubicza	.05
18	Ozzie Guillen	.05
19	Tony Gwynn	.75
20	Rickey Henderson	.40
21	Orel Hershiser	.10
22	Danny Jackson	.05
23	Doug Jones	.05
24	Ricky Jordan	.05
25	Bob Knepper	.05
26	Barry Larkin	.20
27	Vance Law	.05
28	Don Mattingly	.75
29	Mark McGwire	2.00
30	Paul Molitor	.50
31	Gerald Perry	.05
32	Kirby Puckett	.65
33	Johnny Ray	.05
34	Harold Reynolds	.05
35	Cal Ripken, Jr.	1.00
36	Don Robinson	.05
37	Ruben Sierra	.05
38	Dave Smith	.05
39	Darryl Strawberry	.15
40	Dave Steib	.05
41	Alan Trammell	.08
42	Andy Van Slyke	.05
43	Frank Viola	.05
44	Dave Winfield	.30

1989 Fleer Exciting Stars

Sold exclusively in Cumberland Farm stores, this boxed set pictures the game's top stars. The card fronts feature a color player photo surrounded by a blue border with "Baseball's Exciting Stars" along the top. The cards were numbered alphabetically and packed in a special box with a complete checklist on the back.

		MT
Complete Set (44):		3.00
Common Player:		.05
1	Harold Baines	.05
2	Wade Boggs	.65
3	Jose Canseco	.65
4	Joe Carter	.08
5	Will Clark	.50
6	Roger Clemens	1.00
7	Vince Coleman	.05
8	David Cone	.08
9	Eric Davis	.10
10	Glenn Davis	.05
11	Andre Dawson	.10
12	Dwight Evans	.05
13	Andres Galarraga	.10
14	Kirk Gibson	.05
15	Dwight Gooden	.10
16	Jim Gott	.05
17	Mark Grace	.25
18	Mike Greenwell	.05
19	Mark Gubicza	.05
20	Tony Gwynn	.75
21	Rickey Henderson	.40
22	Tom Henke	.05
23	Mike Henneman	.05
24	Orel Hershiser	.10
25	Danny Jackson	.05
26	Gregg Jefferies	.10
27	Ricky Jordan	.05
28	Wally Joyner	.08
29	Mark Langston	.05
30	Tim Leary	.05
31	Don Mattingly	.90
32	Mark McGwire	2.00
33	Dale Murphy	.10
34	Kirby Puckett	.75
35	Chris Sabo	.05
36	Kevin Seitzer	.05
37	Ruben Sierra	.05
38	Ozzie Smith	.50
39	Dave Stewart	.08
40	Darryl Strawberry	.10
41	Alan Trammell	.08
42	Frank Viola	.05
43	Dave Winfield	.40
44	Robin Yount	.50

1989 Fleer Heroes of Baseball

This boxed set was produced by Fleer for the Woolworth store chain. The fronts of the cards are designed in a red and blue color scheme and feature full-color photos that fade into a soft focus on all edges. The set is numbered alphabetically and was packaged in a special box with a checklist on the back.

		MT
Complete Set (44):		4.00
Common Player:		.05
1	George Bell	.05
2	Wade Boggs	.65
3	Barry Bonds	1.00
4	Tom Brunansky	.05
5	Jose Canseco	.75
6	Joe Carter	.08
7	Will Clark	.45
8	Roger Clemens	1.00
9	David Cone	.08
10	Eric Davis	.10
11	Glenn Davis	.05
12	Andre Dawson	.10
13	Dennis Eckersley	.08
14	John Franco	.05
15	Gary Gaetti	.05
16	Andres Galarraga	.10
17	Kirk Gibson	.05
18	Dwight Gooden	.10
19	Mike Greenwell	.05
20	Tony Gwynn	.75
21	Bryan Harvey	.05
22	Orel Hershiser	.08
23	Ted Higuera	.05
24	Danny Jackson	.05
25	Ricky Jordan	.05
26	Don Mattingly	.90
27	Fred McGriff	.20
28	Mark McGwire	2.00
29	Kevin McReynolds	.05
30	Gerald Perry	.05
31	Kirby Puckett	.85
32	Johnny Ray	.05
33	Harold Reynolds	.05
34	Cal Ripken, Jr.	2.00
35	Ryne Sandberg	.65
36	Kevin Seitzer	.05
37	Ruben Sierra	.05
38	Darryl Strawberry	.10
39	Bobby Thigpen	.05
40	Alan Trammell	.08
41	Andy Van Slyke	.05
42	Frank Viola	.05
43	Dave Winfield	.50
44	Robin Yount	.50

1989 Fleer League Leaders

Another of the various small, boxed sets issued by Fleer, "League Leaders" was produced for Walgreen stores. The standard-size cards feature color photos on the front surrounded by a red border with "Fleer League Leaders" across the top. The backs include player stats and data and the team logo. The cards are numbered alphabetically and packaged in a special box that includes the full checklist on the back.

		MT
Complete Set (44):		3.00
Common Player:		.05
1	Allan Anderson	.05
2	Wade Boggs	.70
3	Jose Canseco	.70
4	Will Clark	.50
5	Roger Clemens	1.00
6	Vince Coleman	.05
7	David Cone	.08
8	Kal Daniels	.05
9	Chili Davis	.08
10	Eric Davis	.10
11	Glenn Davis	.05
12	Andre Dawson	.12
13	John Franco	.05
14	Andres Galarraga	.12
15	Kirk Gibson	.05
16	Dwight Gooden	.10
17	Mark Grace	.50
18	Mike Greenwell	.05
19	Tony Gwynn	.75
20	Orel Hershiser	.10
21	Pete Incaviglia	.05
22	Danny Jackson	.05
23	Gregg Jefferies	.15
24	Joe Magrane	.05
25	Don Mattingly	.90
26	Fred McGriff	.20
27	Mark McGwire	2.00
28	Dale Murphy	.10
29	Dan Plesac	.05
30	Kirby Puckett	.80
31	Harold Reynolds	.05
32	Cal Ripken, Jr.	2.00
33	Jeff Robinson	.05
34	Mike Scott	.05
35	Ozzie Smith	.50
36	Dave Stewart	.05
37	Darryl Strawberry	.10
38	Greg Swindell	.05
39	Bobby Thigpen	.05
40	Alan Trammell	.08
41	Andy Van Slyke	.05
42	Frank Viola	.05
43	Dave Winfield	.40
44	Robin Yount	.50

1989 Fleer MVP

Filled with superstars, this boxed set was produced by Fleer in 1989 for the Toys "R" Us chain. The fronts of the cards are designed in a yellow and green color scheme and include a "Fleer Baseball MVP" logo above the color player photo. The backs are printed in shades of green and yellow and include biographical notes and stats. The set was issued in a special box with a checklist on the back.

		MT
Complete Set (44):		4.00
Common Player:		.05
1	Steve Bedrosian	.05
2	George Bell	.05
3	Wade Boggs	.65
4	George Brett	.75
5	Hubie Brooks	.05
6	Jose Canseco	.65
7	Will Clark	.45
8	Roger Clemens	1.00
9	Eric Davis	.10
10	Glenn Davis	.05
11	Andre Dawson	.10
12	Andres Galarraga	.12
13	Kirk Gibson	.05
14	Dwight Gooden	.10
15	Mark Grace	.25
16	Mike Greenwell	.05
17	Tony Gwynn	.75
18	Bryan Harvey	.05
19	Orel Hershiser	.08
20	Ted Higuera	.05
21	Danny Jackson	.05
22	Mike Jackson	.05
23	Doug Jones	.05
24	Greg Maddux	.75
25	Mike Marshall	.05
26	Don Mattingly	.90
27	Fred McGriff	.20
28	Mark McGwire	2.00
29	Kevin McReynolds	.05
30	Jack Morris	.05
31	Gerald Perry	.05
32	Kirby Puckett	.75
33	Chris Sabo	.05
34	Mike Scott	.05
35	Ruben Sierra	.05
36	Darryl Strawberry	.10
37	Danny Tartabull	.05
38	Bobby Thigpen	.05
39	Alan Trammell	.08
40	Andy Van Slyke	.05
41	Frank Viola	.05
42	Walt Weiss	.05
43	Dave Winfield	.45
44	Todd Worrell	.05

Player names in *Italic* type indicate a rookie card.

1989 Fleer Superstars

This boxed set was produced by Fleer for the McCrory store chain. The cards are standard 2-1/2" x 3-1/2" and the full-color player photos are outlined in red with a tan-and-white striped border. The backs carry yellow and white stripes and include the Fleer "SuperStars" logo, player stats and biographical information. The cards are numbered alphabetically and packaged in a special box that includes a checklist on the back.

		MT
Complete Set (44):		4.00
Common Player:		.05
1	Roberto Alomar	.45
2	Harold Baines	.08
3	Tim Belcher	.05
4	Wade Boggs	.60
5	George Brett	.70
6	Jose Canseco	.65
7	Gary Carter	.10
8	Will Clark	.50
9	Roger Clemens	.90
10	Kal Daniels	.05
11	Eric Davis	.10
12	Andre Dawson	.12
13	Tony Fernandez	.05
14	Scott Fletcher	.05
15	Andres Galarraga	.15
16	Kirk Gibson	.05
17	Dwight Gooden	.15
18	Jim Gott	.05
19	Mark Grace	.25
20	Mike Greenwell	.05
21	Tony Gwynn	.75
22	Rickey Henderson	.35
23	Orel Hershiser	.08
24	Ted Higuera	.05
25	Gregg Jefferies	.15
26	Wally Joyner	.08
27	Mark Langston	.05
28	Greg Maddux	1.00
29	Don Mattingly	1.00
30	Fred McGriff	.20
31	Mark McGwire	2.00
32	Dan Plesac	.05
33	Kirby Puckett	.75
34	Jeff Reardon	.05
35	Chris Sabo	.05
36	Mike Schmidt	.60
37	Mike Scott	.05
38	Cory Snyder	.05
39	Darryl Strawberry	.15
40	Alan Trammell	.08
41	Frank Viola	.05
42	Walt Weiss	.05
43	Dave Winfield	.40
44	Todd Worrell	.05

1990 Fleer

Fleer's 1990 set, its 10th annual baseball card offering, again consisted of 660 cards numbered by team. The front of the cards feature mostly action photos surrounded by one of several different color bands and a white border. The set includes various special cards, including a series of "Major League Prospects," Players of the Decade, team checklist cards and a series of multi-player cards. The backs include complete career stats, player data, and a special "Vital Signs" section showing on-base percentage, slugging percentage, etc. for batters; and strikeout and walk ratios, opposing batting averages, etc. for pitchers.

		MT
Complete Set (660):		10.00
Common Player:		.05
Wax Box:		10.00
1	Lance Blankenship	.05
2	Todd Burns	.05
3	Jose Canseco	.25
4	Jim Corsi	.05
5	Storm Davis	.05
6	Dennis Eckersley	.10
7	Mike Gallego	.05
8	Ron Hassey	.05
9	Dave Henderson	.05
10	Rickey Henderson	.25
11	Rick Honeycutt	.05
12	Stan Javier	.05
13	Felix Jose	.05
14	Carney Lansford	.05
15	Mark McGwire	1.00
16	Mike Moore	.05
17	Gene Nelson	.05
18	Dave Parker	.08
19	Tony Phillips	.05
20	Terry Steinbach	.05
21	Dave Stewart	.08
22	Walt Weiss	.08
23	Bob Welch	.05
24	Curt Young	.05
25	Paul Assenmacher	.05
26	Damon Berryhill	.05
27	Mike Bielecki	.05
28	Kevin Blankenship	.05
29	Andre Dawson	.12
30	Shawon Dunston	.08
31	Joe Girardi	.08
32	Mark Grace	.25
33	Mike Harkey	.05
34	Paul Kilgus	.05
35	Les Lancaster	.05
36	Vance Law	.05
37	Greg Maddux	.60
38	Lloyd McClendon	.05
39	Jeff Pico	.05
40	Ryne Sandberg	.30
41	Scott Sanderson	.05
42	Dwight Smith	.05
43	Rick Sutcliffe	.05
44	*Jerome Walton*	.05
45	Mitch Webster	.05
46	Curt Wilkerson	.05
47	*Dean Wilkins*	.05
48	Mitch Williams	.05
49	Steve Wilson	.05
50	Steve Bedrosian	.05
51	*Mike Benjamin*	.08
52	*Jeff Brantley*	.10
53	Brett Butler	.08
54	Will Clark	.25
55	Kelly Downs	.05
56	Scott Garrelts	.05
57	Atlee Hammaker	.05
58	Terry Kennedy	.05
59	Mike LaCoss	.05
60	Craig Lefferts	.05
61	*Greg Litton*	.05
62	Candy Maldonado	.05
63	Kirt Manwaring	.05
64	*Randy McCament*	.05
65	Kevin Mitchell	.05
66	Donell Nixon	.05
67	Ken Oberkfell	.05
68	Rick Reuschel	.05
69	Ernest Riles	.05
70	Don Robinson	.05
71	Pat Sheridan	.05
72	Chris Speier	.05
73	Robby Thompson	.05
74	Jose Uribe	.05
75	Matt Williams	.25
76	George Bell	.05
77	Pat Borders	.05
78	John Cerutti	.05
79	*Junior Felix*	.05
80	Tony Fernandez	.05
81	Mike Flanagan	.05
82	*Mauro Gozzo*	.05
83	Kelly Gruber	.05
84	Tom Henke	.05
85	Jimmy Key	.08
86	Manny Lee	.05
87	Nelson Liriano	.05
88	Lee Mazzilli	.05
89	Fred McGriff	.20
90	Lloyd Moseby	.05
91	Rance Mulliniks	.05
92	Alex Sanchez	.05
93	Dave Steib	.05
94	Todd Stottlemyre	.05
95	Duane Ward	.05
96	David Wells	.08
97	Ernie Whitt	.05
98	Frank Wills	.05
99	Mookie Wilson	.05
100	*Kevin Appier*	.25
101	Luis Aquino	.05
102	Bob Boone	.05
103	George Brett	.30
104	Jose DeJesus	.05
105	Luis de los Santos	.05
106	Jim Eisenreich	.05
107	Steve Farr	.05
108	Tom Gordon	.05
109	Mark Gubicza	.05
110	Bo Jackson	.20
111	Terry Leach	.05
112	Charlie Leibrandt	.05
113	*Rick Luecken*	.05
114	Mike Macfarlane	.05
115	Jeff Montgomery	.05
116	Bret Saberhagen	.08
117	Kevin Seitzer	.05
118	Kurt Stillwell	.05
119	Pat Tabler	.05
120	Danny Tartabull	.05
121	Gary Thurman	.05
122	Frank White	.05
123	Willie Wilson	.05
124	*Matt Winters*	.05
125	Jim Abbott	.08
126	Tony Armas	.05
127	Dante Bichette	.20
128	Bert Blyleven	.05
129	Chili Davis	.08
130	Brian Downing	.05
131	*Mike Fetters*	.08
132	Chuck Finley	.05
133	Willie Fraser	.05
134	Bryan Harvey	.05
135	Jack Howell	.05
136	Wally Joyner	.10
137	*Jeff Manto*	.08
138	Kirk McCaskill	.05
139	Bob McClure	.05
140	Greg Minton	.05
141	Lance Parrish	.05
142	Dan Petry	.05
143	Johnny Ray	.05
144	Dick Schofield	.05
145	*Lee Stevens*	.08
146	Claudell Washington	.05
147	Devon White	.08
148	Mike Witt	.05
149	Roberto Alomar	.25
150	Sandy Alomar, Jr.	.12
151	Andy Benes	.20
152	Jack Clark	.05
153	Pat Clements	.05
154	Joey Cora	.05
155	Mark Davis	.05
156	Mark Grant	.05
157	Tony Gwynn	.40
158	Greg Harris	.05
159	Bruce Hurst	.05
160	Darrin Jackson	.05
161	Chris James	.05
162	Carmelo Martinez	.05
163	Mike Pagliarulo	.05
164	Mark Parent	.05
165	Dennis Rasmussen	.05
166	Bip Roberts	.05
167	Benito Santiago	.05
168	Calvin Schiraldi	.05
169	Eric Show	.05
170	Garry Templeton	.05
171	Ed Whitson	.05
172	Brady Anderson	.12
173	Jeff Ballard	.05
174	Phil Bradley	.05
175	Mike Devereaux	.05
176	*Steve Finley*	.10
177	Pete Harnisch	.10
178	Kevin Hickey	.05
179	Brian Holton	.05
180	*Ben McDonald*	.25
181	Bob Melvin	.05
182	Bob Milacki	.05
183	Randy Milligan	.05
184	Gregg Olson	.05
185	Joe Orsulak	.05
186	Bill Ripken	.05
187	Cal Ripken, Jr.	.60
188	Dave Schmidt	.05
189	Larry Sheets	.05
190	Mickey Tettleton	.05
191	Mark Thurmond	.05
192	Jay Tibbs	.05
193	Jim Traber	.05
194	Mark Williamson	.05
195	Craig Worthington	.05
196	Don Aase	.05
197	*Blaine Beatty*	.05
198	Mark Carreon	.05
199	Gary Carter	.10
200	David Cone	.08
201	Ron Darling	.05
202	Kevin Elster	.05
203	Sid Fernandez	.05
204	Dwight Gooden	.10
205	Keith Hernandez	.05
206	*Jeff Innis*	.05
207	Gregg Jefferies	.12
208	Howard Johnson	.05
209	Barry Lyons	.05
210	Dave Magadan	.05
211	Kevin McReynolds	.05
212	Jeff Musselman	.05
213	Randy Myers	.05
214	Bob Ojeda	.05
215	Juan Samuel	.05
216	Mackey Sasser	.05
217	Darryl Strawberry	.08
218	Tim Teufel	.05
219	Frank Viola	.05
220	Juan Agosto	.05
221	Larry Anderson	.05
222	*Eric Anthony*	.15
223	Kevin Bass	.05
224	Craig Biggio	.15
225	Ken Caminiti	.15
226	Jim Clancy	.05
227	Danny Darwin	.05
228	Glenn Davis	.05
229	Jim Deshaies	.05
230	Bill Doran	.05
231	Bob Forsch	.05
232	Brian Meyer	.05
233	Terry Puhl	.05
234	Rafael Ramirez	.05
235	Rick Rhoden	.05
236	Dan Schatzeder	.05
237	Mike Scott	.05
238	Dave Smith	.05
239	Alex Trevino	.05
240	Glenn Wilson	.05
241	Gerald Young	.05
242	Tom Brunansky	.05
243	Cris Carpenter	.05
244	*Alex Cole*	.05
245	Vince Coleman	.05
246	John Costello	.05
247	Ken Dayley	.05
248	Jose DeLeon	.05
249	Frank DiPino	.05
250	Pedro Guerrero	.05
251	Ken Hill	.05
252	Joe Magrane	.05
253	Willie McGee	.08
254	John Morris	.05
255	Jose Oquendo	.05
256	Tony Pena	.05
257	Terry Pendleton	.05
258	Ted Power	.05
259	Dan Quisenberry	.05
260	Ozzie Smith	.25
261	Scott Terry	.05
262	Milt Thompson	.05
263	Denny Walling	.05
264	Todd Worrell	.05
265	*Todd Zeile*	.15
266	Marty Barrett	.05
267	Mike Boddicker	.05
268	Wade Boggs	.35
269	Ellis Burks	.05
270	Rick Cerone	.05
271	Roger Clemens	.50
272	John Dopson	.05
273	Nick Esasky	.05
274	Dwight Evans	.05
275	Wes Gardner	.05
276	Rich Gedman	.05
277	Mike Greenwell	.05
278	Danny Heep	.05
279	Eric Hetzel	.05
280	Dennis Lamp	.05
281	Rob Murphy	.05
282	Joe Price	.05
283	Carlos Quintana	.05
284	Jody Reed	.05
285	Luis Rivera	.05
286	Kevin Romine	.05
287	Lee Smith	.08
288	Mike Smithson	.05
289	Bob Stanley	.05
290	Harold Baines	.08
291	Kevin Brown	.10
292	Steve Buechele	.05
293	*Scott Coolbaugh*	.05
294	*Jack Daugherty*	.05
295	Cecil Espy	.05
296	Julio Franco	.05
297	*Juan Gonzalez*	3.00
298	Cecilio Guante	.05
299	Drew Hall	.05
300	Charlie Hough	.05
301	Pete Incaviglia	.05
302	Mike Jeffcoat	.05
303	Chad Kreuter	.05
304	Jeff Kunkel	.05
305	Rick Leach	.05
306	Fred Manrique	.05
307	Jamie Moyer	.05
308	Rafael Palmeiro	.15
309	Geno Petralli	.05
310	Kevin Reimer	.05
311	*Kenny Rogers*	.15
312	Jeff Russell	.05
313	Nolan Ryan	.60
314	Ruben Sierra	.05
315	Bobby Witt	.05
316	Chris Bosio	.05
317	Glenn Braggs	.05
318	Greg Brock	.05
319	Chuck Crim	.05
320	Rob Deer	.05
321	Mike Felder	.05
322	Tom Filer	.05
323	*Tony Fossas*	.05
324	Jim Gantner	.05
325	Darryl Hamilton	.05
326	Ted Higuera	.05
327	Mark Knudson	.05
328	Bill Krueger	.05
329	*Tim McIntosh*	.05
330	Paul Molitor	.30
331	*Jaime Navarro*	.15
332	Charlie O'Brien	.05
333	*Jeff Peterek*	.05
334	Dan Plesac	.05
335	Jerry Reuss	.05
336	Gary Sheffield	.25
337	*Bill Spiers*	.05
338	B.J. Surhoff	.08
339	Greg Vaughn	.20
340	Robin Yount	.30
341	Hubie Brooks	.05
342	Tim Burke	.05
343	Mike Fitzgerald	.05
344	Tom Foley	.05
345	Andres Galarraga	.15
346	Damaso Garcia	.05
347	*Marquis Grissom*	.50
348	Kevin Gross	.05
349	Joe Hesketh	.05
350	*Jeff Huson*	.10
351	Wallace Johnson	.05
352	Mark Langston	.05
353	Dave Martinez	.05
354	Dennis Martinez	.08
355	Andy McGaffigan	.05
356	Otis Nixon	.05
357	Spike Owen	.05
358	Pascual Perez	.05
359	Tim Raines	.10
360	Nelson Santovenia	.05
361	Bryn Smith	.05
362	Zane Smith	.05
363	*Larry Walker*	1.25
364	Tim Wallach	.05
365	Rick Aguilera	.05
366	Allan Anderson	.05
367	Wally Backman	.05
368	Doug Baker	.05
369	Juan Berenguer	.05
370	Randy Bush	.05
371	Carmen Castillo	.05
372	*Mike Dyer*	.05
373	Gary Gaetti	.05
374	Greg Gagne	.05
375	Dan Gladden	.05
376	German Gonzalez	.05
377	Brian Harper	.05
378	Kent Hrbek	.08
379	Gene Larkin	.05
380	Tim Laudner	.05
381	John Moses	.05
382	Al Newman	.05
383	Kirby Puckett	.35
384	Shane Rawley	.05
385	Jeff Reardon	.05
386	Roy Smith	.05
387	*Gary Wayne*	.05
388	Dave West	.05
389	Tim Belcher	.05
390	Tim Crews	.05
391	Mike Davis	.05
392	Rick Dempsey	.05
393	Kirk Gibson	.05
394	Jose Gonzalez	.05
395	Alfredo Griffin	.05
396	Jeff Hamilton	.05
397	Lenny Harris	.05
398	Mickey Hatcher	.05
399	Orel Hershiser	.08
400	Jay Howell	.05
401	Mike Marshall	.05
402	Ramon Martinez	.08
403	Mike Morgan	.05
404	Eddie Murray	.25
405	Alejandro Pena	.05
406	Willie Randolph	.05
407	Mike Scioscia	.05
408	Ray Searage	.05
409	Fernando Valenzuela	.08
410	*Jose Vizcaino*	.25
411	*John Wetteland*	.25
412	Jack Armstrong	.05
413	Todd Benzinger	.05
414	Tim Birtsas	.05
415	Tom Browning	.05
416	Norm Charlton	.05
417	Eric Davis	.08
418	Rob Dibble	.05
419	John Franco	.05
420	Ken Griffey, Sr.	.08
421	*Chris Hammond*	.15
422	Danny Jackson	.05
423	Barry Larkin	.15
424	Tim Leary	.05
425	Rick Mahler	.05
426	*Joe Oliver*	.05
427	Paul O'Neill	.15
428	Luis Quinones	.05
429	Jeff Reed	.05
430	Jose Rijo	.05
431	Ron Robinson	.05
432	Rolando Roomes	.05
433	Chris Sabo	.05
434	*Scott Scudder*	.10
435	Herm Winningham	.05
436	Steve Balboni	.05
437	Jesse Barfield	.05
438	*Mike Blowers*	.15
439	Tom Brookens	.05
440	Greg Cadaret	.05
441	Alvaro Espinoza	.05
442	*Bob Geren*	.05
443	Lee Guetterman	.05
444	Mel Hall	.05
445	Andy Hawkins	.05
446	Roberto Kelly	.05
447	Don Mattingly	.40
448	Lance McCullers	.05
449	Hensley Meulens	.05
450	Dale Mohorcic	.05
451	Clay Parker	.05
452	Eric Plunk	.05
453	Dave Righetti	.05
454	Deion Sanders	.25
455	Steve Sax	.05
456	Don Slaught	.05
457	Walt Terrell	.05
458	Dave Winfield	.25
459	Jay Bell	.08
460	Rafael Belliard	.05
461	Barry Bonds	.40
462	Bobby Bonilla	.08
463	Sid Bream	.05
464	Benny Distefano	.05
465	Doug Drabek	.05
466	Jim Gott	.05
467	Billy Hatcher	.05
468	Neal Heaton	.05
469	Jeff King	.08
470	Bob Kipper	.05
471	Randy Kramer	.05
472	Bill Landrum	.05
473	Mike LaValliere	.05
474	Jose Lind	.05
475	Junior Ortiz	.05
476	Gary Redus	.05
477	*Rick Reed*	.05
478	R.J. Reynolds	.05
479	Jeff Robinson	.05
480	John Smiley	.05
481	Andy Van Slyke	.05
482	Bob Walk	.05
483	Andy Allanson	.05
484	Scott Bailes	.05
485	Albert Belle	.50
486	Bud Black	.05
487	Jerry Browne	.05
488	Tom Candiotti	.05
489	Joe Carter	.08
490	David Clark	.05
491	John Farrell	.05
492	Felix Fermin	.05
493	Brook Jacoby	.05
494	Dion James	.05
495	Doug Jones	.05
496	Brad Komminsk	.05
497	Rod Nichols	.05
498	Pete O'Brien	.05
499	*Steve Olin*	.10
500	Jesse Orosco	.05
501	Joel Skinner	.05
502	Cory Snyder	.05
503	Greg Swindell	.05
504	Rich Yett	.05
505	Scott Bankhead	.05
506	Scott Bradley	.05
507	Greg Briley	.05
508	Jay Buhner	.08
509	Darnell Coles	.05
510	Keith Comstock	.05
511	Henry Cotto	.05
512	Alvin Davis	.05
513	Ken Griffey, Jr.	2.00
514	Erik Hanson	.05
515	Gene Harris	.05
516	Brian Holman	.05
517	Mike Jackson	.05
518	Randy Johnson	.35
519	Jeffrey Leonard	.05
520	Edgar Martinez	.08
521	Dennis Powell	.05
522	Jim Presley	.05
523	Jerry Reed	.05
524	Harold Reynolds	.05
525	Mike Schooler	.05
526	Bill Swift	.05
527	David Valle	.05
528	*Omar Vizquel*	.25
529	Ivan Calderon	.05
530	Carlton Fisk	.10
531	Scott Fletcher	.05
532	Dave Gallagher	.05
533	Ozzie Guillen	.05
534	*Greg Hibbard*	.05
535	Shawn Hillegas	.05
536	Lance Johnson	.05
537	Eric King	.05
538	Ron Kittle	.05
539	Steve Lyons	.05
540	Carlos Martinez	.05
541	*Tom McCarthy*	.05
542	*Matt Merullo*	.05
543	Donn Pall	.05
544	Dan Pasqua	.05
545	Ken Patterson	.05
546	Melido Perez	.05
547	Steve Rosenberg	.05
548	*Sammy Sosa*	5.00
549	Bobby Thigpen	.05
550	Robin Ventura	.15
551	Greg Walker	.05
552	Don Carman	.05
553	*Pat Combs*	.10
554	Dennis Cook	.05
555	Darren Daulton	.05
556	Len Dykstra	.08
557	Curt Ford	.05
558	Charlie Hayes	.05
559	Von Hayes	.05

560	Tom Herr	.05
561	Ken Howell	.05
562	Steve Jeltz	.05
563	Ron Jones	.05
564	Ricky Jordan	.05
565	John Kruk	.05
566	Steve Lake	.05
567	Roger McDowell	.05
568	Terry Mulholland	.05
569	Dwayne Murphy	.05
570	Jeff Parrett	.05
571	Randy Ready	.05
572	Bruce Ruffin	.05
573	Dickie Thon	.05
574	Jose Alvarez	.05
575	Geronimo Berroa	.05
576	Jeff Blauser	.05
577	Joe Boever	.05
578	Marty Clary	.05
579	Jody Davis	.05
580	Mark Eichhorn	.05
581	Darrell Evans	.08
582	Ron Gant	.10
583	Tom Glavine	.10
584	*Tommy Greene*	.15
585	Tommy Gregg	.05
586	*Dave Justice*	.40
587	Mark Lemke	.05
588	Derek Lilliquist	.05
589	Oddibe McDowell	.05
590	*Kent Mercker*	.20
591	Dale Murphy	.10
592	Gerald Perry	.05
593	Lonnie Smith	.05
594	Pete Smith	.05
595	John Smoltz	.15
596	*Mike Stanton*	.15
597	Andres Thomas	.05
598	Jeff Treadway	.05
599	Doyle Alexander	.05
600	Dave Bergman	.05
601	*Brian Dubois*	.08
602	Paul Gibson	.05
603	Mike Heath	.05
604	Mike Henneman	.05
605	Guillermo Hernandez	.05
606	*Shawn Holman*	.05
607	Tracy Jones	.05
608	Chet Lemon	.05
609	Fred Lynn	.05
610	Jack Morris	.05
611	Matt Nokes	.05
612	Gary Pettis	.05
613	*Kevin Ritz*	.08
614	Jeff Robinson	.05
615	Steve Searcy	.05
616	Frank Tanana	.05
617	Alan Trammell	.10
618	Gary Ward	.05
619	Lou Whitaker	.05
620	Frank Williams	.05
621a	Players of the Decade - 1980 (George Brett) (... 10 .390 hitting ...)	2.00
621b	Players of the Decade - 1980 (George Brett)	.20
622	Players of the Decade - 1981 (Fernando Valenzuela)	.05
623	Players of the Decade - 1982 (Dale Murphy)	.05
624a	Players of the Decade - 1983 (Cal Ripkin, Jr.) (Ripkin)	3.00
624b	Players of the Decade - 1983 (Cal Ripken, Jr.)	.25
625	Players of the Decade - 1984 (Ryne Sandberg)	.25
626	Players of the Decade - 1985 (Don Mattingly)	.25
627	Players of the Decade - 1986 (Roger Clemens)	.25
628	Players of the Decade - 1987 (George Bell)	.05
629	Players of the Decade - 1988 (Jose Canseco)	.20
630a	Players of the Decade - 1989 (Will Clark) (total bases 32)	.85
630b	Players of the Decade - 1989 (Will Clark) (total bases 321)	.20
631	Game Savers (Mark Davis, Mitch Williams)	.05
632	Boston Igniters (Wade Boggs, Mike Greenwell)	.10
633	Starter & Stopper (Mark Gubicza, Jeff Russell)	.05
634	League's Best Shortstops (Tony Fernandez, Cal Ripken Jr.)	.15
635	Human Dynamos (Kirby Puckett, Bo Jackson)	.20
636	300 Strikeout Club (Mike Scott, Nolan Ryan)	.20
637	The Dymanic Duo (Will Clark, Kevin Mitchell)	.10
638	A.L. All-Stars (Don Mattingly, Mark McGwire)	.50
639	N.L. East Rivals (Howard Johnson, Ryne Sandberg)	.10
640	Major League Prospects (*Rudy Seanez*), (*Colin Charland*)	.15
641	Major League Prospects (*George Canale*), (*Kevin Maas*)	.15
642	Major League Prospects (*Kelly Mann*), (*Dave Hansen*)	.15
643	Major League Prospects (*Greg Smith*), (*Stu Tate*)	.10
644	Major League Prospects (*Tom Drees*), (*Dan Howitt*)	.08
645	Major League Prospects (*Mike Roesler*), (*Derrick May*)	.15
646	Major League Prospects (*Scott Hemond*), (*Mark Gardner*)	.15
647	Major League Prospects (*John Orton*), (*Scott Leius*)	.15
648	Major League Prospects (*Rich Monteleone*), (*Dana Williams*)	.08
649	Major League Prospects (*Mike Huff*), (*Steve Frey*)	.10
650	Major League Prospects (*Chuck McElroy*), (*Moises Alou*)	.50
651	Major League Prospects (*Bobby Rose*), (*Mike Hartley*)	.10
652	Major League Prospects (*Matt Kinzer*), (*Wayne Edwards*)	.08
653	Major League Prospects (*Delino DeShields*), (*Jason Grimsley*)	.20
654	Athletics, Cubs, Giants & Blue Jays (Checklist)	.05
655	Royals, Angels, Padres & Orioles (Checklist)	.05
656	Mets, Astros, Cardinals & Red Sox (Checklist)	.05
657	Rangers, Brewers, Expos & Twins (Checklist)	.05
658	Dodgers, Reds, Yankees & Pirates (Checklist)	.05
659	Indians, Mariners, White Sox & Phillies (Checklist)	.05
660	Braves, Tigers & Special Cards (Checklist)	.05

1990 Fleer All-Stars

The top players at each position, as selected by Fleer, are featured in this 12-card set inserted in cello packs and some wax packs. The cards measure 2-1/2" x 3-1/2" and feature a unique two-photo format on the card fronts.

		MT
Complete Set (12):		5.00
Common Player:		.20
1	Harold Baines	.25
2	Will Clark	.50
3	Mark Davis	.20
4	Howard Johnson	.20
5	Joe Magrane	.20
6	Kevin Mitchell	.20
7	Kirby Puckett	1.50
8	Cal Ripken	3.00
9	Ryne Sandberg	1.50
10	Mike Scott	.20
11	Ruben Sierra	.20
12	Mickey Tettleton	.20

1990 Fleer League Standouts

Fleer's "League Standouts" are six of baseball's top players distributed randomly in Fleer rack packs. Fronts feature full color photos with a six-dimensional effect. A black and gold frame borders the photo. Backs are yellow and describe the player's accomplishments. The cards measure 2-1/2" x 3-1/2".

		MT
Complete Set (6):		4.00
Common Player:		.50
1	Barry Larkin	.50
2	Don Mattingly	1.00
3	Darryl Strawberry	.50
4	Jose Canseco	.75
5	Wade Boggs	.75
6	Mark Grace	.60

1990 Fleer World Series

This 12-card set depicts highlights of the 1989 World Series and was included in the factory-collated Fleer set. Single World Series cards were discovered in cello and rack packs, but this was not intended to happen. Fronts of the 2-1/2" x 3-1/2" cards feature action photos set against a white background with a red and blue "'89 World Series" banner. Backs are pink and white and describe the events of the 1989 Fall Classic.

		MT
Complete Set (12):		1.50
Common Player:		.10
1	The Final Piece To The Puzzle (Mike Moore)	.10
2	Kevin Mitchell	.15
3	Game Two's Crushing Blow	.20
4	Will Clark	.60
5	Jose Canseco	.75
6	Great Leather in the Field	.10
7	Game One And A's Break Out On Top	.10
8	Dave Stewart	.25
9	Parker's Bat Produces Power (Dave Parker)	.25
10	World Series Record Book Game 3	.10
11	Rickey Henderson	.45
12	Oakland A's - Baseball's Best In '89	.25

1990 Fleer Box Panels

For the fifth consecutive year, Fleer issued a series of cards on the bottom panels of its wax pack boxes. This 28-card set features both players and team logo cards. The cards were numbered C-1 to C-28.

		MT
Complete Set, Panels (7):		4.00
Complete Set, Singles (28):		
Common Player:		.05
1	Giants Logo	.05
2	Tim Belcher	.05
3	Roger Clemens	.50
4	Eric Davis	.10
5	Glenn Davis	.05
6	Cubs Logo	.05
7	John Franco	.05
8	Mike Greenwell	.08
9	Athletics logo	.05
10	Ken Griffey, Jr.	2.50
11	Pedro Guerrero	.05
12	Tony Gwynn	.60
13	Blue Jays Logo	.05
14	Orel Hershiser	.10
15	Bo Jackson	.25
16	Howard Johnson	.05
17	Mets Logo	.05
18	Cardinals Logo	.05
19	Don Mattingly	1.00
20	Mark McGwire	1.00
21	Kevin Mitchell	.08
22	Kirby Puckett	.75
23	Royals Logo	.05
24	Orioles Logo	.05
25	Ruben Sierra	.10
26	Dave Stewart	.08
27	Jerome Walton	.05
28	Robin Yount	.25

1990 Fleer "Printed in Canada"

Whether these cards were printed for distribution in Canada or simply the work of a Canadian printer engaged by Fleer to meet U.S. demand is unknown. Each of the 660 cards in the 1990 Fleer issue can be found with a "1990 FLEER LTD./LTEE PTD. IN CANADA" copyright notice on back in the bottom border. Except for various superstar cards, little demand attaches to this variation.

	MT
Complete Set (660):	50.00
Common Player:	.25

(See 1990 Fleer for checklist and base values; stars bring 5X-10X base price.)

1990 Fleer Update

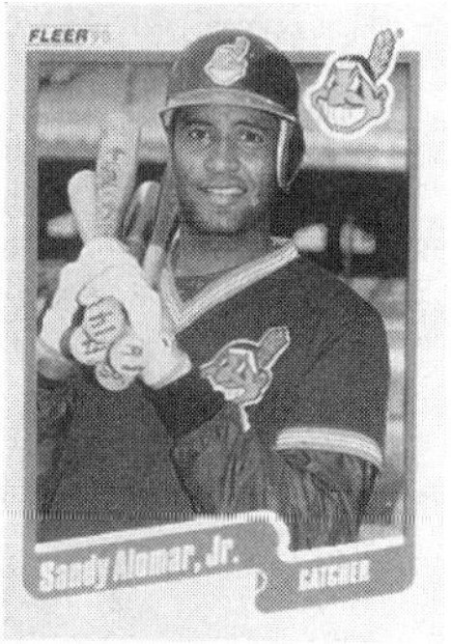

Fleer produced its seventh consecutive "Update" set in 1990. As in the past, the set consists of 132 cards (numbered U-1 through U-132) that were sold by hobby dealers in special collectors boxes. The cards are designed in the same style as the regular issue. A special Nolan Ryan commemorative card is included in the set.

		MT
Complete Set (132):		5.00
Common Player:		.06
1	Steve Avery	.15
2	Francisco Cabrera	.06
3	Nick Esasky	.06
4	Jim Kremers	.06
5	Greg Olson	.06
6	Jim Presley	.06
7	Shawn Boskie	.06
8	Joe Kraemer	.06
9	Luis Salazar	.06
10	Hector Villanueva	.06
11	Glenn Braggs	.06
12	Mariano Duncan	.06
13	Billy Hatcher	.06
14	Tim Layana	.06
15	Hal Morris	.20
16	Javier Ortiz	.06
17	Dave Rohde	.06
18	Eric Yelding	.10
19	Hubie Brooks	.06
20	Kal Daniels	.06
21	Dave Hansen	.06
22	Mike Hartley	.06
23	Stan Javier	.06
24	Jose Offerman	.15
25	Juan Samuel	.06
26	Dennis Boyd	.06
27	Delino DeShields	.10
28	Steve Frey	.06
29	Mark Gardner	.06
30	Chris Nabholz	.06
31	Bill Sampen	.06
32	Dave Schmidt	.06
33	Daryl Boston	.06
34	Chuck Carr	.20
35	John Franco	.06
36	*Todd Hundley*	.75
37	Julio Machado	.06
38	Alejandro Pena	.06
39	Darren Reed	.06
40	Kelvin Torve	.06
41	Darrel Akerfelds	.06
42	Jose DeJesus	.06
43	Dave Hollins	.20
44	Carmelo Martinez	.06
45	Brad Moore	.06
46	Dale Murphy	.15
47	Wally Backman	.06
48	Stan Belinda	.10
49	Bob Patterson	.06
50	Ted Power	.06
51	Don Slaught	.06
52	Geronimo Pena	.15

53	Lee Smith	.08
54	John Tudor	.06
55	Joe Carter	.15
56	Tom Howard	.06
57	Craig Lefferts	.06
58	Rafael Valdez	.06
59	Dave Anderson	.06
60	Kevin Bass	.06
61	John Burkett	.08
62	Gary Carter	.10
63	Rick Parker	.06
64	Trevor Wilson	.10
65	Chris Hoiles	.20
66	Tim Hulett	.06
67	Dave Johnson	.06
68	Curt Schilling	.30
69	David Segui	.15
70	Tom Brunansky	.06
71	Greg Harris	.06
72	Dana Kiecker	.06
73	Tim Naehring	.15
74	Tony Pena	.06
75	Jeff Reardon	.06
76	Jerry Reed	.06
77	Mark Eichhorn	.06
78	Mark Langston	.06
79	John Orton	.06
80	Luis Polonia	.06
81	Dave Winfield	.15
82	Cliff Young	.06
83	Wayne Edwards	.06
84	Alex Fernandez	.20
85	Craig Grebeck	.06
86	Scott Radinsky	.10
87	Frank Thomas	3.00
88	Beau Allred	.06
89	Sandy Alomar, Jr.	.15
90	*Carlos Baerga*	.25
91	Kevin Bearse	.06
92	Chris James	.06
93	Candy Maldonado	.06
94	Jeff Manto	.06
95	Cecil Fielder	.20
96	*Travis Fryman*	.35
97	Lloyd Moseby	.06
98	Edwin Nunez	.06
99	Tony Phillips	.10
100	Larry Sheets	.06
101	Mark Davis	.06
102	Storm Davis	.06
103	Gerald Perry	.06
104	Terry Shumpert	.06
105	Edgar Diaz	.06
106	Dave Parker	.12
107	Tim Drummond	.06
108	Junior Ortiz	.06
109	Park Pittman	.06
110	Kevin Tapani	.25
111	Oscar Azocar	.06
112	Jim Leyritz	.15
113	Kevin Maas	.06
114	Alan Mills	.12
115	Matt Nokes	.06
116	Pascual Perez	.06
117	Ozzie Canseco	.08
118	Scott Sanderson	.06
119	Tino Martinez	.40
120	Jeff Schaefer	.06
121	Matt Young	.06
122	Brian Bohanon	.10
123	Jeff Huson	.06
124	Ramon Manon	.06
125	Gary Mielke	.06
126	Willie Blair	.06
127	Glenallen Hill	.10
128	*John Olerud*	.35
129	Luis Sojo	.06
130	Mark Whiten	.15
131	Three Decades of No Hitters (Nolan Ryan)	.70
132	Checklist	.06

1990 Fleer Award Winners

Hill's department stores and 7-Eleven outlets exclusively sold the 1990 Fleer "Award Winners." This 44-card boxed set includes baseball's statistical leaders of 1989. Card fronts feature a full-color player photo framed by a winner's cup design and blue border. Backs showcase player statistics in blue on a yellow and white background. The cards measure 2-1/2" x 3-1/2". The checklist provided on the back of each box is not correct. It incorrectly lists Bob Boone's team as the Angels and card #10 as Ron Darling. Darryl Strawberry (#38) is not checklisted and all cards #10-38 are off by a number. This is one of the scarcer Fleer box sets of the era.

		MT
Complete Set (44):		7.00
Common Player:		.05
1	Jeff Ballard	.05
2	Tim Belcher	.05
3	Bert Blyleven	.05
4	Wade Boggs	.75
5	Bob Boone	.05
6	Jose Canseco	.75
7	Will Clark	.50
8	Jack Clark	.05
9	Vince Coleman	.05
10	Eric Davis	.10
11	Jose DeLeon	.05
12	Tony Fernandez	.05
13	Carlton Fisk	.15
14	Scott Garrelts	.05
15	Tom Gordon	.08
16	Ken Griffey, Jr.	3.00
17	Von Hayes	.05
18	Rickey Henderson	.50
19	Bo Jackson	.25
20	Howard Johnson	.05
21	Don Mattingly	1.00
22	Fred McGriff	.60
23	Kevin Mitchell	.05
24	Gregg Olson	.05
25	Gary Pettis	.05
26	Kirby Puckett	1.00
27	Harold Reynolds	.05
28	Jeff Russell	.05
29	Nolan Ryan	2.50
30	Bret Saberhagen	.05
31	Ryne Sandberg	.80
32	Benito Santiago	.05
33	Mike Scott	.05
34	Ruben Sierra	.05
35	Lonnie Smith	.05
36	Ozzie Smith	.60
37	Dave Stewart	.05
38	Darryl Strawberry	.25
39	Greg Swindell	.05
40	Andy Van Slyke	.05
41	Tim Wallach	.05
42	Jerome Walton	.05
43	Mitch Williams	.05
44	Robin Yount	.60

1990 Fleer Baseball All Stars

Sold exclusively in Ben Franklin stores, this boxed set showcases the game's top players. Fronts feature a player photo surrounded by a pin-striped tan border. Backs have statistics and data printed in shades of red and dark blue. The cards measure 2-1/2" x 3-1/2" and are packed in a special box with a complete checklist on the back. Like other Fleer boxed sets, the cards are numbered alphabetically. All cards carry a "Printed in Canada" note on back.

		MT
Complete Set (44):		4.00
Common Player:		.05
1	Wade Boggs	.75
2	Bobby Bonilla	.08
3	Tim Burke	.05
4	Jose Canseco	.60
5	Will Clark	.35
6	Eric Davis	.08
7	Glenn Davis	.05
8	Julio Franco	.05
9	Tony Fernandez	.05
10	Gary Gaetti	.08
11	Scott Garrelts	.05
12	Mark Grace	.25
13	Mike Greenwell	.05
14	Ken Griffey, Jr.	2.00
15	Mark Gubicza	.05
16	Pedro Guerrero	.05
17	Von Hayes	.05
18	Orel Hershiser	.08
19	Bruce Hurst	.05
20	Bo Jackson	.25
21	Howard Johnson	.05
22	Doug Jones	.05
23	Barry Larkin	.15
24	Don Mattingly	1.00
25	Mark McGwire	2.00
26	Kevin McReynolds	.05
27	Kevin Mitchell	.05
28	Dan Plesac	.05
29	Kirby Puckett	1.00
30	Cal Ripken, Jr.	1.50
31	Bret Saberhagen	.08
32	Ryne Sandberg	.75
33	Steve Sax	.05
34	Ruben Sierra	.05
35	Ozzie Smith	.50
36	John Smoltz	.08
37	Darryl Strawberry	.08
38	Terry Steinbach	.05
39	Dave Stewart	.08
40	Bobby Thigpen	.05
41	Alan Trammell	.08
42	Devon White	.05
43	Mitch Williams	.05
44	Robin Yount	.50

1990 Fleer League Leaders

For the fifth consecutive year Fleer released a "League Leaders" boxed set of 44 top Major League players. Card number 42 (Jerome Walton) pictures a player other than Walton. The 2-1/2" x 3-1/2" cards display a full-color photo bordered by a blue frame. Backs feature complete statistics. The cards are numbered alphabetically and a complete checklist is displayed on the back of the box. The set was available at Walgreen drug stores. Cards carry a "Printed in Canada" notice in the lower-right corner on back.

		MT
Complete Set (44):		4.00
Common Player:		.05
1	Roberto Alomar	.45
2	Tim Belcher	.05
3	George Bell	.05
4	Wade Boggs	.65
5	Jose Canseco	.55
6	Will Clark	.35
7	David Cone	.08
8	Eric Davis	.08
9	Glenn Davis	.05
10	Nick Esasky	.05
11	Dennis Eckersley	.08
12	Mark Grace	.30
13	Mike Greenwell	.05
14	Ken Griffey, Jr.	1.50
15	Mark Gubicza	.05
16	Pedro Guerrero	.05
17	Tony Gwynn	.65
18	Rickey Henderson	.45
19	Bo Jackson	.25
20	Doug Jones	.05
21	Ricky Jordan	.05
22	Barry Larkin	.20
23	Don Mattingly	1.00
24	Fred McGriff	.25
25	Mark McGwire	1.50
26	Kevin Mitchell	.05
27	Jack Morris	.05
28	Gregg Olson	.05
29	Dan Plesac	.05
30	Kirby Puckett	.75
31	Nolan Ryan	1.25
32	Bret Saberhagen	.08
33	Ryne Sandberg	.65
34	Steve Sax	.05
35	Mike Scott	.05
36	Ruben Sierra	.05
37	Lonnie Smith	.05
38	Darryl Strawberry	.10
39	Bobby Thigpen	.05
40	Andy Van Slyke	.05
41	Tim Wallach	.05
42	Jerome Walton	.05
43	Devon White	.05
44	Robin Yount	.40

1990 Fleer MVP

This 44-card boxed set was produced by Fleer for the Toys R Us chain. Fronts are designed with graduating black-to-white borders, surrounding a color player photo. Backs contain individual data and career statistics. The back of each box carries a checklist of all the players in the set. Six peel-off team logo stickers featuring a baseball trivia quiz on the back are also included with each set. The cards are 2-1/2" x 3-1/2" and numbered alphabetically. All cards carry a "Printed in Canada" notation on the back at bottom.

		MT
Complete Set (44):		4.00
Common Player:		.05
1	George Bell	.05
2	Bert Blyleven	.05
3	Wade Boggs	.65
4	Bobby Bonilla	.08
5	George Brett	.75
6	Jose Canseco	.60
7	Will Clark	.50
8	Roger Clemens	.90
9	Eric Davis	.08
10	Glenn Davis	.05
11	Tony Fernandez	.05
12	Dwight Gooden	.10
13	Mike Greenwell	.05
14	Ken Griffey, Jr.	2.00
15	Pedro Guerrero	.05
16	Tony Gwynn	.75
17	Rickey Henderson	.40
18	Tom Herr	.05
19	Orel Hershiser	.08
20	Kent Hrbek	.05
21	Bo Jackson	.25
22	Howard Johnson	.05
23	Don Mattingly	1.00
24	Fred McGriff	.25
25	Mark McGwire	2.00
26	Kevin Mitchell	.05
27	Paul Molitor	.40
28	Dale Murphy	.10
29	Kirby Puckett	.75
30	Tim Raines	.10
31	Cal Ripken, Jr.	1.50
32	Bret Saberhagen	.08
33	Ryne Sandberg	.65
34	Ruben Sierra	.05
35	Dwight Smith	.05
36	Ozzie Smith	.40
37	Darryl Strawberry	.15
38	Dave Stewart	.08
39	Greg Swindell	.05
40	Bobby Thigpen	.05
41	Alan Trammell	.08
42	Jerome Walton	.05
43	Mitch Williams	.05
44	Robin Yount	.40

1990 Fleer Soaring Stars

Cards from this 12-card set could be found in 1990 Fleer jumbo cello packs. The cards are styled with a cartoon flavor, featuring astronomical graphics surrounding the player. Backs feature information about the promising young player.

		MT
Complete Set (12):		15.00
Common Player:		.25
1	Todd Zeile	.50
2	Mike Stanton	.25
3	Larry Walker	3.00
4	Robin Ventura	2.00
5	Scott Coolbaugh	.25
6	Ken Griffey, Jr.	12.00
7	Tom Gordon	.35
8	Jerome Walton	.25
9	Junior Felix	.25
10	Jim Abbott	.50
11	Ricky Jordan	.25
12	Dwight Smith	.25

1991 Fleer Promo Strip

This three-card strip was issued to introduce Fleer's 1991 baseball card set. The cards on the 7-1/2" x 3-1/2" strip are identical to the players' regular issue cards.

	MT
Three-card Strip: Cal Ripken Jr., Robin Ventura, Bob Milacki	30.00

The election of former players to the Hall of Fame does not always have an immediate upward effect on card prices. The hobby market generally has done a good job of predicting those inductions and adjusting values over the course of several years.

1991 Fleer

Fleer expanded its 1991 set to include 720 cards. The cards feature yellow borders surrounding full-color action photos. Backs feature a circular portrait photo, biographical information, complete statistics, and career highlights. Once again the cards are numbered alphabetically within team. Because Fleer used more than one printer, many minor variations in photo cropping and typography can be found. The most notable are included in the checklist here.

		MT
Unopened Factory Set (732):		10.00
Complete Set (720):		8.00
Common Player:		.05
Wax Box:		8.00
1	*Troy Afenir*	.05
2	Harold Baines	.08
3	Lance Blankenship	.05
4	Todd Burns	.05
5	Jose Canseco	.35
6	Dennis Eckersley	.08
7	Mike Gallego	.05
8	Ron Hassey	.05
9	Dave Henderson	.05
10	Rickey Henderson	.25
11	Rick Honeycutt	.05
12	Doug Jennings	.05
13	*Joe Klink*	.05
14	Carney Lansford	.05
15	*Darren Lewis*	.15
16	Willie McGee	.08
17a	Mark McGwire (six-line career summary)	1.50
17b	Mark McGwire (seven-line career summary)	1.50
18	Mike Moore	.05
19	Gene Nelson	.05
20	Dave Otto	.05
21	Jamie Quirk	.05
22	Willie Randolph	.05
23	Scott Sanderson	.05
24	Terry Steinbach	.05
25	Dave Stewart	.08
26	Walt Weiss	.05
27	Bob Welch	.05
28	Curt Young	.05
29	Wally Backman	.05
30	*Stan Belinda*	.05
31	Jay Bell	.05
32	Rafael Belliard	.05
33	Barry Bonds	.35
34	Bobby Bonilla	.08
35	Sid Bream	.05
36	Doug Drabek	.05
37	*Carlos Garcia*	.15
38	Neal Heaton	.05
39	Jeff King	.05
40	Bob Kipper	.05
41	Bill Landrum	.05
42	Mike LaValliere	.05
43	Jose Lind	.05
44	Carmelo Martinez	.05
45	Bob Patterson	.05
46	Ted Power	.05
47	Gary Redus	.05
48	R.J. Reynolds	.05
49	Don Slaught	.05
50	John Smiley	.05
51	Zane Smith	.05
52	*Randy Tomlin*	.10
53	Andy Van Slyke	.05
54	Bob Walk	.05
55	Jack Armstrong	.05
56	Todd Benzinger	.05
57	Glenn Braggs	.05
58	Keith Brown	.05
59	Tom Browning	.05
60	Norm Charlton	.05
61	Eric Davis	.08
62	Rob Dibble	.05
63	Bill Doran	.05
64	Mariano Duncan	.05
65	Chris Hammond	.05
66	Billy Hatcher	.05
67	Danny Jackson	.05
68	Barry Larkin	.10
69	*Tim Layana*	.05
70	*Terry Lee*	.05
71	Rick Mahler	.05
72	Hal Morris	.05
73	Randy Myers	.05
74	Ron Oester	.05
75	Joe Oliver	.05
76	Paul O'Neill	.10
77	Luis Quinones	.05
78	Jeff Reed	.05
79	Jose Rijo	.05
80	Chris Sabo	.05
81	Scott Scudder	.05
82	Herm Winningham	.05
83	Larry Andersen	.05
84	Marty Barrett	.05
85	Mike Boddicker	.05
86	Wade Boggs	.35
87	Tom Bolton	.05
88	Tom Brunansky	.05
89	Ellis Burks	.05
90	Roger Clemens	.50
91	Scott Cooper	.10
92	John Dopson	.05
93	Dwight Evans	.05
94	Wes Gardner	.05
95	*Jeff Gray*	.05
96	Mike Greenwell	.05
97	Greg Harris	.05
98	*Daryl Irvine*	.05
99	*Dana Kiecker*	.05
100	Randy Kutcher	.05
101	Dennis Lamp	.05
102	Mike Marshall	.05
103	John Marzano	.05
104	Rob Murphy	.05
105a	*Tim Naehring* (seven-line career summary)	.08
105b	*Tim Naehring* (nine-line career summary)	.08
106	Tony Pena	.05
107	*Phil Plantier*	.10
108	Carlos Quintana	.05
109	Jeff Reardon	.05
110	Jerry Reed	.05
111	Jody Reed	.05
112	Luis Rivera	.05
113a	Kevin Romine (one-line career summary)	.05
113b	Kevin Romine (two-line career summary)	.05
114	Phil Bradley	.05
115	Ivan Calderon	.05
116	Wayne Edwards	.05
117	Alex Fernandez	.10
118	Carlton Fisk	.10
119	Scott Fletcher	.05
120	*Craig Grebeck*	.08
121	Ozzie Guillen	.05
122	Greg Hibbard	.05
123	Lance Johnson	.05
124	Barry Jones	.05
125a	Ron Karkovice (two-line career summary)	.05
125b	Ron Karkovice (one-line career summary)	.05
126	Eric King	.05
127	Steve Lyons	.05
128	Carlos Martinez	.05
129	Jack McDowell	.05
130	Donn Pall	.05
131	Dan Pasqua	.05
132	Ken Patterson	.05
133	Melido Perez	.05
134	Adam Peterson	.05
135	*Scott Radinsky*	.08
136	Sammy Sosa	.75
137	Bobby Thigpen	.05
138	Frank Thomas	1.00
139	Robin Ventura	.15
140	Daryl Boston	.05
141	*Chuck Carr*	.15
142	Mark Carreon	.05
143	David Cone	.08
144	Ron Darling	.05
145	Kevin Elster	.05
146	Sid Fernandez	.05
147	John Franco	.05
148	Dwight Gooden	.10
149	Tom Herr	.05
150	Todd Hundley	.10
151	Gregg Jefferies	.10
152	Howard Johnson	.05
153	Dave Magadan	.05
154	Kevin McReynolds	.05
155	Keith Miller	.05
156	Bob Ojeda	.05
157	Tom O'Malley	.05
158	Alejandro Pena	.05
159	*Darren Reed*	.08
160	Mackey Sasser	.05
161	Darryl Strawberry	.10
162	Tim Teufel	.05
163	Kelvin Torve	.05
164	Julio Valera	.05
165	Frank Viola	.05
166	Wally Whitehurst	.05
167	Jim Acker	.05
168	*Derek Bell*	.15
169	George Bell	.05
170	*Willie Blair*	.05
171	Pat Borders	.05
172	John Cerutti	.05
173	Junior Felix	.05
174	Tony Fernandez	.05
175	Kelly Gruber	.05
176	Tom Henke	.05
177	Glenallen Hill	.05
178	Jimmy Key	.08
179	Manny Lee	.05
180	Fred McGriff	.20
181	Rance Mulliniks	.05
182	Greg Myers	.05
183	John Olerud	.15
184	Luis Sojo	.05
185	Dave Steib	.05
186	Todd Stottlemyre	.05
187	Duane Ward	.05
188	David Wells	.08
189	*Mark Whiten*	.15
190	Ken Williams	.05
191	Frank Wills	.05
192	Mookie Wilson	.05
193	Don Aase	.05
194	Tim Belcher	.05
195	Hubie Brooks	.05
196	Dennis Cook	.05
197	Tim Crews	.05
198	Kal Daniels	.05
199	Kirk Gibson	.05
200	Jim Gott	.05
201	Alfredo Griffin	.05
202	Chris Gwynn	.05
203	Dave Hansen	.05
204	Lenny Harris	.05
205	Mike Hartley	.05
206	Mickey Hatcher	.05
207	*Carlos Hernandez*	.10
208	Orel Hershiser	.08
209	Jay Howell	.05
210	Mike Huff	.05
211	Stan Javier	.05
212	Ramon Martinez	.08
213	Mike Morgan	.05
214	Eddie Murray	.20
215	*Jim Neidlinger*	.05
216	Jose Offerman	.05
217	*Jim Poole*	.05
218	Juan Samuel	.05
219	Mike Scioscia	.05
220	Ray Searage	.05
221	Mike Sharperson	.05
222	Fernando Valenzuela	.08
223	Jose Vizcaino	.05
224	Mike Aldrete	.05
225	*Scott Anderson*	.05
226	Dennis Boyd	.05
227	Tim Burke	.05
228	Delino DeShields	.08
229	Mike Fitzgerald	.05
230	Tom Foley	.05
231	Steve Frey	.05
232	Andres Galarraga	.10
233	Mark Gardner	.05
234	Marquis Grissom	.10
235	Kevin Gross	.05
236	Drew Hall	.05
237	Dave Martinez	.05
238	Dennis Martinez	.08
239	Dale Mohorcic	.05
240	*Chris Nabholz*	.05
241	Otis Nixon	.05
242	Junior Noboa	.05
243	Spike Owen	.05
244	Tim Raines	.08
245	*Mel Rojas*	.12
246	*Scott Ruskin*	.05
247	*Bill Sampen*	.05
248	Nelson Santovenia	.05
249	Dave Schmidt	.05
250	Larry Walker	.25
251	Tim Wallach	.05
252	Dave Anderson	.05
253	Kevin Bass	.05
254	Steve Bedrosian	.05
255	Jeff Brantley	.05
256	John Burkett	.08
257	Brett Butler	.08
258	Gary Carter	.08
259	Will Clark	.20
260	*Steve Decker*	.05
261	Kelly Downs	.05
262	Scott Garrelts	.05
263	Terry Kennedy	.05
264	Mike LaCoss (photo on back actually Ken Oberkfell)	.05
265	*Mark Leonard*	.05
266	Greg Litton	.05
267	Kevin Mitchell	.05
268	Randy O'Neal	.05
269	*Rick Parker*	.05
270	Rick Reuschel	.05
271	Ernest Riles	.05
272	Don Robinson	.05
273	Robby Thompson	.05
274	Mark Thurmond	.05
275	Jose Uribe	.05
276	Matt Williams	.20
277	Trevor Wilson	.05
278	*Gerald Alexander*	.05
279	Brad Arnsberg	.05
280	*Kevin Belcher*	.05
281	*Joe Bitker*	.05
282	Kevin Brown	.10
283	Steve Buechele	.05
284	Jack Daugherty	.05
285	Julio Franco	.05
286	Juan Gonzalez	.50
287	*Bill Haselman*	.15
288	Charlie Hough	.05
289	Jeff Huson	.05
290	Pete Incaviglia	.05
291	Mike Jeffcoat	.05
292	Jeff Kunkel	.05
293	Gary Mielke	.05
294	Jamie Moyer	.05
295	Rafael Palmeiro	.12
296	Geno Petralli	.05
297	Gary Pettis	.05
298	Kevin Reimer	.05
299	Kenny Rogers	.05
300	Jeff Russell	.05
301	John Russell	.05
302	Nolan Ryan	.65
303	Ruben Sierra	.05
304	Bobby Witt	.05
305	Jim Abbott	.08
306	Kent Anderson	.05
307	Dante Bichette	.08
308	Bert Blyleven	.05
309	Chili Davis	.08
310	Brian Downing	.05
311	Mark Eichhorn	.05
312	Mike Fetters	.05
313	Chuck Finley	.05
314	Willie Fraser	.05
315	Bryan Harvey	.05
316	Donnie Hill	.05
317	Wally Joyner	.10
318	Mark Langston	.05
319	Kirk McCaskill	.05
320	John Orton	.05
321	Lance Parrish	.08
322	Luis Polonia	.05
323	Johnny Ray	.05
324	Bobby Rose	.05
325	Dick Schofield	.05
326	Rick Schu	.05
327a	Lee Stevens (six-line career summary)	.10
327b	Lee Stevens (seven-line career summary)	.10
328	Devon White	.08
329	Dave Winfield	.20
330	*Cliff Young*	.05
331	Dave Bergman	.05
332	*Phil Clark*	.08
333	Darnell Coles	.05
334	Milt Cuyler	.05
335	Cecil Fielder	.08
336	Travis Fryman	.08
337	Paul Gibson	.05
338	Jerry Don Gleaton	.05
339	Mike Heath	.05
340	Mike Henneman	.05
341	Chet Lemon	.05
342	Lance McCullers	.05
343	Jack Morris	.05
344	Lloyd Moseby	.05
345	Edwin Nunez	.05
346	Clay Parker	.05
347	Dan Petry	.05
348	Tony Phillips	.05
349	Jeff Robinson	.05
350	Mark Salas	.05
351	*Mike Schwabe*	.05
352	Larry Sheets	.05
353	John Shelby	.05
354	Frank Tanana	.05
355	Alan Trammell	.10
356	Gary Ward	.05
357	Lou Whitaker	.08
358	Beau Allred	.05
359	Sandy Alomar,Jr.	.10
360	Carlos Baerga	.05
361	*Kevin Bearse*	.05
362	Tom Brookens	.05
363	Jerry Browne	.05
364	Tom Candiotti	.05
365	Alex Cole	.05
366	John Farrell	.05
367	Felix Fermin	.05
368	Keith Hernandez	.05
369	Brook Jacoby	.05
370	Chris James	.05
371	Dion James	.05
372	Doug Jones	.05
373	Candy Maldonado	.05
374	Steve Olin	.05
375	Jesse Orosco	.05
376	Rudy Seanez	.05
377	Joel Skinner	.05
378	Cory Snyder	.05
379	Greg Swindell	.05
380	Sergio Valdez	.05
381	*Mike Walker*	.05
382	*Colby Ward*	.05
383	*Turner Ward*	.10
384	Mitch Webster	.05
385	Kevin Wickander	.05
386	Darrel Akerfelds	.05
387	Joe Boever	.05
388a	Rod Booker (no 1981 stats)	.05
388b	Rod Booker (1981 stats included)	.10
389	Sil Campusano	.05
390	Don Carman	.05
391	*Wes Chamberlain*	.10
392	Pat Combs	.05
393	Darren Daulton	.05
394	Jose DeJesus	.05
395	Len Dykstra	.08
396	Jason Grimsley	.05
397	Charlie Hayes	.05
398	Von Hayes	.05
399	*Dave Hollins*	.25
400	Ken Howell	.05
401	Ricky Jordan	.05
402	John Kruk	.05
403	Steve Lake	.05
404	*Chuck Malone*	.05
405	Roger McDowell	.05
406	Chuck McElroy	.05
407	*Mickey Morandini*	.10
408	Terry Mulholland	.05
409	Dale Murphy	.10
410	Randy Ready	.05
411	Bruce Ruffin	.05
412	Dickie Thon	.05
413	Paul Assenmacher	.05
414	Damon Berryhill	.05
415	Mike Bielecki	.05
416	*Shawn Boskie*	.08
417	Dave Clark	.05
418	Doug Dascenzo	.05
419a	Andre Dawson (no 1976 stats)	.10
419b	Andre Dawson (1976 stats included)	.10
420	Shawon Dunston	.05
421	Joe Girardi	.05
422	Mark Grace	.20
423	Mike Harkey	.05
424	Les Lancaster	.05
425	Bill Long	.05
426	Greg Maddux	.60
427	Derrick May	.05
428	Jeff Pico	.05
429	Domingo Ramos	.05
430	Luis Salazar	.05
431	Ryne Sandberg	.25
432	Dwight Smith	.05
433	Greg Smith	.05
434	Rick Sutcliffe	.05
435	Gary Varsho	.05
436	*Hector Villanueva*	.05
437	Jerome Walton	.05
438	Curtis Wilkerson	.05
439	Mitch Williams	.05
440	Steve Wilson	.05
441	Marvell Wynne	.05
442	Scott Bankhead	.05
443	Scott Bradley	.05
444	Greg Briley	.05
445	Mike Brumley	.05
446	Jay Buhner	.08
447	*Dave Burba*	.10
448	Henry Cotto	.05
449	Alvin Davis	.05
450	Ken Griffey, Jr.	1.50
451	Erik Hanson	.05
452	Gene Harris	.05
453	Brian Holman	.05
454	Mike Jackson	.05
455	Randy Johnson	.25
456	Jeffrey Leonard	.05
457	Edgar Martinez	.08
458	Tino Martinez	.20
459	Pete O'Brien	.05
460	Harold Reynolds	.05
461	Mike Schooler	.05
462	Bill Swift	.05
463	David Valle	.05
464	Omar Vizquel	.08
465	Matt Young	.05
466	Brady Anderson	.20
467	Jeff Ballard	.05
468	Juan Bell	.05
469a	Mike Devereaux ("six" last word in career summary top line)	.08
469b	Mike Devereaux ("runs" last word in career summary top line)	.08
470	Steve Finley	.05
471	Dave Gallagher	.05
472	*Leo Gomez*	.10
473	Rene Gonzales	.05
474	Pete Harnisch	.05
475	Kevin Hickey	.05
476	*Chris Hoiles*	.10
477	Sam Horn	.05
478	Tim Hulett	.05
479	Dave Johnson	.05
480	Ron Kittle	.05
481	Ben McDonald	.05
482	Bob Melvin	.05
483	Bob Milacki	.05
484	Randy Milligan	.05
485	*John Mitchell*	.05
486	Gregg Olson	.05
487	Joe Orsulak	.05
488	Joe Price	.05
489	Bill Ripken	.05
490	Cal Ripken, Jr.	.75
491	Curt Schilling	.08
492	*David Segui*	.05
493	*Anthony Telford*	.05
494	Mickey Tettleton	.05
495	Mark Williamson	.05
496	Craig Worthington	.05
497	Juan Agosto	.05
498	Eric Anthony	.05
499	Craig Biggio	.12
500	Ken Caminiti	.12
501	Casey Candaele	.05
502	*Andujar Cedeno*	.10

503	Danny Darwin	.05
504	Mark Davidson	.05
505	Glenn Davis	.05
506	Jim Deshaies	.05
507	*Luis Gonzalez*	.25
508	Bill Gullickson	.05
509	Xavier Hernandez	.05
510	Brian Meyer	.05
511	Ken Oberkfell	.05
512	Mark Portugal	.05
513	Rafael Ramirez	.05
514	*Karl Rhodes*	.08
515	Mike Scott	.05
516	*Mike Simms*	.05
517	Dave Smith	.05
518	Franklin Stubbs	.05
519	Glenn Wilson	.05
520	Eric Yelding	.05
521	Gerald Young	.05
522	Shawn Abner	.05
523	Roberto Alomar	.25
524	Andy Benes	.10
525	Joe Carter	.08
526	Jack Clark	.05
527	Joey Cora	.05
528	*Paul Faries*	.05
529	Tony Gwynn	.40
530	Atlee Hammaker	.05
531	Greg Harris	.05
532	*Thomas Howard*	.08
533	Bruce Hurst	.05
534	Craig Lefferts	.05
535	Derek Lilliquist	.05
536	Fred Lynn	.05
537	Mike Pagliarulo	.05
538	Mark Parent	.05
539	Dennis Rasmussen	.05
540	Bip Roberts	.05
541	*Richard Rodriguez*	.05
542	Benito Santiago	.05
543	Calvin Schiraldi	.05
544	Eric Show	.05
545	Phil Stephenson	.05
546	Garry Templeton	.05
547	Ed Whitson	.05
548	Eddie Williams	.05
549	Kevin Appier	.05
550	Luis Aquino	.05
551	Bob Boone	.05
552	George Brett	.25
553	*Jeff Conine*	.30
554	Steve Crawford	.05
555	Mark Davis	.05
556	Storm Davis	.05
557	Jim Eisenreich	.05
558	Steve Farr	.05
559	Tom Gordon	.05
560	Mark Gubicza	.05
561	Bo Jackson	.15
562	Mike Macfarlane	.05
563	*Brian McRae*	.25
564	Jeff Montgomery	.05
565	Bill Pecota	.05
566	Gerald Perry	.05
567	Bret Saberhagen	.08
568	*Jeff Schulz*	.05
569	Kevin Seitzer	.05
570	*Terry Shumpert*	.05
571	Kurt Stillwell	.05
572	Danny Tartabull	.05
573	Gary Thurman	.05
574	Frank White	.05
575	Willie Wilson	.05
576	Chris Bosio	.05
577	Greg Brock	.05
578	George Canale	.05
579	Chuck Crim	.05
580	Rob Deer	.05
581	*Edgar Diaz*	.05
582	*Tom Edens*	.05
583	Mike Felder	.05
584	Jim Gantner	.05
585	Darryl Hamilton	.05
586	Ted Higuera	.05
587	Mark Knudson	.05
588	Bill Krueger	.05
589	Tim McIntosh	.05
590	Paul Mirabella	.05
591	Paul Molitor	.30
592	Jaime Navarro	.05
593	Dave Parker	.05
594	Dan Plesac	.05
595	Ron Robinson	.05
596	Gary Sheffield	.20
597	Bill Spiers	.05
598	B.J. Surhoff	.08
599	Greg Vaughn	.08
600	Randy Veres	.05
601	Robin Yount	.25
602a	Rick Aguilera (five-line career summary)	.08
602b	Rick Aguilera (four-line career summary)	.08
603	Allan Anderson	.05
604	Juan Berenguer	.05
605	Randy Bush	.05
606	Carmen Castillo	.05
607	Tim Drummond	.05
608	*Scott Erickson*	.10
609	Gary Gaetti	.05
610	Greg Gagne	.05
611	Dan Gladden	.05
612	Mark Guthrie	.05
613	Brian Harper	.05
614	Kent Hrbek	.08
615	Gene Larkin	.05
616	Terry Leach	.05
617	Nelson Liriano	.05
618	Shane Mack	.05
619	John Moses	.05
620	*Pedro Munoz*	.10
621	Al Newman	.05
622	Junior Ortiz	.05
623	Kirby Puckett	.40
624	Roy Smith	.05
625	Kevin Tapani	.05
626	Gary Wayne	.05
627	David West	.05
628	Cris Carpenter	.05
629	Vince Coleman	.05
630	Ken Dayley	.05
631	Jose DeLeon	.05
632	Frank DiPino	.05
633	*Bernard Gilkey*	.25
634	Pedro Guerrero	.05
635	Ken Hill	.05
636	Felix Jose	.05
637	*Ray Lankford*	.25
638	Joe Magrane	.05
639	Tom Niedenfuer	.05
640	Jose Oquendo	.05
641	Tom Pagnozzi	.05
642	Terry Pendleton	.05
643	*Mike Perez*	.10
644	Bryn Smith	.05
645	Lee Smith	.08
646	Ozzie Smith	.30
647	Scott Terry	.05
648	Bob Tewksbury	.05
649	Milt Thompson	.05
650	John Tudor	.05
651	Denny Walling	.05
652	*Craig Wilson*	.05
653	Todd Worrell	.05
654	Todd Zeile	.08
655	*Oscar Azocar*	.05
656	Steve Balboni	.05
657	Jesse Barfield	.05
658	Greg Cadaret	.05
659	Chuck Cary	.05
660	Rick Cerone	.05
661	Dave Eiland	.05
662a	Alvaro Espinoza (no 1979-80 stats)	.08
662b	Alvaro Espinoza (1979-80 stats included)	.08
663	Bob Geren	.05
664	Lee Guetterman	.05
665	Mel Hall	.05
666a	Andy Hawkins (no 1978 stats)	.08
666b	Andy Hawkins (1978 stats included)	.08
667	Jimmy Jones	.05
668	Roberto Kelly	.05
669	Dave LaPoint	.05
670	Tim Leary	.05
671	*Jim Leyritz*	.20
672	Kevin Maas	.25
673	Don Mattingly	.40
674	Matt Nokes	.05
675	Pascual Perez	.05
676	Eric Plunk	.05
677	Dave Righetti	.05
678	Jeff Robinson	.05
679	Steve Sax	.05
680	Mike Witt	.05
681	Steve Avery	.05
682	Mike Bell	.05
683	Jeff Blauser	.05
684	Francisco Cabrera	.05
685	Tony Castillo	.05
686	Marty Clary	.05
687	Nick Esasky	.05
688	Ron Gant	.10
689	Tom Glavine	.10
690	Mark Grant	.05
691	Tommy Gregg	.05
692	Dwayne Henry	.05
693	Dave Justice	.25
694	*Jimmy Kremers*	.05
695	Charlie Leibrandt	.05
696	Mark Lemke	.05
697	Oddibe McDowell	.05
698	*Greg Olson*	.05
699	Jeff Parrett	.05
700	Jim Presley	.05
701	*Victor Rosario*	.05
702	Lonnie Smith	.05
703	Pete Smith	.05
704	John Smoltz	.10
705	Mike Stanton	.05
706	Andres Thomas	.05
707	Jeff Treadway	.05
708	*Jim Vatcher*	.05
709	Home Run Kings (Ryne Sandberg, Cecil Fielder)	.15
710	Second Generation Superstars (Barry Bonds, Ken Griffey, Jr.)	.50
711	NLCS Team Leaders (Bobby Bonilla, Barry Larkin)	.15
712	Top Game Savers (Bobby Thigpen, John Franco)	.05
713	Chicago's 100 Club (Andre Dawson, Ryne Sandberg)	.15
714	Checklists (Athletics, Pirates, Reds, Red Sox)	.05
715	Checklists - White Sox, Mets, Blue Jays, Dodgers	.05
716	Checklists (Expos, Giants, Rangers, Angels)	.05
717	Checklists (Tigers, Indians, Phillies, Cubs)	.05
718	Checklists (Mariners, Orioles, Astros, Padres)	.05
719	Checklists (Royals, Brewers, Twins, Cardinals)	.05
720	Checklists (Yankees, Braves, Super Stars)	.05

1991 Fleer All-Stars

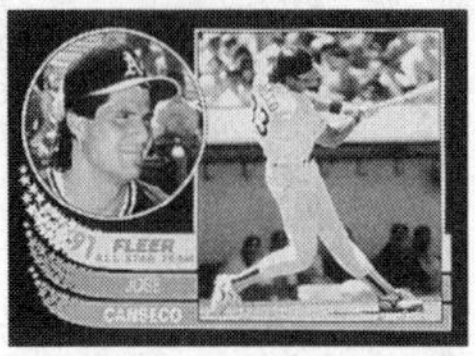

Three player photos are featured on each card in this special insert set. An action shot and portrait close-up are featured on the front, while a full-figure pose is showcased on the back. The cards were inserted into 1991 Fleer cello packs.

		MT
Complete Set (10):		9.00
Common Player:		.50
1	Ryne Sandberg	1.50
2	Barry Larkin	.50
3	Matt Williams	.60
4	Cecil Fielder	.50
5	Barry Bonds	2.00
6	Rickey Henderson	.60
7	Ken Griffey, Jr.	6.00
8	Jose Canseco	.75
9	Benito Santiago	.50
10	Roger Clemens	1.75

1991 Fleer ProVisions

The illustrations of artist Terry Smith are showcased in this special set. Twelve fantasy portraits were produced for cards inserted into rack packs. Four other ProVision cards were inserted into factory sets. The rack pack cards feature black borders, while the factory set cards have white borders. Information on the card backs explains the manner in which Smith painted each player. Factory insert ProVisions are indicated by an "F" suffix in the checklist here.

		MT
Complete Set (12):		3.00
Common Player:		.15
Complete Factory Set (4):		3.00
Common Player:		.40
1	Kirby Puckett	.80
2	Will Clark	.40
3	Ruben Sierra	.15
4	Mark McGwire	1.50
5	Bo Jackson	.25
6	Jose Canseco	.50
7	Dwight Gooden	.25
8	Mike Greenwell	.15
9	Roger Clemens	.75
10	Eric Davis	.20
11	Don Mattingly	1.00
12	Darryl Strawberry	.25
1F	Barry Bonds	1.25
2F	Rickey Henderson	.50
3F	Ryne Sandberg	1.00
4F	Dave Stewart	.40

1991 Fleer ProVisions Souvenir Sheet

In conjunction with its appearance at the 1991 National Sports Collectors Convention, Fleer distributed this two-sport souvenir sheet featuring full-size reproductions of some of its ProVisions insert cards. Cards are pictured in full-color on a blue-to-green graduated background. A yellow and orange ribbon behind the cards identifies the issue. At bottom of the baseball side is a serial number from within an edition of 40,000. All of the ProVision cards feature the artwork of Terry Smith. The players are listed here alphabetically.

	MT
Souvenir Sheet:	10.00

BASEBALL SIDE
Barry Bonds
Jose Canseco
Will Clark
Roger Clemens
Dwight Gooden
Rickey Henderson
FOOTBALL SIDE
Howie Long
Dan Marino
Barry Sanders
Mike Singletary
Lawrence Taylor
Derrick Thomas

1991 Fleer World Series

Once again Fleer released a set in honor of the World Series from the previous season. The 1991 issue features only eight cards compared to twelve in 1990. The cards feature white borders surrounding full-color action shots from the 1990 Fall Classic. The card backs feature an overview of the World Series action.

		MT
Complete Set (8):		1.50
Common Player:		.20
1	Eric Davis	.25
2	Billy Hatcher	.20
3	Jose Canseco	.35
4	Rickey Henderson	.25
5	Chris Sabo, Carney Lansford	.20
6	Dave Stewart	.25
7	Jose Rijo	.20
8	Reds Celebrate	.20

1991 Fleer Box Panels

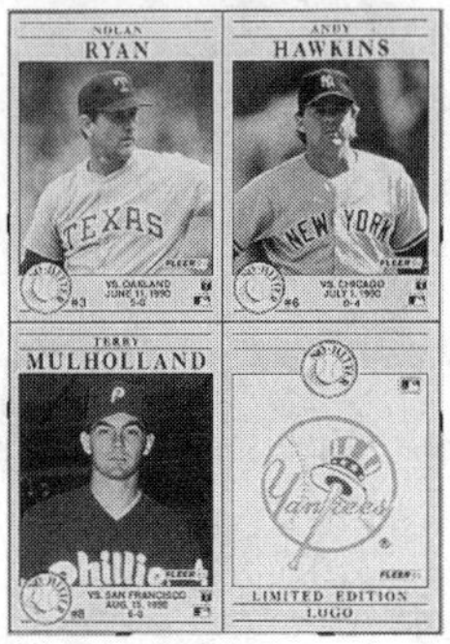

Unlike past box panel sets, the 1991 Fleer box panels feature a theme; 1990 no-hitters are celebrated on the three different boxes. The cards feature blank backs and are numbered in order of no-hitter on the front. A team logo was included on each box. The card fronts are styled after the 1991 Fleer cards. A special no-hitter logo appears in the lower left corner.

		MT
Complete Set (10):		3.00
Common Player:		.10
1	Mark Langston, Mike Witt	.10
2	Randy Johnson	.50
3	Nolan Ryan	2.50
4	Dave Stewart	.20
5	Fernando Valenzuela	.15
6	Andy Hawkins	.10
7	Melido Perez	.10
8	Terry Mulholland	.10
9	Dave Steib	.10
----	Team Logos	.05

1991 Fleer Update

Fleer produced its eighth consecutive "Update" set in 1991 to supplement the company's regular set. As in the past, the set consists of 132 cards that were sold by hobby dealers in special collectors boxes. The cards are designed in the same style as the regular Fleer issue.

		MT
Complete Set (132):		4.00
Common Player:		.06
1	Glenn Davis	.06
2	Dwight Evans	.06
3	Jose Mesa	.12
4	Jack Clark	.06
5	Danny Darwin	.06
6	Steve Lyons	.06
7	Mo Vaughn	.65
8	Floyd Bannister	.06
9	Gary Gaetti	.08
10	Dave Parker	.10
11	Joey Cora	.06
12	Charlie Hough	.06
13	Matt Merullo	.06
14	Warren Newson	.08
15	Tim Raines	.10
16	Albert Belle	.30

17	Glenallen Hill	.08
18	Shawn Hillegas	.06
19	Mark Lewis	.06
20	Charles Nagy	.25
21	Mark Whiten	.06
22	John Cerutti	.06
23	Rob Deer	.06
24	Mickey Tettleton	.06
25	Warren Cromartie	.06
26	Kirk Gibson	.06
27	David Howard	.08
28	Brent Mayne	.10
29	Dante Bichette	.10
30	Mark Lee	.06
31	Julio Machado	.06
32	Edwin Nunez	.06
33	Willie Randolph	.06
34	Franklin Stubbs	.06
35	Bill Wegman	.06
36	Chili Davis	.08
37	Chuck Knoblauch	.50
38	Scott Leius	.06
39	Jack Morris	.06
40	Mike Pagliarulo	.06
41	Lenny Webster	.06
42	John Habyan	.06
43	Steve Howe	.06
44	Jeff Johnson	.06
45	Scott Kamieniecki	.10
46	Pat Kelly	.10
47	Hensley Meulens	.06
48	Wade Taylor	.10
49	Bernie Williams	.30
50	Kirk Dressendorfer	.15
51	Ernest Riles	.06
52	Rich DeLucia	.06
53	Tracy Jones	.06
54	Bill Krueger	.06
55	Alonzo Powell	.06
56	Jeff Schaefer	.06
57	Russ Swan	.06
58	John Barfield	.06
59	Rich Gossage	.08
60	Jose Guzman	.06
61	Dean Palmer	.20
62	*Ivan Rodriguez*	2.00
63	Roberto Alomar	.30
64	Tom Candiotti	.06
65	Joe Carter	.10
66	Ed Sprague	.10
67	Pat Tabler	.06
68	Mike Timlin	.15
69	Devon White	.08
70	Rafael Belliard	.06
71	Juan Berenguer	.06
72	Sid Bream	.06
73	Marvin Freeman	.06
74	Kent Mercker	.06
75	Otis Nixon	.06
76	Terry Pendleton	.06
77	George Bell	.06
78	Danny Jackson	.06
79	Chuck McElroy	.06
80	Gary Scott	.06
81	Heathcliff Slocumb	.06
82	Dave Smith	.06
83	Rick Wilkins	.10
84	Freddie Benavides	.06
85	Ted Power	.06
86	Mo Sanford	.15
87	*Jeff Bagwell*	3.00
88	Steve Finley	.06
89	Pete Harnisch	.06
90	Darryl Kile	.10
91	Brett Butler	.10
92	John Candelaria	.06
93	Gary Carter	.12
94	Kevin Gross	.06
95	Bob Ojeda	.06
96	Darryl Strawberry	.15
97	Ivan Calderon	.06
98	Ron Hassey	.06
99	Gilberto Reyes	.06
100	Hubie Brooks	.06
101	Rick Cerone	.06
102	Vince Coleman	.06
103	Jeff Innis	.06
104	Pete Schourek	.15
105	Andy Ashby	.15
106	Wally Backman	.06
107	Darrin Fletcher	.10
108	Tommy Greene	.08
109	John Morris	.06
110	Mitch Williams	.06
111	Lloyd McClendon	.06
112	Orlando Merced	.25
113	Vicente Palacios	.06
114	Gary Varsho	.06
115	John Wehner	.06
116	Rex Hudler	.06
117	Tim Jones	.06
118	Geronimo Pena	.10
119	Gerald Perry	.06
120	Larry Andersen	.06
121	Jerald Clark	.06
122	Scott Coolbaugh	.06
123	Tony Fernandez	.06
124	Darrin Jackson	.06
125	Fred McGriff	.20
126	Jose Mota	.06
127	Tim Teufel	.06
128	Bud Black	.06
129	Mike Felder	.06
130	Willie McGee	.08
131	Dave Righetti	.06
132	Checklist	.06

1992 Fleer Promo

It has been reported that only 100 of this sample card were made for distribution at the 1991 FanFest event. The card differs from the issued Kirby Puckett card in the '92 Fleer set in the card number, the absence of 1991 stats and the overprinting of a sample card notice, all on the back.

		MT
123	Kirby Puckett	400.00

1992 Fleer

For the second consecutive year, Fleer produced a 720-card set. The standard card fronts feature full-color action photos bordered in green with the player's name, position and team logo on the right border. The backs feature another full-color action photo, biographical information and statistics. A special 12-card Roger Clemens subset is also included in the 1992 Fleer set. Three more Clemens cards were available through a mail-in offer, and 2,000 Roger Clemens autographed cards were inserted in 1992 packs. Once again the cards are numbered according to team. Subsets in the issue included Major League Propects (#652-680), Record Setters (#681-687), League Leaders (#688-697), Superstar Specials (#698-707) and ProVisions (#708-713), which for the first time were part of the regular numbered set rather than limited edition insert cards.

		MT
Complete Set (720):		15.00
Common Player:		.05
Wax Box:		20.00
1	Brady Anderson	.10
2	Jose Bautista	.05
3	Juan Bell	.05
4	Glenn Davis	.05
5	Mike Devereaux	.05
6	Dwight Evans	.05
7	Mike Flanagan	.05
8	Leo Gomez	.05
9	Chris Hoiles	.05
10	Sam Horn	.05
11	Tim Hulett	.05
12	Dave Johnson	.05
13	*Chito Martinez*	.08
14	Ben McDonald	.05
15	Bob Melvin	.05
16	*Luis Mercedes*	.10
17	Jose Mesa	.05
18	Bob Milacki	.05
19	Randy Milligan	.05
20	Mike Mussina	.25
21	Gregg Olson	.05
22	Joe Orsulak	.05
23	Jim Poole	.05
24	*Arthur Rhodes*	.10
25	Billy Ripken	.05
26	Cal Ripken, Jr.	1.00
27	David Segui	.05
28	Roy Smith	.05
29	Anthony Telford	.05
30	Mark Williamson	.05
31	Craig Worthington	.05
32	Wade Boggs	.20
33	Tom Bolton	.05
34	Tom Brunansky	.05
35	Ellis Burks	.05
36	Jack Clark	.05
37	Roger Clemens	.40
38	Danny Darwin	.05
39	Mike Greenwell	.05
40	Joe Hesketh	.05
41	Daryl Irvine	.05
42	Dennis Lamp	.05
43	Tony Pena	.05
44	Phil Plantier	.05
45	Carlos Quintana	.05
46	Jeff Reardon	.05
47	Jody Reed	.05
48	Luis Rivera	.05
49	Mo Vaughn	.30
50	Jim Abbott	.08
51	Kyle Abbott	.05
52	*Ruben Amaro, Jr.*	.05
53	Scott Bailes	.05
54	*Chris Beasley*	.05
55	Mark Eichhorn	.05
56	Mike Fetters	.05
57	Chuck Finley	.05
58	Gary Gaetti	.05
59	Dave Gallagher	.05
60	Donnie Hill	.05
61	Bryan Harvey	.05
62	Wally Joyner	.08
63	Mark Langston	.05
64	Kirk McCaskill	.05
65	John Orton	.05
66	Lance Parrish	.05
67	Luis Polonia	.05
68	Bobby Rose	.05
69	Dick Schofield	.05
70	Luis Sojo	.05
71	Lee Stevens	.05
72	Dave Winfield	.15
73	Cliff Young	.05
74	Wilson Alvarez	.08
75	*Esteban Beltre*	.08
76	Joey Cora	.05
77	*Brian Drahman*	.08
78	Alex Fernandez	.10
79	Carlton Fisk	.12
80	Scott Fletcher	.05
81	Craig Grebeck	.05
82	Ozzie Guillen	.05
83	Greg Hibbard	.05
84	Charlie Hough	.05
85	Mike Huff	.05
86	Bo Jackson	.15
87	Lance Johnson	.05
88	Ron Karkovice	.05
89	Jack McDowell	.05
90	Matt Merullo	.05
91	*Warren Newson*	.10
92	Donn Pall	.05
93	Dan Pasqua	.05
94	Ken Patterson	.05
95	Melido Perez	.05
96	Scott Radinsky	.05
97	Tim Raines	.08
98	Sammy Sosa	.50
99	Bobby Thigpen	.05
100	Frank Thomas	1.00
101	Robin Ventura	.15
102	Mike Aldrete	.05
103	Sandy Alomar, Jr.	.08
104	Carlos Baerga	.05
105	Albert Belle	.35
106	Willie Blair	.05
107	Jerry Browne	.05
108	Alex Cole	.05
109	Felix Fermin	.05
110	Glenallen Hill	.05
111	Shawn Hillegas	.05
112	Chris James	.05
113	Reggie Jefferson	.10
114	Doug Jones	.05
115	Eric King	.05
116	Mark Lewis	.05
117	Carlos Martinez	.05
118	Charles Nagy	.08
119	Rod Nichols	.05
120	Steve Olin	.05
121	Jesse Orosco	.05
122	Rudy Seanez	.05
123	Joel Skinner	.05
124	Greg Swindell	.05
125	Jim Thome	.40
126	Mark Whiten	.05
127	Scott Aldred	.05
128	Andy Allanson	.05
129	John Cerutti	.05
130	Milt Cuyler	.05
131	*Mike Dalton*	.05
132	Rob Deer	.05
133	Cecil Fielder	.08
134	Travis Fryman	.08
135	*Dan Gakeler*	.05
136	Paul Gibson	.05
137	Bill Gullickson	.05
138	Mike Henneman	.05
139	Pete Incaviglia	.05
140	*Mark Leiter*	.05
141	*Scott Livingstone*	.15
142	Lloyd Moseby	.05
143	Tony Phillips	.05
144	Mark Salas	.05
145	Frank Tanana	.05
146	Walt Terrell	.05
147	Mickey Tettleton	.05
148	Alan Trammell	.10
149	Lou Whitaker	.08
150	Kevin Appier	.05

151	Luis Aquino	.05
152	Todd Benzinger	.05
153	Mike Boddicker	.05
154	George Brett	.35
155	Storm Davis	.05
156	Jim Eisenreich	.05
157	Kirk Gibson	.05
158	Tom Gordon	.05
159	Mark Gubicza	.05
160	*David Howard*	.08
161	Mike Macfarlane	.05
162	Brent Mayne	.05
163	Brian McRae	.05
164	Jeff Montgomery	.05
165	Bill Pecota	.05
166	*Harvey Pulliam*	.05
167	Bret Saberhagen	.08
168	Kevin Seitzer	.05
169	Terry Shumpert	.05
170	Kurt Stillwell	.05
171	Danny Tartabull	.05
172	Gary Thurman	.05
173	Dante Bichette	.12
174	Kevin Brown	.05
175	Chuck Crim	.05
176	Jim Gantner	.05
177	Darryl Hamilton	.05
178	Ted Higuera	.05
179	Darren Holmes	.05
180	Mark Lee	.05
181	Julio Machado	.05
182	Paul Molitor	.25
183	Jaime Navarro	.05
184	Edwin Nunez	.05
185	Dan Plesac	.05
186	Willie Randolph	.05
187	Ron Robinson	.05
188	Gary Sheffield	.25
189	Bill Spiers	.05
190	B.J. Surhoff	.08
191	Dale Sveum	.05
192	Greg Vaughn	.08
193	Bill Wegman	.05
194	Robin Yount	.25
195	Rick Aguilera	.05
196	Allan Anderson	.05
197	Steve Bedrosian	.05
198	Randy Bush	.05
199	Larry Casian	.05
200	Chili Davis	.08
201	Scott Erickson	.05
202	Greg Gagne	.05
203	Dan Gladden	.05
204	Brian Harper	.05
205	Kent Hrbek	.08
206	Chuck Knoblauch	.15
207	Gene Larkin	.05
208	Terry Leach	.05
209	Scott Leius	.05
210	Shane Mack	.05
211	Jack Morris	.05
212	Pedro Munoz	.08
213	*Denny Neagle*	.12
214	Al Newman	.05
215	Junior Ortiz	.05
216	Mike Pagliarulo	.05
217	Kirby Puckett	.60
218	Paul Sorrento	.05
219	Kevin Tapani	.05
220	Lenny Webster	.05
221	Jesse Barfield	.05
222	Greg Cadaret	.05
223	Dave Eiland	.05
224	Alvaro Espinoza	.05
225	Steve Farr	.05
226	Bob Geren	.05
227	Lee Guetterman	.05
228	John Habyan	.05
229	Mel Hall	.05
230	Steve Howe	.05
231	*Mike Humphreys*	.05
232	*Scott Kamieniecki*	.10
233	Pat Kelly	.05
234	Roberto Kelly	.05
235	Tim Leary	.05
236	Kevin Maas	.05
237	Don Mattingly	.75
238	Hensley Meulens	.05
239	Matt Nokes	.05
240	Pascual Perez	.05
241	Eric Plunk	.05
242	*John Ramos*	.05
243	Scott Sanderson	.05
244	Steve Sax	.05
245	*Wade Taylor*	.15
246	Randy Velarde	.05
247	Bernie Williams	.20
248	Troy Afenir	.05
249	Harold Baines	.08
250	Lance Blankenship	.05
251	*Mike Bordick*	.10
252	Jose Canseco	.20
253	Steve Chitren	.05
254	Ron Darling	.05
255	Dennis Eckersley	.08
256	Mike Gallego	.05
257	Dave Henderson	.05
258	Rickey Henderson	.20
259	Rick Honeycutt	.05
260	Brook Jacoby	.05
261	Carney Lansford	.05
262	Mark McGwire	1.00
263	Mike Moore	.05
264	Gene Nelson	.05
265	Jamie Quirk	.05
266	*Joe Slusarski*	.15
267	Terry Steinbach	.05
268	Dave Stewart	.08

269	Todd Van Poppel	.08
270	Walt Weiss	.05
271	Bob Welch	.05
272	Curt Young	.05
273	Scott Bradley	.05
274	Greg Briley	.05
275	Jay Buhner	.08
276	Henry Cotto	.05
277	Alvin Davis	.05
278	Rich DeLucia	.05
279	Ken Griffey, Jr.	1.50
280	Erik Hanson	.05
281	Brian Holman	.05
282	Mike Jackson	.05
283	Randy Johnson	.20
284	Tracy Jones	.05
285	Bill Krueger	.05
286	Edgar Martinez	.08
287	Tino Martinez	.12
288	Rob Murphy	.05
289	Pete O'Brien	.05
290	Alonzo Powell	.05
291	Harold Reynolds	.05
292	Mike Schooler	.05
293	Russ Swan	.05
294	Bill Swift	.05
295	Dave Valle	.05
296	Omar Vizquel	.08
297	Gerald Alexander	.05
298	Brad Arnsberg	.05
299	Kevin Brown	.08
300	Jack Daugherty	.05
301	Mario Diaz	.05
302	Brian Downing	.05
303	Julio Franco	.05
304	Juan Gonzalez	.60
305	Rich Gossage	.08
306	Jose Guzman	.05
307	*Jose Hernandez*	.05
308	Jeff Huson	.05
309	Mike Jeffcoat	.05
310	*Terry Mathews*	.05
311	Rafael Palmeiro	.12
312	Dean Palmer	.05
313	Geno Petralli	.05
314	Gary Pettis	.05
315	Kevin Reimer	.05
316	Ivan Rodriguez	.20
317	Kenny Rogers	.05
318	*Wayne Rosenthal*	.05
319	Jeff Russell	.05
320	Nolan Ryan	.45
321	Ruben Sierra	.05
322	Jim Acker	.05
323	Roberto Alomar	.25
324	Derek Bell	.05
325	Pat Borders	.05
326	Tom Candiotti	.05
327	Joe Carter	.08
328	Rob Ducey	.05
329	Kelly Gruber	.05
330	*Juan Guzman*	.25
331	Tom Henke	.05
332	Jimmy Key	.05
333	Manny Lee	.05
334	Al Leiter	.08
335	*Bob MacDonald*	.05
336	Candy Maldonado	.05
337	Rance Mulliniks	.05
338	Greg Myers	.05
339	John Olerud	.20
340	*Ed Sprague*	.10
341	Dave Stieb	.05
342	Todd Stottlemyre	.05
343	*Mike Timlin*	.15
344	Duane Ward	.05
345	David Wells	.08
346	Devon White	.08
347	Mookie Wilson	.05
348	Eddie Zosky	.05
349	Steve Avery	.05
350	Mike Bell	.05
351	Rafael Belliard	.05
352	Juan Berenguer	.05
353	Jeff Blauser	.05
354	Sid Bream	.05
355	Francisco Cabrera	.05
356	Marvin Freeman	.05
357	Ron Gant	.05
358	Tom Glavine	.10
359	*Brian Hunter*	.05
360	Dave Justice	.15
361	Charlie Leibrandt	.05
362	Mark Lemke	.05
363	Kent Mercker	.05
364	*Keith Mitchell*	.05
365	Greg Olson	.05
366	Terry Pendleton	.05
367	*Armando Reynoso*	.05
368	Deion Sanders	.15
369	Lonnie Smith	.05
370	Pete Smith	.05
371	John Smoltz	.10
372	Mike Stanton	.05
373	Jeff Treadway	.05
374	*Mark Wohlers*	.15
375	Paul Assenmacher	.05
376	George Bell	.05
377	Shawn Boskie	.05
378	*Frank Castillo*	.05
379	Andre Dawson	.12
380	Shawon Dunston	.05
381	Mark Grace	.20
382	Mike Harkey	.05
383	Danny Jackson	.05
384	Les Lancaster	.05
385	*Cedric Landrum*	.05
386	Greg Maddux	.60

387 Derrick May .05
388 Chuck McElroy .05
389 Ryne Sandberg .35
390 *Heathcliff Slocumb* .08
391 Dave Smith .05
392 Dwight Smith .05
393 Rick Sutcliffe .05
394 Hector Villanueva .05
395 *Chico Walker* .05
396 Jerome Walton .05
397 *Rick Wilkins* .15
398 Jack Armstrong .05
399 *Freddie Benavides* .10
400 Glenn Braggs .05
401 Tom Browning .05
402 Norm Charlton .05
403 Eric Davis .08
404 Rob Dibble .05
405 Bill Doran .05
406 Mariano Duncan .05
407 *Kip Gross* .05
408 Chris Hammond .05
409 Billy Hatcher .05
410 *Chris Jones* .10
411 Barry Larkin .10
412 Hal Morris .05
413 Randy Myers .05
414 Joe Oliver .05
415 Paul O'Neill .08
416 Ted Power .05
417 Luis Quinones .05
418 Jeff Reed .05
419 Jose Rijo .05
420 Chris Sabo .05
421 Reggie Sanders .15
422 Scott Scudder .05
423 Glenn Sutko .05
424 Eric Anthony .05
425 Jeff Bagwell .75
426 Craig Biggio .15
427 Ken Caminiti .15
428 Casey Candaele .05
429 Mike Capel .05
430 Andujar Cedeno .05
431 Jim Corsi .05
432 Mark Davidson .05
433 Steve Finley .05
434 Luis Gonzalez .08
435 Pete Harnisch .05
436 Dwayne Henry .05
437 Xavier Hernandez .05
438 Jimmy Jones .05
439 *Darryl Kile* .10
440 *Rob Mallicoat* .05
441 *Andy Mota* .08
442 Al Osuna .05
443 Mark Portugal .05
444 *Scott Servais* .10
445 Mike Simms .05
446 Gerald Young .05
447 Tim Belcher .05
448 Brett Butler .08
449 John Candelaria .05
450 Gary Carter .08
451 Dennis Cook .05
452 Tim Crews .05
453 Kal Daniels .05
454 Jim Gott .05
455 Alfredo Griffin .05
456 Kevin Gross .05
457 Chris Gwynn .05
458 Lenny Harris .05
459 Orel Hershiser .08
460 Jay Howell .05
461 Stan Javier .05
462 Eric Karros .15
463 Ramon Martinez .08
464 Roger McDowell .05
465 Mike Morgan .05
466 Eddie Murray .25
467 Jose Offerman .05
468 Bob Ojeda .05
469 Juan Samuel .05
470 Mike Scioscia .05
471 Darryl Strawberry .10
472 *Bret Barberie* .10
473 Brian Barnes .05
474 Eric Bullock .05
475 Ivan Calderon .05
476 Delino DeShields .08
477 *Jeff Fassero* .10
478 Mike Fitzgerald .05
479 Steve Frey .05
480 Andres Galarraga .12
481 Mark Gardner .05
482 Marquis Grissom .10
483 *Chris Haney* .05
484 Barry Jones .05
485 Dave Martinez .05
486 Dennis Martinez .08
487 Chris Nabholz .05
488 Spike Owen .05
489 Gilberto Reyes .05
490 Mel Rojas .05
491 Scott Ruskin .05
492 Bill Sampen .05
493 Larry Walker .20
494 Tim Wallach .05
495 Daryl Boston .05
496 Hubie Brooks .05
497 Tim Burke .05
498 Mark Carreon .05
499 Tony Castillo .05
500 Vince Coleman .05
501 David Cone .08
502 Kevin Elster .05
503 Sid Fernandez .05
504 John Franco .05
505 Dwight Gooden .12
506 Todd Hundley .08
507 Jeff Innis .05
508 Gregg Jefferies .12
509 Howard Johnson .05
510 Dave Magadan .05
511 *Terry McDaniel* .05
512 Kevin McReynolds .05
513 Keith Miller .05
514 Charlie O'Brien .05
515 Mackey Sasser .05
516 *Pete Schourek* .10
517 Julio Valera .05
518 Frank Viola .05
519 Wally Whitehurst .05
520 *Anthony Young* .10
521 *Andy Ashby* .20
522 *Kim Batiste* .05
523 Joe Boever .05
524 Wes Chamberlain .05
525 Pat Combs .05
526 Danny Cox .05
527 Darren Daulton .05
528 Jose DeJesus .05
529 Len Dykstra .08
530 Darrin Fletcher .05
531 Tommy Greene .05
532 Jason Grimsley .05
533 Charlie Hayes .05
534 Von Hayes .05
535 Dave Hollins .08
536 Ricky Jordan .05
537 John Kruk .05
538 Jim Lindeman .05
539 Mickey Morandini .05
540 Terry Mulholland .05
541 Dale Murphy .12
542 Randy Ready .05
543 Wally Ritchie .05
544 Bruce Ruffin .05
545 Steve Searcy .05
546 Dickie Thon .05
547 Mitch Williams .05
548 Stan Belinda .05
549 Jay Bell .05
550 Barry Bonds .35
551 Bobby Bonilla .08
552 Steve Buechele .05
553 Doug Drabek .05
554 Neal Heaton .05
555 Jeff King .05
556 Bob Kipper .05
557 Bill Landrum .05
558 Mike LaValliere .05
559 Jose Lind .05
560 Lloyd McClendon .05
561 Orlando Merced .05
562 Bob Patterson .05
563 *Joe Redfield* .05
564 Gary Redus .05
565 Rosario Rodriguez .05
566 Don Slaught .05
567 John Smiley .05
568 Zane Smith .05
569 Randy Tomlin .05
570 Andy Van Slyke .05
571 Gary Varsho .05
572 Bob Walk .05
573 *John Wehner* .15
574 Juan Agosto .05
575 Cris Carpenter .05
576 Jose DeLeon .05
577 Rich Gedman .05
578 Bernard Gilkey .05
579 Pedro Guerrero .05
580 Ken Hill .05
581 Rex Hudler .05
582 Felix Jose .05
583 Ray Lankford .05
584 Omar Olivares .05
585 Jose Oquendo .05
586 Tom Pagnozzi .05
587 Geronimo Pena .05
588 Mike Perez .05
589 Gerald Perry .05
590 Bryn Smith .05
591 Lee Smith .08
592 Ozzie Smith .25
593 Scott Terry .05
594 Bob Tewksbury .05
595 Milt Thompson .05
596 Todd Zeile .08
597 Larry Andersen .05
598 Oscar Azocar .05
599 Andy Benes .08
600 *Ricky Bones* .08
601 Jerald Clark .05
602 Pat Clements .05
603 Paul Faries .05
604 Tony Fernandez .05
605 Tony Gwynn .35
606 Greg Harris .05
607 Thomas Howard .05
608 Bruce Hurst .05
609 Darrin Jackson .05
610 Tom Lampkin .05
611 Craig Lefferts .05
612 *Jim Lewis* .05
613 Mike Maddux .05
614 Fred McGriff .15
615 *Jose Melendez* .08
616 *Jose Mota* .08
617 Dennis Rasmussen .05
618 Bip Roberts .05
619 Rich Rodriguez .05
620 Benito Santiago .05
621 *Craig Shipley* .05
622 Tim Teufel .05
623 *Kevin Ward* .05
624 Ed Whitson .05
625 Dave Anderson .05
626 Kevin Bass .05
627 *Rod Beck* .10
628 Bud Black .05
629 Jeff Brantley .05
630 John Burkett .05
631 Will Clark .20
632 Royce Clayton .05
633 Steve Decker .05
634 Kelly Downs .05
635 Mike Felder .05
636 Scott Garrelts .05
637 Eric Gunderson .05
638 *Bryan Hickerson* .10
639 Darren Lewis .05
640 Greg Litton .05
641 Kirt Manwaring .05
642 *Paul McClellan* .05
643 Willie McGee .08
644 Kevin Mitchell .05
645 Francisco Olivares .05
646 *Mike Remlinger* .08
647 Dave Righetti .05
648 Robby Thompson .05
649 Jose Uribe .05
650 Matt Williams .15
651 Trevor Wilson .05
652 Tom Goodwin (Prospects) .25
653 Terry Bross (Prospects) .05
654 *Mike Christopher* (Prospects) .10
655 Kenny Lofton (Prospects) 2.50
656 *Chris Cron* (Prospects) .10
657 Willie Banks (Prospects) .10
658 *Pat Rice* (Prospects) .05
659a *Rob Mauer* (Prospects) (last name misspelled) 1.00
659b *Rob Maurer* (Prospects) (corrected) .12
660 Don Harris (Prospects) .12
661 Henry Rodriguez (Prospects) .25
662 *Cliff Brantley* (Prospects) .08
663 *Mike Linskey* (Prospects) .05
664 Gary Disarcina (Prospects) .10
665 *Gil Heredia* (Prospects) .12
666 *Vinny Castilla* (Prospects) 1.00
667 Paul Abbott (Prospects) .08
668 Monty Fariss (Prospects) .08
669 *Jarvis Brown* (Prospects) .08
670 *Wayne Kirby* (Prospects) .15
671 *Scott Brosius* (Prospects) .15
672 Bob Hamelin (Prospects) .10
673 *Joel Johnston* (Prospects) .08
674 *Tim Spehr* (Prospects) .15
675 *Jeff Gardner* (Prospects) .10
676 *Rico Rossy* (Prospects) .10
677 *Roberto Hernandez* (Prospects) .20
678 *Ted Wood* (Prospects) .08
679 Cal Eldred (Prospects) .15
680 Sean Berry (Prospects) .10
681 Rickey Henderson (Stolen Base Record) .15
682 Nolan Ryan (Record 7th No-hitter) .25
683 Dennis Martinez (Perfect Game) .05
684 Wilson Alvarez (Rookie No-hitter) .05
685 Joe Carter (3 100 RBI Seasons) .05
686 Dave Winfield (400 Home Runs) .10
687 David Cone (Ties NL Record Strikeouts) .05
688 Jose Canseco (League Leaders) .15
689 Howard Johnson (League Leaders) .05
690 Julio Franco (League Leaders) .05
691 Terry Pendleton (League Leaders) .05
692 Cecil Fielder (League Leaders) .10
693 Scott Erickson (League Leaders) .05
694 Tom Glavine (League Leaders) .05
695 Dennis Martinez (League Leaders) .05
696 Bryan Harvey (League Leaders) .05
697 Lee Smith (League Leaders) .05
698 Super Siblings (Roberto & Sandy Alomar, Roberto & Sandy Alomar) .15
699 The Indispensables (Bobby Bonilla, Will Clark) .10
700 Teamwork (Mark Wohlers, Kent Mercker, Alejandro Pena) .08
701 Tiger Tandems (Chris Jones, Bo Jackson, Gregg Olson, Frank Thomas) .40
702 The Ignitors (Brett Butler, Paul Molitor) .20
703 The Indispensables II (Cal Ripken Jr., Joe Carter) .15
704 Power Packs (Barry Larkin, Kirby Puckett) .15
705 Today and Tomorrow (Mo Vaughn, Cecil Fielder) .10
706 Teenage Sensations (Ramon Martinez, Ozzie Guillen) .08
707 Designated Hitters (Harold Baines, Wade Boggs) .10
708 Robin Yount (ProVision) .20
709 Ken Griffey, Jr. (ProVision) 1.00
710 Nolan Ryan (ProVision) .85
711 Cal Ripken, Jr. (ProVision) .50
712 Frank Thomas (ProVision) 1.00
713 Dave Justice (ProVision) .20
714 Checklist 1-101 .05
715 Checklist 102-194 .05
716 Checklist 195-296 .05
717 Checklist 297-397 .05
718 Checklist 398-494 .05
719 Checklist 495-596 .05
720a Checklist 597-720 (659 Rob Mauer) .05
720b Checklist 597-720 (659 Rob Maurer) .05

1992 Fleer All-Stars

Black borders with gold highlights are featured on these special wax pack insert cards. The fronts feature glossy action photos with a portrait photo inset. Backs feature career highlights.

		MT
Complete Set (24):		20.00
Common Player:		.20
1	Felix Jose	.20
2	Tony Gwynn	2.00
3	Barry Bonds	1.50
4	Bobby Bonilla	.30
5	Mike LaValliere	.20
6	Tom Glavine	.30
7	Ramon Martinez	.25
8	Lee Smith	.20
9	Mickey Tettleton	.20
10	Scott Erickson	.20
11	Frank Thomas	2.50
12	Danny Tartabull	.20
13	Will Clark	.50
14	Ryne Sandberg	.75
15	Terry Pendleton	.20
16	Barry Larkin	.30
17	Rafael Palmeiro	.50
18	Julio Franco	.20
19	Robin Ventura	.40
20	Cal Ripken, Jr.	3.00
21	Joe Carter	.20
22	Kirby Puckett	2.00
23	Ken Griffey, Jr.	4.50
24	Jose Canseco	.75

1992 Fleer Roger Clemens

This set chronicles the career highlights of Roger Clemens. The initial 12 cards from the set were inserted in 1992 Fleer wax packs. A limited number of autographed cards were inserted as well. The additional three cards from the set were available through a mail-in offer. The card fronts feature black borders with metallic gold type. The flip side is yellow with black borders.

		MT
Complete Set (15):		7.00
Common Card:		.50
Autographed Card:		50.00
1	Quiet Storm	.50
2	Courted by the Mets and Twins	.50
3	The Show	.50
4	A Rocket Launched	.50
5	Time of Trial	.50
6	Break Through	.50
7	Play it Again Roger	.50
8	Business as Usual	.50
9	Heee's Back	.50
10	Blood, Sweat and Tears	.50
11	Prime of Life	.50
12	Man for Every Season	.50
13	Cooperstown Bound	1.00
14	The Heat of the Moment	1.00
15	Final Words	1.00

1992 Fleer Lumber Co.

Baseball's top power hitters at each position are featured in this nine-card set. Fronts feature full-color action photos bordered in black. Backs feature posed player photos and career highlights. The set was included only in factory sets released to the hobby trade.

		MT
Complete Set (9):		7.50
Common Player:		.50
1	Cecil Fielder	.50
2	Mickey Tettleton	.50
3	Darryl Strawberry	.75

4	Ryne Sandberg	1.00
5	Jose Canseco	1.00
6	Matt Williams	.75
7	Cal Ripken, Jr.	2.50
8	Barry Bonds	1.25
9	Ron Gant	.50

1992 Fleer Rookie Sensations

This 20-card set features the top rookies of 1991 and rookie prospects from 1992. The card fronts feature blue borders with "Rookie Sensations" in gold along the top border. The flip sides feature background information on the player. The cards were randomly inserted in 1992 Fleer cello packs. This issue saw very high prices when initially released then suffered long-term declines as the hobby became inundated with more and more insert sets.

		MT
Complete Set (20):		25.00
Common Player:		.50
1	Frank Thomas	7.50
2	Todd Van Poppel	.50
3	Orlando Merced	.50
4	Jeff Bagwell	6.50
5	Jeff Fassero	.50
6	Darren Lewis	1.00
7	Milt Cuyler	.50
8	Mike Timlin	.50
9	Brian McRae	1.00
10	Chuck Knoblauch	2.50
11	Rich DeLucia	.50
12	Ivan Rodriguez	5.00
13	Juan Guzman	.75
14	Steve Chitren	.50
15	Mark Wohlers	.50
16	Wes Chamberlain	.50
17	Ray Lankford	1.00
18	Chito Martinez	.50
19	Phil Plantier	.50
20	Scott Leius	.50

1992 Fleer Smoke 'N Heat

This 12-card set of top pitchers was included in factory sets designated for sale within the general retail trade. Card numbers have an "S" prefix.

		MT
Complete Set (12):		7.50
Common Player:		.25
1	Lee Smith	.25
2	Jack McDowell	.30
3	David Cone	.50
4	Roger Clemens	1.50
5	Nolan Ryan	3.00
6	Scott Erickson	.25
7	Tom Glavine	.40
8	Dwight Gooden	.40
9	Andy Benes	.30
10	Steve Avery	.25
11	Randy Johnson	.75
12	Jim Abbott	.30

1992 Fleer Team Leaders

White and green borders highlight this insert set from Fleer. The card fronts also feature a special gold-foil "team leaders" logo beneath the full-color player photo. The card backs feature player information. The cards were randomly inserted in 1992 Fleer rack packs.

		MT
Complete Set (20):		40.00
Common Player:		.40
1	Don Mattingly	8.00
2	Howard Johnson	.40
3	Chris Sabo	.40
4	Carlton Fisk	.75
5	Kirby Puckett	6.00
6	Cecil Fielder	.50
7	Tony Gwynn	6.00
8	Will Clark	2.50
9	Bobby Bonilla	.50
10	Len Dykstra	.40
11	Tom Glavine	1.25
12	Rafael Palmeiro	1.50
13	Wade Boggs	1.50
14	Joe Carter	.50
15	Ken Griffey, Jr.	12.50
16	Darryl Strawberry	.50
17	Cal Ripken, Jr.	11.00
18	Danny Tartabull	.40
19	Jose Canseco	1.50
20	Andre Dawson	.50

1992 Fleer Update

This 132-card set was released in boxed set form and features traded players, free agents and top rookies from 1992. The cards are styled after the regular 1992 Fleer and are numbered alphabetically according to team. This set marks the ninth year that Fleer has released an update set. The set includes four black-bordered "Headliner" cards.

		MT
Complete Set (136):		140.00
Common Player:		.20
H1	1992 All-Star Game MVP (Ken Griffey, Jr.)	25.00
H2	3000 Career Hits (Robin Yount)	7.00
H3	Major League Career Saves Record (Jeff Reardon)	.25
H4	Record RBI Performance (Cecil Fielder)	1.50
1	Todd Frohwirth	.20
2	Alan Mills	.20
3	Rick Sutcliffe	.20
4	*John Valentin*	3.00
5	Frank Viola	.20
6	Bob Zupcic	.20
7	Mike Butcher	.20
8	*Chad Curtis*	1.50
9	*Damion Easley*	.40
10	Tim Salmon	15.00
11	Julio Valera	.20
12	George Bell	.20
13	Roberto Hernandez	.35
14	Shawn Jeter	.20
15	Thomas Howard	.20
16	Jesse Levis	.40
17	Kenny Lofton	25.00
18	Paul Sorrento	.20
19	Rico Brogna	.35
20	John Doherty	.20
21	Dan Gladden	.20
22	Buddy Groom	.20
23	Shawn Hare	.20
24	John Kiely	.20
25	Kurt Knudsen	.20
26	Gregg Jefferies	.30
27	Wally Joyner	.30
28	Kevin Koslofski	.20
29	Kevin McReynolds	.20
30	Rusty Meacham	.20
31	Keith Miller	.20
32	Hipolito Pichardo	.20
33	James Austin	.20
34	Scott Fletcher	.20
35	*John Jaha*	3.00
36	Pat Listach	.50
37	Dave Nilsson	2.00
38	Kevin Seitzer	.20
39	Tom Edens	.20
40	Pat Mahomes	.65
41	John Smiley	.20
42	Charlie Hayes	.20
43	Sam Militello	.20
44	Andy Stankiewicz	.35
45	Danny Tartabull	.20
46	Bob Wickman	.20
47	Jerry Browne	.20
48	Kevin Campbell	.20
49	Vince Horsman	.20
50	Troy Neel	.50
51	Ruben Sierra	.20
52	Bruce Walton	.20
53	Willie Wilson	.20
54	Bret Boone	3.00
55	Dave Fleming	.65
56	Kevin Mitchell	.20
57	*Jeff Nelson*	.20
58	Shane Turner	.20
59	Jose Canseco	4.00
60	*Jeff Frye*	.30
61	Danilo Leon	.20
62	Roger Pavlik	.30
63	David Cone	.35
64	Pat Hentgen	4.00
65	Randy Knorr	.20
66	Jack Morris	.20
67	Dave Winfield	2.00
68	*David Nied*	.20
69	Otis Nixon	.20
70	Alejandro Pena	.20
71	Jeff Reardon	.20
72	Alex Arias	.25
73	Jim Bullinger	.20
74	Mike Morgan	.20
75	Rey Sanchez	.20
76	Bob Scanlan	.20
77	Sammy Sosa	15.00
78	Scott Bankhead	.20
79	Tim Belcher	.20
80	Steve Foster	.20
81	Willie Greene	.50
82	Bip Roberts	.20
83	Scott Ruskin	.20
84	Greg Swindell	.20
85	Juan Guerrero	.20
86	Butch Henry	.20
87	Doug Jones	.20
88	Brian Williams	.30
89	Tom Candiotti	.20
90	Eric Davis	.25
91	Carlos Hernandez	.20
92	*Mike Piazza*	85.00
93	Mike Sharperson	.20
94	Eric Young	.75
95	Moises Alou	4.00
96	Greg Colbrunn	.20
97	Wil Cordero	3.00
98	Ken Hill	.50
99	John Vander Wal	.40
100	John Wetteland	.20
101	Bobby Bonilla	.35
102	Eric Hilman	.20
103	Pat Howell	.20
104	*Jeff Kent*	4.00
105	Dick Schofield	.20
106	*Ryan Thompson*	.50
107	Chico Walker	.20
108	Juan Bell	.20
109	Mariano Duncan	.20
110	Jeff Grotewold	.25
111	Ben Rivera	.20
112	Curt Schilling	3.00
113	Victor Cole	.20
114	Al Martin	2.00
115	Roger Mason	.20
116	Blas Minor	.35
117	Tim Wakefield	.50
118	*Mark Clark*	2.00
119	Rheal Cormier	.35
120	Donovan Osborne	.20
121	Todd Worrell	.20
122	Jeremy Hernandez	.25
123	Randy Myers	.20
124	Frank Seminara	.20
125	Gary Sheffield	3.00
126	Dan Walters	.20
127	Steve Hosey	.40
128	Mike Jackson	.20
129	Jim Pena	.20
130	Cory Snyder	.20
131	Bill Swift	.20
132	Checklist	.05

1992 Fleer 7-Eleven

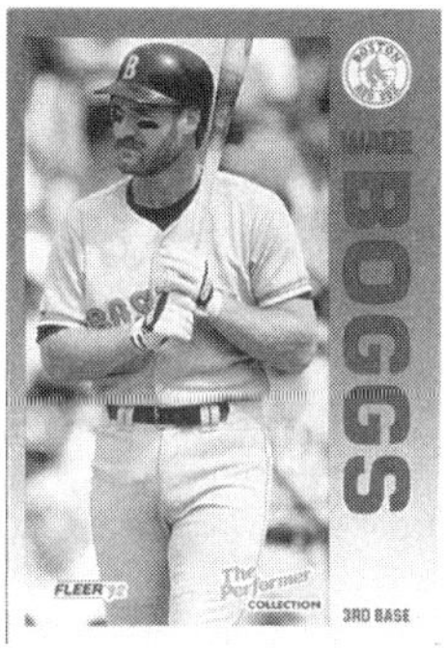

The 1992 Performer Collection was a combined effort from Fleer and 7-11. Customers at 7-11 stores received a packet of five cards with gasoline purchases to build the 24-card set of major stars. The cards are standard size, with virtually the identical design to the regular issue Fleer set of 1992, with only the addition of "The Performer" logo on the lower corner of the card.

		MT
Complete Set (24):		8.00
Common Player:		.20
1	Nolan Ryan	1.50
2	Frank Thomas	1.00
3	Ryne Sandberg	.75
4	Ken Griffey, Jr.	2.00
5	Cal Ripken, Jr.	1.50
6	Roger Clemens	.75
7	Cecil Fielder	.20
8	Dave Justice	.40
9	Wade Boggs	.60
10	Tony Gwynn	.75
11	Kirby Puckett	.75
12	Darryl Strawberry	.30
13	Jose Canseco	.50
14	Barry Larkin	.20
15	Terry Pendleton	.20
16	Don Mattingly	1.00
17	Rickey Henderson	.50
18	Ruben Sierra	.20
19	Jeff Bagwell	.75
20	Tom Glavine	.25
21	Ramon Martinez	.25
22	Will Clark	.45
23	Barry Bonds	.75
24	Roberto Alomar	.40

1993 Fleer

The card fronts feature silver borders with the player's name, team and position in a banner along the left side of the card. The backs feature an action photo of the player with his name in bold behind him. A box featuring biographical information, statistics and player information is located to the right of the action photo. The cards are numbered alphabetically by team. The basic Fleer issue for 1993 was issued in two series of 360 cards each. The 720-card set included a number of subsets and could be found in many different types of packaging with an unprecedented number of insert sets to spice up each offering.

		MT
Complete Set (720):		35.00
Common Player:		.05
Series 1 or 2 Wax Box:		26.00
1	Steve Avery	.05
2	Sid Bream	.05
3	Ron Gant	.10
4	Tom Glavine	.10
5	Brian Hunter	.05
6	Ryan Klesko	.25
7	Charlie Leibrandt	.05
8	Kent Mercker	.05
9	David Nied	.05
10	Otis Nixon	.05
11	Greg Olson	.05
12	Terry Pendleton	.05
13	Deion Sanders	.15
14	John Smoltz	.12
15	Mike Stanton	.05
16	Mark Wohlers	.05
17	Paul Assenmacher	.05
18	Steve Buechele	.05
19	Shawon Dunston	.05
20	Mark Grace	.15
21	Derrick May	.05
22	Chuck McElroy	.05
23	Mike Morgan	.05
24	Rey Sanchez	.05
25	Ryne Sandberg	.30
26	Bob Scanlan	.05
27	Sammy Sosa	.75
28	Rick Wilkins	.05
29	*Bobby Ayala*	.05
30	Tim Belcher	.05
31	*Jeff Branson*	.12
32	Norm Charlton	.05
33	*Steve Foster*	.05
34	Willie Greene	.08
35	Chris Hammond	.05
36	Milt Hill	.05
37	Hal Morris	.05
38	Joe Oliver	.05
39	Paul O'Neill	.15
40	*Tim Pugh*	.12
41	Jose Rijo	.05
42	Bip Roberts	.05
43	Chris Sabo	.05
44	Reggie Sanders	.08
45	Eric Anthony	.05
46	Jeff Bagwell	.75
47	Craig Biggio	.15
48	Joe Boever	.05
49	Casey Candaele	.05
50	Steve Finley	.05
51	Luis Gonzalez	.08
52	Pete Harnisch	.05
53	Xavier Hernandez	.05
54	Doug Jones	.05
55	Eddie Taubensee	.05
56	Brian Williams	.05
57	*Pedro Astacio*	.12
58	Todd Benzinger	.05
59	Brett Butler	.08
60	Tom Candiotti	.05
61	Lenny Harris	.05
62	Carlos Hernandez	.05
63	Orel Hershiser	.08
64	Eric Karros	.12
65	Ramon Martinez	.08
66	Jose Offerman	.05
67	Mike Scioscia	.05
68	Mike Sharperson	.05
69	*Eric Young*	.08
70	Moises Alou	.10
71	Ivan Calderon	.05
72	*Archi Cianfrocco*	.05
73	Wil Cordero	.08
74	Delino DeShields	.08
75	Mark Gardner	.05
76	Ken Hill	.05
77	*Tim Laker*	.08
78	Chris Nabholz	.05
79	Mel Rojas	.05
80	*John Vander Wal*	.12
81	Larry Walker	.20
82	Tim Wallach	.05
83	John Wetteland	.05
84	Bobby Bonilla	.08
85	Daryl Boston	.05

86	Sid Fernandez	.05
87	*Eric Hillman*	.08
88	Todd Hundley	.12
89	Howard Johnson	.05
90	Jeff Kent	.12
91	Eddie Murray	.30
92	Bill Pecota	.05
93	Bret Saberhagen	.08
94	Dick Schofield	.05
95	Pete Schourek	.05
96	Anthony Young	.05
97	Ruben Amaro Jr.	.05
98	Juan Bell	.05
99	Wes Chamberlain	.05
100	Darren Daulton	.05
101	Mariano Duncan	.05
102	Mike Hartley	.05
103	Ricky Jordan	.05
104	John Kruk	.05
105	Mickey Morandini	.05
106	Terry Mulholland	.05
107	*Ben Rivera*	.05
108	Curt Schilling	.08
109	*Keith Shepherd*	.05
110	Stan Belinda	.05
111	Jay Bell	.05
112	Barry Bonds	.40
113	Jeff King	.05
114	Mike LaValliere	.05
115	Jose Lind	.05
116	Roger Mason	.05
117	Orlando Merced	.05
118	Bob Patterson	.05
119	Don Slaught	.05
120	Zane Smith	.05
121	Randy Tomlin	.05
122	Andy Van Slyke	.05
123	*Tim Wakefield*	.08
124	Rheal Cormier	.05
125	Bernard Gilkey	.05
126	Felix Jose	.05
127	Ray Lankford	.05
128	Bob McClure	.05
129	Donovan Osborne	.05
130	Tom Pagnozzi	.05
131	Geronimo Pena	.05
132	Mike Perez	.05
133	Lee Smith	.08
134	Bob Tewksbury	.05
135	Todd Worrell	.05
136	Todd Zeile	.08
137	Jerald Clark	.05
138	Tony Gwynn	.40
139	Greg Harris	.05
140	Jeremy Hernandez	.05
141	Darrin Jackson	.05
142	Mike Maddux	.05
143	Fred McGriff	.20
144	Jose Melendez	.05
145	Rich Rodriguez	.05
146	Frank Seminara	.05
147	Gary Sheffield	.20
148	Kurt Stillwell	.05
149	*Dan Walters*	.10
150	Rod Beck	.05
151	Bud Black	.05
152	Jeff Brantley	.05
153	John Burkett	.05
154	Will Clark	.20
155	Royce Clayton	.05
156	Mike Jackson	.05
157	Darren Lewis	.05
158	Kirt Manwaring	.05
159	Willie McGee	.08
160	Cory Snyder	.05
161	Bill Swift	.05
162	Trevor Wilson	.05
163	Brady Anderson	.10
164	Glenn Davis	.05
165	Mike Devereaux	.05
166	Todd Frohwirth	.05
167	Leo Gomez	.05
168	Chris Hoiles	.05
169	Ben McDonald	.05
170	Randy Milligan	.05
171	Alan Mills	.05
172	Mike Mussina	.30
173	Gregg Olson	.05
174	Arthur Rhodes	.05
175	David Segui	.05
176	Ellis Burks	.08
177	Roger Clemens	.75
178	Scott Cooper	.05
179	Danny Darwin	.05
180	Tony Fossas	.05
181	*Paul Quantrill*	.08
182	Jody Reed	.05
183	*John Valentin*	.15
184	Mo Vaughn	.35
185	Frank Viola	.05
186	Bob Zupcic	.05
187	Jim Abbott	.08
188	Gary DiSarcina	.05
189	*Damion Easley*	.10
190	Junior Felix	.05
191	Chuck Finley	.05
192	Joe Grahe	.05
193	Bryan Harvey	.05
194	Mark Langston	.05
195	John Orton	.05
196	Luis Polonia	.05
197	Tim Salmon	.40
198	Luis Sojo	.05
199	Wilson Alvarez	.05
200	George Bell	.05
201	Alex Fernandez	.08
202	Craig Grebeck	.05
203	Ozzie Guillen	.05
204	Lance Johnson	.05
205	Ron Karkovice	.05
206	Kirk McCaskill	.05
207	Jack McDowell	.05
208	Scott Radinsky	.05
209	Tim Raines	.08
210	Frank Thomas	1.00
211	Robin Ventura	.12
212	Sandy Alomar Jr.	.08
213	Carlos Baerga	.08
214	Dennis Cook	.05
215	Thomas Howard	.05
216	Mark Lewis	.05
217	Derek Lilliquist	.05
218	Kenny Lofton	.50
219	Charles Nagy	.08
220	Steve Olin	.05
221	Paul Sorrento	.05
222	Jim Thome	.25
223	Mark Whiten	.05
224	Milt Cuyler	.05
225	Rob Deer	.05
226	*John Doherty*	.12
227	Cecil Fielder	.08
228	Travis Fryman	.10
229	Mike Henneman	.05
230	*John Kiely*	.05
231	*Kurt Knudsen*	.08
232	Scott Livingstone	.05
233	Tony Phillips	.05
234	Mickey Tettleton	.05
235	Kevin Appier	.05
236	George Brett	.40
237	Tom Gordon	.05
238	Gregg Jefferies	.10
239	Wally Joyner	.08
240	*Kevin Koslofski*	.12
241	Mike Macfarlane	.05
242	Brian McRae	.05
243	Rusty Meacham	.05
244	Keith Miller	.05
245	Jeff Montgomery	.05
246	*Hipolito Pichardo*	.05
247	Ricky Bones	.05
248	Cal Eldred	.05
249	Mike Fetters	.05
250	Darryl Hamilton	.05
251	Doug Henry	.05
252	John Jaha	.05
253	Pat Listach	.05
254	Paul Molitor	.30
255	Jaime Navarro	.05
256	Kevin Seitzer	.05
257	B.J. Surhoff	.08
258	Greg Vaughn	.08
259	Bill Wegman	.05
260	Robin Yount	.30
261	Rick Aguilera	.05
262	Chili Davis	.08
263	Scott Erickson	.05
264	Greg Gagne	.05
265	Mark Guthrie	.05
266	Brian Harper	.05
267	Kent Hrbek	.08
268	Terry Jorgensen	.05
269	Gene Larkin	.05
270	Scott Leius	.05
271	Pat Mahomes	.05
272	Pedro Munoz	.05
273	Kirby Puckett	.50
274	Kevin Tapani	.05
275	Carl Willis	.05
276	Steve Farr	.05
277	John Habyan	.05
278	Mel Hall	.05
279	Charlie Hayes	.05
280	Pat Kelly	.05
281	Don Mattingly	.50
282	Sam Militello	.05
283	Matt Nokes	.05
284	Melido Perez	.05
285	Andy Stankiewicz	.05
286	Danny Tartabull	.05
287	Randy Velarde	.05
288	Bob Wickman	.05
289	Bernie Williams	.40
290	Lance Blankenship	.05
291	Mike Bordick	.05
292	Jerry Browne	.05
293	Dennis Eckersley	.08
294	Rickey Henderson	.20
295	*Vince Horsman*	.12
296	Mark McGwire	2.00
297	Jeff Parrett	.05
298	Ruben Sierra	.05
299	Terry Steinbach	.05
300	Walt Weiss	.05
301	Bob Welch	.05
302	Willie Wilson	.05
303	Bobby Witt	.05
304	Bret Boone	.05
305	Jay Buhner	.08
306	Dave Fleming	.05
307	Ken Griffey, Jr.	2.00
308	Erik Hanson	.05
309	Edgar Martinez	.08
310	Tino Martinez	.15
311	Jeff Nelson	.05
312	Dennis Powell	.05
313	Mike Schooler	.05
314	Russ Swan	.05
315	Dave Valle	.05
316	Omar Vizquel	.08
317	Kevin Brown	.05
318	Todd Burns	.05
319	Jose Canseco	.30
320	Julio Franco	.05
321	Jeff Frye	.08
322	Juan Gonzalez	.50
323	Jose Guzman	.05
324	Jeff Huson	.05
325	Dean Palmer	.08
326	Kevin Reimer	.05
327	Ivan Rodriguez	.40
328	Kenny Rogers	.05
329	Dan Smith	.05
330	Roberto Alomar	.35
331	Derek Bell	.08
332	Pat Borders	.05
333	Joe Carter	.08
334	Kelly Gruber	.05
335	Tom Henke	.05
336	Jimmy Key	.05
337	Manuel Lee	.05
338	Candy Maldonado	.05
339	John Olerud	.15
340	Todd Stottlemyre	.05
341	Duane Ward	.05
342	Devon White	.08
343	Dave Winfield	.15
344	Edgar Martinez (League Leaders)	.05
345	Cecil Fielder (League Leaders)	.05
346	Kenny Lofton (League Leaders)	.15
347	Jack Morris (League Leaders)	.05
348	Roger Clemens (League Leaders)	.25
349	Fred McGriff (Round Trippers)	.10
350	Barry Bonds (Round Trippers)	.15
351	Gary Sheffield (Round Trippers)	.10
352	Darren Daulton (Round Trippers)	.05
353	Dave Hollins (Round Trippers)	.05
354	Brothers In Blue (Pedro Martinez, Ramon Martinez)	.50
355	Power Packs (Ivan Rodriguez, Kirby Puckett)	.35
356	Triple Threats (Ryne Sandberg, Gary Sheffield)	.15
357	Infield Trifecta (Roberto Alomar, Chuck Knoblauch, Carlos Baerga)	.15
358	Checklist	.05
359	Checklist	.05
360	Checklist	.05
361	Rafael Belliard	.05
362	Damon Berryhill	.05
363	Mike Bielecki	.05
364	Jeff Blauser	.05
365	Francisco Cabrera	.05
366	Marvin Freeman	.05
367	Dave Justice	.20
368	Mark Lemke	.05
369	Alejandro Pena	.05
370	Jeff Reardon	.05
371	Lonnie Smith	.05
372	Pete Smith	.05
373	Shawn Boskie	.05
374	Jim Bullinger	.05
375	Frank Castillo	.05
376	Doug Dascenzo	.05
377	Andre Dawson	.12
378	Mike Harkey	.05
379	Greg Hibbard	.05
380	Greg Maddux	1.00
381	Ken Patterson	.05
382	Jeff Robinson	.05
383	Luis Salazar	.05
384	Dwight Smith	.05
385	Jose Vizcaino	.05
386	Scott Bankhead	.05
387	Tom Browning	.05
388	Darnell Coles	.05
389	Rob Dibble	.05
390	Bill Doran	.05
391	Dwayne Henry	.05
392	Cesar Hernandez	.05
393	Roberto Kelly	.05
394	Barry Larkin	.10
395	Dave Martinez	.05
396	Kevin Mitchell	.05
397	Jeff Reed	.05
398	Scott Ruskin	.05
399	Greg Swindell	.05
400	Dan Wilson	.08
401	Andy Ashby	.08
402	Freddie Benavides	.05
403	Dante Bichette	.10
404	Willie Blair	.05
405	Denis Boucher	.05
406	Vinny Castilla	.10
407	Braulio Castillo	.05
408	Alex Cole	.05
409	Andres Galarraga	.15
410	Joe Girardi	.05
411	Butch Henry	.05
412	Darren Holmes	.05
413	Calvin Jones	.05
414	*Steve Reed*	.10
415	Kevin Ritz	.05
416	*Jim Tatum*	.05
417	Jack Armstrong	.05
418	Bret Barberie	.05
419	Ryan Bowen	.05
420	Cris Carpenter	.05
421	Chuck Carr	.05
422	Scott Chiamparino	.05
423	Jeff Conine	.08
424	Jim Corsi	.05
425	Steve Decker	.05
426	Chris Donnels	.05
427	Monty Fariss	.05
428	Bob Natal	.05
429	*Pat Rapp*	.08
430	Dave Weathers	.05
431	*Nigel Wilson*	.10
432	Ken Caminiti	.15
433	Andujar Cedeno	.05
434	Tom Edens	.05
435	Juan Guerrero	.05
436	Pete Incaviglia	.05
437	Jimmy Jones	.05
438	Darryl Kile	.05
439	Rob Murphy	.05
440	Al Osuna	.05
441	Mark Portugal	.05
442	Scott Servais	.05
443	John Candelaria	.05
444	Tim Crews	.05
445	Eric Davis	.08
446	Tom Goodwin	.05
447	Jim Gott	.05
448	Kevin Gross	.05
449	Dave Hansen	.05
450	Jay Howell	.05
451	Roger McDowell	.05
452	Bob Ojeda	.05
453	Henry Rodriguez	.08
454	Darryl Strawberry	.10
455	Mitch Webster	.05
456	Steve Wilson	.05
457	Brian Barnes	.05
458	Sean Berry	.05
459	Jeff Fassero	.05
460	Darrin Fletcher	.05
461	Marquis Grissom	.08
462	Dennis Martinez	.08
463	Spike Owen	.05
464	Matt Stairs	.05
465	Sergio Valdez	.05
466	Kevin Bass	.05
467	Vince Coleman	.05
468	Mark Dewey	.05
469	Kevin Elster	.05
470	Tony Fernandez	.05
471	John Franco	.05
472	Dave Gallagher	.05
473	Paul Gibson	.05
474	Dwight Gooden	.12
475	Lee Guetterman	.05
476	Jeff Innis	.05
477	Dave Magadan	.05
478	Charlie O'Brien	.05
479	Willie Randolph	.05
480	Mackey Sasser	.05
481	Ryan Thompson	.05
482	Chico Walker	.05
483	Kyle Abbott	.05
484	Bob Ayrault	.05
485	Kim Batiste	.05
486	Cliff Brantley	.05
487	Jose DeLeon	.05
488	Len Dykstra	.05
489	Tommy Greene	.05
490	Jeff Grotewold	.05
491	Dave Hollins	.08
492	Danny Jackson	.05
493	Stan Javier	.05
494	Tom Marsh	.05
495	Greg Matthews	.05
496	Dale Murphy	.12
497	*Todd Pratt*	.10
498	Mitch Williams	.05
499	Danny Cox	.05
500	Doug Drabek	.05
501	Carlos Garcia	.05
502	Lloyd McClendon	.05
503	Denny Neagle	.05
504	Gary Redus	.05
505	Bob Walk	.05
506	John Wehner	.05
507	Luis Alicea	.05
508	Mark Clark	.05
509	Pedro Guerrero	.05
510	Rex Hudler	.05
511	Brian Jordan	.10
512	Omar Olivares	.05
513	Jose Oquendo	.05
514	Gerald Perry	.05
515	Bryn Smith	.05
516	Craig Wilson	.05
517	Tracy Woodson	.05
518	Larry Anderson	.05
519	Andy Benes	.05
520	Jim Deshaies	.05
521	Bruce Hurst	.05
522	Randy Myers	.05
523	Benito Santiago	.05
524	Tim Scott	.05
525	Tim Teufel	.05
526	Mike Benjamin	.05
527	Dave Burba	.05
528	Craig Colbert	.05
529	Mike Felder	.05
530	Bryan Hickerson	.05
531	Chris James	.05
532	Mark Leonard	.05
533	Greg Litton	.05
534	Francisco Oliveras	.05
535	John Patterson	.05
536	Jim Pena	.05
537	Dave Righetti	.05
538	Robby Thompson	.05
539	Jose Uribe	.05
540	Matt Williams	.30
541	Storm Davis	.05
542	Sam Horn	.05
543	Tim Hulett	.05
544	Craig Lefferts	.05
545	Chito Martinez	.05
546	Mark McLemore	.05
547	Luis Mercedes	.05
548	Bob Milacki	.05
549	Joe Orsulak	.05
550	Billy Ripken	.05
551	Cal Ripken, Jr.	1.25
552	Rick Sutcliffe	.05
553	Jeff Tackett	.05
554	Wade Boggs	.35
555	Tom Brunansky	.05
556	Jack Clark	.05
557	John Dopson	.05
558	Mike Gardiner	.05
559	Mike Greenwell	.05
560	Greg Harris	.05
561	Billy Hatcher	.05
562	Joe Hesketh	.05
563	Tony Pena	.05
564	Phil Plantier	.05
565	Luis Rivera	.05
566	Herm Winningham	.05
567	Matt Young	.05
568	Bert Blyleven	.05
569	Mike Butcher	.05
570	Chuck Crim	.05
571	*Chad Curtis*	.15
572	Tim Fortugno	.05
573	Steve Frey	.05
574	Gary Gaetti	.05
575	Scott Lewis	.05
576	Lee Stevens	.05
577	Ron Tingley	.05
578	Julio Valera	.05
579	Shawn Abner	.05
580	Joey Cora	.05
581	Chris Cron	.05
582	Carlton Fisk	.10
583	Roberto Hernandez	.05
584	Charlie Hough	.05
585	Terry Leach	.05
586	Donn Pall	.05
587	Dan Pasqua	.05
588	Steve Sax	.05
589	Bobby Thigpen	.05
590	Albert Belle	.40
591	Felix Fermin	.05
592	Glenallen Hill	.05
593	Brook Jacoby	.05
594	Reggie Jefferson	.05
595	Carlos Martinez	.05
596	Jose Mesa	.05
597	Rod Nichols	.05
598	Junior Ortiz	.05
599	Eric Plunk	.05
600	Ted Power	.05
601	Scott Scudder	.05
602	Kevin Wickander	.05
603	Skeeter Barnes	.05
604	Mark Carreon	.05
605	Dan Gladden	.05
606	Bill Gullickson	.05
607	Chad Kreuter	.05
608	Mark Leiter	.05
609	Mike Munoz	.05
610	Rich Rowland	.05
611	Frank Tanana	.05
612	Walt Terrell	.05
613	Alan Trammell	.10
614	Lou Whitaker	.08
615	Luis Aquino	.05
616	Mike Boddicker	.05
617	Jim Eisenreich	.05
618	Mark Gubicza	.05
619	David Howard	.05
620	Mike Magnante	.05
621	Brent Mayne	.05
622	Kevin McReynolds	.05
623	*Eddie Pierce*	.05
624	Bill Sampen	.05
625	Steve Shifflett	.05
626	Gary Thurman	.05
627	Curtis Wikerson	.05
628	Chris Bosio	.05
629	Scott Fletcher	.05
630	Jim Gantner	.05
631	Dave Nilsson	.05
632	Jesse Orosco	.05
633	Dan Plesac	.05
634	Ron Robinson	.05
635	Bill Spiers	.05
636	Franklin Stubbs	.05
637	Willie Banks	.05
638	Randy Bush	.05
639	Chuck Knoblauch	.20
640	Shane Mack	.05
641	Mike Pagliarulo	.05
642	Jeff Reboulet	.05
643	John Smiley	.05
644	*Mike Trombley*	.08
645	Gary Wayne	.05
646	Lenny Webster	.05
647	Tim Burke	.05
648	Mike Gallego	.05
649	Dion James	.05
650	Jeff Johnson	.05
651	Scott Kamieniecki	.05
652	Kevin Maas	.05
653	Rich Monteleone	.05
654	Jerry Nielsen	.05
655	Scott Sanderson	.05
656	Mike Stanley	.05

657	Gerald Williams	.05
658	Curt Young	.05
659	Harold Baines	.08
660	Kevin Campbell	.05
661	Ron Darling	.05
662	Kelly Downs	.05
663	Eric Fox	.05
664	Dave Henderson	.05
665	Rick Honeycutt	.05
666	Mike Moore	.05
667	Jamie Quirk	.05
668	Jeff Russell	.05
669	Dave Stewart	.08
670	Greg Briley	.05
671	Dave Cochrane	.05
672	Henry Cotto	.05
673	Rich DeLucia	.05
674	Brian Fisher	.05
675	Mark Grant	.05
676	Randy Johnson	.35
677	Tim Leary	.05
678	Pete O'Brien	.05
679	Lance Parrish	.08
680	Harold Reynolds	.05
681	Shane Turner	.05
682	Jack Daugherty	.05
683	*David Hulse*	.10
684	Terry Mathews	.05
685	Al Newman	.05
686	Edwin Nunez	.05
687	Rafael Palmeiro	.15
688	Roger Pavlik	.05
689	Geno Petralli	.05
690	Nolan Ryan	.75
691	David Cone	.10
692	Alfredo Griffin	.05
693	Juan Guzman	.08
694	Pat Hentgen	.05
695	Randy Knorr	.05
696	Bob MacDonald	.05
697	Jack Morris	.05
698	Ed Sprague	.05
699	Dave Stieb	.05
700	Pat Tabler	.05
701	Mike Timlin	.05
702	David Wells	.08
703	Eddie Zosky	.05
704	Gary Sheffield (League Leaders)	.10
705	Darren Daulton (League Leaders)	.05
706	Marquis Grissom (League Leaders)	.10
707	Greg Maddux (League Leaders)	.20
708	Bill Swift (League Leaders)	.05
709	Juan Gonzalez (Round Trippers)	.25
710	Mark McGwire (Round Trippers)	1.00
711	Cecil Fielder (Round Trippers)	.10
712	Albert Belle (Round Trippers)	.25
713	Joe Carter (Round Trippers)	.10
714	Power Brokers (Frank Thomas, Cecil Fielder)	.40
715	Unsung Heroes (Larry Walker, Darren Daulton)	.10
716	Hot Corner Hammers (Edgar Martinez, Robin Ventura)	.10
717	Start to Finish (Roger Clemens, Dennis Eckersley)	.25
718	Checklist	.05
719	Checklist	.05
720	Checklist	.05

1993 Fleer All-Stars

Horizontal-format All-Star cards comprised one of the many 1993 Fleer insert issues. Twelve cards of National League All-Stars were included in Series I wax packs, while a dozen American League All-Stars were found in Series II packs. They are among the more popular and valuable of the '93 Fleer inserts.

		MT
Complete Set A.L. (12):		20.00
Complete Set N.L. (12):		12.00
Common Player:		.50
AMERICAN LEAGUE		
1	Frank Thomas	3.50
2	Roberto Alomar	1.50
3	Edgar Martinez	.60
4	Pat Listach	.50
5	Cecil Fielder	.75
6	Juan Gonzalez	3.50
7	Ken Griffey, Jr.	8.00
8	Joe Carter	.60
9	Kirby Puckett	3.00
10	Brian Harper	.50
11	Dave Fleming	.50
12	Jack McDowell	.60
NATIONAL LEAGUE		
1	Fred McGriff	.60
2	Delino DeShields	.50
3	Gary Sheffield	1.00
4	Barry Larkin	.60
5	Felix Jose	.50
6	Larry Walker	1.50
7	Barry Bonds	2.50
8	Andy Van Slyke	.50
9	Darren Daulton	.50
10	Greg Maddux	5.00
11	Tom Glavine	.75
12	Lee Smith	.60

1993 Fleer Tom Glavine Career Highlights

This 15-card insert set spotlighted the career highlights of Fleer's 1993 spokesman, Tom Glavine. Twelve cards were available in Series I and Series II packs; cards #13-15 could be obtained only via a special mail offer. A limited number of certified autograph cards were also inserted into packs. Cards #1-4 and 7-10 can each be found with two variations of the writeups on the back. The versions found in Series II packaging are the "correct" backs. Neither version carries a premium value.

		MT
Complete Set (15):		5.00
Common Card:		.50
Autographed Card:		75.00
1	Tom Glavine	.50
2	Tom Glavine	.50
3	Tom Glavine	.50
4	Tom Glavine	.50
5	Tom Glavine	.50
6	Tom Glavine	.50
7	Tom Glavine	.50
8	Tom Glavine	.50
9	Tom Glavine	.50
10	Tom Glavine	.50
11	Tom Glavine	.50
12	Tom Glavine	.50
13	Tom Glavine	.50
14	Tom Glavine	.50
15	Tom Glavine	.50

1993 Fleer Golden Moments

Three cards of this insert set were available in both series of wax packs. Fronts feature black borders with gold-foil baseballs in the corners. The player's name appears in a "Golden Moments" banner at the bottom of the photo. Backs have a portrait photo of the player at top-center and information on the highlight. The cards are unnumbered and are checklisted here alphabetically within series.

		MT
Complete Set (6):		11.00
Common Player:		.75
	SERIES 1	4.00
(1)	George Brett	3.00
(2)	Mickey Morandini	.75
(3)	Dave Winfield	1.25
	SERIES 2	7.00
(1)	Dennis Eckersley	.75
(2)	Bip Roberts	.75
(3)	Frank Thomas, Juan Gonzalez	4.00

1993 Fleer Major League Prospects

Yet another way to package currently hot rookies and future prospects to increase sales of the base product, there were 18 insert cards found in each series' wax packs. Fronts are bordered in black and have gold-foil highlights. Most of the depicted players were a few seasons away from everyday play in the major leagues.

		MT
Complete Set (36):		25.00
Common Player:		.60
	SERIES 1	18.00
1	Melvin Nieves	.50
2	Sterling Hitchcock	.50
3	Tim Costo	.50
4	Manny Alexander	.50
5	Alan Embree	.50
6	Kevin Young	1.00
7	J.T. Snow	1.50
8	Russ Springer	.50
9	Billy Ashley	.50
10	Kevin Rogers	.50
11	Steve Hosey	.50
12	Eric Wedge	.50
13	Mike Piazza	11.00
14	Jesse Levis	.50
15	Rico Brogna	.50
16	Alex Arias	.50
17	Rod Brewer	.50
18	Troy Neel	.50
	SERIES 2	9.00
1	Scooter Tucker	.50
2	Kerry Woodson	.50
3	Greg Colbrunn	.50
4	Pedro Martinez	3.50
5	Dave Silvestri	.50
6	Kent Bottenfield	.75
7	Rafael Bournigal	.50
8	J.T. Bruett	.50
9	Dave Mlicki	.50
10	Paul Wagner	.50
11	Mike Williams	.50
12	Henry Mercedes	.50
13	Scott Taylor	.50
14	Dennis Moeller	.50
15	Javier Lopez	3.50
16	Steve Cooke	.50
17	Pete Young	.50
18	Ken Ryan	.50

1993 Fleer ProVisions

This three-card insert set in Series I wax packs features the baseball art of Wayne Still. Black-bordered fronts feature a player-fantasy painting at center, with the player's name gold-foil stamped beneath. Backs are also bordered in black and have a white box with a career summary.

		MT
Complete Set (6):		8.00
Common Player:		.75
	SERIES 1	4.00
1	Roberto Alomar	2.00
2	Dennis Eckersley	.75
3	Gary Sheffield	2.00
	SERIES 2	3.00
1	Andy Van Slyke	.75
2	Tom Glavine	1.50
3	Cecil Fielder	1.00

1993 Fleer Rookie Sensations

Ten rookie sensations - some of whom had not been true rookies for several seasons - were featured in this insert issue packaged exclusively in Series 1 and Series 2 cello packs. Card fronts have a player photo set against a silver background and surrounded by a blue border. The player's name and other front printing are in gold foil. Backs are also printed in silver with a blue border. There is a player portrait photo and career summary.

		MT
Complete Set (20):		18.50
Common Player:		.75
	SERIES 1	15.00
1	Kenny Lofton	11.00
2	Cal Eldred	.75
3	Pat Listach	.75
4	Roberto Hernandez	.75
5	Dave Fleming	.75
6	Eric Karros	2.00
7	Reggie Sanders	1.50
8	Derrick May	.75
9	Mike Perez	.75
10	Donovan Osborne	.75
	SERIES 2	7.50
1	Moises Alou	2.75
2	Pedro Astacio	1.25
3	Jim Austin	.75
4	Chad Curtis	.75
5	Gary DiSarcina	.75
6	Scott Livingstone	.75
7	Sam Militello	.75
8	Arthur Rhodes	.75
9	Tim Wakefield	.75
10	Bob Zupcic	.75

1993 Fleer Team Leaders

This 20-card insert issue was exclusive to Series 1 and 2 rack packs. Fronts have a portrait photo, with a small action photo superimposed. At the side is a colored bar with the player's name and "Team Leaders" printed vertically. On back is a career summary. Card borders are a light metallic green and both sides of the card are UV coated.

		MT
Complete Set (20):		45.00
Common Player:		.50
	SERIES 1	35.00
1	Kirby Puckett	5.00
2	Mark McGwire	12.50
3	Pat Listach	.50
4	Roger Clemens	3.00
5	Frank Thomas	4.00
6	Carlos Baerga	.50
7	Brady Anderson	.50
8	Juan Gonzalez	3.00
9	Roberto Alomar	1.25
10	Ken Griffey, Jr.	12.50
	SERIES 2	12.00
1	Will Clark	1.00
2	Terry Pendleton	.50
3	Ray Lankford	.50
4	Eric Karros	.75
5	Gary Sheffield	1.25
6	Ryne Sandberg	2.50
7	Marquis Grissom	.75
8	John Kruk	.50
9	Jeff Bagwell	5.00
10	Andy Van Slyke	.50

1993 Fleer Final Edition

This 310-card set was sold as a complete set in its own box. Card numbers have the prefix "F". The set also includes 10 Diamond Tribute cards, which are numbered DT1-DT10.

		MT
Complete Set (310):		10.00
Common Player:		.05
1	Steve Bedrosian	.05
2	Jay Howell	.05
3	Greg Maddux	1.50
4	*Greg McMichael*	.05
5	*Tony Tarasco*	.05
6	Jose Bautista	.05
7	Jose Guzman	.05
8	Greg Hibbard	.05
9	Candy Maldonado	.05
10	Randy Myers	.05
11	*Matt Walbeck*	.10
12	Turk Wendell	.05
13	Willie Nelson	.05
14	Greg Cadaret	.05
15	Roberto Kelly	.05
16	Randy Milligan	.05
17	Kevin Mitchell	.05
18	Jeff Reardon	.05
19	John Roper	.05
20	John Smiley	.05
21	Andy Ashby	.08
22	Dante Bichette	.30
23	Willie Blair	.05
24	Pedro Castellano	.05
25	Vinny Castilla	.20
26	Jerald Clark	.05
27	Alex Cole	.05
28	*Scott Fredrickson*	.05
29	*Jay Gainer*	.05
30	Andres Galarraga	.25
31	Joe Girardi	.05
32	Ryan Hawblitzel	.05
33	Charlie Hayes	.05
34	Darren Holmes	.05
35	Chris Jones	.05
36	David Nied	.05
37	*J. Owens*	.10
38	*Lance Painter*	.05
39	Jeff Parrett	.05
40	*Steve Reed*	.05
41	Armando Reynoso	.05
42	Bruce Ruffin	.05
43	*Danny Sheaffer*	.08
44	Keith Shepherd	.05
45	Jim Tatum	.05
46	Gary Wayne	.05
47	Eric Young	.10
48	Luis Aquino	.05
49	Alex Arias	.05
50	Jack Armstrong	.05
51	Bret Barberie	.05
52	Geronimo Berroa	.05
53	Ryan Bowen	.05
54	Greg Briley	.05
55	Chris Carpenter	.05
56	Chuck Carr	.05
57	Jeff Conine	.10
58	Jim Corsi	.05
59	Orestes Destrade	.05
60	Junior Felix	.05
61	Chris Hammond	.05
62	Bryan Harvey	.05
63	Charlie Hough	.05
64	Joe Klink	.05
65	*Richie Lewis*	.10
66	*Mitch Lyden*	.05
67	Bob Natal	.05
68	*Scott Pose*	.05
69	Rich Renteria	.05
70	Benito Santiago	.05
71	Gary Sheffield	.40
72	*Matt Turner*	.10
73	Walt Weiss	.05
74	*Darrell Whitmore*	.10
75	Nigel Wilson	.05
76	Kevin Bass	.05
77	Doug Drabek	.05
78	Tom Edens	.05
79	Chris James	.05
80	Greg Swindell	.05
81	*Omar Daal*	.10
82	Raul Mondesi	1.00
83	Jody Reed	.05
84	Cory Snyder	.05
85	Rick Trlicek	.05
86	Tim Wallach	.05
87	Todd Worrell	.05
88	Tavo Alvarez	.05
89	Frank Bolick	.05
90	Kent Bottenfield	.05
91	Greg Colbrunn	.05
92	Cliff Floyd	.15
93	*Lou Frazier*	.08
94	Mike Gardiner	.05
95	*Mike Lansing*	.30
96	Bill Risley	.05
97	Jeff Shaw	.05
98	Kevin Baez	.05
99	*Tim Bogar*	.10
100	Jeromy Burnitz	.15
101	Mike Draper	.05
102	Darrin Jackson	.05
103	Mike Maddux	.05
104	Joe Orsulak	.05
105	Doug Saunders	.05
106	Frank Tanana	.05
107	Dave Telgheder	.05
108	Larry Anderson	.05
109	Jim Eisenreich	.05
110	Pete Incaviglia	.05
111	Danny Jackson	.05
112	David West	.05
113	Al Martin	.10
114	Blas Minor	.05
115	Dennis Moeller	.05
116	Will Pennyfeather	.05
117	Rich Robertson	.05
118	Ben Shelton	.05
119	Lonnie Smith	.05
120	Freddie Toliver	.05
121	Paul Wagner	.05
122	Kevin Young	.08
123	*Rene Arocha*	.10
124	Gregg Jefferies	.10
125	Paul Kilgus	.05
126	Les Lancaster	.05
127	Joe Magrane	.05
128	Rob Murphy	.05
129	Erik Pappas	.05
130	Stan Royer	.10
131	Ozzie Smith	.75
132	Tom Urbani	.05
133	Mark Whiten	.05
134	Derek Bell	.10
135	Doug Brocall	.05
136	Phil Clark	.05
137	*Mark Ettles*	.05
138	Jeff Gardner	.05
139	*Pat Gomez*	.08
140	Ricky Gutierrez	.05
141	Gene Harris	.05
142	*Kevin Higgins*	.05
143	Trevor Hoffman	.05
144	Phil Plantier	.05
145	*Kerry Taylor*	.05
146	Guillermo Velasquez	.05
147	Wally Whitehurst	.05
148	*Tim Worrell*	.05
149	Todd Benzinger	.05
150	Barry Bonds	.90
151	Greg Brummett	.05
152	Mark Carreon	.05
153	Dave Martinez	.05
154	Jeff Reed	.05
155	Kevin Rogers	.05
156	Harold Baines	.08
157	Damon Buford	.05
158	*Paul Carey*	.05
159	Jeffrey Hammonds	.10
160	Jaime Moyer	.05
161	*Sherman Obando*	.10
162	*John O'Donoghue*	.10
163	Brad Pennington	.05
164	Jim Poole	.05
165	Harold Reynolds	.05
166	Fernando Valenzuela	.08
167	*Jack Voight*	.05
168	Mark Williamson	.05
169	Scott Bankhead	.05
170	Greg Blosser	.05
171	*Jim Byrd*	.05
172	Ivan Calderon	.05
173	Andre Dawson	.12
174	Scott Fletcher	.05
175	Jose Melendez	.05
176	Carlos Quintana	.05
177	Jeff Russell	.05
178	Aaron Sele	.10
179	*Rod Correia*	.05
180	Chili Davis	.08
181	*Jim Edmonds*	1.25
182	Rene Gonzales	.05
183	*Hilly Hathaway*	.05
184	Torey Lovullo	.05
185	Greg Myers	.05
186	Gene Nelson	.05
187	Troy Percival	.05
188	Scott Sanderson	.05
189	*Darryl Scott*	.05
190	*J.T. Snow*	.50
191	Russ Springer	.05
192	Jason Bere	.10
193	Rodney Bolton	.05
194	Ellis Burks	.08
195	Bo Jackson	.12
196	Mike LaValliere	.05
197	Scott Ruffcorn	.05
198	*Jeff Schwartz*	.05
199	Jerry DiPoto	.05
200	Alvaro Espinoza	.05
201	Wayne Kirby	.05
202	*Tom Kramer*	.05
203	Jesse Levis	.05
204	Manny Ramirez	1.50
205	Jeff Treadway	.05
206	*Bill Wertz*	.05
207	Cliff Young	.05
208	Matt Young	.05
209	Kirk Gibson	.05
210	Greg Gohr	.05
211	Bill Krueger	.05
212	Bob MacDonald	.05
213	Mike Moore	.05
214	David Wells	.08
215	*Billy Brewer*	.05
216	David Cone	.15
217	Greg Gagne	.05
218	Mark Gardner	.05
219	Chis Haney	.05
220	Phil Hiatt	.05
221	Jose Lind	.05
222	Juan Bell	.05
223	Tom Brunansky	.05
224	Mike Ignasiak	.05
225	Joe Kmak	.05
226	Tom Lampkin	.05
227	*Graeme Lloyd*	.10
228	Carlos Maldonado	.05
229	Matt Mieske	.08
230	Angel Miranda	.05
231	*Troy O'Leary*	.10
232	Kevin Reimer	.05
233	Larry Casian	.05
234	Jim Deshaies	.05
235	*Eddie Guardado*	.10
236	Chip Hale	.05
237	*Mike Maksudian*	.05
238	David McCarty	.05
239	*Pat Meares*	.10
240	*George Tsamis*	.05
241	Dave Winfield	.15
242	Jim Abbott	.10
243	Wade Boggs	.50
244	*Andy Cook*	.05
245	*Russ Davis*	.15
246	Mike Humphreys	.05
247	Jimmy Key	.05
248	Jim Leyritz	.08
249	Bobby Munoz	.05
250	Paul O'Neill	.10
251	Spike Owen	.05
252	Dave Silvestri	.05
253	*Marcos Armas*	.05
254	Brent Gates	.10
255	Goose Gossage	.05
256	*Scott Lydy*	.05
257	Henry Mercedes	.05
258	*Mike Mohler*	.05
259	Troy Neel	.05
260	Edwin Nunez	.05
261	Craig Paquette	.10
262	Kevin Seitzer	.05
263	Rich Amaral	.05
264	Mike Blowers	.05
265	Chris Bosio	.05
266	Norm Charlton	.05
267	*Jim Converse*	.05
268	*John Cummings*	.10
269	Mike Felder	.05
270	Mike Hampton	.05
271	Bill Haselman	.05
272	Dwayne Henry	.05
273	Greg Litton	.05
274	Mackey Sasser	.05
275	Lee Tinsley	.05
276	David Wainhouse	.05
277	*Jeff Bronkey*	.05
278	Benji Gil	.05
279	Tom Henke	.05
280	Charlie Leibrandt	.05
281	Robb Nen	.10
282	Bill Ripken	.05
283	*Jon Shave*	.05
284	Doug Strange	.05
285	*Matt Whiteside*	.10
286	*Scott Brow*	.05
287	*Willie Canate*	.05
288	Tony Castillo	.05
289	*Domingo Cedeno*	.10
290	Darnell Coles	.05
291	Danny Cox	.05
292	Mark Eichhorn	.05
293	Tony Fernandez	.05
294	Al Leiter	.08
295	Paul Molitor	.75
296	Dave Stewart	.08
297	*Woody Williams*	.05
298	Checklist	.05
299	Checklist	.05
300	Checklist	.05

1993 Fleer Atlantic

The Atlantic Collectors Edition set of 1993 featured 24 of the top players in the game (plus one checklist) portrayed in a style matching the regular-issue Fleer set, with the addition of the Atlantic logo and a gold border. The cards were given away five at a time with gasoline purchases at gas stations in New York and Pennsylvania during the summer.

		MT
Complete Set (25):		8.00
Common Player:		.25
1	Roberto Alomar	.60
2	Barry Bonds	1.00
3	Bobby Bonilla	.30
4	Will Clark	.60
5	Roger Clemens	.90
6	Darren Daulton	.25
7	Dennis Eckersley	.30
8	Cecil Fielder	.25
9	Tom Glavine	.30
10	Juan Gonzalez	1.00
11	Ken Griffey Jr.	3.00
12	John Kruk	.25
13	Greg Maddux	1.00
14	Don Mattingly	1.00
15	Fred McGriff	.50
16	Mark McGwire	3.00
17	Terry Pendleton	.25
18	Kirby Puckett	1.00
19	Cal Ripken Jr.	2.00
20	Nolan Ryan	1.50
21	Ryne Sandberg	.90
22	Gary Sheffield	.50
23	Frank Thomas	1.50
24	Andy Van Slyke	.25
25	Checklist	.05

1993 Fleer Fruit of the Loom

Fruit of the Loom and Fleer combined to create a 66-card baseball set in 1993 that featured many of the top players in the game. The cards, with the same design as the regular-issue Fleer cards, also display the Fruit of the Loom logo in the upper-left corner. Three cards were inserted in specially marked packages of the company's products.

		MT
Complete Set (66):		75.00
Common Player:		1.00
1	Roberto Alomar	2.00
2	Brady Anderson	1.25
3	Jeff Bagwell	2.50
4	Albert Belle	2.00
5	Craig Biggio	1.50
6	Barry Bonds	4.00
7	George Brett	5.00
8	Brett Butler	1.00
9	Jose Canseco	2.00
10	Joe Carter	1.00
11	Will Clark	2.00
12	Roger Clemens	3.50
13	Darren Daulton	1.00
14	Andre Dawson	1.50
15	Delino DeShields	1.00
16	Rob Dibble	1.00
17	Doug Drabek	1.00
18	Dennis Eckersley	1.00
19	Cecil Fielder	1.00
20	Travis Fryman	1.50
21	Tom Glavine	1.50
22	Juan Gonzalez	5.00
23	Dwight Gooden	1.25
24	Mark Grace	2.00
25	Ken Griffey, Jr.	8.00
26	Marquis Grissom	1.50
27	Juan Guzman	1.00
28	Tony Gwynn	4.00
29	Rickey Henderson	2.00
30	David Justice	1.75
31	Eric Karros	1.50
32	Chuck Knoblauch	1.75
33	John Kruk	1.00
34	Ray Lankford	1.00
35	Barry Larkin	1.00
36	Pat Listach	1.00
37	Kenny Lofton	2.00
38	Shane Mack	1.00
39	Greg Maddux	4.00
40	Dennis Martinez	1.00
41	Edgar Martinez	1.00
42	Ramon Martinez	1.00
43	Don Mattingly	4.00
44	Jack McDowell	1.00
45	Fred McGriff	2.00
46	Mark McGwire	7.50
47	Jeff Montgomery	1.00
48	Eddie Murray	2.00
49	Charles Nagy	1.00
50	Tom Pagnozzi	1.00
51	Terry Pendleton	1.00
52	Kirby Puckett	3.50
53	Jose Rijo	1.00
54	Cal Ripken, Jr.	7.00
55	Nolan Ryan	7.00
56	Ryne Sandberg	2.50
57	Gary Sheffield	2.00
58	Bill Swift	1.00
59	Danny Tartabull	1.00
60	Mickey Tettleton	1.00
61	Frank Thomas	6.00
62	Andy Van Slyke	1.00
63	Robin Ventura	1.25
64	Larry Walker	1.75
65	Robin Yount	2.00
66	Checklist	.15

Checklists with card numbers in parentheses ( ) indicates the numbers do not appear on the card.

1994 Fleer "Highlights" Promo Sheet

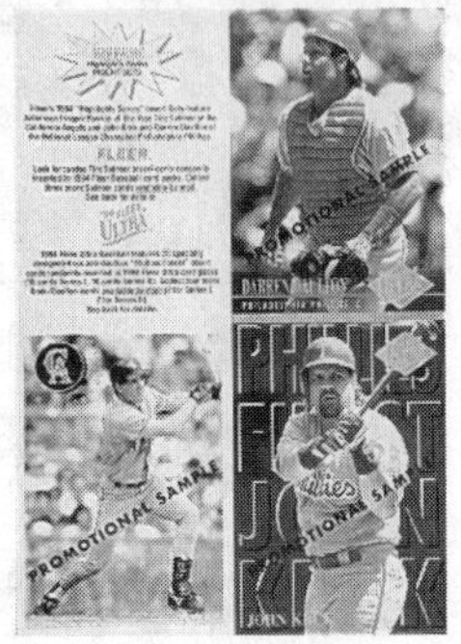

To introduce its special insert card series honoring 1993 A.L. Rookie of the Year Tim Salmon and Phillies stars John Kruk and Darren Daulton, Fleer issued this 5" x 7" promo sheet. The three player cards on the sheet are similar to the issued versions except they have black overprinting on front and back which reads, "PROMOTIONAL SAMPLE". The non-player segment of the sheet has details about the inserts and special mail-in offer for additional cards.

		MT
Complete Set, Sheet:		8.00
Common Card:		3.00
9	John Kruk (Fleer Ultra Phillies Finest)	3.00
69	Tim Salmon (Fleer)	4.00
243	Darren Daulton (Fleer Ultra)	3.00

1994 Fleer

Fleer's 720-card 1994 set, released in one series, includes another 204 insert cards to be pursued by collectors. Every pack includes one of the cards, randomly inserted from among the 12 insert sets. Regular cards have action photos on front, with a team logo in one of the lower corners. The player's name and position is stamped in gold foil around the logo. On back, another color player photo is overprinted with color boxes, data and stats, leaving a clear image of the player's face, 1-1/2" x 1-3/4" in size. Cards are UV coated on both sides.

		MT
Complete Set (720):		45.00
Common Player:		.05
Wax Box:		30.00
1	Brady Anderson	.08
2	Harold Baines	.08
3	Mike Devereaux	.05
4	Todd Frohwirth	.05
5	Jeffrey Hammonds	.08
6	Chris Hoiles	.05
7	Tim Hulett	.05

8	Ben McDonald	.05
9	Mark McLemore	.05
10	Alan Mills	.05
11	Jamie Moyer	.05
12	Mike Mussina	.30
13	Gregg Olson	.05
14	Mike Pagliarulo	.05
15	Brad Pennington	.05
16	Jim Poole	.05
17	Harold Reynolds	.05
18	Arthur Rhodes	.05
19	Cal Ripken, Jr.	3.00
20	David Segui	.05
21	Rick Sutcliffe	.05
22	Fernando Valenzuela	.08
23	Jack Voigt	.05
24	Mark Williamson	.05
25	Scott Bankhead	.05
26	Roger Clemens	1.50
27	Scott Cooper	.05
28	Danny Darwin	.05
29	Andre Dawson	.10
30	Rob Deer	.05
31	John Dopson	.05
32	Scott Fletcher	.05
33	Mike Greenwell	.05
34	Greg Harris	.05
35	Billy Hatcher	.05
36	Bob Melvin	.05
37	Tony Pena	.05
38	Paul Quantrill	.05
39	Carlos Quintana	.05
40	Ernest Riles	.05
41	Jeff Russell	.05
42	Ken Ryan	.05
43	Aaron Sele	.08
44	John Valentin	.10
45	Mo Vaughn	.50
46	Frank Viola	.05
47	Bob Zupcic	.05
48	Mike Butcher	.05
49	Rod Correia	.05
50	Chad Curtis	.10
51	Chili Davis	.08
52	Gary DiSarcina	.05
53	Damion Easley	.10
54	Jim Edmonds	.40
55	Chuck Finley	.05
56	Steve Frey	.05
57	Rene Gonzales	.05
58	Joe Grahe	.05
59	Hilly Hathaway	.05
60	Stan Javier	.05
61	Mark Langston	.05
62	Phil Leftwich	.05
63	Torey Lovullo	.05
64	Joe Magrane	.05
65	Greg Myers	.05
66	Ken Patterson	.05
67	Eduardo Perez	.05
68	Luis Polonia	.05
69	Tim Salmon	.30
69a	Tim Salmon (overprinted PROMOTIONAL SAMPLE)	3.00
70	J.T. Snow	.15
71	Ron Tingley	.05
72	Julio Valera	.05
73	Wilson Alvarez	.05
74	Tim Belcher	.05
75	George Bell	.05
76	Jason Bere	.05
77	Rod Bolton	.05
78	Ellis Burks	.05
79	Joey Cora	.05
80	Alex Fernandez	.08
81	Craig Grebeck	.05
82	Ozzie Guillen	.05
83	Roberto Hernandez	.05
84	Bo Jackson	.15
85	Lance Johnson	.05
86	Ron Karkovice	.05
87	Mike LaValliere	.05
88	Kirk McCaskill	.05
89	Jack McDowell	.05
90	Warren Newson	.05
91	Dan Pasqua	.05
92	Scott Radinsky	.05
93	Tim Raines	.08
94	Steve Sax	.05
95	Jeff Schwarz	.05
96	Frank Thomas	1.50
97	Robin Ventura	.15
98	Sandy Alomar, Jr.	.08
99	Carlos Baerga	.05
100	Albert Belle	.75
101	Mark Clark	.05
102	Jerry DiPoto	.05
103	Alvaro Espinoza	.05
104	Felix Fermin	.05
105	Jeremy Hernandez	.05
106	Reggie Jefferson	.05
107	Wayne Kirby	.05
108	Tom Kramer	.05
109	Mark Lewis	.05
110	Derek Lilliquist	.05
111	Kenny Lofton	.75
112	Candy Maldonado	.05
113	Jose Mesa	.05
114	Jeff Mutis	.05
115	Charles Nagy	.08
116	Bob Ojeda	.05
117	Junior Ortiz	.05
118	Eric Plunk	.05
119	Manny Ramirez	1.50
120	Paul Sorrento	.05
121	Jim Thome	.35
122	Jeff Treadway	.05
123	Bill Wertz	.05
124	Skeeter Barnes	.05
125	Milt Cuyler	.05
126	Eric Davis	.08
127	John Doherty	.05
128	Cecil Fielder	.08
129	Travis Fryman	.10
130	Kirk Gibson	.05
131	Dan Gladden	.05
132	Greg Gohr	.05
133	Chris Gomez	.05
134	Bill Gullickson	.05
135	Mike Henneman	.05
136	Kurt Knudsen	.05
137	Chad Kreuter	.05
138	Bill Krueger	.05
139	Scott Livingstone	.05
140	Bob MacDonald	.05
141	Mike Moore	.05
142	Tony Phillips	.05
143	Mickey Tettleton	.05
144	Alan Trammell	.08
145	David Wells	.08
146	Lou Whitaker	.05
147	Kevin Appier	.05
148	Stan Belinda	.05
149	George Brett	.50
150	Billy Brewer	.05
151	Hubie Brooks	.05
152	David Cone	.08
153	Gary Gaetti	.05
154	Greg Gagne	.05
155	Tom Gordon	.05
156	Mark Gubicza	.05
157	Chris Gwynn	.05
158	John Habyan	.05
159	Chris Haney	.05
160	Phil Hiatt	.05
161	Felix Jose	.05
162	Wally Joyner	.08
163	Jose Lind	.05
164	Mike Macfarlane	.05
165	Mike Magnante	.05
166	Brent Mayne	.05
167	Brian McRae	.05
168	Kevin McReynolds	.05
169	Keith Miller	.05
170	Jeff Montgomery	.05
171	Hipolito Pichardo	.05
172	Rico Rossy	.05
173	Juan Bell	.05
174	Ricky Bones	.05
175	Cal Eldred	.05
176	Mike Fetters	.05
177	Darryl Hamilton	.05
178	Doug Henry	.05
179	Mike Ignasiak	.05
180	John Jaha	.08
181	Pat Listach	.05
182	Graeme Lloyd	.05
183	Matt Mieske	.05
184	Angel Miranda	.05
185	Jaime Navarro	.05
186	Dave Nilsson	.05
187	Troy O'Leary	.05
188	Jesse Orosco	.05
189	Kevin Reimer	.05
190	Kevin Seitzer	.05
191	Bill Spiers	.05
192	B.J. Surhoff	.08
193	Dickie Thon	.05
194	Jose Valentin	.05
195	Greg Vaughn	.10
196	Bill Wegman	.05
197	Robin Yount	.25
198	Rick Aguilera	.05
199	Willie Banks	.05
200	Bernardo Brito	.05
201	Larry Casian	.05
202	Scott Erickson	.05
203	Eddie Guardado	.05
204	Mark Guthrie	.05
205	Chip Hale	.05
206	Brian Harper	.05
207	Mike Hartley	.05
208	Kent Hrbek	.08
209	Terry Jorgensen	.05
210	Chuck Knoblauch	.15
211	Gene Larkin	.05
212	Shane Mack	.05
213	David McCarty	.05
214	Pat Meares	.05
215	Pedro Munoz	.05
216	Derek Parks	.05
217	Kirby Puckett	1.25
218	Jeff Reboulet	.05
219	Kevin Tapani	.05
220	Mike Trombley	.05
221	George Tsamis	.05
222	Carl Willis	.05
223	Dave Winfield	.25
224	Jim Abbott	.08
225	Paul Assenmacher	.05
226	Wade Boggs	.35
227	Russ Davis	.05
228	Steve Farr	.05
229	Mike Gallego	.05
230	Paul Gibson	.05
231	Steve Howe	.05
232	Dion James	.05
233	Domingo Jean	.05
234	Scott Kamieniecki	.05
235	Pat Kelly	.05
236	Jimmy Key	.05
237	Jim Leyritz	.08
238	Kevin Maas	.05
239	Don Mattingly	1.50
240	Rich Monteleone	.05
241	Bobby Munoz	.05
242	Matt Nokes	.05
243	Paul O'Neill	.10
244	Spike Owen	.05
245	Melido Perez	.05
246	Lee Smith	.08
247	Mike Stanley	.05
248	Danny Tartabull	.05
249	Randy Velarde	.05
250	Bob Wickman	.05
251	Bernie Williams	.40
252	Mike Aldrete	.05
253	Marcos Armas	.05
254	Lance Blankenship	.05
255	Mike Bordick	.05
256	Scott Brosius	.05
257	Jerry Browne	.05
258	Ron Darling	.05
259	Kelly Downs	.05
260	Dennis Eckersley	.08
261	Brent Gates	.05
262	Goose Gossage	.08
263	Scott Hemond	.05
264	Dave Henderson	.05
265	Rick Honeycutt	.05
266	Vince Horsman	.05
267	Scott Lydy	.05
268	Mark McGwire	4.00
269	Mike Mohler	.05
270	Troy Neel	.05
271	Edwin Nunez	.05
272	Craig Paquette	.05
273	Ruben Sierra	.05
274	Terry Steinbach	.05
275	Todd Van Poppel	.05
276	Bob Welch	.05
277	Bobby Witt	.05
278	Rich Amaral	.05
279	Mike Blowers	.05
280	Bret Boone	.08
281	Chris Bosio	.05
282	Jay Buhner	.08
283	Norm Charlton	.05
284	Mike Felder	.05
285	Dave Fleming	.05
286	Ken Griffey, Jr.	3.00
287	Erik Hanson	.05
288	Bill Haselman	.05
289	*Brad Holman*	.10
290	Randy Johnson	.40
291	Tim Leary	.05
292	Greg Litton	.05
293	Dave Magadan	.05
294	Edgar Martinez	.08
295	Tino Martinez	.12
296	Jeff Nelson	.05
297	*Erik Plantenberg*	.08
298	Mackey Sasser	.05
299	*Brian Turang*	.08
300	Dave Valle	.05
301	Omar Vizquel	.08
302	Brian Bohanon	.05
303	Kevin Brown	.08
304	Jose Canseco	.35
305	Mario Diaz	.05
306	Julio Franco	.05
307	Juan Gonzalez	1.50
308	Tom Henke	.05
309	David Hulse	.05
310	Manuel Lee	.05
311	Craig Lefferts	.05
312	Charlie Leibrandt	.05
313	Rafael Palmeiro	.15
314	Dean Palmer	.05
315	Roger Pavlik	.05
316	Dan Peltier	.05
317	Geno Petralli	.05
318	Gary Redus	.05
319	Ivan Rodriguez	.40
320	Kenny Rogers	.05
321	Nolan Ryan	2.50
322	Doug Strange	.05
323	Matt Whiteside	.05
324	Roberto Alomar	.75
325	Pat Borders	.05
326	Joe Carter	.08
327	Tony Castillo	.05
328	Darnell Coles	.05
329	Danny Cox	.05
330	Mark Eichhorn	.05
331	Tony Fernandez	.05
332	Alfredo Griffin	.05
333	Juan Guzman	.05
334	Rickey Henderson	.25
335	Pat Hentgen	.05
336	Randy Knorr	.05
337	Al Leiter	.08
338	Paul Molitor	.40
339	Jack Morris	.05
340	John Olerud	.15
341	Dick Schofield	.05
342	Ed Sprague	.05
343	Dave Stewart	.08
344	Todd Stottlemyre	.05
345	Mike Timlin	.05
346	Duane Ward	.05
347	Turner Ward	.05
348	Devon White	.08
349	Woody Williams	.05
350	Steve Avery	.05
351	Steve Bedrosian	.05
352	Rafael Belliard	.05
353	Damon Berryhill	.05
354	Jeff Blauser	.05
355	Sid Bream	.05
356	Francisco Cabrera	.05
357	Marvin Freeman	.05
358	Ron Gant	.08
359	Tom Glavine	.15
360	Jay Howell	.05
361	Dave Justice	.15
362	Ryan Klesko	.40
363	Mark Lemke	.05
364	Javier Lopez	.15
365	Greg Maddux	2.00
366	Fred McGriff	.20
367	Greg McMichael	.05
368	Kent Mercker	.05
369	Otis Nixon	.05
370	Greg Olson	.05
371	Bill Pecota	.05
372	Terry Pendleton	.05
373	Deion Sanders	.40
374	Pete Smith	.05
375	John Smoltz	.12
376	Mike Stanton	.05
377	Tony Tarasco	.05
378	Mark Wohlers	.05
379	Jose Bautista	.05
380	Shawn Boskie	.05
381	Steve Buechele	.05
382	Frank Castillo	.05
383	Mark Grace	.15
384	Jose Guzman	.05
385	Mike Harkey	.05
386	Greg Hibbard	.05
387	Glenallen Hill	.05
388	Steve Lake	.05
389	Derrick May	.05
390	Chuck McElroy	.05
391	Mike Morgan	.05
392	Randy Myers	.05
393	Dan Plesac	.05
394	Kevin Roberson	.05
395	Rey Sanchez	.05
396	Ryne Sandberg	.45
397	Bob Scanlan	.05
398	Dwight Smith	.05
399	Sammy Sosa	.75
400	Jose Vizcaino	.05
401	Rick Wilkins	.05
402	Willie Wilson	.05
403	Eric Yelding	.05
404	Bobby Ayala	.05
405	Jeff Branson	.05
406	Tom Browning	.05
407	Jacob Brumfield	.05
408	Tim Costo	.05
409	Rob Dibble	.05
410	Willie Greene	.05
411	Thomas Howard	.05
412	Roberto Kelly	.05
413	Bill Landrum	.05
414	Barry Larkin	.15
415	*Larry Luebbers*	.05
416	Kevin Mitchell	.05
417	Hal Morris	.05
418	Joe Oliver	.05
419	Tim Pugh	.05
420	Jeff Reardon	.05
421	Jose Rijo	.05
422	Bip Roberts	.05
423	John Roper	.05
424	Johnny Ruffin	.05
425	Chris Sabo	.05
426	Juan Samuel	.05
427	Reggie Sanders	.05
428	Scott Service	.05
429	John Smiley	.05
430	*Jerry Spradlin*	.05
431	Kevin Wickander	.05
432	Freddie Benavides	.05
433	Dante Bichette	.30
434	Willie Blair	.05
435	Daryl Boston	.05
436	Kent Bottenfield	.05
437	Vinny Castilla	.15
438	Jerald Clark	.05
439	Alex Cole	.05
440	Andres Galarraga	.15
441	Joe Girardi	.05
442	Greg Harris	.05
443	Charlie Hayes	.05
444	Darren Holmes	.05
445	Chris Jones	.05
446	Roberto Mejia	.05
447	David Nied	.05
448	J. Owens	.05
449	Jeff Parrett	.05
450	Steve Reed	.05
451	Armando Reynoso	.05
452	Bruce Ruffin	.05
453	Mo Sanford	.05
454	Danny Sheaffer	.05
455	Jim Tatum	.05
456	Gary Wayne	.05
457	Eric Young	.00
458	Luis Aquino	.05
459	Alex Arias	.05
460	Jack Armstrong	.05
461	Bret Barberie	.05
462	Ryan Bowen	.05
463	Chuck Carr	.05
464	Jeff Conine	.08
465	Henry Cotto	.05
466	Orestes Destrade	.05
467	Chris Hammond	.05
468	Bryan Harvey	.05
469	Charlie Hough	.05
470	Joe Klink	.05
471	Richie Lewis	.05
472	*Bob Natal*	.10
473	*Pat Rapp*	.15
474	*Rich Renteria*	.08
475	Rich Rodriguez	.05
476	Benito Santiago	.05
477	Gary Sheffield	.20
478	Matt Turner	.05
479	David Weathers	.05
480	Walt Weiss	.05
481	Darrell Whitmore	.05
482	Eric Anthony	.05
483	Jeff Bagwell	1.00
484	Kevin Bass	.05
485	Craig Biggio	.15
486	Ken Caminiti	.15
487	Andujar Cedeno	.05
488	Chris Donnels	.05
489	Doug Drabek	.05
490	Steve Finley	.05
491	Luis Gonzalez	.08
492	Pete Harnisch	.05
493	Xavier Hernandez	.05
494	Doug Jones	.05
495	Todd Jones	.05
496	Darryl Kile	.05
497	Al Osuna	.05
498	Mark Portugal	.05
499	Scott Servais	.05
500	Greg Swindell	.05
501	Eddie Taubensee	.05
502	Jose Uribe	.05
503	Brian Williams	.05
504	Billy Ashley	.05
505	Pedro Astacio	.10
506	Brett Butler	.05
507	Tom Candiotti	.05
508	Omar Daal	.05
509	Jim Gott	.05
510	Kevin Gross	.05
511	Dave Hansen	.05
512	Carlos Hernandez	.05
513	Orel Hershiser	.08
514	Eric Karros	.12
515	Pedro Martinez	.25
516	Ramon Martinez	.08
517	Roger McDowell	.05
518	Raul Mondesi	.75
519	Jose Offerman	.05
520	Mike Piazza	2.50
521	Jody Reed	.05
522	Henry Rodriguez	.08
523	Mike Sharperson	.05
524	Cory Snyder	.05
525	Darryl Strawberry	.10
526	Rick Trlicek	.05
527	Tim Wallach	.05
528	Mitch Webster	.05
529	Steve Wilson	.05
530	Todd Worrell	.05
531	Moises Alou	.10
532	Brian Barnes	.05
533	Sean Berry	.05
534	Greg Colbrunn	.05
535	Delino DeShields	.05
536	Jeff Fassero	.05
537	Darrin Fletcher	.05
538	Cliff Floyd	.10
539	Lou Frazier	.05
540	Marquis Grissom	.10
541	Butch Henry	.05
542	Ken Hill	.05
543	Mike Lansing	.10
544	*Brian Looney*	.10
545	Dennis Martinez	.08
546	Chris Nabholz	.05
547	Randy Ready	.05
548	Mel Rojas	.05
549	Kirk Rueter	.05
550	Tim Scott	.05
551	Jeff Shaw	.05
552	Tim Spehr	.05
553	John VanderWal	.05
554	Larry Walker	.30
555	John Wetteland	.05
556	Rondell White	.25
557	Tim Bogar	.08
558	Bobby Bonilla	.08
559	Jeremy Burnitz	.08
560	Sid Fernandez	.05
561	John Franco	.05
562	Dave Gallagher	.05
563	Dwight Gooden	.10
564	Eric Hillman	.05
565	Todd Hundley	.12
566	Jeff Innis	.05
567	Darrin Jackson	.05
568	Howard Johnson	.05
569	Bobby Jones	.05
570	Jeff Kent	.05
571	Mike Maddux	.05
572	Jeff McKnight	.05
573	Eddie Murray	.15
574	Charlie O'Brien	.05
575	Joe Orsulak	.05
576	Bret Saberhagen	.08
577	Pete Schourek	.05
578	Dave Telgheder	.05
579	Ryan Thompson	.05
580	Anthony Young	.05
581	Ruben Amaro	.05
582	Larry Andersen	.05
583	Kim Batiste	.05
584	Wes Chamberlain	.05
585	Darren Daulton	.05
586	Mariano Duncan	.05
587	Len Dykstra	.05
588	Jim Eisenreich	.05
589	Tommy Greene	.05
590	Dave Hollins	.08
591	Pete Incaviglia	.05
592	Danny Jackson	.05
593	Ricky Jordan	.05

594	John Kruk	.05
595	Roger Mason	.05
596	Mickey Morandini	.05
597	Terry Mulholland	.05
598	Todd Pratt	.05
599	Ben Rivera	.05
600	Curt Schilling	.08
601	Kevin Stocker	.05
602	Milt Thompson	.05
603	David West	.05
604	Mitch Williams	.05
605	Jay Bell	.05
606	Dave Clark	.05
607	Steve Cooke	.05
608	Tom Foley	.05
609	Carlos Garcia	.05
610	Joel Johnston	.05
611	Jeff King	.05
612	Al Martin	.08
613	Lloyd McClendon	.05
614	Orlando Merced	.05
615	Blas Minor	.05
616	Denny Neagle	.05
617	*Mark Petkovsek*	.10
618	Tom Prince	.05
619	Don Slaught	.05
620	Zane Smith	.05
621	Randy Tomlin	.05
622	Andy Van Slyke	.05
623	Paul Wagner	.05
624	Tim Wakefield	.05
625	Bob Walk	.05
626	Kevin Young	.10
627	Luis Alicea	.05
628	Rene Arocha	.05
629	Rod Brewer	.05
630	Rheal Cormier	.05
631	Bernard Gilkey	.08
632	Lee Guetterman	.05
633	Gregg Jefferies	.08
634	Brian Jordan	.10
635	Les Lancaster	.05
636	Ray Lankford	.08
637	Rob Murphy	.05
638	Omar Olivares	.05
639	Jose Oquendo	.05
640	Donovan Osborne	.05
641	Tom Pagnozzi	.05
642	Erik Pappas	.05
643	Geronimo Pena	.05
644	Mike Perez	.05
645	Gerald Perry	.05
646	Ozzie Smith	.25
647	Bob Tewksbury	.05
648	Allen Watson	.05
649	Mark Whiten	.05
650	Tracy Woodson	.05
651	Todd Zeile	.08
652	Andy Ashby	.08
653	Brad Ausmus	.05
654	Billy Bean	.05
655	Derek Bell	.08
656	Andy Benes	.08
657	Doug Brocail	.05
658	Jarvis Brown	.05
659	Archi Cianfrocco	.05
660	Phil Clark	.05
661	Mark Davis	.05
662	Jeff Gardner	.05
663	Pat Gomez	.05
664	Ricky Gutierrez	.05
665	Tony Gwynn	1.25
666	Gene Harris	.05
667	Kevin Higgins	.05
668	Trevor Hoffman	.10
669	*Pedro A. Martinez*	.05
670	Tim Mauser	.05
671	Melvin Nieves	.05
672	Phil Plantier	.05
673	Frank Seminara	.05
674	Craig Shipley	.05
675	Kerry Taylor	.05
676	Tim Teufel	.05
677	Guillermo Velasquez	.05
678	Wally Whitehurst	.05
679	Tim Worrell	.05
680	Rod Beck	.05
681	Mike Benjamin	.05
682	Todd Benzinger	.05
683	Bud Black	.05
684	Barry Bonds	.60
685	Jeff Brantley	.05
686	Dave Burba	.05
687	John Burkett	.05
688	Mark Carreon	.05
689	Will Clark	.25
690	Royce Clayton	.05
691	Bryan Hickerson	.05
692	Mike Jackson	.05
693	Darren Lewis	.05
694	Kirt Manwaring	.05
695	Dave Martinez	.05
696	Willie McGee	.08
697	John Patterson	.05
698	Jeff Reed	.05
699	Kevin Rogers	.05
700	Scott Sanderson	.05
701	Steve Scarsone	.05
702	Billy Swift	.05
703	Robby Thompson	.05
704	Matt Williams	.15
705	Trevor Wilson	.05
706	"Brave New World" (Fred McGriff, Ron Gant, Dave Justice)	.10
707	"1-2 Punch" (Paul Molitor, John Olerud)	.15
708	"American Heat" (Mike Mussina, Jack McDowell)	.10
709	"Together Again" (Lou Whitaker, Alan Trammell)	.10
710	"Lone Star Lumber" (Rafael Palmeiro, Juan Gonzalez)	.25
711	"Batmen" (Brett Butler, Tony Gwynn)	.10
712	"Twin Peaks" (Kirby Puckett, Chuck Knoblauch)	.25
713	"Back to Back" (Mike Piazza, Eric Karros)	.50
714	Checklist	.05
715	Checklist	.05
716	Checklist	.05
717	Checklist	.05
718	Checklist	.05
719	Checklist	.05
720	Checklist	.05

1994 Fleer All-Stars

Each league's 25 representatives for the 1993 All-Star Game are featured in this insert set. Fronts have a player action photo with a rippling American flag in the top half of the background. The '93 All-Star logo is featured at the bottom, along with a gold-foil impression of the player's name. The flag motif is repeated at top of the card back, along with a player portrait photo set against a red (American League) or blue (National League) background. Odds of finding one of the 50 All-Star inserts are one in every two 15-card foil packs.

		MT
Complete Set (50):		20.00
Common Player:		.25
1	Roberto Alomar	1.00
2	Carlos Baerga	.25
3	Albert Belle	1.00
4	Wade Boggs	.75
5	Joe Carter	.25
6	Scott Cooper	.25
7	Cecil Fielder	.25
8	Travis Fryman	.25
9	Juan Gonzalez	1.50
10	Ken Griffey, Jr.	4.00
11	Pat Hentgen	.25
12	Randy Johnson	.75
13	Jimmy Key	.25
14	Mark Langston	.25
15	Jack McDowell	.25
16	Paul Molitor	.75
17	Jeff Montgomery	.25
18	Mike Mussina	.50
19	John Olerud	.35
20	Kirby Puckett	1.50
21	Cal Ripken, Jr.	4.00
22	Ivan Rodriguez	1.00
23	Frank Thomas	2.00
24	Greg Vaughn	.25
25	Duane Ward	.25
26	Steve Avery	.25
27	Rod Beck	.25
28	Jay Bell	.25
29	Andy Benes	.25
30	Jeff Blauser	.25
31	Barry Bonds	1.00
32	Bobby Bonilla	.25
33	John Burkett	.25
34	Darren Daulton	.25
35	Andres Galarraga	.35
36	Tom Glavine	.35
37	Mark Grace	.50
38	Marquis Grissom	.25
39	Tony Gwynn	1.50
40	Bryan Harvey	.25
41	Dave Hollins	.25
42	Dave Justice	.35
43	Darryl Kile	.25
44	John Kruk	.25
45	Barry Larkin	.35
46	Terry Mulholland	.25
47	Mike Piazza	2.00
48	Ryne Sandberg	1.00
49	Gary Sheffield	.60
50	John Smoltz	.50

1994 Fleer Award Winners

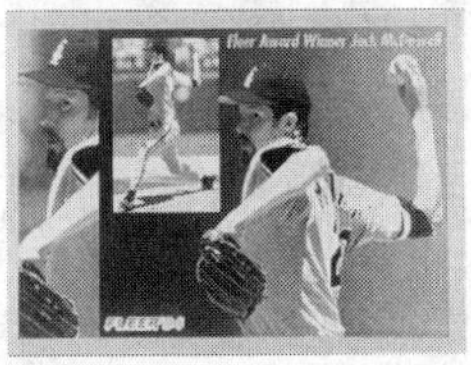

The 1993 MVP, Cy Young and Rookie of the Year award winners from each league are featured in this insert set. Cards are UV coated on both sides. Three different croppings of the same player action photo are featured on the front, with the player's name and other printing in gold foil. Backs have a player portrait and short summary of his previous season's performance. According to the company, odds of finding one of these horizontal-format inserts were one in 37 packs.

		MT
Complete Set (6):		9.00
Common Player:		.75
1	Frank Thomas	3.00
2	Barry Bonds	1.50
3	Jack McDowell	.75
4	Greg Maddux	3.00
5	Tim Salmon	1.00
6	Mike Piazza	3.00

1994 Fleer Golden Moments

Ten highlights from the 1993 Major League baseball season are commemorated in this insert set. Each of the cards has a title which summarizes the historical moment. These inserts were available exclusively in Fleer cards packaged for large retail outlets.

		MT
Complete Set (10):		20.00
Common Player:		.50
1	"Four in One" (Mark Whiten)	.50
2	"Left and Right" (Carlos Baerga)	.50
3	"3,000 Hit Club" (Dave Winfield)	1.50
4	"Eight Straight" (Ken Griffey, Jr.)	10.00
5	"Triumphant Return" (Bo Jackson)	1.50
6	"Farewell to Baseball" (George Brett)	3.00
7	"Farewell to Baseball" (Nolan Ryan)	8.00
8	"Thirty Times Six" (Fred McGriff)	.75
9	"Enters 5th Dimension" (Frank Thomas)	4.00
10	"The No-Hit Parade" (Chris Bosio, Jim Abbott, Darryl Kile)	.50

1994 Fleer Golden Moments Super

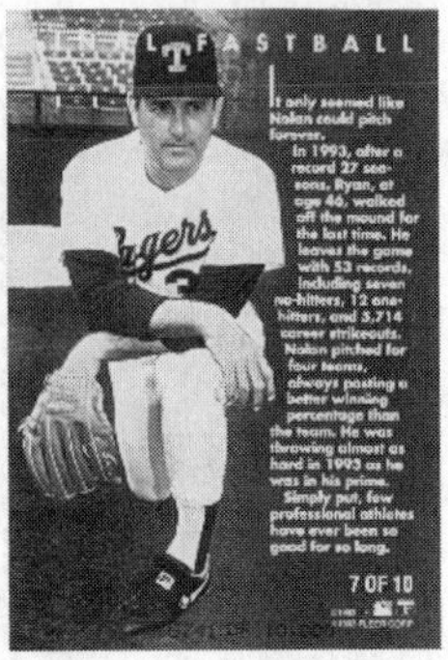

Super-size (3-1/2" x 5") versions of the Golden Moments insert set were included in hobby cases at the rate of one set, in a specially-printed folder, per 20-box case. Each card carries a serial number designating its position in an edition of 10,000.

		MT
Complete Set (10):		37.00
Common Player:		2.50
1	"Four in One" (Mark Whiten)	2.50
2	"Left and Right" (Carlos Baerga)	2.50
3	"3,000 Hit Club" (Dave Winfield)	3.75
4	"Eight Straight" (Ken Griffey, Jr.)	12.00
5	"Triumphant Return" (Bo Jackson)	3.75
6	"Farewell to Baseball" (George Brett)	5.00
7	"Farewell to Baseball" (Nolan Ryan)	7.50
8	"Thirty Times Six" (Fred McGriff)	3.00
9	"Enters 5th Dimension" (Frank Thomas)	5.00
10	"The No-Hit Parade" (Chris Bosio, Jim Abbott, Darryl Kile)	2.50

1994 Fleer League Leaders

Twelve players who led the major leagues in various statistical categories in 1993 are featured in this insert set. Cards are UV coated and have gold-foil stamping on both sides. Within a light metallic green border, card fronts feature a color action photo superimposed over a similar photo in black-and-white. The category in which the player led his league is printed down the right border. Other printing is gold-foil. On back is a color photo and details of the league-leading performance. Stated odds of finding a League Leaders card were one per 17 packs.

		MT
Complete Set (12):		3.00
Common Player:		.10
1	John Olerud	.15
2	Albert Belle	.50
3	Rafael Palmeiro	.25
4	Kenny Lofton	.50
5	Jack McDowell	.10
6	Kevin Appier	.10
7	Andres Galarraga	.25
8	Barry Bonds	.50
9	Len Dykstra	.10
10	Chuck Carr	.10
11	Tom Glavine	.20
12	Greg Maddux	1.25

1994 Fleer Lumber Co.

This insert set features the major leagues' top home run hitters. Inserted only in 21-card jumbo packs, odds of finding one were given as one per five packs. Card fronts feature player action photos against a background resembling the label area of a baseball bat. On back is a background photo of a row of bats on the dirt. A player write-up and close-up photo complete the design.

		MT
Complete Set (10):		11.00
Common Player:		.60
1	Albert Belle	1.25
2	Barry Bonds	1.25
3	Ron Gant	.60
4	Juan Gonzalez	2.00
5	Ken Griffey, Jr.	4.50
6	Dave Justice	.75
7	Fred McGriff	.60
8	Rafael Palmeiro	.75
9	Frank Thomas	1.50
10	Matt Williams	.75

1994 Fleer Major League Prospects

Thirty-five of the game's promising young stars are featured in this insert set. A light green metallic border frames a player photo, with his team logo lightly printed over the background. Most of the printing is gold-foil stamped. Backs have a player photo against a pinstriped background. A light blue box contains career details. Given odds of finding a "Major League Prospects" card are one in six packs.

		MT
Complete Set (35):		9.00
Common Player:		.20
1	Kurt Abbott	.30
2	Brian Anderson	.20
3	Rich Aude	.20
4	Cory Bailey	.20
5	Danny Bautista	.20
6	Marty Cordova	.50
7	Tripp Cromer	.20
8	Midre Cummings	.20
9	Carlos Delgado	1.00
10	Steve Dreyer	.20
11	Steve Dunn	.20
12	Jeff Granger	.20
13	Tyrone Hill	.20
14	Denny Hocking	.20
15	John Hope	.20
16	Butch Huskey	.40
17	Miguel Jimenez	.20
18	Chipper Jones	6.00
19	Steve Karsay	.20
20	Mike Kelly	.20
21	Mike Lieberthal	.50
22	Albie Lopez	.20
23	Jeff McNeely	.20
24	Dan Miceli	.30
25	Nate Minchey	.20
26	Marc Newfield	.20
27	Darren Oliver	.20
28	Luis Ortiz	.20
29	Curtis Pride	.40
30	Roger Salkeld	.25
31	Scott Sanders	.30
32	Dave Staton	.20
33	Salomon Torres	.20
34	Steve Trachsel	.30
35	Chris Turner	.25

1994 Fleer ProVisions

Nine players are featured in this insert set. Cards feature the fantasy artwork of Wayne Still in a format that produces one large image when all nine cards are properly arranged. Besides the art, card fronts feature the player's name in gold-foil. Backs have a background in several shades of red, with the player's name and team at the top in white. A short career summary is printed in black. Odds of finding this particular insert in a pack were one in 12.

		MT
Complete Set (9):		3.00
Common Player:		.20
1	Darren Daulton	.20
2	John Olerud	.25
3	Matt Williams	.50
4	Carlos Baerga	.20
5	Ozzie Smith	.75
6	Juan Gonzalez	1.00
7	Jack McDowell	.20
8	Mike Piazza	2.00
9	Tony Gwynn	1.00

1994 Fleer Rookie Sensations

This insert set features the top rookies from 1993. These inserts were available only in 21-card jumbo packs, with stated odds of one in four packs. Full-bleed fronts have a pair of player photos - one highlighted by a neon outline - superimposed on a graduated background approximating the team colors. Team uniform logo details appear vertically at the right or left side. The player's name is gold-foil stamped in a banner at bottom. The Rookie Sensations and Fleer logos are also gold-imprinted. On back, the team uniform logo is repeated on a white background, along with another player photo and a short write-up.

		MT
Complete Set (20):		15.00
Common Player:		.40
1	Rene Arocha	.40
2	Jason Bere	.40
3	Jeromy Burnitz	.60
4	Chuck Carr	.40
5	Jeff Conine	.50
6	Steve Cooke	.40
7	Cliff Floyd	.60
8	Jeffrey Hammonds	.40
9	Wayne Kirby	.40
10	Mike Lansing	.50
11	Al Martin	.45
12	Greg McMichael	.40
13	Troy Neel	.40
14	Mike Piazza	6.00
15	Armando Reynoso	.40
16	Kirk Rueter	.40
17	Tim Salmon	2.00
18	Aaron Sele	.60
19	J.T. Snow	.75
20	Kevin Stocker	.40

1994 Fleer Tim Salmon A.L. Rookie of the Year

The popular Angels Rookie of the Year is featured in a 15-card set produced in what Fleer terms "metallized" format. The first 12 cards in the set were inserted into foil packs at the rate of about one card per box. Three additional cards could be obtained by sending $1.50 and 10 '94 Fleer wrappers to a mail-in offer. On both front and back, the cards have a color player photo set against a metallic-image background.

		MT
Complete Set (15):		25.00
Common Card:		2.00
Autograph/2,000:		35.00
1	Tim Salmon	2.00
2	Tim Salmon	2.00
3	Tim Salmon	2.00
4	Tim Salmon	2.00
5	Tim Salmon	2.00
6	Tim Salmon	2.00
7	Tim Salmon	2.00
8	Tim Salmon	2.00
9	Tim Salmon	2.00
10	Tim Salmon	2.00
11	Tim Salmon	2.00
12	Tim Salmon	2.00
13	Tim Salmon	3.00
14	Tim Salmon	3.00
15	Tim Salmon	3.00
--	Tim Salmon (autographed edition of 2,000)	75.00

1994 Fleer Smoke 'N Heat

Among the scarcest of the '94 Fleer inserts, available at a stated rate of one per 30 packs, these feature 10 of the top strikeout pitchers in the major leagues. "Metallized" card fronts have a player photo set against an infernal background with large letters, "Smoke 'N Heat". The player's name is in gold foil at bottom. Backs have a similar chaotic hot-red background, a player photo and career summary.

		MT
Complete Set (12):		40.00
Common Player:		.50
1	Roger Clemens	10.00
2	David Cone	1.50
3	Juan Guzman	.50
4	Pete Harnisch	.50
5	Randy Johnson	5.00
6	Mark Langston	.50
7	Greg Maddux	12.50
8	Mike Mussina	3.00
9	Jose Rijo	.50
10	Nolan Ryan	17.50
11	Curt Schilling	1.50
12	John Smoltz	2.50

1994 Fleer Team Leaders

A player from each major league team has been chosen for this 28-card insert set. Fronts feature a team logo against a backgound of graduated team colors. Player portrait and action photos are superimposed. At bottom is the player name, team and position, all in gold foil. Backs have a team logo and player photo set against a white background, with a short write-up justifying the player's selection as a "Team Leader." Odds of finding one of these inserts were given as one in eight packs.

		MT
Complete Set (28):		24.00
Common Player:		.25
1	Cal Ripken, Jr.	5.00
2	Mo Vaughn	1.00
3	Tim Salmon	.75
4	Frank Thomas	2.00
5	Carlos Baerga	.25
6	Cecil Fielder	.25
7	Brian McRae	.25
8	Greg Vaughn	.25
9	Kirby Puckett	2.00
10	Don Mattingly	2.00
11	Mark McGwire	6.00
12	Ken Griffey, Jr.	6.00
13	Juan Gonzalez	2.00
14	Paul Molitor	.75
15	Dave Justice	.35
16	Ryne Sandberg	1.00
17	Barry Larkin	.35
18	Andres Galarraga	.35
19	Gary Sheffield	.75
20	Jeff Bagwell	1.50
21	Mike Piazza	2.50
22	Marquis Grissom	.25
23	Bobby Bonilla	.25
24	Len Dykstra	.25
25	Jay Bell	.25
26	Gregg Jefferies	.25
27	Tony Gwynn	1.50
28	Will Clark	.50

1994 Fleer All-Rookie Team

Sharing the format of the basic 1994 Fleer issue, this nine-card set of rookies was available only by redemption of a trade card randomly inserted into foil packs. The exchange card expired Sept. 30, 1994. The cards are numbered with an "M" prefix.

		MT
Complete Set (9):		5.00
Common Player:		.50
Exchange Card:		.50
1	Kurt Abbott	.75
2	Rich Becker	.75
3	Carlos Delgado	3.00
4	Jorge Fabregas	1.00
5	Bob Hamelin	.50
6	John Hudek	.75
7	Tim Hyers	.50
8	Luis Lopez	.50
9	James Mouton	.50

1994 Fleer Update

Rookies, traded players and free agents who changed teams are included in the annual update issue. Cards are in the same format as the regular-issue '94 Fleer set. Cards are numbered alphabetically within the team.

		MT
Complete Set (200):		50.00
Common Player:		.10
1	Mark Eichhorn	.10
2	Sid Fernandez	.10
3	Leo Gomez	.10
4	Mike Oquist	.10
5	Rafael Palmeiro	.25
6	Chris Sabo	.10
7	Dwight Smith	.10
8	Lee Smith	.12
9	Damon Berryhill	.10
10	Wes Chamberlain	.10
11	Gar Finnvold	.10
12	Chris Howard	.10
13	Tim Naehring	.10
14	Otis Nixon	.10
15	Brian Anderson	.10
16	Jorge Fabregas	.10
17	Rex Hudler	.10
18	Bo Jackson	.20
19	Mark Leiter	.10
20	Spike Owen	.10
21	Harold Reynolds	.10
22	Chris Turner	.10
23	Dennis Cook	.10
24	Jose DeLeon	.10
25	Julio Franco	.10
26	Joe Hall	.10
27	Darrin Jackson	.10
28	Dane Johnson	.10
29	Norberto Martin	.10
30	Scott Sanderson	.10
31	Jason Grimsley	.10
32	Dennis Martinez	.12
33	Jack Morris	.10
34	Eddie Murray	.25
35	Chad Ogea	.10
36	Tony Pena	.10
37	Paul Shuey	.10
38	Omar Vizquel	.12
39	Danny Bautista	.10
40	Tim Belcher	.10
41	Joe Boever	.10
42	Storm Davis	.10
43	Junior Felix	.10
44	Mike Gardiner	.10
45	Buddy Groom	.10
46	Juan Samuel	.10
47	Vince Coleman	.10
48	Bob Hamelin	.10
49	Dave Henderson	.10
50	Rusty Meacham	.10
51	Terry Shumpert	.10
52	Jeff Bronkey	.10
53	Alex Diaz	.10
54	Brian Harper	.10
55	Jose Mercedes	.10
56	Jody Reed	.10
57	Bob Scanlan	.10
58	Turner Ward	.10
59	Rich Becker	.10
60	Alex Cole	.10
61	Denny Hocking	.10
63	Pat Mahomes	.15
64	Carlos Pulido	.10
65	Dave Stevens	.10
66	Matt Walbeck	.10
67	Xavier Hernandez	.10
68	Sterling Hitchcock	.10
69	Terry Mulholland	.10
70	Luis Polonia	.10
71	Gerald Williams	.10
72	Mark Acre	.10
73	Geronimo Berroa	.10
74	Rickey Henderson	.45
75	Stan Javier	.10
76	Steve Karsay	.10
77	Carlos Reyes	.10
78	Bill Taylor	.10
79	Eric Anthony	.10
80	Bobby Ayala	.10
81	Tim Davis	.10
82	Felix Fermin	.10
83	Reggie Jefferson	.10
84	Keith Mitchell	.10
85	Bill Risley	.10
86	*Alex Rodriguez*	45.00
87	Roger Salkeld	.12
88	Dan Wilson	.12
89	Cris Carpenter	.10
90	Will Clark	.40
91	Jeff Frye	.10
92	Rick Helling	.10
93	Chris James	.10
94	Oddibe McDowell	.10
95	Billy Ripken	.10
96	Carlos Delgado	.75
97	Alex Gonzalez	.25
98	Shawn Green	.50
100	Mike Huff	.10
101	Mike Kelly	.10
102	Roberto Kelly	.10
103	Charlie O'Brien	.10
104	Jose Oliva	.10
105	Gregg Olson	.10
106	Willie Banks	.10

107 Jim Bullinger .10
108 Chuck Crim .10
109 Shawon Dunston .10
110 Karl Rhodes .10
111 Steve Trachsel .20
112 Anthony Young .10
113 Eddie Zambrano .10
114 Bret Boone .10
115 Jeff Brantley .10
116 Hector Carrasco .10
117 Tony Fernandez .10
118 Tim Fortugno .10
119 Erik Hanson .10
120 Chuck McElroy .10
121 Deion Sanders 1.00
122 Ellis Burks .10
123 Marvin Freeman .10
124 Mike Harkey .10
125 Howard Johnson .10
126 Mike Kingery .10
127 Nelson Liriano .10
128 Marcus Moore .10
129 Mike Munoz .10
130 Kevin Ritz .10
131 Walt Weiss .10
132 Kurt Abbott .15
133 Jerry Browne .10
134 Greg Colbrunn .10
135 Jeremy Hernandez .10
136 Dave Magadan .10
137 Kurt Miller .10
138 Robb Nen .15
139 Jesus Taverez .10
140 Sid Bream .10
141 Tom Edens .10
142 Tony Eusebio .10
143 John Hudek .10
144 Brian Hunter 1.00
145 Orlando Miller .15
146 James Mouton .10
147 Shane Reynolds .10
148 Rafael Bournigal .10
149 Delino DeShields .10
150 Garey Ingram .10
151 Chan Ho Park .20
152 Wil Cordero .15
153 Pedro Martinez .25
154 Randy Milligan .10
155 Lenny Webster .10
156 Rico Brogna .10
157 Josias Manzanillo .10
158 Kevin McReynolds .10
159 Mike Remlinger .10
160 David Segui .10
161 Pete Smith .10
162 Kelly Stinnett .10
163 Jose Vizcaino .10
164 Billy Hatcher .10
165 Doug Jones .10
166 Mike Lieberthal .20
167 Tony Longmire .10
168 Bobby Munoz .10
169 Paul Quantrill .10
170 Heathcliff Slocumb .10
171 Fernando Valenzuela .12
172 Mark Dewey .10
173 Brian Hunter .10
174 Jon Lieber .10
175 Ravelo Manzanillo .10
176 Dan Miceli .10
177 Rick White .10
178 Bryan Eversgerd .10
179 John Habyan .10
180 Terry McGriff .10
181 Vicente Palacios .10
182 Rich Rodriguez .10
183 Rick Sutcliffe .10
184 Donnie Elliott .10
185 Joey Hamilton .60
186 Tim Hyers .10
187 Luis Lopez .10
188 Ray McDavid .10
189 Bip Roberts .10
190 Scott Sanders .10
191 Eddie Williams .10
192 Steve Frey .10
193 Pat Gomez .10
194 Rich Monteleone .10
195 Mark Portugal .10
196 Darryl Strawberry .15
197 Salomon Torres .10
198 W. Van Landingham .15
199 Checklist .10
200 Checklist .10

1994 Fleer Update Diamond Tribute

These special cards included in the 1994 Fleer Update set feature 10 of baseball's proven superstars. The card front has a color action shot of the player, against a skyline with a baseball pattern among the clouds. The card back is numbered 1 of 8, etc., and includes another photo against a background similar to that used for the card front. A "Diamond Tribute" logo and career summary are also included on the back.

		MT
Complete Set (10):		7.50
Common Player:		.50
1	Barry Bonds	1.00
2	Joe Carter	.50
3	Will Clark	.60
4	Roger Clemens	1.00
5	Tony Gwynn	1.00
6	Don Mattingly	1.00
7	Fred McGriff	.60
8	Eddie Murray	.60
9	Kirby Puckett	1.00
10	Cal Ripken Jr.	3.00

1994 Fleer Atlantic

Five-card packs of this special Fleer set were given away with an eight-gallon premium gasoline purchase at Atlantic/Sunoco stations in the Eastern U.S. between June 1 and July 31. Many of the cards suffered damaged borders from the packaging process. Cards are in the basic 1994 Fleer format, though the name and position around the team logo at top are in white on these cards, rather than gold-foil. Different front and back photos are used in this set. Backs include the gas station logos at bottom.

		MT
Complete Set (25):		8.00
Common Player:		.25
1	Roberto Alomar	.40
2	Carlos Baerga	.25
3	Jeff Bagwell	.75
4	Jay Bell	.25
5	Barry Bonds	.50
6	Joe Carter	.25
7	Roger Clemens	.65
8	Darren Daulton	.25
9	Lenny Dykstra	.25
10	Cecil Fielder	.25
11	Tom Glavine	.30
12	Juan Gonzalez	.75
13	Ken Griffey, Jr.	1.50
14	Dave Justice	.40
15	John Kruk	.25
16	Greg Maddux	1.00
17	Don Mattingly	1.00
18	Jack McDowell	.25
19	John Olerud	.30
20	Mike Piazza	.75
21	Kirby Puckett	.50
22	Tim Salmon	.35
23	Frank Thomas	1.00
24	Andy Van Slyke	.25
25	Checklist	.05

1994 Fleer/Extra Bases

Extra Bases was a 400-card, oversized set, plus 80 insert cards in four different subsets. The cards, 4-11/16" by 2-1/2", have a full-bleed photo on the front and back, as well as UV coating and color coding by team. As was the case in other Fleer products, Extra Bases contained an insert card in every pack. All 80 insert cards feature gold or silver foil stamping.

MT
Complete Set (400): 30.00
Common Player: .10
Wax Box: 30.00
1 Brady Anderson .15
2 Harold Baines .12
3 Mike Devereaux .10
4 Sid Fernandez .10
5 Jeffrey Hammonds .15
6 Chris Hoiles .10
7 Ben McDonald .10
8 Mark McLemore .10
9 Mike Mussina .50
10 Mike Oquist .10
11 Rafael Palmeiro .25
12 Cal Ripken, Jr. 2.50
13 Chris Sabo .10
14 Lee Smith .12
15 Wes Chamberlain .10
16 Roger Clemens .90
17 Scott Cooper .10
18 Danny Darwin .10
19 Andre Dawson .15
20 Mike Greenwell .10
21 Tim Naehring .10
22 Otis Nixon .10
23 Jeff Russell .10
24 Ken Ryan .10
25 Aaron Sele .15
26 John Valentin .15
27 Mo Vaughn .50
28 Frank Viola .10
29 *Brian Anderson* .15
30 Chad Curtis .10
31 Chili Davis .12
32 Gary DiSarcina .10
33 Damion Easley .10
34 Jim Edmonds .30
35 Chuck Finley .10
36 Bo Jackson .15
37 Mark Langston .10
38 Harold Reynolds .10
39 Tim Salmon .40
40 Wilson Alvarez .10
41 James Baldwin .10
42 Jason Bere .10
43 Joey Cora .10
44 *Ray Durham* .60
45 Alex Fernandez .15
46 Julio Franco .10
47 Ozzie Guillen .10
48 Darrin Jackson .10
49 Lance Johnson .10
50 Ron Karkovice .10
51 Jack McDowell .10
52 Tim Raines .12
53 Frank Thomas 1.50
54 Robin Ventura .15
55 Sandy Alomar Jr. .12
56 Carlos Baerga .10
57 Albert Belle .75
58 Mark Clark .10
59 Wayne Kirby .10
60 Kenny Lofton .60
61 Dennis Martinez .12
62 Jose Mesa .10
63 Jack Morris .10
64 Eddie Murray .20
65 Charles Nagy .12
66 Manny Ramirez 1.00
67 Paul Shuey .10
68 Paul Sorrento .10
69 Jim Thome .35
70 Omar Vizquel .12
71 Eric Davis .12
72 John Doherty .10
73 Cecil Fielder .10
74 Travis Fryman .10
75 Kirk Gibson .10
76 Gene Harris .10
77 Mike Henneman .10
78 Mike Moore .10
79 Tony Phillips .10
80 Mickey Tettleton .10
81 Alan Trammell .15
82 Lou Whitaker .10
83 Kevin Appier .10
84 Vince Coleman .10
85 David Cone .15
86 Gary Gaetti .10
87 Greg Gagne .10
88 Tom Gordon .10
89 Jeff Granger .10
90 Bob Hamelin .10
91 Dave Henderson .10
92 Felix Jose .10
93 Wally Joyner .12
94 Jose Lind .10
95 Mike Macfarlane .10
96 Brian McRae .10
97 Jeff Montgomery .10
98 Ricky Bones .10
99 Jeff Bronkey .10
100 Alex Diaz .10
101 Cal Eldred .10
102 Darryl Hamilton .10
103 Brian Harper .10
104 John Jaha .10
105 Pat Listach .10
106 Dave Nilsson .10
107 Jody Reed .10
108 Kevin Seitzer .10
109 Greg Vaughn .15
110 Turner Ward .10
111 Wes Weger .12
112 Bill Wegman .10
113 Rick Aguilera .10
114 Rich Becker .10
115 Alex Cole .10
116 Scott Erickson .10
117 Kent Hrbek .10
118 Chuck Knoblauch .20
119 Scott Leius .10
120 Shane Mack .10
121 Pat Mahomes .10
122 Pat Meares .10
123 Kirby Puckett 1.00
124 Kevin Tapani .10
125 Matt Walbeck .10
126 Dave Winfield .35
127 Jim Abbott .15
128 Wade Boggs .50
129 Mike Gallego .10
130 Xavier Hernandez .10
131 Pat Kelly .10
132 Jimmy Key .10
133 Don Mattingly 1.00
134 Terry Mulholland .10
135 Matt Nokes .10
136 Paul O'Neill .15
137 Melido Perez .10
138 Luis Polonia .10
139 Mike Stanley .10
140 Danny Tartabull .10
141 Randy Velarde .10
142 Bernie Williams .40
143 Mark Acre .10
144 Geronimo Berroa .10
145 Mike Bordick .10
146 Scott Brosius .10
147 Ron Darling .10
148 Dennis Eckersley .12
149 Brent Gates .10
150 Rickey Henderson .40
151 Stan Javier .10
152 Steve Karsay .10
153 Mark McGwire 3.00
154 Troy Neel .10
155 Ruben Sierra .10
156 Terry Steinbach .10
157 Bill Taylor .10
158 Rich Amaral .10
159 Eric Anthony .10
160 Bobby Ayala .10
161 Chris Bosio .10
162 Jay Buhner .10
163 Tim Davis .10
164 Felix Fermin .10
165 Dave Fleming .10
166 Ken Griffey, Jr. 3.00
167 Reggie Jefferson .10
168 Randy Johnson .60
169 Edgar Martinez .12
170 Tino Martinez .15
171 Bill Risley .10
172 Roger Salkeld .10
173 *Mac Suzuki* .20
174 Dan Wilson .10
175 Kevin Brown .20
176 Jose Canseco .40
177 Will Clark .35
178 Juan Gonzalez 1.50
179 Rick Helling .10
180 Tom Henke .10
181 Chris James .10
182 Manuel Lee .10
183 Dean Palmer .10
184 Ivan Rodriguez .40
185 Kenny Rogers .10
186 Roberto Alomar .60
187 Pat Borders .10
188 Joe Carter .15
189 Carlos Delgado .25
190 Juan Guzman .10
191 Pat Hentgen .10
192 Paul Molitor .50
192a Paul Molitor (promotional sample) 6.00
193 John Olerud .15
194 Ed Sprague .10
195 Dave Stewart .12
196 Todd Stottlemyre .12
197 Duane Ward .10
198 Devon White .12
199 Steve Avery .10
200 Jeff Blauser .10
201 Tom Glavine .20
202 Dave Justice .40
203 Mike Kelly .10
204 Roberto Kelly .10
205 Ryan Klesko .25
206 Mark Lemke .10
207 Javier Lopez .25
208 Greg Maddux 1.50
209 Fred McGriff .35
210 Greg McMichael .10
211 Kent Mercker .10
212 Terry Pendleton .10
213 John Smoltz .15
214 Tony Tarasco .10
215 Willie Banks .10
216 Steve Buechele .10
217 Shawon Dunston .10
218 Mark Grace .20
219 *Brooks Kieschnick* .35
220 Derrick May .10
221 Randy Myers .10
222 Karl Rhodes .10
223 Rey Sanchez .10
224 Sammy Sosa 1.50
225 Steve Traschel .20
226 Rick Wilkins .10
227 Bret Boone .10
228 Jeff Brantley .10
229 Tom Browning .10
230 Hector Carrasco .10
231 Rob Dibble .10
232 Erik Hanson .10
233 Barry Larkin .15
234 Kevin Mitchell .10
235 Hal Morris .10
236 Joe Oliver .10
237 Jose Rijo .10
238 Johnny Ruffin .10
239 Deion Sanders .40
240 Reggie Sanders .15
241 John Smiley .10
242 Dante Bichette .30
243 Ellis Burks .10
244 Andres Galarraga .20
245 Joe Girardi .10
246 Greg Harris .10
247 Charlie Hayes .10
248 Howard Johnson .10
249 Roberto Mejia .10
250 Marcus Moore .10
251 David Nied .10
252 Armando Reynoso .10
253 Bruce Ruffin .10
254 Mark Thompson .10
255 Walt Weiss .10
256 *Kurt Abbott* .20
257 Bret Barberie .10
258 Chuck Carr .10
259 Jeff Conine .15
260 Chris Hammond .10
261 Bryan Harvey .10
262 Jeremy Hernandez .10
263 Charlie Hough .10
264 Dave Magadan .10
265 Benito Santiago .10
266 Gary Sheffield .20
267 David Weathers .10
268 Jeff Bagwell 1.00
269 Craig Biggio .15
270 Ken Caminiti .15
271 Andujar Cedeno .10
272 Doug Drabek .10
273 Steve Finley .10
274 Luis Gonzalez .10
275 Pete Harnisch .10
276 John Hudek .10
277 Darryl Kile .10
278 Orlando Miller .10
279 James Mouton .10
280 Shane Reynolds .10
281 Scott Servais .10
282 Greg Swindell .10
283 Pedro Astacio .10
284 Brett Butler .10
285 Tom Candiotti .10
286 Delino DeShields .10
287 Kevin Gross .10
288 Orel Hershiser .12
289 Eric Karros .15
290 Ramon Martinez .12
291 Raul Mondesi .50
292 Jose Offerman .10
293 *Chan Ho Park* .50
294 Mike Piazza 2.00
295 Henry Rodriguez .12
296 Cory Snyder .10
297 Tim Wallach .10
298 Todd Worrell .10
299 Moises Alou .15
300 Sean Berry .10
301 Wil Cordero .10
302 Joey Eischen .10
303 Jeff Fassero .10
304 Darrin Fletcher .10
305 Cliff Floyd .20
306 Marquis Grissom .15
307 Ken Hill .10
308 Mike Lansing .10
309 Pedro Martinez .50
310 Mel Rojas .10
311 Kirk Rueter .10
312 Larry Walker .35
313 John Wetteland .10
314 Rondell White .30
315 Bobby Bonilla .15
316 John Franco .10

317	Dwight Gooden	.15
318	Todd Hundley	.15
319	Bobby Jones	.10
320	Jeff Kent	.10
321	Kevin McReynolds	.10
322	Bill Pulsipher	.10
323	Bret Saberhagen	.10
324	David Segui	.10
325	Pete Smith	.10
326	Kelly Stinnett	.15
327	Ryan Thompson	.10
328	Jose Vizcaino	.10
329	Ricky Bottalico	.10
330	Darren Daulton	.10
331	Mariano Duncan	.10
332	Len Dykstra	.10
333	Tommy Greene	.10
334	Billy Hatcher	.10
335	Dave Hollins	.10
336	Pete Incaviglia	.10
337	Danny Jackson	.10
338	Doug Jones	.10
339	Ricky Jordan	.10
340	John Kruk	.10
341	Curt Schilling	.15
342	Kevin Stocker	.10
343	Jay Bell	.10
344	Steve Cooke	.10
345	Carlos Garcia	.10
346	Brian Hunter	.10
347	Jeff King	.10
348	Al Martin	.10
349	Orlando Merced	.10
350	Denny Neagle	.10
351	Don Slaught	.10
352	Andy Van Slyke	.10
353	Paul Wagner	.10
354	Rick White	.10
355	Luis Alicea	.10
356	Rene Arocha	.10
357	Rheal Cormier	.10
358	Bernard Gilkey	.10
359	Gregg Jefferies	.15
360	Ray Lankford	.10
361	Tom Pagnozzi	.10
362	Mike Perez	.10
363	Ozzie Smith	.50
364	Bob Tewksbury	.10
365	Mark Whiten	.10
366	Todd Zeile	.10
367	Andy Ashby	.12
368	Brad Ausmus	.10
369	Derek Bell	.10
370	Andy Benes	.12
371	Archi Cianfrocco	.10
372	Tony Gwynn	1.00
373	Trevor Hoffman	.12
374	Tim Hyers	.10
375	Pedro Martinez	.20
376	Phil Plantier	.10
377	Bip Roberts	.10
378	Scott Sanders	.10
379	Dave Staton	.10
380	Wally Whitehurst	.10
381	Rod Beck	.10
382	Todd Benzinger	.10
383	Barry Bonds	.75
384	John Burkett	.10
385	Royce Clayton	.10
386	Bryan Hickerson	.10
387	Mike Jackson	.10
388	Darren Lewis	.10
389	Kirt Manwaring	.10
390	Willie McGee	.12
391	Mark Portugal	.10
392	Bill Swift	.10
393	Robby Thompson	.10
394	Salomon Torres	.10
395	Matt Williams	.35
396	Checklist	.10
397	Checklist	.10
398	Checklist	.10
399	Checklist	.10
400	Checklist	.10

1994 Fleer/Extra Bases Game Breakers

Game Breakers featured 30 big-name stars from both leagues who have exhibited offensive firepower. This insert set was done in a horizontal format picturing the player in two different shots, one close-up and one slightly further away. The words "Game Breakers" is written across the bottom, with the player name and team in much smaller letters, printed under it.

		MT
Complete Set (30):		15.00
Common Player:		.25
1	Jeff Bagwell	1.50
2	Rod Beck	.25
3	Albert Belle	1.00
4	Barry Bonds	1.50
5	Jose Canseco	.75
6	Joe Carter	.35
7	Roger Clemens	1.00
8	Darren Daulton	.25
9	Len Dykstra	.25
10	Cecil Fielder	.30
11	Tom Glavine	.30
12	Juan Gonzalez	1.50
13	Mark Grace	.35
14	Ken Griffey, Jr.	4.00
15	Dave Justice	.55
16	Greg Maddux	2.00
17	Don Mattingly	1.75
18	Ben McDonald	.25
19	Fred McGriff	.50
20	Paul Molitor	.65
21	John Olerud	.40
22	Mike Piazza	2.50
23	Kirby Puckett	1.50
24	Cal Ripken, Jr.	3.00
25	Tim Salmon	.75
26	Gary Sheffield	.45
27	Frank Thomas	2.00
28	Mo Vaughn	.75
29	Matt Williams	.50
30	Dave Winfield	.50

1994 Fleer/Extra Bases Major League Hopefuls

Minor league standouts with impressive credentials were showcased in Major League Hopefuls. Each card in this insert set shows the player over a computer-enhanced background, with three smaller photos running down the top half, on the left side of the card. The insert set title runs across the bottom and the player's name is just under it on a black strip.

		MT
Complete Set (10):		4.00
Common Player:		.25
1	James Baldwin	.50
2	Ricky Bottalico	.50
3	Ray Durham	1.00
4	Joey Eischen	.35
5	Brooks Kieschnick	.50
6	Orlando Miller	.35
7	Bill Pulsipher	.25
8	Mac Suzuki	.35
9	Mark Thompson	.25
10	Wes Weger	.35

1994 Fleer/Extra Bases Pitcher's Duel

Pitcher's Duel was available to collectors who mailed in 10 Extra Bases wrappers. The set features 20 of the top pitchers in baseball. Contained in the set were five American League and five National League cards, with two pitchers from the same league on each card. The front background pictures a wide-angle photo of a major league stadium, viewed from above the diamond, behind home plate. Backs have two more action photos set against a sepia-toned background photo of an Old West street to enhance the shootout theme of the set. Cards are numbered with an "M" prefix.

		MT
Complete Set (10):		12.00
Common Player:		.75
1	Roger Clemens, Jack McDowell	3.00
2	Ben McDonald, Randy Johnson	2.00
3	Jimmy Key, David Cone	1.00
4	Mike Mussina, Aaron Sele	1.50
5	Chuck Finley, Wilson Alvarez	.75
6	Steve Avery, Curt Schilling	.75
7	Greg Maddux, Jose Rijo	5.00
8	Bret Saberhagen, Bob Tewksbury	.75
9	Tom Glavine, Bill Swift	1.00
10	Doug Drabek, Orel Hershiser	.75

1994 Fleer/Extra Bases Rookie Standouts

Rookie Standouts highlights 20 of the best and brightest first-year players of the 1994 season. Cards picture the player on a baseball background, with a black, jagged-edged "aura" around the player. Names and teams were placed in the bottom-left corner, running up the side. The Rookie Standouts logo, which is a gold glove with a baseball in it and "Rookie Standouts" printed under it, was placed in the bottom-right corner and the Extra Bases logo appears in the upper-left.

		MT
Complete Set (20):		10.00
Common Player:		.25
1	Kurt Abbott	.50
2	Brian Anderson	.35
3	Hector Carrasco	.35
4	Tim Davis	.25
5	Carlos Delgado	.75
6	Cliff Floyd	.60
7	Bob Hamelin	.30
8	Jeffrey Hammonds	.35
9	Rick Helling	.40
10	Steve Karsay	.30
11	Ryan Klesko	1.00
12	Javier Lopez	1.00
13	Raul Mondesi	2.00
14	James Mouton	.35
15	Chan Ho Park	.75
16	Manny Ramirez	2.00
17	Tony Tarasco	.25
18	Steve Trachsel	.25
19	Rick White	.25
20	Rondell White	1.00

1994 Fleer/Extra Bases Second Year Stars

Second-Year Stars contains 1993 rookies who were expected to have an even bigger impact in the 1994 season. Each card features five photos of the player. Four are in a filmstrip down the left side; the remaining two-thirds of the card contain a larger photo. "Second-Year Stars" is printed across the bottom, along with the player name and team. Backs repeat the film-strip motif.

		MT
Complete Set (20):		9.00
Common Player:		.25
1	Bobby Ayala	.25
2	Jason Bere	.25
3	Chuck Carr	.25
4	Jeff Conine	.40
5	Steve Cooke	.25
6	Wil Cordero	.30
7	Carlos Garcia	.25
8	Brent Gates	.30
9	Trevor Hoffman	.50
10	Wayne Kirby	.25
11	Al Martin	.25
12	Pedro Martinez	1.50
13	Greg McMichael	.25
14	Troy Neel	.25
15	David Nied	.25
16	Mike Piazza	3.50
17	Kirk Rueter	.25
18	Tim Salmon	1.00
19	Aaron Sele	.35
20	Kevin Stocker	.25

1995 Fleer Promos

This eight-player (plus a header card), cello-wrapped promo set was included in a special "Fleer" national newsstand magazine in early 1995. At first glance the cards seem identical to the regularly issued cards of the same players, but there are subtle differences on the back of each card.

		MT
Complete Set (9):		12.50
Common Player:		1.25
26	Roger Clemens (1988 291 SO and 1992 2.41 ERA boxed)	2.50
78	Paul O'Neill (1991 boxed)	1.25
155	David Cone (1990 233 SO boxed, white shadow on team names)	1.25
235	Tim Salmon (No box on 1992 101 R)	2.00
285	Juan Gonzalez (Black stats, 1993 boxed)	2.50
351	Marquis Grissom (No box on 1988 291 AB)	1.25
509	Ozzie Smith (Black stats, no box on 1986 Cardinals)	2.00
514	Dante Bichette (Black stats)	1.25
--	Header card "Different by Design"	.10

1995 Fleer

Fleer baseball arrived in 1995 with six different designs, one for each division. The basic set contains 600 cards and was sold in 12-card and 18-card packs. National League West cards feature many smaller pictures in the background that are identical to the picture in the forefront, while AL West cards contain an action photo over the top of a close-up on the right side and a water colored look on the left side. AL Central cards exhibit numbers pertinent to each player througout the front design, with the player in the middle. NL East players appear in action on the left half of the card with a colorful, encripted look on the rest. National League Central and American League East feature more standard designs with the player in the forefront, with vital numbers and a color background.

		MT
Complete Set (600):		40.00
Common Player:		.05
Wax Box:		35.00
1	Brady Anderson	.15
2	Harold Baines	.08
3	Damon Buford	.05
4	Mike Devereaux	.05
5	Mark Eichhorn	.05
6	Sid Fernandez	.05
7	Leo Gomez	.05
8	Jeffrey Hammonds	.08
9	Chris Hoiles	.05
10	Rick Krivda	.05
11	Ben McDonald	.05
12	Mark McLemore	.05
13	Alan Mills	.05
14	Jamie Moyer	.05
15	Mike Mussina	.30
16	Mike Oquist	.05

17	Rafael Palmeiro	.15
18	Arthur Rhodes	.05
19	Cal Ripken, Jr.	2.50
20	Chris Sabo	.05
21	Lee Smith	.08
22	Jack Voight	.05
23	Damon Berryhill	.05
24	Tom Brunansky	.05
25	Wes Chamberlain	.05
26	Roger Clemens	.75
27	Scott Cooper	.05
28	Andre Dawson	.15
29	Gar Finnvold	.05
30	Tony Fossas	.05
31	Mike Greenwell	.05
32	Joe Hesketh	.05
33	Chris Howard	.05
34	Chris Nabholz	.05
35	Tim Naehring	.05
36	Otis Nixon	.05
37	Carlos Rodriguez	.05
38	Rich Rowland	.05
39	Ken Ryan	.05
40	Aaron Sele	.08
41	John Valentin	.08
42	Mo Vaughn	.60
43	Frank Viola	.05
44	Danny Bautista	.05
45	Joe Boever	.05
46	Milt Cuyler	.05
47	Storm Davis	.05
48	John Doherty	.05
49	Junior Felix	.05
50	Cecil Fielder	.08
51	Travis Fryman	.08
52	Mike Gardiner	.05
53	Kirk Gibson	.05
54	Chris Gomez	.05
55	Buddy Groom	.05
56	Mike Henneman	.05
57	Chad Kreuter	.05
58	Mike Moore	.05
59	Tony Phillips	.05
60	Juan Samuel	.05
61	Mickey Tettleton	.05
62	Alan Trammell	.10
63	David Wells	.08
64	Lou Whitaker	.05
65	Jim Abbott	.10
66	Joe Ausanio	.05
67	Wade Boggs	.30
68	Mike Gallego	.05
69	Xavier Hernandez	.05
70	Sterling Hitchcock	.05
71	Steve Howe	.05
72	Scott Kamieniecki	.05
73	Pat Kelly	.05
74	Jimmy Key	.05
75	Jim Leyritz	.05
76	Don Mattingly	1.00
77	Terry Mulholland	.05
78	Paul O'Neill	.10
79	Melido Perez	.05
80	Luis Polonia	.05
81	Mike Stanley	.05
82	Danny Tartabull	.05
83	Randy Velarde	.05
84	Bob Wickman	.05
85	Bernie Williams	.40
86	Gerald Williams	.05
87	Roberto Alomar	.60
88	Pat Borders	.05
89	Joe Carter	.08
90	Tony Castillo	.05
91	Brad Cornett	.05
92	Carlos Delgado	.40
93	Alex Gonzalez	.10
94	Shawn Green	.20
95	Juan Guzman	.05
96	Darren Hall	.05
97	Pat Hentgen	.05
98	Mike Huff	.05
99	Randy Knorr	.05
100	Al Leiter	.08
101	Paul Molitor	.35
102	John Olerud	.10
103	Dick Schofield	.05
104	Ed Sprague	.05
105	Dave Stewart	.08
106	Todd Stottlemyre	.05
107	Devon White	.05
108	Woody Williams	.05
109	Wilson Alvarez	.05
110	Paul Assenmacher	.05
111	Jason Bere	.05
112	Dennis Cook	.05
113	Joey Cora	.05
114	Jose DeLeon	.05
115	Alex Fernandez	.10
116	Julio Franco	.05
117	Craig Graboeck	.05
118	Ozzie Guillen	.05
119	Roberto Hernandez	.05
120	Darrin Jackson	.05
121	Lance Johnson	.05
122	Ron Karkovice	.05
123	Mike LaValliere	.05
124	Norberto Martin	.05
125	Kirk McCaskill	.05
126	Jack McDowell	.05
127	Tim Raines	.08
128	Frank Thomas	1.00
129	Robin Ventura	.10
130	Sandy Alomar Jr.	.10
131	Carlos Baerga	.05
132	Albert Belle	.60
133	Mark Clark	.05
134	Alvaro Espinoza	.05
135	Jason Grimsley	.05
136	Wayne Kirby	.05
137	Kenny Lofton	.60
138	Albie Lopez	.05
139	Dennis Martinez	.08
140	Jose Mesa	.05
141	Eddie Murray	.35
142	Charles Nagy	.05
143	Tony Pena	.05
144	Eric Plunk	.05
145	Manny Ramirez	1.00
146	Jeff Russell	.05
147	Paul Shuey	.05
148	Paul Sorrento	.05
149	Jim Thome	.40
150	Omar Vizquel	.08
151	Dave Winfield	.25
152	Kevin Appier	.05
153	Billy Brewer	.05
154	Vince Coleman	.05
155	David Cone	.08
156	Gary Gaetti	.05
157	Greg Gagne	.05
158	Tom Gordon	.05
159	Mark Gubicza	.05
160	Bob Hamelin	.05
161	Dave Henderson	.05
162	Felix Jose	.05
163	Wally Joyner	.08
164	Jose Lind	.05
165	Mike Macfarlane	.05
166	Mike Magnante	.05
167	Brent Mayne	.05
168	Brian McRae	.05
169	Rusty Meacham	.05
170	Jeff Montgomery	.05
171	Hipolito Pichardo	.05
172	Terry Shumpert	.05
173	Michael Tucker	.08
174	Ricky Bones	.05
175	*Jeff Cirillo*	.20
176	Alex Diaz	.05
177	Cal Eldred	.05
178	Mike Fetters	.05
179	Darryl Hamilton	.05
180	Brian Harper	.05
181	John Jaha	.05
182	Pat Listach	.05
183	Graeme Lloyd	.05
184	Jose Mercedes	.05
185	Matt Mieske	.05
186	Dave Nilsson	.05
187	Jody Reed	.05
188	Bob Scanlan	.05
189	Kevin Seitzer	.05
190	Bill Spiers	.05
191	B.J. Surhoff	.08
192	Jose Valentin	.05
193	Greg Vaughn	.10
194	Turner Ward	.05
195	Bill Wegman	.05
196	Rick Aguilera	.05
197	Rich Becker	.05
198	Alex Cole	.05
199	Marty Cordova	.08
200	Steve Dunn	.05
201	Scott Erickson	.05
202	Mark Guthrie	.05
203	Chip Hale	.05
204	LaTroy Hawkins	.10
205	Denny Hocking	.05
206	Chuck Knoblauch	.20
207	Scott Leius	.05
208	Shane Mack	.05
209	Pat Mahomes	.05
210	Pat Meares	.05
211	Pedro Munoz	.05
212	Kirby Puckett	.75
213	Jeff Reboulet	.08
214	Dave Stevens	.05
215	Kevin Tapani	.05
216	Matt Walbeck	.05
217	Carl Willis	.05
218	Brian Anderson	.08
219	Chad Curtis	.05
220	Chili Davis	.08
221	Gary DiSarcina	.05
222	Damion Easley	.05
223	Jim Edmonds	.25
224	Chuck Finley	.05
225	Joe Grahe	.05
226	Rex Hudler	.05
227	Bo Jackson	.10
228	Mark Langston	.05
229	Phil Leftwich	.05
230	Mark Leiter	.05
231	Spike Owen	.05
232	Bob Patterson	.05
233	Troy Percival	.05
234	Eduardo Perez	.05
235	Tim Salmon	.25
236	J.T. Snow	.12
237	Chris Turner	.05
238	Mark Acre	.05
239	Geronimo Berroa	.05
240	Mike Bordick	.05
241	John Briscoe	.05
242	Scott Brosius	.05
243	Ron Darling	.05
244	Dennis Eckersley	.08
245	Brent Gates	.05
246	Rickey Henderson	.30
247	Stan Javier	.05
248	Steve Karsay	.10
249	Mark McGwire	3.00
250	Troy Neel	.05
251	Steve Ontiveros	.05
252	Carlos Reyes	.05
253	Ruben Sierra	.05
254	Terry Steinbach	.05
255	Bill Taylor	.05
256	Todd Van Poppel	.05
257	Bobby Witt	.05
258	Rich Amaral	.05
259	Eric Anthony	.05
260	Bobby Ayala	.05
261	Mike Blowers	.05
262	Chris Bosio	.05
263	Jay Buhner	.08
264	John Cummings	.05
265	Tim Davis	.05
266	Felix Fermin	.05
267	Dave Fleming	.05
268	Goose Gossage	.05
269	Ken Griffey, Jr.	3.00
270	Reggie Jefferson	.05
271	Randy Johnson	.50
272	Edgar Martinez	.08
273	Tino Martinez	.15
274	Greg Pirkl	.05
275	Bill Risley	.05
276	Roger Salkeld	.05
277	Luis Sojo	.05
278	Mac Suzuki	.08
279	Dan Wilson	.05
280	Kevin Brown	.12
281	Jose Canseco	.35
282	Cris Carpenter	.05
283	Will Clark	.30
284	Jeff Frye	.05
285	Juan Gonzalez	1.25
286	Rick Helling	.05
287	Tom Henke	.05
288	David Hulse	.05
289	Chris James	.05
290	Manuel Lee	.05
291	Oddibe McDowell	.05
292	Dean Palmer	.05
293	Roger Pavlik	.05
294	Bill Ripken	.05
295	Ivan Rodriguez	.45
296	Kenny Rogers	.05
297	Doug Strange	.05
298	Matt Whiteside	.05
299	Steve Avery	.05
300	Steve Bedrosian	.05
301	Rafael Belliard	.05
302	Jeff Blauser	.05
303	Dave Gallagher	.05
304	Tom Glavine	.15
305	Dave Justice	.20
306	Mike Kelly	.05
307	Roberto Kelly	.05
308	Ryan Klesko	.25
309	Mark Lemke	.05
310	Javier Lopez	.15
311	Greg Maddux	1.00
312	Fred McGriff	.25
313	Greg McMichael	.05
314	Kent Mercker	.05
315	Charlie O'Brien	.05
316	Jose Oliva	.05
317	Terry Pendleton	.05
318	John Smoltz	.20
319	Mike Stanton	.05
320	Tony Tarasco	.05
321	Terrell Wade	.05
322	Mark Wohlers	.05
323	Kurt Abbott	.05
324	Luis Aquino	.05
325	Bret Barberie	.05
326	Ryan Bowen	.05
327	Jerry Browne	.05
328	Chuck Carr	.05
329	Matias Carrillo	.05
330	Greg Colbrunn	.05
331	Jeff Conine	.12
332	Mark Gardner	.05
333	Chris Hammond	.05
334	Bryan Harvey	.05
335	Richie Lewis	.05
336	Dave Magadan	.05
337	Terry Mathews	.05
338	Robb Nen	.05
339	Yorkis Perez	.05
340	Pat Rapp	.05
341	Benito Santiago	.08
342	Gary Sheffield	.35
343	Dave Weathers	.05
344	Moises Alou	.10
345	Sean Berry	.05
346	Wil Cordero	.05
347	Joe Eischen	.05
348	Jeff Fassero	.05
349	Darrin Fletcher	.05
350	Cliff Floyd	.08
351	Marquis Grissom	.10
352	Butch Henry	.05
353	Gil Heredia	.05
354	Ken Hill	.05
355	Mike Lansing	.05
356	Pedro Martinez	.30
357	Mel Rojas	.05
358	Kirk Rueter	.05
359	Tim Scott	.05
360	Jeff Shaw	.05
361	Larry Walker	.30
362	Lenny Webster	.05
363	John Wetteland	.05
364	Rondell White	.12
365	Bobby Bonilla	.08
366	Rico Brogna	.05
367	Jeromy Burnitz	.08
368	John Franco	.05
369	Dwight Gooden	.10
370	Todd Hundley	.15
371	Jason Jacome	.05
372	Bobby Jones	.05
373	Jeff Kent	.05
374	Jim Lindeman	.05
375	Josias Manzanillo	.05
376	Roger Mason	.05
377	Kevin McReynolds	.05
378	Joe Orsulak	.05
379	Bill Pulsipher	.05
380	Bret Saberhagen	.08
381	David Segui	.05
382	Pete Smith	.05
383	Kelly Stinnett	.05
384	Ryan Thompson	.05
385	Jose Vizcaino	.05
386	Toby Borland	.05
387	Ricky Bettalico	.05
388	Darren Daulton	.05
389	Mariano Duncan	.05
390	Len Dykstra	.05
391	Jim Eisenreich	.05
392	Tommy Greene	.05
393	Dave Hollins	.05
394	Pete Incaviglia	.05
395	Danny Jackson	.05
396	Doug Jones	.05
397	Ricky Jordan	.05
398	John Kruk	.05
399	Mike Lieberthal	.08
400	Tony Longmire	.05
401	Mickey Morandini	.05
402	Bobby Munoz	.05
403	Curt Schilling	.10
404	Heathcliff Slocumb	.05
405	Kevin Stocker	.05
406	Fernando Valenzuela	.05
407	David West	.05
408	Willie Banks	.05
409	Jose Bautista	.05
410	Steve Buechele	.05
411	Jim Bullinger	.05
412	Chuck Crim	.05
413	Shawon Dunston	.05
414	Kevin Foster	.05
415	Mark Grace	.20
416	Jose Hernandez	.05
417	Glenallen Hill	.05
418	Brooks Kieschnick	.08
419	Derrick May	.05
420	Randy Myers	.05
421	Dan Plesac	.05
422	Karl Rhodes	.05
423	Rey Sanchez	.05
424	Sammy Sosa	1.00
425	Steve Trachsel	.05
426	Rick Wilkins	.05
427	Anthony Young	.05
428	Eddie Zambrano	.05
429	Bret Boone	.05
430	Jeff Branson	.05
431	Jeff Brantley	.05
432	Hector Carrasco	.05
433	Brian Dorsett	.05
434	Tony Fernandez	.05
435	Tim Fortugno	.05
436	Erik Hanson	.05
437	Thomas Howard	.05
438	Kevin Jarvis	.05
439	Barry Larkin	.15
440	Chuck McElroy	.05
441	Kevin Mitchell	.05
442	Hal Morris	.05
443	Jose Rijo	.05
444	John Roper	.05
445	Johnny Ruffin	.05
446	Deion Sanders	.20
447	Reggie Sanders	.10
448	Pete Schourek	.05
449	John Smiley	.05
450	Eddie Taubensee	.05
451	Jeff Bagwell	.75
452	Kevin Bass	.05
453	Craig Biggio	.15
454	Ken Caminiti	.15
455	Andujar Cedeno	.05
456	Doug Drabek	.05
457	Tony Eusebio	.05
458	Mike Felder	.05
459	Steve Finley	.05
460	Luis Gonzalez	.08
461	Mike Hampton	.05
462	Pete Harnisch	.05
463	John Hudek	.05
464	Todd Jones	.05
465	Darryl Kile	.05
466	James Mouton	.05
467	Shane Reynolds	.05
468	Scott Servais	.05
469	Greg Swindell	.05
470	Dave Veres	.05
471	Brian Williams	.05
472	Jay Bell	.05
473	Jacob Brumfield	.05
474	Dave Clark	.05
475	Steve Cooke	.05
476	Midre Cummings	.05
477	Mark Dewey	.05
478	Tom Foley	.05
479	Carlos Garcia	.05
480	Jeff King	.05
481	Jon Lieber	.05
482	Ravelo Manzanillo	.05
483	Al Martin	.05
484	Orlando Merced	.05
485	Danny Miceli	.05
486	Denny Neagle	.05
487	Lance Parrish	.05
488	Don Slaught	.05
489	Zane Smith	.05
490	Andy Van Slyke	.05
491	Paul Wagner	.05
492	Rick White	.05
493	Luis Alicea	.05
494	Rene Arocha	.05
495	Rheal Cormier	.05
496	Bryan Eversgerd	.05
497	Bernard Gilkey	.08
498	John Habyan	.05
499	Gregg Jefferies	.10
500	Brian Jordan	.10
501	Ray Lankford	.08
502	John Mabry	.05
503	Terry McGriff	.05
504	Tom Pagnozzi	.05
505	Vicente Palacios	.05
506	Geronimo Pena	.05
507	Gerald Perry	.05
508	Rich Rodriguez	.05
509	Ozzie Smith	.35
510	Bob Tewksbury	.05
511	Allen Watson	.08
512	Mark Whiten	.05
513	Todd Zeile	.05
514	Dante Bichette	.25
515	Willie Blair	.05
516	Ellis Burks	.05
517	Marvin Freeman	.05
518	Andres Galarraga	.15
519	Joe Girardi	.05
520	Greg Harris	.05
521	Charlie Hayes	.05
522	Mike Kingery	.05
523	Nelson Liriano	.05
524	Mike Munoz	.05
525	David Nied	.05
526	Steve Reed	.05
527	Kevin Ritz	.05
528	Bruce Ruffin	.05
529	John Vander Wal	.05
530	Walt Weiss	.05
531	Eric Young	.05
532	Billy Ashley	.05
533	Pedro Astacio	.05
534	Rafael Bournigal	.05
535	Brett Butler	.08
536	Tom Candiotti	.05
537	Omar Daal	.05
538	Delino DeShields	.05
539	Darren Dreifort	.05
540	Kevin Gross	.05
541	Orel Hershiser	.08
542	Garey Ingram	.05
543	Eric Karros	.10
544	Ramon Martinez	.08
545	Raul Mondesi	.40
546	Chan Ho Park	.15
547	Mike Piazza	1.50
548	Henry Rodriguez	.08
549	Rudy Seanez	.05
550	Ismael Valdes	.08
551	Tim Wallach	.05
552	Todd Worrell	.05
553	Andy Ashby	.08
554	Brad Ausmus	.05
555	Derek Bell	.10
556	Andy Benes	.08
557	Phil Clark	.05
558	Donnie Elliott	.05
559	Ricky Gutierrez	.05
560	Tony Gwynn	.75
561	Joey Hamilton	.12
562	Trevor Hoffman	.08
563	Luis Lopez	.05
564	Pedro Martinez	.05
565	Tim Mauser	.05
566	Phil Plantier	.05
567	Bip Roberts	.05
568	Scott Sanders	.05
569	Craig Shipley	.05
570	Jeff Tabaka	.05
571	Eddie Williams	.05
572	Rod Beck	.05
573	Mike Benjamin	.05
574	Barry Bonds	.65
575	Dave Burba	.05
576	John Burkett	.05
577	Mark Carreon	.05
578	Royce Clayton	.05
579	Steve Frey	.05
580	Bryan Hickerson	.05
581	Mike Jackson	.05
582	Darren Lewis	.05
583	Kirt Manwaring	.05
584	Rich Monteleone	.05
585	John Patterson	.05
586	J.R. Phillips	.05
587	Mark Portugal	.05
588	Joe Rosselli	.05
589	Darryl Strawberry	.10
590	Bill Swift	.05
591	Robby Thompson	.05
592	William Van Landingham	.05
593	Matt Williams	.20
594	Checklist	.05
595	Checklist	.05
596	Checklist	.05
597	Checklist	.05
598	Checklist	.05
599	Checklist	.05
600	Checklist	.05

Player names in *Italic* type indicate a rookie card.

1995 Fleer All-Stars

All-Stars are a horizontal, two-sided insert set consisting of 25 cards. A National League All-Star is on one side, while an American League All-Star is on the other, by position. All-Stars are the most common insert in Fleer 1995 baseball, with an insertion ratio of one per three packs.

		MT
Complete Set (25):		8.00
Common Player:		.15
1	Ivan Rodriguez, Mike Piazza	1.50
2	Frank Thomas, Gregg Jefferies	1.00
3	Roberto Alomar, Mariano Duncan	.50
4	Wade Boggs, Matt Williams	.50
5	Cal Ripken, Jr., Ozzie Smith	1.75
6	Joe Carter, Barry Bonds	.40
7	Ken Griffey, Jr., Tony Gwynn	2.00
8	Kirby Puckett, Dave Justice	1.00
9	Jimmy Key, Greg Maddux	1.25
10	Chuck Knoblauch, Wil Cordero	.20
11	Scott Cooper, Ken Caminiti	.15
12	Will Clark, Carlos Garcia	.25
13	Paul Molitor, Jeff Bagwell	.40
14	Travis Fryman, Craig Biggio	.20
15	Mickey Tettleton, Fred McGriff	.15
16	Kenny Lofton, Moises Alou	.20
17	Albert Belle, Marquis Grissom	.50
18	Paul O'Neill, Dante Bichette	.15
19	David Cone, Ken Hill	.15
20	Mike Mussina, Doug Drabek	.20
21	Randy Johnson, John Hudek	.35
22	Pat Hentgen, Danny Jackson	.15
23	Wilson Alvarez, Rod Beck	.15
24	Lee Smith, Randy Myers	.15
25	Jason Bere, Doug Jones	.15

1995 Fleer Award Winners

Fleer Award Winners contain Fleer's choices of baseball's most outstanding players. This six-card set was only inserted at a rate of one per 24 packs. Each card has an embossed gold foil design, with the gold strip running up the left side and containing the words "Fleer Award Winner" and the player name.

		MT
Complete Set (6):		7.00
Common Player:		.40
1	Frank Thomas	3.00
2	Jeff Bagwell	2.50
3	David Cone	.50
4	Greg Maddux	3.00
5	Bob Hamelin	.40
6	Raul Mondesi	.75

1995 Fleer League Leaders

League Leaders feature players on a horizontal format from 10 statistical categories from both leagues. "League Leader" is placed in a blue strip down the left-side of the card, with their respective league and their name in it. These were inserted at a rate of one per 12 packs.

		MT
Complete Set (10):		7.50
Common Player:		.40
1	Paul O'Neill	.45
2	Ken Griffey, Jr.	4.00
3	Kirby Puckett	1.25
4	Jimmy Key	.40
5	Randy Johnson	.75
6	Tony Gwynn	1.00
7	Matt Williams	.50
8	Jeff Bagwell	1.25
9	Greg Maddux, Ken Hill	1.50
10	Andy Benes	.40

1995 Fleer Lumber Company

Ten of the top longball hitters were featured in Lumber Company, which were inserted into every 24 12-card retailer packs. They show the power hitter in action, with a wood-grain Lumber Co. logo across the bottom, contain the player's name and team.

		MT
Complete Set (10):		25.00
Common Player:		.75
1	Jeff Bagwell	3.50
2	Albert Belle	3.00
3	Barry Bonds	3.00
4	Jose Canseco	2.00
5	Joe Carter	.75
6	Ken Griffey, Jr.	12.00
7	Fred McGriff	1.50
8	Kevin Mitchell	.75
9	Frank Thomas	4.00
10	Matt Williams	1.00

Checklists with card numbers in parentheses ( ) indicates the numbers do not appear on the card.

1995 Fleer Major League Prospects

Major League Prospects showcases 10 of 1995's most promising young players. The set title is repeatedly printed across the background, with the player's name and team in a grey strip across the bottom. These cards were inserted one every six packs.

		MT
Complete Set (10):		7.00
Common Player:		.25
1	Garret Anderson	.75
2	James Baldwin	.25
3	Alan Benes	.75
4	Armando Benitez	.25
5	Ray Durham	.75
6	Brian Hunter	.35
7a	Derek Jeter (no licensor logos on back)	3.00
7b	Derek Jeter (licensor logos on back)	3.00
8	Charles Johnson	.40
9	Orlando Miller	.25
10	Alex Rodriguez	6.00

1995 Fleer Pro-Visions

Pro-Visions contain six interlocking cards that form one giant picture. These original art cards exhibit the player in a fantasy art background and are inserted into every nine packs.

		MT
Complete Set (6):		2.00
Common Player:		.25
1	Mike Mussina	.25
2	Raul Mondesi	.25
3	Jeff Bagwell	.75
4	Greg Maddux	1.00
5	Tim Salmon	.25
6	Manny Ramirez	.50

1995 Fleer Rookie Sensations

A perennial favorite within Fleer products, Rookie Sensations cards were inserted in 18-card packs only, at a rate of one per 16 packs. This 20-card set featured the top rookies from the 1994 season. The player's name and team run up the right side of the card, while the words "Rookie Sensations" appear in the bottom-left corner, separated by a colorful, zig-zagged image of a player.

		MT
Complete Set (20):		30.00
Common Player:		1.00
1	Kurt Abbott	1.00
2	Rico Brogna	1.00
3	Hector Carrasco	1.00
4	Kevin Foster	1.00
5	Chris Gomez	1.00
6	Darren Hall	1.00
7	Bob Hamelin	1.00
8	Joey Hamilton	1.50
9	John Hudek	1.00
10	Ryan Klesko	1.50
11	Javier Lopez	3.00
12	Matt Mieske	1.00
13	Raul Mondesi	6.00
14	Manny Ramirez	15.00
15	Shane Reynolds	1.00
16	Bill Risley	1.00
17	Johnny Ruffin	1.00
18	Steve Trachsel	1.50
19	William Van Landingham	1.00
20	Rondell White	4.00

1995 Fleer Team Leaders

Team Leaders are two-player cards featuring the leading hitter and pitcher from each major league team, one on each side. Inserted at a rate of one per 24 packs, these are only found in 12-card hobby packs. Team Leaders consisted of 28 cards and included a Team Leader logo in the bottom-left corner.

		MT
Complete Set (28):		150.00
Common Player:		1.25
1	Cal Ripken, Jr., Mike Mussina	20.00
2	Mo Vaughn, Roger Clemens	12.50
3	Tim Salmon, Chuck Finley	2.00
4	Frank Thomas, Jack McDowell	12.50
5	Albert Belle, Dennis Martinez	8.00
6	Cecil Fielder, Mike Moore	1.25
7	Bob Hamelin, David Cone	1.25
8	Greg Vaughn, Ricky Bones	1.25
9	Kirby Puckett, Rick Aguilera	10.00
10	Don Mattingly, Jimmy Key	10.00
11	Ruben Sierra, Dennis Eckersley	1.50
12	Ken Griffey, Jr., Randy Johnson	25.00
13	Jose Canseco, Kenny Rogers	2.50
14	Joe Carter, Pat Hentgen	1.25
15	Dave Justice, Greg Maddux	17.50
16	Sammy Sosa, Steve Trachsel	10.00
17	Kevin Mitchell, Jose Rijo	1.25
18	Dante Bichette, Bruce Ruffin	2.00
19	Jeff Conine, Robb Nen	1.50
20	Jeff Bagwell, Doug Drabek	9.50
21	Mike Piazza, Ramon Martinez	17.50
22	Moises Alou, Ken Hill	1.50
23	Bobby Bonilla, Bret Saberhagen	1.25
24	Darren Daulton, Danny Jackson	1.25
25	Jay Bell, Zane Smith	1.25
26	Gregg Jefferies, Bob Tewksbury	1.25
27	Tony Gwynn, Andy Benes	10.00
28	Matt Williams, Rod Beck	1.50

1995 Fleer All-Fleer 9

Available only by mailing in 10 Fleer wrappers and $3, this set presents an all-star lineup in a unique design. Colored scribbles down one side of the card front offer a background for gold-foil printing of the card title, player name, position and team. Backs repeat the colored scribbles across virtually the entire surface, making it extremely difficult to read the career summary printed in white over it.

		MT
Complete Set (9):		9.00
Common Player:		.50
1	Mike Piazza	1.50
2	Frank Thomas	1.50
3	Roberto Alomar	.75
4	Cal Ripken Jr.	2.00
5	Matt Williams	.50
6	Barry Bonds	1.00
7	Ken Griffey Jr.	2.50
8	Tony Gwynn	1.00
9	Greg Maddux	1.25

1995 Fleer All-Rookies

This mail-in set was available by redeeming a randomly inserted trade card found in packs. The cards feature action player photos on a muted background, with the player ID in gold-foil beneath a huge rookie banner. Horizontal backs have a player photo at left and professional highlights at right. Cards have an "M" prefix to the card number.

		MT
Complete Set (9):		5.00
Common Player:		.50
Trade card (expired Sept. 30, 1995):		.50
1	Edgardo Alfonzo	2.00
2	Jason Bates	.75
3	Brian Boehringer	.50
4	Darren Bragg	.75

5	Brad Clontz	.50
6	Jim Dougherty	.50
7	Todd Hollandsworth	1.00
8	Rudy Pemberton	.50
9	Frank Rodriguez	.75

1995 Fleer Update

Fleer carried its "different by design" concept of six formats (one for each division in each league) from the regular set into its 1995 Update issue. The issue consists of 200 cards of 1995's traded, rookie and free agent players, plus five different insert sets. One insert card was found in each regular (12-card, $1.49) and jumbo (18-card, $2.29) pack. Cards are numbered with a "U" prefix.

		MT
Complete Set (200):		14.00
Common Player:		.10
Wax Box:		35.00
1	Manny Alexander	.10
2	Bret Barberie	.10
3	Armando Benitez	.10
4	Kevin Brown	.10
5	Doug Jones	.10
6	Sherman Obando	.10
7	Andy Van Slyke	.10
8	Stan Belinda	.10
9	Jose Canseco	.30
10	Vaughn Eshelman	.10
11	Mike Macfarlane	.10
12	Troy O'Leary	.10
13	Steve Rodriguez	.10
14	Lee Tinsley	.10
15	Tim Vanegmond	.10
16	Mark Whiten	.10
17	Sean Bergman	.10
18	Chad Curtis	.10
19	John Flaherty	.10
20	*Bob Higginson*	.25
21	Felipe Lira	.10
22	Shannon Penn	.10
23	Todd Steverson	.10
24	Sean Whiteside	.10
25	Tony Fernandez	.10
26	Jack McDowell	.10
27	Andy Pettitte	.12
28	John Wetteland	.10
29	David Cone	.15
30	Mike Timlin	.10
31	Duane Ward	.10
32	Jim Abbott	.15
33	James Baldwin	.10
34	Mike Devereaux	.10
35	Ray Durham	.25
36	Tim Fortugno	.10
37	Scott Ruffcorn	.10
38	Chris Sabo	.10
39	Paul Assenmacher	.10
40	Bud Black	.10
41	Orel Hershiser	.12
42	Julian Tavarez	.10
43	Dave Winfield	.15
44	Pat Borders	.10
45	*Melvin Bunch*	.15
46	Tom Goodwin	.10
47	Jon Nunnally	.10
48	Joe Randa	.10
49	*Dilson Torres*	.10
50	Joe Vitiello	.10
51	David Hulse	.10
52	Scott Karl	.10
53	Mark Kiefer	.10
54	Derrick May	.10
55	Joe Oliver	.10
56	Al Reyes	.10
57	*Steve Sparks*	.15
58	Jerald Clark	.10
59	Eddie Guardado	.10
60	Kevin Maas	.10
61	David McCarty	.10
62	*Brad Radke*	.15
63	Scott Stahoviak	.10
64	Garret Anderson	.15
65	Shawn Boskie	.10
66	Mike James	.10
67	Tony Phillips	.10
68	Lee Smith	.12
69	Mitch Williams	.10
70	Jim Corsi	.10
71	Mark Harkey	.10
72	Dave Stewart	.12
73	Todd Stottlemyre	.10
74	Joey Cora	.10
75	Chad Kreuter	.10
76	Jeff Nelson	.10
77	Alex Rodriguez	1.50
78	Ron Villone	.10
79	*Bob Wells*	.15
80	*Jose Alberro*	.15
81	Terry Burrows	.10
82	Kevin Gross	.10
83	Wilson Heredia	.10
84	Mark McLemore	.10
85	Otis Nixon	.10
86	Jeff Russell	.10
87	Mickey Tettleton	.10
88	Bob Tewksbury	.10
89	Pedro Borbon	.10
90	Marquis Grissom	.12
91	Chipper Jones	.75
92	Mike Mordecai	.10
93	*Jason Schmidt*	.25
94	John Burkett	.10
95	Andre Dawson	.15
96	*Matt Dunbar*	.15
97	Charles Johnson	.15
98	Terry Pendleton	.10
99	Rich Scheid	.10
100	Quilvio Veras	.10
101	Bobby Witt	.10
102	Eddie Zosky	.10
103	Shane Andrews	.10
104	Reid Cornelius	.10
105	*Chad Fonville*	.20
106	*Mark Grudzielanek*	.30
107	Roberto Kelly	.10
108	*Carlos Perez*	.15
109	Tony Tarasco	.10
110	Brett Butler	.15
111	Carl Everett	.10
112	Pete Harnisch	.10
113	Doug Henry	.10
114	Kevin Lomon	.10
115	Blas Minor	.10
116	Dave Mlicki	.10
117	*Ricky Otero*	.15
118	Norm Charlton	.10
119	Tyler Green	.10
120	Gene Harris	.10
121	Charlie Hayes	.10
122	Gregg Jefferies	.15
123	*Michael Mimbs*	.20
124	Paul Quantrill	.10
125	Frank Castillo	.10
126	Brian McRae	.10
127	Jaime Navarro	.10
128	Mike Perez	.10
129	Tanyon Sturtze	.10
130	Ozzie Timmons	.10
131	John Courtright	.10
132	Ron Gant	.15
133	Xavier Hernandez	.10
134	Brian Hunter	.10
135	Benito Santiago	.10
136	Pete Smith	.10
137	Scott Sullivan	.10
138	Derek Bell	.15
139	Doug Brocail	.10
140	Ricky Gutierrez	.10
141	Pedro Martinez	.25
142	Orlando Miller	.10
143	Phil Plantier	.10
144	Craig Shipley	.10
145	Rich Aude	.10
146	*Jason Christiansen*	.15
147	*Freddy Garcia*	.15
148	Jim Gott	.10
149	*Mark Johnson*	.20
150	Esteban Loaiza	.15
151	Dan Plesac	.10
152	*Gary Wilson*	.10
153	Allen Battle	.10
154	Terry Bradshaw	.10
155	Scott Cooper	.10
156	Tripp Cromer	.10
157	John Frascatore	.10
158	John Habyan	.10
159	Tom Henke	.10
160	Ken Hill	.10
161	Danny Jackson	.10
162	Donovan Osborne	.10
163	Tom Urbani	.10
164	Roger Bailey	.10
165	*Jorge Brito*	.15
166	Vinny Castilla	.15
167	Darren Holmes	.10
168	Roberto Mejia	.10
169	Bill Swift	.10
170	Mark Thompson	.10
171	Larry Walker	.40
172	Greg Hansell	.10
173	Dave Hansen	.10
174	Carlos Hernandez	.10
175	*Hideo Nomo*	2.00
176	Jose Offerman	.10
177	Antonio Osuna	.10
178	Reggie Williams	.10
179	Todd Williams	.10
180	Andres Berumen	.10
181	Ken Caminiti	.15
182	Andujar Cedeno	.10
183	Steve Finley	.10
184	Bryce Florie	.10
185	Dustin Hermanson	.15
186	Ray Holbert	.10
187	Melvin Nieves	.10
188	Roberto Petagine	.10
189	Jody Reed	.10
190	Fernando Valenzuela	.10
191	Brian Williams	.10
192	Mark Dewey	.10
193	Glenallen Hill	.10
194	*Chris Hook*	.15
195	Terry Mulholland	.10
196	Steve Scarsone	.10
197	Trevor Wilson	.10
198	Checklist	.10
199	Checklist	.10
200	Checklist	.10

1995 Fleer Update Diamond Tribute

Borderless action photos and gold-foil graphics are front features of this chase set honoring perhaps the 10 top names among baseball's veteran players. Backs have another photo and a few sentences describing what makes the player worthy of inclusion in such a set. The Diamond Tribute cards are found on the average of one per five packs.

		MT
Complete Set (10):		7.00
Common Player:		.25
1	Jeff Bagwell	.75
2	Albert Belle	.75
3	Barry Bonds	.60
4	David Cone	.25
5	Dennis Eckersley	.25
6	Ken Griffey Jr.	2.50
7	Rickey Henderson	.50
8	Greg Maddux	2.00
9	Frank Thomas	2.00
10	Matt Williams	.40

1995 Fleer Update Headliners

The most common of the Fleer Update inserts are the Headliners cards found on average of one per three packs. Fronts have an action photo set against a collage of newspaper clippings. The graphics are gold-foil. Backs have another color photo and a "Fleer Times" newspaper background with career summary and/or quotes about the featured player.

		MT
Complete Set (20):		10.00
Common Player:		.25
1	Jeff Bagwell	.75
2	Albert Belle	.75
3	Barry Bonds	.75
4	Jose Canseco	.50
5	Joe Carter	.25
6	Will Clark	.35
7	Roger Clemens	.75
8	Lenny Dykstra	.25
9	Cecil Fielder	.25
10	Juan Gonzalez	1.50
11	Ken Griffey Jr.	3.00
12	Kenny Lofton	1.00
13	Greg Maddux	2.00
14	Fred McGriff	.40
15	Mike Piazza	2.00
16	Kirby Puckett	1.00
17	Tim Salmon	.40
18	Frank Thomas	2.00
19	Mo Vaughn	.60
20	Matt Williams	.40

1995 Fleer Update Rookie Update

Ten of 1995's top rookies are featured in this horizontally formatted insert set. Fronts have an action photo with a large gold-foil "ROOKIE UPDATE" headline at top. Backs have another photo and career summary. Rookie Update chase cards are found on the average of one per four packs.

		MT
Complete Set (10):		9.00
Common Player:		.15
1	Shane Andrews	.25
2	Ray Durham	.75
3	Shawn Green	2.00
4	Charles Johnson	.75
5	Chipper Jones	3.25
6	Esteban Loaiza	.25
7	Hideo Nomo	1.50
8	Jon Nunnally	.40
9	Alex Rodriguez	4.00
10	Julian Tavarez	.15

1995 Fleer Update Soaring Stars

A metallic foil-etched background behind the color player action photo identifies this chase set as the toughest among those in the 1995 Fleer Update issue. The Soaring Star cards are found at the average rate of one per box. Backs are conventionally printed and featured a colorful posterized version of the front background, along with another color photo and a career summary.

		MT
Complete Set (9):		30.00
Common Player:		1.25
1	Moises Alou	1.50
2	Jason Bere	1.25
3	Jeff Conine	1.25
4	Cliff Floyd	1.25
5	Pat Hentgen	1.25
6	Kenny Lofton	7.00
7	Raul Mondesi	4.00
8	Mike Piazza	9.00
9	Tim Salmon	2.00

1995 Fleer Update Smooth Leather

These inserts featuring top fielders were found only in pre-priced (magazine) foil packs, at an average rate of one card per 12 packs. Fronts are highlighted with gold-foil graphics. Backs have a glove in the background and explain the player's defensive abilities.

		MT
Complete Set (10):		20.00
Common Player:		.50
1	Roberto Alomar	1.25
2	Barry Bonds	1.50
3	Ken Griffey Jr.	7.50
4	Marquis Grissom	.50
5	Darren Lewis	.50
6	Kenny Lofton	1.25
7	Don Mattingly	2.50
8	Cal Ripken Jr.	9.00
9	Ivan Rodriguez	1.00
10	Matt Williams	.90

1995 Fleer-Panini Stickers

Following Fleer's purchase of the well-known Italian sticker company, Panini, it was no surprise to see the companies produce a 1995 baseball issue. Titled "Major League Baseball All-Stars," the set consists of 156 player and team logo stickers. A 36-page color album to house the stickers was sold for $1.19. Sold in six-sticker packs for about .50, the individual stickers measure 1-15/16" x 3". Borders are team color-coded and have the player name and team logo at bottom, with the position abbreviation in a diamond at top-right. Backs are printed in black-and-white and include a sticker number, copyright notice and large logos of the licensors and Fleer/Panini. Each sticker can be found with backs that do, or do not, include a promotional message beginning, "Collect all 156 . . ."

		MT
Complete Set (156):		18.00
Common Player:		.10
Album:		1.25
1	Tom Glavine	.12
2	Doug Drabek	.10
3	Rod Beck	.10
4	Pedro J. Martinez	.15
5	Danny Jackson	.10
6	Greg Maddux	.30
7	Bret Saberhagen	.10
8	Ken Hill	.10
9	Marvin Freeman	.10
10	Andy Benes	.10
11	Wilson Alvarez	.10
12	Jimmy Key	.10
13	Mike Mussina	.12
14	Roger Clemens	.25
15	Pat Hentgen	.10
16	Randy Johnson	.20
17	Lee Smith	.12
18	David Cone	.12
19	Jason Bere	.10
20	Dennis Martinez	.12
21	Darren Daulton	.10
22	Darrin Fletcher	.10
23	Tom Pagnozzi	.10
24	Mike Piazza	.30
25	Benito Santiago	.10
26	Sandy Alomar Jr.	.15
27	Chris Hoiles	.10
28	Ivan Rodriguez	.20
29	Mike Stanley	.10
30	Dave Nilsson	.10
31	Jeff Bagwell	.25
32	Mark Grace	.20
33	Gregg Jefferies	.10
34	Andres Galarraga	.12
35	Fred McGriff	.15
36	Will Clark	.15
37	Mo Vaughn	.20
38	Don Mattingly	.40
39	Frank Thomas	.25
40	Cecil Fielder	.15
41	Robby Thompson	.10
42	Delino DeShields	.10
43	Carlos Garcia	.10
44	Bret Boone	.10
45	Craig Biggio	.15
46	Roberto Alomar	.20
47	Chuck Knoblauch	.15
48	Jose Lind	.10
49	Carlos Baerga	.10
50	Lou Whitaker	.10
51	Bobby Bonilla	.12
52	Tim Wallach	.10
53	Todd Zeile	.10
54	Matt Williams	.12
55	Ken Caminiti	.12
56	Robin Ventura	.12
57	Wade Boggs	.20
58	Scott Cooper	.10
59	Travis Fryman	.10
60	Dean Palmer	.10
61	Jay Bell	.10
62	Barry Larkin	.12
63	Ozzie Smith	.20
64	Wil Cordero	.10
65	Royce Clayton	.10
66	Chris Gomez	.10
67	Ozzie Guillen	.10
68	Cal Ripken Jr.	.50
69	Omar Vizquel	.10
70	Gary DiSarcina	.10
71	Dante Bichette	.15
72	Lenny Dykstra	.10
73	Barry Bonds	.25
74	Gary Sheffield	.15
75	Larry Walker	.20
76	Raul Mondesi	.15
77	Dave Justice	.15
78	Moises Alou	.12
79	Tony Gwynn	.30
80	Deion Sanders	.15
81	Kenny Lofton	.20
82	Kirby Puckett	.40
83	Juan Gonzalez	.30
84	Jay Buhner	.10
85	Joe Carter	.10
86	Ken Griffey Jr.	.50
87	Ruben Sierra	.10
88	Tim Salmon	.15
89	Paul O'Neill	.12
90	Albert Belle	.20
91	Danny Tartabull	.10
92	Jose Canseco	.20
93	Harold Baines	.10
94	Kirk Gibson	.10
95	Chili Davis	.10
96	Eddie Murray	.20
97	Bob Hamelin	.10
98	Paul Molitor	.20
99	Raul Mondesi	.15
100	Ryan Klesko	.15
101	Cliff Floyd	.10
102	William VanLandingham	.10
103	Joey Hamilton	.10
104	John Hudek	.10
105	Manny Ramirez	.20
106	Bob Hamelin	.10
107	Rusty Greer	.10
108	Chris Gomez	.10
	Award Winners	
109	Greg Maddux	.15
110	Jeff Bagwell	.12
111	Raul Mondesi	.15
112	David Cone	.10
113	Frank Thomas	.35
114	Bob Hamelin	.10
	League Leaders	
115	Tony Gwynn	.15
116	Matt Williams	.10
117	Jeff Bagwell	.15
118	Craig Biggio	.10
119	Andy Benes	.10
120	Greg Maddux	.20
121	John Franco	.10
122	Paul O'Neill	.10
123	Ken Griffey Jr.	.35
124	Kirby Puckett	.20
125	Kenny Lofton	.25
126	Randy Johnson	.10
127	Jimmy Key	.10
128	Lee Smith	.10
129	San Francisco Giants logo	.10
130	Montreal Expos logo	.10
131	Cincinnati Reds logo	.10
132	Los Angeles Dodgers logo	.10
133	New York Mets logo	.10
134	San Diego Padres logo	.10
135	Colorado Rockies logo	.10
136	Pittsburgh Pirates logo	.10
137	Florida Marlins logo	.10
138	Philadelphia Phillies logo	.10
139	Atlanta Braves logo	.10
140	Houston Astros logo	.10
141	St. Louis Cardinals logo	.10
142	Chicago Cubs logo	.10
143	Cleveland Indians logo	.10
144	New York Yankees logo	.10
145	Kansas City Royals logo	.10
146	Chicago White Sox logo	.10
147	Baltimore Orioles logo	.10
148	Seattle Mariners logo	.10
149	Boston Red Sox logo	.10
150	California Angels logo	.10
151	Toronto Blue Jays logo	.10
152	Detroit Tigers logo	.10
153	Texas Rangers logo	.10
154	Oakland A's logo	.10
155	Milwaukee Brewers logo	.10
156	Minnesota Twins logo	.10

1995 Fleer-Revco Cleveland Indians

In the midst of their pennant winning season in 1995, the Cleveland Indians were the subject of a special "Update" set produced by Fleer and sold exclusively by Revco stores and the team itself. Seventeen of the 20 cards in the set are virtually identical to the regular-issue 1995 Fleer cards, except for a change in card number on the back, designating each card as "X of 20", and the use of silver foil on front, as opposed to the gold foil found on regular cards. The Dave Winfield card in the Update issue pictures him in an Indians uniform, instead of the Twins uniform in which he appears in the regular set. Logo and checklist cards were added to the team set. Cards were sold in 10-card foil packs.

		MT
Complete Set (20):		7.00
Common Player:		.25
1	Sandy Alomar Jr.	.40
2	Carlos Baerga	.30
3	Albert Belle	1.00
4	Mark Clark	.30
5	Alvaro Espinoza	.25
6	Wayne Kirby	.25
7	Kenny Lofton	.65
8	Dennis Martinez	.35
9	Jose Mesa	.25
10	Eddie Murray	1.00
11	Charles Nagy	.35
12	Tony Pena	.25
13	Eric Plunk	.25
14	Manny Ramirez	.75
15	Paul Sorrento	.25
16	Jim Thome	.40
17	Omar Vizquel	.35
18	Dave Winfield	1.00
19	Indians/Fleer logo card	.05
20	Checklist/Indians logo	.05

1996 Fleer

In a radical departure from the UV-coated standard for even base-brand baseball cards, Fleer's 1996 issue is printed on a matte surface. Fronts feature borderless game-action photos with minimal (player ID, Fleer logo) graphic enhancement in gold foil. Backs have a white background, a portrait photo, full pro stats and a few career highlights. The single-series set was sold in basic 11-card packs with one of nearly a dozen insert-set cards in each $1.49 pack. The set is arranged alphabetically by player within team and league. A glossy-surface Tiffany Collection parallel was included in each pack.

		MT
Complete Set (600):		60.00
Common Player:		.05
Wax Box:		45.00
1	Manny Alexander	.05
2	Brady Anderson	.10
3	Harold Baines	.08
4	Armando Benitez	.05
5	Bobby Bonilla	.10
6	Kevin Brown	.05
7	Scott Erickson	.05
8	Curtis Goodwin	.05
9	Jeffrey Hammonds	.05
10	Jimmy Haynes	.05
11	Chris Hoiles	.05
12	Doug Jones	.05
13	Rick Krivda	.05
14	Jeff Manto	.05
15	Ben McDonald	.05
16	Jamie Moyer	.05
17	Mike Mussina	.30
18	Jesse Orosco	.05
19	Rafael Palmeiro	.20
20	Cal Ripken Jr.	2.50
20 (p)	Cal Ripken Jr. (overprinted "PROMOTIONAL SAMPLE")	8.00
21	Rick Aguilera	.05
22	Luis Alicea	.05
23	Stan Belinda	.05
24	Jose Canseco	.30
25	Roger Clemens	.75
26	Vaughn Eshelman	.05
27	Mike Greenwell	.05
28	Erik Hanson	.05
29	Dwayne Hosey	.05
30	Mike Macfarlane	.05
31	Tim Naehring	.05
32	Troy O'Leary	.05
33	Aaron Sele	.05
34	Zane Smith	.05
35	Jeff Suppan	.05
36	Lee Tinsley	.05
37	John Valentin	.10
38	Mo Vaughn	.75
39	Tim Wakefield	.05
40	Jim Abbott	.10
41	Brian Anderson	.05
42	Garret Anderson	.10
43	Chili Davis	.08
44	Gary DiSarcina	.05
45	Damion Easley	.05
46	Jim Edmonds	.10
47	Chuck Finley	.05
48	Todd Greene	.05
49	Mike Harkey	.05
50	Mike James	.05
51	Mark Langston	.05
52	Greg Myers	.05
53	Orlando Palmeiro	.05
54	Bob Patterson	.05
55	Troy Percival	.05
56	Tony Phillips	.05
57	Tim Salmon	.20
58	Lee Smith	.08
59	J.T. Snow	.10
60	Randy Velarde	.05
61	Wilson Alvarez	.05
62	*Luis Andujar*	.05
63	Jason Bere	.05
64	Ray Durham	.05
65	Alex Fernandez	.05
66	Ozzie Guillen	.05
67	Roberto Hernandez	.05
68	Lance Johnson	.05
69	Matt Karchner	.05
70	Ron Karkovice	.05
71	Norberto Martin	.05
72	Dave Martinez	.05
73	Kirk McCaskill	.05
74	Lyle Mouton	.05
75	Tim Raines	.10
76	Mike Sirotka	.05
77	Frank Thomas	1.00
78	Larry Thomas	.05
79	Robin Ventura	.15
80	Sandy Alomar Jr.	.10
81	Paul Assenmacher	.05
82	Carlos Baerga	.08
83	Albert Belle	.75
84	Mark Clark	.05
85	Alan Embree	.05
86	Alvaro Espinoza	.05
87	Orel Hershiser	.08
88	Ken Hill	.05
89	Kenny Lofton	.75
90	Dennis Martinez	.08
91	Jose Mesa	.05
92	Eddie Murray	.35
93	Charles Nagy	.08
94	Chad Ogea	.05
95	Tony Pena	.05
96	Herb Perry	.05
97	Eric Plunk	.05
98	Jim Poole	.05
99	Manny Ramirez	1.00
100	Paul Sorrento	.05
101	Julian Travarez	.05
102	Jim Thome	.40
103	Omar Vizquel	8.00
104	Dave Winfield	.20
105	Danny Bautista	.05
106	Joe Boever	.05
107	Chad Curtis	.05
108	John Doherty	.05
109	Cecil Fielder	.08
110	John Flaherty	.05
111	Travis Fryman	.08
112	Chris Gomez	.05
113	Bob Higginson	.10
114	Mark Lewis	.05
115	Jose Lima	.08
116	Felipe Lira	.05
117	Brian Maxcy	.05
118	C.J. Nitkowski	.05
119	Phil Plantier	.05
120	Clint Sodowsky	.05
121	Alan Trammell	.10
122	Lou Whitaker	.05
123	Kevin Appier	.05
124	Johnny Damon	.20
125	Gary Gaettl	.05
126	Tom Goodwin	.05
127	Tom Gordon	.05
128	Mark Gubicza	.05
129	Bob Hamelin	.05
130	David Howard	.05
131	Jason Jacome	.05
132	Wally Joyner	.08
133	Keith Lockhart	.05
134	Brent Mayne	.05
135	Jeff Montgomery	.05
136	Jon Nunnally	.05
137	Juan Samuel	.05
138	*Mike Sweeney*	.10
139	Michael Tucker	.08
140	Joe Vitiello	.05
141	Ricky Bones	.05
142	Chuck Carr	.05
143	Jeff Cirillo	.05
144	Mike Fetters	.05
145	Darryl Hamilton	.05
146	David Hulse	.05
147	John Jaha	.05
148	Scott Karl	.05
149	Mark Kiefer	.05
150	Pat Listach	.05
151	Mark Loretta	.05
152	Mike Matheny	.05
153	Matt Mieske	.05
154	Dave Nilsson	.05
155	Joe Oliver	.05
156	Al Reyes	.05
157	Kevin Seitzer	.05
158	Steve Sparks	.05
159	B.J. Surhoff	.08
160	Jose Valentin	.05
161	Greg Vaughn	.10
162	Fernando Vina	.05
163	Rich Becker	.05
164	Ron Coomer	.05
165	Marty Cordova	.10
166	Chuck Knoblauch	.20
167	*Matt Lawton*	.10
168	Pat Meares	.05
169	Paul Molitor	.40
170	Pedro Munoz	.05
171	Jose Parra	.05
172	Kirby Puckett	1.00
173	Brad Radke	.05
174	Jeff Reboulet	.05
175	Rich Robertson	.05
176	Frank Rodriguez	.05
177	Scott Stahoviak	.05
178	Dave Stevens	.05
179	Matt Walbeck	.05
180	Wade Boggs	.30
181	David Cone	.08
182	Tony Fernandez	.05
183	Joe Girardi	.05
184	Derek Jeter	1.50
185	Scott Kamieniecki	.05
186	Pat Kelly	.05
187	Jim Leyritz	.05
188	Tino Martinez	.15
189	Don Mattingly	1.00
190	Jack McDowell	.05
191	Jeff Nelson	.05
192	Paul O'Neill	.10
193	Melido Perez	.05
194	Andy Pettitte	1.00
195	Mariano Rivera	.15
196	Ruben Sierra	.05
197	Mike Stanley	.05
198	Darryl Strawberry	.10
199	John Wetteland	.05
200	Bob Wickman	.05
201	Bernie Williams	.40
202	Mark Acre	.05
203	Geronimo Berroa	.05
204	Mike Bordick	.05
205	Scott Brosius	.05
206	Dennis Eckersley	.08
207	Brent Gates	.05
208	Jason Giambi	.10
209	Rickey Henderson	.30
210	Jose Herrera	.05
211	Stan Javier	.05
212	Doug Johns	.05
213	Mark McGwire	4.00
214	Steve Ontiveros	.05
215	Craig Paquette	.05
216	Ariel Prieto	.05
217	Carlos Reyes	.05
218	Terry Steinbach	.05
219	Todd Stottlemyre	.05
220	Danny Tartabull	.05
221	Todd Van Poppel	.05
222	John Wasdin	.05
223	George Williams	.05
224	Steve Wojciechowski	.05
225	Rich Amaral	.05
226	Bobby Ayala	.05
227	Tim Belcher	.05
228	Andy Benes	.08
229	Chris Bosio	.05
230	Darren Bragg	.05
231	Jay Buhner	.10
232	Norm Charlton	.05
233	Vince Coleman	.05
234	Joey Cora	.05
235	Russ Davis	.05
236	Alex Diaz	.05
237	Felix Fermin	.05
238	Ken Griffey Jr.	3.00
239	Sterling Hitchcock	.05
240	Randy Johnson	.25
241	Edgar Martinez	.08
242	Bill Risley	.05
243	Alex Rodriguez	2.50
244	Luis Sojo	.05
245	Dan Wilson	.05
246	Bob Wolcott	.05
247	Will Clark	.30
248	Jeff Frye	.05
249	Benji Gil	.05
250	Juan Gonzalez	1.00
251	Rusty Greer	.05
252	Kevin Gross	.05
253	Roger McDowell	.05
254	Mark McLemore	.05
255	Otis Nixon	.05
256	Luis Ortiz	.05
257	Mike Pagliarulo	.05
258	Dean Palmer	.05
259	Roger Pavlik	.05
260	Ivan Rodriguez	.65
261	Kenny Rogers	.05
262	Jeff Russell	.05
263	Mickey Tettleton	.05

264	Bob Tewksbury	.05
265	Dave Valle	.05
266	Matt Whiteside	.05
267	Roberto Alomar	.75
268	Joe Carter	.08
269	Tony Castillo	.05
270	Domingo Cedeno	.05
271	Timothy Crabtree	.05
272	Carlos Delgado	.40
273	Alex Gonzalez	.05
274	Shawn Green	.15
275	Juan Guzman	.05
276	Pat Hentgen	.05
277	Al Leiter	.08
278	*Sandy Martinez*	.05
279	Paul Menhart	.05
280	John Olerud	.12
281	Paul Quantrill	.05
282	Ken Robinson	.05
283	Ed Sprague	.05
284	Mike Timlin	.05
285	Steve Avery	.05
286	Rafael Belliard	.05
287	Jeff Blauser	.05
288	Pedro Borbon	.05
289	Brad Clontz	.05
290	Mike Devereaux	.05
291	Tom Glavine	.15
292	Marquis Grissom	.08
293	Chipper Jones	1.75
294	David Justice	.20
295	Mike Kelly	.05
296	Ryan Klesko	.25
297	Mark Lemke	.05
298	Javier Lopez	.15
299	Greg Maddux	1.50
300	Fred McGriff	.35
301	Greg McMichael	.05
302	Kent Mercker	.05
303	Mike Mordecai	.05
304	Charlie O'Brien	.05
305	Eduardo Perez	.05
306	Luis Polonia	.05
307	Jason Schmidt	.05
308	John Smoltz	.20
309	Terrell Wade	.05
310	Mark Wohlers	.05
311	Scott Bullett	.05
312	Jim Bullinger	.05
313	Larry Casian	.05
314	Frank Castillo	.05
315	Shawon Dunston	.05
316	Kevin Foster	.05
317	Matt Franco	.05
318	Luis Gonzalez	.08
319	Mark Grace	.25
320	Jose Hernandez	.05
321	Mike Hubbard	.05
322	Brian McRae	.05
323	Randy Myers	.05
324	Jaime Navarro	.05
325	Mark Parent	.05
326	Mike Perez	.05
327	Rey Sanchez	.05
328	Ryne Sandberg	.75
329	Scott Servais	.05
330	Sammy Sosa	1.50
331	Ozzie Timmons	.05
332	Steve Trachsel	.05
333	Todd Zeile	.08
334	Bret Boone	.05
335	Jeff Branson	.05
336	Jeff Brantley	.05
337	Dave Burba	.05
338	Hector Carrasco	.05
339	Mariano Duncan	.05
340	Ron Gant	.10
341	Lenny Harris	.05
342	Xavier Hernandez	.05
343	Thomas Howard	.05
344	Mike Jackson	.05
345	Barry Larkin	.10
346	Darren Lewis	.05
347	Hal Morris	.05
348	Eric Owens	.05
349	Mark Portugal	.05
350	Jose Rijo	.05
351	Reggie Sanders	.08
352	Benito Santiago	.05
353	Pete Schourek	.05
354	John Smiley	.05
355	Eddie Taubensee	.05
356	Jerome Walton	.05
357	David Wells	.08
358	Roger Bailey	.05
359	Jason Bates	.05
360	Dante Bichette	.15
361	Ellis Burks	.08
362	Vinny Castilla	.12
363	Andres Galarraga	.15
364	Darren Holmes	.05
365	Mike Kingery	.05
366	Curt Leskanic	.05
367	Quinton McCracken	.05
368	Mike Munoz	.05
369	David Nied	.05
370	Steve Reed	.05
371	Bryan Rekar	.05
372	Kevin Ritz	.05
373	Bruce Ruffin	.05
374	Bret Saberhagen	.08
375	Bill Swift	.05
376	John Vander Wal	.05
377	Larry Walker	.30
378	Walt Weiss	.05
379	Eric Young	.05
380	Kurt Abbott	.05
381	Alex Arias	.05

382	Jerry Browne	.05
383	John Burkett	.05
384	Greg Colbrunn	.05
385	Jeff Conine	.10
386	Andre Dawson	.20
387	Chris Hammond	.05
388	Charles Johnson	.10
389	Terry Mathews	.05
390	Robb Nen	.05
391	Joe Orsulak	.05
392	Terry Pendleton	.05
393	Pat Rapp	.05
394	Gary Sheffield	.40
395	Jesus Tavarez	.05
396	Marc Valdes	.05
397	Quilvio Veras	.05
398	Randy Veres	.05
399	Devon White	.05
400	Jeff Bagwell	1.00
401	Derek Bell	.10
402	Craig Biggio	.10
403	John Cangelosi	.05
404	Jim Dougherty	.05
405	Doug Drabek	.05
406	Tony Eusebio	.05
407	Ricky Gutierrez	.05
408	Mike Hampton	.05
409	Dean Hartgraves	.05
410	John Hudek	.05
411	Brian Hunter	.08
412	Todd Jones	.05
413	Darryl Kile	.05
414	Dave Magadan	.05
415	Derrick May	.05
416	Orlando Miller	.05
417	James Mouton	.05
418	Shane Reynolds	.05
419	Greg Swindell	.05
420	Jeff Tabaka	.05
421	Dave Veres	.05
422	Billy Wagner	.10
423	*Donne Wall*	.05
424	Rick Wilkins	.05
425	Billy Ashley	.05
426	Mike Blowers	.05
427	Brett Butler	.08
428	Tom Candiotti	.05
429	Juan Castro	.05
430	John Cummings	.05
431	Delino DeShields	.05
432	Joey Eischen	.05
433	Chad Fonville	.10
434	Greg Gagne	.05
435	Dave Hansen	.05
436	Carlos Hernandez	.05
437	Todd Hollandsworth	.08
438	Eric Karros	.10
439	Roberto Kelly	.05
440	Ramon Martinez	.08
441	Raul Mondesi	.30
442	Hideo Nomo	.45
443	Antonio Osuna	.05
444	Chan Ho Park	.08
445	Mike Piazza	1.75
446	Felix Rodriguez	.05
447	Kevin Tapani	.05
448	Ismael Valdes	.05
449	Todd Worrell	.05
450	Moises Alou	.10
451	Shane Andrews	.05
452	Yamil Benitez	.05
453	Sean Berry	.05
454	Wil Cordero	.05
455	Jeff Fassero	.05
456	Darrin Fletcher	.05
457	Cliff Floyd	.05
458	Mark Grudzielanek	.08
459	Gil Heredia	.05
460	Tim Laker	.05
461	Mike Lansing	.05
462	Pedro Martinez	.25
463	Carlos Perez	.05
464	Curtis Pride	.05
465	Mel Rojas	.05
466	Kirk Rueter	.05
467	*F.P. Santangelo*	.10
468	Tim Scott	.05
469	David Segui	.05
470	Tony Tarasco	.05
471	Rondell White	.10
472	Edgardo Alfonzo	.12
473	Tim Bogar	.05
474	Rico Brogna	.05
475	Damon Buford	.05
476	Paul Byrd	.05
477	Carl Everett	.05
478	John Franco	.05
479	Todd Hundley	.15
480	Butch Huskey	.10
481	Jason Isringhausen	.08
482	Bobby Jones	.05
483	Chris Jones	.05
484	Jeff Kent	.05
485	Dave Mlicki	.05
486	Robert Person	.05
487	Bill Pulsipher	.05
488	Kelly Stinnett	.05
489	Ryan Thompson	.05
490	Jose Vizcaino	.05
491	Howard Battle	.05
492	Toby Borland	.05
493	Ricky Bottalico	.05
494	Darren Daulton	.05
495	Lenny Dykstra	.05
496	Jim Eisenreich	.05
497	Sid Fernandez	.05
498	Tyler Green	.05
499	Charlie Hayes	.05

500	Gregg Jefferies	.10
501	Kevin Jordan	.05
502	Tony Longmire	.05
503	Tom Marsh	.05
504	Michael Mimbs	.05
505	Mickey Morandini	.05
506	Gene Schall	.05
507	Curt Schilling	.08
508	Heathcliff Slocumb	.05
509	Kevin Stocker	.05
510	Andy Van Slyke	.05
511	Lenny Webster	.05
512	Mark Whiten	.05
513	Mike Williams	.05
514	Jay Bell	.05
515	Jacob Brumfield	.05
516	Jason Christiansen	.05
517	Dave Clark	.05
518	Midre Cummings	.05
519	Angelo Encarnacion	.05
520	John Ericks	.05
521	Carlos Garcia	.05
522	Mark Johnson	.08
523	Jeff King	.05
524	Nelson Liriano	.05
525	Esteban Loaiza	.08
526	Al Martin	.05
527	Orlando Merced	.05
528	Dan Miceli	.05
529	Ramon Morel	.05
530	Denny Neagle	.05
531	Steve Parris	.05
532	Dan Plesac	.05
533	Don Slaught	.05
534	Paul Wagner	.05
535	John Wehner	.05
536	Kevin Young	.05
537	Allen Battle	.05
538	David Bell	.05
539	Alan Benes	.10
540	Scott Cooper	.05
541	Tripp Cromer	.05
542	Tony Fossas	.05
543	Bernard Gilkey	.10
544	Tom Henke	.05
545	Brian Jordan	.15
546	Ray Lankford	.10
547	John Mabry	.05
548	T.J. Mathews	.05
549	Mike Morgan	.05
550	Jose Oliva	.05
551	Jose Oquendo	.05
552	Donovan Osborne	.05
553	Tom Pagnozzi	.05
554	Mark Petkovsek	.05
555	Danny Sheaffer	.05
556	Ozzie Smith	.40
557	Mark Sweeney	.05
558	Allen Watson	.05
559	Andy Ashby	.08
560	Brad Ausmus	.05
561	Willie Blair	.05
562	Ken Caminiti	.15
563	Andujar Cedeno	.05
564	Glenn Dishman	.05
565	Steve Finley	.05
566	Bryce Florie	.05
567	Tony Gwynn	.75
568	Joey Hamilton	.10
569	Dustin Hermanson	.10
570	Trevor Hoffman	.08
571	Brian Johnson	.05
572	Marc Kroon	.05
573	Scott Livingstone	.05
574	Marc Newfield	.05
575	Melvin Nieves	.05
576	Jody Reed	.05
577	Bip Roberts	.05
578	Scott Sanders	.05
579	Fernando Valenzuela	.08
580	Eddie Williams	.05
581	Rod Beck	.05
582	*Marvin Benard*	.10
583	Barry Bonds	.75
584	Jamie Brewington	.05
585	Mark Carreon	.05
586	Royce Clayton	.05
587	Shawn Estes	.05
588	Glenallen Hill	.05
589	Mark Leiter	.05
590	Kirt Manwaring	.05
591	David McCarty	.05
592	Terry Mulholland	.05
593	John Patterson	.05
594	J.R. Phillips	.05
595	Deion Sanders	.15
596	Steve Scarsone	.05
597	Robby Thompson	.05
598	Sergio Valdez	.05
599	William VanLandingham	.05
600	Matt Williams	.25

1996 Fleer Tiffany

While Fleer's basic card set for 1996 feature matte-surface cards, a glossy version of each regular card was also issued as a parallel insert set. Other than the UV coating on front and back and the use of silver- rather than gold-foil typography on front, the cards are identical to the regular '96 Fleer player cards. One glossy version card is found in each pack.

	MT
Complete Set (600):	150.00
Common Player:	.15
Stars: 3X	

(See 1996 Fleer for checklist and base card values.)

1996 Fleer Checklists

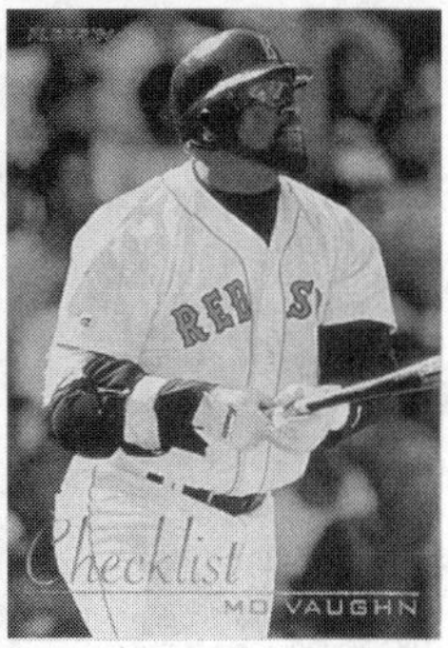

Checklist cards are treated as an insert set in 1996 Fleer, appearing on average once every six packs. Like all other Fleer hobby inserts in the baseball set, the checklists are UV-coated front and back, in contrast to the matte-finish regular issue cards. Checklists have borderless game-action photos on front, with gold-foil typography. Backs have a large Fleer logo and checklist data on a white background.

		MT
Complete Set (10):		3.00
Common Player:		.25
1	Barry Bonds	.40
2	Ken Griffey Jr.	1.50
3	Chipper Jones	.75
4	Greg Maddux	.65
5	Mike Piazza	.75
6	Manny Ramirez	.50
7	Cal Ripken Jr.	1.00
8	Frank Thomas	.50
9	Mo Vaughn	.35
10	Matt Williams	.25

1996 Fleer Golden Memories

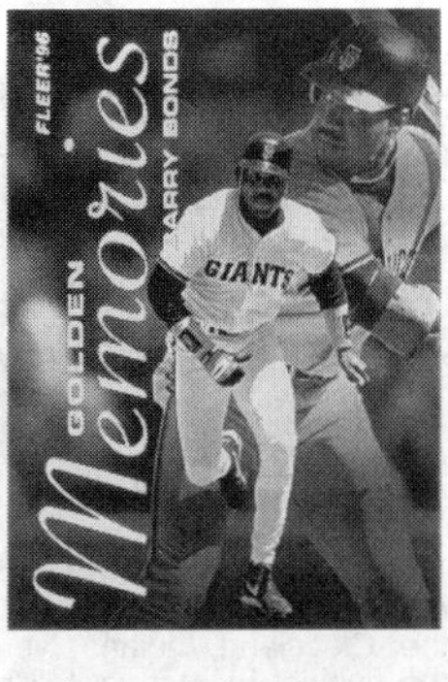

Some of the 1995 season's greatest moments are captured in this insert set, a one per 10 pack pick. Fronts have two photos of the player, one in full color in the foreground and one in monochrome as a backdrop. Typography is in prismatic foil vertically down one side. Backs have another color player photo, along with details of the milestone. Two of the cards feature multiple players.

		MT
Complete Set (10):		6.00
Common Player:		.15
1	Albert Belle	.40
2	Barry Bonds, Sammy Sosa	1.00
3	Greg Maddux	1.00
4	Edgar Martinez	.15
5	Ramon Martinez	.15
6	Mark McGwire	2.50
7	Eddie Murray	.25
8	Cal Ripken Jr.	1.50
9	Frank Thomas	.75
10	Alan Trammell, Lou Whitaker	.15

1996 Fleer Lumber Company

Once again for 1996, a Fleer "Lumber Company" chase set honors the game's top sluggers. The '96 version has a horizontal format with a rather small player action photo on a background resembling the trademark area of a bat. The "trademark" is actually the player and team name along with the "Lumber Company" ID, printed in textured glossy black ink. Backs repeat the trademark motif and also include a close-up player photo and a few words about his power-hitting numbers. Lumber Company cards are a one per nine pack pick, on average, found only in retail packs.

		MT
Complete Set (12):		18.00
Common Player:		.50
1	Albert Belle	1.00
2	Dante Bichette	.75
3	Barry Bonds	1.25
4	Ken Griffey Jr.	5.00
5	Mark McGwire	6.00
6	Mike Piazza	3.00
7	Manny Ramirez	1.50
8	Tim Salmon	.75
9	Sammy Sosa	2.50
10	Frank Thomas	2.00
11	Mo Vaughn	1.00
12	Matt Williams	.75

1996 Fleer Post-Season Glory

Highlights of the 1995 postseason are featured in this small chase card set. Against a stadium background are multiple photos of the featured player, arranged horizontally. The vertical backs have another player photo down one side, and a description of his play-off performance on the other. Stated odds of picking one of these cards are one per five packs.

		MT
Complete Set (5):		2.50
Common Player:		.15
1	Tom Glavine	.20
2	Ken Griffey Jr.	2.00
3	Orel Hershiser	.15
4	Randy Johnson	.30
5	Jim Thome	.20

1996 Fleer Prospects

Minor leaguers who are expected to make it big in the

big time are featured in this insert issue. Fronts feature large portrait photos against pastel backgrounds with player and set ID in prismatic foil. Backs have an action photo and repeat the front background color in a box which details the player's potential and career to date. Average odds of finding a Prospects card are one per six packs.

		MT
Complete Set (10):		3.00
Common Player:		.25
1	Yamil Benitez	.25
2	Roger Cedeno	.50
3	Tony Clark	1.00
4	Micah Franklin	.25
5	Karim Garcia	.75
6	Todd Greene	.25
7	Alex Ochoa	.25
8	Ruben Rivera	.75
9	Chris Snopek	.25
10	Shannon Stewart	.25

1996 Fleer Road Warriors

A black-and-white country highway photo is the background for the color player action photo on this insert set. Front typography is in silver foil. The players featured are those whose performance on the road is considered outstanding. Backs have a white background, portrait photo and stats bearing out the away-game superiority. These inserts are found at an average pace of one per 13 packs.

		MT
Complete Set (10):		9.00
Common Player:		.35
1	Derek Bell	.40
2	Tony Gwynn	1.25
3	Greg Maddux	1.50
4	Mark McGwire	4.00
5	Mike Piazza	2.00
6	Manny Ramirez	1.00
7	Tim Salmon	.50
8	Frank Thomas	1.25
9	Mo Vaughn	.90
10	Matt Williams	.40

1996 Fleer Rookie Sensations

Top rookies of the 1995 season are featured on this chase card set. Horizontally formatted, the cards have an action photo on one side and a large prismatic-foil end strip which displays the player name, team logo and card company identifiers. Backs have a portrait photo on as white background with a few sentences about the player's rookie season. Stated odds of finding one of these inserts is one per 11 packs, on average.

		MT
Complete Set (15):		12.00
Common Player:		.50
1	Garret Anderson	.75
2	Marty Cordova	.75
3	Johnny Damon	.75
4	Ray Durham	.50
5	Carl Everett	.75
6	Shawn Green	1.50
7	Brian Hunter	.50
8	Jason Isringhausen	.50
9	Charles Johnson	.75
10	Chipper Jones	6.00
11	John Mabry	.50
12	Hideo Nomo	1.50
13	Troy Percival	.50
14	Andy Pettitte	3.00
15	Quilvio Veras	.50

1996 Fleer Smoke 'N Heat

Once more using the "Smoke 'N Heat" identifier for a chase set of the game's hardest throwers, Fleer presents these select pitchers in action photos against a black-and-flame background. Front typography is in gold foil. Backs have a large portrait photo, repeat the flame motif as background and have a description of the pitcher's prowess in a black box. The cards are found, on average, once per nine packs.

		MT
Complete Set (10):		5.00
Common Player:		.25
1	Kevin Appier	.25
2	Roger Clemens	2.00
3	David Cone	.25
4	Chuck Finley	.25
5	Randy Johnson	.50
6	Greg Maddux	2.50
7	Pedro Martinez	.50
8	Hideo Nomo	.50
9	John Smoltz	.50
10	Todd Stottlemyre	.25

1996 Fleer Team Leaders

One player from each club has been selected for inclusion in the "Team Leaders" chase set. Fronts have action player photos on a background of metallic foil littered with multiple representations of the team logo. Gold-foil lettering identifies the player, team and chase set. Backs have a white background, portrait photo and description of the player's leadership role. Stated rate of insertion for this set is one card per nine packs, on average, found only in hobby packs.

		MT
Complete Set (28):		50.00
Common Player:		.60
1	Cal Ripken Jr.	10.00
2	Mo Vaughn	2.00
3	Jim Edmonds	.75
4	Frank Thomas	4.00
5	Kenny Lofton	2.00
6	Travis Fryman	.60
7	Gary Gaetti	.60
8	B.J. Surhoff	.60
9	Kirby Puckett	5.00
10	Don Mattingly	5.00
11	Mark McGwire	15.00
12	Ken Griffey Jr.	15.00
13	Juan Gonzalez	6.00
14	Joe Carter	.60
15	Greg Maddux	6.00
16	Sammy Sosa	6.00
17	Barry Larkin	1.00
18	Dante Bichette	1.50
19	Jeff Conine	.75
20	Jeff Bagwell	4.00
21	Mike Piazza	7.50
22	Rondell White	.75
23	Rico Brogna	.60
24	Darren Daulton	.60
25	Jeff King	.60
26	Ray Lankford	.60
27	Tony Gwynn	5.00
28	Barry Bonds	2.50

1996 Fleer Tomorrow's Legends

In this insert set the projected stars of tomorrow are featured in action poses on a busy multi-colored, quartered background of baseball symbols and the globe. Typography is in silver foil. Backs have a portrait photo and large team logo along with an early-career summary. Odds of finding a "Tomorrow's Legends" card are posted at one per 13 packs, on average.

		MT
Complete Set (10):		10.00
Common Player:		.40
1	Garret Anderson	.40
2	Jim Edmonds	.50
3	Brian Hunter	.40
4	Jason Isringhausen	.40
5	Charles Johnson	.40
6	Chipper Jones	5.00
7	Ryan Klesko	.75
8	Hideo Nomo	1.00
9	Manny Ramirez	2.50
10	Rondell White	.40

1996 Fleer Zone

The toughest pull (one in 90 packs, average) among the '96 Fleer chase cards is this set evoking the "zone" that the game's great players seek in which their performance is at its peak. The cards have action photos with a background of prismatic foil. Backs are conventionally printed but simulate the foil background and include a player portrait photo plus quotes about the player.

		MT
Complete Set (12):		75.00
Common Player:		3.00
1	Albert Belle	5.00
2	Barry Bonds	5.00
3	Ken Griffey Jr.	20.00
4	Tony Gwynn	10.00
5	Randy Johnson	5.00
6	Kenny Lofton	5.00
7	Greg Maddux	12.50
8	Edgar Martinez	3.00
9	Mike Piazza	15.00
10	Frank Thomas	7.50
11	Mo Vaughn	4.00
12	Matt Williams	4.00

1996 Fleer Update

Fleer Update Baseball has 250 cards, including more than 55 rookies, plus traded players and free agents in their new uniforms, 35 Encore subset cards and five checklists. Each card in the regular-issue set also has a parallel "Tiffany Collection" version, which has UV coating and holographic foil stamping in contrast to the matte finish and gold foil of the regular cards. Insert cards include Diamond Tribute, New Horizons, Smooth Leather and Soaring Stars. Each pack also contains a Fleer "Thanks a Million" scratch-off game card, redeemable for prizes. Cards are numbered with a "U" prefix.

		MT
Complete Set (250):		20.00
Common Player:		.05
Complete Glossy Set (250):		100.00
Glossy Stars: 3X		
1	Roberto Alomar	.75
2	Mike Devereaux	.05
3	*Scott McClain*	.05
4	Roger McDowell	.05
5	Kent Mercker	.05
6	Jimmy Myers	.05
7	Randy Myers	.05
8	B.J. Surhoff	.08
9	Tony Tarasco	.05
10	David Wells	.08
11	Wil Cordero	.05
12	Tom Gordon	.05
13	Reggie Jefferson	.05
14	Jose Malave	.05
15	Kevin Mitchell	.05
16	Jamie Moyer	.05
17	Heathcliff Slocumb	.05
18	Mike Stanley	.05
19	George Arias	.05
20	Jorge Fabregas	.05
21	Don Slaught	.05
22	Randy Velarde	.05
23	Harold Baines	.05
24	*Mike Cameron*	1.00
25	Darren Lewis	.05
26	Tony Phillips	.05
27	Bill Simas	.05
28	Chris Snopek	.05
29	Kevin Tapani	.05
30	Danny Tartabull	.05
31	Julio Franco	.05
32	Jack McDowell	.08
33	Kimera Bartee	.05
34	Mark Lewis	.05
35	Melvin Nieves	.05
36	Mark Parent	.05
37	Eddie Williams	.05
38	Tim Belcher	.05
39	Sal Fasano	.05
40	Chris Haney	.05
41	Mike Macfarlane	.05
42	Jose Offerman	.05
43	Joe Randa	.05
44	Bip Roberts	.05
45	Chuck Carr	.05
46	Bobby Hughes	.05
47	Graeme Lloyd	.05
48	Ben McDonald	.05
49	Kevin Wickander	.05
50	Rick Aguilera	.05
51	Mike Durant	.05
52	Chip Hale	.05
53	LaTroy Hawkins	.05
54	Dave Hollins	.05
55	Roberto Kelly	.05
56	Paul Molitor	.25
57	*Dan Naulty*	.10
58	Mariano Duncan	.05
59	*Andy Fox*	.05
60	Joe Girardi	.05
61	Dwight Gooden	.10
62	Jimmy Key	.05
63	*Matt Luke*	.08
64	Tino Martinez	.08
65	Jeff Nelson	.05
66	Tim Raines	.08
67	Ruben Rivera	.25
68	Kenny Rogers	.05
69	Gerald Williams	.05
70	*Tony Batista*	1.50
71	Allen Battle	.05
72	Jim Corsi	.05
73	Steve Cox	.05
74	Pedro Munoz	.05
75	Phil Plantier	.05
76	Scott Spiezio	.05
77	Ernie Young	.05
78	Russ Davis	.05
79	Sterling Hitchcock	.05
80	Edwin Hurtado	.05
81	*Raul Ibanez*	.05
82	Mike Jackson	.05
83	Ricky Jordan	.05
84	Paul Sorrento	.05
85	Doug Strange	.05
86	Mark Brandenburg	.05
87	Damon Buford	.05
88	Kevin Elster	.05
89	Darryl Hamilton	.05
90	Ken Hill	.05
91	Ed Vosberg	.05
92	Craig Worthington	.05
93	Tilson Brito	.05
94	Giovanni Carrara	.05
95	Felipe Crespo	.05
96	Erik Hanson	.05
97	*Marty Janzen*	.05
98	Otis Nixon	.05
99	Charlie O'Brien	.05
100	Robert Perez	.05
101	Paul Quantrill	.05
102	Bill Risley	.05
103	Juan Samuel	.05
104	Jermaine Dye	.25
105	Wonderful Monds	.05
106	Dwight Smith	.05
107	Jerome Walton	.05
108	Terry Adams	.05
109	Leo Gomez	.05
110	*Robin Jennings*	.05
111	Doug Jones	.05
112	Brooks Kieschnick	.08
113	Dave Magadan	.05
114	*Jason Maxwell*	.05
115	Rodney Myers	.05
116	Eric Anthony	.05

117 Vince Coleman .05
118 Eric Davis .08
119 Steve Gibralter .05
120 Curtis Goodwin .05
121 Willie Greene .05
122 Mike Kelly .05
123 Marcus Moore .05
124 Chad Mottola .05
125 Chris Sabo .05
126 Roger Salkeld .05
127 Pedro Castellano .05
128 Trenidad Hubbard .05
129 Jayhawk Owens .05
130 Jeff Reed .05
131 Kevin Brown .10
132 Al Leiter .08
133 *Matt Mantei* .75
134 Dave Weathers .05
135 Devon White .05
136 Bob Abreu .15
137 Sean Berry .05
138 Doug Brocail .05
139 Richard Hidalgo .08
140 Alvin Morman .05
141 Mike Blowers .05
142 Roger Cedeno .08
143 Greg Gagne .05
144 Karim Garcia .75
145 *Wilton Guerrero* .50
146 Israel Alcantara .05
147 Omar Daal .05
148 Ryan McGuire .08
149 Sherman Obando .05
150 Jose Paniagua .05
151 Henry Rodriguez .05
152 Andy Stankiewicz .05
153 Dave Veres .05
154 Juan Acevedo .05
155 Mark Clark .05
156 Bernard Gilkey .05
157 Pete Harnisch .05
158 Lance Johnson .05
159 Brent Mayne .05
160 Rey Ordonez .30
161 Kevin Roberson .05
162 Paul Wilson .10
163 *David Doster* .05
164 *Mike Grace* .40
165 *Rich Hunter* .05
166 Pete Incaviglia .05
167 Mike Lieberthal .08
168 Terry Mulholland .05
169 Ken Ryan .05
170 Benito Santiago .05
171 *Kevin Sefcik* .05
172 Lee Tinsley .05
173 Todd Zeile .05
174 *Francisco Cordova* .10
175 Danny Darwin .05
176 Charlie Hayes .05
177 Jason Kendall .08
178 Mike Kingery .05
179 Jon Lieber .05
180 Zane Smith .05
181 Luis Alicea .05
182 Cory Bailey .05
183 Andy Benes .05
184 Pat Borders .05
185 *Mike Busby* .05
186 Royce Clayton .05
187 Dennis Eckersley .08
188 Gary Gaetti .05
189 Ron Gant .10
190 Aaron Holbert .05
191 Willie McGee .05
192 *Miguel Mejia* .05
193 Jeff Parrett .05
194 Todd Stottlemyre .05
195 Sean Bergman .05
196 Archi Cianfrocco .05
197 Rickey Henderson .20
198 Wally Joyner .08
199 Craig Shipley .05
200 Bob Tewksbury .05
201 Tim Worrell .05
202 *Rich Aurilia* .05
203 Doug Creek .05
204 Shawon Dunston .05
205 *Osvaldo Fernandez* .10
206 Mark Gardner .05
207 Stan Javier .05
208 Marcus Jensen .05
209 *Chris Singleton* 6.00
210 Allen Watson .05
211 Jeff Bagwell (Encore) .60
212 Derek Bell (Encore) .05
213 Albert Belle (Encore) .40
214 Wade Boggs (Encore) .15
215 Barry Bonds (Encore) .40
216 Jose Canseco (Encore) .15
217 Marty Cordova (Encore) .08
218 Jim Edmonds (Encore) .10
219 Cecil Fielder (Encore) .08
220 Andres Galarraga (Encore) .15
221 Juan Gonzalez (Encore) .60
222 Mark Grace (Encore) .10
223 Ken Griffey Jr. (Encore) 1.50
224 Tony Gwynn (Encore) .60
225 Jason Isringhausen (Encore) .08
226 Derek Jeter (Encore) .75
227 Randy Johnson (Encore) .35
228 Chipper Jones (Encore) 1.00
229 Ryan Klesko (Encore) .25
230 Barry Larkin (Encore) .15
231 Kenny Lofton (Encore) .50
232 Greg Maddux (Encore) 1.00
233 Raul Mondesi (Encore) .20
234 Hideo Nomo (Encore) .40
235 Mike Piazza (Encore) 1.00
236 Manny Ramirez (Encore) .75
237 Cal Ripken Jr. (Encore) 1.25
238 Tim Salmon (Encore) .15
239 Ryne Sandberg (Encore) .40
240 Reggie Sanders (Encore) .05
241 Gary Sheffield (Encore) .20
242 Sammy Sosa (Encore) 1.00
243 Frank Thomas (Encore) 1.00
244 Mo Vaughn (Encore) .50
245 Matt Williams (Encore) .15
246 Checklist .05
247 Checklist .05
248 Checklist .05
249 Checklist .05
250 Checklist .05

1996 Fleer Update Tiffany

	MT
Complete Set (250):	100.00
Common Player:	.15
Glossy Stars: 3X	

(See 1996 Fleer Update for checklist and base card values.)

1996 Fleer Update Diamond Tribute

These insert cards are the most difficult to pull from 1996 Fleer Update packs; they are seeded one per every 100 packs. The 10-card set features cards of future Hall of Famers on stock utilizing two different holographic foils and a diamond design, similar to the "Zone" insert cards in Fleer Baseball.

		MT
Complete Set (10):		140.00
Common Player:		6.00
1	Wade Boggs	7.50
2	Barry Bonds	10.00
3	Ken Griffey Jr.	40.00
4	Tony Gwynn	20.00
5	Rickey Henderson	6.00
6	Greg Maddux	25.00
7	Eddie Murray	6.00
8	Cal Ripken Jr.	30.00
9	Ozzie Smith	7.50
10	Frank Thomas	15.00

1996 Fleer Update Headliners

These 20 cards feature newsmakers from 1996. The cards were random inserts in 1996 Fleer Update packs, one per every five retail packs.

		MT
Complete Set (20):		35.00
Common Player:		.35
1	Roberto Alomar	1.00
2	Jeff Bagwell	1.75
3	Albert Belle	1.25
4	Barry Bonds	1.25
5	Cecil Fielder	.35
6	Juan Gonzalez	3.00
7	Ken Griffey Jr.	6.00
8	Tony Gwynn	2.00
9	Randy Johnson	1.00
10	Chipper Jones	4.00
11	Ryan Klesko	.50
12	Kenny Lofton	1.25
13	Greg Maddux	3.50
14	Hideo Nomo	.75
15	Mike Piazza	4.00
16	Manny Ramirez	1.50
17	Cal Ripken Jr.	5.00
18	Tim Salmon	.50
19	Frank Thomas	2.00
20	Matt Williams	.50

1996 Fleer Update New Horizons

These 1996 Fleer Update inserts feature 20 promising youngsters with bright futures in the majors. The cards were seeded one per every five hobby packs.

		MT
Complete Set (20):		8.00
Common Player:		.30
1	Bob Abreu	1.50
2	George Arias	.30
3	Tony Batista	.30
4	Steve Cox	.30
5	David Doster	.30
6	Jermaine Dye	1.00
7	Andy Fox	.60
8	Mike Grace	.60
9	Todd Greene	.60
10	Wilton Guerrero	.75
11	Richard Hidalgo	.65
12	Raul Ibanez	.45
13	Robin Jennings	.30
14	Marcus Jensen	.30
15	Jason Kendall	1.00
16	Brooks Kieschnick	.60
17	Ryan McGuire	.45
18	Miguel Mejia	.30
19	Rey Ordonez	2.00
20	Paul Wilson	.60

1996 Fleer Update Smooth Leather

Ten of the game's top fielders are showcased on these 1996 Fleer Update insert cards. The cards were seeded one per every five packs.

		MT
Complete Set (10):		7.50
Common Player:		.40
1	Roberto Alomar	.60
2	Barry Bonds	.60
3	Will Clark	.40
4	Ken Griffey Jr.	3.00
5	Kenny Lofton	.60
6	Greg Maddux	1.50
7	Raul Mondesi	.50
8	Rey Ordonez	.60
9	Cal Ripken Jr.	2.50
10	Matt Williams	.40

1996 Fleer Update Soaring Stars

Ten of the game's top players are spotlighted on these 1996 Fleer Update inserts. The cards were seeded one per every 11 packs.

		MT
Complete Set (10):		20.00
Common Player:		.50
1	Jeff Bagwell	1.50
2	Barry Bonds	1.25
3	Juan Gonzalez	2.50
4	Ken Griffey Jr.	5.00
5	Chipper Jones	3.00
6	Greg Maddux	2.50
7	Mike Piazza	3.00
8	Manny Ramirez	1.50
9	Frank Thomas	2.00
10	Matt Williams	.50

1996 Fleer Baseball '96

For a second consecutive year Fleer issued a special version of its Cleveland Indians cards for sale at Revco stores and Jacobs Field. Sold in 10-card packs with a suggested retail price of $1.49, the Revco version Indians team set differs from the regular Fleer cards in the application of UV coating on front and back, the use of silver—rather than gold-foil highlights and the numbering "X of 20". Following up on the Indians team-set issue, Fleer also issued 20-card sets for several other teams, distributed regionally. They were also sold in 10-card packs ($1.99 SRP) and feature UV coating, silver-foil graphics and special numbering. Some cards were updated and feature new photos reflecting trades, free agent signings, etc.

		MT
Complete Set (180):		48.00
Common Player:		.10
	Atlanta Braves team set:	8.00
1	Steve Avery	.10
2	Jeff Blauser	.10
3	Brad Clontz	.10
4	Tom Glavine	.20
5	Marquis Grissom	.15
6	Chipper Jones	2.00
7	David Justice	.50
8	Ryan Klesko	.40
9	Mark Lemke	.10
10	Javier Lopez	.15
11	Greg Maddux	3.00
12	Fred McGriff	.30
13	Greg McMichael	.10
14	Eddie Perez	.10
15	Jason Schmidt	.10
16	John Smoltz	.25
17	Terrell Wade	.10
18	Mark Wohlers	.10
19	Logo card	.05
20	Checklist	.05
	Baltimore Orioles team set:	8.00
1	Roberto Alomar	1.00
2	Brady Anderson	.15
3	Armando Benitez	.10
4	Bobby Bonilla	.15
5	Scott Erickson	.10
6	Jeffrey Hammonds	.10
7	Jimmy Haynes	.10
8	Chris Hoiles	.10
9	Rick Krivda	.10
10	Kent Mercker	.10
11	Mike Mussina	.20
12	Randy Myers	.10
13	Jesse Orosco	.10
14	Rafael Palmeiro	.40
15	Cal Ripken Jr.	4.00
16	B.J. Surhoff	.10
17	Tony Tarasco	.10
18	David Wells	.10
19	Logo card	.05
20	Checklist	.05
	Boston Red Sox team set:	4.00
1	Stan Belinda	.10
2	Jose Canseco	.75
3	Roger Clemens	1.00
4	Wil Cordero	.10
5	Vaughn Eshelman	.10
6	Tom Gordon	.10
7	Mike Greenwell	.10
8	Dwayne Hosey	.10
9	Kevin Mitchell	.10
10	Tim Naehring	.10
11	Troy O'Leary	.10
12	Aaron Sele	.15
13	Heathcliff Slocumb	.10
14	Mike Stanley	.10
15	Jeff Suppan	.10
16	John Valentin	.15
17	Mo Vaughn	.50
18	Tim Wakefield	.10
19	Logo card	.05
20	Checklist	.05
	Chicago Cubs team set:	4.00
1	Terry Adams	.10
2	Jim Bullinger	.10
3	Frank Castillo	.10
4	Kevin Foster	.10
5	Leo Gomez	.10
6	Luis Gonzalez	.10
7	Mark Grace	.40
8	Jose Hernandez	.10
9	*Robin Jennings*	.10
10	Doug Jones	.10
11	Brooks Kieschnick	.35
12	Brian McRae	.10
13	Jaime Navarro	.10
14	Rey Sanchez	.10
15	Ryne Sandberg	1.50
16	Scott Servais	.10
17	Sammy Sosa	1.00
18	Steve Trachsel	.10
19	Logo card	.05
20	Checklist	.05
	Chicago White Sox team set:	6.00
1	Wilson Alvarez	.10
2	Harold Baines	.10
3	Jason Bere	.10
4	Ray Durham	.15
5	Alex Fernandez	.10
6	Ozzie Guillen	.10
7	Roberto Hernandez	.10
8	Matt Karchner	.10
9	Ron Karkovice	.10
10	Darren Lewis	.10
11	Dave Martinez	.10
12	Lyle Mouton	.10
13	Tony Phillips	.10
14	Chris Snopek	.10
15	Kevin Tapani	.10
16	Danny Tartabull	.10
17	Frank Thomas	1.50

18 Robin Ventura .20
19 Logo card .05
20 Checklist .05
Cleveland Indians team set: 8.00
1 Sandy Alomar Jr. .20
2 Paul Assenmacher .10
3 Carlos Baerga .15
4 Albert Belle 1.00
5 Orel Hershiser .15
6 Kenny Lofton 1.00
7 Dennis Martinez .15
8 Jose Mesa .10
9 Eddie Murray .75
10 Charles Nagy .10
11 Tony Pena .10
12 Herb Perry .10
13 Eric Plunk .10
14 Jim Poole .10
15 Manny Ramirez 2.00
16 Julian Tavarez .10
17 Jim Thome .20
18 Omar Vizquel .10
19 Logo card .05
20 Checklist .05
Colorado Rockies team set: 4.00
1 Jason Bates .10
2 Dante Bichette .75
3 Ellis Burks .15
4 Vinny Castilla .25
5 Andres Galarraga .45
6 Darren Holmes .10
7 Curt Leskanic .10
8 Quinton McCracken .10
9 Mike Munoz .10
10 Jayhawk Owens .10
11 Steve Reed .10
12 Kevin Ritz .10
13 Bret Saberhagen .10
14 Bill Swift .10
15 John Vander Wal .10
16 Larry Walker .30
17 Walt Weiss .10
18 Eric Young .15
19 Logo card .05
20 Checklist .05
L.A. Dodgers team set: 8.00
1 Mike Blowers .10
2 Brett Butler .15
3 Tom Candiotti .10
4 Roger Cedeno .10
5 Delino DeShields .10
6 Chad Fonville .10
7 Greg Gagne .10
8 Karim Garcia .50
9 Todd Hollandsworth .15
10 Eric Karros .15
11 Ramon Martinez .10
12 Raul Mondesi .50
13 Hideo Nomo 1.00
14 Antonio Osuna .10
15 Chan Ho Park .50
16 Mike Piazza 2.50
17 Ismael Valdes .15
18 Todd Worrell .10
19 Logo card .05
20 Checklist .05
Texas Rangers team set: 4.00
1 Mark Brandenburg .10
2 Damon Buford .15
3 Will Clark .60
4 Kevin Elster .10
5 Benji Gil .10
6 Juan Gonzalez 1.50
7 Rusty Greer .10
8 Kevin Gross .10
9 Darryl Hamilton .10
10 Ken Hill .10
11 Mark McLemore .10
12 Dean Palmer .15
13 Roger Pavlik .10
14 Ivan Rodriguez .40
15 Mickey Tettleton .10
16 Dave Valle .10
17 Ed Vosberg .10
18 Matt Whiteside .10
19 Logo card .05
20 Checklist .05

1996 Fleer-Panini Stickers

For the second year of distribution by Fleer/SkyBox, the annual baseball sticker set once again used Panini as the dominant brand identification. Printed in Italy, the stickers were sold in packs of six for 49 cents in the U.S., 69 cents in Canada. At 2-1/8" x 3", the basic player stickers have a green border around the color action photo; a second, ghosted, version of the photo appears in the background. Team logo and player ID are in a bat at bottom. Backs are printed in blue with the sticker number, Panini and licensor logos, along with copyright information. Team logo and special rookie stickers were printed on silver foil. A 60-page album was issued to house the set.

	MT
Complete Set (246):	15.00
Common Player:	.20
Album:	2.00

1 David Justice .30
2 Tom Glavine .25
3 Javier Lopez .25
4 Greg Maddux .75
5 Marquis Grissom .25
6 Braves logo .20
7 Ryan Klesko .25
8 Chipper Jones .75
9 Quilvio Veras .20
10 Chris Hammond .20
11 Charles Johnson .30
12 John Burkett .20
13 Marlins logo .20
14 Jeff Conine .25
15 Gary Sheffield .50
16 Greg Colbrunn .20
17 Moises Alou .25
18 Pedro J. Martinez .30
19 Rondell White .20
20 Tony Tarasco .20
21 Expos logo .20
22 Carlos Perez .20
23 David Segui .20
24 Wil Cordero .20
25 Jason Isringhausen .20
26 Rico Brogna .20
27 Edgardo Alfonzo .25
28 Todd Hundley .25
29 Mets logo .20
30 Bill Pulsipher .20
31 Carl Everett .20
32 Jose Vizcaino .20
33 Lenny Dykstra .20
34 Charlie Hayes .20
35 Heathcliff Slocumb .20
36 Darren Daulton .20
37 Phillies logo .20
38 Mickey Morandini .20
39 Gregg Jefferies .25
40 Jim Eisenreich .20
41 Brian McRae .20
42 Luis Gonzalez .20
43 Randy Myers .20
44 Shawon Dunston .20
45 Cubs logo .20
46 Jaime Navarro .20
47 Mark Grace .50
48 Sammy Sosa .75
49 Barry Larkin .25
50 Pete Schourek .20
51 John Smiley .20
52 Reggie Sanders .20
53 Reds logo .20
54 Hal Morris .20
55 Ron Gant .20
56 Bret Boone .25
57 Craig Biggio .30
58 Brian L. Hunter .20
59 Jeff Bagwell .50
60 Shane Reynolds .20
61 Astros logo .20
62 Derek Bell .20
63 Doug Drabek .20
64 Orlando Miller .20
65 Jay Bell .20
66 Dan Miceli .20
67 Orlando Merced .20
68 Jeff King .20
69 Carlos Garcia .20
70 Pirates logo .20
71 Al Martin .20
72 Denny Neagle .20
73 Ray Lankford .20
74 Ozzie Smith .50
75 Bernard Gilkey .20
76 John Mabry .20
77 Cardinals logo .20
78 Brian Jordan .30
79 Scott Cooper .20
80 Allen Watson .20
81 Dante Bichette .30
82 Bret Saberhagen .20
83 Walt Weiss .20
84 Andres Galarraga .30
85 Rockies logo .20
86 Larry Walker .50
87 Bill Swift .20
88 Vinny Castilla .25
89 Raul Mondesi .40
90 Roger Cedeno .20
91 Chad Fonville .20
92 Hideo Nomo .50
93 Dodgers logo .20
94 Ramon Martinez .25
95 Mike Piazza .75
96 Eric Karros .25
97 Tony Gwynn .50
98 Brad Ausmus .20
99 Trevor Hoffman .20
100 Ken Caminiti .30
101 Padres logo .20
102 Andy Ashby .20
103 Steve Finley .20
104 Joey Hamilton .25
105 Matt Williams .30
106 Rod Beck .20
107 Barry Bonds .50
108 William VanLandingham .20
109 Giants logo .20
110 Deion Sanders .20
111 Royce Clayton .20
112 Glenallen Hill .20
113 Tony Gwynn (League Leader - BA) .20
114 Dante Bichette (League Leader - HR) .20
115 Dante Bichette (League Leader - RBI) .20
116 Quilvio Veras (League Leader - SB) .20
117 Hideo Nomo (League Leader - K) .40
118 Greg Maddux (League Leader - W) .40
119 Randy Myers (League Leader - Saves) .20
120 Edgar Martinez (League Leader - BA) .20
121 Albert Belle (League Leader - HR) .40
122 Mo Vaughn (League Leader - RBI) .20
123 Kenny Lofton (League Leader - SB) .20
124 Randy Johnson (League Leader - K) .20
125 Mike Mussina (League Leader - W) .20
126 Jose Mesa (League Leader - Saves) .20
127 Mike Mussina .25
128 Cal Ripken Jr. 1.50
129 Rafael Palmeiro .25
130 Ben McDonald .20
131 Orioles logo .20
132 Chris Hoiles .20
133 Bobby Bonilla .25
134 Brady Anderson .20
135 Jose Canseco .35
136 Roger Clemens .50
137 Mo Vaughn .35
138 Mike Greenwell .20
139 Red Sox logo .20
140 Tim Wakefield .20
141 John Valentin .20
142 Tim Naehring .20
143 Travis Fryman .20
144 Chad Curtis .20
145 Felipe Lira .20
146 Cecil Fielder .20
147 Tigers logo .20
148 John Flaherty .20
149 Chris Gomez .20
150 Sean Bergman .20
151 Don Mattingly 1.00
152 Andy Pettitte .25
153 Wade Boggs .35
154 Paul O'Neill .20
155 Yankees logo .20
156 Bernie Williams .30
157 Jack McDowell .20
158 David Cone .25
159 Roberto Alomar .35
160 Paul Molitor .50
161 Shawn Green .20
162 Joe Carter .20
163 Blue Jays logo .20
164 Alex Gonzalez .20
165 Al Leiter .20
166 John Olerud .25
167 Alex Fernandez .20
168 Ray Durham .20
169 Lance Johnson .20
170 Ozzie Guillen .20
171 White Sox logo .20
172 Robin Ventura .30
173 Frank Thomas 1.00
174 Tim Raines .25
175 Albert Belle .75
176 Manny Ramirez .50
177 Eddie Murray .40
178 Orel Hershiser .25
179 Indians logo .20
180 Kenny Lofton .50
181 Carlos Baerga .20
182 Jose Mesa .20
183 Gary Gaetti .20
184 Tom Goodwin .20
185 Kevin Appier .20
186 Jon Nunnally .20
187 Royals logo .20
188 Wally Joyner .25
189 Jeff Montgomery .20
190 Johnny Damon .30
191 B.J. Surhoff .20
192 Ricky Bones .20
193 John Jaha .20
194 Dave Nilsson .20
195 Brewers logo .20
196 Greg Vaughn .25
197 Kevin Seitzer .20
198 Joe Oliver .20
199 Chuck Knoblauch .30
200 Kirby Puckett 1.00
201 Marty Cordova .20
202 Pat Meares .20
203 Twins logo .20
204 Scott Stahoviak .20
205 Matt Walbeck .20
206 Pedro Munoz .20
207 Garret Anderson .25
208 Chili Davis .25
209 Tim Salmon .25
210 J.T. Snow .25
211 Angels logo .20
212 Jim Edmonds .25
213 Chuck Finley .20
214 Mark Langston .20
215 Dennis Eckersley .25
216 Todd Stottlemyre .20
217 Geronimo Berroa .20
218 Mark McGwire 1.50
219 A's logo .20
220 Brent Gates .20
221 Terry Steinbach .20
222 Rickey Henderson .40
223 Ken Griffey Jr. 2.00
224 Alex Rodriguez 1.50
225 Tino Martinez .20
226 Randy Johnson .25
227 Mariners logo .20
228 Jay Buhner .25
229 Vince Coleman .20
230 Edgar Martinez .20
231 Will Clark .30
232 Juan Gonzalez .60
233 Kenny Rogers .20
234 Ivan Rodriguez .30
235 Rangers logo .20
236 Mickey Tettleton .20
237 Dean Palmer .20
238 Otis Nixon .20
239 Hideo Nomo (Rookie) .65
240 Quilvio Veras (Rookie) .25
241 Jason Isringhausen (Rookie) .25
242 Andy Pettitte (Rookie) .20
243 Chipper Jones (Rookie) 1.50
244 Garret Anderson (Rookie) .25
245 Charles Johnson (Rookie) .30
246 Marty Cordova (Rookie) .25

1997 Fleer

Fleer maintained its matte-finish coating for 1997 after it debuted in the 1996 product. The regular-issue Series 1 has 500 cards equipped with icons designating All-Stars, League Leaders and World Series cards. There were also 10 checklist cards in the regular-issue set, featuring stars on the front. Fleer arrived in 10-card packs and had a Tiffany Collection parallel set and six different insert sets, including Rookie Sensations, Golden Memories, Team Leaders, Night and Day, Zone and Lumber Company. Series 2 comprises 261 cards plus inserts Decade of Excellence, Bleacher Bashers, Diamond Tributes, Goudey Greats, Headliners, New Horizons and Soaring Stars.

	MT
Complete Set (761):	80.00
Complete Series 1 Set (500):	45.00
Complete Series 2 Set (261):	35.00
Common Player:	.05
A. Jones Circa AU/200:	60.00
Wax Box:	50.00

1 Roberto Alomar .60
2 Brady Anderson .10
3 Bobby Bonilla .08
4 Rocky Coppinger .05
5 Cesar Devarez .05
6 Scott Erickson .05
7 Jeffrey Hammonds .05
8 Chris Hoiles .05
9 Eddie Murray .40
10 Mike Mussina .60
11 Randy Myers .05
12 Rafael Palmeiro .20
13 Cal Ripken Jr. 2.50
14 B.J. Surhoff .08
15 David Wells .08
16 Todd Zeile .05
17 Darren Bragg .05
18 Jose Canseco .25
19 Roger Clemens .75
20 Wil Cordero .05
21 Jeff Frye .05
22 Nomar Garciaparra 2.00
23 Tom Gordon .05
24 Mike Greenwell .05
25 Reggie Jefferson .05
26 Jose Malave .05
27 Tim Naehring .05
28 Troy O'Leary .05
29 Heathcliff Slocumb .05
30 Mike Stanley .05
31 John Valentin .05
32 Mo Vaughn 1.00
33 Tim Wakefield .05
34 Garret Anderson .05
35 George Arias .05
36 Shawn Boskie .05
37 Chili Davis .05
38 Jason Dickson .25
39 Gary DiSarcina .05
40 Jim Edmonds .05
41 Darin Erstad 1.25
42 Jorge Fabregas .05
43 Chuck Finley .05
44 Todd Greene .05
45 *Mike Holtz* .10
46 Rex Hudler .05
47 Mike James .05
48 Mark Langston .05
49 Troy Percival .05
50 Tim Salmon .20
51 Jeff Schmidt .05
52 J.T. Snow .08
53 Randy Velarde .05
54 Wilson Alvarez .05
55 Harold Baines .05
56 James Baldwin .05
57 Jason Bere .05
58 Mike Cameron .05
59 Ray Durham .05
60 Alex Fernandez .05
61 Ozzie Guillen .05
62 Roberto Hernandez .05
63 Ron Karkovice .05
64 Darren Lewis .05
65 Dave Martinez .05
66 Lyle Mouton .05
67 Greg Norton .05
68 Tony Phillips .05
69 Chris Snopek .05
70 Kevin Tapani .05
71 Danny Tartabull .05
72 Frank Thomas 1.50
73 Robin Ventura .10
74 Sandy Alomar Jr. .08
75 Albert Belle .75
76 Mark Carreon .05
77 Julio Franco .05
78 *Brian Giles* 1.50
79 Orel Hershiser .05
80 Kenny Lofton .75
81 Dennis Martinez .05
82 Jack McDowell .05
83 Jose Mesa .05
84 Charles Nagy .08
85 Chad Ogea .05
86 Eric Plunk .05
87 Manny Ramirez 1.00
88 Kevin Seitzer .05
89 Julian Tavarez .05
90 Jim Thome .25
91 Jose Vizcaino .05
92 Omar Vizquel .08
93 Brad Ausmus .05
94 Kimera Bartee .05
95 Raul Casanova .05
96 Tony Clark .60
97 John Cummings .05
98 Travis Fryman .08
99 Bob Higginson .12

100	Mark Lewis	.05
101	Felipe Lira	.05
102	Phil Nevin	.05
103	Melvin Nieves	.05
104	Curtis Pride	.05
105	A.J. Sager	.05
106	Ruben Sierra	.05
107	Justin Thompson	.05
108	Alan Trammell	.05
109	Kevin Appier	.05
110	Tim Belcher	.05
111	Jaime Bluma	.05
112	Johnny Damon	.15
113	Tom Goodwin	.05
114	Chris Haney	.05
115	Keith Lockhart	.05
116	Mike Macfarlane	.05
117	Jeff Montgomery	.05
118	Jose Offerman	.05
119	Craig Paquette	.05
120	Joe Randa	.05
121	Bip Roberts	.05
122	Jose Rosado	.05
123	Mike Sweeney	.05
124	Michael Tucker	.05
125	Jeromy Burnitz	.08
126	Jeff Cirillo	.05
127	Jeff D'Amico	.05
128	Mike Fetters	.05
129	John Jaha	.05
130	Scott Karl	.05
131	Jesse Levis	.05
132	Mark Loretta	.05
133	Mike Matheny	.05
134	Ben McDonald	.05
135	Matt Mieske	.05
136	Marc Newfield	.05
137	Dave Nilsson	.05
138	Jose Valentin	.05
139	Fernando Vina	.05
140	Bob Wickman	.05
141	Gerald Williams	.05
142	Rick Aguilera	.05
143	Rich Becker	.05
144	Ron Coomer	.05
145	Marty Cordova	.10
146	Roberto Kelly	.05
147	Chuck Knoblauch	.10
148	Matt Lawton	.05
149	Pat Meares	.05
150	Travis Miller	.05
151	Paul Molitor	.40
152	Greg Myers	.05
153	Dan Naulty	.05
154	Kirby Puckett	1.00
155	Brad Radke	.05
156	Frank Rodriguez	.05
157	Scott Stahoviak	.05
158	Dave Stevens	.05
159	Matt Walbeck	.05
160	Todd Walker	.50
161	Wade Boggs	.25
162	David Cone	.10
163	Mariano Duncan	.05
164	Cecil Fielder	.08
165	Joe Girardi	.05
166	Dwight Gooden	.08
167	Charlie Hayes	.05
168	Derek Jeter	2.00
169	Jimmy Key	.05
170	Jim Leyritz	.05
171	Tino Martinez	.30
172	*Ramiro Mendoza*	.05
173	Jeff Nelson	.05
174	Paul O'Neill	.10
175	Andy Pettitte	.75
176	Mariano Rivera	.10
177	Ruben Rivera	.25
178	Kenny Rogers	.05
179	Darryl Strawberry	.08
180	John Wetteland	.05
181	Bernie Williams	.40
182	Willie Adams	.05
183	Tony Batista	.05
184	Geronimo Berroa	.05
185	Mike Bordick	.05
186	Scott Brosius	.05
187	Bobby Chouinard	.05
188	Jim Corsi	.05
189	Brent Gates	.05
190	Jason Giambi	.05
191	Jose Herrera	.05
192	*Damon Mashore*	.05
193	Mark McGwire	4.00
194	Mike Mohler	.05
195	Scott Spiezio	.05
196	Terry Steinbach	.05
197	Bill Taylor	.05
198	John Wasdin	.05
199	Steve Wojciechowski	.05
200	Ernie Young	.05
201	Rich Amaral	.05
202	Jay Buhner	.10
203	Norm Charlton	.05
204	Joey Cora	.05
205	Russ Davis	.05
206	Ken Griffey Jr.	3.00
207	Sterling Hitchcock	.05
208	Brian Hunter	.05
209	Raul Ibanez	.05
210	Randy Johnson	.30
211	Edgar Martinez	.05
212	Jamie Moyer	.05
213	Alex Rodriguez	3.00
214	Paul Sorrento	.05
215	Matt Wagner	.05
216	Bob Wells	.05
217	Dan Wilson	.05
218	Damon Buford	.05
219	Will Clark	.25
220	Kevin Elster	.05
221	Juan Gonzalez	1.50
222	Rusty Greer	.05
223	Kevin Gross	.05
224	Darryl Hamilton	.05
225	Mike Henneman	.05
226	Ken Hill	.05
227	Mark McLemore	.05
228	Darren Oliver	.05
229	Dean Palmer	.05
230	Roger Pavlik	.05
231	Ivan Rodriguez	.60
232	Mickey Tettleton	.05
233	Bobby Witt	.05
234	Jacob Brumfield	.05
235	Joe Carter	.08
236	Tim Crabtree	.05
237	Carlos Delgado	.40
238	Huck Flener	.05
239	Alex Gonzalez	.05
240	Shawn Green	.10
241	Juan Guzman	.05
242	Pat Hentgen	.05
243	Marty Janzen	.05
244	Sandy Martinez	.05
245	Otis Nixon	.05
246	Charlie O'Brien	.05
247	John Olerud	.10
248	Robert Perez	.05
249	Ed Sprague	.05
250	Mike Timlin	.05
251	Steve Avery	.05
252	Jeff Blauser	.05
253	Brad Clontz	.05
254	Jermaine Dye	.10
255	Tom Glavine	.10
256	Marquis Grissom	.05
257	Andruw Jones	1.50
258	Chipper Jones	2.00
259	David Justice	.15
260	Ryan Klesko	.25
261	Mark Lemke	.05
262	Javier Lopez	.10
263	Greg Maddux	2.00
264	Fred McGriff	.35
265	Greg McMichael	.05
266	Denny Neagle	.05
267	Terry Pendleton	.05
268	Eddie Perez	.05
269	John Smoltz	.15
270	Terrell Wade	.05
271	Mark Wohlers	.05
272	Terry Adams	.05
273	Brant Brown	.05
274	Leo Gomez	.05
275	Luis Gonzalez	.08
276	Mark Grace	.15
277	Tyler Houston	.05
278	Robin Jennings	.05
279	Brooks Kieschnick	.05
280	Brian McRae	.05
281	Jaime Navarro	.05
282	Ryne Sandberg	.75
283	Scott Servais	.05
284	Sammy Sosa	1.50
285	*Dave Swartzbaugh*	.05
286	Amaury Telemaco	.05
287	Steve Trachsel	.05
288	*Pedro Valdes*	.05
289	Turk Wendell	.05
290	Bret Boone	.05
291	Jeff Branson	.05
292	Jeff Brantley	.05
293	Eric Davis	.08
294	Willie Greene	.05
295	Thomas Howard	.05
296	Barry Larkin	.15
297	Kevin Mitchell	.05
298	Hal Morris	.05
299	Chad Mottola	.05
300	Joe Oliver	.05
301	Mark Portugal	.05
302	Roger Salkeld	.05
303	Reggie Sanders	.05
304	Pete Schourek	.05
305	John Smiley	.05
306	Eddie Taubensee	.05
307	Dante Bichette	.10
308	Ellis Burks	.05
309	Vinny Castilla	.08
310	Andres Galarraga	.15
311	Curt Leskanic	.05
312	Quinton McCracken	.05
313	Neifi Perez	.05
314	Jeff Reed	.05
315	Steve Reed	.05
316	Armando Reynoso	.05
317	Kevin Ritz	.05
318	Bruce Ruffin	.05
319	Larry Walker	.30
320	Walt Weiss	.05
321	Jamey Wright	.05
322	Eric Young	.05
323	Kurt Abbott	.05
324	Alex Arias	.05
325	Kevin Brown	.10
326	Luis Castillo	.15
327	Greg Colbrunn	.05
328	Jeff Conine	.05
329	Andre Dawson	.08
330	Charles Johnson	.08
331	Al Leiter	.08
332	Ralph Milliard	.05
333	Robb Nen	.05
334	Pat Rapp	.05
335	Edgar Renteria	.25
336	Gary Sheffield	.25
337	Devon White	.08
338	Bob Abreu	.08
339	Jeff Bagwell	1.25
340	Derek Bell	.08
341	Sean Berry	.05
342	Craig Biggio	.10
343	Doug Drabek	.05
344	Tony Eusebio	.05
345	Ricky Gutierrez	.05
346	Mike Hampton	.05
347	Brian Hunter	.05
348	Todd Jones	.05
349	Darryl Kile	.05
350	Derrick May	.05
351	Orlando Miller	.05
352	James Mouton	.05
353	Shane Reynolds	.05
354	Billy Wagner	.08
355	Donne Wall	.05
356	Mike Blowers	.05
357	Brett Butler	.05
358	Roger Cedeno	.08
259	Chad Curtis	.05
360	Delino DeShields	.05
361	Greg Gagne	.05
362	Karim Garcia	.50
363	Wilton Guerrero	.08
364	Todd Hollandsworth	.08
365	Eric Karros	.08
366	Ramon Martinez	.08
367	Raul Mondesi	.25
368	Hideo Nomo	.50
369	Antonio Osuna	.05
370	Chan Ho Park	.08
371	Mike Piazza	2.00
372	Ismael Valdes	.05
373	Todd Worrell	.05
374	Moises Alou	.08
375	Shane Andrews	.05
376	Yamil Benitez	.05
377	Jeff Fassero	.05
378	Darrin Fletcher	.05
379	Cliff Floyd	.05
380	Mark Grudzielanek	.05
381	Mike Lansing	.05
382	Barry Manuel	.05
383	Pedro Martinez	.10
384	Henry Rodriguez	.05
385	Mel Rojas	.05
386	F.P. Santangelo	.05
387	David Segui	.05
388	Ugueth Urbina	.05
389	Rondell White	.08
390	Edgardo Alfonzo	.10
391	Carlos Baerga	.08
392	Mark Clark	.05
393	Alvaro Espinoza	.05
394	John Franco	.05
395	Bernard Gilkey	.05
396	Pete Harnisch	.05
397	Todd Hundley	.08
398	Butch Huskey	.05
399	Jason Isringhausen	.05
400	Lance Johnson	.05
401	Bobby Jones	.05
402	Alex Ochoa	.05
403	Rey Ordonez	.20
404	Robert Person	.05
405	Paul Wilson	.08
406	Matt Beech	.05
407	Ron Blazier	.05
408	Ricky Bottalico	.05
409	Lenny Dykstra	.05
410	Jim Eisenreich	.05
411	Bobby Estalella	.05
412	Mike Grace	.05
413	Gregg Jefferies	.05
414	Mike Lieberthal	.08
415	Wendell Magee Jr.	.05
416	Mickey Morandini	.05
417	Ricky Otero	.05
418	Scott Rolen	1.50
419	Ken Ryan	.05
420	Benito Santiago	.05
421	Curt Schilling	.10
422	Kevin Sefcik	.05
423	Jermaine Allensworth	.05
424	Trey Beamon	.05
425	Jay Bell	.05
426	Francisco Cordova	.10
427	Carlos Garcia	.05
428	Mark Johnson	.05
429	Jason Kendall	.08
430	Jeff King	.05
431	Jon Lieber	.05
432	Al Martin	.05
433	Orlando Merced	.05
434	Ramon Morel	.05
435	Matt Ruebel	.05
436	Jason Schmidt	.05
437	*Marc Wilkins*	.05
438	Alan Benes	.10
439	Andy Benes	.05
440	Royce Clayton	.05
441	Dennis Eckersley	.05
442	Gary Gaetti	.05
443	Ron Gant	.10
444	Aaron Holbert	.05
445	Brian Jordan	.05
446	Ray Lankford	.05
447	John Mabry	.05
448	T.J. Mathews	.05
449	Willie McGee	.05
450	Donovan Osborne	.05
451	Tom Pagnozzi	.05
452	Ozzie Smith	.40
453	Todd Stottlemyre	.05
454	Mark Sweeney	.05
455	Dmitri Young	.05
456	Andy Ashby	.05
457	Ken Caminiti	.15
458	Archi Cianfrocco	.05
459	Steve Finley	.05
460	John Flaherty	.05
461	Chris Gomez	.05
462	Tony Gwynn	1.25
463	Joey Hamilton	.05
464	Rickey Henderson	.15
465	Trevor Hoffman	.08
466	Brian Johnson	.05
467	Wally Joyner	.05
468	Jody Reed	.05
469	Scott Sanders	.05
470	Bob Tewksbury	.05
471	Fernando Valenzuela	.05
472	Greg Vaughn	.08
473	Tim Worrell	.05
474	Rich Aurilla	.05
475	Rod Beck	.05
476	Marvin Benard	.05
477	Barry Bonds	.75
478	Jay Canizaro	.05
479	Shawon Dunston	.05
480	Shawn Estes	.05
481	Mark Gardner	.05
482	Glenallen Hill	.05
483	Stan Javier	.05
484	Marcus Jensen	.05
485	*Bill Mueller*	.05
486	William VanLandingham	.05
487	Allen Watson	.05
488	Rick Wilkins	.05
489	Matt Williams	.25
489p	Matt Williams ("PROMOTIONAL SAMPLE")	3.00
490	Desi Wilson	.05
491	Checklist (Albert Belle)	.35
492	Checklist (Ken Griffey Jr.)	1.00
493	Checklist (Andruw Jones)	.50
494	Checklist (Chipper Jones)	.60
495	Checklist (Mark McGwire)	1.50
496	Checklist (Paul Molitor)	.15
497	Checklist (Mike Piazza)	.60
498	Checklist (Cal Ripken Jr.)	.75
499	Checklist (Alex Rodriguez)	1.00
500	Checklist (Frank Thomas)	.75
501	Kenny Lofton	.75
502	Carlos Perez	.05
503	Tim Raines	.05
504	*Danny Patterson*	.10
505	Derrick May	.05
506	Dave Hollins	.05
507	Felipe Crespo	.05
508	Brian Banks	.05
509	Jeff Kent	.05
510	*Bubba Trammell*	.75
511	Robert Person	.05
512	*David Arias* (last name actually Ortiz)	1.00
513	Ryan Jones	.05
514	David Justice	.15
515	Will Cunnane	.05
516	Russ Johnson	.05
517	John Burkett	.05
518	*Robinson Checo*	.25
519	*Ricardo Rincon*	.15
520	Woody Williams	.05
521	Rick Helling	.05
522	Jorge Posada	.05
523	Kevin Orie	.05
524	*Fernando Tatis*	3.00
525	Jermaine Dye	.05
526	Brian Hunter	.05
527	Greg McMichael	.05
528	Matt Wagner	.05
529	Richie Sexson	.05
530	Scott Ruffcorn	.05
531	Luis Gonzalez	.05
532	Mike Johnson	.05
533	Mark Petkovsek	.05
534	Doug Drabek	.05
535	Jose Canseco	.25
536	Bobby Bonilla	.05
537	J.T. Snow	.08
538	Shawon Dunston	.05
539	John Ericks	.05
540	Terry Steinbach	.05
541	Jay Bell	.05
542	Joe Borowski	.05
543	David Wells	.08
544	*Justin Towle*	.25
545	Mike Blowers	.05
546	Shannon Stewart	.05
547	Rudy Pemberton	.05
548	Bill Swift	.05
549	Osvaldo Fernandez	.05
550	Eddie Murray	.35
551	Don Wengert	.05
552	Brad Ausmus	.05
553	Carlos Garcia	.05
554	Jose Guillen	.60
555	Rheal Cormier	.05
556	Doug Brocail	.05
557	Rex Hudler	.05
558	Armando Benitez	.05
559	Elieser Marrero	.05
560	*Ricky Ledee*	3.00
561	Bartolo Colon	.05
562	Quilvio Veras	.05
563	Alex Fernandez	.05
564	Darren Dreifort	.05
565	Benji Gil	.05
566	Kent Mercker	.05
567	Glendon Rusch	.05
568	*Ramon Tatis*	.05
569	Roger Clemens	1.25
570	Mark Lewis	.05
571	*Emil Brown*	.15
572	Jaime Navarro	.05
573	Sherman Obando	.05
574	John Wasdin	.05
575	Calvin Maduro	.05
576	Todd Jones	.05
577	Orlando Merced	.05
578	Cal Eldred	.05
579	Mark Gubicza	.05
580	Michael Tucker	.05
581	*Tony Saunders*	.50
582	Garvin Alston	.05
583	Joe Roa	.05
584	*Brady Raggio*	.05
585	Jimmy Key	.05
586	*Marc Sagmoen*	.05
587	Jim Bullinger	.05
588	Yorkis Perez	.05
589	*Jose Cruz Jr.*	.75
590	Mike Stanton	.05
591	*Deivi Cruz*	.50
592	Steve Karsay	.05
593	Mike Trombley	.05
594	Doug Glanville	.05
595	Scott Sanders	.05
596	Thomas Howard	.05
597	T.J. Staton	.05
598	Garrett Stephenson	.05
599	Rico Brogna	.05
600	Albert Belle	.75
601	Jose Vizcaino	.05
602	Chili Davis	.05
603	Shane Mack	.05
604	Jim Eisenreich	.05
605	Todd Zeile	.05
606	Brian Boehringer	.05
607	Paul Shuey	.05
608	Kevin Tapani	.05
609	John Wetteland	.05
610	Jim Leyritz	.05
611	Ray Montgomery	.05
612	Doug Bochtler	.05
613	Wady Almonte	.05
614	Danny Tartabull	.05
615	Orlando Miller	.05
616	Bobby Ayala	.05
617	Tony Graffanino	.05
618	Marc Valdes	.05
619	Ron Villone	.05
620	Derrek Lee	.05
621	Greg Colbrunn	.05
622	*Felix Heredia*	.25
623	Carl Everett	.05
624	Mark Thompson	.05
625	Jeff Granger	.05
626	Damian Jackson	.05
627	Mark Leiter	.05
628	Chris Holt	.05
629	*Dario Veras*	.15
630	Dave Burba	.05
631	Darryl Hamilton	.05
632	Mark Acre	.05
633	Fernando Hernandez	.05
634	Terry Mulholland	.05
635	Dustin Hermanson	.05
636	Delino DeShields	.05
637	Steve Avery	.05
638	*Tony Womack*	.25
639	Mark Whiten	.05
640	Marquis Grissom	.05
641	Xavier Hernandez	.05
642	Eric Davis	.08
643	Bob Tewksbury	.05
644	Dante Powell	.05
645	Carlos Castillo	.05
646	Chris Widger	.05
647	Moises Alou	.08
648	Pat Listach	.05
649	Edgar Ramos	.05
650	Deion Sanders	.20
651	John Olerud	.10
652	Todd Dunwoody	.30
653	*Randall Simon*	1.50
654	Dan Carlson	.05
655	Matt Williams	.25
656	Jeff King	.05
657	Luis Alicea	.05
658	Brian Moehler	.05
659	Ariel Prieto	.05
660	Kevin Elster	.05
661	Mark Hutton	.05
662	Aaron Sele	.05
663	Graeme Lloyd	.05
664	John Burke	.05
665	Mel Rojas	.05
666	Sid Fernandez	.05
667	Pedro Astacio	.05
668	Jeff Abbott	.05
669	Darren Daulton	.05
670	Mike Bordick	.05
671	Sterling Hitchcock	.05
672	Damion Easley	.05
673	Armando Reynoso	.05
674	Pat Cline	.05

675	*Orlando Cabrera*	.30
676	Alan Embree	.05
677	Brian Bevil	.05
678	David Weathers	.05
679	Cliff Floyd	.05
680	Joe Randa	.05
681	Bill Haselman	.05
682	Jeff Fassero	.05
683	Matt Morris	.05
684	Mark Portugal	.05
685	Lee Smith	.05
686	Pokey Reese	.05
687	Benito Santiago	.05
688	Brian Johnson	.05
689	*Brent Brede*	.05
690	Shigetosi Hasegawa	.05
691	Julio Santana	.05
692	Steve Kline	.05
693	Julian Tavarez	.05
694	John Hudek	.05
695	Manny Alexander	.05
696	Roberto Alomar (Encore)	.30
697	Jeff Bagwell (Encore)	.60
698	Barry Bonds (Encore)	.40
699	Ken Caminiti (Encore)	.10
700	Juan Gonzalez (Encore)	.60
701	Ken Griffey Jr. (Encore)	1.50
702	Tony Gwynn (Encore)	.60
703	Derek Jeter (Encore)	1.00
704	Andruw Jones (Encore)	.75
705	Chipper Jones (Encore)	1.00
706	Barry Larkin (Encore)	.05
707	Greg Maddux (Encore)	1.00
708	Mark McGwire (Encore)	2.00
709	Paul Molitor (Encore)	.15
710	Hideo Nomo (Encore)	.25
711	Andy Pettitte (Encore)	.40
712	Mike Piazza (Encore)	1.00
713	Manny Ramirez (Encore)	.50
714	Cal Ripken Jr. (Encore)	1.25
715	Alex Rodriguez (Encore)	1.50
716	Ryne Sandberg (Encore)	.40
717	John Smoltz (Encore)	.05
718	Frank Thomas (Encore)	.75
719	Mo Vaughn (Encore)	.40
720	Bernie Williams (Encore)	.30
721	Checklist (Tim Salmon)	.05
722	Checklist (Greg Maddux)	.50
723	Checklist (Cal Ripken Jr.)	.75
724	Checklist (Mo Vaughn)	.25
725	Checklist (Ryne Sandberg)	.25
726	Checklist (Frank Thomas)	.50
727	Checklist (Barry Larkin)	.05
728	Checklist (Manny Ramirez)	.30
729	Checklist (Andres Galarraga)	.05
730	Checklist (Tony Clark)	.25
731	Checklist (Gary Sheffield)	.15
732	Checklist (Jeff Bagwell)	.35
733	Checklist (Kevin Appier)	.05
734	Checklist (Mike Piazza)	.50
735	Checklist (Jeff Cirillo)	.05
736	Checklist (Paul Molitor)	.15
737	Checklist (Henry Rodriguez)	.05
738	Checklist (Todd Hundley)	.10
739	Checklist (Derek Jeter)	.50
740	Checklist (Mark McGwire)	.75
741	Checklist (Curt Schilling)	.05
742	Checklist (Jason Kendall)	.05
743	Checklist (Tony Gwynn)	.40
744	Checklist (Barry Bonds)	.25
745	Checklist (Ken Griffey Jr.)	1.00
746	Checklist (Brian Jordan)	.05
747	Checklist (Juan Gonzalez)	.40
748	Checklist (Joe Carter)	.05
749	Arizona Diamondbacks	.05
750	Tampa Bay Devil Rays	.05
751	*Hideki Irabu*	2.00
752	*Jeremi Gonzalez*	.60
753	*Mario Valdez*	.50
754	Aaron Boone	.05
755	Brett Tomko	.05
756	*Jaret Wright*	2.00
757	Ryan McGuire	.05
758	Jason McDonald	.05
759	*Adrian Brown*	.20
760	*Keith Foulke*	.25
761	Checklist	.05

1997 Fleer Tiffany

Insertion odds were considerably lengthened for the UV-coated Tiffany Collection parallels in 1997 Fleer - to one card per 20 packs.

	MT
Complete Set (761):	3500.
Common Player:	2.00
Veteran Stars: 15-25X	
Young Stars/RCs: 10-20X	
(See 1997 Fleer for checklist and base card values.)	

1997 Fleer Bleacher Blasters

This 10-card insert features some of the game's top power hitters and was found in retail packs only. Cards featured a die-cut "burst" pattern on an etched foil background. Backs have a portrait photo and career highlights. Cards were inserted 1:36 packs.

		MT
Complete Set (10):		60.00
Common Player:		2.00
1	Albert Belle	4.00
2	Barry Bonds	5.00
3	Juan Gonzalez	7.00
4	Ken Griffey Jr.	15.00
5	Mark McGwire	15.00
6	Mike Piazza	9.00
7	Alex Rodriguez	15.00
8	Frank Thomas	5.00
9	Mo Vaughn	4.00
10	Matt Williams	2.00

1997 Fleer Decade of Excellence

A 12-card insert found 1:36 in hobby shop packs, cards are in a format similar to the 1987 Fleer set and feature vintage photos of players who started their careers no later than the '87 season. Ten percent of the press run (1:360 packs) received a special foil treatment and designation as "Rare Traditions."

		MT
Complete Set (12):		70.00
Common Player:		3.00
Rare Traditions: 15X		
1	Wade Boggs	5.00
2	Barry Bonds	6.00
3	Roger Clemens	10.00
4	Tony Gwynn	10.00
5	Rickey Henderson	4.00
6	Greg Maddux	12.50
7	Mark McGwire	20.00
8	Paul Molitor	5.00
9	Eddie Murray	4.00
10	Cal Ripken Jr.	15.00
11	Ryne Sandberg	6.00
12	Matt Williams	3.00

1997 Fleer Diamond Tribute

Twelve of the game's top stars are highlighted in this set. Fronts feature an embossed rainbow prismatic foil background and gold lettering. Backs have an action photo and a few sentences about the player. They were inserted 1:288 packs.

		MT
Complete Set (12):		400.00
Common Player:		8.00
1	Albert Belle	15.00
2	Barry Bonds	16.00
3	Juan Gonzalez	35.00
4	Ken Griffey Jr.	75.00
5	Tony Gwynn	35.00
6	Greg Maddux	40.00
7	Mark McGwire	75.00
8	Eddie Murray	8.00
9	Mike Piazza	45.00
10	Cal Ripken Jr.	50.00
11	Alex Rodriguez	50.00
12	Frank Thomas	20.00

1997 Fleer Golden Memories

Golden Memories captures 10 different highlights from the 1996 season, and is inserted one per 16 packs. Moments like Dwight Gooden's no hitter, Paul Molitor's 3000th hit and Eddie Murray's 500th home run are highlighted on a horizontal format.

		MT
Complete Set (10):		10.00
Common Player:		.35
1	Barry Bonds	1.00
2	Dwight Gooden	.40
3	Todd Hundley	.50
4	Mark McGwire	3.00
5	Paul Molitor	1.00
6	Eddie Murray	.75
7	Hideo Nomo	.50
8	Mike Piazza	2.00
9	Cal Ripken Jr.	2.50
10	Ozzie Smith	1.00

1997 Fleer Goudey Greats

Using a 2-3/8" x 2-7/8" format reminiscent of 1933 Goudey cards, this 15-card insert offers today's top players in classic old-time design. Cards were inserted 1:8 packs. A limited number (1% of press run) of cards received a special gold-foil treatment and were found only in hobby packs.

		MT
Complete Set (15):		30.00
Common Player:		.50
Foils: 20-30X		
1	Barry Bonds	1.00
2	Ken Griffey Jr.	5.00
3	Tony Gwynn	2.00
4	Derek Jeter	3.00
5	Chipper Jones	3.00
6	Kenny Lofton	.75
7	Greg Maddux	2.50
8	Mark McGwire	5.00
9	Eddie Murray	.75
10	Mike Piazza	3.00
11	Cal Ripken Jr.	4.00
12	Alex Rodriguez	4.00
13	Ryne Sandberg	1.00
14	Frank Thomas	2.00
15	Mo Vaughn	.75

1997 Fleer Headliners

This 20-card insert highlights the personal achievements of each of the players depicted. Cards were inserted 1:2 packs and feature multicolor foil stamping on the fronts and a newspaper-style account of the player's achievement on the back.

		MT
Complete Set (20):		12.00
Common Player:		.20
1	Jeff Bagwell	.75
2	Albert Belle	.50
3	Barry Bonds	.50
4	Ken Caminiti	.25
5	Juan Gonzalez	.75
6	Ken Griffey Jr.	2.50
7	Tony Gwynn	.75
8	Derek Jeter	1.25
9	Andruw Jones	.75
10	Chipper Jones	1.25
11	Greg Maddux	1.00
12	Mark McGwire	2.50
13	Paul Molitor	.40
14	Eddie Murray	.30
15	Mike Piazza	1.25
16	Cal Ripken Jr.	2.00
17	Alex Rodriguez	2.00
18	Ryne Sandberg	.45
19	John Smoltz	.20
20	Frank Thomas	1.00

1997 Fleer Lumber Company

Lumber Company inserts were found every 48 retail packs. The cards were printed on a die-cut, spherical wood-like pattern, with the player imposed on the left side. Eighteen of the top power hitters in baseball are highlighted.

		MT
Complete Set (18):		150.00
Common Player:		3.00
1	Brady Anderson	3.00
2	Jeff Bagwell	10.00
3	Albert Belle	8.00
4	Barry Bonds	8.00
5	Jay Buhner	4.00
6	Ellis Burks	3.00
7	Andres Galarraga	4.00
8	Juan Gonzalez	15.00
9	Ken Griffey Jr.	30.00
10	Todd Hundley	3.00
11	Ryan Klesko	3.00
12	Mark McGwire	30.00
13	Mike Piazza	20.00
14	Alex Rodriguez	25.00
15	Gary Sheffield	4.00
16	Sammy Sosa	20.00
17	Frank Thomas	10.00
18	Mo Vaughn	6.00

1997-98 Fleer Million Dollar Moments

By assembling a complete set of 50 baseball "Million Dollar Moments" cards prior to July 31, 1998, a collector could win $50,000 a year through 2018. The catch, of course, is that cards #46-50 were printed in very limited quantities, with only one card #50. (Stated odds of winning the million were one in nearly 46,000,000.) The Moments cards have player action photos on front vignetted into a black border. The Fleer Million Dollar Moments logo is at top, with the player name and the date and details of his highlight at bottom in orange and white. Backs have the contest rules in fine print. Instant Win versions of some cards were also issued.

		MT
Complete Set (45):		4.00
Common Player:		.05
1	Checklist	.05
2	Derek Jeter	.10

3	Babe Ruth	.25
4	Barry Bonds	.05
5	Brooks Robinson	.05
6	Todd Hundley	.05
7	Johnny Vander Meer	.05
8	Cal Ripken Jr.	.25
9	Bill Mazeroski	.10
10	Chipper Jones	.15
11	Frank Robinson	.05
12	Roger Clemens	.10
13	Bob Feller	.05
14	Mike Piazza	.10
15	Joe Nuxhall	.05
16	Hideo Nomo	.08
17	Jackie Robinson	.25
18	Orel Hershiser	.05
19	Bobby Thomson	.05
20	Joe Carter	.05
21	Al Kaline	.05
22	Bernie Williams	.05
23	Don Larsen	.05
24	Rickey Henderson	.05
25	Maury Wills	.05
26	Andruw Jones	.10
27	Bobby Richardson	.05
28	Alex Rodriguez	.45
29	Jim Bunning	.05
30	Ken Caminiti	.05
31	Bob Gibson	.05
32	Frank Thomas	.40
33	Mickey Lolich	.05
34	John Smoltz	.05
35	Ron Swoboda	.05
36	Albert Belle	.10
37	Chris Chambliss	.05
38	Juan Gonzalez	.10
39	Ron Blomberg	.05
40	John Wetteland	.05
41	Carlton Fisk	.05
42	Mo Vaughn	.08
43	Bucky Dent	.05
44	Greg Maddux	.10
45	Willie Stargell	.05
46	Tony Gwynn	
47	Joel Youngblood	
48	Andy Pettitte ($500 winner)	
49	Mookie Wilson	
50	Jeff Bagwell ($1 million winner)	

1997 Fleer New Horizons

Rookies and prospects expected to make an impact during the 1996 season were featured in this 15-card insert set. Card fronts feature a rainbow foil background with the words "New Horizon" featured prominently on the bottom under the player's name. Cards were inserted 1:4 packs.

		MT
Complete Set (15):		5.00
Common Player:		.10
1	Bob Abreu	.15
2	Jose Cruz Jr.	.30
3	Darin Erstad	.60
4	Nomar Garciaparra	1.00
5	Vladimir Guerrero	1.00
6	Wilton Guerrero	.10
7	Jose Guillen	.35
8	Hideki Irabu	.50
9	Andruw Jones	1.00
10	Kevin Orie	.10
11	Scott Rolen	.75
12	Scott Spiezio	.10
13	Bubba Trammell	.25
14	Todd Walker	.15
15	Dmitri Young	.10

1997 Fleer Night & Day

Night and Day spotlighted 10 stars with unusual prowess during night or day games. These lenticular cards carried the toughest insert ratios in Fleer Baseball at one per 288 packs.

		MT
Complete Set (10):		200.00
Common Player:		5.00
1	Barry Bonds	9.00
2	Ellis Burks	5.00
3	Juan Gonzalez	15.00
4	Ken Griffey Jr.	40.00
5	Mark McGwire	40.00
6	Mike Piazza	25.00
7	Manny Ramirez	10.00
8	Alex Rodriguez	30.00
9	John Smoltz	5.00
10	Frank Thomas	15.00

1997 Fleer Rookie Sensations

Rookies Sensations showcased 20 of the top up-and-coming stars in baseball. Appearing every six packs, these inserts have the feaured player in the foreground, with the background look of painted brush strokes.

		MT
Complete Set (20):		18.00
Common Player:		.40
1	Jermaine Allensworth	.40
2	James Baldwin	.40
3	Alan Benes	.60
4	Jermaine Dye	.50
5	Darin Erstad	2.00
6	Todd Hollandsworth	.75
7	Derek Jeter	4.00
8	Jason Kendall	.60
9	Alex Ochoa	.50
10	Rey Ordonez	1.00
11	Edgar Renteria	.60
12	Bob Abreu	1.50
13	Nomar Garciaparra	3.50
14	Wilton Guerrero	.50
15	Andruw Jones	3.50
16	Wendell Magee	.75
17	Neifi Perez	.50
18	Scott Rolen	2.50
19	Scott Spiezio	.40
20	Todd Walker	1.00

1997 Fleer Soaring Stars

A 12-card insert found 1:12 packs designed to profile players with outstanding statistical performances early in their careers. Fronts have player action photos set against a background of rainbow holographic stars which appear, disappear and twinkle as the viewing angle is changed. Conventionally printed backs have another player photo and a few sentences about his career. A parallel version on which the background stars glow was issued at a greatly reduced rate.

		MT
Complete Set (12):		35.00
Common Player:		.75
Glowing: 15X		
1	Albert Belle	1.50
2	Barry Bonds	1.50
3	Juan Gonzalez	3.00
4	Ken Griffey Jr.	7.50
5	Derek Jeter	4.00
6	Andruw Jones	3.00
7	Chipper Jones	4.00
8	Greg Maddux	3.00
9	Mark McGwire	7.50
10	Mike Piazza	4.00
11	Alex Rodriguez	5.00
12	Frank Thomas	3.00

1997 Fleer Team Leaders

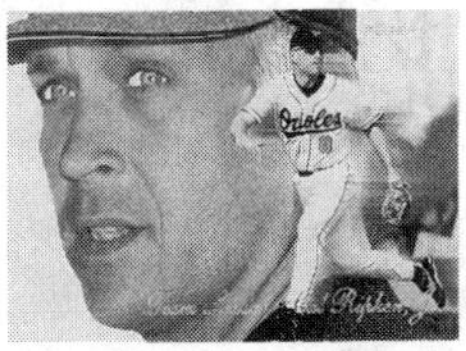

Team Leaders captured the statistical and/or inspirational leaders from all 28 teams. Inserted every 20 packs, these inserts were printed on a horizontal format, with the player's face die-cut in the perimeter of the card.

		MT
Complete Set (28):		90.00
Common Player:		1.50
1	Cal Ripken Jr.	12.50
2	Mo Vaughn	4.00
3	Jim Edmonds	1.50
4	Frank Thomas	5.00
5	Albert Belle	4.00
6	Bob Higginson	1.50
7	Kevin Appier	1.50
8	John Jaha	1.50
9	Paul Molitor	2.50
10	Andy Pettitte	2.00
11	Mark McGwire	17.50
12	Ken Griffey Jr.	17.50
13	Juan Gonzalez	7.50
14	Pat Hentgen	1.50
15	Chipper Jones	9.00
16	Mark Grace	2.50
17	Barry Larkin	1.50
18	Ellis Burks	1.50
19	Gary Sheffield	2.25
20	Jeff Bagwell	7.50
21	Mike Piazza	9.00
22	Henry Rodriguez	1.50
23	Todd Hundley	1.50
24	Curt Schilling	1.50
25	Jeff King	1.50
26	Brian Jordan	1.50
27	Tony Gwynn	7.50
28	Barry Bonds	3.75

1997 Fleer Zone

Twenty of the top hitters in baseball are featured on these holographic cards with the words Zone printed across the front. Zone inserts were found only in hobby packs at a rate of one per 80.

		MT
Complete Set (20):		175.00
Common Player:		3.00
1	Jeff Bagwell	9.00
2	Albert Belle	6.00
3	Barry Bonds	6.00
4	Ken Caminiti	3.50
5	Andres Galarraga	3.00
6	Juan Gonzalez	12.50
7	Ken Griffey Jr.	30.00
8	Tony Gwynn	10.00
9	Chipper Jones	15.00
10	Greg Maddux	12.50
11	Mark McGwire	30.00
12	Dean Palmer	3.00
13	Andy Petitte	4.00
14	Mike Piazza	15.00
15	Alex Rodriguez	20.00
16	Gary Sheffield	4.00
17	John Smoltz	3.00
18	Frank Thomas	9.00
19	Jim Thome	4.00
20	Matt Williams	3.50

1998 Fleer

Fleer was issued in two series in 1998, with 350 cards in Series 1 and 250 in Series 2. Each card features a borderless color action shot, with backs containing player information. Subsets in Series 1 included Smoke 'N Heat (301-310), Golden Memories (311-320) and Tale of the Tape (321-340). Golden Memories (1:6 packs) and Tale of the Tape (1:4) were shortprinted. Series 2 subsets included 25 Unforgettable Moments (571-595). Inserts in Series 1 were Vintage '63, Vintage '63 Classic, Decade of Excellence, Decade of Excellence Rare Traditions, Diamond Ink, Diamond Standouts, Lumber Company, Power Game, Rookie Sensations and Zone. Series 2 inserts include: Vintage '63, Vintage '63 Classic, Promising Forecast, In the Clutch, Mickey Mantle: Monumental Moments, Mickey Mantle: Monumental Moments Gold Edition, Diamond Tribute and Diamond Ink. Card No. 7 in the regular set pictures Mickey Mantle.

		MT
Complete Set (600):		100.00
Complete Series 1 (350):		60.00
Complete Series 2 (250):		40.00
Common Player:		.10
Wax Box:		50.00
1	Ken Griffey Jr.	3.00
2	Derek Jeter	2.00
3	Gerald Williams	.10
4	Carlos Delgado	.40
5	Nomar Garciaparra	2.00
6	Gary Sheffield	.30
7	Jeff King	.10
8	Cal Ripken Jr.	2.50
9	Matt Williams	.25
10	Chipper Jones	2.00
11	Chuck Knoblauch	.25
12	Mark Grudzielanek	.10
13	Edgardo Alfonzo	.15
14	Andres Galarraga	.20
15	Tim Salmon	.25
16	Reggie Sanders	.10
17	Tony Clark	.40
18	Jason Kendall	.12
19	Juan Gonzalez	1.50
20	Ben Grieve	1.00
21	Roger Clemens	1.00
22	Raul Mondesi	.20
23	Robin Ventura	.15
24	Derrek Lee	.10
25	Mark McGwire	4.00
26	Luis Gonzalez	.10
27	Kevin Brown	.20
28	Kirk Rueter	.10
29	Bobby Estalella	.10
30	Shawn Green	.15
31	Greg Maddux	2.00
32	Jorge Velandia	.10
33	Larry Walker	.25
34	Joey Cora	.10
35	Frank Thomas	1.50
36	*Curtis King*	.10
37	Aaron Boone	.10
38	Curt Schilling	.12
39	Bruce Aven	.10
40	Ben McDonald	.10
41	Andy Ashby	.12
42	Jason McDonald	.10
43	Eric Davis	.12
44	Mark Grace	.25
45	Pedro Martinez	.25
46	Lou Collier	.10
47	Chan Ho Park	.12
48	Shane Halter	.10
49	Brian Hunter	.10
50	Jeff Bagwell	1.25
51	Bernie Williams	.50
52	J.T. Snow	.12
53	Todd Greene	.10
54	Shannon Stewart	.10
55	Darren Bragg	.10
56	Fernando Tatis	.20
57	Darryl Kile	.10
58	Chris Stynes	.10
59	Javier Valentin	.10
60	Brian McRae	.10
61	Tom Evans	.10
62	Randall Simon	.20
63	Darrin Fletcher	.10
64	Jaret Wright	1.50
65	Luis Ordaz	.10
66	Jose Canseco	.20
67	Edgar Renteria	.10
68	Jay Buhner	.20
69	Paul Konerko	1.00
70	Adrian Brown	.10
71	Chris Carpenter	.10
72	Mike Lieberthal	.12
73	Dean Palmer	.10
74	Jorge Fabregas	.10
75	Stan Javier	.10
76	Damion Easley	.10
77	David Cone	.20
78	Aaron Sele	.10
79	Antonio Alfonseca	.10
80	Bobby Jones	.10
81	David Justice	.25
82	Jeffrey Hammonds	.10
83	Doug Glanville	.10
84	Jason Dickson	.10
85	Brad Radke	.10
86	David Segui	.10
87	Greg Vaughn	.12
88	*Mike Cather*	.20
89	Alex Fernandez	.10
90	Billy Taylor	.10
91	Jason Schmidt	.10
92	*Mike DeJean*	.10
93	Domingo Cedeno	.10
94	Jeff Cirillo	.10
95	*Manny Aybar*	.25
96	Jaime Navarro	.10
97	Dennis Reyes	.10
98	Barry Larkin	.15
99	Troy O'Leary	.10
100	Alex Rodriguez	2.50
100p	Alex Rodriguez (overprinted PROMOTIONAL SAMPLE)	3.00
101	Pat Hentgen	.10
102	Bubba Trammell	.20
103	Glendon Rusch	.10
104	Kenny Lofton	.75
105	Craig Biggio	.20
106	Kelvim Escobar	.10
107	Mark Kotsay	.40
108	Rondell White	.20
109	Darren Oliver	.10

110	Jim Thome	.40
111	Rich Becker	.10
112	Chad Curtis	.10
113	Dave Hollins	.10
114	Bill Mueller	.10
115	Antone Williamson	.10
116	Tony Womack	.10
117	Randy Myers	.10
118	Rico Brogna	.10
119	Pat Watkins	.10
120	Eli Marrero	.10
121	Jay Bell	.10
122	Kevin Tapani	.10
123	*Todd Erdos*	.20
124	Neifi Perez	.10
125	Todd Hundley	.12
126	Jeff Abbott	.10
127	Todd Zeile	.10
128	Travis Fryman	.12
129	Sandy Alomar	.12
130	Fred McGriff	.20
131	Richard Hidalgo	.10
132	Scott Spiezio	.10
133	John Valentin	.10
134	Quilvio Veras	.10
135	Mike Lansing	.10
136	Paul Molitor	.50
137	Randy Johnson	.40
138	Harold Baines	.10
139	Doug Jones	.10
140	Abraham Nunez	.25
141	Alan Benes	.20
142	Matt Perisho	.10
143	Chris Clemons	.10
144	Andy Pettitte	.50
145	Jason Giambi	.10
146	Moises Alou	.20
147	*Chad Fox*	.25
148	Felix Martinez	.10
149	*Carlos Mendoza*	.25
150	Scott Rolen	1.50
151	*Jose Cabrera*	.20
152	Justin Thompson	.10
153	Ellis Burks	.10
154	Pokey Reese	.10
155	Bartolo Colon	.10
156	Ray Durham	.10
157	Ugueth Urbina	.10
158	Tom Goodwin	.10
159	*David Dellucci*	.50
160	Rod Beck	.10
161	Ramon Martinez	.10
162	Joe Carter	.12
163	Kevin Orie	.10
164	Trevor Hoffman	.10
165	Emil Brown	.10
166	Robb Nen	.10
167	Paul O'Neill	.20
168	Ryan Long	.10
169	Ray Lankford	.10
170	Ivan Rodriguez	.60
171	Rick Aguilera	.10
172	Deivi Cruz	.10
173	Ricky Bottalico	.10
174	Garret Anderson	.10
175	Jose Vizcaino	.10
176	Omar Vizquel	.10
177	Jeff Blauser	.10
178	Orlando Cabrera	.10
179	Russ Johnson	.10
180	Matt Stairs	.10
181	Will Cunnane	.10
182	Adam Riggs	.10
183	Matt Morris	.10
184	Mario Valdez	.10
185	Larry Sutton	.10
186	*Marc Pisciotta*	.10
187	Dan Wilson	.10
188	John Franco	.10
189	Darren Daulton	.10
190	Todd Helton	.75
191	Brady Anderson	.15
192	Ricardo Rincon	.10
193	Kevin Stocker	.10
194	Jose Valentin	.10
195	Ed Sprague	.10
196	Ryan McGuire	.10
197	*Scott Eyre*	.25
198	Steve Finley	.10
199	T.J. Mathews	.10
200	Mike Piazza	2.00
201	Mark Wohlers	.10
202	Brian Giles	.10
203	Eduardo Perez	.10
204	Shigetosi Hasegawa	.10
205	Mariano Rivera	.15
206	Jose Rosado	.10
207	Michael Coleman	.10
208	James Baldwin	.10
209	Russ Davis	.10
210	Billy Wagner	.12
211	Sammy Sosa	1.50
212	*Frank Catalanotto*	.25
213	Delino DeShields	.10
214	John Olerud	.15
215	Heath Murray	.10
216	Jose Vidro	.10
217	Jim Edmonds	.20
218	Shawon Dunston	.10
219	Homer Bush	.10
220	Midre Cummings	.10
221	Tony Saunders	.20
222	Jeromy Burnitz	.10
223	Enrique Wilson	.10
224	Chili Davis	.10
225	Jerry DiPoto	.10
226	Dante Powell	.10
227	Javier Lopez	.20
228	*Kevin Polcovich*	.20
229	Deion Sanders	.15
230	Jimmy Key	.10
231	Rusty Greer	.10
232	Reggie Jefferson	.10
233	Ron Coomer	.10
234	Bobby Higginson	.20
235	*Magglio Ordonez*	2.00
236	Miguel Tejada	.50
237	Rick Gorecki	.10
238	Charles Johnson	.10
239	Lance Johnson	.10
240	Derek Bell	.10
241	Will Clark	.20
242	Brady Raggio	.10
243	Orel Hershiser	.10
244	Vladimir Guerrero	1.25
245	John LeRoy	.10
246	Shawn Estes	.10
247	Brett Tomko	.10
248	Dave Nilsson	.10
249	Edgar Martinez	.10
250	Tony Gwynn	1.50
251	Mark Bellhorn	.10
252	Jed Hansen	.10
253	Butch Huskey	.10
254	Eric Young	.10
255	Vinny Castilla	.10
256	Hideki Irabu	.75
257	Mike Cameron	.10
258	Juan Encarnacion	.25
259	Brian Rose	.25
260	Brad Ausmus	.10
261	Dan Serafini	.10
262	Willie Greene	.10
263	Troy Percival	.10
264	*Jeff Wallace*	.20
265	Richie Sexson	.10
266	Rafael Palmeiro	.20
267	Brad Fullmer	.10
268	Jeremi Gonzalez	.10
269	*Rob Stanifer*	.25
270	Mickey Morandini	.10
271	Andruw Jones	1.50
272	Royce Clayton	.10
273	Takashi Kashiwada	.40
274	*Steve Woodard*	.25
275	Jose Cruz Jr.	.50
276	Keith Foulke	.10
277	Brad Rigby	.10
278	Tino Martinez	.20
279	Todd Jones	.10
280	John Wetteland	.10
281	Alex Gonzalez	.10
282	Ken Cloude	.25
283	Jose Guillen	.40
284	Danny Clyburn	.10
285	David Ortiz	.40
286	John Thomson	.10
287	Kevin Appier	.10
288	Ismael Valdes	.10
289	Gary DiSarcina	.10
290	Todd Dunwoody	.12
291	Wally Joyner	.10
292	Charles Nagy	.10
293	Jeff Shaw	.10
294	*Kevin Millwood*	2.50
295	*Rigo Beltran*	.20
296	Jeff Frye	.10
297	Oscar Henriquez	.10
298	Mike Thurman	.10
299	Garrett Stephenson	.10
300	Barry Bonds	.75
301	Roger Clemens (Smoke 'N Heat)	.50
302	David Cone (Smoke 'N Heat)	.15
303	Hideki Irabu (Smoke 'N Heat)	.40
304	Randy Johnson (Smoke 'N Heat)	.20
305	Greg Maddux (Smoke 'N Heat)	1.00
306	Pedro Martinez (Smoke 'N Heat)	.15
307	Mike Mussina (Smoke 'N Heat)	.30
308	Andy Pettitte (Smoke 'N Heat)	.25
309	Curt Schilling (Smoke 'N Heat)	.15
310	John Smoltz (Smoke 'N Heat)	.15
311	Roger Clemens (Golden Memories)	.50
312	Jose Cruz Jr. (Golden Memories)	.25
313	Nomar Garciaparra (Golden Memories)	1.00
314	Ken Griffey Jr (Golden Memories)	1.50
315	Tony Gwynn (Golden Memories)	.75
316	Hideki Irabu (Golden Memories)	.40
317	Randy Johnson (Golden Memories)	.20
318	Mark McGwire (Golden Memories)	2.00
319	Curt Schilling (Golden Memories)	.15
320	Larry Walker (Golden Memories)	.15
321	Jeff Bagwell (Tale of the Tape)	.60
322	Albert Belle (Tale of the Tape)	.40
323	Barry Bonds (Tale of the Tape)	.40
324	Jay Buhner (Tale of the Tape)	.15
325	Tony Clark (Tale of the Tape)	.20
326	Jose Cruz Jr. (Tale of the Tape)	.25
327	Andres Galarraga (Tale of the Tape)	.15
328	Juan Gonzalez (Tale of the Tape)	.75
329	Ken Griffey Jr. (Tale of the Tape)	1.50
330	Andruw Jones (Tale of the Tape)	.75
331	Tino Martinez (Tale of the Tape)	.15
332	Mark McGwire (Tale of the Tape)	2.00
333	Rafael Palmeiro (Tale of the Tape)	.15
334	Mike Piazza (Tale of the Tape)	1.00
335	Manny Ramirez (Tale of the Tape)	.50
336	Alex Rodriguez (Tale of the Tape)	1.25
337	Frank Thomas (Tale of the Tape)	.75
338	Jim Thome (Tale of the Tape)	.20
339	Mo Vaughn (Tale of the Tape)	.40
340	Larry Walker (Tale of the Tape)	.15
341	Checklist (Jose Cruz Jr.)	.25
342	Checklist (Ken Griffey Jr.)	1.00
343	Checklist (Derek Jeter)	.60
344	Checklist (Andruw Jones)	.50
345	Checklist (Chipper Jones)	.00
346	Checklist (Greg Maddux)	.60
347	Checklist (Mike Piazza)	.60
348	Checklist (Cal Ripken Jr.)	.75
349	Checklist (Alex Rodriguez)	.75
350	Checklist (Frank Thomas)	.50
351	Mo Vaughn	.75
352	Andres Galarraga	.25
353	Roberto Alomar	.50
354	Darin Erstad	.75
355	Albert Belle	.75
356	Matt Williams	.25
357	Darryl Kile	.10
358	Kenny Lofton	.75
359	Orel Hershiser	.10
360	Bob Abreu	.10
361	Chris Widger	.10
362	Glenallen Hill	.10
363	Chili Davis	.10
364	Kevin Brown	.15
365	Marquis Grissom	.12
366	Livan Hernandez	.10
367	Moises Alou	.20
368	Matt Lawton	.10
369	Rey Ordonez	.10
370	Kenny Rogers	.10
371	Lee Stevens	.10
372	Wade Boggs	.20
373	Luis Gonzalez	.10
374	Jeff Conine	.10
375	Esteban Loaiza	.10
376	Jose Canseco	.25
377	Henry Rodriguez	.10
378	Dave Burba	.10
379	Todd Hollandsworth	.10
380	Ron Gant	.20
381	Pedro Martinez	.40
382	Ryan Klesko	.25
383	Derrek Lee	.10
384	Doug Glanville	.10
385	David Wells	.10
386	Ken Caminiti	.20
387	Damon Hollins	.10
388	Manny Ramirez	1.00
389	Mike Mussina	.60
390	Jay Bell	.10
391	Mike Piazza	.40
392	Mike Lansing	.10
393	Mike Hampton	.10
394	Geoff Jenkins	.10
395	Jimmy Haynes	.10
396	Scott Servais	.10
397	Kent Mercker	.10
398	Jeff Kent	.10
399	Kevin Elster	.10
400	*Masato Yoshii*	.40
401	Jose Vizcaino	.10
402	Javier Martinez	.10
403	David Segui	.10
404	Tony Saunders	.10
405	Karim Garcia	.10
406	Armando Benitez	.10
407	Joe Randa	.10
408	Vic Darensbourg	.10
409	Sean Casey	.20
410	Eric Milton	.20
411	Trey Moore	.10
412	Mike Stanley	.10
413	Tom Gordon	.10
414	Hal Morris	.10
415	Braden Looper	.10
416	Mike Kelly	.10
417	John Smoltz	.12
418	Roger Cedeno	.10
419	Al Leiter	.20
420	Chuck Knoblauch	.30
421	Felix Rodriguez	.10
422	Bip Roberts	.10
423	Ken Hill	.10
424	Jermaine Allensworth	.10
425	Esteban Yan	.10
426	Scott Karl	.10
427	Sean Berry	.10
428	Rafael Medina	.10
429	Javier Vazquez	.10
430	Rickey Henderson	.20
431	*Adam Butler*	.10
432	Todd Stottlemyre	.10
433	Yamil Benitez	.10
434	Sterling Hitchcock	.10
435	Paul Sorrento	.10
436	Bobby Ayala	.10
437	Tim Raines	.10
438	Chris Hoiles	.10
439	Rod Beck	.10
440	Donnie Sadler	.10
441	Charles Johnson	.10
442	Russ Ortiz	.10
443	Pedro Astacio	.10
444	Wilson Alvarez	.10
445	Mike Blowers	.10
446	Todd Zeile	.10
447	Mel Rojas	.10
448	F.P. Santangelo	.10
449	Dmitri Young	.10
450	Brian Anderson	.10
451	Cecil Fielder	.12
452	Roberto Hernandez	.10
453	Todd Walker	.20
454	Tyler Green	.10
455	Jorge Posada	.10
456	Geronimo Berroa	.10
457	Jose Silva	.10
458	Bobby Bonilla	.15
459	Walt Weiss	.10
460	Darren Dreifort	.10
461	B.J. Surhoff	.10
462	Quinton McCracken	.10
463	Derek Lowe	.10
464	Jorge Fabregas	.10
465	Joey Hamilton	.10
466	Brian Jordan	.10
467	Allen Watson	.10
468	John Jaha	.10
469	Heathcliff Slocumb	.10
470	Gregg Jefferies	.10
471	Scott Brosius	.10
472	Chad Ogea	.10
473	A.J. Hinch	.20
474	Bobby Smith	.10
475	Brian Moehler	.10
476	DaRond Stovall	.10
477	Kevin Young	.10
478	Jeff Suppan	.10
479	Marty Cordova	.10
480	*John Halama*	.25
481	Bubba Trammell	.10
482	Mike Caruso	.10
483	Eric Karros	.20
484	Jamey Wright	.10
485	Mike Sweeney	.10
486	Aaron Sele	.10
487	Cliff Floyd	.10
488	Jeff Brantley	.10
489	Jim Leyritz	.10
490	Denny Neagle	.10
491	Travis Fryman	.10
492	Carlos Baerga	.10
493	Eddie Taubensee	.10
494	Darryl Strawberry	.15
495	Brian Johnson	.10
496	Randy Myers	.10
497	Jeff Blauser	.10
498	Jason Wood	.10
499	*Rolando Arrojo*	.40
500	Johnny Damon	.10
501	Jose Mercedes	.10
502	Tony Batista	.10
503	Mike Piazza	2.00
504	Hideo Nomo	.25
505	Chris Gomez	.10
506	*Jesus Sanchez*	.25
507	Al Martin	.10
508	Brian Edmondson	.10
509	Joe Girardi	.10
510	Shayne Bennett	.10
511	Joe Carter	.12
512	Dave Mlicki	.10
513	*Rich Butler*	.50
514	Dennis Eckersley	.10
515	Travis Lee	.75
516	John Mabry	.10
517	Jose Mesa	.10
518	Phil Nevin	.10
519	Raul Casanova	.10
520	Mike Fetters	.10
521	Gary Sheffield	.25
522	Terry Steinbach	.10
523	Steve Trachsel	.10
524	Josh Booty	.10
525	Darryl Hamilton	.10
526	Mark McLemore	.10
527	Kevin Stocker	.10
528	Bret Boone	.10
529	Shane Andrews	.10
530	Robb Nen	.10
531	Carl Everett	.10
532	LaTroy Hawkins	.10
533	Fernando Vina	.10
534	Michael Tucker	.10
535	Mark Langston	.10
536	Mickey Mantle	5.00
537	Bernard Gilkey	.10
538	Francisco Cordova	.10
539	Mike Bordick	.10
540	Fred McGriff	.20
541	Cliff Politte	.10
542	Jason Varitek	.10
543	Shawon Dunston	.10
544	Brian Meadows	.10
545	Pat Meares	.10
546	Carlos Perez	.10
547	Desi Relaford	.10
548	Antonio Osuna	.10
549	Devon White	.10
550	Sean Runyan	.10
551	Mickey Morandini	.10
552	Dave Martinez	.10
553	Jeff Fassero	.10
554	*Ryan Jackson*	.25
555	Stan Javier	.10
556	Jaime Navarro	.10
557	Jose Offerman	.10
558	*Mike Lowell*	.40
559	Darrin Fletcher	.10
560	Mark Lewis	.10
561	Dante Bichette	.25
562	Chuck Finley	.10
563	Kerry Wood	1.00
564	Andy Benes	.10
565	Freddy Garcia	.10
566	Tom Glavine	.20
567	Jon Nunnally	.10
568	Miguel Cairo	.10
569	Shane Reynolds	.10
570	Roberto Kelly	.10
571	Checklist (Jose Cruz Jr.)	.25
572	Checklist (Ken Griffey Jr.)	1.50
573	Checklist (Mark McGwire)	1.50
574	Checklist (Cal Ripken Jr.)	1.00
575	Checklist (Frank Thomas)	.50
576	Jeff Bagwell (Unforgettable Moments)	1.50
577	Barry Bonds (Unforgettable Moments)	1.00
578	Tony Clark (Unforgettable Moments)	.75
579	Roger Clemens (Unforgettable Moments)	1.50
580	Jose Cruz Jr. (Unforgettable Moments)	.50
581	Nomar Garciaparra (Unforgettable Moments)	2.50
582	Juan Gonzalez (Unforgettable Moments)	2.00
583	Ben Grieve (Unforgettable Moments)	1.50
584	Ken Griffey Jr. (Unforgettable Moments)	4.00
585	Tony Gwynn (Unforgettable Moments)	2.00
586	Derek Jeter (Unforgettable Moments)	2.50
587	Randy Johnson (Unforgettable Moments)	.75
588	Chipper Jones (Unforgettable Moments)	2.50
589	Greg Maddux (Unforgettable Moments)	2.50
590	Mark McGwire (Unforgettable Moments)	5.00
591	Andy Pettitte (Unforgettable Moments)	.60
592	Paul Molitor (Unforgettable Moments)	.50
593	Cal Ripken Jr. (Unforgettable Moments)	3.00
594	Alex Rodriguez (Unforgettable Moments)	2.50
595	Scott Rolen (Unforgettable Moments)	1.25
596	Curt Schilling (Unforgettable Moments)	.40
597	Frank Thomas (Unforgettable Moments)	1.50
598	Jim Thome (Unforgettable Moments)	.75
599	Larry Walker (Unforgettable Moments)	.50
600	Bernie Williams (Unforgettable Moments)	.75

1998 Fleer Decade of Excellence

Decade of Excellence inserts were found in one per 72 Series 1 hobby packs of Fleer Tradition. The 12-card set features 1988 season photos in Fleer's 1988 card design. The set includes only those current players who have been in baseball for ten years or more. The use of blue and red metallic foil stripes in the background differentiates a scarcer (1:720 hobby packs) "Rare Traditions" parallel to the insert.

		MT
Complete Set (12):		100.00
Common Player:		4.00
Rare Traditions: 5X		
1	Roberto Alomar	6.00
2	Barry Bonds	10.00
3	Roger Clemens	12.00
4	David Cone	4.00
5	Andres Galarraga	4.00
6	Mark Grace	5.00
7	Tony Gwynn	15.00
8	Randy Johnson	6.00
9	Greg Maddux	24.00
10	Mark McGwire	40.00
11	Paul O'Neill	4.00
12	Cal Ripken Jr.	30.00

1998 Fleer Diamond Ink

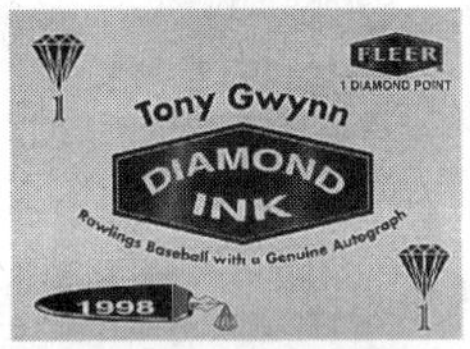

These one-per-pack inserts offer collectors a chance to acquire genuine autographed baseballs. Issued in denominations of 1, 5 and 10 points, the cards had to be accumulated to a total of 500 points of the same player to be redeemed for an autographed ball of that player. Cards are the standard 3-1/2" x 2-1/2" and are printed in black and purple on front and black and yellow on back. The point value of each card is embossed at center to prevent counterfeiting. The rules of the exchange program are printed on back. The deadline for redemption was Dec. 31, 1998. Values shown are for 1-pt. cards, and the unnumbered players in the series are listed alphabetically.

		MT
Complete Set, 1 pt. (11):		1.25
Common Player, 1 pt.:		.05
5-pt. cards: 5X		
10-pt. cards: 12X		
(1)	Jay Buhner	.05
(2)	Roger Clemens	.10
(3)	Jose Cruz Jr.	.15
(4)	Nomar Garciaparra	.10
(5)	Tony Gwynn	.10
(6)	Roberto Hernandez	.05
(7)	Greg Maddux	.10
(8)	Cal Ripken Jr.	.20
(9)	Alex Rodriguez	.20
(10)	Scott Rolen	.10
(11)	Tony Womack	.05

1998 Fleer Diamond Standouts

Diamond Standouts were inserted into Series I packs at a rate of one per 12. The 20-card insert set features players over a diamond design silver foil background.

		MT
Complete Set (20):		50.00
Common Player:		1.50
1	Jeff Bagwell	5.00
2	Barry Bonds	2.50
3	Roger Clemens	5.00
4	Jose Cruz Jr.	1.50
5	Andres Galarraga	1.50
6	Nomar Garciaparra	8.00
7	Juan Gonzalez	6.00
8	Ken Griffey Jr.	15.00
9	Derek Jeter	7.50
10	Randy Johnson	2.00
11	Chipper Jones	8.00
12	Kenny Lofton	2.00
13	Greg Maddux	6.00
14	Pedro Martinez	1.50
15	Mark McGwire	15.00
16	Mike Piazza	8.00
17	Alex Rodriguez	10.00
18	Curt Schilling	1.50
19	Frank Thomas	5.00
20	Larry Walker	2.00

1998 Fleer Diamond Tribute

This 10-card insert was exclusive to Series II packs and seeded one per 300 packs. Cards were printed on a leather-like laminated stock and had silver holofoil stamping.

		MT
Complete Set (10):		400.00
Common Player:		30.00
DT1	Jeff Bagwell	35.00
DT2	Roger Clemens	35.00
DT3	Nomar Garciaparra	50.00
DT4	Juan Gonzalez	40.00
DT5	Ken Griffey Jr.	75.00
DT6	Mark McGwire	75.00
DT7	Mike Piazza	50.00
DT8	Cal Ripken Jr.	60.00
DT9	Alex Rodriguez	60.00
DT10	Frank Thomas	30.00

1998 Fleer In the Clutch

This Series 2 insert features stars who can stand up to pressure of big league ball. Fronts have embossed action photos on a prismatic metallic foil background. Backs have a portrait photo and a few words about the player. Stated insertion rate for the inserts was one per 20 packs on average.

		MT
Complete Set (15):		75.00
Common Player:		1.50
IC1	Jeff Bagwell	5.00
IC2	Barry Bonds	3.00
IC3	Roger Clemens	5.00
IC4	Jose Cruz Jr.	1.50
IC5	Nomar Garciaparra	8.00
IC6	Juan Gonzalez	6.00
IC7	Ken Griffey Jr.	15.00
IC8	Tony Gwynn	6.00
IC9	Derek Jeter	6.00
IC10	Chipper Jones	8.00
IC11	Greg Maddux	6.00
IC12	Mark McGwire	15.00
IC13	Mike Piazza	8.00
IC14	Frank Thomas	5.00
IC15	Larry Walker	1.50

1998 Fleer Lumber Company

This 15-card set was exclusive to Series I retail packs and inserted one per 36 packs. It included power hitters and featured the insert name in large letters across the top.

		MT
Complete Set (15):		100.00
Common Player:		1.50
Inserted 1:36 retail		
1	Jeff Bagwell	6.00
2	Barry Bonds	3.50
3	Jose Cruz Jr.	1.50
4	Nomar Garciaparra	10.00
5	Juan Gonzalez	7.50
6	Ken Griffey Jr.	17.50
7	Tony Gwynn	7.50
8	Chipper Jones	10.00
9	Tino Martinez	1.50
10	Mark McGwire	17.50
11	Mike Piazza	10.00
12	Cal Ripken Jr.	12.50
13	Alex Rodriguez	12.50
14	Frank Thomas	5.00
15	Larry Walker	2.00

1998 Fleer Mickey Mantle Monumental Moments

This 10-card insert honors Hall of Famer Mickey Mantle's legendary career and was seeded one per 68 packs of Series 2. Fleer/SkyBox worked closely with Mantle's family with each photo in the set personally selected by them. A gold-enhanced version was issued with each card serially numbered to 51.

		MT
Complete Set (10):		150.00
Common Card:		20.00
Inserted 1:68		
Golds (51 sets): 10X		
1	Armed and Dangerous	20.00
2	Getting Ready in Spring Training	20.00
3	Mantle and Rizzuto Celebrate	20.00
4	Posed for Action	20.00
5	Signed, Sealed and Ready to Deliver	20.00
6	Triple Crown 1956 Season	20.00
7	Number 7 . . .	20.00
8	Mantle's Powerful Swing . . .	20.00
9	Old-Timers Day Introduction	20.00
10	Portrait of Determination	20.00

1998 Fleer Promising Forecast

Potential future stars are showcased in this Series 2 insert. Both front and back have a background of a colorful weather map. Fronts have a glossy player action photo on a matte-finish background. Backs are all-glossy and have a second photo and a few words about the player's potential. Average odds of pulling a Promising Forecast card were stated as one per 12 packs.

		MT
Complete Set (20):		10.00
Common Player:		.25
Inserted 1:12		
PF1	Rolando Arrojo	.60
PF2	Sean Casey	1.00
PF3	Brad Fullmer	1.00
PF4	Karim Garcia	.25
PF5	Ben Grieve	2.00
PF6	Todd Helton	1.50
PF7	Richard Hidalgo	.25
PF8	A.J. Hinch	.25
PF9	Paul Konerko	.75
PF10	Mark Kotsay	.50
PF11	Derrek Lee	.25
PF12	Travis Lee	1.50
PF13	Eric Milton	.25
PF14	Magglio Ordonez	.75
PF15	David Ortiz	.75
PF16	Brian Rose	.25
PF17	Miguel Tejada	.75
PF18	Jason Varitek	.25
PF19	Enrique Wilson	.25
PF20	Kerry Wood	1.25

1998 Fleer Rookie Sensations

Rookie Sensations included 20 gray-bordered cards of the 1997 most promising players who were eligible for the Rookie of the Year award. Each card contained a multi-colored background and was inserted one per 18 packs.

		MT
Complete Set (20):		45.00
Common Player:		2.00
Inserted 1:18		
1	Mike Cameron	2.00
2	Jose Cruz Jr.	2.00
3	Jason Dickson	2.00
4	Kelvim Escobar	2.00
5	Nomar Garciaparra	12.00
6	Ben Grieve	5.00
7	Vladimir Guerrero	5.00
8	Wilton Guerrero	2.00
9	Jose Guillen	3.00
10	Todd Helton	4.00
11	Livan Hernandez	2.00
12	Hideki Irabu	4.00
13	Andruw Jones	6.00
14	Matt Morris	2.00
15	Magglio Ordonez	2.50
16	Neifi Perez	2.00
17	Scott Rolen	8.00
18	Fernando Tatis	4.00
19	Brett Tomko	2.00
20	Jaret Wright	4.00

1998 Fleer The Power Game

Pitchers and hitters are pictured over a purple metallic background with UV coating in this 20-card insert. Power Game inserts were exclusive to Series I and seeded one per 36 packs.

		MT
Complete Set (20):		130.00
Common Player:		2.25
Inserted 1:36		
1	Jeff Bagwell	9.00
2	Albert Belle	5.00
3	Barry Bonds	6.00
4	Tony Clark	3.50
5	Roger Clemens	7.50
6	Jose Cruz Jr.	2.25
7	Andres Galarraga	2.25

8	Nomar Garciaparra	12.50
9	Juan Gonzalez	12.50
10	Ken Griffey Jr.	25.00
11	Randy Johnson	4.00
12	Greg Maddux	12.50
13	Pedro Martinez	2.25
14	Tino Martinez	2.25
15	Mark McGwire	25.00
16	Mike Piazza	15.00
17	Curt Schilling	2.25
18	Frank Thomas	7.50
19	Jim Thome	3.50
20	Larry Walker	3.00

1998 Fleer Vintage '63

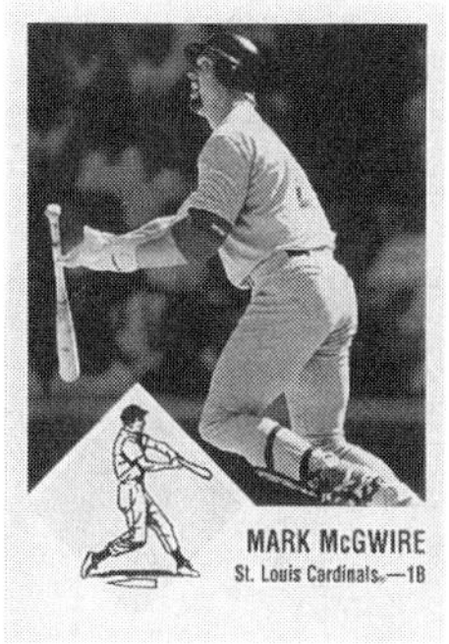

Vintage featured 126 different players, with 63 in Series I and 63 in Series II, on the design of 1963 Fleer cards. The insert commemorated the 35th anniversary of Fleer and was seeded one per hobby pack. In addition, Series II featured Mickey Mantle on card No. 67, which completed the original 1963 Fleer set that ended at card No. 66 and wasn't able to include Mantle for licensing reasons. The Mantle card was printed in vintage looking stock and was purposely made to look and feel like the originals. Fleer also printed a Classic parallel version to this insert that contained gold foil on the front and was sequentially numbered to 63 with a "C" prefix on the back.

		MT
Complete Set (126):		35.00
Complete Series 1 (63):		20.00
Complete Series 2 (63):		15.00
Common Player:		.25
Classics (63 sets): 35-50X		
1	Jason Dickson	.25
2	Tim Salmon	.40
3	Andruw Jones	1.00
4	Chipper Jones	1.50
5	Kenny Lofton	.75
6	Greg Maddux	1.50
7	Rafael Palmeiro	.30
8	Cal Ripken Jr.	2.00
9	Nomar Garciaparra	1.50
10	Mark Grace	.40
11	Sammy Sosa	1.50
12	Frank Thomas	1.50
13	Deion Sanders	.30
14	Sandy Alomar	.25
15	David Justice	.40
16	Jim Thome	.50
17	Matt Williams	.30
18	Jaret Wright	1.00
19	Vinny Castilla	.25
20	Andres Galarraga	.40
21	Todd Helton	.75
22	Larry Walker	.40
23	Tony Clark	.40
24	Moises Alou	.25
25	Kevin Brown	.25
26	Charles Johnson	.25
27	Edgar Renteria	.25
28	Gary Sheffield	.40
29	Jeff Bagwell	1.00
30	Craig Biggio	.25
31	Raul Mondesi	.25
32	Mike Piazza	1.50
33	Chuck Knoblauch	.40
34	Paul Molitor	.50
35	Vladimir Guerrero	1.00
36	Pedro Martinez	.40
37	Todd Hundley	.25
38	Derek Jeter	1.50
39	Tino Martinez	.35
40	Paul O'Neill	.25
41	Andy Pettitte	.35
42	Mariano Rivera	.25
43	Bernie Williams	.35
44	Ben Grieve	1.00
45	Scott Rolen	1.00
46	Curt Schilling	.25
47	Jason Kendall	.25
48	Tony Womack	.25
49	Ray Lankford	.25
50	Mark McGwire	4.00
51	Matt Morris	.25
52	Tony Gwynn	1.25
53	Barry Bonds	.75
54	Jay Buhner	.25
55	Ken Griffey Jr.	4.00
56	Randy Johnson	.40
57	Edgar Martinez	.25
58	Alex Rodriguez	2.00
59	Juan Gonzalez	1.25
60	Rusty Greer	.25
61	Ivan Rodriguez	.75
62	Roger Clemens	1.25
63	Jose Cruz Jr.	.35
	Checklist (Vintage '63)	.25
64	Darin Erstad	.75
65	Jay Bell	.25
66	Andy Benes	.25
67	Mickey Mantle	5.00
68	Travis Lee	1.00
69	Matt Williams	.40
70	Andres Galarraga	.35
71	Tom Glavine	.40
72	Ryan Klesko	.40
73	Denny Neagle	.25
74	John Smoltz	.25
75	Roberto Alomar	.50
76	Joe Carter	.25
77	Mike Mussina	.50
78	B.J. Surhoff	.25
79	Dennis Eckersley	.25
80	Pedro Martinez	.40
81	Mo Vaughn	.60
82	Jeff Blauser	.25
83	Henry Rodriguez	.25
84	Albert Belle	.60
85	Sean Casey	.50
86	Travis Fryman	.25
87	Kenny Lofton	.60
88	Darryl Kile	.25
89	Mike Lansing	.25
90	Bobby Bonilla	.25
91	Cliff Floyd	.25
92	Livan Hernandez	.25
93	Derrek Lee	.25
94	Moises Alou	.25
95	Shane Reynolds	.25
96	Jeff Conine	.25
97	Johnny Damon	.25
98	Eric Karros	.25
99	Hideo Nomo	.25
100	Marquis Grissom	.25
101	Matt Lawton	.25
102	Todd Walker	.25
103	Carlos Baerga	.25
104	Bernard Gilkey	.25
105	Rey Ordonez	.25
106	Chili Davis	.25
107	Jason Giambi	.40
108	Chuck Knoblauch	.40
109	Tim Raines	.25
110	Rickey Henderson	.30
111	Bob Abreu	.25
112	Doug Glanville	.25
113	Gregg Jefferies	.25
114	Al Martin	.25
115	Kevin Young	.25
116	Ron Gant	.25
117	Kevin Brown	.25
118	Ken Caminiti	.25
119	Joey Hamilton	.25
120	Jeff Kent	.25
121	Wade Boggs	.50
122	Quinton McCracken	.25
123	Fred McGriff	.40
124	Paul Sorrento	.25
125	Jose Canseco	.40
126	Randy Myers	.25

1998 Fleer Vintage '63 Classic

Vintage '63 Classic paralleled all 126 Vintage '63 inserts throughout Series 1 and 2, plus the checklist. These cards feature gold-foil stamping on front, specifically around the diamond in the lower-left corner, and are sequentially numbered to 63 sets. Cards have a "C" suffix to the card number.

	MT
Complete Set (127):	3500.
Common Player:	10.00
Stars: 40x to 70x	
Young Stars/RCs: 30x to 60x	
(See 1998 Fleer Vintage '63 for checklist and base card values.)	

Player names in *Italic* type indicate a rookie card.

1998 Fleer Zone

Inserted in one per 288 packs of Series I Fleer Tradition, Zone featured 15 top players printed on rainbow foil and etching.

		MT
Complete Set (15):		350.00
Common Player:		10.00
Inserted 1:288		
1	Jeff Bagwell	12.50
2	Barry Bonds	12.50
3	Roger Clemens	20.00
4	Jose Cruz Jr.	10.00
5	Nomar Garciaparra	30.00
6	Juan Gonzalez	25.00
7	Ken Griffey Jr.	60.00
8	Tony Gwynn	25.00
9	Chipper Jones	30.00
10	Greg Maddux	30.00
11	Mark McGwire	60.00
12	Mike Piazza	35.00
13	Alex Rodriguez	45.00
14	Frank Thomas	17.50
15	Larry Walker	10.00

1998 Fleer Update

Fleer produced its first Update set since 1994 with this 100-card boxed set. It arrived soon after the conclusion of the 1998 World Series and focused on rookies like J.D. Drew, Rich Croushore, Ryan Bradley, John Rocker, Mike Frank and Benj Sampson, who made their major league debut in September and have not yet had a rookie card yet. The set had 70 rookies, including 15 making their major league debut, 20 traded players and free agents. There was one subset called Season's Highlights that focused on feats like Mark McGwire's 70th home run, Sammy Sosa's single-month home run record and Kerry Wood's 20 strikeout performance.

		MT
Complete Set (100):		50.00
Common Player:		.10
U1	Mark McGwire ("Season Highlights" Subset)	3.00
U2	Sammy Sosa ("Season Highlights" Subset)	1.50
U3	Roger Clemens ("Season Highlights" Subset)	.75
U4	Barry Bonds ("Season Highlights" Subset)	.50
U5	Kerry Wood ("Season Highlights" Subset)	.75
U6	Paul Molitor ("Season Highlights" Subset)	.25
U7	Ken Griffey Jr. ("Season Highlights" Subset)	2.50
U8	Cal Ripken Jr. ("Season Highlights" Subset)	1.50
U9	David Wells ("Season Highlights" Subset)	.10
U10	Alex Rodriguez ("Season Highlights" Subset)	1.00
U11	*Angel Pena*	1.00
U12	Bruce Chen	.10
U13	Craig Wilson	.10
U14	*Orlando Hernandez*	5.00
U15	Aramis Ramirez	.25
U16	Aaron Boone	.10
U17	Bob Henley	.10
U18	Juan Guzman	.10
U19	Darryl Hamilton	.10
U20	Jay Payton	.10
U21	*Jeremy Powell*	.25
U22	Ben Davis	.10
U23	Preston Wilson	.10
U24	*Jim Parque*	1.50
U25	*Odalis Perez*	2.00
U26	Ron Belliard	.10
U27	Royce Clayton	.10
U28	George Lombard	.25
U29	Tony Phillips	.10
U30	*Fernando Seguignol*	4.00
U31	*Armando Rios*	.50
U32	*Jerry Hairston*	1.00
U33	*Justin Baughman*	.75
U34	Seth Greisinger	.10
U35	Alex Gonzalez	.10
U36	Michael Barrett	.50
U37	Carlos Beltran	.50
U38	Ellis Burks	.10
U39	Jose Jimenez	.40
U40	Carlos Guillen	.10
U41	Marlon Anderson	.10
U42	Scott Elarton	.10
U43	Glenallen Hill	.10
U44	Shane Monahan	.10
U45	Dennis Martinez	.10
U46	*Carlos Febles*	.20
U47	Carlos Perez	.10
U48	Wilton Guerrero	.10
U49	Randy Johnson	.10
U50	*Brian Simmons*	1.00
U51	Carlton Loewer	.10
U52	*Mark DeRosa*	.25
U53	*Tim Young*	.25
U54	Gary Gaetti	.10
U55	Eric Chavez	1.00
U56	Carl Pavano	.10
U57	Mike Stanley	.10
U58	Todd Stottlemyre	.10
U59	*Gabe Kapler*	6.00
U60	*Mike Jerzembeck*	.25
U61	*Mitch Meluskey*	2.00
U62	Bill Pulsipher	.10
U63	Derrick Gibson	.10
U64	*John Rocker*	1.50
U65	Calvin Pickering	.10
U66	Blake Stein	.10
U67	Fernando Tatis	.15
U68	Gabe Alvarez	.10
U69	Jeffrey Hammonds	.10
U70	Adrian Beltre	.50
U71	*Ryan Bradley*	2.00
U72	*Edgar Clemente*	.20
U73	*Rick Croushore*	.20
U74	Matt Clement	.25
U75	Dermal Brown	.10
U76	Paul Bako	.10
U77	*Placido Polanco*	.75
U78	Jay Tessmer	.10
U79	Jarrod Washburn	.10
U80	Kevin Witt	.10
U81	Mike Metcalfe	.10
U82	Daryle Ward	.10
U83	*Benj Sampson*	.20
U84	*Mike Kinkade*	.50
U85	Randy Winn	.10
U86	Jeff Shaw	.10
U87	*Troy Glaus*	6.00
U88	Hideo Nomo	.15
U89	Mark Grudzielanek	.10
U90	*Mike Frank*	1.50
U91	*Bobby Howry*	.50
U92	*Ryan Minor*	3.00
U93	*Corey Koskie*	1.00
U94	*Matt Anderson*	2.00
U95	Joe Carter	.10
U96	Paul Konerko	.15
U97	Sidney Ponson	.10
U98	*Jeremy Giambi*	4.00
U99	*Jeff Kubenka*	.20
U100	*J.D. Drew*	25.00

1998 Fleer Diamond Skills Commemorative Sheet

In conjunction with its sponsorship of the Diamond Skills program, Fleer and its 2,500 direct dealers distributed this eight-player sheet to 7-14 year olds participating in the event. Participants could get a sheet by redeeming Fleer wrappers at a local card store. The 10" x 9" sheet features full size Fleer Tradition card reproductions. At top is a list of 1997 Diamond Skills winners.

		MT
Complete Sheet:		8.00
2	Derek Jeter	
8	Cal Ripken Jr.	
21	Roger Clemens	
25	Mark McGwire	
50	Jeff Bagwell	
150	Scott Rolen	
200	Mike Piazza	
217	Jim Edmonds	

1998 Fleer Mantle & Sons

As part of its participation in SportsFest in May, 1998, Fleer issued a promotional card featuring a vintage color photo of Mickey Mantle and his sons, David and Danny. The back of the card announced Fleer's first-ever inclusion of Mickey Mantle cards in some of its forthcoming releases.

	MT
Mickey Mantle, Danny Mantle, David Mantle	4.00

1998 Fleer Mickey Mantle promo postcard

This 4-1/4" x 5-1/2" color postcard was sent to Fleer dealers to announce a Mickey Mantle commemorative series in its Series 2 product. The address side has the Fleer Tradition logo in black, blue and red. The picture side has a color photo of one of the Mantle cards to be issued in the format of the 1963 Fleer issue. Cards are individually serial numbered within an edition of 3,500.

	MT
Mickey Mantle	15.00

1998 Fleer National Convention Commemorative Set

In conjunction with its participation at the 19th National Sports Collectors Convention in Chicago in Aug., 1998, Fleer distributed this commemorative set to persons purchasing VIP admission packages. The set includes a specially numbered (NC1) Fleer Tradition Mickey Mantle card, a card picturing Mick with his sons, one of seven large-format (3-1/2" x 5") cards reproducing Mantle Monumental Moments inserts, and an unnumbered header card. The Monumental Moments reproductions are printed on a pinstriped-sky background.

		MT
Complete Set (8):		60.00
Common Card:		10.00
NC1	Mickey Mantle (Fleer Tradition)	10.00
NC2	Mickey Mantle (with sons)	10.00
NC3	Mickey Mantle (Monumental Moments - accepting trophy)	10.00
NC4	Mickey Mantle (Monumental Moments - making a throw)	10.00
NC5	Mickey Mantle (Monumental Moments - in sliding pit)	10.00
NC6	Mickey Mantle (Monumental Moments - batting)	10.00
NC7	Mickey Mantle (Monumental Moments - number retired)	10.00
	Header card	.50

1999 Fleer

Released as a single series in 10-card packs with a suggested retail price of $1.59, the base set consists of 600 cards, including 10 checklists and a 15-card Franchise Futures subset. Cards are UV coated, with borderless photos and gold-foil graphics. Backs have personal bio-information along with year-by-year career stats and a small photo. There are two parallels, Starting Nine, which are hobby-exclusive, numbered to nine sets with blue foil stamping and Warning Track. Found exclusively in retail packs, Warning Tracks can be identified by red foil stamping and a Warning Track logo.

		MT
Complete Set (600):		60.00
Common Player:		.10
Wax Box:		40.00
1	Mark McGwire	4.00
2	Sammy Sosa	2.50
3	Ken Griffey Jr.	3.00
4	Kerry Wood	.75
5	Derek Jeter	2.00
6	Stan Musial	4.00
7	J.D. Drew	1.50
7p	J.D. Drew (overprinted PROMOTIONAL SAMPLE)	3.00
8	Cal Ripken Jr.	2.50
9	Alex Rodriguez	2.00
10	Travis Lee	.75
11	Andres Galarraga	.50
12	Nomar Garciaparra	2.00
13	Albert Belle	.75
14	Barry Larkin	.15
15	Dante Bichette	.20
16	Tony Clark	.40
17	Moises Alou	.20
18	Rafael Palmeiro	.25
19	Raul Mondesi	.25
20	Vladimir Guerrero	1.00
21	John Olerud	.20
22	Bernie Williams	.50
23	Ben Grieve	.75
24	Scott Rolen	.75
25	Jeromy Burnitz	.10
26	Ken Caminiti	.20
27	Barry Bonds	.75
28	Todd Helton	.50
29	Juan Gonzalez	1.50
30	Roger Clemens	1.25
31	Andruw Jones	.75
32	Mo Vaughn	.75
33	Larry Walker	.40
34	Frank Thomas	1.00
35	Manny Ramirez	1.00
36	Randy Johnson	.50
37	Vinny Castilla	.10
38	Juan Encarnacion	.10
39	Jeff Bagwell	.75
40	Gary Sheffield	.25
41	Mike Piazza	2.00
42	Richie Sexson	.10
43	Tony Gwynn	1.50
44	Chipper Jones	1.50
45	Jim Thome	.50
46	Craig Biggio	.30
47	Carlos Delgado	.40
48	Greg Vaughn	.20
49	Greg Maddux	2.00
50	Troy Glaus	.75
51	Roberto Alomar	.50
52	Dennis Eckersley	.10
53	Mike Caruso	.10
54	Bruce Chen	.10
55	Aaron Boone	.10
56	Bartolo Colon	.10
57	Derrick Gibson	.10
58	Brian Anderson	.10
59	Gabe Alvarez	.10
60	Todd Dunwoody	.10
61	Rod Beck	.10
62	Derek Bell	.10
63	Francisco Cordova	.10
64	Johnny Damon	.10
65	Adrian Beltre	.10
66	Garret Anderson	.10
67	Armando Benitez	.10
68	Edgardo Alfonzo	.10
69	Ryan Bradley	.10
70	Eric Chavez	1.00
71	Bobby Abreu	.10
72	Andy Ashby	.10
73	Ellis Burks	.10
74	Jeff Cirillo	.10
75	Jay Buhner	.15
76	Ron Gant	.20
77	Rolando Arrojo	.25
78	Will Clark	.40
79	Chris Carpenter	.10
80	Jim Edmonds	.10
81	Tony Batista	.10
82	Shane Andrews	.10
83	Mark DeRosa	.10
84	Brady Anderson	.10
85	Tony Gordon	.10
86	Brant Brown	.10
87	Ray Durham	.10
88	Ron Coomer	.10
89	Bret Boone	.10
90	Travis Fryman	.10
91	Darryl Kile	.10
92	Paul Bako	.10
93	Cliff Floyd	.10
94	Scott Elarton	.10
95	Jeremy Giambi	.10
96	Darren Dreifort	.10
97	Marquis Grissom	.10
98	Marty Cordova	.10
99	Fernando Seguignol	.25
100	Orlando Hernandez	1.00
101	Jose Cruz Jr.	.50
102	Jason Giambi	.10
103	Damion Easley	.10
104	Freddy Garcia	.10
105	Marlon Anderson	.10
106	Kevin Brown	.20
107	Joe Carter	.20
108	Russ Davis	.10
109	Brian Jordan	.10
110	Wade Boggs	.40
111	Tom Goodwin	.10
112	Scott Brosius	.10
113	Darin Erstad	.75
114	Jay Bell	.10
115	Tom Glavine	.25
116	Pedro Martinez	.50
117	Mark Grace	.25
118	Russ Ortiz	.10
119	Magglio Ordonez	.20
120	Sean Casey	.25
121	*Rafael Roque*	.25
122	Brian Giles	.10
123	Mike Lansing	.10
124	David Cone	.25
125	Alex Gonzalez	.10
126	Carl Everett	.10
127	Jeff King	.10
128	Charles Johnson	.10
129	Geoff Jenkins	.10
130	Corey Koskie	.10
131	Brad Fullmer	.25
132	Al Leiter	.20
133	Rickey Henderson	.25
134	Rico Brogna	.10
135	Jose Guillen	.25
136	Matt Clement	.20
137	Carlos Guillen	.10
138	Orel Hershiser	.10
139	Ray Lankford	.10
140	Miguel Cairo	.10
141	Chuck Finley	.10
142	Rusty Greer	.10
143	Kelvim Escobar	.10
144	Ryan Klesko	.25
145	Andy Benes	.20
146	Eric Davis	.10
147	David Wells	.10
148	Trot Nixon	.25
149	Jose Hernandez	.10
150	Mark Johnson	.10
151	Mike Frank	.10
152	Joey Hamilton	.10
153	David Justice	.30
154	Mike Mussina	.50
155	Neifi Perez	.10
156	Luis Gonzalez	.10
157	Livan Hernandez	.10
158	Dermal Brown	.10
159	Jose Lima	.10
160	Eric Karros	.20
161	Ronnie Belliard	.10
162	Matt Lawton	.10
163	Dustin Hermanson	.10
164	Brian McRae	.10
165	Mike Kinkade	.10
166	A.J. Hinch	.10
167	Doug Glanville	.10
168	Hideo Nomo	.20
169	Jason Kendall	.10
170	Steve Finley	.10
171	Jeff Kent	.10
172	Ben Davis	.10
173	Edgar Martinez	.10
174	Eli Marrero	.10
175	Quinton McCracken	.10
176	Rick Helling	.10
177	Tom Evans	.10
178	Carl Pavano	.10
179	Todd Greene	.10
180	Omar Daal	.10
181	George Lombard	.25
182	Ryan Minor	.40
183	Troy O'Leary	.10
184	Robb Nen	.10
185	Mickey Morandini	.10
186	Robin Ventura	.20
187	Pete Harnisch	.10
188	Kenny Lofton	.60
189	Eric Milton	.10
190	Bobby Higginson	.10
191	Jamie Moyer	.10
192	Mark Kotsay	.25
193	Shane Reynolds	.10
194	Carlos Febles	.10
195	Jeff Kubenka	.10
196	Chuck Knoblauch	.40
197	Kenny Rogers	.10
198	Bill Mueller	.10
199	Shane Monahan	.10
200	Matt Morris	.10
201	Fred McGriff	.30
202	Ivan Rodriguez	.75
203	Kevin Witt	.10
204	Troy Percival	.10
205	David Dellucci	.10
206	Kevin Millwood	.50
207	Jerry Hairston	.50
208	Mike Stanley	.10
209	Henry Rodriguez	.10
210	Trevor Hoffman	.10
211	Craig Wilson	.10
212	Reggie Sanders	.10
213	Carlton Loewer	.10
214	Omar Vizquel	.10
215	Gabe Kapler	1.00
216	Derrek Lee	.10
217	Billy Wagner	.10
218	Dean Palmer	.10
219	Chan Ho Park	.40
220	Fernando Vina	.10
221	Roy Halladay	.50
222	Paul Molitor	.50
223	Ugueth Urbina	.10
224	Rey Ordonez	.10
225	Ricky Ledee	.25
226	Scott Spiezio	.10
227	Wendell Magee Jr.	.10
228	Aramis Ramirez	.10
229	Brian Simmons	.10
230	Fernando Tatis	.10
231	Bobby Smith	.10
232	Aaron Sele	.10
233	Shawn Green	.10
234	Mariano Rivera	.25
235	Tim Salmon	.40
236	Andy Fox	.10
237	Denny Neagle	.10
238	John Valentin	.10
239	Kevin Tapani	.10
240	Paul Konerko	.25
241	Robert Fick	.10
242	Edgar Renteria	.10
243	Brett Tomko	.10
244	Daryle Ward	.10
245	Carlos Beltran	.10
246	Angel Pena	.10
247	Steve Woodard	.10
248	David Ortiz	.10
249	Justin Thompson	.10
250	Rondell White	.25
251	Jaret Wright	.50
252	Ed Sprague	.10
253	Jay Payton	.10
254	Mike Lowell	.25
255	Orlando Cabrera	.10
256	Jason Schmidt	.10
257	David Segui	.10
258	Paul Sorrento	.10
259	John Wetteland	.10
260	Devon White	.10
261	Odalis Perez	.40
262	Calvin Pickering	.10
263	Alex Ramirez	.10
264	Preston Wilson	.10
265	Brad Radke	.10
266	Walt Weiss	.10
267	Tim Young	.10
268	Tino Martinez	.40
269	Matt Stairs	.10
270	Curt Schilling	.20
271	Tony Womack	.10
272	Ismael Valdes	.10
273	Wally Joyner	.10
274	Armando Rios	.10
275	Andy Pettitte	.50
276	Bubba Trammell	.10
277	Todd Zeile	.10
278	Shannon Stewart	.10
279	Matt Williams	.40
280	John Rocker	.10
281	B.J. Surhoff	.10
282	Eric Young	.10
283	Dmitri Young	.10
284	John Smoltz	.25
285	Todd Walker	.25
286	Paul O'Neill	.25
287	Blake Stein	.10
288	Kevin Young	.10
289	Quilvio Veras	.10
290	Kirk Rueter	.10
291	Randy Winn	.10
292	Miguel Tejada	.10
293	J.T. Snow	.10
294	Michael Tucker	.10
295	Jay Tessmer	.10
296	Scott Erickson	.10
297	Tim Wakefield	.10
298	Jeff Abbott	.10
299	Eddie Taubensee	.10
300	Darryl Hamilton	.10
301	Kevin Orie	.10
302	Jose Offerman	.10
303	Scott Karl	.10
304	Chris Widger	.10
305	Todd Hundley	.10
306	Desi Relaford	.10
307	Sterling Hitchcock	.10
308	Delino DeShields	.10
309	Alex Gonzalez	.10
310	Justin Baughman	.10
311	Jamey Wright	.10
312	Wes Helms	.10
313	Dante Powell	.10
314	Jim Abbott	.10
315	Manny Alexander	.10
316	Harold Baines	.10
317	Danny Graves	.10
318	Sandy Alomar	.10
319	Pedro Astacio	.10
320	Jermaine Allensworth	.10
321	Matt Anderson	.10
322	Chad Curtis	.10
323	Antonio Osuna	.10
324	Brad Ausmus	.10
325	Steve Trachsel	.10
326	Mike Blowers	.10
327	Brian Bohanon	.10
328	Chris Gomez	.10
329	Valerio de los Santos	.10
330	Rich Aurilia	.10
331	Michael Barrett	.50
332	Rick Aguilera	.10
333	Adrian Brown	.10
334	Bill Spiers	.10
335	Matt Beech	.10
336	David Bell	.10
337	Juan Acevedo	.10
338	Jose Canseco	.40
339	Wilson Alvarez	.10
340	Luis Alicea	.10
341	Jason Dickson	.10
342	Mike Bordick	.10
343	Ben Ford	.10
344	Keith Lockhart	.10
345	Jason Christiansen	.10
346	Darren Bragg	.10
347	Doug Brocail	.10
348	Jeff Blauser	.10
349	James Baldwin	.10
350	Jeffrey Hammonds	.10
351	Ricky Bottalico	.10
352	Russ Branyon	.10
353	Mark Brownson	.75
354	Dave Berg	.10
355	Sean Bergman	.10
356	Jeff Conine	.10
357	Shayne Bennett	.10
358	Bobby Bonilla	.20
359	Bob Wickman	.10
360	Carlos Baerga	.10
361	Chris Fussell	.10
362	Chili Davis	.10
363	Jerry Spradlin	.10
364	Carlos Hernandez	.10
365	Roberto Hernandez	.10
366	Marvin Benard	.10
367	Ken Cloude	.10
368	Tony Fernandez	.10
369	John Burkett	.10
370	Gary DiSarcina	.10
371	Alan Benes	.10
372	Karim Garcia	.10
373	Carlos Perez	.10
374	Damon Buford	.10
375	Mark Clark	.10
376	*Edgard Clemente*	.10
377	Chad Bradford	.50
378	Frank Catalanotto	.10
379	Vic Darensbourg	.10
380	Sean Berry	.10
381	Dave Burba	.10
382	Sal Fasano	.10
383	Steve Parris	.10
384	Roger Cedeno	.10
385	Chad Fox	.10
386	Wilton Guerrero	.10
387	Dennis Cook	.10
388	Joe Girardi	.10
389	LaTroy Hawkins	.10
390	Ryan Christenson	.10
391	Paul Byrd	.10
392	Lou Collier	.10
393	Jeff Fassero	.10
394	Jim Leyritz	.10
395	Shawn Estes	.10
396	Mike Kelly	.10
397	Rich Croushore	.10
398	Royce Clayton	.10
399	Rudy Seanez	.10
400	Darrin Fletcher	.10
401	Shigetosi Hasegawa	.10
402	Bernard Gilkey	.10
403	Juan Guzman	.10
404	Jeff Frye	.10
405	Marino Santana	.10
406	Alex Fernandez	.10
407	Gary Gaetti	.10
408	Dan Miceli	.10
409	Mike Cameron	.10
410	Mike Remlinger	.10
411	Joey Cora	.10
412	Mark Gardner	.10
413	Aaron Ledesma	.10
414	Jerry Dipoto	.10
415	Ricky Gutierrez	.10
416	John Franco	.10
417	Mendy Lopez	.10
418	Hideki Irabu	.25
419	Mark Grudzielanek	.10
420	Bobby Hughes	.10
421	Pat Meares	.10
422	Jimmy Haynes	.10
423	Bob Henley	.10
424	Bobby Estalella	.10
425	Jon Lieber	.10
426	*Giomar Guevara*	.50
427	Jose Jimenez	.10
428	Deivi Cruz	.10
429	Jonathan Johnson	.10
430	Ken Hill	.10
431	Craig Grebeck	.10
432	Jose Rosado	.10
433	Danny Klassen	.10
434	Bobby Howry	.10
435	Gerald Williams	.10
436	Omar Olivares	.10
437	Chris Hoiles	.10
438	Seth Greisinger	.10
439	Scott Hatteberg	.10
440	Jeremi Gonzalez	.10
441	Wil Cordero	.10
442	Jeff Montgomery	.10
443	Chris Stynes	.10
444	Tony Saunders	.10
445	Einar Diaz	.10
446	Laril Gonzalez	.10
447	Ryan Jackson	.10
448	Mike Hampton	.10
449	Todd Hollandsworth	.10
450	Gabe White	.10

451	John Jaha	.10
452	Bret Saberhagen	.10
453	Otis Nixon	.10
454	Steve Kline	.10
455	Butch Huskey	.10
456	Mike Jerzembeck	.10
457	Wayne Gomes	.10
458	Mike Macfarlane	.10
459	Jesus Sanchez	.10
460	Al Martin	.10
461	Dwight Gooden	.20
462	Ruben Rivera	.10
463	Pat Hentgen	.10
464	Jose Valentin	.10
465	Vladimir Nunez	.10
466	Charlie Hayes	.10
467	Jay Powell	.10
468	Raul Ibanez	.10
469	Kent Mercker	.10
470	John Mabry	.10
471	Woody Williams	.10
472	Roberto Kelly	.10
473	Jim Mecir	.10
474	Dave Hollins	.10
475	Rafael Medina	.10
476	Darren Lewis	.10
477	Felix Heredia	.10
478	Brian Hunter	.10
479	Matt Mantei	.10
480	Richard Hidalgo	.10
481	Bobby Jones	.10
482	Hal Morris	.10
483	Ramiro Mendoza	.10
484	Matt Luke	.10
485	Esteban Loaiza	.10
486	Mark Loretta	.10
487	A.J. Pierzynski	.10
488	Charles Nagy	.10
489	Kevin Sefcik	.10
490	Jason McDonald	.10
491	Jeremy Powell	.10
492	Scott Servais	.10
493	Abraham Nunez	.10
494	Stan Spencer	.10
495	Stan Javier	.10
496	Jose Paniagua	.10
497	Gregg Jefferies	.10
498	Gregg Olson	.10
499	Derek Lowe	.10
500	Willis Otanez	.10
501	Brian Moehler	.10
502	Glenallen Hill	.10
503	Bobby Jones	.10
504	Greg Norton	.10
505	Mike Jackson	.10
506	Kirt Manwaring	.10
507	Eric Weaver	.75
508	Mitch Meluskey	.15
509	Todd Jones	.10
510	Mike Matheny	.10
511	Benj Sampson	.10
512	Tony Phillips	.10
513	Mike Thurman	.10
514	Jorge Posada	.10
515	Bill Taylor	.10
516	Mike Sweeney	.10
517	Jose Silva	.10
518	Mark Lewis	.10
519	Chris Peters	.10
520	Brian Johnson	.10
521	Mike Timlin	.10
522	Mark McLemore	.10
523	Dan Plesac	.10
524	Kelly Stinnett	.10
525	Sidney Ponson	.10
526	Jim Parque	.10
527	Tyler Houston	.10
528	John Thomson	.10
529	Mike Metcalfe	.10
530	Robert Person	.10
531	Marc Newfield	.10
532	Javier Vazquez	.10
533	Terry Steinbach	.10
534	Turk Wendell	.10
535	Tim Raines	.10
536	Brian Meadows	.10
537	Mike Lieberthal	.10
538	Ricardo Rincon	.10
539	Dan Wilson	.10
540	John Johnstone	.10
541	Todd Stottlemyre	.10
542	Kevin Stocker	.10
543	Ramon Martinez	.10
544	Mike Simms	.10
545	Paul Quantrill	.10
546	Matt Walbeck	.10
547	Turner Ward	.10
548	Bill Pulsipher	.10
549	Donnie Sadler	.10
550	Lance Johnson	.10
551	Bill Simas	.10
552	Jeff Reed	.10
553	Jeff Shaw	.10
554	Joe Randa	.10
555	Paul Shuey	.10
556	Mike Redmond	.50
557	Sean Runyan	.10
558	Enrique Wilson	.10
559	Scott Radinsky	.10
560	Larry Sutton	.10
561	Masato Yoshii	.10
562	David Nilsson	.10
563	Mike Trombley	.10
564	Darryl Strawberry	.25
565	Dave Mlicki	.10
566	Placido Polanco	.10
567	Yorkis Perez	.10
568	Esteban Yan	.10
569	Lee Stevens	.10
570	Steve Sinclair	.10
571	Jarrod Washburn	.10
572	Lenny Webster	.10
573	Mike Sirotka	.10
574	Jason Varitek	.10
575	Terry Mulholland	.10
576	Adrian Beltre (Franchise Futures)	.25
577	Eric Chavez (Franchise Futures)	.50
578	J.D. Drew (Franchise Futures)	1.00
579	Juan Encarnacion (Franchise Futures)	.10
580	Nomar Garciaparra (Franchise Futures)	1.00
581	Troy Glaus (Franchise Futures)	.40
582	Ben Grieve (Franchise Futures)	.40
583	Vladimir Guerrero (Franchise Futures)	.50
584	Todd Helton (Franchise Futures)	.40
585	Derek Jeter (Franchise Futures)	1.00
586	Travis Lee (Franchise Futures)	.40
587	Alex Rodriguez (Franchise Futures)	1.00
588	Scott Rolen (Franchise Futures)	.40
589	Richie Sexson (Franchise Futures)	.10
590	Kerry Wood (Franchise Futures)	.40
591	Ken Griffey Jr.	1.50
592	Chipper Jones	.75
593	Alex Rodriguez	1.00
594	Sammy Sosa	1.00
595	Mark McGwire	2.00
596	Cal Ripken Jr.	1.25
597	Nomar Garciaparra	1.00
598	Derek Jeter	1.00
599	Kerry Wood	.40
600	J.D. Drew	.75

1999 Fleer Starting Nine

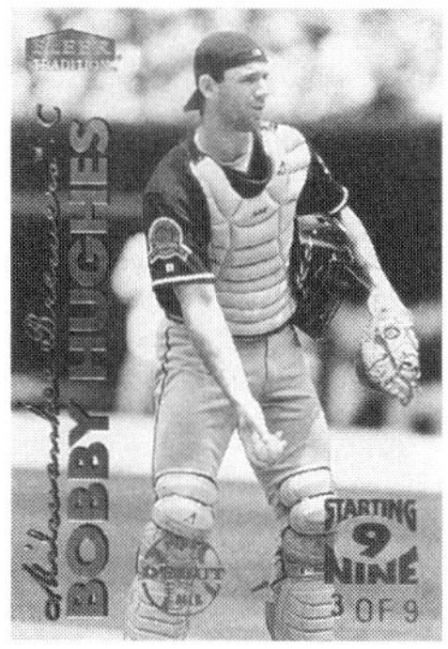

This ultra-scarce, hobby-only parallel insert, found at the rate of about two cards per case, includes just nine cards of each player. Sharing the basic design of the Fleer Traditional set, the cards have blue metallic foil printing on front, including a "STARTING 9 NINE" logo at lower-right. At bottom right, the card's individual serial number from within the edition of nine is printed. Backs have an "S" suffix to the card number.

	MT
Common Player:	20.00
(Star and rookie cards valued at 200-250X base versions.)	

1999 Fleer Warning Track Collection

Each of the cards in '99 Fleer Tradition was paralleled in this retail-only issue found one per pack. Warning Track cards are distinguished by the use of red metallic foil on front for the player's name, team, position that are in gold-foil on the regular version. There is also a special "Warning Track Collection" logo in red foil at bottom-right. On back, WTC cards have a "W" suffix to the card number.

	MT
Complete Set (600):	250.00
Common Player:	.20
Stars: 3X	
(See 1999 Fleer for checklist and base card values.)	

1999 Fleer Date With Destiny

This 10-card set takes a look at what Hall of Fame plaques might look like for some of today's great players. These are serially numbered to 100 sets.

		MT
Complete Set (10):		1000.
Common Player:		40.00
Production: 100 sets		
1	Barry Bonds	50.00
2	Roger Clemens	75.00
3	Ken Griffey Jr.	200.00
4	Tony Gwynn	100.00
5	Greg Maddux	140.00
6	Mark McGwire	250.00
7	Mike Piazza	140.00
8	Cal Ripken Jr.	160.00
9	Alex Rodriguez	140.00
10	Frank Thomas	75.00

1999 Fleer Diamond Magic

A multi-layer card, where collectors turn a "wheel" for a kaleidoscope effect behind the player image. These are seeded 1:96 packs.

		MT
Complete Set (15):		250.00
Common Player:		8.00
Inserted 1:96		
1	Barry Bonds	10.00
2	Roger Clemens	15.00
3	Nomar Garciaparra	25.00
4	Ken Griffey Jr.	40.00
5	Tony Gwynn	20.00
6	Orlando Hernandez	12.00
7	Derek Jeter	20.00
8	Randy Johnson	8.00
9	Chipper Jones	20.00
10	Greg Maddux	25.00
11	Mark McGwire	50.00
12	Alex Rodriguez	25.00
13	Sammy Sosa	25.00
14	Bernie Williams	8.00
15	Kerry Wood	10.00

1999 Fleer Going Yard

This 15-card set features the top home run hitters from the '98 season. These 1:18 pack inserts unfold to be twice as wide as regular cards and takes an unorthodox look at how far the longest home runs went.

		MT
Complete Set (15):		45.00
Common Player:		.75
Inserted 1:18		
1	Moises Alou	.75
2	Albert Belle	2.50
3	Jose Canseco	1.50
4	Vinny Castilla	.75
5	Andres Galarraga	1.50
6	Juan Gonzalez	5.00
7	Ken Griffey Jr.	10.00
8	Chipper Jones	5.00
9	Mark McGwire	12.00
10	Rafael Palmeiro	1.00
11	Mike Piazza	6.00
12	Alex Rodriguez	6.00
13	Sammy Sosa	6.00
14	Greg Vaughn	.75
15	Mo Vaughn	2.50

1999 Fleer Golden Memories

This 15-card set pays tribute to the great moments from the 1998 season including David Wells perfect game and McGwire's record breaking season. These are seeded 1:54 packs on an embossed frame design.

		MT
Complete Set (15):		160.00
Common Player:		4.00
Inserted 1:54		
1	Albert Belle	6.00
2	Barry Bonds	6.00
3	Roger Clemens	10.00
4	Nomar Garciaparra	15.00
5	Juan Gonzalez	12.00
6	Ken Griffey Jr.	25.00
7	Randy Johnson	4.00
8	Greg Maddux	15.00
9	Mark McGwire	30.00
10	Mike Piazza	15.00
11	Cal Ripken Jr.	20.00
12	Alex Rodriguez	15.00
13	Sammy Sosa	15.00
14	David Wells	4.00
15	Kerry Wood	6.00

1999 Fleer Home Run Heroes

These cards were part of an unannounced multi-manufacturer (Fleer, Upper Deck, Topps, Pacific) insert program which was exclusive to Wal-Mart. Each company produced cards of Mark McGwire and Sammy Sosa, along with two other premier sluggers. Each company's cards share a "Power Elite" logo at top and "Home Run Heroes" logo vertically at right.

		MT
Complete Set (4):		9.00
Common Player:		1.50
1	Mark McGwire (Tradition)	4.00
2	Sammy Sosa (Sports Illustrated)	2.50
3	Mike Piazza (SkyBox Thunder)	1.50
4	Nomar Garciaparra (SkyBox Thunder)	1.50

1999 Fleer Stan Musial Monumental Moments

Great moments and insight from and about the St. Louis Cardinals great. This 10-card tribute set chronicles Musial's legendary career. These are seeded 1:36 packs with 500 autographed cards randomly seeded.

		MT
Complete Set (10):		40.00
Common Musial:		5.00
Autographed Card:		95.00
1	Life in Donora	6.00
2	Values	6.00
3	In the Beginning	6.00
4	In the Navy	6.00
5	The 1948 Season (w/ Red Schoendienst)	6.00
6	Success Stories (w/ Pres. Kennedy)	6.00
7	Mr. Cardinal	6.00
8	Most Valuable Player	6.00
9	... baseball's perfect knight	6.00
10	Hall of Fame	6.00

1999 Fleer Rookie Flashback

This 15-card set features the impact rookies from the 1998 season. These are seeded 1:6 packs and feature sculpture embossing.

		MT
Complete Set (15):		18.00
Common Player:		.25
Inserted 1:6		
1	Matt Anderson	.25
2	Rolando Arrojo	.40
3	Adrian Beltre	.75
4	Mike Caruso	.25
5	Eric Chavez	1.50
6	J.D. Drew	3.00
7	Juan Encarnacion	.75
8	Brad Fullmer	.40
9	Troy Glaus	1.50
10	Ben Grieve	1.50
11	Todd Helton	1.00
12	Orlando Hernandez	1.50
13	Travis Lee	1.50
14	Richie Sexson	.50
15	Kerry Wood	1.00

1999 Fleer Vintage '61

This 50-card set takes the first 50 cards from the base set and showcases them in the 1961 Fleer "Baseball Greats" card design. These are seeded one per hobby pack.

		MT
Complete Set (50):		25.00
Common Player:		.20
Inserted 1:1		
1	Mark McGwire	4.00
2	Sammy Sosa	2.50
3	Ken Griffey Jr.	3.00
4	Kerry Wood	.75
5	Derek Jeter	2.00
6	Stan Musial	4.00
7	J.D. Drew	1.50
8	Cal Ripken Jr.	2.50
9	Alex Rodriguez	2.00
10	Travis Lee	.75
11	Andres Galarraga	.50
12	Nomar Garciaparra	2.00
13	Albert Belle	.75
14	Barry Larkin	.40
15	Dante Bichette	.40
16	Tony Clark	.40
17	Moises Alou	.30
18	Rafael Palmeiro	.30
19	Raul Mondesi	.20
20	Vladimir Guerrero	1.00
21	John Olerud	.20
22	Bernie Williams	.40
23	Ben Grieve	.75
24	Scott Rolen	.75
25	Jeromy Burnitz	.20
26	Ken Caminiti	.20
27	Barry Bonds	.75
28	Todd Helton	.75
29	Juan Gonzalez	1.50
30	Roger Clemens	1.25
31	Andruw Jones	.75
32	Mo Vaughn	.75
33	Larry Walker	.50
34	Frank Thomas	1.00
35	Manny Ramirez	1.00
36	Randy Johnson	.50
37	Vinny Castilla	.20
38	Juan Encarnacion	.50
39	Jeff Bagwell	.75
40	Gary Sheffield	.30
41	Mike Piazza	2.00
42	Richie Sexson	.20
43	Tony Gwynn	1.50
44	Chipper Jones	1.50
45	Jim Thome	.50
46	Craig Biggio	.40
47	Carlos Delgado	.50
48	Greg Vaughn	.30
49	Greg Maddux	2.00
50	Troy Glaus	.75

1999 Fleer Update

Distributed as a 150-card boxed set, the main focus for this release is the inclusion of rookie cards of players called up late in the '99 season, including Rick Ankiel. Besides rookies, the set also features 10 traded players/ free agents and a 10-card Season Highlights subset.

		MT
Complete Set (150):		40.00
Common Player:		.10
1	*Rick Ankiel*	15.00
2	*Peter Bergeron*	1.00
3	*Pat Burrell*	4.00
4	*Eric Munson*	5.00
5	*Alfonso Soriano*	6.00
6	*Tim Hudson*	3.00
7	*Erubiel Durazo*	3.00
8	Chad Hermansen	.10
9	Jeff Zimmerman	1.00
10	*Jesus Pena*	.25
11	Ramon Hernandez	.10
12	*Trent Durrington*	.25
13	Tony Armas, Jr.	.15
14	*Mike Fyhrie*	.25
15	*Danny Kolb*	.50
16	*Mike Porzio*	.40
17	*Will Brunson*	.40
18	*Mike Duvall*	.25
19	Doug Mientkiewicz	.10
20	*Gabe Molina*	.50
21	*Luis Vizcaino*	.25
22	*Robinson Cancel*	.50
23	*Brett Laxton*	.50
24	*Joe McEwing*	1.50
25	*Justin Speier*	.40
26	*Kip Wells*	1.00
27	*Armando Almanza*	.25
28	*Joe Davenport*	.50
29	*Yamid Haad*	.25
30	John Halama	.10
31	Adam Kennedy	.10
32	Vicente Padilla	.10
33	*Travis Dawkins*	.75
34	*Ryan Rupe*	.50
35	*B.J. Ryan*	.40
36	*Chance Sanford*	.25
37	*Anthony Shumaker*	.25
38	*Ryan Glynn*	.40
39	Matt Herges	.10
40	Ben Molina	.40
41	Scott Williamson	.10
42	*Eric Gagne*	1.00
43	*John McDonald*	.25
44	*Scott Sauerbeck*	.40
45	*Mike Venafro*	.25
46	*Edwards Guzman*	.50
47	*Richard Barker*	.40
48	Braden Looper	.10
49	*Chad Meyers*	.25
50	*Scott Strickland*	.50
51	Billy Koch	.10
52	*Dave Newhan*	.40
53	*David Riske*	.40
54	Jose Santiago	.10
55	*Miguel Del Toro*	.25
56	*Orber Moreno*	.40
57	Dave Roberts	.10
58	*Tim Byrdak*	.25
59	*David Lee*	.25
60	*Guillermo Mota*	.50
61	*Wilton Veras*	1.50
62	*Mike Colangelo*	.25
63	*Jose Fernandez*	.50
64	*Ray King*	.25
65	*Chris Petersen*	.40
66	Vernon Wells	.25
67	Ruben Mateo	.50
68	Ben Petrick	.10
69	*Chris Tremie*	.25
70	Lance Berkman	.10
71	Dan Smith	.10
72	*Carlos Hernandez*	.10
73	*Chad Harville*	.25
74	Damaso Marte	.10
75	*Aaron Myette*	1.00
76	*Willis Roberts*	.25
77	*Erik Sabel*	.50
78	*Hector Almonte*	.50
79	Kris Benson	.10
80	*Pat Daneker*	.25
81	*Freddy Garcia*	4.00
82	*Byung-Hyun Kim*	1.00
83	*Wily Pena*	2.50
84	*Dan Wheeler*	.25
85	*Tim Harikkala*	.25
86	*Derrin Ebert*	.25
87	*Horacio Estrada*	.50
88	*Liu Rodriguez*	.25
89	*Jordan Zimmerman*	.25
90	*A.J. Burnett*	1.00
91	*Doug Davis*	.25
92	*Robert Ramsey*	.25
93	Ryan Franklin	.10
94	*Charlie Greene*	.25
95	*Bo Porter*	.25
96	*Jorge Toca*	1.00
97	*Casey Blake*	.25
98	*Amaury Garcia*	.50
99	*Jose Molina*	.25
100	*Melvin Mora*	1.50
101	*Joe Nathan*	.10
102	*Juan Pena*	.10
103	*Dave Borkowski*	.10
104	*Eddie Gaillard*	.10
105	Rob Radlosky	.10
106	*Brett Hinchliffe*	.10
107	Carlos Lee	.10
108	*Rob Ryan*	.10
109	*Jeff Weaver*	1.00
110	Ed Yarnall	.10
111	*Nelson Cruz*	.10
112	*Cleatus Davidson*	.25
113	*Tim Kubinski*	.10
114	*Sean Spencer*	.10
115	*Joe Winkelsas*	.10
116	Chris Clapinski	.10
117	*Tom Davey*	.10
118	Warren Morris	.10
119	*Dan Murray*	.10
120	*Jose Nieves*	.10
121	*Mark Quinn*	1.50
122	*Josh Beckett*	4.00
123	*Chad Allen*	.10
124	Mike Figga	.10
125	*Beiker Graterol*	.10
126	*Aaron Scheffer*	.10
127	*Wiki Gonzalez*	.50
128	Ramon E. Martinez	.10
129	*Matt Riley*	1.50
130	*Chris Woodward*	.25
131	Albert Belle	.10
132	Roger Cedeno	.10
133	Roger Clemens	.10
134	Brian Giles	.10
135	Rickey Henderson	.10
136	Randy Johnson	.10
137	Brian Jordan	.10
138	Paul Konerko	.10
139	Hideo Nomo	.10
140	Kenny Rogers	.10
141	Wade Boggs	.25
142	Jose Canseco	.50
143	Roger Clemens	.75
144	David Cone	.10
145	Tony Gwynn	1.00
146	Mark McGwire	2.50
147	Cal Ripken Jr.	1.50
148	Alex Rodriguez	1.00
149	Fernando Tatis	.10
150	Robin Ventura	.10

1999 Fleer Millennium

This special edition of '99 Fleer Tradition was issued only in factory sets, for sale on Shop at Home. Besides the 600 cards in the regular Tradition issue, these sets include 20 renumbered rookie and highlight cards from the Fleer Update set. Each set is sealed with gold-foil on which is a serial number from an edition of 5,000 sets. Each card in the edition has a special gold-foil "2000" logo on front.

		MT
Complete Factory Set (620):		150.00
Common Player:		.50
Stars: 10X		
601	Rick Ankiel	30.00
602	Peter Bergeron	6.00
603	Pat Burrell	12.00
604	Eric Munson	15.00
605	Alfonso Soriano	18.00
606	Tim Hudson	9.00
607	Erubiel Durazo	9.00
608	Chad Hermansen	3.00
609	Jeff Zimmerman	3.00
610	Jesus Pena	3.00
611	Wade Boggs (Highlights)	1.50
612	Jose Canseco (Highlights)	3.00
613	Roger Clemens (Highlights)	4.00
614	David Cone (Highlights)	.75
615	Tony Gwynn (Highlights)	6.00
616	Mark McGwire (Highlights)	12.00
617	Cal Ripken Jr. (Highlights)	8.00
618	Alex Rodriguez (Highlights)	8.00
619	Fernando Tatis (Highlights)	.75
620	Robin Ventura (Highlights)	.75

1999 Fleer Diamond Skills Commemorative Sheet

In conjunction with its sponsorship of the Diamond Skills program, Fleer distributed this eight-player sheet to 7-14 year olds participating in the event. Participants could get a sheet by redeeming Fleer wrappers at a local card store. The 10" x 9" sheet features full size Fleer Tradition cards. At top is a list of 1997 Diamond Skills winners.

		MT
Complete Sheet:		8.00
1	Mark McGwire	
2	Sammy Sosa	
4	Kerry Wood	
5	Derek Jeter	
9	Alex Rodriguez	
12	Nomar Garciaparra	
23	Ben Grieve	
44	Chipper Jones	

1999 Fleer National Convention Commemorative Set

In conjunction with its participation at the 20th National Sports Collectors Convention in Atlanta in July, 1999, Fleer distributed this cello-wrapped commemorative set to persons purchasing VIP admission packages. The set includes a specially numbered (NC1) version of the Stan Musial card from '99 Fleer Tradition, three large-format (3-1/2" x 5") card reproducing Musial Monumental Moments inserts, and an unnumbered header card. The Monumental Moments reproductions are printed on a red background with the famed St. Louis arch.

		MT
Complete Set (5):		20.00
Common Card:		5.00
NC1	Stan Musial (Fleer Tradition)	5.00
NC2	Stan Musial (Life in Donora - Monumental Moment)	5.00
NC3	Stan Musial (The 1948 Season - Monumental Moment)	5.00
NC4	Stan Musial (Hall of Fame - Monumental Season)	5.00
	Header card	.50

1999 Fleer Brilliants Sample

To preview the introduction of its Brilliants brand of premium quality cards into baseball, Fleer issued a promo card of J.D. Drew. Like the issued cards, the sample is printed on plastic with a mirrored silver background on front. Both front and back are overprinted, "PROMOTIONAL SAMPLE".

	MT
SAMPLE J.D. Drew	3.00

1999 Fleer Brilliants

This 175-card set features an action photo on a complete silver-foiled background swirl pattern. The featured player's name, team and postion are stamped in gold foil. Card backs have a small photo, vital information, 1998 statistics and a brief overview of the player's '98 season. Cards numbered 126-175 are part of a short-printed Rookies subset and are seeded 1:2 packs.

		MT
Complete Set (175):		180.00
Common Player:		.40
Common SP (126-175):		1.50
Blues: 2x to 3x		
Production: 24 sets		
Wax Box:		70.00
1	Mark McGwire	8.00
2	Derek Jeter	4.00
3	Nomar Garciaparra	4.00
4	Travis Lee	1.00
5	Jeff Bagwell	1.50
6	Andres Galarraga	.75
7	Pedro Martinez	1.50
8	Cal Ripken Jr.	5.00
9	Vladimir Guerrero	2.00
10	Chipper Jones	3.00
11	Rusty Greer	.40
12	Omar Vizquel	.40
13	Quinton McCracken	.40
14	Jaret Wright	.60
15	Mike Mussina	1.00
16	Jason Giambi	.40
17	Tony Clark	.75
18	Troy O'Leary	.40
19	Troy Percival	.40
20	Kerry Wood	1.00
21	Vinny Castilla	.40
22	Chris Carpenter	.40
23	Richie Sexson	.40
24	Ken Griffey Jr.	6.00
25	Barry Bonds	1.50
26	Carlos Delgado	.75
27	Frank Thomas	2.00
28	Manny Ramirez	2.00
29	Shawn Green	.75
30	Mike Piazza	4.00
31	Tino Martinez	.75
32	Dante Bichette	.75
33	Scott Rolen	1.50
34	Gabe Alvarez	.40
35	Raul Mondesi	.60
36	Damion Easley	.40
37	Jeff Kent	.40
38	Al Leiter	.40
39	Alex Rodriguez	4.00

40	Jeff King	.40
41	Mark Grace	.75
42	Larry Walker	1.00
43	Moises Alou	.60
44	Juan Gonzalez	2.00
45	Rolando Arrojo	.40
46	Tom Glavine	.60
47	Johnny Damon	.40
48	Livan Hernandez	.40
49	Craig Biggio	.75
50	Dmitri Young	.40
51	Chan Ho Park	.60
52	Todd Walker	.40
53	Derrek Lee	.40
54	Todd Helton	1.00
55	Ray Lankford	.40
56	Jim Thome	.75
57	Matt Lawton	.40
58	Matt Anderson	.40
59	Jose Offerman	.40
60	Eric Karros	.40
61	Orlando Hernandez	1.50
62	Ben Grieve	1.00
63	Bobby Abreu	.40
64	Kevin Young	.40
65	John Olerud	.75
66	Sammy Sosa	4.00
67	Andy Ashby	.40
68	Juan Encarnacion	.40
69	Shane Reynolds	.40
70	Bernie Williams	1.00
71	Mike Cameron	.40
72	Troy Glaus	2.00
73	Gary Sheffield	.60
74	Jeromy Burnitz	.40
75	Mike Caruso	.40
76	Chuck Knoblauch	.75
77	Kenny Rogers	.40
78	David Cone	.60
79	Tony Gwynn	3.00
80	Aramis Ramirez	.40
81	Paul O'Neill	.75
82	Charles Nagy	.40
83	Javy Lopez	.60
84	Scott Erickson	.40
85	Trevor Hoffman	.40
86	Andruw Jones	1.50
87	Ray Durham	.40
88	Jorge Posada	.40
89	Edgar Martinez	.40
90	Tim Salmon	.75
91	Bobby Higginson	.40
92	Adrian Beltre	1.00
93	Jason Kendall	.60
94	Henry Rodriguez	.40
95	Greg Maddux	4.00
96	David Justice	.75
97	Ivan Rodriguez	1.50
98	Curt Schilling	.60
99	Matt Williams	.75
100	Darin Erstad	1.00
101	Rafael Palmeiro	.75
102	David Wells	.40
103	Barry Larkin	.75
104	Robin Ventura	.60
105	Edgar Renteria	.40
106	Andy Pettitte	.60
107	Albert Belle	1.50
108	Steve Finley	.40
109	Fernando Vina	.40
110	Rondell White	.60
111	Kevin Brown	.60
112	Jose Canseco	1.00
113	Roger Clemens	2.00
114	Todd Hundley	.40
115	Will Clark	1.00
116	Jim Edmonds	.40
117	Randy Johnson	1.00
118	Denny Neagle	.40
119	Brian Jordan	.40
120	Dean Palmer	.40
121	Roberto Alomar	1.00
122	Ken Caminiti	.60
123	Brian Giles	.40
124	Todd Stottlemyre	.40
125	Mo Vaughn	1.50
126	J.D. Drew	5.00
127	Ryan Minor	2.50
128	Gabe Kapler	3.00
129	Jeremy Giambi	2.00
130	Eric Chavez	1.00
131	Ben Davis	2.00
132	Rob Fick	1.50
133	George Lombard	2.00
134	Calvin Pickering	1.50
135	Preston Wilson	1.50
136	Corey Koskie	1.50
137	Russell Branyan	1.50
138	Bruce Chen	2.00
139	Matt Clement	1.50
140	*Pat Burrell*	15.00
141	*Freddy Garcia*	10.00
142	Brian Simmons	2.00
143	Carlos Febles	3.00
144	Carlos Guillen	1.50
145	Fernando Seguignol	2.00
146	Carlos Beltran	5.00
147	Edgard Clemente	1.50
148	Mitch Meluskey	1.50
149	Ryan Bradley	1.50
150	Marlon Anderson	1.50
151	*A.J. Burnett*	5.00
152	*Scott Hunter*	1.50
153	Mark Johnson	1.50
154	Angel Pena	3.00
155	Roy Halladay	2.00
156	*Chad Allen*	1.50
157	Trot Nixon	1.50
158	Ricky Ledee	1.50
159	*Gary Bennett*	1.50
160	*Micah Bowie*	1.50
161	Doug Mientkiewicz	1.50
162	Danny Klassen	1.50
163	Willis Otanez	1.50
164	Jin Ho Cho	1.50
165	Mike Lowell	2.00
166	Armando Rios	1.50
167	Tom Evans	1.50
168	Michael Barrett	3.00
169	Alex Gonzalez	2.00
170	*Masao Kida*	1.50
171	*Peter Tucci*	1.50
172	Luis Saturria	1.50
173	Kris Benson	1.50
174	*Mario Encarnacion*	4.00
175	*Roosevelt Brown*	2.00

1999 Fleer Brilliants Blue/Golds

The 175 Fleer Brilliants base cards are paralleled in three insert sets of differing degrees of scarcity. Brilliant Blue parallels have a mirrored blue foil background on front and a "B" suffix to the card number on back. They are seeded one per three packs (125 veterans) and one per six packs (50 rookies). Gold parallels are printed with gold foil background and a "G" suffix. Each card is serially numbered on back within an edition of 99. The 24-karat Gold parallels have rainbow holographic foil backgrounds, a 24-karat gold logo and are serially numbered to just 24 of each card.

	MT
Brilliants Blue Common:	1.00
Brilliants Blue Stars: 2X	
Brilliants Blue Rookies: 1.5X	
Brilliants Gold Common:	5.00
Brilliants Gold Stars: 15X	
Brilliants Gold Rookies: 5X	
Brilliants 24K Gold Common:	15.00
Brilliants 24K Gold Stars: 50X	
Brilliants 24K Gold Rookies: 15X	

(See 1999 Fleer Brilliants for checklist and base card values.)

1999 Fleer Brilliants Illuminators

This 15-card set highlights baseball's top young prospects on a team color-coded fully foiled front. Card backs are numbered with an "I" suffix and are inserted 1:10 packs.

		MT
Complete Set (15):		35.00
Common Player:		1.50
Inserted 1:10		
1	Kerry Wood	2.50
2	Ben Grieve	2.50
3	J.D. Drew	5.00
4	Juan Encarnacion	2.50
5	Travis Lee	2.50
6	Todd Helton	3.00
7	Troy Glaus	5.00
8	Ricky Ledee	1.50
9	Eric Chavez	3.00
10	Ben Davis	2.00
11	George Lombard	2.00
12	Jeremy Giambi	1.50
13	Richie Sexson	2.00
14	Corey Koskie	1.50
15		1.50

1999 Fleer Brilliants Shining Stars

Shining Stars is a 15-card set printed on styrene with two-sided mirrored foil. Card backs are numbered with a "S" suffix and are seeded 1:20 packs. Pulsars are a parallel set that are printed on two-sided rainbow holographic foil and styrene with an embossed star pattern in the background. Pulsars are seeded 1:400 packs.

		MT
Complete Set (15):		140.00
Common Player:		4.00
Inserted 1:20		
Pulsars: 4x to 8x		
Inserted 1:400		
1	Ken Griffey Jr.	20.00
2	Mark McGwire	25.00
3	Sammy Sosa	12.00
4	Derek Jeter	12.00
5	Nomar Garciaparra	12.00
6	Alex Rodriguez	12.00
7	Mike Piazza	12.00
8	Juan Gonzalez	10.00
9	Chipper Jones	10.00
10	Cal Ripken Jr.	15.00
11	Frank Thomas	8.00
12	Greg Maddux	12.00
13	Roger Clemens	6.00
14	Vladimir Guerrero	6.00
15	Manny Ramirez	6.00

1999 Fleer Mystique

		MT
Complete Set (160):		350.00
Common Player:		.20
Common SP (1-100):		.75
Common (101-150):		2.50
Production 2,999 sets		
Common (151-160):		10.00
Production 2,500 sets		
1	Ken Griffey Jr.	6.00
2	Livan Hernandez	.20
3	Jeff Kent	.20
4	Brian Jordan	.20
5	Kevin Young	.20
6	Vinny Castilla	.20
7	Orlando Hernandez	.75
8	Bobby Abreu	.20
9	Vladimir Guerrero	2.00
10	Chuck Knoblauch	.50
11	Nomar Garciaparra	4.00
12	Jeff Bagwell	1.00
13	Todd Walker	.20
14	Johnny Damon	.20
15	Mike Caruso	.20
16	Cliff Floyd	.20
17	Andy Pettitte	.40
18	Cal Ripken Jr.	5.00
19	Brian Giles	.20
20	Robin Ventura	.40
21	Alex Gonzalez	.20
22	Randy Johnson	.75
23	Raul Mondesi	.40
24	Ken Caminiti	.40
25	Tom Glavine	.40
26	Derek Jeter	4.00
27	Carlos Delgado	.75
28	Adrian Beltre	.50
29	Tino Martinez	.50
30	Todd Helton	.50
31	Juan Gonzalez	2.00
32	Henry Rodriguez	.20
33	Jim Thome	.50
34	Paul O'Neill	.40
35	Scott Rolen	1.50
36	Rafael Palmeiro	.75
37	Will Clark	.40
38	Todd Hundley	.20
39	Andruw Jones	1.00
40	Luis Holando Arrojo	.20
41	Barry Larkin	.50
42	Tim Salmon	.40
43	Rondell White	.40
44	Curt Schilling	.40
45	Chipper Jones	4.00
46	Jeromy Burnitz	.20
47	Mo Vaughn	1.00
48	Tony Clark	.50
49	Fernando Tatis	.40
50	Dmitri Young	.20
51	Wade Boggs	.50
52	Rickey Henderson	.40
53	Manny Ramirez	2.00
54	Edgar Martinez	.20
55	Jason Giambi	.20
56	Jason Kendall	.20
57	Eric Karros	.20
58	Jose Canseco	1.00
59	Shawn Green	.50
60	Ellis Burks	.20
61	Derek Bell	.20
62	Shannon Stewart	.20
63	Roger Clemens	2.00
64	Sean Casey	1.00
65	Jose Offerman	.20
66	Sammy Sosa	4.00
67	Frank Thomas	1.50
68	Tony Gwynn	3.00
69	Roberto Alomar	.75
70	Mark McGwire	8.00
71	Troy Glaus	1.00
72	Ray Durham	.20
73	Jeff Cirillo	.20
74	Alex Rodriguez	4.00
75	Jose Cruz Jr.	.20
76	Juan Encarnacion	.20
77	Mark Grace	.40
78	Barry Bonds	1.50
79	Ivan Rodriguez	1.50
80	Greg Vaughn	.40
81	Greg Maddux	4.00
82	Albert Belle	1.00
83	John Olerud	.50
84	Kenny Lofton	.75
85	Bernie Williams	.75
86	Matt Williams	.50
87	Ray Lankford	.20
88	Darin Erstad	.50
89	Ben Grieve	.50
90	Craig Biggio	.50
91	Dean Palmer	.20
92	Reggie Sanders	.20
93	Dante Bichette	.40
94	Pedro J. Martinez	1.50
95	Larry Walker	.50
96	David Wells	.20
97	Travis Lee	.75
98	Mike Piazza	2.50
99	Mike Mussina	.75
100	Kevin Brown	.40
101	Ruben Mateo (Rookie)	7.00
102	Roberto Ramirez (Rookie)	2.50
103	*Glen Barker* (Rookie)	2.50
104	*Clay Bellinger* (Rookie)	2.50
105	Carlos Guillen (Rookie)	2.50
106	Scott Schoeneweis (Rookie)	2.50
107	Creighton Gubanich (Rookie)	2.50
108	Scott Williamson (Rookie)	3.00
109	*Edwards Guzman* (Rookie)	4.00
110	*A.J. Burnett* (Rookie)	6.00
111	Jeremy Giambi (Rookie)	3.00
112	Trot Nixon (Rookie)	2.50
113	J.D. Drew (Rookie)	12.00
114	Roy Halladay (Rookie)	3.00
115	*Jose Macias* (Rookie)	4.00
116	Corey Koskie (Rookie)	2.50
117	*Ryan Rupe* (Rookie)	5.00
118	Scott Hunter (Rookie)	4.00
119	Rob Fick (Rookie)	2.50
120	McKay Christensen (Rookie)	4.00
121	Carlos Febles (Rookie)	5.00
122	Gabe Kapler (Rookie)	8.00
123	Jeff Liefer (Rookie)	2.50
124	Warren Morris (Rookie)	3.00
125	Chris Pritchett (Rookie)	2.50
126	Torii Hunter (Rookie)	2.50
127	Armando Rios (Rookie)	5.00
128	Ricky Ledee (Rookie)	2.50
129	*Kelly Dransfeldt* (Rookie)	5.00
130	Jeff Zimmerman (Rookie)	10.00
131	Eric Chavez (Rookie)	5.00
132	Freddy Garcia (Rookie)	25.00
133	Jose Jimenez (Rookie)	2.50
134	*Pat Burrell* (Rookie)	80.00
135	*Joe McEwing* (Rookie)	8.00
136	Kris Benson (Rookie)	2.50
137	*Joe Mays* (Rookie)	8.00
138	Rafael Roque (Rookie)	2.50
139	Cristian Guzman (Rookie)	2.50
140	Michael Barrett (Rookie)	4.00
141	Doug Mientkiewicz (Rookie)	4.00
142	*Jeff Weaver* (Rookie)	10.00
143	Mike Lowell (Rookie)	2.50
144	*Jason Phillips* (Rookie)	2.50
145	Marlon Anderson (Rookie)	2.50
146	*Brett Hinchliffe* (Rookie)	2.50
147	Matt Clement (Rookie)	2.50
148	Terrence Long (Rookie)	2.50
149	Carlos Beltran (Rookie)	10.00
150	Preston Wilson (Rookie)	2.50
151	Ken Griffey Jr. (Stars)	25.00
152	Mark McGwire (Stars)	25.00
153	Sammy Sosa (Stars)	15.00
154	Mike Piazza (Stars)	15.00
155	Alex Rodriguez (Stars)	15.00
156	Nomar Garciaparra (Stars)	15.00
157	Cal Ripken Jr. (Stars)	20.00
158	Greg Maddux (Stars)	12.00
159	Derek Jeter (Stars)	15.00
160	Juan Gonzalez (Stars)	8.00
	Checklist card	.10

1999 Fleer Mystique Destiny

		MT
Complete Set (10):		125.00
Common Player:		8.00
Production 999 sets		
1	Tony Gwynn	25.00
2	Juan Gonzalez	15.00
3	Scott Rolen	12.00
4	Nomar Garciaparra	30.00
5	Orlando Hernandez	10.00
6	Andruw Jones	10.00
7	Vladimir Guerrero	15.00
8	Darin Erstad	10.00
9	Manny Ramirez	15.00
10	Roger Clemens	20.00

1999 Fleer Mystique Established

		MT
Complete Set (10):		900.00
Common Player:		50.00
Production 100 sets		
1	Ken Griffey Jr.	150.00
2	Derek Jeter	100.00
3	Chipper Jones	100.00
4	Greg Maddux	75.00
5	Mark McGwire	200.00
6	Mike Piazza	100.00

7	Cal Ripken Jr.	125.00
8	Alex Rodriguez	100.00
9	Sammy Sosa	100.00
10	Frank Thomas	50.00

1999 Fleer Mystique Feel the Game

	MT
Complete Set (7):	650.00
Common Player:	50.00
Adrian Beltre (shoe, 430)	40.00
J.D. Drew (jersey, 450)	80.00
Juan Gonzalez (bat glove, 415)	80.00
Tony Gwynn (jersey, 435)	125.00
Kevin Millwood (jersey, 435)	60.00
Alex Rodriguez (bat glove, 345)	225.00
Frank Thomas (jersey, 450)	100.00

1999 Fleer Mystique Fresh Ink

	MT
Complete Set (26):	1000.
Common Player:	10.00
Inserted 1:48	
Roberto Alomar (500)	40.00
Michael Barrett (1,000)	15.00
Kris Benson (500)	10.00
Micah Bowie (1,000)	10.00
A.J. Burnett (500)	20.00
Pat Burrell (250)	75.00
Ken Caminiti (250)	30.00
Jose Canseco (250)	120.00
Sean Casey (1,000)	30.00
Edgard Clemente (1,000)	10.00
Bartolo Colon (500)	15.00
J.D. Drew (400)	50.00
Juan Encarnacion (1,000)	10.00
Troy Glaus (400)	25.00
Juan Gonzalez (250)	80.00
Shawn Green (250)	50.00
Tony Gwynn (250)	120.00
Chipper Jones (500)	100.00
Gabe Kapler (750)	30.00
Barry Larkin (250)	40.00
Doug Mientkiewicz (500)	10.00
Alex Rodriguez (200)	250.00
Scott Rolen (140)	80.00
Fernando Tatis (750)	20.00
Robin Ventura (500)	20.00
Todd Walker (1,000)	10.00

Player names in *Italic* type indicate a rookie card.

1999 Fleer Mystique Masterpiece

Each of the cards in Fleer Mystique was also produced in a unique Masterpiece version. The super-rarities are labeled on front "The Only 1 of 1 / Masterpiece".

	MT
Common Player:	100.00
(Because of their unique nature Masterpiece values cannot be determined.)	

1999 Fleer Mystique Prophetic

		MT
Complete Set (10):		60.00
Common Player:		4.00
Production 1,999 sets		
1	Eric Chavez	4.00
2	J.D. Drew	8.00
3	A.J. Burnett	8.00
4	Ben Grieve	6.00
5	Gabe Kapler	8.00
6	Todd Helton	6.00
7	Troy Glaus	8.00
8	Travis Lee	4.00
9	Pat Burrell	25.00
10	Kerry Wood	4.00

1999 Fleer/White Rose Team Trucks

Fleer and White Rose, a die-cast collectible vehicle manufacturer, teamed to produce a set of team pick-up trucks which were packaged with a special-edition Fleer Tradition baseball card. The 1/64th scale (about 2-3/4" long) Ford F-150 pickups are painted in team colors and feature team logos. They are sold in a 6" x 8" blister pack with a card that is identical to the regular-issue Fleer version except for the change in card number and the addition of a White Rose logo on back. Original suggested retail price was about $6. Values shown are for complete, unopened truck/card packages.

		MT
Complete Set (30):		175.00
Common Player:		6.00
1	Cal Ripken Jr.	6.00
2	Nomar Garciaparra	6.00
3	Tim Salmon	6.00
4	Frank Thomas	6.00
5	Jim Thome	6.00
6	Tony Clark	6.00
7	Johnny Damon	6.00
8	Jeromy Burnitz	6.00
9	Brad Radke	6.00
10	Derek Jeter	6.00
11	Ben Grieve	6.00
12	Ken Griffey Jr.	6.00
13	Ivan Rodriguez	6.00
14	Carlos Delgado	6.00
15	Greg Maddux	6.00
16	Sammy Sosa	6.00
17	Sean Casey	6.00
18	Jeff Bagwell	6.00
19	Raul Mondesi	6.00
20	Vladimir Guerrero	6.00
21	Mike Piazza	6.00
22	Scott Rolen	6.00
23	Jose Guillen	6.00
24	Mark McGwire	6.00
25	Tony Gwynn	6.00
26	Barry Bonds	6.00
27	Larry Walker	6.00
28	Livan Hernandez	6.00
29	Matt Williams	6.00
30	Wade Boggs	6.00

2000 Fleer Tradition

The Fleer Tradition base set consists of 450 cards including a 30-card rookies/prospects subset, 30 team cards, 10 league leaders, 6 award winners, 10 postseason recaps and 6 checklists. The card fronts have a close-up photo of the featured player as well as a small action photo surrounded by a white border. Like the fronts the card backs have a "throwback" look, which includes complete year-by-year statistics, a brief career note and vital information. 10-card packs had a SRP of $1.49.

		MT
Complete Set (450):		50.00
Common Player:		.10
Wax Box:		55.00
1	AL HRs	.75
2	NL HRs	.75
3	AL RBIs	.75
4	NL RBIs	.75
5	AL Avg.	.50
6	NL Avg.	.15
7	AL Wins	.20
8	NL Wins	.40
9	AL ERA	.20
10	NL ERA	.25
11	Matt Mantei	.10
12	John Rocker	.10
13	Kyle Farnsworth	.10
14	Juan Guzman	.10
15	Manny Ramirez	1.00
16	Matt Riley-P, Calvin Pickering-1B	.10
17	Tony Clark	.40
18	Brian Meadows	.10
19	Orber Moreno	.10
20	Eric Karros	.20
21	Steve Woodard	.10
22	Scott Brosius	.10
23	Gary Bennett	.10
24	Jason Wood-3B, Dave Borkowski-P	.10
25	Joe McEwing	.10
26	Juan Gonzalez	1.00
27	Roy Halladay	.10
28	Trevor Hoffman	.10
29	Arizona Diamondbacks	.10
30	*Domingo Guzman-P*, Wiki Gonzalez-C	.50
31	Bret Boone	.10
32	Nomar Garciaparra	2.50
33	Bo Porter	.10
34	Eddie Taubensee	.10
35	Pedro Astacio	.10
36	Derek Bell	.10
37	Jacque Jones	.10
38	Ricky Ledee	.20
39	Jeff Kent	.10
40	Matt Williams	.50
41	Alfonso Soriano-SS, D'Angelo Jimenez-3B	2.00
42	B.J. Surhoff	.10
43	Denny Neagle	.10
44	Omar Vizquel	.10
45	Jeff Bagwell	1.00
46	Mark Grudzielanek	.10
47	LaTroy Hawkins	.10
48	Orlando Hernandez	.40
49	Ken Griffey Jr.	4.00
50	Fernando Tatis	.20
51	Quilvio Veras	.10
52	Wayne Gomes	.10
53	Rick Helling	.10
54	Shannon Stewart	.10
55	Dermal Brown-OF, Mark Quinn-OF	.25
56	Randy Johnson	.75
57	Greg Maddux	2.00
58	Mike Cameron	.10
59	Matt Anderson	.10
60	Milwaukee Brewers	.10
61	Derrek Lee	.10
62	Mike Sweeney	.10
63	Fernando Vina	.10
64	Orlando Cabrera	.10
65	Doug Glanville	.10
66	Stan Spencer	.10
67	Ray Lankford	.10
68	Kelly Dransfeldt	.10
69	Alex Gonzalez	.10
70	Russell Branyan-3B, Danny Peoples-OF	.10
71	Jim Edmonds	.10
72	Brady Anderson	.20
73	Mike Stanley	.10
74	Travis Fryman	.20
75	Carlos Febles	.10
76	Bobby Higginson	.10
77	Carlos Perez	.10
78	Steve Cox-1B, Alex Sanchez-OF	.10
79	Dustin Hermanson	.10
80	Kenny Rogers	.10
81	Miguel Tejada	.10
82	Ben Davis	.10
83	Reggie Sanders	.10
84	Eric Davis	.20
85	J.D. Drew	.75
86	Ryan Rupe	.10
87	Bobby Smith	.10
88	Jose Cruz Jr.	.10
89	Carlos Delgado	.75
90	Toronto Blue Jays	.10
91	*Denny Stark-P*, Gil Meche-P	.25
92	Randy Velarde	.10
93	Aaron Boone	.10
94	Javy Lopez	.10
95	Johnny Damon	.10
96	Jon Lieber	.10
97	Montreal Expos	.10
98	Mark Kotsay	.10
99	Luis Gonzalez	.10
100	Larry Walker	.75
101	Adrian Beltre	.25
102	Alex Ochoa	.10
103	Michael Barrett	.10
104	Tampa Bay Devil Rays	.10
105	Rey Ordonez	.10
106	Derek Jeter	2.50
107	Mike Lieberthal	.10
108	Ellis Burks	.10
109	Steve Finley	.10
110	Ryan Klesko	.20
111	Steve Avery	.10
112	Dave Veres	.10
113	Cliff Floyd	.10
114	Shane Reynolds	.10
115	Kevin Brown	.20
116	David Nilsson	.10
117	Mike Trombley	.10
118	Todd Walker	.10
119	John Olerud	.25
120	Chuck Knoblauch	.40
121	Nomar Garciaparra	2.00
122	Trot Nixon	.10
123	Erubiel Durazo	.25
124	Edwards Guzman	.10
125	Curt Schilling	.20
126	Brian Jordan	.10
127	Cleveland Indians	.10
128	Benito Santiago	.10
129	Frank Thomas	1.00
130	Neifi Perez	.10
131	Alex Fernandez	.10
132	Jose Lima	.10
133	Jorge Toca-1B, Melvin Mora-OF	.10
134	Scott Karl	.10
135	Brad Radke	.10
136	Paul O'Neill	.25
137	Kris Benson	.10
138	Colorado Rockies	.10
139	Jason Phillips	.10
140	Robb Nen	.10
141	Ken Hill	.10
142	Charles Johnson	.10
143	Paul Konerko	.10
144	Dmitri Young	.10
145	Justin Thompson	.10
146	Mark Loretta	.10
147	Edgardo Alfonzo	.25
148	Armando Benitez	.10
149	Octavio Dotel	.10
150	Wade Boggs	.50
151	Ramon Hernandez	.10
152	Freddy Garcia	.25
153	Edgar Martinez	.20
154	Ivan Rodriguez	1.00
155	Kansas City Royals	.10
156	Cleatus Davidson-2B, Cristian Guzman-SS	.10
157	Andy Benes	.10
158	Todd Dunwoody	.10
159	Pedro Martinez	1.00
160	Mike Caruso	.10
161	Mike Sirotka	.10
162	Houston Astros	.10
163	Darryl Kile	.10
164	Chipper Jones	2.00
165	Carl Everett	.10
166	Geoff Jenkins	.10
167	Dan Perkins	.10
168	Andy Pettitte	.25
169	Francisco Cordova	.10
170	Jay Buhner	.20
171	Jay Bell	.10
172	Andruw Jones	.75
173	Bobby Howry	.10
174	Chris Singleton	.10
175	Todd Helton	.40
176	A.J. Burnett	.25
177	Marquis Grissom	.10
178	Eric Milton	.10
179	Los Angeles Dodgers	.10
180	Kevin Appier	.10
181	Brian Giles	.10
182	Tom Davey	.10
183	Mo Vaughn	.75
184	Jose Hernandez	.10
185	Jim Parque	.10
186	Derrick Gibson	.10
187	Bruce Aven	.10
188	Jeff Cirillo	.10
189	Doug Mientkiewicz	.10
190	Eric Chavez	.10
191	Al Martin	.10
192	Tom Glavine	.25
193	Butch Huskey	.10
194	Ray Durham	.10
195	Greg Vaughn	.25
196	Vinny Castilla	.10
197	Ken Caminiti	.20
198	Joe Mays	.10
199	Chicago White Sox	.10
200	Mariano Rivera	.25
201	Mark McGwire	4.00
202	Pat Meares	.10
203	Andres Galarraga	.50
204	Tom Gordon	.10
205	Henry Rodriguez	.10
206	Brett Tomko	.10
207	Dante Bichette	.25
208	Craig Biggio	.50
209	Matt Lawton	.10
210	Tino Martinez	.40
211	Aaron Myette-P, Josh Paul-C	.10
212	Warren Morris	.10
213	San Diego Padres	.10
214	Ramon E. Martinez	.10
215	Troy Percival	.10
216	Jason Johnson	.10
217	Carlos Lee	.10
218	Scott Williamson	.10
219	Jeff Weaver	.10
220	Ronnie Belliard	.10
221	Jason Giambi	.10
222	Ken Griffey Jr.	4.00
223	John Halama	.10
224	Brett Hinchliffe	.10
225	Wilson Alvarez	.10
226	Rolando Arrojo	.10
227	Ruben Mateo	.40
228	Rafael Palmeiro	.75
229	David Wells	.10
230	Eric Gagne-P, Jeff Williams-P	.10
231	Tim Salmon	.40
232	Mike Mussina	.75
233	Magglio Ordonez	.25
234	Ron Villone	.10
235	Antonio Alfonseca	.10
236	Jeromy Burnitz	.10
237	Ben Grieve	.40
238	Giomar Guevara	.10
239	Garret Anderson	.10
240	John Smoltz	.20
241	Mark Grace	.25
242	Cole Liniak-3B, Jose Molina-C	.10

243	Damion Easley	.10
244	Jeff Montgomery	.10
245	Kenny Lofton	.60
246	Masato Yoshii	.10
247	Philadelphia Phillies	.10
248	Raul Mondesi	.25
249	Marlon Anderson	.10
250	Shawn Green	.75
251	Sterling Hitchcock	.10
252	Randy Wolf-P, Anthony Shumaker-P	.10
253	Jeff Fassero	.10
254	Eli Marrero	.10
255	Cincinnati Reds	.10
256	Rick Ankiel-P, Adam Kennedy-2B	6.00
257	Darin Erstad	.25
258	Albert Belle	.75
259	Bartolo Colon	.10
260	Bret Saberhagen	.10
261	Carlos Beltran	.50
262	Glenallen Hill	.10
263	Gregg Jefferies	.10
264	Matt Clement	.10
265	Miguel Del Toro	.10
266	Robinson Cancel-C, Kevin Barker-1B	.10
267	San Francisco Giants	.10
268	Kent Bottenfield	.10
269	Fred McGriff	.25
270	Chris Carpenter	.10
271	Atlanta Braves	.10
272	Wilton Veras-3B,*Tomokazu Ohka-P*	.50
273	Will Clark	.50
274	Troy O'Leary	.10
275	Sammy Sosa	2.50
276	Travis Lee	.25
277	Sean Casey	.50
278	Ron Gant	.25
279	Roger Clemens	1.50
280	Phil Nevin	.10
281	Mike Piazza	2.50
282	Mike Lowell	.10
283	Kevin Millwood	.25
284	Joe Randa	.10
285	Jeff Shaw	.10
286	Jason Varitek	.10
287	Harold Baines	.10
288	Gabe Kapler	.25
289	Chuck Finley	.10
290	Carl Pavano	.10
291	Brad Ausmus	.10
292	Brad Fullmer	.10
293	Boston Red Sox	.10
294	Bob Wickman	.10
295	Billy Wagner	.10
296	Shawn Estes	.10
297	Gary Sheffield	.25
298	Fernando Seguignol	.10
299	Omar Olivares	.10
300	Baltimore Orioles	.10
301	Matt Stairs	.10
302	Andy Ashby	.10
303	Todd Greene	.10
304	Jesse Garcia	.10
305	Kerry Wood	.40
306	Roberto Alomar	.75
307	New York Mets	.10
308	Dean Palmer	.10
309	Mike Hampton	.10
310	Devon White	.10
311	Chad Hermansen-OF, Mike Garcia-P	.10
312	Tim Hudson	.40
313	John Franco	.10
314	Jason Schmidt	.10
315	J.T. Snow	.10
316	Ed Sprague	.10
317	Chris Widger	.10
318	Ben Petrick-C,*Luther Hackman-P*	.50
319	Jose Mesa	.10
320	Jose Canseco	1.00
321	John Wetteland	.10
322	Minnesota Twins	.10
323	*Jeff DaVanon-OF,* Brian Cooper-P	.50
324	Tony Womack	.10
325	Rod Beck	.10
326	Mickey Morandini	.10
327	Pokey Reese	.10
328	Jaret Wright	.10
329	Glen Barker	.10
330	Darren Dreifort	.10
331	Torii Hunter	.10
332	Tony Armas, Jr.-P, Peter Bergeron-OF	.10
333	Hideki Irabu	.20
334	Desi Relaford	.10
335	Barry Bonds	1.00
336	Gary DiSarcina	.10
337	Gerald Williams	.10
338	John Valentin	.10
339	David Justice	.25
340	Juan Encarnacion	.10
341	Jeremy Giambi	.10
342	Chan Ho Park	.10
343	Vladimir Guerrero	1.50
344	Robin Ventura	.25
345	Bobby Abreu	.10
346	Tony Gwynn	2.00
347	Jose Jimenez	.10
348	Royce Clayton	.10
349	Kelvim Escobar	.10
350	Chicago Cubs	.10
351	Travis Dawkins-SS, Jason LaRue-C	.10
352	Barry Larkin	.50
353	Cal Ripken Jr.	2.50
354	Alex Rodriguez	2.50
355	Todd Stottlemyre	.20
356	Terry Adams	.10
357	Pittsburgh Pirates	.10
358	Jim Thome	.50
359	Corey Lee-P, Doug Davis-P	.10
360	Moises Alou	.20
361	Todd Hollandsworth	.10
362	Marty Cordova	.10
363	David Cone	.20
364	Joe Nathan-P, Wilson Delgado-SS	.10
365	Paul Byrd	.10
366	Edgar Renteria	.10
367	Rusty Greer	.10
368	David Segui	.10
369	New York Yankees	.50
370	Daryle Ward-OF/1B, Carlos Hernandez-2B	.10
371	Troy Glaus	.40
372	Delino DeShields	.10
373	Jose Offerman	.10
374	Sammy Sosa	2.50
375	Sandy Alomar Jr.	.20
376	Masao Kida	.10
377	Richard Hidalgo	.10
378	Ismael Valdes	.10
379	Ugueth Urbina	.10
380	Darryl Hamilton	.10
381	John Jaha	.10
382	St. Louis Cardinals	.10
383	Scott Sauerbeck	.10
384	Russ Ortiz	.10
385	Jamie Moyer	.10
386	Dave Martinez	.10
387	Todd Zeile	.10
388	Anaheim Angels	.10
389	Rob Ryan-OF, Nick Bierbrodt-P	.10
390	Rickey Henderson	.40
391	Alex Rodriguez	2.50
392	Texas Rangers	.10
393	Roberto Hernandez	.10
394	Tony Batista	.10
395	Oakland Athletics	.10
396	Randall Simon-1B,*David Cortes-P*	.40
397	Gregg Olson	.10
398	Sidney Ponson	.10
399	Micah Bowie	.10
400	Mark McGwire	4.00
401	Florida Marlins	.10
402	Chad Allen	.10
403	Casey Blake-3B, Vernon Wells-OF	.10
404	Pete Harnisch	.10
405	Preston Wilson	.10
406	Richie Sexson	.10
407	Rico Brogna	.10
408	Todd Hundley	.10
409	Wally Joyner	.10
410	Tom Goodwin	.10
411	Joey Hamilton	.10
412	Detroit Tigers	.10
413	*Michael Tejera-P,* Ramon Castro-C	.25
414	Alex Gonzalez	.10
415	Jermaine Dye	.10
416	Jose Rosado	.10
417	Wilton Guerrero	.10
418	Rondell White	.20
419	Al Leiter	.20
420	Bernie Williams	.75
421	A.J. Hinch	.10
422	Pat Burrell	2.50
423	Scott Rolen	1.00
424	Jason Kendall	.25
425	Kevin Young	.10
426	Eric Owens	.10
427	Derek Jeter	2.50
428	Livan Hernandez	.10
429	Russ Davis	.10
430	Dan Wilson	.10
431	Quinton McCracken	.10
432	Homer Bush	.10
433	Seattle Mariners	.10
434	Chad Harville-P, Luis Vizcaino-P	.10
435	Carlos Beltran	.25
436	Scott Williamson	.10
437	Pedro Martinez	.50
438	Randy Johnson	.40
439	Ivan Rodriguez	.50
440	Chipper Jones	1.00
441	AL Division (Bernie Williams)	.40
442	AL Division (Pedro Martinez)	.50
443	AL Champ (Derek Jeter)	1.25
444	NL Division (Brian Jordan)	.10
445	NL Division (Todd Pratt)	.10
446	NL Champ (Kevin Millwood)	.10
447	World Series (Orlando Hernandez)	.20
448	World Series (Derek Jeter)	1.25
449	World Series (Chad Curtis)	.10
450	World Series (Roger Clemens)	.75

2000 Fleer Tradition Club 3000

The Club 3000 inserts are die-cut around the number 3,000, commemmorating their reaching the 3,000 hit achievement. These are seeded 1:36 packs and features George Brett, Rod Carew and Robin Yount.

		MT
Complete Set (3):		10.00
Common Player:		3.00
Inserted 1:36		
GB	George Brett	5.00
RC	Rod Carew	3.00
RY	Robin Yount	3.00

2000 Fleer Tradition Club 3000 Memorabilia

These are a parallel to the base version and has five different memorabilia based tiers. Level 2 (cap), Level 3 (bat), Level 4 (jersey), Level 5 (bat and jersey) and Level 6 (bat, jersey and cap). Each card is hand-numbered.

	MT
Common Card:	75.00
George Brett bat/250	125.00
George Brett hat/100	180.00
George Brett jersey/440	100.00
George Brett bat-jersey/100	200.00
George Brett bat-hat-jersey/25	
Rod Carew bat/250	75.00
Rod Carew hat/100	100.00
Rod Carew jersey/440	75.00
Rod Carew bat-jersey/100	125.00
Rod Carew bat-hat-jersey/25	
Robin Yount bat/250	75.00
Robin Yount hat/100	100.00
Robin Yount jersey/440	75.00
Robin Yount bat-jersey/100	125.00
Robin Yount bat-hat-jersey/25	

2000 Fleer Tradition Dividends

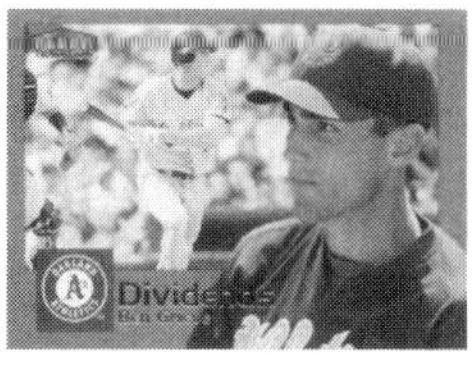

This insert set consists of 15 cards and spotlights the top players on a horizontal format. Card fronts have silver foil stamping, a red border and are seeded 1:6 packs. They are numbered on the back with a "D" suffix.

		MT
Complete Set (15):		30.00
Common Player:		.75
Inserted 1:6		
1	Alex Rodriguez	4.00
2	Ben Grieve	1.00
3	Cal Ripken Jr.	4.00
4	Chipper Jones	3.00
5	Derek Jeter	4.00
6	Frank Thomas	1.50
7	Jeff Bagwell	1.50
8	Sammy Sosa	4.00
9	Tony Gwynn	3.00
10	Scott Rolen	1.50
11	Nomar Garciaparra	4.00
12	Mike Piazza	4.00
13	Mark McGwire	6.00
14	Ken Griffey Jr.	6.00
15	Juan Gonzalez	1.50

2000 Fleer Tradition Fresh Ink

This autographed insert set consists of 38 cards on a vertical format with the autograph on the bottom third of the card below the player image. These were inserted 1:144 packs.

	MT
Common Player:	10.00
Inserted 1:144	
Rick Ankiel	75.00
Carlos Beltran	25.00
Pat Burrell	30.00
Miguel Cairo	10.00
Sean Casey	20.00
Will Clark	25.00
Mike Darr	10.00
J.D. Drew	40.00
Erubiel Durazo	15.00
Carlos Febles	15.00
Freddy Garcia	25.00
Greg Maddux	175.00
Jason Grilli	10.00
Vladimir Guerrero	75.00
Tony Gwynn	120.00
Jerry Hairston Jr.	10.00
Tim Hudson	25.00
John Jaha	10.00
D'Angelo Jimenez	10.00
Andruw Jones	25.00
Gabe Kapler	25.00
Cesar King	10.00
Jason LaRue	10.00
Mike Lieberthal	10.00
Pedro Martinez	75.00
Gary Matthews Jr.	10.00
Orber Moreno	10.00
Eric Munson	35.00
Rafael Palmeiro	35.00
Jim Parque	10.00
Willi Mo Pena	25.00
Cal Ripken Jr.	200.00
Alex Rodriguez	200.00
Tim Salmon	25.00
Chris Singleton	10.00
Alfonso Soriano	40.00
Ed Yarnall	20.00

2000 Fleer Tradition Grasskickers

This 15-card set has a close-up photo of the featured player with holographic silver foil stamping. These are seeded 1:30 packs and are numbered on the back with a "GK" suffix.

		MT
Complete Set (15):		125.00
Common Player:		3.00
Inserted 1:30		
1	Tony Gwynn	10.00
2	Scott Rolen	5.00
3	Nomar Garciaparra	12.00
4	Mike Piazza	12.00
5	Mark McGwire	20.00
6	Frank Thomas	5.00
7	Cal Ripken Jr.	12.00
8	Chipper Jones	10.00
9	Greg Maddux	10.00
10	Ken Griffey Jr.	20.00
11	Juan Gonzalez	5.00
12	Derek Jeter	12.00
13	Sammy Sosa	12.00
14	Roger Clemens	8.00
15	Alex Rodriguez	12.00

2000 Fleer Tradition Hall's Well

This 15-card set spotlights superstars destined for Cooperstown, featured on a transparent plastic stock with overlays of silver foil stamping. These were seeded 1:30 packs and are numbered with a "HW" suffix.

		MT
Complete Set (15):		125.00
Common Player:		3.00
Inserted 1:30		
1	Mark McGwire	20.00
2	Alex Rodriguez	12.00
3	Cal Ripken Jr.	12.00
4	Chipper Jones	10.00
5	Derek Jeter	12.00
6	Frank Thomas	5.00
7	Greg Maddux	10.00
8	Juan Gonzalez	5.00
9	Ken Griffey Jr.	20.00
10	Mike Piazza	12.00
11	Nomar Garciaparra	12.00
12	Sammy Sosa	12.00
13	Roger Clemens	8.00
14	Ivan Rodriguez	5.00
15	Tony Gwynn	10.00

2000 Fleer Tradition Ripken Collection

This 10-card set is devoted to Cal Ripken Jr. and features 10 different Fleer retro designs. These were seeded 1:30 packs.

	MT
Complete Set (10):	70.00
Common Card:	8.00
Inserted 1:30	
(Inserted at the rate of 1:30 packs.)	

2000 Fleer Tradition Ten-4

This 10-card insert set focuses on baseball's home run kings on a die-cut design enhanced with silver foil stamping. These were seeded 1:18 packs and are numbered on the card back with a "TF" suffix.

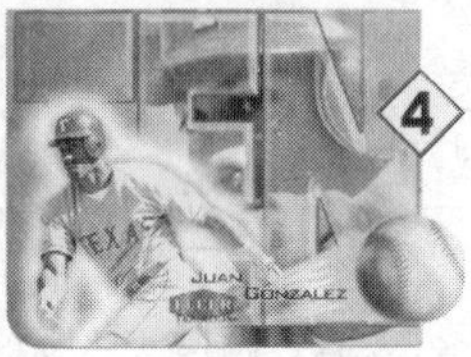

		MT
Complete Set (10):		60.00
Common Player:		2.00
Inserted 1:18		
1	Sammy Sosa	6.00
2	Nomar Garciaparra	6.00
3	Mike Piazza	6.00
4	Mark McGwire	10.00
5	Ken Griffey Jr.	10.00
6	Juan Gonzalez	3.00
7	Derek Jeter	6.00
8	Chipper Jones	5.00
9	Cal Ripken Jr.	6.00
10	Alex Rodriguez	6.00

2000 Fleer Tradition Who To Watch

Top prospects for the 2000 season are highlighted in this 15-card set, including Rick Ankiel. They have a die-cut design with gold foil stamping. These were inserted 1:3 packs and numbered on the back with a "WW" suffix.

		MT
Complete Set (15):		12.00
Common Player:		.50
Inserted 1:3		
1	Rick Ankiel	6.00
2	Matt Riley	.50
3	Wilton Veras	.50
4	Ben Petrick	.50
5	Chad Hermansen	.50
6	Peter Bergeron	1.00
7	Mark Quinn	1.00
8	Russell Branyan	.50
9	Alfonso Soriano	3.00
10	Randy Wolf	.50
11	Ben Davis	.50
12	Jeff DaVanon	.50
13	D'Angelo Jimenez	.50
14	Vernon Wells	1.00
15	Adam Kennedy	.50

2000 Fleer Tradition Opening Day 2K

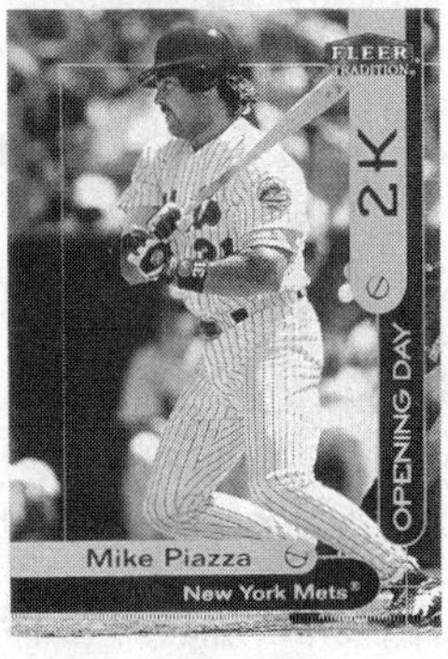

As part of a multi-manufacturer promotion, Fleer issued eight cards of an "Opening Day 2K" set. Packages containing some of the 32 cards in the issue were distributed by MLB teams early in the season. The cards were also available exclusively as inserts in packs sold at KMart stores early in the season. The Fleer Tradition OD2K cards have gold-foil graphic highlights on front. Backs are in the basic format of the rest of the Tradition issue, and are numbered "XX of 32/OD".

		MT
Complete Set (8):		6.00
Common Player:		.50
9	Cal Ripken Jr.	2.00
10	Alex Rodriguez	2.00
11	Mike Piazza	1.00
12	Jeff Bagwell	.75
13	Randy Johnson	.50
14	Jason Kendall	.50
15	Magglio Ordonez	.75
16	Carlos Delgado	.50

2000 Fleer Tradition Japan Commemorative Sheet

To commemorate the opening of the 2000 Major League Baseball season with a Cubs-Mets series in Japan, Fleer created this commemorative sheet for distribution at the opening game on March 29, 2000 and at the Xebio Sporting Goods stores and Pro Pacific Hobby stores in Japan (5,000 each). The 10" x 9" sheets depict on front cards from Fleer's 2000 Tradition set.

	MT
Derek Jeter, Chipper Jones, Pedro Martinez, Mike Piazza, Cal Ripken Jr., Ivan Rodriguez, Sammy Sosa, Mo Vaughn	20.00

2000 Fleer/Twizzlers

A dozen of baseball's biggest stars were reproduced in a format only slightly different from 2000 Fleer Tradition for inclusion in packages of Twizzlers candy. The candy version features UV coating on both front and back, has a small Twizzlers logo at lower-right on back and is numbered "X of 12".

		MT
Complete Set (12):		15.00
Common Player:		.50
1	Mark McGwire	3.00
2	Cal Ripken Jr.	2.00
3	Chipper Jones	1.50
4	Bernie Williams	.50
5	Alex Rodriguez	2.00
6	Curt Schilling	.50
7	Ken Griffey Jr.	3.00
8	Sammy Sosa	2.00
9	Mike Piazza	1.50
10	Pedro Martinez	1.00
11	Kenny Lofton	.50
12	Larry Walker	.50

1992 Flopps Promos

Prior to the 1992 season, Pro Set announced plans to produce a set of 66 cards parodying contemporary baseball stars and teams. The name "Flopps" was used instead of Pro Set, which does not appear anywhere on the cards. While the announced checklist included players such as Craig Piggio, George Brat and Cal Ripped-One, only five promo cards were produced before the players' union whined and the idea was dropped. Pro Set didn't want to offend the union at the time because they were attempting to get a baseball card license. Cards pictured caricatures of the players on front and funny biographies on back, all in color in the standard 2-1/2" x 3-1/2" format.

		MT
Complete Set (5):		30.00
Common Player:		2.00
(1)	Barry Bones	9.00
(2)	Wade Bugs	7.50
(3)	Ken Groovy, Jr.	12.00
(4)	Stickey Henderson	5.00
(5)	Lance Perishable	2.00

1993 Florida Agriculture Dept. Braves/Marlins

A pair of eight-card team panels of the Atlanta Braves and Florida Marlins was issued by the Florida Department of Agriculture and Consumer Services to promote the state's fruit and vegetable products. Individual cards show the player posing - sometimes comically - with one of the state's agricultural products. The photos are bordered in team colors and have a "Fresh 2 U" logo in the upper-left consisting of a fruit or vegetable superimposed on a ball diamond and crossed bats. Backs have the player's name, uniform number, and a short career summary at top. In center is a baseball with the result of an at-bat. In the bottom panel is a statistic about one of the state's crops. A card number is at top. Individual cards measure the standard 2-1/2" x 3-1/2," with the eight-card perforated sheets measuring 10" x 7". The card sheets were distributed during the Sunshine State Games in Tallahassee.

		MT
Complete Set (16):		20.00
Common Player:		1.00
Atlanta Braves Team Set:		12.50
1	Team logo card	1.00
2	Steve Avery	1.00
3	Jeff Blauser	1.00
4	Sid Bream	1.00
5	Tom Glavine	6.00
6	Mark Lemke	1.00
7	Greg Olson	1.00
8	Terry Pendleton	1.50
Florida Marlins Team Set:		9.00
1	Team logo card	1.00
2	Billy the Marlin (mascot)	1.00
3	Ryan Bowen	1.00
4	Benito Santiago	1.00
5	Richie Lewis	1.00
6	Bret Barbarie	1.00
7	Rich Renteria	1.00
8	Jeff Conine	2.50

1994 Florida Marlins Team Issue

These 3-1/2" x 5" black-and-white player portrait cards were issued by the team for publicity use and for player use to honor photo and/or autograph requests from fans. Backs are blank. The unnumbered cards are checklisted here in alphabetical order.

		MT
Complete Set (17):		10.00
Common Player:		.50
(1)	Bret Barberie	.50
(2)	Ryan Bowen	.50
(3)	Chuck Carr	.50
(4)	Jeff Conine	1.00
(5)	Chris Hammond	.50
(6)	Bryan Harvey	.50
(7)	Charlie Hough	.50
(8)	Charles Johnson	1.00
(9)	Richie Lewis	.50
(10)	Dave Magadan	.50
(11)	Rob Natal	.50
(12)	Robb Nen	.50
(13)	Pat Rapp	.50
(14)	Edgar Renteria	1.00
(15)	Benito Santiago	.50
(16)	Gary Sheffield	2.00
(17)	Darrell Whitmore	.50

1987 Red Foley Stickers

Individual player stickers were inserted in sheets within the pages of "Red Foley's Best Baseball Book Ever". The 8-1/2" x 11", 96-page softbound book offered games, quizzes and trivia, with a space to put each sticker. Individual stickers measure about 1-3/8" x 1-3/4". Stickers have color photos on front with a number in the white border at bottom. Player identification does not appear on the sticker. Cover price of the book in 1987 was about $7.

		MT
Complete Book:		9.00
Complete Sticker Set (130):		7.50
Common Player:		.05
1	Julio Franco	.05
2	Willie Randolph	.05
3	Jesse Barfield	.05
4	Mike Witt	.05
5	Orel Hershiser	.05
6	Dwight Gooden	.05
7	Dan Quisenberry	.05
8	Vince Coleman	.05
9	Rich Gossage	.05
10	Kirk Gibson	.05
11	Joaquin Andujar	.05
12	Dave Concepcion	.05
13	Andre Dawson	.05
14	Tippy Martinez	.05
15	Bob James	.05
16	Ryne Sandberg	.25
17	Bob Knepper	.05
18	Bob Stanley	.05
19	Jim Presley	.05
20	Greg Gross	.05
21	Bob Horner	.05
22	Paul Molitor	.25
23	Kirby Puckett	.45
24	Scott Garrelts	.05
25	Tony Pena	.05
26	Charlie Hough	.05
27	Joe Carter	.10
28	Dave Winfield	.25
29	Tony Fernandez	.05
30	Bobby Grich	.05
31	Mike Marshall	.05
32	Keith Hernandez	.05
33	Dennis Leonard	.05
34	John Tudor	.05
35	Kevin McReynolds	.05
36	Lance Parrish	.05
37	Carney Lansford	.05
38	Buddy Bell	.05
39	Tim Raines	.05
40	Mike Boddicker	.05
41	Carlton Fisk	.25
42	Lee Smith	.05
43	Glenn Davis	.05
44	Jim Rice	.10
45	Mark Langston	.05
46	Mike Schmidt	.50
47	Dale Murphy	.40
48	Cecil Cooper	.05
49	Kent Hrbek	.10
50	Will Clark	.15
51	Johnny Ray	.05
52	Darrell Porter	.05
53	Brook Jacoby	.05
54	Ron Guidry	.05
55	Lloyd Moseby	.05
56	Donnie Moore	.05
57	Fernando Valenzuela	.05
58	Darryl Strawberry	.10
59	Hal McRae	.05
60	Tommy Herr	.05
61	Steve Garvey	.20
62	Alan Trammell	.10
63	Jose Canseco	.25
64	Pete Rose	.75
65	Jeff Reardon	.05
66	Eddie Murray	.25
67	Ozzie Guillen	.05
68	Jody Davis	.05
69	Bill Doran	.05
70	Roger Clemens	.25
71	Alvin Davis	.05
72	Von Hayes	.05
73	Zane Smith	.05
74	Ted Higuera	.05
75	Tom Brunansky	.05
76	Chili Davis	.05
77	R.J. Reynolds	.05
78	Oddibe McDowell	.05
79	Brett Butler	.10
80	Rickey Henderson	.25

81	Dave Steib	.05
82	Wally Joyner	.05
83	Pedro Guerrero	.05
84	Jesse Orosco	.05
85	Steve Balboni	.05
86	Willie McGee	.05
87	Graig Nettles	.05
88	Lou Whitaker	.05
89	Jay Howell	.05
90	Dave Parker	.10
91	Hubie Brooks	.05
92	Rick Dempsey	.05
93	Neil Allen	.05
94	Shawon Dunston	.05
95	Jose Cruz	.05
96	Wade Boggs	.25
97	Danny Tartabull	.05
98	Steve Bedrosian	.05
99	Ken Oberkfell	.05
100	Ben Oglivie	.05
101	Bert Blyleven	.05
102	Jeff Leonard	.05
103	Rick Rhoden	.05
104	Larry Parrish	.05
105	Tony Bernazard	.05
106	Don Mattingly	.75
107	Willie Upshaw	.05
108	Reggie Jackson	.50
109	Bill Madlock	.05
110	Gary Carter	.10
111	George Brett	.50
112	Ozzie Smith	.40
113	Tony Gwynn	.45
114	Jack Morris	.05
115	Dave Kingman	.05
116	John Franco	.05
117	Tim Wallach	.05
118	Cal Ripken Jr.	1.00
119	Harold Baines	.05
120	Leon Durham	.05
121	Nolan Ryan	1.00
122	Dennis (Oil Can) Boyd	.05
123	Matt Young	.05
124	Shane Rawley	.05
125	Bruce Sutter	.05
126	Robin Yount	.35
127	Frank Viola	.05
128	Vida Blue	.05
129	Rick Reuschel	.05
130	Pete Incaviglia	.05

1988 Red Foley Stickers

Identical in format to the previous year's issues, the 104 player and 26 team logo stickers in this set were bound into a 96-page, 8-1/2" x 11" softbound book titled "Red Foley's Best Baseball Book Ever". Each 1-3/8" x 1-3/4" sticker could be placed in the book as an answer to trivia questions, quizzes, games, etc. Stickers have color player photos with a number in the white border at bottom. There is no player identification on the stickers. Original issue price was about $8.

		MT
Complete Book:		9.00
Complete Sticker Set (130):		6.00
Common Player:		.05
1	Mike Aldrete	.05
2	Andy Ashby	.05
3	Harold Baines	.05
4	Floyd Bannister	.05
5	Buddy Bell	.05
6	George Bell	.05
7	Barry Bonds	.50
8	Scott Bradley	.05
9	Bob Brower	.05
10	Ellis Burks	.05
11	Casey Candaele	.05
12	Jack Clark	.05
13	Roger Clemens	.25
14	Kal Daniels	.05
15	Eric Davis	.05
16	Mike Davis	.05
17	Andre Dawson	.10
18	Rob Deer	.05
19	Brian Downing	.05
20	Doug Drabek	.05
21	Dwight Evans	.05
22	Sid Fernandez	.05
23	Carlton Fisk	.25
24	Scott Fletcher	.05
25	Julio Franco	.05
26	Gary Gaetti	.05
27	Ken Gerhardt	.05
28	Ken Griffey	.05
29	Pedro Guerrero	.05
30	Billy Hatcher	.05
31	Mike Heath	.05
32	Neal Heaton	.05
33	Tom Henke	.05
34	Larry Herndon	.05
35	Brian Holton	.05
36	Glenn Hubbard	.05
37	Bruce Hurst	.05
38	Bo Jackson	.15
39	Michael Jackson	.05
40	Howard Johnson	.05
41	Wally Joyner	.05
42	Jimmy Key	.05
43	Ray Knight	.05
44	John Kruk	.05
45	Mike Krukow	.05
46	Mark Langston	.05
47	Gene Larkin	.05
48	Jeff Leonard	.05
49	Bill Long	.05
50	Fred Lynn	.05
51	Dave Magadan	.05
52	Joe Magrane	.05
53	Don Mattingly	.75
54	Fred McGriff	.10
55	Mark McGwire	2.00
56	Kevin McReynolds	.05
57	Dave Meads	.05
58	Keith Moreland	.05
59	Dale Murphy	.20
60	Juan Nieves	.05
61	Paul Noce	.05
62	Matt Nokes	.05
63	Pete O'Brien	.05
64	Paul O'Neill	.10
65	Lance Parrish	.05
66	Larry Parrish	.05
67	Tony Pena	.05
68	Terry Pendleton	.05
69	Ken Phelps	.05
70	Dan Plesac	.05
71	Luis Polonia	.05
72	Kirby Puckett	.40
73	Jeff Reardon	.05
74	Rick Rhoden	.05
75	Dave Righetti	.05
76	Cal Ripken Jr.	1.00
77	Bret Saberhagen	.10
78	Benito Santiago	.05
79	Mike Schmidt	.50
80	Dick Schofield	.05
81	Mike Scott	.05
82	John Smiley	.05
83	Cory Snyder	.05
84	Franklin Stubbs	.05
85	B.J. Surhoff	.05
86	Rick Sutcliffe	.05
87	Pat Tabler	.05
88	Jose Tartabull (Danny)	.05
89	Garry Templeton	.05
90	Walt Terrell	.05
91	Andre Thornton	.05
92	Andy Van Slyke	.05
93	Ozzie Virgil	.05
94	Tim Wallach	.05
95	Gary Ward	.05
96	Mark Wasinger	.05
97	Mitch Webster	.05
98	Bob Welch	.05
99	Devon White	.05
100	Frank White	.05
101	Ed Whitson	.05
102	Bill Wilkinson	.05
103	Glenn Wilson	.05
104	Curt Young	.05
105	Braves logo	.05
106	Phillies logo	.05
107	Padres logo	.05
108	Giants logo	.05
109	Orioles logo	.05
110	Tigers logo	.05
111	Pirates logo	.05
112	Royals logo	.05
113	Astros logo	.05
114	Indians logo	.05
115	Brewers logo	.05
116	Cardinals logo	.05
117	White Sox logo	.05
118	Blue Jays logo	.05
119	Red Sox logo	.05
120	Athletics logo	.05
121	Cubs logo	.05
122	Mariners logo	.05
123	Rangers logo	.05
124	Dodgers logo	.05
125	Yankees logo	.05
126	Mets logo	.05
127	Twins logo	.05
128	Expos logo	.05
129	Angels logo	.05
130	Reds logo	.05

1989 Red Foley Stickers

In its third consecutive year of publication, "Red Foley's Best Baseball Book Ever" retained its 96-page softbound 8-1/2" x 11" format of trivia, quizzes and games to be illustrated by placing one of 130 player stickers in the book. Individual stickers are 1-3/8" x 1-3/4" and feature color photos with a white border. Sticker number appears in the bottom-right. There is no player identification on the sticker. Original price of the book was about $8.

		MT
Complete Book:		9.00
Complete Sticker Set (130):		7.50
Common Player:		.05
1	Doyle Alexander	.05
2	Luis Alicea	.05
3	Roberto Alomar	.20
4	Andy Ashby	.05
5	Floyd Bannister	.05
6	Jesse Barfield	.05
7	George Bell	.05
8	Wade Boggs	.25
9	Barry Bonds	.45
10	Bobby Bonilla	.05
11	Chris Bosio	.05
12	George Brett	.50
13	Hubie Brooks	.05
14	Tom Brunansky	.05
15	Tim Burke	.05
16	Ivan Calderon	.05
17	Tom Candiotti	.05
18	Jose Canseco	.25
19	Gary Carter	.10
20	Joe Carter	.05
21	Jack Clark	.05
22	Will Clark	.15
23	Roger Clemens	.25
24	David Cone	.10
25	Ed Correa	.05
26	Kal Daniels	.05
27	Al Davis	.05
28	Chili Davis	.05
29	Eric Davis	.05
30	Glen Davis	.05
31	Jody Davis	.05
32	Mark Davis	.05
33	Andre Dawson	.10
34	Rob Deer	.05
35	Jose DeLeon	.05
36	Bo Diaz	.05
37	Bill Doran	.05
38	Shawon Dunston	.05
39	Dennis Eckersley	.05
40	Dwight Evans	.05
41	Tony Fernandez	.05
42	Brian Fisher	.05
43	Carlton Fisk	.25
44	Mike Flanagan	.05
45	John Franco	.05
46	Gary Gaetti	.05
47	Andres Galarraga	.10
48	Scott Garrelts	.05
49	Kirk Gibson	.05
50	Dan Gladden	.05
51	Dwight Gooden	.05
52	Pedro Guerrero	.05
53	Ozzie Guillen	.05
54	Tony Gwynn	.40
55	Mel Hall	.05
56	Von Hayes	.05
57	Keith Hernandez	.05
58	Orel Hershiser	.05
59	Ted Higuera	.05
60	Charlie Hough	.05
61	Jack Howell	.05
62	Kent Hrbek	.05
63	Pete Incaviglia	.05
64	Bo Jackson	.15
65	Brook Jacoby	.05
66	Chris James	.05
67	Lance Johnson	.05
68	Wally Joyner	.05
69	John Kruk	.05
70	Mike LaCoss	.05
71	Mark Langston	.05
72	Carney Lansford	.05
73	Barry Larkin	.10
74	Mike LaValliere	.05
75	Jose Lind	.05
76	Fred Lynn	.05
77	Greg Maddux	.75
78	Candy Maldonado	.05
79	Don Mattingly	.75
80	Mark McGwire	2.00
81	Paul Molitor	.35
82	Jack Morris	.05
83	Lloyd Moseby	.05
84	Dale Murphy	.25
85	Eddie Murray	.25
86	Matt Nokes	.05
87	Pete O'Brien	.05
88	Rafael Palmeiro	.15
89	Melido Perez	.05
90	Gerald Perry	.05
91	Tim Raines	.05
92	Willie Randolph	.05
93	Johnny Ray	.05
94	Jeff Reardon	.05
95	Jody Reed	.05
96	Harold Reynolds	.05
97	Dave Righetti	.05
98	Billy Ripken	.05
99	Cal Ripken Jr.	1.00
100	Nolan Ryan	1.00
101	Juan Samuel	.05
102	Benito Santiago	.05
103	Steve Sax	.05
104	Mike Schmidt	.45
105	Rick Schu	.05
106	Mike Scott	.05
107	Kevin Seitzer	.05
108	Ruben Sierra	.05
109	Lee Smith	.05
110	Ozzie Smith	.40
111	Zane Smith	.05
112	Dave Stewart	.05
113	Darryl Strawberry	.05
114	Bruce Sutter	.05
115	Bill Swift	.05
116	Greg Swindell	.05
117	Frank Tanana	.05
118	Danny Tartabull	.05
119	Milt Thompson	.05
120	Rob Thompson	.05
121	Alan Trammell	.05
122	John Tudor	.05
123	Fernando Valenzuela	.05
124	Dave Valle	.05
125	Frank Viola	.05
126	Ozzie Virgil	.05
127	Tim Wallach	.05
128	Dave Winfield	.25
129	Mike Witt	.05
130	Robin Yount	.25

1990 Red Foley Stickers

In its fourth consecutive year of publication, "Red Foley's Best Baseball Book Ever" retained its 96-page softbound 8-1/2" x 11" format of trivia, quizzes and games to be illustrated by placing one of 104 player or 26 team logo stickers in the book. Individual stickers are 1-3/8" x 1-3/4" and feature color photos with a white border. Sticker number appears in the bottom-right. There is no player identification on the sticker.

		MT
Complete Book:		9.00
Complete Sticker Set (130):		7.00
Common Player:		.05
1	Allan Anderson	.05
2	Scott Bailes	.05
3	Jeff Ballard	.05
4	Jesse Barfield	.05
5	Bert Blyleven	.05
6	Wade Boggs	.20
7	Barry Bonds	.40
8	Chris Bosio	.05
9	George Brett	.50
10	Tim Burke	.05
11	Ellis Burks	.05
12	Brett Butler	.05
13	Ivan Calderon	.05
14	Jose Canseco	.25
15	Joe Carter	.05
16	Jack Clark	.05
17	Will Clark	.15
18	Roger Clemens	.25
19	Vince Coleman	.05
20	Eric Davis	.05
21	Glenn Davis	.05
22	Mark Davis	.05
23	Andre Dawson	.10
24	Rob Deer	.05
25	Jose DeLeon	.05
26	Jim Deshaies	.05
27	Doug Drabek	.05
28	Lenny Dykstra	.05
29	Dennis Eckersley	.05
30	Steve Farr	.05
31	Tony Fernandez	.05
32	Carlton Fisk	.25
33	John Franco	.05
34	Julio Franco	.05
35	Andres Galarraga	.10
36	Tom Glavine	.10
37	Dwight Gooden	.05
38	Mark Grace	.20
39	Mike Greenwell	.05
40	Ken Griffey Jr.	1.00
41	Kelly Gruber	.05
42	Pedro Guerrero	.05
43	Tony Gwynn	.40
44	Bryan Harvey	.05
45	Von Hayes	.05
46	Willie Hernandez	.05
47	Tommy Herr	.05
48	Orel Hershiser	.05
49	Jay Howell	.05
50	Kent Hrbek	.05
51	Bo Jackson	.10
52	Steve Jeltz	.05
53	Jimmy Key	.05
54	Ron Kittle	.05
55	Mark Langston	.05
56	Carney Lansford	.05
57	Barry Larkin	.05
58	Jeffrey Leonard	.05
59	Don Mattingly	.50
60	Fred McGriff	.10
61	Mark McGwire	1.00
62	Kevin McReynolds	.05
63	Randy Myers	.05
64	Kevin Mitchell	.05
65	Paul Molitor	.30
66	Mike Morgan	.05
67	Dale Murphy	.20
68	Eddie Murray	.20
69	Matt Nokes	.05
70	Greg Olson	.05
71	Paul O'Neill	.10
72	Rafael Palmeiro	.10
73	Lance Parrish	.05
74	Dan Plesac	.05
75	Kirby Puckett	.40
76	Jeff Reardon	.05
77	Rick Reuschel	.05
78	Cal Ripken Jr.	.75
79	Dave Righetti	.05
80	Jeff Russell	.05
81	Nolan Ryan	.75
82	Benito Santiago	.05
83	Steve Sax	.05
84	Mike Schooler	.05
85	Mike Scott	.05
86	Kevin Seitzer	.05
87	Dave Smith	.05
88	Lonnie Smith	.05
89	Ozzie Smith	.25
90	John Smoltz	.10
91	Cory Snyder	.05
92	Darryl Strawberry	.05
93	Greg Swindell	.05
94	Mickey Tettleton	.05
95	Bobby Thigpen	.05
96	Alan Trammell	.05
97	Dave Valle	.05
98	Andy Van Slyke	.05
99	Tim Wallach	.05
100	Jerome Walton	.05
101	Lou Whitaker	.05
102	Devon White	.05
103	Mitch Williams	.05
104	Glen Wilson	.05
105	Indians logo	.05
106	Rangers logo	.05
107	Reds logo	.05
108	Orioles logo	.05
109	Red Sox logo	.05
110	White Sox logo	.05
111	Dodgers logo	.05
112	Tigers logo	.05
113	Mariners logo	.05
114	Blue Jays logo	.05
115	Expos logo	.05
116	Pirates logo	.05
117	Astros logo	.05
118	Cardinals logo	.05
119	Padres logo	.05
120	Angels logo	.05
121	Yankees logo	.05
122	Cubs logo	.05
123	Brewers logo	.05
124	Twins logo	.05
125	Giants logo	.05
126	Royals logo	.05
127	A's logo	.05
128	Mets logo	.05
129	Phillies logo	.05
130	Braves logo	.05

1991 Red Foley Stickers

In its fifth consecutive year of publication, "Red Foley's Best Baseball Book Ever" retained its 96-page softbound 8-1/2" x 11" format of trivia, quizzes and games to be illustrated by placing one of 112 regular player or All-Star (#113-130) stickers in the book. Individual stickers are 1-3/8" x 1-3/4" and feature color photos with a white border. Sticker number appears in the bottom-right. There is no player identification on the sticker.

		MT
Complete Book:		10.00
Comlete Sticker Set (130):		8.00
Common Player:		.05
1	Jim Abbott	.05
2	Rick Aguilera	.05
3	Roberto Alomar	.10
4	Rob Dibble	.05
5	Wally Backman	.05
6	Harold Baines	.05
7	Steve Bedrosian	.05
8	Craig Biggio	.10
9	Wade Boggs	.20
10	Bobby Bonilla	.05
11	George Brett	.50
12	Greg Brock	.05
13	Hubie Brooks	.05
14	Tom Brunansky	.05
15	Tim Burke	.05
16	Tom Candiotti	.05
17	Jose Canseco	.20
18	Jack Clark	.05
19	Will Clark	.15
20	Roger Clemens	.25
21	Vince Coleman	.05
22	Kal Daniels	.05
23	Glenn Davis	.05
24	Mark Davis	.05
25	Andre Dawson	.10
26	Rob Deer	.05
27	Delino DeShields	.05
28	Doug Drabek	.05
29	Shawon Dunston	.05
30	Lenny Dykstra	.05
31	Dennis Eckersley	.05
32	Kevin Elster	.05
33	Tony Fernandez	.05
34	Cecil Fielder	.05
35	Chuck Finley	.05
36	Carlton Fisk	.20
37	Greg Gagne	.05
38	Ron Gant	.05
39	Dan Gladden	.05
40	Dwight Gooden	.05
41	Ken Griffey Jr.	1.00
42	Kelly Gruber	.05
43	Pedro Guerrero	.05
44	Ozzie Guillen	.05
45	Pete Harnisch	.05
46	Billy Hatcher	.05
47	Von Hayes	.05
48	Rickey Henderson	.15
49	Mike Henneman	.05
50	Kent Hrbek	.05
51	Pete Incaviglia	.05
52	Howard Johnson	.05
53	Randy Johnson	.40
54	Doug Jones	.05
55	Ricky Jordan	.05
56	Wally Joyner	.05
57	Roberto Kelly	.05
58	Barry Larkin	.05
59	Craig Lefferts	.05
60	Candy Maldonado	.05
61	Don Mattingly	.65
62	Oddibe McDowell	.05
63	Roger McDowell	.05
64	Willie McGee	.05
65	Fred McGriff	.10
66	Kevin Mitchell	.05
67	Mike Morgan	.05
68	Eddie Murray	.15
69	Gregg Olson	.05
70	Joe Orsulak	.05
71	Dan Petry	.05
72	Dan Plesac	.05
73	Jim Presley	.05
74	Kirby Puckett	.50
75	Tim Raines	.05
76	Jeff Reardon	.05
77	Dave Righetti	.05
78	Cal Ripken Jr.	.75
79	Nolan Ryan	.75
80	Bret Saberhagen	.05
81	Chris Sabo	.05
82	Ryne Sandberg	.25
83	Benito Santiago	.05
84	Steve Sax	.05
85	Mike Schooler	.05
86	Mike Scott	.05
87	Ruben Sierra	.05
88	Cory Snyder	.05
89	Dave Steib	.05
90	Dave Stewart	.05
91	Kurt Stillwell	.05
92	Bobby Thigpen	.05
93	Alan Trammell	.05
94	John Tudor	.05
95	Dave Valle	.05
96	Andy Van Slyke	.05
97	Robin Ventura	.10
98	Frank Viola	.05
99	Tim Wallach	.05
100	Matt Williams	.05
101	Mitch Williams	.05
102	Dave Winfield	.20
103	Eric Yelding	.05
104	Robin Yount	.20
105	Steve Avery	.05
106	Travis Fryman	.05
107	Juan Gonzalez	.60
108	Todd Hundley	.05
109	Ben McDonald	.05
110	Jose Offerman	.05
111	Frank Thomas	.60
112	Bernie Williams	.05
113	Sandy Alomar Jr.	.10
114	Jack Armstrong	.05
115	Wade Boggs	.10
116	Jose Canseco	.10
117	Will Clark	.10
118	Andre Dawson	.05
119	Lenny Dykstra	.05
120	Ken Griffey Jr.	.75
121	Rickey Henderson	.10
122	Mark McGwire	1.00
123	Kevin Mitchell	.05
124	Cal Ripken Jr.	.60
125	Chris Sabo	.05
126	Ryne Sandberg	.15
127	Steve Sax	.05
128	Mike Scoscia	.05
129	Ozzie Smith	.40
130	Bob Welch	.05

1992 Red Foley Stickers

The format was unchanged when "Red Foley's Best Baseball Book Ever" was published in 1992. The 96-page, 8-1/2" x 11" softcover book features 96 pages of quizzes, trivia and games, along with 130 player stickers (#105-130 are All-Star stickers) to be placed on the proper pages. Single stickers measure 1-3/8" x 1-3/4" and have color photos with a white border. A sticker number is in the bottom-right. No player identification appears on the stickers. Issue price of the book was about $9.

		MT
Complete Book:		12.00
Complete Sticker Set (130):		10.00
Common Player:		.05
1	Jim Abbott	.05
2	Roberto Alomar	.15
3	Sandy Alomar Jr.	.10
4	Eric Anthony	.05
5	Kevin Appier	.05
6	Jack Armstrong	.05
7	Steve Avery	.05
8	Carlos Baerga	.05
9	Scott Bankhead	.05
10	George Bell	.05
11	Albert Belle	.15
12	Andy Benes	.05
13	Craig Biggio	.10
14	Wade Boggs	.20
15	Barry Bonds	.50
16	Bobby Bonilla	.05
17	Sid Bream	.05
18	George Brett	.50
19	Hubie Brooks	.05
20	Ellis Burks	.05
21	Brett Butler	.05
22	Jose Canseco	.25
23	Joe Carter	.05
24	Jack Clark	.05
25	Will Clark	.20
26	Roger Clemens	.25
27	Vince Coleman	.05
28	Eric Davis	.05
29	Glenn Davis	.05
30	Andre Dawson	.10
31	Rob Deer	.05
32	Delino DeShields	.05
33	Lenny Dykstra	.05
34	Scott Erickson	.05
35	Cecil Fielder	.05
36	Carlton Fisk	.20
37	Travis Fryman	.05
38	Greg Gagne	.05
39	Juan Gonzalez	.45
40	Tommy Greene	.05
41	Ken Griffey Jr.	1.50
42	Kent Hrbek	.05
43	Kelly Gruber	.05
44	Tony Gwynn	.40
45	Dave Henderson	.05
46	Rickey Henderson	.15
47	Orel Hershiser	.05
48	Marquis Grissom	.05
49	Howard Johnson	.05
50	Felix Jose	.05
51	Wally Joyner	.05
52	David Justice	.10
53	Roberto Kelly	.05
54	Ray Lankford	.05
55	Barry Larkin	.05
56	Mark Lewis	.05
57	Kevin Maas	.05
58	Greg Maddux	.75
59	Dennis Martinez	.05
60	Edgar Martinez	.05
61	Don Mattingly	.75
62	Ben McDonald	.05
63	Jack McDowell	.05
64	Willie McGee	.05
65	Fred McGriff	.10
66	Brian McRae	.05
67	Mark McGwire	1.50
68	Kevin Mitchell	.05
69	Terry Mulholland	.05
70	Dale Murphy	.15
71	Eddie Murray	.15
72	John Olerud	.05
73	Rafael Palmeiro	.10
74	Terry Pendleton	.05
75	Luis Polonia	.05
76	Mark Portugal	.05
77	Kirby Puckett	.40
78	Tim Raines	.05
79	Harold Reynolds	.05
80	Billy Ripken	.05
81	Cal Ripken Jr.	1.00
82	Nolan Ryan	1.00
83	Chris Sabo	.05
84	Ryne Sandberg	.50
85	Benito Santiago	.05
86	Kevin Seitzer	.05
87	Gary Sheffield	.15
88	Ruben Sierra	.05
89	John Smiley	.05
90	Ozzie Smith	.35
91	Darryl Strawberry	.05
92	B.J. Surhoff	.05
93	Frank Thomas	.75
94	Alan Trammell	.05
95	Andy Van Slyke	.05
96	Greg Vaughn	.05
97	Frank Viola	.05
98	Tim Wallach	.05
99	Matt Williams	.05
100	Dave Winfield	.20
101	Mike Witt	.05
102	Eric Yelding	.05
103	Robin Yount	.25
104	Todd Zeile	.05
105	Roberto Alomar	.15
106	Sandy Alomar Jr.	.05
107	Wade Boggs	.15
108	Bobby Bonilla	.05
109	Ivan Calderon	.05
110	Will Clark	.10
111	Andre Dawson	.05
112	Cecil Fielder	.05
113	Carlton Fisk	.05
114	Tom Glavine	.10
115	Ken Griffey Jr.	.75
116	Tony Gwynn	.40
117	Dave Henderson	.05
118	Rickey Henderson	.10
119	Felix Jose	.05
120	Jimmy Key	.05
121	Tony LaRussa	.05
122	Jack Morris	.05
123	Lou Piniella	.05
124	Cal Ripken Jr.	.60
125	Chris Sabo	.05
126	Juan Samuel	.05
127	Ryne Sandberg	.25
128	Benito Santiago	.05
129	Ozzie Smith	.20
130	Danny Tartabull	.05

1993 Red Foley Stickers

The format was unchanged when "Red Foley's Best Baseball Book Ever" was published in 1993. The 96-page, 8-1/2" x 11" softcover book features 96 pages of quizzes, trivia and games, along with 130 player stickers (#105-130 are All-Star stickers) to be placed on the proper pages. Single stickers measure 1-3/8" x 1-3/4" and have color photos with a white border. A sticker number is in the bottom-right. No player identification appears on the stickers.

		MT
Complete Book:		10.00
Complete Sticker Set (130):		9.00
Common Player:		.05
1	Jim Abbott	.05
2	Roberto Alomar	.10
3	Sandy Alomar Jr.	.05
4	Steve Avery	.05
5	Jeff Bagwell	.25
6	Harold Baines	.05
7	Bret Barberie	.05
8	Derek Bell	.05
9	Jay Bell	.05
10	Albert Belle	.20
11	Andy Benes	.05
12	Craig Biggio	.10
13	Wade Boggs	.20
14	Barry Bonds	.40
15	Bobby Bonilla	.05
16	Jose Canseco	.15
17	Joe Carter	.05
18	Wes Chamberlain	.05
19	Will Clark	.15
20	Roger Clemens	.25
21	Milt Cuyler	.05
22	Eric Davis	.05
23	Delino DeShields	.05
24	Rob Dibble	.05
25	Doug Drabek	.05
26	Shawon Dunston	.05
27	Lenny Dykstra	.05
28	Scott Erickson	.05
29	Cecil Fielder	.05
30	Steve Finley	.05
31	Tom Glavine	.10
32	Dwight Gooden	.05
33	Mark Grace	.20
34	Ken Griffey Jr.	1.50
35	Marquis Grissom	.05
36	Kelly Gruber	.05
37	Mark Gubicza	.05
38	Tony Gwynn	.40
39	Mel Hall	.05
40	Pete Harnisch	.05
41	Brian Harper	.05
42	Bryan Harvey	.05
43	Rickey Henderson	.15
44	Orel Hershiser	.05
45	Gregg Jefferies	.05
46	Howard Johnson	.05
47	Felix Jose	.05
48	Wally Joyner	.05
49	David Justice	.10
50	Roberto Kelly	.05
51	Chuck Knoblauch	.05
52	John Kruk	.05
53	Barry Larkin	.05
54	Kenny Lofton	.05
55	Greg Maddux	.65
56	Dennis Martinez	.05
57	Edgar Martinez	.05
58	Tino Martinez	.05
59	Don Mattingly	.50
60	Jack McDowell	.05
61	Willie McGee	.05
62	Fred McGriff	.10
63	Mark McGwire	1.50
64	Brian McRae	.05
65	Randy Milligan	.05
66	Kevin Mitchell	.05
67	Paul Molitor	.20
68	Dale Murphy	.10
69	Mike Mussina	.10
70	Charles Nagy	.05
71	Gregg Olson	.05
72	Rafael Palmeiro	.10
73	Dean Palmer	.05
74	Phil Plantier	.05
75	Luis Polonia	.05
76	Kirby Puckett	.40
77	Tim Raines	.05
78	Cal Ripken Jr.	1.00
79	Bip Roberts	.05
80	Ivan Rodriguez	.20
81	Nolan Ryan	1.00
82	Bret Saberhagen	.05
83	Ryne Sandberg	.25
84	Deion Sanders	.10
85	Reggie Sanders	.05
86	Benito Santiago	.05
87	Mike Scoscia	.05
88	Lee Smith	.05
89	Ozzie Smith	.20
90	Lee Stevens	.05
91	Darryl Strawberry	.05
92	B.J. Surhoff	.05
93	Danny Tartabull	.05
94	Mickey Tettleton	.05
95	Frank Thomas	.90
96	Robby Thompson	.05
97	Alan Trammell	.05
98	Greg Vaughn	.05
99	Mo Vaughn	.10
100	Andy Van Slyke	.05
101	Robin Ventura	.05
102	Matt Williams	.05
103	Robin Yount	.25
104	Todd Zeile	.05
105	Roberto Alomar	.10
106	Sandy Alomar Jr.	.10
107	Wade Boggs	.15
108	Kevin Brown	.05
109	Joe Carter	.05
110	Will Clark	.10
111	Bobby Cox	.05
112	Dennis Eckersley	.05
113	Tony Fernandez	.05
114	Tom Glavine	.05
115	Ken Griffey Jr.	.75
116	Tony Gwynn	.35
117	Tom Kelly	.05
118	John Kruk	.05
119	Fred McGriff	.05
120	Mark McGwire	1.00
121	Kirby Puckett	.25
122	Cal Ripken Jr.	.60
123	Bip Roberts	.05
124	Ivan Rodriguez	.10
125	Gary Sheffield	.05
126	Ruben Sierra	.05
127	Ozzie Smith	.15
128	Andy Van Slyke	.05
129	Robin Ventura	.10
130	Larry Walker	.10

1994 Red Foley

Beginning in 1994, major changes were seen in "Red Foley's Best Baseball Book Ever". The book remained in 8-1/2" x 11" format, but was downsized to 64 pages. The previous years' stickers were replaced with four nine-card sheets of perforated baseball cards. When separated from the sheets, cards measure the standard 2-1/2" x 3-1/2". The unnumbered cards appear in two types. "Superstar" cards feature a single player in a color action photo on front. "Team Leaders" cards have two teammates on front. Red and black printing on backs give personal data and career highlights. Original retail cost of the book was $8.95.

		MT
Complete Book:		15.00
Complete Set (36):		12.00
Common Card:		.50
	SUPERSTARS	
(1)	(Barry Bonds)	1.00
(2)	Joe Carter	.50
(3)	Roger Clemens	1.00
(4)	Juan Gonzalez	1.00
(5)	Ken Griffey Jr.	3.00
(6)	Fred McGriff	.50
(7)	Jose Rijo	.50
(8)	Ryne Sandberg	.75
	TEAM LEADERS	
(9)	Angels (Tim Salmon, Mark Langston)	.50
(10)	Astros (Jeff Bagwell, Doug Drabek)	.50
(11)	Athletics (Mark McGwire, Dennis Eckersley)	1.50
(12)	Blue Jays (Roberto Alomar, John Olerud)	.60
(13)	Braves (Greg Maddux, Tom Glavine)	.75
(14)	Brewers (Robin Yount, Cal Eldred)	.50
(15)	Cardinals (Ray Lankford, Ozzie Smith)	.50
(16)	Cubs (Mark Grace, Randy Myers)	.50
(17)	Dodgers (Mike Piazza, Orel Hershiser)	.50
(18)	Expos (Larry Walker, Marquis Grissom)	.50
(19)	Giants (Will Clark, Matt Williams)	.50
(20)	Indians (Albert Belle, Carlos Baerga)	.50
(21)	Mariners (Jay Buhner, Randy Johnson)	.50

(22)	Marlins (Gary Sheffield, Bryan Harvey)	.50
(23)	Mets (Bobby Bonilla, Dwight Gooden)	.50
(24)	Orioles (Cal Ripken Jr., Mike Mussina)	.75
(25)	Padres (Andy Benes, Tony Gwynn)	.60
(26)	Phillies (John Kruk, Tommy Greene)	.50
(27)	Pirates (Jay Bell, Andy Van Slyke)	.50
(28)	Rangers (Jose Canseco, Kevin Brown)	.50
(29)	Reds (Barry Larkin, Reggie Sanders)	.50
(30)	Red Sox (Mo Vaughn, Frank Viola)	.50
(31)	Rockies (Charlie Hayes, Andres Galarraga)	.50
(32)	Royals (Brian McRae, David Cone)	.50
(33)	Tigers (Cecil Fielder, Mike Henneman)	.50
(34)	Twins (Kirby Puckett, Rick Aguilera)	.60
(35)	White Sox (Frank Thomas, Jack McDowell)	.75
(36)	Yankees (Don Mattingly, Jim Abbott)	.75

1995 Red Foley

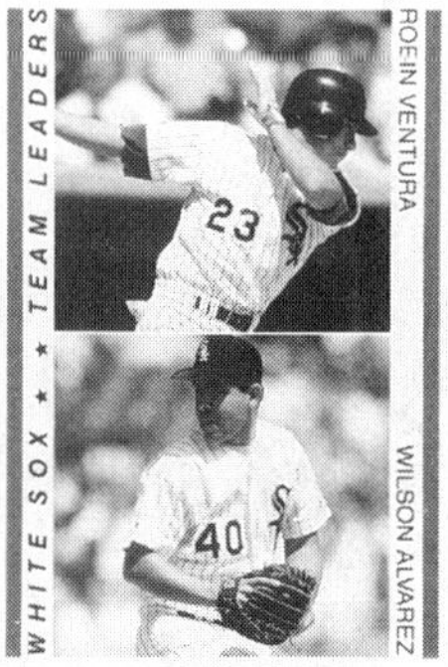

The Red Foley book of children's games, quizzes, trivia and other baseball related entertainment reprised its 1994 format for 1995. The 36 perforated insert cards, 2-1/2" x 3-1/2", were again divided into single-player "Superstar" and two-player "Team Leaders" types. Designs were identical to the previous year, with color action photos on front and career highlights on back. The unnumbered cards are checklisted here in alphabetical order by type.

		MT
Complete Book:		15.00
Complete Set (36):		12.00
Common Card:		.50
	SUPERSTARS	
(1)	(Barry Bonds)	1.00
(2)	Joe Carter	.50
(3)	Roger Clemens	1.00
(4)	Juan Gonzalez	1.00
(5)	Ken Griffey Jr.	3.00
(6)	Fred McGriff	.50
(7)	Cal Ripken Jr.	2.00
(8)	Frank Thomas	1.50
	TEAM LEADERS	
(9)	Angels (Tim Salmon, Steve Finley)	.50
(10)	Astros (Jeff Bagwell, Craig Biggio)	.50
(11)	Athletics (Mark McGwire, Dennis Eckersley)	1.25
(12)	Blue Jays (Roberto Alomar, John Olerud)	.50
(13)	Braves (Greg Maddux, David Justice)	.60
(14)	Brewers (Cal Eldred, Dave Nillson)	.50
(15)	Cardinals (Ozzie Smith, Gregg Jefferies)	.50
(16)	Cubs (Mark Grace, Randy Myers)	.50
(17)	Dodgers (Mike Piazza, Orel Hershiser)	.50
(18)	Expos (Larry Walker, Ken Hill)	.50
(19)	Giants (Matt Williams, Rod Beck)	.50
(20)	Indians (Albert Belle, Carlos Baerga)	.50
(21)	Mariners (Jay Buhner, Randy Johnson)	.50
(22)	Marlins (Gary Sheffield, Benito Santiago)	.50
(23)	Mets (Bret Saberhagen, Bobby Bonilla)	.50
(24)	Orioles (Rafael Palmeiro, Mike Mussina)	.50
(25)	Padres (Tony Gwynn, Andy Benes)	.60
(26)	Phillies (John Kruk, Lenny Dykstra)	.50
(27)	Pirates (Andy Van Slyke, Al Martin)	.50
(28)	Rangers (Jose Canseco, Will Clark)	.50
(29)	Reds (Barry Larkin, Jose Rijo)	.50
(30)	Red Sox (Mo Vaughn, Aaron Sele)	.50
(31)	Rockies (Andres Galarraga, Dante Bichette)	.50
(32)	Royals (Brian McRae, David Cone)	.50
(33)	Tigers (Cecil Fielder, Travis Fryman)	.50
(34)	Twins (Kirby Puckett, Rick Aguilera)	.60
(35)	White Sox (Robin Ventura, Wilson Alvarez)	.50
(36)	Yankees (Don Mattingly, Jimmy Key)	.65

1996 Red Foley

The Red Foley book of children's games, quizzes, trivia and other baseball related entertainment changed little for its 1996 edition. The number of cards was decreased to 32, still in the 2-1/2" x 3-1/2" perforated format. Only single-player cards were produced. Designs were nearly identical to the previous year, with color action photos on front and career highlights on back. The unnumbered cards are checklisted here in alphabetical order.

		MT
Complete Book:		15.00
Complete Set (32):		12.00
Common Player:		.50
(1)	Roberto Alomar	.60
(2)	Moises Alou	.60
(3)	Carlos Baerga	.50
(4)	Jay Bell	.50
(5)	Craig Biggio	.60
(6)	Barry Bonds	.75
(7)	Jeff Conine	.50
(8)	Lenny Dykstra	.50
(9)	Cecil Fielder	.50
(10)	Ken Griffey Jr.	2.00
(11a)	Tony Gwynn (red)	.75
(11b)	Tony Gwynn (purple)	.75
(12)	Rickey Henderson	.60
(13)	Wally Joyner	.50
(14)	Barry Larkin	.50
(15)	Mark McGwire	2.00
(16)	Eddie Murray	.65
(17)	Rafael Palmeiro	.65
(18)	Mike Piazza	.75
(19)	Greg Maddux	.75
(20)	Paul O'Neill	.60
(21)	Kirby Puckett	.65
(22)	Bill Pulsipher	.50
(23)	Cal Ripken Jr.	1.00
(24)	Ivan Rodriguez	.60
(25)	Kenny Rogers	.50
(26)	Tim Salmon	.50
(27)	Kevin Seitzer	.50
(28)	Ozzie Smith	.60
(29)	Sammy Sosa	1.00
(30)	Frank Thomas	1.50
(31)	Mo Vaughn	.60
(32)	Larry Walker	.50

1988 Foot Locker Slam Fest

Two baseball players are among the athletes pictured in this Foot Locker set issued in conjunction with the shoe store chain's Slam Fest competition. Cards were given away at local stores. The 2-1/2" x 3-1/2" cards have color player portrait photos on a semi-gloss front. All athletes are pictured in Slam Dunk basketball style jerseys. A sponsor's banner is at top; the chain's referee logo at lower-left. Backs are printed in blue with information about the televised competition and the player's career.

		MT
Complete Set (9):		3.00
(1)	Bo Jackson	.50
(2)	Devon White	.25

1989 Foot Locker Slam Fest

One baseball player is among the athletes pictured in this Foot Locker set issued in conjunction with the shoe store chain's Slam Fest competition. Cards were given away at local stores. The 2-1/2" x 3-1/2" cards have color player portrait photos on a semi-gloss front. All athletes are pictured in Slam Dunk basketball style jerseys. A sponsor's banner. Backs have information about the televised competition and the player's career.

		MT
Complete Set (10):		4.00
(1)	Vince Coleman	.25

1991 Foot Locker Slam Fest

A number of baseball players were included among the various current and former athletes in this set of three 10-card series produced in conjunction with the sporting gear retailer's Slam Fest charity event. Players are pictured in color on the 2-1/2" x 3-1/2" cards wearing Nike basketball uniforms. Only the baseball players are checklisted here, within series.

		MT
Complete Set (30):		3.00
Common Player:		.12
1-1	Ken Griffey Jr.	1.50
1-2	Delino DeShields	.15
1-3	Barry Bonds	.75
1-4	Jack Armstrong	.15
1-5	Dave Justice	.50
1-6	Deion Sanders	.50
2-2	Bo Jackson	.30

1994 Fox Broadcasting "Hardball"

In conjunction with its short-lived television series "Hardball," Fox issued this set of cards depicting cast members in their roles as members of the fictional Pioneers baseball team. The 2-1/2" x 3-1/2" cards have color photos surrounded by purple border. Backs are blank.

		MT
Complete Set (8):		25.00
Common Card:		4.00
(1)	Lee Emory (Alexandra Wentworth)	4.00
(2)	Lloyd LaCombe (Chris Browning)	4.00
(3)	Dave Logan (Bruce Greenwood)	4.00
(4)	Ernest "Happy" Talbot (Dann Florek)	4.00
(5)	Frank Valente (Joe Rogan)	4.00
(6)	Mike Widmer (Mike Starr)	4.00
(7)	Hardball (mascot)	4.00
(8)	Header card	.50

1989 Foxes Holsum Super Stars Discs

(See 1989 Holsum for checklist and price guide. Distributed in Carolinas)

1981 Franchise 1966 Baltimore Orioles

One of the lesser-known producers of collectors' issues in the early 1980s was "The Franchise". Most of their card sets featured subjects of special interest to their home (Maryland) area. This set, for example, features the 1966 Baltimore Orioles Worlds Champions. In 2-1/2" x 3-1/2" size, cards have black-and-white player photos on front surrounded by orange borders. Black-and-white backs are somewhat in the style of 1953 Bowman, with personal data, career highlights and 1966/Lifetime stats.

		MT
Complete Set (32):		15.00
Common Player:		.25
1	World Champs 1966	.25
2	Team photo	.25
3	Luis Aparicio	1.50
4	Steve Barber	.25
5	Hank Bauer	.35
6	Paul Blair	.25
7	Curt Blefary	.25
8	Sam Bowens	.25
9	Gene Brabender	.25
10	Harry Brecheen	.25
11	Wally Bunker	.25
12	Moe Drabowsky	.25
13	Andy Etchebarren	.25
14	Eddie Fisher	.25
15	Dick Hall	.25
16	Larry Haney	.25
17	Woody Held	.25
18	Billy Hunter	.25
19	Bob Johnson	.25
20	Dave Johnson	.40
21	Sherman Lollar	.25
22	Dave McNally	.25
23	John Miller	.25
24	Stu Miller	.25
25	Jim Palmer	1.50
26	Boog Powell	.85
27	Brooks Robinson	2.00
28	Frank Robinson	2.00
29	Vic Roznovsky	.25
30	Russ Snyder	.25
31	Eddie Watt	.25
32	Gene Woodling	.25

1983 Franchise Brooks Robinson

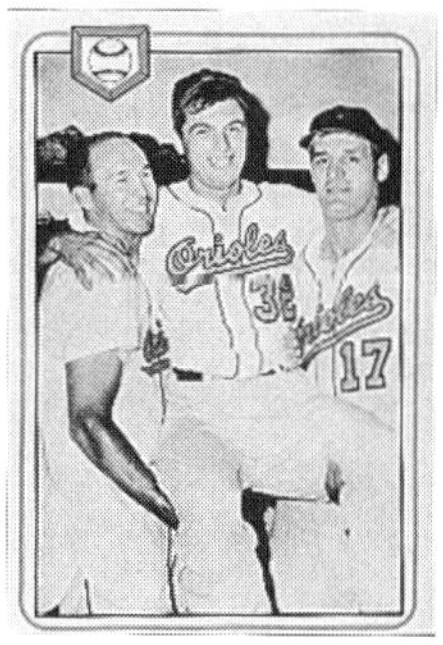

This collectors issue was produced by a Maryland company which specialized in sets of local interest. Cards detail the career of the Orioles Hall of Famer. Fronts of the 2-1/2" x 3-1/2" cards have a black-and-white photo with orange graphics. Backs are printed in black, white and orange and provide a title and details about the front photo.

		MT
Complete Set (40):		16.00
Common Card:		.50
1	Professional record	.50
2	Youngest on team	.50
3	All-state performer	.50
4	Teen-ager in Texas	.50
5	First spring training	.50
6	Another uniform	.50
7	First solid infield	.50
8	Celebration time	.50
9	Instinctive baserunner	.50
10	Wedding day	.50
11	First business partner	.50
12	Second solid infield	.50
13	Two Baltimore heroes	.50
14	Enjoying the kids	.50
15	Playing every game	.50
16	Upsetting the Yankees	.50
17	Tag out at third	.50
18	Getting net results	.50
19	The future MVPs	.75
20	The original Rocky	.50
21	Bauer's gloveman	.50
22	World Series infield	.50
23	Orioles' power parade	.50
24	All Star trio	.75
25	Lethal lumber	.50
26	Belanger joins infield	.50
27	Respect for Oliva	.50
28	Out of Harm's way	.50
29	Master trader	.50
30	Eastern Shore visit	.50
31	Gloves of gold	.50
32	Ripping the Reds	.50
33	Rappin' with Willie	1.00
34	Using the body	.50
35	Getting the umps' attention	.50
36	Respect from teammate	.50
37	Touch of class	.50
38	Bubble never burst	.50
39	Honored by Yankees	.50
40	Two greats at third	.50

1989 Franklin Base Ball Caramels

A step above the usual unlicensed collector issues of its day, this series of cards recreates the look - front and back - of the candy-card issues of the 1910 era, though in current 2-1/2" x 3-1/2" standard size. Fronts have paintings of current stars in vintage uniforms, with identification in the bottom border. Black-and-white backs have artwork of baseball equipment in a large "Base Ball Caramels" logo. The set purports to have been issued by "Franklin Caramel Co. / Chicago," a non-existent firm.

		MT
Complete Set (24)		10.00
Common Player:		.50
	SERIES 1	
1	Bob Uecker	.60
2	Don Mattingly	1.00
3	Jose Canseco	.75
4	Mark McGwire	2.50
5	Bo Jackson	.60
6	Ozzie Smith	.75
7	Nolan Ryan	1.00
8	Gregg Jefferies	.50
9	Gary Sheffield	.50
10	Chris Sabo	.50
11	Pete Rose	1.00
12	Mike Greenwell	.50
	SERIES 2	
1	Jim Abbott	.50
2	Ken Griffey Jr.	2.50
3	Mickey Mantle	1.50
4	Don Mattingly	1.00
5	Darryl Strawberry	.50
6	Kevin Mitchell	.50
7	Rickey Henderson	.50
8	Eric Davis	.50
9	Mark Grace	.75
10	Mike Schmidt	.75
11	Will Clark	.50
12	Willie Mays	1.00

1984 Franklin Glove Hang Tags

Through the last half of the 1980s and into 1990, Franklin Sports Products of Massachusetts issued a series of cards which were hole-punched and attached to baseball gloves as a player endorsement. The series began with a single 1984 issue. The horizontal tag measure about 4-3/4" x 1-5/8". At the left end is a capless portrait photo of Mike Schmidt. A facsimile signature and "NATIONAL LEAGUE M.V.P." appear at right.

	MT
Mike Schmidt	12.00

1987-88 Franklin Glove Hang Tags

Two Star American Leaguers are featured on hang tag cards attached to Franklin Sports Industries baseball gloves in 1987-88. The 1-3/4" x 3" tags have color player photos, with uniform and cap logos removed. Several different types of backs can be found; some referencing the gloves' origins in Korea and Taiwan.

	MT
Wade Boggs	8.00
Don Mattingly	5.00

1989-90 Franklin Glove Hang Tags

In 1989, Franklin Sports Industries switched the format of its hang tag cards. The new design was formatted as a folder. Front of the 2-1/4" x 3-1/4" folders has a color player photo (minus uniform and cap logos) with a black border and gold graphics. Backs have the name and address on the glove company. Inside the folder are career major league stats, highlights and personal data along with an ad for the glove company.

		MT
Complete Set (5):		25.00
Common Player:		4.00
(1)	Wade Boggs (1990)	5.00
(2)	Mike Greenwell (1989)	3.00
(3)	Bo Jackson (1990)	5.00
(4)	Don Mattingly (1989)	6.00
(5)	Mike Schmidt (1989)	10.00

1987 French/Bray Orioles

The Baltimore Orioles and French Bray, Inc. issued a baseball card set to be handed out to fans in attendance at Memorial Stadium on July 26th. Thirty perforated, detachable cards were printed within a three-panel fold-out piece measuring 9-1/2" x 11-1/4". The card fronts feature full-color player photos surrounded by an orange border. The French/Bray logo appears on the card front. The backs are of simple design, containing only the player's name, uniform number, position and professional record.

		MT
Complete Set, Panel:		15.00
Complete Set, Singles (30):		10.00
Common Player:		.25
2	Alan Wiggins	.25
3	Bill Ripken	.25
6	Floyd Rayford	.25
7	Cal Ripken, Sr.	.25
8	Cal Ripken, Jr.	6.00
9	Jim Dwyer	.25
10	Terry Crowley	.25
15	Terry Kennedy	.25
16	Scott McGregor	.25
18	Larry Sheets	.25
19	Fred Lynn	.25
20	Frank Robinson	1.00
24	Dave Schmidt	.25
25	Ray Knight	.25
27	Lee Lacy	.25
31	Mark Wiley	.25
32	Mark Williamson	.25
33	Eddie Murray	4.00
38	Ken Gerhart	.25
39	Ken Dixon	.25
40	Jimmy Williams	.25
42	Mike Griffin	.25
43	Mike Young	.25
44	Elrod Hendricks	.25
45	Eric Bell	.25
46	Mike Flanagan	.25
49	Tom Niedenfuer	.25
52	Mike Boddicker	.25
54	John Habyan	.25
57	Tony Arnold	.25

1988 French/Bray Orioles

French-Bray sponsored a full-color brochure that was distributed to fans during an in-stadium promotion. A blue and orange front cover features inset photos of the Orioles in action on the upper left in a filmstrip motif. To the right is the Orioles logo and their 1988 slogan, "You Gotta Be There" above a baseball glove and ball. The 3-panel foldout measures approximately 9-1/2" x 11-1/4" and includes a team photo on the inside cover, with two perforated pages of individual cards featuring players, coaches and the team manager. Individual cards measure 2-1/4" x 3-1/8", with close-ups framed in white with an orange accent line. The player name and sponsor logo are printed beneath the photo. The black-and-white backs are numbered by player uniform and provide career stats. Additional copies of the brochure were made available from the Orioles Baseball Store following the free give-away.

		MT
Complete Set, Panel:		12.00
Complete Set, Singles (31):		9.00
Common Player:		.25
2	Don Buford	.25
6	Joe Orsulak	.25
7	Bill Ripken	.25
8	Cal Ripken, Jr.	6.00
9	Jim Dwyer	.25
10	Terry Crowley	.25
12	Mike Morgan	.25
14	Mickey Tettleton	.25
15	Terry Kennedy	.25
17	Pete Stanicek	.25
18	Larry Sheets	.25
19	Fred Lynn	.25
20	Frank Robinson	1.00
23	Ozzie Peraza	.25
24	Dave Schmidt	.25
25	Rich Schu	.25
28	Jim Traber	.25
31	Herm Starrette	.25
33	Eddie Murray	3.00
34	Jeff Ballard	.25
38	Ken Gerhart	.25
40	Minnie Mendoza	.25
41	Don Aase	.25
44	Elrod Hendricks	.25
47	John Hart	.25
48	Jose Bautista	.25
49	Tom Niedenfuer	.25
52	Mike Boddicker	.25
53	Jay Tibbs	.25
88	Rene Gonzales	.25
---	Team photo	.40

1989 French/Bray Orioles

This 32-card team set was co-sponsored by French-Bray and the Wilcox Walter Furlong Paper Co., and was distributed as an in-stadium promotion to fans attending the May 12 game. Smaller than standard size, the cards measure 2-1/4" x 3" and feature a full-color player photo with number, name and position below. The backs, done in black-and-white, include brief player data and complete major and minor league stats.

		MT
Complete Set (32):		7.00
Common Player:		.15
3	Bill Ripken	.15
6	Joe Orsulak	.15
7	Cal Ripken, Sr.	.15
8	Cal Ripken, Jr.	5.00
9	Brady Anderson	1.50
10	Steve Finley	.60
11	Craig Worthington	.15
12	Mike Devereaux	.15
14	Mickey Tettleton	.15
15	Randy Milligan	.15
16	Phil Bradley	.15
18	Bob Milacki	.15
19	Larry Sheets	.15
20	Frank Robinson	1.00
21	Mark Thurmond	.15
23	Kevin Hickey	.15
24	Dave Schmidt	.15
28	Jim Traber	.15
29	Jeff Ballard	.15
30	Gregg Olson	.15
31	Al Jackson	.15
32	Mark Williamson	.15
36	Bob Melvin	.15
37	Brian Holton	.15
40	Tom McCraw	.15
42	Pete Harnisch	.35
43	Fransisco Melendez	.15
44	Elrod Hendricks	.15
46	Johnny Oates	.15
48	Jose Bautista	.15
88	Rene Gonzales	.15
---	Sponsor's card	.15

1992 French's Mustard

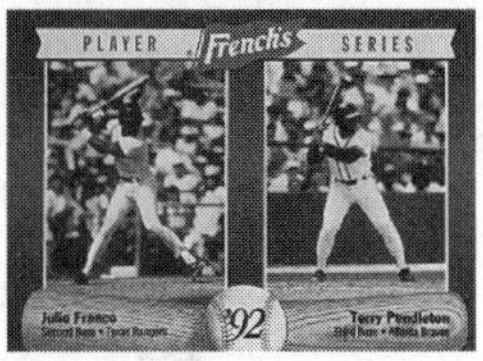

In 1992 French's gave away a promotional card with the purchase of its mustard products. Each of the cards displays photographs of two players. The cards, which have team insignias air-brushed out, feature a green border color photos and the players' statistics on the back.

		MT
Complete Set (18):		10.00
Common Card:		.25
1	Jeff Bagwell, Chuck Knoblauch	.75
2	Roger Clemens, Tom Glavine	.75
3	Julio Franco, Terry Pendleton	.25
4	Howard Johnson, Jose Canseco	.50
5	John Smiley, Scott Erickson	.25
6	Bryan Harvey, Lee Smith	.25
7	Kirby Puckett, Barry Bonds	1.25
8	Robin Ventura, Matt Williams	.50
9	Tony Pena, Tom Pagnozzi	.25
10	Benito Santiago, Sandy Alomar, Jr.	.25
11	Don Mattingly, Will Clark	1.50
12	Ryne Sandberg, Roberto Alomar	1.00
13	Cal Ripken, Jr., Ozzie Smith	2.00
14	Ken Griffey, Jr., Dave Justice	2.00
15	Joe Carter, Tony Gwynn	.75
16	Rickey Henderson, Darryl Strawberry	.50
17	Wade Boggs, Chris Sabo	.50
18	Jack Morris, Steve Avery	.25

1983 Fritsch One-Year Winners

Larry Fritsch Cards continued its series of collector's issues under the banner of "One-Year Winners" with a 64-card color issue in 1983. Most of the player photos featured are unused Topps pictures. As in previous issues, the set features players with short major league careers, few of whom appear on any contemporary baseball card. In the style of 1966 Topps cards, the set has large player photos bordered in white with a diagonal blue strip in an upper corner containing the initials OYW. A blue strip beneath the photo has the player name in black. Backs are in red, black and white with personal data, stats and career highlights.

		MT
Complete Set (64):		12.00
Common Player:		.25
55	Don Prince	.25
56	Tom Gramly	.25
57	Roy Heiser	.25
58	Hank Izquierdo	.25
59	Rex Johnston	.25
60	Jack Damaska	.25
61	John Flavin	.25
62	John Glenn	.25
63	Stan Johnson	.25
64	Don Choate	.25
65	Bill Kern	.25
66	Dick Luebke	.25
67	Glen Clark	.25
68	Lamar Jacobs	.25
69	Rick Herrscher	.25
70	Jim McManus	.25
71	Len Church	.25
72	Larry Stubing	.25
73	Cal Emery	.25
74	Lee Gregory	.25
75	Mike Page	.25
76	Benny Valenzuela	.25
77	John Papa	.25
78	Jim Stump	.25
79	Brian McCall	.25
80	Al Kenders	.25
81	Corky Withrow	.25
82	Verle Tiefenthaler	.25
83	Dave Wissman	.25
84	Tom Fletcher	.25
85	Dale Willis	.25
86	Larry Foster	.25
87	Johnnie Seale	.25
88	Jim Lehew	.25
89	Charlie Shoemaker	.25
90	Don Arlick	.25
91	George Gerberman	.25
92	John Pregenzer	.25
93	Merlin Nippert	.25
94	Steve Demeter	.25
95	John Paciorek	.45
96	Larry Loughlin	.25
97	Alan Brice	.25
98	Chet Boak	.25
99	Alan Koch	.25
100	Danny Walton	.35
101	Elder White	.25
102	Jim Snyder	.25
103	Ted Schreiber	.25
104	Evans Killeen	.25
105	Ray Daviault	.25
106	Larry Foss	.25
107	Wayne Graham	.25
108	Santiago Rosario	.25
109	Bob Sprout	.25
110	Tom Hughes	.25
111	Em Lindbeck	.25
112	Ray Blemker	.25
113	Shaun Fitzmaurice	.25
114	Ron Stillwell	.25
115	Carl Thomas	.25
116	Mike DeGerick	.25
117	Jay Dahl	.25
118	Al Lary	.45

1983 Fritsch 1953 Boston/ Milwaukee Braves

This collectors' issue commemorates the 30th anniversary of the move of the Boston Braves to Milwaukee. The black-and-white photos on the front of the cards (bordered in blue) were taken in spring training, with players still wearing Boston caps. Card backs have personal data and detailed career highlights. Cards measure about 2-5/8" x 3-3/4", which was the standard prior to 1957.

		MT
Complete Set (32):		8.00
Common Player:		.25
1	Joe Adcock	.35
2	John Antonelli	.25
3	Billy Bruton	.25
4	Bob Buhl	.25
5	Lew Burdette	.35
6	Paul Burris	.25
7	Dave Cole	.25
8	Johnny Cooney	.25
9	Walker Cooper	.25
10	Del Crandall	.35
11	George Crowe	.25
12	Jack Dittmer	.25
13	Dick Donovan	.25
14	Sid Gordon	.25
15	Virgil Jester	.25
16	Ernie Johnson	.25
17	Dave Jolly	.25
18	Billy Klaus	.25
19	Don Liddle	.25
20	Johnny Logan	.25
21	Luis Marquez	.25
21s	Luis Marquez (sample overprint)	.25
22	Eddie Mathews	1.00
22s	Eddie Mathews (sample overprint)	.25
23	Andy Pafko	.35
24	Jim Pendleton	.25
25	Ebba St. Claire	.25
26	Sibby Sisti	.25
27	Warren Spahn	1.00
28	Max Surkont	.25
29	Bob Thorpe	.25
30	Murray Wall	.25
31	Bucky Walters	.25
32	Jim Wilson	.25
33	1953 Braves team	.25

1986 Fritsch Negro League Baseball Stars

One of the most comprehensive collectors' issues to feature the stars of the Negro Leagues, the Fritsch set features black-and-white photos of varying quality; most of the photos are contemporary with the players' careers from the 1920s into the 1950s, with a few of the segregated leagues' earlier pioneers also included. Fronts are highlighted with red graphics. Backs are printed in blue and present a brief summary of the player's career and a list of the teams on which he played. Cards are in standard 2-1/2" x 3-1/2" format.

		MT
Complete Set (119):		12.50
Common Player:		.10
1	Buck Leonard	.15
2	Ted Page	.10
3	Cool Papa Bell	.15
4	Oscar Charleston, Josh Gibson, Ted Page, Judy Johnson	.15
5	Judy Johnson	.15
6	Monte Irvin	.15
7	Ray Dandridge	.15
8	Oscar Charleston	.15
9	Josh Gibson	.15
10	Satchel Paige	.25
11	Jackie Robinson	.50
12	Piper Davis	.10
13	Josh Johnson	.10
14	Lou Dials	.15
15	Andy Porter	.10
16	Pop Lloyd	.15
17	Andy Watts	.10
18	Rube Foster	.10
19	Martin Dihigo	.15
20	Lou Dials	.15
21	Satchel Paige	.25
22	Crush Holloway	.10
23	Josh Gibson	.15
24	Oscar Charleston	.15
25	Jackie Robinson	.50
26	Larry Brown	.10
27	Hilton Smith	.10
28	Moses Fleetwood Walker	.25
29	Jimmie Crutchfield	.10
30	Josh Gibson	.15
30s	Josh Gibson (SAMPLE on back)	2.00
31	Josh Gibson	.15
32	Bullet Rogan	.15
33	Clint Thomas	.10
34	Rats Henderson	.10
35	Pat Scantlebury	.10
36	Sidney Morton	.10
37	Larry Kimbrough	.10
38	Sam Jethroe	.10
39	Normal "Tweed" Webb	.10
40	Mahlon Duckett	.10
41	Andy Anderson	.10
42	Buster Haywood	.10
43	Bob Trice	.10
44	Bus Clarkson	.10
45	Buck O'Neil	.15
46	Jim Zapp	.10
47	Piper Davis	.10
48	Ed Steel	.10
49	Bob Boyd	.10
50	Marlin Carter	.10
51	George Giles	.10
52	Bill Byrd	.10
53	Art Pennington	.10
54	Max Manning	.10
55	Ron Teasley	.10
56	Ziggy Marcell	.10
57	Bill Cash	.10
58	Joe Scott	.10
59	Joe Fillmore	.10
60	Bob Thurman	.10
61	Larry Kimbrough	.10
62	Verdell Mathis	.10
63	Josh Johnson	.10
64	Double Duty Radcliffe	.15
65	William Bobby Robinson	.10
66	Bingo DeMoss	.15
67	John Beckwith	.10
68	Bill Jackman	.10
69	Bill Drake	.10
70	Charles Grant	.15
71	Willie Wells	.25
72	Jose Fernandez	.10
73	Isidro Fabri	.10
74	Frank Austin	.10
75	Richard Lundy	.10
76	Junior Gilliam	.15
77	John Donaldson	.10
78	Herb Dixon	.10
79	Slim Jones	.10
80	Sam Jones	.10
81	Dave Hoskins	.10
82	Jerry Benjamin	.10
83	Luke Easter	.10
84	Ramon Herrera	.10
85	Matthew Carlisle	.10
86	Smoky Joe Williams	.25
87	Marv Williams	.10
88	William Yancey	.10
89	Monte Irvin	.15
89s	Monte Irvin (SAMPLE on back)	1.00
90	Cool Papa Bell	.15
91	Biz Mackey	.10
92	Harry Simpson	.10
93	Lazario Salazar	.10
94	Bill Perkins	.10
95	Johnny Davis	.10
96	Jelly Jackson	.10
97	Sam Bankhead	.10
98	Hank Thompson	.10
99	William Bell	.10
100	Cliff Bell	.10
101	Dave Barnhill	.10
102	Dan Bankhead	.10
103	Lloyd Bassett	.10
104	Newt Allen	.10
105	George Jefferson	.10
106	Pat Paterson	.10
107	Goose Tatum	.15
108	Dave Malarcher	.10
109	Home Run Johnson	.10
110	Bill Monroe	.10
111	Sammy Hughes	.10
112	Dick Redding	.10
113	Fats Jenkins	.10
114	Jimmie Lyons	.10
115	Mule Suttles	.10
116	Ted Trent	.10
117	George Sweatt	.10
118	Frank Duncan	.10
119	Checklist	.05

1988 Fritsch Baseball Card Museum Promo Cards

Some of the star attractions of the Larry Fritsch Baseball Card Museum in Cooperstown, N.Y., are featured on this collectors' set. Fronts feature color photos of some of the hobby's rarest and most valuable cards. Backs describe the cards, indicate how they were acquired and provide historical and current value information.

		MT
Complete Set (8):		4.00
Common Card:		.50
1	T206 Honus Wagner	.50
2	T206 Joe Doyle, N.Y. Nat'l	.50
3	T205 Ty Cobb	.50
4	1914 Cracker Jack Joe Jackson	.50
5	T206 Eddie Plank	.50
6	T206 Magie/Magee	.50
7	Colgan's Chips Jim Thorpe	.50
8	Header card	.50

1995 Fritsch All-American Girls Baseball League

The first comprehensive set of cards depicting members of the All-American Girls Professional Baseball League (1943-1954) is this collectors' issue. Contemporary photos with either red or blue graphic highlights are featured on front, along with the Fritsch and AAGPBL logo. Backs are in two styles, depending on the number of stats available; all have personal data and a brief career summary. Backs are printed in either red or blue, plus black on white. Players who are known to have died are indicated by a black name strip on back. The cards are in standard 2-1/2" x 3-1/2" format, printed on semi-gloss cardboard. The set is sold in a red, white and blue collectors' box.

		MT
Complete Set (235):		12.00
Common Player:		.05
1	Dottie Wiltse	.05
2	Wimp Baumgartner	.05
3	Evelyn Adams	.05
4	Ellen Ahrndt	.05
5	Gert Alderfer	.05
6	Bea Allard	.05
7	Isabel Alvarez	.05
8	Amy Irene Applegren	.05
9	Bea Arbour	.05
10	Ange Armato	.05
11	Lou Arnold	.05
12	Norene Arnold	.05
13	Phyllis Baker	.05
14	Chris Ballingall	.05
15	Lois Barker	.05
16	Annastasia Batikis	.05
17	Fern Battaglia	.05
18	Katie Beare	.05
19	Donna Becker	.05
20	Barbara Berger	.05
21	Joan Berger	.05
22	Norma Berger	.05
23	Erma Bergman	.05
24	Betty Berthiaume	.05
25	Mary Beschorner	.05
26	Nalda Bird	.05
27	Maybelle Blair	.05
28	Kay Blumetta	.05
29	Lorraine Borg	.05
30	Ruth Born	.05
31	Wilma Briggs	.05
32	Pat Brown	.05
33	Delores Brumfield	.05
34	Jean Buckley	.05
35	Shirley Burkovich	.05
36	Mary Butcher	.05
37	Helen Callaghan	.05
38	Mary Callaghan	.05
39	Ysora Castillo	.05
40	Ann Cindric	.05
41	Lucille Colacito	.05
42	Donna Cook	.05
43	Doris Cook	.05
44	Gloria Cordes	.05
45	Betty Jane Cornett	.05
46	Pat Courtney	.05
47	Peggy Cramer	.05
48	Eleanor Dapkus	.05
49	Alice DeCambra	.05
50	Lillian DeCambra	.05
51	Millie Deegan	.05
52	Jeanie DesCombes	.05
53	Nancy DeShone	.05
54	Wanita Dokish	.05
55	Terry Donahue	.05
56	Maxine Drinkwater	.05
57	Thelma Eisen	.05
58	Lou Erickson	.05
59	Betty Fabac	.05
60	Jean Faut	.05
61	Dottie Ferguson	.05
62	Helen Filarski	.05
63	Lorraine Fisher	.05
64	Lois Florreich	.05
65	Rose Folder	.05
66	Betty Francis	.05
67	Mary Froning	.05
68	Gertrude Ganote	.05
69	Ann Garman	.05
70	Eileen Gascon	.05
71	Jean Geissinger	.05
72	Bethany Goldsmith	.05
73	Julie Gutz	.05
74	Carol Habben	.05
75	Audrey Haine	.05
76	Beverly Hatzell	.05
77	Jean Havlish	.05
78	Alice Haylett	.05
79	Ruby Heafner	.05
80	Ruth Heverly	.05
81	Irene Hickson	.05
82	Joyce Hill	.05
83	Barb Hoffmann	.05
84	Mabel Holle	.05
85	Alice Hoover	.05
86	Marion Hosbein	.05
87	Dottie Hunter	.05
88	Anna May Hutchison	.05
89	Lillian Jackson	.05
90	Jane Jacobs	.05
91	Janet Jacobs	.05
92	Frances Janssen	.05
93	Marilyn Jenkins	.05
94	Betsy Jochum	.05
95	Arleene Johnson	.05
96	Marilyn Jones	.05
97	Vivian Kellogg	.05
98	Beatty Kemmerer	.05
99	Sue Kidd	.05
100	Audrey Kissel	.05
101	Maxine Kline	.05
102	Phyllis Koehn	.05
103	Mary Lou Kolanko	.05
104	Irene Kotowicz	.05
105	Ruth Kramer	.05
106	Jaynie Krick	.05
107	Marie Kruckel	.05
108	Anna Kunkel	.05
109	Noella Leduc	.05
110	Dolores Lee	.05
111	Rhoda Leonard	.05
112	Joan Lequia	.05
113	Sarah Lonetto	.05
114	Lillian Luckey	.05
115	Helene Machado	.05
116	Lucella MacLean	.05
117	Dorothy Maguire	.05
118	Elizabeth Mahon	.05

119	Marie Mahoney	.05
120	Lenora Mandella	.05
121	Marie Mansfield	.05
122	Jeanie Marlowe	.05
123	Theda Marshall	.05
124	Ruth Matlack	.05
125	Joanne McComb	.05
126	Betty Jean McFadden	.05
127	Terry McKinley	.05
128	Mildred Meacham	.05
129	Norma Metrolis	.05
130	Anna Meyer	.05
131	Rita Meyer	.05
132	Ruth Middleton	.05
133	Betty Moczynski	.05
134	Jane Moffet	.05
135	Dorothy Montgomery	.05
136	Dolores Moore	.05
137	Mary Moore	.05
138	Esther Morrison	.05
139	Nancy Mudge	.05
140	Dolores Mueller	.05
141	Dottie Naum	.05
142	Mary Nesbitt	.05
143	Helen Nordquist	.05
144	Penny O'Brian	.05
145	Annie O'Dowd	.05
146	Shirley Palesh	.05
147	Sue Parsons	.05
148	Barbara Payne	.05
149	Dolly Pearson	.05
150	June Peppas	.05
151	Edie Perlick	.05
152	Marge Peters	.05
153	Betty Jean Peterson	.05
154	Teeny Petras	.05
155	Betty Petryna	.05
156	Alice Pollitt	.05
157	Mary Pratt	.05
158	Charlene Pryer	.05
159	Mamie Redman	.05
160	Dorrie Reid	.05
161	Ruth Richard	.05
162	Ruth Ries	.05
163	Earlene Risinger	.05
164	Jenny Romatowski	.05
165	Eilaine Roth	.05
166	Elaine Roth	.05
167	Mary Rountree	.05
168	Pat Roy	.05
169	Irene Ruhnke	.05
170	Jan Rumsey	.05
171	Maggie Russo	.05
172	Julie Sabo	.05
173	Sarah Jane Sands	.05
174	Blanche Schachter	.05
175	Edna Scheer	.05
176	Claire Schillace	.05
177	Violet Schmidt	.05
178	Dottie Schroeder	.05
179	Gloria Schweigerdt	.05
180	Pat Scott	.05
181	Lillian Shadic	.05
182	Doris Shero	.05
183	Kay Shinen	.05
184	Twila Shively	.05
185	Fern Shollenberger	.05
186	Jo Sindelar	.05
187	Colleen Smith	.05
188	Joyce Steele	.05
189	Rosemary Stevenson	.05
190	Jeanette Stocker	.05
191	Lucille Stone	.05
192	Shirley Stovroff	.05
193	Mary Lou Studnicka	.05
194	Bev Stuhr	.05
195	Lee Surkowski	.05
196	Eunice Taylor	.05
197	Yolande Teillet	.05
198	Doris Tetzlaff	.05
199	Mava Lee Thomas	.05
200	Barbara Thompson	.05
201	Viola Thompson	.05
202	Gene Travis	.05
203	Betty Trezza	.05
204	Ellen Tronnier	.05
205	Betty Tucker	.05
206	Virginia Ventura	.05
207	Marge Villa	.05
208	Georgette Vincent	.05
209	Katie Vonderau	.05
210	Frances Vukovich	.05
211	Helen Waddell	.05
212	Betty Wagoner	.05
213	Helen Walulik	.05
214	Millie Warwick	.05
215	Marion Watson	.05
216	Evie Wawryshyn	.05
217	Mary Weddle	.05
218	Rossey Weeks	.05
219	Marie Wegman	.05
220	Shirley Weierman	.05
221	Helen Westerman	.05
222	Norma Whitney	.05
223	Janet Wiley	.05
224	Connie Wisniewski	.05
225	Marion Wohlwender	.05
226	Sylvia Wronski	.05
227	Renae Youngberg	.05
228	Lois Youngen	.05
229	Marie Zeigler	.05
230	League history card	.05
231	League history card	.05
232	League history card	.05
233	Checklist	.05
234	Checklist	.05
----	Larry Fritsch Cards ad card	.05

1996 Fritsch All-American Girls Baseball League

A second series of AAGPBL cards was issued in 1996 following a similar format to the debut 1995 issue. Cards were sold only as complete boxed sets.

		MT
Complete Set (105):		9.00
Common Player:		.05
235	Angie Allen	.05
236	Vivian Anderson	.05
237	Charlotte Armstrong	.05
238	Mary Baker	.05
239	Pat Barringer	.05
240	Ginger Bell	.05
241	Sonny Berger	.05
242	Jayne Bittner	.05
243	Audrey Bleiler	.05
244	Rita Briggs	.05
245	Eileen Burmeister	.05
246	Helen Campbell	.05
247	Bett Carveth	.05
248	Jean Clone	.05
249	Pauline Crawley	.05
250	JoJo D'Angelo	.05
251	Louella Deitweiler	.05
252	Faye Dancer	.05
253	Shirley Danz	.05
254	Cartha Doyle	.05
255	Gertie Dunn	.05
256	Mid Earp	.05
257	June Emerson	.05
258	Betty Emry	.05
259	Maddy English	.05
260	Liz Farrow	.05
261	Alva Jo Fischer	.05
262	Anita Foss	.05
263	Edna Frank	.05
264	Rose Gacioch	.05
265	Anne Georges	.05
266	Phil Gianfrancisco	.05
267	Mary Lou Graham	.05
268	Dottie Green	.05
269	Dorothy Harrell	.05
270	Kay Helm	.05
271	Joan Holderness	.05
272	Katie Horstman	.05
273	Shirley Jameson	.05
274	Chris Jewett	.05
275	Margaret Johnson	.05
276	Daisy Junor	.05
277	Margaret Jurgensmeier	.05
278	Marie Kazmierczak	.05
279	Jackie Kelley	.05
280	Addie Kerrar	.05
281	Kerry Kerrigan	.05
282	Pepper Kerwin	.05
283	Helen Ketola	.05
284	Erma Keyes	.05
285	Dolores Klosowski	.05
286	Tracy Kobuszewski	.05
287	Riley Kotil	.05
288	Annabelle Lee	.05
289	Barbara Liebrich	.05
290	Alta Little	.05
291	Jackie Mattson	.05
292	Lex McCutchan	.05
293	Betty McKenna	.05
294	Bernie Metesch	.05
295	Sally Meier	.05
296	Ellie Moore	.05
297	Carolyn Morris	.05
298	Dottie Mueller	.05
299	Helen Nelson	.05
300	Dolly Niemiec	.05
301	Eileen O'Brien	.05
302	Janice O'Hara	.05
303	Marilyn Olinger	.05
304	Barbara Parks	.05
305	Dolly Pearson	.05
306	Marge Pieper	.05
307	Pauline Pirok	.05
308	Helen Rauner	.05
309	Mary Reynolds	.05
310	Marty Rommelaere	.05
311	Mary Rudis	.05
312	Terry Rukavina	.05
313	Doris Sams	.05
314	Gig Smith	.05
315	Jean Smith	.05
316	Barb Sowers	.05
317	Elma Steck	.05
318	Dottie Stolze	.05
319	Anne Surkowski	.05
320	Norma Taylor	.05
321	Ginny Tezak	.05
322	Dolly Vanderlip	.05
323	Inez Voyce	.05
324	Betty Waniess	.05
325	Betty Warfel	.05
326	Nancy Warren	.05
327	Betty Weaver	.05
328	Joan Weaver	.05
329	Joanne Weaver	.05
330	Margaret Wigiser	.05
331	Elsie Wingrove	.05
332	Karl Winsch	.05
333	Jo Winter	.05
334	Betty Yahr	.05
335	Alma Ziegler	.05
336	Aggie Zurowski	.05
337	Julie Dusanko	.05
338	Ruth Williams	.05
339	Checklist	.05
340	League logo card	.05

1991 Front Row Ken Griffey Jr.

Production of this collectors' set and related promo cards was reported at 25,000 sets each. Cards trace the three-year career of Junior in photos, stats, highlights and biographic details. Fronts have various posed and color action photos, complete with team logos, and a white border. Horizontal backs are printed in black on a light blue background. Promo cards have a large "PROMO" printed on a baseball at center. Size is 2-1/2" x 3-1/2".

		MT
Complete Set (10):		2.00
Complete Promo Set (5):		1.00
Common Card:		.25
Common Promo:		.25
1	Ken Griffey Jr. (All-Star)	.25
1	Ken Griffey Jr. (All-Star) (promo)	.25
2	Ken Griffey Jr. (The Breakdown)	.25
2	Ken Griffey Jr. (The Breakdown) (promo)	.25
3	Ken Griffey Jr. (Homers)	.25
3	Ken Griffey Jr. (Homers) (promo)	.25
4	Ken Griffey Jr. (Gold Glove)	.25
4	Ken Griffey Jr. (Gold Glove) (promo)	.25
5	Ken Griffey Jr. (Drafted)	.25
5	Ken Griffey Jr. (Drafted) (promo)	.25
6	Ken Griffey Jr. (Up Close and Personal)	.25
7	Ken Griffey Jr. (Background)	.25
8	Ken Griffey Jr. (The Majors)	.25
9	Ken Griffey Jr. (Career Highlights)	.25
10	Ken Griffey Jr. (The American League)	.25

1992-95 Front Row All-Time Great Series

Some of baseball's greatest living former stars were featured in this run of five-card sets. Originally intended to encompass 100 players, the issue was cut considerably short. Each single-player set contains five cards featuring black-and-white and/or color photos on front. Backs have a photo in the background, overprinted with statistical, biographical or career information. Major league uniform logos have been removed from photos for lack of licensing by MLB. Each set was issued in an edition of 25,000, with an illustrated, numbered certificate of authenticity included. Some sets were also produced with the top card authentically autographed. Sets are checklisted here alphabetically; single cards are not listed because the cards are usually sold only as sets.

		MT
Common Player Set:		.25
(1)	Hank Aaron (5-card set)	1.00
(2)	Ernie Banks (5-card set)	.75
(3)	Al Barlick (5-card set)	.25
(4)	Johnny Bench (5-card set)	.75
(5)	Yogi Berra (5-card set)	.75
(6)	Lou Boudreau (5-card set)	.25
(7)	Lou Brock (5-card set)	.25
(8)	Roy Campanella (5-card set)	.75
(9)	Rod Carew (5-card set)	.35
(10)	Ray Dandridge (5-card set)	.25
(11)	Bobby Doerr (5-card set)	.25
(12)	Rick Ferrell (5-card set)	.25
(13)	Rollie Fingers (5-card set)	.25
(14)	Whitey Ford (5-card set)	.50
(15)	George Foster (5-card set)	.25
(16)	Catfish Hunter (5-card set)	.25
(17)	Monte Irvin (5-card set)	.25
(18)	Al Kaline (5-card set)	.50
(19)	George Kell (5-card set)	.25
(20)	Ralph Kiner (5-card set)	.25
(21)	Don Larsen (5-card set)	.25
(22)	Bob Lemon (5-card set)	.25
(23)	Buck Leonard (5-card set)	.25
(24)	Juan Marichal (5-card set)	.35
(25)	Joe Morgan (5-card set)	.25
(26)	Hal Newhouser (5-card set)	.25
(27)	Jim Palmer (5-card set)	.35
(28)	Tony Perez (5-card set)	.25
(29)	Pee Wee Reese (5-card set)	.35
(30)	Phil Rizzuto (5-card set)	.50
(31)	Brooks Robinson (5-card set)	.35
(32)	Frank Robinson (5-card set)	.35
(33)	Red Schoendienst (5-card set)	.25
(34)	Tom Seaver (5-card set)	.35
(35)	Willie Stargell (5-card set)	.25
(36)	Carl Yastrzemski (5-card set)	.35

1992 Front Row Club House Series Ken Griffey, Jr.

Ten cards tracing the life and career of Ken Griffey, Jr. comprise this collectors' issue. Cards are standard 2-1/2" x 3-1/2" with borderless color action and posed photos. Uniform logos have been removed from the photos since the set is not licensed by MLB. A Club House Series logo is on front at bottom-right. Horizontal backs have a color photo of Griffey ghosted in the background. Printed over that are personal data, career highlights and stats.

		MT
Complete Set (10):		2.00
Common Player:		.25
1	Ken Griffey Jr. (Background)	.25
2	Ken Griffey Jr. (Drafted)	.25
3	Ken Griffey Jr. (The Majors)	.25
4	Ken Griffey Jr. (The Breakdown)	.25
5	Ken Griffey Jr. (The American League)	.25
6	Ken Griffey Jr. (All-Star)	.25
7	Ken Griffey Jr. (Gold Glove)	.25
8	Ken Griffey Jr. (Homers)	.25
9	Ken Griffey Jr. (Career Highlights)	.25
10	Ken Griffey Jr. (A Closer Look)	.25

1992 Front Row Holograms

The "career" seasons of three Hall of Famers are remembered in this series of cards. In standard 2-1/2" x 3-1/2" format, fronts have a borderless hologram featuring a vintage action photo. Conventionally printed backs have a color photo, a recap and stats from the named season, and a foil holographic serial number tag designating the card's place in an edition of 100,000 each.

		MT
Complete Set (3):		1.50
Common Player:		.50
(1)	Hank Aaron	.70
(2)	Roy Campanella	.50
(3)	Tom Seaver	.50

Player names in *Italic* type indicate a rookie card.

1992 Front Row Pure Gold

Each of these 2-1/2" x 3-1/2" cards features 23-karat gold borders on front, surrounding a color action photo on which uniform details have been airbrushed away. Backs have player information.

		MT
Complete Set (6):		15.00
Common Player:		3.00
(1)	Hank Aaron	3.00
(2)	Roy Campanella	3.00
(3)	Tom Seaver	3.00
	Frank Thomas strip (3):	10.00
(4)	Frank Thomas (batting)	3.00
(5)	Frank Thomas (standing)	3.00
(6)	Frank Thomas (fielding)	3.00

1992 Front Row Frank Thomas

Budding super slugger Frank Thomas is featured in this collectors issue. Standard-size (2-1/2" x 3-1/2") cards have color photos on front, from which team logos have been airbrushed because the set was licensed only by the player, and not by MLB. Horizontally formatted backs have a second color photo along with a headline and a few sentences about his career to that point. The set was released in an edition of 30,000 and each was sold with a serially numbered certificate of authenticity.

		MT
Complete Set (7):		3.00
Common Card:		.50
1	Frank Thomas (A Good Start)	.50
nno	Frank Thomas (A Good Start- promo overprint on back)	.50
2	Frank Thomas (Multi-Talented)	.50
3	Frank Thomas (Auburn Career)	.50
4	Frank Thomas (Accomplishments)	.50
5	Frnak Thomas (Individual Honors)	.50
6	Frank Thomas (Minor League Stats)	.50
7	Frank Thomas (Major League Stats)	.50

1993 Front Row Gold Collection

Five borderless color photos (uniform logos removed) of Rollie Fingers are featured on the cards in this set. At bottom in a dark green stripe is the player name and, at left, the Front Row logo and the word "PREMIUM". Vertically at left is "The Gold Collection". All front printing is in gold foil. Backs have dark green borders with a ghost-image action photo and a few sentences about the player. A baseball at top carries the legend, "All Time Great / Series".

		MT
Complete Set (5):		2.00
Common Card:		.50
1	Rollie Fingers	.50
2	Rollie Fingers	.50
3	Rollie Fingers	.50
4	Rollie Fingers	.50
5	Rollie Fingers	.50

1999 FroZsnack's High-Screamers Lids

These 3-1/4" plastic lids were found on ice cream snacks sold at ballparks and possibly other outlets. A player photo with uniform logos covered is featured at center with personal data and 1998 stats on the side. The player's name is in a banner at top, his team, position and career highlights are in a banner at bottom.

		MT
Complete Set (40):		40.00
Common Player:		1.00
(1)	Roberto Alomar	1.00
(2)	Jeff Bagwell	1.50
(3)	Albert Belle	1.50
(4)	Dante Bichette	1.00
(5)	Craig Biggio	1.00
(6)	Barry Bonds	1.00
(7)	Kevin Brown	1.00
(8)	Jose Canseco	1.50
(9)	Vinny Castilla	1.00
(10)	Tony Clark	1.00
(11)	Francisco Cordova	1.00
(12)	Eric Davis	1.00
(13)	Nomar Garciaparra	3.00
(14)	Tom Glavine	1.00
(15)	Ben Grieve	1.00
(16)	Ken Griffey Jr.	4.00
(17)	Tony Gwynn	2.00
(18)	Rickey Henderson	1.50
(19)	Livan Hernandez	1.00
(20)	Derek Jeter	3.00
(21)	Jason Kendall	1.00
(22)	Randy Johnson	1.50
(23)	Barry Larkin	1.00
(24)	Greg Maddux	1.50
(25)	Tino Martinez	1.00
(26)	Mark McGwire	3.00
(27)	Robb Nen	1.00
(28)	Mike Piazza	2.50
(29)	Manny Ramirez	2.00
(30)	Cal Ripken Jr.	3.00
(31)	Alex Rodriguez	3.00
(32)	Scott Rolen	1.00
(33)	Sammy Sosa	2.50
(34)	Frank Thomas	2.50
(35)	Greg Vaughn	1.00
(36)	Fernando Vina	1.00
(37)	Omar Vizquel	1.00
(38)	Larry Walker	1.00
(39)	Matt Williams	1.00
(40)	Kerry Wood	1.00

1998 Fruit Roll-Ups All-Stars

Perforated panels of eight small (1-1/2" x 2") cards bearing the Topps logo were found on 38-count boxes of Fruit Roll-Ups snacks early in the 1998 season. The blank-back cards are printed on a 6" x 4" panel which can be removed from the box back. The front of the box pictures Rodriguez, Thomas and McGwire.

		MT
Complete Box:		6.00
Complete Panel:		4.50
Complete Set, Singles (8):		3.50
Common Player:		.50
(1)	Tony Gwynn	.60
(2)	Derek Jeter	.75
(3)	Kenny Lofton	.50
(4)	Mark McGwire	2.00
(5)	Mike Piazza	.75
(6)	Cal Ripken Jr.	1.50
(7)	Ivan Rodriguez	.60
(8)	Frank Thomas	1.25

1992 Fuji/WIZ N.Y. Mets team photo cards

This series of team photo cards was given away as a stadium promotion. The 7" x 5" horizontal cards have color team photos on a purple background. Printed in white in the bottom border are the year and won-loss record. Black-and-white backs have player identification and sponsor logos.

		MT
Complete Set (16):		9.00
Common Card:		1.00
(1)	1977 Mets Team Photo	1.00
(2)	1978 Mets Team Photo	1.00
(3)	1979 Mets Team Photo	1.00
(4)	1980 Mets Team Photo	1.00
(5)	1981 Mets Team Photo	1.00
(6)	1982 Mets Team Photo	1.00
(7)	1983 Mets Team Photo	2.00
(8)	1984 Mets Team Photo	1.50
(9)	1985 Mets Team Photo	1.00
(10)	1986 Mets Team Photo	2.50
(11)	1987 Mets Team Photo	1.00
(12)	1988 Mets Team Photo	1.00
(13)	1989 Mets Team Photo	1.00
(14)	1990 Mets Team Photo	1.00
(15)	1991 Mets Team Photo	1.00
(16)	1992 Mets Team Photo	1.00

1985 Fun Food Buttons

Fun Foods of Little Silver, N.J., issued a set of 133 full-color metal pins in 1985. The buttons, which are 1-1/4" in diameter and have a "safety pin" back, have bright borders which correspond to the player's team colors. The button backs are numbered and contain the player's 1984 batting or earned run average. The buttons were available as complete sets through hobby dealers and were also distributed in packs of three through retail stores. Cardboard 1-1/2" x 1-1/2" square proofs of the buttons' fronts are also seen in the hobby; their value is 5-7x that of the corresponding button, with production reported to be only 2,000 cardboard proofs.

		MT
Complete Set (133):		25.00
Common Player:		.15
1	Dave Winfield	.65
2	Lance Parrish	.15
3	Gary Carter	.35
4	Pete Rose	2.00
5	Jim Rice	.25
6	George Brett	1.25
7	Fernando Valenzuela	.15
8	Darryl Strawberry	.25
9	Steve Garvey	.30
10	Rollie Fingers	.30
11	Mike Schmidt	1.50
12	Kent Tekulve	.15
13	Ryne Sandberg	1.00
14	Bruce Sutter	.15
15	Tom Seaver	.50
16	Reggie Jackson	.75
17	Rickey Henderson	.50
18	Mark Langston	.15
19	Jack Clark	.15
20	Willie Randolph	.15
21	Kirk Gibson	.15
22	Andre Dawson	.30
23	Dave Concepcion	.15
24	Tony Armas	.15
25	Dan Quisenberry	.15
26	Pedro Guerrero	.15
27	Dwight Gooden	.25
28	Tony Gwynn	1.25
29	Robin Yount	.75
30	Steve Carlton	.60
31	Bill Madlock	.15
32	Rick Sutcliffe	.15
33	Willie McGee	.15
34	Greg Luzinski	.15
35	Rod Carew	.60
36	Dave Kingman	.15
37	Alvin Davis	.15
38	Chili Davis	.15
39	Don Baylor	.20
40	Alan Trammell	.25
41	Tim Raines	.30
42	Cesar Cedeno	.15
43	Wade Boggs	1.00
44	Frank White	.15
45	Steve Sax	.15
46	George Foster	.15
47	Terry Kennedy	.15
48	Cecil Cooper	.15
49	John Denny	.15
50	John Candelaria	.15
51	Jody Davis	.15
52	George Hendrick	.15
53	Ron Kittle	.15
54	Fred Lynn	.15
55	Carney Lansford	.15
56	Gorman Thomas	.15
57	Manny Trillo	.15
58	Steve Kemp	.15
59	Jack Morris	.15
60	Dan Petry	.15
61	Mario Soto	.15
62	Dwight Evans	.15
63	Hal McRae	.15
64	Mike Marshall	.15
65	Mookie Wilson	.15
66	Graig Nettles	.15
67	Ben Oglivie	.15
68	Juan Samuel	.15
69	Johnny Ray	.15
70	Gary Matthews	.15
71	Ozzie Smith	.75
72	Carlton Fisk	.45
73	Doug DeCinces	.15
74	Joe Morgan	.60
75	Dave Stieb	.15
76	Buddy Bell	.15
77	Don Mattingly	1.25
78	Lou Whitaker	.15
79	Willie Hernandez	.15
80	Dave Parker	.20
81	Bob Stanley	.15
82	Willie Wilson	.15
83	Orel Hershiser	.25
84	Rusty Staub	.20
85	Goose Gossage	.15
86	Don Sutton	.35
87	Al Holland	.15
88	Tony Pena	.15
89	Ron Cey	.15
90	Joaquin Andujar	.15
91	LaMarr Hoyt	.15
92	Tommy John	.20
93	Dwayne Murphy	.15
94	Willie Upshaw	.15
95	Gary Ward	.15
96	Ron Guidry	.15
97	Chet Lemon	.15
98	Aurelio Lopez	.15
99	Tony Perez	.35
100	Bill Buckner	.15
101	Mike Hargrove	.15
102	Scott McGregor	.15
103	Dale Murphy	.60
104	Keith Hernandez	.15
105	Paul Molitor	.75
106	Bert Blyleven	.15
107	Leon Durham	.15
108	Lee Smith	.20
109	Nolan Ryan	3.00
110	Harold Baines	.20
111	Kent Hrbek	.15
112	Ron Davis	.15
113	George Bell	.15
114	Charlie Hough	.15
115	Phil Niekro	.35
116	Dave Righetti	.15
117	Darrell Evans	.15
118	Cal Ripken, Jr.	3.00
119	Eddie Murray	.75
120	Storm Davis	.15
121	Mike Boddicker	.15
122	Bob Horner	.15
123	Chris Chambliss	.15
124	Ted Simmons	.15
125	Andre Thornton	.15
126	Larry Bowa	.15
127	Bob Dernier	.15
128	Joe Niekro	.15
129	Jose Cruz	.15
130	Tom Brunansky	.15
131a	Garry Gaetti	52.00
131b	Gary Gaetti	.15
132	Lloyd Moseby	.15
133	Frank Tanana	.15

1989-90 Futera Australian Baseball League

Two teams from Australia's professional winter baseball circuit were featured in the inaugural issue by Futera. Just slightly wider than 2-1/2" x 3-1/2", the cards have full color player poses on semi-gloss front stock. Team and league logos are in the upper corners with a kangeroo, player name and position in the bottom white border. Backs are printed in blue on white with a few stats, personal data and career highlights. The Perth team set is not numbered, the Sydney cards are. The cards were issued in boxed team sets. Several players on each team had U.S. minor league experience. Production was 5,000 of each team set.

	MT
Complete Set (45):	18.00
Common Player:	.50
Perth Heat team set:	10.00
(1) Tony Adamson	.50
(2) Kimon Anderson	.50
(3) Lyall Barwick	.50
(4) Mike Borgatti	.50
(5) Ken Burden	.50
(6) Scott Cameron	.50
(7) Kevin Driscoll	.50
(8) Heath Gillard	.50
(9) Greg Harvey	.50
(10) John Hearne	.50
(11) Sean Jones	.50
(12) Andrew Kendray	.50
(13) Ron Malcolm	.50
(14) Trevor Malcolm	.50
(15) Steve Meloncelli	.50
(16) Ray Michell	.50
(17) John Moore	.50
(18) Dean Moyle	.50
(19) Michael Moyle	.50
(20) Shayne Ruscoe	.50
(21) Dave Rusin	.50
(22) Mark Scorer	.50
(23) Scott Steed	.50
(24) Shane Tonkin	.50
(25) James Waddell	.50
Sydney Metros team set:	10.00
1 Stuart Barlow	.50
2 Chris Brown	.50
3 Mike Dennis	.50
4 Matt Everingham	.50
5 Don Franklin	.50
6 Darren Fullerton	.50
7 Karl Hardman	.50
8 Michael Hennessy	.50
9 Nick Kalaf	.50
10 Troy Martin	.50
11 Mike Milmoe	.50
12 Sean Mullins	.50
13 Peter Munro	.50
14 Brian Murphy	.50
15 Jeff Pettett	.50
16 Tad Powers	.50
17 Ross Thomas	.50
18 Greg Turner	.50
19 David Voit	.50
20 Justin Weaver	.50

1990-91 Futera Australian Baseball League

Futera's second effort to chronicle the Australian winter professional baseball league was expanded to eight team sets, as the ABL itself expanded with sponsorship by Pepsi and an influx of players from Major League organizations. The 2-1/2" x 3-1/2" cards feature color photos surrounded by a graduated color border in one of the team's colors. League and team logos are in the top corners; the Futera logo, player name and position are at bottom. Backs retain the color sheme and feature a second player photo along with personal data, career summary and ABL and U.S. stats.

	MT
Complete Set (148):	60.00
Common Player:	.50
Brisbane Bandits team set:	10.00
1 John Bartorillo	.50
2 Allan Albury	.50
3 Gregory Suthers	.50
4 Steven Devlin	.50
5 Chris Welsh	.50
6 Mathew Gates	.50
7 David Kissick	.50
8 Geoff Barden	.50
9 Stuart Roebig	.50
10 Ken MacDonald	.50
11 Cameron Cairncross	.50
12 John Boothby	.50
13 Peter Vogler	.50
14 Tim Worrell	1.00
15 Kim Jessop	.50
16 David Hogan	.50
17 Randy Johnson	.50
18 Royal Thomas	.50
19 Kevin Garner	.50
Clipsal Giants team set:	8.00
1 Glenn Jones	.50
2 Gary Rice	.50
3 Tony Harris	.50
4 Tim Day	.50
5 Nathan Davison	.50
6 James Bushell	.50
7 Dino Ebel	.50
8 Bill Wengert	.50
9 Brett Magnusson	.50
10 John Knapp	.50
11 Darren White	.50
12 Phil Alexander	.50
13 Phil White	.50
14 Mark Van Pelt	.50
15 Troy Scoble	.50
16 Andrew Scott	.50
Daikyo Dolphins team set:	12.00
1 Bob Nilsson, Dave Nilsson, Gary Nilsson	1.00
2 Larry Montgomery	.50
3 Mark Hess	.50
4 David Foxover	.50
5 Ron Johnson	.50
6 Brett Cederblad	.50
7 Gary Nilsson	.50
8 Chris Maguire	.50
9 Peter Yates	.50
10 Bob Nilsson	.50
11 Ian Burns	.50
12 Charles Yang	.50
13 Peter Hartas	.50
14 Paul Gorman	.50
15 Adrian Meagher	.50
16 Travis Nicolau	.50
17 Troy O'Leary	1.00
18 John Jaha	1.50
19 David Nilsson	1.50
Melbourne Bushrangers team set:	9.00
1 Greg Wharton	.50
2 Neil Jones	.50
3 Keith Gogas	.50
4 Larry Gonzales	.50
5 Jeff Oberdank	.50
6 Marcus Moore	.50
7 John Fritz	.50
8 Leigh Walters	.50
9 Mark Guy	.50
10 George Bolin	.50
11 Richard Vagg	.50
12 Malcolm May	.50
13 Mathew Wood	.50
14 Bruce Morrison	.50
15 Terry Reid	.50
16 Howard Norsetter	.50
17 Wayne Pollock	.50
18 Stephen Black	.50
19 Glen Gambrell	.50
Parramatta Patriots team set:	10.00
1 Ken Sharpe	.50
2 Paul Elliot	.50
3 Ben Shelton	.50
4 Darian Lindsay	.50
5 Darren Riley	.50
6 Troy Halliday	.50
7 Chris Hodkinson	.50
8 Gary White	.50
9 Grahame Cassel	.50
10 John Gaynor	.50
11 Gary Wales	.50
12 Greg Johnston	.50
13 Craig Summers	.50
14 Steve Wilson	.50
15 Stewart Bell	.50
16 Scott Tunkin	.50
17 Wayne Harvey	.50
18 Chip Duncan	.50
19 Tim McDowell	.50
20 Austin Manahan	.50
Perth Heat team set:	9.00
1 Simon Eissens	.50
2 Mike Young	.50
3 Shaun Hrabar	.50
4 Dave Rusin	.50
5 John Moore	.50
6 Todd Stephan	.50
7 Pat Leinen	.50
8 Tim Holland	.50
9 Sean Jones	.50
10 T.R. Lewis	.50
11 Michael Moyle	.50
12 Trevor Malcolm	.50
13 Parris Mitchell	.50
14 John Hearne	.50
15 Peter Wood	.50
16 Scott Metcalf	.50
17 James Waddell	.50
18 Tony Adamson	.50
19 Scott Steed	.50
Sydney Wave team set:	10.00
1 Mark Shipley	.50
2 Brian Murphy	.50
3 Matt Everingham	.50
4 Troy Martin	.50
5 Bevan James	.50
6 Gregory Turner	.50
7 Michael Dennis	.50
8 Colin Barnes	.50
9 Darren Fullerton	.50
10 Billy White	.50
11 Craig Johnston	.50
12 Tad Powers	.50
13 Brad DeJardin	.50
14 Dodd Johnson	.50
15 Peter Munro	.50
16 Stuart Barlow	.50
17 Russel Hadden	.50
18 Mike Gabbani	.50
19 David Voit	.50
20 James Donaldson	1.00
Waverly Reds team set:	7.00
1 Geoff Dunn	.50
2 Dave McAuliffe	.50
3 Peter Beeler	.50
4 Mike Anderson	.50
5 Ian Hubble	.50
6 Rob Hogan	.50
7 Craig Kernick	.50
8 David Buckthorpe	.50
9 Mathew Sheldon-Collins	.50
10 Richard King	.50
11 Mark Respondek	.50
12 Ron Carothers	.50
13 Rohan Chapman	.50
14 David Clarkson	.50
--- Phil Dale	.50

G

1981 GAF Steve Garvey Microfiche

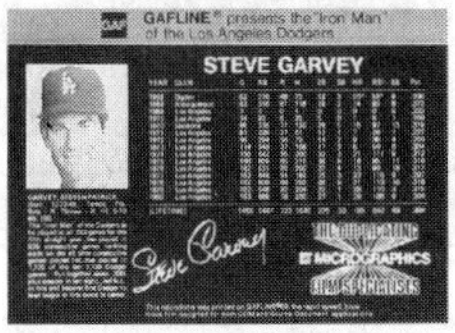

Produced as a microfiche, this 5-7/8" x 4-1/8" transparency features Steve Garvey. A red strip at top carries the company's logo. The blue panel at bottom has Garvey's photo, facsimile autograph, career highlights and stats through the 1980 season.

	MT
Steve Garvey	25.00

1982 Renata Galasso 20 Years of Met Baseball

The original New York Mets team of 1962 is featured on this 20-year anniversary set. The 2-1/2" x 3-1/2" cards have black-and-white photos with blue borders. The player name and position is in orange at bottom. Backs repeat the team colors with blue and orange printing on white cardboard. Card and uniform numbers appear in the top corners, there is a career summary, 1962 and career stats and a trivia question. Production was reported as 2,500 sets.

	MT
Complete Set:	15.00
Common Player:	.35
1 Marv Throneberry	.50
2 Richie Ashburn	2.00
3 Charlie Neal	.35
4 Cliff Cook	.35
5 Elio Chacon	.35
6 Chris Cannizzaro	.35
7 Jim Hickman	.35
8 Rod Kanehl	.35
9 Gene Woodling	.35
10 Gil Hodges	2.00
11 Al Jackson	.35
12 Sammy Taylor	.35
13 Felix Mantilla	.35
14 Ken MacKenzie	.35
15 Craig Anderson	.35
16 Bob Moorhead	.35
17 Joe Christopher	.35
18 Bob Miller	.35
19 Frank Thomas	.50
20 Vinegar Bend Mizell	.35
21 Bill Hunter	.35
22 Roger Craig	.35
23 Jay Hook	.35
24 Meet The Mets (team card)	.50
25 Choo Choo Coleman	.50
26 Casey Stengel	2.00
27 Solly Hemus	.35
28 Rogers Hornsby	1.00
29 Red Ruffing	.35
30 George Weiss	.35

1983 Renata Galasso 1933 All-Stars

The premiere All-Star Game in 1933 is commemorated in this 50th anniversary collectors issue. In standard 2-1/2" x 3-1/2" format (though not uniform cut to exact size), the cards feature black-and-white portrait photos on front. Many of the National League All-Stars are pictured in their special NL uniforms. In the wide white border at bottom is the player's name, position and league. Backs are printed in red, white and blue with a large Galasso ad and a short career summary; there is little mention of the 1933 All-Star Game. Two unnumbered cards issued with the set have N.L. and A.L. team photos on front and blue-tone backs showing A-S managers Connie Mack and John McGraw "choosing up sides."

	MT
Complete Set:	8.00
Common Player:	.25
1 Tony Cuccinello	.25
2 Lon Warenke (Warneke)	.25
3 Hal Schumacher	.25
4 Wally Berger	.25
5 Lefty O'Doul	.25
6 Chuck Klein	.25
7 Chick Hafey	.25
8 Jimmie Wilson	.25
9 John McGraw	.25
10 Max Carey	.25
11 Bill McKechnie	.25
12 Dick Bartell	.25
13 Bill Hallahan	.25
14 Woody English	.25
15 Paul Waner	.25
16 Carl Hubbell	.35
17 Frank Frisch	.35
18 Gabby Hartnett	.25
19 Pie Traynor	.25
20 Bill Terry	.25
21 Pepper Martin	.25
22 Earl Averill	.25
23 Jimmy Dykes	.25
24 Charlie Gehringer	.35
25 Rich Ferrell (Rick)	.25
26 Joe Cronin	.25
27 Ben Chapman	.25
28 Eddie Rommel	.25
29 Lefty Grove	.35
30 Connie Mack	.25
31 Babe Ruth	2.00
32 Sam West	.25
33 Tony Lazzeri	.25
34 Al Simmons	.25
35 Wes Ferrell	.25
36 Bill Dickey	.35
37 General Crowder	.25
38 Oral Hildebrand	.25
39 Lefty Gomez	.25
40 Jimmie Foxx	.40
41 Art Fletcher	.25
42 Eddie Collins	.25
43 Lou Gehrig	1.25
(44) 1933 N.L. All-Star Team	.25
(45) 1933 A.L. All-Star Team	.25

1983 Renata Galasso 1969 Seattle Pilots

The one-year American League franchise in Seattle is recalled with this collectors issue. Full-color photos of the peripatetic Pilots are framed in team-color blue and gold on a beige background in standard 2-1/2" x 3-1/2" size. Backs are printed in red and blue on white and feature a career summary and 1969 stats. For a couple of players this represents their only baseball card appearance and for many more it is their only card in a Pilots' uniform. Many of the sets were originally sold with the #1 Jim Bouton card personally autographed.

	MT
Complete Set:	10.00
Common Player:	.25
1 Jim Bouton	2.00
1 (a) Jim Bouton (autographed)	7.50
2 Joe Schultz	.25
3 Bill Edgerton	.50
4 Gary Timberlake	.50
5 Dick Baney	.25
6 Mike G. Marshall	.50
7 Jim Gosger	.25
8 Mike Hegan	.35
9 Steve Hovley	.25
10 Don Mincher	.25
11 Miguel Fuentes	.25
12 Charlie Bates	.25
13 John O'Donoghue	.25

14	Tommy Davis	.50
15	Jerry McNertney	.25
16	Rich Rollins	.25
17	Fred Talbot	.25
18	John Gelnar	.25
19	Bob Locker	.25
20	Frank Crosetti	.40
21	Sal Maglie	.40
22	Sibby Sisti	.25
23	Ron Plaza	.25
24	Federico Velazquez	.25
25	Diego Segui	.25
26	Steve Barber	.25
27	Jack Aker	.25
28	Marty Pattin	.25
29	Ray Oyler	.25
30	Danny Walton	.40
31	Merritt Ranew	.25
32	John Donaldson	.25
33	Greg Goossen	.25
34	Gary Bell	.25
35	Jim Pagliaroni	.25
36	Mike Ferraro	.25
37	Tommy Harper	.40
38	John Morris	.25
39	Larry Haney	.25
40	Ron Clark	.25
41	Steve Whitaker	.25
42	Wayne Comer	.25
43	Gene Brabender	.25

1984 Renata Galasso Baseball Collector Series

Some of baseball's best are presented in this glossy-front black-and-white, 2-3/8" x 3-1/2", collectors set patterned after the 1953 Bowmans. Backs are in red and black with a career summary and lifetime stats.

		MT
Complete Set (20):		10.00
Common Player:		.25
1	Roberto Clemente	1.00
2	Duke Snider	.40
3	Sandy Koufax	.50
4	Carl Hubbell	.25
5	Ty Cobb	.50
6	Willie Mays	.70
7	Jackie Robinson	.60
8	Joe DiMaggio	1.00
9	Stan Musial	.50
10	Pie Traynor	.25
11	Yogi Berra	.40
12	Babe Ruth	1.50
13	Brooks Robinson	.40
14	Walter Johnson	.25
15	Ted Williams	.70
16	Bill Dickey	.25
17	Lou Gehrig	1.00
18	Hank Aaron	.70
19	Eddie Mathews	.25
20	Mickey Mantle	2.00

1984 Renata Galasso Reggie Jackson

This collectors issue chronicling the career of "Mr. October" was produced in two sizes - the standard 2-1/2" x 3-1/2" and the Topps' "mini" format of 2-1/4" x 3-1/8". Both sizes share the same design of a color or black-and-white photo on a blue border with "Reggie 44" at bottom, along with a photo of his classic swing. Backs have statistical data, career summary or part of a puzzle showing all of Jackson's Topps cards to that point. The full-size set was limited to 10,000, with 500 featuring a genuine autograph on card #1; the mini set was issued in an edition of 5,000.

	MT
Complete Standard-size Set (30):	12.00
Complete Set w/ Autographed #1:	45.00
Complete Mini Set (30):	20.00
Common Card: Reggie Jackson	.50

1984 Renata Galasso Willie Mays Story

Color and black-and-white photos from the Hall of Famer's career and off-field life are featured in this collectors set. Each photo is surrounded by a red frame and white border. Many of the photos will be familiar to collectors as having earlier appeared on Topps cards. Backs of the first 45 cards are in red, black and white, with biographical information or a description of the front photo. Backs of cards #46-90 can be assembled into a full-color puzzle of Mays' baseball cards from Topps, Bowman and others. Card #1 in each set is authentically autographed by Mays. Because of collector interest, cards on which he is pictured with other stars are detailed below. Retail price at issue was $20.

		MT
Complete Set (90):		35.00
Common Card:		.50
1-90 Willie Mays		
13	(w/ Duke Snider)	
19	(w/ Roberto Clemente)	
29	(w/ Mickey Mantle)	
30	(w/ Stan Musial)	
32	(w/ Ernie Banks)	
35	(w/ Don Drysdale)	
39	(w/ Queen Elizabeth, Ronald Reagan)	
40	(w/ Hank Aaron)	
44	(w/ Joe DiMaggio)	
46	(w/ Bill Cosby)	
52	(w/ Hank Aaron)	

1985 Renata Galasso Dwight Gooden

This collectors issue was produced by Brooklyn dealer Renata Galasso as one of several to capitalize on Gooden's early fame. Card #1 features a Ron Lewis painting of Gooden, the others feature color photos from his boyhood and early career. (Card #16 pictures him shaking hands with Henry Aaron.) Photos are surrounded on front with a border of blue squares. A pink "DR. K" logo is at bottom-right. Backs are inblue and white and feature a question and answer session with the pitcher, stats, or part of a nine-piece puzzle. Five thousand sets were produced, with 500 of them featuring Gooden's autograph on Card #1. Issue price was about $11.

	MT
Complete Set (30):	4.00
Complete Set, Autographed:	25.00
Single Card:	.15
1-30 Dwight Gooden	

1986 Renata Galasso Dwight Gooden

Dr. K's Cy Young Season in 1985 is recalled in this collectors set. Numbered from 31-60, picking up where the 1985 set had left off, the series share a similar format. Fronts have black-and-white or color photos surrounded by a frame of blue dots and larger orange squares. A blue "Dr. K" appears in the lower-right corner. Backs are in blue and orange on white and narrate the 1985 season. The final nine cards in the set have pieces forming a puzzle picture of Gooden.

	MT
Complete Set (30):	4.00
Single Card:	.15
31-60 Dwight Gooden	

1986 Renata Galasso Don Mattingly

The life and career of the Yankees superstar is traced in this collectors issue. The 2-1/2" x 3-1/2" cards have a mix of black-and-white and color photos on a white background with blue pinstripes. A yellow circle in a bottom corner of each card front has "THE HIT MAN" in red. Backs are printed in blue, with 21 of them featuring a question-and-answer format and nine forming a puzzle picture of Mattingly.

	MT
Complete Set (30):	9.00
Single Card:	.25
1-30 Don Mattingly	

1986 Renata Galasso 1961 Yankees Black-and-White

Illustrating one of the problems with collectors' issues, a person holding one of these cards might assume it is of 1961 or 1962 vintage because there is no date of actual issue, which occurred around 1986, anywhere on the cards. In a format similar to Topps' 1961 cards, this set features large black-and-white player photos on a 2-1/2" x 3-1/2" glossy stock. The player name and position are in a pair of color bars at bottom. Backs are in red and black and have a few personal data, season and career stats, a 1961 season summary and trivia question. Sometimes referred to a "test set" for the later color issue, this was issued in a reported production of 2,500.

		MT
Complete Set (30):		25.00
Common Player:		.50
1	Roger Maris	3.00
2	Bobby Richardson	.75
3	Tony Kubek	.75
4	Elston Howard	.75
5	Bill Skowron	.75
6	Clete Boyer	.50
7	Mickey Mantle	6.00
8	Yogi Berra	2.00
9	Johnny Blanchard	.50
10	Hector Lopez	.50
11	Whitey Ford	2.00
12	Ralph Terry	.50
13	Bill Stafford	.50
14	Bud Daley	.50
15	Billy Gardner	.50
16	Jim Coates	.50
17	Luis Arroyo	.50
18	Tex Clevenger	.50
19	Bob Cerv	.50
20	Art Ditmar	.50
21	Bob Turley	.50
22	Joe DeMaestri	.50
23	Rollie Sheldon	.50
24	Earl Torgeson	.50
25	Hal Reniff	.50
26	Ralph Houk	.50
27	Jim Hegan	.50
28	Johnny Sain	.60
29	Frank Crosetti	.50
30	Wally Moses	.50

1986 Renata Galasso 1961 Yankees Color

The World Champion N.Y. Yankees of 1961 are remembered in this collectors set. The 2-1/2" x 3-1/2" cards borrow the design of Topps' 1961 issue, with a large color photo at top and red and yellow boxes below with player name and position in contrasting color. Backs are printed in blue and red with a few biographical details, 1961 and career stats and a career summary.

		MT
Complete Set:		12.50
Common Player:		.25
1	Roger Maris	2.00
2	Yogi Berra	1.50
3	Whitey Ford	1.50
4	Hector Lopez	.25
5	Bob Turley	.25
6	Frank Crosetti	.25
7	Bob Cerv	.25
8	Jack Reed	.25
9	Luis Arroyo	.25
10	Danny McDevitt	.25
11	Duke Maas	.25
12	Jesse Gonder	.25
13	Ralph Terry	.25
14	Deron Johnson	.25
15	Johnny Blanchard	.25
16	Bill Stafford	.25
17	Earl Torgeson	.25
18	Tony Kubek	.40
19	Rollie Sheldon	.25
20	Tex Clevenger	.25
21	Art Ditmar	.25
22	Bud Daley	.25
23	Jim Coates	.25
24	Al Downing	.25
25	Johnny Sain	.35
26	Jim Hegan	.25
27	Wally Moses	.25
28	Ralph Houk	.25
29	Bill Skowron	.35
30	Bobby Richardson	.35
31	Johnny James	.25
32	Hal Reniff	.25
33	Mickey Mantle	5.00
34	Clete Boyer	.25
35	Elston Howard	.35
36	Joe DeMaestri	.25
37	Billy Gardner	.25

1994 Garcia Photo Cuban League

The four Cuban professional teams participating in the 1994 Serie Selectiva are featured in this set of cards produced in Canada by Garcia Photo Ltd. Cards are in standard 2-1/2" x 3-1/2" with player action poses on front and portrait photos on back. Personal data, career highlights and stats are printed in Spanish on the back.

		MT
Complete Set (132):		35.00
Common Player:		.10
1	Juan Manrique	.10
2	Lazaro Arturo Castro	.10
3	Pedro Luis Duenas	.10
4	Julio German Fernandez	.10
5	Alberto Peraza	.10
6	Yobal Duenas	.10
7	Alexander Ramos	.10
8	Omar Linares	.10
9	Eduardo Cardenas	.10
10	Reniel Capote	.10
11	Alberto Diaz	.10
12	Lazaro Junco	.10
13	Jose Antonio Estrada	.10
14	Daniel Lazo	.10
15	Juan Carlos Linares	.10
16	Lazaro Madera	.10
17	Felix Isasi	.10
18	Eisler Livan Hernandez	10.00
19	Pedro Luis Lazo	.10
20	Faustino Corrales	.10
21	Omar Ajete	.10
22	Jorge Luis Valdez	.10
23	Carlos Yanes	.10
24	Lazaro Garro	.10
25	Jesus Bosmenier	.10
26	Carlos de la Torre	.10
27	Jorge Antonio Martinez	.10
28	Jorge Fuentes	.10
29	Pablo Pascual Abreu	.10
30	Nestor Perez	.10
31	Roman Suarez	.10
32	Armando Johnson	.10
33	Occidentales team checklist	.10
34	Pedro Luis Rodriguez	.10
35	Francisco Santiesteban	.10
36	Ricardo Miranda	.10
37	Roberto Colina	.10
38	Juan Carlos Millan	.10
39	Juan Padilla	.10
40	Oscar Macias	.10
41	Andy Morales	.10
42	Enrique Diaz	.10
43	German Mesa	.10
44	Juan Carlos Moreno	.10
45	Javier Mendez	.10
46	Geraldo Miranda	.10
47	Romelio Martinez	.10
48	Luis Enrique Piloto	.10
49	Carlos Tabares	.10
50	Orbe Luis Rodriguez	.10
51	Orlando Hernandez	25.00
52	Lazaro Valle	.10
53	Ariel Prieto	3.00
54	Jorge Fumero	.10
55	Jose Ibar	.10
56	Vladimir Nunez	3.00
57	Heriberto Collazo	.10
58	Jorge Garcia	.10
59	Euclides Rojas	.10
60	Osnel Blas Bocourt	.10
61	Jorge Trigoura	.10
62	Rene Bello	.10
63	Jorge Hernandez	.10
64	Antonio Jiminez	.10
65	Rene Rojas	.10
66	Habana team checklist	.10
67	Angel Lopez	.10
68	Jose Raul Delgado	.10
69	Ariel Pestano	.10
70	Lourdes Gurriel	.10
71	Jorge Toca	.10
72	Jorge Diaz	.10
73	Lazaro Lopez	.10
74	Miguel Caldes	.10
75	Eduardo Paret	.10
76	Luis Ulacia	.10
77	Eusebio Miguel Rojas	.10
78	Victor Mesa	.10
79	Oscar Machado	.10
80	Eddy Rojas	.10
81	Pablo Primelles	.10
82	Rey Isaac	.10
83	Edel Pacheco	.10
84	Luis Rolando Arrojo	3.00
85	Jose Ramon Riscart	.10
86	Teofilo Perez	.10
87	Adiel Palma	.10
88	Miguel Arnay Hernandez	.10
89	Omar Luis	.10
90	Felipe Fernandez	.10
91	Ramon Gardon	.10
92	Eliecer Montes de Oca	.10
93	Yovani Aragon	.10
94	Pedro Jova	.10
95	Luis Enrique Gonzalez	.10
96	Roberto Montero	.10
97	Pedro Perez	.10
98	Antonio Munoz	.10
99	Centrales team checklist	.10
100	Alberto Hernandez	.10
101	Luis Enrique Padro	.10
102	Carlos Barrabi	.10
103	Orestes Kindelan	.10
104	Pablo Bejerano	.10
105	Antonio Pacheco	.10
106	Gabriel Pierre	.10
107	Evenecer Godinez	.10
108	Manuel Benavides	.10
109	Marino Moreno	.10
110	Felix Benavides	.10
111	Ermidelio Urrutia	.10
112	Fausto Alvarez	.10
113	Luis Rodriguez	.10
114	Jorge Ochoa	.10
115	Juan Carlos Bruzon	.10
116	Leonel Bueno	.10
117	Osvaldo Fernandez	2.00
118	Ernesto Leonel Guevara	.10
119	Jose Luis Aleman	.10
120	Osmani Tamayo	.10
121	Adolfo Canet	.10
122	Jose Miguel Baez	.10
123	Alfredo Fonseca	.10
124	Miguel Perez	.10
125	Ruben Rodriguez	.10
126	Misael Lopez	.10
127	Frangel Reynaldo	.10
128	Antonio Sanchez	.10
129	Miguel Giro	.10
130	Rafael Ramos	.10
131	Jesus Santiago Guerra	.10
132	Orientales team checklist	.10

1983 Gardner's Brewers

Topps produced in 1983 for Gardner's Bakery of Madison, Wisconsin, a 22-card set featuring the American League champion Milwaukee Brewers. The cards, which measure 2-1/2" x 3-1/2", have colorful fronts which contain the player's name, team and position plus the Brewers and Gardner's logos. The card backs are identical to the regular Topps issue but are numbered 1-22. The cards were inserted in specially marked packages of Gardner's bread products and were susceptible to grease stains.

		MT
Complete Set (22):		10.00
Common Player:		.50
1	Harvey Kuenn	.50
2	Dwight Bernard	.50
3	Mark Brouhard	.50
4	Mike Caldwell	.50
5	Cecil Cooper	.75
6	Marshall Edwards	.50
7	Rollie Fingers	1.50
8	Jim Gantner	.50
9	Moose Haas	.50
10	Bob McClure	.50
11	Paul Molitor	6.00
12	Don Money	.50
13	Charlie Moore	.50
14	Ben Oglivie	.50
15	Ed Romero	.50
16	Ted Simmons	.50
17	Jim Slaton	.50
18	Don Sutton	1.50
19	Gorman Thomas	.50
20	Pete Vuckovich	.50
21	Ned Yost	.50
22	Robin Yount	6.00

1984 Gardner's Brewers

For the second straight year, Gardner's Bakery inserted baseball cards featuring the Milwaukee Brewers with its bread products. The 22-card set, entitled "1984 Series II," have multi-colored fronts that include the Brewers and Gardner's logos. The card backs are identical to the regular 1984 Topps issue except for the 1-22 numbering system. The Topps-produced cards are the standard 2-1/2" x 3-1/2" size. The cards are sometimes found with grease stains, resulting from contact with the bread.

		MT
Complete Set (22):		7.00
Common Player:		.50
1	Rene Lachemann	.50
2	Mark Brouhard	.50
3	Mike Caldwell	.50
4	Bobby Clark	.50
5	Cecil Cooper	.75
6	Rollie Fingers	1.50
7	Jim Gantner	.50
8	Moose Haas	.50
9	Roy Howell	.50
10	Pete Ladd	.50
11	Rick Manning	.50
12	Bob McClure	.50
13	Paul Molitor	5.00
14	Charlie Moore	.50
15	Ben Oglivie	.50
16	Ed Romero	.50
17	Ted Simmons	.50
18	Jim Sundberg	.50
19	Don Sutton	1.50
20	Tom Tellmann	.50
21	Pete Vuckovich	.50
22	Robin Yount	5.00

1985 Gardner's Brewers

Gardner's Bakery issued a 22-card set featuring the Milwaukee Brewers for the third consecutive year in 1985. The set was produced by Topps and is designed in a horizontal format. The card fronts feature color photos inside blue, red and yellow frames. The player's name and position are placed in orange boxes to the right of the photo and are accompanied by the Brewers and Gardner's logos. The card backs are identical to the regular 1985 Topps set but are blue rather than green and are numbered 1-22. The cards, which were inserted in specially marked bread products, are often found with grease stains.

		MT
Complete Set (22):		6.00
Common Player:		.50
1	George Bamberger	.50
2	Mark Brouhard	.50
3	Bob Clark	.50
4	Jaime Cocanower	.50
5	Cecil Cooper	.65
6	Rollie Fingers	1.00
7	Jim Gantner	.50
8	Moose Haas	.50
9	Dion James	.50
10	Pete Ladd	.50
11	Rick Manning	.50
12	Bob McClure	.50
13	Paul Molitor	2.50
14	Charlie Moore	.50
15	Ben Oglivie	.50
16	Chuck Porter	.50
17	Ed Romero	.50
18	Bill Schroeder	.50
19	Ted Simmons	.50
20	Tom Tellmann	.50
21	Pete Vuckovich	.50
22	Robin Yount	2.50

1989 Gardner's Brewers

Returning after a three-year hiatus, Gardner's Bread of Madison, Wis., issued a 15-card Milwaukee Brewers set in 1989. The blue and white-bordered cards are the standard size and feature posed portrait photos with all Brewer logos airbrushed from the players' caps. The Gardner's logo appears at the top of the card, while the player's name is below the photo. The set, which was produced in conjunction with Mike Schechter Associates, was issued with loaves of bread or packages of buns, one card per package.

		MT
Complete Set (15):		5.00
Common Player:		.25
1	Paul Molitor	2.50
2	Robin Yount	2.50
3	Jim Gantner	.25
4	Rob Deer	.25
5	B.J. Surhoff	.35
6	Dale Sveum	.25
7	Ted Higuera	.25
8	Dan Plesac	.25
9	Bill Wegman	.25
10	Juan Nieves	.25
11	Greg Brock	.25
12	Glenn Braggs	.25
13	Joey Meyer	.25
14	Ernest Riles	.25
15	Don August	.25

1986 Gatorade Cubs

Gatorade sponsored this set which was given away at the July 17, 1986 Cubs game. Cards measure 2-7/8" x 4-1/4" and feature color photos inside red and white frames. The Cubs logo appears at the top of the card. Backs include statistical information and the Gatorade logo. This set marked the fifth consecutive year the Cubs had held a baseball card giveaway promotion.

		MT
Complete Set (28):		12.00
Common Player:		.50
4	Gene Michael	.50
6	Keith Moreland	.50
7	Jody Davis	.50
10	Leon Durham	.50
11	Ron Cey	.65
12	Shawon Dunston	.65
15	Davey Lopes	.50
16	Terry Francona	.50
18	Steve Christmas	.50
19	Manny Trillo	.50
20	Bob Dernier	.50
21	Scott Sanderson	.50
22	Jerry Mumphrey	.50
23	Ryne Sandberg	6.00
27	Thad Bosley	.50
28	Chris Speier	.50
29	Steve Lake	.50
31	Ray Fontenot	.50
34	Steve Trout	.50
36	Gary Matthews	.50
39	George Frazier	.50
40	Rick Sutcliffe	.65
43	Dennis Eckersley	2.50
46	Lee Smith	1.00
48	Jay Baller	.50
49	Jamie Moyer	.50
50	Guy Hoffman	.50
---	The Coaching Staff (Ruben Amaro, Billy Connors, Johnny Oates, John Vukovich, Billy Williams)	.50

1987 Gatorade Indians

For the second year in a row, the Indians gave out a perforated set of baseball cards to fans attending the Team Photo/Baseball Card Day promotion. Sponsored by Gatorade, the individual cards measure 2-1/2" x 3-1/8". Fronts contain a color photo surrounded by a red frame inside a white border. The player's name, uniform number and the Gatorade logo are also on front. Backs are printed in black, blue and red and carry a facsimile autograph and the player's stats.

		MT
Complete Set, Foldout:		8.00
Complete Set, Singles (31):		6.00
Common Player:		.25
2	Brett Butler	.50
4	Tony Bernazard	.25
6	Andy Allanson	.25
7	Pat Corrales	.25
8	Carmen Castillo	.25
10	Pat Tabler	.25
11	Jamie Easterly	.25
12	Dave Clark	.25
13	Ernie Camacho	.25
14	Julio Franco	.35
17	Junior Noboa	.25
18	Ken Schrom	.25
20	Otis Nixon	.30
21	Greg Swindell	.25
22	Frank Wills	.25
23	Chris Bando	.25
24	Rick Dempsey	.25
26	Brook Jacoby	.25
27	Mel Hall	.25
28	Cory Snyder	.25
29	Andre Thornton	.35
30	Joe Carter	.75
35	Phil Niekro	.75
36	Ed Vande Berg	.25
42	Rich Yett	.25
43	Scott Bailes	.25
46	Doug Jones	.25
49	Tom Candiotti	.25
54	Tom Waddell	.25
---	Manager and Coaching Staff (Jack Aker, Bobby Bonds, Pat Corrales, Doc Edwards, Johnny Goryl)	.25
---	Team photo	.25

1988 Gatorade Indians

This three-panel foldout was sponsored by Gatorade for distribution during an in-stadium giveaway. The cover includes four game-action photos. One panel of the 9-1/2" x 11-1/4" glossy color foldout features a team photo (with checklist), two panels consist of 30 perforated baseball cards (2-1/4" x 3") featuring team members. Posed portrait photos are framed in red on a white background. The player's name and uniform number are printed below the photo. Backs are printed in red, blue and black. A facsimile autograph appears at the top-right of the card back, opposite the player uniform number, name and position. Both major and minor league stats are listed.

		MT
Complete Set, Foldout:		6.00
Complete Set, Singles (31):		5.00
Common Player:		.25
2	Tom Spencer	.25
6	Andy Allanson	.25
7	Luis Issac	.25
8	Carmen Castillo	.25
9	Charlie Manuel	.25
10	Pat Tabler	.25
11	Doug Jones	.25
14	Julio Franco	.35
15	Ron Washington	.25
16	Jay Bell	.50
17	Bill Laskey	.25
20	Willie Upshaw	.25
21	Greg Swindell	.25
23	Chris Bando	.25
25	Dave Clark	.25
26	Brook Jacoby	.25
27	Mel Hall	.25
28	Cory Snyder	.25
30	Joe Carter	.75
31	Dan Schatzeder	.25
32	Doc Edwards	.25
33	Ron Kittle	.25
35	Mark Wiley	.25
42	Rich Yett	.25
43	Scott Bailes	.25
45	Johnny Goryl	.25
47	Jeff Kaiser	.25
49	Tom Candiotti	.25
50	Jeff Dedmon	.25
52	John Farrell	.25
---	Team photo	.25

1993 Gatorade Detroit Tigers

Color action photos are these oversize (2-7/8" x 4-1/4") cards. The pictures are framed in team-color navy and orange pinstripes with a white border. Player name is in white in a navy border below the photo, with the position printed in orange at bottom. A large team logo appears in the upper-right corner. Backs are printed in orange and black and include a Gatorade logo, player identification and stats. Cards are listed here by uniform number.

		MT
Complete Set (28):		8.00
Common Player:		.25
1	Lou Whitaker	1.00
3	Alan Trammell	2.50
4	Tony Phillips	.50
7	Scott Livingstone	.50
9	Skeeter Barnes	.25
11	Sparky Anderson	1.00
15	Gary Thurman	.25
16	David Wells	2.00
18	David Haas	.25
19	Chad Kreuter	.35
20	Mickey Tettleton	.50
21	Mike Moore	.25
22	Milt Cuyler	.25
23a	Kirk Gibson	1.00
23b	Mark Leiter	.25
24	Travis Fryman	1.50
27	Kurt Knudsen	.25
28	Rob Deer	.25
30	Bill Krueger	.25
32	Dan Gladden	.25
36	Bill Gullickson	.25
38	Bob MacDonald	.25
39	Mike Henneman	.25
42	Buddy Groom	.25
44	John Doherty	.25
45	Cecil Fielder	1.00
49	Tom Bolton	.25
---	Coaches (Dick Tracewkski, Billy Muffett, Larry Herndon, Gene Roof, Dan Whitmer)	.25

1995 Gatorade Cubs

Fans attending the Aug. 24 game at Wrigley Field received a set of oversized (2-7/8" x 4-1/4") cards of the Chicago Cubs, sponsored by Gatorade. Cards feature a color action photo at top, with the player's name, position and uniform number in a blue box at bottom. Backs have a small black-and-white portrait photo, complete minor and major league stats and the team and sponsor logos. Cards are checklisted here by player uniform number.

		MT
Complete Set (27):		7.50
Common Player:		.25
5	Jim Riggleman	.25
9	Scott Servais	.25
10	Scott Bullett	.25
11	Rey Sanchez	.25
12	Shawon Dunston	.30
13	Turk Wendell	.30
16	Anthony Young	.25
17	Mark Grace	1.00
18	Jose Hernandez	.25
20	Howard Johnson	.25
21	Sammy Sosa	4.00
25	Luis Gonzalez	.30
27	Todd Zeile	.40
28	Randy Myers	.30
29	Jose Guzman	.25
30	Ozzie Timmons	.25
32	Kevin Foster	.25
38	Jaime Navarro	.25
46	Steve Trachsel	.30
47	Mike Perez	.25
49	Frank Castillo	.25
52	Jim Bullinger	.25
53	Chris Nabholz	.25
55	Larry Casian	.25
56	Brian McRae	.35
57	Rich Garces	.25
---	Cubs coaches (Dave Bialas, Fergie Jenkins, Tony Muser, Max Oliveras, Dan Radison, Billy Williams)	.25

1985 General Mills Stickers

General Mills of Canada inserted a panel of two cellophane-wrapped baseball stickers in each box of Cheerios in 1985. The full-color sticker panels, measuring 2-3/8" x 3-3/4", are blank-backed and unnumbered and contain the player's name, team and position in both English and French. The General Mills logo appears at the top of each sticker. All team insignias on the players' uniforms and hats have been airbrushed off.

		MT
Complete Panel Set (14):		12.00
Complete Singles Set (28):		7.00
Common Panel:		.50
Common Player:		.25
	Panel (1)	1.00
(1)	Gary Carter	.35
(2)	Tom Brunansky	.25
	Panel (2)	1.00
(3)	Gary Carter	.35
(4)	Dave Steib	.35
	Panel (3)	1.00
(5)	Andre Dawson	.35
(6)	Alvin Davis	.25
	Panel (4)	1.00
(7)	Steve Garvey	.45
(8)	George Bell	.25
	Panel (5)	1.00
(9)	Steve Garvey	.35
(10)	Jim Rice	.30
	Panel (6)	1.00
(11)	Jeffrey Leonard	.25
(12)	Eddie Murray	.40
	Panel (7)	1.50
(13)	Dale Murphy	.40
(14)	Robin Yount	.50
	Panel (8)	1.00
(15)	Terry Puhl	.25
(16)	Reggie Jackson	.50
	Panel (9)	.50
(17)	Johnny Ray	.25
(18)	Lou Whitaker	.25
	Panel (10)	1.00
(19)	Ryne Sandberg	.40
(20)	Mike Hargrove	.25
	Panel (11)	2.00
(21)	Mike Schmidt	.50
(22)	George Brett	.50
	Panel (12)	1.50
(23)	Ozzie Smith	.50
(24)	Dave Winfield	.45
	Panel (13)	1.00
(25)	Mario Soto	.25
(26)	Carlton Fisk	.35
	Panel (14)	1.00
(27)	Fernando Valenzuela	.25
(28)	Dale Murphy	.40

1986 General Mills Booklets

In 1986, General Mills of Canada inserted six different "Baseball Players Booklets" in specially marked boxes of Cheerios. Ten different players are featured in each booklet, with statistics for the 1985 season in both English and French. The booklet, when opened fully, measures 3-3/4" x 15". Also included in the booklet is a contest sponsored by Petro-Canada service stations to win a day with a major league player at his 1987 spring training site in Florida. Team insignias have been airbrushed off the players' uniforms and caps.

		MT
Complete Set (6):		12.50
Common Booklet:		1.25
1	A.L. East (Wade Boggs, Kirk Gibson, Rickey Henderson, Don Mattingly, Jack Morris, Lance Parrish, Jim Rice, Dave Righetti, Cal Ripken, (Lou Whitaker)	4.00
2	A.L. West (Harold Baines, Phil Bradley, George Brett, Carlton Fisk, Ozzie Guillen, Kent Hrbek, Reggie Jackson, Dan Quisenberry, (Bret Saberhagen, Frank White)	2.50
3	Toronto Blue Jays (Jesse Barfield, George Bell, Bill Caudill, Tony Fernandez, Damaso Garcia, Lloyd Moseby, Rance Mulliniks, Dave Steib, (Willie Upshaw, Ernie Whitt)	2.00
4	N.L. East (Gary Carter, Jack Clark, George Foster, Dwight Gooden, Gary Matthews, Willie McGee, Ryne Sanderberg, Mike Schmidt, (Lee Smith, Ozzie Smith)	2.50
5	N.L. West (Dave Concepcion, Pedro Guerrero, Terry Kennedy, Dale Murphy, Graig Nettles, Dave Parker, Tony Perez, Steve Sax, (Bruce Sutter, Fernando Valenzuela)	1.25
6	Montreal Expos (Hubie Brooks, Andre Dawson, Mike Fitzgerald, Vance Law, Tim Raines, Jeff Reardon, Bryn Smith, Jason Thompson, (Tim Wallach, Mitch Webster)	2.00

1987 General Mills Booklets

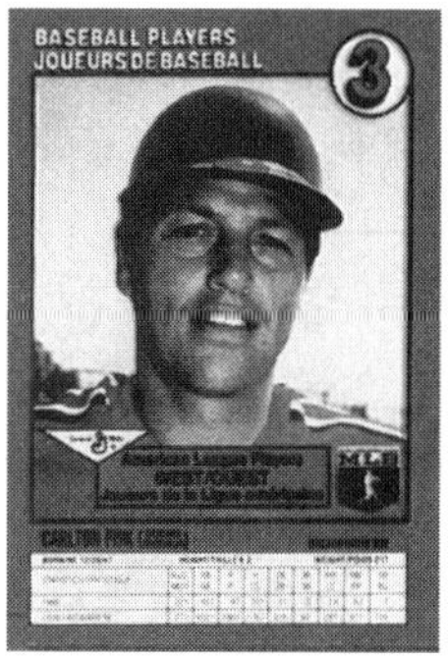

For a second straight year, General Mills of Canada inserted one of six different "Baseball Super-Stars Booklets" in specially marked boxes of Cheerios and Honey Nut Cheerios cereal. Each booklet contains ten full-color photos for a total of 60 players. The booklets, when completely unfolded, measure 15" x 3-3/4". Written in both English and French, the set was produced by Mike Schechter and Associates. All team insignias have been airbrushed off the photos.

		MT
Complete Set (6):		10.00
Common Booklet:		2.00
1	Toronto Blue Jays (Jesse Barfield, George Bell, Tony Fernandez, Kelly Gruber, Tom Henke, Jimmy Key), Lloyd Moseby, Dave Steib, (Willie Upshaw, Ernie Whitt)	2.00
2	A.L. East (Wade Boggs, Roger Clemens, Kirk Gibson, Rickey Henderson, Don Mattingly, Jack Morris, Eddie Murray, Pat Tabler, (Dave Winfield, Robin Yount)	4.00
3	A.L. West (Phil Bradley, George Brett, Jose Canseco, Carlton Fisk, Reggie Jackson, Wally Joyner, Kirk McCaskill, Larry Parrish, (Kirby Puckett, Dan Quisenberry)	2.50
4	Montreal Expos (Hubie Brooks, Mike Fitzgerald, Andres Galarraga, Vance Law, Andy McGaffigan, Bryn Smith), Jason Thompson, Tim	2.00

	Wallach, (Mitch Webster, Floyd Youmans)	
5	N.L. East (Gary Carter, Dwight Gooden, Keith Hernandez, Willie McGee, Tim Raines, R.J. Reynolds, Ryne Sandberg, Mike Schmidt, (Ozzie Smith, Darryl Strawberry)	2.50
6	N.L. West (Kevin Bass, Chili Davis, Bill Doran, Pedro Guerrero, Tony Gwynn, Dale Murphy, Dave Parker), Steve Sax, Mike Scott, (Fernando Valenzuela)	2.00

1990 Giant Eagle Roberto Clemente Stickers

The Giant Eagle food stores in the Pittsburgh issued a collectors' poster and set of 18 stickers circa 1990. Each of the 2-1/2" x 3-1/2" stickers features one of Roberto Clemente's regular-issue Topps cards 1955-72. The stickers were originally issued in strips of three. Backs are blank. The issue was almost certainly not authorized by Topps or the Clemente estate.

	MT
Complete Set, Strips (18):	20.00
Common Sticker:	2.00
Poster:	16.00
(1-18) Roberto Clemente	

1995 GM St. Louis Cardinals Magnets

These 2" x 3" magnets were given away at a series of 1995 games at Busch Stadium. Sponsored by GM Parts/Mr. Goodwrench the magnets have color action photos on front; backs are blank.

		MT
Complete Set (6):		12.00
Common Player:		1.50
1	Ozzie Smith	4.50
2	Gregg Jefferies	2.00
3	Bob Tewksbury	1.50
4	Ray Lankford	2.00
5	Rene Arocha	1.50
6	Tom Pagnozzi	1.50

1992 Gold Entertainment Babe Ruth

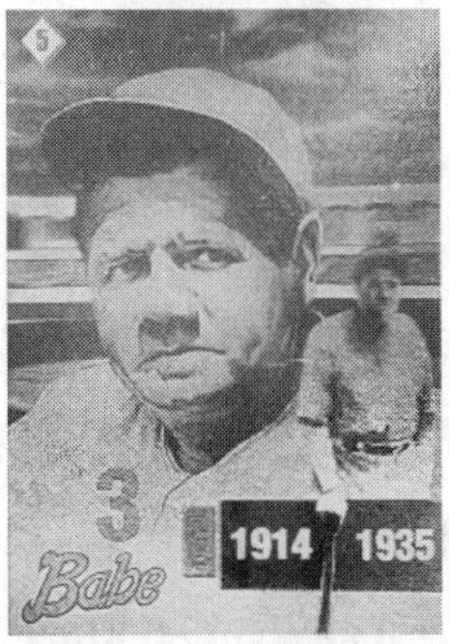

The holography is not state of the art, but the subject matter is popular in this limited edition (250,000 sets) issue. Cards 1, 3, and 5 feature hologram fronts and conventionally printed backs, while 2 and 4 are double-sided holograms. Silver and gold versions of the set were issued, with the silver being four times as common as the gold. Values of the gold cards are 1.5X that of the silver.

		MT
Complete Set, Silver:		2.00
Complete Set, Gold:		3.00
Common Card, Silver:		.50
Common Card, Gold:		.75
1	1914-1919 (Babe Ruth) (Red Sox pitcher)	.50
2	Babe Ruth, Lou Gehrig (Career stats)	.50
3	The Called Shot (Babe Ruth)	.50
3a	The Called Shot (Babe Ruth) (no back printing, rubber-stamped prototype)	2.00
4	61 in '61 - 60 in '27 (Babe Ruth, Roger Maris)	.50
5	1914-1935 (Babe Ruth) (career summary)	.50

1996 Golden Legends

This series of collector issues features some of the game's greatest players. A complete package for each player includes a 2-1/2" x 3-1/2" embossed gold-foil card, a 3-1/8" x 5-1/8" plastic screw-down holder with gold facsimile autograph, a plastic display easel, a 3-7/8" x 5-7/8" black-and-white picture of the player, an assembly instruction sheet and certificate of authenticity which specifies an issue of 50,000. The embossed gold-foil cards have a player portrait on front. Backs have a small action picture and career summary, along with a serial number. Values shown are for complete packages.

		MT
Complete Set (14):		75.00
Common Player:		7.50
(1)	Ty Cobb	10.00
(2)	Dizzy Dean	7.50
(3)	Leo Durocher	7.50
(4)	Bob Feller	7.50
(5)	Jimmie Foxx	7.50
(6)	Lou Gehrig	10.00
(7)	Lefty Grove	7.50
(8)	Rogers Hornsby	7.50
(9)	Joe Jackson	15.00
(10)	Walter Johnson	7.50
(11)	Christy Mathewson	7.50
(12)	Babe Ruth	12.00
(13)	Casey Stengel	7.50
(14)	Honus Wagner	7.50
(15)	Cy Young	7.50

1993 Golden Moments Ken Griffey, Jr.

This two-card set features cartoon images of Ken Griffey, Jr., on front, with backs printed mostly in Japanese.

		MT
Complete Set:		10.00
Common Card:		5.00
(1)	Ken Griffey Jr. (batting)	5.00
(2)	Ken Griffey Jr. (fielding)	5.00

1990 Good Humor Big League Autograph Sticks

These bat-shaped sticks for ice cream bars are collectible in that they feature facsimile autographs of top players. Approximately 4-1/2" x 5/8", the sticks are numbered in alphabetical order.

		MT
Complete Set (26):		9.00
Common Player:		.25
1	Jim Abbott	.25
2	George Bell	.25
3	Wade Boggs	.45
4	Bobby Bonilla	.25
5	Jose Canseco	.45
6	Will Clark	.45
7	Eric Davis	.30
8	Carlton Fisk	.35
9	Kirk Gibson	.25
10	Dwight Gooden	.25
11	Ken Griffey Jr.	2.00
12	Von Hayes	.25
13	Don Mattingly	.75
14	Gregg Olson	.25
15	Kirby Puckett	.65
16	Tim Raines	.25
17	Nolan Ryan	1.50
18	Bret Saberhagen	.25
19	Ryne Sandberg	.50
20	Benito Santiago	.25
21	Mike Scott	.25
22	Zane Smith	.25
23	Ozzie Smith	.45
24	Cory Snyder	.25
25	Alan Trammell	.25
26	Robin Yount	.45

1981 Granny Goose Potato Chips A's

The 1981 Granny Goose set features the Oakland A's. The 2-1/2" x 3-1/2" cards were issued in bags of potato chips and are sometimes found with grease stains. The cards have full color fronts with the graphics done in the team's green and yellow colors. The backs contain the A's logo and a short player biography. The Revering card was withdrawn from the set shortly after he was traded and is in shorter supply than the rest of the cards in the set. The cards are numbered in the checklist that follows by the player's uniform number.

		MT
Complete Set (15):		100.00
Common Player:		2.00
1	Billy Martin	10.00
2	Mike Heath	2.00
5	Jeff Newman	2.00
6	Mitchell Page	2.00
8	Rob Picciolo	2.00
10	Wayne Gross	2.00
13	Dave Revering	45.00
17	Mike Norris	2.00
20	Tony Armas	4.00
21	Dwayne Murphy	2.00
22	Rick Langford	2.00
27	Matt Keough	2.00
35	Rickey Henderson	30.00
39	Dave McKay	2.00
54	Steve McCatty	2.00

1982 Granny Goose Potato Chips A's

Granny Goose repeated its promotion from the previous year and issued another set featuring the Oakland A's. The 2-1/2" x 3-1/2" cards were distributed in two fashions - in bags of potato chips and at Fan Appreciation Day at Oakland-Alameda Coliseum. The cards are identical in design to the 1981 set and can be distinguished from it by the date on the copyright on the bottom of the card reverse. The cards are numbered in the checklist that follows by the player's uniform number.

		MT
Complete Set (15):		12.00
Common Player:		.50
1	Billy Martin	1.50
2	Mike Heath	.50
5	Jeff Newman	.50
8	Rob Picciolo	.50
10	Wayne Gross	.50
11	Fred Stanley	.50
15	Davey Lopes	.65
17	Mike Norris	.50
20	Tony Armas	.65
21	Dwayne Murphy	.50
22	Rick Langford	.50
27	Matt Keough	.50
35	Rickey Henderson	10.00
44	Cliff Johnson, Jr.	.50
54	Steve McCatty	.50

1982 Granny Goose Signature Set

The cards from this very scarce 15-card set are identical to the regular Granny Goose cards, but contain a facsimile autograph on the front. The cards were initially intended as special prize-redemption inserts from Granny Goose potato chips, but were never released in any quantity.

		MT
Complete Set (15):		100.00
Common Player:		5.00
1	Billy Martin	15.00
2	Mike Heath	5.00
5	Jeff Newman	5.00
8	Rob Picciolo	5.00
10	Wayne Gross	5.00
11	Fred Stanley	5.00
15	Davey Lopes	7.50
17	Mike Norris	5.00
20	Tony Armas	5.00
21	Dwayne Murphy	5.00
22	Rick Langford	5.00
27	Matt Keough	5.00
35	Rickey Henderson	35.00
44	Cliff Johnson, Jr.	5.00
54	Steve McCatty	5.00

1983 Granny Goose Potato Chips A's

For the third consecutive year, Granny Goose issued a set of baseball cards featuring the Oakland A's. The cards were issued with or without a detachable coupon found at the bottom of each card. Issued in bags of potato chips were the coupon cards, which contain a scratch-off section offering prizes. The cards without the coupon section were given away to fans at Oakland-Alameda Coliseum on July 3, 1983. Cards with the detachable coupon command a 50 per cent premium over the coupon-less variety. The cards in the following checklist are numbered by the player's uniform number.

		MT
Complete Set (15):		11.00
Common Player:		.50
2	Mike Heath	.50
4	Carney Lansford	.50
10	Wayne Gross	.50
14	Steve Boros	.50
15	Davey Lopes	.65
16	Mike Davis	.50
17	Mike Norris	.50
21	Dwayne Murphy	.50
22	Rick Langford	.50
27	Matt Keough	.50
31	Tom Underwood	.50
33	Dave Beard	.50
35	Rickey Henderson	8.00
39	Tom Burgmeier	.50
54	Steve McCatty	.50

1998 Ken Griffey Jr. Candy Bar

This card was available as a mail-in premium for purchasers of Ken Griffey Jr. MVP candy bars. The cost was $1.50 for shipping and handling. The front features a caricature of Junior in a white tuxedo displaying some of his many awards. The back names him, "Baseball's Most Complete Player," lists his awards, stats and a career summary for the 1997 season, and quotes him, "Play Hard, Have Fun." Back printing is in blue and green on white.

		MT
24	Ken Griffey Jr.	2.00

1982 G.S. Gallery All-Time Favorites

This collectors issue was produced by a Philadelphia-area card dealer and features former stars and superstars. For its time, the use of color photos (thought they were "borrowed" from earlier printed sources) was actually a step up from most collectors sets. The cards are in 2-1/2" x 3-1/8" format (the size of the 1939-41 Play Ball cards). Fronts have only the color photo surrounded by a white border. Backs are printed in blue with player identification and career stats, along with a copyright line and logo.

		MT
Complete Set (24):		6.00
Common Player:		.25
1	Stan Musial	.50
2	Alvin Dark	.25
3	Harry (The Hat) Walker	.25
4	Dom DiMaggio	.35
5	Carl Furillo	.35
6	Joe DiMaggio	2.00
7	Joe Adcock	.25
8	Lou Boudreau	.25
9	Ted Williams	1.50
10	Phil Rizzuto	.35
11	Pee Wee Reese	.35
12	Jimmy Dykes	.25
13	Nellie Fox	.40
14	George Kell	.25
15	Ralph Kiner	.25
16	Roger Maris	1.00
17	Ted Kluszewski	.35
18	Wally Moon	.25
19	Hank Sauer	.25
20	Bobby Thomson	.25
21	Mel Parnell	.25
22	Ewell Blackwell	.25
23	Richie Ashburn	.35
24	Jackie Robinson	.90

1996 GTE Nolan Ryan

To commemorate the 5th anniversary of Nolan Ryan's unprecedented 7th No-Hitter on May 1, 1991. GTE sponsored a commemorative sheet giveaway at the Rangers' game on May 1, 1996. The 8-1/2' x 11" cardboard sheet features the artwork of Vernon Wells with a sepia background of scenes from the no-hitter and, in the foreground, a color picture of a batter's-eye view of the Texas Express. The front carries a serial number from an edition of 50,000. The black-and-white back describes the no-hitter and profiles the artist.

	MT
Commemorative Sheet: Nolan Ryan	15.00

1994 GTS '69 Mets Phone Cards

One of the first multi-player phone card issues was this 32-card series from Global Telecommunications Solutions honoring the 25th anniversary of the "Miracle Mets" 1969 World's Championship. Cards picture team members in color portraits by sports artist Ron Lewis. A gold-foil headline in the top white border reads "'69 Mets Collector Edition". Backs of the 2-1/8" x 3-3/8" plastic cards are printed in black-and-white and contain instructions for use of the phone card. Each of the unnumbered phone cards had a nominal value of five minutes' phone time.

		MT
Complete Set (32):		200.00
Common Player:		6.00
(1)	Tommie Agee	8.00
(2)	Yogi Berra	15.00
(3)	Ken Boswell	6.00
(4)	Don Cardwell	6.00
(5)	Ed Charles	7.50
(6)	Donn Clendenon	8.00
(7)	Jack DiLauro	6.00
(8)	Duffy Dyer	6.00
(9)	Wayne Garrett	6.00
(10)	Rod Gaspar	6.00
(11)	Gary Gentry	6.00
(12)	Jerry Grote	7.50
(13)	Bud Harrelson	7.50
(14)	Gil Hodges	12.00
(15)	Cleon Jones	7.50
(16)	Cal Koonce	7.50
(17)	Jerry Koosman	7.50
(18)	Ed Kranepool	7.50
(19)	J.C. Martin	6.00
(20)	Jim McAndrew	6.00
(21)	Tug McGraw	7.50
(22)	Bobby Pfeil	6.00
(23)	Joe Pignatano	6.00
(24)	Nolan Ryan	60.00
(25)	Tom Seaver	30.00
(26)	Art Shamsky	6.00
(27)	Ron Swoboda	7.50
(28)	Ron Taylor	6.00
(29)	Rube Walker	6.00
(30)	Al Weis	6.00
(31)	Ed Yost	6.00
(32)	Mets logo	6.00

H

1981-89 Hall of Fame Metallic Plaque-cards

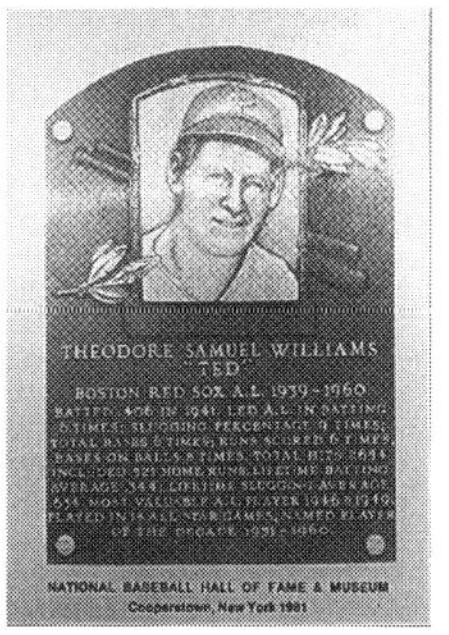

Since 1981, the National Baseball Hall of Fame & Museum has issued a set of metallic baseball cards reproducing the plaques of the baseball greats inducted. The plaques are pictured on 2-1/2" x 3-1/2" blank-backed gold anodized aluminum. Every detail of the plaque is fully and faithfully reproduced. The set was sold in series through the Hall of Fame's gift shop. Plaque-cards for inductees were added annually through at least 1989. Only 1,000 plaques of each player were produced. Values are, to some extent, based not only on player popularity, but on year of issue; later plaques tend to be more expensive.

		MT
Complete Set (205):		2650.
Common Player:		11.00
(1)	Hank Aaron	40.00
(2)	Grover Alexander	18.00
(3)	Walter Alston	16.00
(4)	Cap Anson	16.00
(5)	Luis Aparicio	24.00
(6)	Luke Appling	13.00
(7)	Earl Averill	12.00
(8)	"Home Run" Baker	12.00
(9)	David Bancroft	11.00
(10)	Ernie Banks	30.00
(11)	Al Barlick	17.50
(12)	Ed Barrow	12.00
(13)	Jacob Beckley	12.00
(14)	Cool Papa Bell	20.00
(15)	Johnny Bench	55.00
(16)	"Chief" Bender	14.00
(17)	Yogi Berra	35.00
(18)	Jim Bottomley	16.00
(19)	Lou Boudreau	12.00
(20)	Lou Brock	35.00
(21)	Dan Brouthers	11.00
(22)	Mordecai Brown	16.00
(23)	Morgan Burkeley	12.00
(24)	Jesse Burkett	12.00
(25)	Roger Bresnahan	12.00
(26)	Roy Campanella	30.00
(27)	Rod Carew	12.00
(28)	Max Carey	16.00
(29)	Alexander Cartwright	12.00
(30)	Henry Chadwick	11.00
(31)	Frank Chance	17.50
(32)	Happy Chandler	12.00
(33)	Oscar Charleston	18.00
(34)	Jack Chesbro	13.00
(35)	Fred Clarke	12.00
(36)	John Clarkson	12.00
(37)	Roberto Clemente	60.00
(38)	Ty Cobb	55.00
(39)	Mickey Cochrane	18.00
(40)	Eddie Collins	12.00
(41)	James Collins	12.00
(42)	Earle Combs	12.00
(43)	Charles Comiskey	12.00
(44)	Jocko Conlan	11.00
(45)	Thomas Connolly	11.00
(46)	Roger Connor	12.00
(47)	Stan Coveleski	11.00
(48)	Sam Crawford	13.00
(49)	Joe Cronin	18.00
(50)	Candy Cummings	12.00
(51)	Kiki Cuyler	16.00
(52)	Ray Dandridge	21.00
(53)	Dizzy Dean	35.00
(54)	Ed Delahanty	12.00
(55)	Bill Dickey	18.00
(56)	Martin Dihigo	21.00
(57)	Joe DiMaggio	70.00
(58)	Bobby Doerr	30.00
(59)	Don Drysdale	27.50
(60)	Hugh Duffy	12.00
(61)	Bill Evans	12.00
(62)	John Evers	17.50
(63)	Buck Ewing	12.00
(64)	Urban Faber	12.00
(65)	Bob Feller	22.50
(66)	Rick Ferrell	15.00
(67)	Elmer Flick	12.00
(68)	Whitey Ford	30.00
(69)	Rube Foster	12.00
(70)	Jimmie Foxx	27.50
(71)	Ford Frick	12.00
(72)	Frank Frisch	12.00
(73)	Pud Galvin	12.00
(74)	Lou Gehrig	70.00
(75)	Charles Gehringer	26.00
(76)	Josh Gibson	24.00
(77)	Bob Gibson	22.50
(78)	Warren Giles	12.00
(79)	Lefty Gomez	15.00
(80)	Goose Goslin	16.00
(81)	Hank Greenberg	25.00
(82)	Clark Griffith	12.00
(83)	Burleigh Grimes	12.00
(84)	Lefty Grove	14.00
(85)	Chick Hafey	12.00
(86)	Pop Haines	12.00
(87)	William Hamilton	12.00
(88)	Gabby Hartnett	12.00
(89)	William Harridge	11.00
(90)	Bucky Harris	16.00
(91)	Harry Heilmann	12.00
(92)	Bill Herman	12.00
(93)	Harry Hooper	12.00
(94)	Rogers Hornsby	24.00
(95)	Schoolboy Hoyt	12.00
(96)	Cal Hubbard	12.00
(97)	Carl Hubbell	14.00
(98)	Miller Huggins	13.00
(99)	Catfish Hunter	30.00
(100)	Monte Irvin	14.00
(101)	Travis Jackson	12.00
(102)	Hugh Jennings	12.00
(103)	Ban Johnson	11.00
(104)	Walter Johnson	32.00
(105)	Judy Johnson	12.00
(106)	Addie Joss	12.00
(107)	Al Kaline	27.50
(108)	Timothy Keefe	12.00
(109)	Willie Keeler	16.00
(110)	George Kell	16.00
(111)	Joe Kelley	12.00
(112)	Highpockets Kelly	12.00
(113)	King Kelly	15.00
(114)	Harmon Killebrew	14.00
(115)	Ralph Kiner	12.00
(116)	Bill Klem	12.00
(117)	Chuck Klein	16.00
(118)	Sandy Koufax	30.00
(119)	Nap Lajoie	19.00
(120)	Kenesaw Landis	12.00
(121)	Buck Leonard	14.00
(122)	Bob Lemon	12.00
(123)	Fred Linstrom	12.00
(124)	Pop Lloyd	12.00
(125)	Ernie Lombardi	12.00
(126)	Al Lopez	12.00
(127)	Ted Lyons	12.00
(128)	Connie Mack	12.00
(129)	Larry MacPhail	12.00
(130)	Mickey Mantle	110.00
(131)	Heinie Manush	12.00
(132)	Rabbit Maranville	16.00
(133)	Juan Marichal	18.00
(134)	Rube Marquard	13.00
(135)	Eddie Mathews	14.00
(136)	Christy Mathewson	27.50
(137)	Willie Mays	50.00
(138)	Joe McCarthy	12.00
(139)	Thomas McCarthy	12.00
(140)	Willie McCovey	14.00
(141)	Iron Man McGinnity	12.00
(142)	John McGraw	12.00
(143)	Bill McKechnie	12.00
(144)	Joe Medwick	12.00
(145)	Johnny Mize	12.00
(146)	Stan Musial	42.50
(147)	Kid Nichols	16.00
(148)	James O'Rourke	12.00
(149)	Mel Ott	16.00
(150)	Satchel Paige	29.00
(151)	Herb Pennock	12.00
(152)	Eddie Plank	11.00
(153)	Hoss Radbourne	12.00
(154)	Pee Wee Reese	14.00
(155)	Sam Rice	12.00
(156)	Branch Rickey	12.00
(157)	Eppa Rixey	12.00
(158)	Robin Roberts	19.00
(159)	Brooks Robinson	21.00
(160)	Frank Robinson	23.00
(161)	Jackie Robinson	40.00
(162)	Wilbert Robinson	13.00
(163)	Edd Roush	12.00
(164)	Red Ruffing	16.00
(165)	Amos Rusie	12.00
(166)	Babe Ruth	95.00
(167)	Ray Schalk	12.00
(168)	Red Schoendienst	30.00
(169)	Joe Sewell	12.00
(170)	Al Simmons	18.00
(171)	George Sisler	12.00
(172)	Enos Slaughter	30.00
(173)	Duke Snider	24.00
(174)	Warren Spahn	24.00
(175)	Al Spalding	16.00
(176)	Tris Speaker	23.00
(177)	Willie Stargell	12.00
(178)	Casey Stengel	23.00
(179)	Bill Terry	12.00
(180)	Sam Thompson	12.00
(181)	Joe Tinker	20.00
(182)	Pie Traynor	20.00
(183)	Dazzy Vance	16.00
(184)	Arky Vaughan	12.00
(185)	Rube Waddell	16.00
(186)	Roderick Wallace	12.00
(187)	Ed Walsh	12.00
(188)	Lloyd Waner	16.00
(189)	Paul Waner	18.00
(190)	John Ward	12.00
(191)	Honus Wagner	30.00
(192)	George Weiss	12.00
(193)	Mickey Welch	12.00
(194)	Zack Wheat	16.00
(195)	Hoyt Wilhelm	25.00
(196)	Billy Williams	35.00
(197)	Ted Williams	50.00
(198)	Hack Wilson	15.00
(199)	George Wright	12.00
(200)	Harry Wright	12.00
(201)	Early Wynn	16.00
(202)	Carl Yastrzemski	18.00
(203)	Tom Yawkey	12.00
(204)	Cy Young	26.00
(205)	Ross Youngs	12.00

1998 Hamburger Helper Home Run Heroes

Eight top sluggers are featured in this box-back set from Hamburger Helper. The 2-1/2" x 3-1/2" cards are printed on the backs of various flavors of the skillet meal boxes. Unlike many similar issues these are fully licensed by Major League Baseball, as well as the Players Association, and the player photos have uniform logos.

Also unusual is that the cards have a printed back in black-and-white offering personal data, career highlights and stats.

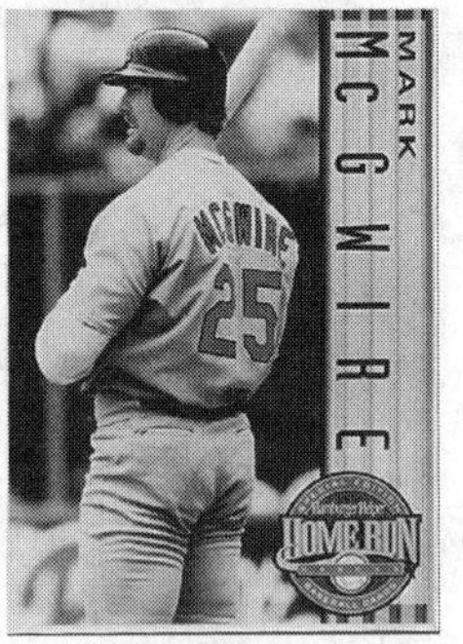

	MT
Complete Set, Boxes (8):	30.00
Complete Set, Singles (8):	7.50
Common Player Box:	3.00
Common Player Single:	.50
1 Mark McGwire	2.00
2 Rafael Palmeiro	.50
3 Tino Martinez	.50
4 Barry Bonds	.75
5 Larry Walker	.50
6 Juan Gonzalez	.75
7 Mike Piazza	1.50
8 Frank Thomas	1.50

1988 Hardee's/Coke Conlon

Regionally issued in a promotion sponsored by Hardee's restaurants and Coca-Cola, this six-card set features the photos of Charles Martin Conlon and is closely related to the Sporting News-Wide World Conlon issues of the time. The cards feature sepia photos on front and career stats and summary on back. The unnumbered cards are checklisted here alphabetically.

	MT
Complete Set (6):	4.00
Common Player:	1.00
(1) Cool Papa Bell	1.00
(2) Ty Cobb	1.50
(3) Lou Gehrig	2.00
(4) Connie Mack	1.00
(5) Casey Stengel	1.00
(6) Rube Waddell	1.00

1996 Hebrew National Detroit Tigers

One of the team's hot dog concessionaires sponsored a set of Tiger cards which was given away at the Sept. 1 game. Originally intended to be 28 cards, only 26 were issued due to late-season trades. Cards are in a larger than normal 2-7/8" x 4-1/4" format with game-action photo on front. Down one side in team colors are the player name and position, with the stalking tiger logo at bottom. Backs have a large light blue gothic "D" in the background with player personal data and major/minor league stats and team/sponsor logos.

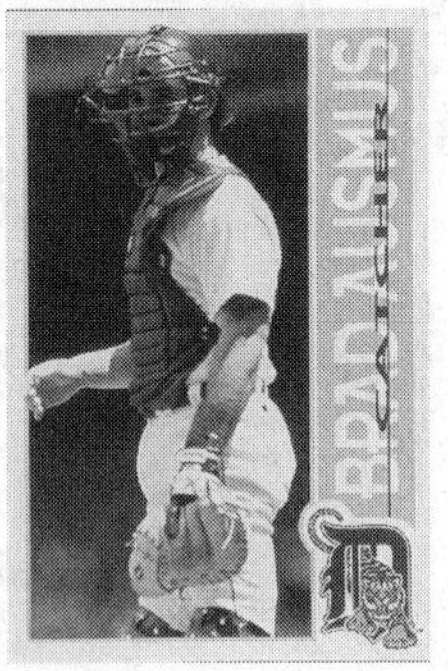

	MT
Complete Set (26):	12.00
Common Player:	.50
1 Kimera Bartee	.50
2 Jose Lima	.50
3 Tony Clark	1.00
4 Not issued	
5 Travis Fryman	.75
6 Not issued	
7 Bobby Higginson	.75
8 Greg Keagle	.50
9 Mark Lewis	.50
10 Richie Lewis	.50
11 Felipe Lira	.50
12 Mike Myers	.50
13 Melvin Nieves	.50
14 Alan Trammell	1.00
15 Tom Urbani	.50
16 Brian Williams	.50
17 Eddie Williams	.50
18 Curtis Pride	.50
19 Mark Parent	.50
20 Raul Casanova	.50
21 Omar Olivares	.50
22 Gregg Olson	.50
23 Justin Thompson	.50
24 Brad Ausmus	.50
25 Andujar Cedeno	.50
26 Buddy Bell	.50
27 Paws (mascot)	.50
28 Detroit Tigers Coaches (Glenn Ezell, Terry Francona, Larry Herndon, Fred Kendall, John (Jon) Matlack, Ron	.50

1997 Hebrew National Detroit Tigers

The hot dog concessionaire at Tiger Stadium produced a second annual team set in 1997, giving the cards away at the June 22 game. Cards feature borderless color action photos on front, with a tiny black-and-white portrait photo at bottom-right. Backs are printed in blue and yellow and have player data, complete major and minor league stats and the team and sponsor logos.

	MT
Complete Set (28):	12.00
Common Player:	.50
1 Jose Bautista	.50
2 Willie Blair	.50
3 Doug Brocail	.50
4 Raul Casanova	.50
5 Tony Clark	.90
6 Deivi Cruz	.50
7 John Cummings	.50
8 Damion Easley	.50
9 Travis Fryman	.60
10 Bobby Higginson	.75
11 Brian Hunter	.60
12 Todd Johnson	.50
13 Todd Jones	.50
14 Felipe Lira	.50
15 Dan Miceli	.50
16 Brian Moehler	.50
17 Mike Myers	.50
18 Phil Nevin	.50
19 Melvin Nieves	.50
20 Omar Oliveras	.50
21 Curtis Pride	.50
22 A.J. Sager	.50
23 Justin Thompson	.50
24 Matt Walbeck	.50
25 Jody Reed	.50
26 Bob Hamelin	.50
27 Buddy Bell	.50
28 Tigers coaches (Rick Adair, Larry Herndon, Perry Hill, Fred Kendall, Larry Parrish, Jerry White)	.50

1993 Highland Mint Mint-Cards

The Highland Mint produced replicas of several Topps rookie cards and other prominent cards in bronze and silver. Limited to 1,000 in silver and 5,000 in bronze, the company produced cards of many current stars along with a replica of Brooks Robinson's 1957 rookie card. The cards carried a suggested retail price of $235 for the silver and $50 for the bronze. Cards measure 2-1/2" x 3-1/2" and are 1/10" thick. Each Mint-Card has a serial number engraved on the edge and is sold in a heavy lucite holder, packaged with a certificate of authenticity in a plastic book-style folder.

	MT
Complete Set, Silver (17):	4000.
Complete Set, Bronze (17):	850.00
Common Player, Silver:	150.00
Common Player, Bronze:	30.00
(1s) Brooks Robinson (1957 Topps, silver edition of 796)	150.00
(1b) Brooks Robinson (1957 Topps, bronze edition of 2,043)	30.00
(2s) Dave Winfield (1974 Topps, silver edition of 266)	275.00
(2b) Dave Winfield (1974 Topps, bronze edition of 1,216)	30.00
(3s) George Brett (1975 Topps, silver edition of 999)	175.00
(3b) George Brett (1975 Topps, bronze edition of 3,560)	50.00
(4s) Robin Yount (1975 Topps silver edition of 349)	200.00
(4b) Robin Yount (1975 Topps, bronze edition of 1,564)	45.00
(5s) Ozzie Smith (1979 Topps, silver edition of 211)	325.00
(5b) Ozzie Smith (1979 Topps, bronze edition of 1,088)	60.00
(6s) Don Mattingly (1984 Topps, silver edition of 414)	225.00
(6b) Don Mattingly (1984 Topps, bronze edition of 1,550)	60.00
(7s) Roger Clemens (1985 Topps, silver edition of 432)	185.00
(7b) Roger Clemens (1985 Topps, bronze edition of 1,789)	30.00
(8s) Kirby Puckett (1985 Topps, silver edition of 359)	200.00
(8b) Kirby Puckett (1985 Topps, bronze edition of 1,723)	45.00
(9s) Barry Bonds (1986 Topps Traded, silver edition of 596)	150.00
(9b) Barry Bonds (1986 Topps Traded, bronze edition of 2,677)	30.00
(10s) Will Clark (1986 Topps Traded, silver edition of 150)	325.00
(10b) Will Clark (1986 Topps Traded, bronze edition of 1,0444)	30.00
(11s) Roberto Alomar (1988 Topps Traded, silver edition of 214)	190.00
(11b) Roberto Alomar (1988 Topps Traded, bronze edition of 928)	30.00
(12s) Juan Gonzalez (1990 Topps, silver edition of 365)	150.00
(12b) Juan Gonzalez (1990 Topps, bronze edition of 1,899)	30.00
(13s) Ken Griffey, Jr. (1992 Topps, silver edition of 1,000)	275.00
(13b) Ken Griffey, Jr. (1992 Topps, bronze edition of 5,000)	65.00
(13g) Ken Griffey, Jr. (1992 Topps, gold edition of 500)	400.00
(14s) Cal Ripken, Jr. (1992 Topps, silver edition of 1,000)	375.00
(14b) Cal Ripken, Jr. (1992 Topps, bronze edition of 4,065)	100.00
(15s) Nolan Ryan (1992 Topps, silver edition of 999)	500.00
(15b) Nolan Ryan (1992 Topps, bronze edition of 5,000)	165.00
(16s) Ryne Sandberg (1992 Topps, silver edition of 430)	195.00
(16b) Ryne Sandberg (1992 Topps, bronze edition of 1,932)	45.00
(17s) Frank Thomas (1992 Topps, silver edition of 1,000)	250.00
(17b) Frank Thomas (1992 Topps, bronze edition of 5,000)	55.00
(17g) Frank Thomas (1992 Topps, gold edition of 500)	350.00

1994 Highland Mint Mint-Cards

In 1994 the Highland Mint continued its production of Mint-Cards, licensed metal replicas of Topps baseball, football and hockey cards. Maximum production of baseball players in the series was reduced to 750 in silver and halved to 2,500 in bronze. Suggested retail prices remained at $235 and $50, respectively. Once again cards were produced in the same 2-1/2" x 3-1/2" format as original Topps cards and were minted to a thickness of 1/10", with a serial number engraved on the edge. Mint-cards were sold in a heavy lucite holder, packaged with a certificate of authenticity in a plastic book-style holder. In mid-year, the company announced it was ceasing production of Topps-replica baseball cards and that henceforth all baseball Mint-Cards would reproduce the designs of Pinnacle brand cards.

	MT
Complete Set, Silver:	2500.
Complete Set, Bronze:	500.00
Complete Set, Gold:	1250.
Common Player, Silver:	150.00
Common Player, Bronze:	30.00
Common Player, Gold:	450.00
(1a) Ernie Banks (1954 Topps, silver edition of 437)	150.00
(1b) Ernie Banks (1954 Topps, bronze edition of 920)	30.00
(2a) Carl Yastrzemski (1960 Topps, silver edition of 500)	150.00
(2b) Carl Yastrzemski (1960 Topps, bronze edition of 1,072)	50.00
(3a) Johnny Bench (1969 Topps, silver edition of 500)	150.00
(3b) Johnny Bench (1969 Topps, bronze edition of 1,384)	30.00
(4a) Mike Schmidt (1974 Topps, silver edition of 500)	150.00
(4b) Mike Schmidt (1974 Topps, bronze edition of 1,641)	30.00
(5a) Paul Molitor (1979 Topps, silver edition of 260)	225.00
(5b) Paul Molitor (1979 Topps, bronze edition of 639)	55.00
(6a) Deion Sanders (1989 Topps, silver edition of 187)	150.00
(6b) Deion Sanders (1989 Topps, bronze edition of 668)	30.00
(7a) Dave Justice (1990 Topps, silver edition of 265)	150.00
(7b) Dave Justice (1990 Topps, bronze edition of 1,396)	30.00
(8a) Jeff Bagwell (1992 Pinnacle, silver edition of 750)	150.00
(8b) Jeff Bagwell (1992 Pinnacle, bronze edition of 2,500)	30.00
(9a) Greg Maddux (1992 Pinnacle, silver edition of 750)	235.00
(9b) Greg Maddux (1992 Pinnacle, bronze edition of 2,500)	55.00
(10a) Mike Piazza (1992 Topps, silver edition of 750)	150.00
(10b) Mike Piazza (1992 Topps, bronze edition of 2,500)	40.00
(10c) Mike Piazza (1992 Topps, gold edition of 374)	400.00
(12a) Nolan Ryan (1992 Pinnacle Then and Now, silver edition of 1,000)	225.00
(12b) Nolan Ryan (1992 Pinnacle Then and Now, bronze edition of 5,000)	45.00
(12c) Nolan Ryan (1992 Pinnacle Then & Now, gold edition 500)	425.00
(13a) Tim Salmon (1993 Topps, silver edition of 264)	150.00
(13b) Tim Salmon (1993 Topps, bronze edition of 768)	30.00

1995 Highland Mint Mint-Cards

For 1995, the Highland Mint continued its series of precious-metal editions of cards in all major team sports. The 2-1/2" x 3-1/2" cards contain 4-1/4 oz. of bronze or silver or 24-karat gold plating on silver. Each Mint-card is sold in a heavy plastic holder within a numbered album and with a certificate of authenticity. Only the firm's baseball cards are listed here.

		MT
Complete Set (Bronze):		100.00
Complete Set (Silver):		470.00
Complete Set (Gold):		1300.
Common Player (Bronze):		55.00
Common Player (Silver):		225.00
Common Player (Gold):		600.00
38b	Michael Jordan (Upper Deck Rare Air, bronze, edition of 5,000)	55.00
38s	Michael Jordan (Upper Deck Rare Air, silver, edition of 1,000)	225.00
38g	Michael Jordan (Upper Deck Rare Air, gold, edition of 500)	600.00
	Mickey Mantle (1992 Pinnacle, bronze edition of 1,000)	70.00
	Mickey Mantle (1992 Pinnacle, silver edition of 1,000)	290.00
	Mickey Mantle (1992 Pinnacle, gold edition of 500)	650.00

1992 High 5 Decals

This issue of peelable, reusable "decals" was sold in both team set and superstar panels. Each $2.99 panel contains five player decals and a team logo decal. The backing paper has a color 5" x 7" photo of a superstar which can be cut out and framed. Overall dimensions of the decal sheet are 7-1/2" x 7". The unnumbered decals are checklisted here in alphabetical order within team.

		MT
Complete Set (156):		40.00
Common Player:		.25
(1)	Baltimore Orioles logo	.25
(2)	Mike Devereaux	.25
(3)	Ben McDonald	.25
(4)	Gregg Olson	.25
(5)	Joe Orsulak	.25
(6)	Cal Ripken Jr.	5.00
(7)	Boston Red Sox logo	.25
(8)	Wade Boggs	1.50
(9)	Roger Clemens	1.50
(10)	Phil Plantier	.25
(11)	Jeff Reardon	.25
(12)	Mo Vaughn	.75
(13)	California Angels logo	.25
(14)	Jim Abbott	.25
(15)	Chuck Finley	.25
(16)	Bryan Harvey	.25
(17)	Mark Langston	.25
(18)	Dave Winfield	.90
(19)	Chicago White Sox logo	.25
(20)	Carlton Fisk	.50
(21)	Jack McDowell	.25
(22)	Bobby Thigpen	.25
(23)	Frank Thomas	3.50
(24)	Robin Ventura	.35
(25)	Cleveland Indians logo	.25
(26)	Sandy Alomar Jr.	.35
(27)	Carlos Baerga	.25
(28)	Albert Belle	1.00
(29)	Alex Cole	.25
(30)	Charles Nagy	.25
(31)	Detroit Tigers logo	.25
(32)	Cecil Fielder	.25
(33)	Travis Fryman	.25
(34)	Tony Phillips	.25
(35)	Alan Trammell	.25
(36)	Lou Whitaker	.25
(37)	Kansas City Royals logo	.25
(38)	George Brett	1.50
(39)	Jim Eisenreich	.25
(40)	Brian McRae	.25
(41)	Jeff Montgomery	.25
(42)	Bret Saberhagen	.25
(43)	Milwaukee Brewers logo	.25
(44)	Chris Bosio	.25
(45)	Paul Molitor	1.25
(46)	B.J. Surhoff	.25
(47)	Greg Vaughn	.25
(48)	Robin Yount	1.50
(49)	Minnesota Twins logo	.25
(50)	Rick Aguilera	.25
(51)	Scott Erickson	.25
(52)	Kent Hrbek	.25
(53)	Kirby Puckett	1.50
(54)	Kevin Tapani	.25
(55)	New York Yankees logo	.25
(56)	Mel Hall	.25
(57)	Roberto Kelly	.25
(58)	Kevin Maas	.25
(59)	Don Mattingly	3.00
(60)	Steve Sax	.25
(61)	Oakland A's logo	.25
(62)	Harold Baines	.25
(63)	Jose Canseco	1.25
(64)	Dennis Eckersley	.25
(65)	Dave Henderson	.25
(66)	Rickey Henderson	.45
(67)	Seattle Mariners logo	.25
(68)	Jay Buhner	.25
(69)	Ken Griffey Jr.	6.00
(70)	Randy Johnson	.75
(71)	Edgar Martinez	.25
(72)	Harold Reynolds	.25
(73)	Texas Rangers logo	.25
(74)	Julio Franco	.25
(75)	Juan Gonzalez	1.50
(76)	Rafael Palmeiro	.40
(77)	Nolan Ryan	5.00
(77p)	Nolan Ryan (prototype)	12.00
(78)	Ruben Sierra	.25
(79)	Toronto Blue Jays logo	.25
(80)	Roberto Alomar	.90
(81)	Joe Carter	.30
(82)	Kelly Gruber	.25
(83)	John Olerud	.30
(84)	Devon White	.25
(85)	Atlanta Braves logo	.25
(86)	Steve Avery	.25
(87)	Ron Gant	.30
(88)	Tom Glavine	.35
(89)	David Justice	.50
(90)	Terry Pendleton	.25
(91)	Chicago Cubs logo	.25
(92)	George Bell	.25
(93)	Andre Dawson	.35
(94)	Mark Grace	.65
(95)	Greg Maddux	3.00
(96)	Ryne Sandberg	1.25
(97)	Cincinnati Reds logo	.25
(98)	Eric Davis	.25
(99)	Barry Larkin	.25
(100)	Hal Morris	.25
(101)	Jose Rijo	.25
(102)	Chris Sabo	.25
(103)	Houston Astros logo	.25
(104)	Jeff Bagwell	1.25
(105)	Craig Biggio	.35
(106)	Ken Caminiti	.35
(107)	Luis Gonzalez	.25
(108)	Pete Harnisch	.25
(109)	Los Angeles Dodgers logo	.25
(110)	Brett Butler	.25
(111)	Lenny Harris	.25
(112)	Ramon Martinez	.25
(113)	Eddie Murray	1.00
(114)	Darryl Strawberry	.50
(115)	Montreal Expos logo	.25
(116)	Ivan Calderon	.25
(117)	Delino DeShields	.25
(118)	Marquis Grissom	.35
(119)	Dennis Martinez	.25
(120)	Larry Walker	.60
(121)	New York Mets logo	.25
(122)	David Cone	.25
(123)	Dwight Gooden	.35
(124)	Gregg Jefferies	.35
(125)	Howard Johnson	.25
(126)	Kevin McReynolds	.25
(127)	Philadelphia Phillies logo	.25
(128)	Wes Chamberlain	.25
(129)	Lenny Dykstra	.25
(130)	John Kruk	.25
(131)	Terry Mulholland	.25
(132)	Mitch Williams	.25
(133)	Pittsburgh Pirates logo	.25
(134)	Barry Bonds	2.00
(135)	Doug Drabek	.25
(136)	John Smiley	.25
(137)	Zane Smith	.25
(138)	Andy Van Slyke	.25
(139)	St. Louis Cardinals logo	.25
(140)	Felix Jose	.25
(141)	Ray Lankford	.30
(142)	Lee Smith	.25
(143)	Ozzie Smith	1.25
(144)	Todd Zeile	.25
(145)	San Diego Padres logo	.25
(146)	Tony Fernandez	.25
(147)	Tony Gwynn	1.50
(148)	Bruce Hurst	.25
(149)	Fred McGriff	.65
(150)	Gary Sheffield	.65
(151)	San Francisco Giants logo	.25
(152)	Will Clark	.75
(153)	Willie McGee	.25
(154)	Kevin Mitchell	.25
(155)	Robby Thompson	.25
(156)	Matt Williams	.35

1989 Hills Team MVP's

This high-gloss, boxed set of superstars was produced by Topps for the Hills department store chain. The words "Hills Team MVP's" appear above the player photos, while the player's name and team are printed below. The front of the card carries a red, white and blue color scheme with yellow and gold accents. The horizontal backs include player data set against a green playing field background.

		MT
Complete Set (33):		5.00
Common Player:		.05
1	Harold Baines	.05
2	Wade Boggs	.35
3	George Brett	.50
4	Tom Brunansky	.05
5	Jose Canseco	.05
6	Joe Carter	.10
7	Will Clark	.35
8	Roger Clemens	.50
9	Dave Cone	.05
10	Glenn Davis	.05
11	Andre Dawson	.10
12	Dennis Eckersley	.05
13	Andres Galarraga	.15
14	Kirk Gibson	.05
15	Mike Greenwell	.05
16	Tony Gwynn	.50
17	Orel Hershiser	.05
18	Danny Jackson	.05
19	Mark Langston	.05
20	Fred McGriff	.25
21	Dale Murphy	.15
22	Eddie Murray	.25
23	Kirby Puckett	.50
24	Johnny Ray	.05
25	Juan Samuel	.05
26	Ruben Sierra	.05
27	Dave Stewart	.05
28	Darryl Strawberry	.10
29	Alan Trammell	.10
30	Andy Van Slyke	.05
31	Frank Viola	.05
32	Dave Winfield	.30
33	Robin Yount	.50

1990 Hills Hit Men

The 33 slugging percentage leaders are featured in this high-gloss set boxed. The cards were produced by Topps for the Hills department store chain. Fronts feature "Hit Men" in a bat design above the photo. The player's name appears on a band below the photo. Horizontal backs feature a breakdown of the player's slugging percentage and also display career statistics.

		MT
Complete Set (33):		5.00
Common Player:		.05
1	Eric Davis	.10
2	Will Clark	.20
3	Don Mattingly	.50
4	Darryl Strawberry	.10
5	Kevin Mitchell	.05
6	Pedro Guerrero	.05
7	Jose Canseco	.30
8	Jim Rice	.05
9	Danny Tartabull	.05
10	George Brett	.50
11	Kent Hrbek	.10
12	George Bell	.05
13	Eddie Murray	.25
14	Fred Lynn	.05
15	Andre Dawson	.15
16	Dale Murphy	.15
17	Dave Winfield	.20
18	Jack Clark	.05
19	Wade Boggs	.25
20	Ruben Sierra	.05
21	Dave Parker	.05
22	Glenn Davis	.05
23	Dwight Evans	.05
24	Jesse Barfield	.05
25	Kirk Gibson	.05
26	Alvin Davis	.05
27	Kirby Puckett	.50
28	Joe Carter	.10
29	Carlton Fisk	.15
30	Harold Baines	.05
31	Andres Galarraga	.10
32	Cal Ripken, Jr.	1.00
33	Howard Johnson	.05

1993 Hills Pirates Kids Club

Stars of the Eastern Division N.L. champions are pictured on this 12-card issue. The set was issued in the form of a perforated 10" x 10-1/2" panel. Fronts have player action photos with orange frames, white borders and a team logo. Black-and-white backs have a player portrait, personal data and stats, and the Hills Pirates Kids Club logo. Cards are numbered by uniform number.

		MT
Complete Set, Sheet:		8.00
Complete Set, Singles (12):		6.00
Common Player:		.50
6	Orlando Merced	.75
7	Jeff King	1.00
10	Jim Leyland	.75
14	Tom Prince	.50
23	Lloyd McClendon	.50
26	Steve Cooke	.75
28	Al Martin	.75
32	Denny Neagle	.75
36	Kevin Young	.50
45	John Candelaria	.50
50	Stan Belinda	.50
55	Blas Minor	.50

1986-90 Hillshire Farm/Kahn's Coins

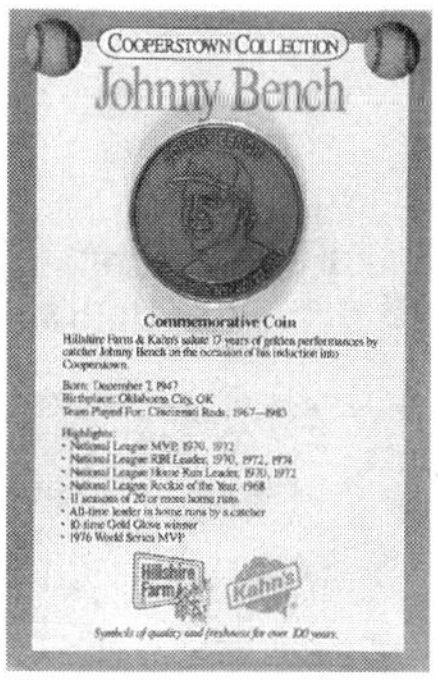

In three years between 1986 and 1990, the Hillshire meat products company issued commemorative medallions honoring former greats of the game. The Rose piece was issued in 1986 to mark his all-time hit record. It is a 1-1/2" bronze medal with his portrait on front. The medal was shrink-wrapper onto a 3-3/4" x 5" card with Rose's career highlights printed in blue and red. The Bench and Yaz coins, which do not include team logos on the caps, are also 1-1/2" bronzes shrink-wrapped onto 3-3/4" x 5-1/2" black, red and green cards and labeled Cooperstown Collection. The Morgan medal is similar in format and attached to a "Legends Collection" card of 3" x 4-1/2", also in red, black and green. All medals were obtained by sending in proofs of purchase from Hillshire/Kahn's products.

		MT
Complete Set (4):		25.00
Common Player:		6.00
(1)	Pete Rose (4,192 hits - 1986)	8.00
(2)	Johnny Bench (Hall of Fame - 1989)	7.50
(3)	Carl Yastrzemski (Hall of Fame - 1989)	7.50
(4)	Joe Morgan (Hall of Fame - 1990)	6.00

1999 Hillshire Farm Home Run Heroes

Via a special offer on packages of Hillshire Farm meats, collectors could order an autographed card of several star sluggers of the 1960s. Cards were available by sending in a package coupon and $4 for handling. The 2-1/2" x 3-1/2" cards have color player photos on which uniform logos have been removed. Borders are black and enhanced with gold foil. Black and gold backs offer lifetime stats and career highlights.

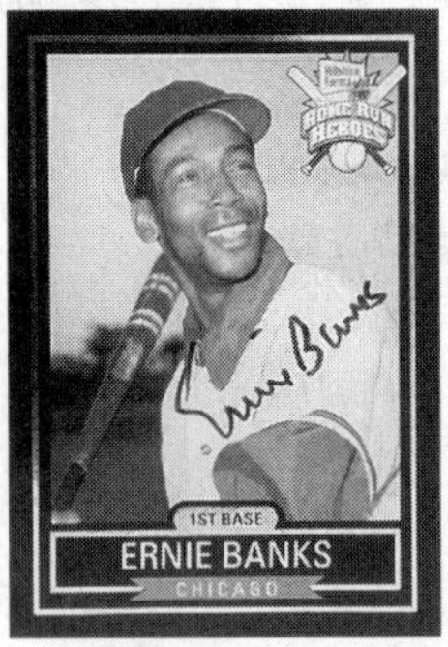

		MT
Complete Set (4):		24.00
Common Player:		6.00
(1)	Ernie Banks	6.00
(2)	Harmon Killebrew	6.00
(3)	Frank Robinson	6.00
(4)	Willie Stargell	6.00

1988 Historic Limited Editions Brooklyn Dodgers

This set of Brooklyn Dodgers postcards features the artwork of Susan Rini, combining on most cards a player portrait and an action pose with Ebbets Field as the background. Fronts of the 5-1/2" x 3-1/2" cards have the artwork at left, bordered in bright blue. In the wide right border, the team name and logo, and the player name, are printed in white. Postcard-style backs are printed in blue. The cards were issued in three series of 12 each, but are checklisted here in alphabetical order. Two different cards each exist for Erskine and Lavagetto. Production of the series was limited to 5,000 sets; 2,000 sets were produced with a low-gloss finish to facilitate autographing, while the remaining 3,000 sets were high-gloss. Either sold for $20 at time of issue. Two hundred uncut sheets of each series were sold for $30 apiece. A special album was also made available.

		MT
Complete Set (36):		10.00
Common Player:		.50
(1)	Cal Abrams	.50
(2)	Sandy Amoros	.50
(3)	Red Barber (announcer)	.50
(4)	Ralph Branca	.50
(5)	Chuck Connors	.75
(6)	Roger Craig	.50
(7)	Roy Campanella	1.50
(8)	Don Drysdale	1.00
(9)	Leo Durocher	.50
(10)	Carl Erskine	.50
(11)	Carl Erskine	.50
(12)	Carl Furillo	.50
(13)	Gene Hermanski	.50
(14)	Gil Hodges	1.00
(15)	Clyde King	.50
(16)	Clem Labine	.50
(17)	Tommy Lasorda	.75
(18)	Cookie Lavagetto	.50
(19)	Cookie Lavagetto	.50
(20)	Larry MacPhail (gm)	.50
(21)	Sal Maglie	.50
(22)	Eddie Miksis	.50
(23)	Don Newcombe	.60
(24)	Walter O'Malley (owner)	.50
(25)	Mickey Owen	.50
(26)	Andy Pafko	.50
(27)	Johnny Podres	.50
(28)	Pee Wee Reese	1.00
(29)	Preacher Roe	.50
(30)	Jackie Robinson	2.50
(31)	George Shuba	.50
(32)	Duke Snider	1.50
(33)	Red Barber, Leo Durocher	.50
(34)	Jackie Robinson, Branch Rickey	1.00
(35)	Ebbets Field	.50
(36)	Dodgers Sym-Phony Band	.50

1988 Historic Limited Editions Brooklyn Dodgers Lithos

The artwork of Susan Rini which had been featured on a series of Brooklyn Dodgers postcards was presented in its unadorned splendor in this series of 10" x 8" lithos. Only 800 sets were produced, originally retailing for $60. As with the postcards, the lithos have a portrait painting of the player on an Ebbets Field background with an action picture. Only Rini's signature and the MLB logo appear on front. Backs have producer and licensor logos and copyright information. Two poses each exist for Erskine and Lavagetto. Cards are checklisted here in alphabetical order.

		MT
Complete Set (36):		40.00
Common Player:		2.00
(1)	Cal Abrams	2.00
(2)	Sandy Amoros	2.00
(3)	Red Barber (announcer)	2.00
(4)	Ralph Branca	2.00
(5)	Chuck Connors	2.50
(6)	Roger Craig	2.00
(7)	Roy Campanella	4.00
(8)	Don Drysdale	3.00
(9)	Leo Durocher	2.00
(10)	Carl Erskine	2.00
(11)	Carl Erskine	2.00
(12)	Carl Furillo	2.00
(13)	Gene Hermanski	2.00
(14)	Gil Hodges	3.00
(15)	Clyde King	2.00
(16)	Clem Labine	2.00
(17)	Tommy Lasorda	2.50
(18)	Cookie Lavagetto	2.00
(19)	Cookie Lavagetto	2.00
(20)	Larry MacPhail (gm)	2.00
(21)	Sal Maglie	2.00
(22)	Eddie Miksis	2.00
(23)	Don Newcombe	2.50
(24)	Walter O'Malley (owner)	2.00
(25)	Mickey Owen	2.00
(26)	Andy Pafko	2.00
(27)	Johnny Podres	2.00
(28)	Pee Wee Reese	3.00
(29)	Preacher Roe	2.00
(30)	Jackie Robinson	6.00
(31)	George Shuba	2.00
(32)	Duke Snider	3.00
(33)	Red Barber, Leo Durocher	2.00
(34)	Jackie Robinson, Branch Rickey	3.50
(35)	Ebbets Field	2.00
(36)	Dodgers Sym-Phony Band	2.00

1989 Historic Limited Editions Lou Gehrig Postcards

This set of postcards combines portrait and action art with a Yankee Stadium backdrop in paintings by Susan Rini. The art is set towards the top of the 3-1/2" x 5-1/2" cards which have a pinstripe background, player name beneath the art and team name and logo at bottom. Horizontal backs are postcard-style and printed in blue with appropriate credit lines, copyright notice and logos. Original issue price was $10 per set, with uncut sheets available for $15.

		MT
Complete Set (8):		6.00
Common Card:		1.00
1-8	Lou Gehrig	1.00

1989 Historic Limited Editions Don Mattingly Series 1

One of the most popular Yankees of the past 25 years is honored on this set of postcards. The 3-1/2" x 5-1/2" cards feature the artwork of Susan Rini on each card. Mattingly is shown in portrait and action art on most of the cards, though sometimes the picture of another Yankee great takes the place of the action picture. Background on the front is white with blue pinstripes. Postcard-style backs are printed in blue and announce an edition of 5,000 sets. Price at issue was about $10, with uncut sheets of the cards available for $24.

		MT
Complete Set (12):		6.00
Common Card:		.50
1-12	Don Mattingly	.50

1989 Historic Limited Editions Negro Leagues Postcards

Both well-known and obscure players of the segregated Negro Leagues are included in this series of color postcards. Fronts of the 3-1/2" x 5-1/2" cards have portrait and action paintings of the players on a peach-colored background. Postcard-style backs are printed in blue and indicate a limit of 5,000 sets were produced. An edition of 200 uncut sheets was also produced.

		MT
Complete Set (12):		4.50
Common Player:		.50
Uncut Sheet:		20.00
1	Monte Irvin	.75
2	Martin Dihigo	.75
3	Clint Thomas	.50
4	Buster Haywood	.50
5	George Giles	.50
6	Isidro Fabri	.50
7	James (Cool Papa) Bell	.65
8	Josh Gibson	1.00
9	Lou Dials	.50
10	Willie Wells	.75
11	Walter (Buck) Leonard	.75
12	Jose Fernandez	.50

1990 Historic Limited Editions Roberto Clemente

This set of 3-1/2" x 5-1/2" postcards graphically details the career of the Pirates outfielder. Background of each card is beige. At top is an approximately 3" x 3-1/2" color painting of Clemente in both portrait and action poses, created by sports artist Susan Rini. Player and team name, and team logo are at bottom. Postcard-style backs are printed in blue with appropriate credit lines and copyright data. Production was reported at 5,000 sets.

		MT
Complete Set (12):		5.00
Common Card:		1.00
1-12	Roberto Clemente	1.00

1990 Historic Limited Editions Thurman Munson Postcards

The late, great Yankees catcher is memorialized in this set of color postcards from sports artist Susan Rini. Fronts of the 3-1/2" x 5-1/2" cards have a combination portrait/action painting toward the top, on a background of pinstripes. Player and team names and the Yankees logo are at bottom. Horizontal backs are in postcard style, printed in blue with appropriate licensing, copyright and credit data, and logos. Production was limited to 5,000 sets and 200 complete-set uncut sheets.

		MT
Complete Set (12):		4.00
Common Card:		.50
Uncut Sheet:		22.00
1-12	Thurman Munson	.50

1990 Historic Limited Editions Nolan Ryan Series 1

The Mets and Rangers years are graphically depicted on this set of postcards in combined portrait and action paintings by sports artist Susan Rini. The 3-1/2" x 5-1/2" cards have a light blue background on front, with the player and team name, and the team logo at bottom. Postcard-style backs are printed in blue and offer copyright and licensing information, along with a notice that the set is limited to an edition of 10,000.

		MT
Complete Set (12):		8.00
Common Card:		1.00
1-12	Nolan Ryan	1.00

1990 Historic Limited Editions Nolan Ryan Series 2

The Astros and Angels years are graphically depicted on this set of postcards in combined portrait and action paintings by sports artist Susan Rini. The 3-1/2" x 5-1/2" cards have a beige background on front, with the player and team name, and the team logo at bottom. Postcard-style backs are printed in blue and offer copyright and licensing information, along with a notice that the set is limited to an edition of 10,000.

	MT
Complete Set (12):	8.00
Common Card:	1.00
1-12 Nolan Ryan	1.00

1990 Historic Limited Editions Yankees Monuments

Those honored with plaques in Monument Park behind the center field wall at Yankee Stadium are presented in this series of postcards. On a pinstriped background, the fronts of the 3-1/2" x 5-1/2" cards have a portrait of the person with his plaque in the background, the work of Susan Rini. The team name and logo are at bottom. Postcard-style backs are printed in blue with various copyright and creator notices, MLB logo and an indication that the cards were produced in an edition of 5,000. At time of issue, complete sets for about $10; uncut sheets were available for $20.

		MT
Complete Set (12):		8.00
Common Player:		.50
1	Lou Gehrig	1.50
2	Babe Ruth	2.00
3	Thurman Munson	1.00
4	Elston Howard	.50
5	Phil Rizzuto	.50
6	Mickey Mantle	3.00
7	Bill Dickey	.50
8	Lefty Gomez	.50
9	Pope Paul VI	1.50
10	Jacob Ruppert	.50
11	Roger Maris	1.50
12	Joe DiMaggio	2.00

1990 Historic Limited Editions 1969 Mets Postcards

This set commemorates the Amazin' Mets Worodl Championship team of 1969. The 5-1/2" x 3-1/2" cards have bright blue front borders. At left is a portrait/action painting of the players by sports artist Susan Rini. Postcard-style backs are printed in blue with copyright and credit data, card number, logos, etc. The issue was limited to 5,000 sets and originally sold for about $20. Uncut sheets were available for $25.

		MT
Complete Set (36):		10.00
Common Player:		.50
1	Championship Trophy	.50
2	Shea Stadium	.50
3	Tommie Agee	.50
4	Ken Boswell	.50
5	Ed Charles	.50
6	Don Cardwell	.50
7	Donn Clendenon	.65
8	Jack DiLauro	.50
9	Duffy Dyer	.50
10	Wayne Garrett	.50
11	Jerry Grote	.50
12	Rod Gaspar	.50
13	Gary Gentry	.50
14	Bud Harrelson	.65
15	Gil Hodges	1.00
16	Cleon Jones	.65
17	Ed Kranepool	.65
18	Cal Koonce	.50
19	Jerry Koosman	.65
20	Jim McAndrew	.50
21	Tug McGraw	.75
22	J.C. Martin	.50
23	Bob Pfeil	.50
24	Nolan Ryan	4.00
25	Ron Swoboda	.50
26	Tom Seaver	1.50
27	Art Shamsky	.50
28	Ron Taylor	.50
29	Al Weis	.50
30	Joe Pignatano	.50
31	Eddie Yost	.50
32	Ralph Kiner (announcer)	.50
33	Bob Murphy (writer)	.50
34	Lindsey Nelson (announcer)	.50
35	Yogi Berra	1.00
36	Rube Walker	.50

1991 Historic Limited Editions Brooklyn Dodgers

Three additional series of 12-card player postcard sets in 1991 were issued as a follow-up to the company's debut issue of 1988. Identical in format, the 5-1/2" x 3-1/2" cards have a Dodger blue background on front. At the left end in artwork by Susan Rini combining portrait and action pictures of the player against a background of Ebbets Field. Player and team identification are in white at right. Postcard backs are printed in blue with credits, copyright data, logos and series and card numbers.

		MT
Complete Set (36):		15.00
Common Player:		.50
	SERIES 2	5.00
1	Charley Dressen	.50
2	John Roseboro	.50
3	Eddie Stanky	.50
4	Goody Rosen	.50
5	Ed Head	.50
6	Dick Williams	.50
7	Clarence (Bud) Podbielan	.50
8	Erv Palica	.50
9	Augie Galan	.50
10	Billy Loes	.50
11	Billy Cox	.50
12	Phil Phifer	.50
	SERIES 3	5.00
1	Joe Black	.75
2	Jack Banta	.50
3	Whitlow Wyatt	.50
4	Gino Cimoli	.50
5	Dolph Camilli (Dolf)	.50
6	Dan Bankhead	.50
7	Henry Behrman	.50
8	Pete Reiser	.50
9	Chris Van Cuyk	.50
10	James (Junior) Gilliam	.75
11	Don Zimmer	.75
12	Ed Roebuck	.50
	SERIES 4	5.00
1	Billy Herman	.50
2	Rube Walker	.50
3	Tommy Brown	.50
4	Charlie Neal	.50
5	Kirby Higbe	.50
6	Bruce Edwards	.50
7	Joe Hatten	.50
8	Rex Barney	.50
9	Al Gionfriddo	.50
10	Luis Olmo	.50
11	Dixie Walker	.50
12	Walter Alston	.75

1991 Historic Limited Editions Don Mattingly Series 2

Two years after the release of the first series, another 12 Mattingly postcards were issued. The 3-1/2" x 5-1/2" cards feature the artwork of Susan Rini on each card. Mattingly is shown in portrait and action art on each of the cards. Background on the front is white with blue pinstripes. Postcard-style backs are printed in blue and announce an edition of 5,000 sets. Price at issue was about $10, with uncut sheets of the cards available for $24.

	MT
Complete Set (12):	6.00
Common Card:	.50
1-12 Don Mattingly	.50

1991 Historic Limited Editions 1961 Yankees Postcards

Three series of 12 postcards each were issued to commemorate the '61 Yanks. All cards are 5-1/2" x 3-1/2", with a pinstriped border design. At left front are combination portrait/action paintings by Susan Rini. Team name and logo are at right, along with player identification. Backs are printed in blue, in postcard style, with copyright, credits, logos, etc.

		MT
Complete Set (36):		12.00
Common Player:		.25
	SERIES 1	3.00
1	Yogi Berra	1.00
2	Tom Tresh	.45
3	Bill Skowron	.45
4	Al Downing	.25
5	Jim Coates	.25
6	Luis Arroyo	.25
7	Johnny Blanchard	.25
8	Hector Lopez	.25
9	Tony Kubek	.50
10	Ralph Houk	.25
11	Bobby Richardson	.50
12	Clete Boyer	.35
	SERIES 2	4.00
1	Roger Maris	2.00
2	Jesse Gonder	.25
3	Danny McDevitt	.25
4	Leroy Thomas	.25
5	Billy Gardner	.25
6	Ralph Terry	.25
7	Hal Reniff	.25
8	Earl Torgeson	.25
9	Art Ditmar	.25
10	Jack Reed	.25
11	Johnny James	.25
12	Elston Howard	.50
	SERIES 3	6.00
1	Mickey Mantle	5.00
2	Deron Johnson	.25
3	Bob Hale	.25
4	Bill Stafford	.25
5	Duke Maas	.25
6	Bob Cerv	.25
7	Roland Sheldon	.25
8	Ryne Duren	.35
9	Bob Turley	.35
10	Whitey Ford	1.00
11	Bud Daley	.25
12	Joe DeMaestri	.25

1989 Holsum Bakeries Super Stars Discs

This set of 2-3/4" diameter discs was manufactured by Mike Schechter Associates for Holsum bakeries' inclusion in various bread brands. Because the cards are licensed only by the players' association and not MLB, the player photos have been airbrushed to remove cap and uniform logos. Cards feature white borders with red, yellow and blue decorations. Backs are printed in dark blue and include a few 1988 and career stats and some player vitals. The set was distributed in Michigan.

		MT
Complete Set (20):		9.00
Common Player:		.25
1	Wally Joyner	.25
2	Wade Boggs	.50
3	Ozzie Smith	.50
4	Don Mattingly	1.00
5	Jose Canseco	.60
6	Tony Gwynn	.75
7	Eric Davis	.25
8	Kirby Puckett	.75
9	Kevin Seitzer	.25
10	Darryl Strawberry	.25
11	Gregg Jefferies	.25
12	Mark Grace	.40
13	Matt Nokes	.25
14	Mark McGwire	3.00
15	Don Mattingly	1.00
16	Roger Clemens	.50
17	Frank Viola	.25
18	Orel Hershiser	.25
19	Dave Cone	.25
20	Kirk Gibson	.25

1989 Holsum/ Schaefer's Super Stars Discs

This version of the 1989 MSA bakeries disc set was issued in Canada by Ben's bakeries. The discs are nearly identical to the other regional variations except for the appearance of a red "Schaefer's" logo at top.

		MT
Complete Set (20):		9.00
Common Player:		.25
1	Wally Joyner	.25
2	Wade Boggs	.50
3	Ozzie Smith	.50
4	Don Mattingly	1.00
5	Jose Canseco	.60
6	Tony Gwynn	.75
7	Eric Davis	.25
8	Kirby Puckett	.75
9	Kevin Seitzer	.25
10	Darryl Strawberry	.25
11	Gregg Jefferies	.25
12	Mark Grace	.45
13	Matt Nokes	.25
14	Mark McGwire	4.00
15	Don Mattingly	1.00
16	Roger Clemens	.50
17	Frank Viola	.25
18	Orel Hershiser	.25
19	Dave Cone	.25
20	Kirk Gibson	.25

1990 Holsum Bakeries Super Stars Discs

Players in this disc set are featured in round portrait photos on which uniform logos have been painted over for lack of a license from Major League Baseball (the set is licensed by the players' union and bears their logo on back). Most of the front border on these 2-3/4" diameter discs is in red, with yellow stars and white baseballs around the portrait and the bakery's logo at top. A yellow banner beneath the photo has the "Superstars" logo. At bottom, in the white portion of the border, the player's name is presented in red, with his team and position in blue. Backs are printed in blue and include 1989 and career stats, a few biographical details, the card number and appropriate copyrights.

		MT
Complete Set (20):		4.00
Common Player:		.25
1	George Bell	.25
2	Tim Raines	.25
3	Tom Henke	.25
4	Andres Galarraga	.30
5	Bret Saberhagen	.30
6	Mark Davis	.25
7	Robin Yount	.50
8	Rickey Henderson	.35
9	Kevin Mitchell	.25
10	Howard Johnson	.25
11	Will Clark	.40
12	Orel Hershiser	.25
13	Fred McGriff	.30
14	Dave Stewart	.25
15	Vince Coleman	.25
16	Steve Sax	.25
17	Kirby Puckett	.50
18	Tony Gwynn	.50

19	Jerome Walton	.25
20	Gregg Olson	.25

1991 Holsum Bakeries Super Stars Discs

Similar to the previous year's issue, the 20 discs in the 1991 bakery set feature a color player photo (uniform logos airbrushed off) at center, with a wide white border to the edge of the 2-3/4" diameter cardboard. The player's name appears in a yellow stripe at bottom, along with his team and position. Backs are printed in dark blue and include a few stats from the previous season.

		MT
Complete Set (20):		90.00
Common Player:		2.00
1	Darryl Strawberry	3.00
2	Eric Davis	2.00
3	Tim Wallach	2.00
4	Kevin Mitchell	2.00
5	Tony Gwynn	9.00
6	Ryne Sandberg	7.50
7	Doug Drabek	2.00
8	Randy Myers	2.00
9	Ken Griffey, Jr.	20.00
10	Alan Trammell	2.00
11	Ken Griffey, Sr.	2.00
12	Rickey Henderson	5.00
13	Roger Clemens	9.00
14	Bob Welch	2.00
15	Kelly Gruber	2.00
16	Mark McGwire	20.00
17	Cecil Fielder	2.50
18	Dave Steib	2.00
19	Nolan Ryan	18.00
20	Cal Ripken, Jr.	18.00

1983 Homeplate Sports Cards Al Kaline Story

Commemorating Al Kaline's 30th anniversary with the Detroit Tigers, this set chronicles his life and career. The 2-1/2" x 3-1/2" cards have either black-and-white front photos with orange borders or color photos with black borders. Backs reverse the color scheme and provide details about the photo on front. The first card in each set has been personally autographed by Kaline.

		MT
Complete Set (73):		15.00
Common Card:		.25
1a	30 Years a Tiger (autographed)	6.00
1b	I'd play baseball for nothing	.25
2	Sandlot days in Baltimore	.25
3	MVP trophy winner	.25
4	Learning the ropes	.25
5	Working for a living	.25
6	Pleasing a young fan	.25
7	Al and Louise - the newlyweds	.25
8	Al and Pat Mullin	.25
9	How Al does it #1	.25
10	How Al does it #2	.25
11	Silver Bat for the Champ	.25
12	Al and George Stark	.25
13	Al watches Gordie Howe swing a bat	2.00
14	Kaline and Mantle - batting champs	1.00
15	Hegan, Martin, Boone, Kuenn, Bunning, Kaline	.25
16	Martin, Kaline, Kuenn, Mantle, Ford	.50
17	Crossing the plate	.25
18	1959 All-Star Game (w/ Bill Skowron)	.25
19	Cash, Colavito, Kaline	.50
20	Kaline slides under Nellie Fox	.25
21	One of many awards	.25
22	Kaline, Jim Campbell, Norm Cash - 1962	.25
23	Costly catch - 1962	.25
24	Jim Bunning, Al, Norm Cash in Japan	.25
25	Perfect form	.25
26	Ernie Harwell, Al, George Kell	.25
27	Life isn't always easy	.25
28	Al, Michael and Mark Kaline	.25
29	Al and Charlie Dressen - 1965	.25
30	George Kell and Al - Fielding masters	.25
31	Al and Hal Newhouser	.25
32	Michael, Louise, Al and Mark Kaline	.25
33	Al, Charlie Gehringer, Bill Freehan	.25
34	Rapping a hit in 1967	.25
35	Veteran rivals Mantle and Kaline	1.00
36	Al homers against Boston - 1968	.25
37	1968 World Series homer	.25
38	Premier fielder	.25
39	All-Time All-Stars (w/ Hank Greenberg, etc.)	.50
40	Part of the game	.25
41	Family portrait	.25
42	Spring training tribute	.25
43	Billy Martin and Al	.25
44	First $100,000 Tiger	.25
45	On deck - 1972	.25
46	A close call	.25
47	On deck in Baltimore - 1974	.25
48	Hit number 3,000 - 1974	.25
49	April 17, 1955 - 3 Homers	.25
50	All-Star Game record	.25
51	1968 Series action - Cepeda	.25
52	Celebrating 1968	.25
53	Al Kaline Day	.25
54	3,000 Hit Day	.25
55	Thank you - Sept. 29, 1974	.25
56	Silver salute - Sept. 29, 1974	.25
57	Al and Kell - a new career	.25
58	Voices of the Tigers	.25
59	Tiger record setter	.25
60	1970 AL All-Star team	.25
61	Pat Mullin and Al	.25
62	Al and Lolich - Aug., 1980	.25
63	Hall of Fame plaque	.25
64	Al and Bowie Kuhn - Aug. 4, 1980	.25
65	Al and parents - Aug., 1980	.25
66	Mike, Mark, Louise, Al at the Hall of Fame	.25
67	"The Man" and the Boy (w/ Stan Musial)	.50
68	Two Kids - Ted Williams and Kaline	.50
69	Master glovemen (w/ Brooks Robinson)	.45
70	Coach and Pupil - Al and Pat Underwood	.25
71	Kaline career records	.25
72	A Tiger Forever	.25

1990 Homers Softball Hall of Fame

The Homers Classic Collection of members of the American Softball Association Hall of Fame was issued by a cookie company. The 2-1/2" x 3-1/2" cards have sepia-toned action photos on front. Backs have career highlights, a checklist, Homers and ASA logos.

		MT
Complete Set (9):		4.00
Common Player:		.50
1	Harold "Shifty" Gears	.50
2	Ruth Sears	.50
3	Bertha Tickey	.50
4	Eddie Zolna	.50
5	Carol Spanks	.50
6	Joan Joyce	.50
7	Dot Wilkinson	.50
8	Herb Dudley	.50
9	Jim Galloway	.50

1991 Homers Cookies

One Hall of Famer's card was inserted in each box of Homers Cookies. The cards measure 2-1/2" x 3-1/2" and feature sepia-toned photos. The card backs feature lifetime statistics and career highlights. The cards are also numbered on the back and a checklist is featured on the back of each card.

		MT
Complete Set (9):		9.00
Common Player:		.50
1	Babe Ruth	1.50
2	Satchel Paige	1.00
3	Lefty Gomez	.50
4	Ty Cobb	1.00
5	Cy Young	.50
6	Bob Feller	.50
7	Roberto Clemente	2.00
8	Dizzy Dean	.75
9	Lou Gehrig	1.50

1999 Homers Cookies

Former stars are featured in this set of cards inserted into specially marked boxes of cookies (suggested retail about $1). The 2-1/2" x 3-1/2" cards have color player photos (without uniform logos) with a white border. At top is player identification, at bottom is is a red stripe with "HOMERS". Horizontal backs have a cartoon, career data, biographical information and a checklist.

		MT
Complete Set (9):		9.00
Common Player:		1.00
1	Vida Blue	1.00
2	Orlando Cepeda	1.50
3	Darrell Evans	1.00
4	Harmon Killebrew	1.50
5	Dave Kingman	1.00
6	Eddie Murray	1.50
7	Frank Robinson	1.50
8	Willie Stargell	1.50
9	Carl Yastrzemski	1.50

1985 Hostess Braves

After a five-year hiatus, Hostess returned to the production of baseball cards in 1985 with an Atlanta Braves team set. The 22 cards in the set were printed by Topps and inserted into packages of snack cake products, three cello-wrapped player cards and a header card per box. The 2-1/2" x 3-1/2" cards share a common back design with the regular-issue Topps cards of 1985.

		MT
Complete Set (22):		6.00
Common Player:		.35
1	Eddie Haas	.35
2	Len Barker	.35
3	Steve Bedrosian	.50
4	Bruce Benedict	.35
5	Rick Camp	.35
6	Rick Cerone	.35
7	Chris Chambliss	.35
8	Terry Forster	.35
9	Gene Garber	.35
10	Albert Hall	.35
11	Bob Horner	.50
12	Glenn Hubbard	.35
13	Brad Komminsk	.35
14	Rick Mahler	.35
15	Craig McMurtry	.35
16	Dale Murphy	3.00
17	Ken Oberkfell	.35
18	Pascual Perez	.50
19	Gerald Perry	.35
20	Rafael Ramirez	.35
21	Bruce Sutter	.60
22	Claudell Washington	.35
---	Header Card	.05

1987 Hostess Stickers

Hostess of Canada issued a 30-card set of stickers in specially marked bags of potato chips. One sticker, measuring 1-3/4" x 1-3/8" in size, was found in each bag. The stickers have full-color fronts with the player's name appearing in black type in a white band. The Hostess logo and the sticker number are also included on the fronts. The backs are written in both English and French and contain the player's name, position and team.

		MT
Complete Set (30):		42.00
Common Player:		.25
1	Jesse Barfield	.25
2	Ernie Whitt	.25
3	George Bell	.25
4	Hubie Brooks	.25
5	Tim Wallach	.25
6	Floyd Youmans	.25
7	Dale Murphy	1.00
8	Ryne Sandberg	2.50
9	Eric Davis	.25
10	Mike Scott	.25
11	Fernando Valenzuela	.25
12	Gary Carter	.75
13	Mike Schmidt	3.00
14	Tony Pena	.25
15	Ozzie Smith	2.50
16	Tony Gwynn	4.00
17	Mike Krukow	.25
18	Eddie Murray	1.00
19	Wade Boggs	2.50
20	Wally Joyner	.35
21	Harold Baines	.25
22	Brook Jacoby	.25
23	Lou Whitaker	.25
24	George Brett	3.00
25	Robin Yount	2.50
26	Kirby Puckett	4.00
27	Don Mattingly	4.00
28	Jose Canseco	2.50
29	Phil Bradley	.25
30	Pete O'Brien	.25

1988 Hostess Potato Chips Expos/Blue Jays

The Expos and Blue Jays are showcased in this set of 24 discs (1-1/2" diameter). Full-color head shots are framed in white, surrounded by red stars. A yellow-banner "1988 Collectors Edition" label is printed (English and French) beneath the photo, followed by the player's name in black. Numbered disc backs are bilingual, blue and white, and include player name and stats. This set was distributed inside Hostess potato chip packages sold in Canada.

		MT
Complete Panel Set (12):		9.00
Complete Singles Set (24):		6.50
Common Panel:		.75
Common Single Player:		.25
	Panel 1	1.25
1	Mitch Webster	.25
20	Lloyd Moseby	.35
	Panel 2	.75
3	Tim Burke	.25
23	Tom Henke	.25
	Panel 3	.75
3	Tom Foley	.25
13	Jim Clancy	.25
	Panel 4	.75
4	Herm Winningham	.25
14	Rance Mulliniks	.25
	Panel 5	1.25
5	Hubie Brooks	.25
24	Jimmy Key	.35
	Panel 6	1.25
6	Mike Fitzgerald	.25
17	Dave Steib	.35
	Panel 7	1.75
7	Tim Wallach	.35
15	Fred McGriff	.50
	Panel 8	1.50
8	Andres Galarraga	.45
21	Tony Fernandez	.30

	Panel 9	.75
9	Floyd Youmans	.25
18	Mark Eichhorn	.25
	Panel 10	1.00
10	Neal Heaton	.25
19	Jesse Barfield	.35
	Panel 11	1.50
11	Tim Raines	.45
16	Ernie Whitt	.25
	Panel 12	1.25
12	Casey Candaele	.25
22	George Bell	.35

1990 Hostess Blue Jays Highlight Stickers

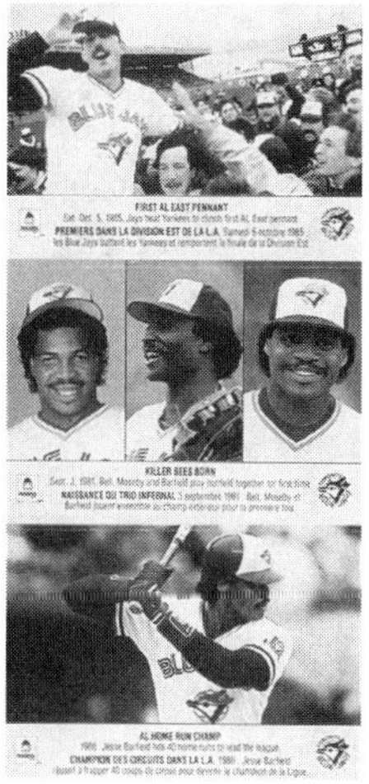

Team history highlights through the 1980 season are featured in this set of stickers. The set was produced in strips of three 2-1/4" x 3-1/4" stickers, some oriented horizontally, some vertically. Fronts have color photos with a light blue box beneath containing the highlight printed in both English and French. Black-and-white Hostess and team logos are at the left and right, respectively. Backs are blank. The set is checklisted here alphabetically based on the title of the sticker at top or left of the strip.

		MT
Complete Set (18):		15.00
Common Sticker:		.50
Panel 1		2.00
(1)	First AL East Pennant (Dave Steib)	.50
(2)	Killer Bees Born (George Bell, Lloyd Moseby, Jesse Barfield)	1.00
(3)	AL Home Run Champ (Jesse Barfield)	1.00
Panel 2		4.00
(4)	First Home Run in Skydome (Fred McGriff)	2.00
(5)	Club Save Leader (Tom Henke)	.50
(6)	Three Winning Openers in a Row (Jimmy Key)	1.00
Panel 3		2.00
(7)	First 100 Wins (Jim Clancy)	.50
(8)	ML Home Run Record (Ernie Whitt)	.50
(9)	AL East Champs Again (Tom Henke)	.50
Panel 4		2.50
(10)	Home Run on First Pitch (Junior Felix)	.50
(11)	Almost Perfect (Dave Steib)	1.00
(12)	First Game at Skydome	1.00
Panel 5		2.50
(13)	Most Double Plays (Damaso Garcia)	.50
(14)	M.V.P. (George Bell)	1.00
(15)	Hits the Cycle (Kelly Gruber)	.75
Panel 6		2.00
(16)	Stolen Bases (Dave Collins)	.50
(17)	Gold Glove Winners (Jesse Barfield, Tony Fernandez)	.75
(18)	Goodbye to Exhibition Stadium	.60

1993 Hostess Twinkies

The Continental Baking Company, makers of Hostess Twinkies and cupcakes, returned to the baseball card market in 1993 with a 32-card set issued in two series. The promotion began around opening day with the first series; the second series was made available after the All-Star break. The cards were packaged in multi-packs with cupcakes that look like baseballs, with three cards in a box of eight cupcakes.

		MT
Complete Set (32):		5.00
Common Player:		.10
1	Andy Van Slyke	.10
2	Ryne Sandberg	.45
3	Bobby Bonilla	.10
4	John Kruk	.10
5	Ray Lankford	.10
6	Gary Sheffield	.30
7	Darryl Strawberry	.15
8	Barry Larkin	.10
9	Terry Pendleton	.10
10	Jose Canseco	.35
11	Dennis Eckersley	.10
12	Brian McRae	.10
13	Frank Thomas	.60
14	Roberto Alomar	.20
15	Cecil Fielder	.10
16	Carlos Baerga	.10
17	Will Clark	.25
18	Andres Galarraga	.20
19	Jeff Bagwell	.40
20	Brett Butler	.10
21	Benito Santiago	.10
22	Tom Glavine	.15
23	Rickey Henderson	.25
24	Wally Joyner	.10
25	Ken Griffey, Jr.	1.00
26	Cal Ripken, Jr.	.75
27	Roger Clemens	.45
28	Don Mattingly	.50
29	Kirby Puckett	.50
30	Larry Walker	.20
31	Jack McDowell	.10
32	Pat Listach	.10

1986 Houston Astros Police

This full-color police safety set was issued by the Houston Police Department and sponsored by Kool-Aid. The set was distributed at the Astrodome on June 14, when 15,000 sets of the first 12 cards were given away. The balance of the set was distributed throughout the summer by police. The cards feature player photos on the fronts and a safety tip on the back. The cards measure 4-1/8" x 2-5/8".

		MT
Complete Set (26):		6.00
Common Player:		.20
1	Jim Pankovits	.20
2	Nolan Ryan	5.00
3	Mike Scott	.30
4	Kevin Bass	.20
5	Bill Doran	.30
6	Hal Lanier	.20
7	Denny Walling	.20
8	Alan Ashby	.20
9	Phil Garner	.20
10	Charlie Kerfeld	.20
11	Dave Smith	.20
12	Jose Cruz	.35
13	Craig Reynolds	.20
14	Mark Bailey	.20
15	Bob Knepper	.20
16	Julio Solano	.20
17	Dickie Thon	.20
18	Mike Madden	.20
19	Jeff Calhoun	.20
20	Tony Walker	.20
21	Terry Puhl	.20
22	Glenn Davis	.20
23	Billy Hatcher	.20
24	Jim Deshaies	.20
25	Frank DiPino	.20
26	Coaching Staff (Yogi Berra, Matt Galante, Denis Menke, Les Moss, Gene Tenace)	.20

1987 Houston Astros Police

The 1987 Astros safety set was produced through the combined efforts of the team, Deer Park Hospital and Sportsmedia Presentations. Cards #1-12 were handed out to youngsters 14 and under at the Astrodome on July 14. The balance of the distribution was handled by Deer Park Hospital. The cards, which measure 2-5/8" x 4-1/8", contain full-color photos. The backs offer a brief team/player history and a "Tips From The Dugout" anti-drug message.

		MT
Complete Set (26):		7.00
Common Player:		.20
1	Larry Andersen	.20
2	Mark Bailey	.20
3	Jose Cruz	.35
4	Danny Darwin	.20
5	Bill Doran	.20
6	Billy Hatcher	.20
7	Hal Lanier	.20
8	Davey Lopes	.30
9	Dave Meads	.20
10	Craig Reynolds	.20
11	Mike Scott	.20
12	Denny Walling	.20
13	Aurelio Lopez	.20
14	Dickie Thon	.20
15	Terry Puhl	.20
16	Nolan Ryan	5.00
17	Dave Smith	.20
18	Julio Solano	.20
19	Jim Deshaies	.20
20	Bob Knepper	.20
21	Alan Ashby	.20
22	Kevin Bass	.20
23	Glenn Davis	.20
24	Phil Garner	.20
25	Jim Pankovits	.20
26	Coaching Staff (Yogi Berra, Matt Galante, Denis Menke, Les Moss, Gene Tenace)	.20

1988 Houston Astros Police

This set of full-color cards highlighting the Houston Astros was produced by the team, in conjunction with Deer Park Hospital and Sportsmedia Promotions for distribution to fans 14 years and younger at a ballpark giveaway. The 2-5/8" x 4-1/8" cards feature full-color player photos framed by a narrow blue border with an orange player/team name block below the photo. Blue-and-white backs have orange borders with player information, career highlights and anti-drug tips.

		MT
Complete Set (26):		6.00
Common Player:		.20
1	Juan Agosto	.20
2	Larry Andersen	.20
3	Joaquin Andujar	.20
4	Alan Ashby	.20
5	Mark Bailey	.20
6	Kevin Bass	.20
7	Danny Darwin	.20
8	Glenn Davis	.20
9	Jim Deshaies	.20
10	Bill Doran	.20
11	Billy Hatcher	.20
12	Jeff Heathcock	.20
13	Steve Henderson	.20
14	Chuck Jackson	.20
15	Bob Knepper	.20
16	Jim Pankovits	.20
17	Terry Puhl	.20
18	Rafael Ramirez	.20
19	Craig Reynolds	.20
20	Nolan Ryan	4.00
21	Mike Scott	.20
22	Dave Smith	.20
23	Denny Walling	.20
24	Gerald Young	.20
25	Hal Lanier	.20
26	Coaching Staff (Yogi Berra, Gene Clines, Matt Galante, Marc Hill, Denis Menke, Les Moss)	.20

1985 Houston Card Show Stan Musial

This collectors' edition set features the Hall of Fame swing of Stan Musial, who was a show autograph guest. The black-and-white cards have front photos of Musial's batting style. The pictures were reproduced from a 1963 booklet which was included in a gas company's promotional record, "Stan-the-Man's Hit Record."

		MT
Complete Set (8):		10.00
Common Card:		2.00
1-8	Stan Musial	2.00

1988 Houston Show Set

This collectors issue of former stars and local favorites was issued in conjunction with a card show. Cards are printed on 2-1/4" x 3-1/8" semi-gloss stock. Black-and-white player photos are surrounded by a starred border in dark blue. Backs are in black-and-white with player name, card number and information about the player's appearance at this or other Houston Superstar Card Shows.

		MT
Complete Set (20):		15.00
Common Player:		.25
1	Brooks Robinson	.50
2	Hank Aaron	2.00
3	Gaylord Perry	.25
4	Stan Musial	1.00
5	Willie Mays	2.00
6	Ernie Banks	.50
7	Rod Carew	.35
8	Duke Snider	.35
9	Mickey Mantle	5.00
10	Lou Brock	.25
11	Yogi Berra	.50
12	Nolan Ryan	3.00
13	Roger Clemens	2.00
14	Jose Cruz	.25
15	Gerald Young	.25
16	Enos Slaughter	.25
17	Glenn Davis	.25
18	J.R. Richard	.25
19	Fergie Jenkins	.25
20	Pete Incaviglia	.25

1989 Houston Colt .45s Fire Safety

The expansion Houston Colt .45s of 1962 are featured in this 1989 fire safety issue. The 2-1/2" x 3-1/2" cards have sepia player photos on front, with blue pistol frames and team logo, an orange name banner and brown Smokey logo. Backs are in black-and-white with a fire prevention cartoon, Forest Service logos and the player name, position and uniform number. Cards numbers are at upper-right.

		MT
Complete Set (29):		12.00
Common Player:		.50
1	Bob Bruce	.50
2	Al Cicotte	.50
3	Dave Giusti	.50

4	Jim Golden	.50
5	Ken Johnson	.50
6	Tom Borland	.50
7	Bobby Shantz	.90
8	Dick Farrell	.50
9	Jim Umbricht	.50
10	Hal Woodeshick	.50
11	Merritt Ranew	.50
12	Hal Smith	.50
13	Jim Campbell	.50
14	Norm Larker	.65
15	Joe Amalfitano	.60
16	Bob Aspromonte	.65
17	Bob Lillis	.60
18	Dick Gernert	.50
19	Don Buddin	.50
20	Pidge Browne	.50
21	Von McDaniel	.50
22	Don Taussig	.50
23	Al Spangler	.50
24	Al Heist	.50
25	Jim Pendleton	.50
26	Johnny Weekly	.50
27	Harry Craft	.50
28	.45s coaches (Lum Harris, Bobby Bragan, Jim Busby, Cot Deal, Jim Adair)	.50
29	Team photo	.50
45	Tim Wakefield	.50
46	Andy Van Slyke	.50
47	Tony Gwynn	2.50
48	Fred McGriff	.65
49	Barry Bonds	2.50
50	Ozzie Smith	1.50
---	Checklist	.25

1993 Humpty Dumpty

The Canadian potato chip company Humpty Dumpty issued a 50-card set of miniature cards in 1993. The UV coated cards measure 1-7/16" x 1-15/16", with a full-bleed color photo on the front along with the team logo. The backs have three-year statistics and biographical information about the player, along with appropriate product and baseball logos and a card number.

		MT
Complete Set (50):		50.00
Common Player:		.50
1	Cal Ripken, Jr.	5.00
2	Mike Mussina	.75
3	Roger Clemens	2.50
4	Chuck Finley	.50
5	Sandy Alomar	.60
6	Frank Thomas	4.00
7	Robin Ventura	.75
8	Cecil Fielder	.50
9	George Brett	3.00
10	Cal Eldred	.50
11	Kirby Puckett	3.00
12	Dave Winfield	.75
13	Jim Abbott	.50
14	Rickey Henderson	.75
15	Ken Griffey, Jr.	6.00
16	Nolan Ryan	5.00
17	Ivan Rodriguez	.75
18	Paul Molitor	2.00
19	John Olerud	.65
20	Joe Carter	.50
21	Jack Morris	.50
22	Roberto Alomar	.75
23	Pat Borders	.50
24	Devon White	.50
25	Juan Guzman	.50
26	Steve Avery	.50
27	John Smoltz	.60
28	Mark Grace	.75
29	Jose Rijo	.50
30	Dave Nied	.50
31	Benito Santiago	.50
32	Jeff Bagwell	2.00
33	Tim Wallach	.50
34	Eric Karros	.50
35	Delino DeShields	.50
36	Wilfredo Cordero	.50
37	Marquis Grissom	.50
38	Ken Hill	.50
39	Moises Alou	.60
40	Chris Nabholz	.50
41	Dennis Martinez	.50
42	Larry Walker	1.00
43	Bobby Bonilla	.50
44	Lenny Dykstra	.50

1995 Hutchinson Cancer Research Center

FRED HUTCHINSON
Manager, Seattle Rainiers, 1955

This card set benefits the Fred Hutchinson Cancer Research Center in Seattle, named after the former big league pitcher and manager and founded by his physician brother. In a throwback to the cards sold in bags of popcorn at Sick's Stadium in the 1950s-1960s, the 2" x 3" cards were given away in a bag of popcorn to fans attending the Aug. 25 game at Tacoma. Fronts have black-and-white photos of Hutchinson while backs have a paragraph about the photo and describe Hutchinson's career and the cancer center's work.

		MT
Complete Set (4):		6.00
Common Card:		1.50
1	Fred Hutchinson (1937 Franklin H.S.)	1.50
2	Fred Hutchinson (1938 Seattle Rainiers)	1.50
3	Fred Hutchinson (1938, w/ Bob Feller)	2.00
4	Fred Hutchinson (1955, Rainiers manager)	1.50

1996 Hutchinson Cancer Research Center

FRED HUTCHINSON
Pitcher (right), Seattle Indians, 1938

For a second year a collectors set was issued to research benefit the Fred Hutchinson Cancer Research Center in Seattle, named after the former big league pitcher and manager and founded by his physician brother. In a throwback to the cards sold in bags of popcorn at Sick's Stadium in the 1950s-1960s, the 2" x 3" cards were given away in a bag of popcorn to fans attending the July 14 game at Tacoma. Fronts have black-and-white photos of Hutchinson while backs have a paragraph about the photo and describe Hutchinson's career and the cancer center's work.

		MT
Complete Set (4):		6.00
Common Card:		1.50
1	Fred Hutchinson (1937 Franklin H.S.)	1.50
2	Fred Hutchinson (1938 Seattle Indians)	1.50
3	Fred Hutchinson (1940s, Detroit Tigers)	2.00
4	Fred Hutchinson (1955, 1959 Rainiers manager)	1.50

1997 Hutchinson Cancer Research Center

FRED HUTCHINSON
Pitcher, Detroit Tigers, 1940s

Four-card sets of the third annual issue commemorating the late Fred Hutchinson were given to fans attending the July 15 Tacoma Rainiers game. The cards are an attempt to raise consciousness of Seattle's Fred Hutchinson Cancer Research Center. In a format similar to the "popcorn" cards issued during the 1950s and 1960s in the Pacific Northwest, these cards measure 2" x 3" and are printed in black-and-white. Fronts have photos of Hutch in his playing and managing days. Backs describe the photo on front and have information about the cancer center and the cards.

		MT
Complete Set (4):		6.00
Common Card:		1.50
1	Fred Hutchinson (Pitcher, Seattle Rainiers, 1938)	1.50
2	Fred Hutchinson (Pitcher, Buffalo, N.Y., Bisons 1941)	1.50
3	Fred Hutchinson (Pitcher, Detroit Tigers, 1940s)	1.50
4	Fred Hutchinson (Manager, Seattle Rainiers, 1955)	1.50

1998 Hutchinson Cancer Research Center

Four-card sets of the fourth annual issue commemorating the late Fred Hutchinson were given to fans attending Aug. 20 and Sept. 6 Tacoma games. The cards are an attempt to raise consciousness of Seattle's Fred Hutchinson Cancer Research Center. For the first time in the series, the card format was changed to 2-3/4" x 3-3/4", printed in black-and-white. Fronts have photos of Hutch in his playing and managing days. Backs describe the photo on front and have information about the cancer center and the cards.

		MT
Complete Set (4):		6.00
Common Card:		1.50
1	Fred Hutchinson (pitcher, Seattle, 1938)	1.50
2	Fred Hutchinson (pitcher, Toledo, 1939)	1.50
3	Fred Hutchinson (manager, Seattle, 1955)	1.50
4	Fred Hutchinson (manager, Cincinnati, 1962)	2.00

1999 Hutchinson Cancer Research Center

Four cards recalling the career of Fred Hutchinson, who died of cancer in 1964, were distributed by the Tacoma Rainiers at the Pacific Coast League team's Aug. 15 game. The 2-3/4" x 3-3/4" black-and-white cards have pictures on front depicting the pitcher at various stages of his career. The issue carries a "HUTCH / Series 5" label on front. Backs have a portrait photo, career highlights and information on the cancer research facility which bears Hutchinson's name.

		MT
Complete Set (4):		6.00
Common Card:		1.50
1	Fred Hutchinson (Brighton School, 1930s)	1.50
2	Fred Hutchinson (Detroit Tigers 1940)	1.50
3	Fred Hutchinson (Cardinals manager 1958)	1.50
4	Fred Hutchinson (1962 All-Star Game)	1.50

1982 Hygrade Expos

This Montreal Expos team set was the object of intense collector speculation when it was first issued. Single cello-wrapped cards were included in packages of Hygrade luncheon meat in the province of Quebec only. A mail-in offer for the complete set appeared later in the season. It remains a relatively scarce issue today. The 2" x 3" cards are printed on heavy paper, with round corners. Backs are printed in French, and contain an offer for an album to house the set.

		MT
Complete Set (24):		30.00
Common Player:		1.00
Album:		10.00
0	Al Oliver	3.00
4	Chris Speier	1.00
5	John Milner	1.00
6	Jim Fanning	1.00
8	Gary Carter	6.00
10	Andre Dawson	6.00
11	Frank Tavaras (Taveras)	1.00
16	Terry Francona	1.00
17	Tim Blackwell	1.00
18	Jerry White	1.00
20	Bob James	1.00
21	Scott Sanderson	1.00
24	Brad Mills	1.00
29	Tim Wallach	3.00
30	Tim Raines	6.00
34	Bill Gullickson	1.00
35	Woodie Fryman	1.00
38	Bryn Smith	1.00
41	Jeff Reardon	1.00
44	Dan Norman	1.00
45	Steve Rogers	1.00
48	Ray Burris	1.00
49	Warren Cromartie	1.00
53	Charlie Lea	1.00

1987 Hygrade Baseball's All-Time Greats

(See "Baseball's All-Time Greats" for checklist and values.)

I

1994 Innovative Confections Sucker Savers

These 2-3/8" diameter discs were included in a plastic snap-top lollipop holder. A yellow strip which intersects the red border at the top contains the player name and team, while a yellow diamond graphic surrounds the player photo. Produced by Michael Schechter Assoc., the discs are licensed by the players' union but not MLB, so team uniform logos are airbrushed off the photos. Backs are printed in blue and have 1993 and career stats.

		MT
Complete Set (20):		24.00
Common Player:		1.00
1	Rickey Henderson	1.00
2	Ken Caminiti	1.00
3	Terry Pendleton	1.00
4	Tim Raines	1.00
5	Joe Carter	1.00
6	Benito Santiago	1.00
7	Jim Abbott	1.00
8	Ozzie Smith	1.50
9	Don Slaught	1.00
10	Tony Gwynn	2.50
11	Mark Langston	1.00
12	Darryl Strawberry	1.25
13	David Justice	1.50
14	Cecil Fielder	1.00
15	Cal Ripken Jr.	4.00
16	Jeff Bagwell	2.00
17	Mike Piazza	3.00
18	Bobby Bonilla	1.00
19	Barry Bonds	2.50
20	Roger Clemens	2.00

1994 International Playing Cards Toronto Blue Jays

Virtually identical to the team and mixed stars playing card sets issued by U.S. Playing Card Co., this Toronto team set was issued for the Canadian market. In playing card format at 2-1/2" x 3-1/2" with rounded corners, the set features Blue Jays players on front with their name and position in white in a blue stripe beneath the photo. Backs are bright blue with the team logo at top-center and sponsors' logos along the bottom. The set was sold in a colorful cardboard box.

		MT
Complete Set (55):		4.00
Common Player:		.05
AC	John Olerud	.30
2C	Al Leiter	.25
3C	Dave Stewart	.10
4C	Pat Borders	.05
5C	Devon White	.15
6C	Joe Carter	.20
7C	Roberto Alomar	.40
8C	Woody Williams	.05
9C	Eddie Zosky	.05
10C	Willie Canate	.05
JC	Danny Cox	.05
QC	Todd Stottlemyre	.10
KC	Ed Sprague	.10
AS	Paul Molitor	.50
2S	Michael Timlin	.05
3S	Randy Knorr	.05
4S	Pat Hentgen	.10
5S	Darnell Coles	.05
6S	Juan Guzman	.05
7S	Roberto Alomar	.40
8S	Joe Carter	.20
9S	Scott Brow	.05
10S	Dick Schofield	.05
JS	Rob Butler	.05
QS	Tony Castillo	.05
KS	Duane Ward	.05
AH	Joe Carter	.20
2H	Woody Williams	.05
3H	Danny Cox	.05
4H	Todd Stottlemyre	.10
5H	Ed Sprague	.10
6H	John Olerud	.30
7H	Paul Molitor	.50
8H	Scott Brow	.05
9H	Pat Hentgen	.10
10H	Al Leiter	.25
JH	Dave Stewart	.10
QH	Pat Borders	.05
KH	Devon White	.10
AD	Roberto Alomar	.40
2D	Eddie Zosky	.05
3D	Rob Butler	.05
4D	Tony Castillo	.05
5D	Duane Ward	.05
6D	Paul Molitor	.50
7D	John Olerud	.30
8D	Carlos Delgado	.40
9D	Michael Timlin	.05
10D	Randy Knorr	.05
JD	Pat Hentgen	.10
QD	Darnell Coles	.05
KD	Juan Guzman	.05
Joker	Team name	.05
Joker	A.L. logo	.05
---	Checklist	.05

1995 International Playing Cards Toronto Blue Jays

For a second year the Canadian affiliate of the U.S. Playing Card Co. issued a team set of Blue Jays. Fronts have color portrait and action photos - up to three for popular players - with player identification and traditional playing card suit and value indicators in opposite corners. Backs have a large team logo. Cards are in 2-1/2" x 3-1/2" round-cornered format and were sold in a colorful flip-top box.

		MT
Complete Set (56):		4.00
Common Player:		.05
AC	John Olerud	.20
2C	Pat Hentgen	.10
3C	Juan Guzman	.05
4C	Cecil Fielder	.25
5C	Roberto Alomar	.45
6C	Joe Carter	.20
7C	Mark Eichhorn	.05
8C	Carlos Delgado	.15
9C	Tom Candiotti	.05
10C	Dave Stewart	.10
JC	Tony Fernandez	.05
QC	Pat Borders	.05
KC	Dave Winfield	.45
AS	Paul Molitor	.50
2S	Todd Stottlemyre	.05
3S	Rickey Henderson	.35
4S	Tom Henke	.05
5S	Fred McGriff	.35
6S	Devon White	.10
7S	Duane Ward	.05
8S	David Wells	.05
9S	David Cone	.15
10S	Mike Timlin	.05
JS	Ed Sprague	.05
QS	Jack Morris	.05
KS	Jimmy Key	.15
AH	Roberto Alomar	.45
2H	Candy Maldonado	.05
3H	Mike Timlin	.05
4H	Ed Sprague	.05
5H	Pat Borders	.05
6H	Jimmy Key	.15
7H	Paul Molitor	.50
8H	Candy Maldonado	.05
9H	Danny Cox	.05
10H	Todd Stottlemyre	.05
JH	Rickey Henderson	.35
QH	Tom Henke	.05
KH	Cecil Fielder	.25
AD	Joe Carter	.20
2D	Duane Ward	.05
3D	Dave Stewart	.10
4D	Tony Fernandez	.05
5D	Jack Morris	.05
6D	Dave Winfield	.45
7D	John Olerud	.20
8D	Manny Lee	.05
9D	Pat Hentgen	.10
10D	Randy Knorr	.05
JD	Juan Guzman	.05
QD	Fred McGriff	.35
KD	Devon White	.10
---	Toronto Blue Jays	.05
---	Team logo card	.05
---	A.L. logo card	.05
---	Checklist	.05

J

1984 Jarvis Press Rangers

For its second annual "Baseball Card Day" game promotional set, the Rangers picked up a new sponsor, Jarvis Press of Dallas. The 30 cards in the set include 27 players, the manager, trainer and a group card of the coaches. Cards measure 2-3/8" x 3-1/2". Color game-action photos make up the card fronts. Backs, printed in black and white, include a portrait photo of the player. A source close to the promotion indicated 10,000 sets were produced.

		MT
Complete Set (30):		4.00
Common Player:		.25
1	Bill Stein	.25
2	Alan Bannister	.25
3	Wayne Tolleson	.25
5	Billy Sample	.25
6	Bobby Jones	.25
7	Ned Yost	.25
9	Pete O'Brien	.25
11	Doug Rader	.25
13	Tommy Dunbar	.25
14	Jim Anderson	.25
15	Larry Parrish	.25
16	Mike Mason	.25
17	Mickey Rivers	.35
19	Curtis Wilkerson	.25
20	Jeff Kunkel	.25
21	Odell Jones	.25
24	Dave Schmidt	.25
25	Buddy Bell	.25
26	George Wright	.25
28	Frank Tanana	.25
30	Marv Foley	.25
31	Dave Stewart	.75
32	Gary Ward	.25
36	Dickie Noles	.25
43	Donnie Scott	.25
44	Danny Darwin	.25
49	Charlie Hough	.25
53	Joey McLaughlin	.25
---	Coaching Staff (Rich Donnelly, Glenn Ezell, Merv Rettenmund, Dick Such, Wayne Terwilliger)	.25
---	Trainer (Bill Zeigler)	.25

1986 Jays Potato Chips

One of a handful of round baseball cards produced for inclusion in boxes of potato chips on a regional basis in 1986, the Jays set of 2-7/8" discs is believed to be the scarcest of the type. The 20 cards in the issue include the most popular Milwaukee Brewers and Chicago Cubs and White Sox players; the set having been distributed in the southern Wisconsin- northern Illinois area. Like many contemporary sets produced by Mike Schechter Associates, the '86 Jays cards feature player photos on which the team logos have been airbrushed off the caps.

		MT
Complete Set (20):		20.00
Common Player:		.60
(1)	Harold Baines	.60
(2)	Cecil Cooper	.60
(3)	Jody Davis	.60
(4)	Bob Dernier	.60
(5)	Richard Dotson	.60
(6)	Shawon Dunston	.60
(7)	Carlton Fisk	1.50
(8)	Jim Gantner	.60
(9)	Ozzie Guillen	.60
(10)	Teddy Higuera	.60
(11)	Ron Kittle	.60
(12)	Paul Molitor	3.00
(13)	Keith Moreland	.60
(14)	Ernie Riles	.60
(15)	Ryne Sandberg	3.00
(16)	Tom Seaver	4.00
(17)	Lee Smith	.60
(18)	Rick Sutcliffe	.60
(19)	Greg Walker	.60
(20)	Robin Yount	3.00

1991 Jesuit High School Alumni

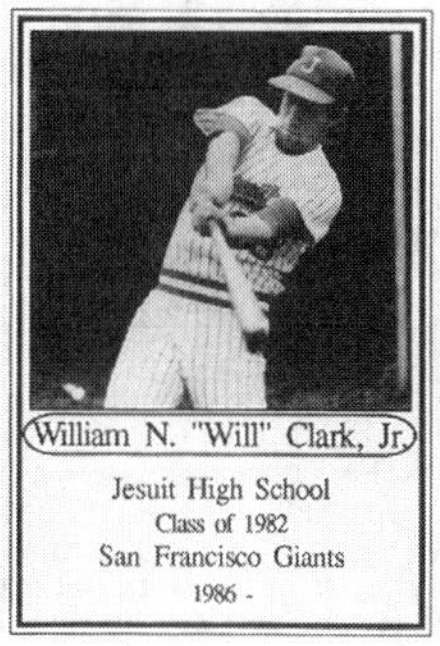

To commemorate the school's 1,000 baseball game, Jesuit High School in New Orleans issued this set of cards featuring alumni who went on to play in the major leagues. The cards have black-and-white photos on front picturing the players in their high school uniform, the year of graduation and the teams and years they played in the major leagues. A large baseball and "M" (thousand) logo apears at top. Backs have career summaries. Sets were given to persons attending ceremonies and the game April 13-14 and were also sold to collectors.

		MT
Complete Set (8):		6.00
Common Player:		.40
(1)	John "Fats" Dantonio	.40
(2)	Charlie Gilbert	.40
(3)	Connie Ryan	.40
(4)	Ralph "Putsy" Caballero	.40
(5)	Harold "Tookie" Gilbert	.40
(6)	Daniel "Rusty" Staub	.75
(7)	Jim Gaudet	.40
(8)	Will Clark	4.50

Player names in *Italic* type indicate a rookie card.

1984 Jewel Food Chicago Cubs/ White Sox

Similar in format to previous issues by the Midwestern food company, these 16-piece sets of Chicago's National and American League teams are printed on 6" x 9" paper. Fronts feature a chest-to-cap color player photo with a black facsimile autograph. A logo and copyright notice by the players' association is at upper-left. Backs are blank. Cards were distributed four per week with the purchase of specific sale products.

		MT
Complete Cubs Set (16):		23.00
Complete White Sox Set (16):		15.00
Common Player:		.75
	CHICAGO CUBS	
(1)	Larry Bowa	.75
(2)	Ron Cey	.90
(3)	Jody Davis	.75
(4)	Bob Dernier	.75
(5)	Leon Durham	.75
(6)	Dennis Eckersley	2.00
(7)	Richie Hebner	.75
(8)	Gary Matthews	.75
(9)	Keith Moreland	.75
(10)	Ryne Sandberg	8.00
(11)	Scott Sanderson	.75
(12)	Lee Smith	2.00
(13)	Tom Stoddard	.75
(14)	Rick Sutcliffe	.75
(15)	Steve Trout	.75
(16)	Gary Woods	.75
	CHICAGO WHITE SOX	
(1)	Harold Baines	1.00
(2)	Alan Bannister	.75
(3)	Julio Cruz	.75
(4)	Richard Dotson	.75
(5)	Jerry Dybzinski	.75
(6)	Carlton Fisk	3.00
(7)	Scott Fletcher	.75
(8)	LaMarr Hoyt	.75
(9)	Ron Kittle	.75
(10)	Rudy Law	.75
(11)	Vance Law	.75
(12)	Greg Luzinski	.75
(13)	Tom Paciorek	.75
(14)	Tom Seaver	3.00
(15)	Mike Squires	.75
(16)	Greg Walker	.75

1987 Jiffy Pop

For a second year, Jiffy Pop inserted player discs in its packages of popcorn. The full-color discs measure 2-7/8" in diameter and were produced by Mike Schechter Associates. Titled "2nd Annual Collectors' Edition," the card fronts feature player photos with all team insignias airbrushed away. Information on the backs of the discs is printed in bright red on white stock. Die-cut press sheets containing all 20 discs were available via a mail-in offer.

		MT
Complete Set (20):		27.50
Common Player:		1.00
1	Ryne Sandberg	2.50
2	Dale Murphy	1.50
3	Jack Morris	1.00
4	Keith Hernandez	1.00
5	George Brett	3.00
6	Don Mattingly	4.00
7	Ozzie Smith	2.50
8	Cal Ripken, Jr.	5.00
9	Dwight Gooden	1.25
10	Pedro Guerrero	1.00
11	Lou Whitaker	1.00
12	Roger Clemens	3.00
13	Lance Parrish	1.00
14	Rickey Henderson	1.25
15	Fernando Valenzuela	1.00
16	Mike Schmidt	2.50
17	Darryl Strawberry	1.00
18	Mike Scott	1.00
19	Jim Rice	1.00
20	Wade Boggs	2.50

1988 Jiffy Pop

This 20-disc set is the third Jiffy Pop issue spotlighting leading players. Discs are 2-1/2" in diameter with a semi-gloss finish and feature full-color closeups on white stock. Team logos have been airbrushed off the player's caps. Fronts have a curved label "3rd Annual Collector's Edition." Disc backs are white, with dark blue lettering, and contain player information, stats and disc number.

		MT
Complete Set (20):		18.00
Common Player:		.60
1	Buddy Bell	.60
2	Wade Boggs	2.00
3	Gary Carter	.90
4	Jack Clark	.60
5	Will Clark	1.50
6	Roger Clemens	2.50
7	Vince Coleman	.60
8	Andre Dawson	.90
9	Keith Hernandez	.60
10	Kent Hrbek	.75
11	Wally Joyner	.75
12	Paul Molitor	2.50
13	Eddie Murray	1.50
14	Tim Raines	.75
15	Bret Saberhagen	.75
16	Alan Trammell	.75
17	Ozzie Virgil	.60
18	Tim Wallach	.60
19	Dave Winfield	1.00
20	Robin Yount	2.50

1986 Jiffy Pop

One of the scarcer of the 1986 regionals, the Jiffy Pop discs were inserted in packages of heat-and-eat popcorn. A production of Mike Schechter Associates, the 2-7/8" diameter discs feature 20 popular stars, many in the same pictures found in other '86 regionals. Like other MSA issues, caps have had the team logos erased, allowing Jiffy Pop to avoid paying a licensing fee to the teams. Backs have a few biographical details and stats.

		MT
Complete Set (20):		30.00
Common Player:		1.00
1	Jim Rice	1.00
2	Wade Boggs	2.50
3	Lance Parrish	1.00
4	George Brett	3.00
5	Robin Yount	3.00
6	Don Mattingly	4.00
7	Dave Winfield	1.50
8	Reggie Jackson	2.00
9	Cal Ripken	5.00
10	Eddie Murray	1.50
11	Pete Rose	4.00
12	Ryne Sandberg	2.50
13	Nolan Ryan	5.00
14	Fernando Valenzuela	1.00
15	Willie McGee	1.00
16	Dale Murphy	1.50
17	Mike Schmidt	3.00
18	Steve Garvey	1.25
19	Gary Carter	1.25
20	Dwight Gooden	1.25

1986 Jiffy Pop/MSA Promos

This 20-card set was produced by Mike Schecter Associates in 1986 to provide attendees at a restaurant and food trade show with examples of his card promotions. The promos have the same fronts as the 1986 Jiffy Pop discs on a 2-7/8" diameter format. The backs have an advertisement for MSA's services. Like the regular issues, the uniform logos have been airbrushed from the discs due to lack of a license from Major League Baseball (the issue is licensed by the players' union). The unnumbered promo discs are checklisted here alphabetically.

		MT
Complete Set (20):		550.00
Common Player:		24.00
(1)	Wade Boggs	40.00
(2)	George Brett	50.00
(3)	Gary Carter	24.00
(4)	Steve Garvey	30.00
(5)	Dwight Gooden	24.00
(6)	Reggie Jackson	30.00
(7)	Don Mattingly	50.00
(8)	Willie McGee	24.00
(9)	Dale Murphy	24.00
(10)	Eddie Murray	30.00
(11)	Lance Parrish	24.00
(12)	Jim Rice	24.00
(13)	Cal Ripken, Jr.	80.00
(14)	Pete Rose	60.00
(15)	Nolan Ryan	80.00
(16)	Ryne Sandberg	40.00
(17)	Mike Schmidt	40.00
(18)	Fernando Valenzuela	24.00
(19)	Dave Winfield	30.00
(20)	Robin Yount	40.00

1990 Jumbo Sunflower Seeds

The 1990 "Autograph Series" of 24 cards came in packages of sunflower seeds and were produced by Mike Schecter Associates for Stagi & Scriven Farms Inc. The cards were found in specially-marked packages of Jumbo California Sunflower Seeds, three cards per package. Standard size with MLB logos airbrushed out, the cards are blue with a white frame. The numbered backs contain yearly statistics and biographical information along with a facsimile autograph.

		MT
Complete Set (24):		20.00
Common Player:		.35
(1)	Kevin Mitchell	.40
(2)	Ken Griffey, Jr.	3.00
(3)	Howard Johnson	.35
(4)	Bo Jackson	.60
(5)	Kirby Puckett	2.00
(6)	Robin Yount	1.50
(7)	Dave Stieb	.35
(8)	Don Mattingly	2.00
(9)	Barry Bonds	2.00
(10)	Pedro Guerrero	.35
(11)	Tony Gwynn	2.00
(12)	Von Hayes	.35
(13)	Rickey Henderson	.75
(14)	Tim Raines	.45
(15)	Alan Trammell	.40
(16)	Dave Stewart	.35
(17)	Will Clark	.75
(18)	Roger Clemens	1.50
(19)	Wally Joyner	.40
(20)	Ryne Sandberg	1.50
(21)	Eric Davis	.40
(22)	Mike Scott	.35
(23)	Cal Ripken, Jr.	2.50
(24)	Eddie Murray	.75

1991 Jumbo Sunflower Seeds

In its second year of baseball card production, Jumbo California Sunflower Seeds maintained the same basic format for its cards. Player photos, with uniform logos airbrushed away, in a white frame are surrounded by a red border with yellow pinstripe. At top left is the issuer's logo; above the photo in white is "Autograph Series II". A facsimile autograph is printed over the photo. Beneath the picture are the player's name, team and position. Backs are printed in red and include major league stats and a career summary.

		MT
Complete Set (24):		13.50
Common Player:		.35
1	Ozzie Smith	.75
2	Wade Boggs	.75
3	Bobby Bonilla	.35
4	George Brett	1.00
5	Kal Daniels	.35
6	Glenn Davis	.35
7	Chuck Finley	.35
8	Cecil Fielder	.35
9	Len Dykstra	.35
10	Dwight Gooden	.35
11	Ken Griffey, Jr.	3.00
12	Kelly Gruber	.35
13	Kent Hrbek	.35
14	Andre Dawson	.35
15	Dave Justice	.60
16	Barry Larkin	.35
17	Ben McDonald	.35
18	Mark McGwire	2.50
19	Roberto Alomar	.40
20	Nolan Ryan	2.50
21	Sandy Alomar, Jr.	.40
22	Bobby Thigpen	.35
23	Tim Wallach	.35
24	Mitch Williams	.35

1992 Jumbo Sunflower Seeds

The basic format used in 1990-91 was returned for 1992 when Michael Schecter Associates produced another 24-card set for inclusion in packages of Jumbo Sunflower Seeds (the "California" identifier was dropped in 1992). Cards feature a player photo on which the uniform logos have been eliminated. Across the photo in black is a facsimile autograph. Around the photo are borders of, successively, white, blue, yellow and white. In the upper-left corner is the issuer's logo. "Autograph Series III" appears in red at upper-right. Beneath the picture, the player's name is printed in red, with his team and position in white. Backs are printed in blue, with major league stats and a career summary, along with a few personal data and the appropriate logos.

		MT
Complete Set (24):		8.00
Common Player:		.25
1	Jeff Reardon	.25
2	Bill Gullickson	.25
3	Todd Zeile	.25
4	Terry Mulholland	.25
5	Kirby Puckett	1.00
6	Howard Johnson	.25
7	Terry Pendleton	.25
8	Will Clark	.45
9	Cal Ripken, Jr.	1.50
10	Chris Sabo	.25
11	Jim Abbott	.25
12	Joe Carter	.25
13	Paul Molitor	.50
14	Ken Griffey, Jr.	2.00
15	Randy Johnson	.45
16	Bobby Bonilla	.25
17	John Smiley	.25
18	Jose Canseco	.40
19	Tom Glavine	.30
20	Darryl Strawberry	.30
21	Brett Butler	.25
22	Devon White	.25
23	Scott Erickson	.25
24	Willie McGee	.25

K

1982 Kmart

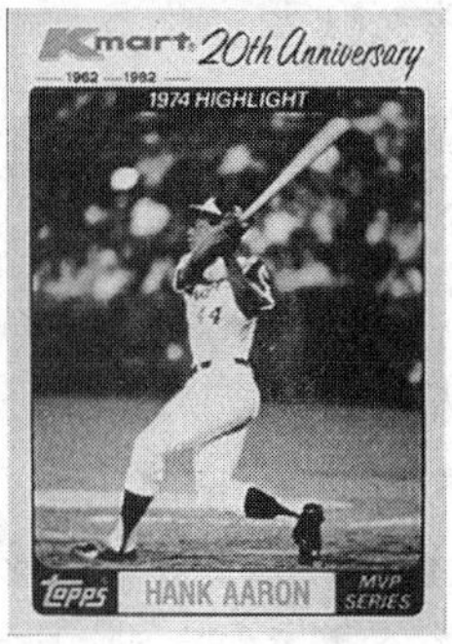

The first of what became dozens of boxed sets specially produced for retail chain stores by the major card producers, the 1982 Kmart set has enjoyed little collector popularity. The theme of the set is Most Valuable Players and selected record- breaking performances of the 1962-1981 seasons. The design used miniature reproductions of Topps cards of the era, except in a few cases where designs had to be created because original cards were never issued (1962 Maury Wills, 1975 Fred Lynn). Originally sold for about $2 per boxed set of 44, large quantities were bought up by speculators who got burned when over-production and lack of demand caused the set to drop as low as 10¢. The 2-1/2" x 3-1/2" cards were printed by Topps.

		MT
Complete Set (44):		2.00
Common Player:		.10
1	Mickey Mantle	1.00
2	Maury Wills	.10
3	Elston Howard	.10
4	Sandy Koufax	.25
5	Brooks Robinson	.10
6	Ken Boyer	.10
7	Zoilo Versalles	.10
8	Willie Mays	.25
9	Frank Robinson	.10
10	Bob Clemente	.50
11	Carl Yastrzemski	.15
12	Orlando Cepeda	.10
13	Denny McLain	.10
14	Bob Gibson	.10
15	Harmon Killebrew	.10
16	Willie McCovey	.10
17	Boog Powell	.10
18	Johnny Bench	.10
19	Vida Blue	.10
20	Joe Torre	.10
21	Rich Allen	.10
22	Johnny Bench	.10
23	Reggie Jackson	.15
24	Pete Rose	.35
25	Jeff Burroughs	.10
26	Steve Garvey	.10
27	Fred Lynn	.10
28	Joe Morgan	.10
29	Thurman Munson	.10
30	Joe Morgan	.10
31	Rod Carew	.10
32	George Foster	.10
33	Jim Rice	.10
34	Dave Parker	.10
35	Don Baylor	.10
36	Keith Hernandez	.10
37	Willie Stargell	.10
38	George Brett	.20
39	Mike Schmidt	.20

40	Rollie Fingers	.10
41	Mike Schmidt	.20
42	Don Drysdale	.10
43	Hank Aaron	.25
44	Pete Rose	.35

1987 Kmart

Produced by Topps for Kmart, the 1987 Kmart set was distributed by the department stores to celebrate their 25th anniversary. Entitled "Baseball's Stars of the Decades," the 33-card set was issued in a special cardboard box with one stick of bubblegum. Fronts feature a full-color photo set diagonally against a red background. The backs contain career highlights plus pitching or batting statistics for the decade in which the player enjoyed his greatest success. Cards are the standard 2-1/2" x 3-1/2".

		MT
Complete Set (33):		3.00
Common Player:		.10
1	Hank Aaron	.40
2	Roberto Clemente	.50
3	Bob Gibson	.10
4	Harmon Killebrew	.10
5	Mickey Mantle	1.00
6	Juan Marichal	.10
7	Roger Maris	.30
8	Willie Mays	.40
9	Brooks Robinson	.15
10	Frank Robinson	.15
11	Carl Yastrzemski	.15
12	Johnny Bench	.15
13	Lou Brock	.10
14	Rod Carew	.15
15	Steve Carlton	.10
16	Reggie Jackson	.20
17	Jim Palmer	.15
18	Jim Rice	.10
19	Pete Rose	.35
20	Nolan Ryan	.50
21	Tom Seaver	.15
22	Willie Stargell	.10
23	Wade Boggs	.30
24	George Brett	.30
25	Gary Carter	.10
26	Dwight Gooden	.10
27	Rickey Henderson	.15
28	Don Mattingly	.40
29	Dale Murphy	.10
30	Eddie Murray	.15
31	Mike Schmidt	.30
32	Darryl Strawberry	.10
33	Fernando Valenzuela	.10

1988 Kmart

This 33-card boxed set, titled "Memorable Moments," was produced by Topps for distribution via Kmart. The 1988 cards are standard-size with red, white and blue borders and a super glossy coating. Numbered card backs are printed in red and blue on white and highlight special events in the featured players' careers. The set was marketed in a bright yellow and green checklist box (gum included).

		MT
Complete Set (33):		4.00
Common Player:		.10
1	George Bell	.10
2	Wade Boggs	.40
3	George Brett	.50
4	Jose Canseco	.35
5	Jack Clark	.10
6	Will Clark	.25
7	Roger Clemens	.45
8	Vince Coleman	.10
9	Andre Dawson	.10
10	Dwight Gooden	.10
11	Pedro Guerrero	.10
12	Tony Gwynn	.50
13	Rickey Henderson	.25
14	Keith Hernandez	.10
15	Don Mattingly	.50
16	Mark McGwire	1.50
17	Paul Molitor	.35
18	Dale Murphy	.10
19	Tim Raines	.10
20	Dave Righetti	.10
21	Cal Ripken, Jr.	1.00
22	Pete Rose	.50
23	Nolan Ryan	1.00
24	Benny Santiago	.10
25	Mike Schmidt	.40
26	Mike Scott	.10
27	Kevin Seitzer	.10
28	Ozzie Smith	.35
29	Darryl Strawberry	.10
30	Rick Sutcliffe	.10
31	Fernando Valenzuela	.10
32	Todd Worrell	.10
33	Robin Yount	.45

1989 Kmart

This 33-card, glossy set was produced by Topps for Kmart, where it was sold in stores nationwide. The standard-size cards feature mostly action shots on the front, and include the Topps "Dream Team" logo at the top, with the K-Mart logo in the lower right corner. The first 11 cards in the set picture the top rookies of 1988, while the next 11 picture the top A.L. rookies of the '80s, and the final 11 cards highlight the top N.L. rookies of the decade.

		MT
Complete Set (33):		2.00
Common Player:		.10
1	Mark Grace	.25
2	Ron Gant	.10
3	Chris Sabo	.10
4	Walt Weiss	.10
5	Jay Buhner	.10
6	Cecil Espy	.10
7	Dave Gallagher	.10
8	Damon Berryhill	.10
9	Tim Belcher	.10
10	Paul Gibson	.10
11	Gregg Jefferies	.15
12	Don Mattingly	.65
13	Harold Reynolds	.10
14	Wade Boggs	.45
15	Cal Ripken, Jr.	1.00
16	Kirby Puckett	.65
17	George Bell	.10
18	Jose Canseco	.35
19	Terry Steinbach	.10
20	Roger Clemens	.50
21	Mark Langston	.10
22	Harold Baines	.10
23	Will Clark	.25
24	Ryne Sandberg	.45
25	Tim Wallach	.10
26	Shawon Dunston	.10
27	Tim Raines	.10
28	Darryl Strawberry	.10
29	Tony Gwynn	.50
30	Tony Pena	.10
31	Doc Gooden	.10
32	Fernando Valenzuela	.10
33	Pedro Guerrero	.10

1990 Kmart

This 33-card glossy set was produced by Topps for Kmart, where it was available nationwide. The set is subtitled "Superstars" and features sixteen A.L. players, sixteen N.L. stars and a managers' card featuring both Tony LaRussa and Roger Craig. A special Superstars logo is featured on the card fronts. The 1990 issue marks the fourth consecutive year that Topps has produced a set in cooperation with Kmart.

		MT
Complete Set (33):		3.00
Common Player:		.10
1	Will Clark	.25
2	Ryne Sandberg	.35
3	Howard Johnson	.10
4	Ozzie Smith	.30
5	Tony Gwynn	.50
6	Kevin Mitchell	.10
7	Jerome Walton	.10
8	Craig Biggio	.10
9	Mike Scott	.10
10	Dwight Gooden	.10
11	Sid Fernandez	.10
12	Joe Magrane	.10
13	Jay Howell	.10
14	Mark Davis	.10
15	Pedro Guerrero	.10
16	Glenn Davis	.10
17	Don Mattingly	.50
18	Julio Franco	.10
19	Wade Boggs	.30
20	Cal Ripken, Jr.	.90
21	Jose Canseco	.30
22	Kirby Puckett	.40
23	Rickey Henderson	.25
24	Mickey Tettleton	.10
25	Nolan Ryan	.90
26	Bret Saberhagen	.15
27	Jeff Ballard	.10
28	Chuck Finley	.10
29	Dennis Eckersley	.10
30	Dan Plesac	.10
31	Fred McGriff	.15
32	Mark McGwire	1.50
33	Managers (Tony LaRussa, Roger Craig)	.10

1987 Kahn's Reds

After a nearly 20-year layoff, Kahn's Wieners sponsored a baseball card set in 1987. The hot dog concessionaire sponsored a 28-card Reds team set that was distributed to fans attending the Aug. 2 game at Riverfront Stadium. Cards are the standard 2-1/2" x 3-1/2" size. The fronts offer a full-color player photo bordered in red and white. Backs carry the Kahn's logo, a portrait photo of the player and career stats.

		MT
Complete Set (28):		10.00
Common Player:		.25
6	Bo Diaz	.25
10	Terry Francona	.25
11	Kurt Stillwell	.25
12	Nick Esasky	.25
13	Dave Concepcion	.25
15	Barry Larkin	3.00
16	Ron Oester	.25
21	Paul O'Neill	2.00
23	Lloyd McClendon	.25
25	Buddy Bell	.25
28	Kal Daniels	.25
29	Tracy Jones	.25
30	Guy Hoffman	.25
31	John Franco	.45
32	Tom Browning	.25
33	Ron Robinson	.25
34	Bill Gullickson	.25
35	Pat Pacillo	.25
39	Dave Parker	1.00
43	Bill Landrum	.25
44	Eric Davis	1.00
46	Rob Murphy	.25
47	Frank Williams	.25
48	Ted Power	.25

1988 Kahn's Mets

Approximately 50,000 Mets fans received this complimentary card set during a ballpark promotion sponsored by Kahn's Wieners. Twenty-five players are featured in the set, along with manager Davey Johnson, four coaches and a team photo. Card fronts have a dark blue border with an orange rectangle framing the color player photo; players' uniform numbers are printed in white in the upper-right corner, beside the team logo. Backs are black-and-white with red accents. In addition to player acquisition date, birthday and residence, a paragraph-style career summary is included. Cards measure 2-1/2" x 3-1/2".

		MT
Complete Set (31):		7.50
Common Player:		.25
1	Mookie Wilson	.25
2	Mackey Sasser	.25
3	Bud Harrelson	.25
4	Lenny Dykstra	.35
5	Davey Johnson	.35
6	Wally Backman	.25
8	Gary Carter	.60
11	Tim Teufel	.25
12	Ron Darling	.25
13	Lee Mazzilli	.25
15	Rick Aguilera	.25
16	Dwight Gooden	.50
17	Keith Hernandez	.25
18	Darryl Strawberry	.50
19	Bob Ojeda	.25
20	Howard Johnson	.25
21	Kevin Elster	.25
22	Kevin McReynolds	.25
26	Terry Leach	.25
28	Bill Robinson	.25
29	Dave Magadan	.25
30	Mel Stottlemyre	.25
31	Gene Walter	.25
33	Barry Lyons	.25
34	Sam Perlozzo	.25
42	Roger McDowell	.25
44	David Cone	.75
48	Randy Myers	.40
50	Sid Fernandez	.25
52	Greg Pavlick	.25
---	Team Photo	.25

1988 Kahn's Reds

This 26-card team set was a giveaway during the Aug. 14, 1988 Cincinnati Reds game. The glossy cards (2-1/2" x 3-1/2") feature color action photos inside red and white borders. The Reds logo, player uniform number, name and position are printed below the photo. The backs are black and white, with small player close-ups and career stats. A promotional 25-cent coupon for Kahn's Wieners was included with each set.

		MT
Complete Set (26):		8.00
Common Player:		.25
6	Bo Diaz	.25
8	Terry McGriff	.25
9	Eddie Milner	.25
10	Leon Durham	.25
11	Barry Larkin	.50
12	Nick Esasky	.25
13	Dave Concepcion	.25
14	Pete Rose	2.00
15	Jeff Treadway	.25
17	Chris Sabo	.30
20	Danny Jackson	.25
21	Paul O'Neill	.50
22	Dave Collins	.25
27	Jose Rijo	.25
28	Kal Daniels	.25
29	Tracy Jones	.25
30	Lloyd McClendon	.25
31	John Franco	.35
32	Tom Browning	.25
33	Ron Robinson	.25
40	Jack Armstrong	.25
44	Eric Davis	.30
46	Rob Murphy	.25
47	Frank Williams	.25
48	Tim Birtsas	.25
---	Coaches (Danny Breeden, Tommy Helms, Bruce Kimm, Jim Lett, Lee May, Tony Perez)	.25

1989 Kahn's Cooperstown Collection

This 11-player card set was available through a mail-in offer. One dollar and three proofs of purchase from Hillshire Farms were needed to obtain the set. The card fronts feature paintings of recent Hall of Fame inductees. A coupon card was also included with each set.

		MT
Complete Set (11):		3.00
Common Player:		.50
(1)	Cool Papa Bell	.50
(2)	Johnny Bench	1.00
(3)	Lou Brock	.60
(4)	Whitey Ford	1.00
(5)	Bob Gibson	.75
(6)	Billy Herman	.50
(7)	Harmon Killebrew	.75
(8)	Eddie Mathews	.65
(9)	Brooks Robinson	.75
(10)	Willie Stargell	.65
(11)	Carl Yastrzemski	.75

1989 Kahn's Mets

This team set was sponsored by Kahn's Wieners and given to fans attending the July 6 game at Shea Stadium. Standard-size cards feature a color photo surrounded by a blue and orange border with the player's name and uniform number across the top. Backs include the Kahn's logo, along with player information and complete Major League stats. Four update cards were later added to the set.

		MT
Complete Set (30):		6.00
Common Player:		.20
1	Mookie Wilson	.20
2	Mackey Sasser	.20
3	Bud Harrelson	.20
5	Davey Johnson	.20
7	Juan Samuel	.20
8	Gary Carter	.50
9	Gregg Jefferies	1.00
12	Ron Darling	.20
13	Lee Mazzilli	.20
16	Dwight Gooden	.50
17	Keith Hernandez	.20
18	Darryl Strawberry	.30
19	Bob Ojeda	.20
20	Howard Johnson	.20
21	Kevin Elster	.20
22	Kevin McReynolds	.20
28	Bill Robinson	.20
29	Dave Magadan	.20
30	Mel Stottlemyre	.20
32	Mark Carreon	.30
33	Barry Lyons	.20
34	Sam Perlozzo	.20
38	Rick Aguilera	.20
44	David Cone	.50
46	Dave West	.20
48	Randy Myers	.30
50	Sid Fernandez	.20
51	Don Aase	.20
52	Greg Pavlick	.20
---	Team card	.20
---	Jeff Innis	.50
----	Keith Miller	.50
----	Jeff Musselman	.50
---	Frank Viola	.50

1989 Kahn's Reds

This team set, sponsored by Kahn's Wieners, was distributed to fans attending the Aug. 6 Reds game at Riverfront Stadium. The standard-size, red-bordered cards feature action photos with the player's name in the upper-left corner, his uniform number in the upper-right and the Reds logo in the middle. Backs include a black-and-white portrait, player data and complete major and minor league stats. The Kahn's logo appears in the upper-right corner of the back.

		MT
Complete Set (26):		7.00
Common Player:		.20
6	Bo Diaz	.20
7	Lenny Harris	.25
11	Barry Larkin	.50
12	Joel Youngblood	.20
14	Pete Rose	1.50
16	Ron Oester	.20
17	Chris Sabo	.20
20	Danny Jackson	.20
21	Paul O'Neill	.40
25	Todd Benzinger	.20
27	Jose Rijo	.20
28	Kal Daniels	.20
29	Herm Winningham	.20
30	Ken Griffey	.30
31	John Franco	.20
32	Tom Browning	.20
33	Ron Robinson	.20
34	Jeff Reed	.20
36	Rolando Roomes	.20
37	Norm Charlton	.20
42	Rick Mahler	.20
43	Kent Tekulve	.20
44	Eric Davis	.30
48	Tim Birtsas	.20
49	Rob Dibble	.25
---	Coaches (Danny Breeden, Dave Bristol, Tommy Helms, Jim Lett, Lee May, Tony Perez)	.20

1990 Kahn's Mets

For the third consecutive year, Kahn's issued a team set of Mets baseball cards. The sets were distrubted at Shea Stadium on May 3, prior to the Mets/Reds game. Cards feature blue and orange (team colors) graphics and are numbered according to uniform number. Two coupon cards were also included with each set.

		MT
Complete Set (34):		8.00
Common Player:		.20
1	Lou Thornton	.20
2	Mackey Sasser	.20
3	Bud Harrelson	.20
4	Mike Cubbage	.20
5	Davey Johnson	.20
6	Mike Marshall	.20
9	Gregg Jefferies	.50
10	Dave Magadan	.20
11	Tim Teufel	.20
13	Jeff Musselman	.20
15	Ron Darling	.20
16	Dwight Gooden	.40
18	Darryl Strawberry	.40
19	Bob Ojeda	.20
20	Howard Johnson	.20
21	Kevin Elster	.20
22	Kevin McReynolds	.20
25	Keith Miller	.20
26	Alejandro Pena	.20
27	Tom O'Malley	.20
29	Frank Viola	.20
30	Mel Stottlemyre	.20
31	John Franco	.20
32	Doc Edwards	.20
33	Barry Lyons	.20
35	Orlando Mercado	.20
40	Jeff Innis	.20
44	David Cone	.35
45	Mark Carreon	.20
47	Wally Whitehurst	.20
48	Julio Machado	.20
50	Sid Fernandez	.20
52	Greg Pavlick	.20
---	Team card	.20

1990 Kahn's Reds

This team set marks the fourth consecutive year in which Kahn's released a modern Reds issue. The cards feature color photos, red and white borders and the player's name, number, and postion on the card front. The flip sides feature biographical information, statistics, a posed photo and the Kahn's logo. The set is numbered by uniform.

		MT
Complete Set (27):		7.00
Common Player:		.25
7	Mariano Duncan	.30
9	Joe Oliver	.25
10	Luis Quinones	.25
11	Barry Larkin	.75
15	Glenn Braggs	.25
16	Ron Oester	.25
17	Chris Sabo	.25
20	Danny Jackson	.25
21	Paul O'Neill	.50
22	Billy Hatcher	.25
23	Hal Morris	.35
25	Todd Benzinger	.25
27	Jose Rijo	.25
28	Randy Myers	.30
29	Herm Winningham	.25
30	Ken Griffey	.35
32	Tom Browning	.25
34	Jeff Reed	.25
37	Norm Charlton	.25
40	Jack Armstrong	.25
41	Lou Pinella	.30
42	Rick Mahler	.25
43	Tim Layana	.25
44	Eric Davis	.35
48	Tim Birtsas	.25
49	Rob Dibble	.25
---	Coaches (Jackie Moore, Tony Perez, Sam Perlozzo, Larry Rothschild, Stan Williams)	.25

1991 Kahn's Mets

Kahn's kept its tradition in 1991 with the release of this set featuring members of the New York Mets. Cards measure 2 1/2" x 3 1/2" and the fronts feature a pinstripe design. The backs are printed horizontally and feature complete statistics. The cards are numbered according to uniform number. The complete set was distributed at a 1991 home game.

		MT
Complete Set (33):		7.50
Common Player:		.20
1	Vince Coleman	.20
2	Mackey Sasser	.20
3	Bud Harrelson	.20
4	Mike Cubbage	.20
5	Charlie O'Brien	.20
7	Hubie Brooks	.20
8	Daryl Boston	.20
9	Gregg Jefferies	.50
10	Dave Magadan	.20
11	Tim Teufel	.20
13	Rick Cerone	.20
15	Ron Darling	.20
16	Dwight Gooden	.30
17	David Cone	.50
20	Howard Johnson	.20
21	Kevin Elster	.20
22	Kevin McReynolds	.20
25	Keith Miller	.20
26	Alejandro Pena	.20
28	Tom Herr	.20
29	Frank Viola	.20
30	Mel Stottlemyre	.20
31	John Franco	.20
32	Doc Edwards	.20
40	Jeff Innis	.20
43	Doug Simons	.20
45	Mark Carreon	.20
47	Wally Whitehurst	.20
48	Pete Schourek	.20
50	Sid Fernandez	.20
51	Tom Spencer	.20
52	Greg Pavlick	.20
---	Team card	.20

1991 Kahn's Reds

The World Champion Cincinnati Reds are showcased in this 28-card set. The card fronts feature small color action photos on white stock. Backs feature statistics, biographical information and the Kahn's logo. A special card of team mascot Schottzie is included in this set.

		MT
Complete Set (28):		7.00
Common Player:		.25
7	Mariano Duncan	.25
9	Joe Oliver	.25
10	Luis Quinones	.25
11	Barry Larkin	.50
15	Glenn Braggs	.25
17	Chris Sabo	.25
19	Bill Doran	.25
21	Paul O'Neill	.45
22	Billy Hatcher	.25
23	Hal Morris	.30
25	Todd Benzinger	.25
27	Jose Rijo	.25
28	Randy Myers	.30
29	Herm Winningham	.25
32	Tom Browning	.25
34	Jeff Reed	.25
36	Don Carman	.25
37	Norm Charlton	.25
40	Jack Armstrong	.25
41	Lou Pinella	.30
44	Eric Davis	.30
45	Chris Hammond	.25
47	Scott Scudder	.25
48	Ted Power	.25
49	Rob Dibble	.25
57	Freddie Benavides	.25
---	Schottzie (mascot)	.25
----	Coaches (Jackie Moore, Tony Perez, Sam Perlozzo, Larry Rothschild, Stan Williams)	.25

1992 Kahn's Mets

A Mets' blue border surrounds the game-action photos in this team set. Backs are horizontally formatted and present full major league stats and the '92 Mets team slogan, "Hardball is Back." A baseball on front carries the uniform number by which the set is checklisted here. Cents-offs coupons for Kahn's hot dogs and corn dogs were packaged with the set when it was distributed at a home game, but are not considered part of the set.

		MT
Complete Set (33):		7.50
Common Player:		.20
1	Vince Coleman	.20
2	Mackey Sasser	.20
3	Junior Noboa	.20
4	Mike Cubbage	.20
6	Daryl Boston	.20
8	Dave Gallagher	.20
9	Todd Hundley	.50
10	Jeff Torborg	.20
11	Dick Schofield	.20
12	Willie Randolph	.20
15	Kevin Elster	.20
16	Dwight Gooden	.40
17	David Cone	.45
18	Bret Saberhagen	.45
19	Anthony Young	.20
20	Howard Johnson	.20
22	Charlie O'Brien	.20
25	Bobby Bonilla	.45
26	Barry Foote	.20
27	Tom McCraw	.20
28	Dave LaRoche	.20
29	Dave Magadan	.20
30	Mel Stottlemyre	.20
31	John Franco	.20
32	Bill Pecota	.20
33	Eddie Murray	.75
40	Jeff Innis	.20
44	Tim Burke	.20
45	Paul Gibson	.20
47	Wally Whitehurst	.20
50	Sid Fernandez	.20
51	John Stephenson	.20
---	Mets Team	.20

1992 Kahn's Reds

This 27-card set (two coupon cards distributed with the

team set are not considered part of the set) was given to fans at a promotional home date. The 2-1/2" x 3-1/2" cards have a red border with the team name at top and player name at bottom in white. The player's uniform number and position in black flank his name. A team logo appears in the lower-left corner of the photo. Backs are printed in red and black and have complete pro stats, a few biographical details and the logo of the Riverfront Stadium hot dog concessionaire. The checklist presented here is in order of uniform number.

		MT
Complete Set (27):		7.00
Common Player:		.25
2	Schottzie (mascot)	.25
9	Joe Oliver	.25
10	Bip Roberts	.30
11	Barry Larkin	.50
12	Freddie Benavides	.25
15	Glenn Braggs	.25
16	Reggie Sanders	.60
17	Chris Sabo	.25
19	Bill Doran	.25
21	Paul O'Neill	.35
23	Hal Morris	.30
25	Scott Bankhead	.25
26	Darnell Coles	.25
27	Jose Rijo	.25
28	Scott Ruskin	.25
29	Greg Swindell	.25
30	Dave Martinez	.25
31	Tim Belcher	.25
32	Tom Browning	.25
34	Jeff Reed	.25
37	Norm Charlton	.25
38	Troy Afenir	.25
41	Lou Piniella	.30
45	Chris Hammond	.25
48	Dwayne Henry	.25
49	Rob Dibble	.25
---	Coaches (Jackie Moore, John McLaren, Sam Perlozzo, Tony Perez, Larry Rothschild)	.25

1993 Kahn's Mets

The Mets distributed the 1993 Kahn's team set to fans on May 23 at Shea Stadium. Cards feature color photos and a white border. The Mets logo is at the bottom center and the player's name, position and uniform number at the top. Backs include career statistics and biography inside a red border. Also included in the set is a team photo card and a title card which features the New York skyline and the stadium. Apparently not all cards, such as those of coaches, were issued in all sets.

		MT
Complete Set (36):		12.00
Common Player:		.25
1	Tony Fernandez	.35
4	Mike Cubbage	.50
6	Joe Orsulak	.25
7	Jeff McKnight	.25
8	Dave Gallagher	.25
9	Todd Hundley	.50
10	Jeff Torborg	.50
11	Vince Coleman	.35
12	Jeff Kent	.45
16	Dwight Gooden	.50
18	Bret Saberhagen	.75
19	Anthony Young	.35
20	Howard Johnson	.25
21	Darren Reed	.25
22	Charlie O'Brien	.25
23	Tim Bogar	.25
25	Bobby Bonilla	.45
26	Barry Foote	.50
27	Tom McCraw	.50
28	Dave LaRoche	.50
29	Frank Tanana	.50
30	Mel Stottlemyre	.50
31	John Franco	.25
33	Eddie Murray	.75
34	Chico Walker	.25
40	Jeff Innis	.25
44	Ryan Thompson	.25
47	Mike Draper	.25
48	Pete Schourek	.25
50	Sid Fernandez	.25
51	Mike Maddux	.25
---	John Stephenson	.50
---	Team photo	.25
---	Header card	.10
---	Corn dog coupon	.05
---	Hot dog coupon	.05

1993 Kahn's Reds

Kahn's produced a Reds team set which was given away to fans at Riverfront Stadium on Aug. 1. The cards, organized by player's uniform number, show a photo of the player on the front with the player's name at the top and the Reds logo in the lower corner, surrounded by a pinstripe border. Card backs have the player's lifetime statistics and biography. Card #2 in the set portrays team owner Marge Schott and her dog Schottzie II. Coupon cards good for discounts on packages of Kahn's hot dogs and corn dogs were packaged with the set but are not considered part of the set.

		MT
Complete Set (20):		7.00
Common Player:		.25
2	Schottzie (mascot) (Marge Schott)	.35
7	Kevin Mitchell	.25
8	Juan Samuel	.25
9	Joe Oliver	.25
10	Bip Roberts	.25
11	Barry Larkin	.40
15	Davey Johnson	.25
16	Reggie Sanders	.50
17	Chris Sabo	.25
19	Randy Milligan	.25
20	Jeff Branson	.25
23	Hal Morris	.25
25	Greg Cadaret	.25
27	Jose Rijo	.25
30	Bobby Kelly	.25
31	Tim Belcher	.25
32	Tom Browning	.25
40	Tim Pugh	.25
41	Jeff Reardon	.25
42	Gary Varsho	.25
43	Bill Landrum	.25
46	Jacob Brumfield	.25
49	Rob Dibble	.25
53	Kevin Wickander	.25
57	John Smiley	.25
59	Bobby Ayala	.25
---	Coaches (Jose Cardenal, Don Gullett, Ray Knight, Bobby Valentine, Dave Miley)	.25
---	Broadcasters (Marty Brennaman, Joe Nuxhall)	.25

1994 Kahn's Reds

Distributed at a promotional game and sponsored by the hot dog concessionaire at Riverfront Stadium this was the eighth consecutive Reds team set produced by Kahn's. Cards feature a player action photo with a red stripe superimposed near the left border. The stripe contains the player name and position at top and the team logo at bottom. Backs are printed in red and black and include full minor and major league stats. Cards are numbered by uniform number printed on back.

		MT
Complete Set (31):		4.00
Common Player:		.10
2	Schottzie (mascot)	.10
4	Jacob Brumfield	.10
7	Kevin Mitchell	.10
9	Joe Oliver	.10
10	Eddie Taubensee	.10
11	Barry Larkin	.35
12	Deion Sanders	.50
15	Davey Johnson	.10
16	Reggie Sanders	.20
19	Jerome Walton	.10
20	Jeff Branson	.10
21	Tony Fernandez	.10
22	Thomas Howard	.15
23	Hal Morris	.15
27	Jose Rijo	.10
28	Lenny Harris	.10
29	Brett Boone	.35
31	Chuck McElroy	.10
32	Tom Browning	.10
33	Brian Dorsett	.10
39	Erik Hanson	.10
40	Tim Pugh	.10
44	John Roper	.10
45	Jeff Brantley	.10
46	Pete Schourek	.10
47	Johnny Ruffin	.10
49	Rob Dibble	.10
55	Tim Fortugno	.10
57	John Smiley	.10
58	Hector Carrasco	.15
	Reds Coaching Staff (Bob Boone, Don Gullett, Grant Jackson, Ray Knight, Joel Youngblood)	.10

1995 Kahn's Mets

Game-action photos are featured in this edition of the annual tradition of cards sponsored by the Mets hot dog concessionaire. In standard 2-1/2" x 3-1/2" format the cards have a gray background with navy pinstripes. The player's name, uniform number and position are in team colors of blue and orange at bottom. Backs are in red, black and white with personal data, previous-year or career stats and team and sponsor logos. The cards are checklisted here by uniform number.

		MT
Complete Set (36):		8.00
Common Player:		.25
1	Ricky Otero	.25
4	Mike Cubbage	.25
5	Chris Jones	.25
6	Joe Orsulak	.25
7	Bobby Wine	.25
8	Steve Swisher	.25
9	Todd Hundley	.40
10	Tom McCraw	.25
11	Aaron Ledesma	.25
12	Jeff Kent	.50
13	Edgardo Alfonzo	.75
15	Jose Vizcaino	.25
17	Bret Saberhagen	.45
18	Jeff Barry	.25
19	Bill Spiers	.25
20	Ryan Thompson	.35
21	Bill Pulsipher	.40
22	Brett Butler	.30
23	Tim Bogar	.25
25	Bobby Bonilla	.40
26	Rico Brogna	.30
27	Pete Harnisch	.35
28	Bobby Jones	.40
31	John Franco	.25
33	Kelly Stinnett	.25
34	Blas Minor	.25
35	Doug Henry	.25
38	Dave Mlicki	.25
40	Eric Gunderson	.25
44	Jason Isringhausen	.50
45	Jerry DiPoto	.25
46	Dallas Green	.25
52	Greg Pavlick	.25
55	Frank Howard	.25
---	50-cent hot dog coupon	.05
---	50-cent corn dog coupon	.05

1995 Kahn's Reds

This team set continues the tradition of baseball card sponsorship by Kahn's Meats. The set was given away at the Aug. 6 game. Team name and the year are printed in red in the white border above the photo; the player's name and position are in white in a red strip at the bottom of the photo. A Reds logo appears in the upper-right corner of the photo, with the player's uniform number below in white. Backs have complete minor and major league stats, along with a few biographical details and the Reds and Kahn's logos. The checklist is presented here by uniform number.

		MT
Complete Set (34):		6.00
Common Player:		.15
02	Schottzie (02)	.15
6	Ron Gant	.45
8	Damon Berryhill	.15
9	Eric Anthony	.15
10	Eddie Taubensee	.15
11	Barry Larkin	.40
12	Willie Greene	.15
15	Davey Johnson	.15
16	Reggie Sanders	.45
17	Mark Lewis	.15
18	Benito Santiago	.20
19	Jerome Walton	.15
20	Jeff Branson	.15
21	Deion Sanders	.45
22	Thomas Howard	.15
23	Hal Morris	.20
26	Johnny Ruffin	.15
27	Jose Rijo	.15
28	Lenny Harris	.15
29	Bret Boone	.35
30	Brian R. Hunter	.15
31	Chuck McElroy	.15
32	Kevin Jarvis	.15
37	Xavier Hernandez	.15
40	Tim Pugh	.15
41	Brad Pennington	.15
42	Mike Jackson	.15
44	John Roper	.15
45	Jeff Brantley	.15
46	Pete Schourek	.15
49	C.J. Nitkowski	.15
57	John Smiley	.15
58	Hector Carrasco	.15
---	Reds coaches (Ray Knight, Don Gullett, Grant Jackson, Hal McRae, Joel Youngblood)	.15

1996 Kahn's Mets

This team set was handed out to attendees at the Aug. 3 game at Shea Stadium. Sponsored by the Mets' hot dog concessionaire, the set features the players, coaches and manager in color action photos. Borders are in dark shades and include a Mets logo at lower-right. The player name and uniform number are in white. Backs are in black, red and white with personal data, 1995 stats and sponsors logos. The uniform number is repeated at lower-left. Cards are checklisted here in alphabetical order.

		MT
Complete Set (32):		8.00
Common Player:		.25
(1)	Edgardo Alfonzo	.50
(2)	Tim Bogar	.25
(3)	Rico Brogna	.25
(4)	Paul Byrd	.25
(5)	Mark Clark	.25
(6)	Mike Cubbage	.25
(7)	Jerry Dipoto	.25
(8)	Carl Everett	.25
(9)	John Franco	.25
(10)	Bernard Gilkey	.40
(11)	Dallas Green	.25
(12)	Pete Harnisch	.25
(13)	Doug Henry	.25
(14)	Frank Howard	.25
(15)	Todd Hundley	.40
(16)	Butch Huskey	.40
(17)	Jason Isringhausen	.30
(18)	Lance Johnson	.25
(19)	Bobby Jones	.25
(20)	Chris Jones	.25
(21)	Brent Mayne	.25
(22)	Tom McCraw	.25
(23)	Dave Mlicki	.25
(24)	Alex Ochoa	.25
(25)	Rey Ordonez	.75
(26)	Greg Pavlick	.25
(27)	Robert Person	.25
(28)	Bill Pulsipher	.25
(29)	Steve Swisher	.25
(30)	Andy Tomberlin	.25
(31)	Paul Wilson	.40
(32)	Bobby Wine	.25

1996 Kahn's Reds

The players, manager, coaches and mascot are once

again featured in a Cincinnati Reds team set sponsored by the team's hot dog concessionaire and given away to fans at the Aug. 4 game. The 2-1/2" x 3-1/2" cards have color game-action photos on front. A team-colors stripe at top has the Reds logo, player name, position and uniform number. A stripe beneath the photo has team name and year. Backs are printed in black and red on white and include personal data and complete major and minor league stats. Cards are checklisted here by uniform number.

		MT
Complete Set (34):		8.00
Common Player:		.25
02	Schottzie (mascot)	.25
7	Curtis Goodwin	.35
9a	Eric Anthony	.25
9b	Joe Oliver	.25
10	Eddie Taubenese	.25
11	Barry Larkin	.50
12	Willie Greene	.25
15	Mike Kelly	.25
16	Reggie Sanders	.35
17	Chris Sabo	.25
18	Eric Owens	.25
20	Jeff Branson	.25
21	Mark Portugal	.25
22	Thomas Howard	.25
23	Hal Morris	.30
25	Ray Knight	.25
26	Johnny Ruffin	.25
27	Jose Rijo	.25
28	Lenny Harris	.25
29	Bret Boone	.35
30	Eduardo Perez	.25
32	Kevin Jarvis	.25
34	Dave Burba	.25
36	Scott Service	.25
41	Jeff Shaw	.25
42	Roger Salkeld	.25
44	Eric Davis	.30
45	Jeff Brantley	.25
46	Pete Schourek	.25
57	John Smiley	.25
58	Hector Carrasco	.25
69	Tim Belk	.25
---	coaches (Marc Bombard, Don Gullett, Tom Hume, Jim Lett, Hal McRae)	.25
---	Bernie Stowe (equipment manager)	.25

1997 Kahn's Reds

This team set was given away to fans at the Aug. 3 game, sponsored by the Reds' hot dog concessionaire. The 2-1/2" x 3-1/2" cards have game action player photos at right and the player's name, position and uniform number in a two-toned red stripe vertically at left. Backs are printed in red and black and include complete major and minor league stats. Cards are listed here according to uniform number.

		MT
Complete Set (34):		8.00
Common Player:		.25
00	Curtis Goodwin	.25
02	Schottzie (mascot)	.25
3	Pokey Reese	.25
6	Brook Fordyce	.25
7	Joe Oliver	.25
9	Terry Pendleton	.25
10	Eddie Taubenese	.25
11	Barry Larkin	.35
12	Willie Greene	.25
15	Mike Kelly	.25
16	Reggie Sanders	.35
17	Aaron Boone	.50
20	Jeff Branson	.25
21	Deion Sanders	.50
23	Hal Morris	.25
25	Ray Knight	.25
27	Jose Rijo	.25
28	Lenny Harris	.25
29	Bret Boone	.35
33	Steve Gibraltar	.25
34	Dave Burba	.25
36	Mike Morgan	.25
37	Stan Belinda	.25
38	Kent Mercker	.25
39	Eduardo Perez	.25
40	Brett Tomko	.25
41	Jeff Shaw	.25
43	Mike Remlinger	.25
45	Jeff Brantley	.25
46	Pete Schourek	.25
56	Scott Sullivan	.25
57	John Smiley	.25
67	Felix Rodriguez	.25
---	Ken Griffey Sr., Don Gullett, Tom Hume, Denis Menke, Joel Youngblood	.25

1998 Kahn's Reds

For the 12th consecutive year, the Reds hot dog concessionaire issued a team set, given away at an Aug. 9 promotional game. The 2-1/2" x 3-1/2" cards have game-action photos at right, borderless at top, bottom and right. At left is a vertical red stripe with player name and uniform number. Horizontal backs have player data and complete major and minor league stats overprinted on a Kahn's logo. Backs are printed in red, black and white.

		MT
Complete Set (34):		8.00
Common Player:		.25
3	Pokey Reese	.35
4	Damian Jackson	.35
6	Brook Fordyce	.25
9	Pat Watkins	.35
10	Ed Taubensee	.25
11	Barry Larkin	.35
12	Willie Greene	.25
15	Jack McKeon	.25
16	Reggie Sanders	.35
17	Aaron Boone	.35
21	Sean Casey	1.00
22	Jon Nunnally	.35
23	Chris Stynes	.35
25	Dmitri Young	.25
26	Steve Cooke	.25
28	Paul Konerko	.75
29	Bret Boone	.35
31	Scott Sullivan	.25
32	Danny Graves	.25
33	John Hudek	.25
34	Mike Frank	.25
36	Gabe White	.25
37	Stan Belinda	.25
38	Pete Harnisch	.25
39	Eduardo Perez	.25
40	Brett Tomko	.25
43	Mike Remlinger	.25
44	Scott Winchester	.25
46	Melvin Nieves	.25
48	Rick Krivda	.25
53	Todd Williams	.25
58	Steve Parris	.25
---	Reds coaches (Harry Dunlop, Ken Griffey, Don Gullett, Tom Hume, Ron Oester)	.25
02	Schottzie (mascot)	.25

1999 Kahn's Reds

Distribution of a Kahn's team set for the Reds attained its 13th annual celebration July 31 when the cards were handed out to fans at Cinergy Field. Cards have player action photos which are borderless at top and right. At left is a ragged-edged red strip with player identification. Team identification is in a red strip at bottom. Backs are in red and black on white with a large Kahn's logo ghosted at center. Player data and complete profession stats are provided. Cards are checklisted here by uniform number.

		MT
Complete Set (34):		8.00
Common Player:		.25
02	Schottzie (mascot)	.35
3	Pokey Reese	.35
4	Jeffrey Hammonds	.35
9	Hal Morris	.35
10	Eddie Taubensee	.25
11	Barry Larkin	.35
12	Chris Stynes	.35
15	Denny Neagle	.25
17	Aaron Boone	.35
21	Sean Casey	.75
23	Greg Vaughn	.50
25	Dmitri Young	.25
26	Jason LaRue	.25
28	Mark Lewis	.25
29	Brian Johnson	.25
31	Jack McKeon	.25
32	Danny Graves	.25
33	Steve Avery	.25
34	Michael Tucker	.25
36	Gabe White	.35
37	Stan Belinda	.25
38	Pete Harnisch	.25
40	Brett Tomko	.25
41	Ron Villone	.25
43	Mark Wohlers	.25
44	Mike Cameron	.25
46	Jason Bere	.25
48	Scott Williamson	.25
49	Dennis Reyes	.25
56	Scott Sullivan	.25
58	Steve Parris	.25
---	Marty Brennaman, Joe Nuxhall (broadcasters)	.25
---	Ken Griffey Sr., Ron Oester, Denis Menke, Dave Collins (Reds coaches)	.25

1981 Kansas City Royals Police

Ten of the most popular Royals players are featured in this 2-1/2" x 4-1/8" set. Card fronts feature full-color photos with player name, position, facsimile autograph and team logo. Backs include player statistics, a tip from the Royals and list the four sponsoring organizations. The set was issued by the Ft. Myers, Fla., police department near the Royals' spring training headquarters.

		MT
Complete Set (10):		40.00
Common Player:		1.50
(1)	Willie Mays Aikens	2.00
(2)	George Brett	20.00
(3)	Rich Gale	1.50
(4)	Clint Hurdle	1.50
(5)	Dennis Leonard	1.50
(6)	Hal McRae	3.00
(7)	Amos Otis	3.00
(8)	U.L. Washington	2.00
(9)	Frank White	2.50
(10)	Willie Wilson	3.00

1982 Kansas City Royals Photocards

Throughout the 1980s, the Royals issued series of player photocards in a blank-backed, black-and-white 3-1/4" x 5" format. The design didn't change over the years and unless a complete set is at hand, distinguishing the year of issue can be impossible. Cards have a photo surrounded with white borders. The bottom margin is extra wide and has the player name and team logotype centered between a pair of team logo shields. The unnumbered cards are checklisted here in alphabetical order.

		MT
Complete Set (25):		12.50
Common Player:		.50
(1)	Willie Aikens	.65
(2)	Mike Armstrong	.50
(3)	Vida Blue	.65
(4)	George Brett	5.00
(5)	Scott Brown	.50
(6)	Onix Concepcion	.50
(7)	Dave Frost	.50
(8)	Cesar Geronimo	.50
(9)	Larry Gura	.50
(10)	Dick Howser	.50
(11)	Dennis Leonard	.50
(12)	Jerry Martin	.50
(13)	Hal McRae	.75
(14)	Amos Otis	.65
(15)	Tom Poquette	.50
(16)	Greg Pryor	.50
(17)	Jamie Quirk	.50
(18)	Dan Quisenberry	.75
(19)	John Schuerholz (gm)	.50
(20)	Paul Splittorff	.50
(21)	U.L. Washington	.60
(22)	John Wathan	.50
(23)	Dennis Werth	.50
(24)	Frank White	.65
(25)	Willie Wilson	1.00

1983 Kansas City Royals Photocards

Throughout the 1980s, the Royals issued series of player photocards in a blank-backed, black-and-white 3-1/4" x 5" format. The design didn't change over the years and unless a complete set is at hand, distinguishing the year of issue can be impossible. Cards have a photo surrounded with white borders. The bottom margin is extra wide and has the player name and team logotype centered between a pair of team logo shields. The unnumbered cards are checklisted here in alphabetical order.

		MT
Complete Set (35):		15.00
Common Player:		.50
(1)	Willie Aikens	.65
(2)	Mike Armstrong	.50
(3)	Bud Black	.50
(4)	Vida Blue	.65
(5)	Cloyd Boyer	.50
(6)	George Brett	5.00
(7)	Bill Castro	.50
(8)	Rocky Colavito	4.00
(9)	Onix Concepcion	.50
(10)	Keith Creel	.50
(11)	Cesar Geronimo	.50
(12)	Larry Gura	.50
(13)	Don Hood	.50
(14)	Dick Howser	.50
(15)	Ron Johnson	.50
(16)	Dennis Leonard	.50
(17)	Jose Martinez	.50
(18)	Jerry Martin	.50
(19)	Hal McRae	.75
(20)	Joe Nossek	.50
(21)	Amos Otis	.65
(22)	Greg Pryor	.50
(23)	Dan Quisenberry	.75
(24)	Steve Renko	.50
(25)	Leon Roberts	.50
(26)	Jim Schaffer	.50
(27)	John Schuerholz (gm)	.50
(28)	Joe Simpson	.50
(29)	Don Slaught	.65
(30)	Paul Splittorff	.50
(31)	Bob Tufts	.50
(32)	U.L. Washington	.60
(33)	John Wathan	.50
(34)	Frank White	.65
(35)	Willie Wilson	1.00

1983 Kansas City Royals Police

After skipping the 1982 season, the Ft. Myers, Fla., police department issued a Royals safety set in 1983 that is almost identical to their 1981 set. Cards are again 2-1/2" x 4-1/8" and include just 10 players. Cards are unnumbered, with vertical fronts and horizontal backs. Fronts have team logos, player name and position and facsimile autographs. Backs list the four sponsoring organizations, a "Tip from the Royals" and a "Kids and Cops Fact" about each player.

		MT
Complete Set (10):		30.00
Common Player:		1.00
(1)	Willie Mays Aikens	2.00
(2)	George Brett	18.00
(3)	Dennis Leonard	1.00
(4)	Hal McRae	2.00
(5)	Amos Otis	2.00
(6)	Dan Quisenberry	2.50
(7)	U.L. Washington	1.00
(8)	John Wathan	1.00
(9)	Frank White	1.50
(10)	Willie Wilson	3.00

1984 Kansas City Royals Photocards

These team-issued photocards feature black-and-white posed portrait photos with white borders in a 3-1/4" x 5" format. In the wide bottom border the player's name and team logotype are centered and flanked by team logos. Backs are blank. The unnumbered cards are checklisted here in alphabetical order.

		MT
Complete Set (37):		15.00
Common Player:		.50
(1)	Steve Balboni	.50
(2)	Howie Bedell	.50
(3)	Joe Beckwith	.50
(4)	Buddy Biancalana	.50
(5)	Bud Black	.50
(6)	Gary Blaylock	.50
(7)	George Brett	5.00
(8)	Onix Concepcion	.50
(9)	Butch Davis	.50
(10)	Mike Ferraro	.50
(11)	Mark Gubicza	1.00
(12)	Larry Gura	.50
(13)	Dick Howser	.50
(14)	Mark Huismann	.50
(15)	Dane Iorg	.50
(16)	Danny Jackson	.65
(17)	Lynn Jones	.50
(18)	Charlie Leibrandt	.60
(19)	Dennis Leonard	.50
(20)	Jose Martinez	.50
(21)	Lee May	.50
(22)	Hal McRae	.75
(23)	Darryl Motley	.50
(24)	Jorge Orta	.65
(25)	Greg Pryor	.50
(26)	Dan Quisenberry	.75
(27)	Leon Roberts	.50
(28)	Bret Saberhagen	1.50
(29)	Jim Schaffer	.50
(30)	John Schuerholz (gm)	.50
(31)	Pat Sheridan	.50
(32)	Don Slaught	.65
(33)	Paul Splittorff	.50
(34)	U.L. Washington	.60
(35)	John Wathan	.50
(36)	Frank White	.65
(37)	Willie Wilson	1.00

1985 Kansas City Royals Photocards

These team-issued photocards feature black-and-white chest-to-cap portrait photos with white borders in a 3-1/2" x 5" format. In the wide bottom border the player's name and team logotype are centered and flanked by team logos. Backs are blank. The unnumbered cards are checklisted here in alphabetical order.

		MT
Complete Set (33):		20.00
Common Player:		1.00
(1)_	Steve Balboni	1.00
(2)	Joe Beckwith	1.00
(3)	Buddy Biancalana	1.00
(4)	Bud Black	1.00
(5)	Gary Blaylock	1.00
(6)	George Brett	6.00
(7)	Onix Concepcion	1.00
(8)	Mike Ferraro	1.00
(9)	Mark Gubicza	1.50
(10)	Larry Gura	1.00
(11)	Dick Howser	1.25
(12)	Dane Iorg	1.00
(13)	Danny Jackson	1.00
(14)	Lynn Jones	1.00
(15)	Mike Jones	1.00
(16)	Mike LaCoss	1.00
(17)	Charlie Leibrandt	1.00
(18)	Dennis Leonard	1.00
(19)	Jose Martinez	1.00
(20)	Lee May	1.00
(21)	Hal McRae	1.50
(22)	Darryl Motley	1.00
(23)	Jorge Orta	1.00
(24)	Dan Quisenberry	1.50
(25)	Greg Pryor	1.00
(26)	Bret Saberhagen	2.50
(27)	Jim Schaffer	1.00
(28)	John Schuerholz (gm)	1.00
(29)	Pat Sheridan	1.00
(30)	Jim Sundberg	1.00
(31)	John Wathan	1.00
(32)	Frank White	1.50
(33)	Willie Wilson	2.50

1986 Kansas City Royals Photocards

Identical in format to sets issued in other years throughout the 1980s, these team-issued black-and-white cards measure about 3-1/4" x 5". Posed player photos are bordered in white with a wider bottom margin that has the players name and team logotype centered between a pair of team logos. Backs are blank. The unnumbered cards are checklisted here in alphabetical order.

		MT
Complete Set (27):		15.00
Common Player:		.50
(1)	Steve Balboni	.50
(2)	Scott Bankhead	.50
(3)	Buddy Biancalana	.50
(4)	Bud Black	.50
(5)	George Brett	4.00
(6)	David Cone	2.50
(7)	Steve Farr	.50
(8)	Mark Gubicza	.75
(9)	Dick Howser	.50
(10)	Danny Jackson	.50
(11)	Lynn Jones	.50
(12)	Mike Kingery	.50
(13)	Rudy Law	.50
(14)	Charlie Leibrandt	.50
(15)	Dennis Leonard	.50
(16)	Hal McRae	.65
(17)	Darryl Motley	.50
(18)	Jorge Orta	.50
(19)	Greg Pryor	.50
(20)	Jamie Quirk	.50
(21)	Dan Quisenberry	.65
(22)	Bret Saberhagen	1.50
(23)	Angel Salazar	.50
(24)	Lonnie Smith	.50
(25)	Jim Sundberg	.50
(26)	Frank White	.75
(27)	Willie Wilson	1.00

1988 Kansas City Royals Fire Safety

This set featuring full-color player caricatures by K.K. Goodale was produced for an in-stadium promotion Aug. 14. The 3" x 5" cards depict players, manager and coaches in action poses against a white background with a Royals logo at upper-left, opposite the Smokey Bear logo. Backs are black-and-white and contain brief player data and a Smokey cartoon.

		MT
Complete Set (28):		9.00
Common Player:		.25
1	John Wathan	.25
2	Coaches (Frank Funk, Adrian Garrett, Mike Lum, Ed Napolean, Bob Schaefer, Jim Schaefer)	.25
3	Willie Wilson	.35
4	Danny Tartabull	.25
5	Bo Jackson	1.50
6	Gary Thurman	.25
7	Jerry Don Gleaton	.25
8	Floyd Bannister	.25
9	Buddy Black	.25
10	Steve Farr	.25
11	Gene Garber	.25
12	Mark Gubicza	.30
13	Charlie Liebrandt	.25
14	Ted Power	.25
15	Dan Quisenberry	.30
16	Bret Saberhagen	.50
17	Mike Macfarlane	.25
18	Scotti Madison	.25
19	Jamie Quirk	.25
20	George Brett	5.00
21	Kevin Seitzer	.25
22	Bill Pecota	.25
23	Kurt Stillwell	.25
24	Brad Wellman	.25
25	Frank White	.25
26	Jim Eisenreich	.25
27	Smokey Bear	.10
---	Checklist	.10

1988 Kansas City Royals Photocards

These team-issued photocards feature black-and-white chest-to-cap portrait photos with white borders in a 3-1/2" x 5" format. In the wide bottom border the player's name and team logotype are centered and flanked by team logos. Backs are blank. The unnumbered cards are checklisted here in alphabetical order.

		MT
Complete Set (38):		12.50
Common Player:		.50
(1)	Rick Anderson	.50
(2)	Steve Balboni	.50
(3)	Floyd Bannister	.50
(4)	Bud Black	.50
(5)	Thad Bosley	.50
(6)	George Brett	3.00
(7)	Bill Buckner	.75
(8)	Jim Eisenreich	.50
(9)	Steve Farr	.50
(10)	Frank Funk	.50
(11)	Gene Garber	.50
(12)	Adrian Garrett	.50
(13)	Jerry Don Gleaton	.50
(14)	Mark Gubicza	.60
(15)	Ed Hearn	.50
(16)	Bo Jackson	2.00
(17)	Charlie Leibrandt	.50
(18)	Mike Lum	.50
(19)	Mike Macfarlane	.50
(20)	Jeff Montgomery	.50
(21)	Ed Napoleon	.50
(22)	Larry Owen	.50
(23)	Bill Pecota	.50
(24)	Ted Power	.50
(25)	Jamie Quirk	.50
(26)	Dan Quisenberry	.75
(27)	Bret Saberhagen	1.25
(28)	Bob Schaefer	.50
(29)	Jim Schaffer	.50
(30)	Kevin Seitzer	.50
(31)	Kurt Stillwell	.50
(32)	Pat Tabler	.50
(33)	Danny Tartabull	.50
(34)	Gary Thurman	.50
(35)	John Wathan	.50
(36)	Brad Wellman	.50
(37)	Frank White	.50
(38)	Willie Wilson	1.00

1989 Kansas City Royals Photocards

This set of player and staff photocards was offered at Royals' souvenir outlets for $2. The 3-1/4" x 5" blank-back cards have a semi-gloss front finish and generally feature portrait poses (some of the pictures are reused from previous years' issues). Player names appear below the photo, with team name and logos at bottom. The unnumbered cards are checklisted here in alphabetical order.

		MT
Complete Set (35):		7.00
Common Player:		.25
(1)	Kevin Appier	.45
(2)	Luis Aquino	.25
(3)	Floyd Bannister	.25
(4)	Buddy Biancalana	.25
(5)	Bob Boone	.35
(6)	George Brett	3.00
(7)	Bill Buckner	.25
(8)	Luis de los Santos	.25
(9)	Jim Eisenreich	.25
(10)	Glenn Ezell	.25
(11)	Steve Farr	.25
(12)	Frank Funk	.25
(13)	Adrian Garrett	.25
(14)	Jerry Don Gleaton	.25
(15)	Tom Gordon	.40
(16)	Mark Gubicza	.45
(17)	Bo Jackson	.50
(18)	Charlie Leibrandt	.25
(19)	Mike Lum	.25
(20)	Mike Macfarlane	.25
(21)	John Mayberry	.25
(22)	Jeff Montgomery	.25
(23)	Rey Palacios	.25
(24)	Bill Pecota	.25
(25)	Bret Saberhagen	.50
(26)	Kevin Seitzer	.25
(27)	Bob Shaeffer	.25
(28)	Kurt Stillwell	.25
(29)	Pat Tabler	.25
(30)	Danny Tartabull	.25
(31)	Gary Thurman	.25
(32)	John Wathan	.25
(33)	Brad Wellman	.25
(34)	Frank White	.25
(35)	Willie Wilson	.40

1991 Kansas City Royals Police

Bo Jackson's release by the Royals in spring training caused his card to be withdrawn from distribution with the other 26 cards in this set. The 2-5/8" x 4-1/8" cards feature a color action photo on front, with the team name in royal blue and the player name and uniform number in black in the bottom border. Backs are printed in blue on white and feature a large cartoon safety message at center, career stats and bio at top, and the logos of the set's sponsors, Kansas City Life Insurance Co., and the Metro Chiefs and Sheriffs Assn., at bottom. Complete sets were distributed in a white paper envelope with team and sponsor logos.

		MT
Complete Set (28) (w/Bo Jackson):		8.00
Complete Set (27) (no Bo Jackson):		5.00
Common Player:		.10
1	Kurt Stillwell	.10
3	Terry Shumpert	.10
4	Danny Tartabull	.10
5	George Brett	2.00
8	Jim Eisenreich	.10
12	John Wathan	.10
14	Storm Davis	.10
15	Mike MacFarlane	.10
16	Bo Jackson	4.00
18	Bret Saberhagen	.25
21	Jeff Montgomery	.10
23	Mark Gubicza	.15
25	Gary Thurman	.10
27	Luis Aquino	.10
28	Steve Crawford	.10
30	Kirk Gibson	.15
32	Bill Pecota	.10
33	Kevin Seitzer	.10
36	Tom Gordon	.15
38	Andy McGaffigan	.10
48	Mark Davis	.10
52	Mike Boddicker	.10
55	Kevin Appier	.15
56	Brian McRae	.40
---	Royals coaches (Pat Dobson, Adrian Garrett)	.10
---	Royals coaches (Glenn Ezell, Lynn Jones, Bob Schaefer)	.10
---	Header card - Royals Stadium	.10

1992 Kansas City Royals Police

Sponsored by K.C. Life Insurance and distributed by the Metropolitan Chiefs and Sheriffs Association, this 27-card set was distributed at a promotional game. Though they are checklisted, it is rumored that the cards of Kevin Seitzer (traded) and Kirk Gibson (released) were withdrawn early in the promotion, though both names appear on the checklist. The cards are numbered to match the player's uniform numbers. Cards are in the popular police-set format of 2-5/8" x 4-1/8" with white borders around color action photos. Backs have player data, stats, a fire safety message and sponsor's information.

		MT
Complete Set (27):		6.00
Common Player:		.25
2	Bob Melvin	.25
3	Terry Shumpert	.25
5	George Brett	1.50
8	Jim Eisenreich	.25
9	Gregg Jefferies	.50
11	Hal McRae	.35
12	Wally Joyner	.40
13	David Howard	.25
15	Mike McFarlane	.25
16	Keith Miller	.25
21	Jeff Montgomery	.25
22	Kevin McReynolds	.25
23	Mark Gubicza	.30
24	Brent Mayne	.25
25	Gary Thomas	.25
27	Luis Aquino	.25
29	Chris Gwynn	.25
30	Kirk Gibson	.50
33	Kevin Seitzer	.25
36	Tom Gordon	.30
37	Joel Johnson	.25
48	Mark Davis	.25
52	Mike Boddicker	.25
55	Kevin Appier	.30
56	Brian McRae	.40
57	Mike Magnante	.25
---	Coaches (Glenn Ezell, Adrian Garrett, Guy Hansen, Lynn Jones, Bruce Kison, Lee May)	.25

1993 Kansas City Royals Police

One of the longest-running police/fire safety issues continued in 1993 with a set marking the team's 25th anniversary season. The 2-5/8" x 4" cards have a light blue border, a color photo at center, an anniversary logo at lower-left and the player's name, position and uniform number at lower-right. All typography is in royal blue. Backs are printed in blue on white and feature career stats and highlights, a few biographical notes and a large safety message. Logos of the set's sponsors, Kansas City Life Insurance and the Metro Police Chiefs and Sheriffs Assn. are featured at bottom.

		MT
Complete Set (27):		5.00
Common Player:		.15
5	George Brett	1.50
7	Greg Gagne	.15
9	Craig Wilson	.15
11	Hal McRae	.15
12	Wally Joyner	.25
13	Jose Lind	.15
14	Chris Gwynn	.15
15	Mike MacFarlane	.15
16	Keith Miller	.15
17	David Cone	.40
19	Curtis Wilkerson	.15
21	Jeff Montgomery	.15
22	Kevin McReynolds	.15
23	Mark Gubicza	.20
24	Brent Mayne	.15
27	Luis Aquino	.15
28	Rusty Meacham	.15
33	Chris Haney	.15
34	Felix Jose	.15
35	Hipolito Pichardo	.15
36	Tom Gordon	.20
37	Mark Gardner	.15
40	Kevin Koslofski	.15
52	Mike Boddicker	.15
55	Kevin Appier	.20
56	Brian McRae	.30
---	Royals coaches (Steve Boros, Glenn Ezell, Guy Hansen, Bruce Kison, Lee May)	.15

1995 Kansas City Royals Police

In 1995, the Royals safety set was sponsored by Kansas City Life Insurance Co., and distributed by law enforcement agencies in the greater Kansas City area. The cards measure about 2-5/8" x 4" and feature action photos on front. The team name is scripted at bottom with logo and the player's last name and "1995" are vertically at right. Backs have a few vital data, a career stats line, a safety message and sponsor's logo. Cards are listed here in alphabetical order.

		MT
Complete Set (12):		6.00
Common Player:		.50
(1)	Kevin Appier	.65
(2)	Bob Boone	.65
(3)	Vince Coleman	.50
(4)	Gary Gaetti	.50
(5)	Greg Gagne	.50
(6)	Tom Gordon	.65
(7)	Mark Gubicza	.65
(8)	Chris Haney	.50
(9)	Wally Joyner	.65
(10)	Brent Mayne	.50
(11)	Jeff Montgomery	.50
(12)	Hipolito Pichardo	.50

1996 Kansas City Royals Police

In 1996 the Royals returned to safety set issue with this 27-card presentation given to fans 14 and under at the April 20 game. The 2-5/8" x 4" cards have game-action color photo bordered in white. Backs are in blue on white with a few personal data, career highlights and record, a cartoon safety message and the logo of sponsoring Kansas City Life Insurance, which provided the cards for distribution by the Metropolitan Chiefs and Sheriffs Assn. Cards are checklisted here by uniform number.

		MT
Complete Set (27):		8.00
Common Player:		.25
1	Bip Roberts	.25
3	Bob Hamelin	.25
4	Keith Lockhart	.40
6	David Howard	.25
8	Bob Boone	.35
15	Mike Macfarlane	.25
16	Joe Randa	.40
17	Kevin Appier	.35
18	Johnny Damon	1.00
21	Jeff Montgomery	.25
22	Jon Nunnally	.40
23	Mark Gubicza	.35
24	Terry Clark	.25
25	Les Norman	.25
28	Rusty Meacham	.25
30	Jose Offerman	.25
31	Michael Tucker	.65
33	Chris Haney	.25
35	Hipolito Pichardo	.25
37	Rick Huisman	.25
38	Jim Converse	.25
41	Tim Belcher	.25
42	Tom Goodwin	.25
44	Joe Vitiello	.40
45	Jason Jacome	.25
50	Melvin Bunch	.25
57	Mike Magnante	.25

1998 Kansas City Royals Police

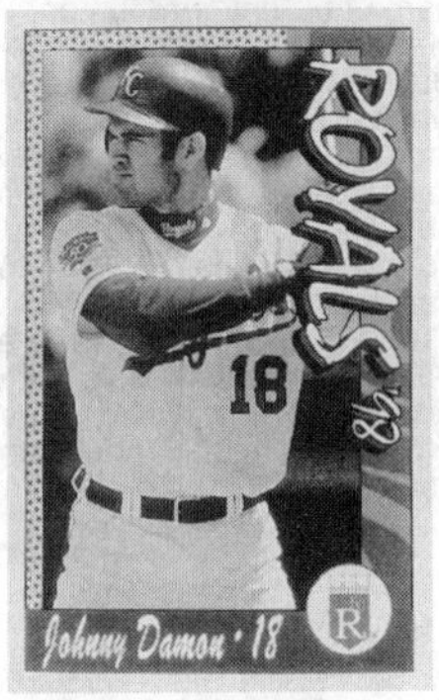

In 1998 the Royals issued this safety set to fans 14 and under at a promotional game. The 2-5/8" x 4" cards have game-action color photo bordered in white. Backs are in blue on white with a few bits of personal data, a cartoon safety message and the logo of sponsoring Kansas City Life Insurance, which provided the cards for distribution by the Metropolitan Chiefs and Sheriffs Assn. Cards are checklisted here by uniform number.

		MT
Complete Set (26):		8.00
Common Player:		.25
2	Jed Hansen	.50
4	Shane Halter	.50
7	Jeff King	.50
14	Felix Martinez	.35
15	Mike Macfarlane	.25
16	Dean Palmer	.25
17	Kevin Appier	.35
18	Johnny Damon	.50
19	Jeff Conine	.50
21	Jeff Montgomery	.25
22	Larry Sutton	.25
23	Hal Morris	.25
24	Jermaine Dye	.25
27	Joe Vitiello	.25
29	Mike Sweeney	.35
30	Jose Offerman	.35
33	Chris Haney	.25
35	Hipolito Pichardo	.25
40	Tony Muser	.25
41	Tim Belcher	.25
43	Roderick Myers	.25
47	Brian Bevil	.25
50	Jose Rosado	.25
53	Glendon Rusch	.25
56	Matt Whisenant	.25
	Sluggerrr (mascot)	.25

1993 Kansas City Star Royals All-Time Team

On the occasion of the team's 25th anniversary the Kansas City Star newspaper issued a sheet honoring the All-Time Team. The 10-3/8" x 14-3/8" sheet is perforated to allow separation of the individual 2-1/2" x 3-1/2" cards. Fronts have color photos at center with royal blue borders at the sides and gold at top and bottom. A Royals 25th anniversary logo is at lower-right. Backs are printed in black and blue on white with a career summary and the player's K.C. stats. The unnumbered cards are checklisted here alphabetically.

		MT
Complete Set:		15.00
Complete Set (16):		12.00
Common Player:		.50
(1)	George Brett	8.00
(2)	Steve Busby	.50
(3)	Al Cowens	.50
(4)	Dick Howser	.50
(5)	Dennis Leonard	.50
(6)	John Mayberry	.50
(7)	Hal McRae	.75
(8)	Amos Otis	.50
(9)	Fred Patek	.50
(10)	Darrell Porter	.50
(11)	Dan Quisenberry	.60
(12)	Bret Saberhagen	2.50
(13)	Paul Splittorff	.50
(14)	Frank White	.75
(15)	Willie Wilson	1.00
(16)	25th Anniversary logo	.50

1985 Kas Potato Chips Discs

One of a pair of nearly identical (see Kitty Clover) sets issued by midwestern potato chip companies, this issue features top stars of the day on 2-3/4" cardboard discs. The discs have a player portrait at center, with uniform logos airbrushed away because the producer was licensed only by the MLB Players Association and not Major League Baseball. The player's name, team and position are printed in a white diamond around the photo. The sponsor's logo is in the orange border. Backs are in black-and-white and have a few biographical data, a 1984 stats line and a Snack Time logo. The unnumbered discs are checklisted here in alphabetical order. Square versions of the discs, which have been cut from press sheets are known within the hobby and carry a small premium. KAS was based in St. Louis.

		MT
Complete Set (20):		125.00
Common Player:		3.00
(1)	Steve Carlton	4.50
(2)	Jack Clark	3.00
(3)	Rich Gossage	3.00
(4)	Tony Gwynn	20.00
(5)	Bob Horner	3.00
(6)	Keith Hernandez	3.00
(7)	Kent Hrbek	3.00
(8)	Willie McGee	3.00
(9)	Dan Quisenberry	3.00
(10)	Cal Ripken Jr.	35.00
(11)	Ryne Sandberg	12.00
(12)	Mike Schmidt	20.00
(13)	Tom Seaver	12.00
(14)	Ozzie Smith	20.00
(15)	Rick Sutcliffe	3.00
(16)	Bruce Sutter	3.00
(17)	Alan Trammell	3.00
(18)	Fernando Valenzuela	3.00
(19)	Willie Wilson	3.00
(20)	Dave Winfield	9.00

1986 Kas Potato Chips Cardinals

One of several of 2-7/8" round baseball card discs created by Mike Schecter Associates for inclusion in packages of potato chips, the 20-card Kas set features players of the defending National League Champion St. Louis Cardinals. Fronts feature color photos on which the team logos have been removed from the caps by airbrushing the photos. uniform logos. Card backs have minimal personal data and 1985 stats.

		MT
Complete Set (20):		16.00
Common Player:		.75
1	Vince Coleman	1.00
2	Ken Dayley	.75
3	Tito Landrum	.75
4	Steve Braun	.75
5	Danny Cox	.75
6	Bob Forsch	.75
7	Ozzie Smith	5.00
8	Brian Harper	.75
9	Jack Clark	.75
10	Todd Worrell	.90
11	Joaquin Andujar	.75
12	Tom Nieto	.75
13	Kurt Kepshire	.75
14	Terry Pendleton	1.50
15	Tom Herr	.75
16	Darrell Porter	.75
17	John Tudor	.75
18	Jeff Lahti	.75
19	Andy Van Slyke	1.00
20	Willie McGee	1.50

1986 Kay Bee Young Superstars

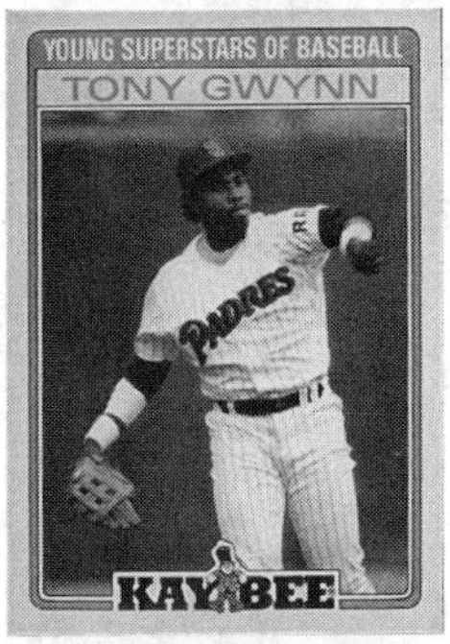

One of the most-widely distributed of the specialty boxed sets of 1986, the Kay Bee toy store chain set of "Young Superstars of Baseball" was produced by Topps. The 2-1/2" x 3-1/2" cards are printed on white stock with a glossy surface finish. Backs, printed in red and black, are strongly reminiscent of the 1971 Topps cards. While the set concentrated on "young" stars of the game, few of the year's top rookies were included.

		MT
Complete Set (33):		3.00
Common Player:		.05
1	Rick Aguilera	.05
2	Chris Brown	.05
3	Tom Browning	.05
4	Tom Brunansky	.05
5	Vince Coleman	.05
6	Ron Darling	.05
7	Alvin Davis	.05
8	Mariano Duncan	.05
9	Shawon Dunston	.05
10	Sid Fernandez	.05
11	Tony Fernandez	.05
12	Brian Fisher	.05
13	John Franco	.05
14	Julio Franco	.05
15	Dwight Gooden	.15
16	Ozzie Guillen	.05
17	Tony Gwynn	1.00
18	Jimmy Key	.05
19	Don Mattingly	1.00
20	Oddibe McDowell	.05
21	Roger McDowell	.05
22	Dan Pasqua	.05
23	Terry Pendleton	.05
24	Jim Presley	.05
25	Kirby Puckett	.75
26	Earnie Riles	.05
27	Bret Saberhagen	.10
28	Mark Salas	.05
29	Juan Samuel	.05
30	Jeff Stone	.05
31	Darryl Strawberry	.15
32	Andy Van Slyke	.05
33	Frank Viola	.05

1987 Kay Bee Superstars of Baseball

For a second year, Topps produced a boxed set for the Kay Bee toy store chain. Called "Superstars of Baseball," cards in the set measure 2-1/2" x 3-1/2". The glossy-coated fronts carry a color player photo plus the Kay Bee logo. Backs, reminiscent of those found in the 1971 Topps set, offer a black-and-white portrait of the player along with his name, postion, personal information, playing record and a brief biography.

		MT
Complete Set (33):		3.00
Common Player:		.05
1	Harold Baines	.10
2	Jesse Barfield	.05
3	Don Baylor	.05
4	Wade Boggs	.50
5	George Brett	1.00
6	Hubie Brooks	.05
7	Jose Canseco	.60
8	Gary Carter	.10
9	Joe Carter	.10
10	Roger Clemens	.65
11	Vince Coleman	.05
12	Glenn Davis	.05
13	Dwight Gooden	.10
14	Pedro Guerrero	.05
15	Tony Gwynn	1.00
16	Rickey Henderson	.15
17	Keith Hernandez	.05
18	Wally Joyner	.10
19	Don Mattingly	1.00
20	Jack Morris	.05
21	Dale Murphy	.10
22	Eddie Murray	.25
23	Dave Parker	.05
24	Kirby Puckett	.75
25	Tim Raines	.10
26	Jim Rice	.05
27	Dave Righetti	.05
28	Ryne Sandberg	.65
29	Mike Schmidt	.65
30	Mike Scott	.05
31	Darryl Strawberry	.10
32	Fernando Valenzuela	.05
33	Dave Winfield	.25

1988 Kay Bee Superstars of Baseball

This boxed set was produced by Topps for exclusive distribution via Kay Bee toy stores nationwide. Card fronts are super glossy and feature color player action photos below a bright red and yellow player name banner. Photos are framed in green above a large, cartoon-style Kay Bee logo. Backs feature player closeups in a horizontal layout in blue ink on a green and white background. Backs are numbered and carry biographical information, career data and major league batting stats.

		MT
Complete Set (33):		4.00
Common Player:		.10
1	George Bell	.10
2	Wade Boggs	.60
3	Jose Canseco	.60
4	Joe Carter	.10
5	Jack Clark	.10
6	Alvin Davis	.10
7	Eric Davis	.10
8	Andre Dawson	.10
9	Darrell Evans	.10
10	Dwight Evans	.10
11	Gary Gaetti	.10
12	Pedro Guerrero	.10
13	Tony Gwynn	.75
14	Howard Johnson	.10
15	Wally Joyner	.10
16	Don Mattingly	.90
17	Willie McGee	.10
18	Mark McGwire	2.00
19	Paul Molitor	.60
20	Dale Murphy	.15
21	Dave Parker	.10
22	Lance Parrish	.10
23	Kirby Puckett	.65
24	Tim Raines	.15
25	Cal Ripken, Jr.	1.00
26	Juan Samuel	.10
27	Mike Schmidt	.65
28	Ruben Sierra	.10
29	Darryl Strawberry	.15
30	Danny Tartabull	.10
31	Alan Trammell	.10
32	Tim Wallach	.10
33	Dave Winfield	.30

1988 Kay Bee Team Leaders

This boxed edition of 44 player and six team logo cards was produced by Fleer for distribution by Kay Bee toy stores nationwide. Color player photos are framed in black against a bright red border. "Fleer Team Leaders 1988" and Kay Bee logos appear on the front. Backs, (red, white and pink) repeat the Team Leaders logo, followed by stats, personal data, team and MLB logos. The player's name, card number and position are listed on the lower border. The set includes six team logo sticker cards that feature black-and-white stadium photos on the backs.

		MT
Complete Set (44):		4.00
Common Player:		.05
1	George Bell	.05
2	Wade Boggs	.60
3	Jose Canseco	.60
4	Will Clark	.50
5	Roger Clemens	.50
6	Eric Davis	.10
7	Andre Dawson	.15
8	Julio Franco	.10
9	Andres Galarraga	.15
10	Dwight Gooden	.10
11	Tony Gwynn	.50
12	Tom Henke	.05
13	Orel Hershiser	.05
14	Kent Hrbek	.10
15	Ted Higuera	.05
16	Wally Joyner	.10
17	Jimmy Key	.05
18	Mark Langston	.05
19	Don Mattingly	.90
20	Willie McGee	.10
21	Mark McGwire	2.00
22	Paul Molitor	.50
23	Jack Morris	.05
24	Dale Murphy	.10
25	Larry Parrish	.05
26	Kirby Puckett	.65
27	Tim Raines	.10
28	Jeff Reardon	.05
29	Dave Righetti	.05
30	Cal Ripken, Jr.	1.00
31	Don Robinson	.05
32	Bret Saberhagen	.05
33	Juan Samuel	.05
34	Mike Schmidt	.75
35	Mike Scott	.05
36	Kevin Seitzer	.05
37	Dave Smith	.05
38	Ozzie Smith	.50
39	Zane Smith	.05
40	Darryl Strawberry	.15
41	Rick Sutcliffe	.05
42	Bobby Thigpen	.05
43	Alan Trammell	.10
44	Andy Van Slyke	.05

1989 Kay Bee Superstars of Baseball

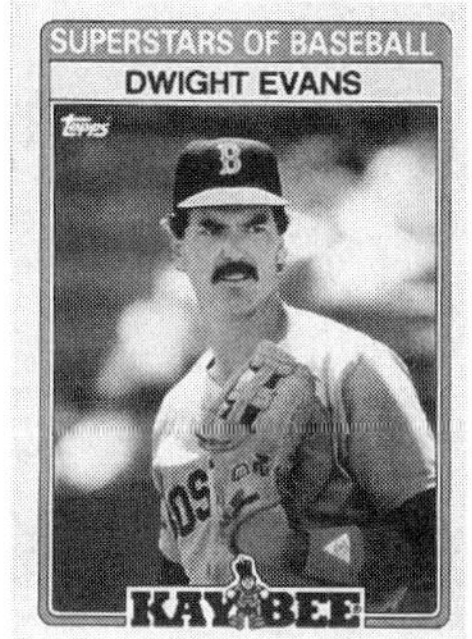

The top stars of baseball are featured in this boxed set produced by Topps for the Kay Bee Toy store chain. The glossy, standard-size cards display the Kay Bee logo below the player photo on the front. The top of the card is headlined "Superstars of Baseball," with the player's name underneath. Backs include a small black-and-white player photo and personal data.

		MT
Complete Set (33):		4.00
Common Player:		.10
1	Wade Boggs	.60
2	George Brett	.75
3	Jose Canseco	.60
4	Gary Carter	.15
5	Jack Clark	.10
6	Will Clark	.50
7	Roger Clemens	.60
8	Eric Davis	.10
9	Andre Dawson	.15
10	Dwight Evans	.10
11	Carlton Fisk	.25
12	Andres Galarraga	.15
13	Kirk Gibson	.10
14	Dwight Gooden	.15
15	Mike Greenwell	.10
16	Pedro Guerrero	.10
17	Tony Gwynn	.75
18	Rickey Henderson	.25
19	Orel Hershiser	.10
20	Don Mattingly	.90
21	Mark McGwire	2.00
22	Dale Murphy	.15
23	Eddie Murray	.25
24	Kirby Puckett	.75
25	Tim Raines	.15
26	Ryne Sandberg	.60
27	Mike Schmidt	.60
28	Ozzie Smith	.60
29	Darryl Strawberry	.15
30	Alan Trammell	.10
31	Frank Viola	.10
32	Dave Winfield	.25
33	Robin Yount	.50

1990 Kay Bee Kings

This boxed set was the fifth annual issue produced by Topps for the Kay Bee toy store chain. The 2-1/2" x 3-1/2" cards feature color action photos on the front and complete statistics on the flip sides. The cards are numbered alphabetically.

		MT
Complete Set (33):		4.00
Common Player:		.10
1	Doyle Alexander	.10
2	Bert Blyleven	.10
3	Wade Boggs	.50
4	George Brett	.75
5	John Candelaria	.10
6	Gary Carter	.15
7	Vince Coleman	.10
8	Andre Dawson	.15
9	Dennis Eckersley	.10
10	Darrell Evans	.10
11	Dwight Evans	.10
12	Carlton Fisk	.25
13	Ken Griffey	.10
14	Tony Gwynn	.75
15	Rickey Henderson	.25
16	Keith Hernandez	.10
17	Charlie Hough	.10
18	Don Mattingly	.75
19	Jack Morris	.10
20	Dale Murphy	.15
21	Eddie Murray	.25
22	Dave Parker	.10
23	Kirby Puckett	.65
24	Tim Raines	.15
25	Rick Reuschel	.10
26	Jerry Reuss	.10
27	Jim Rice	.10
28	Nolan Ryan	1.00
29	Ozzie Smith	.65
30	Frank Tanana	.10
31	Willie Wilson	.10
32	Dave Winfield	.25
33	Robin Yount	.50

1993 Keebler Texas Rangers

Over a series of eight home dates in Arlington Stadium's final season, the Keebler baking company along with a group of rotating co-sponsors produced and distributed a team set featuring "all players, manager and coaches who have ever appeared in a Rangers game." Besides the player cards there were checklists, team photo cards, team-leader cards, logo cards and other specials. The cards were made up into 8-1/2" x 11" booklets, with the cards perforated for removal. Series 2 and 3 booklets had 72 cards; the other series had 54 cards each. Single cards measure 2-1/2" x 3-1/2". Sepia-toned player portraits are featured with red frames. A blue banner at top has the team name. The player name is printed in black in the white bottom border. The Keebler logo is at the photo's lower-left, while the player's position is in a baseball diamond diagram at lower-right. Backs are printed in black, include a few biographical details and the player's Rangers' and major league career stats. The Keebler logo is repreated on the back, along with the logo of the co-sponsor of that particular series. A total of 42,000 of the first series booklets were distributed; 35,000 each of the other seven series were produced.

		MT
Complete Set (468):		35.00
Common Player:		.10
1	Ted Williams	4.00
2	Larry Biitner	.10
3	Rich Billings	.10
4	Dick Bosman	.10
5	Pete Broberg	.10
6	Jeff Burroughs	.10
7	Casey Cox	.10
8	Jim Drixcoll	.10
9	Jan Dukes	.10
10	Bill Fahey	.10
11	Ted Ford	.10
12	Bill Gogolewski	.10
13	Tom Grieve	.10
14	Rich Hand	.10
15	Toby Harrah	.15
16	Vic Harris	.10
17	Rich Hinton	.10
18	Frank Howard	.15
19	Gerry Janeski	.10
20	Dalton Jones	.10
21	Hal King	.10
22	Ted Kubiak	.10
23	Steve Lawson	.10
24	Paul Lindblad	.10
25	Joe Lovitto	.10
26	Elliott Maddox	.10
27	Marty Martinez	.10
28	Jim Mason	.10
29	Don Mincher	.10
30	Dave Nelson	.10
31	Jim Panther	.10
32	Mike Paul	.10
33	Horacio Pina	.10
34	Tom Ragland	.10
35	Lenny Randle	.10
36	Jim Roland	.10
37	Jim Shellenback	.10
38	Don Stanhouse	.10
39	Ken Suarez	.10
40	Joe Camacho	.10
41	Nellie Fox	1.00
42	Sid Hudson	.10
43	George Susce	.10
44	Wayne Terwilliger	.10
45	Darrel Akerfelds	.10
46	Doyle Alexander	.10
47	Gerald Alexander	.10
48	Brian Allard	.10
49	Lloyd Allen	.10
50	Sandy Alomar	.10
51	Wilson Alvarez	.10
52	Jim Anderson	.10
53	Scott Anderson	.10
54	Brad Arnsberg	.10
55	Tucker Ashford	.10
56	Doug Ault	.10
57	Bob Babcock	.10
58	Mike Bacsik	.10
59	Harold Baines	.15
60	Alan Bannister	.10
61	Floyd Bannister	.10
62	John Barfield	.10
63	Len Barker	.10
64	Steve Barr	.10
65	Randy Bass	.10
66	Lew Beasley	.10
67	Kevin Belcher	.10
68	Buddy Bell	.10
69	Juan Beniquez	.10
70	Kurt Bevacqua	.10
71	Jim Bibby	.10
72	Joe Bitker	.10
73	Larvell Blanks	.10
74	Bert Blyleven	.25
75	Terry Bogener	.10
76	Tommy Boggs	.10
77	Dan Boitano	.10
78	Bobby Bonds	.25
79	Thad Bosley	.10
80	Dennis Boyd	.10
81	Nelson Briles	.10
82	Ed Brinkman	.10
83	Bob Brower	.10
84	Jackie Brown	.10
85	Larry Brown	.10
86	Jerry Browne	.10
87	Glenn Brummer	.10
88	Kevin Buckley	.10
89	Steve Buechele	.10
90	Ray Burris	.10

91 John Butcher .10
92 Bert Campaneris .10
93 Mike Campbell .10
94 John Cangelosi .10
95 Nick Capra .10
96 Leo Cardenas .10
97 Don Carman .10
98 Rico Carty .10
99 Don Castle .10
100 Jose Cecena .10
101 Dave Chalk .10
102 Scott Chiamparino .10
103 Ken Clay .10
104 Reggie Cleveland .10
105 Gene Clines .10
106 David Clyde .10
107 Cris Colon .10
108 Merrill Combs .10
109 Steve Comer .10
110 Glen Cook .10
111 Scott Coolbaugh .10
112 Pat Corrales .10
113 Edwin Correa .10
114 Larry Cox .10
115 Keith Creel .10
116 Victor Cruz .10
117 Mike Cubbage .10
118 Bobby Cuellar .10
119 Danny Darwin .10
120 Jack Daugherty .10
121 Doug Davis .10
122 Odie Davis .10
123 Willie Davis .10
124 Bucky Dent .10
125 Adrian Devine .10
126 Mario Diaz .10
127 Rich Donnelly .10
128 Brian Downing .10
129 Tommy Dunbar .10
130 Steve Dunning .10
131 Dan Duran .10
132 Don Durham .10
133 Dick Egan .10
134 Dock Ellis .10
135 John Ellis .10
136 Mike Epstein .10
137 Cecil Espy .10
138 Chuck Estrada .10
139 Glenn Ezell .10
140 Hector Fajardo .10
141 Monty Fariss .10
142 Ed Farmer .10
143 Jim Farr .10
144 Joe Ferguson .10
145 Ed Figueroa .10
146 Steve Fireovid .10
147 Scott Fletcher .10
148 Doug Flynn .10
149 Marv Foley .10
150 Tim Foli .10
151 Tony Fossas .10
152 Steve Foucault .10
153 Art Fowler .10
154 Jim Fregosi .10
155 Pepe Frias .10
156 Oscar Gamble .10
157 Barbaro Garbey .10
158 Dick Gernert .10
159 Jim Gideon .10
160 Jerry Don Gleaton .10
161 Orlando Gomez .10
162 Rich Gossage .15
163 Gary Gray .10
164 Gary Green .10
165 John Grubb .10
166 Cecilio Guante .10
167 Jose Guzman .10
168 Drew Hall .10
169 Bill Hands .10
170 Steve Hargan .10
171 Mike Hargrove .10
172 Toby Harrah .10
173 Bud Harrelson .10
174 Donald Harris .10
175 Greg Harris .10
176 Mike Hart .10
177 Bill Haselman .10
178 Ray Hayward .10
179 Tommy Helms .10
180 Ken Henderson .10
181 Rick Henninger .10
182 Dwayne Henry .10
183 Jose Hernandez .10
184 Whitey Herzog .10
185 Chuck Hiller .10
186 Joe Hoerner .10
187 Guy Hoffman .10
188 Gary Holle .10
189 Rick Honeycutt .10
190 Burt Hooton .10
191 John Hoover .10
192 Willie Horton .10
193 Dave Hostetler .10
194 Charlie Hough .10
195 Tom House .10
196 Art Howe .10
197 Steve Howe .10
198 Roy Howell .10
199 Charles Hudson .10
200 Billy Hunter .10
201 Pete Incaviglia .15
202 Mike Jeffcoat .10
203 Ferguson Jenkins .50
204 Alex Johnson .10
205 Bobby Johnson .10
206 Cliff Johnson .10
207 Darrell Johnson .10
208 John Henry Johnson .10
209 Lamar Johnson .10
210 Bobby Jones .10
211 Odell Jones .10
212 Mike Jorgensen .10
213 Don Kainer .10
214 Mike Kekich .10
215 Steve Kemp .10
216 Jim Kern .10
217 Paul Kilgus .10
218 Ed Kirkpatrick .10
219 Darold Knowles .10
220 Fred Koenig .10
221 Jim Kremmel .10
222 Chad Kreuter .10
223 Jeff Kunkel .10
224 Bob Lacey .10
225 Al Lachowicz .10
226 Joe Lahoud .10
227 Rick Leach .10
228 Danny Leon .10
229 Dennis Lewallyn .10
230 Rick Lisi .10
231 Davey Lopes .10
232 John Lowenstein .10
233 Mike Loynd .10
234 Frank Lucceshi .10
235 Sparky Lyle .10
236 Pete Mackanin .10
237 Bill Madlock .15
238 Greg Mahlberg .10
239 Mickey Mahler .10
240 Bob Malloy .10
241 Ramon Manon .10
242 Fred Manrique .10
243 Barry Manuel .10
244 Mike Marshall .10
245 Billy Martin .35
246 Mike Mason .10
247 Terry Mathews .10
248 Jon Matlack .10
249 Rob Maurer .10
250 Dave May .10
251 Scott May .10
252 Lee Mazzilli .10
253 Larry McCall .10
254 Lance McCullers .10
255 Oddibe McDowell .10
256 Russ McGinnis .10
257 Joey McLaughlin .10
258 Craig McMurtry .10
259 Doc Medich .10
260 Dave Meier .10
261 Mario Mendoza .10
262 Orlando Mercado .10
263 Mark Mercer .10
264 Ron Meridith .10
265 Jim Merritt .10
266 Gary Mielke .10
267 Eddie Miller .10
268 Paul Mirabella .10
269 Dave Moates .10
270 Dale Mohorcic .10
271 Willie Montanez .10
272 Tommy Moore .10
273 Roger Moret .10
274 Jamie Moyer .10
275 Dale Murray .10
276 Al Newman .10
277 Dickie Noles .10
278 Eric Nolte .10
279 Nelson Norman .10
280 Jim Norris .10
281 Edwin Nunez .10
282 Pete O'Brien .10
283 Al Oliver .15
284 Tom O'Malley .10
285 Tom Paciorek .10
286 Ken Pape .10
287 Mark Parent .10
288 Larry Parrish .10
289 Gaylord Perry .50
290 Stan Perzanowski .10
291 Fritz Peterson .10
292 Mark Petkovsek .10
293 Gary Pettis .10
294 Jim Piersall .20
295 John Poloni .10
296 Jim Poole .10
297 Tom Poquette .10
298 Darrell Porter .10
299 Ron Pruitt .10
300 Greg Pryor .10
301 Luis Pujols .10
302 Pat Putnam .10
303 Doug Rader .10
304 Dave Rajsich .10
305 Kevin Reimer .10
306 Merv Rettenmund .10
307 Mike Richardt .10
308 Mickey Rivers .10
309 Dave Roberts .10
310 Leon Roberts .10
311 Jeff Robinson .10
312 Tom Robson .10
313 Wayne Rosenthal .10
314 Dave Rozema .10
315 Jeff Russell .10
316 Connie Ryan .10
317 Billy Sample .10
318 Jim Schaffer .10
319 Calvin Schiraldi .10
320 Dave Schmidt .10
321 Donnie Scott .10
322 Tony Scruggs .10
323 Bob Sebra .10
324 Larry See .10
325 Sonny Siebert .10
326 Ruben Sierra .10
327 Charlie Silvera .10
328 Duke Sims .10
329 Bill Singer .10
330 Craig Skok .10
331 Don Slaught .10
332 Roy Smalley .10
333 Dan Smith .10
334 Keith Smith .10
335 Mike Smithson .10
336 Eric Soderholm .10
337 Sammy Sosa 3.00
338 Jim Spencer .10
339 Dick Such .10
340 Eddie Stanky .10
341 Mike Stanley .10
342 Rusty Staub .20
343 James Steels .10
344 Bill Stein .10
345 Rick Stelmaszek .10
346 Ray Stephens .10
347 Dave Stewart .10
348 Jeff Stone .10
349 Bill Sudakis .10
350 Jim Sundberg .10
351 Rich Surhoff .10
352 Greg Tabor .10
353 Frank Tanana .10
354 Jeff Terpko .10
355 Stan Thomas .10
356 Bobby Thompson .10
357 Danny Thompson .10
358 Dickie Thon .10
359 Dave Tobik .10
360 Wayne Tolleson .10
361 Cesar Tovar .10
362 Jim Umbarger .10
363 Bobby Valentine .10
364 Ellis Valentine .10
365 Ed Vande Berg .10
366 Dewayne Vaughn .10
367 Mark Wagner .10
368 Rick Waits .10
369 Duane Walker .10
370 Mike Wallace .10
371 Denny Walling .10
372 Danny Walton .10
373 Gary Ward .10
374 Claudell Washington .10
375 Larue Wasington .10
376 Chris Welsh .10
377 Don Werner .10
378 Len Whitehouse .10
379 Del Wilber .10
380 Curtis Wilkerson .10
381 Matt Williams .10
382 Mitch Williams .10
383 Bump Wills .10
384 Paul Wilmet .10
385 Steve Wilson .10
386 Bobby Witt .10
387 Clyde Wright .10
388 George Wright .10
389 Ricky Wright .10
390 Ned Yost .10
391 Don Zimmer .10
392 Richie Zisk .10
393 Kevin Kennedy .10
394 Steve Balboni .10
395 Brian Bohanon .10
396 Jeff Bronkey .10
397 Kevin Brown .10
398 Todd Burns .10
399 Jose Canseco .75
400 Cris Carpenter .10
401 Doug Dascenzo .10
402 Butch Davis .10
403 Steve Dreyer .10
404 Rob Ducey .10
405 Julio Franco .10
406 Jeff Frye .10
407 Benji Gil .10
408 Juan Gonzalez 4.00
409 Tom Henke .10
410 David Hulse .10
411 Jeff Huson .10
412 Chris James .10
413 Manuel Lee .10
414 Craig Lefferts .10
415 Charlie Leibrandt .10
416 Gene Nelson .10
417 Robb Nen .10
418 Darren Oliver .10
419 Rafael Palmeiro .75
420 Dean Palmer .20
421 Bob Patterson .10
422 Roger Pavlik .10
423 Dan Peltier .10
424 Geno Petralli .10
425 Gary Redus .10
426 Rick Reed .10
427 Bill Ripken .10
428 Ivan Rodriguez 1.50
429 Kenny Rogers .10
430 John Russell .10
431 Nolan Ryan 4.00
432 Mike Schooler .10
433 Jon Shave .10
434 Doug Strange .10
435 Matt Whiteside .10
436 Mickey Hatcher .10
437 Perry Hill .10
438 Jackie Moore .10
439 Dave Oliver .10
440 Claude Osteen .10
441 Willie Upshaw .10
442 Checklist 1-112 .10
443 Checklist 113-224 .10
444 Checklist 225-336 .10
445 Checklist 337-446 .10
446 Arlington Stadium .10

1SP 1972 Texas Rangers .10
2SP 1972-80 Team Records .10
3SP 1981-83 Team Records .10
4SP 1984-92 Team Records .10
5SP 1993 Logo Card .10
6SP Homerun Leaders .10
7SP RBI Leaders .10
8SP Batting Leaders .10
9SP Win Leaders .10
10SP Save Leaders .10
11SP Hit Leaders .10
12SP Stolen Base Leaders .10
13SP Games Played Leaders .10
14SP Strikeout Leaders .10
15SP ERA Leaders .10
16SP Games Pitched Leaders .10
17SP Innings Pitched Leaders .10
18SP Attendance Records .10
19SP Top 20 Crowds .10
20SP Hitting Streaks .10
21SP All-Star Selections .10
22SP Top Draft Picks .10

1999 Keebler Los Angeles Dodgers

In a promotion similar to those of Mother's Cookies in the past, Keebler sponsored a kids' trading card day Aug. 15 distributing 28-card packs to fans 14 and under. Each pack contained 21 different cards and seven duplicates to trade in an effort to complete the set. The 2-1/2" x 3-1/2" cards have borderless player photos on front with a Dodgers logo and team-color red and blue stripes at bottom in which the player's name appears. Color backs have a team logo, a Keebler's elf logo and a few bits of player biographical data.

		MT
Complete Set (28):		12.00
Common Player:		.25
1	Davey Johnson	.25
2	Eric Karros	.50
3	Gary Sheffield	1.50
4	Raul Mondesi	1.50
5	Kevin Brown	1.00
6	Mark Grudzielanek	.35
7	Todd Hollandsworth	.25
8	Todd Hundley	.35
9	Jeff Shaw	.25
10	Pedro Borbon	.25
11	Chan Ho Park	1.00
12	Jose Vizcaino	.25
13	Devon White	.45
14	Darren Dreifort	.35
15	Onan Masaoka	.25
16	Dave Hansen	.25
17	Adrian Beltre	2.00
18	Ismael Valdes	.35
19	Alan Mills	.25
20	Eric Young	.25
21	Mike Maddux	.25
22	Carlos Perez	.25
23	Tripp Cromer	.25
24	Jamie Arnold	.25
25	Angel Pena	.25
26	Trenidad Hubbard	.25
27	Doug Bochtler	.25
28	Coaches/checklist (Rick Dempsey, Rich Down, Glenn Hoffman, Manny Mota, Claude Osteen, John Shelby, Jim Tracy)	.25

1999 Keebler San Diego Padres

In a promotion similar to those of Mother's Cookies in the past, Keebler sponsored a kids' trading card day Aug. 1 distributing 28-card packs to fans 14 and under. Each pack contained 21 different cards and seven duplicates to trade in an effort to complete the set. The 2-1/2" x 3-1/2" cards have borderless player photos on front with a Padres logo and team-color orange and blue stripes at bottom in which the player's name appears. Color backs have a Padres 1969-1999 logo, a Keebler's elf logo and a few bits of player biographical data.

		MT
Complete Set (28):		15.00
Common Player:		.25
1	Bruce Bochy	.25
2	Tony Gwynn	6.00
3	Wally Joyner	1.00
4	Sterling Hitchcock	.50
5	Jim Leyritz	.35
6	Trevor Hoffman	1.00
7	Quilvio Veras	.35
8	Dave Magadan	.35
9	Andy Ashby	.25
10	Damian Jackson	.25
11	Dan Miceli	.25
12	Reggie Sanders	.35
13	Chris Gomez	.35
14	Ruben Rivera	.35
15	Greg Myers	.25
16	Ed Vosberg	.25
17	John Vander Wal	.25
18	Donne Wall	.25
19	Eric Owens	.25
20	Brian Boehringer	.25
21	Woody Williams	.35
22	Matt Clement	.35
23	Carlos Reyes	.35
24	Stan Spencer	.40
25	George Arias	.25
26	Carlos Almanzar	.45
27	Phil Nevin	.25
28	Greg Booker, Tim Flannery, Davey Lopes, Rob Picciolo, Merv Rettenmund, Dave Smith (Padres coaches)	.25

1986 Keller's Butter Phillies

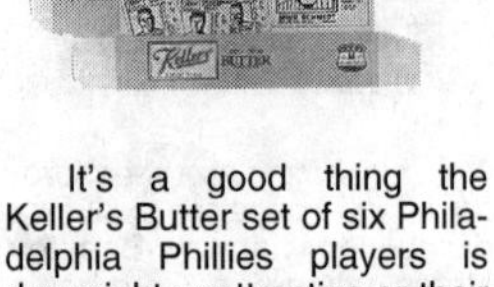

It's a good thing the Keller's Butter set of six Philadelphia Phillies players is downright unattractive or their value would be sky high. One card was printed on each one pound package of butter. The 2-1/2" x 2-3/4" cards feature crude drawings of the players, the backs are blank.

	MT
Complete Set (6):	15.00
Common Player:	1.00

(1)	Steve Carlton	4.00
(2)	Von Hayes	1.00
(3)	Gary Redus	1.00
(4)	Juan Samuel	1.00
(5)	Mike Schmidt	8.00
(6)	Glenn Wilson	1.00

1991 Kellogg's Baseball Greats

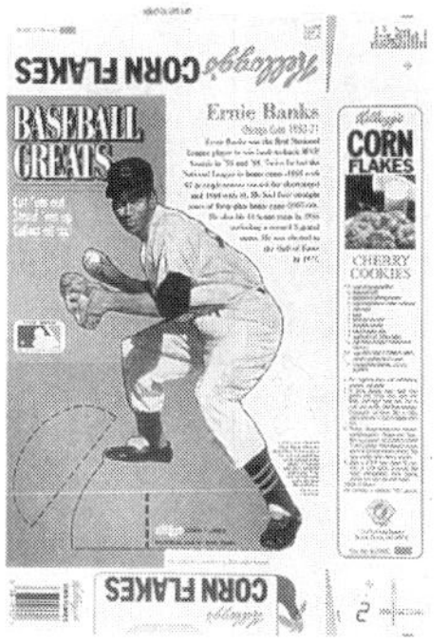

Six Hall of Famers are featured on the backs of 7- and 12-ounce Corn Flakes boxes. The photos are designed to be cut out and assembled as a stand-up figure. A career summary also appears on the box back.

		MT
Complete Set (6):		12.00
Common Player:		2.00
(1)	Hank Aaron	4.00
(2)	Ernie Banks	2.50
(3)	Yogi Berra	2.50
(4)	Lou Brock	2.00
(5)	Steve Carlton	2.00
(6)	Bob Gibson	2.00

1991 Kellogg's Leyendas

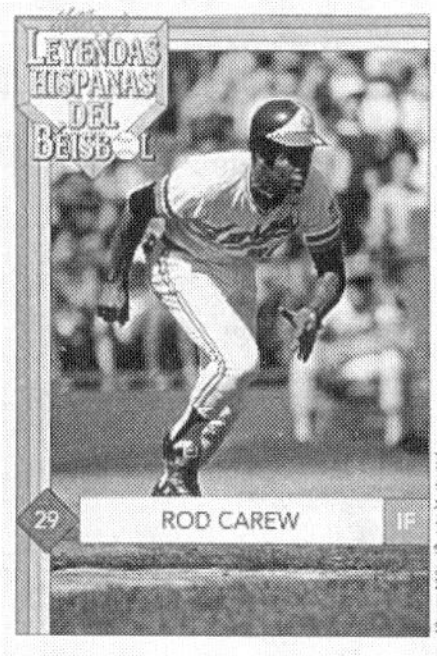

These bilingual (English/ Spanish) cards honoring past Hispanic stars were inserted in several brands of Kellogg's cereal in selected geographic areas. Fronts have an action player photo, while backs have a black-and-white portrait photo, biographical details, career stats and highlights.

		MT
Complete Set (11):		9.00
Common Player:		.50
(1)	Bert Campaneris	.50
(2)	Rod Carew	1.00
(3)	Rico Carty	.50
(4)	Cesar Cedeno	.50
(5)	Orlando Cepeda	1.00
(6)	Roberto Clemente	6.00
(7)	Mike Cuellar	.50
(8)	Ed Figueroa	.50
(9)	Minnie Minoso	.75
(10)	Manny Sanguillen	.50
(11)	Header card	.25

1991 Kellogg's 3-D

In 1991, specially-marked packages of Kellogg's Corn Flakes included 3-D baseball cards, resuming a tradition that began in 1970 and continued without interruption until 1983. In the 1991 edition, there are 15 cards to collect, featuring many of the greatest living retired stars in the game. Most of the players are in the Hall of Fame. The card fronts show two pictures of the player, while the backs include career highlights and a portrait. The cards are 2-1/2" x 3-5/16", numbered and were made by Sportflics. A complete set was available via a mail-in offer for $4.95 plus proofs of purchase.

		MT
Complete Set (15):		5.00
Common Player:		.25
1	Gaylord Perry	.25
2	Hank Aaron	1.00
3	Willie Mays	1.00
4	Ernie Banks	.75
5	Bob Gibson	.50
6	Harmon Killebrew	.50
7	Rollie Fingers	.25
8	Steve Carlton	.50
9	Billy Williams	.25
10	Lou Brock	.25
11	Yogi Berra	.75
12	Warren Spahn	.50
13	Boog Powell	.25
14	Don Baylor	.25
15	Ralph Kiner	.25

1992 Kellogg's 3-D

Kellogg's cereal company created a 10-card 1992 All Star set of retired stars, with one card inserted in specially-marked boxes of corn flakes, and complete sets available by mail. The cards, produced by Sportflics, feature two sequential action images on each front. Red, white and blue designs comprise the border, with yellow bands above and beneath the photo. On back is a black-and-white portrait photo, plus a career summary a few stats, and the logos of the cereal company, the Major League Baseball Players Alumni and Sportflics. As in the previous year, cards are slightly longer, at 2-1/2" x 2-5/16", than standard size. Also available by mail was a large, colorful cardboard display in which the cards could be placed.

		MT
Complete Set (10):		3.00
Common Player:		.25
1	Willie Stargell	.50
2	Tony Perez	.50
3	Jim Palmer	.50
4	Rod Carew	.50
5	Tom Seaver	.65
6	Phil Niekro	.50
7	Bill Madlock	.25
8	Jim Rice	.25
9	Dan Quisenberry	.25
10	Mike Schmidt	1.00

1992 Kellogg's 3-D Canadian

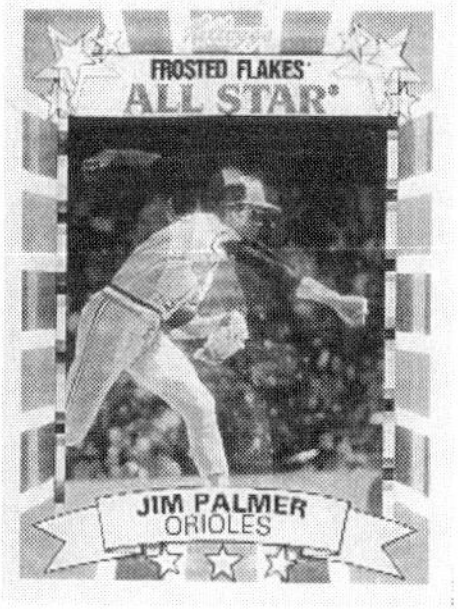

Very similar in format to the American version, 3-D cards of 10 baseball stars of the past were found in packages of Kellogg's Frosted Flakes. Backs of the Canadian cards are printed in both English and French, which left no room for a card number, so the checklist provided here is alphabetical.

		MT
Complete Set (10):		6.00
Common Player:		.50
(1)	Rod Carew	1.00
(2)	Bill Madlock	.50
(3)	Phil Niekro	1.00
(4)	Jim Palmer	1.00
(5)	Tony Perez	1.00
(6)	Dan Quisenberry	.50
(7)	Jim Rice	.50
(8)	Mike Schmidt	2.00
(9)	Tom Seaver	1.00
(10)	Willie Stargell	1.00

1998 Kennett Square Historical Commission

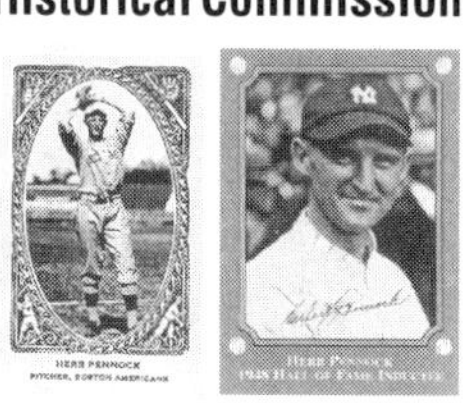

To raise funds for a statue honoring native-son Hall of Famer Herb Pennock, the Kennett Square (Pa.) Historical Commission issued this pair of collectors cards. One card is a virtual reproduction of a 1922 American Caramel card of Pennock as a Red Sox pitcher, it measures 2" x 3-1/4". The other is an original design with a portrait photo of Pennock as a Yankee. It measures 2-1/2" x 3-1/2". Backs have career and biographical highlights and stats. A thousand pair of the cards were issued and offered at $5.

		MT
(1)	Herb Pennock (Red Sox)	2.50
(2)	Herb Pennock (Yankees)	2.50

Player names in *Italic* type indicate a rookie card.

1987 Key Food Discs

(See 1987 Baseball Super Stars Discs for checklist and price guide)

1988 Key Food Discs

(See 1988 Baseball Super Star Discs for checklist and price guide.)

1988 King-B

Created by Mike Schechter Associates, this set consists of 24 numbered discs, 2-3/4" in diameter. The cards were inserted in specially marked 7/16 ounce tubs of Jerky Stuff (shredded beef jerky). Fronts feature full-color photos surrounded by a blue border. The King-B logo appears in the upper left portion of the disc. Backs are printed in blue on white stock and carry player personal and playing information. Team insignias have been airbrushed from the players' caps and jerseys.

		MT
Complete Set (24):		45.00
Common Player:		1.00
1	Mike Schmidt	2.50
2	Dale Murphy	1.50
3	Kirby Puckett	2.50
4	Ozzie Smith	2.50
5	Tony Gwynn	3.00
6	Mark McGwire	5.00
7	George Brett	3.00
8	Darryl Strawberry	1.25
9	Wally Joyner	1.00
10	Cory Snyder	1.00
11	Barry Bonds	3.00
12	Darrell Evans	1.00
13	Mike Scott	1.00
14	Andre Dawson	1.00
15	Don Mattingly	4.00
16	Candy Maldonado	1.00
17	Alvin Davis	1.00
18	Carlton Fisk	1.50
19	Fernando Valenzuela	1.00
20	Roger Clemens	2.50
21	Larry Parrish	1.00
22	Eric Davis	1.00
23	Paul Molitor	2.50
24	Cal Ripken, Jr.	5.00

1989 King-B

The second King-B set created by Mike Schechter Associates again consists of 24 circular baseball cards measuring 2-3/4" in diameter. The cards were inserted into specially-marked tubs of "Jerky Stuff." Fronts feature full-color photos bordered in red. The King-B logo appears in the upper left portion of the disc. Like the 1988 set, the team insignias have airbrushed from uniforms and caps. The backs are printed in red and display personal information and stats.

		MT
Complete Set (24):		25.00
Common Player:		1.00
1	Kirk Gibson	1.00
2	Eddie Murray	1.00
3	Wade Boggs	1.50
4	Mark McGwire	4.00
5	Ryne Sandberg	2.00
6	Ozzie Guillen	1.00
7	Chris Sabo	1.00
8	Joe Carter	1.00
9	Alan Trammell	1.00
10	Nolan Ryan	3.00
11	Bo Jackson	1.25
12	Orel Hershiser	1.00
13	Robin Yount	1.50
14	Frank Viola	1.00
15	Darryl Strawberry	1.00
16	Dave Winfield	1.25
17	Jose Canseco	1.50
18	Von Hayes	1.00
19	Andy Van Slyke	1.00
20	Pedro Guerrero	1.00
21	Tony Gwynn	2.50
22	Will Clark	1.25
23	Danny Jackson	1.00
24	Pete Incaviglia	1.00

1990 King-B

King-B meat products offered baseball player discs inside specially-marked packages in 1990, the third year in a row the company inserted the discs with shredded beef jerky. Each disc measures 2-3/4" across and uses full-color pictures on the front. The backs have biographical information and statistics. Team insignias have been airbrushed from caps and uniforms. As in the first two years of the promotion, there are 24 cards in the set.

		MT
Complete Set (24):		25.00
Common Player:		1.00
1	Mike Scott	1.00
2	Kevin Mitchell	1.00
3	Tony Gwynn	2.00
4	Ozzie Smith	1.50
5	Kirk Gibson	1.00
6	Tim Raines	1.00
7	Von Hayes	1.00
8	Bobby Bonilla	1.00
9	Wade Boggs	1.50
10	Chris Sabo	1.00
11	Dale Murphy	1.25

12	Cory Snyder	1.00
13	Fred McGriff	1.25
14	Don Mattingly	2.00
15	Jerome Walton	1.00
16	Ken Griffey, Jr.	3.00
17	Bo Jackson	1.00
18	Robin Yount	1.50
19	Rickey Henderson	1.25
20	Jim Abbott	1.00
21	Kirby Puckett	2.00
22	Nolan Ryan	3.00
23	Gregg Olson	1.00
24	Lou Whitaker	1.00

1991 King-B

The 1991 release of baseball player discs in cans of shredded beef snack was labeled "Fourth Annual Collectors' Edition". Once again the discs are 2-3/8" in diameter and feature player photos on which uniform logos have been removed for lack of an MLB license. Front border is in green; backs are printed in blue and include 1990 and major league cumulative stats. One player from each major league team is included in the set.

		MT
Complete Set (24):		20.00
Common Player:		.50
1	Willie McGee	.50
2	Kevin Seitzer	.50
3	Kevin Maas	.50
4	Ben McDonald	.50
5	Rickey Henderson	.90
6	Ken Griffey Jr.	4.00
7	John Olerud	.75
8	Dwight Gooden	.60
9	Ruben Sierra	.50
10	Luis Polonia	.50
11	Wade Boggs	2.00
12	Ramon Martinez	.50
13	Craig Biggio	.70
14	Cecil Fielder	.50
15	Will Clark	1.00
16	Matt Williams	.60
17	Sandy Alomar Jr.	.75
18	David Justice	.75
19	Ryne Sandberg	1.50
20	Benito Santiago	.50
21	Barry Bonds	3.00
22	Carlton Fisk	1.00
23	Kirby Puckett	2.50
24	Jose Rijo	.50

1992 King-B

Labeled the "Fifth Annual Collectors Edition," the 1992 King-B discs were again packaged in plastic containers of shredded beef snack. The 2-3/8" diameter discs have a color player portrait at center. Uniform logos have been removed from the photos for lack of an MLB licensing agreement. The player's name and team are in white in a blue banner above his photo. Backs are printed in blue and include previous year and career stats along with a few biographical details and appropriate logos.

		MT
Complete Set (24):		17.50
Common Player:		.50
1	Terry Pendleton	.50
2	Chris Sabo	.50
3	Frank Thomas	2.00
4	Todd Zeile	.50
5	Bobby Bonilla	.50
6	Howard Johnson	.50
7	Nolan Ryan	3.00
8	Ken Griffey Jr.	3.00
9	Roger Clemens	1.50
10	Tony Gwynn	1.50
11	Steve Avery	.50
12	Cal Ripken Jr.	2.50
13	Danny Tartabull	.50
14	Paul Molitor	1.00
15	Willie McGee	.50
16	Wade Boggs	1.50
17	Cecil Fielder	.50
18	Jack Morris	.50
19	Ryne Sandberg	1.50
20	Kirby Puckett	1.50
21	Craig Biggio	.65
22	Harold Baines	.50
23	Scott Erickson	.50
24	Joe Carter	.50

1993 King-B

The sixth annual edition of baseball player discs inserted into packages of King-B meat snacks followed the format of previous issues. Measuring 2-3/8" in diameter, the cards have a photo (with uniform logos airbrushed away) in a yellow baseball diamond design at center. The disc is bordered in black. Backs are printed in red and contain 1992 and career stats.

		MT
Complete Set (24):		12.50
Common Player:		.50
1	Barry Bonds	1.00
2	Ken Griffey, Jr.	1.50
3	Cal Ripken, Jr.	1.25
4	Frank Thomas	1.25
5	Steve Avery	.50
6	Benito Santiago	.50
7	Luis Polonia	.50
8	Jose Rijo	.50
9	George Brett	1.00
10	Darren Daulton	.50
11	Cecil Fielder	.50
12	Ozzie Smith	.75
13	Joe Carter	.50
14	Dwight Gooden	.50
15	Tom Henke	.50
16	Brett Butler	.50
17	Nolan Ryan	1.25
18	Sandy Alomar, Jr.	.50
19	Tom Glavine	.60
20	Rafael Palmeiro	.75
21	Roger Clemens	.75
22	Ryne Sandberg	.75
23	Doug Drabek	.50
24	Chuck Knoblauch	.60

1994 King-B

King-B once again created and inserted discs of 24 major league stars with its products in 1994. The entire set was also available in uncut sheet form which was found in each case. Discs measure 2-3/8" diameter and have a broad purple border with yellow and white typography surrounding the player photo at center. A black glove holds a King-B logo at bottom. Uniform logos have been airbrushed from the photos. Backs are printed in purple and include 1993 and career stats.

		MT
Complete Set (24):		10.00
Common Player:		.50
1	Fred McGriff	.60
2	Paul Molitor	.75
3	Jack McDowell	.50
4	Darren Daulton	.50
5	Wade Boggs	.75
6	Ken Griffey, Jr.	1.50
7	Tim Salmon	.60
8	Dennis Eckersley	.50
9	Albert Belle	.75
10	Travis Fryman	.50
11	Chris Hoiles	.50
12	Kirby Puckett	1.00
13	John Olerud	.60
14	Frank Thomas	1.00
15	Lenny Dykstra	.50
16	Andres Galarraga	.50
17	Barry Larkin	.50
18	Greg Maddux	1.00
19	Mike Piazza	1.00
20	Roberto Alomar	.60
21	Robin Ventura	.60
22	Ryne Sandberg	.75
23	Andy Van Slyke	.50
24	Barry Bonds	.75

1995 King-B

A wood-grain background distinguishes the eighth annual baseball disc issue packaged inside shredded beef snack tins. Because they are licensed only by the players' association, and not MLB, cards in the set have had team logos removed from the color player photos at the center of the 2-3/8" diameter discs. Backs are printed in red and have a few personal bits of data, previous season and career stats and the logos of King-B and the MLBPA.

		MT
Complete Set (24):		20.00
Common Player:		.50
1	Roberto Alomar	.65
2	Jeff Bagwell	1.50
3	Wade Boggs	1.00
4	Barry Bonds	1.50
5	Joe Carter	.50
6	Mariano Duncan	.50
7	Lenny Dykstra	.50
8	Andres Galarraga	.50
9	Matt Williams	.50
10	Raul Mondesi	.60
11	Ken Griffey Jr.	3.00
12	Gregg Jefferies	.50
13	Fred McGriff	.60
14	Paul Molitor	.75
15	Dave Justice	.60
16	Mike Piazza	2.00
17	Kirby Puckett	1.50
18	Cal Ripken Jr.	3.00
19	Ivan Rodriguez	.60
20	Ozzie Smith	1.00
21	Gary Sheffield	.60
22	Frank Thomas	2.50
23	Greg Maddux	1.75
24	Jimmy Key ("JIIMY" on back)	.50

1996 King-B

The "9th Annual Collectors Edition" of King-B discs once again features player photos on which uniform insignia have been airbrushed away. The cards are licensed by Michael Schechter Associates only with the players' union, not MLB, and so cannot display team logos. The 2-5/8" cardboard discs are packaged in plastic cannisters of shredded dried meat. Fronts have the 1996 date at left in a black and gold pinstriped area. The backs are in black and white with 1995 and career stats, along with a few vital data and appropriate logos and copyright information.

		MT
Complete Set (24):		22.00
Common Player:		.50
1	Roger Clemens	1.25
2	Mo Vaughn	1.00
3	Dante Bichette	.75
4	Jeff Bagwell	1.25
5	Randy Johnson	1.00
6	Ken Griffey Jr.	3.00
7	Kirby Puckett	1.25
8	Orel Hershiser	.50
9	Albert Belle	1.00
10	Tony Gwynn	1.50
11	Tom Glavine	.60
12	Jim Abbott	.50
13	Andres Galarraga	.50
14	Frank Thomas	2.00
15	Barry Larkin	.50
16	Mike Piazza	2.00
17	Matt Williams	.50
18	Greg Maddux	1.50
19	Hideo Nomo	1.25
20	Roberto Alomar	.75
21	Ivan Rodriguez	.60
22	Cal Ripken Jr.	2.50
23	Barry Bonds	1.50
24	Mark McGwire	3.00

1997 King-B

The shredded beef product issued its 10th Anniversary set of player discs in 1997. The discs are packed inside the plastic canisters of the snack food and measure 2-3/8" in diameter. The '97 discs have a player action photo on front against a gold and black marbled background. Backs are in black-and-white and repeat the photo in the background, along with a few stats and personal data, logos and a disc number. One player from each team is represented in the checklist.

		MT
Complete Set (28):		28.00
Common Player:		1.00
1	Brady Anderson	1.00
2	Barry Bonds	2.00
3	Travis Fryman	1.00
4	Rey Ordonez	1.00
5	Kenny Lofton	1.00
6	Mark McGwire	4.00
7	Jeff Bagwell	1.50
8	Roger Clemens	1.50
9	Juan Gonzalez	1.50
10	Mike Piazza	2.50
11	Tim Salmon	1.00
12	Jeff Montgomery	1.00
13	Joe Carter	1.00
14	David Cone	1.00
15	Frank Thomas	2.00
16	Mickey Morandini	1.00
17	Ray Lankford	1.00
18	Pedro Martinez	1.00
19	Tom Glavine	1.00
20	Chuck Knoblauch	1.25
21	Dan Wilson	1.00
22	Gary Sheffield	1.25
23	Dante Bichette	1.00
24	Al Martin	1.00
25	Barry Larkin	1.00
26	Ryne Sandberg	1.50
27	Steve Finley	1.00
28	Matt Mieske	1.00

1998 King-B

Except for the expansion teams, each Major League team has one player in this issue of player discs which were packed inside plastic canisters of the snack food. The cards measure 2-3/8" in diameter with a color player action photo on front (uniform logos have been removed). Backs have a few stats and personal data, logos plus a disc number.

		MT
Complete Set (28):		25.00
Common Player:		1.00
1	Brady Anderson	1.00
2	Barry Bonds	1.50
3	Tony Clark	1.00
4	Rey Ordonez	1.00
5	Travis Fryman	1.00
6	Jason Giambi	1.00
7	Jeff Bagwell	1.50
8	Tim Naehring	1.00
9	Juan Gonzalez	1.50
10	Mike Piazza	2.50
11	Tim Salmon	1.00
12	Jeff Montgomery	1.00
13	Tom Glavine	1.00
14	Chuck Knoblauch	1.00
15	Dan Wilson	1.00
16	Gary Sheffield	1.00
17	Dante Bichette	1.00
18	Al Martin	1.00
19	Roger Clemens	1.50
20	David Cone	1.00
21	Frank Thomas	2.50
22	Mike Lieberthal	1.00
23	Ray Lankford	1.00
24	Rondell White	1.00
25	Barry Larkin	1.00
26	Matt Mieske	1.00
27	Steve Finley	1.00
28	Fernando Vina	1.00

1991 Kitchen Sink Press Charms & Hexes Postcards

In 1991, KSP, publisher of underground comics and related collectibles issued a series of postcards which included a five-card series on baseball superstitions. The art and text were by famous comic magazine writer Harvey Kurtzman and illustrator Jack

Davis. The thinly disguised Hall of Famers were originally caricatured in the pages of "Humbug" humor magazine in 1957. The 6" x 4" KSP postcards have color comic sequences on front explaining the superstitions. Black-and-white backs detail the postcards' background.

		MT
Complete Set (5):		11.00
Common Player:		1.00
10	Willie Maze	3.00
11	Robert Robins	1.00
12	Ted Willyums	3.00
13	Pee Wee Reeze	1.00
14	Mickey Mantel	5.00

1985 Kitty Clover Potato Chips Discs

One of a pair of nearly identical (see KAS) sets issued by midwestern potato chip companies, this issue features top stars of the day on 2-3/4" cardboard discs. The discs have a player portrait at center, with uniform logos airbrushed away because the producer was licensed only by the Players Association and not Major League Baseball. The player's name, team and position are printed in a white diamond around the photo. The sponsor's logo is in the yellow border. Backs are in black-and-white and have a few biographical data, a 1984 stats line and a Snack Time logo. The unnumbered discs are checklisted here in alphabetical order. Square versions of the discs, which have been cut from press sheets are known within the hobby and carry a small premium. Kitty Clover was based in Omaha.

		MT
Complete Set (20):		250.00
Common Player:		5.00
(1)	Steve Carlton	7.50
(2)	Jack Clark	5.00
(3)	Rich Gossage	5.00
(4)	Tony Gwynn	25.00
(5)	Bob Horner	5.00
(6)	Keith Hernandez	5.00
(7)	Kent Hrbek	5.00
(8)	Willie McGee	5.00
(9)	Dan Quisenberry	5.00
(10)	Cal Ripken Jr.	95.00
(11)	Ryne Sandberg	20.00
(12)	Mike Schmidt	30.00
(13)	Tom Seaver	20.00
(14)	Ozzie Smith	25.00
(15)	Rick Sutcliffe	5.00
(16)	Bruce Sutter	5.00
(17)	Alan Trammell	6.50
(18)	Fernando Valenzuela	5.00
(19)	Willie Wilson	5.00
(20)	Dave Winfield	10.00

1986 Kitty Clover Potato Chips Royals

Twenty players of the 1985 World's Champion Kansas City Royals are featured in a round card set inserted into packages of potato chips in the K.C. area. The 2-7/8" discs were similar to other contemporary snack issues produced by Mike Schechter Associates in that team logos have been airbrushed off the players' caps. The photos of some of the players can be found on other regional issues of 1986.

		MT
Complete Set (20):		18.00
Common Player:		.75
1	Lonnie Smith	.75
2	Buddy Biancalana	.75
3	Bret Saberhagen	1.50
4	Hal McRae	.90
5	Onix Concepcion	.75
6	Jorge Orta	.75
7	Bud Black	.75
8	Dan Quisenberry	.90
9	Dane Iorg	.75
10	Charlie Leibrandt	.75
11	Pat Sheridan	.75
12	John Wathan	.75
13	Frank White	.75
14	Darryl Motley	.75
15	Willie Wilson	1.00
16	Danny Jackson	.75
17	Steve Balboni	.75
18	Jim Sundberg	.75
19	Mark Gubicza	1.00
20	George Brett	5.00

1996 Klosterman Baking Big Red Machine

Twenty years after The Big Red Machine captured the World's Championship, the 1976 Cincinnati Reds were honored on a card set issued by this Queen City bakery. One card was included with each 20-oz. loaf of bread during the run of the promotion. Cards are 2-3/8" x 3-1/2". Fronts feature color game-action photos with a large headline above and the player's name and position in white on a red strip at bottom. The Reds logo is in an upper corner of the photo, with the player's uniform number beneath. Backs have career summary and stats for the 1976 season and M.L. career, along with sponsors' logos and copyright information.

		MT
Complete Set (10):		6.00
Common Player:		.25
5	Johnny Bench	1.50
8	Joe Morgan	.75
10	Sparky Anderson	.35
13	Dave Concepcion	.25
15	George Foster	.25
20	Cesar Geronimo	.25
24	Tony Perez	.50
30	Ken Griffey	.30
35	Don Gullett	.25
----	The Big Four (Tony Perez, Johnny Bench, Joe Morgan, Pete Rose)	1.50

1988 Kodak White Sox

These blank-back large format (8" x 12") cards feature borderless color action photos of team stars, overprinted with team and sponsor logos and a facsimile autograph. At top is a line of type with the card number and a "1988 Kodak Collectible Series" title.

		MT
Complete Set (5):		10.00
Common Player:		2.00
1	Ozzie Guillen	2.00
2	Carlton Fisk	3.00
3	Rick Horton	2.00
4	Ivan Calderon	2.00
5	Harold Baines	2.00

1989 Kodak White Sox

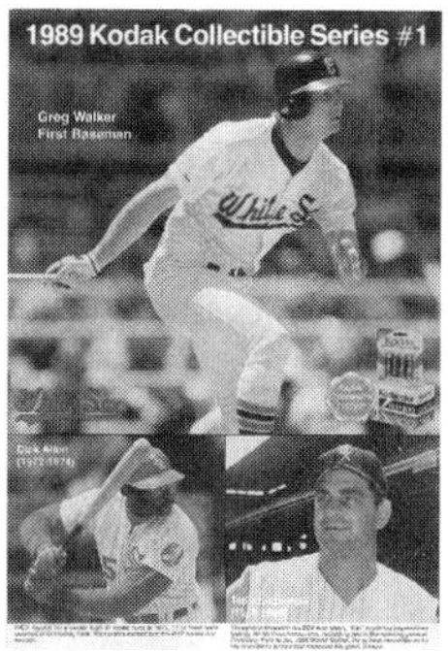

A series of six collectible pictures was given to fans over the course of the 1989 season. Sponsored by Kodak and Osco drug stores, the 8" x 12" sheets combine pictures of a current White Sox star with those of two formers stars who played the same position. Ads for the sponsors appear on the photos' fronts, while there is a modicum of information about the former stars accompanying their portraits, including the years they played for the Sox.

		MT
Complete Set (6):		10.00
Common Card:		2.00
1	Greg Walker, Dick Allen, Ted Kluszewski	2.50
2	Steve Lyons, Eddie Collins, Nellie Fox	2.50
3	Carlton Fisk, Sherm Lollar, Ray Schalk	2.00
4	Harold Baines, Minnie Minoso, Jim Landis	2.00
5	Bobby Thigpen, Gerry Staley, Hoyt Wilhelm	2.00
6	Ozzie Guillen, Luke Appling, Luis Aparicio	2.00

1990 Kodak White Sox

Again utilizing a large format (7" x 11") with borderless color action photos, the "1990 Kodak Collectible Series" features top stars of the South Siders. Player's name and position, along with team and sponsor's logos is superimposed over the photo, along with the title line and card number. The blank-back cards were distributed over the course of the season at various home games.

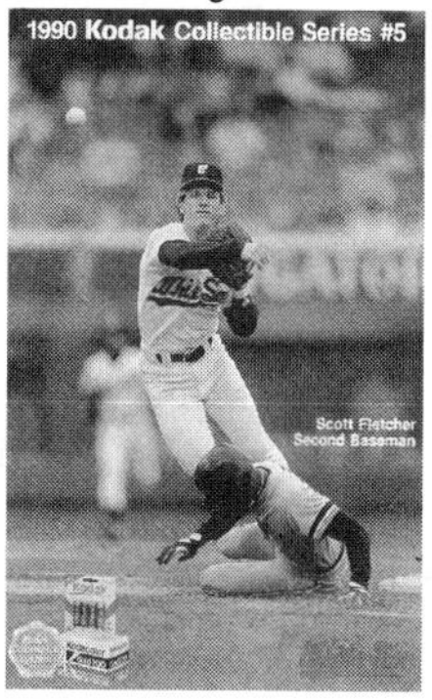

		MT
Complete Set (6):		10.00
Common Player:		2.00
1	Carlton Fisk	3.00
2	Melido Perez	2.00
3	Ozzie Guillen	2.00
4	Ron Kittle	2.00
5	Scott Fletcher	2.00
6	Comiskey Park	2.00

1991 Kodak White Sox

For a fourth year in a row, Kodak sponsored a White Sox team set in 1991. Fronts feature a full-bleed color action photo with the player's name and uniform number at the bottom and a commemorative logo for new Comiskey Park's inaugural season at top. Black-and-white backs have a few stats, personal details and career highlights along with the Kodak logo.

		MT
Complete Set (30):		24.00
Common Player:		.50
1	Lance Johnson	.50
5	Matt Merullo	.50
7	Scott Fletcher	.50
8	Bo Jackson	2.00
10	Jeff Torborg	.50
13	Ozzie Guillen	.50
14	Craig Grebeck	.50
20	Ron Karkovice	.50
21	Joey Cora	.50
22	Donn Pall	.50
23	Robin Ventura	2.00
25	Sammy Sosa	8.00
27	Greg Hibbard	.50
28	Cory Snyder	.50
29	Jack McDowell	.50
30	Tim Raines	1.50
31	Scott Radinsky	.50
32	Alex Fernandez	1.75
33	Melido Perez	.50
34	Ken Patterson	.50
35	Frank Thomas	6.00
37	Bobby Thigpen	.50
44	Dan Pasqua	.50
45	Wayne Edwards	.50
49	Charlie Hough	.50
50	Brian Drahman	.50
72	Carlton Fisk	2.00
---	White Sox Coaches (Terry Bevington, Sammy Ellis, Barry Foote, Walt Hriniak, Dave Laroche, Joe Nossek),	.50
---	Co-captains (Ozzie Guillen, Carlton Fisk)	.50
---	No. 1 Draft Choices (Alex Fernandez, Jack McDowell, Frank Thomas, Robin Ventura)	2.00

1992 Kodak White Sox

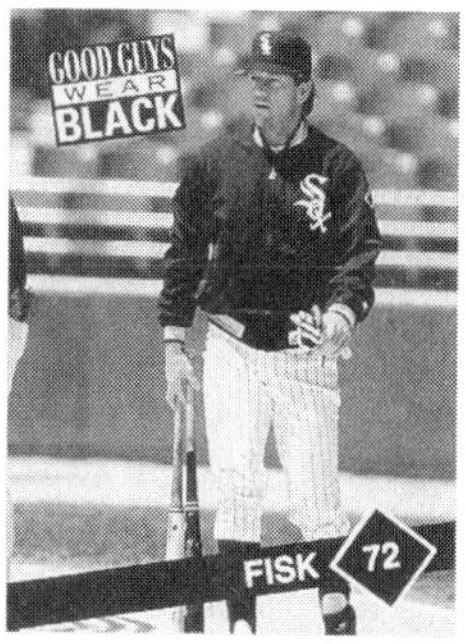

With the theme of "Good Guys Wear Black," this set depicts the Chicago southsiders in photos featuring the team's Sunday-best black uniform jerseys. Photos on the cards are full-bleed with the GGWB logo in the upper-left corner of each card. At bottom is a black strip with the player's last name and uniform number. On back are the player's 1991 and career stats, a few biographical details, a trivia question and Kodak logo. At 2-5/8" x 3-1/2", the cards are slightly wider than current standard.

		MT
Complete Set (30):		12.00
Common Player:		.25
1	Lance Johnson	.25
5	Matt Merullo	.25
7	Steve Sax	.25
12	Mike Huff	.25
13	Ozzie Guillen	.25
14	Craig Grebeck	.25
20	Ron Karkovice	.25
21	George Bell	.30
22	Donn Pall	.25
23	Robin Ventura	1.00
24	Warren Newson	.25
25	Kirk McCaskill	.25
27	Greg Hibbard	.25
28	Joey Cora	.25
29	Jack McDowell	.25
30	Tim Raines	.50
31	Scott Radinsky	.25
32	Alex Fernandez	.50
33	Gene Lamont	.25
34	Terry Leach	.25
35	Frank Thomas	4.00
37	Bobby Thigpen	.25
39	Roberto Hernandez	.25
40	Wilson Alvarez	.25
44	Dan Pasqua	.25
45	Shawn Abner	.25
49	Charlie Hough	.25
72	Carlton Fisk	1.00
00	Waldo (Cartoon mascot)	.25
---	Mike Squires, Terry Bevington, Gene Lamont, Joe Nossek, Jackie Brown, Walt Hriniak, Doug Mansolino, Dave Huppert	.25

1993 Kodak White Sox

Kodak produced a White Sox set of 30 cards in 1993 that was given away prior to the July 23 game between Chicago and Milwaukee. The full color cards are slightly oversized at 2-5/8" x 3-1/2" and are printed on a very heavy card stock. The photo on the front is full bleed, with the White Sox logo appearing in the upper corner and a metallic blue stripe at the card bottom displaying the player's uniform number, name and position. The backs are white with gray borders and a Kodak logo, with year and career statistics and biographical information. The cards are unnumbered.

		MT
Complete Set (30):		14.00
Common Player:		.25
1	Lance Johnson	.25
7	Steve Sax	.25
8	Bo Jackson	.75
10	Mike LaValliere	.25
12	Mike Huff	.25
13	Ozzie Guillen	.25
14	Craig Grebeck	.25
20	Ron Karkovice	.25
21	George Bell	.25
22	Donn Pall	.25
23	Robin Ventura	.60
25	Kirk McCaskill	.25
26	Ellis Burks	.40
28	Joey Cora	.25
29	Jack McDowell	.25
30	Tim Raines	.50
31	Scott Radinsky	.25
32	Alex Fernandez	.45
33	Gene Lamont	.25
34	Terry Leach	.25
35	Frank Thomas	4.00
37	Bobby Thigpen	.25
39	Roberto Hernandez	.25
40	Wilson Alvarez	.25
42	Rod Bolton	.25
44	Dan Pasqua	.25
45	Chuck Cary	.25
49	Jeff Schwartz	.25
51	Jason Bere	.25
---	1993 Coaching Staff (Gene Lamont, Jackie Brown, Terry Bevington, Joe Nossek, Walt Hriniak, Doug Mansolino, Dewey Robinson, Jose Antigua)	.25

1995 Kodak Pittsburgh Pirates

This 13-1/2" x 20-1/4" perforated sheet containing 30 player and staff cards and sponsor advertising was issued to persons attending a July 23 promotional game. Individual cards measure 2-1/4" x 3-1/4." Player photos at center are flanked by the team name in gold with the player name in yellow in a red banner above. Backs are in black-and-white with just a few biographical notes and team and sponsor logos. The unnumbered cards are checklisted here alphabetically.

		MT
Complete Set, Sheet:		10.00
Complete Set, Singles (30):		7.00
Common Player:		.25
(1)	Rich Aude	.25
(2)	Jay Bell	.50
(3)	Jacob Brumfield	.25
(4)	Jason Christiansen	.25
(5)	Dave Clark	.25
(6)	Steve Cooke	.25
(7)	Midre Cummings	.45
(8)	Mike Dyer	.25
(9)	Angelo Encarnacion	.25
(10)	Carlos Garcia	.40
(11)	Freddy Garcia	.25
(12)	Jim Gott	.25
(13)	Mark Johnson	.35
(14)	Jeff King	.35
(15)	Jim Leyland	.25
(16)	Jon Lieber	.25
(17)	Nelson Liriano	.25
(18)	Esteban Loaiza	.35
(19)	Al Martin	.35
(20)	Jeff McCurry	.25
(21)	Orlando Merced	.35
(22)	Dan Miceli	.25
(23)	Denny Neagle	.45
(24)	Mark Parent	.25
(25)	Steve Pegues	.25
(26)	Dan Plesac	.25
(27)	Don Slaught	.25
(28)	Paul Wagner	.25
(29)	Rick White	.25
(30)	Gary Wilson	.25

1995 Kodak White Sox

Fans attending the July 21 game at Comiskey Park received a cello-wrapped 30-card team set. Fronts of the 2-5/8" x 3-1/2" cards have color player photos that are borderless at top and sides. At bottom the player's name appears in black-and-white. Backs are in black-and-white and feature the sponsor's logo and the team's 95-year anniversary logo. There are also a few biographical details, 1994 and career stats and a player trivia question. Cards are numbered by player uniform number.

		MT
Complete Set (30):		12.00
Common Player:		.15
1	Lance Johnson	.15
5	Ray Durham	.40
7	Norberto Martin	.15
8	Mike Devereaux	.15
10	Mike Lavalliere	.15
12	Craig Grebeck	.15
13	Ozzie Guillen	.15
14	Dave Martinez	.15
15	Kirk McCaskill	.15
18	Terry Bevington	.15
20	Ron Karkovice	.15
23	Robin Ventura	.50
24	Warren Newson	.15
25	Jim Abbott	.30
26	Brian Keyser	.15
29	John Kruk	.25
30	Tim Raines	.40
31	Scott Radinsky	.15
32	Alex Fernandez	.30
35	Frank Thomas	6.00
39	Roberto Hernandez	.15
40	Wilson Alvarez	.15
46	Jason Bere	.15
48	Jose DeLeon	.15
49	Rob Dibble	.15
51	Tim Fortugno	.15
---	Frank Thomas (1995 All-Star)	3.50
---	White Sox Coaching Staff (Terry Bevington, Don Cooper, Roly DeArmas, Walt Hriniak, Ron Jackson, Doug Mansolino, Joe Nossek, (Mark Salas)	.15
---	Trainers (Herm Schneider, Mark Anderson)	.15
---	Director of Conditioning (Steve Odgers)	.15

1999 Kodak Cooperstown Collection

Six great moments in baseball history are presented in this series of "magic motion" cards. Each 4-7/8" x 3-5/8" card is sold in a 7" x 5" blister pack and includes a clip-on plastic stand which allows the card to be easily moved to observe the action photos on front. Each card front has appropriate player identification and highlight graphics. Backs are blank. The unnumbered cards are checklisted here alphabetically. Retail price at issue was $12.95.

		MT
Complete Set (6):		75.00
Common Player:		12.50
(1)	Hank Aaron	12.50
(2)	Lou Gehrig	12.50
(3)	Reggie Jackson	12.50
(4)	Mickey Mantle	12.50
(5)	Jackie Robinson	12.50
(6)	Babe Ruth	12.50

1985 Kondritz Vince Coleman

The debut season of 1985 N.L. Rookie of the Year Vince Coleman is traced in this 20-card set issued by Illinois dealer Kondritz Trading Cards. Fronts of the 2-1/2" x 3-1/2" cards have player posed or action photos surrounded by a wide red border. Backs are in black-and-white with a few sentences about Coleman, a card number, large "Invincible" and copyright data. Sets were originally sold for about $10.

	MT
Complete Set (20):	5.00
Common Card:	.25
1-20 Vince Coleman	.25

1986 Kondritz Ozzie Smith

The career of future Hall of Fame Cardinals' shortstop Ozzie Smith is traced in this 20-card set issued by Illinois dealer Kondritz Trading Cards. Fronts of the 2-1/2" x 3-1/2" cards have player posed or action photos surrounded by a wide red border. Backs are in black-and-white with a few sentences about Smith, a card number, a large "THE WIZARD" and copyright data. Sets were originally sold for about $10.

	MT
Complete Set (20):	10.00
Common Card:	.50
1-20 Ozzie Smith	.50

1987 Kraft

Kraft Foods issued a 48-card set on specially marked packages of macaroni & cheese dinners. Titled "Home Plate Heroes," 24 two-card panels measuring 3-1/2" x 7-1/8" make up the set. Individual cards measure 2-1/4" x 3-1/2". The blank-backed cards feature fronts with full-color photos, although all team insignias have been erased. In conjunction with the card set, Kraft offered a contest to "Win A Day With A Major Leaguer." Mike Schechter Associates produced the set for Kraft. A total of 120 different panel combinations (five with each player) can be found.

		MT
Complete Set, Panels:		22.00
Complete Set, Singles (48):		18.00
Common Player:		.25
1	Eddie Murray	.65
2	Dale Murphy	.50
3	Cal Ripken, Jr.	1.00
4	Mike Scott	.25
5	Jim Rice	.30
6	Jody Davis	.25
7	Wade Boggs	.65
8	Ryne Sandberg	.75
9	Wally Joyner	.25
10	Eric Davis	.25
11	Ozzie Guillen	.25
12	Tony Pena	.25
13	Harold Baines	.25
14	Johnny Ray	.25
15	Joe Carter	.25
16	Ozzie Smith	.50
17	Cory Snyder	.25
18	Vince Coleman	.25
19	Kirk Gibson	.25
20	Steve Garvey	.35
21	George Brett	.90
22	John Tudor	.25
23	Robin Yount	.75
24	Von Hayes	.25
25	Kent Hrbek	.25
26	Darryl Strawberry	.30
27	Kirby Puckett	.80
28	Ron Darling	.25
29	Don Mattingly	.90
30	Mike Schmidt	.80
31	Rickey Henderson	.45
32	Fernando Valenzuela	.25
33	Dave Winfield	.45
34	Pete Rose	.80
35	Jose Canseco	.65
36	Glenn Davis	.25
37	Alvin Davis	.25
38	Steve Sax	.25
39	Pete Incaviglia	.25
40	Jeff Reardon	.25
41	Jesse Barfield	.25
42	Hubie Brooks	.25
43	George Bell	.25
44	Tony Gwynn	.75
45	Roger Clemens	.65
46	Chili Davis	.25
47	Mike Witt	.25
48	Nolan Ryan	1.00

1993 Kraft Pop-Up Action

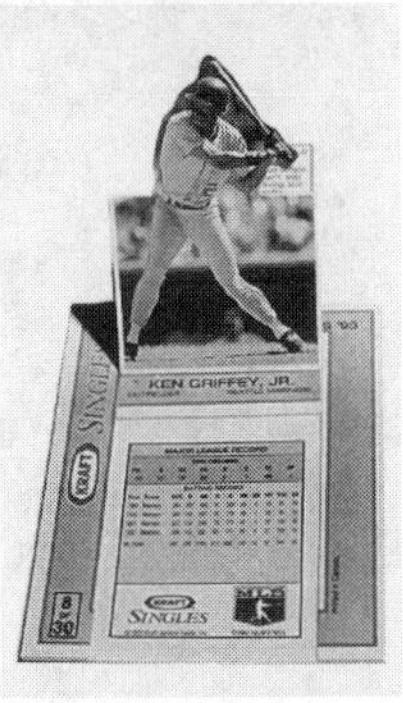

Kraft released a set of Pop-Up Action baseball cards in 1993 that was available in specially-marked packages of Kraft Singles. The cards are similar to the 1992 Canadian Post Cereal cards with a pop-up tab. The set is made up of 15 players each from the American and National leagues.

		MT
Complete Set (30):		20.00
Common Player:		.35
American League		
(1)	Jim Abbott	.35
(2)	Roberto Alomar	.80
(3)	Sandy Alomar Jr.	.35
(4)	George Brett	1.00
(5)	Roger Clemens	1.00
(6)	Dennis Eckersley	.35
(7)	Cecil Fielder	.35
(8)	Ken Griffey, Jr.	3.00
(9)	Don Mattingly	1.25
(10)	Mark McGwire	3.00
(11)	Kirby Puckett	1.00
(12)	Cal Ripken, Jr.	2.50
(13)	Nolan Ryan	2.50
(14)	Robin Ventura	.35
(15)	Robin Yount	1.00
National League		
(1)	Bobby Bonilla	.35
(2)	Ken Caminiti	.35
(3)	Will Clark	.75
(4)	Darren Daulton	.35
(5)	Doug Drabek	.35
(6)	Delino DeShields	.35
(7)	Tom Glavine	.40
(8)	Tony Gwynn	1.00
(9)	Orel Hershiser	.35
(10)	Barry Larkin	.35
(11)	Terry Pendleton	.35
(12)	Ryne Sandberg	1.00
(13)	Gary Sheffield	.50
(14)	Lee Smith	.35
(15)	Andy Van Slyke	.35

1994 Kraft Pop-Ups

Kraft offered a 30-card set in 1994 featuring major stars in a pop-up format. The cards show the players in action shots front and back, with the front picture "popping up." Kraft Singles consumers could find one 2-1/2" x 3-3/8" card in each package of cheese, with 15 players from each league. The cards were licensed by the Major League Baseball Players Association, but not by Major League Baseball, so the team logos were airbrushed from player's caps and uniforms. Through an on-pack and in-store mail-in offer, collectors could order complete sets of the cards for $1.95 per league (15 cards), plus the appropriate proofs of purchase. In a somewhat unusual move, officials of Kraft USA announced that the print run would be eight million cards, which works out to about 266,000 sets.

		MT
Complete Set (30):		11.00
Common Player:		.25
1	Carlos Baerga	.25
2	Dennis Eckersley	.25
3	Cecil Fielder	.25
4	Juan Gonzalez	.90
5	Ken Griffey Jr.	1.50
6	Mark Langston	.25
7	Brian McRae	.25
8	Paul Molitor	.60
9	Kirby Puckett	.75
10	Cal Ripken Jr.	1.25
11	Danny Tartabull	.25
12	Frank Thomas	1.00
13	Greg Vaughn	.30
14	Mo Vaughn	.45
15	Dave Winfield	.35
16	Jeff Bagwell	.50
17	Barry Bonds	.75
18	Bobby Bonilla	.25
19	Delino DeShields	.25
20	Lenny Dykstra	.25
21	Andres Galarraga	.30
22	Tom Glavine	.25
23	Mark Grace	.35
24	Tony Gwynn	.75
25	David Justice	.35
26	Barry Larkin	.25
27	Mike Piazza	1.00
28	Gary Sheffield	.45
29	Ozzie Smith	.60
30	Andy Van Slyke	.25

1995 Kraft Singles Superstars

Once again incorporating a pop-up center action figure, these cards were available both in packages of cheese slices and via a mail-in offer. The 2-1/2" x 3-1/2" cards have a second player photo in the center which is revealed by pushing down the hinged front and back of the card, creating a stand. All photos have had uniform logos removed. A baseball design is at the bottom of each player photo. Back of the card has abbreviated stats and career highlights. The back of the pop-up figure has a paragraph about the player titled, "What Singles Him Out". Besides being packaged with cheese, the cards were available by sending in proofs of purchase and $1.95 for each 15-player A.L. or N.L. set.

		MT
Complete Set (30):		11.00
Common Player:		.25
1	Roberto Alomar	.40
2	Joe Carter	.25
3	Cecil Fielder	.25
4	Juan Gonzalez	.75
5	Ken Griffey Jr.	2.00
6	Jimmy Key	.25
7	Chuck Knoblauch	.35
8	Kenny Lofton	.45
9	Mike Mussina	.30
10	Paul O'Neill	.25
11	Kirby Puckett	.75
12	Cal Ripken Jr.	1.50
13	Ivan Rodriguez	.40
14	Frank Thomas	1.00
15	Mo Vaughn	.45
16	Moises Alou	.25
17	Jeff Bagwell	.75
18	Barry Bonds	.75
19	Jeff Conine	.25
20	Lenny Dykstra	.25
21	Andres Galarraga	.25
22	Tony Gwynn	.75
23	Gregg Jefferies	.25
24	Barry Larkin	.25
25	Greg Maddux	1.00
26	Mike Piazza	1.00
27	Bret Saberhagen	.25
28	Ozzie Smith	.50
29	Sammy Sosa	1.50
30	Matt Williams	.35

1994 KVTU-TV San Francisco Giants

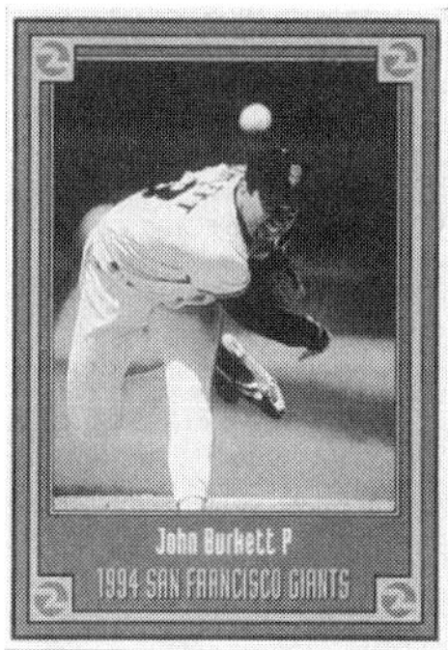

This short set was sponsored by the Giants' television broadcasting partner. Eight of the team's top names are featured on the 2-1/2" x 3-1/2" cards. Fronts have action photos framed in orange and brown with white borders. Black-and-white backs have a few career highlights and the TV station's logo.

		MT
Complete Set (9):		12.00
Common Player:		1.00
(1)	Dusty Baker	1.00
(2)	Rod Beck	1.00
(3)	Barry Bonds	6.00
(4)	Bobby Bonds	1.00
(5)	John Burkett	1.00
(6)	Billy Swift	1.00
(7)	Robby Thompson	1.00
(8)	Matt Williams	2.50
(9)	Header card	.50

L

1981 L.A. Dodgers Police

Similar in format to the previous year's set, the Dodgers 1981 police set grew to 32 cards due to the acquisitions of Ken Landreaux and Dave Stewart shortly before printing of the sets. These two cards may even have been added after the initial printing run, making them slightly more difficult to obtain. The full-color cards are again 2-13/16" x 4-1/8", with a safety tip on the card back. Each card front has the line "LAPD Salutes the 1981 Dodgers."

		MT
Complete Set (32):		15.00
Common Player:		.35
2	Tom Lasorda	.75
3	Rudy Law	.40
6	Steve Garvey	2.00
7	Steve Yeager	.40
8	Reggie Smith	.60
10	Ron Cey	.50
12	Dusty Baker	.50
13	Joe Ferguson	.40
14	Mike Scioscia	.40
15	Davey Lopes	.40
16	Rick Monday	.40
18	Bill Russell	.40
21	Jay Johnstone	.40
26	Don Stanhouse	.40
27	Joe Beckwith	.40
28	Pete Guerrero	.40
30	Derrel Thomas	.40
34	Fernando Valenzuela	1.50
35	Bob Welch	.40
36	Pepe Frias	.40
37	Robert Castillo	.40
38	Dave Goltz	.40
41	Jerry Reuss	.40
43	Rick Sutcliffe	.40
44a	Mickey Hatcher	.40
44b	Ken Landreaux	1.25
46	Burt Hooton	.40
48	Dave Stewart	2.25
51	Terry Forster	.40
57	Steve Howe	.50
---	Coaching Staff (Monty Basgall, Mark Cresse, Tom Lasorda, Manny Mota, Danny Ozark, Ron Perranoski)	.40
---	Team Photo/Checklist	.40

1981 L.A. Dodgers Postcards

A change in publishers to Crocker is noted by the eagle logo on the back of the 1981 team-issued postcards. Fronts are again borderless glossy photos with facsimile autographs. The size remains at 3-1/2" x 5-1/2".

		MT
Complete Set (11):		30.00
Common Player:		3.00
D-1	Steve Garvey	6.00
D-2	Davey Lopes	3.00
D-3	Mike Scioscia	3.00
D-4	Steve Yeager	3.00
D-5	Dusty Baker	4.00
D-6	Steve Howe	4.00
D-7	Pedro Guerrero	3.00
D-8	Robert Welch	3.00
D-9	Ken Landreaux	3.00
D-10	Fernando Valenzuela	4.50
D-11	Jerry Reuss	3.00

1982 L.A. Dodger Police

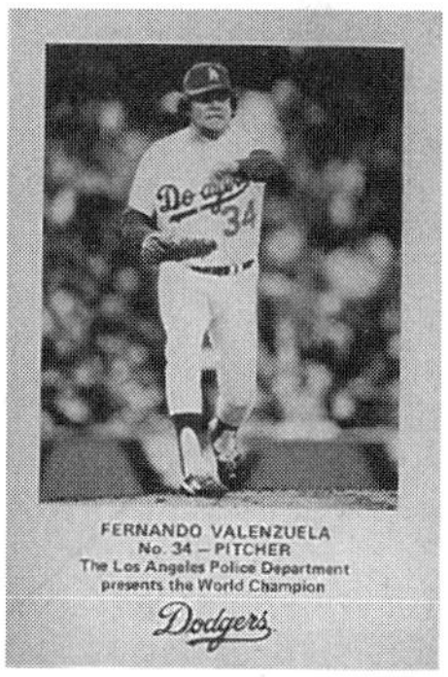

Again issued in the same 2-13/16" x 4-1/8" size of the '80 and '81 sets, the 1982 Los Angeles set commemorates the team's 1981 World Championship. In addition to the 26 cards numbered by uniform for players and manager Tom Lasorda, there are four unnumbered cards which feature the team winning the division, league and World Series titles, plus one of the World Series trophy. The full-color card photos are once again vivid portraits on a clean white card stock. Card backs offer brief biographies and stadium information in addition to a safety tip.

		MT
Complete Set (30):		12.00
Common Player:		.30
2	Tom Lasorda	.75
6	Steve Garvey	2.00
7	Steve Yeager	.30
8	Mark Belanger	.30
10	Ron Cey	.30
12	Dusty Baker	.40
14	Mike Scioscia	.30
16	Rick Monday	.30
18	Bill Russell	.30
21	Jay Johnstone	.30
26	Alejandro Pena	.30
28	Pedro Guerrero	.30
30	Derrel Thomas	.30
31	Jorge Orta	.30
34	Fernando Valenzuela	.75
35	Bob Welch	.30
38	Dave Goltz	.30
40	Ron Roenicke	.30
41	Jerry Reuss	.30
44	Ken Landreaux	.30
46	Burt Hooton	.30
48	Dave Stewart	.75
49	Tom Niedenfuer	.30
51	Terry Forster	.30
52	Steve Sax	.40
57	Steve Howe	.30
---	Division Championship	.30
---	League Championship	.30
---	World Series Championship	.30
---	Trophy Card/Checklist	.30

1982 L.A. Dodgers Postcards

Retaining the 3-1/2" x 5-1/2" borderless color format with facsimile autograph on front, 16 new player cards were issued in 1982. The '82 cards can be detected by the appearance of two numbers, one in the stamp box in the range of C34507-C34521, and one in the lower-left corner, as shown on the checklist here.

		MT
Complete Set (16):		48.00
Common Player:		3.00
M-1	Jerry Reuss	3.00
M-2	Burt Hooton	3.00
M-3	Steve Garvey	6.00
M-4	Steve Howe	3.00
M-5	Pedro Guerrero	3.00
M-6	Fernando Valenzuela	4.00
M-7	Bob Welch	3.00
M-8	Derrel Thomas	3.00
M-9	Bill Russell	3.00
M-10	Tom Niedenfuer	3.00
M-11	Steve Sax	4.00
M-12	Ron Cey	3.00
M-13	Dusty Baker	4.00
M-14	Rick Monday	3.00
M-15	Tommy Lasorda	4.00
M-16	Mike Scioscia	3.00

1983 L.A. Dodgers Police

While these full-color cards remained 2-13/16" x 4-1/8" and card fronts were similar to those of previous years, the card backs are quite different. Card backs are in a horizontal design for the first time, and include a small head portrait photo of the player in the upper left corner. Fairly complete player statistics are included but there is no safety tip. The 30 cards are numbered by uniform number, with an unnumbered coaches card also included. Fronts include the year, team logo, player name and number.

		MT
Complete Set (30):		8.00
Common Player:		.30
2	Tom Lasorda	.75
3	Steve Sax	.40
5	Mike Marshall	.40
7	Steve Yeager	.30
12	Dusty Baker	.50
14	Mike Scioscia	.30
16	Rick Monday	.30
17	Greg Brock	.30
18	Bill Russell	.30
20	Candy Maldonado	.30
21	Ricky Wright	.30
22	Mark Bradley	.30
23	Dave Sax	.30
26	Alejandro Pena	.30
27	Joe Beckwith	.30
28	Pedro Guerrero	.30
30	Derrel Thomas	.30
34	Fernando Valenzuela	.75
35	Bob Welch	.30
38	Pat Zachry	.30
40	Ron Roenicke	.30
41	Jerry Reuss	.30
43	Jose Morales	.30
44	Ken Landreaux	.30
46	Burt Hooton	.30
47	Larry White	.30
48	Dave Stewart	.50
49	Tom Niedenfuer	.30
57	Steve Howe	.30
---	Coaches Card (Joe Amalfitano, Monty Basgall, Mark Cresse, Manny Mota, Ron Perranoski)	.30

The election of former players to the Hall of Fame does not always have an immediate upward effect on card prices. The hobby market generally has done a good job of predicting those inductions and adjusting values over the course of several years.

1983 L.A. Dodgers Postcards

The tradition of team-issued postcards which had begun in 1959 ended with this series of 1983 issues. A new printer, Mike Roberts Color, maintained the basic format of the 3-1/2" x 5-1/2" cards in their final year. Fronts have borderless color poses with a facsimile autograph. Postcard style backs note the change in printer and have individual card numbers printed at lower-left.

		MT
Complete Set (12):		35.00
Common Player:		3.00
C35508	Dusty Baker	3.00
C35509	Burt Hooton	3.00
C35510	Steve Howe	3.00
C35511	Dave Stewart	4.00
C35512	Mike Marshall	3.00
C35513	Bob Welch	3.00
C35514	Bill Russell	3.00
C35515	Fernando Valenzuela	4.00
C35516	Mike Scioscia	3.00
C35517	Steve Sax	3.00
C35518	Steve Yeager	3.00
C35519	Greg Brock	3.00

1984 L.A. Dodgers Fire Safety

Unlike the California Angels and San Diego Padres sets issued in conjunction with the Forestry Service in 1984, the Los Angeles Dodgers set contains only three players, pictured on much larger 5" x 7" cards. Each player is pictured with Smokey in a forest scene on the full-color fronts. Backs of the unnumbered cards have brief biographical information and lifetime statistics. The cards were distributed at a Dodgers home game.

		MT
Complete Set (4):		7.00
Common Player:		2.50
(1)	Ken Landreaux	2.50
(2)	Tom Niedenfuer	2.50
(3)	Steve Sax	2.50
(4)	Smokey Bear	.50

1984 L.A. Dodgers Police

This was the fifth yearly effort of the Dodgers and the Los Angeles Police Department. There are 30 cards in the set, which remains 2-13/16" x 4-1/8". Card fronts are designed somewhat differently than previous years, with more posed photos, bolder player names and numbers and a different team logo. Card backs again feature a small portrait photo in the upper left corner, along with brief biographical information and an anti-drug tip. Card backs are in Dodger blue. Cards are numbered by uniform number, with an unnumbered coaches card also included.

		MT
Complete Set (30):		10.00
Common Player:		.30
2	Tom Lasorda	.75
3	Steve Sax	.40
5	Mike Marshall	.40
7	Steve Yeager	.30
9	Greg Brock	.30
10	Dave Anderson	.30
14	Mike Scioscia	.30
16	Rick Monday	.30
17	Rafael Landestoy	.30
18	Bill Russell	.30
20	Candy Maldonado	.30
21	Bob Bailor	.30
25	German Rivera	.30
26	Alejandro Pena	.30
27	Carlos Diaz	.30
28	Pedro Guerrero	.40
31	Jack Fimple	.30
34	Fernando Valenzuela	.75
35	Bob Welch	.50
38	Pat Zachry	.30
40	Rick Honeycutt	.30
41	Jerry Reuss	.30
43	Jose Morales	.30
44	Ken Landreaux	.30
45	Terry Whitfield	.30
46	Burt Hooton	.30
49	Tom Niedenfuer	.30
55	Orel Hershiser	4.00
56	Richard Rodas	.30
---	Coaches Card (Joe Amalfitano, Monty Basgall, Mark Cresse, Manny Mota, Ron Perranoski)	.30

1986 L.A. Dodgers Police

After skipping the 1985 season, the Los Angeles Dodgers once again issued baseball cards related to police safety. The 1986 set features 30 full-color glossy cards measuring 2-1/4" x 4-1/8", numbered according to player uniforms. The backs feature brief player data and a safety tip from the Los Angeles Police Department. The sets were given away May 18 during Baseball Card Day at Dodger Stadium.

		MT
Complete Set (30):		6.00
Common Player:		.15
2	Tom Lasorda	.40
3	Steve Sax	.15
5	Mike Marshall	.15
9	Greg Brock	.15
10	Dave Anderson	.15
12	Bill Madlock	.20
14	Mike Scioscia	.15
17	Len Matuszek	.15
18	Bill Russell	.15
22	Franklin Stubbs	.15
23	Enos Cabell	.15
25	Mariano Duncan	.25
26	Alejandro Pena	.15
27	Carlos Diaz	.15
28	Pedro Guerrero	.15
29	Alex Trevino	.15
31	Ed Vande Berg	.15
34	Fernando Valenzuela	.45
35	Bob Welch	.15
40	Rick Honeycutt	.15
41	Jerry Reuss	.15
43	Ken Howell	.15
44	Ken Landreaux	.15
45	Terry Whitfield	.15
48	Dennis Powell	.15
49	Tom Niedenfuer	.15
51	Reggie Williams	.15
55	Orel Hershiser	.50
---	Team photo/checklist	.15
---	Coaching Staff (Joe Amalfitano, Monty Basgall, Mark Cresse, Ben Hines, Don McMahon, Manny Mota, Ron Perranoski)	.15

1987 L.A. Dodgers All-Stars Fire Safety

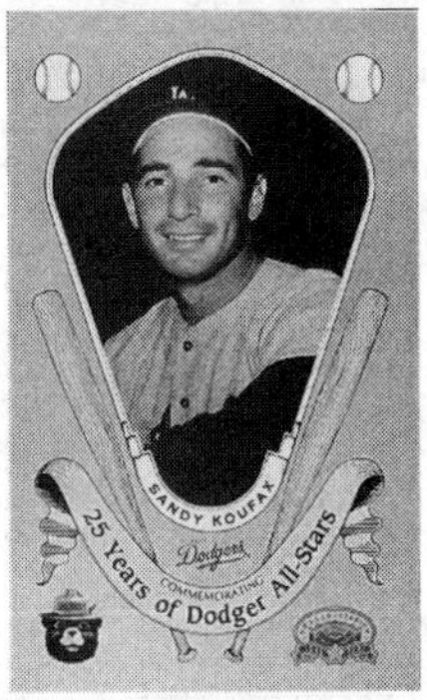

This fire safety set features "25 Years of Dodger All-Stars." The cards, which measure 2-1/2" x 3-3/4", were given out to fans 14 and younger at the Sept. 18 game at Dodgers Stadium. Fronts have full-color photos set in the shape of Dodger Stadium and have attractive silver borders. Backs carry the player's All-Star Game record plus a fire prevention message. Many of the photos used in the set were from team-issued picture packs sold by the Dodgers in the past.

		MT
Complete Set (40):		10.00
Common Player:		.25
(1)	Walt Alston	.40
(2)	Dusty Baker	.25
(3)	Jim Brewer	.25
(4)	Ron Cey	.25
(5)	Tommy Davis	.25
(6)	Willie Davis	.25
(7)	Don Drysdale	1.50
(8)	Steve Garvey	.75
(9)	Bill Grabarkewitz	.25
(10)	Pedro Guerrero	.25
(11)	Tom Haller	.25
(12)	Orel Hershiser	.45
(13)	Burt Hooton	.25
(14)	Steve Howe	.25
(15)	Tommy John	.40
(16)	Sandy Koufax	4.00
(17)	Tom Lasorda	.40
(18)	Jim Lefebvre	.25
(19)	Davey Lopes	.25
(20)	Mike Marshall (outfielder)	.25
(21)	Mike Marshall (pitcher)	.25
(22)	Andy Messersmith	.25
(23)	Rick Monday	.25
(24)	Manny Mota	.25
(25)	Claude Osteen	.25
(26)	Johnny Podres	.30
(27)	Phil Regan	.25
(28)	Jerry Reuss	.25
(29)	Rick Rhoden	.25
(30)	John Roseboro	.25
(31)	Bill Russell	.25
(32)	Steve Sax	.25
(33)	Bill Singer	.25
(34)	Reggie Smith	.25
(35)	Don Sutton	1.00
(36)	Fernando Valenzuela	.50
(37)	Bob Welch	.25
(38)	Maury Wills	.40
(39)	Jim Wynn	.25
(40)	Logo Card/Checklist	.10

1987 L.A. Dodgers Police

Producing a police set for the seventh time in eight years, the 1987 edition contains 30 cards which measure 2-13/16" x 4-1/8". The set includes a special Dodger Stadium 25th Anniversary card. The card fronts contain a full-color photo plus the Dodger Stadium 25th Anniversay logo. The photos are a mix of action and posed shots. The backs contain personal player data plus a police safety tip. The cards were given out April 24th at Dodger Stadium and were distributed by the Los Angeles police department at a rate of two cards per week.

		MT
Complete Set (30):		6.00
Common Player:		.20
2	Tom Lasorda	.40
3	Steve Sax	.25
5	Mike Marshall	.25
10	Dave Anderson	.25
12	Bill Madlock	.25
14	Mike Scioscia	.25
15	Gilberto Reyes	.25
17	Len Matuszek	.25
21	Reggie Williams	.25
22	Franklin Stubbs	.25
23	Tim Leary	.25
25	Mariano Duncan	.25
26	Alejandro Pena	.25
28	Pedro Guerrero	.25
29	Alex Trevino	.25
33	Jeff Hamilton	.25
34	Fernando Valenzuela	.60
35	Bob Welch	.25
36	Matt Young	.25
40	Rick Honeycutt	.25
41	Jerry Reuss	.25
43	Ken Howell	.25
44	Ken Landreaux	.25
46	Ralph Bryant	.25
47	Jose Gonzalez	.25
49	Tom Niedenfuer	.25
51	Brian Holton	.25
55	Orel Hershiser	.70
---	Coaching Staff (Joe Amalfitano, Mark Cresse, Tom Lasorda, Don McMahon, Manny Mota, Ron Perranoski, Bill Russell)	.25
---	Dodger Stadium/ Checklist	.25

1988 L.A. Dodgers Fire Safety

Record-breaking Dodgers from the past three decades are featured on this perforated sheet. Individual cards measure 2-1/2" x 4" and are printed on a light blue background in a design similar to the previous year's All-Star set. Black-and-white card backs contain the player name, a summary of the player's record-breaking performance and a reproduction of one of a number of Smokey Bear fire prevention posters printed during the 1950s-1980s. The sheets were distributed to fans in Dodger Stadium.

		MT
Complete Set, Foldout:		10.00
Complete Set, Singles (32):		7.00
Common Player:		.25
1	Walter Alston	.30
2	John Roseboro	.25
3	Frank Howard	.30
4	Sandy Koufax	4.00
5	Manny Mota	.25
6	Record Pitchers (Sandy Koufax, Jerry Reuss, Bill Singer)	.35
7	Maury Wills	.30
8	Tommy Davis	.25
9	Phil Regan	.25
10	Wes Parker	.25
11	Don Drysdale	1.50
12	Willie Davis	.25
13	Bill Russell	.25
14	Jim Brewer	.25
15	Record Fielders (Ron Cey, Steve Garvey, Davey Lopes, Bill Russell)	.30
16	Mike Marshall (pitcher)	.25
17	Steve Garvey	.75
18	Davey Lopes	.25
19	Burt Hooton	.25
20	Jim Wynn	.25
21	Record Hitters (Dusty Baker, Ron Cey, Steve Garvey, Reggie Smith)	.30
22	Dusty Baker	.25
23	Tom Lasorda	.45
24	Fernando Valenzuela	.40
25	Steve Sax	.25
26	Dodger Stadium	.25
27	Ron Cey	.25
28	Pedro Guerrero	.25
29	Mike Marshall (outfielder)	.25
30	Don Sutton	1.00
---	Logo Card/Checklist	.10
---	Smokey Bear	.10

1988 L.A. Dodgers Police

The Los Angeles police department sponsored this 30-card set (2-3/4" x 4-1/8") for use in a local crime prevention promotion. The sets include an unnumbered manager/coaches photo and three double-photo cards. The double cards feature posed closeups; the rest are action photos. The card fronts have white borders, with the team logo lower right and a bold black player name lower left. Card backs are black and white with a small closeup photo of the player, followed by personal and career info, a crime prevention tip and a LAPD badge logo. Card numbers refer to players' uniform numbers (the double-photo cards carry two numbers on both front and back).

		MT
	Complete Set (30):	4.00
	Common Player:	.15
2	Tom Lasorda	.25
3	Steve Sax	.15
5	Mike Marshall	.15
7	Alfredo Griffin	.15
9	Mickey Hatcher	.15
10	Dave Anderson	.15
12	Danny Heep	.15
14	Mike Scioscia	.15
17/21	Tito Landrum, Len Matuszek	.15
20	Don Sutton	.75
22	Franklin Stubbs	.15
23	Kirk Gibson	.30
25	Mariano Duncan	.15
26	Alejandro Pena	.15
27/52	Tim Crews, Mike Sharperson	.25
28	Pedro Guerrero	.15
29	Alex Trevino	.15
31	John Shelby	.15
33	Jeff Hamilton	.15
34	Fernando Valenzuela	.35
37	Mike Davis	.15
41	Brad Havens	.15
43	Ken Howell	.15
47	Jesse Orosco	.15
49/57	Tim Belcher, Shawn Hillegas	.15
50	Jay Howell	.15
51	Brian Holton	.15
54	Tim Leary	.15
55	Orel Hershiser	.40
---	Manager/Coaches (Joe Amalfitano, Steve Boros, Mark Cresse, Joe Ferguson, Tom Lasorda, Manny Mota, Ron Perranoski, Bill Russell)	.15

1989 L.A. Dodgers Greats Fire Safety

The largest baseball card set ever issued in conjunction with the U.S. Forest Service's Smokey the Bear fire prevention campaign was this 104-card issue featuring great players of the Brooklyn and L.A. Dodgers. Issued on perforated sheets, individual cards measure 2-1/2" x 3-1/2". White-bordered fronts have a sepia-toned photo of the player, with Dodger blue rules on the top and sides. Beneath the photo is a baseball-and-banner logo, "A Century of Dodger Greats." The player's name is beneath the ball with Smokey at left and the team logo at right. Backs are printed in blue, feature career stats and highlights and include a Smokey fire safety cartoon.

		MT
	Complete Set (104):	20.00
	Common Player:	.10
1	Tommy Lasorda, Walter Alston, Burt Shotton	.25
2	David Bancroft	.10
3	Dan Brouthers	.10
4	Roy Campanella	.45
5	Max Carey	.10
6	Hazen "Kiki" Cuyler	.10
7	Don Drysdale	.50
8	Burleigh Grimes	.10
9	Billy Herman	.10
10	Waite Hoyt	.10
11	Hughie Jennings	.10
12	Willie Keeler	.10
13	Joseph Kelley	.10
14	George Kelly	.10
15	Sandy Koufax	3.00
16	Heinie Manush	.10
17	Juan Marichal	.25
18	Walter Maranville	.10
19	Rube Marquard	.10
20	Thomas McCarthy	.10
21	Joseph McGinnity	.10
22	Joe Medwick	.10
23	Pee Wee Reese	.50
24	Frank Robinson	.25
25	Jackie Robinson	3.00
26	Babe Ruth	3.00
27	Duke Snider	.50
28	Casey Stengel	.15
29	Dazzy Vance	.10
30	Arky Vaughan	.10
31	Mike Scioscia	.10
32	Lloyd Waner, Paul Waner	.10
33	John Monte Ward	.10
34	Zack Wheat	.10
35	Hoyt Wilhelm	.10
36	Hack Wilson	.10
37	Tony Cuccinello	.10
38	Al Lopez	.10
39	Leo Durocher	.15
40	Cookie Lavagetto	.10
41	Babe Phelps	.10
42	Dolf Camilli	.10
43	Whit Wyatt	.10
44	Mickey Owen	.10
45	Van Mungo	.10
46	Pete Coscarart	.10
47	Pete Reiser	.10
48	Augie Galan	.10
49	Dixie Walker	.10
50	Kirby Higbe	.10
51	Ralph Branca	.10
52	Bruce Edwards	.10
53	Eddie Stanky	.10
54	Gil Hodges	.35
55	Don Newcombe	.15
56	Preacher Roe	.15
57	Willie Randolph	.10
58	Carl Furillo	.25
59	Charles Dressen	.10
60	Carl Erskine	.15
61	Clem Labine	.10
62	Gino Cimoli	.10
63	Johnny Podres	.15
64	Johnny Roseboro	.15
65	Wally Moon	.10
66	Charlie Neal	.10
67	Norm Larker	.10
68	Stan Williams	.10
69	Maury Wills	.15
70	Tommy Davis	.15
71	Jim Lefebvre	.10
72	Phil Regan	.10
73	Claude Osteen	.10
74	Tom Haller	.10
75	Bill Singer	.10
76	Bill Grabarkewitz	.10
77	Willie Davis	.15
78	Don Sutton	.25
79	Jim Brewer	.10
80	Manny Mota	.10
81	Bill Russell	.10
82	Ron Cey	.10
83	Steve Garvey	.25
84	Mike G. Marshall	.10
85	Andy Messersmith	.10
86	Jimmy Wynn	.10
87	Rick Rhoden	.10
88	Reggie Smith	.15
89	Jay Howell	.10
90	Rick Monday	.10
91	Tommy John	.15
92	Bob Welch	.10
93	Dusty Baker	.15
94	Pedro Guerrero	.10
95	Burt Hooton	.10
96	Davey Lopes	.10
97	Fernando Valenzuela	.15
98	Steve Howe	.10
99	Steve Sax	.10
100	Orel Hershiser	.20
101	Mike A. Marshall	.10
102	Wilbert Robinson	.10
103	Fred Lindstrom	.10
104	Ernie Lombardi	.10

Checklists with card numbers in parentheses ( ) indicates the numbers do not appear on the card.

1989 L.A. Dodgers Police

The Los Angeles Dodgers and the L.A. Police Department teamed up in 1989 to produce a 30-card police set. The cards, which measure 4-1/4" x 2-5/8", feature color action photos with the player's name and uniform number below. The Dodgers logo and "1989" appear in the upper left. The backs include player information plus a safety message.

		MT
	Complete Set (30):	6.00
	Common Player:	.20
2	Tom Lasorda	.40
3	Jeff Hamilton	.25
5	Mike Marshall	.25
7	Alfredo Griffin	.25
9	Mickey Hatcher	.25
10	Dave Anderson	.25
12	Willie Randolph	.25
14	Mike Scioscia	.25
17	Rick Dempsey	.25
20	Mike Davis	.25
21	Tracy Woodson	.25
22	Franklin Stubbs	.25
23	Kirk Gibson	.45
25	Mariano Duncan	.25
26	Alejandro Pena	.25
27	Mike Sharperson	.25
29	Ricky Horton	.25
30	John Tudor	.25
31	John Shelby	.25
33	Eddie Murray	1.25
34	Fernando Valenzuela	.45
36	Mike Morgan	.25
48	Ramon Martinez	2.25
49	Tim Belcher	.25
50	Jay Howell	.25
52	Tim Crews	.25
54	Tim Leary	.25
55	Orel Hershiser	.50
57	Ray Searage	.25
---	Dodger coaches (Joe Amalfitano, Mark Cresse, Joe Ferguson, Ben Hines, Tommy Lasorda, Manny Mota, Ron Perranoski, Bill Russell)	.25

1990 L.A. Dodgers Police

This set honors the centennial celebration of the Los Angeles Dodgers. A special 100 Anniversary logo appears on the card fronts. The cards measure 2-3/4" x 4-1/4" and feature full-color photos. The card backs are printed horizontally and contain a special safety tip or anti-drug message along with player information. The L.A.P.D. logo is featured on the bottom of the card back.

		MT
	Complete Set (30):	6.00
	Common Player:	.30
2	Tommy Lasorda	.50
3	Jeff Hamilton	.30
7	Alfredo Griffin	.30
9	Mickey Hatcher	.30
10	Juan Samuel	.30
12	Willie Randolph	.30
14	Mike Scioscia	.30
15	Chris Gwynn	.30
17	Rick Dempsey	.30
21	Hubie Brooks	.30
22	Franklin Stubbs	.30
23	Kirk Gibson	.50
27	Mike Sharperson	.30
28	Kal Daniels	.30
29	Lenny Harris	.40
31	John Shelby	.30
33	Eddie Murray	1.50
34	Fernando Valenzuela	.50
35	Jim Gott	.30
36	Mike Morgan	.30
38	Jose Gonzalez	.30
46	Mike Hartley	.30
48	Ramon Martinez	1.25
49	Tim Belcher	.30
50	Jay Howell	.30
52	Tim Crews	.30
55	Orel Hershiser	.75
57	John Wetteland	1.00
59	Ray Searage	.30
---	Dodgers coaches (Joe Amalfitano, Mark Cresse, Joe Ferguson, Ben Hines, Tommy Lasorda, Manny Mota, Ron Perranoski, Bill Russell)	.30

1991 L.A. Dodgers Police

One of the longest-running police/fire safety sets continued in 1991 with this 30-card set. Players are featured in color action photos set in a tombstone shape against a white background. The date is in a banner at top with the player name, team logo and uniform number at bottom. All typography is printed in Dodger blue. Backs are printed in black-and-white and include biographical data, an anti-drug message and an LAPD badge. Cards measure 2-13/16" x 4-1/8".

		MT
	Complete Set (30):	6.00
	Common Player:	.15
3	Jeff Hamilton	.15
5	Stan Javier	.15
7	Alfredo Griffin	.15
10	Juan Samuel	.15
12	Gary Carter	.60
14	Mike Scioscia	.15
15	Chris Gwynn	.15
17	Bob Ojeda	.15
22	Brett Butler	.40
25	Dennis Cook	.15
27	Mike Sharperson	.15
28	Kal Daniels	.15
29	Lenny Harris	.15
30	Jose Offerman	.25
31	Jim Neidlinger	.15
33	Eddie Murray	.75
35	Jim Gott	.15
36	Mike Morgan	.15
38	Jose Gonzalez	.15
40	Barry Lyons	.15
44	Darryl Strawberry	.45
45	Kevin Gross	.15
46	Mike Hartley	.15
48	Ramon Martinez	.25
49	Tim Belcher	.15
50	Jay Howell	.15
52	Tim Crews	.15
54	John Candelaria	.15
55	Orel Hershiser	.40
---	Dodgers coaches (Ben Hines, Ron Perranoski, Mark Cresse, Manny Mota, Tommy Lasorda, Joe Amalfitano), Joe Ferguson, Bill Russell)	.15

1992 L.A. Dodgers Police

The 1992 Dodgers Police set consists of 30 cards numbered to correspond to the player's uniform number. The set includes a card of manager Tommy Lasorda and Dodgers coaches. They were given out at promotional dates at Dodger Stadium.

		MT
	Complete Set (30):	9.00
	Common Player:	.50
2	Tommy Lasorda	.60
3	Jeff Hamilton	.50
5	Stan Javier	.50
10	Juan Samuel	.50
14	Mike Scioscia	.50
15	Dave Hansen	.50
17	Bob Ojeda	.50
20	Mitch Webster	.50
22	Brett Butler	.50
23	Eric Karros	1.50
27	Mike Sharperson	.50
28	Kal Daniels	.50
29	Lenny Harris	.50
30	Jose Offerman	.50
31	Roger McDowell	.50
33	Eric Davis	.50
35	Jim Gott	.50
36	Todd Benzinger	.50
38	Steve Wilson	.50
41	Carlos Hernandez	.50
44	Darryl Strawberry	.90
46	Kevin Gross	.50
48	Ramon Martinez	.75
49	Tom Candiotti	.50
50	Jay Howell	.50
52	Tim Crews	.50
54	John Candelaria	.50
55	Orel Hershiser	.60
57	Kip Gross	.50
---	Coaches (Joe Amalfitano, Mark Cresse, Joe Ferguson, Ben Hines, Tommy Lasorda, Manny Mota, Ron Roenicke)	.50

1993 L.A. Dodgers Police

The 1993 Los Angeles Dodgers Police Set consisted of 29 cards, including cards of manager Tommy Lasorda and his coaches. The fronts of the cards have a photo surrounded by a blue border, with the Dodgers logo and the player's name on the bottom. The set is not numbered, but the player's uniform number does appear on the front of the cards.

		MT
Complete Set (29):		9.00
Common Player:		.35
2	Tommy Lasorda	.45
3	Jody Reed	.40
5	Dave Hansen	.40
12	Lance Parrish	.40
17	Roger McDowell	.40
20	Mitch Webster	.40
22	Brett Butler	.50
23	Eric Karros	.75
25	Tim Wallach	.40
26	Henry Rodriguez	.50
27	Mike Sharperson	.40
28	Cory Snyder	.40
29	Lenny Harris	.40
30	Jose Offerman	.40
31	Mike Piazza	4.00
33	Eric Davis	.50
35	Jim Gott	.40
38	Todd Worrell	.40
41	Carlos Hernandez	.40
45	Pedro Martinez	1.50
46	Kevin Gross	.40
47	Tom Goodwin	.40
48	Ramon Martinez	.50
49	Tom Candiotti	.40
50	Steve Wilson	.40
55	Orel Hershiser	.50
56	Pedro Astacio	.45
57	Kip Gross	.40
---	Coaches (Joe Amalfitano, Mark Cresse, Joe Ferguson, Ben Hines, Tommy Lasorda, Manny Mota, Ron Roenicke)	.40

1994 L.A. Dodgers Police

This 30-card set was distributed to all fans attending the Dodgers May 27 home game. Cards were produced in the form of a perforated sheet. Fronts have mostly game-action photos surrounded by a Dodger-blue border. The player's uniform number is in red in a baseball in the upper-left corner. At bottom is the team logo and the player's name in black on a yellow strip. Backs are in black on white, have a few career and biographical notes and an anti-drug message from the L.A.P.D. and the D.A.R.E. program. When removed from the sheet, cards measure the standard 2-1/2" x 3-1/2". They are checklisted here by uniform number.

		MT
Complete Set (30):		7.50
Common Player:		.15
2	Tommy Lasorda	.40
5	Dave Hansen	.15
7	Billy Ashley	.30
10	Chris Gwynn	.15
12	Jeff Treadway	.15
14	Delino DeShields	.30
15	Tom Prince	.15
17	Roger McDowell	.15
20	Mitch Webster	.15
21	Rafael Bournigal	.15
22	Brett Butler	.25
23	Eric Karros	.30
26	Carlos Hernandez	.15
28	Cory Snyder	.15
29	Tim Wallach	.15
30	Jose Offerman	.25
31	Mike Piazza	1.50
35	Jim Gott	.15
37	Darren Dreifort	.25
38	Todd Worrell	.15
40	Henry Rodriguez	.40
43	Raul Mondesi	.90
46	Kevin Gross	.15
47	Garey Wayne	.15
48	Ramon Martinez	.40
49	Tom Candiotti	.15
55	Orel Hershiser	.25
56	Pedro Astacio	.15
61	Chan Ho Park	.75
---	Coaches (Mark Cresse, Manny Mota, Bill Russell, Reggie Smith, Joe Ferguson, Ron Perranoski, Tommy Lasorda, Joe Amalfitano)	.15

1995 L.A. Dodgers Limited Edition

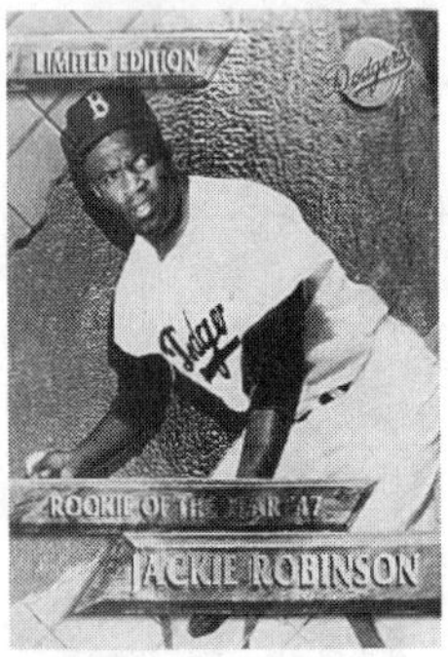

This special high-tech set of Brooklyn/Los Angeles Dodgers rookie of the year winners between 1947-94 was given to Dodger season ticket purchasers prior to the strike-shortened 1995 baseball season. Produced in a technique similar to Topps Finest, the cards have on front metallic backgrounds in red, green, blue and purple. A color player action photo is featured. Faux granite strips at bottom have the player's name and year of his ROY award in gold. Backs have a color portrait photo in a gold frame at left with career stats and highlights and a few personal details at right. The primary front background color is repeated on the back. A header card printed in blue on white linen-texture paper accompanies the set.

		MT
Complete Set (14):		60.00
Common Player:		2.00
1	Jackie Robinson	15.00
2	Don Newcombe	4.00
3	Joe Black	4.50
4	Jim Gilliam	4.50
5	Frank Howard	4.00
6	Jim Lefebvre	3.00
7	Ted Sizemore	2.00
8	Rick Sutcliffe	3.00
9	Steve Howe	3.00
10	Fernando Valenzuela	5.00
11	Steve Sax	2.00
12	Eric Karros	4.00
13	Mike Piazza	15.00
14	Raul Mondesi	7.50

1995 L.A. Dodgers Police

Action photos of the L.A. Dodgers are featured on this 30-card safety set which was given away to some 40,000 fans attending an early-season game. The set was produced as a perforated sheet measuring 14-13/16" x 17-1/2", with individual cards measuring 2-1/2" x 3-1/2". Fronts feature a Dodger-blue border with the player name in black in a yellow stripe at bottom. The player's uniform number is in red in a baseball in the upper-right. Backs are in black-and-white and have a few player biographical details along with an anti-drug safety message and the logos of the LAPD and D.A.R.E.

		MT
Complete Set (30):		9.00
Common Player:		.15
2	Tommy Lasorda	.40
3	Eddie Pye	.15
5	Dave Hansen	.15
7	Billy Ashley	.30
12	Jeff Treadway	.15
14	Delino DeShields	.30
16	Hideo Nomo	3.75
21	Rafael Bournigal	.15
23	Eric Karros	.40
25	Ron Coomer	.15
26	Carlos Hernandez	.15
28	Todd Hollandsworth	.45
29	Tim Wallach	.15
30	Jose Offerman	.15
31	Mike Piazza	2.00
38	Todd Worrell	.15
40	Henry Rodriguez	.40
43	Raul Mondesi	.75
45	Al Osuna	.15
48	Ramon Martinez	.25
49	Tom Candiotti	.15
50	Antonio Osuna	.15
52	Greg Hansell	.15
54	Omar Daal	.25
56	Pedro Astacio	.15
57	Rudy Seanez	.25
59	Ismael Valdes	.40
61	Chan Ho Park	.60
66	Todd Williams	.15
---	Coaches (Mark Cresse, Manny Mota, Bill Russell, Reggie Smith, Tommy Lasorda, Joe Amalfitano, Dave Wallace, Ralph Avila)	.15

1996 L.A. Dodgers Police

For the 16th time in 17 years (they skipped 1985), the Dodgers issued a safety set to fans attending the April 11 game. As in recent years, the set was issued in the form of a perforated 30-card sheet. Each card measures just under 2-1/2" wide and is 3-1/2" tall; sheet dimensions are 14-7/8" x 17-1/2". Game-action photos are bordered in Dodger blue with the uniform number in red at upper-left. Backs are in black-and-white with a few vital stats and an anti-drug abuse, anti-gang message from D.A.R.E.

		MT
Complete Set (30):		7.00
Common Player:		.10
2	Tommy Lasorda	.25
3	Chad Fonville	.10
5	Dave Hansen	.10
7	Greg Gagne	.15
12	Karim Garcia	1.50
13	Antonio Osuna	.10
14	Delino DeShields	.15
16	Hideo Nomo	1.50
20	Mike Blowers	.10
21	Billy Ashley	.10
22	Brett Butler	.15
23	Eric Karros	.35
25	Mike Busch	.15
26	Carlos Hernandez	.10
27	Roger Cedeno	.25
28	Todd Hollandsworth	.25
29	Milt Thompson	.10
31	Mike Piazza	2.00
33	Garey Ingram	.10
38	Todd Worrell	.10
41	John Cummings	.10
43	Raul Mondesi	.90
44	Mark Guthrie	.10
48	Ramon Martinez	.30
49	Tom Candiotti	.15
51	Joey Eischen	.10
52	Darren Hall	.10
56	Pedro Astacio	.10
59	Ismael Valdes	.15
---	Dodgers coaches (Joe Amalfitano, Mark Cresse, Tommy Lasorda, Manny Mota, Bill Russell, Reggie Smith, Dave Wallace)	.15

1996 L.A. Dodgers Rookies of the Year

This card was inserted into a die-cut space in the 1996 holiday greetings card sent out by the L.A. Dodgers. In 2-1/2" x 3-1/2" format it features portrait photos of the 1992-96 National League Rookies of the Year - all Dodgers. Overall background of the front is green. Back has information on previous Dodgers ROYs and the rookie season stats of the 1992-96 winners.

	MT
Dodger Rookies of the Year (Eric Karros (1992), Mike Piazza (1993), Raul Mondesi (1994), Hideo Nomo (1995), Todd Hollandsworth (1996)	15.00

1997 L.A. Dodgers Fan Appreciation Days

Fans attending the Sept. 21 game were given this 11" x 8-1/2" sheet announcing a one-day sale of Dodgers souvenirs. At bottom are three differently styled cards of some of the team's most popular players. All are in color and standard 2-1/2" x 3-1/2" size, perforated for easy separation from the sheet. Card backs are in black-and-white with drawings of the players in the upper-left, biographical data and trivia. Cards are numbered by uniform number.

		MT
Complete Sheet:		7.50
Complete Set, Singles (3):		2.00
16	Hideo Nomo	4.00
31	Mike Piazza	6.00
61	Chan Ho Park	2.00

1997 L.A. Dodgers Police

Action photos of the 1997 Dodgers are featured on this set distributed at the April 23 game to nearly 30,500 fans. The 14-3/4" x 17-1/2" sheet has 30 cards, perforated on two, three or four sides, depending on position on the sheet. Individual cards measure 2-1/2" x 3-1/2". A central photo is surrounded with a white border. A ball with the player's uniform number in red is at top-left. At bottom is the team logo and player name. Backs are in black-and-white with biographical notes, an anti-drug message from each player and the logos of LAPD and DARE. Cards are checklisted here by uniform number.

		MT
Complete Set, Sheet:		12.00
Complete Set, Singles (30):		10.00
Common Player:		.25
3	Chad Fonville	.40
5	Chip Hale	.25

7	Greg Gagne	.40
12	Karim Garcia	1.00
13	Anthony Osuna	.25
15	Tom Prince	.25
16	Hideo Nomo	1.00
18	Bill Russell	.25
21	Billy Ashley	.25
22	Brett Butler	.40
23	Eric Karros	.50
25	Juan Castro	.25
27	Todd Zeile	.40
28	Todd Hollandsworth	.40
30	Wilton Guerrero	.40
31	Mike Piazza	2.50
35	Wayne Kirby	.25
36	Scott Radinsky	.25
37	Darren Dreifort	.25
38	Todd Worrell	.25
43	Raul Mondesi	.90
44	Mark Guthrie	.25
46	Nelson Liriano	.25
48	Ramon Martinez	.50
49	Tom Candiotti	.25
52	Darren Hall	.25
56	Pedro Astacio	.25
59	Ismael Valdes	.40
61	Chan Ho Park	.60
---	Coaches (Joe Amalfitano, Mark Cresse, Manny Mota, Mike Scioscia, Reggie Smith, Dave Wallace)	.25

1998 L.A. Dodgers Fan Appreciation Days

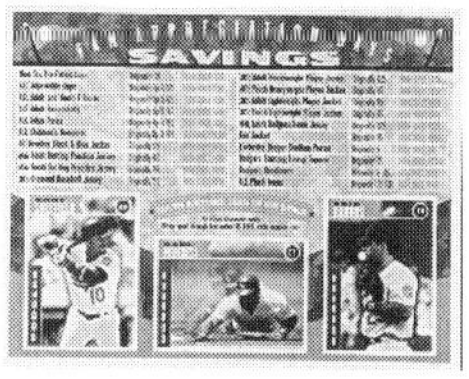

Fans attending the Dodgers' final homestand were given this 11" x 8-1/2" sheet announcing a sale of Dodgers souvenirs. At bottom are three cards of some of the team's most popular players. All are in color and standard 2-1/2" x 3-1/2" size, perforated for easy separation from the sheet. Card backs are in black-and-white with personal data, a facsimile autograph and trivia. Cards are numbered by uniform number.

		MT
Complete Sheet:		6.00
Complete Set (3):		4.00
Common Player:		2.00
10	Gary Sheffield	2.50
23	Eric Karros	2.00
43	Raul Mondesi	2.00

1998 L.A. Dodgers Police

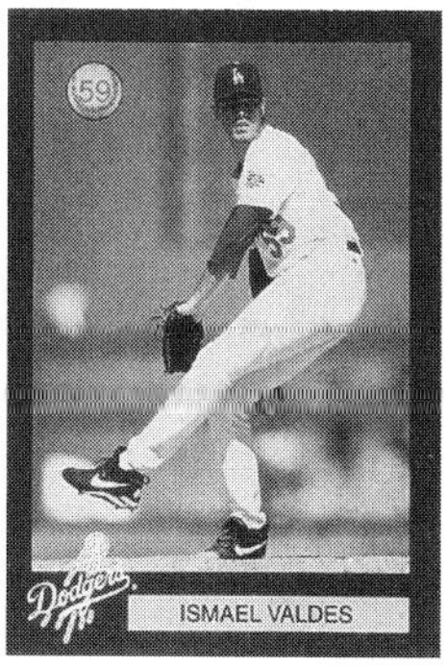

Repeating the format used in recent years, a 30-card perforated sheet, the Dodgers issued their annual D.A.R.E. drug-awareness set in April. Individual cards are the standard 2-1/2" x 3-1/2" on the 15" x 17-1/2" sheet. Fronts have action photos with blue borders. A baseball at top-left has the player's uniform number, by which the set is checklisted here.

		MT
Complete Set, Sheet:		16.00
Complete Set, Singles (30):		12.00
Common Player:		.25
7	Paul Konerko	3.00
10	Jose Vizcaino	.25
12	Mike Devereaux	.25
13	Antonio Osuna	.25
15	Tom Prince	.25
16	Hideo Nomo	2.00
18	Bill Russell	.25
22	Thomas Howard	.25
23	Eric Karros	.50
25	Juan Castro	.25
26	Eric Young	.75
27	Todd Zeile	.35
28	Todd Hollandsworth	.50
30	Wilton Guerrero	.25
31	Mike Piazza	4.00
36	Scott Radinsky	.25
37	Darren Dreifort	.25
40	Matt Luke	.25
41	Tripp Cromer	.25
43	Raul Mondesi	2.00
44	Mark Guthrie	.25
45	Roger Cedeno	.35
46	Jim Bruske	.25
47	Trenidad Hubbard	.25
48	Ramon Martinez	.50
49	Frank Lankford	.25
52	Darren Hall	.25
59	Ismael Valdes	.25
61	Chan Ho Park	.75
---	Joe Amalfitano, Mark Cresse, Glenn Gregson, Manny Mota, Mike Scioscia, Reggie Smith	.25

1998 L.A. Dodgers Record Breakers

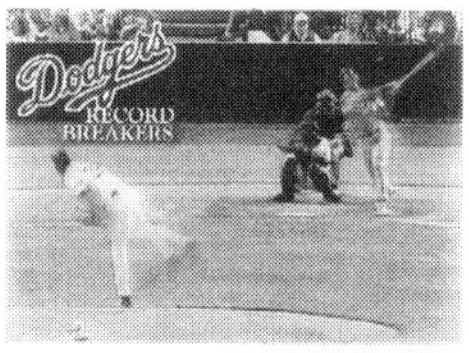

This set of motion cards was distributed one per month to members of the Dodgers Kids Clubhouse when they attended a game. The 3-1/2" x 2-1/2" cards have a borderless front with an action scene viewed by changing the angle of the card. The team logo appears in an upper corner. Backs repeat the logo and have personal data and details of the record performance. The cards are unnumbered.

		MT
Complete Set (5):		20.00
Common Player:		4.00
(1)	Ramon Martinez	4.00
(2)	Raul Mondesi (action)	5.00
(3)	Raul Mondesi (portrait, membership card)	4.00
(4)	Hideo Nomo	5.00
(5)	Mike Piazza	8.00

1999 L.A. Dodgers Concession Stand Cards

During the first five home games of the 1999 season, fans visiting the concession stands at Dodgers Stadium could receive a free player card. Fronts have color action photos on a white background with blue borders. The player's first name is printed at bottom, and a catchword at top. Backs are horizontal in black-and-white with a portrait photo career highlights and personal data, plus team and Dodger Stadium logos.

		MT
Complete Set (5):		4.00
Common Player:		1.00
1	Kevin Brown	1.00
2	Chan Ho Park	1.50
3	Ismael Valdes	1.00
4	Carlos Perez	1.00
5	Darren Dreifort	1.00

1999 L.A. Dodgers Fan Appreciation Days

Fans attending the Dodgers' final homestand were given this 11" x 8-1/2" sheet announcing special sales of Dodgers souvenirs. At bottom are three cards of some of the team's most popular players. All are in color and standard 2-1/2" x 3-1/2" size, perforated for easy separation from the sheet. The card fronts are in the style of 1953 Topps while backs are in black-and-white 1951-Bowman format with personal data, and a career summary.

		MT
Complete Sheet:		5.00
Complete Set (3):		4.00
1	Adrian Beltre	2.00
2	Kevin Brown	1.50
3	Eric Karros	1.00

1999 L.A. Dodgers Police

Repeating the format used in recent years, a 30-card perforated sheet, the Dodgers issued their annual D.A.R.E. drug-awareness set in April. Individual cards are the standard 2-1/2" x 3-1/2" on the 15" x 17-1/2" sheet. Fronts have action photos with blue borders. A baseball at top-left has the player's uniform number, by which the set is checklisted here. Backs are in black-and-white with LAPD and D.A.R.E. logos, player data and a safety message.

		MT
Complete Set, Sheet:		12.50
Complete Set, Singles (30):		10.00
Common Player:		.25
5	Jose Vizcaino	.25
7	Tripp Cromer	.25
8	Mark Grudzielanek	.35
9	Todd Hundley	.50
10	Gary Sheffield	.75
13	Antonio Osuna	.25
14	Adam Riggs	.25
15	Davey Johnson	.25
16	Paul Loduca	.40
17	Juan Castro	.25
21	Eric Young	.40
22	Devon White	.35
23	Eric Karros	.50
25	Dave Hansen	.25
27	Kevin Brown	1.50
28	Todd Hollandsworth	.25
29	Adrian Beltre	1.50
33	Carlos Perez	.25
37	Darren Dreifort	.25
41	Jeff Shaw	.25
43	Raul Mondesi	.75
46	Rick Wilkins	.25
48	Jacob Brumfield	.25
50	Pedro Borbon	.25
55	Onan Masaoka	.50
59	Ismael Valdes	.25
61	Chan Ho Park	.75
63	Angel Pena	.25
75	Alan Mills	.25
	Coaches (Rick Dempsey, Rick Down, Glenn Hoffman, Charlie Hough, Manny Mota, John Shelby, Jim Tracy)	.25

1997 LaSalle Bank Ryne Sandberg

This card was part of a souvenir tribute distributed to more than 30,000 persons attending Ryne Sandberg's final game at Wrigley Field on Sept. 20. A commemorative program and this card marked Ryno's 15 years as a Chicago Cub. The 2-1/2" x 3-1/2" card is printed on heavy, UV-coated cardboard. The front features a borderless color action photo. On the full-color back are portrait and action photos, career highlights and stats through Sept. 14.

	MT
Ryne Sandberg	7.50

1983 LCF/JAF

(See listings under Larry Fritsch Cards)

1985 Leaf-Donruss

In an attempt to share in the Canadian baseball card market, Donruss issued a 264-card version of its regular set to be sold in Canada. Fronts of the 2-1/2" x 3-1/2" cards are virtually identical to the regular '85 Donruss cards of the same players, except that a green stylized leaf has been added to the logo in the upper-left. On back, player biographies have been re-written to accomodate both English and French versions, and new card numbers have been assigned. The 264 cards in this shortened set concentrate on star-caliber players, as well as those of Canada's two major league teams. A special two-card subset, "Canadian Greats," featured paintings of Dave Stieb and Tim Raines. The Leaf-Donruss cards were widely distributed in the U.S. through hobby dealers.

		MT
Complete Set (264):		60.00
Common Player:		.08
1	Ryne Sandberg (Diamond King)	2.50
2	Doug DeCinces (DK)	.08
3	Rich Dotson (DK)	.08
4	Bert Blyleven (DK)	.08
5	Lou Whitaker (DK)	.10
6	Dan Quisenberry (DK)	.08
7	Don Mattingly (DK)	3.00
8	Carney Lansford (DK)	.08
9	Frank Tanana (DK)	.08
10	Willie Upshaw (DK)	.10
11	Claudell Washington (DK)	.08
12	Mike Marshall (DK)	.10
13	Joaquin Andujar (DK)	.08
14	Cal Ripken, Jr. (DK)	9.00
15	Jim Rice (DK)	.25
16	Don Sutton (DK)	.50
17	Frank Viola (DK)	.10
18	Alvin Davis (DK)	.08
19	Mario Soto (DK)	.08
20	Jose Cruz (DK)	.08
21	Charlie Lea (DK)	.08
22	Jesse Orosco (DK)	.08
23	Juan Samuel (DK)	.08
24	Tony Pena (DK)	.08
25	Tony Gwynn (DK)	3.00
26	Bob Brenly (DK)	.08
27	Steve Kiefer (Rated Rookie)	.08
28	Joe Morgan	.25
29	Luis Leal	.08
30	Dan Gladden	.08
31	Shane Rawley	.08
32	Mark Clear	.08
33	Terry Kennedy	.08
34	Hal McRae	.08
35	Mickey Rivers	.08
36	Tom Brunansky	.08
37	LaMarr Hoyt	.08
38	Orel Hershiser	1.50
39	Chris Bando	.08
40	Lee Lacy	.08
41	Lance Parrish	.10
42	George Foster	.10
43	Kevin McReynolds	.08
44	Robin Yount	2.00
45	Craig McMurtry	.08
46	Mike Witt	.08
47	Gary Redus	.08
48	Dennis Rasmussen	.08
49	Gary Woods	.08
50	Phil Bradley	.08
51	Steve Bedrosian	.08
52	Duane Walker	.08
53	Geoff Zahn	.08
54	Dave Stieb	.10
55	Pascual Perez	.08
56	Mark Langston	1.50
57	Bob Dernier	.08
58	Joe Cowley	.08

59	Dan Schatzeder	.08
60	Ozzie Smith	2.00
61	Bob Knepper	.08
62	Keith Hernandez	.08
63	Rick Rhoden	.08
64	Alejandro Pena	.08
65	Damaso Garcia	.08
66	Chili Davis	.10
67	Al Oliver	.10
68	Alan Wiggins	.08
69	Darryl Motley	.08
70	Gary Ward	.08
71	John Butcher	.08
72	Scott McGregor	.08
73	Bruce Hurst	.08
74	Dwayne Murphy	.08
75	Greg Luzinski	.10
76	Pat Tabler	.08
77	Chet Lemon	.08
78	Jim Sundberg	.08
79	Wally Backman	.08
80	Terry Puhl	.08
81	Storm Davis	.08
82	Jim Wohlford	.08
83	Willie Randolph	.08
84	Ron Cey	.10
85	Jim Beattie	.08
86	Rafael Ramirez	.08
87	Cesar Cedeno	.08
88	Bobby Grich	.08
89	Jason Thompson	.08
90	Steve Sax	.08
91	Tony Fernandez	.15
92	Jeff Leonard	.08
93	Von Hayes	.08
94	Steve Garvey	.30
95	Steve Balboni	.08
96	Larry Parrish	.08
97	Tim Teufel	.08
98	Sammy Stewart	.08
99	Roger Clemens	40.00
100	Steve Kemp	.08
101	Tom Seaver	.90
102	Andre Thornton	.08
103	Kirk Gibson	.08
104	Ted Simmons	.08
105	David Palmer	.08
106	Roy Lee Jackson	.08
107	Kirby Puckett	40.00
108	Charlie Hough	.08
109	Mike Boddicker	.08
110	Willie Wilson	.08
111	Tim Lollar	.08
112	Tony Armas	.08
113	Steve Carlton	.60
114	Gary Lavelle	.08
115	Cliff Johnson	.08
116	Ray Burris	.08
117	Rudy Law	.08
118	Mike Scioscia	.08
119	Kent Tekulve	.08
120	George Vukovich	.08
121	Barbaro Garbey	.08
122	Mookie Wilson	.08
123	Ben Oglivie	.08
124	Jerry Mumphrey	.08
125	Willie McGee	.10
126	Jeff Reardon	.10
127	Dave Winfield	1.50
128	Lee Smith	.15
129	Ken Phelps	.08
130	Rick Camp	.08
131	Dave Concepcion	.08
132	Rod Carew	.40
133	Andre Dawson	.25
134	Doyle Alexander	.08
135	Miguel Dilone	.08
136	Jim Gott	.08
137	Eric Show	.08
138	Phil Niekro	.40
139	Rick Sutcliffe	.08
140	Two For The Title (Don Mattingly, Dave Winfield)	3.25
141	Ken Oberkfell	.08
142	Jack Morris	.10
143	Lloyd Moseby	.10
144	Pete Rose	2.00
145	Gary Gaetti	.10
146	Don Baylor	.15
147	Bobby Meacham	.08
148	Frank White	.08
149	Mark Thurmond	.08
150	Dwight Evans	.08
151	Al Holland	.08
152	Joel Youngblood	.08
153	Rance Mulliniks	.08
154	Bill Caudill	.08
155	Carlton Fisk	.35
156	Rick Honeycutt	.08
157	John Candelaria	.08
158	Alan Trammell	.15
159	Darryl Strawberry	.50
160	Aurelio Lopez	.08
161	Enos Cabell	.08
162	Dion James	.08
163	Bruce Sutter	.08
164	Razor Shines	.08
165	Butch Wynegar	.08
166	Rich Bordi	.08
167	Spike Owen	.08
168	Chris Chambliss	.08
169	Dave Parker	.10
170	Reggie Jackson	1.00
171	Bryn Smith	.08
172	Dave Collins	.08
173	Dave Engle	.08
174	Buddy Bell	.08
175	Mike Flanagan	.08
176	George Brett	3.50
177	Graig Nettles	.08
178	Jerry Koosman	.08
179	Wade Boggs	2.00
180	Jody Davis	.08
181	Ernie Whitt	.08
182	Dave Kingman	.08
183	Vance Law	.08
184	Fernando Valenzuela	.10
185	Bill Madlock	.08
186	Brett Butler	.10
187	Doug Sisk	.08
188	Dan Petry	.08
189	Joe Niekro	.08
190	Rollie Fingers	.20
191	David Green	.08
192	Steve Rogers	.08
193	Ken Griffey	.08
194	Scott Sanderson	.08
195	Barry Bonnell	.08
196	Bruce Benedict	.08
197	Keith Moreland	.08
198	Fred Lynn	.10
199	Tim Wallach	.20
200	Kent Hrbek	.10
201	Pete O'Brien	.08
202	Bud Black	.08
203	Eddie Murray	1.50
204	Goose Gossage	.10
205	Mike Schmidt	3.00
206	Mike Easler	.08
207	Jack Clark	.08
208	Rickey Henderson	.75
209	Jesse Barfield	.15
210	Ron Kittle	.08
211	Pedro Guerrero	.08
212	Johnny Ray	.08
213	Julio Franco	.10
214	Hubie Brooks	.08
215	Darrell Evans	.08
216	Nolan Ryan	9.00
217	Jim Gantner	.08
218	Tim Raines	.20
219	Dave Righetti	.10
220	Gary Matthews	.08
221	Jack Perconte	.08
222	Dale Murphy	.30
223	Brian Downing	.08
224	Mickey Hatcher	.08
225	Lonnie Smith	.08
226	Jorge Orta	.08
227	Milt Wilcox	.08
228	John Denny	.08
229	Marty Barrett	.08
230	Alfredo Griffin	.08
231	Harold Baines	.10
232	Bill Russell	.08
233	Marvell Wynne	.08
234	Dwight Gooden	1.00
235	Willie Hernandez	.08
236	Bill Gullickson	.08
237	Ron Guidry	.10
238	Leon Durham	.08
239	Al Cowens	.08
240	Bob Horner	.08
241	Gary Carter	.30
242	Glenn Hubbard	.08
243	Steve Trout	.08
244	Jay Howell	.08
245	Terry Francona	.08
246	Cecil Cooper	.08
247	Larry McWilliams	.08
248	George Bell	.15
249	Larry Herndon	.08
250	Ozzie Virgil	.08
251	Dave Stieb (Canadian Great)	.45
252	Tim Raines (Canadian Great)	2.00
253	Ricky Horton	.08
254	Bill Buckner	.08
255	Dan Driessen	.08
256	Ron Darling	.08
257	Doug Flynn	.08
258	Darrell Porter	.08
259	George Hendrick	.08
653	Lou Gehrig Puzzle Card	.08
----	Checklist 1-26 DK	.08
----	Checklist 27-102	.08
----	Checklist 103-178	.08
----	Checklist 179-259	.08

1986 Leaf

For its second Canadian card set the Donruss name was removed from the front of the company's 264-card issue, identifying the cards as "Leaf '86." Again concentrating on big-name stars and players from the Expos and Blue Jays, the 2-1/2" x 3-1/2" cards feature a design identical to the 1986 Donruss cards. Backs were altered to allow the publication of career highlights in both English and French, and card numbers were changed. The "Canadian Greats" cards in the 1986 Leaf set, painted portraits rather than photos, were Jesse Barfield and Jeff Reardon. Besides being sold in its intended market in Canada, the set was widely distributed in the U.S. through hobby vendors.

		MT
Complete Set (260):		45.00
Common Player:		.08
1	Kirk Gibson (Diamond King)	.10
2	Goose Gossage (DK)	.10
3	Willie McGee (DK)	.10
4	George Bell (DK)	.15
5	Tony Armas (DK)	.08
6	Chili Davis (DK)	.10
7	Cecil Cooper (DK)	.08
8	Mike Boddicker (DK)	.08
9	Davey Lopes (DK)	.08
10	Bill Doran (DK)	.08
11	Bret Saberhagen (DK)	.15
12	Brett Butler (DK)	.15
13	Harold Baines (DK)	.10
14	Mike Davis (DK)	.08
15	Tony Perez (DK)	.25
16	Willie Randolph (DK)	.08
17	Bob Boone (DK)	.10
18	Orel Hershiser (DK)	.15
19	Johnny Ray (DK)	.08
20	Gary Ward (DK)	.08
21	Rick Mahler (DK)	.08
22	Phil Bradley (DK)	.08
23	Jerry Koosman (DK)	.08
24	Tom Brunansky (DK)	.08
25	Andre Dawson (DK)	.25
26	Dwight Gooden (DK)	.75
27	Andres Galarraga (Rated Rookie)	15.00
28	Fred McGriff (RR)	25.00
29	Dave Shipanoff (RR)	.08
30	Danny Jackson	.08
31	Robin Yount	2.00
32	Mike Fitzgerald	.08
33	Lou Whitaker	.08
34	Alfredo Griffin	.08
35	"Oil Can" Boyd	.08
36	Ron Guidry	.08
37	Rickey Henderson	.75
38	Jack Morris	.10
39	Brian Downing	.08
40	Mike Marshall	.08
41	Tony Gwynn	2.50
42	George Brett	3.00
43	Jim Gantner	.08
44	Hubie Brooks	.08
45	Tony Fernandez	.15
46	Oddibe McDowell	.08
47	Ozzie Smith	2.00
48	Ken Griffey	.08
49	Jose Cruz	.08
50	Mariano Duncan	.08
51	Mike Schmidt	3.00
52	Pat Tabler	.08
53	Pete Rose	2.50
54	Frank White	.08
55	Carney Lansford	.08
56	Steve Garvey	.30
57	Vance Law	.08
58	Tony Pena	.08
59	Wayne Tolleson	.08
60	Dale Murphy	.30
61	LaMarr Hoyt	.08
62	Ryne Sandberg	2.00
63	Gary Carter	.40
64	Lee Smith	.08
65	Alvin Davis	.08
66	Edwin Nunez	.08
67	Kent Hrbek	.10
68	Dave Stieb	.10
69	Kirby Puckett	6.00
70	Paul Molitor	2.00
71	Glenn Hubbard	.08
72	Lloyd Moseby	.08
73	Mike Smithson	.08
74	Jeff Leonard	.08
75	Danny Darwin	.08
76	Kevin McReynolds	.08
77	Bill Buckner	.08
78	Ron Oester	.08
79	Tommy Herr	.08
80	Mike Pagliarulo	.08
81	Ron Romanick	.08
82	Brook Jacoby	.08
83	Eddie Murray	1.50
84	Gary Pettis	.08
85	Chet Lemon	.08
86	Toby Harrah	.08
87	Mike Scioscia	.08
88	Bert Blyleven	.08
89	Dave Righetti	.08
90	Bob Knepper	.08
91	Fernando Valenzuela	.15
92	Dave Dravecky	.08
93	Julio Franco	.08
94	Keith Moreland	.08
95	Darryl Motley	.08
96	Jack Clark	.08
97	Tim Wallach	.10
98	Steve Balboni	.08
99	Storm Davis	.08
100	Jay Howell	.08
101	Alan Trammell	.10
102	Willie Hernandez	.08
103	Don Mattingly	3.00
104	Lee Lacy	.08
105	Pedro Guerrero	.08
106	Willie Wilson	.08
107	Craig Reynolds	.08
108	Tim Raines	.25
109	Shane Rawley	.08
110	Larry Parrish	.08
111	Eric Show	.08
112	Mike Witt	.08
113	Dennis Eckersley	.10
114	Mike Moore	.08
115	Vince Coleman	.10
116	Damaso Garcia	.08
117	Steve Carlton	.50
118	Floyd Bannister	.08
119	Mario Soto	.08
120	Fred Lynn	.08
121	Bob Horner	.08
122	Rick Sutcliffe	.08
123	Walt Terrell	.08
124	Keith Hernandez	.08
125	Dave Winfield	1.50
126	Frank Viola	.08
127	Dwight Evans	.08
128	Willie Upshaw	.08
129	Andre Thornton	.08
130	Donnie Moore	.08
131	Darryl Strawberry	.35
132	Nolan Ryan	6.00
133	Garry Templeton	.08
134	John Tudor	.08
135	Dave Parker	.10
136	Larry McWilliams	.08
137	Terry Pendleton	.08
138	Terry Puhl	.08
139	Bob Dernier	.08
140	Ozzie Guillen	.08
141	Jim Clancy	.08
142	Cal Ripken, Jr.	6.00
143	Mickey Hatcher	.08
144	Dan Petry	.08
145	Rich Gedman	.08
146	Jim Rice	.08
147	Butch Wynegar	.08
148	Donnie Hill	.08
149	Jim Sundberg	.08
150	Joe Hesketh	.08
151	Chris Codiroli	.08
152	Charlie Hough	.08
153	Herman Winningham	.08
154	Dave Rozema	.08
155	Don Slaught	.08
156	Juan Beniquez	.08
157	Ted Higuera	.08
158	Andy Hawkins	.08
159	Don Robinson	.08
160	Glenn Wilson	.08
161	Earnest Riles	.08
162	Nick Esasky	.08
163	Carlton Fisk	.50
164	Claudell Washington	.08
165	Scott McGregor	.08
166	Nate Snell	.08
167	Ted Simmons	.08
168	Wade Boggs	2.00
169	Marty Barrett	.08
170	Bud Black	.08
171	Charlie Leibrandt	.08
172	Charlie Lea	.08
173	Reggie Jackson	.75
174	Bryn Smith	.08
175	Glenn Davis	.08
176	Von Hayes	.08
177	Danny Cox	.08
178	Sam Khalifa	.08
179	Tom Browning	.08
180	Scott Garrelts	.08
181	Shawon Dunston	.08
182	Doyle Alexander	.08
183	Jim Presley	.08
184	Al Cowens	.08
185	Mark Salas	.08
186	Tom Niedenfuer	.08
187	Dave Henderson	.08
188	Lonnie Smith	.08
189	Bruce Bochte	.08
190	Leon Durham	.08
191	Terry Francona	.08
192	Bruce Sutter	.08
193	Steve Crawford	.08
194	Bob Brenly	.08
195	Dan Pasqua	.08
196	Juan Samuel	.08
197	Floyd Rayford	.08
198	Tim Burke	.08
199	Ben Oglivie	.08
200	Don Carman	.08
201	Lance Parrish	.08
202	Terry Forster	.08
203	Neal Heaton	.08
204	Ivan Calderon	.08
205	Jorge Orta	.08
206	Tom Henke	.10
207	Rick Reuschel	.08
208	Dan Quisenberry	.08
209	Ty-Breaking Hit (Pete Rose)	.50
210	Floyd Youmans	.08
211	Tom Filer	.08
212	R.J. Reynolds	.08
213	Gorman Thomas	.08
214	Canadian Great (Jeff Reardon) (Canadian Great)	.75
215	Chris Brown	.08
216	Rick Aguilera	.08
217	Ernie Whitt	.08
218	Joe Orsulak	.08
219	Jimmy Key	.10
220	Atlee Hammaker	.08
221	Ron Darling	.08
222	Zane Smith	.08
223	Bob Welch	.08
224	Reid Nichols	.08
225	Fleet Feet (Vince Coleman, Willie McGee)	.15
226	Mark Gubicza	.10
227	Tim Birtsas	.08
228	Mike Hargrove	.08
229	Randy St. Claire	.08
230	Larry Herndon	.08
231	Dusty Baker	.08
232	Mookie Wilson	.08
233	Jeff Lahti	.08
234	Tom Seaver	.85
235	Mike Scott	.08
236	Don Sutton	.35
237	Roy Smalley	.08
238	Bill Madlock	.08
239	Charles Hudson	.08
240	John Franco	.08
241	Frank Tanana	.08
242	Sid Fernandez	.08
243	Knuckle Brothers (Joe Niekro, Phil Niekro)	.25
244	Dennis Lamp	.08
245	Gene Nelson	.08
246	Terry Harper	.08
247	Vida Blue	.08
248	Roger McDowell	.08
249	Tony Bernazard	.08
250	Cliff Johnson	.08
251	Hal McRae	.08
252	Garth Iorg	.08
253	Mitch Webster	.10
254	Jesse Barfield (Canadian Great)	.60
255	Dan Driessen	.08
256	Mike Brown	.08
257	Ron Kittle	.08
258	Bo Diaz	.08
259	Hank Aaron Puzzle Card	.08
260	Pete Rose (King of Kings)	2.00
----	Checklist 1-26 DK	.08
----	Checklist 27-106	.08
----	Checklist 107-186	.08
----	Checklist 187-260	.08

1987 Leaf

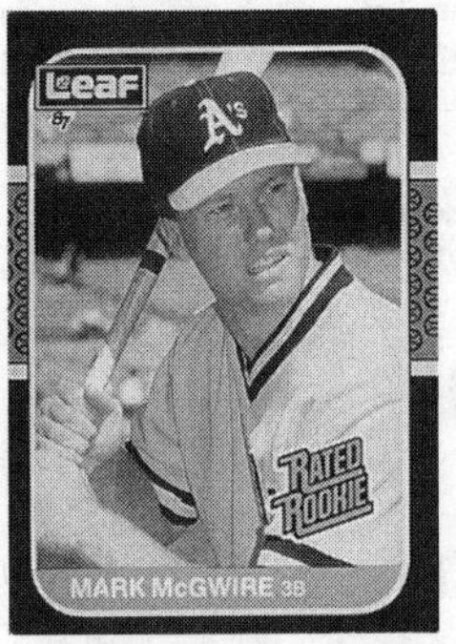

For the third consecutive season, Leaf-Donruss issued a Canadian baseball card set. These cards are nearly identical to the American set except for the name "Leaf" which appears on the front in place of "Donruss." The set contains 264 cards, each measuring 2-1/2" x 3-1/2", with a special emphasis being placed on players from the Montreal and Toronto teams. Backs feature career highlights in both English and French. As in the previous years, two "Canadian Greats" cards appear in the set. These painted portraits feature Mark Eichhorn and Floyd Youmans.

		MT
Complete Set (264):		35.00
Common Player:		.08
1	Wally Joyner (Diamond King)	.30
2	Roger Clemens (DK)	2.50
3	Dale Murphy (DK)	.30
4	Darryl Strawberry (DK)	.30
5	Ozzie Smith (DK)	.90
6	Jose Canseco (DK)	1.00
7	Charlie Hough (DK)	.08
8	Brook Jacoby (DK)	.08
9	Fred Lynn (DK)	.08
10	Rick Rhoden (DK)	.08
11	Chris Brown (DK)	.08
12	Von Hayes (DK)	.08
13	Jack Morris (DK)	.15
14	Kevin McReynolds (DK)	.08
15	George Brett (DK)	1.50
16	Ted Higuera (DK)	.08
17	Hubie Brooks (DK)	.08
18	Mike Scott (DK)	.08
19	Kirby Puckett (DK)	2.50
20	Dave Winfield (DK)	1.00
21	Lloyd Moseby (DK)	.15
22	Eric Davis (DK)	.25
23	Jim Presley (DK)	.08
24	Keith Moreland (DK)	.08
25	Greg Walker (DK)	.08
26	Steve Sax (DK)	.08
27	Checklist 1-27	.08
28	B.J. Surhoff (Rated Rookie)	.15
29	Randy Myers (RR)	.20
30	Ken Gerhart (RR)	.08
31	Benito Santiago (RR)	.15
32	Greg Swindell (RR)	.15
33	Mike Birkbeck (RR)	.08
34	Terry Steinbach (RR)	.25
35	Bo Jackson (RR)	1.00
36	Greg Maddux (RR)	15.00
37	Jim Lindeman (RR)	.08
38	Devon White (RR)	1.75
39	Eric Bell (RR)	.08
40	Will Fraser (RR)	.08
41	Jerry Browne (RR)	.08
42	Chris James (RR)	.08
43	Rafael Palmeiro (RR)	3.00
44	Pat Dodson (RR)	.08
45	Duane Ward (RR)	.50
46	Mark McGwire (RR)	20.00
47	Bruce Fields (RR) (photo actually Darnell Coles)	.08
48	Jody Davis	.08
49	Roger McDowell	.08
50	Jose Guzman	.08
51	Oddibe McDowell	.08
52	Harold Baines	.10
53	Dave Righetti	.08
54	Moose Haas	.08
55	Mark Langston	.10
56	Kirby Puckett	1.00
57	Dwight Evans	.08
58	Willie Randolph	.08
59	Wally Backman	.08
60	Bryn Smith	.08
61	Tim Wallach	.10
62	Joe Hesketh	.08
63	Garry Templeton	.08
64	Rob Thompson	.08
65	Canadian Greats (Floyd Youmans)	.15
66	Ernest Riles	.08
67	Robin Yount	1.00
68	Darryl Strawberry	.25
69	Ernie Whitt	.08
70	Dave Winfield	.50
71	Paul Molitor	1.00
72	Dave Stieb	.10
73	Tom Henke	.10
74	Frank Viola	.08
75	Scott Garrelts	.08
76	Mike Boddicker	.08
77	Keith Moreland	.08
78	Lou Whitaker	.10
79	Dave Parker	.10
80	Lee Smith	.10
81	Tom Candiotti	.08
82	Greg Harris	.08
83	Fred Lynn	.08
84	Dwight Gooden	.25
85	Ron Darling	.08
86	Mike Krukow	.08
87	Spike Owen	.08
88	Len Dykstra	.10
89	Rick Aguilera	.08
90	Jim Clancy	.08
91	Joe Johnson	.08
92	Damaso Garcia	.08
93	Sid Fernandez	.08
94	Bob Ojeda	.08
95	Ted Higuera	.08
96	George Brett	1.00
97	Willie Wilson	.08
98	Cal Ripken	3.00
99	Kent Hrbek	.10
100	Bert Blyleven	.08
101	Ron Guidry	.08
102	Andy Allanson	.08
103	Dave Henderson	.08
104	Kirk Gibson	.08
105	Lloyd Moseby	.08
106	Tony Fernandez	.10
107	Lance Parrish	.10
108	Ozzie Smith	.90
109	Gary Carter	.50
110	Eddie Murray	.65
111	Mike Witt	.08
112	Bobby Witt	.08
113	Willie McGee	.10
114	Steve Garvey	.20
115	Glenn Davis	.08
116	Jose Cruz	.08
117	Ozzie Guillen	.08
118	Alvin Davis	.08
119	Jose Rijo	.08
120	Bill Madlock	.08
121	Tommy Herr	.08
122	Mike Schmidt	1.00
123	Mike Scioscia	.08
124	Terry Pendleton	.08
125	Leon Durham	.08
126	Alan Trammell	.10
127	Jesse Barfield	.10
128	Shawon Dunston	.08
129	Pete Rose	1.50
130	Von Hayes	.08
131	Julio Franco	.08
132	Juan Samuel	.08
133	Joe Carter	.50
134	Brook Jacoby	.08
135	Jack Morris	.10
136	Bob Horner	.08
137	Calvin Schiraldi	.08
138	Tom Browning	.08
139	Shane Rawley	.08
140	Mario Soto	.08
141	Dale Murphy	.30
142	Hubie Brooks	.08
143	Jeff Reardon	.10
144	Will Clark	3.00
145	Ed Correa	.08
146	Glenn Wilson	.08
147	Johnny Ray	.08
148	Fernando Valenzuela	.10
149	Tim Raines	.25
150	Don Mattingly	2.50
151	Jose Canseco	1.50
152	Gary Pettis	.08
153	Don Sutton	.15
154	Jim Presley	.08
155	Checklist 28-105	.08
156	Dale Sveum	.08
157	Cory Snyder	.08
158	Jeff Sellers	.08
159	Denny Walling	.08
160	Danny Cox	.08
161	Bob Forsch	.08
162	Joaquin Andujar	.08
163	Roberto Clemente Puzzle Card	.15
164	Paul Assenmacher	.08
165	Marty Barrett	.08
166	Ray Knight	.08
167	Rafael Santana	.08
168	Bruce Ruffin	.08
169	Buddy Bell	.08
170	Kevin Mitchell	.08
171	Ken Oberkfell	.08
172	Gene Garber	.08
173	Canadian Greats (Mark Eichhorn)	.25
174	Don Carman	.08
175	Jesse Orosco	.08
176	Mookie Wilson	.08
177	Gary Ward	.08
178	John Franco	.08
179	Eric Davis	.10
180	Walt Terrell	.08
181	Phil Niekro	.20
182	Pat Tabler	.08
183	Brett Butler	.10
184	George Bell	.20
185	Pete Incaviglia	.08
186	Pete O'Brien	.08
187	Jimmy Key	.10
188	Frank White	.08
189	Mike Pagliarulo	.08
190	Roger Clemens	2.00
191	Rickey Henderson	.75
192	Mike Easler	.08
193	Wade Boggs	1.00
194	Vince Coleman	.08
195	Charlie Kerfeld	.08
196	Dickie Thon	.08
197	Bill Doran	.08
198	Alfredo Griffin	.08
199	Carlton Fisk	.35
200	Phil Bradley	.08
201	Reggie Jackson	.60
202	Bob Boone	.08
203	Steve Sax	.08
204	Tom Niedenfuer	.08
205	Tim Burke	.08
206	Floyd Youmans	.08
207	Jay Tibbs	.08
208	Chili Davis	.10
209	Larry Parrish	.08
210	John Cerutti	.10
211	Kevin Bass	.08
212	Andre Dawson	.25
213	Bob Sebra	.08
214	Kevin McReynolds	.08
215	Jim Morrison	.08
216	Candy Maldonado	.08
217	John Kruk	.10
218	Todd Worrell	.08
219	Barry Bonds	6.00
220	Andy McGaffigan	.08
221	Andres Galarraga	.15
222	Mike Fitzgerald	.08
223	Kirk McCaskill	.08
224	Dave Smith	.08
225	Ruben Sierra	.08
226	Scott Fletcher	.08
227	Chet Lemon	.08
228	Dan Petry	.08
229	Mark Eichhorn	.10
230	Cecil Cooper	.08
231	Willie Upshaw	.08
232	Don Baylor	.10
233	Keith Hernandez	.08
234	Ryne Sandberg	1.00
235	Tony Gwynn	1.00
236	Chris Brown	.08
237	Pedro Guerrero	.08
238	Mark Gubicza	.08
239	Sid Bream	.08
240	Joe Cowley	.08
241	Bill Buckner	.08
242	John Candelaria	.08
243	Scott McGregor	.08
244	Tom Brunansky	.08
245	Gary Gaetti	.08
246	Orel Hershiser	.20
247	Jim Rice	.08
248	Oil Can Boyd	.08
249	Bob Knepper	.08
250	Danny Tartabull	.08
251	John Cangelosi	.08
252	Wally Joyner	.15
253	Bruce Hurst	.08
254	Rich Gedman	.08
255	Jim Deshaies	.08
256	Tony Pena	.08
257	Nolan Ryan	3.00
258	Mike Scott	.08
259	Checklist 106-183	.08
260	Dennis Rasmussen	.08
261	Bret Saberhagen	.10
262	Steve Balboni	.08
263	Tom Seaver	.50
264	Checklist 184-264	.08

1987 Leaf Candy City Team

Leaf produced this set as part of its endorsement for the Special Olympics. Twelve cards feature Baseball Hall of Famers. The cards measure 2-1/2" x 3-1/2" and are numbered H1-H12. The remaining six cards in the set are numbered S1-S6 and feature unnamed Special Olympics champions. All cards feature the artwork of Dick Perez. The cards were available through a mail-in offer advertised at special store displays. Only the baseball-related subjects are listed in the checklist.

		MT
Complete Set (12):		4.00
Common Player:		.15
H1	Mickey Mantle	1.00
H2	Yogi Berra	.40
H3	Roy Campanella	.40
H4	Stan Musial	.50
H5	Ted Williams	.60
H6	Duke Snider	.40
H7	Hank Aaron	.50
H8	Pee Wee Reese	.30
H9	Brooks Robinson	.30
H10	Al Kaline	.30
H11	Willie McCovey	.25
H12	Cool Papa Bell	.15

1988 Leaf

This 264-card set features color player photos from among the 1988 Donruss 660-card standard issue, with emphasis on players from Montreal and Toronto. A border of red, blue and black stripes duplicates the design of the Donruss set, with the exception of a "Leaf '88" logo in the upper-left corner that replaces the Donruss logo. Two special Canadian Greats cards are included in this set: Perez-Steele portraits of Tim Wallach and George Bell. The set also includes the portrait-style Diamond Kings cards (the set's first 26 cards, one for each team). The DK's carry the Donruss logo above the gold DK banner. All card backs are bilingual (French/English), numbered, and printed in black on white stock with a light blue border. This set was sold in 10-card wax packs with one triple-piece puzzle card per pack and was distributed via larger hobby and retail shops in the U.S. and Canada.

		MT
Complete Set (264):		10.00
Common Player:		.08
1	Mark McGwire (Diamond King)	5.00
2	Tim Raines (DK)	.20
3	Benito Santiago (DK)	.08
4	Alan Trammell (DK)	.10
5	Danny Tartabull (DK)	.08
6	Ron Darling (DK)	.08
7	Paul Molitor (DK)	.50
8	Devon White (DK)	.15
9	Andre Dawson (DK)	.15
10	Julio Franco (DK)	.08
11	Scott Fletcher (DK)	.08
12	Tony Fernandez (DK)	.10
13	Shane Rawley (DK)	.08
14	Kal Daniels (DK)	.08
15	Jack Clark (DK)	.08
16	Dwight Evans (DK)	.08
17	Tommy John (DK)	.08
18	Andy Van Slyke (DK)	.08
19	Gary Gaetti (DK)	.08
20	Mark Langston (DK)	.08
21	Will Clark (DK)	.35
22	Glenn Hubbard (DK)	.08
23	Billy Hatcher (DK)	.08
24	Bob Welch (DK)	.08
25	Ivan Calderon (DK)	.08
26	Cal Ripken, Jr. (DK)	2.00
27	Checklist 1-27	.08
28	Mackey Sasser (Rated Rookie)	.08
29	Jeff Treadway (RR)	.08
30	Mike Campbell (RR)	.08
31	Lance Johnson (RR)	.15
32	Nelson Liriano (RR)	.08
33	Shawn Abner (RR)	.08
34	Roberto Alomar (RR)	3.00
35	Shawn Hillegas (RR)	.08
36	Joey Meyer (RR)	.08
37	Kevin Elster (RR)	.08
38	Jose Lind (RR)	.08
39	Kirt Manwaring (RR)	.10
40	Mark Grace (RR)	1.50
41	Jody Reed (RR)	.20
42	John Farrell (RR)	.08
43	Al Leiter (RR)	.25
44	Gary Thurman (RR)	.08
45	Vincente Palacios (RR)	.08
46	Eddie Williams (RR)	.08
47	Jack McDowell (RR)	.40
48	Dwight Gooden	.15
49	Mike Witt	.08
50	Wally Joyner	.15
51	Brook Jacoby	.08
52	Bert Blyleven	.08
53	Ted Higuera	.08
54	Mike Scott	.08
55	Jose Guzman	.08
56	Roger Clemens	1.00
57	Dave Righetti	.08
58	Benito Santiago	.08
59	Ozzie Guillen	.08
60	Matt Nokes	.08
61	Fernando Valenzuela	.10
62	Orel Hershiser	.15
63	Sid Fernandez	.08
64	Ozzie Virgil	.08
65	Wade Boggs	.60
66	Floyd Youmans	.08
67	Jimmy Key	.10
68	Bret Saberhagen	.08
69	Jody Davis	.08
70	Shawon Dunston	.08
71	Julio Franco	.08
72	Danny Cox	.08
73	Jim Clancy	.08
74	Mark Eichhorn	.08
75	Scott Bradley	.08
76	Charlie Liebrandt	.08
77	Nolan Ryan	1.50
78	Ron Darling	.08
79	John Franco	.08
80	Dave Stieb	.08
81	Mike Fitzgerald	.08
82	Steve Bedrosian	.08
83	Dale Murphy	.20
84	Tim Burke	.08
85	Jack Morris	.10
86	Greg Walker	.08
87	Kevin Mitchell	.08
88	Doug Drabek	.08
89	Charlie Hough	.08
90	Tony Gwynn	.60
91	Rick Sutcliffe	.08
92	Shane Rawley	.08
93	George Brett	.50
94	Frank Viola	.08
95	Tony Pena	.08
96	Jim Deshaies	.08
97	Mike Scioscia	.08
98	Rick Rhoden	.08
99	Terry Kennedy	.08
100	Cal Ripken	1.50
101	Pedro Guerrero	.08
102	Andy Van Slyke	.08
103	Willie McGee	.10
104	Mike Kingery	.08
105	Kevin Seitzer	.08
106	Robin Yount	.40
107	Tracy Jones	.08
108	Dave Magadan	.08
109	Mel Hall	.08
110	Billy Hatcher	.08
111	Todd Benzinger	.08
112	Mike LaValliere	.08
113	Barry Bonds	1.00
114	Tim Raines	.20
115	Ozzie Smith	.75
116	Dave Winfield	.65
117	Keith Hernandez	.08
118	Jeffrey Leonard	.08
119	Larry Parrish	.08
120	Rob Thompson	.08
121	Andres Galarraga	.30
122	Mickey Hatcher	.08
123	Mark Langston	.08
124	Mike Schmidt	.75
125	Cory Snyder	.08
126	Andre Dawson	.15
127	Devon White	.15
128	Vince Coleman	.08
129	Bryn Smith	.08
130	Lance Parrish	.08
131	Willie Upshaw	.08
132	Pete O'Brien	.08
133	Tony Fernandez	.10
134	Billy Ripken	.08
135	Len Dykstra	.08
136	Kirk Gibson	.08
137	Kevin Bass	.08
138	Jose Canseco	.60
139	Kent Hrbek	.08
140	Lloyd Moseby	.08
141	Marty Barrett	.08
142	Carmelo Martinez	.08
143	Tom Foley	.08
144	Kirby Puckett	.75
145	Rickey Henderson	.35
146	Juan Samuel	.08
147	Pete Incaviglia	.08
148	Greg Brock	.08
149	Eric Davis	.10
150	Kal Daniels	.08
151	Bob Boone	.08
152	John Cerutti	.08
153	Mike Greenwell	.08
154	Oddibe McDowell	.08
155	Scott Fletcher	.08
156	Gary Carter	.30
157	Harold Baines	.08
158	Greg Swindell	.08
159	Mark McLemore	.08
160	Keith Moreland	.08
161	Jim Gantner	.08
162	Willie Randolph	.08
163	Fred Lynn	.08
164	B.J. Surhoff	.08
165	Ken Griffey	.08
166	Chet Lemon	.08
167	Alan Trammell	.10

168	Paul Molitor	.50
169	Lou Whitaker	.08
170	Will Clark	.50
171	Dwight Evans	.08
172	Eddie Murray	.35
173	Darrell Evans	.08
174	Ellis Burks	.10
175	Ivan Calderon	.08
176	John Kruk	.08
177	Don Mattingly	.75
178	Dick Schofield	.08
179	Bruce Hurst	.08
180	Ron Guidry	.08
181	Jack Clark	.08
182	Franklin Stubbs	.08
183	Bill Doran	.08
184	Joe Carter	.15
185	Steve Sax	.08
186	Glenn Davis	.08
187	Bo Jackson	.20
188	Bobby Bonilla	.10
189	Willie Wilson	.08
190	Danny Tartabull	.08
191	Bo Diaz	.08
192	Buddy Bell	.08
193	Tim Wallach	.10
194	Mark McGwire	3.00
195	Carney Lansford	.08
196	Alvin Davis	.08
197	Von Hayes	.08
198	Mitch Webster	.08
199	Casey Candaele	.08
200	Gary Gaetti	.08
201	Tommy Herr	.08
202	Wally Backman	.08
203	Brian Downing	.08
204	Rance Mulliniks	.08
205	Craig Reynolds	.08
206	Ruben Sierra	.08
207	Ryne Sandberg	.60
208	Carlton Fisk	.25
209	Checklist 28-107	.08
210	Gerald Young	.08
211	MVP (Tim Raines)	.25
212	John Tudor	.08
213	Canadian Greats (George Bell)	.60
214	MVP (George Bell)	.25
215	Jim Rice	.08
216	Gerald Perry	.08
217	Dave Stewart	.08
218	Jose Uribe	.08
219	Rick Rueschel	.08
220	Darryl Strawberry	.20
221	Chris Brown	.08
223	Lee Mazzilli	.08
224	Denny Walling	.08
225	Jesse Barfield	.10
226	Barry Larkin	.10
227	Harold Reynolds	.08
228	Kevin McReynolds	.08
229	Todd Worrell	.08
230	Tommy John	.08
231	Rick Aguilera	.08
232	Bill Madlock	.08
233	Roy Smalley	.08
234	Jeff Musselman	.08
235	Mike Dunne	.08
236	Jerry Browne	.08
237	Sam Horn	.08
238	Howard Johnson	.08
239	Candy Maldonado	.08
240	Nick Esasky	.08
241	Geno Petralli	.08
242	Herm Winningham	.08
243	Roger McDowell	.08
244	Brian Fisher	.08
245	John Marzano	.08
246	Terry Pendleton	.08
247	Rick Leach	.08
248	Pascual Perez	.08
249	Mookie Wilson	.08
250	Ernie Whitt	.08
251	Ron Kittle	.08
252	Oil Can Boyd	.08
253	Jim Gott	.08
254	George Bell	.15
255	Canadian Greats (Tim Wallach)	.60
256	Luis Polonia	.08
257	Hubie Brooks	.08
258	Mickey Brantley	.08
259	Gregg Jefferies	.50
260	Johnny Ray	.08
261	Checklist 108-187	.08
262	Dennis Martinez	.08
263	Stan Musial Puzzle Card	.08
264	Checklist 188-264	.08

1990 Leaf Previews

This 12-card set was produced for dealer distribution to introduce Leaf as Donruss' premium-quality brand in mid-1990. Cards have the same format as the regular-issue versions with metallic silver ink highlights on front and back. The preview cards have a white undertype on back over the stats and career highlights. It reads "Special Preview Card".

		MT
Complete Set (12):		800.00
Common Player:		20.00
1	Steve Sax	20.00
2	Joe Carter	35.00
3	Dennis Eckersley	65.00
4	Ken Griffey, Jr.	450.00
5	Barry Larkin	50.00
6	Mark Langston	25.00
7	Eric Anthony	20.00
8	Robin Ventura	60.00
9	Greg Vaughn	35.00
10	Bobby Bonilla	25.00
11	Gary Gaetti	20.00
12	Ozzie Smith	150.00

1990 Leaf

This 528-card set was issued in two 264-card series. The cards were printed on heavy quality stock and both the card fronts and backs have full color player photos. Cards also have an ultra-glossy finish on both the fronts and the backs. A high-tech foil Hall of Fame puzzle features former Yankee great Yogi Berra is included.

		MT
Complete Set (528):		240.00
Complete Series 1 (264):		100.00
Complete Series 2 (264):		140.00
Common Player:		.25
Series 1 Wax Box:		220.00
Series 2 Wax Box:		300.00
1	Introductory card	.25
2	Mike Henneman	.25
3	Steve Bedrosian	.25
4	Mike Scott	.25
5	Allan Anderson	.25
6	Rick Sutcliffe	.25
7	Gregg Olson	.25
8	Kevin Elster	.25
9	Pete O'Brien	.25
10	Carlton Fisk	.50
11	Joe Magrane	.25
12	Roger Clemens	4.00
13	Tom Glavine	2.00
14	Tom Gordon	.25
15	Todd Benzinger	.25
16	Hubie Brooks	.25
17	Roberto Kelly	.25
18	Barry Larkin	1.00
19	Mike Boddicker	.25
20	Roger McDowell	.25
21	Nolan Ryan	10.00
22	John Farrell	.25
23	Bruce Hurst	.25
24	Wally Joyner	.40
25	Greg Maddux	15.00
26	Chris Bosio	.25
27	John Cerutti	.25
28	Tim Burke	.25
29	Dennis Eckersley	.40
30	Glenn Davis	.25
31	Jim Abbott	.50
32	Mike LaValliere	.25
33	Andres Thomas	.25
34	Lou Whitaker	.35
35	Alvin Davis	.25
36	Melido Perez	.25
37	Craig Biggio	1.25
38	Rick Aguilera	.25
39	Pete Harnisch	.35
40	David Cone	1.00
41	Scott Garrelts	.25
42	Jay Howell	.25
43	Eric King	.25
44	Pedro Guerrero	.25
45	Mike Bielecki	.25
46	Bob Boone	.35
47	Kevin Brown	2.00
48	Jerry Browne	.25
49	Mike Scioscia	.25
50	Chuck Cary	.25
51	Wade Boggs	1.00
52	Von Hayes	.25
53	Tony Fernandez	.25
54	Dennis Martinez	.35
55	Tom Candiotti	.25
56	Andy Benes	1.00
57	Rob Dibble	.25
58	Chuck Crim	.25
59	John Smoltz	3.00
60	Mike Heath	.25
61	Kevin Gross	.25
62	Mark McGwire	20.00
63	Bert Blyleven	.25
64	Bob Walk	.25
65	Mickey Tettleton	.25
66	Sid Fernandez	.25
67	Terry Kennedy	.25
68	Fernando Valenzuela	.40
69	Don Mattingly	3.00
70	Paul O'Neill	.50
71	Robin Yount	1.00
72	Bret Saberhagen	.30
73	Geno Petralli	.25
74	Brook Jacoby	.25
75	Roberto Alomar	2.50
76	Devon White	.35
77	Jose Lind	.25
78	Pat Combs	.25
79	Dave Steib	.25
80	Tim Wallach	.25
81	Dave Stewart	.30
82	*Eric Anthony*	.25
83	Randy Bush	.25
84	Checklist	.25
85	Jaime Navarro	.25
86	Tommy Gregg	.25
87	Frank Tanana	.25
88	Omar Vizquel	1.50
89	Ivan Calderon	.25
90	Vince Coleman	.25
91	Barry Bonds	2.50
92	Randy Milligan	.25
93	Frank Viola	.25
94	Matt Williams	2.00
95	Alfredo Griffin	.25
96	Steve Sax	.25
97	Gary Gaetti	.30
98	Ryne Sandberg	2.00
99	Danny Tartabull	.25
100	Rafael Palmeiro	1.50
101	Jesse Orosco	.25
102	Garry Templeton	.25
103	Frank DiPino	.25
104	Tony Pena	.25
105	Dickie Thon	.25
106	Kelly Gruber	.25
107	*Marquis Grissom*	3.00
108	Jose Canseco	.75
109	Mike Blowers	.25
110	Tom Browning	.25
111	Greg Vaughn	4.00
112	Oddibe McDowell	.25
113	Gary Ward	.25
114	Jay Buhner	1.50
115	Eric Show	.25
116	Bryan Harvey	.25
117	Andy Van Slyke	.25
118	Jeff Ballard	.25
119	Barry Lyons	.25
120	Kevin Mitchell	.25
121	Mike Gallego	.25
122	Dave Smith	.25
123	Kirby Puckett	2.00
124	Jerome Walton	.25
125	Bo Jackson	.75
126	Harold Baines	.35
127	Scott Bankhead	.25
128	Ozzie Guillen	.25
129	Jose Oquendo	.25
130	John Dopson	.25
131	Charlie Hayes	.25
132	Fred McGriff	.75
133	Chet Lemon	.25
134	Gary Carter	.40
135	Rafael Ramirez	.25
136	Shane Mack	.25
137	Mark Grace	1.00
138	Phil Bradley	.25
139	Dwight Gooden	.40
140	Harold Reynolds	.25
141	Scott Fletcher	.25
142	Ozzie Smith	1.50
143	Mike Greenwell	.30
144	Pete Smith	.25
145	Mark Gubicza	.30
146	Chris Sabo	.25
147	Ramon Martinez	.35
148	Tim Leary	.25
149	Randy Myers	.25
150	Jody Reed	.25
151	Bruce Ruffin	.25
152	Jeff Russell	.25
153	Doug Jones	.25
154	Tony Gwynn	4.00
155	Mark Langston	.30
156	Mitch Williams	.25
157	Gary Sheffield	4.00
158	Tom Henke	.25
159	Oil Can Boyd	.25
160	Rickey Henderson	.50
161	Bill Doran	.25
162	Chuck Finley	.25
163	Jeff King	.35
164	Nick Esasky	.25
165	Cecil Fielder	.45
166	Dave Valle	.25
167	Robin Ventura	2.00
168	Jim Deshaies	.25
169	Juan Berenguer	.25
170	Craig Worthington	.25
171	Gregg Jefferies	.50
172	Will Clark	.75
173	Kirk Gibson	.25
174	Checklist	.25
175	Bobby Thigpen	.25
176	John Tudor	.25
177	Andre Dawson	.50
178	George Brett	2.50
179	Steve Buechele	.25
180	Albert Belle	15.00
181	Eddie Murray	1.00
182	Bob Geren	.25
183	Rob Murphy	.25
184	Tom Herr	.25
185	George Bell	.25
186	Spike Owen	.25
187	Cory Snyder	.25
188	Fred Lynn	.30
189	Eric Davis	.40
190	Dave Parker	.35
191	Jeff Blauser	.25
192	Matt Nokes	.25
193	*Delino DeShields*	.50
194	Scott Sanderson	.25
195	Lance Parrish	.25
196	Bobby Bonilla	.40
197	Cal Ripken, Jr.	10.00
198	Kevin McReynolds	.25
199	Robby Thompson	.25
200	Tim Belcher	.25
201	Jesse Barfield	.25
202	Mariano Duncan	.25
203	Bill Spiers	.25
204	Frank White	.25
205	Julio Franco	.25
206	Greg Swindell	.25
207	Benito Santiago	.25
208	Johnny Ray	.25
209	Gary Redus	.25
210	Jeff Parrett	.25
211	Jimmy Key	.35
212	Tim Raines	.35
213	Carney Lansford	.25
214	Gerald Young	.25
215	Gene Larkin	.25
216	Dan Plesac	.25
217	Lonnie Smith	.25
218	Alan Trammell	.40
219	Jeffrey Leonard	.25
220	*Sammy Sosa*	80.00
221	Todd Zeile	.30
222	Bill Landrum	.25
223	Mike Devereaux	.25
224	Mike Marshall	.25
225	Jose Uribe	.25
226	Juan Samuel	.25
227	Mel Hall	.25
228	Kent Hrbek	.35
229	Shawon Dunston	.25
230	Kevin Seitzer	.25
231	Pete Incaviglia	.25
232	Sandy Alomar	.35
233	Bip Roberts	.25
234	Scott Terry	.25
235	Dwight Evans	.25
236	Ricky Jordan	.25
237	*John Olerud*	7.50
238	Zane Smith	.25
239	Walt Weiss	.25
240	Alvaro Espinoza	.25
241	Billy Hatcher	.25
242	Paul Molitor	2.00
243	Dale Murphy	.30
244	Dave Bergman	.25
245	Ken Griffey, Jr.	30.00
246	Ed Whitson	.25
247	Kirk McCaskill	.25
248	Jay Bell	.25
249	*Ben McDonald*	1.50
250	Darryl Strawbrry	.50
251	Brett Butler	.30
252	Terry Steinbach	.25
253	Ken Caminiti	2.00
254	Dan Gladden	.25
255	Dwight Smith	.25
256	Kurt Stillwell	.25
257	Ruben Sierra	.25
258	Mike Schooler	.25
259	Lance Johnson	.25
260	Terry Pendleton	.25
261	Ellis Burks	.35
262	Len Dykstra	.25
263	Mookie Wilson	.25
264	Checklist (Nolan Ryan)	.25
265	Nolan Ryan (No-Hit King)	4.00
266	Brian DuBois	.25
267	Don Robinson	.25
268	Glenn Wilson	.25
269	*Kevin Tapani*	.75
270	Marvell Wynne	.25
271	Billy Ripken	.25
272	Howard Johnson	.25
273	Brian Holman	.25
274	Dan Pasqua	.25
275	Ken Dayley	.25
276	Jeff Reardon	.25
277	Jim Presley	.25
278	Jim Eisenreich	.25
279	Danny Jackson	.25
280	Orel Hershiser	.35
281	Andy Hawkins	.25
282	Jose Rijo	.25
283	Luis Rivera	.25
284	John Kruk	.25
285	Jeff Huson	.25
286	Joel Skinner	.25
287	Jack Clark	.25
288	Chili Davis	.35
289	Joe Girardi	.30
290	B.J. Surhoff	.30
291	Luis Sojo	.25
292	Tom Foley	.25
293	Mike Moore	.25
294	Ken Oberkfell	.25
295	Luis Polonia	.25
296	Doug Drabek	.25
297	*Dave Justice*	4.00
298	Paul Gibson	.25
299	Edgar Martinez	1.50
300	*Frank Thomas*	40.00
301	Eric Yelding	.25
302	Greg Gagne	.25
303	Brad Komminsk	.25
304	Ron Darling	.25
305	Kevin Bass	.25
306	Jeff Hamilton	.25
307	Ron Karkovice	.25
308	Milt Thompson	.25
309	Mike Harkey	.25
310	Mel Stottlemyre	.25
311	Kenny Rogers	.35
312	Mitch Webster	.25
313	Kal Daniels	.25
314	Matt Nokes	.25
315	Dennis Lamp	.25
316	Ken Howell	.25
317	Glenallen Hill	.25
318	Dave Martinez	.25
319	Chris James	.25
320	Mike Pagliarulo	.25
321	Hal Morris	.25
322	Rob Deer	.25
323	Greg Olson	.25
324	Tony Phillips	.30
325	*Larry Walker*	15.00
326	Ron Hassey	.25
327	Jack Howell	.25
328	John Smiley	.25
329	Steve Finley	.45
330	Dave Magadan	.25
331	Greg Litton	.25
332	Mickey Hatcher	.25
333	Lee Guetterman	.25
334	Norm Charlton	.25
335	Edgar Diaz	.25
336	Willie Wilson	.25
337	Bobby Witt	.25
338	Candy Maldonado	.25
339	Craig Lefferts	.25
340	Dante Bichette	2.00
341	Wally Backman	.25
342	Dennis Cook	.25
343	Pat Borders	.25
344	Wallace Johnson	.25
345	Willie Randolph	.25
346	Danny Darwin	.25
347	Al Newman	.25
348	Mark Knudson	.25
349	Joe Boever	.25
350	Larry Sheets	.25
351	Mike Jackson	.25
352	Wayne Edwards	.25
353	*Bernard Gilkey*	2.50
354	Don Slaught	.25
355	Joe Orsulak	.25
356	John Franco	.25
357	Jeff Brantley	.25
358	Mike Morgan	.25
359	Deion Sanders	2.00
360	Terry Leach	.25
361	Les Lancaster	.25
362	Storm Davis	.25
363	Scott Coolbaugh	.25
364	Checklist	.25
365	Cecilio Guante	.25
366	Joey Cora	.25
367	Willie McGee	.35
368	Jerry Reed	.25
369	Darren Daulton	.25
370	Manny Lee	.25
371	Mark Gardner	.25
372	Rick Honeycutt	.25
373	Steve Balboni	.25
374	Jack Armstrong	.25
375	Charlie O'Brien	.25
376	Ron Gant	.75
377	Lloyd Moseby	.25
378	Gene Harris	.25
379	Joe Carter	.30

380	Scott Bailes	.25
381	R.J. Reynolds	.25
382	Bob Melvin	.25
383	Tim Teufel	.25
384	John Burkett	.30
385	Felix Jose	.25
386	Larry Andersen	.25
387	David West	.25
388	Luis Salazar	.25
389	Mike Macfarlane	.25
390	Charlie Hough	.25
391	Greg Briley	.25
392	Donn Pall	.25
393	Bryn Smith	.25
394	Carlos Quintana	.25
395	Steve Lake	.25
396	*Mark Whiten*	.50
397	Edwin Nunez	.25
398	Rick Parker	.25
399	Mark Portugal	.25
400	Roy Smith	.25
401	Hector Villanueva	.25
402	Bob Milacki	.25
403	Alejandro Pena	.25
404	Scott Bradley	.25
405	Ron Kittle	.25
406	Bob Tewksbury	.25
407	Wes Gardner	.25
408	Ernie Whitt	.25
409	Terry Shumpert	.25
410	Tim Layana	.25
411	Chris Gwynn	.25
412	Jeff Robinson	.25
413	Scott Scudder	.25
414	Kevin Romine	.25
415	Jose DeJesus	.25
416	Mike Jeffcoat	.25
417	Rudy Seanez	.25
418	Mike Dunne	.25
419	Dick Schofield	.25
420	Steve Wilson	.25
421	Bill Krueger	.25
422	Junior Felix	.25
423	Drew Hall	.25
424	Curt Young	.25
425	Franklin Stubbs	.25
426	Dave Winfield	.50
427	Rick Reed	.25
428	Charlie Leibrandt	.25
429	Jeff Robinson	.25
430	Erik Hanson	.25
431	Barry Jones	.25
432	Alex Trevino	.25
433	John Moses	.25
434	Dave Johnson	.25
435	Mackey Sasser	.25
436	Rick Leach	.25
437	Lenny Harris	.25
438	Carlos Martinez	.25
439	Rex Hudler	.25
440	Domingo Ramos	.25
441	Gerald Perry	.25
442	John Russell	.25
443	*Carlos Baerga*	2.00
444	Checklist	.25
445	Stan Javier	.25
446	*Kevin Maas*	.25
447	Tom Brunansky	.25
448	Carmelo Martinez	.25
449	*Willie Blair*	.25
450	Andres Galarraga	1.50
451	Bud Black	.25
452	Greg Harris	.25
453	Joe Oliver	.25
454	Greg Brock	.25
455	Jeff Treadway	.25
456	Lance McCullers	.25
457	Dave Schmidt	.25
458	Todd Burns	.25
459	Max Venable	.25
460	Neal Heaton	.25
461	Mark Williamson	.25
462	Keith Miller	.25
463	Mike LaCoss	.25
464	*Jose Offerman*	.50
465	*Jim Leyritz*	.50
466	Glenn Braggs	.25
467	Ron Robinson	.25
468	Mark Davis	.25
469	Gary Pettis	.25
470	Keith Hernandez	.25
471	Dennis Rasmussen	.25
472	Mark Eichhorn	.25
473	Ted Power	.25
474	Terry Mulholland	.30
475	Todd Stottlemyre	.30
476	Jerry Goff	.25
477	Gene Nelson	.25
478	Rich Gedman	.25
479	Brian Harper	.25
480	Mike Felder	.25
481	Steve Avery	.25
482	Jack Morris	.25
483	Randy Johnson	4.00
484	Scott Radinsky	.25
485	Jose DeLeon	.25
486	*Stan Belinda*	.25
487	Brian Holton	.25
488	Mark Carreon	.40
489	Trevor Wilson	.25
490	Mike Sharperson	.25
491	*Alan Mills*	.25
492	John Candelaria	.25
493	Paul Assenmacher	.25
494	Steve Crawford	.25
495	Brad Arnsberg	.25
496	Sergio Valdez	.25
497	Mark Parent	.25
498	Tom Pagnozzi	.25
499	Greg Harris	.25
500	Randy Ready	.25
501	Duane Ward	.25
502	Nelson Santovenia	.25
503	Joe Klink	.25
504	Eric Plunk	.25
505	Jeff Reed	.25
506	Ted Higuera	.25
507	Joe Hesketh	.25
508	Dan Petry	.25
509	Matt Young	.25
510	Jerald Clark	.25
511	*John Orton*	.25
512	Scott Ruskin	.25
513	*Chris Hoiles*	.75
514	Daryl Boston	.25
515	Francisco Oliveras	.25
516	Ozzie Canseco	.30
517	*Xavier Hernandez*	.40
518	Fred Manrique	.25
519	Shawn Boskie	.30
520	Jeff Montgomery	.30
521	Jack Daugherty	.25
522	Keith Comstock	.25
523	*Greg Hibbard*	.30
524	Lee Smith	.30
525	Dana Kiecker	.25
526	Darrel Akerfelds	.25
527	Greg Myers	.25
528	Checklist	.25

1991 Leaf Previews

Cello packs of four cards previewing the 1991 Leaf set were included in each 1991 Donruss hobby factory set. The cards are identical in format to the regular 1991 Leafs, except there is a notation, "1991 PREVIEW CARD" in white print beneath the statistics and career information on the back.

		MT
Complete Set (26):		55.00
Common Player:		1.00
1	Dave Justice	3.00
2	Ryne Sandberg	5.00
3	Barry Larkin	1.50
4	Craig Biggio	1.50
5	Ramon Martinez	1.50
6	Tim Wallach	1.00
7	Dwight Gooden	1.50
8	Len Dykstra	1.00
9	Barry Bonds	6.00
10	Ray Lankford	1.00
11	Tony Gwynn	6.00
12	Will Clark	2.50
13	Leo Gomez	1.00
14	Wade Boggs	3.50
15	Chuck Finley	1.00
16	Carlton Fisk	1.50
17	Sandy Alomar, Jr.	1.50
18	Cecil Fielder	1.50
19	Bo Jackson	2.00
20	Paul Molitor	3.50
21	Kirby Puckett	6.00
22	Don Mattingly	6.00
23	Rickey Henderson	2.00
24	Tino Martinez	2.00
25	Nolan Ryan	9.00
26	Dave Steib	1.00

1991 Leaf

Silver borders and black insets surround the color action photos on the 1991 Leaf cards. The set was once again released in two series. Series I consists of cards 1-264. Card backs feature an additional player photo, biographical information, statistics and career highlights. The 1991 issue is not considered as scarce as the 1990 release.

		MT
Complete Set (528):		25.00
Common Player:		.05
Series 1 or 2 Wax Box:		28.00
1	The Leaf Card	.05
2	Kurt Stillwell	.05
3	Bobby Witt	.05
4	Tony Phillips	.05
5	Scott Garrelts	.05
6	Greg Swindell	.05
7	Billy Ripken	.05
8	Dave Martinez	.05
9	Kelly Gruber	.05
10	Juan Samuel	.05
11	Brian Holman	.05
12	Craig Biggio	.25
13	Lonnie Smith	.05
14	Ron Robinson	.05
15	Mike LaValliere	.05
16	Mark Davis	.05
17	Jack Daugherty	.05
18	Mike Henneman	.05
19	Mike Greenwell	.05
20	Dave Magadan	.05
21	Mark Williamson	.05
22	Marquis Grissom	.15
23	Pat Borders	.05
24	Mike Scioscia	.05
25	Shawon Dunston	.05
26	Randy Bush	.05
27	John Smoltz	.20
28	Chuck Crim	.05
29	Don Slaught	.05
30	Mike Macfarlane	.05
31	Wally Joyner	.05
32	Pat Combs	.05
33	Tony Pena	.05
34	Howard Johnson	.05
35	Leo Gomez	.05
36	Spike Owen	.05
37	Eric Davis	.10
38	Roberto Kelly	.05
39	Jerome Walton	.05
40	Shane Mack	.05
41	Kent Mercker	.05
42	B.J. Surhoff	.10
43	Jerry Browne	.05
44	Lee Smith	.05
45	Chuck Finley	.05
46	Terry Mulholland	.05
47	Tom Bolton	.05
48	Tom Herr	.05
49	Jim Deshaies	.05
50	Walt Weiss	.05
51	Hal Morris	.05
52	Lee Guetterman	.05
53	Paul Assenmacher	.05
54	Brian Harper	.05
55	Paul Gibson	.05
56	John Burkett	.05
57	Doug Jones	.05
58	Jose Oquendo	.05
59	Dick Schofield	.05
60	Dickie Thon	.05
61	Ramon Martinez	.10
62	Jay Buhner	.10
63	Mark Portugal	.05
64	Bob Welch	.05
65	Chris Sabo	.05
66	Chuck Cary	.05
67	Mark Langston	.10
68	Joe Boever	.05
69	Jody Reed	.05
70	Alejandro Pena	.05
71	Jeff King	.05
72	Tom Pagnozzi	.05
73	Joe Oliver	.05
74	Mike Witt	.05
75	Hector Villanueva	.05
76	Dan Gladden	.05
77	Dave Justice	.25
78	Mike Gallego	.05
79	Tom Candiotti	.05
80	Ozzie Smith	.50
81	Luis Polonia	.05
82	Randy Ready	.05
83	Greg Harris	.05
84	Checklist (Dave Justice)	.15
85	Kevin Mitchell	.05
86	Mark McLemore	.05
87	Terry Steinbach	.05
88	Tom Browning	.05
89	Matt Nokes	.05
90	Mike Harkey	.05
91	Omar Vizquel	.10
92	Dave Bergman	.05
93	Matt Williams	.40
94	Steve Olin	.05
95	Craig Wilson	.05
96	Dave Stieb	.05
97	Ruben Sierra	.05
98	Jay Howell	.05
99	Scott Bradley	.05
100	Eric Yelding	.05
101	Rickey Henderson	.25
102	Jeff Reed	.05
103	Jimmy Key	.10
104	Terry Shumpert	.05
105	Kenny Rogers	.05
106	Cecil Fielder	.10
107	Robby Thompson	.05
108	Alex Cole	.05
109	Randy Milligan	.05
110	Andres Galarraga	.15
111	Bill Spiers	.05
112	Kal Daniels	.05
113	Henry Cotto	.05
114	Casy Candaele	.05
115	Jeff Blauser	.05
116	Robin Yount	.40
117	Ben McDonald	.05
118	Bret Saberhagen	.10
119	Juan Gonzalez	1.25
120	Lou Whitaker	.05
121	Ellis Burks	.10
122	Charlie O'Brien	.05
123	John Smiley	.05
124	Tim Burke	.05
125	John Olerud	.20
126	Eddie Murray	.30
127	Greg Maddux	1.50
128	Kevin Tapani	.05
129	Ron Gant	.15
130	Jay Bell	.05
131	Chris Hoiles	.05
132	Tom Gordon	.05
133	Kevin Seitzer	.05
134	Jeff Huson	.05
135	Jerry Don Gleaton	.05
136	Jeff Brantley	.05
137	Felix Fermin	.05
138	Mike Devereaux	.05
139	Delino DeShields	.05
140	David Wells	.10
141	Tim Crews	.05
142	Erik Hanson	.05
143	Mark Davidson	.05
144	Tommy Gregg	.05
145	Jim Gantner	.05
146	Jose Lind	.05
147	Danny Tartabull	.05
148	Geno Petralli	.05
149	Travis Fryman	.15
150	Tim Naehring	.05
151	Kevin McReynolds	.05
152	Joe Orsulak	.05
153	Steve Frey	.05
154	Duane Ward	.05
155	Stan Javier	.05
156	Damon Berryhill	.05
157	Gene Larkin	.05
158	Greg Olson	.05
159	Mark Knudson	.05
160	Carmelo Martinez	.05
161	Storm Davis	.05
162	Jim Abbott	.10
163	Len Dykstra	.05
164	Tom Brunansky	.05
165	Dwight Gooden	.15
166	Jose Mesa	.05
167	Oil Can Boyd	.05
168	Barry Larkin	.15
169	Scott Sanderson	.05
170	Mark Grace	.15
171	Mark Guthrie	.05
172	Tom Glavine	.40
173	Gary Sheffield	.25
174	Checklist (Roger Clemens)	.15
175	Chris James	.05
176	Milt Thompson	.05
177	Donnie Hill	.05
178	Wes Chamberlain	.05
179	John Marzano	.05
180	Frank Viola	.05
181	Eric Anthony	.05
182	Jose Canseco	.50
183	Scott Scudder	.05
184	Dave Eiland	.05
185	Luis Salazar	.05
186	Pedro Munoz	.05
187	Steve Searcy	.05
188	Don Robinson	.05
189	Sandy Alomar	.10
190	Jose DeLeon	.05
191	John Orton	.05
192	Darren Daulton	.05
193	Mike Morgan	.05
194	Greg Briley	.05
195	Karl Rhodes	.05
196	Harold Baines	.10
197	Bill Doran	.05
198	Alvaro Espinoza	.05
199	Kirk McCaskill	.05
200	Jose DeJesus	.05
201	Jack Clark	.05
202	Daryl Boston	.05
203	Randy Tomlin	.05
204	Pedro Guerrero	.05
205	Billy Hatcher	.05
206	Tim Leary	.05
207	Ryne Sandberg	.60
208	Kirby Puckett	.75
209	Charlie Leibrandt	.05
210	Rick Honeycutt	.05
211	Joel Skinner	.05
212	Rex Hudler	.05
213	Bryan Harvey	.05
214	Charlie Hayes	.05
215	Matt Young	.05
216	Terry Kennedy	.05
217	Carl Nichols	.05
218	Mike Moore	.05
219	Paul O'Neill	.10
220	Steve Sax	.05
221	Shawn Boskie	.05
222	Rich DeLucia	.05
223	Lloyd Moseby	.05
224	Mike Kingery	.05
225	Carlos Baerga	.10
226	Bryn Smith	.05
227	Todd Stottlemyre	.05
228	Julio Franco	.10
229	Jim Gott	.05
230	Mike Schooler	.05
231	Steve Finley	.05
232	Dave Henderson	.05
233	Luis Quinones	.05
234	Mark Whiten	.05
235	Brian McRae	.10
236	Rich Gossage	.05
237	Rob Deer	.05
238	Will Clark	.25
239	Albert Belle	.50
240	Bob Melvin	.05
241	Larry Walker	.30
242	Dante Bichette	.20
243	Orel Hershiser	.15
244	Pete O'Brien	.05
245	Pete Harnisch	.10
246	Jeff Treadway	.05
247	Julio Machado	.05
248	Dave Johnson	.05
249	Kirk Gibson	.05
250	Kevin Brown	.05
251	Milt Cuyler	.05
252	Jeff Reardon	.05
253	David Cone	.10
254	Gary Redus	.05
255	Junior Noboa	.05
256	Greg Myers	.05
257	Dennis Cook	.05
258	Joe Girardi	.05
259	Allan Anderson	.05
260	Paul Marak	.05
261	Barry Bonds	.75
262	Juan Bell	.05
263	Russ Morman	.05
264	Checklist (George Brett)	.20
265	Jerald Clark	.05
266	Dwight Evans	.05
267	Roberto Alomar	.50
268	Danny Jackson	.05
269	Brian Downing	.05
270	John Cerutti	.05
271	Robin Ventura	.20
273	Wade Boggs	.40
274	Dennis Martinez	.15
275	Andy Benes	.10
276	Tony Fossas	.05
277	Franklin Stubbs	.05
278	John Kruk	.05
279	Kevin Gross	.05
280	Von Hayes	.05
281	Frank Thomas	1.50
282	Rob Dibble	.05
283	Mel Hall	.05
284	Rick Mahler	.05
285	Dennis Eckersley	.15
286	Bernard Gilkey	.10
287	Dan Plesac	.05
288	Jason Grimsley	.05
289	Mark Lewis	.10
290	Tony Gwynn	.75
291	Jeff Russell	.05
292	Curt Schilling	.10
293	Pascual Perez	.05
294	Jack Morris	.05
295	Hubie Brooks	.05
296	Alex Fernandez	.40
297	Harold Reynolds	.05
298	Craig Worthington	.05
299	Willie Wilson	.05
300	Mike Maddux	.05
301	Dave Righetti	.05
302	Paul Molitor	.40
303	Gary Gaetti	.10
304	Terry Pendleton	.05
305	Kevin Elster	.05
306	Scott Fletcher	.05
307	Jeff Robinson	.05
308	Jesse Barfield	.05
309	Mike LaCoss	.05
310	Andy Van Slyke	.05
311	Glenallen Hill	.05
312	Bud Black	.05
313	Kent Hrbek	.10
314	Tim Teufel	.05
315	Tony Fernandez	.05
316	Beau Allred	.05
317	Curtis Wilkerson	.05
318	Bill Sampen	.05
319	Randy Johnson	.40
320	Mike Heath	.05
321	Sammy Sosa	2.00

322 Mickey Tettleton .05
323 Jose Vizcaino .05
324 John Candelaria .05
325 David Howard .05
326 Jose Rijo .05
327 Todd Zeile .10
328 Gene Nelson .05
329 Dwayne Henry .05
330 Mike Boddicker .05
331 Ozzie Guillen .05
332 Sam Horn .05
333 Wally Whitehurst .05
334 Dave Parker .10
335 George Brett .40
336 Bobby Thigpen .05
337 Ed Whitson .05
338 Ivan Calderon .05
339 Mike Pagliarulo .05
340 Jack McDowell .05
341 Dana Kiecker .05
342 Fred McGriff .40
343 Mark Lee .05
344 Alfredo Griffin .05
345 Scott Bankhead .05
346 Darrin Jackson .05
347 Rafael Palmeiro .25
348 Steve Farr .05
349 Hensley Meulens .05
350 Danny Cox .05
351 Alan Trammell .15
352 Edwin Nunez .05
353 Joe Carter .10
354 Eric Show .05
355 Vance Law .05
356 Jeff Gray .05
357 Bobby Bonilla .15
358 Ernest Riles .05
359 Ron Hassey .05
360 Willie McGee .12
361 Mackey Sasser .05
362 Glenn Braggs .05
363 Mario Diaz .05
364 Checklist (Barry Bonds) .15
365 Kevin Bass .05
366 Pete Incaviglia .05
367 Luis Sojo .05
368 Lance Parrish .10
369 Mark Leonard .05
370 Heathcliff Slocumb .05
371 Jimmy Jones .05
372 Ken Griffey, Jr. 3.50
373 Chris Hammond .05
374 Chili Davis .10
375 Joey Cora .05
376 Ken Hill .10
377 Darryl Strawberry .15
378 Ron Darling .05
379 Sid Bream .05
380 Bill Swift .05
381 Shawn Abner .05
382 Eric King .05
383 Mickey Morandini .05
384 Carlton Fisk .15
385 Steve Lake .05
386 Mike Jeffcoat .05
387 Darren Holmes .05
388 Tim Wallach .05
389 George Bell .05
390 Craig Lefferts .05
391 Ernie Whitt .05
392 Felix Jose .05
393 Kevin Maas .05
394 Devon White .12
395 Otis Nixon .05
396 Chuck Knoblauch .40
397 Scott Coolbaugh .05
398 Glenn Davis .05
399 Manny Lee .05
400 Andre Dawson .15
401 Scott Chiamparino .05
402 Bill Gullickson .05
403 Lance Johnson .05
404 Juan Agosto .05
405 Danny Darwin .05
406 Barry Jones .05
407 Larry Andersen .05
408 Luis Rivera .05
409 Jaime Navarro .05
410 Roger McDowell .05
411 Brett Butler .10
412 Dale Murphy .15
413 Tim Raines .15
414 Norm Charlton .05
415 Greg Cadaret .05
416 Chris Nabholz .05
417 Dave Stewart .05
418 Rich Gedman .05
419 Willie Randolph .05
420 Mitch Williams .05
421 Brook Jacoby .05
422 Greg Harris .05
423 Nolan Ryan 2.00
424 Dave Rohde .05
425 Don Mattingly .75
426 Greg Gagne .05
427 Vince Coleman .05
428 Dan Pasqua .05
429 Alvin Davis .05
430 Cal Ripken, Jr. 2.00
431 Jamie Quirk .05
432 Benito Santiago .05
433 Jose Uribe .05
434 Candy Maldonado .05
435 Junior Felix .05
436 Deion Sanders .45
437 John Franco .05
438 Greg Hibbard .05
439 Floyd Bannister .05
440 Steve Howe .05
441 Steve Decker .05
442 Vicente Palacios .05
443 Pat Tabler .05
444 Checklist (Darryl Strawberry) .10
445 Mike Felder .05
446 Al Newman .05
447 Chris Donnels .05
448 Rich Rodriguez .05
449 Turner Ward .05
450 Bob Walk .05
451 Gilberto Reyes .05
452 Mike Jackson .05
453 Rafael Belliard .05
454 Wayne Edwards .05
455 Andy Allanson .05
456 Dave Smith .05
457 Gary Carter .15
458 Warren Cromartie .05
459 Jack Armstrong .05
460 Bob Tewksbury .10
461 Joe Klink .05
462 Xavier Hernandez .05
463 Scott Radinsky .05
464 Jeff Robinson .05
465 Gregg Jefferies .15
466 Denny Neagle .05
467 Carmelo Martinez .05
468 Donn Pall .05
469 Bruce Hurst .05
470 Eric Bullock .05
471 Rick Aguilera .05
472 Charlie Hough .05
473 Carlos Quintana .05
474 Marty Barrett .05
475 Kevin Brown .10
476 Bobby Ojeda .05
477 Edgar Martinez .10
478 Bip Roberts .05
479 Mike Flanagan .05
480 John Habyan .05
481 Larry Casian .05
482 Wally Backman .05
483 Doug Dascenzo .05
484 Rick Dempsey .05
485 Ed Sprague .10
486 Steve Chitren .05
487 Mark McGwire 3.00
488 Roger Clemens .65
489 Orlando Merced .05
490 Rene Gonzales .05
491 Mike Stanton .05
492 Al Osuna .05
493 Rick Cerone .05
494 Mariano Duncan .05
495 Zane Smith .05
496 John Morris .05
497 Frank Tanana .05
498 Junior Ortiz .05
499 Dave Winfield .35
500 Gary Varsho .05
501 Chico Walker .05
502 Ken Caminiti .25
503 Ken Griffey, Sr. .10
504 Randy Myers .05
505 Steve Bedrosian .05
506 Cory Snyder .05
507 Cris Carpenter .05
508 Tim Belcher .05
509 Jeff Hamilton .05
510 Steve Avery .05
511 Dave Valle .05
512 Tom Lampkin .05
513 Shawn Hillegas .05
514 Reggie Jefferson .10
515 Ron Karkovice .05
516 Doug Drabek .05
517 Tom Henke .05
518 Chris Bosio .05
519 Gregg Olson .05
520 Bob Scanlan .05
521 Alonzo Powell .05
522 Jeff Ballard .05
523 Ray Lankford .10
524 Tommy Greene .05
525 Mike Timlin .10
526 Juan Berenguer .05
527 Scott Erickson .10
528 Checklist (Sandy Alomar Jr.) .05

1991 Leaf Gold Rookies

Special gold rookie and gold bonus cards were randomly inserted in 1991 Leaf packs. Backs have a design similar to the regular-issue cards, but have gold, rather than silver background. Fronts have gold-foil highlights. Card numbers of the issued version have a "BC" prefix, but there is a much rarer second version of the Series 1 cards, which carry card numbers between 265-276.

		MT
Complete Set (26):		30.00
Common Player:		.50
1	Scott Leius	.50
2	Luis Gonzalez	.75
3	Wil Cordero	.75
4	Gary Scott	.50
5	Willie Banks	.50
6	Arthur Rhodes	.50
7	Mo Vaughn	8.00
8	Henry Rodriguez	.75
9	Todd Van Poppel	.50
10	Reggie Sanders	.75
11	Rico Brogna	.50
12	Mike Mussina	7.50
13	Kirk Dressendorfer	.50
14	Jeff Bagwell	12.00
15	Pete Schourek	.50
16	Wade Taylor	.50
17	Pat Kelly	.50
18	Tim Costo	.50
19	Roger Salkeld	.50
20	Andujar Cedeno	.50
21	Ryan Klesko	1.50
22	Mike Huff	.50
23	Anthony Young	.75
24	Eddie Zosky	.50
25	Nolan Ryan (7th no-hitter)	10.00
26	Rickey Henderson (record steal)	2.00
265	Scott Leius	9.00
266	Luis Gonzalez	12.00
267	Wil Cordero	12.00
268	Gary Scott	9.00
269	Willie Banks	9.00
270	Arthur Rhodes	9.00
271	Mo Vaughn	65.00
272	Henry Rodriguez	9.00
273	Todd Van Poppel	9.00
274	Reggie Sanders	12.00
275	Rico Brogna	9.00
276	Mike Mussina	60.00

1992 Leaf Previews

In a format identical to the regular-issue 1992 Leaf cards, this 26-card preview set was issued as a bonus in packs of four cards in each 1992 Donruss hobby factory set.

		MT
Complete Set (26):		150.00
Common Player:		1.00
1	Steve Avery	1.00
2	Ryne Sandberg	9.00
3	Chris Sabo	1.00
4	Jeff Bagwell	15.00
5	Darryl Strawberry	2.50
6	Bret Barberie	1.00
7	Howard Johnson	1.00
8	John Kruk	1.00
9	Andy Van Slyke	1.00
10	Felix Jose	1.00
11	Fred McGriff	6.00
12	Will Clark	7.50
13	Cal Ripken, Jr.	20.00
14	Phil Plantier	1.00
15	Lee Stevens	1.00
16	Frank Thomas	15.00
17	Mark Whiten	1.00
18	Cecil Fielder	2.00
19	George Brett	10.00
20	Robin Yount	7.50
21	Scott Erickson	1.00
22	Don Mattingly	10.00
23	Jose Canseco	7.50
24	Ken Griffey, Jr.	25.00
25	Nolan Ryan	20.00
26	Joe Carter	2.00

1992 Leaf

Two 264-card series comprise this 528-card set. The cards feature action photos on both the front and the back. Silver borders surround the photo on the card front. Each leaf card was also produced in a gold foil version. One gold card was issued per pack and a complete Leaf Gold Edition set can be assembled. Traded players and free agents are shown in uniform with their new teams.

		MT
Complete Set (528):		20.00
Common Player:		.05
Series 1 or 2 Wax Box:		20.00
1	Jim Abbott	.10
2	Cal Eldred	.05
3	Bud Black	.05
4	Dave Howard	.05
5	Luis Sojo	.05
6	Gary Scott	.05
7	Joe Oliver	.05
8	Chris Gardner	.05
9	Sandy Alomar	.12
10	Greg Harris	.05
11	Doug Drabek	.05
12	Darryl Hamilton	.10
13	Mike Mussina	.60
14	Kevin Tapani	.10
15	Ron Gant	.10
16	Mark McGwire	2.50
17	Robin Ventura	.25
18	Pedro Guerrero	.05
19	Roger Clemens	.65
20	Steve Farr	.05
21	Frank Tanana	.05
22	Joe Hesketh	.05
23	Erik Hanson	.05
24	Greg Cadaret	.05
25	Rex Hudler	.05
26	Mark Grace	.15
27	Kelly Gruber	.05
28	Jeff Bagwell	1.00
29	Darryl Strawberry	.10
30	Dave Smith	.05
31	Kevin Appier	.10
32	Steve Chitren	.05
33	Kevin Gross	.05
34	Rick Aguilera	.05
35	Juan Guzman	.10
36	Joe Orsulak	.05
37	Tim Raines	.15
38	Harold Reynolds	.05
39	Charlie Hough	.05
40	Tony Phillips	.05
41	Nolan Ryan	1.50
42	Vince Coleman	.05
43	Andy Van Slyke	.05
44	Tim Burke	.05
45	Luis Polonia	.05
46	Tom Browning	.05
47	Willie McGee	.10
48	Gary DiSarcina	.05
49	Mark Lewis	.10
50	Phil Plantier	.05
51	Doug Dascenzo	.05
52	Cal Ripken, Jr.	2.00
53	Pedro Munoz	.05
54	Carlos Hernandez	.05
55	Jerald Clark	.05
56	Jeff Brantley	.05
57	Don Mattingly	.60
58	Roger McDowell	.05
59	Steve Avery	.05
60	John Olerud	.20
61	Bill Gullickson	.05
62	Juan Gonzalez	.75
63	Felix Jose	.05
64	Robin Yount	.25
65	Greg Briley	.05
66	Steve Finley	.05
67	Checklist	.05
68	Tom Gordon	.05
69	Rob Dibble	.05
70	Glenallen Hill	.05
71	Calvin Jones	.05
72	Joe Girardi	.05
73	Barry Larkin	.15
74	Andy Benes	.05
75	Milt Cyler	.05
76	Kevin Bass	.05
77	Pete Harnisch	.05
78	Wilson Alvarez	.05
79	Mike Devereaux	.05
80	Doug Henry	.05
81	Orel Hershiser	.15
82	Shane Mack	.05
83	Mike Macfarlane	.05
84	Thomas Howard	.05
85	Alex Fernandez	.05
86	Reggie Jefferson	.10
87	Leo Gomez	.05
88	Mel Hall	.05
89	Mike Greenwell	.05
90	Jeff Russell	.05
91	Steve Buechele	.05
92	David Cone	.12
93	Kevin Reimer	.05
94	Mark Lemke	.05
95	Bob Tewksbury	.05
96	Zane Smith	.05
97	Mark Eichhorn	.05
98	Kirby Puckett	.75
99	Paul O'Neill	.12
100	Dennis Eckersley	.10
101	Duane Ward	.05
102	Matt Nokes	.05
103	Mo Vaughn	.50
104	Pat Kelly	.05
105	Ron Karkovice	.05
106	Bill Spiers	.05
107	Gary Gaetti	.10
108	Mackey Sasser	.05
109	Robby Thompson	.05
110	Marvin Freeman	.05
111	Jimmy Key	.05
112	Dwight Gooden	.12
113	Charlie Leibrandt	.05
114	Devon White	.10
115	Charles Nagy	.10
116	Rickey Henderson	.25
117	Paul Assenmacher	.05
118	Junior Felix	.05
119	Julio Franco	.05
120	Norm Charlton	.05
121	Scott Servais	.05
122	Gerald Perry	.05
123	Brian McRae	.10
124	Don Slaught	.05
125	Juan Samuel	.05
126	Harold Baines	.12
127	Scott Livingstone	.05
128	Jay Buhner	.10
129	Darrin Jackson	.05
130	Luis Mercedes	.05
131	Brian Harper	.05
132	Howard Johnson	.05
133	Checklist	.05
134	Dante Bichette	.10
135	Dave Righetti	.05
136	Jeff Montgomery	.05
137	Joe Grahe	.05
138	Delino DeShields	.10
139	Jose Rijo	.05
140	Ken Caminiti	.15
141	Steve Olin	.05
142	Kurt Stillwell	.05
143	Jay Bell	.05
144	Jaime Navarro	.05
145	Ben McDonald	.05
146	Greg Gagne	.05
147	Jeff Blauser	.05
148	Carney Lansford	.05
149	Ozzie Guillen	.05
150	Milt Thompson	.05
151	Jeff Reardon	.05
152	Scott Sanderson	.05
153	Cecil Fielder	.10
154	Greg Harris	.05
155	Rich DeLucia	.05
156	Roberto Kelly	.05
157	Bryn Smith	.05
158	Chuck McElroy	.05
159	Tom Henke	.05
160	Luis Gonzalez	.10
161	Steve Wilson	.05
162	Shawn Boskie	.05
163	Mark Davis	.05
164	Mike Moore	.05
165	Mike Scioscia	.05
166	Scott Erickson	.10
167	Todd Stottlemyre	.10
168	Alvin Davis	.05
169	Greg Hibbard	.05
170	David Valle	.05
171	Dave Winfield	.25
172	Alan Trammell	.12
173	Kenny Rogers	.05
174	John Franco	.05
175	Jose Lind	.05
176	Pete Schourek	.05
177	Von Hayes	.05
178	Chris Hammond	.05
179	John Burkett	.05
180	Dickie Thon	.05
181	Joel Skinner	.05
182	Scott Cooper	.05
183	Andre Dawson	.15

184	Billy Ripken	.05
185	Kevin Mitchell	.05
186	Brett Butler	.10
187	Tony Fernandez	.05
188	Cory Snyder	.05
189	John Habyan	.05
190	Dennis Martinez	.12
191	John Smoltz	.15
192	Greg Myers	.05
193	Rob Deer	.05
194	Ivan Rodriguez	.50
195	Ray Lankford	.10
196	Bill Wegman	.05
197	Edgar Martinez	.10
198	Darryl Kile	.10
199	Checklist	.05
200	Brent Mayne	.05
201	Larry Walker	.25
202	Carlos Baerga	.10
203	Russ Swan	.05
204	Mike Morgan	.05
205	Hal Morris	.10
206	Tony Gwynn	.75
207	Mark Leiter	.05
208	Kirt Manwaring	.05
209	Al Osuna	.05
210	Bobby Thigpen	.05
211	Chris Hoiles	.05
212	B.J. Surhoff	.10
213	Lenny Harris	.05
214	Scott Leius	.05
215	Gregg Jefferies	.10
216	Bruce Hurst	.05
217	Steve Sax	.05
218	Dave Otto	.05
219	Sam Horn	.05
220	Charlie Hayes	.05
221	Frank Viola	.05
222	Jose Guzman	.05
223	Gary Redus	.05
224	Dave Gallagher	.05
225	Dean Palmer	.05
226	Greg Olson	.05
227	Jose DeLeon	.05
228	Mike LaValliere	.05
229	Mark Langston	.05
230	Chuck Knoblauch	.20
231	Bill Doran	.05
232	Dave Henderson	.05
233	Roberto Alomar	.50
234	Scott Fletcher	.05
235	Tim Naehring	.05
236	Mike Gallego	.05
237	Lance Johnson	.05
238	Paul Molitor	.25
239	Dan Gladden	.05
240	Willie Randolph	.05
241	Will Clark	.30
242	Sid Bream	.05
243	Derek Bell	.10
244	Bill Pecota	.05
245	Terry Pendleton	.05
246	Randy Ready	.05
247	Jack Armstrong	.05
248	Todd Van Poppel	.10
249	Shawon Dunston	.05
250	Bobby Rose	.05
251	Jeff Huson	.05
252	Bip Roberts	.05
253	Doug Jones	.05
254	Lee Smith	.10
255	George Brett	.40
256	Randy Tomlin	.05
257	Todd Benzinger	.05
258	Dave Stewart	.05
259	Mark Carreon	.05
260	Pete O'Brien	.05
261	Tim Teufel	.05
262	Bob Milacki	.05
263	Mark Guthrie	.05
264	Darrin Fletcher	.05
265	Omar Vizquel	.10
266	Chris Bosio	.05
267	Jose Canseco	.25
268	Mike Boddicker	.05
269	Lance Parrish	.10
270	Jose Vizcaino	.05
271	Chris Sabo	.05
272	Royce Clayton	.05
273	Marquis Grissom	.10
274	Fred McGriff	.25
275	Barry Bonds	.60
276	Greg Vaughn	.15
277	Gregg Olson	.05
278	Dave Hollins	.10
279	Tom Glavine	.15
280	Bryan Hickerson	.05
281	Scott Radinsky	.05
282	Omar Olivares	.05
283	Ivan Calderon	.05
284	Kevin Maas	.05
285	Mickey Tettleton	.05
286	Wade Boggs	.25
287	Stan Belinda	.05
288	Bret Barberie	.05
289	Jose Oquendo	.05
290	Frank Castillo	.05
291	Dave Stieb	.05
292	Tommy Greene	.05
293	Eric Karros	.10
294	Greg Maddux	1.50
295	Jim Eisenreich	.05
296	Rafael Palmeiro	.15
297	Ramon Martinez	.10
298	Tim Wallach	.05
299	Jim Thome	.50
300	Chito Martinez	.05
301	Mitch Williams	.05

302	Randy Johnson	.30
303	Carlton Fisk	.10
304	Travis Fryman	.10
305	Bobby Witt	.05
306	Dave Magadan	.05
307	Alex Cole	.05
308	Bobby Bonilla	.12
309	Bryan Harvey	.05
310	Rafael Belliard	.05
311	Mariano Duncan	.05
312	Chuck Crim	.05
313	John Kruk	.05
314	Ellis Burks	.10
315	Craig Biggio	.15
316	Glenn Davis	.05
317	Ryne Sandberg	.35
318	Mike Sharperson	.05
319	Rich Rodriguez	.05
320	Lee Guetterman	.05
321	Benito Santiago	.05
322	Jose Offerman	.05
323	Tony Pena	.05
324	Pat Borders	.05
325	Mike Henneman	.05
326	Kevin Brown	.15
327	Chris Nabholz	.05
328	Franklin Stubbs	.05
329	Tino Martinez	.15
330	Mickey Morandini	.05
331	Checklist	.05
332	Mark Gubicza	.05
333	Bill Landrum	.05
334	Mark Whiten	.05
335	Darren Daulton	.05
336	Rick Wilkins	.05
337	*Brian Jordan*	1.50
338	Kevin Ward	.05
339	Ruben Amaro	.05
340	Trevor Wilson	.05
341	Andujar Cedeno	.05
342	Michael Huff	.05
343	Brady Anderson	.10
344	Craig Grebeck	.05
345	Bobby Ojeda	.05
346	Mike Pagliarulo	.05
347	Terry Shumpert	.05
348	Dann Bilardello	.05
349	Frank Thomas	2.00
350	Albert Belle	.40
351	Jose Mesa	.05
352	Rich Monteleone	.05
353	Bob Walk	.05
354	Monty Fariss	.05
355	Luis Rivera	.05
356	Anthony Young	.05
357	Geno Petralli	.05
358	Otis Nixon	.05
359	Tom Pagnozzi	.05
360	Reggie Sanders	.10
361	Lee Stevens	.05
362	Kent Hrbek	.10
363	Orlando Merced	.05
364	Mike Bordick	.05
365	Dion James	.05
366	Jack Clark	.05
367	Mike Stanley	.05
368	Randy Velarde	.05
369	Dan Pasqua	.05
370	Pat Listach	.05
371	Mike Fitzgerald	.05
372	Tom Foley	.05
373	Matt Williams	.20
374	Brian Hunter	.05
375	Joe Carter	.10
376	Bret Saberhagen	.10
377	Mike Stanton	.05
378	Hubie Brooks	.05
379	Eric Bell	.05
380	Walt Weiss	.05
381	Danny Jackson	.05
382	Manuel Lee	.05
383	Ruben Sierra	.10
384	Greg Swindell	.05
385	Ryan Bowen	.05
386	Kevin Ritz	.05
387	Curtis Wilkerson	.05
388	Gary Varsho	.05
389	Dave Hansen	.05
390	Bob Welch	.05
391	Lou Whitaker	.05
392	Ken Griffey, Jr.	3.00
393	Mike Maddux	.05
394	Arthur Rhodes	.05
395	Chili Davis	.10
396	Eddie Murray	.20
397	Checklist	.05
398	Dave Cochrane	.05
399	Kevin Seitzer	.05
400	Ozzie Smith	.25
401	Paul Sorrento	.05
402	Les Lancaster	.05
403	Junior Noboa	.05
404	Dave Justice	.25
405	Andy Ashby	.10
406	Danny Tartabull	.05
407	Bill Swift	.05
408	Craig Lefferts	.05
409	Tom Candiotti	.05
410	Lance Blankenship	.05
411	Jeff Tackett	.05
412	Sammy Sosa	2.00
413	Jody Reed	.05
414	Bruce Ruffin	.05
415	Gene Larkin	.05
416	John Vanderwal	.05
417	Tim Belcher	.05
418	Steve Frey	.05
419	Dick Schofield	.05

420	Jeff King	.05
421	Kim Batiste	.05
422	Jack McDowell	.05
423	Damon Berryhill	.05
424	Gary Wayne	.05
425	Jack Morris	.05
426	Moises Alou	.10
427	Mark McLemore	.05
428	Juan Guerrero	.05
429	Scott Scudder	.05
430	Eric Davis	.10
431	Joe Slusarski	.05
432	Todd Zeile	.15
433	Dwayne Henry	.05
434	Cliff Brantley	.05
435	Butch Henry	.05
436	Todd Worrell	.05
437	Bob Scanlan	.05
438	Wally Joyner	.10
439	John Flaherty	.05
440	Brian Downing	.05
441	Darren Lewis	.05
442	Gary Carter	.10
443	Wally Ritchie	.05
444	Chris Jones	.05
445	Jeff Kent	.10
446	Gary Sheffield	.25
447	Ron Darling	.05
448	Deion Sanders	.15
449	Andres Galarraga	.20
450	Chuck Finley	.05
451	Derek Lilliquist	.05
452	Carl Willis	.05
453	Wes Chamberlain	.05
454	Roger Mason	.05
455	Spike Owen	.05
456	Thomas Howard	.05
457	Dave Martinez	.05
458	Pete Incaviglia	.05
459	Keith Miller	.05
460	Mike Fetters	.05
461	Paul Gibson	.05
462	George Bell	.05
463	Checklist	.05
464	Terry Mulholland	.05
465	Storm Davis	.05
466	Gary Pettis	.05
467	Randy Bush	.05
468	Ken Hill	.05
469	Rheal Cormier	.05
470	Andy Stankiewicz	.05
471	Dave Burba	.05
472	Henry Cotto	.05
473	Dale Sveum	.05
474	Rich Gossage	.05
475	William Suero	.05
476	Doug Strange	.05
477	Bill Krueger	.05
478	John Wetteland	.10
479	Melido Perez	.05
480	Lonnie Smith	.05
481	Mike Jackson	.05
482	Mike Gardiner	.05
483	David Wells	.10
484	Barry Jones	.05
485	Scott Bankhead	.05
486	Terry Leach	.05
487	Vince Horsman	.05
488	Dave Eiland	.05
489	Alejandro Pena	.05
490	Julio Valera	.05
491	Joe Boever	.05
492	Paul Miller	.05
493	*Arci Cianfrocco*	.10
494	Dave Fleming	.05
495	Kyle Abbott	.10
496	Chad Kreuter	.05
497	Chris James	.05
498	Donnie Hill	.05
499	Jacob Brumfield	.05
500	Ricky Bones	.05
501	Terry Steinbach	.05
502	Bernard Gilkey	.10
503	Dennis Cook	.05
504	Len Dykstra	.05
505	Mike Bielecki	.05
506	Bob Kipper	.05
507	Jose Melendez	.05
508	Rick Sutcliffe	.05
509	Ken Patterson	.05
510	Andy Allanson	.05
511	Al Newman	.05
512	Mark Gardner	.05
513	Jeff Schaefer	.05
514	Jim McNamara	.05
515	Peter Hoy	.05
516	Curt Schilling	.12
517	Kirk McCaskill	.05
518	Chris Gwynn	.05
519	Sid Fernandez	.05
520	Jeff Parrett	.05
521	Scott Ruskin	.05
522	Kevin McReynolds	.05
523	Rick Cerone	.05
524	Jesse Orosco	.05
525	Troy Afenir	.05
526	John Smiley	.05
527	Dale Murphy	.12
528	Leaf Set Card	.05

1992 Leaf Gold Previews

In the same format as the chase cards which would be included in the regular 1992 Leaf packs, this preview set was produced for distribution to the Donruss dealer network. Cards feature the same black borders and gold highlights as the regular-issue Leaf Gold cards, but are numbered "X of 33" on the back.

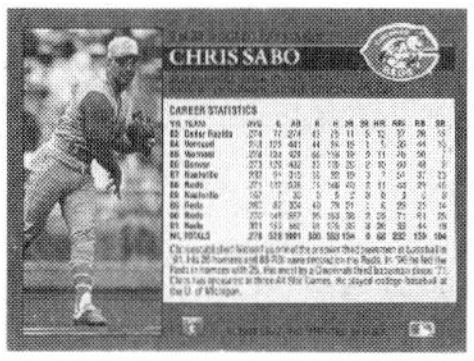

		MT
Complete Set (33):		100.00
Common Player:		1.50
1	Steve Avery	1.50
2	Ryne Sandberg	4.50
3	Chris Sabo	1.50
4	Jeff Bagwell	4.50
5	Darryl Strawberry	2.50
6	Bret Barbarie	1.50
7	Howard Johnson	1.50
8	John Kruk	1.50
9	Andy Van Slyke	1.50
10	Felix Jose	1.50
11	Fred McGriff	2.00
12	Will Clark	3.00
13	Cal Ripken, Jr.	8.00
14	Phil Plantier	1.50
15	Lee Stevens	1.50
16	Frank Thomas	5.00
17	Mark Whiten	1.50
18	Cecil Fielder	2.00
19	George Brett	6.00
20	Robin Yount	3.50
21	Scott Erickson	1.50
22	Don Mattingly	5.00
23	Jose Canseco	3.75
24	Ken Griffey, Jr.	9.00
25	Nolan Ryan	8.00
26	Joe Carter	2.00
27	Deion Sanders	3.00
28	Dean Palmer	1.50
29	Andy Benes	1.50
30	Gary DiSarcina	1.50
31	Chris Hoiles	1.50
32	Mark McGwire	9.00
33	Reggie Sanders	1.50

1992 Leaf Gold Edition

This set is a parallel version of Leaf's regular 1992 set. Card fronts do not have silver borders like the regular cards do; black borders and gold foil highlights are seen instead. A Gold Edition card was inserted in each 15-card 1992 Leaf foil pack.

	MT
Complete Set (528):	100.00
Common Player:	.10
Veteran Stars: 4X	
Young Stars: 2X	

(See 1992 Leaf for checklist and base card values)

1992 Leaf Gold Rookies

Two dozen of the major leagues' most promising players are featured in this insert set. Cards 1-12 were randomly included in Series I foil packs, while cards 13-24 were in Series II packs. Cards, numbered with a BC prefix, are standard size and enhanced with gold foil.

		MT
Complete Set (24):		10.00
Common Player:		.25
1	Chad Curtis	.25
2	Brent Gates	.40
3	Pedro Martinez	2.50
4	Kenny Lofton	4.00
5	Turk Wendell	.25
6	Mark Hutton	.25
7	Todd Hundley	.75
8	Matt Stairs	.25
9	Ed Taubensee	.25
10	David Nied	.25
11	Salomon Torres	.25
12	Bret Boone	.40
13	John Ruffin	.25
14	Ed Martel	.25
15	Rick Trlicek	.25
16	Raul Mondesi	2.00
17	Pat Mahomes	.35
18	Dan Wilson	.25
19	Donovan Osborne	.25
20	Dave Silvestri	.25
21	Gary DiSarcina	.25
22	Denny Neagle	.25
23	Steve Hosey	.25
24	John Doherty	.25

1993 Leaf

Leaf issued this set in three series: two 220-card series and a 110-card update set. Card fronts have full-bleed action photos and players' names stamped in gold foil. Color-coded slate corners are used to differentiate teams. Backs have player photos against cityscapes or landmarks from the team's home city, a holographic embossed team logo and 1992 and career statistics. Players from the National League's expansion teams, the Colorado Rockies and Florida Marlins, along with the Cincinnati Reds, California Angels and Seattle Mariners were featured in Series II packs so they could be pictured in their new uniforms. The Update series included a specially numbered "DW" insert card honoring Dave Winfield's 3,000-hit landmark, plus 3,500 special Frank Thomas autographed cards.

		MT
Complete Set (550):		35.00
Common Player:		.10
Series 1 or 2 Wax Box:		30.00
Update Wax Box:		45.00
1	Ben McDonald	.10
2	Sid Fernandez	.10
3	Juan Guzman	.10
4	Curt Schilling	.15
5	Ivan Rodriguez	.65
6	Don Slaught	.10
7	Terry Steinbach	.10
8	Todd Zeile	.15
9	Andy Stankiewicz	.10
10	Tim Teufel	.10
11	Marvin Freeman	.10
12	Jim Austin	.10
13	Bob Scanlan	.10
14	Rusty Meacham	.10
15	Casey Candaele	.10
16	Travis Fryman	.20
17	Jose Offerman	.10
18	Albert Belle	.75
19	John Vander Wahl (Vander Wal)	.10
20	Dan Pasqua	.10
21	Frank Viola	.10
22	Terry Mulholland	.10
23	Gregg Olson	.10
24	Randy Tomlin	.10
25	Todd Stottlemyre	.10
26	Jose Oquendo	.10
27	Julio Franco	.10
28	Tony Gwynn	1.25
29	Ruben Sierra	.10
30	Bobby Thigpen	.10
31	Jim Bullinger	.10
32	Rick Aguilera	.10
33	Scott Servais	.10
34	Cal Eldred	.10
35	Mike Piazza	2.00
36	Brent Mayne	.10
37	Wil Cordero	.10
38	Milt Cuyler	.10
39	Howard Johnson	.10
40	Kenny Lofton	.75
41	Alex Fernandez	.15
42	Denny Neagle	.10
43	Tony Pena	.10
44	Bob Tewksbury	.10
45	Glenn Davis	.10
46	Fred McGriff	.25
47	John Olerud	.20
48	Steve Hosey	.10
49	Rafael Palmeiro	.20
50	Dave Justice	.20
51	Pete Harnisch	.10
52	Sam Militello	.10
53	Orel Hershiser	.15
54	Pat Mahomes	.10
55	Greg Colbrunn	.10
56	Greg Vaughn	.15
57	Vince Coleman	.10
58	Brian McRae	.10
59	Len Dykstra	.10
60	Dan Gladden	.10
61	Ted Power	.10
62	Donovan Osborne	.10
63	Ron Karkovice	.10
64	Frank Seminara	.10
65	Bob Zupcic	.10
66	Kirt Manwaring	.10
67	Mike Devereaux	.10
68	Mark Lemke	.10
69	Devon White	.10
70	Sammy Sosa	1.50
71	Pedro Astacio	.10
72	Dennis Eckersley	.15
73	Chris Nabholz	.10
74	Melido Perez	.10
75	Todd Hundley	.20
76	Kent Hrbek	.10
77	Mickey Morandini	.10
78	Tim McIntosh	.10
79	Andy Van Slyke	.10
80	Kevin McReynolds	.10
81	Mike Henneman	.10
82	Greg Harris	.10
83	Sandy Alomar Jr.	.15
84	Mike Jackson	.10
85	Ozzie Guillen	.10
86	Jeff Blauser	.10
87	John Valentin	.20
88	Rey Sanchez	.10
89	Rick Sutcliffe	.10
90	Luis Gonzalez	.10
91	Jeff Fassero	.10
92	Kenny Rogers	.10
93	Bret Saberhagen	.10
94	Bob Welch	.10
95	Darren Daulton	.10
96	Mike Gallego	.10
97	Orlando Merced	.10
98	Chuck Knoblauch	.25
99	Bernard Gilkey	.10
100	Billy Ashley	.10
101	Kevin Appier	.10
102	Jeff Brantley	.10
103	Bill Gullickson	.10
104	John Smoltz	.20
105	Paul Sorrento	.10
106	Steve Buechele	.10
107	Steve Sax	.10
108	Andujar Cedeno	.10
109	Billy Hatcher	.10
110	Checklist	.10
111	Alan Mills	.10
112	John Franco	.10
113	Jack Morris	.10
114	Mitch Williams	.10
115	Nolan Ryan	2.00
116	Jay Bell	.10
117	Mike Bordick	.10
118	Geronimo Pena	.10
119	Danny Tartabull	.10
120	Checklist	.10
121	Steve Avery	.10
122	Ricky Bones	.10
123	Mike Morgan	.10
124	Jeff Montgomery	.10
125	Jeff Bagwell	1.00
126	Tony Phillips	.10
127	Lenny Harris	.10
128	Glenallen Hill	.10
129	Marquis Grissom	.15
130	Bernie Williams (name on front is Gerald Williams)	.60
131	Greg Harris	.10
132	Tommy Greene	.10
133	Chris Hoiles	.10
134	Bob Walk	.10
135	Duane Ward	.10
136	Tom Pagnozzi	.10
137	Jeff Huson	.10
138	Kurt Stillwell	.10
139	Dave Henderson	.10
140	Darrin Jackson	.10
141	Frank Castillo	.10
142	Scott Erickson	.10
143	Darryl Kile	.10
144	Bill Wegman	.10
145	Steve Wilson	.10
146	George Brett	.75
147	Moises Alou	.15
148	Lou Whitaker	.10
149	Chico Walker	.10
150	Jerry Browne	.10
151	Kirk McCaskill	.10
152	Zane Smith	.10
153	Matt Young	.10
154	Lee Smith	.15
155	Leo Gomez	.10
156	Dan Walters	.10
157	Pat Borders	.10
158	Matt Williams	.25
159	Dean Palmer	.15
160	John Patterson	.10
161	Doug Jones	.10
162	John Habyan	.10
163	Pedro Martinez	.35
164	Carl Willis	.10
165	Darrin Fletcher	.10
166	B.J. Surhoff	.10
167	Eddie Murray	.40
168	Keith Miller	.10
169	Ricky Jordan	.10
170	Juan Gonzalez	1.25
171	Charles Nagy	.10
172	Mark Clark	.10
173	Bobby Thigpen	.10
174	Tim Scott	.10
175	Scott Cooper	.10
176	Royce Clayton	.10
177	Brady Anderson	.15
178	Sid Bream	.10
179	Derek Bell	.15
180	Otis Nixon	.10
181	Kevin Gross	.10
182	Ron Darling	.10
183	John Wetteland	.10
184	Mike Stanley	.10
185	Jeff Kent	.10
186	Brian Harper	.10
187	Mariano Duncan	.10
188	Robin Yount	.50
189	Al Martin	.10
190	Eddie Zosky	.10
191	Mike Munoz	.10
192	Andy Benes	.10
193	Dennis Cook	.10
194	Bill Swift	.10
195	Frank Thomas	1.50
196	Damon Berryhill	.10
197	Mike Greenwell	.10
198	Mark Grace	.20
199	Darryl Hamilton	.10
200	Derrick May	.10
201	Ken Hill	.10
202	Kevin Brown	.15
203	Dwight Gooden	.15
204	Bobby Witt	.10
205	Juan Bell	.10
206	Kevin Maas	.10
207	Jeff King	.10
208	Scott Leius	.10
209	Rheal Cormier	.10
210	Darryl Strawberry	.15
211	Tom Gordon	.10
212	Bud Black	.10
213	Mickey Tettleton	.10
214	Pete Smith	.10
215	Felix Fermin	.10
216	Rick Wilkins	.10
217	George Bell	.10
218	Eric Anthony	.10
219	Pedro Munoz	.10
220	Checklist	.10
221	Lance Blankenship	.10
222	Deion Sanders	.40
223	Craig Biggio	.20
224	Ryne Sandberg	.60
225	Ron Gant	.15
226	Tom Brunansky	.10
227	Chad Curtis	.10
228	Joe Carter	.15
229	Brian Jordan	.15
230	Brett Butler	.10
231	Frank Bolick	.10
232	Rod Beck	.10
233	Carlos Baerga	.10
234	Eric Karros	.15
235	Jack Armstrong	.10
236	Bobby Bonilla	.15
237	Don Mattingly	1.00
238	Jeff Gardner	.10
239	Dave Hollins	.10
240	Steve Cooke	.10
241	Jose Canseco	.25
242	Ivan Calderon	.10
243	Tim Belcher	.10
244	Freddie Benavides	.10
245	Roberto Alomar	.50
246	Rob Deer	.10
247	Will Clark	.25
248	Mike Felder	.10
249	Harold Baines	.15
250	David Cone	.15
251	Mark Guthrie	.10
252	Ellis Burks	.10
253	Jim Abbott	.15
254	Chili Davis	.10
255	Chris Bosio	.10
256	Bret Barberie	.10
257	Hal Morris	.10
258	Dante Bichette	.25
259	Storm Davis	.10
260	Gary DiSarcina	.10
261	Ken Caminiti	.25
262	Paul Molitor	.50
263	Joe Oliver	.10
264	Pat Listach	.10
265	Gregg Jefferies	.15
266	Jose Guzman	.10
267	Eric Davis	.15
268	Delino DeShields	.10
269	Barry Bonds	.75
270	Mike Bielecki	.10
271	Jay Buhner	.15
272	*Scott Pose*	.15
273	Tony Fernandez	.10
274	Chito Martinez	.10
275	Phil Plantier	.10
276	Pete Incaviglia	.10
277	Carlos Garcia	.10
278	Tom Henke	.10
279	Roger Clemens	1.00
280	Rob Dibble	.10
281	Daryl Boston	.10
282	Greg Gagne	.10
283	Cecil Fielder	.10
284	Carlton Fisk	.15
285	Wade Boggs	.25
286	Damion Easley	.10
287	Norm Charlton	.10
288	Jeff Conine	.15
289	Roberto Kelly	.10
290	Jerald Clark	.10
291	Rickey Henderson	.25
292	Chuck Finley	.10
293	Doug Drabek	.10
294	Dave Stewart	.10
295	Tom Glavine	.20
296	Jaime Navarro	.10
297	Ray Lankford	.15
298	Greg Hibbard	.10
299	Jody Reed	.10
300	Dennis Martinez	.10
301	Dave Martinez	.10
302	Reggie Jefferson	.10
303	*John Cummings*	.25
304	Orestes Destrade	.10
305	Mike Maddux	.10
306	David Segui	.10
307	Gary Sheffield	.30
308	Danny Jackson	.10
309	Craig Lefferts	.10
310	Andre Dawson	.15
311	Barry Larkin	.15
312	Alex Cole	.10
313	Mark Gardner	.10
314	Kirk Gibson	.10
315	Shane Mack	.10
316	Bo Jackson	.15
317	Jimmy Key	.10
318	Greg Myers	.10
319	Ken Griffey, Jr.	3.00
320	Monty Fariss	.10
321	Kevin Mitchell	.10
322	Andres Galarraga	.20
323	Mark McGwire	3.00
324	Mark Langston	.10
325	Steve Finley	.10
326	Greg Maddux	1.50
327	Dave Nilsson	.10
328	Ozzie Smith	.50
329	Candy Maldonado	.10
330	Checklist	.10
331	*Tim Pugh*	.10
332	Joe Girardi	.10
333	Junior Feliz	.10
334	Greg Swindell	.10
335	Ramon Martinez	.15
336	Sean Berry	.10
337	Joe Orsulak	.10
338	Wes Chamberlain	.10
339	Stan Belinda	.10
340	Checklist	.10
341	Bruce Hurst	.10
342	John Burkett	.10
343	Mike Mussina	.60
344	Scott Fletcher	.10
345	Rene Gonzales	.10
346	Roberto Hernandez	.10
347	Carlos Martinez	.10
348	Bill Krueger	.10
349	Felix Jose	.10
350	John Jaha	.15
351	Willie Banks	.10
352	Matt Nokes	.10
353	Kevin Seitzer	.10
354	Erik Hanson	.10
355	*David Hulse*	.10
356	*Domingo Martinez*	.10
357	Greg Olson	.10
358	Randy Myers	.10
359	Tom Browning	.10
360	Charlie Hayes	.10
361	Bryan Harvey	.10
362	Eddie Taubensee	.10
363	Tim Wallach	.10
364	Mel Rojas	.10
365	Frank Tanana	.10
366	John Kruk	.10
367	*Tim Laker*	.10
368	Rich Rodriguez	.10
369	Darren Lewis	.10
370	Harold Reynolds	.10
371	Jose Melendez	.10
372	Joe Grahe	.10
373	Lance Johnson	.10
374	Jose Mesa	.10
375	Scott Livingstone	.10
376	Wally Joyner	.10
377	Kevin Reimer	.10
378	Kirby Puckett	1.00
379	Paul O'Neill	.20
380	Randy Johnson	.40
381	Manuel Lee	.10
382	Dick Schofield	.10
383	Darren Holmes	.10
384	Charlie Hough	.10
385	John Orton	.10
386	Edgar Martinez	.10
387	Terry Pendleton	.10
388	Dan Plesac	.10
389	Jeff Reardon	.10
390	David Nied	.10
391	Dave Magadan	.10
392	Larry Walker	.25
393	Ben Rivera	.10
394	Lonnie Smith	.10
395	Craig Shipley	.10
396	Willie McGee	.10
397	Arthur Rhodes	.10
398	Mike Stanton	.10
399	Luis Polonia	.10
400	Jack McDowell	.10
401	Mike Moore	.10
402	Jose Lind	.10
403	Bill Spiers	.10
404	Kevin Tapani	.10
405	Spike Owen	.10
406	Tino Martinez	.25
407	Charlie Leibrandt	.10
408	Ed Sprague	.10
409	Bryn Smith	.10
410	Benito Santiago	.10
411	Jose Rijo	.10
412	Pete O'Brien	.10
413	Willie Wilson	.10
414	Bip Roberts	.10
415	Eric Young	.15
416	Walt Weiss	.10
417	Milt Thompson	.10
418	Chris Sabo	.10
419	Scott Sanderson	.10
420	Tim Raines	.15
421	Alan Trammell	.15
422	Mike Macfarlane	.10
423	Dave Winfield	.30
424	Bob Wickman	.10
425	David Valle	.10
426	Gary Redus	.10
427	Turner Ward	.10
428	Reggie Sanders	.10
429	Todd Worrell	.10
430	Julio Valera	.10
431	Cal Ripken, Jr.	2.50
432	Mo Vaughn	.65
433	John Smiley	.10
434	Omar Vizquel	.10
435	Billy Ripken	.10
436	Cory Snyder	.10
437	Carlos Quintana	.10
438	Omar Olivares	.10
439	Robin Ventura	.15
440	Checklist	.10
441	Kevin Higgins	.10
442	Carlos Hernandez	.10
443	Dan Peltier	.10
444	Derek Lilliquist	.10
445	Tim Salmon	.50
446	*Sherman Obando*	.10
447	Pat Kelly	.10
448	Todd Van Poppel	.10
449	Mark Whiten	.10
450	Checklist	.10
451	Pat Meares	.10
452	*Tony Tarasco*	.10
453	Chris Gwynn	.10
454	Armando Reynoso	.10
455	Danny Darwin	.10
456	Willie Greene	.10
457	Mike Blowers	.10
458	*Kevin Roberson*	.15
459	*Graeme Lloyd*	.10
460	David West	.10
461	Joey Cora	.10
462	Alex Arias	.10
463	Chad Kreuter	.10
464	Mike Lansing	.15
465	Mike Timlin	.10
466	Paul Wagner	.10
467	Mark Portugal	.10
468	Jim Leyritz	.10
469	Ryan Klesko	.25
470	Mario Diaz	.10
471	Guillermo Velasquez	.10
472	Fernando Valenzuela	.10
473	Raul Mondesi	1.50
474	Mike Pagliarulo	.10
475	Chris Hammond	.10
476	Torey Lovullo	.10
477	Trevor Wilson	.10
478	*Marcos Armas*	.10
479	Dave Gallagher	.10
480	Jeff Treadway	.10
481	Jeff Branson	.10
482	Dickie Thon	.10
483	Eduardo Perez	.10
484	David Wells	.15
485	Brian Williams	.10
486	Domingo Cedeno	.10
487	Tom Candiotti	.10
488	Steve Frey	.10
489	Greg McMichael	.10
490	Marc Newfield	.10
491	Larry Andersen	.10
492	Damon Buford	.15
493	Ricky Gutierrez	.10
494	Jeff Russell	.10
495	Vinny Castilla	.20
496	Wilson Alvarez	.10
497	Scott Bullett	.10
498	Larry Casian	.10
499	Jose Vizcaino	.10
500	*J.T. Snow*	.75
501	Bryan Hickerson	.10
502	Jeremy Hernandez	.10
503	Jeromy Burnitz	.15
504	Steve Farr	.10
505	J. Owens	.10
506	Craig Paquette	.10
507	Jim Eisenreich	.10
508	Matt Whiteside	.10
509	Luis Aquino	.10
510	Mike LaValliere	.10
511	Jim Gott	.10
512	Mark McLemore	.10
513	Randy Milligan	.10
514	Gary Gaetti	.10
515	Lou Frazier	.10
516	Rich Amaral	.10
517	Gene Harris	.10
518	Aaron Sele	.15
519	Mark Wohlers	.10
520	Scott Kamieniecki	.10
521	Kent Mercker	.10
522	Jim Deshaies	.10
523	Kevin Stocker	.10
524	Jason Bere	.10
525	Tim Bogar	.10
526	Brad Pennington	.15
527	*Curt Leskanic*	.15
528	Wayne Kirby	.10
529	Tim Costo	.10
530	Doug Henry	.10
531	Trevor Hoffman	.20
532	Kelly Gruber	.10
533	Mike Harkey	.10
534	John Doherty	.10
535	Erik Pappas	.10
536	Brent Gates	.15
537	Roger McDowell	.10
538	Chris Haney	.10
539	Blas Minor	.10
540	Pat Hentgen	.10
541	Chuck Carr	.10
542	Doug Strange	.10
543	Xavier Hernandez	.10
544	Paul Quantrill	.10
545	Anthony Young	.10
546	Bret Boone	.15
547	Dwight Smith	.10
548	Bobby Munoz	.10
549	Russ Springer	.10
550	Roger Pavlik	.10
----	Dave Winfield (3000 Hits)	4.00
----	Frank Thomas (Autograph)	200.00

1993 Leaf Fasttrack

This 20-card insert set was released in two series; cards 1-10 were randomly included in Leaf Series I retail packs, while 11-20 were in Series II packs. Card fronts and backs are similar with a player photo and a diagonal white strip with "on the Fasttrack" printed in black and red. Fronts have the gold embossed Leaf logo, backs have the silver holographic team logo.

		MT
Complete Set (20):		60.00
Common Player:		1.50
1	Frank Thomas	12.00
2	Tim Wakefield	1.50
3	Kenny Lofton	6.00
4	Mike Mussina	4.00
5	Juan Gonzalez	8.00
6	Chuck Knoblauch	3.00
7	Eric Karros	2.00
8	Ray Lankford	1.50
9	Juan Guzman	1.50
10	Pat Listach	1.50
11	Carlos Baerga	1.50
12	Felix Jose	1.50
13	Steve Avery	1.50
14	Robin Ventura	2.50
15	Ivan Rodriguez	6.00
16	Cal Eldred	1.50
17	Jeff Bagwell	10.00
18	Dave Justice	3.00
19	Travis Fryman	1.50
20	Marquis Grissom	1.50

1993 Leaf Gold All-Stars

Cards 1-10 in this insert set were randomly inserted one per Leaf Series I jumbo packs, while cards 11-20 were in Series II jumbo packs. Cards feature two players per card, one on each side. Only one side is numbered, but both sides have gold foil.

		MT
Complete Set (20):		35.00
Common Player:		.50
1	Ivan Rodriguez, Darren Daulton	1.50
2	Don Mattingly, Fred McGriff	2.50
3	Cecil Fielder, Jeff Bagwell	3.00
4	Carlos Baerga, Ryne Sandberg	2.00
5	Chuck Knoblauch, Delino DeShields	.50
6	Robin Ventura, Terry Pendleton	.75
7	Ken Griffey, Jr., Andy Van Slyke	7.50
8	Joe Carter, Dave Justice	1.00
9	Jose Canseco, Tony Gwynn	2.50
10	Dennis Eckersley, Rob Dibble	.50
11	Mark McGwire, Will Clark	7.50
12	Frank Thomas, Mark Grace	4.00
13	Roberto Alomar, Craig Biggio	2.00
14	Barry Larkin, Cal Ripken, Jr.	6.00
15	Gary Sheffield, Edgar Martinez	1.50
16	Juan Gonzalez, Barry Bonds	3.00
17	Kirby Puckett, Marquis Grissom	2.50
18	Jim Abbott, Tom Glavine	1.00
19	Nolan Ryan, Greg Maddux	7.50
20	Roger Clemens, Doug Drabek	2.00

1993 Leaf Gold Rookies

These cards, numbered 1 of 20 etc., feature 1993 rookies and were randomly inserted into hobby foil packs, 10 players per series. Card fronts feature action photos, while the backs show a player photo against a landmark from his team's city.

		MT
Complete Set (20):		40.00
Common Player:		.50
1	Kevin Young	.50
2	Wil Cordero	1.00
3	Mark Kiefer	.50
4	Gerald Williams	1.00
5	Brandon Wilson	.50
6	Greg Gohr	.50
7	Ryan Thompson	1.50
8	Tim Wakefield	.50
9	Troy Neel	1.00
10	Tim Salmon	8.00
11	Kevin Rogers	.50
12	Rod Bolton	.50
13	Ken Ryan	.50
14	Phil Hiatt	.50
15	Rene Arocha	1.00
16	Nigel Wilson	.50
17	J.T. Snow	3.00
18	Benji Gil	.50
19	Chipper Jones	18.00
20	Darrell Sherman	.50

1993 Leaf Heading for the Hall

Ten players on the way to the Baseball Hall of Fame are featured in this insert set. Series I Leaf packs had cards 1-5 randomly included; Series II packs had cards 6-10.

		MT
Complete Set (10):		30.00
Common Player:		2.00
1	Nolan Ryan	9.00
2	Tony Gwynn	5.00
3	Robin Yount	2.50
4	Eddie Murray	2.00
5	Cal Ripken, Jr.	12.00
6	Roger Clemens	4.00
7	George Brett	4.00
8	Ryne Sandberg	3.00
9	Kirby Puckett	6.00
10	Ozzie Smith	3.00

1993 Leaf Frank Thomas

Leaf signed Frank Thomas as its spokesman for 1993, and honored him with a 10-card insert set. Cards 1-5 were randomly included in Series I packs; cards 6-10 were in Series II packs. A custom designed "Frank" logo in a holographic foil stamp is featured on each card front which includes a one-word character trait. On back is a color portrait photo of Thomas superimposed on a Chicago skyline. A paragraph on back describes how the character trait on front applies to Thomas.

		MT
Complete Set:		25.00
Common Card:		3.00
Autographed Card:		200.00
1	Aggressive (Frank Thomas)	3.00
2	Serious (Frank Thomas)	3.00
3	Intense (Frank Thomas)	3.00
4	Confident (Frank Thomas)	3.00
5	Assertive (Frank Thomas)	3.00
6	Power (Frank Thomas)	3.00
7	Control (Frank Thomas)	3.00
8	Strength (Frank Thomas)	3.00
9	Concentration (Frank Thomas)	3.00
10	Preparation (Frank Thomas)	3.00

1993 Leaf Update Gold All-Stars

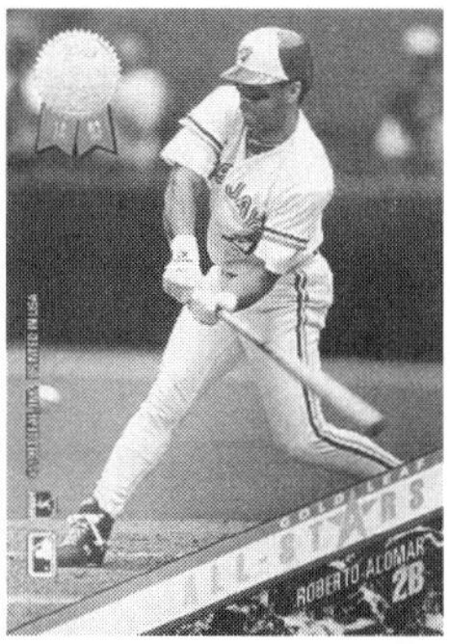

These 10 cards, featuring 20 all stars, were randomly inserted in Leaf Update packs. Each card features two players, one on each side. Cards are distinguished from the regular Gold All-Stars by indicating on the front the card is number X of 10, with a tiny white "Update" in the red stripe above the card number.

		MT
Complete Set (10):		15.00
Common Player:		.50
1	Mark Langston, Terry Mulholland	.50
2	Ivan Rodriguez, Darren Daulton	1.00
3	John Olerud, John Kruk	.50
4	Roberto Alomar, Ryne Sandberg	2.00
5	Wade Boggs, Gary Sheffield	1.00
6	Cal Ripken, Jr., Barry Larkin	6.00
7	Kirby Puckett, Barry Bonds	4.00
8	Marquis Grissom, Ken Griffey Jr.	7.50
9	Joe Carter, Dave Justice	1.00
10	Mark Grace, Paul Molitor	1.50

1993 Leaf Update Gold Rookies

These five cards were randomly inserted in Leaf Update packs. Cards are similiar in design to the regular Gold Rookies cards, except the logo on the back indicates they are from the Update series.

		MT
Complete Set (5):		22.00
Common Player:		2.00
1	Allen Watson	2.00
2	Jeffrey Hammonds	2.00
3	David McCarty	2.00
4	Mike Piazza	20.00
5	Roberto Meija	2.00

1993 Leaf Update Frank Thomas Autograph

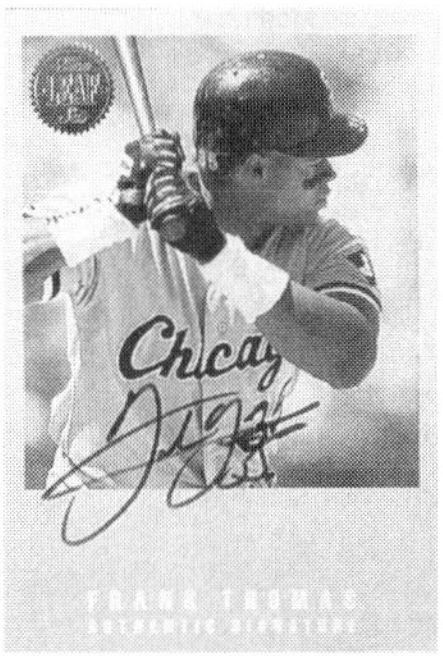

This card was a random insert in '93 Leaf Update packs and features a genuine Frank Thomas autograph on front. Unlike the other cards in the set, this has a silver-gray border on front and back. Front has a gold-foil seal in upper-left. Back has a photo of Thomas in his batting follow-through. At bottom on back is a white strip bearing the card's individual serial number from within an edition of 3,500.

		MT
FT	Frank Thomas	125.00

Player names in *Italic* type indicate a rookie card.

1993 Leaf Update Frank Thomas Super

This 10-card insert set features Leaf's 1993 spokesman, Frank Thomas. Cards, which measure 5" x 7", were included one per every Leaf Update foil box and are identical to the inserts found in Series I and II except in size. Cards are individually numbered. Thomas autographed 3,500 cards.

		MT
Complete Set (10):		45.00
Common Thomas:		5.00
1	Aggressive (Frank Thomas)	5.00
2	Serious (Frank Thomas)	5.00
3	Intense (Frank Thomas)	5.00
4	Confident (Frank Thomas)	5.00
5	Assertive (Frank Thomas)	5.00
6	Power (Frank Thomas)	5.00
7	Control (Frank Thomas)	5.00
8	Strength (Frank Thomas)	5.00
9	Concentration (Frank Thomas)	5.00
10	Preparation (Frank Thomas)	5.00

1994 Leaf Promos

Identical in format to the regular issue, this nine-card set was produced as a preview for the 1994 Leaf cards. The only differences on the promo cards are a large, black "Promotional Sample" notice overprinted diagonally on both the front and back of the cards. Instead of the regular card numbers, the promos are numbered "X of 9" at top to the left of the team logo hologram.

		MT
Complete Set (9):		20.00
Common Player:		1.00
1	Roberto Alomar	2.00
2	Darren Daulton	1.00
3	Ken Griffey, Jr.	6.00
4	David Justice	2.00
5	Don Mattingly	4.00
6	Mike Piazza	4.00
7	Cal Ripken, Jr.	5.00
8	Ryne Sandberg	3.00
9	Frank Thomas	3.00

1994 Leaf

Donruss returned its premium-brand Leaf set in 1994 with an announced 25% production cut from the previous season - fewer than 20,000 20-box cases of each 220-card series. Game-action photos dominate the fronts of the cards, borderless at the top and sides. At bottom are team color-coded faux-marble borders with the player's name (last name in gold foil) and team. Backs have a background of the player's home stadium with another action photo superimposed. In a ticket-stub device at upper-left is a portrait photo and a few personal numbers. Previous season and career stats are in white stripes at bottom. The team logo is presented in holographic foil at upper-right. To feature 1994's new stadiums and uniforms, cards of the Indians, Rangers, Brewers and Astros were included only in the second series. Seven different types of insert cards were produced and distributed among the various types of Leaf packaging.

		MT
Complete Set (440):		32.00
Complete Series 1 (220):		15.00
Complete Series 2 (220):		17.00
Common Player:		.10
Series 1 or 2 Wax Box:		40.00
1	Cal Ripken, Jr.	2.50
2	Tony Tarasco	.10
3	Joe Girardi	.10
4	Bernie Williams	.60
5	Chad Kreuter	.10
6	Troy Neel	.15
7	Tom Pagnozzi	.10
8	Kirk Rueter	.10
9	Chris Bosio	.10
10	Dwight Gooden	.15
11	Mariano Duncan	.10
12	Jay Bell	.10
13	Lance Johnson	.10
14	Richie Lewis	.10
15	Dave Martinez	.10
16	Orel Hershiser	.15
17	Rob Butler	.10
18	Glenallen Hill	.10
19	Chad Curtis	.10
20	Mike Stanton	.10
21	Tim Wallach	.10
22	Milt Thompson	.10
23	Kevin Young	.10
24	John Smiley	.10
25	Jeff Montgomery	.10
26	Robin Ventura	.20
27	Scott Lydy	.10
28	Todd Stottlemyre	.10
29	Mark Whiten	.10
30	Robby Thompson	.10
31	Bobby Bonilla	15.00
32	Andy Ashby	.10
33	Greg Myers	.10
34	Billy Hatcher	.10
35	Brad Holman	.10
36	Mark McLemore	.10
37	Scott Sanders	.10
38	Jim Abbott	.10
39	David Wells	.15
40	Roberto Kelly	.10
41	Jeff Conine	.10
42	Sean Berry	.10
43	Mark Grace	.20
44	Eric Young	.10
45	Rick Aguilera	.10
46	Chipper Jones	1.50
47	Mel Rojas	.10
48	Ryan Thompson	.10
49	Al Martin	.10
50	Cecil Fielder	.15
51	Pat Kelly	.10
52	Kevin Tapani	.10
53	Tim Costo	.10
54	Dave Hollins	.10
55	Kirt Manwaring	.10
56	Gregg Jefferies	.15
57	Ron Darling	.10
58	Bill Haselman	.10
59	Phil Plantier	.10
60	Frank Viola	.10
61	Todd Zeile	.10
62	Bret Barberie	.10
63	Roberto Mejia	.10
64	Chuck Knoblauch	.15
65	Jose Lind	.10
66	Brady Anderson	.15
67	Ruben Sierra	.10
68	Jose Vizcaino	.10
69	Joe Grahe	.10
70	Kevin Appier	.10
71	Wilson Alvarez	.10
72	Tom Candiotti	.10
73	John Burkett	.10
74	Anthony Young	.10
75	Scott Cooper	.10
76	Nigel Wilson	.10
77	John Valentin	.10
78	Dave McCarty	.10
79	Archi Cianfrocco	.10
80	Lou Whitaker	.10
81	Dante Bichette	.15
82	Mark Dewey	.10
83	Danny Jackson	.10
84	Harold Baines	.10
85	Todd Benzinger	.10
86	Damion Easley	.10
87	Danny Cox	.10
88	Jose Bautista	.10
89	Mike Lansing	.10
90	Phil Hiatt	.10
91	Tim Pugh	.10
92	Tino Martinez	.15
93	Raul Mondesi	.60
94	Greg Maddux	1.50
95	Al Leiter	.15
96	Benito Santiago	.10
97	Len Dykstra	.10
98	Sammy Sosa	1.50
99	Tim Bogar	.10
100	Checklist	.10
101	Deion Sanders	.20
102	Bobby Witt	.10
103	Wil Cordero	.10
104	Rich Amaral	.10
105	Mike Mussina	.40
106	Reggie Sanders	.10
107	Ozzie Guillen	.10
108	Paul O'Neill	.15
109	Tim Salmon	.35
110	Rheal Cormier	.10
111	Billy Ashley	.10
112	Jeff Kent	.10
113	Derek Bell	.15
114	Danny Darwin	.10
115	Chip Hale	.10
116	Tim Raines	.10
117	Ed Sprague	.10
118	Darrin Fletcher	.10
119	Darren Holmes	.10
120	Alan Trammell	.15
121	Don Mattingly	1.00
122	Greg Gagne	.10
123	Jose Offerman	.10
124	Joe Orsulak	.10
125	Jack McDowell	.10
126	Barry Larkin	.15
127	Ben McDonald	.10
128	Mike Bordick	.10
129	Devon White	.10
130	Mike Perez	.10
131	Jay Buhner	.10
132	Phil Leftwich	.10
133	Tommy Greene	.10
134	Charlie Hayes	.10
135	Don Slaught	.10
136	Mike Gallego	.10
137	Dave Winfield	.25
138	Steve Avery	.10
139	Derrick May	.10
140	Bryan Harvey	.10
141	Wally Joyner	.10
142	Andre Dawson	.15
143	Andy Benes	.10
144	John Franco	.10
145	Jeff King	.10
146	Joe Oliver	.10
147	Bill Gullickson	.10
148	Armando Reynoso	.10
149	Dave Fleming	.10
150	Checklist	.10
151	Todd Van Poppel	.10
152	Bernard Gilkey	.10
153	Kevin Gross	.10
154	Mike Devereaux	.10
155	Tim Wakefield	.10
156	Andres Galarraga	.15
157	Pat Meares	.10
158	Jim Leyritz	.10
159	Mike Macfarlane	.10
160	Tony Phillips	.10
161	Brent Gates	.10
162	Mark Langston	.10
163	Allen Watson	.10
164	Randy Johnson	.35
165	Doug Brocail	.10
166	Rob Dibble	.10
167	Roberto Hernandez	.10
168	Felix Jose	.10
169	Steve Cooke	.10
170	Darren Daulton	.10
171	Eric Karros	.10
172	Geronimo Pena	.10
173	Gary DiSarcina	.10
174	Marquis Grissom	.10
175	Joey Cora	.10
176	Jim Eisenreich	.10
177	Brad Pennington	.10
178	Terry Steinbach	.10
179	Pat Borders	.10
180	Steve Buechele	.10
181	Jeff Fassero	.10
182	Mike Greenwell	.10
183	Mike Henneman	.10
184	Ron Karkovice	.10
185	Pat Hentgen	.10
186	Jose Guzman	.10
187	Brett Butler	.10
188	Charlie Hough	.10
189	Terry Pendleton	.10
190	Melido Perez	.10
191	Orestes Destrade	.10
192	Mike Morgan	.10
193	Joe Carter	.10
194	Jeff Blauser	.10
195	Chris Hoiles	.10
196	Ricky Gutierrez	.10
197	Mike Moore	.10
198	Carl Willis	.10
199	Aaron Sele	.10
200	Checklist	.10
201	Tim Naehring	.10
202	Scott Livingstone	.10
203	Luis Alicea	.10
204	*Torey Lovullo*	.10
205	Jim Gott	.10
206	Bob Wickman	.10
207	Greg McMichael	.10
208	Scott Brosius	.10
209	Chris Gwynn	.10
210	Steve Sax	.10
211	Dick Schofield	.10
212	Robb Nen	.10
213	Ben Rivera	.10
214	Vinny Castilla	.15
215	Jamie Moyer	.10
216	Wally Whitehurst	.10
217	Frank Castillo	.10
218	Mike Blowers	.10
219	Tim Scott	.10
220	Paul Wagner	.10
221	Jeff Bagwell	1.00
222	Ricky Bones	.10
223	Sandy Alomar Jr.	.15
224	Rod Beck	.10
225	Roberto Alomar	.65
226	Jack Armstrong	.10
227	Scott Erickson	.10
228	Rene Arocha	.10
229	Eric Anthony	.10
230	Jeromy Burnitz	.15
231	Kevin Brown	.15
232	Tim Belcher	.10
233	Bret Boone	.10
234	Dennis Eckersley	.10
235	Tom Glavine	.20
236	Craig Biggio	.15
237	Pedro Astacio	.10
238	Ryan Bowen	.10
239	Brad Ausmus	.10
240	Vince Coleman	.10
241	Jason Bere	.10
242	Ellis Burks	.10
243	Wes Chamberlain	.10
244	Ken Caminiti	.15
245	Willie Banks	.10
246	Sid Fernandez	.10
247	Carlos Baerga	.10
248	Carlos Garcia	.10
249	Jose Canseco	.30
250	Alex Diaz	.10
251	Albert Belle	.75
252	Moises Alou	.15
253	Bobby Ayala	.10
254	Tony Gwynn	1.00
255	Roger Clemens	1.00
256	Eric Davis	.15
257	Wade Boggs	.30
258	Chili Davis	.10
259	Rickey Henderson	.35
260	Andujar Cedeno	.10
261	Cris Carpenter	.10
262	Juan Guzman	.10
263	Dave Justice	.20
264	Barry Bonds	.75
265	Pete Incaviglia	.10
266	Tony Fernandez	.10
267	Cal Eldred	.10
268	Alex Fernandez	.10
269	Kent Hrbek	.10
270	Steve Farr	.10
271	Doug Drabek	.10
272	Brian Jordan	.15
273	Xavier Hernandez	.10
274	David Cone	.15
275	Brian Hunter	.10
276	Mike Harkey	.10
277	Delino DeShields	.10
278	David Hulse	.10
279	Mickey Tettleton	.10
280	Kevin McReynolds	.10
281	Darryl Hamilton	.10
282	Ken Hill	.10
283	Wayne Kirby	.10
284	Chris Hammond	.10
285	Mo Vaughn	.60
286	Ryan Klesko	.25
287	Rick Wilkins	.10
288	Bill Swift	.10
289	Rafael Palmeiro	.15
290	Brian Harper	.10
291	Chris Turner	.10
292	Luis Gonzalez	.10
293	Kenny Rogers	.10
294	Kirby Puckett	1.00
295	Mike Stanley	.10
296	Carlos Reyes	.10
297	Charles Nagy	.10
298	Reggie Jefferson	.10
299	Bip Roberts	.10
300	Darrin Jackson	.10
301	Mike Jackson	.10
302	Dave Nilsson	.10
303	Ramon Martinez	.15
304	Bobby Jones	.10
305	Johnny Ruffin	.10
306	Brian McRae	.10
307	Bo Jackson	.15
308	Dave Stewart	.10
309	John Smoltz	.15
310	Dennis Martinez	.10
311	Dean Palmer	.10
312	David Nied	.10
313	Eddie Murray	.25
314	Darryl Kile	.10
315	Rick Sutcliffe	.10
316	Shawon Dunston	.10
317	John Jaha	.10
318	Salomon Torres	.10
319	Gary Sheffield	.15
320	Curt Schilling	.15
321	Greg Vaughn	.10
322	Jay Howell	.10
323	Todd Hundley	.15
324	Chris Sabo	.10
325	Stan Javier	.10
326	Willie Greene	.10
327	Hipolito Pichardo	.10
328	Doug Strange	.10
329	Dan Wilson	.10
330	Checklist	.10
331	Omar Vizquel	.10
332	Scott Servais	.10
333	Bob Tewksbury	.10
334	Matt Williams	.30
335	Tom Foley	.10
336	Jeff Russell	.10
337	Scott Leius	.10
338	Ivan Rodriguez	.50
339	Kevin Seitzer	.10
340	Jose Rijo	.10
341	Eduardo Perez	.10
342	Kirk Gibson	.10
343	Randy Milligan	.10
344	Edgar Martinez	.10
345	Fred McGriff	.25
346	Kurt Abbott	.10
347	John Kruk	.10
348	Mike Felder	.10
349	Dave Staton	.10
350	Kenny Lofton	.60
351	Graeme Lloyd	.10
352	David Segui	.10
353	Danny Tartabull	.10
354	Bob Welch	.10
355	Duane Ward	.10
356	Tuffy Rhodes	.10
357	Lee Smith	.10
358	Chris James	.10
359	Walt Weiss	.10
360	Pedro Munoz	.10
361	Paul Sorrento	.10
362	Todd Worrell	.10
363	Bob Hamelin	.10
364	Julio Franco	.10
365	Roberto Petagine	.10
366	Willie McGee	.10
367	Pedro Martinez	.25
368	Ken Griffey, Jr.	3.00
369	B.J. Surhoff	.10
370	Kevin Mitchell	.10
371	John Doherty	.10
372	Manuel Lee	.10
373	Terry Mulholland	.10
374	Zane Smith	.10
375	Otis Nixon	.10
376	Jody Reed	.10
377	Doug Jones	.10
378	John Olerud	.20
379	Greg Swindell	.10
380	Checklist	.10
381	Royce Clayton	.10
382	Jim Thome	.40
383	Steve Finley	.10
384	Ray Lankford	.10
385	Henry Rodriguez	.10
386	Dave Magadan	.10
387	Gary Redus	.10
388	Orlando Merced	.10
389	Tom Gordon	.10
390	Luis Polonia	.10
391	Mark McGwire	3.00
392	Mark Lemke	.10
393	Doug Henry	.10
394	Chuck Finley	.10
395	Paul Molitor	.40
396	Randy Myers	.10
397	Larry Walker	.20
398	Pete Harnisch	.10
399	Darren Lewis	.10
400	Frank Thomas	1.00
401	Jack Morris	.10
402	Greg Hibbard	.10
403	Jeffrey Hammonds	.10
404	Will Clark	.25
405	Travis Fryman	.15
406	Scott Sanderson	.10
407	Gene Harris	.10
408	Chuck Carr	.10
409	Ozzie Smith	.50
410	Kent Mercker	.10
411	Andy Van Slyke	.10
412	Jimmy Key	.10
413	Pat Mahomes	.10
414	John Wetteland	.10
415	Todd Jones	.10
416	Greg Harris	.10
417	Kevin Stocker	.10
418	Juan Gonzalez	1.00
419	Pete Smith	.10
420	Pat Listach	.10
421	Trevor Hoffman	.15
422	Scott Fletcher	.10
423	Mark Lewis	.10
424	Mickey Morandini	.10
425	Ryne Sandberg	.75
426	Erik Hanson	.10
427	Gary Gaetti	.10
428	Harold Reynolds	.10
429	Mark Portugal	.10
430	David Valle	.10
431	Mitch Williams	.10
432	Howard Johnson	.10
433	Hal Morris	.10
434	Tom Henke	.10
435	Shane Mack	.10
436	Mike Piazza	1.50
437	Bret Saberhagen	.10
438	Jose Mesa	.10
439	Jaime Navarro	.10
440	Checklist	.10

1994 Leaf Clean-Up Crew

The number four spot in the line-up is featured on this 12-card insert set (six per series) found only in magazine distributor packaging. Fronts are gold-foil enhanced; backs feature an action photo set against a background of a lineup card on which the player is pencilled into the #4 spot. His 1993 stats when batting clean-up are presented.

		MT
Complete Set (12):		20.00
Common Player:		1.00
1	Larry Walker	1.50
2	Andres Galarraga	1.50
3	Dave Hollins	1.00
4	Bobby Bonilla	1.00
5	Cecil Fielder	1.00
6	Danny Tartabull	1.00
7	Juan Gonzalez	7.50
8	Joe Carter	1.00
9	Fred McGriff	2.00
10	Matt Williams	2.00
11	Albert Belle	3.00
12	Harold Baines	1.00

1994 Leaf Gamers

Leaf jumbo packs are the exclusive venue for the six cards of this insert set which were issued in each series.

		MT
Complete Set (12):		75.00
Common Player:		1.50
1	Ken Griffey, Jr.	20.00
2	Len Dykstra	1.00
3	Juan Gonzalez	12.50
4	Don Mattingly	9.00
5	Dave Justice	2.00
6	Mark Grace	2.00
7	Frank Thomas	12.50
8	Barry Bonds	4.00
9	Kirby Puckett	9.00
10	Will Clark	2.00
11	John Kruk	1.00
12	Mike Piazza	15.00

1994 Leaf Gold Rookies

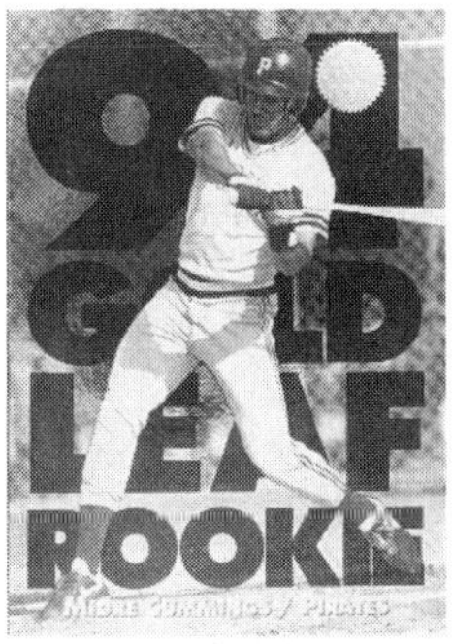

A gold-foil rendered stadium background and huge black "94 Gold Leaf Rookie" serve as a backdrop for a player photo on these insert cards found at the rate of about one per 18 foil packs. The player's name and team are in silver at bottom. Horizontal backs have a ghosted action photo of the player in the background. A portrait photo is in the upper-right corner, above some personal data and stats. Cards are numbered "X of 20".

		MT
Complete Set (20):		16.00
Common Player:		.50
1	Javier Lopez	2.00
2	Rondell White	2.50
3	Butch Huskey	.75
4	Midre Cummings	.50
5	Scott Ruffcorn	.50
6	Manny Ramirez	7.50
7	Danny Bautista	.50
8	Russ Davis	.50
9	Steve Karsay	.50
10	Carlos Delgado	2.50
11	Bob Hamelin	.50
12	Marcus Moore	.50
13	Miguel Jimenez	.50
14	Matt Walbeck	.50
15	James Mouton	.50
16	Rich Becker	.50
17	Brian Anderson	.50
18	Cliff Floyd	.75
19	Steve Trachsel	.75
20	Hector Carrasco	.50

1994 Leaf Gold Stars

The "Cadillac" of 1994 Leaf inserts, this 15-card series (#1-8 in Series I; 9-15 in Series II) is found on average only one card per 90 packs. The edition of 10,000 of each player's card is serially numbered. Fronts feature a rather small photo in a diamond-shaped frame against a green marble-look background. The border, facsimile autograph and several other graphic elements are presented in prismatic foil. The back repeats the basic front design with a few sentences about the player and a serial number strip at bottom.

		MT
Complete Set (15):		150.00
Common Player:		5.00
1	Roberto Alomar	10.00
2	Barry Bonds	10.00
3	Dave Justice	6.00
4	Ken Griffey, Jr.	40.00
5	Len Dykstra	5.00
6	Don Mattingly	17.50
7	Andres Galarraga	6.00
8	Greg Maddux	25.00
9	Carlos Baerga	5.00
10	Paul Molitor	7.50
11	Frank Thomas	20.00
12	John Olerud	7.50
13	Juan Gonzalez	17.50
14	Fred McGriff	6.00
15	Jack McDowell	5.00

1994 Leaf MVP Contenders

Found on an average of about once per 36-pack foil box, these inserts were produced in an edition of 10,000 each. Cards found in packs were marked "Silver Collection" on the horizontal fronts, and featured a silver-foil Leaf seal and other enhancements. Persons holding cards of the players selected as N.L. and A.L. MVPs could trade in their Contender card for an individually numbered 5" x 7" card of Leaf spokesman Frank Thomas and be entered in a drawing for one of 5,000 Gold Collection MVP Contender 28-card sets. Winning cards were punch-cancelled and returned to the winner along with his prize.

		MT
Complete Set, Silver:		150.00
Complete Set, Gold:		200.00
Common Player, Silver:		1.00
Common Player, Gold:		2.00
AMERICAN LEAGUE		8.00
1a	Albert Belle (silver)	4.00
1b	Albert Belle (gold)	8.00
2a	Jose Canseco (silver)	3.00
2b	Jose Canseco (gold)	6.00
3a	Joe Carter (silver)	2.00
3b	Joe Carter (gold)	4.00
4a	Will Clark (silver)	2.00
4b	Will Clark (gold)	4.00
5a	Cecil Fielder (silver)	1.00
5b	Cecil Fielder (gold)	2.00
6a	Juan Gonzalez (silver)	8.00
6b	Juan Gonzalez (gold)	15.00
7a	Ken Griffey, Jr. (silver)	35.00
7b	Ken Griffey, Jr. (gold)	60.00
8a	Paul Molitor (silver)	4.00
8b	Paul Molitor (gold)	8.00
9a	Rafael Palmeiro (silver)	2.00
9b	Rafael Palmeiro (gold)	4.00
10a	Kirby Puckett (silver)	8.00
10b	Kirby Puckett (gold)	15.00
11a	Cal Ripken, Jr. (silver)	25.00
11b	Cal Ripken, Jr. (gold)	50.00
12a	Frank Thomas (silver)	12.50
12b	Frank Thomas (gold)	25.00
13a	Mo Vaughn (silver)	2.00
13b	Mo Vaughn (gold)	4.00
14a	Carlos Baerga (silver)	1.00
14b	Carlos Baerga (gold)	2.00
15	AL Bonus Card (silver)	2.00
NATIONAL LEAGUE		2.50
1a	Gary Sheffield (silver)	2.50
1b	Gary Sheffield (gold)	5.00
2a	Jeff Bagwell (silver)	12.00
2b	Jeff Bagwell (gold)	24.00
3a	Dante Bichette (silver)	1.00
3b	Dante Bichette (gold)	2.00
4a	Barry Bonds (silver)	5.00
4b	Barry Bonds (gold)	10.00
5a	Darren Daulton (silver)	1.00
5b	Darren Daulton (gold)	2.00
6a	Andres Galarraga (silver)	1.50
6b	Andres Galarraga (gold)	3.00
7a	Gregg Jefferies (silver)	1.00
7b	Gregg Jefferies (gold)	2.00
8a	Dave Justice (silver)	2.00
8b	Dave Justice (gold)	4.00
9a	Ray Lankford (silver)	1.00
9b	Ray Lankford (gold)	2.00
10a	Fred McGriff (silver)	2.00
10b	Fred McGriff (gold)	4.00
11a	Barry Larkin (silver)	1.00
11b	Barry Larkin (gold)	2.00
12a	Mike Piazza (silver)	12.00
12b	Mike Piazza (gold)	24.00
13a	Deion Sanders (silver)	2.50
13b	Deion Sanders (gold)	5.00
14a	Matt Williams (silver)	2.00
14b	Matt Williams (gold)	4.00
15	NL Bonus Card (silver)	2.50

1994 Leaf Power Brokers

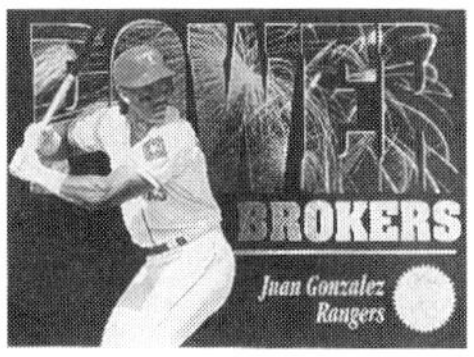

This insert set was unique to Leaf Series II packs and features the game's top sluggers. Horizontal-format fronts have a player photo at left, depicting his power stroke. A fireworks display is featured in the large letters of "POWER" at top. Other gold and silver foil highlights are featured on the black background. Backs have pie charts showing home run facts along with another player photo and a few stats. Stated odds of finding a Power Brokers insert card were one per dozen packs, on average.

		MT
Complete Set (10):		30.00
Common Player:		1.00
1	Frank Thomas	5.00
2	Dave Justice	1.00
3	Barry Bonds	2.00
4	Juan Gonzalez	3.00
5	Ken Griffey, Jr.	10.00
6	Mike Piazza	5.00
7	Cecil Fielder	1.00
8	Fred McGriff	1.00
9	Joe Carter	1.00
10	Albert Belle	2.50

1994 Leaf Slide Show

A new level of high-tech insert card production values was reached with the creation of Leaf's "Slide Show" chase cards. The cards feature a printed acetate center sandwiched between cardboard front and back. The see-through acetate portion of the card is bordered in white to give it the appearance of a slide. The player's name, location and date of the photo are printed on the front of the "slide," with the card number on back. The pseudo-slide is bordered in black (Series I) or white (Series II), with a blue "Slide Show" logo at bottom and a silver-foil Leaf logo. Backs of the Slide Show inserts have a few sentences about the featured player from Frank Thomas, Leaf's official spokesman again in 1994. The first five cards were released in Series I; cards 6-10 in Series II. Stated odds of finding a Slide Show insert are one per 54 packs.

		MT
Complete Set (10):		50.00
Common Player:		1.00
1	Frank Thomas	8.00
2	Mike Piazza	10.00
3	Darren Daulton	1.00
4	Ryne Sandberg	5.00
5	Roberto Alomar	5.00
6	Barry Bonds	5.00
7	Juan Gonzalez	8.00
8	Tim Salmon	2.50
9	Ken Griffey, Jr.	20.00
10	Dave Justice	1.00

1994 Leaf Statistical Standouts

Significant statistical acheivements from the 1993 season are marked in this insert set found in both retail and hobby packs at a rate of about once every 12 packs. Fronts feature player action photos set against a foil background of silver at right and a team color at left. A gold embossed Leaf seal is at upper left. Backs are bordered in the complementary team color at right, silver at left and have a vertical player photo along with the statistical achievement. Cards are numbered "x-10".

		MT
Complete Set (10):		24.00
Common Player:		1.00
1	Frank Thomas	4.50
2	Barry Bonds	2.50
3	Juan Gonzalez	4.00
4	Mike Piazza	5.00
5	Greg Maddux	5.00
6	Ken Griffey, Jr.	7.50
7	Joe Carter	1.00
8	Dave Winfield	1.50
9	Tony Gwynn	4.00
10	Cal Ripken, Jr.	6.00

1994 Leaf Frank Thomas Super

An edition of 20,000 super-size versions of Frank Thomas' 1994 Leaf card was produced for inclusion in Series II hobby boxes as a bonus. Except for its 5" x 7" format and a white strip on back bearing a serial number, the card is identical to the normal-size issue.

		MT
400	Frank Thomas	8.00

1994 Leaf Frank Thomas Poster

This large (24" x 28") poster was distributed by Leaf in a mail-in promotional offer. The blank-back sheet is printed on heavy gloss paper. A black-and-white photo of Thomas dominates the piece. In the bottom border is an embossed gold-foil Leaf seal.

		MT
	Frank Thomas	20.00

1994 Leaf 5th Anniversary

The card which insured the success of the Leaf brand name when it was re-introduced in 1990, the Frank Thomas rookie card, was re-issued in a 5th anniversary commemorative form as an insert in the 1994 set. On the chase card, silver foil rays emanate from the White Sox logo at lower-left, while a silver-foil 5th anniversary logo at upper-right replaces the Leaf script on the 1990 version. The card back carries a 1994 copyright. The Thomas anniversary card is found on average of once every 36 Series I hobby packs.

		MT
300	Frank Thomas	2.50

1994 Leaf/Limited

Leaf Limited was a 160-card high-end, super premium set printed on the highest quality board stock ever used by Donruss. Production was limited to 3,000 20-box case equivalents, making this the most limited product up to that point in 1994 by Donruss. Card fronts feature silver holographic Spectra Tech foiling and a silhouetted layer action photo over full silver foil. Cards have the team name and logo in silver and player name written in black at the bottom of the card. Leaf Limited appears in silver at the top and the player is bordered in silver on the front. The backs are dull grey or silver with a quote from a baseball personality and a player picture in the top-right corner. Leaf Limited and the card number are printed above the player photo. This card set was highly sought after and very limited. The cards look very unique and truly can't be described in words.

		MT
Complete Set (160):		75.00
Common Player:		.25
Wax Box:		100.00
1	Jeffrey Hammonds	.25
2	Ben McDonald	.25
3	Mike Mussina	2.00
4	Rafael Palmeiro	1.00
5	Cal Ripken, Jr.	8.00
6	Lee Smith	.45
7	Roger Clemens	5.00
8	Scott Cooper	.25
9	Andre Dawson	.75
10	Mike Greenwell	.25
11	Aaron Sele	.25
12	Mo Vaughn	2.00
13	*Brian Anderson*	1.00
14	Chad Curtis	.25
15	Chili Davis	.25
16	Gary DiSarcina	.25
17	Mark Langston	.25
18	Tim Salmon	1.00
19	Wilson Alvarez	.25
20	Jason Bere	.25
21	Julio Franco	.25
22	Jack McDowell	.25
23	Tim Raines	.25
24	Frank Thomas	4.00
25	Robin Ventura	1.00
26	Carlos Baerga	.25
27	Albert Belle	3.00
28	Kenny Lofton	3.00
29	Eddie Murray	1.00
30	Manny Ramirez	3.00
31	Cecil Fielder	.25
32	Travis Fryman	.35
33	Mickey Tettleton	.25
34	Alan Trammell	.50
35	Lou Whitaker	.25
36	David Cone	.40
37	Gary Gaetti	.25
38	Greg Gagne	.25
39	Bob Hamelin	.25
40	Wally Joyner	.40
41	Brian McRae	.25
42	Ricky Bones	.25
43	Brian Harper	.25
44	John Jaha	.25
45	Pat Listach	.25
46	Dave Nilsson	.25
47	Greg Vaughn	.40
48	Kent Hrbek	.25
49	Chuck Knoblauch	.75
50	Shane Mack	.25
51	Kirby Puckett	2.50
52	Dave Winfield	1.00
53	Jim Abbott	.50
54	Wade Boggs	1.50
55	Jimmy Key	.25
56	Don Mattingly	2.50
57	Paul O'Neill	.40
58	Danny Tartabull	.25
59	Dennis Eckersley	.60
60	Rickey Henderson	1.00
61	Mark McGwire	12.50
62	Troy Neel	.25
63	Ruben Sierra	.25
64	Eric Anthony	.25
65	Jay Buhner	.50
66	Ken Griffey, Jr.	12.50
67	Randy Johnson	1.50
68	Edgar Martinez	.35
69	Tino Martinez	.50
70	Jose Canseco	1.25
71	Will Clark	1.00
72	Juan Gonzalez	5.00
73	Dean Palmer	.25
74	Ivan Rodriguez	2.00
75	Roberto Alomar	1.50
76	Joe Carter	.50
77	Carlos Delgado	.75
78	Paul Molitor	1.50
79	John Olerud	.45
80	Devon White	.25
81	Steve Avery	.25
82	Tom Glavine	.75
83	Dave Justice	.75
84	Roberto Kelly	.25
85	Ryan Klesko	.75
86	Javier Lopez	.75
87	Greg Maddux	6.00
88	Fred McGriff	.75
89	Shawon Dunston	.25
90	Mark Grace	.75
91	Derrick May	.25
92	Sammy Sosa	8.00
93	Rick Wilkins	.25
94	Bret Boone	.25
95	Barry Larkin	.50
96	Kevin Mitchell	.25
97	Hal Morris	.25
98	Deion Sanders	.75
99	Reggie Sanders	.25
100	Dante Bichette	.50
101	Ellis Burks	.25
102	Andres Galarraga	.75
103	Joe Girardi	.25
104	Charlie Hayes	.25
105	Chuck Carr	.25
106	Jeff Conine	.25
107	Bryan Harvey	.25
108	Benito Santiago	.25
109	Gary Sheffield	.75
110	Jeff Bagwell	3.00
111	Craig Biggio	.75
112	Ken Caminiti	.75
113	Andujar Cedeno	.25
114	Doug Drabek	.25
115	Luis Gonzalez	.25
116	Brett Butler	.25
117	Delino DeShields	.25
118	Eric Karros	.25
119	Raul Mondesi	1.00
120	Mike Piazza	7.50
121	Henry Rodriguez	.25
122	Tim Wallach	.25
123	Moises Alou	.50
124	Cliff Floyd	.25
125	Marquis Grissom	.25
126	Ken Hill	.25
127	Larry Walker	.75
128	John Wetteland	.25
129	Bobby Bonilla	.25
130	John Franco	.25
131	Jeff Kent	.25
132	Bret Saberhagen	.25
133	Ryan Thompson	.25
134	Darren Daulton	.25
135	Mariano Duncan	.25
136	Len Dykstra	.25
137	Danny Jackson	.25
138	John Kruk	.25
139	Jay Bell	.25
140	Jeff King	.25
141	Al Martin	.25
142	Orlando Merced	.25
143	Andy Van Slyke	.25
144	Bernard Gilkey	.25
145	Gregg Jefferies	.35
146	Ray Lankford	.25
147	Ozzie Smith	1.50
148	Mark Whiten	.25
149	Todd Zeile	.25
150	Derek Bell	.25
151	Andy Benes	.25
152	Tony Gwynn	5.00
153	Phil Plantier	.25
154	Bip Roberts	.25
155	Rod Beck	.25
156	Barry Bonds	2.50
157	John Burkett	.25
158	Royce Clayton	.25
159	Bill Swift	.25
160	Matt Williams	1.00

1994 Leaf/Limited Gold

Leaf Limited Gold was an 18-card insert set randomly packed into Leaf Limited. All cards are individually numbered and feature the starting lineups at each position in both the National League and American League for the 1994 All-Star Game. There were only 10,000 cards of each player produced in this insert set.

		MT
Complete Set (18):		125.00
Common Player:		1.00
1	Frank Thomas	15.00
2	Gregg Jefferies	1.00
3	Roberto Alomar	5.00
4	Mariano Duncan	1.00
5	Wade Boggs	4.00
6	Matt Williams	4.00
7	Cal Ripken, Jr.	25.00
8	Ozzie Smith	6.00
9	Kirby Puckett	8.00
10	Barry Bonds	8.00
11	Ken Griffey, Jr.	30.00
12	Tony Gwynn	15.00
13	Joe Carter	1.00
14	Dave Justice	3.00
15	Ivan Rodriguez	6.00
16	Mike Piazza	20.00
17	Jimmy Key	1.00
18	Greg Maddux	20.00

1994 Leaf/Limited Rookies

Similar in format to the super-premium Leaf Limited issue, this separate issue features 80 of baseball's brightest young talents.

		MT
Complete Set (80):		25.00
Common Player:		.35
Wax Box:		60.00
1	Charles Johnson	2.00
2	Rico Brogna	.50
3	Melvin Nieves	.35
4	Rich Becker	.35
5	Russ Davis	.50
6	Matt Mieske	.50
7	Paul Shuey	.35
8	Hector Carrasco	.50
9	J.R. Phillips	1.00
10	Scott Ruffcorn	.35
11	Kurt Abbott	.35
12	Danny Bautista	.35
13	Rick White	.35
14	Steve Dunn	.35
15	Joe Ausanio	.35
16	Salomon Torres	.35
17	Rick Bottalico	.50
18	Johnny Ruffin	.35
19	Kevin Foster	.35
20	*W. Van Landingham*	.50
21	Troy O'Leary	.40
22	Mark Acre	.35
23	Norberto Martin	.35
24	*Jason Jacome*	.40
25	Steve Trachsel	.75
26	Denny Hocking	.35
27	Mike Lieberthal	.50
28	Gerald Williams	.50
29	John Mabry	.50
30	Greg Blosser	.35
31	Carl Everett	.50
32	Steve Karsay	.40
33	Jose Valentin	.35
34	Jon Lieber	.35
35	Chris Gomez	.50
36	Jesus Tavarez	.35
37	Tony Longmire	.50
38	Luis Lopez	.35
39	Matt Walbeck	.35
40	Rikkert Faneyte	.35
41	Shane Reynolds	.45
42	Joey Hamilton	1.50
43	Ismael Valdes	1.00
44	Danny Miceli	.40
45	Darren Bragg	.35
46	Alex Gonzalez	1.00
47	Rick Helling	.35
48	Jose Oliva	.35
49	Jim Edmonds	2.50
50	Miguel Jimenez	.35
51	Tony Eusebio	.45
52	Shawn Green	5.00
53	Billy Ashley	.35
54	Rondell White	3.00
55	Cory Bailey	.45
56	Tim Davis	.35
57	John Hudek	.35
58	Darren Hall	.35
59	Darren Dreifort	.35
60	Mike Kelly	.35
61	Marcus Moore	.35
62	Garret Anderson	1.00
63	Brian Hunter	1.00
64	Mark Smith	.45
65	Garey Ingram	.35
66	*Rusty Greer*	1.50
67	Marc Newfield	.35
68	Gar Finnvold	.35
69	Paul Spoljaric	.35
70	Ray McDavid	.35
71	Orlando Miller	.75
72	Jorge Fabregas	.45
73	Ray Holbert	.35
74	Armando Benitez	.50
75	Ernie Young	.35
76	James Mouton	.35
77	*Robert Perez*	.45
78	*Chan Ho Park*	2.00
79	Roger Salkeld	.35
80	Tony Tarasco	.35

1994 Leaf/Limited Rookies Rookie Phenoms

Similar in format to the other Leaf Limited cards for 1994, these Phenom inserts feature gold-foil background and graphics, rather than silver. Each card is numbered from within an edition of 5,000 of each player.

		MT
Complete Set (10):		125.00
Common Player:		3.00
1	Raul Mondesi	20.00
2	Bob Hamelin	3.00
3	Midre Cummings	3.00
4	Carlos Delgado	12.00
5	Cliff Floyd	4.00
6	Jeffrey Hammonds	3.00
7	Ryan Klesko	10.00
8	Javier Lopez	15.00
9	Manny Ramirez	30.00
10	Alex Rodriguez	50.00

1995 Leaf Promos

The lack of a "Sample" or "Promotional Card" notice makes these promos somewhat difficult to spot. The promos can be detected bu the placement of the Registered symbol farther down and to the right compared to regular-issue cards. Also the thin line inside the gld-foil stamping enclosing the Leaf logo and inner "95" diamond is missing on the promos.

		MT
Complete Set (9):		65.00
Common Player:		3.00
1	Frank Thomas	10.00
10	Joe Carter	3.00
28	Matt Williams	3.00
40	Wade Boggs	6.00
60	Raul Mondesi	4.50
115	Greg Maddux	15.00
119	Jeff Bagwell	10.00
134	Cal Ripken Jr.	25.00
183	Kirby Puckett	10.00

1995 Leaf

Two series of 200 basic cards each, plus numerous insert sets, are featured in 1995 Leaf. The basic card design has a borderless action photo on front, with a small portrait photo printed at upper-left on holographic silver foil. The team name is printed in the same foil in large letters down the left side. A script rendition of the player's name is at bottom-right, with the Leaf logo under the portrait photo; both elements are in gold foil. Backs have a couple more player photos. The card number is in white in a silver-foil seal at upper-right. Previous season and career stats are at lower-left. Several of the inserts sets are unique to various package configurations, while others are found in all types of packs.

		MT
Complete Set (400):		40.00
Complete Series 1 (200):		15.00
Complete Series 2 (200):		25.00
Common Player:		.10
Series 1 or 2 Wax Box:		60.00
1	Frank Thomas	1.00
2	Carlos Garcia	.10
3	Todd Hundley	.15

4	Damion Easley	.10
5	Roberto Mejia	.10
6	John Mabry	.10
7	Aaron Sele	.10
8	Kenny Lofton	.75
9	John Doherty	.10
10	Joe Carter	.15
11	Mike Lansing	.10
12	John Valentin	.15
13	Ismael Valdes	.15
14	Dave McCarty	.10
15	Melvin Nieves	.10
16	Bobby Jones	.10
17	Trevor Hoffman	.15
18	John Smoltz	.25
19	Leo Gomez	.10
20	Roger Pavlik	.10
21	Dean Palmer	.10
22	Rickey Henderson	.25
23	Eddie Taubensee	.10
24	Damon Buford	.10
25	Mark Wohlers	.10
26	Jim Edmonds	.15
27	Wilson Alvarez	.10
28	Matt Williams	.35
29	Jeff Montgomery	.10
30	Shawon Dunston	.10
31	Tom Pagnozzi	.10
32	Jose Lind	.10
33	Royce Clayton	.10
34	Cal Eldred	.10
35	Chris Gomez	.10
36	Henry Rodriguez	.10
37	Dave Fleming	.10
38	Jon Lieber	.10
39	Scott Servais	.10
40	Wade Boggs	.30
41	John Olerud	.15
42	Eddie Williams	.10
43	Paul Sorrento	.10
44	Ron Karkovice	.10
45	Kevin Foster	.10
46	Miguel Jimenez	.10
47	Reggie Sanders	.10
48	Rondell White	.15
49	Scott Leius	.10
50	Jose Valentin	.10
51	William Van Landingham	.10
52	Denny Hocking	.10
53	Jeff Fassero	.10
54	Chris Hoiles	.10
55	Walt Weiss	.10
56	Geronimo Berroa	.10
57	Rich Rowland	.10
58	Dave Weathers	.10
59	Sterling Hitchcock	.10
60	Raul Mondesi	.50
61	Rusty Greer	.10
62	Dave Justice	.25
63	Cecil Fielder	.10
64	Brian Jordan	.15
65	Mike Lieberthal	.10
66	Rick Aguilera	.10
67	Chuck Finley	.10
68	Andy Ashby	.10
69	Alex Fernandez	.15
70	Ed Sprague	.10
71	Steve Buechele	.10
72	Willie Greene	.10
73	Dave Nilsson	.10
74	Bret Saberhagen	.10
75	Jimmy Key	.10
76	Darren Lewis	.10
77	Steve Cooke	.10
78	Kirk Gibson	.10
79	Ray Lankford	.10
80	Paul O'Neill	.15
81	Mike Bordick	.10
82	Wes Chamberlain	.10
83	Rico Brogna	.10
84	Kevin Appier	.10
85	Juan Guzman	.10
86	Kevin Seitzer	.10
87	Mickey Morandini	.10
88	Pedro Martinez	.20
89	Matt Mieske	.10
90	Tino Martinez	.15
91	Paul Shuey	.10
92	Bip Roberts	.10
93	Chili Davis	.10
94	Deion Sanders	.25
95	Darrell Whitmore	.10
96	Joe Orsulak	.10
97	Bret Boone	.10
98	Kent Mercker	.10
99	Scott Livingstone	.10
100	Brady Anderson	.15
101	James Mouton	.10
102	Jose Rijo	.10
103	Bobby Munoz	.10
104	Ramon Martinez	.15
105	Bernie Williams	.60
106	Troy Neel	.10
107	Ivan Rodriguez	.50
108	Salomon Torres	.10
109	Johnny Ruffin	.10
110	Darryl Kile	.10
111	Bobby Ayala	.10
112	Ron Darling	.10
113	Jose Lima	.10
114	Joey Hamilton	.15
115	Greg Maddux	1.50
116	Greg Colbrunn	.10
117	Ozzie Guillen	.10
118	Brian Anderson	.10
119	Jeff Bagwell	1.00
120	Pat Listach	.10
121	Sandy Alomar	.15
122	Jose Vizcaino	.10
123	Rick Helling	.10
124	Allen Watson	.10
125	Pedro Munoz	.10
126	Craig Biggio	.15
127	Kevin Stocker	.10
128	Wil Cordero	.10
129	Rafael Palmeiro	.25
130	Gar Finnvold	.10
131	Darren Hall	.10
132	Heath Slocumb	.10
133	Darrin Fletcher	.10
134	Cal Ripken Jr.	2.50
135	Dante Bichette	.15
136	Don Slaught	.10
137	Pedro Astacio	.10
138	Ryan Thompson	.10
139	Greg Gohr	.10
140	Javier Lopez	.20
141	Lenny Dykstra	.10
142	Pat Rapp	.10
143	Mark Kiefer	.10
144	Greg Gagne	.10
145	Eduardo Perez	.10
146	Felix Fermin	.10
147	Jeff Frye	.10
148	Terry Steinbach	.10
149	Jim Eisenreich	.10
150	Brad Ausmus	.10
151	Randy Myers	.10
152	Rick White	.10
153	Mark Portugal	.10
154	Delino DeShields	.10
155	Scott Cooper	.10
156	Pat Hentgen	.10
157	Mark Gubicza	.10
158	Carlos Baerga	.10
159	Joe Girardi	.10
160	Rey Sanchez	.10
161	Todd Jones	.10
162	Luis Polonia	.10
163	Steve Trachsel	.10
164	Roberto Hernandez	.10
165	John Patterson	.10
166	Rene Arocha	.10
167	Will Clark	.30
168	Jim Leyritz	.10
169	Todd Van Poppel	.10
170	Robb Nen	.10
171	Midre Cummings	.10
172	Jay Buhner	.15
173	Kevin Tapani	.10
174	Mark Lemke	.10
175	Marcus Moore	.10
176	Wayne Kirby	.10
177	Rich Amaral	.10
178	Lou Whitaker	.10
179	Jay Bell	.10
180	Rick Wilkins	.10
181	Paul Molitor	.40
182	Gary Sheffield	.40
183	Kirby Puckett	1.00
184	Cliff Floyd	.10
185	Darren Oliver	.10
186	Tim Naehring	.10
187	John Hudek	.10
188	Eric Young	.10
189	Roger Salkeld	.10
190	Kirt Manwaring	.10
191	Kurt Abbott	.10
192	David Nied	.10
193	Todd Zeile	.10
194	Wally Joyner	.10
195	Dennis Martinez	.10
196	Billy Ashley	.10
197	Ben McDonald	.10
198	Bob Hamelin	.10
199	Chris Turner	.10
200	Lance Johnson	.10
201	Willie Banks	.10
202	Juan Gonzalez	1.50
203	Scott Sanders	.10
204	Scott Brosius	.10
205	Curt Schilling	.15
206	Alex Gonzalez	.10
207	Travis Fryman	.15
208	Tim Raines	.15
209	Steve Avery	.10
210	Hal Morris	.10
211	Ken Griffey Jr.	3.00
212	Ozzie Smith	.40
213	Chuck Carr	.10
214	Ryan Klesko	.25
215	Robin Ventura	.20
216	Luis Gonzalez	.10
217	Ken Ryan	.10
218	Mike Piazza	1.50
219	Matt Walbeck	.10
220	Jeff Kent	.10
221	Orlando Miller	.10
222	Kenny Rogers	.10
223	J.T. Snow	.15
224	Alan Trammell	.15
225	John Franco	.10
226	Gerald Williams	.10
227	Andy Benes	.10
228	Dan Wilson	.10
229	Dave Hollins	.10
230	Vinny Castilla	.10
231	Devon White	.10
232	Fred McGriff	.35
233	Quilvio Veras	.10
234	Tom Candiotti	.10
235	Jason Bere	.10
236	Mark Langston	.10
237	Mel Rojas	.10
238	Chuck Knoblauch	.20
239	Bernard Gilkey	.10
240	Mark McGwire	3.00
241	Kirk Rueter	.10
242	Pat Kelly	.10
243	Ruben Sierra	.10
244	Randy Johnson	.40
245	Shane Reynolds	.10
246	Danny Tartabull	.10
247	Darryl Hamilton	.10
248	Danny Bautista	.10
249	Tom Gordon	.10
250	Tom Glavine	.20
251	Orlando Merced	.10
252	Eric Karros	.15
253	Benji Gil	.10
254	Sean Bergman	.10
255	Roger Clemens	1.00
256	Roberto Alomar	.60
257	Benito Santiago	.10
258	Robby Thompson	.10
259	Marvin Freeman	.10
260	Jose Offerman	.10
261	Greg Vaughn	.15
262	David Segui	.10
263	Geronimo Pena	.10
264	Tim Salmon	.25
265	Eddie Murray	.40
266	Mariano Duncan	.10
267	*Hideo Nomo*	2.00
268	Derek Bell	.10
269	Mo Vaughn	.75
270	Jeff King	.10
271	Edgar Martinez	.10
272	Sammy Sosa	1.50
273	Scott Ruffcorn	.10
274	Darren Daulton	.10
275	John Jaha	.10
276	Andres Galarraga	.20
277	Mark Grace	.20
278	Mike Moore	.10
279	Barry Bonds	.75
280	Manny Ramirez	1.00
281	Ellis Burks	.10
282	Greg Swindell	.10
283	Barry Larkin	.20
284	Albert Belle	.75
285	Shawn Green	.20
286	John Roper	.10
287	Scott Erickson	.10
288	Moises Alou	.15
289	Mike Blowers	.10
290	Brent Gates	.10
291	Sean Berry	.10
292	Mike Stanley	.10
293	Jeff Conine	.10
294	Tim Wallach	.10
295	Bobby Bonilla	.15
296	Bruce Ruffin	.10
297	Chad Curtis	.10
298	Mike Greenwell	.10
299	Tony Gwynn	1.00
300	Russ Davis	.10
301	Danny Jackson	.10
302	Pete Harnisch	.10
303	Don Mattingly	1.00
304	Rheal Cormier	.10
305	Larry Walker	.30
306	Hector Carrasco	.10
307	Jason Jacome	.10
308	Phil Plantier	.10
309	Harold Baines	.10
310	Mitch Williams	.10
311	Charles Nagy	.10
312	Ken Caminiti	.20
313	Alex Rodriguez	3.00
314	Chris Sabo	.10
315	Gary Gaetti	.10
316	Andre Dawson	.15
317	Mark Clark	.10
318	Vince Coleman	.10
319	Brad Clontz	.10
320	Steve Finley	.10
321	Doug Drabek	.10
322	Mark McLemore	.10
323	Stan Javier	.10
324	Ron Gant	.15
325	Charlie Hayes	.10
326	Carlos Delgado	.50
327	Ricky Bottalico	.10
328	Rod Beck	.10
329	Mark Acre	.10
330	Chris Bosio	.10
331	Tony Phillips	.10
332	Garret Anderson	.15
333	Pat Meares	.10
334	Todd Worrell	.10
335	Marquis Grissom	.10
336	Brent Mayne	.10
337	Lee Tinsley	.10
338	Terry Pendleton	.10
339	David Cone	.15
340	Tony Fernandez	.10
341	Jim Bullinger	.10
342	Armando Benitez	.10
343	John Smiley	.10
344	Dan Miceli	.10
345	Charles Johnson	.15
346	Lee Smith	.15
347	Brian McRae	.10
348	Jim Thome	.35
349	Jose Oliva	.10
350	Terry Mulholland	.10
351	Tom Henke	.10
352	Dennis Eckersley	.15
353	Sid Fernandez	.10
354	Paul Wagner	.10
355	John Dettmer	.10
356	John Wetteland	.10
357	John Burkett	.10
358	Marty Cordova	.15
359	Norm Charlton	.10
360	Mike Devereaux	.10
361	Alex Cole	.10
362	Brett Butler	.10
363	Mickey Tettleton	.10
364	Al Martin	.10
365	Tony Tarasco	.10
366	Pat Mahomes	.10
367	Gary DiSarcina	.10
368	Bill Swift	.10
369	Chipper Jones	1.50
370	Orel Hershiser	.15
371	Kevin Gross	.10
372	Dave Winfield	.25
373	Andujar Cedeno	.10
374	Jim Abbott	.10
375	Glenallen Hill	.10
376	Otis Nixon	.10
377	Roberto Kelly	.10
378	Chris Hammond	.10
379	Mike Macfarlane	.10
380	J.R. Phillips	.10
381	Luis Alicea	.10
382	Bret Barberie	.10
383	Tom Goodwin	.10
384	Mark Whiten	.10
385	Jeffrey Hammonds	.10
386	Omar Vizquel	.10
387	Mike Mussina	.35
388	Rickey Bones	.10
389	Steve Ontiveros	.10
390	Jeff Blauser	.10
391	Jose Canseco	.30
392	Bob Tewksbury	.10
393	Jacob Brumfield	.10
394	Doug Jones	.10
395	Ken Hill	.10
396	Pat Borders	.10
397	Carl Everett	.10
398	Gregg Jefferies	.15
399	Jack McDowell	.10
400	Denny Neagle	.10

1995 Leaf Checklists

Honoring the major 1994 award winners in the American (Series I) and National (Series II) Leagues, checklists for the 1995 Leaf set are not numbered among the regular issue. Horizontal cards have a player action photo at left with his name and team in gold foil at bottom. The award is printed vertically at left with the checklist beginning on the right. Backs continue the checklist on a graduated purple background with the checklist number in a silver-foil seal at top-right.

		MT
	Complete Set (8):	3.00
	Common Player:	.25
1	Checklist 1-67 (Bob Hamelin) (Rookie of the Year)	.25
2	Checklist 68-134 (David Cone) (Cy Young)	.25
3	Checklist 135-200 (Frank Thomas) (MVP)	.75
4	Series II inserts checklist (Paul O'Neill) (Batting title)	.25
5	Checklist 201-267 (Raul Mondesi) (Rookie of the Year)	.50
6	Checklist 268-334 (Greg Maddux) (Cy Young)	.60
7	Checklist 335-400 (Jeff Bagwell) (MVP)	.50
8	Series 2 inserts checklist (Tony Gwynn) (Batting title)	.75

Player names in *Italic* type indicate a rookie card.

1995 Leaf Cornerstones

Cornerstones, six of the best first baseman-third baseman combos in baseball, are a six-card insert series found, on average, once every 18 packs in Series I Leaf. Card fronts are horizontally oriented and have a silver prismatic border and player names. Player defensive action photos are set against a background resembling their team logo chiseled into a stone block. Backs have player batting photos at each end with offensive and defensive stats from 1994, and a few words about the duo.

		MT
	Complete Set (6):	7.50
	Common Player:	.50
1	Frank Thomas, Robin Ventura	2.00
2	Cecil Fielder, Travis Fryman	.50
3	Don Mattingly, Wade Boggs	2.00
4	Jeff Bagwell, Ken Caminiti	2.00
5	Will Clark, Dean Palmer	.75
6	J.R. Phillips, Matt Williams	.50

1995 Leaf Gold Stars

Once again the toughest pull among the Leaf inserts are the Gold Leaf Stars found in both series. Found on average of one card per 90-270 packs, depending on pack card count, each of these chase cards is numbered on back within an edition of 10,000. Cards have fronts printed on metallic foil with the player name at top, the series title at bottom and a vertical stars and stripe device at right all printed in gold foil. A die-cut star appears at bottom-left. Backs are coventionally printed with another player photo and a few sentences about the star. The serial number is in gold foil in a white strip at top.

		MT
	Complete Set (14):	150.00
	Common Player:	5.00
1	Jeff Bagwell	15.00
2	Albert Belle	10.00
3	Tony Gwynn	20.00
4	Ken Griffey Jr.	30.00
5	Barry Bonds	10.00
6	Don Mattingly	15.00
7	Raul Mondesi	8.00
8	Joe Carter	5.00

9	Greg Maddux	20.00
10	Frank Thomas	15.00
11	Mike Piazza	25.00
12	Jose Canseco	8.00
13	Kirby Puckett	15.00
14	Matt Williams	5.00

1995 Leaf Gold Rookies

Every other pack of Series I Leaf Series I is seeded with a Gold Leaf Rookie card. Fronts have a largely white background with a large player photo at left-center and a smaller picture in a rectangle at upper-right. A team-color stripe is at left, while a smaller gray stripe is at top-right. The team name is printed in large gray letters across the center of the card, with the player name in a team color beneath that and above the gold-foil Leaf logo at lower-left. "Gold Leaf Rookies" is printed in gold foil down the right side. Backs repeat the team-color motif with a large action photo of the player in a single color and a smaller color portrait. Full career stats are at bottom.

		MT
Complete Set (16):		5.00
Common Player:		.25
1	Alex Rodriguez	4.00
2	Garret Anderson	.50
3	Shawn Green	1.00
4	Armando Benitez	.35
5	Darren Dreifort	.25
6	Orlando Miller	.25
7	Jose Oliva	.25
8	Ricky Bottalico	.25
9	Charles Johnson	.50
10	Brian Hunter	.35
11	Ray McDavid	.25
12	Chan Ho Park	.75
13	Mike Kelly	.25
14	Cory Bailey	.25
15	Alex Gonzalez	.75
16	Andrew Lorraine	.25

1995 Leaf Great Gloves

While the stated emphasis is on fielding prowess in this Series II chase set, players who don't also swing a big stick are ignored. Found as frequently as one per two packs, cards have a detail photo of a glove at left, with an action photo at right. The player name in the Great Gloves logo at bottom-right is in gold foil, as are the Leaf logo at top-left and the team name vertically at right. Backs repeat the glove photo and series logo as background for another player photo and a few words and stats about the player's defense.

		MT
Complete Set (16):		7.50
Common Player:		.25
1	Jeff Bagwell	.65
2	Roberto Alomar	.40
3	Barry Bonds	.40
4	Wade Boggs	.50
5	Andres Galarraga	.25
6	Ken Griffey Jr.	3.00
7	Marquis Grissom	.25
8	Kenny Lofton	.40
9	Barry Larkin	.25
10	Don Mattingly	.75
11	Greg Maddux	1.50
12	Kirby Puckett	.75
13	Ozzie Smith	.50
14	Cal Ripken Jr.	2.50
15	Matt Williams	.25
16	Ivan Rodriguez	.50

1995 Leaf Heading For The Hall

Series II hobby packs were the home of this scarce (one per 75 packs, average) chase set. Eight players deemed to be sure shots for Cooperstown are pictured in a semblance of the famed tombstone-shaped plaque they will someday adorn at the Hall of Fame; in fact the cards are die-cut to that shape. Backs have a sepia-toned photo, career stats and a serial number placing the card within an edition of 5,000.

		MT
Complete Set (8):		125.00
Common Player:		10.00
1	Frank Thomas	15.00
2	Ken Griffey Jr.	40.00
3	Jeff Bagwell	15.00
4	Barry Bonds	10.00
5	Kirby Puckett	15.00
6	Cal Ripken Jr.	30.00
7	Tony Gwynn	20.00
8	Paul Molitor	10.00

1995 Leaf Slideshow

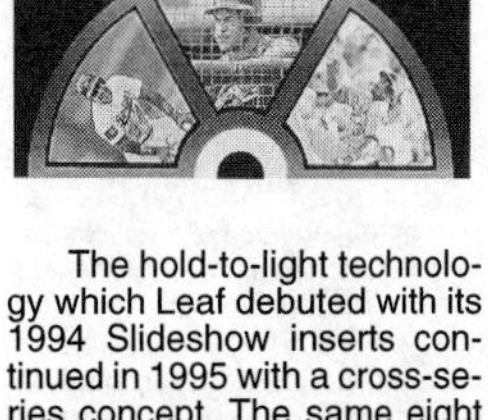

The hold-to-light technology which Leaf debuted with its 1994 Slideshow inserts continued in 1995 with a cross-series concept. The same eight players are featured on these cards in both Series I and II. Each has three clear photos at center, between the spokes of a silver-foil wheel. When both the player's cards are placed side-by-side, the six-picture see-through photo device is complete. Silver-foil and black borders surround the photo wheel on each side of the card. The Slideshow inserts are found on average of just over one per box among all types of pack configurations. Cards were issued with a peelable plastic protector on the front.

		MT
Complete Set (16):		80.00
Complete Series 1 (1a-8a):		40.00
Complete Series 2 (1b-8b):		40.00
Same CL and prices for both series		
Common Player:		4.00
1a	Raul Mondesi	5.00
1b	Raul Mondesi	5.00
2a	Frank Thomas	6.00
2b	Frank Thomas	6.00
3a	Fred McGriff	4.00
3b	Fred McGriff	4.00
4a	Cal Ripken Jr.	12.00
4b	Cal Ripken Jr.	12.00
5a	Jeff Bagwell	7.50
5b	Jeff Bagwell	7.50
6a	Will Clark	4.00
6b	Will Clark	4.00
7a	Matt Williams	4.00
7b	Matt Williams	4.00
8a	Ken Griffey Jr.	15.00
8b	Ken Griffey Jr.	15.00

1995 Leaf Statistical Standouts Promos

Each of the popular Statistical Standouts insert cards can also be found in a promo card version. The promos have their upper-right corner clipped off and lack the individual card serial number in gold-foil on back (though the "/ 5000" remains).

		MT
Complete Set (9):		175.00
Common Player:		10.00
1	Joe Carter	10.00
2	Ken Griffey Jr.	60.00
3	Don Mattingly	20.00
4	Fred McGriff	10.00
5	Paul Molitor	12.00
6	Kirby Puckett	20.00
7	Cal Ripken Jr.	50.00
8	Frank Thomas	15.00
9	Matt Williams	10.00

1995 Leaf Statistical Standouts

Embossed red stitches on the large baseball background make the Statistical Standouts chase cards stand out among the inserts in Series I hobby packs (one per 70, average). The leather surface of the ball is also lightly textured, as is the player action photo at center. Printed in gold foil on front are the series name at top, the player's facsimile autograph at lower-center and the Leaf logo and team name at bottom. Backs have a graduated black background with a large team logo at bottom, and a circular player portrait at center. A few words explain why the player's stats stand out among his peers.

		MT
Complete Set (9):		350.00
Common Player:		10.00
1	Joe Carter	10.00
2	Ken Griffey Jr.	125.00
3	Don Mattingly	40.00
4	Fred McGriff	10.00
5	Paul Molitor	25.00
6	Kirby Puckett	40.00
7	Cal Ripken Jr.	100.00
8	Frank Thomas	40.00
9	Matt Williams	12.50

1995 Leaf Special Edition Jumbos

As a dealer incentive, each case of 1995 Leaf Series I cards contained one of two 3" x 5" jumbos. Similar in format to the players' regular Leaf cards, each is individually serially numbered within an edition of 5,000.

		MT
Complete Set (2):		10.00
Common Player:		5.00
1	Frank Thomas	7.50
2	Barry Bonds	5.00

1995 Leaf Frank Thomas

The Big Hurt's six seasons in the major leagues are chronicled in this flashy insert set. Silver and gold foil squares are the background for a photo of Thomas on front. Backs repeat the motif with standard print technology and another photo, along with a few words about Thomas' season. The Frank Thomas inserts are found in all types of Series II packs, with odds varying from one in 42 packs to one in 14 packs, depending on card count per pack.

		MT
Complete Set (6):		25.00
Common Thomas:		5.00
1	The Rookie	5.00
2	Sophomore Stardom	5.00
3	Super Star	5.00
4	AL MVP	5.00
5	Back-To-Back	5.00
6	The Big Hurt	5.00

1995 Leaf 300 Club

Issued in both Series I and II Leaf, but only in the retail and magazine packs, at a rate of one per 12-30 packs, depending on pack configuration, 300 Club inserts feature the 18 active players with lifetime .300+ batting averages in a minimum of 1,000 AB. Fronts have color player photos with a large white "300" in the background and "club" in gold foil near the bottom. The player name is in gold foil in an arc above the silver Leaf logo at bottom-center. Large embossed silver triangles in each bottom corner have the team name and player position (left) and career BA (right). Backs have another player photo and highlight his place on the list of .300+ batters.

		MT
Complete Set (18):		80.00
Common Player:		1.00
1	Frank Thomas	12.50
2	Paul Molitor	4.00
3	Mike Piazza	15.00
4	Moises Alou	1.50
5	Mike Greenwell	1.00
6	Will Clark	2.50
7	Hal Morris	1.00
8	Edgar Martinez	1.00
9	Carlos Baerga	1.00
10	Ken Griffey Jr.	25.00
11	Wade Boggs	3.50
12	Jeff Bagwell	8.00
13	Tony Gwynn	12.50
14	John Kruk	1.00
15	Don Mattingly	6.00
16	Mark Grace	3.00
17	Kirby Puckett	7.50
18	Kenny Lofton	4.00

1995 Leaf/Limited

Issued in two series of 96 basic cards each, plus inserts, Leaf Limited was a hobby-only product limited to 90,000 numbered 20-pack boxes. Five-card packs had a suggested retail price of $4.99. Fronts of the basic cards have a player action photo on a background of silver holographic foil highlighted with team colors and a gold-foil Leaf Limited logo. Horizontal-format backs have two more player photos, career stats and holographic foil team logos and card numbers.

		MT
Complete Set (192):		50.00
Complete Series 1 (96):		30.00
Complete Series 2 (96):		30.00
Common Player:		.25
Series 1 or 2 Wax Box:		65.00
1	Frank Thomas	2.50
2	Geronimo Berroa	.25
3	Tony Phillips	.25
4	Roberto Alomar	1.25
5	Steve Avery	.25
6	Darryl Hamilton	.25
7	Scott Cooper	.25
8	Mark Grace	.60
9	Billy Ashley	.25
10	Wil Cordero	.25
11	Barry Bonds	1.50
12	Kenny Lofton	1.25
13	Jay Buhner	.35
14	Alex Rodriguez	5.00
15	Bobby Bonilla	.40
16	Brady Anderson	.45
17	Ken Caminiti	.50
18	Charlie Hayes	.25
19	Jay Bell	.25
20	Will Clark	.50
21	Jose Canseco	.50
22	Bret Boone	.25
23	Dante Bichette	.40
24	Kevin Appier	.25
25	Chad Curtis	.25
26	Marty Cordova	.25
27	Jason Bere	.25
28	Jimmy Key	.25
29	Rickey Henderson	.40
30	Tim Salmon	.60
31	Joe Carter	.25
32	Tom Glavine	.40
33	Pat Listach	.25
34	Brian Jordan	.35
35	Brian McRae	.25
36	Eric Karros	.35
37	Pedro Martinez	.65
38	Royce Clayton	.25
39	Eddie Murray	.75
40	Randy Johnson	1.00
41	Jeff Conine	.25
42	Brett Butler	.25
43	Jeffrey Hammonds	.25
44	Andujar Cedeno	.25
45	Dave Hollins	.25
46	Jeff King	.25
47	Benji Gil	.25
48	Roger Clemens	2.00
49	Barry Larkin	.40
50	Joe Girardi	.25
51	Bob Hamelin	.25
52	Travis Fryman	.25
53	Chuck Knoblauch	.50
54	Ray Durham	.35
55	Don Mattingly	2.00
56	Ruben Sierra	.25
57	J.T. Snow	.40
58	Derek Bell	.25
59	David Cone	.35
60	Marquis Grissom	.35
61	Kevin Seitzer	.25
62	Ozzie Smith	1.00
63	Rick Wilkins	.25
64	*Hideo Nomo*	2.50
65	Tony Tarasco	.25
66	Manny Ramirez	2.00
67	Charles Johnson	.35
68	Craig Biggio	.50
69	Bobby Jones	.25
70	Mike Mussina	.75
71	Alex Gonzalez	.25
72	Gregg Jefferies	.25
73	Rusty Greer	.25
74	Mike Greenwell	.25
75	Hal Morris	.25
76	Paul O'Neill	.40
77	Luis Gonzalez	.25
78	Chipper Jones	4.00
79	Mike Piazza	4.00
80	Rondell White	.50
81	Glenallen Hill	.25
82	Shawn Green	.60
83	Bernie Williams	1.25
84	Jim Thome	.75
85	Terry Pendleton	.25
86	Rafael Palmeiro	.50
87	Tony Gwynn	3.00
88	Mickey Tettleton	.25
89	John Valentin	.25
90	Deion Sanders	.50
91	Larry Walker	.75
92	Michael Tucker	.25
93	Alan Trammell	.25
94	Tim Raines	.25
95	Dave Justice	.50
96	Tino Martinez	.40
97	Cal Ripken Jr.	5.00
98	Deion Sanders	.75
99	Darren Daulton	.25
100	Paul Molitor	1.00
101	Randy Myers	.25
102	Wally Joyner	.25
103	Carlos Perez	.25
104	Brian Hunter	.25
105	Wade Boggs	.75
106	*Bobby Higginson*	3.00
107	Jeff Kent	.25
108	Jose Offerman	.25
109	Dennis Eckersley	.35
110	Dave Nilsson	.25
111	Chuck Finley	.25
112	Devon White	.25
113	Bip Roberts	.25
114	Ramon Martinez	.25
115	Greg Maddux	4.00
116	Curtis Goodwin	.25
117	John Jaha	.25
118	Ken Griffey Jr.	6.00
119	Geronimo Pena	.25
120	Shawon Dunston	.25
121	Ariel Prieto	.25
122	Kirby Puckett	2.00
123	Carlos Baerga	.25
124	Todd Hundley	.50
125	Tim Naehring	.25
126	Gary Sheffield	.60
127	Dean Palmer	.25
128	Rondell White	.50
129	Greg Gagne	.25
130	Jose Rijo	.25
131	Ivan Rodriguez	1.00
132	Jeff Bagwell	2.00
133	Greg Vaughn	.35
134	Chili Davis	.25
135	Al Martin	.25
136	Kenny Rogers	.25
137	Aaron Sele	.25
138	Raul Mondesi	.50
139	Cecil Fielder	.25
140	Tim Wallach	.25
141	Andres Galarraga	.50
142	Lou Whitaker	.25
143	Jack McDowell	.25
144	Matt Williams	.50
145	Ryan Klesko	.40
146	Carlos Garcia	.25
147	Albert Belle	1.50
148	Ryan Thompson	.25
149	Roberto Kelly	.25
150	Edgar Martinez	.25
151	Robby Thompson	.25
152	Mo Vaughn	1.25
153	Todd Zeile	.25
154	Harold Baines	.25
155	Phil Plantier	.25
156	Mike Stanley	.25
157	Ed Sprague	.25
158	Moises Alou	.35
159	Quilvio Veras	.25
160	Reggie Sanders	.25
161	Delino DeShields	.25
162	Rico Brogna	.25
163	Greg Colbrunn	.25
164	Steve Finley	.25
165	Orlando Merced	.25
166	Mark McGwire	6.00
167	Garret Anderson	.25
168	Paul Sorrento	.25
169	Mark Langston	.25
170	Danny Tartabull	.25
171	Vinny Castilla	.25
172	Javier Lopez	.40
173	Bret Saberhagen	.25
174	Eddie Williams	.25
175	Scott Leius	.25
176	Juan Gonzalez	3.00
177	Gary Gaetti	.25
178	Jim Edmonds	.40
179	John Olerud	.35
180	Lenny Dykstra	.25
181	Ray Lankford	.25
182	Ron Gant	.25
183	Doug Drabek	.25
184	Fred McGriff	.50
185	Andy Benes	.25
186	Kurt Abbott	.25
187	Bernard Gilkey	.25
188	Sammy Sosa	3.00
189	Lee Smith	.25
190	Dennis Martinez	.25
191	Ozzie Guillen	.25
192	Robin Ventura	.35

Checklists with card numbers in parentheses ( ) indicates the numbers do not appear on the card.

1995 Leaf/Limited Bat Patrol

Yet another insert of the game's top veteran hitters was featured as chase cards in Series 2 Leaf Limited. The cards have player action photos on front with large silver-foil "BAT / PATROL" lettering at lower-left. Backs are printed on a silver background and include career stats plus another color player photo. The cards were seeded at the rate of one per pack.

		MT
Complete Set (24):		20.00
Common Player:		.25
1	Frank Thomas	2.00
2	Tony Gwynn	2.50
3	Wade Boggs	.75
4	Larry Walker	.60
5	Ken Griffey Jr.	5.00
6	Jeff Bagwell	2.00
7	Manny Ramirez	1.50
8	Mark Grace	.60
9	Kenny Lofton	1.00
10	Mike Piazza	3.00
11	Will Clark	.50
12	Mo Vaughn	1.00
13	Carlos Baerga	.25
14	Rafael Palmeiro	.50
15	Barry Bonds	1.25
16	Kirby Puckett	2.00
17	Roberto Alomar	1.00
18	Barry Larkin	.35
19	Eddie Murray	.75
20	Tim Salmon	.45
21	Don Mattingly	1.50
22	Fred McGriff	.45
23	Albert Belle	1.00
24	Dante Bichette	.40

1995 Leaf/Limited Gold

Seeded one per pack in Series I only, this insert set follows the format of the basic Leaf Limited cards, but is distinguished by the presence of gold, rather than silver, holographic foil.

		MT
Complete Set (24):		30.00
Common Player:		.50
1	Frank Thomas	2.50
2	Jeff Bagwell	2.00
3	Raul Mondesi	.75
4	Barry Bonds	1.25
5	Albert Belle	1.25
6	Ken Griffey Jr.	5.00
7	Cal Ripken Jr.	4.00
8	Will Clark	.75
9	Jose Canseco	.75
10	Larry Walker	.75
11	Kirby Puckett	1.50
12	Don Mattingly	1.50
13	Tim Salmon	.50
14	Roberto Alomar	1.00
15	Greg Maddux	2.50
16	Mike Piazza	3.00
17	Matt Williams	.50
18	Kenny Lofton	1.00
19	Alex Rodriquez (Rodriguez)	4.00
20	Tony Gwynn	2.50
21	Mo Vaughn	1.00
22	Chipper Jones	3.00
23	Manny Ramirez	1.50
24	Deion Sanders	.50

1995 Leaf/Limited Lumberjacks

Among the scarcest of 1995 chase cards are the Lumberjacks inserts found in both Series 1 and 2 Leaf Limited at a rate of one per 23 packs on average (less than one per box). Fronts are printed on woodgrain veneer with a large team logo behind a batting action photo of the game's top sluggers. Backs have another photo against a background of tree trunks. A white stripe at bottom carries each card's unique serial number within an edition of 5,000. An even more limited version with black background is limited to 500 numbered cards of each player. Each player can also be found in a promo version.

		MT
Complete Set (16):		250.00
Common Player:		8.00
Black: 5X		
Promo: 25-50%		
1	Albert Belle	12.00
2	Barry Bonds	12.00
3	Juan Gonzalez	25.00
4	Ken Griffey Jr.	50.00
5	Fred McGriff	8.00
6	Mike Piazza	30.00
7	Kirby Puckett	15.00
8	Mo Vaughn	10.00
9	Frank Thomas	20.00
10	Jeff Bagwell	20.00
11	Matt Williams	8.00
12	Jose Canseco	10.00
13	Raul Mondesi	8.00
14	Manny Ramirez	15.00
15	Cecil Fielder	8.00
16	Cal Ripken Jr.	40.00

1995 Leaf/ Opening Day

Issued in celebration of the 1995's season's delayed debut, this set was only available via a mail-in offer for $2 and eight wrappers. Cards were advertised as featuring front and back photos shot on opening day. Fronts have a player photo bordered on the left with a vertical "1995 Opening Day" stripe featuring exploding fireworks at the bottom. The player's name and position appear in a silver-foil strip at bottom; a silver-foil Leaf logo is at upper-right. Backs have a player action photo set against a background of exploding fireworks and a re-cap of the player's 1995 Opening Day performance.

		MT
Complete Set (8):		8.00
Common Player:		.50
1	Frank Thomas	1.50
2	Jeff Bagwell	1.50
3	Barry Bonds	1.00
5	Ken Griffey Jr.	3.00
5	Mike Piazza	2.00
6	Cal Ripken Jr.	2.50
7	Jose Canseco	.50
8	Larry Walker	.50

1996 Leaf

Reverting to a single-series issue of 220 basic cards, plus numerous insert set bells and whistles, this was the final Leaf set under Donruss' ownership. Regular cards offer large action photos on front and back with a side and bottom border subdued through darkening (front) or lightening (back). Fronts feature silver prismatic-foil graphic highlights while the back includes a circular portrait photo with vital data around. Leaf was sold in both hobby and retail versions, each with some unique inserts. Basic unit was the 12-card foil pack, with suggested retail of $2.49.

		MT
Complete Set (220):		20.00
Common Player:		.10
Complete Gold Set (220):		2000.
Wax Box:		50.00
1	John Smoltz	.25
2	Dennis Eckersley	.15
3	Delino DeShields	.10
4	Cliff Floyd	.10
5	Chuck Finley	.10
6	Cecil Fielder	.15
7	Tim Naehring	.10
8	Carlos Perez	.10
9	Brad Ausmus	.10
10	*Matt Lawton*	.10
11	Alan Trammell	.15
12	Steve Finley	.10
13	Paul O'Neill	.15
14	Gary Sheffield	.40
15	Mark McGwire	3.00
16	Bernie Williams	.50
17	Jeff Montgomery	.10
18	Chan Ho Park	.15
19	Greg Vaughn	.15
20	Jeff Kent	.10
21	Cal Ripken Jr.	2.50
22	Charles Johnson	.10

23	Eric Karros	.10
24	Alex Rodriguez	2.50
25	Chris Snopek	.10
26	Jason Isringhausen	.10
27	Chili Davis	.10
28	Chipper Jones	2.00
29	Bret Saberhagen	.10
30	Tony Clark	.35
31	Marty Cordova	.10
32	Dwayne Hosey	.10
33	Fred McGriff	.35
34	Deion Sanders	.25
35	Orlando Merced	.10
36	Brady Anderson	.15
37	Ray Lankford	.15
38	Manny Ramirez	1.00
39	Alex Fernandez	.15
40	Greg Colbrunn	.10
41	Ken Griffey Jr.	3.00
42	Mickey Morandini	.10
43	Chuck Knoblauch	.20
44	Quinton McCracken	.10
45	Tim Salmon	.25
46	Jose Mesa	.10
47	Marquis Grissom	.10
48	Checklist	.10
49	Raul Mondesi	.25
50	Mark Grudzielanek	.10
51	Ray Durham	.10
52	Matt Williams	.25
53	Bob Hamelin	.10
54	Lenny Dykstra	.10
55	Jeff King	.10
56	LaTroy Hawkins	.10
57	Terry Pendleton	.10
58	Kevin Stocker	.10
59	Ozzie Timmons	.10
60	David Justice	.20
61	Ricky Bottalico	.10
62	Andy Ashby	.10
63	Larry Walker	.35
64	Jose Canseco	.25
65	Bret Boone	.10
66	Shawn Green	.15
67	Chad Curtis	.10
68	Travis Fryman	.10
69	Roger Clemens	.75
70	David Bell	.10
71	Rusty Greer	.10
72	Bob Higginson	.10
73	Joey Hamilton	.10
74	Kevin Seitzer	.10
75	Julian Tavarez	.10
76	Troy Percival	.10
77	Kirby Puckett	1.00
78	Barry Bonds	.75
79	Michael Tucker	.10
80	Paul Molitor	.35
81	Carlos Garcia	.10
82	Johnny Damon	.15
83	Mike Hampton	.10
84	Ariel Prieto	.10
85	Tony Tarasco	.10
86	Pete Schourek	.10
87	Tom Glavine	.20
88	Rondell White	.15
89	Jim Edmonds	.10
90	Robby Thompson	.10
91	Wade Boggs	.35
92	Pedro Martinez	.15
93	Gregg Jefferies	.15
94	Albert Belle	.75
95	Benji Gil	.10
96	Denny Neagle	.10
97	Mark Langston	.10
98	Sandy Alomar	.15
99	Tony Gwynn	1.25
100	Todd Hundley	.20
101	Dante Bichette	.15
102	Eddie Murray	.40
103	Lyle Mouton	.10
104	John Jaha	.10
105	Checklist	.10
106	Jon Nunnally	.10
107	Juan Gonzalez	1.50
108	Kevin Appier	.10
109	Brian McRae	.10
110	Lee Smith	.10
111	Tim Wakefield	.10
112	Sammy Sosa	1.50
113	Jay Buhner	.15
114	Garret Anderson	.10
115	Edgar Martinez	.10
116	Edgardo Alfonzo	.15
117	Billy Ashley	.10
118	Joe Carter	.10
119	Javy Lopez	.15
120	Bobby Bonilla	.15
121	Ken Caminiti	.25
122	Barry Larkin	.15
123	Shannon Stewart	.10
124	Orel Hershiser	.10
125	Jeff Conine	.10
126	Mark Grace	.20
127	Kenny Lofton	.60
128	Luis Gonzalez	.10
129	Rico Brogna	.10
130	Mo Vaughn	.60
131	Brad Radke	.10
132	Jose Herrera	.10
133	Rick Aguilera	.10
134	Gary DiSarcina	.10
135	Andres Galarraga	.15
136	Carl Everett	.10
137	Steve Avery	.10
138	Vinny Castilla	.10
139	Dennis Martinez	.10
140	John Wetteland	.10
141	Alex Gonzalez	.10
142	Brian Jordan	.15
143	Todd Hollandsworth	.15
144	Terrell Wade	.10
145	Wilson Alvarez	.10
146	Reggie Sanders	.10
147	Will Clark	.25
148	Hideo Nomo	.50
149	J.T. Snow	.10
150	Frank Thomas	1.50
151	Ivan Rodriguez	.60
152	Jay Bell	.10
153	Checklist	.10
154	David Cone	.15
155	Roberto Alomar	.75
156	Carlos Delgado	.50
157	Carlos Baerga	.10
158	Geronimo Berroa	.10
159	Joe Vitiello	.10
160	Terry Steinbach	.10
161	Doug Drabek	.10
162	David Segui	.10
163	Ozzie Smith	.40
164	Kurt Abbott	.10
165	Randy Johnson	.40
166	John Valentin	.10
167	Mickey Tettleton	.10
168	Ruben Sierra	.10
169	Jim Thome	.35
170	Mike Greenwell	.10
171	Quilvio Veras	.10
172	Robin Ventura	.15
173	Bill Pulsipher	.10
174	Rafael Palmeiro	.20
175	Hal Morris	.10
176	Ryan Klesko	.25
177	Eric Young	.10
178	Shane Andrews	.10
179	Brian Hunter	.10
180	Brett Butler	.10
181	John Olerud	.15
182	Moises Alou	.10
183	Glenallen Hill	.10
184	Ismael Valdes	.10
185	Andy Pettitte	.75
186	Yamil Benitez	.10
187	Jason Bere	.10
188	Dean Palmer	.10
189	Jimmy Haynes	.10
190	Trevor Hoffman	.10
191	Mike Mussina	.30
192	Greg Maddux	1.50
193	Ozzie Guillen	.10
194	Pat Listach	.10
195	Derek Bell	.10
196	Darren Daulton	.10
197	John Mabry	.10
198	Ramon Martinez	.10
199	Jeff Bagwell	1.25
200	Mike Piazza	2.00
201	Al Martin	.10
202	Aaron Sele	.10
203	Ed Sprague	.10
204	Rod Beck	.10
205	Checklist	.10
206	Mike Lansing	.10
207	Craig Biggio	.15
208	Jeffrey Hammonds	.10
209	Dave Nilsson	.10
210	Checklist, Inserts (Dante Bichette, Albert Belle)	.10
211	Derek Jeter	2.00
212	Alan Benes	.10
213	Jason Schmidt	.10
214	Alex Ochoa	.10
215	Ruben Rivera	.15
216	Roger Cedeno	.20
217	Jeff Suppan	.10
218	Billy Wagner	.10
219	Mark Loretta	.10
220	Karim Garcia	.50

1996 Leaf Press Proofs

Carrying the parallel edition concept to its inevitable next level, '96 Leaf offered the Press Proof insert cards in three degrees of scarcity, each highlighted with appropriate holographic foil. Like the other '96 Leaf inserts, these are individually serially numbered within its edition limit. At the top of the line are Gold Press Proofs in an edition of only 500 of each card. Silver and Bronze versions were produced in editions of 1,000 and 2,000, respectively. Press Proofs are inserted into both hobby and retail packs at an average rate of one card per 10 packs.

	MT
Complete Set, Gold (220):	2000.
Complete Set, Silver (220):	1000.
Complete Set, Bronze (220):	500.00
Common Player, Gold:	4.00
Common Player, Silver:	2.50
Common Player, Bronze:	1.00
(Press Proof stars valued as follows in comparison to regular-issue '96 Leaf - Gold: 20-30X; Silver: 10-15X;	

1996 Leaf All-Star MVP Contenders

A surprise insert in Leaf boxes was this interactive redemption issue. Twenty leading candidates for MVP honors at the 1996 All-Star Game in Philadelphia were presented in a silver-foil highlighted horizontal format. The player's league logo serves as a background to the color action photo on front; the All-Star logo is in the lower-left corner. Backs have details of the redemption offer. Persons who sent in the Mike Piazza card for redemption received a gold version of the set and had their Piazza card punch-cancelled and returned.

		MT
Complete Set (20):		30.00
Common Card:		1.00
Expired: 8-15-96		
Golds: 1.5X		
1	Frank Thomas	3.00
2	Mike Piazza	4.00
2c	Mike Piazza (redeemed and punch-cancelled)	3.00
3	Sammy Sosa	3.00
4	Cal Ripken Jr.	5.00
5	Jeff Bagwell	2.00
6	Reggie Sanders	.75
7	Mo Vaughn	1.00
8	Tony Gwynn	3.00
9	Dante Bichette	1.00
10	Tim Salmon	1.00
11	Chipper Jones	4.00
12	Kenny Lofton	1.00
13	Manny Ramirez	2.00
14	Barry Bonds	1.50
15	Raul Mondesi	1.00
16	Kirby Puckett	1.50
17	Albert Belle	1.50
18	Ken Griffey Jr.	6.00
19	Greg Maddux	3.00
20	Bonus card	.75

1996 Leaf All-Star MVP Contenders Gold

A surprise insert in Leaf boxes was an interactive redemption issue of 20 leading candidates for MVP honors at the 1996 All-Star Game in Philadelphia. The first 5,000 persons who sent in the Mike Piazza card for redemption received a gold version of the set and had their Piazza card punch-cancelled and returned.

		MT
Complete Set (19):		45.00
Common Card:		1.00
1	Frank Thomas	5.00
2	Mike Piazza	6.00
3	Sammy Sosa	5.00
4	Cal Ripken Jr.	7.50
5	Jeff Bagwell	7.50
6	Reggie Sanders	1.00
7	Mo Vaughn	2.00
8	Tony Gwynn	7.50
9	Dante Bichette	1.00
10	Tim Salmon	1.00
11	Chipper Jones	6.00
12	Kenny Lofton	2.00
13	Manny Ramirez	10.00
14	Barry Bonds	3.00
15	Raul Mondesi	2.00
16	Kirby Puckett	3.00
17	Albert Belle	2.00
18	Ken Griffey Jr.	10.00
19	Greg Maddux	5.00

1996 Leaf Gold Leaf Stars

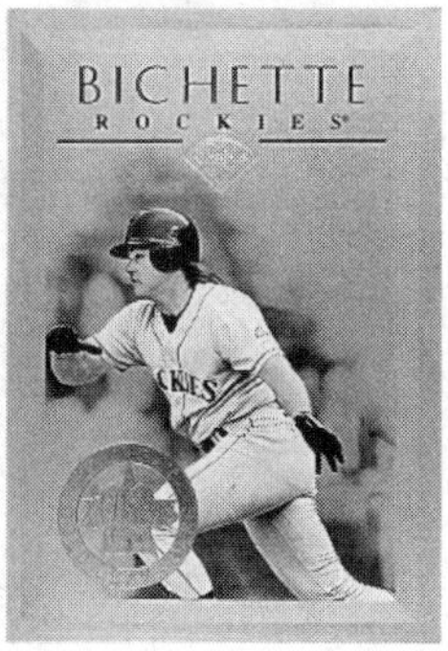

A vignetted background of embossed gold metallic cardboard and a Gold Leaf Stars logo in 22-karat gold foil are featured on this limited (2,500 of each) edition insert. Backs include a second color photo of the player and a serial number from within the edition. Gold Leaf Stars were included in both hobby and retail packaging, with an average insertion rate of one per 210 packs.

		MT
Complete Set (15):		300.00
Common Player:		7.50
1	Frank Thomas	25.00
2	Dante Bichette	7.50
3	Sammy Sosa	40.00
4	Ken Griffey Jr.	60.00
5	Mike Piazza	40.00
6	Tim Salmon	7.50
7	Hideo Nomo	7.50
8	Cal Ripken Jr.	50.00
9	Chipper Jones	40.00
10	Albert Belle	12.00
11	Tony Gwynn	30.00
12	Mo Vaughn	10.00
13	Barry Larkin	7.50
14	Manny Ramirez	15.00
15	Greg Maddux	30.00

1996 Leaf Hats Off

The most technically innovative inserts of 1996 have to be the Hats Off series exclusive to Leaf retail packs. Front player photos are on a background that is both flocked to simulate the cloth of a baseball cap, plus enhanced with a stiched team logo. The graphics are all in raised textured gold foil. Backs are conventionally printed and include a gold-foil serial number placing each card within an edition of 5,000 per player.

		MT
Complete Set (8):		120.00
Common Player:		5.00
1	Cal Ripken Jr.	30.00
2	Barry Larkin	5.00
3	Frank Thomas	20.00
4	Mo Vaughn	8.00
5	Ken Griffey Jr.	40.00
6	Hideo Nomo	6.00
7	Albert Belle	10.00
8	Greg Maddux	20.00

1996 Leaf Picture Perfect Promos

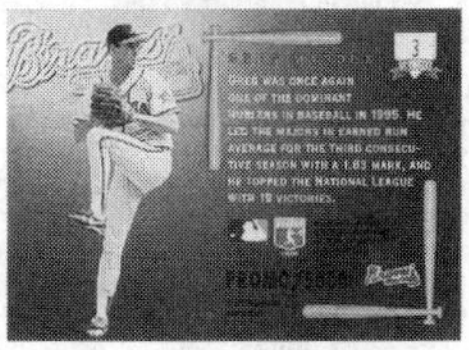

Because of technical considerations it was unfeasible for Leaf to print a promo card of just one player from its Picture Perfect insert set. Thus, each of the 12 cards in the issue can be found in a version which has a black "PROMOTIONAL CARD" printed diagonally over the front. On back, the promos have "PROMO/5000" printed instead of the individual serial number found on issued cards.

		MT
Complete Set (12):		200.00
Common Player:		7.50
1	Frank Thomas	15.00
2	Cal Ripken Jr.	25.00
3	Greg Maddux	15.00
4	Manny Ramirez	7.50
5	Chipper Jones	20.00
6	Tony Gwynn	12.50
7	Ken Griffey Jr.	30.00
8	Albert Belle	7.50
9	Jeff Bagwell	12.50
10	Mike Piazza	20.00
11	Mo Vaughn	7.50
12	Barry Bonds	10.00

1996 Leaf Picture Perfect

Leaf calls the glossy central area of these inserts "pearlized foil," which allows the player action photo to stand out in contrast to the actual wood veneer background. Gold foil graphic highlights complete the design. Backs are conventionally printed and include a gold-foil serial number from within the edition of 5,000 of each player's card. Cards #1-6 are hobby-only inserts, while #7-12 are found in retail packs. Average insertion rate is one per 140 packs.

		MT
Complete Set (12):		220.00
Common Player:		5.00
1	Frank Thomas	15.00
2	Cal Ripken Jr.	30.00
3	Greg Maddux	20.00
4	Manny Ramirez	12.00
5	Chipper Jones	25.00
6	Tony Gwynn	20.00
7	Ken Griffey Jr.	40.00
8	Albert Belle	10.00
9	Jeff Bagwell	15.00
10	Mike Piazza	25.00
11	Mo Vaughn	10.00
12	Barry Bonds	12.00

1996 Leaf Statistical Standouts

The feel of leather complements the game-used baseball background on these hobby-only inserts featuring the game's top names. Backs offer statistical data and a gold-foil serial number placing the card within an edition of 2,500 for each player. Average insertion rate is one per 210 packs.

		MT
Complete Set (8):		150.00
Common Player:		10.00
1	Cal Ripken Jr.	35.00
2	Tony Gwynn	20.00
3	Frank Thomas	20.00
4	Ken Griffey Jr.	45.00
5	Hideo Nomo	10.00
6	Greg Maddux	20.00
7	Albert Belle	10.00
8	Chipper Jones	25.00

1996 Leaf Frank Thomas' Greatest Hits

Die-cut plastic with a background of prismatic foil to simulate a segment of a compact disc is the format for this insert issue chronicling the career-to-date of Frank Thomas. Backs include a few stats and a portrait photo, plus a gold-foil serial number from within an edition of 5,000. Cards #1-4 are found only in hobby packs; cards #5-7 are exclusive to retail packs (average insertion rate one per 210 packs) and card #8 could be had only through a wrapper redemption.

		MT
Complete Set (8):		145.00
Common Card:		20.00
1	1990	20.00
2	1991	20.00
3	1992	20.00
4	1993	20.00
5	1994	20.00
6	1995	20.00
7	Career	20.00
8	MVP	20.00

1996 Leaf Total Bases Promos

Because the complex production process for its "canvas" baseball card inserts precluded featuring the same player on each promo card for the series, all 12 players in the Total Bases set can be found in a promo card version. Otherwise identical to the issued cards, the promos have a diagonal black "PROMOTIONAL CARD" overprint on front. On back, in place of the normal serial number line is a black "PROMO/5000" line.

		MT
Complete Set (12):		75.00
Common Player:		2.50
1	Frank Thomas	7.50
2	Albert Belle	4.00
3	Rafael Palmeiro	3.00
4	Barry Bonds	5.00
5	Kirby Puckett	6.00
6	Joe Carter	2.50
7	Paul Molitor	3.50
8	Fred McGriff	3.00
9	Ken Griffey Jr.	17.50
10	Carlos Baerga	2.50
11	Juan Gonzalez	6.00
12	Cal Ripken Jr.	15.00

1996 Leaf Total Bases

Total-base leaders from 1991-95 are featured in this hobby-only insert set. Card fronts are printed on textured canvas to simulate a base. Fronts are highlighted with gold foil. Backs have stats ranking the player in this category plus a gold-foil serial number from an edition of 5,000 of each player. Total Bases inserts are seeded at an average rate of one per 72 packs.

		MT
Complete Set (12):		110.00
Common Player:		3.00
1	Frank Thomas	15.00
2	Albert Belle	8.00
3	Rafael Palmeiro	5.00
4	Barry Bonds	8.00
5	Kirby Puckett	12.50
6	Joe Carter	3.00
7	Paul Molitor	5.00
8	Fred McGriff	5.00
9	Ken Griffey Jr.	30.00
10	Carlos Baerga	3.00
11	Juan Gonzalez	12.50
12	Cal Ripken Jr.	25.00

1996 Leaf/Limited

Leaf's 1996 Limited set contains 90 of the top rookies and veterans in baseball. There is also a 100-card Limited Gold parallel set which includes the 90 main cards, plus 10 cards from a Limited Rookies insert set. The gold parallel cards are seeded one per every 11 packs. Regular Limited Rookies inserts were seeded one per every seven packs. Two other insert sets were also made - two versions of Lumberjacks and Pennant Craze.

		MT
Complete Set (90):		50.00
Common Player:		.25
Limited Gold Set (90):		250.00
Limited Golds: 5X		
Unlisted Stars: .50 to .75		
Wax Box:		75.00
1	Ivan Rodriguez	1.50
2	Roger Clemens	2.50
3	Gary Sheffield	1.00
4	Tino Martinez	.35
5	Sammy Sosa	5.00
6	Reggie Sanders	.25
7	Ray Lankford	.25
8	Manny Ramirez	2.50
9	Jeff Bagwell	3.00
10	Greg Maddux	4.50
11	Ken Griffey Jr.	8.00
12	Rondell White	.25
13	Mike Piazza	5.00
14	Marc Newfield	.25
15	Cal Ripken Jr.	6.00
16	Carlos Delgado	.50
17	Tim Salmon	.50
18	Andres Galarraga	.50
19	Chuck Knoblauch	.50
20	Matt Williams	.50
21	Mark McGwire	8.00
22	Ben McDonald	.25
23	Frank Thomas	3.00
24	Johnny Damon	.25
25	Gregg Jefferies	.25
26	Travis Fryman	.25
27	Chipper Jones	5.00
28	David Cone	.35
29	Kenny Lofton	2.00
30	Mike Mussina	1.00
31	Alex Rodriguez	7.50
32	Carlos Baerga	.25
33	Brian Hunter	.25
34	Juan Gonzalez	4.00
35	Bernie Williams	1.50
36	Wally Joyner	.25
37	Fred McGriff	.75
38	Randy Johnson	1.00
39	Marty Cordova	.25
40	Garret Anderson	.25
41	Albert Belle	2.00
42	Edgar Martinez	.25
43	Barry Larkin	.40
44	Paul O'Neill	.40
45	Cecil Fielder	.25
46	Rusty Greer	.25
47	Mo Vaughn	2.00
48	Dante Bichette	.75
49	Ryan Klesko	.50
50	Roberto Alomar	2.00
51	Raul Mondesi	.75
52	Robin Ventura	.40
53	Tony Gwynn	3.00
54	Mark Grace	.50
55	Jim Thome	1.00
56	Jason Giambi	.25
57	Tom Glavine	.50
58	Jim Edmonds	.40
59	Pedro Martinez	.40
60	Charles Johnson	.25
61	Wade Boggs	.50
62	Orlando Merced	.25
63	Craig Biggio	.40
64	Brady Anderson	.25
65	Hideo Nomo	.75
66	Ozzie Smith	1.00
67	Eddie Murray	.75
68	Will Clark	.75
69	Jay Buhner	.25
70	Kirby Puckett	3.00
71	Barry Bonds	2.50
72	Ray Durham	.25
73	Sterling Hitchcock	.25
74	John Smoltz	.75
75	Andre Dawson	.35
76	Joe Carter	.25
77	Ryne Sandberg	1.50
78	Rickey Henderson	.40
79	Brian Jordan	.25
80	Greg Vaughn	.35
81	Andy Pettitte	1.50
82	Dean Palmer	.25
83	Paul Molitor	1.00
84	Rafael Palmeiro	.50
85	Henry Rodriguez	.25
86	Larry Walker	.75
87	Ismael Valdes	.25
88	Derek Bell	.25
89	J.T. Snow	.25
90	Jack McDowell	.25

1996 Leaf/Limited Lumberjacks Samples

Each of the Lumberjacks insert cards can be found in a sample version distributed to card retailers prior to the Leaf Limited issue. These promos are virtually identical to the issued version of the Lumberjacks except they have a diagonal black overprint on front and back, "SAMPLE CARD", and "PROMO" where the serial number would be found on a regular card.

		MT
Complete Set (10):		220.00
Common Player:		12.00
1	Ken Griffey Jr.	35.00
2	Sammy Sosa	20.00
3	Cal Ripken Jr.	30.00
4	Frank Thomas	20.00
5	Alex Rodriguez	30.00
6	Mo Vaughn	12.50
7	Chipper Jones	25.00
8	Mike Piazza	25.00
9	Jeff Bagwell	15.00
10	Mark McGwire	35.00

1996 Leaf/Limited Lumberjacks

Lumberjacks inserts return to Leaf Limited, but the 1996 versions feature an improved maple stock that puts wood grains on both sides of the card. Ten different Lumberjacks are available in two different versions. Regular versions are serial numbered to 5,000, while a special black-bordered Limited Edition version is numbered to 500.

		MT
Complete Set (10):		180.00
Common Player:		6.00
Lumberjack Blacks (500): 3X		
1	Ken Griffey Jr.	35.00
2	Sammy Sosa	20.00
3	Cal Ripken Jr.	30.00
4	Frank Thomas	20.00
5	Alex Rodriguez	30.00
6	Mo Vaughn	10.00
7	Chipper Jones	25.00
8	Mike Piazza	25.00
9	Jeff Bagwell	15.00
10	Mark McGwire	35.00

1996 Leaf/Limited Lumberjacks - black

The normal maple front and back borders of the Lumberjacks insert set gives way to black in this super-scarce chase set within a chase set. Each black Lumberjacks card is individually serial numbered on back from within an edition of 500.

		MT
Complete Set (10):		500.00
Common Player:		24.00
1	Ken Griffey Jr.	90.00
2	Sammy Sosa	50.00
3	Cal Ripken Jr.	75.00
4	Frank Thomas	40.00
5	Alex Rodriguez	75.00
6	Mo Vaughn	25.00
7	Chipper Jones	50.00
8	Mike Piazza	60.00
9	Jeff Bagwell	25.00
10	Mark McGwire	90.00

1996 Leaf/Limited Pennant Craze Samples

Each card in the Pennant Craze insert set can also be found in a sample version originally distributed to hobby dealers. Samples are identical to the issued version except for the silver-foil "XXXX" instead of a serial number on back.

		MT
Complete Set (10):		75.00
Common Player:		4.00
1	Juan Gonzalez	5.00
2	Cal Ripken Jr.	10.00
3	Frank Thomas	6.00
4	Ken Griffey Jr.	12.50
5	Albert Belle	4.00

6	Greg Maddux	6.00
7	Paul Molitor	4.00
8	Alex Rodriguez	10.00
9	Barry Bonds	4.00
10	Chipper Jones	7.50

1996 Leaf/Limited Pennant Craze

Each card in this insert set is sequentially numbered to 2,500 in silver foil on the back. The top-front of the cards have a die-cut pennant shape and is felt-textured.

		MT
Complete Set (10):		150.00
Common Player:		7.50
1	Juan Gonzalez	20.00
2	Cal Ripken Jr.	30.00
3	Frank Thomas	15.00
4	Ken Griffey Jr.	35.00
5	Albert Belle	7.50
6	Greg Maddux	20.00
7	Paul Molitor	7.50
8	Alex Rodriguez	30.00
9	Barry Bonds	10.00
10	Chipper Jones	25.00

1996 Leaf/Limited Rookies

There are two versions of this 1996 Limited insert set. The cards are reprinted as part of a Limited Gold parallel set, which also includes the regular issue's 90 cards. The gold cards are seeded one per every 11 packs. The top young players are also featured on regular Limited Rookies inserts; these versions are seeded one per every seven packs.

		MT
Complete Set (10):		40.00
Common Player:		2.00
Limited Gold: 5X		
1	Alex Ochoa	2.00
2	Darin Erstad	10.00
3	Ruben Rivera	2.00
4	Derek Jeter	15.00
5	Jermaine Dye	2.00
6	Jason Kendall	2.50
7	Mike Grace	2.00
8	Andruw Jones	10.00
9	Rey Ordonez	5.00
10	George Arias	2.00

1996 Leaf/Preferred Leaf Gold Promos

Each of the 77 gold cards in the Preferred Steel set can also be found in a promo card version. The samples differ from the issued versions only in an overprint diagonally on the back which reads "PROMOTIONAL CARD". This parallel promo edition represents one of the largest promo card issues of the mid-1990s.

		MT
Complete Set (77):		750.00
Common Player:		5.00
1	Frank Thomas	15.00
2	Paul Molitor	15.00
3	Kenny Lofton	15.00
4	Travis Fryman	5.00
5	Jeff Conine	5.00
6	Barry Bonds	30.00
7	Gregg Jefferies	5.00
8	Alex Rodriguez	40.00
9	Wade Boggs	12.50
10	David Justice	7.50
11	Hideo Nomo	12.50
12	Roberto Alomar	2.00
13	Todd Hollandsworth	7.50
14	Mark McGwire	45.00
15	Rafael Palmeiro	7.50
16	Will Clark	7.50
17	Cal Ripken Jr.	40.00
18	Derek Bell	5.00
19	Gary Sheffield	12.50
20	Juan Gonzalez	25.00
21	Garret Anderson	5.00
22	Mo Vaughn	15.00
23	Robin Ventura	5.00
24	Carlos Baerga	5.00
25	Tim Salmon	10.00
26	Matt Williams	7.50
27	Fred McGriff	10.00
28	Rondell White	5.00
29	Ray Lankford	5.00
30	Lenny Dykstra	5.00
31	J.T. Snow	5.00
32	Sammy Sosa	15.00
33	Chipper Jones	35.00
34	Bobby Bonilla	5.00
35	Paul Wilson	5.00
36	Darren Daulton	5.00
37	Larry Walker	7.50
38	Raul Mondesi	7.50
39	Jeff Bagwell	25.00
40	Derek Jeter	25.00
41	Kirby Puckett	25.00
42	Jason Isringhausen	5.00
43	Vinny Castilla	5.00
44	Jim Edmonds	7.50
45	Ron Gant	5.00
46	Carlos Delgado	5.00
47	Jose Canseco	10.00
48	Tony Gwynn	25.00
49	Mike Mussina	7.50
50	Charles Johnson	5.00
51	Mike Piazza	35.00
52	Ken Griffey Jr.	50.00
53	Greg Maddux	32.00
54	Mark Grace	10.00
55	Ryan Klesko	7.50
56	Dennis Eckersley	5.00
57	Rickey Henderson	7.50
58	Michael Tucker	5.00
59	Joe Carter	7.50
60	Randy Johnson	12.50
61	Brian Jordan	5.00
62	Shawn Green	5.00
63	Roger Clemens	20.00
64	Andres Galarraga	7.50
65	Johnny Damon	7.50
66	Ryne Sandberg	15.00
67	Alan Benes	5.00
68	Albert Belle	20.00
69	Barry Larkin	7.50
70	Marty Cordova	6.25
71	Dante Bichette	7.50
72	Craig Biggio	5.00
73	Reggie Sanders	5.00
74	Moises Alou	5.00
75	Chuck Knoblauch	7.50
76	Cecil Fielder	7.50
77	Manny Ramirez	7.50

1996 Leaf/Preferred

Leaf Preferred consists of 150 cards, a Press Proof parallel set and three insert sets, one of which has its own parallel set, too. While no individual odds are given for insert sets, the overall odds of getting an insert card are one per 10 packs. The Press Proof inserts replace the silver foil name and strip down the left side of the card with gold foil. Press Proof parallels were limited to 250 sets. Another insert set, Silver Leaf Steel, has a card seeded one per pack. This insert set is paralleled by a Gold Leaf Steel set, which appears in much more limited numbers. The two other insert sets are Steel Power and Staremaster.

		MT
Complete Set (150):		40.00
Common Player:		.15
Gold Press Proofs: 25X		
Unlisted Stars: .25 to .50		
Wax Box:		65.00
1	Ken Griffey Jr.	4.00
2	Rico Brogna	.15
3	Gregg Jefferies	.15
4	Reggie Sanders	.15
5	Manny Ramirez	1.50
6	Shawn Green	.15
7	Tino Martinez	.15
8	Jeff Bagwell	2.00
9	Marc Newfield	.15
10	Ray Lankford	.15
11	Jay Bell	.15
12	Greg Maddux	2.50
13	Frank Thomas	1.50
14	Travis Fryman	.15
15	Mark McGwire	4.00
16	Chuck Knoblauch	.25
17	Sammy Sosa	2.00
18	Matt Williams	.35
19	Roger Clemens	1.00
20	Rondell White	.15
21	Ivan Rodriguez	.75
22	Cal Ripken Jr.	3.00
23	Ben McDonald	.15
24	Kenny Lofton	1.00
25	Mike Piazza	2.50
26	David Cone	.25
27	Gary Sheffield	.75
28	Tim Salmon	.40
29	Andres Galarraga	.30
30	Johnny Damon	.20
31	Ozzie Smith	1.00
32	Carlos Baerga	.20
33	Raul Mondesi	.35
34	Moises Alou	.15
35	Alex Rodriguez	5.00
36	Mike Mussina	1.00
37	Jason Isringhausen	.40
38	Barry Larkin	.40
39	Bernie Williams	.75
40	Chipper Jones	2.50
41	Joey Hamilton	.15
42	Charles Johnson	.15
43	Juan Gonzalez	2.00
44	Greg Vaughn	.15
45	Robin Ventura	.15
46	Albert Belle	1.00
47	Rafael Palmeiro	.25
48	Brian Hunter	.15
49	Mo Vaughn	1.50
50	Paul O'Neill	.15
51	Mark Grace	.25
52	Randy Johnson	.60
53	Pedro Martinez	.15
54	Marty Cordova	.20
55	Garret Anderson	.20
56	Joe Carter	.40
57	Jim Thome	.75
58	Edgardo Alfonzo	.15
59	Dante Bichette	.40
60	Darryl Hamilton	.15
61	Roberto Alomar	1.25
62	Fred McGriff	.60
63	Kirby Puckett	2.00
64	Hideo Nomo	.75
65	Alex Fernandez	.15
66	Ryan Klesko	.40
67	Wade Boggs	.25
68	Eddie Murray	.50
69	Eric Karros	.15
70	Jim Edmonds	.25
71	Edgar Martinez	.15
72	Andy Pettitte	1.00
73	Mark Grudzielanek	.15
74	Tom Glavine	.25
75	Ken Caminiti	.50
76	Will Clark	.30
77	Craig Biggio	.15
78	Brady Anderson	.20
79	Tony Gwynn	2.00
80	Larry Walker	.40
81	Brian Jordan	.25
82	Lenny Dykstra	.15
83	Butch Huskey	.15
84	Jack McDowell	.15
85	Cecil Fielder	.25
86	Jose Canseco	.30
87	Jason Giambi	.20
88	Rickey Henderson	.15
89	Kevin Seitzer	.15
90	Carlos Delgado	.75
91	Ryne Sandberg	1.25
92	Dwight Gooden	.15
93	Michael Tucker	.15
94	Barry Bonds	1.25
95	Eric Young	.15
96	Dean Palmer	.15
97	Henry Rodriguez	.15
98	John Mabry	.15
99	J.T. Snow	.15
100	Andre Dawson	.15
101	Ismael Valdes	.15
102	Charles Nagy	.15
103	Jay Buhner	.40
104	Derek Bell	.15
105	Paul Molitor	.75
106	Hal Morris	.15
107	Ray Durham	.15
108	Bernard Gilkey	.15
109	John Valentin	.15
110	Melvin Nieves	.15
111	John Smoltz	.40
112	Terrell Wade	.15
113	Chad Mottola	.15
114	Tony Clark	.75
115	John Wasdin	.15
116	Derek Jeter	2.00
117	Rey Ordonez	.50
118	Jason Thompson	.15
119	*Robin Jennings*	.15
120	*Rocky Coppinger*	.40
121	Billy Wagner	.30
122	Steve Gibralter	.15
123	Jermaine Dye	.40
124	Jason Kendall	.15
125	*Mike Grace*	.50
126	Jason Schmidt	.15
127	Paul Wilson	.25
128	Alan Benes	.25
129	Justin Thompson	.15
130	Brooks Kieschnick	.15
131	George Arias	.15
132	*Osvaldo Fernandez*	.40
133	Todd Hollandsworth	.20
134	Eric Owens	.15
135	Chan Ho Park	.15
136	Mark Loretta	.15
137	Ruben Rivera	.75
138	Jeff Suppan	.15
139	Ugueth Urbina	.15
140	LaTroy Hawkins	.15
141	Chris Snopek	.15
142	Edgar Renteria	.40
143	Raul Casanova	.15
144	Jose Herrera	.15
145	*Matt Lawton*	.15
146	*Ralph Milliard*	.15
147	Checklist	.15
148	Checklist	.15
149	Checklist	.15
150	Checklist	.15

1996 Leaf/Preferred Press Proofs

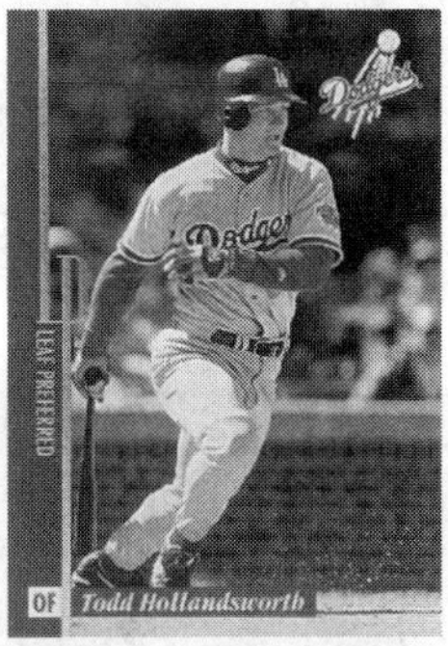

Inserted at a rate of about one per 48 packs, Press Proof parallels of the 150 cards in Leaf Preferred are identifiable only by the use of gold foil, rather than silver, on the card fronts, and gold ink on back. The cards are not otherwise marked or numbered. It is believed the issue was limited to 250-500 of each card.

	MT
Complete Set (150):	1500.
Common Player:	2.00
Stars: 25X	

(See 1996 Leaf Preferred for checklist and base card values.)

1996 Leaf/Preferred Leaf Steel

This 77-card insert set has two versions - a silver one and a much more limited gold one. A Silver Leaf Steel card is included in every pack; the parallel versions appear about one per 24 packs.

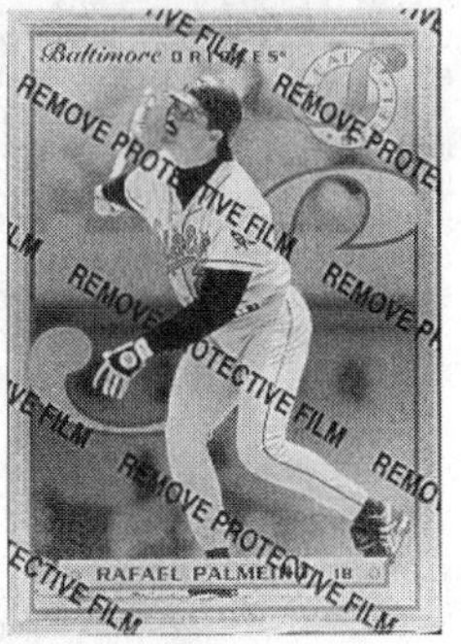

		MT
Complete Set (77):		100.00
Common Player:		.25
Golds: 6X		
1	Frank Thomas	5.00
2	Paul Molitor	2.00
3	Kenny Lofton	1.50
4	Travis Fryman	.25
5	Jeff Conine	.25
6	Barry Bonds	2.50
7	Gregg Jefferies	.25
8	Alex Rodriguez	7.50
9	Wade Boggs	.50
10	David Justice	1.00
11	Hideo Nomo	1.00
12	Roberto Alomar	2.00
13	Todd Hollandsworth	.25
14	Mark McGwire	10.00
15	Rafael Palmeiro	1.00
16	Will Clark	1.00
17	Cal Ripken Jr.	8.00
18	Derek Bell	.25
19	Gary Sheffield	1.50
20	Juan Gonzalez	5.00
21	Garret Anderson	.25
22	Mo Vaughn	1.50
23	Robin Ventura	.50
24	Carlos Baerga	.25
25	Tim Salmon	1.00
26	Matt Williams	1.00
27	Fred McGriff	.75
28	Rondell White	.75
29	Ray Lankford	.25
30	Lenny Dykstra	.25
31	J.T. Snow	.25
32	Sammy Sosa	6.00
33	Chipper Jones	6.00
34	Bobby Bonilla	.25
35	Paul Wilson	.25
36	Darren Daulton	.25
37	Larry Walker	1.50
38	Raul Mondesi	1.00
39	Jeff Bagwell	3.00
40	Derek Jeter	5.00
41	Kirby Puckett	2.50
42	Jason Isringhausen	.25
43	Vinny Castilla	.25
44	Jim Edmonds	.50
45	Ron Gant	.25
46	Carlos Delgado	.75
47	Jose Canseco	1.00
48	Tony Gwynn	5.00
49	Mike Mussina	2.00
50	Charles Johnson	.25
51	Mike Piazza	6.00
52	Ken Griffey Jr.	10.00
53	Greg Maddux	5.00
54	Mark Grace	1.00
55	Ryan Klesko	.75
56	Dennis Eckersley	.25
57	Rickey Henderson	.50
58	Michael Tucker	.25
59	Joe Carter	.50
60	Randy Johnson	1.50
61	Brian Jordan	.25
62	Shawn Green	.50
63	Roger Clemens	3.00
64	Andres Galarraga	.50
65	Johnny Damon	.25
66	Ryne Sandberg	2.50
67	Alan Benes	.25
68	Albert Belle	2.00
69	Barry Larkin	.50
70	Marty Cordova	.25
71	Dante Bichette	.50
72	Craig Biggio	.75
73	Reggie Sanders	.25
74	Moises Alou	.50
75	Chuck Knoblauch	1.00
76	Cecil Fielder	.25
77	Manny Ramirez	3.00

1996 Leaf/Preferred Staremaster

These 1996 Leaf Preferred inserts provide a photographic tribute to the stares of

12 top players. Each card is printed on silver holographic card stock and is numbered up to 2,500.

		MT
Complete Set (12):		300.00
Common Player:		10.00
1	Chipper Jones	30.00
2	Alex Rodriguez	40.00
3	Derek Jeter	25.00
4	Tony Gwynn	25.00
5	Frank Thomas	20.00
6	Ken Griffey Jr.	50.00
7	Cal Ripken Jr.	40.00
8	Greg Maddux	30.00
9	Albert Belle	12.00
10	Barry Bonds	12.00
11	Jeff Bagwell	15.00
12	Mike Piazza	35.00

1996 Leaf/Preferred Steel Power

This eight-card Leaf Steel insert set combines micro-etched foil with interior die-cutting to honor the game's top power hitters. Each insert card carries a serial number up to 5,000.

		MT
Complete Set (8):		125.00
Common Player:		6.00
1	Albert Belle	10.00
2	Mo Vaughn	6.00
3	Ken Griffey Jr.	40.00
4	Cal Ripken Jr.	30.00
5	Mike Piazza	25.00
6	Barry Bonds	7.50
7	Jeff Bagwell	15.00
8	Frank Thomas	20.00

1996 Leaf/ Signature Series

There were 245 Major League players who autographed cards for Leaf's Signature Series. At least one authentic signature is guaranteed in every pack. There were 235 players who signed cards in these quantities: Gold (500 autographs), Silver (1,000) and Bronze (3,500). The other 10 players signed fewer autographs - 100 Gold, 200 Silver and 700 Bronze. Each major leaguer signed his cards, including an affidavit that was notarized to guarantee each signature was authentic. In addition, Pinnacle used team clubhouse officials to witness autographs. One out of every 48 packs is a super pack containing nothing but autographed cards. In addition, the regular-issue base set is paralleled in Gold and Platinum Press Proof insert sets. The gold version is seeded one per 12 packs in Series 1 and one per eight in the Extended Series. Platinums are found only in the Extended Series packs at the rate of one per 24 packs. Four-card packs of Leaf Signature Series carried a suggested retail price at issue of $9.99.

		MT
Complete Set (150):		75.00
Complete 1st Series (100):		50.00
Complete Extended Series (50):		25.00
Common Player:		.20
Gold Press Proofs Set (150):		900.00
Gold PP Stars: 10X		
Complete Platinum Set (150):		3000.
Platinum PP Ser.1 Stars: 30X		
Platinum PP Ser.2 Stars: 15X		
Platinum PP Ser. 1 Yng Stars: 20X		
Platinum PP Ser. 2 Yng Stars: 12X		
Wax Box:		100.00
1	Mike Piazza	3.00
2	Juan Gonzalez	2.50
3	Greg Maddux	3.00
4	Marc Newfield	.20
5	Wade Boggs	.50
6	Ray Lankford	.20
7	Frank Thomas	2.00
8	Rico Brogna	.20
9	Tim Salmon	.40
10	Ken Griffey Jr.	5.00
11	Manny Ramirez	1.50
12	Cecil Fielder	.25
13	Gregg Jefferies	.20
14	Rondell White	.40
15	Cal Ripken Jr.	4.00
16	Alex Rodriguez	4.00
17	Bernie Williams	1.00
18	Andres Galarraga	.40
19	Mike Mussina	1.00
20	Chuck Knoblauch	.30
21	Joe Carter	.25
22	Jeff Bagwell	2.50
23	Mark McGwire	5.00
24	Sammy Sosa	2.00
25	Reggie Sanders	.20
26	Chipper Jones	3.00
27	Jeff Cirillo	.20
28	Roger Clemens	1.25
29	Craig Biggio	.35
30	Gary Sheffield	.50
31	Paul O'Neill	.35
32	Johnny Damon	.50
33	Jason Isringhausen	.20
34	Jay Bell	.20
35	Henry Rodriguez	.20
36	Matt Williams	.40
37	Randy Johnson	.75
38	Fred McGriff	.50
39	Jason Giambi	.20
40	Ivan Rodriguez	.75
41	Raul Mondesi	.50
42	Barry Larkin	.50
43	Ryan Klesko	.40
44	Joey Hamilton	.20
45	Todd Hundley	.25
46	Jim Edmonds	.50
47	Dante Bichette	.35
48	Roberto Alomar	1.25
49	Mark Grace	.40
50	Brady Anderson	.30
51	Hideo Nomo	1.00
52	Ozzie Smith	1.00
53	Robin Ventura	.35
54	Andy Pettitte	1.00
55	Kenny Lofton	1.00
56	John Mabry	.20
57	Paul Molitor	.75
58	Rey Ordonez	.75
59	Albert Belle	1.00
60	Charles Johnson	.20
61	Edgar Martinez	.20
62	Derek Bell	.20
63	Carlos Delgado	.75
64	Raul Casanova	.20
65	Ismael Valdes	.20
66	J.T. Snow	.20
67	Derek Jeter	3.00
68	Jason Kendall	.20
69	John Smoltz	.50
70	Chad Mottola	.20
71	Jim Thome	.30
72	Will Clark	.50
73	Mo Vaughn	1.00
74	John Wasdin	.20
75	Rafael Palmeiro	.50
76	Mark Grudzielanek	.20
77	Larry Walker	.40
78	Alan Benes	.25
79	Michael Tucker	.20
80	Billy Wagner	.25
81	Paul Wilson	.25
82	Greg Vaughn	.25
83	Dean Palmer	.20
84	Ryne Sandberg	1.25
85	Eric Young	.20
86	Jay Buhner	.25
87	Tony Clark	.35
88	Jermaine Dye	.20
89	Barry Bonds	1.25
90	Ugueth Urbina	.20
91	Charles Nagy	.20
92	Ruben Rivera	.25
93	Todd Hollandsworth	.20
94	*Darin Erstad*	5.00
95	Brooks Kieschnick	.20
96	Edgar Renteria	.35
97	Lenny Dykstra	.20
98	Tony Gwynn	2.00
99	Kirby Puckett	1.50
100	Checklist	.20
101	Andruw Jones	2.50
102	Alex Ochoa	.20
103	David Cone	.20
104	Rusty Greer	.20
105	Jose Canseco	.40
106	Ken Caminiti	.40
107	Mariano Rivera	.50
108	Ron Gant	.20
109	Darryl Strawberry	.20
110	Vladimir Guerrero	1.50
111	George Arias	.20
112	Jeff Conine	.20
113	Bobby Higginson	.20
114	Eric Karros	.20
115	Brian Hunter	.20
116	Eddie Murray	.50
117	Todd Walker	.75
118	Chan Ho Park	.20
119	John Jaha	.20
120	David Justice	.40
121	Makoto Suzuki	.20
122	Scott Rolen	1.50
123	Tino Martinez	.20
124	Kimera Bartee	.20
125	Garret Anderson	.20
126	Brian Jordan	.20
127	Andre Dawson	.20
128	Javier Lopez	.30
129	Bill Pulsipher	.20
130	Dwight Gooden	.20
131	Al Martin	.20
132	Terrell Wade	.20
133	Steve Gibralter	.20
134	Tom Glavine	.30
135	Kevin Appier	.20
136	Tim Raines	.20
137	Curtis Pride	.20
138	Todd Greene	.20
139	Bobby Bonilla	.20
140	Trey Beamon	.20
141	Marty Cordova	.20
142	Rickey Henderson	.35
143	Ellis Burks	.20
144	Dennis Eckersley	.20
145	Kevin Brown	.25
146	Carlos Baerga	.20
147	Brett Butler	.20
148	Marquis Grissom	.20
149	Karim Garcia	.75
150	Checklist	.20

1996 Leaf/ Signature Series Autograph Promos

To introduce its Autograph Series, Leaf sent dealers one of two promo card versions of the Frank Thomas card. Most received a card with a pre-printed facsimile autograph, duly noted in small type beneath the signature. Others (500) received a genuine Frank Thomas autograph on their promo. All of the cards are marked "PROMOTIONAL CARD" diagonally on both front and back.

	MT
Frank Thomas (facsimile signature)	5.00
Frank Thomas (genuine autograph)	150.00

1996 Leaf/ Signature Series Autographs

Every pack of 1996 Leaf Signature Series includes at least one authentically signed card from one of 245 players. There were 235 players who signed three versions in these quantities - 500 Gold, 1,000 Silver and 3,500 Bronze. There are also short-printed autographs for 10 players in quantities of 100 Gold, 200 Silver and 700 Bronze. The short-printed players are designated with an "SP" in the checklist. Cards are numbered alphabetically in the checklist since the autographed cards are unnumbered. Each major leaguer signed a notarized affidavit to guarantee each signature was authentic. Series 1 cards of Carlos Delgado, Brian Hunter, Phil Plantier, Jim Thome, Terrell Wade and Ernie Young were signed too late for inclusion in Series 1 packs, and were inserted with Extended. No Bronze cards of Thome were signed.

		MT
Complete Bronze Set (251):		2000.
Common Bronze Player:		2.00
Silver: 2X		
Gold: 3X-4X		
SP Signatures: 100 Gold, 200 Silver, 700 Bronze		
(1)	Kurt Abbott	3.00
(2)	Juan Acevedo	2.00
(3)	Terry Adams	2.00
(4)	Manny Alexander	2.00
(5)	Roberto Alomar (SP)	60.00
(6)	Moises Alou	12.00
(7)	Wilson Alvarez	4.00
(8)	Garret Anderson	3.00
(9)	Shane Andrews	4.00
(10)	Andy Ashby	4.00
(11)	Pedro Astacio	3.00
(12)	Brad Ausmus	3.00
(13)	Bobby Ayala	2.00
(14)	Carlos Baerga	2.00
(15)	Harold Baines	5.00
(16)	Jason Bates	2.00
(17)	Allen Battle	2.00
(18)	Rich Becker	2.00
(19)	David Boll	2.00
(20)	Rafael Belliard	2.00
(21)	Andy Benes	4.00
(22)	Armando Benitez	2.00
(23)	Jason Bere	2.00
(24)	Geronimo Berroa	2.00
(25)	Willie Blair	2.00
(26)	Mike Blowers	2.00
(27)	Wade Boggs (SP)	140.00
(28)	Ricky Bones	2.00
(29)	Mike Bordick	2.00
(30)	Toby Borland	2.00
(31)	Ricky Bottalico	2.00
(32)	Darren Bragg	2.00
(33)	Jeff Branson	2.00
(34)	Tilson Brito	2.00
(35)	Rico Brogna	3.00
(36)	Scott Brosius	4.00
(37)	Damon Buford	4.00
(38)	Mike Busby	2.00
(39)	Tom Candiotti	2.00
(40)	Frank Castillo	2.00
(41)	Andujar Cedeno	2.00
(42)	Domingo Cedeno	2.00
(43)	Roger Cedeno	5.00
(44)	Norm Charlton	2.00
(45)	Jeff Cirillo	3.00
(46)	Will Clark	20.00
(47)	Jeff Conine	3.00
(48)	Steve Cooke	4.00
(49)	Joey Cora	3.00
(50)	Marty Cordova	3.00
(51)	Rheal Cormier	2.00
(52)	Felipe Crespo	2.00
(53)	Chad Curtis	4.00
(54)	Johnny Damon	12.00
(55)	Russ Davis	3.00
(56)	Andre Dawson	20.00
(57a)	Carlos Delgado (black autograph)	20.00
(57b)	Carlos Delgado (blue autograph)	20.00
(58)	Doug Drabek	4.00
(59)	Darren Dreifort	4.00
(60)	Shawon Dunston	3.00
(61)	Ray Durham	4.00
(62)	Jim Edmonds	5.00
(63)	Joey Eischen	2.00
(64)	Jim Eisenreich	4.00
(65)	Sal Fasano	2.00
(66)	Jeff Fassero	2.00
(67)	Alex Fernandez	7.50
(68)	Darrin Fletcher	4.00
(69)	Chad Fonville	4.00
(70)	Kevin Foster	4.00
(71)	John Franco	4.00
(72)	Julio Franco	3.00
(73)	Marvin Freeman	2.00
(74)	Travis Fryman	3.00
(75)	Gary Gaetti	3.00
(76)	Carlos Garcia	4.00
(77)	Jason Giambi	3.00
(78)	Benji Gil	2.00
(79)	Greg Gohr	2.00
(80)	Chris Gomez	2.00
(81)	Leo Gomez	2.00
(82)	Tom Goodwin	3.00
(83)	Mike Grace	2.00
(84)	Mike Greenwell	4.00
(85)	Rusty Greer	3.00
(86)	Mark Grudzielanek	2.00
(87)	Mark Gubicza	4.00
(88)	Juan Guzman	4.00
(89)	Darryl Hamilton	4.00
(90)	Joey Hamilton	3.00
(91)	Chris Hammond	4.00
(92)	Mike Hampton	2.00
(93)	Chris Haney	2.00
(94)	Todd Haney	2.00
(95)	Erik Hanson	2.00
(96)	Pete Harnisch	3.00
(97)	LaTroy Hawkins	2.00
(98)	Charlie Hayes	2.00
(99)	Jimmy Haynes	2.00
(100)	Roberto Hernandez	4.00
(101)	Bobby Higginson	9.00
(102)	Glenallen Hill	3.00
(103)	Ken Hill	4.00
(104)	Sterling Hitchcock	4.00
(105)	Trevor Hoffman	6.00
(106)	Dave Hollins	4.00
(107)	Dwayne Hosey	3.00
(108)	Thomas Howard	2.00
(109)	Steve Howe	6.00
(110)	John Hudek	2.00
(111)	Rex Hudler	2.00
(112)	Brian Hunter	2.00
(113)	Butch Huskey	5.00
(114)	Mark Hutton	2.00
(115)	Jason Jacome	2.00
(116)	John Jaha	4.00
(117)	Reggie Jefferson	4.00
(118)	Derek Jeter (SP)	175.00
(119)	Bobby Jones	4.00
(120)	Todd Jones	3.00
(121)	Brian Jordan	4.00
(122)	Kevin Jordan	2.00
(123)	Jeff Juden	3.00
(124)	Ron Karkovice	3.00
(125)	Roberto Kelly	3.00
(126)	Mark Kiefer	2.00
(127)	Brooks Kieschnick	2.00
(128)	Jeff King	4.00
(129)	Mike Lansing	4.00
(130)	Matt Lawton	4.00
(131)	Al Leiter	4.00
(132)	Mark Leiter	2.00
(133)	Curtis Leskanic	4.00
(134)	Darren Lewis	3.00
(135)	Mark Lewis	4.00
(136)	Felipe Lira	2.00
(137)	Pat Listach	3.00
(138)	Keith Lockhart	3.00
(139)	Kenny Lofton (SP)	50.00
(140)	John Mabry	4.00
(141)	Mike Macfarlane	3.00
(142)	Kirt Manwaring	3.00
(143)	Al Martin	4.00
(144)	Norberto Martin	3.00
(145)	Dennis Martinez	5.00
(146)	Pedro Martinez	50.00
(147)	Sandy Martinez	4.00
(148)	Mike Matheny	4.00
(149)	T.J. Mathews	2.00
(150)	David McCarty	3.00
(151)	Ben McDonald	4.00
(152)	Pat Meares	4.00
(153)	Orlando Merced	4.00

(154) Jose Mesa 3.00
(155) Matt Mieske 4.00
(156) Orlando Miller 4.00
(157) Mike Mimbs 2.00
(158) Paul Molitor (SP) 60.00
(159) Raul Mondesi (SP) 50.00
(160) Jeff Montgomery 4.00
(161) Mickey Morandini 3.00
(162) Lyle Mouton 2.00
(163) James Mouton 2.00
(164) Jamie Moyer 4.00
(165) Rodney Myers 2.00
(166) Denny Neagle 2.00
(167) Robb Nen 3.00
(168) Marc Newfield 2.00
(169) Dave Nilsson 4.00
(170) Jon Nunnally 4.00
(171) Chad Ogea 4.00
(172) Troy O'Leary 4.00
(173) Rey Ordonez 7.50
(174) Jayhawk Owens 2.00
(175) Tom Pagnozzi 3.00
(176) Dean Palmer 4.00
(177) Roger Pavlik 3.00
(178) Troy Percival 4.00
(179) Carlos Perez 4.00
(180) Robert Perez 2.00
(181) Andy Pettitte 20.00
(182) Phil Plantier 4.00
(183) Mike Potts 2.00
(184) Curtis Pride 4.00
(185) Ariel Prieto 2.00
(186) Bill Pulsipher 3.00
(187) Brad Radke 4.00
(188) Manny Ramirez (SP) 75.00
(189) Joe Randa 4.00
(190) Pat Rapp 4.00
(191) Bryan Rekar 2.00
(192) Shane Reynolds 4.00
(193) Arthur Rhodes 4.00
(194) Mariano Rivera 6.00
(195a) Alex Rodriguez (SP, black autograph) 275.00
(195b) Alex Rodriguez (SP, blue autograph) 275.00
(196) Frank Rodriguez 3.00
(197) Mel Rojas 2.00
(198) Ken Ryan 3.00
(199) Bret Saberhagen 6.00
(200) Tim Salmon 6.00
(201) Rey Sanchez 3.00
(202) Scott Sanders 2.00
(203) Steve Scarsone 2.00
(204) Curt Schilling 6.00
(205) Jason Schmidt 2.00
(206) David Segui 4.00
(207) Kevin Seitzer 4.00
(208) Scott Servais 2.00
(209) Don Slaught 3.00
(210) Zane Smith 3.00
(211) Paul Sorrento 2.00
(212) Scott Stahoviak 2.00
(213) Mike Stanley 2.00
(214) Terry Steinbach 4.00
(215) Kevin Stocker 2.00
(216) Jeff Suppan 3.00
(217) Bill Swift 2.00
(218) Greg Swindell 3.00
(219) Kevin Tapani 4.00
(220) Danny Tartabull 3.00
(221) Julian Tavarez 2.00
(222) Frank Thomas (SP) 150.00
(223) Ozzie Timmons 2.00
(224a) Michael Tucker (black autograph) 4.00
(224b) Michael Tucker (blue autograph) 4.00
(225) Ismael Valdez 3.00
(226) Jose Valentin 2.00
(227) Todd Van Poppel 4.00
(228) Mo Vaughn (SP) 50.00
(229) Quilvio Veras 3.00
(230) Fernando Vina 3.00
(231) Joe Vitiello 3.00
(232) Jose Vizcaino 2.00
(233) Omar Vizquel 5.00
(234) Terrell Wade 2.00
(235) Paul Wagner 2.00
(236) Matt Walbeck 3.00
(237) Jerome Walton 2.00
(238) Turner Ward 2.00
(239) Allen Watson 2.00
(240) David Weathers 2.00
(241) Walt Weiss 4.00
(242) Turk Wendell 4.00
(243) Rondell White 5.00
(244) Brian Williams 2.00
(245) George Williams 2.00
(246) Paul Wilson 2.00
(247) Bobby Witt 3.00
(248) Bob Wolcott 2.00
(249) Eric Young 4.00
(250) Ernie Young 2.00
(251) Greg Zaun 4.00
--- Frank Thomas (Autographed jumbo) 60.00

1996 Leaf/ Signature Series Extended Autographs

Leaf Signature Series Exended Autograph cards consist of 31 stars and rising prospects, six autographs from Series 1 that were late inclusions and 186 other major leaguers. The 186 regular players signed 5,000 each, while other signees' totals are listed in parentheses. Signature cards for Alex Rodriguez, Juan Gonzalez and Andruw Jones were only available through redemption cards. Autographed versions are different designs from the regular-issue cards, with two available in each pack. The unnumbered cards are checklisted here in alphabetical order.

	MT
Complete Set (217):	1300.
Common Player:	2.00
Extended Box:	150.00
(1) Scott Aldred	2.00
(2) Mike Aldrete	2.00
(3) Rich Amaral	2.00
(4) Alex Arias	2.00
(5) Paul Assenmacher	2.00
(6) Roger Bailey	2.00
(7) Erik Bennett	2.00
(8) Sean Bergman	2.00
(9) Doug Bochtler	2.00
(10) Tim Bogar	2.00
(11) Pat Borders	2.00
(12) Pedro Borbon	2.00
(13) Shawn Boskie	2.00
(14) Rafael Bournigal	2.00
(15) Mark Brandenburg	2.00
(16) John Briscoe	2.00
(17) Jorge Brito	2.00
(18) Doug Brocail	2.00
(19) Jay Buhner (SP, 1000)	20.00
(20) Scott Bullett	2.00
(21) Dave Burba	2.00
(22) Ken Caminiti (SP, 1000)	25.00
(23) John Cangelosi	2.00
(24) Cris Carpenter	2.00
(25) Chuck Carr	2.00
(26) Larry Casian	2.00
(27) Tony Castillo	2.00
(28) Jason Christiansen	2.00
(29) Archi Cianfrocco	2.00
(30) Mark Clark	2.00
(31) Terry Clark	2.00
(32) Roger Clemens (SP, 1000)	80.00
(33) Jim Converse	2.00
(34) Dennis Cook	2.00
(35) Francisco Cordova	3.00
(36) Jim Corsi	2.00
(37) Tim Crabtree	2.00
(38) Doug Creek (SP, 1950)	3.00
(39) John Cummings	2.00
(40) Omar Daal	2.00
(41) Rich DeLucia	2.00
(42) Mark Dewey	2.00
(43) Alex Diaz	2.00
(44) Jermaine Dye (SP, 2500)	8.00
(45) Ken Edenfield	2.00
(46) Mark Eichhorn	2.00
(47) John Ericks	2.00
(48) Darin Erstad	30.00
(49) Alvaro Espinoza	2.00
(50) Jorge Fabregas	2.00
(51) Mike Fetters	2.00
(52) John Flaherty	2.00
(53) Bryce Florie	2.00
(54) Tony Fossas	2.00
(55) Lou Frazier	2.00
(56) Mike Gallego	2.00
(57) Karim Garcia (SP, 2500)	20.00
(58) Jason Giambi	2.00
(59) Ed Giovanola	2.00
(60) Tom Glavine (SP, 1250)	25.00
(61) Juan Gonzalez (SP, 1000)	75.00
(62) Craig Grebeck	2.00
(63) Buddy Groom	2.00
(64) Kevin Gross	2.00
(65) Eddie Guardado	2.00
(66) Mark Guthrie	2.00
(67) Tony Gwynn (SP, 1000)	70.00
(68) Chip Hale	2.00
(69) Darren Hall	2.00
(70) Lee Hancock	2.00
(71) Dave Hansen	2.00
(72) Bryan Harvey	2.00
(73) Bill Haselman	2.00
(74) Mike Henneman	2.00
(75) Doug Henry	2.00
(76) Gil Heredia	2.00
(77) Carlos Hernandez	2.00
(78) Jose Hernandez	2.00
(79) Darren Holmes	2.00
(80) Mark Holzemer	2.00
(81) Rick Honeycutt	2.00
(82) Chris Hook	2.00
(83) Chris Howard	2.00
(84) Jack Howell	2.00
(85) David Hulse	2.00
(86) Edwin Hurtado	2.00
(87) Jeff Huson	2.00
(88) Mike James	2.00
(89) Derek Jeter (SP, 1000)	65.00
(90) Brian Johnson	2.00
(91) Randy Johnson (SP, 1000)	30.00
(92) Mark Johnson	2.00
(93) Andruw Jones (SP, 2000)	30.00
(94) Chris Jones	2.00
(95) Ricky Jordan	2.00
(96) Matt Karchner	2.00
(97) Scott Karl	2.00
(98) Jason Kendall (SP, 2500)	7.50
(99) Brian Keyser	2.00
(100) Mike Kingery	2.00
(101) Wayne Kirby	2.00
(102) Ryan Klesko (SP, 1000)	10.00
(103) Chuck Knoblauch (SP, 1000)	30.00
(104) Chad Kreuter	2.00
(105) Tom Lampkin	2.00
(106) Scott Leius	2.00
(107) Jon Lieber	2.00
(108) Nelson Liriano	2.00
(109) Scott Livingstone	2.00
(110) Graeme Lloyd	2.00
(111) Kenny Lofton (SP, 1000)	30.00
(112) Luis Lopez	2.00
(113) Torey Lovullo	2.00
(114) Greg Maddux (SP, 500)	125.00
(115) Mike Maddux	2.00
(116) Dave Magadan	2.00
(117) Mike Magnante	2.00
(118) Joe Magrane	2.00
(119) Pat Mahomes	2.00
(120) Matt Mantei	2.00
(121) John Marzano	2.00
(122) Terry Matthews	2.00
(123) Chuck McElroy	2.00
(124) Fred McGriff (SP, 1000)	15.00
(125) Mark McLemore	2.00
(126) Greg McMichael	2.00
(127) Blas Minor	2.00
(128) Dave Mlicki	2.00
(129) Mike Mohler	2.00
(130) Paul Molitor (SP, 1000)	40.00
(131) Steve Montgomery	2.00
(132) Mike Mordecai	2.00
(133) Mike Morgan	2.00
(134) Mike Munoz	2.00
(135) Greg Myers	2.00
(136) Jimmy Myers	2.00
(137) Mike Myers	2.00
(138) Bob Natal	2.00
(139) Dan Naulty	2.00
(140) Jeff Nelson	2.00
(141) Warren Newson	2.00
(142) Chris Nichting	2.00
(143) Melvin Nieves	2.00
(144) Charlie O'Brien	2.00
(145) Alex Ochoa	2.00
(146) Omar Olivares	2.00
(147) Joe Oliver	2.00
(148) Lance Painter	2.00
(149) Rafael Palmeiro (SP, 2000)	17.50
(150) Mark Parent	2.00
(151) Steve Parris (SP, 1800)	6.00
(152) Bob Patterson	2.00
(153) Tony Pena	2.00
(154) Eddie Perez	2.00
(155) Yorkis Perez	2.00
(156) Robert Person	2.00
(157) Mark Petkovsek	2.00
(158) Andy Pettitte (SP, 1000)	25.00
(159) J.R. Phillips	2.00
(160) Hipolito Pichardo	2.00
(161) Eric Plunk	2.00
(162) Jimmy Poole	2.00
(163) Kirby Puckett (SP, 1000)	75.00
(164) Paul Quantrill	2.00
(165) Tom Quinlan	2.00
(166) Jeff Reboulet	2.00
(167) Jeff Reed	2.00
(168) Steve Reed	2.00
(169) Carlos Reyes	2.00
(170) Bill Risley	2.00
(171) Kevin Ritz	2.00
(172) Kevin Roberson	2.00
(173) Rich Robertson	2.00
(174) Alex Rodriguez (SP, 500)	150.00
(175) Ivan Rodriguez (SP, 1250)	40.00
(176) Bruce Ruffin	2.00
(177) Juan Samuel	2.00
(178) Tim Scott	2.00
(179) Kevin Sefcik	2.00
(180) Jeff Shaw	2.00
(181) Danny Sheaffer	2.00
(182) Craig Shipley	2.00
(183) Dave Silvestri	2.00
(184) Aaron Small	2.00
(185) John Smoltz (SP, 1000)	25.00
(186) Luis Sojo	2.00
(187) Sammy Sosa (SP, 1000)	80.00
(188) Steve Sparks	2.00
(189) Tim Spehr	2.00
(190) Russ Springer	2.00
(191) Matt Stairs	2.00
(192) Andy Stankiewicz	2.00
(193) Mike Stanton	2.00
(194) Kelly Stinnett	2.00
(195) Doug Strange	2.00
(196) Mark Sweeney	2.00
(197) Jeff Tabaka	2.00
(198) Jesus Tavarez	2.00
(199) Frank Thomas (SP, 1000)	75.00
(200) Larry Thomas	2.00
(201) Mark Thompson	2.00
(202) Mike Timlin	2.00
(203) Steve Trachsel	4.00
(204) Tom Urbani	2.00
(205) Julio Valera	2.00
(206) Dave Valle	2.00
(207) William VanLandingham	2.00
(208) Mo Vaughn (SP, 1000)	35.00
(209) Dave Veres	2.00
(210) Ed Vosberg	2.00
(211) Don Wengert	2.00
(212) Matt Whiteside	2.00
(213) Bob Wickman	2.00
(214) Matt Williams (SP, 1250)	22.00
(215) Mike Williams	2.00
(216) Woody Williams	2.00
(217) Craig Worthington	2.00
--- Frank Thomas (Autographed jumbo)	40.00

1996 Leaf/ Signature Extended Autographs - Century Marks

Century Marks represent the first 100 autographs by the 31 stars and top prospects, and are designated with a "Century Marks" blue holographic foil logo. Several players' autographed cards were available only by mail-in redemption cards.

	MT
Common Player:	20.00
(1) Jay Buhner	25.00
(2) Ken Caminiti	25.00
(3) Roger Clemens	150.00
(4) Jermaine Dye	20.00
(5) Darin Erstad	60.00
(6) Karim Garcia	20.00
(7) Jason Giambi	20.00
(8) Tom Glavine	25.00
(9) Juan Gonzalez	100.00
(9) Juan Gonzalez (redemption card)	25.00
(10) Tony Gwynn	135.00
(11) Derek Jeter	135.00
(11) Derek Jeter (redemption card)	30.00
(12) Randy Johnson	50.00
(13) Andruw Jones	60.00
(13) Andruw Jones (redemption card)	15.00
(14) Jason Kendall	20.00
(15) Ryan Klesko	20.00
(16) Chuck Knoblauch	35.00
(17) Kenny Lofton	50.00
(18) Greg Maddux	150.00
(19) Fred McGriff	30.00
(20) Paul Molitor	50.00
(21) Alex Ochoa	20.00
(22) Rafael Palmeiro	20.00
(22) Rafael Palmeiro (redemption card)	5.00
(23) Andy Pettitte	25.00
(24) Kirby Puckett	100.00
(25) Alex Rodriguez	200.00
(25) Alex Rodriguez (redemption card)	40.00
(26) Ivan Rodriguez	75.00
(27) John Smoltz	25.00
(28) Sammy Sosa	175.00
(29) Frank Thomas	50.00
(30) Mo Vaughn	40.00
(31) Matt Williams	30.00

1997 Leaf

Leaf produced a 400-card set in two series in 1997. The cards feature a grey border with the player photo vignetted at center. The player's name, team and a Leaf logo are displayed at bottom in silver foil. A team logo is in the upper-right corner. Besides the base cards, 10-card packs retailing for $2.99 could contain one of the following inserts: Banner Season, Dress for Success, Get-A-Grip, Knot-hole Gang, Statistical Standouts, Fractal Matrix or Fractal Matrix Die-cut.

	MT
Complete Set (400):	40.00
Common Player:	.10
Jackie Robinson 1948 Leaf Reprint:	60.00
Wax Box:	45.00
1 Wade Boggs	.30
2 Brian McRae	.10
3 Jeff D'Amico	.10
4 George Arias	.10
5 Billy Wagner	.15
6 Ray Lankford	.10
7 Will Clark	.25
8 Edgar Renteria	.10
9 Alex Ochoa	.10
10 Roberto Hernandez	.10
11 Joe Carter	.15
12 Gregg Jefferies	.10
13 Mark Grace	.25
14 Roberto Alomar	.75
15 Joe Randa	.10
16 Alex Rodriguez	3.00
17 Tony Gwynn	1.25
18 Steve Gibralter	.10
19 Scott Stahoviak	.10
20 Matt Williams	.25
21 Quinton McCracken	.10
22 Ugueth Urbina	.10
23 Jermaine Allensworth	.10
24 Paul Molitor	.40
25 Carlos Delgado	.40
26 Bob Abreu	.10
27 John Jaha	.10
28 Rusty Greer	.10
29 Kimera Bartee	.10
30 Ruben Rivera	.15
31 Jason Kendall	.10
32 Lance Johnson	.10
33 Robin Ventura	.15
34 Kevin Appier	.10
35 John Mabry	.10
36 Ricky Otero	.10
37 Mike Lansing	.10
38 Mark McGwire	4.00
39 Tim Naehring	.10
40 Tom Glavine	.20
41 Rey Ordonez	.25
42 Tony Clark	.50
43 Rafael Palmeiro	.25
44 Pedro Martinez	.30
45 Keith Lockhart	.10
46 Dan Wilson	.10
47 John Wetteland	.10
48 Chan Ho Park	.15
49 Gary Sheffield	.40
50 Shawn Estes	.10
51 Royce Clayton	.10
52 Jaime Navarro	.10
53 Raul Casanova	.10
54 Jeff Bagwell	1.25
55 Barry Larkin	.20
56 Charles Nagy	.10
57 Ken Caminiti	.30

58	Todd Hollandsworth	.10
59	Pat Hentgen	.10
60	Jose Valentin	.10
61	Frank Rodriguez	.10
62	Mickey Tettleton	.10
63	Marty Cordova	.10
64	Cecil Fielder	.15
65	Barry Bonds	.75
66	Scott Servais	.10
67	Ernie Young	.10
68	Wilson Alvarez	.10
69	Mike Grace	.10
70	Shane Reynolds	.10
71	Henry Rodriguez	.10
72	Eric Karros	.10
73	Mark Langston	.10
74	Scott Karl	.10
75	Trevor Hoffman	.15
76	Orel Hershiser	.10
77	John Smoltz	.20
78	Raul Mondesi	.25
79	Jeff Brantley	.10
80	Donne Wall	.10
81	Joey Cora	.10
82	Mel Rojas	.10
83	Chad Mottola	.10
84	Omar Vizquel	.10
85	Greg Maddux	2.00
86	Jamey Wright	.10
87	Chuck Finley	.10
88	Brady Anderson	.10
89	Alex Gonzalez	.10
90	Andy Benes	.10
91	Reggie Jefferson	.10
92	Paul O'Neill	.15
93	Javier Lopez	.20
94	Mark Grudzielanek	.10
95	Marc Newfield	.10
96	Kevin Ritz	.10
97	Fred McGriff	.25
98	Dwight Gooden	.10
99	Hideo Nomo	.50
100	Steve Finley	.10
101	Juan Gonzalez	1.25
102	Jay Buhner	.15
103	Paul Wilson	.10
104	Alan Benes	.10
105	Manny Ramirez	1.00
106	Kevin Elster	.10
107	Frank Thomas	1.50
108	Orlando Miller	.10
109	Ramon Martinez	.10
110	Kenny Lofton	.75
111	Bernie Williams	.50
112	Robby Thompson	.10
113	Bernard Gilkey	.10
114	Ray Durham	.10
115	Jeff Cirillo	.10
116	Brian Jordan	.10
117	Rich Becker	.10
118	Al Leiter	.10
119	Mark Johnson	.10
120	Ellis Burks	.10
121	Sammy Sosa	1.50
122	Willie Greene	.10
123	Michael Tucker	.10
124	Eddie Murray	.40
125	Joey Hamilton	.10
126	Antonio Osuna	.10
127	Bobby Higginson	.10
128	Tomas Perez	.10
129	Tim Salmon	.25
130	Mark Wohlers	.10
131	Charles Johnson	.10
132	Randy Johnson	.50
133	Brooks Kieschnick	.10
134	Al Martin	.10
135	Dante Bichette	.20
136	Andy Pettitte	.75
137	Jason Giambi	.10
138	James Baldwin	.10
139	Ben McDonald	.10
140	Shawn Green	.15
141	Geronimo Berroa	.10
142	Jose Offerman	.10
143	Curtis Pride	.10
144	Terrell Wade	.10
145	Ismael Valdes	.10
146	Mike Mussina	.60
147	Mariano Rivera	.20
148	Ken Hill	.10
149	Darin Erstad	1.25
150	Jay Bell	.10
151	Mo Vaughn	.75
152	Ozzie Smith	.50
153	Jose Mesa	.10
154	Osvaldo Fernandez	.10
155	Vinny Castilla	.10
156	Jason Isringhausen	.10
157	B.J. Surhoff	.10
158	Robert Perez	.10
159	Ron Coomer	.10
160	Darren Oliver	.10
161	Mike Mohler	.10
162	Russ Davis	.10
163	Bret Boone	.10
164	Ricky Bottalico	.10
165	Derek Jeter	2.00
166	Orlando Merced	.10
167	John Valentin	.10
168	Andruw Jones	1.50
169	Angel Echevarria	.10
170	Todd Walker	.75
171	Desi Relaford	.10
172	Trey Beamon	.10
173	*Brian Giles*	1.50
174	Scott Rolen	1.25
175	Shannon Stewart	.10
176	Dmitri Young	.10
177	Justin Thompson	.10
178	Trot Nixon	.10
179	Josh Booty	.10
180	Robin Jennings	.10
181	Marvin Benard	.10
182	Luis Castillo	.15
183	Wendell Magee	.10
184	Vladimir Guerrero	1.50
185	Nomar Garciaparra	2.00
186	Ryan Hancock	.10
187	Mike Cameron	.10
188	Cal Ripken Jr. (Legacy)	1.25
189	Chipper Jones (Legacy)	1.00
190	Albert Belle (Legacy)	.50
191	Mike Piazza (Legacy)	1.00
192	Chuck Knoblauch (Legacy)	.10
193	Ken Griffey Jr. (Legacy)	1.50
194	Ivan Rodriguez (Legacy)	.25
195	Jose Canseco (Legacy)	.20
196	Ryne Sandberg (Legacy)	.35
197	Jim Thome (Legacy)	.20
198	Andy Pettitte (Checklist)	.35
199	Andruw Jones (Checklist)	.75
200	Derek Jeter (Checklist)	.60
201	Chipper Jones	2.00
202	Albert Belle	.75
203	Mike Piazza	2.00
204	Ken Griffey Jr.	4.00
205	Ryne Sandberg	.75
206	Jose Canseco	.25
207	Chili Davis	.10
208	Roger Clemens	1.00
209	Deion Sanders	.15
210	Darryl Hamilton	.10
211	Jermaine Dye	.10
212	Matt Williams	.25
213	Kevin Elster	.10
214	John Wetteland	.10
215	Garret Anderson	.10
216	Kevin Brown	.10
217	Matt Lawton	.10
218	Cal Ripken Jr.	2.50
219	Moises Alou	.10
220	Chuck Knoblauch	.20
221	Ivan Rodriguez	.60
222	Travis Fryman	.10
223	Jim Thome	.40
224	Eddie Murray	.35
225	Eric Young	.10
226	Ron Gant	.10
227	Tony Phillips	.10
228	Reggie Sanders	.10
229	Johnny Damon	.10
230	Bill Pulsipher	.10
231	Jim Edmonds	.10
232	Melvin Nieves	.10
233	Ryan Klesko	.25
234	David Cone	.20
235	Derek Bell	.10
236	Julio Franco	.10
237	Juan Guzman	.10
238	Larry Walker	.25
239	Delino DeShields	.10
240	Troy Percival	.10
241	Andres Galarraga	.15
242	Rondell White	.15
243	John Burkett	.10
244	J.T. Snow	.10
245	Alex Fernandez	.10
246	Edgar Martinez	.10
247	Craig Biggio	.15
248	Todd Hundley	.15
249	Jimmy Key	.10
250	Cliff Floyd	.10
251	Jeff Conine	.10
252	Curt Schilling	.10
253	Jeff King	.10
254	Tino Martinez	.15
255	Carlos Baerga	.10
256	Jeff Fassero	.10
257	Dean Palmer	.10
258	Robb Nen	.10
259	Sandy Alomar Jr.	.15
260	Carlos Perez	.10
261	Rickey Henderson	.20
262	Bobby Bonilla	.10
263	Darren Daulton	.10
264	Jim Leyritz	.10
265	Dennis Martinez	.10
266	Butch Huskey	.10
267	Joe Vitiello	.10
268	Steve Trachsel	.10
269	Glenallen Hill	.10
270	Terry Steinbach	.10
271	Mark McLemore	.10
272	Devon White	.10
273	Jeff Kent	.10
274	Tim Raines	.10
275	Carlos Garcia	.10
276	Hal Morris	.10
277	Gary Gaetti	.10
278	John Olerud	.15
279	Wally Joyner	.10
280	Brian Hunter	.10
281	Steve Karsay	.10
282	Denny Neagle	.10
283	Jose Herrera	.10
284	Todd Stottlemyre	.10
285	Bip Roberts	.10
286	Kevin Seitzer	.10
287	Benji Gil	.10
288	Dennis Eckersley	.10
289	Brad Ausmus	.10
290	Otis Nixon	.10
291	Darryl Strawberry	.10
292	Marquis Grissom	.10
293	Darryl Kile	.10
294	Quilvio Veras	.10
295	Tom Goodwin	.10
296	Benito Santiago	.10
297	Mike Bordick	.10
298	Roberto Kelly	.10
299	David Justice	.20
300	Carl Everett	.10
301	Mark Whiten	.10
302	Aaron Sele	.10
303	Darren Dreifort	.10
304	Bobby Jones	.10
305	Fernando Vina	.10
306	Ed Sprague	.10
307	Andy Ashby	.10
308	Tony Fernandez	.10
309	Roger Pavlik	.10
310	Mark Clark	.10
311	Mariano Duncan	.10
312	Tyler Houston	.10
313	Eric Davis	.10
314	Greg Vaughn	.15
315	David Segui	.10
316	Dave Nilsson	.10
317	F.P. Santangelo	.10
318	Wilton Guerrero	.10
319	Jose Guillen	1.00
320	Kevin Orie	.10
321	Derrek Lee	.10
322	*Bubba Trammell*	.75
323	Pokey Reese	.10
324	*Hideki Irabu*	1.50
325	Scott Spiezio	.10
326	Bartolo Colon	.10
327	Damon Mashore	.10
328	Ryan McGuire	.10
329	Chris Carpenter	.10
330	*Jose Cruz Jr.*	.75
331	Todd Greene	.10
332	Brian Moehler	.10
333	Mike Sweeney	.10
334	Neifi Perez	.10
335	Matt Morris	.10
336	Marvin Benard	.10
337	Karim Garcia	.10
338	Jason Dickson	.10
339	Brant Brown	.10
340	Jeff Suppan	.10
341	*Deivi Cruz*	.50
342	Antone Williamson	.10
343	Curtis Goodwin	.10
344	Brooks Kieschnick	.10
345	*Tony Womack*	.25
346	Rudy Pemberton	.10
347	Todd Dunwoody	.30
348	Frank Thomas (Legacy)	.75
349	Andruw Jones (Legacy)	.75
350	Alex Rodriguez (Legacy)	1.25
351	Greg Maddux (Legacy)	1.00
352	Jeff Bagwell (Legacy)	.75
353	Juan Gonzalez (Legacy)	.75
354	Barry Bonds (Legacy)	.40
355	Mark McGwire (Legacy)	2.00
356	Tony Gwynn (Legacy)	.75
357	Gary Sheffield (Legacy)	.20
358	Derek Jeter (Legacy)	1.00
359	Manny Ramirez (Legacy)	.50
360	Hideo Nomo (Legacy)	.25
361	Sammy Sosa (Legacy)	.75
362	Paul Molitor (Legacy)	.20
363	Kenny Lofton (Legacy)	.40
364	Eddie Murray (Legacy)	.20
365	Barry Larkin (Legacy)	.10
366	Roger Clemens (Legacy)	.50
367	John Smoltz (Legacy)	.10
368	Alex Rodriguez (Gamers)	1.25
369	Frank Thomas (Gamers)	.75
370	Cal Ripken Jr. (Gamers)	1.25
371	Ken Griffey Jr. (Gamers)	1.50
372	Greg Maddux (Gamers)	1.00
373	Mike Piazza (Gamers)	1.00
374	Chipper Jones (Gamers)	1.00
375	Albert Belle (Gamers)	.40
376	Chuck Knoblauch (Gamers)	.15
377	Brady Anderson (Gamers)	.10
378	David Justice (Gamers)	.10
379	Randy Johnson (Gamers)	.20
380	Wade Boggs (Gamers)	.15
381	Kevin Brown (Gamers)	.10
382	Tom Glavine (Gamers)	.10
383	Raul Mondesi (Gamers)	.10
384	Ivan Rodriguez (Gamers)	.30
385	Larry Walker (Gamers)	.10
386	Bernie Williams (Gamers)	.30
387	Rusty Greer (Gamers)	.10
388	Rafael Palmeiro (Gamers)	.10
389	Matt Williams (Gamers)	.15
390	Eric Young (Gamers)	.10
391	Fred McGriff (Gamers)	.10
392	Ken Caminiti (Gamers)	.10
393	Roberto Alomar (Gamers)	.30
394	Brian Jordan (Gamers)	.10
395	Mark Grace (Gamers)	.10
396	Jim Edmonds (Gamers)	.10
397	Deion Sanders (Gamers)	.10
398	Checklist (Vladimir Guerrero)	.50
399	Checklist (Darin Erstad)	.60
400	Checklist (Nomar Garciaparra)	.75

1997 Leaf Fractal Matrix

Leaf introduced Fractal Matrix inserts, a 400-card parallel set broken down into three colors and three unique die-cuts. Two fractures break the insert set down by foil background color only (80 Golds, 120 Silvers and 200 Bronze). A second fracture breaks those cards down into color and die-cutting variations. No production numbers or insert ratios were released for either fracture. Each player is available in only one color.

		MT
	Common Bronze:	1.00
	Common Silver:	2.00
	Common Gold:	4.00
	Common Gold Z-Axis:	5.00
	Common Gold Y-Axis:	10.00
	Common Gold X-Axis:	20.00
1	Wade Boggs G/Y	17.50
2	Brian McRae B/Y	1.00
3	Jeff D'Amico B/Y	1.00
4	George Arias S/Y	2.00
5	Billy Wagner S/Y	2.00
6	Ray Lankford B/Z	1.00
7	Will Clark S/Y	5.00
8	Edgar Renteria S/Y	2.00
9	Alex Ochoa S/Y	2.00
10	Roberto Hernandez	2.00
11	Joe Carter S/Y	3.00
12	Gregg Jefferies B/Y	1.00
13	Mark Grace S/Y	4.00
14	Roberto Alomar G/Y	25.00
15	Joe Randa B/X	1.00
16	Alex Rodriguez G/Z	65.00
17	Tony Gwynn G/Z	35.00
18	Steve Gibralter B/Y	1.00
19	Scott Stahoviak B/X	1.00
20	Matt Williams S/Z	7.50
21	Quinton McCracken B/Y	1.00
22	Ugueth Urbina B/X	1.00
23	Jermaine Allensworth S/X	3.00
24	Paul Molitor G/X	30.00
25	Carlos Delgado S/Y	4.00
26	Bob Abreu S/Y	3.00
27	John Jaha S/Y	3.00
28	Rusty Greer S/Z	2.00
29	Kimera Bartee B/X	1.00
30	Ruben Rivera S/Y	3.00
31	Jason Kendall S/Y	3.00
32	Lance Johnson B/X	1.00
33	Robin Ventura B/Y	1.00
34	Kevin Appier S/X	2.00
35	John Mabry S/Y	2.00
36	Ricky Otero B/X	1.00
37	Mike Lansing B/X	1.00
38	Mark McGwire G/Z	75.00
39	Tim Naehring B/X	1.00
40	Tom Glavine S/Z	3.00
41	Rey Ordonez S/Y	3.00
42	Tony Clark S/Y	10.00
43	Rafael Palmeiro S/Z	5.00
44	Pedro Martinez B/X	2.00
45	Keith Lockhart B/X	1.00
46	Dan Wilson B/Y	1.00
47	John Wetteland B/Y	1.00
48	Chan Ho Park B/X	1.00
49	Gary Sheffield G/Z	12.50
50	Shawn Estes B/X	1.00
51	Royce Clayton B/X	1.00
52	Jaime Navarro B/X	1.00
53	Raul Casanova B/X	1.00
54	Jeff Bagwell G/Z	30.00
55	Barry Larkin G/X	15.00
56	Charles Nagy B/Y	1.00
57	Ken Caminiti G/Y	20.00
58	Todd Hollandsworth S/Z	2.00
59	Pat Hentgen S/X	2.00
60	Jose Valentin B/X	1.00
61	Frank Rodriguez B/X	1.00
62	Mickey Tettleton B/X	1.00
63	Marty Cordova G/X	15.00
64	Cecil Fielder S/X	4.00
65	Barry Bonds G/Z	20.00
66	Scott Servais B/X	1.00
67	Ernie Young B/X	1.00
68	Wilson Alvarez B/X	1.00
69	Mike Grace B/X	1.00
70	Shane Reynolds S/X	3.00
71	Henry Rodriguez S/Y	2.00
72	Eric Karros B/X	1.00
73	Mark Langston B/X	1.00
74	Scott Karl B/X	1.00
75	Trevor Hoffman B/X	1.00
76	Orel Hershiser S/X	2.00
77	John Smoltz G/Y	15.00
78	Raul Mondesi G/Z	12.50
79	Jeff Brantley B/X	1.00
80	Donne Wall B/X	1.00
81	Joey Cora B/X	1.00
82	Mel Rojas B/X	1.00
83	Chad Mottola B/X	1.00
84	Omar Vizquel B/X	1.00
85	Greg Maddux G/Z	60.00
86	Jamey Wright S/Y	3.00
87	Chuck Finley B/X	1.00
88	Brady Anderson G/Y	10.00
89	Alex Gonzalez S/X	3.00
90	Andy Benes B/X	1.00
91	Reggie Jefferson B/X	1.00
92	Paul O'Neill B/Y	2.00
93	Javier Lopez S/X	4.00
94	Mark Grudzielanek S/X	3.00
95	Marc Newfield B/X	1.00
96	Kevin Ritz B/X	1.00
97	Fred McGriff G/Y	12.50
98	Dwight Gooden S/X	3.00
99	Hideo Nomo S/Y	12.50
100	Steve Finley B/X	1.00
101	Juan Gonzalez G/Z	35.00
102	Jay Buhner S/Z	4.00
103	Paul Wilson S/Y	2.00
104	Alan Benes B/Y	2.00
105	Manny Ramirez G/Z	15.00
106	Kevin Elster B/X	1.00
107	Frank Thomas G/Z	30.00
108	Orlando Miller B/X	1.00
109	Ramon Martinez B/X	2.00
110	Kenny Lofton G/Z	20.00
111	Bernie Williams G/Y	25.00
112	Robby Thompson B/X	1.00
113	Bernard Gilkey B/Z	1.00
114	Ray Durham B/X	1.00
115	Jeff Cirillo S/Z	2.00
116	Brian Jordan G/Z	5.00
117	Rich Becker S/Y	2.00
118	Al Leiter B/X	1.00
119	Mark Johnson B/X	1.00
120	Ellis Burks B/Y	2.00
121	Sammy Sosa G/Z	40.00
122	Willie Greene B/X	1.00
123	Michael Tucker B/X	1.00
124	Eddie Murray G/Y	20.00
125	Joey Hamilton S/Y	2.00
126	Antonio Osuna B/X	1.00
127	Bobby Higginson S/Y	3.00
128	Tomas Perez B/X	1.00
129	Tim Salmon G/Z	10.00
130	Mark Wohlers B/X	1.00
131	Charles Johnson S/X	2.00
132	Randy Johnson S/Y	10.00
133	Brooks Kieschnick S/X	3.00
134	Al Martin S/Y	2.00

135 Dante Bichette B/X 2.00
136 Andy Pettitte G/Z 20.00
137 Jason Giambi G/Y 10.00
138 James Baldwin S/X 2.00
139 Ben McDonald B/X 1.00
140 Shawn Green S/X 2.00
141 Geronimo Berroa B/Y 1.00
142 Jose Offerman B/X 1.00
143 Curtis Pride B/X 1.00
144 Terrell Wade B/X 1.00
145 Ismael Valdes S/X 2.00
146 Mike Mussina S/Y 12.50
147 Mariano Rivera S/X 5.00
148 Ken Hill B/Y 1.00
149 Darin Erstad G/Z 35.00
150 Jay Bell B/X 1.00
151 Mo Vaughn G/Z 20.00
152 Ozzie Smith G/Y 30.00
153 Jose Mesa B/X 1.00
154 Osvaldo Fernandez B/X 1.00
155 Vinny Castilla B/Y 1.00
156 Jason Isringhausen S/Y 2.00
157 B.J. Surhoff B/X 1.00
158 Robert Perez B/X 1.00
159 Ron Coomer B/X 1.00
160 Darren Oliver B/X 1.00
161 Mike Mohler B/X 1.00
162 Russ Davis B/X 1.00
163 Bret Boone B/X 1.00
164 Ricky Bottalico B/X 1.00
165 Derek Jeter G/Z 50.00
166 Orlando Merced B/X 1.00
167 John Valentin B/X 1.00
168 Andruw Jones G/Z 40.00
169 Angel Echevarria B/X 1.00
170 Todd Walker G/Z 15.00
171 Desi Relaford B/Y 1.00
172 Trey Beamon S/X 2.00
173 Brian Giles S/Y 2.00
174 Scott Rolen G/Z 35.00
175 Shannon Stewart S/Z 2.00
176 Dmitri Young G/Z 5.00
177 Justin Thompson B/X 1.00
178 Trot Nixon S/Y 2.00
179 Josh Booty S/Y 2.00
180 Robin Jennings B/X 1.00
181 Marvin Benard B/X 1.00
182 Luis Castillo B/Y 1.00
183 Wendell Magee B/X 1.00
184 Vladimir Guerrero G/X 50.00
185 Nomar Garciaparra G/X 60.00
186 Ryan Hancock B/X 1.00
187 Mike Cameron S/X 6.00
188 Cal Ripken Jr. B/Z (Legacy) 15.00
189 Chipper Jones S/Z (Legacy) 25.00
190 Albert Belle S/Z (Legacy) 10.00
191 Mike Piazza B/Z (Legacy) 12.50
192 Chuck Knoblauch S/Y (Legacy) 6.00
193 Ken Griffey Jr. B/Z (Legacy) 20.00
194 Ivan Rodriguez G/Z (Legacy) 15.00
195 Jose Canseco S/X (Legacy) 10.00
196 Ryne Sandberg S/X (Legacy) 20.00
197 Jim Thome G/Y (Legacy) 20.00
198 Checklist (Andy Pettitte B/Y) 6.00
199 Checklist (Andruw Jones B/Y) 10.00
200 Checklist (Derek Jeter S/Y) 30.00
201 Chipper Jones G/X 60.00
202 Albert Belle G/Y 25.00
203 Mike Piazza G/Y 50.00
204 Ken Griffey Jr. G/X 175.00
205 Ryne Sandberg G/Z 12.50
206 Jose Canseco S/Y 4.00
207 Chili Davis B/X 1.00
208 Roger Clemens G/Z 15.00
209 Deion Sanders G/Z 7.50
210 Darryl Hamilton B/X 1.00
211 Jermaine Dye S/X 2.00
212 Matt Williams G/Y 12.50
213 Kevin Elster B/X 1.00
214 John Wetteland S/X 2.00
215 Garret Anderson G/Z 5.00
216 Kevin Brown G/Y 10.00
217 Matt Lawton S/Y 2.00
218 Cal Ripken Jr. G/X 125.00
219 Moises Alou G/Y 10.00
220 Chuck Knoblauch G/Z 7.50
221 Ivan Rodriguez G/Y 20.00
222 Travis Fryman B/Y 1.00
223 Jim Thome G/Z 10.00
224 Eddie Murray S/Z 7.50
225 Eric Young G/Z 5.00
226 Ron Gant S/X 2.00
227 Tony Phillips B/X 1.00
228 Reggie Sanders B/Y 1.00
229 Johnny Damon S/Z 2.00
230 Bill Pulsipher B/X 1.00
231 Jim Edmonds G/Z 5.00
232 Melvin Nieves B/X 1.00
233 Ryan Klesko G/Z 7.50
234 David Cone S/X 2.00
235 Derek Bell B/Y 1.00
236 Julio Franco S/X 2.00
237 Juan Guzman B/X 1.00
238 Larry Walker G/Z 7.50
239 Delino DeShields B/X 1.00
240 Troy Percival B/Y 1.00
241 Andres Galarraga G/Z 6.00
242 Rondell White G/Z 5.00
243 John Burkett B/X 1.00
244 J.T. Snow B/Y 1.00
245 Alex Fernandez S/Y 2.00
246 Edgar Martinez G/Z 5.00
247 Craig Biggio G/Z 5.00
248 Todd Hundley G/Y 10.00
249 Jimmy Key S/X 2.00
250 Cliff Floyd B/Y 1.00
251 Jeff Conine B/Y 1.00
252 Curt Schilling B/X 1.00
253 Jeff King B/X 1.00
254 Tino Martinez G/Z 7.50
255 Carlos Baerga S/Y 2.00
256 Jeff Fassero B/Y 1.00
257 Dean Palmer S/Y 2.00
258 Robb Nen B/X 1.00
259 Sandy Alomar Jr. S/Y 2.00
260 Carlos Perez B/X 1.00
261 Rickey Henderson S/Y 2.00
262 Bobby Bonilla S/Y 2.00
263 Darren Daulton B/X 1.00
264 Jim Leyritz B/X 1.00
265 Dennis Martinez B/X 1.00
266 Butch Huskey B/X 1.00
267 Joe Vitiello S/Y 2.00
268 Steve Trachsel B/X 1.00
269 Glenallen Hill B/X 1.00
270 Terry Steinbach B/X 1.00
271 Mark McLemore B/X 1.00
272 Devon White B/X 1.00
273 Jeff Kent B/X 1.00
274 Tim Raines B/X 1.00
275 Carlos Garcia B/X 1.00
276 Hal Morris B/X 1.00
277 Gary Gaetti B/X 1.00
278 John Olerud S/Y 2.00
279 Wally Joyner B/X 1.00
280 Brian Hunter S/X 2.00
281 Steve Karsay B/X 1.00
282 Denny Neagle S/X 2.00
283 Jose Herrera B/X 1.00
284 Todd Stottlemyre B/X 1.00
285 Bip Roberts S/X 2.00
286 Kevin Seitzer B/X 1.00
287 Benji Gil B/X 1.00
288 Dennis Eckersley S/X 2.00
289 Brad Ausmus B/X 1.00
290 Otis Nixon B/X 1.00
291 Darryl Strawberry B/X 1.00
292 Marquis Grissom S/Y 2.00
293 Darryl Kile B/X 1.00
294 Quilvio Veras B/X 1.00
295 Tom Goodwin B/X 1.00
296 Benito Santiago B/X 1.00
297 Mike Bordick B/X 1.00
298 Roberto Kelly B/X 1.00
299 David Justice G/Z 7.50
300 Carl Everett B/X 1.00
301 Mark Whiten B/X 1.00
302 Aaron Sele B/X 1.00
303 Darren Dreifort B/X 1.00
304 Bobby Jones B/X 1.00
305 Fernando Vina B/X 1.00
306 Ed Sprague B/X 1.00
307 Andy Ashby S/X 2.00
308 Tony Fernandez B/X 1.00
309 Roger Pavlik B/X 1.00
310 Mark Clark B/X 1.00
311 Mariano Duncan B/X 1.00
312 Tyler Houston B/X 1.00
313 Eric Davis S/Y 2.00
314 Greg Vaughn B/Y 1.00
315 David Segui S/Y 2.00
316 Dave Nilsson S/X 2.00
317 F.P. Santangelo S/X 2.00
318 Wilton Guerrero G/Z 5.00
319 Jose Guillen G/Z 12.50
320 Kevin Orie S/Y 2.00
321 Derrek Lee G/Z 5.00
322 Bubba Trammell S/Y 7.50
323 Pokey Reese G/Z 5.00
324 Hideki Irabu G/X 30.00
325 Scott Spiezio S/Z 2.00
326 Bartolo Colon G/Z 5.00
327 Damon Mashore S/Y 2.00
328 Ryan McGuire S/Y 2.00
329 Chris Carpenter B/X 1.00
330 Jose Cruz, Jr. G/X 20.00
331 Todd Greene S/Z 3.00
332 Brian Moehler B/X 1.00
333 Mike Sweeney B/Y 1.00
334 Neifi Perez G/Z 5.00
335 Matt Morris S/Y 2.00
336 Marvin Benard B/Y 1.00
337 Karim Garcia S/Z 2.00
338 Jason Dickson S/Y 2.00
339 Brant Brown S/Y 2.00
340 Jeff Suppan S/Z 2.00
341 Deivi Cruz B/X 2.00
342 Antone Williamson G/Z 5.00
343 Curtis Goodwin B/X 1.00
344 Brooks Kieschnick S/Y 2.00
345 Tony Womack B/X 1.00
346 Rudy Pemberton B/X 1.00
347 Todd Dunwoody B/X 1.00
348 Frank Thomas S/Y (Legacy) 12.50
349 Andruw Jones S/X (Legacy) 12.50
350 Alex Rodriguez B/Y (Legacy) 15.00
351 Greg Maddux S/Y (Legacy) 20.00
352 Jeff Bagwell B/Y (Legacy) 10.00
353 Juan Gonzalez S/Y (Legacy) 15.00
354 Barry Bonds B/Y (Legacy) 5.00
355 Mark McGwire B/Y (Legacy) 15.00
356 Tony Gwynn B/Y (Legacy) 10.00
357 Gary Sheffield B/X (Legacy) 2.00
358 Derek Jeter S/X (Legacy) 15.00
359 Manny Ramirez S/Y (Legacy) 7.50
360 Hideo Nomo G/Z (Legacy) 7.50
361 Sammy Sosa B/X (Legacy) 10.00
362 Paul Molitor S/Z (Legacy) 4.00
363 Kenny Lofton B/Y (Legacy) 5.00
364 Eddie Murray B/X (Legacy) 3.00
365 Barry Larkin S/Z (Legacy) 3.00
366 Roger Clemens S/Y (Legacy) 10.00
367 John Smoltz B/Z (Legacy) 1.00
368 Alex Rodriguez S/X (Gamers) 20.00
369 Frank Thomas B/X (Gamers) 7.50
370 Cal Ripken Jr. S/Y (Gamers) 25.00
371 Ken Griffey Jr. S/Y (Gamers) 35.00
372 Greg Maddux B/X (Gamers) 10.00
373 Mike Piazza S/X (Gamers) 15.00
374 Chipper Jones B/Y (Gamers) 10.00
375 Albert Belle B/X (Gamers) 5.00
376 Chuck Knoblauch B/X (Gamers) 2.00
377 Brady Anderson B/Z (Gamers) 1.00
378 David Justice S/X (Gamers) 4.00
379 Randy Johnson B/Z (Gamers) 4.00
380 Wade Boggs B/X (Gamers) 2.00
381 Kevin Brown B/X (Gamers) 1.00
382 Tom Glavine G/Y (Gamers) 10.00
383 Raul Mondesi S/X (Gamers) 3.00
384 Ivan Rodriguez S/X (Gamers) 5.00
385 Larry Walker B/Y (Gamers) 2.00
386 Bernie Williams B/Z (Gamers) 3.00
387 Rusty Greer G/Y (Gamers) 10.00
388 Rafael Palmeiro G/Y (Gamers) 10.00
389 Matt Williams B/X (Gamers) 2.00
390 Eric Young B/X (Gamers) 1.00
391 Fred McGriff B/X (Gamers) 2.00
392 Ken Caminiti B/X (Gamers) 1.50
393 Roberto Alomar B/Z (Gamers) 4.00
394 Brian Jordan B/X (Gamers) 1.00
395 Mark Grace G/Z (Gamers) 7.50
396 Jim Edmonds B/Y (Gamers) 1.00
397 Deion Sanders S/Y (Gamers) 3.00
398 Checklist (Vladimir Guerrero S/Z) 7.50
399 Checklist (Darin Erstad S/Y) 10.00
400 Checklist (Nomar Garciaparra S/Z) 12.50

1997 Leaf Fractal Matrix Die-Cut

A second parallel set to the Leaf product, the Fractal Matrix Die-Cuts offer three different die-cut designs with three different styles for each. The Axis-X die-cuts consist of 200 cards (150 bronze, 40 silver and 10 gold), the Axis-Y die-cuts consist of 120 cards (60 silver, 40 bronze, 20 gold), and the Axis-Z die-cuts consist of 80 cards (50 gold, 20 silver, 10 bronze). Odds of finding any of these inserts are 1:6 packs. Each player was issued in only one color/cut combination.

	MT
Complete Set (400):	
Common X-Axis:	4.00
Common Y-Axis:	6.00
Y-Axis Unlisted Stars:	10.00
Common Z-Axis:	10.00
Z-Axis Unlisted Stars:	15.00

1 Wade Boggs G/Y 17.50
2 Brian McRae B/Y 6.00
3 Jeff D'Amico B/Y 6.00
4 George Arias S/Y 6.00
5 Billy Wagner S/Y 6.00
6 Ray Lankford B/Z 10.00
7 Will Clark S/Y 10.00
8 Edgar Renteria S/Y 6.00
9 Alex Ochoa S/Y 6.00
11 Joe Carter S/Y 6.00
12 Gregg Jefferies B/Y 6.00
13 Mark Grace S/Y 9.00
14 Roberto Alomar G/Y 25.00
15 Joe Randa B/X 4.00
16 Alex Rodriguez G/Z 125.00
17 Tony Gwynn G/Z 75.00
18 Steve Gibralter B/Y 6.00
19 Scott Stahoviak B/X 4.00
20 Matt Williams S/Z 25.00
21 Quinton McCracken B/Y 6.00
22 Ugueth Urbina B/X 4.00
23 Jermaine Allensworth S/X 4.00
24 Paul Molitor G/X 12.50
25 Carlos Delgado S/Y 6.00
26 Bob Abreu S/Y 6.00
27 John Jaha S/Y 6.00
28 Rusty Greer S/Z 10.00
29 Kimera Bartee B/X 4.00
30 Ruben Rivera S/Y 6.00
31 Jason Kendall S/Y 6.00
32 Lance Johnson B/X 4.00
33 Robin Ventura B/Y 6.00
34 Kevin Appier S/X 4.00
35 John Mabry S/Y 6.00
36 Ricky Otero B/X 4.00
37 Mike Lansing B/X 4.00
38 Mark McGwire G/Z 150.00
39 Tim Naehring B/X 4.00
40 Tom Glavine S/Z 12.50
41 Rey Ordonez S/Y 6.00
42 Tony Clark S/Y 20.00
43 Rafael Palmeiro S/Z 12.50
44 Pedro Martinez B/X 5.00
45 Keith Lockhart B/X 4.00
46 Dan Wilson B/Y 6.00
47 John Wetteland B/Y 6.00
48 Chan Ho Park B/X 4.00
49 Gary Sheffield G/Z 30.00
50 Shawn Estes B/X 4.00
51 Royce Clayton B/X 4.00
52 Jaime Navarro B/X 4.00
53 Raul Casanova B/X 4.00
54 Jeff Bagwell G/Z 75.00
55 Barry Larkin G/X 6.00
56 Charles Nagy B/Y 6.00
57 Ken Caminiti G/Y 20.00
58 Todd Hollandsworth S/Z 10.00
59 Pat Hentgen S/X 4.00
60 Jose Valentin B/X 4.00
61 Frank Rodriguez B/X 4.00
62 Mickey Tettleton B/X 4.00
63 Marty Cordova G/X 5.00
64 Cecil Fielder S/X 6.00
65 Barry Bonds G/Z 40.00
66 Scott Servais B/X 4.00
67 Ernie Young B/X 4.00
68 Wilson Alvarez B/X 4.00
69 Mike Grace B/X 6.00
70 Shane Reynolds S/X 4.00
71 Henry Rodriguez S/Y 6.00
72 Eric Karros B/X 4.00
73 Mark Langston B/X 4.00
74 Scott Karl B/X 4.00
75 Trevor Hoffman B/X 4.00
76 Orel Hershiser S/X 4.00
77 John Smoltz G/Y 20.00
78 Raul Mondesi G/Z 15.00
79 Jeff Brantley B/X 4.00
80 Donne Wall B/X 4.00
81 Joey Cora B/X 4.00
82 Mel Rojas B/X 4.00
83 Chad Mottola B/X 4.00
84 Omar Vizquel B/X 4.00
85 Greg Maddux G/Z 100.00
86 Jamey Wright S/Y 6.00
87 Chuck Finley B/X 4.00
88 Brady Anderson G/Y 7.50
89 Alex Gonzalez S/X 4.00
90 Andy Benes B/X 4.00
91 Reggie Jefferson B/X 4.00
92 Paul O'Neill B/Y 7.50
93 Javier Lopez S/X 6.00
94 Mark Grudzielanek S/X 4.00
95 Marc Newfield B/X 4.00
96 Kevin Ritz B/X 4.00
97 Fred McGriff G/Y 10.00
98 Dwight Gooden S/X 5.00
99 Hideo Nomo S/Y 25.00
100 Steve Finley B/X 4.00
101 Juan Gonzalez G/Z 75.00
102 Jay Buhner S/Z 12.50
103 Paul Wilson S/Y 6.00
104 Alan Benes B/Y 6.00
105 Manny Ramirez G/Z 30.00
106 Kevin Elster B/X 4.00
107 Frank Thomas G/Z 60.00
108 Orlando Miller B/X 4.00
109 Ramon Martinez B/X 4.00
110 Kenny Lofton G/Z 40.00
111 Bernie Williams G/Y 25.00
112 Robby Thompson B/X 4.00
113 Bernard Gilkey B/Z 10.00
114 Ray Durham B/X 4.00
115 Jeff Cirillo S/Z 10.00
116 Brian Jordan G/Z 10.00
117 Rich Becker S/Y 6.00
118 Al Leiter B/X 4.00
119 Mark Johnson B/X 4.00
120 Ellis Burks B/Y 6.00
121 Sammy Sosa G/Z 65.00
122 Willie Greene B/X 4.00
123 Michael Tucker B/X 4.00
124 Eddie Murray G/Y 20.00
125 Joey Hamilton S/Y 6.00
126 Antonio Osuna B/X 4.00
127 Bobby Higginson S/Y 7.50
128 Tomas Perez B/X 4.00
129 Tim Salmon G/Z 15.00
130 Mark Wohlers B/X 4.00
131 Charles Johnson S/X 4.00
132 Randy Johnson S/Y 20.00
133 Brooks Kieschnick S/X 4.00
134 Al Martin S/Y 4.00
135 Dante Bichette B/X 6.00
136 Andy Pettitte G/Z 30.00
137 Jason Giambi G/Y 10.00
138 James Baldwin S/X 4.00
139 Ben McDonald B/X 4.00
140 Shawn Green S/X 4.00
141 Geronimo Berroa B/Y 6.00
142 Jose Offerman B/X 4.00
143 Curtis Pride B/X 4.00
144 Terrell Wade B/X 4.00
145 Ismael Valdes S/X 4.00
146 Mike Mussina S/Y 20.00
147 Mariano Rivera S/X 7.50
148 Ken Hill B/Y 6.00
149 Darin Erstad G/Z 50.00
150 Jay Bell B/X 4.00
151 Mo Vaughn G/Z 40.00
152 Ozzie Smith G/Y 30.00
153 Jose Mesa B/X 4.00
154 Osvaldo Fernandez B/X 4.00
155 Vinny Castilla B/Y 6.00
156 Jason Isringhausen S/Y 6.00
157 B.J. Surhoff B/X 4.00
158 Robert Perez B/X 4.00
159 Ron Coomer B/X 4.00
160 Darren Oliver B/X 4.00
161 Mike Mohler B/X 4.00
162 Russ Davis B/X 4.00
163 Bret Boone B/X 4.00
164 Ricky Bottalico B/X 4.00
165 Derek Jeter G/Z 100.00
166 Orlando Merced B/X 4.00
167 John Valentin B/X 4.00
168 Andruw Jones G/Z 80.00
169 Angel Echevarria B/X 4.00
170 Todd Walker G/Z 25.00
171 Desi Relaford B/Y 6.00
172 Trey Beamon S/X 4.00
173 Brian Giles S/Y 6.00
174 Scott Rolen G/Z 50.00
175 Shannon Stewart S/Z 10.00
176 Dmitri Young G/Z 10.00
177 Justin Thompson B/X 4.00
178 Trot Nixon S/Y 6.00
179 Josh Booty S/Y 5.00
180 Robin Jennings B/X 4.00
181 Marvin Benard B/X 4.00
182 Luis Castillo B/Y 6.00
183 Wendell Magee B/X 4.00
184 Vladimir Guerrero G/X 25.00

185	Nomar Garciaparra G/X	30.00
186	Ryan Hancock B/X	4.00
187	Mike Cameron S/X	7.50
188	Cal Ripken Jr. B/Z (Legacy)	125.00
189	Chipper Jones S/Z (Legacy)	100.00
190	Albert Belle S/Z (Legacy)	40.00
191	Mike Piazza B/Z (Legacy)	100.00
192	Chuck Knoblauch S/Y (Legacy)	10.00
193	Ken Griffey Jr. B/Z (Legacy)	150.00
194	Ivan Rodriguez G/Z (Legacy)	30.00
195	Jose Canseco S/X (Legacy)	10.00
196	Ryne Sandberg S/X (Legacy)	20.00
197	Jim Thome G/Y (Legacy)	25.00
198	Checklist (Andy Pettitte B/Y)	20.00
199	Checklist (Andruw Jones B/Y)	50.00
200	Checklist (Derek Jeter S/Y)	60.00
201	Chipper Jones G/X	30.00
202	Albert Belle G/Y	35.00
203	Mike Piazza G/Y	60.00
204	Ken Griffey Jr. G/X	50.00
205	Ryne Sandberg G/Z	35.00
206	Jose Canseco S/Y	10.00
207	Chili Davis B/X	4.00
208	Roger Clemens G/Z	50.00
209	Deion Sanders G/Z	15.00
210	Darryl Hamilton B/X	4.00
211	Jermaine Dye S/X	4.00
212	Matt Williams G/Y	17.50
213	Kevin Elster B/X	4.00
214	John Wetteland S/X	4.00
215	Garret Anderson G/Z	10.00
216	Kevin Brown G/Y	6.00
217	Matt Lawton S/Y	6.00
218	Cal Ripken Jr. G/X	35.00
219	Moises Alou G/Y	7.50
220	Chuck Knoblauch G/Z	20.00
221	Ivan Rodriguez G/Y	25.00
222	Travis Fryman B/Y	6.00
223	Jim Thome G/Z	25.00
224	Eddie Murray S/Z	25.00
225	Eric Young G/Z	10.00
226	Ron Gant S/X	4.00
227	Tony Phillips B/X	4.00
228	Reggie Sanders B/Y	6.00
229	Johnny Damon S/Z	10.00
230	Bill Pulsipher B/X	4.00
231	Jim Edmonds G/Z	12.50
232	Melvin Nieves B/X	4.00
233	Ryan Klesko G/Z	25.00
234	David Cone S/X	4.00
235	Derek Bell B/Y	6.00
236	Julio Franco S/X	4.00
237	Juan Guzman B/X	4.00
238	Larry Walker G/Z	20.00
239	Delino DeShields B/X	4.00
240	Troy Percival B/Y	6.00
241	Andres Galarraga G/Z	15.00
242	Rondell White G/Z	10.00
243	John Burkett B/X	4.00
244	J.T. Snow B/Y	6.00
245	Alex Fernandez S/Y	6.00
246	Edgar Martinez G/Z	10.00
247	Craig Biggio G/Z	10.00
248	Todd Hundley G/Y	7.50
249	Jimmy Key S/X	4.00
250	Cliff Floyd B/Y	6.00
251	Jeff Conine B/Y	6.00
252	Curt Schilling B/X	4.00
253	Jeff King B/X	4.00
254	Tino Martinez G/Z	17.50
255	Carlos Baerga S/Y	6.00
256	Jeff Fassero B/Y	6.00
257	Dean Palmer S/Y	6.00
258	Robb Nen B/X	4.00
259	Sandy Alomar Jr. S/Y	6.00
260	Carlos Perez B/X	4.00
261	Rickey Henderson S/Y	6.00
262	Bobby Bonilla S/Y	6.00
263	Darren Daulton B/X	4.00
264	Jim Leyritz B/X	4.00
265	Dennis Martinez B/X	4.00
266	Butch Huskey B/X	4.00
267	Joe Vitiello S/Y	6.00
268	Steve Trachsel B/X	4.00
269	Glenallen Hill B/X	4.00
270	Terry Steinbach B/X	4.00
271	Mark McLemore B/X	4.00
272	Devon White B/X	4.00
273	Jeff Kent B/X	4.00
274	Tim Raines B/X	4.00
275	Carlos Garcia B/X	4.00
276	Hal Morris B/X	4.00
277	Gary Gaetti B/X	4.00
278	John Olerud S/Y	6.00
279	Wally Joyner B/X	4.00
280	Brian Hunter S/X	4.00
281	Steve Karsay B/X	4.00
282	Denny Neagle S/X	4.00
283	Jose Herrera B/X	4.00
284	Todd Stottlemyre B/X	4.00
285	Bip Roberts S/X	4.00
286	Kevin Seitzer B/X	4.00
287	Benji Gil B/X	4.00
288	Dennis Eckersley S/X	4.00
289	Brad Ausmus B/X	4.00
290	Otis Nixon B/X	4.00
291	Darryl Strawberry B/X	4.00
292	Marquis Grissom S/Y	6.00
293	Darryl Kile B/X	4.00
294	Quilvio Veras B/X	4.00
295	Tom Goodwin B/X	4.00
296	Benito Santiago B/X	4.00
297	Mike Bordick B/X	4.00
298	Roberto Kelly B/X	4.00
299	David Justice G/Z	15.00
300	Carl Everett B/X	4.00
301	Mark Whiten B/X	4.00
302	Aaron Sele B/X	4.00
303	Darren Dreifort B/X	4.00
304	Bobby Jones B/X	4.00
305	Fernando Vina B/X	4.00
306	Ed Sprague B/X	4.00
307	Andy Ashby S/X	4.00
308	Tony Fernandez B/X	4.00
309	Roger Pavlik B/X	4.00
310	Mark Clark B/X	4.00
311	Mariano Duncan B/X	4.00
312	Tyler Houston B/X	4.00
313	Eric Davis S/Y	6.00
314	Greg Vaughn B/Y	6.00
315	David Segui S/Y	6.00
316	Dave Nilsson S/X	4.00
317	F.P. Santangelo S/X	4.00
318	Wilton Guerrero G/Z	10.00
319	Jose Guillen G/Z	35.00
320	Kevin Orie S/Y	6.00
321	Derrek Lee G/Z	10.00
322	Bubba Trammell S/Y	25.00
323	Pokey Reese G/Z	10.00
324	Hideki Irabu G/X	20.00
325	Scott Spiezio S/Z	10.00
326	Bartolo Colon G/Z	10.00
327	Damon Mashore S/Y	6.00
328	Ryan McGuire S/Y	6.00
329	Chris Carpenter B/X	4.00
330	Jose Cruz, Jr. G/X	12.50
331	Todd Greene S/Z	15.00
332	Brian Moehler B/X	4.00
333	Mike Sweeney B/Y	6.00
334	Neifi Perez G/Z	10.00
335	Matt Morris S/Y	6.00
336	Marvin Benard B/Y	6.00
337	Karim Garcia S/Z	12.50
338	Jason Dickson S/Y	6.00
339	Brant Brown S/Y	6.00
340	Jeff Suppan S/Z	10.00
341	Deivi Cruz B/X	5.00
342	Antone Williamson G/Z	10.00
343	Curtis Goodwin B/X	4.00
344	Brooks Kieschnick S/Y	6.00
345	Tony Womack B/X	4.00
346	Rudy Pemberton B/X	4.00
347	Todd Dunwoody B/X	4.00
348	Frank Thomas S/Y (Legacy)	35.00
349	Andruw Jones S/X (Legacy)	20.00
350	Alex Rodriguez B/Y (Legacy)	60.00
351	Greg Maddux S/Y (Legacy)	50.00
352	Jeff Bagwell B/Y (Legacy)	35.00
353	Juan Gonzalez S/Y (Legacy)	35.00
354	Barry Bonds B/Y (Legacy)	25.00
355	Mark McGwire B/Y (Legacy)	75.00
356	Tony Gwynn B/Y (Legacy)	35.00
357	Gary Sheffield B/X (Legacy)	6.00
358	Derek Jeter S/X (Legacy)	20.00
359	Manny Ramirez S/Y (Legacy)	17.50
360	Hideo Nomo G/Z (Legacy)	15.00
361	Sammy Sosa B/X (Legacy)	15.00
362	Paul Molitor S/Z (Legacy)	15.00
363	Kenny Lofton B/Y (Legacy)	25.00
364	Eddie Murray B/X (Legacy)	7.50
365	Barry Larkin S/Z (Legacy)	12.50
366	Roger Clemens S/Y (Legacy)	25.00
367	John Smoltz B/Z (Legacy)	10.00
368	Alex Rodriguez S/X (Gamers)	35.00
369	Frank Thomas B/X (Gamers)	20.00
370	Cal Ripken Jr. S/Y (Gamers)	60.00
371	Ken Griffey Jr. S/Y (Gamers)	85.00
372	Greg Maddux B/X (Gamers)	20.00
373	Mike Piazza S/X (Gamers)	20.00
374	Chipper Jones B/Y (Gamers)	45.00
375	Albert Belle B/X (Gamers)	7.50
376	Chuck Knoblauch B/X (Gamers)	7.50
377	Brady Anderson B/Z (Gamers)	10.00
378	David Justice S/X (Gamers)	6.00
379	Randy Johnson B/Z (Gamers)	20.00
380	Wade Boggs B/X (Gamers)	6.00
381	Kevin Brown B/X (Gamers)	4.00
382	Tom Glavine G/Y (Gamers)	6.00
383	Raul Mondesi S/X (Gamers)	6.00
384	Ivan Rodriguez S/X (Gamers)	7.50
385	Larry Walker B/Y (Gamers)	10.00
386	Bernie Williams B/Z (Gamers)	20.00
387	Rusty Greer G/Y (Gamers)	6.00
388	Rafael Palmeiro G/Y (Gamers)	7.50
389	Matt Williams B/X (Gamers)	6.00
390	Eric Young B/X (Gamers)	4.00
391	Fred McGriff B/X (Gamers)	6.00
392	Ken Caminiti B/X (Gamers)	5.00
393	Roberto Alomar B/Z (Gamers)	20.00
394	Brian Jordan B/X (Gamers)	4.00
395	Mark Grace G/Z (Gamers)	15.00
396	Jim Edmonds B/Y (Gamers)	6.00
397	Deion Sanders S/Y (Gamers)	9.00
398	Checklist (Vladimir Guerrero S/Z)	25.00
399	Checklist (Darin Erstad S/Y)	25.00
400	Checklist (Nomar Garciaparra S/Z)	35.00

1997 Leaf Banner Season

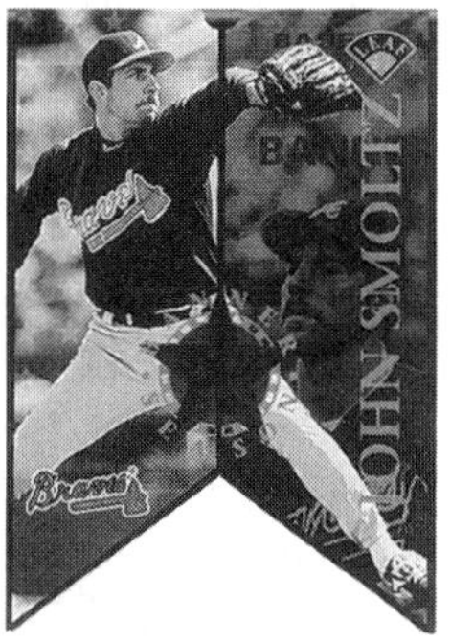

Banner Season was a 15-card insert set that was die-cut and printed on a canvas card stock. Only 2,500 individually numbered sets were produced, with cards only found in pre-priced packs.

		MT
Complete Set (15):		200.00
Common Player:		2.50
1	Jeff Bagwell	20.00
2	Ken Griffey Jr.	50.00
3	Juan Gonzalez	25.00
4	Frank Thomas	20.00
5	Alex Rodriguez	40.00
6	Kenny Lofton	12.00
7	Chuck Knoblauch	5.00
8	Mo Vaughn	12.00
9	Chipper Jones	30.00
10	Ken Caminiti	5.00
11	Craig Biggio	5.00
12	John Smoltz	2.50
13	Pat Hentgen	2.50
14	Derek Jeter	25.00
15	Todd Hollandsworth	2.50

1997 Leaf Dress for Success

Exclusive to retail packs was an insert called Dress for Success. It included 18 players printed on nylon and flocking card stock. Dress for Success was limited to 3,500 individually numbered sets.

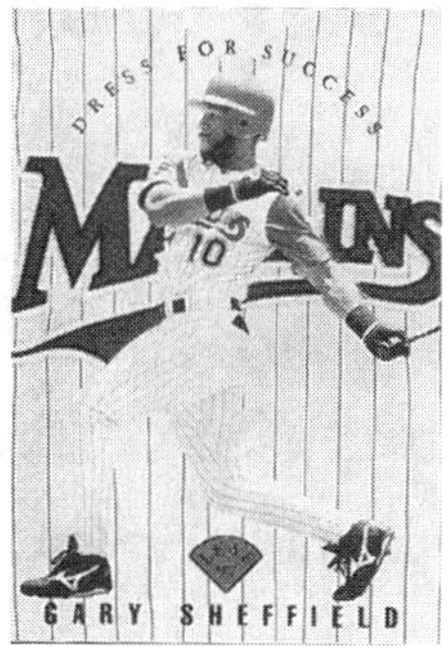

		MT
Complete Set (18):		150.00
Common Player:		2.50
1	Greg Maddux	10.00
2	Cal Ripken Jr.	15.00
3	Albert Belle	5.00
4	Frank Thomas	10.00
5	Dante Bichette	2.50
6	Gary Sheffield	4.00
7	Jeff Bagwell	9.00
8	Mike Piazza	12.50
9	Mark McGwire	25.00
10	Ken Caminiti	4.00
11	Alex Rodriguez	15.00
12	Ken Griffey Jr.	25.00
13	Juan Gonzalez	9.00
14	Brian Jordan	2.50
15	Mo Vaughn	5.00
16	Ivan Rodriguez	4.00
17	Andruw Jones	10.00
18	Chipper Jones	12.50

1997 Leaf Get-A-Grip

Get a Grip included 16 double-sided cards, with a star hitter on one side and a star pitcher on the other. The card slated the two stars against each other and explained how the hitter would hit against the pitcher, while featuring the pitcher's top pitch. This insert was printed on silver foilboard with the right side die-cut, and limited to 3,500 numbered sets found only in hobby packs.

		MT
Complete Set (16):		250.00
Common Player:		6.00
1	Ken Griffey Jr., Greg Maddux	40.00
2	John Smoltz, Frank Thomas	15.00
3	Mike Piazza, Andy Pettitte	25.00
4	Randy Johnson, Chipper Jones	25.00
5	Tom Glavine, Alex Rodriguez	35.00
6	Pat Hentgen, Jeff Bagwell	15.00
7	Kevin Brown, Juan Gonzalez	15.00
8	Barry Bonds, Mike Mussina	12.00
9	Hideo Nomo, Albert Belle	9.00
10	Troy Percival, Andruw Jones	15.00
11	Roger Clemens, Brian Jordan	15.00
12	Paul Wilson, Ivan Rodriguez	10.00
13	Andy Benes, Mo Vaughn	6.00
14	Al Leiter, Derek Jeter	25.00
15	Bill Pulsipher, Cal Ripken Jr.	30.00
16	Mariano Rivera, Ken Caminiti	6.00

1997 Leaf Knot-Hole Gang Samples

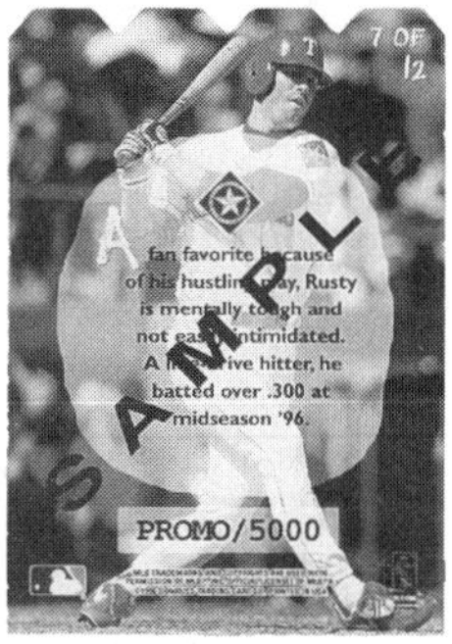

Because of the die-cutting and wooden "fence" overlay, it was impractical to produce a sample of just one card for this insert set, so each of the regularly issued cards can also be found with a "SAMPLE" overprint on front and back, and a "PROMO/5000" serial number on back.

		MT
Complete Set (12):		32.00
Common Player:		2.00
1	Chuck Knoblauch	2.00
2	Ken Griffey Jr.	7.50
3	Frank Thomas	4.00
4	Tony Gwynn	3.50
5	Mike Piazza	5.00
6	Jeff Bagwell	3.00
7	Rusty Greer	2.00
8	Cal Ripken Jr.	6.00
9	Chipper Jones	5.00
10	Ryan Klesko	2.00
11	Barry Larkin	2.00
12	Paul Molitor	3.00

1997 Leaf Knot-Hole Gang

Knot-Hole Gang pictured 12 hitters against a wood picket fence in the background. Cards were die-cut along the top of the fence and printed on a wood card stock. Set production was limited to 5,000 and these inserts were found in all types of packs.

		MT
Complete Set (12):		90.00
Common Player:		2.50
1	Chuck Knoblauch	3.00
2	Ken Griffey Jr.	20.00
3	Frank Thomas	10.00
4	Tony Gwynn	10.00
5	Mike Piazza	15.00
6	Jeff Bagwell	10.00
7	Rusty Greer	2.50
8	Cal Ripken Jr.	17.50
9	Chipper Jones	15.00
10	Ryan Klesko	2.50
11	Barry Larkin	2.50
12	Paul Molitor	5.00

-07571997 Leaf Leagues of the Nation

A 15-card insert set featuring a double-sided die-cut design. The players on each card represent matchups from the initial rounds of inter-league play. Cards were numbered to 2,500 and feature a flocked texture.

		MT
	Complete Set (15):	300.00
	Common Player:	10.00
1	Juan Gonzalez, Barry Bonds	20.00
2	Cal Ripken Jr., Chipper Jones	35.00
3	Mark McGwire, Ken Caminiti	40.00
4	Derek Jeter, Kenny Lofton	25.00
5	Ivan Rodriguez, Mike Piazza	25.00
6	Ken Griffey Jr., Larry Walker	45.00
7	Frank Thomas, Sammy Sosa	30.00
8	Paul Molitor, Barry Larkin	10.00
9	Albert Belle, Deion Sanders	10.00
10	Matt Williams, Jeff Bagwell	15.00
11	Mo Vaughn, Gary Sheffield	10.00
12	Alex Rodriguez, Tony Gwynn	35.00
13	Tino Martinez, Scott Rolen	15.00
14	Darin Erstad, Wilton Guerrero	15.00
15	Tony Clark, Vladimir Guerrero	15.00

1997 Leaf Statistical Standouts

Statistical Standouts were limited to only 1,000 individually numbered sets. Inserts were printed on leather and die-cut. The set included 15 top stars who excelled beyond their competition in many statistical categories.

		MT
	Complete Set (15):	450.00
	Common Player:	10.00
1	Albert Belle	15.00
2	Juan Gonzalez	30.00
3	Ken Griffey Jr.	65.00
4	Alex Rodriguez	50.00
5	Frank Thomas	30.00
6	Chipper Jones	40.00
7	Greg Maddux	35.00
8	Mike Piazza	40.00
9	Cal Ripken Jr.	50.00
10	Mark McGwire	65.00
11	Barry Bonds	15.00
12	Derek Jeter	40.00
13	Ken Caminiti	10.00
14	John Smoltz	10.00
15	Paul Molitor	10.00

1997 Leaf Thomas Collection

This six-card insert from Series II features pieces of various game-used Frank Thomas items built into the texture of each card. Jerseys, bats, hats, batting gloves and sweatbands are all featured on the various cards, which are numbered to 100 each.

		MT
	Complete Set (6):	2000.
	Common Thomas:	350.00
1	Frank Thomas Hat	300.00
2	Frank Thomas Home Jersey	400.00
3	Frank Thomas Batting Glove	300.00
4	Frank Thomas Bat	300.00
5	Frank Thomas Sweatband	300.00
6	Frank Thomas Away Jersey	400.00

1997 Leaf Warning Track

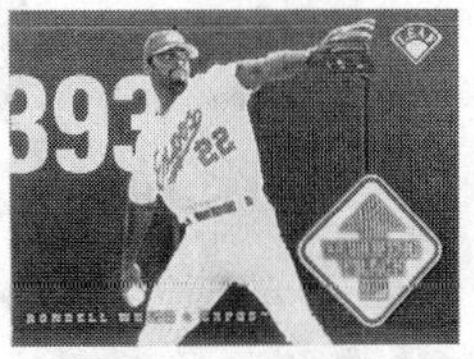

A 12-card insert printed on embossed canvas depicting players who are known for making tough catches. Cards were numbered to 3,500.

		MT
	Complete Set (18):	100.00
	Common Player:	2.00
1	Ken Griffey Jr.	30.00
2	Albert Belle	8.00
3	Barry Bonds	8.00
4	Andruw Jones	8.00
5	Kenny Lofton	6.00
6	Tony Gwynn	15.00
7	Manny Ramirez	10.00
8	Rusty Greer	2.00
9	Bernie Williams	6.00
10	Gary Sheffield	5.00
11	Juan Gonzalez	15.00
12	Raul Mondesi	5.00
13	Brady Anderson	2.00
14	Rondell White	2.00
15	Sammy Sosa	20.00
16	Deion Sanders	3.00
17	David Justice	3.00
18	Jim Edmonds	2.00

1997 Leaf 22kt Gold Stars

A 36-card insert from Series II Leaf, each card features a special 22kt. gold foil embossed stamp on front which is printed on gold foil cardboard. Horizontal backs have a portrait photo on a dark background and are serially numbered to a limit of 2,500 each.

		MT
	Complete Set (36):	300.00
	Common Player:	2.50
1	Frank Thomas	15.00
2	Alex Rodriguez	25.00
3	Ken Griffey Jr.	30.00
4	Andruw Jones	12.50
5	Chipper Jones	20.00
6	Jeff Bagwell	10.00
7	Derek Jeter	17.50
8	Deion Sanders	2.50
9	Ivan Rodriguez	7.50
10	Juan Gonzalez	15.00
11	Greg Maddux	17.50
12	Andy Pettitte	6.00
13	Roger Clemens	12.50
14	Hideo Nomo	5.00
15	Tony Gwynn	15.00
16	Barry Bonds	7.50
17	Kenny Lofton	6.00
18	Paul Molitor	6.00
19	Jim Thome	4.00
20	Albert Belle	7.50
21	Cal Ripken Jr.	25.00
22	Mark McGwire	30.00
23	Barry Larkin	3.00
24	Mike Piazza	20.00
25	Darin Erstad	10.00
26	Chuck Knoblauch	3.00
27	Vladimir Guerrero	10.00
28	Tony Clark	4.00
29	Scott Rolen	15.00
30	Nomar Garciaparra	20.00
31	Eric Young	2.50
32	Ryne Sandberg	7.50
33	Roberto Alomar	6.00
34	Eddie Murray	3.00
35	Rafael Palmeiro	3.00
36	Jose Guillen	4.00

1998 Leaf

The 50th Anniversary edition of Leaf Baseball consists of a 200-card base set with three subsets, three parallels and four inserts. The base set has 147 regular cards, a 10-card Curtain Calls subset, Gold Leaf Stars subset (20 cards), Gold Leaf Rookies subset (20 cards) and three checklists. Card #42 does not exist because Leaf retired the number in honor of Jackie Robinson. The base set was paralleled in Fractal Matrix, Fractal Matrix Die-Cuts and Fractal Diamond Axis. Inserts include Crusade, Heading for the Hall, State Representatives and Statistical Standouts.

		MT
	Complete Set (200):	200.00
	Common Player:	.10
	Wax Box:	65.00
1	Rusty Greer	.10
2	Tino Martinez	.25
3	Bobby Bonilla	.15
4	Jason Giambi	.10
5	Matt Morris	.20
6	Craig Counsell	.10
7	Reggie Jefferson	.10
8	Brian Rose	.20
9	Ruben Rivera	.10
10	Shawn Estes	.10
11	Tony Gwynn	1.50
12	Jeff Abbott	.10
13	Jose Cruz Jr.	.20
14	Francisco Cordova	.10
15	Ryan Klesko	.25
16	Tim Salmon	.30
17	Brett Tomko	.10
18	Matt Williams	.25
19	Joe Carter	.15
20	Harold Baines	.10
21	Gary Sheffield	.25
22	Charles Johnson	.15
23	Aaron Boone	.20
24	Eddie Murray	.20
25	Matt Stairs	.10
26	David Cone	.20
27	Jon Nunnally	.10
28	Chris Stynes	.10
29	Enrique Wilson	.10
30	Randy Johnson	.50
31	Garret Anderson	.10
32	Manny Ramirez	1.00
33	Jeff Suppan	.10
34	Rickey Henderson	.20
35	Scott Spiezio	.10
36	Rondell White	.20
37	Todd Greene	.20
38	Delino DeShields	.10
39	Kevin Brown	.20
40	Chili Davis	.10
41	Jimmy Key	.10
42	NOT ISSUED	
43	Mike Mussina	.60
44	Joe Randa	.10
45	Chan Ho Park	.20
46	Brad Radke	.10
47	Geronimo Berroa	.10
48	Wade Boggs	.25
49	Kevin Appier	.10
50	Moises Alou	.20
51	David Justice	.25
52	Ivan Rodriguez	.75
53	J.T. Snow	.20
54	Brian Giles	.10
55	Will Clark	.25
56	Justin Thompson	.10
57	Javier Lopez	.20
58	Hideki Irabu	.30
59	Mark Grudzielanek	.10
60	Abraham Nunez	.10
61	Todd Hollandsworth	.10
62	Jay Bell	.10
63	Nomar Garciaparra	2.00
64	Vinny Castilla	.10
65	Lou Collier	.10
66	Kevin Orie	.10
67	John Valentin	.10
68	Robin Ventura	.20
69	Denny Neagle	.10
70	Tony Womack	.10
71	Dennis Reyes	.10
72	Wally Joyner	.10
73	Kevin Brown	.20
74	Ray Durham	.10
75	Mike Cameron	.15
76	Dante Bichette	.15
77	Jose Guillen	.25
78	Carlos Delgado	.50
79	Paul Molitor	.40
80	Jason Kendall	.10
81	Mark Belhorn	.10
82	Damian Jackson	.10
83	Bill Mueller	.10
84	Kevin Young	.10
85	Curt Schilling	.20
86	Jeffrey Hammonds	.10
87	Sandy Alomar Jr.	.20
88	Bartolo Colon	.10
89	Wilton Guerrero	.10
90	Bernie Williams	.50
91	Deion Sanders	.20
92	Mike Piazza	2.00
93	Butch Huskey	.10
94	Edgardo Alfonzo	.10
95	Alan Benes	.20
96	Craig Biggio	.20
97	Mark Grace	.25
98	Shawn Green	.20
99	Derrek Lee	.20
100	Ken Griffey Jr.	3.00
101	Tim Raines	.10
102	Pokey Reese	.10
103	Lee Stevens	.10
104	Shannon Stewart	.10
105	John Smoltz	.20
106	Frank Thomas	1.00
107	Jeff Fassero	.10
108	Jay Buhner	.15
109	Jose Canseco	.25
110	Omar Vizquel	.10
111	Travis Fryman	.10
112	Dave Nilsson	.10
113	John Olerud	.15
114	Larry Walker	.25
115	Jim Edmonds	.15
116	Bobby Higginson	.20
117	Todd Hundley	.10
118	Paul O'Neill	.20
119	Bip Roberts	.10
120	Ismael Valdes	.10
121	Pedro Martinez	.25
122	Jeff Cirillo	.10
123	Andy Benes	.15
124	Bobby Jones	.10
125	Brian Hunter	.10
126	Darryl Kile	.10
127	Pat Hentgen	.10
128	Marquis Grissom	.10
129	Eric Davis	.10
130	Chipper Jones	2.00
131	Edgar Martinez	.10
132	Andy Pettitte	.40
133	Cal Ripken Jr.	2.50
134	Scott Rolen	1.50
135	Ron Coomer	.10
136	Luis Castillo	.10
137	Fred McGriff	.20
138	Neifi Perez	.10
139	Eric Karros	.20
140	Alex Fernandez	.10
141	Jason Dickson	.10
142	Lance Johnson	.10
143	Ray Lankford	.10
144	Sammy Sosa	3.00
145	Eric Young	.10
146	Bubba Trammell	.20
147	Todd Walker	.20
148	Mo Vaughn (Curtain Calls)	3.00
149	Jeff Bagwell (Curtain Calls)	5.00
150	Kenny Lofton (Curtain Calls)	3.00
151	Raul Mondesi (Curtain Calls)	1.50
152	Mike Piazza (Curtain Calls)	10.00
153	Chipper Jones (Curtain Calls)	8.00
154	Larry Walker (Curtain Calls)	1.50
155	Greg Maddux (Curtain Calls)	10.00
156	Ken Griffey Jr. (Curtain Calls)	15.00
157	Frank Thomas (Curtain Calls)	6.00
158	Darin Erstad (Gold Leaf Stars)	3.00
159	Roberto Alomar (Gold Leaf Stars)	2.00
160	Albert Belle (Gold Leaf Stars)	3.00
161	Jim Thome (Gold Leaf Stars)	1.50
162	Tony Clark (Gold Leaf Stars)	2.00
163	Chuck Knoblauch (Gold Leaf Stars)	1.50
164	Derek Jeter (Gold Leaf Stars)	8.00
165	Alex Rodriguez (Gold Leaf Stars)	8.00
166	Tony Gwynn (Gold Leaf Stars)	6.00
167	Roger Clemens (Gold Leaf Stars)	5.00
168	Barry Larkin (Gold Leaf Stars)	1.00
169	Andres Galarraga (Gold Leaf Stars)	1.00
170	Vladimir Guerrero (Gold Leaf Stars)	3.00
171	Mark McGwire (Gold Leaf Stars)	20.00
172	Barry Bonds (Gold Leaf Stars)	3.00
173	Juan Gonzalez (Gold Leaf Stars)	6.00
174	Andruw Jones (Gold Leaf Stars)	6.00
175	Paul Molitor (Gold Leaf Stars)	2.00
176	Hideo Nomo (Gold Leaf Stars)	1.50
177	Cal Ripken Jr. (Gold Leaf Stars)	12.00
178	Brad Fullmer (Gold Leaf Rookies)	1.50
179	Jaret Wright (Gold Leaf Rookies)	8.00
180	Bobby Estalella (Gold Leaf Rookies)	.75
181	Ben Grieve (Gold Leaf Rookies)	5.00
182	Paul Konerko (Gold Leaf Rookies)	4.00
183	David Ortiz (Gold Leaf Rookies)	1.00
184	Todd Helton (Gold Leaf Rookies)	3.00
185	Juan Encarnacion (Gold Leaf Rookies)	.75
186	Miguel Tejada (Gold Leaf Rookies)	3.00
187	Jacob Cruz (Gold Leaf Rookies)	1.00
188	Mark Kotsay (Gold Leaf Rookies)	1.50
189	Fernando Tatis (Gold Leaf Rookies)	1.00
190	Ricky Ledee (Gold Leaf Rookies)	1.50
191	Richard Hidalgo (Gold Leaf Rookies)	.75
192	Richie Sexson (Gold Leaf Rookies)	.75
193	Luis Ordaz (Gold Leaf Rookies)	.75
194	Eli Marrero (Gold Leaf Rookies)	.75
195	Livan Hernandez (Gold Leaf Rookies)	1.50
196	Homer Bush (Gold Leaf Rookies)	.75
197	Raul Ibanez (Gold Leaf Rookies)	.75
198	Checklist (Nomar Garciaparra)	1.50
199	Checklist (Scott Rolen)	1.00

200 Checklist (Jose Cruz Jr.) .10
201 Al Martin

1998 Leaf Fractal Foundation

Fractal Foundations is a stand-alone product but it parallels the 1998 Leaf set. It contains the Curtain Calls, Gold Leaf Stars and Gold Leaf Rookies subsets and is missing card #42 which Leaf retired in honor of Jackie Robinson. The set was printed on foil board and each card is numbered to 3,999. The set is paralleled in Fractal Materials, Fractal Materials Die-Cuts and Fractal Materials Z2 Axis.

		MT
Complete Set (200):		250.00
Common Player:		.50
Semistars:		1.50
Unlisted Stars:		2.50
Wax Box:		62.00
1	Rusty Greer	.50
2	Tino Martinez	1.50
3	Bobby Bonilla	1.00
4	Jason Giambi	.50
5	Matt Morris	1.00
6	Craig Counsell	.50
7	Reggie Jefferson	.50
8	Brian Rose	1.50
9	Ruben Rivera	.50
10	Shawn Estes	.50
11	Tony Gwynn	5.00
12	Jeff Abbott	.50
13	Jose Cruz Jr.	1.00
14	Francisco Cordova	.50
15	Ryan Klesko	1.50
16	Tim Salmon	1.50
17	Brett Tomko	.50
18	Matt Williams	1.50
19	Joe Carter	1.00
20	Harold Baines	.50
21	Gary Sheffield	1.50
22	Charles Johnson	1.00
23	Aaron Boone	.50
24	Eddie Murray	1.50
25	Matt Stairs	.50
26	David Cone	1.00
27	Jon Nunnally	.50
28	Chris Stynes	.50
29	Enrique Wilson	.50
30	Randy Johnson	2.00
31	Garret Anderson	.50
32	Manny Ramirez	2.50
33	Jeff Suppan	.50
34	Rickey Henderson	.50
35	Scott Spiezio	.50
36	Rondell White	1.00
37	Todd Greene	.50
38	Delino DeShields	.50
39	Kevin Brown	1.00
40	Chili Davis	.50
41	Jimmy Key	.50
42	NOT ISSUED	
43	Mike Mussina	2.50
44	Joe Randa	.50
45	Chan Ho Park	1.00
46	Brad Radke	.50
47	Geronimo Berroa	.50
48	Wade Boggs	1.50
49	Kevin Appier	.50
50	Moises Alou	1.00
51	David Justice	1.50
52	Ivan Rodriguez	2.50
53	J.T. Snow	.50
54	Brian Giles	.50
55	Will Clark	1.50
56	Justin Thompson	.50
57	Javier Lopez	1.00
58	Hideki Irabu	1.00
59	Mark Grudzielanek	.50
60	Abraham Nunez	.50
61	Todd Hollandsworth	.50
62	Jay Bell	.50
63	Nomar Garciaparra	6.00
64	Vinny Castilla	1.00
65	Lou Collier	.50
66	Kevin Orie	.50
67	John Valentin	.50
68	Robin Ventura	1.00
69	Denny Neagle	1.00
70	Tony Womack	.50
71	Dennis Reyes	.50
72	Wally Joyner	.50
73	Kevin Brown	1.00
74	Ray Durham	.50
75	Mike Cameron	1.00
76	Dante Bichette	1.50
77	Jose Guillen	1.50
78	Carlos Delgado	1.50
79	Paul Molitor	2.00
80	Jason Kendall	.50
81	Mark Belhorn	.50
82	Damian Jackson	.50
83	Bill Mueller	.50
84	Kevin Young	.50
85	Curt Schilling	1.00
86	Jeffrey Hammonds	.50
87	Sandy Alomar Jr.	1.00
88	Bartolo Colon	.50
89	Wilton Guerrero	.50
90	Bernie Williams	2.00
91	Deion Sanders	1.50
92	Mike Piazza	6.00
93	Butch Huskey	.50
94	Edgardo Alfonzo	.50
95	Alan Benes	1.00
96	Craig Biggio	1.00
97	Mark Grace	1.25
98	Shawn Green	.50
99	Derrek Lee	1.50
100	Ken Griffey Jr.	10.00
101	Tim Raines	.50
102	Pokey Reese	.50
103	Lee Stevens	.50
104	Shannon Stewart	.50
105	John Smoltz	1.00
106	Frank Thomas	4.00
107	Jeff Fassero	.50
108	Jay Buhner	1.50
109	Jose Canseco	1.50
110	Omar Vizquel	.50
111	Travis Fryman	.50
112	Dave Nilsson	.50
113	John Olerud	.50
114	Larry Walker	1.50
115	Jim Edmonds	1.00
116	Bobby Higginson	1.00
117	Todd Hundley	.50
118	Paul O'Neill	1.00
119	Bip Roberts	.50
120	Ismael Valdes	.50
121	Pedro Martinez	2.00
122	Jeff Cirillo	.50
123	Andy Benes	1.00
124	Bobby Jones	.50
125	Brian Hunter	.50
126	Darryl Kile	.50
127	Pat Hentgen	.50
128	Marquis Grissom	.50
129	Eric Davis	.50
130	Chipper Jones	6.00
131	Edgar Martinez	.50
132	Andy Pettitte	1.50
133	Cal Ripken Jr.	7.50
134	Scott Rolen	4.00
135	Ron Coomer	.50
136	Luis Castillo	.50
137	Fred McGriff	1.00
138	Neifi Perez	.50
139	Eric Karros	1.00
140	Alex Fernandez	.50
141	Jason Dickson	.50
142	Lance Johnson	.50
143	Ray Lankford	.50
144	Sammy Sosa	5.00
145	Eric Young	.50
146	Bubba Trammell	1.00
147	Todd Walker	1.00
148	Mo Vaughn (Curtain Calls)	3.00
149	Jeff Bagwell (Curtain Calls)	4.00
150	Kenny Lofton (Curtain Calls)	2.50
151	Raul Mondesi (Curtain Calls)	1.00
152	Mike Piazza (Curtain Calls)	6.00
153	Chipper Jones (Curtain Calls)	6.00
154	Larry Walker (Curtain Calls)	1.50
155	Greg Maddux (Curtain Calls)	6.00
156	Ken Griffey Jr. (Curtain Calls)	10.00
157	Frank Thomas (Curtain Calls)	4.00
158	Darin Erstad (Gold Leaf Stars)	2.50
159	Roberto Alomar (Gold Leaf Stars)	2.00
160	Albert Belle (Gold Leaf Stars)	2.50
161	Jim Thome (Gold Leaf Stars)	1.50
162	Tony Clark (Gold Leaf Stars)	1.50
163	Chuck Knoblauch (Gold Leaf Stars)	1.25
164	Derek Jeter (Gold Leaf Stars)	5.00
165	Alex Rodriguez (Gold Leaf Stars)	6.00
166	Tony Gwynn (Gold Leaf Stars)	5.00
167	Roger Clemens (Gold Leaf Stars)	4.00
168	Barry Larkin (Gold Leaf Stars)	1.50
169	Andres Galarraga (Gold Leaf Stars)	1.50
170	Vladimir Guerrero (Gold Leaf Stars)	2.50
171	Mark McGwire (Gold Leaf Stars)	12.50
172	Barry Bonds (Gold Leaf Stars)	2.50
173	Juan Gonzalez (Gold Leaf Stars)	5.00
174	Andruw Jones (Gold Leaf Stars)	3.00
175	Paul Molitor (Gold Leaf Stars)	2.00
176	Hideo Nomo (Gold Leaf Stars)	2.00
177	Cal Ripken Jr. (Gold Leaf Stars)	7.50
178	Brad Fullmer (Gold Leaf Rookies)	1.50
179	Jaret Wright (Gold Leaf Rookies)	4.00
180	Bobby Estalella (Gold Leaf Rookies)	.50
181	Ben Grieve (Gold Leaf Rookies)	4.00
182	Paul Konerko (Gold Leaf Rookies)	2.00
183	David Ortiz (Gold Leaf Rookies)	1.00
184	Todd Helton (Gold Leaf Rookies)	2.50
185	Juan Encarnacion (Gold Leaf Rookies)	.50
186	Miguel Tejada (Gold Leaf Rookies)	2.00
187	Jacob Cruz (Gold Leaf Rookies)	.50
188	Mark Kotsay (Gold Leaf Rookies)	1.00
189	Fernando Tatis (Gold Leaf Rookies)	.50
190	Ricky Ledee (Gold Leaf Rookies)	1.00
191	Richard Hidalgo (Gold Leaf Rookies)	.50
192	Richie Sexson (Gold Leaf Rookies)	.50
193	Luis Ordaz (Gold Leaf Rookies)	.50
194	Eli Marrero (Gold Leaf Rookies)	.50
195	Livan Hernandez (Gold Leaf Rookies)	1.00
196	Homer Bush (Gold Leaf Rookies)	.50
197	Raul Ibanez (Gold Leaf Rookies)	.50
198	Checklist (Nomar Garciaparra)	3.00
199	Checklist (Scott Rolen)	2.00
200	Checklist (Jose Cruz Jr.)	.50

1998 Leaf Diamond Axis

	MT
Common Player:	10.00
Diamond Axis Stars: 50X	
Young Stars/RCs: 30X	
SP (148-177): 12X	
(See 1998 Leaf for checklist and base card values.)	

1998 Leaf Fractal Foundation Z2 Axis

This 200-card set parallels Leaf Fractal Materials and was numbered to 20 sets.

	MT
Common Player:	15.00
Z2 Stars: 15-20X	
Production 20 sets	
(See 1998 Leaf Fractal Foundation for checklist and base card prices.)	

1998 Leaf Fractal Materials

The Fractal Materials set parallels 1998 Leaf Fractal Foundations. Every card in the set is sequentially numbered. The 200 card set was printed on four different materials: 100 plastic cards (numbered to 3,250), 50 leather (numbered to 1,000), 30 nylon (500) and 20 wood (250). This set was inserted one per pack.

		MT
Common Plastic (3,250):		.50
Common Leather (1,000):		2.00
Common Nylon (500):		5.00
Common Wood (250):		20.00
Wax Box:		120.00
1	Rusty Greer N	5.00
2	Tino Martinez W	15.00
3	Bobby Bonilla N	7.50
4	Jason Giambi N	5.00
5	Matt Morris L	4.00
6	Craig Counsell P	.50
7	Reggie Jefferson P	.50
8	Brian Rose P	.50
9	Ruben Rivera L	2.00
10	Shawn Estes L	4.00
11	Tony Gwynn W	50.00
12	Jeff Abbott P	.50
13	Jose Cruz Jr. W	15.00
14	Francisco Cordova P	.50
15	Ryan Klesko L	7.50
16	Tim Salmon W	15.00
17	Brett Tomko L	2.00
18	Matt Williams N	10.00
19	Joe Carter P	.50
20	Harold Baines P	.50
21	Gary Sheffield N	12.50
22	Charles Johnson L	4.00
23	Aaron Boone P	.50
24	Eddie Murray N	12.50
25	Matt Stairs P	.50
26	David Cone P	1.00
27	Jon Nunnally P	.50
28	Chris Stynes P	.50
29	Enrique Wilson P	.50
30	Randy Johnson W	20.00
31	Garret Anderson N	5.00
32	Manny Ramirez W	25.00
33	Jeff Suppan L	2.00
34	Rickey Henderson N	10.00
35	Scott Spiezio P	.50
36	Rondell White L	4.00
37	Todd Greene N	5.00
38	Delino DeShields P	.50
39	Kevin Brown L	4.00
40	Chili Davis P	.50
41	Jimmy Key P	.50
42	NOT ISSUED	
43	Mike Mussina N	15.00
44	Joe Randa P	.50
45	Chan Ho Park N	7.50
46	Brad Radke P	.50
47	Geronimo Berroa P	.50
48	Wade Boggs N	12.50
49	Kevin Appier P	.50
50	Moises Alou N	7.50
51	David Justice N	10.00
52	Ivan Rodriguez W	25.00
53	J.T. Snow L	3.00
54	Brian Giles P	.50
55	Will Clark L	7.50
56	Justin Thompson N	5.00
57	Javier Lopez P	1.00
58	Hideki Irabu L	7.50
59	Mark Grudzielanek P	.50
60	Abraham Nunez P	.50
61	Todd Hollandsworth P	.50
62	Jay Bell P	.50
63	Nomar Garciaparra W	60.00
64	Vinny Castilla P	1.00
65	Lou Collier P	.50
66	Kevin Orie L	2.00
67	John Valentin P	.50
68	Robin Ventura P	1.00
69	Denny Neagle P	.50
70	Tony Womack L	2.00
71	Dennis Reyes L	2.00
72	Wally Joyner P	.50
73	Kevin Brown P	1.00
74	Ray Durham P	.50
75	Mike Cameron N	7.50
76	Dante Bichette L	6.00
77	Jose Guillen N	7.50
78	Carlos Delgado L	4.00
79	Paul Molitor W	20.00
80	Jason Kendall P	.50
81	Mark Belhorn L	2.00
82	Damian Jackson P	.50
83	Bill Mueller P	.50
84	Kevin Young P	.50
85	Curt Schilling P	1.00
86	Jeffrey Hammonds P	.50
87	Sandy Alomar Jr. L	4.00
88	Bartolo Colon P	1.00
89	Wilton Guerrero L	2.00
90	Bernie Williams N	15.00
91	Deion Sanders N	10.00
92	Mike Piazza W	65.00
93	Butch Huskey L	2.00
94	Edgardo Alfonzo L	2.00
95	Alan Benes L	4.00
96	Craig Biggio N	10.00
97	Mark Grace L	6.00
98	Shawn Green L	2.00
99	Derrek Lee L	5.00
100	Ken Griffey Jr. W	100.00
101	Tim Raines P	.50
102	Pokey Reese P	.50
103	Lee Stevens P	.50
104	Shannon Stewart N	5.00
105	John Smoltz L	5.00
106	Frank Thomas W	40.00
107	Jeff Fassero P	.50
108	Jay Buhner L	6.00
109	Jose Canseco L	7.50
110	Omar Vizquel P	.50
111	Travis Fryman P	.50
112	Dave Nilsson P	.50
113	John Olerud P	.75
114	Larry Walker W	15.00
115	Jim Edmonds N	7.50
116	Bobby Higginson L	2.00
117	Todd Hundley L	4.00
118	Paul O'Neill P	1.00
119	Bip Roberts P	.50
120	Ismael Valdes P	.50
121	Pedro Martinez N	12.50
122	Jeff Cirillo P	.50
123	Andy Benes P	.50
124	Bobby Jones P	.50
125	Brian Hunter P	.50
126	Darryl Kile P	.50
127	Pat Hentgen P	.50
128	Marquis Grissom P	.50
129	Eric Davis P	.50
130	Chipper Jones W	65.00
131	Edgar Martinez N	7.50
132	Andy Pettitte W	20.00
133	Cal Ripken Jr. W	75.00
134	Scott Rolen W	40.00
135	Ron Coomer P	.50
136	Luis Castillo L	2.00
136	Luis Castillo ("SAMPLE" overprint on back)	1.50
137	Fred McGriff L	6.00
138	Neifi Perez L	2.00
139	Eric Karros P	1.00
140	Alex Fernandez P	.50
141	Jason Dickson P	.50
142	Lance Johnson P	.50
143	Ray Lankford P	.50
144	Sammy Sosa N	25.00
145	Eric Young P	.50
146	Bubba Trammell L	4.00
147	Todd Walker L	4.00
148	Mo Vaughn P (Curtain Calls)	3.00
149	Jeff Bagwell P (Curtain Calls)	4.00
150	Kenny Lofton P (Curtain Calls)	3.00
151	Raul Mondesi P (Curtain Calls)	1.00
152	Mike Piazza P (Curtain Calls)	7.50
153	Chipper Jones P (Curtain Calls)	7.50
154	Larry Walker P (Curtain Calls)	2.00
155	Greg Maddux P (Curtain Calls)	7.50
156	Ken Griffey Jr. P (Curtain Calls)	12.50
157	Frank Thomas P (Curtain Calls)	6.00
158	Darin Erstad L (Gold Leaf Stars)	10.00
159	Roberto Alomar P (Gold Leaf Stars)	2.50
160	Albert Belle L (Gold Leaf Stars)	3.00
161	Jim Thome L (Gold Leaf Stars)	2.00
162	Tony Clark L (Gold Leaf Stars)	2.50
163	Chuck Knoblauch L (Gold Leaf Stars)	2.00
164	Derek Jeter P (Gold Leaf Stars)	6.00
165	Alex Rodriguez P (Gold Leaf Stars)	7.50
166	Tony Gwynn P (Gold Leaf Stars)	6.00
167	Roger Clemens L (Gold Leaf Stars)	17.50
168	Barry Larkin P (Gold Leaf Stars)	1.50
169	Andres Galarraga P (Gold Leaf Stars)	1.50
170	Vladimir Guerrero L (Gold Leaf Stars)	7.50
171	Mark McGwire L (Gold Leaf Stars)	40.00

172 Barry Bonds L 12.50
(Gold Leaf Stars)
173 Juan Gonzalez P 6.00
(Gold Leaf Stars)
174 Andruw Jones P 4.00
(Gold Leaf Stars)
175 Paul Molitor P 2.50
(Gold Leaf Stars)
176 Hideo Nomo L 10.00
(Gold Leaf Stars)
177 Cal Ripken Jr. P 10.00
(Gold Leaf Stars)
178 Brad Fullmer P 1.50
(Gold Leaf Rookies)
179 Jaret Wright N 30.00
(Gold Leaf Rookies)
180 Bobby Estalella P .50
(Gold Leaf Rookies)
181 Ben Grieve W 30.00
(Gold Leaf Rookies)
182 Paul Konerko W 12.50
(Gold Leaf Rookies)
183 David Ortiz N 6.00
(Gold Leaf Rookies)
184 Todd Helton W 20.00
(Gold Leaf Rookies)
185 Juan Encarnacion N 5.00
(Gold Leaf Rookies)
186 Miguel Tejada N 12.50
(Gold Leaf Rookies)
187 Jacob Cruz P .50
(Gold Leaf Rookies)
188 Mark Kotsay N 12.50
(Gold Leaf Rookies)
189 Fernando Tatis L 5.00
(Gold Leaf Rookies)
190 Ricky Ledee P 1.00
(Gold Leaf Rookies)
191 Richard Hidalgo P .50
(Gold Leaf Rookies)
192 Richie Sexson P .50
(Gold Leaf Rookies)
193 Luis Ordaz P .50
(Gold Leaf Rookies)
194 Eli Marrero L 4.00
(Gold Leaf Rookies)
195 Livan Hernandez L 4.00
(Gold Leaf Rookies)
196 Homer Bush P .50
(Gold Leaf Rookies)
197 Raul Ibanez P .50
(Gold Leaf Rookies)
198 Checklist (Nomar 5.00
Garciaparra P)
199 Checklist 2.50
(Scott Rolen P)
200 Checklist 2.50
(Jose Cruz Jr. P)

1998 Leaf Fractal Materials Die-Cut

This parallel set adds a die-cut to the Fractal Materials set. The first 200 of 75 plastic, 15 Leather, 5 nylon and 5 wood cards have an x-axis die-cut. The first 100 of 20 plastic, 25 leather, 10 nylon and 5 wood cards have a y-axis die-cut. The first 50 of 5 plastic, 10 leather, 15 nylon and 10 wood cards have a z-axis die-cut.

MT
Common X (200 of each): 4.00
Common Y (100): 10.00
Common Z (50): 20.00
1 Rusty Greer Z 20.00
2 Tino Martinez Y 20.00
3 Bobby Bonilla Y 15.00
4 Jason Giambi Z 20.00
5 Matt Morris Y 15.00
6 Craig Counsell X 4.00
7 Reggie Jefferson X 4.00
8 Brian Rose X 12.50
9 Ruben Rivera Y 10.00
10 Shawn Estes Y 10.00
11 Tony Gwynn X 50.00
12 Jeff Abbott Y 10.00
13 Jose Cruz Jr. Z 20.00
14 Francisco Cordova Y 10.00
15 Ryan Klesko X 12.50
16 Tim Salmon Y 20.00
17 Brett Tomko Y 10.00
18 Matt Williams Y 20.00
19 Joe Carter X 10.00
20 Harold Baines X 4.00
21 Gary Sheffield Z 40.00
22 Charles Johnson Y 15.00
23 Aaron Boone Y 10.00
24 Eddie Murray Y 20.00
25 Matt Stairs X 4.00
26 David Cone X 10.00
27 Jon Nunnally X 4.00
28 Chris Stynes X 4.00
29 Enrique Wilson Y 10.00
30 Randy Johnson Y 20.00
31 Garret Anderson Y 10.00
32 Manny Ramirez Y 35.00
33 Jeff Suppan Y 10.00
34 Rickey Henderson X 7.50
35 Scott Spiezio Y 10.00
36 Rondell White Y 15.00
37 Todd Greene Z 30.00
38 Delino DeShields Y 10.00
39 Kevin Brown X 7.50
40 Chili Davis X 4.00
41 Jimmy Key X 4.00
42 NOT ISSUED
43 Mike Mussina Z 60.00
44 Joe Randa X 4.00
45 Chan Ho Park Y 12.50
46 Brad Radke X 4.00
47 Geronimo Berroa X 4.00
48 Wade Boggs Y 15.00
49 Kevin Appier X 4.00
50 Moises Alou X 7.50
51 David Justice Z 35.00
52 Ivan Rodriguez X 20.00
53 J.T. Snow X 7.50
54 Brian Giles Y 10.00
55 Will Clark X 10.00
56 Justin Thompson Y 12.50
57 Javier Lopez Y 12.50
58 Hideki Irabu X 10.00
59 Mark Grudzielanek X 4.00
60 Abraham Nunez Z 20.00
61 Todd Hollandsworth 4.00
X
62 Jay Bell X 4.00
63 Nomar Garciaparra Z 175.00
64 Vinny Castilla Y 12.50
65 Lou Collier Y 10.00
66 Kevin Orie X 4.00
67 John Valentin X 4.00
68 Robin Ventura X 7.50
69 Denny Neagle X 7.50
70 Tony Womack X 4.00
71 Dennis Reyes Y 10.00
72 Wally Joyner X 4.00
73 Kevin Brown X 4.00
74 Ray Durham X 4.00
75 Mike Cameron Y 15.00
76 Dante Bichette X 12.50
77 Jose Guillen Z 30.00
78 Carlos Delgado Y 15.00
79 Paul Molitor X 20.00
80 Jason Kendall X 4.00
81 Mark Belhorn X 4.00
82 Damian Jackson Y 10.00
83 Bill Mueller X 4.00
84 Kevin Young X 4.00
85 Curt Schilling X 10.00
86 Jeffrey Hammonds X [illegible]
87 Sandy Alomar Jr. Y 15.00
88 Bartolo Colon Y 10.00
89 Wilton Guerrero Y 10.00
90 Bernie Williams Z 60.00
91 Deion Sanders Y 15.00
92 Mike Piazza Z 200.00
93 Butch Huskey X 4.00
94 Edgardo Alfonzo Y 10.00
95 Alan Benes Z 20.00
96 Craig Biggio X 10.00
97 Mark Grace Y 20.00
98 Shawn Green Y 10.00
99 Derrek Lee Y 15.00
100 Ken Griffey Jr. Z 300.00
101 Tim Raines X 4.00
102 Pokey Reese Y 10.00
103 Lee Stevens X 4.00
104 Shannon Stewart X 4.00
105 John Smoltz Y 15.00
106 Frank Thomas Z 125.00
107 Jeff Fassero X 4.00
108 Jay Buhner Y 20.00
109 Jose Canseco X 12.50
110 Omar Vizquel X 4.00
111 Travis Fryman X 4.00
112 Dave Nilsson X 4.00
113 John Olerud X 7.50
114 Larry Walker X 15.00
115 Jim Edmonds Z 20.00
116 Bobby Higginson Y 10.00
117 Todd Hundley Z 20.00
118 Paul O'Neill X 10.00
119 Bip Roberts X 4.00
120 Ismael Valdes X 7.50
121 Pedro Martinez X 12.50
122 Jeff Cirillo X 4.00
123 Andy Benes X 10.00
124 Bobby Jones X 4.00
125 Brian Hunter X 4.00
126 Darryl Kile X 4.00
127 Pat Hentgen X 4.00
128 Marquis Grissom X 4.00
129 Eric Davis X 4.00
130 Chipper Jones Z 200.00
131 Edgar Martinez Z 30.00
132 Andy Pettitte Y 30.00
133 Cal Ripken Jr. Z 225.00
134 Scott Rolen X 40.00
135 Ron Coomer X 4.00
136 Luis Castillo X 4.00
137 Fred McGriff X 12.50
138 Neifi Perez Y 10.00
139 Eric Karros X 10.00
140 Alex Fernandez X 4.00
141 Jason Dickson X 4.00
142 Lance Johnson X 4.00
143 Ray Lankford Y 10.00
144 Sammy Sosa Y 40.00
145 Eric Young Y 10.00
146 Bubba Trammell Z 20.00
147 Todd Walker Z 30.00
148 Mo Vaughn X 20.00
(Curtain Calls)
149 Jeff Bagwell X 40.00
(Curtain Calls)
150 Kenny Lofton X 20.00
(Curtain Calls)
151 Raul Mondesi X 10.00
(Curtain Calls)
152 Mike Piazza X 60.00
(Curtain Calls)
153 Chipper Jones X 60.00
(Curtain Calls)
154 Larry Walker X 15.00
(Curtain Calls)
155 Greg Maddux X 60.00
(Curtain Calls)
156 Ken Griffey Jr. X 100.00
(Curtain Calls)
157 Frank Thomas X 40.00
(Curtain Calls)
158 Darin Erstad Y 35.00
(Gold Leaf Stars)
159 Roberto Alomar X 20.00
(Gold Leaf Stars)
160 Albert Belle X 20.00
(Gold Leaf Stars)
161 Jim Thome X 15.00
(Gold Leaf Stars)
162 Tony Clark Z 50.00
(Gold Leaf Stars)
163 Chuck Knoblauch Z 35.00
(Gold Leaf Stars)
164 Derek Jeter X 50.00
(Gold Leaf Stars)
165 Alex Rodriguez Y 90.00
(Gold Leaf Stars)
166 Tony Gwynn X 50.00
(Gold Leaf Stars)
167 Roger Clemens Y 60.00
(Gold Leaf Stars)
168 Barry Larkin Y 20.00
(Gold Leaf Stars)
169 Andres Galarraga Y 20.00
(Gold Leaf Stars)
170 Vladimir Guerrero Y 30.00
(Gold Leaf Stars)
171 Mark McGwire Z 200.00
(Gold Leaf Stars)
172 Barry Bonds Y 35.00
(Gold Leaf Stars)
173 Juan Gonzalez Y 75.00
(Gold Leaf Stars)
174 Andruw Jones X 20.00
(Gold Leaf Stars)
175 Paul Molitor X 17.50
(Gold Leaf Stars)
176 Hideo Nomo Z 50.00
(Gold Leaf Stars)
177 Cal Ripken Jr. X 75.00
(Gold Leaf Stars)
178 Brad Fullmer Z 30.00
(Gold Leaf Rookies)
179 Jaret Wright Z 120.00
(Gold Leaf Rookies)
180 Bobby Estalella Y 10.00
(Gold Leaf Rookies)
181 Ben Grieve Z 90.00
(Gold Leaf Rookies)
182 Paul Konerko Z 50.00
(Gold Leaf Rookies)
183 David Ortiz Z 30.00
(Gold Leaf Rookies)
184 Todd Helton Z 60.00
(Gold Leaf Rookies)
185 Juan Encarnacion Z 20.00
(Gold Leaf Rookies)
186 Miguel Tejada Z 40.00
(Gold Leaf Rookies)
187 Jacob Cruz X 4.00
(Gold Leaf Rookies)
188 Mark Kotsay Z 40.00
(Gold Leaf Rookies)
189 Fernando Tatis Y 20.00
(Gold Leaf Rookies)
190 Ricky Ledee X 12.50
(Gold Leaf Rookies)
191 Richard Hidalgo Z 20.00
(Gold Leaf Rookies)
192 Richie Sexson Z 20.00
(Gold Leaf Rookies)
193 Luis Ordaz X 4.00
(Gold Leaf Rookies)
194 Eli Marrero Z 20.00
(Gold Leaf Rookies)
195 Livan Hernandez Z 30.00
(Gold Leaf Rookies)
196 Homer Bush X 4.00
(Gold Leaf Rookies)
197 Raul Ibanez X 4.00
(Gold Leaf Rookies)
198 Checklist (Nomar 30.00
Garciaparra X)
199 Checklist 60.00
(Scott Rolen Z)
200 Checklist 7.50
(Jose Cruz Jr. X)

1998 Leaf Fractal Matrix

Fractal Matrix parallels the 1998 Leaf set. The cards have a metallic-colored finish, with 100 done in bronze, 60 in silver and 40 in gold, and each color having some cards in X, Y and Z axis. Stated print runs are: Bronze: X - 1,600; Y - 1,800; Z - 1,900. Silver: X - 600; Y - 800; Z - 900. Gold: X - 100; Y - 300; Z - 400. Each player is found only in a single color/axis combination.

MT
Complete Set (200): 750.00
Common Bronze: .75
Common Silver: 2.50
Common Gold: 5.00
1 Rusty Greer G/Z 5.00
2 Tino Martinez G/Z 5.00
3 Bobby Bonilla S/Y 2.50
4 Jason Giambi S/Y 2.50
5 Matt Morris S/Y 2.50
6 Craig Counsell B/X .75
7 Reggie Jefferson B/X .75
8 Brian Rose S/Y 3.50
9 Ruben Rivera B/X .75
10 Shawn Estes S/Y 2.50
11 Tony Gwynn G/Z 20.00
12 Jeff Abbott B/Y .75
13 Jose Cruz Jr. G/Z 6.50
14 Francisco Cordova .75
B/X
15 Ryan Klesko B/X 1.00
16 Tim Salmon G/Y 7.50
17 Brett Tomko B/X [illegible]
18 Matt Williams S/Y 3.00
19 Joe Carter B/X .75
20 Harold Baines B/X .75
21 Gary Sheffield S/Z 5.00
22 Charles Johnson S/X 2.50
23 Aaron Boone B/X 1.00
24 Eddie Murray G/Y 5.00
25 Matt Stairs B/X .75
26 David Cone B/X 1.00
27 Jon Nunnally B/X .75
28 Chris Stynes B/X .75
29 Enrique Wilson B/Y .75
30 Randy Johnson S/Z 7.50
31 Garret Anderson S/Y 2.50
32 Manny Ramirez G/Z 9.00
33 Jeff Suppan S/X 2.50
34 Rickey Henderson 1.00
B/X
35 Scott Spiezio B/X .75
36 Rondell White S/Y 2.50
37 Todd Greene S/Z 2.50
38 Delino DeShields B/X .75
39 Kevin Brown S/X 3.00
40 Chili Davis B/X .75
41 Jimmy Key B/X .75
42 NOT ISSUED
43 Mike Mussina G/Y 10.00
44 Joe Randa B/X .75
45 Chan Ho Park S/Z 3.00
46 Brad Radke B/X .75
47 Geronimo Berroa B/X .75
48 Wade Boggs S/Y 5.00
49 Kevin Appier B/X .75
50 Moises Alou S/Y 2.50
51 David Justice G/Y 5.00
52 Ivan Rodriguez G/Z 10.00
53 J.T. Snow B/X .75
54 Brian Giles B/X .75
55 Will Clark B/Y 1.25
56 Justin Thompson S/Y 2.50
57 Javier Lopez S/X 3.50
58 Hideki Irabu B/Z 2.00
59 Mark Grudzielanek .75
B/X
60 Abraham Nunez S/X 2.50
61 Todd Hollandsworth .75
B/X
62 Jay Bell B/X .75
63 Nomar Garciaparra 25.00
G/Z
64 Vinny Castilla B/Y .75
65 Lou Collier B/Y .75
66 Kevin Orie S/X 2.50
67 John Valentin B/X .75
68 Robin Ventura B/X 1.00
69 Denny Neagle B/X .75
70 Tony Womack S/Y 2.50
71 Dennis Reyes S/Y 2.50
72 Wally Joyner B/X .75
73 Kevin Brown B/Y 1.00
74 Ray Durham B/X .75
75 Mike Cameron S/Z 2.50
76 Dante Bichette B/X 1.00
77 Jose Guillen G/Y 5.00
78 Carlos Delgado B/Y .75
79 Paul Molitor G/Z 7.50
80 Jason Kendall B/X .75
81 Mark Belhorn B/X .75
82 Damian Jackson B/X .75
83 Bill Mueller B/X .75
84 Kevin Young B/X .75
85 Curt Schilling B/X 1.00
86 Jeffrey Hammonds .75
B/X
87 Sandy Alomar Jr. S/Y 3.50
88 Bartolo Colon B/Y .75
89 Wilton Guerrero B/Y .75
90 Bernie Williams G/Y 10.00
91 Deion Sanders S/Y 3.00
92 Mike Piazza G/X 75.00
93 Butch Huskey B/X .75
94 Edgardo Alfonzo S/X 3.00
95 Alan Benes S/Y 2.50
96 Craig Biggio S/Y 3.50
97 Mark Grace S/Y 3.00
98 Shawn Green S/Y 3.00
99 Derrek Lee S/Y 2.50
100 Ken Griffey Jr. G/Z 40.00
101 Tim Raines B/X .75
102 Pokey Reese S/X 2.50
103 Lee Stevens B/X .75
104 Shannon Stewart S/Y 2.50
105 John Smoltz S/Y 3.50
106 Frank Thomas G/X 45.00
107 Jeff Fassero B/X .75
108 Jay Buhner B/Y 1.00
109 Jose Canseco B/X 1.00
110 Omar Vizquel B/X .75
111 Travis Fryman B/X .75
112 Dave Nilsson B/X .75
113 John Olerud B/X 1.00
114 Larry Walker G/Z 6.50
115 Jim Edmonds S/Y 2.50
116 Bobby Higginson S/X 2.50
117 Todd Hundley S/X 3.50
118 Paul O'Neill B/X 1.00
119 Bip Roberts B/X .75
120 Ismael Valdes B/X .75
121 Pedro Martinez S/Y 5.00
122 Jeff Cirillo B/X .75
123 Andy Benes B/X .75
124 Bobby Jones B/X .75
125 Brian Hunter B/X .75
126 Darryl Kile B/X .75
127 Pat Hentgen B/X .75
128 Marquis Grissom B/X .75
129 Eric Davis B/X [illegible]
130 Chipper Jones G/Z 25.00
131 Edgar Martinez S/Z 2.50
132 Andy Pettitte G/Z 7.50
133 Cal Ripken Jr. G/X 100.00
134 Scott Rolen G/Z 18.50
135 Ron Coomer B/X .75
136 Luis Castillo B/Y .75
137 Fred McGriff B/Y 1.00
138 Neifi Perez S/Y 2.50
139 Eric Karros B/X .75
140 Alex Fernandez B/X .75
141 Jason Dickson B/X .75
142 Lance Johnson B/X .75
143 Ray Lankford B/Y .75
144 Sammy Sosa G/Y 18.50
145 Eric Young B/Y .75
146 Bubba Trammell S/Y 2.50
147 Todd Walker S/Y 2.50
148 Mo Vaughn S/X 5.00
(Curtain Calls)
149 Jeff Bagwell S/X 7.50
(Curtain Calls)
150 Kenny Lofton S/X 5.00
(Curtain Calls)
151 Raul Mondesi S/X 2.50
(Curtain Calls)
152 Mike Piazza S/X 12.50
(Curtain Calls)
153 Chipper Jones S/X 12.50
(Curtain Calls)
154 Larry Walker S/X 2.50
(Curtain Calls)
155 Greg Maddux S/X 12.50
(Curtain Calls)
156 Ken Griffey Jr. S/X 20.00
(Curtain Calls)
157 Frank Thomas S/X 7.50
(Curtain Calls)
158 Darin Erstad B/Z 2.00
(Gold Leaf Stars)
159 Roberto Alomar B/Y 1.50
(Gold Leaf Stars)

160	Albert Belle G/Y (Gold Leaf Stars)	6.50
161	Jim Thome G/Y (Gold Leaf Stars)	5.00
162	Tony Clark G/Y (Gold Leaf Stars)	5.00
163	Chuck Knoblauch B/Y (Gold Leaf Stars)	1.00
164	Derek Jeter G/Z (Gold Leaf Stars)	12.50
165	Alex Rodriguez G/Z (Gold Leaf Stars)	12.50
166	Tony Gwynn B/X (Gold Leaf Stars)	6.50
167	Roger Clemens G/Z (Gold Leaf Stars)	7.50
168	Barry Larkin B/Y (Gold Leaf Stars)	1.00
169	Andres Galarraga B/Y (Gold Leaf Stars)	1.00
170	Vladimir Guerrero G/Z (Gold Leaf Stars)	6.50
171	Mark McGwire B/Z (Gold Leaf Stars)	7.50
172	Barry Bonds B/Z (Gold Leaf Stars)	3.00
173	Juan Gonzalez G/Z (Gold Leaf Stars)	10.00
174	Andruw Jones G/Z (Gold Leaf Stars)	10.00
175	Paul Molitor B/X (Gold Leaf Stars)	1.50
176	Hideo Nomo B/Z (Gold Leaf Stars)	2.50
177	Cal Ripken Jr. B/X (Gold Leaf Stars)	5.00
178	Brad Fullmer S/Z (Gold Leaf Rookies)	3.00
179	Jaret Wright G/Z (Gold Leaf Rookies)	12.50
180	Bobby Estalella B/Y (Gold Leaf Rookies)	.75
181	Ben Grieve G/X (Gold Leaf Rookies)	30.00
182	Paul Konerko G/Z (Gold Leaf Rookies)	7.50
183	David Ortiz G/Z (Gold Leaf Rookies)	5.00
184	Todd Helton G/X (Gold Leaf Rookies)	20.00
185	Juan Encarnacion G/Z (Gold Leaf Rookies)	5.00
186	Miguel Tejada G/Z (Gold Leaf Rookies)	6.50
187	Jacob Cruz B/Y (Gold Leaf Rookies)	.75
188	Mark Kotsay G/Z (Gold Leaf Rookies)	5.00
189	Fernando Tatis S/Z (Gold Leaf Rookies)	2.50
190	Ricky Ledee S/Y (Gold Leaf Rookies)	3.00
191	Richard Hidalgo S/Y (Gold Leaf Rookies)	2.50
192	Richie Sexson S/Y (Gold Leaf Rookies)	2.50
193	Luis Ordaz B/X (Gold Leaf Rookies)	.75
194	Eli Marrero S/Z (Gold Leaf Rookies)	2.50
195	Livan Hernandez S/Z (Gold Leaf Rookies)	2.50
196	Homer Bush B/X (Gold Leaf Rookies)	.75
197	Raul Ibanez B/X (Gold Leaf Rookies)	.75
198	Checklist (Nomar Garciaparra B/X)	4.00
199	Checklist (Scott Rolen B/X)	2.50
200	Checklist (Jose Cruz Jr. B/X)	2.50

1998 Leaf Fractal Matrix Die-Cut

This parallel set adds a die-cut to the Fractal Matrix set. Three different die-cut versions were created: X-axis, Y-axis and Z-axis. An X-axis die-cut was added to 75 bronze, 20 silver and 5 gold cards. A Y-axis die-cut was added to 20 bronze, 30 silver and 10 gold cards. Of the 40 Z-axis cards, 5 are bronze, 10 silver and 25 gold. Stated print runs were 400 of each X-axis card; 200 Y and 100 Z.

		MT
	Complete Set (200):	1875.
	Common X-Axis:	3.00
	Common Y-Axis:	5.00
	Common Z-Axis:	10.00
1	Rusty Greer G/Z	10.00
2	Tino Martinez G/Z	15.00
3	Bobby Bonilla S/Y	7.50
4	Jason Giambi S/Y	6.00
5	Matt Morris S/Y	7.50
6	Craig Counsell B/X	3.00
7	Reggie Jefferson B/X	3.00
8	Brian Rose S/Y	7.50
9	Ruben Rivera B/X	5.00
10	Shawn Estes S/Y	5.00
11	Tony Gwynn G/Z	75.00
12	Jeff Abbott B/Y	5.00
13	Jose Cruz Jr. G/Z	20.00
14	Francisco Cordova B/X	3.00
15	Ryan Klesko B/X	4.00
16	Tim Salmon G/Y	12.50
17	Brett Tomko B/X	3.00
18	Matt Williams S/Y	10.00
19	Joe Carter B/X	5.00
20	Harold Baines B/X	3.00
21	Gary Sheffield S/Z	20.00
22	Charles Johnson S/X	4.00
23	Aaron Boone B/X	4.00
24	Eddie Murray G/Y	10.00
25	Matt Stairs B/X	3.00
26	David Cone B/X	5.00
27	Jon Nunnally B/X	3.00
28	Chris Stynes B/X	3.00
29	Enrique Wilson B/Y	5.00
30	Randy Johnson S/Z	25.00
31	Garret Anderson S/Y	5.00
32	Manny Ramirez G/Z	30.00
33	Jeff Suppan S/X	3.00
34	Rickey Henderson B/X	3.00
35	Scott Spiezio B/X	3.00
36	Rondell White S/Y	10.00
37	Todd Greene S/Z	15.00
38	Delino DeShields B/X	3.00
39	Kevin Brown S/X	4.00
40	Chili Davis B/X	3.00
41	Jimmy Key B/X	3.00
42	NOT ISSUED	
43	Mike Mussina G/Y	20.00
44	Joe Randa B/X	3.00
45	Chan Ho Park S/Z	15.00
46	Brad Radke B/X	3.00
47	Geronimo Berroa B/X	3.00
48	Wade Boggs S/Y	12.50
49	Kevin Appier B/X	3.00
50	Moises Alou S/Y	7.50
51	David Justice G/Y	12.50
52	Ivan Rodriguez G/Z	40.00
53	J.T. Snow B/X	4.00
54	Brian Giles B/X	3.00
55	Will Clark B/Y	10.00
56	Justin Thompson S/Y	5.00
57	Javier Lopez S/X	4.00
58	Hideki Irabu B/Z	20.00
59	Mark Grudzielanek B/X	3.00
60	Abraham Nunez S/X	5.00
61	Todd Hollandsworth B/X	3.00
62	Jay Bell B/X	3.00
63	Nomar Garciaparra G/Z	100.00
64	Vinny Castilla B/Y	5.00
65	Lou Collier B/Y	5.00
66	Kevin Orie S/X	3.00
67	John Valentin B/X	3.00
68	Robin Ventura B/X	4.00
69	Denny Neagle B/X	4.00
70	Tony Womack S/Y	5.00
71	Dennis Reyes S/Y	5.00
72	Wally Joyner B/X	3.00
73	Kevin Brown B/Y	7.50
74	Ray Durham B/X	3.00
75	Mike Cameron S/Z	15.00
76	Dante Bichette B/X	5.00
77	Jose Guillen G/Y	10.00
78	Carlos Delgado B/Y	7.50
79	Paul Molitor G/Z	30.00
80	Jason Kendall B/X	3.00
81	Mark Belhorn B/X	3.00
82	Damian Jackson B/X	3.00
83	Bill Mueller B/X	3.00
84	Kevin Young B/X	3.00
85	Curt Schilling B/X	5.00
86	Jeffrey Hammonds B/X	3.00
87	Sandy Alomar Jr. S/Y	10.00
88	Bartolo Colon B/Y	5.00
89	Wilton Guerrero B/Y	5.00
90	Bernie Williams G/Y	20.00
91	Deion Sanders S/Y	10.00
92	Mike Piazza G/X	40.00
93	Butch Huskey B/X	3.00
94	Edgardo Alfonzo S/X	3.00
95	Alan Benes S/Y	7.50
96	Craig Biggio S/Y	10.00
97	Mark Grace S/Y	12.50
98	Shawn Green S/Y	7.50
99	Derrek Lee S/Y	10.00
100	Ken Griffey Jr. G/Z	150.00
101	Tim Raines B/X	3.00
102	Pokey Reese S/X	3.00
103	Lee Stevens B/X	3.00
104	Shannon Stewart S/Y	5.00
105	John Smoltz S/Y	10.00
106	Frank Thomas G/X	25.00
107	Jeff Fassero B/X	3.00
108	Jay Buhner B/Y	10.00
109	Jose Canseco B/X	5.00
110	Omar Vizquel B/X	3.00
111	Travis Fryman B/X	4.00
112	Dave Nilsson B/X	3.00
113	John Olerud B/X	5.00
114	Larry Walker G/Z	20.00
115	Jim Edmonds S/Y	10.00
116	Bobby Higginson S/X	5.00
117	Todd Hundley S/X	4.00
118	Paul O'Neill B/X	5.00
119	Bip Roberts B/X	3.00
120	Ismael Valdes B/X	3.00
121	Pedro Martinez S/Y	12.50
122	Jeff Cirillo B/X	3.00
123	Andy Benes B/X	3.00
124	Bobby Jones B/X	3.00
125	Brian Hunter B/X	3.00
126	Darryl Kile B/X	3.00
127	Pat Hentgen B/X	3.00
128	Marquis Grissom B/X	3.00
129	Eric Davis B/X	3.00
130	Chipper Jones G/Z	100.00
131	Edgar Martinez S/Z	10.00
132	Andy Pettitte G/Z	30.00
133	Cal Ripken Jr. G/X	50.00
134	Scott Rolen G/Z	75.00
135	Ron Coomer B/X	3.00
136	Luis Castillo B/Y	5.00
137	Fred McGriff B/Y	10.00
138	Neifi Perez S/Y	5.00
139	Eric Karros B/X	4.00
140	Alex Fernandez B/X	3.00
141	Jason Dickson B/X	3.00
142	Lance Johnson B/X	3.00
143	Ray Lankford B/Y	5.00
144	Sammy Sosa G/Y	40.00
145	Eric Young B/Y	5.00
146	Bubba Trammell S/Y	7.50
147	Todd Walker S/Y	10.00
148	Mo Vaughn S/X (Curtain Calls)	7.50
149	Jeff Bagwell S/X (Curtain Calls)	12.50
150	Kenny Lofton S/X (Curtain Calls)	7.50
151	Raul Mondesi S/X (Curtain Calls)	5.00
152	Mike Piazza S/X (Curtain Calls)	20.00
153	Chipper Jones S/X (Curtain Calls)	20.00
154	Larry Walker S/X (Curtain Calls)	5.00
155	Greg Maddux S/X (Curtain Calls)	20.00
156	Ken Griffey Jr. S/X (Curtain Calls)	40.00
157	Frank Thomas S/X (Curtain Calls)	15.00
158	Darin Erstad B/Z (Gold Leaf Stars)	20.00
159	Roberto Alomar B/Y (Gold Leaf Stars)	10.00
160	Albert Belle G/Y (Gold Leaf Stars)	12.50
161	Jim Thome G/Y (Gold Leaf Stars)	9.00
162	Tony Clark G/Y (Gold Leaf Stars)	9.00
163	Chuck Knoblauch B/Y (Gold Leaf Stars)	10.00
164	Derek Jeter G/Z (Gold Leaf Stars)	50.00
165	Alex Rodriguez G/Z (Gold Leaf Stars)	50.00
166	Tony Gwynn B/X (Gold Leaf Stars)	17.50
167	Roger Clemens G/Z (Gold Leaf Stars)	30.00
168	Barry Larkin B/Y (Gold Leaf Stars)	10.00
169	Andres Galarraga B/Y (Gold Leaf Stars)	10.00
170	Vladimir Guerrero G/Z (Gold Leaf Stars)	25.00
171	Mark McGwire B/Z (Gold Leaf Stars)	50.00
172	Barry Bonds B/Z (Gold Leaf Stars)	20.00
173	Juan Gonzalez G/Z (Gold Leaf Stars)	35.00
174	Andruw Jones G/Z (Gold Leaf Stars)	35.00
175	Paul Molitor B/X (Gold Leaf Stars)	7.50
176	Hideo Nomo B/Z (Gold Leaf Stars)	30.00
177	Cal Ripken Jr. B/X (Gold Leaf Stars)	25.00
178	Brad Fullmer S/Z (Gold Leaf Rookies)	17.50
179	Jaret Wright G/Z (Gold Leaf Rookies)	35.00
180	Bobby Estalella B/Y (Gold Leaf Rookies)	5.00
181	Ben Grieve G/X (Gold Leaf Rookies)	15.00
182	Paul Konerko G/Z (Gold Leaf Rookies)	25.00
183	David Ortiz G/Z (Gold Leaf Rookies)	15.00
184	Todd Helton G/X (Gold Leaf Rookies)	7.50
185	Juan Encarnacion G/Z (Gold Leaf Rookies)	15.00
186	Miguel Tejada G/Z (Gold Leaf Rookies)	20.00
187	Jacob Cruz B/Y (Gold Leaf Rookies)	7.50
188	Mark Kotsay G/Z (Gold Leaf Rookies)	17.50
189	Fernando Tatis S/Z (Gold Leaf Rookies)	12.50
190	Ricky Ledee S/Y (Gold Leaf Rookies)	10.00
191	Richard Hidalgo S/Y (Gold Leaf Rookies)	5.00
192	Richie Sexson S/Y (Gold Leaf Rookies)	5.00
193	Luis Ordaz B/X (Gold Leaf Rookies)	3.00
194	Eli Marrero S/Z (Gold Leaf Rookies)	10.00
195	Livan Hernandez S/Z (Gold Leaf Rookies)	15.00
196	Homer Bush B/X (Gold Leaf Rookies)	3.00
197	Raul Ibanez B/X (Gold Leaf Rookies)	3.00
198	Checklist (Nomar Garciaparra B/X)	20.00
199	Checklist (Scott Rolen B/X)	15.00
200	Checklist (Jose Cruz Jr. B/X)	5.00

1998 Leaf Crusade

Thirty cards from the cross-brand Crusade insert appear in 1998 Leaf. The cards had Green (250 sets), Purple (100 sets) and Red (25 sets) versions. Forty Crusade cards were in 1998 Donruss and 30 each in 1998 Donruss Update and Leaf Rookies & Stars.

		MT
	Complete Set (30):	475.00
	Common Player:	5.00
	Purples: 1.5X	
	Reds: 5X	
3	Jim Edmonds	5.00
4	Darin Erstad	25.00
11	Mike Mussina	20.00
15	Albert Belle	30.00
18	Manny Ramirez	25.00
19	Jim Thome	20.00
24	Bubba Trammell	7.50
26	Bobby Higginson	5.00
28	Paul Molitor	20.00
30	Todd Walker	10.00
34	Andy Pettitte	20.00
35	Wade Boggs	25.00
40	Alex Rodriguez	75.00
41	Randy Johnson	20.00
46	Ivan Rodriguez	30.00
48	Roger Clemens	50.00
54	John Smoltz	10.00
56	Andruw Jones	60.00
58	Javier Lopez	7.50
59	Fred McGriff	10.00
64	Pokey Reese	5.00
66	Andres Galarraga	12.50
70	Eric Young	5.00
73	Moises Alou	5.00
76	Ben Grieve	30.00
79	Mike Piazza	75.00
91	Jason Kendall	5.00
95	Alan Benes	5.00
97	Tony Gwynn	60.00
98	Ken Caminiti	15.00

1998 Leaf Heading for the Hall

This 20-card insert features players destined for the Hall of Fame. The set is sequentially numbered to 3,500.

		MT
	Complete Set (20):	185.00
	Common Player:	4.50
1	Roberto Alomar	6.00
2	Jeff Bagwell	12.50
3	Albert Belle	7.50
4	Wade Boggs	6.00
5	Barry Bonds	7.50
6	Roger Clemens	12.50
7	Juan Gonzalez	15.00
8	Ken Griffey Jr.	30.00
9	Tony Gwynn	15.00
10	Barry Larkin	4.50
11	Kenny Lofton	6.00
12	Greg Maddux	17.50
13	Mark McGwire	30.00
14	Paul Molitor	6.00
15	Eddie Murray	4.50
16	Mike Piazza	20.00
16s	Mike Piazza (SAMPLE overprint on back)	4.00
17	Cal Ripken Jr.	25.00
18	Ivan Rodriguez	7.50
19	Ryne Sandberg	7.50
20	Frank Thomas	12.50

1998 Leaf State Representatives

This 30-card insert features top players. The background has a picture of the state in which he plays. "State Representatives" is printed at the top with the player's name at the bottom. This set is sequentially numbered to 5,000.

		MT
	Complete Set (30):	200.00
	Common Player:	2.00
1	Ken Griffey Jr.	30.00
2	Frank Thomas	10.00
3	Alex Rodriguez	20.00
4	Cal Ripken Jr.	20.00
5	Chipper Jones	15.00
6	Andruw Jones	12.00
7	Scott Rolen	12.00
8	Nomar Garciaparra	15.00
9	Tim Salmon	5.00
10	Manny Ramirez	8.00
11	Jose Cruz Jr.	2.00
12	Vladimir Guerrero	10.00
13	Tino Martinez	5.00
14	Larry Walker	6.00
15	Mo Vaughn	6.00
16	Jim Thome	5.00
17	Tony Clark	5.00
18	Derek Jeter	15.00
19	Juan Gonzalez	12.00

20	Jeff Bagwell	10.00
21	Ivan Rodriguez	8.00
22	Mark McGwire	30.00
23	David Justice	3.00
24	Chuck Knoblauch	5.00
25	Andy Pettitte	5.00
26	Raul Mondesi	5.00
27	Randy Johnson	5.00
28	Greg Maddux	12.00
29	Bernie Williams	5.00
30	Rusty Greer	2.00

1998 Leaf Statistical Standouts

This 24-card insert features players with impressive statistics. The cards have a horizontal layout and the feel of leather. The background has a ball and glove with the player's facsimile signature on the ball. Statistical Standouts is numbered to 2,500. A parallel die-cut version of each card was produced to the number of 250.

		MT
Complete Set (24):		300.00
Common Player:		5.00
Die-Cuts: 2X		
1	Frank Thomas	15.00
2	Ken Griffey Jr.	30.00
3	Alex Rodriguez	20.00
4	Mike Piazza	20.00
5	Greg Maddux	17.50
6	Cal Ripken Jr.	25.00
7	Chipper Jones	20.00
8	Juan Gonzalez	15.00
9	Jeff Bagwell	12.50
10	Mark McGwire	30.00
11	Tony Gwynn	15.00
12	Mo Vaughn	7.50
13	Nomar Garciaparra	20.00
14	Jose Cruz Jr.	5.00
15	Vladimir Guerrero	10.00
16	Scott Rolen	12.50
17	Andy Pettitte	6.00
18	Randy Johnson	6.00
19	Larry Walker	6.00
20	Kenny Lofton	6.00
21	Tony Clark	5.00
22	David Justice	6.00
23	Derek Jeter	20.00
24	Barry Bonds	7.50

1998 Leaf Limited Star Factor Sample

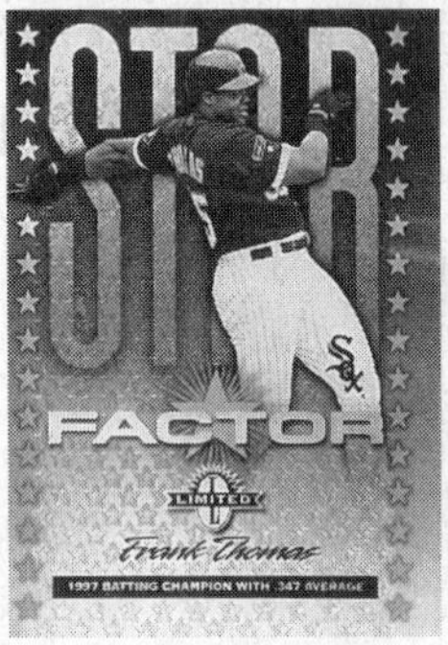

This sample card was intended to preview the 1998 Leaf Limited issue which was never released due to Pinnacle's bankruptcy. The card is printed with a refractive foil background and hundreds of embossed stars front and back. The back has a large "SAMPLE" overprint and is numbered "000".

		MT
000	Frank Thomas	6.00

1998 Leaf Rookies & Stars

This 339-card set consists of three subsets: Power Tools, Lineup Card and Rookies. Fronts feature full-bleed photos and silver-foil graphics.Backs have complete year-by-year statistics and a small photo. The base set has short-printed base cards, numbers 131-230, 301-339, which are seeded 1:2 packs. Rookies and Stars has two parallels to the base set: True Blue and Longevity. True Blue's feature blue foil stamping and are each numbered "1 0f 500" on the card back. Longevity's are printed on a full-foiled card front with gold foil stamping and limited to 50 serially numbered sets.

		MT
Complete Set (339):		600.00
Common Player:		.10
Common SP (131-230):		.40
Common SP (301-339):		1.00
1	Andy Pettitte	.30
2	Roberto Alomar	.30
3	Randy Johnson	.30
4	Manny Ramirez	.60
5	Paul Molitor	.30
6	Mike Mussina	.30
7	Jim Thome	.25
8	Tino Martinez	.20
9	Gary Sheffield	.15
10	Chuck Knoblauch	.20
11	Bernie Williams	.30
12	Tim Salmon	.15
13	Sammy Sosa	1.25
14	Wade Boggs	.15
15	Andres Galarraga	.30
16	Pedro Martinez	.30
17	David Justice	.20
18	Chan Ho Park	.20
19	Jay Buhner	.15
20	Ryan Klesko	.15
21	Barry Larkin	.15
22	Will Clark	.20
23	Raul Mondesi	.15
24	Rickey Henderson	.12
25	Jim Edmonds	.10
26	Ken Griffey Jr.	2.00
27	Frank Thomas	1.00
28	Cal Ripken Jr.	1.50
29	Alex Rodriguez	1.25
30	Mike Piazza	1.25
31	Greg Maddux	1.25
32	Chipper Jones	1.00
33	Tony Gwynn	1.00
34	Derek Jeter	1.00
35	Jeff Bagwell	.45
36	Juan Gonzalez	1.00
37	Nomar Garciaparra	1.25
38	Andruw Jones	.45
39	Hideo Nomo	.15
40	Roger Clemens	.75
41	Mark McGwire	2.50
42	Scott Rolen	.45
43	Vladimir Guerrero	.60
44	Barry Bonds	.45
45	Darin Erstad	.45
46	Albert Belle	.45
47	Kenny Lofton	.45
48	Mo Vaughn	.45
49	Ivan Rodriguez	.45
50	Jose Cruz Jr.	.30
51	Tony Clark	.30
52	Larry Walker	.25
53	Mark Grace	.15
54	Edgar Martinez	.10
55	Fred McGriff	.15
56	Rafael Palmeiro	.15
57	Matt Williams	.15
58	Craig Biggio	.15
59	Ken Caminiti	.12
60	Jose Canseco	.20
61	Brady Anderson	.10
62	Moises Alou	.15
63	Justin Thompson	.10
64	John Smoltz	.12
65	Carlos Delgado	.30
66	J.T. Snow	.10
67	Jason Giambi	.10
68	Garret Anderson	.10
69	Rondell White	.15
70	Eric Karros	.10
71	Javier Lopez	.15
72	Pat Hentgen	.10
73	Dante Bichette	.15
74	Charles Johnson	.10
75	Tom Glavine	.15
76	Rusty Greer	.10
77	Travis Fryman	.10
78	Todd Hundley	.10
79	Ray Lankford	.10
80	Denny Neagle	.10
81	Henry Rodriguez	.10
82	Sandy Alomar Jr.	.10
83	Robin Ventura	.10
84	John Olerud	.15
85	Omar Vizquel	.10
86	Darren Dreifort	.10
87	Kevin Brown	.15
88	Curt Schilling	.15
89	Francisco Cordova	.10
90	Brad Radke	.10
91	David Cone	.15
92	Paul O'Neill	.15
93	Vinny Castilla	.10
94	Marquis Grissom	.10
95	Brian Hunter	.10
96	Kevin Appier	.10
97	Bobby Bonilla	.10
98	Eric Young	.10
99	Jason Kendall	.15
100	Shawn Green	.10
101	Edgardo Alfonzo	.10
102	Alan Benes	.10
103	Bobby Higginson	.10
104	Todd Greene	.10
105	Jose Guillen	.15
106	Neifi Perez	.10
107	Edgar Renteria	.10
108	Chris Stynes	.10
109	Todd Walker	.15
110	Brian Jordan	.10
111	Joe Carter	.15
112	Ellis Burks	.10
113	Brett Tomko	.10
114	Mike Cameron	.10
115	Shannon Stewart	.10
116	Kevin Orie	.10
117	Brian Giles	.10
118	Hideki Irabu	.20
119	Delino DeShields	.10
120	David Segui	.10
121	Dustin Hermanson	.10
122	Kevin Young	.10
123	Jay Bell	.10
124	Doug Glanville	.10
125	*John Roskos*	.10
126	*Damon Hollins*	.10
127	Matt Stairs	.10
128	Cliff Floyd	.10
129	Derek Bell	.10
130	Darryl Strawberry	.10
131	Ken Griffey Jr. (Power Tools)	9.00
132	Tim Salmon (Power Tools)	.75
133	Manny Ramirez (Power Tools)	3.00
134	Paul Konerko (Power Tools)	.60
135	Frank Thomas (Power Tools)	3.50
136	Todd Helton (Power Tools)	2.50
137	Larry Walker (Power Tools)	1.25
138	Mo Vaughn (Power Tools)	2.50
139	Travis Lee (Power Tools)	2.00
140	Ivan Rodriguez (Power Tools)	2.50
141	Ben Grieve (Power Tools)	2.50
142	Brad Fullmer (Power Tools)	.60
143	Alex Rodriguez (Power Tools)	6.00
144	Mike Piazza (Power Tools)	6.00
145	Greg Maddux (Power Tools)	6.00
146	Chipper Jones (Power Tools)	5.00
147	Kenny Lofton (Power Tools)	2.50
148	Albert Belle (Power Tools)	2.50
149	Barry Bonds (Power Tools)	2.50
150	Vladimir Guerrero (Power Tools)	3.00
151	Tony Gwynn (Power Tools)	5.00
152	Derek Jeter (Power Tools)	5.00
153	Jeff Bagwell (Power Tools)	3.00
154	Juan Gonzalez (Power Tools)	5.00
155	Nomar Garciaparra (Power Tools)	6.00
156	Andruw Jones (Power Tools)	2.50
157	Hideo Nomo (Power Tools)	.75
158	Roger Clemens (Power Tools)	3.50
159	Mark McGwire (Power Tools)	12.00
160	Scott Rolen (Power Tools)	2.50
161	Travis Lee (Team Line-Up)	2.00
162	Ben Grieve (Team Line-Up)	2.50
163	Jose Guillen (Team Line-Up)	.40
164	John Olerud (Team Line-Up)	.50
165	Kevin Appier (Team Line-Up)	.40
166	Marquis Grissom (Team Line-Up)	.40
167	Rusty Greer (Team Line-Up)	.40
168	Ken Caminiti (Team Line-Up)	.50
169	Craig Biggio (Team Line-Up)	.60
170	Ken Griffey Jr. (Team Line-Up)	9.00
171	Larry Walker (Team Line-Up)	1.25
172	Barry Larkin (Team Line-Up)	.60
173	Andres Galarraga (Team Line-Up)	1.50
174	Wade Boggs (Team Line-Up)	.60
175	Sammy Sosa (Team Line-Up)	7.50
176	Mike Piazza (Team Line-Up)	6.00
177	Jim Thome (Team Line-Up)	1.50
178	Paul Molitor (Team Line-Up)	2.00
179	Tony Clark (Team Line-Up)	1.00
180	Jose Cruz Jr. (Team Line-Up)	1.00
181	Darin Erstad (Team Line-Up)	2.50
182	Barry Bonds (Team Line-Up)	2.50
183	Vladimir Guerrero (Team Line-Up)	3.00
184	Scott Rolen (Team Line-Up)	2.50
185	Mark McGwire (Team Line-Up)	12.00
186	Nomar Garciaparra (Team Line-Up)	6.00
187	Gary Sheffield (Team Line-Up)	.60
188	Cal Ripken Jr. (Team Line-Up)	7.50
189	Frank Thomas (Team Line-Up)	3.50
190	Andy Pettitte (Team Line-Up)	1.00
191	Paul Konerko	.60
192	Todd Helton	2.50
193	Mark Kotsay	.45
194	Brad Fullmer	.45
195	*Kevin Millwood*	30.00
196	David Ortiz	.45
197	Kerry Wood	1.50
198	Miguel Tejada	.60
199	Fernando Tatis	.45
200	Jaret Wright	2.00
201	Ben Grieve	2.50
202	Travis Lee	2.00
203	Wes Helms	.40
204	Geoff Jenkins	.40
205	Russell Branyan	.40
206	*Esteban Yan*	.40
207	*Ben Ford*	.40
208	*Rich Butler*	2.50
209	*Ryan Jackson*	.40
210	A.J. Hinch	.40
211	*Magglio Ordonez*	40.00
212	*David Dellucci*	2.50
213	Billy McMillon	.40
214	*Mike Lowell*	3.50
215	*Todd Erdos*	.40
216	*Carlos Mendoza*	1.00
217	*Frank Catalanotto*	.40
218	*Julio Ramirez*	6.00
219	*John Halama*	.40
220	Wilson Delgado	.40
221	*Mike Judd*	2.50
222	*Rolando Arrojo*	4.00
223	*Jason LaRue*	2.50
224	*Manny Aybar*	.45
225	Jorge Velandia	.40
226	*Mike Kinkade*	1.50
227	*Carlos Lee*	15.00
228	Bobby Hughes	.40
229	*Ryan Christenson*	1.50
230	*Masato Yoshii*	.60
231	Richard Hidalgo	.10
232	Rafael Medina	.10
233	Damian Jackson	.10
234	Derek Lowe	.10
235	Mario Valdez	.10
236	Eli Marrero	.10
237	Juan Encarnacion	.10
238	Livan Hernandez	.10
239	Bruce Chen	.40
240	Eric Milton	.10
241	Jason Varitek	.10
242	Scott Elarton	.10
243	*Manuel Barrios*	.20
244	Mike Caruso	.10
245	Tom Evans	.10
246	Pat Cline	.10
247	Matt Clement	.10
248	Karim Garcia	.10
249	Richie Sexson	.15
250	Sidney Ponson	.10
251	Randall Simon	.15
252	Tony Saunders	.10
253	Javier Valentin	.10
254	Danny Clyburn	.10
255	Michael Coleman	.10
256	*Hanley Frias*	.15
257	Miguel Cairo	.10
258	*Rob Stanifer*	.10
259	Lou Collier	.10
260	Abraham Nunez	.10
261	Ricky Ledee	.40
262	Carl Pavano	.10
263	Derrek Lee	.10
264	Jeff Abbott	.10
265	Bob Abreu	.10
266	Bartolo Colon	.10
267	Mike Drumright	.10
268	Daryle Ward	.10
269	Gabe Alvarez	.10
270	Josh Booty	.10
271	Damian Moss	.10
272	Brian Rose	.10
273	Jarrod Washburn	.10
274	Bobby Estalella	.10
275	Enrique Wilson	.10
276	Derrick Gibson	.10
277	Ken Cloude	.10
278	Kevin Witt	.10
279	Donnie Sadler	.10
280	Sean Casey	.15
281	Jacob Cruz	.10
282	Ron Wright	.10
283	Jeremi Gonzalez	.10
284	Desi Relaford	.10
285	Bobby Smith	.10
286	Javier Vazquez	.10
287	*Steve Woodard*	.15
288	Greg Norton	.10
289	Cliff Politte	.10
290	Felix Heredia	.10
291	Braden Looper	.10
292	Felix Martinez	.10
293	Brian Meadows	.10
294	Edwin Diaz	.10
295	Pat Watkins	.10
296	*Marc Pisciotta*	.10
297	Rick Gorecki	.10
298	DaRond Stovall	.10
299	Andy Larkin	.10
300	Felix Rodriguez	.10
301	Blake Stein	1.00
302	*John Rocker*	5.00
303	*Justin Baughman*	1.50
304	*Jesus Sanchez*	2.50
305	Randy Winn	1.00
306	Lou Merloni	1.00
307	*Jim Parque*	3.50
308	Dennis Reyes	1.00
309	*Orlando Hernandez*	20.00
310	Jason Johnson	1.00
311	Torii Hunter	1.00
312	Mike Piazza	9.00
313	*Mike Frank*	2.50
314	*Troy Glaus*	75.00
315	*Jin Cho*	.45
316	*Ruben Mateo*	40.00
317	*Ryan Minor*	20.00
318	Aramis Ramirez	1.50
319	Adrian Beltre	3.00
320	*Matt Anderson*	8.00
321	*Gabe Kapler*	40.00
322	*Jeremy Giambi*	9.00
323	Carlos Beltran	6.00
324	Dermal Brown	.60
325	Ben Davis	2.00
326	Eric Chavez	9.00
327	*Bob Howry*	3.00
328	Roy Halladay	.45
329	George Lombard	3.00
330	Michael Barrett	4.00
331	*Fernando Seguignol*	15.00
332	*J.D. Drew*	60.00
333	*Odalis Perez*	8.00
334	*Alex Cora*	3.00
335	*Placido Polanco*	2.50
336	*Armando Rios*	.60
337	Sammy Sosa (HR commemorative)	15.00
338	Mark McGwire (HR commemorative)	25.00
339	Sammy Sosa, Mark McGwire (Checklist)	18.00

1998 Leaf Rookies & Stars Longevity

Only 50 sets of this parallel edition were issued. Each card is serially numbered on back. Fronts are printed with gold foil background and have LONGEVITY printed at top. Special Longevity holographic 1 of 1 cards exist, but cannot be priced due to rarity.

	MT
Common Player:	7.50
Stars: 40-60X	
SP Stars (131-230): 10-15X	
SP Stars (301-339): 5-7X	
(See 1998 Leaf Rookies & Stars for checklist and base card values.)	

1998 Leaf Rookies & Stars True Blue

This parallel edition of the Rookies & Stars base set is labeled at top-back "1 of 500". The parallels feature blue foil graphic highlights on front with TRUE BLUE at top.

	MT
Complete Set (339):	2000.
Common Player:	2.00
Stars: 8-12X	
SP Stars (131-230): 2X	
SP Stars (301-339): 1.5X	
(See 1998 Leaf Rookies & Stars for checklist and base card values.)	

1998 Leaf Rookies & Stars Cross Training

This 10-card insert set highlights players who excel at multiple aspects of the game. Card fronts are full-foiled and sequentially numbered on the card back to 1,000.

		MT
Complete Set (10):		180.00
Common Player:		7.50
Production 1,000 sets		
1	Kenny Lofton	7.50
2	Ken Griffey Jr.	45.00
3	Alex Rodriguez	30.00
4	Greg Maddux	20.00
5	Barry Bonds	10.00
6	Ivan Rodriguez	10.00
7	Chipper Jones	25.00
8	Jeff Bagwell	10.00
9	Nomar Garciaparra	20.00
10	Derek Jeter	25.00

1998 Leaf Rookies & Stars Crusade

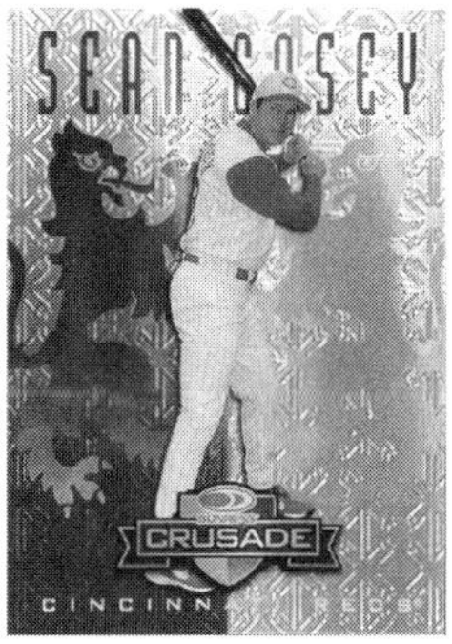

This 30-card set is a continuation of this cross-brand insert. Cards are printed on a holographic green foil front and limited to 250 serial numbered sets. Two parallels are also randomly seeded: Purple and Red. Purples have purple holographic foil fronts and limited to 100 serial numbered sets. Reds are printed on red holographic foil fronts and limited to 25 serial numbered sets.

		MT
Complete Green Set (30):		400.00
Common Player:		4.00
Production 250 sets		
Purples: 2X		
Production 100 sets		
Reds: 4X		
Production 25 sets		
101	Richard Hidalgo	4.00
102	Paul Konerko	10.00
103	Miguel Tejada	12.50
104	Fernando Tatis	4.00
105	Travis Lee	20.00
106	Wes Helms	4.00
107	Rich Butler	10.00
108	Mark Kotsay	7.50
109	Eli Marrero	4.00
110	David Ortiz	4.00
111	Juan Encarnacion	4.00
112	Jaret Wright	20.00
113	Livan Hernandez	4.00
114	Ron Wright	7.50
115	Ryan Christenson	4.00
116	Eric Milton	4.00
117	Brad Fullmer	7.50
118	Karim Garcia	4.00
119	Abraham Nunez	4.00
120	Ricky Ledee	12.50
121	Carl Pavano	4.00
122	Derrek Lee	4.00
123	A.J. Hinch	4.00
124	Brian Rose	4.00
125	Bobby Estalella	4.00
126	Kevin Millwood	30.00
127	Kerry Wood	25.00
128	Sean Casey	12.50
129	Russell Branyan	4.00
130	Magglio Ordonez	20.00

1998 Leaf Rookies & Stars Donruss MVPs

This 20-card set is printed on a full silver-foil card stock and sequentially numbered to 5,000. The first 500 of each card is treated with a "Pennant Edition" logo and unique color coating.

		MT
Complete Set (20):		75.00
Common Player:		1.00
Production 4,500 sets		
Pennant Editions: 5X		
Production 500 sets		
1	Frank Thomas	5.00
2	Chuck Knoblauch	1.00
3	Cal Ripken Jr.	7.50
4	Alex Rodriguez	7.50
5	Ivan Rodriguez	2.50
6	Albert Belle	2.50
7	Ken Griffey Jr.	10.00
8	Juan Gonzalez	5.00
9	Roger Clemens	4.00
10	Mo Vaughn	2.00
11	Jeff Bagwell	2.50
12	Craig Biggio	1.00
13	Chipper Jones	6.00
14	Barry Larkin	1.00
15	Mike Piazza	6.00
16	Barry Bonds	2.50
17	Andruw Jones	2.50
18	Tony Gwynn	5.00
19	Greg Maddux	6.00
20	Mark McGwire	10.00

1998 Leaf Rookies & Stars Extreme Measures

These inserts are each printed on a full-foiled card front. Each card highlights an outstanding statistic for the featured player. Each card is sequentially numbered to 1,000.

		MT
Complete Set (10):		150.00
Common Player:		10.00
1	Ken Griffey Jr. (944)	30.00
2	Frank Thomas (653)	20.00
3	Tony Gwynn (628)	20.00
4	Mark McGwire (942)	30.00
5	Larry Walker (280)	10.00
6	Mike Piazza (960)	25.00
7	Roger Clemens (708)	15.00
8	Greg Maddux (980)	20.00
9	Jeff Bagwell (873)	10.00
10	Nomar Garciaparra (989)	20.00

1998 Leaf Rookies & Stars Extreme Measures Die-Cut

Each card highlights an outstanding statistic for each featured player, is die-cut and limited to the featured statistic.

		MT
Complete Set (10):		950.00
Common Player:		5.00
Die-Cut to featured stat		
1	Ken Griffey Jr. (56)	200.00
2	Frank Thomas (347)	25.00
3	Tony Gwynn (372)	30.00
4	Mark McGwire (58)	250.00
5	Larry Walker (720)	5.00
6	Mike Piazza (40)	135.00
7	Roger Clemens (292)	25.00
8	Greg Maddux (20)	250.00
9	Jeff Bagwell (127)	45.00
10	Nomar Garciaparra (11)	325.00

1998 Leaf Rookies & Stars Freshman Orientation

Card fronts are printed on holographic foil with silver foil stamping and features top young prospects. Card backs highlight the date of the featured player's Major League debut, have a small photo and are serially numbered to 5,000 sets.

		MT
Complete Set (20):		20.00
Common Player:		.70
Production 5,000 sets		
1	Todd Helton	3.00
2	Ben Grieve	3.00
3	Travis Lee	2.50
4	Paul Konerko	1.25
5	Jaret Wright	2.00
6	Livan Hernandez	.75
7	Brad Fullmer	1.25
8	Carl Pavano	.75
9	Richard Hidalgo	.75
10	Miguel Tejada	1.50
11	Mark Kotsay	1.00
12	David Ortiz	.75
13	Juan Encarnacion	.75
14	Fernando Tatis	.75
15	Kevin Millwood	3.50
15s	Kevin Millwood ("SAMPLE" overprint on back)	2.50
16	Kerry Wood	2.50
16s	Kerry Wood ("SAMPLE" overprint on back)	2.50
17	Magglio Ordonez	1.50
18	Derrek Lee	.75
19	Jose Cruz Jr.	.75
20	A.J. Hinch	.75

1998 Leaf Rookies & Stars Great American Heroes

Card fronts are stamped with a holographic silver foil and done on a horizontal format. Card backs have a photo and are serially numbered to 2,500.

		MT
Complete Set (20):		100.00
Common Player:		2.00
Production 2,500 sets		
1	Frank Thomas	7.50
2	Cal Ripken Jr.	12.50
3	Ken Griffey Jr.	15.00
4	Alex Rodriguez	12.50
5	Greg Maddux	9.00
6	Mike Piazza	10.00
7	Chipper Jones	10.00
8	Tony Gwynn	7.50
9	Jeff Bagwell	4.00
10	Juan Gonzalez	7.50
11	Hideo Nomo	2.00
12	Roger Clemens	6.00
13	Mark McGwire	15.00
14	Barry Bonds	4.00
15	Kenny Lofton	3.00
16	Larry Walker	2.00
17	Paul Molitor	3.00
18	Wade Boggs	2.00
19	Barry Larkin	2.00
20	Andres Galarraga	3.00

1998 Leaf Rookies & Stars Greatest Hits

These inserts feature holographic silver foil stamping on the card front done on a horizontal format. Card backs have a photo and serially numbered to 2,500.

		MT
Complete Set (20):		125.00
Common Player:		2.00
Production 2,500 sets		
1	Ken Griffey Jr.	17.50
2	Frank Thomas	7.50
3	Cal Ripken Jr.	12.50
4	Alex Rodriguez	12.50
5	Ben Grieve	4.00
6	Mike Piazza	10.00
7	Chipper Jones	10.00
8	Tony Gwynn	7.50
9	Derek Jeter	9.00
10	Jeff Bagwell	4.00
11	Tino Martinez	2.00
12	Juan Gonzalez	7.50
13	Nomar Garciaparra	10.00
14	Mark McGwire	17.50
15	Scott Rolen	4.00
16	David Justice	2.00
17	Darin Erstad	4.00
18	Mo Vaughn	3.00
19	Ivan Rodriguez	4.00
20	Travis Lee	3.00

1998 Leaf Rookies & Stars Home Run Derby

This 20-card set spotlights the top home run hitters on a bronze full-foiled card front. Card backs have a small photo and are serially numbered to 2,500.

		MT
Complete Set (20):		100.00
Common Player:		2.00
Production 2,500 sets		
1	Tino Martinez	2.00
2	Jim Thome	3.00
3	Larry Walker	3.00
4	Tony Clark	3.00
5	Jose Cruz Jr.	2.00
6	Barry Bonds	4.00
7	Scott Rolen	4.00
8	Paul Konerko	2.00
9	Travis Lee	3.00
10	Todd Helton	4.00
11	Mark McGwire	15.00
12	Andruw Jones	4.00
13	Nomar Garciaparra	10.00
14	Juan Gonzalez	7.50
15	Jeff Bagwell	4.00
16	Chipper Jones	12.50
17	Mike Piazza	12.50
18	Frank Thomas	7.50
19	Ken Griffey Jr.	15.00
20	Albert Belle	4.00

Player names in *Italic* type indicate a rookie card.

1998 Leaf Rookies & Stars ML Hard Drives

Card fronts are stamped with silver holographic foil. Card backs detail which field (left, center and right) the featured player hit each of his singles, doubles, triples and homeruns. Each card is serially numbered to 2,500.

		MT
Complete Set (20):		110.00
Common Player:		2.00
Production 2,500 sets		
1	Jeff Bagwell	4.00
2	Juan Gonzalez	7.50
3	Nomar Garciaparra	10.00
4	Ken Griffey Jr.	15.00
5	Frank Thomas	7.50
6	Cal Ripken Jr.	12.50
7	Alex Rodriguez	12.50
8	Mike Piazza	10.00
9	Chipper Jones	10.00
10	Tony Gwynn	7.50
11	Derek Jeter	9.00
12	Mo Vaughn	2.00
13	Ben Grieve	4.00
14	Manny Ramirez	5.00
15	Vladimir Guerrero	5.00
16	Scott Rolen	4.00
17	Darin Erstad	4.00
18	Kenny Lofton	3.00
19	Brad Fullmer	2.00
20	David Justice	2.00

1998 Leaf Rookies & Stars Standing Ovation

Card fronts are stamped with silver holographic foil and card backs have a small photo of the featured player and serially numbered to 5,000.

		MT
Complete Set (10):		45.00
Common Player:		2.00
Production 5,000 sets		
1	Barry Bonds	2.50
2	Mark McGwire	12.50
3	Ken Griffey Jr.	12.50
4	Frank Thomas	5.00
5	Tony Gwynn	5.00
6	Cal Ripken Jr.	7.50
7	Greg Maddux	6.00
8	Roger Clemens	4.00
9	Paul Molitor	2.00
10	Ivan Rodriguez	2.50

Player names in *Italic* type indicate a rookie card.

1998 Leaf Rookies & Stars Ticket Masters

Card fronts are printed on a full-foiled card stock with silver foil stamping and have a photo of one of the two players featured from the same team. Card backs have a photo of the other featured player and are serially numbered to 2,500. The first 250 of each card are die-cut.

		MT
Complete Set (20):		110.00
Common Player:		2.00
Production 2,250 sets		
Die-Cuts: 2X		
Production 250 sets		
1	Ken Griffey Jr., Alex Rodriguez	20.00
2	Frank Thomas, Albert Belle	7.50
3	Cal Ripken Jr., Roberto Alomar	12.50
4	Greg Maddux, Chipper Jones	10.00
5	Tony Gwynn, Ken Caminiti	7.50
6	Derek Jeter, Andy Pettitte	9.00
7	Jeff Bagwell, Craig Biggio	4.00
8	Juan Gonzalez, Ivan Rodriguez	7.50
9	Nomar Garciaparra, Mo Vaughn	10.00
10	Vladimir Guerrero, Brad Fullmer	5.00
11	Andruw Jones, Andres Galarraga	4.00
12	Tino Martinez, Chuck Knoblauch	3.00
13	Raul Mondesi, Paul Konerko	2.00
14	Roger Clemens, Jose Cruz Jr.	2.00
15	Mark McGwire, Brian Jordan	20.00
16	Kenny Lofton, Manny Ramirez	5.00
17	Larry Walker, Todd Helton	4.00
18	Darin Erstad, Tim Salmon	4.00
19	Travis Lee, Matt Williams	2.00
20	Ben Grieve, Jason Giambi	2.00

1993-94 Legendary Foils Baseball Legends

Embossed portraits on thin metal plates was the technology used in production of this series of collectors issues. Several different sizes and formats were used for promo cards and issued versions. The promo cards measure about 2-5/8" x 3-3/4", as does the Babe Ruth Hawaii giveaway. The regular-issue pieces, which were packaged in a cardboard folder, are about 3-1/2" x 5". Other pieces than those listed here may have been produced and would have similar value. Production was reported at 100,000 each with 5,000 gold pieces each serially numbered. Issue price was about $7.95 apiece.

		MT
	PROMOS (2-5/8" x 3-3/4")	
(1)	Hank Aaron	2.00
(2)	Satchel Paige	2.00
(3)	Honus Wagner	2.00
	PROMO 3-1/2" x 5" (Honus Wagner)	4.00
	HAWAII IX GIVEAWAY	
	Babe Ruth (2-5/8" x 3-3/4")	6.00
	REGULAR ISSUE - GOLD ON GOLD (serially numbered to 5,000)	
(1)	Roberto Clemente	24.00
(2)	Dizzy Dean	12.00
(3)	Lou Gehrig	20.00
(4)	Rogers Hornsby	12.00
(5)	Carl Hubbell	12.00
(6)	Walter Johnson	12.00
(7)	Tony Lazzeri	12.00
(8)	Satchel Paige	15.00
(9)	Babe Ruth	24.00
(10)	Casey Stengel	12.00
(11)	Pie Traynor	12.00
(12)	Honus Wagner	12.00
	REGULAR-ISSUE GOLD ON BLUE (serially numbered edition of 95,000)	
(1)	Roberto Clemente	6.00
(2)	Dizzy Dean	3.00
(3)	Lou Gehrig	5.00
(4)	Rogers Hornsby	3.00
(5)	Carl Hubbell	3.00
(6)	Walter Johnson	3.00
(7)	Tony Lazzeri	3.00
(8)	Satchel Paige	4.00
(9)	Babe Ruth	6.00
(10)	Casey Stengel	3.00
(11)	Pie Traynor	3.00
(12)	Honus Wagner	3.00

1990 Legends Magazine Insert Cards

Beginning in 1990, Legends Sports Memorabilia magazine - devoted to feature articles and a price guide to limited edition sports collectibles - bound collectors' issue sportscards into each issue. Rather high-tech for the time, the first series of Legends insert cards featured gold-foil borders on front. Cards had large color action or posed photos. At bottom was a red Legends logo and player identification. Cards were printed on heavy stock in 8-1/4" x 11" sheets, with nine per issue. Individual cards measure 2-1/2" x 3-1/2". Full-color backs present a career summary. Only the baseball cards from the series are listed here. Prices are for single cards; complete magazines retail for $2 to $10 apiece, depending on cover subject.

		MT
Complete Baseball Set (19):		10.00
Common Player:		.50
1	Joe Morgan	.50
2	Jim Palmer	.50
3	Bo Jackson	.50
5	Nolan Ryan	2.00
6	Tony Gwynn	1.00
10	(Will Clark)	.50
11	(Don Mattingly)	.75
12	(Roger Clemens)	.75
13	(Dale Murphy)	.50
14	(Wade Boggs)	.75
19	(Ryne Sandberg)	.75
20	(Rickey Henderson)	.75
21	(Carlton Fisk)	.50
22	(Cal Ripken Jr.)	2.00
23	(Ken Griffey, Jr.)	2.50
24	(George Brett)	1.00

1990-92 Legends Magazine Postcard Inserts

In addition to standard-format insert cards, Legends Sports Memorabilia - a magazine devoted to features and price guide for collectors of limited edition sports collectibles - also issued several series of postcards depicting current and former star athletes. The postcards were printed three per 7" x 11" sheet on thin cardboard. Individual cards are 3-1/2" x 5-1/2". The first two series feature color artwork by noted sports artists Christopher Paluso and Michael Taylor. Black-and-white backs have standard postcard indicia and include a career summary. Only the baseball players are listed here. Values shown are for single cards; complete magazines retail between $2-10, usually depending on cover subject. The 1991 cards #4-6 bear on back the logo of the 12th annual National Sports Collectors Convention and were inserted in the official show program.

		MT
Complete Baseball Set (18):		20.00
Common Player:		1.00
	FIRST SERIES by CHRIS PALUSO	
1	Mike Schmidt	1.00
6	Stan Musial	1.00
	SECOND SERIES by MICHAEL J. TAYLOR	
1	(Nolan Ryan)	3.00
3	(Reggie Jackson)	1.00
4	(Brooks Robinson)	1.00
5	(Don Drysdale)	1.00
6	(Harmon Killebrew)	1.00
7	(Rod Carew)	1.00
8	(Gaylord Perry)	1.00
9	(Fergie Jenkins)	1.00
10	(Mickey Mantle)	6.00
11	(Ted Williams)	3.00
15	(Joe DiMaggio)	3.00
	THIRD SERIES by MICHAEL J. TAYLOR	
2	(Hank Aaron)	2.50
4	(Willie Mays)	2.50
9	(Johnny Bench)	1.00
10	Tom Seaver	1.00
11	Rollie Fingers	1.00

1991 Legends Magazine Insert Cards

In 1991, Legends Sports Memorabilia magazine - devoted to feature articles and a price guide to limited edition sports collectibles - began a new series of collectors' sportscards bound into each issue. Rather high-tech for the time, the second series of Legends insert cards features silver-foil borders on front. Cards have color action or posed photos. In the black background at top is a large Legends logo. Cards are printed on heavy stock in 8-1/4" x 11" sheets, with nine per issue. Individual cards measure 2-1/2" x 3-1/2". Backs are in red, black and white and present a career summary. Only the baseball cards from the series are listed here. Prices are for single cards; complete magazines retail for $2 to $10 apiece, depending on cover subject. Cards #19-27 were inserts in the 1991 National Convention program (reported production of 7,000) and have a gold-foil convention logo at lower-right. Cards #46-54 could also be found in a gold-foil version inserted into a special 15,000-production gold-cover version of Vol. 4, No. 5.

		MT
Complete Baseball Set (26):		12.50
Common Player:		.50
		.50
2	(Cecil Fielder)	.50
3	(Sandy Alomar Jr.)	.50
4	(Jose Canseco)	.75
6	(Dave Justice)	.50
10	(Rickey Henderson)	.60
15	(Darryl Strawberry)	.50
16	(Dave Stewart)	.50
17	(Alex Fernandez)	.50
	1991 Nat'l Convention Issue (Carew, Jabbar, Starr, Hull)	
19	(Warren Spahn)	.50
20	(Brooks Robinson)	.50
21	(Hank Aaron)	1.50
22	(Rod Carew)	.50
24	(Duke Snider)	.50
25	(Harmon Killebrew)	.50
27	(Willie Stargell)	.50
	Vol. 4, No. 3 (Griffey or Carew, Jenkins, Perry)	
28	(Ken Griffey Jr.)	3.00
29	(Kelly Gruber)	.50
30	(Frank Thomas)	1.50
31	(Kirby Puckett)	.75
33	(Mark McGwire)	3.00
	Vol. 4, No. 4 (Ryan or David Robinson)	
37	(Nolan Ryan)	2.00

39	(Bo Jackson) (White Sox)	.50
41	(Ramon Martinez)	.50
45	(Kevin Costner) (Texas Rangers)	1.50
	Vol. 4, No. 5 (Ripken, Brett Hull or Canseco)	
50	(Cal Ripken, Jr.)	2.00
53	(Tony Gwynn)	1.50

1996 Legends of the Negro Leagues Playing Cards

This set of playing cards depicting ballplayers of the pre-integration Negro Leagues was issued as a fundraiser by the International Society of Athletes in conjunction with a re-union of the players. In standard playing card finish and round-corner format, the cards have black-and-white photos at center. Backs are in black with gold printing. Size is 2-1/2" x 3-1/2". The deck's queens feature notable females of the Negro Leagues and the sponsor. No 2 of Diamonds was issued.

		MT
Complete Set (55):		10.00
Common Player:		.05
AS	Satchel Paige	1.00
2S	James "Joe" Greene	.05
3S	James "Red" Moore	.05
4S	Othello "Chico" Renfroe	.15
5S	William "Judy" Johnson	.15
6S	Willie "The Devil" Wells	.15
7S	Gene Benson	.05
8S	Willard "Sunnie" Brown	.05
9S	Martin Dihigo	.15
10S	Don Newcombe	.15
JS	Ray "Hooks" Dandridge	.15
QS	Billie Harden	.05
KS	Roy "Campy" Campanella	.75
AD	Jack "Jackie" Robinson	2.00
2D	not issued	
3D	Bob "The Rope" Boyd	.10
4D	William "Bonnie" Serrell	.05
5D	Orestes "Minnie" Minoso	.15
6D	Pop Lloyd	.15
7D	Art "Superman" Pennington	.05
8D	Francisco "Pancho" Coimbre	.15
9D	Sam "Jet" Jethroe	.10
10D	Joe Black	.15
JD	Monte Irvin	.15
QD	Effa "Effie" Manley	.05
KD	Henry "Hank" Aaron	1.50
AC	Joshua "Josh" Gibson	.25
2C	William "Bill" Cash	.05
3C	Francis "Fran" Matthews	.15
4C	Fred "Leap" Bankhead	.15
5C	Alex Radcliffe	.15
6C	Authur "Artie" Wilson (Arthur)	.10
7C	James "Jim" Zapp	.05
8C	Henry "Kimmie" Kimbro	.05
9C	Chester "Chet" Brewer	.05
10C	Verdell "Lefty" Mathis	.05
JC	James "Junior" Gilliam	.15
QC	Marcenia "Toni" Stone	.15
KC	Willie Mays	1.50
AH	James "Cool Papa" Bell	.15
2H	Samuel "Harriston" Hairston	.10
3H	John "Buck" O'Neil	.15
4H	Lorenzo "Piper" Davis	.05
5H	Parnell Woods	.05
6H	Thomas "Pee Wee" Butts	.05
7H	Oscar Charleston	.15
8H	Lawrence "Larry" Doby	1.00
9H	Hilton Smith	.05
10H	Leon Day	.15
JH	Walter "Buck" Leonard	.15
QH	Pamela Pryor-Fuller	.05
KH	Ernest "Ernie" Banks	.75
---	Joker (Ted "Double Duty" Radcliffe)	.15
---	Super Joker (Andrew "Rube" Foster)	.15
---	Wilmer "Red" Fields	.05
---	Clifford "Connie" Johnson	.05

1989 Lennox/HSE Astros

Formatted similar to a police/fire safety set, this Astros team issue is sponsored instead by a furnace company and the team's cable TV outlet. Cards measure 2-5/8" x 4-1/8" and feature portrait photos on front with orange and black team color pinstripes. Backs have biographical data, career summary and sponsors' logos.

		MT
Complete Set (26):		5.00
Common Player:		.25
1	Billy Hatcher	.25
2	Greg Gross	.25
3	Rick Rhoden	.25
4	Mike Scott	.25
5	Kevin Bass	.25
6	Alex Trevino	.25
7	Jim Clancy	.25
8	Bill Doran	.25
9	Dan Schatzeder	.25
10	Bob Knepper	.25
11	Jim Deshaies	.25
12	Eric Yelding	.25
13	Danny Darwin	.25
14	Coaches	.25
15	Craig Reynolds	.25
16	Rafael Ramirez	.25
17	Juan Agosto	.25
18	Larry Andersen	.25
19	Dave Smith	.25
20	Gerald Young	.25
21	Ken Caminiti	1.00
22	Terry Puhl	.25
23	Bob Forsch	.25
24	Craig Biggio	1.00
25	Art Howe	.25
26	Glenn Davis	.25

1990 Lennox/HSE Astros

For a second straight year Lennox, the furnace people, and HSE, the Astros cable TV outlet, sponsored a team set in an oversize (3-1/2" x 5") format. Fronts feature color player portrait photos, backs have a few biographical notes and logos for all parties. Cards are checklisted here by uniform numbers which appear on front and back.

		MT
Complete Set (28):		12.00
Common Player:		.50
1	Casey Candaele	.50
6	David Rohde	.50
7	Craig Biggio	1.00
9	Alex Trevino	.50
11	Ken Caminiti	1.00
12	Glenn Wilson	.50
13	Gerald Young	.50
15	Eric Yelding	.50
16	Rafael Ramirez	.50
18	Art Howe	.50
19	Bill Doran	.50
20	Dan Schatzeder	.50
21	Terry Puhl	.50
22	Mark Davidson	.50
23	Eric Anthony	.50
24	Franklin Stubbs	.50
27	Glenn Davis	.50
31	Xavier Hernandez	.50
33	Mike Scott	.50
36	Bill Gullickson	.50
38	Jim Clancy	.50
39	Jose Cano	.50
43	Jim Deshaies	.50
44	Danny Darwin	.50
45	Dave Smith	.50
47	Larry Andersen	.50
49	Juan Agosto	.50
51	Mark Portugal	.50

1989-91 Ron Lewis Living Legends

This series of Ron Lewis' portraits was issued in five four-card series over a period of three years. The 8" x 10" cards have color portraits on a white background. Lewis' signature, the year of issue and MLB licensing logo appear at bottom-right. Backs have player identification, another Lewis signature and distributor (Capital Cards) information. Also on back is a serial number from within an edition of 5,000. Issue price was about $7 apiece.

		MT
Complete Set (20):		150.00
Common Player:		6.00
1	Mickey Mantle	24.00
2	Frank Robinson	9.00
3	Duke Snider	10.00
4	Mike Schmidt	12.50
5	Reggie Jackson	7.50
6	Eddie Mathews	6.00
7	Nolan Ryan	20.00
8	Pete Rose	17.50
9	Sandy Koufax	15.00
10	Whitey Ford	9.00
11	Warren Spahn	6.00
12	Bob Feller	6.00
13	Willie Mays	15.00
14	Johnny Bench	8.00
15	Enos Slaughter	6.00
16	Tom Seaver	7.50
17	Harmon Killebrew	6.00
18	Yogi Berra	7.50
19	Red Schoendienst	6.00
20	Don Drysdale	6.00

1990 Ron Lewis 1961 N.Y. Yankees

The World's Champion 1961 N.Y. Yankees are featured in this set of cards by sports artist Ron Lewis. The 42-card set contains cards of individual players, coaches and the manager, plus a team picture. The 3-1/2" x 5-1/2" cards were sold only in a complete boxed set edition of 10,000. Cards have oil painted portraits of the players set against a blue background. The card borders are pin-striped in dark blue. At bottom is a blank panel for autographing. Backs are printed in red and blue and have personal data, career summary, 1961 and career stats.

		MT
Complete Boxed Set (42):		10.00
Common Player:		.50
1	1961 N.Y. Yankees team	3.00
2	Bobby Richardson	.75
3	Roger Maris	2.00
4	Elston Howard	.75
5	Bill Skowron	.60
6	Clete Boyer	.50
7	Mickey Mantle	4.00
8	Yogi Berra	1.00
9	Johnny Blanchard	.50
10	Hector Lopez	.50
11	Whitey Ford	1.00
12	Ralph Terry	.50
13	Bill Stafford	.50
14	Bud Daley	.50
15	Billy Gardner	.50
16	Jim Coates	.50
17	Luis Arroyo	.50
18	Tex Clevenger	.50
19	Bob Cerv	.50
20	Art Ditmar	.50
21	Bob Turley	.50
22	Joe DeMaestri	.50
23	Rollie Sheldon	.50
24	Earl Torgeson	.50
25	Hal Reniff	.50
26	Ralph Houk	.50
27	Johnny James	.50
28	Bob Hale	.50
29	Danny McDevitt	.50
30	Duke Maas	.50
31	Jim Hegan	.50
32	Wally Moses	.50
33	Frank Crosetti	.50
34	Lee Thomas	.50
35	Al Downing	.50
36	Jack Reed	.50
37	Ryne Duren	.50
38	Tom Tresh	.50
39	Johnny Sain	.50
40	Jesse Gonder	.50
41	Deron Johnson	.50
42	Tony Kubek	.60

1991 Ron Lewis Negro Leagues Postcards

Willie Mays

The 1991 Negro League Living Legends Postcard Set features paintings by artist Ron Lewis. Cards measure 3-1/2" x 5-1/2" and are stamped with a number within the 10,000 sets produced. Between each player's image and the player's name at the bottom of the card, is ample space for an autograph. The set, originally sold for $27, was created as a fund raiser for the Negro League Baseball Players Association. Two hundred uncut sheets were offered at $100 each.

		MT
Complete Set (30):		20.00
Common Player:		.40
1	George Giles	.40
2	Bill Cash	.40
3	Bob Harvey	.40
4	Lyman Bostock Sr.	.60
5	Ray Dandridge	1.50
6	Leon Day	1.25
7	Verdell "Lefty" Mathis	.40
8	Jimmie Crutchfield	.60
9	Clyde McNeal	.40
10	Bill Wright	.40
11	Mahlon Duckett	.40
12	William "Bobby" Robinson	.40
13	Max Manning	.40
14	Armando Vazquez	.40
15	Jehosie Heard	.60
16	Quincy Trouppe	.60
17	Wilmer Fields	.40
18	Lonnie Blair	.40
19	Garnett Blair	.60
20	Monte Irvin	1.50
21	Willie Mays	4.75
22	Buck Leonard	3.25
23	Frank Evans	.40
24	Josh Gibson Jr.	3.25
25	Ted "Double Duty" Radcliffe	.90
26	Josh Johnson	.40
27	Gene Benson	.60
28	Lester Lockett	.40
29	Cowan "Bubba" Hyde	.40
30	Rufus Lewis	.40

1994 Ron Lewis Negro Leagues Postcards

BUCK O'NEILL

A second series of postcards honoring players of the Negro Leagues was produced by artist Ron Lewis in September, 1994. In this set, more emphasis was placed on multi-player cards. Many of the cards also feature detailed backgrounds of street scenes with vintage vehicles, old-time stadiums, etc. Cards measure 3-1/2" x 5-1/2" and have a wide front border with the player (s) name printed at bottom and space above for autographing. Postcard backs are printed in black and include a few career stats, a card number and the card's position among the limited edition of 10,000.

		MT
Complete Set (32):		25.00
Common Card:		1.00
1	Willie Mays, Ernie Banks, Hank Aaron	4.00
1p	Mays, Banks, Aaron promo card (3-1/2" x 2-1/2")	2.00

2	Bill Wright, Lester Lockett, Lyman Bostock, Sr.	1.00
3	Josh Gibson, Josh Gibson, Jr., Buck Leonard	2.50
4	Max Manning, Monte Irvin, Leon Day	1.50
5	Armando Vazquez, Minnie Minoso, Martin Dihigo	1.50
6	Ted "Double Duty" Radcliffe	1.50
7	Bill Owens, Turkey Stearnes, Bobby Robinson	1.00
8	Wilmer Fields, Edsall Walker, Josh Johnson	1.00
9	Artie Wilson, Lionel Hampton	1.50
10	Earl Taborn	1.00
11	Barney "Bonnie" Serrell	1.00
12	Rodolfo "Rudy" Fernandez	1.00
13	Willie Pope	1.00
14	Ray Noble	1.00
15	Jim "Fireball" Cohen	1.00
16	Henry Kimbro	1.00
17	Charlie Biot	1.00
18	Al Wilmore	1.00
19	Sam Jethroe	1.50
20	Tommy Sampson	1.00
21	Charlie Rivera	1.00
22	Claro Duany	1.00
23	Russell Awkard	1.00
24	Art "Superman" Pennington	1.00
25	Wilmer Harris	1.00
26	Napoleon "Nap" Gulley	1.00
27	Emilio Navarro	1.00
28	Andy Porter	1.00
29	Willie Grace	1.00
30	Red Moore	1.00
31	Buck O'Neill	2.00
32	Stanley Glenn	1.00

1994 Life in America

In the same size (4-3/4" x 6-1/4") and style as as the better-known Sportscaster cards, these American history cards were also sold by mail in series. A number of sports-related cards are part of the issue. Only the baseball-related cards are checklisted here.

	MT
Jackie Robinson	6.00
Babe Ruth	8.00

1992 Lime Rock Griffey Baseball Holograms

This set of three hologram cards features the Griffey family of pro players. Each card carries a "GRIFFEY BASEBALL" headline at top, with a large central action photo of one of the family and his facsimile autograph. The backs have a color photo, career highlights and stats. The cards were issued in several different versions as noted below.

		MT
	Complete Set, Silver Holograms (3):	4.00
	Complete Set, Gold Holograms (3):	12.50
	Complete Set, Autographed (3):	70.00
	Complete Set, Blank-backed Promos (3):	12.50
	Three-card strip, edition of 5,000:	9.00
1	Ken Griffey Sr. (silver hologram, edition of 250,000)	.50
1	Ken Griffey Sr. (gold hologram, edition of 1,000)	2.00
1	Ken Griffey Sr. (autographed edition of 2,500)	12.00
1	Ken Griffey Sr. (blank-back promo, edition of 750)	2.00
2	Ken Griffey Jr. (silver)	3.00
2	Ken Griffey Jr. (gold)	12.00
2	Ken Griffey Jr. (autographed)	60.00
2	Ken Griffey Jr. (promo)	12.00
3	Craig Griffey (silver)	.50
3	Craig Griffey (gold)	2.00
3	Craig Griffey (autographed)	8.00
3	Craig Griffey (promo)	2.00

1993 Lime Rock Winter Baseball Promos

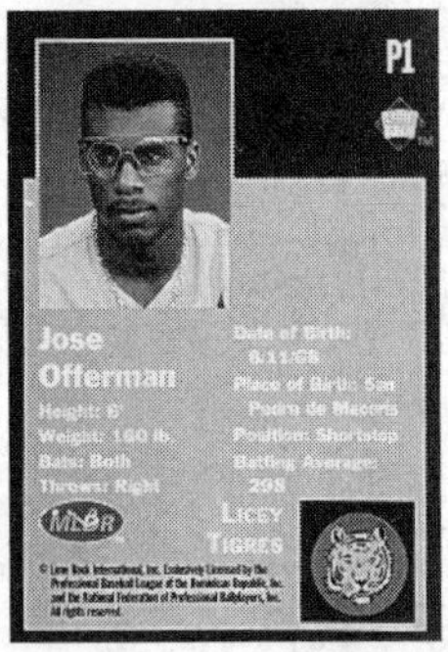

Four of the cards from the Dominican Republic League set are found with card numbers P1-P4, indicating promo card status. Besides being given away as samples, the cards could also be found in foil packs. They are otherwise identical to the regular-issue versions of the same players.

		MT
	Complete Set (4):	.25
	Common Player:	.05
P1	Jose Offerman	.15
P2	Denio Gonzalez	.10
P3	Omar Ramirez	.05
P4	Yorkis Perez	.10

1993 Lime Rock Winter Baseball

The players of the 1993-94 Dominican Winter League are featured in this set. Many of the players are former, current or future U.S. Major Leaguers. The set was issued in nine-card foil packs. The basic design of the 2-1/2" x 3-1/2" cards offers a player pose on front, which is repeated as a close-up head shot on back, both in color. Fronts borders are in gray speckled with white. The player's last name is in white block letters in the right margin. Backs are in black and a team color and include a few vital stats and team logo. The checklist is arranged in team order. Besides the basic player cards there are rookie and "Top Ten" subsets. Each of the player cards can also be found as a "Diamond Star" parallel chase card featruing a large gold-foil Lime Rock logo at top-back. The chase cards are seeded about one per four packs and have premium value.

		MT
	Complete Set (161):	12.00
	Common Player:	.05
1	Luis Encarnacion	.05
2	Alberto Reyes	.05
3	Victor Silverio	.05
4	Wilfredo Tejada	.10
5	Bienvenido Figueroa	.05
6	Daniel Bautista	.10
7	Fidel Compres	.05
8	Miguel Batista	.05
9	Mario Brito	.05
10	Mariano de los Santos	.05
11	Jose Nunez	.05
12	Ramon Manon	.05
13	Rafael Quirico	.05
14	Mel Rojas	.15
15	Sergio Valdez	.05
16	Tony Eusebio	.10
17	Carlos Mota	.05
18	Fausto Cruz	.10
19	Luis de los Santos	.05
20	Mike Guerrero	.05
21	Nelson Liriano	.10
22	Junior Noboa	.05
23	Ruben Santana	.05
24	Domingo Martinez	.05
25	Jose Oliva	.05
26	Julio Peguero	.05
27	Raul Mondesi	.50
28	Juan de la Rosa	.05
29	Geronimo Berroa	.10
30	Jesus Tavares	.05
31	Samuel Cruz	[illegible]
32	Carlos de la Cruz	.05
33	Julian Martinez	.05
34	Norberto Martin	.10
35	Luis Ortiz	.05
36	Miguel Sabino	.05
37	Mauricio Nunez	.05
38	Roberto Rojas	.05
39	Francisco de la Rosa	.05
40	Armando Benitez	.10
41	Julian Heredia	.05
42	Josias Manzanillo	.10
43	Jose Mercedes	.05
44	Bienvenido Rivera	.05
45	Pedro Borbon	.10
46	Francisco Cabrera	.05
47	Ruben Rodriguez	.05
48	Cesar Devarez	.05
49	Manny Alexander	.10
50	Hector Roa	.10
51	Cesar Bernhardt	.05
52	Luis Mercedes	.10
53	Sergio Cairo	.05
54	Cesar Hernandez	.05
55	Jose Luis Garcia	.05
56	Jose Parra	.05
57	Carlos Perez	.25
58	Tito Bell	.05
59	Miguel Santana	.05
60	Pedro Julio Astacio	.15
61	Balvino Galvez	.05
62	Jose Mesa	.15
63	Gabriel Ozuna	.05
64	Hipolito Pena	.05
65	Vladimir Perez	.05
66	Salomon Torres	.05
67	Rafael Valdez	.05
68	Yorkis Perez	.10
69	Jose Segura	.05
70	Efrain Valdez	.05
71	Gilberto Reyes	.05
72	Juan Guerrero	.05
73	Jorge Alvarez	.05
74	Gregorio Carmona	.05
75	Freddy Gonzalez	.05
76	Willie Otanez	.05
77	Jose Offerman	.15
78	Geronimo Pena	.15
79	Bernie Brito	.05
80	Braulio Castillo	.10
81	Silvestre Campusano	.05
82	Felix Jose	.05
83	Jose Rafael Gonzalez	.05
84	Henry Rodriguez	.25
85	Mateo Ozuna	.05
86	Miguel Jimenez	.05
87	Jose Lima	.10
88	Arturo Pena	.05
89	Julian Tavarez	.10
90	Elvin Paulino	.05
91	Patricio Claudio	.05
92	Miguel Garcia	.05
93	Carmelo Castillo	.05
94	Miguel Dilone	.05
95	Jose Sued	.05
96	Bernie Tatis	.05
97	Miguel Fermin	.05
98	Apolinar Garcia	.05
99	Jose Joaquin Bautista	.05
100	Johnny Guzman	.05
101	Manuel Fulcar	.05
102	Victor Garcia	.05
103	Fernando Hernandez	.05
104	Jose Martinez	.05
105	Tony Pena	.15
106	Esteban Beltre	.05
107	Felix Fermin	.10
108	Carlos Fermin	.05
109	William Suero	.05
110	Quilvio Veras	.20
111	Luis Polonia	.10
112	Moises Alou	.50
113	Omar Ramirez	.05
114	Andy Araujo	.05
115	Andres Lopez	.05
116	Jose Cano	.05
117	Cecilio Guante	.05
118	Jesus Martinez	.05
119	Sandy Guerrero	.05
120	Domingo Michel	.05
121	Manolo Mota	.10
122	Ramon Sambo	.05
123	Manny Jose	.05
124	Wilson Heredia	.05
125	Dario Perez	.05
126	Pedro A. Martinez	.05
127	Melido Perez	.10
128	Hipolito Pichardo	.10
129	Jose Ventura	.05
130	Roberto Delgado	.05
131	Henry Mercedes	.10
132	Carlos Capellan	.05
133	Domingo Cedeno	.10
134	Julian Yan	.05
135	Victor Rosario	.05
136	Andujar Cedeno	.15
137	Denio Gonzalez	.05
138	Alberto de los Santos	.05
139	Hensley Meulens	.05
140	Miguel Batista (Top Ten)	.05
141	Fausto Cruz (Top Ten)	.10
142	Raul Mondesi (Top Ten)	.25
143	Jose Lima (Top Ten)	.20
144	Luis Ortiz (Top Ten)	.10
145	Manny Alexander (Top Ten)	.20
146	Jose Oliva (Top Ten)	.05
147	Salomon Torres (Top Ten)	.05
148	Ruben Santana (Top Ten)	.10
149	Omar Ramirez (Top Ten)	.10
150	League history card (checklist 140-149)	.05
151	League history card (checklist 150-161)	.05
152	Escogido Leones logo (checklist 1-15)	.05
153	Escogido Leones logo (checklist 16-31)	.05
154	Estrellas de Oriente logo (checklist 32-43)	.05
155	Estrellas de Oriente logo (checklist 44-54)	.05
156	Licey Tigres logo (checklist 55-70)	.05
157	Licey Tigres logo (checklist 71-86)	.05
158	Aguilas Cibaenas logo (checklist 87-99)	.05
159	Aguilas Cibaenas logo (checklist 100-113)	.05
160	Azucareros del Este logo (checklist 114-126)	.05
161	Azucareros del Estes logo (checklist 127-139)	.05

1991 Line Drive Collect A Books

In their second year, the Collect A Books were produced under the Line Drive brand name. (See CMC for 1990 Collect-A-Books). In similar format, 2-1/2" x 3-1/2" 8-pagers have cardboard covers with a glossy paper insert. The cover and inside cover have action player photos. Page 1 has a portrait photo and personal data. The centerspread has an action photo and career summary. Page 6 has career stats. The inside back cover has another portrait photo, a quote by the player and a trivia fact. The back cover features a cartoon caricature and a couple of career highlights. The books were sold individually for 1991.

		MT
	Complete Set (36):	6.00
	Common Player:	.10
1	Roger Clemens	.45
2	Cal Ripken Jr.	1.50
3	Nolan Ryan	1.50
4	Ken Griffey Jr.	2.00
5	Bob Welch	.10
6	Kevin Mitchell	.10
7	Kirby Puckett	.75
8	Lenny Dykstra	.10
9	Ben McDonald	.10
10	Don Drysdale	.15
11	Lou Brock	.10
12	Ralph Kiner	.10
13	Jose Canseco	.25
14	Cecil Fielder	.15
15	Ryne Sandberg	.50
16	Wade Boggs	.45
17	Dwight Gooden	.15
18	Ramon Martinez	.10
19	Tony Gwynn	.50
20	Mark Grace	.25
21	Kevin Maas	.10
22	Thurman Munson	.25
23	Bob Gibson	.10
24	Bill Mazeroski	.10
25	Rickey Henderson	.15
26	Barry Bonds	.75
27	Jose Rijo	.10
28	George Brett	.50
29	Doug Drabek	.10
30	Matt Williams	.15
31	Barry Larkin	.10
32	Dave Stewart	.10
33	Dave Justice	.15
34	Harmon Killebrew	.10
35	Yogi Berra	.15
36	Billy Williams	.10

1991 Line Drive Mickey Mantle

This 20-card set was part of a collectors kit featuring the Yankees superstar. Fronts of the 2-1/2" x 3-1/2" cards have sepia or color poses or action photos. The player's name appears in white in a blue panel at bottom. Red striping separates the graphics from the white border. The Line Drive logo appears in an upper corner. Backs are printed in red and blue and feature a facsimile autograph, a few sentences about Mantle's career, manufacturer's and licensor's logos, and a card number. The same basic cards were included in a Collectors Marketing Corp. (see CMC) in 1989, lacking the Line Drive logo on front and the Impel logo and 1991 dates on back.

	MT
Complete Set (20):	24.00
Common Card:	2.00
1-20 Mickey Mantle	2.00

1991 Line Drive Ryne Sandberg

This 20-card set was part of a collectors kit featuring the Cubs Hall of Fame second baseman. Fronts of the 2-1/2" x 3-1/2" cards have color poses or action photos. The player's name appears in blue and red in the white border above the photo. Backs are printed in red and blue and feature a few sentences about Sandberg's career, along with manufacturer's and licensor's logos, and a card number.

	MT
Complete Set (20):	10.00
Common Card:	.50
1-20 Ryne Sandberg	.50

1993-94 Line Up Venezuelan Baseball

With names like Aparicio, Valenzuela, Armas, Galarraga and Cedeno, the 1993-94 LineUp Venezuelan Baseball Spanish language set has a certain major league flavor, and the cards could also boast a quality that rivals the myriad sets produced each year in North America. The set contains 350 cards, full color front and back and UV coating, all in a card design reminiscent of Upper Deck issues. The backs of the cards are in Spanish, with a portrait of the player, biographical information, statistics and a large team logo at the bottom of the card. There are two subsets within the regular issue; seven cards honoring former major leaguer and home run champion Tony Armas and 27 cards picturing the Caribbean Series. Randomly inserted into the 14-card foil packs are 250 autographed cards each of Andres Galarraga, Omar Vizquel, Wilson Alvarez, Luis Salazar, William Canate and legendary announcer Musiu Lacavalerie.

		MT
Complete Set (350):		36.00
Common Player:		.10
1	Luis Salazar	.10
2	Antonio Castillo	.10
3	Pedro J. Chavez	.10
4	Felix Leon (Eric Ojeta data on back)	.10
5	Ivan Arteaga	.10
6	Wilson Alvarez	.75
7	Ismael Rodriguez	.10
8	Urbano Lugo	.10
9	Todd Pratt	.35
10	Jose Cardona	.10
11	Luis Aparicio	2.00
12	Frank Campos	.10
13	Pedro P. Belmonte	.10
14	Alejandro Alvarez	.10
15	Juan F. Castillo	.10
16	Jay Baller	.10
17	Jose L. Zambrano	.10
18	Argenis Conde	.10
19	Yonni Naveda	.10
20	Damaso Betancourt	.10
21	Giovanni Carrara	.10
22	Julio Franco	.25
23	Omar Vizquel	.50
24	Jose Marchan	.10
25	Edgar Naveda	.10
26	Pedro Castellano	.10
27	Jairo Ramos	.10
28	Dave Burba	.20
29	Pat Hentgen	.50
30	Ramon Garcia	.10
31	Robinson Garces	.10
32	Remigio Hermoso	.10
33	Malvin Matos	.10
34	Miguel A. Garcia	.10
35	Brad Holman	.10
36	Johnny Malaver	.10
37	Omar Daal	.35
38	Edwin Hurtado	.20
39	Ifrain Linares	.10
40	Richard Delgado	.10
41	Quinn Mack	.20
42	Luis Lunar	.10
43	Luis Gonzalez	.20
44	Gilberto Clisanchez	.10
45	Dave Masters	.10
46	Jesus Hernandez	.10
47	Johanne Manaure	.10
48	Dean Hartgraves	.15
49	Henrique A. Gomez	.10
50	Oscar Azocar	.15
51	Edgar Herrera	.10
52	Luis Dorante	.10
53	Carlos Landines	.10
54	Marcos Manrique	.10
55	Dave Pavlas	.10
56	Jose Garcia	.10
57	Mark Ohlms	.10
58	Todd Jones	.25
59	Julio Machado	.10
60	Jose G. Urdaneta	.10
61	Antonio Lopez	.10
62	Alfredo Ortiz	.10
63	Scott Cepicky	.10
64	Gustavo Pinto	.10
65	Tom McGraw	.15
66	Oswald Peraza	.15
67	Benito Malave	.10
68	Esmily Guerra	.10
69	Todd Trafton	.10
70	Jesus Mendez	.10
71	Amalio Carreno	.10
72	Graciano Ravelo	.10
73	Jose L. Ramos	.10
74	Paul Marak	.10
75	Oscar Sarmiento	.10
76	Alfonzo Osuna	.10
77	Felix Perez	.10
78	Marlon Nava	.10
79	Melvin Mora	.10
80	Steve Wapnick	.10
81	Ricky Rojas	.10
82	Flores Bolivar	.10
83	Donald Strange	.10
84	Mike Soper	.10
85	Juan C. Pulido	.10
86	Daniel Rambo	.10
87	Jorge Velandia	.10
88	Silverio Navas	.10
89	Trent Hubbard	.10
90	Cliff Young	.10
91	Julio C. Strauss	.10
92	Cesar Tovar	.15
93	Dilson Torres	.10
94	Jose Villa	.10
95	Jose Solarte	.10
96	Francisco Munoz	.10
97	Jesus Garces	.10
98	Luis M. Sanchez	.10
99	Jose Monzon	.10
100	Luis Sojo	.10
101	Ugueth Urbina	.25
102	William Ereu	.10
103	Mike Maksudian	.10
104	Clemente Alvarez	.35
105	Luis Portillo	.10
106	Dan Urbina	.10
107	Lester Straker	.10
108	Jose Guarache	.10
109	Miguel Soto	.10
110	Henry Contreras	.10
111	Jose Moreno	.10
112	Luis Leal	.10
113	Jesus Laya	.10
114	Heberto Andrade	.10
115	Angel Escovar	.10
116	Jim Bruske	.10
117	Edgar Marquez	.10
118	Miguel Castellanos	.10
119	Howard Battle	.25
120	Amador Arias	.10
121	Alexander Delgado	.10
122	Omar Malave	.10
123	Lipso Nava	.10
124	Omar Bencomo	.10
125	Oswaldo Olivares	.10
126	Mahaly Carrera	.10
127	Jesus Gonzalez	.10
128	Doug Jennings	.15
129	Egardo Alfonzo	.75
130	Rob Natal	.10
131	Joel Cartaya	.10
132	Antonio Torres	.10
133	Jose Betancourt	.10
134	Carlos Lopez	.10
135	Mario Gonzalez	.10
136	Jose Stella	.10
137	Oscar Ecobar	.10
138	Eddy Diaz	.10
139	Mario Labastidas	.10
140	Rafael DeLima	.10
141	Edgar Tovar	.10
142	Gregorio Machado	.10
143	Harry Guanchez	.10
144	Jesus Alfaro	.10
145	Asdrubal Estrada	.10
146	Henry Centeno	.10
147	Pedro Blanco	.10
148	Kevin Noriega	.10
149	Julio Armas	.10
150	Cristobal Colon	.20
151	Edgar Alfonzo	.10
152	Pablo Torrealba	.10
153	Alexis Infante	.20
154	Andres Espinoza	.10
155	Jeff Grotewold	.15
156	Robert Machado	.10
157	Sherman Obando	.20
158	Wilfredo Polidor	.10
159	Henry Blanco	.10
160	Jeff Kent	.75
161	Alexander Sutherland	.10
162	Noe Maduro	.10
163	Jose G. Gil	.10
164	Fernando Soto	.10
165	Jose Leiva	.10
166	Carlos Subero	.10
167	Edgar Caceres	.10
168	Rodolfo Hernandez	.10
169	William Mota	.10
170	Jesus Acevedo	.10
171	Jose Leon	.10
172	Cesar Gutierrez	.10
173	Blas Cedeno	.10
174	Fernando Ramsey	.10
175	Marcos Armas	.10
176	Roberto Castillo	.10
177	Felipe Lira	.10
178	Joe Hall	.10
179	Freddy Torres	.10
180	Juan Querecuto	.10
181	Douglas Odor	.10
182	Ruben Amaro	.30
183	Matt Maysey	.15
184	Eduardo Perez	.50
185	Freddy Gonzalez	.10
186	Donald Harris	.30
187	Ernesto Gomez	.10
188	William Canate	.10
189	Hector Rincones	.10
190	Johnny Paredes	.10
191	Roberto Espinoza	.10
192	Jesus M. Trillo	.30
193	Jaime Torres	.10
194	Bob K. Abreu	.35
195	Jeff Frye	.20
196	Shawn Jeter	.25
197	Jesus Marquez	.10
198	Scott Bryant	.10
199	Robert Taylor	.10
200	Carlos Garcia	.40
201	Temis Liendo	.10
202	Mauro Mendez	.10
203	Jerry Kutzler	.10
204	Troy O'Leary	.15
205	Phil Regan	.20
206	Lino Conell	.10
207	Luis R. Salazar	.10
208	Len Picota	.10
209	William Magallanes	.10
210	Luis Gonzalez	.50
211	Carlos Burgillos	.10
212	Justo Massaro	.10
213	Carlos T. Trillo	.10
214	Richard Garces	.10
215	Rick Sweet	.10
216	Jim Newlin	.10
217	Hector Ortega	.10
218	Roger Cedeno	.25
219	Eric Anthony	.50
220	Jason Grimsley	.20
221	Juan C. Abreu	.10
222	Leonel Carrion	.10
223	Alejandro Rodriguez	.10
224	Jeff Pierce	.10
225	Gustavo Polidor	.10
226	Steve Pegues	.10
227	William Pennyfeather	.10
228	Eminson Soto	.10
229	Karl Rhodes	.20
230	Barry Manuel	.10
231	Simon Pinango	.10
232	Elias Lugo	.10
233	Raul P. Tovar	.10
234	Roberto Petaguine	.10
235	Oswaldo Virgil	.20
236	Gregory O'Halloran	.10
237	Adrian Jordan	.10
238	Orangel Lopez	.10
239	Roberto Zambrano	.10
240	Mauricio Ruiz	.10
241	Igor Oviedo	.10
242	Angel Leon	.10
243	Wilfredo Romero	.10
244	Richard Romero	.10
245	Pompeyo Davalillo	.20
246	Jack Voigt	.20
247	Danilo Leon	.10
248	Mike Draper	.10
249	Dan Urbina	.10
250	Carlos Hernandez	.20
251	Carlos Martinez	.20
252	Brian Keyser	.10
253	Jorge Uribe	.15
254	Jesus Delgado	.10
255	Garth Iorg	.10
256	Jose Centeno	.10
257	Douglas Moreno	.10
258	Jose F. Malave	.10
259	Oscar Henriquez	.10
260	Eduardo Zembrano	.10
261	Doug Linton	.10
262	Robert Perez	.10
263	Raul Chavez	.10
264	Darrin Chapin	.10
265	Mike Hart	.10
266	Ender Perozo	.10
267	Rick Polak	.10
268	Orlando Munoz	.10
269	Carlos Quintana	.20
270	Oswaldo Guillen	.50
271	Todd Stephan	.10
272	Manuel Gonzalez	.10
273	Terry Francona	.10
274	Jorge Mitchell	.10
275	Alfredo Pedrique	.10
276	Andres Galarraga, Cesar Tovar, Oswaldo Olivares, Alvaro Espinoza	.20
277	Roger Cedeno, Bob Abreau, Rob Natal, Jay Baller, Doug Jennings	.10
278	Roger Cedeno (Novato Del Ano '92-'93)	.15
279	William Canate (Jugador Mas Valioso '92-'93)	.10
280	Andres Galarraga	.75
281	Antonio Armas	.15
282	Tony Armas (El Slugger de Venezuela)	.15
283	Tony Armas (El Slugger de Venezuela)	.15
284	Tony Armas (El Slugger de Venezuela)	.15
285	Tony Armas (El Slugger de Venezuela)	.15
286	Tony Armas (El Slugger de Venezuela)	.15
287	Tony Armas (El Slugger de Venezuela)	.15
288	Todd Pratt, Rob Natal, Gregory O'Halloran, Eduardo Perez, Carlos Hernandez	.10
289	Aguilas del Zulia BBC (team photo)	.10
290	Cangrejeros de Santurce BBC (team photo)	.10
291	Aguilas Cibaenas BBC (team photo)	.10
292	Venados de Mazatlan BBC (team photo)	.10
293	Refuerzos Pitchers (Jason Grimsley, Urbano Lugo, Juan C. Pulido, Felipe Lira)	.10
294	Refuerzos Jugadores (William Canate, Edgar Naveda, Robert Perez)	.10
295	Las Maximas Autoridades (umpires)	.10
296	(Scott Bryant, Jeff Grotewold)	.10
297	Hector Villanueva	.10
298	Tony Pena	.20
299	Jose Munoz	.10
300	Andujar Cedeno	.20
301	Cristobal Colon	.20
302	Edwin Alicea	.30
303	Moises Alou	.75
304	Matias Carrillo	.10
305	Dickie Thon	.20
306	Angel Moreno	.10
307	Mike Cook	.10
308	Luis Polonia	.20
309	Felix Fermin	.20
310	Adalberto Ortiz (Junior)	.20
311	Alex Arias	.20
312	Fernando Valenzuela	.40
313	Johnny Paredes, Moises Alou	.30
314	Scott Bryant, Hector Villanueva	.10
315	Jimmy Wilson, Nelson Simmons	.10
316	(Mako Olivares, Pompeyo Davalillo, Ramon Montaya, Miguel Dilone)	.10
317	Hector Villanueva, Alexander Delgado, Tony Pena	.10
318	William Suero, Edgar Naveda, Guillermo Velazquez	.10
319	Cristobal Colon, Luis Lopez, Andujar Cedeno	.10
320	Luis Polonia, Ruben Escalera, Robert Perez	.10
321	Moises Alou, William Canate, Eric Fox	.15
322	Urbano Lugo, Fernando Valenzuela	.10
323	Liga Venezolana de Beisbol Profesional	.10
324	Asociacion Unica de Peloteros Profesionales de Venezuela	.10
325	Aguilas del Zulia logo	.10
326	Navegantes del Magallanes logo	.10
327	Leones del Caracas logo	.10
328	Cardenenales de Lara logo	.10
329	Tiburones de la Guaira logo	.10
330	Tigres de Aragua logo	.10
331	Caribes de Oriente logo	.10
332	Petroleros de Cabimas logo	.10
333	Checklist: Zulia	.10
334	Checklist: Magallanes	.10
335	Checklist: Caracas	.10
336	Checklist: Lara	.10
337	Checklist: La Guaria	.10
338	Checklist: Aragua	.10
339	Checklist: Caribes	.10
340	Checklist: Cabimas	.10
341	Omar Vizquel	.30
341a	Omar Vizquel (autographed)	35.00
342	William Canate	.10
342a	William Canate (autographed)	5.00
343	Luis Salazar	.10
343a	Luis Salazar (autographed)	5.00
344	Andres Galarraga	.75
344a	Andres Galarraga (autographed)	45.00
345	(Musiu Lacavalerie)	.10
345a	(Musiu Lacavalerie) (autographed)	5.00
346	Wilson Alzarez	.60
346a	Wilson Alvarez (autographed)	20.00
347	La Gran Serie Checklist	.10
348	Checklist 1-122	.10
349	Checklist 123-246	.10
350	Checklist 247-350	.10

1994-95 Line Up Venezuelan Baseball

Line Up followed its debut set for the Venezuelan professional winter baseball league with a 300-card set for the 1994-95 season. Cards have borderless front photos, color photos on back and are UV coated on both sides. Many Major Leaguers are included in the checklist. Besides 14-card foil packs, a factory set was also issued.

		MT
Complete Set (300):		40.00
Common Player:		.10
1	Carlos Garcia	.25
2	Ivan Arteaga	.10
3	Billy Hatcher	.15
4	Erick Ojeda	.10
5	Raul Chavez	.10
6	Cesar Morillo	.10
7	Brian Hunter	1.50
8	Edgar Naveda	.10
9	Luis Raven	.10
10	R. "Tucupita" Marcano	.10
11	Jose Villa	.10
12	Oscar Azocar	.10
13	John Hudek	.25
14	Andres Espinoza	.10
15	Eddy Diaz	.10
16	Edgardo Alfonzo	1.00
17	Juan F. Castillo	.10
18	Melvin Mora	.10
19	Melcher Pacheco	.10
20	Richard Hidalgo	.50
21	Clemente Alvarez	.20
22	Juan Carlos Pulido	.10
23	Al Osuna	.10
24	Ifrain Linares	.10
25	Jason Grimsley	.10
26	Alvaro Espinoza	.10
27	Tim Tolman	.10
28	Coaches Magallanes	.10
29	Henry Blanco	.10
30	Jose Centeno	.10
31	Francisco Munoz	.10
32	Ugueth Urbina	.10
33	Julio Strauss	.10
34	Terry Clark	.10
35	Omar Daal	.20
36	Kip Gross	.10
37	Bill Wertz	.10
38	Jeff Shaw	.10
39	Brad Holman	.10
40	Urbano Lugo	.10
41	Andres Galarraga	2.50
42	Omar Vizquel	2.00
43	Tim Spehr	.10
44	E. "Charallave" Rios	.10
45	Rodolfo Hernandez	.10
46	Jose Stella	.10
47	Miguel Cairo	.25
48	Greg Briley	.10
49	Edgar Caceres	.10
50	Roberto Petagine	.10
51	Bob Abreu	.50
52	Edgar Alfonzo	.10
53	Roger Cedeno	.75
54	Carlos Hernandez	.20
55	Jesus Alfaro	.10
56	Jorge Uribe	.10
57	Roger Cedeno, Omar Vizquel	.25
58	Phil Regan	.15
59	Coaches Caracas	.10
60	Luis Salazar	.10
61	Carlos "Cafe" Martinez	.15
62	Jose Monzon	.10
63	Miguel Soto	.10
64	Gustavo Polidor	.10
65	Alejandro Alvarez	.10
66	Juan Carlos Quero	.10
67	Andrew Lorraine	.10
68	Luis Gonzalez	.50
69	Gustavo Pinto	.10
70	Frank Campos	.10
71	Mark Zappelli	.10
72	Alejandro Prieto	.10
73	Igor Oropeza	.10
74	Steve Pegues	.10
75	Luis Dorante	.10
76	Johanne Manaure	.10
77	Jose Cardona	.10
78	Felipe Lira	.10
79	Dennis Moeller	.10
80	Raul Perez Tovar	.10
81	Freddy Torres	.10
82	Keith Lockhart	.20
83	Mickey Malos	.10
84	Hector Ortega	.10
85	Harry Guanchez	.10
86	Ronny Benavente	.10
87	Karl Rhodes	.20
88	Terry Shumpert	.10
89	Jairo Ramos	.10
90	Oswaldo Guillen	.50
91	Mario Gonzalez	.10
92	Carlos Subero	.10
93	Luis Vasquez	.10
94	Miguel Castellanos	.10
95	Jose Machan	.10
96	Edwin Marquez	.10
97	Robert Guerra	.10
98	James Hurst	.10
99	Jeff Cox	.10
100	Coaches La Guaira	.10
101	Derek Bell	1.50
102	William Canate	.10
103	Jesus Marquez	.10
104	Alex Ramirez	.10
105	Howard Battle	.20
106	Asdrubal Estrada	.10
107	Jesus Azuaje	.10
108	Luis Sojo	.20
109	Alexis Infante	.20
110	Domingo Carrasquel	.10
111	Dilson Torres	.10
112	Oswaldo Peraza	.15
113	Juan Querecuto	.10
114	Woody Williams	.10
115	Scott Brown	.10
116	Gilberto Clisanchez	.10
117	Jose Moreno	.10
118	Omar Sanchez	.10
119	Alex Gonzalez	1.00
120	Mackey Sasser	.10
121	Edwin Hurtado	.15
122	Jose Montilla	.10
123	Marcos Armas	.10
124	Giovanni Carrara	.10
125	Robert Perez	.10
126	Doug Linton	.10
127	Antonio Castillo	.10
128	Huck Flener	.10
129	McLaren	.10
130	Coaches Cardenales	.10
131	Luis Gallardo	.10
132	Jesus Gonzalez	.10
133	Oscar Sarmiento	.10
134	Tow Maynard	.10
135	Todd Pratt	.30
136	Wilfredo Polidor	.10
137	Marcos Manrique	.10
138	L. Mercedes Sanchez	.10
139	Al Levine	.10
140	Augustine Gomez	.10
141	Familia Armas	.10
142	Rolando Caridad	.10
143	Simon Pinango	.10
144	Gilberto Roca	.10
145	Ronaldo Caridad	.10
146	Frank Merigliano	.10
147	Mike Robertson	.10
148	Nigel Alejo	.10
149	Maglio Ordonez	1.50
150	Johnny Paredes	.10
151	Carlos Lopez	.10
152	Brian Keyser	.10
[illegible]	[illegible]	.10
154	Argenis Conde	.10
155	Fred Manrique	.10
156	Jorge Mitchell	.10
157	Wilmer Montoya	.10
158	Julio Franco	.75
159	Felix Perez	.10
160	Pedro Jose Chavez	.10
161	Stuart Ruiz	.10
162	Victor Oramas	.10
163	Julio Armas	.10
164	Jeff Frye	.10
165	William Magallanes	.10
166	Fred Kendall	.10
167	Coaches Caribes	.10
168	Prospectos	.10
'69	Alexis Infante	.20
170	Alfredo Pedrique	.10
171	Fernando Soto	.10
172	Matt Dunbar	.20
173	Marcos Bolanos	.10
174	Jesus "Chalao" Mendez	.10
175	Brad Woodall	.35
176	Jose Leon	.10
177	Jose Correa	.10
178	Jesus Garces	.10
179	Jalal Leach	.10
180	Edgar Tovar	.10
181	Kevin Jordan	.10
182	Leo Hernandez	.10
183	Luis Gallardo	.10
184	Ernesto Gomez	.10
185	Roberto Zambrano	.10
186	Miguel Angel Garcia	.10
187	Rafael DeLima	.10
188	German Gonzalez	.10
189	Lester Straker	.10
190	Robert Castillo	.10
191	Temistocles Liendo	.10
192	Jaime Torres	.10
193	Silverio Navas	.10
194	Eduardo Perez	.35
195	Alexis Santaella	.10
196	Richard Garces	.10
197	Zambrano, Armas	.10
198	Rick Down	.10
199	Coaches Aragua	.10
200	Eduardo Zambrano	.15
201	Wilson Alvarez	.35
202	Jose Solarte	.10
203	Omar Bencomo	.10
204	Lipso Nava	.10
205	Henrique Gomez	.10
206	Jose Luis Zambrano	.10
207	Frank Gonzalez	.10
208	Robinson Garces	.10
209	Jimmy Williams	.10
210	Esmily Guerra	.10
211	Julio Machado	.10
212	Heath Haynes	.10
213	Jeremis Gonzalez	.10
214	Jose Gil	.10
215	Alexander Delgado	.10
216	Eminson Soto	.10
217	Ender Perozo	.10
218	Angel Escobar	.10
219	Jack Voight	.15
220	Cesar Vargas	.10
221	Jeff Tackett	.15
222	Jesse Lewis	.10
223	Dan Masteller	.10
224	Ken Ramos	.10
225	Pedro Castellanos	.10
226	Jorge Velandia	.10
227	Cristobal Colon	.20
228	William Mota	.10
229	Blas Cedeno	.10
230	Luis Portillo	.10
231	Omar Munoz	.10
232	Carlos Burguillos	.10
233	Carlos Quintana	.15
234	Jason Satre	.10
235	Richard Perez	.10
236	Pompeyo Davalillo	.15
237	Coaches Zulia	.10
238	Edgar Herrera	.10
239	Len Picota	.10
240	Nelson Portales	.10
241	Jose Amado	.10
242	Johan Strauss	.10
243	Oswaldo Villalobos	.10
244	David Mosquera	.10
245	Omar Munoz	.10
246	Johnny Gonzalez	.10
247	Danilo Leon	.10
248	Ismel Zabala	.10
249	Joel Pozo	.10
250	Carlos Tovar Trillo	.10
251	Robert Machado	.10
252	Teo Mejias	.10
253	Benito Malave	.10
254	Raul Herrera	.10
255	Luis Salazar	.10
256	Jose Graterol	.10
257	Joe Hall	.10
258	Mario Labastidas	.10
259	Rouglas Odor	.10
260	Jose "Cheo" Garcia	.10
261	Adrian Jordan	.10
262	Jose G. Gil	.10
263	Luis Gallardo	.10
264	Mario Nava	.10
265	Steve Carter	.10
266	Jamie Dismuke	.10
267	Jeff Carter	.10
268	Jimmy Kremers	.10
[illegible]	[illegible]	.10
270	Coaches Petroleros	.10
271	Magallanes checklist	.10
272	Caracas checklist	.10
273	La Guaira checklist	.10
274	Lara checklist	.10
275	Caribes checklist	.10
276	Tigres checklist	.10
277	Zulia checklist	.10
278	Petroleros checklist	.10
279	Clasico La Chinita	.10
280	Garcia, Espinoza	.10
281	Calendario Magallanes	.10
282	Calendario Caracas	.10
283	Calendario La Guaira	.10
284	Calendario Lara	.10
285	Calendario Caribes	.10
286	Calendario Aragua	.10
287	Calendario Zulia	.10
288	Calendario Cabimas	.10
289	Juego de las Estrellas	.10
290	Juego de las Estrellas	.10
291	Juego de las Estrellas	.10
292	Juego de las Estrellas	.10
293	Juego de las Estrellas	.10
294	Juego de las Estrellas	.10
295	Juego de las Estrellas	.10
296	Juego de las Estrellas	.10
297	Juego de las Estrellas	.10
298	Checklist 1-100	.10
299	Checklist 101-200	.10
300	Checklist 201-300	.10

1995-96 Line Up Venezuelan Baseball

The 50th anniversary of Venezuela's winter Professional Baseball League is celebrated in the annual card set from Line Up. Many special subsets are featured along with the basic player cards. The set is rife with current, former and future U.S. major leaguers, as well as local heroes. The basic design features poses and game-action photos with team logos in the lower-left corner of the black borders. Backs have another photo and the player's 1994-95 record against the other teams in the league. Among the subsets are cards commemorating the 1994 and 1995 All-Star Games, cards honoring league award winners, cards honoring the Caimanera (Caymans), a baseball writer's group and a lengthy series featuring the teams and players of the Caribbean Series (#300-325).

		MT
Complete Set (330):		45.00
Common Player:		.10
1	Roger Cedeno	.45
2	Curtis Goodwin	.20
3	Reggie Williams	.20
4	David Davalillo	.10
5	Wiklenman Gonzalez	.25
6	Carlos Mendez	.10
7	Edgar Alfonzo	.10
8	Urbano Lugo	.10
9	Miguel Cairo	.15
10	Jorge Uribe	.10
11	Bob Abreu	.45
12	Tyrone Woods	.15
13	Omar Vizquel	.50
14	Andres Galarraga	.50
15	Wilfredo Romero	.10
16	Henry Blanco	.10
17	Guiomar Guevara	.10
18	Jesus Alfaro	.10
19	Edgar Caceres	.10
20	E. "Charallave" Rios	.10
21	Omar Daal	.20
22	Jose Centeno	.10
23	John DeSilva	.10
24	Pedro P. Belmonte	.10
25	Calvin Jones	.10
26	Carlos Hernandez	.20
27	Roberto Petaguine	.15
28	Jesus Hernandez	.10
29	Ugueth Urbina	.10
30	Dan Urbina	.10
31	Johann Lopez	.10
32	Terry Clark	.10
33	Marcos Ferreira	.10
34	Damaso Betancourt	.10
35	Flores Bolivar, Henry Contreras, Dave Jauss	.10
36	Pompeyo Davalillo	.10
37	Phil Regan	.20
38	Emison Soto	.10
39	Lipso Nava	.10
40	Wilson Alvarez	.45
41	Johnny Carvajal	.10
42	Carlos Quintana	.10
43	Cristobal Colon	.20
44	Jose L. Zambrano	.10
45	David Montiel	.10
46	Orlando Munoz	.10
47	Alexander Delgado	.10
48	Pedro Castellano	.10
49	Jorge Velandia	.10
50	Lino Connell	.10
51	Carlos Burguillos	.10
52	A. Sutherland	.10
53	Jose Gil	.10
54	Ender Perozo	.10
55	William Mota	.10
56	Richard Perez	.10
57	Jose Solarte	.10
58	Geremy Gonzalez	.10
59	Heath Haynes (Heynes on front)	.10
60	Frank Gonzalez	.10
61	Hugo Pinero	.10
62	Blas Cedeno	.10
63	Omar Bencomo	.10
64	Danilo Leon	.10
65	Esmily Guerra	.10
66	Robinson Garces	.10
67	Ruben Amaro, Jr.	.20
68	Luis H. Silva	.10
69	Clasico de la Chinita	.10
70	Cesar Gutierrez, Noel Maduro	.10
71	Ruben Amaro	.20
72	Raul "Tucupita" Marcano	.10
73	Oscar Azocar	.10
74	Edgar Naveda	.10
75	Melvin Mora	.10
76	Edgardo Alfonzo	.75
77	Orlando Miller	.30
78	Eddy Diaz	.10
79	Alvaro Espinoza	.10
80	Carlos Garcia	.20
81	Richard Hidalgo	.50
82	Luis Raven	.10
83	Andres Espinoza	.10
84	Jose F. Malave	.10
85	Amador Arias	.10
86	Clemente Alvarez	.15
87	Raul Chavez	.10
88	Cesar Morillo	.10
89	Cesar Diaz	.10
90	Luis Gonzalez	.35
91	Oscar Padron	.10
92	Ifrain Linares	.10
93	J. Carlos Pulido	.10
94	Melchor Pacheco	.10
95	Ramon Garcia	.10
96	Ivan Arteaga	.10
97	Jose Villa	.10
98	Erick Ojeda	.10
99	Juan F. Castillo	.10
100	Antonio "Loco" Torres, Pablo Torrealba, Hector Rincones	.10
101	Tim Tolman	.10
102	Alvaro Espinoza	.10
103	Chip Hale	.20
104	Silverio Navas	.10
105	Rafael De Lima	.10
106	Jose "Cheo" Garcia	.10
107	J.T. Snow	.50
108	Jesus Mendez	.10
109	Mike Mordecai	.30
110	Jesus Garces	.10
111	Kevin Noriega	.10
112	Jaime Torres	.10
113	Edgar Tovar	.10
114	Rodolfo Hernandez	.10
115	Temis Liendo	.10
116	Eduardo Zambrano	.10
117	Roberto Zambrano	.10
118	Eduardo Perez	.30
119	Rene Pinto	.10
120	Richard Garces	.30
121	M. Angel Garcia	.10
[illegible]	[illegible]	.10
123	Argenis Conde	.10
124	Julio Cesar Strauss	.10
125	Fernando Mejias	.15
126	Lester Straker	.10
127	Alexis Santaella	.10
128	Darwin Cubillan	.10
129	Carlos Aguilar	.10
130	Angel Leon, Alfredo Ortiz, Elias Lugo, Nelson Portales	.10
131	Nigel Alejo	.10
132	Luis M. Sanchez	.10
133	Tony Armas, Jr.	.20
134	Brian Keyser	.10
135	Augustin Gomez	.10
136	Wilmer Montoya	.10
137	Francisco Munoz	.10
138	Al Levine	.10
139	Roberto Castillo	.10
140	Richard Negrete	.10
141	Mauricio Ruiz	.10
142	Alexander Portillo	.10
143	Joe Hall	.10
144	Jesus Lugo	.10
145	Darren Bragg	.30
146	Carlos Lopez	.10
147	Wilfredo Polidor	.10
148	Luis Galindo	.10
149	William Magallanes	.10
150	Mike Robertson	.10
151	Maglio Ordonez	.75
152	Olmedo Saenz	.10
153	Henry Centeno	.10
154	Marcos Manrique	.10
155	Joe Oliver	.20
156	Alexander Ramirez	.10
157	Pedro J. Chavez	.10
158	Rafael Betancourt	.10
159	Jesus Mendoza	.10
160	Carlos Alvarez	.10
161	Daniel Alzualde	.10

162 Antonio Armas, Angel Hernandez, Arquimides Rojas, Jesus Tiamo .10
163 Luis Aponte .10
164 Luis Sojo .20
165 Alexis Infante .20
166 Rob Butler .10
167 Shawn Green 1.00
168 Robert Perez .20
169 Marcos Armas .10
170 Howard Battle .20
171 Jason Townley .10
172 D.E. Carrasqual .10
173 Juan Querecuto .10
174 Omar Sanchez .10
175 Jesus Marquez .10
176 Jesus Gonzalez .10
177 William Canate .10
178 Richard Romero .10
179 Jose Montilla .10
180 Erick Perez .10
181 Isbel Cardona .10
182 Tim Crabtree .20
183 Dilson Torres .10
184 Edwin Hurtado .20
185 Antonio Castillo .10
186 Giovanni Carrara .10
187 Doug Linton .10
188 Jesus Delgado .10
189 Kelvin Escobar .10
190 William Ereu, Juan Escobar, Luis Leal .10
191 Omar Malave .10
192 Jesus Ugueto .10
193 Miguel Soto .10
194 Derek Wachter .10
195 Jose Stella .10
196 Asdrubal Estrada .10
197 Robert Machado .10
198 Jose Marchan .10
199 Luis Ordaz .15
200 Tomas Perez .30
201 Jose Gratorol .10
202 Malvin Matos .10
203 Rouglas Odor .10
204 Jose Amado .10
205 Marlon Nava .10
206 Vicente Garcia .10
207 Quinn Mack .10
208 Adrian Jordan .10
209 Luis Tinoco .10
210 Luis R. Salazar .20
211 Luis Lunar .10
212 Nelson Canas .10
213 Benito Malave .10
214 Carlos T. Trillo .10
215 Ismel Zabala .10
216 Ivan Paz Montiel .10
217 Johnny Gonzalez .10
218 Jose Gonzalez .10
219 Terry Burrows .10
220 Cesar Heredia, Mauro Mendez, Amilcar Medina (El Buchon - mascot) .10
221 William Oropeza .10
222 "Cafe" Martinez .10
223 Jairo Ramos .10
224 Carlos Subero .10
225 Alexander Cabrera .10
226 Hector Ortega .10
227 Johnny Paredes .10
228 Homy Ovalles .10
229 Luis Cartaya .10
230 Mahali Carrera .10
231 Miguel Castellanos .10
232 Jose Monzon .10
233 Harry Guanchez .10
234 Frank Campos .10
235 Edwin Marquez .10
236 Heberto Andrade .10
237 Robert Guerra .10
238 Jorge Melendez .10
239 Victor Lunar .10
240 Alejandro Alvarez .10
241 Gustavo Polidor .10
242 Felipe Lira .15
243 Jose L. Ramos .10
244 James Hurst .10
245 Gustavo Pinto .10
246 Johanne Manaure .10
247 Mario Gonzalez .10
248 Igor Oropeza .10
249 Luis Vazquez .10
250 Oswaldo Guillen .50
251 Victor Colina, Jeff Cox, Evelio Ovalles .10
252 Luis Salazar .10
253 Juego de las Estrellas XXIX (Luis Salazar) (29th All-Star Game) .10
254 Juego de las Estrellas XXIX (Roberto Alomar) (special guest) .50
255 Juego de las Estrellas XXIX - Los Criollos team photo .10
256 Juego de las Estrellas XXIX - Los Extranjeros team photo .10
257 Juego de las Estrellas XXIX (Marcos Armas) (Home run champion) .20
258 Juego de las Estrellas XXIX (Robert Machado, Carlos Hernandez) (All-Star catchers) .10
259 Juego de las Estrellas XXIX (Emilo Velasquez, Humberto Castillo, Henry Leon, "Musulungo" Herrera) (All-Star Umpires) .10
260 Juego de las Estrellas XXIX (Derek Wachter) (All-Star MVP) .10
261 Juego de las Estrellas XXX (Cecil Fielder) (special guest) .45
262 Los Compadres (Caracas teammates) .10
263 El Gran Dia (team photos) .10
264 Leones del Caracas B.B.C. Campeon 1994-1995 (team photo) .10
265 Roberto Petaugine (Gold Glove 1B) .15
266 Carlos Garcia (Gold Glove 2B) .15
267 Omar Vizquel (Gold Glove SS) .50
268 Carlos Martinez (Gold Glove 3B) .20
269 Eduardo Perez (Gold Glove C) .20
270 Darren Bragg (Gold Glove LF) .30
271 J.D. Noland (Gold Glove CF) .10
272 Robert Perez (Gold Glove RF) .15
273 Antonio Castillo (Gold Glove P) .10
274 Caimanera (Andres Galarraga, Victor Davalillo) .20
275 Caimanera (Cesar Tovar) (retiring Tovar's uniform #12) .10
276 Caimanera Los mas Valiosos .10
277 Caimanera (mascot) .10
278 Caimanera (group photo) .10
279 Caimanera (log and history) .10
280 Premio Vitico Davalillo (Victor Davalillo Award - league MVP) .10
281 Victor Davalillo, Eduardo Perez .10
282 Premio Carrao Bracho (Carrao Bracho pitcher of the year award) .10
283 Victor Davalillo, Richard Garces .10
284 Lider Bate 94-95 (Luis Sojo) (batting average leader) .20
285 Novato del Ano 94-95 (Fernando Mejias) (Rookie of the Year) .20
286 Jugado mas Valioso 94-95 (Eduardo Perez) (MVP) .20
287 Pitcher de Ano 94-95 (Richard Garces) (Pitcher of the Year) .20
288 Productor del Ano 94-95 (Carlos Martinez) .10
289 Regreso del Ano 94-95 (Carlos Martinez) .10
290 Caracas Leones logo/checklist .10
291 Aguilas del Zulia logo/checklist .10
292 Magallanes logo/checklist .10
293 Tigres de Aragua logo/checklist .10
294 Caribes de Oriente logo/checklist .10
295 Cardenales logo/checklist .10
296 Pastora logo/checklist .10
297 Tiburones La Guaira logo/checklist .10
298 50 Anos Liga Venezolana de Beisbol Profesional logo/list of presidents .10
299 50 Victorias (Urbano Lugo) .10
300 Senadores de San Juan team photo .10
301 Azucareros del Este team photo .10
302 Naranjeros de Hermosillo team photo .10
303 Leones del Caracas team photo .10
304 Art Howe, Pompeyo Davalillo, Ralph Bryant, Luis Melendez, Luis Tiant .20
305 Los Refuerzos (Caracas teammates) .10
306 Los Refuerzos (Luis Sojo, Eduardo Perez, Carlos Martinez) .10
307 Edgar Alfonzo, Henry Blanco, Roberto Petaguine, Omar Vizquel .20
308 Jose Rijo, Urbano Lugo, Raul Mondesi .30
309 Andujar Cedeno, Domingo Cedeno .25
310 Eduardo Perez, Carlos Delgado, Carlos Hernandez .30
311 Carmelo Martinez, Bob Abreu, Juan Gonzalez, Jesus Alfaro .50
312 Vinny Castilla, Omar Vizquel .40
313 Ruben Sierra, Carlos Delgado .25
314 Roberto Petaguine, Carlos Hernandez, Henry Rodriguez, Henry Blanco .30
315 Roger Cedeno, Raul Mondesi .45
316 Edgar Alfonzo, Jose Offerman, Omar Vizquel, Henry Blanco .30
317 Carlos Baerga, Omar Vizquel .40
318 Jose Rijo, Carlos Martinez .30
319 Jose Rijo, Urbano Lugo .20
320 Rey Sanchez, Omar Vizquel, Roberto Alomar, Luis Sojo .50
321 Carmelo Martinez, Ruben Sierra .25
322 Jose Rijo, Vinny Castilla .40
323 Raul Mondesi, Henry Blanco .40
324 Juan Gonzalez 2.00
325 Roberto Alomar, Carlos Baerga .75
326 Checklist 1-84 .10
327 Checklist 85-168 .10
328 Checklist 169-252 .10
329 Checklist 253-330 .10
330 El Gran #14 (Gus Polidor) (In memoriam) .10

1996-97 Line Up Venezuelan Baseball

Line Up borrowed heavily from Upper Deck's 1994 design in its 1996-97 Venezuelan winter league card set. For the first time, no Anglos are included in the set, only Latino players. Fronts have a large color photo which is repeated at left in a small monotone version. Horizontal backs have a portrait photo, a large team logo and winter league stats.

	MT
Complete Set (300):	35.00
Common Player:	.10

1 Checklist Navegantes .10
2 Alvaro Espinoza .10
3 Eddy Diaz .10
4 Carlos Hernandez .10
5 Cesar Morillo .10
6 Luis Raven .10
7 Melvin Mora .10
8 Carlos Guillen .15
9 Jose Francisco Malave .10
10 Alejandro Freire .10
11 Edgardo Alfonzo .75
12 Carlos Mendoza .25
13 Carlos Garcia .15
14 Raul Chavez .10
15 Richard Hidalgo .50
16 Cesar Diaz .10
17 Clemente Alvarez .15
18 Andres Espinoza .10
19 Ifrain Linares .10
20 Melchor Pacheco .10
21 Oscar Henriquez .10
22 Juan Carlos Pulido .10
23 Erick Ojeda .10
24 Juan Francisco Castillo .10
25 Ramon Garcia .10
26 Mauro Zerpa .10
27 Ivan Arteaga .10
28 Roberto Espinoza .10
29 Hector Rincones .10
30 Jesus Laya .10
31 Gregorio Machado .10
32 Luis Burelli .10
33 Freddy Garcia .20
34 Andy Vicentino .10
35 Checklist Lara .10
36 Juan Munoz .10
37 Miguel Cairo .15
38 Luis Sojo .10
39 Robert Perez .10
40 Alexis Infante .10
41 Juan Querecuto .10
42 Jesus Gonzalez .10
43 Raul Perez Tovar .10
44 Jesus Marquez .10
45 Omar Sanchez .10
46 Domingo E. Carrasqual .10
47 Jose Alguacil .10
48 Jesus Azuaje .10
49 Marcos Armas .10
50 Antonio Castillo .10
51 Giovanni Carrara .10
52 Edwin Hurtado .15
53 Erick Perez .10
54 Jesus Delgado .10
55 Kelvin Escobar .10
56 Isbel Cardona .10
57 Luis Leal .10
58 Graterol, Vargas .10
59 Omar Malave .10
60 Checklist Aragua .10
61 Oscar Azocar .10
62 Roberto Zambrano .10
63 Jose Cheo Garcia .10
64 Temis Liendo .10
65 Rene Pinto .10
66 Silverio Navas .10
67 Jesus Chalao Mendez .10
68 Marlon Nava .10
69 Jaime Torres .10
70 Edgar Naveda .10
71 Eduardo Perez .15
72 Edgar Tovar .10
73 Hector Ugueto .10
74 Jesus Garces .10
75 Eduardo Zambrano .10
76 Amador Arias .10
77 Carlos Aguilar .10
78 Simon Pinango .10
79 Alejandro Bracho .10
80 Luis Colmenares .10
81 Richard Garces .10
82 Ronald Caridad .10
83 Alexis Santaella .10
84 Darwin Cubillan .10
85 Fernando Mejias .10
86 Julio Cesar Strauss .10
87 Jose Correa .10
88 Miguel Angel Garcia .10
89 Les Straker .10
90 Argenis Conde .10
91 Ismel Zabala .10
92 Jesus Avila .10
93 Elias Lugo .10
94 Nelson Porte .10
95 Angel Pocho Gomez .10
96 Alfredo Ortiz .10
97 Checklist Zulia .10
98 Cristobal Colon .10
99 Ruben Amaro, Jr. .15
100 Jose Gil Urdaneta .10
101 Carlos Burguillos .10
102 Lino Connell .10
103 Emison Soto .10
104 Carlos Quintana .10
105 Lipso Nava .10
106 Orlando Munoz .10
107 Jose Luis Zambrano .10
108 Alexander Delgado .15
109 Pedro Castellano .10
110 Jorge Velandia .10
111 Jhonny Carvajal .10
112 David Montiel .10
113 Johnny Paredes .10
114 Hugo Pinero .10
115 Omar Bencomo .10
116 Wilson Alvarez .20
117 Julio Machado .10
118 Jose Solarte .10
119 Danilo Leon .10
120 Jeremy Gonzalez .10
121 Blas Cedeno .10
122 Esmili Guerra .10
123 Noe Maduro .10
124 Cesar Gutierrez .10
125 Ruben Amaro .10
126 Clasico La Chinita .10
127 Boanerge Corzo .10
128 Campos Miguel .10
129 Didimo Bracho .10
130 Checklist Caracas .10
131 Roger Cedeno .25
132 Bob Abreu .45
133 Carlos Hernandez .15
134 Roberto Petagine .10
135 Eduardo Rios .10
136 Edgar Alfonzo .10
137 Wilfredo Romero .10
138 Giomar Guevara .10
139 Edgar Caceres .10
140 Alex Gonzalez .25
141 Luis Rodriguez .10
142 Jorge Uribe .10
143 Nestor Serrano .10
144 Wiklenman Gonzalez .25
145 Henry Blanco .10
146 Carlos Mendez .10
147 David Davalillo .10
148 Omar Vizquel .35
149 Andres Galarraga .75
150 Urbano Lugo .10
151 Jesus Hernandez .10
152 Ronnie Sorzano .10
153 Omar Daal .15
154 Pedro Belmonte .10
155 Jose Centeno .10
156 Johan Lopez .10
157 Ugueth Urbina .15
158 Damaso Betancourt .10
159 Gustavo Jose Gil .10
160 Dilson Torres .10
161 Dan Urbina .10
162 David Jauss .10
163 Jesus Alfaro .10
164 Manuel Gonzalez .10
165 Phil Regan .10
166 Checklist Pastora .10
167 Robert Machado .10
168 Malvin Matos .10
169 Tomas Perez .25
170 Vincente Garcia .10
171 Kevin Noriega .10
172 Rafael DeLima .10
173 Jose Amado .10
174 Richard Romero .10
175 Asdrubal Estrada .10
176 Luis Ordaz .10
177 Jesus Ugueto .10
178 Ender Perozo .10
179 Ramon Hernandez .10
180 Luis Tinoco .10
181 Adrian Jordan .10
182 Darwin Bracho .10
183 Raul Marval .10
184 Jose Villa .10
185 Luis Lunar .10
186 Douglas Aguiar .10
187 Benito Malave .10
188 Luis Rafael Salazar .10
189 Nelson Canas .10
190 Guillermo Larreal .10
191 Robinson Garces .10
192 Jose Gonzalez .10
193 Johnny Gonzalez .10
194 Oswaldo Villalobos .10
195 Massaro, Humphryes .10
196 Domingo Carrasquel .10
197 Checklist Caribes .10
198 Raul Marcano .10
199 Marcos Manrique .10
200 Edwin Marquez .10
201 Maglio Ordonez .75
202 Victor Oramas .10
203 Jesus Mendoza .10
204 Alexander Ramirez .10
205 Miguel Nieves .10
206 Wuarnner Rincones .10
207 Carlos Alvarez .10
208 Marco Scutaro .10
209 Jesus Lugo .10
210 Fernando Lunar .10
211 Henry Centeno .10
212 Freddy Gonzalez .10
213 Antonio Armas, Jr .10
214 Jose Luis Ramos .10
215 Nigel Alejo .10
216 William Martinez .10
217 Wilmer Montoya .10
218 Richard Negrete .10
219 Francisco Munoz .10
220 Mauricio Ruiz .10
221 Agustin Gomez .10
222 Alexander Portillo .10
223 Tomas Salazar .10
224 Mendoza, Tiamo .10
225 Rojas, Marcano .10
226 Pompeyo Davalillo .10
227 Checklist La Guara .10
228 William Oropeza .10
229 Jairo Ramos .10
230 Miguel Rendon .10
231 Wilfredo Polidor .10
232 Alexander Cabrera .10
233 Carlos Martinez .10

234	Mario Gonzalez	.10
235	Jose Monzon	.10
236	Carlos Subero	.10
237	Rouglas Odor	.10
238	William Canate	.10
239	Hector Ortega	.10
240	William Magallanes	.10
241	Alejandro Prieto	.10
242	Rafael Alvarez	.10
243	Miguel Castellanos	.10
244	Heberto Andrade	.10
245	Ozwaldo Guillen	.40
246	Ivan Paz Montiel	.10
247	Frank Campos	.10
248	Carlos Tovar Trillo	.10
249	Igor Oropeza	.10
250	Alex Oviedo	.10
251	Juan Carlos Moreno	.10
252	Richard Fernandez	.10
253	Felipe Lira	.15
254	Alejandro Alvarez	.10
255	Homer Baez	.10
256	Remigio Hermoso	.10
257	Dorante, Moreno	.10
258	Los Hermanos Zambrano (Alexander Delgado, Eduardo Perez)	.10
259	Checklist Equipos	.10
260	Premio Vitico Davalillo	.15
261	Premio Carrao Bracho	.15
262	Premio Pitcher Del Ano	.15
263	Premio Relevista Del Ano	.15
264	Premio Novato Del Ano	.25
265	Premio Productor Del Ano	.15
266	Premio Regreso Del Ano	.15
267	J.E. Fielder/Leal	.15
268	J.E. Criollos/ Importados	.15
269	J.E. Competencias	.15
270	J.E. Jonrrones/ Umpires	.15
271	J.E. Directiva/ Delgados	.15
272	Sojo, Vitico	.15
273	Los Grandes en la Serie	.15
274	Los Grandes en la Serie	.15
275	Los Grandes en la Serie	.15
276	Los Grandes en la Serie	.15
277	Los Grandes en la Serie	.15
278	Los Grandes en la Serie	.15
279	Los Grandes en la Serie	.15
280	G.O. Omar Daal	.15
281	G.O. Robert Machado	.15
282	G.O. Carlos Quintana	.15
283	G.O. Eddy Diaz	.15
284	G.O. Miguel Cairo	.15
285	G.O. Tomas Perez	.25
286	G.O. Robert Perez	.25
287	G.O. Roger Cedeno	.25
288	G.O. Marvin Benard	[illegible]
289	David Concepcion	.25
290	David Concepcion	.25
291	David Concepcion	.25
292	David Concepcion	.25
293	David Concepcion	.25
294	David Concepcion	.25
295	David Concepcion	.25
296	David Concepcion	.25
297	David Concepcion	.25
298	Check List General 1-100	.10
299	Check List General 101-200	.10
300	Check List General 201-300	.10

1997-98 Line Up Venezuelan Baseball

Many current, former and future major leaguers are included in this set of players in Venezuela's winter league. Cards fronts (some horizontal, some vertical) have one color action photo over another. Backs have a portrait photo and league stats. Both team and manufacturer logos appear on front and back.

		MT
	Complete Set (350):	35.00
	Common Player:	.10
1	Checklist Magallanes	.10
2	Carlos Guillen	.15
3	Erick Ojeda	.10
4	Melvin Mora	.10
5	Eddy Diaz	.15
6	Richard Hidalgo	.50
7	Clemente Alvarez	.10
8	Marvin Benard	.25
9	Edgardo Alfonzo	.75
10	Alvaro Espinoza	.10
11	Juan Francisco Castillo	.10
12	Carlos Hernandez	.15
13	Carlos Garcia	.15
14	Richard Paz	.10
15	Juan Penalver	.10
16	Marlon Roche	.10
17	Oscar Henriquez	.10
18	Luis Raven	.10
19	Melcher Pacheco	.10
20	Roger Blanco	.10
21	Al Osuna	.10
22	Ivan Arteaga	.10
23	Jose Francisco Malave	.10
24	Jeff Tam	.10
25	Raul Chavez	.10
26	Edgar Ramos	.10
27	Alejandro Freire	.10
28	Carlos Mendoza	.25
29	Alberto Blanco	.10
30	Ramon Garcia	.10
31	Andy Abad	.10
32	Leonaldo Oliveros	.10
33	Jose Luis Avila	.10
34	Freddy Garcia	.20
35	Juan Carlos Pulido	.10
36	Alexander Rondon	.10
37	Alfredo Pedrique	.10
38	Gregorio Machado	.10
39	John Tamargo	.10
40	Checklist Caracas	.10
41	Giomar Guevara	.10
42	Henry Blanco	.10
43	Wiklenman Gonzalez	.25
44	Roberto Petagine	.10
45	Roger Cedeno	.25
46	Edgar Alfonzo	.10
47	Alex Gonzalez	.25
48	Wilfredo Romero	.10
49	Carlos Mendez	.10
50	Carlos Hernandez	.15
51	David Davalillo	.10
52	Liu Rodriguez	.10
53	Bob Abreu	.35
54	Howard Battle	.15
55	Ken Huckaby	.10
56	Edwin Centeno	.10
57	Daniel Delgado	.10
58	Oswaldo Flores	.10
59	Gary Thurman	.10
60	Omar Daal	.15
61	Jose Centeno	.10
62	Dilson Torres	.10
63	Ronnie Sorzano	.10
64	Renny Duarte	.10
65	Matt Herges	.10
66	John Hudek	.10
67	Johan Lopez	.10
68	Urbano Lugo	.10
69	Orber Moreno	.10
70	Jean Morillo	.10
71	Jimmy Myers	.10
72	Pedro Ortiz	.10
73	Klisber Parra	.10
74	Jesus Hernandez	.10
75	Ugueth Urbina	.15
76	Andres Galarraga	.50
77	Omar Vizquel	.40
78	A. Colmenares, C. Gil	.10
79	Manuel Gonzalez	.10
80	Jesus Alfaro	.10
81	Antonio Armas, Jr.	.15
82	Phil Regan	.10
83	Checklist Lara	.10
84	Alexis Infante	.10
85	Marcos Armas	.10
86	Juan Querecuto	.10
87	Jose Alguacil	.10
88	Luis Sojo	.10
89	Jesus Azuaje	.10
90	Miguel Cairo	.20
91	Shannon Stewart	.25
92	Edgar Naveda	.10
93	Wilfredo Polidor	.10
94	Alexander Ramirez	.10
95	Andres Espinoza	.10
96	Cesar Diaz	.10
97	Curtis Charles	.10
98	Selwyn Langaine	.10
99	Juan Nieves	.10
100	Robert Perez	.15
101	Nelson Prada	.10
102	Lonell Roberts	.10
103	Giovanni Carrara	.10
104	Antonio Castillo	.10
105	Edwin Hurtado	.15
106	Kelvim Escobar	.10
107	Beiker Graterol	.10
108	Erick Perez	.10
109	Alexander Portillo	.10
110	Travis Baptist	.10
111	Luis Silva	.10
112	Carlos Hernandez	.10
113	Los Broncos/Los Prospectos	.10
114	Luis Leal	.10
115	Omar Malave	.10
116	Checklist Caribes	.10
117	Raul Marcano	.10
118	Marcos Manrique	.10
119	Edwin Marquez	.10
120	Magglio Ordonez	.75
121	Nigel Alejo	.10
122	Jesus Mendoza	.10
123	Miguel Nieves	.10
124	Antonio Armas, Jr.	.15
125	Alexander Delgado	.15
126	Henry Centeno	.10
127	Marco Scutaro	.10
128	Jesus Lugo	.10
129	Richard Negrete	.10
130	Jackson Melian	.50
131	Fernando Lunar	.10
132	Rafael Betancourt	.10
133	Eduardo Rios	.10
134	Jack Voight	.10
135	Tomas Perez	.15
136	Omar Sanchez	.10
137	Luis Gonzalez	.15
138	Chris Clapinski	.10
139	Pedro Belmonte	.10
140	Luis Aponte	.10
141	Benji Simonton	.10
142	Anaximandro Morales	.10
143	Casey Candaele	.10
144	Horacio Estrada	.10
145	Les Norman	.10
146	Jose Luis Ramos	.10
147	William Pennyfeather	.10
148	Javier Gutierrez	.10
149	Wilmer Sanchez	.10
150	Maycol Anez	.10
151	Antonio Vasquez	.10
152	Rouglas Odor	.10
153	Pompeyo Davalillo	.10
154	Checklist Aragua	.10
155	Jose Garcia	.10
156	Rene Pinto	.10
157	Marlon Nava	.10
158	Jaime Torres	.10
159	Willie Banks	.10
160	Oscar Azocar	.10
161	Edgar Tovar	.10
162	Hector Ugueto	.10
163	Julio Cesar Strauss	.10
164	Ronald Caridad	.10
165	Jesus Mendez	.10
166	David Concepcion Jr.	.15
167	Jose Lobaton	.10
168	Fernando Mejias	.10
169	Jesus Paraqueima	.10
170	Richard Garces	.10
171	Franklin Font	.15
172	[illegible]	.10
173	Victor Valencia	.10
174	Juan Carlos Orta	.10
175	Eduardo Zambrano	.10
176	Alejandro Bracho	.10
177	Jorge Cordova	.10
178	Luis Colmenares	.10
179	Carlos Aguilar	.10
180	Roberto Zambrano	.10
181	Jorby Sosa	.10
182	Pedro Castellano	.10
183	Blas Cedeno	.10
184	El Aguinaldazo de los Tigres	.10
185	Coaches	.10
186	Alfredo Ortiz	.10
187	Checklist Zulia	.10
188	Carlos Burguillos	.10
189	Ruben Amaro, Jr.	.15
190	Cristobal Colon	.10
191	Omar Bencomo	.10
192	Lino Connell	.10
193	Gary Bennett	.10
194	Lipso Nava	.10
195	Geremi Gonzalez	.10
196	Emison Soto	.10
197	Danilo Leon	.10
198	Orlando Munoz	.10
199	Carlos Quintana	.10
200	Wilson Alvarez	.15
201	Jose Luis Zambrano	.10
202	Elvis Polanco	.10
203	Hugo Pinero	.10
204	Jhonny Carvajal	.10
205	Jorge Velandia	.10
206	Richard Perez	.10
207	Dennis Abreu	.10
208	Didimo Bracho	.10
209	Jesus Marquez	.10
210	Eduardo Perez	.15
211	Eric Owens	.10
212	Felipe Jiminez	.10
213	Clasico "La Chinita"	.10
214	Labastidas, Andrade	.10
215	Ruben Amaro	.15
216	Noe Maduro	.10
217	Checklist Pastora	.10
218	Elkin Barrios	.10
219	Felix Blanco	.10
220	Robert Machado	.10
221	Nelson Canas	.10
222	Darwin Bracho	.10
223	Douglas Aguiar	.10
224	Alexander Cabrera	.10
225	Ramon Hernandez	.10
226	Ifrain Linares	.10
227	Ronald Machado	.10
228	Domingo Carrasquel	.10
229	Jacob Cruz	.20
230	Luis Tinoco	.10
231	Esmili Guerra	.10
232	Argenis Conde	.10
233	Rafael Delima	.10
234	Guillermo Larreal	.10
235	Jose Montilla	.10
236	Kevin Noriega	.10
237	Erwin Oquendo	.10
238	Wilmer Montoya	.10
239	Jose Villa	.10
240	Richard Romero	.10
241	Carlos Valderrama	.10
242	Desi Wilson	.25
243	Dan Carlson	.10
244	Luis Ordaz	.10
245	Hector Ortega	.10
246	Yolvit Torrealba	.10
247	Luis Lunar	.10
248	Vincente Garcia	.10
249	Nasty Boys/ Hermanos Machado	.10
250	Humphreys, Gutierrez	.10
251	Domingo Carrasquel	.10
252	Checklist La Guaria	.10
253	Daniel Agli	.10
254	Rafael Alvarez	.10
255	Igor Oropeza	.10
256	Igor Oviedo	.10
257	Johnatan Arraiz	.10
258	Wesley Helms	.50
259	Carl Shultz	.10
260	Oswaldo Guillen	.45
261	Angel Juarez	.10
262	Carlos Tovar Trillo	.10
263	Rendy Espina	.10
264	Luis Landaeta	.10
265	William Oropeza	.10
266	Bronson Heflin	.10
267	Homy Ovalles	.10
268	John Saffer	.10
269	Jose Monzon	.10
270	Andruw Jones	5.00
271	Luis Lopez	.10
272	Ben VanRyn	.10
273	Raul Marval	.10
274	Juan Carlos Moreno	.10
275	Bobby Jones	.25
276	Alejandro Prieto	.10
277	Carlos Subero	.10
278	Kerry Valrie	.10
279	Luis Rafael Salazar	.10
280	Carlos Martinez	.10
281	Rodolfo Veitia	.10
282	Robinson Romero	.10
283	Grabriel Luckert	.10
284	Delvis Pacheco	.10
285	William Canate	.10
286	Mike Hostetler	.10
287	Rene Arocha	.15
288	Homer Baez	.10
289	Frank Campos	.10
290	Felipe Lira	.10
291	Jairo Ramos	.10
292	Milton D'Abreu	.10
293	Dorante, Hernandez	.10
294	Carlos Moreno	.10
295	Antonio Torres	.10
296	Checklist Line Up	.10
297	Juego de las Estrellas	.10
298	J.E. D. Acosta/ Premier Bola	.10
299	J.E. M. Benard/ Comp. Jonrones	.10
300	J.E. J. Monzon/ Comp. Tiro A 2DA.	.10
301	J.E. Turino Gran Gato / I. Saez	.10
302	Premio Vitico Davalillo	.10
303	Premio Carrao Bracho	.10
304	Premio Novato Del Ano	.25
305	Premio Productor Del Ano	.10
306	Premio Regreso Del Ano	.10
307	G.O. Omar Daal	.10
308	G.O. Robert Machado	.10
309	G.O. Jesus Mendez	.10
310	G.O. Henry Centeno	.10
311	G.O. Edgardo Alfonzo	.20
312	G.O. Alex Gonzalez	.20
313	G.O. Magglio Ordonez	.20
314	G.O. Roger Cedeno	.15
315	G.O. Robert Perez	.20
316	Checklist Serie del Caribe	.10
317	S.C. Alex Arias	.10
318	S.C. Alomar, Alfonzo, Alfanzo, Pena	.25
319	S.C. Abreu, Polonia, Mora, Alvarez, Pacheco, Velasquez, Malave	.25
320	S.C. Rafel Montalvo	.10
321	S.C. Alomar, Carrara, Carrara, Fermin, Sojo	.25
322	S.C. Jose Offerman	.15
323	S.C. Castillo, Hector Villanueva, Olivares	.10
324	S.C. Luis Polonia	.10
325	S.C. Munoz, Hidalgo, Diaz, Sojo, Munoz	.10
326	S.C. Mike Perez	.10
327	S.C. Perez, Henriquez, Henriquez, Lima	.10
328	S.C. Tony Batista, Neifi Perez	.20
329	S.C. Tavares, Ramos, Roberto Alomar	.35
330	S.C. Malave, Hamelin, Jose Rosado	.15
331	S.C. Roberto Alomar	1.00
332	S.C. La Tacomania Abreu / Perez	.25
333	S.C. Alvarez, Chavez, Abreu y Ahijado	.20
334	Luis Aparicio	.50
335	Luis Aparicio	.50
336	Luis Aparicio	.50
337	Luis Aparicio	.50
338	Luis Aparicio	.50
339	Luis Aparicio	.50
340	Luis Aparicio	.50
341	Luis Aparicio	.50
342	Luis Aparicio	.50
343	Caribes Al Round Robin	.10
344	Homenajea Galarraga	.30
345	Trainers	.10
346	Asoda	.10
347	Checklist General 1-92	.10
348	Checklist General 93-183	.10
349	Checklist General 184-273	.10
350	Checklist General 274-350	.10

1991 Line Up Productions Minnesota Twins Playmakers

The World Champion Minnesota Twins of 1991 are featured on a line-up of what can best be described as huge cards or small posters. The 7" x 18" "Playmakers" posters were sold by Twin Cities Federal Banks' 57 branches for $2 apiece with three or four different posters available each week from Oct. 4 through Oct. 21; the promotion ended Nov. 8. The posters feature bold artwork and colors, the work of Minneapolis artist Mark Herman. A Twins' championship season logo appears beneath the player picture. At bottom are logos of the bank, Major

League Baseball and the team's media flagship. Backs are blank.

		MT
Complete Set (14):		45.00
Common Player:		3.00
(1)	Rick Aguilera	3.00
(2)	Chili Davis	4.00
(3)	Scott Erickson	4.00
(4)	Greg Gagne	4.00
(5)	Dan Gladden	3.00
(6)	Brian Harper	3.00
(7)	Kent Hrbek	5.00
(8)	Tom Kelly	3.00
(9)	Chuck Knoblauch	7.50
(10)	Shane Mack	3.00
(11)	Jack Morris	4.00
(12)	Mike Pagliarulo	3.00
(13)	Kirby Puckett	15.00
(14)	Kevin Tapani	3.00

1992 Line Up Productions Atlanta Braves Playmakers

Following up on its series of '91 Twins posters, Line Up issued a set to commemorate the Braves' 1992 National League championship. Sponsored by Target stores and Coca-Cola, the Braves posters were sold at all Target stores in Georgia. Retail price at issue was $2.97. The 7" x 18" blank-back posters feature the bold colors and artwork of artist Mark Herman. A championship logo is beneath the player picture, with sponsors' and licensors' logos and copyright information at bottom.

		MT
Complete Set (8):		32.00
Common Player:		3.00
111	Tom Glavine	4.50
112	Sid Bream	3.00
113	Deion Sanders	7.50
114	John Smoltz	4.50
115	David Justice	6.00
116	Terry Pendleton	3.00
117	Greg Olson	3.00
118	Ron Gant	4.50

1985 Lion Photo Chicago Cubs

Sponsored by a Chicago photography store chain, this set features the players, coaches and manager on large-format (3-1/2" x 5") cards. Fronts have a color portrait photo of the player, with his name in blue at the bottom. Backs are printed in dark blue and have an ad for Lion Photo and its product lines. The unnumbered cards are checklisted here alphabetically.

		MT
Complete Set (27):		15.00
Common Player:		.50
(1)	Thad Bosley	.50
(2)	Larry Bowa	.50
(3)	Warren Brusstar	.50
(4)	Ron Cey	.75
(5)	Jody Davis	.50
(6)	Brian Dayett	.50
(7)	Bob Dernier	.50
(8)	Shawon Dunston	.75
(9)	Leon Durham	.50
(10)	Dennis Eckersley	2.00
(11)	Ray Fontenot	.50
(12)	George Frazier	.50
(13)	Jim Frey	.50
(14)	Steve Lake	.50
(15)	Davy Lopes	.50
(16)	Gary Matthews	.50
(17)	Keith Moreland	.50
(18)	Dick Ruthven	.50
(19)	Ryne Sandberg	6.00
(20)	Scott Sanderson	.50
(21)	Lee Smith	.75
(22)	Lary Sorenson	.50
(23)	Chris Speier	.50
(24)	Rick Sutcliffe	.50
(25)	Steve Trout	.50
(26)	Gary Woods	.50
(27)	Don Zimmer	.50

1984 Lite Beer Tony Gwynn

Fans attending the Padres game on Sept. 23 received a 5" x 7" card honoring Tony Gwynn, who won the N.L. batting championship that season. The card features a color photo on front of Gwynn posing with a huge baseball bat. The photo is surrounded by a gold border with his name and team at bottom and Lite logos in the lower corners. The back has personal data and Gwynn's stats through the 1983 season.

		MT
(1)	Tony Gwynn	12.00

1986 Lite Beer Astros

This regional set of the Houston Astros was sponsored by Lite Beer and given away in a special stadium promotion. The 4-1/2" x 6-3/4" cards feature full-color photos surrounded by a wide, white border. Diagonal color bands of yellow, orange, red and purple extend throught the upper-right and lower-left corners of the card, which also displays the Astros' 25th Anniversary logo and the Lite Beer logo in opposite corners. The backs include player information and statistics.

		MT
Complete Set (22):		35.00
Common Player:		1.50
3	Phil Garner	1.50
6	Mark Bailey	1.50
10	Dickie Thon	1.50
11	Frank DiPino	1.50
12	Craig Reynolds	1.50
14	Alan Ashby	1.50
17	Kevin Bass	1.50
19	Bill Doran	1.50
20	Jim Pankovits	1.50
21	Terry Puhl	1.50
22	Hal Lanier	1.50
25	Jose Cruz	2.00
27	Glenn Davis	1.50
28	Billy Hatcher	1.50
29	Denny Walling	1.50
33	Mike Scott	1.50
34	Nolan Ryan	15.00
37	Charlie Kerfeld	1.50
39	Bob Knepper	1.50
43	Jim Deshaies	1.50
45	Dave Smith	1.50
53	Mike Madden	1.50

1986 Lite Beer Rangers

This postcard-size (approximately 4" x 6") set of Texas Rangers cards was sponsored by Lite Beer and was available by mail directly from the team. Fronts feature full-color photos surrounded by a wide, white border with the player's name, uniform number and postion appearing below. The Rangers logo is displayed in the lower-left corner, while the Lite Beer logo is in the lower-right. Backs offer personal information and stats.

		MT
Complete Set (28):		30.00
Common Player:		1.50
0	Oddibe McDowell	1.50
1	Scott Fletcher	1.50
2	Bobby Valentine	1.50
4	Don Slaught	1.50
5	Pete Incaviglia	2.00
9	Pete O'Brien	1.50
10	Art Howe	1.50
11	Toby Harrah	1.50
12	Geno Petralli	1.50
13	Joe Ferguson	1.50
14	Tim Foli	1.50
15	Larry Parrish	1.50
16	Mike Mason	1.50
17	Darrell Porter	1.50
18	Ed Correa	1.50
19	Curtis Wilkerson	1.50
22	Steve Buechele	1.50
23	Jose Guzman	1.50
24	Ricky Wright	1.50
27	Greg Harris	1.50
31	Tom Robson	1.50
32	Gary Ward	1.50
35	Tom House	1.50
44	Tom Paciorek	1.50
45	Dwayne Henry	1.50
48	Bobby Witt	2.00
49	Charlie Hough	2.50
---	Arlington Stadium	1.50

1988 Lite Beer All Stars (large)

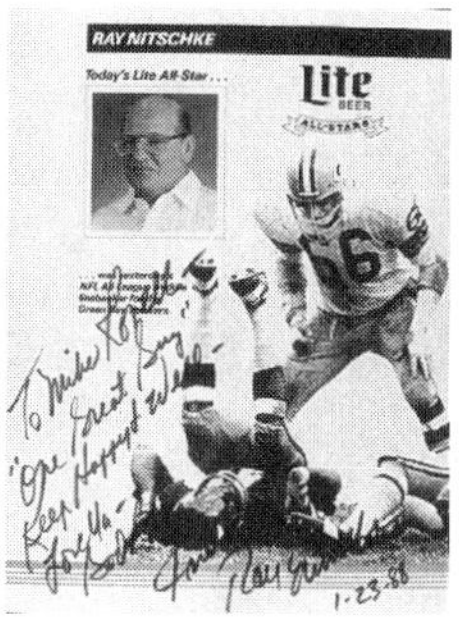

One of two types of photo cards produced in conjunction with its series of late-1980s television commercials featuring former athletes, this series from Lite Beer is printed in a 6" x 7-3/4" format. Card fronts feature a color head shot of the spokesman as he appeared at the time of issue, and a larger black-and-white action photo from his playing days. Backs of the larger-format series include biographical details, career summary and/or stats.

		MT
Complete Set (4):		24.00
Common Player:		6.00
(1)	Ken Brett	6.00
(2)	Boog Powell	9.00
(3)	Luis Tiant	7.50
(4)	Bob Uecker	9.00

1988 Lite Beer All Stars (small)

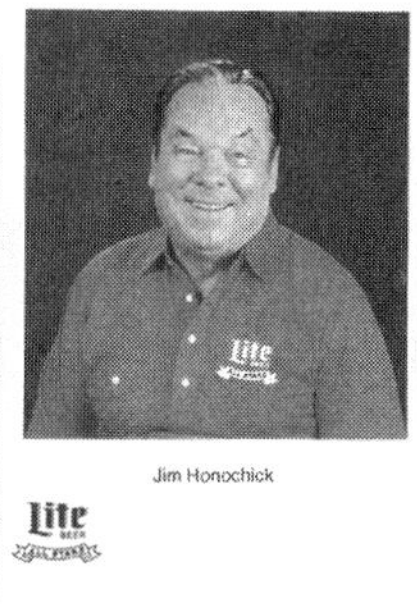

In the late 1980s, in conjunction with its series of television commercials featuring former athletes, Lite Beer created this set of 5" x 7" photocards, presumably for use as autograph items at personal appearances. Cards feature the athletes in color portraits wearing Lite Beer golf shirts. Their name appears in black in the wide white bottom border, which also contains a Lite Beer All Stars logo at left. The cards are blank backed. Only the baseball players from the set are included in the checklist here, presented alphabetically.

		MT
Complete Set (5):		24.00
Common Player:		4.00
(1)	Jim Honochick	4.00
(2)	Sparky Lyle	4.00
(3)	Frank Robinson	9.00
(4)	Marv Throneberry	4.00
(5)	Dick Williams	4.00

1994 Lite Beer Milwaukee Brewers

The 1994 baseball strike interrupted the issue of this four-series commemorative set advertised as including "Every Player in the Brewers Twenty-Five Year History." The set was produced in four booklets of 94 cards each. Individual 2-1/2" x 3-1/2" cards were perforated for easy detachment from the 13" x 7" booklets. Cards feature black-and-white player photos against a gold border. A blue, green and gold Brewers 25th anniversary logo is in the upper-left corner on front. Half of the cards (Series I, II) have a Lite beer logo at top, while half (Series III, IV) have a Miller Genuine Draft logo. Backs are in black-and-white and include a few biographical bits, a line of career stats, the years played with the Brewers and team and brewery logos. Books I and II were issued as planned to adults attending the April 24 and June 26, 1994 games. The Series IV book, containing 10 special cards honoring the Brewers 25th Anniversary Team, was given away at a June, 1995, game and Book III was distributed in August of 1995. Individual cards are unnumbered and are presented here in alphabetical order within series. Cards of Bobby Clark, Tom Edens, Ken McMullen and Danny Walton, which appear in Series I or III are repeated in Series IV.

		MT
Complete Set, Booklets (4):		30.00
Complete Set, Singles (376):		24.00
Common Player:		.10
Series I		.10
	Complete book:	10.00
(1)	Hank Aaron	3.00
(2)	Jim Adduci	.10
(3)	Jay Aldrich	.10
(4)	Andy Allanson	.10
(5)	Dave Baldwin	.10
(6)	Sal Bando	.10
(7)	Len Barker	.10
(8)	Kevin Bass	.10
(9)	Ken Berry	.10
(10)	George Canale	.10
(11)	Tom Candiotti	.10
(12)	Mike Capel	.10
(13)	Bobby Darwin	.10
(14)	Danny Darwin	.10
(15)	Brock Davis	.10
(16)	Dick Davis	.10
(17)	Jamie Easterley	.10
(18)	Tom Edens	.10
(19)	Marshall Edwards	.10
(20)	Cal Eldred	.15
(21)	Bob Ellis	.10
(22)	Ed Farmer	.10
(23)	Mike Felder	.10

(24) John Felske .10
(25) Mike Ferraro .10
(26) Mike Fetters .10
(27) Danny Frisella .10
(28) Bob Galasso .10
(29) Jim Gantner .10
(30) Pedro Garcia .10
(31) Bob Gardner .10
(32) John Gelnar .10
(33) Moose Haas .10
(34) Darryl Hamilton .10
(35) Larry Haney .10
(36) Jim Hannan .10
(37) Bob Hansen .10
(38) Mike Ignasiak .10
(39) John Jaha .10
(40) Dion James .10
(41) Deron Johnson .10
(42) John Henry Johnson .10
(43) Tim Johnson .10
(44) Rickey Keeton .10
(45) John Kennedy .10
(46) Jim Kern .10
(47) Pete Ladd .10
(48) Joe Lahoud .10
(49) Tom Lampkin .10
(50) Dave LaPoint .10
(51) George Lauzerique .10
(52) Julio Machado .10
(53) Alex Madrid .10
(54) Candy Maldonado .10
(55) Carlos Maldonado .10
(56) Rick Manning .10
(57) Jaime Navarro .10
(58) Ray Newman .10
(59) Juan Nieves .10
(60) Dave Nilsson .10
(61) Charlie O'Brien .10
(62) Syd O'Brien .10
(63) John O'Donoghue .10
(64) Jim Paciorek .10
(65) Dave Parker .15
(66) Bill Parsons .10
(67) Marty Pattin .10
(68) Jamie Quirk .10
(69) Willie Randolph .10
(70) Paul Ratliff .10
(71) Lance Rautzhan .10
(72) Randy Ready .10
(73) Ray Sadecki .10
(74) Lenn Sakata .10
(75) Ken Sanders .10
(76) Ted Savage .10
(77) Dick Schofield .10
(78) Jim Tatum .10
(79) Chuck Taylor .10
(80) Tom Tellmann .10
(81) Frank Tepedino .10
(82) Sandy Valdespino .10
(83) Jose Valentin .10
(84) Greg Vaughn .25
(85) Carlos Velazquez .10
(86) Rick Waits .10
(87) Danny Walton .10
(88) Floyd Weaver .10
(89) Bill Wegman .10
(90) Floyd Wicker .10
(91) Al Yates .10
(92) Ned Yost .10
(93) Mike Young .10
(94) Robin Yount 2.00
Series II .10
Complete book: 8.00
(95) Hank Allen .10
(96) Felipe Alou .20
(97) Max Alvis .10
(98) Larry Andersen .10
(99) Rick Auerbach .10
(100) Don August .10
(101) Billy Bates .10
(102) Gary Beare .10
(103) Larry Bearnarth .10
(104) Andy Beene .10
(105) Jerry Bell .10
(106) Juan Bell .10
(107) Dwight Bernard .10
(108) Bernie Carbo .10
(109) Jose Cardenal .10
(110) Matias Carrillo .10
(111) Juan Castillo .10
(112) Bill Castro .10
(113) Rick Cerone .10
(114) Rob Deer .10
(115) Rick Dempsey .10
(116) Alex Diaz .10
(117) Dick Ellsworth .10
(118) Narciso Elvira .10
(119) Tom Filer .10
(120) Rollie Fingers .50
(121) Scott Fletcher .10
(122) John Flinn .10
(123) Rich Folkers .10
(124) Tony Fossas .10
(125) Chris George .10
(126) Bob L. Gibson .10
(127) Gus Gil .10
(128) Tommy Harper .10
(129) Vic Harris .10
(130) Paul Hartzell .10
(131) Tom Hausman .10
(132) Neal Heaton .10
(133) Mike Hegan .10
(134) Jack Heidemann .10
(135) Doug Jones .10
(136) Mark Kiefer .10
(137) Steve Kiefer .10
(138) Ed Kirkpatrick .10
(139) Joe Kmak .10
(140) Mark Knudson .10
(141) Kevin Kobel .10
(142) Pete Koegel .10
(143) Jack Lazorko .10
(144) Tim Leary .10
(145) Mark Lee .10
(146) Jeffrey Jo Leonard .10
(147) Randy Lerch .10
(148) Brad Lesley .10
(149) Sixto Lezcano .10
(150) Josias Manzanillo .10
(151) Buck Martinez .10
(152) Tom Matchick .10
(153) Davey May .10
(154) Matt Maysey .10
(155) Bob McClure .10
(156) Tim McIntosh .10
(157) Tim Nordbrook .10
(158) Ben Oglivie .10
(159) Jim Olander .10
(160) Troy O'Leary .10
(161) Roberto Pena .10
(162) Jeff Peterek .10
(163) Ray Peters .10
(164) Rob Picciolo .10
(165) John Poff .10
(166) Gus Polidor .10
(167) Dan Plesac .10
(168) Kevin Reimer .10
(169) Andy Replogle .10
(170) Jerry Reuss .10
(171) Archie Reynolds .10
(172) Bob Reynolds .10
(173) Ken Reynolds .10
(174) Tommie Reynolds .10
(175) Ernest Riles .10
(176) Bill Schroeder .10
(177) George Scott .15
(178) Ray Searage .10
(179) Bob Sebra .10
(180) Kevin Seitzer .10
(181) Dick Selma .10
(182) Bill Sharp .10
(183) Ron Theobald .10
(184) Dan Thomas .10
(185) Gorman Thomas .12
(186) Randy Veres .10
(187) Bill Voss .10
(188) Jim Wohlford .10
Series III .10
Complete book: 8.00
(189) Jerry Augustine .10
(190) James Austin .10
(191) Rick Austin .10
(192) Kurt Bevacqua .10
(193) Tom Bianco .10
(194) Dante Bichette .30
(195) Mike Birkbeck .10
(196) Dan Boitano .10
(197) Bobby Bolin .10
(198) Mark Bomback .10
(199) Ricky Bones .10
(200) Chris Bosio .10
(201) Thad Bosley .10
(202) Steve Bowling .10
(203) Gene Brabender .10
(204) Glenn Braggs .10
(205) Mike Caldwell .10
(206) Billy Champion .10
(207) Mark Ciardi .10
(208) Bobby Clark .10
(209) Ron Clark .10
(210) Mark Clear .10
(211) Reggie Cleveland .10
(212) Bryan Clutterbuck .10
(213) Jaime Cocanower .10
(214) Jim Colborn .10
(215) Cecil Cooper .15
(216) Edgar Diaz .10
(217) Frank DiPino .10
(218) Dave Engle .10
(219) Ray Fosse .10
(220) Terry Francona .10
(221) Tito Francona .10
(222) LaVel Freeman .10
(223) Brian Giles .10
(224) Bob Heise .10
(225) Doug Henry .10
(226) Mike Hershberger .10
(227) Teddy Higuera .10
(228) Sam Hinds .10
(229) Fred Holdsworth .10
(230) Darren Holmes .10
(231) Paul Householder .10
(232) Odell Jones .10
(233) Brad Komminsk .10
(234) Andy Kosco .10
(235) Lew Krausse .10
(236) Ray Krawczyk .10
(237) Bill Krueger .10
(238) Ted Kubiak .10
(239) Jack Lind .10
(240) Frank Linzy .10
(241) Pat Listach .10
(242) Graeme Lloyd .10
(243) Bob Locker .10
(244) Skip Lockwood .10
(245) Ken McMullen .10
(246) Jerry McNertney .10
(247) Doc Medich .10
(248) Bob Meyer .10
(249) Joey Meyer .10
(250) Matt Mieske .10
(251) Roger Miller .10
(252) Paul Mirabella .10
(253) Angel Miranda .10
(254) Bobby Mitchell .10
(255) Paul Mitchell .10
(256) Paul Molitor 2.00
(257) Rafael Novoa .10
(258) Jesse Orosco .10
(259) Carlos Ponce .10
(260) Chuck Porter .10
(261) Darrell Porter .10
(262) Billy Jo Robidoux .10
(263) Ron Robinson .10
(264) Eduardo Rodriguez .10
(265) Ellie Rodriguez .10
(266) Rich Rollins .10
(267) Ed Romero .10
(268) Gary Sheffield .50
(269) Bob Sheldon .10
(270) Chris Short .10
(271) Bob Skube .10
(272) Jim Slaton .10
(273) Bernie Smith .10
(274) Russ Snyder .10
(275) Lary Sorenson .10
(276) Billy Spiers .10
(277) Ed Sprague .10
(278) Dickie Thon .10
(279) Bill Travers .10
(280) Pete Vuckovich .10
(281) Clyde Wright .10
(282) Jeff Yurak .10
Series IV .10
Complete book: 8.00
(283) Joe Azcue .10
(284) Mike Boddicker .10
(285) Ken Brett .10
(286) John Briggs .10
(287) Pete Broberg .10
(288) Greg Brock .10
(289) Jeff Bronkey .10
(290) Mark Brouhard .10
(291) Kevin Brown .10
(292) Ollie Brown .10
(293) Bruce Brubaker .10
(294) Tom Brunansky .10
(295) Steve Brye .10
(296) Bob Burda .10
(297) Ray Burris .10
(298) Jeff Cirillo .10
(299) Bobby Clark .10
(300) Bob Coluccio .10
(301) Wayne Comer .10
(302) Billy Conigliaro .10
(303) Cecil Cooper (25th Anniversary Team) .10
(304) Barry Cort .10
(305) Chuck Crim .10
(306) Lafayette Currence .10
(307) Kiki Diaz .10
(308) Bill Doran .10
(309) Al Downing .10
(310) Tom Edens .10
(311) Andy Etchebarren .10
(312) Rollie Fingers (25th) .25
(313) Jim Gantner (25th) .10
(314) Greg Goossen .10
(315) Brian Harper .10
(316) Larry Hisle .10
(317) Steve Hovley .10
(318) Wilbur Howard .10
(319) Roy Howell .10
(320) Bob Humphreys .10
(321) Jim Hunter .10
(322) Dave Huppert .10
(323) Von Joshua .10
(324) Art Kusnyer .10
(325) Doug Loman .10
(326) Jim Lonborg .10
(327) Marcelino Lopez .10
(328) Willie Lozado .10
(329) [illegible]
(330) Ken McMullen .10
(331) Jose Mercedes .10
(332) Paul Molitor (25th) 1.00
(333) Don Money .10
(334) Don Money (25th) .10
(335) Charlie Moore .10
(336) Donnie Moore .10
(337) John Morris .10
(338) Curt Motton .10
(339) Willie Mueller .10
(340) Tom Murphy .10
(341) Tony Muser .10
(342) Edwin Nunez .10
(343) Ben Oglivie (25th) .10
(344) Pat Osborn (Osburn) .10
(345) Dennis Powell .10
(346) Jody Reed .10
(347) Phil Roof .10
(348) Jimmy Rosario .10
(349) Bruce Ruffin .10
(350) Gary Ryerson .10
(351) Bob Scanlan .10
(352) Ted Simmons .10
(353) Ted Simmons (25th) .10
(354) Duane Singleton .10
(355) Steve Stanicek .10
(356) Fred Stanley .10
(357) Dave Stapleton .10
(358) Randy Stein .10
(359) Earl Stephenson .10
(360) Franklin Stubbs .10
(361) William Suero .10
(362) Jim Sundberg .10
(363) B.J. Surhoff .10
(364) Gary Sutherland .10
(365) Don Sutton .25
(366) Dale Sveum .10
(367) Gorman Thomas (25th) .10
(368) Wayne Twitchell .10
(369) Dave Valle .10
(370) Greg Vaughn (25th) .10
(371) John Vukovich .10
(372) Danny Walton .10
(373) Turner Ward .10
(374) Rick Wrona .10
(375) Jim Wynn .10
(376) Robin Yount (25th) 1.50

1990 Little Big Leaguers

This set was issued on a series of five nine-card perforated panels at the back of a book titled, "little BIG LEAGUERS / Amazing Boyhood Stories of Today's Baseball Stars." The 96 text pages of the book offer inspiring boyhood baseball tales as well as childhood and major league photos of the players. The tear-out cards measure 2-1/2" x 3-1/2" and are perforated on all four sides. Fronts have a black-and-white childhood photo of the player, nearly all in baseball uniform. The player's name is in white in a red strip at top, with the set name at bottom. Backs have the same red strips. At center in black-and-white are biographical data and career highlights. The unnumbered cards are checklisted here alphabetically.

	MT
Complete Set, Book:	8.00
Complete Set, Singles (45):	8.00
Common Player:	.25
(1) Todd Benzinger	.25
(2) Bud Black	.25
(3) Wade Boggs	2.00
(4) Chris Bosio	.25
(5) George Brett	2.00
(6) Brett Butler	.35
(7) Jose Canseco	1.00
(8) Gary Carter	.50
(9) [illegible]	[illegible]
(10) Eric Davis	.35
(11) Glenn Davis	.25
(12) Storm Davis	.25
(13) Kevin Elster	.25
(14) Tony Fernandez	.25
(15) John Franco	.25
(16) Gary Gaetti	.25
(17) Mark Gubicza	.25
(18) Tony Gwynn	1.00
(19) Bruce Hurst	.25
(20) Bo Jackson	.60
(21) Bob Kipper	.25
(22) Ron Kittle	.25
(23) Carney Lansford	.25
(24) Jeffrey Leonard	.25
(25) Mike A. Marshall	.25
(26) Lloyd McClendon	.25
(27) Andy McGaffigan	.25
(28) Keith Moreland	.25
(29) Lloyd Moseby	.25
(30) Dale Murphy	.50
(31) Pete O'Brien	.25
(32) Mike Pagliarulo	.25
(33) Tim Raines	.40
(34) Dennis Rasmussen	.25
(35) Harold Reynolds	.25
(36) Billy Ripken	.25
(37) Nolan Ryan	3.00
(38) Steve Sax	.25
(39) Ozzie Smith	.75
(40) Jim Sundberg	.25
(41) Rick Sutcliffe	.25
(42) Dave Valle	.25
(43) Andy Van Slyke	.25
(44) Glenn Wilson	.25
(45) Todd Worrell	.25

Player names in *Italic* type indicate a rookie card.

1998 Little League Mark McGwire

During his record-breaking season, Little League Baseball issued a pair of cards featuring Mark McGwire, a "graduate" of the youth program. A red-bordered card was issued early in the season; a green-bordered card was issued with the purchase of a program at the Little League World Series later in the year. Each card has on front a color action photo of McGwire and includes the Cardinals and Little League logos. Backs have six safety tips for youngsters.

	MT
Complete Set (2):	20.00
(1) Mark McGwire (red borders)	10.00
(2) Mark McGwire (green borders)	10.00

1989 Little Simon Hall of Fame Stickers

These stickers were issued with an album in which to mount them and feature 100 members of Baseball's Hall of Fame. The 1-5/8" x 2-1/8" stickers have large player pictures on front with blank backs. They were arranged in the book by position.

	MT
Complete Book:	15.00
Complete Singles Set (100):	12.00
Common Sticker:	.50
(1) Lou Gehrig	3.00
(2) Bill Terry	[illegible]
(3) Johnny Mize	.50
(4) Willie McCovey	.50
(5) Cap Anson	.50
(6) Ernie Banks	.75
(7) Dan Brouthers	.50
(8) George Kelly	.50
(9) Roger Connor	.50
(10) Nap Lajoie	.50
(11) Bobby Doerr	.50
(12) Jackie Robinson	2.00
(13) Frankie Frisch	.50
(14) Honus Wagner	1.00
(15) George Wright	.50
(16) Hughie Jennings	.50
(17) Rabbit Maranville	.50
(18) Luis Aparicio	.50
(19) Joe Cronin	.50
(20) Dave Bancroft	.50
(21) Arky Vaughan	.50
(22) Joe Sewell	.50
(23) Jimmy Collins	.50
(24) George Kell	.50
(25) Eddie Mathews	.50
(26) Ray Dandridge	.50
(27) Willie Stargell	.50
(28) Ted Williams	3.00
(29) Billy Williams	.50
(30) Stan Musial	2.00
(31) Ed Delahanty	.50
(32) Monte Irvin	.50
(33) Jesse Burkett	.50
(34) Chick Hafey	.50
(35) Joe Kelley	.50
(36) Heinie Manush	.50
(37) Ty Cobb	2.50
(38) Max Carey	.50
(39) Joe DiMaggio	3.00
(40) Mickey Mantle	6.00
(41) Tris Speaker	.50
(42) Lloyd Waner	.50
(43) Billy Hamilton	.50

(44)	Hank Aaron	2.00
(45)	Paul Waner	.50
(46)	Roberto Clemente	4.00
(47)	Babe Ruth	4.00
(48)	Chuck Klein	.50
(49)	Mel Ott	.50
(50)	Sam Crawford	.50
(51)	Willie Keeler	.50
(52)	Harry Hooper	.50
(53)	Elmer Flick	.50
(54)	Roy Campanella	.75
(55)	Roger Bresnahan	.50
(56)	Mickey Cochrane	.50
(57)	Buck Ewing	.50
(58)	Ernie Lombardi	.50
(59)	Cy Young	.60
(60)	Mordecai Brown	.50
(61)	Red Faber	.50
(62)	Bob Feller	.50
(63)	Martin Dihigo	.50
(64)	Candy Cummings	.50
(65)	Christy Mathewson	.60
(66)	Rube Marquard	.50
(67)	Herb Pennock	.50
(68)	Bob Lemon	.50
(69)	Eppa Rixey	.50
(70)	Whitey Ford	.50
(71)	Waite Hoyt	.50
(72)	Grover Alexander	.50
(73)	Dazzy Vance	.50
(74)	Lefty Grove	.50
(75)	Carl Hubbell	.50
(76)	Lefty Gomez	.50
(77)	Ed Walsh	.50
(78)	Ed Plank	.50
(79)	Sandy Koufax	2.50
(80)	Pud Galvin	.50
(81)	Hoyt Wilhelm	.50
(82)	Catfish Hunter	.50
(83)	Red Ruffing	.50
(84)	Warren Spahn	.50
(85)	Connie Mack	.50
(86)	Wilbert Robinson	.50
(87)	Joe McCarthy	.50
(88)	Bill McKechnie	.50
(89)	John McGraw	.50
(90)	Alexander Cartwright	.50
(91)	Branch Rickey	.50
(92)	Warren Giles	.50
(93)	Tom Yawkey	.50
(94)	Ed Barrow	.50
(95)	Kenesaw Landis	.50
(96)	Ban Johnson	.50
(97)	Happy Chandler	.50
(98)	Jocko Conlan	.50
(99)	Cal Hubbard	.50
(100)	Billy Evans	.50

1990 Little Simon Stickers

These baseball player stickers feature color artwork of both star and journeyman players throughout the game's history. The 1-5/8" x 2-1/8" stickers were issued with an album to house them and present more of the story of baseball. The album is titled "The Official Hall of Fame Sticker Book of Records" and was published by the juvenile division of Simon & Schuster in New York. Stickers have a number and player name in the bottom border. Backs are, of course, blank.

		MT
Complete Album:		20.00
Complete Singles Set (100):		15.00
Common Player:		.50
1	George Bradley	.50
2	Old Hoss Radbourn	.50
3	Guy Hecker	.50
4	Tim Keefe	.50
5	Curt Welch	.50
6	George Gore	.50
7	Tip O'Neill	.50
8	Hugh Duffy	.50
9	Cap Anson	.50
10	Christy Mathewson	.60
11	Joe McGinnity	.50
12	Ed Reulbach	.50
13	Jack Taylor	.50
14	Cy Young	.60
15	Ernie Shore	.50
16	Smoky Joe Wood	.50
17	Fred Toney, Hippo Vaughn	.50
18	Chief Wilson	.50
19	Ty Cobb	2.00
20	Fielder Jones	.50
21	George Stallings	.50
22	Leon Cadore, Joe Oeschger	.50
23	George Sisler	.50
24	Bill Wambsganss	.50
25	Babe Ruth	4.00
26	Jim Bottomley	.50
27	Rogers Hornsby	.60
28	Walter Johnson	.60
29	unknown	.50
30	Wes Ferrell	.50
31	Lefty Grove	.50
32	Carl Hubbell	.50
33	Joe Sewell	.50
34	Johnny Frederick	.50
35	Rudy York	.50
36	Johnny Vander Meer	.50
37	Pinky Higgins	.50
38	Lou Gehrig	3.00
39	Joe DiMaggio	3.00
40	Ted Williams	3.00
41	Jim Tobin	.50
42	Hal Newhouser	.50
43	Cookie Lavagetto	.50
44	Jim Konstanty	.50
45	Connie Mack	.50
46	Bobby Thomson	.50
47	Bobo Holloman	.50
48	Gene Stephens	.50
49	Mickey Mantle	6.00
50	Joe Adcock	.50
51	Stan Musial	2.00
52	Al Kaline	.75
53	Dale Long	.50
54	Don Larsen	.50
55	Dave Philley	.50
56	Vic Power	.50
57	Harvey Haddix	.50
58	Elroy Face	.50
59	Larry Sherry	.50
60	Casey Stengel	.50
61	Bobby Richardson	.50
62	Bill Mazeroski	.50
63	Roger Maris	1.50
64	Bill Fischer	.50
65	Willie Mays	3.00
66	Maury Wills	.50
67	Bert Campaneris	.50
68	Warren Spahn	.50
69	Sandy Koufax	2.50
70	Tony Cloninger	.50
71	Carl Yastrzemski	1.00
72	Denny McLain	.50
73	Don Drysdale	.50
74	Bob Gibson	.50
75	Frank Howard	.50
76	Tom Seaver	.50
77	Nolan Ryan	4.00
78	Steve Carlton	.50
79	Mike Marshall	.50
80	Nate Colbert	.50
81	Hank Aaron	3.00
82	Rennie Stennett	.50
83	Fred Lynn	.50
84	Pete Rose	2.50
85	Pedro Guerrero	.50
86	Lou Brock	.50
87	Rickey Henderson	.50
88	Reggie Jackson	.50
89	Bob Horner	.50
90	Don Mattingly	.60
91	Mark McGwire	5.00
92	Benito Santiago	.50
93	George Brett	.75
94	Mike Schmidt	.75
95	Jose Canseco	.65
96	Andre Dawson	.50
97	Ron Guidry	.50
98	Dwight Gooden	.50
99	Orel Hershiser	.50
100	Vince Coleman	.50

1988 Little Sun Black Sox

The members of the 1919 Chicago White Sox, the team which conspired to lose the World Series, is featured in this collectors' issue. The 2-1/2" x 3-1/2" cards have sepia player photos (along with photos of other figures in the scandal) on a bright green background. Player identification and team logo are in black. Black-and-white backs have biographical data, regular-season and World Series stats for 1919, and a summary of the person's role in the scandal. Cards were sold only in complete sets, with 5,000 reported produced.

		MT
Complete Set (16):		6.00
Common Player:		.25
1	Black Sox Scandal	.25
2	Chick Gandil	.50
3	Ed Cicotte	.50
4	Joe Jackson	2.00
5	Buck Weaver	.50
6	Swede Risberg	.50
7	Happy Felsch	.50
8	Lefty Williams	.50
9	Fred McMullin	.50
10	Eddie Collins	.25
11	Kid Gleason	.25
12	Charles Comiskey	.25
13	Abe Attell	.25
14	Arnold Rothstein	.25
15	Judge Landis	.25
---	Title card	.25

1990 Little Sun Baseball Writers

Nearly two dozen of the best-known baseball writers of the past two centuries are featured in this collectors' issue. A number of former players appear in the set. The 2-1/2" x 3-1/2" cards have black-and-white portrait photos on front, with borders of beige and green. Backs are in black-and-white with a lengthy biographical sketch and a trivia question.

		MT
Complete Set (24):		5.00
Common Card:		.25
1	Checklist	.25
2	Henry Chadwick	.50
3	Jacob C. Morse	.25
4	Francis Richter	.25
5	Grantland Rice	.25
6	Lee Allen	.25
7	Joe Reichler	.25
8	Ned Smith	.25
9	Dick Young	.25
10	Jim Brosnan	.40
11	Charles Einstein	.25
12	Lawrence Ritter	.35
13	Roger Kahn	.35
14	Robert Creamer	.35
15	W.P. Kinsella	.35
16	Harold Seymour	.25
17	Ron Shelton	.25
18	Tom Clark	.25
19	Mark Harris	.25
20	John Holway	.25
21	Peter Golenbock	.25
22	Jim Bouton	.50
23	John Thorn	.25
24	Mike Shannon	.25

1992 LK Star Decals

A small hoard of these player decals surfaced in the mid 1990s. About 3-5/8" x 3-5/8", each player's decals come in two parts. A front has a player portrait photo (cap logo removed) against a stylized star and ball diamond. There is also a facsimile autograph, player and team identification and a Major League Baseball Players Association logo. The back decal has another facsimile autograph, player stats and the manufacturer's logo. These were evidently intended for use on coffee mugs, drinking glasses and similar items. Values quoted are for unused decals in pairs only. The Ryne Sandberg decal was reported pulled from production with few outstanding pieces.

		MT
Complete Set (30):		375.00
Common Player:		10.00
(1)	Wade Boggs	15.00
(2)	Barry Bonds	25.00
(3)	George Brett	25.00
(4)	Will Clark	15.00
(5)	Jose Canseco	15.00
(6)	Roger Clemens	25.00
(7)	David Cone	10.00
(8)	Andre Dawson	10.00
(9)	Rob Dibble	10.00
(10)	Lenny Dykstra	10.00
(11)	Cecil Fielder	10.00
(12)	Julio Franco	10.00
(13)	Dwight Gooden	10.00
(14)	Ken Griffey Jr.	75.00
(15)	Ken Griffey Sr.	10.00
(16)	Tony Gwynn	25.00
(17)	Rickey Henderson	12.00
(18)	Orel Hershiser	10.00
(19)	Howard Johnson	10.00
(20)	David Justice	12.00
(21)	Don Mattingly	25.00
(22)	Fred McGriff	10.00
(23)	Cal Ripken Jr.	60.00
(24)	Nolan Ryan	75.00
(25)	Ryne Sandberg	125.00
(26)	Steve Sax	10.00
(27)	Ozzie Smith	25.00
(28)	Darryl Strawberry	10.00
(29)	Frank Viola	10.00
(30)	Dave Winfield	15.00

1981-90 Louisville Slugger

Hillerich & Bradsby, makers of Louisville Slugger bats and gloves, produced these cards to be attached to the company's baseball gloves. A small round hole is punched in the upper-left corner of each standard-size card to enable them to be attached to the gloves. Undamaged cards are hard ot find. All cards follow the same basic design - bright blue and green borders, player name and position above the full-color photo (with autograph overprint), yellow Louisville Slugger logo across the bottom border. Beneath the logo are the words "Member Louisville Slugger Bat & Glove Advisory Staff." The card backs are blue and green and include the player name, short biography and a list of personal records and information. Cards were printed with a glossy finish through 1987, when a flat finish was adopted as production moved from Taiwan to the Philippines.

		MT
Complete Set (20):		120.00
Common Player:		5.00
	1981	
(1)	Steve Garvey (Dodgers)	12.00
(2)	Graig Nettles (Yankees)	10.00
	1982	
(1)	Pedro Guerrero (Dodgers)	5.00
(2)	Fred Lynn (Angels)	5.00
	1984	
(1)	Ray Knight (Astros)	15.00
(2)	Ray Knight (Mets)	6.00
(3)	Graig Nettles (Padres)	8.00
	1985	
(1)	Steve Garvey (Padres)	8.00
(2)	Gary Matthews (Cubs)	5.00
	1986	
(1)	Orel Hershiser (Dodgers)	5.00
(2)	Rick Rhoden (Pirates)	5.00
	1987	
(1)	Eric Davis (Reds)	5.00
	1988	
(1)	(Eric Davis) (Reds)	5.00
(2)	Steve Garvey (Padres)	10.00
(3)	Orel Hershiser (Dodgers)	5.00
(4)	Mike Pagliarulo (Yankees)	5.00
	1989	
(1)	Orel Hershiser (Dodgers)	5.00
	1990	
(1)	Orel Hershiser (Dodgers)	5.00
(2)	Andy Van Slyke (Pirates)	5.00
(3)	Lou Whitaker (Tigers)	7.50

1992 Lyke's Braves

Though Braves players no longer appeared at an autograph booth on card giveaway days in 1992, the team's hot dog vendor, Lyke's, continued to offer small groups of cards to kids attending Tuesday home games. This distribution makes assembling complete sets very challenging. In standard 2-1/2" x 3-1/2" size, the cards have a player photo border in, successively, white, dark blue, red and white. A red-and-blue Lyke's logo is at lower-right. Above is a blue ball with the year of issue, and the team and player name printed in white. Backs are in black with the player's uniform number, full minor and major league stats, and biographical vitae.

		MT
Complete Set (37):		24.00
Common Player:		.50
(1)	Steve Avery	.50
(2)	Jim Beauchamp	.50
(3)	Rafael Belliard	.50
(4)	Juan Berenguer	.50
(5)	Damon Berryhill	.50
(6)	Mike Bielecki	.50

(7)	Jeff Blauser	.50
(8)	Sid Bream	.50
(9)	Francisco Cabrera	.50
(10)	Pat Corrales	.50
(11)	Bobby Cox	.50
(12)	Marvin Freeman	.50
(13)	Ron Gant	1.00
(14)	Tom Glavine	1.50
(15)	Tommy Gregg	.50
(16)	Brian Hunter	.50
(17)	Clarence Jones	.50
(18)	David Justice	2.50
(19)	Charlie Leibrandt	.50
(20)	Mark Lemke	.50
(21)	Leo Mazzone	.50
(22)	Kent Mercker	.50
(23)	Otis Nixon	.50
(24)	Greg Olson	.50
(25)	Alejandro Pena	.50
(26)	Terry Pendleton	.50
(27)	Deion Sanders	2.00
(28)	Lonnie Smith	.50
(29)	John Smoltz	1.00
(30)	Mike Stanton	.50
(31)	Jeff Treadway	.50
(32)	Jerry Willard	.50
(33)	Jimy Williams	.50
(34)	Mark Wohlers	.50
(35)	Ned Yost	.50
(36)	Homer the Brave (mascot)	.50
(37)	Rally (mascot)	.50

1992 Lyke's Braves Team Photo Set

When Lykes Meats was awarded the Braves hot dog contract for 1992 they continued the previous years' baseball card promotions, including this early-May team photo/player card panel. Three 9-1/2" x 10-1/2" panels feature a team photo and 30 player cards. The cards have player portraits against a blue background in a tombstone shape. A blue ball at lower-left has the player's uniform number, while his name is in white in a red strip beneath the photo. Red logos of the team and hot dog vendor are at bottom. Backs are printed in red and dark blue and feature full stats, player data and a facsimile autograph. These cards are much more common than the Lykes singles distributed later in the season. The checklist here is alphabetized.

		MT
Complete Set, Foldout:		12.00
Complete Set, Singles (31):		8.00
Common Player:		.25
(1)	Steve Avery	.25
(2)	Rafael Belliard	.25
(3)	Juan Berenguer	.25
(4)	Damon Berryhill	.25
(5)	Mike Bielecki	.25
(6)	Jeff Blauser	.25
(7)	Sid Bream	.25
(8)	Francisco Cabrera	.25
(9)	Bobby Cox	.25
(10)	Nick Esasky	.25
(11)	Marvin Freeman	.25
(12)	Ron Gant	.50
(13)	Tom Glavine	.75
(14)	Tommy Gregg	.25
(15)	Brian Hunter	.25
(16)	David Justice	2.00
(17)	Charlie Leibrandt	.25
(18)	Mark Lemke	.25
(19)	Kent Mercker	.25
(20)	Otis Nixon	.25
(21)	Greg Olson	.25
(22)	Alejandro Pena	.25
(23)	Terry Pendleton	.35
(24)	Deion Sanders	1.00
(25)	Lonnie Smith	.25
(26)	John Smoltz	.60
(27)	Mike Stanton	.25
(28)	Jeff Treadway	.25
(29)	Jerry Willard	.25
(30)	Mark Wohlers	.25
(31)	Team Photo	1.00

1993 Lyke's Braves

Each home Tuesday during the 1993 season, three player cards were distributed to youngsters, sponsored by the team's hot dog vendor, Lyke's. This style of distribution makes collecting a complete 38-card set very challenging. Standard 2-1/2" x 3-1/2" size cards have a player portrait photo against a blue background. The card's front border is a darker blue separated from the photo by a yellow stripe. Red-white-and-blue team and vendor logos appear at the corners and the player's name and position are in white at lower-left. Backs are printed in black with complete career stats, biographical data and sponsors' logos. The unnumbered cards are checklisted here alphabetically. The final Tuesday's handouts, Lopez, McGriff and Tarasco have slightly different back printing and are somewhat scarcer than other cards.

		MT
Complete Set (38):		55.00
Common Player:		1.00
(1)	Steve Avery	1.00
(2)	Jim Beauchamp	1.00
(3)	Steve Bedrosian	1.00
(4)	Rafael Belliard	1.00
(5)	Damon Berryhill	1.00
(6)	Jeff Blauser	1.00
(7)	Sid Bream	1.00
(8)	Francisco Cabrera	1.00
(9)	Pat Corrales	1.00
(10)	Bobby Cox	1.00
(11)	Marvin Freeman	1.00
(12)	Ron Gant	1.50
(13)	Tom Glavine	2.00
(14)	Jay Howell	1.00
(15)	Brian Hunter	1.00
(16)	Clarence Jones	1.00
(17)	David Justice	3.00
(18)	Mark Lemke	1.00
(19)	Javier Lopez	3.00
(20)	Greg Maddux	5.00
(21)	Leo Mazzone	1.00
(22)	Fred McGriff	5.00
(23)	Greg McMichael	1.00
(24)	Kent Mercker	1.00
(25)	Otis Nixon	1.00
(26)	Greg Olson	1.00
(27)	Bill Pecota	1.00
(28)	Terry Pendleton	1.00
(29)	Deion Sanders	4.00
(30)	Pete Smith	1.00
(31)	John Smoltz	3.00
(32)	Mike Stanton	1.00
(33)	Tony Tarasco	3.00
(34)	Jimy Williams	1.00
(35)	Mark Wohlers	1.00
(36)	Ned Yost	1.00
(37)	Homer the Brave (mascot)	1.00
(38)	Rally (mascot)	1.00

1993 Lyke's Braves Team Photo Set

The Atlanta Braves offered a perforated, uncut sheet team set in 1992 that was handed out in an early season game. The set, sponsored by Lykes, includes 30 cards and a team photo and carries the player's name and uniform number on the front of the card along with the Braves and Lykes logos. The backs contain the player's biography, career statistics and a facsimile autograph. The first card of Fred McGriff as a Brave appears in this promotional set issued later in the season than in previous years. The 30 individual player cards also include Ryan Klesko, who was not in the single-card season-long giveaways. Three 9-1/2" x 10-1/2" panels comprise this issue, with each of the player cards perforated at the edges. Also for the first time in 1992, the same photos were used for the team sheet and single card promotions. Single cards measure 2-1/4" x 3-1/2" and are checklisted alphabetically here.

		MT
Complete Set, Foldout:		12.00
Complete Set, Singles (31):		8.00
Common Player:		.25
(1)	Steve Avery	.25
(2)	Steve Bedrosian	.25
(3)	Rafael Belliard	.25
(4)	Damon Berryhill	.25
(5)	Jeff Blauser	.25
(6)	Sid Bream	.25
(7)	Francisco Cabrera	.25
(8)	Bobby Cox	.25
(9)	Marvin Freeman	.25
(10)	Ron Gant	1.00
(11)	Tom Glavine	1.00
(12)	Jay Howell	.25
(13)	Brian Hunter	.25
(14)	David Justice	2.00
(15)	Ryan Klesko	2.00
(16)	Mark Lemke	.25
(17)	Greg Maddux	3.00
(18)	Fred McGriff	1.50
(19)	Greg McMichael	.25
(20)	Kent Mercker	.25
(21)	Otis Nixon	.25
(22)	Greg Olson	.25
(23)	Bill Pecota	.25
(24)	Terry Pendleton	.35
(25)	Deion Sanders	1.50
(26)	Pete Smith	.25
(27)	John Smoltz	1.00
(28)	Mike Stanton	.25
(29)	Tony Tarasco	.25
(30)	Mark Wohlers	.25
(31)	Team Photo	1.00

1994 Lyke's Braves

While 34 cards were printed, only 27 were publicly released prior to the beginning of the 1994 baseball strike. Sponsored by the Braves' stadium hot dog concessionaire, the cards were given away at the rate of three per Tuesday home game. Because of the strike, the cards of Cox, Hill, Chipper Jones, Mike Kelly, Klesko, McGriff and Sanders were not officially released and are scarcer than the other 27. Card fronts feature a chest-to-cap player portrait photo set agaonst a blue background with an orange border and vertical blue stripe at right bearing the player's name. Backs are printed in black-and-white and have full major and minor league stats along with a few biographical details. There is no card or uniform number on the cards. They are presented here alphabetically.

		MT
Complete Set (34):		80.00
Common Player:		.50
(1)	Steve Avery	.50
(2)	Jim Beauchamp	.50
(3)	Steve Bedrosian	.50
(4)	Rafael Belliard	.50
(5)	Mike Bielecki	.50
(6)	Jeff Blauser	.50
(7)	Pat Corrales	.50
(8)	Bobby Cox	4.00
(9)	Dave Gallagher	.50
(10)	Tom Glavine	2.00
(11)	Milt Hill	4.00
(12)	Chipper Jones	18.00
(13)	Clarence Jones	.50
(14)	David Justice	5.00
(15)	Mike Kelly	6.00
(16)	Ryan Klesko	12.00
(17)	Mark Lemke	.50
(18)	Javy Lopez	2.00
(19)	Greg Maddux	4.00
(20)	Leo Mazzone	.50
(21)	Greg McMichael	.50
(22)	Fred McGriff	10.00
(23)	Kent Mercker	.50
(24)	Charlie O'Brien	.50
(25)	Gregg Olson	.50
(26)	Bill Pecota	.50
(27)	Terry Pendleton	.50
(28)	Deion Sanders	12.00
(29)	John Smoltz	2.50
(30)	Mike Stanton	.50
(31)	Tony Tarasco	.50
(32)	Jimy Williams	.50
(33)	Mark Wohlers	.50
(34)	Ned Yost	.50

1994 Lyke's Braves Team Photo Set

Few of these team photo/player card sets have found their way into the hobby because they were intended for distribution at the Aug. 14 Sunday home game which fell after the beginning of the 1994 baseball strike. As in past years, the set was produced as a fold-out containing a team photo and 35 player cards. Unlike previous editions, however, the player cards are identical in format to the single cards given away during the season, except that they are printed in red and blue on the back and are slightly smaller, at 2-1/8" x 3-1/8". The cards are checklisted here alphabeitcally.

		MT
Complete Set, Foldout:		45.00
Complete Set, Singles (36):		40.00
Common Player:		.50
(1)	Steve Avery	.50
(2)	Jim Beauchamp	.50
(3)	Steve Bedrosian	.50
(4)	Rafael Belliard	.50
(5)	Mike Bielecki	.50
(6)	Jeff Blauser	.50
(7)	Pat Corrales	.50
(8)	Bobby Cox	.50
(9)	Dave Gallagher	.50
(10)	Tom Glavine	2.00
(11)	Chipper Jones	6.00
(12)	Clarence Jones	.50
(13)	David Justice	4.00
(14)	Mike Kelly	.50
(15)	Roberto Kelly	.50
(16)	Ryan Klesko	3.00
(17)	Mark Lemke	.50
(18)	Javy Lopez	2.00
(19)	Greg Maddux	5.00
(20)	Leo Mazzone	.50
(21)	Greg McMichael	.50
(22)	Fred McGriff	3.00
(23)	Kent Mercker	.50
(24)	Mike Mordecai	.50
(25)	Charlie O'Brien	.50
(26)	Jose Oliva	.50
(27)	Gregg Olson	.50
(28)	Bill Pecota	.50
(29)	Terry Pendleton	.50
(30)	John Smoltz	2.50
(31)	Mike Stanton	.50
(32)	Tony Tarasco	.50
(33)	Jimy Williams	.50
(34)	Mark Wohlers	.50
(35)	Ned Yost	.50
(36)	Team Photo Team Photo	1.00

1995 Lyke's Braves Team Photo Set

Once again this promotional giveaway by the team's hot dog concessionaire took the form of a three-panel cardboard poster. Overall 10-3/4" x 28", the foldout features a color team photo at top and 30 individual player portrait cards below. Each card is 2-1/8" x 3-1/8" and perforated for separation. Backs are printed in red, white and blue with a few stats and vital data, along with team and sponsor logos. The unnumbered cards are checklisted here alphabetically.

		MT
Complete Foldout Set:		8.00
Complete Singles Set (31):		7.50
Common Player:		.10
(1)	Steve Avery	.10
(2)	Jim Beauchamp	.10
(3)	Rafael Belliard	.10
(4)	Jeff Blauser	.10
(5)	Pedro Borbon	.10
(6)	Brad Clontz	.10
(7)	Pat Corrales	.10
(8)	Bobby Cox	.10
(9)	Tom Glavine	.25
(10)	Marquis Grissom	.25
(11)	Chipper Jones	[illegible]
(12)	Clarence Jones	.10
(13)	David Justice	.75
(14)	Mike Kelly	.10
(15)	Ryan Klesko	.60
(16)	Mark Lemke	.10
(17)	Javier Lopez	.25
(18)	Greg Maddux	1.50
(19)	Leo Mazzone	.10
(20)	Fred McGriff	.60
(21)	Greg McMichael	.10
(22)	Kent Mercker	.10
(23)	Mike Mordecai	.10
(24)	Charlie O'Brien	.10
(25)	Jason Schmidt	.10
(26)	Dwight Smith	.10
(27)	John Smoltz	.25
(28)	Jimy Williams	.10
(29)	Mark Wohlers	.10
(30)	Ned Yost	.10
---	Team photo	.25

M

1987 M & M's

The M&M's "Star Lineup" set consists of 12 two card panels inserted in specially marked packages of large M&M's candy. The two-card panels measure 5" x 3-1/2" with individual cards measuring 2-1/2" x 3-1/2" in size. The full-color photos are enclosed by a wavy blue frame and a white border. Card backs are printed in red ink on white stock and carry the player's career statistics and highlights. All team insignias have been airbrushed away. The set was designed and produced by Mike Schechter and Associates.

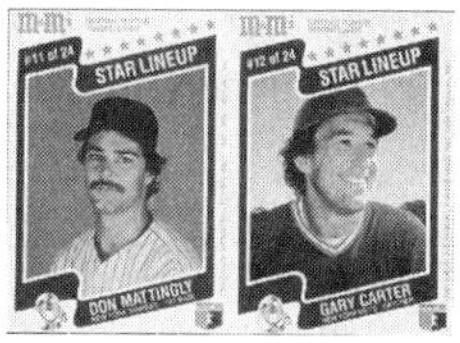

		MT
Complete Panel Set (12):		6.00
Complete Singles Set (24):		3.00
Common Panel:		.70
Common Single Player:		.06
Panel 1		.25
1	Wally Joyner	.10
2	Tony Pena	.05
Panel 2		.70
3	Mike Schmidt	.25
4	Ryne Sandberg	.20
Panel 3		.45
5	Wade Boggs	.25
6	Jack Morris	.05
Panel 4		.60
7	Roger Clemens	.35
8	Harold Baines	.10
Panel 5		.60
9	Dale Murphy	.15
10	Jose Canseco	.30
Panel 6		.90
11	Don Mattingly	.50
12	Gary Carter	.10
Panel 7		1.25
13	Cal Ripken, Jr.	.50
14	George Brett	.25
Panel 8		.85
15	Kirby Puckett	.45
16	Joe Carter	.10
Panel 9		.25
17	Mike Witt	.05
18	Mike Scott	.05
Panel 10		.35
19	Fernando Valenzuela	.05
20	Steve Garvey	.15
Panel 11		1.00
21	Steve Sax	.05
22	Nolan Ryan	.50
Panel 12		1.00
23	Tony Gwynn	.40
24	Ozzie Smith	.35

1990 Major League Baseball All-Star Masks

This unusual series of player memorabilia allows the user to assume the identity of one of more than a dozen big league stars of the day. The cardboard punch-out masks, in full color, were issued in four books of four, grouped along specific themes. The 11-1/2" x 13-1/8" books have player photos and career highlights inside the covers. Values shown are for unpunched masks and complete books.

		MT
Complete Set, Books (4):		
Common Player:		1.00
	BIG HITTERS book:	6.00
(1)	Jose Canseco	1.50
(2)	Will Clark	1.00
(3)	Don Mattingly	3.00
(4)	Darryl Strawberry	1.00
	GOLD GLOVERS book:	6.00
(5)	Mark Grace	1.50
(6)	Wally Joyner	1.00
(7)	Ryne Sandberg	2.00
(8)	Ozzie Smith	2.50
	HOT ROOKIES book:	8.00
(9)	Jim Abbott	1.00
(10)	Ken Griffey Jr.	6.00
(11)	Gregg Jefferies	1.00
(12)	Jerome Walton	1.00
	POWER PITCHERS book:	8.00
(13)	Roger Clemens	2.00
(14)	Dwight Gooden	1.00
(15)	Orel Hershiser	1.00
(16)	Nolan Ryan	5.00

1990 Major League Baseball Photocards

No indication of who produced or marketed these photocards is found on the cards. Printed on thin, glossy cardboard in 8" x 10" format, the cards have a color player photo which is borderless at top and sides. At bottom is a color bar with player name, team logo and the licensors' logos. Backs are blank. The unnumbered cards are checklisted here alphabetically.

		MT
Complete Set (95):		65.00
Common Player:		.50
(1)	Jim Abbott	.50
(2)	Harold Baines	.50
(3)	George Bell	.50
(4)	Bert Blyleven	.50
(5)	Wade Boggs	.75
(6)	Barry Bonds	1.00
(7)	Bobby Bonilla	.50
(8)	Bob Boone	.50
(9)	George Brett	1.00
(10)	Ellis Burks	.50
(11)	Jose Canseco	.75
(12)	Gary Carter	.50
(13)	Joe Carter	.50
(14)	Will Clark	.60
(15)	Roger Clemens	.75
(16)	Vince Coleman	.50
(17)	David Cone	.50
(18)	Ron Darling	.50
(19)	Alvin Davis	.50
(20)	Eric Davis	.50
(21)	Glenn Davis	.50
(22)	Andre Dawson	.50
(23)	Mike Devereaux	.50
(24)	Bill Doran	.50
(25)	Shawon Dunston	.50
(26)	Dennis Eckersley	.50
(27)	Dwight Evans	.50
(28)	Junior Felix	.50
(29)	Carlton Fisk	.60
(30)	Julio Franco	.50
(31)	Gary Gaetti	.50
(32)	Andres Galarraga	.60
(33)	Ron Gant	.50
(34)	Kirk Gibson	.50
(35)	Tom Gordon	.50
(36)	Mark Grace	.65
(37)	Mike Greenwell	.50
(38)	Ken Griffey Jr.	2.00
(39)	Kelly Gruber	.50
(40)	Pedro Guerrero	.50
(41)	Tony Gwynn	1.00
(42)	Von Hayes	.50
(43)	Dave Henderson	.50
(44)	Rickey Henderson	.50
(45)	Orel Hershiser	.50
(46)	Kent Hrbek	.50
(47)	Bo Jackson	.50
(48)	Gregg Jefferies	.50
(49)	Ricky Jordan	.50
(50)	Wally Joyner	.50
(51)	Mark Langston	.50
(52)	Barry Larkin	.50
(53)	Joe Magrane	.50
(54)	Don Mattingly	1.00
(55)	Jack McDowell	.50
(56)	Willie McGee	.50
(57)	Fred McGriff	.55
(58)	Mark McGwire	2.00
(59)	Kevin Mitchell	.50
(60)	Dale Murphy	.55
(61)	Eddie Murray	.60
(62)	Rafael Palmeiro	.55
(63)	Dave Parker	.50
(64)	Kirby Puckett	1.00
(65)	Tim Raines	.50
(66)	Willie Randolph	.50
(67)	Jim Rice	.50
(68)	Dave Righetti	.50
(69)	Cal Ripken Jr.	1.50
(70)	Bret Saberhagen	.50
(71)	Chris Sabo	.50
(72)	Ryne Sandberg	1.00
(73)	Benito Santiago	.50
(74)	Steve Sax	.50
(75)	Mike Schmidt	1.00
(76)	Mike Scott	.50
(77)	Kevin Seitzer	.50
(78)	Ruben Sierra	.50
(79)	Ozzie Smith	.75
(80)	Zane Smith	.50
(81)	John Smoltz	.50
(82)	Terry Steinbach	.50
(83)	Dave Stewart	.50
(84)	Dave Steib	.50
(85)	Darryl Strawberry	.60
(86)	Rick Sutcliffe	.50
(87)	Bobby Thigpen	.50
(88)	Fernando Valenzuela	.50
(89)	Andy Van Slyke	.50
(90)	Frank Viola	.50
(91)	Tim Wallach	.50
(92)	Walt Weiss	.50
(93)	Bob Welch	.50
(94)	Dave Winfield	.60
(95)	Todd Worrell	.50

1988 Mickey Mantle's Restaurant

To promote the grand opening of Mickey Mantle's restaurant in New York City, this promotional card was issued by an Oklahoma public relations firm to members of the media. In round-cornered 2-1/2" x 3-1/2" format on thin, semi-gloss cardboard, the front has a posed color photo of Mantle. The back has details of the restaurant opening and a design reminiscent of the Yankee Stadium facade, printed in white on a dark blue background.

	MT
Mickey Mantle	12.00

1989 Marathon Cubs

This colorful 25-card Cubs team set was sponsored by Marathon and was distributed as a stadium promotion to fans attending the August 10, 1989, game at Chicago's Wrigley Field. The oversize (2-3/4" x 4-1/4") feature an action photo inside a diagonal box on the card front, with the Chicago Cubs logo at the top and the player's uniform number, name and position along the bottom. The backs include a small black-and-white photo, player data and the Cubs and Marathon logos.

		MT
Complete Set (25):		15.00
Common Player:		.50
2	Vance Law	.50
4	Don Zimmer	.50
7	Joe Girardi	.75
8	Andre Dawson	1.75
9	Damon Berryhill	.50
10	Lloyd McClendon	.50
12	Shawon Dunston	.65
15	Domingo Ramos	.50
17	Mark Grace	2.00
18	Dwight Smith	.50
19	Curt Wilkerson	.50
20	Jerome Walton	.50
21	Scott Sanderson	.50
23	Ryne Sandberg	4.00
28	Mitch Williams	.50
31	Greg Maddux	6.00
32	Calvin Schiraldi	.50
33	Mitch Webster	.50
36	Mike Bielecki	.50
39	Paul Kilgus	.50
40	Rick Sutcliffe	.50
41	Jeff Pico	.50
44	Steve Wilson	.50
50	Les Lancaster	.50
---	Coaches (Joe Altobelli, Chuck Cottier, Larry Cox, Jose Martinez, Dick Pole)	.50

1989 Marathon Tigers

Marathon sponsored this give-away set for a 1989 Tigers home game. The oversized cards feature thin white stock and full-color player photos. The cards are numbered according to uniform number.

		MT
Complete Set (28):		12.00
Common Player:		.50
1	Lou Whitaker	1.00
3	Alan Trammell	1.75
8	Mike Heath	.50
9	Fred Lynn	.60
10	Keith Moreland	.50
11	Sparky Anderson	.80
12	Mike Brumley	.50
14	Dave Bergman	.50
15	Pat Sheridan	.50
17	Al Pedrique	.50
18	Ramon Pena	.50
19	Doyle Alexander	.50
21	Guillermo Hernandez	.50
23	Torey Lovullo	.50
24	Gary Pettis	.50
25	Ken Williams	.50
26	Frank Tanana	.50
27	Charles Hudson	.50
32	Gary Ward	.50
33	Matt Nokes	.50
34	Chet Lemon	.50
35	Rick Schu	.50
36	Frank Williams	.50
39	Mike Henneman	.60
44	Jeff Robinson	.50
47	Jack Morris	.80
48	Paul Gibson	.50
---	Coaches (Billy Consolo, Alex Grammas, Billy Muffett, Vada Pinson, Dick Tracewksi)	.50

1990 Marathon Cubs

Marathon sponsored its second consecutive Chicago Cubs team set. The oversized cards feature thin white stock and full-color photos. The cards are numbered according to uniform number, and were distributed at a Cubs home game.

		MT
Complete Set (28):		15.00
Common Player:		.50
4	Don Zimmer	.50
7	Joe Girardi	.50
8	Andre Dawson	1.50
10	Lloyd McClendon	.50
11	Luis Salazar	.50
12	Shawon Dunston	.50
15	Domingo Ramos	.50
17	Mark Grace	2.00
18	Dwight Smith	.50
19	Curtis Wilkerson	.50
20	Jerome Walton	.50
22	Mike Harkey	.50
23	Ryne Sandberg	5.00
25	Marvell Wynne	.50
28	Mitch Williams	.50
29	Doug Dascenzo	.50
30	Dave Clark	.50
31	Greg Maddux	6.00
32	Hector Villanueva	.50
36	Mike Bielecki	.50
37	Bill Long	.50
40	Rick Sutcliffe	.50
41	Jeff Pico	.50
44	Steve Wilson	.50
45	Paul Assenmacher	.50
47	Shawn Boskie	.50
50	Les Lancaster	.50
---	Coaches (Joe Altobelli, Chuck Cottier, Jose Martinez, Dick Pole, Phil Roof)	.50

1991 Marathon Cubs

Marathon Oil once again sponsored a set featuring the Chicago Cubs. This 28-card release features oversized cards measuring 2-7/8" x 4-1/4". The card fronts feature full-color action photos. The flip sides feature complete statistics. The cards are numbered according to uniform number. This number appears on both the front and back of the card.

	MT
Complete Set (28):	15.00
Common Player:	.50

7	Joe Girardi	.50
8	Andre Dawson	1.50
9	Damon Berryhill	.50
10	Luis Salazar	.50
11	George Bell	.60
12	Shawon Dunston	.50
16	Jose Vizcaino	.50
17	Mark Grace	2.00
18	Dwight Smith	.50
19	Hector Villanueva	.50
20	Jerome Walton	.50
22	Mike Harkey	.50
23	Ryne Sandberg	5.00
24	Chico Walker	.50
29	Doug Dascenzo	.50
30	Bob Scanlan	.50
31	Greg Maddux	6.00
32	Danny Jackson	.50
35	Chuck McElroy	.50
36	Mike Bielecki	.50
40	Rick Sutcliffe	.50
41	Jim Essian	.50
42	Dave Smith	.50
45	Paul Assenmacher	.50
47	Shawn Boskie	.50
50	Les Lancaster	.50
51	Heathcliff Slocumb	.50
---	Coaches (Joe Altobelli, Billy Connors, Chuck Cottier, Jose Martinez, Phil Roof, Richie Zisk)	.50

1992 Marathon Cubs

The fourth consecutive year of a Cubs team set sponsored by Marathon Oil consists of 28 cards, including manager Jim Lefebvre and his coaching staff. The set was originally given away at the July 10, 1993 game at Wrigley Field. Cards are checklisted here by uniform number.

		MT
	Complete Set (28):	10.00
	Common Player:	.25
1	Doug Strange	.30
2	Frank Castillo	.30
5	Jim Lefebvre	.30
6	Rey Sanchez	.30
7	Joe Girardi	.40
8	Andre Dawson	.75
10	Luis Salazar	.30
12	Shawon Dunston	.40
16	Jose Vazcaino	.30
17	Mark Grace	1.00
18	Dwight Smith	.30
19	Hector Villanueva	.30
20	Jerome Walton	.30
21	Sammy Sosa	4.00
23	Ryne Sandberg	2.00
27	Derrick May	.30
29	Doug Dascenzo	.30
30	Bob Scanlan	.30
31	Greg Maddux	2.50
32	Danny Jackson	.30
34	Ken Patterson	.30
35	Chuck McElroy	.30
36	Mike Morgan	.30
38	Jeff Robinson	.30
42	Dave Smith	.30
45	Paul Assenmacher	.30
47	Shawn Boskie	.30
---	Coaches (Tom Treblehorn, Jose Martinez, Billy Williams, Sammy Ellis, Chuck Cottier, Billy Connors)	.30

1993 Marathon Cubs

The Cubs distributed the 1993 Marathon Oil set on July 28 in a game against the Padres. The cards, measuring an oversized 4-1/4" x 2-7/8", are unnumbered, with uniform numbers appearing on the back. The cards have a vertical blue stripe down the right side with the player's last name in large, white letters. Backs carry complete major and minor league statistics. There are 27 cards in the set. The checklist is presented here by uniform number.

		MT
	Complete Set (27):	6.00
	Common Player:	.25
2	Rick Wilkins	.40
5	Jim Lefebvre	.25
6	Willie Wilson	.30
10	Steve Lake	.25
11	Rey Sanchez	.25
16	Jose Vizcaino	.25
17	Mark Grace	1.00
18	Dwight Smith	.25
20	Eric Yelding	.25
21	Sammy Sosa	4.00
22	Mike Harkey	.25
23	Ryne Sandberg	2.00
24	Steve Buechele	.25
25	Candy Maldonado	.25
27	Derrick May	.25
28	Randy Myers	.30
29	Jose Guzman	.25
30	Bob Scanlan	.25
32	Dan Plesac	.25
36	Mike Morgan	.25
37	Greg Hibbard	.25
38	Jose Bautista	.25
45	Paul Assenmacher	.25
49	Frank Castillo	.25
53	Doug Jennings	.25
---	Coaches (Billy Williams, Jose Martinez, Billy Connors, Tony Muser)	.25
---	Coaches (Dan Simonds, Tom Treblehorn, Chuck Cottier)	.25

1994 Chris Martin Enterprises Pro Mags

Borderless color player action photos are featured on this set of blank-backed, round-cornered 2-1/8" x 3-3/8" magnets produced by former NFL player Chris Martin (sets were also made of football and basketball player magnets). The flexible, UV-coated magnets have a color team logo in an upper corner and a "Pro Mags" logo in the other. At bottom is the player's name, magnet number, the logos of the MLBPA and MLB licensors and a Chris Martin Enterprises copyright line. Magnets were sold in blister packs of five with a 2-1/8" x 3/4" team logo magnet and a checklist card of Joe Carter at about $5. Autographed magnets of Joe Carter were randomly inserted into packs.

		MT
	Complete Set (140):	100.00
	Common Player:	1.00
1	Terry Pendleton	1.00
2	Ryan Klesko	1.00
3	Fred McGriff	1.25
4	Dave Justice	1.25
5	Greg Maddux	2.00
6	Brady Anderson	1.00
7	Ben McDonald	1.00
8	Cal Ripken Jr.	2.50
9	Mike Mussina	1.00
10	Jeffrey Hammonds	1.00
11	Roger Clemens	1.50
12	Andre Dawson	1.00
13	Mike Greenwell	1.00
14	Mo Vaughn	1.00
15	Otis Nixon	1.00
16	Chad Curtis	1.00
17	Mark Langston	1.00
18	Tim Salmon	1.00
19	Chuck Finley	1.00
20	Eduardo Perez	1.00
21	Steve Buechele	1.00
22	Mark Grace	1.50
23	Sammy Sosa	2.00
24	Derrick May	1.00
25	Shawon Dunston	1.00
26	Jack McDowell	1.00
27	Tim Raines	1.00
28	Frank Thomas	2.00
29	Robin Ventura	1.00
30	Julio Franco	1.00
31	John Smiley	1.00
32	Barry Larkin	1.00
33	Jose Rijo	1.00
34	Reggie Sanders	1.00
35	Kevin Mitchell	1.00
36	Sandy Alomar Jr.	1.00
37	Carlos Baerga	1.00
38	Albert Belle	1.25
39	Manny Ramirez	1.50
40	Eddie Murray	1.25
41	Dante Bichette	1.25
42	Ellis Burks	1.00
43	Andres Galarraga	1.25
44	Greg W. Harris	1.00
45	David Nied	1.00
46	Cecil Fielder	1.00
47	Kirk Gibson	1.00
48	Mickey Tettleton	1.00
49	Lou Whitaker	1.00
50	Travis Fryman	1.00
51	Jeff Conine	1.00
52	Charlie Hough	1.00
53	Benito Santiago	1.00
54	Gary Sheffield	1.25
55	Dave Magadan	1.00
56	Jeff Bagwell	1.75
57	Luis Gonzalez	1.00
58	Andujar Cedeno	1.00
59	Craig Biggio	1.00
60	Doug Drabek	1.00
61	Tom Gordon	1.00
62	Brian McRae	1.00
63	David Cone	1.00
64	Wally Joyner	1.00
65	Jeff Montgomery	1.00
66	Eric Karros	1.00
67	Tom Candiotti	1.00
68	Delino DeShields	1.00
69	Orel Hershiser	1.00
70	Mike Piazza	2.00
71	Darryl Hamilton	1.00
72	Kevin Seitzer	1.00
73	B.J. Surhoff	1.00
74	John Jaha	1.00
75	Greg Vaughn	1.00
76	Kent Hrbek	1.00
77	Kirby Puckett	2.00
78	Kevin Tapani	1.00
79	Dave Winfield	1.50
80	Chuck Knoblauch	1.00
81	Moises Alou	1.00
82	Wil Cordero	1.00
83	Marquis Grissom	1.00
84	Pedro J. Martinez	1.50
85	Larry Walker	1.25
86	Jim Abbott	1.00
87	Wade Boggs	1.50
88	Don Mattingly	2.00
89	Luis Polonia	1.00
90	Danny Tartabull	1.00
91	Bobby Bonilla	1.00
92	Todd Hundley	1.00
93	Dwight Gooden	1.00
94	Jeromy Burnitz	1.00
95	Bret Saberhagen	1.00
96	Dennis Eckersley	1.00
97	Mark McGwire	3.00
98	Ruben Sierra	1.00
99	Terry Steinbach	1.00
100	Rickey Henderson	1.50
101	Darren Daulton	1.00
102	Lenny Dykstra	1.00
103	Dave Hollins	1.00
104	John Kruk	1.00
105	Curt Schilling	1.00
106	Carlos Garcia	1.00
107	Jay Bell	1.00
108	Don Slaught	1.00
109	Andy Van Slyke	1.00
110	Orlando Merced	1.00
111	Ray Lankford	1.00
112	Mark Whiten	1.00
113	Todd Zeile	1.00
114	Ozzie Smith	1.50
115	Gregg Jefferies	1.00
116	Derek Bell	1.00
117	Andy Benes	1.00
118	Phil Plantier	1.00
119	Tony Gwynn	1.50
120	Bip Roberts	1.00
121	Barry Bonds	1.50
122	John Burkett	1.00
123	Robby Thompson	1.00
124	Darren Lewis	1.00
125	Willie McGee	1.00
126	Jay Buhner	1.00
127	Ken Griffey Jr.	3.00
128	Randy Johnson	1.50
129	Eric Anthony	1.00
130	Edgar Martinez	1.00
131	Kevin Brown	1.50
132	Jose Canseco	1.50
133	Juan Gonzalez	1.75
134	Will Clark	1.50
135	Ivan Rodriguez	1.50
136	Roberto Alomar	1.25
137	Joe Carter	1.00
137a	Joe Carter (autographed)	15.00
138	Juan Guzman	1.00
139	Paul Molitor	1.25
140	John Olerud	1.25

1996 Chris Martin Enterprises Pro Mags

Large team logos on silver metallic foil are the background for the action player photos in this set of card-like magnets. At left is a color strip with the team nickname in a combination of colors approximating team standards. The player name is in gold foil. Backs of the 2-1/4" x 3-1/2" magnets are, of course, blank. The basic unit of sale for the product is foil packs containing five player magnets. While packaging advertises 140 players, only 137 were issued. The unnumbered magnets are checklisted here in alphabetical order.

		MT
	Complete Set (137):	50.00
	Common Player:	.25
(1)	Brady Anderson	.35
(2)	Brian Anderson	.25
(3)	Kevin Appier	.25
(4)	Andy Ashby	.25
(5)	Jeff Bagwell	1.00
(6)	Derek Bell	.40
(7)	Jay Bell	.25
(8)	Albert Belle	1.00
(9)	Geronimo Berroa	.25
(10)	Dante Bichette	.45
(11)	Craig Biggio	.50
(12)	Wade Boggs	.75
(13)	Barry Bonds	2.00
(14)	Bobby Bonilla	.25
(15)	Bret Boone	.25
(16)	Rico Brogna	.25
(17)	Jay Buhner	.25
(18)	Ken Caminiti	.35
(19)	Jose Canseco	.75
(20)	Joe Carter	.25
(21)	Vinny Castilla	.35
(22)	Andujar Cedeno	.25
(23)	Will Clark	.60
(24)	Roger Clemens	.75
(25)	Greg Colbrunn	.25
(26)	David Cone	.25
(27)	Jeff Conine	.25
(28)	Wil Cordero	.25
(29)	Marty Cordova	.25
(30)	Chad Curtis	.25
(31)	Darren Daulton	.25
(32)	Chili Davis	.25
(33)	Carlos Delgado	.25
(34)	Delino DeShields	.25
(35)	Gary DiSarcina	.25
(36)	Doug Drabek	.25
(37)	Shawon Dunston	.25
(38)	Jim Eisenreich	.25
(39)	Alex Fernandez	.25
(40)	Cecil Fielder	.25
(41)	Darrin Fletcher	.25
(42)	Travis Fryman	.25
(43)	Andres Galarraga	.35
(44)	Carlos Garcia	.25
(45)	Benji Gil	.25
(46)	Bernard Gilkey	.25
(47)	Tom Glavine	.35
(48)	Alex Gonzalez	.35
(49)	Juan Gonzalez	1.00
(50)	Tom Goodwin	.25
(51)	Mark Grace	.50
(52)	Ken Griffey Jr.	4.00
(53)	Mark Gubicza	.25
(54)	Tony Gwynn	1.00
(55)	Chris Hammond	.25
(56)	Glenallen Hill	.25
(57)	Todd Hundley	.35
(58)	John Jaha	.25
(59)	Gregg Jefferies	.35
(60)	Randy Johnson	.50
(61)	Bobby Jones	.25
(62)	Brian Jordan	.25
(63)	David Justice	.35
(64)	Ron Karkovice	.25
(65)	Eric Karros	.25
(66)	Jeff Kent	.25
(67)	Jimmy Key	.25
(68)	Ryan Klesko	.40
(69)	Chuck Knoblauch	.40
(70)	Ray Lankford	.25
(71)	Barry Larkin	.25
(72)	Mark Leiter	.25
(73)	Scott Leius	.25
(74)	Pat Listach	.25
(75)	Keith Lockhart	.25
(76)	Kenny Lofton	.40
(77)	Greg Maddux	2.50
(78)	Dave Magadan	.25
(79)	Al Martin	.25
(80)	Edgar Martinez	.25
(81)	Pedro Martinez	.50
(82)	Fred McGriff	.35
(83)	Mark McGwire	4.00
(84)	Brian McRae	.25
(85)	Orlando Merced	.25
(86)	Raul Mondesi	.40
(87)	Mickey Morandini	.25
(88)	Pedro Munoz	.25
(89)	Eddie Murray	.50
(90)	Mike Mussina	.35
(91)	Charles Nagy	.25
(92)	Jaime Navarro	.25
(93)	Denny Neagle	.25
(94)	Phil Nevin	.25
(95)	Hideo Nomo	1.00
(96)	Jon Nunnally	.25
(97)	John Olerud	.35
(98)	Paul O'Neill	.25
(99)	Tom Pagnozzi	.25
(100)	Rafael Palmeiro	.40
(101)	Terry Pendleton	.25
(102)	Mike Piazza	2.00
(103)	Kirby Puckett	1.50
(104)	Paul Quantrill	.25
(105)	Tim Raines	.30
(106)	Manny Ramirez	.60
(107)	Jody Reed	.25
(108)	Jose Rijo	.25
(109)	Cal Ripken Jr.	3.00
(110)	Carlos Rodriguez	.25
(111)	Ivan Rodriguez	.60
(112)	Tim Salmon	.40
(113)	Deion Sanders	.40
(114)	Reggie Sanders	.25
(115)	Benito Santiago	.25
(116)	David Segui	.25
(117)	Kevin Seitzer	.25
(118)	Gary Sheffield	.40
(119)	Ozzie Smith	.75
(120)	J.T. Snow	.35
(121)	Sammy Sosa	1.25
(122)	Ed Sprague	.25
(123)	Terry Steinbach	.25
(124)	Todd Stottlemyre	.25
(125)	Danny Tartabull	.25
(126)	Frank Thomas	2.50
(127)	Alan Trammell	.25
(128)	John Valentin	.25
(129)	Mo Vaughn	.40
(130)	Robin Ventura	.35
(131)	Jose Vizcaino	.25
(132)	Larry Walker	.35
(133)	Walt Weiss	.25
(134)	Rondell White	.25
(135)	Bob Wickman	.25
(136)	Matt Williams	.30
(137)	Dan Wilson	.25

Player names in *Italic* type indicate a rookie card.

1996 Chris Martin Enterprises Die-cut Magnets

A die-cut team logo and player surname form the background for the action photo on these magnets. The player's first name is printed in gold foil. Varying in size, but about 3-1/2" x 3-1/2", the magnets are blank-backed. The die-cut magnets are sold in single-player blister packs. The unnumbered magnets are checklisted here alphabetically.

		MT
Complete Set (25):		60.00
Common Player:		2.50
(1)	Albert Belle	2.50
(2)	Dante Bichette	2.50
(3)	Barry Bonds	4.00
(4)	Bobby Bonilla	2.50
(5)	Joe Carter	2.50
(6)	Will Clark	2.50
(7)	Cecil Fielder	2.50
(8)	Andres Galarraga	2.50
(9)	Juan Gonzalez	4.00
(10)	Ken Griffey Jr.	6.00
(11)	Tony Gwynn	3.50
(12)	Randy Johnson	2.50
(13)	David Justice	2.50
(14)	Ryan Klesko	2.50
(15)	Barry Larkin	2.50
(16)	Don Mattingly	4.00
(17)	Fred McGriff	2.50
(18)	Eddie Murray	2.50
(19)	Hideo Nomo	2.50
(20)	Mike Piazza	4.00
(21)	Kirby Puckett	3.50
(22)	Cal Ripken Jr.	5.00
(23)	Tim Salmon	2.50
(24)	Frank Thomas	5.00
(25)	Mo Vaughn	2.50

1996 Chris Martin Enterprises Pro Stamps

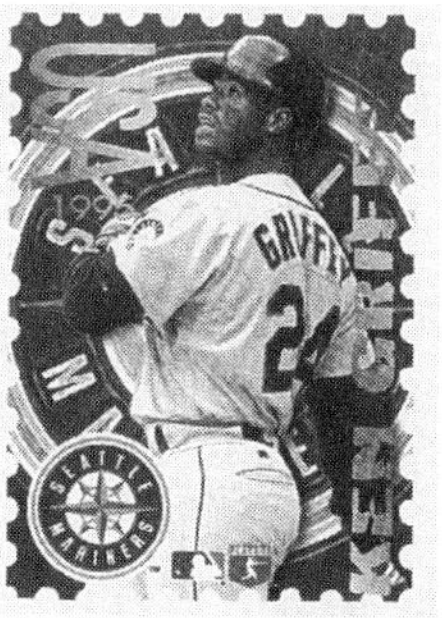

Large team logos are the background for the action player photos in this set of stamp-shaped stickers. Down one side is a gold-foil "USA" and small team logo at bottom. Vertically on the other side is the player name in gold foil. Backs of the 1-1/2" x 2-1/2" stamps are blank. The stamps are sold in 12-piece cello packs. Although the pack header advertises 140 players, only 137 were issued. The unnumbered magnets are checklisted here in alphabetical order.

		MT
Complete Set (137):		50.00
Common Player:		.25
(1)	Brady Anderson	.30
(2)	Brian Anderson	.25
(3)	Kevin Appier	.25
(4)	Andy Ashby	.25
(5)	Jeff Bagwell	1.50
(6)	Derek Bell	.40
(7)	Jay Bell	.25
(8)	Albert Belle	1.00
(9)	Geronimo Berroa	.25
(10)	Dante Bichette	.50
(11)	Craig Biggio	.40
(12)	Wade Boggs	.60
(13)	Barry Bonds	2.00
(14)	Bobby Bonilla	.25
(15)	Bret Boone	.25
(16)	Rico Brogna	.25
(17)	Jay Buhner	.25
(18)	Ken Caminiti	.35
(19)	Jose Canseco	.65
(20)	Joe Carter	.30
(21)	Vinny Castilla	.35
(22)	Andujar Cedeno	.25
(23)	Will Clark	.45
(24)	Roger Clemens	1.00
(25)	Greg Colbrunn	.25
(26)	David Cone	.25
(27)	Jeff Conine	.25
(28)	Wil Cordero	.25
(29)	Marty Cordova	.25
(30)	Chad Curtis	.25
(31)	Darren Daulton	.25
(32)	Chili Davis	.25
(33)	Carlos Delgado	.25
(34)	Delino DeShields	.25
(35)	Gary DiSarcina	.25
(36)	Doug Drabek	.25
(37)	Shawon Dunston	.25
(38)	Jim Eisenreich	.25
(39)	Alex Fernandez	.25
(40)	Cecil Fielder	.25
(41)	Darrin Fletcher	.25
(42)	Travis Fryman	.25
(43)	Andres Galarraga	.35
(44)	Carlos Garcia	.25
(45)	Benji Gil	.25
(46)	Bernard Gilkey	.25
(47)	Tom Glavine	.35
(48)	Alex Gonzalez	.35
(49)	Juan Gonzalez	.75
(50)	Tom Goodwin	.25
(51)	Mark Grace	.45
(52)	Ken Griffey Jr.	4.00
(53)	Mark Gubicza	.25
(54)	Tony Gwynn	1.00
(55)	Chris Hammond	.25
(56)	Glenallen Hill	.25
(57)	Todd Hundley	.35
(58)	John Jaha	.25
(59)	Gregg Jefferies	.35
(60)	Randy Johnson	.50
(61)	Bobby Jones	.25
(62)	Brian Jordan	.25
(63)	David Justice	.35
(64)	Ron Karkovice	.25
(65)	Eric Karros	.25
(66)	Jeff Kent	.25
(67)	Jimmy Key	.25
(68)	Ryan Klesko	.25
(69)	Chuck Knoblauch	.45
(70)	Ray Lankford	.25
(71)	Barry Larkin	.25
(72)	Mark Leiter	.25
(73)	Scott Leius	.25
(74)	Pat Listach	.25
(75)	Keith Lockhart	.25
(76)	Kenny Lofton	.40
(77)	Greg Maddux	2.50
(78)	Dave Magadan	.25
(79)	Al Martin	.25
(80)	Edgar Martinez	.25
(81)	Pedro Martinez	.50
(82)	Fred McGriff	.35
(83)	Mark McGwire	4.00
(84)	Brian McRae	.25
(85)	Orlando Merced	.25
(86)	Raul Mondesi	.40
(87)	Mickey Morandini	.25
(88)	Pedro Munoz	.25
(89)	Eddie Murray	.45
(90)	Mike Mussina	.35
(91)	Charles Nagy	.25
(92)	Jaime Navarro	.25
(93)	Denny Neagle	.25
(94)	Phil Nevin	.25
(95)	Hideo Nomo	.75
(96)	Jon Nunnally	.25
(97)	John Olerud	.35
(98)	Paul O'Neill	.30
(99)	Tom Pagnozzi	.25
(100)	Rafael Palmeiro	.40
(101)	Terry Pendleton	.25
(102)	Mike Piazza	2.50
(103)	Kirby Puckett	1.50
(104)	Paul Quantrill	.25
(105)	Tim Raines	.30
(106)	Manny Ramirez	.60
(107)	Jody Reed	.25
(108)	Jose Rijo	.25
(109)	Cal Ripken Jr.	3.00
(110)	Carlos Rodriguez	.25
(111)	Ivan Rodriguez	.60
(112)	Tim Salmon	.40
(113)	Deion Sanders	.35
(114)	Reggie Sanders	.30
(115)	Benito Santiago	.25
(116)	David Segui	.25
(117)	Kevin Seitzer	.25
(118)	Gary Sheffield	.35
(119)	Ozzie Smith	.50
(120)	J.T. Snow	.30
(121)	Sammy Sosa	.75
(122)	Ed Sprague	.25
(123)	Terry Steinbach	.25
(124)	Todd Stottlemyre	.25
(125)	Danny Tartabull	.25
(126)	Frank Thomas	2.00
(127)	Alan Trammell	.25
(128)	John Valentin	.25
(129)	Mo Vaughn	.40
(130)	Robin Ventura	.35
(131)	Jose Vizcaino	.25
(132)	Larry Walker	.40
(133)	Walt Weiss	.25
(134)	Rondell White	.25
(135)	Bob Wickman	.25
(136)	Matt Williams	.35
(137)	Dan Wilson	.25

1999 Maryland Baseball Legends Lottery Tickets

Former Baltimore Orioles' greats are pictured in this series of $1 scratch-off lottery tickets. Appropriately, funds generated from the game benefit the Maryland Stadium Authority. Measuring about 4" x 2", the tickets have postage-stamp sized color player portraits (minus MLB logos) with facsimile autograph on an orange metallic background. At right is a green scratch-off area with chances to win prizes up to $2,500. Backs are in black-and-white with lottery rules. Values shown are for unscratched tickets; used tickets are worth about 25%.

		MT
Complete Set (6):		8.00
Common Player:		1.50
(1)	Paul Blair	1.50
(2)	Rick Dempsey	1.50
(3)	Eddie Murray	1.50
(4)	Boog Powell	1.50
(5)	Brooks Robinson	1.50
(6)	Earl Weaver	1.50

1998 Maryvale Baseball Park Inauguration

This commemorative card marking the inaugural season of the Milwaukee Brewers' new spring training base in Arizona was given to fans attending the first game. The 4" x 6-1/2" card has a game-action photo of Robin Yount on front, with the ballpark and sponsor's logos at top in the dark blue border. Career highlights are at bottom. The back is blank.

	MT
Robin Yount	7.50

1988 Master Bread Twins

This set of 12 cardboard discs (2-3/4" diameter) features full-color photos of Minnesota Twins team members. Fronts have a bright blue background with red, yellow and black printing. The player photo (with team logos air-brushed off) is centered beneath a "Master Is Good Bread" headliner and a vivid yellow player/team name banner. Backs are black-and-white with five stars printed above the player's name, team, personal data, disc number, stats and "1988 Collector's Edition" banner. The discs were printed in Canada and marketed exclusively in Minnesota in packages of Master Bread, one disc per loaf.

		MT
Complete Set (12):		15.00
Common Player:		.50
1	Bert Blyleven	.75
2	Frank Viola	.75
3	Juan Berenguer	.50
4	Jeff Reardon	.75
5	Tim Laudner	.50
6	Steve Lombardozzi	.50
7	Randy Bush	.50
8	Kirby Puckett	8.00
9	Gary Gaetti	1.00
10	Kent Hrbek	2.00
11	Greg Gagne	1.00
12	Tom Brunansky	.50

1989 Master Bread

For a second year Master Bread packages in the Twin Cities area contained a baseball player disc in 1989. The 2-3/4" discs are in the familiar Mike Schechter Associates format and, unlike the '88 set, featured American League players other than Twins. The issue is among the scarcer of the MSA disc issues. Fronts are trimmed in yellow banners and blue stars. Backs are in blue and have a few stats and player data, along with a disc number.

		MT
Complete Set (12):		40.00
Common Player:		2.50
1	Frank Viola	2.50
2	Kirby Puckett	8.00
3	Gary Gaetti	2.50
4	Alan Trammell	3.00
5	Wade Boggs	6.00
6	Don Mattingly	8.00
7	Wally Joyner	3.00
8	Paul Molitor	5.00
9	George Brett	7.00
10	Jose Canseco	4.00
11	Julio Franco	2.50
12	Cal Ripken Jr.	12.00

1999 MasterCard Aaron Anniversary

The 25th anniversary of Hank Aaron's record-setting 715th career home run is commemorated on this "magic motion" card given away in an edition of 50,000 as part of "A Salute to Hank Aaron Night" on April 8, 1999, at Turner Field. The 5" x 3" card has a borderless action shot of Aaron's historic homer. The team, anniversary and sponsor logos are on front. The back has information on receiving a commemorative baseball.

	MT
Hank Aaron	6.00

1999 MasterCard Ted Williams

In conjunction with the 1999 All-Star Game at Boston's Fenway Park, 40,000 "magic motion" cards honoring Ted Williams were given away. The front of the 4" x 3" card has a borderless color action sequence of Williams' swing. On back, on a green-toned background, is a black-and-white photo of Williams, information on his web site and a facsimile autograph.

	MT
Ted Williams	5.00

1992 Maxwell House Toronto Blue Jays

The first 16 years of Toronto Blue Jays teams are commemorated in this mail-in premium from the coffee company. Each 3-1/2" x 2-1/2" card has a color team photo on front, with a blue frame and white borders. A team logo is at top-center. Backs are in blue on white with player identification, team highlights for that season, and team and sponsor logos. An album to house the collection was available for $6.

		MT
Complete Set (18):		15.00
Common Card:		1.00
(1)	1977 Toronto Blue Jays	1.00
(2)	1978 Toronto Blue Jays	1.00
(3)	1979 Toronto Blue Jays	1.00
(4)	1980 Toronto Blue Jays	1.00
(5)	1981 Toronto Blue Jays	1.00
(6)	1982 Toronto Blue Jays	1.00
(7)	1983 Toronto Blue Jays	1.00
(8)	1984 Toronto Blue Jays	1.00
(9)	1985 Toronto Blue Jays	1.00
(10)	1986 Toronto Blue Jays	1.00
(11)	1987 Toronto Blue Jays	1.00
(12)	1988 Toronto Blue Jays	1.00
(13)	1989 Toronto Blue Jays	1.00
(14)	1990 Toronto Blue Jays	1.00
(15)	1991 Toronto Blue Jays	1.00
(16)	1992 Toronto Blue Jays	1.00
(17)	Title card	1.00
(18)	Album offer card	1.00

1985 Thom McAn Discs

One of the more obscure 1985 issues, this 47-card set of "Pro Player Discs" was issued by Thom McAn as a promotion for its "Jox" tennis shoes, which are advertised on the back of the cards. The discs, which measure 2-3/4" in diameter, feature black-and-white player photos against a background of either gold, yellow, red, pink, green or blue. Although not included in the "official" checklist released by the company, cards of George Brett have also been reported. Many of the Latin players' discs are quite scarce and are believed to have been issued in more limited quantities in Hispanic communities. The discs are unnumbered and checklisted here alphabetically.

		MT
Complete Set (47):		600.00
Common Player:		12.50
(1)	Benny Ayala	18.50
(2)	Buddy Bell	12.50
(3)	Juan Beniquez	18.50
(4)	Tony Bernazard	18.50
(5)	Mike Boddicker	12.50
(6)	George Brett	100.00
(7)	Bill Buckner	12.50
(8)	Rod Carew	45.00
(9)	Steve Carlton	45.00
(10)	Caesar Cedeno (Cesar)	12.50
(11)	Onix Concepcion	12.50
(12)	Cecil Cooper	12.50
(13)	Al Cowens	12.50
(14)	Jose Cruz	18.50
(15)	Ivan DeJesus	18.50
(16)	Luis DeLeon	18.50
(17)	Rich Gossage	15.00
(18)	Pedro Guerrero	12.50
(19)	Ron Guidry	12.50
(20)	Tony Gwynn	90.00
(21)	Mike Hargrove	12.50
(22)	Keith Hernandez	18.50
(23)	Bob Horner	12.50
(24)	Kent Hrbek	18.50
(25)	Rick Langford	12.50
(26)	Jeff Leonard	12.50
(27)	Willie McGee	12.50
(28)	Jack Morris	12.50
(29)	Jesse Orosco	18.50
(30)	Junior Ortiz	18.50
(31)	Terry Puhl	12.50
(32)	Dan Quisenberry	12.50
(33)	Johnny Ray	12.50
(34)	Cal Ripken	150.00
(35)	Ed Romero	18.50
(36)	Ryne Sandberg	60.00
(37)	Mike Schmidt	75.00
(38)	Tom Seaver	45.00
(39)	Rick Sutcliffe	12.50
(40)	Bruce Sutter	12.50
(41)	Alan Trammell	18.50
(42)	Fernando Valenzuela	20.00
(43)	Ozzie Virgil	18.50
(44)	Greg Walker	12.50
(45)	Willie Wilson	12.50
(46)	Dave Winfield	40.00
(47)	Geoff Zahn	12.50

1992 John McClean

These cards were issued ostensibly to showcase the work of sports artist John McClean. Multiple player views are included on each 2-1/4" x 3-3/4" card. Backs are blank and the players are not identified anywhere on the cards. Besides the six baseball players listed here, the set includes nine hockey players and Michael Jordan.

		MT
Complete Set (16):		7.50
Common Baseball Player:		.25
(1)	Roberto Alomar	.25
(2)	Jose Canseco	.50
(3)	Joe Carter	.25
(4)	Kirby Puckett	.75
(5)	Cal Ripken Jr.	2.00
(6)	Nolan Ryan	2.00

1990 McDonald's

This 25-card set was released exclusively in the Boise, Idaho area. The set features baseball all-stars and was very limited in production. The cards have front borders of graduated purple shades. The McDonald's logo appears on front and back.

		MT
Complete Set (25):		450.00
Common Player:		5.00
1	Will Clark	45.00
2	Sandy Alomar, Jr.	20.00
3	Julio Franco	5.00
4	Carlton Fisk	35.00
5	Rickey Henderson	35.00
6	Matt Williams	25.00
7	John Franco	5.00
8	Ryne Sandberg	60.00
9	Kelly Gruber	5.00
10	Andre Dawson	10.00
11	Barry Bonds	50.00
12	Gary Sheffield	25.00
13	Ramon Martinez	10.00
14	Len Dykstra	5.00
15	Benito Santiago	5.00
16	Cecil Fielder	7.50
17	John Olerud	20.00
18	Roger Clemens	60.00
19	George Brett	60.00
20	George Bell	5.00
21	Ozzie Guillen	5.00
22	Steve Sax	5.00
23	Dave Stewart	5.00
24	Ozzie Smith	60.00
25	Robin Yount	60.00

1991 McDonald's Cleveland Indians

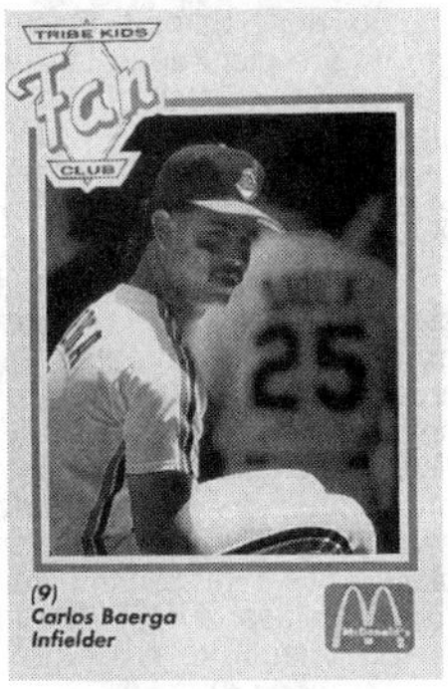

Distributed only at northern Ohio area McDonalds, this set features the players, coaches and manager of the Indians on an oversize (2-7/8" x 4-1/4") format. Color photos on front are framed in white and red with a white border all around. In the upper-left corner is a "Tribe Kids Fan Club" logo, while the McDonald's logo appears at lower-right. The player's uniform number, name and position are in black at lower-left. Backs are printed in black and have complete major and minor league statistics.

		MT
Complete Set (30):		7.00
Common Player:		.25
1	John McNamara	.25
2	Alex Cole	.25
4	Joel Skinner	.25
6	Jose Escobar	.25
7	Chris James	.25
8	Albert Belle	4.00
9	Carlos Baerga	.50
11	Doug Jones	.25
14	Jerry Browne	.25
15	Sandy Alomar	1.50
16	Felix Fermin	.25
20	Turner Ward	.25
21	Greg Swindell	.25
23	Mitch Webster	.25
26	Brook Jacoby	.25
27	Dave Otto	.25
31	Steve Olin	.25
37	Beau Allred	.25
38	Shawn Hillegas	.25
40	Eric King	.25
41	Charles Nagy	.40
44	Mike Huff	.25
45	Jeff Manto	.25
46	Bruce Egloff	.25
47	Jesse Orosco	.25
48	Mike Walker	.25
49	Tom Candiotti	.25
52	John Farrell	.25
54	Rod Nichols	.25
---	Coaches (Billy Williams, Jose Morales, Rich Dauer, Mike Hargrove, Luis Isaac, Mark Wiley)	.25

1992 McDonald's Baseball's Best

Sold in five-card cello packs with a food purchase at McDonald's stores in New York, New Jersey and Connecticut, this 44-card set was produced by Topps and carries the Topps logo, along with the Golden Arches, on front and back. Player photos on front are framed in yellow, surrounded by a black border. A red and blue "Baseball's Best" logo appears at top-right of the photo. Above that is a gold-foil stripe announcing "Limited Edition". At lower-right is another gold-foil stripe with the McDonald's logo and the player's name embossed thereon. On cards #34-44, which were distributed one per pack, there is an additional gold embossed "Rookie" shield at upper-left. Backs have a red border with a yellow stat box at center framed in white.

		MT
Complete Set (44):		20.00
Common Player:		.25
1	Cecil Fielder	.40
2	Benito Santiago	.25
3	Rickey Henderson	.60
4	Roberto Alomar	.75
5	Ryne Sandberg	1.00
6	George Brett	1.50
7	Terry Pendleton	.25
8	Ken Griffey, Jr.	3.00
9	Bobby Bonilla	.25
10	Roger Clemens	1.00
11	Ozzie Smith	.65
12	Barry Bonds	1.50
13	Cal Ripken, Jr.	2.50
14	Ron Gant	.25
15	Carlton Fisk	.50
16	Steve Avery	.25
17	Robin Yount	1.00
18	Will Clark	.65
19	Kirby Puckett	1.50
20	Jim Abbott	.25
21	Barry Larkin	.35
22	Jose Canseco	.65
23	Howard Johnson	.25
24	Nolan Ryan	2.50
25	Frank Thomas	2.00
26	Danny Tartabull	.25
27	Julio Franco	.25
28	David Justice	.50
29	Joe Carter	.25
30	Dale Murphy	.35
31	Andre Dawson	.30
32	Dwight Gooden	.25
33	Bo Jackson	.35
34	Jeff Bagwell	.75
35	Chuck Knoblauch	.40
36	Derek Bell	.25
37	Jim Thome	.45
38	Royce Clayton	.25
39	Ryan Klesko	.50
40	Chito Martinez	.25
41	Ivan Rodriguez	.50
42	Todd Hundley	.25
43	Eric Karros	.25
44	Todd Van Poppel	.25

1992 McDonald's Cardinals

Pacific Trading Cards and McDonald's combined in 1992 to produce this 55-card (plus checklist) team set for the benefit of Ronald McDonald Children's Charities on the occasion of the St. Louis Cardinals' 100th anniversary. Sets were sold initially for $1.49. Cards are standard 2-1/2" x 3-1/2" size and UV coated on each side. There is a sepia-toned or color photo on both front and back; generally an action photo on front and a portrait on back. Player selection is largely weighted to the last half of the 20th Century, with only a few cards of players pre-dating the Gashouse Gang era. The front design is completed with a Cardinals anniversary logo in the upper-left corner, a McDonalds logo at lower-right and gold stripes top and bottom. The player's name and position appear in red at the bottom of the photo. Besides the portrait photo, backs have a career summary stats for the player's Cardinals year and major league career and all appropriate logos.

		MT
Complete Set (55):		18.00
Common Player:		.25
1	Jim Bottomley	.35
2	Rip Collins	.25
3	Johnny Mize	.50
4	Rogers Hornsby	.75
5	Miller Huggins	.30
6	Marty Marion	.30
7	Frank Frisch	.35
8	Whitey Kurowski	.25
9	Joe Medwick	.25
10	Terry Moore	.25
11	Chick Hafey	.25
12	Pepper Martin	.35
13	Bob O'Farrell	.25
14	Walker Cooper	.25
15	Dizzy Dean	1.00
16	Grover Cleveland Alexander	.75
17	Jesse Haines	.25
18	Bill Hallahan	.25
19	Mort Cooper	.25
20	Burleigh Grimes	.25
21	Red Schoendienst	.35
22	Stan Musial	3.00
23	Enos Slaughter	.35
24	Keith Hernandez	.30
25	Bill White	.25
26	Orlando Cepeda	.50
27	Julian Javier	.25
28	Dick Groat	.25
29	Ken Boyer	.35
30	Lou Brock	.40
31	Mike Shannon	.30
32	Curt Flood	.30
33	Joe Cunningham	.25
34	Reggie Smith	.25
35	Ted Simmons	.25
36	Tim McCarver	.35
37	Tom Herr	.25
38	Ozzie Smith	2.00
39	Joe Torre	.45
40	Terry Pendleton	.25
41	Ken Reitz	.25
42	Vince Coleman	.30
43	Willie McGee	.30
44	Bake McBride	.25
45	George Hendrick	.25
46	Bob Gibson	1.00
47	Whitey Herzog	.25
48	Harry Brecheen	.25
49	Howard Pollet	.25
50	John Tudor	.25
51	Bob Forsch	.25
52	Bruce Sutter	.25
53	Lee Smith	.30
54	Todd Worrell	.25
55	Al Hrabosky	.25
---	Checklist	.05

1992 McDonald's Ken Griffey, Jr.

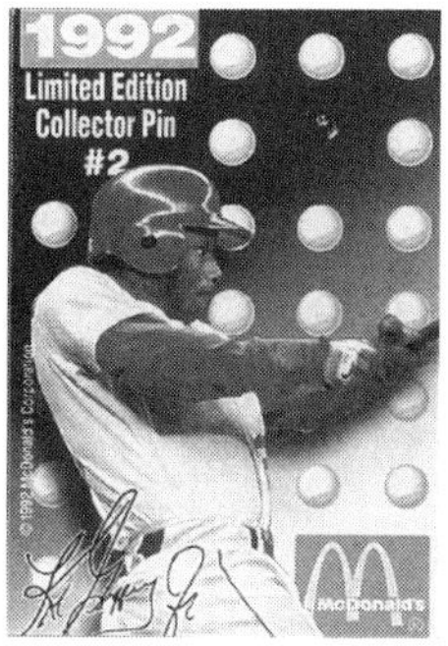

This set of three card-pin combinations saw limited distribution in the Northwestern U.S., with sales benefitting the Ronald McDonald Children's Charities. Cards measure 2-1/2" x 3-1/2" and have color photos of Ken Griffey, Jr. on the front. Fronts also have a McDonald's logo and facsimile autograph. Uniform logos have been removed from the player's photo. Backs have a description of the benefitting charity and the logo "Griffey's Golden Moments," along with a 1992 Alrak Enterprises copyright. The pins were fastened through the cardboard of the card, leaving each with a hole. Prices quoted are for card/pin combinations.

		MT
Complete Set (3):		10.00
Common Card/Pin:		4.00
1	Ken Griffey, Jr.	4.00
2	Ken Griffey, Jr.	4.00
3	Ken Griffey, Jr.	4.00

1992 McDonald's MVP

McDonald's restaurants in Ontario released a 26-card All-Star baseball card set in 1992 featuring many of the top players in the game. The cards were sold at Canadian McDonald's in packs of four with the purchase of a meal. Additionally, the company offered a six-card Toronto Blue Jays subset. The cards were produced by Donruss.

		MT
Complete Set (33):		10.00
Common Player:		.25
1	Cal Ripken, Jr.	1.00
2	Frank Thomas	.90
3	George Brett	.75
4	Roberto Kelly	.25
5	Nolan Ryan	1.00
6	Ryne Sandberg	.60
7	Darryl Strawberry	.25
8	Len Dykstra	.25
9	Fred McGriff	.30
10	Roger Clemens	.50
11	Sandy Alomar Jr.	.30
12	Robin Yount	.60
13	Jose Canseco	.35
14	Jimmy Key	.25
15	Barry Larkin	.25
16	Dennis Martinez	.25
17	Andy Van Slyke	.25
18	Will Clark	.30
19	Mark Langston	.25
20	Cecil Fielder	.30
21	Kirby Puckett	.50
22	Ken Griffey Jr.	1.50
23	David Justice	.30
24	Jeff Bagwell	.30
25	Howard Johnson	.25
26	Ozzie Smith	.50
	GOLD BLUE JAYS	
1	Roberto Alomar	.50
2	Joe Carter	.30
3	Kelly Gruber	.25
4	Jack Morris	.25
5	Tom Henke	.25
6	Devon White	.25
1	Roberto Alomar	.75
2	Joe Carter	.50
3	Kelly Gruber	.25
4	Jack Morris	.35
5	Tom Henke	.25
6	Devon White	.45

1993 McDonald's Blue Jays

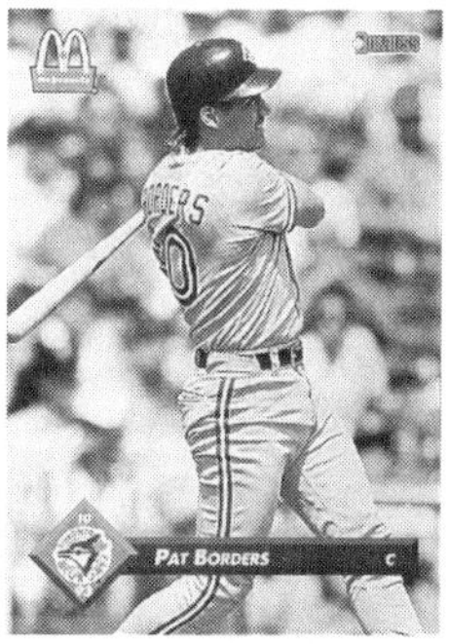

This 36-card set was produced by Donruss and distributed by McDonald's of Canada. The set features two distinct styles of cards. The first 26 are "Great Moments" cards which feature team highlights of the 1985-1992 seasons. These cards have gold-foil embossed on front with a team logo/Great Moments seal. Backs have a description of the highlight. Cards #27-35 are individual player cards. They feature full-bleed color action photos on front. Backs have a second photo and recent stats. All cards have the McDonald's and Donruss logos on front. The 36th card in the set is a header card with a checklist on back.

		MT
Complete Set (36):		9.00
Common Card:		.25
	GREAT MOMENTS	
1	First Title - 1985 (Doyle Alexander)	.25
2	Home Run King - 1986 (Jesse Barfield)	.25
3	Major League Home Run Record - 1987 (Fred McGriff)	.35
4	Opening Bell - 1988 (George Bell)	.35
5	First Cycle - 1989 (Kelly Gruber)	.25
6	Unbelievable Comeback - 1989 (Ernie Whitt)	.25
7	Winners Again - 1989 (Tom Henke)	.25
8	First No-Hitter - 1990 (Dave Stieb)	.25
9	First 20-Gamer (Jack Morris)	.25
10	FANtastic - 1992	.25
11	Sudden Impact - 1992 (Pat Borders, Mark McGwire)	.25
12	The Turning Point - 1992 (Roberto Alomar)	.35
13	On to Atlanta - 1992 (Candy Maldonado)	.25
14	Instant Hero - 1992 (Ed Sprague)	.25
15	Old Friends - 1992 (Cito Gaston, Bobby Cox)	.25
16	The Catch - 1992 (Devon White)	.25
17	Near Triple Play - 1992 (Kelly Gruber, Deion Sanders)	.25
18	Winning Welcome - 1992 (Roberto Alomar)	.35
19	Winning Slide - 1992 (Kelly Gruber)	.25
20	Final Farewell - 1992 (Jimmy Key)	.25
21	Winning RBI - 1992 (Devon White, Candy Maldonado)	.25
22	Clincher - 1992 (Joe Carter)	.35
23	World Chamions - 1992	.25
24	Trophy Presentation - 1992 (Cito Gaston, Bobby Brown)	.25
25	MVP - 1992 (Pat Borders)	.25
26	Heroes' Welcome - 1992 (Roberto Alomar)	.35
27	John Olerud	.35
28	Roberto Alomar	.50
29	Ed Sprague	.25
30	Dick Schofield	.25
31	Devon White	.25
32	Joe Carter	.25
33	Darrin Jackson	.25
34	Pat Borders	.25
35	Paul Molitor	.50
36	Checklist	.25

1993 McDonald's Expos

Top players and manager's from the team's 25 years were featured in a 33-card set produced by Donruss and distributed by Canadian McDonald's outlets. Card fronts feature a full-color borderless photo with the McDonald's and Donruss logos at top. A blue strip at bottom contains the player name and uniform number. At lower-left is an embossed silver-foil 25th anniversary logo. Fronts of the 2-1/2" x 3-1/2" cards are UV coated. Backs are printed in English and French and include a career summary and the player's stats while with the Expos. Appropriate sponsor, team and licensor logos also appear. Autographed cards of Expos manager Felipe Alou were randomly packaged.

		MT
Complete Set (33):		18.00
Common Player:		.40
1	Moises Alou	2.00
2	Andre Dawson	2.50
3	Delino DeShields	.45
4	Andres Galarraga	2.50
5	Marquis Grissom	1.25
6	Tim Raines	.80
7	Larry Walker	4.00
8	Tim Wallach	.45
9	Ken Hill	.45
10	Dennis Martinez	.90
11	Jeff Reardon	.40
12	Gary Carter	2.50
13	Dave Cash	.40
14	Warren Cromartie	.40
15	Mack Jones	.40
16	Al Oliver	.60
17	Larry Parrish	.40
18	Rodney Scott	.40
19	Ken Singleton	.40
20	Rusty Staub	.70
21	Ellis Valentine	.40
22	Woody Fryman	.40
23	Charlie Lea	.40
24	Bill Lee	.40
25	Mike G. Marshall	.40
26	Claude Raymond	.40
27	Steve Renko	.40
28	Steve Rogers	.40
29	Bill Stoneman	.40
30	Gene Mauch	.40
31	Felipe Alou	.40
31a	Felipe Alou (autographed)	24.00
32	Buck Rodgers	.40
33	Checklist	.08

1993 McDonald's/ Topps Glasses

A promotion at McDonald's outlets in 1993 offered a set of drinking glasses with pictures of Topps baseball cards printed on them. The promotion was in conjunction with the All-Star Game in Boston, which was the exclusive area of distribution for the Yaz glass. The 16-oz. glasses were 89 cents with purchase of an Extra Value Meal. The 10 players in the set form an "All-Time Greatest Baseball Team". Besides the card pictures, the glasses include player and card identification and a facsimile autograph.

		MT
Complete Set (10):		100.00
Common Glass:		6.00
1	Nolan Ryan (1969)	20.00
2	Johnny Bench (1970)	6.00
3	Lou Gehrig (1961)	6.00
4	Joe Morgan (1973)	6.00
5	Cal Ripken Jr. (1985)	20.00
6	Brooks Robinson (1961)	6.00
7	Roberto Clemente (1961)	18.00
8	Willie Mays (1957)	8.00
9	Babe Ruth (1962)	6.00
10	Carl Yastrzemski (1969)	16.00

1997 McDonald's N.Y. Yankees

Three popular Yankees stars of the 1996 World Championship team are featured in this issue which raised funds for Ronald McDonald House Charities. The 2-1/2" x 3-1/2" cards have color action photos on front with dark blue borders, a facsimile autograph and McDonald's logo. Uniform and cap logos have been removed from the photos. Backs are printed in blue with a cartoon of Ronald McDonald in baseball gear, a few biographical details about the player and some information about the charity.

		MT
Complete Set (3):		10.00
Common Player:		4.00
(1)	Dwight Gooden	4.00
(2)	Tino Martinez	4.00
(3)	Andy Pettitte	4.00

1998 McDonald's Arizona Diamondbacks

Marking the team's first year in the National League, this card set was given away to children 14 and under at an Aug. 14 promotional game. In standard 2-1/2" x 3-1/2" format, the cards feature color portrait photos. Team and sponsor logos are in the left corners, with player identification in a green stripe at bottom. Backs have a desert scene background over which is printed personal data and professional stats. At bottom is a "Diamondbacks' Fact".

Cards are listed here according to uniform number appearing on front.

		MT
Complete Set (24):		9.00
Common Player:		.50
5	Andy Stankiewicz	.50
6	Andy Fox	.50
9	Matt Williams	1.00
10	Tony Batista	.50
11	Buck Showalter	.50
12	Jorge Fabregas	.50
15	Brent Brede	.50
16	Travis Lee	3.00
19	Willie Blair	.50
20	Jeff Suppan	.50
22	Devon White	.60
24	Karim Garcia	1.50
25	David Dellucci	.50
26	Damian Miller	.50
30	Gregg Olson	.50
33	Jay Bell	.60
34	Brian Anderson	.50
35	Kelly Stinnett	.50
36	Clint Sodowsky	.50
37	Omar Daal	.50
38	Joel Adamson	.50
40	Andy Benes	.75
43	Yamil Benitez	.50
47	Felix Rodriguez	.50

1999 McDonald's Mark McGwire Milestones

A late-season promotion at McDonald's restaurants in the St. Louis area offered six-card packs of Upper Deck Cardinal cards at $2.49, or $1.99 with a purchase. Each foil pack contains four of the 15 player cards, plus two special Mark McGwire Milestone inserts. Horizontally formatted, the Milestones inserts have an action photo of McGwire on a silver metallic-foil background with red, blue and black high-tech graphic designs. The cards mark one of McGwire important home runs of 1998. Backs have a portrait photo and recount some of his career highlights. A McDonald's logo appears in the lower-right corner.

		MT
Complete Set (9):		20.00
Common Card:		2.00
M1	Mark McGwire (#50)	2.00
M2	Mark McGwire (#60)	2.50
M3	Mark McGwire (#61)	2.50
M4	Mark McGwire (#62)	3.50
M5	Mark McGwire (#63)	2.00
M6	Mark McGwire (#67)	2.00
M7	Mark McGwire (#68)	2.00
M8	Mark McGwire (#69)	2.00
M9	Mark McGwire (#70)	3.50

1999 McDonald's St. Louis Cardinals

A late-season promotion at McDonald's restaurants in the St. Louis area offered six-card packs of Upper Deck Cardinal cards at $2.49, or $1.99 with a purchase. Cards are in the basic style of UD's 1999 MVP issue, but lack the silver-foil highlights on front. Backs are also nearly identical, but include a McDonald's logo at bottom-right. Both front and back photos on the McDonald's cards differ from those used on UD MVP. Each foil pack contains four of the 15 player cards, plus two of the special Mark McGwire Milestone inserts. Checklist cards are a one-in-nine pack insert.

		MT
Complete Set (16):		6.00
Common Player:		.25
1	J.D. Drew	.75
2	Jose Jiminez	.35
3	Mark McGwire	2.00
4	Fernando Tatis	.45
5	Edgar Renteria	.35
6	Ray Lankford	.35
7	Willie McGee	.35
8	Ricky Bottalico	.25
9	Eli Marrero	.25
10	Kent Bottenfield	.25
11	Eric Davis	.25
12	Darren Bragg	.25
13	Joe McEwing	.35
14	Shawon Dunston	.25
15	Darren Oliver	.25
---	Checklist	.25

1990 Mark McGwire Fan Club

Persons purchasing a membership in the "Official Mark McGwire Fan Club received this two-card set among their benefits. Licensed by Major League Baseball and limited to 3,500 sets, the cards feature the photography of Barry Colla on the UV-coated front. Backs are printed in black-and-white with a few career highlights.

		MT
Complete Set (2):		8.00
Common Card:		4.00
1	Mark McGwire (pose)	4.00
2	Mark McGwire (action)	4.00

1992 MCI Ambassadors

Issued in conjunction with the MCI-sponsored Ambassadors of Baseball World Tour of overseas military bases, this set features retired players who participated in the tour. Cards feature color photos with a white border, a color tour logo in the lower-left and a banner across the upper-left reading, "Support MWR With MCI." The player's name and position appear in the bottom border. Horizontally oriented backs have career stats and highlights and the logos of MCI and the Major League Baseball Players Alumni in black-and-white.

		MT
Complete Set (16):		45.00
Common Player:		2.00
1	Earl Weaver	4.00
2	Steve Garvey	8.00
3	Doug Flynn	2.00
4	Bert Campaneris	2.00
5	Bill Madlock	2.00
6	Graig Nettles	2.00
7	Dave Kingman	5.00
8	Paul Blair	2.00
9	Jeff Burroughs	2.00
10	Rick Waits	2.00
11	Elias Sosa	2.00
12	Tug McGraw	5.00
13	Ferguson Jenkins (photo)	6.00
14	Bob Feller	8.00
---	Ferguson Jenkins (art)	6.00
---	Header card	.50

1993 MCI Ambassadors

The Major League Baseball Players Alumni Association produced a set of 13 former players who were featured in 1993's MCI Ambassadors of Baseball World Tour. The card set was available free to military personnel who completed an MCI application. The tour of military bases worldwide included appearances by the players at base exchanges, clinics for dependent children and a softball game against base all-stars. The cards feature a photo of the player on the front with logos from the Ambassador tour and MCI in opposite corners.

		MT
Complete Set (14):		50.00
Common Player:		3.00
1	Vida Blue	3.00
2	Paul Blair	3.00
3	Mudcat Grant	3.00
4	Phil Niekro	5.00
5	Bob Feller	6.00
6	Joe Charboneau	4.00
7	Joe Rudi	3.00
8	Catfish Hunter	5.00
9	Manny Sanguillen	3.00
10	Harmon Killebrew	6.00
11	Al Oliver	3.50
12	Bob Dernier	3.00
13	Graig Nettles, Sparky Lyle	3.00
----	Header card	.40

1994 MCI Ambassadors

Once again in 1994, the old-timers' tour of overseas military bases sponsored by MCI spawned a card set. The '94 set is similar to previous years' issues except that color player photos have had the uniform logos airbrushed away. MCI and tour logos appear in color on the front; backs are in black-and-white and contain career data and highlights along with MCI and Major League Baseball Players Alumni logos. Besides 11 numbered cards, there are four unnumbered cards in the 1994 set which include a pair honoring major leaguers who served in the military during World War II.

		MT
Complete Set (15):		30.00
Common Player:		2.00
1	Sparky Lyle	2.00
2	John Stearns	2.00
3	Bobby Thomson	2.50
4	Jimmy Wynn	2.00
5	Ferguson Jenkins	4.00
6	Tug McGraw	2.50
7	Paul Blair	2.00
8	Ron LeFlore	2.00
9	Manny Sanguillen	2.00
10	Doug Flynn	2.00
11	Bill North	2.00
----	Manny Sanguillen (signing autographs)	2.00
----	Doug Flynn (instructing children)	2.00
----	American Leaguers in WWII	2.00
----	National Leaguers in WWII	2.00

1995 MCI Ambassadors

For a fourth year, Major League Basaeball, the players' union and the long distance phone provider issued a card set in conjunction with its series of softball games at military bases. Approximately 2,000 sets were issued. The 2-1/2" x 3-1/2" cards have player photos on front with MCI and the baseball tour logos in opposite corners. Backs have biographical and career information about the retired stars.

		MT
Complete Set (16):		30.00
Common Player:		2.00
1	Vida Blue	2.00
2	Bert Campaneris	2.00
3	Tug McGraw	2.00
4	Doug Flynn	2.00
5	Paul Blair	2.00
6	Harmon Killebrew	4.00
7	Sparky Lyle	2.00
8	Steve Garvey	4.00
9	Bert Blyleven	2.00
10	Omar Moreno	2.00
11	Bill Lee	2.00
12	Maury Wills	2.00
13	Dave Parker	2.00
14	Luis Aparicio	4.00
15	Brooks Robinson	6.00
16	George Foster	2.00

1996 MCI Ambassadors

This set of former players' cards was issued in conjunction with a tour of overseas U.S. military bases by members of the Major League Baseball Players Alumni Association. Players taking part in the tour are featured on the card fronts in photos contemporary with their major league days. Backs have career summaries and stats along with sponsors logos. The cards were virtually all distributed overseas.

		MT
Complete Set (8):		30.00
Common Player:		5.00
(1)	Tommy Davis	6.00
(2)	Darrell Evans	6.00
(3)	Jay Howell	5.00
(4)	John Montefusco	5.00
(5)	Graig Nettles	6.00
(6)	Jim Sundberg	5.00
(7)	Header card	.60
(8)	American Airlines sponsor card	.60

1991 MDA All-Stars

Though the Muscular Dystrophy Association isn't mentioned on the player cards, it was the beneficiary of this set produced by SmithKline Beecham. Card fronts feature color photos of the players during their active careers. Because the set was not licensed by MLB, team uniform logos have been airbrushed off the photos. Black-and-white backs have a recent portrait photo of the player, along with biographical and career data. The set was available by mail for $3.99 plus proofs of purchase from Tums antacid.

		MT
Complete Set (20):		12.00
Common Player:		.50
1	Steve Carlton	.75
2	Ted Simmons	.50
3	Willie Stargell	.75
4	Bill Mazeroski	.60
5	Ron Santo	.60
6	Dave Concepcion	.50
7	Bobby Bonds	.60
8	George Foster	.50
9	Billy Williams	.75
10	Whitey Ford	1.00

11	Yogi Berra	1.00
12	Boog Powell	.60
13	Davey Johnson	.50
14	Brooks Robinson	1.00
15	Jim Fregosi	.50
16	Harmon Killebrew	.75
17	Ted Williams	2.00
18	Al Kaline	1.00
---	MDA Fact Card (Brooks Robinson)	.50
---	Header card	.50

1986 Meadow Gold Blank Backs

This was the second set to be distributed by Meadow Gold Dairy (Beatrice Foods) in 1986. It was issued on Double Play ice cream cartons, one card per package. Full-color player photos have team logos and insignias airbrushed away. This 16-card set is very similar to the Meadow Gold popsicle set, but the photos are different in some instances. The cards measure 2-3/8" x 3-1/2". The Willie McGee card is reportedly tougher to find than other cards in the set.

		MT
Complete Singles Set (16):		45.00
Complete Carton Set (16):		100.00
Common Player:		2.00
(1)	George Brett	4.00
(2)	Wade Boggs	3.00
(3)	Carlton Fisk	2.50
(4)	Steve Garvey	2.50
(5)	Dwight Gooden	2.00
(6)	Pedro Guerrero	2.00
(7)	Reggie Jackson	3.00
(8)	Don Mattingly	4.00
(9)	Willie McGee	2.00
(10)	Dale Murphy	2.50
(11)	Cal Ripken, Jr.	6.00
(12)	Pete Rose	5.00
(13)	Ryne Sandberg	3.00
(14)	Mike Schmidt	3.00
(15)	Fernando Valenzuela	2.00
(16)	Dave Winfield	2.50

1986 Meadow Gold Milk

The third set from Meadow Gold from 1986 came on milk cartons; on pint, quart and half-gallon size containers. The cards measure 2-1/2" x 3-1/2" and feature drawings instead of photographs. Different dairies distributed the cards in various colors of ink. The cards can be found printed in red, brown or black ink. The crude drawings have prevented this rare set from being higher in price.

		MT
Complete Set (11):		95.00
Common Player:		4.00
(1)	Wade Boggs	9.00
(2)	George Brett	10.00
(3)	Steve Carlton	6.00
(4)	Dwight Gooden	5.00
(5)	Willie McGee	4.00
(6)	Dale Murphy	7.00
(7)	Cal Ripken, Jr.	16.00
(8)	Pete Rose	15.00
(9)	Ryne Sandberg	9.00
(10)	Mike Schmidt	12.00
(11)	Fernando Valenzuela	5.00

1986 Meadow Gold Statistic Backs

Beatrice Foods produced this set of 20 cards on specially marked boxes of Meadow Gold Double Play popsicles, fudgesicles and bubble gum coolers. They came in two-card panels and have full-color player pictures with player name, team and position printed below the photo. Card backs are printed in red ink and feature player career highlights. The cards measure 2-3/8" x 3-1/2" and were distributed in the West and Midwest. It is considered one of the toughest 1986 regional sets to complete.

		MT
Complete Panel Set (10):		24.00
Complete Singles Set (20):		15.00
Common Panel:		1.00
Common Single:		.30
	PANEL 1	3.00
1	George Brett	1.50
2	Fernando Valenzuela	.30
	PANEL 2	4.00
3	Dwight Gooden	.50
4	Dale Murphy	1.00
	PANEL 3	5.00
5	Don Mattingly	2.00
6	Reggie Jackson	1.00
	PANEL 4	4.00
7	Dave Winfield	.75
8	Pete Rose	2.00
	PANEL 5	2.50
9	Wade Boggs	1.00
10	Willie McGee	.30
	PANEL 6	5.00
11	Cal Ripkin (Ripken)	3.00
12	Ryne Sandberg	1.50
	PANEL 7	3.00
13	Carlton Fisk	.75
14	Jim Rice	.45
	PANEL 8	2.50
15	Steve Garvey	.50
16	Mike Schmidt	1.00
	PANEL 9	1.00
17	Bruce Sutter	.30
18	Pedro Guerrero	.30
	PANEL 10	1.00
19	Rick Sutcliff (Sutcliffe)	.30
20	Rich Gossage	.30
1	George Brett	2.00
2	Fernando Valenzuela	.40
3	Dwight Gooden	.60
4	Dale Murphy	1.50
5	Don Mattingly	2.00
6	Reggie Jackson	1.50
7	Dave Winfield	1.00
8	Pete Rose	2.00
9	Wade Boggs	1.00
10	Willie McGee	.50
11	Cal Ripkin (Ripken)	5.00
12	Ryne Sandberg	1.50
13	Carlton Fisk	.80
14	Jim Rice	.30
15	Steve Garvey	.50
16	Mike Schmidt	2.00
17	Bruce Sutter	.30
18	Pedro Guerrero	.30
19	Rick Sutcliff (Sutcliffe)	.30
20	Rich Gossage	.30

1991 Medford Phillies

In 1991 Medford Foods took over sponsorship of the Phillies' traditional large-format (4-1/8" x 6") baseball card series. The main body of 35 cards of players and coaches was issued early in the season. Later, a three-card set highlighting career milestones was issued. The three-card update set differs from the regular issue in that the cards feature a white border on front with the player's name in white on a red strip at top-center. Still later another eight cards, including the manager and mascot, were produced, following the basic format of borderless color photos with the player's name in white on a red strip somewhere on the front of the card. Backs are printed in red and black and include biographical details, full major and minor league stats and the Phillies and Medford logos. While the cards feature a uniform number on back, the checklist is presented here alphabetically.

		MT
Complete Set (46):		13.50
Common Player:		.25
(1)	Darrel Akerfelds	.25
(2)	Andy Ashby	.35
(3)	Wally Backman	.25
(4)	Joe Boever	.25
(5)	Rod Booker	.25
(6)	Larry Bowa	.30
(7)	Sil Campusano	.25
(8)	Wes Chamberlain	.25
(9)	Pat Combs	.25
(10)	Danny Cox	.25
(11)	Darren Daulton	.50
(12)	Jose DeJesus	.25
(13)	Len Dykstra	.75
(14)	Darrin Fletcher	.25
(15)	Jim Fregosi	.35
(16a)	Tommy Greene	.35
(16b)	Tommy Greene (5-23-91 no-hitter)	.45
(17)	Jason Grimsley	.25
(18)	Charlie Hayes	.35
(19)	Von Hayes	.25
(20)	Dave Hollins	.45
(21)	Ken Howell	.25
(22)	Ron Jones	.25
(23)	Ricky Jordan	.25
(24)	John Kruk	.50
(25)	Steve Lake	.25
(26)	Hal Lanier	.25
(27)	Jim Lindeman	.25
(28)	Tim Mauser	.25
(29)	Roger McDowell	.25
(30)	Denis Menke	.25
(31)	Mickey Morandini	.35
(32)	John Morris	.25
(33a)	Terry Mulholland	.35
(33b)	Terry Mulholland (8-15-90 no-hitter)	.50
(34a)	Dale Murphy	2.00
(34b)	Dale Murphy (5-29-91 2,000 hit)	2.50
(35)	Johnny Podres	.35
(36)	Randy Ready	.25
(37)	Wally Ritchie	.25
(38)	Bruce Ruffin	.25
(39)	Steve Searcy	.25
(40)	Dickie Thon	.25
(41)	John Vukovich	.25
(42)	Mitch Williams	.30
(43)	Phillie Phanatic (mascot)	.25

1992 Medford Phillies

Issued in two series, a 36-card release early in the season and a 10-card update (Terry Mulholland appears in each), these cards continue the Phillies' tradition of large-format presenations. Measuring 4-1/8" x 6" they feature full-bleed color studio portrait photos on front. The player's name appears in white letters on a red strip somewhere on the card front. Backs are printed in red and black and include full major and minor league stats and some biographical data, along with the logos of the Phillies and the sponsoring Medford food company. The cards are checklisted here by uniform numbers on back.

		MT
Complete Set (46):		11.00
Common Player:		.25
2	Larry Bowa	.30
3	Dale Murphy	2.00
4	Len Dykstra	.75
5	Kim Batiste	.25
6	Wally Backman	.25
7	Mariano Duncan	.30
8	Dale Sveum	.25
9	Tom Marsh	.25
10	Darren Daulton	.50
11	Jim Fregosi	.30
12	Mickey Morandini	.35
14	Denis Menke	.25
15	Dave Hollins	.40
17	Ricky Jordan	.25
18	John Vukovich	.25
19	Jim Lindeman	.25
21	Pat Combs	.25
23	Brad Brink	.25
24	Steve Searcy	.25
25	Mike Ryan	.25
26	Mel Roberts	.25
28	Mitch Williams	.20
29	John Kruk	.50
30	Steve Lake	.25
33	Ruben Amaro	.25
34a	Danny Cox	.25
34b	Ben Rivera	.25
35	Don Robinson	.25
38	Curt Schilling	.45
39	Wally Ritchie	.25
40	Andy Ashby	.35
42	Mike Hartley	.25
44	Wes Chamberlain	.25
45a	Terry Mulholland (cap-to-chest photo)	.35
45b	Terry Mulholland (cap-to-waist photo)	.35
46	Johnny Podres	.30
47	Kyle Abbott	.30
48	Jeff Grotewold	.25
49	Tommy Greene	.30
50	Barry Jones	.25
51	Cliff Brantley	.25
55	Bob Ayrault	.25
---	Phillie Phanatic (mascot)	.25
---	1992 Philadelphia Phillies (team photo)	.25
---	Uniforms Through The Years	.25
---	Veterans Stadium	.25

1993 Medford Phillies

The third in an annual series of large-format (4-1/8" x 6") cards issued by Medford Foods, this set retains the same basic format as previous issues. Cards feature a borderless color photo on front with the player's name in white on a red strip. Several of the cards in the 1993 issue feature players in turn-back-the-clock uniforms and there are a few horizontal-format photos included. Backs are printed in red and black and feature the Phillies and sponsor's logos, biographical data and major and minor league stats. Cards are checklisted here by the player number which appears at top on the back. An update set of five cards was issued later in the season.

		MT
Complete Set (35):		11.00
Common Player:		.25
2	Larry Bowa	.30
4	Lenny Dykstra	.75
5	Kim Batiste	.25
7	Mariano Duncan	.25
8	Jim Eisenreich	.25
9	Mike Ryan	.25
10	Darren Daulton	.50
11	Jim Fregosi	.30
12	Mickey Morandini	.30
14	Denis Menke	.25
15	Dave Hollins	.35
17	Ricky Jordan	.25
18	John Vukovich	.25
22	Pete Incaviglia	.25
23	Todd Pratt	.25
24	Juan Bell	.25
25	Milt Thompson	.25
26	Mel Roberts	.25
27	Danny Jackson	.25
28	Tyler Green	.30
29	John Kruk	.50
33	Ruben Amaro	.25
34	Ben Rivera	.25
37	Kyle Abbott	.25
38	Curt Schilling	.45
40	David West	.25
44	Wes Chamberlain	.25
45	Terry Mulholland	.30
46	Johnny Podres	.30
47	Larry Andersen	.25
49	Tommy Greene	.25
50	Jose DeLeon	.25
53	Bob Ayrault	.25
99	Mitch Williams	.25
---	Phillie Phanatic (mascot)	.25
UPDATE SET (5):		
19	Kevin Stocker	.50
30	Jeff Manto	.25
41	Mike Williams	.25
48	Roger Mason	.25
---	'93 Phils NL All-Stars (Terry Mulholland, Darren Daulton, Jim Fregosi, John Kruk, Dave Hollins)	.35

1991 Media Materials Sports Stars

This set of classroom materials uses sports figures to teach reading and other skills to grade schoolers. Sold in a boxed set featuring 30 athletes, only the baseball players are listed here. The 4-3/4" x 8" black-and-white cards come in pairs. One has the Sports Stars logo on front and a player biography on back. The second has a player photo on front and a series of questions on back. The values shown below are for each pair of cards.

		MT
Complete (Baseball) Set (8):		24.00
Common Player:		1.00
4	Wade Boggs	4.00
5	Gary Carter	2.00
6	Roger Clemens	5.00
18	Mark McGwire	11.00
24	Cal Ripken, Jr.	9.00
25	Ozzie Smith	4.00
26	Darryl Strawberry	2.00
27	Frank Viola	1.00

1992 Megacards Babe Ruth Prototypes

Basically identical to the regularly issued versions, these sample cards were distributed to hobby dealers to introduce Megacards Babe Ruth Collection. Most of the prototypes have different card numbers than those in the regular set, and all carry a large gray diagonal "PROTOTYPE" on back.

		MT
Complete Set (9):		15.00
Common Card:		2.00
14	Year in Review - 1921 (Babe Ruth)	2.00
31	World Series - 1916 (Babe Ruth)	2.00
75	Place in History - 1928 (Babe Ruth)	2.00
106	Career Highlights - 1927 (Babe Ruth)	2.00
124	Trivia - 1926 (Babe Ruth)	2.00
129	Sultan of Swat - 1925 (Babe Ruth)	2.00
134	Being Remembered - 1948 - George Bush (Babe Ruth)	2.00
138	Being Remembered - 1923 - Grantland Rice (Babe Ruth)	2.00
154	The Bambino - The Man (Babe Ruth, Lou Gehrig)	2.50

1992 Megacards Babe Ruth

This 165-card set chronicles the life and times of Babe Ruth. The set was produced by Megacards and is officially entitled "The Babe Ruth Collection". The cards feature classic black and white photos with black borders and captions below the photo. The card backs feature coordinating statistics and information.

		MT
Complete Set (165):		20.00
Common Card:		.10
1	Lifetime Pitching Statistics	.10
2	Lifetime Batting Statistics	.10
3	Lifetime - World Series Pitching	.10
4	Lifetime World Series Batting	.10
5	22-9 Record in the Minors	.10
6	2-1 Record First Year in the Majors	.10
7	Won 17 of his Last 21 Decisions	.10
8	Led League with 1.75 ERA and 9 Shutouts	.10
9	Defeats Walter Johnson for 6th Time	.10
10	Doubles as Pitcher and a Regular	.10
11	First Season in the Outfield	.10
12	Sold to Yankees for $100,000	.10
13	The Best Year Any Batter Ever Had	.10
14	Suspended for First 38 Games	.10
15	Wins American League MVP	.10
16	Wins Only Batting Title - .378	.10
17	The "Million Dollar Stomachache"	.10
18	Bats .372 with a .737 Slugging Average	.10
19	The Best Baseball Team in History	.20
20	Tops 50 Home Runs - 4th Time	.10
21	Clubs 500th Home Run	.10
22	Bam Bams Nine in a Week	.10
23	.700 Slugging Average for 9th Time	.10
24	Blasts Over 40 Homers for 11th Time	.10
25	Over 100 RBIs for 13th Time	.10
26	Tops 2,000 Career Walks	.10
27	Babe Retires	.10
28	Babe Coaches the Dodgers	.10
29	The Babe in Retirement	.10
30	1915 World Series - Warms Bench	.10
31	1916 World Series - Hurls 14-Inning Win	.10
32	1918 World Series - Scoreless Innings	.10
33	1921 World Series - Yankees' First	.10
34	1922 World Series - Back to the Farm	.10
35	1923 World Series - First Championship	.10
36	1926 World Series - 4 HR in Losing Cause	.15
37	1927 World Series - Destroy Bucs in Four	.15
38	1928 World Series - .625 BA and 1.375 SA	.10
39	1932 World Series - Yanks Sweep Cubs	.15
40	Lifetime - 2,056 Walks	.10
41	First to Fan 1,000 Times	.10
42	Lifetime - 2,174 Runs Scored	.15
43	Lifetime - 5,793 Total Bases	.15
44	Lifetime - 1,356 Extra-Base Hits	.10
45	Lifetime - 714 Home Runs	.10
46	Lifetime - 16 Grand Slams	.10
47	Lifetime - 8.5 Home Run Percentage	.15
48	Lifetime - Most Games, 2 or More HR	.10
49	Lifetime - 11 Seasons with 40+ HRs	.10
50	Lifetime - 2,211 RBIs	.15
51	Lifetime - .342 Batting Average	.15
52	Lifetime - .690 Slugging Average	.15
53	Season - Nine Shutouts	.10
54	Season - 170 Walks	.10
55	Season - 177 Runs Scored	.20
56	Season - .545 On-Base Percentage	.10
57	Season - 457 Total Bases	.15
58	Season - 119 Extra-Base Hits	.15
59	Season - 171 Runs Batted In	.15
60	Season - 60 Home Runs	.10
61	Season - 11.8 Home Run Percentage	.10
62	Season - .847 Slugging Average	.15
63	World Series 3-0 Record	.10
64	World Series - 0.87 ERA	.10
65	World Series - 33 Walks	.10
66	World Series - 37 Runs	.10
67	World Series - 96 Total Bases	.10
68	World Series - 15 Home Runs	.10
69	World Series - 33 RBIs	.10
70	World Series - .744 Slugging Average	.20
71	1914 - First Major League Victory	.10
72	1915 - First Major League Home Run	.10
73	1916 - Babe Derails "Big Train"	.10
74	1919 - Leads League in Fielding	.10
75	1919 First Home Run Record	.10
76	1920 - Babe Becomes a Yankee	.10
77	1923 - First Home Run in Yankee Stadium	.10
78	1923 - American League MVP	.10
79	1924 - Wins Only Batting Title	.15
80	1926 - Hits 3 Home Runs in Series Game	.10
81	1927 - Babe and Lou Smack 107 Home Runs (Lou Gehrig)	.20
82	1927 - The Babe's 60th Home Run	.20
83	1928 - Three HR in World Series Game	.10
84	1932 - Early "Called Shots" by the Bam	.10
85	1932 - The "Called Shot" - The Legend	.10
86	1932 - The "Called Shot" - The Believers	.10
87	1932 - The "Called Shot" - The Doubters	.10
88	1932 - The "Called Shot" - Babe's View	.10
89	1933 - First HR in an All-Star Game	.15
90	1933 - Last Time on the Mound	.10
91	1934 - Babe Hits 700th Home Run	.10
92	1934 - The Babe in Japan	.10
93	1935 - Last Major League Homers	.10
94	1939 - Inaugurated into Hall of Fame	.10
95	1942 - Faces Johnson Again in Exhibition	.10
96	1947 - Babe Ruth Day	.10
97	1948 - Babe's Farewell	.25
98	A Perfect Punch	.10
99	Yankees Best Base Thief	.10
100	Hub Pruett: Babe Buster	.10
101	Babe Caught Stealing, Ends 1926 Series	.10
102	Never Won a Triple Crown	.10
103	Babe Used a 54-Ounce Bat	.10
104	Babe Bats Righty	.10
105	Babe's Greatness	.10
106	The Babe's Best	.10
107	Outslugged Entire Teams	.10
108	First to Hit 30, 40, 50 and 60 Home Runs	.10
109	The Pitkin Study	.10
110	First to Put the Ball Into Orbit	.10
111	Afraid to Kill Somebody	.10
112	The Wonder Years: 1926-31	.10
113	Hit .422 With 7 Homers on Opening Days	.10
114	Babe at Bat	.10
115	"Greatest Ballplayer the Game Has Known"	.10
116	The Babe's Early Childhood	.10
117	St. Mary's Industrial School	.10
118	Babe and Brother Matthias	.10
119	The Babe's Nicknames	.10
120	Babe's First Wife, Helen	.10
121	Babe's Second Wife, Claire	.10
122	Lou Gehrig Appreciation Day	.20
123	Babe's Friendship With Herb Pennock	.10
124	The Babe and Miller Huggins	.10
125	The Babe and Ty Cobb	.15
126	Babe and Walter Johnson	.15
127	Baseball's Biggest Drawing Card	.10
128	Babe's Barnstorming	.10
129	Costly Confrontation	.10
130	He Often Played Hurt	.10
131	Babe's Big Bucks	.10
132	Want to be a Manager	.10
133	The Babe on the Links	.10
134	Babe in the Movies	.10
135	Babe Contributes to War Effort	.10
136	The Babe - Peace Negotiator	.10
137	Everyone Loved the Babe	.10
138	He Brought Children Joy	.10
139	He Always Had Time for Kids	.10
140	The Johnny Sylvester Story	.10
141	Moving with the Great	.10
142	Babe Ruth and the American Dream	.10
143	Being Remembered - Bill James	.10
144	Being Remembered - Bill James	.10
145	Being Remembered - Bill James	.10
146	Being Remembered - Mel Allen	.10
147	Being Remembered - Mel Allen	.10
148	Being Remembered - Wes Ferrell	.10
149	Being Remembered - George Bush	.50
150	Being Remembered - Ethan Allen	.20
151	Being Remembered - Daughter Dorothy	.10
152	Being Remembered - Daughter Julia	.10
153	Being Remembered - Daughter Julia	.10
154	Being Remembered - Mark Koenig	.10
155	Being Remembered - Donald Honig	.10
156	Being Remembered - L. Waner, Waite Hoyt	.10
157	Being Remembered - Waite Hoyt	.10
158	Being Remembered - Bill Dickey	.10
159	Being Remembered - Bob Meusel	.10
160	Being Remembered - Jim Chapman	.10
161	Being Remembered - Christy Walsh	.10
162	Being Remembered - The Babe Passes Away	.10
163	Being Remembered - Grantland Rice	.10
164	Checklist 1-83	.10
165	Checklist 84-165	.10

1995 Megacards Babe Ruth 100th Anniversary

Marking the centennial of Babe Ruth's birth, Megacards issued this 25-card set chronicling the life and career of baseball's all-time greatest player. Most of the cards feature on front black-and-white photos of Ruth, although there are several colorized pictures scattered through the set. Fronts have gold-foil frames, captions and Ruth Centennial logo. Reverses have a background photo of Ruth's classic swing and a detailed vignette pertinent to the card's theme. The Babe Ruth 100th Anniversary Collection set was sold in a plastic clam-shell package containing one of three Babe Ruth "Mega-caps". The edition was limited to 100,000 sets.

		MT
Complete Set (27):		5.00
Common Card:		.25
1	Baseball's Greatest Ever? (Babe Ruth)	.25
2	60 Home Run Club (Babe Ruth)	.25
3	No Slugger Comes Close (Babe Ruth) (with Jimmie Foxx, Lou Gehrig, Al Simmons)	.25
4	History's Most Frequent Home Run Threat (Babe Ruth)	.25
5	He Knew the Way Home (Babe Ruth)	.25
6	He Didn't Leave Them Stranded (Babe Ruth) (with Lou Gehrig)	.25
7	50 Home Run King (Babe Ruth)	.25
8	Long Ball Legend (Babe Ruth)	.25
9	.342 Plus Power (Babe Ruth) (with Lloyd Waner, Paul Waner, Lou Gehrig)	.25
10	No One Hit 'Em More Often (Babe Ruth)	.25
11	Greatest Pitching Prospect (Babe Ruth) (colorized, Red Sox pitcher)	.25
12	Career Year (Babe Ruth) (colorized, fishing with Lou Gehrig)	.25
13	Mr. Yankee (Babe Ruth) (with Lou Gehrig; Don Mattingly superimposed)	.50
14	Babe and "The Kid" (Babe Ruth) (Ken Griffey, Jr., superimposed)	.50
15	Everyone Loved the Babe (Babe Ruth)	.25
16	The Babe Played Hurt (Babe Ruth)	.25

17	He Did It His Way (Babe Ruth)	.25
18	The Rewards of Greatness (Babe Ruth)	.25
19	Babe and Today's Rules (Babe Ruth)	.25
20	Babe in Today's Ballparks (Babe Ruth)	.25
21	Babe and Today's Best (Babe Ruth) (colorized, Ken Griffey Jr. superimposed)	.75
22	Babe vs. Today's Pitching (Babe Ruth)	.25
23	The Babe and Father Time (Babe Ruth)	.25
24	How He Changed the Game (Babe Ruth) (colorized, with Dizzy Dean, Frank Frisch, Mickey Cochrane, Schoolboy Rowe)	.25
25	Will There Be Another Babe? (Babe Ruth)	.25
---	Sweepstakes card	.05
---	Babe Ruth merchandise order card	.05

1995 Megacards Babe Ruth MegaCaps

One of three different 1-5/8" "MegaCaps" picturing Babe Ruth was packaged in each set of Babe Ruth 100th Anniversary Collection cards. The discs feature a photo of Ruth on front and trademark information on the back. Each cap was produced in an edition of 34,000.

		MT
Complete Set (3):		1.50
Common Cap:		.50
1	Babe Ruth	.50
2	Babe Ruth	.50
3	Babe Ruth	.50

1995 Megacards Ken Griffey, Jr. MegaCaps

Three different "MegaCaps" picturing Ken Griffey, Jr., were prepared for insertion into blister packs containing full sets of the Ken Griffey, Jr., Wish List Collection. Each of the 1-5/8" diameter cardboard discs has a color photo of Junior on front. Backs have trademark information. Reported print run for each of the three versions was 34,000.

		MT
Complete Set:		1.50
Common Cap:		.50
		.50
1	Ken Griffey Jr.	.50
2	Ken Griffey Jr.	.50
3	Ken Griffey Jr.	.50

1995 Megacards Ken Griffey, Jr. Wish List

Sold only as a complete set in a clam-shell plastic blister pack, this set has two areas of focus. The first 14 cards details Griffey's hopes for his baseball career and his life; the second 11 cards feature projections on Junior's possible career stats based on numbers generated by baseball statstician Bill James. Each card has a different action photo of Griffey on the front. Backs have a smaller version of the front photo in the upper-right corner, and a muted background photo of Griffey at bat. Card fronts are gold-foil enhanced. Packed with each set was one of three "MegaCaps" with Griffey's picture. With a reported print run of 100,000 sets, the issue sold for about $10 retail, with part of the purchase price going to the Make a Wish Foundation for seriously ill children.

		MT
Complete Set (27):		7.50
Common Card:		.50
1	Introduction (Ken Griffey Jr.)	.50
2	Make-A-Wish Foundation (Ken Griffey Jr.)	.50
3	To Make Dreams Come True (Ken Griffey Jr.)	.50
4	To Play With Dad (Ken Griffey Jr.) (w/ Ken Griffey, Sr.)	.50
5	"The Best I Can Be" (Ken Griffey Jr.)	.50
6	To Make the Majors (Ken Griffey Jr.)	.50
7	To Play for a Winner (Ken Griffey Jr.)	.50
8	To Assist B.A.T. (Ken Griffey Jr.)	.50
9	To Enrich Inner-City Baseball (Ken Griffey Jr.)	.50
10	A Lot to Live For (Ken Griffey Jr.)	.50
11	To Be an All-Around Player (Ken Griffey Jr.)	.50
12	To Be #1 in the Draft (Ken Griffey Jr.)	.50
13	To Win the Gold (Ken Griffey Jr.)	.50
14	Most Home Runs by Father/Son (Ken Griffey Jr.) (w/ Ken Griffey, Sr.)	.50
15	The Field of Possibilities (Ken Griffey Jr.)	.50
16	The Griffey Forecast (Ken Griffey Jr.)	.50
17	3,598 Career Games (Ken Griffey Jr.)	.50
18	2,361 Career Runs (Ken Griffey Jr.)	.50
19	3,947 Career Hits (Ken Griffey Jr.)	.50
20	777 Career Doubles (Ken Griffey Jr.)	.50
21	699 Career Home Runs (Ken Griffey Jr.)	.50
22	2,234 Career RBIs (Ken Griffey Jr.)	.50
24	1,541 Career Extra Base Hits (Ken Griffey Jr.)	.50
24	40 or More Home Runs 5 Times (Ken Griffey Jr.)	.50
25	28 Career Grand Slams (Ken Griffey Jr.)	.50
---	Contest card	.05
---	Merchandise order card	.05

1996 Metal Universe Sample Sheet

To introduce its premiere edition of Metal Universe baseball cards, Fleer sent a nine-card sample sheet to dealers. The 8" x 11" sheet has a black border on each side of each card. The cards are identical in format to the issued version, printed on etched foil and overprinted "PROMOTIONAL SAMPLE" in gold diagonally on front and back.

		MT
Complete Sheet:		24.00
28	Todd Greene	
67	Jon Nunnally	
81	Brad Radke	
90	Don Mattingly	
110	Alex Rodriguez	
116	Ivan Rodriguez	
129	Chipper Jones	
183	Eric Karros	
216	Jeff King	

1996 Metal Universe

Certainly one of the most unusual baseball card issues of its era, Fleer's Metal Universe set is distinguished by its colored, textured metallic-foil backgrounds created by comic book illustrators. The effects range from gaudy to grotesque. Glossy player action photos are featured on front, with a steel-colored metallic strip at bottom carrying set and player ID. Conventionally printed backs have a heavy-metal theme with a color player portrait photo at top and a few stats and person data around. The issue was sold in hobby and retail packaging with the basic hobby pack containing eight cards at a suggested retail price of $2.49. Several insert sets were included, along with a platinum parallel edition of the player cards.

		MT
Complete Set (250):		30.00
Common Player:		.10
Platinum Set (250):		100.00
Common Platinum:		.25
Platinums: 3X		
Wax Box:		40.00
1	Roberto Alomar	1.00
2	Brady Anderson	.20
3	Bobby Bonilla	.15
4	Chris Holles	.10
5	Ben McDonald	.10
6	Mike Mussina	.40
7	Randy Myers	.10
8	Rafael Palmeiro	.25
9	Cal Ripken Jr.	2.50
10	B.J. Surhoff	.12
11	Luis Alicea	.10
12	Jose Canseco	.30
13	Roger Clemens	1.00
14	Wil Cordero	.10
15	Tom Gordon	.10
16	Mike Greenwell	.10
17	Tim Naehring	.10
18	Troy O'Leary	.10
19	Mike Stanley	.10
20	John Valentin	.15
21	Mo Vaughn	.75
22	Tim Wakefield	.10
23	Garret Anderson	.15
24	Chili Davis	.12
25	Gary DiSarcina	.10
26	Jim Edmonds	.15
27	Chuck Finley	.10
28	Todd Greene	.10
29	Mark Langston	.10
30	Troy Percival	.10
31	Tony Phillips	.10
32	Tim Salmon	.30
33	Lee Smith	.12
34	J.T. Snow	.15
35	Ray Durham	.10
36	Alex Fernandez	.15
37	Ozzie Guillen	.10
38	Roberto Hernandez	.10
39	Lyle Mouton	.10
40	Frank Thomas	1.50
41	Robin Ventura	.20
42	Sandy Alomar	.20
43	Carlos Baerga	.10
44	Albert Belle	.75
45	Orel Hershiser	.12
46	Kenny Lofton	.75
47	Dennis Martinez	.12
48	Jack McDowell	.10
49	Jose Mesa	.10
50	Eddie Murray	.40
51	Charles Nagy	.12
52	Manny Ramirez	1.00
53	Julian Tavarez	.10
54	Jim Thome	.50
55	Omar Vizquel	.12
56	Chad Curtis	.10
57	Cecil Fielder	.15
58	John Flaherty	.10
59	Travis Fryman	.12
60	Chris Gomez	.10
61	Felipe Lira	.10
62	Kevin Appier	.10
63	Johnny Damon	.15
64	Tom Goodwin	.10
65	Mark Gubicza	.10
66	Jeff Montgomery	.10
67	Jon Nunnally	.10
68	Ricky Bones	.10
69	Jeff Cirillo	.10
70	John Jaha	.10
71	Dave Nilsson	.10
72	Joe Oliver	.10
73	Kevin Seitzer	.10
74	Greg Vaughn	.15
75	Marty Cordova	.15
76	Chuck Knoblauch	.20
77	Pat Meares	.10
78	Paul Molitor	.40
79	Pedro Munoz	.10
80	Kirby Puckett	1.25
81	Brad Radke	.10
82	Scott Stahoviak	.10
83	Matt Walbeck	.10
84	Wade Boggs	.40
85	David Cone	.12
86	Joe Girardi	.10
87	Derek Jeter	2.00
88	Jim Leyritz	.10
89	Tino Martinez	.15
90	Don Mattingly	1.50
91	Paul O'Neill	.15
92	Andy Pettitte	1.00
93	Tim Raines	.15
94	Kenny Rogers	.10
95	Ruben Sierra	.10
96	John Wetteland	.10
97	Bernie Williams	.60
98	Geronimo Berroa	.10
99	Dennis Eckersley	.12
100	Brent Gates	.10
101	Mark McGwire	4.00
102	Steve Ontiveros	.10
103	Terry Steinbach	.10
104	Jay Buhner	.15
105	Vince Coleman	.10
106	Joey Cora	.10
107	Ken Griffey Jr.	4.00
108	Randy Johnson	.40
109	Edgar Martinez	.12
110	Alex Rodriguez	3.00
111	Paul Sorrento	.10
112	Will Clark	.30
113	Juan Gonzalez	1.25
114	Rusty Greer	.10
115	Dean Palmer	.10
116	Ivan Rodriguez	.75
117	Mickey Tettleton	.10
118	Joe Carter	.15
119	Alex Gonzalez	.15
120	Shawn Green	.15
121	Erik Hanson	.10
122	Pat Hentgen	.10
123	Sandy Martinez	.10
124	Otis Nixon	.10
125	John Olerud	.20
126	Steve Avery	.10
127	Tom Glavine	.20
128	Marquis Grissom	.15
129	Chipper Jones	2.00
130	David Justice	.20
131	Ryan Klesko	.20
132	Mark Lemke	.10
133	Javier Lopez	.20
134	Greg Maddux	2.00
135	Fred McGriff	.50
136	John Smoltz	.25
137	Mark Wohlers	.10
138	Frank Castillo	.10
139	Shawon Dunston	.10
140	Luis Gonzalez	.10
141	Mark Grace	.20
142	Brian McRae	.10
143	Jaime Navarro	.10
144	Rey Sanchez	.10
145	Ryne Sandberg	.90
146	Sammy Sosa	2.00
147	Bret Boone	.10
148	Curtis Goodwin	.10
149	Barry Larkin	.20
150	Hal Morris	.10
151	Reggie Sanders	.10
152	Pete Schourek	.10
153	John Smiley	.10
154	Dante Bichette	.30
155	Vinny Castilla	.15
156	Andres Galarraga	.20
157	Bret Saberhagen	.10
158	Bill Swift	.10
159	Larry Walker	.40
160	Walt Weiss	.10
161	Kurt Abbott	.10
162	John Burkett	.10
163	Greg Colbrunn	.10
164	Jeff Conine	.15
165	Chris Hammond	.10
166	Charles Johnson	.15
167	Al Leiter	.12
168	Pat Rapp	.10
169	Gary Sheffield	.50
170	Quilvio Veras	.10
171	Devon White	.10
172	Jeff Bagwell	1.25
173	Derek Bell	.15
174	Sean Berry	.10
175	Craig Biggio	.15
176	Doug Drabek	.10
177	Tony Eusebio	.10
178	Brian Hunter	.10
179	Orlando Miller	.10
180	Shane Reynolds	.10
181	Mike Blowers	.10
182	Roger Cedeno	.10
183	Eric Karros	.15
184	Ramon Martinez	.12
185	Raul Mondesi	.25
186	Hideo Nomo	.50
187	Mike Piazza	2.00
188	Moises Alou	.15
189	Yamil Benitez	.10
190	Darrin Fletcher	.10
191	Cliff Floyd	.10
192	Pedro Martinez	.15
193	Carlos Perez	.10
194	David Segul	.10
195	Tony Tarasco	.10
196	Rondell White	.15
197	Edgardo Alfonzo	.12
198	Rico Brogna	.10
199	Carl Everett	.10
200	Todd Hundley	.20
201	Jason Isringhausen	.10
202	Lance Johnson	.10
203	Bobby Jones	.10
204	Jeff Kent	.10
205	Bill Pulsipher	.10
206	Jose Vizcaino	.10
207	Ricky Bottalico	.10
208	Darren Daulton	.10
209	Lenny Dykstra	.10
210	Jim Eisenreich	.10

211	Gregg Jefferies	.15
212	Mickey Morandini	.10
213	Heathcliff Slocumb	.10
214	Jay Bell	.10
215	Carlos Garcia	.10
216	Jeff King	.10
217	Al Martin	.10
218	Orlando Merced	.10
219	Dan Miceli	.10
220	Denny Neagle	.10
221	Andy Benes	.12
222	Royce Clayton	.10
223	Gary Gaetti	.10
224	Ron Gant	.15
225	Bernard Gilkey	.10
226	Brian Jordan	.20
227	Ray Lankford	.10
228	John Mabry	.10
229	Ozzie Smith	.40
230	Todd Stottlemyre	.10
231	Andy Ashby	.12
232	Brad Ausmus	.10
233	Ken Caminiti	.20
234	Steve Finley	.10
235	Tony Gwynn	1.25
236	Joey Hamilton	.10
237	Rickey Henderson	.30
238	Trevor Hoffman	.12
239	Wally Joyner	.15
240	Rod Beck	.10
241	Barry Bonds	.75
242	Glenallen Hill	.10
243	Stan Javier	.10
244	Mark Leiter	.10
245	Deion Sanders	.20
246	William VanLandingham	.10
247	Matt Williams	.25
248	Checklist	.10
249	Checklist	.10
250	Checklist	.10

1996 Metal Universe Platinum Edition

One of the eight cards in each pack of Fleer Metal baseball is a Platinum Edition parallel insert. Each of the 247 player cards (no checklists) in this special version has the textured foil background rendered only in silver. The second line of the logo/ID strip at bottom also identifies the card as part of the Platinum Edition.

	MT
Complete Set (247):	100.00
Common Player:	.25
Stars: 3X	

(See 1996 Metal Universe for checklist and base card values.)

1996 Metal Universe Heavy Metal

Some of the game's biggest hitters are included in this insert set. Action photos of players at bat are set on a silver-foil background on front. Backs have a close-up photo down one side, with praise for the player's power potential down the other. The Heavy Metal inserts can be expected to turn up at an average rate of one per eight packs.

		MT
Complete Set (10):		20.00
Common Player:		1.00
1	Albert Belle	1.25
2	Barry Bonds	1.25
3	Juan Gonzalez	2.50
4	Ken Griffey Jr.	6.00
5	Mark McGwire	6.00
6	Mike Piazza	3.00
7	Sammy Sosa	3.00
8	Frank Thomas	2.50
9	Mo Vaughn	1.00
10	Matt Williams	1.00

1996 Metal Universe Mining for Gold

Available only in retail packs, at an average rate of one per dozen packs, the Mining for Gold insert series focuses on 1995's top rookies. Fronts have player action photos frame and backgrounded with several different gold tones in etched metal foil. Backs are conventionally printed, carrying on the same format with a portrait photo and a few words about the player.

		MT
Complete Set (12):		[illegible]
Common Player:		1.00
1	Yamil Benitez	1.00
2	Marty Cordova	2.00
3	Shawn Green	3.00
4	Todd Greene	1.50
5	Brian Hunter	1.00
6	Derek Jeter	10.00
7	Charles Johnson	1.00
8	Chipper Jones	10.00
9	Hideo Nomo	4.00
10	Alex Ochoa	1.00
11	Andy Pettitte	4.50
12	Quilvio Veras	1.00

1996 Metal Universe Mother Lode

Medieval designs rendered in textured silver-foil on a plain white background are the setting for the color player photos in this hobby-only insert. Backs also have a silver and white background along with another player photo and some kind words about his skills. The cards are found at an average rate of one per 12 packs.

		MT
Complete Set (12):		40.00
Common Player:		1.50
1	Barry Bonds	4.00
2	Jim Edmonds	1.50
3	Ken Griffey Jr.	15.00
4	Kenny Lofton	3.00
5	Raul Mondesi	2.00
6	Rafael Palmeiro	2.50
7	Manny Ramirez	5.00
8	Cal Ripken Jr.	12.00
9	Tim Salmon	1.50
10	Ryne Sandberg	4.00
11	Frank Thomas	6.00
12	Matt Williams	2.00

1996 Metal Universe Platinum Portraits

Close-up color photos on a plain metallic-foil background are featured in this insert set. The checklist is heavy in rookie and sophomore players, who are featured in an action photo on back, with a few career details. Platinum Portraits inserts are found in every fourth pack, on average.

		MT
Complete Set (10):		10.00
Common Player:		.50
1	Garret Anderson	.50
2	Marty Cordova	.50
3	Jim Edmonds	.50
4	Jason Isringhausen	.50
5	Chipper Jones	6.00
6	Ryan Klesko	.75
7	Hideo Nomo	2.00
8	Carlos Perez	.50
9	Manny Ramirez	4.00
10	Rondell White	[illegible]

1996 Metal Universe Titanium

A huge purple-highlighted silver baseball in a star-studded night sky is the background for the action photos of the game's biggest names in this insert series. Backs have a second, more up-close, photo and a few words about the player. Titanium inserts are found in Metal Universe packs at an average rate of one per 24 packs.

		MT
Complete Set (10):		100.00
Common Player:		4.00
1	Albert Belle	6.00
2	Barry Bonds	6.00
3	Ken Griffey Jr.	25.00
4	Tony Gwynn	12.00
5	Greg Maddux	15.00
6	Mike Piazza	15.00
7	Cal Ripken Jr.	20.00
8	Frank Thomas	10.00
9	Mo Vaughn	4.00
10	Matt Williams	4.00

1997 Metal Universe

Metal Universe Baseball arrived in a 250-card set, including three checklists. Each card is printed on 100-percent etched foil with "comic book" art full-bleed backgrounds, with the player's name, team, position and the Metal Universe logo near the bottom of the card. Backs contain another player photo and key statistics. Metal Universe sold in eight-card packs and contained six different insert sets. They included: Blast Furnace, Magnetic Field, Mining for Gold, Mother Lode, Platinum Portraits and Titanium.

		MT
Complete Set (250):		35.00
Common Player:		.10
Wax Box:		45.00
1	Roberto Alomar	.60
2	Brady Anderson	.15
3	Rocky Coppinger	.10
4	Chris Hoiles	.10
5	Eddie Murray	.40
6	Mike Mussina	.50
7	Rafael Palmeiro	.25
8	Cal Ripken Jr.	2.50
9	B.J. Surhoff	.15
10	Brant Brown	.10
11	Mark Grace	.25
12	Brian McRae	.10
13	Jaime Navarro	.10
14	Ryne Sandberg	.75
15	Sammy Sosa	1.50
16	Amaury Telemaco	.10
17	Steve Trachsel	.10
18	Darren Bragg	.10
19	Jose Canseco	.25
20	Roger Clemens	1.00
21	Nomar Garciaparra	2.00
22	Tom Gordon	.10
23	Tim Naehring	.10
24	Mike Stanley	.10
25	John Valentin	.10
26	Mo Vaughn	.75
27	Jermaine Dye	.10
28	Tom Glavine	.20
29	Marquis Grissom	.10
30	Andruw Jones	1.50
31	Chipper Jones	2.00
32	Ryan Klesko	.25
33	Greg Maddux	2.00
34	Fred McGriff	.30
35	John Smoltz	.25
36	Garret Anderson	.10
37	George Arias	.10
38	Gary DiSarcina	.10
39	Jim Edmonds	.10
40	Darin Erstad	1.00
41	Chuck Finley	.10
42	Troy Percival	.10
43	Tim Salmon	.25
44	Bret Boone	.10
45	Jeff Brantley	.10
46	Eric Davis	.10
47	Barry Larkin	.20
48	Hal Morris	.10
49	Mark Portugal	.10
50	Reggie Sanders	.10
51	John Smiley	.10
52	Wilson Alvarez	.10
53	Harold Baines	.10
54	James Baldwin	.10
55	Albert Belle	.75
56	Mike Cameron	.10
57	Ray Durham	.10
58	Alex Fernandez	.10
59	Roberto Hernandez	.10
60	Tony Phillips	.10
61	Frank Thomas	1.50
62	Robin Ventura	.15
63	Jeff Cirillo	.10
64	Jeff D'Amico	.10
65	John Jaha	.10
66	Scott Karl	.10
67	Ben McDonald	.10
68	Marc Newfield	.10
69	Dave Nilsson	.10
70	Jose Valentin	.10
71	Dante Bichette	.20
72	Ellis Burks	.10
73	Vinny Castilla	.10
74	Andres Galarraga	.20
75	Kevin Ritz	.10
76	Larry Walker	.40
77	Walt Weiss	.10
78	Jamey Wright	.10
79	Eric Young	.10
80	Julio Franco	.10
81	Orel Hershiser	.10
82	Kenny Lofton	.60
83	Jack McDowell	.10
84	Jose Mesa	.10
85	Charles Nagy	.10
86	Manny Ramirez	1.00
87	Jim Thome	.40
88	Omar Vizquel	.10
89	Matt Williams	.25
90	Kevin Appier	.10
91	Johnny Damon	.10
92	Chili Davis	.10
93	Tom Goodwin	.10
94	Keith Lockhart	.10
95	Jeff Montgomery	.10
96	Craig Paquette	.10
97	Jose Rosado	.10
98	Michael Tucker	.10
99	Wilton Guerrero	.10
100	Todd Hollandsworth	.10
101	Eric Karros	.10
102	Ramon Martinez	.10
103	Raul Mondesi	.25
104	Hideo Nomo	.50
105	Mike Piazza	2.00
106	Ismael Valdes	.10
107	Todd Worrell	.10
108	Tony Clark	.50
109	Travis Fryman	.10
110	Bob Higginson	.10
111	Mark Lewis	.10
112	Melvin Nieves	.10
113	Justin Thompson	.10
114	Wade Boggs	.30
115	David Cone	.15
116	Cecil Fielder	.15
117	Dwight Gooden	.10
118	Derek Jeter	2.00
119	Tino Martinez	.35
120	Paul O'Neill	.10
121	Andy Pettitte	.60
122	Mariano Rivera	.15
123	Darryl Strawberry	.10
124	John Wetteland	.10
125	Bernie Williams	.40
126	Tony Batista	.10
127	Geronimo Berroa	.10
128	Scott Brosius	.10
129	Jason Giambi	.10
130	Jose Herrera	.10
131	Mark McGwire	4.00
132	John Wasdin	.10
133	Bob Abreu	.10
134	Jeff Bagwell	1.25
135	Derek Bell	.10
136	Craig Biggio	.10
137	Brian Hunter	.10
138	Darryl Kile	.10
139	Orlando Miller	.10
140	Shane Reynolds	.10
141	Billy Wagner	.10
142	Donne Wall	.10
143	Jay Buhner	.15
144	Jeff Fassero	.10
145	Ken Griffey Jr.	4.00
146	Sterling Hitchcock	.10
147	Randy Johnson	.40
148	Edgar Martinez	.10
149	Alex Rodriguez	3.00
149p	Alex Rodriguez ("PROMOTIONAL SAMPLE")	3.00
150	Paul Sorrento	.10
151	Dan Wilson	.10
152	Moises Alou	.10
153	Darrin Fletcher	.10
154	Cliff Floyd	.10
155	Mark Grudzielanek	.10
156	Vladimir Guerrero	1.00
157	Mike Lansing	.10
158	Pedro Martinez	.15
159	Henry Rodriguez	.10
160	Rondell White	.10
161	Will Clark	.25
162	Juan Gonzalez	1.25
163	Rusty Greer	.10
164	Ken Hill	.10
165	Mark McLemore	.10
166	Dean Palmer	.10
167	Roger Pavlik	.10

168	Ivan Rodriguez	.75
169	Mickey Tettleton	.10
170	Bobby Bonilla	.10
171	Kevin Brown	.15
172	Greg Colbrunn	.10
173	Jeff Conine	.10
174	Jim Eisenreich	.10
175	Charles Johnson	.10
176	Al Leiter	.10
177	Robb Nen	.10
178	Edgar Renteria	.20
179	Gary Sheffield	.40
180	Devon White	.10
181	Joe Carter	.15
182	Carlos Delgado	.40
183	Alex Gonzalez	.10
184	Shawn Green	.15
185	Juan Guzman	.10
186	Pat Hentgen	.10
187	Orlando Merced	.10
188	John Olerud	.15
189	Robert Perez	.10
190	Ed Sprague	.10
191	Mark Clark	.10
192	John Franco	.10
193	Bernard Gilkey	.10
194	Todd Hundley	.10
195	Lance Johnson	.10
196	Bobby Jones	.10
197	Alex Ochoa	.10
198	Rey Ordonez	.20
199	Paul Wilson	.10
200	Ricky Bottalico	.10
201	Gregg Jefferies	.10
202	Wendell Magee Jr.	.10
203	Mickey Morandini	.10
204	Ricky Otero	.10
205	Scott Rolen	1.25
206	Benito Santiago	.10
207	Curt Schilling	.15
208	Rich Becker	.10
209	Marty Cordova	.10
210	Chuck Knoblauch	.10
211	Pat Meares	.10
212	Paul Molitor	.40
213	Frank Rodriguez	.10
214	Terry Steinbach	.10
215	Todd Walker	.60
216	Andy Ashby	.10
217	Ken Caminiti	.25
218	Steve Finley	.10
219	Tony Gwynn	1.00
220	Joey Hamilton	.10
221	Rickey Henderson	.20
222	Trevor Hoffman	.10
223	Wally Joyner	.10
224	Scott Sanders	.10
225	Fernando Valenzuela	.10
226	Greg Vaughn	.15
227	Alan Benes	.10
228	Andy Benes	.10
229	Dennis Eckersley	.10
230	Ron Gant	.10
231	Brian Jordan	.10
232	Ray Lankford	.10
233	John Mabry	.10
234	Tom Pagnozzi	.10
235	Todd Stottlemyre	.10
236	Jermaine Allensworth	.10
237	Francisco Cordova	.15
238	Jason Kendall	.10
239	Jeff King	.10
240	Al Martin	.10
241	Rod Beck	.10
242	Barry Bonds	.75
243	Shawn Estes	.10
244	Mark Gardner	.10
245	Glenallen Hill	.10
246	Bill Mueller	.10
247	J.T. Snow	.10
248	Checklist	.10
249	Checklist	.10
250	Checklist	.10

1997 Metal Universe Blast Furnace

Blast Furnace inserts were found only in hobby packs, at a rate of one per 48 packs. The 12-card set was printed on a red-tinted plastic, with the words "Blast Furnace" near the bottom in gold foil with a fire-like border.

		MT
Complete Set (12):		125.00
Common Player:		3.00
1	Jeff Bagwell	12.00
2	Albert Belle	6.00
3	Barry Bonds	7.50
4	Andres Galarraga	3.00
5	Juan Gonzalez	15.00
6	Ken Griffey Jr.	30.00
7	Todd Hundley	3.00
8	Mark McGwire	30.00
9	Mike Piazza	20.00
10	Alex Rodriguez	25.00
11	Frank Thomas	10.00
12	Mo Vaughn	6.00

1997 Metal Universe Emerald Autograph Redemption

Six different young stars were featured in this insert, which was found every 480 hobby packs of Metal Universe. The cards are similar to regular-issue cards, but have green foil highlights. Redemption cards are numbered AU1-AU6. The redemption period expired Jan. 15, 1998.

		MT
Complete Set (6):		50.00
Common Player:		3.00
1	Darin Erstad	7.50
2	Todd Hollandsworth	3.00
3	Alex Ochoa	3.00
4	Alex Rodriguez	25.00
5	Scott Rolen	7.50
6	Todd Walker	5.00

1997 Metal Universe Emerald Autographs

Six different young stars were featured in this insert, which was found every 480 hobby packs of Metal Universe. The cards are similar to regular-issue cards, but have a green foil finish and autograph on the front. Redemption cards are numbered AU1-AU6, the autographed cards have a notation on back, "Certified Emerald Autograph Card".

		MT
Complete Set (6):		175.00
Common Autograph:		12.50
1	Darin Erstad	30.00
2	Todd Hollandsworth	12.50
3	Alex Ochoa	12.50
4	Alex Rodriguez	100.00
5	Scott Rolen	35.00
6	Todd Walker	15.00

1997 Metal Universe Magnetic Field

Magnetic Field inserts are printed in a horizontal format with prismatic foil backgrounds. This 10-card insert was found every 12 packs of Metal Universe.

		MT
Complete Set (10):		20.00
Common Player:		1.00
1	Roberto Alomar	1.25
2	Jeff Bagwell	2.00
3	Barry Bonds	1.25
4	Ken Griffey Jr.	7.50
5	Derek Jeter	3.00
6	Kenny Lofton	1.00
7	Edgar Renteria	1.00
8	Cal Ripken Jr.	5.00
9	Alex Rodriguez	5.00
10	Matt Williams	1.00

1997 Metal Universe Mining for Gold

Mining for Gold was a 10-card insert that featured some of baseball's brightest stars on a die-cut "ingot" design with pearlized gold coating. This insert was found every nine packs.

		MT
Complete Set (10):		20.00
Common Player:		.75
1	Bob Abreu	1.00
2	Kevin Brown	.75
3	Nomar Garciaparra	5.00
4	Vladimir Guerrero	3.00
5	Wilton Guerrero	.75
6	Andruw Jones	4.00
7	Curt Lyons	.75
8	Neifi Perez	.75
9	Scott Rolen	3.00
10	Todd Walker	2.00

Player names in *Italic* type indicate a rookie card.

1997 Metal Universe Mother Lode

Mother Lode was the most difficult insert out of Metal Universe with a one per 288 pack insertion ratio. Each card in this 10-card inert was printed on etched foil with a plant-type monument in back of the player.

		MT
Complete Set (12):		250.00
Common Player:		7.50
1	Roberto Alomar	10.00
2	Jeff Bagwell	15.00
3	Barry Bonds	12.50
4	Ken Griffey Jr.	45.00
5	Andruw Jones	12.50
6	Chipper Jones	30.00
7	Kenny Lofton	10.00
8	Mike Piazza	30.00
9	Cal Ripken Jr.	35.50
10	Alex Rodriguez	35.00
11	Frank Thomas	15.00
12	Matt Williams	7.50

1997 Metal Universe Platinum Portraits

Each card in the Platinum Portraits insert is printed on a background of platinum-colored etched foil. The 10-card set includes some of the top prospects and rising stars in baseball, and is included every 36 packs.

		MT
Complete Set (10):		30.00
Common Player:		1.25
1	James Baldwin	1.00
2	Jermaine Dye	1.00
3	Todd Hollandsworth	1.00
4	Derek Jeter	10.00
5	Chipper Jones	10.00
6	Jason Kendall	1.00
7	Rey Ordonez	2.00
8	Andy Pettitte	3.00
9	Edgar Renteria	2.00
10	Alex Rodriguez	12.50

1997 Metal Universe Titanium

These retail exclusive inserts include 10 cards and were found every 24 packs. Each card is die-cut on the top-left and bottom-right corner with a silver foil background. Titanium includes some of the most popular players in baseball on cards that are also embossed.

		MT
Complete Set (10):		90.00
Common Player:		4.00
1	Jeff Bagwell	7.00
2	Albert Belle	4.00
3	Ken Griffey Jr.	20.00
4	Chipper Jones	10.00
5	Greg Maddux	10.00
6	Mark McGwire	20.00
7	Mike Piazza	10.00
8	Cal Ripken Jr.	15.00
9	Alex Rodriguez	15.00
10	Frank Thomas	8.00

1998 Metal Universe

This 220-card single series release captured players over a foil etched, art background that related in some way to them or the city they played in. Metal Universe included a 15-card Hardball Galaxy subset and dealers and media were given an Alex Rodriguez promo card that was identical the base card except for the words "Promotional Sample" written across the back. The set arrived with a parallel called Precious Metal Gems, and included the following insert sets: All-Galactic Team, Diamond Heroes, Platinum Portraits, Titanium and Universal Language.

		MT
Complete Set (220):		30.00
Common Player:		.10
Wax Box:		55.00
1	Jose Cruz Jr.	.25
2	Jeff Abbott	.10
3	Rafael Palmeiro	.25
4	Ivan Rodriguez	.75
5	Jaret Wright	.75
6	Derek Bell	.10
7	Chuck Finley	.10
8	Travis Fryman	.10
9	Randy Johnson	.50
10	Derrek Lee	.20
11	Bernie Williams	.50
12	Carlos Baerga	.10
13	Ricky Bottalico	.10
14	Ellis Burks	.10
15	Russ Davis	.10
16	Nomar Garciaparra	2.00
17	Joey Hamilton	.10
18	Jason Kendall	.20
19	Darryl Kile	.10
20	Edgardo Alfonzo	.15
21	Moises Alou	.20
22	Bobby Bonilla	.20
23	Jim Edmonds	.20

24	Jose Guillen	.25
25	Chuck Knoblauch	.40
26	Javy Lopez	.20
27	Billy Wagner	.10
28	Kevin Appier	.10
29	Joe Carter	.15
30	Todd Dunwoody	.10
31	Gary Gaetti	.10
32	Juan Gonzalez	1.50
33	Jeffrey Hammonds	.10
34	Roberto Hernandez	.10
35	Dave Nilsson	.10
36	Manny Ramirez	.75
37	Robin Ventura	.20
38	Rondell White	.20
39	Vinny Castilla	.20
40	Will Clark	.25
41	Scott Hatteberg	.10
42	Russ Johnson	.10
43	Ricky Ledee	.50
44	Kenny Lofton	.75
45	Paul Molitor	.50
46	Justin Thompson	.10
47	Craig Biggio	.20
48	Damion Easley	.10
49	Brad Radke	.10
50	Ben Grieve	1.00
51	Mark Bellhorn	.10
52	*Henry Blanco*	.10
53	Mariano Rivera	.20
54	Reggie Sanders	.10
55	Paul Sorrento	.10
56	Terry Steinbach	.10
57	Mo Vaughn	.75
58	Brady Anderson	.20
59	Tom Glavine	.20
60	Sammy Sosa	2.00
61	Larry Walker	.30
62	Rod Beck	.10
63	Jose Canseco	.25
64	Steve Finley	.10
65	Pedro Martinez	.50
66	John Olerud	.20
67	Scott Rolen	1.00
68	Ismael Valdes	.10
69	Andrew Vessel	.10
70	Mark Grudzielanek	.10
71	Eric Karros	.10
72	Jeff Shaw	.10
73	Lou Collier	.10
74	Edgar Martinez	.10
75	Vladimir Guerrero	1.50
76	Paul Konerko	.50
77	Kevin Orie	.10
78	Kevin Polcovich	.10
79	Brett Tomko	.10
80	Jeff Bagwell	1.00
81	Barry Bonds	.75
82	David Justice	.25
83	Hideo Nomo	.50
84	Ryne Sandberg	.75
85	Shannon Stewart	.10
86	Derek Wallace	.10
87	Tony Womack	.10
88	Jason Giambi	.10
89	Mark Grace	.25
90	Pat Hentgen	.10
91	Raul Mondesi	.25
92	Matt Morris	.20
93	Matt Perisho	.10
94	Tim Salmon	.25
95	Jeremi Gonzalez	.10
96	Shawn Green	.15
97	Todd Greene	.10
98	Ruben Rivera	.10
99	Deion Sanders	.20
100	Alex Rodriguez	2.50
101	Will Cunnane	.10
102	Ray Lankford	.10
103	Ryan McGuire	.10
104	Charles Nagy	.10
105	Rey Ordonez	.10
106	Mike Piazza	2.00
107	Tony Saunders	.10
108	Curt Schilling	.20
109	Fernando Tatis	.10
110	Mark McGwire	4.00
111	*David Dellucci*	.50
112	Garret Anderson	.10
113	Shane Bowers	.10
114	David Cone	.20
115	Jeff King	.10
116	Matt Williams	.25
117	Aaron Boone	.10
118	Dennis Eckersley	.20
119	Livan Hernandez	.15
120	Richard Hidalgo	.10
121	Bobby Higginson	.10
122	Tino Martinez	.40
123	Tim Naehring	.10
124	Jose Vidro	.10
125	John Wetteland	.10
126	Jay Bell	.10
127	Albert Belle	.75
128	Marty Cordova	.10
129	Chili Davis	.10
130	Jason Dickson	.10
131	Rusty Greer	.15
132	Hideki Irabu	.40
133	Greg Maddux	2.00
134	Billy Taylor	.10
135	Jim Thome	.50
136	Gerald Williams	.10
137	Jeff Cirillo	.10
138	Delino DeShields	.10
139	Andres Galarraga	.40
140	Willie Greene	.10
141	John Jaha	.10
142	Charles Johnson	.15
143	Ryan Klesko	.25
144	Paul O'Neill	.20
145	Robinson Checo	.10
146	Roberto Alomar	.50
147	Wilson Alvarez	.10
148	Bobby Jones	.10
149	Raul Casanova	.10
150	Andruw Jones	1.00
151	Mike Lansing	.10
152	Mickey Morandini	.10
153	Neifi Perez	.10
154	Pokey Reese	.10
155	Edgar Renteria	.10
156	Eric Young	.10
157	Darin Erstad	1.00
158	Kelvim Escobar	.10
159	Carl Everett	.10
160	Tom Gordon	.10
161	Ken Griffey Jr.	4.00
162	Al Martin	.10
163	Bubba Trammell	.20
164	Carlos Delgado	.40
165	Kevin Brown	.20
166	Ken Caminiti	.20
167	Roger Clemens	1.00
168	Ron Gant	.20
169	Jeff Kent	.10
170	Mike Mussina	.60
171	Dean Palmer	.10
172	Henry Rodriguez	.10
173	Matt Stairs	.10
174	Jay Buhner	.20
175	Frank Thomas	1.50
176	Mike Cameron	.10
177	Johnny Damon	.10
178	Tony Gwynn	1.50
179	John Smoltz	.20
180	B.J. Surhoff	.10
181	Antone Williamson	.10
182	Alan Benes	.20
183	Jeromy Burnitz	.10
184	Tony Clark	.40
185	Shawn Estes	.10
186	Todd Helton	.75
187	Todd Hundley	.10
188	Chipper Jones	2.00
189	Mark Kotsay	.25
190	Barry Larkin	.20
191	Mike Lieberthal	.10
192	Andy Pettitte	.50
193	Gary Sheffield	.30
194	Jeff Suppan	.10
195	Mark Wohlers	.10
196	Dante Bichette	.25
197	Trevor Hoffman	.10
198	J.T. Snow	.20
199	Derek Jeter	2.00
200	Cal Ripken Jr.	2.50
201	*Steve Woodard*	.40
202	Ray Durham	.10
203	Barry Bonds (Hardball Galaxy)	.40
204	Tony Clark (Hardball Galaxy)	.20
205	Roger Clemens (Hardball Galaxy)	.50
206	Ken Griffey Jr. (Hardball Galaxy)	1.50
207	Tony Gwynn (Hardball Galaxy)	.75
208	Derek Jeter (Hardball Galaxy)	1.00
209	Randy Johnson (Hardball Galaxy)	.20
210	Mark McGwire (Hardball Galaxy)	[illegible]
211	Hideo Nomo (Hardball Galaxy)	.25
212	Mike Piazza (Hardball Galaxy)	1.00
213	Cal Ripken Jr. (Hardball Galaxy)	1.25
214	Alex Rodriguez (Hardball Galaxy)	1.00
215	Frank Thomas (Hardball Galaxy)	.75
216	Mo Vaughn (Hardball Galaxy)	.40
217	Larry Walker (Hardball Galaxy)	.15
218	Checklist (Ken Griffey Jr.)	1.00
219	Checklist (Alex Rodriguez)	.60
220	Checklist (Frank Thomas)	.50

1998 Metal Universe Precious Metal Gems

Precious Metal Gems includes 217 (no checklists) player cards from Metal Universe and are serial numbered to 50 sets. Because there were five Ultimate Metal Gems redemption cards (good for a complete set of Metal Gems) available, only serial numbers 1-45 were found in packs (46-50 were held back for the exchage program).

	MT
Common Player:	10.00
Stars: 25-40X	
Production 50 sets	

(See 1998 Metal Universe for checklist and base card values.)

1998 Metal Universe All-Galactic Team

This 18-card insert captures players over a planet holofoil background. Cards were inserted one per 192 packs.

		MT
Complete Set (18):		400.00
Common Player:		10.00
Inserted 1:192		
1	Ken Griffey Jr.	60.00
2	Frank Thomas	20.00
3	Chipper Jones	30.00
4	Albert Belle	12.50
5	Juan Gonzalez	25.00
6	Jeff Bagwell	15.00
7	Andruw Jones	12.50
8	Cal Ripken Jr.	40.00
9	Derek Jeter	25.00
10	Nomar Garciaparra	30.00
11	Darin Erstad	15.00
12	Greg Maddux	25.00
13	Alex Rodriguez	40.00
14	Mike Piazza	30.00
15	Vladimir Guerrero	12.50
16	Jose Cruz Jr.	10.00
17	Mark McGwire	60.00
18	Scott Rolen	15.00

1998 Metal Universe Diamond Heroes

Diamond Heroes displayed six players in a comic book setting. This insert was seeded one per 18 packs and contained a foil etched image of a Marvel comic in the background.

		MT
Complete Set (6):		20.00
Common Player:		1.50
Inserted 1:18		
1	Ken Griffey Jr.	7.50
2	Frank Thomas	4.00
3	Andruw Jones	4.00
4	Alex Rodriguez	6.00
5	Jose Cruz Jr.	1.50
6	Cal Ripken Jr.	6.00

Checklists with card numbers in parentheses ( ) indicates the numbers do not appear on the card.

1998 Metal Universe Platinum Portraits

This 12-card insert set featured color portraits of top players highlighted with a platinum-colored etched foil frame over it. Platinum Portraits are seeded one per 360 packs of Metal Universe.

		MT
Complete Set (12):		350.00
Common Player:		12.50
Inserted 1:360		
1	Ken Griffey Jr.	60.00
2	Frank Thomas	20.00
3	Chipper Jones	40.00
4	Jose Cruz Jr.	12.50
5	Andruw Jones	15.00
6	Cal Ripken Jr.	45.00
7	Derek Jeter	35.00
8	Darin Erstad	15.00
9	Greg Maddux	35.00
10	Alex Rodriguez	45.00
11	Mike Piazza	40.00
12	Vladimir Guerrero	15.00

1998 Metal Universe Titanium

This die-cut 15-card insert contained color photos printed on embossed, sculpted cards on etched foil. Titanium inserts were seeded one per 96 packs.

		MT
Complete Set (15):		175.00
Common Player:		5.00
Inserted 1:96		
1	Ken Griffey Jr.	30.00
2	Frank Thomas	12.50
3	Chipper Jones	20.00
4	Jose Cruz Jr.	5.00
5	Juan Gonzalez	12.50
6	Scott Rolen	10.00
7	Andruw Jones	10.00
8	Cal Ripken Jr.	25.00
9	Derek Jeter	20.00
10	Nomar Garciaparra	15.00
11	Darin Erstad	7.50
12	Greg Maddux	15.00
13	Alex Rodriguez	25.00
14	Mike Piazza	20.00
15	Vladimir Guerrero	7.50

1998 Metal Universe Universal Language

This 20-card insert features illustration and copy done in the player's native language. Cards were die-cut and inserted one per six packs.

		MT
Complete Set (20):		40.00
Common Player:		1.00
Inserted 1:6		
1	Ken Griffey Jr.	7.50
2	Frank Thomas	2.50
3	Chipper Jones	3.50
4	Albert Belle	1.50
5	Juan Gonzalez	3.00
6	Jeff Bagwell	2.50
7	Andruw Jones	2.50
8	Cal Ripken Jr.	5.00
9	Derek Jeter	3.50
10	Nomar Garciaparra	3.50
11	Darin Erstad	1.75
12	Greg Maddux	3.00
13	Alex Rodriguez	3.50
14	Mike Piazza	3.50
15	Vladimir Guerrero	1.75
16	Jose Cruz Jr.	1.00
17	Hideo Nomo	1.00
18	Kenny Lofton	1.00
19	Tony Gwynn	3.00
20	Scott Rolen	3.00

1999 Metal Universe Sample Sheet

To introduce its annual issue of embossed cards this six-card sheet of Metal Universe samples was issued. The 5" x 10-1/2" sheet has five regular cards and an example of the Building Blocks insert set. Cards on the sheet are virtually identical to the issued versions except they have the word "SAMPLE" on back in place of card numbers.

		MT
Complete Sheet:		15.00
	Albert Belle	
	Derek Jeter	
	Mark McGwire (Building Blocks)	
	Mike Piazza	
	Alex Rodriguez	
	Sammy Sosa	

1999 Metal Universe

The 300-card base set offers 232 player cards and three subsets: Building Blocks, M.L.P.D. and Caught on the Fly. Base cards feature an action photo framed in an etched-foil and metallic, embossed name plate. Packs consist of eight cards with a S.R.P. of $2.69. There are two parallels, Precious Metal Gems and Gem Masters. Metal Gems are numbered to 50 with gold-foil etching. Gem Masters are limited to only one set, with silver foil etching and serial numbered "one of one".

		MT
Complete Set (300):		35.00
Common Player:		.15
Wax Box:		35.00
1	Mark McGwire	4.00
2	Jim Edmonds	.25
3	Travis Fryman	.15
4	Tom Gordon	.15
5	Jeff Bagwell	1.00
6	Rico Brogna	.15
7	Tom Evans	.15
8	John Franco	.15
9	Juan Gonzalez	1.50
10	Paul Molitor	.50
11	Roberto Alomar	.50
12	Mike Hampton	.15
13	Orel Hershiser	.15
14	Todd Stottlemyre	.15
15	Robin Ventura	.25
16	Todd Walker	.25
17	Bernie Williams	.50
18	Shawn Estes	.15
19	Richie Sexson	.25
20	Kevin Millwood	.40
21	David Ortiz	.15
22	Mariano Rivera	.25
23	Ivan Rodriguez	.75
24	Mike Sirotka	.15
25	David Justice	.30
26	Carl Pavano	.15
27	Albert Belle	.75
28	Will Clark	.40
29	Jose Cruz Jr.	.15
30	Trevor Hoffman	.15
31	Dean Palmer	.15
32	Edgar Renteria	.15
33	David Segui	.15
34	B.J. Surhoff	.15
35	Miguel Tejada	.30
36	Bob Wickman	.15
37	Charles Johnson	.15
38	Andruw Jones	.75
39	Mike Lieberthal	.15
40	Eli Marrero	.15
41	Neifi Perez	.15
42	Jim Thome	.50
43	Barry Bonds	.75
44	Carlos Delgado	.40
45	Chuck Finley	.15
46	Brian Meadows	.15
47	Tony Gwynn	1.50
48	Jose Offerman	.15
49	Cal Ripken Jr.	2.50
50	Alex Rodriguez	2.50
51	Esteban Yan	.15
52	Matt Stairs	.15
53	Fernando Vina	.15
54	Rondell White	.25
55	Kerry Wood	.75
56	Dmitri Young	.15
57	Ken Caminiti	.25
58	Alex Gonzalez	.15
59	Matt Mantei	.15
60	Tino Martinez	.30
61	Hal Morris	.15
62	Rafael Palmeiro	.30
63	Troy Percival	.15
64	Bobby Smith	.15
65	Ed Sprague	.15
66	Brett Tomko	.15
67	Steve Trachsel	.15
68	Ugueth Urbina	.15
69	Jose Valentin	.15
70	Kevin Brown	.25
71	Shawn Green	.25
72	Dustin Hermanson	.15
73	Livan Hernandez	.15
74	Geoff Jenkins	.15
75	Jeff King	.15
76	Chuck Knoblauch	.30
77	Edgar Martinez	.15
78	Fred McGriff	.25
79	Mike Mussina	.50
80	Dave Nilsson	.15
81	Kenny Rogers	.15
82	Tim Salmon	.30
83	Reggie Sanders	.15
84	Wilson Alvarez	.15
85	Rod Beck	.15
86	Jose Guillen	.25
87	Bob Higginson	.15
88	Gregg Olson	.15
89	Jeff Shaw	.15
90	Masato Yoshii	.25
91	Todd Helton	.75
92	David Dellucci	.15
93	Johnny Damon	.15
94	Cliff Floyd	.15
95	Ken Griffey Jr.	4.00
96	Juan Guzman	.15
97	Derek Jeter	2.00
98	Barry Larkin	.30
99	Quinton McCracken	.15
100	Sammy Sosa	2.50
101	Kevin Young	.15
102	Jay Bell	.15
103	Jay Buhner	.20
104	Jeff Conine	.15
105	Ryan Jackson	.15
106	Sidney Ponson	.15
107	Jeromy Burnitz	.15
108	Roberto Hernandez	.15
109	A.J. Hinch	.15
110	Hideki Irabu	.25
111	Paul Konerko	.25
112	Henry Rodriguez	.15
113	Shannon Stewart	.15
114	Tony Womack	.15
115	Wilton Guerrero	.15
116	Andy Benes	.15
117	Jeff Cirillo	.15
118	Chili Davis	.15
119	Eric Davis	.15
120	Vladimir Guerrero	1.00
121	Dennis Reyes	.15
122	Rickey Henderson	.30
123	Mickey Morandini	.15
124	Jason Schmidt	.15
125	J.T. Snow	.15
126	Justin Thompson	.15
127	Billy Wagner	.15
128	Armando Benitez	.15
129	Sean Casey	.25
130	Brad Fullmer	.25
131	Ben Grieve	.75
132	Robb Nen	.15
133	Shane Reynolds	.15
134	Todd Zeile	.15
135	Brady Anderson	.15
136	Aaron Boone	.15
137	Orlando Cabrera	.15
138	Jason Giambi	.15
139	Randy Johnson	.50
140	Jeff Kent	.15
141	John Wetteland	.15
142	Rolando Arrojo	.15
143	Scott Brosius	.15
144	Mark Grace	.30
145	Jason Kendall	.25
146	Travis Lee	.75
147	Gary Sheffield	.30
148	David Cone	.25
149	Jose Hernandez	.15
150	Todd Jones	.15
151	Al Martin	.15
152	Ismael Valdes	.15
153	Wade Boggs	.30
154	Garret Anderson	.15
155	Bobby Bonilla	.20
156	Darryl Kile	.15
157	Ryan Klesko	.25
158	Tim Wakefield	.15
159	Kenny Lofton	.60
160	Jose Canseco	.40
161	Doug Glanville	.15
162	Todd Hundley	.15
163	Brian Jordan	.15
164	Steve Finley	.15
165	Tom Glavine	.25
166	Al Leiter	.25
167	Raul Mondesi	.30
168	Desi Relaford	.15
169	Bret Saberhagen	.15
170	Omar Vizquel	.15
171	Larry Walker	.40
172	Bobby Abreu	.15
173	Moises Alou	.25
174	Mike Caruso	.15
175	Royce Clayton	.15
176	Bartolo Colon	.25
177	Marty Cordova	.15
178	Darin Erstad	.75
179	Nomar Garciaparra	2.00
180	Andy Ashby	.15
181	Dan Wilson	.15
182	Larry Sutton	.15
183	Tony Clark	.40
184	Andres Galarraga	.50
185	Ray Durham	.15
186	Hideo Nomo	.25
187	Steve Woodard	.15
188	Scott Rolen	.75
189	Mike Stanley	.15
190	Jaret Wright	.50
191	Vinny Castilla	.15
192	Jason Christiansen	.15
193	Paul Bako	.15
194	Carlos Perez	.15
195	Mike Piazza	2.00
196	Fernando Tatis	.15
197	Mo Vaughn	.75
198	Devon White	.15
199	Ricky Gutierrez	.15
200	Charlie Hayes	.15
201	Brad Radke	.15
202	Rick Helling	.15
203	John Smoltz	.25
204	Frank Thomas	1.00
205	David Wells	.15
206	Roger Clemens	1.25
207	Mark Grudzielanek	.15
208	Chipper Jones	1.50
209	Ray Lankford	.15
210	Pedro Martinez	.50
211	Manny Ramirez	1.00
212	Greg Vaughn	.25
213	Craig Biggio	.30
214	Rusty Greer	.15
215	Greg Maddux	2.00
216	Rick Aguilera	.15
217	Andy Pettitte	.50
218	Dante Bichette	.30
219	Damion Easley	.15
220	Matt Morris	.15
221	John Olerud	.25
222	Chan Ho Park	.40
223	Curt Schilling	.25
224	John Valentin	.15
225	Matt Williams	.40
226	Ellis Burks	.15
227	Tom Goodwin	.15
228	Javy Lopez	.25
229	Eric Milton	.15
230	Paul O'Neill	.30
231	Magglio Ordonez	.15
232	Derrek Lee	.15
233	Ken Griffey Jr. (Caught on the Fly)	1.50
234	Randy Johnson (Caught on the Fly)	.25
235	Alex Rodriguez (Caught on the Fly)	1.00
236	Darin Erstad (Caught on the Fly)	.40
237	Juan Gonzalez (Caught on the Fly)	.75
238	Derek Jeter (Caught on the Fly)	1.00
239	Tony Gwynn (Caught on the Fly)	.75
240	Kerry Wood (Caught on the Fly)	.40
241	Cal Ripken Jr. (Caught on the Fly)	1.25
242	Sammy Sosa (Caught on the Fly)	1.25
243	Greg Maddux (Caught on the Fly)	1.00
244	Mark McGwire (Caught on the Fly)	2.00
245	Chipper Jones (Caught on the Fly)	.75
246	Barry Bonds (Caught on the Fly)	.40
247	Ben Grieve (Caught on the Fly)	.40
248	Ben Davis (Building Blocks)	.15
249	Robert Fick (Building Blocks)	.25
250	Carlos Guillen (Building Blocks)	.15
251	Mike Frank (Building Blocks)	.25
252	Ryan Minor (Building Blocks)	.40
253	Troy Glaus (Building Blocks)	1.00
254	Matt Anderson (Building Blocks)	.25
255	Josh Booty (Building Blocks)	.15
256	Gabe Alvarez (Building Blocks)	.15
257	Gabe Kapler (Building Blocks)	1.50
258	Enrique Wilson (Building Blocks)	.15
259	Alex Gonzalez (Building Blocks)	.25
260	Preston Wilson (Building Blocks)	.15
261	Eric Chavez (Building Blocks)	.30
262	Adrian Beltre (Building Blocks)	.30
263	Corey Koskie (Building Blocks)	.25
264	*Robert Machado* (Building Blocks)	.50
265	Orlando Hernandez (Building Blocks)	2.00
266	Matt Clement (Building Blocks)	.15
267	Luis Ordaz (Building Blocks)	.15
268	Jeremy Giambi (Building Blocks)	.25
269	J.D. Drew (Building Blocks)	1.00
270	Cliff Politte (Building Blocks)	.15
271	Carlton Loewer (Building Blocks)	.15
272	Aramis Ramirez (Building Blocks)	.25
273	Ken Griffey Jr. (M.I.P.D.)	1.50
274	Randy Johnson (M.I.P.D.)	.25
275	Alex Rodriguez (M.I.P.D.)	1.00
276	Darin Erstad (M.I.P.D.)	.40
277	Scott Rolen (M.I.P.D.)	.40
278	Juan Gonzalez (M.I.P.D.)	.75
279	Jeff Bagwell (M.I.P.D.)	.40
280	Mike Piazza (M.I.P.D.)	1.00
281	Derek Jeter (M.I.P.D.)	1.00
282	Travis Lee (M.I.P.D.)	.40
283	Tony Gwynn (M.I.P.D.)	.75
284	Kerry Wood (M.I.P.D.)	.40
285	Albert Belle (M.I.P.D.)	.40
286	Sammy Sosa (M.I.P.D.)	1.25
287	Mo Vaughn (M.I.P.D.)	.40
288	Nomar Garciaparra (M.I.P.D.)	1.00
289	Frank Thomas (M.I.P.D.)	.50
290	Cal Ripken Jr. (M.I.P.D.)	1.25
291	Greg Maddux (M.I.P.D.)	1.00
292	Chipper Jones (M.I.P.D.)	.75
293	Ben Grieve (M.I.P.D.)	.40
294	Andruw Jones (M.I.P.D.)	.40
295	Mark McGwire (M.I.P.D.)	2.00
296	Roger Clemens (M.I.P.D.)	.60
297	Barry Bonds (M.I.P.D.)	.40
298	Ken Griffey Jr.-Checklist (M.I.P.D.)	1.00
299	Kerry Wood-Checklist (M.I.P.D.)	.25
300	Alex Rodriguez-Checklist (M.I.P.D.)	.75

1999 Metal Universe Precious Metal Gems

A 300-card parallel of the base set, these cards feature gold-foil etching and are inserted exclusively in hobby packs. Each card is serially numbered to 50. A Gem Master 1 of 1 parallel was also issued, but is too rare to value.

	MT
Common Player:	10.00
Stars: 25-40X	
Gem Master 1 of 1:	
(Value undetermined)	

(See 1999 Metal Universe for checklist and base card values.)

1999 Metal Universe Boyz With The Wood

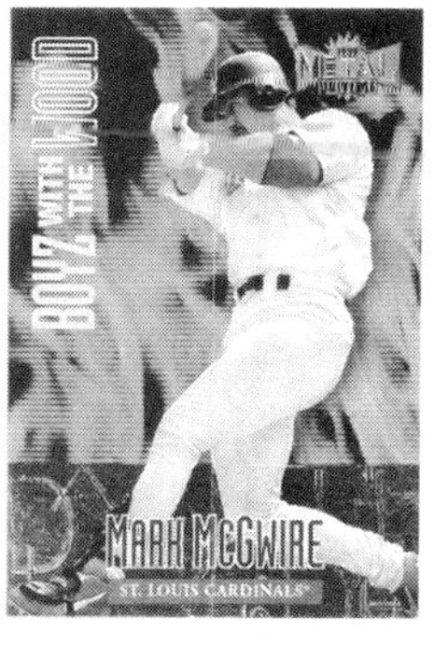

The top hitters in the game are featured on these folded cards with four sides. These are inserted 1:18.

		MT
Complete Set (15):		75.00
Common Player:		2.00
Inserted 1:18		
1	Ken Griffey Jr.	15.00
2	Frank Thomas	5.00
3	Jeff Bagwell	4.00
4	Juan Gonzalez	6.00
5	Mark McGwire	15.00
6	Scott Rolen	3.00
7	Travis Lee	2.00
8	Tony Gwynn	6.00
9	Mike Piazza	7.50
10	Chipper Jones	7.50
11	Nomar Garciaparra	7.50
12	Derek Jeter	7.50
13	Cal Ripken Jr.	10.00
14	Andruw Jones	3.00
15	Alex Rodriguez	10.00

1999 Metal Universe Diamond Soul

Utilizing lenticular technology these inserts showcase a soulful "galactic" design. The set consists of 15 cards which are seeded at 1:72 packs.

		MT
Complete Set (15):		140.00
Common Player:		3.00
Inserted 1:72		
1	Cal Ripken Jr.	20.00
2	Alex Rodriguez	20.00
3	Chipper Jones	15.00
4	Derek Jeter	12.50
5	Frank Thomas	10.00
6	Greg Maddux	12.50
7	Juan Gonzalez	10.00
8	Ken Griffey Jr.	25.00
9	Kerry Wood	3.00
10	Mark McGwire	25.00
11	Mike Piazza	15.00
12	Nomar Garciaparra	15.00
13	Scott Rolen	5.00
14	Tony Gwynn	10.00
15	Travis Lee	3.00

1999 Metal Universe Linchpins

This 10-card set features a laser die-cut design and highlights key players who hold their teams together on the field and in the clubhouse. These are seeded 1:360 packs.

		MT
Complete Set (10):		300.00
Common Player:		12.50
Inserted 1:360		
1	Mike Piazza	30.00
2	Mark McGwire	60.00
3	Kerry Wood	12.50
4	Ken Griffey Jr.	60.00
5	Greg Maddux	25.00
6	Frank Thomas	20.00
7	Derek Jeter	30.00
8	Chipper Jones	30.00
9	Cal Ripken Jr.	40.00
10	Alex Rodriguez	40.00

1999 Metal Universe Neophytes

This 15-card insert set showcases young stars like J.D. Drew and Troy Glaus.

The cards feature silver foil stamping on a horizontal format, found on an average of 1:6 packs.

		MT
Complete Set (15):		20.00
Common Player:		.50
Inserted 1:6		
1	Troy Glaus	4.00
2	Travis Lee	1.50
3	Scott Elarton	.50
4	Ricky Ledee	.50
5	Richard Hidalgo	.50
6	J.D. Drew	3.00
7	Paul Konerko	1.00
8	Orlando Hernandez	5.00
9	Mike Caruso	.50
10	Mike Frank	.50
11	Miguel Tejada	1.00
12	Matt Anderson	.75
13	Kerry Wood	1.50
14	Gabe Alvarez	.50
15	Adrian Beltre	1.50

1999 Metal Universe Planet Metal

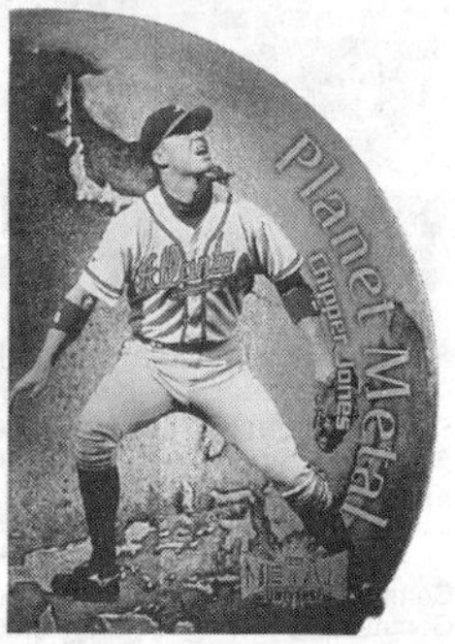

These die-cut cards feature a metallic view of the planet behind pop-out action photography. The 15-card set features the top players in the game and are seeded 1:36 packs.

		MT
Complete Set (15):		150.00
Common Player:		5.00
Inserted 1:36		
1	Alex Rodriguez	20.00
2	Andruw Jones	6.00
3	Cal Ripken Jr.	20.00
4	Chipper Jones	15.00
5	Darin Erstad	6.00
6	Derek Jeter	15.00
7	Frank Thomas	10.00
8	Travis Lee	5.00
9	Scott Rolen	6.00
10	Nomar Garciaparra	15.00
11	Mike Piazza	15.00
12	Mark McGwire	30.00
13	Ken Griffey Jr.	30.00
14	Juan Gonzalez	12.00
15	Jeff Bagwell	8.00

2000 Metal

		MT
Complete Set (250):		
Common Player:		.15
Common Prospect (201-250):		.75
Inserted 1:2		
1	Tony Gwynn	1.50
2	Derek Jeter	2.00
3	Johnny Damon	.15
4	Javy Lopez	.25
5	Preston Wilson	.15
6	Derek Bell	.15
7	Richie Sexson	.25
8	Vinny Castilla	.25
9	Billy Wagner	.15
10	Carlos Beltran	.40
11	Chris Singleton	.15
12	Nomar Garciaparra	2.00
13	Carlos Febles	.15
14	Jason Varitek	.15
15	Luis Gonzalez	.15
16	Jon Lieber	.15
17	Mo Vaughn	.50
18	Dave Burba	.15
19	Brady Anderson	.25
20	Carlos Lee	.25
21	Chuck Finley	.15
22	Alex Gonzalez	.15
23	Matt Williams	.40
24	Chipper Jones	1.50
25	Pokey Reese	.15
26	Todd Helton	.40
27	Mike Mussina	.50
28	Butch Huskey	.15
29	Jeff Bagwell	.75
30	Juan Encarnacion	.15
31	A.J. Burnett	.15
32	Micah Bowie	.15
33	Brian Jordan	.15
34	Scott Erickson	.15
35	Sean Casey	.30
36	John Smoltz	.15
37	Edgard Clemente	.15
38	Mike Hampton	.15
39	Tom Glavine	.25
40	Albert Belle	.50
41	Jim Thome	.30
42	Jermaine Dye	.15
43	Sammy Sosa	2.00
44	Pedro Martinez	.75
45	Paul Konerko	.15
46	Damion Easley	.15
47	Cal Ripken Jr.	2.50
48	Jose Lima	.15
49	Mike Lowell	.15
50	Randy Johnson	.50
51	Dean Palmer	.25
52	Tim Salmon	.30
53	Kevin Millwood	.25
54	Mark Grace	.25
55	Aaron Boone	.15
56	Omar Vizquel	.15
57	Moises Alou	.25
58	Travis Fryman	.25
59	Erubiel Durazo	.25
60	Carl Everett	.15
61	Charles Johnson	.15
62	Trot Nixon	.15
63	Andres Galarraga	.40
64	Magglio Ordonez	.25
65	Pedro Astacio	.15
66	Roberto Alomar	.50
67	Pete Harnisch	.15
68	Scott Williamson	.15
69	Alex Fernandez	.15
70	Robin Ventura	.25
71	Chad Allen	.15
72	Darin Erstad	.25
73	Ron Coomer	.15
74	Ellis Burks	.25
75	Kent Bottenfield	.15
76	Ken Griffey Jr.	3.00
77	Mike Piazza	2.00
78	Jorge Posada	.25
79	Dante Bichette	.25
80	Adrian Beltre	.25
81	Andruw Jones	.50
82	Wilson Alvarez	.15
83	Edgardo Alfonzo	.25
84	Brian Giles	.25
85	Gary Sheffield	.30
86	Matt Stairs	.15
87	Bret Boone	.15
88	Kenny Rogers	.15
89	Barry Bonds	.75
90	Scott Rolen	.75
91	Edgar Renteria	.15
92	Larry Walker	.50
93	Roger Cedeno	.15
94	Kevin Brown	.25
95	Lee Stevens	.15
96	Brad Radke	.15
97	Andy Pettitte	.25
98	Bobby Higginson	.15
99	Eric Chavez	.25
100	Alex Rodriguez	2.00
101	Shannon Stewart	.15
102	Ryan Rupe	.15
103	Freddy Garcia	.25
104	John Jaha	.15
105	Greg Maddux	1.50
106	Hideki Irabu	.15
107	Rey Ordonez	.15
108	Troy O'Leary	.15
109	Frank Thomas	1.00
110	Corey Koskie	.15
111	Bernie Williams	.50
112	Barry Larkin	.40
113	Kevin Appier	.15
114	Curt Schilling	.25
115	Bartolo Colon	.15
116	Edgar Martinez	.15
117	Ray Lankford	.15
118	Todd Walker	.15
119	John Wetteland	.15
120	David Nilsson	.15
121	Tino Martinez	.30
122	Phil Nevin	.15
123	Ben Grieve	.25
124	Ron Gant	.25
125	Jeff Kent	.15
126	Rick Helling	.15
127	Russ Ortiz	.15
128	Troy Glaus	.30
129	Chan Ho Park	.25
130	Jeromy Burnitz	.15
131	Aaron Sele	.15
132	Mike Sirotka	.15
133	Brad Ausmus	.15
134	Jose Rosado	.15
135	Mariano Rivera	.25
136	Jason Giambi	.15
137	Mike Lieberthal	.15
138	Chris Carpenter	.15
139	Henry Rodriguez	.15
140	Mike Sweeney	.15
141	Vladimir Guerrero	1.00
142	Charles Nagy	.15
143	Jason Kendall	.25
144	Matt Lawton	.15
145	Michael Barrett	.15
146	David Cone	.25
147	Bobby Abreu	.15
148	Fernando Tatis	.25
149	Jose Canseco	.75
150	Craig Biggio	.40
151	Matt Mantei	.15
152	Jacque Jones	.15
153	John Halama	.15
154	Trevor Hoffman	.15
155	Rondell White	.25
156	Reggie Sanders	.15
157	Steve Finley	.15
158	Roberto Hernandez	.15
159	Geoff Jenkins	.25
160	Chris Widger	.15
161	Orel Hershiser	.15
162	Tim Hudson	.25
163	Kris Benson	.15
164	Kevin Young	.15
165	Rafael Palmeiro	.40
166	David Wells	.15
167	Ben Davis	.15
168	Jamie Moyer	.15
169	Randy Wolf	.15
170	Jeff Cirillo	.15
171	Warren Morris	.15
172	Billy Koch	.15
173	Marquis Grissom	.15
174	Geoff Blum	.15
175	Octavio Dotel	.15
176	Orlando Hernandez	.40
177	J.D. Drew	.40
178	Carlos Delgado	.50
179	Sterling Hitchcock	.15
180	Shawn Green	.50
181	Tony Clark	.30
182	Joe McEwing	.15
183	Fred McGriff	.25
184	Tony Batista	.25
185	Al Leiter	.25
186	Roger Clemens	1.00
187	Al Martin	.15
188	Eric Milton	.15
189	Bobby Smith	.15
190	Rusty Greer	.15
191	Shawn Estes	.15
192	Ken Caminiti	.25
193	Eric Karros	.25
194	Manny Ramirez	.75
195	Jim Edmonds	.15
196	Paul O'Neill	.25
197	Rico Brogna	.15
198	Ivan Rodriguez	.75
199	Doug Glanville	.15
200	Mark McGwire	3.00
201	Mark Quinn (Prospect)	1.00
202	Norm Hutchins (Prospect)	.75
203	Ramon Ortiz (Prospect)	1.00
204	Brett Laxton (Prospect)	.75
205	Jimmy Anderson (Prospect)	.75
206	Calvin Murray (Prospect)	.75
207	Wilton Veras (Prospect)	1.50
208	Chad Hermansen (Prospect)	.75
209	Nick Johnson (Prospect)	2.50
210	Kevin Barker (Prospect)	.75
211	Casey Blake (Prospect)	1.00
212	Chad Meyers (Prospect)	.75
213	Kip Wells (Prospect)	.75
214	Eric Munson (Prospect)	4.00
215	Lance Berkman (Prospect)	.75
216	Wily Pena (Prospect)	3.00
217	Gary Matthews Jr. (Prospect)	.75
218	Travis Dawkins (Prospect)	1.00
219	Josh Beckett (Prospect)	4.00
220	Tony Armas, Jr. (Prospect)	.75
221	Alfonso Soriano (Prospect)	4.00
222	Pat Burrell (Prospect)	4.00
223	*Danys Baez* (Prospect)	1.50
224	Adam Kennedy (Prospect)	.75
225	Ruben Mateo (Prospect)	1.50
226	Vernon Wells (Prospect)	1.00
227	Brian Cooper (Prospect)	.75
228	*Jeff DaVanon* (Prospect)	.75
229	Glen Barker (Prospect)	.75
230	Robinson Cancel (Prospect)	.75
231	D'Angelo Jimenez (Prospect)	.75
232	Adam Piatt (Prospect)	2.00
233	Buddy Carlyle (Prospect)	.75
234	Chad Hutchinson (Prospect)	1.00
235	Matt Riley (Prospect)	1.50
236	Cole Liniak (Prospect)	.75
237	Ben Petrick (Prospect)	.75
238	Peter Bergeron (Prospect)	.75
239	Cesar King (Prospect)	.75
240	Aaron Myette (Prospect)	.75
241	Eric Gagne (Prospect)	.75
242	Joe Nathan (Prospect)	.75
243	Bruce Chen (Prospect)	.75
244	Rob Bell (Prospect)	.75
245	*Juan Sosa* (Prospect)	1.00
246	Julio Ramirez (Prospect)	.75
247	Wade Miller (Prospect)	.75
248	*Trace Coquillette* (Prospect)	1.00
249	Robert Ramsay (Prospect)	.75
250	Rick Ankiel (Prospect)	10.00

2000 Metal Fusion

		MT
Complete Set (15):		25.00
Common Player:		.50
Inserted 1:4		
1	Ken Griffey Jr., Alex Rodriguez	4.00
2	Mark McGwire, Rick Ankiel	5.00
3	Scott Rolen, Curt Schilling	1.00
4	Pedro Martinez, Nomar Garciaparra	2.50
5	Carlos Beltran, Carlos Febles	.50
6	Sammy Sosa, Mark Grace	2.50
7	Vladimir Guerrero, Ugueth Urbina	1.50
8	Roger Clemens, Derek Jeter	2.50
9	Jeff Bagwell, Craig Biggio	1.00
10	Chipper Jones, Andruw Jones	2.00
11	Cal Ripken Jr., Mike Mussina	3.00
12	Manny Ramirez, Roberto Alomar	1.00
13	Sean Casey, Barry Larkin	.50
14	Ivan Rodriguez, Rafael Palmeiro	1.00
15	Mike Piazza, Robin Ventura	2.50

Checklists with card numbers in parentheses ( ) indicates the numbers do not appear on the card.

2000 Metal Base Shredders

	MT
Complete Set (18):	
Common Player:	
Roberto Alomar	
Michael Barrett	
Tony Clark	
Ben Davis	
Erubiel Durazo	
Troy Glaus	
Ben Grieve	
Vladimir Guerrero	
Tony Gwynn	
Todd Helton	
Eric Munson	
Rafael Palmeiro	
Manny Ramirez	
Ivan Rodriguez	
Miguel Tejada	
Mo Vaughn	
Larry Walker	
Matt Williams	

2000 Metal Heavy Metal

		MT
Complete Set (10):		60.00
Common Player:		2.00
Inserted 1:20		
1	Sammy Sosa	8.00
2	Mark McGwire	12.00
3	Ken Griffey Jr.	12.00
4	Mike Piazza	8.00
5	Nomar Garciaparra	8.00
6	Alex Rodriguez	8.00
7	Manny Ramirez	3.00
8	Jeff Bagwell	3.00
9	Chipper Jones	6.00
10	Vladimir Guerrero	4.00

2000 Metal Hit Machines

		MT
Complete Set (10):		50.00
Common Player:		2.00
Inserted 1:20		
1	Ken Griffey Jr.	12.00
2	Mark McGwire	12.00
3	Frank Thomas	4.00
4	Tony Gwynn	6.00
5	Rafael Palmeiro	2.00
6	Bernie Williams	2.50
7	Derek Jeter	8.00
8	Sammy Sosa	8.00
9	Mike Piazza	8.00
10	Chipper Jones	6.00

2000 Metal Platinum Portraits

		MT
Complete Set (10).		15.00
Common Player:		.50
Inserted 1:8		
1	Carlos Beltran	.75
2	Vladimir Guerrero	2.00
3	Manny Ramirez	1.50
4	Ivan Rodriguez	1.50
5	Sean Casey	.75
6	Alex Rodriguez	4.00
7	Derek Jeter	4.00
8	Nomar Garciaparra	4.00
9	Vernon Wells	.50
10	Shawn Green	1.00

2000 Metal Talent Show

		MT
Complete Set (15):		10.00
Common Player:		.25
Inserted 1:4		
1	Rick Ankiel	6.00
2	Matt Riley	.25
3	Chad Hermansen	.25
4	Ruben Mateo	.50
5	Eric Munson	2.00
6	Alfonso Soriano	1.50
7	Wilton Veras	.25
8	Vernon Wells	.50
9	Erubiel Durazo	.25
10	Pat Burrell	1.50
11	Ben Davis	.25
12	A.J. Burnett	.50
13	Peter Bergeron	.50
14	Mark Quinn	.50
15	Ben Petrick	.25

1993 Metallic Images Cooperstown Collection

A company known as Metallic Images Inc. created the Cooperstown Collection in 1993, a unique, 20-card set of retired players produced of durable, embossed metal with rolled edges. The set, limited to 49,900 came packaged in a collector's tin with a numbered certificate of authenticity. The cards feature full-color photos on the front and back and statistics on the reverse. Half of the players in the set are members of the Hall of Fame.

		MT
Complete Set (20):		25.00
Common Player:		.50
1	Hank Aaron	7.50
2	Vida Blue	.50
3	Yogi Berra	2.00
4	Bobby Bonds	.50
5	Lou Brock	1.00
6	Lew Burdette	.50
7	Rod Carew	1.00
8	Rocky Colavito	1.00
9	George Foster	.50
10	Bob Gibson	1.00
11	Mickey Lolich	.50
12	Willie Mays	7.50
13	Johnny Mize	1.00
14	Don Newcombe	.75
15	Gaylord Perry	1.00
16	Boog Powell	.50
17	Bill Skowron	.50
18	Warren Spahn	1.50
19	Willie Stargell	1.00
20	Luis Tiant	.50
P1	Willie Mays	6.00

1995 Metallic Images Babe Ruth

This five-card set of metal cards honors Babe Ruth in the 100th anniversary of his birth. The cards are 2-5/8" x 3-9/16" and featured gold-toned rolled edges. Fronts have familiar sepia-toned photos of the Babe with colorized backgrounds. "Cooperstown Collection" logos appear on front and back. Backs have an overall background of a ghost-image picture of Ruth at bat, along with a small sepia portrait photo, career summary and, on some cards, a few stats. The set was issued in a black embossed tin box, with cards in a cello wrapper.

		MT
Complete Boxed Set (5):		12.00
Common Card:		3.00
1	Babe Ruth (batting follow-through)	3.00
2	Babe Ruth (seated with bat on shoulders)	3.00
3	Babe Ruth (batting follow-through)	3.00
4	Babe Ruth (standing behind 10 bats)	3.00
5	Babe Ruth (batting follow-through)	3.00

1996 Metallic Impressions Cal Ripken, Jr.

Highlights of Cal Ripken's career are presented in this set of metallic baseball cards. Each 2-5/8" x 3-5/8" card has a color photo at center, surrounded by team-colored borders. Embossed at the bottom is a script version of Ripken's name with an oriole atop. In the lower-right corner is a metallic-looking home plate with "Iron Oriole". Backs repeat some of the front graphics and have identical portrait and action photos of Ripken and the magic number "2131" in lights at top. A paragraph at bottom describes a career milestone or highlight. The set was sold in an embossed lithographed metal box. Each set is accompanied by a serial numbered certificate from an edition of 29,950.

		MT
Complete Boxed Set:		25.00
Single Card:		2.00
1	Cal Ripken Jr. (Major League debut)	3.00
2	Cal Ripken Jr. (1982 - Opening Day 3B)	3.00
3	Cal Ripken Jr. (Streak begins)	3.00
4	Cal Ripken Jr. (Rookie of the Year)	3.00
5	Cal Ripken Jr. (1983)	3.00
6	Cal Ripken Jr. (Consecutive innings streak)	3.00
7	Cal Ripken Jr. (1991 MVP)	3.00
8	Cal Ripken Jr. (Gold Glover)	3.00
9	Cal Ripken Jr. (Game 2,130)	3.00
10	Cal Ripken Jr. (Game 2,131)	3.00

1997 Metallic Impressions Jackie Robinson

As part of its Cooperstown Collection series of embossed metal cards, this set was released in the 50th anniversary year of Jackie Robinson's entry into the major leagues. The set was sold in a lithographed steel box with pictures of Robinson on the top and sides. Each of the cards inside was sealed in a cellophane wrapper. Cards measure about 2-5/8" x 3-5/8" and feature monochrome or color photos lithographed on steel. Borders and other design details are embossed. A black-and-white photo of Robinson is on back, along with a few sentences about his life and career.

		MT
Complete Boxed Set (5):		20.00
Common Card:		5.00
1	Jackie Robinson (thigh-to-cap portrait)	5.00
2	Jackie Robinson (chest-to-cap portrait)	5.00
3	Jackie Robinson (batting, color)	5.00
4	Jackie Robinson (fielding)	5.00
5	Jackie Robinson (batting, b/w)	5.00

1993 Metz Bakeries

Metz Baking Company of Sioux City, Iowa produced a 40-card set utilizing drawings of players rather than photos. The company also made available uncut sheets of the sets via a mail-in offer. Cards have either a yellow background with blue pinstripes or a blue background with yellow pinstripes. Players are shown in a red, white and black porthole at center. Backs are printed in black-and-white with complete major and minor league stats. Because the cards are licensed only by the players' union and not Major League Baseball, the player paintings omit uniform logos. The unnumbered cards are checklisted here in alphabetical order. A special collectors tin to house the set was also available.

		MT
Complete Set (40):		9.00
Common Player:		.20
(1)	Dante Bichette	.25
(2)	Wade Boggs	.50
(3)	Barry Bonds	.75
(4)	Bobby Bonilla	.20
(5)	Jose Canseco	.40
(6)	Joe Carter	.20
(7)	Will Clark	.30
(8)	Roger Clemens	.75
(9)	Doug Drabek	.20
(10)	Shawon Dunston	.20
(11)	Dennis Eckersley	.20
(12)	Cecil Fielder	.20
(13)	Carlton Fisk	.50
(14)	Andres Galarraga	.30
(15)	Kirk Gibson	.20
(16)	Dwight Gooden	.25
(17)	Mark Grace	.30
(18)	Ken Griffey, Jr.	1.50
(19)	Tony Gwynn	.75
(20)	Rickey Henderson	.30
(21)	Kent Hrbek	.20
(22)	Howard Johnson	.20
(23)	Wally Joyner	.25
(24)	Dave Justice	.30
(25)	Barry Larkin	.20
(26)	Don Mattingly	.75
(27)	Jack McDowell	.20
(28)	Paul Molitor	.40
(29)	Terry Pendleton	.20
(30)	Kirby Puckett	.50
(31)	Cal Ripken, Jr.	1.25
(32)	Nolan Ryan	1.25
(33)	Ryne Sandberg	.50
(34)	Ozzie Smith	.50
(35)	Darryl Strawberry	.25
(36)	Danny Tartabull	.20
(37)	Mickey Tettleton	.20
(38)	Alan Trammell	.20
(39)	Andy Van Slyke	.20
(40)	Dave Winfield	.30

1995 Micro Stars

		MT
Complete Set:		3.25
1	Roberto Alomar	3.25
2	Moises Alou	3.25
3	Jeff Bagwell	4.75
4	Jay Bell	3.25
5	Albert Belle	4.25
6	Dante Bichette	3.25
7	Craig Biggio	3.25
8	Wade Boggs	3.25
9	Barry Bonds	3.75
10	Jose Canseco	3.25
11	Joe Carter	3.25
12	Will Clark	3.25
13	Roger Clemens	3.25
14	David Cone	3.25
15	Darren Daulton	3.25
16	Len Dykstra	3.25
17	Cecil Fielder	3.25
18	Travis Fryman	3.25
19	Andres Galarraga	3.25
20	Juan Gonzalez	3.75
21	Ken Griffey Jr.	5.00
22	Tony Gwynn	3.25
23	Rickey Henderson	3.25
24	Ken Hill	3.25
25	Randy Johnson	3.25
26	Dave Justice	3.25
27	Jimmy Key	3.25
28	Mark Langston	3.25
29	Barry Larkin	3.25
30	Kenny Lofton	4.75
31	Greg Maddux	5.00
32	Don Mattingly	4.25
33	Fred McGriff	3.25
34	Paul Molitor	3.25
35	Raul Mondesi	3.75
36	David Nied	3.25
37	Rafael Palmeiro	3.25
38	Mike Piazza	5.00
39	Kirby Puckett	4.25
40	Cal Ripken Jr.	7.00
41	Bret Saberhagen	3.25
42	Deion Sanders	4.50
43	Gary Sheffield	3.25
44	Ozzie Smith	3.25
45	Sammy Sosa	6.00
46	Frank Thomas	5.00
47	Greg Vaughn	3.25
48	Mo Vaughn	3.25
49	Robin Ventura	3.25
50	Matt Williams	4.25

1998 Midwest Sports Channel Milwaukee Brewers

For 1998, the Brewers cable television outlet sponsored the team's annual safety set, given away to kids at the June 21 game. Card fronts have player action photos vignetted on a close-up baseball background. Team and sponsor logos appear in opposite corners. Backs have a few bits of player data, a safety tip, sponsor's logo and uniform number.

		MT
Complete Set (30):		8.00
Common Player:		.25
1	Fernando Vina	.25
2	Jose Valentin	.25
3	Phil Garner	.25
5	Geoff Jenkins	.65
7	Dave Nillson	.25
8	Mark Loretta	.25
9	Marquis Grissom	.50
10	Marc Newfield	.25
13	Jeff D'Amico	.25
14	Jeff Juden	.25
16	Jesse Levis	.25
20	Jeromy Burnitz	.45
21	Cal Eldred	.25
22	Mike Matheny	.25
24	Darrin Jackson	.25
26	Jeff Cirillo	.35
27	Bob Wickman	.25
28	Mike Myers	.25
30	Bob Hamelin	.25
32	John Jaha	.35
33/39	Bobby Hughes, Eric Owens	.50
37	Steve Woodard	.25
40	Chad Fox	.25
41	Jose Mercedes	.25
42	Scott Karl	.25
43	Doug Jones	.25
46	Paul Wagner	.25
47	Al Reyes	.25
48/30	Brad Woodall, Bronswell Patrick	.50
---	Coaches (Chris Bando, Bill Castro, Lamar Johnson, Doug Mansolino, Don Rowe, Joel Youngblood)	.25

1999 Midwest Sports Channel Milwaukee Brewers

The regional cable station which carries Brewers games was the principal sponsor of the team's safety set given to fans on May 29. Cards feature color player poses against a sepia background showing Milwaukee County Stadium throughout the course of its 46-year history. Sponsor and team logos are in various corners on front along with the player's name and uniform number. Backs have a few bits of personal data, a safety message and an ad from the sponsor. Cards are checklisted here in order of uniform number.

		MT
Complete Set (30):		8.00
Common Player:		.25
1	Fernando Vina	.25
2	Jose Valentin	.25
3	Phil Garner	.25
5	Geoff Jenkins	.65
7	Sean Berry	.25
8	Mark Loretta	.25
9	Marquis Grissom	.50
14	David Nilsson	.25
16	Lou Collier	.25
20	Jeromy Burnitz	.35
21	Cal Eldred	.25
22/48	Rich Becker, Steve Falteisek	.35
23	Brian Banks	.25
24	Alex Ochoa	.25
25	Jim Abbott	.35
26	Jeff Cirillo	.35
27	Bob Wickman	.25
28	Mike Myers	.25
31	Bobby Hughes	.25
37	Steve Woodard	.25
38	Eric Plunk	.25
40	Chad Fox	.25
42	Scott Karl	.25
46	Bill Pulsipher	.25
47	Al Reyes	.25
49	David Weathers	.25
52	Rafael Roque	.25
58	Valerio de los Santos	.25
---	Coaches (Bill Campbell, Bill Castro, Ron Jackson, Jim Lefebvre, Doug Mansolino, Bob Melvin)	.25
---	Milwaukee County Stadium	.25

1993 Milk Bone Super Stars

Milk Bone Flavor Snacks and Dog Treats issued a 20-card Super Stars set in 1993 in a format comparable to the NFL Pro Line cards. The cards show the player at home with his dog, with the player shown in an action photo in the lower left corner of the card. The card backs have the player's stats and biography, along with information about the pet and a quote from the player about his dog. The cards were available, two at a time, in specially-marked packages of the company's products. The set also could be obtained through the mail by following instructions on the boxes.

		MT
Complete Set (20):		10.00
Common Player:		.50
(1)	Paul Molitor	1.00
(2)	Tom Glavine	.80
(3)	Barry Larkin	.50
(4)	Mark McGwire	1.00
(5)	Bill Swift	.50
(6)	Ken Caminiti	.60
(7)	Will Clark	.75
(8)	Rafael Palmeiro	.75
(9)	Matt Young	.50
(10)	Todd Zeile	.50
(11)	Wally Joyner	.50
(12)	Cal Ripken Jr.	3.00
(13)	Tom Foley	.50
(14)	Ben McDonald	.50
(15)	Larry Walker	.90
(16)	Rob Dibble	.50
(17)	Brett Butler	.50
(18)	Joe Girardi	.50
(19)	Brady Anderson	.65
(20)	Craig Biggio	.60

1989 Milk Duds Pittsburgh Pirates

This set of Pirates photo-cards carries on its backs advertising for various brands of Leaf candies, principally Milk Duds. The 3-3/8" x 5-1/2" cards have color portrait photo on front with the player's name near the bottom and a team logo at bottom center. Backs have a few vital statistics, candy advertising and/or free ticket or contest offers. The cards are numbered by uniform number, but are listed here in alphabetical order.

		MT
Complete Set (38):		24.00
Common Player:		.75
(1)	Pirate Parrot (mascot)	.75
(2)	Rafael Belliard	.75
(3)	Dann Bilardello	.75
(4)	Barry Bonds	6.00
(5)	Sid Bream	.75
(6)	Bobby Bonilla	2.00
(7)	John Cangelosi	.75
(8)	Benny Distefano	.75
(9)	Rich Donnelly	.75
(10)	Doug Drabek	.90
(11)	Brian Fisher	.75
(12)	Miguel Garcia	.75
(13)	Jim Gott	.75
(14)	Neal Heaton	.75
(15)	Bruce Kimm	.75
(16)	Jeff King	.90
(17)	Bob Kipper	.75
(18)	Randy Kramer	.75
(19)	Gene Lamont	.75
(20)	Bill Landrum	.75
(21)	Mike LaValliere	.75
(22)	Jim Leyland	.75
(23)	Jose Lind	.75
(24)	Morris Madden	.75
(25)	Milt May	.75
(26)	Ray Miller	.75
(27)	Junior Ortiz	.75
(28)	Tom Prince	.75
(29)	Rey Quinones	.75
(30)	Gary Redus	.75
(31)	R.J. Reynolds	.75
(32)	Jeff Robinson	.75
(33)	Tommy Sandt	.75
(34)	John Smiley	.75
(35)	Dorn Taylor	.75
(36)	Andy Van Slyke	1.00
(37)	Bob Walk	.75
(38)	Glenn Wilson	.75

1997 Milk Mustache Trading Cards

Sponsored by the National Fluid Milk Processor Promotion Board (really), this nine-card panel was an advertising insert in the Oct., 1997, issue of Sports Illustrated for Kids. The perforated panel measures about 7-1/2" x 10-1/2", with each card measuring the standard 2-1/2" x 3-1/2" and perforated on two, three or four sides, depending on its placement on the sheet. Player portrait photos are set on a silver-look background. Cap and uniform logos have been eliminated and a milk moustache added. "MILK" appears in white in a purple stripe at the top of each player's card. Backs have a baseball tip and a milk tip ascribed to each player.

		MT
Complete Sheet:		10.00
Complete Set (9):		6.00
Common Player:		.50
1	Alex Rodriguez	4.00
2	Nomar Garciaparra	2.00
3	Andy Pettitte	.50
4	Darin Erstad	1.00
5	Jason Kendall	.50
6	Vladimir Guerrero	1.50
7	Scott Rolen	1.25
8	Tony Clark	.70
--	Header card	.50

1990 Miller Beer Milwaukee Brewers

This 32-card set was given away with an album to adults attending an August Brewers game. Cards are standard 2-1/2" x 3-1/2" and feature borderless color photos above gold and black bottom stripes. The beer company's logo is featured in the upper-right corner, with the team logo at lower-left. Black-and-white backs feature player stats. The set has been checklisted below in alphabetical order. Cards are not numbered.

		MT
Complete Set w/Album (32):		12.00
Common Player:		.25
(1)	Chris Bosio	.25
(2)	Greg Brock	.25
(3)	Chuck Crim	.25
(4)	Rob Deer	.25
(5)	Edgar Diaz	.25
(6)	Tom Edens	.25
(7)	Mike Felder	.25
(8)	Tom Filer	.25
(9)	Jim Gantner	.25
(10)	Darryl Hamilton	.40
(11)	Teddy Higuera	.25
(12)	Mark Knudson	.25
(13)	Bill Krueger	.25
(14)	Paul Mirabella	.25
(15)	Paul Molitor	3.00
(16)	Jaime Navarro	.25
(17)	Charlie O'Brien	.25
(18)	Dave Parker	.75
(19)	Dan Plesac	.25
(20)	Dennis Powell	.25
(21)	Ron Robinson	.25
(22)	Bob Sebra	.25
(23)	Gary Sheffield	2.50
(24)	Bill Spiers	.25
(25)	B.J. Surhoff	.35
(26)	Dale Sveum	.25
(27)	Tom Trebelhorn	.25
(28)	Greg Vaughn	1.00
(29)	Randy Veres	.25
(30)	Bill Wegman	.25
(31)	Robin Yount	4.00
(32)	Coaches (Don Baylor, Ray Burris, Duffy Dyer, Andy Etchebarren, Larry Haney)	.25

1991 Miller Beer Milwaukee Brewers

The Miller High Life Brewing Company, in conjunction with the Milwaukee Brewers, sponsored a 32-card limited edition baseball card set in 1991. The set, which features 30 cards of Brewer players plus additional cards of manager Tom Trebelhorn and his coaching staff, employs a home plate window for the front photo, with the player's name and words "Miller High Life" along the bottom of the card. Complete major and minor league stats are printed on the black-and-white backs, which also include sponsors' logos.

		MT
Complete Set w/Album (32):		12.00
Common Player:		.25
(1)	Don August	.25
(2)	James Austin	.25
(3)	Dante Bichette	1.50
(4)	Chris Bosio	.25
(5)	Kevin Brown	.25
(6)	Chuck Crim	.25
(7)	Rick Dempsey	.25
(8)	Jim Gantner	.25
(9)	Darryl Hamilton	.30
(10)	Teddy Higuera	.25
(11)	Darren Holmes	.25
(12)	Jim Hunter	.25
(13)	Mark Knudson	.25
(14)	Mark Lee	.25
(15)	Julio Machado	.25
(16)	Candy Maldonado	.25
(17)	Paul Molitor	3.00
(18)	Jaime Navarro	.25
(19)	Edwin Nunez	.25
(20)	Dan Plesac	.25
(21)	Willie Randolph	.25
(22)	Ron Robinson	.25
(23)	Gary Sheffield	2.00
(24)	Bill Spiers	.25
(25)	Franklin Stubbs	.25
(26)	B.J. Surhoff	.35
(27)	Dale Sveum	.25
(28)	Tom Treblehorn	.25
(29)	Greg Vaughn	.65
(30)	Bill Wegman	.25
(31)	Robin Yount	4.00
----	Coaches (Don Baylor, Ray Burris, Duffy Dyer, Andy Etchebarren, Larry Haney, Fred Stanley)	

1994 Miller Genuine Draft Milwaukee Brewers

MT

(See 1994 Lite Beer Milwaukee Brewers)

1982 Milwaukee Brewers Police

The inaugural Milwaukee Brewers police set contains 30 cards in a 2-13/16" x 4-1/8" format. There are 26 players included in the set, which is numbered by player uniform number. Unnumbered cards were also issued for general manager Harry Dalton, manager Buck Rodgers, the coaches and a team card with checklist. The full-color photos are especially attractive, printed on the cards' crisp white stock. A number of Wisconsin law enforcement agencies distributed the cards and credit lines on the card fronts were changed accordingly.

		MT
Complete Set (30):		10.00
Common Player:		.25
4	Paul Molitor	2.00
5	Ned Yost	.25
7	Don Money	.25
9	Larry Hisle	.25
10	Bob McClure	.25
11	Ed Romero	.25
13	Roy Howell	.25
15	Cecil Cooper	.35
17	Jim Gantner	.25
19	Robin Yount	3.00
20	Gorman Thomas	.25
22	Charlie Moore	.25
23	Ted Simmons	.25
24	Ben Oglivie	.25
26	Kevin Bass	.25
28	Jamie Easterly	.25
29	Mark Brouhard	.25
30	Moose Haas	.25
34	Rollie Fingers	1.00
35	Randy Lerch	.25
37	Buck Rodgers	.25
41	Jim Slaton	.25
45	Doug Jones	.25
46	Jerry Augustine	.25
47	Dwight Bernard	.25
48	Mike Caldwell	.25
50	Pete Vuckovich	.25
---	Team photo/checklist	.25
---	Harry Dalton (general mgr.)	.25
---	Coaches card (Pat Dobson, Larry Haney, Ron Hansen, Cal McLish, Buck Rogers, Harry Warner)	.25

1983 Milwaukee Brewers Police

16 MARSHALL EDWARDS — OF
The Milwaukee Police Department
Presents The 1983
Milwaukee Brewers

Similar to 1982, a number of issuer variations exist for the 1983 Brewers police set, as law enforcement agencies throughout the state distributed the set with their own credit lines on the cards. At least 28 variations are known to exist, with those issued by smaller agencies being scarcest. Prices quoted below are for the most common variations, generally the Milwaukee police department and a few small-town departments whose entire supply of police cards seem to have fallen into dealers' hands. Some specialists are willing to pay a premium for the scarcer departments' issues. The 30, 2-13/16" x 4-1/8" cards include 29 players and coaches, along with a team card (with a checklist back). The team card and group coaches' card are unnumbered, while the others are numbered by uniform number.

		MT
Complete Set (30):		10.00
Common Player:		.25
4	Paul Molitor	2.50
5	Ned Yost	.25
7	Don Money	.25
8	Rob Picciolo	.25
10	Bob McClure	.25
11	Ed Romero	.25
13	Roy Howell	.25
15	Cecil Cooper	.25
16	Marshall Edwards	.25
17	Jim Gantner	.25
19	Robin Yount	3.00
20	Gorman Thomas	.25
21	Don Sutton	1.50
22	Charlie Moore	.25
23	Ted Simmons	.25
24	Ben Oglivie	.25
26	Bob Skube	.25
27	Pete Ladd	.25
28	Jamie Easterly	.25
30	Moose Haas	.25
32	Harvey Kuenn	.30
34	Rollie Fingers	1.50
40	Bob L. Gibson	.25
41	Jim Slaton	.25
42	Tom Tellmann	.25
46	Jerry Augustine	.25
48	Mike Caldwell	.25
50	Pete Vuckovich	.25
---	Team photo/checklist	.25
---	Coaches Card (Pat Dobson, Dave Garcia, Larry Haney, Ron Hansen)	.25

1984 Milwaukee Brewers Police

20 DON SUTTON — P
The Winneconne Police Department
Presents The 1984
MILWAUKEE BREWERS

The king of the variations again in 1984, the Milwaukee Brewers set has been found with more than 50 different police agencies' credit lines on the front of the cards. Once again, law enforcement agencies statewide participated in distributing the sets. Some departments also include a badge of the participating agency on the card backs. The full-color cards measure 2-13/16" x 4-1/8". There are 28 numbered player and manager cards, along with an unnumbered coaches card and a team card. Player names, uniform numbers and positions are listed on each card front. Prices listed are for the most common variety (Milwaukee police department); sets issued by smaller departments may be worth a premium to specialists.

		MT
Complete Set (30):		7.50
Common Player:		.15
2	Randy Ready	.15
4	Paul Molitor	2.00
8	Jim Sundberg	.15
9	Rene Lachemann	.15
10	Bob McClure	.15
11	Ed Romero	.15
13	Roy Howell	.15
14	Dion James	.15
15	Cecil Cooper	.20
17	Jim Gantner	.15
19	Robin Yount	3.00
20	Don Sutton	1.00
21	Bill Schroeder	.15
22	Charlie Moore	.15
23	Ted Simmons	.15
24	Ben Oglivie	.15
25	Bobby Clark	.15
27	Pete Ladd	.15
28	Rick Manning	.15
29	Mark Brouhard	.15
30	Moose Haas	.15
34	Rollie Fingers	1.00
42	Tom Tellmann	.15
43	Chuck Porter	.15
46	Jerry Augustine	.15
47	Jaime Cocanower	.15
48	Mike Caldwell	.15
50	Pete Vuckovich	.15
---	Team photo/checklist	.15
---	Coaches Card (Pat Dobson, Dave Garcia, Larry Haney, Tom Trebelhorn)	.15

1985 Milwaukee Brewers Police

49 Ted Higuera P
The Milwaukee Police Department
and The Milwaukee Journal
present the 1985
Milwaukee Brewers

The Brewers changed the size of their annual police set in 1985, but almost imperceptibly. The full-color cards are 2-3/4" x 4-1/8", a slight 1/16" narrower than the four previous efforts. Player and team name on the card fronts are much bolder than in previous years. Once again, numerous area police groups distributed the sets, leading to nearly 60 variations, as each agency put their own credit line on the cards. Card backs include the Brewers logo, a safety tip and, in some cases, a badge of the participating law enforcement group. There are 27 numbered player cards (by uniform number) and three unnumbered cards - team roster, coaches and a newspaper carrier card. Prices are for the most common departments.

		MT
Complete Set (30):		6.00
Common Player:		.15
2	Randy Ready	.15
4	Paul Molitor	1.50
5	Doug Loman	.15
7	Paul Householder	.15
10	Bob McClure	.15
11	Ed Romero	.15
14	Dion James	.15
15	Cecil Cooper	.15
17	Jim Gantner	.15
18	Danny Darwin	.15
19	Robin Yount	2.50
21	Bill Schroeder	.15
22	Charlie Moore	.15
23	Ted Simmons	.15
24	Ben Oglivie	.15
26	Brian Giles	.15
27	Pete Ladd	.15
28	Rick Manning	.15
29	Mark Brouhard	.15
30	Moose Haas	.15
31	George Bamberger	.15
34	Rollie Fingers	.90
40	Bob L. Gibson	.15
41	Ray Searage	.15
47	Jaime Cocanower	.15
48	Ray Burris	.15
49	Ted Higuera	.25
50	Pete Vuckovich	.15
---	Coaches Card (Andy Etchebarren, Larry Haney, Frank Howard, Tony Muser, Herm Starrette)	.15
---	Team Photo	.15

1986 Milwaukee Brewers Police

45 Rob Deer OF
The Fond du Lac Police Dept, KFIZ Radio,
and National Exchange Bank & Trust
present the 1986
Milwaukee Brewers

The Milwaukee Brewers, in conjunction with the Milwaukee Police Department, WTMJ Radio and Kinney Shoes, produced this attractive police safety set of 30 cards. The cards measure 2-13/16" x 4-1/2". A thin black border encloses a full-color Player photo on the front. The card backs give a safety tip and promos for the sponsor. The cards were distributed throughout the state of Wisconsin by numerous police departments; those of the smaller departments generally being scarcer than those issued in the big cities. Prices quoted below are for the most common departments' issues.

		MT
Complete Set (30):		6.50
Common Player:		.15
1	Ernest Riles	.20
2	Randy Ready	.15
3	Juan Castillo	.15
4	Paul Molitor	1.50
7	Paul Householder	.15
10	Bob McClure	.15
11	Rick Cerone	.15
13	Billy Jo Robidoux	.15
15	Cecil Cooper	.20
16	Mike Felder	.15
17	Jim Gantner	.15
18	Danny Darwin	.15
19	Robin Yount	2.00
20	Juan Nieves	.15
21	Bill Schroeder	.15
22	Charlie Moore	.15
24	Ben Oglivie	.20
25	Mark Clear	.15
28	Rick Manning	.15
31	George Bamberger	.15
37	Dan Plesac	.20
39	Tim Leary	.15
41	Ray Searage	.15
43	Chuck Porter	.15
45	Rob Deer	.15
46	Bill Wegman	.15
47	Jamie Cocanower	.15
49	Ted Higuera	.20
---	Coaches Card (Andy Etchebarren, Larry Haney, Frank Howard, Tony Muser, Herm Starrette)	.15
---	Team Photo/Roster	.15

1987 Milwaukee Brewers Police

The Milwaukee Brewers issued a safety set in 1987 for the sixth consecutive year. As in the past, many local police departments throughout Wisconsin participated in the giveaway program. The Milwaukee version was sponsored by Kinney Shoe Stores and WTMJ Radio and was handed out to youngsters attending the Baseball Card Day at County Stadium on May 9th. The cards, which measure 2-1/4" x 4-1/8", feature full-color photos plus a safety tip on the backs. Chris Bosio can be found with a uniform number of 26 or 29. The card was corrected to #29 in later printings.

		MT
Complete Set (30):		5.00
Common Player:		.15
1	Ernest Riles	.15
2	Edgar Diaz	.15
3	Juan Castillo	.15
4	Paul Molitor	1.50
5	B.J. Surhoff	.50
7	Dale Sveum	.15
9	Greg Brock	.15
13	Billy Jo Robidoux	.15
14	Jim Paciorek	.15
15	Cecil Cooper	.15
16	Mike Felder	.15
17	Jim Gantner	.15
19	Robin Yount	2.50
20	Juan Nieves	.15
21	Bill Schroeder	.15
25	Mark Clear	.15
26a	Glenn Braggs	.15
26b	Chris Bosio	.30
28	Rick Manning	.15
29	Chris Bosio	.30
32	Chuck Crim	.15
34	Mark Ciardi	.15
37	Dan Plesac	.15
38	John Henry Johnson	.15
40	Mike Birbeck	.15
42	Tom Trebelhorn	.15
45	Rob Deer	.15
46	Bill Wegman	.15
49	Ted Higuera	.15
---	Coaches Card (Andy Etchebarren, Larry Haney, Chuck Hartenstein, Dave Hilton, Tony Muser)	.15
---	Team Photo/Roster	.15

1988 Milwaukee Brewers Police

3 Juan Castillo IF
The Marathon County Sheriff's Dept. and
Brickner Chrysler Center Inc.
2525 Grand Avenue, Wausau, WI 54401
present the 1988
Milwaukee Brewers

This 30-card set is the seventh annual issue sponsored by the Milwaukee Police Department for local distribution during a crime prevention promotion. The full-color card fronts (2-3/4" x 4-1/8") feature the same design as the 1987 set with white borders and a black frame outling the player photo and name. Sponsor credits and the team name are listed below the photo. The vertical card backs are blue on white with messages from the player and sponsors. Two group photos - one of the team's five coaches and one of the team (with a checklist back) - are unnumbered and printed horizontally. Card numbers refer to the players uniform numbers.

		MT
Complete Set (30):		4.00
Common Player:		.15
1	Ernest Riles	.15
3	Juan Castillo	.15
4	Paul Molitor	1.25
5	B.J. Surhoff	.30
7	Dale Sveum	.15
9	Greg Brock	.15
11	Charlie O'Brien	.15
14	Jim Adduci	.15
16	Mike Felder	.15
17	Jim Gantner	.15
19	Robin Yount	2.00
20	Juan Nieves	.15

21	Bill Schroeder	.15
23	Joey Meyer	.15
25	Mark Clear	.15
26	Glenn Braggs	.15
28	Odell Jones	.15
29	Chris Bosio	.15
30	Steve Kiefer	.15
32	Chuck Crim	.15
33	Jay Aldrich	.15
37	Dan Plesac	.15
40	Mike Birkbeck	.15
42	Tom Trebelhorn	.15
43	Dave Stapleton	.15
45	Rob Deer	.15
46	Bill Wegman	.15
49	Ted Higuera	.15
---	Coaches Card (Andy Etchebarren, Larry Haney, Chuck Hartenstein, Dave Hilton, Tony Muser)	.15
---	Team photo	.15

1988 Milwaukee Brewers team issue

These 4" x 5-1/2" black-and-white cards were available from the team at $5 per set or 50 cents per card. All players except Mike Felder are pictured in portrait photos with white borders. In the bottom border are the player's name, position and team name. Felder's card shows him in a batting pose. Backs are blank. Cards are checklisted here alphabetically.

		MT
Complete Set (37):		20.00
Common Player:		1.00
(1)	Jim Adduci	1.00
(2)	Don August	1.00
(3)	Mike Birkbeck	1.00
(4)	Chris Bosio	1.00
(5)	Glenn Braggs	1.00
(6)	Greg Brock	1.00
(7)	Juan Castillo	1.00
(8)	Mark Clear	1.00
(9)	Chuck Crim	1.00
(10)	Rob Deer	1.00
(11)	Andy Etchebarren	1.00
(12)	Mike Felder	1.00
(13)	Tom Filer	1.00
(14)	Jim Gantner	1.00
(15)	Darryl Hamilton	1.50
(16)	Larry Haney	1.00
(17)	Chuck Hartenstein	1.00
(18)	Teddy Higuera	1.00
(19)	Dave Hilton	1.00
(20)	Odell Jones	1.00
(21)	Steve Kiefer	1.00
(22)	Jeffrey Leonard	1.00
(23)	Joey Meyer	1.00
(24)	Paul Mirabella	1.00
(25)	Paul Molitor	4.00
(26)	Tony Muser	1.00
(27)	Juan Nieves	1.00
(28)	Charlie O'Brien	1.00
(29)	Dan Plesac	1.00
(30)	Billy Jo Robidoux	1.00
(31)	Bill Schroeder	1.00
(32)	Dave Stapleton	1.00
(33)	B.J. Surhoff	2.00
(34)	Dale Sveum	1.00
(35)	Tom Trebelhorn	1.00
(36)	Bill Wegman	1.00
(37)	Robin Yount	5.00

1989 Milwaukee Brewers Police

30 Terry Francona OF
Iola, Manawa & Marion Police Depts., and Wisconsin Power and Light present the 1989
Milwaukee Brewers

The Milwaukee Brewers, in conjunction with various corporate and civic sponsors, issued a 30-card police set in 1989, the eighth consecutive police set issued by the club. Some 95 law enforcement agencies in Wisconsin participated in the program, each releasing their own version of the same set. The cards measure 2-13/16" x 4-1/8" and feature full-color action photos with the player's name, uniform number and position below, along with the sponsoring agencies. The backs include the traditional safety messages. The cards were distributed in complete sets at a stadium promotion and also handed out individually over the course of the summer by uniformed police officers in various Wisconsin cities and counties.

		MT
Complete Set (30):		5.00
Common Player:		.15
1	Gary Sheffield	1.50
4	Paul Molitor	1.00
5	B.J. Surhoff	.25
6	Bill Spiers	.15
7	Dale Sveum	.15
9	Greg Brock	.15
14	Gus Polidor	.15
16	Mike Felder	.15
17	Jim Gantner	.15
19	Robin Yount	1.50
20	Juan Nieves	.15
22	Charlie O'Brien	.15
23	Joey Meyer	.15
25	Dave Engle	.15
26	Glenn Braggs	.15
27	Paul Mirabella	.15
29	Chris Bosio	.15
30	Terry Francona	.15
32	Chuck Crim	.15
37	Dan Plesac	.15
40	Mike Birkbeck	.15
41	Mark Knudson	.15
42	Tom Trebelhorn	.15
45	Rob Deer	.15
46	Bill Wegman	.15
48	Bryan Clutterbuck	.15
49	Teddy Higuera	.15
---	Team photo	.15
---	Coaching staff	.15

1989 Milwaukee Brewers Yearbook Cards

Included in the team's special 20th anniversary edition yearbook was a set of 18 player cards stapled into the center of the book. Printed on a 16-1/2" x 11" cardboard sheet, there are nine cards per page, perforated on two, three or four sides, depending on sheet position. Cards have a pale yellow background. A blue and bright yellow 20th Anniversary team logo appears in the lower-right corner with the player's uniform number, name and position stacked at left in black. All but one of the photos are game-action shots. Backs are printed in black and include complete major and minor league stats. Cards are checklisted here by uniform number.

	MT
Complete Set, Singles (18):	8.00
Complete Yearbook:	10.00
Common Player:	.25

1	Gary Sheffield	1.50
4	Paul Molitor	2.50
5	B.J. Surhoff	.50
7	Dale Sveum	.25
9	Greg Brock	.25
17	Jim Gantner	.25
19	Robin Yount	4.00
20	Juan Nieves	.25
26	Glenn Braggs	.25
29	Chris Bosio	.25
32	Chuck Crim	.25
37	Dan Plesac	.25
38	Don August	.25
40	Mike Birkbeck	.25
42	Tom Trebelhorn	.25
45	Rob Deer	.25
46	Bill Wegman	.25
49	Teddy Higuera	.25

1990 Milwaukee Brewers Police

Brewers
4 Paul Molitor IF
The Chilton Police Department
Chilton Food Mart & Valley Bank-Chilton
present the 1990
Milwaukee Brewers

Blue borders are featured on the front of the 1990 Brewers Police/Fire Safety set. The cards are numbered according to uniform number and public service messages appear on the card backs. The 2-13/16" x 4-1/8" cards were distributed by various Wisconsin police departments.

		MT
Complete Set (30):		5.00
Common Player:		.20
2	Eddie Diaz	.20
4	Paul Molitor	1.00
5	B. J. Surhoff	.30
6	Bill Spiers	.20
7	Dale Sveum	.20
9	Greg Brock	.20
11	Gary Sheffield	.60
14	Gus Polidor	.20
16	Mike Felder	.20
17	Jim Gantner	.20
19	Robin Yount	1.50
22	Charlie O'Brien	.20
23	Greg Vaughn	.45
26	Glenn Braggs	.20
27	Paul Mirabella	.20
28	Tom Filer	.20
29	Chris Bosio	.20
31	Jaime Navarro	.20
32	Chuck Crim	.20
34	Billy Bates	.20
36	Tony Fossas	.20
37	Dan Plesac	.20
38	Don August	.20
39	Dave Parker	.30
41	Mark Knudson	.20
42	Tom Trebelhorn	.20
45	Rob Deer	.20
49	Ted Higuera	.20
---	Coaches (Don Baylor, Ray Burris, Duffy Dyer, Larry Haney, Andy Etchebarren)	.20
---	Team photo/roster card	.20

1990 Milwaukee Brewers team issue

These 4" x 5-1/2" black-and-white, blank-back cards were produced by the Brewers for distribution to media and for use by players in answering fan requests. All photos are neck-to-cap portraits with players in pinstriped jerseys. The unnumbered cards have player name in the border at bottom-left, his position at center and team name at right. The photos are checklisted here in alphabetical order.

		MT
Complete Set (29):		19.00
Common Player:		.50
(1)	Don Baylor	1.00
(2)	Chris Bosio	.50
(3)	Greg Brock	.50
(4)	Ray Burris	.50
(5)	Chuck Crim	.50
(6)	Rob Deer	.50
(7)	Duffy Dyer	.50
(8)	Andy Etchebarren	.50
(9)	Mike Felder	.50
(10)	Tom Filer	.50
(11)	Jim Gantner	.50
(12)	Darryl Hamilton	.65
(13)	Larry Haney	.50
(14)	Teddy Higuera	.50
(15)	Mark Knudson	.50
(16)	Bill Krueger	.50
(17)	Paul Mirabella	.50
(18)	Paul Molitor	3.00
(19)	Charlie O'Brien	.50
(20)	Dave Parker	1.00
(21)	Dan Plesac	.50
(22)	Gary Sheffield	1.50
(23)	Bill Spiers	.50
(24)	B.J. Surhoff	.65
(25)	Dale Sveum	.50
(26)	Tom Trebelhorn	.50
(27)	Greg Vaughn	1.50
(28)	Bill Wegman	.50
(29)	Robin Yount	3.00

1990 Milwaukee Brewers Yearbook Cards

Printed on cardboard stock and stapled into the center of the team's 1990 yearbook was a set of 18 cards. The sheet is 16-1/2" x 11" overall. Each page has nine 2-5/8" x 3-1/2" cards perforated on two, three or four sides, depending on sheet position. Above-left and below-right of the color player poses are yellow triangles with blue pinstripes. The team's scrip logo is in the same team colors in the lower-left of the photo. The player's name, position abbreviation and uniform number are in yellow in the upper-right corner. Backs are printed in blue and include complete major and minor league stats. The checklist is presented here by uniform number.

	MT
Complete Set, Singles (18):	8.00
Complete Yearbook:	10.00
Common Player:	.25

4	Paul Molitor	2.50
5	B.J. Surhoff	.50
6	Bill Spiers	.25
7	Dale Sveum	.25
9	Greg Brock	.25
17	Jim Gantner	.25
19	Robin Yount	4.00
26	Glenn Braggs	.25
28	Tom Filer	.25
29	Chris Bosio	.25
31	Jaime Navarro	.25
32	Chuck Crim	.25
37	Dan Plesac	.25
38	Don August	.25
39	Dave Parker	.35
42	Tom Trebelhorn	.25
45	Rob Deer	.25
49	Ted Higuera	.25

1991 Milwaukee Brewers Police

The Milwaukee Brewers are featured on a 1991 team set sponsored by several Milwaukee area police departments and Delicious Brand Cookies and Crackers. The 30-card set is in full color with light gray border on the front and the backs are unnumbered and contain safety tips from the players.

		MT
Complete Set (30):		5.00
Common Player:		.25
(1)	Robin Yount	1.50
(2)	Rick Dempsey	.25
(3)	Jamie Navarro	.25
(4)	Darryl Hamilton	.25
(5)	Bill Spiers	.25
(6)	Dante Bichette	.65
(7)	Dan Plesac	.25
(8)	Don August	.25
(9)	Willie Randolph	.25
(10)	Franklin Stubbs	.25
(11)	Julio Machado	.25
(12)	Greg Vaughn	.40
(13)	Chris Bosio	.25
(14)	Mark Knudson	.25
(15)	Paul Molitor	1.00
(16)	Kevin Brown	.25
(17)	Ron Robinson	.25
(18)	Bill Wegman	.25
(19)	Teddy Higuera	.25
(20)	Mark Lee	.25
(21)	B.J. Surhoff	.35
(22)	Candy Maldonado	.25
(23)	Chuck Crim	.25
(24)	Dale Sveum	.25
(25)	Jim Gantner	.25
(26)	Greg Brock	.25
(27)	Gary Sheffield	.50
(28)	Edwin Nunez	.25
(29)	Tom Trebelhorn	.25
(30)	Coaches (Don Baylor, Ray Burris, Duffy Dyer, Andy Etchebarren, Larry Haney, Fred Stanley)	.25

1992 Milwaukee Brewers Police

The 1992 Milwaukee Brewers Police set consists of 30-cards in the standard, 2-1/2" x 3-1/2" format. The yellow-bordered cards were produced by Delicious Brand Cookies and Crackers and distributed by local Wisconsin police departments in cooperation with the Brewers.

	MT
Complete Set (30):	4.00
Common Player:	.25
(1) Andy Allanson	.25
(2) James Austin	.25
(3) Dante Bichette	.50
(4) Ricky Bones	.25
(5) Chris Bosio	.25
(6) Mike Fetters	.25
(7) Scott Fletcher	.25
(8) Jim Gantner	.25
(9) Phil Garner	.25
(10) Darryl Hamilton	.25
(11) Doug Henry	.25
(12) Teddy Higuera	.25
(13) Pat Listach	.25
(14) Jamie Navarro	.25
(15) Edwin Nunez	.25
(16) Tim McIntosh	.25
(17) Paul Molitor	.75
(18) Jesse Orosco	.25
(19) Dan Plesac	.25
(20) Ron Robinson	.25
(21) Bruce Ruffin	.25
(22) Kevin Seitzer	.25
(23) Bill Spiers	.25
(24) Franklin Stubbs	.25
(25) William Suero	.25
(26) B.J. Surhoff	.35
(27) Greg Vaughn	.30
(28) Bill Wegman	.25
(29) Robin Yount	1.00
(30) Coaches (Bill Castro, Duffy Dyer, Mike Easler, Tim Foli, Don Rowe)	.25

1992 Milwaukee Brewers team-issue 5x7s

These 5" x 7" black-and-white blank-back photos were produced by the Brewers for distribution to media and for use by players in answering fan requests. All photos are portrait, with most showing players in blue mesh warm-up jerseys. Some photos were re-issued the following year and some variations exist, presumably where inventories ran out. The unnumbered pictures have player name in the border at bottom-left, his position at center and team name at right. The photos are checklisted here in alphabetical order.

	MT
Complete Set (44):	35.00
Common Player:	.50
(1) Andy Allanson	.50
(2) James Austin	.50
(3) Dante Bichette	1.00
(4) Ricky Bones	.50
(5) Chris Bosio	.50
(6) Bill Castro	.50
(7) Duffy Dyer	.50
(8) Mike Easler	.50
(9) Cal Eldred (mesh jersey)	.75
(10) Cal Eldred (pinstripes)	.90
(11) Mike Fetters	.50
(12) Scott Fletcher	.50
(13) Tim Foli	.50
(14) Jim Gantner	.50
(15) Phil Garner	.50
(16) Chris George	.50
(17) Darryl Hamilton (mesh jersey)	.65
(18) Darryl Hamilton (pinstripes)	.85
(19) Doug Henry	.50
(20) Ted Higuera	.50
(21) Mark Kiefer	.50
(22) Joe Kmak	.50
(23) Jeff Kunkel	.50
(24) Pat Listach	.50
(25) Tim McIntosh	.50
(26) Paul Molitor	3.00
(27) Jamie Navarro	.50
(28) Edwin Nunez	.50
(29) Jesse Orosco	.50
(30) Dan Plesac	.50
(31) Ron Robinson	.50
(32) Don Rowe	.50
(33) Bruce Ruffin	.50
(34) Kevin Seitzer	.50
(35) Bill Spiers	.50
(36) Franklin Stubbs	.50
(37) William Suero	.50
(38) B.J. Surhoff	.75
(39) Greg Vaughn (mesh jersey)	1.50
(40) Greg Vaughn (pinstripes)	2.50
(41) Bill Wegman (mesh jersey)	.50
(42) Bill Wegman (pinstripes)	.75
(43) Robin Yount (mesh jersey)	3.00
(44) Robin Yount (pinstripes)	4.50

1993 Milwaukee Brewers Police

The 1993 Milwaukee Brewers Police set included 30 cards with a graduated blue border. The left side has a '93 Brewers flag along the border in yellow, with the player's name in the upper right corner in white. The backs, which are white with black print, feature quotes from the player pictured. The cards are not numbered and the set also includes a card commemorating Robin Yount's 3,000th hit.

	MT
Complete Set (30):	6.00
Common Player:	.25
(1) Bernie Brewer (mascot)	.25
(2) Phil Garner	.25
(3) Yount's 3,000th Hit (Robin Yount)	.50
(4) Mark Kiefer	.25
(5) Bill Spiers	.25
(6) John Jaha	.40
(7) Bill Wegman	.25
(8) Ted Higuera	.25
(9) Greg Vaughn	.40
(10) Kevin Reimer	.25
(11) Doug Henry	.25
(12) William Suero	.25
(13) Dave Nilsson	.30
(14) James Austin	.25
(15) Mike Fetters	.25
(16) Ricky Bones	.25
(17) Jaime Navarro	.25
(18) Jesse Orosco	.25
(19) Darryl Hamilton	.25
(20) Cal Eldred	.30
(21) Tim McIntosh	.25
(22) Dickie Thon	.25
(23) Graeme Lloyd	.25
(24) Pat Listach	.25
(25) Joe Kmak	.25
(26) Alex Diaz	.25
(27) Robin Yount	1.00
(28) Tom Brunansky	.25
(29) B.J. Surhoff	.30
(30) Bill Doran	.25

1993 Milwaukee Brewers team-issue 5x7s

These 5" x 7" black-and-white, blank-back photos were produced by the team for distribution to media and for use by players in answering fan requests. All photos are portraits showing players in dark mesh warm-up jerseys. The unnumbered pictures have player name in the border at bottom-left, position at center and team name at right. The photos are checklisted here in alphabetical order.

	MT
Complete Set (41):	24.00
Common Player:	.50
(1) James Austin	.50
(2) Juan Bell	.50
(3) Mike Boddicker	.50
(4) Ricky Bones	.50
(5) Tom Brunansky	.50
(6) Bill Castro	.50
(7) Gene Clines	.50
(8) Alex Diaz	.50
(9) Bill Doran	.50
(10) Duffy Dyer	.50
(11) Cal Eldred	.75
(12) Mike Fetters	.50
(13) Tim Foli	.50
(14) Phil Garner	.50
(15) Darryl Hamilton	.65
(16) Doug Henry	.50
(17) Ted Higuera	.50
(18) John Jaha	.90
(19) Joe Kmak	.50
(20) Tom Lampkin	.50
(21) Pat Listach	.50
(22) Graeme Lloyd	.50
(23) Carlos Maldonado	.50
(24) Josias Manzanillo	.50
(25) Tim McIntosh	.50
(26) Angel Miranda	.50
(27) Jamie Navarro	.50
(28) David Nilsson	.50
(29) Rafael Novoa	.50
(30) Troy O'Leary	.50
(31) Jesse Orosco	.50
(32) Kevin Reimer	.50
(33) Don Rowe	.50
(34) Kevin Seitzer	.50
(35) Bill Spiers	.50
(36) William Suero	.50
(37) B.J. Surhoff	.75
(38) Dickie Thon	.50
(39) Greg Vaughn	1.50
(40) Bill Wegman	.50
(41) Robin Yount	3.00

1994 Milwaukee Brewers Police

All youngsters attending the April 23 Brewers game received this 30-card set sponsored by Pick'n Save supermarkets and Snickers candy bar, whose logos appear on both front and back. Cards featured posed player photos in their new 25th anniversary uniforms, against a lime green fabric backdrop or game action photos. Two green borders surround the photos. Navy blue bars above and below the photo have the player's name, team and uniform number. A 25th anniversary logo is at lower-right. The name of one of the many Wisconsin police agencies which distributed the cards is printed in black at bottom. Backs are printed in black-on-white and feature full major and minor league stats. The traditional safety message or anti-drug warning is not included on this issue. Cards are checklisted here by uniform number. Cards are inthe 2-1/2" x 3-1/2" format.

	MT
Complete Set (30):	4.00
Common Player:	.20
2 Jose Valentin	.20
3 Phil Garner	.20
5 B.J. Surhoff	.25
8 Jody Reed	.25
9 Bill Spiers	.20
11 Dave Nilsson	.25
12 Brian Harper	.20
16 Pat Listach	.25
18 Tom Brunansky	.20
20 Kevin Seitzer	.20
21 Cal Eldred	.25
23 Greg Vaughn	.45
24 Darryl Hamilton	.20
25 Ricky Bones	.20
27 Turner Ward	.20
28 Doug Henry	.20
29 Jeff Bronkey	.20
30 Matt Mieske	.30
31 Jaime Navarro	.20
32 John Jaha	.30
36 Mike Fetters	.20
37 Graeme Lloyd	.20
39 Bob Scanlan	.20
40 Mike Ignasiak	.20
43 Mark Kiefer	.20
46 Bill Wegman	.20
47 Jesse Orosco	.20
49 Teddy Higuera	.20
63 Jeff D'Amico, Kelly Wunsch	.50
--- Bernie Brewer (mascot)	.20

1994 Milwaukee Brewers team issue

These 4" x 5-1/2" black-and-white, blank-back cards were apparently produced by the Brewers for use by players in answering fan requests. All photos are chest-to-cap portraits with players in dark mesh jerseys, with or without turtlenecks beneath. The unnumbered cards have player name in the border at bottom-left, his position at center and team name at right. The photos are checklisted here in alphabetical order.

	MT
Complete Set (28):	15.00
Common Player:	.50
(1) Ricky Bones	.50
(2) Jeff Bronkey	.50
(3) Tom Brunansky	.50
(4) Alex Diaz	.50
(5) Cal Eldred	.65
(6) Mike Fetters	.50
(7) Phil Garner	.50
(8) Brian Harper	.50
(9) Doug Henry	.50
(10) Ted Higuera	.50
(11) John Jaha	.75
(12) Mark Kiefer	.50
(13) Pat Listach	.50
(14) Graeme Lloyd	.50
(15) Matt Mieske	.50
(16) Angel Miranda	.50
(17) Dave Nilsson	.65
(18) Jesse Orosco	.50
(19) Jody Reed	.50
(20) Bob Scanlan	.50
(21) Kevin Seitzer	.50
(22) Bill Spiers	.50
(23) B.J. Surhoff	.75
(24) Greg Vaughn	.90
(25) Jose Valentin	.50
(26) Turner Ward	.50
(27) Bill Wegman	.50
(28) Robin Yount	4.00

1994 Milwaukee Brewers team-issue 5x7s

These 5" x 7" black-and-white, blank-back photos were produced by the team for distribution to media and for use by players in answering fan requests. All photos are portraits showing players in dark mesh warm-up jerseys. The unnumbered pictures have player name in the border at bottom-left, position at center and team name at right. The photos are checklisted here in alphabetical order.

	MT
Complete Set (37):	16.00
Common Player:	.50
(1) Ricky Bones	.50
(2) Jeff Bronkey	.65
(3) Tom Brunansky	.50
(4) Bill Castro	.50
(5) Gene Clines	.50
(6) Alex Diaz	.50
(7) Duffy Dyer	.50
(8) Cal Eldred	.65
(9) Mike Fetters	.50
(10) Tim Foli	.50
(11) Phil Garner	.50
(12) Darryl Hamilton	.65
(13) Brian Harper	.50
(14) Doug Henry	.50
(15) Ted Higuera	.50
(16) Mike Ignasiak	.50
(17) John Jaha	.75
(18) Mark Kiefer	.50
(19) Pat Listach	.50
(20) Graeme Lloyd	.50
(21) Mike Matheny	.50
(22) Matt Mieske	.50

(23)	Angel Miranda	.50
(24)	Jamie Navarro	.50
(25)	David Nilsson	.50
(26)	Jesse Orosco	.50
(27)	Jody Reed	.50
(28)	Don Rowe	.50
(29)	Bob Scanlan	.50
(30)	Kevin Seitzer	.50
(31)	Bill Spiers	.50
(32)	B.J. Surhoff	.75
(33)	Jose Valentin	.50
(34)	Greg Vaughn	1.00
(35)	Turner Ward	.50
(36)	Bill Wegman	.50
(37)	Rob Wine	.50

1995 Milwaukee Brewers Police

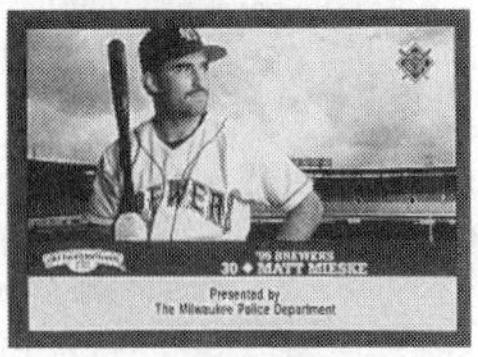

Some of the finest portrait photos seen on modern baseball cards are combined with game-action shots in the annual Brewers police set, sponsored by Old Fashioned Foods (makers of Squeeze Cheese). The 2-1/2" x 3-1/2" cards feature forest green borders with the player and team name, and uniform number in white on a deep blue band beneath. A tan panel at bottom has the name of the Milwaukee P.D. Many of the cards are presented in horizontal format. Backs are in black-and-white and include career stats and a safety tip. Cards are checklisted here according to uniform number.

		MT
Complete Set (33):		8.00
Common Player:		.25
1	Fernando Vina	.25
2	Jose Valentin	.25
3	Phil Garner	.25
5	B.J. Surhoff	.45
9	Joe Oliver	.25
10	Brewers Coaches (Bill Castro, Duffy Dyer, Tim Foli, Lamar Johnson, Don Rowe)	.25
11	Dave Nilsson	.30
12	Derrick May	.25
15	Dave Hulse	.25
16	Pat Listach	.25
20	Kevin Seitzer	.25
21	Cal Eldred	.35
22	Mike Matheny, Jeff Cirillo	.40
23	Greg Vaughn	.45
24	Darryl Hamilton	.25
25	Ricky Bones	.25
27	Turner Ward	.25
29	Jeff Bronkey	.25
30	Matt Mieske	.35
32	John Jaha	.35
36	Mike Fetters	.25
37	Graeme Lloyd	.25
38	Angel Miranda	.25
39	Bob Scanlan	.25
40	Michael Ignasiak	.25
41	Jose Mercedes, Mark Kiefer	.25
42	Scott Karl, Al Reyes, Steve Sparks	.30
46	Bill Wegman	.25
---	Bob Uecker (announcer)	1.50
---	Charlie the Mouse (sponsor)	.05
---	Iris the Cow (sponsor)	.05
---	Squeezasaurus (sponsor)	.05
---	Squeeze Cheese (coupon)	.05

1995 Milwaukee Brewers team-issue 5x7s

These 5" x 7" black-and-white, blank-back photos were produced by the team for distribution to media and for use by players in answering fan requests. All photos are portraits. Most players are posed in home white uniforms, a few are in dark mesh warm-up jerseys. The unnumbered pictures have player name in the border at bottom-left, position at center and team name at right. The photos are checklisted here in alphabetical order.

		MT
Complete Set (35):		15.00
Common Player:		.50
(1)	Ricky Bones	.50
(2)	Jeff Bronkey	.50
(3)	Bill Castro	.50
(4)	Jeff Cirillo	1.50
(5)	Duffy Dyer	.50
(6)	Cal Eldred	.65
(7)	Mike Fetters	.50
(8)	Tim Foli	.50
(9)	Phil Garner	.50
(10)	Darryl Hamilton	.65
(11)	Dave Hulse	.50
(12)	Mike Ignasiak	.50
(13)	John Jaha	.75
(14)	Lamar Johnson	.50
(15)	Mark Kiefer	.50
(16)	Pat Listach	.50
(17)	Graeme Lloyd	.50
(18)	Mike Matheny	.50
(19)	Derrick May	.50
(20)	Jose Mercedes	.50
(21)	Matt Mieske	.50
(22)	Angel Miranda	.50
(23)	Dave Nilsson	.50
(24)	Joe Oliver	.50
(25)	Al Reyes	.50
(26)	Don Rowe	.50
(27)	Bob Scanlan	.50
(28)	Kevin Seitzer	.50
(29)	Steve Sparks	.50
(30)	B.J. Surhoff	.75
(31)	Jose Valentin	.50
(32)	Greg Vaughn	1.00
(33)	Fernando Vina	.50
(34)	Turner Ward	.50
(35)	Bill Wegman	.50

1996 Milwaukee Brewers Police

Metallic gold borders are featured on the Brewers' 14th annual safety set issued June 16 as a stadium giveaway. Cards are a mix of horizontal and vertical design with a large color photo at left. In a gold strip at right is the team logotype, player name, position and uniform number. Backs are in black-and-white with a safety message from the pictured player and the team logo. No sponsoring company or police agency is mentioned on the card. A special card in the set illustrates the proposed new Brewers stadium. Cards are listed here by uniform number.

		MT
Complete Set (30):		5.00
Common Player:		.15
1	Fernando Vina	.15
2	Jose Valentin	.15
3	Phil Garner	.15
4	Pat Listach	.15
8	Mark Loretta	.15
14	Dave Nilsson	.25
15	David Hulse	.15
16	Jesse Levis	.15
20	Kevin Seitzer	.15
21	Cal Eldred	.20
22	Mike Matheny	.15
23	Greg Vaughn	.35
24	Chuckie Carr	.15
25	Ricky Bones	.15
26	Jeff Cirillo	.15
27	Turner Ward	.15
30	Matt Mieske	.20
32	John Jaha	.25
36	Mike Fetters	.15
37	Graeme Lloyd	.15
38	Angel Miranda	.15
40	Ben McDonald	.25
42	Scott Karl	.15
48	Marshall Boze	.15
49	Mike Potts	.15
50	Steve Sparks	.15
51	Ramon Garcia	.15
52	Kevin Wickander	.15
---	Brewers coaches	.15
---	Miller Park	.15

1996 Milwaukee Brewers team-issue 5x7s

These 5" x 7" black-and-white blank-back photos were produced by the team for distribution to media and for use by players in answering fan requests. All photos are chest-to-cap portraits showing players and staff either in dark mesh warm-up jerseys or home whites. The unnumbered pictures have player name in the border at bottom-left, his position at center and team name at right. The photos are checklisted here in alphabetical order.

		MT
Complete Set (38):		18.00
Common Player:		.50
(1)	Chris Bando	.50
(2)	Ricky Bones	.50
(3)	Marshall Boze	.75
(4)	Chuck Carr	.50
(5)	Bill Castro	.50
(6)	Jeff Cirillo	.75
(7)	Jeff D'Amico	.65
(8)	Cal Eldred	.50
(9)	Mike Fetters	.50
(10)	Jim Gantner	.50
(11)	Ramon Garcia	.50
(12)	Phil Garner	.50
(13)	Brian Givens	.55
(14)	Dave Hulse	.50
(15)	John Jaha	.65
(16)	Lamar Johnson	.50
(17)	Scott Karl	.50
(18)	Kevin Koslofski	.65
(19)	Jesse Levis	.50
(20)	Pat Listach	.50
(21)	Graeme Lloyd	.50
(22)	Mark Loretta	.60
(23)	Mike Matheny	.50
(24)	Ben McDonald	.50
(25)	Matt Mieske	.50
(26)	Jose Mercedes	.50
(27)	Angel Miranda	.50
(28)	David Nilsson	.50
(29)	Mike Potts	.50
(30)	Don Rowe	.50
(31)	Kevin Seitzer	.50
(32)	Steve Sparks	.50
(33)	Tim Unroe	.50
(34)	Jose Valentin	.50
(35)	Greg Vaughn	.85
(36)	Fernando Vina	.50
(37)	Turner Ward	.50
(38)	Kevin Wickander	.50

1997 Milwaukee Brewers Police

One of the more attractive safety sets of recent years, the 1997 Brewers team issue features action photos of each player in the standard 2-1/2" x 3-1/2" format. Down one side of the photo is the player's name in outline type. A team logo is at bottom-right. Backs are in black-and-white with a few bits of personal data and a cartoon figure presenting a safety tip for youngsters. The set was distributed to children attending the May 30 game at County Stadium. The checklist here is arranged by uniform number.

		MT
Complete Set (30):		7.00
Common Player:		.25
1	Fernando Vina	.25
2	Jose Valentin	.25
3	Phil Garner	.25
8	Mark Loretta	.30
9	Tim Unroe	.25
10	Marc Newfield	.25
13	Jeff D'Amico	.25
14	Dave Nillson	.25
15	Jeff Huson	.25
16	Jesse Levis	.25
20	Jeromy Burnitz	.25
21	Cal Eldred	.25
22	Mike Matheny	.25
24	Chuckie Carr	.25
25	Angel Miranda	.25
26	Jeff Cirillo	.35
27	Bob Wickman	.25
29	Gerald Williams	.35
30	Matt Mieske	.25
32	John Jaha	.40
36	Mike Fetters	.25
39	Bryce Florie	.25
40	Ben McDonald	.30
41	Jose Mercedes	.25
42a	Scott Karl	.25
42b	Jackie Robinson (tribute)	2.00
43	Doug Jones	.25
49	Ron Villone	.25
51	Eddy Diaz	.25
---	Coaches (Chris Bando, Bill Castro, Jim Gantner, Lamar Johnson, Don Rowe)	.25

1997 Milwaukee Brewers team-issue 5x7s

These 5" x 7" black-and-white blank-back photos were produced by the Brewers for distribution to media and for use by players in answering fan requests. All photos are cap-to-chest portraits, showing players in dark mesh warm-up jerseys. The unnumbered pictures have player name in the border at bottom-left, his position at center and team name at right. The photos are checklisted here in alphabetical order.

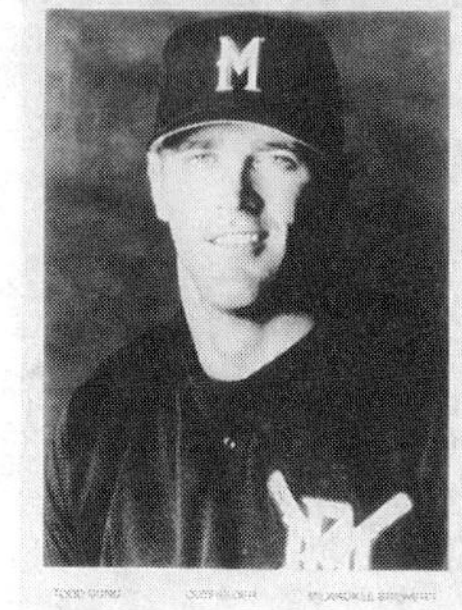

		MT
Complete Set (40):		21.00
Common Player:		.50
(1)	Joel Adamson	.65
(2)	Chris Bando	.50
(3)	Brian Banks	.65
(4)	Jeromy Burnitz	.80
(5)	Chuckie Carr	.50
(6)	Bill Castro	.50
(7)	Jeff Cirillo	.65
(8)	Jeff D'Amico	.50
(9)	Todd Dunn	1.50
(10)	Cal Eldred	.65
(11)	Mike Fetters	.50
(12)	Bryce Florie	.50
(13)	Jim Gantner	.50
(14)	Phil Garner	.50
(15)	Jeff Huson	.50
(16)	John Jaha	.65
(17)	Lamar Johnson	.50
(18)	Doug Jones	.50
(19)	Scott Karl	.50
(20)	Jesse Levis	.50
(21)	Mark Loretta	.50
(22)	Mike Matheny	.50
(23)	Jamie McAndrew	.50
(24)	Ben McDonald	.50
(25)	Jose Mercedes	.50
(26)	Matt Mieske	.50
(27)	Angel Miranda	.50
(28)	Marc Newfield	.50
(29)	David Nilsson	.50
(30)	Don Rowe	.50
(31)	Steve Sparks	.50
(32)	Tim Unroe	.50
(33)	Jose Valentin	.50
(34)	Tim Van Egmond	.65
(35)	Ron Villone	.50
(36)	Fernando Vina	.50
(37)	Jack Voight	.50
(38)	Bob Wickman	.50
(39)	Gerald Williams	.65
(40)	Antone Williamson	.75

1998 Milwaukee Brewers team-issue 5x7s

Virtually every player, coach and the manager of the '98 Brew Crew is included in this team-issued promotional photo set distributed for media and player use. Each photo has a chest-to-cap portrait with players wearing dark mesh warm-up jerseys. Some pictures are re-issues from the previous season, and have only a single line of identification in the bottom border; new pictures have the player name, position and team in three lines at bottom-left. The unnumbered photos are checklisted here in alphabetical order.

		MT
	Complete Set (50):	25.00
	Common Player:	.50
(1)	Jeff Alfano	.65
(2)	Chris Bando	.50
(3)	Brian Banks	.60
(4)	Ron Belliard	.60
(5)	Jeromy Burnitz	.65
(6)	Bill Castro	.50
(7)	Jeff Cirillo	.65
(8)	Jeff D'Amico	.50
(9)	Valerio de los Santos	.65
(10)	Eddy Diaz	.50
(11)	Andres Duncan	.65
(12)	Todd Dunn	.65
(13)	Cal Eldred	.50
(14)	Horacio Estrada	.50
(15)	Ken Felder	.50
(16)	Chad Fox	.65
(17)	Phil Garner	.50
(18)	Chad Green	.50
(19)	Marquis Grissom	.75
(20)	Bob Hamelin	.50
(21)	Bobby Hughes	.75
(22)	Darrin Jackson	.60
(23)	John Jaha	.65
(24)	Geoff Jenkins	1.50
(25)	Lamar Johnson	.50
(26)	Doug Jones	.50
(27)	Jeff Juden	.65
(28)	Scott Karl	.50
(29)	Scott Krause	.50
(30)	Jesse Levis	.50
(31)	Mark Loretta	.50
(32)	Doug Mansolino	.50
(33)	Pablo Martinez	.65
(34)	Mike Matheny	.50
(35)	Jose Mercedes	.50
(36)	Mike Myers	.50
(37)	Marc Newfield	.50
(38)	David Nilsson	.50
(39)	Al Reyes	.50
(40)	Don Rowe	.50
(41)	Jose Valentin	.50
(42)	Tim Van Egmond	.50
(43)	Fernando Vina	.50
(44)	Paul Wagner	.50
(45)	Bob Wickman	.50
(46)	Antone Williamson	.65
(47)	Brad Woodall	.50
(48)	Steve Woodard	.50
(49)	Joel Youngblood	.50
(50)	Eddie Zosky	.50

1998 Milwaukee Brewers Diamond Celebration

Persons attending a Jan. 30 banquet in Milwaukee received a set of these cards highlighting the team's award winners for 1997. The set was sponsored by the Milwaukee Metropolitan Association of Commerce; their logo appears on the back. Fronts have color photos centered on a white background. The players are pictured in action, the staff in portraits. "Diamond Celebration" and the name are in script. The banquet date and specific honor also appear on front. Backs are in black-and-white with season highlights. The unnumbered cards are checklisted here alphabetically.

		MT
	Complete Set (10):	20.00
	Common Card:	.50
(1)	Hank Aaron	6.00
(2)	Jeromy Burnitz	3.00
(3)	Jeff Cirillo	3.00
(4)	Dick Hackett (staff)	.50
(5)	Bill Haig (staff)	.50
(6)	John Jaha	3.00
(7)	Doug Jones (MV Pitcher)	1.50
(8)	Doug Jones (MVP)	1.50
(9)	Bob Uecker (MC)	3.00
(10)	Bob Wickman	1.50

1999 Milwaukee Brewers Diamond Celebration

Persons attending a Jan. 22 banquet in Milwaukee received a set of these cards highlighting the team's award winners for 1997. The set was sponsored by the Milwaukee Metropolitan Association of Commerce, whose logo appears on the back. Fronts have color photos. The players are pictured in action, the staff in portraits. "Diamond Celebration" and team logo are at left. The specific honor also appears on front. Backs are in black-and-white with season highlights. The unnumbered cards are checklisted here alphabetically.

		MT
	Complete Set (11):	20.00
	Common Player:	.50
(1)	Bob Betts (P.A. announcer)	.50
(2)	Jeromy Burnitz (HR Champ)	3.00
(3)	Jeromy Burnitz (MVP)	3.00
(4)	Jeff Cirillo	3.00
(5)	Peter Gammons (writer)	.50
(6)	Mark Loretta (manager's award)	2.00
(7)	Mark Loretta (community service)	2.00
(8)	Bud Selig (owner)	.50
(9)	Bob Wickman	1.50
(10)	Steve Woodard	3.00
(11)	Robin Yount	6.00

2000 Milwaukee Brewers Diamond Celebration

Winners of various annual awards by the Milwaukee Brewers are featured in this standard-size card set which was issued at the team's Diamond Celebration dinner on Jan. 21. Fronts have large portrait photos featured along the left or right edge on front. Down the other side is player identification and the name of the award won. Backs have season highlights. The unnumbered cards are checklisted here alphabetically.

		MT
	Complete Set (10):	18.00
	Common Player:	.50
(1)	Kevin Barker	3.00
(2)	Ron Belliard	2.00
(3)	Jeromy Burnitz (HR Champ)	3.00
(4)	Jeromy Burnitz (MVP)	3.00
(5)	Jeff Cirillo	3.00
(6)	Marquis Grissom	2.50
(7)	Geoff Jenkins	3.00
(8)	Tim Kurkjian	.50
(9)	Dean Taylor, Davey Lopes	.50
(10)	Bob Wickman	1.00

1981 Minnesota Twins Postcards

The photography of Barry Fritz is again featured on the Twins' 1981 color postcard issue. Players are posed on front of the borderless, 3-1/2" x 5-1/2" cards. A black facsimile autograph appears on front, as well. A few biographical details appear on the back. The unnumbered cards are checklisted here in alphabetical order.

		MT
	Complete Set (34):	50.00
	Common Player:	2.00
(1)	Glenn Adams	2.00
(2)	Fernando Arroyo	2.00
(3)	Chuck Baker	2.00
(4)	Sal Butera	2.00
(5)	John Castino	2.00
(6)	Don Cooper	2.00
(8)	Doug Corbett	2.00
(9)	David Engle	2.00
(10)	Roger Erickson	2.00
(11)	Billy Gardner	2.00
(12)	Danny Goodwin	2.00
(13)	Johnny Goryl	2.00
(14)	Mickey Hatcher	2.00
(15)	Darrell Jackson	2.00
(16)	Ron Jackson	2.00
(17)	Greg Johnston	2.00
(18)	Jerry Koosman	2.50
(19)	Karl Kuehl	2.00
(20)	Pete Mackanin	2.00
(21)	Jack O'Connor	2.00
(22)	Johnny Podres	2.50
(23)	Hosken Powell	2.00
(24)	Pete Redfern	2.00
(25)	Roy Smalley	2.00
(26)	Ray Smith	2.00
(27)	Rick Sofield	2.00
(28)	Rick Stelmaszek	2.00
(29)	John Verhoeven	2.00
(30)	Gary Ward	2.00
(31)	Rob Wilfong	2.00
(32)	Al Williams	2.00
(33)	Butch Wynegar	2.00
(34)	Metropolitan Stadium	2.50

1982 Minnesota Twins Postcards

Again produced by collector Barry Fritz, the Twins' 1982 color player postcards are similar in format to earlier efforts. The 3-1/2" x 5-1/2" cards have borderless color poses on front. Cards in the 1982 series can be found either with or without facsimile autographs. Postcard-style backs are printed in blue with a large script team name, player identification and, on most cards, a 1982 dateline. The unnumbered cards are checklisted here alphabetically. Prices shown are for cards with facsimile signatures; those without sell for about twice those prices.

		MT
	Complete Set (39):	55.00
	Common Player:	2.00
(1)	Fernando Arroyo	2.00
(2)	Sal Butera	2.00
(3)	Bobby Castillo	2.00
(4)	John Castino	2.00
(5)	Doug Corbett	2.00
(6)	Ron Davis	2.00
(7)	Jim Eisenreich	2.00
(8)	Dave Engle	2.00
(9)	Roger Erickson	2.00
(10)	Len Faedo	2.00
(11)	Terry Felton	2.00
(12)	Gary Gaetti	2.00
(13)	Billy Gardner	2.00
(14)	Calvin Griffith (president)	2.00
(15)	Mickey Hatcher	2.00
(16)	Brad Havens	2.00
(17)	Kent Hrbek	2.00
(18)	Darrell Jackson	2.00
(19)	Randy Johnson	2.00
(20)	Karl Kuehl	2.00
(21)	Tim Laudner	2.00
(22)	Jim Lemon	2.00
(23)	Ivan Mesa	2.00
(24)	Bobby Mitchell	2.00
(25)	Jack O'Conner	2.00
(26)	Tony Oliva	2.00
(27)	Johnny Podres	2.00
(28)	Pete Redfern	2.00
(29)	Rick Stelmaszek	2.00
(30)	Jesus Vega	2.00
(31)	Frank Viola	2.00
(32)	Gary Ward	2.00
(33)	Ron Washington	2.00
(34)	Rob Wilfong	2.00
(35)	Al Williams	2.00
(36)	Butch Wynegar	2.00
(37)	1982 Twins team photo	2.00
(38)	Metrodome - outside view	2.00
(39)	Metrodome - inside view	2.00

1983 Minnesota Twins Postcards

The familiar team postcard format of a 3-1/2" x 5-1/2" card with borderless color player poses on front was continued in Barry Fritz' production of the 1983 set. To allow for in-person or personalized autographing, each player card can also be found without the facsimile signature. Postcard backs have a few player details, a team script logo and credits for the photographer and printer. The unnumbered cards are checklisted here in alphabetical order.

		MT
	Complete Set (36):	22.00
	Common Player:	1.00
(1)	Tom Brunansky	1.00
(2)	Randy Bush	1.00
(3)	Bobby Castillo	1.00
(4)	John Castino	1.00
(5)	Catchers (Ray Smith, Dave Engle, Tim Laudner)	1.00
(6)	(Ron Davis)	1.00
(7)	Jim Eisenreich	1.25
(8)	Dave Engle	1.00
(9)	Len Faedo	1.00
(10)	Pete Filson	1.00
(11)	Gary Gaetti	1.50
(12)	Billy Gardner	1.00
(13)	Mickey Hatcher	1.00
(14)	Brad Havens	1.00
(15)	Kent Hrbek	2.00
(16)	Tom Kelly	1.00
(17)	Tim Laudner	1.00
(18)	Jim Lemon	1.00
(19)	Lumber Company (Tom Brunansky, Gary Gaetti, Kent Hrbek, Gary Ward)	1.25
(20)	Rick Lysander	1.00
(21)	Manager and Coaches (Billy Gardner, Tom Kelly, Jim Lemon, Johnny Podres, Rick Stelmaszek)	1.00
(22)	Bobby Mitchell	1.00
(23)	Native Sons (Jim Eisenreich, Kent Hrbek, Tim Laudner)	1.00
(24)	Jack O'Connor	1.00
(25)	Bryan Oelkers	1.00
(26)	Johnny Podres	1.25
(27)	Ray Smith	1.00
(28)	Rick Stelmaszek	1.00
(29)	Scott Ullger	1.00
(30)	Frank Viola	1.00
(31)	Gary Ward	1.00
(32)	Ron Washington	1.00
(33)	Len Whitehouse	1.00
(34)	Al Williams	1.00
(35)	Team photo	1.00
(36)	Metrodome/checklist	1.00

1983 Minnesota Twins team issue

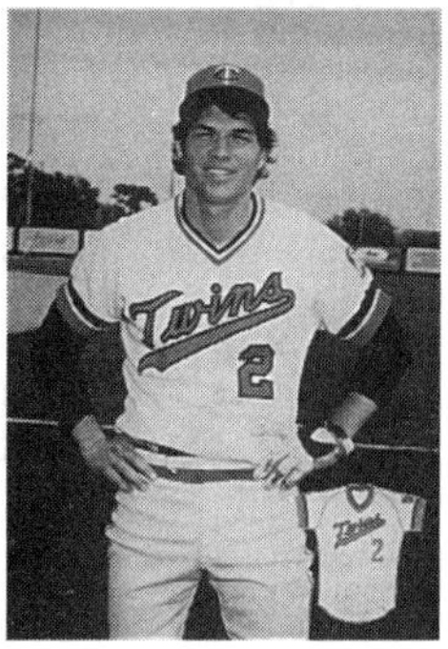

The Minnesota Twins produced a 36-card set in 1983 to be sold at concession stands and through the mail. The full-color borderless cards measure 2-1/2" x 3-1/2" and displayed the player's uniform number on a white Twins jersey at the bottom of the card. The backs contain full career statistics.

		MT
	Complete Set (36):	10.00
	Common Player:	.25
1	John Castino	.25
2	Jim Eisenreich	.50
3	Ray Smith	.25
4	Scott Ullger	.25
5	Gary Gaetti	1.00
6	Mickey Hatcher	.25
7	Bobby Mitchell	.25
8	Len Faedo	.25
9	Kent Hrbek	2.00
10	Tim Laudner	.25
11	Frank Viola	1.50
12	Bryan Oelkers	.25
13	Rick Lysander	.25
14	Dave Engle	.25
15	Len Whitehouse	.25
16	Pete Filson	.25
17	Tom Brunansky	.25
18	Randy Bush	.25
19	Brad Havens	.25
20	Al Williams	.25
21	Gary Ward	.25
22	Jack O'Connor	.25
23	Bobby Castillo	.25
24	Ron Washington	.25
25	Ron Davis	.25
26	Tom Kelly	.25
27	Billy Gardner	.25
28	Rick Stelmaszek	.25
29	Jim Lemon	.25
30	Johnny Podres	.50
31	Minnesota's Native Sons (Jim Eisenreich, Kent Hrbek, Tim Laudner)	.60
32	Twins' Catchers (Dave Engle, Tim Laudner)	.25
33	The Lumber Company (Tom Brunansky, Gary Gaetti, Kent Hrbek, Gary Ward)	.60
34	Twins' Coaches (Billy Gardner, Tom Kelly, Jim Lemon, Johnny Podres, Rick Stelmaszek)	.25
35	Team Photo	.40
36	Metrodome/Checklist	.25

1984 Minnesota Twins team issue

This team-issued set from the Minnesota Twins consists of 36 full-color, borderless cards, each measuring 2-1/2" x 3-1/2". As in the previous year, the player's uniform number appears on a white Twins jersey at the bottom of the card. The backs are printed in red and blue on white stock and include career stats. The set features several special cards, including one of Harmon Killebrew.

		MT
Complete Set (36):		10.00
Common Player:		.25
1	John Castino	.25
2	Jim Eisenreich	.35
3	Al Jimenez	.25
4	Dave Meier	.25
5	Gary Gaetti	.90
6	Mickey Hatcher	.25
7	Jeff Reed	.25
8	Tim Teufel	.25
9	Len Faedo	.25
10	Kent Hrbek	1.50
11	Tim Laudner	.25
12	Frank Viola	.60
13	Ken Schrom	.25
14	Larry Pashnick	.25
15	Dave Engle	.25
16	Keith Comstock	.25
17	Pete Filson	.25
18	Tom Brunansky	.25
19	Randy Bush	.25
20	Darrell Brown	.25
21	Al Williams	.25
22	Mike Walters	.25
23	John Butcher	.25
24	Bobby Castillo	.25
25	Ron Washington	.25
26	Ron Davis	.25
27	Tom Kelly	.25
28	Billy Gardner	.25
29	Rick Stelmaszek	.25
30	Jim Lemon	.25
31	Johnny Podres	.40
32	Mike Smithson	.25
33	Harmon Killebrew	2.50
34	Team Photo	.50
35	Logo Card	.25
36	Metrodome/Checklist	.25

1985 Minnesota Twins Postcards

The 1985 All-Star Game logo (played at the Metrodome) appears on the front of this team-issued color postcard set. Borderless color photos on the fronts of the 3-1/2" x 5-1/2" cards were taken by Barry Fritz. Postcard backs have standard indicia, a team name in script and player name and position. The unnumbered cards are checklisted here in alphabetical order.

		MT
Complete Set (33):		24.00
Common Player:		1.00
(1)	Tom Brunansky	1.00
(2)	Randy Bush	1.00
(3)	John Butcher	1.00
(4)	Andre David	1.00
(5)	Ron Davis	1.00
(6)	Dave Engle	1.00
(7)	Alvaro Espinoza	1.00
(8)	Pete Filson	1.00
(9)	Gary Gaetti	2.50
(10)	Greg Gagne	1.50
(11)	Billy Gardner	1.00
(12)	Mickey Hatcher	1.00
(13)	Kent Hrbek	2.50
(14)	Tom Kelly	1.00
(15)	Tom Klawitter	1.00
(16)	Tim Laudner	1.00
(17)	Rick Lysander	1.00
(18)	Dave Meier	1.00
(19)	Tony Oliva	2.50
(20)	Johnny Podres	1.50
(21)	Kirby Puckett	15.00
(22)	Mark Salas	1.00
(23)	Ken Schrom	1.00
(24)	Roy Smalley	1.00
(25)	Mike Smithson	1.00
(26)	Rick Stelmaszek	1.00
(27)	Mike Stenhouse	1.00
(28)	Tim Teufel	1.00
(29)	Frank Viola	1.00
(30)	Curt Wardle	1.00
(31)	Ron Washington	1.00
(32)	Len Whitehouse	1.00
(33)	Rich Yett	1.00

1985 Minnesota Twins team issue

Similar in format to the previous two years, this 36-card team-issued set features full-color, borderless cards. The player's uniform number is again displayed on a white Twins jersey in the lower right corner, and the 1985 All-Star Game logo is shown in the lower left. The All-Star Game logo also appears on a special card in the set that lists on the back all Twins who have been selected for previous All-Star Games. The set was sold at ballpark concession stands and through the mail.

		MT
Complete Set (36):		15.00
Common Player:		.20
1	Alvaro Espinoza	.25
2	Roy Smalley	.25
3	Pedro Oliva	.75
4	Dave Meier	.25
5	Gary Gaetti	.50
6	Mickey Hatcher	.25
7	Jeff Reed	.25
8	Tim Teufel	.25
9	Mark Salas	.25
10	Kent Hrbek	1.00
11	Tim Laudner	.25
12	Frank Viola	.50
13	Ken Schrom	.25
14	Rick Lysander	.25
15	Dave Engle	.25
16	Andre David	.25
17	Len Whitehouse	.25
18	Pete Filson	.25
19	Tom Brunansky	.25
20	Randy Bush	.25
21	Greg Gagne	.90
22	John Butcher	.25
23	Mike Stenhouse	.25
24	Kirby Puckett	10.00
25	Tom Klawitter	.25
26	Curt Wardle	.25
27	Rich Yett	.25
28	Ron Washington	.25
29	Ron Davis	.25
30	Tom Kelly	.25
31	Billy Gardner	.25
32	Rick Stelmaszek	.25
33	Johnny Podres	.40
34	Mike Smithson	.25
35	1985 All-Star Game Logo Card	.25
36	Twins Logo/Checklist	.25

1986 Minnesota Twins Postcards

In the team's 25th anniversary season, this set of color postcards was issued. The 3-1/2" x 5-1/2" semi-gloss cards have borderless color poses on the front, along with a facsimile autograph and a color 25th anniversary logo. Backs have standard postcard indicia, a few player details and credit lines of the photographer, printer and producer. The unnumbered cards are checklisted here in alphabetical order.

		MT
Complete Set (36):		35.00
Common Player:		1.00
(1)	Billy Beane	1.00
(2)	Bert Blyleven	2.00
(3)	Tom Brunansky	1.00
(4)	Dennis Burtt	1.00
(5)	Randy Bush	1.00
(6)	John Butcher	1.00
(7)	Mark Davidson	1.00
(8)	Ron Davis	1.00
(9)	Frank Eufemia	1.00
(10)	Pete Filson	1.00
(11)	Gary Gaetti	2.00
(12)	Greg Gagne	1.50
(13)	Mickey Hatcher	1.00
(14a)	Kent Hrbek (facsimile autograph)	3.00
(14b)	Kent Hrbek (no facsimile autograph)	12.00
(15)	Tom Kelly	1.00
(16)	Bill Latham	1.00
(17)	Tim Laudner	1.00
(18)	Steve Lombardozzi	1.00
(19)	Ray Miller	1.00
(20)	Tony Oliva	2.50
(21)	Chris Pittaro	1.00
(22)	Kirby Puckett	9.00
(23)	Jeff Reed	1.00
(24)	Mark Salas	1.00
(25)	Alex Sanchez	1.00
(26)	Roy Smalley	1.00
(27)	Roy Smith	1.00
(28)	Mike Smithson	1.00
(29)	Rick Stelmaszek	1.00
(30)	Dick Such	1.00
(31)	Wayne Terwilliger	1.00
(32)	Frank Viola	1.00
(33)	Ron Washington	1.00
(34)	Al Woods	1.00
(35)	Twins Team Photo	1.50
(36)	Twins anniversary logo	1.00

1986 Minnesota Twins team issue

This team-issued set contains 36 2-9/16" x 3-1/2" full-color cards. Fronts feature the Twins 25th anniversary logo and a jersey at the bottom of each card with the player's uniform number. All cards, except an action shot of Bert Blyleven, are posed photos, with a facsimile autograph on each. The set also includes a checklist and a team photo.

		MT
Complete Set (36):		10.00
Common Player:		.15
1	Chris Pittaro	.15
2	Steve Lombardozzi	.15
3	Roy Smalley	.15
4	Pedro Oliva	.50
5	Gary Gaetti	.40
6	Mickey Hatcher	.15
7	Jeff Reed	.15
8	Mark Salas	.15
9	Kent Hrbek	.60
10	Tim Laudner	.15
11	Frank Viola	.45
12	Dennis Burtt	.15
13	Alex Sanchez	.15
14	Roy Smith	.15
15	Billy Beane	.15
16	Pete Filson	.15
17	Tom Brunansky	.15
18	Randy Bush	.15
19	Frank Eufemia	.15
20	Mark Davidson	.15
21	Bert Blyleven	.40
22	Greg Gagne	.25
23	John Butcher	.15
24	Kirby Puckett	5.00
25	Bill Latham	.15
26	Ron Washington	.15
27	Ron Davis	.15
28	Tom Kelly	.15
29	Dick Such	.15
30	Rick Stelmaszek	.15
31	Ray Miller	.15
32	Wayne Terwilliger	.15
33	Mike Smithson	.15
34	Alvis Woods	.15
35	Team Photo	.25
36	Twins Logo/Checklist	.15

1987 Minnesota Twins Postcards

Collector Barry Fritz, who worked with the Twins on many baseball card and postcard issues in the 1970s and 1980s produced this set. It was the Twins' last team-issued postcard set until 1992. The 3-1/2" x 5-1/2" cards are printed on thin, semi-gloss cardboard. Fronts have borderless poses with a facsimile autograph printed in blue. Each card, except the team logo card, can be found in versions with and without a 1987 World's Champions logo. Backs are printed in blue with a team logo, player ID, photo and printer credit lines and an MLB logo, along with standard postcard indicia. The unnumbered cards are checklisted here in alphabetical order.

		MT
Complete Set (31):		17.50
Common Player:		1.00
(1)	Keith Atherton	1.00
(2)	Juan Berenguer	1.00
(3)	Bert Blyleven	1.50
(4)	Tom Brunansky	1.00
(5)	Randy Bush	1.00
(6)	Mark Davidson	1.00
(7)	George Frazier	1.00
(8)	Gary Gaetti	1.50
(9)	Greg Gagne	1.25
(10)	Dan Gladden	1.00
(11)	Kent Hrbek	2.00
(12)	Tom Kelly	1.00
(13)	Joe Klink	1.00
(14)	Tim Laudner	1.00
(15)	Steve Lombardozzi	1.00
(16)	Al Newman	1.00
(17)	Tom Nieto	1.00
(18)	Tony Oliva	2.00
(19)	Mark Portugal	1.00
(20)	Kirby Puckett	6.00
(21)	Jeff Reardon	1.00
(22)	Rick Renick	1.00
(23)	Mark Salas	1.00
(24)	Roy Smalley	1.00
(25)	Mike Smithson	1.00
(26)	Rick Stelmaszek	1.00
(27)	Les Straker	1.00
(28)	Dick Such	1.00
(29)	Wayne Terwilliger	1.00
(30)	Frank Viola	1.00
(31)	1986 Minnesota Twins Team Photo	1.50
(32)	World's Champions logo	1.00

1987 Minnesota Twins team issue

The Minnesota Twins produced a 32-card set of 2-1/2" x 3-1/2" full-color baseball cards to be sold at the ballpark and through their souvenir catalog. The card fronts are borderless, containing only the player photo. The backs are printed in blue and red on white card stock and carry the player's personal data and career record. The Twins also produced a post card set which was similar in design to the standard-size card set, but utilized different photos.

		MT
Complete Set (32):		9.00
Common Player:		.15
1	Steve Lombardozzi	.15
2	Roy Smalley	.15
3	Pedro Oliva	.50
4	Greg Gagne	.20
5	Gary Gaetti	.30
6	Tom Kelly	.15
7	Tom Nieto	.15
8	Mark Salas	.15
9	Kent Hrbek	.50
10	Tim Laudner	.15
11	Frank Viola	.35
12	Les Straker	.15
13	George Frazier	.15
14	Keith Atherton	.15
15	Tom Brunansky	.15
16	Randy Bush	.15
17	Al Newman	.15
18	Mark Davidson	.15
19	Bert Blyleven	.35
20	Dan Gladden	.25
21	Kirby Puckett	5.00
22	Mark Portugal	.15
23	Juan Berenguer	.15
24	Jeff Reardon	.20
25	Dick Such	.15
26	Rick Stelmaszek	.15
27	Rick Renick	.15
28	Wayne Terwilliger	.15
29	Joe Klink	.15
30	Mike Smithson	.15
31	Team Photo	.25
32	Twins Logo/Checklist	.15

1988 Minnesota Twins Fire Safety

This 8-1/4" x 3-3/4" booklet contains a dozen postcards called Color-Grams featuring caricatures (suitable for coloring) of star players. Postcards are attached along a perforated edge to a baseball card-size stub with a black-and-white photo of the featured player. Backs include the player name and personal information. The card stubs include the same information, along with a fire prevention tip. Twins Color-Grams were produced as a public service by the U.S. Forest Service and Dept. of Agriculture and were distributed to fans at the Metrodome.

		MT
Complete Booklet:		12.00
Complete Set, Singles (12):		9.00
Common Player:		.50
(1)	Bert Blyleven	.75
(2)	Randy Bush	.50
(3)	Gary Gaetti	.60
(4)	Greg Gagne	.50
(5)	Dan Gladden	.50
(6)	Kent Hrbek	1.00
(7)	Gene Larkin	.50
(8)	Tim Laudner	.50
(9)	Al Newman	.50
(10)	Kirby Puckett	4.00
(11)	Jeff Reardon	.50
(12)	Frank Viola	.50

1988 Minnesota Twins team issue

The Twins issued this set to commemorate the team's 1987 World Series victory. The slightly oversized cards (2-5/8" x 3-7/16") feature color player photos printed on heavy stock with a gold-embossed "1987 World Champions" logo in the lower-left corner. Numbered card backs are red, white and blue and contain player name, personal info and stats. A limited edition of 5000 sets were printed but only a few hundred were sold before the cards were taken off the market due to Major League Baseball licensing restrictions on the use of the World Series logo.

		MT
Complete Set (33):		80.00
Common Player:		1.50
1	Steve Lombardozzi	1.50
2	Roy Smalley	1.50
3	Pedro Oliva	3.00
4	Greg Gagne	3.00
5	Gary Gaetti	4.00
6	Gene Larkin	2.00
7	Tom Kelly	2.00
8	Kent Hrbek	9.00
9	Tim Laudner	2.00
10	Frank Viola	4.00
11	Les Straker	1.50
12	Don Baylor	4.00
13	George Frazier	1.50
14	Keith Atherton	1.50
15	Tom Brunansky	1.50
16	Randy Bush	1.50
17	Al Newman	1.50
18	Mark Davidson	1.50
19	Bert Blyleven	4.00
20	Dan Schatzeder	1.50
21	Dan Gladden	3.00
22	Sal Butera	1.50
23	Kirby Puckett	25.00
24	Joe Niekro	2.00
25	Juan Berenguer	1.50
26	Jeff Reardon	3.00
27	Dick Such	1.50
28	Rick Stelmaszek	1.50
29	Rick Renick	1.50
30	Wayne Terwilliger	1.50
31	Team Photo	1.50
32	World Champions Team Logo Card	1.50
33	Team Logo Card/ Checklist	1.50

1995 Minnesota Twins POGs

Over the course of three games in July, 1995, the Twins issued a three-sheet series of POGs, 15,000 at each game. The souvenir measures about 10-1/4" x 9-1/2" and features a large color game photo, around and above which are POGs, about 1-1/8" diameter, of players, coaches and sponsors. The POGs are die-cut for removal from the sheets. Each sheet has 11 players or coaches, and each has the same four sponsors' POGs. Fronts have player portrait photos while backs have a repeating Coca-Cola logo. The POGs are unnumbered and listed here alphabetically by sheet. The players are not identified on the POGs themselves.

		MT
Complete Set, Sheets (3):		12.00
Complete Set, Singles (33):		9.00
Common Player:		.25
	Series 1, July 1	4.00
(1)	Rick Aguilera	.25
(2)	Rich Becker	.40
(3)	Marty Cordova	.40
(4)	Terry Crowley	.25
(5)	Eddie Guardado	.25
(6)	Jeff Reboulet	.25
(7)	Rich Robertson	.25
(8)	Scott Stahoviak	.25
(9)	Dick Such	.25
(10)	Kevin Tapani	.35
(11)	Matt Walbeck	.25
	Series 2, July 17	4.00
(12)	Alex Cole	.25
(13)	Scott Erickson	.35
(14)	Ron Gardenhire	.25
(15)	Chip Hale	.25
(16)	Chuck Knoblauch	1.00
(17)	Scott Leius	.25
(18)	Pat Mahomes	.25
(19)	Pedro Munoz	.25
(20)	Erik Schullstrom	.25
(21)	Dave Stevens	.25
(22)	Scott Ullger	.25
	Series 3, July 28	5.00
(23)	Jerald Clark	.25
(24)	Mark Guthrie	.25
(25)	Tom Kelly	.25
(26)	Kevin Maas	.25
(27)	Pat Meares	.25
(28)	Matt Merullo	.25
(29)	Kirby Puckett	2.00
(30)	Brad Radke	.25
(31)	Rick Stelmaszek	.25
(32)	Mike Trombley	.25
(33)	Jerry White	.25
	Sponsors' POGs	
---	Coca-Cola	.05
---	Fox 29 TV	.05
---	Minnesota Twins logo	.10
---	Nestle	.05

1997 Minnesota Twins 10th Anniversary

The 10th anniversary of the team's 1987 World Series victory is recalled with this set given to fans on Aug. 8 during the reunion weekend at the Metrodome. The 2-1/2" x 3-1/2" cards have 10-year-old color action photos on front with the anniversary logo and player identification. On back are a black-and-white portrait photo, uniform number, biographical details, the player's 1987 season and post-season performance and the sponsor's logo. The cards are checklisted here in alphabetical order.

		MT
Complete Set (25):		12.00
Common Player:		.25
(1)	Keith Atherton	.25
(2)	Don Baylor	.40
(3)	Juan Berenguer	.25
(4)	Bert Blyleven	.35
(5)	Tom Brunansky	.25
(6)	Randy Bush	.25
(7)	Sal Butera	.25
(8)	Mark Davidson	.25
(9)	George Frazier	.25
(10)	Gary Gaetti	.50
(11)	Greg Gagne	.50
(12)	Dan Gladden	.25
(13)	Kent Hrbek	1.00
(14)	Tom Kelly	.25
(15)	Gene Larkin	.25
(16)	Tim Laudner	.25
(17)	Steve Lombardozzi	.25
(18)	Al Newman	.25
(19)	Joe Niekro	.40
(20)	Kirby Puckett	5.00
(21)	Jeff Reardon	.25
(22)	Dan Schatzeder	.25
(23)	Roy Smalley	.25
(24)	Les Straker	.25
(25)	Frank Viola	.40

1982 Mizuno

This is a one-card "set" promoting Pete Rose as an endorser of Mizuno baseball equipment. The blank-backed card is black-and-white and measures 3-1/4" x 5-1/2".

		MT
(1)	Pete Rose	5.00

Player names in *Italic* type indicate a rookie card.

1992 MJB Holoprisms

The Holoprism set consists of two 4-card hologram sets of Rookies of the Year Jeff Bagwell and Chuck Knoblauch. Each player set was packaged in a special plastic case. The production was limited to 250,000 of each set, numbered and with a letter of authenticity. Each player autographed 500 cards which were randomly inserted.

		MT
Complete Bagwell Set (4):		6.00
Common Bagwell Card:		1.50
Complete Knoblauch Set (4):		6.00
Common Knoblauch Card:		1.00
Autographed Bagwell Card:		75.00
Autographed Knoblauch Card:		40.00
R1	Jeff Bagwell (batting)	1.50
R1a	Jeff Bagwell (overprinted "PROTOTYPE" on back)	2.00
R2	Jeff Bagwell (fielding)	1.50
R3	Jeff Bagwell (batting)	1.50
R4	Jeff Bagwell (batting)	1.50
R1	Chuck Knoblauch (batting)	1.00
R1a	Chuck Knoblauch (overprinted "PROTOTYPE" on back)	1.50
R2	Chuck Knoblauch (fielding)	1.00
R3	Chuck Knoblauch (batting)	1.00
R4	Chuck Knoblauch (batting)	1.00

1992 Modell's Team Mets

Team Mets, the junior fan club, included in its 1992 membership benefits a nine-card perforated sheet sponsored by Modell's Sporting Goods. Cards feature color action photos highlighted by team-color stripes of blue and orange, with a white outer border. The 7-1/2" x 10-1/2" sheet can be separated into standard-size 2-1/2" x 3-1/2" cards. Team Mets and Modell's logos are featured on back, along with 1991 stats and highlights, career numbers and personal data. Cards are checklisted here according to the uniform numbers found on the front.

		MT
Complete Set (9):		5.00
Common Player:		.50
1	Vince Coleman	.50
9	Todd Hundley	.75
12	Willie Randolph	.50
16	Dwight Gooden	.75
17	David Cone	.60
18	Bret Saberhagen	.60
20	Howard Johnson	.50
25	Bobby Bonilla	.60
33	Eddie Murray	1.00

1990 Modern Publishing Poster Books

This series of books offers individual mini-posters of the game's top players arranged in four categories. Each of the 11" x 17" books has a dozen color posters inside, perforated for easy separation. Fronts of each poster have borderless game-action photos with a facsimile autograph identifying the player. Backs have a large logo identifying the particular poster book from which the piece originated, along with player ID and a few sentences about him. Licensors logos and copyright data are at bottom. Original cover price was $10.95 each.

		MT
Complete Set, Books (4):		40.00
	Complete Poster Book, Big Hitters:	10.00
(1)	Wade Boggs	
(2)	Jose Canseco	
(3)	Will Clark	
(4)	Tony Gwynn	
(5)	Rickey Henderson	
(6)	Bo Jackson	
(7)	Howard Johnson	
(8)	Don Mattingly	
(9)	Kirby Puckett	
(10)	Kevin Mitchell	
(11)	Darryl Strawberry	
(12)	Robin Yount	
	Complete Poster Book, Gold Gloves:	10.00
(1)	Eric Davis	
(2)	Andre Dawson	
(3)	Dwight Evans	
(4)	Tony Fernandez	
(5)	Gary Gaetti	
(6)	Harold Reynolds	
(7)	Ryne Sandberg	
(8)	Benito Santiago	
(9)	Ozzie Smith	
(10)	Andy Van Slyke	
(11)	Devon White	
(12)	Dave Winfield	
	Complete Poster Book, Hot Rookies:	12.00
(1)	Jim Abbott	
(2)	Greg Briley	
(3)	Kevin Brown	
(4)	Junior Felix	
(5)	Bob Geren	
(6)	Tom Gordon	
(7)	Ken Griffey Jr.	
(8)	Gregg Jefferies	
(9)	Gregg Olson	
(10)	Dwight Smith	
(11)	Jerome Walton	
(12)	Craig Worthington	
	Complete Poster Book, Power Pitchers:	12.00
(1)	Roger Clemens	
(2)	Dennis Eckersley	
(3)	Doc Gooden	
(4)	Orel Hershiser	
(5)	Mark Langston	
(6)	Nolan Ryan	
(7)	Bret Saberhagen	
(8)	Mike Scott	
(9)	Dave Stewart	
(10)	Dave Steib	
(11)	Frank Viola	
(12)	Mitch Williams	

1992 Montoursville Rotary Mike Mussina

This collectors issue card was produced in conjunction

with a 1992 card show sponsored by the Rotary Club in Mussina's hometown of Montoursville, Pa. The card has a color action photo on front with Mussina's name, position and the sponsor club's logo in gold-foil. Back has a photo of the pitcher in his high school uniform, along with his 1991-92 Orioles stats.

	MT
Mike Mussina	20.00

1984 Montreal Expos Postcards

With its 1984 club issue, the Expos adopted a new format for its color player postcards. Fronts of the 3-9/16" x 5-7/16" cards are borderless, with no player identification or other graphics. Black-and-white backs have a team logo, uniform number and player name in the upper left. Vertically at center is the name of the printer. At upper-right is a dotted-line stamp box with "1984" beneath and a card number corresponding to the uniform number, with a "4000" prefix; four horizontal lines are printed for the address. Several cards can be found with back variations and three players are found on unnumbered cards printed in the spring training program.

		MT
Complete Set (35):		35.00
Common Player:		1.00
2	Billy DeMars	1.00
3	Bryan Little	1.00
4	Chris Speier	1.00
5	Jim Wohlford	1.00
6	Argenis Salazar	1.00
7	Bill Virdon	1.00
8	Gary Carter	3.00
10a	Andre Dawson	3.00
10b	Andre Dawson ("Printed in Canada" in stamp box)	3.00
12	Russ Nixon	1.00
13	Derrel Thomas	1.00
14	Pete Rose	6.00
15	Mike Fuentes	1.00
16a	Terry Francona	1.00
16b	Terry Francona ("Printed in Canada" in stamp box)	1.00
17	Felipe Alou	2.00
18	Miguel Dilone	1.00
19	Fred Breining	1.00
23	Doug Flynn	1.00
25a	Gary Lucas	1.00
25b	Gary Lucas (blank-back)	1.00
27	Ron Johnson	1.00
28	Bryn Smith	1.00
29a	Tim Wallach	1.00
29b	Tim Wallach ("Printed in Canada" in stamp box)	1.00
30a	Tim Raines	2.50
30b	Tim Raines ("Printed in Canada" in stamp box)	2.50
32	Mike Stenhouse	1.00
33	Mike Vail	1.00
34	Bill Gullickson	1.00
36	Galen Cisco	1.00
37	Andy McGaffigan	1.00
40	Joe Kerrigan	1.00
41	Jeff Reardon	1.00
42	Bob James	1.00
43	Dan Schatzeder	1.00
44	Bobby Ramos	1.00
45a	Steve Rogers	1.00
45b	Steve Rogers ("Printed in Canada" in stamp box)	1.00
46	David Palmer	1.00
48	Greg Harris	1.00
53a	Charlie Lea	1.00
53b	Charlie Lea ("Printed in Canada" in stamp box)	1.00
---	Andre Dawson (spring training program)	5.00
---	Tim Raines (spring training program)	5.00
---	Bill Virdon (spring training program)	3.00

1985 Montreal Expos Postcards

The second year of issue for the reformatted Expos color player postcards saw no change on the fronts of the 3-1/2" x 5-1/2" cards. Borderless player poses are featured without identification or other graphic elements. Backs feature considerably more black-and-white typography than the previous year, with team logo and copyright information at top- and bottom-left. The uniform number and player name are also at top. The printer is identified by a line of vertical type at center. Postcard indicia at right is in English and French. The year "1985" is printed beneath the stamp box. The cards are checklisted here by uniform number.

		MT
Complete Set (24):		16.00
Common Player:		1.00
1	U.L. Washington	1.00
2	Vance Law	1.00
3	Herm Winningham	1.00
4	Al Newman	1.00
6	Steve Nicosia	1.00
7	Hubie Brooks	1.00
11	Sal Butera	1.00
17	Skeeter Barnes	1.00
20a	Mike Fitzgerald (wearing cap)	1.00
20b	Mike Fitzgerald (wearing helmet)	1.00
22	Dan Driessen	1.00
24	Mickey Mahler	1.00
26	Ron Hansen	1.00
28	Bryn Smith	1.00
31	Razor Shines	1.00
32	Jack O'Conner	1.00
35	Rick Renick	1.00
36	Larry Bearnarth	1.00
37	Buck Rodgers	1.00
38	Joe Hesketh	1.00
42	Bert Roberge	1.00
44	Tim Burke	1.00
46	David Palmer	1.00
51	Randy St. Claire	1.00

1986 Montreal Expos Postcards

A new format was adopted for Montreal player postcards in 1986, eliminating the stamp box, date and other postcard elements from the back. Backs of the 1986 cards feature only the team logo, player uniform number and name, all in blue. Fronts of the 3-1/2" x 5-1/2" cards remained the same as in recent years, borderless color poses with no name box or facsimile autograph. Cards are listed here by uniform number.

		MT
Complete Set (20):		19.00
Common Player:		1.00
1	Bobby Winkles	1.00
4	Al Newman	1.00
11	Dann Bilardello	1.00
12	Andres Galarraga	6.00
15	Wayne Krenchicki	1.00
20	Mike Fitzgerald	1.00
23	Mitch Webster	1.00
24	Jason Thompson	1.00
27	Andy McGaffigan	1.00
28	Bryn Smith	1.00
29	Tim Wallach	1.00
31	Ken Macha	1.00
33	Floyd Youmans	1.00
34	Tom Nieto	1.00
38	Joe Hesketh	1.00
39	Jay Tibbs	1.00
43	Dan Schatzeder	1.00
44	Tim Burke	1.00
46	George Riley	1.00
49	Jeff Parrett	1.00

1987 Montreal Expos Postcards

Continuing a format adopted in 1986, the Expos annual postcard issue in 1987 added 26 new players. Fronts of the 3-1/2" x 5-1/2" cards are borderless with posed color photos; there is no name or facsimile autograph. Backs are printed in blue with a team logo at upper-left, and the player's uniform number and name to the right. The 1987 cards are checklisted here in uniform-number order.

		MT
Complete Set (26):		22.00
Common Player:		1.00
2	Vance Law	1.00
3	Herm Winningham	1.00
4	Dave Engle	1.00
5	Reid Nichols	1.00
6	Wallace Johnson	1.00
7	Hubie Brooks	1.00
9	Casey Candaele	1.00
12	Luis Rivera	1.00
14	Andres Galarraga	4.50
16	Tom Foley	1.00
17	Floyd Youmans	1.00
18	Ron Hansen	1.00
19	John Stefero	1.00
21	Alonzo Powell	1.00
22	Bob McClure	1.00
23	Mitch Webster	1.00
24	Jeff Reed	1.00
26	Neal Heaton	1.00
27	Andy McGaffigan	1.00
30	Tim Raines	2.50
36	Larry Bearnarth	1.00
37	Buck Rodgers	1.00
40	Lary Sorensen	1.00
42	Jackie Moore	1.00
48	Bob Sebra	1.00
51	Randy St. Claire	1.00

1991 MooTown Snackers

Produced by the Sargento Cheese Co., this 24-card set features the superstars of baseball. Cards were available in MooTown Snacker packages or by sending in a special set redemption coupon from a package to obtain the entire set for $5.95 and three UPC codes. The card fronts feature full-color action photos, but uniform logos are airbrushed off. Photos are bordered at top and bottom in red. Backs are in red, black and white and feature statistics and a facsimile autograph. Each player card is attached to a perforated panel on its right which has the checklist and a coupon to order the complete set. Cards with the offer coupon still attached are worth a premium of 50% over the values quoted here.

		MT
Complete Set (24):		8.00
Common Player:		.25
1	Jose Canseco	.50
2	Kirby Puckett	.75
3	Barry [illegible]	[illegible]
4	Ken Griffey, Jr.	2.00
5	Ryne Sandberg	.50
6	Tony Gwynn	.65
7	Kal Daniels	.25
8	Ozzie Smith	.45
9	Dave Justice	.40
10	Sandy Alomar, Jr.	.35
11	Wade Boggs	.40
12	Ozzie Guillen	.25
13	Dave Magadan	.25
14	Cal Ripken, Jr.	1.25
15	Don Mattingly	.75
16	Ruben Sierra	.25
17	Robin Yount	.65
18	Len Dykstra	.25
19	George Brett	.75
20	Lance Parrish	.25
21	Chris Sabo	.25
22	Craig Biggio	.35
23	Kevin Mitchell	.25
24	Cecil Fielder	.25

1992 MooTown Snackers

The unusual venue of cheese snack packs was the source for these cards. Produced as two-piece panels, there is a player card attached via perforations to an offer card for a complete set for $7 and proofs of purchase. The player cards have cheese-yellow borders at top and bottom with a player action photo at center. Produced by Michael Schecter Assoc., the cards have had uniform and cap logos removed because they are licensed only by the Players Association and not by MLB. Backs are printed in black and yellow on white and include a facsimile autograph. Cards with the complete set offer card still attached are worth a 50% premium above the values shown here.

		MT
Complete Set (24):		9.00
Common Player:		.25
1	Albert Belle	.50
2	Jeff Bagwell	.65
3	Jose Rijo	.25
4	Roger Clemens	.65
5	Kevin Maas	.25
6	Kirby Puckett	.75
7	Ken Griffey Jr.	2.00
8	Will Clark	.35
9	Felix Jose	.25
10	Cecil Fielder	.25
11	Darryl Strawberry	.30
12	John Smiley	.25
13	Roberto Alomar	.40
14	Paul Molitor	.50
15	Andre Dawson	.25
16	Terry Mulholland	.25
17	Fred McGriff	.35
18	Dwight Gooden	.30
19	Rickey Henderson	.35
20	Nolan Ryan	1.25
21	George Brett	.65
22	Tom Glavine	.35
23	Cal Ripken Jr.	1.25
24	Frank Thomas	.75

1983 Mother's Cookies Giants

After putting out Pacific Coast League sets in 1952-53 Mother's Cookies distributed this full-color set of 20 San Francisco Giants cards three decades later. The 2-1/2" x 3-1/2" cards were produced by hobbyist Barry Colla and include the Giants logo and player's name on the card fronts. Backs are numbered and contain biographical information, sponsor's logo and a space for the player's autograph. Fifteen cards were given to every fan at the Aug. 7, 1983, Giants game, with each fan also receiving a coupon good for five additional cards.

	MT
Complete Set (20):	30.00
Common Player:	1.00

1	Frank Robinson	6.00
2	Jack Clark	2.50
3	Chili Davis	2.50
4	Johnnie LeMaster	1.00
5	Greg Minton	1.00
6	Bob Brenly	1.00
7	Fred Breining	1.00
8	Jeff Leonard	1.00
9	Darrell Evans	2.50
10	Tom O'Malley	1.00
11	Duane Kuiper	1.00
12	Mike Krukow	1.00
13	Atlee Hammaker	1.00
14	Gary Lavelle	1.00
15	Bill Laskey	1.00
16	Max Venable	1.00
17	Joel Youngblood	1.00
18	Dave Bergman	1.00
19	Mike Vail	1.00
20	Andy McGaffigan	1.00

1984 Mother's Cookies Astros

Mother's Cookies issued a full-color team set for the Astros in 1984. Cards measure 2-1/2" x 3-1/2" with rounded corners. Card fronts feature unbordered color photos. Horizontal backs have biographical data, card number, Mother's Cookies logo and space for player autograph. There are 28 cards in the Astros set, with 20 of the cards distributed during a stadium promotion. Fans also received a coupon redeemable for eight additional cards. Since those cards did not necessarily complete collectors' sets, Mother's Cookies cards became very popular among traders. The Astros set includes one card for the coaches and a checklist.

		MT
Complete Set (28):		25.00
Common Player:		.50
1	Nolan Ryan	18.00
2	Joe Niekro	.65
3	Alan Ashby	.50
4	Bill Doran	.50
5	Phil Garner	.50
6	Ray Knight	.50
7	Dickie Thon	.50
8	Jose Cruz	.50
9	Jerry Mumphrey	.50
10	Terry Puhl	.50
11	Enos Cabell	.50
12	Harry Spilman	.50
13	Dave Smith	.50
14	Mike Scott	.50
15	Bob Lillis	.50
16	Bob Knepper	.50
17	Frank DiPino	.50
18	Tom Wieghaus	.50
19	Denny Walling	.50
20	Tony Scott	.50
21	Alan Bannister	.50
22	Bill Dawley	.50
23	Vern Ruhle	.50
24	Mike LaCoss	.50
25	Mike Madden	.50
26	Craig Reynolds	.50
27	Astros Coaches (Cot Deal, Don Leppert, Denis Menke, Les Moss, Jerry Walker)	.50
28	Astros Logo/Checklist	.50

1984 Mother's Cookies A's

Following the success of their one set in 1983, Mother's Cookies issued five more team sets of cards in 1984. Cards measure 2-1/2" x 3-1/2" with rounded corners. Fronts feature unbordered color photos. Horizontal backs have biographical data, card number, Mother's Cookies logo and space for player autograph. There are 28 cards in the A's set, with 20 of the cards distributed during a stadium promotion. Fans also received a coupon redeemable for eight additional cards. Since those cards did not necessarily complete collectors' sets, Mother's Cookies cards become very popular among card traders. The A's set includes cards for the manager, coaches and a checklist.

		MT
Complete Set (28):		25.00
Common Player:		.75
1	Steve Boros	.75
2	Rickey Henderson	5.00
3	Joe Morgan	2.50
4	Dwayne Murphy	.75
5	Mike Davis	.75
6	Bruce Bochte	.75
7	Carney Lansford	.75
8	Steve McCatty	.75
9	Mike Heath	.75
10	Chris Codiroli	.75
11	Bill Almon	.75
12	Bill Caudill	.75
13	Donnie Hill	.75
14	Lary Sorenson	.75
15	Dave Kingman	1.00
16	Garry Hancock	.75
17	Jeff Burroughs	.75
18	Tom Burgmeier	.75
19	Jim Essian	.75
20	Mike Warren	.75
21	Davey Lopes	.75
22	Ray Burris	.75
23	Tony Phillips	1.00
24	Tim Conroy	.75
25	Jeff Bettendorf	.75
26	Keith Atherton	.75
27	A's Coaches (Clete Boyer, Bob Didier, Jackie Moore, Ron Schueler, Billy Williams)	.75
28	Oakland Coliseum/ Checklist	.75

1984 Mother's Cookies Giants

Mother's Cookies issued a second annual full-color card set for the S.F. Giants in 1984. Cards measure 2-1/2" x 3-1/2" with rounded corners. Fronts feature drawings of former Giant All-Star team selections. Horizontal backs have brief biographical information, card number and Mother's Cookies logo and autograph space. There are 28 cards in the Giants set, with 20 of the cards distributed during a stadium promotion. Fans also received a coupon redeemable for eight additional cards. Since those cards did not necessarily complete collectors' sets, Mother's Cookies cards became very popular among card traders.

		MT
Complete Set (28):		27.50
Common Player:		.50
1	Willie Mays	9.00
2	Willie McCovey	4.00
3	Juan Marichal	2.50
4	Gaylord Perry	2.00
5	Tom Haller	.50
6	Jim Davenport	.50
7	Jack Clark	1.00
8	Greg Minton	.50
9	Atlee Hammaker	.50
10	Gary Lavelle	.50
11	Orlando Cepeda	2.50
12	Bobby Bonds	1.00
13	John Antonelli	.50
14	Bob Schmidt (photo actually Wes Westrum)	.50
15	Sam Jones	.50
16	Mike McCormick	.50
17	Ed Bailey	.50
18	Stu Miller	.50
19	Felipe Alou	1.00
20	Jim Hart	.50
21	Dick Dietz	.50
22	Chris Speier	.50
23	Bobby Murcer	.50
24	John Montefusco	.50
25	Vida Blue	.50
26	Ed Whitson	.50
27	Darrell Evans	1.00
28	All-Star Game Logo/ Checklist	.50

1984 Mother's Cookies Mariners

Mother's Cookies issued a full-color set for the Mariners Mariners in 1984. Cards measure 2-1/2" x 3-1/2" with rounded corners. Fronts feature unbordered color photos. Horizontal backs have brief biographical data, card number, Mother's Cookies logo and space for player autograph. There are 28 cards in the set with 20 of the cards distributed during a stadium promotion. Fans also received a coupon redeemable for eight additional cards. Since those cards did not necessarily complete collectors' sets, Mother's Cookies cards became very popular among traders. The set includes one card each for the manager, coaches and a checklist.

		MT
Complete Set (28):		20.00
Common Player:		.75
1	Del Crandall	.75
2	Barry Bonnell	.75
3	Dave Henderson	.75
4	Bob Kearney	.75
5	Mike Moore	.75
6	Spike Owen	.75
7	Gorman Thomas	.75
8	Ed VandeBerg	.75
9	Matt Young	.75
10	Larry Milbourne	.75
11	Dave Beard	.75
12	Jim Beattie	.75
13	Mark Langston	2.50
14	Orlando Mercado	.75
15	Jack Perconte	.75
16	Pat Putnam	.75
17	Paul Mirabella	.75
18	Domingo Ramos	.75
19	Al Cowens	.75
20	Mike Stanton	.75
21	Steve Henderson	.75
22	Bob Stoddard	.75
23	Alvin Davis	.75
24	Phil Bradley	.75
25	Roy Thomas	.75
26	Darnell Coles	.75
27	Mariners Coaches (Chuck Cottier, Frank Funk, Ben Hines, Phil Roof, Rick Sweet)	.75
28	Seattle Kingdome/ Checklist	.75

1984 Mother's Cookies Padres

Mother's Cookies issued a full-color set for the Padres in 1984. Cards measure 2-1/2" x 3-1/2", with rounded corners. Fronts feature unbordered color photos. Horizontal backs have brief biographical data, card number, sponsor's logo and space for player autograph. There are 28 cards in the set, with 20 of the cards distributed during a stadium promotion. Fans also received a coupon redeemable for eight additional cards. Since those cards did not necessarily complete collector's sets, Mother's Cookies cards became very popular among traders. The Padres set includes one card each for the manager, coaches and a checklist.

		MT
Complete Set (28):		30.00
Common Player:		.75
1	Dick Williams	.75
2	Rich Gossage	1.00
3	Tim Lollar	.75
4	Eric Show	.75
5	Terry Kennedy	.75
6	Kurt Bevacqua	.75
7	Steve Garvey	3.00
8	Garry Templeton	.75
9	Tony Gwynn	15.00
10	Alan Wiggins	.75
11	Dave Dravecky	.75
12	Tim Flannery	.75
13	Kevin McReynolds	.75
14	Bobby Brown	.75
15	Ed Whitson	.75
16	Doug Gwosdz	.75
17	Luis DeLeon	.75
18	Andy Hawkins	.75
19	Craig Lefferts	.75
20	Carmelo Martinez	.75
21	Sid Monge	.75
22	Graig Nettles	.75
23	Mario Ramirez	.75
24	Luis Salazar	.75
25	Champ Summers	.75
26	Mark Thurmond	.75
27	Padres Coaches (Harry Dunlop, Deacon Jones, Jack Krol, Norm Sherry, Ozzie Virgil)	.75
28	Jack Murphy Stadium/Checklist	.75

1985 Mother's Cookies Astros

Mother's Cookies issued a second annual full-color set for the Astros in 1985. Cards measure 2-1/2" x 3-1/2" with roundee corners. Fronts feature unbordered color photos. Horizontal backs have biographical information, card number, Mother's Cookies logo and space for player autograph. The set was distributed in its entirety during a stadium promotion.

		MT
Complete Set (28):		30.00
Common Player:		.50
1	Bob Lillis	.50
2	Nolan Ryan	21.00
3	Phil Garner	.50
4	Jose Cruz	.50
5	Denny Walling	.50
6	Joe Niekro	.60
7	Terry Puhl	.50
8	Bill Doran	.50
9	Dickie Thon	.50
10	Enos Cabell	.50
11	Frank Dipino (DiPino)	.50
12	Julio Solano	.50
13	Alan Ashby	.50
14	Craig Reynolds	.50
15	Jerry Mumphrey	.50
16	Bill Dawley	.50
17	Mark Bailey	.50
18	Mike Scott	.50
19	Harry Spilman	.50
20	Bob Knepper	.50
21	Dave Smith	.50
22	Kevin Bass	.50
23	Tim Tolman	.50
24	Jeff Calhoun	.50
25	Jim Pankovits	.50
26	Ron Mathis	.50
27	Astros Coaches (Cot Deal, Matt Galante, Don Leppert, Denis Menke, Jerry Walker)	.50
28	Astros Logo/Checklist	.50

1985 Mother's Cookies A's

Mother's Cookies again issued five full-color sets for Major League teams in 1985. Cards measure 2-1/2" x 3-1/2" with rounded corners. Fronts feature unbordered color photos. Horizontal backs have brief biographical data, card number, Mother's Cookies logo and space for player autograph. The set was distributed in its entirety during a stadium promotion.

		MT
Complete Set (28):		17.50
Common Player:		.50
1	Jackie Moore	.50
2	Dave Kingman	1.00
3	Don Sutton	3.00
4	Mike Heath	.50
5	Alfredo Griffin	.50
6	Dwayne Murphy	.50
7	Mike Davis	.50
8	Carney Lansford	.50
9	Chris Codiroli	.50
10	Bruce Bochte	.50
11	Mickey Tettleton	1.00
12	Donnie Hill	.50
13	Rob Picciolo	.50
14	Dave Collins	.50
15	Dusty Baker	.75
16	Tim Conroy	.50
17	Keith Atherton	.50
18	Jay Howell	.50
19	Mike Warren	.50
20	Steve McCatty	.50
21	Bill Krueger	.50
22	Curt Young	.50
23	Dan Meyer	.50
24	Mike Gallego	.60
25	Jeff Kaiser	.50
26	Steve Henderson	.50
27	A's Coaches (Clete Boyer, Bob Didier, Dave McKay, Wes Stock, Billy Williams)	.50
28	Oakland Coliseum/ Checklist	.50

1985 Mother's Cookies Giants

Mother's Cookies issued a third annual full-color set for the Giants in 1985. Cards measure 2-1/2" x 3-1/2" with rounded corners. Fronts feature unbordered color photos. Horizontal backs have brief biographical information, card number, Mother's Cookies logo and space for player autograph. The set was distributed in its entirety during a stadium promotion.

		MT
Complete Set (28):		14.00
Common Player:		.50
1	Jim Davenport	.50
2	Chili Davis	.75
3	Dan Gladden	.50
4	Jeff Leonard	.50
5	Manny Trillo	.50
6	Atlee Hammaker	.50
7	Bob Brenly	.50
8	Greg Minton	.50
9	Bill Laskey	.50
10	Vida Blue	.60
11	Mike Krukow	.50
12	Frank Williams	.50
13	Jose Uribe	.50
14	Johnnie LeMaster	.50
15	Scot Thompson	.50
16	Dave LaPoint	.50
17	David Green	.50
18	Chris Brown	.50
19	Joel Youngblood	.50
20	Mark Davis	.50
21	Jim Gott	.50
22	Doug Gwosdz	.50

23	Scott Garrelts	.50
24	Gary Rajsich	.50
25	Rob Deer	.50
26	Brad Wellman	.50
27	Coaches (Rocky Bridges, Chuck Hiller, Tom McCraw, Bob Miller, Jack Mull)	.50
28	Candlestick Park/ Checklist	.50

1985 Mother's Cookies Mariners

Mother's Cookies issued a second annual full-color set for the Mariners in 1985. Cards measure 2-1/2" x 3-1/2" with rounded corners. Fronts feature unbordered color photos. Horizontal backs have biographical information, card number, Mother's Cookies logo and space for player autograph. The set was distributed in its entirety during a stadium promotion.

		MT
Complete Set (28):		14.00
Common Player:		.50
1	Chuck Cottier	.50
2	Alvin Davis	.50
3	Mark Langston	1.00
4	Dave Henderson	.50
5	Ed VandeBerg	.50
6	Al Cowens	.50
7	Spike Owen	.50
8	Mike Moore	.50
9	Gorman Thomas	.50
10	Barry Bonnell	.50
11	Jack Perconte	.50
12	Domingo Ramos	.50
13	Bob Kearney	.50
14	Matt Young	.50
15	Jim Beattie	.50
16	Mike Stanton	.50
17	David Valle	.50
18	Ken Phelps	.50
19	Salome Barojas	.50
20	Jim Presley	.50
21	Phil Bradley	.50
22	Dave Geisel	.50
23	Harold Reynolds	1.00
24	Edwin Nunez	.50
25	Mike Morgan	.50
26	Ivan Calderon	.50
27	Mariners Coaches (Deron Johnson, Jim Mahoney, Marty Martinez, Phil Regan, Phil Roof)	.50
28	Seattle Kingdome/ Checklist	.50

1985 Mother's Cookies Padres

Mother's Cookies issued a second annual full-color Padres team set in 1985. Cards have rounded corners and measure 2-1/2" x 3-1/2". Glossy fronts feature unbordered color photos. Horizontal backs have biographical data, card number, Mother's Cookies logo and space for player autograph. The set was distributed in its entirety during a stadium promotion.

		MT
Complete Set (28):		22.00
Common Player:		.50
1	Dick Williams	.50
2	Tony Gwynn	10.00
3	Kevin McReynolds	.50
4	Graig Nettles	.50
5	Rich Gossage	.75
6	Steve Garvey	2.50
7	Garry Templeton	.50
8	Dave Dravecky	.50
9	Eric Show	.50
10	Terry Kennedy	.50
11	Luis DeLeon	.50
12	Bruce Bochy	.50
13	Andy Hawkins	.50
14	Kurt Bevacqua	.50
15	Craig Lefferts	.50
16	Mario Ramirez	.50
17	LaMarr Hoyt	.50
18	Jerry Royster	.50
19	Tim Stoddard	.50
20	Tim Flannery	.50
21	Mark Thurmond	.50
22	Greg Booker	.50
23	Bobby Brown	.50
24	Carmelo Martinez	.50
25	Al Bumbry	.50
26	Jerry Davis	.50
27	Padres Coaches (Galen Cisco, Harry Dunlop, Deacon Jones, Jack Krol, Ozzie Virgil)	.50
28	Jack Murphy Stadium/Checklist	.50

1986 Mother's Cookies Astros

Mother's Cookies produced a third annual Astros team set in 1985. The round-cornered, glossy front 2-1/2" x 3-1/2" cards feature unbordered color paintings of Houston's past All-Star Game performers Back have biographical information, card number and Mother's Cookies logo. There are 28 cards in the set, with 20 of the cards distributed during a stadium promotion. Each fan also received a coupon redeemable for eight additional cards which could be traded to complete a set.

		MT
Complete Set (28):		25.00
Common Player:		.50
1	Dick Farrell	.50
2	Hal Woodeschick (Woodeshick)	.50
3	Joe Morgan	2.00
4	Claude Raymond	.50
5	Mike Cuellar	.50
6	Rusty Staub	.50
7	Jimmy Wynn	.50
8	Larry Dierker	.50
9	Denis Menke	.50
10	Don Wilson	.50
11	Cesar Cedeno	.50
12	Lee May	.50
13	Bob Watson	.50
14	Ken Forsch	.50
15	Joaquin Andujar	.50
16	Terry Puhl	.50
17	Joe Niekro	.75
18	Craig Reynolds	.50
19	Joe Sambito	.50
20	Jose Cruz	.50
21	J.R. Richard	.60
22	Bob Knepper	.50
23	Nolan Ryan	17.50
24	Ray Knight	.50
25	Bill Dawley	.50
26	Dickie Thon	.50
27	Jerry Mumphrey	.50
28	Astros Logo/Checklist	.50

1986 Mother's Cookies A's

Mother's Cookies produced four full-color team sets in 1986, with only the San Diego Padres not repeating from the 1985 group. The third annual set for the Oakland A's measures 2-1/2" x 3-1/2" with rounded corners. Glossy fronts feature unbordered color photos. Horizontal backs have brief biographical information, card number and Mother's Cookies logo. There are 28 cards in the A's set, with 20 of the cards distributed during a stadium promotion. Each fan also received a coupon redeemable for eight additional cards which could be traded to complete a set.

		MT
Complete Set (28):		30.00
Common Player:		.50
1	Jackie Moore	.50
2	Dave Kingman	1.00
3	Dusty Baker	.75
4	Joaquin Andujar	.50
5	Alfredo Griffin	.50
6	Dwayne Murphy	.50
7	Mike Davis	.50
8	Carney Lansford	.50
9	Jose Canseco	16.00
10	Bruce Bochte	.50
11	Mickey Tettleton	.60
12	Donnie Hill	.50
13	Jose Rijo	.50
14	Rick Langford	.50
15	Chris Codiroli	.50
16	Moose Haas	.50
17	Keith Atherton	.50
18	Jay Howell	.50
19	Tony Phillips	.75
20	Steve Henderson	.50
21	Bill Krueger	.50
22	Steve Ontiveros	.50
23	Bill Bathe	.50
24	Rickey Peters	.50
25	Tim Birtsas	.50
26	Trainers (Frank Ciensczyk, Larry Davis, Steve Vucinich, Barry Weinberg)	.50
27	Coaches (Bob Didier, Dave McKay, Jeff Newman, Ron Plaza, Wes Stock, Bob Watson)	.50
28	Oakland Coliseum/ Checklist	.50

1986 Mother's Cookies Giants

Mother's Cookies produced a fourth annual set for the Giants in 1985. Round-cornered, glossy front cards measure 2-1/2" x 3-1/2" and feature unbordered color photos. Horizontal backs have biographical data, card number, and Mother's Cookies logo. There are 28 cards in the set, with 20 of the cards distributed during a stadium promotion. Each fan also received a coupon redeemable for eight additional cards which could be traded to complete the set.

		MT
Complete Set (28):		21.00
Common Player:		.50
1	Roger Craig	.50
2	Chili Davis	1.00
3	Dan Gladden	.50
4	Jeff Leonard	.50
5	Bob Brenly	.50
6	Atlee Hammaker	.50
7	Will Clark	8.00
8	Greg Minton	.50
9	Candy Maldonado	.50
10	Vida Blue	.60
11	Mike Krukow	.50
12	Bob Melvin	.50
13	Jose Uribe	.50
14	Dan Driessen	.50
15	Jeff Robinson	.50
16	Rob Thompson	.60
17	Mike LaCoss	.50
18	Chris Brown	.50
19	Scott Garrelts	.50
20	Mark Davis	.50
21	Jim Gott	.50
22	Brad Wellman	.50
23	Roger Mason	.50
24	Bill Laskey	.50
25	Brad Gulden	.50
26	Joel Youngblood	.50
27	Juan Berenguer	.50
28	Coaches/Checklist (Bill Fahey, Bob Lillis, Gordy MacKenzie, Jose Morales, Norm Sherry)	.50

1986 Mother's Cookies Mariners

Mother's Cookies produced a third annual set for the M's in 1985. Round-cornered, glossy front cards measure 2-1/2" x 3-1/2" and feature unbordered color photos. Horizontal backs have brief biographical information, card number and sponsor's logo. There are 28 cards in the set, with 20 distributed during a stadium promotion. Each fan also received a coupon redeemable for eight additional cards which could be traded to complete the set.

		MT
Complete Set (28):		14.00
Common Player:		.50
1	Dick Williams	.50
2	Alvin Davis	.50
3	Mark Langston	.75
4	Dave Henderson	.50
5	Steve Yeager	.50
6	Al Cowens	.50
7	Jim Presley	.50
8	Phil Bradley	.50
9	Gorman Thomas	.50
10	Barry Bonnell	.50
11	Milt Wilcox	.50
12	Domingo Ramos	.50
13	Paul Mirabella	.50
14	Matt Young	.50
15	Ivan Calderon	.50
16	Bill Swift	.50
17	Pete Ladd	.50
18	Ken Phelps	.50
19	Karl Best	.50
20	Spike Owen	.50
21	Mike Moore	.50
22	Danny Tartabull	.50
23	Bob Kearney	.50
24	Edwin Nunez	.50
25	Mike Morgan	.50
26	Roy Thomas	.50
27	Jim Beattie	.50
28	Coaches/Checklist (Deron Johnson, Marty Martinez, Phil Regan, Phil Roof, Ozzie Virgil)	.50

1987 Mother's Cookies Astros

Twenty of 28 cards featuring Astros players were given out to the first 25,000 fans attending the July 17 game at the Astrodome. An additional eight cards (though not necessarily the exact eight needed to complete a set) were available from the sponsor by redeeming a mail-in certificate. The cards have rounded corners, glossy fronts and measure 2-1/2" x 3-1/2". Backs are printed in purple and orange and contain personal data, the Mother's Cookies logo, card number and a spot for the player's autograph.

		MT
Complete Set (28):		27.50
Common Player:		.50
1	Hal Lanier	.50
2	Mike Scott	.50
3	Jose Cruz	.50
4	Bill Doran	.50
5	Bob Knepper	.50
6	Phil Garner	.50
7	Terry Puhl	.50
8	Nolan Ryan	17.50
9	Kevin Bass	.50
10	Glenn Davis	.50
11	Alan Ashby	.50
12	Charlie Kerfeld	.50
13	Denny Walling	.50
14	Danny Darwin	.50
15	Mark Bailey	.50
16	Davey Lopes	.50
17	Dave Meads	.50
18	Aurelio Lopez	.50
19	Craig Reynolds	.50
20	Dave Smith	.50
21	Larry Anderson (Andersen)	.50
22	Jim Pankovits	.50
23	Jim Deshaies	.50
24	Bert Pena	.50
25	Dickie Thon	.50
26	Billy Hatcher	.50
27	Coaches (Yogi Berra, Matt Galante, Denis Menke, Les Moss, Gene Tenace)	.50
28	Houston Astrodome/ Checklist	.50

1987 Mother's Cookies A's

Continuing with a tradition of producing beautiful baseball cards, Mother's Cookies of Oakland, Calif. issued a 28-card set featuring every Oakland A's player to have been elected to the All-Star Game since 1968. The full-color photos came from the private collection of nationally known photographer Doug McWilliams. Twenty of the 28 cards were given out to fans attending the A's game on July 5. An additional eight cards were available by redeeming a mail-in certificate. The cards measure 2-1/2" x 3-1/2" and feature rounded corners. Backs carry the player's All-Star Game statistics.

		MT
Complete Set (28):		27.50
Common Player:		.50
1	Bert Campaneris	.50
2	Rick Monday	.50
3	John Odom	.50
4	Sal Bando	.50
5	Reggie Jackson	4.00
6	Catfish Hunter	2.00
7	Vida Blue	.50
8	Dave Duncan	.50
9	Joe Rudi	.50
10	Rollie Fingers	1.50
11	Ken Holtzman	.50
12	Dick Williams	.50
13	Alvin Dark	.50
14	Gene Tenace	.50
15	Claudell Washington	.50
16	Phil Garner	.50
17	Wayne Gross	.50
18	Matt Keough	.50
19	Jeff Newman	.50
20	Rickey Henderson	3.00
21	Tony Armas	.50
22	Mike Norris	.50
23	Billy Martin	.75
24	Bill Caudill	.50
25	Jay Howell	.50
26	Jose Canseco	5.00
27	Jose and Reggie (Jose Canseco, Reggie Jackson)	5.00
28	A's Logo/Checklist	.50

The values of some parallel-card issues will have to be calculated based on figures presented in the heading for the regular-issue card set.

1987 Mother's Cookies Dodgers

Mother's Cookies produced for the first time in 1987 a team set featuring the L.A. Dodgers. Twenty of the 28 cards were given to youngsters 14 and under at Dodger Stadium on Aug. 9. An additional eight cards were available from Mother's Cookies via a mail-in coupon. The borderless, full-color cards measure 2-1/2" x 3-1/2" and have rounded corners. A special album designed to house the set was available for $3.95 through a mail-in offer.

		MT
Complete Set (28):		12.00
Common Player:		.50
1	Tom Lasorda	.75
2	Pedro Guerrero	.50
3	Steve Sax	.50
4	Fernando Valenzuela	.75
5	Mike Marshall	.50
6	Orel Hershiser	1.00
7	Mariano Duncan	.50
8	Bill Madlock	.50
9	Bob Welch	.50
10	Mike Scioscia	.50
11	Mike Ramsey	.50
12	Matt Young	.50
13	Franklin Stubbs	.50
14	Tom Niedenfuer	.50
15	Reggie Williams	.50
16	Rick Honeycutt	.50
17	Dave Anderson	.50
18	Alejandro Pena	.50
19	Ken Howell	.50
20	Len Matuszek	.50
21	Tim Leary	.50
22	Tracy Woodson	.50
23	Alex Trevino	.50
24	Ken Landreaux	.50
25	Mickey Hatcher	.50
26	Brian Holton	.50
27	Coaches (Joey Amalfitano, Mark Cresse, Don McMahon, Manny Mota, Ron Perranoski, Bill Russell)	.50
28	Dodger Stadium/ Checklist	.50

1987 Mother's Cookies Giants

Distribution of the 1987 Mother's Cookies Giants, cards took place at Candlestick Park on June 27. Twenty of the 28 cards in the set were given to the first 25,000 fans entering the park. The starter packet of 20 cards contained a mail-in coupon card which was good for an additional eight cards. The glossy-front cards measure 2-1/2" x 3-1/2" with rounded corners. Backs are printed in red and purple and contain personal and statistical information along with the Mother's Cookies logo.

		MT
Complete Set (28):		16.00
Common Player:		.50
1	Roger Craig	.50
2	Will Clark	3.00
3	Chili Davis	.75
4	Bob Brenly	.50
5	Chris Brown	.50
6	Mike Krukow	.50
7	Candy Maldonado	.50
8	Jeffrey Leonard	.50
9	Greg Minton	.50
10	Robby Thompson	.50
11	Scott Garrelts	.50
12	Bob Melvin	.50
13	Jose Uribe	.50
14	Mark Davis	.50
15	Eddie Milner	.50
16	Harry Spilman	.50
17	Kelly Downs	.50
18	Chris Speier	.50
19	Jim Gott	.50
20	Joel Youngblood	.50
21	Mike LaCoss	.50
22	Matt Williams	3.00
23	Roger Mason	.50
24	Mike Aldrete	.50
25	Jeff Robinson	.50
26	Mark Grant	.50
27	Coaches (Bill Fahey, Bob Lillis, Gordon MacKenzie, Jose Morales, Norm Sherry, Don Zimmer)	.50
28	Candlestick Park/ Checklist	.50

1987 Mother's Cookies Mariners

For the fourth consecutive year, Mother's Cookies issued a team set featuring the Mariners. Twenty of the 28 cards were distributed to the first 20,000 fans entering the Kingdome on Aug. 9. An additional eight cards (though not necessarily the eight cards needed to complete the set) were available by redeeming a mail-in certificate. Collectors were encouraged to trade to complete a set. The 2-1/2" x 3-1/2" full-color cards feature glossy fronts and rounded corners. A specially designed album to house the set was available.

		MT
Complete Set (28):		14.00
Common Player:		.50
1	Dick Williams	.50
2	Alvin Davis	.50
3	Mike Moore	.50
4	Jim Presley	.50
5	Mark Langston	.75
6	Phil Bradley	.50
7	Ken Phelps	.50
8	Mike Morgan	.50
9	David Valle	.50
10	Harold Reynolds	.75
11	Edwin Nunez	.50
12	Bob Kearney	.50
13	Scott Bankhead	.50
14	Scott Bradley	.50
15	Mickey Brantley	.50
16	Mark Huismann	.50
17	Mike Kingery	.50
18	John Moses	.50
19	Donell Nixon	.50
20	Rey Quinones	.50
21	Domingo Ramos	.50
22	Jerry Reed	.50
23	Rich Renteria	.50
24	Rich Monteleone	.50
25	Mike Trujillo	.50
26	Bill Wilkinson	.50
27	John Christensen	.50
28	Coaches/Checklist (Billy Connors, Frank Howard, Phil Roof, Bobby Tolan, Ozzie Virgil)	.50

1987 Mother's Cookies Rangers

While Mother's Cookies of Oakland had produced high-quality baseball card sets of various teams since 1983, the Rangers participated in the promotion for the first time in 1987. Twenty cards from the 28-card set were handed out to the first 25,000 fans entering Arlington Stadium on July 17. An additional eight cards (though not necessarily the eight needed to complete a set) were available by redeeming a mail-in certificate. The cards measure 2-1/2" x 3-1/2" with rounded corners and glossy finish, like all Mother's Cookies issued in 1987.

		MT
Complete Set (28):		14.00
Common Player:		.50
1	Bobby Valentine	.50
2	Pete Incaviglia	.75
3	Charlie Hough	.50
4	Oddibe McDowell	.50
5	Larry Parrish	.50
6	Scott Fletcher	.60
7	Steve Buechele	.50
8	Tom Paciorek	.50
9	Pete O'Brien	.50
10	Darrell Porter	.50
11	Greg Harris	.50
12	Don Slaught	.50
13	Ruben Sierra	.75
14	Curtis Wilkerson	.50
15	Dale Mohorcic	.50
16	Ron Meredith	.50
17	Mitch Williams	.75
18	Bob Brower	.50
19	Edwin Correa	.50
20	Geno Petralli	.50
21	Mike Loynd	.50
22	Jerry Browne	.50
23	Jose Guzman	.50
24	Jeff Kunkel	.50
25	Bobby Witt	.60
26	Jeff Russell	.50
27	Trainers (Danny Wheat, Bill Zeigler)	.50
28	Coaches/Checklist (Joe Ferguson, Tim Foli, Tom House, Art Howe, Dave Oliver, Tom Robson)	.50

1987 Mother's Cookies Mark McGwire

A four-card set featuring outstanding rookie Mark McGwire of the Oakland A's was produced by Mother's Cookies in 1987. Cards are 2-1/2" x 3-1/2" and have rounded corners and glossy finish like other Mother's issues. The set was obtainable by sending in eight proof-of-purchase seals or could be secured at the National Sports Collectors Convention held July 9-12 in San Francisco. Convention goers received one card as a bonus for each Mother's Cookies baseball card album purchased.

		MT
Complete Set (4):		75.00
Common Card:		20.00
1	Mark McGwire (portrait)	20.00
2	Mark McGwire (leaning on bat rack)	20.00
3	Mark McGwire (beginning batting swing)	20.00
4	Mark McGwire (batting follow-through)	20.00

1987-93 Mother's Cookies Advertising Display Signs

Used as point of purchase advertising displays, these colorful cardboard signs are of interest to card collectors because many of them picture the Mother's Cookies cards which could be found in packages. Two basic sizes are found, 18" x 18" and 18" x 27". The larger displays usually feature star players from the card sets, while the smaller signs picture only the cards.

	MT
Common 18" x 18" sign:	40.00
Common 18" x 27" sign:	50.00
1987 Bay Area Trading Card Days (Jose Canseco, Will Clark) (18x27)	50.00
1988 Bay Area Trading Card Days (Mark McGwire, Will Clark) (18x27)	70.00
1988 Mark McGwire - shows four cards (18x18)	80.00
1989 Bay Area Trading Card Days (Mark McGwire, Will Clark) (18x27)	70.00
1989 40/40 (Jose Canseco - shows four cards) (18x18)	40.00
1989 A.L. R.O.Y.s (Jose Canseco, Mark McGwire, Walt Weiss - shows four cards) (18x18)	75.00
1989 (Ken Griffey Jr. - shows four cards) (18x18)	80.00
1990 Bay Area Trading Card Days (Mark McGwire, Will Clark) (18x27)	70.00
1990 Jose Canseco, Mark McGwire - holding four card sets (18x27)	70.00
1990 5,000K (Nolan Ryan - pulling cards from bag) (18x27)	50.00
1990 5,000K (Nolan Ryan - shows four cards) (18x18)	40.00
1990 5,000K (Nolan Ryan - holding bags of cookies) (18x18)	40.00
1991 300 Wins (Nolan Ryan - pulling card from bag) (18x27)	50.00
1991 300 Wins (Nolan Ryan - shows four single cards) (18x18)	40.00
1991 300 Wins (Nolan Ryan - shows uncut sheet of four) (18x18)	40.00
1991 Ken Griffey Sr., Ken Griffey Jr. (18x27)	50.00
1991 Ken Griffey Sr., Ken Griffey Jr. - shows four cards (18x18)	50.00
1991 Ken Griffey Sr., Ken Griffey Jr. - shows uncut panel (18x18)	40.00
1993 Fired Up (Nolan Ryan) (18x27)	50.00
1993 Farewell (Nolan Ryan - shows nine cards) (18x18)	40.00
1993 Farewell (Nolan Ryan - shows 10 card sheet) (18x18)	40.00
1993 Farewell (Nolan Ryan - holding cookies) (18x18)	40.00

1988 Mother's Cookies Astros

One of six team sets issued by Mother's Cookies in 1988, the 28-card Astros set is similar in design to other Mother's Cookies sets. Glossy-front cards are 2-1/2" x 3-1/2" size with rounded corners and feature full-color, borderless photos on the fronts. Backs feature red and purple printing and include brief biographical information, the Mother's logo and card number. Twenty of the cards were distributed in a stadium promotion, along with a redemption card that could be exchanged for an additional eight cards (but not necessarily the eight needed to complete the set). An album was also available to house the set.

		MT
Complete Set (28):		25.00
Common Player:		.50
1	Hal Lanier	.50
2	Mike Scott	.50
3	Gerald Young	.50
4	Bill Doran	.50
5	Bob Knepper	.50
6	Billy Hatcher	.50
7	Terry Puhl	.50
8	Nolan Ryan	17.50
9	Kevin Bass	.50
10	Glenn Davis	.50
11	Alan Ashby	.50
12	Steve Henderson	.50
13	Denny Walling	.50
14	Danny Darwin	.50
15	Mark Bailey	.50
16	Ernie Camacho	.50
17	Rafael Ramirez	.50
18	Jeff Heathcock	.50
19	Craig Reynolds	.50
20	Dave Smith	.50
21	Larry Andersen	.50
22	Jim Pankovits	.50
23	Jim Deshaies	.50
24	Juan Agosto	.50
25	Chuck Jackson	.50
26	Joaquin Andujar	.50
27	Coaches (Yogi Berra, Gene Clines, Matt Galante, Marc Hill, Denis Menke, Les Moss)	.50
28	Trainers/Checklist (Doc Ewell, Dave Labossiere, Dennis Liborio)	.50

1988 Mother's Cookies A's

Complete at 28 cards, the 1988 Mother's Cookies A's set features full-color, borderless cards with rounded corners in the standard 2-1/2" x 3-1/2" format. Backs are printed in red and purple and include biographical information, the Mother's Cookies logo and card number. Starter sets of 20 cards were distributed at the stadium along with a promotional card redeemable for another eights cards (not necessarily those needed to complete the set). An album to house the cards was also available.

		MT
Complete Set (28):		35.00
Common Player:		.50
1	Tony LaRussa	.60
2	Mark McGwire	15.00
3	Dave Stewart	.75
4	Mickey Tettleton	.50
5	Dave Parker	.75
6	Carney Lansford	.50
7	Jose Canseco	5.00
8	Don Baylor	.75
9	Bob Welch	.50
10	Dennis Eckersley	1.50
11	Walt Weiss	1.00
12	Tony Phillips	.60
13	Steve Ontiveros	.50
14	Dave Henderson	.50
15	Stan Javier	.50
16	Ron Hassey	.50
17	Curt Young	.50
18	Glenn Hubbard	.50
19	Storm Davis	.50
20	Eric Plunk	.50
21	Matt Young	.50
22	Mike Gallego	.50
23	Rick Honeycutt	.50
24	Doug Jennings	.50
25	Gene Nelson	.50
26	Greg Cadaret	.50
27	Coaches (Dave Duncan, Rene Lachemann, Jim Lefebvre, Dave McKay, Mike Paul, Bob Watson)	.50
28	Jose Canseco, Mark McGwire	7.50

1988 Mother's Cookies Dodgers

Similar in design to other Mother's Cookies sets, the 1988 Dodgers issue features full-color, borderless photos with backs printed in red and purple. The 28 cards in the set measure 2-1/2" x 3-1/2" with rounded corners. Starter packs of 20 cards were distributed at a ballpark promotion along with a coupon card that could be exchanged for an additional eight cards at a local card show or through the mail. Backs include brief player information, the Mother's Cookies logo and card number. The promotion also included a special album to house the set.

		MT
Complete Set (28):		12.00
Common Player:		.50
1	Tom Lasorda	.75
2	Pedro Guerrero	.50
3	Steve Sax	.50
4	Fernando Valenzuela	.65
5	Mike Marshall	.50
6	Orel Hershiser	.75
7	Alfredo Griffin	.50
8	Kirk Gibson	.75
9	Don Sutton	1.00
10	Mike Scioscia	.50
11	Franklin Stubbs	.50
12	Mike Davis	.50
13	Jesse Orosco	.50
14	John Shelby	.50
15	Rick Dempsey	.50
16	Jay Howell	.50
17	Dave Anderson	.50
18	Alejandro Pena	.50
19	Jeff Hamilton	.50
20	Danny Heep	.50
21	Tim Leary	.50
22	Brad Havens	.50
23	Tim Belcher	.50
24	Ken Howell	.50
25	Mickey Hatcher	.50
26	Brian Holton	.50
27	Mike Devereaux	.50
28	Coaches/Checklist (Joe Amalfitano, Mark Cresse, Joe Ferguson, Ben Hines, Manny Mota, Ron Perranoski, Bill Russell)	.50

1988 Mother's Cookies Giants

One of six team sets issued in 1988 by Mother's Cookies, this 28-card Giants set featured full-color borderless photos on a standard-size card with rounded corners. Backs, printed in red and purple, include brief player data, the Mother's Cookies logo and card number. Twenty different cards were distributed as a starter set at a stadium promotion along with a coupon card that could be redeemed for an additional eight cards (not necessarily those needed to complete the set). The redemption cards could be exchanged through the mail or redeemed at a local card show.

		MT
Complete Set (28):		15.00
Common Player:		.50
1	Roger Craig	.50
2	Will Clark	2.50
3	Kevin Mitchell	.50
4	Bob Brenly	.50
5	Mike Aldrete	.50
6	Mike Krukow	.50
7	Candy Maldonado	.50
8	Jeffrey Leonard	.50
9	Dave Dravecky	.50
10	Robby Thompson	.50
11	Scott Garrelts	.50
12	Bob Melvin	.50
13	Jose Uribe	.50
14	Brett Butler	.75
15	Rick Reuschel	.50
16	Harry Spilman	.50
17	Kelly Downs	.50
18	Chris Speier	.50
19	Atlee Hammaker	.50
20	Joel Youngblood	.50
21	Mike LaCoss	.50
22	Don Robinson	.50
23	Mark Wasinger	.50
24	Craig Lefferts	.50
25	Phil Garner	.50
26	Joe Price	.50
27	Coaches (Dusty Baker, Bill Fahey, Bob Lillis, Gordie MacKenzie, Jose Morales, Norm Sherry)	.50
28	Logo Card/Checklist	.50

1988 Mother's Cookies Mariners

Similar in design to other Mother's Cookies sets, the 28-card Mariners issue features full-color, borderless photos on a 2-1/2" x 3-1/2" card with rounded corners. Backs, printed in red and purple, include brief biographical information, the Mother's Cookies logo and card number. Twenty-card starter packs were distributed at a stadium promotion, where fans also received a coupon card that could be exchanged for an additional eight cards (not necessarily those needed to complete the set). The coupon card could be redeemed through the mail or exchanged at a local baseball card show. As with the rest of the 1988 Mother's Cookies sets, an album was also available to house the cards.

		MT
Complete Set (28):		14.00
Common Player:		.50
1	Dick Williams	.50
2	Alvin Davis	.50
3	Mike Moore	.50
4	Jim Presley	.50
5	Mark Langston	.75
6	Henry Cotto	.50
7	Ken Phelps	.50
8	Steve Trout	.50
9	David Valle	.50
10	Harold Reynolds	.75
11	Edwin Nunez	.50
12	Glenn Wilson	.50
13	Scott Bankhead	.50
14	Scott Bradley	.50
15	Mickey Brantley	.50
16	Bruce Fields	.50
17	Mike Kingery	.50
18	Mike Campbell	.50
19	Mike Jackson	.50
20	Rey Quinones	.50
21	Mario Diaz	.50
22	Jerry Reed	.50
23	Rich Renteria	.50
24	Julio Solano	.50
25	Bill Swift	.50
26	Bill Wilkinson	.50
27	Coaches (Billy Connors, Frank Howard, Phil Roof, Jim Snyder, Ozzie Virgil)	.50
28	Trainers/Checklist (Henry Genzale, Rick Griffin)	.50

1988 Mother's Cookies Rangers

This 28-card issue was one of six team sets issued in 1988 by Mother's Cookies. The Rangers issue features full-color, borderless cards printed in standard 2-1/2" x 3-1/2" format with rounded corners. Backs are printed in red and purple and include player information, Mother's Cookies logo and card number. Twenty-card starter packs were distributed as a stadium promotion that included a redemption card good for another eight cards (not necessarily those needed to complete the set) either through the mail or at a local card show.

		MT
Complete Set (28):		14.00
Common Player:		.50
1	Bobby Valentine	.50
2	Pete Incaviglia	.50
3	Charlie Hough	.50
4	Oddibe McDowell	.50
5	Larry Parrish	.50
6	Scott Fletcher	.50
7	Steve Buechele	.50
8	Steve Kemp	.50
9	Pete O'Brien	.50
10	Ruben Sierra	.50
11	Mike Stanley	.50
12	Jose Cecena	.50
13	Cecil Espy	.50
14	Curtis Wilkerson	.50
15	Dale Mohorcic	.50
16	Ray Hayward	.50
17	Mitch Williams	.50
18	Bob Brower	.50
19	Paul Kilgus	.50
20	Geno Petralli	.50
21	James Steels	.50
22	Jerry Browne	.50
23	Jose Guzman	.50
24	DeWayne Vaughn	.50
25	Bobby Witt	.50
26	Jeff Russell	.50
27	Coaches (Richard Egan, Tom House, Art Howe, Davey Lopes, David Oliver, Tom Robson)	.50
28	Trainers/Checklist (Danny Wheat, Bill Zeigler)	.50

1988 Mother's Cookies Will Clark

In a baseball spring training-related promotion, Mother's Cookies of Oakland, Calif. produced a full-color four-card set featuring San Francisco Giants first baseman Will Clark. The cards, which have glossy finishes and rounded corners, came cellophane-wrapped in specially marked 18-ounce packages of Mother's Cookies products. The cards are identical in style to the other Mother's Cookies issues.

		MT
Complete Set (4):		10.00
Common Card:		2.50
1	Will Clark (bat on shoulder)	2.50
2	Will Clark (kneeling)	2.50
3	Will Clark (batting follow-thru)	2.50
4	Will Clark (heading for first base)	2.50

1988 Mother's Cookies Mark McGwire

For the second consecutive year, Mother's Cookies devoted a four-card set to Oakland A's slugger Mark McGwire. The full-color cards have rounded corners and measure 2-1/2" x 3-1/2". The cards were issued in specially marked 18-ounce packages of Mother's Cookies products in the northern California area. The cards are identical in design to the team issues produced by Mother's.

		MT
Complete Set (4):		30.00
Common Card:		7.50
1	Mark McGwire (holding oversized bat)	7.50
2	Mark McGwire (fielding)	7.50
3	Mark McGwire (kneeling)	7.50
4	Mark McGwire (bat in air)	7.50

1989 Mother's Cookies Astros

The 1989 Astros team set issued by Mother's Cookies consists of 28 cards in 2-1/2" x 3-1/2" format in the traditional style of glossy borderless photos and rounded corners. Partial sets were distributed to fans attending the July 22 game at the Astrodome. The cards feature the photography of Barry Colla and display the Mother's Cookies logo on the back.

		MT
Complete Set (28):		20.00
Common Player:		.50
1	Art Howe	.50
2	Mike Scott	.50
3	Gerald Young	.50
4	Bill Doran	.50
5	Billy Hatcher	.50
6	Terry Puhl	.50
7	Bob Knepper	.50
8	Kevin Bass	.50
9	Glenn Davis	.50
10	Alan Ashby	.50
11	Bob Forsch	.50
12	Greg Gross	.50
13	Danny Darwin	.50
14	Craig Biggio	4.00
15	Jim Clancy	.50
16	Rafael Ramirez	.50
17	Alex Trevino	.50
18	Craig Reynolds	.50
19	Dave Smith	.50
20	Larry Andersen	.50
21	Eric Yelding	.50
22	Jim Deshaies	.50
23	Juan Agosto	.50
24	Rick Rhoden	.50
25	Ken Caminiti	3.00
26	Dave Meads	.50
27	Astros coaches (Yogi Berra, Matt Galante, Phil Garner, Les Moss, Ed Napoleon, Ed Ott)	.50
28	Trainers/checklist (Dave Labossiere, Doc Ewell, Dennis Liborio)	.50

1989 Mother's Cookies A's

The 1989 Mother's Cookies A's set consists of 28 cards designed in the traditional style: a glossy 2-1/2" x 3-1/2" card with a borderless photo and rounded corners. A starter set of the cards was used as a stadium promotion and distributed to fans attending the July 30 Oakland game.

		MT
Complete Set (28):		30.00
Common Player:		.50
1	Tony LaRussa	.50
2	Mark McGwire	10.00
3	Terry Steinbach	.75
4	Dave Parker	.60
5	Carney Lansford	.50
6	Dave Stewart	.60
7	Jose Canseco	5.00
8	Walt Weiss	.75
9	Bob Welch	.50
10	Dennis Eckersley	.60
11	Tony Phillips	.75
12	Mike Moore	.50
13	Dave Henderson	.50
14	Curt Young	.50
15	Ron Hassey	.50
16	Eric Plunk	.50
17	Luis Polonia	.50
18	Storm Davis	.50
19	Glenn Hubbard	.50
20	Greg Cadaret	.50
21	Stan Javier	.50
22	Felix Jose	.50
23	Mike Gallego	.50
24	Todd Burns	.50
25	Rick Honeycutt	.50
26	Gene Nelson	.50
27	A's Coaches (Dave Duncan, Rene Lacheman, Art Kusnyer, Tommie Reynolds, Merv Rettenmund)	.50
28	Walt Weiss, Mark McGwire, Jose Canseco	5.00

1989 Mother's Cookies Dodgers

This 28-card set features the players and coaches of the L.A. Dodgers. The cards follow the traditional Mother's Cookies style featuring rounded corners, borderless color photos, horizontal backs and 2-1/2" x 3-1/2" size. Initially 20 cards were given away as starter sets at Dodger Stadium.

		MT
Complete Set (28):		12.00
Common Player:		.50
1	Tom Lasorda	.75
2	Eddie Murray	3.00
3	Mike Scioscia	.50
4	Fernando Valenzuela	.65
5	Mike Marshall	.50
6	Orel Hershiser	.75
7	Alfredo Griffin	.50
8	Kirk Gibson	.75
9	John Tudor	.50
10	Willie Randolph	.50
11	Franklin Stubbs	.50
12	Mike Davis	.50
13	Mike Morgan	.50
14	John Shelby	.50
15	Rick Dempsey	.50
16	Jay Howell	.50
17	Dave Anderson	.50
18	Alejandro Pena	.50
19	Jeff Hamilton	.50
20	Ricky Horton	.50
21	Tim Leary	.50
22	Ray Searage	.50
23	Tim Belcher	.50
24	Tim Crews	.50
25	Mickey Hatcher	.50
26	Mariano Duncan	.50
27	Coaches (Joe Amalfitano, Mark Cresse, Joe Ferguson, Ben Hines, Manny Mota, Ron Perranoski, Bill Russell)	.50
28	Checklist	.50

1989 Mother's Cookies Giants

The 1989 Mother's Cookies Giants set consists of 28 cards, all featuring borderless, color photos with rounded corners. Starter sets of the cards were distributed as a stadium promotion to fans attending the Aug. 6, game at Candlestick Park.

		MT
Complete Set (28):		16.00
Common Player:		.50
1	Roger Craig	.50
2	Will Clark	2.50
3	Kevin Mitchell	.50
4	Kelly Downs	.50
5	Brett Butler	.75
6	Mike Krukow	.50
7	Candy Maldonado	.50
8	Terry Kennedy	.50
9	Dave Dravecky	.50
10	Robby Thompson	.50
11	Scott Garrelts	.50
12	Matt Williams	2.50
13	Jose Uribe	.50
14	Tracy Jones	.50
15	Rick Reuschel	.50
16	Ernest Riles	.50
17	Jeff Brantley	.50
18	Chris Speier	.50
19	Atlee Hammaker	.50
20	Ed Jurak	.50
21	Mike LaCoss	.50
22	Don Robinson	.50
23	Kirt Manwaring	.50
24	Craig Lefferts	.50
25	Donnell Nixon	.50
26	Joe Price	.50
27	Rich Gossage	.75
28	Coaches/Checklist (Bill Fahey, Dusty Baker, Bob Lillis, Wendell Kim, Norm Sherry)	.50

1989 Mother's Cookies Mariners

For the sixth straight season Mother's Cookies released a Mariners team set. The 1989 issue features 28 cards. Starter sets of 20 cards were distributed at a Mariner home game. The cards are 2-1/2" x 3-1/2" and feature borderless, glossy full color photos. Card backs are horizontal. Rookie sensation Ken Griffey Jr. was included in the 1989 issue.

		MT
Complete Set (28):		50.00
Common Player:		.50
1	Jim Lefebvre	.50
2	Alvin Davis	.50
3	Ken Griffey, Jr.	35.00
4	Jim Presley	.50
5	Mark Langston	.75
6	Henry Cotto	.50
7	Mickey Brantley	.50
8	Jeffrey Leonard	.50
9	Dave Valle	.50
10	Harold Reynolds	.75
11	Edgar Martinez	2.00
12	Tom Niedenfuer	.50
13	Scott Bankhead	.50
14	Scott Bradley	.50
15	Omar Vizquel	.50
16	Erik Hanson	.50
17	Bill Swift	.50
18	Mike Campbell	.50
19	Mike Jackson	.50
20	Rich Renteria	.50
21	Mario Diaz	.50
22	Jerry Reed	.50
23	Darnell Coles	.50
24	Steve Trout	.50
25	Mike Schooler	.50
26	Julio Solano	.50
27	Coaches (Gene Clines, Bob Didier, Rusty Kuntz, Mike Paul, Bill Plummer)	.50
28	Checklist/Trainers (Henry Genzale, Rick Griffin)	.50

Player names in *Italic* type indicate a rookie card.

1989 Mother's Cookies Rangers

The 1989 Mother's Cookies Rangers team set features the traditional glossy borderless photos and rounded corners. The 2-1/2" x 3-1/2" set of 28 cards features the photography of Barry Colla. Partial sets were distributed to fans attending the July 30 game at Arlington Stadium.

		MT
Complete Set (28):		27.50
Common Player:		.50
1	Bobby Valentine	.50
2	Nolan Ryan	12.00
3	Julio Franco	.50
4	Charlie Hough	.50
5	Rafael Palmeiro	6.00
6	Jeff Russell	.50
7	Ruben Sierra	.50
8	Steve Buechele	.50
9	Buddy Bell	.50
10	Pete Incaviglia	.50
11	Geno Petralli	.50
12	Cecil Espy	.50
13	Scott Fletcher	.50
14	Bobby Witt	.50
15	Brad Arnsberg	.50
16	Rick Leach	.50
17	Jamie Moyer	.50
18	Kevin Brown	.50
19	Jeff Kunkel	.50
20	Craig McMurtry	.50
21	Kenny Rogers	1.50
22	Mike Stanley	.50
23	Cecilio Guante	.50
24	Jim Sundberg	.50
25	Jose Guzman	.50
26	Jeff Stone	.50
27	Coaches (Dick Egan, Tom Robson, Toby Harrah, Dave Oliver, Tom House, Davey Lopes)	.50
28	Trainers/Checklist (Bill Ziegler, Danny Wheat)	.50

1989 Mother's Cookies Jose Canseco

This special insert glossy set features Canseco in two posed (one standing, one kneeling) and two action (one batting, one running) shots. Full-color card fronts have rounded corners. Flip sides are numbered, printed in red and purple, and carry 1988 stats and career notes. Cards are individually cello-wrapped and inserted in Mother's Fudge 'N Chips, Oatmeal Raisin and Cocadas cookie bags.

		MT
Complete Set (4):		20.00
Common Card:		5.00
1	Jose Canseco (ball in hand)	5.00
2	Jose Canseco (on one knee grasping bat)	5.00
3	Jose Canseco (swinging-in action)	5.00
4	Jose Canseco (baserunning)	5.00

1989 Mother's Cookies Will Clark

Will Clark is featured on a special-edition glossy set inserted in Mother's big bag chocolate chip cookies. The standard-size (2-1/2" x 3-1/2") cards feature Clark in two posed (batting and catching) and two action (batting and running) shots. Purple and red backs list 1986-88 stats.

		MT
Complete Set (4):		10.00
Common Card:		2.50
1	Will Clark (displaying ball in glove)	2.50
2	Will Clark (batting stance)	2.50
3	Will Clark (in action-after swing)	2.50
4	Will Clark (heading towards first)	2.50

1989 Mother's Cookies Ken Griffey, Jr.

This set featuring Ken Griffey, Jr. was issued by Mother's Cookies and was available only in cookie packages in Washington and Oregon. The cards were also available at a Seattle Mariners Kingdome baseball card show on Aug. 20, where the set was introduced. The cards were then packed inside specially marked bags of cookies, one card per bag.

		MT
Complete Set (4):		40.00
Common Card:		10.00
1	Ken Griffey, Jr. (arms folded)	10.00
2	Ken Griffey, Jr. (ball in hand)	10.00
3	Ken Griffey, Jr. (bat over left shoulder)	10.00
4	Ken Griffey, Jr. (back of jersey showing)	10.00

1989 Mother's Cookies Mark McGwire

This special edition features full-color glossy player photos by Barry Colla on standard-size (2 1/2" x 3-1/2") cards with rounded corners. Photos feature four different batting poses. Numbered flip sides, printed in purple and red, carry 1987-88 statistics. Cards are individually cello-wrapped and were inserted in Mother's Cookie Parade variety cookie bags.

		MT
Complete Set (4):		30.00
Common Player:		7.50
1	Mark McGwire (bat on shoulder)	7.50
2	Mark McGwire (batting stance)	7.50
3	Mark McGwire (bat in front)	7.50
4	Mark McGwire (batting follow through)	7.50

1989 Mother's Cookies Rookies of the Year

This four-card set features the American League Rookies of the Year for 1986, 1987 and 1988, all members of the Oakland A's. The 2-1/2" x 3-1/2" cards feature full color photos in the traditional Mother's Cookies format. One card was devoted to each player along with a special card showcasing all three players. The cards were distributed one per box in Mother's Cookies.

		MT
Complete Set (4):		25.00
Common Card:		1.00
1	Jose Canseco	5.00
2	Mark McGwire	15.00
3	Walt Weiss	1.00
4	Walt Weiss, Mark McGwire, Jose Canseco	8.00

1990 Mother's Cookies Astros

This 28-card set features cards styled like past Mother's Cookies releases. The cards were distributed in 20-card packs at an Astro home game. The cards were never distributed in complete set form.

		MT
Complete Set (28):		15.00
Common Player:		.50
1	Art Howe	.50
2	Glenn Davis	.50
3	Eric Anthony	.50
4	Mike Scott	.50
5	Craig Biggio	2.00
6	Ken Caminiti	1.00
7	Bill Doran	.50
8	Gerald Young	.50
9	Terry Puhl	.50
10	Mark Portugal	.50
11	Mark Davidson	.50
12	Jim Deshaies	.50
13	Bill Gullickson	.50
14	Franklin Stubbs	.50
15	Danny Darwin	.50
16	Ken Oberkfell	.50
17	Dave Smith	.50
18	Dan Schatzeder	.50
19	Rafael Ramirez	.50
20	Larry Andersen	.50
21	Alex Trevino	.50
22	Glenn Wilson	.50
23	Jim Clancy	.50
24	Eric Yelding	.50
25	Casey Candaele	.50
26	Juan Agosto	.50
27	Coaches (Bill Bowman, Bob Cluck, Phil Garner, Matt Galante, Rudy Jaramillo, Ed Napoleon)	.50
28	Checklist/Trainers (Doc Ewell, Dave Labossiere, Dennis Liborio)	.50

1990 Mother's Cookies A's

This 28-card set features cards distributed at an A's home game. Cards measure 2-1/2" x 3-1/2" and feature rounded corners. Backs include biographical information and autograph space.

		MT
Complete Set (28):		22.00
Common Player:		.50
1	Tony LaRussa	.50
2	Mark McGwire	7.50
3	Terry Steinbach	.50
4	Rickey Henderson	1.50
5	Dave Stewart	.75
6	Jose Canseco	3.00
7	Dennis Eckersley	.75
8	Carney Lansford	.50
9	Mike Moore	.50
10	Walt Weiss	.50
11	Scott Sanderson	.50
12	Ron Hassey	.50
13	Rick Honeycutt	.50
14	Ken Phelps	.50
15	Jamie Quirk	.50
16	Bob Welch	.50
17	Felix Jose	.50
18	Dave Henderson	.50
19	Mike Norris	.50
20	Todd Burns	.50
21	Lance Blankenship	.50
22	Gene Nelson	.50
23	Stan Javier	.50
24	Curt Young	.50
25	Mike Gallego	.50
26	Joe Klink	.50
27	Coaches (Dave Duncan, Art Kuysner, Rene Lacheman, Dave McKay, Merv Rettenmund, Tommie Reynolds)	.50
28	Checklist/Trainers (Frank Ciensczyk, Larry Davis, Steve Vucinich, Barry Weinberg)	.50

1990 Mother's Cookies Dodgers

Distributed as a promotional item, these cards are styled like past Mother's Cookies releases. Fans 14 and under received a 20-card pack at a Dodger home game. Cards were also available at a Labor Day card show in Anaheim. The cards were not distributed in complete set form.

		MT
Complete Set (28):		14.00
Common Player:		.50
1	Tom Lasorda	.75
2	Fernando Valenzuela	.65
3	Kal Daniels	.50
4	Mike Scioscia	.50
5	Eddie Murray	3.00
6	Mickey Hatcher	.60
7	Juan Samuel	.50
8	Alfredo Griffin	.50
9	Tim Belcher	.50
10	Hubie Brooks	.50
11	Jose Gonzalez	.50
12	Orel Hershiser	.65
13	Kirk Gibson	.75
14	Chris Gwynn	.50
15	Jay Howell	.50
16	Rick Dempsey	.50
17	Ramon Martinez	2.00
18	Lenny Harris	.50
19	John Wetteland	.75
20	Mike Sharperson	.50
21	Mike Morgan	.50
22	Ray Searage	.50
23	Jeff Hamilton	.50
24	Jim Gott	.50
25	John Shelby	.50
26	Tim Crews	.50
27	Don Aase	.50
28	Coaches (Joe Amalfitano, Mark Cresse, Joe Ferguson, Ben Hines, Manny Mota, Ron Perranoski, Bill Russell)	.50

1990 Mother's Cookies Giants

Like the other Mother's Cookies issues of 1990, Giants cards were distributed as a promotional item. Fans 14 and under were given a 20-card starter set at a Giants game. Cards could also be obtained at the Labor Day card show in San Francisco. The cards were not released in complete set form.

		MT
Complete Set (28):		15.00
Common Player:		.50
1	Roger Craig	.50
2	Will Clark	2.00
3	Gary Carter	1.50
4	Kelly Downs	.50
5	Kevin Mitchell	.50
6	Steve Bedrosian	.50
7	Brett Butler	.65
8	Rick Reuschel	.50
9	Matt Williams	1.50
10	Robby Thompson	.50
11	Mike LaCoss	.50
12	Terry Kennedy	.50
13	Atlee Hammaker	.50
14	Rick Leach	.50
15	Ernest Riles	.50
16	Scott Garrelts	.50
17	Jose Uribe	.50
18	Greg Litton	.50
19	Dave Anderson	.50
20	Don Robinson	.50

21	Coaches (Dusty Baker, Bill Fahey, Wendell Kim, Bob Lillis, Norm Sherry)	.50
22	Bill Bathe	.50
23	Randy O'Neal	.50
24	Kevin Bass	.50
25	Jeff Brantley	.50
26	John Burkett	.75
27	Ernie Camacho	.50
28	Checklist	.50

1990 Mother's Cookies Mariners

This 28-card set features the traditional Mother's Cookies style with borderless full-color photos with rounded corners. Backs feature biographical information and autograph space. The cards were released as a promotion at a Mariners home game and at a Kingdome card show.

		MT
Complete Set (28):		37.50
Common Player:		.50
1	Jim Lefebvre	.50
2	Alvin Davis	.50
3	Ken Griffey, Jr.	20.00
4	Jeffrey Leonard	.50
5	David Valle	.50
6	Harold Reynolds	.50
7	Jay Buhner	2.00
8	Erik Hanson	.50
9	Henry Cotto	.50
10	Edgar Martinez	.75
11	Bill Swift	.50
12	Omar Vizquel	1.00
13	Randy Johnson	5.00
14	Greg Briley	.50
15	Gene Harris	.50
16	Matt Young	.50
17	Pete O'Brien	.50
18	Brent Knackert	.50
19	Mike Jackson	.50
20	Brian Holman	.50
21	Mike Schooler	.50
22	Darnell Coles	.50
23	Keith Comstock	.50
24	Scott Bankhead	.50
25	Scott Bradley	.50
26	Mike Brumley	.50
27	Coaches (Gene Clines, Bob Didier, Rusty Kuntz, Mike Paul, Bill Plummer)	.50
28	Checklist/Trainers (Henry Genzale, Rick Griffin, Tom Newberg)	.50

1990 Mother's Cookies Rangers

Putting together a complete set of these cards was not an easy task. The cards were distributed in 20-card packs at a Ranger home game and also could be obtained at a Dallas card convention. The cards were not released in complete set form. The cards feature the traditional Mother's Cookies style of glossy photos and rounded corners.

		MT
Complete Set (28):		27.50
Common Player:		.50
1	Bobby Valentine	.50
2	Nolan Ryan	17.50
3	Ruben Sierra	.50
4	Pete Incaviglia	.50
5	Charlie Hough	.50
6	Harold Baines	.60
7	Gino Petralli	.50
8	Jeff Russell	.50
9	Rafael Palmeiro	2.50
10	Julio Franco	.50
11	Jack Daugherty	.50
12	Gary Pettis	.50
13	Brian Bohanon	.50
14	Steve Buechele	.50
15	Bobby Witt	.50
16	Thad Bosley	.50
17	Gary Mielke	.50
18	Jeff Kunkel	.50
19	Mike Jeffcoat	.50
20	Mike Stanley	.50
21	Kevin Brown	.50
22	Kenny Rogers	.50
23	Jeff Huson	.50
24	Jamie Moyer	.50
25	Cecil Espy	.50
26	John Russell	.50

27	Coaches (Toby Harrah, Tom House, Davey Lopes, Dave Oliver, Tom Robson)	.50
28	Checklist/Trainers (Joe Macko, Marty Stajduhar, Danny Wheat, Bill Zeigler)	.50

1990 Mother's Cookies Jose Canseco

This special insert glossy set features Canseco in four posed shots. Full-color card fronts have rounded corners. Flip sides are numbered, printed in red and purple and feature the Mother's Cookies logo. The cards are individually cello-wrapped and inserted one per Mother's Cookies bag.

		MT
Complete Set (4):		16.00
Common Card:		4.00
1	Jose Canseco (sitting, bat on shoulder)	5.00
2	Jose Canseco (bat behind neck)	5.00
3	Jose Canseco (batting stance)	5.00
4	Jose Canseco (on dugout step)	5.00

1990 Mother's Cookies Will Clark

1990 marks the third consecutive year that Mother's Cookies devoted a set to Giants slugger Will Clark. The set features four posed full-color shots. The cards follow the same design as all recent Mother's Cookies cards.

		MT
Complete Set (4):		6.00
Common Card:		1.50
1	Will Clark (bat on shoulder)	1.50
2	Will Clark (closeup in stance)	1.50
3	Will Clark (open in stance)	1.50
4	Will Clark (bat behind neck)	1.50

1990 Mother's Cookies Mark McGwire

1990 marks the fourth year that A's slugger Mark McGwire was featured on a special four-card Mother's Cookies set. The photos for the cards were once again by Barry Colla. Four different posed shots of McGwire are showcased.

		MT
Complete Set (4):		30.00
Common Card:		7.50
1	Mark McGwire (bat on shoulder)	7.50
2	Mark McGwire (leaning against bat rack)	7.50
3	Mark McGwire (glove in hand)	7.50
4	Mark McGwire (on dugout step)	7.50

1990 Mother's Cookies Nolan Ryan

Unlike other special Mother's Cookies player sets, the Nolan Ryan cards feature "5000 K's" along with his name and team on the card fronts. The set honors the strikout king's monumental feat. The cards follow the classic Mother's Cookies style.

		MT
Complete Set (4):		15.00
Common Card:		5.00
1	Nolan Ryan (facing with ball in hand)	4.50
2	Nolan Ryan (standing in dugout)	4.50
3	Nolan Ryan (gripping ball behind back)	4.50
4	Nolan Ryan (sitting on dugout step)	4.50

1990 Mother's Cookies Matt Williams

Matt Williams made his Mother's Cookies single-player card set debut in 1990. Four posed shots of the Giants third baseman are showcased. Williams is featured twice in batting poses and twice as a fielder on the glossy, round-cornered 2-1/2" x 3-1/2" cards.

		MT
Complete Set (4):		6.00
Common Card:		1.50
1	Matt Williams (bat on shoulder)	1.25
2	Matt Williams (in batting stance)	1.25
3	Matt Williams (glove in hand)	1.25
4	Matt Williams (fielding)	1.25

1991 Mother's Cookies Astros

This 28-card set was produced in the now-familiar Mother's Cookies card format. Glossy fronts feature rounded corners and full-bleed posed color photos (apparently taken at San Francisco's Candlestick Park, home base of photographer Barry Colla) with the player's name and team in white in an upper corner. Backs are printed in red and purple and include a few biographical details, along with cookie company and MLB logos, uniform and card numbers and a line for autographing.

		MT
Complete Set (28):		22.00
Common Player:		.50
1	Art Howe	.50
2	Steve Finley	.60
3	Pete Harnisch	.75
4	Mike Scott	.50
5	Craig Biggio	2.00
6	Ken Caminiti	1.00
7	Eric Yelding	.50
8	Jeff Bagwell	7.50
9	Jim Deshaies	.50
10	Mark Portugal	.50
11	Mark Davidson	.50
12	Jimmy Jones	.50
13	Luis Gonzalez	.50
14	Karl Rhodes	.50
15	Curt Schilling	.75
16	Ken Oberkfell	.50
17	Mark McLemore	.50
18	David Rohde	.50
19	Rafael Ramirez	.50
20	Al Osuna	.50
21	Jim Corsi	.50
22	Carl Nichols	.50
23	Jim Clancy	.50
24	Dwayne Henry	.50
25	Casey Candaele	.50
26	Xavier Hernandez	.50
27	Darryl Kile	.50
28	Coaches/Checklist (Cluck Galante, Rudy Jaramillo, Phil Garner, Bob Cluck, Ed Ott)	.50

1991 Mother's Cookies A's

The incomparable photography of Barry Colla captures the Oakland A's in their home-field environs for the 28 cards in this set. Glossy fronts feature borderless posed photos. The player's name and team appear in white in an upper corner. Backs have minimal biographical data, player position, uniform and card numbers and appropriate logos.

		MT
Complete Set (28):		25.00
Common Player:		.50
1	Tony LaRussa	.50
2	Mark McGwire	10.00
3	Terry Steinbach	.50
4	Rickey Henderson	1.50
5	Dave Stewart	.75
6	Jose Canseco	5.00
7	Dennis Eckersley	.75
8	Carney Lansford	.50
9	Bob Welch	.50
10	Walt Weiss	.50
11	Mike Moore	.50
12	Vance Law	.50
13	Rick Honeycutt	.50
14	Harold Baines	.50
15	Jamie Quirk	.50
16	Ernest Riles	.50
17	Willie Wilson	.50
18	Dave Henderson	.50
19	Kirk Dressendorfer	.50
20	Todd Burns	.50
21	Lance Blankenship	.50
22	Gene Nelson	.50
23	Eric Show	.50
24	Curt Young	.50
25	Mike Gallego	.50
26	Joe Klink	.50
27	Steve Chitren	.50
28	Coaches/Checklist (Rene Lachemann, Dave Duncan, Dave McKay, Tommie Reynolds, Art Kuysner, Reggie Jackson, Rick Burleson)	.50

1991 Mother's Cookies Dodgers

Dodger Stadium is the background for Barry Colla's portraits of the Los Angeles manager, coaches and players appearing in this 28-card set. Standard-size cards with rounded corners feature borderless UV-coated fronts on which the only printing is the player's name and team in white in an upper corner. Backs are in red and purple and include a few biographical details, position, uniform and card numbers, a space for an autograph and the logos of the cookie company and MLB.

		MT
Complete Set (28):		15.00
Common Player:		.50
1	Tom Lasorda	.75
2	Darryl Strawberry	.75
3	Kal Daniels	.50
4	Mike Scioscia	.50
5	Eddie Murray	2.00
6	Brett Butler	.50
7	Juan Samuel	.50
8	Alfredo Griffin	.50
9	Tim Belcher	.50
10	Ramon Martinez	.75
11	Jose Gonzalez	.50
12	Orel Hershiser	.75
13	Bob Ojeda	.50
14	Chris Gwynn	.50
15	Jay Howell	.50
16	Gary Carter	.75
17	Kevin Gross	.50
18	Lenny Harris	.50
19	Mike Hartley	.50
20	Mike Sharperson	.50
21	Mike Morgan	.50
22	John Candelaria	.50
23	Jeff Hamilton	.50
24	Jim Gott	.50
25	Barry Lyons	.50
26	Tim Crews	.50
27	Stan Javier	.50
28	Coaches/Checklist (Ron Perranoski, Bill Russell, Manny Mota, Joe Ferguson, Ben Hines, Joe Amalfitano, Mark Cresse)	.50

1991 Mother's Cookies Giants

For the ninth consecutive year Mother's Cookies sponsored a promotional card set for the Giants. As in the beginning, the cards highlight the work of photographer Barry Colla with posed portraits of the personnel in Candlestick Park. Fronts of the round-cornered borderless cards are UV-coated and have the player's name and team printed in white in an upper corner. Backs are in red and purple and include cookie company and Major League Baseball logos along with a few biographical details and both uniform and card numbers.

		MT
Complete Set (28):		16.00
Common Player:		.50
1	Roger Craig	.50
2	Will Clark	2.00
3	Steve Decker	.50
4	Kelly Downs	.50
5	Kevin Mitchell	.50
6	Willie McGee	.75
7	Buddy Black	.50
8	Dave Righetti	.50
9	Matt Williams	1.00
10	Robby Thompson	.50
11	Mike LaCoss	.50
12	Terry Kennedy	.50
13	Mark Leonard	.50
14	Rick Reuschel	.50
15	Mike Felder	.50
16	Scott Garrelts	.50
17	Jose Uribe	.50
18	Greg Litton	.50
19	Dave Anderson	.50
20	Don Robinson	.50
21	Mike Kingery	.50
22	Trevor Wilson	.50
23	Kirt Manwaring	.50
24	Kevin Bass	.50
25	Jeff Brantley	.50
26	John Burkett	.50
27	Coaches (Norm Sherry, Wendell Kim, Bob Lillis, Dusty Baker, Bill Fahey)	.50
28	Trainers/Checklist (Mark Letendre, Greg Lynn)	.50

1991 Mother's Cookies Rangers

The unusual venue of the players' locker room provides the backdrop for photos for this 28-card set sponsored by Mother's Cookies. Besides a look at the player's wardrobe, the full-bleed glossy front photos feature the player's name and position vertically along the left side. Backs have uniform and card numbers, some biographical data and logos of the cookie company and Major League Baseball.

		MT
Complete Set (28):		35.00
Common Player:		.50
1	Bobby Valentine	.50
2	Nolan Ryan	17.50
3	Ruben Sierra	.50
4	Juan Gonzalez	12.50
5	Steve Buechele	.50
6	Bobby Witt	.50
7	Geno Petralli	.50
8	Jeff Russell	.50
9	Rafael Palmeiro	2.00
10	Julio Franco	.50
11	Jack Daugherty	.50
12	Gary Pettis	.50
13	John Barfield	.50
14	Scott Chiamparino	.50
15	Kevin Reimer	.50
16	Rich Gossage	.75
17	Brian Downing	.50
18	Denny Walling	.50
19	Mike Jeffcoat	.50
20	Mike Stanley	.50
21	Kevin Brown	.50
22	Kenny Rogers	.50
23	Jeff Huson	.50
24	Mario Diaz	.50
25	Brad Arnsberg	.50
26	John Russell	.50
27	Gerald Alexander	.50
28	Coaches/Checklist (Orlando Gomez, Toby Harrah, Tom House, Davey Lopes, Dave Oliver, Tom Robson)	.50

1991 Mother's Cookies Griffeys

This four-card set was packaged with Mother's Cookies sold in the Pacific Northwest. Each card features a borderless glossy posed photo on front. The traditional rounded corners of Mother's cards are found on the issue. Backs have a few stats and career notes.

		MT
Complete Set, Singles (4):		20.00
Complete Set, Uncut Strip:		24.00
Common Card:		5.00
1	Ken Griffey, Jr.	10.00
2	Ken Griffey, Sr.	5.00
3	Ken Griffey, Jr., Ken Griffey, Sr. (holding gloves)	5.00
4	Ken Griffey, Jr., Ken Griffey, Sr. (holding bats)	5.00

1991 Mother's Cookies Nolan Ryan 300 Wins

Mother's Cookies in 1991 created a four-card Nolan Ryan set honoring baseball's most recent 300-game winner. One card was included in specially-marked packages of cookies. Card fronts have the traditional Mother's Cookies look: Barry Colla photography on full-bleed cards with rounded corners. Backs have a few statistics and career notes.

		MT
Complete Set (4):		8.00
Common Card:		2.00
1	Nolan Ryan (standing, front view)	2.00
2	Nolan Ryan (kneeling)	2.00
3	Nolan Ryan (standing, side view)	2.00
4	Nolan Ryan (gripping "300" ball)	2.00

1992 Mother's Cookies Astros

The Astrodome provides the backdrop for Barry Colla's photos of Astros personnel seen on this 28-card set sponsored by Mother's Cookies. Cards are in standard 2-1/2" x 3-1/2" and feature rounded corners. Glossy fronts are borderless and have no graphics except the player's name and team in an upper corner. Backs are printed in red and purple and have a few biographical details along with uniform and card numbers, the player's position, an autograph line and the logos of the cookie company and MLB.

		MT
Complete Set (28):		16.00
Common Player:		.50
1	Art Howe	.50
2	Steve Finley	.50
3	Pete Harnisch	.50
4	Pete Incaviglia	.50
5	Craig Biggio	1.00
6	Ken Caminiti	.75
7	Eric Anthony	.50
8	Jeff Bagwell	4.50
9	Andujar Cedeno	.50
10	Mark Portugal	.50
11	Eddie Taubensee	.50
12	Jimmy Jones	.50
13	Joe Boever	.50
14	Benny Distefano	.50
15	Juan Guerrero	.50
16	Doug Jones	.50
17	Scott Servais	.50
18	Butch Henry	.50
19	Rafael Ramirez	.50
20	Al Osuna	.50
21	Rob Murphy	.50
22	Chris Jones	.50
23	Rob Mallicoat	.50
24	Darryl Kile	.50
25	Casey Candaele	.50
26	Xavier Hernandez	.50
27	Coaches (Bob Cluck, Matt Galante, Rudy Jaramillo, Ed Ott, Tom Spencer)	.50
28	Trainers / Checklist (Doc Ewell, Dennis Liborio, Dave Labossiere)	.50

1992 Mother's Cookies A's

The commemorative patch marking the Oakland A's 25th season on the West Coast is visible on several of Barry Colla's photos in this 28-card issue. The traditional Mother's Cookies card format of 2-1/2" x 3-1/2", round-cornered cards with UV-coated borderless front photos is followed in this set. The player's name and team are in white in an upper corner. Backs have cookie company and Major League Baseball logos, along with the player's position, uniform and card numbers, space for an autograph and minimal biographical data. Back printing is in red and purple on white.

		MT
Complete Set (28):		25.00
Common Player:		.50
1	Tony LaRussa	.50
2	Mark McGwire	9.00
3	Terry Steinbach	.50
4	Rickey Henderson	1.50
5	Dave Stewart	.75
6	Jose Canseco	4.50
7	Dennis Eckersley	.75
8	Carney Lansford	.50
9	Bob Welch	.50
10	Walt Weiss	.50
11	Mike Moore	.50
12	Goose Gossage	.50
13	Rick Honeycutt	.50
14	Harold Baines	.50
15	Jamie Quirk	.50
16	Jeff Parrett	.50
17	Willie Wilson	.50
18	Dave Henderson	.50
19	Joe Slusarski	.50
20	Mike Bordick	.50
21	Lance Blankenship	.50
22	Gene Nelson	.50
23	Vince Horsman	.50
24	Ron Darling	.50
25	Randy Ready	.50
26	Scott Hemond	.50
27	Scott Brosius	.50
28	Coaches/Checklist (Tommie Reynolds, Dave Duncan, Doug Rader, Rene Lachemann, Art Kusnyer, Dave McKay)	.50

1992 Mother's Cookies Dodgers

A commemorative patch marking Dodger Stadium's 30th anniversay is featured on some of the Barry Colla photos seen on this 28-card set. Cards have the now-traditional round-corner, glossy-front borderless format with player name and team in white in an upper corner. Printed in red and purple, the backs have a few biographical details along with uniform and card numbers and appropriate logos.

		MT
Complete Set (28):		15.00
Common Player:		.50
1	Tom Lasorda	.75
2	Brett Butler	.75
3	Tom Candiotti	.50
4	Eric Davis	.60
5	Lenny Harris	.50
6	Orel Hershiser	.65
7	Ramon Martinez	.75
8	Jose Offerman	.50
9	Mike Scioscia	.50
10	Darryl Strawberry	.75
11	Todd Benzinger	.50
12	John Candelaria	.50
13	Tim Crews	.50
14	Kal Daniels	.50
15	Jim Gott	.50
16	Kevin Gross	.50
17	Dave Hansen	.50
18	Carlos Hernandez	.50
19	Jay Howell	.50
20	Stan Javier	.50
21	Eric Karros	2.00
22	Roger McDowell	.50
23	Bob Ojeda	.50
24	Juan Samuel	.50
25	Mike Sharperson	.50
26	Mitch Webster	.50
27	Steve Wilson	.50
28	Coaches/Checklist (Joe Amalfitano, Mark Cresse, Joe Ferguson, Ben Hines, Manny Mota, Ron Perranoski),	.50

1992 Mother's Cookies Giants

In 1983 Mother's Cookies re-entered the baseball card world with a set of S.F. Giants cards. In 1992, the company sponsored its 10th consecutive Giants team issue. As in the '83 set, the cards feature the photography of Barry Colla. In 2-1/2" x 3-1/2" size with rounded corners and UV-coating on the borderless fronts, the cards continue the format used since 1984. Backs are also in the familiar style, with a bit of biographical data and appropriate logos.

		MT
Complete Set (28):		15.00
Common Player:		.50
1	Roger Craig	.50
2	Will Clark	2.00
3	Bill Swift	.50
4	Royce Clayton	.75
5	John Burkett	.50
6	Willie McGee	.60
7	Buddy Black	.50
8	Dave Righetti	.50
9	Matt Williams	1.50
10	Robby Thompson	.50
11	Darren Lewis	.60
12	Mike Jackson	.50
13	Mark Leonard	.50
14	Rod Beck	.75
15	Mike Felder	.50
16	Bryan Hickerson	.50
17	Jose Uribe	.50
18	Greg Litton	.50
19	Cory Snyder	.50
20	Jim McNamara	.50
21	Kelly Downs	.50
22	Trevor Wilson	.50
23	Kirt Manwaring	.50
24	Kevin Bass	.50
25	Jeff Brantley	.50
26	Dave Burba	.50
27	Chris James	.50
28	Coaches/Checklist (Carlos Alfonso, Dusty Baker, Bob Brenly, Wendell Kim, Bob Lillis)	.50

1992 Mother's Cookies Mariners

After a one-year absence from the Mother's Cookies lineup, the M's returned in 1992 with a set. Standard-size cards have rounded corners and UV-coated fronts. The only graphics appearing on the borderless photos are the player and team name in white in an upper corner. Backs are printed in red and purple and have basic biographical data, uniform and cards numbers, space for an autograph and appropriate sponsor and licensor logos.

		MT
Complete Set (28):		25.00
Common Player:		.50
1	Bill Plummer	.50
2	Ken Griffey, Jr.	7.50
3	Harold Reynolds	.60
4	Kevin Mitchell	.50
5	David Valle	.50
6	Jay Buhner	1.00
7	Erik Hanson	.50
8	Pete O'Brien	.50
9	Henry Cotto	.50
10	Mike Schooler	.50
11	Tino Martinez	2.00
12	Dennis Powell	.50
13	Randy Johnson	2.50
14	Dave Cochrane	.50
15	Greg Briley	.50
16	Omar Vizquel	.60
17	Dave Fleming	.50
18	Matt Sinatro	.50
19	Jeff Nelson	.50
20	Edgar Martinez	.75
21	Calvin Jones	.50
22	Russ Swan	.50
23	Jim Acker	.50
24	Jeff Schaffer	.50
25	Clay Parker	.50
26	Brian Holman	.50
27	Coaches (Marty Martinez, Gene Clines, Roger Hansen, Dan Warthen, Russ Nixon, Rusty Kuntz)	.50
28	Mascot/Checklist	.50

1992 Mother's Cookies Padres

The Padres ended a six-year hiatus when they re-appeared in the Mother's Cookies lineup for 1992. The 28-card set follows the traditional Mother's format: 2-1/2" x 3-1/2" cards with rounded corners, glossy borderless front photos and the player and team name in white in an upper corner. Backs have appropriate logos, uniform and card numbers, player data and room for an autograph, all printed in red and purple.

		MT
Complete Set (28):		25.00
Common Player:		.50
1	Greg Riddoch	.50
2	Greg Harris	.50
3	Gary Sheffield	4.00
4	Fred McGriff	4.00
5	Kurt Stillwell	.50
6	Benito Santiago	.50
7	Tony Gwynn	7.50
8	Tony Fernandez	.50
9	Jerald Clark	.50
10	Dave Eiland	.50
11	Randy Myers	.60
12	Oscar Azocar	.50
13	Dann Bilardello	.50
14	Jose Melendez	.50
15	Darrin Jackson	.50
16	Andy Benes	.90
17	Tim Teufel	.50
18	Jeremy Hernandez	.50
19	Kevin Ward	.50
20	Bruce Hurst	.50
21	Larry Andersen	.50
22	Rich Rodriguez	.50
23	Pat Clements	.50
24	Craig Lefferts	.50
25	Craig Shipley	.50
26	Mike Maddux	.50
27	Coaches (Bruce Kimm, Rob Picciolo, Merv Rettenmund, Mike Roarke, Jim Snyder)	.50
28	Team logo/checklist	.50

1992 Mother's Cookies Rangers

The clubhouse wall provides the universal backdrop for the posed photos in this 28-card set. Standard-size cards have a high-gloss borderless front photo with rounded corners and the player and team name in white in an upper corner. Backs are in red and purple and have a few player biographical details along with uniform and card numbers, space for an autograph and the logos of the sponsor and licensor.

		MT
Complete Set (28):		35.00
Common Player:		.50
1	Bobby Valentine	.50
2	Nolan Ryan	15.00
3	Ruben Sierra	.50
4	Juan Gonzalez	8.00
5	Ivan Rodriguez	5.00
6	Bobby Witt	.50
7	Geno Petralli	.50
8	Jeff Russell	.50
9	Rafael Palmeiro	1.50
10	Julio Franco	.50
11	Jack Daugherty	.50
12	Dickie Thon	.50
13	Floyd Bannister	.50
14	Scott Chiamparino	.50
15	Kevin Reimer	.50
16	Jeff Robinson	.50
17	Brian Downing	.50
18	Brian Bohanon	.50
19	Jose Guzman	.50
20	Terry Mathews	.50
21	Kevin Brown	.50
22	Kenny Rogers	.50
23	Jeff Huson	.50
24	Monty Fariss	.50
25	Al Newman	.50
26	Dean Palmer	.50
27	John Cangelosi	.50
28	Coaches/Checklist (Ray Burris, Orlando Gomez, Toby Harrah, Tom House, Dave Oliver, Tom Robson)	.50

Player names in *Italic* type indicate a rookie card.

1992 Mother's Cookies Jeff Bagwell

The set consists of four standard-size cards with a full-bleed color photo on the fronts of the cards and rounded corners. Bagwell's name appears horizontally in white on the front of the card and the backs are printed in purple and red. Along with the Major League merchandise logo on the bottom of the card there is an area for the player's autograph.

		MT
Complete Set (4):		16.00
Common Card:		4.00
1	Jeff Bagwell (head and shoulders)	4.00
2	Jeff Bagwell (bat on shoulder)	4.00
3	Jeff Bagwell (waist-up)	4.00
4	Jeff Bagwell (ball in glove)	4.00

1992 Mother's Cookies Chuck Knoblauch

American League 1991 Rookie of the Year Chuck Knoblauch is featured in this four-card set. Similar in format to other Mother's cards, the glossy fronts have rounded corners and feature full-bleed color photos. The red and purple backs have statistical and biographical data along with appropriate logos.

		MT
Complete Set (4):		12.00
Common Card:		3.00
1	Chuck Knoblauch (bat on shoulder)	3.00
2	Chuck Knoblauch (head and shoulders)	3.00
3	Chuck Knoblauch (waist-up)	3.00
4	Chuck Knoblauch (fielding)	3.00

1992 Mother's Cookies Nolan Ryan 7 No-Hitter

Mother's Cookie Company produced an eight-card set in 1992 commemorating Nolan Ryan's seven no-hitters. Cards were found in specially-marked packages of Mother's Cookies. The company also made available uncut sheets of the eight cards through the mail. Fronts feature photos contemporary with Ryan's no-hitters in a borderless, round-cornered format with glossy surface. "Nolan Ryan/7 No-Hitters" appears in white vertically in the upper-left corner. Backs are printed in red and purple and include a bit of biographical data along with details of each no-hitter. The eighth card in the set offers room to write in information about a future no-hitter which never materialized prior to Ryan's retirement following the 1993 season.

		MT
Complete Set (8):		25.00
Common Card:		4.00
1	Nolan Ryan (Angels, portrait)	4.00
2	Nolan Ryan (Angels, pitching)	4.00
3	Nolan Ryan (Angels, waving)	4.00
4	Nolan Ryan (Angels, holding four "0" balls)	4.00
5	Nolan Ryan (Astros)	4.00
6	Nolan Ryan (Rangers, pitching)	4.00
7	Nolan Ryan (Rangers, pointing)	4.00
8	Nolan Ryan (Rangers, palms up)	4.00

1993 Mother's Cookies Angels

In its 11th year of renewed baseball card production, Mother's Cookies sponsored trading card promotions with seven major league teams including, for the first time, the California Angels. At special promotional games, youngsters entering the ballpark were given packs of 28 cards. Each of the paper envelopes contained 20 different player cards and eight cards of another player. Instructions on the envelope encouraged trading to complete a set of 28. All of the team sets were identical in format. Cards measure the standard 2-1/2" x 3-1/2" with rounded corners. Fronts feature borderless posed photos, the work of photographer Barry Colla. The only graphic elements on the front are the player's name and team in white, generally in an upper corner. In 1993 the Mother's cards featured a somewhat less glossy front finish than in previous years. Backs are printed in red and purple. Data includes the player's position, uniform and card numbers, a few biographical bits, a "How Obtained" statement and a space for an autograph, along with the logos of the cookie company and Major League Baseball.

		MT
Complete Set (28):		20.00
Common Player:		.50
1	Buck Rodgers	.50
2	Gary DiSarcina	.50
3	Chuck Finley	.50
4	J.T. Snow	2.00
5	Gary Gaetti	.50
6	Chili Davis	.75
7	Tim Salmon	4.00
8	Mark Langston	.65
9	Scott Sanderson	.50
10	John Orton	.50
11	Julio Valera	.50
12	Chad Curtis	.75
13	Kelly Gruber	.50
14	Rene Gonzalez	.50
15	Luis Polonia	.50
16	Greg Myers	.50
17	Gene Nelson	.50
18	Torey Lovullo	.50
19	Scott Lewis	.50
20	Chuck Crim	.50
21	John Farrell	.50
22	Steve Frey	.50
23	Stan Javier	.50
24	Ken Patterson	.50
25	Ron Tingley	.50
26	Damion Easley	.50
27	Joe Grahe	.50
28	Coaches/Checklist (Jimmie Reese, Rod Carew, Bobby Knoop, Chuck Hernandez, Ken Macha, John Wathan, Rick Turner)	.50

1993 Mother's Cookies Astros

		MT
Complete Set (28):		16.00
Common Player:		.50
1	Art Howe	.50
2	Steve Finley	.50
3	Pete Harnisch	.50
4	Craig Biggio	1.00
5	Doug Drabek	.65
6	Scott Servais	.50
7	Jeff Bagwell	3.00
8	Eric Anthony	.50
9	Ken Caminiti	.75
10	Andujar Cedeno	.50
11	Mark Portugal	.50
12	Jose Uribe	.50
13	Rick Parker	.50
14	Doug Jones	.50
15	Luis Gonzalez	.50
16	Kevin Bass	.50
17	Greg Swindell	.50
18	Eddie Taubensee	.50
19	Darryl Kile	.50
20	Brian Williams	.50
21	Chris James	.50
22	Chris Donnels	.50
23	Xavier Hernandez	.50
24	Casey Candaele	.50
25	Eric Bell	.50
26	Mark Grant	.50
27	Tom Edens	.50
28	Coaches/Checklist (Bill Bowman, Bob Cluck, Matt Galante, Rudy Jaramillo, Ed Ott, Tom Spencer)	.50

1993 Mother's Cookies A's

		MT
Complete Set (28):		17.50
Common Player:		.50
1	Tony LaRussa	.50
2	Mark McGwire	5.00
3	Terry Steinbach	.50
4	Dennis Eckersley	.75
5	Ruben Sierra	.50
6	Rickey Henderson	1.00
7	Mike Bordick	.50
8	Rick Honeycutt	.50
9	Dave Henderson	.50
10	Bob Welch	.50
11	Dale Sveum	.50
12	Ron Darling	.50
13	Jerry Browne	.50
14	Bobby Witt	.50
15	Troy Neel	.50
16	Goose Gossage	.50
17	Brent Gates	.75
18	Storm Davis	.50
19	Scott Hemond	.50
20	Kelly Downs	.50
21	Kevin Seitzer	.50
22	Lance Blankenship	.50
23	Mike Mohler	.50
24	Edwin Nunez	.50
25	Joe Boever	.50
26	Shawn Hillegas	.50
27	Coaches (Dave Duncan, Art Kusnyer, Greg Luzinski, Dave McKay, Tommie Reynolds)	.50
28	Checklist (Frank Ciensczyk) (equipment manager)	.50

1993 Mother's Cookies Dodgers

		MT
Complete Set (28):		20.00
Common Player:		.50
1	Tommy Lasorda	.75
2	Eric Karros	.75
3	Brett Butler	.75
4	Mike Piazza	10.00
5	Jose Offerman	.50
6	Tim Wallach	.50
7	Eric Davis	.65
8	Darryl Strawberry	.75
9	Jody Reed	.50
10	Orel Hershiser	.65
11	Tom Candiotti	.50
12	Ramon Martinez	.75
13	Lenny Harris	.50
14	Mike Sharperson	.50
15	Omar Daal	.50
16	Pedro Martinez	3.00
17	Jim Gott	.50
18	Carlos Hernandez	.50
19	Kevin Gross	.50
20	Cory Snyder	.50
21	Todd Worrell	.50
22	Mitch Webster	.50
23	Steve Wilson	.50
24	Dave Hansen	.50
25	Roger McDowell	.50
26	Pedro Astacio	.50
27	Rick Trlicek	.50
28	Coaches/Checklist (Joe Amalfitano, Mark Cresse, Joe Ferguson, Ben Hines, Manny Mota, Ron Perranoski),	.50

1993 Mother's Cookies Giants

		MT
Complete Set (28):		24.00
Common Player:		.50
1	Dusty Baker	.75
2	Will Clark	2.00
3	Matt Williams	1.00
4	Barry Bonds	9.00
5	Bill Swift	.50
6	Royce Clayton	.60
7	John Burkett	.50
8	Willie McGee	.75
9	Kirt Manwaring	.50
10	Dave Righetti	.50
11	Todd Benzinger	.50
12	Rod Beck	.50
13	Darren Lewis	.50
14	Robby Thompson	.50
15	Mark Carreon	.50
16	Dave Martinez	.50
17	Jeff Brantley	.50
18	Dave Burba	.50
19	Mike Benjamin	.50
20	Mike Jackson	.50
21	Craig Colbert	.50
22	Bud Black	.50
23	Trevor Wilson	.50
24	Kevin Rogers	.50
25	Jeff Reed	.50
26	Bryan Hickerson	.50
27	Gino Minutelli	.50
28	Coaches / Checklist (Bobby Bonds, Bob Brenly, Wendell Kim, Bob Lillis, Dick Pole, Denny Sommers)	.50

1993 Mother's Cookies Mariners

		MT
Complete Set (28):		20.00
Common Player:		.50
1	Lou Piniella	.65
2	Dave Fleming	.50
3	Pete O'Brien	.50
4	Ken Griffey, Jr.	10.00
5	Henry Cotto	.50
6	Jay Buhner	1.00
7	David Valle	.50
8	Dwayne Henry	.50
9	Mike Felder	.50
10	Norm Charlton	.50
11	Edgar Martinez	.75
12	Erik Hanson	.50
13	Mike Blowers	.50
14	Omar Vizquel	.50
15	Randy Johnson	2.00
16	Russ Swan	.50
17	Tino Martinez	.75
18	Rich DeLucia	.50
19	Jeff Nelson	.50
20	Chris Bosio	.50
21	Tim Leary	.50
22	Mackey Sasser	.50
23	Dennis Powell	.50
24	Mike Hampton	.50
25	Fernando Vina	.50
26	John Cummings	.50
27	Rich Amaral	.50
28	Coaches/Checklist (Sammy Ellis, John McLaren, Ken Griffey Sr., Sam Perlozzo, Sam Mejias, Lee Elia)	.50

1993 Mother's Cookies Padres

		MT
Complete Set (28):		20.00
Common Player:		.50
1	Jim Riggleman	.50
2	Gary Sheffield	2.50
3	Tony Gwynn	4.00
4	Fred McGriff	2.50
5	Greg Harris	.50
6	Tim Teufel	.50
7	Dave Eiland	.50
8	Phil Plantier	.50
9	Bruce Hurst	.50
10	Ricky Gutierrez	.50
11	Rich Rodriguez	.50
12	Derek Bell	1.00
13	Bob Geren	.50
14	Andy Benes	.75
15	Darrell Sherman	.50
16	Frank Seminara	.50
17	Guillermo Velasquez	.50
18	Gene Harris	.50
19	Dan Walters	.50
20	Craig Shipley	.50
21	Phil Clark	.50
22	Jeff Gardner	.50
23	Mike Scioscia	.50
24	Wally Whitehurst	.50
25	Roger Mason	.50
26	Kerry Taylor	.50
27	Tim Scott	.50
28	Coaches/Checklist (Dave Bialas, Bruce Bochy, Rob Picciolo, Dan Radison, Merv Rettenmund, Mike Roarke)	.50

1993 Mother's Cookies Nolan Ryan Farewell

Nolan Ryan's final 10 major league seasons with the Astros and Rangers are captured in this set. Cards are in standard Mother's Cookies format: 2-1/2" x 3-1/2" with rounded corners, borderless front photos and UV-coated. Each card has a "Nolan Ryan Farewell Set" diamond logo in an upper corner. Backs are printed in red and purple and have a few biographical details along with the year the picture on front was created. Each card has stats for one year from 1984-1992 or cumulative All-Star stats along with Major League totals. Cards were available either cello-wrapped singly in cookie packages or as a complete set via a mail-in offer.

		MT
Complete Set (9):		15.00
Common Card:		1.50
1	Nolan Ryan (1984 Astros)	1.50
2	Nolan Ryan (1985 Astros)	1.50
3	Nolan Ryan (1986 Astros)	1.50
4	Nolan Ryan (1987 Astros)	1.50
5	Nolan Ryan (1988 Astros)	1.50
6	Nolan Ryan (1989 Rangers)	1.50
7	Nolan Ryan (1990 Rangers)	1.50
8	Nolan Ryan (1991 Rangers)	1.50
9	Nolan Ryan (1992 Rangers)	1.50

1994 Mother's Cookies Angels

Originally scheduled to be given away at a promotional date during the 1994 season, these cards were caught in the strike and not distributed until the March 30-April 1 home-and-home series between the replacement players of the Angels and those of the Oakland A's. The cards were distributed in a paper envelope containing 20 different cards and eight cards of a 21st player. The idea was to trade to complete a set. The 2-1/2" x 3-1/2" cards have rounded corners and feature borderless color photos on front with the player's name and team in one of the corners. Backs are printed in red and purple and include some biographical data, uniform and card numbers, logos of Mother's Cookies and Major League Baseball and a line for an autograph.

		MT
Complete Set (28):		20.00
Common Player:		.50
1	Marcel Lacheman	.50
2	Mark Langston	.50
3	J.T. Snow	2.00
4	Chad Curtis	.50
5	Tim Salmon	3.00
6	Gary DiSarcina	.50
7	Bo Jackson	2.00
8	Dwight Smith	.50
9	Chuck Finley	.50
10	Rod Correia	.50
11	Spike Owen	.50
12	Harold Reynolds	.50
13	Chris Turner	.50
14	Chili Davis	.60
15	Bob Patterson	.50
16	Jim Edmonds	3.00
17	Joe Magrane	.50
18	Craig Lefferts	.50
19	Scott Lewis	.50
20	Rex Hudler	.50
21	Mike Butcher	.50
22	Brian Anderson	.50
23	Greg Myers	.50
24	Mark Leiter	.50
25	Joe Grahe	.50
26	Jorge Fabregas	.65
27	John Dopson	.50
28	Angels Coaches/Checklist (Chuck Hernandez, Ken Macha, Bobby Knoop, Joe Maddon, Rod Carew, Max Oliveras)	.50

1994 Mother's Cookies Astros

Distributed at an early 1995 game because the 1994 strike wiped out the planned promotional date, these cards were handed out in packages that contained 20 different cards and eight cards of a 21st player. The idea was to trade the duplicates to form a team set. The round-cornered 2-1/2" x 3-1/2" cards have a borderless color photo on front. Backs are printed in red and purple and include a few biographical notes, uniform and card numbers, a line for an autograph and logos of Mother's Cookies and Major League Baseball.

		MT
Complete Set (28):		15.00
Common Player:		.50
1	Terry Collins	.50
2	Mitch Williams	.50
3	Jeff Bagwell	3.50
4	Luis Gonzalez	.50
5	Craig Biggio	1.00
6	Darryl Kile	.50
7	Ken Caminiti	.75
8	Steve Finley	.50
9	Pete Harnisch	.50
10	Sid Bream	.50
11	Mike Felder	.50
12	Tom Edens	.50
13	James Mouton	.50
14	Doug Drabek	.50
15	Greg Swindell	.50
16	Chris Donnels	.50
17	John Hudek	.50
18	Andujar Cedeno	.50
19	Scott Servais	.50
20	Todd Jones	.50
21	Kevin Bass	.50
22	Shane Reynolds	.60
23	Brian Williams	.50
24	Tony Eusebio	.50
25	Mike Hampton	.50
26	Andy Stankiewicz	.50
27	Astros Coaches (Ben Hines, Julio Linares, Matt Galante, Steve Henderson, Mel Stottlemyre, Sr.)	.50
28	Astros Trainers/Checklist (Dave Labossiere, Dennis Liborio, Rex Jones)	.50

1994 Mother's Cookies A's

Departing little from previous years, this 28-card set of the players, manager and coaches of the Oakland A's features the inimitable photography of Barry Colla. Cards are 2-1/2" x 3-1/2" with rounded corners and borderless photos. The player's name and team are in white in one of the corners. Backs are printed in red and purple and feature a few biographical bits, a uniform number and card number, a line for an autograph and the logos of Mother's Cookies and Major League Baseball. Originally intended to be given away at a game during the strike-shortened 1994 season, the cards were instead given out at the March 30-April 1 home-and-home exhibition series between the A's and the California Angels. To promote old-fashioned card trading, each package of cards contained 20 different cards, plus eight cards of a 21st player. Considerable trading was thus required to complete a set.

		MT
Complete Set (28):		17.50
Common Player:		.50
1	Tony LaRussa	.50
2	Mark McGwire	5.00
3	Terry Steinbach	.50
4	Dennis Eckersley	.75
5	Mike Bordick	.50
6	Rickey Henderson	1.00
7	Ruben Sierra	.50
8	Stan Javier	.50
9	Todd Van Poppel	.50
10	Bob Welch	.50
11	Miguel Jiminez	.50
12	Steve Karsay	.50
13	Geronimo Berroa	.50
14	Bobby Witt	.50
15	Troy Neel	.50
16	Ron Darling	.50
17	Scott Hemond	.50
18	Steve Ontiveros	.50
19	Mike Aldrete	.50
20	Carlos Reyes	.50
21	Brent Gates	.50
22	Mark Acre	.50
23	Eric Helfand	.50
24	Vince Horsman	.50
25	Bill Taylor	.50
26	Scott Brosius	.75
27	John Briscoe	.50
28	Athletics' Coaches/Checklist (Dave Duncan, Jim Lefebvre, Carney Lansford, Tommie Reynolds, Art Kusnyer, Dave McKay)	.50

1994 Mother's Cookies Dodgers

Plans to distribute this set were postponed when the players' strike wiped out the latter part of the 1994 season. Instead, the cards were distributed at an early 1995 promotional contest. Each package of 28 cards contained 20 different cards and eight cards of a 21st player. This required extensive trading to complete a team set. Cards feature borderless color photos on a 2-1/2" x 3-1/2" round-cornered format. Backs are printed in red and purple and include uniform and card numbers, biographical data, an autograph line and the logos of Mother's Cookies and Major League Baseball.

		MT
Complete Set (28):		24.00
Common Player:		.50
1	Tommy Lasorda	.75
2	Mike Piazza	8.00
3	Delino DeShields	.60
4	Eric Karros	.75
5	Jose Offerman	.50
6	Brett Butler	.75
7	Orel Hershiser	.75
8	Henry Rodriguez	.60
9	Raul Mondesi	5.00
10	Tim Wallach	.50
11	Ramon Martinez	.80
12	Mitch Webster	.50
13	Todd Worrell	.50
14	Jeff Treadway	.50
15	Tom Candiotti	.50
16	Pedro Astacio	.50
17	Chris Gwynn	.50
18	Jim Gott	.50
19	Omar Daal	.50
20	Cory Snyder	.50
21	Kevin Gross	.50
22	Dave Hansen	.50
23	Al Osuna	.50
24	Darren Dreifort	.50
25	Roger McDowell	.50
26	Carlos Hernandez	.50
27	Gary Wayne	.50
28	Dodgers Coaches/Checklist (Ron Perranoski, Joe Amalfitano, Reggie Smith, Joe Ferguson, Bill Russell, Mark Cresse)	.50

1994 Mother's Cookies Giants

Unable to distribute these cards in 1994 because the strike wiped out a promotional date, the Giants gave away the cards at an early 1995 game. Cards were distributed in packages containing 20 different players and eight cards of a 21st player; requiring extensive trading to complete a team set. The 2-1/2" x 3-1/2" round-cornered cards feature borderless color photos on front. Backs have red and purple printing and include a few biographical notes, card and uniform numbers, Mother's Cookies and Major League Baseball logos and a line for an autograph.

		MT
Complete Set (28):		17.50
Common Player:		.50
1	Dusty Baker	.75
2	Robby Thompson	.50
3	Barry Bonds	4.50
4	Royce Clayton	.60
5	John Burkett	.50
6	Bill Swift	.50
7	Matt Williams	1.50
8	Rod Beck	.50
9	Steve Scarsone	.50
10	Mark Portugal	.50
11	John Patterson	.50
12	Darren Lewis	.50
13	Kirt Manwaring	.50
14	Salomon Torres	.50
15	Willie McGee	.60
16	Dave Martinez	.50
17	Darryl Strawberry	.75
18	Steve Frey	.50
19	Rich Monteleone	.50
20	Todd Benzinger	.50
21	Jeff Reed	.50
22	Mike Benjamin	.50
23	Mike Jackson	.50
24	Pat Gomez	.50
25	Dave Burba	.50
26	Bryan Hickerson	.50
27	Mark Carreon	.50
28	Giants Coaches/Checklist (Bobby Bonds, Bob Lillis, Wendell Kim, Bob Brenly, Dick Pole, Denny Sommers)	.50

1994 Mother's Cookies Mariners

When the players struck on Aug. 12, 1994, it killed the Mariners' plans to distribute these cards at a promotional date. Instead, packages of the cards were given away during the winter as players and management toured the Northwest drumming up fan interest. Cards were issued in a group containing 20 different players and eight cards of a 21st player. It was necessary to trade the duplicates to finish a team set. Cards are 2-1/2" x 3-1/2" with round corners and feature borderless color photos on front. Backs are in red and purple and include biographical bits, uniform and card numbers and the logos of Mother's Cookies and Major League Baseball.

		MT
Complete Set (28):		20.00
Common Player:		.50
1	Lou Piniella	.60
2	Randy Johnson	2.00
3	Eric Anthony	.50
4	Ken Griffey Jr.	5.00
5	Felix Fermin	.50
6	Jay Buhner	.75
7	Chris Bosio	.50
8	Reggie Jefferson	.50
9	Greg Hibbard	.50
10	Dave Fleming	.50
11	Rich Amaral	.50
12	Rich Gossage	.50
13	Edgar Martinez	.75
14	Bobby Ayala	.50
15	Darren Bragg	.50
16	Tino Martinez	1.00
17	Mike Blowers	.50
18	John Cummings	.50
19	Keith Mitchell	.50
20	Bill Haselman	.50
21	Greg Pirkl	.50
22	Mackey Sasser	.50
23	Tim Davis	.50
24	Dan Wilson	.50
25	Jeff Nelson	.50
26	Kevin King	.50
27	Torey Lovullo	.50
28	Mariners Coaches/Checklist (Sam Perlozzo, Lee Elia, Sammy Ellis, John McLaren, Sam Mejias)	.50

1994 Mother's Cookies Padres

The cancellation of the latter part of the 1994 season by the players' strike wiped out a planned promotional date on which these cards were to have been given out. Instead, the cards were distributed at an early 1995 game. Packages were given out consisting of 20 different cards plus eight cards of a 21st player, which could be traded to complete a team set. Cards are 2-1/2" x 3-1/2" with rounded corners and a borderless color photo on front. Backs are printed in red and purple and have a few biographical notes, card and uniform numbers, an autograph line and logos of Mother's Cookies and Major League Baseball.

		MT
Complete Set (28):		15.00
Common Player:		.50
1	Jim Riggleman	.50
2	Tony Gwynn	4.50
3	Andy Benes	.75
4	Bip Roberts	.50
5	Phil Clark	.50
6	Wally Whitehurst	.50
7	Archi Cianfrocco	.50
8	Derek Bell	.75
9	Ricky Gutierrez	.50
10	Mark Davis	.50
11	Phil Plantier	.50
12	Brian Johnson	.50
13	Billy Bean	.50
14	Craig Shipley	.50
15	Tim Hyers	.50
16	Gene Harris	.50
17	Scott Sanders	.50
18	A.J. Sager	.50
19	Keith Lockhart	.50
20	Tim Mauser	.50
21	Andy Ashby	.50
22	Brad Ausmus	.50
23	Trevor Hoffman	.50
24	Luis Lopez	.50
25	Doug Brocail	.50
26	Dave Staton	.50
27	Pedro A. Martinez	.50
28	Padres Coaches/Checklist (Sonny Siebert, Rob Picciolo, Dave Bialas, Dan Radison, Merv Rettenmund, Bruce Bochy)	.50

1994 Mother's Cookies Nolan Ryan Final Farewell

A virtual reprint of the 1993 Farewell Set, the 1994 version uses the same photos and, except for card #10, presents the same information on the card backs. Card #10 in the 1994 set offers 1993 season and final Major League stats instead of the All-Star stats on the 1993 version. Some minor differences in photo cropping between the two sets will be noticed, as well as the fact that many of the back elements which had been printed in red on the 1993 cards are in purple on the 1994 cards, and vice versa. Cards can be distinguished by the presence of a 1993 or 1994 copyright line on the back.

		MT
Complete Set (10):		24.00
Common Card:		3.00
1	Nolan Ryan (1984 Astros)	3.00
2	Nolan Ryan (1985 Astros)	3.00
3	Nolan Ryan (1986 Astros)	3.00
4	Nolan Ryan (1987 Astros)	3.00
5	Nolan Ryan (1988 Astros)	3.00
6	Nolan Ryan (1989 Rangers)	3.00
7	Nolan Ryan (1990 Rangers)	3.00
8	Nolan Ryan (1991 Rangers)	3.00
9	Nolan Ryan (1992 Rangers)	3.00
10	Nolan Ryan (1993 Rangers)	3.00

1994 Mother's Cookies Rookies of the Year

In 1994 Mother's Cookies issued three different four-card sets of the 1993 Rookies of the Year. Cards of Mike Piazza of the Dodgers and Tim Salmon of California were available, one per package, in each of six varieties of Mother's Big Cookies. There was also a four-card set featuring both players on each of the four cards. These cards were packaged one per bag of Mother's Major League Double Headers. The specially-marked packages with the trading cards inside also carried details about Mother's Commemorative Uncut Strips of each of the three different sets in a mail-in offer. In addition, the company created two chase cards designed to put the real cookie fans to the test. The "One in a Thousand - Rookies of the Year" - foil trading cards were inserted one in every 1,000 packages, with either blue or red foil, and fewer than 10,000 of the foil cards were produced.

		MT
Complete Set (12):		30.00
Common Card:		1.50
1	Tim Salmon (bat on shoulder)	2.00
2	Tim Salmon (batting stance)	2.00
3	Tim Salmon (dugout pose)	2.00
4	Tim Salmon (fielding)	2.00
5	Mike Piazza (bat on shoulder)	4.00
6	Mike Piazza (batting stance)	4.00
7	Mike Piazza (dugout pose)	4.00
8	Mike Piazza (catching)	4.00
9	Tim Salmon, Mike Piazza (bats on shoulders)	2.00
10	Tim Salmon, Mike Piazza (arm around shoulder)	2.00
11	Tim Salmon, Mike Piazza (shaking hands)	2.00
12	Tim Salmon, Mike Piazza (back to back)	2.00
BF	Tim Salmon, Mike Piazza (shaking hands; 1 in 1,000 blue foil)	25.00
RF	Tim Salmon, Mike Piazza (kneeling; 1 in 1,000 red foil)	25.00

1995 Mother's Cookies Angels

Seven teams in the Western U.S. participated in Mother's Cookies 13th season of sponsoring team sets. Virtually identical in format to previous years, the 2-1/2" x 3-1/2" round-cornered cards were given away at promotional dates. To promote old-fashioned card trading, the cards were distributed in a paper envelope containing 20 different cards, plus eight cards of a 21st player. Considerable trading was thus required to complete a team set. As in previous years, Barry Colla's superb photos capture the players, manager and coaches of each team in a 28-card set. Backs are again printed in red and purple with a few bits of biographical data, uniform and card numbers and space for an autograph, along with the sponsor's logo.

		MT
Complete Set (28):		17.50
Common Player:		.50
1	Marcel Lachemann	.50
2	Mark Langston	.75
3	J.T. Snow	1.00
4	Tim Salmon	3.00
5	Chili Davis	.65
6	Gary DiSarcina	.50
7	Tony Phillips	.65
8	Jim Edmonds	1.50
9	Chuck Finley	.50
10	Mark Dalesandro	.50
11	Greg Myers	.50
12	Spike Owen	.50
13	Lee Smith	.75
14	Eduardo Perez	.50
15	Bob Patterson	.50
16	Mitch Williams	.50
17	Garret Anderson	1.00
18	Mike Bielecki	.50
19	Shawn Boskie	.50
20	Damion Easley	.50
21	Mike Butcher	.50
22	Brian Anderson	.50
23	Andy Allanson	.50
24	Scott Sanderson	.50
25	Troy Percival	.50
26	Rex Hudler	.50
27	Mike James	.50
28	Coaches/checklist (Mick Billmeyer, Rick Burleson, Rod Carew, Chuck Hernandez, Bobby Knoop, Bill Lachemann, Joe Maddon)	.50

1995 Mother's Cookies Astros

		MT
Complete Set (28):		16.00
Common Player:		.50
1	Terry Collins	.50
2	Jeff Bagwell	3.00
3	Luis Gonzalez	.60
4	Darryl Kile	.50
5	Derek Bell	.75
6	Scott Servais	.50
7	Craig Biggio	1.00
8	Dave Magadan	.50
9	Milt Thompson	.50
10	Derrick May	.50
11	Doug Drabek	.50
12	Tony Eusebio	.50
13	Phil Nevin	.50
14	James Mouton	.50
15	Phil Plantier	.50
16	Pedro Martinez	.50
17	Orlando Miller	.60
18	John Hudek	.50
19	Doug Brocail	.50
20	Craig Shipley	.50
21	Shane Reynolds	.50
22	Mike Hampton	.50
23	Todd Jones	.50
24	Greg Swindell	.50
25	Jim Dougherty	.50
26	Brian Hunter	.75
27	Dave Veres	.50
28	Coaches/checklist (Jesse Barfield, Matt Galante, Steve Henderson, Julio Linares, Mel Stottlemyre)	.50

1995 Mother's Cookies A's

		MT
Complete Set (29):		20.00
Common Player:		.50
1	Tony LaRussa	.50
2	Mark McGwire	5.00
3	Terry Steinbach	.50
4	Dennis Eckersley	.75
5	Rickey Henderson	2.00
6	Ron Darling	.50
7	Ruben Sierra	.50
8	Mike Aldrete	.50
9	Stan Javier	.50
10	Mike Bordick	.50
11	Dave Stewart	.75
12	Geronimo Berroa	.50
13	Todd Van Poppel	.50
14	Todd Stottlemyre	.50
15	Eric Helfand	.50
16	Dave Leiper	.50
17	Rick Honeycutt	.50
18	Steve Ontiveros	.50
19	Mike Gallego	.50
20	Carlos Reyes	.50
21	Brent Gates	.50
22	Craig Paquette	.50
23	Mike Harkey	.50
24	Andy Tomberlin	.50
25	Jim Corsi	.50
26	Mark Acre	.50
27	Scott Brosius	.50
28	Coaches/checklist (Dave Duncan, Art Kusnyer, Carney Lansford, Jim Lefebvre, Dave McKay, Tommie Reynolds)	.50
29	Ariel Prieto (late-season update)	2.00
---	Mother's coupon (Spanish)	.10

1995 Mother's Cookies Dodgers

		MT
Complete Set (28):		20.00
Common Player:		.50
1	Tommy Lasorda	.75
2	Mike Piazza	8.00
3	Raul Mondesi	2.00
4	Ramon Martinez	.75
5	Eric Karros	.75
6	Roberto Kelly	.50
7	Tim Wallach	.50
8	Jose Offerman	.50
9	Delino DeShields	.50
10	Dave Hansen	.50
11	Pedro Astacio	.50
12	Mitch Webster	.50
13	Hideo Nomo	6.00
14	Billy Ashley	.50
15	Chris Gwynn	.50
16	Todd Hollandsworth	1.00
17	Omar Daal	.50
18	Todd Worrell	.50
19	Todd Williams	.50
20	Carlos Hernandez	.50
21	Tom Candiotti	.50
22	Antonio Osuna	.50
23	Ismael Valdes	.75
24	Rudy Seanez	.50
25	Joey Eischen	.50
26	Greg Hansell	.50
27	Rick Parker	.50
28	Coaches/checklist (Joe Amalfitano, Mark Cresse, Manny Mota, Bill Russell, Reggie Smith, Dave Wallace)	.50

1995 Mother's Cookies Giants

		MT
Complete Set (28):		19.00
Common Player:		.50
1	Dusty Baker	.75
2	Robby Thompson	.50
3	Barry Bonds	5.00
4	Royce Clayton	.75
5	Glenallen Hill	.50
6	Terry Mulholland	.50
7	Matt Williams	1.50
8	Mark Portugal	.50
9	John Patterson	.50
10	Rod Beck	.50
11	Mark Leiter	.50
12	Kirt Manwaring	.50
13	Steve Scarsone	.50
14	Darren Lewis	.50
15	Tom Lampkin	.50
16	William Van Landingham	.50
17	Joe Rosselli	.50
18	Chris Hook	.50
19	Mark Dewey	.50
20	J.R. Phillips	1.00
21	Jeff Reed	.50
22	Pat Gomez	.50
23	Mike Benjamin	.50
24	Trevor Wilson	.50
25	Dave Burba	.50
26	Jose Bautista	.50
27	Mark Carreon	.50
28	Coaches/checklist (Bobby Bonds, Bob Brenly, Wendell Kim, Bob Lillis, Dick Pole)	.50

1995 Mother's Cookies Mariners

		MT
Complete Set (28):		27.50
Common Player:		.50
1	Lou Piniella	.60
2	Randy Johnson	2.00
3	Dave Fleming	.50
4	Ken Griffey Jr.	6.00
5	Edgar Martinez	.75
6	Jay Buhner	.75
7	Alex Rodriguez	12.50
8	Joey Cora	.50
9	Tim Davis	.50
10	Mike Blowers	.50
11	Chris Bosio	.50
12	Dan Wilson	.50
13	Rich Amaral	.50
14	Bobby Ayala	.50
15	Darren Bragg	.50
16	Bob Wells	.50
17	Doug Strange	.50
18	Chad Kreuter	.50
19	Rafael Carmona	.50
20	Luis Sojo	.50
21	Tim Belcher	.50
22	Steve Frey	.50
23	Tino Martinez	.80
24	Felix Fermin	.50
25	Jeff Nelson	.50
26	Alex Diaz	.50
27	Bill Risley	.50
28	Coaches/checklist (Bobby Cuellar, Lee Elia, John McLaren, Sam Mejias, Sam Perlozzo, Matt Sinatro)	.50

1995 Mother's Cookies Padres

		MT
Complete Set (28):		15.00
Common Player:		.50
1	Bruce Bochy	.50
2	Tony Gwynn	3.00
3	Ken Caminiti	.75
4	Bip Roberts	.50
5	Andujar Cedeno	.50
6	Andy Benes	.75
7	Phil Clark	.50
8	Fernando Valenzuela	.60
9	Roberto Petagine	.50
10	Brian Johnson	.50
11	Scott Livingstone	.50
12	Brian Williams	.50
13	Jody Reed	.50
14	Steve Finley	.50
15	Jeff Tabaka	.50
16	Ray Holbert	.50
17	Tim Worrell	.50
18	Eddie Williams	.50
19	Brad Ausmus	.50
20	Willie Blair	.50
21	Trevor Hoffman	.50
22	Scott Sanders	.50
23	Andy Ashby	.50
24	Joey Hamilton	.75
25	Andres Berumen	.50
26	Melvin Nieves	.50
27	Bryce Florie	.50
28	Coaches/checklist (Davey Lopes, Graig Nettles, Rob Picciolo, Merv Rettenmund, Sonny Siebert)	.50

1996 Mother's Cookies Angels

After a four-year absence, the Texas Rangers returned to participate in Mother's Cookies 14th season of sponsoring team sets. Virtually identical in format to previous years, the 2-1/2" x 3-1/2" round-cornered cards were given away at promotional dates. To promote old-fashioned card trading, the cards were distributed in a paper envelope containing 20 different cards, plus eight cards of a 21st player. Considerable trading was thus required to complete a team set. As in previous years, superb photos capture the players, manager and coaches of each team in a 28-card set. Backs are again printed in red and purple with a few bits of biographical data, uniform and card numbers and space for an autograph, along with the sponsor's logo.

		MT
Complete Set (28):		17.50
Common Player:		.50
1	Marcel Lachemann	.50
2	Chili Davis	.60
3	Mark Langston	.75
4	Tim Salmon	3.00
5	Jim Abbott	.65
6	Jim Edmonds	2.00
7	Gary DiSarcina	.50
8	J.T. Snow	1.50
9	Chuck Finley	.60
10	Tim Wallach	.50
11	Lee Smith	.75
12	George Arias	.50
13	Troy Percival	.50
14	Randy Velarde	.50
15	Garret Anderson	.75
16	Jorge Fabregas	.60
17	Shawn Boskie	.50
18	Mark Eichhorn	.50
19	Jack Howell	.50
20	Jason Grimsley	.50
21	Rex Hudler	.50
22	Mike Aldrete	.50
23	Mike James	.50
24	Scott Sanderson	.50
25	Don Slaught	.50
26	Mark Holzemer	.50
27	Dick Schofield	.50
28	Coaches/checklist (Mick Billmeyer, Rick Burleson, Rod Carew, Chuck Hernandez, Bobby Knoop, Bill Lachemann, Joe Maddon)	.50

1996 Mother's Cookies Astros

		MT
Complete Set (28):		16.00
Common Player:		.50
1	Terry Collins	.50
2	Jeff Bagwell	3.00
3	Craig Biggio	1.50
4	Derek Bell	.60
5	Darryl Kile	.50
6	Sean Berry	.50
7	Doug Drabek	.60
8	Derrick May	.50
9	Orlando Miller	.50
10	Mike Hampton	.50
11	Rick Wilkins	.50
12	Brian Hunter	.75
13	Shane Reynolds	.50
14	James Mouton	.50
15	Greg Swindell	.50
16	Bill Spiers	.50
17	Alvin Morman	.50
18	Tony Eusebio	.50
19	John Hudek	.50
20	Doug Brocail	.50
21	Anthony Young	.50
22	John Cangelosi	.50
23	Jeff Tabaka	.50
24	Mike Simms	.50
25	Todd Jones	.50
26	Ricky Gutierrez	.50
27	Mark Small	.50
28	Coaches/checklist (Matt Galante, Steve Henderson, Julio Linares, Brent Strom, Rick Sweet)	.50

1996 Mother's Cookies A's

		MT
Complete Set (28):		17.00
Common Player:		.50
1	Art Howe	.50
2	Mark McGwire	5.00
3	Jason Giambi	2.50
4	Terry Steinbach	.50
5	Mike Bordick	.50
6	Brent Gates	.50
7	Scott Brosius	.50
8	Doug Johns	.50
9	Jose Herrera	.50
10	John Wasdin	.50
11	Ernie Young	.50
12	Pedro Munoz	.50
13	Steve Wojciechowski	.50
14	Geronimo Berroa	.50
15	Phil Plantier	.50
16	Bobby Chouinard	.50
17	George Williams	.50
18	Jim Corsi	.50
19	Mike Mohler	.50
20	Torey Lovullo	.50
21	Carlos Reyes	.50
22	Buddy Groom	.50
23	Don Wengert	.50
24	Bill Taylor	.50
25	Todd Van Poppel	.50
26	Rafael Bournigal	.50
27	Damon Mashore	.50
28	Coaches/checklist (Bob Alejo, Bob Cluck, Duffy Dyer, Brad Fischer, Denny Walling, Ron Washington)	.50

1996 Mother's Cookies Dodgers

		MT
Complete Set (28):		17.60
Common Player:		.50
1	Tommy Lasorda	.75
2	Mike Piazza	5.00
3	Hideo Nomo	2.00
4	Raul Mondesi	1.50
5	Eric Karros	.75
6	Delino DeShields	.50
7	Greg Gagne	.50
8	Brett Butler	.60
9	Todd Hollandsworth	.60
10	Mike Blowers	.50
11	Ismael Valdes	.60
12	Pedro Astacio	.50
13	Billy Ashley	.50
14	Tom Candiotti	.50
15	Dave Hansen	.50
16	Joey Eischen	.50
17	Milt Thompson	.50
18	Chan Ho Park	1.50
19	Antonio Osuna	.50
20	Carlos Hernandez	.50
21	Ramon Martinez	.75
22	Scott Radinsky	.50
23	Chad Fonville	.50
24	Darren Hall	.50
25	Todd Worrell	.50
26	Mark Guthrie	.50
27	Roger Cedeno	.60
28	Coaches/checklist (Joe Amalfitano, Mark Cresse, Manny Mota, Bill Russell, Reggie Smith, Dave Wallace)	.50

1996 Mother's Cookies Giants

		MT
Complete Set (28):		16.00
Common Player:		.50
1	Dusty Baker	.75
2	Barry Bonds	4.00
3	Rod Beck	.50
4	Matt Williams	1.00
5	Robby Thompson	.50
6	Glenallen Hill	.50
7	Kirt Manwaring	.50
8	Mark Carreon	.50
9	Osvaldo Fernandez	.50
10	J.R. Phillips	.50
11	Shawon Dunston	.50
12	Mark Leiter	.50
13	William VanLandingham	.50
14	Stan Javier	.50
15	Allen Watson	.50
16	Mel Hall	.50
17	Doug Creek	.50
18	Steve Scarsone	.50
19	Mark Dewey	.50
20	Mark Gardner	.50
21	David McCarty	.50
22	Tom Lampkin	.50
23	Jeff Juden	.50
24	Steve Decker	.50
25	Rich DeLucia	.50
26	Kim Batiste	.50
27	Steve Bourgeois	.50
28	Checklist/coaches (Carlos Alfonso, Bobby Bonds, Jim Davenport, Wendell Kim, Bob Lillis, Juan Lopez), Dick Pole, Mike Sadek	.50

1996 Mother's Cookies Mariners

		MT
Complete Set (28):		25.00
Common Player:		.50
1	Lou Piniella	.50
2	Randy Johnson	1.00
3	Jay Buhner	.75
4	Ken Griffey Jr.	8.00
5	Ricky Jordan	.50
6	Rich Amaral	.50
7	Edgar Martinez	.65
8	Joey Cora	.50
9	Alex Rodriguez	0.00
10	Sterling Hitchcock	.50
11	Chris Bosio	.50
12	John Marzano	.50
13	Bob Wells	.50
14	Rafael Carmona	.50
15	Dan Wilson	.50
16	Norm Charlton	.50
17	Paul Sorrento	.50
18	Mike Jackson	.50
19	Luis Sojo	.50
20	Bobby Ayala	.50
21	Alex Diaz	.50
22	Doug Strange	.50
23	Bob Wolcott	.50
24	Darren Bragg	.50
25	Paul Menhart	.50
26	Edwin Hurtado	.50
27	Russ Davis	.50
28	Cocahes/checklist (Bobby Cuellar, Lee Elia, John McLaren, Sam Mejias, Matt Sinatro, Steve Smith)	.50

1996 Mother's Cookies Padres

		MT
Complete Set (28):		16.00
Common Player:		.50
1	Bruce Bochy	.50
2	Tony Gwynn	3.00
3	Wally Joyner	.75
4	Rickey Henderson	1.00
5	Ken Caminiti	.75
6	Scott Sanders	.50
7	Steve Finley	.50
8	Fernando Valenzuela	.60
9	Brian Johnson	.50
10	Jody Reed	.50
11	Bob Tewksbury	.50
12	Andujar Cedeno	.50
13	Sean Bergman	.50
14	Marc Newfield	.50
15	Craig Shipley	.50
16	Scott Livingstone	.50
17	Trevor Hoffman	.50
18	Doug Bochtler	.50
19	Archi Cianfrocco	.50
20	Joey Hamilton	.50
21	Andy Ashby	.50
22	Chris Gwynn	.50
23	Luis Lopez	.50
24	Tim Worrell	.50
25	Brad Ausmus	.50
26	Willie Blair	.50
27	Bryce Florie	.50
28	Coaches/checklist (Tim Flannery, Grady Little, Davey Lopes, Rob Picciolo, Merv Rettenmund, Dan Warthen)	.50

Misspellings of names are not uncommon on modern minor league cards. Unless a corrected version was issued, such errors have no effect on value.

1996 Mother's Cookies Rangers

		MT
Complete Set (28):		18.00
Common Player:		.50
1	Johnny Oates	.50
2	Will Clark	1.50
3	Juan Gonzalez	4.00
4	Ivan Rodriguez	1.50
5	Darryl Hamilton	.50
6	Dean Palmer	.50
7	Mickey Tettleton	.50
8	Craig Worthington	.50
9	Rusty Greer	.50
10	Kevin Gross	.50
11	Rick Helling	.50
12	Kevin Elster	.50
13	Bobby Witt	.50
14	Mark McLemore	.50
15	Warren Newson	.50
16	Mike Henneman	.50
17	Ken Hill	.50
18	Gil Heredia	.50
19	Roger Pavlik	.50
20	Dave Valle	.50
21	Mark Brandenburg	.50
22	Kurt Stillwell	.50
23	Ed Vosberg	.50
24	Dennis Cook	.50
25	Damon Buford	.50
26	Benji Gil	.50
27	Darren Oliver	.50
28	Cocahes/checklist (Dick Bosman, Bucky Dent, Larry Hardy, Rudy Jaramillo, Ed Napoleon, Jerry Narron)	.50

1997 Mother's Cookies

Fans attending promotional games during the season received a starter set of 21 of the 28 cards in their local team set, plus seven duplicates. They were encouraged to trade to fill their sets. The 2-1/2" x 3-1/2" round-corner cards have player portrait photos on front. To the left and bottom are team-color stripes. The player name is at bottom in white, and the team logo is at bottom-right. Backs have minimal player data, a sponsor's logo and space for an autograph.

(Team sets checklisted below)

1997 Mother's Cookies Angels

Fans attending the Aug. 3 game at Anaheim Stadium received a starter set of 21 of the 28 cards in this team set, plus seven duplicates. They were encouraged to trade to fill their sets. The 2-1/2" x 3-1/2" round-corner cards have player portrait photos on front. To the left and bottom are red and blue stripes. The player name is at bottom in white, and the team logo is at bottom-right. Backs have minimal player data, a sponsor's logo and space for an autograph.

		MT
Complete Set (28):		17.50
Common Player:		.50
1	Terry Collins	.50
2	Tim Salmon	1.00
3	Eddie Murray	1.50
4	Mark Langston	.50
5	Jim Edmonds	.75
6	Tony Phillips	.50
7	Gary DiSarcina	.50
8	Garret Anderson	.50
9	Chuck Finley	.50
10	Darin Erstad	3.00
11	Jim Leyritz	.50
12	Shigetosi Hasegawa	.75
13	Luis Alicea	.50
14	Troy Percival	.50
15	Allen Watson	.50
16	Craig Grebeck	.50
17	Mike Holtz	.50
18	Chad Kreuter	.50
19	Dennis Springer	.50
20	Jason Dickson	.50
21	Mike James	.50
22	Orlando Palmeiro	.50
23	Dave Hollins	.50
24	Mark Gubicza	.50
25	Pep Harris	.50
26	Jack Howell	.50
27	Rich DeLucia	.50
28	Angels coaches/checklist (Larry Bowa, Rod Carew, Joe Coleman, Marcel Lachemann, Joe Maddon, Dave Parker)	.50

1997 Mother's Cookies Astros

Children attending a promotional game at the Astrodome received a starter set of 21 of the 28 cards in this team set, plus seven duplicates. They were encouraged to trade to fill their sets. The 2-1/2" x 3-1/2" round-corner cards have portrait photos on front. To the left and bottom are navy and gold stripes. The player name is at bottom in white, and the team logo is at bottom-right. Backs have minimal player data, a sponsor's logo and space for an autograph.

		MT
Complete Set (28):		16.00
Common Player:		.50
1	Larry Dierker	.50
2	Jeff Bagwell	2.00
3	Craig Biggio	1.00
4	Darryl Kile	.50
5	Luis Gonzalez	.60
6	Shane Reynolds	.50
7	James Mouton	.50
8	Sean Berry	.50
9	Billy Wagner	1.00
10	Ricky Gutierrez	.50
11	Mike Hampton	.50
12	Tony Eusebio	.50
13	Derek Bell	.75
14	Ray Montgomery	.50
15	Bill Spiers	.50
16	Sid Fernandez	.50
17	Brad Ausmus	.50
18	John Hudek	.50
19	Bob Abreu	.75
20	Russ Springer	.50
21	Chris Holt	.50
22	Tom Martin	.50
23	Donne Wall	.50
24	Thomas Howard	.50
25	Jose Lima	.50
26	Pat Listach	.50
27	Ramon Garcia	.50
28	Astros coache4s/checklist (Alan Ashby, Jose Cruz, Mike Cubbage, Tom McCraw, Vern Ruhle, Bill Virdon)	.50

1997 Mother's Cookies A's

Fans attending the Aug. 10 game at the Coliseum received a starter set of 21 of the 28 cards in this team set, plus seven duplicates. They were encouraged to trade to fill their sets. The 2-1/2" x 3-1/2" round-corner cards have player portrait photos on front. To the left and bottom are green and gold stripes. The player name is at bottom in white, and the team logo is at bottom-right. Backs have minimal player data, a sponsor's logo and space for an autograph.

		MT
Complete Set (28):		20.00
Common Player:		.50
1	Art Howe	.50
2	Mark McGwire	8.00
3	Jose Canseco	3.00
4	Jason Giambi	1.00
5	Geronimo Berroa	.50
6	Ernie Young	.50
7	Scott Brosius	.65
8	Dave Magadan	.50
9	Mike Mohler	.50
10	George Williams	.50
11	Tony Batista	.50
12	Steve Karsay	.50
13	Rafael Bournigal	.50
14	Ariel Prieto	.50
15	Buddy Groom	.50
16	Matt Stairs	.50
17	Brent Mayne	.50
18	Bill Taylor	.50
19	Scott Spiezio	.50
20	Richie Lewis	.50
21	Mark Acre	.50
22	Dave Telgheder	.50
23	Willie Adams	.50
24	Izzy Molina	.50
25	Don Wengert	.50
26	Damon Mashore	.50
27	Aaron Small	.50
28	A's coaches/checklist (Bob Alejo, Bob Cluck, Duffy Dyer, Brad Fischer, Denny Walling, Ron Washington)	.50

1997 Mother's Cookies Dodgers

Children attending the July 13 game at Dodger Stadium received a starter set of 21 of the 28 cards in this team set, plus seven duplicates. They were encouraged to trade to fill their sets. The 2-1/2" x 3-1/2" round-corner cards have player portrait photos on front. To the left and bottom are red and blue stripes. The player name is at bottom in white, and the team logo is at bottom-right. Backs have minimal player data, a sponsor's logo and space for an autograph.

		MT
Complete Set (28):		17.50
Common Player:		.50
1	Bill Russell	.50
2	Eric Karros	.75
3	Mike Piazza	4.00
4	Raul Mondesi	.75
5	Hideo Nomo	1.00
6	Todd Hollandsworth	.60
7	Greg Gagne	.50
8	Brett Butler	.60
9	Ramon Martinez	.65
10	Todd Zeile	.50
11	Ismael Valdes	.50
12	Chip Hale	.50
13	Tom Candiotti	.50
14	Billy Ashley	.50
15	Chan Ho Park	.75
16	Wayne Kirby	.50
17	Mark Guthrie	.50
18	Juan Castro	.50
19	Todd Worrell	.50
20	Tom Prince	.50
21	Scott Radinsky	.50
22	Pedro Astacio	.50
23	Wilton Guerrero	.50
24	Darren Hall	.50
25	Darren Dreifort	.50
26	Nelson Liriano	.50
27	Dodgers coaches (Joe Amalfitano, Mark Cresse, Manny Mota, Mike Scioscia, Reggie Smith, Dave Wallace)	.50
28	Robinson 50th anniversary logo/checklist	.50

1997 Mother's Cookies Giants

Twenty thousand fans attending the July 27 game at 3Com Park received a starter set of 21 of the 28 cards in this team set, plus seven duplicates. They were encouraged to trade to fill their sets. The 2-1/2" x 3-1/2" round-corner cards have player portrait photos on front. To the left and bottom are black and orange stripes. The player name is at bottom in white, and the team logo is at bottom-right. Backs have minimal player data, a sponsor's logo and space for an autograph.

		MT
Complete Set (28)		15.00
Common Player:		.50
1	Dusty Baker	.50
2	Barry Bonds	3.00
3	J.T. Snow	.75
4	Rod Beck	.50
5	Glenallen Hill	.50
6	Rick Wilkins	.50
7	Jeff Kent	.50
8	Shawn Estes	.50
9	Darryl Hamilton	.50
10	Jose Vizcaino	.50
11	Julian Tavares	.50
12	Mark Gardner	.50
13	Stan Javier	.50
14	Osvaldo Fernandez	.50
15	Jim Poole	.50
16	Marvin Benard	.50
17	William VanLandingham	.50
18	Bill Mueller	.50
19	Mark Lewis	.50
20	Damon Berryhill	.50
21	Doug Henry	.50
22	Rich Rodriguez	.50
23	Kirk Rueter	.50
24	Rich Aurilia	.50
25	Joe Roa	.50
26	Marcus Jensen	.50
27	Miguel Murphy (equipment manager)	.50
28	Giants coaches/checklist (Carlos Alfonso, Gene Clines, Sonny Jackson, Juan Lopez, Ron Perranoski, Dick Pole)	.50

1997 Mother's Cookies Padres

Partial sets of Mother's Cookies Padres were given to children 14 and under attending the June 22 game at Jack Murphy Stadium. Team colors of royal blue and orange form border strips to the left and bottom of the posed photo. A team logo appears at lower-right.

		MT
Complete Set (28):		18.00
Common Player:		.50
1	Bruce Bochy	.50
2	Tony Gwynn	3.00
3	Ken Caminiti	1.00
4	Wally Joyner	.75
5	Rickey Henderson	1.50
6	Greg Vaughn	.60
7	Steve Finley	.50
8	Fernando Valenzuela	.60
9	John Flaherty	.50
10	Sterling Hitchcock	.50
11	Quilvio Veras	.50
12	Don Slaught	.50
13	Sean Bergman	.50
14	Chris Gomez	.50
15	Craig Shipley	.50
16	Joey Hamilton	.65
17	Scott Livingstone	.50
18	Trevor Hoffman	.50
19	Doug Bochtler	.50
20	Chris Jones	.50
21	Andy Ashby	.50
22	Archi Cianfrocco	.50
23	Tim Worrell	.50
24	Will Cunnane	.50
25	Carlos Hernandez	.50
26	Tim Scott	.50
27	Dario Veras	.50
28	Coaches/checklist (Greg Booker, Tim Flannery, Davey Lopes, Rob Picciolo, Merv Rettenmund, Dan Warthen)	.50

1997 Mother's Cookies Rangers

Fans attending a promotional game at the Ballpark in Arlington received a starter set of 21 of the 28 cards in this team set, plus seven duplicates. They were encouraged to trade to fill their sets. The 2-1/2" x 3-1/2" round-corner cards have player portrait photos on front. To the left and bottom are red and blue stripes. The player name is at bottom in white, and the team logo is at bottom-right. Backs have minimal player data, a sponsor's logo and space for an autograph.

		MT
Complete Set (28):		20.00
Common Player:		.50
1	Johnny Oates	.50
2	Will Clark	2.00
3	Juan Gonzalez	5.00
4	Ivan Rodriguez	2.50
5	John Wetteland	.50
6	Mickey Tettleton	.50
7	Dean Palmer	.65
8	Rusty Greer	.50
9	Ed Vosberg	.50
10	Lee Stevens	.50
11	Benji Gil	.50
12	Mike Devereaux	.50
13	Bobby Witt	.50
14	Mark McLemore	.50
15	Warren Newson	.50
16	Eric Gunderson	.50
17	Ken Hill	.50
18	Damon Buford	.50
19	Roger Pavlik	.50
20	Billy Ripken	.50
21	John Burkett	.50
22	Darren Oliver	.50
23	Mike Simms	.50
24	Julio Santana	.50
25	Henry Mercedes	.50
26	Xavier Hernandez	.50
27	Danny Patterson	.50
28	Rangers coaches/checklist (Dick Bosman, Bucky Dent, Larry Hardy, Rudy Jaramillo, Ed Napoleon, Jerry Narron)	.50

1998 Mother's Cookies Astros

The first 25,000 fans at the Sept. 13 game at the Astrodome received a starter set of 21 of the 28 cards in this team set, plus seven duplicates. They were encouraged to trade to fill their sets. The 2-1/2" x 3-1/2" round-corner cards have player portrait photos on front. To the left and bottom are team-color blue and gold stripes. The player name is at the bottom in white, and the team logo is at bottom-left. Backs have minimal player data, a sponsor's logo and space for an autograph, all printed in red and purple on a purple background.

		MT
Complete Set (28):		20.00
Common Player:		.50
1	Larry Dierker	.50
2	Jeff Bagwell	3.00
3	Craig Biggio	2.00
4	Derek Bell	1.00
5	Shane Reynolds	.50
6	Sean Berry	.50
7	Moises Alou	1.00
8	Carl Everett	.50
9	Billy Wagner	1.00
10	Tony Eusebio	.50
11	Mike Hampton	.50
12	Ricky Gutierrez	.50
13	Jose Lima	.50
14	Brad Ausmus	.50
15	Bill Spiers	.50
16	C.J. Nitkowski	.50
17	Randy Johnson	5.00
18	Mike Magnante	.50
19	Dave Clark	.50
20	Sean Bergman	.50
21	Richard Hidalgo	.65
22	Pete Shourek	.50
23	Jay Powell	.50
24	Trever Miller	.50
25	Tim Bogar	.50
26	Doug Henry	.50
27	Scott Elarton	.50
28	Coaches (Jose Cruz, Mike Cubbage, Dave Engle, Matt Galante, Tom McCraw, Vern Ruhle)	.50

1998 Mother's Cookies A's

The first 25,000 fans at the Aug. 2 game in Oakland received a starter set of 21 of the 28 cards in this team set, plus seven duplicates. They were encouraged to trade to fill their sets. The 2-1/2" x 3-1/2" round-corner cards have player portrait photos on front. To the left and bottom are green and gold stripes. The player name is at the bottom in white, and the team logo is at bottom-left. Backs have minimal player data, a sponsor's logo and space for an autograph, all printed in red and purple on a purple background.

		MT
Complete Set (28):		15.00
Common Player:		.50
1	Art Howe	.50
2	Rickey Henderson	1.00
3	Jason Giambi	1.50
4	Tom Candiotti	.50
5	Matt Stairs	.50
6	Kenny Rogers	.50
7	Scott Spiezio	.50
8	Ben Grieve	2.50
9	Kevin Mitchell	.50
10	A.J. Hinch	.50
11	Bill Taylor	.50
12	Rafael Bournigal	.50
13	Miguel Tejada	1.50
14	Kurt Abbott	.50
15	Buddy Groom	.50
16	Dave Magadan	.50
17	Mike Oquist	.50
18	Mike Macfarlane	.50
19	Mike Fetters	.50
20	Ryan Christenson	.50
21	T.J. Mathews	.50
22	Mike Mohler	.50
23	Jason McDonald	.50
24	Blake Stein	.50
25	Mike Blowers	.50
26	Jimmy Haynes	.50
27	Aaron Small	.50
28	Coaches/checklist (Duffy Dyer, Brad Fischer, Gary Jones, Rick Peterson, Denny Walling, Ron Washington)	.50

1998 Mother's Cookies Dodgers

The first 25,000 kids at the Aug. 16 game in Los Angeles received a starter set of 21 of the 28 cards in this team set, plus seven duplicates. They were encouraged to trade to fill their sets. The 2-1/2" x 3-1/2" round-corner cards have player portrait photos on front. To the left and bottom are red and blue stripes. The player name is at the bottom in white, and the team logo is at bottom-left. Backs have minimal player data, a sponsor's logo and space for an autograph, all printed in red and purple on a purple background.

		MT
Complete Set (28):		16.00
Common Player:		.50
1	Glenn Hoffman	.50
2	Eric Karros	.75
3	Bobby Bonilla	.75
4	Raul Mondesi	.75
5	Gary Sheffield	1.00
6	Ramon Martinez	.75
7	Charles Johnson	1.00
8	Jose Vizcaino	.50
9	Scott Radinsky	.50
10	Jim Eisenreich	.50
11	Ismael Valdes	.60
12	Eric Young	.50
13	Chan Ho Park	.75
14	Roger Cedeno	.50
15	Antonio Osuna	.50
16	Dave Mlicki	.50
17	Mark Guthrie	.50
18	Juan Castro	.50
19	Darren Dreifort	.50
20	Tom Prince	.50
21	Jeff Shaw	.60
22	Alex Cora	.50
23	Matt Luke	.50
24	Darren Hall	.50
25	Trenidad Hubbard	.50
26	Jim Bruske	.50
27	Tripp Cromer	.50
28	Dodgers coaches (Joe Amalfitano, Mickey Hatcher, Charlie Hough, Manny Mota, Mike Scioscia, John Shelby)	.50

1998 Mother's Cookies Giants

The first 25,000 fans at the July 26 game at 3Com Park received a starter set of 21 of the 28 cards in this team set, plus seven duplicates. They were encouraged to trade to fill their sets. The 2-1/2" x 3-1/2" round-corner cards have player portrait photos on front. To the left and bottom are black and orange stripes. The player name is at the bottom in white, and the team logo is at bottom-left. Backs have minimal player data, a sponsor's logo and space for an autograph, all printed in red and purple on a purple background.

	MT
Complete Set (28):	15.00
Common Player:	.50

1	Dusty Baker	.60
2	Barry Bonds	3.00
3	Shawn Estes	.75
4	Jeff Kent	.75
5	Orel Hershiser	.75
6	Brian Johnson	.60
7	J.T. Snow	.75
8	Bill Mueller	.65
9	Kirk Rueter	.50
10	Darryl Hamilton	.50
11	Rich Aurilia	.50
12	Mark Gardner	.50
13	Stan Javier	.50
14	Robb Nen	.50
15	Rich Rodriguez	.50
16	Brent Mayne	.50
17	Julian Tavares	.50
18	Rey Sanchez	.50
19	Chris Jones	.50
20	Charlie Hayes	.50
21	Danny Darwin	.50
22	Jim Poole	.50
23	Marvin Benard	.50
24	Steve Reed	.50
25	Alex Diaz	.50
26	John Johnstone	.50
27	Rene De La Rosa, Mike Krukow, Duane Kuiper, Jon Miller, Amaury Pi-Gonzalez, Ted Robinson (broadcasters)	.50
28	Giants coaches/ checklist (Carlos Alfonso, Gene Clines, Sonny Jackson, Juan Lopez, Ron Perranoski, Ron Wotus)	.50

1998 Mother's Cookies Padres

Fans at a designated Pads' home game received a starter set of 21 of the 28 cards in this team set, plus seven duplicates. They were encouraged to trade to fill their sets. The 2-1/2" x 3-1/2" round-corner cards have player portrait photos on front. To the left and bottom are blue and orange stripes. The player name is at the bottom in white, and the team logo is at bottom-left. Backs have minimal player data, a sponsor's logo and space for an autograph, all printed in red and purple on a purple background.

		MT
Complete Set (28):		16.00
Common Player:		.50
1	Bruce Bochy	.50
2	Tony Gwynn	3.00
3	Ken Caminiti	1.00
4	Kevin Brown	1.00
5	Wally Joyner	.75
6	Sterling Hitchcock	.50
7	Greg Vaughn	.60
8	Steve Finley	.50
9	Joey Hamilton	.60
10	Carlos Hernandez	.50
11	Quilvio Veras	.50
12	Trevor Hoffman	.65
13	Chris Gomez	.50
14	Andy Ashby	.50
15	Greg Myers	.50
16	Mark Langston	.60
17	Andy Sheets	.50
18	Dan Miceli	.50
19	James Mouton	.50
20	Brian Boehringer	.50
21	Archi Cianfrocco	.50
22	Mark Sweeney	.50
23	Pete Smith	.50
24	Eddie Williams	.50
25	Ed Giovanola	.50
26	Carlos Reyes	.50
27	Donne Wall	.50
28	Padres coaches (Greg Booker, Tim Flannery, Davey Lopes, Rob Picciolo, Merv Rettenmund, Dave Stewart)	.50

1992 Mr. Turkey

Mr. Turkey, a division of Sara Lee, offered a set of Major League Superstar cards during the 1992 season. A total of 26 cards, one player representing each team, were included in various Mr. Turkey meat packages. The cardboard packaging allows for the printing directly on the carton instead of inserting the cards inside the package. Collectors were able to collect the cards individually or as an uncut sheet, available by sending to the company.

		MT
Complete Set (26):		10.00
Uncut Sheet:		25.00
Common Player:		.25
1	Jim Abbott	.25
2	Roberto Alomar	.65
3	Sandy Alomar, Jr.	.25
4	Craig Biggio	.35
5	George Brett	1.00
6	Will Clark	.60
7	Roger Clemens	.90
8	Cecil Fielder	.25
9	Carlton Fisk	.50
10	Andres Galarraga	.40
11	Dwight Gooden	.30
12	Ken Griffey, Jr.	3.00
13	Tony Gwynn	1.00
14	Rickey Henderson	.60
15	Dave Justice	.50
16	Don Mattingly	1.00
17	Dale Murphy	.45
18	Kirby Puckett	1.00
19	Cal Ripken, Jr.	2.50
20	Nolan Ryan	2.50
21	Chris Sabo	.25
22	Ryne Sandberg	.90
23	Ozzie Smith	.75
24	Darryl Strawberry	.30
25	Andy Van Slyke	.25
26	Robin Yount	.75

1983 Mr. Z's Pizza Milwaukee Brewers

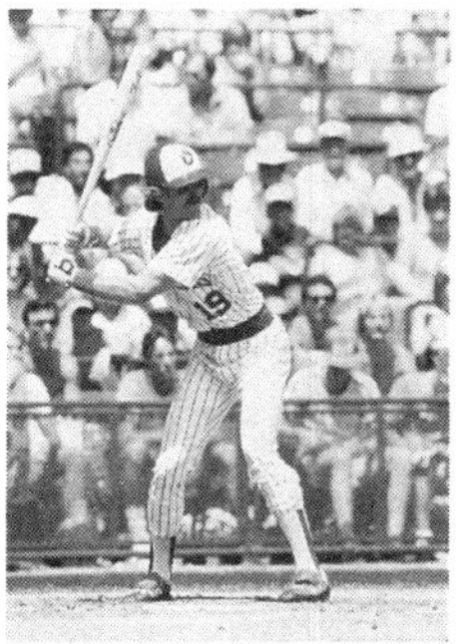

These 5" x 7" color cards were given away (bagged in cellophane) with the purchase of frozen pizzas.

		MT
Complete Set (3):		12.00
Common Player:		2.00
(1)	Cecil Cooper	2.00
(2)	Paul Molitor	6.00
(3)	Robin Yount	7.50

1984 Mr. Z's Pizza Milwaukee Brewers

These 5"x7" color cards were given away with the purchase of frozen pizza and other Brewer-logo food products.

		MT
Complete Set (3):		7.00
Common Player:		2.00
(1)	George Bamberger	2.00
(2)	Rollie Fingers	4.00
(3)	Jim Gantner	2.00

1985 Mr. Z's Pizza Pete Rose

These 5" x 7" cards were issued in Mr. Z's pizzas, each one picturing Pete Rose. Fronts have borderless action photos with a headline in black or white and a facsimile autograph. Backs have a red border with photos of Reds team merchandise which could be obtained by saving pizza labels.

		MT
Complete Set (11):		35.00
Common Card:		4.00
(1)	Another Hit! (Pete Rose)	4.00
(2)	Classic Rose (Pete Rose)	4.00
(3)	Lay One Down (Pete Rose)	4.00
(4)	Line Up Time (Pete Rose)	4.00
(5)	On Deck (Pete Rose)	4.00
(6)	One Hit Closer! (Pete Rose) (no facsimile autograph)	4.00
(7)	Pete's Back (Pete Rose)	4.00
(8)	Play Ball! (Pete Rose)	4.00
(9)	Player-Manager (Pete Rose)	4.00
(10)	Rounding Third Heading for Home (Pete Rose)	4.00
(11)	Send in the Lefty (Pete Rose)	4.00

N

1989 Nabisco Don Mattingly

Issued as a mail-in premium for Ritz cracker proofs of purchase this sheet measures 10-5/8" x 13-15/16" and includes eight 2-1/2" x 3-1/2" cards and a 5" x 7" card. The individual cards are not perforated and are seldom seen cut from the sheet. For lack of licensing by Major League Baseball, the photos on front have generally had the team logos airbrushed away. Cards are numbered on front and back with a year identifying the photo. Backs are printed in red, white and blue and contain biographical data and career highlights on the small cards, while the large card offers complete major and minor league stats and major awards won. The sheet was produced for Nabisco by Topps.

		MT
Complete Sheet:		20.00
Common Card:		2.00
72	Don Mattingly (boyhood photo)	2.00
81	Don Mattingly (minor league photo)	2.00
84	Don Mattingly (fielding)	2.00
85	Don Mattingly (batting)	2.00
86	Don Mattingly (batting)	2.00
87	Don Mattingly (batting)	2.00
88	Don Mattingly (batting)	2.00
89	Don Mattingly (batting)	2.00
----	Don Mattingly (5" x 7" pose)	2.00

1992 Nabisco Canadian Tradition

Nabisco released a 36-card set of former Toronto Blue Jays and Montreal Expos inside several of its products in 1992. Three cards were included per box, and the company also made available a collectors' album for the cards which are artist renderings of the various players, similar in style to the famous sports drawings that appeared on the pages of the Sporting News over the years. Text on the drawings is in both English and French. Backs are printed in red, white and blue and include the team and Nabisco logos along with English and French descriptions of the Famous Moment.

		MT
Complete Set (36):		25.00
Common Player:		.75
1	Bill Lee	.90
2	Cliff Johnson	.75
3	Ken Singleton	.90
4	Al Woods	.75
5	Ron Hunt	.75
6	Barry Bonnell	.75
7	Tony Perez	3.00
8	Willie Upshaw	.75
9	Coco Laboy	.75
10	Famous Moments (Blue Jays Win A.L. East - 1985)	.75
11	Bob Bailey	.75
12	Dave McKay	.75
13	Rodney Scott	.75
14	Jerry Garvin	.75
15	Famous Moments (Expos Win N.L. East - 1981)	.75
16	Rick Bosetti	.75
17	Larry Parrish	.75
18	Bill Singer	.75
19	Ron Fairly	.75
20	Damaso Garcia	.90
21	Al Oliver	1.25
22	Famous Moments (Blue Jays Win Eastern Division - 1989)	.75
23	Claude Raymond	.75
24	Buck Martinez	.75
25	Rusty Staub	1.25
26	Otto Velez	.75
27	Mack Jones	.75
28	Garth Iorg	.75
29	Bill Stoneman	.75
30	Doug Ault	.75
31	Famous Moments (Expos Host All-Star Game 1982)	.75
32	Jesse Jefferson	.75
33	Steve Rogers	.90
34	Ernie Whitt	.75
35	John Boccabella	.75
36	Bob Bailor	.75

1993 Nabisco All-Star Autographs

In a promotion with the Major League Baseball Players Alumni, Nabisco produced this six-card set of former stars. For $5 and proofs of purchase, collectors could receive an authentically autographed card. The 2-1/2" x 3-1/2" cards featured color photos on front on which the team logos have been airbrushed away, since Major League Baseball did not license the issue. Backs gave biographical and career information along with a black-and-white childhood photo of the player. The unnumbered cards are checklisted here in alphabetical order. Don Drysdale's death on July 3 in the midst of the promotion curtailed availability of cards with his autograph.

		MT
Complete Set (6):		70.00
Common Player:		6.00
(1)	Ernie Banks	10.00
(2)	Don Drysdale	35.00
(3)	Catfish Hunter	6.00
(4)	Phil Niekro	6.00
(5)	Brooks Robinson	10.00
(6)	Willie Stargell	6.00

1994 Nabisco All-Star Legends

For a second year in 1994, Nabisco continued its program of offering autographed cards of former stars for $5 and proofs of purchase from its snack products. Cards retained the same basic format of using airbrushed color photos on front and black-and-white childhood photos on back. Fronts have a "Nabisco All-Star Legends" logo in the upper-left. Backs have career and biographical data and the logos of the sponsor and the Major League Baseball Players Alumni. The unnumbered cards are checklisted here alphabetically. Each card came with a certificate of authenticity. The Sparky Lyle card was not part of the mail-in promotion but was distributed in person during the Legends' tour.

		MT
Complete Set (5):		32.00
Common Player:		6.00
(1)	Bob Gibson	6.00
(2)	Sparky Lyle	9.00
(3)	Jim Palmer	6.00
(4)	Frank Robinson	8.00
(5)	Duke Snider	8.00

1983 Nalley Potato Chips Mariners

These large (8-11/16" x 10-11/16") photo cards were issued only in the area of Washington state by Nalley Potato Chips. The six Seattle Mariners are pictured in full color on the entire back panel of each box. On the side panels, detailed player stats and biographies are listed on one side, with a Mariners schedule and ticket discount offer on the other side.

		MT
Complete Set (6):		45.00
Common Player:		7.50
8	Rick Sweet	7.50
16	Al Cowens	7.50
21	Todd Cruz	7.50
22	Richie Zisk	7.50
36	Gaylord Perry	20.00
37	Bill Caudill	7.50

1987 Nash & Zullo Baseball Hall of Shame

In conjunction with a book of the same name, authors Nash & Zullo contracted with Star Co. to produce this Hall of Shame set. The 2-1/2" x 3-1/2" cards have color cartoons on front. A description of the particular bizarre bit of baseball history is printed in green on the pink and yellow backs in the form of a date-lined "Blooperstown News" article. Cards were sold in packs of five labeled as First Series, but no others were issued.

		MT
Complete Set (32):		10.00
Common Card:		.35
1	John McGraw	.35
2	N.Y. Giants Players	.35
3	Cincinnati Reds Players	.35
4	Clarence Blethen	.35
5	Bruno Haas	.35
6	Roger Peckinpaugh	.35
7	1885 World Series	.35
8	Harley "Doc" Parker	.35
9	Bill Bergen	.35
10	Dutch Leonard	.35
11	Timothy Hurst	.35
12	"The Tabasco Kid" (Kid Elberfeld)	.35
13	New York Fans	.35
14	Ducky Medwick	.35
15	Chicago Fans	.35
16	Phenomenal Smith	.35
17	John Anderson	.35
18	Chicken Wolf	.35
19	George Harper	.35
20	Ping Bodie	.35
21	Hank Gowdy	.35
22	Bob "Fats" Fothergill	.35
23	Ed Delahanty	.35
24	Harry Heilmann	.35
25	N.Y. Giants Infield	.35
26	Jack Chesbro	.35
27	Al Selbach	.35
28	First Ladies Day	.35
29	Cleveland Spiders	.35
30	Jimmy St. Vrain	.35
31	Cy Rigler	.35
32	Brooklyn Fans	.35

1995 National Packtime

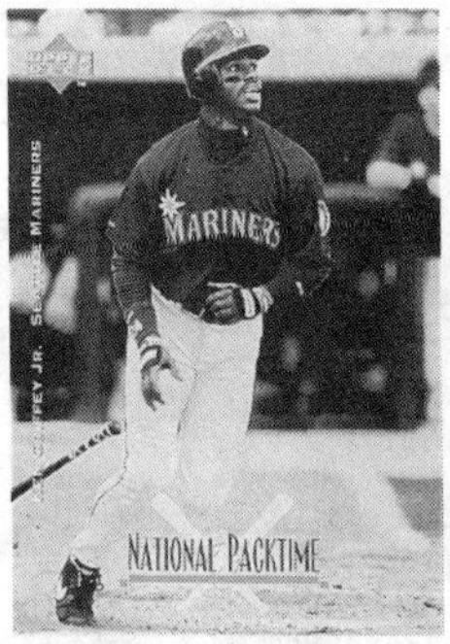

An unusual joint venture by the six major baseball card licensees resulted in this 18-card set which was available only via a mail-in offer. The set was obtained by sending in $2 and 28 wrappers from any of the companies' 1995 baseball cards prior to June 30, 1995. Most of the card designs were similar to the respective company's regular issues of the same brand. Each card is gold-foil enhanced and each carries the crossed-bats National Packtime logo on front. Cards are numbered on back from 1-18. A reported 130,000 of the sets were exchanged for wrappers.

		MT
Complete Set (18):		7.50
Common Player:		.25
1	Frank Thomas (Donruss)	1.50
2	Matt Williams (Fleer Ultra)	.35
3	Juan Gonzalez (Pacific Crown)	.65
4	Bob Hamelin (Pinnacle)	.25
5	Mike Piazza (Topps)	1.25
6	Ken Griffey Jr. (Upper Deck)	2.00
7	Barry Bonds (Donruss)	.75
8	Tim Salmon (Fleer Ultra)	.35
9	Jose Canseco (Pacific Crown)	.35
10	Cal Ripken Jr. (Pinnacle)	2.00
11	Raul Mondesi (Topps)	.50
12	Alex Rodriguez (Upper Deck)	1.50
13	Will Clark (Donruss)	.50
14	Fred McGriff (Fleer Ultra)	.35
15	Tony Gwynn (Pacific Crown)	.50
16	Kenny Lofton (Pinnacle)	.40
17	Deion Sanders (Topps)	.35
18	Jeff Bagwell (Upper Deck)	.75

1995 National Packtime Welcome to the Show

This special set was another joint venture by the major card manufacturers, Major League Baseball and the players' association. Sets of six cards were given to attendees at the National Sports Collectors Convention. In designs similar to the companies' regular-issue cards of 1995, these handouts carry a National Packtime logo on front and a red, white and black "WELCOME TO THE SHOW" logo on back. Cards are various numbered "of" 5, 6 or 8, though only six were issued. A paper accompanying the six-card packs assured collectors they were receiving the entire set.

		MT
Complete Set (6):		6.00
Common Player:		.50
1/6	Greg Maddux (Leaf)	2.00
1/8	Albert Belle (Upper Deck)	1.00
2 of 6	Darren Daulton (Ultra)	.50
2 of 6	Don Mattingly (Topps)	1.50
3 of 5	Hideo Nomo (Pinnacle)	1.00
3 of 6	Randy Johnson (Pacific)	1.50

1986 National Photo Royals

These 2-7/8" x 4-1/4" cards were a team issue produced in conjunction with National Photo. The 24-card set includes 21 players, manager Dick Howser, a Royals' 1985 World Championship commemorative card and a discount offer card from National Photo. Card fronts feature full-color action photos with a blue "Kansas City Royals" at the top of each card. Each player's name, number and position are also included. Card backs list complete professional career statistics, along with the National Photo logo.

		MT
Complete Set (24):		8.00
Common Player:		.25
1	Buddy Biancalana	.25
3	Jorge Orta	.25
4	Greg Pryor	.25
5	George Brett	4.00
6	Willie Wilson	.50
8	Jim Sundberg	.25
10	Dick Howser	.25
11	Hal McRae	.50
20	Frank White	.40
21	Lonnie Smith	.25
22	Dennis Leonard	.25
23	Mark Gubicza	.50
24	Darryl Motley	.25
25	Danny Jackson	.35
26	Steve Farr	.25
29	Dan Quisenberry	.35
31	Bret Saberhagen	1.00
35	Lynn Jones	.25
37	Charlie Leibrandt	.25
38	Mark Huismann	.25
40	Buddy Black	.25
45	Steve Balboni	.25
----	Header Card	.25
----	Discount Card	.25

1981 National Sports Collectors Convention

BOB FOTHERGILL
Outfield
1922-30
11
1981 2nd National Sports Collectors Convention · Plymouth, Michigan

Detroit Tigers from the turn of the century through the early 1950s are featured in this collector's set issued in conjunction with the 2nd annual National Sports Collectors Convention in Plymouth, Mich. The 2-3/4" x 4-1/4" cards feature black-and-white photos of the players with identification and card number in the wide white border at bottom. Backs are blank. Issue price was $3.

		MT
Complete Set (32):		10.00
Common Player:		.25
1	Ty Cobb	2.00
2	Hughie Jennings	.25
3	Heinie Manush	.25
4	George Mullin	.25
5	Donie Bush	.25
6	Bobby Veach	.25
7	Wild Bill Donovan	.25
8	Harry Heilmann	.25
9	Sam Crawford	.25
10	Lu Blue	.25
11	Bob Fothergill	.25
12	Harry Coveleski	.25
13	Dale Alexander	.25
14	Charlie Gehringer	.45
15	Tommy Bridges	.25
16	1935 Tigers	.25
17	Hank Greenberg	1.00
18	Goose Goslin	.25
19	Firpo Marberry	.25
20	Hal Newhouser	.25
21	Schoolboy Rowe	.25
22	Mickey Cochrane	.35
23	Gee Walker	.25
24	Marv Owen	.25
25	Barney McCosky	.25
26	Rudy York	.25
27	Pete Fox	.25
28	Al Benton	.25
29	Billy Rogell	.25
30	Jo-Jo White	.25
31	Dizzy Trout	.25
32	1945 Tigers	.25

1992 Nationwide Insurance Pirates

Nationwide Insurance sponsored a Pittsburgh Pirates set. Released in June of 1993, the set includes a card of by-then departed MVP Barry Bonds. Each of the cards in the set includes a fire safety tip on the reverse. Measuring 3-1/2" x 5-3/4", the cards have color action photos on front. In color at bottom are a team logo, a ribbon with the player name and a baseball with his uniform number. Backs have personal data, a fire safety message and a sponsor's logo. The unnumbered cards are checklisted here in alphabetical order.

		MT
Complete Set (25):		9.00
Common Player:		.50
(1)	Stan Belinda	.50
(2)	Jay Bell	.75
(3)	Barry Bonds	4.00
(4)	Steve Buechele	.50
(5)	Terry Collins	.50
(6)	Rich Donnelly	.50
(7)	Doug Drabek	.60
(8)	Cecil Espy	.50
(9)	Jeff King	.60
(10)	Mike LaValliere	.50
(11)	Jim Leyland	.75
(12)	Jose Lind	.50
(13)	Roger Mason	.50
(14)	Milt May	.50
(15)	Lloyd McClendon	.50
(16)	Orlando Merced	.60
(17)	Denny Neagle	.75
(18)	Bob Patterson	.50
(19)	Gary Redus	.50
(20)	Don Slaught	.50
(21)	Zane Smith	.50
(22)	Randy Tomlin	.50
(23)	Andy Van Slyke	.65
(24)	Gary Varsho	.50
(25)	Bob Walk	.50

1993 Nationwide/Quintex Pirates

Backs of these 3-1/2" x 5-3/4" player photocards can be found bearing the advertising of either Nationwide Insurance or Quintex Mobile

Communications. The cards were given away at a June 27 promotional date. Cards have large action photos on front with a red stripe above and below. The player's name is in white at bottom, along with a color logo marking the team's N.L. East division championships of 1990-92. Backs are in black-and-white with a sponsor's ad at bottom and player data, including uniform number, at top. Cards are checklisted here in alphabetical order.

		MT
	Complete Set (40):	9.00
	Common Player:	.25
(1)	Stan Belinda	.25
(2)	Jay Bell	.75
(3)	Steve Blass (broadcaster)	.25
(4)	John Candelaria	.40
(5)	Dave Clark	.25
(6)	Terry Collins	.25
(7)	Steve Cooke	.35
(8)	Kent Derdivannis (broadcaster)	.25
(9)	Rich Donnelly	.25
(10)	Tom Foley	.25
(11)	Lanny Frattare (broadcaster)	.25
(12)	Carlos Garcia	.35
(13)	Jeff King	.50
(14)	Jim Leyland	.50
(15)	Al Martin	.40
(16)	Milt May	.25
(17)	Lloyd McClendon	.25
(18)	Orlando Merced	.40
(19)	Ray Miller	.25
(20)	Blas Minor	.25
(21)	Dennis Moeller	.25
(22)	Denny Neagle	.50
(23)	Dave Otto	.25
(24)	Tom Prince	.25
(25)	Jim Rooker (broadcaster)	.25
(26)	Tommy Sandt	.25
(27)	Ted Simmons (office)	.35
(28)	Don Slaught	.25
(29)	Lonnie Smith	.25
(30)	Zane Smith	.25
(31)	Randy Tomlin	.25
(32)	Andy Van Slyke	.35
(33)	Bill Virdon	.35
(34)	Paul Wagner	.25
(35)	Tim Wakefield	.30
(36)	Bob Walk	.25
(37)	John Wehner	.25
(38)	Kevin Young	.25
(39)	Pirate Parrot (mascot) (Nationwide only)	.25
(40)	Three Rivers Stadium (Nationwide only)	.25

1994 Nationwide/ Quintex Pirates

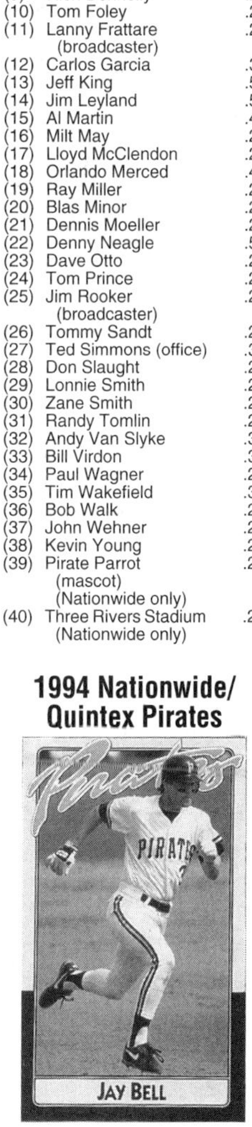

This set of Pirate photo-cards was issued as a stadium give-away on July 31. The 3-1/2" x 5-3/4" cards have color game-action photos on front with borders of team-color black and yellow. Team name is at top in red and white. Backs are in black-and-white and feature biographical data, a team logo and an ad for one of the set's co-sponsors, Quintex or Nationwide. Player uniform numbers are also presented. The checklist here is arranged in alphabetical order.

		MT
	Complete Set (30):	7.00
	Common Player:	.25
(1)	Jay Bell	.75
(2)	Dave Clark	.25
(3)	Steve Cooke	.35
(4)	Mark Dewey	.25
(5)	Rich Donnelly	.25
(6)	Tom Foley	.25
(7)	Carlos Garcia	.35
(8)	Brian Hunter	.25
(9)	Jeff King	.40
(10)	Jim Leyland	.50
(11)	Ravelo Manzanillo	.25
(12)	Al Martin	.50
(13)	Milt May	.25
(14)	Lloyd McClendon	.25
(15)	Orlando Merced	.35
(16)	Dan Miceli	.25
(17)	Ray Miller	.25
(18)	Denny Neagle	.50
(19)	Tommy Sandt	.25
(20)	Don Slaught	.25
(21)	Zane Smith	.25
(22)	Andy Van Slyke	.45
(23)	Bill Virdon	.35
(24)	Paul Wagner	.25
(25)	Rick White	.25
(26)	Spin Williams	.25
(27)	Kevin Young	.25
(28)	Lanny Frattare (radio announcer)	.25
(29)	Pirate Parrot (mascot)	.25
(30)	Three Rivers Stadium	.25

1988 Negro League Stars

Players associated with the segregated Negro Leagues around Pittsburgh are featured on this set sponsored by the Duquesne Light Co., and the Pittsburgh Pirates and handed out at the Sept. 10 Pirates game. The 2-1/2" x 3-1/2" cards were issued on a perforated sheet. Fronts have sepia photos. A yellow banner at top reads "NEGRO LEAGUE STARS", a commemorative circle logo appears at lower-right. Backs are in black-and-white with a career summary, biographical data, and the Pirates logo.

		MT
	Complete Set (20):	15.00
	Common Player:	.50
1	Rube Foster	.75
2	1913 Homestead Grays	.50
3	Cum Posey	.50
4	1926 Pittsburgh Crawford	.50
5	Gus Greenlee	.50
6	Pop Lloyd	.75
7	Oscar Charleston	.75
8	Smoky Joe Williams	.75
9	Judy Johnson	.75
10	Martin Dihigo	.75
11	Satchel Paige	2.00
12	Josh Gibson	2.00
13	Sam Streeter	.50
14	Cool Papa Bell	.75
15	Ted Page	.50
16	Buck Leonard	1.00
17	Ray Dandridge	.75
18	Lefty Melix, Willis Moody	.50
19	Harold Tinker	.50
20	Monte Irvin	1.00

1995 Negro Leagues Museum Buck O'Neil Mini-poster

On July 28, 1995, the Kansas City Royals held a Buck O'Neil Appreciation Night at which the former Negro Leagues star and major league coach was honored. This 8-3/8" x 10-3/4" glossy cardboard mini-poster pictures O'Neil as he appeared in 1995 in a color painting by John Boyd Martin. On back is a career summary and the logo of the Negro Leagues Baseball Musuem, which sponsored the give-away.

	MT
John "Buck" O'Neil	6.00

1984 Nestle

The 792 cards in the 1984 Nestle set are identical to the Topps regular issue except that the candy company's logo replaces the Topps logo in the upper-right corner of the front. The set was offered as a premium in uncut 132-card sheet form (24" x 48"). A few enterprising individuals bought up the majority of the reported 4,000 set production and had the sheets cut into single cards. Due to the ease in handling individual cards, as opposed to large press sheets, sets of single cards sell for more than sheet sets.

	MT
Complete Set, Sheets (6)	350.00
Complete Set, Singles (792)	500.00
Common Player:	.25
Sheet A:	175.00
Sheet B:	30.00
Sheet C:	30.00
Sheet D:	30.00
Sheet E:	30.00
Sheet F:	30.00
(Star cards valued at 7X-10X same card in regular 1984 Topps set.)	

1984 Nestle Dream Team

This set was issued by the Nestle candy company in conjunction with Topps. Cards are in standard 2-1/2" x 3-1/2" size and feature the top 22 players of 1984, 11 from each league. This full-color "Dream Team" includes one player at each position, plus right- and left-handed starting pitchers and one reliever. Card fronts and backs each have a Nestle logo. An unnumbered checklist was included with the set.

		MT
	Complete Set (23):	21.00
	Common Player:	.60
1	Eddie Murray	2.00
2	Lou Whitaker	.60
3	George Brett	4.00
4	Cal Ripken	6.00
5	Jim Rice	.75
6	Dave Winfield	2.00
7	Lloyd Moseby	.60
8	Lance Parrish	.60
9	LaMarr Hoyt	.60
10	Ron Guidry	.60
11	Dan Quisenberry	.60
12	Steve Garvey	1.50
13	Johnny Ray	.60
14	Mike Schmidt	4.00
15	Ozzie Smith	3.00
16	Andre Dawson	1.00
17	Tim Raines	.75
18	Dale Murphy	1.50
19	Tony Pena	.60
20	John Denny	.60
21	Steve Carlton	2.00
22	Al Holland	.60
----	Checklist	.05

1987 Nestle

Nestle, in conjunction with Topps, issued a 33-card set in 1987. Cards #1-11 feature black-and-white photos of players from the "Golden Era." Cards #12-33 feature full-color photos of American (12-22) and National League (23-33) players from the "Modern Era" of baseball. The cards measure 2-1/2" x 3-1/2" and have all team emblems airbrushed away. Three cards were inserted in specially marked six-packs of various Nestle candy bars. Two complete sets were available through a mail-in offer for $1.50 and three proofs of purchase.

		MT
	Complete Set (33):	10.00
	Common Player:	.25
1	Lou Gehrig	.50
2	Rogers Hornsby	.25
3	Pie Traynor	.25
4	Honus Wagner	.30
5	Babe Ruth	1.00
6	Tris Speaker	.25
7	Ty Cobb	.50
8	Mickey Cochrane	.25
9	Walter Johnson	.25
10	Carl Hubbell	.25
11	Jimmie Foxx	.25
12	Rod Carew	.25
13	Nellie Fox	.25
14	Brooks Robinson	.25
15	Luis Aparicio	.25
16	Frank Robinson	.25
17	Mickey Mantle	1.50
18	Ted Williams	.75
19	Yogi Berra	.25
20	Bob Feller	.25
21	Whitey Ford	.25
22	Harmon Killebrew	.25
23	Stan Musial	.45
24	Jackie Robinson	.75
25	Eddie Mathews	.25
26	Ernie Banks	.25
27	Roberto Clemente	1.00
28	Willie Mays	.45
29	Hank Aaron	.45
30	Johnny Bench	.25
31	Bob Gibson	.25
32	Warren Spahn	.25
33	Duke Snider	.25

1988 Nestle

This 44-card set was produced by Mike Schechter Associates for Nestle. "Dream Team" packets of three player cards and one checklist card were inserted in six-packs of Nestle's candy bars. The issue features current players divided into four Dream Teams (East and West teams for each league). The "1988 Nestle" header appears at the top of the red and yellow-bordered cards. Below the player closeup (in an airbrushed cap) is a blue oval player name banner. Card backs are red, white and blue with personal stats, career highlights and major league totals. The bright red, blue and yellow checklist card outlines two special offers; one for an uncut sheet of all 44 player cards and one for a 1988 replica autographed baseball.

		MT
	Complete Set, Singles (44):	15.00
	Complete Set, Uncut Sheet:	18.00
	Common Player:	.25
1	Roger Clemens	1.00
2	Dale Murphy	.40
3	Eric Davis	.25
4	Gary Gaetti	.25
5	Ozzie Smith	.65
6	Mike Schmidt	1.50

7	Ozzie Guillen	.25
8	John Franco	.25
9	Andre Dawson	.35
10	Mark McGwire	2.50
11	Bret Saberhagen	.30
12	Benny Santiago	.25
13	Jose Uribe	.25
14	Will Clark	.75
15	Don Mattingly	1.25
16	Juan Samuel	.25
17	Jack Clark	.25
18	Darryl Strawberry	.35
19	Bill Doran	.25
20	Pete Incaviglia	.25
21	Dwight Gooden	.35
22	Willie Randolph	.25
23	Tim Wallach	.25
24	Pedro Guerrero	.25
25	Steve Bedrosian	.25
26	Gary Carter	.40
27	Jeff Reardon	.25
28	Dave Righetti	.25
29	Frank White	.25
30	Buddy Bell	.25
31	Tim Raines	.35
32	Wade Boggs	.75
33	Dave Winfield	.90
34	George Bell	.25
35	Alan Trammell	.25
36	Joe Carter	.25
37	Jose Canseco	.55
38	Carlton Fisk	.65
39	Kirby Puckett	1.00
40	Tony Gwynn	.90
41	Matt Nokes	.25
42	Keith Hernandez	.25
43	Nolan Ryan	2.00
44	Wally Joyner	.35

1992 NewSport

This set of glossy player cards was issued in France; hence all of the text is in French. The approximately 4" x 6" cards were evidently issued in series, as a month of issue appears in tiny type on the back. Fronts have large color game-action photos or poses bordered in white. At top is the player's last name and initial, and his position. The NewSport and MLB logos are at bottom. Backs are in black-and-white with biographical details, major league stats and career summary. The unnumbered cards are checklisted here in alphabetical order.

		MT
Complete Set (30):		250.00
Common Player:		4.00
(1)	Roberto Alomar	10.00
(2)	Wade Boggs	15.00
(3)	George Brett	25.00
(4)	Will Clark	12.00
(5)	Eric Davis	4.00
(6)	Rob Dibble	4.00
(7)	Doug Drabek	4.00
(8)	Julio Franco	4.00
(9)	Ken Griffey Jr.	65.00
(10)	Rickey Henderson	6.00
(11)	Kent Hrbek	4.00
(12)	Bo Jackson	6.00
(13)	Howard Johnson	4.00
(14)	Barry Larkin	5.00
(15)	Don Mattingly	15.00
(16)	Fred McGriff	5.00
(17)	Mark McGwire	60.00
(18)	Jack Morris	4.00
(19)	Lloyd Moseby	4.00
(20)	Terry Pendleton	4.00
(21)	Cal Ripken Jr.	50.00
(22)	Nolan Ryan	50.00
(23)	Bret Saberhagen	4.00
(24)	Ryne Sandberg	15.00
(25)	Benito Santiago	4.00
(26)	Mike Scioscia	4.00
(27)	Ozzie Smith	20.00
(28)	Darryl Strawberry	5.00
(29)	Andy Van Slyke	4.00
(30)	Frank Viola	4.00

1983 Nike Poster Cards

Nike issued these counter cards as samples to illustrate its line of sports posters. A total of 27 individual and group posters and cards were issued with an emphasis on baseball, football and basketball subjects. The 5" x 7" cards feature a reproduction of the poster on the high-gloss front. A small die-cut hole appears at the top of each card. Backs are blank except for the poster stock number and title. Only the baseball subjects are checklisted here. All cards have a "290" prefix to the number shown.

		MT
Complete (Baseball) Set (10):		125.00
Common Card:		3.00
218	MVP & CY (Mike Schmidt, Steve Carlton)	15.00
223	Fingers & Sutter (Rollie Fingers, Bruce Sutter)	12.00
224	Penguin Power (Ron Cey)	12.00
231	K-Lord (Gaylord Perry)	15.00
237	Power Alley (Dale Murphy)	15.00
238	Tigerrr Catcher (Lance Parrish)	15.00
239	Dodger Kid (Steve Sax)	15.00
245	Blue Thunder (Pedro Guerrero)	12.00
852	Dr. K (Dwight Gooden)	15.00
855	Rick's World (Rick Sutcliffe)	12.00

1985 Nike Poster Cards

Nike, the athletic shoe company, produced posters and counter display cards of its posters for several years, but in 1985 issued a five-card set. The cards are borderless, color miniature versions (3-1/16" x 5-1/16") of the Nike posters. Backs feature personal data and career highlights, along with the warning, "Promotional Use Only/Not For Resale." The five-card set includes two baseball players.

		MT
Complete Set (5):		40.00
Common Player:		2.50
(1)	Dwight Gooden (baseball)	4.50
(2)	Michael Jordan (basketball)	35.00
(3)	James Lofton (football)	2.50
(4)	John McEnroe (tennis)	6.00
(5)	Lance Parrish (baseball)	2.50

1986 Nike Poster Cards

Nike issued these counter cards as samples to illustrate its line of sports posters. The 4-3/4" x 6-3/4" cards feature a reproduction of the poster on the high-gloss front. A small die-cut hole appears at the top of each card. Backs are blank except for the poster stock number and title. Only the baseball subjects are checklisted here. All cards have a "290" prefix to the number shown.

		MT
863	Hitting Machine - Tony Gwynn	15.00
865	Wally World - Wally Joyner	12.00

1987 Nike Poster Cards

Nike issued these counter cards as samples to illustrate its line of sports posters. The 5" x 7" pieces are printed on heavy semi-gloss paper and feature a reproduction of the poster on front. Backs are blank except for the poster stock number and title. Only the baseball subjects are checklisted here. All cards have a "290" prefix to the number shown.

		MT
876	Mark McGwire	20.00

1991 Nike Poster Cards

Nike issued these counter cards as samples to illustrate its line of sports posters. The approximately 4-3/4" x 6-3/4" cards feature a reproduction of the poster on the front, along with its stock number and title. Backs are blank. Only the baseball subjects are checklisted here.

		MT
290911	Out of the Blue - Kirby Puckett	9.00
290912	Grace Under Pressure - Mark Grace	9.00

1989 J.J. Nissen Super Stars

Distributed with bakery products, these standard-size cards feature central color photos on which uniform logos have been airbrushed away due to lack of a Major League Baseball license by Michael Schechter Associates, the cards' manufacturer. Front graphics are in shades of red, orange and yellow. Backs are printed in black-and-white. The complete set price does not include the Mark Grace card with Vance Law's photo.

		MT
Complete Set (20):		18.00
Common Player:		.50
1	Wally Joyner	.60
2	Wade Boggs	1.50
3	Ellis Burks	.50
4	Don Mattingly	2.50
5	Jose Canseco	1.50
6	Mike Greenwell	.50
7	Eric Davis	.50
8	Kirby Puckett	2.00
9	Kevin Seitzer	.50
10	Darryl Strawberry	.75
11	Gregg Jefferies	.50
12a	Mark Grace (photo actually Vance Law)	8.00
12b	Mark Grace (correct photo)	.75
13	Matt Nokes	.50
14	Mark McGwire	4.00
15	Bobby Bonilla	.50
16	Roger Clemens	2.00
17	Frank Viola	.50
18	Orel Hershiser	.50
19	David Cone	.50
20	Ted Williams	2.50

1994 North American Telephone Phone Cards

These phone cards honoring top Hall of Famers were issued in the standard round-cornered plastic format in 2-1/2" x 3-3/8" size. Fronts have black-and-white player photos, a facsimile autograph and $5 value. Backs are also in black-and-white and have details for use of the card to make calls. Original retail price of the cards was $8. Announced production of each "TeleTrading Card" was 5,000.

		MT
Complete Set (4):		18.00
Common Player:		3.00
(1)	Ty Cobb	4.00
(2)	Lou Gehrig	4.00
(3)	Satchel Paige	3.00
(4)	Babe Ruth	6.00

1997 N.Y. Lottery Legends

Five stars who played some or all of their careers with New York teams are featured in this series of $1 scratch-off lottery tickets. The 4" x 2" tickets have color player pictures at left. Because the tickets are licensed only by the players, and not Major League Baseball, the photos have had uniform logos removed. Tickets have dark blue borders and are perforated at top and bottom. Backs are printed in black-and-white.

		MT
Complete Set:		10.00
Common Player:		2.00
(1)	Yogi Berra	2.00
(2)	Keith Hernandez	2.00
(3)	Gil Hodges	2.00
(4)	Monte Irvin	2.00
(5)	Don Larsen	2.00

1984 N.Y. Mets M.V.P. Club

This nine-card, uncut panel was issued - along with other souvenir items - as a promotion by the New York Mets M.V.P. (Most Valuable Person) Club. Available from the club by mail, the perforated panel features eight full-color player cards, plus a special promotional card in the center. The full panel measures 7-1/2" x 10-1/2", with individual cards measuring the standard 2-1/2" x 3-1/2". Card backs are numbered in the upper right corner and include player stats and career highlights.

		MT
Complete Singles Set (9):		3.00
Common Player:		.25
Panel:		9.00
1	Dave Johnson	.30
2	Ron Darling	.25
3	George Foster	.25
4	Keith Hernandez	.30
5	Jesse Orosco	.25
6	Rusty Staub	.30
7	Darryl Strawberry	2.00
8	Mookie Wilson	.25
----	Membership Card	.05

1985 N.Y. Mets Police

This unauthorized collectors' issue came out of Florida, where the Mets conducted spring training. The cards were not authorized by the teams, the Kiwanis Club or any police agency; they were manufactured strictly for sale to unsuspecting collectors. In format they resemble contemporary safety issues, measuring 2-5/8" x 4-1/4" with color player photos on front and an anti-drug message on back (ironic, considering the percentage of players in the set who had well-publicized substance abuse problems). Cards are checklisted here in alphabetical order. Because distribution was quickly halted these cards are not commonly encountered in hobby channels.

		MT
Complete Set (6):		7.00
Common Player:		1.00
1	George Foster, Bill Robinson	1.00
2	Gary Carter, Davey Johnson	1.50
3	Dwight Gooden	1.50
4	Mookie Wilson	1.00
5	Keith Hernandez	1.00
6	Darryl Strawberry	1.25

1985 N.Y. Mets Super Fan Club

This specially-produced nine-card panel was issued as part of a souvenir package by the New York Mets Super Fan Club. The full-color, perforated panel measures 7-1/2" x 10-1/2" and features eight standard-size player cards, plus a special promotional card in the center. The uncut sheet was available by mail directly from the club. The backs are numbered in the upper right corner and include player statistics and career highlights.

		MT
Complete Singles Set (9):		4.00
Common Player:		.25
Panel:		9.00
1	Wally Backman	.25
2	Bruce Berenyi	.25
3	Gary Carter	.60
4	George Foster	.25
5	Dwight Gooden	1.50
6	Keith Hernandez	.30
7	Doug Sisk	.25
8	Darryl Strawberry	.75
----	Membership Card	.05

1986 N.Y. Mets Super Fan Club

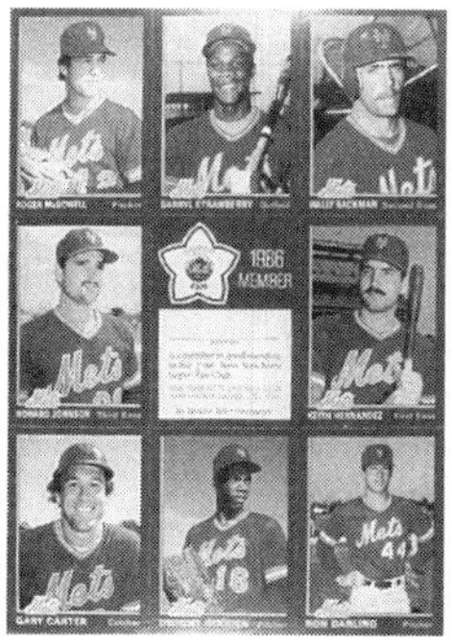

This special nine-card panel was issued by the fan club of the 1986 World Champion New York Mets, along with other souvenir items gained with membership in the club. Included in the full-color set are eight top Mets players, with a promotional card in the center of the panel. Individual cards measure 2-1/2" x 3-1/2", and are perforated at the edges to facilitate separation. The full panel measures 70-1/2" x 10-1/2". Card fronts feature posed photos of each player, along with name, position and team logo. Backs feature career and personal data, and are printed in the team's blue and orange colors.

		MT
Complete Singles Set (9):		4.00
Common Player:		.15
Panel:		6.00
1	Wally Backman	.25
2	Gary Carter	.60
3	Ron Darling	.25
4	Dwight Gooden	.90
5	Keith Hernandez	.30
6	Howard Johnson	.25
7	Roger McDowell	.25
8	Darryl Strawberry	.75
----	Membership Card	.05

1987 N.Y. Mets Darryl Strawberry Sheet

This souvenir sheet was a stadium giveaway at a special promotional home date at Shea during the peak of Strawberry's career in New York. The blank-back 8-1/2" x 11" sheet has five baseball designs of varying sizes with color action photos of Strawberry in each.

	MT
Darryl Strawberry	2.00

1992 N.Y. Mets Spring Training Superstars

A series of large-format (13-3/4" x 22-3/4") color pictures of Mets players was issued during spring training 1992 by The Port St. Lucie News and The Stuart News in Florida. The pictures are printed on heavy newspaper stock and feature color action photos with a light blue frame and white border. A box at bottom has the player's major league career stats. Various advertisements appear on back. The unnumbered pictures are listed here alphabetically and it is possible this list is not complete.

		MT
Complete Set (9):		35.00
Common Player:		4.00
(1)	Bobby Bonilla	5.00
(2)	Kevin Elster	4.00
(3)	John Franco	4.00
(4)	Todd Hundley	4.00
(5)	Howard Johnson	4.00
(6)	Dave Magadan	4.00
(7)	Eddie Murray	8.00
(8)	Willie Randolph	4.00
(9)	Bret Saberhagen	6.00

1996 N.Y. Mets Photocards

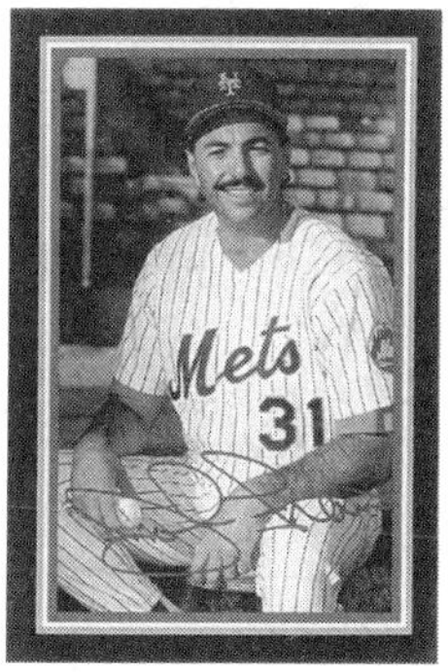

This series of player photocards was apparently provided by the team to answer fan autograph requests. In 3-3/4" x 5-1/2" size the cards are printed on thin cardboard. Player photos are framed in team colors of blue, white and orange with a wide black border. A large facsimile autograph is printed in blue across the photo. Black-and-white backs have a large team logo at center, overprinted with the player's personal data. Name and uniform number are at top. The unnumbered cards are listed here in alphabetical order.

		MT
Complete Set (25):		24.00
Common Player:		1.00
(1)	Edgardo Alfonzo	2.50
(2)	Tim Bogar	1.00
(3)	Rico Brogna	1.00
(4)	Paul Byrd	1.00
(5)	Mark Clark	1.00
(6)	Jerry DiPoto	1.00
(7)	Carl Everett	1.50
(8)	John Franco	1.00
(9)	Bernard Gilkey	1.50
(10)	Pete Harnisch	1.00
(11)	Doug Henry	1.00
(12)	Todd Hundley	2.50
(13)	Butch Huskey	2.00
(14)	Jason Isringhausen	1.50
(15)	Lance Johnson	1.00
(16)	Bobby Jones	1.00
(17)	Chris Jones	1.00
(18)	Jeff Kent	1.00
(19)	Brent Mayne	1.00
(20)	Dave Mlicki	1.00
(21)	Rey Ordonez	2.50
(22)	Robert Person	1.00
(23)	Bill Pulsipher	1.00
(24)	Jose Vizcaino	1.00
(25)	Paul Wilson	1.50

1997 N.Y. Mets Motion Cards

This issue was handed out to fans as a stadium promotion. The 3-1/2" x 2-1/2" cards have a borderless action scene on front, in which the players move when the card is tilted. Backs are conventionally printed with another player action photo, 1996 stats and biographical details.

		MT
Complete Set (4):		9.00
Common Player:		2.00
0	Rey Ordonez	3.00
1	Lance Johnson	2.00
9	Todd Hundley	2.50
31	John Franco	2.00

1982 N.Y. Yankees Photo Album

This stadium giveaway is an album measuring approximately 7-7/8" square. The cover is printed in red, white and blue. Inside the album are color portrait photos of the players, manager and coaches. Except for group pages of the coaches and bench-warmers, each of the blank-back pages has a single player picture with a white border and facsimile autograph. The individual pictures are perforated so they could be easily removed for display. The pictures are mostly arranged alphabetically and checklisted here in that fashion.

		MT
Complete Album:		10.00
Common Player:		.50
(1)	Gene Michael	.50
(2)	Clyde King, Joe Altobelli, Joe Pepitone, Mike Ferraro, Jeff Torborg, Yogi Berra	.50
(3)	Rick Cerone	.50
(4)	Dave Collins	.50
(5)	Bucky Dent	.60
(6)	George Frazier	.50
(7)	Oscar Gamble	.50
(8)	Goose Gossage	.60
(9)	Ken Griffey	.60
(10)	Ron Guidry	.75
(11)	Butch Hobson	.50
(12)	Tommy John	.75
(13)	Rudy May	.50
(14)	John Mayberry	.50
(15)	Mike Morgan	.50
(16)	Jerry Mumphrey	.50
(17)	Bobby Murcer	.60
(18)	Graig Nettles	.60
(19)	Lou Piniella	.65
(20)	Willie Randolph	.65
(21)	Shane Rawley	.50
(22)	Dave Righetti	.50
(23)	Andre Robertson	.50
(24)	Roy Smalley	.50
(25)	Dave Winfield	2.00
(26)	Butch Wynegar	.50
(27)	Roger Erickson, Barry Foote, Dave LaRoche, Doyle Alexander	.50

1995 N.Y. Yankees Pogs

Date of issue is conjecture because this is an unlicensed collectors issue bearing no copyright date. The set was issued as a 10" x 8" blank-back cardboard sheet with 11 individual pogs of Yankee greats die cut for removal. The loose pogs measure 1-5/8" in diameter. Background of the sheet is a game-action photo of Yankee Stadium. The unnumbered pogs are checklisted here alphabetically.

		MT
Complete Sheet:		6.00
Common Player:		.50
(1)	Yogi Berra	.50
(2)	Joe DiMaggio	1.00
(3)	Whitey Ford	.50
(4)	Lou Gehrig	.75
(5)	Reggie Jackson	.50
(6)	Mickey Mantle	2.00
(7)	Roger Maris	1.00
(8)	Billy Martin	.50
(9)	Don Mattingly	1.00
(10)	Thurman Munson	.50
(11)	Babe Ruth	2.00

1982 N.Y. Yankees Yearbook

American League stars of the 1940s-1960s are featured in a two-page cardboard panel stapled into the Yankees yearbook in 1982. The cards were the work of TCMA and done in the style of early-1950s Bowman cards, although the size is the standard 2-1/2" x 3-1/2". Like the '51 Bowmans, the yearbook cards have a color painting of the player on front with his name in a black strip near the bottom. Backs have a career summary and a bit of personal data along with the TCMA copyright notice. The yearbook originally sold for $3.

		MT
Complete Yearbook:		24.00
Complete Set, Singles (18):		16.00
Common Player:		1.00
1	Joe DiMaggio	6.00
2	Billy Pierce	1.00
3	Phil Rizzuto	2.00
4	Ted Williams	5.00
5	Billy Martin	1.50
6	Mel Parnell	1.00
7	Harmon Killebrew	1.50
8	Yogi Berra	2.00
9	Roy Sievers	1.00
10	Bill Dickey	1.50
11	Hank Greenberg	2.00
12	Allie Reynolds	1.00
13	Joe Sewell	1.00
14	Virgil Trucks	1.00
15	Mickey Mantle	8.00
16	Boog Powell	1.00
17	Whitey Ford	1.50
18	Lou Boudreau	1.00

1985 N.Y. Yankees Police

This unauthorized collectors' issue came out of Florida, where the Yankees conducted spring training. The cards were not authorized by the teams, the Kiwanis Club or any police agency; they were manufactured strictly for sale to unsuspecting collectors. In format they resemble contemporary safety issues, measuring 2-5/8" x 4-1/4" with color player photos on front and an anti-drug message on back. Cards are checklisted here in alphabetical order. Because distribution was quickly halted these cards are not commonly encountered in hobby channels.

		MT
Complete Set (6):		7.00
Common Player:		1.00
1	(Willie Randolph)	1.00
2	Phil Niekro	2.00
3	Ron Guidry (photo actually Righetti)	1.00
4	Dave Winfield	2.00
5	Dave Righetti (photo actually Guidry)	1.00
6	Billy Martin	1.00

1987 N.Y. Yankees Season Tickets

Current and former Yankee greats were depicted on season tickets during the 1987 campaign. Each 1-3/4" x 6" ticket has on front a 1-1/2" square color or blue duo-tone picture of one or more unidentified Yankees. Backs are printed in red and blue with advertising for WABC radio. Tickets were issued in strips of eight.

		MT
Complete Strip:		24.00
Complete Set (8):		20.00
Common Ticket:		2.00
(1)	Yogi Berra, Don Larsen	3.00
(2)	Joe DiMaggio, Mickey Mantle	6.00
(3)	Lou Gehrig	4.00
(4)	Rickey Henderson	2.00
(5)	Don Mattingly	3.00
(6)	Dave Righetti	2.00
(7)	Babe Ruth	5.00
(8)	Dave Winfield	2.00

O

1981 O-Pee-Chee

The Canadian version of the 1981 Topps set consists of 374 cards. This O-Pee-Chee set features many cards which note a player team change on front. These notations could be accomplished as the OPC cards were printed after the Topps. The cards measure 2-1/2" x 3-1/2" and have texts that are written in both English and French. The cards were printed on both white and gray stock. Cards with gray stock are valued three times greater than those with white stock.

		MT
Complete Set (374):		48.00
Common Player:		.15
1	Frank Pastore	.15
2	Phil Huffman	.15
3	Len Barker	.15
4	Robin Yount	4.00
5	Dave Stieb	.40
6	Gary Carter	2.00
7	Butch Hobson	.15
8	Lance Parrish	.15
9	Bruce Sutter	.15
10	Mike Flanagan	.15
11	Paul Mirabella	.15
12	Craig Reynolds	.15
13	Joe Charboneau	.50
14	Dan Driessen	.15
15	Larry Parrish	.15
16	Ron Davis	.15
17	Cliff Johnson	.15
18	Bruce Bochte	.15
19	Jim Clancy	.15
20	Bill Russell	.15
21	Ron Oester	.15
22	Danny Darwin	.15
23	Willie Aikens	.15
24	Don Stanhouse	.15
25	Sixto Lezcano	.15
26	U.L. Washington	.15
27	Champ Summers	.15
28	Enrique Romo	.15
29	Gene Tenace	.15
30	Jack Clark	.15
31	Checklist 1-125	.15
32	Ken Oberkfell	.15
33	Rick Honeycutt	.15
34	Al Bumbry	.15
35	John Tamargo	.15
36	Ed Farmer	.15
37	Gary Roenicke	.15
38	Tim Foli	.15
39	Eddie Murray	4.00
40	Roy Howell	.15
41	Bill Gullickson	.25
42	Jerry White	.15
43	Tim Blackwell	.15
44	Steve Henderson	.15
45	Enos Cabell	.15
46	Rick Bossetti	.15
47	Bill North	.15
48	Rich Gossage	.30
49	Bob Shirley	.15
50	Dave Lopes	.15
51	Shane Rawley	.15
52	Lloyd Moseby	.75
53	Burt Hooton	.15
54	Ivan DeJesus	.15
55	Mike Norris	.15
56	Del Unser	.15
57	Dave Revering	.15
58	Joel Youngblood	.15
59	Steve McCatty	.15
60	Willie Randolph	.15
61	Butch Wynegar	.15
62	Gary Lavelle	.15
63	Willie Montanez	.15
64	Terry Puhl	.15
65	Scott McGregor	.15
66	Buddy Bell	.15
67	Toby Harrah	.15
68	Jim Rice	.45
69	Darrell Evans	.15
70	Al Oliver	.15
71	Hal Dues	.15
72	Barry Evans	.15
73	Doug Bair	.15
74	Mike Hargrove	.15
75	Reggie Smith	.15
76	Mario Mendoza	.15
77	Mike Barlow	.15
78	Garth Iorg	.15
79	Jeff Reardon	1.50
80	Roger Erickson	.15
81	Dave Stapleton	.15
82	Barry Bonnell	.15
83	Dave Concepcion	.15
84	Johnnie LeMaster	.15
85	Mike Caldwell	.15
86	Wayne Gross	.15
87	Rick Camp	.15
88	Joe Lefebvre	.15
89	Darrell Jackson	.15
90	Bake McBride	.15
91	Tim Stoddard	.15
92	Mike Easler	.15
93	Jim Bibby	.15
94	Kent Tekulve	.15
95	Jim Sundberg	.15
96	Tommy John	.40
97	Chris Speier	.15
98	Clint Hurdle	.15
99	Phil Garner	.15
100	Rod Carew	2.00
101	Steve Stone	.15
102	Joe Niekro	.15
103	Jerry Martin	.15
104	Ron LeFlore	.15
105	Jose Cruz	.15
106	Don Money	.15
107	Bobby Brown	.15
108	Larry Herndon	.15
109	Dennis Eckersley	1.00
110	Carl Yastrzemski	2.00
111	Greg Minton	.15
112	Dan Schatzeder	.15
113	George Brett	5.50
114	Tom Underwood	.15
115	Roy Smalley	.15
116	Carlton Fisk	1.50
117	Pete Falcone	.15
118	Dale Murphy	2.00
119	Tippy Martinez	.15
120	Larry Bowa	.15
121	Julio Cruz	.15
122	Jim Gantner	.15
123	Al Cowens	.15
124	Jerry Garvin	.15
125	Andre Dawson	3.00
126	Charlie Leibrandt	.15
127	Willie Stargell	1.50
128	Andre Thornton	.15
129	Art Howe	.15
130	Larry Gura	.15
131	Jerry Remy	.15
132	Rick Dempsey	.15
133	Alan Trammell	.75
134	Mike LaCoss	.15
135	Gorman Thomas	.15
136	Expos Future Stars (Bobby Pate, Tim Raines, Roberto Ramos)	7.50
137	Bill Madlock	.15
138	Rich Dotson	.15
139	Oscar Gamble	.15
140	Bob Forsch	.15
141	Miguel Dilone	.15
142	Jackson Todd	.15
143	Dan Meyer	.15
144	Garry Templeton	.15
145	Mickey Rivers	.15
146	Alan Ashby	.15
147	Dale Berra	.15
148	Randy Jones	.15
149	Joe Nolan	.15
150	Mark Fidrych	.20
151	Tony Armas	.15
152	Steve Kemp	.15
153	Jerry Reuss	.15
154	Rick Langford	.15
155	Chris Chambliss	.15
156	Bob McClure	.15
157	John Wathan	.15
158	John Curtis	.15
159	Steve Howe	.15
160	Garry Maddox	.15
161	Dan Graham	.15
162	Doug Corbett	.15
163	Rob Dressler	.15
164	Bucky Dent	.15
165	Alvis Woods	.15
166	Floyd Bannister	.15
167	Lee Mazzilli	.15
168	Don Robinson	.15
169	John Mayberry	.15
170	Woodie Fryman	.15
171	Gene Richards	.15
172	Rick Burleson	.15
173	Bump Wills	.15
174	Glenn Abbott	.15
175	Dave Collins	.15
176	Mike Krukow	.15
177	Rick Monday	.15
178	Dave Parker	.40
179	Rudy May	.15
180	Pete Rose	6.00
181	Elias Sosa	.15
182	Bob Grich	.15
183	Fred Norman	.15
184	Jim Dwyer	.15
185	Dennis Leonard	.15
186	Gary Matthews	.15
187	Ron Hassey	.15
188	Doug DeCinces	.15
189	Craig Swan	.15
190	Cesar Cedeno	.15
191	Rick Sutcliffe	.15
192	Kiko Garcia	.15
193	Pete Vuckovich	.15
194	Tony Bernazard	.15
195	Keith Hernandez	.20
196	Jerry Mumphrey	.15
197	Jim Kern	.15
198	Jerry Dybzinski	.15
199	John Lowenstein	.15
200	George Foster	.15
201	Phil Niekro	1.50
202	Bill Buckner	.15
203	Steve Carlton	2.50
204	John D'Acquisto	.15
205	Rick Reuschel	.15
206	Dan Quisenberry	.15
207	Mike Schmidt	3.00
208	Bob Watson	.15
209	Jim Spencer	.15
210	Jim Palmer	2.00
211	Derrel Thomas	.15
212	Steve Nicosia	.15
213	Omar Moreno	.15
214	Richie Zisk	.15
215	Larry Hisle	.15
216	Mike Torrez	.15
217	Rich Hebner	.15
218	Britt Burns	.15
219	Ken Landreaux	.15
220	Tom Seaver	2.50
221	Bob Davis	.15
222	Jorge Orta	.15
223	Bobby Bonds	.15
224	Pat Zachry	.15
225	Ruppert Jones	.15
226	Duane Kuiper	.15
227	Rodney Scott	.15
228	Tom Paciorek	.15
229	Rollie Fingers	1.50
230	George Hendrick	.15
231	Tony Perez	1.50
232	Grant Jackson	.15
233	Damaso Garcia	.15
234	Lou Whitaker	.25
235	Scott Sanderson	.15
236	Mike Ivie	.15
237	Charlie Moore	.15
238	Blue Jays Future Stars (Luis Leal, Brian Milner, Ken Schrom)	.45
239	Rick Miller	.15
240	Nolan Ryan	12.00
241	Checklist 126-250	.15
242	Chet Lemon	.15
243	Dave Palmer	.15
244	Ellis Valentine	.15
245	Carney Lansford	.15
246	Ed Ott	.15
247	Glenn Hubbard	.15
248	Joey McLaughlin	.15
249	Jerry Narron	.15
250	Ron Guidry	.40
251	Steve Garvey	.75
252	Victor Cruz	.15
253	Bobby Murcer	.15
254	Ozzie Smith	4.00
255	John Stearns	.15
256	Bill Campbell	.15
257	Rennie Stennett	.15
258	Rick Waits	.15
259	Gary Lucas	.15
260	Ron Cey	.15
261	Rickey Henderson	8.00
262	Sammy Stewart	.15
263	Brian Downing	.15
264	Mark Bomback	.15
265	John Candelaria	.15
266	Renie Martin	.15
267	Stan Bahnsen	.15
268	Expos Team	.25
269	Ken Forsch	.15
270	Greg Luzinski	.15
271	Ron Jackson	.15
272	Wayne Garland	.15
273	Milt May	.15
274	Rick Wise	.15
275	Dwight Evans	.15
276	Sal Bando	.15
277	Alfredo Griffin	.15
278	Rick Sofield	.15
279	Bob Knepper	.15
280	Ken Griffey	.15
281	Ken Singleton	.15
282	Ernie Whitt	.15
283	Billy Sample	.15
284	Jack Morris	.25
285	Dick Ruthven	.15
286	Johnny Bench	2.50
287	Dave Smith	.15
288	Amos Otis	.15
289	Dave Goltz	.15
290	Bob Boone	.15
291	Aurelio Lopez	.15
292	Tom Hume	.15
293	Charlie Lea	.15
294	Bert Blyleven	.15
295	Hal McRae	.15
296	Bob Stanley	.15
297	Bob Bailor	.15
298	Jerry Koosman	.15
299	Eliott Maddox	.15
300	Paul Molitor	4.00
301	Matt Keough	.15
302	Pat Putnam	.15
303	Dan Ford	.15
304	John Castino	.15
305	Barry Foote	.15
306	Lou Piniella	.20
307	Gene Garber	.15
308	Rick Manning	.15
309	Don Baylor	.20
310	Vida Blue	.15
311	Doug Flynn	.15
312	Rick Rhoden	.15
313	Fred Lynn	.25
314	Rich Dauer	.15
315	Kirk Gibson	2.00
316	Ken Reitz	.15
317	Lonnie Smith	.15
318	Steve Yeager	.15
319	Rowland Office	.15
320	Tom Burgmeier	.15
321	Leon Durham	.15
322	Neil Allen	.15
323	Ray Burris	.15
324	Mike Willis	.15
325	Ray Knight	.15
326	Rafael Landestoy	.15
327	Moose Haas	.15
328	Ross Baumgarten	.15
329	Joaquin Andujar	.15
330	Frank White	.15
331	Blue Jays Team	.50
332	Dick Drago	.15
333	Sid Monge	.15
334	Joe Sambito	.15
335	Rick Cerone	.15
336	Eddie Whitson	.15
337	Sparky Lyle	.15
338	Checklist 251-374	.15
339	Jon Matlack	.15
340	Ben Oglivie	.15
341	Dwayne Murphy	.15
342	Terry Crowley	.15
343	Frank Taveras	.15
344	Steve Rogers	.15
345	Warren Cromartie	.15
346	Bill Caudill	.15
347	Harold Baines	2.00
348	Frank LaCorte	.15
349	Glenn Hoffman	.15
350	J.R. Richard	.20
351	Otto Velez	.15
352	Ted Simmons	.15
353	Terry Kennedy	.15
354	Al Hrabosky	.15
355	Bob Horner	.15
356	Cecil Cooper	.15
357	Bob Welch	.15
358	Paul Moskau	.15
359	Dave Rader	.15
360	Willie Wilson	.15
361	Dave Kingman	.15
362	Joe Rudi	.15
363	Rich Gale	.15

364	Steve Trout	.15
365	Graig Nettles	.15
366	Lamar Johnson	.15
367	Denny Martinez	.15
368	Manny Trillo	.15
369	Frank Tanana	.15
370	Reggie Jackson	2.25
371	Bill Lee	.15
372	Jay Johnstone	.15
373	Jason Thompson	.15
374	Tom Hutton	.15

1981 O-Pee-Chee Posters

Inserted inside the regular 1081 O-Pee-Chee wax packs, these full-color posters measure approximately 4-7/8" x 6-7/8". The set is complete at 24 posters and includes 12 players each from the Blue Jays and Expos. The blank-backed posters are numbered in the border below the photo where the caption is written in both French and English. The photos are surrounded by a blue border for Blue Jays players or a red border for Expos. Because they were inserted in wax packs, the posters generally contain folds.

		MT
Complete Set (24):		11.00
Common Player:		.50
1	Willie Montanez	.50
2	Rodney Scott	.50
3	Chris Speier	.50
4	Larry Parrish	.50
5	Warren Cromartie	.50
6	Andre Dawson	4.00
7	Ellis Valentine	.50
8	Gary Carter	4.00
9	Steve Rogers	.50
10	Woodie Fryman	.50
11	Jerry White	.50
12	Scott Sanderson	.50
13	John Mayberry	.50
14	Damasa Garcia (Damaso)	.50
15	Alfredo Griffin	.50
16	Garth Iorg	.50
17	Alvis Woods	.50
18	Rick Bosetti	.50
19	Barry Bonnell	.50
20	Ernie Whitt	.50
21	Jim Clancy	.50
22	Dave Stieb	1.50
23	Otto Velez	.50
24	Lloyd Moseby	.50

1982 O-Pee-Chee

The 1982 O-Pee-Chee set, complete at 396 cards, is nearly identical in design to the 1982 Topps set, except the Canadian-issued cards display the O-Pee-Chee logo on the front of the card and list the player's position in both French and English. The backs of the cards, which measure the standard 2-1/2" x 3-1/2", are also bilingual. Some of the cards carry an extra line on the front indicating an off-season team change.

		MT
Complete Set (396):		55.00
Common Player:		.12
1	Dan Spillner	.12
2	Ken Singleton (All-Star)	.12
3	John Candelaria	.12
4	Frank Tanana	.12
5	Reggie Smith	.12
6	Rick Monday	.12
7	Scott Sanderson	.12
8	Rich Dauer	.12
9	Ron Guidry	.25
10	Ron Guidry (In Action)	.12
11	Tom Brookens	.12
12	Moose Haas	.12
13	Chet Lemon	.12
14	Steve Howe	.12
15	Ellis Valentine	.12
16	Toby Harrah	.12
17	Darrell Evans	.12
18	Johnny Bench	1.75
19	Ernie Whitt	.12
20	Garry Maddox	.12
21	Graig Nettles (IA)	.12
22	Al Oliver (IA)	.12
23	Bob Boone	.12
24	Pete Rose (IA)	1.00
25	Jerry Remy	.12
26	Jorge Orta	.12
27	Bobby Bonds	.12
28	Jim Clancy	.12
29	Dwayne Murphy	.12
30	Tom Seaver	1.50
31	Tom Seaver (IA)	.75
32	Claudell Washington	.12
33	Bob Shirley	.12
34	Bob Forsch	.12
35	Willie Aikens	.12
36	Rod Carew (AS)	.30
37	Willie Randolph	.12
38	Charlie Lea	.12
39	Lou Whitaker	.15
40	Dave Parker	.20
41	Dave Parker (IA)	.12
42	Mark Belanger	.12
43	Rick Langford	.12
44	Rollie Fingers (IA)	.12
45	Rick Cerone	.12
46	Johnny Wockenfuss	.12
47	Jack Morris (AS)	.12
48	Cesar Cedeno	.12
49	Alvis Woods	.12
50	Buddy Bell	.12
51	Mickey Rivers (IA)	.12
52	Steve Rogers	.12
53	Blue Jays Team	.50
54	Ron Hassey	.12
55	Rick Burleson	.12
56	Harold Baines	.12
57	Craig Reynolds	.12
58	Carlton Fisk (AS)	.35
59	Jim Kern	.12
60	Tony Armas	.12
61	Warren Cromartie	.12
62	Graig Nettles	.12
63	Jerry Koosman	.12
64	Pat Zachry	.12
65	Terry Kennedy	.12
66	Richie Zisk	.12
67	Rich Gale	.12
68	Steve Carlton	.75
69	Greg Luzinski (IA)	.12
70	Tim Raines	2.50
71	Roy Lee Jackson	.12
72	Carl Yastrzemski	1.50
73	John Castino	.12
74	Joe Niekro	.12
75	Tommy John	.20
76	Dave Winfield AS	.20
77	Miguel Dilone	.12
78	Gary Gray	.12
79	Tom Hume	.12
80	Jim Palmer	1.00
81	Jim Palmer (IA)	.25
82	Vida Blue (IA)	.12
83	Garth Iorg	.12
84	Rennie Stennett	.12
85	Davey Lopes (IA)	.12
86	Dave Concepcion	.15
87	Matt Keough	.12
88	Jim Spencer	.12
89	Steve Henderson	.12
90	Nolan Ryan	10.00
91	Carney Lansford	.12
92	Bake McBride	.12
93	Dave Stapleton	.12
94	Expos Team	.50
95	Ozzie Smith	3.00
96	Rich Hebner	.12
97	Tim Foli	.12
98	Darrell Porter	.12
99	Barry Bonnell	.12
100	Mike Schmidt	3.00
101	Mike Schmidt (IA)	1.50
102	Dan Briggs	.12
103	Al Cowens	.12
104	Grant Jackson	.12
105	Kirk Gibson	.30
106	Dan Schatzeder	.12
107	Juan Berenguer	.12
108	Jack Morris	.25
109	Dave Revering	.12
110	Carlton Fisk	1.00
111	Carlton Fisk (IA)	.50
112	Billy Sample	.12
113	Steve McCatty	.12
114	Ken Landreaux	.12
115	Gaylord Perry	.75
116	Elias Sosa	.12
117	Rich Gossage (IA)	.12
118	Expos Future Stars (Terry Francona, Brad Mills, Bryn Smith)	.25
119	Billy Almon	.12
120	Gary Lucas	.12
121	Ken Oberkfell	.12
122	Steve Carlton (IA)	.30
123	Jeff Reardon	1.00
124	Bill Buckner	.15
125	Danny Ainge	2.25
126	Paul Splittorff	.12
127	Lonnie Smith	.12
128	Rudy May	.12
129	Checklist 1-132	.12
130	Julio Cruz	.12
131	Stan Bahnsen	.12
132	Pete Vuckovich	.12
133	Luis Salazar	.12
134	Dan Ford	.12
135	Denny Martinez	.20
136	Lary Sorensen	.12
137	Fergie Jenkins	.75
138	Rick Camp	.12
139	Wayne Nordhagen	.12
140	Ron LeFlore	.12
141	Rick Sutcliffe	.12
142	Rick Waits	.12
143	Mookie Wilson	.12
144	Greg Minton	.12
145	Bob Horner	.12
146	Joe Morgan (IA)	.15
147	Larry Gura	.12
148	Alfredo Griffin	.12
149	Pat Putnam	.12
150	Ted Simmons	.12
151	Gary Matthews	.12
152	Greg Luzinski	.15
153	Mike Flanagan	.12
154	Jim Morrison	.12
155	Otto Velez	.12
156	Frank White	.12
157	Doug Corbett	.12
158	Brian Downing	.12
159	Willie Randolph (IA)	.12
160	Luis Tiant	.15
161	Andre Thornton	.12
162	Amos Otis	.12
163	Paul Mirabella	.12
164	Bert Blyleven	.12
165	Rowland Office	.12
166	Gene Tenace	.12
167	Cecil Cooper	.12
168	Bruce Benedict	.12
169	Mark Clear	.12
170	Jim Bibby	.12
171	Ken Griffey Sr. (IA)	.12
172	Bill Gullickson	.12
173	Mike Scioscia	.12
174	Doug DeCinces	.12
175	Jerry Mumphrey	.12
176	Rollie Fingers	.75
177	George Foster (IA)	.12
178	Mitchell Page	.12
179	Steve Garvey	.65
180	Steve Garvey (IA)	.25
181	Woodie Fryman	.12
182	Larry Herndon	.12
183	Frank White (IA)	.12
184	Alan Ashby	.12
185	Phil Niekro	1.00
186	Leon Roberts	.12
187	Rod Carew	2.00
188	Willie Stargell (IA)	.30
189	Joel Youngblood	.12
190	J.R. Richard	.12
191	Tim Wallach	1.75
192	Broderick Perkins	.12
193	Johnny Grubb	.12
194	Larry Bowa	.12
195	Paul Molitor	3.00
196	Willie Upshaw	.12
197	Roy Smalley	.12
198	Chris Speier	.12
199	Don Aase	.12
200	George Brett	3.50
201	George Brett (IA)	2.00
202	Rick Manning	.12
203	Blue Jays Future Stars (Jesse Barfield, Brian Milner, Boomer Wells)	2.00
204	Rick Reuschel	.12
205	Neil Allen	.12
206	Leon Durham	.12
207	Jim Gantner	.12
208	Joe Morgan	.30
209	Gary Lavelle	.12
210	Keith Hernandez	.12
211	Joe Charboneau	.15
212	Mario Mendoza	.12
213	Willie Randolph (AS)	.12
214	Lance Parrish	.12
215	Mike Krukow	.12
216	Ron Cey	.12
217	Ruppert Jones	.12
218	Dave Lopes	.12
219	Steve Yeager	.12
220	Manny Trillo	.12
221	Dave Concepcion (IA)	.12
222	Butch Wynegar	.12
223	Lloyd Moseby	.20
224	Bruce Bochte	.12
225	Ed Ott	.12
226	Checklist 133-264	.12
227	Ray Burris	.12
228	Reggie Smith (IA)	.12
229	Oscar Gamble	.12
230	Willie Wilson	.12
231	Brian Kingman	.12
232	John Stearns	.12
233	Duane Kuiper	.12
234	Don Baylor	.12
235	Mike Easler	.12
236	Lou Piniella	.12
237	Robin Yount	2.50
238	Kevin Saucier	.12
239	Jon Matlack	.12
240	Bucky Dent	.12
241	Bucky Dent (IA)	.12
242	Milt May	.12
243	Lee Mazzilli	.12
244	Gary Carter	.75
245	Ken Reitz	.12
246	Scott McGregor (AS)	.12
247	Pedro Guerrero	.12
248	Art Howe	.12
249	Dick Tidrow	.12
250	Tug McGraw	.12
251	Fred Lynn	.15
252	Fred Lynn (IA)	.12
253	Gene Richards	.12
254	Jorge Bell	4.25
255	Tony Perez	.75
256	Tony Perez (IA)	.12
257	Rich Dotson	.12
258	Bo Diaz	.12
259	Rodney Scott	.12
260	Bruce Sutter	.12
261	George Brett (AS)	.75
262	Rick Dempsey	.12
263	Mike Phillips	.12
264	Jerry Garvin	.12
265	Al Bumbry	.12
266	Hubie Brooks	.12
267	Vida Blue	.12
268	Rickey Henderson	2.50
269	Rick Peters	.12
270	Rusty Staub	.15
271	Sixto Lezcano	.12
272	Bump Wills	.12
273	Gary Allenson	.12
274	Randy Jones	.12
275	Bob Watson	.12
276	Dave Kingman	.15
277	Terry Puhl	.12
278	Jerry Reuss	.12
279	Sammy Stewart	.12
280	Ben Oglivie	.12
281	Kent Tekulve	.12
282	Ken Macha	.12
283	Ron Davis	.12
284	Bob Grich	.12
285	Sparky Lyle	.12
286	Rich Gossage (AS)	.12
287	Dennis Eckersley	.50
288	Garry Templeton	.12
289	Bob Stanley	.12
290	Ken Singleton	.12
291	Mickey Hatcher	.12
292	Dave Palmer	.12
293	Damaso Garcia	.12
294	Don Money	.12
295	George Hendrick	.12
296	Steve Kemp	.12
297	Dave Smith	.12
298	Bucky Dent (AS)	.12
299	Steve Trout	.12
300	Reggie Jackson	2.00
301	Reggie Jackson (IA)	1.00
302	Doug Flynn	.12
303	Wayne Gross	.12
304	Johnny Bench (IA)	.40
305	Don Sutton	.75
306	Don Sutton (IA)	.20
307	Mark Bomback	.12
308	Charlie Moore	.12
309	Jeff Burroughs	.12
310	Mike Hargrove	.12
311	Enos Cabell	.12
312	Lenny Randle	.12
313	Ivan DeJesus	.12
314	Buck Martinez	.12
315	Burt Hooton	.12
316	Scott McGregor	.12
317	Dick Ruthven	.12
318	Mike Heath	.12
319	Ray Knight	.12
320	Chris Chambliss	.12
321	Chris Chambliss (IA)	.12
322	Ross Baumgarten	.12
323	Bill Lee	.12
324	Gorman Thomas	.12
325	Jose Cruz	.12
326	Al Oliver	.12
327	Jackson Todd	.12
328	Ed Farmer	.12
329	U.L. Washington	.12
330	Ken Griffey	.12
331	John Milner	.12
332	Don Robinson	.12
333	Cliff Johnson	.12
334	Fernando Valenzuela	.60
335	Jim Sundberg	.12
336	George Foster	.15
337	Pete Rose (AS)	.75
338	Davey Lopes (AS)	.12
339	Mike Schmidt (AS)	.40
340	Dave Concepcion (AS)	.12
341	Andre Dawson (AS)	.20
342	George Foster (AS)	.12
343	Dave Parker (AS)	.15
344	Gary Carter (AS)	.30
345	Fernando Valenzuela (AS)	.20
346	Tom Seaver (AS)	.30
347	Bruce Sutter (AS)	.12
348	Darrell Porter (IA)	.12
349	Dave Collins	.12
350	Amos Otis (IA)	.12
351	Frank Taveras	.12
352	Dave Winfield	3.00
353	Larry Parrish	.12
354	Roberto Ramos	.12
355	Dwight Evans	.12
356	Mickey Rivers	.12
357	Butch Hobson	.12
358	Carl Yastrzemski (IA)	.30
359	Ron Jackson	.12
360	Len Barker	.12
361	Pete Rose	4.00
362	Kevin Hickey	.12
363	Rod Carew (IA)	.30
364	Hector Cruz	.12
365	Bill Madlock	.12
366	Jim Rice	.25
367	Ron Cey (IA)	.12
368	Luis Leal	.12
369	Dennis Leonard	.12
370	Mike Norris	.12
371	Tom Paciorek	.12
372	Willie Stargell	.75
373	Dan Driessen	.12
374	Larry Bowa (IA)	.12
375	Dusty Baker	.12
376	Joey McLaughlin	.12
377	Reggie Jackson (AS)	.40
378	Mike Caldwell	.12
379	Andre Dawson	2.25
380	Dave Stieb	.15
381	Alan Trammell	.20
382	John Mayberry	.12
383	John Wathan	.12
384	Hal McRae	.12
385	Ken Forsch	.12
386	Jerry White	.12
387	Tom Veryzer	.12
388	Joe Rudi	.12
389	Bob Knepper	.12
390	Eddie Murray	2.75
391	Dale Murphy	.80
392	Bob Boone (IA)	.12
393	Al Hrabosky	.12
394	Checklist 265-396	.12
395	Omar Moreno	.12
396	Rich Gossage	.25

1982 O-Pee-Chee Posters

The 24 posters in this Canadian set, which features 12 players from the Expos and 12 from the Blue Jays, were inserted in regular 1982 O-Pee-Chee wax packs. The posters measure approximately 4-7/8" x 6-7/8" and are usually found with fold marks. The blank-backed posters are numbered in the bottom border where the captions appear in both French and English. Red borders surround the photos of Blue Jays players, while blue borders are used for the Expos.

		MT
Complete Set (24):		14.00
Common Player:		.50
1	John Mayberry	.50
2	Damaso Garcia	.50
3	Ernie Whitt	.50
4	Lloyd Moseby	.50
5	Alvis Woods	.50
6	Dave Stieb	.75
7	Roy Lee Jackson	.50
8	Joey McLaughlin	.50
9	Luis Leal	.50
10	Aurelio Rodriguez	.50
11	Otto Velez	.50
12	Juan Berenger (Berenguer)	.50
13	Warren Cromartie	.50
14	Rodney Scott	.50
15	Larry Parrish	.50
16	Gary Carter	3.00
17	Tim Raines	3.00
18	Andre Dawson	3.00
19	Terry Francona	.50
20	Steve Rogers	.50
21	Bill Gullickson	.50
22	Scott Sanderson	.50
23	Jeff Reardon	.50
24	Jerry White	.50

1983 O-Pee-Chee

Again complete at 396 cards, the 1983 O-Pee-Chee set borrows its design from the 1983 Topps set, except the Canadian-issued cards display the O-Pee-Chee logo on the front of the card and show the player's position in both French and English. The backs of the cards are also printed in both languages. The cards measure the standard 2-1/2" x 3-1/2". Some cards carry the extra line on the front indicating an off-season trade.

		MT
Complete Set (396):		68.00
Common Player:		.12
1	Rusty Staub	.15
2	Larry Parrish	.12
3	George Brett	3.50
4	Carl Yastrzemski	1.50
5	Al Oliver (Super Veteran)	.12
6	Bill Virdon	.12
7	Gene Richards	.12
8	Steve Balboni	.12
9	Joey McLaughlin	.12
10	Gorman Thomas	.12
11	Chris Chambliss	.12
12	Ray Burris	.12
13	Larry Herndon	.12
14	Ozzie Smith	2.50
15	Ron Cey	.12
16	Willie Wilson	.12
17	Kent Tekulve	.12
18	Kent Tekulve (Super Veteran)	.12
19	Oscar Gamble	.12
20	Carlton Fisk	1.50
21	Dale Murphy (All-Star)	.30
22	Randy Lerch	.12
23	Dale Murphy	.60
24	Steve Mura	.12
25	Hal McRae	.12
26	Dennis Lamp	.12
27	Ron Washington	.12
28	Bruce Bochte	.12
29	Randy Jones	.12
30	Jim Rice	.25
31	Bill Gullickson	.12
32	Dave Concepcion (AS)	.12
33	Ted Simmons (Super Veteran)	.12
34	Bobby Cox	.12
35	Rollie Fingers	.75
36	Rollie Fingers (Super Veteran)	.15
37	Mike Hargrove	.12
38	Roy Smalley	.12
39	Terry Puhl	.12
40	Fernando Valenzuela	.15
41	Garry Maddox	.12
42	Dale Murray	.12
43	Bob Dernier	.12
44	Don Robinson	.12
45	John Mayberry	.12
46	Richard Dotson	.12
47	Wayne Nordhagen	.12
48	Lary Sorenson	.12
49	Willie McGee	1.50
50	Bob Horner	.12
51	Rusty Staub (Super Veteran)	.12
52	Tom Seaver	1.75
53	Chet Lemon	.12
54	Scott Sanderson	.12
55	Mookie Wilson	.12
56	Reggie Jackson	1.75
57	Tim Blackwell	.12
58	Keith Moreland	.12
59	Alvis Woods	.12
60	Johnny Bench	1.75
61	Johnny Bench (Super Veteran)	.75
62	Jim Gott	.12
63	Rick Monday	.12
64	Gary Matthews	.12
65	Jack Morris	.50
66	Lou Whitaker	.12
67	U.L. Washington	.12
68	Eric Show	.12
69	Lee Lacy	.12
70	Steve Carlton	1.50
71	Steve Carlton (Super Veteran)	.25
72	Tom Paciorek	.12
73	Manny Trillo	.12
74	Tony Perez (Super Veteran)	.12
75	Amos Otis	.12
76	Rick Mahler	.12
77	Hosken Powell	.12
78	Bill Caudill	.12
79	Dan Petry	.12
80	George Foster	.12
81	Joe Morgan	.30
82	Burt Hooton	.12
83	Ryne Sandberg	35.00
84	Alan Ashby	.12
85	Ken Singleton	.12
86	Tom Hume	.12
87	Dennis Leonard	.12
88	Jim Gantner	.12
89	Leon Roberts	.12
90	Jerry Reuss	.12
91	Ben Oglivie	.12
92	Sparky Lyle (Super Veteran)	.12
93	John Castino	.12
94	Phil Niekro	.75
95	Alan Trammell	.25
96	Gaylord Perry	.30
97	Tom Herr	.12
98	Vance Law	.12
99	Dickie Noles	.12
100	Pete Rose	4.00
101	Pete Rose (Super Veteran)	.70
102	Dave Concepcion	.12
103	Darrell Porter	.12
104	Ron Guidry	.12
105	Don Baylor	.12
106	Steve Rogers (AS)	.12
107	Greg Minton	.12
108	Glenn Hoffman	.12
109	Luis Leal	.12
110	Ken Griffey	.12
111	Expos Team	.30
112	Luis Pujols	.12
113	Julio Cruz	.12
114	Jim Slaton	.12
115	Chili Davis	.15
116	Pedro Guerrero	.12
117	Mike Ivie	.12
118	Chris Welsh	.12
119	Frank Pastore	.12
120	Len Barker	.12
121	Chris Speier	.12
122	Bobby Murcer	.12
123	Bill Russell	.12
124	Lloyd Moseby	.12
125	Leon Durham	.12
126	Carl Yastrzemski (Super Veteran)	.30
127	John Candelaria	.12
128	Phil Garner	.12
129	Checklist 1-132	.12
130	Dave Stieb	.15
131	Geoff Zahn	.12
132	Todd Cruz	.12
133	Tony Pena	.12
134	Hubie Brooks	.12
135	Dwight Evans	.12
136	Willie Aikens	.12
137	Woodie Fryman	.12
138	Rick Dempsey	.12
139	Bruce Berenyi	.12
140	Willie Randolph	.12
141	Eddie Murray	2.50
142	Mike Caldwell	.12
143	Tony Gwynn	60.00
144	Tommy John (Super Veteran)	.12
145	Don Sutton	.75
146	Don Sutton (Super Veteran)	.15
147	Rick Manning	.12
148	George Hendrick	.12
149	Johnny Ray	.12
150	Bruce Sutter	.12
151	Bruce Sutter (Super Veteran)	.12
152	Jay Johnstone	.12
153	Jerry Koosman	.12
154	Johnnie LeMaster	.12
155	Dan Quisenberry	.12
156	Luis Salazar	.12
157	Steve Bedrosian	.12
158	Jim Sundberg	.12
159	Gaylord Perry (Super Veteran)	.15
160	Dave Kingman	.15
161	Dave Kingman (Super Veteran)	.12
162	Mark Clear	.12
163	Cal Ripken	50.00
164	Dave Palmer	.12
165	Dan Driessen	.12
166	Tug McGraw	.12
167	Denny Martinez	.20
168	Juan Eichelberger	.12
169	Doug Flynn	.12
170	Steve Howe	.12
171	Frank White	.12
172	Mike Flanagan	.12
173	Andre Dawson (AS)	.15
174	Manny Trillo (AS)	.12
175	Bo Diaz	.12
176	Dave Righetti	.12
177	Harold Baines	.12
178	Vida Blue	.12
179	Luis Tiant (Super Veteran)	.12
180	Rickey Henderson	2.50
181	Rick Rhoden	.12
182	Fred Lynn	.15
183	Ed Vande Berg	.12
184	Dwayne Murphy	.12
185	Tim Lollar	.12
186	Dave Tobik	.12
187	Tug McGraw (Super Veteran)	.12
188	Rick Miller	.12
189	Dan Schatzeder	.12
190	Cecil Cooper	.12
191	Jim Beattie	.12
192	Rich Dauer	.12
193	Al Cowens	.12
194	Roy Lee Jackson	.12
195	Mike Gates	.12
196	Tommy John	.15
197	Bob Forsch	.12
198	Steve Garvey	.60
199	Brad Mills	.12
200	Rod Carew	1.25
201	Rod Carew (Super Veteran)	.30
202	Blue Jays Team	.30
203	Floyd Bannister	.12
204	Bruce Benedict	.12
205	Dave Parker	.20
206	Ken Oberkfell	.12
207	Graig Nettles (Super Veteran)	.12
208	Sparky Lyle	.12
209	Jason Thompson	.12
210	Jack Clark	.15
211	Jim Kaat	.15
212	John Stearns	.12
213	Tom Burgmeier	.12
214	Jerry White	.12
215	Mario Soto	.12
216	Scott McGregor	.12
217	Tim Stoddard	.12
218	Bill Laskey	.12
219	Reggie Jackson (Super Veteran)	.30
220	Dusty Baker	.12
221	Joe Niekro	.12
222	Damaso Garcia	.12
223	John Montefusco	.12
224	Mickey Rivers	.12
225	Enos Cabell	.12
226	LaMarr Hoyt	.12
227	Tim Raines	.40
228	Joaquin Andujar	.12
229	Tim Wallach	.25
230	Fergie Jenkins	.30
231	Fergie Jenkins (Super Veteran)	.12
232	Tom Brunansky	.12
233	Ivan DeJesus	.12
234	Bryn Smith	.12
235	Claudell Washington	.12
236	Steve Renko	.12
237	Dan Norman	.12
238	Cesar Cedeno	.12
239	Dave Stapleton	.12
240	Rich Gossage	.20
241	Rich Gossage (Super Veteran)	.12
242	Bob Stanley	.12
243	Rich Gale	.12
244	Sixto Lezcano	.12
245	Steve Sax	.12
246	Jerry Mumphrey	.12
247	Dave Smith	.12
248	Bake McBride	.12
249	Checklist 133-264	.12
250	Bill Buckner	.12
251	Kent Hrbek	.15
252	Gene Tenace	.12
253	Charlie Lea	.12
254	Rick Cerone	.12
255	Gene Garber	.12
256	Gene Garber (Super Veteran)	.12
257	Jesse Barfield	.75
258	Dave Winfield	2.00
259	Don Money	.12
260	Steve Kemp	.12
261	Steve Yeager	.12
262	Keith Hernandez	.12
263	Tippy Martinez	.12
264	Joe Morgan (Super Veteran)	.12
265	Joel Youngblood	.12
266	Bruce Sutter (AS)	.12
267	Terry Francona	.12
268	Neil Allen	.12
269	Ron Oester	.12
270	Dennis Eckersley	.60
271	Dale Berra	.12
272	Al Bumbry	.12
273	Lonnie Smith	.12
274	Terry Kennedy	.12
275	Ray Knight	.12
276	Mike Norris	.12
277	Rance Mulliniks	.12
278	Dan Spillner	.12
279	Bucky Dent	.12
280	Bert Blyleven	.12
281	Barry Bonnell	.12
282	Reggie Smith	.12
283	Reggie Smith (Super Veteran)	.12
284	Ted Simmons	.12
285	Lance Parrish	.12
286	Larry Christenson	.12
287	Ruppert Jones	.12
288	Bob Welch	.12
289	John Wathan	.12
290	Jeff Reardon	.12
291	Dave Revering	.12
292	Craig Swan	.12
293	Graig Nettles	.12
294	Alfredo Griffin	.12
295	Jerry Remy	.12
296	Joe Sambito	.12
297	Ron LeFlore	.12
298	Brian Downing	.12
299	Jim Palmer	1.25
300	Mike Schmidt	2.50
301	Mike Schmidt (Super Veteran)	1.25
302	Ernie Whitt	.12
303	Andre Dawson	2.00
304	Bobby Murcer (Super Veteran)	.12
305	Larry Bowa	.12
306	Lee Mazzilli	.12
307	Lou Piniella	.12
308	Buck Martinez	.12
309	Jerry Martin	.12
310	Greg Luzinski	.12
311	Al Oliver	.12
312	Mike Torrez	.12
313	Dick Ruthven	.12
314	Gary Carter (AS)	.30
315	Rick Burleson	.12
316	Phil Niekro (Super Veteran)	.15
317	Moose Haas	.12
318	Carney Lansford	.12
319	Tim Foli	.12
320	Steve Rogers	.12
321	Kirk Gibson	.12
322	Glenn Hubbard	.12
323	Luis DeLeon	.12
324	Mike Marshall	.12
325	Von Hayes	.12
326	Garth Iorg	.12
327	Jose Cruz	.12
328	Jim Palmer (Super Veteran)	.15
329	Darrell Evans	.12
330	Buddy Bell	.12
331	Mike Krukow	.12
332	Omar Moreno	.12
333	Dave LaRoche	.12
334	Dave LaRoche (Super Veteran)	.12
335	Bill Madlock	.12
336	Garry Templeton	.12
337	John Lowenstein	.12
338	Willie Upshaw	.12
339	Dave Hostetler	.12
340	Larry Gura	.12
341	Doug DeCinces	.12
342	Mike Schmidt (AS)	.40
343	Charlie Hough	.12
344	Andre Thornton	.12
345	Jim Clancy	.12
346	Ken Forsch	.12
347	Sammy Stewart	.12
348	Alan Bannister	.12
349	Checklist 265-396	.12
350	Robin Yount	2.00
351	Warren Cromartie	.12
352	Tim Raines (AS)	.30
353	Tony Armas	.12
354	Tom Seaver (Super Veteran)	.75
355	Tony Perez	.75
356	Toby Harrah	.12
357	Dan Ford	.12
358	Charlie Puleo	.12
359	Dave Collins	.12
360	Nolan Ryan	15.00
361	Nolan Ryan (Super Veteran)	7.50
362	Bill Almon	.12
363	Eddie Milner	.12
364	Gary Lucas	.12
365	Dave Lopes	.12
366	Bob Boone	.12
367	Biff Pocoroba	.12
368	Richie Zisk	.12
369	Tony Bernazard	.12
370	Gary Carter	.65
371	Paul Molitor	3.00
372	Art Howe	.12
373	Pete Rose (AS)	.75
374	Glenn Adams	.12
375	Pete Vukovich	.12
376	Gary Lavelle	.12
377	Lee May	.12
378	Lee May (Super Veteran)	.12
379	Butch Wynegar	.12
380	Ron Davis	.12
381	Bob Grich	.12
382	Gary Roenicke	.12
383	Jim Kaat	.15
384	Steve Carlton (AS)	.30
385	Mike Easler	.12
386	Rod Carew (AS)	.30
387	Bobby Grich (AS)	.12
388	George Brett (AS)	.40
389	Robin Yount (AS)	.30
390	Reggie Jackson (AS)	.30
391	Rickey Henderson (AS)	.45
392	Fred Lynn (AS)	.12
393	Carlton Fisk (AS)	.12
394	Pete Vuckovich (AS)	.12
395	Larry Gura (AS)	.12
396	Dan Quisenberry (AS)	.12

1984 O-Pee-Chee

Almost identical in design to the 1984 Topps set, the 1984 O-Pee-Chee set contains 396 cards. The O-Pee-Chee cards display the Canadian company's logo in the upper right corner and the backs of the cards are printed in both English and French. The cards measure 2-1/2" x 3-1/2", and some include the extra line on the front of the card to indicate a trade.

		MT
Complete Set (396):		36.00
Common Player:		.12
1	Pascual Perez	.20
2	Cal Ripken	15.00
3	Lloyd Moseby	.20
4	Mel Hall	.12
5	Willie Wilson	.12
6	Mike Morgan	.12
7	Gary Lucas	.12
8	Don Mattingly	12.00
9	Jim Gott	.12
10	Robin Yount	2.00
11	Joey McLaughlin	.12
12	Billy Sample	.12
13	Oscar Gamble	.12
14	Bill Russell	.12
15	Burt Hooton	.12
16	Omar Moreno	.12
17	Dave Lopes	.12
18	Dale Berra	.12
19	Rance Mulliniks	.12
20	Greg Luzinski	.12
21	Doug Sisk	.12
22	Don Robinson	.12
23	Keith Moreland	.12
24	Richard Dotson	.12
25	Glenn Hubbard	.12
26	Rod Carew	1.50
27	Alan Wiggins	.12
28	Frank Viola	.12

29	Phil Niekro	1.50
30	Wade Boggs	3.00
31	Dave Parker	.50
32	Bobby Ramos	.12
33	Tom Burgmeier	.12
34	Eddie Milner	.12
35	Don Sutton	1.50
36	Glenn Wilson	.12
37	Mike Krukow	.12
38	Dave Collins	.12
39	Garth Iorg	.12
40	Dusty Baker	.12
41	Tony Bernazard	.12
42	Claudell Washington	.12
43	Cecil Cooper	.12
44	Dan Driessen	.12
45	Jerry Mumphrey	.12
46	Rick Rhoden	.12
47	Rudy Law	.12
48	Julio Franco	.30
49	Mike Norris	.12
50	Chris Chambliss	.12
51	Pete Falcone	.12
52	Mike Marshall	.12
53	Amos Otis	.12
54	Jesse Orosco	.12
55	Dave Concepcion	.12
56	Gary Allenson	.12
57	Dan Schatzeder	.12
58	Jerry Remy	.12
59	Carney Lansford	.12
60	Paul Molitor	2.00
61	Chris Codiroli	.12
62	Dave Hostetler	.12
63	Ed Vande Berg	.12
64	Ryne Sandberg	6.00
65	Kirk Gibson	.12
66	Nolan Ryan	12.50
67	Gary Ward	.12
68	Luis Salazar	.12
69	Dan Quisenberry	.12
70	Gary Matthews	.12
71	Pete O'Brien	.12
72	John Wathan	.12
73	Jody Davis	.12
74	Kent Tekulve	.12
75	Bob Forsch	.12
76	Alfredo Griffin	.12
77	Bryn Smith	.12
78	Mike Torrez	.12
79	Mike Hargrove	.12
80	Steve Rogers	.12
81	Bake McBride	.12
82	Doug DeCinces	.12
83	Richie Zisk	.12
84	Randy Bush	.12
85	Atlee Hammaker	.12
86	Chet Lemon	.12
87	Frank Pastore	.12
88	Alan Trammell	.20
89	Terry Francona	.12
90	Pedro Guerrero	.12
91	Dan Spillner	.12
92	Lloyd Moseby	.12
93	Bob Knepper	.12
94	Ted Simmons	.12
95	Aurelio Lopez	.12
96	Bill Buckner	.12
97	LaMarr Hoyt	.12
98	Tom Brunansky	.12
99	Ron Oester	.12
100	Reggie Jackson	2.00
101	Ron Davis	.12
102	Ken Oberkfell	.12
103	Dwayne Murphy	.12
104	Jim Slaton	.12
105	Tony Armas	.12
106	Ernie Whitt	.12
107	Johnnie LeMaster	.12
108	Randy Moffitt	.12
109	Terry Forster	.12
110	Ron Guidry	.12
111	Bill Virdon	.12
112	Doyle Alexander	.12
113	Lonnie Smith	.12
114	Checklist	.12
115	Andre Thornton	.12
116	Jeff Reardon	.15
117	Tom Herr	.12
118	Charlie Hough	.12
119	Phil Garner	.12
120	Keith Hernandez	.12
121	Rich Gossage	.25
122	Ted Simmons	.12
123	Butch Wynegar	.12
124	Damaso Garcia	.12
125	Britt Burns	.12
126	Bert Blyleven	.12
127	Carlton Fisk	1.50
128	Rick Manning	.12
129	Bill Lackey	.12
130	Ozzie Smith	2.00
131	Bo Diaz	.12
132	Tom Paciorek	.12
133	Dave Rozema	.12
134	Dave Stieb	.20
135	Brian Downing	.12
136	Rick Camp	.12
137	Willie Aikens	.12
138	Charlie Moore	.12
139	George Frazier	.12
140	Storm Davis	.12
141	Glenn Hoffman	.12
142	Charlie Lea	.12
143	Mike Vail	.12
144	Steve Sax	.12
145	Gary Lavelle	.12
146	Gorman Thomas	.12
147	Dan Petry	.12
148	Mark Clear	.12
149	Dave Beard	.12
150	Dale Murphy	.75
151	Steve Trout	.12
152	Tony Pena	.12
153	Geoff Zahn	.12
154	Dave Henderson	.12
155	Frank White	.12
156	Dick Ruthven	.12
157	Gary Gaetti	.12
158	Lance Parrish	.12
159	Joe Price	.12
160	Mario Soto	.12
161	Tug McGraw	.12
162	Bob Ojeda	.12
163	George Hendrick	.12
164	Scott Sanderson	.12
165	Ken Singleton	.12
166	Terry Kennedy	.12
167	Gene Garber	.12
168	Juan Bonilla	.12
169	Larry Parrish	.12
170	Jerry Reuss	.12
171	John Tudor	.12
172	Dave Kingman	.15
173	Garry Templeton	.12
174	Bob Boone	.12
175	Graig Nettles	.12
176	Lee Smith	.15
177	LaMarr Hoyt	.12
178	Bill Krueger	.12
179	Buck Martinez	.12
180	Manny Trillo	.12
181	Lou Whitaker	.12
182	Darryl Strawberry	4.00
183	Neil Allen	.12
184	Jim Rice	.15
185	Sixto Lezcano	.12
186	Tom Hume	.12
187	Garry Maddox	.12
188	Bryan Little	.12
189	Jose Cruz	.12
190	Ben Oglivie	.12
191	Cesar Cedeno	.12
192	Nick Esasky	.12
193	Ken Forsch	.12
194	Jim Palmer	1.50
195	Jack Morris	.20
196	Steve Howe	.12
197	Harold Baines	.12
198	Bill Doran	.12
199	Willie Hernandez	.12
200	Andre Dawson	.80
201	Bruce Kison	.12
202	Bobby Cox	.12
203	Matt Keough	.12
204	Ron Guidry	.12
205	Greg Minton	.12
206	Al Holland	.12
207	Luis Leal	.12
208	Jose Oquendo	.12
209	Leon Durham	.12
210	Joe Morgan	1.50
211	Lou Whitaker (All-Star)	.12
212	George Brett (AS)	.40
213	Bruce Hurst	.12
214	Steve Carlton	1.50
215	Tippy Martinez	.12
216	Ken Landreaux	.12
217	Alan Ashby	.12
218	Dennis Eckersley	.60
219	Craig McMurtry	.12
220	Fernando Valenzuela	.25
221	Cliff Johnson	.12
222	Rick Honeycutt	.12
223	George Brett	2.00
224	Rusty Staub	.20
225	Lee Mazzilli	.12
226	Pat Putnam	.12
227	Bob Welch	.12
228	Rick Cerone	.12
229	Lee Lacy	.12
230	Rickey Henderson	1.50
231	Gary Redus	.12
232	Tim Wallach	.25
233	Checklist	.12
234	Rafael Ramirez	.12
235	Matt Young	.12
236	Ellis Valentine	.12
237	John Castino	.12
238	Eric Show	.12
239	Bob Horner	.12
240	Eddie Murray	1.50
241	Billy Almon	.12
242	Greg Brock	.12
243	Bruce Sutter	.12
244	Dwight Evans	.12
245	Rick Sutcliffe	.12
246	Terry Crowley	.12
247	Fred Lynn	.25
248	Bill Dawley	.12
249	Dave Stapleton	.12
250	Bill Madlock	.12
251	Jim Sundberg	.12
252	Steve Yeager	.12
253	Jim Wohlford	.12
254	Shane Rawley	.12
255	Bruce Benedict	.12
256	Dave Geisel	.12
257	Julio Cruz	.12
258	Luis Sanchez	.12
259	Von Hayes	.12
260	Scott McGregor	.12
261	Tom Seaver	2.00
262	Doug Flynn	.12
263	Wayne Gross	.12
264	Larry Gura	.12
265	John Montefusco	.12
266	Dave Winfield	1.50
267	Tim Lollar	.12
268	Ron Washington	.12
269	Mickey Rivers	.12
270	Mookie Wilson	.12
271	Moose Haas	.12
272	Rick Dempsey	.12
273	Dan Quisenberry	.12
274	Steve Henderson	.12
275	Len Matuszek	.12
276	Frank Tanana	.12
277	Dave Righetti	.12
278	Jorge Bell	.40
279	Ivan DeJesus	.12
280	Floyd Bannister	.12
281	Dale Murray	.12
282	Andre Robertson	.12
283	Rollie Fingers	1.00
284	Tommy John	.20
285	Darrell Porter	.12
286	Lary Sorensen	.12
287	Warren Cromartie	.12
288	Jim Beattie	.12
289	Blue Jays Team	.25
290	Dave Dravecky	.12
291	Eddie Murray (AS)	.50
292	Greg Bargar	.12
293	Tom Underwood	.12
294	U.L. Washington	.12
295	Mike Flanagan	.12
296	Rich Gedman	.12
297	Bruce Berenyi	.12
298	Jim Gantner	.12
299	Bill Caudill	.12
300	Pete Rose	3.00
301	Steve Kemp	.12
302	Barry Bonnell	.12
303	Joel Youngblood	.12
304	Rick Langford	.12
305	Roy Smalley	.12
306	Ken Griffey	.12
307	Al Oliver	.12
308	Ron Hassey	.12
309	Len Barker	.12
310	Willie McGee	.15
311	Jerry Koosman	.12
312	Jorge Orta	.12
313	Pete Vuckovich	.12
314	George Wright	.12
315	Bob Grich	.12
316	Jesse Barfield	.40
317	Willie Upshaw	.12
318	Bill Gullickson	.20
319	Ray Burris	.12
320	Bob Stanley	.12
321	Ray Knight	.12
322	Ken Schrom	.12
323	Johnny Ray	.12
324	Brian Giles	.12
325	Darrell Evans	.15
326	Mike Caldwell	.12
327	Ruppert Jones	.12
328	Chris Speier	.12
329	Bobby Castillo	.12
330	John Candelaria	.12
331	Bucky Dent	.12
332	Expos Team	.25
333	Larry Herndon	.12
334	Chuck Rainey	.12
335	Don Baylor	.12
336	Bob James	.12
337	Jim Clancy	.12
338	Duane Kuiper	.12
339	Roy Lee Jackson	.12
340	Hal McRae	.12
341	Larry McWilliams	.12
342	Tim Foli	.12
343	Fergie Jenkins	1.00
344	Dickie Thon	.12
345	Kent Hrbek	.15
346	Larry Bowa	.12
347	Buddy Bell	.12
348	Toby Harrah	.12
349	Dan Ford	.12
350	George Foster	.12
351	Lou Piniella	.12
352	Dave Stewart	.25
353	Mike Easler	.12
354	Jeff Burroughs	.12
355	Jason Thompson	.12
356	Glenn Abbott	.12
357	Ron Cey	.12
358	Bob Dernier	.12
359	Jim Acker	.12
360	Willie Randolph	.12
361	Mike Schmidt	2.00
362	David Green	.12
363	Cal Ripken Jr. (AS)	3.00
364	Jim Rice (AS)	.12
365	Steve Bedrosian	.12
366	Gary Carter	1.00
367	Chili Davis	.15
368	Hubie Brooks	.12
369	Steve McCatty	.12
370	Tim Raines	.40
371	Joaquin Andujar	.12
372	Gary Roenicke	.12
373	Ron Kittle	.12
374	Rich Dauer	.12
375	Dennis Leonard	.12
376	Rick Burleson	.12
377	Eric Rasmussen	.12
378	Dave Winfield	1.50
379	Checklist	.12
380	Steve Garvey	1.00
381	Jack Clark	.12
382	Odell Jones	.12
383	Terry Puhl	.12
384	Joe Niekro	.12
385	Tony Perez	1.00
386	George Hendrick (AS)	.12
387	Johnny Ray (AS)	.12
388	Mike Schmidt (AS)	.60
389	Ozzie Smith (AS)	.20
390	Tim Raines (AS)	.30
391	Dale Murphy (AS)	.20
392	Andre Dawson (AS)	.30
393	Gary Carter (AS)	.40
394	Steve Rogers (AS)	.20
395	Steve Carlton (AS)	.40
396	Jesse Orosco (AS)	.12

1985 O-Pee-Chee

This 396-card set is almost identical in design to the 1985 Topps set. Measuring 2-1/2" x 3-1/2", the fronts of the Canadian-issued cards display the O-Pee-Chee logo in the upper left corner, and the backs of the cards are printed in both French and English. A "traded" line appears on the front of some of the cards to indicate a change in teams.

		MT
Complete Set (396):		28.00
Common Player:		.10
1	Tom Seaver	.45
2	Gary Lavelle	.10
3	Tim Wallach	.12
4	Jim Wohlford	.10
5	Jeff Robinson	.10
6	Willie Wilson	.10
7	Cliff Johnson	.10
8	Willie Randolph	.10
9	Larry Herndon	.10
10	Kirby Puckett	15.00
11	Mookie Wilson	.10
12	Dave Lopes	.10
13	Tim Lollar	.10
14	Chris Bando	.10
15	Jerry Koosman	.10
16	Bobby Meacham	.10
17	Mike Scott	.10
18	Rich Gedman	.10
19	George Frazier	.10
20	Chet Lemon	.10
21	Dave Concepcion	.10
22	Jason Thompson	.10
23	Bret Saberhagen	.75
24	Jesse Barfield	.15
25	Steve Bedrosian	.10
26	Roy Smalley	.10
27	Bruce Berenyi	.10
28	Butch Wynegar	.10
29	Alan Ashby	.10
30	Cal Ripken	7.50
31	Luis Leal	.10
32	Dave Dravecky	.10
33	Tito Landrum	.10
34	Pedro Guerrero	.10
35	Graig Nettles	.10
36	Fred Breining	.10
37	Roy Lee Jackson	.10
38	Steve Henderson	.10
39	Gary Pettis	.10
40	Phil Niekro	.45
41	Dwight Gooden	1.50
42	Luis Sanchez	.10
43	Lee Smith	.10
44	Dickie Thon	.10
45	Greg Minton	.10
46	Mike Flanagan	.10
47	Bud Black	.10
48	Tony Fernandez	.50
49	Carlton Fisk	1.00
50	John Candelaria	.10
51	Bob Watson	.10
52	Rick Leach	.10
53	Rick Rhoden	.10
54	Cesar Cedeno	.10
55	Frank Tanana	.10
56	Larry Bowa	.10
57	Willie McGee	.12
58	Rich Dauer	.10
59	Jorge Bell	.35
60	George Hendrick	.10
61	Donnie Moore	.10
62	Mike Ramsey	.10
63	Nolan Ryan	7.50
64	Mark Bailey	.10
65	Bill Buckner	.10
66	Jerry Reuss	.10
67	Mike Schmidt	1.50
68	Von Hayes	.10
69	Phil Bradley	.10
70	Don Baylor	.10
71	Julio Cruz	.10
72	Rick Sutcliffe	.10
73	Storm Davis	.10
74	Mike Krukow	.10
75	Willie Upshaw	.10
76	Craig Lefferts	.10
77	Lloyd Moseby	.10
78	Ron Davis	.10
79	Rick Mahler	.10
80	Keith Hernandez	.12
81	Vance Law	.10
82	Joe Price	.10
83	Dennis Lamp	.10
84	Gary Ward	.10
85	Mike Marshall	.10
86	Marvell Wynne	.10
87	David Green	.10
88	Bryn Smith	.10
89	Sixto Lezcano	.10
90	Rich Gossage	.15
91	Jeff Burroughs	.10
92	Bobby Brown	.10
93	Oscar Gamble	.10
94	Rick Dempsey	.10
95	Jose Cruz	.10
96	Johnny Ray	.10
97	Joel Youngblood	.10
98	Eddie Whitson	.10
99	Milt Wilcox	.10
100	George Brett	1.50
101	Jim Acker	.10
102	Jim Sundberg	.10
103	Ozzie Virgil	.10
104	Mike Fitzgerald	.10
105	Ron Kittle	.10
106	Pascual Perez	.10
107	Barry Bonnell	.10
108	Lou Whitaker	.10
109	Gary Roenicke	.10
110	Alejandro Pena	.10
111	Doug DeCinces	.10
112	Doug Flynn	.10
113	Tom Herr	.10
114	Bob James	.10
115	Rickey Henderson	.75
116	Pete Rose	2.50
117	Greg Gross	.10
118	Eric Show	.10
119	Buck Martinez	.10
120	Steve Kemp	.10
121	Checklist 1-132	.10
122	Tom Brunansky	.10
123	Dave Kingman	.12
124	Garry Templeton	.10
125	Kent Tekulve	.10
126	Darryl Strawberry	.35
127	Mark Gubicza	.10
128	Ernie Whitt	.10
129	Don Robinson	.10
130	Al Oliver	.10
131	Mario Soto	.10
132	Jeff Leonard	.10
133	Andre Dawson	.25
134	Bruce Hurst	.10
135	Bobby Cox	.10
136	Matt Young	.10
137	Bob Forsch	.10
138	Ron Darling	.10
139	Steve Trout	.10
140	Geoff Zahn	.10
141	Ken Forsch	.10
142	Jerry Willard	.10
143	Bill Gullickson	.10
144	Mike Mason	.10
145	Alvin Davis	.10
146	Gary Redus	.10
147	Willie Aikens	.10
148	Steve Yeager	.10
149	Dickie Noles	.10
150	Jim Rice	.25
151	Moose Haas	.10
152	Steve Balboni	.10
153	Frank LaCorte	.10
154	Argenis Salazar	.10
155	Bob Grich	.10
156	Craig Reynolds	.10
157	Bill Madlock	.10
158	Pat Tabler	.10
159	Don Slaught	.10
160	Lance Parrish	.10
161	Ken Schrom	.10
162	Wally Backman	.10
163	Dennis Eckersley	.10
164	Dave Collins	.10
165	Dusty Baker	.10
166	Claudell Washington	.10
167	Rick Camp	.10
168	Garth Iorg	.10
169	Shane Rawley	.10
170	George Foster	.10
171	Tony Bernazard	.10
172	Don Sutton	.45
173	Jerry Remy	.10
174	Rick Honeycutt	.10
175	Dave Parker	.15

176	Buddy Bell	.10
177	Steve Garvey	.30
178	Miguel Dilone	.10
179	Tommy John	.15
180	Dave Winfield	.90
181	Alan Trammell	.15
182	Rollie Fingers	.45
183	Larry McWilliams	.10
184	Carmen Castillo	.10
185	Al Holland	.10
186	Jerry Mumphrey	.10
187	Chris Chambliss	.10
188	Jim Clancy	.10
189	Glenn Wilson	.10
190	Rusty Staub	.10
191	Ozzie Smith	1.00
192	Howard Johnson	.40
193	Jimmy Key	1.50
194	Terry Kennedy	.10
195	Glenn Hubbard	.10
196	Pete O'Brien	.10
197	Keith Moreland	.10
198	Eddie Milner	.10
199	Dave Engle	.10
200	Reggie Jackson	.85
201	Burt Hooton	.10
202	Gorman Thomas	.10
203	Larry Parrish	.10
204	Bob Stanley	.10
205	Steve Rogers	.10
206	Phil Garner	.10
207	Ed Vande Berg	.10
208	Jack Clark	.12
209	Bill Campbell	.10
210	Gary Matthews	.10
211	Dave Palmer	.10
212	Tony Perez	.90
213	Sammy Stewart	.10
214	John Tudor	.10
215	Bob Brenly	.10
216	Jim Gantner	.10
217	Bryan Clark	.10
218	Doyle Alexander	.10
219	Bo Diaz	.10
220	Fred Lynn	.15
221	Eddie Murray	.90
222	Hubie Brooks	.10
223	Tom Hume	.10
224	Al Cowens	.10
225	Mike Boddicker	.10
226	Len Matuszek	.10
227	Danny Darwin	.10
228	Scott McGregor	.10
229	Dave LaPoint	.10
230	Gary Carter	.30
231	Joaquin Andujar	.10
232	Rafael Ramirez	.10
233	Wayne Gross	.10
234	Neil Allen	.10
235	Gary Maddox	.10
236	Mark Thurmond	.10
237	Julio Franco	.12
238	Ray Burris	.10
239	Tim Teufel	.10
240	Dave Stieb	.12
241	Brett Butler	.12
242	Greg Brock	.10
243	Barbaro Garbey	.10
244	Greg Walker	.10
245	Chili Davis	.12
246	Darrell Porter	.10
247	Tippy Martinez	.10
248	Terry Forster	.10
249	Harold Baines	.10
250	Jesse Orosco	.10
251	Brad Gulden	.10
252	Mike Hargrove	.10
253	Nick Esasky	.10
254	Frank Williams	.10
255	Lonnie Smith	.10
256	Daryl Sconiers	.10
257	Bryan Little	.10
258	Terry Francona	.10
259	Mark Langston	.85
260	Dave Righetti	.10
261	Checklist 133-264	.10
262	Bob Horner	.10
263	Mel Hall	.10
264	John Shelby	.10
265	Juan Samuel	.10
266	Frank Viola	.10
267	Jim Fanning	.10
268	Dick Ruthven	.10
269	Bobby Ramos	.10
270	Dan Quisenberry	.10
271	Dwight Evans	.10
272	Andre Thornton	.10
273	Orel Hershiser	.85
274	Ray Knight	.10
275	Bill Caudill	.10
276	Charlie Hough	.10
277	Tim Raines	.30
278	Mike Squires	.10
279	Alex Trevino	.10
280	Ron Romanick	.10
281	Tom Niedenfuer	.10
282	Mike Stenhouse	.10
283	Terry Puhl	.10
284	Hal McRae	.10
285	Dan Driessen	.10
286	Rudy Law	.10
287	Walt Terrell	.10
288	Jeff Kunkel	.10
289	Bob Knepper	.10
290	Cecil Cooper	.10
291	Bob Welch	.10
292	Frank Pastore	.10
293	Dan Schatzeder	.10
294	Tom Nieto	.10
295	Joe Niekro	.10
296	Ryne Sandberg	2.50
297	Gary Lucas	.10
298	John Castino	.10
299	Bill Doran	.10
300	Rod Carew	.45
301	John Montefusco	.10
302	Johnnie LeMaster	.10
303	Jim Beattie	.10
304	Gary Gaetti	.10
305	Dale Berra	.10
306	Rick Reuschel	.10
307	Ken Oberkfell	.10
308	Kent Hrbek	.15
309	Mike Witt	.10
310	Manny Trillo	.10
311	Jim Gott	.10
312	LaMarr Hoyt	.10
313	Dave Schmidt	.10
314	Ron Oester	.10
315	Doug Sisk	.10
316	John Lowenstein	.10
317	Derrel Thomas	.10
318	Ted Simmons	.10
319	Darrell Evans	.12
320	Dale Murphy	.50
321	Ricky Horton	.10
322	Ken Phelps	.10
323	Lee Mazzilli	.10
324	Don Mattingly	4.50
325	John Denny	.10
326	Ken Singleton	.10
327	Brook Jacoby	.10
328	Greg Luzinski	.10
329	Bob Ojeda	.10
330	Leon Durham	.10
331	Bill Laskey	.10
332	Ben Oglivie	.10
333	Willie Hernandez	.10
334	Bob Dernier	.10
335	Bruce Benedict	.10
336	Rance Mulliniks	.10
337	Rick Cerone	.10
338	Britt Burns	.10
339	Danny Heep	.10
340	Robin Yount	1.00
341	Andy Van Slyke	.10
342	Curt Wilkerson	.10
343	Bill Russell	.10
344	Dave Henderson	.10
345	Charlie Lea	.10
346	Terry Pendleton	.40
347	Carney Lansford	.10
348	Bob Boone	.10
349	Mike Easler	.10
350	Wade Boggs	1.00
351	Atlee Hammaker	.10
352	Joe Morgan	.35
353	Damaso Garcia	.10
354	Floyd Bannister	.10
355	Bert Blyleven	.10
356	John Butcher	.10
357	Fernando Valenzuela	.15
358	Tony Pena	.10
359	Mike Smithson	.10
360	Steve Carlton	.45
361	Alfredo Griffin	.10
362	Craig McMurtry	.10
363	Bill Dawley	.10
364	Richard Dotson	.10
365	Carmelo Martinez	.10
366	Ron Cey	.10
367	Tony Scott	.10
368	Dave Bergman	.10
369	Steve Sax	.10
370	Bruce Sutter	.10
371	Mickey Rivers	.10
372	Kirk Gibson	.10
373	Scott Sanderson	.10
374	Brian Downing	.10
375	Jeff Reardon	.12
376	Frank DiPino	.10
377	Checklist 265-396	.10
378	Alan Wiggins	.10
379	Charles Hudson	.10
380	Ken Griffey	.10
381	Tom Paciorek	.10
382	Jack Morris	.15
383	Tony Gwynn	3.50
384	Jody Davis	.10
385	Jose DeLeon	.10
386	Bob Kearney	.10
387	George Wright	.10
388	Ron Guidry	.10
389	Rick Manning	.10
390	Sid Fernandez	.15
391	Bruce Bochte	.10
392	Dan Petry	.10
393	Tim Stoddard	.10
394	Tony Armas	.10
395	Paul Molitor	1.00
396	Mike Heath	.10

1985 O-Pee-Chee Posters

The 1985 O-Pee-Chee poster set consists of 12 players each from the Expos and Blue Jays. The blank-backed posters measure approximately 4-7/8" x 6-7/8" and generally have fold marks because they were inserted in the OPC wax packs. The card number, written in both French and English, appears in the bottom border. The full-color player photos are surrounded by a red border for Expos and a blue border for Blue Jays.

		MT
Complete Set (24):		13.50
Common Player:		.50
1	Mike Fitzgerald	.50
2	Dan Driessen	.50
3	Dave Palmer	.50
4	U.L. Washington	.50
5	Hubie Brooks	.50
6	Tim Wallach	.75
7	Tim Raines	2.50
8	Herm Winningham	.50
9	Andre Dawson	3.00
10	Charlie Lea	.50
11	Steve Rogers	.50
12	Jeff Reardon	.60
13	Buck Martinez	.50
14	Willie Upshaw	.50
15	Damaso Garcia	.50
16	Tony Fernandez	1.00
17	Rance Mulliniks	.50
18	George Bell	1.00
19	Lloyd Moseby	.50
20	Jesse Barfield	.60
21	Doyle Alexander	.50
22	Dave Stieb	.85
23	Bill Caudill	.50
24	Gary Lavelle	.50

1986 O-Pee-Chee

As usual, the 1986 O-Pee-Chee set was issued in close simulation of the Topps cards for the same year. The 396 cards in the set are 2-1/2" x 3-1/2" and use almost all of the same pictures as the Topps set. The O-Pee-Chee cards, being a Canadian issue, list player information in both English and French. There is an abundance of players from the two Canadian teams - Toronto and Montreal. As the O-Pee-Chee set was issued later in the year than the Topps regular issue, players who changed teams after the printing date are noted with a traded line at the bottom of the player photo. O-Pee-Chee's logo appears in the upper right of each card front.

		MT
Complete Set (396):		18.00
Common Player:		.10
1	Pete Rose	3.00
2	Ken Landreaux	.10
3	Rob Picciolo	.10
4	Steve Garvey	.25
5	Andy Hawkins	.10
6	Rudy Law	.10
7	Lonnie Smith	.10
8	Dwayne Murphy	.10
9	Moose Haas	.10
10	Tony Gwynn	2.50
11	Bob Ojeda	.10
12	Jose Uribe	.10
13	Bob Kearney	.10
14	Julio Cruz	.10
15	Eddie Whitson	.10
16	Rick Schu	.10
17	Mike Stenhouse	.10
18	Lou Thornton	.10
19	Ryne Sandberg	2.00
20	Lou Whitaker	.10
21	Mark Brouhard	.10
22	Gary Lavelle	.10
23	Manny Lee	.10
24	Don Slaught	.10
25	Willie Wilson	.10
26	Mike Marshall	.10
27	Ray Knight	.10
28	Mario Soto	.10
29	Dave Anderson	.10
30	Eddie Murray	1.00
31	Dusty Baker	.10
32	Steve Yeager	.10
33	Andy Van Slyke	.10
34	Dave Righetti	.10
35	Jeff Reardon	.10
36	Burt Hooton	.10
37	Johnny Ray	.10
38	Glenn Hoffman	.10
39	Rick Mahler	.10
40	Ken Griffey	.10
41	Brad Wellman	.10
42	Joe Hesketh	.10
43	Mark Salas	.10
44	Jorge Orta	.10
45	Damaso Garcia	.10
46	Jim Acker	.10
47	Bill Madlock	.10
48	Bill Almon	.10
49	Rick Manning	.10
50	Dan Quisenberry	.10
51	Jim Gantner	.10
52	Kevin Bass	.10
53	Len Dykstra	1.00
54	John Franco	.10
55	Fred Lynn	.12
56	Jim Morrison	.10
57	Bill Doran	.10
58	Leon Durham	.10
59	Andre Thornton	.10
60	Dwight Evans	.10
61	Larry Herndon	.10
62	Bob Boone	.10
63	Kent Hrbek	.12
64	Floyd Bannister	.10
65	Harold Baines	.10
66	Pat Tabler	.10
67	Carmelo Martinez	.10
68	Ed Lynch	.10
69	George Foster	.10
70	Dave Winfield	.65
71	Ken Schrom	.10
72	Toby Harrah	.10
73	Jackie Gutierrez	.10
74	Rance Mulliniks	.10
75	Jose DeLeon	.10
76	Ron Romanick	.10
77	Charlie Leibrandt	.10
78	Bruce Benedict	.10
79	Dave Schmidt	.10
80	Darryl Strawberry	.15
81	Wayne Krenchicki	.10
82	Tippy Martinez	.10
83	Phil Garner	.10
84	Darrell Porter	.10
85	Tony Perez	.65
86	Tom Waddell	.10
87	Tim Hulett	.10
88	Barbaro Garbey	.10
89	Randy St. Claire	.10
90	Garry Templeton	.10
91	Tim Teufel	.10
92	Al Cowens	.10
93	Scot Thompson	.10
94	Tom Herr	.10
95	Ozzie Virgil	.10
96	Jose Cruz	.10
97	Gary Gaetti	.10
98	Roger Clemens	3.00
99	Vance Law	.10
100	Nolan Ryan	4.00
101	Mike Smithson	.10
102	Rafael Santana	.10
103	Darrell Evans	.12
104	Rich Gossage	.12
105	Gary Ward	.10
106	Jim Gott	.10
107	Rafael Ramirez	.10
108	Ted Power	.10
109	Ron Guidry	.10
110	Scott McGregor	.10
111	Mike Scioscia	.10
112	Glenn Hubbard	.10
113	U.L. Washington	.10
114	Al Oliver	.10
115	Jay Howell	.10
116	Brook Jacoby	.10
117	Willie McGee	.12
118	Jerry Royster	.10
119	Barry Bonnell	.10
120	Steve Carlton	.40
121	Alfredo Griffin	.10
122	David Green	.10
123	Greg Walker	.10
124	Frank Tanana	.10
125	Dave Lopes	.10
126	Mike Krukow	.10
127	Jack Howell	.10
128	Greg Harris	.10
129	Herm Winningham	.10
130	Alan Trammell	.15
131	Checklist 1-132	.10
132	Razor Shines	.10
133	Bruce Sutter	.10
134	Carney Lansford	.10
135	Joe Niekro	.10
136	Ernie Whitt	.10
137	Charlie Moore	.10
138	Mel Hall	.10
139	Roger McDowell	.10
140	John Candelaria	.10
141	Bob Rodgers	.10
142	Manny Trillo	.10
143	Dave Palmer	.10
144	Robin Yount	.75
145	Pedro Guerrero	.10
146	Von Hayes	.10
147	Lance Parrish	.10
148	Mike Heath	.10
149	Brett Butler	.12
150	Joaquin Andujar	.10
151	Graig Nettles	.10
152	Pete Vuckovich	.10
153	Jason Thompson	.10
154	Bert Roberge	.10
155	Bob Grich	.10
156	Roy Smalley	.10
157	Ron Hassey	.10
158	Bob Stanley	.10
159	Orel Hershiser	.15
160	Chet Lemon	.10
161	Terry Puhl	.10
162	Dave LaPoint	.10
163	Onix Concepcion	.10
164	Steve Balboni	.10
165	Mike Davis	.10
166	Dickie Thon	.10
167	Zane Smith	.10
168	Jeff Burroughs	.10
169	Alex Trevino	.10
170	Gary Carter	.25
171	Tito Landrum	.10
172	Sammy Stewart	.10
173	Wayne Gross	.10
174	Britt Burns	.10
175	Steve Sax	.10
176	Jody Davis	.10
177	Joel Youngblood	.10
178	Fernando Valenzuela	.12
179	Storm Davis	.10
180	Don Mattingly	2.00
181	Steve Bedrosian	.10
182	Jesse Orosco	.10
183	Gary Roenicke	.10
184	Don Baylor	.10
185	Rollie Fingers	.40
186	Ruppert Jones	.10
187	Scott Fletcher	.10
188	Bob Dernier	.10
189	Mike Mason	.10
190	George Hendrick	.10
191	Wally Backman	.10
192	Oddibe McDowell	.10
193	Bruce Hurst	.10
194	Ron Cey	.10
195	Dave Concepcion	.10
196	Doyle Alexander	.10
197	Dale Murray	.10
198	Mark Langston	.10
199	Dennis Eckersley	.20
200	Mike Schmidt	1.00
201	Nick Esasky	.10
202	Ken Dayley	.10
203	Rick Cerone	.10
204	Larry McWilliams	.10
205	Brian Downing	.10
206	Danny Darwin	.10
207	Bill Caudill	.10
208	Dave Rozema	.10
209	Eric Show	.10
210	Brad Komminsk	.10
211	Chris Bando	.10
212	Chris Speier	.10
213	Jim Clancy	.10
214	Randy Bush	.10
215	Frank White	.10
216	Dan Petry	.10
217	Tim Wallach	.10
218	Mitch Webster	.10
219	Dennis Lamp	.10
220	Bob Horner	.10
221	Dave Henderson	.10
222	Dave Smith	.10
223	Willie Upshaw	.10
224	Cesar Cedeno	.10
225	Ron Darling	.10
226	Lee Lacy	.10
227	John Tudor	.10
228	Jim Presley	.10
229	Bill Gullickson	.10
230	Terry Kennedy	.10
231	Bob Knepper	.10
232	Rick Rhoden	.10
233	Richard Dotson	.10
234	Jesse Barfield	.12
235	Butch Wynegar	.10
236	Jerry Reuss	.10
237	Juan Samuel	.10

238	Larry Parrish	.10
239	Bill Buckner	.10
240	Pat Sheridan	.10
241	Tony Fernandez	.10
242	Rich Thompson	.10
243	Rickey Henderson	.50
244	Craig Lefferts	.10
245	Jim Sundberg	.10
246	Phil Niekro	.40
247	Terry Harper	.10
248	Spike Owen	.10
249	Bret Saberhagen	.15
250	Dwight Gooden	.20
251	Rich Dauer	.10
252	Keith Hernandez	.12
253	Bo Diaz	.10
254	Ozzie Guillen	.10
255	Tony Armas	.10
256	Andre Dawson	.20
257	Doug DeCinces	.10
258	Tim Burke	.10
259	Dennis Boyd	.10
260	Tony Pena	.10
261	Sal Butera	.10
262	Wade Boggs	.75
263	Checklist 133-254	.10
264	Ron Oester	.10
265	Ron Davis	.10
266	Keith Moreland	.10
267	Paul Molitor	.75
268	John Denny	.10
269	Frank Viola	.10
270	Jack Morris	.12
271	Dave Collins	.10
272	Bert Blyleven	.10
273	Jerry Willard	.10
274	Matt Young	.10
275	Charlie Hough	.10
276	Dave Dravecky	.10
277	Garth Iorg	.10
278	Hal McRae	.10
279	Curt Wilkerson	.10
280	Tim Raines	.25
281	Bill Laskey	.10
282	Jerry Mumphrey	.10
283	Pat Clements	.10
284	Bob James	.10
285	Buddy Bell	.10
286	Tom Brookens	.10
287	Dave Parker	.12
288	Ron Kittle	.10
289	Johnnie LeMaster	.10
290	Carlton Fisk	.65
291	Jimmy Key	.10
292	Gary Matthews	.10
293	Marvell Wynne	.10
294	Danny Cox	.10
295	Kirk Gibson	.10
296	Mariano Duncan	.10
297	Ozzie Smith	.75
298	Craig Reynolds	.10
299	Bryn Smith	.10
300	George Brett	1.00
301	Walt Terrell	.10
302	Greg Gross	.10
303	Claudell Washington	.10
304	Howard Johnson	.10
305	Phil Bradley	.10
306	R.J. Reynolds	.10
307	Bob Brenly	.10
308	Hubie Brooks	.10
309	Alvin Davis	.10
310	Donnie Hill	.10
311	Dick Schofield	.10
312	Tom Filer	.10
313	Mike Fitzgerald	.10
314	Marty Barrett	.10
315	Mookie Wilson	.10
316	Alan Knicely	.10
317	Ed Romero	.10
318	Glenn Wilson	.10
319	Bud Black	.10
320	Jim Rice	.25
321	Terry Pendleton	.12
322	Dave Kingman	.10
323	Gary Pettis	.10
324	Dan Schatzeder	.10
325	Juan Beniquez	.10
326	Kent Tekulve	.10
327	Mike Pagliarulo	.10
328	Pete O'Brien	.10
329	Kirby Puckett	3.00
330	Rick Sutcliffe	.10
331	Alan Ashby	.10
332	Willie Randolph	.10
333	Tom Henke	.10
334	Ken Oberkfell	.10
335	Don Sutton	.40
336	Dan Gladden	.10
337	George Vuckovich	.10
338	Jorge Bell	.25
339	Jim Dwyer	.10
340	Cal Ripken	4.00
341	Willie Hernandez	.10
342	Gary Redus	.10
343	Jerry Koosman	.10
344	Jim Wohlford	.10
345	Donnie Moore	.10
346	Floyd Youmans	.10
347	Gorman Thomas	.10
348	Cliff Johnson	.10
349	Ken Howell	.10
350	Jack Clark	.10
351	Gary Lucas	.10
352	Bob Clark	.10
353	Dave Stieb	.10
354	Tony Bernazard	.10
355	Lee Smith	.10
356	Mickey Hatcher	.10
357	Ed Vande Berg	.10
358	Rick Dempsey	.10
359	Bobby Cox	.10
360	Lloyd Moseby	.10
361	Shane Rawley	.10
362	Garry Maddox	.10
363	Buck Martinez	.10
364	Ed Nunez	.10
365	Luis Leal	.10
366	Dale Berra	.10
367	Mike Boddicker	.10
368	Greg Brock	.10
369	Al Holland	.10
370	Vince Coleman	.15
371	Rod Carew	.40
372	Ben Oglivie	.10
373	Lee Mazzilli	.10
374	Terry Francona	.10
375	Rich Gedman	.10
376	Charlie Lea	.10
377	Joe Carter	1.50
378	Bruce Bochte	.10
379	Bobby Meacham	.10
380	LaMarr Hoyt	.10
381	Jeff Leonard	.10
382	Ivan Calderon	.10
383	Chris Brown	.10
384	Steve Trout	.10
385	Cecil Cooper	.10
386	Cecil Fielder	5.00
387	Tim Flannery	.10
388	Chris Codiroli	.10
389	Glenn Davis	.10
390	Tom Seaver	.40
391	Julio Franco	.10
392	Tom Brunansky	.10
393	Rob Wilfong	.10
394	Reggie Jackson	.65
395	Scott Garrelts	.10
396	Checklist 255-396	.10

1986 O-Pee-Chee Box Panels

The Canadian card company licensed by Topps to distribute cards in Canada is O-Pee-Chee. In 1986, O-Pee-Chee issued wax pack boxes with baseball cards printed on the box bottoms. Four cards appear on four different boxes making a complete set of 16. The cards are identical to the 1986 Topps wax box issue with the exception of the OPC logo replacing Topps' and the addition of French on the card backs. These bilingual cards were issued in Canada but are readily available in the USA. The cards are the standard 2-1/2" x 3-1/2" size, printed in full-color with black and red backs. The panel cards are not numbered but instead are lettered from A through P.

		MT
Complete Panel Set (4):		12.00
Complete Singles Set (16):		7.00
Common Panel:		3.00
Common Single Player:		.15
Panel		3.50
A	Jorge Bell	.30
B	Wade Boggs	.75
C	George Brett	1.00
D	Vince Coleman	.20
Panel		3.00
E	Carlton Fisk	.75
F	Dwight Gooden	.30
G	Pedro Guerrero	.20
H	Ron Guidry	.20
Panel		3.50
I	Reggie Jackson	.60
J	Don Mattingly	1.00
K	Oddibe McDowell	.15
L	Willie McGee	.15
Panel		3.50
M	Dale Murphy	.40
N	Pete Rose	1.00
O	Bret Saberhagen	.30
P	Fernando Valenzuela	.15

1986 O-Pee-Chee Stickers

Bilingual backs are the only difference between the OPC 1986 sticker set and the Topps issue. The sets share a checklist and, generally, values, although some Blue Jays and Expos stars may command a small premium in the Canadian version.

	MT
Complete Set:	15.00
Common Player:	.05
Album:	2.00

(See 1986 Topps Stickers for checklist and individual sticker values.)

1987 O-Pee-Chee

O-Pee-Chee of London, Ont., under license from the Topps Chewing Gum Co., continued a practice started in 1965 by issuing a baseball card set for 1987. The 396-card set is identical in design to the regular Topps set, save the name "O-Pee-Chee" replacing "Topps" in the lower right corner. Because the set is issued after its American counterpart, several cards appear with trade notations and corrected logos on the fronts. The cards, which are printed on white stock and are the standard 2-1/2" x 3-1/2", feature backs written in both English and French.

		MT
Complete Set (396):		12.00
Common Player:		.10
1	Ken Oberkfell	.10
2	Jack Howell	.10
3	Hubie Brooks	.10
4	Bob Grich	.10
5	Rick Leach	.10
6	Phil Niekro	.40
7	Rickey Henderson	.30
8	Terry Pendleton	.10
9	Jay Tibbs	.10
10	Cecil Cooper	.10
11	Mario Soto	.10
12	George Bell	.15
13	Nick Esasky	.10
14	Larry McWilliams	.10
15	Dan Quisenberry	.10
16	Ed Lynch	.10
17	Pete O'Brien	.10
18	Luis Aguayo	.10
19	Matt Young	.10
20	Gary Carter	.20
21	Tom Paciorek	.10
22	Doug DeCinces	.10
23	Lee Smith	.10
24	Jesse Barfield	.10
25	Bert Blyleven	.10
26	Greg Brock	.10
27	Dan Petry	.10
28	Rick Dempsey	.10
29	Jimmy Key	.10
30	Tim Raines	.20
31	Bruce Hurst	.10
32	Manny Trillo	.10
33	Andy Van Slyke	.10
34	Ed Vande Berg	.10
35	Sid Bream	.10
36	Dave Winfield	.35
37	Scott Garrelts	.10
38	Dennis Leonard	.10
39	Marty Barrett	.10
40	Dave Righetti	.10
41	Bo Diaz	.10
42	Gary Redus	.10
43	Tom Niedenfuer	.10
44	Greg Harris	.10
45	Jim Presley	.10
46	Danny Gladden	.10
47	Roy Smalley	.10
48	Wally Backman	.10
49	Tom Seaver	.40
50	Dave Smith	.10
51	Mel Hall	.10
52	Tim Flannery	.10
53	Julio Cruz	.10
54	Dick Schofield	.10
55	Tim Wallach	.10
56	Glenn Davis	.10
57	Darren Daulton	.10
58	Chico Walker	.10
59	Garth Iorg	.10
60	Tony Pena	.10
61	Ron Hassey	.10
62	Dave Dravecky	.10
63	Jorge Orta	.10
64	Al Nipper	.10
65	Tom Browning	.10
66	Marc Sullivan	.10
67	Todd Worrell	.10
68	Glenn Hubbard	.10
69	Carney Lansford	.10
70	Charlie Hough	.10
71	Lance McCullers	.10
72	Walt Terrell	.10
73	Bob Kearney	.10
74	Dan Pasqua	.10
75	Ron Darling	.10
76	Robin Yount	.40
77	Pat Tabler	.10
78	Tom Foley	.10
79	Juan Nieves	.10
80	Wally Joyner	.15
81	Wayne Krenchicki	.10
82	Kirby Puckett	1.00
83	Bob Ojeda	.10
84	Mookie Wilson	.10
85	Kevin Bass	.10
86	Kent Tekulve	.10
87	Mark Salas	.10
88	Brian Downing	.10
89	Ozzie Guillen	.10
90	Dave Stieb	.10
91	Rance Mulliniks	.10
92	Mike Witt	.10
93	Charlie Moore	.10
94	Jose Uribe	.10
95	Oddibe McDowell	.10
96	Ray Soff	.10
97	Glenn Wilson	.10
98	Brook Jacoby	.10
99	Darryl Motley	.10
100	Steve Garvey	.15
101	Frank White	.10
102	Mike Moore	.10
103	Rick Aguilera	.10
104	Buddy Bell	.10
105	Floyd Youmans	.10
106	Lou Whitaker	.10
107	Ozzie Smith	.40
108	Jim Gantner	.10
109	R.J. Reynolds	.10
110	John Tudor	.10
111	Alfredo Griffin	.10
112	Mike Flanagan	.10
113	Neil Allen	.10
114	Ken Griffey	.10
115	Donnie Moore	.10
116	Bob Horner	.10
117	Ron Shepherd	.10
118	Cliff Johnson	.10
119	Vince Coleman	.10
120	Eddie Murray	.40
121	Dwayne Murphy	.10
122	Jim Clancy	.10
123	Ken Landreaux	.10
124	Tom Nieto	.10
125	Bob Brenly	.10
126	George Brett	.75
127	Vance Law	.10
128	Checklist 1-132	.10
129	Bob Knepper	.10
130	Dwight Gooden	.20
131	Juan Bonilla	.10
132	Tim Burke	.10
133	Bob McClure	.10
134	Scott Bailes	.10
135	Mike Easler	.10
136	Ron Romanick	.10
137	Rich Gedman	.10
138	Bob Dernier	.10
139	John Denny	.10
140	Bret Saberhagen	.15
141	Herm Winningham	.10
142	Rick Sutcliffe	.10
143	Ryne Sandberg	.75
144	Mike Scioscia	.10
145	Charlie Kerfeld	.10
146	Jim Rice	.20
147	Steve Trout	.10
148	Jesse Orosco	.10
149	Mike Boddicker	.10
150	Wade Boggs	.45
151	Dane Iorg	.10
152	Rick Burleson	.10
153	Duane Ward	.15
154	Rick Reuschel	.10
155	Nolan Ryan	2.00
156	Bill Caudill	.10
157	Danny Darwin	.10
158	Ed Romero	.10
159	Bill Almon	.10
160	Julio Franco	.10
161	Kent Hrbek	.10
162	Chill Davis	.10
163	Kevin Gross	.10
164	Carlton Fisk	.45
165	Jeff Reardon	.10
166	Bob Boone	.10
167	Rick Honeycutt	.10
168	Dan Schatzeder	.10
169	Jim Wohlford	.10
170	Phil Bradley	.10
171	Ken Schrom	.10
172	Ron Oester	.10
173	Juan Beniquez	.10
174	Tony Armas	.10
175	Bob Stanley	.10
176	Steve Buechele	.10
177	Keith Moreland	.10
178	Cecil Fielder	.50
179	Gary Gaetti	.10
180	Chris Brown	.10
181	Tom Herr	.10
182	Lee Lacy	.10
183	Ozzie Virgil	.10
184	Paul Molitor	.40
185	Roger McDowell	.10
186	Mike Marshall	.10
187	Ken Howell	.10
188	Rob Deer	.10
189	Joe Hesketh	.10
190	Jim Sundberg	.10
191	Kelly Gruber	.15
192	Cory Snyder	.10
193	Dave Concepcion	.10
194	Kirk McCaskill	.10
195	Mike Pagliarulo	.10
196	Rick Manning	.10
197	Brett Butler	.10
198	Tony Gwynn	1.00
199	Mariano Duncan	.10
200	Pete Rose	1.50
201	John Cangelosi	.10
202	Danny Cox	.10
203	Butch Wynegar	.10
204	Chris Chambliss	.10
205	Graig Nettles	.10
206	Chet Lemon	.10
207	Don Aase	.10
208	Mike Mason	.10
209	Alan Trammell	.15
210	Lloyd Moseby	.10
211	Richard Dotson	.10
212	Mike Fitzgerald	.10
213	Darrell Porter	.10
214	Checklist 133-264	.10
215	Mark Langston	.10
216	Steve Farr	.10
217	Dann Bilardello	.10
218	Gary Ward	.10
219	Cecilio Guante	.10
220	Joe Carter	.25
221	Ernie Whitt	.10
222	Denny Walling	.10
223	Charlie Leibrandt	.10
224	Wayne Tolleson	.10
225	Mike Smithson	.10
226	Zane Smith	.10
227	Terry Puhl	.10
228	Eric Davis	.15
229	Don Mattingly	1.00
230	Don Baylor	.10
231	Frank Tanana	.10
232	Tom Brookens	.10
233	Steve Bedrosian	.10
234	Wallace Johnson	.10
235	Alvin Davis	.10
236	Tommy John	.10
237	Jim Morrison	.10
238	Ricky Horton	.10
239	Shane Rawley	.10
240	Steve Balboni	.10
241	Mike Krukow	.10
242	Rick Mahler	.10
243	Bill Doran	.10
244	Mark Clear	.10
245	Willie Upshaw	.10
246	Hal McRae	.10
247	Jose Canseco	.60
248	George Hendrick	.10
249	Doyle Alexander	.10
250	Teddy Higuera	.10
251	Tom Hume	.10
252	Denny Martinez	.10
253	Eddie Milner	.10
254	Steve Sax	.10
255	Juan Samuel	.10
256	Dave Bergman	.10
257	Bob Forsch	.10
258	Steve Yeager	.10
259	Don Sutton	.40
260	Vida Blue	.10
261	Tom Brunansky	.10
262	Joe Sambito	.10
263	Mitch Webster	.10
264	Checklist 265-396	.10
265	Darrell Evans	.10
266	Dave Kingman	.10
267	Howard Johnson	.10
268	Greg Pryor	.10
269	Tippy Martinez	.10
270	Jody Davis	.10
271	Steve Carlton	.40

272	Andres Galarraga	.20
273	Fernando Valenzuela	.10
274	Jeff Hearron	.10
275	Ray Knight	.10
276	Bill Madlock	.10
277	Tom Henke	.10
278	Gary Pettis	.10
279	Jimy Williams	.10
280	Jeffrey Leonard	.10
281	Bryn Smith	.10
282	John Cerutti	.10
283	Gary Roenicke	.10
284	Joaquin Andujar	.10
285	Dennis Boyd	.10
286	Tim Hulett	.10
287	Craig Lefferts	.10
288	Tito Landrum	.10
289	Manny Lee	.10
290	Leon Durham	.10
291	Johnny Ray	.10
292	Franklin Stubbs	.10
293	Bob Rodgers	.10
294	Terry Francona	.10
295	Len Dykstra	.10
296	Tom Candiotti	.10
297	Frank DiPino	.10
298	Craig Reynolds	.10
299	Jerry Hairston	.10
300	Reggie Jackson	.40
301	Luis Aquino	.10
302	Greg Walker	.10
303	Terry Kennedy	.10
304	Phil Garner	.10
305	John Franco	.10
306	Bill Buckner	.10
307	Kevin Mitchell	.10
308	Don Slaught	.10
309	Harold Baines	.10
310	Frank Viola	.10
311	Dave Lopes	.10
312	Cal Ripken	2.00
313	John Candelaria	.10
314	Bob Sebra	.10
315	Bud Black	.10
316	Brian Fisher	.10
317	Clint Hurdle	.10
318	Ernie Riles	.10
319	Dave LaPoint	.10
320	Barry Bonds	3.00
321	Tim Stoddard	.10
322	Ron Cey	.10
323	Al Newman	.10
324	Jerry Royster	.10
325	Garry Templeton	.10
326	Mark Gubicza	.10
327	Andre Thornton	.10
328	Bob Welch	.10
329	Tony Fernandez	.10
330	Mike Scott	.10
331	Jack Clark	.10
332	Danny Tartabull	.10
333	Greg Minton	.10
334	Ed Correa	.10
335	Candy Maldonado	.10
336	Dennis Lamp	.10
337	Sid Fernandez	.10
338	Greg Gross	.10
339	Willie Hernandez	.10
340	Roger Clemens	1.00
341	Mickey Hatcher	.10
342	Bob James	.10
343	Jose Cruz	.10
344	Bruce Sutter	.10
345	Andre Dawson	.15
346	Shawon Dunston	.10
347	Scott McGregor	.10
348	Carmelo Martinez	.10
349	Storm Davis	.10
350	Keith Hernandez	.10
351	Andy McGaffigan	.10
352	Dave Parker	.10
353	Ernie Camacho	.10
354	Eric Show	.10
355	Don Carman	.10
356	Floyd Bannister	.10
357	Willie McGee	.10
358	Atlee Hammaker	.10
359	Dale Murphy	.30
360	Pedro Guerrero	.10
361	Will Clark	1.00
362	Bill Campbell	.10
363	Alejandro Pena	.10
364	Dennis Rasmussen	.10
365	Rick Rhoden	.10
366	Randy St. Claire	.10
367	Willie Wilson	.10
368	Dwight Evans	.10
369	Moose Haas	.10
370	Fred Lynn	.10
371	Mark Eichhorn	.10
372	Dave Schmidt	.10
373	Jerry Reuss	.10
374	Lance Parrish	.10
375	Ron Guidry	.10
376	Jack Morris	.10
377	Willie Randolph	.10
378	Joel Youngblood	.10
379	Darryl Strawberry	.15
380	Rich Gossage	.10
381	Dennis Eckersley	.10
382	Gary Lucas	.10
383	Ron Davis	.10
384	Pete Incaviglia	.10
385	Orel Hershiser	.15
386	Kirk Gibson	.10
387	Don Robinson	.10
388	Darnell Coles	.10
389	Von Hayes	.10
390	Gary Matthews	.10
391	Jay Howell	.10
392	Tim Laudner	.10
393	Rod Scurry	.10
394	Tony Bernazard	.10
395	Damasco Garcia	.10
396	Mike Schmidt	.65

1987 O-Pee-Chee Box Panels

For the second consecutive year, O-Pee-Chee placed baseball cards on the bottoms of its wax pack boxes. The 2-1/8" x 3" cards were issued in panels of four and are slightly smaller in size than the regular issue OPC cards. The card fronts are identical in design to the regular issue, while the backs contain a newspaper-type commentary in both French and English. Collectors may note the 1987 Topps wax box cards were issued on side panels as opposed to box bottoms. Because the OPC wax boxes are smaller in size than their U.S. counterparts, printing cards on side panels was not possible.

		MT
Complete Panel Set (2):		5.00
Complete Singles Set (8):		2.00
Common Single Player:		.15
Panel		2.00
A	Don Baylor	.15
B	Steve Carlton	.30
C	Ron Cey	.15
D	Cecil Cooper	.15
Panel		3.50
E	Rickey Henderson	.40
F	Jim Rice	.25
G	Don Sutton	.35
H	Dave Winfield	.40

1988 O-Pee-Chee

Under license from Topps, O-Pee-Chee uses the same player photos as the Topps issue, but the Canadian edition includes only 396 cards (one-half the number in the Topps set). The OPC set was printed after the U.S. press run, so several cards carry overprints on the fronts, indicating changes in players' teams. New teams are named in the overprints; card headers bear the former team names. This set follows the same basic design as the 1988 Topps cards. The OPC logo appears in place of the Topps logo, both front and back. A four-card subset consists of #1 and #2 draft choices for the Expos (Nathan Minchey and Delino DeShields) and Blue Jays (Alex Sanchez and Derek Bell). These cards are distinguished by a yellow or orange triangle in the lower-right corner bearing the player's name above the words "Choisi au repecharge." Card backs are bilingual (English-French) and printed in black on orange. This series was marketed primarily in Canada in four separate display boxes, with four cards printed one each box bottom. Individual card packs contain seven cards and one stick of gum.

		MT
Complete Set (396):		11.00
Common Player:		.08
1	Chris James	.08
2	Steve Buechele	.08
3	Mike Henneman	.08
4	Eddie Murray	.30
5	Bret Saberhagen	.15
6	Nathan Minchey (Draft Pick)	.10
7	Harold Reynolds	.08
8	Bo Jackson	.20
9	Mike Easler	.08
10	Ryne Sandberg	.40
11	Mike Young	.08
12	Tony Phillips	.08
13	Andres Thomas	.08
14	Tim Burke	.08
15	Chili Davis	.10
16	Jim Lindeman	.08
17	Ron Oester	.08
18	Craig Reynolds	.08
19	Juan Samuel	.08
20	Kevin Gross	.08
21	Cecil Fielder	.25
22	Greg Swindell	.08
23	Jose DeLeon	.08
24	Jim Deshaies	.08
25	Andres Galarraga	.15
26	Mitch Williams	.08
27	R.J. Reynolds	.08
28	Jose Nunez	.08
29	Angel Salazar	.08
30	Sid Fernandez	.08
31	Keith Moreland	.08
32	John Kruk	.08
33	Rob Deer	.08
34	Ricky Horton	.08
35	Harold Baines	.08
36	Jamie Moyer	.08
37	Kevin McReynolds	.08
38	Ozzie Smith	.30
39	Ron Darling	.08
40	Orel Hershiser	.10
41	Bob Melvin	.08
42	Alfredo Griffin	.08
43	Dick Schofield	.08
44	Terry Steinbach	.10
45	Kent Hrbek	.10
46	Darnell Coles	.08
47	Jimmy Key	.10
48	Alan Ashby	.08
49	Julio Franco	.10
50	Hubie Brooks	.08
51	Chris Bando	.08
52	Fernando Valenzuela	.10
53	Kal Daniels	.08
54	Jim Clancy	.08
55	Phil Bradley	.08
56	Andy McGaffigan	.08
57	Mike LaVaillere	.08
58	Dave Magadan	.08
59	Danny Cox	.08
60	Rickey Henderson	.25
61	Jim Rice	.15
62	Calvin Schiraldi	.08
63	Jerry Mumphrey	.08
64	Ken Caminiti	.15
65	Leon Durham	.08
66	Shane Rawley	.08
67	Ken Oberkfell	.08
68	Keith Hernandez	.08
69	Bob Brenly	.08
70	Roger Clemens	.50
71	Gary Pettis	.08
72	Dennis Eckersley	.10
73	Dave Smith	.08
74	Cal Ripken	1.00
75	Joe Carter	.15
76	Denny Martinez	.10
77	Juan Beniquez	.08
78	Tim Laudner	.08
79	Ernie Whitt	.08
80	Mark Langston	.10
81	Dale Sveum	.08
82	Dion James	.08
83	Dave Valle	.08
84	Bill Wegman	.08
85	Howard Johnson	.08
86	Benito Santiago	.10
87	Casey Candaele	.08
88	Delino DeShields (Draft Pick)	2.00
89	Dave Winfield	.25
90	Dale Murphy	.15
91	Jay Howell	.08
92	Ken Williams	.08
93	Bob Sebra	.08
94	Tim Wallach	.10
95	Lance Parrish	.08
96	Todd Benzinger	.08
97	Scott Garrelts	.08
98	Jose Guzman	.08
99	Jeff Reardon	.08
100	Jack Clark	.08
101	Tracy Jones	.08
102	Barry Larkin	.15
103	Curt Young	.08
104	Juan Nieves	.08
105	Terry Pendleton	.08
106	Rob Ducey	.08
107	Scott Bailes	.08
108	Eric King	.08
109	Mike Pagliarulo	.08
110	Teddy Higuera	.08
111	Pedro Guerrero	.08
112	Chris Brown	.08
113	Kelly Gruber	.08
114	Jack Howell	.08
115	Johnny Ray	.08
116	Mark Eichhorn	.08
117	Tony Pena	.08
118	Bob Welch	.08
119	Mike Kingery	.08
120	Kirby Puckett	.50
121	Charlie Hough	.08
122	Tony Bernazard	.08
123	Tom Candiotti	.08
124	Ray Knight	.08
125	Bruce Hurst	.08
126	Steve Jeltz	.08
127	Ron Guidry	.08
128	Duane Ward	.08
129	Greg Minton	.08
130	Buddy Bell	.08
131	Denny Walling	.08
132	Donnie Hill	.08
133	Wayne Tolleson	.08
134	Bob Rodgers	.08
135	Todd Worrell	.08
136	Brian Dayett	.08
137	Chris Bosio	.08
138	Mitch Webster	.08
139	Jerry Browne	.08
140	Jesse Barfield	.08
141	Doug DeCinces	.08
142	Andy Van Slyke	.08
143	Doug Drabek	.08
144	Jeff Parrett	.08
145	Bill Madlock	.08
146	Larry Herndon	.08
147	Bill Buckner	.08
148	Carmelo Martinez	.08
149	Ken Howell	.08
150	Eric Davis	.08
151	Randy Ready	.08
152	Jeffrey Leonard	.08
153	Dave Steib	.08
154	Jeff Stone	.08
155	Dave Righetti	.08
156	Gary Matthews	.08
157	Gary Carter	.15
158	Bob Boone	.08
159	Glenn Davis	.08
160	Willie McGee	.08
161	Bryn Smith	.08
162	Mark McLemore	.08
163	Dale Mohorcic	.08
164	Mike Flanagan	.08
165	Robin Yount	.40
166	Bill Doran	.08
167	Rance Mulliniks	.08
168	Wally Joyner	.10
169	Cory Snyder	.08
170	Rich Gossage	.08
171	Rick Mahler	.08
172	Henry Cotto	.08
173	George Bell	.15
174	B.J. Surhoff	.08
175	Kevin Bass	.08
176	Jeff Reed	.08
177	Frank Tanana	.08
178	Darryl Strawberry	.15
179	Lou Whitaker	.08
180	Terry Kennedy	.08
181	Mariano Duncan	.08
182	Ken Phelps	.08
183	Bob Dernier	.08
184	Ivan Calderon	.08
185	Rick Rhoden	.08
186	Rafael Palmeiro	.30
187	Kelly Downs	.08
188	Spike Owen	.08
189	Bobby Bonilla	.15
190	Candy Maldonado	.08
191	John Cerutti	.08
192	Devon White	.15
193	Brian Fisher	.08
194	Alex Sanchez (Draft Pick)	.20
195	Dan Quisenberry	.08
196	Dave Engle	.08
197	Lance McCullers	.08
198	Franklin Stubbs	.08
199	Scott Bradley	.08
200	Wade Boggs	.35
201	Kirk Gibson	.08
202	Brett Butler	.08
203	Dave Anderson	.08
204	Donnie Moore	.08
205	Nelson Liriano	.08
206	Danny Gladden	.08
207	Dan Pasqua	.08
208	Robbie Thompson	.08
209	Richard Dotson	.08
210	Willie Randolph	.08
211	Danny Tartabull	.08
212	Greg Brock	.08
213	Albert Hall	.08
214	Dave Schmidt	.08
215	Von Hayes	.08
216	Herm Winningham	.08
217	Mike Davis	.08
218	Charlie Leibrandt	.08
219	Mike Stanley	.08
220	Tom Henke	.08
221	Dwight Evans	.08
222	Willie Wilson	.08
223	Stan Jefferson	.08
224	Mike Dunne	.08
225	Mike Scioscia	.08
226	Larry Parrish	.08
227	Mike Scott	.08
228	Wallace Johnson	.08
229	Jeff Musselman	.08
230	Pat Tabler	.08
231	Paul Molitor	.35
232	Bob James	.08
233	Joe Niekro	.08
234	Oddibe McDowell	.08
235	Gary Ward	.08
236	Ted Power	.08
237	Pascual Perez	.08
238	Luis Polonia	.08
239	Mike Diaz	.08
240	Lee Smith	.08
241	Willie Upshaw	.08
242	Tom Neidenfuer	.08
243	Tim Raines	.20
244	Jeff Robinson	.08
245	Rich Gedman	.08
246	Scott Bankhead	.08
247	Andre Dawson	.15
248	Brook Jacoby	.08
249	Mike Marshall	.08
250	Nolan Ryan	1.00
251	Tom Foley	.08
252	Bob Brower	.08
253	Checklist 1-132	.08
254	Scott McGregor	.08
255	Ken Griffey	.08
256	Ken Schrom	.08
257	Gary Gaetti	.08
258	Ed Nunez	.08
259	Frank Viola	.08
260	Vince Coleman	.08
261	Reid Nichols	.08
262	Tim Flannery	.08
263	Glenn Braggs	.08
264	Garry Templeton	.08
265	Bo Diaz	.08
266	Matt Nokes	.08
267	Barry Bonds	.60
268	Bruce Ruffin	.08
269	Ellis Burks	.10
270	Mike Witt	.08
271	Ken Gerhart	.08
272	Lloyd Moseby	.08
273	Garth Iorg	.08
274	Mike Greenwell	.08
275	Kevin Seitzer	.08
276	Luis Salazar	.08
277	Shawon Dunston	.08
278	Rick Reuschel	.08
279	Randy St. Claire	.08
280	Pete Incaviglia	.08
281	Mike Boddicker	.08
282	Jay Tibbs	.08
283	Shane Mack	.08
284	Walt Terrell	.08
285	Jim Presley	.08
286	Greg Walker	.08
287	Dwight Gooden	.15
288	Jim Morrison	.08
289	Gene Garber	.08
290	Tony Fernandez	.08
291	Ozzie Virgil	.08
292	Carney Lansford	.08
293	Jim Acker	.08
294	Tommy Hinzo	.08
295	Bert Blyleven	.08
296	Ozzie Guillen	.08
297	Zane Smith	.08
298	Milt Thompson	.08
299	Len Dykstra	.08
300	Don Mattingly	.60
301	Bud Black	.08
302	Jose Uribe	.08
303	Manny Lee	.08
304	Sid Bream	.08
305	Steve Sax	.08
306	Billy Hatcher	.08
307	John Shelby	.08
308	Lee Mazzilli	.08
309	Bill Long	.08
310	Tom Herr	.08
311	Derek Bell (Draft Pick)	4.50
312	George Brett	.50
313	Bob McClure	.08
314	Jimy Williams	.08
315	Dave Parker	.10
316	Doyle Alexander	.08

317	Dan Plesac	.08
318	Mel Hall	.08
319	Ruben Sierra	.08
320	Alan Trammell	.10
321	Mike Schmidt	.35
322	Wally Ritchie	.08
323	Rick Leach	.08
324	Danny Jackson	.08
325	Glenn Hubbard	.08
326	Frank White	.08
327	Larry Sheets	.08
328	John Cangelosi	.08
329	Bill Gullickson	.08
330	Eddie Whitson	.08
331	Brian Downing	.08
332	Gary Redus	.08
333	Wally Backman	.08
334	Dwayne Murphy	.08
335	Claudell Washington	.08
336	Dave Concepcion	.08
337	Jim Gantner	.08
338	Marty Barrett	.08
339	Mickey Hatcher	.08
340	Jack Morris	.08
341	John Franco	.08
342	Ron Robinson	.08
343	Greg Gagne	.08
344	Steve Bedrosian	.08
345	Scott Fletcher	.08
346	Vance Law	.08
347	Joe Johnson	.08
348	Jim Eisenreich	.08
349	Alvin Davis	.08
350	Will Clark	.35
351	Mike Aldrete	.08
352	Billy Ripken	.08
353	Dave Stewart	.08
354	Neal Heaton	.08
355	Roger McDowell	.08
356	John Tudor	.08
357	Floyd Bannister	.08
358	Rey Quinones	.08
359	Glenn Wilson	.08
360	Tony Gwynn	.75
361	Greg Maddux	1.00
362	Juan Castillo	.08
363	Willie Fraser	.08
364	Nick Esasky	.08
365	Floyd Youmans	.08
366	Chet Lemon	.08
367	Matt Young	.08
368	Gerald Young	.08
369	Bob Stanley	.08
370	Jose Canseco	.45
371	Joe Hesketh	.08
372	Rick Sutcliffe	.08
373	Checklist 133-264	.08
374	Checklist 265-396	.08
375	Tom Brunansky	.08
376	Jody Davis	.08
377	Sam Horn	.08
378	Mark Gubicza	.08
379	Rafael Ramirez	.08
380	Joe Magrane	.08
381	Pete O'Brien	.08
382	Lee Guetterman	.08
383	Eric Bell	.08
384	Gene Larkin	.08
385	Carlton Fisk	.35
386	Mike Fitzgerald	.08
387	Kevin Mitchell	.08
388	Jim Winn	.08
389	Mike Smithson	.08
390	Darrell Evans	.08
391	Terry Leach	.08
392	Charlie Kerfeld	.08
393	Mike Krukow	.08
394	Mark McGwire	2.00
395	Fred McGriff	.30
396	DeWayne Buice	.08

1988 O-Pee-Chee Box Panels

A Topps licensee, O-Pee-Chee of Canada issued this 16-card set on wax display box bottoms. Cards feature popular current players and are identified by alphabet (A-P) rather than numbers. Player photos are the same ones used on the Topps U.S. issue and cards follow the same design as Topps' regular issue set. The OPC logo replaces the Topps logo on both front and back. Orange and black card backs are bilingual (French/English) and include complete major and minor league career stats.

		MT
Complete Panel Set (4):		8.00
Complete Singles Set (16):		3.50
Common Single Player:		.08
Panel		1.00
A	Don Baylor	.10
B	Steve Bedrosian	.08
C	Juan Beniquez	.08
D	Bob Boone	.08
Panel		2.00
E	Darrell Evans	.10
F	Tony Gwynn	.75
G	John Kruk	.08
H	Marvell Wynne	.08
Panel		1.50
I	Joe Carter	.20
J	Eric Davis	.15
K	Howard Johnson	.08
L	Darryl Strawberry	.15
Panel		3.50
M	Rickey Henderson	.25
N	Nolan Ryan	1.00
O	Mike Schmidt	.50
P	Kent Tekulve	.08

1988 O-Pee-Chee Stickers/Stickercards

This is the Canadian version of Topps' sticker issue for 1988, virtually identical except for the substitution of the OPC logo and copyright notice on the front of the stickercard. The Canadian version shares the Topps' checklists and, essentially, the price structure, although Canadian star players command a small premium in the OPC version.

	MT
Complete Set:	17.50
Common Sticker/Stickercard:	.10
Album:	1.50

(See 1988 Topps Stickers, Stickercards for checklist and value information.)

1989 O-Pee-Chee

At 396 cards, the 1989 O-Pee-Chee issue is half the size of the corresponding Topps set. As in previous years, the design of the OPC cards is virtually identical to the Topps version, though the Topps logo on front has been replaced with an O-Pee-Chee logo in one of the upper corners and the backs are printed in both English and French for the Canadian market. Cards of players who changed teams often contain an overprint indicating the player's new team and date of the transaction.

		MT
Complete Set (396):		11.00
Common Player:		.05
1	Brook Jacoby	.05
2	Atlee Hammaker	.05
3	Jack Clark	.05
4	Dave Steib	.10
5	Bud Black	.05
6	Damon Berryhill	.05
7	Mike Scioscia	.05
8	Jose Uribe	.05
9	Mike Aldrete	.05
10	Andre Dawson	.10
11	Bruce Sutter	.05
12	Dale Sveum	.05
13	Dan Quisenberry	.05
14	Tom Niedenfeur	.05
15	Robby Thompson	.05
16	Ron Robinson	.05
17	Brian Downing	.05
18	Rick Rhoden	.05
19	Greg Gagne	.05
20	Allan Anderson	.05
21	Eddie Whitson	.05
22	Billy Ripken	.05
23	Mike Fitzgerald	.05
24	Shane Rawley	.05
25	Frank White	.05
26	Don Mattingly	.75
27	Fred Lynn	.05
28	Mike Moore	.05
29	Kelly Gruber	.05
30	Dwight Gooden	.10
31	Dan Pasqua	.05
32	Dennis Rasmussen	.05
33	B.J. Surhoff	.05
34	Sid Fernandez	.05
35	John Tudor	.05
36	Mitch Webster	.05
37	Doug Drabek	.05
38	Bobby Witt	.05
39	Mike Maddux	.05
40	Steve Sax	.05
41	Orel Hershiser	.10
42	Pete Incaviglia	.05
43	Guillermo Hernandez	.05
44	Kevin Coffman	.05
45	Kal Daniels	.05
46	Carlton Fisk	.25
47	Carney Lansford	.05
48	Tim Burke	.05
49	Alan Trammell	.05
50	George Bell	.12
51	Tony Gwynn	.65
52	Bob Brenly	.05
53	Ruben Sierra	.05
54	Otis Nixon	.05
55	Julio Franco	.05
56	Pat Tabler	.05
57	Alvin Davis	.05
58	Kevin Seitzer	.05
59	Mark Davis	.05
60	Tom Brunansky	.05
61	Jeff Treadway	.05
62	Alfredo Griffin	.05
63	Keith Hernandez	.05
64	Alex Trevino	.05
65	Rick Reuschel	.05
66	Bob Walk	.05
67	Dave Palmer	.05
68	Pedro Guerrero	.05
69	Jose Oquendo	.05
70	Mark McGwire	2.00
71	Mike Boddicker	.05
72	Wally Backman	.05
73	Pascual Perez	.05
74	Joe Hesketh	.05
75	Tom Henke	.05
76	Nelson Liriano	.05
77	Doyle Alexander	.05
78	Tim Wallach	.10
79	Scott Bankhead	.05
80	Cory Snyder	.05
81	Dave Magadan	.05
82	Randy Ready	.05
83	Steve Buechele	.05
84	Bo Jackson	.10
85	Kevin McReynolds	.05
86	Jeff Reardon	.05
87	Tim Raines	.25
88	Melido Perez	.05
89	Dave LaPoint	.05
90	Vince Coleman	.05
91	Floyd Youmans	.05
92	Buddy Bell	.05
93	Andres Galarraga	.15
94	Tony Pena	.05
95	Gerald Young	.05
96	Rick Cerone	.05
97	Ken Oberkfell	.05
98	Larry Sheets	.05
99	Chuck Crim	.05
100	Mike Schmidt	.50
101	Ivan Calderon	.05
102	Kevin Bass	.05
103	Chili Davis	.05
104	Randy Myers	.05
105	Ron Darling	.05
106	Willie Upshaw	.05
107	Jose DeLeon	.05
108	Fred Manrique	.05
109	Johnny Ray	.05
110	Paul Molitor	.35
111	Rance Mulliniks	.05
112	Jim Presley	.05
113	Lloyd Moseby	.05
114	Lance Parrish	.05
115	Jody Davis	.05
116	Matt Nokes	.05
117	Dave Anderson	.05
118	Checklist	.05
119	Rafael Belliard	.05
120	Frank Viola	.05
121	Roger Clemens	.50
122	Luis Salazar	.05
123	Mike Stanley	.05
124	Jim Traber	.05
125	Mike Krukow	.05
126	Sid Bream	.05
127	Joel Skinner	.05
128	Milt Thompson	.05
129	Terry Clark	.05
130	Gerald Perry	.05
131	Bryn Smith	.05
132	Kirby Puckett	.45
133	Bill Long	.05
134	Jim Gantner	.05
135	Jose Rijo	.05
136	Joey Meyer	.05
137	Geno Petralli	.05
138	Wallace Johnson	.05
139	Mike Flanagan	.05
140	Shawon Dunston	.05
141	Eric Plunk	.05
142	Bobby Bonilla	.05
143	Jack McDowell	.05
144	Mookie Wilson	.05
145	Dave Stewart	.10
146	Gary Pettis	.05
147	Eric Show	.05
148	Eddie Murray	.30
149	Lee Smith	.05
150	Fernando Valenzuela	.05
151	Bob Walk	.05
152	Harold Baines	.05
153	Albert Hall	.05
154	Don Carman	.05
155	Marty Barrett	.05
156	Chris Sabo	.05
157	Bret Saberhagen	.05
158	Danny Cox	.05
159	Tom Foley	.05
160	Jeffrey Leonard	.05
161	Brady Anderson	.05
162	Rich Gossage	.05
163	Greg Brock	.05
164	Joe Carter	.20
165	Mike Dunne	.05
166	Jeff Russell	.05
167	Dan Plesac	.05
168	Willie Wilson	.05
169	Mike Jackson	.05
170	Tony Fernandez	.05
171	Jamie Moyer	.05
172	Jim Gott	.05
173	Mel Hall	.05
174	Mark McGwire	1.50
175	John Shelby	.05
176	Jeff Parrett	.05
177	Tim Belcher	.05
178	Rich Gedman	.05
179	Ozzie Virgil	.05
180	Mike Scott	.05
181	Dickie Thon	.05
182	Rob Murphy	.05
183	Oddibe McDowell	.05
184	Wade Boggs	.35
185	Claudell Washington	.05
186	Randy Johnson	.40
187	Paul O'Neill	.10
188	Todd Benzinger	.05
189	Kevin Mitchell	.05
190	Mike Witt	.05
191	Sil Campusano	.05
192	Ken Gerhart	.05
193	Bob Rodgers	.05
194	Floyd Bannister	.05
195	Ozzie Guillen	.05
196	Ron Gant	.10
197	Neal Heaton	.05
198	Bill Swift	.05
199	Dave Parker	.10
200	George Brett	.45
201	Bo Diaz	.05
202	Brad Moore	.05
203	Rob Ducey	.05
204	Bert Blyleven	.05
205	Dwight Evans	.05
206	Roberto Alomar	.90
207	Henry Cotto	.05
208	Harold Reynolds	.05
209	Jose Guzman	.05
210	Dale Murphy	.10
211	Mike Pagliarulo	.05
212	Jay Howell	.05
213	Rene Gonzalez	.05
214	Scott Garrelts	.05
215	Kevin Gross	.05
216	Jack Howell	.05
217	Kurt Stillwell	.05
218	Mike LaValliere	.05
219	Jim Clancy	.05
220	Gary Gaetti	.05
221	Hubie Brooks	.05
222	Bruce Ruffin	.05
223	Jay Buhner	.10
224	Cecil Fielder	.20
225	Willie McGee	.05
226	Bill Doran	.05
227	John Farrell	.05
228	Nelson Santovenia	.05
229	Jimmy Key	.05
230	Ozzie Smith	.30
231	Dave Schmidt	.05
232	Jody Reed	.05
233	Gregg Jefferies	.25
234	Tom Browning	.05
235	John Kruk	.05
236	Charles Hudson	.05
237	Todd Stottlemyre	.10
238	Don Slaught	.05
239	Tim Laudner	.05
240	Greg Maddux	.75
241	Brett Butler	.05
242	Checklist	.05
243	Bob Boone	.05
244	Willie Randolph	.05
245	Jim Rice	.05
246	Rey Quinonez	.05
247	Checklist	.05
248	Stan Javier	.05
249	Tim Leary	.05
250	Cal Ripken, Jr.	1.00
251	John Dopson	.05
252	Billy Hatcher	.05
253	Robin Yount	.40
254	Mickey Hatcher	.05
255	Bob Horner	.05
256	Benito Santiago	.05
257	Luis Rivera	.05
258	Fred McGriff	.20
259	Dave Wells	.05
260	Dave Winfield	.30
261	Rafael Ramirez	.05
262	Nick Esasky	.05
263	Barry Bonds	.60
264	Joe Magrane	.05
265	Kent Hrbek	.05
266	Jack Morris	.05
267	Jeff Robinson	.05
268	Ron Kittle	.05
269	Candy Maldonado	.05
270	Wally Joyner	.10
271	Glenn Braggs	.05
272	Ron Hassey	.05
273	Jose Lind	.05
274	Mark Eichhorn	.05
275	Danny Tartabull	.05
276	Paul Kilgus	.05
277	Mike Davis	.05
278	Andy McGaffigan	.05
279	Scott Bradley	.05
280	Bob Knepper	.05
281	Gary Redus	.05
282	Rickey Henderson	.25
283	Andy Allenson	.05
284	Rick Leach	.05
285	John Candelaria	.05
286	Dick Schofield	.05
287	Bryan Harvey	.05
288	Randy Bush	.05
289	Ernie Whitt	.05
290	John Franco	.05
291	Todd Worrell	.05
292	Teddy Higuera	.05
293	Keith Moreland	.05
294	Juan Berenguer	.05
295	Scott Fletcher	.05
296	Roger McDowell	.05
297	Mark Grace	.25
298	Chris James	.05
299	Frank Tanana	.05
300	Darryl Strawberry	.10
301	Charlie Leibrandt	.05
302	Gary Ward	.05
303	Brian Fisher	.05
304	Terry Steinbach	.05
305	Dave Smith	.05
306	Greg Minton	.05
307	Lance McCullers	.05
308	Phil Bradley	.05
309	Terry Kennedy	.05
310	Rafael Palmeiro	.12
311	Ellis Burks	.05
312	Doug Jones	.05
313	Dennis Martinez	.10
314	Pete O'Brien	.05
315	Greg Swindell	.05
316	Walt Weiss	.05
317	Pete Stanicek	.05
318	Gene Nelson	.05
319	Danny Jackson	.05
320	Lou Whitaker	.05
321	Will Clark	.25
322	John Smiley	.05
323	Mike Marshall	.05
324	Gary Carter	.20
325	Jesse Barfield	.05
326	Dennis Boyd	.05
327	Dave Henderson	.05
328	Chet Lemon	.05
329	Bob Melvin	.05
330	Eric Davis	.05
331	Ted Power	.05
332	Carmelo Martinez	.05
333	Bob Ojeda	.05
334	Steve Lyons	.05
335	Dave Righetti	.05
336	Steve Balboni	.05
337	Calvin Schiraldi	.05
338	Vance Law	.05
339	Zane Smith	.05
340	Kirk Gibson	.05
341	Jim Deshaies	.05
342	Tom Brookens	.05
343	Pat Borders	.10
344	Devon White	.10
345	Charlie Hough	.05
346	Rex Hudler	.05
347	John Cerutti	.05
348	Kirk McCaskill	.05

349 Len Dykstra .05
350 Andy Van Slyke .05
351 Jeff Robinson .05
352 Rick Schu .05
353 Bruce Benedict .05
354 Bill Wegman .05
355 Mark Langston .05
356 Steve Farr .05
357 Richard Dotson .05
358 Andres Thomas .05
359 Alan Ashby .05
360 Ryne Sandberg .60
361 Kelly Downs .05
362 Jeff Musselman .05
363 Barry Larkin .12
364 Rob Deer .05
365 Mike Henneman .05
366 Nolan Ryan 1.00
367 Johnny Paredes .05
368 Bobby Thigpen .05
369 Mickey Brantley .05
370 Dennis Eckersley .10
371 Manny Lee .05
372 Juan Samuel .05
373 Tracy Jones .05
374 Mike Greenwell .05
375 Terry Pendleton .05
376 Steve Lombardozzi .05
377 Mitch Williams .05
378 Glenn Davis .05
379 Mark Gubicza .05
380 Orel Hershiser .10
381 Jimy Williams .05
382 Kirk Gibson .05
383 Howard Johnson .05
384 Dave Cone .10
385 Von Hayes .05
386 Luis Polonia .05
387 Dan Gladden .05
388 Pete Smith .05
389 Jose Canseco .35
390 Mickey Hatcher .05
391 Wil Tejada .10
392 Duane Ward .05
393 Rick Mahler .05
394 Rick Sutcliffe .05
395 Dave Martinez .05
396 Ken Dayley .05

1989 O-Pee-Chee Box Panels

Continuing its practice of printing baseball cards on the bottom panels of its wax pack boxes, OPC in 1989 issued a special 16-card set, printing four cards on each of four different box-bottom panels. The cards are identical in design to the regular 1989 OPC cards. They are designated by letter (from A through P) rather than by number.

	MT
Complete Panel Set (4):	10.00
Complete Singles Set (16):	7.50
Common Panel:	1.50
Common Single Player:	.10

Panel 2.50
A George Brett 1.00
B Bill Buckner .10
C Darrell Evans .15
D Rich Gossage .10
Panel 1.50
E Greg Gross .10
F Rickey Henderson .25
G Keith Hernandez .10
H Tom Lasorda .25
Panel 7.50
I Jim Rice .20
J Cal Ripken, Jr. 2.00
K Nolan Ryan 2.00
L Mike Schmidt 1.00
Panel 2.00
M Bruce Sutter .10
N Don Sutton .25
O Kent Tekulve .10
P Dave Winfield .50

1989 O-Pee-Chee Stickers/Stickercards

Once again sharing a checklist with the 1989 Topps sticker issue, the OPC version differs only in the substitution of the O-Pee-Chee logo and copyright notice on the front of the stickercard. Values are also essentially the same, although Expos and Blue Jays stars carry a small premium in the OPC version.

	MT
Complete Set:	24.00
Common Sticker/Stickercard:	.15
Album:	2.00

(See 1989 Topps stickers/stickercards for checklist and value information.)

1990 O-Pee-Chee

Virtually identical to the contemporary 1990 Topps set, the OPC issue features the same 792 cards. On most cards the fronts are indistinguishable, even to the use of a Topps logo on the Canadian product. A number of the OPC cards differ from their Topps counterparts in that there is a notice of team change printed in black on the front. Backs of the OPC cards feature a few lines of French in areas such as the stat headings, the career summary and monthly scoreboard. The OPC cards omit the Topps copyright line and feature an OPC copyright line on back.

	MT
Complete Set (792):	18.00
Common Player:	.05

(See 1990 Topps for checklist and base card values. Star cards valued about .75X-1X corresponding Topps card.)

1990 O-Pee-Chee Stickers

Once again sharing a checklist with the 1990 Topps sticker issue, the OPC version differs only in the substitution of the O-Pee-Chee logo and copyright notice on the stickercard. Values are also essentially the same, although Expos and Blue Jays stars carry a small premium in the OPC version.

(See 1990 Topps stickers for checklist and base values.)

1991 O-Pee-Chee Sample Sheet

This 7-1/2" x 10-1/2" sample sheet debuts the 1991 OPC set. Fronts reproduce the basic design while the back, printed in blue on white, contains an ad for OPC.

	MT
Complete Sheet:	5.00

Bill Bathe
Jeff Blauser
Jose Canseco (All-Star)
Wes Chamberlain (photo actually Louie Meadows)
Norm Charlton
Mike Dunne
Craig Grebeck
Carmelo Martinez
Mike Scioscia (All-Star)

1991 O-Pee-Chee

Once again for 1991, OPC utilized the contemporary Topps set of 792 cards as the basis for its own issue. The OPC cards are again printed on a lighter, whiter stock and differ from the Topps cards in the addition of French to the card backs, along with the OPC copyright. Many card fronts in OPC carry a small black typographical notice concerning team changes by the players.

	MT
Complete Set (792):	18.00
Common Player:	.05

(See 1991 Topps for checklist and base values. Star cards worth .75X-1X Topps.)

1991 O-Pee-Chee Premier

The O-Pee-Chee Co. of London, Ontario, Canada produced this 132-card set. The card fronts feature action photos, while the flip sides display a posed photo and career statistics. The cards were packaged seven cards per pack in a tamper-proof foil wrap. Several Expo and Blue Jay players are featured. Two special cards are included in this set. Card #62 honors Rickey Henderson's stolen base record, while card #102 commemorates Nolan Ryan's seventh no-hitter. Traded players and free agents are featured with their new teams.

	MT
Complete Set (132):	9.00
Common Player:	.05
Wax Box:	10.00

1 Roberto Alomar .40
2 Sandy Alomar .10
3 Moises Alou .40
4 Brian Barnes .05
5 Steve Bedrosian .05
6 George Bell .05
7 Juan Bell .05
8 Albert Belle .40
9 Bud Black .05
10 Mike Boddicker .05
11 Wade Boggs .35
12 Barry Bonds .65
13 Denis Boucher .15
14 George Brett .50
15 Hubie Brooks .05
16 Brett Butler .05
17 Ivan Calderon .05
18 Jose Canseco .35
19 Gary Carter .15
20 Joe Carter .25
21 Jack Clark .05
22 Will Clark .25
23 Roger Clemens .40
24 Alex Cole .05
25 Vince Coleman .05
26 Jeff Conine .10
27 Milt Cuyler .05
28 Danny Darwin .05
29 Eric Davis .05
30 Glenn Davis .05
31 Andre Dawson .12
32 Ken Dayley .05
33 Steve Decker .05
34 Delino DeShields .10
35 Lance Dickson .05
36 Kirk Dressendorfer .05
37 Shawon Dunston .05
38 Dennis Eckersley .05
39 Dwight Evans .05
40 Howard Farmer .05
41 Junior Felix .05
42 Alex Fernandez .10
43 Tony Fernandez .05
44 Cecil Fielder .25
45 Carlton Fisk .25
46 Willie Fraser .05
47 Gary Gaetti .05
48 Andres Galarraga .15
49 Ron Gant .10
50 Kirk Gibson .05
51 Bernard Gilkey .05
52 Leo Gomez .05
53 Rene Gonzalez .05
54 Juan Gonzalez .75
55 Doc Gooden .10
56 Ken Griffey, Jr. 2.00
57 Kelly Gruber .05
58 Pedro Guerrero .05
59 Tony Gwynn .50
60 Chris Hammond .05
61 Ron Hassey .05
62 Rickey Henderson .25
63 Tom Henke .05
64 Orel Hershiser .10
65 Chris Hoiles .05
66 Todd Hundley .05
67 Pete Incaviglia .05
68 Danny Jackson .05
69 Barry Jones .05
70 David Justice .30
71 Jimmy Key .05
72 Ray Lankford .05
73 Darren Lewis .05
74 Kevin Maas .05
75 Denny Martinez .10
76 Tino Martinez .10
77 Don Mattingly .50
78 Willie McGee .05
79 Fred McGriff .25
80 Hensley Meulens .05
81 Kevin Mitchell .05
82 Paul Molitor .40
83 Mickey Morandini .05
84 Jack Morris .05
85 Dale Murphy .10
86 Eddie Murray .20
87 Chris Nabholz .05
88 Tim Naehring .05
89 Otis Nixon .05
90 Jose Offerman .05
91 Bob Ojeda .05
92 John Olerud .15
93 Gregg Olson .05
94 Dave Parker .05
95 Terry Pendleton .05
96 Kirby Puckett .65
97 Rock Raines .10
98 Jeff Reardon .05
99 Dave Righetti .05
100 Cal Ripken 1.50
101 Mel Rojas .12
102 Nolan Ryan 1.50
103 Ryne Sandberg .50
104 Scott Sanderson .05
105 Benito Santiago .05
106 Pete Schourek .05
107 Gary Scott .05
108 Terry Shumpert .05
109 Ruben Sierra .05
110 Doug Simons .05
111 Dave Smith .05
112 Ozzie Smith .35
113 Cory Snyder .05
114 Luis Sojo .05
115 Dave Stewart .10
116 Dave Stieb .05
117 Darryl Strawberry .10
118 Pat Tabler .05
119 Wade Taylor .05
120 Bobby Thigpen .05
121 Frank Thomas 1.00
122 Mike Timlin .05
123 Alan Trammell .05
124 Mo Vaughn .30
125 Tim Wallach .05
126 Devon White .10
127 Mark Whiten .05
128 Bernie Williams .25
129 Willie Wilson .05
130 Dave Winfield .15
131 Robin Yount .40
132 Checklist .05

1992 O-Pee-Chee

Once again closely following the format of the 1992 Topps set, and for the most part corresponding to its 792-card checklist, the 1992 OPCs differ on the front only in the substitution of an O-Pee-Chee logo for the Topps logo, and in the inclusion of team-change information for many of the players who moved after the Topps cards were printed. On backs, the light blue "Topps" logo printed behind the stats has been removed, and the logo beneath the card number changed from "Topps" to "O-Pee-Chee". The addition of a few lines of French above the stats and in the career summary can be seen on the OPC cards, as well as the substitution of an OPC copyright line for that of Topps. Where the 1992 Topps set features All-Star cards in the number range 386-407, the OPC set has a group of player cards who are not represented in the Topps set, including four "Tribute" cards honoring Gary Carter. Card #45 in the OPC set is also a Carter Trbitue card, whereas in the Topps set it is a regular card.

		MT
Complete Set (792):		18.00
Common Player:		.08
45	Gary Carter - Tribute	.25
386	Lance Blankenship	.08
387	Gary Carter - Tribute	.25
388	Ron Tingley	.08
389	Gary Carter - Tribute	.25
390	Gene Harris	.08
391	Jeff Schaefer	.08
392	Mark Grant	.08
393	Carl Willis	.08
394	Al Leiter	.25
395	Ron Robinson	.08
396	Tim Hullett	.08
397	Craig Worthington	.08
398	John Orton	.08
399	Gary Carter - Tribute	.25
400	John Dopson	.08
401	Moises Alou	.50
402	Gary Carter - Tribute	.25
403	Matt Young	.08
404	Wayne Edwards	.08
405	Nick Esasky	.08
406	Dave Eiland	.08
407	Mike Brumley	.08

1992 O-Pee-Chee Premier

O-Pee-Chee increased the number of cards in its premier set to 198 for 1992. The cards feature white borders surrounding full-color player photos. The O-Pee-Chee banner appears at the top of the card and the player's name and position appear at the bottom. The backs feature an additional player photo, statistics and player information. Traded players and free agents are featured with their new teams.

		MT
Complete Set (198):		11.00
Common Player:		.08
Wax Box:		9.00
1	Wade Boggs	.40
2	John Smiley	.08
3	Checklist	.08
4	Ron Gant	.15
5	Mike Bordick	.08
6	Charlie Hayes	.08
7	Kevin Morton	.08
8	Checklist	.08
9	Chris Gwynn	.08
10	Melido Perez	.08
11	Danny Gladden	.08
12	Brian McRae	.10
13	Denny Martinez	.10
14	Bob Scanlan	.08
15	Julio Franco	.10
16	Ruben Amaro	.08
17	Mo Sanford	.08
18	Scott Bankhead	.08
19	Dickie Thon	.08
20	Chris James	.08
21	Mike Huff	.08
22	Orlando Merced	.08
23	Chris Sabo	.08
24	Jose Canseco	.50
25	Reggie Sanders	.10
26	Chris Nabholz	.08
27	Kevin Seitzer	.08
28	Ryan Bowen	.08
29	Gary Carter	.15
30	Wayne Rosenthal	.08
31	Alan Trammell	.10
32	Doug Drabek	.08
33	Craig Shipley	.08
34	Ryne Sandberg	.40
35	Chuck Knoblauch	.10
36	Bret Barberie	.08
37	Tim Naehring	.08
38	Omar Olivares	.08
39	Royce Clayton	.08
40	Brent Mayne	.08
41	Darrin Fletcher	.08
42	Howard Johnson	.08
43	Steve Sax	.08
44	Greg Swindell	.08
45	Andre Dawson	.15
46	Kent Hrbek	.10
47	Doc Gooden	.10
48	Mark Leiter	.08
49	Tom Glavine	.10
50	Mo Vaughn	.30
51	Doug Jones	.08
52	Brian Barnes	.08
53	Rob Dibble	.08
54	Kevin McReynolds	.08
55	Ivan Rodriguez	.45
56	Scott Livingstone	.08
57	Mike Magnante	.08
58	Pete Schourek	.08
59	Frank Thomas	1.00
60	Kirk McCaskill	.08
61	Wally Joyner	.10
62	Rick Aguilera	.08
63	Eric Karros	.25
64	Tino Martinez	.10
65	Bryan Hickerson	.08
66	Ruben Sierra	.08
67	Willie Randolph	.08
68	Bill Landrum	.08
69	Bip Roberts	.08
70	Cecil Fielder	.15
71	Pat Kelly	.10
72	Kenny Lofton	.65
73	John Franco	.08
74	Phil Plantier	.08
75	Dave Martinez	.08
76	Warren Newson	.08
77	Chito Martinez	.08
78	Brian Hunter	.08
79	Jack Morris	.08
80	Eric King	.08
81	Nolan Ryan	1.50
82	Bret Saberhagen	.10
83	Roberto Kelly	.08
84	Ozzie Smith	.40
85	Chuck McElroy	.08
86	Carlton Fisk	.50
87	Mike Mussina	.25
88	Mark Carreon	.08
89	Ken Hill	.08
90	Rick Cerone	.08
91	Deion Sanders	.20
92	Don Mattingly	.65
93	Danny Tartabull	.08
94	Keith Miller	.08
95	Gregg Jefferies	.10
96	Barry Larkin	.10
97	Kevin Mitchell	.08
98	Rick Sutcliffe	.08
99	Mark McGwire	2.00
100	Albert Belle	.50
101	Gregg Olson	.08
102	Kirby Puckett	.60
103	Luis Gonzalez	.08
104	Randy Myers	.08
105	Roger Clemens	.75
106	Tony Gwynn	.75
107	Jeff Bagwell	.50
108	John Wetteland	.08
109	Bernie Williams	.25
110	Scott Kamieniecki	.08
111	Robin Yount	.50
112	Dean Palmer	.08
113	Tim Belcher	.08
114	George Brett	.50
115	Frank Viola	.08
116	Kelly Gruber	.08
117	David Justice	.20
118	Scott Leius	.08
119	Jeff Fassero	.08
120	Sammy Sosa	1.00
121	Al Osuna	.08
122	Wilson Alvarez	.08
123	Jose Offerman	.10
124	Mel Rojas	.10
125	Shawon Dunston	.08
126	Pete Incaviglia	.08
127	Von Hayes	.08
128	Dave Gallagher	.08
129	Eric Davis	.08
130	Roberto Alomar	.35
131	Mike Gallego	.08
132	Robin Ventura	.15
133	Bill Swift	.08
134	John Kruk	.08
135	Craig Biggio	.15
136	Eddie Taubensee	.08
137	Cal Ripken, Jr.	1.50
138	Charles Nagy	.08
139	Jose Melendez	.08
140	Jim Abbott	.10
141	Paul Molitor	.40
142	Tom Candiotti	.08
143	Bobby Bonilla	.10
144	Matt Williams	.15
145	Brett Butler	.10
146	Will Clark	.30
147	Rickey Henderson	.25
148	Ray Lankford	.08
149	Bill Pecota	.08
150	Dave Winfield	.25
151	Darren Lewis	.08
152	Bob MacDonald	.08
153	David Segui	.10
154	Benny Santiago	.10
155	Chuck Finley	.08
156	Andujar Cedeno	.08
157	Barry Bonds	.65
158	Joe Grahe	.08
159	Frank Castillo	.08
160	Dave Burba	.08
161	Leo Gomez	.08
162	Orel Hershiser	.10
163	Delino DeShields	.15
164	Sandy Alomar	.15
165	Denny Neagle	.10
166	Fred McGriff	.30
167	Ken Griffey, Jr.	2.00
168	Juan Guzman	.10
169	Bobby Rose	.08
170	Steve Avery	.08
171	Rich DeLucia	.08
172	Mike Timlin	.08
173	Randy Johnson	.15
174	Paul Gibson	.08
175	David Cone	.10
176	Marquis Grissom	.15
177	Kurt Stillwell	.08
178	Mark Whiten	.10
179	Darryl Strawberry	.10
180	Mike Morgan	.08
181	Scott Scudder	.08
182	George Bell	.08
183	Alvin Davis	.08
184	Len Dykstra	.08
185	Kyle Abbott	.08
186	Chris Haney	.08
187	Junior Noboa	.08
188	Dennis Eckersley	.05
189	Derek Bell	.25
190	Lee Smith	.10
191	Andres Galarraga	.15
192	Jack Armstrong	.08
193	Eddie Murray	.25
194	Joe Carter	.20
195	Terry Pendleton	.08
196	Darryl Kile	.10
197	Rod Beck	.08
198	Hubie Brooks	.08

1993 O-Pee-Chee

For the first time in history, the 1993 O-Pee-Chee set differed significantly from the Topps set; photographs and designs are entirely different. Team names are scripted across the top, but a yellow triangle with a new team name appears on the front for players who have been traded. Two insert sets honoring the 1992 World Champion Toronto Blue Jays were also produced.

		MT
Complete Set (396):		37.50
Common Player:		.15
Wax Box:		30.00
1	Jim Abbott	.15
2	Eric Anthony	.15
3	Harold Baines	.15
4	Roberto Alomar	.65
5	Steve Avery	.15
6	James Austin	.15
7	Mark Wohlers	.15
8	Steve Buechele	.15
9	Pedro Astacio	.15
10	Moises Alou	.40
11	Rod Beck	.15
12	Sandy Alomar	.20
13	Brett Boone	.20
14	Bryan Harvey	.15
15	Bobby Bonilla	.20
16	Brady Anderson	.15
17	Andy Benes	.20
18	Ruben Amaro	.15
19	Jay Bell	.15
20	Kevin Brown	.25
21	Scott Bankhead	.15
22	Denis Boucher	.15
23	Kevin Appier	.15
24	Pat Kelly	.15
25	Rick Aguilera	.15
26	George Bell	.15
27	Steve Farr	.15
28	Chad Curtis	.20
29	Jeff Bagwell	.90
30	Lance Blankenship	.15
31	Derek Bell	.35
32	Damon Berryhill	.15
33	Ricky Bones	.15
34	Rheal Cormier	.15
35	Andre Dawson	.20
36	Brett Butler	.15
37	Sean Berry	.15
38	Bud Black	.15
39	Carlos Baerga	.15
40	Jay Buhner	.20
41	Charlie Hough	.15
42	Sid Fernandez	.15
43	Luis Mercedes	.15
44	Jerald Clark	.15
45	Wes Chamberlain	.15
46	Barry Bonds	.90
47	Jose Canseco	.50
48	Tim Belcher	.15
49	David Nied	.15
50	George Brett	1.50
51	Cecil Fielder	.50
52	Chili Davis	.15
53	Alex Fernandez	.20
54	Charlie Hayes	.15
55	Rob Ducey	.15
56	Craig Biggio	.25
57	Mike Bordick	.15
58	Pat Borders	.15
59	Jeff Blauser	.15
60	Chris Bosio	.15
61	Bernard Gilkey	.15
62	Shawon Dunston	.15
63	Tom Candiotti	.15
64	Darrin Fletcher	.15
65	Jeff Brantley	.15
66	Albert Belle	.75
67	Dave Fleming	.15
68	John Franco	.15
69	Glenn Davis	.15
70	Tony Fernandez	.15
71	Darren Daulton	.15
72	Doug Drabek	.15
73	Julio Franco	.15
74	Tom Browning	.15
75	Tom Gordon	.15
76	Travis Fryman	.15
77	Scott Erickson	.15
78	Carlton Fisk	.40
79	Roberto Kelly	.15
80	Gary DiSarcina	.15
81	Ken Caminiti	.20
82	Ron Darling	.15
83	Joe Carter	.20
84	Sid Bream	.15
85	Cal Eldred	.15
86	Mark Grace	.35
87	Eric Davis	.15
88	Ivan Calderon	.15
89	John Burkett	.15
90	Felix Fermin	.15
91	Ken Griffey Jr.	4.00
92	Doc Gooden	.20
93	Mike Devereaux	.15
94	Tony Gwynn	.75
95	Mariano Duncan	.15
96	Jeff King	.15
97	Juan Gonzalez	1.00
98	Norm Charlton	.15
99	Mark Gubicza	.15
100	Danny Gladden	.15
101	Greg Gagne	.15
102	Ozzie Guillen	.15
103	Don Mattingly	.90
104	Damion Easley	.15
105	Casey Candaele	.15
106	Dennis Eckersley	.20
107	David Cone	.15
108	Ron Gant	.20
109	Mike Fetters	.15
110	Mike Harkey	.15
111	Kevin Gross	.15
112	Archi Cianfrocco	.15
113	Will Clark	.50
114	Glenallen Hill	.15
115	Erik Hanson	.15
116	Todd Hundley	.15
117	Leo Gomez	.15
118	Bruce Hurst	.15
119	Len Dykstra	.15
120	Jose Lind	.15
121	Jose Guzman	.15
122	Rob Dibble	.15
123	Gregg Jefferies	.20
124	Bill Gulickson	.15
125	Brian Harper	.15
126	Roberto Hernandez	.15
127	Sam Militello	.15
128	Junior Felix	.15
129	Andujar Cedeno	.15
130	Rickey Henderson	.20
131	Bob MacDonald	.15
132	Tom Glavine	.20
133	Scott Fletcher	.15
134	Brian Jordan	.20
135	Greg Maddux	.90
136	Orel Hershiser	.20
137	Greg Colbrunn	.15
138	Royce Clayton	.15
139	Thomas Howard	.15
140	Randy Johnson	.30
141	Jeff Innis	.15
142	Chris Hoiles	.15
143	Darrin Jackson	.15
144	Tommy Greene	.15
145	Mike LaValliere	.15
146	David Hulse	.15
147	Barry Larkin	.20
148	Wally Joyner	.20
149	Mike Henneman	.15
150	Kent Hrbek	.15
151	Bo Jackson	.20
152	Rich Monteleone	.15
153	Chuck Finley	.15
154	Steve Finley	.15
155	Dave Henderson	.15
156	Kelly Gruber	.15
157	Brian Hunter	.15
158	Darryl Hamilton	.15
159	Derrick May	.15
160	Jay Howell	.15
161	Wil Cordero	.20
162	Bryan Hickerson	.15
163	Reggie Jefferson	.15
164	Edgar Martinez	.15
165	Nigel Wilson	.15
166	Howard Johnson	.15
167	Tim Hulett	.15
168	Mike Maddux	.15
169	Dave Hollins	.15
170	Zane Smith	.15
171	Rafael Palmeiro	.25
172	Dave Martinez	.15
173	Rusty Meacham	.15
174	Mark Leiter	.15
175	Chuck Knoblauch	.20
176	Lance Johnson	.15
177	Matt Nokes	.15
178	Luis Gonzalez	.15
179	Jack Morris	.15
180	David Justice	.40
181	Doug Henry	.15
182	Felix Jose	.15
183	Delino DeShields	.25
184	Rene Gonzales	.15
185	Pete Harnisch	.15
186	Mike Moore	.15
187	Juan Guzman	.15
188	John Olerud	.30
189	Ryan Klesko	.40
190	John Jaha	.15
191	Ray Lankford	.15
192	Jeff Fassero	.15
193	Darren Lewis	.15
194	Mark Lewis	.15
195	Alan Mills	.15
196	Wade Boggs	.50
197	Hal Morris	.15
198	Ron Karkovice	.15
199	John Grahe	.15
200	Butch Henry	.15
201	Mark McGwire	4.00
202	Tom Henke	.15
203	Ed Sprague	.15
204	Charlie Leibrandt	.15
205	Pat Listach	.15
206	Omar Olivares	.15
207	Mike Morgan	.15
208	Eric Karros	.15
209	Marquis Grissom	.25
210	Willie McGee	.15
211	Derek Lilliquist	.15
212	Tino Martinez	.20
213	Jeff Kent	.15
214	Mike Mussina	.25
215	Randy Myers	.15
216	John Kruk	.15
217	Tom Brunansky	.15
218	Paul O'Neill	.20
219	Scott Livingstone	.15
220	John Valentin	.15
221	Eddie Zosky	.15
222	Pete Smith	.15
223	Bill Wegman	.15
224	Todd Zeile	.15
225	Tim Wallach	.15
226	Mitch Williams	.15
227	Tim Wakefield	.15
228	Frank Viola	.15
229	Nolan Ryan	3.50
230	Kirk McCaskill	.15
231	Melido Perez	.15
232	Mark Langston	.15
233	Xavier Hernandez	.15
234	Jerry Browne	.15
235	Dave Stieb	.15
236	Mark Lemke	.15
237	Paul Molitor	.50
238	Geronimo Pena	.15
239	Ken Hill	.15
240	Jack Clark	.15
241	Greg Myers	.15
242	Pete Incaviglia	.15
243	Ruben Sierra	.15
244	Todd Stottlemyre	.15
245	Pat Hentgen	.15
246	Melvin Nieves	.15
247	Jaime Navarro	.15
248	Donovan Osborne	.15
249	Brian Barnes	.15
250	Cory Snyder	.15
251	Kenny Lofton	.50
252	Kevin Mitchell	.15
253	Dave Magadan	.15
254	Ben McDonald	.15
255	Fred McGriff	.40
256	Mickey Morandini	.15
257	Randy Tomlin	.15
258	Dean Palmer	.15
259	Roger Clemens	.75
260	Joe Oliver	.15

261	Jeff Montgomery	.15
262	Tony Phillips	.15
263	Shane Mack	.15
264	Jack McDowell	.15
265	Mike Macfarlane	.15
266	Luis Polonia	.15
267	Doug Jones	.15
268	Terry Steinbach	.15
269	Jimmy Key	.15
270	Pat Tabler	.15
271	Otis Nixon	.15
272	Dave Nilsson	.15
273	Tom Pagnozzi	.15
274	Ryne Sandberg	.75
275	Ramon Martinez	.20
276	Tim Laker	.15
277	Bill Swift	.15
278	Charles Nagy	.15
279	Harold Reynolds	.15
280	Eddie Murray	.25
281	Gregg Olson	.15
282	Frank Seminara	.15
283	Terry Mulholland	.15
284	Kevin Palmer	.15
285	Mike Greenwell	.15
286	Jose Rijo	.15
287	Brian McRae	.15
288	Frank Tanana	.15
289	Pedro Munoz	.15
290	Tim Raines	.20
291	Andy Stankiewicz	.15
292	Tim Salmon	1.50
293	Jimmy Jones	.15
294	Dave Stewart	.20
295	Mike Timlin	.15
296	Greg Olson	.15
297	Dan Plesac	.15
298	Mike Perez	.15
299	Jose Offerman	.20
300	Denny Martinez	.20
301	Robby Thompson	.15
302	Bret Saberhagen	.20
303	Joe Orsulak	.15
304	Tim Naehring	.15
305	Bip Roberts	.15
306	Kirby Puckett	.80
307	Steve Sax	.15
308	Danny Tartabull	.15
309	Jeff Juden	.15
310	Duane Ward	.15
311	Alejandro Pena	.15
312	Kevin Seitzer	.15
313	Ozzie Smith	.75
314	Mike Piazza	2.50
315	Chris Nabholz	.15
316	Tony Pena	.15
317	Gary Sheffield	.35
318	Mark Portugal	.15
319	Walt Weiss	.15
320	Manuel Lee	.15
321	David Wells	.25
322	Terry Pendleton	.15
323	Billy Spiers	.15
324	Lee Smith	.20
325	Bob Scanlan	.15
326	Mike Scioscia	.15
327	Spike Owen	.15
328	Mackey Sasser	.15
329	Arthur Rhodes	.15
330	Ben Rivera	.15
331	Ivan Rodriguez	.40
332	Phil Plantier	.15
333	Chris Sabo	.15
334	Mickey Tettleton	.15
335	John Smiley	.15
336	Bobby Thigpen	.15
337	Randy Velarde	.15
338	Luis Sojo	.15
339	Scott Servais	.15
340	Bob Welch	.15
341	Devon White	.20
342	Jeff Reardon	.15
343	B.J. Surhoff	.15
344	Bob Tewksbury	.15
345	Jose Vizcaino	.15
346	Mike Sharperson	.15
347	Mel Rojas	.20
348	Matt Williams	.45
349	Steve Olin	.15
350	Mike Schooler	.15
351	Ryan Thompson	.20
352	Cal Ripken	3.00
353	Benny Santiago	.15
354	Curt Schilling	.15
355	Andy Van Slyke	.15
356	Kenny Rogers	.15
357	Jody Reed	.15
358	Reggie Sanders	.15
359	Kevin McReynolds	.15
360	Alan Trammell	.20
361	Kevin Tapani	.15
362	Frank Thomas	1.50
363	Bernie Williams	.40
364	John Smoltz	.20
365	Robin Yount	.40
366	John Wetteland	.15
367	Bob Zupcic	.15
368	Julio Valera	.15
369	Brian Williams	.15
370	Willie Wilson	.15
371	Dave Winfield	.40
372	Deion Sanders	.45
373	Greg Vaughn	.25
374	Todd Worrell	.15
375	Darryl Strawberry	.20
376	John Vander Wal	.20
377	Mike Benjamin	.15
378	Mark Whiten	.15
379	Omar Vizquel	.15
380	Anthony Young	.15
381	Rick Sutcliffe	.15
382	Candy Maldonado	.15
383	Francisco Cabrera	.15
384	Larry Walker	.25
385	Scott Cooper	.15
386	Gerald Williams	.15
387	Robin Ventura	.20
388	Carl Willis	.15
389	Lou Whitaker	.15
390	Hipolito Pichardo	.15
391	Rudy Seanez	.15
392	Greg Swindell	.15
393	Mo Vaughn	.50
394	Checklist 1 of 3	.15
395	Checklist 2 of 3	.15
396	Checklist 3 of 3	.15

1993 O-Pee-Chee World Champs

This 18-card insert set commemorates the Toronto Blue Jays' 1992 World Series victory; seventeen players and Manager Cito Gaston are featured. Cards were randomly inserted, one World Champs or World Series Heroes card per every 69-cent, eight-card pack. Fronts and backs each feature the World's Championship logo. Backs include stats from the 1992 ALCS and World Series.

		MT
Complete Set (18):		7.00
Common Player:		.25
1	Roberto Alomar	1.00
2	Pat Borders	.30
3	Joe Carter	.65
4	David Cone	.50
5	Kelly Gruber	.25
6	Juan Guzman	.35
7	Tom Henke	.25
8	Jimmy Key	.50
9	Manuel Lee	.25
10	Candy Maldonado	.25
11	Jack Morris	.35
12	John Olerud	.60
13	Ed Sprague	.30
14	Todd Stottlemyre	.25
15	Duane Ward	.35
16	Devon White	.40
17	Dave Winfield	.75
18	Cito Gaston	.35

1993 O-Pee-Chee World Series Heroes

This insert set honors four of the Toronto Blue Jays' World Series stars. Cards were randomly inserted in every 69-cent, eight-card pack, one World Champs or World Series Heroes card per pack.

		MT
Complete Set (4):		2.00
Common Player:		.50
1	Pat Borders	.50
2	Jimmy Key	.75
3	Ed Sprague	.50
4	Dave Winfield	1.00

1993 O-Pee-Chee Premier

For the third consecutive year, O-Pee-Chee produced a set under its Premier brand name. The regular set, issued in three series, has 132 cards and 48 insert cards. The insert sets are titled Star Performers (gold borders), Foil Star Performers (full-bleed photos and gold stamping), and Top Draft Picks (two each featuring the Toronto Blue Jays and Montreal Expos top picks). O-Pee-Chee announced it produced only 4,000 cases for this set.

		MT
Complete Set (132):		8.00
Common Player:		.10
Wax Box:		10.00
1	Barry Bonds	.75
2	Chad Curtis	.10
3	Chris Bosio	.10
4	Cal Eldred	.10
5	Dan Walter	.10
6	Rene Arocha	.10
7	Delino DeShields	.10
8	Spike Owen	.10
9	Jeff Russell	.10
10	Phil Plantier	.10
11	Mike Christopher	.10
12	Darren Daulton	.10
13	Scott Cooper	.10
14	Paul O'Neill	.15
15	Jimmy Key	.10
16	Dickie Thon	.10
17	Greg Gohr	.10
18	Andre Dawson	.15
19	Steve Cooke	.10
20	Tony Fernandez	.10
21	Mark Gardner	.10
22	Dave Martinez	.10
23	Jose Guzman	.10
24	Chili Davis	.10
25	Randy Knorr	.10
26	Mike Piazza	1.50
27	Benji Gil	.10
28	Dave Winfield	.30
29	Wil Cordero	.15
30	Butch Henry	.10
31	Eric Young	.10
32	Orestes Destrade	.10
33	Randy Myers	.10
34	Tom Brunansky	.10
35	Dan Wilson	.10
36	Juan Guzman	.15
37	Tim Salmon	.40
38	Bill Krueger	.10
39	Larry Walker	.25
40	David Hulse	.10
41	Ken Ryan	.10
42	Jose Lind	.10
43	Benny Santiago	.10
44	Ray Lankford	.10
45	Dave Stewart	.10
46	Don Mattingly	.50
47	Fernando Valenzuela	.10
48	Scott Fletcher	.10
49	Wade Boggs	.25
50	Norm Charlton	.10
51	Carlos Baerga	.10
52	John Olerud	.25
53	Willie Wilson	.10
54	Dennis Moeller	.10
55	Joe Orsulak	.10
56	John Smiley	.10
57	Al Martin	.10
58	Andres Galarraga	.15
59	Billy Ripken	.10
60	Dave Stieb	.10
61	Dave Magadan	.10
62	Todd Worrell	.10
63	Sherman Obando	.10
64	Kent Bottenfield	.10
65	Vinny Castilla	.25
66	Charlie Hayes	.10
67	Mike Hartley	.10
68	Harold Baines	.10
69	John Cummings	.10
70	J.T. Snow	.20
71	Graeme Lloyd	.10
72	Frank Bolick	.10
73	Doug Drabek	.10
74	Milt Thompson	.10
75	Tim Pugh	.10
76	John Kruk	.10
77	Tom Henke	.10
78	Kevin Young	.10
79	Ryan Thompson	.15
80	Mike Hampton	.10
81	Jose Canseco	.40
82	Mike Lansing	.15
83	Candy Maldonado	.10
84	Alex Arias	.10
85	Troy Neel	.10
86	Greg Swindell	.10
87	Tim Wallach	.10
88	Andy Van Slyke	.10
89	Harold Baines	.10
90	Bryan Harvey	.10
91	Jerald Clark	.10
92	David Cone	.15
93	Ellis Burks	.10
94	Scott Bankhead	.10
95	Pete Incaviglia	.10
96	Cecil Fielder	.15
97	Sean Berry	.10
98	Gregg Jefferies	.15
99	Billy Brewer	.10
100	Scott Sanderson	.10
101	Walt Weiss	.10
102	Travis Fryman	.10
103	Barry Larkin	.10
104	Darren Holmes	.10
105	Ivan Calderon	.10
106	Terry Jorgensen	.10
107	David Nied	.10
108	Tim Bogar	.10
109	Roberto Kelly	.10
110	Mike Moore	.10
111	Carlos Garcia	.10
112	Mike Bielecki	.10
113	Trevor Hoffman	.10
114	Rich Amaral	.10
115	Jody Reed	.10
116	Charlie Leibrandt	.10
117	Greg Gagne	.10
118	Darrell Sherman	.10
119	Jeff Conine	.10
120	Tim Laker	.10
121	Kevin Seitzer	.10
122	Jeff Mutis	.10
123	Rico Rossy	.10
124	Paul Molitor	.50
125	Cal Ripken	2.00
126	Greg Maddux	1.50
127	Greg McMichael	.10
128	Felix Jose	.10
129	Dick Schofield	.10
130	Jim Abbott	.10
131	Kevin Reimer	.10
132	Checklist	.10

1993 O-Pee-Chee Premier Star Performers

O-Pee-Chee released a 22-card insert set in two forms: Star Performers (featuring a gold border design) and Foil Star Performers (featuring full-bleed photos and gold stamping). The players are identical in both sets, but foil cards are generally worth more. There are 34 Star Performers per 36-card wax box and one Foil Star Performer card per box.

		MT
Complete Set (22):		7.50
Common Player:		.10
1	Frank Thomas	1.00
2	Fred McGriff	.20
3	Roberto Alomar	.35
4	Ryne Sandberg	.40
6	Gary Sheffield	.25
7	Juan Gonzalez	.65
8	Eric Karros	.15
9	Ken Griffey, Jr.	2.00
10	Deion Sanders	.15
11	Kirby Puckett	.50
12	Will Clark	.20
13	Joe Carter	.15
14	Barry Bonds	.65
15	Pat Listach	.10
16	Mark McGwire	2.00
17	Kenny Lofton	.20
18	Roger Clemens	.50
19	Greg Maddux	1.00
20	Nolan Ryan	1.50
21	Tom Glavine	.10
22	Checklist	.05

1993 O-Pee-Chee Premier Star Performers Foil

O-Pee-Chee released a 22-card insert set in two forms: Star Performers (featuring a gold border design) and Foil Star Performers (featuring full-bleed photos and gold stamping). The players are identical in both sets, but foil cards are generally worth more. There are 34 Star Performers per 36-card wax box and one Foil Star Performer card per box.

		MT
Complete Set (22):		250.00
Common Player:		2.50
1	Frank Thomas	25.00
2	Fred McGriff	7.50
3	Roberto Alomar	7.50
4	Ryne Sandberg	10.00
6	Gary Sheffield	7.50
7	Juan Gonzalez	15.00
8	Eric Karros	3.00
9	Ken Griffey, Jr.	55.00
10	Deion Sanders	3.00
11	Kirby Puckett	12.00
12	Will Clark	7.50
13	Joe Carter	2.50
14	Barry Bonds	25.00
15	Pat Listach	2.50
16	Mark McGwire	50.00
17	Kenny Lofton	7.50
18	Roger Clemens	15.00
19	Greg Maddux	35.00
20	Nolan Ryan	45.00
21	Tom Glavine	3.00
22	Checklist	.50

1993 O-Pee-Chee Premier Top Draft Picks

These randomly inserted cards feature four prospects; two each for Montreal and Toronto. Card fronts are foil-stamped and have a vertical banner with the player's name. The OPC Premier logo is in the corner. On back is another player photo, a team logo and a bilingual rationale for the player's draft status.

		MT
Complete Set (4):		4.00
Common Player:		1.00
1	B.J. Wallace	1.00
2	Shannon Stewart	1.50
3	Rod Henderson	1.00
4	Todd Steverson	1.00

1994 O-Pee-Chee Sample Sheet

The basic '94 OPC card set and all of its chase card sets were previewed on this sample sheet sent to dealers. Measuring 8" x 11", the sheet's card vary slightly from issued cards in terms of foil highlights. Card fronts on the sample sheet are highlighted in red foil while there is no foil on the backs. Each of the card backs (except the jumbo All-Star) includes the notation "Pre-Production Sample."

		MT
Complete Sheet:		12.00
Complete Set (9):		9.00
Common Player:		2.00
0	Paul Molitor (Blue Jays insert)	6.00
5	Carlos Delgado (Hot Prospects)	4.00
9	Mike Piazza (jumbo All-Stars)	6.00
12	Jeff Conine (Diamond Dynamos)	2.00
14	Jack McDowell (All-Star)	2.00
123	Darren Daulton	2.00

1994 O-Pee-Chee

Limited to 2,500 cases (about 112,000 of each card in the regular 270-card set) the '94 OPC issue features color photos on front and back along with complete major league stats (and some minor league stats) on back. Team names are in a color-coded strip at left. Career summaries and some other data are printed in both English and French.

		MT
Complete Set (270):		18.00
Common Player:		.05
Wax Box:		30.00
1	Paul Molitor	.45
2	Kirt Manwaring	.05
3	Brady Anderson	.05
4	Scott Cooper	.05
5	Kevin Stocker	.05
6	Alex Fernandez	.15
7	Jeff Montgomery	.05
8	Danny Tartabull	.05
9	Damion Easley	.05
10	Andujar Cedeno	.05
11	Steve Karsay	.05
12	Dave Stewart	.10
13	Fred McGriff	.25
14	Jaime Navarro	.05
15	Allen Watson	.05
16	Ryne Sandberg	.75
17	Arthur Rhodes	.05
18	Marquis Grissom	.15
19	John Burkett	.05
20	Robby Thompson	.05
21	Denny Martinez	.10
22	Ken Griffey, Jr.	3.00
23	Orestes Destrade	.05
24	Dwight Gooden	.10
25	Rafael Palmeiro	.20
26	Pedro Martinez	.25
27	Wes Chamberlain	.05
28	Juan Gonzalez	1.00
29	Kevin Mitchell	.05
30	Dante Bichette	.25
31	Howard Johnson	.05
32	Mickey Tettleton	.05
33	Robin Ventura	.10
34	Terry Mulholland	.05
35	Bernie Williams	.40
36	Eduardo Perez	.05
37	Rickey Henderson	.15
38	Terry Pendleton	.05
39	John Smoltz	.10
40	Derrick May	.05
41	Pedro Martinez	.25
42	Mark Portugal	.05
43	Albert Belle	.60
44	Edgar Martinez	.05
45	Gary Sheffield	.20
46	Bret Saberhagen	.10
47	Ricky Gutierrez	.05
48	Orlando Merced	.05
49	Mike Greenwell	.05
50	Jose Rijo	.05
51	Jeff Granger	.05
52	Mike Henneman	.05
53	Dave Winfield	.15
54	Don Mattingly	.90
55	J.T. Snow	.20
56	Todd Van Poppel	.10
57	Chipper Jones	2.00
58	Darryl Hamilton	.05
59	Delino DeShields	.10
60	Rondell White	.15
61	Eric Anthony	.05
62	Charlie Hough	.05
63	Sid Fernandez	.05
64	Derek Bell	.15
65	Phil Plantier	.05
66	Curt Schilling	.10
67	Roger Clemens	.65
68	Jose Lind	.05
69	Andres Galarraga	.15
70	Tim Belcher	.05
71	Ron Karkovice	.05
72	Alan Trammell	.10
73	Pete Harnisch	.05
74	Mark McGwire	3.00
75	Ryan Klesko	.25
76	Ramon Martinez	.10
77	Gregg Jefferies	.10
78	Steve Buechele	.05
79	Bill Swift	.05
80	Matt Williams	.20
81	Randy Johnson	.25
82	Mike Mussina	.20
83	Andy Benes	.10
84	Dave Staton	.05
85	Steve Cooke	.05
86	Andy Van Slyke	.05
87	Ivan Rodriguez	.50
88	Frank Viola	.05
89	Aaron Sele	.10
90	Ellis Burks	.05
91	Wally Joyner	.10
92	Rick Aguilera	.05
93	Kirby Puckett	1.00
94	Roberto Hernandez	.05
95	Mike Stanley	.05
96	Roberto Alomar	.40
97	James Mouton	.05
98	Chad Curtis	.05
99	Mitch Williams	.05
100	Carlos Delgado	.40
101	Greg Maddux	2.00
102	Brian Harper	.05
103	Tom Pagnozzi	.05
104	Jose Offerman	.05
105	John Wetteland	.05
106	Carlos Baerga	.05
107	Dave Madagan	.05
108	Bobby Jones	.10
109	Tony Gwynn	1.00
110	Jeromy Burnitz	.05
111	Bip Roberts	.05
112	Carlos Garcia	.05
113	Jeff Russell	.05
114	Armando Reynoso	.05
115	Ozzie Guillen	.05
116	Bo Jackson	.20
117	Terry Steinbach	.05
118	Deion Sanders	.35
119	Randy Myers	.05
120	Mark Whiten	.05
121	Manny Ramirez	.75
122	Ben McDonald	.05
123	Darren Daulton	.05
124	Kevin Young	.10
125	Barry Larkin	.10
126	Cecil Fielder	.15
127	Frank Thomas	1.50
128	Luis Polonia	.05
129	Steve Finley	.05
130	John Olerud	.20
131	John Jaha	.05
132	Darren Lewis	.05
133	Orel Hershiser	.10
134	Chris Bosio	.05
135	Ryan Thompson	.05
136	Chris Sabo	.05
137	Tommy Greene	.05
138	Andre Dawson	.15
139	Bobby Kelly	.05
140	Ken Hill	.05
141	Greg Gagne	.05
142	Julio Franco	.05
143	Chili Davis	.05
144	Dennis Eckersley	.10
145	Joe Carter	.15
146	Mark Grace	.20
147	Mike Piazza	2.00
148	J.R. Phillips	.05
149	Rich Amaral	.05
150	Benny Santiago	.05
151	Jeff King	.05
152	Dean Palmer	.05
153	Hal Morris	.05
154	Mike MacFarlane	.05
155	Chuck Knoblauch	.10
156	Pat Kelly	.05
157	Greg Swindell	.05
158	Chuck Finley	.05
159	Devon White	.15
160	Duane Ward	.05
161	Sammy Sosa	1.00
162	Javier Lopez	.10
163	Eric Karros	.10
164	Royce Clayton	.05
165	Salomon Torres	.05
166	Jeff Kent	.05
167	Chris Hoiles	.05
168	Len Dykstra	.05
169	Jose Canseco	.25
170	Bret Boone	.10
171	Charlie Hayes	.05
172	Lou Whitaker	.05
173	Jack McDowell	.05
174	Jimmy Key	.05
175	Mark Langston	.05
176	Darryl Kile	.05
177	Juan Guzman	.10
178	Pat Borders	.05
179	Cal Eldred	.05
180	Jose Guzman	.05
181	Ozzie Smith	.40
182	Rod Beck	.05
183	Dave Fleming	.05
184	Eddie Murray	.35
185	Cal Ripken	2.50
186	Dave Hollins	.05
187	Will Clark	.25
188	Otis Nixon	.05
189	Joe Oliver	.05
190	Roberto Mejia	.05
191	Felix Jose	.05
192	Tony Phillips	.05
193	Wade Boggs	.25
194	Tim Salmon	.30
195	Ruben Sierra	.05
196	Steve Avery	.05
197	B.J. Surhoff	.05
198	Todd Zeile	.05
(199)	Raul Mondesi (no card number on back)	.50
200	Barry Bonds	.75
201	Sandy Alomar	.10
202	Bobby Bonilla	.10
203	Mike Devereaux	.05
204	Rickey Bottalico	.05
205	Kevin Brown	.10
206	Jason Bere	.10
207	Reggie Sanders	.10
208	David Nied	.05
209	Travis Fryman	.10
210	James Baldwin	.10
211	Jim Abbott	.10
212	Jeff Bagwell	.75
213	Bob Welch	.05
214	Jeff Blauser	.05
215	Brett Butler	.05
216	Pat Listach	.05
217	Bob Tewksbury	.05
218	Mike Lansing	.10
219	Wayne Kirby	.05
220	Chuck Carr	.05
221	Harold Baines	.05
222	Jay Bell	.05
223	Cliff Floyd	.20
224	Rob Dibble	.05
225	Kevin Appier	.05
226	Eric Davis	.05
227	Matt Walbeck	.05
228	Tim Raines	.15
229	Paul O'Neill	.10
230	Craig Biggio	.10
231	Brent Gates	.10
232	Rob Butler	.05
233	Dave Justice	.35
234	Rene Arocha	.05
235	Mike Morgan	.05
236	Denis Boucher	.05
237	Kenny Lofton	.40
238	Jeff Conine	.10
239	Bryan Harvey	.05
240	Danny Jackson	.05
241	Al Martin	.05
242	Tom Henke	.05
243	Erik Hanson	.05
244	Walt Weiss	.05
245	Brian McRae	.05
246	Kevin Tapani	.05
247	David McCarty	.05
248	Doug Drabek	.05
249	Troy Neel	.05
250	Tom Glavine	.10
251	Ray Lankford	.05
252	Wil Cordero	.10
253	Larry Walker	.25
254	Charles Nagy	.05
255	Kirk Rueter	.05
256	John Franco	.05
257	John Kruk	.05
258	Alex Gonzalez	.15
259	Mo Vaughn	.40
260	David Cone	.05
261	Kent Hrbek	.10
262	Lance Johnson	.05
263	Luis Gonzalez	.05
264	Mike Bordick	.05
265	Ed Sprague	.05
266	Moises Alou	.15
267	Omar Vizquel	.05
268	Jay Buhner	.10
269	Checklist	.05
270	Checklist	.05

1994 O-Pee-Chee All-Star Redemption Cards

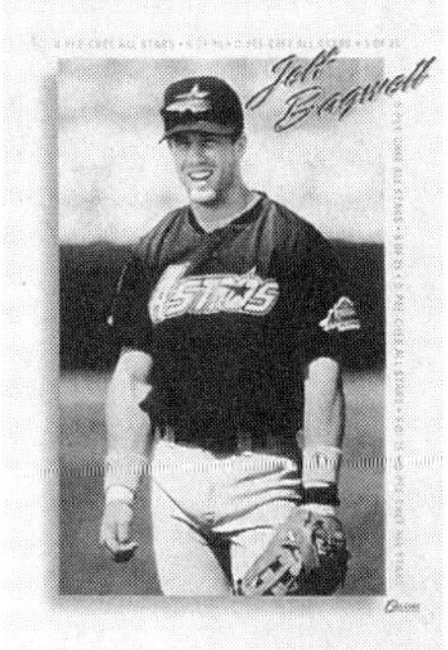

A series of 25 All-Star redemption cards was one of the several inserts which were found at the rate of one per pack in '94 OPC foil. Fronts feature a color photo floating over a white background. The player's name is displayed in gold script at top and the card number is repeated along the top and left or right of the photo. Backs have information on how to redeem the cards for a super-size version of the set. Approximately 78,000 of each of the 25 cards in the insert set were produced.

		MT
Complete Set (25):		15.00
Common Player:		1.00
1	Frank Thomas	2.00
2	Paul Molitor	2.50
3	Barry Bonds	3.00
4	Juan Gonzalez	3.00
5	Jeff Bagwell	3.00
6	Carlos Baerga	1.00
7	Ryne Sandberg	1.50
8	Ken Griffey, Jr.	5.00
9	Mike Piazza	4.00
10	Tim Salmon	1.00
11	Marquis Grissom	1.00
12	Albert Belle	2.00
13	Fred McGriff	1.50
14	Jack McDowell	1.00
14p	Jack McDowell ("Pre-Production Sample")	2.00
15	Cal Ripken, Jr.	5.00
16	John Olerud	1.50
17	Kirby Puckett	3.00
18	Roger Clemens	3.00
19	Larry Walker	2.00
20	Cecil Fielder	1.00
21	Roberto Alomar	1.50
22	Greg Maddux	2.50
23	Joe Carter	1.00
24	Dave Justice	1.00
25	Kenny Lofton	1.00

1994 O-Pee-Chee Diamond Dynamos

"Baseball's brightest new stars" was the stated criteria for inclusion in this chase card set. Fronts feature a full-bleed action photo with the player's name and "Diamond Dynamos" logo at bottom in red foil. Backs have a second player photo, personal data, a bi-lingual career summary and gold-foil presentation of the player's name and "Twenty-first Century Stars." An average of 1-2 of the cards was inserted per foil box, creating a production run of 5,000 of each card.

		MT
Complete Set (18):		16.00
Common Player:		.75
1	Mike Piazza	7.50
2	Roberto Mejia	.75
3	Wayne Kirby	.75
4	Kevin Stocker	.75
5	Chris Gomez	.75
6	Bobby Jones	.75
7	David McCarty	.75
8	Kirk Rueter	.75
9	J.T. Snow	2.00
10	Wil Cordero	1.00
11	Tim Salmon	3.00
12	Jeff Conine	1.00
13	Jason Bere	.75
14	Greg McMichael	.75
15	Brent Gates	.75
16	Allen Watson	.75
17	Aaron Sele	.75
18	Carlos Garcia	.75

1994 O-Pee-Chee Hot Prospects

Nine of 1994's hottest rookies are featured in this insert set. Fronts feature full-bleed photos with the player's name in gold foil at bottom. An "O-Pee-Chee Hot Prospects" logo appears in an upper corner. Backs are in shades of red, yellow and orange and include another player photo, biographical data, a career summary and complete minor league stats.

		MT
Complete Set (9):		15.00
Common Player:		.50
1	Cliff Floyd	1.50
2	James Mouton	.50
3	Salomon Torres	.50
4	Raul Mondesi	2.00
5	Carlos Delgado	1.50
6	Manny Ramirez	3.00
7	Javier Lopez	2.00
8	Alex Gonzalez	1.50
9	Ryan Klesko	2.00

Player names in *Italic* type indicate a rookie card.

1994 O-Pee-Chee Jumbo All-Stars

Each of the 60,000 foil-pack boxes of '94 OPC contained one jumbo (5" x 7") All-Star card from a set of 25. Fronts are identical to the All-Star redemption card inserts found in foil packs, with a UV coating. Backs are blank. Each of the jumbo All-Stars was produced in a quantity of 2,400.

		MT
Complete Set (25):		150.00
Common Player:		3.25
1	Frank Thomas	10.00
2	Paul Molitor	6.00
3	Barry Bonds	8.00
4	Juan Gonzalez	10.00
5	Jeff Bagwell	5.00
6	Carlos Baerga	3.00
7	Ryne Sandberg	6.50
8	Ken Griffey, Jr.	20.00
9	Mike Piazza	12.00
10	Tim Salmon	4.00
11	Marquis Grissom	3.00
12	Albert Belle	4.00
13	Fred McGriff	4.00
14	Jack McDowell	3.00
15	Cal Ripken	18.00
16	John Olerud	3.50
17	Kirby Puckett	8.00
18	Roger Clemens	7.50
19	Larry Walker	4.00
20	Cecil Fielder	3.00
21	Roberto Alomar	4.00
22	Greg Maddux	12.00
23	Joe Carter	3.00
24	Dave Justice	4.00
25	Kenny Lofton	3.00

1994 O-Pee-Chee Jumbo All-Stars Factory Set

A special gold-foil enhanced edition of the jumbo All-Stars cards was made available via a mail-in redemption program. By sending in five of the pack-insert All-Star cards and $20, a collector could receive a specially boxed factory set from a limited edition of 5,000.

		MT
Complete Set (25):		45.00
Common Player:		4.00
1	Frank Thomas	6.50
2	Paul Molitor	5.00
3	Barry Bonds	6.00
4	Juan Gonzalez	6.00
5	Jeff Bagwell	5.00
6	Carlos Baerga	3.00
7	Ryne Sandberg	4.00
8	Ken Griffey, Jr.	10.00
9	Mike Piazza	7.00
10	Tim Salmon	3.00
11	Marquis Grissom	3.00
12	Albert Belle	3.00
13	Fred McGriff	3.00
14	Jack McDowell	3.00
15	Cal Ripken, Jr.	8.00
16	John Olerud	3.50
17	Kirby Puckett	5.00
18	Roger Clemens	5.00
19	Larry Walker	4.00
20	Cecil Fielder	3.00
21	Roberto Alomar	3.00
22	Greg Maddux	7.00
23	Joe Carter	3.00
24	Dave Justice	3.00
25	Kenny Lofton	3.00

1994 O-Pee-Chee Toronto Blue Jays

The Blue Jays' starting line-up for the final game of the 1993 World Series is honored on this insert set. Fronts have a blue typographic background of "World Series Champions '92 & '93." There is a color player photo with his name in red foil at bottom. Backs repeat the typographic background in black and include 1992 and 1993 World Series stats along with the player's Series highlights in both English and French. A gold-foil seal marking the back-to-back championships is at top center. Stated odds of finding a Blue Jays insert card are one per foil box, indicating a production of about 6,666 of each card.

		MT
Complete Set (9):		12.00
Common Player:		1.00
1	Rickey Henderson	2.00
2	Devon White	1.00
3	Paul Molitor	4.00
4	Joe Carter	1.50
5	John Olerud	2.00
6	Roberto Alomar	3.00
7	Ed Sprague	1.00
8	Pat Borders	1.00
9	Tony Fernandez	1.00

1987 Oakland Athletics Fire Safety

The 1987 Smokey Bear A's set is not comparable to earlier Forestry Service issues. The cards are bound together in a book titled "Smokey Bear's Fire Prevention Color-Grams." Each Color-Gram features two cards in one. A near-standard size (2-1/2" x 3-3/4") black-and-white card is attached to a large perforated (3-3/4" x 6") card, also black-and-white. The large card, which has a postcard back, features a caricature of the player and is intended to be colored and mailed. Backs contain personal and statistical information and carry a Smokey the Bear cartoon fire safety message. The books were distributed at an A's game during the 1987 season.

		MT
Complete Book:		6.00
Complete Singles Set (12):		3.00
Common Player:		.25
(1)	Joaquin Andujar	.25
(2)	Jose Canseco	1.50
(3)	Mike Davis	.25
(4)	Alfredo Griffin	.25
(5)	Moose Haas	.25
(6)	Jay Howell	.25
(7)	Reggie Jackson	1.50
(8)	Carney Lansford	.25
(9)	Dwayne Murphy	.25
(10)	Tony Phillips	.25
(11)	Dave Stewart	.50
(12)	Curt Young	.25

1992 Oakland A's Dream Team

Following fan balloting in 1991, the Oakland A's named an all-time Dream Team for their 25th anniversary season in 1992 and issued a card set of those players. Cards were distributed in two versions. Perforated sheets of eight cards each were included in the second and third editions of the team's magazine. Imperforate four-card strips were also handed out to the first 10,000 fans attending each of four selected home games in 1992. Cards measure 2-9/16" x 3-3/4". Fronts have gray borders. At upper-left is a green and yellow Dream Team pennant; a 25th anniversary logo at lower-right is also in team colors. A red box beneath the color player photo has the name and position in red and white. Black-and-white backs have uniform and card numbers, career stats and highlights and a few biographical bits.

		MT
Complete Set (16):		45.00
Common Player:		2.00
1	Mark McGwire	12.00
2	Mike Gallego	2.00
3	Bert Campaneris	2.00
4	Carney Lansford	2.00
5	Reggie Jackson	7.50
6	Rickey Henderson	5.00
7	Jose Canseco	6.00
8	Dave Parker	3.00
9	Terry Steinbach	2.00
10	Dave Stewart	2.50
11	Jim "Catfish" Hunter	4.00
12	Vida Blue	2.00
13	Bob Welch	2.00
14	Dennis Eckersley	4.00
15	Rollie Fingers	4.00
16	Tony LaRussa	2.00

1999 Generation '99 A's

Borrowing from the concept used for many years by Mother's Cookies, this team set was designed to encourage trading when it was distributed to 15,000 fans on May 2. Cards were given away in shrink-wrapped packs of 28, containing 20 single cards and eight of one of the others. Sponsored by a trade union, the Plumbers Steamfitters Refrigeration Local 342, the set has color photos on front, surrounded by borders which morph from yellow to dark green. A "Generation '99 A's" logo is at lower-left. Backs have minimal player data.

		MT
Complete Set (28):		15.00
Common Player:		.25
1	Art Howe	.25
2	Ben Grieve	3.00
3	Jason Giambi	1.50
4	Kenny Rogers	.25
5	Matt Stairs	.50
6	Tom Candiotti	.25
7	Tony Phillips	.35
8	Eric Chavez	2.50
9	Tim Raines	1.50
10	A.J. Hinch	1.00
11	Bill Taylor	.25
12	Miguel Tejada	.75
13	Tim Worrell	.25
14	Scott Spezio	.25
15	Buddy Groom	.25
16	Olmedo Saenz	.25
17	T.J. Mathews	.25
18	Mike Macfarlane	.25
19	Brad Rigby	.25
20	Ryan Christenson	.25
21	Doug Jones	.25
22	Terry Clark	.25
23	Jorge Velandia	.25
24	Gil Heredia	.25
25	John Jaha	.35
26	Jimmy Haynes	.25
27	Jason McDonald	.50
28	A's coaches/checklist (Thad Bosley, Brad Fischer, Dave Hudgens, Ken Macha, Rick Peterson, Ron	.25

1983 O'Connell & Son Ink Baseball Greats

This set of 4-1/2" x 6-1/2" blank-back cards features the artwork of T.S. O'Connell done in the style of 1959 Topps cards. Player portraits are in black-and-white, while backgrounds and team logos are in color. Production was limited to 2,000 sets.

		MT
Complete Set (20):		50.00
Common Player:		1.00
(1)	Hank Aaron	6.00
(2)	Johnny Bench	2.00
(3)	Yogi Berra	3.00
(4)	George Brett	4.00
(5)	Roy Campanella	3.00
(6)	Rod Carew	2.00
(7)	Roberto Clemente	10.00
(8)	Bob Gibson	1.00
(9)	Al Kaline	3.00
(10)	Mickey Mantle	12.00
(11)	Joe Morgan	1.00
(12)	Stan Musial	3.00
(13)	Jim Rice	1.00
(14)	Frank Robinson	2.00
(15)	Pete Rose	6.00
(16)	Tom Seaver	2.00
(17)	Duke Snider	2.00
(18)	Honus Wagner	1.00
(19)	Carl Yastrzemski	2.00
(20)	Robin Yount	2.00

1984-91 O'Connell & Son Ink Mini Prints

This series of 2-1/2" x 3-1/2" blank-backed cards was issued over the period of 1984-91. Cards #1-180 were sold in annual series of 36 each from 1984-88; the 21-card Sixth Series was issued in 1990. The final 43 cards, plus unnumbered checklists for the fist six series were distributed in issues of the company's newsletter, "The Infield Dirt." All cards feature black-and-white pen-and-ink player portraits by T.S. O'Connell and have only the player name and card number on front. Several styles of background, some in color, are found among the various series. Production was limited to 2,000 of each card.

		MT
Complete Set (250):		145.00
Common Player:		.75
	First Series	15.00
1	Ted Williams	2.50
2	Minnie Minoso	.75
3	Sandy Koufax	3.00
4	Al Kaline	.75
5	Whitey Ford	.75
6	Wade Boggs	1.00
7	Nolan Ryan	4.00
9	Greg Luzinski	.75
10	Cal Ripken	4.00
11	Carl Yastrzemski	1.00
12	Dale Murphy	.75
13	Rocky Colavito	1.00
14	George Brett	1.50
15	Rod Carew	.75
16	Bob Gibson	.75
17	Robin Yount	1.00
18	Steve Carlton	.75
19	Harmon Killebrew	.75
20	Willie Mays	2.50
21	Reggie Jackson	1.00
22	Eddie Mathews	.75
23	Eddie Murray	.75
24	Johnny Bench	.75
25	Mickey Mantle	6.00

26	Willie Stargell	.75
27	Rickey Henderson	.75
28	Roger Maris	2.50
29	Darryl Strawberry	.75
30	Pete Rose	3.00
31	Jim Rice	.75
32	Thurman Munson	1.00
33	Brooks Robinson	.75
34	Fernando Valenzuela	.75
35	Tony Oliva	.75
36	Hank Aaron	2.50
	Second Series	15.00
37	Joe Morgan	.75
38	Kent Hrbek	.75
39	Yogi Berra	1.00
40	Stan Musial	2.50
41	Gary Matthews	.75
42	Larry Doby	.75
43	Steve Garvey	.75
44	Bob Horner	.75
45	Ron Guidry	.75
46	Ernie Banks	1.00
47	Carlton Fisk	.75
48	"Pee Wee" Reese	.75
49	Bobby Shantz	.75
50	Joe DiMaggio	4.00
51	Enos Slaughter	.75
52	Gary Carter	.75
53	Bob Feller	.75
54	Phil Rizzuto	.75
55	Dave Concepcion	.75
56	Ron Kittle	.75
57	Dwight Evans	.75
58	Johnny Mize	.75
59	Richie Ashburn	.75
60	Roberto Clemente	4.00
61	Fred Lynn	.75
62	Billy Williams	.75
63	Dave Winfield	.75
64	Robin Roberts	.75
65	Billy Martin	.75
66	Duke Snider	1.00
67	Luis Aparicio	.75
68	Mickey Vernon	.75
69	Mike Schmidt	1.00
70	Frank Robinson	.75
71	Bill Madlock	.75
72	Rollie Fingers	.75
	Third Series	15.00
73	Rod Carew	.75
74	Carl Erskine	.75
75	Lou Brock	.75
76	Brooks Robinson	.75
77	Roberto Clemente	4.00
78	Nellie Fox	.75
79	Bud Harrelson	.75
80	Ted Williams	2.50
81	Walter Johnson	.75
82	Cal Ripken	4.00
83	Lefty Grove	.75
84	Lou Whitaker	.75
85	Johnny Bench	.75
86	Ty Cobb	2.00
87	Mike Schmidt	1.00
88	George Brett	1.50
89	Jim Bunning	.75
90	Babe Ruth	4.00
91	Satchel Paige	1.00
92	Warren Spahn	.75
93	Dale Murphy	.75
94	Early Wynn	.75
95	Reggie Jackson	.75
96	Charlie Gehringer	.75
97	Jackie Robinson	3.00
98	Lou Gehrig	2.50
99	Hank Aaron	2.50
100	Mickey Mantle	6.00
101	Sandy Koufax	3.00
102	Ryne Sandberg	.75
103	Don Mattingly	2.50
104	Darryl Strawberry	.75
105	Tom Seaver	.75
106	Bill Klem	.75
107	Dwight Gooden	.75
108	Pete Rose	3.00
	Fourth Series	15.00
109	Elston Howard	.75
110	Honus Wagner	.75
111	Waite Hoyt	.75
112	Bill Bruton	.75
113	Gil Hodges	.75
114	Vic Power	.75
115	Al Kaline	.75
116	Al Lopez	.75
117	Rocky Bridges	.75
118	Jim Gilliam	.75
119	Christy Mathewson	.75
120	Hank Greenberg	1.00
121	Eddie Mathews	.75
122	Van Mungo	.75
123	Harry Simpson	.75
124	Carl Yastrzemski	.75
125	Pete Rose	3.00
126	Dizzy Dean	1.00
127	Chi Chi Olivo	.75
128	Johnny Vander Meer	.75
129	Roberto Clemente	4.00
130	Carl Hubbell	.75
131	Willie Mays	2.50
132	Willie Stargell	.75
133	Sam Jethroe	.75
134	Pete Rose	3.00
135	Jackie Robinson	3.00
136	Yogi Berra	1.00
137	Grover Alexander	.75
138	Joe Morgan	.75
139	Rube Foster	.75
140	Mickey Mantle	6.00
141	Ted Williams	2.50
142	Jimmie Foxx	.75
143	Pepper Martin	.75
144	Hank Aaron	2.50
	Fifth Series	15.00
145	Vida Blue	.75
146	Carl Furillo	.75
147	Lloyd Waner	.75
148	Eddie Dyer	.75
149	Casey Stengel	.75
150	Mickey Mantle	6.00
151	Gil Hodges	.75
152	Don Mossi	.75
153	Ron Swoboda	.75
154	Hoyt Wilhelm	.75
155	Ed Roush (Edd)	.75
156	Mickey Lolich	.75
157	Jim Palmer	.75
158	Thurman Munson	1.00
159	Don Zimmer	.75
160	Hank Aaron	2.50
161	Johnny Bench	.75
162	Orlando Cepeda	.75
163	Honus Wagner	.75
164	Tom Seaver	.75
165	Willie Mays	2.50
166	Elmer Riddle	.75
167	Tony Oliva	.75
168	Elmer Flick	.75
169	Curt Flood	.75
170	Carl Yastrzemski	.75
171	Charlie Keller	.75
172	Christy Mathewson	.75
173	Eddie Plank	.75
174	Lou Gehrig	2.50
175	John McGraw	.75
176	Mule Haas	.75
177	Paul Waner	.75
178	Steve Blass	.75
179	Honus Wagner	.75
180	Jack Barry	.75
	Sixth Series	15.00
181	Rocky Colavito	.75
182	Danny Murtaugh	.75
183	John Edwards	.75
184	Pete Rose	3.00
185	Roy Campanella	1.00
186	Jerry Grote	.75
187	Leo Durocher	.75
188	Rollie Fingers	.75
189	Wes Parker	.75
190	Joe Rudi	.75
191	Bill Veeck	.75
192	Mark Fidrych	.75
193	George Foster	.75
194	Early Wynn	.75
195	Frank Howard	.75
196	Graig Nettles	.75
197	Juan Pizzaro	.75
198	Jose Cruz	.75
199	Joe Jackson	3.00
200	Stan Musial	2.50
201	Chuck Klein	.75
	Seventh Series	15.00
202	Ryne Sandberg	.75
203	Richie Allen	.75
204	Bo Jackson	.75
205	Kevin Mitchell	.75
206	Al Smith, Early Wynn, Larry Doby	.75
207	Mickey Mantle	6.00
208	Will Clark	.75
209	Cecil Fielder	.75
210	Bobby Richardson	.75
211	Nolan Ryan	4.00
212	Casey Stengel	.75
213	Ted Kluszewski	1.00
214	Gaylord Perry	.75
215	Johnny Vander Meer	.75
216	Willie Mays	2.50
217	Goose Goslin	.75
218	Bobby Shantz	.75
219	Terry Pendleton	.75
220	Richie Ashburn	.75
221	Robin Yount	1.00
222	Cal Ripken	4.00
223	Danny Ainge	.75
224	Bob Friend	.75
225	Orel Hershiser	.75
226	Wade Boggs	.75
227	Bill Mazeroski (1960 World Series home run)	.75
228	Stan Musial	2.50
229	Chris Short	.75
230	Johnny Bench	.75
231	Nellie Fox	.75
232	Ron Santo	.75
233	Tony Gwynn	1.50
234	Phil Niekro	.75
235	Frank Thomas	2.50
236	Greg Gross	.75
237	Ken Griffey Jr.	5.00
238	Benito Santiago	.75
239	Dwight Gooden	.75
240	Darryl Strawberry	.75
241	Roy Campanella	1.00
242	Roger Clemens	1.50
243	Kirby Puckett	1.00
244	Nolan Ryan	4.00
---	First Series checklist	.75
---	Second Series checklist	.75
---	Third Series checklist	.75
---	Fourth Series checklist	.75
---	Fifth Series checklist	.75
---	Sixth Series checklist	.75

1986 Oh Henry! Cleveland Indians

This 30-card set of Cleveland Indians players was distributed by the team at a special Photo/Baseball Card Day at Municipal Stadium. The cards were printed on an 11" x 29" three-panel, perforated foldout piece which featured four action shots of the Indians on the cover. Unfolded, there are two panels containing the baseball cards and a third which contains a team photo. Cards measure 2-1/4" x 3-1/8". The players' studio portraits are framed in blue with a white border and list player name, number and position. Card fronts also include a picture of the sponsoring candy bar. Card backs include facsimile autograph and professional records. Each card is perforated for separation.

		MT
	Complete Set, Foldout:	12.00
	Common Player:	.40
2	Brett Butler	.75
4	Tony Bernazard	.40
6	Andy Allanson	.40
7	Pat Corrales	.40
8	Carmen Castillo	.40
10	Pat Tabler	.40
13	Ernie Camacho	.40
14	Julio Franco	.90
15	Dan Rohn	.40
18	Ken Schrom	.40
20	Otis Nixon	.40
22	Fran Mullins	.40
23	Chris Bando	.40
24	Ed Williams	.40
26	Brook Jacoby	.40
27	Mel Hall	.40
29	Andre Thornton	.50
30	Joe Carter	1.50
35	Phil Niekro	2.00
36	Jamie Easterly	.40
37	Don Schulze	.40
42	Rich Yett	.40
43	Scott Bailes	.40
44	Neal Heaton	.40
46	Jim Kern	.40
48	Dickie Noles	.40
49	Tom Candiotti	.50
53	Reggie Ritter	.40
54	Tom Waddell	.40
----	Coaching Staff (Jack Aker, Bobby Bonds, Doc Edwards, John Goryl)	.40

1996 Oh Henry! Toronto Blue Jays

In celebration of the team's 20th anniversary, Oh Henry! sponsored a card set giveaway at SkyDome on June 11. The first 25,000 fans received a boxed set of current and former players. The 2-1/2" x 3-1/2" cards have a borderless photo on front. The central portion of the picture is in color, the edges are in black-and-white. The player name and uniform number are overprinted at bottom. The team's anniversary logo is in the upper-left corner. On former players' cards there is a gold "ALUMNI" banner under the logo ball. Backs are printed in blue and white with career summary and stats, a few bits of personal data and logos of the team and sponsor. Cards are listed here alphabetically.

		MT
	Complete Set (36):	8.00
	Common Player:	.25
(1)	George Bell	.35
(2)	Brian Bohanon	.25
(3)	Joe Carter	.40
(4)	Tony Castillo	.25
(5)	Domingo Cedeno	.25
(6)	Tim Crabtree	.25
(7)	Felipe Crespo	.25
(8)	Carlos Delgado	.75
(9)	Cito Gaston	.25
(10)	Alex Gonzalez	.35
(11)	Shawn Green	1.00
(12)	Alfredo Griffin	.25
(13)	Kelly Gruber	.25
(14)	Juan Guzman	.25
(15)	Erik Hanson	.25
(16)	Pat Hentgen	.35
(17)	Marty Janzen	.25
(18)	Nick Leyva	.25
(19)	Sandy Martinez	.25
(20)	Lloyd Moseby	.35
(21)	Otis Nixon	.25
(22)	Charlie O'Brien	.25
(23)	John Olerud	.75
(24)	Robert Perez	.25
(25)	Paul Quantrill	.25
(26)	Mel Queen	.25
(27)	Bill Risley	.25
(28)	Juan Samuel	.25
(29)	Ed Sprague	.25
(30)	Dave Steib	.35
(31)	Gene Tenace	.25
(32)	Mike Timlin	.25
(33)	Willie Upshaw	.25
(34)	Jeffrey Ware	.25
(35)	Ernie Whitt	.25
(36)	Woody Williams	.25

1997 Oh Henry! Toronto Blue Jays

The first 25,000 fans entering SkyDome for the Blue Jays' May 6 game received a team card set sponsored by the candy bar company. In 2-1/2" x 3-1/2" size, fronts feature color action photos with a splash of "infield dirt" vertically at left. The player's name and uniform number appear at top-left. "Oh!" and the team logo are printed in bottom corners. Backs are printed in blue and white with a few personal data, stats and career highlights.

		MT
	Complete Set (36):	8.00
	Common Player:	.25
2	Otis Nixon	.25
3	Felipe Crespo	.25
4	Alfredo Griffin	.25
5	Jacob Brumfield	.25
6	Orlando Merced	.25
7	Shannon Stewart	.50
8	Alex Gonzalez	.40
10	Jim Lett	.25
11	Juan Samuel	.25
12	Tilson Brito	.25
13	Carlos Garcia	.25
15	Shawn Green	1.00
16	Nick Leyva	.25
17	Robert Perez	.25
18	Benito Santiago	.25
19	Dan Plesac	.25
21	Roger Clemens	2.00
22	Charlie O'Brien	.25
24	Paul Spoljaric	.25
25	Carlos Delgado	.75
26	Willie Upshaw	.25
29	Joe Carter	.40
31	Robert Person	.25
33	Ed Sprague	.25
34	Mel Queen	.25
37	Tim Crabtree	.25
39	Erik Hanson	.25
40	Mike Timlin	.25
41	Pat Hentgen	.35
43	Cito Gaston	.25
44	Gene Tenace	.25
48	Paul Quantrill	.25
49	Luis Andujar	.25
54	Woody Williams	.25
55	Bill Risley	.25
57	Juan Guzman	.25

1982 Ohio Baseball Hall of Fame

Ohio natives and players who made their mark playing in the Buckeye State are featured in this collectors issue, along with executives and a few other figures. Fronts of the 3-3/8" x 5-5/8" cards have black-and-white player photos surrounded by red borders. The player's name and year of induction are at bottom. Black-and-white backs have lengthy career summaries. Original production was 2,500 sets which were sold into the hobby at $7 apiece. Later inductees were added to the set through at least 1985, but the checklist after #65 is unknown.

		MT
	Complete Set (75):	60.00
	Common Player:	2.00
1	Ohio Baseball Hall of Fame	2.00
2	Checklist	2.00
3	Nick Cullop	2.00
4	Dean Chance	2.00
5	Bob Feller	3.00
6	Jesse Haines	2.00
7	Waite Hoyt	2.00
8	Ernie Lombardi	2.00
9	Mike Powers	2.00
10	Edd Roush	2.00
11	Red Ruffing	2.00
12	Luke Sewell	2.00
13	Tris Speaker	2.00
14	Cy Young	3.00
15	Walter Alston	2.00
16	Lou Boudreau	2.00
17	Warren Giles	2.00
18	Ted Kluszewski	3.00
19	William McKinley	2.00
20	Roger Peckinpaugh	2.00
21	Johnny Vander Meer	2.00
22	Early Wynn	2.00
23	Earl Averill	2.00
24	Stan Coveleski	2.00
25	Lefty Grove	2.00
26	Nap Lajoie	2.00
27	Al Lopez	2.00
28	Eddie Onslow	2.00
29	Branch Rickey	2.00
30	Frank Robinson	3.00
31	George Sisler	2.00
32	Bob Lemon	2.00
33	Satchel Paige	3.00
34	Bucky Walters	2.00
35	Gus Bell	2.00
36	Rocky Colavito	3.00
37	Mel Harder	2.00
38	Tommy Henrich	2.00
39	Miller Huggins	2.00
40	Fred Hutchinson	2.00
41	Eppa Rixey	2.00
42	Joe Sewell	2.00
43	George Uhle	2.00
44	Bill Veeck	2.00
45	Estel Crabtree	2.00

46	Harvey Haddix	2.00
47	Noodles Hahn	2.00
48	Joe Jackson	4.00
49	Kenesaw Landis	2.00
50	Thurman Munson	3.00
51	Gabe Paul	2.00
52	Vada Pinson	2.00
53	Wally Post	2.00
54	Vic Wertz	2.00
55	Paul Derringer	2.00
56	John Galbreath	2.00
57	Richard Marquard	2.00
58	Bill McKechnie	2.00
59	Rocky Nelson	2.00
60	Al Rosen	2.00
61	Lew Fonseca	2.00
62	Larry MacPhail	2.00
63	Joe Nuxhall	2.00
64	Birdie Tebbetts	2.00
65	Gene Woodling	2.00
66		
67		
68		
69		
70		
71		
72		
73		
74		
75	Bill Mazeroski	3.00

1997 Ohio Casualty Milwaukee Brewers

This set of black-and-white player/staff pictures was distributed in conjunction with Friday home-game autograph appearances. The portraits are printed on 5" x 7" heavy paper and are blank-backed. The unnumbered pictures are checklisted here alphabetically.

		MT
Complete Set (37):		25.00
Common Player:		.50
(1)	Chris Bando	.50
(2)	Sal Bando	.50
(3)	Jeromy Burnitz	1.25
(4)	Chuck Carr	.50
(5)	Bill Castro	.50
(6)	Jeff Cirillo	1.00
(7)	Cecil Cooper	.75
(8)	Jeff D'Amico	.50
(9)	Cal Eldred	.75
(10)	Mike Fetters	.50
(11)	Bryce Florie	.50
(12)	Jim Gantner	.50
(13)	Phil Garner	.50
(14)	John Jaha	.50
(15)	Doug Jones	.50
(16)	Scott Karl	.50
(17)	Jesse Levis	.50
(18)	Mark Loretta	.50
(19)	Mike Matheny	.50
(20)	Jamie McAndrew	.50
(21)	Ben McDonald	.50
(22)	Jose Mercedes	.50
(23)	Matt Mieske	.50
(24)	Angel Miranda	.50
(25)	Marc Newfield	.50
(26)	David Nilsson	.50
(27)	Don Rowe	.50
(28)	Allan H. (Bud) Selig	.50
(29)	Steve Sparks	.50
(30)	Jose Valentin	.50
(31)	Ron Villone	.50
(32)	Fernando Vina	.75
(33)	Bob Wickman	.50
(34)	Gerald Williams	.50
(35)	Robin Yount	6.00
(36)	Bernie Brewer (mascot)	.50
(37)	County Stadium	.50

1998 Ohio Casualty Milwaukee Brewers

For a second consectuvie season, the insurance company sponsored an issue of Brewers' players and staff cards. The cards were given away on Friday nights when groups of players would sign autographs along the box seats prior to the game. Cards are virtualty identical in format to the '97s, featuring black-and-white portrait photos in a 5" x 7" blank-back format. Year of issue can be differentiated by final line of type at bottom. The 1997 issue begins, "Where Extra Effort . . ." The 1998 cards read, "Call a Local . . ." It is possible cards of Bob Uecker and a few other non-players may have also been issued.

		MT
Complete Set (53):		30.00
Common Player:		.50
(1)	Chris Bando	.50
(2)	Sal Bando	.50
(3)	Brian Banks	.50
(4)	Ron Belliard	.50
(5)	Bernie Brewer (mascot)	.50
(6)	Jeromy Burnitz	.75
(7)	Bill Campbell	.50
(8)	Bill Castro	.50
(9)	Jeff Cirillo	.75
(10)	Cecil Cooper	.75
(11)	Jeff D'Amico	.50
(12)	Valerio de los Santos	.50
(13)	Eddy Diaz	.50
(14)	Todd Dunn	1.00
(15)	Cal Eldred	.75
(16)	Chad Fox	.75
(17)	Phil Garner	.50
(18)	Marquis Grissom	.75
(19)	Darrin Jackson	.50
(20)	Bob Hamelin	.50
(21)	John Jaha	.50
(22)	Geoff Jenkins	1.50
(23)	Lamar Johnson	.50
(24)	Doug Jones	.50
(25)	Jeff Juden	.50
(26)	Bobby Hughes	1.00
(27)	Scott Karl	.50
(28)	Jim Lefebvre	.50
(29)	Jesse Levis	.50
(30)	Mark Loretta	.50
(31)	Doug Mansolino	.50
(32)	Mike Matheny	.50
(33)	Jose Mercedes	.50
(34)	Mike Myers	.50
(35)	Marc Newfield	.50
(36)	Eric Owens	.50
(37)	Bronswell Patrick	.50
(38)	Jim Powell (announcer)	.50
(39)	Bill Pulsipher	.50
(40)	Al Reyes	.50
(41)	Rafael Roque	.50
(42)	Don Rowe	.50
(43)	Ken Sanders	.50
(44)	The Sausages (mascots)	.50
(45)	Bill Schroeder (announcer)	.50
(46)	Allan H. (Bud) Selig	.50
(47)	Jose Valentin	.50
(48)	Bob Wickman	.50
(49)	Paul Wagner	.50
(50)	Brad Woodall	.50
(51)	Steve Woodward	.50
(52)	Joel Youngblood	.50
(53)	Robin Yount	5.00

1997 Ohio Lottery Baseball Legends

Five stars who played all or part of their careers with the Indians or Reds are featured in this series of $1 scratch-off lottery tickets. The 4" x 2-1/4" tickets have color player portraits on a background of pinstripes, a baseball and diamond. There are black facsimile autographs toward the bottom. Blue-foil vertical strips are along the perforated top and bottom edges. Backs are printed in black, white and green. Values quoted are for unscratched tickets.

		MT
Complete Set:		10.00
Common Player:		2.00
(1)	Rocky Colavito	2.00
(2)	Larry Doby	2.00
(3)	George Foster	2.00
(4)	Tony Perez	2.00
(5)	Gaylord Perry	2.00

1992 Old Style Chicago Cubs

More than two dozen Cubs stars are featured in this set of 2-1/2" x 3-1/2" cards. Front have sepia player photos with their years at Chicago indicated on top. Backs are printed in black, red and blue on white with a few stats and career highlights, sponsor and team logos and a picture of the Cubs uniform in the player's debut year. The unnumbered cards are checklisted here in alphabetical order.

		MT
Complete Set (28):		15.00
Common Player:		.50
(1)	Grover Alexander	.75
(2)	Cap Anson	.50
(3)	Ernie Banks	2.00
(4)	Mordecai Brown	.50
(5)	Phil Cavarretta	.50
(6)	Frank Chance	.75
(7)	Kiki Cuyler	.50
(8)	Johnny Evers	.75
(9)	Charlie Grimm	.50
(10)	Stan Hack	.50
(11)	Gabby Hartnett	.50
(12)	Billy Herman	.50
(13)	Rogers Hornsby	.75
(14)	Ken Hubbs	.75
(15)	Randy Hundley	.50
(16)	Fergie Jenkins	.50
(17)	Bill Lee	.50
(18)	Andy Pafko	.50
(19)	Rick Reuschel	.50
(20)	Charlie Root	.50
(21)	Ron Santo	.60
(22)	Hank Sauer	.50
(23)	Riggs Stephenson	.50
(24)	Bruce Sutter	.50
(25)	Joe Tinker	.75
(26)	Hippo Vaughn	.50
(27)	Billy Williams	.75
(28)	Hack Wilson	.50

1993 Old Style Billy Williams

The career of long-time Cubs star, batting coach and Hall of Famer Billy Williams is traced in this four-card set given to fans attending the Aug. 17, 1993, game at Wrigley Field between the Cubs and Expos. Fronts of the first three cards have black-and-white photos, the last card is in color. Backs have biographical and career information along with the sponsor's logo.

		MT
Complete Set:		8.00
Common Card:		2.00
(1)	Billy Williams (batting - personal)	2.00
(2)	Billy Williams (fielding - playing career)	2.00
(3)	Billy Williams (batting - playing career)	2.00
(4)	Billy Williams (portrait - coaching career)	2.00

1982 On Deck Cookies Discs

These 2-3/4" discs were packaged with a large cookie and sold for 25-29 cents in areas including Florida and New Jersey. The fronts have a 1981 copyright date, but the backs indicate "1982 Collectors Series." Fronts have black-and-white player portraits in the center panel of a baseball design. The end panels can be any one of several pastel colors. Backs are in red and black and repeat the baseball motif and include a copyright for "All Sports Baking Co., Inc." Each side carries the players' union logo through which the discs were licensed by Michael Schechter Associates. Because they are not licensed through Major League Baseball, player pictures have no uniform logos.

		MT
Complete Set (32):		95.00
Common Player:		3.00
(1)	Buddy Bell	3.00
(2)	Johnny Bench	9.00
(3)	Bruce Bochte	3.00
(4)	George Brett	12.00
(5)	Bill Buckner	3.00
(6)	Rod Carew	7.00
(7)	Steve Carlton	7.00
(8)	Cesar Cedeno	3.00
(9)	Jack Clark	3.00
(10)	Cecil Cooper	3.00
(11)	Bucky Dent	3.00
(12)	Carlton Fisk	6.00
(13)	Steve Garvey	4.00
(14)	Goose Gossage	3.00
(15)	Mike Hargrove	3.00
(16)	Keith Hernandez	3.00
(17)	Bob Horner	3.00
(18)	Reggie Jackson	8.00
(19)	Steve Kemp	3.00
(20)	Ron LeFlore	3.00
(21)	Fred Lynn	3.00
(22)	Lee Mazilli	3.00
(23)	Eddie Murray	7.00
(24)	Mike Norris	3.00
(25)	Dave Parker	3.00
(26)	J.R. Richard	3.00
(27)	Pete Rose	15.00
(28)	Mike Schmidt	9.00
(29)	Tom Seaver	8.00
(30)	Willie Stargell	7.00
(31)	Roy Smalley	3.00
(32)	Garry Templeton	3.00

1997 Ontario Special Olympics Roger Clemens

"Rocket Boosters" - donors to Ontario's Special Olympics - received this 3-1/2" x 5" card. The front is bordered in red and has a stylized Blue Jays logo in the background. Horizontal backs have a color portrait photo of Clemens, career highlights printed on a blue background and color logos of the program's sponsors.

	MT
Roger Clemens	6.00

1988 Orion Pictures Bull Durham

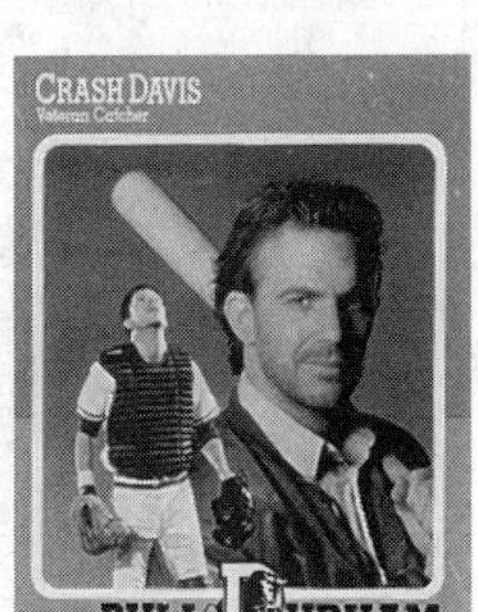

This set was distributed with a single-serving packet of Gatorade drink mix in a cello bag. The oversize (4" x 5") cards feature color photos at center, combining both portrait and full-length poses. The character's name and "position" are printed in white in the red border at top. In the blue border at bottom is the movie logo, which is similar to that of the Durham Bulls minor league team. Backs are in black-and-white and contain the actor's or actress' name and several quotes from the movie character on topics as diverse as strikeouts and sex. There is also an ad for the movie.

		MT
Complete Set (4):		10.00
Common Card:		2.00
(1)	Crash Davis (Kevin Costner)	4.00
(2)	Ebby "Nuke" LaLoosh (Tim Robbins)	2.00
(3)	Millie (Jenny Robertson)	2.00
(4)	Annie Savoy (Susan Sarandon)	2.50

1994 Oscar Mayer Superstar Pop-Ups

Oscar Mayer Bologna packages in 1994 included one pop-up card in each, but unlike the similar Kraft cards, in this case it was 30 round cards (2-1/2 inches in diameter), with the Oscar Mayer logo on the front and trivia questions on the backs. The promotion ran from April through May, or as long as the supplies lasted. The cards were licensed by the Major League Baseball Players Association, but not by Major League Baseball, so the team logos were airbrushed from player's caps and uniforms. Through an on-pack and in-store mail-in offer, collectors could order complete sets of cards for $1.95 per league (15 cards), plus the appropriate proofs of purchase. Officials of Kraft USA, parent company of Oscar Mayer, announced that they printed 266,000 sets.

		MT
Complete Set (30):		20.00
Common Player:		.40
1	Jim Abbott	.50
2	Kevin Appier	.40
3	Roger Clemens	1.50
4	Cecil Fielder	.50
5	Juan Gonzalez	2.00
6	Ken Griffey Jr.	4.00
7	Kenny Lofton	.50
8	Jack McDowell	.40
9	Paul Molitor	1.25
10	Kirby Puckett	1.50
11	Cal Ripken Jr.	3.50
12	Tim Salmon	.80
13	Ruben Sierra	.40
14	Frank Thomas	3.00
15	Greg Vaughn	.60
16	Jeff Bagwell	1.25
17	Barry Bonds	2.00
18	Bobby Bonilla	.50
19	Jeff Conine	.40
20	Lenny Dykstra	.40
21	Andres Galarraga	.60
22	Marquis Grissom	.40
23	Tony Gwynn	1.25
24	Gregg Jefferies	.40
25	John Kruk	.40
26	Greg Maddux	2.00
27	Mike Piazza	2.50
28	Jose Rijo	.40
29	Ryne Sandberg	1.25
30	Andy Van Slyke	.40

1987 Our Own Tea Discs

(See 1987 Super Stars Discs for checklist and price guide.)

1988 Our Own Tea Discs

(See 1988 Superstar Discs for checklist and price guide.)

1989 Ozzie's Restaurant

This card promotes the restaurant and sports bar owned by Cardinals' shortstop Ozzie Smith in a western St. Louis suburban mall. The front has a color photo of Smith and an ad for the business. The black-and-white back has biographical data and stats through the 1989 season. The 3-1/2" x 4-1/2" card is printed on thin cardboard with a semi-glossy front surface.

	MT
Ozzie Smith	8.00

P

1992 Paccar/Alrak Ken Griffey Jr.

Ken Griffey Jr. was the subject of a 1992, five-card set of plastic trading cards issued by ALRAK Enterprises and PACCAR Automotive Inc. The cards were available at PACCAR retail outlets in the West. Each purchaser was limited to three cards purchased per store visit.

		MT
Complete Set (5):		15.00
Common Card:		3.00
(1)	Ken Griffey Jr. (Golden Moments)	3.00
(2)	Ken Griffey Jr. (Golden Moments)	3.00
(3)	Ken Griffey Jr. (Golden Moments)	3.00
(4)	Ken Griffey Jr. (Golden Moments)	3.00
(5)	Ken Griffey Jr. (Golden Moments)	3.00

1988 Pacific Baseball Legends

Pacific Trading Cards rounded up 110 photos of the greatest baseball players from the past 40 years for its 1988 "Baseball Legends" set. All players featured in the set are (or were) members of the Major League Baseball Alumni Association. Card fronts feature silver outer borders and large, clear full-color player photos outlined in black against colorful banner-style inner borders of red, blue, green, orange or gold. The player's name and position are printed in white letters on the lower portion of the banner. Card backs are numbered and carry the Baseball Legends logo, player biography, major league career stats, and personal information. The cards were sold in boxed sets via candy wholesalers, with emphasis on Midwest and New England states. Complete collector sets in clear plastic boxes were made available via dealers or directly from Pacific Trading Cards. Pacific

		MT
Complete Set (110) (no checklist):		14.00
Common Player:		.05
1	Hank Aaron	.50
2	Red Shoendienst (Schoendienst)	.15
3	Brooks Robinson	.25
4	Luke Appling	.15
5	Gene Woodling	.05
6	Stan Musial	.50
7	Mickey Mantle	3.00
8	Richie Ashburn	.25
9	Ralph Kiner	.20
10	Phil Rizzuto	.25
11	Harvey Haddix	.05
12	Ken Boyer	.10
13	Clete Boyer	.05
14	Ken Harrelson	.05
15	Robin Roberts	.20
16	Catfish Hunter	.20
17	Frank Howard	.10
18	Jim Perry	.05
19	Elston Howard	.10
20	Jim Bouton	.10
21	Pee Wee Reese	.25
22	Mel Stottlemyer (Stottlemyre)	.10
23	Hank Sauer	.05
24	Willie Mays	.50
25	Tom Tresh	.05
26	Roy Sievers	.05
27	Leo Durocher	.15
28	Al Dark	.10
29	Tony Kubek	.15
30	Johnny Vander Meer	.10
31	Joe Adcock	.10
32	Bob Lemon	.20
33	Don Newcombe	.15
34	Thurman Munson	.25
35	Earl Battey	.05
36	Ernie Banks	.30
37	Matty Alou	.05
38	Dave McNally	.05
39	Mickey Lolich	.10
40	Jackie Robinson	.50
41	Allie Reynolds	.15
42	Don Larson (Larsen)	.10
43	Fergie Jenkins	.15
44	Jim Gilliam	.10
45	Bobby Thomson	.10
46	Sparky Anderson	.10
47	Roy Campanella	.30
48	Marv Throneberry	.10
49	Bill Virdon	.05
50	Ted Williams	.50
51	Minnie Minoso	.10
52	Bob Turley	.10
53	Yogi Berra	.30
54	Juan Marichal	.20
55	Duke Snider	.30
56	Harvey Kuenn	.10
57	Nellie Fox	.20
58	Felipe Alou	.05
59	Tony Oliva	.10
60	Bill Mazeroski	.10
61	Bobby Shantz	.10
62	Mark Fidrych	.05
63	Johnny Mize	.15
64	Ralph Terry	.05
65	Gus Bell	.05
66	Jerry Koosman	.10
67	Mike McCormick	.05
68	Lou Burdette	.10
69	George Kell	.15
70	Vic Raschi	.10
71	Chuck Connors	.20
72	Ted Kluszewski	.15
73	Bobby Doerr	.15
74	Bobby Richardson	.15
75	Carl Erskine	.15
76	Hoyt Wilhelm	.20
77	Bob Purkey	.05
78	Bob Friend	.05
79	Monte Irvin	.15
80	Jim Longborg (Lonborg)	.05
81	Wally Moon	.05
82	Moose Skowron	.10
83	Tommy Davis	.10
84	Enos Slaughter	.20
85	Sal Maglie	.10
86	Harmon Killebrew	.25
87	Gil Hodges	.25
88	Jim Kaat	.10
89	Roger Maris	.30
90	Billy Williams	.20
91	Luis Aparicio	.20
92	Jim Bunning	.20
93	Bill Freehan	.05
94	Orlando Cepeda	.10
95	Early Wynn	.20
96	Tug McGraw	.10
97	Ron Santo	.10
98	Del Crandall	.05
99	Sal Bando	.05
100	Joe DiMaggio	.75
101	Bob Feller	.25
102	Larry Doby	.20
103	Rollie Fingers	.15
104	Al Kaline	.30
105	Johnny Podres	.10
106	Lou Boudreau	.15
107	Zoilo Versalles	.05
108	Dick Groat	.05
109	Warren Spahn	.25
110	Johnny Bench	.30
----	Checklist	3.00

1988 Pacific "Eight Men Out"

Trading Cards produced this 110-card set featuring actual players from the 1919 World Series (#78-110) and actors from Orion's movie (#1-77) "Eight Men Out." Card fronts feature a burgundy outer border and thin silver inner border framing the player photos (actor photos are full-color, vintage photos are sepia-toned). A silver banner beneath the photo, outlined in black, bears a brief photo caption. The Eight Men Out logo appears lower right. The card backs are printed in burgundy and black on white, with a gray border, and include the actor/player's name and a paragraph-style biography or description of the action. Pacific Trading Cards' "Eight Men Out" set was distributed by hobby stores nationwide in 10-card wax packs and in complete boxed sets.

		MT
Complete Set (110):		7.00
Common Player:		.05
1	We're going to see the Sox!	.05
2	White Sox Win the Pennant!	.05
3	The Series	.05
4	1919 Chicago White Sox	.05
5	The Black Sox Scandal	.05
6	Eddie Cicotte - 29-7 in 1919	.05
7	"Buck's there faverit"	.05
8	Eddie Collins	.05
9	Michael Rooker as Arnold "Chick" Gandil	.05
10	Charlie Sheen as Oscar "Happy" Felsch	.05
11	James Read as Claude "Lefty" Williams	.05
12	John Cusack as George Buck Weaver	.05
13	D.B. Sweeney as "Shoeless" Joe Jackson	.05
14	David Strathairn as Eddie Cicotte	.05
15	Perry Lang as Fred McMullin	.05
16	Don Harvey as Charles "Swede" Risberg	.05
17	The Gamblers - Burns and Maharg	.05
18	Sleepy Bill Burns	.05
19	The Key is Cicotte	.05
20	C'moan, Betsy	.05
21	The Fix	.05
22	Chick approaches Cicotte	.05
23	"Kid" Gleason	.05
24	Charles Comiskey - Owner	.05
25	Arnold "Chick" Gandil - First Baseman	.05
26	Charles "Swede" Risberg	.05
27	Sport Sullivan	.05
28	Abe Attell/Arnold Rothstein	.05
29	Hugh Fullerton - Sports Writer	.05
30	Ring Lardner - Sports Writer	.05
31	"Shoeless" Joe's batting eye	.05
32	"Shoeless" Joe	.05
33	Buck can't sleep	.05
34	George "Buck" Weaver	.05
35	Hugh and Ring confront Kid	.05
36	Joe doesn't want to play.	.05
37	"Shoeless" Joe Jackson	.05
38	"Sore Arm, Cicotte", "Old Man Cicotte"	.05
39	The fix is on.	.05
40	Buck's playing to win.	.05
41	Hap makes a great catch.	.05
42	Hugh and Ring suspect!	.05
43	Ray gets things going.	.05
44	Lefty loses Game Two	.05
45	Lefty crosses up Ray Schalk's signals.	.05
46	Chick's RBI wins Game Three	.05
47	Dickie Kerr Wins Game Three	.05
48	Chick leaves Buck stranded at third.	.05

49	Williams loses Game Five	.05
50	Ray Schalk	.05
51	Schalk blocks the plate.	.05
52	Schalk is thrown out.	.05
53	Chicago stick ball game.	.05
54	I'm forever blowing ballgames.	.05
55	Felsch Scores Jackson	.05
56	Kerr wins Game Six.	.05
57	Where's the money?	.05
58	Cicotte wins Game Seven.	.05
59	Kid watches Eddie.	.05
60	Lefty is threatened	.05
61	James! Get your arm ready! Fast!	.05
62	"Shoeless" Joe's Home Run	.05
63	Buck played his best	.05
64	Hugh exposes the fix.	.05
65	Sign the petition	.05
66	Baseball owners hire a commissioner	.05
67	Judge Kenesaw Mountain Landis	.05
68	Grand jury summoned	.05
69	Say it ain't so, Joe!	.05
70	"The Swede's a Hard Guy"	.05
71	Buck loves the game.	.05
72	The trial.	.05
73	Kid Gleason take the stand.	.05
74	The Verdict	.05
75	Eight Men Out	.05
76	Oscar "Happy" Felsch	.05
77	Who's Joe Jackson?	.05
78	Ban Johnson - President	.05
79	Judge Landis - Commissioner of Baseball	.05
80	Charles A. Comiskey - Owner	.05
81	Heinie Groh - Third Baseman	.05
82	Slim Sallee - Pitcher	.05
83	Dutch Ruether - Pitcher	.05
84	Edd Roush - Outfielder	.05
85	Morrie Rath - Second Baseman	.05
86	Bill Rariden - Catcher	.05
87	Jimmy Ring - Pitcher	.05
88	Greasy Neale - Outfielder	.05
89	Pat Moran - Manager	.05
90	Adolfo Luque - Pitcher	.05
91	Larry Kopf - Shortstop	.05
92	Ray Fisher - Pitcher	.05
93	Hod Eller - Pitcher	.05
94	Pat Duncan - Outfielder	.05
95	Jake Daubert - First Baseman	.05
96	Red Faber - Pitcher	.05
97	Dickie Kerr - Pitcher	.05
98	Shano Collins - Outfielder	.05
99	Eddie Collins - Second Baseman	.05
100	Ray Schalk - Catcher	.05
101	Nemo Liebold - Outfielder	.05
102	Kid Gleason - Manager	.05
103	Swede Risberg - Shortstop	.05
104	Eddie Cicotte - Pitcher	.05
105	Fred McMullin - Infielder	.05
106	Chick Gandil - First Baseman	.05
107	Buck Weaver - Third Baseman	.05
108	Lefty Williams - Pitcher	.05
109	Happy Felsch - Outfielder	.05
110	Shoeless Joe Jackson - Outfielder	.05

1989 Pacific Ken Griffey, Jr. Candy Bar Promo

Coinciding with the introduction of the Ken Griffey, Jr. milk chocolate bar in 1989, Pacific issued this card to promote the new candy treat. Front of the 2-1/2" x 3-1/2" card has a batting pose of Griffey on a yellow background with a silver border, similar to the actual wrapper. Back is in blue and red with the player's early 1989 highlights and appropriate logos and copyright data. An ad at bottom says, "Available At Fine Stores Throughout the Northwest."

	MT
Ken Griffey, Jr.	8.00

1989 Pacific Legends II

Pacific Trading Cards issued its Baseball Legends II set as a carry over of its initial set. The photos are printed on silver background and have colorful inner borders of red, blue, orange or gold. Players' names and positions are printed in white letters below the photos. The card backs once again present the "Baseball Legends" logo, player biography, major league career statistics, and personal information. The Baseball Legends II are numbered 110-220 and were available in wax packs at a limited number of retail chains. The complete set was also made available via dealers or could be ordered directly from Pacific Trading Cards.

		MT
Complete Set (110) (no checklist):		10.00
Common Player:		.05
111	Reggie Jackson	.25
112	Rich Reese	.05
113	Frankie Frisch	.15
114	Ed Kranepool	.05
115	Al Hrabosky	.05
116	Eddie Mathews	.20
117	Ty Cobb	.50
118	Jim Davenport	.05
119	Buddy Lewis	.05
120	Virgil Trucks	.05
121	Del Ennis	.05
122	Dick Radatz	.05
123	Andy Pafko	.05
124	Wilbur Wood	.05
125	Joe Sewell	.15
126	Herb Score	.10
127	Paul Waner	.10
128	Lloyd Waner	.10
129	Brooks Robinson	.20
130	Bo Belinsky	.10
131	Phil Cavaretta	.05
132	Claude Osteen	.05
133	Tito Francona	.05
134	Billy Pierce	.05
135	Roberto Clemente	1.00
136	Spud Chandler	.05
137	Enos Slaughter	.15
138	Ken Holtzman	.05
139	John Hopp	.05
140	Tony LaRussa	.05
141	Ryne Duren	.05
142	Glenn Beckert	.05
143	Ken Keltner	.05
144	Hank Bauer	.15
145	Roger Craig	.10
146	Frank Baker	.10
147	Jim O'Toole	.05
148	Rogers Hornsby	.20
149	Jose Cardenal	.05
150	Bobby Doerr	.10
151	Mickey Cochrane	.10
152	Gaylord Perry	.10
153	Frank Thomas	.05
154	Ted Williams	.50
155	Sam McDowell	.10
156	Bob Feller	.20
157	Bert Campaneris	.05
158	Thornton Lee	.05
159	Gary Peters	.05
160	Joe Medwick	.10
161	Joe Nuxhall	.10
162	Joe Schultz	.05
163	Harmon Killebrew	.15
164	Bucky Walters	.05
165	Bobby Allison	.10
166	Lou Boudreau	.15
167	Joe Cronin	.10
168	Mike Torrez	.10
169	Rich Rollins	.05
170	Tony Cuccinello	.05
171	Hoyt Wilhelm	.15
172	Ernie Harwell	.10
173	George Foster	.05
174	Lou Gehrig	.75
175	Dave Kingman	.05
176	Babe Ruth	1.00
177	Joe Black	.10
178	Roy Face	.10
179	Earl Weaver	.10
180	Johnny Mize	.15
181	Roger Cramer	.05
182	Jim Piersall	.10
183	Ned Garver	.05
184	Billy Williams	.15
185	Lefty Grove	.15
186	Jim Grant	.05
187	Elmer Valo	.05
188	Ewell Blackwell	.10
189	Mel Ott	.20
190	Harry Walker	.05
191	Bill Campbell	.05
192	Walter Johnson	.25
193	Jim "Catfish" Hunter	.10
194	Charlie Keller	.10
195	Hank Greenberg	.25
196	Bobby Murcer	.10
197	Al Lopez	.10
198	Vida Blue	.10
199	Shag Crawford	.05
200	Arky Vaughan	.10
201	Smoky Burgess	.05
202	Rip Sewell	.05
203	Earl Averill	.10
204	Milt Pappas	.05
205	Mel Harder	.05
206	Sam Jethroe	.05
207	Randy Hundley	.05
208	Jessie Haines	.10
209	Jack Brickhouse	.10
210	Whitey Ford	.20
211	Honus Wagner	.75
212	Phil Niekro	.10
213	Gary Bell	.05
214	Jon Matlack	.05
215	Moe Drabowsky	.05
216	Edd Roush	.10
217	Joel Horlen	.05
218	Casey Stengel	.20
219	Burt Hooton	.05
220	Joe Jackson	1.00
----	Checklist	3.00

1990 Pacific Legends

The cards in this 110-card set feature the same style as the previous Pacific Legends releases. The cards were available in wax packs as well as in complete set form. Several players found in the first two legends releases are also found in this issue along with new players.

		MT
Complete Set (110):		10.00
Common Player:		.05
1	Hank Aaron	.50
2	Tommie Agee	.05
3	Luke Appling	.15
4	Sal Bando	.05
5	Ernie Banks	.40
6	Don Baylor	.10
7	Yogi Berra	.40
8	Vida Blue	.05
9	Lou Boudreau	.10
10	Clete Boyer	.05
11	George Bamberger	.05
12	Lou Brock	.30
13	Ralph Branca	.05
14	Carl Erskine	.05
15	Bert Campaneris	.05
16	Steve Carlton	.30
17	Rod Carew	.35
18	Rocky Colovito	.15
19	Frank Crosetti	.10
20	Larry Doby	.15
21	Bobby Doerr	.10
22	Walt Dropo	.05
23	Rick Ferrell	.05
24	Joe Garagiola	.25
25	Ralph Garr	.05
26	Dick Groat	.10
27	Steve Garvey	.20
28	Bob Gibson	.25
29	Don Drysdale	.20
30	Billy Herman	.10
31	Bobby Grich	.05
32	Monte Irvin	.15
33	Dave Johnson	.05
34	Don Kessinger	.05
35	Harmon Killebrew	.25
36	Ralph Kiner	.15
37	Vern Law	.05
38	Ed Lopat	.05
39	Bill Mazeroski	.15
40	Rick Monday	.05
41	Manny Mota	.05
42	Don Newcombe	.10
43	Gaylord Perry	.15
44	Jim Piersall	.10
45	Johnny Podres	.05
46	Boog Powell	.10
47	Robin Roberts	.15
48	Ron Santo	.15
49	Herb Score	.10
50	Enos Slaughter	.15
51	Warren Spahn	.35
52	Rusty Staub	.05
53	Frank Torre	.10
54	Bob Horner	.05
55	Lee May	.05
56	Bill White	.10
57	Hoyt Wilhelm	.15
58	Billy Williams	.15
59	Ted Williams	.50
60	Tom Seaver	.35
61	Carl Yastrzemski	.50
62	Marv Throneberry	.10
63	Steve Stone	.05
64	Rico Petrocelli	.05
65	Orlando Cepeda	.20
66	Eddie Mathews	.25
67	Joe Sewell	.10
68	Jim "Catfish" Hunter	.15
69	Alvin Dark	.05
70	Richie Ashburn	.15
71	Dusty Baker	.05
72	George Foster	.05
73	Eddie Yost	.05
74	Buddy Bell	.05
75	Manny Sanguillen	.05
76	Jim Bunning	.15
77	Smokey Burgess	.10
78	Al Rosen	.10
79	Gene Conley	.05
80	Dave Dravecky	.05
81	Charlie Gehringer	.15
82	Billy Pierce	.05
83	Willie Horton	.05
84	Ron Hunt	.05
85	Bob Feller	.20
86	George Kell	.10
87	Dave Kingman	.10
88	Jerry Koosman	.05
89	Clem Labine	.05
90	Tony LaRussa	.05
91	Dennis Leonard	.05
92	Dale Long	.05
93	Sparky Lyle	.05
94	Gil McDougald	.05
95	Don Mossi	.05
96	Phil Niekro	.25
97	Tom Paciorek	.05
98	Mel Parnell	.05
99	Lou Pinella	.05
100	Bobby Richardson	.10
101	Phil Rizzuto	.30
102	Brooks Robinson	.20
103	Pete Runnels	.05
104	Diego Segui	.05
105	Bobby Shantz	.05
106	Bobby Thomson	.10
107	Joe Torre	.15
108	Earl Weaver	.15
109	Willie Wilson	.05
110	Jesse Barfield	.05

1990 Pacific Senior League

An early supporter of the short-lived "old-timers" league, Pacific issued a card set depicting the players of the Senior Professional Baseball Association. Sold in wax packs as well as complete boxed sets, the cards have silver borders on front with yellow stars above and to the right of the player photo. Color team logos are at bottom-left. Red, white and blue backs have appropriate logos, card number, a few biographical details and a short career summary in a horizontal format. The cards were issued with a set of 15 team logo stickers with a puzzle back. Shades of the 1989 Fleer Billy Ripken card, the card of Jim Nettles contains a photo which shows a vulgarity written on the knob of his bat. A cleaned-up version was issued later, and is much scarcer. Many other errors from the regular-edition set were corrected in a glossy edition of 20,000 complete sets, while several new errors were created.

		MT
Complete Set (220):		5.00
Common Player:		.05
Glossy: 2X		
1	Bobby Tolan	.05
2	Sergio Ferrer	.05
3	David Rajsich	.05
4	Ron LeFlore	.10
5	Steve Henderson	.05
6	Jerry Martin	.05
7	Gary Rajsich	.05
8	Elias Sosa	.05
9	Jon Matlack	.05
10	Steve Kemp	.05
11	Lenny Randle	.05
12	Roy Howell	.05
13	Milt Wilcox	.05
14	Alan Bannister	.05
15	Dock Ellis	.05
16	Mike Williams	.05
17	Luis Gomez	.05
18	Joe Sambito	.05
19	Bake McBride	.05
20a	Pat Zachry (photo actually Dick Bosman)	.05
20b	Dick Bosman	.10
21	Dwight Lowry	.05
22	Ozzie Virgil Sr.	.05
23	Randy Lerch	.05
24	Butch Benton	.05
25	Tom Zimmer	.05
26a	Al Holland (photo actually Nardi Contreras)	.05
26b	Nardi Contreras	.10
27	Sammy Stewart	.05
28	Bill Lee	.05
29	Ferguson Jenkins	.50
30	Leon Roberts	.05
31	Rick Wise	.05
32	Butch Hobson	.05
33	Pete LaCock	.05
34	Bill Campbell	.05
35	Doug Simunic	.05
36	Mario Guerrero	.05
37	Jim Willoughby	.05
38	Joe Pittman	.05
39	Mark Bomback	.05
40	Tommy McMillian	.05
41	Gary Allanson	.05
42	Cecil Cooper	.10
43	John LaRosa	.05
44	Darrell Brandon	.05
45	Bernie Carbo	.05
46	Mike Cuellar	.10
47	Al Bumbry	.05
48a	Gene Richards (photo actually Tony Scott)	.05
49b	Tony Scott	.10
49	Pedro Borbon	.05
50	Julio Solo	.05
51a	Ed Nottle (back reads Sun Sox)	.05
51b	Ed Nottle (back reads Super Sox)	.10
52	Jim Bibby	.05
53	Doug Griffin	.05

54	Ed Clements	.05
55	Dalton Jones	.05
56	Earl Weaver	.25
57	Jesus DeLaRosa	.05
58	Paul Casanova	.05
59	Frank Riccelli	.05
60	Rafael Landestoy	.05
61	George Hendrick	.05
62	Cesar Cedeno	.10
63	Bert Campaneris	.10
64	Derrel Thomas	.05
65	Bobby Ramos	.05
66	Grant Jackson	.05
67	Steve Whitaker	.05
68	Pedro Ramos	.05
69	Joe Hicks	.05
70	Taylor Duncan	.05
71	Tom Shopay	.05
72	Ken Clay	.05
73	Mike Kekich	.05
74	Ed Halicki	.05
75	Ed Figueroa	.05
76	Paul Blair	.05
77	Luis Tiant	.10
78	Stan Bahnsen	.05
79	Rennie Stennett	.05
80	Bobby Molinaro	.05
81	Jim Gideon	.05
82	Orlando Gonzalez	.05
83	Amos Otis	.05
84	Dennis Leonard	.05
85	Pat Putman	.05
86	Rick Manning	.05
87	Pat Dobson	.05
88	Marty Castillo	.05
89	Steve McCatty	.05
90	Doug Bird	.05
91	Rick Waits	.05
92	Ron Jackson	.05
93	Tim Hosley	.05
94	Steve Luebber	.05
95	Rich Gale	.05
96	Champ Summers	.05
97	Dave LaRoche	.05
98	Bobby Jones	.05
99	Kim Allen	.05
100	Wayne Garland	.05
101	Tom Spencer	.05
102	Dan Driessen	.05
103	Ron Pruitt	.05
104	Tim Ireland	.05
105	Dan Driessen	.05
106	Pepe Frias	.05
107	Eric Rasmussen	.05
108	Don Hood	.05
109a	Joe Coleman (photo actually Tony Torchia)	.05
109b	Tony Torchia	.10
110	Jim Slaton	.05
111	Clint Hurdle	.05
112	Larry Milbourne	.05
113	Al Holland	.05
114	George Foster	.10
115	Graig Nettles	.10
116	Oscar Gamble	.05
117	Ross Grimsley	.05
118	Bill Travers	.05
119	Jose Beniquez	.05
120a	Jerry Grote (In Action)	.05
120b	Jerry Grote (catcher)	.10
121	John D'Acquisto	.05
122	Tom Murphy	.05
123	Walt Williams	.05
124	Roy Thomas	.05
125a	Jerry Grote (photo actually Fred Stanley)	.05
125b	Fred Stanley (Jerry Grote back)	.10
126a	Jim Nettles (vulgarity on bat knob)	.50
126b	Jim Nettles (no vulgarity)	3.00
127	Randy Niemann	.05
128a	Bobby Bonds	.10
128b	Bobby Bonds (no name/position on front)	.50
129	Ed Glynn	.05
130	Ed Hicks	.05
131	Ivan Murrell	.05
132	Graig Nettles	.10
133	Hal McRae	.20
134	Pat Kelly	.05
135	Sammy Stewart	.05
136	Bruce Kison	.05
137	Jim Morrison	.05
138	Omar Moreno	.05
139	Tom Brown	.05
140	Steve Dillard	.05
141	Gary Alexander	.05
142	Al Oliver	.10
143	Rick Lysander	.05
144	Tippy Martinez	.05
145	Al Cowens	.05
146	Gene Clines	.05
147	Willie Aikens	.05
148	Tommy Moore	.05
149	Clete Boyer	.05
150	Stan Cliburn	.05
151	Ken Kravec	.05
152	Garth Iorg	.05
153	Rick Peterson	.05
154	Wayne Nordhagen	.05
155	Danny Meyer	.05
156	Wayne Garrett	.05
157	Wayne Krenchicki	.05
158	Graig Nettles	.10
159	Earl Stephenson	.05
160	Carl Taylor	.05
161	Rollie Fingers	.50
162	Toby Harrah	.10
163	Mickey Rivers	.05
164	Dave Kingman	.10
165	Paul Mirabella	.05
166	Dick Williams	.05
167	Luis Pujols	.05
168	Tito Landrum	.05
169	Tom Underwood	.05
170	Mark Wagner	.05
171	Odell Jones	.05
172	Doug Capilla	.05
173	Alfie Rondon	.05
174	Lowell Palmer	.05
175	Juan Eichelberger	.05
176	Wes Clements	.05
177	Rodney Scott	.05
178	Ron Washington	.05
179	Al Hrabosky	.05
180	Sid Monge	.05
181	Randy Johnson	.05
182	Tim Stoddard	.05
183	Dick Williams	.05
184	Lee Lacy	.05
185	Jerry White	.05
186	Dave Kingman	.10
187	Checklistt 1-110	.05
188	Jose Cruz	.10
189	Jamie Easterly	.05
190	Ike Blessit	.05
191	Johnny Grubb	.05
192	Dave Cash	.05
193	Doug Corbett	.05
194	Bruce Bochy	.05
195	Mark Corey	.05
196	Gil Rondon	.05
197	Jerry Martin	.05
198	Gerry Pirtle	.05
199	Gates Brown	.05
200	Bob Galasso	.05
201	Bake McBride	.05
202	Wayne Granger	.05
203	Larry Milbourne	.05
204	Tom Paciorek	.05
205	U.L. Washington	.05
206	Larvell Blanks	.05
207	Bob Shirley	.05
208	Pete Falcone	.05
209	Sal Butera	.05
210	Roy Branch	.05
211	Dyar Miller	.05
212	Paul Siebert	.05
213	Ken Reitz	.05
214	Bill Madlock	.10
215	Vida Blue	.15
216	Dave Hilton	.05
217	Pedro Ramos, Charlie Bree	.05
218	Checklist 111-220	.05
219	Pat Dobson, Earl Weaver	.25
220	Curt Flood	.15

1991 Pacific Senior League

In 1991 Pacific Trading Cards produced its second set of cards of Senior Professional Baseball Association players. The cards feature color photos on the front, with the player's name and position along the bottom and team nickname and logo on a banner vertically on the left side. There are 160 cards in the glossy set, with some multi-player and in-action cards included. For reasons unknown, some of the cards (including those of Rice, Fingers, Blue, Dave Cash, Dan Norman, Ron LeFlore, Cesar Cedeno, Rafael Landestoy and Dan Driessen) were apparently printed in two versions.

		MT
	Complete Set (160):	5.00
	Common Player:	.05
1	Dan Driessen	.05
2	Marty Castillo	.05
3	Jerry White	.05
4	Bud Anderson	.05
5	Ron Jackson	.05
6	Fred Stanley	.05
7	Steve Luebber	.05
8	Jery Terrell	.05
9	Pat Dobson	.05
10	Ken Kravec	.05
11	Gil Rondon	.05
12	Dyar Miller	.05
13	Bobby Molinaro	.05
14	Jerry Martin	.05
15	Rick Waits	.05
16	Steve McCatty	.05
17	Roger Slagle	.05
18	Mike Ramsey	.05
19	Rich Gale	.05
20	Larry Harlow	.05
21	Dan Rohn	.05
22	Don Cooper	.05
23	Marv Foley	.05
24	Rafael Landestoy	.05
25	Eddie Milner	.05
26	Amos Otis	.05
27	Odell Jones	.05
28	Tippy Martinez	.05
29	Stu Cliburn	.05
30	Stan Cliburn	.05
31	Tony Cloninger	.05
32	Jeff Jones	.05
33	Ken Reitz	.05
34	Dave Sax	.05
35	Orlando Gonzalez	.05
36	Jose Cruz	.10
37	Mickey Mahler	.05
38	Derek Botelho	.05
39	Rick Lysander	.05
40	Cesar Cedeno	.10
41	Garth Iorg	.05
42	Wayne Krenchicki	.05
43	Clete Boyer	.05
44	Dan Boone	.05
45	George Vukovich	.05
46	Omar Moreno	.05
47	Ron Washington	.05
48	Ron Washington (MVP)	.05
49	Rick Peterson	.05
50	Tack Wilson	.05
51	Stan Cliburn, Stu Cliburn	.05
52	Rick Lysander (POY)	.05
53	Cesar Cedeno, Pete LaCock	.05
54	Jim Marshall, Clete Boyer	.05
55	Doug Simunic	.05
56	Pat Kelly	.05
57	Roy Branch	.05
58	Dave Cash	.05
59	Bobby Jones	.05
60	Hector Cruz	.05
61	Reggie Cleveland	.05
62	Gary Lance	.05
63	Ron LeFlore	.05
64	Dan Norman	.05
65	Renie Martin	.05
66	Pete Mackanin	.05
67	Frank Riccelli	.05
68	Alfie Rondon	.05
69	Rodney Scott	.05
70	Jim Tracy	.05
71	Ed Dennis	.05
72	Rick Lindell	.05
73	Stu Pepper	.05
74	Jeff Youngbauer	.05
75	Russ Foster	.05
76	Jeff Capriati	.05
77	Art DeFreites	.05
78	Alfie Rondon (Action)	.05
79	Reggie Cleveland (Action)	.05
80	Dave Cash (Action)	.05
81	Vida Blue	.15
82	Ed Glynn	.05
83	Bob Owchinko	.05
84	Bill Fleming	.05
85	Ron Roenicke, Gary Roenicke	.05
86	Tom Thompson	.05
87	Derrell Thomas	.05
88	Jim Willoughby	.05
89	Jim Pankovits	.05
90	Jack Cooley	.05
91	Lenn Sakata	.05
92	Mike Brocki	.05
93	Chuck Fick	.05
94	Tom Benedict	.05
95	Anthony Davis	.05
96	Cardell Camper	.05
97	Leon Roberts	.05
98	Roger Erickson	.05
99	Kim Allen	.05
100	Dave Skaggs	.05
101	Joe Decker	.05
102	U.L. Washington	.05
103	Don Fletcher	.05
104	Gary Roenicke	.05
105	Rich Dauer	.05
106	Ron Roenicke	.05
107	Mike Norris	.05
108	Ferguson Jenkins	.50
109	Ronn Reynolds	.05
110	Pete Falcone	.05
111	Gary Allenson	.05
112	Mark Wagner	.05
113	Jack Lazorko	.05
114	Bob Galasso	.05
115	Ron Davis	.05
116	Lenny Randle	.05
117	Ricky Peters	.05
118	Jim Dwyer	.05
119	Juan Eichelberger	.05
120	Pete LaCock	.05
121	Tony Scott	.05
122	Rick Lancellotti	.05
123	Barry Bonnell	.05
124	Dave Hilton	.05
125	Bill Campbell	.05
126	Rollie Fingers	.50
127	Jim Marshall	.05
128	Razor Shines	.05
129	Guy Sularz	.05
130	Roy Thomas	.05
131	Joel Youngblood	.05
132	Ernie Camacho	.05
133	Dave Hilton, Jim Marshall, Fred Stanley	.05
134	Ken Landreaux	.05
135	Dave Rozema	.05
136	Tom Zimmer	.05
137	Elias Sosa	.05
138	Ozzie Virgil Sr.	.05
139	Al Holland	.05
140	Milt Wilcox	.05
141	Jerry Reed	.05
142	Chris Welch	.05
143	Luis Gomez	.05
144	Steve Henderson	.05
145	Butch Benton	.05
146	Bill Lee	.05
147	Todd Cruz	.05
148	Jim Rice	.45
149	Tito Landrum	.05
150	Ozzie Virgil Jr.	.05
151	Joe Pittman	.05
152	Bobby Tolan	.05
153	Len Barker	.05
154	Dave Rajsich	.05
155	Glenn Gulliver	.05
156	Gary Rajsich	.05
157	Joe Sambito	.05
158	Frank Vito	.05
159	Ozzie Virgil Sr., Ozzie Virgil Jr.	.05
160	Dave Rajsich, Gary Rajsich	.05

1991 Pacific Nolan Ryan

The career and family life of Nolan Ryan (to 1991) were the subject matter of this 110-card set by Pacific Trading Card Co. Sold in both foil packs and factory sets, the cards have a UV-coated front featuring a photo flanked on the left by "Nolan Ryan" printed vertically in a color accent stripe. At lower left is a flaming baseball "Texas Express" logo. A photo caption appears beneath the photo. On back the blazing ball motif is repeated, with a photo or career highlights in its center.

		MT
	Complete Set (110):	8.00
	Common Player:	.10
1	Future Hall of Famer	.10
2	From Little League to the Major Leagues	.10
3	A Dream Come True	.10
4	Signed by the Mets	.10
5	Fireball Pitcher	.10
6	Mets Rookie Pitcher	.10
7	First Major League Win	.10
8	Early in 1969	.10
9	Tensions of a Pennant Race	.10
10	Mets Clinch NL East	.10
11	Keep the Ball Down	.10
12	Playoff Victory	.10
13	World Series Victory	.10
14	The Amazin' Mets	.10
15	Met Strikeout Record	.10
16	One of the Worst Trades in Baseball	.10
17	Slow Start with Mets	.10
18	Pitcher New York Mets	.10
19	Traded to the Angels	.10
20	Meeting New Friends	.10
21	Throwing Fast Balls	.10
22	Move the Ball Around	.10
23	Nolan Heat	.10
24	No-Hitter Number 1	.10
25	Looking Back on Number 1	.10
26	No-Hitter Number 2	.10
27	Single Season Strikeout Record	.10
28	21 Wins in 1973	.10
29	Fastest Pitch Ever Thrown at 100.9 MPH	.10
30	No-Hitter Number 3	.10
31	No-Hitter Number 4	.10
32	Ryan and Tanana	.10
33	Learning Change-Up	.10
34	Pitcher California Angels	.10
35	Nolan Joins Astros	.10
36	Starting Pitcher Nolan Ryan	.10
37	Taking Batting Practice	.10
38	The Game's Greatest Power Pitcher	.10
39	3000 Career Strikeouts	.10
40	A Ryan Home Run	.10
41	The Fast Ball Grip	.10
42	Record 5th No-Hitter	.10
43	No-Hitter Number 5	.10
44	A Dream Fulfilled	.10
45	Nolan Passes Walter Johnson	.10
46	Strikeout 4000	.10
47	Astros Win Western Division Title	.10
48	Pitcher Houston Astros	.10
49	Milestone Strikeouts	.10
50	Post Season Participant	.10
51	Hurling for Houston	.10
52	135 N.L. Wins	.10
53	Through with Chew	.10
54	Signed by Rangers 1989	.10
55	Pleasant Change for Nolan	.10
56	Real Special Moment	.10
57	1989 All-Star Game	.10
58	Pitching in 1989 All-Star Game	.10
59	5000 Strikeouts; A Standing Ovation	.10
60	Great Moments in 1989	.10
61	Nolan with Dan Smith, Rangers First Pic	.10
62	Ranger Club Record 16 Strikeouts	.10
63	Last Pitch No-Hitter Number 6	.10
64	Sweet Number 6	.10
65	Oldest to Throw No-Hitter	.10
66	Another Ryan Win	.10
67	20th Pitcher to Win 300	.10
68	300 Win Battery	.10
69	300 Game Winner	.10
70	Perfect Mechanics	.10
71	22 Seasons with 100 or more Strikeouts	.10
72	11th Strikeout Title	.10
73	232 Strikeouts, 1990	.10
74	The 1990 Season	.10
75	Pitcher Texas Rangers	.10
76	1991, Nolan's 25th Season	.10
77	Throwing Spirals	.10
78	Running the Steps	.10
79	Hard Work and Conditioning	.10
80	The Rigid Workout	.10
81	Ryan's Routine	.10
82	Ryan's Routine Between Starts	.10
83	Running in Outfield	.10
84	B.P. in Texas	.10
85	18 Career Low-Hitters	.10
86	My Job is to Give My Team/Chance to Win	.10
87	The Spring Workout	.10
88	Power versus Power	.10

89	Awesome Power	.10
90	Blazing Speed	.10
91	The Pick Off	.10
92	Real Gamer	.10
93	Ranger Battery Mates	.10
94	The Glare	.10
95	The High Leg Kick	.10
96	Day Off	.10
97	A New Ball	.10
98	Going to Rosin Bag	.10
99	Time for Relief	.10
100	Lone Star Legend	.10
101	Fans' Favorite	.10
102	Watching Nolan Pitch	.10
103	Our Family of Five	.10
104	Texas Beefmaster	.10
105	Gentleman Rancher	.10
106	Texas Cowboy Life	.10
107	The Ryan Family	.10
108	Participating in Cutting Horse Contest	.10
109	Nolan Interviews	.10
110	Lynn Nolan Ryan	.10

1991 Pacific Nolan Ryan Milestones

Issued as inserts in the 1991 Nolan Ryan foil packs was this set of eight career highlight cards. The format is basically the same as the regular-issue cards, except that the inserts are bordered in either silver (edition of 10,000) or gold (edition of 1,000). The unnumbered cards are checklisted here in chronolgical order. The inserts were found only in foil and wax packs.

		MT
Complete Set, Silver (8):		100.00
Complete Set, Gold (8):		225.00
Common Ryan, Silver:		12.00
Common Ryan, Gold:		40.00
(1a)	Rookie Pitcher (silver)	15.00
(1b)	Rookie Pitcher (gold)	50.00
(2a)	No-Hitter 1 (silver)	15.00
(2b)	No-Hitter 1 (gold)	50.00
(3a)	No-Hitter 2 (silver)	15.00
(3b)	No-Hitter 2 (gold)	50.00
(4a)	No-Hitter 3 (silver)	15.00
(4b)	No-Hitter 3 (gold)	50.00
(5a)	No-Hitter 4 (silver)	15.00
(5b)	No-Hitter 4 (gold)	50.00
(6a)	No-Hitter 5 (silver)	15.00
(6b)	No-Hitter 5 (gold)	50.00
(7a)	Sweet 6 (silver)	15.00
(7b)	Sweet 6 (gold)	50.00
(8a)	25th Season (silver)	15.00
(8b)	25th Season (gold)	50.00

1991 Pacific Nolan Ryan 7th No-Hitter

On May 1, 1991, before the home crowd at Arlington, Nolan Ryan posted his seventh career no-hitter, blanking the Blue Jays. In commemoration of the event, Pacific produced a seven-card insert set for random inclusion in its Nolan Ryan "Texas Express" foil packs. Each card was produced in an edition of 10,000 silver-foil bordered cards and 1,000 with gold-foil borders. The design follows the basic format of the regular Ryan issue, with the flaming baseball series logo at lower-left on the front, the card's title in a colored stripe beneath the photo, and Ryan's name printed vertically in a colored stripe at left. Backs repeat the flaming ball design at center, containing information about the no-hitter.

		MT
Complete Set, Silver (7):		80.00
Complete Set, Gold (7):		225.00
Common Card, Silver:		12.00
Common Card, Gold:		35.00
1a	Last Pitch (silver)	15.00
1b	Last Pitch (gold)	50.00
2a	No-Hitter #7 (silver)	15.00
2b	No-Hitter #7 (gold)	50.00
3a	The Best (silver)	15.00
3b	The Best (gold)	50.00
4a	Time to Celebrate (silver)	15.00
4b	Time to Celebrate (gold)	50.00
5a	Congratulations from Rangers Fans (silver))	15.00
5b	Congratulations from Rangers Fans (gold))	50.00
6a	Catcher Mike Stanley (silver)	15.00
6b	Catcher Mike Stanley (gold)	50.00
7a	All in a Day's Work (silver)	15.00
7b	All in a Day's Work (gold)	50.00

1991 Pacific Nolan Ryan 7th No-Hitter Hologram

Even more elusive and exclusive than the gold- and silver-foil bordered "7th No-Hitter" inserts found in wax and foil packs was this edition produced with gold and silver holographic borders (1,000 each in gold and silver. The hologram 7th No-Hitter inserts were found only in 99-cent cello packs.

		MT
Complete Set, Silver (7):		300.00
Complete Set, Gold (7):		300.00
Common Card, Silver:		50.00
Common Card, Gold:		50.00
1a	Last Pitch (silver)	50.00
1b	Last Pitch (gold)	50.00
2a	No-Hitter #7 (silver)	50.00
2b	No-Hitter #7 (gold)	50.00
3a	The Best (silver)	50.00
3b	The Best (gold)	50.00
4a	Time to Celebrate (silver)	50.00
4b	Time to Celebrate (gold)	50.00
5a	Congratulations from Rangers Fans (silver)	50.00
5b	Congratulations from Rangers Fans (gold)	50.00
6a	Catcher Mike Stanley (silver)	50.00
6b	Catcher Mike Stanley (gold)	50.00
7a	All in a Day's Work (silver)	50.00
7b	All in a Day's Work (gold)	50.00

Player names in *Italic* type indicate a rookie card.

1992 Pacific Nolan Ryan

The 1992 Nolan Ryan "Texas Express" Series II is numbered 111 to 220, featuring the same design as the original 110-card issue of 1991. The set includes photos of Ryan from boyhood to his seventh no-hitter, and two bonus subsets were also randomly inserted in the foil packs.

		MT
Complete Set (110):		10.00
Common Player:		.10
111	The Golden Arm	.10
112	Little League All-Star	.10
113	All-State Pitcher	.10
114	Nolan Ryan Field	.10
115	Nolan at Age 20	.10
116	Nolan Ryan Jacksonville Suns	.10
117	Surrounded By Friends	.10
118	Nolan the Cowboy	.10
119	The Simple Life	.10
120	Nolan Loves Animals	.10
121	Growing Up in New York	.10
122	New York Strikeout Record	.10
123	Traded	.10
124	Hall of Fame Victims	.10
125	Number 500	.10
126	California Victory	.10
127	20 Win Season	.10
128	Throwing Heat	.10
129	Strikeout Record	.10
130	Number One	.10
131	1,000th Strikeout	.10
132	Number Two	.10
133	2,000th Strikeout	.10
134	Number Three	.10
135	Pure Speed	.10
136	Independence Day Fireworks	.10
137	Fast Ball Pitcher	.10
138	Number Four	.10
139	Free Agent	.10
140	Houston Bound	.10
141	Big Dollars	.10
142	Strong Houston Staff	.10
143	Number Five	.10
144	Astro MVP	.10
145	Western Divison Game	.10
146	National League All-Star	.10
147	Major League Record	.10
148	Nolan Breaks Johnson's Record	.10
149	Reese and Nolan	.10
150	100th National League Win	.10
151	4,000th Strikeout	.10
152	League Leader	.10
153	250th Career Win	.10
154	The Seldom of Swat	.10
155	4,500th Strikeout	.10
156	Like Father Like Son	.10
157	Spoiled in the Ninth	.10
158	Leaving Houston	.10
159	Houston Star	.10
160	Ryan Test Free Agency	.10
161	Awesome Heat	.10
162	Brotherly Love	.10
163	Astros Return	.10
164	Texas Size Decision	.10
165	Texas Legend	.10
166	Drawing a Crowd	.10
167	Great Start	.10
168	5,000th Strikeout	.10
169	Texas All-Star	.10
170	Number Six	.10
171	300th Win	.10
172	1990 League Leader	.10
173	Man of the Year	.10
174	Spring Training 1991	.10
175	Fast Ball Grip	.10
176	Strong Arm	.10
177	Stanley's Delight	.10
178	After Nolan's 7th No-Hitter	.10
179	Stretching Before the Game	.10
180	The Rangers Sign Nolan for 1992 and 1993	.10
181	Heading to the Bullpen	.10
182	Nolan Ryan - Banker	.10
183	Time with Fans	.10
184	Solid 1992 Season	.10
185	Ranger Team Leader	.10
186	More Records	.10
187	Number Seven	.10
188	Nolan Passes Niekro	.10
189	Ryan Trails Sutton	.10
190	Ranger Strikeout Mark	.10
191	Consectutive K's	.10
192	5,500th Strikeout	.10
193	Twenty-Five First Timers	.10
194	No-Hitters Ended in the Ninth	.10
195	Constant Work-Outs	.10
196	Nolan in Motion	.10
197	Pitching in Fenway Park	.10
198	Goose and Nolan	.10
199	Talking Over Strategy	.10
200	Don't Mess With Texas	.10
201	314-278 Thru 1991	.10
202	All-Time Leader	.10
203	High Praise	.10
204	Manager's Delight	.10
205	733 Major League Starts	.10
206	Ryan the Quarterback	.10
207	Hard Work Pays Off	.10
208	Passing Along Wisdom	.10
209	Still Dominant	.10
210	Nolan's Fast Ball	.10
211	Seven No-Hitters	.10
212	Training for Perfection	.10
213	Nolan's Edge - Speed	.10
214	This One was for Them	.10
215	Another Day's Work	.10
216	Pick Off at Third	.10
217	Ready to Pitch	.10
218	Spring Training 1992	.10
219	Nolan Receives The Victor Award	.10
220	Nolan's 26th Season	.10

1992 Pacific Nolan Ryan Gold Inserts

Pacific produced this insert set for the 1992 Nolan Ryan "Texas Express" sequel. There are eight different gold-foil bordered cards, one for each of Ryan's no-hitters, plus an additional card combining all seven. Design is similar to the 1991-92 Ryan cards from Pacific. Backs feature box scores of the no-hitters. The cards are unnumbered. According to the manufacturer, 10,000 of each insert were produced.

		MT
Complete Set (8):		80.00
Common Ryan:		15.00
(1)	Number One	15.00
(2)	Number Two	15.00
(3)	Number Three	15.00
(4)	Number Four	15.00
(5)	Number Five	15.00
(6)	Number Six	15.00
(7)	Number Seven	15.00
(8)	Seven No-Hitters	15.00

1992 Pacific Nolan Ryan Limited

One of two insert sets included in both regular and jumbo foil packs of 1992 Pacific Nolan Ryan cards was this six-card presentation. Cards have the basic format of the regular issue except the "Texas Express" logo on front has been replaced by a Rangers team logo. Vertically formatted backs have a color photo at left and a few paragraphs of career summary at center. Each card was printed in an edition of 3,000, and Ryan personally autographed 1,000 of card #1. A second version of these cards, without the words "Limited Edition" on back beneath the Rangers and MLB logos, was produced for inclusion in the July, 1992, issue of "Trading Cards" magazine. The magazine versions of these cards are worth about 10% of the inserts.

		MT
Complete Set (6):		90.00
Common Ryan:		20.00
1	Nolan Ryan	20.00
1a	Nolan Ryan (autographed)	200.00
2	Nolan Ryan	20.00
3	The Texas Express	20.00
4	Seventh No-Hitter	20.00
5	Texas Legacy	20.00
6	Quarter Century	20.00

1992 Pacific Tom Seaver

In a style similar to its popular Nolan Ryan sets, Pacific produced a Tom Seaver set of 110 cards in 1992. The company also produced two limited edition subsets as part of the "Tom Terrific" card series. Cards were sold in both foil packs and factory sets. UV-coated fronts have white borders with silver, violet or magenta highlight stripes. A baseball symbol at lower-left has "Tom" above and "Terrific" beneath. This image is duplicated on back, with the ball containing either a photo or career highlights.

		MT
Complete Set (110):		9.00
Common Player:		.10
1	Stand-out High School Basketball Player	.10
2	Pro Ball Player	.10
3	Destined to be a Met	.10
4	Brave or Met	.10
5	Mets Luck of the Draw	.10
6	Sent to Jacksonville	.10
7	First Major League Win	.10
8	1967 Rookie of the Year	.10
9	Humble Beginnings	.10
10	Predicting the Future	.10
11	Rookie All-Star	.10
12	16 Wins in 1968	.10
13	1968 N.L. All-Star	.10
14	The Amazing Mets	.10
15	1969 Cy Young Winner	.10
16	Pitcher of the Year	.10
17	Strikeout Leader	.10
18	Ties Major League Record	.10
19	Mr. Consistency	.10
20	Finishing in Style	.10
21	Twenty-Game Winner	.10
22	Second Cy Young Award	.10
23	Batting Star	.10
24	At Bat in the World Series	.10
25	Championship Series Record	.10

26	Injury Plagued Season	.10
27	Comeback	.10
28	Super September	.10
29	Sporting News All-Star	.10
30	Strikeout Record	.10
31	USC Alumni Star	.10
32	Winning Smile	.10
33	One-Hitter	.10
34	Traded to the Reds	.10
35	New York Mets Pitcher	.10
36	Winning with the Reds	.10
37	No-Hitter	.10
38	N.L. Leader	.10
39	Smooth Swing	.10
40	No Decision in the Championship Series	.10
41	Injury Shortened Season	.10
42	Bouncing Back	.10
43	Eighth All-Star Appearance	.10
44	Spring Training 1982	.10
45	Back to New York	.10
46	Cincinnati Reds Pitcher	.10
47	Back in the Big Apple	.10
48	Opening Day Star	.10
49	Not Much Run Support	.10
50	Pair of Shutouts	.10
51	4,000 Inning Mark	.10
52	One Season in New York	.10
53	Chicago Bound	.10
54	Chicago White Sox Pitcher	.10
55	Win 300	.10
56	16 Wins in 1985	.10
57	Blast From the Past	.10
58	Moving Up in the Record Book	.10
59	Cy Young Winners	.10
60	Two Legends of the Game	.10
61	Singing Praise	.10
62	300th Win Tribute	.10
63	The Seaver Family	.10
64	20th Major League Season	.10
65	Traded to the Red Sox	.10
66	Chicago White Sox Career Record	.10
67	Red Sox Man	.10
68	Boston Red Sox Pitcher	.10
69	One Last Try	.10
70	Major League Records	.10
71	Lowest N.L. Career ERA	.10
72	Pitching in Comsikey Park	.10
73	273 N.L. Wins	.10
74	300 Win Honors	.10
75	311 Major League Wins	.10
76	41 Retired	.10
77	Championship Series 2.84 ERA	.10
78	June 1976 Age 32	.10
79	8-Time N.L. All-Star	.10
80	Broadcasting Career	.10
81	300th Win Celebration	.10
82	Tom and Nolan	.10
83	4th Best ERA All-Time	.10
84	15th All-Time in Victories	.10
85	300 Win Club	.10
86	Hall of Fame	.10
87	Pitching in Wrigley Field	.10
88	Power Pitching	.10
89	Spring Training 1980	.10
90	Pitching in Riverfront Stadium 1980	.10
91	Tom Terrific	.10
92	Super Seaver	.10
93	Top 10 All-Time	.10
94	16 Opening Day Starts	.10
95	3,272 Strikeouts	.10
96	Six Opening Day Wins	.10
97	239 Innings Pitched in 1985	.10
98	A Day Off	.10
99	Concentration (You Can't Let Up)	.10
100	Velocity, Movement, and Location	.10
101	Strikeout King	.10
102	The Most Important Pitch	.10
103	Cincinnati Reds Number 41	.10
104	George Thomas Seaver	.10
105	Dazzling Dean of the Reds' Staff	.10
106	Tom Receives the Judge Emil Fuchs Award	.10
107	Boston Mound Ace	.10
108	Fly Ball to Center	.10
109	August 4, 1985 Yankee Stadium	.10
110	Breaking Walter Johnson's Record	.10

1992 Pacific Tom Seaver Milestones

Inserted into foil packs of its 1992 Seaver set, Pacific produced a gold-foil bordered set limited to 10,000 each of six different cards featuring career milestones. A white-bordered version of 3,000 cards each was also produced. One thousand of the "Rookie Phenomenon" cards were personally autographed by Seaver among the inserts. On each card, an action photo of Seaver is flanked at left with his name vertically printed in a fading color stripe. The "Tom Terrific" baseball logo is carried over from the regular set at lower-left. Backs have a second photo at left, and a summary of the career highlight.

		MT
Complete Set (6):		50.00
Complete Set, Gold (6):		60.00
Common Seaver:		10.00
Common Seaver, Gold:		12.50
1a	Rookie Phenomenon	10.00
1b	Rookie Phenomenon (gold)	12.50
2a	Miracle Mets	10.00
2b	Miracle Mets (gold)	12.50
3a	Strikeout Record	10.00
3b	Strikeout Record (gold)	12.50
4a	No-Hitter	10.00
4b	No-Hitter (gold)	12.50
5a	300th Win	10.00
5b	300th Win (gold)	12.50
6a	Hall of Fame	10.00
6b	Hall of Fame (gold)	12.50

1993 Pacific/ Nolan Ryan 27th Season

The Pacific Trading Card Company marked the record-breaking 27th season of Nolan Ryan's career by re-issuing all 220 cards in its popular Nolan Ryan set with a special logo. The first series of the set (110 cards) had been issued in 1991 and the second series was issued in 1992 and numbered 111-220. In 1993 the company released a 30-card update for the pitcher's final season, complete with the special logo. Later the company decided to reissue cards 1-220 with the same logo because of the demand for the cards. Refer to 1991 and 1992 sets for card 1-220 checklists.

		MT
Complete Set (250):		22.00
Common Player:		.10
221	Rangers' Opening Night	.10
222	Slow Start in 1992	.10
223	Still Productive	.10
224	Getting Hot	.10
225	Closing Strong	.10
226	No Decision	.10
227	No Run Support	.10
228	Two Complete Games	.10
229	8-2/3 Inning Shutout	.10
230	Multiple Stikeout Games	.10
231	Ejected!	.10
232	319 and Counting	.10
233	Strikeout	.10
234	24 of 26 Seasons	.10
235	Smile, Nolan	.10
236	Texas Ranger Marks	.10
237	Ranger Ace	.10
238	Another Record	.10
239	6th Place All-Time Innings Pitched	.10
240	27 Games Started in 1992	.10
241	Seaver & Ryan	.10
242	Angels' Number 30 Retired	.10
243	Angels' Nolan Ryan Night	.10
244	Angels' Hall of Fame	.10
245	Great Friends	.10
246	Cowboys	.10
247	Spring Training	.10
248	Smokin' Fastball	.10
249	The Texas Express	.10
250	Pacific Pride	.10

1993 Pacific/ Nolan Ryan Prism

An insert set unique to the 1993 Pacific Nolan Ryan 27th Season set was this issue of 20 prism cards. Fronts feature an action photo of Ryan against a prismatic background. Backs have another photo and a few brief biographical notes on a marbled background. Each prism card was produced in a silver edition of 10,000 and a gold edition of 1,500. The prism cards were inserted into 25-cent foil packs of Pacific's 1993 Nolan Ryan issue.

		MT
Complete Set (Silver) (20):		200.00
Common Card (Silver):		12.50
1	Nolan Ryan (silver)	12.50
1a	Nolan Ryan (gold)	25.00
2	Nolan Ryan (silver)	12.50
2a	Nolan Ryan (gold)	25.00
3	Nolan Ryan (silver)	12.50
3a	Nolan Ryan (gold)	25.00
4	Nolan Ryan (silver)	12.50
4a	Nolan Ryan (gold)	25.00
5	Nolan Ryan (silver)	12.50
5a	Nolan Ryan (gold)	25.00
6	Nolan Ryan (silver)	12.50
6a	Nolan Ryan (gold)	25.00
7	Nolan Ryan (silver)	12.50
7a	Nolan Ryan (gold)	25.00
8	Nolan Ryan (silver)	12.50
8a	Nolan Ryan (gold)	25.00
9	Nolan Ryan (silver)	12.50
9a	Nolan Ryan (gold)	25.00
10	Nolan Ryan (silver)	12.50
10a	Nolan Ryan (gold)	25.00
11	Nolan Ryan (silver)	12.50
11a	Nolan Ryan (gold)	25.00
12	Nolan Ryan (silver)	12.50
12a	Nolan Ryan (gold)	25.00
13	Nolan Ryan (silver)	12.50
13a	Nolan Ryan (gold)	25.00
14	Nolan Ryan (silver)	12.50
14a	Nolan Ryan (gold)	25.00
15	Nolan Ryan (silver)	12.50
15a	Nolan Ryan (gold)	25.00
16	Nolan Ryan (silver)	12.50
16a	Nolan Ryan (gold)	25.00
17	Nolan Ryan (silver)	12.50
17a	Nolan Ryan (gold)	25.00
18	Nolan Ryan (silver)	12.50
18a	Nolan Ryan (gold)	25.00
19	Nolan Ryan (silver)	12.50
19a	Nolan Ryan (gold)	25.00
20	Nolan Ryan (silver)	12.50
20a	Nolan Ryan (gold)	25.00

1993 Pacific/ Nolan Ryan 27th Season Limited

Continuing with its "Limited Edition" insert set from the 1992 Nolan Ryan issue, this insert set picks up with numbers 7-12, featuring 1992 highlights in Ryan's career.

		MT
Complete Set (6):		65.00
Common Player:		15.00
7	Nolan Ryan	15.00
8	Nolan Ryan	15.00
9	Nolan Ryan	15.00
10	Nolan Ryan	15.00
11	Nolan Ryan	15.00
12	Nolan Ryan	15.00

1993 Pacific/ Nolan Ryan 27th Season Gold Limited

A gold-foil bordered version of the six 1993 Nolan Ryan "Limited Edition" insert cards was created as a card show give-away and random pack insert. Gold versions of cards #7-9 were given out at a Bellevue, Wash., show, while gold cards of #10-12 were found in foil packs. Just 3,000 of each foil-pack insert was produced.

		MT
Complete Set (6):		65.00
Common Player:		15.00
7	Nolan Ryan	15.00
8	Nolan Ryan	15.00
9	Nolan Ryan	15.00
10	Nolan Ryan	15.00
11	Nolan Ryan	15.00
12	Nolan Ryan	15.00

1993 Pacific

This set marks the first time a major league set was designed entirely for the Spanish-speaking market. Distribution areas included retail markets in the United States, Mexico, South America and the Caribbean. The cards are glossy and are written in Spanish on both sides. Cards are numbered in alphabetical order by team, beginning with Atlanta. Insert sets are titled Prism (20 cards featuring Spanish players and their accomplishments), Beisbol De Estralla (Stars of Baseball), Hot Players and Amigos (a 30-card set which features two players per card).

		MT
Complete Set (660):		20.00
Common Player:		.05
1	Rafael Belliard	.05
2	Sid Bream	.05
3	Francisco Cabrera	.05
4	Marvin Freeman	.05
5	Ron Gant	.10
6	Tom Glavine	.15
7	Brian Hunter	.05
8	Dave Justice	.20
9	Ryan Klesko	.20
10	Melvin Nieves	.05
11	Deion Sanders	.15
12	John Smoltz	.15
13	Mark Wohlers	.05
14	Brady Anderson	.15
15	Glenn Davis	.05
16	Mike Devereaux	.05
17	Leo Gomez	.05
18	Chris Hoiles	.05
19	Chito Martinez	.05
20	Ben McDonald	.05
21	Mike Mussina	.15
22	Gregg Olson	.05
23	Joe Orsulak	.05
24	Cal Ripken, Jr.	1.50
25	David Segui	.05
26	Rick Sutcliffe	.05
27	Wade Boggs	.40
28	Tom Brunansky	.05
29	Ellis Burks	.10
30	Roger Clemens	.50
31	John Dopson	.05
32	John Flaherty	.05
33	Mike Greenwell	.05
34	Tony Pena	.05
35	Carlos Quintana	.05
36	Luis Rivera	.05
37	Mo Vaughn	.40
38	Frank Viola	.05
39	Matt Young	.05
40	Scott Bailes	.05
41	Bert Blyleven	.05
42	Chad Curtis	.10
43	Gary DiSarcina	.05
44	Chuck Finley	.05
45	Mike Fitzgerald	.05
46	Gary Gaetti	.05

47	Rene Gonzales	.05
48	Mark Langston	.05
49	Scott Lewis	.05
50	Luis Polonia	.05
51	Tim Salmon	.50
52	Lee Stevens	.05
53	Steve Buechele	.05
54	Frank Castillo	.05
55	Doug Dascenzo	.05
56	Andre Dawson	.15
57	Shawon Dunston	.05
58	Mark Grace	.15
59	Mike Morgan	.05
60	Luis Salazar	.05
61	Rey Sanchez	.05
62	Ryne Sandberg	.50
63	Dwight Smith	.05
64	Jerome Walton	.05
65	Rick Wilkins	.05
66	Wilson Alvarez	.05
67	George Bell	.05
68	Joey Cora	.05
69	Alex Fernandez	.10
70	Carlton Fisk	.10
71	Craig Grebeck	.05
72	Ozzie Guillen	.05
73	Jack McDowell	.05
74	Scott Radinsky	.05
75	Tim Raines	.10
76	Bobby Thigpen	.05
77	Frank Thomas	1.00
78	Robin Ventura	.20
79	Tom Browning	.05
80	Jacob Brumfield	.05
81	Rob Dibble	.05
82	Bill Doran	.05
83	Billy Hatcher	.05
84	Barry Larkin	.15
85	Hal Morris	.05
86	Joe Oliver	.05
87	Jeff Reed	.05
88	Jose Rijo	.05
89	Bip Roberts	.05
90	Chris Sabo	.05
91	Sandy Alomar, Jr.	.10
92	Brad Arnsberg	.05
93	Carlos Baerga	.10
94	Albert Belle	.60
95	Felix Fermin	.05
96	Mark Lewis	.05
97	Kenny Lofton	.40
98	Carlos Martinez	.05
99	Rod Nicholos	.05
100	Dave Rohde	.05
101	Scott Scudder	.05
102	Paul Sorrento	.05
103	Mark Whiten	.05
104	Mark Carreon	.05
105	Milt Cuyler	.05
106	Rob Deer	.05
107	Cecil Fielder	.10
108	Travis Fryman	.10
109	Dan Gladden	.05
110	Bill Gullickson	.05
111	Les Lancaster	.05
112	Mark Leiter	.05
113	Tony Phillips	.05
114	Mickey Tettleton	.05
115	Alan Trammell	.10
116	Lou Whitaker	.05
117	Jeff Bagwell	.50
118	Craig Biggio	.20
119	Joe Boever	.05
120	Casey Candaele	.05
121	Andujar Cedeno	.05
122	Steve Finley	.05
123	Luis Gonzalez	.05
124	Pete Harnisch	.05
125	Jimmy Jones	.05
126	Mark Portugal	.05
127	Rafael Ramirez	.05
128	Mike Simms	.05
129	Eric Yelding	.05
130	Luis Aquino	.05
131	Kevin Appier	.05
132	Mike Boddicker	.05
133	George Brett	.50
134	Tom Gordon	.05
135	Mark Gubicza	.05
136	David Howard	.05
137	Gregg Jefferies	.10
138	Wally Joyner	.10
139	Brian McRae	.05
140	Jeff Montgomery	.05
141	Terry Shumpert	.05
142	Curtis Wilkerson	.05
143	Brett Butler	.10
144	Eric Davis	.10
145	Kevin Gross	.05
146	Dave Hansen	.05
147	Lenny Harris	.05
148	Carlos Hernandez	.05
149	Orel Hershiser	.10
150	Jay Howell	.05
151	Eric Karros	.10
152	Ramon Martinez	.10
153	Jose Offerman	.05
154	Mike Sharperson	.05
155	Darryl Strawberry	.10
156	Jim Gantner	.05
157	Darryl Hamilton	.05
158	Doug Henry	.05
159	John Jaha	.05
160	Pat Listach	.05
161	Jaime Navarro	.05
162	Dave Nilsson	.05
163	Jesse Orosco	.05
164	Kevin Seitzer	.05
165	B.J. Surhoff	.10
166	Greg Vaughn	.10
167	Robin Yount	.30
168	Rick Aguilera	.05
169	Scott Erickson	.05
170	Mark Guthrie	.05
171	Kent Hrbek	.10
172	Chuck Knoblauch	.15
173	Gene Larkin	.05
174	Shane Mack	.05
175	Pedro Munoz	.05
176	Mike Pagliarulo	.05
177	Kirby Puckett	.60
178	Kevin Tapani	.05
179	Gary Wayne	.05
180	Moises Alou	.10
181	Brian Barnes	.05
182	Archie Cianfrocco	.05
183	Delino DeShields	.10
184	Darrin Fletcher	.05
185	Marquis Grissom	.10
186	Ken Hill	.05
187	Dennis Martinez	.10
188	Bill Sampen	.05
189	John VanderWal	.05
190	Larry Walker	.15
191	Tim Wallach	.05
192	Bobby Bonilla	.10
193	Daryl Boston	.05
194	Vince Coleman	.05
195	Kevin Elster	.05
196	Sid Fernandez	.05
197	John Franco	.05
198	Dwight Gooden	.10
199	Howard Johnson	.05
200	Willie Randolph	.05
201	Bret Saberhagen	.05
202	Dick Schofield	.05
203	Pete Schourek	.05
204	Greg Cadaret	.05
205	John Habyan	.05
206	Pat Kelly	.05
207	Kevin Maas	.05
208	Don Mattingly	.45
209	Matt Nokes	.05
210	Melido Perez	.05
211	Scott Sanderson	.05
212	Andy Stankiewicz	.05
213	Danny Tartabull	.05
214	Randy Velarde	.05
215	Bernie Williams	.40
216	Harold Baines	.10
217	Mike Bordick	.05
218	Scott Brosius	.05
219	Jerry Browne	.05
220	Ron Darling	.05
221	Dennis Eckersley	.10
222	Rickey Henderson	.30
223	Rick Honeycutt	.05
224	Mark McGwire	1.50
225	Ruben Sierra	.05
226	Terry Steinbach	.05
227	Bob Welch	.05
228	Willie Wilson	.05
229	Ruben Amaro	.05
230	Kim Batiste	.05
231	Juan Bell	.05
232	Wes Chamberlain	.05
233	Darren Daulton	.05
234	Mariano Duncan	.05
235	Len Dykstra	.05
236	Dave Hollins	.05
237	Stan Javier	.05
238	John Kruk	.05
239	Mickey Morandini	.05
240	Terry Mulholland	.05
241	Mitch Williams	.05
242	Stan Belinda	.05
243	Jay Bell	.05
244	Carlos Garcia	.05
245	Jeff King	.05
246	Mike LaValliere	.05
247	Lloyd McClendon	.05
248	Orlando Merced	.05
249	Paul Miller	.05
250	Gary Redus	.05
251	Don Slaught	.05
252	Zane Smith	.05
253	Andy Van Slyke	.05
254	Tim Wakefield	.05
255	Andy Benes	.05
256	Dann Bilardello	.05
257	Tony Gwynn	.50
258	Greg Harris	.05
259	Darrin Jackson	.05
260	Mike Maddux	.05
261	Fred McGriff	.25
262	Rich Rodriguez	.05
263	Benito Santiago	.05
264	Gary Sheffield	.25
265	Kurt Stillwell	.05
266	Tim Teufel	.05
267	Bud Black	.05
268	John Burkett	.05
269	Will Clark	.30
270	Royce Calyton	.05
271	Bryan Hickerson	.05
272	Chris James	.05
273	Darren Lewis	.05
274	Willie McGee	.05
275	Jim McNamara	.05
276	Francisco Oliveras	.05
277	Robby Thompson	.05
278	Matt Williams	.25
279	Trevor Wilson	.05
280	Bret Boone	.10
281	Greg Briley	.05
282	Jay Buhner	.10
283	Henry Cotto	.05
284	Rich DeLucia	.05
285	Dave Fleming	.05
286	Ken Griffey, Jr.	2.00
287	Erik Hanson	.05
288	Randy Johnson	.25
289	Tino Martinez	.15
290	Edgar Martinez	.10
291	Dave Valle	.05
292	Omar Vizquel	.10
293	Luis Alicea	.05
294	Bernard Gilkey	.10
295	Felix Jose	.05
296	Ray Lankford	.10
297	Omar Olivares	.05
298	Jose Oquendo	.05
299	Tom Pagnozzi	.05
300	Geronimo Pena	.05
301	Gerald Perry	.05
302	Ozzie Smith	.40
303	Lee Smith	.10
304	Bob Tewksbury	.05
305	Todd Zeile	.10
306	Kevin Brown	.10
307	Todd Burns	.05
308	Jose Canseco	.40
309	Hector Fajardo	.05
310	Julio Franco	.05
311	Juan Gonzalez	.65
312	Jeff Huson	.05
313	Rob Maurer	.05
314	Rafael Palmeiro	.15
315	Dean Palmer	.10
316	Ivan Rodriguez	.40
317	Nolan Ryan	1.00
318	Dickie Thon	.05
319	Roberto Alomar	.50
320	Derek Bell	.10
321	Pat Borders	.05
322	Joe Carter	.10
323	Kelly Gruber	.05
324	Juan Guzman	.05
325	Manny Lee	.05
326	Jack Morris	.05
327	John Olerud	.15
328	Ed Sprague	.05
329	Todd Stottlemyre	.05
330	Duane Ward	.05
331	Steve Avery	.05
332	Damon Berryhill	.05
333	Jeff Blauser	.05
334	Mark Lemke	.05
335	Greg Maddux	1.00
336	Kent Mercker	.05
337	Otis Nixon	.05
338	Greg Olson	.05
339	Bill Pecota	.05
340	Terry Pendleton	.05
341	Mike Stanton	.05
342	Todd Frohwirth	.05
343	Tim Hulett	.05
344	Mark McLemore	.05
345	Luis Mercedes	.05
346	Alan Mills	.05
347	Sherman Obando	.05
348	Jim Poole	.05
349	Harold Reynolds	.05
350	Arthur Rhodes	.05
351	Jeff Tackett	.05
352	Fernando Valenzuela	.05
353	Scott Bankhead	.05
354	Ivan Calderon	.05
355	Scott Cooper	.05
356	Danny Darwin	.05
357	Scott Fletcher	.05
358	Tony Fossas	.05
359	Greg Harris	.05
360	Joe Hesketh	.05
361	Jose Melendez	.05
362	Paul Quantrill	.05
363	John Valentin	.10
364	Mike Butcher	.05
365	Chuck Crim	.05
366	Chili Davis	.05
367	Damion Easley	.05
368	Steve Frey	.05
369	Joe Grahe	.05
370	Greg Myers	.05
371	John Orton	.05
372	J.T. Snow	.25
373	Ron Tingley	.05
374	Julio Valera	.05
375	Paul Assenmacher	.05
376	Jose Bautista	.05
377	Jose Guzman	.05
378	Greg Hibbard	.05
379	Candy Maldonado	.05
380	Derrick May	.05
381	Dan Plesac	.05
382	Tommy Shields	.05
383	Sammy Sosa	1.00
384	Jose Vizcaino	.05
385	Greg Walbeck	.05
386	Ellis Burks	.10
387	Roberto Hernandez	.05
388	Mike Huff	.05
389	Bo Jackson	.15
390	Lance Johnson	.05
391	Ron Karkovice	.05
392	Kirk McCaskill	.05
393	Donn Pall	.05
394	Dan Pasqua	.05
395	Steve Sax	.05
396	Dave Stieb	.05
397	Bobby Ayala	.05
398	Tim Belcher	.05
399	Jeff Branson	.05
400	Cesar Hernandez	.05
401	Roberto Kelly	.05
402	Randy Milligan	.05
403	Kevin Mitchell	.05
404	Juan Samuel	.05
405	Reggie Sanders	.10
406	John Smiley	.05
407	Dan Wilson	.05
408	Mike Christopher	.05
409	Dennis Cook	.05
410	Alvaro Espinoza	.05
411	Glenallen Hill	.05
412	Reggie Jefferson	.05
413	Derek Lilliquist	.05
414	Jose Mesa	.05
415	Charles Nagy	.05
416	Junior Ortiz	.05
417	Eric Plunk	.05
418	Ted Power	.05
419	Scott Aldred	.05
420	Andy Ashby	.05
421	Freddie Benavides	.05
422	Dante Bichette	.10
423	Willie Blair	.05
424	Vinny Castilla	.10
425	Jerald Clark	.05
426	Alex Cole	.05
427	Andres Galarraga	.10
428	Joe Girardi	.05
429	Charlie Hayes	.05
430	Butch Henry	.05
431	Darren Holmes	.05
432	Dale Murphy	.15
433	David Nied	.05
434	Jeff Parrett	.05
435	*Steve Reed*	.05
436	Armando Reynoso	.05
437	Bruce Ruffin	.05
438	Bryn Smith	.05
439	Jim Tatum	.05
440	Eric Young	.10
441	Skeeter Barnes	.05
442	Tom Bolton	.05
443	Kirk Gibson	.05
444	Chad Krueter	.05
445	Bill Krueger	.05
446	Scott Livingstone	.05
447	Bob MacDonald	.05
448	Mike Moore	.05
449	Mike Munoz	.05
450	Gary Thurman	.05
451	David Wells	.10
452	Alex Arias	.05
453	Jack Armstrong	.05
454	Bret Barberie	.05
455	Ryan Bowen	.05
456	Cris Carpenter	.05
457	Chuck Carr	.05
458	Jeff Conine	.10
459	Steve Decker	.05
460	Orestes Destrade	.05
461	Monty Fariss	.05
462	Junior Felix	.05
463	Bryan Harvey	.05
464	Trevor Hoffman	.10
465	Charlie Hough	.05
466	Dave Magadan	.05
467	Bob McClure	.05
468	Rob Natal	.05
469	Scott Pose	.05
470	Rich Renteria	.05
471	Benito Santiago	.05
472	Matt Turner	.05
473	Walt Weiss	.05
474	Eric Anthony	.05
475	Chris Donnels	.05
476	Doug Drabek	.05
477	Xavier Hernandez	.05
478	Doug Jones	.05
479	Darryl Kile	.05
480	Scott Servais	.05
481	Greg Swindell	.05
482	Eddie Taubensee	.05
483	Jose Uribe	.05
484	Brian Williams	.05
485	Billy Brewer	.05
486	David Cone	.10
487	Greg Gagne	.05
488	Phil Hiatt	.05
489	Jose Lind	.05
490	Brent Mayne	.05
491	Kevin McReynolds	.05
492	Keith Miller	.05
493	Hipolito Pichardo	.05
494	Harvey Pulliam	.05
495	Rico Rossay	.05
496	Pedro Astacio	.05
497	Tom Candiotti	.05
498	Tom Goodwin	.05
499	Jim Gott	.05
500	Pedro Martinez	.15
501	Roger McDowell	.05
502	Mike Piazza	1.00
503	Jody Reed	.05
504	Rick Trlicek	.05
505	Mitch Weber	.05
506	Steve Wilson	.05
507	James Austin	.05
508	Ricky Bones	.05
509	Alex Diaz	.05
510	Mike Fetters	.05
511	Teddy Higuera	.05
512	Graeme Lloyd	.05
513	Carlos Maldonado	.05
514	Josias Manzanillo	.05
515	Kevin Reimer	.05
516	Bill Spiers	.05
517	Bill Wegman	.05
518	Willie Banks	.05
519	J.T. Bruett	.05
520	Brian Harper	.05
521	Terry Jorgensen	.05
522	Scott Leius	.05
523	Pat Mahomes	.05
524	Dave McCarty	.05
525	Jeff Reboulet	.10
526	Mike Trombley	.05
527	Carl Willis	.05
528	Dave Winfield	.25
529	Sean Berry	.05
530	Frank Bolick	.05
531	Kent Bottenfield	.05
532	Wil Cordero	.05
533	Jeff Fassero	.05
534	Tim Laker	.05
535	Mike Lansing	.10
536	Chris Nabholz	.05
537	Mel Rojas	.05
538	John Wetteland	.05
539	Ted Wood (Front photo actually Frank Bollick)	.05
540	Mike Draper	.05
541	Tony Fernandez	.05
542	Todd Hundley	.10
543	Jeff Innis	.05
544	Jeff McKnight	.05
545	Eddie Murray	.30
546	Charlie O'Brien	.05
547	Frank Tanana	.05
548	Ryan Thompson	.10
549	Chico Walker	.05
550	Anthony Young	.05
551	Jim Abbott	.10
552	Wade Boggs	.40
553	Steve Farr	.05
554	Neal Heaton	.05
555	Steve Howe	.05
556	Dion James	.05
557	Scott Kamieniecki	.05
558	Jimmy Key	.05
559	Jim Leyritz	.05
560	Paul O'Neill	.15
561	Spike Owen	.05
562	Lance Blankenship	.05
563	Joe Boever	.05
564	Storm Davis	.05
565	Kelly Downs	.05
566	Eric Fox	.05
567	Rich Gossage	.05
568	Dave Henderson	.05
569	Shawn Hillegas	.05
570	*Mike Mohler*	.05
571	Troy Neel	.10
572	Dale Sveum	.05
573	Larry Anderson	.05
574	Bob Ayrault	.05
575	Jose DeLeon	.05
576	Jim Eisenreich	.05
577	Pete Incaviglia	.05
578	Danny Jackson	.05
579	Ricky Jordan	.05
580	Ben Rivera	.05
581	Curt Schilling	.10
582	Milt Thompson	.05
583	David West	.05
584	John Candelaria	.05
585	Steve Cooke	.05
586	Tom Foley	.05
587	Al Martin	.05
588	Blas Minor	.05
589	Dennis Moeller	.05
590	Denny Neagle	.05
591	Tom Prince	.05
592	Randy Tomlin	.05
593	Bob Walk	.05
594	Kevin Young	.05
595	Pat Gomez	.05
596	Ricky Gutierrez	.05
597	Gene Harris	.05
598	Jeremy Hernandez	.05
599	Phil Plantier	.05
600	Tim Scott	.05
601	Frank Seminara	.05
602	Darrell Sherman	.05
603	Craig Shipley	.05
604	Guillermo Velasquez	.05
605	Dan Walters	.05
606	Mike Benjamin	.05
607	Barry Bonds	.35
608	Jeff Brantley	.05
609	Dave Burba	.05
610	Craig Colbert	.05
611	Mike Jackson	.05
612	Kirt Manwaring	.05
613	Dave Martinez	.05
614	Dave Righetti	.05
615	Kevin Rogers	.05
616	Bill Swift	.05
617	Rich Amaral	.05
618	Mike Blowers	.05
619	Chris Bosio	.05
620	Norm Charlton	.05
621	John Cummings	.05
622	Mike Felder	.05
623	Bill Haselman	.05
624	Tim Leary	.05
625	Pete O'Brien	.05
626	Russ Swan	.05
627	Fernando Vina	.05
628	Rene Arocha	.05
629	Rod Brewer	.05
630	Ozzie Canseco	.05
631	Rheal Cormier	.05
632	Brian Jordan	.10
633	Joe Magrane	.05
634	Donovan Osborne	.05

635	Mike Perez	.05
636	Stan Royer	.05
637	Hector Villanueva	.05
638	Tracy Woodson	.05
639	Benji Gil	.05
640	Tom Henke	.05
641	David Hulse	.05
642	Charlie Leibrandt	.05
643	Robb Nen	.05
644	Dan Peltier	.05
645	Billy Ripken	.05
646	Kenny Rogers	.05
647	John Russell	.05
648	Dan Smith	.05
649	Matt Whiteside	.05
650	William Canate	.05
651	Darnell Coles	.05
652	Al Leiter	.10
653	Dominigo Martinez	.05
654	Paul Molitor	.30
655	Luis Sojo	.05
656	Dave Stewart	.05
657	Mike Timlin	.05
658	Turner Ward	.05
659	Devon White	.10
660	Eddie Zosky	.05

1993 Pacific Beisbol Amigos

In groups of two, three or more, and generally from the same team, Latin players are paired in this second series insert set. The cards feature player photos (sometimes posed, sometimes superimposed) on a background of red, white and black baseballs. The players' last names and a card title are printed in Spanish on front and repeated on back. Also on back a few career highlights and stats are printed in red on a marbled background - again all in Spanish.

		MT
	Complete Set (30):	12.00
	Common Player:	.50
1	Edgar Martinez	.70
2	Luis Polonia, Stan Javier	.50
3	George Bell, Julio Franco	.50
4	Ozzie Guillen, Ivan Rodriguez	.75
5	Carlos Baerga, Sandy Alomar Jr.	.50
6	Sandy Alomar Jr., Alvaro Espinoza, Paul Sorrento, Carlos Baerga, Felix Fermin, Junior Ortiz, Jose Mesa, Carlos Martinez	.50
7	Sandy Alomar Jr., Roberto Alomar	1.00
8	Jose Lind, Felix Jose	.50
9	Ricky Bones, Jaime Navarro	.50
10	Jaime Navarro, Jesse Orosco	.50
11	Tino Martinez, Edgar Martinez	.50
12	Juan Gonzalez, Ivan Rodriguez	1.50
13	Juan Gonzalez, Julio Franco	.75
14	Julio Franco, Jose Canseco, Rafael Palmeiro	.60
15	Juan Gonzalez, Jose Canseco	1.00
16	Ivan Rodriguez, Benji Gil	.60
17	Jose Guzman, Frank Castillo	.50
18	Rey Sanchez, Jose Vizcaino	.50
19	Derrick May, Sammy Sosa	1.50
20	Sammy Sosa, Candy Maldonado	1.50
21	Jose Rijo, Juan Samuel	.50
22	Freddie Benavides, Andres Galarraga	.50
23	Guillermo Velasquez, Benito Santiago	.50
24	Luis Gonzalez, Andujar Cedeno	.50
25	Wil Cordero, Dennis Martinez	.50
26	Moises Alou, Wil Cordero	.50
27	Ozzie Canseco, Jose Canseco	.75
28	Jose Oquendo, Luis Alicea	.50
29	Luis Alicea, Rene Arocha	.50
30	Geronimo Pena, Luis Alicea	.50

1993 Pacific Estrellas de Beisbol

Pacific produced a gold-foil "Stars of Baseball" set of 20 that was randomly inserted as part of the company's first series Spanish language Major League set in 1993. Each card features a color action photo on the front surrounded by a gold-foil border. Production was limited to 10,000 of each card.

		MT
	Complete Set (20):	37.00
	Common Player:	1.50
1	Moises Alou	2.00
2	Bobby Bonilla	2.00
3	Tony Fernandez	1.50
4	Felix Jose	1.50
5	Dennis Martinez	2.00
6	Orlando Merced	1.50
7	Jose Oquendo	1.50
8	Geronimo Pena	1.50
9	Jose Rijo	1.50
10	Benito Santiago	1.50
11	Sandy Alomar Jr.	3.00
12	Carlos Baerga	1.50
13	Jose Canseco	4.00
14	Juan "Igor" Gonzalez	6.00
15	Juan Guzman	1.50
16	Edgar Martinez	1.50
17	Rafael Palmeiro	3.00
18	Ruben Sierra	1.50
19	Danny Tartabull	1.50
20	Omar Vizquel	1.50

1993 Pacific Jugadores Calientes

Three dozen "hot players" with a decidedly Hispanic predominance are featured in this glittery Series II insert set. Player action photos appear in front of a silver prismatic foil background. Names appear at bottom in boldly styled but hard to read letters in bright colors. Horizontal backs have a pair of player photos and a large team logo, along with a few stats, all printed in Spanish.

		MT
	Complete Set (36):	25.00
	Common Player:	.50
1	Rich Amaral	.50
2	George Brett	2.00
3	Jay Buhner	.50
4	Roger Clemens	1.20
5	Kirk Gibson	.50
6	Juan Gonzalez	1.50
7	Ken Griffey Jr.	3.00
8	Bo Jackson	.50
9	Kenny Lofton	.75
10	Mark McGwire	3.00
11	Sherman Obando	.50
12	John Olerud	.60
13	Carlos Quintana	.50
14	Ivan Rodriguez	.75
15	Nolan Ryan	2.50
16	J.T. Snow	.75
17	Fernando Valenzuela	.50
18	Dave Winfield	.75
19	Moises Alou	.60
20	Jeff Bagwell	1.25
21	Barry Bonds	1.25
22	Bobby Bonilla	.50
23	Vinny Castilla	.50
24	Andujar Cedeno	.50
25	Orestes Destrade	.50
26	Andres Galarraga	.60
27	Mark Grace	.75
28	Tony Gwynn	1.20
29	Roberto Kelly	.50
30	John Kruk	.50
31	Dave Magadan	.50
32	Derrick May	.50
33	Orlando Merced	.50
34	Mike Piazza	2.00
35	Armadno Reynoso	.50
36	Jose Vizcaino	.50

1993 Pacific Prism Insert

Pacific produced a prism card that was randomly inserted in its Series I Spanish-language set in 1993. Each of the 20 cards has a color photo of a star Latino player on the front superimposed over a prismatic silver-foil background. Card backs contain an action photo and a brief player biography on a marbled background. Production was limited to 10,000 of each card.

		MT
	Complete Set (20):	125.00
	Common Player:	6.00
1	Francisco Cabrera	6.00
2	Jose Lind	6.00
3	Dennis Martinez	6.00
4	Ramon Martinez	7.00
5	Jose Rijo	6.00
6	Benito Santiago	6.00
7	Roberto Alomar	12.50
8	Sandy Alomar Jr.	7.00
9	Carlos Baerga	6.00
10	George Bell	6.00
11	Jose Canseco	10.00
12	Alex Fernandez	6.00
13	Julio Franco	6.00
14	Igor (Juan) Gonzalez	22.00
15	Ozzie Guillen	6.00
16	Teddy Higuera	6.00
17	Edgar Martinez	6.00
18	Hipolito Pichardo	6.00
19	Luis Polonia	6.00
20	Ivan Rodriguez	8.00

Player names in *Italic* type indicate a rookie card.

1993 Pacific/ McCormick Nolan Ryan Milestones

Great moments in Nolan Ryan's career are featured in this set produced by Pacific for McCormick & Co., a food products company. Fronts are similar to several of Pacific's other Ryan issues and include a "Farewell to a Legend" logo in the lower-left corner. The career highlight represented by the photo is named in a red strip at bottom. Backs share an action photo of Ryan over which are printed stats, information about the highlight or other data. Sponsors logos are in the corners. Cards are UV coated on both sides.

		MT
	Complete Set (21):	10.00
	Common Player:	.50
1	No-Hitter #1 (Nolan Ryan)	.50
2	No-Hitter #2 (Nolan Ryan)	.50
3	No-Hitter #3 (Nolan Ryan)	.50
4	No-Hitter #4 (Nolan Ryan)	.50
5	No-Hitter #5 (Nolan Ryan)	.50
6	Last Pitch No-Hitter #6 (Nolan Ryan)	.50
7	No-Hitter #7 (Nolan Ryan)	.50
8	1st Strikeout (Nolan Ryan)	.50
9	1,000 Strikeout (Nolan Ryan)	.50
10	2,000 Strikeout (Nolan Ryan)	.50
11	3,000 Strikeout (Nolan Ryan)	.50
12	Nolan Breaks Johnson's Record (Nolan Ryan)	.50
13	4,000 Strikeout (Nolan Ryan)	.50
14	5,000 Strikeout (Nolan Ryan)	.50
15	5,500th Strikeout (Nolan Ryan)	.50
16	First Major League Win (Nolan Ryan)	.50
17	250th Career Win (Nolan Ryan)	.50
18	300th Win (Nolan Ryan)	.50
19	100.9 MPH Pitch (Nolan Ryan)	.50
20	Lone Star Legend (Nolan Ryan)	.50
---	Header card	.10

1994 Pacific Crown Promos

Virtually identical in format to the regular 1994 Pacific Crown issue, the eight cards in the promo set have a "P-" prefix to the card number. Each side has a large "For Promotional Use Only" printed diagonally in black. The cards were sent to dealers as a preview to Pacific's 1994 bilingual issue.

		MT
	Complete Set (8):	20.00
	Common Player:	1.50
1	Carlos Baerga	1.50
2	Joe Carter	1.50
3	Juan Gonzalez	3.00
4	Ken Griffey, Jr.	4.00
5	Greg Maddux	3.00
6	Mike Piazza	3.00
7	Tim Salmon	2.00
8	Frank Thomas	3.00

1994 Pacific Crown

Following its 1993 Spanish-language set, Pacific's 1994 "Crown Collection" offering is bi-lingual, featuring both English and Spanish for most of the back printing. Fronts have an action photo which is borderless at the top and sides. A gold-foil line separates the bottom of the photo from a marbled strip that is color-coded by team. The player's name appears in two lines at the left of the strip, a gold-foil crown logo is at left. A Pacific logo appears in one of the upper corners of the photo. Backs have a photo, again borderless at top and sides, with a Pacific logo in one upper corner and the card number and MLB logos in the lower corners. At bottom is a gray marble strip with a few biographical details, 1993 and career stats and a ghost-image color team logo. The 660 cards in the set were issued in a single series.

		MT
	Complete Set (660):	35.00
	Common Player:	.05
	Wax Box:	25.00
1	Steve Avery	.05
2	Steve Bedrosian	.05
3	Damon Berryhill	.05
4	Jeff Blauser	.05
5	Sid Bream	.05
6	Francisco Cabrera	.05
7	Ramon Caraballo	.05
8	Ron Gant	.10
9	Tom Glavine	.15
10	Chipper Jones	1.50
11	Dave Justice	.25
12	Ryan Klesko	.20
13	Mark Lemke	.05
14	Javier Lopez	.20
15	Greg Maddux	1.25
16	Fred McGriff	.25
17	Greg McMichael	.05

18	Kent Mercker	.05
19	Otis Nixon	.05
20	Terry Pendleton	.05
21	Deion Sanders	.15
22	John Smoltz	.15
23	Tony Tarasco	.05
24	Manny Alexander	.05
25	Brady Anderson	.15
26	Harold Baines	.05
27	Damion Buford (Damon)	.10
28	Paul Carey	.05
29	Mike Devereaux	.05
30	Todd Frohwirth	.05
31	Leo Gomez	.05
32	Jeffrey Hammonds	.05
33	Chris Hoiles	.05
34	Tim Hullett	.05
35	Ben McDonald	.05
36	Mark McLemore	.05
37	Alan Mills	.05
38	Mike Mussina	.20
39	Sherman Obando	.05
40	Gregg Olson	.05
41	Mike Pagliarulo	.05
42	Jim Poole	.05
43	Harold Reynolds	.05
44	Cal Ripken, Jr.	2.00
45	David Segui	.05
46	Fernando Valenzuela	.05
47	Jack Voight	.05
48	Scott Bankhead	.05
49	Roger Clemens	.75
50	Scott Cooper	.05
51	Danny Darwin	.05
52	Andre Dawson	.10
53	John Dopson	.05
54	Scott Fletcher	.05
55	Tony Fossas	.05
56	Mike Greenwell	.05
57	Billy Hatcher	.05
58	Jeff McNeely	.05
59	Jose Melendez	.05
60	Tim Naehring	.05
61	Tony Pena	.05
62	Carlos Quintana	.05
63	Paul Quantrill	.05
64	Luis Rivera	.05
65	Jeff Russell	.05
66	Aaron Sele	.05
67	John Valentin	.05
68	Mo Vaughn	.40
69	Frank Viola	.05
70	Bob Zupcic	.05
71	Mike Butcher	.05
72	Ron Correia	.05
73	Chad Curtis	.05
74	Chili Davis	.05
75	Gary DiSarcia	.05
76	Damion Easley	.05
77	John Farrell	.05
78	Chuck Finley	.05
79	Joe Grahe	.05
80	Stan Javier	.05
81	Mark Langston	.05
82	Phil Leftwich	.05
83	Torey Lovullo	.05
84	Joe Magrane	.05
85	Greg Myers	.05
86	Eduardo Perez	.05
87	Luis Polonia	.05
88	Tim Salmon	.25
89	J.T. Snow	.15
90	Kurt Stillwell	.05
91	Ron Tingley	.05
92	Chris Turner	.05
93	Julio Valera	.05
94	Jose Bautista	.05
95	Shawn Boskie	.05
96	Steve Buechele	.05
97	Frank Castillo	.05
98	Mark Grace	.15
99	Jose Guzman	.05
100	Mike Harkey	.05
101	Greg Hibbard	.05
102	Doug Jennings	.05
103	Derrick May	.05
104	Mike Morgan	.05
105	Randy Myers	.05
106	Karl Rhodes	.05
107	Kevin Robinson	.05
108	Rey Sanchez	.05
109	Ryne Sandberg	.50
110	Tommy Shields	.05
111	Dwight Smith	.05
112	Sammy Sosa	1.00
113	Jose Vizcaino	.05
114	Turk Wendell	.05
115	Rick Wilkins	.05
116	Willie Wilson	.05
117	Eddie Zambrano	.05
118	Wilson Alvarez	.05
119	Tim Belcher	.05
120	Jason Bere	.05
121	Rodney Bolton	.05
122	Ellis Burks	.10
123	Joey Cora	.05
124	Alex Fernandez	.10
125	Ozzie Guillen	.05
126	Craig Grebeck	.05
127	Roberto Hernandez	.05
128	Bo Jackson	.15
129	Lance Johnson	.05
130	Ron Karkovice	.05
131	Mike Lavalliere	.05
132	Norberto Martin	.05
133	Kirk McCaskill	.05
134	Jack McDowell	.05
135	Scott Radinsky	.05
136	Tim Raines	.10
137	Steve Sax	.05
138	Frank Thomas	1.00
139	Dan Pasqua	.05
140	Robin Ventura	.15
141	Jeff Branson	.05
142	Tom Browning	.05
143	Jacob Brumfield	.05
144	Tim Costo	.05
145	Rob Dibble	.05
146	Brian Dorsett	.05
147	Steve Foster	.05
148	Cesar Hernandez	.05
149	Roberto Kelly	.05
150	Barry Larkin	.15
151	Larry Luebbers	.05
152	Kevin Mitchell	.05
153	Joe Oliver	.05
154	Tim Pugh	.05
155	Jeff Reardon	.05
156	Jose Rijo	.05
157	Bip Roberts	.05
158	Chris Sabo	.05
159	Juan Samuel	.05
160	Reggie Sanders	.05
161	John Smiley	.05
162	Jerry Spradlin	.05
163	Gary Varsho	.05
164	Sandy Alomar Jr.	.10
165	Carlos Baerga	.05
166	Albert Belle	.60
167	Mark Clark	.05
168	Alvaro Espinoza	.05
169	Felix Fermin	.05
170	Reggie Jefferson	.05
171	Wayne Kirby	.05
172	Tom Kramer	.05
173	Jesse Levis	.05
174	Kenny Lofton	.50
175	Candy Maldonado	.05
176	Carlos Martinez	.05
177	Jose Mesa	.05
178	Jeff Mutis	.05
179	Charles Nagy	.05
180	Bob Ojeda	.05
181	Junior Ortiz	.05
182	Eric Plunk	.05
183	Manny Ramirez	.75
184	Paul Sorrento	.05
185	Jeff Treadway	.05
186	Bill Wertz	.05
187	Freddie Benavides	.05
188	Dante Bichette	.25
189	Willie Blair	.05
190	Daryl Boston	.05
191	Pedro Castellano	.05
192	Vinny Castilla	.10
193	Jerald Clark	.05
194	Alex Cole	.05
195	Andres Galarraga	.10
196	Joe Girardi	.05
197	Charlie Hayes	.05
198	Darren Holmes	.05
199	Chris Jones	.05
200	Curt Leskanic	.05
201	Roberto Mejia	.05
202	David Nied	.05
203	J. Owens	.05
204	Steve Reed	.05
205	Armando Reynoso	.05
206	Bruce Ruffin	.05
207	Keith Shepherd	.05
208	Jim Tatum	.05
209	Eric Young	.05
210	Skeeter Barnes	.05
211	Danny Bautista	.05
212	Tom Bolton	.05
213	Eric Davis	.10
214	Storm Davis	.05
215	Cecil Fielder	.10
216	Travis Fryman	.10
217	Kirk Gibson	.05
218	Dan Gladden	.05
219	John Doherty	.05
220	Chris Gomez	.05
221	David Haas	.05
222	Bill Krueger	.05
223	Chad Kreuter	.05
224	Mark Leiter	.05
225	Bob MacDonald	.05
226	Mike Moore	.05
227	Tony Phillips	.05
228	Rich Rowland	.05
229	Mickey Tettleton	.05
230	Alan Trammell	.10
231	David Wells	.10
232	Lou Whitaker	.05
233	Luis Aquino	.05
234	Alex Arias	.05
235	Jack Armstrong	.05
236	Ryan Bowen	.05
237	Chuck Carr	.05
238	Matias Carrillo	.05
239	Jeff Conine	.10
240	Henry Cotto	.05
241	Orestes Destrade	.05
242	Chris Hammond	.05
243	Bryan Harvey	.05
244	Charlie Hough	.05
245	Richie Lewis	.05
246	Mitch Lyden	.05
247	Dave Magadan	.05
248	Bob Natal	.05
249	Benito Santiago	.05
250	Gary Sheffield	.20
251	Matt Turner	.05
252	David Weathers	.05
253	Walt Weiss	.05
254	Darrell Whitmore	.05
255	Nigel Wilson	.05
256	Eric Anthony	.05
257	Jeff Bagwell	.75
258	Kevin Bass	.05
259	Craig Biggio	.15
260	Ken Caminiti	.15
261	Andujar Cedeno	.05
262	Chris Donnels	.05
263	Doug Drabek	.05
264	Tom Edens	.05
265	Steve Finley	.05
266	Luis Gonzalez	.05
267	Pete Harnisch	.05
268	Xavier Hernandez	.05
269	Todd Jones	.05
270	Darryl Kile	.05
271	Al Osuna	.05
272	Rick Parker	.05
273	Mark Portugal	.05
274	Scott Servais	.05
275	Greg Swindell	.05
276	Eddie Taubensee	.05
277	Jose Uribe	.05
278	Brian Williams	.05
279	Kevin Appier	.05
280	Billy Brewer	.05
281	David Cone	.10
282	Greg Gagne	.05
283	Tom Gordon	.05
284	Chris Gwynn	.05
285	John Habyan	.05
286	Chris Haney	.05
287	Phil Hiatt	.05
288	David Howard	.05
289	Felix Jose	.05
290	Wally Joyner	.05
291	Kevin Koslofski	.05
292	Jose Lind	.05
293	Brent Mayne	.05
294	Mike Mcfarlane	.05
295	Brian McRae	.05
296	Kevin McReynolds	.05
297	Keith Miller	.05
298	Jeff Montgomery	.05
299	Hipolito Pichardo	.05
300	Rico Rossy	.05
301	Curtis Wilkerson	.05
302	Pedro Astacio	.05
303	Rafael Bournigal	.05
304	Brett Butler	.10
305	Tom Candiotti	.05
306	Omar Daal	.05
307	Jim Gott	.05
308	Kevin Gross	.05
309	Dave Hansen	.05
310	Carlos Hernandez	.05
311	Orel Hershiser	.10
312	Eric Karros	.10
313	Pedro Martinez	.15
314	Ramon Martinez	.10
315	Roger McDowell	.05
316	Raul Mondesi	.40
317	Jose Offerman	.05
318	Mike Piazza	1.50
319	Jody Reed	.05
320	Henry Rodriguez	.05
321	Cory Snyder	.05
322	Darryl Strawberry	.10
323	Tim Wallach	.05
324	Steve Wilson	.05
325	Juan Bell	.05
326	Ricky Bones	.05
327	Alex Diaz	.05
328	Cal Eldred	.05
329	Darryl Hamilton	.05
330	Doug Henry	.05
331	John Jaha	.05
332	Pat Listach	.05
333	Graeme Lloyd	.05
334	Carlos Maldonado	.05
335	Angel Miranda	.05
336	Jaime Navarro	.05
337	Dave Nilsson	.05
338	Rafael Novoa	.05
339	Troy O'Leary	.05
340	Jesse Orosco	.05
341	Kevin Seitzer	.05
342	Bill Spiers	.05
343	William Suero	.05
344	B.J. Surhoff	.10
345	Dickie Thon	.05
346	Jose Valentin	.05
347	Greg Vaughn	.10
348	Robin Yount	.30
349	Willie Banks	.05
350	Bernardo Brito	.05
351	Scott Erickson	.05
352	Mark Guthrie	.05
353	Chip Hale	.05
354	Brian Harper	.05
355	Kent Hrbek	.10
356	Terry Jorgenson	.05
357	Chuck Knoblauch	.15
358	Gene Larkin	.05
359	Scott Leius	.05
360	Shane Mack	.05
361	David McCarty	.05
362	Pat Meares	.05
363	Pedro Munoz	.05
364	Derek Parks	.05
365	Kirby Puckett	.75
366	Jeff Reboulet	.05
367	Kevin Tapani	.05
368	Mike Trombley	.05
369	George Tsamis	.05
370	Carl Willis	.05
371	Dave Winfield	.20
372	Moises Alou	.10
373	Brian Barnes	.05
374	Sean Berry	.05
375	Frank Bolick	.05
376	Wil Cordero	.05
377	Delino DeShields	.05
378	Jeff Fassero	.05
379	Darren Fletcher	.05
380	Cliff Floyd	.05
381	Lou Frazier	.05
382	Marquis Grissom	.10
383	Gil Heredia	.05
384	Mike Lansing	.05
385	Oreste Marrero	.05
386	Dennis Martinez	.10
387	Curtis Pride	.10
388	Mel Rojas	.05
389	Kirk Rueter	.05
390	Joe Siddall	.05
391	John Vander Wal	.05
392	Larry Walker	.20
393	John Wetteland	.05
394	Rondell White	.10
395	Tom Bogar	.05
396	Bobby Bonilla	.10
397	Jeromy Burnitz	.05
398	Mike Draper	.05
399	Sid Fernandez	.05
400	John Franco	.05
401	Dave Gallagher	.05
402	Dwight Gooden	.10
403	Eric Hillman	.05
404	Todd Hundley	.10
405	Butch Huskey	.10
406	Jeff Innis	.05
407	Howard Johnson	.05
408	Jeff Kent	.05
409	Ced Landrum	.05
410	Mike Maddux	.05
411	Josias Manzanillo	.05
412	Jeff McKnight	.05
413	Eddie Murray	.25
414	Tito Navarro	.05
415	Joe Orsulak	.05
416	Bret Saberhagen	.05
417	Dave Telgheder	.05
418	Ryan Thompson	.05
419	Chico Walker	.05
420	Jim Abbott	.10
421	Wade Boggs	.30
422	Mike Gallego	.05
423	Mark Hutton	.05
424	Dion James	.05
425	Domingo Jean	.05
426	Pat Kelly	.05
427	Jimmy Key	.05
428	Jim Leyritz	.05
429	Kevin Maas	.05
430	Don Mattingly	1.00
431	Bobby Munoz	.05
432	Matt Nokes	.05
433	Paul O'Neill	.10
434	Spike Owen	.05
435	Melido Perez	.05
436	Lee Smith	.10
437	Andy Stankiewicz	.05
438	Mike Stanley	.05
439	Danny Tartabull	.05
440	Randy Velarde	.05
441	Bernie Williams	.35
442	Gerald Williams	.10
443	Mike Witt	.05
444	Marcos Armas	.05
445	Lance Blankenship	.05
446	Mike Bordick	.05
447	Ron Darling	.05
448	Dennis Eckersley	.10
449	Brent Gates	.05
450	Goose Gossage	.05
451	Scott Hemond	.05
452	Dave Henderson	.05
453	Shawn Hillegas	.05
454	Rick Honeycutt	.05
455	Scott Lydy	.05
456	Mark McGwire	3.00
457	Henry Mercedes	.05
458	Mike Mohler	.05
459	Troy Neel	.10
460	Edwin Nunez	.05
461	Craig Paquette	.05
462	Ruben Sierra	.05
463	Terry Steinbach	.05
464	Todd Van Poppel	.05
465	Bob Welch	.05
466	Bobby Witt	.05
467	Ruben Amaro	.05
468	Larry Anderson	.05
469	Kim Batiste	.05
470	Wes Chamberlain	.05
471	Darren Daulton	.05
472	Mariano Duncan	.05
473	Len Dykstra	.05
474	Jim Eisenreich	.05
475	Tommy Greene	.05
476	Dave Hollins	.05
477	Pete Incaviglia	.05
478	Danny Jackson	.05
479	John Kruk	.05
480	Tony Longmire	.05
481	Jeff Manto	.05
482	Mike Morandini	.05
483	Terry Mulholland	.05
484	Todd Pratt	.05
485	Ben Rivera	.05
486	Curt Shilling	.10
487	Kevin Stocker	.05
488	Milt Thompson	.05
489	David West	.05
490	Mitch Williams	.05
491	Jeff Ballard	.05
492	Jay Bell	.05
493	Scott Bullett	.05
494	Dave Clark	.05
495	Steve Cooke	.05
496	Midre Cummings	.05
497	Mark Dewey	.05
498	Carlos Garcia	.05
499	Jeff King	.05
500	Al Martin	.05
501	Lloyd McClendon	.05
502	Orlando Merced	.05
503	Blas Minor	.05
504	Denny Neagle	.05
505	Tom Prince	.05
506	Don Slaught	.05
507	Zane Smith	.05
508	Randy Tomlin	.05
509	Andy Van Slyke	.05
510	Paul Wagner	.05
511	Tim Wakefield	.05
512	Bob Walk	.05
513	John Wehner	.05
514	Kevin Young	.10
515	Billy Bean	.05
516	Andy Benes	.10
517	Derek Bell	.10
518	Doug Brocail	.05
519	Jarvis Brown	.05
520	Phil Clark	.05
521	Mark Davis	.05
522	Jeff Gardner	.05
523	Pat Gomez	.05
524	Ricky Gutierrez	.05
525	Tony Gwynn	.40
526	Gene Harris	.05
527	Kevin Higgins	.05
528	Trevor Hoffman	.10
529	Luis Lopez	.05
530	Pedro A. Martinez	.05
531	Melvin Nieves	.05
532	Phil Plantier	.05
533	Frank Seminara	.05
534	Craig Shipley	.05
535	Tim Tuefel	.05
536	Guillermo Velasquez	.05
537	Wally Whitehurst	.05
538	Rod Beck	.05
539	Todd Benzinger	.05
540	Barry Bonds	.50
541	Jeff Brantley	.05
542	Dave Burba	.05
543	John Burkett	.05
544	Will Clark	.25
545	Royce Clayton	.05
546	Brian Hickerson (Bryan)	.05
547	Mike Jackson	.05
548	Darren Lewis	.05
549	Kirt Manwaring	.05
550	Dave Martinez	.05
551	Willie McGee	.05
552	Jeff Reed	.05
553	Dave Righetti	.05
554	Kevin Rogers	.05
555	Steve Scarsone	.05
556	Bill Swift	.05
557	Robby Thompson	.05
558	Salomon Torres	.05
559	Matt Williams	.20
560	Trevor Wilson	.05
561	Rich Amaral	.05
562	Mike Blowers	.05
563	Chris Bosio	.05
564	Jay Buhner	.10
565	Norm Charlton	.05
566	Jim Converse	.05
567	Rich DeLucia	.05
568	Mike Felder	.05
569	Dave Fleming	.05
570	Ken Griffey, Jr.	3.00
571	Bill Haselman	.05
572	Dwayne Henry	.05
573	Brad Holman	.05
574	Randy Johnson	.25
575	Greg Litton	.05
576	Edgar Martinez	.10
577	Tino Martinez	.10
578	Jeff Nelson	.05
579	Mark Newfield	.05
580	Roger Salkeld	.05
581	Mackey Sasser	.05
582	Brian Turang	.05
583	Omar Vizquel	.05
584	Dave Valle	.05
585	Luis Alicea	.05
586	Rene Arocha	.05
587	Rheal Cormier	.05
588	Tripp Cromer	.05
589	Bernard Gilkey	.05
590	Lee Guetterman	.05
591	Gregg Jefferies	.10
592	Tim Jones	.05
593	Paul Kilgus	.05
594	Les Lancaster	.05
595	Omar Olivares	.05
596	Jose Oquendo	.05
597	Donovan Osborne	.05
598	Tom Pagnozzi	.05
599	Erik Pappas	.05
600	Geronimo Pena	.05
601	Mike Perez	.05
602	Gerald Perry	.05
603	Stan Royer	.05
604	Ozzie Smith	.25
605	Bob Tewksbury	.05

606	Allen Watson	.05
607	Mark Whiten	.05
608	Todd Zeile	.05
609	Jeff Bronkey	.05
610	Kevin Brown	.10
611	Jose Canseco	.25
612	Doug Dascenzo	.05
613	Butch Davis	.05
614	Mario Diaz	.05
615	Julio Franco	.05
616	Benji Gil	.05
617	Juan Gonzalez	1.00
618	Tom Henke	.05
619	Jeff Huson	.05
620	David Hulse	.05
621	Craig Lefferts	.05
622	Rafael Palmeiro	.15
623	Dean Palmer	.05
624	Bob Patterson	.05
625	Roger Pavlik	.05
626	Gary Redus	.05
627	Ivan Rodriguez	.40
628	Kenny Rogers	.05
629	Jon Shave	.05
630	Doug Strange	.05
631	Matt Whiteside	.05
632	Roberto Alomar	.50
633	Pat Borders	.05
634	Scott Brow	.05
635	Rob Butler	.05
636	Joe Carter	.10
637	Tony Castillo	.05
638	Mark Eichhorn	.05
639	Tony Fernandez	.05
640	*Huck Flener*	.05
641	Alfredo Griffin	.05
642	Juan Guzman	.05
643	Rickey Henderson	.25
644	Pat Hentgen	.05
645	Randy Knorr	.05
646	Al Leiter	.10
647	Dominigo Martinez	.05
648	Paul Molitor	.40
649	Jack Morris	.05
650	John Olerud	.15
651	Ed Sprague	.05
652	Dave Stewart	.05
653	Devon White	.10
654	Woody Williams	.05
655	Barry Bonds (MVP)	.40
656	Greg Maddux (CY)	.75
657	Jack McDowell (CY)	.05
658	Mike Piazza (ROY)	.75
659	Tim Salmon (ROY)	.25
660	Frank Thomas (MVP)	1.00

1994 Pacific Crown All Latino All-Star Team

Latino All-Stars is the theme of the third insert set found randomly packed in Pacific Spanish for 1994. Cards feature a player action photo on front, with a gold foil pinstripe around the sides and top. The player's name appears in gold script at bottom and there is a baseball logo in the corner. On backs a portrait photo of the player is set against a background of his native flag. Season highlights of 1993 are presented in English and Spanish. Eight thousand sets were produced.

		MT
Complete Set (20):		13.00
Common Player:		.50
1	Benito Santiago	.50
2	Dave Magadan	.50
3	Andres Galarraga	.75
4	Luis Gonzalez	.50
5	Jose Offerman	.50
6	Bobby Bonilla	.60
7	Dennis Martinez	.50
8	Mariano Duncan	.50
9	Orlando Merced	.50
10	Jose Rijo	.50
11	Danny Tartabull	.50
12	Ruben Sierra	.50
13	Ivan Rodriguez	2.00
14	Juan Gonzalez	4.00
15	Jose Canseco	1.50
16	Rafael Palmeiro	1.00
17	Roberto Alomar	2.00
18	Eduardo Perez	.50
19	Alex Fernandez	.50
20	Omar Vizquel	.60

1994 Pacific Crown Homerun Leaders

A gold prismatic background behind a color action player photo is the featured design on this Pacific insert set. Backs have another player photo against a ballfield backdrop. A huge baseball is overprinted with the player's name and number of 1993 homers. A league designation is among the logos featured on back. A total of 8,000 of these inserts sets was the announced production.

		MT
Complete Set (20):		30.00
Common Player:		1.00
1	Juan Gonzalez	4.50
2	Ken Griffey, Jr.	7.50
3	Frank Thomas	3.00
4	Albert Belle	2.50
5	Rafael Palmeiro	1.50
6	Joe Carter	1.50
7	Dean Palmer	1.00
8	Mickey Tettleton	1.00
9	Tim Salmon	1.50
10	Danny Tartabull	1.00
11	Barry Bonds	2.50
12	Dave Justice	2.00
13	Matt Williams	1.50
14	Fred McGriff	1.50
15	Ron Gant	1.00
16	Mike Piazza	4.50
17	Bobby Bonilla	1.00
18	Phil Plantier	1.00
19	Sammy Sosa	5.00
20	Rick Wilkins	1.00

1994 Pacific Crown Jewels of the Crown

One of three inserts into 1994 Pacific Spanish foil packs. The design features a player action photo set against a silver prismatic background. On back is another color player photo against a background of colored silk and a large jewel. Season highlight stats and awards won are presented in both English and Spanish. The announced production run of these inserts was 8,000 sets.

		MT
Complete Set (36):		60.00
Common Player:		1.00
1	Robin Yount	2.00
2	Juan Gonzalez	5.00
3	Rafael Palmeiro	1.50
4	Paul Molitor	2.50
5	Roberto Alomar	2.50
6	John Olerud	1.50
7	Randy Johnson	2.50
8	Ken Griffey, Jr.	9.00
9	Wade Boggs	2.50
10	Don Mattingly	4.00
11	Kirby Puckett	4.00
12	Tim Salmon	2.00
13	Frank Thomas	4.00
14	Fernando Valenzuela (Comeback Player)	1.00
15	Cal Ripken, Jr.	7.50
16	Carlos Baerga	1.00
17	Kenny Lofton	3.00
18	Cecil Fielder	1.00
19	John Burkett	1.00
20	Andres Galarraga (Comeback Player)	1.00
21	Charlie Hayes	1.00
22	Orestes Destrade	1.00
23	Jeff Conine	1.00
24	Jeff Bagwell	3.00
25	Mark Grace	1.50
26	Ryne Sandberg	2.50
27	Gregg Jefferies	1.00
28	Barry Bonds	2.50
29	Mike Piazza	6.00
30	Greg Maddux	5.00
31	Darren Daulton	1.00
32	John Kruk	1.00
33	Len Dykstra	1.00
34	Orlando Merced	1.00
35	Tony Gwynn	4.50
36	Robby Thompson	1.00

1994 Pacific Crown Jewels of the Crown - Retail

Using the same design, photos, graphics and card numbers, the retail version of the Jewels of the Crown insert set varies only in the silver prismatic foil background on front. While the scarcer hobby version has a diamond-shaped pattern to the foil, the retail version has numerous circles as a background pattern. The retail cards were inserted one per pack of retail product and are thus much more common than the hobby version.

		MT
Complete Set (36):		60.00
Common Player:		1.00
1	Robin Yount	2.00
2	Juan Gonzalez	4.50
3	Rafael Palmeiro	2.00
4	Paul Molitor	2.00
5	Roberto Alomar	2.50
6	John Olerud	1.50
7	Randy Johnson	2.00
8	Ken Griffey, Jr.	9.00
9	Wade Boggs	2.00
10	Don Mattingly	4.00
11	Kirby Puckett	4.00
12	Tim Salmon	1.50
13	Frank Thomas	5.00
14	Fernando Valenzuela (Comeback Player)	1.00
15	Cal Ripken, Jr.	7.50
16	Carlos Baerga	1.00
17	Kenny Lofton	1.50
18	Cecil Fielder	1.00
19	John Burkett	1.00
20	Andres Galarraga (Comeback Player)	1.00
21	Charlie Hayes	1.00
22	Orestes Destrade	1.00
23	Jeff Conine	1.00
24	Jeff Bagwell	3.00
25	Mark Grace	1.50
26	Ryne Sandberg	2.50
27	Gregg Jefferies	1.00
28	Barry Bonds	2.50
29	Mike Piazza	6.00
30	Greg Maddux	5.00
31	Darren Daulton	1.00
32	John Kruk	1.00
33	Len Dykstra	1.00
34	Orlando Merced	1.00
35	Tony Gwynn	4.50
36	Robby Thompson	1.00

1995 Pacific

The base cards in Pacific's Crown Collection baseball issue for 1995 feature borderless color action photos on front, graphically highlighted by the player name at bottom in gold foil and a color team logo in a baseball at lower-left. Backs have a playing field design in the background with a portrait photo at left. At right are 1994 stats, career highlights and a ghosted image of the team logo. Most back printing is in both English and Spanish. The 450 cards in the series are arranged alphabetically within team, with the teams arranged in city-alpha order. Several chase cards series are found in the 12-card foil packs.

		MT
Complete Set (450):		22.00
Common Player:		.05
Unlisted Stars: .25 to .50		
1	Steve Avery	.05
2	Rafael Belliard	.05
3	Jeff Blauser	.05
4	Tom Glavine	.10
5	Dave Justice	.35
6	Mike Kelly	.05
7	Roberto Kelly	.05
8	Ryan Klesko	.20
9	Mark Lemke	.05
10	Javier Lopez	.15
11	Greg Maddux	1.50
12	Fred McGriff	.25
13	Greg McMichael	.05
14	Jose Oliva	.05
15	John Smoltz	.10
16	Tony Tarasco	.05
17	Brady Anderson	.10
18	Harold Baines	.05
19	Armando Benitez	.05
20	Mike Devereaux	.05
21	Leo Gomez	.05
22	Jeffrey Hammonds	.05
23	Chris Hoiles	.05
24	Ben McDonald	.05
25	Mark McLemore	.05
26	Jamie Moyer	.05
27	Mike Mussina	.20
28	Rafael Palmeiro	.15
29	Jim Poole	.05
30	Cal Ripken Jr.	2.50
31	Lee Smith	.05
32	Mark Smith	.05
33	Jose Canseco	.30
34	Roger Clemens	.60
35	Scott Cooper	.05
36	Andre Dawson	.10
37	Tony Fossas	.05
38	Mike Greenwell	.05
39	Chris Howard	.05
40	Jose Melendez	.05
41	Nate Minchey	.05
42	Tim Naehring	.05
43	Otis Nixon	.05
44	Carlos Rodriguez	.05
45	Aaron Sele	.05
46	Lee Tinsley	.05
47	Sergio Valdez	.05
48	John Valentin	.05
49	Mo Vaughn	.50
50	Brian Anderson	.05
51	Garret Anderson	.05
52	Rod Correia	.05
53	Chad Curtis	.05
54	Mark Dalesandro	.05
55	Chili Davis	.05
56	Gary DiSarcina	.05
57	Damion Easley	.05
58	Jim Edmonds	.10
59	Jorge Fabregas	.05
60	Chuck Finley	.05
61	Bo Jackson	.10
62	Mark Langston	.05
63	Eduardo Perez	.05
64	Tim Salmon	.15
65	J.T. Snow	.10
66	Willie Banks	.05
67	Jose Bautista	.05
68	Shawon Dunston	.05
69	Kevin Foster	.05
70	Mark Grace	.20
71	Jose Guzman	.05
72	Jose Hernandez	.05
73	Blaise Ilsley	.05
74	Derrick May	.05
75	Randy Myers	.05
76	Karl Rhodes	.05
77	Kevin Roberson	.05
78	Rey Sanchez	.05
79	Sammy Sosa	1.00
80	Steve Trachsel	.05
81	Eddie Zambrano	.05
82	Wilson Alvarez	.05
83	Jason Bere	.05
84	Joey Cora	.05
85	Jose DeLeon	.05
86	Alex Fernandez	.05
87	Julio Franco	.05
88	Ozzie Guillen	.05
89	Joe Hall	.05
90	Roberto Hernandez	.05
91	Darrin Jackson	.05
92	Lance Johnson	.05
93	Norberto Martin	.05
94	Jack McDowell	.05
95	Tim Raines	.10
96	Olmedo Saenz	.05
97	Frank Thomas	1.00
98	Robin Ventura	.10
99	Bret Boone	.05
100	Jeff Brantley	.05
101	Jacob Brumfield	.05
102	Hector Carrasco	.05
103	Brian Dorsett	.05
104	Tony Fernandez	.05
105	Willie Greene	.05
106	Erik Hanson	.05
107	Kevin Jarvis	.05
108	Barry Larkin	.15
109	Kevin Mitchell	.05
110	Hal Morris	.05
111	Jose Rijo	.05
112	Johnny Ruffin	.05
113	Deion Sanders	.15
114	Reggie Sanders	.05
115	Sandy Alomar Jr.	.10
116	Ruben Amaro	.05
117	Carlos Baerga	.05
118	Albert Belle	.60
119	Alvaro Espinoza	.05
120	Rene Gonzales	.05
121	Wayne Kirby	.05
122	Kenny Lofton	.45
123	Candy Maldonado	.05
124	Dennis Martinez	.05
125	Eddie Murray	.25
126	Charles Nagy	.05
127	Tony Pena	.05
128	Manny Ramirez	.50
129	Paul Sorrento	.05
130	Jim Thome	.20
131	Omar Vizquel	.05
132	Dante Bichette	.25
133	Ellis Burks	.10
134	Vinny Castilla	.10
135	Marvin Freeman	.05
136	Andres Galarraga	.10
137	Joe Girardi	.05
138	Charlie Hayes	.05
139	Mike Kingery	.05
140	Nelson Liriano	.05
141	Roberto Mejia	.05
142	David Nied	.05
143	Steve Reed	.05
144	Armando Reynoso	.05
145	Bruce Ruffin	.05
146	John Vander Wal	.05
147	Walt Weiss	.05
148	Skeeter Barnes	.05
149	Tim Belcher	.05
150	Junior Felix	.05
151	Cecil Fielder	.10
152	Travis Fryman	.10
153	Kirk Gibson	.05
154	Chris Gomez	.05
155	Buddy Groom	.05
156	Chad Kreuter	.05
157	Mike Moore	.05
158	Tony Phillips	.05
159	Juan Samuel	.05
160	Mickey Tettleton	.05

161	Alan Trammell	.10
162	David Wells	.10
163	Lou Whitaker	.05
164	Kurt Abbott	.05
165	Luis Aquino	.05
166	Alex Arias	.05
167	Bret Barberie	.05
168	Jerry Browne	.05
169	Chuck Carr	.05
170	Matias Carrillo	.05
171	Greg Colbrunn	.05
172	Jeff Conine	.05
173	Carl Everett	.05
174	Robb Nen	.05
175	Yorkis Perez	.05
176	Pat Rapp	.05
177	Benito Santiago	.05
178	Gary Sheffield	.15
179	Darrell Whitmore	.05
180	Jeff Bagwell	.75
181	Kevin Bass	.05
182	Craig Biggio	.10
183	Andujar Cedeno	.05
184	Doug Drabek	.05
185	Tony Eusebio	.05
186	Steve Finley	.05
187	Luis Gonzalez	.05
188	Pete Harnisch	.05
189	John Hudek	.05
190	Orlando Miller	.05
191	James Mouton	.05
192	Roberto Petagine	.05
193	Shane Reynolds	.05
194	Greg Swindell	.05
195	Dave Veres	.05
196	Kevin Appier	.05
197	Stan Belinda	.05
198	Vince Coleman	.05
199	David Cone	.10
200	Gary Gaetti	.05
201	Greg Gagne	.05
202	Mark Gubicza	.05
203	Bob Hamelin	.05
204	Dave Henderson	.05
205	Felix Jose	.05
206	Wally Joyner	.05
207	Jose Lind	.05
208	Mike Macfarlane	.05
209	Brian McRae	.05
210	Jeff Montgomery	.05
211	Hipolito Pichardo	.05
212	Pedro Astacio	.05
213	Brett Butler	.10
214	Omar Daal	.05
215	Delino DeShields	.05
216	Darren Dreifort	.05
217	Carlos Hernandez	.05
218	Orel Hershiser	.05
219	Garey Ingram	.05
220	Eric Karros	.10
221	Ramon Martinez	.10
222	Raul Mondesi	.50
223	Jose Offerman	.05
224	Mike Piazza	1.50
225	Henry Rodriguez	.05
226	Ismael Valdes	.10
227	Tim Wallach	.05
228	Jeff Cirillo	.05
229	Alex Diaz	.05
230	Cal Eldred	.05
231	Mike Fetters	.05
232	Brian Harper	.05
233	Ted Higuera	.05
234	John Jaha	.05
235	Graeme Lloyd	.05
236	Jose Mercedes	.05
237	Jaime Navarro	.05
238	Dave Nilsson	.05
239	Jesse Orosco	.05
240	Jody Reed	.05
241	Jose Valentin	.05
242	Greg Vaughn	.10
243	Turner Ward	.05
244	Rick Aguilera	.05
245	Rich Becker	.05
246	Jim Deshaies	.05
247	Steve Dunn	.05
248	Scott Erickson	.05
249	Kent Hrbek	.05
250	Chuck Knoblauch	.15
251	Scott Leius	.05
252	David McCarty	.05
253	Pat Meares	.05
254	Pedro Munoz	.05
255	Kirby Puckett	.75
256	Carlos Pulido	.05
257	Kevin Tapani	.05
258	Matt Walbeck	.05
259	Dave Winfield	.15
260	Moises Alou	.10
261	Juan Bell	.05
262	Freddie Benavides	.05
263	Sean Berry	.05
264	Wil Cordero	.05
265	Jeff Fassero	.05
266	Darrin Fletcher	.05
267	Cliff Floyd	.05
268	Marquis Grissom	.05
269	Gil Heredia	.05
270	Ken Hill	.05
271	Pedro Martinez	.15
272	Mel Rojas	.05
273	Larry Walker	.25
274	John Wetteland	.05
275	Rondell White	.15
276	Tim Bogar	.05
277	Bobby Bonilla	.10
278	Rico Brogna	.05
279	Jeromy Burnitz	.05
280	John Franco	.05
281	Eric Hillman	.05
282	Todd Hundley	.10
283	Jeff Kent	.05
284	Mike Maddux	.05
285	Joe Orsulak	.05
286	Luis Rivera	.05
287	Bret Saberhagen	.05
288	David Segui	.05
289	Ryan Thompson	.05
290	Fernando Vina	.05
291	Jose Vizcaino	.05
292	Jim Abbott	.05
293	Wade Boggs	.25
294	Russ Davis	.05
295	Mike Gallego	.05
296	Xavier Hernandez	.05
297	Steve Howe	.05
298	Jimmy Key	.05
299	Don Mattingly	.75
300	Terry Mulholland	.05
301	Paul O'Neill	.10
302	Luis Polonia	.05
303	Mike Stanley	.05
304	Danny Tartabull	.05
305	Randy Velarde	.05
306	Bob Wickman	.05
307	Bernie Williams	.35
308	Mark Acre	.05
309	Geronimo Berroa	.05
310	Mike Bordick	.05
311	Dennis Eckersley	.05
312	Rickey Henderson	.20
313	Stan Javier	.05
314	Miguel Jimenez	.05
315	Francisco Matos	.05
316	Mark McGwire	3.00
317	Troy Neel	.05
318	Steve Ontiveros	.05
319	Carlos Reyes	.05
320	Ruben Sierra	.05
321	Terry Steinbach	.05
322	Bob Welch	.05
323	Bobby Witt	.05
324	Larry Andersen	.05
325	Kim Batiste	.05
326	Darren Daulton	.05
327	Mariano Duncan	.05
328	Lenny Dykstra	.05
329	Jim Eisenreich	.05
330	Danny Jackson	.05
331	John Kruk	.05
332	Tony Longmire	.05
333	Tom Marsh	.05
334	Mickey Morandini	.05
335	Bobby Munoz	.05
336	Todd Pratt	.05
337	Tom Quinlan	.05
338	Kevin Stocker	.05
339	Fernando Valenzuela	.05
340	Jay Bell	.05
341	Dave Clark	.05
342	Steve Cooke	.05
343	Carlos Garcia	.05
344	Jeff King	.05
345	Jon Lieber	.05
346	Ravelo Manzanillo	.05
347	Al Martin	.05
348	Orlando Merced	.05
349	Denny Neagle	.05
350	Alejandro Pena	.05
351	Don Slaught	.05
352	Zane Smith	.05
353	Andy Van Slyke	.05
354	Rick White	.05
355	Kevin Young	.05
356	Andy Ashby	.05
357	Derek Bell	.10
358	Andy Benes	.10
359	Phil Clark	.05
360	Donnie Elliott	.05
361	Ricky Gutierrez	.05
362	Tony Gwynn	.50
363	Trevor Hoffman	.10
364	Tim Hyers	.05
365	Luis Lopez	.05
366	Jose Martinez	.05
367	Pedro A. Martinez	.05
368	Phil Plantier	.05
369	Bip Roberts	.05
370	A.J. Sager	.05
371	Jeff Tabaka	.05
372	Todd Benzinger	.05
373	Barry Bonds	.50
374	John Burkett	.05
375	Mark Carreon	.05
376	Royce Clayton	.05
377	Pat Gomez	.05
378	Erik Johnson	.05
379	Darren Lewis	.05
380	Kirt Manwaring	.05
381	Dave Martinez	.05
382	John Patterson	.05
383	Mark Portugal	.05
384	Darryl Strawberry	.10
385	Salomon Torres	.05
386	Bill Van Landingham	.05
387	Matt Williams	.20
388	Rich Amaral	.05
389	Bobby Ayala	.05
390	Mike Blowers	.05
391	Chris Bosio	.05
392	Jay Buhner	.10
393	Jim Converse	.05
394	Tim Davis	.05
395	Felix Fermin	.05
396	Dave Fleming	.05
397	Goose Gossage	.05
398	Ken Griffey Jr.	3.00
399	Randy Johnson	.25
400	Edgar Martinez	.05
401	Tino Martinez	.10
402	Alex Rodriguez	2.50
403	Dan Wilson	.05
404	Luis Alicea	.05
405	Rene Arocha	.05
406	Bernard Gilkey	.05
407	Gregg Jefferies	.05
408	Ray Lankford	.10
409	Terry McGriff	.05
410	Omar Olivares	.05
411	Jose Oquendo	.05
412	Vicente Palacios	.05
413	Geronimo Pena	.05
414	Mike Perez	.05
415	Gerald Perry	.05
416	Ozzie Smith	.35
417	Bob Tewksbury	.05
418	Mark Whiten	.05
419	Todd Zeile	.05
420	Esteban Beltre	.05
421	Kevin Brown	.10
422	Cris Carpenter	.05
423	Will Clark	.25
424	Hector Fajardo	.05
425	Jeff Frye	.05
426	Juan Gonzalez	.50
427	Rusty Greer	.05
428	Rick Honeycutt	.05
429	David Hulse	.05
430	Manny Lee	.05
431	Junior Ortiz	.05
432	Dean Palmer	.05
433	Ivan Rodriguez	.45
434	Dan Smith	.05
435	Roberto Alomar	.50
436	Pat Borders	.05
437	Scott Brow	.05
438	Rob Butler	.05
439	Joe Carter	.10
440	Tony Castillo	.05
441	Domingo Cedeno	.05
442	Brad Cornett	.05
443	Carlos Delgado	.20
444	Alex Gonzalez	.10
445	Juan Guzman	.05
446	Darren Hall	.05
447	Paul Molitor	.25
448	John Olerud	.10
449	Robert Perez	.05
450	Devon White	.05

1995 Pacific Gold Crown Die-cut

A die-cut gold holographic foil crown in the background is featured in this chase set. The player's name at bottom is rendered in the same foil. Backs have a dark blue background, a portrait photo and a 1994 season recap.

		MT
Complete Set (20):		125.00
Common Player:		1.50
1	Greg Maddux	12.50
2	Fred McGriff	2.50
3	Rafael Palmeiro	2.50
4	Cal Ripken Jr.	16.00
5	Jose Canseco	2.50
6	Frank Thomas	6.00
7	Albert Belle	5.00
8	Manny Ramirez	5.00
9	Andres Galarraga	1.50
10	Jeff Bagwell	7.50
11	Chan Ho Park	1.50
12	Raul Mondesi	2.00
13	Mike Piazza	12.50
14	Kirby Puckett	7.50
15	Barry Bonds	5.00
16	Ken Griffey Jr.	20.00
17	Alex Rodriguez	16.00
18	Juan Gonzalez	10.00
19	Roberto Alomar	4.00
20	Carlos Delgado	1.50

1995 Pacific Hot Hispanics

Acknowledging its bi-lingual card license and market niche, this insert set of Latinos Destacados (Hot Hispanics) features top Latin players in the majors. The series logo and a gold-foil holographic player name rise from a row of flames at bottom-front. On the reverse is another player photo, on an inferno background, along with 1994 season highlights and a large team logo.

		MT
Complete Set (36):		45.00
Common Player:		1.25
1	Roberto Alomar	5.00
2	Moises Alou	1.50
3	Wilson Alvarez	1.25
4	Carlos Baerga	1.25
5	Geronimo Berroa	1.25
6	Jose Canseco	3.00
7	Hector Carrasco	1.25
8	Wil Cordero	1.25
9	Carlos Delgado	1.50
10	Damion Easley	1.25
11	Tony Eusebio	1.25
12	Hector Fajardo	1.25
13	Andres Galarraga	2.00
14	Carlos Garcia	1.25
15	Chris Gomez	1.25
16	Alex Gonzalez	1.25
17	Juan Gonzalez	8.00
18	Luis Gonzalez	1.25
19	Felix Jose	1.25
20	Javier Lopez	2.00
21	Luis Lopez	1.25
22	Dennis Martinez	1.25
23	Orlando Miller	1.25
24	Raul Mondesi	2.00
25	Jose Oliva	1.25
26	Rafael Palmeiro	2.00
27	Yorkis Perez	1.25
28	Manny Ramirez	8.00
29	Jose Rijo	1.25
30	Alex Rodriguez	16.00
31	Ivan Rodriguez	5.00
32	Carlos Rodriguez	1.25
33	Sammy Sosa	10.00
34	Tony Tarasco	1.25
35	Ismael Valdes	1.25
36	Bernie Williams	4.00

1995 Pacific Marquee Prism

Etched gold holographic foil is the background to the action photos in this insert set. Player names at bottom-front are shadowed in team colors. Backs repeat the front photo in miniature version in a box at one side that offers career stats and a highlight. On the other end is a portrait photo on a background of baseballs.

		MT
Complete Set (36):		125.00
Common Player:		1.50
1	Jose Canseco	2.50
2	Gregg Jefferies	1.50
3	Fred McGriff	2.00
4	Joe Carter	2.00
5	Tim Salmon	2.50
6	Wade Boggs	4.00
7	Dave Winfield	2.50
8	Bob Hamelin	1.50
9	Cal Ripken Jr.	15.00
10	Don Mattingly	8.00
11	Juan Gonzalez	8.00
12	Carlos Delgado	1.75
13	Barry Bonds	7.50
14	Albert Belle	6.00
15	Raul Mondesi	3.00
16	Jeff Bagwell	8.00
17	Mike Piazza	10.00
18	Rafael Palmeiro	2.50
19	Frank Thomas	8.00
20	Matt Williams	2.50
21	Ken Griffey Jr.	20.00
22	Will Clark	3.00
23	Bobby Bonilla	1.50
24	Kenny Lofton	5.00
25	Paul Molitor	6.00
26	Kirby Puckett	8.00
27	Dave Justice	2.00
28	Jeff Conine	1.50
29	Bret Boone	1.50
30	Larry Walker	2.50
31	Cecil Fielder	1.50
32	Manny Ramirez	7.50
33	Javier Lopez	2.00
34	Jimmy Key	1.50
35	Andres Galarraga	2.00
36	Tony Gwynn	8.00

1995 Pacific Prism

The rainbow prismatic foil which is the background ot the action photos on the card fronts provides the visual punch to Pacific's premium brand cards. In a throwback to the 1950s, the cards were sold in single-card packs for $1.75. Production was limited to 2,999 cases of 36-pack boxes. Backs have a large portrait photo on a conventionally printed rainbow background. In keeping with the company's license, the 1994 season summary printed at bottom on back is in both English and Spanish. One checklist, team or Pacific logo was inserted into each pack to protect the Prism card.

		MT
Complete Set (144):		150.00
Common Player:		.50
Wax Box:		48.00
Unlisted Stars:		1.50
1	Dave Justice	1.00
2	Ryan Klesko	1.00
3	Javier Lopez	.75
4	Greg Maddux	10.00
5	Fred McGriff	1.00
6	Tony Tarasco	.50
7	Jeffrey Hammonds	.50
8	Mike Mussina	1.50
9	Rafael Palmeiro	.75
10	Cal Ripken Jr.	12.00
11	Lee Smith	.50
12	Roger Clemens	2.50
13	Scott Cooper	.50
14	Mike Greenwell	.50
15	Carlos Rodriguez	.50
16	Mo Vaughn	4.00

17	Chili Davis	.50
18	Jim Edmonds	.50
19	Jorge Fabregas	.50
20	Bo Jackson	.60
21	Tim Salmon	.60
22	Mark Grace	.75
23	Jose Guzman	.50
24	Randy Myers	.50
25	Rey Sanchez	.50
26	Sammy Sosa	8.00
27	Wilson Alvarez	.50
28	Julio Franco	.50
29	Ozzie Guillen	.50
30	Jack McDowell	.50
31	Frank Thomas	6.00
32	Bret Boone	.50
33	Barry Larkin	1.00
34	Hal Morris	.50
35	Jose Rijo	.50
36	Deion Sanders	1.50
37	Carlos Baerga	.50
38	Albert Belle	4.00
39	Kenny Lofton	2.00
40	Dennis Martinez	.50
41	Manny Ramirez	4.00
42	Omar Vizquel	.50
43	Dante Bichette	1.00
44	Marvin Freeman	.50
45	Andres Galarraga	.60
46	Mike Kingery	.50
47	Danny Bautista	.50
48	Cecil Fielder	.50
49	Travis Fryman	.50
50	Tony Phillips	.50
51	Alan Trammell	.50
52	Lou Whitaker	.50
53	Alex Arias	.50
54	Bret Barberie	.50
55	Jeff Conine	.50
56	Charles Johnson	.50
57	Gary Sheffield	3.00
58	Jeff Bagwell	6.00
59	Craig Biggio	.50
60	Doug Drabek	.50
61	Tony Eusebio	.50
62	Luis Gonzalez	.50
63	David Cone	.60
64	Bob Hamelin	.50
65	Felix Jose	.50
66	Wally Joyner	.50
67	Brian McRae	.50
68	Brett Butler	.50
69	Garey Ingram	.50
70	Ramon Martinez	.50
71	Raul Mondesi	1.00
72	Mike Piazza	10.00
73	Henry Rodriguez	.50
74	Ricky Bones	.50
75	Pat Listach	.50
76	Dave Nilsson	.50
77	Jose Valentin	.50
78	Rick Aguilera	.50
79	Denny Hocking	.50
80	Shane Mack	.50
81	Pedro Munoz	.50
82	Kirby Puckett	6.00
83	Dave Winfield	.75
84	Moises Alou	.60
85	Wil Cordero	.50
86	Cliff Floyd	.50
87	Marquis Grissom	.50
88	Pedro Martinez	.75
89	Larry Walker	.75
90	Bobby Bonilla	.50
91	Jeromy Burnitz	.50
92	John Franco	.50
93	Jeff Kent	.50
94	Jose Vizcaino	.50
95	Wade Boggs	1.50
96	Jimmy Key	.50
97	Don Mattingly	7.00
98	Paul O'Neill	.60
99	Luis Polonia	.50
100	Danny Tartabull	.50
101	Geronimo Berroa	.50
102	Rickey Henderson	.75
103	Ruben Sierra	.50
104	Terry Steinbach	.50
105	Darren Daulton	.50
106	Mariano Duncan	.50
107	Lenny Dykstra	.50
108	Mike Lieberthal	.50
109	Tony Longmire	.50
110	Tom Marsh	.50
111	Jay Bell	.50
112	Carlos Garcia	.50
113	Orlando Merced	.50
114	Andy Van Slyke	.50
115	Derek Bell	.50
116	Tony Gwynn	6.00
117	Luis Lopez	.50
118	Bip Roberts	.50
119	Rod Beck	.50
120	Barry Bonds	5.00
121	Darryl Strawberry	.60
122	Bill Van Landingham	.50
123	Matt Williams	1.00
124	Jay Buhner	.50
125	Felix Fermin	.50
126	Ken Griffey Jr.	15.00
127	Randy Johnson	1.00
128	Edgar Martinez	.50
129	Alex Rodriguez	15.00
130	Rene Arocha	.50
131	Gregg Jefferies	.50
132	Mike Perez	.50
133	Ozzie Smith	3.00
134	Jose Canseco	.75
135	Will Clark	.75
136	Juan Gonzalez	6.00
137	Ivan Rodriguez	3.00
138	Roberto Alomar	3.00
139	Joe Carter	.50
140	Carlos Delgado	.50
141	Alex Gonzalez	.50
142	Juan Guzman	.50
143	Paul Molitor	2.00
144	John Olerud	.65

1995 Pacific Prism Team Logos

Inserted one card per pack to provide some protection to the Prism card was a checklist, team or Pacific logo card. The large color logos are on a background of a playing field. Backs have a short English/Spanish history of the team.

		MT
Complete Set (31):		2.00
Common Player:		.10
1	Baltimore Orioles	.10
2	Boston Red Sox	.10
3	California Angels	.10
4	Chicago White Sox	.10
5	Cleveland Indians	.10
6	Detroit Tigers	.10
7	Kansas City Royals	.10
8	Milwaukee Brewers	.10
9	Minnesota Twins	.10
10	New York Yankees	.10
11	Oakland Athletics	.10
12	Seattle Mariners	.10
13	Texas Rangers	.10
14	Toronto Blue Jays	.10
15	Atlanta Braves	.10
16	Chicago Cubs	.10
17	Cincinnati Reds	.10
18	Colorado Rockies	.10
19	Florida Marlins	.10
20	Houston Astros	.10
21	Los Angeles Dodgers	.10
22	Montreal Expos	.10
23	New York Mets	.10
24	Philadelphia Phillies	.10
25	Pittsburgh Pirates	.10
26	St. Louis Cardinals	.10
27	San Diego Padres	.10
28	San Francisco Giants	.10
1	Checklist 1-72	.05
2	Checklist 73-144	.05
---	Pacific logo card	.05

1995 Pacific Harvey Riebe

This card was produced as a favor for a former major leaguer who had never had a card issued of him during his career as a catcher with the Detroit Tigers (1942, 1947-49). The front has a sepia action photo, a portrait photo, also sepia, is on back along with Riebe's major league stats.

	MT
Harvey Riebe	3.00

1995 Pacific Mariners Memories

To commemorate the M's magical 1995 season leading up to the A.L. Western Division pennant and the American League championship series, Pacific issued this boxed set. The first 17 cards in the set depict post-season action, with backs done in newspaper style. The rest of the set features the individual players in borderless action photos on front and smaller color portraits on back. All cards feature silver-foil highlights on front. The set was sold in a team-colors cardboard box. The set was released in late December and includes full 1995 stats for the players.

		MT
Complete Set (50):		15.00
Common Player:		.10
1	Griffey slams M's to brink (Ken Griffey Jr.)	.50
2	Mariners clinch tie in Texas (Vince Coleman)	.10
3	Mariners win the West (Luis Sojo)	.10
4	At last, something to celebrate (Randy Johnson)	.15
5	Johnson stands tall (Randy Johnson)	.15
6	Griffey has big debut (Ken Griffey Jr.)	.50
7	Tino ignites Mariners (Edgar Martinez, Tino Martinez)	.10
8	Mariners tie Yankee series (Edgar Martinez)	.10
9	Griffey scores winning run (Ken Griffey Jr.)	.50
10	Thunder in the Kingdome	.10
11	Series win ends years of futility	.10
12	Bob who? beats Cleveland (Bob Wolcott)	.10
13	Buhner rocks Cleveland (Jay Buhner)	.15
14	Johnson salutes Kingdome crowd (Randy Johnson)	.15
15	Fans give their all (Lou Piniella)	.10
16	Cora eludes tag (Joey Cora)	.10
17	Voice of M's calls winner (Dave Niehaus)	.10
18	Rich Amaral	.10
19	Bobby Ayala	.10
20	Tim Belcher	.10
21	Andy Benes	.20
22	Mike Blowers	.10
23	Chris Bosio	.10
24	Darren Bragg	.10
25	Jay Buhner	1.00
26	Rafael Carmona	.10
27	Norm Charlton	.10
28	Vince Coleman	.25
29	Joey Cora	.10
30	Alex Diaz	.10
31	Felix Fermin	.10
32	Ken Griffey Jr.	6.00
33	Lee Guetterman	.10
34	Randy Johnson	3.00
35	Edgar Martinez	.75
36	Tino Martinez	.50
37	Jeff Nelson	.10
38	Warren Newson	.10
39	Greg Pirkl	.10
40	Arquimedez Pozo	.10
41	Bill Risley	.10
42	Alex Rodriquez (Rodriguez)	4.00
43	Luis Sojo	.10
44	Doug Strange	.10
45	Salomon Torres	.10
46	Bob Wells	.10
47	Chris Widger	.10
48	Dan Wilson	.10
49	Bob Wolcott	.10
50	Lou Piniella	.25

1996 Pacific Crown Collection

Pacific's base set for 1996 features 450 gold-foil enhanced cards. Fronts have borderless game-action photos with the issuer's logo in an upper corner and the player's name at bottom center in gold. Horizontal backs have a portrait photo at right, career highlights in both English and Spanish at left, and 1995 stats at top. Cards were sold in 12-card foil packs which could include one of six types of insert cards.

		MT
Complete Set (450):		30.00
Common Player:		.05
Wax Box:		50.00
1	Steve Avery	.05
2	Ryan Klesko	.20
3	Pedro Borbon	.05
4	Chipper Jones	2.00
5	Kent Mercker	.05
6	Greg Maddux	2.00
7	Greg McMichael	.05
8	Mark Wohlers	.05
9	Fred McGriff	.20
10	John Smoltz	.20
11	Rafael Belliard	.05
12	Mark Lemke	.05
13	Tom Glavine	.15
14	Javier Lopez	.15
15	Jeff Blauser	.05
16	Dave Justice	.25
17	Marquis Grissom	.05
18	Greg Maddux (NL Cy Young)	1.00
19	Randy Myers	.05
20	Scott Servais	.05
21	Sammy Sosa	1.50
22	Kevin Foster	.05
23	Jose Hernandez	.05
24	Jim Bullinger	.05
25	Mike Perez	.05
26	Shawon Dunston	.05
27	Rey Sanchez	.05
28	Frank Castillo	.05
29	Jaime Navarro	.05
30	Brian McRae	.05
31	Mark Grace	.15
32	Roberto Rivera	.05
33	Luis Gonzalez	.05
34	Hector Carrasco	.05
35	Bret Boone	.05
36	Thomas Howard	.05
37	Hal Morris	.05
38	John Smiley	.05
39	Jeff Brantley	.05
40	Barry Larkin	.15
41	Mariano Duncan	.05
42	Xavier Hernandez	.05
43	Pete Schourek	.05
44	Reggie Sanders	.05
45	Dave Burba	.05
46	Jeff Branson	.05
47	Mark Portugal	.05
48	Ron Gant	.10
49	Benito Santiago	.05
50	Barry Larkin (NL MVP)	.05
51	Steve Reed	.05
52	Kevin Ritz	.05
53	Dante Bichette	.20
54	Darren Holmes	.05
55	Ellis Burks	.05
56	Walt Weiss	.05
57	Armando Reynoso	.05
58	Vinny Castilla	.05
59	Jason Bates	.05
60	Mike Kingery	.05
61	Bryan Rekar	.05
62	Curtis Leskanic	.05
63	Bret Saberhagen	.05
64	Andres Galarraga	.10
65	Larry Walker	.25
66	Joe Girardi	.05
67	Quilvio Veras	.05
68	Robb Nen	.05
69	Mario Diaz	.05
70	Chuck Carr	.05
71	Alex Arias	.05
72	Pat Rapp	.05
73	Rich Garces	.05
74	Kurt Abbott	.05
75	Andre Dawson	.10
76	Greg Colbrunn	.05
77	John Burkett	.05
78	Terry Pendleton	.05
79	Jesus Tavarez	.05
80	Charles Johnson	.10
81	Yorkis Perez	.05
82	Jeff Conine	.05
83	Gary Sheffield	.35
84	Brian Hunter	.05
85	Derrick May	.05
86	Greg Swindell	.05
87	Derek Bell	.05
88	Dave Veres	.05
89	Jeff Bagwell	.75
90	Todd Jones	.05
91	Orlando Miller	.05
92	Pedro A. Martinez	.05
93	Tony Eusebio	.05
94	Craig Biggio	.15
95	Shane Reynolds	.05
96	James Mouton	.05
97	Doug Drabek	.05
98	Dave Magadan	.05
99	Ricky Gutierrez	.05
100	Hideo Nomo	.50
101	Delino DeShields	.05
102	Tom Candiotti	.05
103	Mike Piazza	2.00
104	Ramon Martinez	.10
105	Pedro Astacio	.05
106	Chad Fonville	.05
107	Raul Mondesi	.20
108	Ismael Valdes	.05
109	Jose Offerman	.05
110	Todd Worrell	.05
111	Eric Karros	.10
112	Brett Butler	.05
113	Juan Castro	.05
114	Roberto Kelly	.05
115	Omar Daal	.05
116	Antonio Osuna	.05
117	Hideo Nomo (NL Rookie of Year)	.25
118	Mike Lansing	.05
119	Mel Rojas	.05
120	Sean Berry	.05
121	David Segui	.05
122	Tavo Alvarez	.05
123	Pedro Martinez	.15
124	*F.P. Santangelo*	.10
125	Rondell White	.10
126	Cliff Floyd	.05
127	Henry Rodriguez	.05
128	Tony Tarasco	.05
129	Yamil Benitez	.05
130	Carlos Perez	.05
131	Wil Cordero	.05
132	Jeff Fassero	.05
133	Moises Alou	.10
134	John Franco	.05
135	Rico Brogna	.05
136	Dave Mlicki	.05
137	Bill Pulsipher	.05
138	Jose Vizcaino	.05
139	Carl Everett	.05
140	Edgardo Alfonzo	.10
141	Bobby Jones	.05
142	Alberto Castillo	.05
143	Joe Orsulak	.05
144	Jeff Kent	.05
145	Ryan Thompson	.05
146	Jason Isringhausen	.05
147	Todd Hundley	.15
148	Alex Ochoa	.05
149	Charlie Hayes	.05
150	Michael Mimbs	.05
151	Darren Daulton	.05
152	Toby Borland	.05
153	Andy Van Slyke	.05
154	Mickey Morandini	.05
155	Sid Fernandez	.05
156	Tom Marsh	.05
157	Kevin Stocker	.05
158	Paul Quantrill	.05
159	Gregg Jefferies	.05
160	Ricky Bottalico	.05
161	Lenny Dykstra	.05
162	Mark Whiten	.05
163	Tyler Green	.05
164	Jim Eisenreich	.05
165	Heathcliff Slocumb	.05
166	Esteban Loaiza	.10
167	Rich Aude	.05
168	Jason Christiansen	.05

169	Ramon Morel	.05
170	Orlando Merced	.05
171	Paul Wagner	.05
172	Jeff King	.05
173	Jay Bell	.05
174	Jacob Brumfield	.05
175	Nelson Liriano	.05
176	Dan Miceli	.05
177	Carlos Garcia	.05
178	Denny Neagle	.05
179	Angelo Encarnacion	.05
180	Al Martin	.05
181	Midre Cummings	.05
182	Eddie Williams	.05
183	Roberto Petagine	.05
184	Tony Gwynn	.75
185	Andy Ashby	.05
186	Melvin Nieves	.05
187	Phil Clark	.05
188	Brad Ausmus	.05
189	Bip Roberts	.05
190	Fernando Valenzuela	.05
191	Marc Newfield	.05
192	Steve Finley	.05
193	Trevor Hoffman	.05
194	Andujar Cedeno	.05
195	Jody Reed	.05
196	Ken Caminiti	.25
197	Joey Hamilton	.05
198	Tony Gwynn (NL Batting Champ)	.30
199	Shawn Barton	.05
200	Deion Sanders	.15
201	Rikkert Faneyte	.05
202	Barry Bonds	.75
203	Matt Williams	.25
204	Jose Bautista	.05
205	Mark Leiter	.05
206	Mark Carreon	.05
207	Robby Thompson	.05
208	Terry Mulholland	.05
209	Rod Beck	.05
210	Royce Clayton	.05
211	J.R. Phillips	.05
212	Kirt Manwaring	.05
213	Glenallen Hill	.05
214	William Van Landingham	.05
215	Scott Cooper	.05
216	Bernard Gilkey	.05
217	Allen Watson	.05
218	Donovan Osborne	.05
219	Ray Lankford	.05
220	Tony Fossas	.05
221	Tom Pagnozzi	.05
222	John Mabry	.05
223	Tripp Cromer	.05
224	Mark Petkovsek	.05
225	Mike Morgan	.05
226	Ozzie Smith	.40
227	Tom Henke	.05
228	Jose Oquendo	.05
229	Brian Jordan	.05
230	Cal Ripken Jr.	2.50
231	Scott Erickson	.05
232	Harold Baines	.05
233	Jeff Manto	.05
234	Jesse Orosco	.05
235	Jeffrey Hammonds	.05
236	Brady Anderson	.10
237	Manny Alexander	.05
238	Chris Hoiles	.05
239	Rafael Palmeiro	.15
240	Ben McDonald	.05
241	Curtis Goodwin	.05
242	Bobby Bonilla	.05
243	Mike Mussina	.40
244	Kevin Brown	.10
245	Armando Benitez	.05
246	Jose Canseco	.35
247	Erik Hanson	.05
248	Mo Vaughn	.50
249	Tim Naehring	.05
250	Vaughn Eshelman	.05
251	Mike Greenwell	.05
252	Troy O'Leary	.05
253	Tim Wakefield	.05
254	Dwayne Hosey	.05
255	John Valentin	.05
256	Rick Aguilera	.05
257	Mike MacFarlane	.05
258	Roger Clemens	.75
259	Luis Alicea	.05
260	Mo Vaughn (AL MVP)	.25
261	Mark Langston	.05
262	Jim Edmonds	.10
263	Rod Correia	.05
264	Tim Salmon	.25
265	J.T. Snow	.10
266	Orlando Palmeiro	.05
267	Jorge Fabregas	.05
268	Jim Abbott	.05
269	Eduardo Perez	.05
270	Lee Smith	.05
271	Gary DiSarcina	.05
272	Damion Easley	.05
273	Tony Phillips	.05
274	Garret Anderson	.05
275	Chuck Finley	.05
276	Chili Davis	.05
277	Lance Johnson	.05
278	Alex Fernandez	.10
279	Robin Ventura	.15
280	Chris Snopek	.05
281	Brian Keyser	.05
282	Lyle Mouton	.05
283	*Luis Andujar*	.05
284	Tim Raines	.10

285	Larry Thomas	.05
286	Ozzie Guillen	.05
287	Frank Thomas	1.50
288	Roberto Hernandez	.05
289	Dave Martinez	.05
290	Ray Durham	.05
291	Ron Karkovice	.05
292	Wilson Alvarez	.05
293	Omar Vizquel	.05
294	Eddie Murray	.40
295	Sandy Alomar	.10
296	Orel Hershiser	.05
297	Jose Mesa	.05
298	Julian Tavarez	.05
299	Dennis Martinez	.05
300	Carlos Baerga	.05
301	Manny Ramirez	1.00
302	Jim Thome	.25
303	Kenny Lofton	.50
304	Tony Pena	.05
305	Alvaro Espinoza	.05
306	Paul Sorrento	.05
307	Albert Belle	.75
308	Danny Bautista	.05
309	Chris Gomez	.05
310	Jose Lima	.10
311	Phil Nevin	.05
312	Alan Trammell	.10
313	Chad Curtis	.05
314	John Flaherty	.05
315	Travis Fryman	.05
316	Todd Steverson	.05
317	Brian Bohanon	.05
318	Lou Whitaker	.05
319	Bobby Higginson	.15
320	Steve Rodriguez	.05
321	Cecil Fielder	.10
322	Felipe Lira	.05
323	Juan Samuel	.05
324	Bob Hamelin	.05
325	Tom Goodwin	.05
326	Johnny Damon	.15
327	Hipolito Pichardo	.05
328	Dilson Torres	.05
329	Kevin Appier	.05
330	Mark Gubicza	.05
331	Jon Nunnally	.05
332	Gary Gaetti	.05
333	Brent Mayne	.05
334	Brent Cookson	.05
335	Tom Gordon	.05
336	Wally Joyner	.05
337	Greg Gagne	.05
338	Fernando Vina	.05
339	Joe Oliver	.05
340	John Jaha	.05
341	Jeff Cirillo	.05
342	Pat Listach	.05
343	Dave Nilsson	.05
344	Steve Sparks	.05
345	Ricky Bones	.05
346	David Hulse	.05
347	Scott Karl	.05
348	Darryl Hamilton	.05
349	B.J. Surhoff	.10
350	Angel Miranda	.05
351	Sid Roberson	.05
352	Matt Mieske	.05
353	*Jose Valentin*	.05
354	*Matt Lawton*	.05
355	Eddie Guardado	.05
356	Brad Radke	.05
357	Pedro Munoz	.05
358	Scott Stahoviak	.05
359	Erik Schullstrom	.05
360	Pat Meares	.05
361	Marty Cordova	.10
362	Scott Leius	.05
363	Matt Walbeck	.05
364	Rich Becker	.05
365	Kirby Puckett	.75
366	Oscar Munoz	.05
367	Chuck Knoblauch	.20
368	Marty Cordova (AL Rookie of Year)	.10
369	Bernie Williams	.40
370	Mike Stanley	.05
371	Andy Pettitte	.60
372	Jack McDowell	.05
373	Sterling Hitchcock	.05
374	David Cone	.10
375	Randy Velarde	.05
376	Don Mattingly	1.00
377	Melido Perez	.05
378	Wade Boggs	.25
379	Ruben Sierra	.05
380	Tony Fernandez	.05
381	John Wetteland	.05
382	Mariano Rivera	.15
383	Derek Jeter	2.00
384	Paul O'Neill	.10
385	Mark McGwire	3.00
386	Scott Brosius	.05
387	Don Wengert	.05
388	Terry Steinbach	.05
389	Brent Gates	.05
390	Craig Paquette	.05
391	Mike Bordick	.05
392	Ariel Prieto	.05
393	Dennis Eckersley	.05
394	Carlos Reyes	.05
395	Todd Stottlemyre	.05
396	Rickey Henderson	.25
397	Geronimo Berroa	.05
398	Steve Ontiveros	.05
399	Mike Gallego	.05
400	Stan Javier	.05
401	Randy Johnson	.30

402	Norm Charlton	.05
403	Mike Blowers	.05
404	Tino Martinez	.10
405	Dan Wilson	.05
406	Andy Benes	.05
407	Alex Diaz	.05
408	Edgar Martinez	.05
409	Chris Bosio	.05
410	Ken Griffey Jr.	2.50
411	Luis Sojo	.05
412	Bob Wolcott	.05
413	Vince Coleman	.05
414	Rich Amaral	.05
415	Jay Buhner	.10
416	Alex Rodriguez	2.50
417	Joey Cora	.05
418	Randy Johnson (AL Cy Young)	.20
419	Edgar Martinez (AL Batting Champ)	.05
420	Ivan Rodriguez	.40
421	Mark McLemore	.05
422	Mickey Tettleton	.05
423	Juan Gonzalez	1.25
424	Will Clark	.25
425	Kevin Gross	.05
426	Dean Palmer	.05
427	Kenny Rogers	.05
428	Bob Tewksbury	.05
429	Benji Gil	.05
430	Jeff Russell	.05
431	Rusty Greer	.05
432	Roger Pavlik	.05
433	Esteban Beltre	.05
434	Otis Nixon	.05
435	Paul Molitor	.40
436	Carlos Delgado	.25
437	Ed Sprague	.05
438	Juan Guzman	.05
439	Domingo Cedeno	.05
440	Pat Hentgen	.05
441	Tomas Perez	.05
442	John Olerud	.10
443	Shawn Green	.20
444	Al Leiter	.10
445	Joe Carter	.10
446	Robert Perez	.05
447	Devon White	.05
448	Tony Castillo	.05
449	Alex Gonzalez	.05
450	Roberto Alomar	.60
450p	Roberto Alomar (unmarked promo card, "Games: 128" on back)	7.50

1996 Pacific Crown Cramer's Choice

One of the most unusually shaped baseball cards of all time is the Cramer's Choice insert set from the 1996 Pacific Crown Collection. The set features the 10 best players as chosen by Pacific founder and president Mike Cramer. Cards are in a die-cut pyramidal design 3-1/2" tall and 2-1/2" at the base. The player picture on front is set against a silver-foil background, while the player name and other information is in gold foil on a faux marble base at bottom; the effect is a simulation of a trophy. Backs repeat the marbled background and have a bi-lingual justification from Cramer concerning his choice of the player as one of the 10 best. Average insertion rate is one card per case (720 packs). Cards are numbered with a "CC" prefix.

		MT
Complete Set (10):		800.00
Common Player:		40.00
1	Roberto Alomar	50.00
2	Wade Boggs	50.00
3	Cal Ripken Jr.	200.00
4	Greg Maddux	125.00
5	Frank Thomas	100.00
6	Tony Gwynn	110.00
7	Mike Piazza	150.00
8	Ken Griffey Jr.	225.00
9	Manny Ramirez	60.00
10	Edgar Martinez	40.00

1996 Pacific Crown Estrellas Latinas

Three dozen of the best contemporary Latino ballplayers are honored in this chase set. Cards feature action photos silhouetted on a black background shot through with gold-foil streaks and stars. The player name, set and insert set logos are in gold at left. Backs have a player portrait photo and English/Spanish career summary. The Latino Stars insert cards are inserted at an average rate of one per nine packs; about four per foil box. Cards are numbered with an "EL" prefix.

		MT
Complete Set (36):		35.00
Common Player:		.75
1	Roberto Alomar	4.50
2	Moises Alou	.90
3	Carlos Baerga	.75
4	Geronimo Berroa	.75
5	Ricky Bones	.75
6	Bobby Bonilla	.75
7	Jose Canseco	1.50
8	Vinny Castilla	.90
9	Pedro Martinez	1.50
10	John Valentin	.75
11	Andres Galarraga	1.25
12	Juan Gonzalez	6.00
13	Ozzie Guillen	.75
14	Esteban Loaiza	.90
15	Javier Lopez	1.50
16	Dennis Martinez	.75
17	Edgar Martinez	.75
18	Tino Martinez	.90
19	Orlando Merced	.75
20	Jose Mesa	.75
21	Raul Mondesi	1.50
22	Jaime Navarro	.75
23	Rafael Palmeiro	1.50
24	Carlos Perez	.75
25	Manny Ramirez	4.00
26	Alex Rodriguez	10.00
27	Ivan Rodriguez	3.00
28	David Segui	.75
29	Ruben Sierra	.75
30	Sammy Sosa	7.50
31	Julian Tavarez	.75
32	Ismael Valdes	.75
33	Fernando Valenzuela	.75
34	Quilvio Veras	.75
35	Omar Vizquel	.75
36	Bernie Williams	2.00

1996 Pacific Crown Gold Crown Die-Cuts

One of Pacific's most popular inserts of the previous year returns in 1996. The Gold Crown die-cuts have the top of the card cut away to form a gold-foil crown design with an action photo below. The player's name is also in gold foil. Backs repeat the gold crown design at top, have a portrait photo at lower-right and a few words about the player, in both English and Spanish. Insertion rate was advertised as one per 37 packs, on average. Cards are numbered with a "DC" prefix.

		MT
Complete Set (36):		195.00
Common Player:		2.50
1	Roberto Alomar	5.00
2	Will Clark	3.50
3	Johnny Damon	2.50
4	Don Mattingly	7.50
5	Edgar Martinez	2.50
6	Manny Ramirez	7.50
7	Mike Piazza	15.00
8	Quilvio Veras	2.50
9	Rickey Henderson	3.50
10	Jeff Bagwell	9.00
11	Andres Galarraga	2.50
12	Tim Salmon	3.00
13	Ken Griffey Jr.	25.00
14	Sammy Sosa	15.00
15	Cal Ripken Jr.	20.00
16	Raul Mondesi	3.00
17	Jose Canseco	3.50
18	Frank Thomas	9.00
19	Hideo Nomo	4.50
20	Wade Boggs	3.50
21	Reggie Sanders	2.50
22	Carlos Baerga	2.50
23	Mo Vaughn	5.00
24	Ivan Rodriguez	6.00
25	Kirby Puckett	9.00
26	Albert Belle	6.00
27	Vinny Castilla	2.50
28	Greg Maddux	15.00
29	Dante Bichette	3.00
30	Deion Sanders	3.00
31	Chipper Jones	15.00
32	Cecil Fielder	2.50
33	Randy Johnson	4.50
34	Mark McGwire	25.00
35	Tony Gwynn	12.00
36	Barry Bonds	6.00

1996 Pacific Crown Hometown of the Players

The hometown roots of 20 top players are examined in this chase set. Fronts have action photos with large areas of the background replaced with textured gold foil, including solid and outline versions of the player's name. Backs have a portrait photo, a representation of the player's native flag and a few words about his hometown. Card numbers have an "HP" prefix and are inserted at an average rate of one per 18 packs; about two per box.

		MT
Complete Set (20):		50.00
Common Player:		1.50
1	Mike Piazza	6.00
2	Greg Maddux	6.00
3	Tony Gwynn	4.00
4	Carlos Baerga	1.50
5	Don Mattingly	4.00
6	Cal Ripken Jr.	7.50
7	Chipper Jones	6.00
8	Andres Galarraga	1.50
9	Manny Ramirez	3.00
10	Roberto Alomar	3.50
11	Ken Griffey Jr.	9.00
12	Jose Canseco	2.50
13	Frank Thomas	4.00
14	Vinny Castilla	1.50
15	Roberto Kelly	1.50
16	Dennis Martinez	1.50
17	Kirby Puckett	3.50
18	Raul Mondesi	2.00
19	Hideo Nomo	2.50
20	Edgar Martinez	1.50

1996 Pacific Crown Milestones

A textured metallic blue-foil background is featured in this insert set. Behind the player action photo is a spider's web design with flying baseballs, team logo and a number representing the milestone. The player's name is in purple foil, outlined in white, vertically at right. Backs have a portrait photo and bi-lingual description of the milestone. Average insertion rate for this insert series is one per 37 packs. Cards are numbered with a "M" prefix.

		MT
Complete Set (10):		35.00
Common Player:		1.50
1	Albert Belle	3.00
2	Don Mattingly	5.00
3	Tony Gwynn	5.00
4	Jose Canseco	2.50
5	Marty Cordova	1.50
6	Wade Boggs	2.00
7	Greg Maddux	6.00
8	Eddie Murray	2.50
9	Ken Griffey Jr.	10.00
10	Cal Ripken Jr.	7.50

1996 Pacific Crown October Moments

Post-season baseball has never been better represented on a card than in Pacific's "October Moments" chase set. Color action photos are set again a background of a stadium decked in the traditional Fall Classic bunting, all rendered in metallic copper foil. At bottom is a textured silver strip with the player name in copper and a swirl of fallen leaves. Backs have a repeat of the leaves and bunting themes with a player portrait at center and English/Spanish description of his October heroics. These cards are found at an average rate of once per 37 packs. Cards are numbered with an "OM" prefix.

		MT
Complete Set (20):		75.00
Common Player:		1.50
1	Carlos Baerga	1.50
2	Albert Belle	4.50
3	Dante Bichette	2.00
4	Jose Canseco	2.50
5	Tom Glavine	2.00
6	Ken Griffey Jr.	15.00
7	Randy Johnson	3.00
8	Chipper Jones	10.00
9	Dave Justice	1.50
10	Ryan Klesko	1.50
11	Kenny Lofton	3.00
12	Javier Lopez	1.50
13	Greg Maddux	10.00
14	Edgar Martinez	1.50
15	Don Mattingly	7.50
16	Hideo Nomo	4.00
17	Mike Piazza	10.00
18	Manny Ramirez	6.00
19	Reggie Sanders	1.50
20	Jim Thome	1.50

1996 Pacific Prism

Only the best in baseball make the cut for the Prism checklist. Sold in one-card foil packs the cards feature action photos set against an etched silver-foil background highlighted by slashes approximating team colors. Backs are conventionally printed in a horizontal format with a player portrait photo at left center on a purple background. A short 1995 season recap is feature in both English and Spanish. Card numbers are prefixed with a "P".

		MT
Complete Set (144):		150.00
Common Player:		1.00
Wax Box:		45.00
1	Tom Glavine	1.50
2	Chipper Jones	10.00
3	David Justice	1.50
4	Ryan Klesko	1.50
5	Javier Lopez	1.50
6	Greg Maddux	10.00
7	Fred McGriff	1.50
8	Frank Castillo	1.00
9	Luis Gonzalez	1.00
10	Mark Grace	2.00
11	Brian McRae	1.00
12	Jaime Navarro	1.00
13	Sammy Sosa	9.00
14	Bret Boone	1.00
15	Ron Gant	1.50
16	Barry Larkin	1.50
17	Reggie Sanders	1.00
18	Benito Santiago	1.00
19	Dante Bichette	1.50
20	Vinny Castilla	1.25
21	Andres Galarraga	1.50
22	Bryan Rekar	1.00
23	Roberto Alomar	3.00
23p	Roberto Alomar ("Azulejos" rather than "Los Azulajos" on back, unmarked promo card)	7.50
24	Jeff Conine	1.00
25	Andre Dawson	1.00
26	Charles Johnson	1.50
27	Gary Sheffield	2.00
28	Quilvio Veras	1.00
29	Jeff Bagwell	6.00
30	Derek Bell	1.00
31	Craig Biggio	1.25
32	Tony Eusebio	1.00
33	Karim Garcia	2.50
34	Eric Karros	1.00
35	Ramon Martinez	1.00
36	Raul Mondesi	1.50
37	Hideo Nomo	2.00
38	Mike Piazza	10.00
39	Ismael Valdes	1.00
40	Moises Alou	1.00
41	Wil Cordero	1.00
42	Pedro Martinez	1.50
43	Mel Rojas	1.00
44	David Segui	1.00
45	Edgardo Alfonzo	1.25
46	Rico Brogna	1.00
47	John Franco	1.00
48	Jason Isringhausen	1.00
49	Jose Vizcaino	1.00
50	Ricky Bottalico	1.00
51	Darren Daulton	1.00
52	Lenny Dykstra	1.00
53	Tyler Green	1.00
54	Gregg Jefferies	1.00
55	Jay Bell	1.00
56	Jason Christiansen	1.00
57	Carlos Garcia	1.00
58	Esteban Loaiza	1.25
59	Orlando Merced	1.00
60	Andujar Cedeno	1.00
61	Tony Gwynn	6.00
62	Melvin Nieves	1.00
63	Phil Plantier	1.00
64	Fernando Valenzuela	1.00
65	Barry Bonds	5.00
66	J.R. Phillips	1.00
67	Deion Sanders	1.50
68	Matt Williams	1.50
69	Bernard Gilkey	1.00
70	Tom Henke	1.00
71	Brian Jordan	1.00
72	Ozzie Smith	3.00
73	Manny Alexander	1.00
74	Bobby Bonilla	1.00
75	Mike Mussina	1.50
76	Rafael Palmeiro	2.00
77	Cal Ripken Jr.	12.00
78	Jose Canseco	2.00
79	Roger Clemens	5.00
80	John Valentin	1.00
81	Mo Vaughn	4.00
82	Tim Wakefield	1.00
83	Garret Anderson	1.00
84	Damion Easley	1.00
85	Jim Edmonds	1.50
86	Tim Salmon	1.50
87	Wilson Alvarez	1.00
88	Alex Fernandez	1.00
89	Ozzie Guillen	1.00
90	Roberto Hernandez	1.00
91	Frank Thomas	5.00
92	Robin Ventura	1.50
93	Carlos Baerga	1.00
94	Albert Belle	4.00
95	Kenny Lofton	3.00
96	Dennis Martinez	1.00
97	Eddie Murray	2.00
98	Manny Ramirez	3.00
99	Omar Vizquel	1.00
100	Chad Curtis	1.00
101	Cecil Fielder	1.00
102	Felipe Lira	1.00
103	Alan Trammell	1.00
104	Kevin Appier	1.00
105	Johnny Damon	1.00
106	Gary Gaetti	1.00
107	Wally Joyner	1.00
108	Ricky Bones	1.00
109	John Jaha	1.00
110	B.J. Surhoff	1.00
111	Jose Valentin	1.00
112	Fernando Vina	1.00
113	Marty Cordova	1.00
114	Chuck Knoblauch	1.50
115	Scott Leius	1.00
116	Pedro Munoz	1.00
117	Kirby Puckett	6.00
118	Wade Boggs	2.00
119	Don Mattingly	8.00
120	Jack McDowell	1.00
121	Paul O'Neill	1.25
122	Ruben Rivera	1.00
123	Bernie Williams	3.00
124	Geronimo Berroa	1.00
125	Rickey Henderson	2.00
126	Mark McGwire	15.00
127	Terry Steinbach	1.00
128	Danny Tartabull	1.00
129	Jay Buhner	1.00
130	Joey Cora	1.00
131	Ken Griffey Jr.	15.00
132	Randy Johnson	2.00
133	Edgar Martinez	1.00
134	Tino Martinez	1.50
135	Will Clark	2.00
136	Juan Gonzalez	8.00
137	Dean Palmer	1.00
138	Ivan Rodriguez	3.00
139	Mickey Tettleton	1.00
140	Larry Walker	1.50
141	Joe Carter	1.00
142	Carlos Delgado	2.00
143	Alex Gonzalez	1.00
144	Paul Molitor	2.00

1996 Pacific Prism Gold

Exactly paralleling the cards in the regular Prism set, this chase card insert replaces the silver foil on front with gold foil. All else remains the same. Stated odds of picking a Gold Prism parallel card are about one per 18 packs, on average (two per box).

	MT
Complete Set (144):	500.00
Common Player:	2.50
Stars: 2.5X	

(See 1996 Pacific Prism for checklist and base card values.)

1996 Pacific Prism Fence Busters

Home run heroes are featured in this insert set. The player's big swing is photographed in the foreground while a baseball flies out of the etched metallic foil stadium background. The player's name is in blue foil. Backs have another player photo and details of his 1995 season home run output, in both English and Spanish. Cards are numbered with an FB prefix. Stated odds of finding a Fence Busters insert are one per 37 packs, on average.

		MT
Complete Set (19):		130.00
Common Player:		4.50
1	Albert Belle	7.50
2	Dante Bichette	5.00
3	Barry Bonds	7.50
4	Jay Buhner	4.50
5	Jose Canseco	6.00
6	Ken Griffey Jr.	30.00
7	Chipper Jones	20.00
8	David Justice	5.00
9	Eric Karros	4.50
10	Edgar Martinez	4.50
11	Mark McGwire	30.00
12	Eddie Murray	6.00
10	Mike Piazza	20.00
14	Kirby Puckett	10.00
15	Cal Ripken Jr.	25.00
16	Tim Salmon	6.00
17	Sammy Sosa	15.00
18	Frank Thomas	10.00
19	Mo Vaughn	6.00

1996 Pacific Prism Flame Throwers

Burning baseballs are the background for the game's best pitchers in this die-cut insert set. The gold-foil highlighted flames have their tails die-cut at the card's left end. The featured pitcher is shown in action in the foreground. The name at bottom and company logo are in gold foil. Backs are conventionally printed with another action photo and 1995 highlight printed in both English and Spanish. Card numbers carry an FT prefix. Stated odds of finding a Flame Throwers card are one in 73 boxes, about every two boxes.

		MT
Complete Set (10):		95.00
Common Player:		6.00
1	Roger Clemens	25.00
2	David Cone	8.00
3	Tom Glavine	8.00
4	Randy Johnson	15.00
5	Greg Maddux	30.00
6	Ramon Martinez	6.00
7	Jose Mesa	6.00
8	Mike Mussina	12.00
9	Hideo Nomo	15.00
10	Jose Rijo	6.00

1996 Pacific Prism Red Hot Stars

Bright red metallic foil provides the background for these inserts. Color action photos are in the foreground, while player name and multiple team logos are worked into the background. Backs are conventionally printed with another player photo and a few words - in both English and Spanish - about the player's 1995 season. Card numbers have an RH prefix. Stated odds of finding a Red Hot Stars insert are one per 37 packs.

		MT
Complete Set (19):		175.00
Common Player:		3.00
1	Roberto Alomar	5.00
2	Jeff Bagwell	10.00
3	Albert Belle	7.50
4	Wade Boggs	3.50
5	Barry Bonds	7.50
6	Jose Canseco	3.50
7	Ken Griffey Jr.	27.50
8	Tony Gwynn	10.00
9	Randy Johnson	4.50
10	Chipper Jones	15.00
11	Greg Maddux	12.50
12	Edgar Martinez	3.00
13	Don Mattingly	12.50
14	Mike Piazza	15.00
15	Kirby Puckett	9.00
16	Manny Ramirez	6.00
17	Cal Ripken Jr.	20.00
18	Tim Salmon	3.00
19	Frank Thomas	10.00

1996 Pacific Carlos Baerga Celebrities Softball

This set was produced for distribution to fans attending the second annual Carlos Baerga Celebrities Softball Game in Puerto Rico. Packs were handed out containing two of the cards from this set, a regular Pacific Crown Collection card, a Pacific logo card and an information card about card shops on the island. The softball celebrities cards have a blue and red marbled border with player names at bottom in gold foil. Players are shown in action during the '95 game. Backs feature a portrait photo of the player and English/Spanish description of his participation in the event.

		MT
Complete Set (8):		35.00
Common Player:		2.00
1	Carlos Baerga	2.00
2	Mike Piazza	9.00
3	Bernie Williams	2.00
4	Frank Thomas	7.00
5	Roberto Alomar	5.00
6	Edgar Martinez	2.00
7	Kenny Lofton	2.00
8	Sammy Sosa	10.00

1996 Pacific Nolan Ryan Career Highlights

Highlights of Ryan's career with the Texas Rangers are featured in this 11-card set given to fans attending the Sept. 13 game at Arlington during Nolan Ryan Appreciation Week, when the team retired his jersey. Ten cards feature action photos on front with gold-foil graphics. Backs share a background photo of Ryan's classic windup and describe the action pictured on front. Sponsors' and licensors' logos are at top and bottom. An 11th unnumbered card is a checklist.

		MT
Complete Set (11):		9.00
Common Player:		1.00
---	Header card/checklist	.25
1	King of K's (Nolan Ryan)	1.00
2	324 Career Wins (Nolan Ryan)	1.00
3	Miracle Man (Nolan Ryan)	1.00
4	Low-Hit Nolan (Nolan Ryan)	1.00
5	Milestone K's (Nolan Ryan)	1.00
6	Pure Heat (Nolan Ryan)	1.00
7	No-Hit Nolan (Nolan Ryan)	1.00
8	Ryan's Farewell (Nolan Ryan)	1.00
9	Legendary Career (Nolan Ryan)	1.00
10	Retiring #34 (Nolan Ryan)	1.00

1996 Pacific/Advil Nolan Ryan

Nolan Ryan, who starred in TV commericals for Advil pain reliever at the end of his career continued his association with the product via a baseball card set in 1996. A pair of cards marking the all-time strikeout leader's first and last Ks were available in-store with the purchase of a bottle of Advil. A 27-card set of career highlight cards was available by mail for $5.50 and proof of purchase. All of the Ryan cards have full-bleed front photos with gold-foil highlights and the Advil and Pacific logos. Backs have a background photo of Ryan pitching, with a description of the highlight. Cards are UV coated on each side. The mail-in set was issued in a collectors box.

		MT
Complete Set (28):		9.00
Common Player:		.50
IN-STORE CARDS		
1a	First Strikeout (Nolan Ryan)	.50
2a	Last strikeout (Nolan Ryan)	.50
MAIL-IN SET		
1	New York Mets Rookie Pitcher (Nolan Ryan)	.50
2	California Angels (Nolan Ryan)	.50
3	Houston Astros (Nolan Ryan)	.50
4	Texas Rangers (Nolan Ryan)	.50
5	No-Hitter #1 (Nolan Ryan)	.50
6	No-Hitter #2 (Nolan Ryan)	.50
7	No-Hitter #3 (Nolan Ryan)	.50
8	No-Hitter #4 (Nolan Ryan)	.50
9	No-Hitter #5 (Nolan Ryan)	.50
10	No-Hitter #6 (Nolan Ryan)	.50
11	No-Hitter #7 (Nolan Ryan)	.50
12	First Major League Win (Nolan Ryan)	.50
13	250th Win (Nolan Ryan)	.50
14	300th Win (Nolan Ryan)	.50
15	324th Win (Nolan Ryan)	.50
16	1,000th Strikeout (Nolan Ryan)	.50
17	2,000th Strikeout (Nolan Ryan)	.50
18	3,000th Strikeout (Nolan Ryan)	.50
19	Nolan Breaks Johnson Record (Nolan Ryan)	.50
20	4,000th Strikeout (Nolan Ryan)	.50
21	5,000th Strikeout (Nolan Ryan)	.50
22	World Series Victory (Nolan Ryan)	.50
23	Fastest Pitch Ever Thrown (Nolan Ryan)	.50
24	Ryan Home Run (Nolan Ryan)	.50
25	The Greatest Power Pitcher (Nolan Ryan)	.50
26	1989 All-Star Game (Nolan Ryan)	.50
27	Last Appearance (Nolan Ryan)	.50

1997 Pacific Crown

The 450-card, regular-sized set was available in 12-card packs. The card fronts feature the player's name in gold foil along the left border with the team logo in the bottom right corner. The card backs feature a head shot of the player in the lower left quadrant with a short highlight in both Spanish and English. Inserted in packs were: Card-Supials, Cramer's Choice, Latinos Of The Major Leagues, Fireworks Die-Cuts, Gold Crown Die-Cuts and Triple Crown Die-Cuts. A parallel silver version (67 sets) was available.

		MT
Complete Set (450):		35.00
Common Player:		.05
Wax Box:		60.00
1	Garret Anderson	.05
2	George Arias	.05
3	Chili Davis	.05
4	Gary DiSarcina	.05
5	Jim Edmonds	.05
6	Darin Erstad	1.25
7	Jorge Fabregas	.05
8	Chuck Finley	.05
9	Rex Hudler	.05
10	Mark Langston	.05
11	Orlando Palmeiro	.05
12	Troy Percival	.05
13	Tim Salmon	.25
14	J.T. Snow	.05
15	Randy Velarde	.05
16	Manny Alexander	.05
17	Roberto Alomar	.60
18	Brady Anderson	.10
19	Armando Benitez	.05
20	Bobby Bonilla	.10
21	Rocky Coppinger	.05
22	Scott Erickson	.05
23	Jeffrey Hammonds	.05
24	Chris Hoiles	.05
25	Eddie Murray	.35
26	Mike Mussina	.60
27	Randy Myers	.05
28	Rafael Palmeiro	.15
29	Cal Ripken Jr.	2.50
30	B.J. Surhoff	.05
31	Tony Tarasco	.05
32	Esteban Beltre	.05
33	Darren Bragg	.05
34	Jose Canseco	.25
35	Roger Clemens	1.00
36	Wil Cordero	.05
37	Alex Delgado	.05
38	Jeff Frye	.05
39	Nomar Garciaparra	1.50
40	Tom Gordon	.05
41	Mike Greenwell	.05
42	Reggie Jefferson	.05
43	Tim Naehring	.05
44	Troy O'Leary	.05
45	Heathcliff Slocumb	.05
46	Lee Tinsley	.05
47	John Valentin	.05
48	Mo Vaughn	1.00
49	Wilson Alvarez	.05
50	Harold Baines	.05
51	Ray Durham	.05
52	Alex Fernandez	.05
53	Ozzie Guillen	.05
54	Roberto Hernandez	.05
55	Ron Karkovice	.05
56	Darren Lewis	.05
57	Norberto Martin	.05
58	Dave Martinez	.05
59	Lyle Mouton	.05
60	Jose Munoz	.05
61	Tony Phillips	.05
62	Rich Sauveur	.05
63	Danny Tartabull	.05
64	Frank Thomas	1.00
65	Robin Ventura	.15
66	Sandy Alomar Jr.	.10
67	Albert Belle	.75
68	Julio Franco	.05
69	*Brian Giles*	1.00
70	Danny Graves	.05
71	Orel Hershiser	.05
72	Jeff Kent	.05
73	Kenny Lofton	.65
74	Dennis Martinez	.05
75	Jack McDowell	.05
76	Jose Mesa	.05
77	Charles Nagy	.05
78	Manny Ramirez	1.00
79	Julian Tavarez	.05
80	Jim Thome	.25
81	Jose Vizcaino	.05
82	Omar Vizquel	.05
83	Brad Ausmus	.05
84	Kimera Bartee	.05
85	Raul Casanova	.05
86	Tony Clark	.25
87	Travis Fryman	.05
88	Bobby Higginson	.10
89	Mark Lewis	.05
90	Jose Lima	.05
91	Felipe Lira	.05
92	Phil Nevin	.05
93	Melvin Nieves	.05
94	Curtis Pride	.05
95	Ruben Sierra	.05
96	Alan Trammell	.05
97	Kevin Appier	.05
98	Tim Belcher	.05
99	Johnny Damon	.20
100	Tom Goodwin	.05
101	Bob Hamelin	.05
102	David Howard	.05
103	Jason Jacome	.05
104	Keith Lockhart	.05
105	Mike Macfarlane	.05
106	Jeff Montgomery	.05
107	Jose Offerman	.05
108	Hipolito Pichardo	.05
109	Joe Randa	.05
110	Bip Roberts	.05
111	Chris Stynes	.05
112	Mike Sweeney	.05
113	Joe Vitiello	.05
114	Jeromy Burnitz	.05
115	Chuck Carr	.05
116	Jeff Cirillo	.05
117	Mike Fetters	.05
118	David Hulse	.05
119	John Jaha	.05
120	Scott Karl	.05
121	Jesse Levis	.05
122	Mark Loretta	.05
123	Mike Matheny	.05
124	Ben McDonald	.05
125	Matt Mieske	.05
126	Angel Miranda	.05
127	Dave Nilsson	.05
128	Jose Valentin	.05
129	Fernando Vina	.05
130	Ron Villone	.05
131	Gerald Williams	.05
132	Rick Aguilera	.05
133	Rich Becker	.05
134	Ron Coomer	.05
135	Marty Cordova	.05
136	Eddie Guardado	.05
137	Denny Hocking	.05
138	Roberto Kelly	.05
139	Chuck Knoblauch	.10
140	Matt Lawton	.05
141	Pat Meares	.05
142	Paul Molitor	.35
143	Greg Myers	.05
144	Jeff Reboulet	.05
145	Scott Stahoviak	.05
146	Todd Walker	.50
147	Wade Boggs	.25
148	David Cone	.10
149	Mariano Duncan	.05
150	Cecil Fielder	.10
151	Dwight Gooden	.05
152	Derek Jeter	2.00
153	Jim Leyritz	.05
154	Tino Martinez	.25
155	Paul O'Neill	.10
156	Andy Pettitte	.65
157	Tim Raines	.05
158	Mariano Rivera	.15
159	Ruben Rivera	.10
160	Kenny Rogers	.05
161	Darryl Strawberry	.05
162	John Wetteland	.05
163	Bernie Williams	.50
164	Tony Batista	.05
165	Geronimo Berroa	.05
166	Mike Bordick	.05
167	Scott Brosius	.05
168	Brent Gates	.05
169	Jason Giambi	.05
170	Jose Herrera	.05
171	Brian Lesher	.05
172	*Damon Mashore*	.05
173	Mark McGwire	3.00
174	Ariel Prieto	.05
175	Carlos Reyes	.05
176	Matt Stairs	.05
177	Terry Steinbach	.05
178	John Wasdin	.05
179	Ernie Young	.05
180	Rich Amaral	.05
181	Bobby Ayala	.05
182	Jay Buhner	.10
183	Rafael Carmona	.05
184	Norm Charlton	.05
185	Joey Cora	.05
186	Ken Griffey Jr.	3.00
187	Sterling Hitchcock	.05
188	Dave Hollins	.05
189	Randy Johnson	.35
190	Edgar Martinez	.05
191	Jamie Moyer	.05
192	Alex Rodriguez	2.50
193	Paul Sorrento	.05
194	Salomon Torres	.05
195	Bob Wells	.05
196	Dan Wilson	.05
197	Will Clark	.25
198	Kevin Elster	.05
199	Rene Gonzales	.05
200	Juan Gonzalez	1.50
201	Rusty Greer	.05
202	Darryl Hamilton	.05
203	Mike Henneman	.05
204	Ken Hill	.05
205	Mark McLemore	.05
206	Darren Oliver	.05
207	Dean Palmer	.05
208	Roger Pavlik	.05
209	Ivan Rodriguez	.65
210	Kurt Stillwell	.05
211	Mickey Tettleton	.05
212	Bobby Witt	.05
213	Tilson Brito	.05
214	Jacob Brumfield	.05
215	Miguel Cairo	.10
216	Joe Carter	.10
217	Felipe Crespo	.05
218	Carlos Delgado	.25
219	Alex Gonzalez	.05
220	Shawn Green	.15
221	Juan Guzman	.05
222	Pat Hentgen	.05
223	Charlie O'Brien	.05
224	John Olerud	.10
225	Robert Perez	.05
226	Tomas Perez	.05
227	Juan Samuel	.05
228	Ed Sprague	.05
229	Mike Timlin	.05
230	Rafael Belliard	.05
231	Jermaine Dye	.10
232	Tom Glavine	.10
233	Marquis Grissom	.05
234	Andruw Jones	1.50
235	Chipper Jones	2.00
236	David Justice	.20
237	Ryan Klesko	.20
238	Mark Lemke	.05
239	Javier Lopez	.15
240	Greg Maddux	2.00
241	Fred McGriff	.35
242	Denny Neagle	.05
243	Eddie Perez	.05
244	John Smoltz	.15
245	Mark Wohlers	.05
246	Brant Brown	.05
247	Scott Bullett	.05
248	Leo Gomez	.05
249	Luis Gonzalez	.05
250	Mark Grace	.15
251	Jose Hernandez	.05
252	Brooks Kieschnick	.05
253	Brian McRae	.05
254	Jaime Navarro	.05
255	Mike Perez	.05
256	Rey Sanchez	.05
257	Ryne Sandberg	.75
258	Scott Servais	.05
259	Sammy Sosa	1.50
260	*Pedro Valdes*	.05
261	Turk Wendell	.05
262	Bret Boone	.05
263	Jeff Branson	.05
264	Jeff Brantley	.05
265	Dave Burba	.05
266	Hector Carrasco	.05
267	Eric Davis	.05
268	Willie Greene	.05
269	Lenny Harris	.05
270	Thomas Howard	.05
271	Barry Larkin	.15
272	Hal Morris	.05
273	Joe Oliver	.05
274	Eric Owens	.05
275	Jose Rijo	.05

276	Reggie Sanders	.05
277	Eddie Taubensee	.05
278	Jason Bates	.05
279	Dante Bichette	.20
280	Ellis Burks	.05
281	Vinny Castilla	.05
282	Andres Galarraga	.15
283	Quinton McCracken	.05
284	Jayhawk Owens	.05
285	Jeff Reed	.05
286	Bryan Rekar	.05
287	Armando Reynoso	.05
288	Kevin Ritz	.05
289	Bruce Ruffin	.05
290	John Vander Wal	.05
291	Larry Walker	.25
292	Walt Weiss	.05
293	Eric Young	.05
294	Kurt Abbott	.05
295	Alex Arias	.05
296	Miguel Batista	.05
297	Kevin Brown	.10
298	Luis Castillo	.05
299	Greg Colbrunn	.05
300	Jeff Conine	.05
301	Charles Johnson	.05
302	Al Leiter	.05
303	Robb Nen	.05
304	Joe Orsulak	.05
305	Yorkis Perez	.05
306	Edgar Renteria	.25
307	Gary Sheffield	.25
308	Jesus Tavarez	.05
309	Quilvio Veras	.05
310	Devon White	.05
311	Jeff Bagwell	1.25
312	Derek Bell	.05
313	Sean Berry	.05
314	Craig Biggio	.10
315	Doug Drabek	.05
316	Tony Eusebio	.05
317	Ricky Gutierrez	.05
318	Xavier Hernandez	.05
319	Brian L. Hunter	.05
320	Darryl Kile	.05
321	Derrick May	.05
322	Orlando Miller	.05
323	James Mouton	.05
324	Bill Spiers	.05
325	Pedro Astacio	.05
326	Brett Butler	.05
327	Juan Castro	.05
328	Roger Cedeno	.05
329	Delino DeShields	.05
330	Karim Garcia	.50
331	Todd Hollandsworth	.05
332	Eric Karros	.05
333	Oreste Marrero	.05
334	Ramon Martinez	.05
335	Raul Mondesi	.25
336	Hideo Nomo	.50
337	Antonio Osuna	.05
338	Chan Ho Park	.05
339	Mike Piazza	2.00
340	Ismael Valdes	.05
341	Moises Alou	.05
342	Omar Daal	.05
343	Jeff Fassero	.05
344	Cliff Floyd	.05
345	Mark Grudzielanek	.05
346	Mike Lansing	.05
347	Pedro Martinez	.15
348	Sherman Obando	.05
349	Jose Paniagua	.05
350	Henry Rodriguez	.05
351	Mel Rojas	.05
352	F.P. Santangelo	.05
353	Dave Segui	.05
354	Dave Silvestri	.05
355	Ugueth Urbina	.05
356	Rondell White	.05
357	Edgardo Alfonzo	.05
358	Carlos Baerga	.05
359	Tim Bogar	.05
360	Rico Brogna	.05
361	Alvaro Espinoza	.05
362	Carl Everett	.05
363	John Franco	.05
364	Bernard Gilkey	.05
365	Todd Hundley	.05
366	Butch Huskey	.05
367	Jason Isringhausen	.05
368	Bobby Jones	.05
369	Lance Johnson	.05
370	Brent Mayne	.05
371	Alex Ochoa	.05
372	Rey Ordonez	.20
373	Ron Blazier	.05
374	Ricky Bottalico	.05
375	David Doster	.05
376	Lenny Dykstra	.05
377	Jim Eisenreich	.05
378	Bobby Estalella	.05
379	Gregg Jefferies	.05
380	Kevin Jordan	.05
381	Ricardo Jordan	.05
382	Mickey Morandini	.05
383	Ricky Otero	.05
384	Benito Santiago	.05
385	Gene Schall	.05
386	Curt Schilling	.10
387	Kevin Sefcik	.05
388	Kevin Stocker	.05
389	Jermaine Allensworth	.05
390	Jay Bell	.05
391	Jason Christiansen	.05
392	Francisco Cordova	.05
393	Mark Johnson	.05
394	Jason Kendall	.05
395	Jeff King	.05
396	Jon Lieber	.05
397	Nelson Liriano	.05
398	Esteban Loaiza	.10
399	Al Martin	.05
400	Orlando Merced	.05
401	Ramon Morel	.05
402	Luis Alicea	.05
403	Alan Benes	.10
404	Andy Benes	.05
405	Terry Bradshaw	.05
406	Royce Clayton	.05
407	Dennis Eckersley	.05
408	Gary Gaetti	.05
409	Mike Gallego	.05
410	Ron Gant	.10
411	Brian Jordan	.05
412	Ray Lankford	.05
413	John Mabry	.05
414	Willie McGee	.05
415	Tom Pagnozzi	.05
416	Ozzie Smith	.40
417	Todd Stottlemyre	.05
418	Mark Sweeney	.05
419	Andy Ashby	.05
420	Ken Caminiti	.10
421	Archi Cianfrocco	.05
422	Steve Finley	.05
423	Chris Gomez	.05
424	Tony Gwynn	1.25
425	Joey Hamilton	.05
426	Rickey Henderson	.20
427	Trevor Hoffman	.05
428	Brian Johnson	.05
429	Wally Joyner	.05
430	Scott Livingstone	.05
431	Jody Reed	.05
432	Craig Shipley	.05
433	Fernando Valenzuela	.05
434	Greg Vaughn	.10
435	Rich Aurilia	.05
436	Kim Batiste	.05
437	Jose Bautista	.05
438	Rod Beck	.05
439	Marvin Benard	.05
440	Barry Bonds	.75
441	Shawon Dunston	.05
442	Shawn Estes	.05
443	Osvaldo Fernandez	.05
444	Stan Javier	.05
445	David McCarty	.05
446	*Bill Mueller*	.05
447	Steve Scarsone	.05
448	Robby Thompson	.05
449	Rick Wilkins	.05
450	Matt Williams	.25

1997 Pacific Crown Light Blue

This parallel insert was produced exclusively for insertion in Wal-Mart/Sam's jumbo packs at the rate of one per pack. Following the format of the regular-issue, they use light blue foil, rather than the standard gold. Light blue inserts should not be confused with the much scarcer silver inserts which are visually similar.

	MT
Complete Set (450):	250.00
Common Player:	.25
Stars: 2X	

(See 1997 Pacific Crown for checklist and base card values.)

1997 Pacific Crown Silver

This parallel insert was produced in an edition of only 67 cards per player. Following the format of the regular-issue, they use silver foil, rather than the standard gold. Silver parallels were inserted at an advertised rate of one per 73 packs. Silver inserts should not be confused with the much more common light blue inserts which are visually similar.

	MT
Common Player:	5.00
Stars: 35-50X	
Rookies: 25-40X	

(See 1997 Pacific Crown for checklist and base card values.)

1997 Pacific Crown Card-Supials

The 36-card, regular-sized set was inserted every 37 packs of 1997 Pacific Crown baseball. The card fronts feature a gold-foil spiral with the player's name printed along a curve on the bottom edge. The team logo appears in the lower right corner. The card backs feature an action shot and are numbered "x of 36." The cards come with a mini (1-1/4" x 1-3/4") card that slides into a pocket on the back. The mini cards are of a different player, but depict the same action shot as the larger card backs.

		MT
Complete Set (72):		250.00
Complete Large Set (36):		175.00
Complete Small Set (36):		90.00
Common Large:		2.00
Small Cards: 50%		
1	Roberto Alomar	3.00
2	Brady Anderson	2.00
3	Eddie Murray	3.00
4	Cal Ripken Jr.	12.50
5	Jose Canseco	2.50
6	Mo Vaughn	3.50
7	Frank Thomas	7.50
8	Albert Belle	4.00
9	Omar Vizquel	2.00
10	Chuck Knoblauch	2.00
11	Paul Molitor	3.00
12	Wade Boggs	2.50
13	Derek Jeter	10.00
14	Andy Pettitte	3.50
15	Mark McGwire	15.00
16	Jay Buhner	2.00
17	Ken Griffey Jr.	15.00
18	Alex Rodriguez	12.50
19	Juan Gonzalez	7.50
20	Ivan Rodriguez	3.00
21	Andruw Jones	7.50
22	Chipper Jones	10.00
23	Ryan Klesko	2.00
24	Greg Maddux	10.00
25	Ryne Sandberg	4.00
26	Andres Galarraga	2.00
27	Gary Sheffield	2.50
28	Jeff Bagwell	7.50
29	Todd Hollandsworth	2.00
30	Hideo Nomo	2.50
31	Mike Piazza	10.00
32	Todd Hundley	2.00
33	Dennis Eckersley	2.00
34	Ken Caminiti	2.00
35	Tony Gwynn	7.50
36	Barry Bonds	4.00

1997 Pacific Crown Cramer's Choice Awards

The 10-card, regular-sized set was inserted every 721 packs and features a die-cut pyramid design. A color player photo is imaged over silver foil with the player's name and position in gold foil over a green marble background along the bottom. The card backs feature a headshot with a brief career highlight in both Spanish and English. The cards are numbered with a "CC" prefix.

		MT
Complete Set (10):		450.00
Common Player:		20.00
1	Roberto Alomar	20.00
2	Frank Thomas	45.00
3	Albert Belle	25.00
4	Andy Pettitte	20.00
5	Ken Griffey Jr.	100.00
6	Alex Rodriguez	75.00
7	Chipper Jones	60.00
8	John Smoltz	20.00
9	Mike Piazza	60.00
10	Tony Gwynn	50.00

1997 Pacific Crown Fireworks Die-Cuts

The 20-card, regular-sized, die-cut set was inserted every 73 packs of 1997 Crown. The card fronts feature a color action shot with generic fireworks over a stadium on the upper half. The horizontal card backs contain close-up shots with highlights in Spanish and English. The cards are numbered with the "FW" prefix.

		MT
Complete Set (20):		240.00
Common Player:		3.50
1	Roberto Alomar	7.50
2	Brady Anderson	3.50
3	Eddie Murray	4.50
4	Cal Ripken Jr.	25.00
5	Frank Thomas	15.00
6	Albert Belle	7.50
7	Derek Jeter	20.00
8	Andy Pettitte	6.00
9	Bernie Williams	6.00
10	Mark McGwire	30.00
11	Ken Griffey Jr.	30.00
12	Alex Rodriguez	25.00
13	Juan Gonzalez	12.50
14	Andruw Jones	15.00
15	Chipper Jones	20.00
16	Hideo Nomo	4.50
17	Mike Piazza	20.00
18	Henry Rodriguez	3.50
19	Tony Gwynn	15.00
20	Barry Bonds	7.50

1997 Pacific Crown Gold Crown Die-Cuts

The 36-card, regular-sized, die-cut set was inserted every 37 packs. The card fronts feature a die-cut, gold-foil crown on the top border and the player's name appears in gold along the bottom edge. The card backs contain a headshot and a Spanish/English highlight and are numbered with the "GC" prefix.

		MT
Complete Set (36):		240.00
Common Player:		2.50
1	Roberto Alomar	6.00
2	Brady Anderson	2.50
3	Mike Mussina	4.00
4	Eddie Murray	4.50
5	Cal Ripken Jr.	20.00
6	Jose Canseco	3.50
7	Frank Thomas	12.50
8	Albert Belle	6.00
9	Omar Vizquel	2.50
10	Wade Boggs	3.50
11	Derek Jeter	12.50
12	Andy Pettitte	5.00
13	Mariano Rivera	2.50
14	Bernie Williams	4.00
15	Mark McGwire	25.00
16	Ken Griffey Jr.	25.00
17	Edgar Martinez	2.50
18	Alex Rodriguez	20.00
19	Juan Gonzalez	12.00
20	Ivan Rodriguez	7.50
21	Andruw Jones	12.00
22	Chipper Jones	15.00
23	Ryan Klesko	2.50
24	John Smoltz	3.00
25	Ryne Sandberg	6.00
26	Andres Galarraga	2.50
27	Edgar Renteria	3.50
28	Jeff Bagwell	10.00
29	Todd Hollandsworth	2.50
30	Hideo Nomo	3.50
31	Mike Piazza	15.00
32	Todd Hundley	2.50
33	Brian Jordan	2.50
34	Ken Caminiti	3.00
35	Tony Gwynn	10.00
36	Barry Bonds	6.00

Player names in *Italic* type indicate a rookie card.

1997 Pacific Crown Latinos of the Major Leagues

The 36-card, regular-sized set was inserted twice every 37 packs. The card fronts feature a color action shot over the player's name in gold foil. The card backs have another action shot and a Spanish/English highlight.

		MT
Complete Set (36):		60.00
Common Player:		1.50
1	George Arias	1.50
2	Roberto Alomar	4.00
3	Rafael Palmeiro	3.00
4	Bobby Bonilla	2.00
5	Jose Canseco	2.50
6	Wilson Alvarez	1.50
7	Dave Martinez	1.50
8	Julio Franco	1.50
9	Manny Ramirez	6.00
10	Omar Vizquel	1.50
11	Marty Cordova	1.50
12	Roberto Kelly	1.50
13	Tino Martinez	2.00
14	Mariano Rivera	2.50
15	Ruben Rivera	1.50
16	Bernie Williams	4.00
17	Geronimo Berroa	1.50
18	Joey Cora	1.50
19	Edgar Martinez	1.50
20	Alex Rodriguez	12.50
21	Juan Gonzalez	10.00
22	Ivan Rodriguez	7.50
23	Andruw Jones	10.00
24	Javier Lopez	2.00
25	Sammy Sosa	10.00
26	Vinny Castilla	2.00
27	Andres Galarraga	2.00
28	Ramon Martinez	2.00
29	Raul Mondesi	3.00
30	Ismael Valdes	1.50
31	Pedro Martinez	6.00
32	Henry Rodriguez	1.50
33	Carlos Baerga	1.50
34	Rey Ordonez	2.00
35	Fernando Valenzuela	1.50
36	Osvaldo Fernandez	1.50

1997 Pacific Crown Triple Crown Die-Cuts

The 20-card, regular-sized, die-cut set was inserted every 145 packs of Crown baseball. The horizontal card fronts feature the same gold-foil, die-cut crown as on the Gold Crown Die-Cut inserts. The card backs feature a headshot, Spanish/English text and are numbered with the "TC" prefix.

		MT
Complete Set (20):		450.00
Common Player:		10.00
1	Brady Anderson	8.00
2	Rafael Palmeiro	12.50
3	Mo Vaughn	20.00
4	Frank Thomas	45.00
5	Albert Belle	20.00
6	Jim Thome	8.00
7	Cecil Fielder	8.00
8	Mark McGwire	75.00
9	Ken Griffey Jr.	75.00
10	Alex Rodriguez	60.00
11	Juan Gonzalez	40.00
12	Andruw Jones	25.00
13	Chipper Jones	50.00
14	Dante Bichette	8.00
15	Ellis Burks	8.00
16	Andres Galarraga	10.00
17	Jeff Bagwell	25.00
18	Mike Piazza	50.00
19	Ken Caminiti	10.00
20	Barry Bonds	20.00

1997 Pacific Invincible

The 1997 Pacific Invincible 150-card set was sold in three-card packs. The card fronts feature gold foil parallel lines with a color action shot. The bottom right quadrant contains a transparent cel headshot. The card backs have Spanish/English text and another color action shot. The reverse cel has the player's hat team logo air-brushed off to prevent reverse print. Insert sets are: Sluggers & Hurlers, Sizzling Lumber, Gate Attractions, Gems of the Diamond (2:1), and Light Blue (retail only) and Platinum (hobby) parallel sets of the 150 baseball cards.

		MT
Complete Set (150):		150.00
Common Player:		1.00
Light Blues: 2X		
Platinums: 2X		
Wax Box:		70.00
1	Chili Davis	1.00
2	Jim Edmonds	1.50
3	Darin Erstad	5.00
4	Orlando Palmeiro	1.00
5	Tim Salmon	2.00
6	J.T. Snow	1.00
7	Roberto Alomar	2.50
8	Brady Anderson	1.50
9	Eddie Murray	2.00
10	Mike Mussina	2.50
11	Rafael Palmeiro	2.00
12	Cal Ripken Jr.	12.00
13	Jose Canseco	2.00
14	Roger Clemens	5.00
15	Nomar Garciaparra	7.00
16	Reggie Jefferson	1.00
17	Mo Vaughn	2.50
18	Wilson Alvarez	1.00
19	Harold Baines	1.00
20	Alex Fernandez	1.00
21	Danny Tartabull	1.00
22	Frank Thomas	6.00
23	Robin Ventura	1.50
24	Sandy Alomar Jr.	1.50
25	Albert Belle	4.00
26	Kenny Lofton	2.50
27	Jim Thome	1.50
28	Omar Vizquel	1.00
29	Raul Casanova	1.00
30	Tony Clark	1.50
31	Travis Fryman	1.00
32	Bobby Higginson	1.00
33	Melvin Nieves	1.00
34	Justin Thompson	1.00
35	Johnny Damon	1.00
36	Tom Goodwin	1.00
37	Jeff Montgomery	1.00
38	Jose Offerman	1.00
39	John Jaha	1.00
40	Jeff Cirillo	1.00
41	Dave Nilsson	1.00
42	Jose Valentin	1.00
43	Fernando Vina	1.00
44	Marty Cordova	1.00
45	Roberto Kelly	1.00
46	Chuck Knoblauch	1.50
47	Paul Molitor	2.50
48	Todd Walker	3.00
49	Wade Boggs	2.00
50	Cecil Fielder	1.00
51	Derek Jeter	10.00
52	Tino Martinez	1.50
53	Andy Pettitte	3.00
54	Mariano Rivera	1.50
55	Bernie Williams	2.50
56	Tony Batista	1.00
57	Geronimo Berroa	1.00
58	Jason Giambi	1.00
59	Mark McGwire	15.00
60	Terry Steinbach	1.00
61	Jay Buhner	1.00
62	Joey Cora	1.00
63	Ken Griffey Jr.	15.00
64	Edgar Martinez	1.00
65	Alex Rodriguez	12.00
66	Paul Sorrento	1.00
67	Will Clark	1.50
68	Juan Gonzalez	7.00
69	Rusty Greer	1.00
70	Dean Palmer	1.00
71	Ivan Rodriguez	3.00
72	Joe Carter	1.00
73	Carlos Delgado	2.00
74	Juan Guzman	1.00
75	Pat Hentgen	1.00
76	Ed Sprague	1.00
77	Jermaine Dye	1.00
78	Andruw Jones	7.00
79	Chipper Jones	10.00
80	Ryan Klesko	1.50
81	Javier Lopez	1.50
82	Greg Maddux	10.00
83	John Smoltz	2.00
84	Mark Grace	1.50
85	Luis Gonzalez	1.00
86	Brooks Kieschnick	1.00
87	Jaime Navarro	1.00
88	Ryne Sandberg	4.00
89	Sammy Sosa	8.00
90	Bret Boone	1.00
91	Jeff Brantley	1.00
92	Eric Davis	1.00
93	Barry Larkin	1.50
94	Reggie Sanders	1.00
95	Ellis Burks	1.00
96	Dante Bichette	1.50
97	Vinny Castilla	1.00
98	Andres Galarraga	1.50
99	Eric Young	1.00
100	Kevin Brown	1.50
101	Jeff Conine	1.00
102	Charles Johnson	1.00
103	Edgar Renteria	1.50
104	Gary Sheffield	2.00
105	Jeff Bagwell	7.00
106	Derek Bell	1.00
107	Sean Berry	1.00
108	Craig Biggio	1.50
109	Shane Reynolds	1.00
110	Karim Garcia	2.00
111	Todd Hollandsworth	1.00
112	Ramon Martinez	1.00
113	Raul Mondesi	2.00
114	Hideo Nomo	2.00
115	Mike Piazza	10.00
116	Ismael Valdes	1.00
117	Moises Alou	1.00
118	Mark Grudzielanek	1.00
119	Pedro Martinez	2.00
120	Henry Rodriguez	1.00
121	F.P. Santangelo	1.00
122	Carlos Baerga	1.00
123	Bernard Gilkey	1.00
124	Todd Hundley	1.00
125	Lance Johnson	1.00
126	Alex Ochoa	1.00
127	Rey Ordonez	1.50
128	Lenny Dykstra	1.00
129	Gregg Jefferies	1.00
130	Ricky Otero	1.00
131	Benito Santiago	1.00
132	Jermaine Allensworth	1.00
133	Francisco Cordova	1.00
134	Carlos Garcia	1.00
135	Jason Kendall	1.00
136	Al Martin	1.00
137	Dennis Eckersley	1.00
138	Ron Gant	1.00
139	Brian Jordan	1.00
140	John Mabry	1.00
141	Ozzie Smith	3.00
142	Ken Caminiti	2.00
143	Steve Finley	1.00
144	Tony Gwynn	6.00
145	Wally Joyner	1.00
146	Fernando Valenzuela	1.00
147	Barry Bonds	5.00
148	Jacob Cruz	2.00
149	Osvaldo Fernandez	1.00
150	Matt Williams	2.00

1997 Pacific Invincible Gate Attractions

The 32-card, regular-sized set was inserted every 73 packs of Pacific Invincible baseball. The card fronts feature a generic baseball glove background with the player's name and position in a gold-foil circle. The center of the card is a cel action shot within a common baseball image. The player's team logo appears in the upper right corner. The card backs contain a headshot in the upper left corner with highlights in Spanish and English. The player's image in the cel is etched in gray in reverse. The cards are numbered with the "GA" prefix.

		MT
Complete Set (32):		350.00
Common Player:		4.00
1	Roberto Alomar	7.50
2	Brady Anderson	4.00
3	Cal Ripken Jr.	30.00
4	Frank Thomas	18.00
5	Kenny Lofton	5.00
6	Omar Vizquel	4.00
7	Paul Molitor	7.50
8	Wade Boggs	7.50
9	Derek Jeter	25.00
10	Andy Pettitte	5.00
11	Bernie Williams	5.00
12	Geronimo Berroa	4.00
13	Mark McGwire	35.00
14	Ken Griffey Jr.	35.00
15	Alex Rodriguez	30.00
16	Juan Gonzalez	20.00
17	Andruw Jones	18.00
18	Chipper Jones	25.00
19	Greg Maddux	24.00
20	Ryne Sandberg	9.00
21	Sammy Sosa	18.00
22	Andres Galarraga	4.00
23	Jeff Bagwell	15.00
24	Todd Hollandsworth	4.00
25	Hideo Nomo	4.00
26	Mike Piazza	25.00
27	Todd Hundley	4.00
28	Lance Johnson	4.00
29	Ozzie Smith	9.00
30	Ken Caminiti	6.00
31	Tony Gwynn	20.00
32	Barry Bonds	9.00

1997 Pacific Invincible Gems of the Diamond

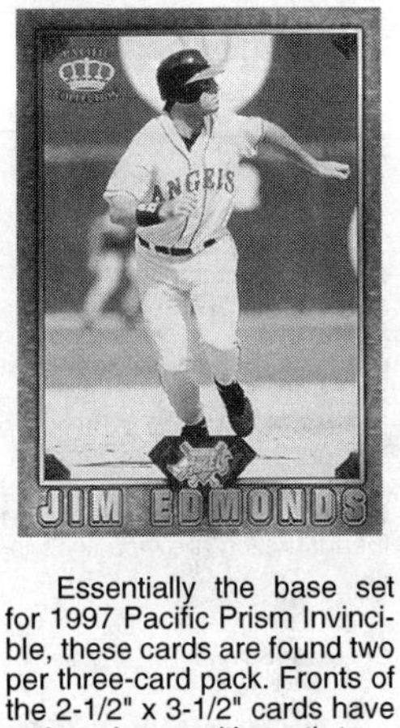

Essentially the base set for 1997 Pacific Prism Invincible, these cards are found two per three-card pack. Fronts of the 2-1/2" x 3-1/2" cards have action photos with earth-tone borders and a color team logo at bottom. Backs have a large player portrait photos in a diamond at right-center and are numbered with a "GD-" prefix.

		MT
Complete Set (220):		50.00
Common Player:		.15
1	Jim Abbott	.15
2	Shawn Boskie	.15
3	Gary DiSarcina	.15
4	Jim Edmonds	.25
5	Todd Greene	.15
6	Jack Howell	.15
7	Jeff Schmidt	.15
8	Shad Williams	.15
9	Roberto Alomar	.50
10	Cesar Devarez	.15
11	Alan Mills	.15
12	Eddie Murray	.30
13	Jesse Orosco	.15
14	Arthur Rhodes	.15
15	Bill Ripken	.15
16	Cal Ripken Jr.	3.00
17	Mark Smith	.15
18	Roger Clemens	1.50
19	Vaughn Eshelman	.15
20	Rich Garces	.15
21	Bill Haselman	.15
22	Dwayne Hosey	.15
23	Mike Maddux	.15
24	Jose Malave	.15
25	Aaron Sele	.15
26	James Baldwin	.15
27	Pat Borders	.15
28	Mike Cameron	.15
29	Tony Castillo	.15
30	Domingo Cedeno	.15
31	Greg Norton	.15
32	Frank Thomas	1.50
33	Albert Belle	.75
34	Einar Diaz	.15
35	Alan Embree	.15
36	Albie Lopez	.15
37	Chad Ogea	.15
38	Tony Pena	.15
39	Joe Roa	.15
40	Fausto Cruz	.15
41	Joey Eischen	.15
42	Travis Fryman	.15
43	Mike Myers	.15
44	A.J. Sager	.15
45	Duane Singleton	.15
46	Justin Thompson	.15
47	Jeff Granger	.15
48	Les Norman	.15
49	Jon Nunnally	.15
50	Craig Paquette	.15
51	Michael Tucker	.15
52	Julio Valera	.15
53	Kevin Young	.15
54	Cal Eldred	.15
55	Ramon Garcia	.15
56	Marc Newfield	.15
57	Al Reyes	.15
58	Tim Unroe	.15
59	Tim Vanegmond	.15
60	Turner Ward	.15
61	Bob Wickman	.15
62	Chuck Knoblauch	.25
63	Paul Molitor	.50
64	Kirby Puckett	.75
65	Tom Quinlan	.15
66	Rich Robertson	.15
67	Dave Stevens	.15
68	Matt Walbeck	.15
69	Wade Boggs	.50
70	Tony Fernandez	.15
71	Andy Fox	.15
72	Joe Girardi	.15
73	Charlie Hayes	.15
74	Pat Kelly	.15
75	Jeff Nelson	.15
76	Melido Perez	.15
77	Mark Acre	.15
78	Allen Battle	.15
79	Rafael Bournigal	.15
80	Mark McGwire	5.00
81	Pedro Munoz	.15
82	Scott Spiezio	.15
83	Don Wengert	.15
84	Steve Wojciechowski	.15
85	Alex Diaz	.15
86	Ken Griffey Jr.	5.00
87	Raul Ibanez	.25
88	Mike Jackson	.15
89	John Marzano	.15
90	Greg McCarthy	.15
91	Alex Rodriguez	3.00
92	Andy Sheets	.15
93	Makoto Suzuki	.15
94	Benji Gil	.15
95	Juan Gonzalez	2.00
96	Kevin Gross	.15
97	Gil Heredia	.15
98	Luis Ortiz	.15
99	Jeff Russell	.15
100	Dave Valle	.15
101	Marty Janzen	.15
102	Sandy Martinez	.15
103	Julio Mosquera	.15
104	Otis Nixon	.15
105	Paul Spoljaric	.15
106	Shannon Stewart	.15
107	Woody Williams	.15
108	Steve Avery	.15
109	Mike Bielecki	.15
110	Pedro Borbon	.15
111	Ed Giovanola	.15
112	Chipper Jones	2.50
113	Greg Maddux	2.50
114	Mike Mordecai	.15
115	Terrell Wade	.15
116	Terry Adams	.15
117	Brian Dorsett	.15
118	Doug Glanville	.15
119	Tyler Houston	.15
120	Robin Jennings	.15

121	Ryne Sandberg	.75
122	Terry Shumpert	.15
123	Amaury Telemaco	.15
124	Steve Trachsel	.15
125	Curtis Goodwin	.15
126	Mike Kelly	.15
127	Chad Mottola	.15
128	Mark Portugal	.15
129	Roger Salkeld	.15
130	John Smiley	.15
131	Lee Smith	.20
132	Roger Bailey	.15
133	Andres Galarraga	.25
134	Darren Holmes	.15
135	Curtis Leskanic	.15
136	Mike Munoz	.15
137	Jeff Reed	.15
138	Mark Thompson	.15
139	Jamey Wright	.15
140	Andre Dawson	.20
141	Craig Grebeck	.15
142	Matt Mantei	.15
143	Billy McMillon	.15
144	Kurt Miller	.15
145	Ralph Milliard	.15
146	Bob Natal	.15
147	Joe Siddall	.15
148	Bob Abreu	.20
149	Doug Brocail	.15
150	Danny Darwin	.15
151	Mike Hampton	.15
152	Todd Jones	.15
153	Kirt Manwaring	.15
154	Alvin Morman	.15
155	Billy Ashley	.15
156	Tom Candiotti	.15
157	Darren Dreifort	.15
158	Greg Gagne	.15
159	Wilton Guerrero	.15
160	Hideo Nomo	.50
161	Mike Piazza	2.50
162	Tom Prince	.15
163	Todd Worrell	.15
164	Moises Alou	.20
165	Shane Andrews	.15
166	Derek Aucoin	.15
167	Raul Chavez	.15
168	Darrin Fletcher	.15
169	Mark Leiter	.15
170	Henry Rodriguez	.15
171	Dave Veres	.15
172	Paul Byrd	.15
173	Alberto Castillo	.15
174	Mark Clark	.15
175	Rey Ordonez	.20
176	Roberto Petagine	.15
177	Andy Tomberlin	.15
178	Derek Wallace	.15
179	Paul Wilson	.15
180	Ruben Amaro, Jr.	.15
181	Toby Borland	.15
182	Rich Hunter	.15
183	Tony Longmire	.15
184	Wendell Magee Jr.	.15
185	Bobby Munoz	.15
186	Scott Rolen	.75
187	Mike Williams	.15
188	Trey Beamon	.15
189	Jason Christiansen	.15
190	Elmer Dessens	.15
191	Angelo Encarnacion	.25
192	Carlos Garcia	.15
193	Mike Kingery	.15
194	Chris Peters	.15
195	Tony Womack	.20
196	Brian Barber	.15
197	David Bell	.15
198	Tony Fossas	.15
199	Rick Honeycutt	.15
200	T.J. Mathews	.15
201	Miguel Mejia	.15
202	Donovan Osborne	.15
203	Ozzie Smith	.50
204	Andres Berumen	.15
205	Ken Caminiti	.25
206	Chris Gwynn	.15
207	Tony Gwynn	2.00
208	Rickey Henderson	.30
209	Scott Sanders	.15
210	Jason Thompson	.15
211	Fernando Valenzuela	.15
212	Tim Worrell	.15
213	Barry Bonds	.75
214	Jay Canizaro	.15
215	Doug Creek	.15
216	Jacob Cruz	.15
217	Glenallen Hill	.15
218	Tom Lampkin	.15
219	Jim Poole	.15
220	Desi Wilson	.15

1997 Pacific Invincible Sizzling Lumber

The 36-card, regular-sized, die-cut set was inserted every 37 packs of Invinceable. The cards have die-cut flames along the right border with a bat running parallel. The player's name appears in gold foil along the top border with his position in English and Spanish in gold foil along the bottom. The card backs feature a headshot in the upper half and contain Spanish and English text. The cards are numbered with the "SL" prefix.

		MT
Complete Set (36):		200.00
Common Player:		2.50
1A	Cal Ripken Jr.	20.00
1B	Rafael Palmeiro	3.00
1C	Roberto Alomar	4.00
2A	Frank Thomas	10.00
2B	Robin Ventura	2.50
2C	Harold Baines	2.50
3A	Albert Belle	6.00
3B	Manny Ramirez	6.00
3C	Kenny Lofton	4.50
4A	Derek Jeter	15.00
4B	Bernie Williams	3.50
4C	Wade Boggs	3.00
5A	Mark McGwire	25.00
5B	Jason Giambi	2.50
5C	Geronimo Berroa	2.50
6A	Ken Griffey Jr.	25.00
6B	Alex Rodriguez	20.00
6C	Jay Buhner	2.50
7A	Juan Gonzalez	12.50
7B	Dean Palmer	2.50
7C	Ivan Rodriguez	6.00
8A	Ryan Klesko	2.50
8B	Chipper Jones	15.00
8C	Andruw Jones	12.50
9A	Dante Bichette	2.50
9B	Andres Galarraga	2.50
9C	Vinny Castilla	2.50
10A	Jeff Bagwell	12.50
10B	Craig Biggio	2.50
10C	Derek Bell	2.50
11A	Mike Piazza	15.00
11B	Raul Mondesi	3.50
11C	Karim Garcia	3.50
12A	Tony Gwynn	12.50
12B	Ken Caminiti	3.50
12C	Greg Vaughn	2.50

1997 Pacific Invincible Sluggers & Hurlers

The 24-card, regular-sized set was inserted every 145 packs of Pacific Invincible baseball. The cards are numbered with an "SH-xA" or "SH-xaB." Each "A" card is the left half of a two-card set with the two players from the same team having their logo in the fit-together center. Each card has the player's name printed in gold foil along the bottom border with gold-foil swirls around the team logo. The card backs have a circular headshot with text in English and Spanish.

		MT
Complete Set (24):		500.00
Common Player:		7.50
SH-1a	Cal Ripken Jr.	40.00
SH-1b	Mike Mussina	10.00
SH-2a	Jose Canseco	10.00
SH-2b	Roger Clemens	15.00
SH-3a	Frank Thomas	20.00
SH-3b	Wilson Alvarez	7.50
SH-4a	Kenny Lofton	10.00
SH-4b	Orel Hershiser	7.50
SH-5a	Derek Jeter	30.00
SH-5b	Andy Pettitte	10.00
SH-6a	Ken Griffey Jr.	50.00
SH-6b	Randy Johnson	10.00
SH-7a	Alex Rodriguez	40.00
SH-7b	Jamie Moyer	7.50
SH-8a	Andruw Jones	25.00
SH-8b	Greg Maddux	30.00
SH-9a	Chipper Jones	30.00
SH-9b	John Smoltz	9.00
SH-10a	Jeff Bagwell	20.00
SH-10b	Shane Reynolds	7.50
SH-11a	Mike Piazza	30.00
SH-11b	Hideo Nomo	10.00
SH-12a	Tony Gwynn	20.00
SH-12b	Fernando Valenzuela	7.50

1997 Pacific Carlos Baerga Celebrities Softball

This set was produced for distribution to fans attending the third annual Carlos Baerga Celebrities Softball Game in Puerto Rico on Dec. 14. Packs were handed out containing two cards from this set, a 1997 Pacific Crown Collection card, a '97 Pacific Invincible card, a Pacific logo card and an information card about card shops on the island. The softball celebrities cards have gold-foil highlighted borderless action photos from the 1996 game. Pacific and the charity game's logos are in upper-right and lower left. Horizontal backs have a player portrait photo at left and English/Spanish description of his participation in the event.

		MT
Complete Set (10):		30.00
Common Player:		2.00
1	Carlos Baerga	2.00
2	Bernie Williams	2.00
3	Ivan Rodriguez	4.00
4	Sandy Alomar Jr.	2.50
5	Joey Cora	2.00
6	Roberto Alomar	5.00
7	Moises Alou	2.00
8	Rey Ordonez	2.00
9	Derek Jeter	9.00
10	David Justice	3.00

1997 Pacific/ NationsBank Florida Marlins

Certainly one of the nicest team card sets ever given away at a promotional game was this Marlins set produced by Pacific and sponsored by NationsBank. The cello-wrapped set was given out to the first 16,000 children attending the June 27 Marlins game. The 2-1/2" x 3-1/2" cards are UV-coated on both sides with a gold-foil "wave" containing the player names on front. The producer, sponsor and team logos also appear on front. Backs have a swirling teal background with a player color portrait in the upper-right. Personal data, 1996 and career stats and a short career summary - in both English and Spanish - are also found on back.

		MT
Complete Set (33):		12.00
Common Player:		.30
1	Kurt Abbott	.30
2	Moises Alou	.45
3	Alex Arias	.30
4	Bobby Bonilla	1.00
5	Kevin Brown	.60
6	John Cangelosi	.30
7	Luis Castillo	.30
8	Jeff Conine	.45
9	Jim Eisenreich	.30
10	Alex Fernandez	.40
11	Cliff Floyd	.40
12	Rick Helling	.30
13	Felix Heredia	.30
14	Mark Hutton	.30
15	Charles Johnson	.45
16	Al Leiter	.30
17	Robb Nen	.30
18	Jay Powell	.30
19	Pat Rapp	.30
20	Edgar Renteria	.60
21	Tony Saunders	.30
22	Gary Sheffield	1.00
23	Devon White	.40
24	Gregg Zaun	.30
25	Jim Leyland	.30
26	Rich Donnelly	.30
27	Bruce Kimm	.30
28	Jerry Manuel	.30
29	Milt May	.30
30	Larry Rothschild	.30
31	Tommy Sandt	.30
32	Billy the Marlin (mascot)	.30
(33)	Header card/checklist	.30

1998 Pacific

1998 Pacific Baseball is a 450-card, bilingual set. The base set features full-bleed photos with the Pacific Crown Collection logo in the upper left and the player's name, position and team at the bottom. Inserts include Cramer's Choice Awards, In The Cage Laser-Cuts, Home Run Hitters, Team Checklist Laser-Cuts, Gold Crown Die-Cuts and Latinos of the Major Leagues.

		MT
Complete Set (450):		35.00
Common Player:		.10
Inserted 1:73		
1	Luis Alicea	.10
2	Garret Anderson	.10
3	Jason Dickson	.10
4	Gary DiSarcina	.10
5	Jim Edmonds	.20
6	Darin Erstad	.75
7	Chuck Finley	.10
8	Shigetosi Hasegawa	.10
9	Rickey Henderson	.20
10	Dave Hollins	.10
11	Mark Langston	.10
12	Orlando Palmeiro	.10
13	Troy Percival	.10
14	Tony Phillips	.10
15	Tim Salmon	.30
16	Allen Watson	.10
17	Roberto Alomar	.60
18	Brady Anderson	.10
19	Harold Baines	.10
20	Armando Benitez	.10
21	Geronimo Berroa	.10
22	Mike Bordick	.10
23	Eric Davis	.10
24	Scott Erickson	.10
25	Chris Hoiles	.10
26	Jimmy Key	.10
27	Aaron Ledesma	.10
28	Mike Mussina	.60
29	Randy Myers	.10
30	Jesse Orosco	.10
31	Rafael Palmeiro	.25
32	Jeff Reboulet	.10
33	Cal Ripken Jr.	2.50
34	B.J. Surhoff	.10
35	Steve Avery	.10
36	Darren Bragg	.10
37	Wil Cordero	.10
38	Jeff Frye	.10
39	Nomar Garciaparra	2.00
40	Tom Gordon	.10
41	Bill Haselman	.10
42	Scott Hatteberg	.10
43	Butch Henry	.10
44	Reggie Jefferson	.10
45	Tim Naehring	.10
46	Troy O'Leary	.10
47	Jeff Suppan	.10
48	John Valentin	.10
49	Mo Vaughn	.60
50	Tim Wakefield	.10
51	James Baldwin	.10
52	Albert Belle	.75
53	Tony Castillo	.10
54	Doug Drabek	.10
55	Ray Durham	.10
56	Jorge Fabregas	.10
57	Ozzie Guillen	.10
58	Matt Karchner	.10
59	Norberto Martin	.10
60	Dave Martinez	.10
61	Lyle Mouton	.10
62	Jaime Navarro	.10
63	Frank Thomas	1.00
64	Mario Valdez	.10
65	Robin Ventura	.20
66	Sandy Alomar Jr.	.20
67	Paul Assenmacher	.10
68	Tony Fernandez	.10
69	Brian Giles	.10
70	Marquis Grissom	.10
71	Orel Hershiser	.10
72	Mike Jackson	.10
73	David Justice	.30
74	Albie Lopez	.10
75	Jose Mesa	.10
76	Charles Nagy	.10
77	Chad Ogea	.10
78	Manny Ramirez	.75
79	Jim Thome	.25
80	Omar Vizquel	.10
81	Matt Williams	.25
82	Jaret Wright	.75
83	Willie Blair	.10
84	Raul Casanova	.10
85	Tony Clark	.25
86	Deivi Cruz	.10
87	Damion Easley	.10
88	Travis Fryman	.10
89	Bobby Higginson	.15
90	Brian Hunter	.10
91	Todd Jones	.10
92	Dan Miceli	.10
93	Brian Moehler	.10
94	Melvin Nieves	.10
95	Jody Reed	.10
96	Justin Thompson	.10
97	Bubba Trammell	.10
98	Kevin Appier	.10
99	Jay Bell	.10
100	Yamil Benitez	.10
101	Johnny Damon	.10
102	Chili Davis	.10
103	Jermaine Dye	.10
104	Jed Hansen	.10
105	Jeff King	.10
106	Mike Macfarlane	.10
107	Felix Martinez	.10
108	Jeff Montgomery	.10
109	Jose Offerman	.10
110	Dean Palmer	.10
111	Hipolito Pichardo	.10
112	Jose Rosado	.10
113	Jeromy Burnitz	.10
114	Jeff Cirillo	.10
115	Cal Eldred	.10
116	John Jaha	.10
117	Doug Jones	.10

118	Scott Karl	.10
119	Jesse Levis	.10
120	Mark Loretta	.10
121	Ben McDonald	.10
122	Jose Mercedes	.10
123	Matt Mieske	.10
124	Dave Nilsson	.10
125	Jose Valentin	.10
126	Fernando Vina	.10
127	Gerald Williams	.10
128	Rick Aguilera	.10
129	Rich Becker	.10
130	Ron Coomer	.10
131	Marty Cordova	.10
132	Eddie Guardado	.10
133	LaTroy Hawkins	.10
134	Denny Hocking	.10
135	Chuck Knoblauch	.30
136	Matt Lawton	.10
137	Pat Meares	.10
138	Paul Molitor	.60
139	David Ortiz	.30
140	Brad Radke	.10
141	Terry Steinbach	.10
142	Bob Tewksbury	.10
143	Javier Valentin	.10
144	Wade Boggs	.25
145	David Cone	.15
146	Chad Curtis	.10
147	Cecil Fielder	.10
148	Joe Girardi	.10
149	Dwight Gooden	.10
150	Hideki Irabu	.50
151	Derek Jeter	2.00
152	Tino Martinez	.10
153	Ramiro Mendoza	.10
154	Paul O'Neill	.20
155	Andy Pettitte	.60
156	Jorge Posada	.10
157	Mariano Rivera	.20
158	Rey Sanchez	.10
159	Luis Sojo	.10
160	David Wells	.10
161	Bernie Williams	.50
162	Rafael Bournigal	.10
163	Scott Brosius	.10
164	Jose Canseco	.20
165	Jason Giambi	.10
166	Ben Grieve	1.00
167	Dave Magadan	.10
168	Brent Mayne	.10
169	Jason McDonald	.10
170	Izzy Molina	.10
171	Ariel Prieto	.10
172	Carlos Reyes	.10
173	Scott Spiezio	.10
174	Matt Stairs	.10
175	Bill Taylor	.10
176	Dave Telgheder	.10
177	Steve Wojciechowski	.10
178	Rich Amaral	.10
179	Bobby Ayala	.10
180	Jay Buhner	.15
181	Rafael Carmona	.10
182	Ken Cloude	.10
183	Joey Cora	.10
184	Russ Davis	.10
185	Jeff Fassero	.10
186	Ken Griffey Jr.	3.50
187	Raul Ibanez	.10
188	Randy Johnson	.50
189	Roberto Kelly	.10
190	Edgar Martinez	.10
191	Jamie Moyer	.10
192	Omar Olivares	.10
193	Alex Rodriguez	2.00
194	Heathcliff Slocumb	.10
195	Paul Sorrento	.10
196	Dan Wilson	.10
197	Scott Bailes	.10
198	John Burkett	.10
199	Domingo Cedeno	.10
200	Will Clark	.25
201	*Hanley Frias*	.10
202	Juan Gonzalez	1.50
203	Tom Goodwin	.10
204	Rusty Greer	.10
205	Wilson Heredia	.10
206	Darren Oliver	.10
207	Billy Ripken	.10
208	Ivan Rodriguez	.60
209	Lee Stevens	.10
210	Fernando Tatis	.25
211	John Wetteland	.10
212	Bobby Witt	.10
213	Jacob Brumfield	.10
214	Joe Carter	.10
215	Roger Clemens	1.00
216	Felipe Crespo	.10
217	Jose Cruz Jr.	.30
218	Carlos Delgado	.40
219	Mariano Duncan	.10
220	Carlos Garcia	.10
221	Alex Gonzalez	.10
222	Juan Guzman	.10
223	Pat Hentgen	.10
224	Orlando Merced	.10
225	Tomas Perez	.10
226	Paul Quantrill	.10
227	Benito Santiago	.10
228	Woody Williams	.10
229	Rafael Belliard	.10
230	Jeff Blauser	.10
231	Pedro Borbon	.10
232	Tom Glavine	.20
233	Tony Graffanino	.10
234	Andruw Jones	1.50
235	Chipper Jones	2.00
236	Ryan Klesko	.20
237	Mark Lemke	.10
238	Kenny Lofton	.60
239	Javier Lopez	.20
240	Fred McGriff	.25
241	Greg Maddux	2.00
242	Denny Neagle	.10
243	John Smoltz	.20
244	Michael Tucker	.10
245	Mark Wohlers	.10
246	Manny Alexander	.10
247	Miguel Batista	.10
248	Mark Clark	.10
249	Doug Glanville	.10
250	Jeremi Gonzalez	.10
251	Mark Grace	.25
252	Jose Hernandez	.10
253	Lance Johnson	.10
254	Brooks Kieschnick	.10
255	Kevin Orie	.10
256	Ryne Sandberg	.75
257	Scott Servais	.10
258	Sammy Sosa	2.00
259	Kevin Tapani	.10
260	Ramon Tatis	.10
261	Bret Boone	.10
262	Dave Burba	.10
263	Brook Fordyce	.10
264	Willie Greene	.10
265	Barry Larkin	.15
266	Pedro A. Martinez	.10
267	Hal Morris	.10
268	Joe Oliver	.10
269	Eduardo Perez	.10
270	Pokey Reese	.10
271	Felix Rodriguez	.10
272	Deion Sanders	.15
273	Reggie Sanders	.10
274	Jeff Shaw	.10
275	Scott Sullivan	.10
276	Brett Tomko	.10
277	Roger Bailey	.10
278	Dante Bichette	.20
279	Ellis Burks	.10
280	Vinny Castilla	.15
281	Frank Castillo	.10
282	*Mike DeJean*	.10
283	Andres Galarraga	.15
284	Darren Holmes	.10
285	Kirt Manwaring	.10
286	Quinton McCracken	.10
287	Neifi Perez	.10
288	Steve Reed	.10
289	John Thomson	.10
290	Larry Walker	.30
291	Walt Weiss	.10
292	Kurt Abbott	.10
293	Antonio Alfonseca	.10
294	Moises Alou	.20
295	Alex Arias	.10
296	Bobby Bonilla	.10
297	Kevin Brown	.20
298	Craig Counsell	.10
299	Darren Daulton	.10
300	Jim Eisenreich	.10
301	Alex Fernandez	.10
302	Felix Heredia	.10
303	Livan Hernandez	.15
304	Charles Johnson	.10
305	Al Leiter	.10
306	Robb Nen	.10
307	Edgar Renteria	.15
308	Gary Sheffield	.30
309	Devon White	.10
310	Bob Abreu	.10
311	Brad Ausmus	.10
312	Jeff Bagwell	1.25
313	Derek Bell	.10
314	Sean Berry	.10
315	Craig Biggio	.20
316	Ramon Garcia	.10
317	Luis Gonzalez	.10
318	Ricky Gutierrez	.10
319	Mike Hampton	.10
320	Richard Hidalgo	.10
321	Thomas Howard	.10
322	Darryl Kile	.10
323	Jose Lima	.10
324	Shane Reynolds	.10
325	Bill Spiers	.10
326	Tom Candiotti	.10
327	Roger Cedeno	.15
328	Greg Gagne	.10
329	Karim Garcia	.15
330	Wilton Guerrero	.10
331	Todd Hollandsworth	.10
332	Eric Karros	.15
333	Ramon Martinez	.10
334	Raul Mondesi	.25
335	Otis Nixon	.10
336	Hideo Nomo	.50
337	Antonio Osuna	.10
338	Chan Ho Park	.20
339	Mike Piazza	2.00
340	Dennis Reyes	.10
341	Ismael Valdes	.10
342	Todd Worrell	.10
343	Todd Zeile	.10
344	Darrin Fletcher	.10
345	Mark Grudzielanek	.10
346	Vladimir Guerrero	1.50
347	Dustin Hermanson	.10
348	Mike Lansing	.10
349	Pedro Martinez	.25
350	Ryan McGuire	.10
351	Jose Paniagua	.10
352	Carlos Perez	.10
353	Henry Rodriguez	.10
354	F.P. Santangelo	.10
355	David Segui	.10
356	Ugueth Urbina	.10
357	Marc Valdes	.10
358	Jose Vidro	.10
359	Rondell White	.15
360	Juan Acevedo	.10
361	Edgardo Alfonzo	.15
362	Carlos Baerga	.10
363	Carl Everett	.10
364	John Franco	.10
365	Bernard Gilkey	.10
366	Todd Hundley	.20
367	Butch Huskey	.10
368	Bobby Jones	.10
369	Takashi Kashiwada	.40
370	Greg McMichael	.10
371	Brian McRae	.10
372	Alex Ochoa	.10
373	John Olerud	.15
374	Rey Ordonez	.15
375	Turk Wendell	.10
376	Ricky Bottalico	.10
377	Rico Brogna	.10
378	Lenny Dykstra	.10
379	Bobby Estalella	.10
380	Wayne Gomes	.10
381	Tyler Green	.10
382	Gregg Jefferies	.10
383	Mark Leiter	.10
384	Mike Lieberthal	.10
385	Mickey Morandini	.10
386	Scott Rolen	1.50
387	Curt Schilling	.20
388	Kevin Stocker	.10
389	Danny Tartabull	.10
390	Jermaine Allensworth	.10
391	Adrian Brown	.10
392	Jason Christiansen	.10
393	Steve Cooke	.10
394	Francisco Cordova	.10
395	Jose Guillen	.40
396	Jason Kendall	.10
397	Jon Lieber	.10
398	Esteban Loaiza	.10
399	Al Martin	.10
400	*Kevin Polcovich*	.15
401	Joe Randa	.10
402	Ricardo Rincon	.10
403	Tony Womack	.10
404	Kevin Young	.10
405	Andy Benes	.10
406	Royce Clayton	.10
407	Delino DeShields	.10
408	Mike Difelice	.10
409	Dennis Eckersley	.10
410	John Frascatore	.10
411	Gary Gaetti	.10
412	Ron Gant	.10
413	Brian Jordan	.10
414	Ray Lankford	.10
415	Willie McGee	.10
416	Mark McGwire	3.50
417	Matt Morris	.10
418	Luis Ordaz	.10
419	Todd Stottlemyre	.10
420	Andy Ashby	.10
421	Jim Bruske	.10
422	Ken Caminiti	.25
423	Will Cunnane	.10
424	Steve Finley	.10
425	John Flaherty	.10
426	Chris Gomez	.10
427	Tony Gwynn	1.50
428	Joey Hamilton	.10
429	Carlos Hernandez	.10
430	Sterling Hitchcock	.10
431	Trevor Hoffman	.10
432	Wally Joyner	.10
433	Greg Vaughn	.15
434	Quilvio Veras	.10
435	Wilson Alvarez	.10
436	Rod Beck	.10
437	Barry Bonds	.75
438	Jacob Cruz	.10
439	Shawn Estes	.10
440	Darryl Hamilton	.10
441	Roberto Hernandez	.10
442	Glenallen Hill	.10
443	Stan Javier	.10
444	Brian Johnson	.10
445	Jeff Kent	.10
446	Bill Mueller	.10
447	Kirk Rueter	.10
448	J.T. Snow	.10
449	Julian Tavarez	.10
450	Jose Vizcaino	.10

1998 Pacific Red/ Silver

Red and Silver parallels reprinted all 450 cards in Pacific, with the gold foil used on base cards replaced by red or silver foil. Red foil versions were inserted one per Wal-Mart pack (retail), while Silver versions were inserted one per hobby pack.

Reds: 2x to 4x
Inserted 1:1 Retail
Silvers: 2x to 4x
Inserted 1:1 Hobby
(See 1998 Pacific for checklist and base card values.)

1998 Pacific Cramer's Choice

Cramer's Choice Awards is a 10-card die-cut insert. The cards feature the top player at each position as selected by Pacific CEO Mike Cramer. Each card is shaped like a trophy. Cramer's Choice Awards were inserted one per 721 packs of 1998 Pacific Baseball.

		MT
Complete Set (10):		900.00
Common Player:		30.00
Inserted 1:721		
1	Greg Maddux	100.00
2	Roberto Alomar	30.00
3	Cal Ripken Jr.	150.00
4	Nomar Garciaparra	115.00
5	Larry Walker	30.00
6	Mike Piazza	125.00
7	Mark McGwire	200.00
8	Tony Gwynn	100.00
9	Ken Griffey Jr.	200.00
10	Roger Clemens	75.00

1998 Pacific Gold Crown Die-Cuts

Gold Crown Die-Cuts is a 36-card insert seeded one per 37 packs. Each card has a holographic silver foil background and gold etching. The cards are die-cut around a crown design at the top.

		MT
Complete Set (36):		400.00
Common Player:		4.00
1	Chipper Jones	25.00
2	Greg Maddux	25.00
3	Denny Neagle	4.00
4	Roberto Alomar	8.00
5	Rafael Palmeiro	6.00
6	Cal Ripken Jr.	30.00
7	Nomar Garciaparra	25.00
8	Mo Vaughn	6.00
9	Frank Thomas	20.00
10	Sandy Alomar Jr.	5.00
11	David Justice	5.00
12	Manny Ramirez	12.00
13	Andres Galarraga	5.00
14	Larry Walker	6.00
15	Moises Alou	4.00
16	Livan Hernandez	4.00
17	Gary Sheffield	6.00
18	Jeff Bagwell	15.00
19	Raul Mondesi	6.00
20	Hideo Nomo	5.00
21	Mike Piazza	25.00
22	Derek Jeter	25.00
23	Tino Martinez	4.00
24	Bernie Williams	5.00
25	Ben Grieve	12.00
26	Mark McGwire	45.00
27	Tony Gwynn	20.00
28	Barry Bonds	10.00
29	Ken Griffey Jr.	45.00
30	Randy Johnson	8.00
31	Edgar Martinez	4.00
32	Alex Rodriguez	30.00
33	Juan Gonzalez	20.00
34	Ivan Rodriguez	8.00
35	Roger Clemens	15.00
36	Jose Cruz Jr.	4.00

1998 Pacific Home Run Hitters

This 20-card set was inserted one per 73 packs. The full-foil cards feature a color player photo with their home run total from 1997 embossed in the background.

		MT
Complete Set (20):		220.00
Common Player:		6.00
1	Rafael Palmeiro	6.00
2	Mo Vaughn	10.00
3	Sammy Sosa	25.00
4	Albert Belle	10.00
5	Frank Thomas	20.00
6	David Justice	6.00
7	Jim Thome	8.00
8	Matt Williams	6.00
9	Vinny Castilla	6.00
10	Andres Galarraga	6.00
11	Larry Walker	8.00
12	Jeff Bagwell	15.00
13	Mike Piazza	25.00
14	Tino Martinez	6.00
15	Mark McGwire	40.00
16	Barry Bonds	10.00
17	Jay Buhner	6.00
18	Ken Griffey Jr.	40.00
19	Alex Rodriguez	30.00
20	Juan Gonzalez	20.00

1998 Pacific In the Cage

This 20-card insert features top players in a die-cut batting cage. The netting on the cage is laser-cut. In The Cage Laser-Cuts were inserted one per 145 packs.

		MT
Complete Set (20):		450.00
Common Player:		8.00
1	Chipper Jones	40.00
2	Roberto Alomar	12.00
3	Cal Ripken Jr.	50.00
4	Nomar Garciaparra	40.00
5	Frank Thomas	35.00
6	Sandy Alomar Jr.	8.00
7	David Justice	8.00
8	Larry Walker	10.00
9	Bobby Bonilla	8.00
10	Mike Piazza	40.00
11	Tino Martinez	8.00
12	Bernie Williams	8.00
13	Mark McGwire	60.00
14	Tony Gwynn	35.00
15	Barry Bonds	16.00
16	Ken Griffey Jr.	60.00
17	Edgar Martinez	8.00
18	Alex Rodriguez	50.00
19	Juan Gonzalez	35.00
20	Ivan Rodriguez	12.00

Checklists with card numbers in parentheses ( ) indicates the numbers do not appear on the card.

1998 Pacific Latinos of the Major Leagues

This 36-card set (2:37) features Major League players of Hispanic descent. The background has a world map on the left, the player's team logo in the center and an American flag on the right.

		MT
Complete Set (36):		75.00
Common Player:		1.50
Inserted 2:37		
1	Andruw Jones	8.00
2	Javier Lopez	1.50
3	Roberto Alomar	4.00
4	Geronimo Berroa	1.50
5	Rafael Palmeiro	2.00
6	Nomar Garciaparra	9.00
7	Sammy Sosa	10.00
8	Ozzie Guillen	1.50
9	Sandy Alomar Jr.	1.50
10	Manny Ramirez	7.50
11	Omar Vizquel	1.50
12	Vinny Castilla	1.50
13	Andres Galarraga	2.50
14	Moises Alou	1.50
15	Bobby Bonilla	1.50
16	Livan Hernandez	1.50
17	Edgar Renteria	1.50
18	Wilton Guerrero	1.50
19	Raul Mondesi	2.50
20	Ismael Valdes	1.50
21	Fernando Vina	1.50
22	Pedro Martinez	2.00
23	Edgardo Alfonzo	1.50
24	Carlos Baerga	1.50
25	Rey Ordonez	1.50
26	Tino Martinez	1.50
27	Mariano Rivera	1.50
28	Bernie Williams	4.00
29	Jose Canseco	3.00
30	Joey Cora	1.50
31	Roberto Kelly	1.50
32	Edgar Martinez	1.50
33	Alex Rodriguez	10.00
34	Juan Gonzalez	8.00
35	Ivan Rodriguez	5.00
36	Jose Cruz Jr.	1.50

1998 Pacific Team Checklists

Team Checklists is a 30-card insert in the bilingual Pacific Baseball set. One card was created for each team. A player photo is featured on the right with the team logo laser-cut into a bat barrel design on the left.

		MT
Complete Set (30):		240.00
Common Player:		3.00
1	Tim Salmon, Jim Edmonds	4.00
2	Cal Ripken Jr, Roberto Alomar	25.00
3	Nomar Garciaparra, Mo Vaughn	20.00
4	Frank Thomas, Albert Belle	20.00
5	Sandy Alomar Jr., Manny Ramirez	8.00
6	Justin Thompson, Tony Clark	5.00
7	Johnny Damon, Jermaine Dye	3.00
8	Dave Nilsson, Jeff Cirillo	3.00
9	Paul Molitor, Chuck Knoblauch	5.00
10	Tino Martinez, Derek Jeter	10.00
11	Ben Grieve, Jose Canseco	12.00
12	Ken Griffey Jr., Alex Rodriguez	30.00
13	Juan Gonzalez, Ivan Rodriguez	15.00
14	Jose Cruz Jr., Roger Clemens	3.00
15	Greg Maddux, Chipper Jones	20.00
16	Sammy Sosa, Mark Grace	15.00
17	Barry Larkin, Deion Sanders	4.00
18	Larry Walker, Andres Galarraga	4.00
19	Moises Alou, Bobby Bonilla	3.00
20	Jeff Bagwell, Craig Biggio	15.00
21	Mike Piazza, Hideo Nomo	20.00
22	Pedro Martinez, Henry Rodriguez	4.00
23	Rey Ordonez, Carlos Baerga	3.00
24	Curt Schilling, Scott Rolen	10.00
25	Al Martin, Tony Womack	3.00
26	Mark McGwire, Dennis Eckersley	30.00
27	Tony Gwynn, Wally Joyner	15.00
28	Barry Bonds, J.T. Snow	8.00
29	Matt Williams, Jay Bell	5.00
30	Fred McGriff, Roberto Hernandez	4.00

1998 Pacific Aurora

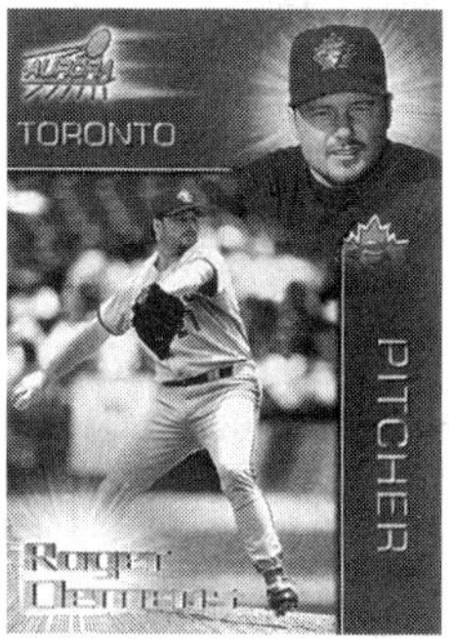

The Aurora base set consists of 200 cards printed on 24-point board. The cards have a color photo bordered on two sides by a thick green border. A headshot of the player appears in the corner of the border. Inserts include Pennant Fever (with three parallels), Hardball Cel-Fusions, Kings of the Major Leagues, On Deck Laser-Cuts and Pacific Cubes.

		MT
Complete Set (200):		40.00
Common Player:		.15
Wax Box:		90.00
1	Garret Anderson	.15
2	Jim Edmonds	.25
3	Darin Erstad	.75
4	Cecil Fielder	.15
5	Chuck Finley	.15
6	Todd Greene	.15
7	Ken Hill	.15
8	Tim Salmon	.40
9	Roberto Alomar	.60
10	Brady Anderson	.15
11	Joe Carter	.15
12	Mike Mussina	.60
13	Rafael Palmeiro	.25
14	Cal Ripken Jr.	2.50
15	B.J. Surhoff	.15
16	Steve Avery	.15
17	Nomar Garciaparra	2.00
18	Pedro Martinez	.50
19	John Valentin	.15
20	Jason Varitek	.15
21	Mo Vaughn	.60
22	Albert Belle	.75
23	Ray Durham	.15
24	*Magglio Ordonez*	1.00
25	Frank Thomas	1.50
26	Robin Ventura	.25
27	Sandy Alomar Jr.	.25
28	Travis Fryman	.15
29	Dwight Gooden	.25
30	David Justice	.50
31	Kenny Lofton	.60
32	Manny Ramirez	1.00
33	Jim Thome	.30
34	Omar Vizquel	.15
35	Enrique Wilson	.15
36	Jaret Wright	.75
37	Tony Clark	.30
38	Bobby Higginson	.15
39	Brian Hunter	.15
40	Bip Roberts	.15
41	Justin Thompson	.15
42	Jeff Conine	.15
43	Johnny Damon	.15
44	Jermaine Dye	.15
45	Jeff King	.15
46	Jeff Montgomery	.15
47	Hal Morris	.15
48	Dean Palmer	.15
49	Terry Pendleton	.15
50	Rick Aguilera	.15
51	Marty Cordova	.15
52	Paul Molitor	.50
53	Otis Nixon	.15
54	Brad Radke	.15
55	Terry Steinbach	.15
56	Todd Walker	.40
57	Chili Davis	.15
58	Derek Jeter	2.00
59	Chuck Knoblauch	.40
60	Tino Martinez	.30
61	Paul O'Neill	.40
62	Andy Pettitte	.60
63	Mariano Rivera	.25
64	Bernie Williams	.60
65	Jason Giambi	.15
66	Ben Grieve	1.00
67	Rickey Henderson	.25
68	A.J. Hinch	.40
69	Kenny Rogers	.15
70	Jay Buhner	.20
71	Joey Cora	.15
72	Ken Griffey Jr.	3.50
73	Randy Johnson	.60
74	Edgar Martinez	.20
75	Jamie Moyer	.15
76	Alex Rodriguez	2.50
77	David Segui	.15
78	*Rolando Arrojo*	.50
79	Wade Boggs	.40
80	Roberto Hernandez	.15
81	Dave Martinez	.15
82	Fred McGriff	.40
83	Paul Sorrento	.15
84	Kevin Stocker	.15
85	Will Clark	.40
86	Juan Gonzalez	1.50
87	Tom Goodwin	.15
88	Rusty Greer	.20
89	Ivan Rodriguez	.75
90	John Wetteland	.15
91	Jose Canseco	.40
92	Roger Clemens	1.00
93	Jose Cruz Jr.	.25
94	Carlos Delgado	.40
95	Pat Hentgen	.15
96	Jay Bell	.15
97	Andy Benes	.25
98	Karim Garcia	.20
99	Travis Lee	.75
100	Devon White	.15
101	Matt Williams	.40
102	Andres Galarraga	.40
103	Tom Glavine	.25
104	Andruw Jones	.75
105	Chipper Jones	2.00
106	Ryan Klesko	.25
107	Javy Lopez	.25
108	Greg Maddux	2.00
109	Walt Weiss	.15
110	Rod Beck	.15
111	Jeff Blauser	.15
112	Mark Grace	.40
113	Lance Johnson	.15
114	Mickey Morandini	.15
115	Henry Rodriguez	.15
116	Sammy Sosa	1.50
117	Kerry Wood	.75
118	Lenny Harris	.15
119	Damian Jackson	.15
120	Barry Larkin	.30
121	Reggie Sanders	.15
122	Brett Tomko	.15
123	Dante Bichette	.30
124	Ellis Burks	.15
125	Vinny Castilla	.25
126	Todd Helton	.75
127	Darryl Kile	.15
128	Larry Walker	.40
129	Bobby Bonilla	.20
130	Livan Hernandez	.20
131	Charles Johnson	.15
132	Derrek Lee	.15
133	Edgar Renteria	.20
134	Gary Sheffield	.50
135	Moises Alou	.25
136	Jeff Bagwell	1.00
137	Derek Bell	.15
138	Craig Biggio	.40
139	*John Halama*	.40
140	Mike Hampton	.15
141	Richard Hidalgo	.15
142	Wilton Guerrero	.15
143	Todd Hollandsworth	.15
144	Eric Karros	.20
145	Paul Konerko	.40
146	Raul Mondesi	.40
147	Hideo Nomo	.50
148	Chan Ho Park	.40
149	Mike Piazza	2.00
150	Jeromy Burnitz	.15
151	Todd Dunn	.15
152	Marquis Grissom	.15
153	John Jaha	.15
154	Dave Nilsson	.15
155	Fernando Vina	.15
156	Mark Grudzielanek	.15
157	Vladimir Guerrero	.75
158	F.P. Santangelo	.15
159	Jose Vidro	.15
160	Rondell White	.25
161	Edgardo Alfonzo	.20
162	Carlos Baerga	.15
163	John Franco	.15
164	Todd Hundley	.15
165	Brian McRae	.15
166	John Olerud	.25
167	Rey Ordonez	.15
168	*Masato Yoshii*	.50
169	Ricky Bottalico	.15
170	Doug Glanville	.15
171	Gregg Jefferies	.15
172	Desi Relaford	.15
173	Scott Rolen	1.00
174	Curt Schilling	.25
175	Jose Guillen	.25
176	Jason Kendall	.15
177	Al Martin	.15
178	Abraham Nunez	.15
179	Kevin Young	.15
180	Royce Clayton	.15
181	Delino DeShields	.15
182	Gary Gaetti	.15
183	Ron Gant	.15
184	Brian Jordan	.15
185	Ray Lankford	.15
186	Willie McGee	.15
187	Mark McGwire	3.50
188	Kevin Brown	.25
189	Ken Caminiti	.25
190	Steve Finley	.15
191	Tony Gwynn	1.60
192	Wally Joyner	.15
193	Ruben Rivera	.15
194	Quilvio Veras	.15
195	Barry Bonds	.75
196	Shawn Estes	.15
197	Orel Hershiser	.15
198	Jeff Kent	.15
199	Robb Nen	.15
200	J.T. Snow	.15

1998 Pacific Aurora Cubes

A cardboard cube presenting player photos on top and three sides, plus a side of stats was created as a hobby-only insert for Pacific Aurora. The assembled, shrink-wrapped cubes were packed one per box.

		MT
Complete Set (20):		140.00
Common Player:		3.00
Inserted 1:box		
1	Travis Lee	4.00
2	Chipper Jones	12.00
3	Greg Maddux	12.00
4	Cal Ripken Jr.	15.00
5	Nomar Garciaparra	12.00
6	Frank Thomas	10.00
7	Manny Ramirez	5.00
8	Larry Walker	3.00
9	Hideo Nomo	3.00
10	Mike Piazza	12.00
11	Derek Jeter	10.00
12	Ben Grieve	6.00
13	Mark McGwire	20.00
14	Tony Gwynn	10.00
15	Barry Bonds	5.00
16	Ken Griffey Jr.	20.00
17	Alex Rodriguez	15.00
18	Wade Boggs	3.00
19	Juan Gonzalez	10.00
20	Jose Cruz Jr.	3.00

1998 Pacific Aurora Hardball

Hardball Cel-Fusions is a 20-card insert seeded one per 73 packs. The cards feature a die-cut cel baseball fused to a foiled and etched card.

		MT
Complete Set (20):		500.00
Common Player:		10.00
Inserted 1:73		
1	Travis Lee	12.00
2	Chipper Jones	40.00
3	Greg Maddux	40.00
4	Cal Ripken Jr.	50.00
5	Nomar Garciaparra	40.00
6	Frank Thomas	25.00
7	David Justice	10.00
8	Jeff Bagwell	20.00
9	Hideo Nomo	10.00
10	Mike Piazza	40.00
11	Derek Jeter	40.00
12	Ben Grieve	20.00
13	Scott Rolen	20.00
14	Mark McGwire	60.00
15	Tony Gwynn	30.00
16	Ken Griffey Jr.	60.00
17	Alex Rodriguez	50.00
18	Ivan Rodriguez	15.00
19	Roger Clemens	20.00
20	Jose Cruz Jr.	10.00

1998 Pacific Aurora Kings of the Major Leagues

This 10-card insert features star players on fully-foiled cards. Kings of the Major Leagues was seeded one per 361 packs.

		MT
Complete Set (10):		425.00
Common Player:		35.00
Inserted 1:361		
1	Chipper Jones	45.00
2	Greg Maddux	45.00
3	Cal Ripken Jr.	55.00
4	Nomar Garciaparra	45.00
5	Frank Thomas	35.00
6	Mike Piazza	45.00
7	Mark McGwire	75.00
8	Tony Gwynn	35.00
9	Ken Griffey Jr.	75.00
10	Alex Rodriguez	55.00

1998 Pacific Aurora On Deck Laser-Cut

On Deck Laser-Cuts is a 20-card insert seeded four per 37 packs of 1998 Pacific Aurora Baseball.

		MT
Complete Set (20):		70.00
Common Player:		1.00
Inserted 1:9		
1	Travis Lee	2.00
2	Chipper Jones	6.00
3	Greg Maddux	6.00
4	Cal Ripken Jr.	8.00
5	Nomar Garciaparra	6.00
6	Frank Thomas	5.00
7	Manny Ramirez	4.00
8	Larry Walker	1.00
9	Hideo Nomo	1.50
10	Mike Piazza	6.00
11	Derek Jeter	6.00
12	Ben Grieve	4.00
13	Mark McGwire	12.50
14	Tony Gwynn	5.00
15	Barry Bonds	2.50
16	Ken Griffey Jr.	12.50
17	Alex Rodriguez	8.00
18	Wade Boggs	1.50
19	Juan Gonzalez	5.00
20	Jose Cruz Jr.	1.00

1998 Pacific Aurora Pennant Fever

Pennant Fever is a 50-card insert seeded one per pack. Each card is fully foiled and etched. The color player image is duplicated in the upper-left corner with an image stamped in gold foil. Pennant Fever has four parallels. Red cards are a 1:4 retail insert. The Silver retail parallel is numbered to 250, Platinum Blue is numbered to 100 and the Copper hobby parallel is numbered to 20. Tony Gwynn signed his card serially numbered one in each insert.

		MT
Complete Set (50):		20.00
Common Player:		.25
Inserted 1:1		
Reds: 2.5X		
Inserted 1:4 Retail		
Silvers: 15-25X		
Production 250 sets		
Platinum Blues: 35-50X		
Production 100 sets		
Coppers: 75-125X		
Production 20 sets		
1	Tony Gwynn	1.00
2	Derek Jeter	1.50
3	Alex Rodriguez	2.00
4	Paul Molitor	.40
5	Nomar Garciaparra	1.25
6	Jeff Bagwell	.75
7	Ivan Rodriguez	.50
8	Cal Ripken Jr.	2.00
9	Matt Williams	.25
10	Chipper Jones	1.25
11	Edgar Martinez	.25
12	Wade Boggs	.35
13	Paul Konerko	.25
14	Ben Grieve	.75
15	Sandy Alomar Jr.	.25
16	Travis Lee	.50
17	Scott Rolen	.75
18	Ryan Klesko	.25
19	Juan Gonzalez	1.00
20	Albert Belle	.50
21	Roger Clemens	1.00
22	Javy Lopez	.25
23	Jose Cruz Jr.	.25
24	Ken Griffey Jr.	2.50
25	Mark McGwire	2.50
26	Brady Anderson	.25
27	Jaret Wright	.50
28	Roberto Alomar	.40
29	Joe Carter	.25
30	Hideo Nomo	.40
31	Mike Piazza	1.50
32	Andres Galarraga	.25
33	Larry Walker	.35
34	Tim Salmon	.25
35	Frank Thomas	1.00
36	Moises Alou	.25
37	David Justice	.40
38	Manny Ramirez	.75
39	Jim Edmonds	.25
40	Barry Bonds	.50
41	Jim Thome	.40
42	Mo Vaughn	.50
43	Rafael Palmeiro	.35
44	Darin Erstad	.50
45	Pedro Martinez	.50
46	Greg Maddux	1.25
47	Jose Canseco	.35
48	Vladimir Guerrero	.75
49	Bernie Williams	.40
50	Randy Johnson	.40

1998 Pacific Crown Royale

The Crown Royale base set consists of 144 die-cut cards. The cards have a horizontal layout and are die-cut around a crown design at the top. The cards are double-foiled and etched. Inserts include Diamond Knights, Pillars of the Game, Race to the Record, All-Star Die-Cuts, Firestone on Baseball and Cramer's Choice Awards.

		MT
Complete Set (144):		125.00
Common Player:		.50
1	Garret Anderson	.50
2	Jim Edmonds	.75
3	Darin Erstad	2.50
4	Tim Salmon	1.00
5	Jarrod Washburn	.50
6	David Dellucci	.50
7	Travis Lee	2.00
8	Devon White	.50
9	Matt Williams	1.00
10	Andres Galarraga	1.00
11	Tom Glavine	.75
12	Andruw Jones	2.50
13	Chipper Jones	6.00
14	Ryan Klesko	.75
15	Javy Lopez	.75
16	Greg Maddux	6.00
17	Walt Weiss	.50
18	Roberto Alomar	1.50
19	Harold Baines	.50
20	Eric Davis	.50
21	Mike Mussina	2.00
22	Rafael Palmeiro	1.00
23	Cal Ripken Jr.	8.00
24	Nomar Garciaparra	6.00
25	Pedro Martinez	2.50
26	Troy O'Leary	.50
27	Mo Vaughn	2.00
28	Tim Wakefield	.50
29	Mark Grace	1.00
30	Mickey Morandini	.50
31	Sammy Sosa	8.00
32	Kerry Wood	2.50
33	Albert Belle	2.50
34	Mike Caruso	.50
35	Ray Durham	.50
36	Frank Thomas	5.00
37	Robin Ventura	.75
38	Bret Boone	.50
39	Sean Casey	.75
40	Barry Larkin	.75
41	Reggie Sanders	.50
42	Sandy Alomar Jr.	.50
43	David Justice	1.00
44	Kenny Lofton	2.00
45	Manny Ramirez	4.00
46	Jim Thome	.75
47	Omar Vizquel	.50
48	Jaret Wright	1.50
49	Dante Bichette	.75
50	Ellis Burks	.50
51	Vinny Castilla	.75
52	Todd Helton	2.00
53	Larry Walker	1.00
54	Tony Clark	.75
55	Damion Easley	.50
56	Bobby Higginson	.50
57	Cliff Floyd	.50
58	Livan Hernandez	.50
59	Derrek Lee	.50
60	Edgar Renteria	.50
61	Moises Alou	.75
62	Jeff Bagwell	3.00
63	Derek Bell	.50
64	Craig Biggio	.75
65	Johnny Damon	.50
66	Jeff King	.50
67	Hal Morris	.50
68	Dean Palmer	.50
69	Bobby Bonilla	.50
70	Eric Karros	.75
71	Raul Mondesi	.75
72	Gary Sheffield	.75
73	Jeromy Burnitz	.50
74	Jeff Cirillo	.50
75	Marquis Grissom	.50
76	Fernando Vina	.50
77	Marty Cordova	.50
78	Pat Meares	.50
79	Paul Molitor	1.50
80	Terry Steinbach	.50
81	Todd Walker	.75
82	Brad Fullmer	1.00
83	Vladimir Guerrero	2.50
84	Carl Pavano	.50
85	Rondell White	.75
86	Carlos Baerga	.50
87	Hideo Nomo	1.00
88	John Olerud	.75
89	Rey Ordonez	.50
90	Mike Piazza	6.00
91	*Masato Yoshii*	1.50
92	*Orlando Hernandez*	5.00
93	Hideki Irabu	.75
94	Derek Jeter	6.00
95	Chuck Knoblauch	1.00
96	Ricky Ledee	.75
97	Tino Martinez	.75
98	Paul O'Neill	.75
99	Bernie Williams	1.00
100	Jason Giambi	.50
101	Ben Grieve	3.00
102	Rickey Henderson	1.00
103	Matt Stairs	.50
104	Bob Abreu	.50
105	Doug Glanville	.50
106	Scott Rolen	3.00
107	Curt Schilling	.75
108	Jose Guillen	.50
109	Jason Kendall	.75
110	Jason Schmidt	.50
111	Kevin Young	.50
112	Delino DeShields	.50
113	Brian Jordan	.50
114	Ray Lankford	.50
115	Mark McGwire	12.00
116	Tony Gwynn	5.00
117	Wally Joyner	.50
118	Ruben Rivera	.50
119	Greg Vaughn	.75
120	Rich Aurilia	.50
121	Barry Bonds	2.50
122	Bill Mueller	.50
123	Robb Nen	.50
124	Jay Buhner	.50
125	Ken Griffey Jr.	12.00
126	Edgar Martinez	.50
127	Shane Monahan	.50
128	Alex Rodriguez	8.00
129	David Segui	.50
130	*Rolando Arrojo*	2.00
131	Wade Boggs	.75
132	Quinton McCracken	.50
133	Fred McGriff	.75
134	Bobby Smith	.50
135	Will Clark	1.00
136	Juan Gonzalez	5.00
137	Rusty Greer	.50
138	Ivan Rodriguez	2.50
139	Aaron Sele	.50
140	John Wetteland	.50
141	Jose Canseco	1.00
142	Roger Clemens	4.00
143	Carlos Delgado	.75
144	Shawn Green	1.00

1998 Pacific Crown Royale All-Star

This 20-card insert was seeded one per 25 packs. The featured players all participated in the 1998 All-Star Game. The background features the sun rising over a mountain with a die-cut at the top of the card.

		MT
Complete Set (20):		350.00
Common Player:		5.00
1	Roberto Alomar	10.00
2	Cal Ripken Jr.	40.00
3	Kenny Lofton	10.00
4	Jim Thome	8.00
5	Derek Jeter	30.00
6	David Wells	5.00
7	Ken Griffey Jr.	50.00
8	Alex Rodriguez	40.00
9	Juan Gonzalez	25.00
10	Ivan Rodriguez	15.00
11	Gary Sheffield	5.00
12	Chipper Jones	30.00
13	Greg Maddux	30.00
14	Walt Weiss	5.00
15	Larry Walker	8.00
16	Craig Biggio	5.00
17	Mike Piazza	30.00
18	Mark McGwire	50.00
19	Tony Gwynn	25.00
20	Barry Bonds	15.00

1998 Pacific Crown Royale Cramer's Choice Awards

Premium-sized Cramer's Choice Awards were inserted one per box. The ten players in the set are featured on a die-cut card designed to resemble a trophy. Pacific CEO Mike Cramer signed and hand-numbered ten sets of Cramer's Choice Awards.

		MT
Complete Set (10):		100.00
Common Player:		5.00
Inserted 1:box		
1	Cal Ripken Jr.	15.00
2	Ken Griffey Jr.	20.00
3	Alex Rodriguez	15.00
4	Juan Gonzalez	10.00
5	Travis Lee	5.00
6	Chipper Jones	12.00
7	Greg Maddux	12.00
8	Kerry Wood	5.00
9	Mark McGwire	20.00
10	Tony Gwynn	10.00

1998 Pacific Crown Royale Diamond Knights

Diamond Knights is a 25-card, one per pack insert. Each card features a color action photo and the player's name, team and position listed in a Medieval-type border at the bottom.

		MT
Complete Set (25):		40.00
Common Player:		.75
1	Andres Galarraga	1.00
2	Chipper Jones	3.00
3	Greg Maddux	3.00
4	Cal Ripken Jr.	4.00
5	Nomar Garciaparra	3.00
6	Mo Vaughn	1.00
7	Kerry Wood	1.50
8	Frank Thomas	2.50
9	Vinny Castilla	.75
10	Jeff Bagwell	1.50
11	Craig Biggio	1.00
12	Paul Molitor	1.00
13	Mike Piazza	3.00
14	Orlando Hernandez	3.00
15	Derek Jeter	3.00
16	Ricky Ledee	.75
17	Mark McGwire	6.00
18	Tony Gwynn	2.50
19	Barry Bonds	1.25
20	Ken Griffey Jr.	6.00
21	Alex Rodriguez	4.00
22	Wade Boggs	1.00
23	Juan Gonzalez	2.50
24	Ivan Rodriguez	1.25
25	Jose Canseco	1.00

1998 Pacific Crown Royale Firestone on Baseball

This 26-card insert features star players with commentary by sports personality Roy Firestone. The fronts have a color photo of the player and a portrait of Firestone in the lower right corner. The card backs have text by Firestone on what makes the featured player great. Firestone signed a total of 300 cards in this insert.

		MT
Complete Set (26):		200.00
Common Player:		2.00
1	Travis Lee	4.00
2	Chipper Jones	15.00
3	Greg Maddux	15.00
4	Cal Ripken Jr.	20.00
5	Nomar Garciaparra	15.00
6	Mo Vaughn	5.00
7	Kerry Wood	5.00
8	Frank Thomas	10.00
9	Manny Ramirez	6.50
10	Larry Walker	3.00
11	Gary Sheffield	2.00
12	Paul Molitor	4.00
13	Hideo Nomo	2.50
14	Mike Piazza	15.00
15	Ben Grieve	7.50
16	Mark McGwire	25.00
17	Tony Gwynn	12.50
18	Barry Bonds	5.00
19	Ken Griffey Jr.	25.00
20	Randy Johnson	4.00
21	Alex Rodriguez	20.00
22	Wade Boggs	2.50
23	Juan Gonzalez	12.50
24	Ivan Rodriguez	5.00
25	Roger Clemens	10.00
26	Roy Firestone	2.00

1998 Pacific Crown Royale Home Run Fever

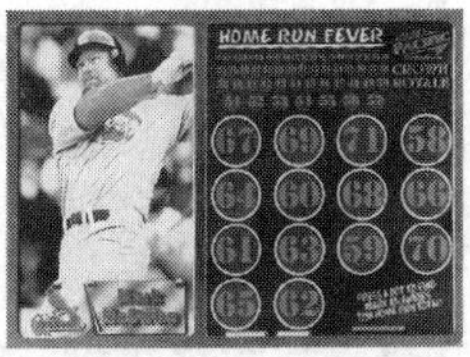

Home Run Fever (10 cards, 1:73) features players who had a shot at breaking Roger Maris' home run record in 1998. The card fronts have a player photo on the left and a blackboard with numbers from 1 to 60 on the right. Ten circles featuring disappearing ink contained numbers 61 through 70. Collectors could rub the circles to reveal the player's potential record home run total.

		MT
Complete Set (10):		225.00
Common Player:		7.50
1	Andres Galarraga	7.50
2	Sammy Sosa	35.00
3	Albert Belle	15.00
4	Jim Thome	7.50
5	Mark McGwire	60.00
6	Greg Vaughn	7.50
7	Ken Griffey Jr.	60.00
8	Alex Rodriguez	50.00
9	Juan Gonzalez	30.00
10	Jose Canseco	10.00

1998 Pacific Crown Royale Pillars of the Game

This 25-card insert was seeded one per pack. Each card features a star player with a background of holographic silver foil.

		MT
Complete Set (25):		40.00
Common Player:		.75
1	Jim Edmonds	.75
2	Travis Lee	1.00
3	Chipper Jones	3.00
4	Tom Glavine, John Smoltz, Greg Maddux	2.00
5	Cal Ripken Jr.	4.00
6	Nomar Garciaparra	3.00
7	Mo Vaughn	1.25
8	Sammy Sosa	4.00
9	Kerry Wood	1.50
10	Frank Thomas	2.50
11	Jim Thome	1.00
12	Larry Walker	1.00
13	Moises Alou	.75
14	Raul Mondesi	1.00
15	Mike Piazza	3.00
16	Hideki Irabu	1.00
17	Bernie Williams	1.00
18	Ben Grieve	1.50
19	Scott Rolen	1.50
20	Mark McGwire	6.00
21	Tony Gwynn	2.50
22	Ken Griffey Jr.	6.00
23	Alex Rodriguez	4.00
24	Juan Gonzalez	2.50
25	Roger Clemens	2.00

1998 Pacific Invincible

Invincible Baseball consists of a 150-card base set. The base cards have a horizontal layout and feature a player photo on the left and a headshot in a cel window on the right. The regular cards were inserted one per five-card pack. Silver (2:37) and Platinum Blue (1:73) parallels were also created. Inserts include Moments in Time, Team Checklists, Photoengravings, Interleague Players, Gems of the Diamond and Cramer's Choice Awards.

		MT
Complete Set (150):		175.00
Common Player:		1.00
Silvers: 3X		
Inserted 2:37		
Platinum Blues: 8X		
Inserted 1:73		
Wax Box:		90.00
1	Garret Anderson	1.00
2	Jim Edmonds	1.50
3	Darin Erstad	4.00
4	Chuck Finley	1.00
5	Tim Salmon	2.00
6	Roberto Alomar	3.00
7	Brady Anderson	1.50
8	Geronimo Berroa	1.00
9	Eric Davis	1.00
10	Mike Mussina	3.00
11	Rafael Palmeiro	2.50
12	Cal Ripken Jr.	12.00
13	Steve Avery	1.00
14	Nomar Garciaparra	9.00
15	John Valentin	1.00
16	Mo Vaughn	3.00
17	Albert Belle	4.00
18	Ozzie Guillen	1.00
19	Norberto Martin	1.00
20	Frank Thomas	7.00
21	Robin Ventura	1.50
22	Sandy Alomar Jr.	1.00
23	David Justice	1.50
24	Kenny Lofton	3.00
25	Manny Ramirez	5.00
26	Jim Thome	1.50
27	Omar Vizquel	1.00
28	Matt Williams	2.00
29	Jaret Wright	6.00
30	Raul Casanova	1.00
31	Tony Clark	1.50
32	Deivi Cruz	1.00
33	Bobby Higginson	1.00
34	Justin Thompson	1.00
35	Yamil Benitez	1.00
36	Johnny Damon	1.00
37	Jermaine Dye	1.00
38	Jed Hansen	1.00
39	Larry Sutton	1.00
40	Jeromy Burnitz	1.00
41	Jeff Cirillo	1.00
42	Dave Nilsson	1.00
43	Jose Valentin	1.00
44	Fernando Vina	1.00
45	Marty Cordova	1.00
46	Chuck Knoblauch	2.00
47	Paul Molitor	3.00
48	Brad Radke	1.00
49	Terry Steinbach	1.00
50	Wade Boggs	2.00
51	Hideki Irabu	1.00
52	Derek Jeter	10.00
53	Tino Martinez	1.50
54	Andy Pettitte	3.00
55	Mariano Rivera	1.50
56	Bernie Williams	3.00
57	Jose Canseco	1.50
58	Jason Giambi	1.00
59	Ben Grieve	6.00
60	Aaron Small	1.00
61	Jay Buhner	1.00
62	Ken Cloude	1.00
63	Joey Cora	1.00
64	Ken Griffey Jr.	15.00
65	Randy Johnson	3.00
66	Edgar Martinez	1.00
67	Alex Rodriguez	12.00
68	Will Clark	1.50
69	Juan Gonzalez	8.00
70	Rusty Greer	1.00
71	Ivan Rodriguez	4.00
72	Joe Carter	1.00
73	Roger Clemens	5.00
74	Jose Cruz Jr.	1.00
75	Carlos Delgado	1.50
76	Andruw Jones	7.00
77	Chipper Jones	9.00
78	Ryan Klesko	1.00
79	Javier Lopez	1.50
80	Greg Maddux	9.00
81	Miguel Batista	1.00
82	Jeremi Gonzalez	1.00
83	Mark Grace	2.50
84	Kevin Orie	1.00
85	Sammy Sosa	10.00
86	Barry Larkin	1.50
87	Deion Sanders	1.50
88	Reggie Sanders	1.00
89	Chris Stynes	1.00
90	Dante Bichette	1.50
91	Vinny Castilla	1.00
92	Andres Galarraga	2.00
93	Neifi Perez	1.00
94	Larry Walker	2.50
95	Moises Alou	1.00
96	Bobby Bonilla	1.00
97	Kevin Brown	1.50
98	Craig Counsell	1.00
99	Livan Hernandez	1.50
100	Edgar Renteria	1.00
101	Gary Sheffield	2.00
102	Jeff Bagwell	7.00
103	Craig Biggio	1.50
104	Luis Gonzalez	1.00
105	Darryl Kile	1.00
106	Wilton Guerrero	1.00
107	Eric Karros	1.50
108	Ramon Martinez	1.50
109	Raul Mondesi	2.00
110	Hideo Nomo	3.00
111	Chan Ho Park	1.50
112	Mike Piazza	9.00
113	Mark Grudzielanek	1.00
114	Vladimir Guerrero	5.00
115	Pedro Martinez	3.00
116	Henry Rodriguez	1.00
117	David Segui	1.00
118	Edgardo Alfonzo	1.00
119	Carlos Baerga	1.00
120	John Franco	1.00
121	John Olerud	1.50
122	Rey Ordonez	1.00
123	Ricky Bottalico	1.00
124	Gregg Jefferies	1.00
125	Mickey Morandini	1.00
126	Scott Rolen	6.00
127	Curt Schilling	1.50
128	Jose Guillen	2.00
129	Esteban Loaiza	1.00
130	Al Martin	1.00
131	Tony Womack	1.00
132	Dennis Eckersley	1.00
133	Gary Gaetti	1.00
134	Curtis King	1.00
135	Ray Lankford	1.00
136	Mark McGwire	15.00
137	Ken Caminiti	1.50
138	Steve Finley	1.00
139	Tony Gwynn	7.00
140	Carlos Hernandez	1.00
141	Wally Joyner	1.00
142	Barry Bonds	4.00
143	Jacob Cruz	1.00
144	Shawn Estes	1.00
145	Stan Javier	1.00
146	J.T. Snow	1.50
147	Nomar Garciaparra	7.00
148	Scott Rolen	4.00
149	Ken Griffey Jr.	10.00
150	Larry Walker	1.50

1998 Pacific Invincible Cramer's Choice

The 10-card Cramer's Choice Awards insert features top players on cards with a die-cut trophy design. This set has six different foil variations, each with a different production number. Green (99 hand-numbered sets), Dark Blue (80), Light Blue (50), Red (25), Gold (15) and Purple (10) versions were included in Invincible.

		MT
Complete Green Set (10):		1100.
Common Green (99 sets):		50.00
Dark Blues (80 sets): 1X		
Light Blues (50 sets): 1.5X		
Reds (25 sets): 2X		
Golds (15 sets): 3X		
Purples (10 sets): 5X		
1	Greg Maddux	125.00
2	Roberto Alomar	50.00
3	Cal Ripken Jr.	200.00
4	Nomar Garciaparra	125.00
5	Larry Walker	50.00
6	Mike Piazza	150.00
7	Mark McGwire	250.00
8	Tony Gwynn	125.00
9	Ken Griffey Jr.	250.00
10	Roger Clemens	100.00

1998 Pacific Invincible Gems of the Diamond

Gems of the Diamond is a 220-card insert seeded four per pack. The cards feature a color photo inside a white border.

		MT
Complete Set (220):		30.00
Common Player:		.10
1	Jim Edmonds	.20
2	Todd Greene	.20
3	Ken Hill	.10
4	Mike Holtz	.10
5	Mike James	.10
6	Chad Kreuter	.10
7	Tim Salmon	.30
8	Roberto Alomar	.60
9	Brady Anderson	.15
10	David Dellucci	.10
11	Jeffrey Hammonds	.10
12	Mike Mussina	.60
13	Rafael Palmeiro	.25
14	Arthur Rhodes	.10
15	Cal Ripken Jr.	2.50
16	Nerio Rodriguez	.10
17	Tony Tarasco	.10
18	Lenny Webster	.10
19	Mike Benjamin	.10
20	Rich Garces	.10
21	Nomar Garciaparra	2.00
22	Shane Mack	.10
23	Jose Malave	.10
24	Jesus Tavarez	.10
25	Mo Vaughn	.60
26	John Wasdin	.10
27	Jeff Abbott	.10
28	Albert Belle	.75
29	Mike Cameron	.25
30	Al Levine	.10
31	Robert Machado	.10
32	Greg Norton	.10
33	Magglio Ordonez	.35
34	Mike Sirotka	.10
35	Frank Thomas	1.25
36	Mario Valdez	.10
37	Sandy Alomar Jr.	.20
38	David Justice	.25
39	Jack McDowell	.10
40	Eric Plunk	.10
41	Manny Ramirez	.75
42	Kevin Seitzer	.10
43	Paul Shuey	.10
44	Omar Vizquel	.10
45	Kimera Bartee	.10
46	Glenn Dishman	.10
47	Orlando Miller	.10
48	Mike Myers	.10
49	Phil Nevin	.10
50	A.J. Sager	.10
51	Ricky Bones	.10
52	Scott Cooper	.10
53	Shane Halter	.10
54	David Howard	.10
55	Glendon Rusch	.10
56	Joe Vitiello	.10
57	Jeff D'Amico	.10
58	Mike Fetters	.10
59	Mike Matheny	.10
60	Jose Mercedes	.10
61	Ron Villone	.10
62	Jack Voigt	.10
63	Brent Brede	.10
64	Chuck Knoblauch	.25
65	Paul Molitor	.50
66	Todd Ritchie	.10
67	Frankie Rodriguez	.10
68	Scott Stahoviak	.10
69	Greg Swindell	.10
70	Todd Walker	.20
71	Wade Boggs	.25
72	Hideki Irabu	.30
73	Derek Jeter	2.00
74	Pat Kelly	.10
75	Graeme Lloyd	.10
76	Tino Martinez	.25
77	Jeff Nelson	.10
78	Scott Pose	.10
79	Mike Stanton	.10
80	Darryl Strawberry	.10
81	Bernie Williams	.50
82	Tony Batista	.10
83	Mark Bellhorn	.10
84	Ben Grieve	1.25
85	Pat Lennon	.10
86	Brian Lesher	.10
87	Miguel Tejada	.75
88	George Williams	.10
89	Joey Cora	.10
90	Rob Ducey	.10
91	Ken Griffey Jr.	3.50
92	Randy Johnson	.50
93	Edgar Martinez	.10
94	John Marzano	.10
95	Greg McCarthy	.10
96	Alex Rodriguez	2.50
97	Andy Sheets	.10
98	Mike Timlin	.10
99	Lee Tinsley	.10
100	Damon Buford	.10
101	Alex Diaz	.10
102	Benji Gil	.10
103	Juan Gonzalez	1.50
104	Eric Gunderson	.10
105	Danny Patterson	.10
106	Ivan Rodriguez	.75
107	Mike Simms	.10
108	Luis Andujar	.10
109	Joe Carter	.15
110	Roger Clemens	1.00
111	Jose Cruz Jr.	.40
112	Shawn Green	.15
113	Robert Perez	.10
114	Juan Samuel	.10
115	Ed Sprague	.10
116	Shannon Stewart	.10
117	Danny Bautista	.10
118	Chipper Jones	2.00
119	Ryan Klesko	.20
120	Keith Lockhart	.10
121	Javier Lopez	.15
122	Greg Maddux	2.00
123	Kevin Millwood	.75
124	Mike Mordecai	.10
125	Eddie Perez	.10
126	Randall Simon	.25
127	Miguel Cairo	.10
128	Dave Clark	.10
129	Kevin Foster	.10
130	Mark Grace	.25
131	Tyler Houston	.10
132	Mike Hubbard	.10
133	Kevin Orie	.10
134	Ryne Sandberg	.75
135	Sammy Sosa	1.50
136	Lenny Harris	.10
137	Kent Mercker	.10
138	Mike Morgan	.10
139	Deion Sanders	.15
140	Chris Stynes	.10
141	Gabe White	.10
142	Jason Bates	.10
143	Vinny Castilla	.10
144	Andres Galarraga	.25
145	Curtis Leskanic	.10
146	Jeff McCurry	.10
147	Mike Munoz	.10
148	Larry Walker	.30
149	Jamey Wright	.10
150	Moises Alou	.20
151	Bobby Bonilla	.10
152	Kevin Brown	.15
153	John Cangelosi	.10
154	Jeff Conine	.10
155	Cliff Floyd	.10
156	Jay Powell	.10
157	Edgar Renteria	.10
158	Tony Saunders	.10
159	Gary Sheffield	.25
160	Jeff Bagwell	1.25
161	Tim Bogar	.10
162	Tony Eusebio	.10
163	Chris Holt	.10
164	Ray Montgomery	.10
165	Luis Rivera	.10
166	Eric Anthony	.10
167	Brett Butler	.10
168	Juan Castro	.10
169	Tripp Cromer	.10
170	Raul Mondesi	.25
171	Hideo Nomo	.50
172	Mike Piazza	2.00
173	Tom Prince	.10
174	Adam Riggs	.10
175	Shane Andrews	.10
176	Shayne Bennett	.10
177	Raul Chavez	.10
178	Pedro Martinez	.30
179	Sherman Obando	.10
180	Andy Stankiewicz	.10
181	Alberto Castillo	.10
182	Shawn Gilbert	.10
183	Luis Lopez	.10
184	Roberto Petagine	.10
185	Armando Reynoso	.10
186	Midre Cummings	.10
187	Kevin Jordan	.10
188	Desi Relaford	.10
189	Scott Rolen	1.25
190	Ken Ryan	.10
191	Kevin Sefcik	.10
192	Emil Brown	.10
193	Lou Collier	.10
194	Francisco Cordova	.10
195	Kevin Elster	.10
196	Mark Smith	.10
197	Marc Wilkins	.10
198	Manny Aybar	.25
199	Jose Bautista	.10
200	David Bell	.10
201	Rigo Beltran	.10
202	Delino DeShields	.10
203	Dennis Eckersley	.10
204	John Mabry	.10
205	Eli Marrero	.10
206	Willie McGee	.10
207	Mark McGwire	3.50
208	Ken Caminiti	.20
209	Tony Gwynn	1.50
210	Chris Jones	.10
211	Craig Shipley	.10
212	Pete Smith	.10
213	Jorge Velandia	.10
214	Dario Veras	.10
215	Rich Aurilia	.10
216	Damon Berryhill	.10
217	Barry Bonds	.75
218	Osvaldo Fernandez	.10
219	Dante Powell	.10
220	Rich Rodriguez	.10

1998 Pacific Invincible Interleague Players

Interleague Players is a 30-card insert featuring 15 sets of players - one National League and one American League player. The dark blue backgrounds have red lightning bolts and the white borders are made of a leather-like material. When a set of players is placed next to each other, they form the MLB Interleague logo in the center. Interleague Players cards were inserted one per 73 packs.

	MT
Complete Set (30):	475.00
Common Player:	4.00

Inserted 1:73

1A	Roberto Alomar	10.00
1N	Craig Biggio	6.00
2A	Cal Ripken Jr.	40.00
2N	Chipper Jones	30.00
3A	Nomar Garciaparra	30.00
3N	Scott Rolen	20.00
4A	Mo Vaughn	10.00
4N	Andres Galarraga	6.00
5A	Frank Thomas	20.00
5N	Tony Gwynn	25.00
6A	Albert Belle	12.50
6N	Barry Bonds	12.50
7A	Hideki Irabu	5.00
7N	Hideo Nomo	7.50
8A	Derek Jeter	30.00
8N	Rey Ordonez	5.00
9A	Tino Martinez	7.50
9N	Mark McGwire	50.00
10A	Alex Rodriguez	40.00
10N	Edgar Renteria	5.00
11A	Ken Griffey Jr.	50.00
11N	Larry Walker	7.50
12A	Randy Johnson	10.00
12N	Greg Maddux	30.00
13A	Ivan Rodriguez	12.50
13N	Mike Piazza	30.00
14A	Roger Clemens	20.00
14N	Pedro Martinez	7.50
15A	Jose Cruz Jr.	4.00
15N	Wilton Guerrero	4.00

1998 Pacific Invincible Moments in Time

Moments in Time (20 cards, 1:145) is designed as a baseball scoreboard. The cards have a horizontal layout with the date of an important game in the player's career at the top. The player's stats from the game are featured and a picture is located on the scoreboard screen.

		MT
Complete Set (20):		500.00
Common Player:		9.00
Inserted 1:145		
1	Chipper Jones	45.00
2	Cal Ripken Jr.	60.00
3	Frank Thomas	30.00
4	David Justice	9.00
5	Andres Galarraga	9.00
6	Larry Walker	15.00
7	Livan Hernandez	9.00
8	Wilton Guerrero	9.00
9	Hideo Nomo	18.00
10	Mike Piazza	45.00
11	Pedro Martinez	15.00
12	Bernie Williams	9.00
13	Ben Grieve	25.00
14	Scott Rolen	25.00
15	Mark McGwire	75.00
16	Tony Gwynn	35.00
17	Ken Griffey Jr.	75.00
18	Alex Rodriguez	60.00
19	Juan Gonzalez	35.00
20	Jose Cruz Jr.	9.00

1998 Pacific Invincible Photoengravings

Photoengravings is an 18-card insert seeded one per 37 packs. Each card has a unique "old-style" design with a player photo in a frame in the center.

		MT
Complete Set (18):		150.00
Common Player:		2.00
Inserted 1:37		
1	Greg Maddux	12.50
2	Cal Ripken Jr.	15.00
3	Nomar Garciaparra	12.50
4	Frank Thomas	9.00
5	Larry Walker	4.00
6	Mike Piazza	12.50
7	Hideo Nomo	3.00
8	Pedro Martinez	4.00
9	Derek Jeter	12.50
10	Tino Martinez	2.00
11	Mark McGwire	20.00
12	Tony Gwynn	10.00
13	Barry Bonds	5.00
14	Ken Griffey Jr.	20.00
15	Alex Rodriguez	15.00
16	Ivan Rodriguez	5.00
17	Roger Clemens	7.50
18	Jose Cruz Jr.	2.00

1998 Pacific Invincible Team Checklists

Team Checklists is a 30-card insert seeded 2:37. The fronts feature a player collage with the team logo in the background. The back has a complete checklist for that team in Invincible.

		MT
Complete Set (30):		200.00
Common Player:		3.00
Inserted 2:37		
1	Anaheim Angels	6.00
2	Atlanta Braves	15.00
3	Baltimore Orioles	20.00
4	Boston Red Sox	15.00
5	Chicago Cubs	10.00
6	Chicago White Sox	20.00
7	Cincinnati Reds	3.00
8	Cleveland Indians	5.00
9	Colorado Rockies	4.00
10	Detroit Tigers	5.00
11	Florida Marlins	4.00
12	Houston Astros	10.00
13	Kansas City Royals	3.00
14	Los Angeles Dodgers	15.00
15	Milwaukee Brewers	3.00
16	Minnesota Twins	5.00
17	Montreal Expos	6.00
18	New York Mets	3.00
19	New York Yankees	15.00
20	Oakland Athletics	10.00
21	Philadelphia Phillies	10.00
22	Pittsburgh Pirates	3.00
23	St. Louis Cardinals	10.00
24	San Diego Padres	12.00
25	San Francisco Giants	6.00
26	Seattle Mariners	25.00
27	Texas Rangers	12.00
28	Toronto Blue Jays	15.00
29	Arizona Diamondbacks	5.00
30	Tampa Bay Devil Rays	5.00

1998 Pacific Omega

The Omega base set consists of 250 three-image cards. The horizontal cards feature a color player photo in the center with the image duplicated in foil on the right. Another color photo is on the left. The photos are divided by a baseball seam design. Inserts in the set include Prisms, Face to Face, EO Portraits, Online and Rising Stars.

		MT
Complete Set (250):		35.00
Common Player:		.10
Reds: 6-8X		
Wax Box:		60.00
1	Garret Anderson	.10
2	Gary DiSarcina	.10
3	Jim Edmonds	.20
4	Darin Erstad	.75
5	Cecil Fielder	.15
6	Chuck Finley	.10
7	Shigetosi Hasegawa	.10
8	Tim Salmon	.25
9	Brian Anderson	.10
10	Jay Bell	.10
11	Andy Benes	.10
12	Yamil Benitez	.10
13	Jorge Fabregas	.10
14	Travis Lee	.75
15	Devon White	.10
16	Matt Williams	.30
17	Andres Galarraga	.25
18	Tom Glavine	.20
19	Andruw Jones	.75
20	Chipper Jones	2.00
21	Ryan Klesko	.25
22	Javy Lopez	.15
23	Greg Maddux	2.00
24	*Kevin Millwood*	2.50
25	Denny Neagle	.10
26	John Smoltz	.20
27	Roberto Alomar	.60
28	Brady Anderson	.10
29	Joe Carter	.15
30	Eric Davis	.10
31	Jimmy Key	.10
32	Mike Mussina	.60
33	Rafael Palmeiro	.25
34	Cal Ripken Jr.	2.50
35	B.J. Surhoff	.10
36	Dennis Eckersley	.10
37	Nomar Garciaparra	2.00
38	Reggie Jefferson	.10
39	Derek Lowe	.10
40	Pedro Martinez	.50
41	Brian Rose	.10
42	John Valentin	.10
43	Jason Varitek	.15
44	Mo Vaughn	.60
45	Jeff Blauser	.10
46	Jeremi Gonzalez	.10
47	Mark Grace	.25
48	Lance Johnson	.10
49	Kevin Orie	.10
50	Henry Rodriguez	.10
51	Sammy Sosa	1.50
52	Kerry Wood	.75
53	Albert Belle	.75
54	Mike Cameron	.10
55	Mike Caruso	.10
56	Ray Durham	.10
57	Jaime Navarro	.10
58	Greg Norton	.10
59	*Magglio Ordonez*	1.00
60	Frank Thomas	1.50
61	Robin Ventura	.20
62	Bret Boone	.10
63	Willie Greene	.10
64	Barry Larkin	.20
65	Jon Nunnally	.10
66	Eduardo Perez	.10
67	Reggie Sanders	.10
68	Brett Tomko	.10
69	Sandy Alomar Jr.	.20
70	Travis Fryman	.10
71	David Justice	.25
72	Kenny Lofton	.60
73	Charles Nagy	.10
74	Manny Ramirez	.75
75	Jim Thome	.40
76	Omar Vizquel	.10
77	Enrique Wilson	.10
78	Jaret Wright	.60
79	Dante Bichette	.25
80	Ellis Burks	.10
81	Vinny Castilla	.20
82	Todd Helton	.75
83	Darryl Kile	.10
84	Mike Lansing	.10
85	Neifi Perez	.10
86	Larry Walker	.40
87	Raul Casanova	.10
88	Tony Clark	.30
89	Luis Gonzalez	.10
90	Bobby Higginson	.10
91	Brian Hunter	.10
92	Bip Roberts	.10
93	Justin Thompson	.10
94	Josh Booty	.10
95	Craig Counsell	.10
96	Livan Hernandez	.10
97	*Ryan Jackson*	.50
98	Mark Kotsay	.25
99	Derrek Lee	.10
100	Mike Piazza	2.00
101	Edgar Renteria	.10
102	Cliff Floyd	.10
103	Moises Alou	.20
104	Jeff Bagwell	1.00
105	Derrick Bell	.10
106	Sean Berry	.10
107	Craig Biggio	.20
108	*John Halama*	.25
109	Richard Hidalgo	.10
110	Shane Reynolds	.10
111	Tim Belcher	.10
112	Brian Bevil	.10
113	Jeff Conine	.10
114	Johnny Damon	.10
115	Jeff King	.10
116	Jeff Montgomery	.10
117	Dean Palmer	.10
118	Terry Pendleton	.10
119	Bobby Bonilla	.15
120	Wilton Guerrero	.15
121	Todd Hollandsworth	.10
122	Charles Johnson	.10
123	Eric Karros	.15
124	Paul Konerko	.25
125	Ramon Martinez	.10
126	Raul Mondesi	.25
127	Hideo Nomo	.40
128	Gary Sheffield	.30
129	Ismael Valdes	.10
130	Jeromy Burnitz	.10
131	Jeff Cirillo	.10
132	Todd Dunn	.10
133	Marquis Grissom	.10
134	John Jaha	.10
135	Scott Karl	.10
136	Dave Nilsson	.10
137	Jose Valentin	.10
138	Fernando Vina	.10
139	Rick Aguilera	.10
140	Marty Cordova	.10
141	Pat Meares	.10
142	Paul Molitor	.50
143	David Ortiz	.20
144	Brad Radke	.10
145	Terry Steinbach	.10
146	Todd Walker	.20
147	Shane Andrews	.10
148	Brad Fullmer	.25
149	Mark Grudzielanek	.10
150	Vladimir Guerrero	.75
151	F.P. Santangelo	.10
152	Jose Vidro	.10
153	Rondell White	.20
154	Carlos Baerga	.10
155	Bernard Gilkey	.10
156	Todd Hundley	.10
157	Butch Huskey	.10
158	Bobby Jones	.10
159	Brian McRae	.10
160	John Olerud	.20
161	Rey Ordonez	.10
162	*Masato Yoshii*	.50
163	David Cone	.20
164	Hideki Irabu	.25
165	Derek Jeter	2.00
166	Chuck Knoblauch	.30
167	Tino Martinez	.25
168	Paul O'Neill	.20
169	Andy Pettitte	.35
170	Mariano Rivera	.20
171	Darryl Strawberry	.20
172	David Wells	.10
173	Bernie Williams	.25
174	*Ryan Christenson*	.20
175	Jason Giambi	.10
176	Ben Grieve	1.00
177	Rickey Henderson	.20
178	A.J. Hinch	.30
179	Kenny Rogers	.10
180	Ricky Bottalico	.10
181	Rico Brogna	.10
182	Doug Glanville	.10
183	Gregg Jefferies	.10
184	Mike Lieberthal	.10
185	Scott Rolen	1.00
186	Curt Shilling	.20
187	Jermaine Allensworth	.10
188	Lou Collier	.10
189	Jose Guillen	.25
190	Jason Kendall	.10
191	Al Martin	.10
192	Tony Womack	.10
193	Kevin Young	.10
194	Royce Clayton	.10
195	Delino DeShields	.10
196	Gary Gaetti	.10
197	Ron Gant	.15
198	Brian Jordan	.10
199	Ray Lankford	.10
200	Mark McGwire	3.50
201	Todd Stottlemyre	.10
202	Kevin Brown	.20
203	Ken Caminiti	.20
204	Steve Finley	.10
205	Tony Gwynn	1.50
206	Carlos Hernandez	.10
207	Wally Joyner	.10
208	Greg Vaughn	.25
209	Barry Bonds	.75
210	Shawn Estes	.10
211	Orel Hershiser	.10
212	Stan Javier	.10
213	Jeff Kent	.10
214	Bill Mueller	.10
215	Robb Nen	.10
216	J.T. Snow	.10
217	Jay Buhner	.15
218	Ken Cloude	.25
219	Joey Cora	.10
220	Ken Griffey Jr.	3.50
221	Glenallen Hill	.10
222	Randy Johnson	.50
223	Edgar Martinez	.10
224	Jamie Moyer	.10
225	Alex Rodriguez	2.50
226	David Segui	.10
227	Dan Wilson	.10
228	*Rolando Arrojo*	.40
229	Wade Boggs	.25
230	Miguel Cairo	.10
231	Roberto Hernandez	.10
232	Quinton McCracken	.10
233	Fred McGriff	.20
234	Paul Sorrento	.10
235	Kevin Stocker	.10
236	Will Clark	.20
237	Juan Gonzalez	1.50
238	Rusty Greer	.10
239	Rick Helling	.10
240	Roberto Kelly	.10
241	Ivan Rodriguez	.75
242	Aaron Sele	.10
243	John Wetteland	.10
244	Jose Canseco	.25
245	Roger Clemens	1.00
246	Jose Cruz Jr.	.15
247	Carlos Delgado	.25
248	Alex Gonzalez	.10
249	Ed Sprague	.10
250	Shannon Stewart	.10

1998 Pacific Omega EO Portraits

EO Portraits is a 20-card insert seeded 1:73. Each card has a color action photo with a player portrait laser-cut into the card. A "1-of-1" parallel features a laser-cut number on the card as well. The "EO" stands for "Electro Optical" technology.

		MT
Complete Set (20):		350.00
Common Player:		5.00
1	Cal Ripken Jr.	30.00
2	Nomar Garciaparra	25.00
3	Mo Vaughn	10.00
4	Frank Thomas	15.00
5	Manny Ramirez	12.50
6	Ben Grieve	15.00
7	Ken Griffey Jr.	40.00
8	Alex Rodriguez	30.00
9	Juan Gonzalez	20.00
10	Ivan Rodriguez	10.00
11	Travis Lee	8.00
12	Greg Maddux	25.00
13	Chipper Jones	25.00
14	Kerry Wood	10.00
15	Larry Walker	5.00
16	Jeff Bagwell	15.00
17	Mike Piazza	25.00
18	Mark McGwire	40.00
19	Tony Gwynn	20.00
20	Barry Bonds	10.00

1998 Pacific Omega Face to Face

Face to Face features two star players on each card. It is a 10-card insert seeded one per 145 packs.

		MT
Complete Set (10):		200.00
Common Player:		8.00
1	Alex Rodriguez, Nomar Garciaparra	30.00
2	Mark McGwire, Ken Griffey Jr.	60.00
3	Mike Piazza, Sandy Alomar Jr.	25.00
4	Kerry Wood, Roger Clemens	20.00
5	Cal Ripken Jr., Paul Molitor	30.00
6	Tony Gwynn, Wade Boggs	20.00
7	Frank Thomas, Chipper Jones	20.00
8	Travis Lee, Ben Grieve	15.00
9	Hideo Nomo, Hideki Irabu	5.00
10	Juan Gonzalez, Manny Ramirez	20.00

1998 Pacific Omega Online

Online is a 36-card insert seeded about one per nine packs. The foiled and etched cards feature a color player photo in front of a hi-tech designed background. The card fronts also include the internet address for the player's web site on bigleaguers.com.

		MT
Complete Set (36):		140.00
Common Player:		1.00
1	Cal Ripken Jr.	10.00
2	Nomar Garciaparra	8.00
3	Pedro Martinez	2.00
4	Mo Vaughn	2.00
5	Frank Thomas	6.00
6	Sandy Alomar Jr.	1.00
7	Manny Ramirez	5.00
8	Jaret Wright	1.50
9	Paul Molitor	2.50
10	Derek Jeter	6.00
11	Bernie Williams	1.50
12	Ben Grieve	4.00
13	Ken Griffey Jr.	15.00
14	Edgar Martinez	1.00
15	Alex Rodriguez	10.00
16	Wade Boggs	2.00
17	Juan Gonzalez	6.00
18	Ivan Rodriguez	3.00
19	Roger Clemens	5.00
20	Travis Lee	2.50
21	Matt Williams	1.50
22	Andres Galarraga	1.50
23	Chipper Jones	8.00
24	Greg Maddux	7.50
25	Sammy Sosa	6.00
26	Kerry Wood	3.00
27	Barry Larkin	1.50
28	Larry Walker	2.00
29	Derrek Lee	1.00
30	Jeff Bagwell	4.00
31	Hideo Nomo	1.00
32	Mike Piazza	8.00
33	Scott Rolen	4.00
34	Mark McGwire	15.00
35	Tony Gwynn	6.00
36	Barry Bonds	3.00

1998 Pacific Omega Prism

This 20-card insert was seeded one per 37 packs. Horizontal card fronts feature prismatic foil technology.

		MT
Complete Set (20):		145.00
Common Player:		2.00
1	Cal Ripken Jr.	12.00
2	Nomar Garciaparra	10.00
3	Pedro Martinez	2.50
4	Frank Thomas	8.00
5	Manny Ramirez	5.00
6	Brian Giles	2.00
7	Derek Jeter	9.00
8	Ben Grieve	5.00
9	Ken Griffey Jr.	16.00
10	Alex Rodriguez	12.00
11	Juan Gonzalez	8.00
12	Travis Lee	3.00
13	Chipper Jones	10.00
14	Greg Maddux	9.00
15	Kerry Wood	4.00
16	Larry Walker	2.50
17	Hideo Nomo	2.00
18	Mike Piazza	10.00
19	Mark McGwire	16.00
20	Tony Gwynn	8.00

1998 Pacific Omega Rising Stars

Rising Stars is a four-tiered hobby-only insert. The 20 cards were seeded four per 37 packs. Each card featured three rookies and each tier has a different foil color. A parallel of the insert is sequentially numbered. Tier One cards are numbered to 100, Tier Two to 50, Tier Three to 25 and Tier 4 to one.

		MT
Complete Set (30):		55.00
Common Player:		1.00
1	Nerio Rodriguez, Sidney Ponson	1.00
2	Frank Catalanotto, Roberto Duran, Sean Runyan	1.00
3	Kevin L. Brown, Carlos Almanzar	1.00
4	Aaron Boone, Pat Watkins, Scott Winchester	1.00
5	Brian Meadows, Andy Larkin, Antonio Alfonseca	1.00
6	DaRond Stovall, Trey Moore, Shayne Bennett	1.00
7	Felix Martinez, Larry Sutton, Brian Bevil	1.00
8	Homer Bush, Mike Buddie	1.00
9	Rich Butler, Esteban Yan	2.50
10	Damon Hollins, Brian Edmondson	1.00
11	Lou Collier, Jose Silva, Javier Martinez	1.00
12	Steve Sinclair, Mark Dalesandro	1.00
13	Jason Varitek, Brian Rose, Brian Shouse	2.00
14	Mike Caruso, Jeff Abbott, Tom Fordham	2.00
15	Jason Johnson, Bobby Smith	1.00
16	Dave Berg, Mark Kotsay, Jesus Sanchez	3.00
17	Richard Hidalgo, John Halama, Trever Miller	2.00
18	Geoff Jenkins, Bobby Hughes, Steve Woodard	2.00
19	Eli Marrero, Cliff Politte, Mike Busby	1.00
20	Desi Relaford, Darrin Winston	1.00
21	Todd Helton, Bobby Jones	4.00
22	Rolando Arrojo, Miguel Cairo, Dan Carlson	3.00
23	David Ortiz, Javier Valentin, Eric Milton	2.00
24	Magglio Ordonez, Greg Norton	3.00
25	Brad Fullmer, Javier Vazquez, Rick DeHart	2.00
26	Paul Konerko, Matt Luke	3.00
27	Derrek Lee, Ryan Jackson, John Roskos	2.00
28	Ben Grieve, A.J. Hinch, Ryan Christenson	5.00
29	Travis Lee, Karim Garcia, David Dellucci	6.00
30	Kerry Wood, Marc Pisciotta	4.00

1998 Pacific Online

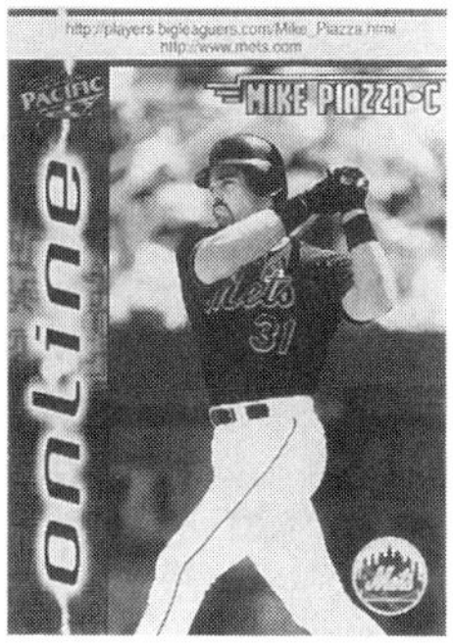

Online Baseball consists of an 800-card base set with one parallel. The base set features 750 players on cards that list the internet address of the player's home page on the bigleaguers.com web site. Twenty players have two cards and each of the 30 teams has a checklist that lists the team's web site. The Web Cards set parallels the 750 player cards. It has a serial number that can be entered at the big leaguers.com web site to determine if a prize has been won.

		MT
Complete Set (780):		100.00
Common Player:		.15
Inserted 1:1		
1	Garret Anderson	.15
2	*Rich DeLucia*	.40
3	Jason Dickson	.15
4	Gary DiSarcina	.15
5	Jim Edmonds	.15
6	Darin Erstad	1.50
7	Cecil Fielder	.15
8	Chuck Finley	.15
9	Carlos Carcia	.15
10	Shigetosi Hasegawa	.15
11	Ken Hill	.15
12	Dave Hollins	.15
13	Mike Holtz	.15
14	Mike James	.15
15	Norberto Martin	.15
16	Damon Mashore	.15
17	Jack McDowell	.15
18	Phil Nevin	.15
19	Omar Olivares	.15
20	Troy Percival	.15
21	Rich Robertson	.15
22	Tim Salmon	.30
23	Craig Shipley	.15
24	Matt Walbeck	.15
25	Allen Watson	.15
26	Jim Edmonds	.15
27	Brian Anderson	.15
28	Tony Batista	.15
29	Jay Bell	.15
30	Andy Benes	.15
31	Yamil Benitez	.15
32	Willie Blair	.15
33	Brent Brede	.15
34	Scott Brow	.15
35	Omar Daal	.15
36	David Dellucci	.15
37	Edwin Diaz	.15
38	Jorge Fabregas	.15
39	Andy Fox	.15
40	Karim Garcia	.20
41	Travis Lee	.75
42	Barry Manuel	.15
43	Gregg Olson	.15
44	Felix Rodriguez	.15
45	Clint Sodowsky	.15
46	Russ Springer	.15
47	Andy Stankiewicz	.15
48	Kelly Stinnett	.15
49	Jeff Suppan	.15
50	Devon White	.15
51	Matt Williams	.20
52	Travis Lee	.75
53	Danny Bautista	.15
54	Rafael Belliard	.15
55	*Adam Butler*	.30
56	Mike Cather	.15
57	Brian Edmondson	.15
58	Alan Embree	.15
59	Andres Galarraga	.40
60	Tom Glavine	.30
61	Tony Graffanino	.15
62	Andruw Jones	1.00
63	Chipper Jones	2.50
64	Ryan Klesko	.25
65	Keith Lockhart	.15
66	Javy Lopez	.20
67	Greg Maddux	2.50
68	Dennis Martinez	.15
69	*Kevin Millwood*	3.00
70	Denny Neagle	.15
71	Eddie Perez	.15
72	Curtis Pride	.15
73	John Smoltz	.25
74	Michael Tucker	.15
75	Walt Weiss	.15
76	Gerald Williams	.15
77	Mark Wohlers	.15
78	Chipper Jones	2.50
79	Roberto Alomar	.40
80	Brady Anderson	.15
81	Harold Baines	.15
82	Armando Benitez	.15
83	Mike Bordick	.15
84	Joe Carter	.15
85	Norm Charlton	.15
86	Eric Davis	.15
87	Doug Drabek	.15
88	Scott Erickson	.15
89	Jeffrey Hammonds	.15
90	Chris Hoiles	.15
91	Scott Kamieniecki	.15
92	Jimmy Key	.15
93	Terry Mathews	.15
94	Alan Mills	.15
95	Mike Mussina	.75
96	Jesse Orosco	.15
97	Rafael Palmeiro	.25
98	Sidney Ponson	.15
99	Jeff Reboulet	.15
100	Arthur Rhodes	.15
101	Cal Ripken Jr.	3.00
102	Nerio Rodriguez	.15
103	B.J. Surhoff	.15
104	Lenny Webster	.15
105	Cal Ripken Jr.	3.00
106	Steve Avery	.15
107	Mike Benjamin	.15
108	Darren Bragg	.15
109	Damon Buford	.15
110	Jim Corsi	.15
111	Dennis Eckersley	.15
112	Rich Garces	.15
113	Nomar Garciaparra	2.50
114	Tom Gordon	.15
115	Scott Hatteberg	.15
116	Butch Henry	.15
117	Reggie Jefferson	.15
118	Mark Lemke	.15
119	Darren Lewis	.15
120	Jim Leyritz	.15
121	Derek Lowe	.15
122	Pedro Martinez	.75
123	Troy O'Leary	.15
124	Brian Rose	.15
125	Bret Saberhagen	.15
126	Donnie Sadler	.15
127	Brian Shouse	.15
128	John Valentin	.15
129	Jason Varitek	.15
130	Mo Vaughn	1.00
131	Tim Wakefield	.15
132	John Wasdin	.15
133	Nomar Garciaparra	2.50
134	Terry Adams	.15
135	Manny Alexander	.15
136	Rod Beck	.15
137	Jeff Blauser	.15
138	Brant Brown	.15
139	Mark Clark	.15
140	Jeremi Gonzalez	.15
141	Mark Grace	.25
142	Jose Hernandez	.15
143	Tyler Houston	.15
144	Lance Johnson	.15
145	Sandy Martinez	.15
146	Matt Mieske	.15
147	Mickey Morandini	.15
148	Terry Mulholland	.15
149	Kevin Orie	.15
150	Bob Patterson	.15
151	Marc Pisciotta	.15
152	Henry Rodriguez	.15
153	Scott Servais	.15
154	Sammy Sosa	2.50
155	Kevin Tapani	.15
156	Steve Trachsel	.15
157	Kerry Wood	1.00
158	Kerry Wood	1.00
159	Jeff Abbott	.15
160	James Baldwin	.15
161	Albert Belle	1.00
162	Jason Bere	.15
163	Mike Cameron	.15
164	Mike Caruso	.15
165	Carlos Castillo	.15
166	Tony Castillo	.15
167	Ray Durham	.15
168	Scott Eyre	.15
169	Tom Fordham	.15
170	Keith Foulke	.15
171	Lou Frazier	.15
172	Matt Karchner	.15
173	Chad Kreuter	.15
174	Jaime Navarro	.15
175	Greg Norton	.15
176	Charlie O'Brien	.15
177	Magglio Ordonez	.50
178	Ruben Sierra	.15
179	Bill Simas	.15
180	Mike Sirotka	.15
181	Chris Snopek	.15
182	Frank Thomas	1.50
183	Robin Ventura	.25
184	Frank Thomas	1.50
185	Stan Belinda	.15
186	Aaron Boone	.15
187	Bret Boone	.15
188	Brook Fordyce	.15
189	Willie Greene	.15
190	Pete Harnisch	.15
191	Lenny Harris	.15
192	Mark Hutton	.15
193	Damian Jackson	.15
194	Ricardo Jordan	.15
195	Barry Larkin	.30
196	Eduardo Perez	.15
197	Pokey Reese	.15
198	Mike Remlinger	.15
199	Reggie Sanders	.15
200	Jeff Shaw	.15
201	Chris Stynes	.15
202	Scott Sullivan	.15
203	Eddie Taubensee	.15
204	Brett Tomko	.15
205	Pat Watkins	.15
206	David Weathers	.15
207	Gabe White	.15
208	Scott Winchester	.15
209	Barry Larkin	.25
210	Sandy Alomar Jr.	.20
211	Paul Assenmacher	.15
212	Geronimo Berroa	.15
213	Pat Borders	.15
214	Jeff Branson	.15
215	Dave Burba	.15
216	Bartolo Colon	.30
217	Shawon Dunston	.15
218	Travis Fryman	.15
219	Brian Giles	.15
220	Dwight Gooden	.15
221	Mike Jackson	.15
222	David Justice	.40
223	Kenny Lofton	1.00
224	Jose Mesa	.15
225	Alvin Morman	.15
226	Charles Nagy	.15
227	Chad Ogea	.15
228	Eric Plunk	.15
229	Manny Ramirez	1.50
230	Paul Shuey	.15
231	Jim Thome	.60
232	Ron Villone	.15
233	Omar Vizquel	.15
234	Enrique Wilson	.15
235	Jaret Wright	1.00
236	Manny Ramirez	1.50
237	Pedro Astacio	.15
238	Jason Bates	.15
239	Dante Bichette	.30
240	Ellis Burks	.15
241	Vinny Castilla	.25
242	Greg Colbrunn	.15
243	Mike DeJean	.15
244	Jerry Dipoto	.15
245	Curtis Goodwin	.15
246	Todd Helton	.75
247	Bobby Jones	.15
248	Darryl Kile	.15
249	Mike Lansing	.15
250	Curtis Leskanic	.15
251	Nelson Liriano	.15
252	Kirt Manwaring	.15
253	Chuck McElroy	.15
254	Mike Munoz	.15
255	Neifi Perez	.15
256	Jeff Reed	.15
257	Mark Thompson	.15
258	John Vander Wal	.15
259	Dave Veres	.15
260	Larry Walker	.40
261	Jamey Wright	.15
262	Larry Walker	.25
263	Kimera Bartee	.15
264	Doug Brocail	.15
265	Raul Casanova	.15
266	Frank Castillo	.15
267	Frank Catalanotto	.15
268	Tony Clark	.40
269	Deivi Cruz	.15
270	Roberto Duran	.15
271	Damion Easley	.15
272	Bryce Florie	.15
273	Luis Gonzalez	.15
274	Bob Higginson	.15
275	Brian Hunter	.15
276	Todd Jones	.15
277	Greg Keagle	.15
278	Jeff Manto	.15
279	Brian Moehler	.15
280	Joe Oliver	.15
281	Joe Randa	.15
282	Billy Ripken	.15
283	Bip Roberts	.15

284	Sean Runyan	.15
285	A.J. Sager	.15
286	Justin Thompson	.15
287	Tony Clark	.50
288	Antonio Alfonseca	.15
289	Dave Berg	.15
290	Josh Booty	.15
291	John Cangelosi	.15
292	Craig Counsell	.15
293	Vic Darensbourg	.15
294	Cliff Floyd	.15
295	Oscar Henriquez	.15
296	Felix Heredia	.15
297	*Ryan Jackson*	.15
298	Mark Kotsay	.40
299	Andy Larkin	.15
300	Derrek Lee	.15
301	Brian Meadows	.15
302	Rafael Medina	.15
303	Jay Powell	.15
304	Edgar Renteria	.15
305	*Jesus Sanchez*	.30
306	Rob Stanifer	.15
307	Greg Zaun	.15
308	Derrek Lee	.15
309	Moises Alou	.25
310	Brad Ausmus	.15
311	Jeff Bagwell	1.50
312	Derek Bell	.15
313	Sean Bergman	.15
314	Sean Berry	.15
315	Craig Biggio	.25
316	Tim Bogar	.15
317	Jose Cabrera	.15
318	Dave Clark	.15
319	Tony Eusebio	.15
320	Carl Everett	.15
321	Ricky Gutierrez	.15
322	John Halama	.15
323	Mike Hampton	.15
324	Doug Henry	.15
325	Richard Hidalgo	.15
326	Jack Howell	.15
327	Jose Lima	.15
328	Mike Magnante	.15
329	Trever Miller	.15
330	C.J. Nitkowski	.15
331	Shane Reynolds	.15
332	Bill Spiers	.15
333	Billy Wagner	.20
334	Jeff Bagwell	1.50
335	Tim Belcher	.15
336	Brian Bevil	.15
337	Johnny Damon	.15
338	Jermaine Dye	.15
339	Sal Fasano	.15
340	Shane Halter	.15
341	Chris Haney	.15
342	Jed Hansen	.15
343	Jeff King	.15
344	Jeff Montgomery	.15
345	Hal Morris	.15
346	Jose Offerman	.15
347	Dean Palmer	.15
348	Terry Pendleton	.15
349	Hipolito Pichardo	.15
350	Jim Pittsley	.15
351	Pat Rapp	.15
352	Jose Rosado	.15
353	Glendon Rusch	.15
354	Scott Service	.15
355	Larry Sutton	.15
356	Mike Sweeney	.15
357	Joe Vitiello	.15
358	Matt Whisenant	.15
359	Ernie Young	.15
360	Jeff King	.15
361	Bobby Bonilla	.15
362	Jim Bruske	.15
363	Juan Castro	.15
364	Roger Cedeno	.15
365	Mike Devereaux	.15
366	Darren Dreifort	.15
367	Jim Eisenreich	.15
368	Wilton Guerrero	.15
369	Mark Guthrie	.15
370	Darren Hall	.15
371	Todd Hollandsworth	.15
372	Thomas Howard	.15
373	Trenidad Hubbard	.15
374	Charles Johnson	.15
375	Eric Karros	.15
376	Paul Konerko	.40
377	Matt Luke	.15
378	Ramon Martinez	.15
379	Raul Mondesi	.30
380	Hideo Nomo	.50
381	Antonio Osuna	.15
382	Chan Ho Park	.30
383	Tom Prince	.15
384	Scott Radinsky	.15
385	Gary Sheffield	.40
386	Ismael Valdes	.15
387	Jose Vizcaino	.15
388	Eric Young	.15
389	Gary Sheffield	.40
390	Jeromy Burnitz	.15
391	Jeff Cirillo	.15
392	Cal Eldred	.15
393	Chad Fox	.15
394	Marquis Grissom	.15
395	Bob Hamelin	.15
396	Bobby Hughes	.15
397	Darrin Jackson	.15
398	John Jaha	.15
399	Geoff Jenkins	.15
400	Doug Jones	.15
401	Jeff Juden	.15
402	Scott Karl	.15
403	Jesse Levis	.15
404	Mark Loretta	.15
405	Mike Matheny	.15
406	Jose Mercedes	.15
407	Mike Myers	.15
408	Marc Newfield	.15
409	Dave Nilsson	.15
410	Al Reyes	.15
411	Jose Valentin	.15
412	Fernando Vina	.15
413	Paul Wagner	.15
414	Bob Wickman	.15
415	Steve Woodard	.15
416	Marquis Grissom	.15
417	Rick Aguilera	.15
418	Ron Coomer	.15
419	Marty Cordova	.15
420	Brent Gates	.15
421	Eddie Guardado	.15
422	Denny Hocking	.15
423	Matt Lawton	.15
424	Pat Meares	.15
425	Orlando Merced	.15
426	Eric Milton	.15
427	Paul Molitor	.75
428	Mike Morgan	.15
429	Dan Naulty	.15
430	Otis Nixon	.15
431	Alex Ochoa	.15
432	David Ortiz	.15
433	Brad Radke	.15
434	Todd Ritchie	.15
435	Frank Rodriguez	.15
436	Terry Steinbach	.15
437	Greg Swindell	.15
438	Bob Tewksbury	.15
439	Mike Trombley	.15
440	Javier Valentin	.15
441	Todd Walker	.40
442	Paul Molitor	.75
443	Shane Andrews	.15
444	Miguel Batista	.15
445	Shayne Bennett	.15
446	Rick DeHart	.15
447	Brad Fullmer	.40
448	Mark Grudzielanek	.15
449	Vladimir Guerrero	1.25
450	Dustin Hermanson	.15
451	Steve Kline	.15
452	Scott Livingstone	.15
453	Mike Maddux	.15
454	Derrick May	.15
455	Ryan McGuire	.15
456	Trey Moore	.15
457	Mike Mordecai	.15
458	Carl Pavano	.15
459	Carlos Perez	.15
460	F.P. Santangelo	.15
461	DaRond Stovall	.15
462	Anthony Telford	.15
463	Ugueth Urbina	.15
464	Marc Valdes	.15
465	Jose Vidro	.15
466	Rondell White	.25
467	Chris Widger	.15
468	Vladimir Guerrero	1.25
469	Edgardo Alfonzo	.20
470	Carlos Baerga	.15
471	Rich Becker	.15
472	Brian Bohanon	.15
473	Alberto Castillo	.15
474	Dennis Cook	.15
475	John Franco	.15
476	Matt Franco	.15
477	Bernard Gilkey	.15
478	John Hudek	.15
479	Butch Huskey	.15
480	Bobby Jones	.15
481	Al Leiter	.25
482	Luis Lopez	.15
483	Brian McRae	.15
484	Dave Mlicki	.15
485	John Olerud	.25
486	Rey Ordonez	.20
487	Craig Paquette	.15
488	Mike Piazza	2.50
489	Todd Pratt	.15
490	Mel Rojas	.15
491	Tim Spehr	.15
492	Turk Wendell	.15
493	*Masato Yoshii*	.40
494	Mike Piazza	2.50
495	Willie Banks	.15
496	Scott Brosius	.15
497	Mike Buddie	.15
498	Homer Bush	.15
499	David Cone	.20
500	Chad Curtis	.15
501	Chili Davis	.15
502	Joe Girardi	.15
503	Darren Holmes	.15
504	Hideki Irabu	.40
505	Derek Jeter	2.50
506	Chuck Knoblauch	.50
507	Graeme Lloyd	.15
508	Tino Martinez	.40
509	Ramiro Mendoza	.15
510	Jeff Nelson	.15
511	Paul O'Neill	.40
512	Andy Pettitte	.60
513	Jorge Posada	.25
514	Tim Raines	.15
515	Mariano Rivera	.25
516	Luis Sojo	.15
517	Mike Stanton	.15
518	Darryl Strawberry	.25
519	Dale Sveum	.15
520	David Wells	.20
521	Bernie Williams	.75
522	Bernie Williams	.40
523	Kurt Abbott	.15
524	Mike Blowers	.15
525	Rafael Bournigal	.15
526	Tom Candiotti	.15
527	Ryan Christenson	.15
528	Mike Fetters	.15
529	Jason Giambi	.15
530	Ben Grieve	1.25
531	Buddy Groom	.15
532	Jimmy Haynes	.15
533	Rickey Henderson	.25
534	A.J. Hinch	.15
535	Mike Macfarlane	.15
536	Dave Magadan	.15
537	T.J. Mathews	.15
538	Jason McDonald	.15
539	Kevin Mitchell	.15
540	Mike Mohler	.15
541	Mike Oquist	.15
542	Ariel Prieto	.15
543	Kenny Rogers	.15
544	Aaron Small	.15
545	Scott Spiezio	.15
546	Matt Stairs	.15
547	Bill Taylor	.15
548	Dave Telgheder	.15
549	Jack Voigt	.15
550	Ben Grieve	1.25
551	Bob Abreu	.15
552	Ruben Amaro	.15
553	Alex Arias	.15
554	Matt Beech	.15
555	Ricky Bottalico	.15
556	Billy Brewer	.15
557	Rico Brogna	.15
558	Doug Glanville	.15
559	Wayne Gomes	.15
560	Mike Grace	.15
561	Tyler Green	.15
562	Rex Hudler	.15
563	Gregg Jefferies	.15
564	Kevin Jordan	.15
565	Mark Leiter	.15
566	Mark Lewis	.15
567	Mike Lieberthal	.15
568	Mark Parent	.15
569	Yorkis Perez	.15
570	Desi Relaford	.15
571	Scott Rolen	1.25
572	Curt Schilling	.25
573	Kevin Sefcik	.15
574	Jerry Spradlin	.15
575	Garrett Stephenson	.15
576	Darrin Winston	.15
577	Scott Rolen	1.25
578	Jermaine Allensworth	.15
579	Jason Christiansen	.15
580	Lou Collier	.15
581	Francisco Cordova	.15
582	Elmer Dessens	.15
583	Freddy Garcia	.15
584	Jose Guillen	.25
585	Jason Kendall	.15
586	Jon Lieber	.15
587	Esteban Loaiza	.15
588	Al Martin	.15
589	Javier Martinez	.15
590	*Chris Peters*	.15
591	Kevin Polcovich	.15
592	Ricardo Rincon	.15
593	Jason Schmidt	.15
594	Jose Silva	.15
595	Mark Smith	.15
596	Doug Strange	.15
597	Turner Ward	.15
598	Marc Wilkins	.15
599	Mike Williams	.15
600	Tony Womack	.15
601	Kevin Young	.15
602	Tony Womack	.15
603	Manny Aybar	.25
604	Kent Bottenfield	.15
605	Jeff Brantley	.15
606	Mike Busby	.15
607	Royce Clayton	.15
608	Delino DeShields	.15
609	John Frascatore	.15
610	Gary Gaetti	.15
611	Ron Gant	.15
612	David Howard	.15
613	Brian Hunter	.15
614	Brian Jordan	.15
615	Tom Lampkin	.15
616	Ray Lankford	.15
617	Braden Looper	.15
618	John Mabry	.15
619	Eli Marrero	.15
620	Willie McGee	.15
621	Mark McGwire	4.00
622	Kent Mercker	.15
623	Matt Morris	.15
624	Donovan Osborne	.15
625	Tom Pagnozzi	.15
626	Lance Painter	.15
627	Mark Petkovsek	.15
628	Todd Stottlemyre	.15
629	Mark McGwire	4.00
630	Andy Ashby	.15
631	Brian Boehringer	.15
632	Kevin Brown	.25
633	Ken Caminiti	.25
634	Steve Finley	.15
635	Ed Giovanola	.15
636	Chris Gomez	.15
637	Tony Gwynn	2.00
SAMPLE	Tony Gwynn (SAMPLE overprint on back)	3.00
638	Joey Hamilton	.15
639	Carlos Hernandez	.15
640	Sterling Hitchcock	.15
641	Trevor Hoffman	.15
642	Wally Joyner	.15
643	Dan Miceli	.15
644	James Mouton	.15
645	Greg Myers	.15
646	Carlos Reyes	.15
647	Andy Sheets	.15
648	Pete Smith	.15
649	Mark Sweeney	.15
650	Greg Vaughn	.20
651	Quilvio Veras	.15
652	Tony Gwynn	2.00
653	Rich Aurilla	.15
654	Marvin Benard	.15
655	Barry Bonds	1.00
656	Danny Darwin	.15
657	Shawn Estes	.15
658	Mark Gardner	.15
659	Darryl Hamilton	.15
660	Charlie Hayes	.15
661	Orel Hershiser	.15
662	Stan Javier	.15
663	Brian Johnson	.15
664	John Johnstone	.15
665	Jeff Kent	.15
666	Brent Mayne	.15
667	Bill Mueller	.15
668	Robb Nen	.15
669	Jim Poole	.15
670	Steve Reed	.15
671	Rich Rodriguez	.15
672	Kirk Rueter	.15
673	Rey Sanchez	.15
674	J.T. Snow	.15
675	Julian Tavarez	.15
676	Barry Bonds	1.00
677	Rich Amaral	.15
678	Bobby Ayala	.15
679	Jay Buhner	.30
680	Ken Cloude	.15
681	Joey Cora	.15
682	Russ Davis	.15
683	Rob Ducey	.15
684	Jeff Fassero	.15
685	Tony Fossas	.15
686	Ken Griffey Jr.	4.00
687	Glenallen Hill	.15
688	Jeff Huson	.15
689	Randy Johnson	.75
690	Edgar Martinez	.15
691	John Marzano	.15
692	Jamie Moyer	.15
693	Alex Rodriguez	3.00
694	David Segui	.15
695	Heathcliff Slocumb	.15
696	Paul Spoljaric	.15
697	Bill Swift	.15
698	Mike Timlin	.15
699	Bob Wells	.15
700	Dan Wilson	.15
701	Ken Griffey Jr.	4.00
702	Wilson Alvarez	.15
703	*Rolando Arrojo*	.75
704	Wade Boggs	.30
705	Rich Butler	.15
706	Miguel Cairo	.15
707	Mike Difelice	.15
708	John Flaherty	.15
709	Roberto Hernandez	.15
710	Mike Kelly	.15
711	Aaron Ledesma	.15
712	Albie Lopez	.15
713	Dave Martinez	.15
714	Quinton McCracken	.15
715	Fred McGriff	.25
716	Jim Mecir	.15
717	Tony Saunders	.15
718	Bobby Smith	.15
719	Paul Sorrento	.15
720	Dennis Springer	.15
721	Kevin Stocker	.15
722	Ramon Tatis	.15
723	Bubba Trammell	.15
724	Esteban Yan	.15
725	Wade Boggs	.30
726	Luis Alicea	.15
727	Scott Bailes	.15
728	John Burkett	.15
729	Domingo Cedeno	.15
730	Will Clark	.40
731	Kevin Elster	.15
732	Juan Gonzalez	2.00
733	Tom Goodwin	.15
734	Rusty Greer	.15
735	Eric Gunderson	.15
736	Bill Haselman	.15
737	Rick Helling	.15
738	Roberto Kelly	.15
739	Mark McLemore	.15
740	Darren Oliver	.15
741	Danny Patterson	.15
742	Roger Pavlik	.15
743	Ivan Rodriguez	1.00
744	Aaron Sele	.15
745	Mike Simms	.15
746	Lee Stevens	.15
747	Fernando Tatis	.25
748	John Wetteland	.15
749	Bobby Witt	.15
750	Juan Gonzalez	2.00
751	Carlos Almanzar	.15
752	Kevin Brown	.25
753	Jose Canseco	.40
754	Chris Carpenter	.15
755	Roger Clemens	1.50
756	Felipe Crespo	.15
757	Jose Cruz Jr.	.15
758	Mark Dalesandro	.15
759	Carlos Delgado	.40
760	Kelvim Escobar	.15
761	Tony Fernandez	.15
762	Darrin Fletcher	.15
763	Alex Gonzalez	.15
764	Craig Grebeck	.15
765	Shawn Green	.25
766	Juan Guzman	.15
767	Erik Hanson	.15
768	Pat Hentgen	.15
769	Randy Myers	.15
770	Robert Person	.15
771	Dan Plesac	.15
772	Paul Quantrill	.15
773	Bill Risley	.15
774	Juan Samuel	.15
775	Steve Sinclair	.15
776	Ed Sprague	.15
777	Mike Stanley	.15
778	Shannon Stewart	.15
779	Woody Williams	.15
780	Roger Clemens	1.50

1998 Pacific Online Web Cards

This 800-card parallel set allowed collectors to use Pacific's web site to find out the prize they had won. The cards used gold foil on the front instead of the silver foil used on base cards, and contained an eight-digit code on the back that was the claim number. These were inserted one per pack in Online Baseball.

Web Stars: 3X
Young Stars/RCs: 2X
Inserted 1:1
(See 1998 Pacific Online for checklist and base card values.)

1998 Pacific Paramount

Paramount was Pacific's first fully-licensed baseball card product. The 250 base cards feature full-bleed photos with the player's name and team listed at the bottom. The base set is paralleled three times. Gold retail (1:1), Copper hobby (1:1) and Platinum Blue (1:73) versions were included. Inserts in the product are Special Delivery Die-Cuts, Team Checklist Die-Cuts,

Cooperstown Bound, Fielder's Choice Laser-Cuts and Inaugural Issue.

		MT
Complete Set (250):		20.00
Common Player:		.10
Wax Box:		48.00
1	Garret Anderson	.10
2	Gary DiSarcina	.10
3	Jim Edmonds	.15
4	Darin Erstad	.50
5	Cecil Fielder	.10
6	Chuck Finley	.10
7	Todd Greene	.15
8	Shigetosi Hasegawa	.10
9	Tim Salmon	.30
10	Roberto Alomar	.50
11	Brady Anderson	.15
12	Joe Carter	.15
13	Eric Davis	.10
14	Ozzie Guillen	.10
15	Mike Mussina	.50
16	Rafael Palmeiro	.30
17	Cal Ripken Jr.	2.00
18	B.J. Surhoff	.10
19	Steve Avery	.10
20	Nomar Garciaparra	1.50
21	Reggie Jefferson	.10
22	Pedro Martinez	.25
23	Tim Naehring	.10
24	John Valentin	.10
25	Mo Vaughn	.60
26	James Baldwin	.10
27	Albert Belle	.60
28	Ray Durham	.10
29	Benji Gil	.10
30	Jaime Navarro	.10
31	*Magglio Ordonez*	1.00
32	Frank Thomas	1.25
33	Robin Ventura	.20
34	Sandy Alomar Jr.	.20
35	Geronimo Berroa	.10
36	Travis Fryman	.10
37	David Justice	.25
38	Kenny Lofton	.60
39	Charles Nagy	.10
40	Manny Ramirez	.75
41	Jim Thome	.25
42	Omar Vizquel	.10
43	Jaret Wright	.75
44	Raul Casanova	.10
45	*Frank Catalanotto*	.20
46	Tony Clark	.25
47	Bobby Higginson	.10
48	Brian Hunter	.10
49	Todd Jones	.10
50	Bip Roberts	.10
51	Justin Thompson	.10
52	Kevin Appier	.10
53	Johnny Damon	.10
54	Jermaine Dye	.10
55	Jeff King	.10
56	Jeff Montgomery	.10
57	Dean Palmer	.10
58	Jose Rosado	.10
59	Larry Sutton	.10
60	Rick Aguilera	.10
61	Marty Cordova	.10
62	Pat Meares	.10
63	Paul Molitor	.40
64	Otis Nixon	.10
65	Brad Radke	.10
66	Terry Steinbach	.10
67	Todd Walker	.25
68	Hideki Irabu	.25
69	Derek Jeter	1.50
70	Chuck Knoblauch	.30
71	Tino Martinez	.25
72	Paul O'Neill	.20
73	Andy Pettitte	.25
74	Mariano Rivera	.25
75	Bernie Williams	.35
76	Mark Bellhorn	.10
77	Tom Candiotti	.10
78	Jason Giambi	.10
79	Ben Grieve	1.00
80	Rickey Henderson	.20
81	Jason McDonald	.10
82	Aaron Small	.10
83	Miguel Tejada	.10
84	Jay Buhner	.15
85	Joey Cora	.10
86	Jeff Fassero	.10
87	Ken Griffey Jr.	3.00
88	Randy Johnson	.40
89	Edgar Martinez	.10
90	Alex Rodriguez	2.00
91	David Segui	.10
92	Dan Wilson	.10
93	Wilson Alvarez	.10
94	Wade Boggs	.25
95	Miguel Cairo	.10
96	John Flaherty	.10
97	Dave Martinez	.10
98	Quinton McCracken	.10
99	Fred McGriff	.25
100	Paul Sorrento	.10
101	Kevin Stocker	.10
102	John Burkett	.10
103	Will Clark	.25
104	Juan Gonzalez	1.25
105	Rusty Greer	.10
106	Roberto Kelly	.10
107	Ivan Rodriguez	.60
108	Fernando Tatis	.15
109	John Wetteland	.10
110	Jose Canseco	.25
111	Roger Clemens	1.00
112	Jose Cruz Jr.	.20
113	Carlos Delgado	.20
114	Alex Gonzalez	.10
115	Pat Hentgen	.10
116	Ed Sprague	.10
117	Shannon Stewart	.10
118	Brian Anderson	.10
119	Jay Bell	.10
120	Andy Benes	.15
121	Yamil Benitez	.10
122	Jorge Fabregas	.10
123	Travis Lee	.75
124	Devon White	.10
125	Matt Williams	.25
126	Bob Wolcott	.10
127	Andres Galarraga	.25
128	Tom Glavine	.20
129	Andruw Jones	.60
130	Chipper Jones	1.50
131	Ryan Klesko	.25
132	Javy Lopez	.15
133	Greg Maddux	1.50
134	Denny Neagle	.10
135	John Smoltz	.20
136	Rod Beck	.10
137	Jeff Blauser	.10
138	Mark Grace	.25
139	Lance Johnson	.10
140	Mickey Morandini	.10
141	Kevin Orie	.10
142	Sammy Sosa	1.50
143	Aaron Boone	.10
144	Bret Boone	.10
145	Dave Burba	.10
146	Lenny Harris	.10
147	Barry Larkin	.15
148	Reggie Sanders	.10
149	Brett Tomko	.10
150	Pedro Astacio	.10
151	Dante Bichette	.20
152	Ellis Burks	.10
153	Vinny Castilla	.20
154	Todd Helton	.50
155	Darryl Kile	.10
156	Jeff Reed	.10
157	Larry Walker	.30
158	Bobby Bonilla	.10
159	Todd Dunwoody	.15
160	Livan Hernandez	.15
161	Charles Johnson	.15
162	Mark Kotsay	.35
163	Derrek Lee	.10
164	Edgar Renteria	.15
165	Gary Sheffield	.30
166	Moises Alou	.20
167	Jeff Bagwell	1.00
168	Derek Bell	.10
169	Craig Biggio	.20
170	Mike Hampton	.10
171	Richard Hidalgo	.10
172	Chris Holt	.10
173	Shane Reynolds	.10
174	Wilton Guerrero	.10
175	Eric Karros	.15
176	Paul Konerko	.25
177	Ramon Martinez	.20
178	Raul Mondesi	.25
179	Hideo Nomo	.40
180	Chan Ho Park	.20
181	Mike Piazza	1.50
182	Ismael Valdes	.10
183	Jeromy Burnitz	.10
184	Jeff Cirillo	.10
185	Todd Dunn	.10
186	Marquis Grissom	.10
187	John Jaha	.10
188	Doug Jones	.10
189	Dave Nilsson	.10
190	Jose Valentin	.10
191	Fernando Vina	.10
192	Orlando Cabrera	.10
193	Steve Falteisek	.10
194	Mark Grudzielanek	.10
195	Vladimir Guerrero	.50
196	Carlos Perez	.10
197	F.P. Santangelo	.10
198	Jose Vidro	.10
199	Rondell White	.20
200	Edgardo Alfonzo	.15
201	Carlos Baerga	.10
202	John Franco	.10
203	Bernard Gilkey	.10
204	Todd Hundley	.20
205	Butch Huskey	.10
206	Bobby Jones	.10
207	Brian McRae	.10
208	John Olerud	.20
209	Rey Ordonez	.15
210	Ricky Bottalico	.10
211	Bobby Estalella	.10
212	Doug Glanville	.10
213	Gregg Jefferies	.10
214	Mike Lieberthal	.10
215	Desi Relaford	.10
216	Scott Rolen	.75
217	Curt Schilling	.25
218	Adrian Brown	.10
219	Emil Brown	.10
220	Francisco Cordova	.10
221	Jose Guillen	.40
222	Al Martin	.10
223	Abraham Nunez	.10
224	Tony Womack	.10
225	Kevin Young	.10
226	Alan Benes	.15
227	Royce Clayton	.10
228	Gary Gaetti	.10
229	Ron Gant	.10
230	Brian Jordan	.10
231	Ray Lankford	.10
232	Mark McGwire	3.00
233	Todd Stottlemyre	.10
234	Kevin Brown	.20
235	Ken Caminiti	.20
236	Steve Finley	.10
237	Tony Gwynn	1.25
238	Wally Joyner	.10
239	Ruben Rivera	.10
240	Greg Vaughn	.15
241	Quilvio Veras	.10
242	Barry Bonds	.60
243	Jacob Cruz	.10
244	Shawn Estes	.10
245	Orel Hershiser	.10
246	Stan Javier	.10
247	Brian Johnson	.10
248	Jeff Kent	.10
249	Robb Nen	.10
250	J.T. Snow	.10

1998 Pacific Paramount Gold/ Copper/Red

Gold, Copper and Red foil versions of all 250 cards in Paramount were reprinted and inserted at a rate of one per pack. Gold versions were retail exclusive, Copper versions were hobby exclusive and Red versions were ANCO pack exclusive. The only difference is these parallels use a different color foil than the base cards.

	MT
Common Gold/Copper Player:	.25
Gold/Copper Stars: 2X	
Inserted 1:1	
Common Red Player:	.30
Red Stars: 3X	
Inserted 1:ANCO pack	

(See 1998 Pacific Paramount for checklist and base card values.)

1998 Pacific Paramount Holographic Silver

Holographics Silver parallel cards were issued for all 250 cards in the Paramount set. These were inserted into hobby packs, while only 99 sets were produced.

	MT
Common Player:	5.00
Holographic Silver Stars: 40-60X	
Production 99 sets	

(See 1998 Pacific Paramount for checklist and base card values.)

1998 Pacific Paramount Platinum Blue

This paralled set reprinted all 250 cards in Paramount using blue foil stamping on the card front. These were inserted one per 73 packs.

	MT
Common Platinum Blue Player:	3.00
Platinum Blue Stars: 15-30X	
Inserted 1:73	

(See 1998 Pacific Paramount for checklist and base card values.)

1998 Pacific Paramount Cooperstown Bound

Cooperstown Bound is a 10-card insert seeded one per 361 packs. Each card features a color player photo with a silver foil column on the left. The cards are fully foiled and etched.

		MT
Complete Set (10):		450.00
Common Player:		15.00
Pacific Proofs: 6X		
Production 20 sets		
1	Greg Maddux	60.00
2	Cal Ripken Jr.	80.00
3	Frank Thomas	40.00
4	Mike Piazza	60.00
5	Paul Molitor	20.00
6	Mark McGwire	100.00
7	Tony Gwynn	50.00
8	Barry Bonds	25.00
9	Ken Griffey Jr.	100.00
10	Wade Boggs	15.00

1998 Pacific Paramount Fielder's Choice

Fielder's Choice Laser-Cuts is a 20-card insert seeded one per 73 packs. Each card is die-cut around a baseball glove that appears in the background. The webbing of the glove is laser-cut.

		MT
Complete Set (20):		400.00
Common Player:		5.00
1	Chipper Jones	30.00
2	Greg Maddux	30.00
3	Cal Ripken Jr.	40.00
4	Nomar Garciaparra	30.00
5	Frank Thomas	25.00
6	David Justice	5.00
7	Larry Walker	7.50
8	Jeff Bagwell	20.00
9	Hideo Nomo	5.00
10	Mike Piazza	30.00
11	Derek Jeter	30.00
12	Ben Grieve	15.00
13	Mark McGwire	50.00
14	Tony Gwynn	25.00
15	Barry Bonds	15.00
16	Ken Griffey Jr.	50.00
17	Alex Rodriguez	40.00
18	Wade Boggs	6.00
19	Ivan Rodriguez	15.00
20	Jose Cruz Jr.	5.00

1998 Pacific Paramount Inaugural Issue

A special edition of Pacific's premiere Paramount issue was created to mark the new brand's introduction on May 27 at the debut SportsFest '98 show in Philadelphia. Each of the cards from the Paramount issue was printed with a gold-foil "INAUGURAL ISSUE May 27, 1998" logo, and was embossed with Pacific and SportsFest logos at center and hand-numbered at bottom from within an edition of just 20 cards each.

	MT
Common Player:	6.00

(Stars and rookies valued at 50-75X regular Paramount version.)

1998 Pacific Paramount Special Delivery

Special Delivery cards are die-cut to resemble a postage stamp. Each card front is foiled and etched and features three photos of the player. Special Delivery is a 20-card insert seeded one per 37 packs.

		MT
Complete Set (20):		150.00
Common Player:		1.50
1	Chipper Jones	10.00
2	Greg Maddux	10.00
3	Cal Ripken Jr.	12.50
4	Nomar Garciaparra	10.00
5	Pedro Martinez	3.00
6	Frank Thomas	7.50
7	David Justice	2.00
8	Larry Walker	2.50
9	Jeff Bagwell	6.00
10	Hideo Nomo	2.00
11	Mike Piazza	10.00
12	Vladimir Guerrero	5.00
13	Derek Jeter	10.00
14	Ben Grieve	5.00
15	Mark McGwire	15.00
16	Tony Gwynn	7.50
17	Barry Bonds	4.00
18	Ken Griffey Jr.	15.00
19	Alex Rodriguez	12.50
20	Jose Cruz Jr.	1.50

1998 Pacific Paramount Team Checklist

Team Checklists (30 cards, 2:37) feature a player photo surrounded by two bats. The card is die-cut around the photo and the bats at the top. The bottom has the player's name, position and team.

		MT
Complete Set (30):		150.00
Common Player:		1.50
1	Tim Salmon	3.00
2	Cal Ripken Jr.	15.00
3	Nomar Garciaparra	12.00
4	Frank Thomas	10.00
5	Manny Ramirez	7.50
6	Tony Clark	4.00
7	Dean Palmer	1.50
8	Paul Molitor	4.00
9	Derek Jeter	12.00
10	Ben Grieve	8.00
11	Ken Griffey Jr.	25.00
12	Wade Boggs	2.50
13	Ivan Rodriguez	6.00
14	Roger Clemens	8.00
15	Matt Williams	2.50
16	Chipper Jones	12.00
17	Sammy Sosa	10.00
18	Barry Larkin	2.00
19	Larry Walker	3.00
20	Livan Hernandez	1.50
21	Jeff Bagwell	8.00
22	Mike Piazza	12.00
23	John Jaha	1.50
24	Vladimir Guerrero	5.00
25	Todd Hundley	1.50
26	Scott Rolen	8.00
27	Kevin Young	1.50
28	Mark McGwire	25.00
29	Tony Gwynn	10.00
30	Barry Bonds	5.00

1998 Pacific Revolution

Pacific Revolution Baseball consists of a 150-card base set. The base cards are dual-foiled, etched and embossed. Inserts include Showstoppers, Prime Time Performers Laser-Cuts, Foul Pole Laser-Cuts, Major League Icons and Shadow Series.

		MT
Complete Set (150):		90.00
Common Player:		.40
Wax Box:		80.00
1	Garret Anderson	.40
2	Jim Edmonds	.40
3	Darin Erstad	1.50
4	Chuck Finley	.40
5	Tim Salmon	1.00
6	Jay Bell	.40
7	Travis Lee	2.00
8	Devon White	.40
9	Matt Williams	1.00
10	Andres Galarraga	1.00
11	Tom Glavine	.60
12	Andruw Jones	2.50
13	Chipper Jones	6.00
14	Ryan Klesko	.50
15	Javy Lopez	.60
16	Greg Maddux	6.00
17	Walt Weiss	.40
18	Roberto Alomar	2.00
19	Joe Carter	.60
20	Mike Mussina	2.00
21	Rafael Palmeiro	1.00
22	Cal Ripken Jr.	8.00
23	B.J. Surhoff	.40
24	Nomar Garciaparra	6.00
25	Reggie Jefferson	.40
26	Pedro Martinez	2.00
27	Troy O'Leary	.40
28	Mo Vaughn	1.50
29	Mark Grace	1.00
30	Mickey Morandini	.40
31	Henry Rodriguez	.40
32	Sammy Sosa	5.00
33	Kerry Wood	2.50
34	Albert Belle	2.50
35	Ray Durham	.40
36	*Magglio Ordonez*	4.00
37	Frank Thomas	5.00
38	Robin Ventura	.60
39	Bret Boone	.40
40	Barry Larkin	.60
41	Reggie Sanders	.40
42	Brett Tomko	.40
43	Sandy Alomar	.60
44	David Justice	.75
45	Kenny Lofton	1.50
46	Manny Ramirez	4.00
47	Jim Thome	1.50
48	Omar Vizquel	.40
49	Jaret Wright	1.50
50	Dante Bichette	.75
51	Ellis Burks	.40
52	Vinny Castilla	.40
53	Todd Helton	2.50
54	Larry Walker	1.50
55	Tony Clark	1.00
56	Deivi Cruz	.40
57	Damion Easley	.40
58	Bobby Higginson	.40
59	Brian Hunter	.40
60	Cliff Floyd	.40
61	Livan Hernandez	.40
62	Derrek Lee	.40
63	Edgar Renteria	.50
64	Moises Alou	.75
65	Jeff Bagwell	3.00
66	Derek Bell	.40
67	Craig Biggio	.75
68	Richard Hidalgo	.40
69	Johnny Damon	.40
70	Jeff King	.40
71	Hal Morris	.40
72	Dean Palmer	.40
73	Bobby Bonilla	.40
74	Charles Johnson	.40
75	Paul Konerko	.75
76	Raul Mondesi	.75
77	Gary Sheffield	1.00
78	Jeromy Burnitz	.40
79	Marquis Grissom	.40
80	Dave Nilsson	.40
81	Fernando Vina	.40
82	Marty Cordova	.40
83	Pat Meares	.40
84	Paul Molitor	2.00
85	Brad Radke	.40
86	Terry Steinbach	.40
87	Todd Walker	.75
88	Brad Fullmer	.75
89	Vladimir Guerrero	2.50
90	Carl Pavano	.40
91	Rondell White	.75
92	Bernard Gilkey	.40
93	Hideo Nomo	1.00
94	John Olerud	.75
95	Rey Ordonez	.50
96	Mike Piazza	6.00
97	*Masato Yoshii*	1.50
98	Hideki Irabu	1.00
99	Derek Jeter	6.00
100	Chuck Knoblauch	1.00
101	Tino Martinez	.75
102	Paul O'Neill	.75
103	Darryl Strawberry	.60
104	Bernie Williams	1.50
105	Jason Giambi	.40
106	Ben Grieve	3.00
107	Rickey Henderson	.75
108	Matt Stairs	.40
109	Doug Glanville	.40
110	Desi Relaford	.40
111	Scott Rolen	3.00
112	Curt Schilling	.75
113	Jason Kendall	.75
114	Al Martin	.40
115	Jason Schmidt	.40
116	Kevin Young	.40
117	Delino DeShields	.40
118	Gary Gaetti	.40
119	Brian Jordan	.40
120	Ray Lankford	.40
121	Mark McGwire	12.00
122	Kevin Brown	.60
123	Steve Finley	.40
124	Tony Gwynn	5.00
125	Wally Joyner	.40
126	Greg Vaughn	.50
127	Barry Bonds	2.50
128	Orel Hershiser	.40
129	Jeff Kent	.40
130	Bill Mueller	.40
131	Jay Buhner	.75
132	Ken Griffey Jr.	12.00
133	Randy Johnson	2.00
134	Edgar Martinez	.40
135	Alex Rodriguez	8.00
136	David Segui	.40
137	*Rolando Arrojo*	3.00
138	Wade Boggs	.75
139	Quinton McCracken	.40
140	Fred McGriff	.60
141	Will Clark	.75
142	Juan Gonzalez	5.00
143	Tom Goodwin	.40
144	Ivan Rodriguez	2.50
145	Aaron Sele	.40
146	John Wetteland	.40
147	Jose Canseco	1.00
148	Roger Clemens	3.00
149	Jose Cruz Jr.	.50
150	Carlos Delgado	.75

1998 Pacific Revolution Shadows

Shadows is a full parallel of the Revolution base set. Limited to 99 sequentially numbered sets, each card is embossed with a special "Shadow Series" stamp.

	MT
Common Player:	5.00
Veteran Stars: 12X	
Young Stars: 8X	

(See 1998 Pacific Revolution for checklist and base card values.)

1998 Pacific Revolution Foul Pole

Foul Pole Laser-Cuts is a 20-card insert seeded one per 49 packs. Each card features a color player photo on the left and a foul pole on the right. The foul pole design includes netting that is laser cut.

		MT
Complete Set (20):		350.00
Common Player:		6.00
1	Cal Ripken Jr.	35.00
2	Nomar Garciaparra	30.00
3	Mo Vaughn	12.00
4	Frank Thomas	20.00
5	Manny Ramirez	15.00
6	Bernie Williams	8.00
7	Ben Grieve	15.00
8	Ken Griffey Jr.	50.00
9	Alex Rodriguez	35.00
10	Juan Gonzalez	25.00
11	Ivan Rodriguez	12.00
12	Travis Lee	10.00
13	Chipper Jones	30.00
14	Sammy Sosa	25.00
15	Vinny Castilla	6.00
16	Moises Alou	6.00
17	Gary Sheffield	6.00
18	Mike Piazza	30.00
19	Mark McGwire	50.00
20	Barry Bonds	12.00

Player names in *Italic* type indicate a rookie card.

1998 Pacific Revolution Major League Icons

Major League Icons is a 10-card insert seeded one per 121 packs. Each card features a player photo on a die-cut shield, with the shield on a flaming stand.

		MT
Complete Set (10):		400.00
Common Player:		20.00
1	Cal Ripken Jr.	50.00
2	Nomar Garciaparra	40.00
3	Frank Thomas	25.00
4	Ken Griffey Jr.	75.00
5	Alex Rodriguez	50.00
6	Chipper Jones	40.00
7	Kerry Wood	20.00
8	Mike Piazza	40.00
9	Mark McGwire	75.00
10	Tony Gwynn	30.00

1998 Pacific Revolution Prime Time Performers

Prime Time Performers is a 20-card insert seeded one per 25 packs. The cards are designed like a TV program guide with the team logo laser-cut on the TV screen. The color player photo is located on the left.

		MT
Complete Set (20):		250.00
Common Player:		4.00
1	Cal Ripken Jr.	20.00
2	Nomar Garciaparra	17.50
3	Frank Thomas	12.50
4	Jim Thome	4.00
5	Hideki Irabu	4.00
6	Derek Jeter	17.50
7	Ben Grieve	7.50
8	Ken Griffey Jr.	25.00
9	Alex Rodriguez	20.00
10	Juan Gonzalez	15.00
11	Ivan Rodriguez	7.50
12	Travis Lee	5.00
13	Chipper Jones	17.50
14	Greg Maddux	17.50
15	Kerry Wood	5.00
16	Larry Walker	4.00
17	Jeff Bagwell	10.00
18	Mike Piazza	17.50
19	Mark McGwire	25.00
20	Tony Gwynn	15.00

1998 Pacific Revolution Rookies and Hardball Heroes

This hobby-only insert combines 20 hot prospects with 10 veteran stars. Horizontal cards have action photos on a flashy metallic-foil background. A portrait photo is on back. The first 20 cards in the set, the youngsters, are paralleled in a gold edition which was limited to just 50 cards of each.

		MT
Complete Set (30):		100.00
Common Player:		.50
Inserted 1:6		
Gold (1-20): 15X		
Production 50 sets		
1	Justin Baughman	.50
2	Jarrod Washburn	.50
3	Travis Lee	4.00
4	Kerry Wood	8.00
5	Magglio Ordonez	2.00
6	Todd Helton	2.50
7	Derrek Lee	1.50
8	Richard Hidalgo	1.00
9	Mike Caruso	1.00
10	David Ortiz	1.00
11	Brad Fullmer	2.00
12	Masato Yoshii	1.00
13	Orlando Hernandez	8.00
14	Ricky Ledee	1.00
15	Ben Grieve	5.00
16	Carlton Loewer	.50
17	Desi Relaford	.50
18	Ruben Rivera	.50
19	Rolando Arrojo	3.00
20	Matt Perisho	.50
21	Chipper Jones	8.00
22	Greg Maddux	8.00
23	Cal Ripken Jr.	10.00
24	Nomar Garciaparra	8.00
25	Frank Thomas	6.00
26	Mark McGwire	15.00
27	Tony Gwynn	6.00
28	Ken Griffey Jr.	15.00
29	Alex Rodriguez	10.00
30	Juan Gonzalez	6.00

1998 Pacific Revolution Showstoppers

This 36-card insert was seeded two per 25 packs. The cards feature holographic foil. The color photo is centered above the team logo and the Showstoppers logo.

		MT
Complete Set (36):		275.00
Common Player:		2.00
1	Cal Ripken Jr.	20.00
2	Nomar Garciaparra	15.00
3	Pedro Martinez	5.00
4	Mo Vaughn	4.00
5	Frank Thomas	10.00
6	Manny Ramirez	9.00
7	Jim Thome	4.00
8	Jaret Wright	4.00
9	Paul Molitor	6.00
10	Orlando Hernandez	12.00
11	Derek Jeter	15.00
12	Bernie Williams	3.00
13	Ben Grieve	7.50
14	Ken Griffey Jr.	25.00
15	Alex Rodriguez	20.00
16	Wade Boggs	3.00
17	Juan Gonzalez	12.00
18	Ivan Rodriguez	6.00
19	Jose Canseco	4.00
20	Roger Clemens	10.00
21	Travis Lee	5.00
22	Andres Galarraga	3.00
23	Chipper Jones	15.00
24	Greg Maddux	15.00
25	Sammy Sosa	12.00
26	Kerry Wood	6.00
27	Vinny Castilla	2.00
28	Larry Walker	4.00
29	Moises Alou	2.00
30	Raul Mondesi	3.00
31	Gary Sheffield	3.00
32	Hideo Nomo	3.00
33	Mike Piazza	15.00
34	Mark McGwire	25.00
35	Tony Gwynn	12.00
36	Barry Bonds	6.00

1998 Pacific Home Run Heroes

This retail exclusive product was sold as a complete set sealed in a tin lithographed can. The 2-1/2" x 3-1/2" cards have color action photos on front of the players in the followthrough of their home run swing. The figures are set on an artificial background which includes a sign giving the date and distance of their final home run of the 1998 season. Their team logo is in the "turf" at their feet. Fronts are highlighted with gold foil. On back are a portrait photo, a season summary and 1998 stats, along with appropriate licensor and manufacturer logos.

		MT
Complete Set (6):		5.00
Common Player:		.50
1	Mark McGwire	2.00
2	Sammy Sosa	1.00
3	Ken Griffey Jr.	2.00
4	Greg Vaughn	.50
5	Albert Belle	.50
6	Jose Canseco	.50

1998 Pacific Mariners Baseball Card Calendar

For an April 3 stadium promotion in which calendars were given away to 20,000 fans, Pacific Trading Cards produced a 12-month calendar featuring enlarged pictures of several types of its Mariners' trading cards. The calendar pad beneath each card picture has a team schedule and color advertising for one or more of the team's sponsors. The calendar pages are each 11" x 8-1/2". Titled "You Gotta Love These Guys," the cover has a model of the team's future domed stadium and action photos of five players.

	MT
Complete Calendar:	12.00
4/98 Rich Amaral	
5/98 Jeff Fassero, Randy Johnson, Jamie Moyer	
6/98 Joey Cora	
7/98 Bobby Ayala, Heathcliff Slocumb, Mike Timlin	
8/98 Edgar Martinez	
9/98 Jay Buhner	
10/98Ken Griffey Jr.	
11/98Russ Davis	
12/98David Segui	
1/99 Lou Piniella	
2/99 Alex Rodriguez	
3/99 Dan Wilson	

1998 Pacific National Convention Redemption

This card of Pacific spokesman Tony Gwynn was given away at the card company's booth in a redemption program during the 1998 National Sports Collectors Convention in August, 1998. The card front has a color photo of Gwynn on red and yellow rayed background. At lower-right is a gold-foil convention logo. Back has an action photo, copyright information and logos.

	MT
1998 Tony Gwynn	8.00

1998 Pacific Nestle's Latinos

Produced by Pacific this set of Latino ballplayers' cards was issued in three-card packs with the purchase of certain Nestle's food products in Los Angeles, Miami, Houston and San Antonio. Cards are found in two styles. Five of the cards have gold-foil graphic highlights on both top and bottom on front. On back the card number is in a white circle. The second style has foil only at bottom front and on back the card number is in a black circle. Both types have Pacific and Nestle logos on front and back.

		MT
Complete Set (20):		8.00
Common Player:		.25
	TYPE 1	
1	Ismael Valdes	.25
2	Juan Gonzalez	1.00
3	Ivan Rodriguez	.50
4	Joey Cora	.25
5	Livan Hernandez	.25
	TYPE 2	
1	Bernie Williams	.25
2	Tino Martinez	.25
3	Alex Rodriguez	1.50
4	Edgar Martinez	.25
5	Andres Galarraga	.35
6	Manny Ramirez	.50
7	Carlos Baerga	.25
8	Pedro Martinez	.25
9	Vinny Castilla	.30
10	Sammy Sosa	1.50
11	Nomar Garciaparra	.50
12	Javy Lopez	.45
13	Sandy Alomar	.25
14	Roberto Alomar	.35
15	Jose Canseco	.45

1999 Pacific Sample

This card of Pacific spokesman Tony Gwynn introduces the 1999 series. The sample card follows the format of the issued version but is overprinted "SAMPLE" on back and lacks Gwynn's 1998 season and career stats.

	MT
Tony Gwynn	3.00

1999 Pacific

The 450-card base set features full bleed fronts enhanced with silver foil stamping. Card backs have year-by-year statistics, a small photo and a brief career highlight caption. There are two parallels, Platinum Blues and Reds. Platinum Blues have blue foil stamping and are seeded 1:73 packs. Reds are retail exclusive with red foil stamping and are seeded one per retail pack.

		MT
Complete Set (500):		40.00
Common Player:		.10
Wax Box:		60.00
1	Garret Anderson	.10
2	Jason Dickson	.10
3	Gary DiSarcina	.10
4	Jim Edmonds	.20
5	Darin Erstad	.75
6	Chuck Finley	.10
7	Shigetosi Hasegawa	.10
8	Ken Hill	.10
9	Dave Hollins	.10
10	Phil Nevin	.10
11	Troy Percival	.10
12	Tim Salmon (action)	.25
12	Tim Salmon (portrait)	.25
13	Brian Anderson	.10
14	Tony Batista	.10
15	Jay Bell	.10
16	Andy Benes	.10
17	Yamil Benitez	.10
18	Omar Daal	.10
19	David Dellucci	.10
20	Karim Garcia	.15
21	Bernard Gilkey	.10
22	Travis Lee (action)	.60
22	Travis Lee (portrait)	.60
23	Aaron Small	.10
24	Kelly Stinnett	.10
25	Devon White	.10
26	Matt Williams	.25
27	Bruce Chen (action)	.15
27	Bruce Chen (portrait)	.15
28	Andres Galarraga (action)	.35
28	Andres Galarraga (portrait)	.35
29	Tom Glavine	.20
30	Ozzie Guillen	.10
31	Andruw Jones	.75
32	Chipper Jones (action)	2.00
32	Chipper Jones (portrait)	2.00
33	Ryan Klesko	.20
34	George Lombard	.10
35	Javy Lopez	.15
36	Greg Maddux (action)	2.00
36	Greg Maddux (portrait)	2.00
37	Marty Malloy (action)	.10
37	Marty Malloy (portrait)	.10
38	Dennis Martinez	.10
39	Kevin Millwood	.25
40	Alex Rodriguez (action)	2.50
40	Alex Rodriguez (portrait)	2.50
41	Denny Neagle	.10
42	John Smoltz	.20
43	Michael Tucker	.10
44	Walt Weiss	.10
45	Roberto Alomar (action)	.50
45	Roberto Alomar (portrait)	.50
46	Brady Anderson	.10
47	Harold Baines	.10
48	Mike Bordick	.10
49	Danny Clyburn (action)	.10
49	Danny Clyburn (portrait)	.10
50	Eric Davis	.10
51	Scott Erickson	.10
52	Chris Hoiles	.10
53	Jimmy Key	.10
54	Ryan Minor (action)	.40
54	Ryan Minor (portrait)	.40
55	Mike Mussina	.50
56	Jesse Orosco	.10
57	Rafael Palmeiro (action)	.25
57	Rafael Palmeiro (portrait)	.25
58	Sidney Ponson	.10
59	Arthur Rhodes	.10
60	Cal Ripken Jr. (action)	2.50
60	Cal Ripken Jr. (portrait)	2.50
61	B.J. Surhoff	.10
62	Steve Avery	.10
63	Darren Bragg	.10
64	Dennis Eckersley	.10
65	Nomar Garciaparra (action)	2.00
65	Nomar Garciaparra (portrait)	2.00
66	Sammy Sosa (action)	2.50
66	Sammy Sosa (portrait)	2.50
67	Tom Gordon	.10
68	Reggie Jefferson	.10
69	Darren Lewis	.10
70	Mark McGwire (action)	3.50
70	Mark McGwire (portrait)	3.50
71	Pedro Martinez	.50
72	Troy O'Leary	.10
73	Bret Saberhagen	.10
74	Mike Stanley	.10
75	John Valentin	.10
76	Jason Varitek	.10
77	Mo Vaughn	.60
78	Tim Wakefield	.10
79	Manny Alexander	.10
80	Rod Beck	.10
81	Brant Brown	.10
82	Mark Clark	.10
83	Gary Gaetti	.10
84	Mark Grace	.25
85	Jose Hernandez	.10
86	Lance Johnson	.10
87	Jason Maxwell (action)	.10
87	Jason Maxwell (portrait)	.10
88	Mickey Morandini	.10
89	Terry Mulholland	.10
90	Henry Rodriguez	.10
91	Scott Servais	.10
92	Kevin Tapani	.10
93	Pedro Valdes	.10
94	Kerry Wood	.75
95	Jeff Abbott	.10
96	James Baldwin	.10
97	Albert Belle	.75
98	Mike Cameron	.10
99	Mike Caruso	.10
100	Wil Cordero	.10
101	Ray Durham	.10
102	Jaime Navarro	.10
103	Greg Norton	.10
104	Magglio Ordonez	.20
105	Mike Sirotka	.10
106	Frank Thomas (action)	1.00
106	Frank Thomas (portrait)	1.00
107	Robin Ventura	.15
108	Craig Wilson	.10
109	Aaron Boone	.10
110	Bret Boone	.10
111	Sean Casey	.20
112	Pete Harnisch	.10
113	John Hudek	.10
114	Barry Larkin	.15
115	Eduardo Perez	.10
116	Mike Remlinger	.10
117	Reggie Sanders	.10
118	Chris Stynes	.10
119	Eddie Taubensee	.10
120	Brett Tomko	.10
121	Pat Watkins	.10
122	Dmitri Young	.10
123	Sandy Alomar Jr.	.15
124	Dave Burba	.10
125	Bartolo Colon	.15
126	Joey Cora	.10
127	Brian Giles	.10
128	Dwight Gooden	.10
129	Mike Jackson	.10
130	David Justice	.25
131	Kenny Lofton	.60
132	Charles Nagy	.10
133	Chad Ogea	.10
134	Manny Ramirez (action)	1.00
134	Manny Ramirez (portrait)	1.00
135	Richie Sexson	.20
136	Jim Thome (action)	.40
136	Jim Thome (portrait)	.40
137	Omar Vizquel	.10
138	Jaret Wright	.40
139	Pedro Astacio	.10
140	Jason Bates	.10
141	Dante Bichette (action)	.25
141	Dante Bichette (portrait)	.25
142	Vinny Castilla (action)	.10
142	Vinny Castilla (portrait)	.10
143	Edgar Clemente (action)	.10
143	Edgar Clemente (portrait)	.10
144	Derrick Gibson (action)	.10
144	Derrick Gibson (portrait)	.10
145	Curtis Goodwin	.10
146	Todd Helton (action)	.60
146	Todd Helton (portrait)	.60
147	Bobby Jones	.10
148	Darryl Kile	.10
149	Mike Lansing	.10
150	Chuck McElroy	.10
151	Neifi Perez	.10
152	Jeff Reed	.10
153	John Thomson	.10
154	Larry Walker (action)	.30
154	Larry Walker (portrait)	.30
155	Jamey Wright	.10
156	Kimera Bartee	.10
157	Geronimo Berroa	.10
158	Raul Casanova	.10
159	Frank Catalanotto	.10
160	Tony Clark	.40
161	Deivi Cruz	.10
162	Damion Easley	.10
163	Juan Encarnacion	.10
164	Luis Gonzalez	.10
165	Seth Greisinger	.10
166	Bob Higginson	.10
167	Brian Hunter	.10
168	Todd Jones	.10
169	Justin Thompson	.10
170	Antonio Alfonseca	.10
171	Dave Berg	.10
172	John Cangelosi	.10
173	Craig Counsell	.10
174	Todd Dunwoody	.10
175	Cliff Floyd	.10
176	Alex Gonzalez	.10
177	Livan Hernandez	.10
178	Ryan Jackson	.10
179	Mark Kotsay	.20
180	Derrek Lee	.10
181	Matt Mantei	.10

182 Brian Meadows .10
183 Edgar Renteria .10
184 Moises Alou (action) .25
184 Moises Alou (portrait) .25
185 Brad Ausmus .10
186 Jeff Bagwell (action) 1.00
186 Jeff Bagwell (portrait) 1.00
187 Derek Bell .10
188 Sean Berry .10
189 Craig Biggio .25
190 Carl Everett .10
191 Ricky Gutierrez .10
192 Mike Hampton .10
193 Doug Henry .10
194 Richard Hidalgo .10
195 Randy Johnson .50
196 Russ Johnson (action) .10
196 Russ Johnson (portrait) .10
197 Shane Reynolds .10
198 Bill Spiers .10
199 Kevin Appier .10
200 Tim Belcher .10
201 Jeff Conine .10
202 Johnny Damon .10
203 Jermaine Dye .10
204 Jeremy Giambi (batting stance) .20
204 Jeremy Giambi (follow-through) .20
205 Jeff King .10
206 Shane Mack .10
207 Jeff Montgomery .10
208 Hal Morris .10
209 Jose Offerman .10
210 Dean Palmer .10
211 Jose Rosado .10
212 Glendon Rusch .10
213 Larry Sutton .10
214 Mike Sweeney .10
215 Bobby Bonilla .15
216 Alex Cora .10
217 Darren Dreifort .10
218 Mark Grudzielanek .10
219 Todd Hollandsworth .10
220 Trenidad Hubbard .10
221 Charles Johnson .10
222 Eric Karros .15
223 Matt Luke .10
224 Ramon Martinez .20
225 Raul Mondesi .25
226 Chan Ho Park .20
227 Jeff Shaw .10
228 Gary Sheffield .25
229 Eric Young .10
230 Jeromy Burnitz .10
231 Jeff Cirillo .10
232 Marquis Grissom .10
233 Bobby Hughes .10
234 John Jaha .10
235 Geoff Jenkins .10
236 Scott Karl .10
237 Mark Loretta .10
238 Mike Matheny .10
239 Mike Myers .10
240 Dave Nilsson .10
241 Bob Wickman .10
242 Jose Valentin .10
243 Fernando Vina .10
244 Rick Aguilera .10
245 Ron Coomer .10
246 Marty Cordova .10
247 Denny Hocking .10
248 Matt Lawton .10
249 Pat Meares .10
250 Paul Molitor (action) .50
250 Paul Molitor (portrait) .50
251 Otis Nixon .10
252 Alex Ochoa .10
253 David Ortiz .20
254 A.J. Pierzynski .10
255 Brad Radke .10
256 Terry Steinbach .10
257 Bob Tewksbury .10
258 Todd Walker .25
259 Shane Andrews .10
260 Shayne Bennett .10
261 Orlando Cabrera .10
262 Brad Fullmer .25
263 Vladimir Guerrero 1.00
264 Wilton Guerrero .10
265 Dustin Hermanson .10
266 Terry Jones .10
267 Steve Kline .10
268 Carl Pavano .10
269 F.P. Santangelo .10
270 Fernando Seguignol (action) .15
270 Fernando Seguignol (portrait) .15
271 Ugueth Urbina .10
272 Jose Vidro .10
273 Chris Widger .10
274 Edgardo Alfonzo .15
275 Carlos Baerga .10
276 John Franco .10
277 Todd Hundley .10
278 Butch Huskey .10
279 Bobby Jones .10
280 Al Leiter .20
281 Greg McMichael .10
282 Brian McRae .10
283 Hideo Nomo .25
284 John Olerud .20
285 Rey Ordonez .15
286 Mike Piazza (action) 2.00
286 Mike Piazza (portrait) 2.00
287 Turk Wendell .10
288 Masato Yoshii .10
289 David Cone .20
290 Chad Curtis .10
291 Joe Girardi .10
292 Orlando Hernandez 1.50
293 Hideki Irabu (action) .20
293 Hideki Irabu (portrait) .20
294 Derek Jeter (action) 2.00
294 Derek Jeter (portrait) 2.00
295 Chuck Knoblauch .25
296 Mike Lowell (action) .20
296 Mike Lowell (portrait) .20
297 Tino Martinez .25
298 Ramiro Mendoza .20
299 Paul O'Neill .25
300 Andy Pettitte .40
301 Jorge Posada .15
302 Tim Raines .10
303 Mariano Rivera .20
304 David Wells .20
305 Bernie Williams (action) .50
305 Bernie Williams (portrait) .50
306 Mike Blowers .10
307 Tom Candiotti .10
308 Eric Chavez (action) .40
308 Eric Chavez (portrait) .40
309 Ryan Christenson .10
310 Jason Giambi .10
311 Ben Grieve (action) .75
311 Ben Grieve (portrait) .75
312 Rickey Henderson .20
313 A.J. Hinch .10
314 Jason McDonald .10
315 Bip Roberts .10
316 Kenny Rogers .10
317 Scott Spiezio .10
318 Matt Stairs .10
319 Miguel Tejada .25
320 Bob Abreu .10
321 Alex Arias .10
322 *Gary Bennett* (action) .25
322 *Gary Bennett* (portrait) .25
323 Ricky Bottalico .10
324 Rico Brogna .10
325 Bobby Estalella .10
326 Doug Glanville .10
327 Kevin Jordan .10
328 Mark Leiter .10
329 Wendell Magee .10
330 Mark Portugal .10
331 Desi Relaford .10
332 Scott Rolen .75
333 Curt Schilling .20
334 Kevin Sefcik .10
335 Adrian Brown .10
336 Emil Brown .10
337 Lou Collier .10
338 Francisco Cordova .10
339 Freddy Garcia .10
340 Jose Guillen .20
341 Jason Kendall .20
342 Al Martin .10
343 Abraham Nunez .10
344 Aramis Ramirez .20
345 Ricardo Rincon .10
346 Jason Schmidt .10
347 Turner Ward .10
348 Tony Womack .10
349 Kevin Young .10
350 Juan Acevedo .10
351 Delino DeShields .10
352 J.D. Drew (action) 1.00
352 J.D. Drew (portrait) 1.00
353 Ron Gant .15
354 Brian Jordan .10
355 Ray Lankford .15
356 Eli Marrero .10
357 Kent Mercker .10
358 Matt Morris .10
359 Luis Ordaz .10
360 Donovan Osborne .10
361 Placido Polanco .10
362 Fernando Tatis .15
363 Andy Ashby .10
364 Kevin Brown .20
365 Ken Caminiti .20
366 Steve Finley .10
367 Chris Gomez .10
368 Tony Gwynn (action) 1.50
368 Tony Gwynn (portrait) 1.50
369 Joey Hamilton .10
370 Carlos Hernandez .10
371 Trevor Hoffman .10
372 Wally Joyner .10
373 Jim Leyritz .10
374 Ruben Rivera .10
375 Greg Vaughn .20
376 Quilvio Veras .10
377 Rich Aurilla .10
378 Barry Bonds (action) .75
378 Barry Bonds (portrait) .75
379 Ellis Burks .10
380 Joe Carter .15
381 Stan Javier .10
382 Brian Johnson .10
383 Jeff Kent .10
384 Jose Mesa .10
385 Bill Mueller .10
386 Robb Nen .10
387 Armando Rios (action) .10
387 Armando Rios (portrait) .10
388 Kirk Rueter .10
389 Rey Sanchez .10
390 J.T. Snow .10
391 David Bell .10
392 Jay Buhner .15
393 Ken Cloude .10
394 Russ Davis .10
395 Jeff Fassero .10
396 Ken Griffey Jr. (action) 3.50
396 Ken Griffey Jr. (portrait) 3.50
397 *Giomar Guevara* .25
398 Carlos Guillen .10
399 Edgar Martinez .10
400 Shane Monahan .10
401 Jamie Moyer .10
402 David Segui .10
403 Makoto Suzuki .10
404 Mike Timlin .10
405 Dan Wilson .10
406 Wilson Alvarez .10
407 Rolando Arrojo .25
408 Wade Boggs .25
409 Miguel Cairo .10
410 Roberto Hernandez .10
411 Mike Kelly .10
412 Aaron Ledesma .10
413 Albie Lopez .10
414 Dave Martinez .10
415 Quinton McCracken .10
416 Fred McGriff .25
417 Bryan Rekar .10
418 Paul Sorrento .10
419 Randy Winn .10
420 John Burkett .10
421 Will Clark .25
422 Royce Clayton .10
423 Juan Gonzalez (action) 1.50
423 Juan Gonzalez (portrait) 1.50
424 Tom Goodwin .10
425 Rusty Greer .10
426 Rick Helling .10
427 Roberto Kelly .10
428 Mark McLemore .10
429 Ivan Rodriguez (action) .75
429 Ivan Rodriguez (portrait) .75
430 Aaron Sele .10
431 Lee Stevens .10
432 Todd Stottlemyre .10
433 John Wetteland .10
434 Todd Zeile .10
435 Jose Canseco .40
436 Roger Clemens (action) 1.50
436 Roger Clemens (portrait) 1.50
437 Felipe Crespo .10
438 Jose Cruz Jr. (action) .15
438 Jose Cruz Jr. (portrait) .15
438 (portrait)
439 Carlos Delgado .40
440 Tom Evans (action) .10
440 Tom Evans (portrait) .10
441 Tony Fernandez .10
442 Darrin Fletcher .10
443 Alex Gonzalez .10
444 Shawn Green .15
445 Roy Halladay .25
446 Pat Hentgen .10
447 Juan Samuel .10
448 Benito Santiago .10
449 Shannon Stewart .10
450 Woody Williams .10

1999 Pacific Platinum Blue

This 450-card parallel set reprinted each card in Pacific, but used a platinum blue foil on the front instead of the gold foil used on base cards. These were inserted one per 73 packs.

Platinum Blue Stars: 40x to 80x
Yng Stars & RCs: 30x to 60x
Inserted 1:73
(See 1999 Pacific for checklist and base card values.)

1999 Pacific Cramer's Choice

Pacific CEO/President Michael Cramer personally chose this 10-card set. Die-cut into a trophy shape, the cards are enhanced with silver holographic etching and gold foil stamping across the card bottom. These are seeded 1:721 packs.

MT
Complete Set (10): 600.00
Common Player: 25.00
Inserted 1:721
1 Cal Ripken Jr. 75.00
2 Nomar Garciaparra 60.00
3 Frank Thomas 50.00
4 Ken Griffey Jr. 100.00
5 Alex Rodriguez 75.00
6 Greg Maddux 60.00
7 Sammy Sosa 75.00
8 Kerry Wood 25.00
9 Mark McGwire 125.00
10 Tony Gwynn 50.00

1999 Pacific Dynagon Diamond

Dynagon Diamond captures 20 of baseball's biggest stars in action against a mirror-patterned full-foil background. These are seeded 4:37.

MT
Complete Set (20): 75.00
Common Player: 1.00
Inserted 1:9
1 Cal Ripken Jr. 7.50
2 Nomar Garciaparra 6.00
3 Frank Thomas 4.00
4 Derek Jeter 6.00
5 Ben Grieve 2.00
6 Ken Griffey Jr. 10.00
7 Alex Rodriguez 7.50
8 Juan Gonzalez 4.00
9 Travis Lee 1.50
10 Chipper Jones 6.00
11 Greg Maddux 5.00
12 Sammy Sosa 7.50
13 Kerry Wood 2.00
14 Jeff Bagwell 3.00
15 Hideo Nomo 1.00
16 Mike Piazza 6.00
17 J.D. Drew 3.00
18 Mark McGwire 10.00
19 Tony Gwynn 4.00
20 Barry Bonds 2.00

1999 Pacific Dynagon Diamond Titanium

A parallel to Dynagon Diamond, these are serially numbered to 99 sets and exclusive to hobby packs.

MT
Common Player: 7.50
Titanium Stars: 8X
Production 99 sets
(See 1999 Pacific Dynagon Diamond for checklist and base card values.)

1999 Pacific Gold Crown Die-Cuts

This 36-card die-cut set is shaped like a crown at the top and features dual foiling, 24-pt. stock and gold foil stamping. These are seeded 1:37 packs.

MT
Complete Set (36): 400.00
Common Player: 4.00
Inserted 1:37
1 Darin Erstad 10.00
2 Cal Ripken Jr. 30.00
3 Nomar Garciaparra 25.00
4 Pedro Martinez 8.00
5 Mo Vaughn 6.00
6 Frank Thomas 20.00
7 Kenny Lofton 6.00
8 Manny Ramirez 12.50
9 Jaret Wright 6.00
10 Paul Molitor 8.00
11 Derek Jeter 25.00
12 Bernie Williams 6.00
13 Ben Grieve 10.00
14 Ken Griffey Jr. 45.00
15 Alex Rodriguez 30.00
16 Rolando Arrojo 4.00
17 Wade Boggs 5.00
18 Juan Gonzalez 20.00
19 Ivan Rodriguez 10.00
20 Roger Clemens 20.00
21 Travis Lee 8.00
22 Chipper Jones 25.00
23 Greg Maddux 20.00
24 Sammy Sosa 30.00
25 Kerry Wood 10.00
26 Todd Helton 8.00
27 Jeff Bagwell 10.00
28 Craig Biggio 5.00
29 Vladimir Guerrero 10.00
30 Hideo Nomo 5.00
31 Mike Piazza 25.00
32 Scott Rolen 10.00
33 J.D. Drew 10.00
34 Mark McGwire 45.00
35 Tony Gwynn 20.00
36 Barry Bonds 10.00

1999 Pacific Hot Cards

This dealer-only 10-card set was awarded to any dealer that had sold any packs/boxes that produced a card for the Pacific Hot Cards Registry Program. Sets are limited to 500 serial numbered sets.

MT
Complete Set (10): 200.00
Common Player: 8.00
1 Alex Rodriguez 30.00
2 Tony Gwynn 20.00
3 Ken Griffey Jr. 45.00
4 Sammy Sosa 25.00
5 Ivan Rodriguez 10.00
6 Derek Jeter 25.00
7 Cal Ripken Jr. 30.00
8 Mark McGwire 45.00
9 J.D. Drew 15.00
10 Bernie Williams 8.00

1999 Pacific Team Checklists

This 30-card horizontal insert set features a star player from each team on the card front, with each team's complete checklist on the card back. Fronts feature a holographic silver-foiled and embossed logo of the player's respective team. These are seeded 2:37 packs.

		MT
Complete Set (30):		100.00
Common Player:		1.50
Inserted 1:18		
1	Darin Erstad	3.00
2	Cal Ripken Jr.	9.00
3	Nomar Garciaparra	8.00
4	Frank Thomas	5.00
5	Manny Ramirez	3.00
6	Damion Easley	1.50
7	Jeff King	1.50
8	Paul Molitor	2.50
9	Derek Jeter	8.00
10	Ben Grieve	3.00
11	Ken Griffey Jr.	15.00
12	Wade Boggs	2.00
13	Juan Gonzalez	6.00
14	Roger Clemens	6.00
15	Travis Lee	2.00
16	Chipper Jones	6.00
17	Sammy Sosa	10.00
18	Barry Larkin	2.00
19	Todd Helton	2.50
20	Mark Kotsay	1.50
21	Jeff Bagwell	3.00
22	Raul Mondesi	2.00
23	Jeff Cirillo	1.50
24	Vladimir Guerrero	4.00
25	Mike Piazza	8.00
26	Scott Rolen	3.00
27	Jason Kendall	1.50
28	Mark McGwire	15.00
29	Tony Gwynn	5.00
30	Barry Bonds	3.00

1999 Pacific Timelines

Timelines features 20 superstars, giving a chronological history of each player complete with photos from early in their careers. Three photos of the player are on the card front. Inserted exclusively in hobby packs these are limited to 199 serially numbered sets.

		MT
Complete Set (20):		900.00
Common Player:		15.00
Inserted 1:181 H		
1	Cal Ripken Jr.	90.00
2	Frank Thomas	50.00
3	Jim Thome	15.00
4	Paul Molitor	20.00
5	Bernie Williams	15.00
6	Derek Jeter	75.00
7	Ken Griffey Jr.	125.00
8	Alex Rodriguez	90.00
9	Wade Boggs	15.00
10	Jose Canseco	15.00
11	Roger Clemens	60.00
12	Andres Galarraga	15.00
13	Chipper Jones	75.00
14	Greg Maddux	75.00
15	Sammy Sosa	90.00
16	Larry Walker	15.00
17	Randy Johnson	15.00
18	Mike Piazza	75.00
19	Mark McGwire	125.00
20	Tony Gwynn	60.00

Player names in *Italic* type indicate a rookie card.

1999 Pacific Aurora

The 200-card set features two photos on the card front and one on the back. Card backs also have '98 and career stats along with personal information. The player's name and Aurora logo are stamped with gold foil.

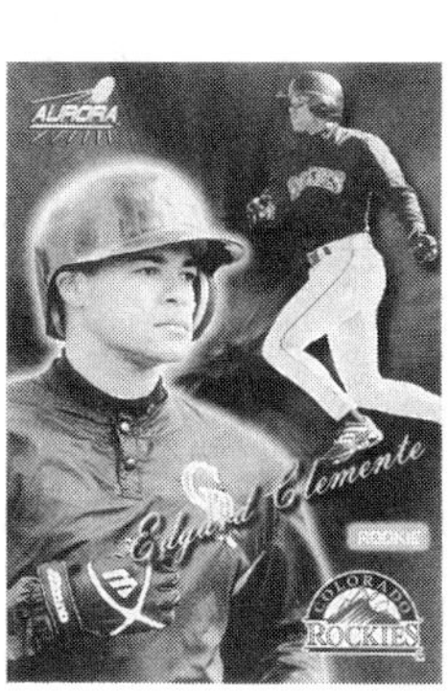

		MT
Complete Set (200):		55.00
Common Player:		.20
1	Garret Anderson	.20
2	Jim Edmonds	.40
3	Darin Erstad	1.00
4	Matt Luke	.20
5	Tim Salmon	.50
6	Mo Vaughn	.75
7	Jay Bell	.20
8	David Dellucci	.20
9	Steve Finley	.20
10	Bernard Gilkey	.20
11	Randy Johnson	.75
12	Travis Lee	.75
13	Matt Williams	.50
14	Andres Galarraga	.50
15	Tom Glavine	.40
16	Andruw Jones	1.00
17	Chipper Jones	2.50
18	Brian Jordan	.20
19	Javy Lopez	.40
20	Greg Maddux	2.50
21	Albert Belle	1.00
22	Will Clark	.50
23	Scott Erickson	.20
24	Mike Mussina	.75
25	Cal Ripken Jr.	3.00
26	B.J. Surhoff	.20
27	Nomar Garciaparra	2.50
28	Reggie Jefferson	.20
29	Darren Lewis	.20
30	Pedro Martinez	.75
31	John Valentin	.20
32	Rod Beck	.20
33	Mark Grace	.40
34	Lance Johnson	.20
35	Mickey Morandini	.20
36	Sammy Sosa	2.50
37	Kerry Wood	1.00
38	James Baldwin	.20
39	Mike Caruso	.20
40	Ray Durham	.20
41	Magglio Ordonez	.35
42	Frank Thomas	2.00
43	Aaron Boone	.20
44	Sean Casey	.30
45	Barry Larkin	.35
46	Hal Morris	.20
47	Denny Neagle	.20
48	Greg Vaughn	.40
49	Pat Watkins	.20
50	Roberto Alomar	.75
51	Sandy Alomar Jr.	.30
52	David Justice	.40
53	Kenny Lofton	.75
54	Manny Ramirez	1.00
55	Richie Sexson	.40
56	Jim Thome	.60
57	Omar Vizquel	.20
58	Dante Bichette	.50
59	Vinny Castilla	.40
60	*Edgard Clemente*	.50
61	Derrick Gibson	.20
62	Todd Helton	.75
63	Darryl Kile	.20
64	Larry Walker	.75
65	Tony Clark	.60
66	Damion Easley	.20
67	Bob Higginson	.40
68	Brian Hunter	.20
69	Dean Palmer	.20
70	Justin Thompson	.20
71	Craig Counsell	.20
72	Todd Dunwoody	.25
73	Cliff Floyd	.20
74	Alex Gonzalez	.20
75	Livan Hernandez	.20
76	Mark Kotsay	.25
77	Derrek Lee	.20
78	Moises Alou	.40
79	Jeff Bagwell	1.00
80	Derek Bell	.20
81	Craig Biggio	.75
82	Ken Caminiti	.40
83	Richard Hidalgo	.20
84	Shane Reynolds	.20
85	Jeff Conine	.20
86	Johnny Damon	.20
87	Jermaine Dye	.20
88	Jeff King	.20
89	Jeff Montgomery	.20
90	Mike Sweeney	.20
91	Kevin Brown	.40
92	Mark Grudzielanek	.20
93	Eric Karros	.20
94	Raul Mondesi	.40
95	Chan Ho Park	.40
96	Gary Sheffield	.40
97	Jeromy Burnitz	.20
98	Jeff Cirillo	.20
99	Marquis Grissom	.20
100	Geoff Jenkins	.20
101	Dave Nilsson	.20
102	Jose Valentin	.20
103	Fernando Vina	.20
104	Marty Cordova	.20
105	Matt Lawton	.20
106	David Ortiz	.20
107	Brad Radke	.20
108	Todd Walker	.40
109	Shane Andrews	.20
110	Orlando Cabrera	.20
111	Brad Fullmer	.40
112	Vladimir Guerrero	1.50
113	Wilton Guerrero	.20
114	Carl Pavano	.20
115	Fernando Seguignol	.45
116	Ugueth Urbina	.20
117	Edgardo Alfonzo	.25
118	Bobby Bonilla	.20
119	Rickey Henderson	.40
120	Hideo Nomo	.35
121	John Olerud	.40
122	Rey Ordonez	.25
123	Mike Piazza	2.50
124	Masato Yoshii	.20
125	Scott Brosius	.20
126	Orlando Hernandez	1.50
127	Hideki Irabu	.50
128	Derek Jeter	2.50
129	Chuck Knoblauch	.50
130	Tino Martinez	.35
131	Jorge Posada	.50
132	Bernie Williams	.60
133	Eric Chavez	.50
134	Ryan Christenson	.20
135	Jason Giambi	.20
136	Ben Grieve	1.00
137	A.J. Hinch	.20
138	Matt Stairs	.20
139	Miguel Tejada	.30
140	Bob Abreu	.20
141	*Gary Bennett*	.40
142	Desi Relaford	.20
143	Scott Rolen	1.00
144	Curt Schilling	.40
145	Kevin Sefcik	.20
146	Brian Giles	.20
147	Jose Guillen	.20
148	Jason Kendall	.40
149	Aramis Ramirez	.20
150	Tony Womack	.20
151	Kevin Young	.20
152	Eric Davis	.20
153	J.D. Drew	1.00
154	Ray Lankford	.20
155	Eli Marrero	.20
156	Mark McGwire	4.00
157	Luis Ordaz	.20
158	Edgar Renteria	.20
159	Andy Ashby	.20
160	Tony Gwynn	2.00
161	Trevor Hoffman	.20
162	Wally Joyner	.20
163	Jim Leyritz	.20
164	Ruben Rivera	.20
165	Reggie Sanders	.20
166	Quilvio Veras	.20
167	Rich Aurilia	.20
168	Marvin Benard	.20
169	Barry Bonds	1.00
170	Ellis Burks	.20
171	Jeff Kent	.30
172	Bill Mueller	.20
173	J.T. Snow	.20
174	Jay Buhner	.30
175	Jeff Fassero	.20
176	Ken Griffey Jr.	4.00
177	Carlos Guillen	.20
178	Edgar Martinez	.25
179	Alex Rodriguez	3.00
180	David Segui	.20
181	Dan Wilson	.20
182	Rolando Arrojo	.40
183	Wade Boggs	.50
184	Jose Canseco	1.00
185	Aaron Ledesma	.20
186	Dave Martinez	.20
187	Quinton McCracken	.20
188	Fred McGriff	.50
189	Juan Gonzalez	2.00
190	Tom Goodwin	.20
191	Rusty Greer	.20
192	Roberto Kelly	.20
193	Rafael Palmeiro	.75
194	Ivan Rodriguez	1.00
195	Roger Clemens	1.50
196	Jose Cruz Jr.	.25
197	Carlos Delgado	.75
198	Alex Gonzalez	.20
199	Roy Halladay	.50
200	Pat Hentgen	.20

1999 Pacific Aurora Complete Players

The 10 players featured in this serial numbered 20-card set each have two cards, designed to fit together. Card fronts feature a red border on the top and bottom with the rest of the card done in gold foil etching. Each card is serially numbered to 299.

		MT
Complete Set (10):		325.00
Common Player:		15.00
Production 299 sets		
1	Cal Ripken Jr.	50.00
2	Nomar Garciaparra	40.00
3	Sammy Sosa	40.00
4	Kerry Wood	15.00
5	Frank Thomas	25.00
6	Mike Piazza	40.00
7	Mark McGwire	60.00
8	Tony Gwynn	30.00
9	Ken Griffey Jr.	60.00
10	Alex Rodriguez	50.00

1999 Pacific Aurora Kings of the Major Leagues

The full foiled card fronts also utilize gold foil stamping. Pacific's crown as well as the featured player's team are shadow boxed in the background with the player's image in the foreground. These are seeded 1:361.

		MT
Complete Set (10):		750.00
Common Player:		30.00
Inserted 1:361		
1	Cal Ripken Jr.	90.00
2	Nomar Garciaparra	75.00
3	Sammy Sosa	75.00
4	Kerry Wood	30.00
5	Frank Thomas	60.00
6	Mike Piazza	75.00
7	Mark McGwire	125.00
8	Tony Gwynn	60.00
9	Ken Griffey Jr.	125.00
10	Alex Rodriguez	90.00

1999 Pacific Aurora On Deck

Twenty of the game's hottest players are featured in this laser-cut and silver foil stamped set. The player's team logo is laser cut into the bottom half of the card beneath the player photo. These are seeded 4:37 packs.

		MT
Complete Set (20):		100.00
Common Player:		2.00
Inserted 1:9		
1	Chipper Jones	8.00
2	Cal Ripken Jr.	10.00
3	Nomar Garciaparra	8.00
4	Sammy Sosa	8.00
5	Frank Thomas	6.00
6	Manny Ramirez	4.00
7	Todd Helton	2.50
8	Larry Walker	2.00
9	Jeff Bagwell	3.00
10	Vladimir Guerrero	4.00
11	Mike Piazza	8.00
12	Derek Jeter	8.00
13	Bernie Williams	2.00
14	J.D. Drew	3.00
15	Mark McGwire	15.00
16	Tony Gwynn	6.00
17	Ken Griffey Jr.	15.00
18	Alex Rodriguez	10.00
19	Juan Gonzalez	6.00
20	Ivan Rodriguez	3.00

1999 Pacific Aurora Pennant Fever

Regular Pennant Fever inserts feature gold foil stamping of 20 of the hottest players in the hobby. These are seeded 4:37 packs. There are also three parallel versions which consist of: Platinum Blue, Silver and Copper. Platinum Blues are limited to 100 serial numbered sets, Silvers are retail exclusive and limited to 250 numbered sets and Coppers are hobby exclusive and limited to 20 numbered sets. Pacific spokesman Tony Gwynn autographed 97 regular Pennant Fever cards and one each of the Silver, Blue and Copper.

		MT
Complete Set (20):		90.00
Common Player:		1.00
Silver Stars (250 each): 2X		
Platinum Blue Stars (100 each): 6X		
Copper Stars (20 each): 20X		
Tony Gwynn Autograph:		200.00
1	Chipper Jones	6.00
2	Greg Maddux	6.00
3	Cal Ripken Jr.	8.00
4	Nomar Garciaparra	6.00
5	Sammy Sosa	6.00
6	Kerry Wood	2.50
7	Frank Thomas	5.00
8	Manny Ramirez	3.00
9	Todd Helton	2.00
10	Jeff Bagwell	3.00
11	Mike Piazza	6.00
12	Derek Jeter	6.00
13	Bernie Williams	2.00
14	J.D. Drew	3.00
15	Mark McGwire	12.00
16	Tony Gwynn	5.00
17	Ken Griffey Jr.	12.00
18	Alex Rodriguez	8.00
19	Juan Gonzalez	5.00
20	Ivan Rodriguez	2.50

1999 Pacific Aurora Styrotechs

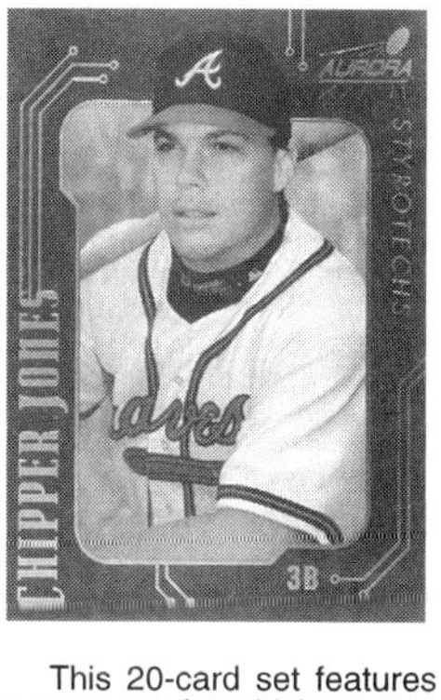

This 20-card set features styrene stock, which makes the cards more resilient. Fronts have a black border and stamped with gold foil. Backs have a photo and a brief career highlight caption. These are seeded 1:37 packs.

		MT
Complete Set (20):		300.00
Common Player:		5.00

Inserted 1:37

1	Chipper Jones	20.00
2	Greg Maddux	20.00
3	Cal Ripken Jr.	25.00
4	Nomar Garciaparra	20.00
5	Sammy Sosa	20.00
6	Kerry Wood	6.00
7	Frank Thomas	12.50
8	Manny Ramirez	10.00
9	Larry Walker	5.00
10	Jeff Bagwell	8.00
11	Mike Piazza	20.00
12	Derek Jeter	20.00
13	Bernie Williams	5.00
14	J.D. Drew	6.00
15	Mark McGwire	40.00
16	Tony Gwynn	15.00
17	Ken Griffey Jr.	40.00
18	Alex Rodriguez	25.00
19	Juan Gonzalez	15.00
20	Ivan Rodriguez	8.00

1999 Pacific Crown Collection Sample

This card of Pacific spokesman Tony Gwynn introduces the 1999 Crown series. The sample card follows the format of the issued version but is overprinted "SAMPLE" on back.

	MT
Tony Gwynn	3.00

1999 Pacific Crown Collection

Released in one series the 300-card set has white borders and gold foil stamping on the card fronts. Backs have a small photo along with English and Spanish translation. There is one parallel to the base set Platinum Blues, which are stamped with a platinum blue holographic tint and are seeded 1:73. Packs consist of 12 cards with a S.R.P. of $2.49.

		MT
Complete Set (300):		30.00
Common Player:		.10
Platinum Blue Stars: 30X		
Inserted 1:73		
1	Garret Anderson	.10
2	Gary DiSarcina	.10
3	Jim Edmonds	.20
4	Darin Erstad	.75
5	Shigetosi Hasegawa	.10
6	Norberto Martin	.10
7	Omar Olivares	.10
8	Orlando Palmeiro	.10
9	Tim Salmon	.25
10	Randy Velarde	.10
11	Tony Batista	.10
12	Jay Bell	.10
13	Yamil Benitez	.10
14	Omar Daal	.10
15	David Dellucci	.10
16	Karim Garcia	.15
17	Travis Lee	.60
18	Felix Rodriguez	.10
19	Devon White	.10
20	Matt Williams	.25
21	Andres Galarraga	.50
22	Tom Glavine	.20
23	Ozzie Guillen	.10
24	Andruw Jones	.75
25	Chipper Jones	2.00
26	Ryan Klesko	.25
27	Javy Lopez	.20
28	Greg Maddux	2.00
29	Dennis Martinez	.10
30	Odaliz Perez	.10
31	Rudy Seanez	.10
32	John Smoltz	.20
33	Roberto Alomar	.50
34	Armando Benitez	.10
35	Scott Erickson	.10
36	Juan Guzman	.10
37	Mike Mussina	.50
38	Jesse Orosco	.10
39	Rafael Palmeiro	.40
40	Sidney Ponson	.10
41	Cal Ripken Jr.	2.50
42	B.J. Surhoff	.10
43	Lenny Webster	.10
44	Dennis Eckersley	.10
45	Nomar Garciaparra	2.00
46	Darren Lewis	.10
47	Pedro Martinez	.50
48	Troy O'Leary	.10
49	Bret Saberhagen	.10
50	John Valentin	.10
51	Mo Vaughn	.60
52	Tim Wakefield	.10
53	Manny Alexander	.10
54	Rod Beck	.10
55	Gary Gaetti	.10
56	Mark Grace	.25
57	Felix Heredia	.10
58	Jose Hernandez	.10
59	Henry Rodriguez	.10
60	Sammy Sosa	2.50
61	Kevin Tapani	.10
62	Kerry Wood	.75
63	James Baldwin	.10
64	Albert Belle	.75
65	Mike Caruso	.10
66	Carlos Castillo	.10
67	Wil Cordero	.10
68	Jaime Navarro	.10
69	Magglio Ordonez	.20
70	Frank Thomas	1.50
71	Robin Ventura	.20
72	Bret Boone	.10
73	Sean Casey	.25
74	*Guillermo Garcia*	.10
75	Barry Larkin	.15
76	Melvin Nieves	.10
77	Eduardo Perez	.10
78	Roberto Petagine	.10
79	Reggie Sanders	.10
80	Eddie Taubensee	.10
81	Brett Tomko	.10
82	Sandy Alomar Jr.	.15
83	Bartolo Colon	.10
84	Joey Cora	.10
85	Einar Diaz	.10
86	David Justice	.25
87	Kenny Lofton	.60
88	Manny Ramirez	1.00
89	Jim Thome	.30
90	Omar Vizquel	.10
91	Enrique Wilson	.10
92	Pedro Astacio	.10
93	Dante Bichette	.30
94	Vinny Castilla	.15
95	*Edgard Clemente*	.15
96	Todd Helton	.60
97	Darryl Kile	.10
98	Mike Munoz	.10
99	Neifi Perez	.10
100	Jeff Reed	.10
101	Larry Walker	.40
102	Gabe Alvarez	.10
103	Kimera Bartee	.10
104	Frank Castillo	.10
105	Tony Clark	.25
106	Deivi Cruz	.10
107	Damion Easley	.10
108	Luis Gonzalez	.10
109	Marino Santana	.10
110	Justin Thompson	.10
111	Antonio Alfonseca	.10
112	Alex Fernandez	.10
113	Cliff Floyd	.10
114	Alex Gonzalez	.10
115	Livan Hernandez	.10
116	Mark Kotsay	.20
117	Derrek Lee	.10
118	Edgar Renteria	.15
119	Jesus Sanchez	.10
120	Moises Alou	.20
121	Jeff Bagwell	1.00
122	Derek Bell	.10
123	Craig Biggio	.25
124	Tony Eusebio	.10
125	Ricky Gutierrez	.10
126	Richard Hidalgo	.10
127	Randy Johnson	.50
128	Jose Lima	.10
129	Shane Reynolds	.10
130	Johnny Damon	.10
131	Carlos Febles	.10
132	Jeff King	.10
133	Mendy Lopez	.10
134	Hal Morris	.10
135	Jose Offerman	.10
136	Jose Rosado	.10
137	Jose Santiago	.10
138	Bobby Bonilla	.10
139	Roger Cedeno	.10
140	Alex Cora	.10
141	Eric Karros	.15
142	Raul Mondesi	.25
143	Antonio Osuna	.10
144	Chan Ho Park	.20
145	Gary Sheffield	.25
146	Ismael Valdes	.10
147	Jeromy Burnitz	.10
148	Jeff Cirillo	.10
149	Valerio de los Santos	.10
150	Marquis Grissom	.10
151	Scott Karl	.10
152	Dave Nilsson	.10
153	Al Reyes	.10
154	Rafael Roque	.10
155	Jose Valentin	.10
156	Fernando Vina	.10
157	Rick Aguilera	.10
158	Hector Carrasco	.10
159	Marty Cordova	.10
160	Eddie Guardado	.10
161	Paul Molitor	.50
162	Otis Nixon	.10
163	Alex Ochoa	.10
164	David Ortiz	.10
165	Frank Rodriguez	.10
166	Todd Walker	.25
167	Miguel Batista	.10
168	Orlando Cabrera	.10
169	Vladimir Guerrero	1.00
170	Wilton Guerrero	.10
171	Carl Pavano	.10
172	Robert Perez	.10
173	F.P. Santangelo	.10
174	Fernando Seguignol	.20
175	Ugueth Urbina	.10
176	Javier Vazquez	.10
177	Edgardo Alfonzo	.15
178	Carlos Baerga	.10
179	John Franco	.10
180	Luis Lopez	.10
181	Hideo Nomo	.25
182	John Olerud	.20
183	Rey Ordonez	.15
184	Mike Piazza	2.00
185	Armando Reynoso	.10
186	Masato Yoshii	.10
187	David Cone	.20
188	Orlando Hernandez	2.00
189	Hideki Irabu	.20
190	Derek Jeter	2.00
191	Ricky Ledee	.25
192	Tino Martinez	.25
193	Ramiro Mendoza	.10
194	Paul O'Neill	.25
195	Jorge Posada	.20
196	Mariano Rivera	.20
197	Luis Sojo	.10
198	Bernie Williams	.35
199	Rafael Bournigal	.10
200	Eric Chavez	.40
201	Ryan Christenson	.10
202	Jason Giambi	.10
203	Ben Grieve	.75
204	Rickey Henderson	.25
205	A.J. Hinch	.10
206	Kenny Rogers	.10
207	Miguel Tejada	.20
208	Jorge Velandia	.10
209	Bobby Abreu	.10
210	Marlon Anderson	.10
211	Alex Arias	.10
212	Bobby Estalella	.10
213	Doug Glanville	.10
214	Scott Rolen	.75
215	Curt Schilling	.20
216	Kevin Sefcik	.10
217	Adrian Brown	.10
218	Francisco Cordova	.10
219	Freddy Garcia	.10
220	Jose Guillen	.20
221	Jason Kendall	.10
222	Al Martin	.10
223	Abraham Nunez	.10
224	Aramis Ramirez	.25
225	Ricardo Rincon	.10
226	Kevin Young	.10
227	J.D. Drew	1.00
228	Ron Gant	.10
229	Jose Jimenez	.10
230	Brian Jordan	.10
231	Ray Lankford	.10
232	Eli Marrero	.10
233	Mark McGwire	4.00
234	Luis Ordaz	.10
235	Placido Polanco	.10
236	Fernando Tatis	.15
237	Andy Ashby	.10
238	Kevin Brown	.15
239	Ken Caminiti	.20
240	Steve Finley	.10
241	Chris Gomez	.10
242	Tony Gwynn	1.50
243	Carlos Hernandez	.10
244	Trevor Hoffman	.10
245	Wally Joyner	.10
246	Ruben Rivera	.10
247	Greg Vaughn	.20
248	Quilvio Veras	.10
249	Rich Aurilia	.10
250	Barry Bonds	.75
251	Stan Javier	.10
252	Jeff Kent	.10
253	Ramon Martinez	.10
254	Jose Mesa	.10
255	Armando Rios	.10
256	Rich Rodriguez	.10
257	Rey Sanchez	.10
258	J.T. Snow	.10
259	Julian Tavarez	.10
260	Jeff Fassero	.10
261	Ken Griffey Jr.	4.00
262	*Giomar Guevara*	.10
263	Carlos Guillen	.10
264	Raul Ibanez	.10
265	Edgar Martinez	.10
266	Jamie Moyer	.10
267	Alex Rodriguez	2.50
268	David Segui	.10
269	Makoto Suzuki	.10
270	Wilson Alvarez	.10
271	Rolando Arrojo	.10
272	Wade Boggs	.25
273	Miguel Cairo	.10
274	Roberto Hernandez	.10
275	Aaron Ledesma	.10
276	Albie Lopez	.10
277	Quinton McCracken	.10
278	Fred McGriff	.25
279	Esteban Yan	.10
280	Luis Alicea	.10
281	Will Clark	.40
282	Juan Gonzalez	1.50
283	Rusty Greer	.10
284	Rick Helling	.10
285	Xavier Hernandez	.10
286	Roberto Kelly	.10
287	Esteban Loaiza	.10
288	Ivan Rodriguez	.75
289	Aaron Sele	.10
290	John Wetteland	.10
291	Jose Canseco	.40
292	Roger Clemens	1.00
293	Felipe Crespo	.10
294	Jose Cruz Jr.	.20
295	Carlos Delgado	.40
296	Kelvim Escobar	.10
297	Tony Fernandez	.10
298	Alex Gonzalez	.10
299	Tomas Perez	.10
300	Juan Samuel	.10

1999 Pacific Crown Collection In The Cage

These die-cut inserts have a netting like background with laser cutting, giving the look that the player is hitting in a batting cage. These are seeded 1:145 packs.

		MT
Complete Set (20):		600.00
Common Player:		10.00
Inserted 1:145		
1	Chipper Jones	40.00
2	Cal Ripken Jr.	50.00
3	Nomar Garciaparra	40.00
4	Sammy Sosa	50.00
5	Frank Thomas	30.00
6	Manny Ramirez	20.00
7	Todd Helton	15.00
8	Moises Alou	10.00
9	Vladimir Guerrero	20.00
10	Mike Piazza	40.00
11	Derek Jeter	40.00
12	Ben Grieve	15.00
13	J.D. Drew	15.00
14	Mark McGwire	75.00
15	Tony Gwynn	30.00
16	Ken Griffey Jr.	75.00
17	Edgar Martinez	10.00
18	Alex Rodriguez	50.00
19	Juan Gonzalez	25.00
20	Ivan Rodriguez	15.00

1999 Pacific Crown Collection Latinos/ Major Leagues

This 36-card set salutes the many latino players in the major league including Roberto Alomar, Manny Ramirez and Juan Gonzalez. These are seeded 2:37 packs.

		MT
Complete Set (36):		80.00
Common Player:		1.25
Inserted 1:18		
1	Roberto Alomar	3.00
2	Rafael Palmeiro	2.50
3	Nomar Garciaparra	10.00
4	Pedro Martinez	4.00
5	Magglio Ordonez	2.00
6	Sandy Alomar Jr.	2.00
7	Bartolo Colon	1.50
8	Manny Ramirez	6.00
9	Omar Vizquel	1.50
10	Enrique Wilson	1.50
11	David Ortiz	1.50
12	Orlando Hernandez	10.00
13	Tino Martinez	1.50
14	Mariano Rivera	2.00
15	Bernie Williams	2.50
16	Edgar Martinez	1.50
17	Alex Rodriguez	15.00
18	David Segui	1.50
19	Rolando Arrojo	2.00
20	Juan Gonzalez	7.50
21	Ivan Rodriguez	4.00
22	Jose Canseco	3.00
23	Jose Cruz Jr.	1.50
24	Andres Galarraga	3.00
25	Andruw Jones	4.00
26	Javy Lopez	2.00
27	Sammy Sosa	12.50
28	Vinny Castilla	1.50
29	Alex Gonzalez	1.50
30	Moises Alou	2.00
31	Bobby Bonilla	1.50
32	Raul Mondesi	2.00
33	Fernando Vina	1.50
34	Vladimir Guerrero	5.00
35	Carlos Baerga	1.50
36	Rey Ordonez	1.50

1999 Pacific Crown Collection Pacific Cup

These die-cut inserts are shaped like a trophy with the featured player's photo in the foreground. These are seeded 1:721 packs.

		MT
Complete Set (10):		700.00
Common Player:		30.00
Inserted 1:721		
1	Cal Ripken Jr.	90.00
2	Nomar Garciaparra	75.00
3	Frank Thomas	50.00
4	Ken Griffey Jr.	125.00
5	Alex Rodriguez	90.00
6	Greg Maddux	75.00
7	Sammy Sosa	90.00
8	Kerry Wood	30.00
9	Mark McGwire	125.00
10	Tony Gwynn	60.00

1999 Pacific Crown Collection Tape Measure

This 20-card insert set is fully foiled in platinum blue with rainbow highlights in the background of the player photo. Saluting the top power hitters in the game today, these are seeded 1:73 packs.

		MT
Complete Set (20):		325.00
Common Player:		6.00
Inserted 1:73		
1	Andres Galarraga	6.00
2	Chipper Jones	25.00
3	Nomar Garciaparra	25.00
4	Sammy Sosa	35.00
5	Frank Thomas	15.00
6	Manny Ramirez	15.00
7	Vinny Castilla	6.00
8	Moises Alou	6.00
9	Jeff Bagwell	12.50
10	Raul Mondesi	6.00
11	Vladimir Guerrero	15.00
12	Mike Piazza	25.00
13	J.D. Drew	10.00
14	Mark McGwire	45.00
15	Greg Vaughn	6.00
16	Ken Griffey Jr.	45.00
17	Alex Rodriguez	35.00
18	Juan Gonzalez	20.00
19	Ivan Rodriguez	10.00
20	Jose Canseco	6.00

1999 Pacific Crown Collection Team Checklists

This 30-card set feature is highlighted with holographic silver foil stamping and done in a horizontal format. The backs have a complete team checklist for the featured player's team. These have an insertion rate of 1:37 packs.

		MT
Complete Set (30):		275.00
Common Player:		4.00
Inserted 1:37		
1	Darin Erstad	8.00
2	Travis Lee	6.00
3	Chipper Jones	20.00
4	Cal Ripken Jr.	25.00
5	Nomar Garciaparra	20.00
6	Sammy Sosa	25.00
7	Frank Thomas	15.00
8	Barry Larkin	5.00
9	Manny Ramirez	12.50
10	Larry Walker	6.00
11	Bob Higginson	4.00
12	Livan Hernandez	4.00
13	Moises Alou	5.00
14	Jeff King	4.00
15	Raul Mondesi	5.00
16	Marquis Grissom	4.00
17	David Ortiz	4.00
18	Vladimir Guerrero	10.00
19	Mike Piazza	20.00
20	Derek Jeter	20.00
21	Ben Grieve	8.00
22	Scott Rolen	8.00
23	Jason Kendall	4.00
24	Mark McGwire	40.00
25	Tony Gwynn	15.00
26	Barry Bonds	8.00
27	Ken Griffey Jr.	40.00
28	Wade Boggs	6.00
29	Juan Gonzalez	15.00
30	Jose Canseco	6.00

1999 Pacific Crown Royale

The Crown Royale 144-card base set has a horizontal format die-cut around a crown design at the top. The cards are double foiled and etched. There are two parallels: Limited Series and Opening Day. Limited Series is produced on 24-point stock with silver foil and limited to 99 numbered sets. Opening Day is limited to 72 numbered sets.

		MT
Complete Set (144):		275.00
Common Player:		.50
Common SP:		4.00
Limited Series: 8X		
SPs: 2X		
Production 99 sets		
Opening Day: 15X		
SPs: 3X		
Production 72 sets		
1	Jim Edmonds	.50
2	Darin Erstad	2.00
3	Troy Glaus	3.00
4	Tim Salmon	1.00
5	Mo Vaughn	2.00
6	Jay Bell	.50
7	Steve Finley	.50
8	Randy Johnson	2.00
9	Travis Lee	2.00
10	Matt Williams	1.00
11	Andruw Jones	2.50
12	Chipper Jones	6.00
13	Brian Jordan	.50
14	Ryan Klesko	.50
15	Javy Lopez	.75
16	Greg Maddux	6.00
17	Randall Simon	.50
18	Albert Belle	2.50
19	Will Clark	1.00
20	Delino DeShields	.50
21	Mike Mussina	2.00
22	Cal Ripken Jr.	8.00
23	Nomar Garciaparra	6.00
24	Pedro Martinez	2.50
25	Jose Offerman	.50
26	John Valentin	.50
27	Mark Grace	1.00
28	Lance Johnson	.50
29	Henry Rodriguez	.50
30	Sammy Sosa	6.00
31	Kerry Wood	2.00
32	Mike Caruso	.50
33	Ray Durham	.50
34	Magglio Ordonez	.75
35	Brian Simmons	.50
36	Frank Thomas	5.00
37	Mike Cameron	.50
38	Barry Larkin	.75
39	Greg Vaughn	.50
40	Dmitri Young	.50
41	Roberto Alomar	2.00
42	Sandy Alomar Jr.	.50
43	David Justice	.75
44	Kenny Lofton	2.00
45	Manny Ramirez	3.00
46	Jim Thome	.75
47	Dante Bichette	1.00
48	Vinny Castilla	.50
49	Todd Helton	2.00
50	Larry Walker	2.00
51	Tony Clark	1.00
52	Damion Easley	.50
53	Bob Higginson	.50
54	Brian Hunter	.50
55	Gabe Kapler	8.00
56	*Jeff Weaver*	15.00
57	Cliff Floyd	.50
58	Alex Gonzalez	.50
59	Mark Kotsay	.50
60	Derrek Lee	.50
61	Preston Wilson	4.00
62	Moises Alou	.75
63	Jeff Bagwell	2.50
64	Derek Bell	.50
65	Craig Biggio	1.50
66	Ken Caminiti	.75
67	Carlos Beltran	10.00
68	Johnny Damon	.50
69	Carlos Febles	6.00
70	Jeff King	.50
71	Kevin Brown	.75
72	Todd Hundley	.50
73	Eric Karros	.50
74	Raul Mondesi	.75
75	Gary Sheffield	.75
76	Jeromy Burnitz	.50
77	Jeff Cirillo	.50
78	Marquis Grissom	.50
79	Fernando Vina	.50
80	*Chad Allen*	4.00
81	Matt Lawton	.50
82	Doug Mientkiewicz	4.00
83	Brad Radke	.50
84	Todd Walker	.50
85	Michael Barrett	6.00
86	Brad Fullmer	.50
87	Vladimir Guerrero	3.00
88	Wilton Guerrero	.50
89	Ugueth Urbina	.50
90	Bobby Bonilla	.50
91	Rickey Henderson	1.00
92	Rey Ordonez	.50
93	Mike Piazza	6.00
94	Robin Ventura	.75
95	Roger Clemens	3.00
96	Orlando Hernandez	2.50
97	Derek Jeter	6.00
98	Chuck Knoblauch	1.00
99	Tino Martinez	.75
100	Bernie Williams	1.00
101	Eric Chavez	5.00
102	Jason Giambi	.50
103	Ben Grieve	2.00
104	Tim Raines	.50
105	Marlon Anderson	4.00
106	Doug Glanville	.50
107	Scott Rolen	2.50
108	Curt Schilling	.75
109	Brian Giles	.50
110	Jose Guillen	.50
111	Jason Kendall	.75
112	Kevin Young	.50
113	J.D. Drew	10.00
114	Jose Jimenez	4.00
115	Ray Lankford	.50
116	Mark McGwire	12.00
117	Fernando Tatis	.50
118	Matt Clement	4.00
119	Tony Gwynn	5.00
120	Trevor Hoffman	.50
121	Wally Joyner	.50
122	Reggie Sanders	.50
123	Barry Bonds	2.50
124	Ellis Burks	.50
125	Jeff Kent	.50
126	J.T. Snow	.50
127	Freddy Garcia	25.00
128	Ken Griffey Jr.	12.00
129	Edgar Martinez	.50
130	Alex Rodriguez	8.00
131	David Segui	.50
132	Rolando Arrojo	.50
133	Wade Boggs	1.50
134	Jose Canseco	2.00
135	Quinton McCracken	.50
136	Fred McGriff	.75
137	Juan Gonzalez	5.00
138	Rusty Greer	.50
139	Rafael Palmeiro	1.50
140	Ivan Rodriguez	2.50
141	Jose Cruz Jr.	.50
142	Carlos Delgado	.75
143	Shawn Green	.75
144	Roy Halladay	5.00

1999 Pacific Crown Royale Century 21

This 10-card set features some of baseball's most dominating players, on a full silver foil front. These are seeded 1:25 packs.

		MT
Complete Set (10):		100.00
Common Player:		10.00
Inserted 1:25		
1	Cal Ripken Jr.	25.00
2	Nomar Garciaparra	20.00
3	Sammy Sosa	20.00
4	Frank Thomas	15.00
5	Mike Piazza	20.00
6	J.D. Drew	6.00
7	Mark McGwire	30.00
8	Tony Gwynn	15.00
9	Ken Griffey Jr.	30.00
10	Alex Rodriguez	25.00

1999 Pacific Crown Royale Cramer's Choice Premiums

This enlarged 10-card set is die-cut into a trophy shape. Cards are enhanced with silver holographic fronts with silver holographic etching and gold foil stamping across the card bottom. They are seeded one per box. Six serially numbered parallels are also randomly seeded: Dark Blue (35 each), Green (30), Red (25), Light Blue (20), Gold (10) and Purple (1).

		MT
Complete Set (10):		120.00
Common Player:		10.00
Inserted 1:box		
Dark Blue (35 each): 5X		
Green (30 each): 6X		
Red (25 each): 8X		
Light Blue (20 each): 10X		
Gold (10 each): 15X		
Purple (one set produced)		
1	Cal Ripken Jr.	15.00
2	Nomar Garciaparra	12.00
3	Sammy Sosa	12.00
4	Frank Thomas	10.00
5	Mike Piazza	12.00
6	Derek Jeter	12.00
7	J.D. Drew	5.00
8	Mark McGwire	25.00
9	Tony Gwynn	10.00
10	Ken Griffey Jr.	25.00

1999 Pacific Crown Royale Gold Crown Die-Cut Premiums

This enlarged six-card set is identical to Crown Die-cuts besides their larger size. These were limited to 1,036 numbered sets.

		MT
Complete Set (6):		65.00
Common Player:		8.00
Inserted 6:10 boxes		
1	Cal Ripken Jr.	15.00
2	Mike Piazza	10.00
3	Ken Griffey Jr.	20.00
4	Tony Gwynn	8.00
5	Mark McGwire	20.00
6	J.D. Drew	8.00

1999 Pacific Crown Royale Living Legends

This 10-card set spotlights baseball's top stars on an full foiled card front. These are serial numbered to 375 sets.

		MT
Complete Set (10):		225.00
Common Player:		20.00
Production 375 sets		
1	Greg Maddux	25.00
2	Cal Ripken Jr.	30.00
3	Nomar Garciaparra	25.00
4	Sammy Sosa	25.00
5	Frank Thomas	20.00
6	Mike Piazza	25.00
7	Mark McGwire	40.00
8	Tony Gwynn	20.00
9	Ken Griffey Jr.	40.00
10	Alex Rodriguez	30.00

1999 Pacific Crown Royale Master Performers

This 20-card set features a full foiled front with the player photo in a frame like border. Master Performers are seeded 2:25 packs.

		MT
Complete Set (20):		150.00
Common Player:		2.50
Inserted 2:25		
1	Chipper Jones	12.00
2	Greg Maddux	12.00
3	Cal Ripken Jr.	15.00
4	Nomar Garciaparra	12.00
5	Sammy Sosa	12.00
6	Frank Thomas	9.00
7	Raul Mondesi	2.50
8	Vladimir Guerrero	6.00
9	Mike Piazza	12.00
10	Roger Clemens	8.00
11	Derek Jeter	12.00
12	Scott Rolen	4.00
13	J.D. Drew	4.00
14	Mark McGwire	20.00
15	Tony Gwynn	9.00
16	Barry Bonds	4.00
17	Ken Griffey Jr.	20.00
18	Alex Rodriguez	15.00
19	Juan Gonzalez	9.00
20	Ivan Rodriguez	4.00

1999 Pacific Crown Royale Pillars of the Game

This 25-card set features holographic silver foil fronts on a horizontal format. These are seeded one per pack.

		MT
Complete Set (25):		30.00
Common Player:		.60
Inserted 1:1		
1	Mo Vaughn	.75
2	Chipper Jones	2.00
3	Greg Maddux	2.00
4	Albert Belle	.75
5	Cal Ripken Jr.	2.50
6	Nomar Garciaparra	2.00
7	Sammy Sosa	2.00
8	Frank Thomas	1.50
9	Manny Ramirez	1.00
10	Jeff Bagwell	.75
11	Raul Mondesi	.60
12	Vladimir Guerrero	1.25
13	Mike Piazza	2.00
14	Roger Clemens	1.25
15	Derek Jeter	2.00
16	Bernie Williams	.60
17	Ben Grieve	.60
18	J.D. Drew	1.50
19	Mark McGwire	3.50
20	Tony Gwynn	1.50
21	Barry Bonds	.75
22	Ken Griffey Jr.	3.50
23	Alex Rodriguez	2.50
24	Juan Gonzalez	1.50
25	Ivan Rodriguez	.75

1999 Pacific Crown Royale Pivotal Players

This 25-card set features holographic silver foil fronts

with a flame in the background of the player photo. These are seeded one per pack.

		MT
Complete Set (25):		30.00
Common Player:		.60
Inserted 1:1		
1	Mo Vaughn	.75
2	Chipper Jones	2.00
3	Greg Maddux	2.00
4	Albert Belle	.75
5	Cal Ripken Jr.	2.50
6	Nomar Garciaparra	2.00
7	Sammy Sosa	2.00
8	Frank Thomas	1.50
9	Manny Ramirez	1.00
10	Craig Biggio	.60
11	Raul Mondesi	.60
12	Vladimir Guerrero	1.25
13	Mike Piazza	2.00
14	Roger Clemens	1.25
15	Derek Jeter	2.00
16	Bernie Williams	.60
17	Ben Grieve	.60
18	Scott Rolen	.75
19	J.D. Drew	1.50
20	Mark McGwire	3.50
21	Tony Gwynn	1.50
22	Ken Griffey Jr.	3.50
23	Alex Rodriguez	2.50
24	Juan Gonzalez	1.50
25	Ivan Rodriguez	.75

1999 Pacific Invincible

The base set consists of 150 base cards and feature a player photo and a headshot in a cel window on the bottom right portion of the card. There are also two parallels to the base set: Opening Day and Platinum Blue. Both parallels are limited to 67 serial numbered sets.

		MT
Complete Set (150):		175.00
Common Player:		.75
Opening Day: 9X		
Production 67 sets		
Platinum Blues: 9X		
Production 67 sets		
Wax Box:		60.00
1	Jim Edmonds	.75
2	Darin Erstad	3.00
3	Troy Glaus	4.00
4	Tim Salmon	1.50
5	Mo Vaughn	2.00
6	Steve Finley	.75
7	Randy Johnson	2.00
8	Travis Lee	2.50
9	Dante Powell	.75
10	Matt Williams	1.50
11	Bret Boone	.75
12	Andruw Jones	2.00
13	Chipper Jones	8.00
14	Brian Jordan	.75
15	Ryan Klesko	.75
16	Javy Lopez	.75
17	Greg Maddux	7.50
18	Brady Anderson	.75
19	Albert Belle	3.00
20	Will Clark	1.50
21	Mike Mussina	2.00
22	Cal Ripken Jr.	10.00
23	Nomar Garciaparra	8.00
24	Pedro Martinez	2.50
25	Trot Nixon	.75
26	Jose Offerman	.75
27	Donnie Sadler	.75
28	John Valentin	.75
29	Mark Grace	1.00
30	Lance Johnson	.75
31	Henry Rodriguez	.75
32	Sammy Sosa	8.00
33	Kerry Wood	3.00
34	McKay Christensen	.75
35	Ray Durham	.75
36	Jeff Liefer	.75
37	Frank Thomas	6.00
38	Mike Cameron	.75
39	Barry Larkin	1.00
40	Greg Vaughn	1.00
41	Dmitri Young	.75
42	Roberto Alomar	2.50
43	Sandy Alomar Jr.	.75
44	David Justice	1.00
45	Kenny Lofton	2.00
46	Manny Ramirez	5.00
47	Jim Thome	1.00
48	Dante Bichette	1.00
49	Vinny Castilla	1.00
50	Darryl Hamilton	.75
51	Todd Helton	2.00
52	Neifi Perez	.75
53	Larry Walker	2.00
54	Tony Clark	1.50
55	Damion Easley	.75
56	Bob Higginson	.75
57	Brian Hunter	.75
58	Gabe Kapler	4.00
59	Cliff Floyd	.75
60	Alex Gonzalez	.75
61	Mark Kotsay	.75
62	Derrek Lee	.75
63	Braden Looper	.75
64	Moises Alou	1.00
65	Jeff Bagwell	3.00
66	Craig Biggio	1.50
67	Ken Caminiti	1.00
68	Scott Elarton	.75
69	Mitch Meluskey	.75
70	Carlos Beltran	1.50
71	Johnny Damon	.75
72	Carlos Febles	1.00
73	Jeremy Giambi	.75
74	Kevin Brown	1.00
75	Todd Hundley	.75
76	Paul Loduca	.75
77	Raul Mondesi	1.00
78	Gary Sheffield	1.00
79	Geoff Jenkins	.75
80	Jeromy Burnitz	.75
81	Marquis Grissom	.75
82	Jose Valentin	.75
83	Fernando Vina	.75
84	Corey Koskie	.75
85	Matt Lawton	.75
86	Christian Guzman	.75
87	Torii Hunter	.75
88	Doug Mientkiewicz	.75
89	Michael Barrett	.75
90	Brad Fullmer	.75
91	Vladimir Guerrero	4.00
92	Fernando Seguignol	1.00
93	Ugueth Urbina	.75
94	Bobby Bonilla	.75
95	Rickey Henderson	1.50
96	Rey Ordonez	.75
97	Mike Piazza	8.00
98	Robin Ventura	.75
99	Roger Clemens	4.00
100	Derek Jeter	8.00
101	Chuck Knoblauch	1.00
102	Tino Martinez	1.00
103	Paul O'Neill	1.00
104	Bernie Williams	1.50
105	Eric Chavez	3.00
106	Ryan Christenson	.75
107	Jason Giambi	.75
108	Ben Grieve	3.00
109	Miguel Tejada	.75
110	Marlon Anderson	.75
111	Doug Glanville	.75
112	Scott Rolen	3.00
113	Curt Schilling	1.00
114	Brian Giles	.75
115	Warren Morris	.75
116	Jason Kendall	1.00
117	Kris Benson	.75
118	J.D. Drew	3.00
119	Ray Lankford	.75
120	Mark McGwire	12.50
121	Matt Clement	.75
122	Tony Gwynn	6.00
123	Trevor Hoffman	.75
124	Wally Joyner	.75
125	Reggie Sanders	.75
126	Barry Bonds	3.00
127	Ellis Burks	.75
128	Jeff Kent	.75
129	Stan Javier	.75
130	J.T. Snow	.75
131	Jay Buhner	.75
132	Freddy Garcia	.75
133	Ken Griffey Jr.	12.50
134	Russ Davis	.75
135	Edgar Martinez	.75
136	Alex Rodriguez	10.00
137	David Segui	.75
138	Rolando Arrojo	.75
139	Wade Boggs	1.50
140	Jose Canseco	2.50
141	Quinton McCracken	.75
142	Fred McGriff	1.00
143	Juan Gonzalez	6.00
144	Tom Goodwin	.75
145	Rusty Greer	.75
146	Ivan Rodriguez	3.00
147	Jose Cruz Jr.	.75
148	Carlos Delgado	1.50
149	Shawn Green	1.00
150	Roy Halladay	1.00

1999 Pacific Invincible Diamond Magic

This 10-card set features a horizontal format with silver foil stamping on the front. Diamond Magic's are seeded 1:49 packs.

		MT
Complete Set (10):		80.00
Common Player:		7.50
Inserted 1:49		
1	Cal Ripken Jr.	12.50
2	Nomar Garciaparra	10.00
3	Sammy Sosa	10.00
4	Frank Thomas	7.50
5	Mike Piazza	10.00
6	J.D. Drew	6.00
7	Mark McGwire	15.00
8	Tony Gwynn	7.50
9	Ken Griffey Jr.	15.00
10	Alex Rodriguez	12.50

1999 Pacific Invincible Flash Point

This 20-card set features gold etching and gold foil stamping on the card front. These were seeded 1:25 packs.

		MT
Complete Set (20):		200.00
Common Player:		4.00
Inserted 1:25		
1	Mo Vaughn	4.00
2	Chipper Jones	15.00
3	Greg Maddux	15.00
4	Cal Ripken Jr.	20.00
5	Nomar Garciaparra	15.00
6	Sammy Sosa	15.00
7	Frank Thomas	12.50
8	Manny Ramirez	9.00
9	Vladimir Guerrero	8.00
10	Mike Piazza	15.00
11	Roger Clemens	8.00
12	Derek Jeter	15.00
13	Ben Grieve	4.00
14	Scott Rolen	4.00
15	J.D. Drew	5.00
16	Mark McGwire	25.00
17	Tony Gwynn	12.50
18	Ken Griffey Jr.	25.00
19	Alex Rodriguez	20.00
20	Juan Gonzalez	12.50

1999 Pacific Invincible Giants of the Game

This insert set features 10 of baseball's top stars and are limited to 10 serially numbered sets. Due to their scarcity no pricing is available.

		MT
Complete Set (10):		
Common Player:		
Production 10 sets		
1	Cal Ripken Jr.	
2	Nomar Garciaparra	
3	Sammy Sosa	
4	Frank Thomas	
5	Mike Piazza	
6	J.D. Drew	
7	Mark McGwire	
8	Tony Gwynn	
9	Ken Griffey Jr.	
10	Alex Rodriguez	

1999 Pacific Invincible Sandlot Heroes

Sandlot Heroes salutes baseball's top players on a horizontal format with holographic silver foil stamping on the card front. These were inserted one per pack.

		MT
Complete Set (20):		25.00
Common Player:		.75
Inserted 1:1		
1	Mo Vaughn	.75
2	Chipper Jones	2.00
3	Greg Maddux	2.00
4	Cal Ripken Jr.	2.50
5	Nomar Garciaparra	2.00
6	Sammy Sosa	2.00
7	Frank Thomas	1.50
8	Manny Ramirez	1.00
9	Vladimir Guerrero	1.00
10	Mike Piazza	2.00
11	Roger Clemens	1.00
12	Derek Jeter	2.00
13	Eric Chavez	.75
14	Ben Grieve	.75
15	J.D. Drew	.75
16	Mark McGwire	4.00
17	Tony Gwynn	1.50
18	Ken Griffey Jr.	4.00
19	Alex Rodriguez	2.50
20	Juan Gonzalez	1.50

1999 Pacific Invincible Seismic Force

This 20-card set has a dot pattern behind the featured player with the left side and bottom of the card in a gold border. These were seeded one per pack.

		MT
Complete Set (20):		25.00
Common Player:		.50
Inserted 1:1		
1	Mo Vaughn	.50
2	Chipper Jones	2.00
3	Greg Maddux	2.00
4	Cal Ripken Jr.	2.50
5	Nomar Garciaparra	2.00
6	Sammy Sosa	2.00
7	Frank Thomas	1.50
8	Manny Ramirez	1.00
9	Vladimir Guerrero	1.00
10	Mike Piazza	2.00
11	Bernie Williams	.50
12	Derek Jeter	2.00
13	Ben Grieve	.50
14	J.D. Drew	.75
15	Mark McGwire	3.50
16	Tony Gwynn	1.50
17	Ken Griffey Jr.	3.50
18	Alex Rodriguez	2.50
19	Juan Gonzalez	1.50
20	Ivan Rodriguez	.75

1999 Pacific Invincible Thunder Alley

Thunder Alley focuses on baseball's top power hitters. These were inserted 1:121 packs.

		MT
Complete Set (20):		500.00
Common Player:		10.00
Inserted 1:121		
1	Mo Vaughn	10.00
2	Chipper Jones	40.00
3	Cal Ripken Jr.	50.00
4	Nomar Garciaparra	40.00
5	Sammy Sosa	40.00
6	Frank Thomas	25.00
7	Manny Ramirez	20.00
8	Todd Helton	10.00
9	Vladimir Guerrero	12.50
10	Mike Piazza	40.00
11	Derek Jeter	40.00
12	Ben Grieve	12.50
13	Scott Rolen	15.00
14	J.D. Drew	15.00
15	Mark McGwire	60.00
16	Tony Gwynn	30.00
17	Ken Griffey Jr.	60.00
18	Alex Rodriguez	50.00
19	Juan Gonzalez	30.00
20	Ivan Rodriguez	15.00

1999 Pacific Omega Sample

The Omega brand for '99 was launched with this sample card of Pacific spokesman Tony Gwynn. The card is in the same format as the regular-issue cards, except for the SAMPLE overprint on back and in the card-number circle at bottom-right.

		MT
SAMPLE	Tony Gwynn	3.00

1999 Pacific Omega

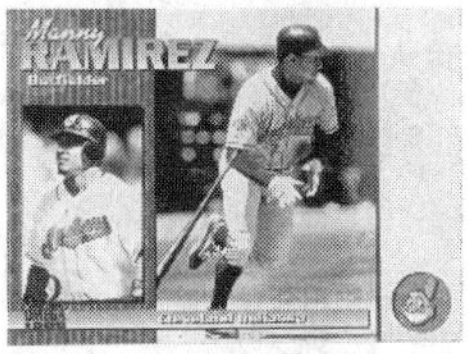

		MT
Complete Set (250):		35.00
Common Player:		.10
Copper Stars: 20X		
Young Stars/RCs: 8X		
Production 99 sets H		
Platinum Blue Stars: 30X		
Young Stars/RCs: 10X		
Production 75 sets		
Wax Box:		65.00
1	Garret Anderson	.10
2	Jim Edmonds	.10
3	Darin Erstad	.40
4	Chuck Finley	.10
5	Troy Glaus	.50
6	Troy Percival	.10
7	Chris Pritchett	.10
8	Tim Salmon	.25
9	Mo Vaughn	.50
10	Jay Bell	.10
11	Steve Finley	.10
12	Luis Gonzalez	.10
13	Randy Johnson	.50
14	*Byung-Hyun Kim*	2.00
15	Travis Lee	.40
16	Matt Williams	.40
17	Tony Womack	.10
18	Bret Boone	.10
19	Mark DeRosa	.10
20	Tom Glavine	.25
21	Andruw Jones	.50
22	Chipper Jones	2.00
23	Brian Jordan	.10
24	Ryan Klesko	.20
25	Javy Lopez	.20
26	Greg Maddux	1.50
27	John Smoltz	.15
28	Bruce Chen, Odalis Perez	.10

29	Brady Anderson	.10
30	Harold Baines	.10
31	Albert Belle	.75
32	Will Clark	.40
33	Delino DeShields	.10
34	Jerry Hairston Jr.	.25
35	Charles Johnson	.10
36	Mike Mussina	.50
37	Cal Ripken Jr.	2.50
38	B.J. Surhoff	.10
39	Jin Ho Cho	.10
40	Nomar Garciaparra	2.00
41	Pedro Martinez	1.00
42	Jose Offerman	.10
43	Troy O'Leary	.10
44	John Valentin	.10
45	Jason Varitek	.10
46	*Juan Pena*, Brian Rose	.10
47	Mark Grace	.25
48	Glenallen Hill	.10
49	Tyler Houston	.10
50	Mickey Morandini	.10
51	Henry Rodriguez	.10
52	Sammy Sosa	2.00
53	Kevin Tapani	.10
54	Mike Caruso	.10
55	Ray Durham	.10
56	Paul Konerko	.10
57	Carlos Lee	.10
58	Magglio Ordonez	.20
59	Mike Sirotka	.10
60	Frank Thomas	1.50
61	Mark L. Johnson, Chris Singleton	.10
62	Mike Cameron	.10
63	Sean Casey	.25
64	Pete Harnisch	.10
65	Barry Larkin	.20
66	Pokey Reese	.10
67	Greg Vaughn	.25
68	Scott Williamson	.10
69	Dmitri Young	.10
70	Roberto Alomar	.50
71	Sandy Alomar Jr.	.20
72	Travis Fryman	.20
73	David Justice	.20
74	Kenny Lofton	.50
75	Manny Ramirez	1.00
76	Richie Sexson	.10
77	Jim Thome	.30
78	Omar Vizquel	.10
79	Jaret Wright	.10
80	Dante Bichette	.25
81	Vinny Castilla	.10
82	Todd Helton	.50
83	Darryl Hamilton	.10
84	Darryl Kile	.10
85	Neifi Perez	.10
86	Larry Walker	.50
87	Tony Clark	.30
88	Damion Easley	.10
89	Juan Encarnacion	.10
90	Bobby Higginson	.10
91	Gabe Kapler	.75
92	Dean Palmer	.10
93	Justin Thompson	.10
94	*Masao Kida,Jeff Weaver*	.30
95	Bruce Aven	.10
96	Luis Castillo	.10
97	Alex Fernandez	.10
98	Cliff Floyd	.10
99	Alex Gonzalez	.10
100	Mark Kotsay	.10
101	Preston Wilson	.10
102	Moises Alou	.15
103	Jeff Bagwell	.75
104	Derek Bell	.10
105	Craig Biggio	.40
106	Mike Hampton	.10
107	Richard Hidalgo	.10
108	Jose Lima	.10
109	Billy Wagner	.10
110	Russ Johnson, Daryle Ward	.10
111	Carlos Beltran	1.00
112	Johnny Damon	.10
113	Jermaine Dye	.10
114	Carlos Febles	.40
115	Jeremy Giambi	.10
116	Joe Randa	.10
117	Mike Sweeney	.10
118	*Orber Moreno*, Jose Santiago	.10
119	Kevin Brown	.20
120	Todd Hundley	.10
121	Eric Karros	.20
122	Raul Mondesi	.20
123	Chan Ho Park	.20
124	Angel Pena	.10
125	Gary Sheffield	.25
126	Devon White	.10
127	Eric Young	.10
128	Ron Belliard	.25
129	Jeromy Burnitz	.20
130	Jeff Cirillo	.10
131	Marquis Grissom	.10
132	Geoff Jenkins	.10
133	David Nilsson	.10
134	Hideo Nomo	.15
135	Fernando Vina	.10
136	Ron Coomer	.10
137	Marty Cordova	.10
138	Corey Koskie	.10
139	Brad Radke	.10
140	Todd Walker	.20
141	*Chad Allen*, Torii Hunter	.10
142	Cristian Guzman, Jacque Jones	.10
143	Michael Barrett	.40
144	Orlando Cabrera	.10
145	Vladimir Guerrero	1.00
146	Wilton Guerrero	.10
147	Ugueth Urbina	.10
148	Rondell White	.20
149	Chris Widger	.10
150	Edgardo Alfonzo	.25
151	Roger Cedeno	.10
152	Octavio Dotel	.10
153	Rickey Henderson	.25
154	John Olerud	.25
155	Rey Ordonez	.10
156	Mike Piazza	2.00
157	Robin Ventura	.25
158	Scott Brosius	.10
159	Roger Clemens	1.00
160	David Cone	.25
161	Chili Davis	.10
162	Orlando Hernandez	.50
163	Derek Jeter	2.00
164	Chuck Knoblauch	.25
165	Tino Martinez	.20
166	Paul O'Neill	.25
167	Bernie Williams	.60
168	Jason Giambi	.10
169	Ben Grieve	.50
170	*Chad Harville*	.10
171	*Tim Hudson*	2.00
172	Tony Phillips	.10
173	Kenny Rogers	.10
174	Matt Stairs	.10
175	Miguel Tejada	.20
176	Eric Chavez	.25
177	Bobby Abreu	.10
178	Ron Gant	.15
179	Doug Glanville	.10
180	Mike Lieberthal	.10
181	Desi Relaford	.10
182	Scott Rolen	.75
183	Curt Schilling	.25
184	Marlon Anderson, Randy Wolf	.10
185	Brant Brown	.10
186	Brian Giles	.10
187	Jason Kendall	.20
188	Al Martin	.10
189	Ed Sprague	.10
190	Kevin Young	.10
191	Kris Benson, Warren Morris	.10
192	Kent Bottenfield	.10
193	Eric Davis	.10
194	J.D. Drew	1.00
195	Ray Lankford	.10
196	*Joe McEwing*	.75
197	Mark McGwire	3.50
198	Edgar Renteria	.10
199	Fernando Tatis	.25
200	Andy Ashby	.10
201	Ben Davis	.20
202	Tony Gwynn	1.50
203	Trevor Hoffman	.10
204	Wally Joyner	.10
205	Gary Matthews Jr.	.10
206	Ruben Rivera	.10
207	Reggie Sanders	.10
208	Rich Aurilia	.10
209	Marvin Benard	.10
210	Barry Bonds	.75
211	Ellis Burks	.10
212	Stan Javier	.10
213	Jeff Kent	.10
214	Robb Nen	.10
215	J.T. Snow	.10
216	David Bell	.10
217	Jay Buhner	.15
218	Freddy Garcia	.40
219	Ken Griffey Jr.	3.50
220	Brian Hunter	.10
221	Butch Huskey	.10
222	Edgar Martinez	.10
223	Jamie Moyer	.10
224	Alex Rodriguez	2.50
225	David Segui	.10
226	Rolando Arrojo	.10
227	Wade Boggs	.40
228	Miguel Cairo	.10
229	Jose Canseco	.75
230	Dave Martinez	.10
231	Fred McGriff	.25
232	Kevin Stocker	.10
233	*Mike Duvall*, David Lamb	.10
234	Royce Clayton	.10
235	Juan Gonzalez	1.00
236	Rusty Greer	.10
237	Ruben Mateo	.25
238	Rafael Palmeiro	.50
239	Ivan Rodriguez	.75
240	John Wetteland	.10
241	Todd Zeile	.10
242	Jeff Zimmerman	.10
243	Homer Bush	.10
244	Jose Cruz Jr.	.10
245	Carlos Delgado	.30
246	Tony Fernandez	.10
247	Shawn Green	.25
248	Shannon Stewart	.10
249	David Wells	.15
250	Roy Halladay, Billy Koch	.15

1999 Pacific Omega Debut Duos

		MT
Complete Set (10):		275.00
Common Player:		10.00
Inserted 1:145		
1	Nomar Garciaparra, Vladimir Guerrero	30.00
2	Derek Jeter, Andy Pettitte	35.00
3	Garret Anderson, Alex Rodriguez	30.00
4	Chipper Jones, Raul Mondesi	30.00
5	Pedro Martinez, Mike Piazza	35.00
6	Mo Vaughn, Bernie Williams	10.00
7	Juan Gonzalez, Ken Griffey Jr.	50.00
8	Sammy Sosa, Larry Walker	30.00
9	Barry Bonds, Mark McGwire	50.00
10	Wade Boggs, Tony Gwynn	25.00

1999 Pacific Omega Diamond Masters

		MT
Complete Set (24):		75.00
Common Player:		1.00
Inserted 4:37		
1	Darin Erstad	1.50
2	Mo Vaughn	1.00
3	Matt Williams	1.00
4	Andruw Jones	2.50
5	Chipper Jones	8.00
6	Greg Maddux	7.50
7	Cal Ripken Jr.	10.00
8	Nomar Garciaparra	8.00
9	Pedro Martinez	4.00
10	Sammy Sosa	8.00
11	Frank Thomas	6.00
12	Kenny Lofton	2.50
13	Manny Ramirez	5.00
14	Larry Walker	2.50
15	Gabe Kapler	2.50
16	Jeff Bagwell	3.00
17	Craig Biggio	2.00
18	Raul Mondesi	1.00
19	Vladimir Guerrero	4.00
20	Mike Piazza	8.00
21	Roger Clemens	4.00
22	Derek Jeter	8.00
23	Bernie Williams	2.00
24	Scott Rolen	3.00

1999 Pacific Omega EO Portraits

		MT
Complete Set (20):		350.00
Common Player:		5.00
Inserted 1:73		
1	Mo Vaughn	5.00
2	Chipper Jones	25.00
3	Greg Maddux	20.00
4	Cal Ripken Jr.	30.00
5	Nomar Garciaparra	25.00
6	Sammy Sosa	25.00
7	Frank Thomas	20.00
8	Manny Ramirez	12.50
9	Jeff Bagwell	10.00
10	Mike Piazza	25.00
11	Roger Clemens	15.00
12	Derek Jeter	25.00
13	Scott Rolen	10.00
14	Mark McGwire	40.00
15	Tony Gwynn	20.00
16	Barry Bonds	10.00
17	Ken Griffey Jr.	40.00
18	Alex Rodriguez	30.00
19	Jose Canseco	7.50
20	Juan Gonzalez	10.00

1999 Pacific Omega Hit Machine 3000

Within days of Tony Gwynn's 3,000 hit on Aug. 6, Pacific had rushed into production a special insert set honoring the achievement of its long-time spokesman. A total of 3,000 serially numbered sets of 20 cards were issued as random packs inserts in Omega. Fronts feature various game-action and studio photos of Gwynn, and are highlighted in silver foil. Backs have two more color photos of Gwynn and a few sentences about the player. A serial number in printed on front.

		MT
Complete Set (20):		150.00
Common Card:		15.00
1	The Hitting Machine	15.00
2	The Eyes Have It	15.00
3	The Art of Hitting	15.00
4	Solid as a Rock	15.00
5	Seeing Doubles	15.00
6	Pithcer's Worst Nightmare	15.00
7	Portrait of an All-Star	15.00
8	An American Hero	15.00
9	Fan Favorite	15.00
10	Mr. Batting Title	15.00
11	4-for-5!	15.00
12	Mission Accomplished	15.00
13	One Hit Away	15.00
14	A Tip of the Hat	15.00
15	It's a Base Hit!	15.00
16	2997th - Grand Slam!	15.00
17	2998th Hit	15.00
18	2999th Hit - 2-Run Double	15.00
19	3000th Hit!	15.00
20	3000 Hits, 8874 At-Bats, 18 Years	15.00

1999 Pacific Omega HR '99

		MT
Complete Set (20):		125.00
Common Player:		2.50
Inserted 1:37		
1	Mo Vaughn	2.50
2	Matt Williams	2.50
3	Chipper Jones	12.50
4	Albert Belle	4.00
5	Nomar Garciaparra	12.50
6	Sammy Sosa	12.50
7	Frank Thomas	6.00
8	Manny Ramirez	5.00
9	Jeff Bagwell	4.00
10	Raul Mondesi	2.50
11	Vladimir Guerrero	6.00
12	Mike Piazza	12.50
13	Derek Jeter	12.50
14	Mark McGwire	20.00
15	Fernando Tatis	2.50
16	Barry Bonds	4.00
17	Ken Griffey Jr.	20.00
18	Alex Rodriguez	15.00
19	Jose Canseco	4.00
20	Juan Gonzalez	5.00

1999 Pacific Omega 5-Tool Talents

		MT
Complete Set (30):		100.00
Common Player:		1.00
Inserted 4:37		
1	Randy Johnson	2.00
2	Carlos Lee	1.00
3	Chipper Jones	8.00
4	Nomar Garciaparra	8.00
5	Barry Bonds	3.00
6	Jeff Bagwell	3.00
7	Greg Maddux	6.00
8	Gabe Kapler	2.50
9	Manny Ramirez	4.00
10	Frank Thomas	5.00
11	Ivan Rodriguez	3.00
12	Ken Griffey Jr.	15.00
13	Pedro Martinez	4.00
14	Carlos Beltran	2.00
15	Mark McGwire	15.00
16	Larry Walker	2.50
17	Cal Ripken Jr.	10.00
18	Derek Jeter	8.00
19	Kevin Brown	1.00
20	J.D. Drew	4.00
21	Sammy Sosa	8.00
22	Tony Gwynn	6.00
23	Alex Rodriguez	10.00
24	Jose Canseco	3.00
25	Roger Clemens	4.00
26	Ruben Mateo	1.50
27	Vladimir Guerrero	4.00
28	Mike Piazza	8.00
29	Scott Rolen	2.50
30	Juan Gonzalez	3.00

1999 Pacific Omega 5-Tool Talents Tiered

A parallel of the 5-Tool Talents inserts is fractured into five tiers of increasing scarcity, differentiated by the color of foil highlights and the serially numbered limited edition. The breakdown is: Tier 1, blue, 100 sets; Tier 2, red, 75 sets; Tier 3, green, 50 sets; Tier 4, purple, 25 sets; Tier 5, gold, 1 set. The unique gold cards are not priced due to their rarity.

		MT
	TIER 1 (BLUE, 100 SETS)	
1	Randy Johnson	6.00
6	Carlos Lee	3.00
11	Chipper Jones	15.00
18	Nomar Garciaparra	15.00
21	Jeff Bagwell	9.00
28	Barry Bonds	9.00
	TIER 2 (RED, 75 SETS)	
2	Greg Maddux	25.00
7	Gabe Kapler	5.00
13	Manny Ramirez	15.00
16	Ken Griffey Jr.	50.00
19	Frank Thomas	15.00
30	Ivan Rodriguez	12.50
	TIER 3 (GREEN, 50 SETS)	
3	Pedro Martinez	25.00
8	Carlos Beltran	15.00
15	Mark McGwire	100.00
20	Larry Walker	15.00
25	Cal Ripken Jr.	80.00
26	Derek Jeter	60.00
	TIER 4 (PURPLE, 25 SETS)	
4	Kevin Brown	15.00
9	J.D. Drew	30.00
12	Sammy Sosa	60.00
17	Jose Canseco	40.00
23	Tony Gwynn	50.00
29	Alex Rodriguez	75.00
	TIER 5 (GOLD 1 SET)	
5	Roger Clemens	
10	Ruben Mateo	
14	Vladimir Guerrero	
22	Mike Piazza	
24	Juan Gonzalez	
27	Scott Rolen	

The election of former players to the Hall of Fame does not always have an immediate upward effect on card prices. The hobby market generally has done a good job of predicting those inductions and adjusting values over the course of several years.

1999 Pacific Paramount Sample

Pacific spokesman Tony Gwynn is featured on the sample card issued to introduce the brand for 1999. The card carries a large "SAMPLE" overprint diagonally on back.

	MT
Tony Gwynn	3.00

1999 Pacific Paramount

The 250-card base set is highlighted by silver foil stamping and a white border. Card backs have a small photo along with 1998 statistics and career totals and a a brief career note. There are six parallels to the base set: Copper, Platinum Blue, Holographic Silver, Opening Day Issue, Gold and Holographic Gold. Each parallel is enhanced with the appropriate foil color. Coppers are found exclusively in hobby packs at a rate of one per pack. Platinum Blues are seeded one per 73 packs, Holographic Silvers are hobby only and limited to 99 serial numbered sets. Opening Day Issue is limited to 74 numbered sets. Golds are found one per retail pack. Holographic Golds are limited to 199 numbered sets.

		MT
Complete Set (250):		35.00
Common Player:		.10
Common Copper:		.25
Copper Stars: 3X		
Common Platinum Blue:		3.00
Platinum Blue Stars: 20X		
Common Holographic Silver:		4.00
Holographic Silver Stars: 30X		
Common Opening Day:		5.00
Opening Day Stars: 40X		
Common Gold:		.35
Gold Stars: 4X		
Common Holographic Gold:		2.50
Holographic Gold Stars: 20X		
Wax Box:		45.00
1	Garret Anderson	.10
2	Gary DiSarcina	.10
3	Jim Edmonds	.20
4	Darin Erstad	.60
5	Chuck Finley	.10
6	Troy Glaus	.75
7	Troy Percival	.10
8	Tim Salmon	.25
9	Mo Vaughn	.40
10	Tony Batista	.10
11	Jay Bell	.10
12	Andy Benes	.10
13	Steve Finley	.10
14	Luis Gonzalez	.10
15	Randy Johnson	.50
16	Travis Lee	.60
17	Todd Stottlemyre	.10
18	Matt Williams	.25
19	David Dellucci	.10
20	Bret Boone	.10
21	Andres Galarraga	.40
22	Tom Glavine	.25
23	Andruw Jones	.50
24	Chipper Jones	1.50
25	Brian Jordan	.10
26	Ryan Klesko	.15
27	Javy Lopez	.20
28	Greg Maddux	1.50
29	John Smoltz	.20
30	Brady Anderson	.10
31	Albert Belle	.60
32	Will Clark	.30
33	Delino DeShields	.10
34	Charles Johnson	.10
35	Mike Mussina	.50
36	Cal Ripken Jr.	2.00
37	B.J. Surhoff	.10
38	Nomar Garciaparra	1.50
39	Reggie Jefferson	.10
40	Darren Lewis	.10
41	Pedro Martinez	.50
42	Troy O'Leary	.10
43	Jose Offerman	.10
44	Donnie Sadler	.10
45	John Valentin	.10
46	Rod Beck	.10
47	Gary Gaetti	.10
48	Mark Grace	.25
49	Lance Johnson	.10
50	Mickey Morandini	.10
51	Henry Rodriguez	.10
52	Sammy Sosa	1.50
53	Kerry Wood	.60
54	Mike Caruso	.10
55	Ray Durham	.10
56	Paul Konerko	.20
57	Jaime Navarro	.10
58	Greg Norton	.10
59	Magglio Ordonez	.10
60	Frank Thomas	1.00
61	Aaron Boone	.10
62	Mike Cameron	.10
63	Barry Larkin	.15
64	Hal Morris	.10
65	Pokey Reese	.10
66	Brett Tomko	.10
67	Greg Vaughn	.20
68	Dmitri Young	.10
69	Roberto Alomar	.50
70	Sandy Alomar Jr.	.20
71	Bartolo Colon	.10
72	Travis Fryman	.10
73	David Justice	.25
74	Kenny Lofton	.40
75	Manny Ramirez	1.00
76	Richie Sexson	.10
77	Jim Thome	.25
78	Omar Vizquel	.10
79	Dante Bichette	.30
80	Vinny Castilla	.20
81	Darryl Hamilton	.10
82	Todd Helton	.50
83	Darryl Kile	.10
84	Mike Lansing	.10
85	Neifi Perez	.10
86	Larry Walker	.50
87	Tony Clark	.30
88	Damion Easley	.10
89	Bob Higginson	.10
90	Brian Hunter	.10
91	Dean Palmer	.10
92	Justin Thompson	.10
93	Todd Dunwoody	.10
94	Cliff Floyd	.10
95	Alex Gonzalez	.10
96	Livan Hernandez	.10
97	Mark Kotsay	.10
98	Derrek Lee	.10
99	Kevin Orie	.10
100	Moises Alou	.20
101	Jeff Bagwell	.75
102	Derek Bell	.10
103	Craig Biggio	.40
104	Ken Caminiti	.20
105	Ricky Gutierrez	.10
106	Richard Hidalgo	.10
107	Billy Wagner	.15
108	Jeff Conine	.10
109	Johnny Damon	.10
110	Carlos Febles	.20
111	Jeremy Giambi	.10
112	Jeff King	.10
113	Jeff Montgomery	.10
114	Joe Randa	.10
115	Kevin Brown	.25
116	Mark Grudzielanek	.10
117	Todd Hundley	.10
118	Eric Karros	.10
119	Raul Mondesi	.25
120	Chan Ho Park	.25
121	Gary Sheffield	.25
122	Devon White	.10
123	Eric Young	.10
124	Jeromy Burnitz	.10
125	Jeff Cirillo	.10
126	Marquis Grissom	.10
127	Geoff Jenkins	.10
128	Dave Nilsson	.10
129	Jose Valentin	.10
130	Fernando Vina	.10
131	Rick Aguilera	.10
132	Ron Coomer	.10
133	Marty Cordova	.10
134	Matt Lawton	.10
135	David Ortiz	.10
136	Brad Radke	.10
137	Terry Steinbach	.10
138	Javier Valentin	.10
139	Todd Walker	.10
140	Orlando Cabrera	.10
141	Brad Fullmer	.10
142	Vladimir Guerrero	.75
143	Wilton Guerrero	.10
144	Carl Pavano	.10
145	Ugueth Urbina	.10
146	Rondell White	.15
147	Chris Widger	.10
148	Edgardo Alfonzo	.15
149	Bobby Bonilla	.10
150	Rickey Henderson	.25
151	Brian McRae	.10
152	Hideo Nomo	.25
153	John Olerud	.25
154	Rey Ordonez	.15
155	Mike Piazza	1.50
156	Robin Ventura	.20
157	Masato Yoshii	.10
158	Roger Clemens	1.00
159	David Cone	.20
160	Orlando Hernandez	.75
161	Hideki Irabu	.15
162	Derek Jeter	1.50
163	Chuck Knoblauch	.25
164	Tino Martinez	.20
165	Paul O'Neill	.25
166	Darryl Strawberry	.20
167	Bernie Williams	.40
168	Eric Chavez	.60
169	Ryan Christenson	.10
170	Jason Giambi	.10
171	Ben Grieve	.60
172	Tony Phillips	.10
173	Tim Raines	.10
174	Scott Spiezio	.10
175	Miguel Tejada	.25
176	Bobby Abreu	.10
177	Rico Brogna	.10
178	Ron Gant	.15
179	Doug Glanville	.10
180	Desi Relaford	.10
181	Scott Rolen	.75
182	Curt Schilling	.25
183	Brant Brown	.10
184	Brian Giles	.15
185	Jose Guillen	.10
186	Jason Kendall	.20
187	Al Martin	.10
188	Ed Sprague	.10
189	Kevin Young	.10
190	Eric Davis	.10
191	J.D. Drew	1.00
192	Ray Lankford	.10
193	Eli Marrero	.10
194	Mark McGwire	3.00
195	Edgar Renteria	.10
196	Fernando Tatis	.15
197	Andy Ashby	.10
198	Tony Gwynn	1.25
199	Carlos Hernandez	.10
200	Trevor Hoffman	.10
201	Wally Joyner	.10
202	Jim Leyritz	.10
203	Ruben Rivera	.10
204	Matt Clement	.10
205	Quilvio Veras	.10
206	Rich Aurilia	.10
207	Marvin Benard	.10
208	Barry Bonds	.60
209	Ellis Burks	.10
210	Jeff Kent	.10
211	Bill Mueller	.10
212	Robb Nen	.10
213	J.T. Snow	.10
214	Jay Buhner	.20
215	Jeff Fassero	.10
216	Ken Griffey Jr.	3.00
217	Carlos Guillen	.10
218	Butch Huskey	.10
219	Edgar Martinez	.10
220	Alex Rodriguez	2.00
221	David Segui	.10
222	Dan Wilson	.10
223	Rolando Arrojo	.10
224	Wade Boggs	.25
225	Jose Canseco	.50
226	Roberto Hernandez	.10
227	Dave Martinez	.10
228	Quinton McCracken	.10
229	Fred McGriff	.20
230	Kevin Stocker	.10
231	Randy Winn	.10
232	Royce Clayton	.10
233	Juan Gonzalez	1.25
234	Tom Goodwin	.10
235	Rusty Greer	.10
236	Rick Helling	.10
237	Rafael Palmeiro	.25
238	Ivan Rodriguez	.60
239	Aaron Sele	.10
240	John Wetteland	.10
241	Todd Zeile	.10
242	Jose Cruz Jr.	.15
243	Carlos Delgado	.40
244	Tony Fernandez	.10
245	Cecil Fielder	.10
246	Alex Gonzalez	.10
247	Shawn Green	.20
248	Roy Halladay	.15
249	Shannon Stewart	.10
250	David Wells	.15

1999 Pacific Paramount Cooperstown Bound

This 10-card set focuses on players who seem destined for the Hall of Fame. These inserts feature silver foil stamping and are seeded 1:361 packs.

		MT
Complete Set (10):		500.00
Common Player:		40.00
Inserted 1:361		
1	Greg Maddux	60.00
2	Cal Ripken Jr.	75.00
3	Nomar Garciaparra	60.00
4	Sammy Sosa	60.00
5	Frank Thomas	40.00
6	Mike Piazza	60.00
7	Mark McGwire	90.00
8	Tony Gwynn	50.00
9	Ken Griffey Jr.	90.00
10	Alex Rodriguez	75.00

1999 Pacific Paramount Fielder's Choice

This 20-card set is die-cut into a glove shape and enhanced with gold foil stamping. These are seeded 1:73 packs.

		MT
Complete Set (20):		400.00
Common Player:		7.50
Inserted 1:73		
1	Chipper Jones	30.00
2	Greg Maddux	30.00
3	Cal Ripken Jr.	40.00
4	Nomar Garciaparra	30.00
5	Sammy Sosa	30.00
6	Kerry Wood	10.00
7	Frank Thomas	20.00
8	Manny Ramirez	15.00
9	Todd Helton	7.50
10	Jeff Bagwell	12.50
11	Mike Piazza	30.00
12	Derek Jeter	30.00
13	Bernie Williams	7.50
14	J.D. Drew	10.00
15	Mark McGwire	50.00
16	Tony Gwynn	25.00
17	Ken Griffey Jr.	50.00
18	Alex Rodriguez	40.00
19	Juan Gonzalez	20.00
20	Ivan Rodriguez	10.00

1999 Pacific Paramount Personal Bests

This 36-card set features holographic silver foil stamping on the card front. Card backs include a close-up photo of the featured player and a career note. These are seeded 1:37 packs.

		MT
Complete Set (36):		475.00
Common Player:		3.00
Inserted 1:37		
1	Darin Erstad	10.00
2	Mo Vaughn	6.00
3	Travis Lee	8.00
4	Chipper Jones	25.00
5	Greg Maddux	25.00
6	Albert Belle	10.00
7	Cal Ripken Jr.	30.00
8	Nomar Garciaparra	25.00
9	Sammy Sosa	25.00
10	Kerry Wood	10.00
11	Frank Thomas	20.00
12	Greg Vaughn	3.00
13	Manny Ramirez	12.00
14	Todd Helton	8.00
15	Larry Walker	8.00
16	Jeff Bagwell	12.00
17	Craig Biggio	5.00
18	Raul Mondesi	3.00
19	Vladimir Guerrero	10.00
20	Hideo Nomo	3.00
21	Mike Piazza	25.00
22	Roger Clemens	15.00
23	Derek Jeter	25.00
24	Bernie Williams	4.50
25	Eric Chavez	10.00
26	Ben Grieve	8.00
27	Scott Rolen	10.00
28	J.D. Drew	10.00
29	Mark McGwire	40.00
30	Tony Gwynn	20.00
31	Barry Bonds	10.00
32	Ken Griffey Jr.	40.00
33	Alex Rodriguez	30.00
34	Jose Canseco	7.50
35	Juan Gonzalez	20.00
36	Ivan Rodriguez	10.00

1999 Pacific Paramount Team Checklists

This 30-card set features gold foil etching and stamping on the card front. Card backs feature the featured player's team checklist for the main set. These were seeded 2:37 packs.

		MT
Complete Set (30):		150.00
Common Player:		1.50
Inserted 2:37		
1	Mo Vaughn	5.00
2	Travis Lee	4.00
3	Chipper Jones	12.00
4	Cal Ripken Jr.	15.00
5	Nomar Garciaparra	12.00
6	Sammy Sosa	12.00
7	Frank Thomas	8.00
8	Greg Vaughn	1.50
9	Manny Ramirez	5.00
10	Larry Walker	4.00
11	Damion Easley	1.50

12	Mark Kotsay	1.50
13	Jeff Bagwell	6.00
14	Jeremy Giambi	1.50
15	Raul Mondesi	2.50
16	Marquis Grissom	1.50
17	Brad Radke	1.50
18	Vladimir Guerrero	6.00
19	Mike Piazza	12.00
20	Roger Clemens	8.00
21	Ben Grieve	5.00
22	Scott Rolen	5.00
23	Brian Giles	2.00
24	Mark McGwire	20.00
25	Tony Gwynn	10.00
26	Barry Bonds	5.00
27	Ken Griffey Jr.	20.00
28	Jose Canseco	4.00
29	Juan Gonzalez	10.00
30	Jose Cruz Jr.	1.50

1999 Pacific Prism Sample

This card of Pacific spokesman Tony Gwynn introduces the 1999 Prism series. The sample card follows the format of the issued version but is overprinted "SAMPLE" on back.

	MT
Tony Gwynn	3.00

1999 Pacific Prism

This 150-card base set has a full, holographic silver card front. Card backs feature two more player photos along with 1998 and career statistics. Hobby packs consist of five cards. There are also five parallels including Holographic Gold, Holographic Mirror, Holographic Blue, Holographic Purple and Red. Golds are limited to 480 serial numbered sets, Mirrors 160 sets, Blues 80 numbered sets, and, Purples 320 sets. Red parallels are a retail-only insert and are seeded at a rate of one per 12.5 packs.

		MT
Complete Set (150):		80.00
Common Player:		.50
1	Garret Anderson	.50
2	Jim Edmonds	.50
3	Darin Erstad	1.50
4	Chuck Finley	.50
5	Tim Salmon	1.00
6	Jay Bell	.50
7	David Dellucci	.50
8	Travis Lee	1.00
9	Matt Williams	1.00
10	Andres Galarraga	1.00
11	Tom Glavine	.75
12	Andruw Jones	1.50
13	Chipper Jones	4.00
14	Ryan Klesko	.75
15	Javy Lopez	.75
16	Greg Maddux	4.00
17	Roberto Alomar	1.00
18	Ryan Minor	.50
19	Mike Mussina	.75
20	Rafael Palmeiro	1.00
21	Cal Ripken Jr.	5.00
22	Nomar Garciaparra	4.00
23	Pedro Martinez	1.00
24	John Valentin	.50
25	Mo Vaughn	.75
26	Tim Wakefield	.50
27	Rod Beck	.50
28	Mark Grace	.75
29	Lance Johnson	.50
30	Sammy Sosa	4.00
31	Kerry Wood	1.50
32	Albert Belle	1.50
33	Mike Caruso	.50
34	Magglio Ordonez	.75
35	Frank Thomas	3.00
36	Robin Ventura	.75
37	Aaron Boone	.50
38	Barry Larkin	.60
39	Reggie Sanders	.50
40	Brett Tomko	.50
41	Sandy Alomar Jr.	.65
42	Bartolo Colon	.50
43	David Justice	.75
44	Kenny Lofton	.75
45	Manny Ramirez	2.50
46	Richie Sexson	.50
47	Jim Thome	1.00
48	Omar Vizquel	.50
49	Dante Bichette	.75
50	Vinny Castilla	.50
51	*Edgard Clemente*	.50
52	Todd Helton	1.00
53	Quinton McCracken	.50
54	Larry Walker	1.00
55	Tony Clark	1.00
56	Damion Easley	.50
57	Luis Gonzalez	.50
58	Bob Higginson	.50
59	Brian Hunter	.50
60	Cliff Floyd	.50
61	Alex Gonzalez	.50
62	Livan Hernandez	.50
63	Derrek Lee	.50
64	Edgar Renteria	.50
65	Moises Alou	.75
66	Jeff Bagwell	1.50
67	Derek Bell	.50
68	Craig Biggio	1.00
69	Randy Johnson	1.00
70	Johnny Damon	.50
71	Jeff King	.50
72	Hal Morris	.50
73	Dean Palmer	.50
74	Eric Karros	.50
75	Raul Mondesi	.75
76	Chan Ho Park	1.00
77	Gary Sheffield	.75
78	Jeromy Burnitz	.50
79	Jeff Cirillo	.50
80	Marquis Grissom	.50
81	Jose Valentin	.50
82	Fernando Vina	.50
83	Paul Molitor	1.00
84	Otis Nixon	.50
85	David Ortiz	.50
86	Todd Walker	.75
87	Vladimir Guerrero	1.50
88	Carl Pavano	.50
89	Fernando Seguignol	.50
90	Ugueth Urbina	.50
91	Carlos Baerga	.50
92	Bobby Bonilla	.50
93	Hideo Nomo	.60
94	John Olerud	.75
95	Rey Ordonez	.65
96	Mike Piazza	4.00
97	David Cone	.75
98	Orlando Hernandez	1.50
99	Hideki Irabu	.75
100	Derek Jeter	4.00
101	Tino Martinez	.60
102	Bernie Williams	1.00
103	Eric Chavez	.50
104	Jason Giambi	.50
105	Ben Grieve	.75
106	Rickey Henderson	.75
107	Bob Abreu	.50
108	Doug Glanville	.50
109	Scott Rolen	1.00
110	Curt Schilling	.75
111	Emil Brown	.50
112	Jose Guillen	.50
113	Jason Kendall	.50
114	Al Martin	.50
115	Aramis Ramirez	.50
116	Kevin Young	.50
117	J.D. Drew	2.00
118	Ron Gant	.50
119	Brian Jordan	.50
120	Eli Marrero	.50
121	Mark McGwire	7.50
122	Kevin Brown	.75
123	Tony Gwynn	3.00
124	Trevor Hoffman	.50
125	Wally Joyner	.50
126	Greg Vaughn	.60
127	Barry Bonds	1.50
128	Ellis Burks	.50
129	Jeff Kent	.50
130	Robb Nen	.50
131	J.T. Snow	.50
132	Jay Buhner	.50
133	Ken Griffey Jr.	7.50
134	Edgar Martinez	.50
135	Alex Rodriguez	5.00
136	David Segui	.50
137	Rolando Arrojo	.75
138	Wade Boggs	.75
139	Aaron Ledesma	.50
140	Fred McGriff	.75
141	Will Clark	1.00
142	Juan Gonzalez	3.00
143	Rusty Greer	.50
144	Ivan Rodriguez	1.50
145	Aaron Sele	.50
146	Jose Canseco	1.00
147	Roger Clemens	2.00
148	Jose Cruz Jr.	.50
149	Carlos Delgado	1.00
150	Alex Gonzalez	.50

1999 Pacific Prism Red

This retail-only parallel is found on average of one per 12.5 packs.

	MT
Complete Set (150):	300.00
Common Player:	.75
Prism Red Stars: 3X	

(See 1999 Pacific Prism for checklist and base card values.)

1999 Pacific Prism Holographic Parallels

Four parallel versions of each of the base cards in '99 Prism were issued as random pack inserts. All share the same front and back design and photos, except for the use of special holographic colored foil background on the inserts. Each of the parallels carries at bottom front an individual serial number from within its prescribed edition. The Holographic purple parallels are a hobby-only insert. Rates of insertion were not stated by Pacific.

	MT
Common Gold (edition/480):	2.00
Gold Stars: 5X	
Common Purple (edition/320):	2.50
Purple Stars: 6X	
Common Mirror (edition/160):	5.00
Mirror Stars: 10X	
Common Blue (edition/80):	7.50
Blue Stars: 20X	

(See 1999 Pacific Prism for checklist and base card values.)

1999 Pacific Prism Ahead of the Game

Each card features full gold foil and etching with a close- up photo of baseball's top 20 stars. These are seeded 1:49 packs.

		MT
Complete Set (20):		200.00
Common Player:		4.00
Inserted 1:49		
1	Darin Erstad	6.00
2	Travis Lee	5.00
3	Chipper Jones	12.50
4	Cal Ripken Jr.	15.00
5	Nomar Garciaparra	12.50
6	Sammy Sosa	12.50
7	Kerry Wood	5.00
8	Frank Thomas	10.00
9	Manny Ramirez	8.00
10	Todd Helton	5.00
11	Jeff Bagwell	6.00
12	Mike Piazza	12.50
13	Derek Jeter	12.50
14	Bernie Williams	4.00
15	J.D. Drew	6.00
16	Mark McGwire	25.00
17	Tony Gwynn	10.00
18	Ken Griffey Jr.	25.00
19	Alex Rodriguez	15.00
20	Ivan Rodriguez	6.00

1999 Pacific Prism Ballpark Legends

This 10 card set salutes baseball's biggest stars. These inserts feature silver foil stamping and etching with an image of a ballpark in the background of the player photo. These are seeded 1:193 packs.

		MT
Complete Set (10):		200.00
Common Player:		10.00
Inserted 1:193		
1	Cal Ripken Jr.	30.00
2	Nomar Garciaparra	25.00
3	Frank Thomas	17.50
4	Ken Griffey Jr.	40.00
5	Alex Rodriguez	30.00
6	Greg Maddux	25.00
7	Sammy Sosa	25.00
8	Kerry Wood	10.00
9	Mark McGwire	40.00
10	Tony Gwynn	17.50

1999 Pacific Prism Diamond Glory

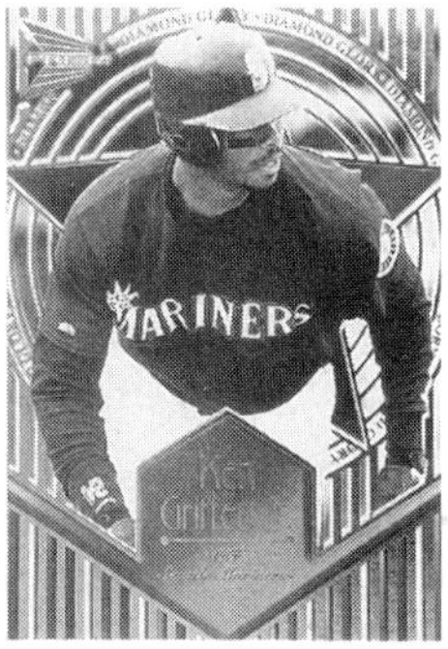

Card fronts feature full copper foil stamping with a star in the background of the player's photo. The 20-card set features 20 of baseball's most exciting players including several top 1999 rookies. These are seeded 2:25 packs.

		MT
Complete Set (20):		125.00
Common Player:		2.50
Inserted 2:25		
1	Darin Erstad	4.00
2	Travis Lee	3.00
3	Chipper Jones	10.00
4	Greg Maddux	10.00
5	Cal Ripken Jr.	12.00
6	Nomar Garciaparra	10.00
7	Sammy Sosa	10.00
8	Kerry Wood	4.00
9	Frank Thomas	8.00
10	Todd Helton	4.00
11	Jeff Bagwell	4.00
12	Mike Piazza	10.00
13	Derek Jeter	10.00
14	Bernie Williams	2.50
15	J.D. Drew	3.00
16	Mark McGwire	15.00
17	Tony Gwynn	8.00
18	Ken Griffey Jr.	15.00
19	Alex Rodriguez	12.00
20	Juan Gonzalez	8.00

1999 Pacific Prism Epic Performers

This hobby-only set features 10 of the top hobby favorites and seeded at 1:97 packs.

		MT
Complete Set (10):		185.00
Common Player:		10.00
Inserted 1:97 H		
1	Cal Ripken Jr.	25.00
2	Nomar Garciaparra	20.00
3	Frank Thomas	20.00
4	Ken Griffey Jr.	35.00
5	Alex Rodriguez	25.00
6	Greg Maddux	20.00
7	Sammy Sosa	20.00
8	Kerry Wood	10.00
9	Mark McGwire	35.00
10	Tony Gwynn	15.00

1999 Pacific Private Stock

The premiere issue of Private Stock base cards features holographic silver foil on 30-pt. cardboard. Card backs have selected box scores from the '98 season, with a brief commentary on the player. Packs consist of six cards.

		MT
Complete Set (150):		60.00
Common Player:		.25
1	Jeff Bagwell	1.50
2	Roger Clemens	2.00
3	J.D. Drew	1.00
4	Nomar Garciaparra	3.00
5	Juan Gonzalez	2.50
6	Ken Griffey Jr.	5.00
7	Tony Gwynn	2.50
8	Derek Jeter	3.00
9	Chipper Jones	3.00
10	Travis Lee	1.00
11	Greg Maddux	3.00
12	Mark McGwire	5.00
13	Mike Piazza	3.00
14	Manny Ramirez	1.50
15	Cal Ripken Jr.	4.00
16	Alex Rodriguez	4.00
17	Ivan Rodriguez	1.25
18	Sammy Sosa	3.00
19	Frank Thomas	2.50
20	Kerry Wood	1.50
21	Roberto Alomar	.75
22	Moises Alou	.40
23	Albert Belle	1.25
24	Craig Biggio	.30
25	Wade Boggs	.50
26	Barry Bonds	1.25
27	Jose Canseco	.75
28	Jim Edmonds	.25
29	Darin Erstad	1.25
30	Andres Galarraga	.75
31	Tom Glavine	.40
32	Ben Grieve	1.25
33	Vladimir Guerrero	1.50
34	Wilton Guerrero	.25
35	Todd Helton	1.25
36	Andruw Jones	1.25
37	Ryan Klesko	.30
38	Kenny Lofton	.75
39	Javy Lopez	.40
40	Pedro Martinez	1.00
41	Paul Molitor	1.00

42	Raul Mondesi	.40
43	Rafael Palmeiro	.50
44	Tim Salmon	.40
45	Jim Thome	.75
46	Mo Vaughn	.75
47	Larry Walker	.75
48	David Wells	.25
49	Bernie Williams	.75
50	Jaret Wright	.75
51	Bobby Abreu	.25
52	Garret Anderson	.25
53	Rolando Arrojo	.25
54	Tony Batista	.25
55	Rod Beck	.25
56	Derek Bell	.25
57	Marvin Benard	.25
58	Dave Berg	.25
59	Dante Bichette	.50
60	Aaron Boone	.25
61	Bret Boone	.25
62	Scott Brosius	.25
63	Brant Brown	.25
64	Kevin Brown	.40
65	Jeromy Burnitz	.25
66	Ken Caminiti	.40
67	Mike Caruso	.25
68	Sean Casey	.40
69	Vinny Castilla	.25
70	Eric Chavez	.75
71	Ryan Christenson	.25
72	Jeff Cirillo	.25
73	Tony Clark	.75
74	Will Clark	.50
75	*Edgard Clemente*	.25
76	David Cone	.40
77	Marty Cordova	.25
78	Jose Cruz Jr.	.25
79	Eric Davis	.25
80	Carlos Delgado	.50
81	David Dellucci	.25
82	Delino DeShields	.25
83	Gary DiSarcina	.25
84	Damion Easley	.25
85	Dennis Eckersley	.25
86	Cliff Floyd	.25
87	Jason Giambi	.25
88	Doug Glanville	.25
89	Alex Gonzalez	.25
90	Mark Grace	.50
91	Rusty Greer	.25
92	Jose Guillen	.40
93	Carlos Guillen	.25
94	Jeffrey Hammonds	.25
95	Rick Helling	.25
96	Bob Henley	.25
97	Livan Hernandez	.25
98	Orlando Hernandez	2.00
99	Bob Higginson	.25
100	Trevor Hoffman	.25
101	Randy Johnson	.75
102	Brian Jordan	.25
103	Wally Joyner	.25
104	Eric Karros	.25
105	Jason Kendall	.40
106	Jeff Kent	.25
107	Jeff King	.25
108	Mark Kotsay	.40
109	Ray Lankford	.25
110	Barry Larkin	.30
111	Mark Loretta	.25
112	Edgar Martinez	.25
113	Tino Martinez	.50
114	Quinton McCracken	.25
115	Fred McGriff	.40
116	Ryan Minor	.75
117	Hal Morris	.25
118	Bill Mueller	.25
119	Mike Mussina	.75
120	Dave Nilsson	.25
121	Otis Nixon	.25
122	Hideo Nomo	.50
123	Paul O'Neill	.50
124	Jose Offerman	.25
125	John Olerud	.40
126	Rey Ordonez	.25
127	David Ortiz	.25
128	Dean Palmer	.25
129	Chan Ho Park	.50
130	Aramis Ramirez	.50
131	Edgar Renteria	.25
132	Armando Rios	.25
133	Henry Rodriguez	.25
134	Scott Rolen	1.25
135	Curt Schilling	.40
136	David Segui	.25
137	Richie Sexson	.25
138	Gary Sheffield	.50
139	John Smoltz	.40
140	Matt Stairs	.25
141	Justin Thompson	.25
142	Greg Vaughn	.40
143	Omar Vizquel	.25
144	Tim Wakefield	.25
145	Todd Walker	.40
146	Devon White	.25
147	Rondell White	.40
148	Matt Williams	.50
149	*Enrique Wilson*	.25
150	Kevin Young	.25

1999 Pacific Private Stock Exclusive Series

This 20-card set is a partial parallel to the base set. Taking the first 20 cards from the set and serially numbering them to 299 sets. These are inserted exclusively in hobby packs.

		MT
Complete Set (20):		350.00
Common Player:		7.50
Production 299 sets H		
1	Jeff Bagwell	10.00
2	Roger Clemens	15.00
3	J.D. Drew	6.00
4	Nomar Garciaparra	25.00
5	Juan Gonzalez	20.00
6	Ken Griffey Jr.	40.00
7	Tony Gwynn	20.00
8	Derek Jeter	25.00
9	Chipper Jones	25.00
10	Travis Lee	7.50
11	Greg Maddux	25.00
12	Mark McGwire	40.00
13	Mike Piazza	25.00
14	Manny Ramirez	10.00
15	Cal Ripken Jr.	30.00
16	Alex Rodriguez	30.00
17	Ivan Rodriguez	10.00
18	Sammy Sosa	25.00
19	Frank Thomas	15.00
20	Kerry Wood	10.00

1999 Pacific Private Stock Homerun History

This holographic silver foiled commemorative set honors Mark McGwire and Sammy Sosa's historic '98 seasons. Two cards were added to the end of the set, which are Silver Crown Die-Cuts honoring Ripken Jr.'s consecutive games streak and McGwire's 70 home runs. These are inserted 2:25 packs.

		MT
Complete Set (22):		200.00
Common McGwire:		12.00
Common Sosa:		8.00
Inserted 1:12		
1	Home Run #61 (Mark McGwire)	15.00
2	Home Run #59 (Sammy Sosa)	10.00
3	Home Run #62 (Mark McGwire)	15.00
4	Home Run #60 (Sammy Sosa)	10.00
5	Home Run #63 (Mark McGwire)	15.00
6	Home Run #61 (Sammy Sosa)	10.00
7	Home Run #64 (Mark McGwire)	15.00
8	Home Run #62 (Sammy Sosa)	10.00
9	Home Run #65 (Mark McGwire)	15.00
10	Home Run #63 (Sammy Sosa)	10.00
11	Home Run #67 (Mark McGwire)	15.00
12	Home Run #64 (Sammy Sosa)	10.00
13	Home Run #68 (Mark McGwire)	15.00
14	Home Run #65 (Sammy Sosa)	10.00
15	Home Run #70 (Mark McGwire)	15.00
16	Home Run #66 (Sammy Sosa)	10.00
17	A Season of Celebration (Mark McGwire)	15.00
18	A Season of Celebration (Sammy Sosa)	10.00
19	Awesome Power (Sammy Sosa, Mark McGwire)	15.00
20	Transcending Sports (Mark McGwire, Sammy Sosa)	15.00
21	Crown Die-Cut (Mark McGwire)	15.00
22	Crown Die-Cut (Cal Ripken Jr.)	10.00

1999 Pacific Private Stock Preferred Series

Another partial parallel of the first 20 base cards. Each card is stamped with a holographic Preferred logo and are numbered to 399 sets.

		MT
Complete Set (20):		400.00
Common Player:		5.00
Production 399 sets		
1	Jeff Bagwell	7.50
2	Roger Clemens	15.00
3	J.D. Drew	10.00
4	Nomar Garciaparra	30.00
5	Juan Gonzalez	10.00
6	Ken Griffey Jr.	50.00
7	Tony Gwynn	20.00
8	Derek Jeter	30.00
9	Chipper Jones	30.00
10	Travis Lee	5.00
11	Greg Maddux	30.00
12	Mark McGwire	50.00
13	Mike Piazza	30.00
14	Manny Ramirez	10.00
15	Cal Ripken Jr.	40.00
16	Alex Rodriguez	40.00
17	Ivan Rodriguez	7.50
18	Sammy Sosa	30.00
19	Frank Thomas	15.00
20	Kerry Wood	5.00

1999 Pacific Private Stock Vintage Series

This insert set is a partial parallel of the first 50 cards in the base set and have a Vintage holograpic stamp on the card fronts. These are limited to 99 numbered sets.

		MT
Complete Set (50):		900.00
Common Player:		5.00
Production 99 sets		
1	Jeff Bagwell	20.00
2	Roger Clemens	30.00
3	J.D. Drew	20.00
4	Nomar Garciaparra	50.00
5	Juan Gonzalez	35.00
6	Ken Griffey Jr.	80.00
7	Tony Gwynn	35.00
8	Derek Jeter	50.00
9	Chipper Jones	50.00
10	Travis Lee	10.00
11	Greg Maddux	45.00
12	Mark McGwire	80.00
13	Mike Piazza	50.00
14	Manny Ramirez	20.00
15	Cal Ripken Jr.	65.00
16	Alex Rodriguez	65.00
17	Ivan Rodriguez	20.00
18	Sammy Sosa	50.00
19	Frank Thomas	30.00
20	Kerry Wood	10.00
21	Roberto Alomar	15.00
22	Moises Alou	5.00
23	Albert Belle	15.00
24	Craig Biggio	12.50
25	Wade Boggs	12.50
26	Barry Bonds	15.00
27	Jose Canseco	12.50
28	Jim Edmonds	5.00
29	Darin Erstad	12.50
30	Andres Galarraga	5.00
31	Tom Glavine	12.50
32	Ben Grieve	7.50
33	Vladimir Guerrero	20.00
34	Wilton Guerrero	5.00
35	Todd Helton	12.50
36	Andruw Jones	15.00
37	Ryan Klesko	5.00
38	Kenny Lofton	5.00
39	Javy Lopez	5.00
40	Pedro Martinez	12.50
41	Paul Molitor	12.50
42	Raul Mondesi	7.50
43	Rafael Palmeiro	12.50
44	Tim Salmon	5.00
45	Jim Thome	5.00
46	Mo Vaughn	5.00
47	Larry Walker	5.00
48	David Wells	5.00
49	Bernie Williams	5.00
50	Jaret Wright	5.00

1999 Pacific Private Stock Platinum Series

Another partial parallel of the first 50 cards in the base set. Cards have a platinum holographic sheen to them with a Platinum stamp on the front. These are limited to 199 numbered sets.

		MT
Complete Set (50):		700.00
Common Player:		4.00
Production 199 sets		
1	Jeff Bagwell	25.00
2	Roger Clemens	25.00
3	J.D. Drew	10.00
4	Nomar Garciaparra	40.00
5	Juan Gonzalez	30.00
6	Ken Griffey Jr.	65.00
7	Tony Gwynn	30.00
8	Derek Jeter	40.00
9	Chipper Jones	40.00
10	Travis Lee	12.50
11	Greg Maddux	35.00
12	Mark McGwire	65.00
13	Mike Piazza	40.00
14	Manny Ramirez	20.00
15	Cal Ripken Jr.	50.00
16	Alex Rodriguez	50.00
17	Ivan Rodriguez	15.00
18	Sammy Sosa	40.00
19	Frank Thomas	25.00
20	Kerry Wood	15.00
21	Roberto Alomar	12.50
22	Moises Alou	5.00
23	Albert Belle	15.00
24	Craig Biggio	10.00
25	Wade Boggs	10.00
26	Barry Bonds	15.00
27	Jose Canseco	10.00
28	Jim Edmonds	5.00
29	Darin Erstad	15.00
30	Andres Galarraga	10.00
31	Tom Glavine	5.00
32	Ben Grieve	10.00
33	Vladimir Guerrero	20.00
34	Wilton Guerrero	4.00
35	Todd Helton	12.50
36	Andruw Jones	15.00
37	Ryan Klesko	5.00
38	Kenny Lofton	10.00
39	Javy Lopez	5.00
40	Pedro Martinez	12.50
41	Paul Molitor	12.50
42	Raul Mondesi	7.50
43	Rafael Palmeiro	7.50
44	Tim Salmon	5.00
45	Jim Thome	10.00
46	Mo Vaughn	10.00
47	Larry Walker	10.00
48	David Wells	4.00
49	Bernie Williams	10.00
50	Jaret Wright	10.00

1999 Pacific Private Stock PS-206

This 150-card set takes reverent reach back into collecting history with its smaller format (1.5" x 2.5"). Card fronts have a white border with silver foil stamping and a blue back, these are found one per pack. A parallel also exists with a red back, which are seeded 1:25 packs.

		MT
Complete Set (150):		25.00
Common Player:		.25
Inserted 1:1		
Red Parallels: 4X		
Inserted 1:25		
1	Jeff Bagwell	.75
2	Roger Clemens	1.00
3	J.D. Drew	1.00
4	Nomar Garciaparra	2.00
5	Juan Gonzalez	1.50
6	Ken Griffey Jr.	3.50
7	Tony Gwynn	1.50
8	Derek Jeter	2.00
9	Chipper Jones	2.00
10	Travis Lee	.75
11	Greg Maddux	2.00
12	Mark McGwire	3.50
13	Mike Piazza	2.00
14	Manny Ramirez	1.00
15	Cal Ripken Jr.	2.50
16	Alex Rodriguez	2.50
17	Ivan Rodriguez	.75
18	Sammy Sosa	2.00
19	Frank Thomas	1.50
20	Kerry Wood	.75
21	Roberto Alomar	.50
22	Moises Alou	.25
23	Albert Belle	.75
24	Craig Biggio	.35
25	Wade Boggs	.40
26	Barry Bonds	.75
27	Jose Canseco	.40
28	Jim Edmonds	.25
29	Darin Erstad	.75
30	Andres Galarraga	.50
31	Tom Glavine	.40
32	Ben Grieve	.75
33	Vladimir Guerrero	1.00
34	Wilton Guerrero	.25
35	Todd Helton	.75
36	Andruw Jones	.75
37	Ryan Klesko	.30
38	Kenny Lofton	.60
39	Javy Lopez	.30
40	Pedro Martinez	.60
41	Paul Molitor	.50
42	Raul Mondesi	.35
43	Rafael Palmeiro	.35
44	Tim Salmon	.40
45	Jim Thome	.50
46	Mo Vaughn	.60
47	Larry Walker	.40
48	David Wells	.25
49	Bernie Williams	.60
50	Jaret Wright	.50
51	Bobby Abreu	.25
52	Garret Anderson	.25
53	Rolando Arrojo	.25
54	Tony Batista	.25
55	Rod Beck	.25
56	Derek Bell	.25
57	Marvin Benard	.25
58	Dave Berg	.25
59	Dante Bichette	.40
60	Aaron Boone	.25
61	Bret Boone	.25
62	Scott Brosius	.25
63	Brant Brown	.25
64	Kevin Brown	.35
65	Jeromy Burnitz	.25
66	Ken Caminiti	.35
67	Mike Caruso	.35
68	Sean Casey	.35
69	Vinny Castilla	.25
70	Eric Chavez	.50
71	Ryan Christenson	.25
72	Jeff Cirillo	.25
73	Tony Clark	.50
74	Will Clark	.40
75	Edgard Clemente	.25
76	David Cone	.25
77	Marty Cordova	.25
78	Jose Cruz Jr.	.25
79	Eric Davis	.25
80	Carlos Delgado	.50
81	David Dellucci	.25
82	Delino DeShields	.25
83	Gary DiSarcina	.25
84	Damion Easley	.25
85	Dennis Eckersley	.25
86	Cliff Floyd	.25
87	Jason Giambi	.25
88	Doug Glanville	.25
89	Alex Gonzalez	.25
90	Mark Grace	.40
91	Rusty Greer	.25
92	Jose Guillen	.25
93	Carlos Guillen	.25
94	Jeffrey Hammonds	.25
95	Rick Helling	.25
96	Bob Henley	.25
97	Livan Hernandez	.25
98	Orlando Hernandez	1.50
99	Bob Higginson	.25
100	Trevor Hoffman	.25
101	Randy Johnson	.50
102	Brian Jordan	.25
103	Wally Joyner	.25
104	Eric Karros	.25
105	Jason Kendall	.40
106	Jeff Kent	.25
107	Jeff King	.25
108	Mark Kotsay	.40
109	Ray Lankford	.25
110	Barry Larkin	.30
111	Mark Loretta	.25
112	Edgar Martinez	.25
113	Tino Martinez	.30
114	Quinton McCracken	.25
115	Fred McGriff	.40
116	Ryan Minor	.75
117	Hal Morris	.25
118	Bill Mueller	.25
119	Mike Mussina	.50
120	Dave Nilsson	.25
121	Otis Nixon	.25
122	Hideo Nomo	.40
123	Paul O'Neill	.40
124	Jose Offerman	.25
125	John Olerud	.40
126	Rey Ordonez	.25
127	David Ortiz	.25
128	Dean Palmer	.25
129	Chan Ho Park	.40
130	Aramis Ramirez	.40
131	Edgar Renteria	.25
132	Armando Rios	.25
133	Henry Rodriguez	.25
134	Scott Rolen	.75
135	Curt Schilling	.35
136	David Segui	.25
137	Richie Sexson	.25
138	Gary Sheffield	.40
139	John Smoltz	.25

140	Matt Stairs	.25
141	Justin Thompson	.25
142	Greg Vaughn	.40
143	Omar Vizquel	.25
144	Tim Wakefield	.25
145	Todd Walker	.40
146	Devon White	.25
147	Rondell White	.35
148	Matt Williams	.40
149	Enrique Wilson	.25
150	Kevin Young	.25

1999 Pacific Revolution

The 150-card set features dual foiled etching and embossing enhanced by gold-foil stamping. Card backs have year-by- year statistics along with a close-up photo. There are three parallels to the base set: Opening Day, Red and Shadow. Reds are retail exclusive and are limited to 299 numbered sets. Shadows have light blue foil stamping and are limited to 99 numbered sets. Opening Day are seeded exclusively in hobby packs at a rate of 1:25 packs.

		MT
Complete Set (150):		125.00
Common Player:		.50
1	Jim Edmonds	.50
2	Darin Erstad	2.00
3	Troy Glaus	3.00
4	Tim Salmon	1.00
5	Mo Vaughn	1.50
6	Steve Finley	.50
7	Luis Gonzalez	.50
8	Randy Johnson	2.00
9	Travis Lee	2.00
10	Matt Williams	1.00
11	Andruw Jones	2.50
12	Chipper Jones	6.00
13	Brian Jordan	.50
14	Javy Lopez	.75
15	Greg Maddux	6.00
16	*Kevin McGlinchy*	.50
17	John Smoltz	.50
18	Brady Anderson	.50
19	Albert Belle	2.50
20	Will Clark	1.00
21	*Willis Otanez*	.50
22	*Calvin Pickering*	.50
23	Cal Ripken Jr.	8.00
24	Nomar Garciaparra	6.00
25	Pedro Martinez	2.50
26	Troy O'Leary	.50
27	Jose Offerman	.50
28	Mark Grace	.75
29	Mickey Morandini	.50
30	Henry Rodriguez	.50
31	Sammy Sosa	6.00
32	Ray Durham	.50
33	Carlos Lee	.50
34	*Jeff Liefer*	.50
35	Magglio Ordonez	.75
36	Frank Thomas	4.00
37	Mike Cameron	.50
38	Sean Casey	.75
39	Barry Larkin	.75
40	Greg Vaughn	.75
41	Roberto Alomar	2.00
42	Sandy Alomar Jr.	.50
43	David Justice	.75
44	Kenny Lofton	1.50
45	Manny Ramirez	3.00
46	Richie Sexson	.50
47	Jim Thome	1.50
48	Dante Bichette	1.00
49	Vinny Castilla	.50
50	Darryl Hamilton	.50
51	Todd Helton	1.50
52	Larry Walker	2.00
53	Tony Clark	1.00
54	Damion Easley	.50
55	Bob Higginson	.50
56	*Gabe Kapler*	5.00
57	*Alex Gonzalez*	.50
58	Mark Kotsay	.50
59	Kevin Orie	.50
60	Preston Wilson	.50
61	Jeff Bagwell	3.00
62	Derek Bell	.50
63	Craig Biggio	1.00
64	Ken Caminiti	.75
65	Carlos Beltran	1.00
66	Johnny Damon	.50
67	Jermaine Dye	.50
68	Carlos Febles	.50
69	Kevin Brown	.75
70	Todd Hundley	.50
71	Eric Karros	.50
72	Raul Mondesi	.75
73	Gary Sheffield	.75
74	Jeromy Burnitz	.50
75	Jeff Cirillo	.50
76	Marquis Grissom	.50
77	Fernando Vina	.50
78	*Chad Allen*	.50
79	*Corey Koskie*	.50
80	*Doug Mientkiewicz*	.50
81	Brad Radke	.50
82	Todd Walker	.50
83	*Michael Barrett*	.75
84	Vladimir Guerrero	3.00
85	Wilton Guerrero	.50
86	*Guillermo Mota*	.50
87	Rondell White	.75
88	Edgardo Alfonzo	.50
89	Rickey Henderson	.75
90	John Olerud	.75
91	Mike Piazza	6.00
92	Robin Ventura	.75
93	Roger Clemens	3.00
94	Chili Davis	.50
95	Derek Jeter	6.00
96	Chuck Knoblauch	1.00
97	Tino Martinez	.75
98	Paul O'Neill	.75
99	Bernie Williams	1.50
100	Eric Chavez	1.50
101	Jason Giambi	.50
102	Ben Grieve	2.00
103	John Jaha	.50
104	*Olmedo Saenz*	.50
105	Bobby Abreu	.50
106	Doug Glanville	.50
107	Desi Relaford	.50
108	Scott Rolen	2.50
109	Curt Schilling	.75
110	Brian Giles	.50
111	Jason Kendall	.75
112	Pat Meares	.50
113	Kevin Young	.50
114	J.D. Drew	5.00
115	Ray Lankford	.50
116	Eli Marrero	.50
117	*Joe McEwing*	.50
118	Mark McGwire	12.00
119	Fernando Tatis	.50
120	Tony Gwynn	5.00
121	Trevor Hoffman	.50
122	Wally Joyner	.50
123	Reggie Sanders	.50
124	Barry Bonds	2.50
125	Ellis Burks	.50
126	Jeff Kent	.50
127	*Ramon Martinez*	.50
128	*Joe Nathan*	.50
129	*Freddy Garcia*	15.00
130	Ken Griffey Jr.	12.00
131	Brian Hunter	.50
132	Edgar Martinez	.50
133	Alex Rodriguez	8.00
134	David Segui	.50
135	Wade Boggs	1.00
136	Jose Canseco	1.50
137	Quinton McCracken	.50
138	Fred McGriff	.75
139	*Kelly Dransfeldt*	.50
140	Juan Gonzalez	5.00
141	Rusty Greer	.50
142	Rafael Palmeiro	1.00
143	Ivan Rodriguez	2.50
144	Lee Stevens	.50
145	Jose Cruz Jr.	.50
146	Carlos Delgado	1.00
147	Shawn Green	.75
148	*Roy Halladay*	1.00
149	Shannon Stewart	.50
150	*Kevin Witt*	.50

1999 Pacific Revolution Premiere Date

A Premiere Date seal and a serial number from within an edition of 49 sets differentiates these inserts from the base cards they parallel. This version is a 1:25 pack hobby-only insert.

	MT
Common Player:	6.00
Stars: 15X	
SPs: 6X	

(See 1999 Pacific Revolution for checklist and base card values.)

1999 Pacific Revolution Red

Serially numbered within an edition of 299 each, the Red parallels are a retail-only insert. They feature red metallic-foil background and highlights on front, but otherwise are identical to the base cards, except for the serial number printed on back.

	MT
Common Player:	1.50
Stars: 3X	
SPs: 1.5X	

(See 1999 Pacific Revolution for checklist and base card values.)

1999 Pacific Revolution Shadow

This hobby-only parallel insert features blue metallic-foil background and graphics on front. Backs are identical to the base version except they include a dot-matrix applied serial number at left within an edition of 99.

	MT
Common Player:	4.00
Stars: 6X	
SPs: 3X	

(See 1999 Pacific Revolution for checklist and base card values.)

1999 Pacific Revolution Diamond Legacy

This 36-card set features a holographic patterned foil card front. Card backs have a small close-up photo along with a career note. These were seeded 2:25 packs.

		MT
Complete Set (36):		250.00
Common Player:		2.00
Inserted 2:25		
1	Troy Glaus	8.00
2	Mo Vaughn	4.00
3	Matt Williams	3.00
4	Chipper Jones	15.00
5	Andruw Jones	6.00
6	Greg Maddux	15.00
7	Albert Belle	6.00
8	Cal Ripken Jr.	20.00
9	Nomar Garciaparra	15.00
10	Sammy Sosa	15.00
11	Frank Thomas	12.00
12	Manny Ramirez	10.00
13	Todd Helton	4.00
14	Larry Walker	4.00
15	Gabe Kapler	8.00
16	Jeff Bagwell	8.00
17	Craig Biggio	4.00
18	Raul Mondesi	2.00
19	Vladimir Guerrero	8.00
20	Mike Piazza	15.00
21	Roger Clemens	10.00
22	Derek Jeter	15.00
23	Bernie Williams	3.00
24	Ben Grieve	4.00
25	Scott Rolen	6.00
26	J.D. Drew	5.00
27	Mark McGwire	30.00
28	Fernando Tatis	2.00
29	Tony Gwynn	12.00
30	Barry Bonds	6.00
31	Ken Griffey Jr.	30.00
32	Alex Rodriguez	20.00
33	Jose Canseco	4.00
34	Juan Gonzalez	12.00
35	Ivan Rodriguez	6.00
36	Shawn Green	6.00

1999 Pacific Revolution Foul Pole

This 20-card set features netting down the right side of each card, with the player photo on the left side. The player name, position and logo are stamped with gold foil. These were seeded 1:49 packs.

		MT
Complete Set (20):		450.00
Common Player:		5.00
Inserted 1:49		
1	Chipper Jones	30.00
2	Andruw Jones	15.00
3	Cal Ripken Jr.	40.00
4	Nomar Garciaparra	30.00
5	Sammy Sosa	30.00
6	Frank Thomas	25.00
7	Manny Ramirez	20.00
8	Jeff Bagwell	15.00
9	Raul Mondesi	5.00
10	Vladimir Guerrero	20.00
11	Mike Piazza	30.00
12	Derek Jeter	30.00
13	Bernie Williams	5.00
14	Scott Rolen	15.00
15	J.D. Drew	12.00
16	Mark McGwire	50.00
17	Tony Gwynn	25.00
18	Ken Griffey Jr.	50.00
19	Alex Rodriguez	40.00
20	Juan Gonzalez	25.00

1999 Pacific Revolution Icons

This 10-card set spotlights the top players, each card is die-cut in the shape of a shield with silver foil etching and stamping. These were seeded 1:121 packs.

		MT
Complete Set (10):		450.00
Common Player:		40.00
Inserted 1:121		
1	Cal Ripken Jr.	60.00
2	Nomar Garciaparra	50.00
3	Sammy Sosa	50.00
4	Frank Thomas	40.00
5	Mike Piazza	50.00
6	Derek Jeter	50.00
7	Mark McGwire	80.00
8	Tony Gwynn	40.00
9	Ken Griffey Jr.	80.00
10	Alex Rodriguez	60.00

1999 Pacific Revolution Thorn in the Side

This 20-card set features full holographic silver foil and is die-cut in the upper right portion. Card backs analyzes the featured player's success against a certain opponent over the years. These were seeded 1:25 packs.

		MT
Complete Set (20):		250.00
Common Player:		5.00
Inserted 1:25		
1	Mo Vaughn	5.00
2	Chipper Jones	20.00
3	Greg Maddux	20.00
4	Cal Ripken Jr.	25.00
5	Nomar Garciaparra	20.00
6	Sammy Sosa	20.00
7	Frank Thomas	15.00
8	Manny Ramirez	10.00
9	Jeff Bagwell	8.00
10	Mike Piazza	20.00
11	Derek Jeter	20.00
12	Bernie Williams	5.00
13	J.D. Drew	6.00
14	Mark McGwire	35.00
15	Tony Gwynn	15.00
16	Barry Bonds	8.00
17	Ken Griffey Jr.	35.00
18	Alex Rodriguez	25.00
19	Juan Gonzalez	15.00
20	Ivan Rodriguez	8.00

1999 Pacific Revolution Tripleheader

This 30-card set features spotted gold foil blotching around the player image with the name, postion, team and logo stamped in gold foil. These were seeded 4:25 hobby packs. The set is also broken down into three separate tiers of 10 cards. Tier 1 (cards 1-10) are limited to 99 numbered sets. Tier 2 (11-20) 199 numbered sets and Tier 3 (21-30) 299 numbered sets.

		MT
Complete Set (30):		120.00
Common Player:		1.00
Inserted 4:25 H		
Tier 1 (1-10): 6X		
Production 99 sets H		
Tier 2 (11-20): 3X		
Production 199 sets H		
Tier 3 (21-30): 1.5X		
Production 299 sets H		
1	Greg Maddux	8.00
2	Cal Ripken Jr.	10.00
3	Nomar Garciaparra	8.00
4	Sammy Sosa	8.00
5	Frank Thomas	6.00
6	Mike Piazza	8.00
7	Mark McGwire	15.00
8	Tony Gwynn	6.00
9	Ken Griffey Jr.	15.00
10	Alex Rodriguez	10.00
11	Mo Vaughn	2.00
12	Chipper Jones	6.00
13	Manny Ramirez	4.00
14	Larry Walker	1.00
15	Jeff Bagwell	3.00
16	Vladimir Guerrero	3.00
17	Derek Jeter	8.00
18	J.D. Drew	2.50
19	Barry Bonds	3.00
20	Juan Gonzalez	6.00
21	Troy Glaus	4.00
22	Andruw Jones	3.00
23	Matt Williams	1.00
24	Craig Biggio	1.00
25	Raul Mondesi	1.00
26	Roger Clemens	4.00
27	Bernie Williams	1.00
28	Scott Rolen	3.00
29	Jose Canseco	1.50
30	Ivan Rodriguez	3.00

1999 Pacific Home Run Heroes

These cards were part of an unannounced multi-manufacturer (Fleer, Upper Deck, Topps, Pacific) insert program which was exclusive to Wal-Mart. Each company produced cards of Mark McGwire and Sammy Sosa, along with two other premier sluggers. Each company's cards share a "Power Elite" logo at top and "Home Run Heroes" logo vertically at right.

		MT
Complete Set (4):		7.00
Common Player:		1.00
13	Mark McGwire	4.00
14	Sammy Sosa	2.50
15	Juan Gonzalez	1.00
16	Manny Ramirez	1.00

2000 Pacific Sample

Tony Gwynn was once again the spokesman for Pacific's 2000 line-up of baseball cards products. To showcase its base brand for the year, Pacific produced this sample card, so overprinted and "numbered" on back, but otherwise virtually identical to the issued version.

		MT
SAMPLE	Tony Gwynn	3.00

2000 Pacific

		MT
Complete Set (500):		60.00
Common Player:		.10
Wax Box:		50.00
1	Garret Anderson	.10
2	Tim Belcher	.10
3	Gary DiSarcina	.10
4	Trent Durrington	.10
5	Jim Edmonds	.10
6	Darin Erstad	.25
6b	Darin Erstad	.25
7	Chuck Finley	.10
8	Troy Glaus	.25
9	Todd Greene	.10
10	Bret Hemphill	.10
11	Ken Hill	.10
12	Ramon Ortiz	.10
13	Troy Percival	.10
14	Mark Petkovsek	.10
15	Tim Salmon	.20
16	Mo Vaughn	.50
16b	Mo Vaughn	.50
17	Jay Bell	.10
18	Omar Daal	.10
19	Erubiel Durazo	.10
20	Steve Finley	.10
21	Bernard Gilkey	.10
22	Luis Gonzalez	.20
23	Randy Johnson	.50
24	Byung-Hyun Kim	.10
25	Travis Lee	.25
26	Matt Mantei	.10
27	Armando Reynoso	.10
28	Rob Ryan	.10
29	Kelly Stinnett	.10
30	Todd Stottlemyre	.10
31	Matt Williams	.30
31b	Matt Williams	.30
32	Tony Womack	.10
33	Bret Boone	.10
34	Andres Galarraga	.40
35	Tom Glavine	.25
36	Ozzie Guillen	.10
37	Andruw Jones	.40
37b	Andruw Jones	.40
38	Chipper Jones	1.50
38b	Chipper Jones	1.50
39	Brian Jordan	.10
40	Ryan Klesko	.20
41	Javy Lopez	.20
42	Greg Maddux	1.50
42b	Greg Maddux	1.50
43	Kevin Millwood	.10
44	John Rocker	.10
45	Randall Simon	.10
46	John Smoltz	.20
47	Gerald Williams	.10
48	Brady Anderson	.20
49	Albert Belle	.60
49b	Albert Belle	.60
50	Mike Bordick	.10
51	Will Clark	.25
52	Jeff Conine	.10
53	Delino DeShields	.10
54	Jerry Hairston Jr.	.10
55	Charles Johnson	.10
56	Eugene Kingsale	.10
57	Ryan Minor	.20
58	Mike Mussina	.50
59	Sidney Ponson	.10
60	Cal Ripken Jr.	2.00
60b	Cal Ripken Jr.	2.00
61	B.J. Surhoff	.10
62	Mike Timlin	.10
63	Rod Beck	.10
64	Nomar Garciaparra	2.00
64b	Nomar Garciaparra	2.00
65	Tom Gordon	.10
66	Butch Huskey	.10
67	Derek Lowe	.10
68	Pedro Martinez	.75
68b	Pedro Martinez	.75
69	Trot Nixon	.10
70	Jose Offerman	.10
71	Troy O'Leary	.10
72	Pat Rapp	.10
73	Donnie Sadler	.10
74	Mike Stanley	.10
75	John Valentin	.10
76	Jason Varitek	.10
77	Wilton Veras	.25
78	Tim Wakefield	.10
79	Rick Aguilera	.10
80	Mann Alexander	.10
81	Roosevelt Brown	.10
82	Mark Grace	.20
83	Glenallen Hill	.10
84	Lance Johnson	.10
85	Jon Lieber	.10
86	Cole Liniak	.10
87	Chad Meyers	.10
88	Mickey Morandini	.10
89	Jose Nieves	.10
90	Henry Rodriguez	.10
91	Sammy Sosa	2.00
91b	Sammy Sosa	2.00
92	Kevin Tapani	.10
93	Kerry Wood	.40
94	Mike Caruso	.10
95	Ray Durham	.10
96	Brook Fordyce	.10
97	Bobby Howry	.10
98	Paul Konerko	.10
99	Carlos Lee	.10
100	Aaron Myette	.10
101	Greg Norton	.10
102	Magglio Ordonez	.25
103	Jim Parque	.10
104	Liu Rodriguez	.10
105	Chris Singleton	.10
106	Mike Sirotka	.10
107	Frank Thomas	.75
107b	Frank Thomas	.75
108	Kip Wells	.10
109	Aaron Boone	.10
110	Mike Cameron	.10
111	Sean Casey	.40
111b	Sean Casey	.40
112	Jeffrey Hammonds	.10
113	Pete Harnisch	.10
114	Barry Larkin	.40
114b	Barry Larkin	.40
115	Jason LaRue	.10
116	Denny Neagle	.10
117	Pokey Reese	.10
118	Scott Sullivan	.10
119	Eddie Taubensee	.10
120	Greg Vaughn	.20
121	Scott Williamson	.10
122	Dmitri Young	.10
123	Roberto Alomar	.50
123b	Roberto Alomar	.50
124	Sandy Alomar Jr.	.10
125	Harold Baines	.10
126	Russell Branyan	.10
127	Dave Burba	.10
128	Bartolo Colon	.10
129	Travis Fryman	.20
130	Mike Jackson	.10
131	David Justice	.25
132	Kenny Lofton	.50
132b	Kenny Lofton	.50
133	Charles Nagy	.10
134	Manny Ramirez	.75
134b	Manny Ramirez	.75
135	Dave Roberts	.10
136	Richie Sexson	.10
137	Jim Thome	.40
138	Omar Vizquel	.10
139	Jaret Wright	.10
140	Pedro Astacio	.10
141	Dante Bichette	.25
142	Brian Bohanon	.10
143	Vinny Castilla	.10
143b	Vinny Castilla	.10
144	Edgard Clemente	.10
145	Derrick Gibson	.10
146	Todd Helton	.40
147	Darryl Kile	.10
148	Mike Lansing	.10
149	Kirt Manwaring	.10
150	Neifi Perez	.10
151	Ben Petrick	.10
152	*Juan Sosa*	.40
153	Dave Veres	.10
154	Larry Walker	.50
154b	Larry Walker	.50
155	Brad Ausmus	.10
156	Dave Borkowski	.10
157	Tony Clark	.25
158	Francisco Cordero	.10
159	Deivi Cruz	.10
160	Damion Easley	.10
161	Juan Encarnacion	.10
162	Robert Fick	.10
163	Bobby Higginson	.10
164	Gabe Kapler	.25
165	Brian Moehler	.10
166	Dean Palmer	.10
167	Luis Polonia	.10
168	Justin Thompson	.10
169	Jeff Weaver	.10
170	Antonio Alfonseca	.10
171	Bruce Aven	.10
172	A.J. Burnett	.25
173	Luis Castillo	.10
174	Ramon Castro	.10
175	Ryan Dempster	.10
176	Alex Fernandez	.10
177	Cliff Floyd	.10
178	Amaury Garcia	.10
179	Alex Gonzalez	.10
180	Mark Kotsay	.10
181	Mike Lowell	.10
182	Brian Meadows	.10
183	Kevin Orie	.10
184	Julio Ramirez	.10
185	Preston Wilson	.10
186	Moises Alou	.20
187	Jeff Bagwell	.75
187b	Jeff Bagwell	.75
188	Glen Barker	.10
189	Derek Bell	.10
190	Craig Biggio	.40
190b	Craig Biggio	.40
191	Ken Caminiti	.20
192	Scott Elarton	.10
193	Carl Everett	.10
194	Mike Hampton	.10
195	Carlos Hernandez	.10
196	Richard Hidalgo	.10
197	Jose Lima	.10
198	Shane Reynolds	.20
199	Bill Spiers	.10
200	Billy Wagner	.10
201	Carlos Beltran	.40
201b	Carlos Beltran	.40
202	Dermal Brown	.10
203	Johnny Damon	.10
204	Jermaine Dye	.10
205	Carlos Febles	.10
206	Jeremy Giambi	.10
207	Mark Quinn	.10
208	Joe Randa	.10
209	Dan Reichert	.10
210	Jose Rosado	.10
211	Rey Sanchez	.10
212	Jeff Suppan	.10
213	Mike Sweeney	.10
214	Kevin Brown	.20
214b	Kevin Brown	.20
215	Darren Dreifort	.10
216	Eric Gagne	.10
217	Mark Grudzielanek	.10
218	Todd Hollandsworth	.10
219	Todd Hundley	.10
220	Eric Karros	.20
221	Raul Mondesi	.20
222	Chan Ho Park	.20
223	Jeff Shaw	.10
224	Gary Sheffield	.25
224b	Gary Sheffield	.25
225	Ismael Valdes	.10
226	Devon White	.10
227	Eric Young	.10
228	Kevin Barker	.10
229	Ron Belliard	.10
230	Jeromy Burnitz	.10
230b	Jeromy Burnitz	.10
231	Jeff Cirillo	.10
232	Marquis Grissom	.10
233	Geoff Jenkins	.10
234	Mark Loretta	.10
235	David Nilsson	.10
236	Hideo Nomo	.10
237	Alex Ochoa	.10
238	Kyle Peterson	.10
239	Fernando Vina	.10
240	Bob Wickman	.10
241	Steve Woodard	.10
242	Chad Allen	.10
243	Ron Coomer	.10
244	Marty Cordova	.10
245	Cristian Guzman	.10
246	Denny Hocking	.10
247	Jacque Jones	.10
248	Corey Koskie	.10
249	Matt Lawton	.10
250	Joe Mays	.10
251	Eric Milton	.10
252	Brad Radke	.10
253	Mark Redman	.10
254	Terry Steinbach	.10
255	Todd Walker	.10
256	Tony Armas, Jr.	.10
257	Michael Barrett	.10
258	Peter Bergeron	.10
259	Geoff Blum	.10
260	Orlando Cabrera	.10
261	*Trace Coquillette*	.25
262	Brad Fullmer	.10
263	Vladimir Guerrero	1.00
263b	Vladimir Guerrero	1.00
264	Wilton Guerrero	.10
265	Dustin Hermanson	.10
266	Manny Martinez	.10
267	Ryan McGuire	.10
268	Ugueth Urbina	.10
269	Jose Vidro	.10
270	Rondell White	.20
271	Chris Widger	.10
272	Edgardo Alfonzo	.25
273	Armando Benitez	.10
274	Roger Cedeno	.10
275	Dennis Cook	.10
276	Octavio Dotel	.10
277	John Franco	.10
278	Darryl Hamilton	.10
279	Rickey Henderson	.25
280	Orel Hershiser	.10
281	Al Leiter	.20
282	John Olerud	.25
282b	John Olerud	.25
283	Rey Ordonez	.10
284	Mike Piazza	2.00
284b	Mike Piazza	2.00
285	Kenny Rogers	.10
286	Jorge Toca	.10
287	Robin Ventura	.20
288	Scott Brosius	.10
289	Roger Clemens	1.00
289b	Roger Clemens	1.00
290	David Cone	.20
291	Chili Davis	.10
292	Orlando Hernandez	.25
293	Hideki Irabu	.10
294	Derek Jeter	2.00
294b	Derek Jeter	2.00
295	Chuck Knoblauch	.25
296	Ricky Ledee	.10
297	Jim Leyritz	.10
298	Tino Martinez	.40
299	Paul O'Neill	.25
300	Andy Pettitte	.25
301	Jorge Posada	.10
302	Mariano Rivera	.25
303	Alfonso Soriano	.75
304	Bernie Williams	.50
304b	Bernie Williams	.50
305	Ed Yarnall	.10
306	Kevin Appier	.10
307	Rich Becker	.10
308	Eric Chavez	.10
309	Jason Giambi	.10
310	Ben Grieve	.25
311	Ramon Hernandez	.10
312	Tim Hudson	.40
313	John Jaha	.10
314	Doug Jones	.10
315	Omar Olivares	.10
316	Mike Oquist	.10
317	Matt Stairs	.10
318	Miguel Tejada	.10
319	Randy Velarde	.10
320	Bobby Abreu	.10
321	Marlon Anderson	.10
322	Alex Arias	.10
323	Rico Brogna	.10
324	Paul Byrd	.10
325	Ron Gant	.10
326	Doug Glanville	.10
327	Wayne Gomes	.10
328	Mike Lieberthal	.10
329	Robert Person	.10
330	Desi Relaford	.10
331	Scott Rolen	.75
331b	Scott Rolen	.75
332	Curt Schilling	.20
332b	Curt Schilling	.20
333	Kris Benson	.10
334	Adrian Brown	.10
335	Brant Brown	.10
336	Brian Giles	.10
337	Chad Hermansen	.10
338	Jason Kendall	.20
339	Al Martin	.10
340	Pat Meares	.10
341	Warren Morris	.10
341b	Warren Morris	.10
342	Todd Ritchie	.10
343	Jason Schmidt	.10
344	Ed Sprague	.10
345	Mike Williams	.10
346	Kevin Young	.10
347	Rick Ankiel	2.50
348	Ricky Bottalico	.10
349	Kent Bottenfield	.10
350	Darren Bragg	.10
351	Eric Davis	.20
352	J.D. Drew	.50
352b	J.D. Drew	.50
353	Adam Kennedy	.10
354	Ray Lankford	.10
355	Joe McEwing	.10
356	Mark McGwire	3.00
356b	Mark McGwire	3.00
357	Matt Morris	.10
358	Darren Oliver	.10
359	Edgar Renteria	.10
360	Fernando Tatis	.25
361	Andy Ashby	.10
362	Ben Davis	.10
363	Tony Gwynn	1.50
363b	Tony Gwynn	1.50
364	Sterling Hitchcock	.10
365	Trevor Hoffman	.10
366	Damian Jackson	.10
367	Wally Joyner	.10
368	Dave Magadan	.10
369	Gary Matthews Jr.	.10
370	Phil Nevin	.10
371	Eric Owens	.10
372	Ruben Rivera	.10
373	Reggie Sanders	.10
373b	Reggie Sanders	.10
374	Quilvio Veras	.10
375	Rich Aurilia	.10
376	Marvin Benard	.10
377	Barry Bonds	.75
377b	Barry Bonds	.75
378	Ellis Burks	.10
379	Shawn Estes	.10
380	Livan Hernandez	.10
381	Jeff Kent	.10
381b	Jeff Kent	.10
382	Brent Mayne	.10
383	Bill Mueller	.10
384	Calvin Murray	.10
385	Robb Nen	.10
386	Russ Ortiz	.10
387	Kirk Rueter	.10
388	J.T. Snow	.10
389	David Bell	.10
390	Jay Buhner	.20
391	Russ Davis	.10
392	Freddy Garcia	.25
392b	Freddy Garcia	.25
393	Ken Griffey Jr.	3.00
393b	Ken Griffey Jr.	3.00
394	Carlos Guillen	.10
395	John Halama	.10
396	Brian Hunter	.10
397	Ryan Jackson	.10
398	Edgar Martinez	.10
399	Gil Meche	.10
400	Jose Mesa	.10
401	Jamie Moyer	.10
402	Alex Rodriguez	2.00
402b	Alex Rodriguez	2.00
403	Dan Wilson	.10
404	Wilson Alvarez	.10
405	Rolando Arrojo	.10
406	Wade Boggs	.25
406b	Wade Boggs	.25
407	Miguel Cairo	.10
408	Jose Canseco	.75
408b	Jose Canseco	.75
409	John Flaherty	.10
410	Jose Guillen	.10
411	Roberto Hernandez	.10
412	Terrell Lowery	.10
413	Dave Martinez	.10
414	Quinton McCracken	.10
415	Fred McGriff	.25
415b	Fred McGriff	.25
416	Ryan Rupe	.10
417	Kevin Stocker	.10
418	Bubba Trammell	.10
419	Royce Clayton	.10
420	Juan Gonzalez	.75
420b	Juan Gonzalez	.75
421	Tom Goodwin	.10
422	Rusty Greer	.10
423	Rick Helling	.10
424	Roberto Kelly	.10
425	Ruben Mateo	.10
426	Mark McLemore	.10
427	Mike Morgan	.10
428	Rafael Palmeiro	.40
429	Ivan Rodriguez	.75
429b	Ivan Rodriguez	.75
430	Aaron Sele	.10
431	Lee Stevens	.10
432	John Wetteland	.10
433	Todd Zeile	.10
434	Jeff Zimmerman	.10
435	Tony Batista	.10
436	Casey Blake	.10
437	Homer Bush	.10
438	Chris Carpenter	.10
439	Jose Cruz Jr.	.10
440	Carlos Delgado	.50
440b	Carlos Delgado	.50
441	Tony Fernandez	.10
442	Darrin Fletcher	.10
443	Alex Gonzalez	.10
444	Shawn Green	.50
444b	Shawn Green	.50
445	Roy Halladay	.10
446	Billy Koch	.10
447	David Segui	.10
448	Shannon Stewart	.10
449	David Wells	.10
450	Vernon Wells	.10

2000 Pacific Ruby Red (Seven-11)

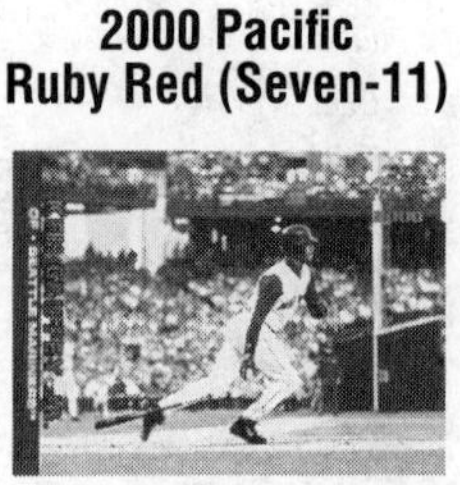

This parallel to the base set of 2000 Pacific was available only in 10-card retail "Jewel Collection" packs at Seven-11 convenience stores. Other than the use of red metallic foil for the player name and Pacific logo, the cards are identical to the regular-issue version.

	MT
Complete Set (500):	75.00
Common Player:	.15
Stars/Rookies 1.5X	

(See 2000 Pacific for checklist and base card values.)

2000 Pacific Cramer's Choice Awards

		MT
Complete Set (10):		575.00
Common Player:		25.00
Inserted 1:721		
1	Chipper Jones	50.00
2	Cal Ripken Jr.	60.00
3	Nomar Garciaparra	60.00
4	Sammy Sosa	60.00
5	Mike Piazza	60.00
6	Derek Jeter	60.00
7	Mark McGwire	100.00
8	Tony Gwynn	50.00
9	Ken Griffey Jr.	100.00
10	Alex Rodriguez	60.00

2000 Pacific Diamond Leaders

		MT
Complete Set (30):		60.00
Common Player:		1.00
Inserted 2:25		
1	Anaheim Angels (Garret Anderson, Chuck Finley, Troy Percival, Mo Vaughn)	2.00
2	Baltimore Orioles (Albert Belle, Mike Mussina, B.J. Surhoff)	2.00
3	Boston Red Sox (Nomar Garciaparra, Pedro J. Martinez, Troy O'Leary)	6.00
4	Chicago White Sox (Ray Durham, Magglio Ordonez, Frank Thomas)	2.50
5	Cleveland Indians (Bartolo Colon, Manny Ramirez, Omar Vizquel)	2.50
6	Detroit Tigers (Deivi Cruz, Dave Mlicki, David Palmer)	1.00
7	Kansas City Royals (Johnny Damon, Jermaine Dye, Jose Rosado, Mike Sweeney)	1.00
8	Minnesota Twins (Corey Koskie, Eric Milton, Brad Radke)	1.00
9	New York Yankees (Orlando Hernandez, Derek Jeter, Mariano Rivera, Bernie Williams)	6.00
10	Oakland Athletics (Jeremy Giambi, Tim Hudson, Matt Stairs)	1.00
11	Seattle Mariners (Freddy Garcia, Ken Griffey Jr., Edgar Martinez)	10.00
12	Tampa Bay Devil Rays (Jose Canseco, Roberto Hernandez, Fred McGriff)	2.00
13	Texas Rangers (Rafael Palmeiro, Ivan Rodriguez, John Wetteland)	2.50
14	Toronto Blue Jays (Carlos Delgado, Shannon Stewart, David Wells)	1.50
15	Arizona Diamondbacks (Luis Gonzalez, Randy Johnson, Matt Williams)	2.00
16	Atlanta Braves (Chipper Jones, Brian Jordan, Greg Maddux)	5.00
17	Chicago Cubs (Mark Grace, Jon Lieber, Sammy Sosa)	6.00
18	Cincinnati Reds (Sean Casey, Pete Harnisch, Greg Vaughn)	1.00
19	Colorado Rockies (Pedro Astacio, Dante Bichette, Larry Walker)	2.00
20	Florida Marlins (Luis Castillo, Alex Fernandez, Preston Wilson)	1.00
21	Houston Astros (Jeff Bagwell, Mike Hampton, Billy Wagner)	2.50
22	Los Angeles Dodgers (Kevin Brown, Mark Grudzielanek, Eric Karros)	1.00
23	Milwaukee Brewers (Jeromy Burnitz, Jeff Cirillo, Marquis Grissom, Hideo Nomo)	1.00
24	Montreal Expos (Vladimir Guerrero, Dustin Hermanson, Ugueth Urbina)	3.00
25	New York Mets (Roger Cedeno, Rickey Henderson, Mike Piazza)	6.00
26	Philadelphia Phillies (Bobby Abreu, Mike Lieberthal, Curt Schilling)	1.00
27	Pittsburgh Pirates (Brian Giles, Jason Kendall, Kevin Young)	1.00
28	St. Louis Cardinals (Kent Bottenfield, Ray Lankford, Mark McGwire)	10.00
29	San Diego Padres (Tony Gwynn, Trevor Hoffman, Reggie Sanders)	5.00
30	San Francisco Giants (Barry Bonds, Jeff Kent, Russ Ortiz)	2.50

2000 Pacific Gold Crown Die-Cuts

		MT
Complete Set (36):		250.00
Common Player:		3.00
Inserted 1:25		
1	Mo Vaughn	5.00
2	Matt Williams	4.00
3	Andruw Jones	4.00
4	Chipper Jones	15.00
5	Greg Maddux	12.00
6	Cal Ripken Jr.	15.00
7	Nomar Garciaparra	15.00
8	Pedro Martinez	6.00
9	Sammy Sosa	15.00
10	Magglio Ordonez	4.00
11	Frank Thomas	6.00
12	Sean Casey	4.00
13	Roberto Alomar	5.00
14	Manny Ramirez	6.00
15	Larry Walker	5.00
16	Jeff Bagwell	6.00
17	Craig Biggio	4.00
18	Carlos Beltran	5.00
19	Vladimir Guerrero	8.00
20	Mike Piazza	15.00
21	Roger Clemens	10.00
22	Derek Jeter	15.00
23	Bernie Williams	5.00
24	Scott Rolen	6.00
25	Warren Morris	3.00
26	J.D. Drew	6.00
27	Mark McGwire	25.00
28	Tony Gwynn	12.00
29	Barry Bonds	6.00
30	Ken Griffey Jr.	25.00
31	Alex Rodriguez	15.00
32	Jose Canseco	6.00
33	Juan Gonzalez	6.00
34	Rafael Palmeiro	5.00
35	Ivan Rodriguez	6.00
36	Shawn Green	4.00

2000 Pacific Ornaments

		MT
Complete Set (20):		140.00
Common Player:		3.00
Inserted 2:25		
1	Mo Vaughn	4.00
2	Chipper Jones	12.00
3	Greg Maddux	10.00
4	Cal Ripken Jr.	12.00
5	Nomar Garciaparra	12.00
6	Sammy Sosa	12.00
7	Frank Thomas	5.00
8	Manny Ramirez	5.00
9	Larry Walker	4.00
10	Jeff Bagwell	5.00
11	Mike Piazza	12.00
12	Roger Clemens	8.00
13	Derek Jeter	12.00
14	Scott Rolen	5.00
15	J.D. Drew	5.00
16	Mark McGwire	20.00
17	Tony Gwynn	10.00
18	Ken Griffey Jr.	20.00
19	Alex Rodriguez	12.00
20	Ivan Rodriguez	5.00

2000 Pacific Past & Present

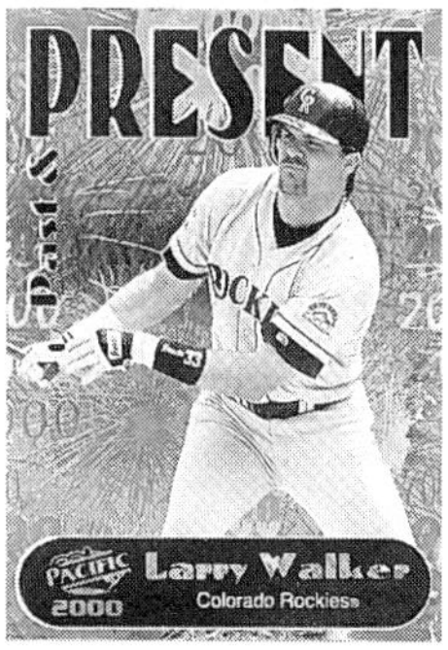

		MT
Complete Set (20):		240.00
Common Player:		4.00
Inserted 1:49 H		
1	Chipper Jones	20.00
2	Greg Maddux	15.00
3	Cal Ripken Jr.	20.00
4	Nomar Garciaparra	20.00
5	Pedro Martinez	8.00
6	Sammy Sosa	20.00
7	Frank Thomas	8.00
8	Manny Ramirez	8.00
9	Larry Walker	6.00
10	Jeff Bagwell	8.00
11	Mike Piazza	20.00
12	Roger Clemens	10.00
13	Derek Jeter	20.00
14	Mark McGwire	30.00
15	Tony Gwynn	15.00
16	Barry Bonds	8.00
17	Ken Griffey Jr.	30.00
18	Alex Rodriguez	20.00
19	Wade Boggs	6.00
20	Ivan Rodriguez	8.00

Checklists with card numbers in parentheses ( ) indicates the numbers do not appear on the card.

2000 Pacific Reflections

		MT
Complete Set (20):		350.00
Common Player:		8.00
Inserted 1:97		
1	Andruw Jones	8.00
2	Chipper Jones	30.00
3	Cal Ripken Jr.	30.00
4	Nomar Garciaparra	30.00
5	Sammy Sosa	30.00
6	Frank Thomas	12.00
7	Manny Ramirez	12.00
8	Jeff Bagwell	12.00
9	Vladimir Guerrero	15.00
10	Mike Piazza	30.00
11	Derek Jeter	30.00
12	Bernie Williams	10.00
13	Scott Rolen	12.00
14	J.D. Drew	12.00
15	Mark McGwire	50.00
16	Tony Gwynn	25.00
17	Ken Griffey Jr.	50.00
18	Alex Rodriguez	30.00
19	Juan Gonzalez	12.00
20	Ivan Rodriguez	12.00

2000 Pacific Aurora Sample

Nearly identical to the issued version of spokesman Tony Gwynn's card, this features a large white diagonal "SAMPLE" overprint on back and in the space where a card number usually appears.

	MT
Tony Gwynn	3.00

2000 Pacific Aurora

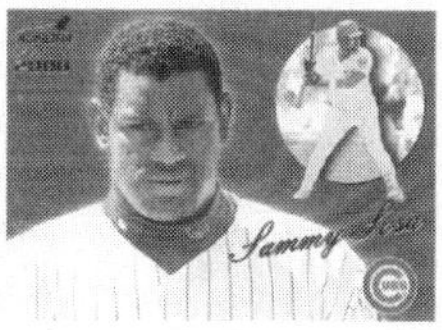

		MT
Complete Set (151):		50.00
Common Player:		.15
Wax Box:		70.00
1	Darin Erstad	.25
2	Troy Glaus	.50
3	Tim Salmon	.40
4	Mo Vaughn	.75
5	Jay Bell	.15
6	Erubiel Durazo	.50
7	Luis Gonzalez	.15
8	Randy Johnson	.75
9	Matt Williams	.50
10	Tom Glavine	.40
11	Andruw Jones	.75
12	Chipper Jones	2.00
13	Brian Jordan	.15
14	Greg Maddux	2.00
15	Kevin Millwood	.25
16	Albert Belle	.75
17	Will Clark	.50
18	Mike Mussina	.75
19	Cal Ripken Jr.	3.00
20	B.J. Surhoff	.15
21	Nomar Garciaparra	2.50
22	Pedro Martinez	1.00
23	Troy O'Leary	.15
24	Wilton Veras	.40
25	Mark Grace	.40
26	Henry Rodriguez	.15
27	Sammy Sosa	2.50
28	Kerry Wood	.40
29	Ray Durham	.15
30	Paul Konerko	.25
31	Carlos Lee	.15
32	Magglio Ordonez	.40
33	Chris Singleton	.15
34	Frank Thomas	1.25
35	Mike Cameron	.15
36	Sean Casey	.40
37	Barry Larkin	.50
38	Pokey Reese	.15
39	Eddie Taubensee	.15
40	Roberto Alomar	.75
41	David Justice	.40
42	Kenny Lofton	.50
43	Manny Ramirez	1.00
44	Richie Sexson	.15
45	Jim Thome	.50
46	Omar Vizquel	.15
47	Todd Helton	.50
48	Mike Lansing	.15
49	Neifi Perez	.15
50	Ben Petrick	.15
51	Larry Walker	.75
52	Tony Clark	.40
53	Damion Easley	.15
54	Juan Encarnacion	.15
55	Juan Gonzalez	1.25
56	Dean Palmer	.15
57	Luis Castillo	.15
58	Cliff Floyd	.15
59	Alex Gonzalez	.15
60	Mike Lowell	.15
61	Preston Wilson	.15
62	Jeff Bagwell	1.00
63	Craig Biggio	.50
64	Ken Caminiti	.25
65	Jose Lima	.15
66	Billy Wagner	.15
67	Carlos Beltran	.40
68	Johnny Damon	.15
69	Jermaine Dye	.15
70	Mark Quinn	.15
71	Mike Sweeney	.15
72	Kevin Brown	.25
73	Shawn Green	.75
74	Eric Karros	.25
75	Chan Ho Park	.15
76	Gary Sheffield	.40
77	Ron Belliard	.15
78	Jeromy Burnitz	.15
79	Marquis Grissom	.15
80	Geoff Jenkins	.15
81	David Nilsson	.15
82	Ron Coomer	.15
83	Jacque Jones	.15
84	Brad Radke	.15
85	Todd Walker	.15
86	Michael Barrett	.15
87	Peter Bergeron	.15
88	Vladimir Guerrero	1.50
89	Jose Vidro	.15
90	Rondell White	.25
91	Edgardo Alfonzo	.25
92	Darryl Hamilton	.15
93	Rey Ordonez	.15
94	Mike Piazza	2.50
95	Robin Ventura	.25
96	Roger Clemens	1.50
97	Orlando Hernandez	.50
98	Derek Jeter	2.50
99	Tino Martinez	.40
100	Mariano Rivera	.25
101	Bernie Williams	.75
102	Eric Chavez	.40
103	Jason Giambi	.15
104	Ben Grieve	.40
105	Tim Hudson	.50
106	John Jaha	.15
107	Matt Stairs	.15
108	Bobby Abreu	.15
109	Doug Glanville	.15
110	Mike Lieberthal	.15
111	Scott Rolen	1.00
112	Curt Schilling	.25
113	Brian Giles	.15
114	Chad Hermansen	.15
115	Jason Kendall	.25
116	Warren Morris	.15
117	Kevin Young	.15
118	Rick Ankiel	4.00
119	J.D. Drew	.75
120	Ray Lankford	.15
121	Mark McGwire	4.00
122	Edgar Renteria	.15
123	Fernando Tatis	.25
124	Ben Davis	.15
125	Tony Gwynn	2.00
126	Trevor Hoffman	.15
127	Phil Nevin	.15
128	Barry Bonds	1.00
129	Ellis Burks	.15
130	Jeff Kent	.15
131	J.T. Snow	.15
132	Freddy Garcia	.40
133	Ken Griffey Jr.	4.00
133a	Ken Griffey Jr. Reds	10.00
134	Edgar Martinez	.15
135	Alex Rodriguez	2.50
136	Dan Wilson	.15
137	Jose Canseco	1.00
138	Roberto Hernandez	.15
139	Dave Martinez	.15
140	Fred McGriff	.40
141	Rusty Greer	.15
142	Ruben Mateo	.40
143	Rafael Palmeiro	.75
144	Ivan Rodriguez	1.00
145	Jeff Zimmerman	.15
146	Homer Bush	.15
147	Carlos Delgado	.75
148	Raul Mondesi	.40
149	Shannon Stewart	.15
150	Vernon Wells	.25

2000 Pacific Aurora At-Bat Styrotechs

		MT
Complete Set (20):		375.00
Common Player:		8.00
Production 299 sets		
1	Chipper Jones	25.00
2	Cal Ripken Jr.	40.00
3	Nomar Garciaparra	30.00
4	Sammy Sosa	30.00
5	Frank Thomas	15.00
6	Manny Ramirez	12.00
7	Larry Walker	10.00
8	Jeff Bagwell	12.00
9	Carlos Beltran	10.00
10	Vladimir Guerrero	20.00
11	Mike Piazza	30.00
12	Derek Jeter	30.00
13	Bernie Williams	10.00
14	Mark McGwire	50.00
15	Tony Gwynn	25.00
16	Barry Bonds	12.00
17	Ken Griffey Jr.	50.00
18	Alex Rodriguez	30.00
19	Jose Canseco	12.00
20	Ivan Rodriguez	12.00

2000 Pacific Aurora Dugout View Net-Fusions

		MT
Complete Set (20):		160.00
Common Player:		4.00
Inserted 1:37		
1	Mo Vaughn	5.00
2	Chipper Jones	12.00
3	Cal Ripken Jr.	20.00
4	Nomar Garciaparra	15.00
5	Sammy Sosa	15.00
6	Manny Ramirez	6.00
7	Larry Walker	5.00
8	Juan Gonzalez	8.00
9	Jeff Bagwell	6.00
10	Craig Biggio	5.00
11	Shawn Green	4.00
12	Vladimir Guerrero	8.00
13	Mike Piazza	15.00
14	Derek Jeter	15.00
15	Scott Rolen	6.00
16	Mark McGwire	8.00
17	Tony Gwynn	12.00
18	Ken Griffey Jr.	25.00
19	Alex Rodriguez	15.00
20	Rafael Palmeiro	4.00

2000 Pacific Aurora Pennant Fever

		MT
Complete Set (20):		60.00
Common Player:		1.00
T. Gwynn Auto./147		100.00
Inserted 4:37		
1	Andruw Jones	1.50
2	Chipper Jones	4.00
3	Greg Maddux	4.00
4	Cal Ripken Jr.	6.00
5	Nomar Garciaparra	5.00
6	Pedro Martinez	2.00
7	Sammy Sosa	5.00
8	Manny Ramirez	2.00
9	Jim Thome	1.00
10	Jeff Bagwell	2.00
11	Mike Piazza	5.00
12	Roger Clemens	3.00
13	Derek Jeter	5.00
14	Bernie Williams	1.50
15	Mark McGwire	8.00
16	Tony Gwynn	4.00
17	Ken Griffey Jr.	8.00
18	Alex Rodriguez	5.00
19	Rafael Palmeiro	1.00
20	Ivan Rodriguez	2.00

2000 Pacific Aurora Pinstripes

		MT
Complete Set (50):		200.00
Common Player:		1.00
Premiere Date: 4x-8x		
Production 51 sets		
4	Mo Vaughn	2.00
8	Randy Johnson	2.50
9	Matt Williams	2.50
11	Andruw Jones	2.50
12	Chipper Jones	6.00
14	Greg Maddux	6.00
19	Cal Ripken Jr.	10.00
21	Nomar Garciaparra	8.00
22	Pedro Martinez	4.00
27	Sammy Sosa	8.00
32	Magglio Ordonez	1.00
34	Frank Thomas	4.00
36	Sean Casey	1.50
37	Barry Larkin	2.00
42	Kenny Lofton	1.50
43	Manny Ramirez	3.00
45	Jim Thome	2.50
47	Todd Helton	2.00
51	Larry Walker	2.00
55	Juan Gonzalez	4.00
62	Jeff Bagwell	3.00
63	Craig Biggio	2.00
67	Carlos Beltran	2.00
73	Shawn Green	3.00
76	Gary Sheffield	1.50
78	Jeromy Burnitz	1.00
88	Vladimir Guerrero	4.00
91	Edgardo Alfonzo	2.00
94	Mike Piazza	8.00
96	Roger Clemens	5.00
97	Orlando Hernandez	1.50
98	Derek Jeter	8.00
101	Bernie Williams	2.00
102	Eric Chavez	1.00
105	Tim Hudson	1.50
111	Scott Rolen	3.00
112	Curt Schilling	1.50
113	Brian Giles	1.00
114	Rick Ankiel	10.00
121	Mark McGwire	12.00
125	Tony Gwynn	6.00
128	Barry Bonds	3.00
130	Jeff Kent	1.00
133	Ken Griffey Jr.	2.00
135	Alex Rodriguez	8.00
137	Jose Canseco	3.00
140	Fred McGriff	2.00
143	Rafael Palmeiro	2.00
144	Ivan Rodriguez	3.00
147	Carlos Delgado	2.50

The election of former players to the Hall of Fame does not always have an immediate upward effect on card prices. The hobby market generally has done a good job of predicting those inductions and adjusting values over the course of several years.

2000 Pacific Aurora Star Factor

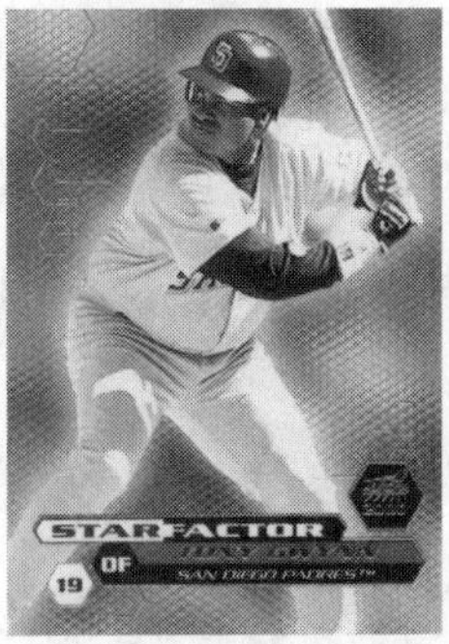

		MT
Complete Set (10):		675.00
Common Player:		25.00
Inserted 1:361		
1	Chipper Jones	60.00
2	Cal Ripken Jr.	100.00
3	Nomar Garciaparra	75.00
4	Sammy Sosa	75.00
5	Mike Piazza	75.00
6	Derek Jeter	75.00
7	Mark McGwire	120.00
8	Tony Gwynn	60.00
9	Ken Griffey Jr.	120.00
10	Alex Rodriguez	75.00

2000 Pacific Crown Collection Sample

Nearly identical to the issued version of spokesman Tony Gwynn's card, this features a large white diagonal "SAMPLE" overprint on back and in the space where a card number usually appears.

	MT
Tony Gwynn	3.00

2000 Pacific Crown Collection

		MT
Complete Set (300):		35.00
Common Player:		.10
Wax Box:		75.00
1	Garret Anderson	.10
2	Darin Erstad	.25
3	Ben Molina	.10
4	(Ramon Ortiz)	.10
5	Orlando Palmeiro	.10
6	Troy Percival	.10
7	Tim Salmon	.20
8	Mo Vaughn	.50
9	Checklist (Mo Vaughn)	.25
10	Jay Bell	.10
11	Omar Daal	.10
12	Erubiel Durazo	.25
13	Steve Finley	.10
14	Hanley Frias	.10
15	Luis Gonzalez	.10
16	Randy Johnson	.50
17	Matt Williams	.40
18	Checklist (Matt Williams)	.20
19	Andres Galarraga	.40
20	Tom Glavine	.20
21	Andruw Jones	.40
22	Chipper Jones	1.50
23	Brian Jordan	.10
24	Javy Lopez	.10
25	Greg Maddux	1.50
26	Kevin Millwood	.20
27	Eddie Perez	.10
28	John Smoltz	.20
29	Checklist (Chipper Jones)	.75
30	Albert Belle	.50
31	Jesse Garcia	.10
32	Jerry Hairston Jr.	.10
33	Charles Johnson	.10
34	Mike Mussina	.50
35	Sidney Ponson	.10
36	Cal Ripken Jr.	2.00
37	B.J. Surhoff	.10
38	Checklist (Cal Ripken Jr.)	1.00
39	Nomar Garciaparra	2.00
40	Pedro Martinez	.75
41	Ramon Martinez	.10
42	Trot Nixon	.10
43	Jose Offerman	.10
44	Troy O'Leary	.10
45	John Valentin	.10
46	Wilton Veras	.10
47	Checklist (Nomar Garciaparra)	1.00
48	Mark Grace	.20
49	Felix Heredia	.10
50	Jose Molina	.10
51	Jose Nieves	.10
52	Henry Rodriguez	.10
53	Sammy Sosa	2.00
54	Kerry Wood	.40
55	Checklist (Sammy Sosa)	1.00
56	Mike Caruso	.10
57	Carlos Castillo	.10
58	Jason Dellaero	.10
59	Carlos Lee	.10
60	Magglio Ordonez	.25
61	Jesus Pena	.10
62	Liu Rodriguez	.10
63	Frank Thomas	1.00
64	Checklist (Magglio Ordonez)	.15
65	Aaron Boone	.10
66	Mike Cameron	.10
67	Sean Casey	.40
68	Juan Guzman	.10
69	Barry Larkin	.40
70	Pokey Reese	.10
71	Eddie Taubensee	.10
72	Greg Vaughn	.25
73	Checklist (Sean Casey)	.20
74	Roberto Alomar	.25
75	Sandy Alomar Jr.	.15
76	Bartolo Colon	.10
77	Jacob Cruz	.10
78	Einar Diaz	.10
79	David Justice	.20
80	Kenny Lofton	.50
81	Manny Ramirez	.75
82	Richie Sexson	.10
83	Jim Thome	.40
84	Omar Vizquel	.10
85	Enrique Wilson	.10
86	Checklist (Manny Ramirez)	.40
87	Pedro Astacio	.10
88	Henry Blanco	.10
89	Vinny Castilla	.20
90	Edgard Clemente	.10
91	Todd Helton	.40
92	Neifi Perez	.10
93	Terry Shumpert	.10
94	*Juan Sosa*	.40
95	Larry Walker	.50
96	Checklist (Vinny Castilla)	.10
97	Tony Clark	.25
98	Deivi Cruz	.10
99	Damion Easley	.10
100	Juan Encarnacion	.10
101	Karim Garcia	.10
102	Luis Garcia	.10
103	Juan Gonzalez	1.00
104	Jose Macias	.10
105	Dean Palmer	.10
106	Checklist (Juan Encarnacion)	.10
107	Antonio Alfonseca	.10
108	Armando Almanza	.10
109	Bruce Aven	.10
110	Luis Castillo	.10
111	Ramon Castro	.10
112	Alex Fernandez	.10
113	Cliff Floyd	.10
114	Alex Gonzalez	.10
115	*Michael Tejera*	.10
116	Preston Wilson	.10
117	Checklist (Luis Castillo)	.10
118	Jeff Bagwell	.75
119	Craig Biggio	.50
120	Jose Cabrera	.10
121	Tony Eusebio	.10
122	Carl Everett	.10
123	Ricky Gutierrez	.10
124	Mike Hampton	.10
125	Richard Hidalgo	.10
126	Jose Lima	.10
127	Billy Wagner	.10
128	Checklist (Jeff Bagwell)	.40
129	Carlos Beltran	.25
130	Johnny Damon	.10
131	Jermaine Dye	.10
132	Carlos Febles	.10
133	Jeremy Giambi	.10
134	Jose Rosado	.10
135	Rey Sanchez	.10
136	Jose Santiago	.10
137	Checklist (Carlos Beltran)	.10
138	Kevin Brown	.20
139	Craig Counsell	.10
140	Shawn Green	.40
141	Eric Karros	.20
142	Angel Pena	.10
143	Gary Sheffield	.25
144	Ismael Valdes	.10
145	Jose Vizcaino	.10
146	Devon White	.10
147	Checklist (Eric Karros)	.10
148	Ron Belliard	.10
149	Jeromy Burnitz	.10
150	Jeff Cirillo	.10
151	Marquis Grissom	.10
152	Geoff Jenkins	.10
153	Dave Nilsson	.10
154	Rafael Roque	.10
155	Jose Valentin	.10
156	Fernando Vina	.10
157	Jeromy Burnitz	.10
158	Chad Allen	.10
159	Ron Coomer	.10
160	Eddie Guardado	.10
161	Cristian Guzman	.10
162	Jacque Jones	.10
163	Javier Valentin	.10
164	Todd Walker	.10
165	Checklist (Ron Coomer)	.10
166	Michael Barrett	.10
167	Miguel Batista	.10
168	Vladimir Guerrero	1.00
169	Wilton Guerrero	.10
170	Fernando Seguignol	.10
171	Ugueth Urbina	.10
172	Javier Vazquez	.10
173	Jose Vidro	.10
174	Rondell White	.20
175	Checklist (Vladimir Guerrero)	.50
176	Edgardo Alfonzo	.25
177	Armando Benitez	.10
178	Roger Cedeno	.10
179	Octavio Dotel	.10
180	Melvin Mora	.10
181	Rey Ordonez	.10
182	Mike Piazza	2.00
183	Jorge Toca	.10
184	Robin Ventura	.25
185	Checklist (Edgardo Alfonzo)	.15
186	Roger Clemens	1.00
187	David Cone	.20
188	Orlando Hernandez	.25
189	Derek Jeter	2.00
190	Ricky Ledee	.10
191	Tino Martinez	.25
192	Ramiro Mendoza	.10
193	Jorge Posada	.20
194	Mariano Rivera	.25
195	Alfonso Soriano	2.00
196	Bernie Williams	.50
197	Checklist (Derek Jeter)	1.00
198	Eric Chavez	.10
199	Jason Giambi	.10
200	Ben Grieve	.25
201	Ramon Hernandez	.10
202	Tim Hudson	.40
203	John Jaha	.10
204	Omar Olivares	.10
205	Olmedo Saenz	.10
206	Matt Stairs	.10
207	Miguel Tejada	.10
208	Checklist (Tim Hudson)	.25
209	Rico Brogna	.10
210	Bobby Abreu	.10
211	Marlon Anderson	.10
212	Alex Arias	.10
213	Doug Glanville	.10
214	Robert Person	.10
215	Scott Rolen	.75
216	Curt Schilling	.20
217	Checklist (Scott Rolen)	.40
218	Francisco Cordova	.10
219	Brian Giles	.10
220	Jason Kendall	.20
221	Warren Morris	.10
222	Abraham Nunez	.10
223	Aramis Ramirez	.10
224	Jose Silva	.10
225	Kevin Young	.10
226	Checklist (Brian Giles)	.10
227	Rick Ankiel	5.00
228	Ricky Bottalico	.10
229	J.D. Drew	.50
230	Ray Lankford	.10
231	Mark McGwire	3.00
232	Eduardo Perez	.10
233	Placido Polanco	.10
234	Edgar Renteria	.10
235	Fernando Tatis	.10
236	Checklist (Mark McGwire)	1.50
237	Carlos Almanzar	.10
238	Wiki Gonzalez	.10
239	Tony Gwynn	1.50
240	Trevor Hoffman	.10

241 Damian Jackson .10
242 Wally Joyner .10
243 Ruben Rivera .10
244 Reggie Sanders .10
245 Quilvio Veras .10
246 Checklist (Tony Gwynn) .75
247 Rich Aurilia .10
248 Marvin Benard .10
249 Barry Bonds .75
250 Ellis Burks .10
251 Miguel Del Toro .10
252 Edwards Guzman .10
253 Livan Hernandez .10
254 Jeff Kent .10
255 Russ Ortiz .10
256 Armando Rios .10
257 Checklist (Barry Bonds) .40
258 Rafael Bournigal .10
259 Freddy Garcia .50
260 Ken Griffey Jr. 3.00
261 Carlos Guillen .10
262 Raul Ibanez .10
263 Edgar Martinez .20
264 Jose Mesa .10
265 Jamie Moyer .10
266 John Olerud .25
267 Jose Paniagua .10
268 Alex Rodriguez 2.00
269 Checklist (Alex Rodriguez) 1.00
270 Wilson Alvarez .10
271 Rolando Arrojo .10
272 Wade Boggs .40
273 Miguel Cairo .10
274 Jose Canseco .75
275 Jose Guillen .10
276 Roberto Hernandez .10
277 Albie Lopez .10
278 Fred McGriff .25
279 Esteban Yan .10
280 Checklist (Jose Canseco) .40
281 Rusty Greer .10
282 Roberto Kelly .10
283 Esteban Loaiza .10
284 Ruben Mateo .25
285 Rafael Palmeiro .50
286 Ivan Rodriguez .75
287 Aaron Sele .10
288 John Wetteland .10
289 Checklist (Ivan Rodriguez) .40
290 Tony Batista .10
291 Jose Cruz Jr. .10
292 Carlos Delgado .50
293 Kelvim Escobar .10
294 Tony Fernandez .10
295 Billy Koch .10
296 Raul Mondesi .20
297 Willis Otanez .10
298 David Segui .10
299 David Wells .10
300 Checklist (Carlos Delgado) .25

2000 Pacific Crown Collection In The Cage

		MT
Complete Set (20):		600.00
Common Player:		10.00
Inserted 1:145		
1	Mo Vaughn	15.00
2	Chipper Jones	40.00
3	Cal Ripken Jr.	50.00
4	Nomar Garciaparra	50.00
5	Sammy Sosa	50.00
6	Frank Thomas	20.00
7	Roberto Alomar	15.00
8	Manny Ramirez	20.00
9	Larry Walker	15.00
10	Jeff Bagwell	20.00
11	Vladimir Guerrero	25.00
12	Mike Piazza	50.00
13	Derek Jeter	50.00
14	Bernie Williams	15.00
15	Mark McGwire	80.00
16	Tony Gwynn	40.00
17	Ken Griffey Jr.	80.00
18	Alex Rodriguez	50.00
19	Rafael Palmeiro	15.00
20	Ivan Rodriguez	20.00

2000 Pacific Crown Coll. Latinos of the Major Leagues

MT

Complete Set (36):
Common Player:
1 Erubiel Durazo
2 Luis Gonzalez
3 Andruw Jones
4 Nomar Garciaparra
5 Pedro Martinez
6 Sammy Sosa
7 Carlos Lee
8 Magglio Ordonez
9 Roberto Alomar
10 Manny Ramirez
11 Omar Vizquel
12 Vinny Castilla
13 Juan Gonzalez
14 Luis Castillo
15 Jose Lima
16 Carlos Beltran
17 Vladimir Guerrero
18 Edgardo Alfonzo
19 Roger Cedeno
20 Rey Ordonez
21 Orlando Hernandez
22 Tino Martinez
23 Mariano Rivera
24 Bernie Williams
25 Miguel Tejada
26 Bobby Abreu
27 Fernando Tatis
28 Freddy Garcia
29 Edgar Martinez
30 Alex Rodriguez
31 Jose Canseco
32 Ruben Mateo
33 Rafael Palmeiro
34 Ivan Rodriguez
35 Carlos Delgado
36 Raul Mondesi

2000 Pacific Crown Collection Moment of Truth

		MT
Complete Set (30):		300.00
Common Player:		3.00
Inserted 1:37		
1	Mo Vaughn	6.00
2	Chipper Jones	18.00
3	Greg Maddux	18.00
4	Albert Belle	6.00
5	Cal Ripken Jr.	20.00
6	Nomar Garciaparra	20.00
7	Pedro Martinez	8.00
8	Sammy Sosa	20.00
9	Frank Thomas	8.00
10	Barry Larkin	5.00
11	Kenny Lofton	5.00
12	Manny Ramirez	8.00
13	Larry Walker	6.00
14	Juan Gonzalez	8.00
15	Jeff Bagwell	8.00
16	Craig Biggio	5.00
17	Carlos Beltran	4.00
18	Vladimir Guerrero	10.00
19	Mike Piazza	20.00
20	Roger Clemens	12.00
21	Derek Jeter	20.00
22	Bernie Williams	6.00
23	Mark McGwire	35.00
24	Tony Gwynn	18.00
25	Barry Bonds	8.00
26	Ken Griffey Jr.	35.00
27	Alex Rodriguez	20.00
28	Rafael Palmeiro	6.00
29	Ivan Rodriguez	8.00
30	Carlos Delgado	6.00

2000 Pacific Crown Collection Pacific Cup

		MT
Complete Set (10):		650.00
Common Player:		25.00
Inserted 1:721		
1	Cal Ripken Jr.	80.00
2	Nomar Garciaparra	80.00
3	Pedro Martinez	30.00
4	Sammy Sosa	80.00
5	Vladimir Guerrero	40.00
6	Derek Jeter	80.00
7	Mark McGwire	120.00
8	Tony Gwynn	60.00
9	Ken Griffey Jr.	120.00
10	Alex Rodriguez	80.00

2000 Pacific Crown Collection Timber 2000

		MT
Complete Set (20):		275.00
Common Player:		5.00
Inserted 1:73		
1	Chipper Jones	25.00
2	Nomar Garciaparra	30.00
3	Sammy Sosa	30.00
4	Magglio Ordonez	5.00
5	Manny Ramirez	12.00
6	Vinny Castilla	5.00
7	Juan Gonzalez	12.00
8	Jeff Bagwell	12.00
9	Shawn Green	8.00
10	Vladimir Guerrero	15.00
11	Mike Piazza	20.00
12	Derek Jeter	20.00
13	Bernie Williams	10.00
14	Mark McGwire	50.00
15	Ken Griffey Jr.	50.00
16	Alex Rodriguez	30.00
17	Jose Canseco	12.00
18	Rafael Palmeiro	8.00
19	Ivan Rodriguez	12.00
20	Carlos Delgado	8.00

2000 Pacific Paramount Sample

Nearly identical to the issued version of spokesman Tony Gwynn's card, this features a large white diagonal "SAMPLE" overprint on back and in the space where a card number usually appears.

	MT
Tony Gwynn	3.00

2000 Pacific Paramount

		MT
Complete Set (250):		35.00
Common Player:		.10
Wax Box:		50.00
1	Garret Anderson	.10
2	Jim Edmonds	.10
3	Darin Erstad	.20
4	Chuck Finley	.10
5	Troy Glaus	.25
6	Troy Percival	.10
7	Tim Salmon	.20
8	Mo Vaughn	.40
9	Jay Bell	.10
10	Erubiel Durazo	.20
11	Steve Finley	.10
12	Luis Gonzalez	.10
13	Randy Johnson	.40
14	Travis Lee	.20
15	Matt Mantei	.10
16	Matt Williams	.25
17	Tony Womack	.10
18	Bret Boone	.10
19	Tom Glavine	.20
20	Andruw Jones	.40
21	Chipper Jones	1.00
22	Brian Jordan	.10
23	Javy Lopez	.15
24	Greg Maddux	1.00
25	Kevin Millwood	.20
26	John Rocker	.10
27	John Smoltz	.15
28	Brady Anderson	.15
29	Albert Belle	.40
30	Will Clark	.25
31	Charles Johnson	.10
32	Mike Mussina	.40
33	Cal Ripken Jr.	1.25
34	B.J. Surhoff	.10
35	Nomar Garciaparra	1.25
36	Derek Lowe	.10
37	Pedro Martinez	.50
38	Trot Nixon	.10
39	Troy O'Leary	.10
40	Jose Offerman	.10
41	John Valentin	.10
42	Jason Varitek	.10
43	Mark Grace	.20
44	Glenallen Hill	.10
45	Jon Lieber	.10
46	Cole Liniak	.10
47	Jose Nieves	.10
48	Henry Rodriguez	.10
49	Sammy Sosa	1.25
50	Kerry Wood	.40
51	Jason Dellaero	.10
52	Ray Durham	.10
53	Paul Konerko	.10
54	Carlos Lee	.10
55	Greg Norton	.10
56	Magglio Ordonez	.25
57	Chris Singleton	.10
58	Frank Thomas	.60
59	Aaron Boone	.10
60	Mike Cameron	.10
61	Sean Casey	.40
62	Pete Harnisch	.10
63	Barry Larkin	.25
64	Pokey Reese	.10
65	Greg Vaughn	.25
66	Scott Williamson	.10
67	Roberto Alomar	.40
68	*Sean DePaula*	.25
69	Travis Fryman	.20
70	David Justice	.20
71	Kenny Lofton	.40
72	Manny Ramirez	.50
73	Richie Sexson	.10
74	Jim Thome	.25
75	Omar Vizquel	.10
76	Pedro Astacio	.10
77	Vinny Castilla	.15
78	Derrick Gibson	.10
79	Todd Helton	.20
80	Neifi Perez	.10
81	Ben Petrick	.10
82	Larry Walker	.40
83	Brad Ausmus	.10
84	Tony Clark	.20
85	Deivi Cruz	.10
86	Damion Easley	.10
87	Juan Encarnacion	.10
88	Juan Gonzalez	.50
89	Bobby Higginson	.10
90	Dave Mlicki	.10
91	Dean Palmer	.15
92	Bruce Aven	.10
93	Luis Castillo	.10
94	Ramon Castro	.10
95	Cliff Floyd	.10
96	Alex Gonzalez	.10
97	Mike Lowell	.10
98	Preston Wilson	.10
99	Jeff Bagwell	.50
100	Derek Bell	.10
101	Craig Biggio	.30
102	Ken Caminiti	.15
103	Carl Everett	.15
104	Mike Hampton	.10
105	Jose Lima	.10
106	Billy Wagner	.10
107	Daryle Ward	.10
108	Carlos Beltran	.20
109	Johnny Damon	.10
110	Jermaine Dye	.10
111	Carlos Febles	.10
112	Mark Quinn	.10
113	Joe Randa	.10
114	Jose Rosado	.10
115	Mike Sweeney	.10
116	Kevin Brown	.15
117	Shawn Green	.40
118	Mark Grudzielanek	.10
119	Todd Hollandsworth	.10
120	Eric Karros	.15
121	Chan Ho Park	.15
122	Gary Sheffield	.25
123	Devon White	.10
124	Eric Young	.10
125	Kevin Barker	.10
126	Ron Belliard	.10
127	Jeromy Burnitz	.10
128	Jeff Cirillo	.10
129	Marquis Grissom	.10
130	Geoff Jenkins	.10
131	David Nilsson	.10
132	Chad Allen	.10
133	Ron Coomer	.10
134	Jacque Jones	.10
135	Corey Koskie	.10
136	Matt Lawton	.10
137	Brad Radke	.10
138	Todd Walker	.10
139	Michael Barrett	.10
140	Peter Bergeron	.10
141	Brad Fullmer	.10
142	Vladimir Guerrero	.60
143	Ugueth Urbina	.10
144	Jose Vidro	.10
145	Rondell White	.15
146	Edgardo Alfonzo	.20
147	Armando Benitez	.10
148	Roger Cedeno	.10
149	Rickey Henderson	.30
150	Melvin Mora	.10
151	John Olerud	.25
152	Rey Ordonez	.10
153	Mike Piazza	1.25
154	Jorge Toca	.10
155	Robin Ventura	.20
156	Roger Clemens	.75
157	David Cone	.20
158	Orlando Hernandez	.20
159	Derek Jeter	1.25
160	Chuck Knoblauch	.25
161	Ricky Ledee	.10
162	Tino Martinez	.25
163	Paul O'Neill	.20
164	Mariano Rivera	.20
165	Alfonso Soriano	.50
166	Bernie Williams	.40
167	Eric Chavez	.10
168	Jason Giambi	.10
169	Ben Grieve	.20
170	Tim Hudson	.20
171	John Jaha	.10
172	Matt Stairs	.10
173	Miguel Tejada	.10
174	Randy Velarde	.10
175	Bobby Abreu	.10
176	Marlon Anderson	.10
177	Rico Brogna	.10
178	Ron Gant	.20
179	Doug Glanville	.10
180	Mike Lieberthal	.10
181	Scott Rolen	.50
182	Curt Schilling	.15
183	Brian Giles	.10
184	Chad Hermansen	.10
185	Jason Kendall	.10
186	Al Martin	.10
187	Pat Meares	.10
188	Warren Morris	.10
189	Ed Sprague	.10
190	Kevin Young	.10
191	Rick Ankiel	5.00
192	Kent Bottenfield	.10
193	Eric Davis	.20
194	J.D. Drew	.50
195	Adam Kennedy	.10
196	Ray Lankford	.10
197	Joe McEwing	.10
198	Mark McGwire	2.00
199	Edgar Renteria	.10
200	Fernando Tatis	.20
201	Mike Darr	.10
202	Ben Davis	.10
203	Tony Gwynn	1.00
204	Trevor Hoffman	.10
205	Damian Jackson	.10
206	Phil Nevin	.10
207	Reggie Sanders	.10
208	Quilvio Veras	.10
209	Rich Aurilia	.10
210	Marvin Benard	.10
211	Barry Bonds	.50
212	Ellis Burks	.10
213	Livan Hernandez	.10
214	Jeff Kent	.10
215	Russ Ortiz	.10
216	J.T. Snow	.10
217	Paul Abbott	.10
218	David Bell	.10
219	Freddy Garcia	.25
220	Ken Griffey Jr.	2.00
221	Carlos Guillen	.10
222	Brian Hunter	.10
223	Edgar Martinez	.15
224	Jamie Moyer	.10
225	Alex Rodriguez	1.25
226	Wade Boggs	.25
227	Miguel Cairo	.10
228	Jose Canseco	.50
229	Roberto Hernandez	.10
230	Dave Martinez	.10
231	Quinton McCracken	.10
232	Fred McGriff	.20
233	Kevin Stocker	.10
234	Royce Clayton	.10
235	Rusty Greer	.10
236	Ruben Mateo	.10
237	Rafael Palmeiro	.30
238	Ivan Rodriguez	.50
239	Aaron Sele	.10
240	John Wetteland	.10
241	Todd Zeile	.10
242	Tony Batista	.10
243	Homer Bush	.10
244	Carlos Delgado	.40
245	Tony Fernandez	.10
246	Billy Koch	.10
247	Raul Mondesi	.20
248	Shannon Stewart	.10
249	David Wells	.10
250	Vernon Wells	.10

2000 Pacific Paramount Cooperstown Bound

	MT
Complete Set (10):	550.00
Common Player:	30.00

Inserted 1:361

1	Greg Maddux	50.00
2	Cal Ripken Jr.	70.00
3	Nomar Garciaparra	60.00
4	Sammy Sosa	60.00
5	Roger Clemens	40.00
6	Derek Jeter	60.00
7	Mark McGwire	100.00
8	Tony Gwynn	50.00
9	Ken Griffey Jr.	100.00
10	Alex Rodriguez	60.00

2000 Pacific Paramount Double Vision

		MT
Complete Set (36):		350.00
Common Player:		3.00
Inserted 1:37		
1	Chipper Jones	15.00
2	Cal Ripken Jr.	15.00
3	Nomar Garciaparra	15.00
4	Pedro Martinez	6.00
5	Sammy Sosa	15.00
6	Manny Ramirez	6.00
7	Jeff Bagwell	6.00
8	Craig Biggio	3.00
9	Vladimir Guerrero	8.00
10	Mike Piazza	15.00
11	Roger Clemens	10.00
12	Derek Jeter	15.00
13	Mark McGwire	25.00
14	Tony Gwynn	12.00
15	Ken Griffey Jr.	25.00
16	Alex Rodriguez	15.00
17	Rafael Palmeiro	4.00
18	Ivan Rodriguez	6.00
19	Chipper Jones	12.00
20	Cal Ripken Jr.	15.00
21	Nomar Garciaparra	15.00
22	Pedro Martinez	6.00
23	Sammy Sosa	15.00
24	Manny Ramirez	6.00
25	Jeff Bagwell	6.00
26	Craig Biggio	3.00
27	Vladimir Guerrero	8.00
28	Mike Piazza	15.00
29	Roger Clemens	10.00
30	Derek Jeter	15.00
31	Mark McGwire	25.00
32	Tony Gwynn	12.00
33	Ken Griffey Jr.	25.00
34	Alex Rodriguez	15.00
35	Rafael Palmeiro	4.00
36	Ivan Rodriguez	6.00

2000 Pacific Paramount Fielder's Choice

		MT
Complete Set (20):		400.00
Common Player:		8.00
Inserted 1:73		
1	Andruw Jones	10.00
2	Chipper Jones	25.00
3	Greg Maddux	25.00
4	Cal Ripken Jr.	30.00
5	Nomar Garciaparra	30.00
6	Sammy Sosa	30.00
7	Sean Casey	8.00
8	Manny Ramirez	15.00
9	Larry Walker	12.00
10	Jeff Bagwell	15.00
11	Mike Piazza	30.00
12	Derek Jeter	30.00
13	Bernie Williams	12.00
14	Scott Rolen	15.00
15	Mark McGwire	50.00
16	Tony Gwynn	25.00
17	Barry Bonds	15.00
18	Ken Griffey Jr.	50.00
19	Alex Rodriguez	30.00
20	Ivan Rodriguez	15.00

2000 Pacific Paramount Season in Review

		MT
Complete Set (30):		125.00
Common Player:		2.00
Inserted 2:37		
1	Randy Johnson	3.00
2	Matt Williams	2.00
3	Chipper Jones	8.00
4	Greg Maddux	8.00
5	Cal Ripken Jr.	10.00
6	Nomar Garciaparra	10.00
7	Pedro Martinez	4.00
8	Sammy Sosa	10.00
9	Manny Ramirez	4.00
10	Larry Walker	3.00
11	Jeff Bagwell	4.00
12	Craig Biggio	2.00
13	Carlos Beltran	2.00
14	Mark Quinn	2.00
15	Vladimir Guerrero	5.00
16	Mike Piazza	10.00
17	Robin Ventura	2.00
18	Roger Clemens	5.00
19	David Cone	2.00
20	Derek Jeter	10.00
21	Mark McGwire	15.00
22	Fernando Tatis	2.00
23	Tony Gwynn	8.00
24	Barry Bonds	4.00
25	Ken Griffey Jr.	15.00
26	Alex Rodriguez	10.00
27	Wade Boggs	2.50
28	Jose Canseco	4.00
29	Rafael Palmeiro	3.00
30	Ivan Rodriguez	4.00

2000 Pacific Prism

		MT
Complete Set (150):		75.00
Common Player:		.50
1	*Jeff DaVanon*	.50
2	Troy Glaus	1.50
3	Tim Salmon	.75
4	Mo Vaughn	1.50
5	Jay Bell	.50
6	Erubiel Durazo	.75
7	Luis Gonzalez	.75
8	Randy Johnson	1.50
9	Matt Williams	1.00
10	Andres Galarraga	1.00
11	Andruw Jones	1.50
12	Chipper Jones	4.00
13	Brian Jordan	.50
14	Greg Maddux	4.00
15	Kevin Millwood	.75
16	John Smoltz	.50
17	Albert Belle	1.50
18	Mike Mussina	1.50
19	Calvin Pickering	.50
20	Cal Ripken Jr.	6.00
21	B.J. Surhoff	.50
22	Nomar Garciaparra	5.00
23	Pedro Martinez	2.00
24	Troy O'Leary	.50
25	John Valentin	.50
26	Jason Varitek	.50
27	Mark Grace	.75
28	Henry Rodriguez	.50
29	Sammy Sosa	5.00
30	Kerry Wood	1.00
31	Ray Durham	.50
32	Carlos Lee	.50
33	Magglio Ordonez	.75
34	Chris Singleton	.50
35	Frank Thomas	2.50
36	Sean Casey	.75
37	Travis Dawkins	.50
38	Barry Larkin	1.00
39	Pokey Reese	.50
40	Scott Williamson	.50
41	Roberto Alomar	1.50
42	Bartolo Colon	.50
43	David Justice	.75
44	Manny Ramirez	2.00
45	Richie Sexson	.50
46	Jim Thome	1.50
47	Omar Vizquel	.50
48	Pedro Astacio	.50
49	Todd Helton	1.00
50	Neifi Perez	.50
51	Ben Petrick	.50
52	Larry Walker	1.50
53	Tony Clark	1.00
54	Damion Easley	.50
55	Juan Gonzalez	2.50
56	Dean Palmer	.50
57	A.J. Burnett	.50
58	Luis Castillo	.50
59	Cliff Floyd	.50
60	Alex Gonzalez	.50
61	Preston Wilson	.50
62	Jeff Bagwell	2.00
63	Craig Biggio	1.00
64	Ken Caminiti	.60
65	Jose Lima	.50
66	Billy Wagner	.50
67	Carlos Beltran	.75
68	Johnny Damon	.50
69	Jermaine Dye	.50
70	Carlos Febles	.50
71	Mike Sweeney	.50
72	Kevin Brown	.75
73	Shawn Green	1.00
74	Eric Karros	.75
75	Chan Ho Park	.75
76	Gary Sheffield	.75
77	Ron Belliard	.50
78	Jeromy Burnitz	.50
79	Marquis Grissom	.50
80	Geoff Jenkins	.50
81	Mark Loretta	.50
82	Ron Coomer	.50
83	Jacque Jones	.50
84	Corey Koskie	.50
85	Brad Radke	.50
86	Todd Walker	.50
87	Michael Barrett	.50
88	Peter Bergeron	.50
89	Vladimir Guerrero	2.50
90	Jose Vidro	.50
91	Rondell White	.75
92	Edgardo Alfonzo	.75
93	Rickey Henderson	1.00
94	Rey Ordonez	.50
95	Mike Piazza	5.00
96	Robin Ventura	.75
97	Roger Clemens	3.00
98	Orlando Hernandez	1.00
99	Derek Jeter	5.00
100	Tino Martinez	.75
101	Mariano Rivera	.75
102	Alfonso Soriano	2.00
103	Bernie Williams	1.50
104	Eric Chavez	.50
105	Jason Giambi	.50
106	Ben Grieve	.75
107	Tim Hudson	.75
108	John Jaha	.50
109	Bobby Abreu	.50
110	Doug Glanville	.50
111	Mike Lieberthal	.50
112	Scott Rolen	2.00
113	Curt Schilling	.75
114	Brian Giles	.50
115	Jason Kendall	.75
116	Warren Morris	.50
117	Kevin Young	.50
118	Rick Ankiel	10.00
119	J.D. Drew	1.00
120	Chad Hutchinson	.50
121	Ray Lankford	.50
122	Mark McGwire	8.00
123	Fernando Tatis	.50
124	Bret Boone	.50
125	Ben Davis	.50
126	Tony Gwynn	4.00
127	Trevor Hoffman	.50
128	Barry Bonds	2.00
129	Ellis Burks	.50
130	Jeff Kent	.50
131	J.T. Snow	.50
132	Freddy Garcia	1.00
133	Ken Griffey Jr.	8.00
134	Edgar Martinez	.50
135	John Olerud	.75
136	Alex Rodriguez	5.00
137	Jose Canseco	2.00
138	Vinny Castilla	.75
139	Roberto Hernandez	.50
140	Fred McGriff	.75
141	Rusty Greer	.50
142	Ruben Mateo	1.00
143	Rafael Palmeiro	1.00
144	Ivan Rodriguez	2.00
145	Lee Stevens	.50
146	Tony Batista	.50
147	Carlos Delgado	1.50
148	Shannon Stewart	.50
149	David Wells	.50
150	Vernon Wells	.50

2000 Pacific Prism A.L. Legends

		MT
Complete Set (10):		60.00
Common Player:		2.00
Inserted 1:25		
1	Mo Vaughn	3.00
2	Cal Ripken Jr.	12.00
3	Nomar Garciaparra	10.00
4	Manny Ramirez	4.00
5	Roger Clemens	5.00
6	Derek Jeter	10.00
7	Ken Griffey Jr.	15.00
8	Alex Rodriguez	10.00
9	Jose Canseco	4.00
10	Rafael Palmeiro	3.00

2000 Pacific Prism Center Stage

		MT
Complete Set (20):		180.00
Common Player:		4.00
Inserted 1:25		
1	Chipper Jones	12.00
2	Cal Ripken Jr.	20.00
3	Nomar Garciaparra	15.00
4	Pedro Martinez	6.00
5	Sammy Sosa	15.00
6	Sean Casey	4.00
7	Manny Ramirez	6.00
8	Jim Thome	5.00
9	Jeff Bagwell	6.00
10	Carlos Beltran	4.00
11	Vladimir Guerrero	8.00
12	Mike Piazza	15.00
13	Derek Jeter	15.00
14	Bernie Williams	5.00
15	Scott Rolen	6.00
16	Mark McGwire	25.00
17	Tony Gwynn	12.00
18	Ken Griffey Jr.	25.00
19	Alex Rodriguez	15.00
20	Ivan Rodriguez	6.00

2000 Pacific Prism Diamond Dial-A-Stats

		MT
Complete Set (10):		400.00
Common Player:		10.00
Inserted 1:193		
1	Chipper Jones	40.00
2	Greg Maddux	40.00
3	Cal Ripken Jr.	60.00
4	Sammy Sosa	50.00
5	Mike Piazza	50.00
6	Roger Clemens	30.00
7	Mark McGwire	75.00
8	Tony Gwynn	35.00
9	Ken Griffey Jr.	75.00
10	Alex Rodriguez	50.00

2000 Pacific Prism N.L. Legends

		MT
Complete Set (10):		60.00
Common Player:		2.00
Inserted 1:25		
1	Chipper Jones	8.00
2	Greg Maddux	8.00
3	Sammy Sosa	10.00
4	Larry Walker	3.00
5	Jeff Bagwell	4.00
6	Vladimir Guerrero	5.00
7	Mike Piazza	10.00
8	Mark McGwire	15.00
9	Tony Gwynn	8.00
10	Barry Bonds	4.00

2000 Pacific Prism Prospects

		MT
Complete Set (10):		70.00
Common Player:		4.00
Inserted 1:97		
1	Erubiel Durazo	6.00
2	Wilton Veras	5.00
3	Ben Petrick	4.00
4	Mark Quinn	6.00
5	Peter Bergeron	4.00
6	Alfonso Soriano	15.00
7	Tim Hudson	8.00
8	Chad Hermansen	4.00
9	Rick Ankiel	25.00
10	Ruben Mateo	6.00

2000 Pacific Private Stock

		MT
Complete Set (150):		125.00
Common Player:		.25

Common SP Prospect:		2.00
Inserted 1:4		
Wax Box:		85.00
1	Darin Erstad	.50
2	Troy Glaus	.50
3	Tim Salmon	.40
4	Mo Vaughn	1.00
5	Jay Bell	.25
6	Luis Gonzalez	.25
7	Randy Johnson	1.00
8	Matt Williams	.75
9	Andruw Jones	1.00
10	Chipper Jones	2.50
11	Brian Jordan	.25
12	Greg Maddux	2.50
13	Kevin Millwood	.50
14	Albert Belle	1.00
15	Mike Mussina	1.00
16	Cal Ripken Jr.	3.00
17	B.J. Surhoff	.25
18	Nomar Garciaparra	3.00
19	Butch Huskey	.25
20	Pedro Martinez	1.50
21	Troy O'Leary	.25
22	Mark Grace	.50
23	Bo Porter (SP)	2.00
24	Henry Rodriguez	.25
25	Sammy Sosa	3.00
26	Kerry Wood	.75
27	Jason Dellaero (SP)	3.00
28	Ray Durham	.25
29	Paul Konerko	.25
30	Carlos Lee	.25
31	Magglio Ordonez	.50
32	Frank Thomas	1.50
33	Mike Cameron	.25
34	Sean Casey	.75
35	Barry Larkin	.75
36	Greg Vaughn	.50
37	Roberto Alomar	1.00
38	Russell Branyan (SP)	3.00
39	Kenny Lofton	1.00
40	Manny Ramirez	1.50
41	Richie Sexson	.25
42	Jim Thome	.75
43	Omar Vizquel	.25
44	Dante Bichette	.50
45	Vinny Castilla	.40
46	Todd Helton	.50
47	Ben Petrick (SP)	3.00
48	Juan Sosa (SP)	3.00
49	Larry Walker	1.00
50	Tony Clark	.50
51	Damion Easley	.25
52	Juan Encarnacion	.25
53	Robert Fick (SP)	2.00
54	Dean Palmer	.25
55	A.J. Burnett (SP)	4.00
56	Luis Castillo	.25
57	Alex Gonzalez	.25
58	Julio Ramirez (SP)	3.00
59	Preston Wilson	.25
60	Jeff Bagwell	1.50
61	Craig Biggio	.75
62	Ken Caminiti	.40
63	Carl Everett	.25
64	Mike Hampton	.25
65	Billy Wagner	.25
66	Carlos Beltran	.50
67	Dermal Brown (SP)	2.00
68	Jermaine Dye	.25
69	Carlos Febles	.25
70	Mark Quinn (SP)	4.00
71	Mike Sweeney	.25
72	Kevin Brown	.40
73	Eric Gagne (SP)	2.00
74	Eric Karros	.40
75	Raul Mondesi	.40
76	Gary Sheffield	.50
77	Jeromy Burnitz	.25
78	Jeff Cirillo	.25
79	Geoff Jenkins	.25
80	David Nilsson	.25
81	Ron Coomer	.25
82	Jacque Jones	.25
83	Corey Koskie	.25
84	Brad Radke	.25
85	Tony Armas, Jr. (SP)	3.00
86	Peter Bergeron (SP)	3.00
87	Vladimir Guerrero	1.50
88	Jose Vidro	.25
89	Rondell White	.40
90	Edgardo Alfonzo	.50
91	Roger Cedeno	.25
92	Rickey Henderson	.75
93	Jay Payton (SP)	2.00
94	Mike Piazza	3.00
95	Jorge Toca (SP)	4.00
96	Robin Ventura	.50
97	Roger Clemens	2.00
98	David Cone	.40
99	Derek Jeter	3.00
100	D'Angelo Jimenez (SP)	2.00
101	Tino Martinez	.50
102	Alfonso Soriano (SP)	6.00
103	Bernie Williams	1.00
104	Jason Giambi	.25
105	Ben Grieve	.50
106	Tim Hudson	.50
107	Matt Stairs	.25
108	Bobby Abreu	.25
109	Doug Glanville	.25
110	Scott Rolen	1.50
111	Curt Schilling	.40
112	Brian Giles	.25
113	Chad Hermansen (SP)	3.00
114	Jason Kendall	.25
115	Warren Morris	.25
116	Rick Ankiel (SP)	20.00
117	J.D. Drew	1.00
118	Adam Kennedy (SP)	2.00
119	Ray Lankford	.25
120	Mark McGwire	5.00
121	Fernando Tatis	.50
122	Mike Darr (SP)	2.00
123	Ben Davis	.25
124	Tony Gwynn	2.50
125	Trevor Hoffman	.25
126	Reggie Sanders	.25
127	Barry Bonds	1.50
128	Ellis Burks	.25
129	Jeff Kent	.25
130	J.T. Snow	.25
131	Freddy Garcia	.75
132	Ken Griffey Jr.	5.00
133	Carlos Guillen (SP)	2.00
134	Edgar Martinez	.25
135	Alex Rodriguez	3.00
136	Miguel Cairo	.25
137	Jose Canseco	1.00
138	Steve Cox (SP)	2.00
139	Roberto Hernandez	.25
140	Fred McGriff	.50
141	Juan Gonzalez	1.50
142	Rusty Greer	.25
143	Ruben Mateo (SP)	4.00
144	Rafael Palmeiro	.75
145	Ivan Rodriguez	1.50
146	Carlos Delgado	.75
147	Tony Fernandez	.25
148	Shawn Green	1.00
149	Shannon Stewart	.25
150	Vernon Wells (SP)	3.00

2000 Pacific Private Stock Extreme Action

		MT
Complete Set (20):		100.00
Common Player:		2.50
Inserted 2:25		
1	Andruw Jones	3.00
2	Chipper Jones	8.00
3	Cal Ripken Jr.	10.00
4	Nomar Garciaparra	10.00
5	Sammy Sosa	10.00
6	Frank Thomas	4.00
7	Roberto Alomar	3.00
8	Manny Ramirez	4.00
9	Larry Walker	3.00
10	Jeff Bagwell	4.00
11	Vladimir Guerrero	5.00
12	Mike Piazza	10.00
13	Derek Jeter	10.00
14	Bernie Williams	3.00
15	Scott Rolen	4.00
16	Mark McGwire	15.00
17	Tony Gwynn	8.00
18	Ken Griffey Jr.	15.00
19	Alex Rodriguez	10.00
20	Ivan Rodriguez	4.00

2000 Pacific Private Stock Private Stock Canvas

		MT
Complete Set (20):		400.00
Common Player:		10.00
Inserted 1:49		
1	Chipper Jones	25.00
2	Greg Maddux	25.00
3	Cal Ripken Jr.	30.00
4	Nomar Garciaparra	30.00
5	Sammy Sosa	30.00
6	Frank Thomas	15.00
7	Manny Ramirez	15.00
8	Larry Walker	10.00
9	Jeff Bagwell	15.00
10	Vladimir Guerrero	18.00
11	Mike Piazza	30.00
12	Roger Clemens	20.00
13	Derek Jeter	30.00
14	Mark McGwire	50.00
15	Tony Gwynn	25.00
16	Barry Bonds	15.00
17	Ken Griffey Jr.	50.00
18	Alex Rodriguez	30.00
19	Juan Gonzalez	15.00
20	Ivan Rodriguez	15.00

2000 Pacific Private Stock Private Stock Reserve

		MT
Complete Set (20):		175.00
Common Player:		4.00
Inserted 1:25		
1	Chipper Jones	12.00
2	Greg Maddux	12.00
3	Cal Ripken Jr.	15.00
4	Nomar Garciaparra	15.00
5	Sammy Sosa	15.00
6	Frank Thomas	6.00
7	Manny Ramirez	6.00
8	Larry Walker	5.00
9	Jeff Bagwell	6.00
10	Vladimir Guerrero	8.00
11	Mike Piazza	15.00
12	Roger Clemens	10.00
13	Derek Jeter	15.00
14	Mark McGwire	25.00
15	Tony Gwynn	12.00
16	Barry Bonds	6.00
17	Ken Griffey Jr.	25.00
18	Alex Rodriguez	15.00
19	Ivan Rodriguez	6.00
20	Shawn Green	4.00

2000 Pacific Private Stock PS-2000

		MT
Complete Set (60):		40.00
Common Player:		.25
Inserted 2:pack		
1	Mo Vaughn	.75
2	Greg Maddux	2.00
3	Andruw Jones	.75
4	Chipper Jones	2.00
5	Cal Ripken Jr.	2.50
6	Nomar Garciaparra	2.50
7	Pedro Martinez	1.00
8	Sammy Sosa	2.50
9	Jason Dellaero	.25
10	Magglio Ordonez	.25
11	Frank Thomas	1.00
12	Sean Casey	.50
13	Russell Branyan	.25
14	Manny Ramirez	1.00
15	Richie Sexson	.25
16	Ben Petrick	.25
17	Juan Sosa	.25
18	Larry Walker	.75
19	Robert Fick	.25
20	Craig Biggio	.50
21	Jeff Bagwell	1.00
22	Carlos Beltran	.50
23	Dermal Brown	.25
24	Mark Quinn	.25
25	Eric Gagne	.25
26	Jeromy Burnitz	.25
27	Tony Armas, Jr.	.25
28	Peter Bergeron	.25
29	Vladimir Guerrero	1.50
30	Edgardo Alfonzo	.50
31	Mike Piazza	2.50
32	Jorge Toca	.25
33	Roger Clemens	1.50
34	Alfonso Soriano	1.00
35	Bernie Williams	.75
36	Derek Jeter	2.50
37	Tim Hudson	.50
38	Bobby Abreu	.25
39	Scott Rolen	1.00
40	Brian Giles	.25
41	Chad Hermansen	.25
42	Warren Morris	.25
43	Rick Ankiel	5.00
44	J.D. Drew	1.00
45	Adam Kennedy	.25
46	Mark McGwire	4.00
47	Mike Darr	.25
48	Tony Gwynn	2.00
49	Barry Bonds	1.00
50	Ken Griffey Jr.	4.00
51	Carlos Guillen	.25
52	Alex Rodriguez	2.50
53	Juan Gonzalez	1.00
54	Ruben Mateo	.50
55	Ivan Rodriguez	1.00
56	Rafael Palmeiro	.50
57	Jose Canseco	1.00
58	Steve Cox	.25
59	Shawn Green	.75
60	Vernon Wells	.25

2000 Pacific Private Stock PS-2000 New Wave

		MT
Complete Set (20):		160.00
Common Player:		3.00
Production 199 sets		
1	Andruw Jones	8.00
2	Chipper Jones	20.00
3	Nomar Garciaparra	30.00
4	Magglio Ordonez	5.00
5	Sean Casey	8.00
6	Manny Ramirez	12.00
7	Richie Sexson	3.00
8	Carlos Beltran	5.00
9	Jeromy Burnitz	3.00
10	Vladimir Guerrero	15.00
11	Edgardo Alfonzo	5.00
12	Derek Jeter	30.00
13	Tim Hudson	3.00
14	Bobby Abreu	3.00
15	Scott Rolen	12.00
16	Brian Giles	3.00
17	Warren Morris	3.00
18	J.D. Drew	10.00
19	Alex Rodriguez	30.00
20	Shawn Green	8.00

2000 Pacific Private Stock PS-2000 Rookies

		MT
Complete Set (20):		160.00
Common Player:		8.00
Inserted 99 sets		
1	Jason Dellaero	8.00
2	Russell Branyan	8.00
3	Ben Petrick	8.00
4	Juan Sosa	8.00
5	Robert Fick	8.00
6	Dermal Brown	8.00
7	Mark Quinn	12.00
8	Eric Gagne	8.00
9	Tony Armas, Jr.	8.00
10	Peter Bergeron	8.00
11	Jorge Toca	8.00
12	Alfonso Soriano	20.00
13	Chad Hermansen	8.00
14	Rick Ankiel	50.00
15	Adam Kennedy	8.00
16	Mike Darr	8.00
17	Carlos Guillen	8.00
18	Steve Cox	8.00
19	Ruben Mateo	12.00
20	Vernon Wells	10.00

2000 Pacific Private Stock PS-2000 Stars

		MT
Complete Set (20):		260.00
Common Player:		6.00
Production 299 sets		
1	Mo Vaughn	8.00
2	Greg Maddux	20.00
3	Cal Ripken Jr.	25.00
4	Pedro Martinez	10.00
5	Sammy Sosa	25.00
6	Frank Thomas	10.00
7	Larry Walker	8.00
8	Craig Biggio	6.00
9	Jeff Bagwell	10.00
10	Mike Piazza	25.00
11	Roger Clemens	15.00
12	Bernie Williams	8.00
13	Mark McGwire	40.00
14	Tony Gwynn	20.00
15	Barry Bonds	10.00
16	Ken Griffey Jr.	40.00
17	Juan Gonzalez	10.00
18	Ivan Rodriguez	10.00
19	Rafael Palmeiro	6.00
20	Jose Canseco	10.00

2000 Pacific Opening Day 2K

As part of a multi-manufacturer promotion, Pacific issued eight cards of an "Opening Day 2K" set. Packages containing some of the 32 cards in the issue were distributed by MLB teams early in the season. The cards were also available exclusively as inserts in Pacific Crown Collection and Pacific Aurora packs sold at Kmart stores early in the season. The Paciic OD2K cards have gold-foil graphic highlights on front. Backs have a portrait photo and are numbered with an "OD" prefix.

		MT
Complete Set (8):		4.00
Common Player:		.50
25	Mo Vaughn	.50
26	Chipper Jones	1.00
27	Nomar Garciaparra	1.00
28	Larry Walker	.65
29	Corey Koskie	.50
30	Scott Rolen	.75
31	Tony Gwynn	.75
32	Jose Canseco	.65

1991 Pacific Gas & Electric S.F. Giants

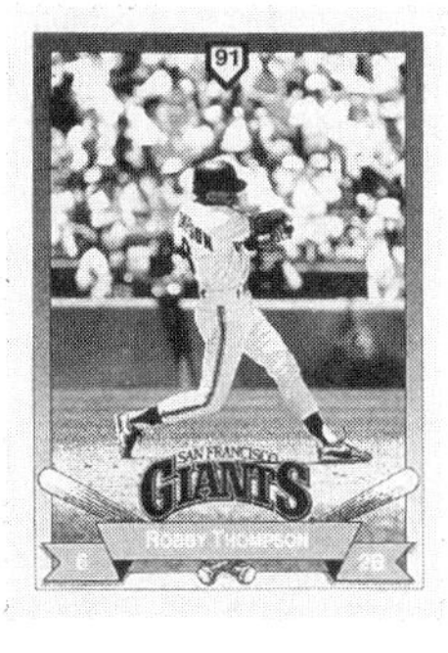

Perforated panels of six 2-3/4" x 3-3/4" Giants cards were included in each of five editions of Giants Magazine, the team's official program, for 1991. The set was sponsored by PG&E. Cards have color action photos on front with a graduated gray frame and white borders. At bottom is a team typographical logo, crossed bats and a red ribbon with player identification. A pentagon at top has the date "91". Backs are in black-and-white with a large sponsor's ad, the player's career stats, a few biographical details and uniform and card numbers.

		MT
Complete Set (30):		15.00
Common Player:		.50
1	Kevin Mitchell	.50
2	Robby Thompson	.50
3	John Burkett	.65
4	Kelly Downs	.50
5	Terry Kennedy	.50
6	Roger Craig	.50
7	Jeff Brantley	.50
8	Greg Litton	.50
9	Trevor Wilson	.50
10	Kevin Bass	.50
11	Matt Williams	1.50
12	Jose Uribe	.50
13	Steve Decker	.50
14	Will Clark	3.00
15	Dave Righetti	.50
16	Mike Kingery	.50
17	Mike LaCoss	.50
18	Dave Anderson	.50
19	Bud Black	.50
20	Mike Benjamin	.50
21	Don Robinson	.50
22	Mark Leonard	.50
23	Willie McGee	.75
24	Francisco Oliveras	.50
25	Kirt Manwaring	.50
26	Rick Parker	.50
27	Mike Remlinger	.50
28	Mike Felder	.50
29	Scott Garrelts	.50
30	Tony Perezchica	.50

1988 Pacific Northwest Bell Seattle Mariners

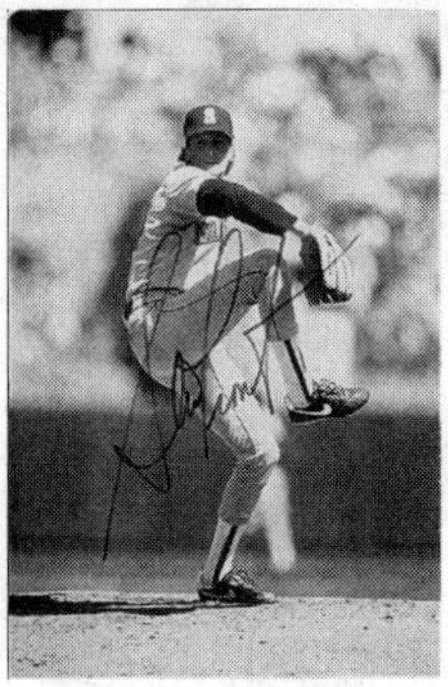

This set of photocards was intended for player use in responding to autograph requests (as on the card shown here) and was not sold as a set. The 3-3/4" x 5-1/2" cards rae printed on thin, glossy stock. Fronts have borderless color action shots with no extraneous graphic elements. Backs are in black-and-white with team and sponsor logos, the player's name and position. The unnumbered cards are checklisted here in alphabetical order.

		MT
Complete Set (29):		45.00
Common Player:		1.50
(1)	Scott Bankhead	1.50
(2)	Scott Bradley	1.50
(3)	Mickey Brantley	1.50
(4)	Mike Campbell	1.50
(5)	Billy Connors	1.50
(6)	Henry Cotto	1.50
(7)	Alvin Davis	1.50
(8)	Bruce Fields	1.50
(9)	Frank Howard	2.00
(10)	Mike Jackson	1.50
(11)	Mike Kingery	1.50
(12)	Mark Langston	3.00
(13)	Mike Moore	1.50
(14)	Ken Phelps	1.50
(15)	Jim Presley	1.50
(16)	Jerry Reed	1.50
(17)	Rich Renteria	1.50
(18)	Harold Reynolds	2.50
(19)	Phil Roof	1.50
(20)	Rey Quinones	1.50
(21)	Jim Snyder	1.50
(22)	Julio Solano	1.50
(23)	Bill Swift	1.50
(24)	Steve Trout	1.50
(25)	Dave Valle	1.50
(26)	Ozzie Virgil	1.50
(27)	Bill Wilkinson	1.50
(28)	Dick Williams	1.50
(29)	Glenn Wilson	1.50

Player names in *Italic* type indicate a rookie card.

1990 Jim Palmer Hall of Fame pin/card

On the occasion of his induction into the Hall of Fame, Orioles' pitcher Jim Palmer was honored with the issue of a card and pin combination sponsored by The One Book, a Baltimore area phone directory. As issued, the card measures 2-1/2" x 5-1/4". There is a perforation at the 3-1/2" mark to allow a telephone information sticker to be removed from the bottom. The top half has an action photo of Palmer. Attached to the card is a 1-1/4" x 1" shield-shaped bronze pin with the pitcher's name, team, number and "Hall of Fame" printed. The pin covers a small Orioles logo. The back of the card is in black-and-white and has career highlights.

	MT
Jim Palmer	6.00

1988 Panini Stickers

This set of 480 stickers features 312 major league players, both rookies and superstar veterans. The full-color stickers measure 2-11/16" x 1-7/8" (team emblem and uniform stickers are slightly larger). Individual players, duos and group action shots are included in the set which also contains 14 stickers that depict 1987 season highlights such as Paul Molitor's 39-game hitting streak. Panini produced a 64-page album with two pages devoted to each team and a space marked for each sticker in the set. Individual sticker packets contained a total of six stickers; four players, one team logo, one uniform sticker. Panini offered a collectors' sticker exchange service in which up to 30 stickers could be traded or specific stickers purchased for 10 cents each. The 26 team logo/pennant stickers (numbered A-1 through Z-1) are checklisted as #'s 455 through 480 in the following checklist.

		MT
Complete Set (480):		20.00
Common Player:		.05
Sticker Album:		.90
1	World Series Trophy	.05
2	Orioles Logo	.05
3	Orioles Uniform	.05
4	Eric Bell	.05
5	Mike Boddicker	.05
6	Dave Schmidt	.05
7	Terry Kennedy	.05
8	Eddie Murray	.25
9	Bill Ripken	.05
10	Orioles Action (Tony Armas, Cal Ripken Jr.)	.45
11	Orioles Action (Tony Armas, Cal Ripken Jr.)	.45
12	Ray Knight	.05
13	Cal Ripken, Jr.	1.25
14	Ken Gerhart	.05
15	Fred Lynn	.05
16	Larry Sheets	.05
17	Mike Young	.05
18	Red Sox Logo	.05
19	Red Sox Uniform	.05
20	Oil Can Boyd	.05
21	Roger Clemens	.50
22	Bruce Hurst	.05
23	Bob Stanley	.05
24	Rich Gedman	.05
25	Dwight Evans	.05
26	Red Sox Action (Marty Barrett, Tim Laudner)	.05
27	Red Sox Action (Marty Barrett, Tim Laudner)	.05
28	Marty Barrett	.05
29	Wade Boggs	.50
30	Spike Owen	.05
31	Ellis Burks	.05
32	Mike Greenwell	.05
33	Jim Rice	.10
34	Angels Logo	.05
35	Angels Uniform	.05
36	Kirk McCaskill	.05
37	Don Sutton	.10
38	Mike Witt	.05
39	Bob Boone	.05
40	Wally Joyner	.10
41	Mark McLemore	.05
42	Angels Action (Juan Bonilla, Devon White)	.05
43	Angels Action (Juan Bonilla, Devon White)	.05
44	Jack Howell	.05
45	Dick Schofield	.05
46	Brian Downing	.05
47	Ruppert Jones	.05
48	Gary Pettis	.05
49	Devon White	.05
50	White Sox Logo	.05
51	White Sox Uniform	.05
52	Floyd Bannister	.05
53	Richard Dotson	.05
54	Bob James	.05
55	Carlton Fisk	.30
56	Greg Walker	.05
57	Fred Manrique	.05
58	White Sox Action (Ozzie Guillen, Donnie Hill, Pat Sheridan)	.05
59	White Sox Action (Ozzie Guillen, Donnie Hill, Pat Sheridan)	.05
60	Steve Lyons	.05
61	Ozzie Guillen	.05
62	Harold Baines	.10
63	Ivan Calderon	.05
64	Gary Redus	.05
65	Ken Williams	.05
66	Indians Logo	.05
67	Indians Uniform	.05
68	Scott Bailes	.05
69	Tom Candiotti	.05
70	Greg Swindell	.05
71	Chris Bando	.05
72	Joe Carter	.10
73	Tommy Hinzo	.05
74	Indians Action (Juan Bonilla, Joe Carter)	.05
75	Indians Action (Juan Bonilla, Joe Carter)	.05
76	Brook Jacoby	.05
77	Julio Franco	.05
78	Brett Butler	.05
79	Mel Hall	.05
80	Cory Snyder	.05
81	Pat Tabler	.05
82	Tigers Logo	.05
83	Tigers Uniform	.05
84	Willie Hernandez	.05
85	Jack Morris	.05
86	Frank Tanana	.05
87	Walt Terrell	.05
88	Matt Nokes	.05
89	Darrell Evans	.05
90	Tigers Action (Darrell Evans, Carlton Fisk)	.10
91	Tigers Action (Darrell Evans, Carlton Fisk)	.10
92	Lou Whitaker	.05
93	Tom Brookens	.05
94	Alan Trammell	.10
95	Kirk Gibson	.05
96	Chet Lemon	.05
97	Pat Sheridan	.05
98	Royals Logo	.05
99	Royals Uniform	.05
100	Charlie Leibrandt	.05
101	Dan Quisenberry	.05
102	Bret Saberhagen	.05
103	Jamie Quirk	.05
104	George Brett	.75
105	Frank White	.05
106	Royals Action (Bret Saberhagen)	.05
107	Royals Action (Bret Saberhagen)	.05
108	Kevin Seitzer	.05
109	Angel Salazar	.05
110	Bo Jackson	.15
111	Lonnie Smith	.05
112	Danny Tartabull	.05
113	Willie Wilson	.05
114	Brewers Logo	.05
115	Brewers Uniform	.05
116	Ted Higuera	.05
117	Juan Nieves	.05
118	Dan Plesac	.05
119	Bill Wegman	.05
120	B.J. Surhoff	.05
121	Greg Brock	.05
122	Brewers Action (Jim Gantner, Lou Whitaker)	.05
123	Brewers Action (Jim Gantner, Lou Whitaker)	.05
124	Jim Gantner	.05
125	Paul Molitor	.50
126	Dale Sveum	.05
127	Glenn Braggs	.05
128	Rob Deer	.05
129	Robin Yount	.75
130	Twins Logo	.05
131	Twins Uniform	.05
132	Bert Blyleven	.05
133	Jeff Reardon	.05
134	Frank Viola	.05
135	Tim Laudner	.05
136	Kent Hrbek	.05
137	Steve Lombardozzi	.05
138	Twins Action (Steve Lombardozzi, Frank White)	.05
139	Twins Action (Steve Lombardozzi, Frank White)	.05
140	Gary Gaetti	.05
141	Greg Gagne	.05
142	Tom Brunansky	.05
143	Dan Gladden	.05
144	Kirby Puckett	.75
145	Gene Larkin	.05
146	Yankees Logo	.05
147	Yankees Uniform	.05
148	Tommy John	.05
149	Rick Rhoden	.05
150	Dave Righetti	.05
151	Rick Cerone	.05
152	Don Mattingly	.75
153	Willie Randolph	.05
154	Yankees Action (Scott Fletcher, Don Mattingly)	.30
155	Yankees Action (Scott Fletcher, Don Mattingly)	.30
156	Mike Pagliarulo	.05
157	Wayne Tolleson	.05
158	Rickey Henderson	.25
159	Dan Pasqua	.05
160	Gary Ward	.05
161	Dave Winfield	.35
162	Athletics Logo	.05
163	Athletics Uniform	.05
164	Dave Stewart	.05
165	Curt Young	.05
166	Terry Steinbach	.05
167	Mark McGwire	1.50
168	Tony Phillips	.05
169	Carney Lansford	.05
170	Athletics Action (Mike Gallego, Tony Phillips)	.05
171	Athletics Action (Mike Gallego, Tony Phillips)	.05
172	Alfredo Griffin	.05
173	Jose Canseco	.35
174	Mike Davis	.05
175	Reggie Jackson	.45
176	Dwayne Murphy	.05
177	Luis Polonia	.05
178	Mariners Logo	.05
179	Mariners Uniform	.05
180	Scott Bankhead	.05
181	Mark Langston	.05
182	Edwin Nunez	.05
183	Scott Bradley	.05
184	Dave Valle	.05
185	Alvin Davis	.05
186	Mariners Action (Jack Howell, Rey Quinones)	.05
187	Mariners Action (Jack Howell, Rey Quinones)	.05
188	Harold Reynolds	.05
189	Jim Presley	.05
190	Rey Quinones	.05
191	Phil Bradley	.05
192	Mickey Brantley	.05
193	Mike Kingery	.05
194	Rangers Logo	.05
195	Rangers Uniform	.05
196	Edwin Correa	.05
197	Charlie Hough	.05
198	Bobby Witt	.05
199	Mike Stanley	.05
200	Pete O'Brien	.05
201	Jerry Browne	.05
202	Rangers Action (Steve Buechele, Eddie Murray)	.05
203	Rangers Action (Steve Buechele, Eddie Murray)	.05
204	Steve Buechele	.05
205	Larry Parrish	.05
206	Scott Fletcher	.05
207	Pete Incaviglia	.05
208	Oddibe McDowell	.05
209	Ruben Sierra	.05
210	Blue Jays Logo	.05
211	Blue Jays Uniform	.05
212	Mark Eichhorn	.05
213	Tom Henke	.05
214	Jimmy Key	.05
215	Dave Stieb	.05
216	Ernie Whitt	.05
217	Willie Upshaw	.05
218	Blue Jays Action (Harold Reynolds, Willie Upshaw)	.05
219	Blue Jays Action (Harold Reynolds, Willie Upshaw)	.05
220	Garth Iorg	.05
221	Kelly Gruber	.05
222	Tony Fernandez	.05
223	Jesse Barfield	.05
224	George Bell	.05
225	Lloyd Moseby	.05
226	American League Logo National League Logo	.05
227	Terry Kennedy, Don Mattingly	.25
228	Wade Boggs, Willie Randolph	.10
229	Bret Saberhagen	.05
230	George Bell, Cal Ripken Jr.	.45
231	Rickey Henderson, Dave Winfield	.20
232	Gary Carter, Jack Clark	.05
233	Mike Scott	.05
234	Ryne Sandberg, Mike Schmidt	.20
235	Ozzie Smith, Eric Davis	.25
236	Andre Dawson, Darryl Strawberry	.10
237	Braves Logo	.05
238	Braves Uniform	.05
239	Rick Mahler	.05
240	Zane Smith	.05
241	Ozzie Virgil	.05
242	Gerald Perry	.05
243	Glenn Hubbard	.05
244	Ken Oberkfell	.05
245	Braves Action (Glenn Hubbard, Jeffrey Leonard)	.05
246	Braves Action (Glenn Hubbard, Jeffrey Leonard)	.05
247	Rafael Ramirez	.05
248	Ken Griffey	.05
249	Albert Hall	.05
250	Dion James	.05
251	Dale Murphy	.15
252	Gary Roenicke	.05
253	Cubs Logo	.05
254	Cubs Uniform	.05
255	Jamie Moyer	.05
256	Lee Smith	.05
257	Rick Sutcliffe	.05
258	Jody Davis	.05
259	Leon Durham	.05
260	Ryne Sandberg	.50
261	Cubs Action (Jody Davis)	.05
262	Cubs Action (Jody Davis)	.05
263	Keith Moreland	.05
264	Shawon Dunston	.05
265	Andre Dawson	.15
266	Dave Martinez	.05
267	Jerry Mumphrey	.05
268	Rafael Palmeiro	.20
269	Reds Logo	.05
270	Reds Uniform	.05
271	John Franco	.05
272	Ted Power	.05
273	Bo Diaz	.05
274	Nick Esasky	.05

275 Dave Concepcion .05
276 Kurt Stillwell .05
277 Reds Action (Bob Melvin, Dave Parker) .05
278 Reds Action (Bob Melvin, Dave Parker) .05
279 Buddy Bell .05
280 Barry Larkin .10
281 Kal Daniels .05
282 Eric Davis .05
283 Tracy Jones .05
284 Dave Parker .05
285 Astros Logo .05
286 Astros Uniform .05
287 Jim Deshaies .05
288 Nolan Ryan 1.00
289 Mike Scott .05
290 Dave Smith .05
291 Alan Ashby .05
292 Glenn Davis .05
293 Astros Action (Alan Ashby, Gary Carter) .05
294 Astros Action (Alan Ashby, Gary Carter) .05
295 Bill Doran .05
296 Denny Walling .05
297 Craig Reynolds .05
298 Kevin Bass .05
299 Jose Cruz .05
300 Billy Hatcher .05
301 Dodgers Logo .05
302 Dodgers Uniform .05
303 Orel Hershiser .10
304 Fernando Valenzuela .05
305 Bob Welch .05
306 Matt Young .05
307 Mike Scioscia .05
308 Franklin Stubbs .05
309 Dodgers Action (Mariano Duncan, Junior Ortiz) .05
310 Dodgers Action (Mariano Duncan, Junior Ortiz) .05
311 Steve Sax .05
312 Jeff Hamilton .05
313 Dave Anderson .05
314 Pedro Guerrero .05
315 Mike Marshall .05
316 John Shelby .05
317 Expos Logo .05
318 Expos Uniform .05
319 Neal Heaton .05
320 Bryn Smith .05
321 Floyd Youmans .05
322 Mike Fitzgerald .05
323 Andres Galarraga .15
324 Vance Law .05
325 Expos Action (John Kruk, Tim Raines) .05
326 Expos Action (John Kruk, Tim Raines) .05
327 Tim Wallach .05
328 Hubie Brooks .05
329 Casey Candaele .05
330 Tim Raines .10
331 Mitch Webster .05
332 Herm Winningham .05
333 Mets Logo .05
334 Mets Uniform .05
335 Ron Darling .05
336 Sid Fernandez .05
337 Dwight Gooden .10
338 Gary Carter .15
339 Keith Hernandez .05
340 Wally Backman .05
341 Mets Action (Mike Diaz, Darryl Strawberry, Tim Teufel, Mookie Wilson) .10
342 Mets Action (Mike Diaz, Darryl Strawberry, Tim Teufel, Mookie Wilson) .10
343 Howard Johnson .05
344 Rafael Santana .05
345 Lenny Dykstra .05
346 Kevin McReynolds .05
347 Darryl Strawberry .15
348 Mookie Wilson .05
349 Phillies Logo .05
350 Phillies Uniform .05
351 Steve Bedrosian .05
352 Shane Rawley .05
353 Bruce Ruffin .05
354 Kent Tekulve .05
355 Lance Parrish .05
356 Von Hayes .05
357 Phillies Action (Tony Pena, Glenn Wilson) .05
358 Phillies Action (Tony Pena, Glenn Wilson) .05
359 Juan Samuel .05
360 Mike Schmidt .75
361 Steve Jeltz .05
362 Chris James .05
363 Milt Thompson .05
364 Glenn Wilson .05
365 Pirates Logo .05
366 Pirates Uniform .05
367 Mike Dunne .05
368 Brian Fisher .05
369 Mike LaValliere .05
370 Sid Bream .05
371 Jose Lind .05
372 Bobby Bonilla .10
373 Pirates Action (Bobby Bonilla) .05
374 Pirates Action (Bobby Bonilla) .05
375 Al Pedrique .05
376 Barry Bonds .75
377 John Cangelosi .05
378 Mike Diaz .05
379 R.J. Reynolds .05
380 Andy Van Slyke .05
381 Cardinals Logo .05
382 Cardinals Uniform .05
383 Danny Cox .05
384 Bob Forsch .05
385 Joe Magrane .05
386 Todd Worrell .05
387 Tony Pena .05
388 Jack Clark .05
389 Cardinals Action (Jody Davis, Tom Herr) .05
390 Cardinals Action (Jody Davis, Tom Herr) .05
391 Tom Herr .05
392 Terry Pendleton .05
393 Ozzie Smith .50
394 Vince Coleman .05
395 Curt Ford .05
396 Willie McGee .05
397 Padres Logo .05
398 Padres Uniform .05
399 Lance McCullers .05
400 Eric Show .05
401 Ed Whitson .05
402 Benito Santiago .05
403 John Kruk .05
404 Tim Flannery .05
405 Padres Action (Randy Ready, Benito Santiago) .05
406 Padres Action (Randy Ready, Benito Santiago) .05
407 Randy Ready .05
408 Chris Brown .05
409 Garry Templeton .05
410 Tony Gwynn .75
411 Stan Jefferson .05
412 Carmelo Martinez .05
413 Giants Logo .05
414 Giants Uniform .05
415 Kelly Downs .05
416 Scott Garrelts .05
417 Mike Krukow .05
418 Mike LaCoss .05
419 Bob Brenly .05
420 Will Clark .35
421 Giants Action (Will Clark, Mike Fitzgerald) .10
422 Giants Action (Will Clark, Mike Fitzgerald) .10
423 Robby Thompson .05
424 Kevin Mitchell .05
425 Jose Uribe .05
426 Mike Aldrete .05
427 Jeffrey Leonard .05
428 Candy Maldonado .05
429 Mike Schmidt .75
430 Don Mattingly .75
431 Juan Nieves .05
432 Paul Molitor .50
433 Benito Santiago .05
434 Rickey Henderson .25
435 Nolan Ryan 1.00
436 Kevin Seitzer .05
437 Tony Gwynn .75
438 Mark McGwire 1.50
439 Howard Johnson .05
440 Steve Bedrosian .05
441 Darrell Evans .05
442 Eddie Murray .25
443 1987 A.L. Championship Series (Kirby Puckett, Alan Trammell, Lou Whitaker) .10
444 1987 A.L. Championship Series (Kirby Puckett, Alan Trammell, Lou Whitaker) .10
445 American League Championship Series MVP (Gary Gaetti) .05
446 National League Championship Series MVP (Jeffrey Leonard) .05
447 1987 N.L. Championship Series (Kevin Mitchell, Tony Pena) .05
448 1987 N.L. Championship Series (Kevin Mitchell, Tony Pena) .05
449 1987 World Series (Tom Brunansky, Tony Pena) .05
450 1987 World Series (Tom Brunansky, Tony Pena) .05
451 World Series Celebration .05
452 World Series Celebration .05
453 World Series Celebration .05
454 World Series Celebration .05
(455) Orioles Logo/Pennant .05
(456) Red Sox Logo/Pennant .05
(457) Angels Logo/Pennant .05
(458) White Sox Logo/Pennant .05
(459) Indians Logo/Pennant .05
(460) Tigers Logo/Pennant .05
(461) Royals Logo/Pennant .05
(462) Brewers Logo/Pennant .05
(463) Twins Logo/Pennant .05
(464) Yankees Logo/Pennant .05
(465) Athletics Logo/Pennant .05
(466) Mariners Logo/Pennant .05
(467) Rangers Logo/Pennant .05
(468) Blue Jays Logo/Pennant .05
(469) Braves Logo/Pennant .05
(470) Cubs Logo/Pennant .05
(471) Reds Logo/Pennant .05
(472) Astros Logo/Pennant .05
(473) Dodgers Logo/Pennant .05
(474) Expos Logo/Pennant .05
(475) Mets Logo/Pennant .05
(476) Phillies Logo/Pennant .05
(477) Pirates Logo/Pennant .05
(478) Cardinals Logo/Pennant .05
(479) Padres Logo/Pennant .05
(480) Giants Logo/Pennant .05

1989 Panini Stickers

For a second straight year, the Italian sticker manufacturer produced a 480-piece set for the American market. The 1-7/8" x 2-11/16" stickers were sold in packs of six for 30 cents. Packs contain five player stickers and a foil depicting team logos, lettering or ballparks. A 64-page album depicting Jose Canseco on the cover was offered for 69 cents. The 1989 Panini stickers used more action photos than the previous year. Color photos had banners at the bottom with team and player name. Backs had appropriate logos, sticker number and ads for Panini's sticker book.

	MT
Complete Set (480):	20.00
Common Player:	.05
Sticker Album:	2.00

1 World Series Trophy .05
2 World Series Trophy .05
3 Mike Schmidt .25
4 Tom Browning .05
5 Doug Jones .05
6 Wrigley Field .05
7 Wade Boggs .20
8 Jose Canseco .20
9 Orel Hershiser .05
10 Oakland A's Win ALCS .05
11 Oakland A's Win ALCS .05
12 Dennis Eckersley (ALCS MVP) .05
13 Orel Hershiser (NLCS MVP) .05
14 Dodgers Win NLCS .05
15 Dodgers Win NLCS .05
16 Kirk Gibson .05
17 Kirk Gibson .05
18 Orel Hershiser .05
19 Orel Hershiser .05
20 Mark McGwire 1.50
21 Tim Belcher .05
22 Jay Howell .05
23 Mickey Hatcher .05
24 Mike Davis .05
25 Orel Hershiser (World Series MVP) .05
26 Dodgers Win World Series .05
27 Dodgers Win World Series .05
28 Dodgers Win World Series .05
29 Dodgers Win World Series .05
30 Braves Logo .05
31 Jose Alvarez .05
32 Tommy Gregg .05
33 Paul Assenmacher .05
34 Tom Glavine .15
35 Rick Mahler .05
36 Pete Smith .05
37 Atlanta Stadium .05
38 Braves Script .05
39 Bruce Sutter .05
40 Gerald Perry .05
41 Jeff Blauser .05
42 Ron Gant .05
43 Andres Thomas .05
44 Dion James .05
45 Dale Murphy .15
46 Cubs Logo .05
47 Doug Dascenzo .05
48 Mike Harkey .05
49 Greg Maddux .60
50 Jeff Pico .05
51 Rick Sutcliffe .05
52 Damon Berryhill .05
53 Wrigley Field .05
54 Cubs Script .05
55 Mark Grace .20
56 Ryne Sandberg .35
57 Vance Law .05
58 Shawon Dunston .05
59 Andre Dawson .10
60 Rafael Palmeiro .20
61 Mitch Webster .05
62 Reds Logo .05
63 Jack Armstrong .05
64 Chris Sabo .05
65 Tom Browning .05
66 John Franco .05
67 Danny Jackson .05
68 Jose Rijo .05
69 Riverfront Stadium .05
70 Reds Script .05
71 Bo Diaz .05
72 Nick Esasky .05
73 Jeff Treadway .05
74 Barry Larkin .10
75 Kal Daniels .05
76 Eric Davis .05
77 Paul O'Neill .10
78 Astros Logo .05
79 Craig Biggio .10
80 John Fishel .05
81 Juan Agosto .05
82 Bob Knepper .05
83 Nolan Ryan .75
84 Mike Scott .05
85 The Astrodome .05
86 Astros Script .05
87 Dave Smith .05
88 Glenn Davis .05
89 Bill Doran .05
90 Rafael Ramirez .05
91 Kevin Bass .05
92 Billy Hatcher .05
93 Gerald Young .05
94 Dodgers Logo .05
95 Tim Belcher .05
96 Tim Crews .05
97 Orel Hershiser .05
98 Jay Howell .05
99 Tim Leary .05
100 John Tudor .05
101 Dodgers Stadium .05
102 Dodgers Script .05
103 Fernando Valenzuela .05
104 Mike Scioscia .05
105 Mickey Hatcher .05
106 Steve Sax .05
107 Kirk Gibson .05
108 Mike Marshall .05
109 John Shelby .05
110 Expos Logo .05
111 Randy Johnson .20
112 Nelson Santovenia .05
113 Tim Burke .05
114 Dennis Martinez .05
115 Pascual Perez .05
116 Bryn Smith .05
117 Olympic Stadium .05
118 Expos Script .05
119 Andres Galarraga .15
120 Wallace Johnson .05
121 Tom Foley .05
122 Tim Wallach .05
123 Hubie Brooks .05
124 Tracy Jones .05
125 Tim Raines .10
126 Mets Logo .05
127 Kevin Elster .05
128 Gregg Jefferies .05
129 David Cone .10
130 Ron Darling .05
131 Dwight Gooden .10
132 Roger McDowell .05
133 Shea Stadium .05
134 Mets Script .05
135 Randy Myers .05
136 Gary Carter .10
137 Keith Hernandez .05
138 Lenny Dykstra .05
139 Kevin McReynolds .05
140 Darryl Strawberry .10
141 Mookie Wilson .05
142 Phillies Logo .05
143 Ron Jones .05
144 Ricky Jordan .05
145 Steve Bedrosian .05
146 Don Carman .05
147 Kevin Gross .05
148 Bruce Ruffin .05
149 Veterans Stadium .05
150 Phillies Script .05
151 Von Hayes .05
152 Juan Samuel .05
153 Mike Schmidt .25
154 Phil Bradley .05
155 Bob Dernier .05
156 Chris James .05
157 Milt Thompson .05
158 Pirates Logo .05
159 Randy Kramer .05
160 Scott Medvin .05
161 Doug Drabek .05
162 Mike Dunne .05
163 Jim Gott .05
164 Jeff Robinson .05
165 Three Rivers Stadium .05
166 Pirates Script .05
167 John Smiley .05
168 Mike LaValliere .05
169 Sid Bream .05
170 Jose Lind .05
171 Bobby Bonilla .10
172 Barry Bonds .60
173 Andy Van Slyke .05
174 Cardinals Logo .05
175 Luis Alicea .05
176 John Costello .05
177 Jose DeLeon .05
178 Joe Magrane .05
179 Todd Worrell .05
180 Tony Pena .05
181 Busch Stadium .05
182 Cardinals Script .05
183 Pedro Guerrero .05
184 Jose Oquendo .05
185 Terry Pendleton .05
186 Ozzie Smith .35
187 Tom Brunansky .05
188 Vince Coleman .05
189 Willie McGee .05
190 Padres Logo .05
191 Roberto Alomar .20
192 Sandy Alomar, Jr. .10
193 Mark Davis .05
194 Andy Hawkins .05
195 Dennis Rasmussen .05
196 Eric Show .05
197 Jack Murphy Stadium .05
198 Padres Script .05
199 Benito Santiago .05
200 John Kruk .05
201 Randy Ready .05
202 Garry Templeton .05
203 Tony Gwynn .60
204 Carmelo Martinez .05
205 Marvell Wynne .05
206 Giants Logo .05
207 Dennis Cook .05
208 Kirt Manwaring .05
209 Kelly Downs .05
210 Rick Reuschel .05
211 Don Robinson .05
212 Will Clark .30
213 Candlestick Park .05
214 Giants Script .05
215 Robby Thompson .05
216 Kevin Mitchell .05
217 Jose Uribe .05
218 Matt Williams .15
219 Mike Aldrete .05
220 Brett Butler .05
221 Candy Maldonado .05
222 Tony Gwynn .60
223 Darryl Strawberry .10
224 Andres Galarraga .10
225 Orel Hershiser, Danny Jackson .05
226 Nolan Ryan .75
227 Dwight Gooden (All-Star) .05
228 Gary Carter (All-Star) .05
229 Vince Coleman (All-Star) .05
230 Andre Dawson (All-Star) .05
231 Darryl Strawberry (All-Star) .05
232 Will Clark (All-Star) .10
233 Ryne Sandberg (All-Star) .15
234 Bobby Bonilla (All-Star) .05

235 Ozzie Smith (All-Star) .20
236 Terry Steinbach (All-Star) .05
237 Frank Viola (All-Star) .05
238 Jose Canseco (All-Star) .15
239 Rickey Henderson (All-Star) .10
240 Dave Winfield (All-Star) .10
241 Cal Ripken, Jr. (All-Star) .35
242 Wade Boggs (All-Star) .15
243 Paul Molitor (All-Star) .15
244 Mark McGwire (All-Star) .50
245 Wade Boggs .20
246 Jose Canseco .20
247 Kirby Puckett .50
248 Frank Viola .05
249 Roger Clemens .45
250 Orioles Logo .05
251 Bob Milacki .05
252 Craig Worthington .05
253 Jeff Ballard .05
254 Tom Niedenfeuer .05
255 Dave Schmidt .05
256 Terry Kennedy .05
257 Memorial Stadium .05
258 Orioles Script .05
259 Mickey Tettleton .05
260 Eddie Murray .20
261 Billy Ripken .05
262 Cal Ripken, Jr. 1.00
263 Joe Orsulak .05
264 Larry Sheets .05
265 Pete Stanicek .05
266 Red Sox Logo .05
267 Steve Curry .05
268 Jody Reed .05
269 "Oil Can" Boyd .05
270 Roger Clemens .40
271 Bruce Hurst .05
272 Lee Smith .05
273 Fenway Park .05
274 Red Sox Script .05
275 Todd Benzinger .05
276 Marty Barrett .05
277 Wade Boggs .20
278 Ellis Burks .05
279 Dwight Evans .05
280 Mike Greenwell .05
281 Jim Rice .10
282 Angels Logo .05
283 Dante Bichette .10
284 Bryan Harvey .05
285 Kirk McCaskill .05
286 Mike Witt .05
287 Bob Boone .05
288 Brian Downing .05
289 Anaheim Stadium .05
290 Angels Script .05
291 Wally Joyner .10
292 Johnny Ray .05
293 Jack Howell .05
294 Dick Schofield .05
295 Tony Armas .05
296 Chili Davis .05
297 Devon White .05
298 White Sox Logo .05
299 Dave Gallagher .05
300 Melido Perez .05
301 Shawn Hillegas .05
302 Jack McDowell .05
303 Bobby Thigpen .05
304 Carlton Fisk .20
305 Comiskey Park .05
306 White Sox Script .05
307 Greg Walker .05
308 Steve Lyons .05
309 Ozzie Guillen .05
310 Harold Baines .05
311 Daryl Boston .05
312 Lance Johnson .05
313 Dan Pasqua .05
314 Indians Logo .05
315 Luis Medina .05
316 Ron Tingley .05
317 Tom Candiotti .05
318 John Farrell .05
319 Doug Jones .05
320 Greg Swindell .05
321 Cleveland Stadium .05
322 Indians Script .05
323 Andy Allanson .05
324 Willie Upshaw .05
325 Julio Franco .05
326 Brook Jacoby .05
327 Joe Carter .05
328 Mel Hall .05
329 Cory Snyder .05
330 Tigers Logo .05
331 Paul Gibson .05
332 Torey Luvello .05
333 Mike Henneman .05
334 Jack Morris .05
335 Jeff Robinson .05
336 Frank Tanana .05
337 Tiger Stadium .05
338 Tigers Script .05
339 Matt Nokes .05
340 Tom Brookens .05
341 Lou Whitaker .05
342 Luis Salazar .05
343 Alan Trammell .10
344 Chet Lemon .05
345 Gary Pettis .05
346 Royals Logo .05
347 Luis de los Santos .05
348 Gary Thurman .05
349 Steve Farr .05
350 Mark Gubicza .05
351 Charlie Leibrandt .05
352 Bret Saberhagen .05
353 Royals Stadium .05
354 Royals Script .05
355 George Brett .60
356 Frank White .05
357 Kevin Seitzer .05
358 Bo Jackson .20
359 Pat Tabler .05
360 Danny Tartabull .05
361 Willie Wilson .05
362 Brewers Logo .05
363 Joey Meyer .05
364 Gary Sheffield .20
365 Don August .05
366 Ted Higuera .05
367 Dan Plesac .05
368 B.J. Surhoff .05
369 County Stadium .05
370 Brewers Script .05
371 Greg Brock .05
372 Jim Gantner .05
373 Paul Molitor .35
374 Dale Sveum .05
375 Glenn Braggs .05
376 Rob Deer .05
377 Robin Yount .50
378 Twins Logo .05
379 German Gonzalez .05
380 Kelvin Torve .05
381 Allan Anderson .05
382 Jeff Reardon .05
383 Frank Viola .05
384 Tim Laudner .05
385 HHH Metrodome .05
386 Twins Script .05
387 Kent Hrbek .05
388 Gene Larkin .05
389 Gary Gaetti .05
390 Greg Gagne .05
391 Randy Bush .05
392 Dan Gladden .05
393 Kirby Puckett .50
394 Yankees Logo .05
395 Roberto Kelly .05
396 Al Leiter .10
397 John Candelaria .05
398 Rich Dotson .05
399 Rick Rhoden .05
400 Dave Righetti .05
401 Yankee Stadium .05
402 Yankees Script .05
403 Don Slaught .05
404 Don Mattingly .60
405 Willie Randolph .05
406 Mike Pagliarulo .05
407 Rafael Santana .05
408 Rickey Henderson .15
409 Dave Winfield .20
410 A's Logo .05
411 Todd Burns .05
412 Walt Weiss .05
413 Storm Davis .05
414 Dennis Eckersley .05
415 Dave Stewart .05
416 Bob Welch .05
417 Oakland Coliseum .05
418 A's Script .05
419 Terry Steinbach .05
420 Mark McGwire 1.50
421 Carney Lansford .05
422 Jose Canseco .20
423 Dave Henderson .05
424 Dave Parker .05
425 Luis Polonia .05
426 Mariners Logo .05
427 Mario Diaz .05
428 Edgar Martinez .05
429 Scott Bankhead .05
430 Mark Langston .05
431 Mike Moore .05
432 Scott Bradley .05
433 The Kingdome .05
434 Mariners Script .05
435 Alvin Davis .05
436 Harold Reynolds .05
437 Jim Presley .05
438 Rey Quinonez .05
439 Mickey Brantley .05
440 Jay Buhner .10
441 Henry Cotto .05
442 Rangers Logo .05
443 Cecil Espy .05
444 Chad Kreuter .05
445 Jose Guzman .05
446 Charlie Hough .05
447 Jeff Russell .05
448 Bobby Witt .05
449 Arlington Stadium .05
450 Rangers Script .05
451 Geno Petralli .05
452 Pete O'Brien .05
453 Steve Buechele .05
454 Scott Fletcher .05
455 Pete Incaviglia .05
456 Oddibe McDowell .05
457 Ruben Sierra .05
458 Blue Jays Logo .05
459 Rob Ducey .05
460 Todd Stottlemyre .05
461 Tom Henke .05
462 Jimmy Key .05
463 Dave Steib .05
464 Pat Borders .05
465 Exhibition Stadium .05
466 Blue Jays Script .05
467 Fred McGriff .15
468 Manny Lee .05
469 Kelly Gruber .05
470 Tony Fernandez .05
471 Jesse Barfield .05
472 George Bell .05
473 Lloyd Moseby .05
474 Orel Hershiser .05
475 Frank Viola .05
476 Chris Sabo .05
477 Jose Canseco .20
478 Walt Weiss .05
479 Kirk Gibson .05
480 Jose Canseco .20

1990 Panini Stickers

Nearly 400 individual player and specialty stickers comprise the 1990 issue from this Italian company. Sold in packs of five regular and one foil sticker, the set includes 388 2-1/8" x 3" stickers. Fronts feature color action photos. Backs are printed in black-and-white and include a sticker number and appropriate logos. A 68-page album with Nolan Ryan on the cover was sold as an adjunct to the stickers. Among the foil stickers in the set are those featuring the team logo and batting helmet of each team.

		MT
Complete Set (388):		9.00
Common Player:		.05
Sticker Album:		2.00

1 Randy Milligan .05
2 Gregg Olson .05
3 Bill Ripken .05
4 Phil Bradley .05
5 Joe Orsulak .05
6 Bob Milacki .05
7 Cal Ripken, Jr. 1.00
8 Mickey Tettleton .05
9 Orioles Logo (foil) .05
10 Orioles Helmet (foil) .05
11 Craig Worthington .05
12 Mike Devereaux .05
13 Jeff Ballard .05
14 Lee Smith .05
15 Marty Barrett .05
16 Mike Greenwell .05
17 Dwight Evans .05
18 John Dopson .05
19 Wade Boggs .25
20 Mike Boddicker .05
21 Ellis Burks .10
22 Red Sox Logo (foil) .05
23 Red Sox Helmet (foil) .05
24 Roger Clemens .60
25 Jody Reed .05
26 Nick Esasky .05
27 Brian Downing .05
28 Bert Blyleven .05
29 Devon White .05
30 Claudell Washington .05
31 Wally Joyner .10
32 Chuck Finley .05
33 Johnny Ray .05
34 Jim Abbott .05
35 Angels Logo (foil) .05
36 Angels Helmet (foil) .05
37 Kirk McCaskill .05
38 Lance Parrish .05
39 Chili Davis .05
40 Steve Lyons .05
41 Ozzie Guillen .05
42 Melido Perez .05
43 Scott Fletcher .05
44 Carlton Fisk .45
45 Greg Walker .05
46 Dave Gallagher .05
47 Ivan Calderon .05
48 White Sox Logo (foil) .05
49 White Sox Helmet (foil) .05
50 Bobby Thigpen .05
51 Ron Kittle .05
52 Daryl Boston .05
53 John Farrell .05
54 Jerry Browne .05
55 Pete O'Brien .05
56 Cory Snyder .05
57 Tom Candiotti .05
58 Brook Jacoby .05
59 Greg Swindell .05
60 Felix Fermin .05
61 Indians Logo (foil) .05
62 Indians Helmet (foil) .05
63 Doug Jones .05
64 Dion James .05
65 Joe Carter .10
66 Mike Heath .05
67 Dave Bergman .05
68 Gary Ward .05
69 Mike Henneman .05
70 Alan Trammell .10
71 Lou Whitaker .05
72 Frank Tanana .05
73 Fred Lynn .05
74 Tigers Logo (foil) .05
75 Tigers Helmet (foil) .05
76 Jack Morris .05
77 Chet Lemon .05
78 Gary Pettis .05
79 Kurt Stillwell .05
80 Jim Eisenreich .05
81 Bret Saberhagen .05
82 Mark Gubicza .05
83 Frank White .05
84 Bo Jackson .25
85 Jeff Montgomery .05
86 Kevin Seitzer .05
87 Royals Logo (foil) .05
88 Royals Helmet (foil) .05
89 Tom Gordon .05
90 Danny Tartabull .05
91 George Brett .75
92 Robin Yount .60
93 B.J. Surhoff .05
94 Jim Gantner .05
95 Dan Plesac .05
96 Ted Higuera .05
97 Glenn Braggs .05
98 Paul Molitor .40
99 Chris Bosio .05
100 Brewers Logo (foil) .05
101 Brewers Helmet (foil) .05
102 Rob Deer .05
103 Chuck Crim .05
104 Greg Brock .05
105 Kirby Puckett .75
106 Gary Gaetti .05
107 Roy Smith .05
108 Jeff Reardon .05
109 Randy Bush .05
110 Al Newman .05
111 Dan Gladden .05
112 Kent Hrbek .10
113 Twins Logo (foil) .05
114 Twins Helmet (foil) .05
115 Greg Gagne .05
116 Brian Harper .05
117 Allan Anderson .05
118 Lee Guetterman .05
119 Roberto Kelly .05
120 Jesse Barfield .05
121 Alvaro Espinoza .05
122 Mel Hall .05
123 Chuck Cary .05
124 Dave Righetti .05
125 Don Mattingly .75
126 Yankees Logo (foil) .05
127 Yankees Helmet (foil) .05
128 Bob Geren .05
129 Steve Sax .05
130 Andy Hawkins .05
131 Bob Welch .05
132 Mark McGwire 1.50
133 Dave Henderson .05
134 Carney Lansford .05
135 Walt Weiss .05
136 Mike Moore .05
137 Dennis Eckersley .05
138 Rickey Henderson .20
139 A's Logo (foil) .05
140 A's Helmet (foil) .05
141 Dave Stewart .05
142 Jose Canseco .35
143 Terry Steinbach .05
144 Harold Reynolds .05
145 Darnell Coles .05
146 Brian Holman .05
147 Scott Bankhead .05
148 Greg Briley .05
149 Alvin Davis .05
150 Jeffrey Leonard .05
151 Mike Schooler .05
152 Mariners Logo (foil) .05
153 Mariners Helmet (foil) .05
154 Randy Johnson .15
155 Ken Griffey, Jr. 1.50
156 Dave Valle .05
157 Pete Incaviglia .05
158 Fred Manrique .05
159 Jeff Russell .05
160 Nolan Ryan 1.00
161 Geno Petralli .05
162 Ruben Sierra .05
163 Julio Franco .05
164 Rafael Palmeiro .15
165 Rangers Logo (foil) .05
166 Rangers Helmet (foil) .05
167 Harold Baines .05
168 Kevin Brown .15
169 Steve Buechele .05
170 Fred McGriff .35
171 Kelly Gruber .05
172 Todd Stottlemyre .05
173 Dave Steib .05
174 Mookie Wilson .05
175 Pat Borders .05
176 Tony Fernandez .05
177 John Cerutti .05
178 Blue Jays Logo (foil) .05
179 Blue Jays Helmet (foil) .05
180 George Bell .05
181 Jimmy Key .05
182 Nelson Liriano .05
183 Kirby Puckett (BA leader) .15
184 Carney Lansford (stats leader) .05
185 Nolan Ryan (K leader) .90
186 American League Logo (foil) .05
187 National League Logo (foil) .05
188 World's Championship Trophy (foil) .05
189 1988 L.A. Dodgers World Series Ring (foil) .05
190 1987 Minnesota Twins World Series Ring (foil) .05
191 1986 N.Y. Mets World Series Ring (foil) .05
192 1985 K.C. Royals World Series Ring (foil) .05
193 1984 Detroit Tigers World Series Ring (foil) .05
194 1983 Baltimore Orioles World Series Ring (foil) .05
195 1982 Cardinals World Series Ring (foil) .05
196 1981 L.A. Dodgers World Series Ring (foil) .05
197 19890 Phillies World Series Ring (foil) .05
198 Dave Stewart, Bo Jackson (All-Star) .05
199 Wade Boggs, Kirby Puckett (All-Star) .10
200 Harold Baines (All-Star) .05
201 Julio Franco (All-Star) .05
202 Cal Ripken, Jr. (All-Star) .50
203 Ruben Sierra (All-Star) .05
204 Mark McGwire (All-Star) .75
205 Terry Steinbach (All-Star) .05
206 Rick Reuschel, Ozzie Smith (All-Star) .05
207 Tony Gwynn, Will Clark (All-Star) .10
208 Kevin Mitchell (All-Star) .05
209 Eric Davis (All-Star) .05
210 Howard Johnson (All-Star) .05
211 Pedro Guerrero (All-Star) .05
212 Ryne Sandberg (All-Star) .15
213 Benito Santiago (All-Star) .05
214 Kevin Mitchell (HR leaders) .05
215 Mark Davis (Saves leader) .05
216 Vince Coleman (SB leader) .05
217 Jeff Blauser .05
218 Jeff Treadway .05
219 Tom Glavine .10
220 Joe Boever .05
221 Oddibe McDowell .05
222 Dale Murphy .20
223 Derek Lilliquist .05
224 Tommy Gregg .05
225 Braves Logo (foil) .05
226 Braves Helmet (foil) .05
227 Lonnie Smith .05
228 John Smoltz .10
229 Andres Thomas .05
230 Jerome Walton .05
231 Ryne Sandberg .40
232 Mitch Williams .05
233 Rick Sutcliffe .05
234 Damon Berryhill .05
235 Dwight Smith .05
236 Shawon Dunston .05
237 Greg Maddux .75
238 Cubs Logo (foil) .05
239 Cubs Helmet (foil) .05
240 Andre Dawson .20
241 Mark Grace .20
242 Mike Bielecki .05

243	Jose Rijo	.05
244	John Franco	.05
245	Paul O'Neill	.10
246	Eric Davis	.10
247	Tom Browning	.05
248	Chris Sabo	.05
249	Rob Dibble	.05
250	Todd Benzinger	.05
251	Reds Logo (foil)	.05
252	Reds Helmet (foil)	.05
253	Barry Larkin	.10
254	Rolando Roomes	.05
255	Danny Jackson	.05
256	Terry Puhl	.05
257	Dave Smith	.05
258	Glenn Davis	.05
259	Craig Biggio	.10
260	Ken Caminiti	.15
261	Kevin Bass	.05
262	Mike Scott	.05
263	Gerald Young	.05
264	Astros Logo (foil)	.05
265	Astros Helmet (foil)	.05
266	Rafael Ramirez	.05
267	Jim Deshaies	.05
268	Bill Doran	.05
269	Fernando Valenzuela	.05
270	Alfredo Griffin	.05
271	Kirk Gibson	.05
272	Mike Marshall	.05
273	Eddie Murray	.20
274	Jay Howell	.05
275	Orel Hershiser	.10
276	Mike Scioscia	.05
277	Dodgers Logo (foil)	.05
278	Dodgers Helmet (foil)	.05
279	Willie Randolph	.05
280	Kal Daniels	.05
281	Tim Belcher	.05
282	Pascual Perez	.05
283	Tim Raines	.10
284	Andres Galarraga	.10
285	Spike Owen	.05
286	Tim Wallach	.05
287	Mark Langston	.05
288	Dennis Martinez	.05
289	Nelson Santovenia	.05
290	Expos Logo (foil)	.05
291	Expos Helmet (foil)	.05
292	Tom Foley	.05
293	Dave Martinez	.05
294	Tim Burke	.05
295	Ron Darling	.05
296	Kevin Elster	.05
297	Dwight Gooden	.10
298	Gregg Jefferies	.10
299	Sid Fernandez	.05
300	Dave Magadan	.05
301	David Cone	.10
302	Darryl Strawberry	.10
303	Mets Logo (foil)	.05
304	Mets Helmet (foil)	.05
305	Kevin McReynolds	.05
306	Howard Johnson	.05
307	Randy Myers	.05
308	Roger McDowell	.05
309	Tom Herr	.05
310	John Kruk	.05
311	Randy Ready	.05
312	Jeff Parrett	.05
313	Lenny Dykstra	.05
314	Ken Howell	.05
315	Ricky Jordan	.05
316	Phillies Logo (foil)	.05
317	Phillies Helmet (foil)	.05
318	Dickie Thon	.05
319	Von Hayes	.05
320	Dennis Cook	.05
321	Jay Bell	.05
322	Barry Bonds	.75
323	John Smiley	.05
324	Andy Van Slyke	.05
325	Bobby Bonilla	.10
326	Bill Landrum	.05
327	Randy Kramer	.05
328	Jose Lind	.05
329	Pirates Logo (foil)	.05
330	Pirates Helmet (foil)	.05
331	Gary Redus	.05
332	Doug Drabek	.05
333	Mike LaValliere	.05
334	Jose DeLeon	.05
335	Pedro Guerrero	.05
336	Vince Coleman	.05
337	Terry Pendleton	.05
338	Ozzie Smith	.40
339	Willie McGee	.05
340	Todd Worrell	.05
341	Jose Oquendo	.05
342	Cardinals Logo (foil)	.05
343	Cardinals Helmet (foil)	.05
344	Tom Brunansky	.05
345	Milt Thompson	.05
346	Joe Magrane	.05
347	Ed Whitson	.05
348	Jack Clark	.05
349	Roberto Alomar	.15
350	Chris James	.05
351	Tony Gwynn	.75
352	Mark Davis	.05
353	Greg W. Harris	.05
354	Garry Templeton	.05
355	Padres Logo (foil)	.05
356	Padres Helmet (foil)	.05
357	Bruce Hurst	.05
358	Benito Santiago	.05
359	Bip Roberts	.05
360	Dave Dravecky	.05
361	Kevin Mitchell	.05
362	Craig Lefferts	.05
363	Will Clark	.20
364	Steve Bedrosian	.05
365	Brett Butler	.10
366	Matt Williams	.10
367	Scott Garrelts	.05
368	Giants Logo (foil)	.05
369	Giants Helmet (foil)	.05
370	Rick Reuschel	.05
371	Robby Thompson	.05
372	Jose Uribe	.05
373	Ben McDonald (Headliner)	.05
374	Carlos Martinez (Headliner)	.05
375	Steve Olin (Headliner)	.05
376	Bill Spiers (Headliner)	.05
377	Junior Felix (Headliner)	.05
378	Joe Oliver (Headliner)	.05
379	Eric Anthony (Headliner)	.05
380	Ramon Martinez (Headliner)	.05
381	Todd Zeile (Headliner)	.05
382	Andy Benes (Headliner)	.05
383	Vince Coleman (Highlight)	.05
384	Bo Jackson (Highlight)	.05
385	Howard Johnson (Highlight)	.05
386	Dave Dravecky (Highlight)	.05
387	Nolan Ryan (Highlight)	.75
388	Cal Ripken, Jr. (Highlight)	.75

1991 Panini Stickers

For 1991 the Panini stickers were considerable downsized in both the number of pieces in the set (271) and in the size of each sticker (1-1/2" x 2-9/16"). Player stickers have a color action photo at center with a few stats at bottom. There are foil pennant and team logo stickers for each team as well as 1990 season highlights kicking off the set. Backs are printed in black-and-white and have MLB and players' association logos, along with Panini advertising. A colorful album was available to house the stickers.

		MT
Complete Set (271):		20.00
Common Player:		.10
Album:		2.00
1	Mark Langston, Mike Witt (no-hitter)	.10
2	Randy Johnson (no-hitter)	.15
3	Nolan Ryan (no-hitter)	.60
4	Dave Stewart (no-hitter)	.10
5	Fernando Valenzuela (no-hitter)	.10
6	Andy Hawkins (no-hitter)	.10
7	Melido Perez (no-hitter)	.10
8	Terry Mullholland (no-hitter)	.10
9	Dave Steib (no-hitter)	.10
10	Craig Biggio	.15
11	Jim Deshaies	.10
12	Dave Smith	.10
13	Eric Yelding	.10
14	Astros pennant	.10
15	Astros logo	.10
16	Mike Scott	.10
17	Ken Caminiti	.15
18	Danny Darwin	.10
19	Glenn Davis	.10
20	Braves pennant	.10
21	Braves logo	.10
22	Lonnie Smith	.10
23	Charlie Leibrandt	.10
24	Jim Presley	.10
25	Greg Olson	.10
26	John Smoltz	.10
27	Ron Gant	.10
28	Jeff Treadway	.10
29	Dave Justice	.15
30	Jose Oquendo	.10
31	Joe Magrane	.10
32	Cardinals pennant	.10
33	Cardinals logo	.10
34	Todd Zeile	.10
35	Vince Coleman	.10
36	Bob Tewksbury	.10
37	Pedro Guerrero	.10
38	Lee Smith	.10
39	Ozzie Smith	.25
40	Ryne Sandberg	.35
41	Andre Dawson	.10
42	Cubs pennant	.10
43	Greg Maddux	.75
44	Jerome Walton	.10
45	Cubs logo	.10
46	Mike Harkey	.10
47	Shawon Dunston	.10
48	Mark Grace	.20
49	Joe Girardi	.10
50	Ramon Martinez	.10
51	Lenny Harris	.10
52	Mike Morgan	.10
53	Eddie Murray	.20
54	Dodgers pennant	.10
55	Dodgers logo	.10
56	Hubie Brooks	.10
57	Mike Scioscia	.10
58	Kal Daniels	.10
59	Fernando Valenzuela	.10
60	Expos pennant	.10
61	Expos logo	.10
62	Spike Owen	.10
63	Tim Raines	.10
64	Tim Wallach	.10
65	Larry Walker	.20
66	Dave Martinez	.10
67	Mark Gardner	.10
68	Dennis Martinez	.10
69	Delino DeShields	.10
70	Jeff Brantley	.10
71	Kevin Mitchell	.10
72	Giants pennant	.10
73	Giants logo	.10
74	Don Robinson	.10
75	Brett Butler	.10
76	Matt Williams	.10
77	Robby Thompson	.10
78	John Burkett	.10
79	Will Clark	.20
80	David Cone	.15
81	Dave Magadan	.10
82	Mets pennant	.10
83	Gregg Jefferies	.10
84	Frank Viola	.10
85	Mets logo	.10
86	Howard Johnson	.10
87	John Franco	.10
88	Darryl Strawberry	.10
89	Dwight Gooden	.10
90	Joe Carter	.10
91	Ed Whitson	.10
92	Andy Benes	.10
93	Benito Santiago	.10
94	Padres pennant	.10
95	Padres logo	.10
96	Roberto Alomar	.15
97	Bip Roberts	.10
98	Jack Clark	.10
99	Tony Gwynn	.50
100	Phillies pennant	.10
101	Phillies logo	.10
102	Charlie Hayes	.10
103	Lenny Dykstra	.10
104	Dale Murphy	.15
105	Von Hayes	.10
106	Dickie Thon	.10
107	John Kruk	.10
108	Ken Howell	.10
109	Darren Daulton	.10
110	Jay Bell	.10
111	Bobby Bonilla	.10
112	Pirates pennant	.10
113	Pirates logo	.10
114	Barry Bonds	.50
115	Neal Heaton	.10
116	Doug Drabek	.10
117	Jose Lind	.10
118	Andy Van Slyke	.10
119	Sid Bream	.10
120	Paul O'Neill	.15
121	Randy Myers	.10
122	Reds pennant	.10
123	Mariano Duncan	.10
124	Eric Davis	.10
125	Red logo	.10
126	Jack Armstrong	.10
127	Chris Sabo	.10
128	Rob Dibble	.10
129	Barry Larkin	.10
130	National League logo	.10
131	American League logo	.10
132	Dave Winfield	.15
133	Lance Parrish	.10
134	Chili Davis	.10
135	Chuck Finley	.10
136	Angels pennant	.10
137	Angels logo	.10
138	Johnny Ray	.10
139	Dante Bichette	.15
140	Jim Abbott	.10
141	Wally Joyner	.10
142	A's pennant	.10
143	A's logo	.10
144	Dave Stewart	.10
145	Mark McGwire	2.00
146	Rickey Henderson	.15
147	Walt Weiss	.10
148	Dennis Eckersley	.10
149	Jose Canseco	.25
150	Dave Henderson	.10
151	Bob Welch	.10
152	Tony Fernandez	.10
153	David Wells	.10
154	Blue Jays pennant	.10
155	Blue Jays logo	.10
156	Pat Borders	.10
157	Fred McGriff	.15
158	George Bell	.10
159	John Olerud	.15
160	Dave Steib	.10
161	Kelly Gruber	.10
162	Billy Spiers	.10
163	Dan Plesac	.10
164	Brewers pennant	.10
165	Mark Knudson	.10
166	Robin Yount	.40
167	Brewers logo	.10
168	Paul Molitor	.30
169	B.J. Surhoff	.10
170	Gary Sheffield	.20
171	Dave Parker	.10
172	Sandy Alomar	.15
173	Doug Jones	.10
174	Tom Candiotti	.10
175	Mitch Webster	.10
176	Indians pennant	.10
177	Indians logo	.10
178	Brook Jacoby	.10
179	Candy Maldonado	.10
180	Carlos Baerga	.10
181	Chris James	.10
182	Mariners pennant	.10
183	Mariners logo	.10
184	Mike Schooler	.10
185	Alvin Davis	.10
186	Erik Hanson	.10
187	Edgar Martinez	.10
188	Randy Johnson	.20
189	Ken Griffey Jr.	2.00
190	Jay Buhner	.10
191	Harold Reynolds	.10
192	Cal Ripken Jr.	1.50
193	Gregg Olson	.10
194	Orioles pennant	.10
195	Orioles logo	.10
196	Mike Devereaux	.10
197	Ben McDonald	.10
198	Craig Worthington	.10
199	Dave Johnson	.10
200	Joe Orsulak	.10
201	Randy Milligan	.10
202	Ruben Sierra	.10
203	Bobby Witt	.10
204	Rangers pennant	.10
205	Nolan Ryan	1.50
206	Jeff Huson	.10
207	Rangers logo	.10
208	Kevin Brown	.15
209	Steve Buechele	.10
210	Julio Franco	.10
211	Rafael Palmeiro	.15
212	Ellis Burks	.10
213	Dwight Evans	.10
214	Wade Boggs	.25
215	Roger Clemens	.45
216	Red Sox pennant	.10
217	Red Sox logo	.10
218	Jeff Reardon	.10
219	Tony Pena	.10
220	Jody Reed	.10
221	Carlos Quintana	.10
222	Royals pennant	.10
223	Royals logo	.10
224	George Brett	.45
225	Bret Saberhagen	.15
226	Bo Jackson	.15
227	Kevin Seitzer	.10
228	Mark Gubicza	.10
229	Jim Eisenreich	.10
230	Gerald Perry	.10
231	Tom Gordon	.10
232	Cecil Fielder	.10
233	Lou Whitaker	.10
234	Tigers pennant	.10
235	Tigers logo	.10
236	Mike Henneman	.10
237	Mike Heath	.10
238	Alan Trammell	.10
239	Lloyd Moseby	.10
240	Dan Petry	.10
241	Dave Bergman	.10
242	Brian Harper	.10
243	Rick Aguilera	.10
244	Twins pennant	.10
245	Greg Gagne	.10
246	Gene Larkin	.10
247	Twins logo	.10
248	Kirby Puckett	.45
249	Kevin Tapani	.10
250	Gary Gaetti	.10
251	Kent Hrbek	.10
252	Bobby Thigpen	.10
253	Lance Johnson	.10
254	Greg Hibbard	.10
255	Carlton Fisk	.25
256	White Sox pennant	.10
257	White Sox logo	.10
258	Ivan Calderon	.10
259	Barry Jones	.10
260	Robin Ventura	.15
261	Ozzie Guillen	.10
262	Yankees pennant	.10
263	Yankees logo	.10
264	Kevin Maas	.10
265	Bob Geren	.10
266	Dave Righetti	.10
267	Don Mattingly	.75
268	Roberto Kelly	.10
269	Alvaro Espinosa	.10
270	Oscar Azocar	.10
271	Steve Sax	.10

1991 Panini Stickers - Canadian

While the U.S. sticker set from Panini was downsized both in physical format and number of stickers in the set, a special issue for the Canadian market was produced in the 2-1/8" x 3" size to a total of 360 pieces. The relatively simple design has a color game-action photo with a wide white border. The black player name and team at bottom are highlighted by a red (American League) or blue (National League) splash of color at lower-left. Black-and-white backs have a sticker number and a few words about the collection in English and French. Besides player stickers there are foil specialty stickers for the teams and a subset of All-Star stickers.

		MT
Complete Set (360):		24.00
Common Player:		.05
Album:		3.00
1	Major League Baseball logo (foil)	.05
2	MLB Players Association logo (foil)	.05
3	Panini logo (foil)	.05
4	Houston Astros pennant (foil)	.05
5	Houston Astros logo (foil)	.05
6	Craig Biggio	.15
7	Glenn Davis	.05
8	Casey Candaele	.05
9	Ken Caminiti	.15
10	Rafael Ramirez	.05
11	Glenn Wilson	.05
12	Eric Yelding	.05
13	Franklin Stubbs	.05
14	Mike Scott	.05
15	Danny Darwin	.05
16	Atlanta Braves pennant (foil)	.05
17	Atlanta Braves logo (foil)	.05
18	Greg Olson	.05
19	Tommy Gregg	.05
20	Jeff Treadway	.05
21	Jim Presley	.05
22	Jeff Blauser	.05
23	Ron Gant	.10
24	Lonnie Smith	.05
25	Dave Justice	.15
26	John Smoltz	.10
27	Charlie Leibrandt	.05
28	St. Louis Cardinals pennant (foil)	.05

29	St. Louis Cardinals logo (foil)	.05
30	Tom Pagnozzi	.05
31	Pedro Guerrero	.05
32	Jose Oquendo	.05
33	Todd Zeile	.05
34	Ozzie Smith	.25
35	Vince Coleman	.05
36	Milt Thompson	.05
37	Rex Hudler	.05
38	Joe Magrane	.05
39	Lee Smith	.05
40	Chicago Cubs pennant (foil)	.05
41	Chicago Cubs logo (foil)	.05
42	Joe Girardi	.05
43	Mark Grace	.20
44	Ryne Sandberg	.25
45	Luis Salazar	.05
46	Shawon Dunston	.05
47	Dwight Smith	.05
48	Jerome Walton	.05
49	Andre Dawson	.10
50	Greg Maddux	.75
51	Mike Harkey	.05
52	Los Angeles Dodgers pennant (foil)	.05
53	Los Angeles Dodgers logo (foil)	.05
54	Mike Scioscia	.05
55	Eddie Murray	.15
56	Juan Samuel	.05
57	Lenny Harris	.05
58	Alfredo Griffin	.05
59	Hubie Brooks	.05
60	Kal Daniels	.05
61	Stan Javier	.05
62	Ramon Martinez	.10
63	Mike Morgan	.05
64	San Francisco Giants pennant (foil)	.05
65	San Francisco Giants logo (foil)	.05
66	Terry Kennedy	.05
67	Will Clark	.15
68	Robby Thompson	.05
69	Matt Williams	.10
70	Jose Uribe	.05
71	Kevin Mitchell	.05
72	Brett Butler	.05
73	Don Robinson	.05
74	John Burkett	.05
75	Jeff Brantley	.05
76	New York Mets pennant (foil)	.05
77	New York Mets logo (foil)	.05
78	Mackey Sasser	.05
79	Dave Magadan	.05
80	Gregg Jefferies	.10
81	Howard Johnson	.05
82	Kevin Elster	.05
83	Kevin McReynolds	.05
84	Daryl Boston	.05
85	Darryl Strawberry	.10
86	Dwight Gooden	.10
87	Frank Viola	.05
88	San Diego Padres pennant (foil)	.05
89	San Diego Padres logo (foil)	.05
90	Benito Santiago	.05
91	Jack Clark	.05
92	Roberto Alomar	.15
93	Mike Pagliarulo	.05
94	Garry Templeton	.05
95	Joe Carter	.10
96	Bip Roberts	.05
97	Tony Gwynn	.45
98	Ed Whitson	.05
99	Andy Benes	.10
100	Philadelphia Phillies pennant (foil)	.05
101	Philadelphia Phillies logo (foil)	.05
102	Darren Daulton	.05
103	Ricky Jordan	.05
104	Randy Ready	.05
105	Charlie Hayes	.05
106	Dickie Thon	.05
107	Von Hayes	.05
108	Lenny Dykstra	.05
109	Dale Murphy	.15
110	Ken Howell	.05
111	Roger McDowell	.05
112	Pittsburgh Pirates pennant (foil)	.05
113	Pittsburgh Pirates logo (foil)	.05
114	Mike LaValliere	.05
115	Sid Bream	.05
116	Jose Lind	.05
117	Jeff King	.05
118	Jay Bell	.05
119	Barry Bonds	.50
120	Bobby Bonilla	.10
121	Andy Van Slyke	.05
121	Doug Drabek	.05
123	Neal Heaton	.05
124	Cincinnati Reds pennant (foil)	.05
125	Cincinnati Reds logo (foil)	.05
126	Joe Oliver	.05
127	Todd Benzinger	.05
128	Mariano Duncan	.05
129	Chris Sabo	.05
130	Barry Larkin	.10
131	Eric Davis	.10
132	Billy Hatcher	.05
133	Paul O'Neill	.10
134	Jose Rijo	.05
135	Randy Myers	.05
136	Montreal Expos pennant (foil)	.05
137	Montreal Expos logo (foil)	.05
138	Mike Fitzgerald	.05
139	Andres Galarraga	.10
140	Delino DeShields	.05
141	Tim Wallach	.05
142	Spike Owen	.05
143	Tim Raines	.10
144	Dave Martinez	.05
145	Larry Walker	.20
146	Expos batting helmet	.05
147	Dennis Boyd	.05
148	Tim Burke	.05
149	Bill Sampen	.05
150	Dennis Martinez	.05
151	Marquis Grissom	.10
152	Otis Nixon	.05
153	Jerry Goff	.05
154	Steve Frey	.05
155	National League logo (foil)	.05
156	American League logo (foil)	.05
157	Benito Santiago (All-Star)	.05
158	Will Clark (All-Star)	.05
159	Ryne Sandberg (All-Star)	.10
160	Chris Sabo (All-Star)	.05
161	Ozzie Smith (All-Star)	.10
162	Kevin Mitchell (All-Star)	.05
163	Lenny Dykstra (All-Star)	.05
164	Darryl Strawberry (All-Star)	.05
165	Jack Armstrong (All-Star)	.05
166	Sandy Alomar, Jr. (All-Star)	.05
167	Mark McGwire (All-Star)	.50
168	Steve Sax (All-Star)	.05
169	Wade Boggs (All-Star)	.10
170	Cal Ripken, Jr. (All-Star)	.35
171	Rickey Henderson (All-Star)	.05
172	Ken Griffey, Jr. (All-Star)	.50
173	Jose Canseco (All-Star)	.10
174	Bob Welch (All-Star)	.05
175	All-Star Game - Wrigley Field	.05
176	World's Championship Trophy (foil)	.05
177	California Angels pennant (foil)	.05
178	California Angels logo (foil)	.05
179	Lance Parrish	.05
180	Wally Joyner	.10
181	Johnny Ray	.05
182	Jack Howell	.05
183	Dick Schofield	.05
184	Dave Winfield	.15
185	Devon White	.05
186	Dante Bichette	.10
187	Chuck Finley	.05
188	Jim Abbott	.05
189	Oakland A's pennant (foil)	.05
190	Oakland A's logo (foil)	.05
191	Terry Steinbach	.05
192	Mark McGwire	1.00
193	Willie Randolph	.05
194	Carney Lansford	.05
195	Walt Weiss	.05
196	Rickey Henderson	.20
197	Dave Henderson	.05
198	Jose Canseco	.20
199	Dave Stewart	.05
200	Dennis Eckersley	.05
201	Milwaukee Brewers pennant (foil)	.05
202	Milwaukee Brewers logo (foil)	.05
203	B.J. Surhoff	.05
204	Greg Brock	.05
205	Paul Molitor	.25
206	Gary Sheffield	.20
207	Billy Spiers	.05
208	Robin Yount	.40
209	Rob Deer	.05
210	Dave Parker	.05
211	Mark Knudson	.05
212	Dan Plesac	.05
213	Cleveland Indians pennant (foil)	.05
214	Cleveland Indians logo (foil)	.05
215	Sandy Alomar, Jr.	.10
216	Brook Jacoby	.05
217	Jerry Browne	.05
218	Carlos Baerga	.05
219	Felix Fermin	.05
220	Candy Maldonado	.05
221	Cory Snyder	.05
222	Alex Cole, Jr.	.05
223	Tom Candiotti	.05
224	Doug Jones	.05
225	Seattle Mariners pennant (foil)	.05
226	Seattle Mariners logo (foil)	.05
227	Dave Valle	.05
228	Pete O'Brien	.05
229	Harold Reynolds	.05
230	Edgar Martinez	.05
231	Omar Vizquel	.05
232	Henry Cotto	.05
233	Ken Griffey, Jr.	1.00
234	Jay Buhner	.05
235	Eric Hanson (Erik)	.05
236	Mike Schooler	.05
237	Baltimore Orioles pennant (foil)	.05
238	Baltimore Orioles logo (foil)	.05
239	Mickey Tettleton	.05
240	Randy Milligan	.05
241	Billy Ripken	.05
242	Craig Worthington	.05
243	Cal Ripken, Jr.	.90
244	Steve Finley	.05
245	Mike Devereaux	.05
246	Joe Orsulak	.05
247	Ben McDonald	.05
248	Gregg Olson	.05
249	Texas Rangers pennant (foil)	.05
250	Texas Rangers logo (foil)	.05
251	Geno Petralli	.05
252	Rafael Palmeiro	.15
253	Julio Franco	.05
254	Steve Buechele	.05
255	Jeff Huson	.05
256	Gary Pettis	.05
257	Ruben Sierra	.05
258	Pete Incaviglia	.05
259	Nolan Ryan	.90
260	Bobby Witt	.05
261	Boston Red Sox pennant (foil)	.05
262	Boston Red Sox logo (foil)	.05
263	Tony Pena	.05
264	Carlos Quintana	.05
265	Jody Reed	.05
266	Wade Boggs	.20
267	Luis Rivera	.05
268	Mike Greenwell	.05
269	Ellis Burks	.05
270	Tom Brunansky	.05
271	Roger Clemens	.45
272	Jeff Reardon	.05
273	Kansas City Royals pennant (foil)	.05
274	Kansas City Royals logo (foil)	.05
275	Mike Macfarlane	.05
276	George Brett	.45
277	Bill Pecota	.05
278	Kevin Seitzer	.05
279	Kurt Stillwell	.05
280	Jim Eisenreich	.05
281	Bo Jackson	.10
282	Danny Tartabull	.05
283	Bret Saberhagen	.05
284	Tom Gordon	.05
285	Detroit Tigers pennant (foil)	.05
286	Detroit Tigers logo (foil)	.05
287	Mike Heath	.05
288	Cecil Fielder	.10
289	Lou Whitaker	.05
290	Tony Phillips	.05
291	Alan Trammell	.05
292	Chet Lemon	.05
293	Lloyd Moseby	.05
294	Gary Ward	.05
295	Dan Petry	.05
296	Jack Morris	.05
297	Minnesota Twins pennant (foil)	.05
298	Minnesota Twins logo (foil)	.05
299	Brian Harper	.05
300	Kent Hrbek	.05
301	Al Newman	.05
302	Gary Gaetti	.05
303	Greg Gagne	.05
304	Dan Gladden	.05
305	Kirby Puckett	.45
306	Gene Larkin	.05
307	Kevin Tapani	.05
308	Rick Aguilera	.05
309	Chicago White Sox pennant (foil)	.05
310	Chicago White Sox logo (foil)	.05
311	Carlton Fisk	.25
312	Carlos Martinez	.05
313	Scott Fletcher	.05
314	Robin Ventura	.10
315	Ozzie Guillen	.05
316	Sammy Sosa	.60
317	Lance Johnson	.05
318	Ivan Calderon	.05
319	Greg Hibbard	.05
320	Bobby Thigpen	.05
321	New York Yankees pennant (foil)	.05
322	New York Yankees logo (foil)	.05
323	Bob Geren	.05
324	Don Mattingly	.45
325	Steve Sax	.05
326	Jim Leyritz	.05
327	Alvaro Espinoza	.05
328	Roberto Kelly	.05
329	Oscar Azocar	.05
330	Jesse Barfield	.05
331	Chuck Cary	.05
332	Dave Righetti	.05
333	Toronto Blue Jays pennant (foil)	.05
334	Toronto Blue Jays logo (foil)	.05
335	Pat Borders	.05
336	Fred McGriff	.15
337	Manny Lee	.05
338	Kelly Gruber	.05
339	Tony Fernandez	.05
340	George Bell	.05
341	Mookie Wilson	.05
342	Junior Felix	.05
343	Blue Jays batting helmet (foil)	.05
344	Dave Steib	.05
345	Tom Henke	.05
346	Greg Myers	.05
347	Glenallen Hill	.05
348	John Olerud	.10
349	Todd Stottlemyre	.05
350	David Wells	.10
351	Jimmy Key	.05
352	Mark Langston (no-hitter)	.05
353	Randy Johnson (no-hitter)	.10
354	Nolan Ryan (no-hitter)	.45
355	Dave Stewart (no-hitter)	.05
356	Fernando Valenzuela (no-hitter)	.05
357	Andy Hawkins (no-hitter)	.05
358	Melido Perez (no-hitter)	.05
359	Terry Mulholland (no-hitter)	.05
360	Dave Stieb (no-hitter)	.05

1991 Panini Top 15 Stickers (Canadian)

The four leaders from each league in major statistical categories from the 1990 season are featured in this set of stickers marketed in Canada. The 2-1/2" x 3-1/2" stickers feature a large color photo at top. In the white border at bottom is the player's name and team, the stat in which he excelled (printed in both English and French), the number achieved, and, at lower-left, his rank among the top 4. Gold Glove winners in each league are also recognized. A series of team logo metallic stickers honors the teams which led in various stats. Backs are printed in black with appropriate logos and sticker number. A colorful album could be purchased to the house the sticker collection.

		MT
Complete Set (136):		20.00
Common Player:		.07
1	Willie McGee	.07
2	Eddie Murray	.15
3	Dave Magadan	.07
4	Lenny Dykstra	.07
5	George Brett	.40
6	Rickey Henderson	.15
7	Rafael Palmeiro	.15
8	Alan Trammell	.07
9	Ryne Sandberg	.30
10	Darryl Strawberry	.10
11	Kevin Mitchell	.07
12	Barry Bonds	.40
13	Cecil Fielder	.07
14	Mark McGwire	.75
15	Jose Canseco	.15
16	Fred McGriff	.10
17	Matt Williams	.10
18	Bobby Bonilla	.10
19	Joe Carter	.07
20	Barry Bonds	.40
21	Cecil Fielder	.10
22	Kelly Gruber	.07
23	Mark McGwire	.75
24	Jose Canseco	.15
25	Brett Butler	.07
26	Lenny Dykstra	.07
27	Ryne Sandberg	.30
28	Barry Larkin	.10
29	Rafael Palmeiro	.15
30	Wade Boggs	.15
31	Roberto Kelly	.07
32	Mike Greenwell	.07
33	Barry Bonds	.40
34	Ryne Sandberg	.30
35	Kevin Mitchell	.07
36	Ron Gant	.07
37	Cecil Fielder	.10
38	Rickey Henderson	.15
39	Jose Canseco	.15
40	Fred McGriff	.10
41	Vince Coleman	.07
42	Eric Yelding	.07
43	Barry Bonds	.40
44	Brett Butler	.07
45	Rickey Henderson	.15
46	Steve Sax	.07
47	Roberto Kelly	.07
48	Alex Cole, Jr.	.07
49	Ryne Sandberg	.30
50	Bobby Bonilla	.07
51	Brett Butler	.07
52	Ron Gant	.07
53	Rickey Henderson	.15
54	Cecil Fielder	.10
55	Harold Reynolds	.07
56	Robin Yount	.25
57	Doug Drabek	.07
58	Ramon Martinez	.10
59	Frank Viola	.07
60	Dwight Gooden	.10
61	Bob Welch	.07
62	Dave Stewart	.07
63	Roger Clemens	.25
64	Dave Stieb	.07
65	Danny Darwin	.07
66	Zane Smith	.07
67	Ed Whitson	.07
68	Frank Viola	.07
69	Roger Clemens	.25
70	Chuck Finley	.07
71	Dave Stewart	.07
72	Kevin Appier	.07
73	David Cone	.10
74	Dwight Gooden	.10
75	Ramon Martinez	.07
76	Frank Viola	.07
77	Nolan Ryan	.90
78	Bobby Witt	.07
79	Erik Hanson	.07
80	Roger Clemens	.25
81	John Franco	.07
82	Randy Myers	.07
83	Lee Smith	.07
84	Craig Lefferts	.07
85	Bobby Thigpen	.07
86	Dennis Eckersley	.07
87	Doug Jones	.07
88	Gregg Olson	.07
89	Mike Morgan	.07
90	Bruce Hurst	.07
91	Mark Gardner	.07
92	Doug Drabek	.07
93	Dave Stewart	.07
94	Roger Clemens	.25
95	Kevin Appier	.07
96	Melido Perez	.07
97	National League logo	.07
98	Greg Maddux	.45
99	Benito Santiago	.07
100	Andres Galarraga	.10
101	Ryne Sandberg	.30
102	Tim Wallach	.07
103	Ozzie Smith	.25
104	Tony Gwynn	.45
105	Barry Bonds	.40
106	Andy Van Slyke	.07
107	American League logo	.07
108	Mike Boddicker	.07
109	Sandy Alomar Jr.	.10
110	Mark McGwire	.75
111	Harold Reynolds	.07
112	Kelly Gruber	.07
113	Ozzie Guillen	.07
114	Ellis Burks	.07
115	Gary Pettis	.07
116	Ken Griffey Jr.	1.00
117	Cincinnati Reds logo	.07
118	New York Mets logo	.07
119	New York Mets script	.07
120	Chicago Cubs logo	.07
121	Montreal Expos logo	.07
122	Boston Red Sox logo	.07

123 Detroit Tigers logo .07
124 Toronto Blue Jays logo .07
125 Boston Red Sox script .07
126 Milwaukee Brewers logo .07
127 Philadelphia Phillies logo .07
128 Cincinnati Reds logo .07
129 Montreal Expos logo .07
130 New York Mets logo .07
131 Cincinnati Reds logo .07
132 California Angels logo .07
133 Toronto Blue Jays logo .07
134 Oakland A's logo .07
135 Oakland A's script .07
136 Chicago White Sox logo .07

1992 Panini Stickers

A 288-piece set comprised Panini's annual baseball issue in 1992. Stickers were sold in packs of six for 39 cents. A colorful album for housing the stickers was also availabe. Individual stickers measured 2-1/8" x 3". Player stickers feature a color action photo at center, with a shark's tooth border at right. The player's name and position are printed in the white bottom border, with the sticker number in the lower-right. A colored diamond is overprinted on the first letters of the name, while a rule of the same color is printed around the photo. On American League stickers the color highlights are in magenta; teal for N.L. Stickers are numbered by position within team, and each team set includes a foil-glitter team logo stickers. Similar special stickers honor the 1991 All-Star Game starters and a few other special themes. Backs of the foils are printed in blue and promote sticker collecting. Backs of the player stickers are special themes. Backs of the foils are printed in blue and in full color and include trivia questions, "Play Ball" game situations and score cards for the game.

MT
Complete Set (288): 15.00
Common Player: .05
1 Panini logo (foil) .05
2 Major League Baseball logo (foil) .05
3 Players Association logo (foil) .05
4 Lance Parrish .05
5 Wally Joyner .08
6 Luis Sojo .05
7 Gary Gaetti .08
8 Dick Schofield .05
9 Junior Felix .05
10 Luis Polonia .05
11 Mark Langston .08
12 Jim Abbott .08
13 California Angels logo (foil) .05
14 Terry Steinbach .05
15 Mark McGwire 1.00
16 Mike Gallego .05
17 Carney Lansford .05
18 Walt Weiss .05
19 Jose Canseco .30
20 Dave Henderson .05
21 Rickey Henderson .25
22 Dennis Eckersley .08
23 Oakland A's logo (foil) .05
24 Pat Borders .05
25 John Olerud .12
26 Roberto Alomar .15
27 Kelly Gruber .05
28 Manuel Lee .05
29 Joe Carter .10
30 Devon White .05
31 Candy Maldonado .05
32 Jimmy Key .05
33 Toronto Blue Jays logo (foil) .05
34 B.J. Surhoff .05
35 Franklin Stubbs .05
36 Willie Randolph .05
37 Jim Gantner .05
38 Bill Spiers .05
39 Dante Bichette .15
40 Robin Yount .35
41 Greg Vaughn .12
42 Jaime Navarro .05
43 Milwaukee Brewers logo (foil) .05
44 Sandy Alomar Jr. .08
45 Mike Aldrete .05
46 Mark Lewis .05
47 Carlos Baerga .10
48 Felix Fermin .05
49 Mark Whiten .05
50 Alex Cole .05
51 Albert Belle .30
52 Greg Swindell .05
53 Cleveland Indians logo (foil) .05
54 Dave Valle .05
55 Pete O'Brien .05
56 Harold Reynolds .05
57 Edgar Martinez .08
58 Omar Vizquel .05
59 Jay Buhner .10
60 Ken Griffey Jr. 1.00
61 Greg Briley .05
62 Randy Johnson .15
63 Seattle Mariners logo (foil) .05
64 Chris Hoiles .05
65 Randy Milligan .05
66 Billy Ripken .05
67 Leo Gomez .05
68 Cal Ripken Jr. .90
69 Dwight Evans .05
70 Mike Devereaux .05
71 Joe Orsulak .05
72 Gregg Olson .05
73 Baltimore Orioles logo (foil) .05
74 Ivan Rodriguez .25
75 Rafael Palmeiro .15
76 Julio Franco .05
77 Dean Palmer .05
78 Jeff Huson .05
79 Ruben Sierra .05
80 Gary Pettis .05
81 Juan Gonzalez .50
82 Nolan Ryan .90
83 Texas Rangers logo (foil) .05
84 Tony Pena .05
85 Carlos Quintana .05
86 Jody Reed .05
87 Wade Boggs .30
88 Luis Rivera .05
89 Tom Brunansky .05
90 Ellis Burks .10
91 Mike Greenwell .05
92 Roger Clemens .40
93 Boston Red Sox logo (foil) .05
94 Todd Benzinger .05
95 Terry Shumpert .05
96 Bill Pecota .05
97 Kurt Stillwell .05
98 Danny Tartabull .05
99 Brian McRae .05
100 Kirk Gibson .05
101 Bret Saberhagen .08
102 George Brett .50
103 Kansas City Royals logo (foil) .05
104 Mickey Tettleton .05
105 Cecil Fielder .10
106 Lou Whitaker .05
107 Travis Fryman .08
108 Alan Trammell .10
109 Rob Deer .05
110 Milt Cuyler .05
111 Lloyd Moseby .05
112 Bill Gullickson .05
113 Detroit Tigers logo (foil) .05
114 Brian Harper .05
115 Kent Hrbek .10
116 Chuck Knoblauch .12
117 Mike Pagliarulo .05
118 Greg Gagne .05
119 Shane Mack .05
120 Kirby Puckett .50
121 Dan Gladden .05
122 Jack Morris .05
123 Minnesota Twins logo (foil) .05
124 Carlton Fisk .25
125 Frank Thomas .90
126 Joey Cora .05
127 Robin Ventura .20
128 Ozzie Guillen .05
129 Sammy Sosa .65
130 Lance Johnson .05
131 Tim Raines .08
132 Bobby Thigpen .05
133 Chicago White Sox logo (foil) .05
134 Matt Nokes .05
135 Don Mattingly .50
136 Steve Sax .05
137 Pat Kelly .05
138 Alvaro Espinoza .05
139 Jesse Barfield .05
140 Roberto Kelly .05
141 Mel Hall .05
142 Scott Sanderson .05
143 New York Yankees logo (foil) .05
144 A.L. HR Leaders (Cecil Fielder, Jose Canseco) .08
145 A.L. BA Leader (Julio Franco) .05
146 A.L. ERA Leader (Roger Clemens) .15
147 N.L. HR Leader (Howard Johnson) .05
148 N.L. BA Leader (Terry Pendleton) .05
149 N.L. ERA Leader (Dennis Martinez) .05
150 Houston Astros logo (foil) .05
151 Craig Biggio .10
152 Jeff Bagwell .40
153 Casey Candaele .05
154 Ken Caminiti .15
155 Andujar Cedeno .05
156 Mike Simms .05
157 Steve Finley .05
158 Luis Gonzalez .05
159 Pete Harnisch .05
160 Atlanta Braves logo (foil) .05
161 Greg Olson .05
162 Sid Bream .05
163 Mark Lemke .05
164 Terry Pendleton .05
165 Rafael Belliard .05
166 Dave Justice .15
167 Ron Gant .08
168 Lonnie Smith .05
169 Steve Avery .05
170 St. Louis Cardinals logo (foil) .05
171 Tom Pagnozzi .05
172 Pedro Guerrero .05
173 Jose Oquendo .05
174 Todd Zeile .08
175 Ozzie Smith .35
176 Felix Jose .05
177 Ray Lankford .08
178 Jose DeLeon .05
179 Lee Smith .08
180 Chicago Cubs logo (foil) .05
181 Hector Villanueva .05
182 Mark Grace .20
183 Ryne Sandberg .45
184 Luis Salazar .05
185 Shawon Dunston .08
186 Andre Dawson .10
187 Jerome Walton .05
188 George Bell .05
189 Greg Maddux .75
190 Los Angeles Dodgers logo (foil) .05
191 Mike Scioscia .05
192 Eddie Murray .25
193 Juan Samuel .05
194 Lenny Harris .05
195 Alfredo Griffin .05
196 Darryl Strawberry .08
197 Brett Butler .08
198 Kal Daniels .05
199 Orel Hershiser .08
200 Montreal Expos logo (foil) .05
201 Gilberto Reyes .05
202 Andres Galarraga .08
203 Delino DeShields .05
204 Tim Wallach .05
205 Spike Owen .05
206 Larry Walker .12
207 Marquis Grissom .08
208 Ivan Calderon .05
209 Dennis Martinez .08
210 San Francisco Giants logo (foil) .05
211 Steve Decker .05
212 Will Clark .20
213 Robby Thompson .05
214 Matt Williams .10
215 Jose Uribe .05
216 Kevin Bass .05
217 Willie McGee .08
218 Kevin Mitchell .08
219 Dave Righetti .05
220 New York Mets logo (foil) .05
221 Rick Cerone .05
222 Dave Magadan .05
223 Gregg Jefferies .08
224 Howard Johnson .05
225 Kevin Elster .05
226 Hubie Brooks .05
227 Vince Coleman .05
228 Kevin McReynolds .05
229 Frank Viola .05
230 San Diego Padres logo (foil) .05
231 Benito Santiago .05
232 Fred McGriff .15
233 Bip Roberts .05
234 Jack Howell .05
235 Tony Fernandez .05
236 Tony Gwynn .40
237 Darrin Jackson .05
238 Bruce Hurst .05
239 Craig Lefferts .05
240 Philadelphia Phillies logo (foil) .05
241 Darren Daulton .05
242 John Kruk .05
243 Mickey Morandini .05
244 Charlie Hayes .05
245 Dickie Thon .05
246 Dale Murphy .25
247 Lenny Dykstra .05
248 Von Hayes .05
249 Terry Mulholland .05
250 Pittsburgh Pirates logo (foil) .05
251 Mike LaValliere .05
252 Orlando Merced .05
253 Jose Lind .05
254 Steve Buechele .05
255 Jay Bell .05
256 Bobby Bonilla .10
257 Andy Van Slyke .05
258 Barry Bonds .40
259 Doug Drabek .05
260 Cincinnati Reds logo (foil) .05
261 Joe Oliver .05
262 Hal Morris .05
263 Bill Doran .05
264 Chris Sabo .05
265 Barry Larkin .12
266 Paul O'Neill .12
267 Eric Davis .12
268 Glenn Braggs .05
269 Jose Rijo .05
270 Toronto Sky Dome (foil) .05
271 Sandy Alomar Jr. (All-Star foil) .05
272 Cecil Fielder (All-Star foil) .08
273 Roberto Alomar (All-Star foil) .10
274 Wade Boggs (All-Star foil) .25
275 Cal Ripken Jr. (All-Star foil) .75
276 Dave Henderson (All-Star foil) .05
277 Ken Griffey Jr. (All-Star foil) 1.00
278 Rickey Henderson (All-Star foil) .10
279 Jack Morris (All-Star foil) .05
280 Benito Santiago (All-Star foil) .05
281 Will Clark (All-Star foil) .10
282 Ryne Sandberg (All-Star foil) .25
283 Chris Sabo (All-Star foil) .05
284 Ozzie Smith (All-Star foil) .25
285 Andre Dawson (All-Star foil) .10
286 Tony Gwynn (All-Star foil) .25
287 Ivan Calderon (All-Star foil) .05
288 Tom Glavine (All-Star foil) .10

1992 Panini Stickers - Canadian

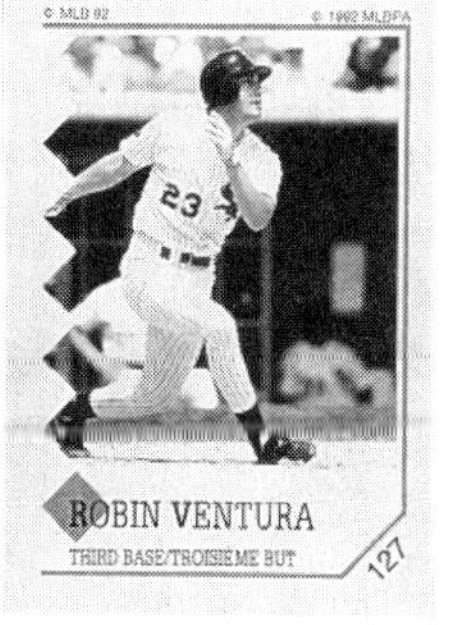

The Canadian version of the 1992 Panini stickers mirrors the U.S. set's checklist (and price guide). In the same size (2-1/8" x 3") and format, the Canadian stickers differ from the U.S. version in the addition of French position on front and bilingual back.

MT
Complete Set (288): 15.00
Common Player: .05
Album: 2.50
(See 1992 Panini Stickers for checklist and price guide)

1993 Panini Stickers

The 1993 issue is complete at 300 stickers. Besides 10 player stickers for each major league team, there are stickers for league leaders and major 1992-season award winners. There is a gold-foil team logo sticker for each team and one of the player stickers on each team is produced in a glitter technology. Sticers measure 2-3/8" x 3-3/8". Fronts have an action photo at center with team logo in the lower-left corner. Backs are printed in green and include the sticker number and appropriate Panini and baseball logos. A 58-page album was available to house the stickers.

MT
Complete Set (300): 18.00
Common Player: .05
Sticker Album: 2.00
1 California Angels logo .05
2 Mark Langston .05
3 Ron Tingley .05
4 Gary Gaetti .05
5 Kelly Gruber .05
6 Gary Disarcina .05
7 Damion Easley (glitter) .05
8 Luis Polonia .05
9 Lee Stevens .05
10 Chad Curtis .05
11 Rene Gonzales .05
12 Oakland A's logo .05
13 Dennis Eckersley .05
14 Terry Steinbach .05
15 Mark McGwire 1.25
16 Mike Bordick (glitter) .05
17 Carney Lansford .05
18 Jerry Browne .05
19 Rickey Henderson .15
20 Dave Henderson .05
21 Ruben Sierra .05
22 Ron Darling .05
23 Toronto Blue Jays logo .05
24 Jack Morris .05
25 Pat Borders .05
26 John Olerud .15
27 Roberto Alomar .15
28 Luis Sojo .05
29 Dave Stewart .05
30 Devon White .05
31 Joe Carter .10
32 Derek Bell .05
33 Juan Guzman (glitter) .05
34 Milwaukee Brewers logo .05
35 Jaime Navarro .05
36 B.J. Surhoff .05
37 Franklin Stubbs .05
38 Billy Spiers .05
39 Pat Listach (glitter) .05
40 Kevin Seitzer .05
41 Darryl Hamilton .05
42 Robin Yount .35
43 Kevin Reimer .05
44 Greg Vaughn .10
45 Cleveland Indians logo .05
46 Charles Nagy .05
47 Sandy Alomar Jr. .10
48 Reggie Jefferson .05

49 Mark Lewis .05
50 Felix Fermin .05
51 Carlos Baerga .05
52 Albert Belle .40
53 Kenny Lofton (glitter) .30
54 Mark Whiten .05
55 Paul Sorrento .05
56 Seattle Mariners logo .05
57 Dave Fleming .05
58 Dave Valle .05
59 Pete O'Brien .05
60 Randy Johnson .15
61 Omar Vizquel .05
62 Edgar Martinez .05
63 Ken Griffey Jr. (glitter) 1.50
64 Henry Cotto .05
65 Jay Buhner .10
66 Tino Martinez .15
67 Baltimore Orioles logo .05
68 Ben McDonald .05
69 Mike Mussina (glitter) .30
70 Chris Hoiles .05
71 Randy Milligan .05
72 Billy Ripken .05
73 Cal Ripken Jr. 1.00
74 Leo Gomez .05
75 Mike Devereaux .05
76 Brady Anderson .10
77 Joe Orsulak .05
78 Texas Rangers logo .05
79 Kevin Brown .10
80 Ivan Rodriguez (glitter) .30
81 Rafael Palmeiro .15
82 Julio Franco .05
83 Jeff Huson .05
84 Dean Palmer .05
85 Jose Canseco .25
86 Juan Gonzalez .60
87 Nolan Ryan 1.00
88 Brian Downing .05
89 Boston Red Sox logo .05
90 Roger Clemens .40
91 Tony Pena .05
92 Mo Vaughn .20
93 Scott Cooper .05
94 Luis Rivera .05
95 Ellis Burks .10
96 Mike Greenwell .05
97 Andre Dawson .15
98 Ivan Calderon .05
99 Phil Plantier (glitter) .05
100 Kansas City Royals logo .05
101 Kevin Appier .05
102 Mike MacFarlane .05
103 Wally Joyner .10
104 Jim Eisenreich .05
105 Greg Gagne .05
106 Gregg Jefferies .15
107 Kevin McReynolds .05
108 Brian McRae (glitter) .05
109 Keith Miller .05
110 George Brett .75
111 Detroit Tigers logo .05
112 Bill Gullickson .05
113 Mickey Tettleton .05
114 Cecil Fielder .10
115 Tony Phillips .05
116 Scott Livingstone .05
117 Travis Fryman (glitter) .10
118 Dan Gladden .05
119 Rob Deer .05
120 Frank Tanana .05
121 Skeeter Barnes .05
122 Minnesota Twins logo .05
123 Scott Erickson .05
124 Brian Harper .05
125 Kent Hrbek .05
126 Chuck Knoblauch (glitter) .30
127 Willie Banks .05
128 Scott Leius .05
129 Shane Mack .05
130 Kirby Puckett .50
131 Chili Davis .05
132 Pedro Munoz .05
133 Chicago White Sox logo .05
134 Jack McDowell .05
135 Carlton Fisk .25
136 Frank Thomas (glitter) 1.00
137 Steve Sax .05
138 Ozzie Guillen .05
139 Robin Ventura .10
140 Tim Raines .10
141 Lance Johnson .05
142 Ron Karkovice .05
143 George Bell .05
144 New York Yankees logo .05
145 Scott Sanderson .05
146 Matt Nokes .05
147 Kevin Maas (glitter) .05
148 Randy Velarde .05
149 Andy Stankiewicz .05
150 Pat Kelly .05
151 Paul O'Neill .10
152 Wade Boggs .35
153 Danny Tartabull .05
154 Don Mattingly .75
155 Edgar Martinez (B.A. leader) .05
156 Kevin Brown (W-L record) .05
157 Dennis Eckersley (Saves leader) .05
158 Gary Sheffield (B.A. leader) .05
159 Tom Glavine, Greg Maddux (W-L leaders) .20
160 Lee Smith (Saves leader) .05
161 Dennis Eckersley (Cy Young) .05
162 Dennis Eckersley (MVP) .05
163 Pat Listach (Rookie/ year) .05
164 Greg Maddux (Cy Young) .45
165 Barry Bonds (MVP) .30
166 Eric Karros (Rookie/ year) .20
167 Houston Astros logo .05
168 Pete Harnisch .05
169 Eddie Taubenese .05
170 Jeff Bagwell (glitter) .40
171 Craig Biggio .10
172 Andujar Cedeno .05
173 Ken Caminiti .15
174 Steve Finley .05
175 Luis Gonzalez .05
176 Eric Anthony .05
177 Casey Candaele .05
178 Atlanta Braves logo .05
179 Tom Glavine .10
180 Greg Olson .05
181 Sid Bream .05
182 Mark Lemke .05
183 Jeff Blauser .05
184 Terry Pendleton .05
185 Ron Gant .10
186 Otis Nixon .05
187 Dave Justice .15
188 Deion Sanders (glitter) .30
189 St. Louis Cardinals logo .05
190 Bob Tewksbury .05
191 Tom Pagnozzi .05
192 Lee Smith .05
193 Geronimo Pena .05
194 Ozzie Smith .35
195 Todd Zeile .10
196 Ray Lankford .15
197 Bernard Gilkey .10
198 Felix Jose .05
199 Donovan Osborne (glitter) .05
200 Chicago Cubs logo .05
201 Mike Morgan .05
202 Rick Wilkins .05
203 Mark Grace (glitter) .30
204 Ryne Sandberg .35
205 Shawon Dunston .05
206 Steve Buechele .05
207 Kal Daniels .05
208 Sammy Sosa .75
209 Derrick May .05
210 Doug Dascenzo .05
211 Los Angeles Dodgers logo .05
212 Ramon Martinez .10
213 Mike Scioscia .05
214 Eric Karros (glitter) .15
215 Tim Wallach .05
216 Jose Offerman .05
217 Mike Sharperson .05
218 Brett Butler .10
219 Darryl Strawberry .15
220 Lenny Harris .05
221 Eric Davis .10
222 Montreal Expos logo .05
223 Ken Hill .05
224 Darrin Fletcher .05
225 Greg Colbrunn (glitter) .10
226 Delino DeShields .05
227 Wil Cordero .05
228 Dennis Martinez .05
229 John Vander Wal .05
230 Marquis Grissom .10
231 Larry Walker .15
232 Moises Alou .10
233 San Francisco Giants logo .05
234 Billy Swift .05
235 Kirt Manwaring .05
236 Will Clark .20
237 Robby Thompson .05
238 Royce Clayton (glitter) .10
239 Matt Williams .15
240 Willie McGee .05
241 Mark Leonard .05
242 Cory Snyder .05
243 Barry Bonds .60
244 New York Mets logo .05
245 Dwight Gooden .10
246 Todd Hundley (glitter) .10
247 Eddie Murray .25
248 Sid Fernandez .05
249 Tony Fernandez .05
250 Dave Magadan .05
251 Howard Johnson .05
252 Vince Coleman .05
253 Bobby Bonilla .10
254 Daryl Boston .05
255 San Diego Padres logo .05
256 Bruce Hurst .05
257 Dan Walters .05
258 Fred McGriff .15
259 Kurt Stillwell .05
260 Craig Shipley .05
261 Gary Sheffield (glitter) .30
262 Tony Gwynn .45
263 Oscar Azocar .05
264 Darrin Jackson .05
265 Andy Benes .10
266 Philadelphia Phillies logo .05
267 Terry Mulholland .05
268 Curt Schilling .05
269 Darren Daulton .05
270 John Kruk .05
271 Mickey Morandini (glitter) .05
272 Mariano Duncan .05
273 Dave Hollins .05
274 Lenny Dykstra .05
275 Wes Chamberlain .05
276 Stan Javier .05
277 Pittsburgh Pirates logo .05
278 Zane Smith .05
279 Tim Wakefield (glitter) .10
280 Mike LaValliere .05
281 Orlando Merced .05
282 Stan Belinda .05
283 Jay Bell .05
284 Jeff King .05
285 Andy Van Slyke .05
286 Bob Walk .05
287 Gary Varsho .05
288 Cincinnati Reds logo .05
289 Jose Rijo .05
290 Joe Oliver .05
291 Hal Morris .05
292 Bip Roberts .05
293 Barry Larkin .10
294 Chris Sabo .05
295 Roberto Kelly .05
296 Kevin Mitchell .05
297 Rob Dibble .05
298 Reggie Sanders (glitter) .10
299 Florida Marlins logo .05
300 Colorado Rockies logo .05

1994 Panini Stickers

With set size at the reduced count of 268, Panini retained the larger format 2-3/8" x 3-3/8" sticker size. Stickers featured green borders surrounding a color action photo on front. Below the player photo is a pennant with the team logo and player name. Backs have a sticker number at center, with appropriate licensor logos and Panini advertising in black-and-white. The set includes 16 foil stickers honoring major 1993 season award winners in the A.L. and N.L. and four World Series action stickers. The set is arranged alphabetically within team and league. Stickers were sold in packs of six for 49 cents. A colorful album to house the stickers was also available.

MT
Complete Set (268): 18.00
Common Player: .05
1 World Series Action (foil) .05
2 World Series Action (foil) .05
3 World Series Action (foil) .05
4 World Series Action (foil) .05
5 BA Leader (John Olerud) (foil) .10
6 HR Leader (Juan Gonzalez) (foil) .25
7 RBI Leader (Albert Belle) (foil) .35
8 Wins Leader (Jack McDowell) (foil) .05
9 K Leader (Randy Johnson) (foil) .25
10 Saves Leader (Jeff Montgomery) (foil) .05
11 BA Leader (Andres Galarraga) (foil) .10
12 HR Leader (Barry Bonds) (foil) .35
13 RBI Leader (Barry Bonds) (foil) .35
14 Wins Leaders (Tom Glavine, John Burkett) (foil) .05
15 K Leader (Jose Rijo) (foil) .05
16 Saves Leader (Randy Myers) (foil) .05
17 Brady Anderson .10
18 Harold Baines .10
19 Mike Devereaux .05
20 Chris Hoiles .05
21 Mike Mussina .15
22 Harold Reynolds .05
23 Cal Ripken Jr. .90
24 David Segui .05
25 Fernando Valenzuela .05
26 Roger Clemens .40
27 Scott Cooper .05
28 Andre Dawson .10
29 Scott Fletcher .05
30 Mike Greenwell .05
31 Billy Hatcher .05
32 Tony Pena .05
33 John Valentin .10
34 Mo Vaughn .25
35 Chad Curtis .05
36 Gary DiSarcina .05
37 Damion Easley .05
38 Mark Langston .05
39 Torey Lovullo .05
40 Greg Myers .05
41 Luis Polonia .05
42 Tim Salmon .15
43 J.T. Snow .15
44 George Bell .05
45 Ellis Burks .05
46 Joey Cora .05
47 Ozzie Guillen .05
48 Roberto Hernandez .05
49 Bo Jackson .15
50 Jack McDowell .05
51 Frank Thomas .90
52 Robin Ventura .20
53 Sandy Alomar Jr. .10
54 Carlos Baerga .05
55 Albert Belle .25
56 Felix Fermin .05
57 Wayne Kirby .05
58 Kenny Lofton .25
59 Charles Nagy .05
60 Paul Sorrento .05
61 Jeff Treadway .05
62 Eric Davis .10
63 Cecil Fielder .20
64 Travis Fryman .05
65 Bill Gullickson .05
66 Mike Moore .05
67 Tony Phillips .05
68 Mickey Tettleton .05
69 Alan Trammell .05
70 Lou Whitaker .05
71 Kevin Appier .05
72 Greg Gagne .05
73 Tom Gordon .05
74 Felix Jose .05
75 Wally Joyner .10
76 Jose Lind .05
77 Mike Macfarlane .05
78 Brian McRae .05
79 Kevin McReynolds .05
80 Darryl Hamilton .05
81 Teddy Higuera .05
82 John Jaha .05
83 Pat Listach .05
84 Dave Nilsson .05
85 Kevin Reimer .05
86 Kevin Seitzer .05
87 B. J. Surhoff .05
88 Greg Vaughn .10
89 Willie Banks .05
90 Brian Harper .05
91 Kent Hrbek .05
92 Chuck Knoblauch .15
93 Shane Mack .05
94 Pat Meares .05
95 Pedro Munoz .05
.5 Kirby Puckett .60
97 Dave Winfield .25
98 Jim Abbott .05
99 Wade Boggs .35
100 Mike Gallego .05
101 Pat Kelly .05
102 Don Mattingly .50
103 Paul O'Neill .10
104 Mike Stanley .05
105 Danny Tartabull .05
106 Bernie Williams .25
107 Mike Bordick .05
108 Dennis Eckersley .05
109 Dave Henderson .05
110 Mark McGwire 1.00
111 Troy Neel .05
112 Ruben Sierra .05
113 Terry Steinbach .05
114 Todd Van Poppel .05
115 Bob Welch .05
116 Bret Boone .05
117 Jay Buhner .10
118 Ken Griffey Jr. 1.00
119 Randy Johnson .20
120 Rich Amaral .05
121 Edgar Martinez .05
122 Tino Martinez .15
123 Dave Valle .05
124 Omar Vizquel .05
125 Jose Canseco .25
126 Julio Franco .05
127 Juan Gonzalez .50
128 Tom Henke .05
129 Manuel Lee .05
130 Rafael Palmeiro .15
131 Dean Palmer .05
132 Ivan Rodriguez .25
133 Doug Strange .05
134 Roberto Alomar .25
135 Pat Borders .05
136 Joe Carter .05
137 Tony Fernandez .05
138 Juan Guzman .05
139 Rickey Henderson .25
140 Paul Molitor .30
141 John Olerud .15
142 Devon White .05
143 Jeff Blauser .05
144 Ron Gant .10
145 Tom Glavine .10
146 Dave Justice .25
147 Greg Maddux .75
148 Fred McGriff .20
149 Terry Pendleton .05
150 Deion Sanders .15
151 John Smoltz .10
152 Shawon Dunston .05
153 Mark Grace .15
154 Derrick May .05
155 Randy Myers .05
156 Ryne Sandberg .30
157 Dwight Smith .05
158 Sammy Sosa .75
159 Jose Vizcaino .05
160 Rick Wilkins .05
161 Tom Browning .05
162 Roberto Kelly .05
163 Barry Larkin .10
164 Kevin Mitchell .05
165 Hal Morris .05
166 Joe Oliver .05
167 Jose Rijo .05
168 Chris Sabo .05
169 Reggie Sanders .05
170 Freddie Benavides .05
171 Dante Bichette .10
172 Vinny Castilla .10
173 Jerald Clark .05
174 Andres Galarraga .15
175 Charlie Hayes .05
176 Chris Jones .05
177 Roberto Mejia .05
178 Eric Young .10
179 Bret Barberie .05
180 Chuck Carr .05
181 Jeff Conine .05
182 Orestes Destrade .05
183 Bryan Harvey .05
184 Rich Renteria .05
185 Benito Santiago .05
186 Gary Sheffield .20
187 Walt Weiss .05
188 Eric Anthony .05
189 Jeff Bagwell .40
190 Craig Biggio .10
191 Ken Caminiti .15
192 Andujar Cedeno .05
193 Doug Drabek .05
194 Steve Finley .05
195 Doug Jones .05
196 Darryl Kile .05
197 Brett Butler .05
198 Tom Candiotti .05
199 Dave Hansen .05
200 Orel Hershiser .05
201 Eric Karros .10
202 Jose Offerman .05
203 Mike Piazza .75
204 Cory Snyder .05
205 Darryl Strawberry .15
206 Moises Alou .10
207 Sean Berry .05
208 Wil Cordero .05
209 Delino DeShields .05
210 Marquis Grissom .15
211 Ken Hill .05
212 Mike Lansing .05
213 Larry Walker .15
214 John Wetteland .05
215 Bobby Bonilla .05
216 Jeromy Burnitz .10
217 Dwight Gooden .10
218 Todd Hundley .10
219 Howard Johnson .05
220 Jeff Kent .05
221 Eddie Murray .25
222 Bret Saberhagen .10
223 Ryan Thompson .05
224 Darren Daulton .05
225 Mariano Duncan .05
226 Lenny Dykstra .05
227 Jim Eisenreich .05
228 Dave Hollins .05
229 John Kruk .05
230 Curt Schilling .05
231 Kevin Stocker .05

232	Mitch Williams	.05
233	Jay Bell	.05
234	Steve Cooke	.05
235	Carlos Garcia	.05
236	Jeff King	.05
237	Orlando Merced	.05
238	Don Slaught	.05
239	Zane Smith	.05
240	Andy Van Slyke	.05
241	Kevin Young	.05
242	Bernard Gilkey	.10
243	Gregg Jefferies	.10
244	Brian Jordan	.10
245	Ray Lankford	.10
246	Tom Pagnozzi	.05
247	Geronimo Pena	.05
248	Ozzie Smith	.35
249	Bob Tewksbury	.05
250	Mark Whiten	.05
251	Brad Ausmus	.05
252	Derek Bell	.05
253	Andy Benes	.10
254	Phil Clark	.05
255	Jeff Gardner	.05
256	Tony Gwynn	.30
257	Trevor Hoffman	.10
258	Phil Plantier	.05
259	Craig Shipley	.05
260	Rod Beck	.05
261	Barry Bonds	.50
262	John Burkett	.05
263	Will Clark	.20
264	Royce Clayton	.05
265	Willie McGee	.05
266	Bill Swift	.05
267	Robby Thompson	.05
268	Matt Williams	.20

1988 Pepsi-Cola/ Kroger Tigers

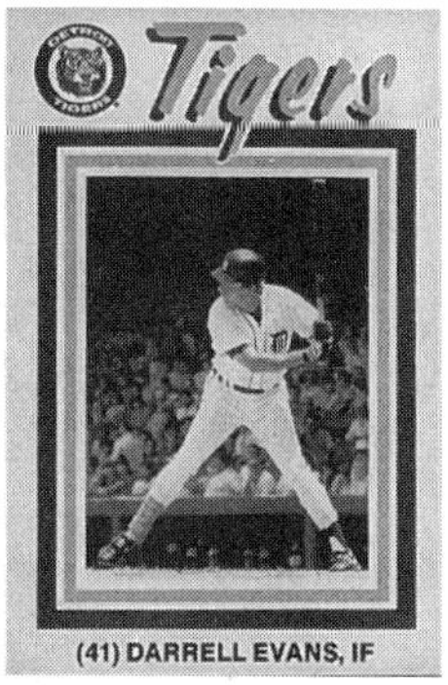

Approximately 38,000 sets of cards were given to fans at Tiger Stadium on July 30th, 1988. The set, sponsored by Pepsi-Cola and Kroger, includes 25 oversized (2-7/8" x 4-1/4") cards printed on glossy white stock with blue and orange borders. The card backs include small black and white close-up photos, the players' professional records and sponsor logos. The numbers in the following checklist refer to the players' uniform.

		MT
Complete Set (25):		8.00
Common Player:		.25
1	Lou Whitaker	.75
2	Alan Trammell	1.50
8	Mike Heath	.25
11	Sparky Anderson	.75
12	Luis Salazar	.25
14	Dave Bergman	.25
15	Pat Sheridan	.25
16	Tom Brookens	.25
19	Doyle Alexander	.25
21	Guillermo Hernandez	.25
22	Ray Knight	.25
24	Gary Pettis	.25
25	Eric King	.25
26	Frank Tanana	.25
31	Larry Herndon	.25
32	Jim Walewander	.25
33	Matt Nokes	.25
34	Chet Lemon	.25
35	Walt Terrell	.25
39	Mike Henneman	.45
41	Darrell Evans	.60
44	Jeff Robinson	.25
47	Jack Morris	.40
48	Paul Gibson	.25
---	Coaches (Billy Consolo, Alex Grammas, Billy Muffett, Vada Pinson, Dick Tracewski)	.25

1989 Pepsi-Cola Mark McGwire

During the summer of 1989, selected Pepsi products in the Northern California area carried these special McGwire cards. Photos were posed with McGwire wearing a generic white uniform trimmed in A's colors and bearing his number 25 and a Pepsi logo patch. Backs have the same biographical details, recent stats and career highlights. A card number is printed at lower-right.

		MT
Complete Set (12):		40.00
Common Card:		4.00
1	Mark McGwire (batting, left foot raised)	4.00
2	Mark McGwire (fielding)	4.00
3	Mark McGwire (reaching for ball with glove)	4.00
4	Mark McGwire (batting, foot down)	4.00
5	Mark McGwire (kneeling with bat)	4.00
6	Mark McGwire (stretching for throw at first)	4.00
7	Mark McGwire (bat on shoulder)	4.00
8	Mark McGwire (holding bat)	4.00
9	Mark McGwire (bat on shoulder)	4.00
10	Mark McGwire (holding bat)	4.00
11	Mark McGwire (holding bat)	4.00
12	Mark McGwire (batting follow-through)	4.00

1990 Pepsi-Cola Jose Canseco

Single cards from this issue were distributed in packs of Pepsi products in the San Francisco Bay area. Each card has a photo of Canseco in a generic red, white and blue uniform. Fronts have a blue border with a Pepsi logo. Backs have biographical data, recent stats and career highlights. The cards are numbered in the lower-right corner.

		MT
Complete Set (10):		7.00
Common Card:		1.00
1	Jose Canseco (batting follow-through)	1.00
2	Jose Canseco (batting follow-through)	1.00
3	Jose Canseco (fielding)	1.00
4	Jose Canseco (batting)	1.00
5	Jose Canseco (holding glove)	1.00
6	Jose Canseco (batting follow-through)	1.00
7	Jose Canseco (on dugout steps)	1.00
8	Jose Canseco (batting)	1.00
9	Jose Canseco (portrait)	1.00
10	Jose Canseco (portrait)	1.00

1990 Pepsi-Cola Red Sox

Pepsi combined with Score to produce this special 20-card Boston Red Sox team set. Cards were inserted regionally in 12-packs of Pepsi and Diet Pepsi. The card fronts feature full-color action photos with the team name across the top border and the player's name along the bottom border. The Pepsi and Diet Pepsi logos also appear on the bottom border. The card backs represent standard Score card backs, but are not numbered and also once again feature the Pepsi and Diet Pepsi logos.

		MT
Complete Set (20):		8.00
Common Player:		.25
(1)	Marty Barrett	.25
(2)	Mike Boddicker	.25
(3)	Wade Boggs	2.50
(4)	Bill Buckner	.35
(5)	Ellis Burks	.50
(6)	Roger Clemens	4.00
(7)	John Dopson	.25
(8)	Dwight Evans	.35
(9)	Wes Gardner	.25
(10)	Rich Gedman	.25
(11)	Mike Greenwell	.35
(12)	Dennis Lamp	.25
(13)	Rob Murphy	.25
(14)	Tony Pena	.25
(15)	Carlos Quintana	.25
(16)	Jeff Reardon	.35
(17)	Jody Reed	.35
(18)	Luis Rivera	.25
(19)	Kevin Romine	.25
(20)	Lee Smith	.40

1991 Pepsi-Cola Cincinnati Reds

This team set was produced for inclusion in packages of Pepsi products in the Ohio area by Michael Schechter Assoc. Like most MSA issues, the cards have had cap and uniform logos airbrushed away because they are licensed only by the players' union, and not MLB. Fronts have red borders with Pepsi, Diet Pepsi and MLBPA logos. Backs are in red, white and blue with the soda logos at top a few biographical notes, complete major and minor league stats and a facsimile autograph. The unnumbered cards are checklisted here alphabetically.

		MT
Complete Set (20):		12.00
Common Player:		.50
(1)	Jack Armstrong	.50
(2)	Todd Benzinger	.50
(3)	Glenn Braggs	.50
(4)	Tom Browning	.60
(5)	Norm Charlton	.50
(6)	Eric Davis	.75
(7)	Rob Dibble	.60
(8)	Bill Doran	.50
(9)	Mariano Duncan	.50
(10)	Billy Hatcher	.50
(11)	Barry Larkin	2.00
(12)	Hal Morris	.60
(13)	Randy Myers	.75
(14)	Joe Oliver	.50
(15)	Paul O'Neill	3.00
(16)	Lou Piniella	.60
(17)	Jeff Reed	.50
(18)	Jose Rijo	.50
(19)	Chris Sabo	.50
(20)	Herm Winningham	.50

1991 Pepsi-Cola Griffeys

This regionally released set features Ken Griffey, Sr. and Jr. and was distributed in Pepsi products. In the photos the players are shown in generic white uniforms with Pepsi logo patches. Backs are printed in black-and-white and include biographical data, recent stats and career highlights. Card numbers are in the lower-right.

		MT
Complete Set (8):		10.00
Common Card:		.50
1	Ken Griffey, Jr. (swinging bat)	3.00
2	Ken Griffey, Jr. (throwing)	3.00
3	Ken Griffey, Jr. (catching)	3.00
4	Ken Griffey, Jr. (bat on shoulder)	3.00
5	Ken Griffey, Jr. (leaning on father)	1.00
6	Ken Griffey, Jr. (standing with father)	1.00
7	Ken Griffey Sr. (batting)	.50
8	Ken Griffey Sr. (fielding)	.50

1991 Pepsi-Cola Rickey Henderson

A third annual issue distributed with Pepsi products in the San Francisco Bay area this set features photos of the all-time base stealing king in airbrushed uniforms. Borders are red, white and blue pinstripes. A line-art figure of a base runner appears in the lower-right. Backs have a few bits of biographical data, career stats and a career highlight. Card numbers are printed in the lower-right.

		MT
Complete Set (10):		9.00
Common Card:		1.00
1	Rickey Henderson (batting follow-through)	1.00
2	Rickey Henderson (base running)	1.00
3	Rickey Henderson (warm-up stretches)	1.00
4	Rickey Henderson (taking lead-off)	1.00
5	Rickey Henderson (bat on shoulder)	1.00
6	Rickey Henderson (batting follow-through)	1.00
7	Rickey Henderson (squatting with bat)	1.00
8	Rickey Henderson (throwing follow-through)	1.00
9	Rickey Henderson (leading off)	1.00
10	Rickey Henderson (warm-up swings)	1.00

1991 Pepsi-Cola Rickey Henderson Discs

Intended as a giveaway with Pepsi fountain drinks, this four-piece set of "3-D" discs pictures Rickey Henderson in a generic Pepsi-logo uniform. Each 2-1/4" diameter disc has two pictures of Henderson which change when the disc is moved. There is a purple border around the color photos, with "Pepsi," decorative stars and Henderson's name in white. Backs are printed in red and blue on white and are identical and unnumbered. The date and Pepsi logo are at top with 1990 season and career stats beneath.

		MT
Complete Set (4):		2.50
Common Disc:		1.00
(1)	Rickey Henderson (bat on shoulder/ follow-through)	1.00
(2)	Rickey Henderson (warm-up swing/ batting follow-through)	1.00
(3)	Rickey Henderson (lead-off/running for 2nd)	1.00
(4)	Rickey Henderson (lead-off/headfirst slide)	1.00

1991 Pepsi-Cola Red Sox

For the second consecutive year, Pepsi/Diet Pepsi sponsored Boston Red Sox trading cards. The cards were inserted in specially marked packs of Pepsi and Diet Pepsi and were made available from July 1 through August 10. A consumer sweepstakes was also included with this promotion. Player jersey numbers are featured on the backs of the cards. Danny Darwin's jersey is incorrectly listed as #46. He actually wears #44 for the

BoSox. Wade Boggs is not featured on a 1991 Pepsi-Cola Red Sox card.

		MT
Complete Set (20):		6.00
Common Player:		.25
2	Luis Rivera	.25
3	Jody Reed	.25
6	Tony Pena	.25
11	Tim Naehring	.25
12	Ellis Burks	.75
15	Dennis Lamp	.25
18	Carlos Quintana	.25
19	Dana Kiecker	.25
20	John Marzano	.25
21	Roger Clemens	4.00
23	Tom Brunansky	.25
25	Jack Clark	.35
27	Greg Harris	.25
29	Phil Plantier	.25
30	Matt Young	.25
38	Jeff Gray	.25
39	Mike Greenwell	.35
41	Jeff Reardon	.35
46	Danny Darwin	.25
50	Tom Bolton	.25

1991 Pepsi-Cola Superstars

This Florida regional issue was distributed by gluing cards inside of specially marked Pepsi products. Both front and back feature a "Flavor of Baseball" headline and logo of a glove catching a flying Pepsi can. Fronts have an action photo with colored strips at top and bottom. Player photos have uniform logos deleted. Backs have career stats, a few biographical details and a card number. The cards are slightly larger than current standards, measuring 2-5/8" x 3-1/2".

		MT
Complete Set (17):		95.00
Common Player:		2.00
1	Dwight Gooden	3.00
2	Andre Dawson	3.00
3	Ryne Sandberg	9.00
4	Dave Steib	2.00
5	Jose Rijo	2.00
6	Roger Clemens	12.00
7	Barry Bonds	12.00
8	Cal Ripken, Jr.	20.00
9	Dave Justice	7.50
10	Cecil Fielder	3.00
11	Don Mattingly	10.00
12	Ozzie Smith	9.00
13	Kirby Puckett	9.00
14	Rafael Palmeiro	6.00
15	Bobby Bonilla	3.00
16	Len Dykstra	2.00
17	Jose Canseco	5.00

1996 Pepsi-Cola Cubs Convention

In conjunction with the Chicago Cubs 11th annual winter fan convention, Pepsi issued this boxed set featuring past and current Cubs with an emphasis on those appearing as convention guests. Individual cards are 4" x 5-1/2" and feature black-and-white or color photos inside a black border with white piping. The team and convention logos are printed in red, white and blue. Backs are printed in black on white and feature stats and biographical data plus the team and sponsor logos. The unnumbered cards are checklisted here in alphabetical order.

		MT
Complete Set (24):		8.00
Common Player:		.25
(1)	Ernie Banks	3.00
(2)	Glenn Beckert	.25
(3)	Larry Bowa	.25
(4)	Harry Caray	.25
(5)	Frank Castillo	.25
(6)	Jody Davis	.25
(7)	Dynamic Duo (Scott Bullett, Ozzie Timmons)	.25
(8)	Flashback Favorites (Milt Pappas, Tim Stoddard)	.25
(9)	Golden Voices (Jack Brickhouse, Vince Lloyd)	.25
(10)	Randy Hundley	.25
(11)	Fergie Jenkins	.50
(12)	Don Kessinger	.35
(13)	Gary Matthews	.25
(14)	Brian McRae	.40
(15)	Jim Riggleman	.25
(16)	Ron Santo	.45
(17)	Sensational 70's (Jose Cardenal, Rick Monday)	.25
(18)	Scott Servais	.25
(19)	Rick Sutcliffe	.25
(20)	Steve Trachsel	.35
(21)	Billy Williams	.50
(22)	Wrigleyville Sluggers (Keith Moreland, Richie Hebner)	.25
(23)	Young Guns (Turk Wendell, Terry Adams)	.35
(24)	Vine Line subscription offer (Ernie Banks)	.25

1998 Pepsi-Cola Arizona Diamondbacks

Pepsi-Cola and Circle K stores ran a baseball-season promotion to distribute 15 cards of Arizona Diamondback players on a regional basis. By use of a punchcard to record the purchase of five 20-oz. or 1-liter Pepsi products a customer could receive a series of three players cards each month. Produced by Pinnacle, the D'back cards have action photos on front against a stylized semi-circular background. Team, Pinnacle and Pepsi logos are in three of the corners with the player name at lower-right. Backs have a red-white and blue Pepsi-style whirlpool background, another player photo, major league stats, a careeer highlight and licensor logos. Final production of the cards differs considerably from the player checklist provided on the punchcard and ads.

		MT
Complete Set (15):		10.00
Common Player:		.50
1	Andy Benes	.75
2	Willie Blair	.50
3	Jorge Fabregas	.50
4	Jay Bell	.75
5	Travis Lee	2.00
6	Matt Williams	1.00
7	Devon White	.75
8	Karim Garcia	.85
9	Yamil Benitez	.75
10	Brian Anderson	.75
11	Scott Brow	.50
12	Felix Rodriguez	.50
13	Jeff Suppan	.50
14	Andy Fox	.50
15	Andy Stankiewicz	.50

1999 Pepsi-Cola Arizona Diamondbacks

Sponsored by Pepsi and produced by Fleer, this team-set promotion features action photos on front on a metallic-foil background which approximates the colors and design of the soft drink logo, which also appears at lower-left. The player's uniform is at top-left. On back is a portrait photo on a repeat of the red, white and blue background. Full Major League stats are provided, along with career highlights and biographical data. At bottom is a row of licensor and sponsor logos.

		MT
Complete Set (15):		15.00
Common Player:		.50
1	Jay Bell	1.50
2	Andy Benes	1.00
3	Randy Johnson	3.00
4	Matt Williams	2.50
5	Steve Finley	.75
6	Todd Stottlemyre	.50
7	Omar Daal	.50
8	Travis Lee	1.50
9	Armando Reynoso	.50
10	Gregg Olson	.50
11	Tony Batista	.50
12	Greg Swindell	.50
13	Greg Colbrunn	.50
14	Damian Miller	.50
15	Kelly Stinnett	.50
---	Checklist 1	.10
---	Checklist 2	.10
---	Checklist 3	.10
---	Checklist 4	.10

1980-98 Perez-Steele Hall of Fame Postcards

In 1980, Perez-Steele Galleries of Ft. Washington, Pa., produced the first in an ongoing series of limited-edition (10,000 each) postcards devoted to members of the Hall of Fame. The company updates its series regularly to add new inductees. The 3-1/2" x 5-1/2" cards feature color portrait and smaller sepia action watercolor paintings by Dick Perez. Decorative postcard backs have a few words about the player, card and series number and individual set number from within the edition of 10,000. Cards were sold by series only, in a color-coded box which includes a checklist. To a great degree, value of unsigned Perez-Steele cards depends on whether the player is still alive to autograph them.

		MT
Complete Set (240):		1100.
Common Player:		4.00
	First Series, 1980	
1	Ty Cobb	35.00
2	Walter Johnson	16.00
3	Christy Mathewson	8.00
4	Babe Ruth	50.00
5	Honus Wagner	8.00
6	Morgan Bulkeley	4.00
7	Ban Johnson	4.00
8	Nap Lajoie	6.00
9	Connie Mack	6.00
10	John McGraw	4.00
11	Tris Speaker	6.00
12	George Wright	4.00
13	Cy Young	8.00
14	Grover Alexander	6.00
15	Alexander Cartwright	4.00
16	Henry Chadwick	4.00
17	Cap Anson	4.00
18	Eddie Collins	4.00
19	Candy Cummings	4.00
20	Charles Comiskey	4.00
21	Buck Ewing	4.00
22	Lou Gehrig	35.00
23	Willie Keeler	4.00
24	Hoss Radbourne	4.00
25	George Sisler	4.00
26	A.G. Spalding	4.00
27	Rogers Hornsby	6.00
28	Kenesaw Landis	4.00
29	Roger Breshnahan	4.00
30	Dan Brouthers	4.00
---	First Series Checklist	4.00
	Second Series, 1980	
31	Fred Clarke	4.00
32	Jimmy Collins	4.00
33	Ed Delahanty	4.00
34	Hugh Duffy	4.00
35	Hughie Jennings	4.00
36	King Kelly	4.00
37	Jim O'Rourke	4.00
38	Wilbert Robinson	4.00
39	Jesse Burkett	4.00
40	Frank Chance	4.00
41	Jack Chesbro	4.00
42	Johnny Evers	4.00
43	Clark Griffith	4.00
44	Thomas McCarthy	4.00
45	Joe McGinnity	4.00
46	Eddie Plank	4.00
47	Joe Tinker	4.00
48	Rube Waddell	4.00
49	Ed Walsh	4.00
50	Mickey Cochrane	4.00
51	Frankie Frisch	4.00
52	Lefty Grove	15.00
53	Carl Hubbell	10.00
54	Herb Pennock	4.00
55	Pie Traynor	4.00
56	Mordecai Brown	4.00
57	Charlie Gehringer	15.00
58	Kid Nichols	4.00
59	Jimmie Foxx	8.00
60	Mel Ott	4.00
---	Second Series Checklist	4.00
	Third Series, 1980	
61	Harry Heilmann	4.00
62	Paul Waner	4.00
63	Ed Barrow	4.00
64	Chief Bender	4.00
65	Tom Connolly	4.00
66	Dizzy Dean	15.00
67	Bill Klem	4.00
68	Al Simmons	4.00
69	Bobby Wallace	4.00
70	Harry Wright	4.00
71	Bill Dickey	12.00
72	Rabbit Maranville	4.00
73	Bill Terry	12.00
74	Frank Baker	4.00
75	Joe DiMaggio	35.00
76	Gabby Hartnett	4.00
77	Ted Lyons	4.00
78	Ray Schalk	4.00
79	Dazzy Vance	4.00
80	Joe Cronin	8.00
81	Hank Greenberg	12.00
82	Sam Crawford	4.00
83	Joe McCarthy	4.00
84	Zack Wheat	4.00
85	Max Carey	4.00
86	Billy Hamilton	4.00
87	Bob Feller	8.00
88	Bill McKechnie	4.00
89	Jackie Robinson	15.00
90	Edd Roush	4.00
---	Third Series Checklist	4.00
	Fourth Series, 1981	
91	John Clarkson	4.00
92	Elmer Flick	4.00
93	Sam Rice	4.00
94	Eppa Rixey	4.00
95	Luke Appling	5.00
96	Red Faber	4.00
97	Burleigh Grimes	5.00
98	Miller Huggins	5.00
99	Tim Keefe	4.00
100	Heinie Manush	4.00
101	John Ward	4.00
102	Pud Galvin	4.00
103	Casey Stengel	10.00
104	Ted Williams	35.00
105	Branch Rickey	4.00
106	Red Ruffing	4.00
107	Lloyd Waner	5.00
108	Kiki Cuyler	4.00
109	Goose Goslin	5.00
110	Joe Medwick	5.00
111	Roy Campanella	20.00
112	Stan Coveleski	5.00
113	Waite Hoyt	5.00
114	Stan Musial	35.00
115	Lou Boudreau	6.00
116	Earle Combs	4.00
117	Ford Frick	4.00
118	Jesse Haines	4.00
119	David Bancroft	4.00
120	Jake Beckley	4.00
---	Fourth Series Checklist	4.00
	Fifth Series, 1981	
121	Chick Hafey	4.00
122	Harry Hooper	4.00
123	Joe Kelley	4.00
124	Rube Marquard	4.00
125	Satchel Paige	25.00
126	George Weiss	4.00
127	Yogi Berra	12.00
128	Josh Gibson	6.00
129	Lefty Gomez	10.00
130	William Harridge	4.00
131	Sandy Koufax	35.00
132	Buck Leonard	6.00
133	Early Wynn	6.00
134	Ross Youngs	4.00
135	Roberto Clemente	35.00
136	Billy Evans	4.00
137	Monte Irvin	5.00
138	George Kelly	4.00
139	Warren Spahn	5.00
140	Mickey Welch	4.00
141	Cool Papa Bell	6.00
142	Jim Bottomley	4.00
143	Jocko Conlan	4.00
144	Whitey Ford	12.00
145	Mickey Mantle	50.00
146	Sam Thompson	4.00
147	Earl Averill	4.00
148	Bucky Harris	4.00
149	Billy Herman	6.00
150	Judy Johnson	8.00
---	Fifth Series Checklist	4.00
	Sixth Series, 1981	
151	Ralph Kiner	7.00
152	Oscar Charleston	4.00
153	Roger Connor	4.00
154	Cal Hubbard	4.00
155	Bob Lemon	6.00
156	Freddie Lindstrom	4.00
157	Robin Roberts	6.00
158	Ernie Banks	9.00
159	Martin DiHigo	4.00
160	John Lloyd	4.00
161	Al Lopez	4.00
162	Amos Rusie	4.00
163	Joe Sewell	8.00
164	Addie Joss	4.00
165	Larry MacPhail	4.00
166	Eddie Mathews	6.00
167	Warren Giles	4.00
168	Willie Mays	30.00
169	Hack Wilson	7.00
170	Al Kaline	9.00
171	Chuck Klein	4.00
172	Duke Snider	10.00
173	Tom Yawkey	4.00
174	Rube Foster	4.00
175	Bob Gibson	6.00
176	Johnny Mize	8.00

A Abner Doubleday 4.00
B Stephen Clark 4.00
C Paul Kerr 4.00
D Edward W. Stack 4.00
--- Sixth Series Checklist 4.00
Seventh Series, 1983
177 Hank Aaron 20.00
178 Happy Chandler 4.00
179 Travis Jackson 4.00
180 Frank Robinson 8.00
181 Walter Alston 9.00
182 George Kell 6.00
183 Juan Marichal 6.00
184 Brooks Robinson 9.00
185 Luis Aparicio 6.00
Eighth Series, 1985
186 Don Drysdale 6.00
187 Rick Ferrell 4.00
188 Harmon Killebrew 10.00
189 Pee Wee Reese 10.00
190 Lou Brock 6.00
191 Enos Slaughter 6.00
192 Arky Vaughn 4.00
193 Hoyt Wilhelm 5.00
Ninth Series, 1987
194 Bobby Doerr 6.00
195 Ernie Lombardi 4.00
196 Willie McCovey 6.00
197 Ray Dandridge 4.00
198 Catfish Hunter 4.00
199 Billy Williams 5.00
E Frank Steele, Peggy Steele, Dick Perez 4.00
Tenth Series, 1989
200 Willie Stargell 6.00
201 Al Barlick 4.00
202 Johnny Bench 7.00
203 Red Schoendienst 5.00
204 Carl Yastrzemski 9.00
F George Bush, Edward Stack 10.00
Eleventh Series, 1981
205 Joe Morgan 5.00
206 Jim Palmer 5.00
207 Rod Carew 5.00
208 Ferguson Jenkins 5.00
209 Tony Lazzeri 4.00
210 Gaylord Perry 5.00
211 Bill Veeck 4.00
212 Rollie Fingers 5.00
213 Bill McGowan 4.00
214 Hal Newhouser 6.00
215 Tom Seaver 6.00
216 Reggie Jackson 6.00
217 Steve Carlton 5.00
218 Leo Durocher 4.00
219 Phil Rizzuto 6.00
220 Vic Willis 4.00
221 William Hulbert 4.00
222 Bill Foster 4.00
223 Ned Hanlon 4.00
224 Mike Schmidt 10.00
225 Richie Ashburn 6.00
226 Earl Weaver 6.00
227 Jim Bunning 6.00
228 Leon Day 4.00

1980-98 Perez-Steele Hall of Fame Postcards - Autographed

Because the cards are so popular with autograph collectors, a listing of Perez-Steele Hall of Fame postcards which are possible to acquire in authentically autographed form is provided here, along with current retail values. Only those players who were alive at the time of their cards' issue are included in this listings; no cards from Series 1 and very few from Series 2 are available in autographed form.

MT
Common Player: 10.00
Second Series, 1980
53 Carl Hubbell 75.00
57 Charlie Gehringer 65.00
Third Series, 1980
71 Bill Dickey 85.00
73 Bill Terry 70.00
75 Joe DiMaggio 300.00
77 Ted Lyons 145.00
80 Joe Cronin 750.00
81 Hank Greenberg 250.00
87 Bob Feller 21.00
90 Edd Roush 75.00
Fourth Series, 1981
95 Luke Appling 40.00
97 Burleigh Grimes 200.00
104 Ted Williams 195.00
106 Red Ruffing 450.00
107 Lloyd Waner 2500.
111 Roy Campanella 185.00
112 Stan Coveleski 300.00
113 Waite Hoyt 495.00
114 Stan Musial 65.00
115 Lou Boudreau 20.00
Fifth Series, 1981
125 Satchel Paige 2500.
127 Yogi Berra 27.50
129 Lefty Gomez 70.00
131 Sandy Koufax 65.00
132a Buck Leonard (pre-stroke) 50.00
132b Buck Leonard (post-stroke) 25.00
133 Early Wynn 35.00
137 Monte Irvin 20.00
138 George Kelly 350.00
139 Warren Spahn 19.00
141 Cool Papa Bell 75.00
143 Jocko Conlan 55.00
144 Whitey Ford 30.00
145 Mickey Mantle 300.00
147 Earl Averill 525.00
149 Billy Herman 30.00
150 Judy Johnson 75.00
Sixth Series, 1981
151 Ralph Kiner 20.00
155 Bob Lemon 20.00
157 Robin Roberts 20.00
158 Ernie Banks 30.00
161 Al Lopez 70.00
163 Joe Sewell 50.00
166 Eddie Mathews 20.00
168 Willie Mays 60.00
170 Al Kaline 22.00
172 Duke Snider 25.00
175 Bob Gibson 20.00
176 Johnny Mize 30.00
D Edward W. Stack 12.50
Seventh Series, 1983
177 Hank Aaron 40.00
178 Happy Chandler 45.00
179 Travis Jackson 75.00
180 Frank Robinson 20.00
181 Walter Alston 700.00
182 George Kell 15.00
183 Juan Marichal 15.00
184 Brooks Robinson 20.00
185 Luis Aparicio 20.00
Eighth Series, 1985
186 Don Drysdale 50.00
187 Rick Ferrell 20.00
188 Harmon Killebrew 22.00
189 Pee Wee Reese 35.00
190 Lou Brock 20.00
191 Enos Slaughter 20.00
193 Hoyt Wilhelm 15.00
Ninth Series, 1987
194 Bobby Doerr 15.00
196 Willie McCovey 15.00
197 Ray Dandridge 25.00
198 Catfish Hunter 30.00
199 Billy Williams 15.00
E Frank Steele, Peggy Steele, Dick Perez 10.00
Tenth Series, 1989
200 Willie Stargell 12.50
201 Al Barlick 17.50
202 Johnny Bench 25.00
203 Red Schoendienst 15.00
204 Carl Yastrzemski 20.00
F George Bush, Edward Stack 60.00
Eleventh Series, 1981
205 Joe Morgan 24.00
206 Jim Palmer 20.00
207 Rod Carew 25.00
208 Ferguson Jenkins 15.00
210 Gaylord Perry 16.00
212 Rollie Fingers 25.00
214 Hal Newhouser 25.00
215 Tom Seaver 40.00
216 Reggie Jackson 55.00
217 Steve Carlton 35.00
219 Phil Rizzuto 25.00
224 Mike Schmidt 45.00
225 Richie Ashburn 30.00
226 Earl Weaver 25.00
227 Jim Bunning 30.00

1985-95 Perez-Steele Great Moments Postcards

Yet another collectors issue devoted solely to Hall of Fame players, the Great Moments series borrows the form and format of the 1911 Turkey Red cabinet cards. The 5-3/4" x 8" cards are printed on textured cardboard (which was noticeably downgraded beginning with the 1993 series). Fronts have Dick Perez player paintings surrounded by a greenish-brown border; backs are in black-and-white. Each card carries a series checklist on back and an individual set serial number from within an edition of 5,000. Cards are issued in series of 12.

MT
Complete Set (108): 550.00
Common Player: 6.00
First Series, 1985 6.00
1 Babe Ruth 30.00
2 Al Kaline 12.00
3 Jackie Robinson 15.00
4 Lou Gehrig 25.00
5 Whitey Ford 12.00
6 Christy Mathewson 10.00
7 Roy Campanella 15.00
8 Walter Johnson 12.00
9 Hank Aaron 20.00
10 Cy Young 10.00
11 Stan Musial 25.00
12 Ty Cobb 25.00
Second Series, 1987 6.00
13 Ted Williams 65.00
14 Warren Spahn 4.00
15 Lloyd Waner, Paul Waner 4.00
16 Sandy Koufax 17.50
17 Robin Roberts 4.00
18 Dizzy Dean 9.00
19 Mickey Mantle 65.00
20 Satchel Paige 24.00
21 Ernie Banks 12.50
22 Willie McCovey 4.00
23 Johnny Mize 4.00
24 Honus Wagner 12.00
Third Series, 1988 6.00
25 Willie Keeler 4.00
26 Pee Wee Reese 10.00
27 Monte Irvin 4.00
28 Eddie Mathews 4.00
29 Enos Slaughter 4.00
30 Rube Marquard 4.00
31 Charlie Gehringer 5.00
32 Roberto Clemente 20.00
33 Duke Snider 10.00
34 Ray Dandridge 4.00
35 Carl Hubbell 4.00
36 Bobby Doerr 4.00
Fourth Series, 1988 6.00
37 Bill Dickey 4.00
38 Willie Stargell 4.00
39 Brooks Robinson 7.50
40 Joe Tinker, Johnny Evers, Frank Chance 10.00
41 Billy Herman 4.00
42 Grover Alexander 8.00
43 Luis Aparicio 4.00
44 Lefty Gomez 4.00
45 Eddie Collins 4.00
46 Judy Johnson 4.00
47 Harry Heilmann 4.00
48 Harmon Killebrew 6.00
Fifth Series, 1990 6.00
49 Johnny Bench 9.00
50 Max Carey 4.00
51 Cool Papa Bell 4.00
52 Rube Waddell 4.00
53 Yogi Berra 10.00
54 Herb Pennock 4.00
55 Red Schoendienst 4.00
56 Juan Marichal 4.00
57 Frankie Frisch 4.00
58 Buck Leonard 4.00
59 George Kell 4.00
60 Chuck Klein 4.00
Sixth Series, 1990 6.00
61 King Kelly 4.00
62 Jim Hunter 4.00
63 Lou Boudreau 4.00
64 Al Lopez 4.00
65 Willie Mays 15.00
66 Lou Brock 5.00
67 Bob Lemon 4.00
68 Joe Sewell 4.00
69 Billy Williams 4.00
70 Rick Ferrell 4.00
71 Arky Vaughn 4.00
72 Carl Yastrzemski 9.00
Seventh Series, 1991 6.00
73 Tom Seaver 10.00
74 Rollie Fingers 4.00
75 Ralph Kiner 4.00
76 Frank Baker 4.00
77 Rod Carew 7.50
78 Goose Goslin 4.00
79 Gaylord Perry 4.00
80 Hack Wilson 4.00
81 Hal Newhouser 4.00
82 Early Wynn 4.00
83 Bob Feller 8.00
84 Branch Rickey (w/ Jackie Robinson) 4.00
Eighth Series, 1992 6.00
85 Jim Palmer 4.00
86 Al Barlick 4.00
87 Willie Mays, Mickey Mantle, Duke Snider 20.00
88 Hank Greenberg 12.00
89 Joe Morgan 4.00
90 Chief Bender 4.00
91 Pee Wee Reese, Jackie Robinson 10.00
92 Jim Bottomley 4.00
93 Ferguson Jenkins 4.00
94 Frank Robinson 8.00
95 Hoyt Wilhelm 4.00
96 Cap Anson 4.00
97 Jim Bunning 8.00
98 Richie Ashburn 8.00
99 Steve Carlton 8.00
100 Mike Schmidt 12.00
101 Nellie Fox 8.00
102 Tommy Lasorda 8.00
103 Leo Durocher 8.00
104 Reggie Jackson 10.00
105 Phil Rizzuto 10.00
106 Phil Niekro 8.00
107 Willie Wells 8.00
108 Earl Weaver 8.00

1985-95 Perez-Steele Great Moments Postcards - Autographed

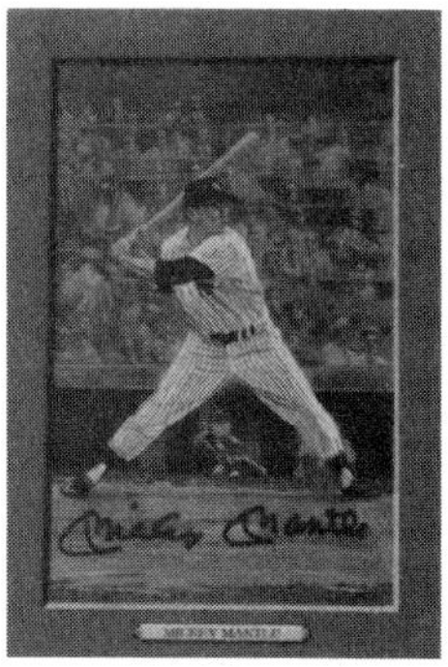

Because the Perez-Steele postcards are so popular with autograph collectors, separate listings for authentically autographed examples of the cards are provided here. Those cards not listed cannot possibly have been signed because the player was deceased prior to issue.

MT
Common Player: 10.00
First Series, 1985
2 Al Kaline 24.00
5 Whitey Ford 25.00
7 Roy Campanella 250.00
9 Hank Aaron 30.00
11 Stan Musial 70.00
Second Series, 1987
13 Ted Williams 125.00
14 Warren Spahn 15.00
16 Sandy Koufax 50.00
17 Robin Roberts 15.00
19 Mickey Mantle 200.00
21 Ernie Banks 25.00
22 Willie McCovey 15.00
23 Johnny Mize 18.00
Third Series, 1988
26 Pee Wee Reese 35.00
27 Monte Irvin 15.00
28 Eddie Mathews 22.00
29 Enos Slaughter 22.00
31 Charlie Gehringer 40.00
33 Duke Snider 27.50
34 Ray Dandridge 30.00
35 Carl Hubbell 45.00
36 Bobby Doerr 12.50
Fourth Series, 1988
37 Bill Dickey 45.00
38 Willie Stargell 16.00
39 Brooks Robinson 20.00
41 Billy Herman 17.50
43 Luis Aparicio 22.00
44 Lefty Gomez 40.00
48 Harmon Killebrew 22.00
Fifth Series, 1990
49 Johnny Bench 20.00
51 Cool Papa Bell 95.00
53 Yogi Berra 20.00
55 Red Schoendienst 10.00
56 Juan Marichal 12.00
58 Buck Leonard 18.00
59 George Kell 12.50
Sixth Series, 1990
62 Jim Hunter 12.00
63 Lou Boudreau 17.50
64 Al Lopez 55.00
65 Willie Mays 45.00
66 Lou Brock 15.00
67 Bob Lemon 15.00
68 Joe Sewell 50.00
69 Billy Williams 15.00
70 Rick Ferrell 15.00
72 Carl Yastrzemski 18.00
Seventh Series, 1991
73 Tom Seaver 35.00
74 Rollie Fingers 17.50
75 Ralph Kiner 17.50
77 Rod Carew 20.00
79 Gaylord Perry 15.00
81 Hal Newhouser 20.00
82 Early Wynn 15.00
83 Bob Feller 20.00
Eighth Series, 1992
85 Jim Palmer 20.00
86 Al Barlick 15.00
87 Willie Mays, Mickey Mantle, Duke Snider 325.00
89 Joe Morgan 15.00
93 Ferguson Jenkins 15.00
94 Frank Robinson 25.00
95 Hoyt Wilhelm 12.50
97 Jim Bunning 15.00
98 Richie Ashburn 15.00
99 Steve Carlton 15.00
100 Mike Schmidt 18.00
102 Tommy Lasorda 15.00
104 Reggie Jackson 20.00
105 Phil Rizzuto 20.00
106 Phil Niekro 15.00
108 Earl Weaver 15.00

1989 Perez-Steele Celebration Postcards

The Celebrations postcard issue from Perez-Steele was an attempt to offer collectors an original medium on which to obtain autographs of Hall of Famers. All 44 of the players included in the issue were alive when the set was conceived and most were still around when it was actually issued. The 3-1/2" x 5-1/2" cards have color portrait and action paintings by Dick Perez on front, which features a linen texture. Backs have postcard indicia, Perez-Steele and Hall of Fame logos, card number and individual serial number from within the edition limit of 10,000. Cards were originally sold only as complete sets.

MT
Complete Set (45): 200.00
Common Player: 5.00
1 Hank Aaron 20.00
2 Luis Aparicio 5.00
3 Ernie Banks 12.00
4 Cool Papa Bell 5.00
5 Johnny Bench 5.00
6 Yogi Berra 12.00
7 Lou Boudreau 5.00

8	Roy Campanella	15.00
9	Happy Chandler	5.00
10	Jocko Conlan	5.00
11	Ray Dandridge	5.00
12	Bill Dickey	9.00
13	Bobby Doerr	5.00
14	Rick Ferrell	5.00
15	Charlie Gehringer	9.00
16	Lefty Gomez	9.00
17	Billy Herman	5.00
18	Catfish Hunter	5.00
19	Monte Irvin	5.00
20	Judy Johnson	5.00
21	Al Kaline	12.00
22	George Kell	5.00
23	Harmon Killebrew	5.00
24	Ralph Kiner	5.00
25	Bob Lemon	5.00
26	Buck Leonard	5.00
27	Al Lopez	5.00
28	Mickey Mantle	35.00
29	Juan Marichal	5.00
30	Eddie Mathews	5.00
31	Willie McCovey	5.00
32	Johnny Mize	5.00
33	Stan Musial	15.00
34	Pee Wee Reese	12.00
35	Brooks Robinson	5.00
36	Joe Sewell	5.00
37	Enos Slaughter	5.00
38	Duke Snider	12.00
39	Warren Spahn	5.00
40	Willie Stargell	5.00
41	Bill Terry	5.00
42	Billy Williams	5.00
43	Ted Williams	17.50
44	Carl Yastrzemski	5.00
---	Checklist	2.00

1989 Perez-Steele Celebration Postcards - Autographed

Because of their popularity as an autograph vehicle, values for authentically signed examples of the Perez-Steele Celebrations postcards are presented here. Cards of Lefty Gomez (#16), Judy Johnson (#20) and Bill Terry (#41) cannot exist with genuine autographs because those players were deceased by the time the cards were issued.

		MT
Complete Set (41):		1100.
Common Player:		10.00
1	Hank Aaron	24.00
2	Luis Aparicio	15.00
3	Ernie Banks	22.00
4	Cool Papa Bell	50.00
5	Johnny Bench	20.00
6	Yogi Berra	17.50
7	Lou Boudreau	10.00
8	Roy Campanella	225.00
9	Happy Chandler	17.50
10	Jocko Conlan	300.00
11	Ray Dandridge	20.00
12	Bill Dickey	50.00
13	Bobby Doerr	10.00
14	Rick Ferrell	15.00
15	Charlie Gehringer	30.00
17	Billy Herman	15.00
18	Catfish Hunter	12.00
19	Monte Irvin	15.00
21	Al Kaline	15.00
22	George Kell	10.00
23	Harmon Killebrew	15.00
24	Ralph Kiner	15.00
25	Bob Lemon	12.00
26	Buck Leonard	20.00
27	Al Lopez	45.00
28	Mickey Mantle	200.00
29	Juan Marichal	10.00
30	Eddie Mathews	15.00
31	Willie McCovey	15.00
32	Johnny Mize	15.00
33	Stan Musial	35.00
34	Pee Wee Reese	22.00
35	Brooks Robinson	12.50
36	Joe Sewell	27.50
37	Enos Slaughter	10.00
38	Duke Snider	20.00
39	Warren Spahn	15.00
40	Willie Stargell	10.00
42	Billy Williams	10.00
43	Ted Williams	100.00
44	Carl Yastrzemski	15.00

1990-92 Perez-Steele Master Works Postcards

A blending of the designs of classic early baseball cards with the artwork of one of today's most recognized baseball artists produced the Perez-Steele Master Works postcard series. Each of the players in the collection (living players selected for inclusion on the basis of autograph possibilities) is shown on five different cards, one of original design and four adapting the formats of the 1909 Ramly (T204), 1911 "Gold Borders" (T205) and 1908 Rose Co. postcards (PC760) and 1888 Goodwin Champions (N162). The Ramly and Rose takeoffs feature gold-foil embossing. Postcard backs are printed in brown (#1-25) or dark green (#26-50). Information on back includes a description of the card set on which the design is based, card and series number and the individual set serial number from within the edition of 10,000. Series 1 (#1-25) was issued in 1990; Series 2 (#26-50) in 1992. Each was available only as a complete boxed set.

		MT
Complete Set (52):		225.00
Common Player:		3.00
1	Charlie Gehringer (Ramly)	3.00
2	Charlie Gehringer (Goodwin)	3.00
3	Charlie Gehringer (Rose)	3.00
4	Charlie Gehringer (Gold Border)	3.00
5	Charlie Gehringer (Perez-Steele)	3.00
6	Mickey Mantle (Ramly)	20.00
7	Mickey Mantle (Goodwin)	20.00
8	Mickey Mantle (Rose)	20.00
9	Mickey Mantle (Gold Border)	20.00
10	Mickey Mantle (Perez-Steele)	20.00
11	Willie Mays (Ramly)	9.00
12	Willie Mays (Goodwin)	9.00
13	Willie Mays (Rose)	9.00
14	Willie Mays (Gold Border)	9.00
15	Willie Mays (Perez-Steele)	9.00
16	Duke Snider (Ramly)	6.00
17	Duke Snider (Goodwin)	6.00
18	Duke Snider (Rose)	6.00
19	Duke Snider (Gold Border)	6.00
20	Duke Snider (Perez-Steele)	6.00
21	Warren Spahn (Ramly)	3.00
22	Warren Spahn (Goodwin)	3.00
23	Warren Spahn (Rose)	3.00
24	Warren Spahn (Gold Border)	3.00
25	Warren Spahn (Perez-Steele)	3.00
---	Checklist 1-25	1.00
26	Yogi Berra (Ramly)	5.00
27	Yogi Berra (Goodwin)	5.00
28	Yogi Berra (Rose)	5.00
29	Yogi Berra (Gold Border)	5.00
30	Yogi Berra (Perez-Steele)	5.00
31	Johnny Mize (Ramly)	3.00
32	Johnny Mize (Goodwin)	3.00
33	Johnny Mize (Rose)	3.00
34	Johnny Mize (Gold Border)	3.00
35	Johnny Mize (Perez-Steele)	3.00
36	Willie Stargell (Ramly)	3.00
37	Willie Stargell (Goodwin)	3.00
38	Willie Stargell (Rose)	3.00
39	Willie Stargell (Gold Border)	3.00
40	Willie Stargell (Perez-Steele)	3.00
41	Ted Williams (Ramly)	12.00
42	Ted Williams (Goodwin)	12.00
43	Ted Williams (Rose)	12.00
44	Ted Williams (Gold Border)	12.00
45	Ted Williams (Perez-Steele)	12.00
46	Carl Yastrzemski (Ramly)	4.00
47	Carl Yastrzemski (Goodwin)	4.00
48	Carl Yastrzemski (Rose)	4.00
49	Carl Yastrzemski (Gold Border)	4.00
50	Carl Yastrzemski (Perez-Steele)	4.00
---	Checklist 26-50	1.00

1985 Performance Printing Texas Rangers

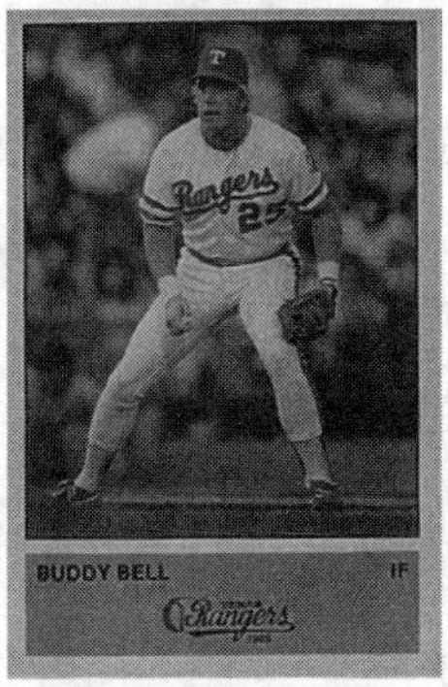

A local printing company sponsored this 28-card set of the Texas Rangers. The 2-3/8" x 3-1/2" cards are in full color and are numbered on the back by uniform number. Card fronts feature full-color, game-action photos. The 25 players on the Rangers' active roster at press time are included, along with manager Bobby Valentine and unnumbered coaches and trainer cards. The black and white card backs have a smaller portrait photo of each player, as well as biographical information and career statistics.

		MT
Complete Set (28):		6.00
Common Player:		.25
0	Oddibe McDowell	.25
1	Bill Stein	.25
2	Bobby Valentine	.25
3	Wayne Tolleson	.25
4	Don Slaught	.35
5	Alan Bannister	.25
6	Bobby Jones	.25
7	Glenn Brummer	.25
8	Luis Pujols	.25
9	Pete O'Brien	.25
11	Toby Harrah	.25
13	Tommy Dunbar	.25
15	Larry Parrish	.25
16	Mike Mason	.25
19	Curtis Wilkerson	.25
24	Dave Schmidt	.25
25	Buddy Bell	.35
27	Greg Harris	.25
30	Dave Rozema	.25
32	Gary Ward	.25
36	Dickie Noles	.25
41	Chris Welsh	.25
44	Cliff Johnson	.25
46	Burt Hooton	.25
48	Dave Stewart	.50
49	Charlie Hough	.30
----	Trainers (Danny Wheat, Bill Ziegler)	.25
----	Rangers Coaches (Rich Donnelly, Glenn Ezell, Tom House, Art Howe, Wayne Terwilliger)	.25

1986 Performance Printing Texas Rangers

For the second time, the Texas Rangers issued a full-color card set in conjunction with this local printing company. Fronts of the 28-card set include player name, position and team logo beneath the color photo. Backs of the 2-3/8" x 3-1/2" cards are in black and white, with a small portrait photo of each player along with personal and professional statistics. Cards were distributed at the August 23 Rangers home game, and the set includes all of the Rangers' fine rookies such as Bobby Witt, Pete Incaviglia, Edwin Correa and Ruben Sierra.

		MT
Complete Set (28):		6.00
Common Player:		.25
0	Oddibe McDowell	.25
1	Scott Fletcher	.35
2	Bobby Valentine	.25
3	Ruben Sierra	.45
4	Don Slaught	.35
9	Pete O'Brien	.25
11	Toby Harrah	.25
12	Geno Petralli	.25
15	Larry Parrish	.25
16	Mike Mason	.25
17	Darrell Porter	.25
18	Edwin Correa	.25
19	Curtis Wilkerson	.25
22	Steve Buechele	.25
23	Jose Guzman	.25
24	Ricky Wright	.25
27	Greg Harris	.25
28	Mitch Williams	.30
29	Pete Incaviglia	.50
32	Gary Ward	.25
34	Dale Mohorcic	.25
40	Jeff Russell	.25
44	Tom Paciorek	.25
46	Mike Loynd	.25
48	Bobby Witt	.50
49	Charlie Hough	.25
----	Coaching Staff (Joe Ferguson, Tim Foli, Tom House, Art Howe, Tom Robson)	.25
----	Trainers (Danny Wheat, Bill Zeigler)	.25

1989 Performance Printing Texas Rangers

The photographs taken by Barry Colla for the 1989 Mother's Cookies team set did double-duty, being featured on a stadium giveaway poster sponsored by a Dallas printer. The 17" x 24" poster is printed on heavy semi-gloss paper. Both fronts and backs are printed in a style similar to Mother's format, but with the sponsor's logo instead of the bakery's. Backs are printed in blue and red.

	MT
Complete Set, Sheet: (See 1989 Mother's Cookies for checklist)	30.00

1981 Perma-Graphics All-Star Credit Cards

Using the same "credit card" style of its previous 1981 issue, Perma-Graphics issued an 18-card set in the fall of 1981 featuring the starting players from the 1981 All-Star Game. The front of the card contains a full-color photo, plus the player's name, position and team. The back includes personal data, career records, highlights and an "autograph panel."

		MT
Complete Set (18):		60.00
Common Player:		2.00
1	Gary Carter	2.50
2	Dave Concepcion	2.00
3	Andre Dawson	2.50
4	George Foster	2.00
5	Davey Lopes	2.00
6	Dave Parker	2.00
7	Pete Rose	12.50
8	Mike Schmidt	8.00
9	Fernando Valenzuela	2.50
10	George Brett	8.00
11a	Rod Carew (outfield)	5.00
12	Bucky Dent	2.00
13	Carlton Fisk	4.00
14	Reggie Jackson	5.00
15	Jack Morris	2.00
16	Willie Randolph	2.00
17	Ken Singleton	2.00
18	Dave Winfield	4.00

1981 Perma-Graphics Super Star Credit Cards

Issued in 1981 by Perma-Graphics of Maryland Heights, Mo., this innovative 32-card set was printed on high-impact, permanently laminated vinyl to give the appearance of a real credit card. The front of the wallet-sized cards includes career statistics and highlights, along with an "autograph panel" for obtaining the player's signature.

		MT
Complete Set (32):		95.00
Common Player:		2.00
1	Johnny Bench	7.50
2	Mike Schmidt	8.00
3	George Brett	8.00
4	Carl Yastrzemski	6.00
5	Pete Rose	12.50
6	Bob Horner	2.00
7	Reggie Jackson	5.00
8	Keith Hernandez	2.00
9	George Foster	2.00
10	Garry Templeton	2.00
11	Tom Seaver	5.00
12	Steve Garvey	3.00
13	Dave Parker	2.00
14	Willie Stargell	4.00
15	Cecil Cooper	2.00
16	Steve Carlton	4.00
17	Ted Simmons	2.00
18	Dave Kingman	2.50
19	Rickey Henderson	4.00
20	Fred Lynn	2.00
21	Dave Winfield	5.00
22a	Rod Carew (uniform #20 on back)	5.00
22b	Rod Carew (uniform #29 on back)	5.00
23	Jim Rice	2.50
24	Bruce Sutter	2.00
25	Cesar Cedeno	2.00
26	Nolan Ryan	16.00
27	Dusty Baker	2.00
28	Jim Palmer	4.00
29	Gorman Thomas	2.00
30	Ben Oglivie	2.00
31	Willie Wilson	2.00
32	Gary Carter	2.50

1982 Perma-Graphics All-Star Credit Cards

Perma-Graphics issued its second "All-Star Credit Card" set in the fall of 1982. Consisting of 18 cards, the set pictured the starters from both leagues in the 1982 All-Star Game. It was also available in a limited-edition "gold" version, which is generally two to three times the value of the regular edition.

		MT
Complete Set (18):		55.00
Common Player:		2.00
1	Dennis Eckersley	2.00
2	Cecil Cooper	2.00
3	Carlton Fisk	4.00
4	Robin Yount	6.50
5	Bobby Grich	2.00
6	Rickey Henderson	4.00
7	Reggie Jackson	5.00
8	Fred Lynn	2.00
9	George Brett	7.50
10	Gary Carter	2.50
11	Dave Concepcion	2.00
12	Andre Dawson	2.50
13	Tim Raines	2.00
14	Dale Murphy	2.50
15	Steve Rogers	2.00
16	Pete Rose	10.00
17	Mike Schmidt	7.50
18	Manny Trillo	2.00

1982 Perma-Graphics Super Star Credit Cards

Perma-Graphics reduced its "Superstar Credit Card Set" to 24 players in 1982, maintaining the same basic credit card appearance. The player photos on the front of the cards are surrounded by a wood-tone border and the backs include the usual personal data, career statistics, highlights and autograph panel. The set was also issued in a limited-edition "gold" version. The special "gold" cards are generally worth two to three times the value of a regular-edition card.

		MT
Complete Set (24):		70.00
Common Player:		2.00
1	Johnny Bench	5.00
2	Tom Seaver	4.00
3	Mike Schmidt	6.00
4	Gary Carter	2.50
5	Willie Stargell	3.00
6	Tim Raines	2.00
7	Bill Madlock	2.00
8	Keith Hernandez	2.00
9	Pete Rose	9.00
10	Steve Carlton	3.00
11	Steve Garvey	2.50
12	Fernando Valenzuela	2.00
13	Carl Yastrzemski	4.00
14	Dave Winfield	3.00
15	Carney Lansford	2.00
16	Rollie Fingers	3.00
17	Tony Armas	2.00
18	Cecil Cooper	2.00
19	George Brett	6.00
20	Reggie Jackson	3.00
21	Rod Carew	3.00
22	Eddie Murray	3.00
23	Rickey Henderson	3.00
24	Kirk Gibson	2.00

1983 Perma-Graphics All-Star Credit Cards

The final issue from Perma-Graphics, this 18-card set was produced in the fall of 1983 and features the 18 starting players from the 1983 All-Star Game. Similar to other Perma-Graphics sets, the cards were printed on wallet-size vinyl to give the appearance of a real credit card. The set was also available in a limited-edition "gold" version, which carries a value two to three times a regular set or card.

		MT
Complete Set (18):		40.00
Common Player:		2.00
1	George Brett	4.00
2	Rod Carew	2.50
3	Fred Lynn	2.00
4	Jim Rice	2.00
5	Ted Simmons	2.00
6	Dave Stieb	2.00
7	Manny Trillo	2.00
8	Dave Winfield	3.00
9	Robin Yount	3.00
10	Gary Carter	2.50
11	Andre Dawson	2.50
12	Dale Murphy	2.50
13	Al Oliver	2.00
14	Tim Raines	2.00
15	Steve Sax	2.00
16	Mike Schmidt	4.00
17	Ozzie Smith	3.00
18	Mario Soto	2.00

1983 Perma-Graphics Super Star Credit Cards

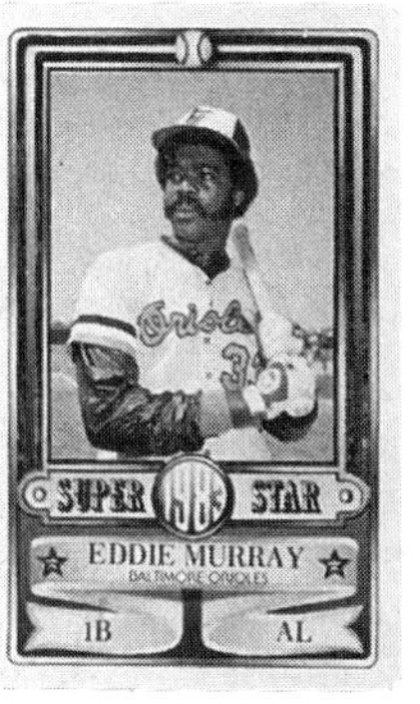

Similar in design to its previous sets, Perma-Graphics increased the number of cards in its 1983 "Superstar" set to 36, including 18 players from each league. The front of the vinyl card has a full-color photo with the player's name, team, league and position below. The backs contain career records, highlights and autograph panel. The cards were also issued in a special "gold" edition, which are valued at two to three times a regular edition card.

		MT
Complete Set (36):		95.00
Common Player:		2.00
1	Bill Buckner	2.00
2	Steve Carlton	5.00
3	Gary Carter	2.50
4	Andre Dawson	2.50
5	Pedro Guerrero	2.00
6	George Hendrick	2.00
7	Keith Hernandez	2.00
8	Bill Madlock	2.00
9	Dale Murphy	2.50
10	Al Oliver	2.00
11	Dave Parker	2.00
12	Darrell Porter	2.00
13	Pete Rose	9.00
14	Mike Schmidt	7.50
15	Lonnie Smith	2.00
16	Ozzie Smith	5.00
17	Bruce Sutter	2.00
18	Fernando Valenzuela	2.00
19	George Brett	8.00
20	Rod Carew	4.00
21	Cecil Cooper	2.00
22	Doug DeCinces	2.00
23	Rollie Fingers	3.00
24	Damaso Garcia	2.00
25	Toby Harrah	2.00
26	Rickey Henderson	4.00
27	Reggie Jackson	4.00
28	Hal McRae	2.00
29	Eddie Murray	4.00
30	Lance Parrish	2.00
31	Jim Rice	2.00
32	Gorman Thomas	2.00
33	Willie Wilson	2.00
34	Dave Winfield	4.50
35	Carl Yastrzemski	6.00
36	Robin Yount	7.00

1983 Gaylord Perry Career Highlights

Although their name does not appear anywhere on the six cards in this set, Topps was the manufacturer of this career highlights issue which was distributed by Perry's own memorabilia company. In standard 2-1/2" x 3-1/2" format, card fronts feature a color photo with various colored borders and name plates. The year of the career highlight printed on back is presented in the lower-right. Backs have a card number in a peanut and a write-up of the career accomplishment, printed in brown and orange.

		MT
Complete Set (6):		9.00
Common Card:		1.50
1	Gaylord Perry (First win)	1.50
2	Gaylord Perry (No-hitter)	1.50
3	Gaylord Perry (Cy Young Award)	1.50
4	Gaylord Perry (2,500th K)	1.50
5	Gaylord Perry (Cy Young/3,000th K)	1.50
6	Gaylord Perry (300th win)	1.50

1991 Petro Canada All-Star FanFest Standups

1991 Petro-Canada Standups are vaguely reminiscent of the 1964 Topps Standups. The set was distributed at Fanfest in Toronto in conjunction with the All-Star Game. There are 26 players in the set, with the folded card measuring 2-7/8" x 3-7/8". Unfolded, the card shows a cutout figure of the player superimposed in front of a photo of stadium surroundings. The base which the player stands on has major league and All-Star Game statistics, with career highlights on the back and a player quiz.

		MT
Complete Set (26):		16.00
Common Player:		.25
1	Cal Ripken, Jr.	3.00
2	Greg Olson	.25
3	Roger Clemens	1.50
4	Ryne Sandberg	1.00
5	Dave Winfield	.50
6	Eric Davis	.25
7	Carlton Fisk	.75
8	Mike Scott	.25
9	Sandy Alomar, Jr.	.35
10	Tim Wallach	.25
11	Cecil Fielder	.25
12	Dwight Gooden	.35
13	George Brett	1.50
14	Dale Murphy	.45
15	Paul Molitor	.75
16	Barry Bonds	2.00
17	Kirby Puckett	1.00
18	Ozzie Smith	.75
19	Don Mattingly	1.20
20	Will Clark	.50
21	Rickey Henderson	.40
22	Orel Hershiser	.25
23	Ken Griffey, Jr.	4.00
24	Tony Gwynn	1.50
25	Nolan Ryan	3.00
26	Kelly Gruber	.25

1998 Philadelphia A's Historical Society

A major undertaking by the Philadelphia A's Historical Society was the creation of this collectors card set in conjunction with the group's fourth reunion in 1998. Card designs are strongly reminiscent of the classic Topps and Bowman cards of the early 1950s. Fronts have a painting of each player by Ron Joyner, noted sports artist. Backs have a cartoon, career stats with the A's and lifetime, biographical data and career highlights. Backs are printed in blue and black on white. A card of 1908-09 A's Joe Jackson has been printed in a limited edition of 500 numbered cards and is available only in those sets sold directly through the Society at its original $18.50 price. Seventy-five sets of the cards, which included a sample Joe Jackson card and a pair of large-format cards of Jimmie Foxx and Roger Cramer, were sold as uncut sheets.

		MT
Complete Set, w/Jackson (41):		24.00
Complete Set, no/Jackson (40):		18.50
Complete Set, uncut sheet:		60.00
Common Player:		.50
1	Connie Mack	.75
2	Sam Chapman	.50
3	Bobby Shantz	.60
4	Al Brancato	.50
5	Bob Dillinger	.50
6	Irv Hall	.50
7	Joe Hauser	.50
8	Taffy Wright	.50
9	Gus Zernial	.60
10	Ray Murray	.50
11	Skeeter Kell	.50
12	Morrie Martin	.50
13	Pete Suder	.50
14	Pinky Higgins	.50
15	Allie Clark	.50
16	Hank Wyse	.50
17	George Kell	.75
18	Hank Majeski	.50
19	Jimmie Foxx	1.00
20	Crash Davis	.50
21	Elmer Valo	.50
22	Ray Coleman	.50
23	Carl Scheib	.50
24	Billy Hitchcock	.50
25	Earle Brucker Jr.	.50
26	Dave Philley	.50
27	Joe DeMaestri	.50
28	Eddie Collins Jr.	.50
29	Eddie Joost	.50

30	Spook Jacobs	.50
31	Ferris Fain	.60
32	Eddie Robinson	.50
33	Vic Power	.60
34	Lou Brissie	.50
35	Bill Renna	.50
36	Nellie Fox	1.00
37	Lou Limmer	.50
38	Eddie Collins Sr.	1.00
39	Roger Cramer	.50
40	Joe Astroth	.50
---	Joe Jackson (# of 500)	8.00
---	Joe Jackson (sample overprint)	4.00
	FAN FAVORITES	
---	Roger Cramer (3-1/2" x 6")	2.00
---	Jimmie Foxx (3-1/2" x 8-1/2")	4.00

1985 Philadelphia Phillies Police

This is a brilliantly colored 2-5/8" x 4-1/8" set, co-sponsored by the Phillies and Cigna Corporation. Card fronts include the player name, number, position and team logo. The 16 cards are numbered on the back and include biographical information and a safety tip. The cards were distributed by several Philadelphia area police departments.

		MT
Complete Set (16):		6.00
Common Player:		.15
1	Juan Samuel	.25
2	Von Hayes	.20
3	Ozzie Virgil	.15
4	Mike Schmidt	2.50
5	Greg Gross	.15
6	Tim Corcoran	.15
7	Jerry Koosman	.20
8	Jeff Stone	.15
9	Glenn Wilson	.15
10	Steve Jeltz	.15
11	Garry Maddox	.15
12	Steve Carlton	1.25
13	John Denny	.15
14	Kevin Gross	.15
15	Shane Rawley	.15
16	Charlie Hudson	.15

1986 Philadelphia Phillies Fire Safety

For the second straight year, the Philadelphia Phillies issued a 16-card safety set. However, in 1986 the set was issued in conjunction with the Philadelphia Fire Department rather than the police. Cigna Corporation remained a sponsor. The cards, which measure 2-5/8" x 4-1/8" in size, feature full color photos. Along with other pertinent information, the card backs contain a short player biography and a "Tips From The Dugout" fire safety hint.

		MT
Complete Set (16):		6.00
Common Player:		.15
1	Juan Samuel	.20
2	Don Carman	.15
3	Von Hayes	.15
4	Kent Tekulve	.15
5	Greg Gross	.15
6	Shane Rawley	.15
7	Darren Daulton	.45
8	Kevin Gross	.15
9	Steve Jeltz	.15
10	Mike Schmidt	1.50
11	Steve Bedrosian	.15
12	Gary Redus	.15
13	Charles Hudson	.15
14	John Russell	.15
15	Fred Toliver	.15
16	Glenn Wilson	.15

1990 Philadelphia Phillies Photocards

Identical in format to the prior year's Tastykake issue, but bearing no sponsor's advertising, these borderless large-format (4-1/8" x 6") cards have the player's name in white on a red strip. Black, white and red backs have complete major and minor league stats, along with the Phillies logo, a few biographical details and information on the player's acquisition. Besides the current manager, players and coaches, the set included several stars of the past. The set is checklisted here alphabetically.

		MT
Complete Set (45):		12.50
Common Player:		.15
(1)	Darrel Ackerfelds	.15
(2)	Richie Ashburn	1.50
(3)	Rod Booker	.15
(4)	Sil Campusano	.15
(5)	Steve Carlton	1.50
(6)	Don Carman	.15
(7)	Pat Combs	.15
(8)	Dennis Cook	.15
(9)	Darren Daulton	.20
(10)	Lenny Dykstra	.30
(11)	Curt Ford	.15
(12)	Jason Grimsley	.15
(13)	Charlie Hayes	.20
(14)	Von Hayes	.15
(15)	Tommy Herr	.15
(16)	Dave Hollins	.45
(17)	Ken Howell	.15
(18)	Ron Jones	.15
(19)	Ricky Jordan	.15
(20)	John Kruk	.15
(21)	Steve Lake	.15
(22)	Nick Levya	.15
(23)	Carmelo Martinez	.15
(24)	Roger McDowell	.15
(25)	Chuck McElroy	.15
(26)	Terry Mulholland	.25
(27)	Jeff Parrett	.15
(28)	Randy Ready	.15
(29)	Robin Roberts	1.25
(30)	Bruce Ruffin	.15
(31)	Mike Schmidt	2.00
(32)	Dickie Thon	.15
(33)	Phillie Phanatic (mascot)	.15
(34)	Coaches (Larry Bowa, Darold Knowles, Hal Lanier, Denis Menke, Mike Ryan, John Vukovich)	.15
(35)	Broadcasters (Richie Ashburn, Harry Kalas, Andy Musser, Chris Wheeler)	.20
(36)	Broadcasters (Jim Barniak, Garry Maddox, Mike Schmidt)	.50
	UPDATE SET	
(37)	Joe Boever	.15
(38)	Jose DeJesus	.15
(39)	Marvin Freeman	.15
(40)	Tommy Greene	.45
(41)	Chuck Malone	.15
(42)	Brad Moore	.15
(43)	Dale Murphy	1.50
(44)	Dickie Noles	.15

1994 Philadelphia Phillies Photocards

For 1994 the team took over full sponsorship for its traditional large-format photocard issue. The 4" x 6" cards are in the same style as previous years, with a borderless color photo on front and the player's name in white on a red strip. Red and black backs feature the Phillies' 1993 N.L. Championship logo, biographical data and full major and minor league stats. The cards are numbered according to the player's uniform number at upper-left.

		MT
Complete Set (36):		8.00
Common Player:		.25
2	Larry Bowa	.25
4	Lenny Dykstra	.50
5	Kim Batiste	.25
6	Todd Pratt	.25
7	Mariano Duncan	.30
8	Jim Eisenreich	.25
9	Mike Ryan	.25
10	Darren Daulton	.30
11	Jim Fregosi	.25
12	Mickey Morandini	.40
14	Denis Menke	.25
15	Dave Hollins	.45
16	Tony Longmire	.30
17	Ricky Jordan	.25
18	John Vukovich	.25
19	Kevin Stocker	.30
22	Pete Incaviglia	.25
23	Doug Jones	.25
25	Milt Thompson	.25
26	Mel Roberts	.25
27	Danny Jackson	.25
28	Tyler Green	.45
29	John Kruk	.30
34	Ben Rivera	.25
35	Bobby Munoz	.30
37	Norm Charlton	.25
38	Curt Schilling	.50
40	David West	.25
41	Mike Williams	.25
43	Jeff Juden	.35
44	Wes Chamberlain	.25
46	Johnny Podres	.30
47	Larry Andersen	.25
48	Roger Mason	.25
49	Tommy Greene	.30
51	Heathcliff Slocumb	.25

1995 Philadelphia Phillies Photocards

Hall of Fame inductees Mike Schmidt and Richie Ashburn were honored by inclusion in the Phils' annual photocard issue for 1995. In its 13th edition, the cards measure 4" x 6" and feature borderless color photos on front. The player's name appears in white in a red stripe. Backs are printed in red and black and include a few biographical bits and complete career stats. Cards are numbered by uniform number. The Schmidt and Ashburn cards carry black facsimile autographs on front. Sets were sold by the team for $8.

		MT
Complete Set (36):		7.00
Common Player:		.25
1	Richie Ashburn	1.50
2	Larry Bowa	.25
4	Lenny Dykstra	.35
5	Gary Varsho	.25
7	Mariano Duncan	.25
8	Jim Eisenreich	.25
9	Mike Ryan	.25
10	Darren Daulton	.25
11	Jim Fregosi	.25
12	Mickey Morandini	.35
13	Charlie Hayes	.25
14	Denis Menke	.25
15	Dave Hollins	.35
16	Tony Longmire	.25
17	Dave Gallagher	.25
18	John Vukovich	.25
19	Kevin Stocker	.25
20	Mike Schmidt	3.00
23	Randy Ready	.25
25	Gregg Jefferies	.35
26	Mel Roberts	.25
27	Lenny Webster	.25
28	Tyler Green	.35
33	Gene Harris	.25
35	Bobby Munoz	.25
37	Norm Charlton	.25
38	Curt Schilling	.45
39	Kyle Abbott	.25
40	David West	.25
42	Toby Borland	.25
45	Michael Mimbs	.25
46	Johnny Podres	.25
48	Paul Quantrill	.25
51	Heathcliff Slocumb	.25
52	Ricky Bottalico	.25
---	Team photo	.50

1996 Philadelphia Phillies Photocards

An annual tradition for the Phillies continued in 1996 with the issue of a set of player/coach photocards. Once again in 4" x 6" format, the cards feature borderless color photos (generally game-action) on the front. The player's name is printed vertically in one of the corners in scruffy white lettering. Backs are printed in red and black and feature the 1996 All-Star Game logo, personal data and complete major and minor league stats. Complete sets of the cards were sold by the team for $9.

		MT
Complete Set (36):		8.00
Common Player:		.25
2	Larry Bowa	.25
3	John Vukovich	.25
4	Lenny Dykstra	.30
5	Mike Benjamin	.25
8	Jim Eisenreich	.25
9	Pete Incaviglia	.25
10	Darren Daulton	.25
11	Jim Fregosi	.25
12	Mickey Morandini	.25
14	Denis Menke	.25
18	Benito Santiago	.30
19	Kevin Stocker	.25
22	Mark Whiten	.25
23	Kevin Jordan	.25
24	Mike Lieberthal	.25
25	Gregg Jefferies	.45
26	Lee Tinsley	.25
27	Todd Zeile	.35
28	Tyler Green	.25
30	Dave Cash	.25
33	Russ Springer	.25
34	Howard Battle	.25
37	Steve Frey	.25
41	Mike Williams	.25
42	Toby Borland	.25
43	Dave Leiper	.25
44	Mike Grace	.25
45	Terry Mulholland	.35
46	Johnny Podres	.25
47	Michael Mimbs	.25
50	Sid Fernandez	.25
51	Ken Ryan	.25
52	Ricky Bottalico	.30
54	Carlos Crawford	.25
59	Joe Rigoli	.25
---	Phillie Phanatic (mascot)	.25

1997 Philadelphia Phillies Photocards

The initial release of player/staff photocards by the team in 1997 was a 36-card issue sold for $10. As in past years, it is likely some cards were withdrawn and other issued to reflect roster changes during the season. The 1997 series features posed or action photos on borderless 4" x 6" format. The player's name is in gray in a red stripe at top. In a lower corner of each card's front is a logo marking 1997 as the inaugural year of interleague play. Backs are printed in red and blue and feature personal data, full professional stats, team logo and photo credit. Cards are listed here according to uniform number, also found on back.

		MT
Complete Set (36):		10.00
Common Player:		.25
2	Rico Brogna	.25
3	Chuck Cottier	.25
7	Terry Francona	.25
8	Mark Parent	.25
9	Brad Mills	.25
10	Darren Daulton	.25
12	Mickey Morandini	.35

14 Rex Hudler .25
17 Scott Rolen 3.00
18 John Vukovich .25
19 Kevin Stocker .25
20 Mark Portugal .25
22 Ron Blazier .25
23 Kevin Jordan .25
24 Mike Lieberthal .25
25 Gregg Jefferies .50
29 Wendell Magee Jr. 1.50
31 Mark Leiter .25
31 Kevin Sefcik .25
33 Scott Ruffcorn .25
34 Derrick May .25
35 Bobby Munoz .25
37 Ruben Amaro .25
38 Curt Schilling .50
40 Reggie Harris .25
41 Erik Plantenberg .25
42 Galen Cisco .25
45 Danny Tartabull .25
47 Michael Mimbs .25
48 Jerry Spradlin .25
50 Calvin Maduro .25
51 Ken Ryan .25
52 Ricky Bottalico .40
56 Hal McRae .25
59 Joe Rigoli .25
--- Phillie Phanatic (mascot) .25

1989 Phoenix Holsum Super Stars Discs

(See 1989 Holsum for checklist and price guide. Distributed in Arizona.)

1989 Phoenix Magnetables

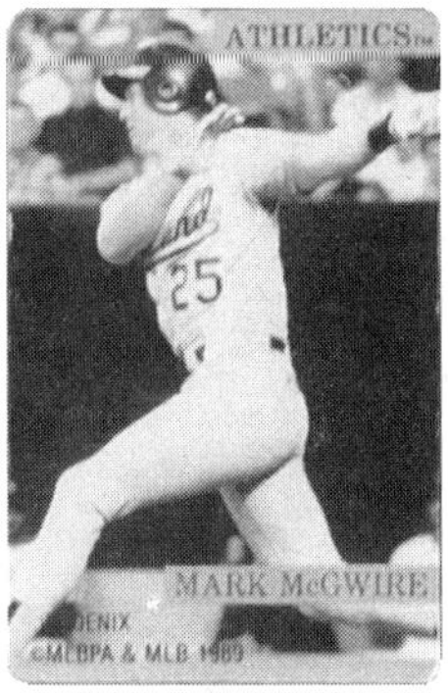

The first of what was intended to be a long line of sports-themed "magnetables" (magnetic collectables), this 156-piece set of baseball players never caught on and the line ended. Measuring 2" x 3" with rounded corners, these items feature color player photos attached to a magnetic backing. Fronts include the player and team name in orange strips, and in the lower-left corner the word "Phoenix" and a copyright line for Major League Baseball and the players' association. The unnumbered pieces are checklisted here alphabetically.

MT
Complete Set (156): 80.00
Common Player: .50
(1) Andy Allanson .50
(2) Roberto Alomar 1.00
(3) Sandy Alomar, Jr. .60
(4) Harold Baines .60
(5) Marty Barrett .50
(6) Kevin Bass .50
(7) Dave Bergman .50
(8) Mike Boddicker .50
(9) Wade Boggs 1.50
(10) Phil Bradley .50
(11) Mickey Brantley .50
(12) George Brett 3.00
(13) Tom Brookens .50
(14) Hubie Brooks .50
(15) Tom Browning .50
(16) Tom Brunansky .50
(17) Ellis Burks .50
(18) Randy Bush .50
(19) Brett Butler .50
(20) Jose Canseco 1.50
(21) Gary Carter .75
(22) Joe Carter .60
(23) Jack Clark .50
(24) Will Clark 1.00
(25) Roger Clemens 1.50
(26) Vince Coleman .50
(27) David Cone .60
(28) Kal Daniels .50
(29) Eric Davis .50
(30) Chili Davis .50
(31) Glenn Davis .50
(32) Jody Davis .50
(33) Andre Dawson .65
(34) Jose DeJesus .50
(35) Rick Dempsey .50
(36) Bob Dernier .50
(37) Brian Downing .50
(38) Cameron Drew .50
(39) Kevin Elster .50
(40) Dwight Evans .50
(41) Felix Fermin .50
(42) Tony Fernandez .50
(43) Carlton Fisk 1.25
(44) Tim Flannery .50
(45) Julio Franco .50
(46) Greg Gagne .50
(47) Andres Galarraga .65
(48) Dave Gallagher .50
(49) Ron Gant .50
(50) Jim Gantner .50
(51) Kirk Gibson .50
(52) Paul Gibson .50
(53) Dan Gladden .50
(54) Dwight Gooden .75
(55) Mark Grace .90
(56) Mike Greenwell .50
(57) Ken Griffey, Jr. 4.00
(58) Pedro Guerrero .50
(59) Ozzie Guillen .50
(60) Tony Gwynn 2.00
(61) Jeff Hamilton .50
(62) Lenny Harris .50
(63) Billy Hatcher .50
(64) Mickey Hatcher .50
(65) Dave Henderson .50
(66) Rickey Henderson 1.00
(67) Keith Hernandez .50
(68) Orel Hershiser .50
(69) Jack Howell .50
(70) Kent Hrbek .50
(71) Bo Jackson .75
(72) Brook Jacoby .50
(73) Chris James .50
(74) Dion James .50
(75) Gregg Jefferies .60
(76) Steve Jeltz .50
(77) Doug Jennings .50
(78) Tommy John .50
(79) Wally Joyner .60
(80) Carney Lansford .50
(81) Barry Larkin .60
(82) Tim Laudner .50
(83) Vance Law .50
(84) Manny Lee .50
(85) Chet Lemon .50
(86) Jeffrey Leonard .50
(87) Jose Lind .50
(88) Steve Lyons .50
(89) Candy Maldonado .50
(90) Mike Marshall .50
(91) Ramon Martinez .60
(92) Don Mattingly 3.00
(93) Willie McGee .50
(94) Fred McGriff .90
(95) Mark McGwire 4.00
(96) Kevin McReynolds .50
(97) Bobby Meacham .50
(98) Luis Medina .50
(99) Kevin Mitchell .50
(100) Paul Molitor 1.50
(101) Lloyd Moseby .50
(102) Darryl Motley .50
(103) Rance Mulliniks .50
(104) Dale Murphy .75
(105) Matt Nokes .50
(106) Jose Oquendo .50
(107) Joe Orsulak .50
(108) Rafael Palmeiro .75
(109) Tony Pena .50
(110) Terry Pendleton .50
(111) Gerald Perry .50
(112) Tom Prince .50
(113) Kirby Puckett 1.50
(114) Tim Raines .60
(115) Rafael Ramirez .50
(116) Johnny Ray .50
(117) Jody Reed .50
(118) Kevin Reimer .50
(119) Bill Ripken .50
(120) Cal Ripken, Jr. 3.50
(121) Nolan Ryan 3.50
(122) Chris Sabo .50
(123) Luis Salazar .50
(124) Juan Samuel .50
(125) Ryne Sandberg 1.25
(126) Rafael Santana .50
(127) Mike Schmidt 2.00
(128) Steve Sax .50
(129) Dick Schofield .50
(130) Kevin Seitzer .50
(131) John Shelby .50
(132) Ruben Sierra .50
(133) Don Slaught .50
(134) Ozzie Smith 1.25
(135) Van Snider .50
(136) Cory Snyder .50
(137) Darryl Strawberry .80
(138a) B.J. Surhoff (batting) .50
(138b) B.J. Surhoff (throwing) .50
(139) Pat Tabler .50
(140) Danny Tartabull .50
(141) Wayne Tolleson .50
(142) Jim Traber .50
(143) Alan Trammell .50
(144) Andy Van Slyke .50
(145) Frank Viola .50
(146) Greg Walker .50
(147) Walt Weiss .50
(148) Lou Whitaker .50
(149) Devon White .60
(150) Frank White .50
(151) Mookie Wilson .50
(152) Willie Wilson .50
(153) Dave Winfield 1.00
(154) Craig Worthington .50
(155) Gerald Young .50
(156) Robin Yount 1.50

1993 Photo File Nolan Ryan No-Hitter Highlights

This series of large-format (10" x 8") cards was produced in commemoration of Ryan's record seven career no hit games. Besides photos of Ryan in action or being congratulated, each card presents the box score from the no-hitter depicted along with the date and location. Otherwise blank backs have a trademark notice at center. Cards of no-hitters 1-5 have black-and-white photos; the others are in color.

MT
Complete Set (8): 16.00
Common Card: 3.00
Header card 2.00
(1) 1st No-Hitter (5/15/73) 3.00
(2) 2nd No-Hitter (7/15/73) 3.00
(3) 3rd No-Hitter (9/28/74) 3.00
(4) 4th No-Hitter (6/1/75) 3.00
(5) 5th No-Hitter (9/26/81) 3.00
(6) 6th No-Hitter (6/11/90) 3.00
(7) 7th No-Hitter (5/1/91) 3.00

1993 Photo File 500 Home Run Club

Photo File produced a set of 8" x 10" cards of members of the 500 Home Run Club. The Supercards feature all 14 current members of the club, plus a header card with all 14 players. The card fronts feature a photo of the player plus statistics and biographical information. Backs have a trademark notice.

MT
Complete Set (15): 20.00
Common Player: 1.50
1 Hank Aaron 2.50
2 Willie Mays 2.50
3 Mickey Mantle 6.00
4 Reggie Jackson 2.00
5 Ted Williams 2.50
6 Mel Ott 1.50
7 Babe Ruth 4.00
8 Frank Robinson 1.50
9 Harmon Killebrew 1.50
10 Ed Mathews 1.50
11 Jimmie Foxx 1.50
12 Ernie Banks 1.50
13 Mike Schmidt 2.00
14 Willie McCovey 1.50
--- Header card 1.50

1989 Photomation California Angels

These large-format (4" x 8") black-and-white glossy player cards were provided to players for use in answering fan requests for pictures and autographs. The cards have portrait photos which are borderless at top and sides. In the wide white bottom border are the player's uniform number and name, with the team and sponsor logos beneath. Backs are blank. Complete sets were not available from the team.

MT
Complete Set (32): 30.00
Common Player: 1.00
1 Bobby Knoop 1.00
2 Deron Johnson 1.00
3 Johnny Ray 1.00
5 Brian Downing 1.00
7 Kent Anderson 1.00
9 Glenn Hoffman 1.00
12 Doug Rader 1.00
13 Lance Parrish 1.25
15 Kirk McCaskill 1.50
16 Jack Howell 1.50
18 Claudell Washington 1.00
19 Dante Bichette 2.50
20 Tony Armas 1.50
21 Wally Joyner 2.50
22 Dick Schofield 1.00
23 Bill Schroeder 1.00
24 Chili Davis 1.50
25 Jim Abbott 2.50
27 Willie Fraser 1.00
28 Bert Blyleven 1.50
30 Devon White 2.00
31 Chuck Finley 1.50
34 Bryan Harvey 1.00
37 Bob McClure 1.00
38 Greg Minton 1.00
39 Mike Witt 1.50
40 Joe Coleman 1.00
44 Rich Monteleone 1.00
46 Dan Petry 1.00
47 Moose Stubing 1.00
50 Jimmie Reese 1.50
53 Marcel Lachemann 1.00

1992 Pinnacle

Score entered the high-end card market with the release of this 620-card set. The cards feature black borders surrounding a white frame with a full-color action photo inside. The player extends beyond the natural background. The backs are horizontal and feature a closeup photo, statistics, team logo, biographical information and player information. Several subsets can be found within the set including "Idols, Sidelines, Grips, Shades" and "Technicians".

MT
Complete Set (620): 45.00
Common Player: .10
1 Frank Thomas 1.50
2 Benito Santiago .10
3 Carlos Baerga .10
4 Cecil Fielder .15
5 Barry Larkin .15
6 Ozzie Smith .50
7 Willie McGee .10
8 Paul Molitor .50
9 Andy Van Slyke .10
10 Ryne Sandberg .75
11 Kevin Seitzer .10
12 Len Dykstra .15
13 Edgar Martinez .10
14 Ruben Sierra .10
15 Howard Johnson .10
16 Dave Henderson .10
17 Devon White .10
18 Terry Pendleton .10
19 Steve Finley .10
20 Kirby Puckett .75
21 Orel Hershiser .10
22 Hal Morris .10
23 Don Mattingly .75
24 Delino DeShields .15
25 Dennis Eckersley .15
26 Ellis Burks .10
27 Jay Buhner .10
28 Matt Williams .25
29 Lou Whitaker .10
30 Alex Fernandez .15
31 Albert Belle .75
32 Todd Zeile .10
33 Tony Pena .10
34 Jay Bell .10
35 Rafael Palmeiro .30
36 Wes Chamberlain .10
37 George Bell .10
38 Robin Yount .75
39 Vince Coleman .10
40 Bruce Hurst .10
41 Harold Baines .10
42 Chuck Finley .10
43 Ken Caminiti .20
44 Ben McDonald .10
45 Roberto Alomar .60
46 Chili Davis .10
47 Bill Doran .10
48 Jerald Clark .10
49 Jose Lind .10
50 Nolan Ryan 2.00
51 Phil Plantier .10
52 Gary DiSarcina .10
53 Kevin Bass .10
54 Pat Kelly .10
55 Mark Wohlers .10
56 Walt Weiss .10
57 Lenny Harris .10
58 Ivan Calderon .10
59 Harold Reynolds .10
60 George Brett .75
61 Gregg Olson .10
62 Orlando Merced .10
63 Steve Decker .10
64 John Franco .10
65 Greg Maddux 1.50
66 Alex Cole .10
67 Dave Hollins .10
68 Kent Hrbek .10
69 Tom Pagnozzi .10
70 Jeff Bagwell 1.50
71 Jim Gantner .10
72 Matt Nokes .10
73 Brian Harper .10
74 Andy Benes .15
75 Tom Glavine .25
76 Terry Steinbach .10
77 Dennis Martinez .10
78 John Olerud .20
79 Ozzie Guillen .10
80 Darryl Strawberry .15
81 Gary Gaetti .10
82 Dave Righetti .10
83 Chris Hoiles .10
84 Andujar Cedeno .10
85 Jack Clark .10
86 David Howard .10
87 Bill Gullickson .10
88 Bernard Gilkey .15
89 Kevin Elster .10
90 Kevin Maas .10
91 Mark Lewis .10
92 Greg Vaughn .15
93 Bret Barberie .10
94 Dave Smith .10
95 Roger Clemens .75
96 Doug Drabek .10
97 Omar Vizquel .15
98 Jose Guzman .10
99 Juan Samuel .10
100 Dave Justice .25
101 Tom Browning .10
102 Mark Gubicza .10
103 Mickey Morandini .10
104 Ed Whitson .10
105 Lance Parrish .10
106 Scott Erickson .10
107 Jack McDowell .10
108 Dave Stieb .10
109 Mike Moore .10
110 Travis Fryman .10

111	Dwight Gooden	.15
112	Fred McGriff	.35
113	Alan Trammell	.15
114	Roberto Kelly	.10
115	Andre Dawson	.15
116	Bill Landrum	.10
117	Brian McRae	.10
118	B.J. Surhoff	.15
119	Chuck Knoblauch	.15
120	Steve Olin	.10
121	Robin Ventura	.30
122	Will Clark	.25
123	Tino Martinez	.15
124	Dale Murphy	.20
125	Pete O'Brien	.10
126	Ray Lankford	.10
127	Juan Gonzalez	.75
128	Ron Gant	.15
129	Marquis Grissom	.15
130	Jose Canseco	.40
131	Mike Greenwell	.10
132	Mark Langston	.10
133	Brett Butler	.10
134	Kelly Gruber	.10
135	Chris Sabo	.10
136	Mark Grace	.25
137	Tony Fernandez	.10
138	Glenn Davis	.10
139	Pedro Munoz	.10
140	Craig Biggio	.20
141	Pete Schourek	.10
142	Mike Boddicker	.10
143	Robby Thompson	.10
144	Mel Hall	.10
145	Bryan Harvey	.10
146	Mike LaValliere	.10
147	John Kruk	.10
148	Joe Carter	.15
149	Greg Olson	.10
150	Julio Franco	.10
151	Darryl Hamilton	.10
152	Felix Fermin	.10
153	Jose Offerman	.10
154	Paul O'Neill	.15
155	Tommy Greene	.10
156	Ivan Rodriguez	.60
157	Dave Stewart	.15
158	Jeff Reardon	.10
159	Felix Jose	.10
160	Doug Dascenzo	.10
161	Tim Wallach	.10
162	Dan Plesac	.10
163	Luis Gonzalez	.10
164	Mike Henneman	.10
165	Mike Devereaux	.10
166	Luis Polonia	.10
167	Mike Sharperson	.10
168	Chris Donnels	.10
169	Greg Harris	.10
170	Deion Sanders	.30
171	Mike Schooler	.10
172	Jose DeJesus	.10
173	Jeff Montgomery	.10
174	Milt Cuyler	.10
175	Wade Boggs	.45
176	Kevin Tapani	.10
177	Bill Spiers	.10
178	Tim Raines	.15
179	Randy Milligan	.10
180	Rob Dibble	.10
181	Kirt Manwaring	.10
182	Pascual Perez	.10
183	Juan Guzman	.15
184	John Smiley	.10
185	David Segui	.10
186	Omar Olivares	.10
187	Joe Slusarski	.10
188	Erik Hanson	.10
189	Mark Portugal	.10
190	Walt Terrell	.10
191	John Smoltz	.15
192	Wilson Alvarez	.15
193	Jimmy Key	.10
194	Larry Walker	.25
195	Lee Smith	.10
196	Pete Harnisch	.10
197	Mike Harkey	.10
198	Frank Tanana	.10
199	Terry Mulholland	.10
200	Cal Ripken, Jr.	2.50
201	Dave Magadan	.10
202	Bud Black	.10
203	Terry Shumpert	.10
204	Mike Mussina	.50
205	Mo Vaughn	.50
206	Steve Farr	.10
207	Darrin Jackson	.10
208	Jerry Browne	.10
209	Jeff Russell	.10
210	Mike Scioscia	.10
211	Rick Aguilera	.10
212	Jaime Navarro	.10
213	Randy Tomlin	.10
214	Bobby Thigpen	.10
215	Mark Gardner	.10
216	Norm Charlton	.10
217	Mark McGwire	3.00
218	Skeeter Barnes	.10
219	Bob Tewksbury	.10
220	Junior Felix	.10
221	Sam Horn	.10
222	Jody Reed	.10
223	Luis Sojo	.10
224	Jerome Walton	.10
225	Darryl Kile	.10
226	Mickey Tettleton	.10
227	Dan Pasqua	.10
228	Jim Gott	.10
229	Bernie Williams	.30
230	Shane Mack	.10
231	Steve Avery	.10
232	Dave Valle	.10
233	Mark Leonard	.10
234	Spike Owen	.10
235	Gary Sheffield	.25
236	Steve Chitren	.10
237	Zane Smith	.10
238	Tom Gordon	.10
239	Jose Oquendo	.10
240	Todd Stottlemyre	.10
241	Darren Daulton	.10
242	Tim Naehring	.10
243	Tony Phillips	.10
244	Shawon Dunston	.10
245	Manuel Lee	.10
246	Mike Pagliarulo	.10
247	Jim Thome (Rookie Prospect)	.30
248	Luis Mercedes (Rookie Prospect)	.15
249	Cal Eldred (Rookie Prospect)	.15
250	Derek Bell (Rookie Prospect)	.20
251	Arthur Rhodes (Rookie Prospect)	.15
252	Scott Cooper (Rookie Prospect)	.10
253	Roberto Hernandez (Rookie Prospect)	.15
254	Mo Sanford (Rookie Prospect)	.15
255	Scott Servais (Rookie Prospect)	.10
256	Eric Karros (Rookie Prospect)	.15
257	Andy Mota	.10
258	Keith Mitchell	.10
259	Joel Johnston (Rookie Prospect)	.10
260	John Wehner (Rookie Prospect)	.10
261	Gino Minutelli (Rookie Prospect)	.10
262	Greg Gagne	.10
263	Stan Royer (Rookie Prospect)	.15
264	Carlos Garcia (Rookie Prospect)	.15
265	Andy Ashby (Rookie Prospect)	.20
266	Kim Batiste (Rookie Prospect)	.10
267	Julio Valera (Rookie Prospect)	.10
268	Royce Clayton (Rookie Prospect)	.10
269	Gary Scott (Rookie Prospect)	.10
270	Kirk Dressendorfer (Rookie Prospect)	.10
271	Sean Berry (Rookie Prospect)	.15
272	Lance Dickson (Rookie Prospect)	.15
273	Rob Maurer (Rookie Prospect)	.10
274	Scott Brosius (Rookie Prospect)	.15
275	Dave Fleming (Rookie Prospect)	.10
276	Lenny Webster (Rookie Prospect)	.15
277	Mike Humphreys	.10
278	Freddie Benavides (Rookie Prospect)	.15
279	Harvey Pulliam (Rookie Prospect)	.10
280	Jeff Carter (Rookie Prospect)	.15
281	Jim Abbott, Nolan Ryan (Idols)	.25
282	Wade Boggs, George Brett (Idols)	.20
283	Ken Griffey Jr., Rickey Henderson (Idols)	.75
284	Dale Murphy, Wally Joyner (Idols)	.15
285	Chuck Knoblauch, Ozzie Smith (Idols)	.15
286	Robin Ventura, Lou Gehrig (Idols)	.35
287	Robin Yount (Sidelines - Motocross)	.35
288	Bob Tewksbury (Sidelines - Cartoonist)	.10
289	Kirby Puckett (Sidelines - Pool Player)	.40
290	Kenny Lofton (Sidelines - Basketball Player)	.50
291	Jack McDowell (Sidelines - Guitarist)	.10
292	John Burkett (Sidelines - Bowler)	.10
293	Dwight Smith (Sidelines - Singer)	.10
294	Nolan Ryan (Sidelines - Cattle Rancher)	1.00
295	*Manny Ramirez* (1st Round Draft Pick)	6.00
296	*Cliff Floyd* (1st Round Draft Pick)	.50
297	*Al Shirley* (1st Round Draft Pick)	.10
298	*Brian Barber* (1st Round Draft Pick)	.15
299	*Jon Farrell* (1st Round Draft Pick)	.15
300	*Scott Ruffcorn* (1st Round Draft Pick)	.25
301	*Tyrone Hill* (1st Round Draft Pick)	.15
302	*Benji Gil* (1st Round Draft Pick)	.25
303	*Tyler Green* (1st Round Draft Pick)	.30
304	Allen Watson (Shades)	.15
305	Jay Buhner (Shades)	.15
306	Roberto Alomar (Shades)	.35
307	Chuck Knoblauch (Shades)	.15
308	Darryl Strawberry (Shades)	.10
309	Danny Tartabull (Shades)	.15
310	Bobby Bonilla (Shades)	.10
311	Mike Felder	.10
312	Storm Davis	.10
313	Tim Teufel	.10
314	Tom Brunansky	.10
315	Rex Hudler	.10
316	Dave Otto	.10
317	Jeff King	.10
318	Dan Gladden	.10
319	Bill Pecota	.10
320	Franklin Stubbs	.10
321	Gary Carter	.20
322	Melido Perez	.10
323	Eric Davis	.15
324	Greg Myers	.10
325	Pete Incaviglia	.10
326	Von Hayes	.10
327	Greg Swindell	.10
328	Steve Sax	.10
329	Chuck McElroy	.10
330	Gregg Jefferies	.20
331	Joe Oliver	.10
332	Paul Faries	.10
333	David West	.10
334	Craig Grebeck	.10
335	Chris Hammond	.10
336	Billy Ripken	.10
337	Scott Sanderson	.10
338	Dick Schofield	.10
339	Bob Milacki	.10
340	Kevin Reimer	.10
341	Jose DeLeon	.10
342	Henry Cotto	.10
343	Daryl Boston	.10
344	Kevin Gross	.10
345	Milt Thompson	.10
346	Luis Rivera	.10
347	Al Osuna	.10
348	Rob Deer	.10
349	Tim Leary	.10
350	Mike Stanton	.10
351	Dean Palmer	.10
352	Trevor Wilson	.10
353	Mark Eichhorn	.10
354	Scott Aldred	.10
355	Mark Whiten	.15
356	Leo Gomez	.10
357	Rafael Belliard	.10
358	Carlos Quintana	.10
359	Mark Davis	.10
360	Chris Nabholz	.10
361	Carlton Fisk	.25
362	Joe Orsulak	.10
363	Eric Anthony	.10
364	Greg Hibbard	.10
365	Scott Leius	.10
366	Hensley Meulens	.10
367	Chris Bosio	.10
368	Brian Downing	.10
369	Sammy Sosa	2.00
370	Stan Belinda	.10
371	Joe Grahe	.10
372	Luis Salazar	.10
373	Lance Johnson	.10
374	Kal Daniels	.10
375	Dave Winfield	.50
376	Brook Jacoby	.10
377	Mariano Duncan	.10
378	Ron Darling	.10
379	Randy Johnson	.50
380	Chito Martinez	.10
381	Andres Galarraga	.15
382	Willie Randolph	.10
383	Charles Nagy	.10
384	Tim Belcher	.10
385	Duane Ward	.10
386	Vicente Palacios	.10
387	Mike Gallego	.10
388	Rich DeLucia	.10
389	Scott Radinsky	.10
390	Damon Berryhill	.10
391	Kirk McCaskill	.10
392	Pedro Guerrero	.10
393	Kevin Mitchell	.10
394	Dickie Thon	.10
395	Bobby Bonilla	.15
396	Bill Wegman	.10
397	Dave Martinez	.10
398	Rick Sutcliffe	.10
399	Larry Andersen	.10
400	Tony Gwynn	1.00
401	Rickey Henderson	.45
402	Greg Cadaret	.10
403	Keith Miller	.10
404	Bip Roberts	.10
405	Kevin Brown	.15
406	Mitch Williams	.10
407	Frank Viola	.10
408	Darren Lewis	.10
409	Bob Walk	.10
410	Bob Walk	.10
411	Todd Frohwirth	.10
412	Brian Hunter	.10
413	Ron Karkovice	.10
414	Mike Morgan	.10
415	Joe Hesketh	.10
416	Don Slaught	.10
417	Tom Henke	.10
418	Kurt Stillwell	.10
419	Hector Villanueva	.10
420	Glenallen Hill	.10
421	Pat Borders	.10
422	Charlie Hough	.10
423	Charlie Leibrandt	.10
424	Eddie Murray	.35
425	Jesse Barfield	.10
426	Mark Lemke	.10
427	Kevin McReynolds	.10
428	Gilberto Reyes	.10
429	Ramon Martinez	.15
430	Steve Buechele	.10
431	David Wells	.15
432	Kyle Abbott (Rookie Prospect)	.15
433	John Habyan	.10
434	Kevin Appier	.10
435	Gene Larkin	.10
436	Sandy Alomar, Jr.	.15
437	Mike Jackson	.10
438	Todd Benzinger	.10
439	Teddy Higuera	.10
440	Reggie Sanders (Rookie Prospect)	.15
441	Mark Carreon	.10
442	Bret Saberhagen	.10
443	Gene Nelson	.10
444	Jay Howell	.10
445	Roger McDowell	.10
446	Sid Bream	.10
447	Mackey Sasser	.10
448	Bill Swift	.10
449	Hubie Brooks	.10
450	David Cone	.15
451	Bobby Witt	.10
452	Brady Anderson	.15
453	Lee Stevens	.10
454	Luis Aquino	.10
455	Carney Lansford	.10
456	Carlos Hernandez (Rookie Prospect)	.15
457	Danny Jackson	.10
458	Gerald Young	.10
459	Tom Candiotti	.10
460	Billy Hatcher	.10
461	John Wetteland	.15
462	Mike Bordick	.10
463	Don Robinson	.10
464	Jeff Johnson	.10
465	Lonnie Smith	.10
466	Paul Assenmacher	.10
467	Alvin Davis	.10
468	Jim Eisenreich	.10
469	Brent Mayne	.10
470	Jeff Brantley	.10
471	Tim Burke	.10
472	*Pat Mahomes* (Rookie Prospect)	.25
473	Ryan Bowen	.10
474	Bryn Smith	.10
475	Mike Flanagan	.10
476	Reggie Jefferson (Rookie Prospect)	.15
477	Jeff Blauser	.10
478	Craig Lefferts	.10
479	Todd Worrell	.10
480	Scott Scudder	.10
481	Kirk Gibson	.10
482	Kenny Rogers	.10
483	Jack Morris	.10
484	Russ Swan	.10
485	Mike Huff	.10
486	Ken Hill	.10
487	Geronimo Pena	.10
488	Charlie O'Brien	.10
489	Mike Maddux	.10
490	Scott Livingstone (Rookie Prospect)	.15
491	Carl Willis	.10
492	Kelly Downs	.10
493	Dennis Cook	.10
494	Joe Magrane	.10
495	Bob Kipper	.10
496	Jose Mesa	.10
497	Charlie Hayes	.10
498	Joe Girardi	.10
499	Doug Jones	.10
500	Barry Bonds	.75
501	Bill Krueger	.10
502	Glenn Braggs	.10
503	Eric King	.10
504	Frank Castillo	.10
505	Mike Gardiner	.10
506	Cory Snyder	.10
507	Steve Howe	.10
508	Jose Rijo	.10
509	Sid Fernandez	.10
510	*Archi Cianfrocco* (Rookie Prospect)	.15
511	Mark Guthrie	.10
512	Bob Ojeda	.10
513	John Doherty (Rookie Prospect)	.15
514	Dante Bichette	.10
515	Juan Berenguer	.10
516	Jeff Robinson	.10
517	Mike MacFarlane	.10
518	Matt Young	.10
519	Otis Nixon	.10
520	Brian Holman	.10
521	Chris Haney	.10
522	*Jeff Kent* (Rookie Prospect)	.50
523	*Chad Curtis* (Rookie Prospect)	.50
524	Vince Horsman	.10
525	Rod Nichols	.10
526	*Peter Hoy* (Rookie Prospect)	.10
527	Shawn Boskie	.10
528	Alejandro Pena	.10
529	Dave Burba (Rookie Prospect)	.10
530	Ricky Jordan	.10
531	David Silvestri (Rookie Prospect)	.15
532	John Patterson (Rookie Prospect)	.20
533	Jeff Branson (Rookie Prospect)	.15
534	Derrick May (Rookie Prospect)	.15
535	Esteban Beltre (Rookie Prospect)	.10
536	Jose Melendez	.10
537	Wally Joyner	.10
538	Eddie Taubensee (Rookie Prospect)	.15
539	Jim Abbott	.15
540	*Brian Williams* (Rookie Prospect)	.15
541	Donovan Osborne (Rookie Prospect)	.10
542	Patrick Lennon (Rookie Prospect)	.10
543	*Mike Groppuso* (Rookie Prospect)	.10
544	*Jarvis Brown* (Rookie Prospect)	.10
545	*Shawn Livesy* (1st Round Draft Pick)	.20
546	Jeff Ware (1st Round Draft Pick)	.15
547	Danny Tartabull	.10
548	*Bobby Jones* (1st Round Draft Pick)	.60
549	Ken Griffey, Jr.	3.00
550	*Rey Sanchez* (Rookie Prospect)	.25
551	*Pedro Astacio* (Rookie Prospect)	.25
552	*Juan Guerrero* (Rookie Prospect)	.10
553	*Jacob Brumfield* (Rookie Prospect)	.15
554	*Ben Rivera* (Rookie Prospect)	.10
555	*Brian Jordan* (Rookie Prospect)	1.00
556	Denny Neagle (Rookie Prospect)	.10
557	Cliff Brantley (Rookie Prospect)	.15
558	Anthony Young (Rookie Prospect)	.10
559	*John VanderWal* (Rookie Prospect)	.15
560	*Monty Fariss* (Rookie Prospect)	.10
561	*Russ Springer* (Rookie Prospect)	.20
562	*Pat Listach* (Rookie Prospect)	.15
563	Pat Hentgen (Rookie Prospect)	.10
564	Andy Stankiewicz (Rookie Prospect)	.10
565	Mike Perez (Rookie Prospect)	.15
566	Mike Bielecki	.10
567	Butch Henry (Rookie Prospect)	.10
568	*Dave Nilsson* (Rookie Prospect)	.30
569	*Scott Hatteberg* (Rookie Prospect)	.20
570	Ruben Amaro, Jr. (Rookie Prospect)	.15
571	Todd Hundley (Rookie Prospect)	.15
572	Moises Alou (Rookie Prospect)	.20
573	Hector Fajardo (Rookie Prospect)	.15
574	Todd Van Poppel (Rookie Prospect)	.15
575	Willie Banks (Rookie Prospect)	.15
576	Bob Zupcic (Rookie Prospect)	.10
577	*J.J. Johnson* (1st Round Draft Pick)	.15
578	John Burkett	.10
579	Trever Miller (1st Round Draft Pick)	.15

580	Scott Bankhead	.10
581	Rich Amaral (Rookie Prospect)	.10
582	Kenny Lofton (Rookie Prospect)	.50
583	Matt Stairs (Rookie Prospect)	.20
584	Don Mattingly, Rod Carew (Idols)	.25
585	Jack Morris, Steve Avery (Idols)	.10
586	Roberto Alomar, Sandy Alomar (Idols)	.25
587	Scott Sanderson, Catfish Hunter (Idols)	.10
588	Dave Justice, Willie Stargell (Idols)	.30
589	Rex Hudler, Roger Staubach (Idols)	.10
590	David Cone, Jackie Gleason (Idols)	.10
591	Willie Davis, Tony Gwynn (Idols)	.15
592	Orel Hershiser (Sidelines - Golfer)	.15
593	John Wetteland (Sidelines - Musician)	.15
594	Tom Glavine (Sidelines - Hockey Player)	.15
595	Randy Johnson (Sidelines - Photographer)	.20
596	Jim Gott (Sidelines - Black Belt)	.10
597	Donald Harris	.10
598	*Shawn Hare*	.15
599	Chris Gardner	.10
600	Rusty Meacham	.10
601	Benito Santiago (Shades)	.10
602	Eric Davis (Shades)	.15
603	Jose Lind (Shades)	.10
604	Dave Justice (Shades)	.30
605	Tim Raines (Shades)	.15
606	Randy Tomlin (Grips -Vulcan Change)	.10
607	Jack McDowell (Grips - Split-finger)	.10
608	Greg Maddux (Grips - Circle change)	.30
609	Charles Nagy (Grips - Slider)	.10
610	Tom Candiotti (Grips - Knuckleball)	.10
611	David Cone (Grips - Curveball)	.10
612	Steve Avery (Grips - Fastball)	.10
613	*Rod Beck*	.30
614	Rickey Henderson (Technician - Base Stealing)	.25
615	Benito Santiago (Technician - Catching)	.10
616	Ruben Sierra (Technician - Outfield)	.10
617	Ryne Sandberg (Technician - Infield)	.40
618	Nolan Ryan (Technician - Pitching)	.75
619	Brett Butler (Technician - Bunting)	.10
620	Dave Justice (Technician - Hitting)	.30

1992 Pinnacle Rookie Idols

Carrying on with the Idols subset theme in the regular issue, these Series II foil-pack inserts feature 18 of the year's rookie prospects sharing cards with their baseball heroes. Both front and back are horizontal in format and include photos of both the rookie and his idol.

		MT
Complete Set (18):		95.00
Common Player:		2.00
1	Reggie Sanders, Eric Davis	2.00
2	Hector Fajardo, Jim Abbott	2.00
3	Gary Cooper, George Brett	10.00
4	Mark Wohlers, Roger Clemens	8.00
5	Luis Mercedes, Julio Franco	2.00
6	Willie Banks, Dwight Gooden	2.00
7	Kenny Lofton, Rickey Henderson	10.00
8	Keith Mitchell, Dave Henderson	2.00
9	Kim Batiste, Barry Larkin	2.00
10	Thurman Munson, Todd Hundley	7.50
11	Eddie Zosky, Cal Ripken Jr.	20.00
12	Todd Van Poppel, Nolan Ryan	20.00
13	Ryne Sandberg, Jim Thome	10.00
14	Dave Fleming, Bobby Murcer	2.00
15	Royce Clayton, Ozzie Smith	7.50
16	Don Harris, Darryl Strawberry	2.00
17	Alan Trammell, Chad Curtis	2.00
18	Derek Bell, Dave Winfield	4.00

1992 Pinnacle Rookies

Styled after the regular 1992 Score Pinnacle cards, this 30-card boxed set features the top rookies of 1992. The cards have a player action photo which is borderless on the top and sides. Beneath the photo a team color-coded strip carries the player's name in gold foil, with a round gold-bordered team logo at left. A black strip at bottom has the notation "1992 Rookie". Horizontal-format backs follow a similar design and include a bit of player information, Pinnacle's anti-counterfeiting strip and some gold-foil enhancements.

		MT
Complete Set (30):		6.00
Common Player:		.15
1	Luis Mercedes	.25
2	Scott Cooper	.15
3	Kenny Lofton	2.00
4	John Doherty	.20
5	Pat Listach	.20
6	Andy Stankiewicz	.15
7	Derek Bell	.45
8	Gary DiSarcina	.15
9	Roberto Hernandez	.25
10	Joel Johnston	.15
11	Pat Mahomes	.25
12	Todd Van Poppel	.15
13	Dave Fleming	.15
14	Monty Fariss	.15
15	Gary Scott	.15
16	Moises Alou	.50
17	Todd Hundley	.35
18	Kim Batiste	.15
19	Denny Neagle	.20
20	Donovan Osborne	.15
21	Mark Wohlers	.15
22	Reggie Sanders	.30
23	Brian Williams	.15
24	Eric Karros	.75
25	Frank Seminara	.15
26	Royce Clayton	.15
27	Dave Nilsson	.30
28	Matt Stairs	.20
29	Chad Curtis	.35
30	Carlos Hernandez	.15

1992 Pinnacle Slugfest

Each specially marked Slugfest jumbo pack of '92 Pinnacle contained one of these horizontal-format cards of the game's top hitters. The player's name is printed in gold foil at the bottom of the card, along with a red and white Slugfest logo. Backs, which are vertical in orientation, have a color player photo, a career summary and a few lifetime stats.

		MT
Complete Set (15):		35.00
Common Player:		.50
1	Cecil Fielder	.75
2	Mark McGwire	10.00
3	Jose Canseco	1.50
4	Barry Bonds	3.00
5	Dave Justice	1.00
6	Bobby Bonilla	.75
7	Ken Griffey, Jr.	10.00
8	Ron Gant	.75
9	Ryne Sandberg	3.00
10	Ruben Sierra	.50
11	Frank Thomas	7.50
12	Will Clark	2.00
13	Kirby Puckett	4.00
14	Cal Ripken, Jr.	6.00
15	Jeff Bagwell	4.00

1992 Pinnacle Team Pinnacle

The most sought-after and valuable of the 1992 Pinnacle insert cards is this 12-piece set of "two-headed" cards. An American and a National League superstar at each position are featured on each card, with two cards each for starting and relief pitchers. The ultra-realistic artwork of Chris Greco is featured on the cards, which were inserted into Series I foil packs.

		MT
Complete Set (12):		60.00
Common Player:		2.50
1	Roger Clemens, Ramon Martinez	6.00
2	Jim Abbott, Steve Avery	2.00
3	Benito Santiago, Ivan Rodriguez	3.00
4	Frank Thomas, Will Clark	7.50
5	Roberto Alomar, Ryne Sandberg	9.00
6	Robin Ventura, Matt Williams	4.00
7	Cal Ripken, Jr., Barry Larkin	12.50
8	Danny Tartabull, Barry Bonds	5.00
9	Brett Butler, Ken Griffey Jr.	15.00
10	Ruben Sierra, Dave Justice	4.00
11	Dennis Eckersley, Rob Dibble	2.00
12	Scott Radinsky, John Franco	2.00

1992 Pinnacle Team 2000

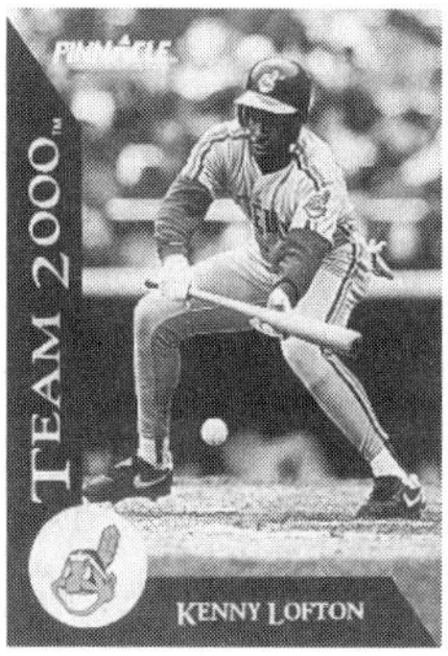

Young stars who were projected to be the game's superstars in the year 2000 were chosen for this 80-card insert set found three at a time in jumbo packs. Cards #1-40 were included in Series I packaging, while cards #41-80 were inserted with Series II Pinnacle. Cards feature gold foil highlights on both front and back.

		MT
Complete Set (80):		30.00
Common Player:		.10
1	Mike Mussina	1.00
2	Phil Plantier	.10
3	Frank Thomas	2.50
4	Travis Fryman	.10
5	Kevin Appier	.10
6	Chuck Knoblauch	.50
7	Pat Kelly	.10
8	Ivan Rodriguez	1.25
9	Dave Justice	.25
10	Jeff Bagwell	2.00
11	Marquis Grissom	.15
12	Andy Benes	.10
13	Gregg Olson	.10
14	Kevin Morton	.10
15	Tim Naehring	.10
16	Dave Hollins	.10
17	Sandy Alomar Jr.	.20
18	Albert Belle	1.50
19	Charles Nagy	.15
20	Brian McRae	.10
21	Larry Walker	.65
22	Delino DeShields	.10
23	Jeff Johnson	.10
24	Bernie Williams	1.00
25	Jose Offerman	.10
26	Juan Gonzalez	2.00
27	Juan Guzman	.10
28	Eric Anthony	.10
29	Brian Hunter	.10
30	John Smoltz	.30
31	Deion Sanders	.25
32	Greg Maddux	2.50
33	Andujar Cedeno	.10
34	Royce Clayton	.10
35	Kenny Lofton	1.00
36	Cal Eldred	.10
37	Jim Thome	.60
38	Gary DiSarcina	.10
39	Brian Jordan	.50
40	Chad Curtis	.10
41	Ben McDonald	.10
42	Jim Abbott	.15
43	Robin Ventura	.25
44	Milt Cuyler	.10
45	Gregg Jefferies	.15
46	Scott Radinsky	.10
47	Ken Griffey, Jr.	5.00
48	Roberto Alomar	1.50
49	Ramon Martinez	.15
50	Bret Barberie	.10
51	Ray Lankford	.15
52	Leo Gomez	.10
53	Tommy Greene	.10
54	Mo Vaughn	1.00
55	Sammy Sosa	3.00
56	Carlos Baerga	.10
57	Mark Lewis	.10
58	Tom Gordon	.10
59	Gary Sheffield	.65
60	Scott Erickson	.10
61	Pedro Munoz	.10
62	Tino Martinez	.15
63	Darren Lewis	.10
64	Dean Palmer	.10
65	John Olerud	.25
66	Steve Avery	.10
67	Pete Harnisch	.10
68	Luis Gonzalez	.15
69	Kim Batiste	.10
70	Reggie Sanders	.15
71	Luis Mercedes	.10
72	Todd Van Poppel	.10
73	Gary Scott	.10
74	Monty Fariss	.10
75	Kyle Abbott	.10
76	Eric Karros	.15
77	Mo Sanford	.10
78	Todd Hundley	.50
79	Reggie Jefferson	.10
80	Pat Mahomes	.15

1992 Pinnacle Mickey Mantle

This boxed set highlighting the career of Mickey Mantle was issued in a reported edition of 180,000 sets. Fronts and backs feature an assortment of black-and-white, color and colorized photos. Fronts have gold-foil stamped highlights. Card backs have a few sentences about Mantle's life or career.

		MT
Complete Set:		15.00
Common Player:		1.00
1	Father and Son	1.00
2	High School	1.00
3	Commerce Comet	1.00
4	Spring Training	1.00
5	The Beginning	1.00
6	No. 6	1.00
7	The Rookie	1.00
8	Tape-Measure Shots	1.00
9	Shortstop	1.00
10	Outfield	1.00
11	Speed, Speed, Speed	1.00
12	Contracts	1.00
13	Three-time MVP	1.00
14	Triple Crown	1.00
15	Series Slam	1.00
16	Series Star	1.00
17	Switch Hitter	1.00
18	Fan Favorite	1.00
19	Milestones	1.00
20	Enthuiasm	1.00
21	Hitting	1.00
22	First Base	1.00
23	Courage	1.00
24	Mick & Stan (w/ Stan Musial)	1.00
25	Whitey & Yogi (w/ Whitey Ford, Yogi Berra)	1.00
26	Mick & Billy (w/ Billy Martin)	1.00
27	Mick & Casey (w/ Casey Stengel)	1.00
28	Awards	1.00
29	Retirement	1.00
30	Cooperstown	1.00

1993 Pinnacle Promos

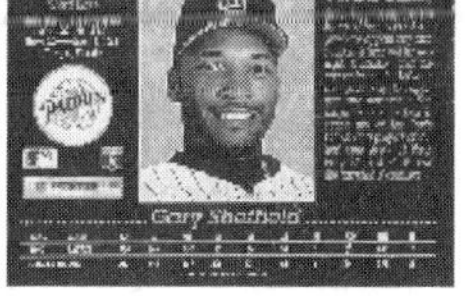

On six of the eight cards issued to premiere Pinnacle's '93 set, the difference between the promo version and the issued version is so slight it can easily go unnoticed - the "TM" in the upper-right corner on front is larger on the promo than on the regular card. Promo cards #3 and #5 are easier to spot because the team logos on back of the promos are the old Expos and Mariners logos, rather than the new versions found on issued cards.

		MT
Complete Set (8):		50.00
Common Player:		5.00
1	Gary Sheffield	10.00
2	Cal Eldred	5.00
3	Larry Walker	9.00
4	Deion Sanders	10.00
5	Dave Fleming	5.00
6	Carlos Baerga	5.00
7	Bernie Williams	9.00
8	John Kruk	5.00

1993 Pinnacle

This 620-card set offers many of the same features which made the first Pinnacle set so popular in 1992. Subsets are titled Rookies, Now & Then (which shows the player as he looks now and as a rookie), Idols (active players and their heroes on the same card), Hometown Heroes (players who are playing with their hometown team), Draft Picks and Rookies. More than 100 rookies and 10 draft picks are featured. All regular cards have an action photo, a black border and the Pinnacle name stamped in gold. Series I cards feature portraits of players on the two new expansion teams; Series II cards feature action shots of them. Team Pinnacle insert cards return, while Rookie Team Pinnacle cards make their debut. Other insert sets are titled Team 2001, Slugfest and Tribute, which features five cards each of Nolan Ryan and George Brett.

		MT
Complete Set (620):		50.00
Complete Series 1 (310):		25.00
Complete Series 2 (310):		25.00
Common Player:		.05
Series 1 or 2 Wax Box:		45.00
1	Gary Sheffield	.30
2	Cal Eldred	.10
3	Larry Walker	.25
4	Deion Sanders	.15
5	Dave Fleming	.05
6	Carlos Baerga	.05
7	Bernie Williams	.40
8	John Kruk	.05
9	Jimmy Key	.05
10	Jeff Bagwell	1.00
11	Jim Abbott	.05
12	Terry Steinbach	.05
13	Bob Tewksbury	.05
14	Eric Karros	.10
15	Ryne Sandberg	.75
16	Will Clark	.30
17	Edgar Martinez	.10
18	Eddie Murray	.30
19	Andy Van Slyke	.05
20	Cal Ripken, Jr.	2.50
21	Ivan Rodriguez	.60
22	Barry Larkin	.20
23	Don Mattingly	1.00
24	Gregg Jefferies	.05
25	Roger Clemens	1.00
26	Cecil Fielder	.10
27	Kent Hrbek	.05
28	Robin Ventura	.15
29	Rickey Henderson	.30
30	Roberto Alomar	.60
31	Luis Polonia	.05
32	Andujar Cedeno	.05
33	Pat Listach	.05
34	Mark Grace	.20
35	Otis Nixon	.05
36	Felix Jose	.05
37	Mike Sharperson	.05
38	Dennis Martinez	.05
39	Willie McGee	.05
40	Kenny Lofton	.60
41	Randy Johnson	.40
42	Andy Benes	.05
43	Bobby Bonilla	.10
44	Mike Mussina	.60
45	Len Dykstra	.10
46	Ellis Burks	.05
47	Chris Sabo	.05
48	Jay Bell	.05
49	Jose Canseco	.35
50	Craig Biggio	.20
51	Wally Joyner	.05
52	Mickey Tettleton	.05
53	Tim Raines	.10
54	Brian Harper	.05
55	Rene Gonzales	.05
56	Mark Langston	.05
57	Jack Morris	.05
58	Mark McGwire	3.00
59	Ken Caminiti	.20
60	Terry Pendleton	.05
61	Dave Nilsson	.05
62	Tom Pagnozzi	.05
63	Mike Morgan	.05
64	Darryl Strawberry	.10
65	Charles Nagy	.05
66	Ken Hill	.05
67	Matt Williams	.25
68	Jay Buhner	.10
69	Vince Coleman	.05
70	Brady Anderson	.10
71	Fred McGriff	.30
72	Ben McDonald	.05
73	Terry Mulholland	.05
74	Randy Tomlin	.05
75	Nolan Ryan	2.50
76	Frank Viola	.05
77	Jose Rijo	.05
78	Shane Mack	.05
79	Travis Fryman	.15
80	Jack McDowell	.05
81	Mark Gubicza	.05
82	Matt Nokes	.05
83	Bert Blyleven	.05
84	Eric Anthony	.05
85	Mike Bordick	.05
86	John Olerud	.15
87	B.J. Surhoff	.05
88	Bernard Gilkey	.05
89	Shawon Dunston	.05
90	Tom Glavine	.15
91	Brett Butler	.05
92	Moises Alou	.15
93	Albert Belle	.75
94	Darren Lewis	.05
95	Omar Vizquel	.05
96	Dwight Gooden	.10
97	Gregg Olson	.05
98	Tony Gwynn	1.00
99	Darren Daulton	.05
100	Dennis Eckersley	.05
101	Rob Dibble	.05
102	Mike Greenwell	.05
103	Jose Lind	.05
104	Julio Franco	.05
105	Tom Gordon	.05
106	Scott Livingstone	.05
107	Chuck Knoblauch	.20
108	Frank Thomas	1.50
109	Melido Perez	.05
110	Ken Griffey, Jr.	3.00
111	Harold Baines	.05
112	Gary Gaetti	.05
113	Pete Harnisch	.05
114	David Wells	.10
115	Charlie Leibrandt	.05
116	Ray Lankford	.10
117	Kevin Seitzer	.05
118	Robin Yount	.45
119	Lenny Harris	.05
120	Chris James	.05
121	Delino DeShields	.05
122	Kirt Manwaring	.05
123	Glenallen Hill	.05
124	Hensley Meulens	.05
125	Darrin Jackson	.05
126	Todd Hundley	.15
127	Dave Hollins	.10
128	Sam Horn	.05
129	Roberto Hernandez	.05
130	Vicente Palacios	.05
131	George Brett	.75
132	Dave Martinez	.05
133	Kevin Appier	.10
134	Pat Kelly	.05
135	Pedro Munoz	.05
136	Mark Carreon	.05
137	Lance Johnson	.05
138	Devon White	.05
139	Julio Valera	.05
140	Eddie Taubensee	.05
141	Willie Wilson	.05
142	Stan Belinda	.05
143	John Smoltz	.15
144	Darryl Hamilton	.05
145	Sammy Sosa	1.50
146	Carlos Hernandez	.05
147	Tom Candiotti	.05
148	Mike Felder	.05
149	Rusty Meacham	.05
150	Ivan Calderon	.05
151	Pete O'Brien	.05
152	Erik Hanson	.05
153	Billy Ripken	.05
154	Kurt Stillwell	.05
155	Jeff Kent	.05
156	Mickey Morandini	.05
157	Randy Milligan	.05
158	Reggie Sanders	.10
159	Luis Rivera	.05
160	Orlando Merced	.05
161	Dean Palmer	.05
162	Mike Perez	.05
163	Scott Erikson	.05
164	Kevin McReynolds	.05
165	Kevin Maas	.05
166	Ozzie Guillen	.05
167	Rob Deer	.05
168	Danny Tartabull	.05
169	Lee Stevens	.05
170	Dave Henderson	.05
171	Derek Bell	.05
172	Steve Finley	.05
173	Greg Olson	.05
174	Geronimo Pena	.05
175	Paul Quantrill	.05
176	Steve Buechele	.05
177	Kevin Gross	.05
178	Tim Wallach	.05
179	Dave Valle	.05
180	Dave Silvestri	.05
181	Bud Black	.05
182	Henry Rodriguez	.05
183	Tim Teufel	.05
184	Mark McLemore	.05
185	Bret Saberhagen	.05
186	Chris Hoiles	.05
187	Ricky Jordan	.05
188	Don Slaught	.05
189	Mo Vaughn	.60
190	Joe Oliver	.05
191	Juan Gonzalez	1.00
192	Scott Leius	.05
193	Milt Cuyler	.05
194	Chris Haney	.05
195	Ron Karkovice	.05
196	Steve Farr	.05
197	John Orton	.05
198	Kelly Gruber	.05
199	Ron Darling	.05
200	Ruben Sierra	.05
201	Chuck Finley	.05
202	Mike Moore	.05
203	Pat Borders	.05
204	Sid Bream	.05
205	Todd Zeile	.05
206	Rick Wilkins	.05
207	Jim Gantner	.05
208	Frank Castillo	.05
209	Dave Hansen	.05
210	Trevor Wilson	.05
211	Sandy Alomar, Jr.	.15
212	Sean Berry	.05
213	Tino Martinez	.25
214	Chito Martinez	.05
215	Dan Walters	.05
216	John Franco	.05
217	Glenn Davis	.05
218	Mariano Duncan	.05
219	Mike LaValliere	.05
220	Rafael Palmeiro	.20
221	Jack Clark	.05
222	Hal Morris	.05
223	Ed Sprague	.05
224	John Valentin	.10
225	Sam Militello	.05
226	Bob Wickman	.05
227	Damion Easley	.10
228	John Jaha	.10
229	Bob Ayrault	.05
230	Mo Sanford (Expansion Draft)	.05
231	Walt Weiss (Expansion Draft)	.05
232	Dante Bichette (Expansion Draft)	.35
233	Steve Decker (Expansion Draft)	.05
234	Jerald Clark (Expansion Draft)	.05
235	Bryan Harvey (Expansion Draft)	.05
236	Joe Girardi (Expansion Draft)	.05
237	Dave Magadan (Expansion Draft)	.05
238	David Nied (Rookie Prospect)	.05
239	*Eric Wedge* (Rookie Prospect)	.05
240	Rico Brogna (Rookie Prospect)	.10
241	J.T. Bruett (Rookie Prospect)	.05
242	Jonathan Hurst (Rookie Prospect)	.05
243	Bret Boone (Rookie Prospect)	.25
244	Manny Alexander (Rookie Prospect)	.15
245	Scooter Tucker (Rookie Prospect)	.05
246	Troy Neel (Rookie Prospect)	.10
247	Eddie Zosky (Rookie Prospect)	.05
248	Melvin Nieves (Rookie Prospect)	.05
249	Ryan Thompson (Rookie Prospect)	.15
250	Shawn Barton (Rookie Prospect)	.10
251	Ryan Klesko (Rookie Prospect)	.50
252	Mike Piazza (Rookie Prospect)	2.00
253	Steve Hosey (Rookie Prospect)	.10
254	Shane Reynolds (Rookie Prospect)	.15
255	Dan Wilson (Rookie Prospect)	.15
256	Tom Marsh (Rookie Prospect)	.05
257	Barry Manuel (Rookie Prospect)	.05
258	Paul Miller (Rookie Prospect)	.05
259	Pedro Martinez (Rookie Prospect)	.25
260	Steve Cooke (Rookie Prospect)	.10
261	Johnny Guzman (Rookie Prospect)	.05
262	Mike Butcher (Rookie Prospect)	.10
263	Bien Figueroa (Rookie Prospect)	.10
264	Rich Rowland (Rookie Prospect)	.05
265	Shawn Jeter (Rookie Prospect)	.10
266	Gerald Williams (Rookie Prospect)	.15
267	Derek Parks (Rookie Prospect)	.05
268	Henry Mercedes (Rookie Prospect)	.10
269	*David Hulse* (Rookie Prospect)	.10
270	*Tim Pugh* (Rookie Prospect)	.10
271	William Suero (Rookie Prospect)	.05
272	Ozzie Canseco (Rookie Prospect)	.05
273	Fernando Ramsey (Rookie Prospect)	.10
274	Bernardo Brito (Rookie Prospect)	.05
275	Dave Mlicki (Rookie Prospect)	.10
276	Tim Salmon (Rookie Prospect)	.60
277	Mike Raczka (Rookie Prospect)	.05
278	*Ken Ryan* (Rookie Prospect)	.25
279	Rafael Bournigal (Rookie Prospect)	.10
280	Wil Cordero (Rookie Prospect)	.15
281	Billy Ashley (Rookie Prospect)	.10
282	Paul Wagner (Rookie Prospect)	.10
283	Blas Minor (Rookie Prospect)	.10
284	Rick Trlicek (Rookie Prospect)	.05
285	Willie Greene (Rookie Prospect)	.05
286	Ted Wood (Rookie Prospect)	.05
287	Phil Clark (Rookie Prospect)	.05
288	Jesse Levis (Rookie Prospect)	.10
289	Tony Gwynn (Now & Then)	.40
290	Nolan Ryan (Now & Then)	1.00
291	Dennis Martinez (Now & Then)	.05
292	Eddie Murray (Now & Then)	.15
293	Robin Yount (Now & Then)	.30
294	George Brett (Now & Then)	.40
295	Dave Winfield (Now & Then)	.15
296	Bert Blyleven (Now & Then)	.05
297	Jeff Bagwell (Idols - Carl Yastrzemski)	.40
298	John Smoltz (Idols - Jack Morris)	.10
299	Larry Walker (Idols - Mike Bossy)	.20
300	Gary Sheffield (Idols - Barry Larkin)	.15
301	Ivan Rodriguez (Idols - Carlton Fisk)	.25
302	Delino DeShields (Idols - Malcolm X)	.05
303	Tim Salmon (Idols - Dwight Evans)	.25
304	Bernard Gilkey (Hometown Heroes)	.05
305	Cal Ripken, Jr. (Hometown Heroes)	1.00
306	Barry Larkin (Hometown Heroes)	.10
307	Kent Hrbek (Hometown Heroes)	.05
308	Rickey Henderson (Hometown Heroes)	.10
309	Darryl Strawberry (Hometown Heroes)	.05
310	John Franco (Hometown Heroes)	.05
311	Todd Stottlemyre	.05
312	Luis Gonzalez	.10
313	Tommy Greene	.05
314	Randy Velarde	.05
315	Steve Avery	.05
316	Jose Oquendo	.05
317	Rey Sanchez	.05
318	Greg Vaughn	.10
319	Orel Hershiser	.05
320	Paul Sorrento	.05
321	Royce Clayton	.05
322	John Vander Wal	.05
323	Henry Cotto	.05
324	Pete Schourek	.05
325	David Segui	.05
326	Arthur Rhodes	.05
327	Bruce Hurst	.05
328	Wes Chamberlain	.05
329	Ozzie Smith	.45
330	Scott Cooper	.05
331	Felix Fermin	.05
332	Mike Macfarlane	.05
333	Dan Gladden	.05
334	Kevin Tapani	.05
335	Steve Sax	.05
336	Jeff Montgomery	.05
337	Gary DiSarcina	.05
338	Lance Blankenship	.05
339	Brian Williams	.05
340	Duane Ward	.05
341	Chuck McElroy	.05
342	Joe Magrane	.05
343	Jaime Navarro	.05
344	Dave Justice	.25
345	Jose Offerman	.05
346	Marquis Grissom	.10
347	Bill Swift	.05
348	Jim Thome	.50
349	Archi Cianfrocco	.05
350	Anthony Young	.05
351	Leo Gomez	.05
352	Bill Gullickson	.05
353	Alan Trammell	.10
354	Dan Pasqua	.05
355	Jeff King	.05
356	Kevin Brown	.10
357	Tim Belcher	.05
358	Bip Roberts	.05
359	Brent Mayne	.05
360	Rheal Cormier	.05
361	Mark Guthrie	.05
362	Craig Grebeck	.05
363	Andy Stankiewicz	.05
364	Juan Guzman	.05
365	Bobby Witt	.05
366	Mark Portugal	.05
367	Brian McRae	.05
368	Mark Lemke	.05
369	Bill Wegman	.05
370	Donovan Osborne	.05
371	Derrick May	.05
372	Carl Willis	.05
373	Chris Nabholz	.05
374	Mark Lewis	.05
375	John Burkett	.05
376	Luis Mercedes	.05
377	Ramon Martinez	.15
378	Kyle Abbott	.05
379	Mark Wohlers	.05
380	Bob Walk	.05
381	Kenny Rogers	.05
382	Tim Naehring	.05
383	Alex Fernandez	.05
384	Keith Miller	.05
385	Mike Henneman	.05
386	Rick Aguilera	.05
387	George Bell	.05
388	Mike Gallego	.05
389	Howard Johnson	.05
390	Kim Batiste	.05
391	Jerry Browne	.05
392	Damon Berryhill	.05
393	Ricky Bones	.05
394	Omar Olivares	.05
395	Mike Harkey	.05
396	Pedro Astacio	.05
397	John Wetteland	.05
398	Rod Beck	.05
399	Thomas Howard	.05
400	Mike Devereaux	.05
401	Tim Wakefield	.05
402	Curt Schilling	.10
403	Zane Smith	.05
404	Bob Zupcic	.05
405	Tom Browning	.05
406	Tony Phillips	.05
407	John Doherty	.05
408	Pat Mahomes	.05
409	John Habyan	.05
410	Steve Olin	.05
411	Chad Curtis	.10
412	Joe Grahe	.05
413	John Patterson	.05
414	Brian Hunter	.05
415	Doug Henry	.05
416	Lee Smith	.05

duced as a subdued background photo, over which are printed recent stats and a few biographical details. A different player photo is featured at left. Pinnacle's trademarks appear at lower-right, while the brand's optical-variable anti-counterfeiting device is at bottom center. Subsets include major award winners, Rookie Prospects and Draft Picks which are appropriately noted with gold-foil lettering on front. The issue was produced in two series of 270 cards each.

		MT
Complete Set (540):		35.00
Complete Series 1 (270):		20.00
Complete Series 2 (270):		15.00
Common Player:		.10
Artist's Proof Stars: 20X		
Younng Stars/RCs: 15X		
Museum Stars: 8X		
Young Stars/RCs: 5X		
Series 1 & 2 Wax Box:		38.00
1	Frank Thomas	1.50
2	Carlos Baerga	.10
3	Sammy Sosa	1.50
4	Tony Gwynn	1.00
5	John Olerud	.20
6	Ryne Sandberg	.75
7	Moises Alou	.15
8	Steve Avery	.10
9	Tim Salmon	.40
10	Cecil Fielder	.15
11	Greg Maddux	2.00
12	Barry Larkin	.20
13	Mike Devereaux	.10
14	Charlie Hayes	.10
15	Albert Belle	.75
16	Andy Van Slyke	.10
17	Mo Vaughn	.50
18	Brian McRae	.10
19	Cal Eldred	.10
20	Craig Biggio	.20
21	Kirby Puckett	1.00
22	Derek Bell	.10
23	Don Mattingly	1.00
24	John Burkett	.10
25	Roger Clemens	1.00
26	Barry Bonds	.75
27	Paul Molitor	.40
28	Mike Piazza	1.50
29	Robin Ventura	.20
30	Jeff Conine	.15
31	Wade Boggs	.30
32	Dennis Eckersley	.10
33	Bobby Bonilla	.10
34	Len Dykstra	.10
35	Manny Alexander	.10
36	Ray Lankford	.10
37	Greg Vaughn	.15
38	Chuck Finley	.10
39	Todd Benzinger	.10
40	Dave Justice	.40
41	Rob Dibble	.10
42	Tom Henke	.10
43	David Nied	.10
44	Sandy Alomar Jr.	.15
45	Pete Harnisch	.10
46	Jeff Russell	.10
47	Terry Mulholland	.10
48	Kevin Appier	.10
49	Randy Tomlin	.10
50	Cal Ripken, Jr.	2.50
51	Andy Benes	.10
52	Jimmy Key	.10
53	Kirt Manwaring	.10
54	Kevin Tapani	.10
55	Jose Guzman	.10
56	Todd Stottlemyre	.10
57	Jack McDowell	.10
58	Orel Hershiser	.10
59	Chris Hammond	.10
60	Chris Nabholz	.10
61	Ruben Sierra	.10
62	Dwight Gooden	.10
63	John Kruk	.10
64	Omar Vizquel	.10
65	Tim Naehring	.10
66	Dwight Smith	.10
67	Mickey Tettleton	.10
68	J.T. Snow	.20
69	Greg McMichael	.10
70	Kevin Mitchell	.10
71	Kevin Brown	.15
72	Scott Cooper	.10
73	Jim Thome	.30
74	Joe Girardi	.10
75	Eric Anthony	.10
76	Orlando Merced	.10
77	Felix Jose	.10
78	Tommy Greene	.10
79	Bernard Gilkey	.10
80	Phil Plantier	.10
81	Danny Tartabull	.10
82	Trevor Wilson	.10
83	Chuck Knoblauch	.15
84	Rick Wilkins	.10
85	Devon White	.10
86	Lance Johnson	.10
87	Eric Karros	.15
88	Gary Sheffield	.15
89	Wil Cordero	.10
90	Ron Darling	.10
91	Darren Daulton	.10
92	Joe Orsulak	.10
93	Steve Cooke	.10
94	Darryl Hamilton	.10
95	Aaron Sele	.15
96	John Doherty	.10
97	Gary DiSarcina	.10
98	Jeff Blauser	.10
99	John Smiley	.10
100	Ken Griffey, Jr.	3.00
101	Dean Palmer	.10
102	Felix Fermin	.10
103	Jerald Clark	.10
104	Doug Drabek	.10
105	Curt Schilling	.15
106	Jeff Montgomery	.10
107	Rene Arocha	.10
108	Carlos Garcia	.10
109	Wally Whitehurst	.10
110	Jim Abbott	.15
111	Royce Clayton	.10
112	Chris Hoiles	.10
113	Mike Morgan	.10
114	Joe Magrane	.10
115	Tom Candiotti	.10
116	Ron Karkovice	.10
117	Ryan Bowen	.10
118	Rod Beck	.10
119	John Wetteland	.10
120	Terry Steinbach	.10
121	Dave Hollins	.10
122	Jeff Kent	.10
123	Ricky Bones	.10
124	Brian Jordan	.10
125	Chad Kreuter	.10
126	John Valentin	.10
127	Billy Hathaway	.10
128	Wilson Alvarez	.10
129	Tino Martinez	.10
130	Rodney Bolton	.10
131	David Segui	.10
132	Wayne Kirby	.10
133	Eric Young	.10
134	Scott Servais	.10
135	Scott Radinsky	.10
136	Bret Barberie	.10
137	John Roper	.10
138	Ricky Gutierrez	.10
139	Bernie Williams	.50
140	Bud Black	.10
141	Jose Vizcaino	.10
142	Gerald Williams	.10
143	Duane Ward	.10
144	Danny Jackson	.10
145	Allen Watson	.10
146	Scott Fletcher	.10
147	Delino DeShields	.10
148	Shane Mack	.10
149	Jim Eisenreich	.10
150	Troy Neel	.15
151	Jay Bell	.10
152	B.J. Surhoff	.10
153	Mark Whiten	.10
154	Mike Henneman	.10
155	Todd Hundley	.15
156	Greg Myers	.10
157	Ryan Klesko	.50
158	Dave Fleming	.10
159	Mickey Morandini	.10
160	Blas Minor	.10
161	Reggie Jefferson	.10
162	David Hulse	.10
163	Greg Swindell	.10
164	Roberto Hernandez	.10
165	Brady Anderson	.10
166	Jack Armstrong	.10
167	Phil Clark	.10
168	Melido Perez	.10
169	Darren Lewis	.10
170	Sam Horn	.10
171	Mike Harkey	.10
172	Juan Guzman	.10
173	Bob Natal	.10
174	Deion Sanders	.25
175	Carlos Quintana	.10
176	Mel Rojas	.10
177	Willie Banks	.10
178	Ben Rivera	.10
179	Kenny Lofton	.60
180	Leo Gomez	.10
181	Roberto Mejia	.10
182	Mike Perez	.10
183	Travis Fryman	.15
184	Ben McDonald	.10
185	Steve Frey	.10
186	Kevin Young	.10
187	Dave Magadan	.10
188	Bobby Munoz	.10
189	Pat Rapp	.10
190	Jose Offerman	.10
191	Vinny Castilla	.15
192	Ivan Calderon	.10
193	Ken Caminiti	.20
194	Benji Gil	.10
195	Chuck Carr	.10
196	Derrick May	.10
197	Pat Kelly	.10
198	Jeff Brantley	.10
199	Jose Lind	.10
200	Steve Buechele	.10
201	Wes Chamberlain	.10
202	Eduardo Perez	.10
203	Bret Saberhagen	.10
204	Gregg Jefferies	.15
205	Darrin Fletcher	.10
206	Kent Hrbek	.10
207	Kim Batiste	.10
208	Jeff King	.10
209	Donovan Osborne	.10
210	Dave Nilsson	.10
211	Al Martin	.10
212	Mike Moore	.10
213	Sterling Hitchcock	.15
214	Geronimo Pena	.10
215	Kevin Higgins	.10
216	Norm Charlton	.10
217	Don Slaught	.10
218	Mitch Williams	.10
219	Derek Lilliquist	.10
220	Armando Reynoso	.10
221	Kenny Rogers	.10
222	Doug Jones	.10
223	Luis Aquino	.10
224	Mike Oquist	.10
225	Darryl Scott	.10
226	Kurt Abbott	.10
227	Andy Tomberlin	.10
228	Norberto Martin	.10
229	Pedro Castellano	.10
230	*Curtis Pride*	.25
231	Jeff McNeely	.15
232	Scott Lydy	.10
233	Darren Oliver	.10
234	Danny Bautista	.10
235	Butch Huskey	.10
236	Chipper Jones	1.50
237	Eddie Zambrano	.10
238	Jean Domingo	.10
239	Javier Lopez	.30
240	Nigel Wilson	.15
241	*Drew Denson*	.15
242	Raul Mondesi	.50
243	Luis Ortiz	.10
244	Manny Ramirez	1.00
245	Greg Blosser	.10
246	Rondell White	.20
247	Steve Karsay	.10
248	Scott Stahoviak	.10
249	Jose Valentin	.10
250	Marc Newfield	.10
251	Keith Kessinger	.10
252	Carl Everett	.10
253	John O'Donoghue	.10
254	Turk Wendell	.10
255	Scott Ruffcorn	.10
256	Tony Tarasco	.10
257	Andy Cook	.10
258	Matt Mieske	.10
259	Luis Lopez	.10
260	Ramon Caraballo	.10
261	Salomon Torres	.10
262	*Brooks Kieschnick*	.50
263	*Daron Kirkreit*	.25
264	*Bill Wagner*	.40
265	*Matt Drews*	.15
266	Scott Christman	.10
267	*Torii Hunter*	.25
268	*Jamey Wright*	.25
269	Jeff Granger	.10
270	*Trot Nixon*	.75
271	Randy Myers	.10
272	Trevor Hoffman	.15
273	Bob Wickman	.10
274	Willie McGee	.10
275	Hipolito Pichardo	.10
276	Bobby Witt	.10
277	Gregg Olson	.10
278	Randy Johnson	.25
279	Robb Nen	.10
280	Paul O'Neill	.15
281	Lou Whitaker	.10
282	Chad Curtis	.10
283	Doug Henry	.10
284	Tom Glavine	.15
285	Mike Greenwell	.10
286	Roberto Kelly	.10
287	Roberto Alomar	.60
288	Charlie Hough	.10
289	Alex Fernandez	.15
290	Jeff Bagwell	1.00
291	Wally Joyner	.10
292	Andujar Cedeno	.10
293	Rick Aguilera	.10
294	Darryl Strawberry	.15
295	Mike Mussina	.40
296	Jeff Gardner	.10
297	Chris Gwynn	.10
298	Matt Williams	.30
299	Brent Gates	.15
300	Mark McGwire	3.00
301	Jim Deshaies	.10
302	Edgar Martinez	.10
303	Danny Darwin	.10
304	Pat Meares	.10
305	Benito Santiago	.10
306	Jose Canseco	.30
307	Jim Gott	.10
308	Paul Sorrento	.10
309	Scott Kamieniecki	.10
310	Larry Walker	.25
311	Mark Langston	.10
312	John Jaha	.10
313	Stan Javier	.10
314	Hal Morris	.10
315	Robby Thompson	.10
316	Pat Hentgen	.10
317	Tom Gordon	.10
318	Joey Cora	.10
319	Luis Alicea	.10
320	Andre Dawson	.15
321	Darryl Kile	.10
322	Jose Rijo	.10
323	Luis Gonzalez	.15
324	Billy Ashley	.10
325	David Cone	.15
326	Bill Swift	.10
327	Phil Hiatt	.10
328	Craig Paquette	.10
329	Bob Welch	.10
330	Tony Phillips	.10
331	Archi Cianfrocco	.10
332	Dave Winfield	.25
333	David McCarty	.15
334	Al Leiter	.15
335	Tom Browning	.10
336	Mark Grace	.20
337	Jose Mesa	.10
338	Mike Stanley	.10
339	Roger McDowell	.10
340	Damion Easley	.10
341	Angel Miranda	.10
342	John Smoltz	.10
343	Jay Buhner	.10
344	Bryan Harvey	.10
345	Joe Carter	.15
346	Dante Bichette	.30
347	Jason Bere	.10
348	Frank Viola	.10
349	Ivan Rodriguez	.65
350	Juan Gonzalez	1.00
351	Steve Finley	.10
352	Mike Felder	.10
353	Ramon Martinez	.15
354	Greg Gagne	.10
355	Ken Hill	.10
356	Pedro Munoz	.10
357	Todd Van Poppel	.10
358	Marquis Grissom	.15
359	Milt Cuyler	.10
360	Reggie Sanders	.15
361	Scott Erickson	.10
362	Billy Hatcher	.10
363	Gene Harris	.10
364	Rene Gonzales	.10
365	Kevin Rogers	.10
366	Eric Plunk	.10
367	Todd Zeile	.10
368	John Franco	.10
369	Brett Butler	.10
370	Bill Spiers	.10
371	Terry Pendleton	.10
372	Chris Bosio	.10
373	Orestes Destrade	.10
374	Dave Stewart	.10
375	Darren Holmes	.10
376	Doug Strange	.10
377	Brian Turang	.15
378	Carl Willis	.10
379	Mark McLemore	.10
380	Bobby Jones	.15
381	Scott Sanders	.10
382	Kirk Rueter	.15
383	Randy Velarde	.10
384	Fred McGriff	.35
385	Charles Nagy	.10
386	Rich Amaral	.10
387	Geronimo Berroa	.10
388	Eric Davis	.10
389	Ozzie Smith	.25
390	Alex Arias	.10
391	Brad Ausmus	.10
392	Cliff Floyd	.15
393	Roger Salkeld	.10
394	Jim Edmonds	.30
395	Jeromy Burnitz	.15
396	Dave Staton	.10
397	Rob Butler	.10
398	Marcos Armas	.10
399	Darrell Whitmore	.10
400	Ryan Thompson	.15
401	*Ross Powell*	.10
402	Joe Oliver	.10
403	Paul Carey	.10
404	Bob Hamelin	.10
405	Chris Turner	.10
406	Nate Minchey	.10
407	*Lonnie Maclin*	.10
408	Harold Baines	.10
409	Brian Williams	.15
410	Johnny Ruffin	.10
411	*Julian Tavarez*	.25
412	Mark Hutton	.10
413	Carlos Delgado	.50
414	Chris Gomez	.10
415	Mike Hampton	.10
416	Alex Diaz	.10
417	Jeffrey Hammonds	.10
418	Jayhawk Owens	.10
419	J.R. Phillips	.10
420	*Cory Bailey*	.15
421	Denny Hocking	.10
422	Jon Shave	.10
423	Damon Buford	.15
424	Troy O'Leary	.10
425	Tripp Cromer	.10
426	Albie Lopez	.10
427	Tony Fernandez	.10
428	Ozzie Guillen	.10
429	Alan Trammell	.10
430	*John Wasdin*	.40
431	Marc Valdes	.10
432	*Brian Anderson*	.25
433	*Matt Brunson*	.25
434	*Wayne Gomes*	.50
435	*Jay Powell*	.25
436	*Kirk Presley*	.50
437	*Jon Ratliff*	.25
438	*Derrek Lee*	1.50
439	Tom Pagnozzi	.10
440	Kent Mercker	.10
441	*Phil Leftwich*	.20
442	Jamie Moyer	.10
443	John Flaherty	.10
444	Mark Wohlers	.10
445	Jose Bautista	.10
446	Andres Galarraga	.15
447	Mark Lemke	.10
448	Tim Wakefield	.10
449	Pat Listach	.10
450	Rickey Henderson	.25
451	Mike Gallego	.10
452	Bob Tewksbury	.10
453	Kirk Gibson	.10
454	Pedro Astacio	.10
455	Mike Lansing	.10
456	Sean Berry	.10
457	Bob Walk	.10
458	Chili Davis	.10
459	Ed Sprague	.10
460	Kevin Stocker	.10
461	Mike Stanton	.10
462	Tim Raines	.15
463	Mike Bordick	.10
464	David Wells	.15
465	Tim Laker	.10
466	Cory Snyder	.10
467	Alex Cole	.10
468	Pete Incaviglia	.10
469	Roger Pavlik	.10
470	Greg W. Harris	.10
471	Xavier Hernandez	.10
472	Erik Hanson	.10
473	Jesse Orosco	.10
474	Greg Colbrunn	.10
475	Harold Reynolds	.10
476	Greg Harris	.10
477	Pat Borders	.10
478	Melvin Nieves	.10
479	Mariano Duncan	.10
480	Greg Hibbard	.10
481	Tim Pugh	.10
482	Bobby Ayala	.10
483	Sid Fernandez	.10
484	Tim Wallach	.10
485	Randy Milligan	.10
486	Walt Weiss	.10
487	Matt Walbeck	.20
488	Mike Macfarlane	.10
489	Jerry Browne	.10
490	Chris Sabo	.10
491	Tim Belcher	.10
492	Spike Owen	.10
493	Rafael Palmeiro	.20
494	Brian Harper	.10
495	Eddie Murray	.20
496	Ellis Burks	.10
497	Karl Rhodes	.10
498	Otis Nixon	.10
499	Lee Smith	.10
500	Bip Roberts	.10
501	Pedro Martinez	.10
502	Brian L. Hunter	.15
503	Tyler Green	.15
504	Bruce Hurst	.10
505	Alex Gonzalez	.30
506	Mark Portugal	.10
507	Bob Ojeda	.10
508	Dave Henderson	.10
509	Bo Jackson	.20
510	Bret Boone	.15
511	Mark Eichhorn	.10
512	Luis Polonia	.10
513	Will Clark	.35
514	Dave Valle	.10
515	Dan Wilson	.10
516	Dennis Martinez	.10
517	Jim Leyritz	.10
518	Howard Johnson	.10
519	Jody Reed	.10
520	Julio Franco	.10
521	Jeff Reardon	.10
522	Willie Greene	.10
523	Shawon Dunston	.10
524	Keith Mitchell	.10
525	Rick Helling	.10
526	Mark Kiefer	.10
527	*Chan Ho Park*	.75
528	Tony Longmire	.15
529	Rich Becker	.10
530	Tim Hyers	.10
531	Darrin Jackson	.10
532	Jack Morris	.10
533	Rick White	.10
534	Mike Kelly	.15
535	James Mouton	.10
536	Steve Trachsel	.30
537	Tony Eusebio	.10
538	Kelly Stinnett	.10
539	Paul Spoljaric	.10
540	Darren Dreifort	.15

1994 Pinnacle Artist's Proof

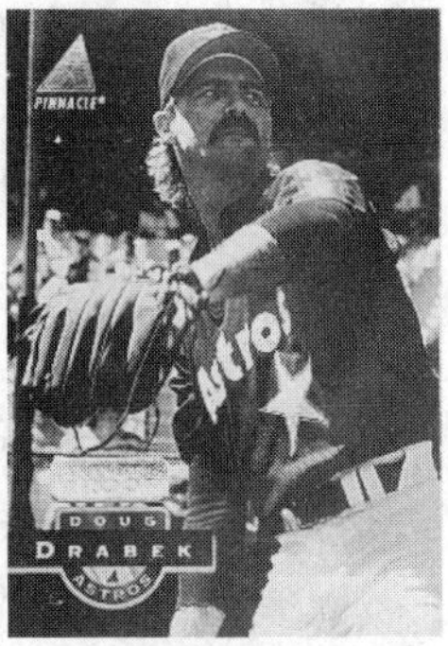

A specially designated version of the regular Pinnacle set, described as the first day's production of the first 1,000 of each card, was issued as a random pack insert. Cards feature a small gold-foil "Artist's Proof" rectangle embossed above the player/team name shield on front. In all other respects the cards are identical to the regular-issue versions.

	MT
Complete Set (540):	1600.
Common Player:	1.00
Stars: 20X	
Young Stars/RCs: 15X	

(See 1994 Pinnacle for checklist and base card values.)

1994 Pinnacle Museum Collection

Each card in the 1994 Pinnacle set was produced in a parallel "Museum Collection" version. The inserts were produced utilizing the company's Dufex foil-printing technology on front, with rays emanating from the Pinnacle logo. Backs are virtually identical to the regular-issue version except for the substitution of a "1994 Museum Collection" logo for the optical-variable anti-counterfeiting bar at bottom-center. Museums were random package inserts, appearing at the rate of about once per four packs.

	MT
Complete Set (540):	500.00
Common Player:	1.00
Stars: 8X	
Young Stars/RCs: 5X	

(See 1994 Pinnacle for checklist and base card values.)

1994 Pinnacle Rookie Team Pinnacle

The very popular Rookie Team Pinnacle insert card tradition continued in 1994 with a series of nine "two-headed" cards featuring the top prospect from each league at each position. The cards again feature the ultra-realistic artwork of Chris Greco. Each side is enhanced with gold-foil presentations of the player's name, the Pinnacle logo and the Rookie Team Pinnacle logo. The inserts were packaged, on average, one per 90 packs of hobby foil only.

		MT
Complete Set (9):		50.00
Common Player:		2.50
1	Carlos Delgado, Javier Lopez	12.50
2	Bob Hamelin, J.R. Phillips	3.00
3	Jon Shave, Keith Kessinger	2.50
4	Butch Huskey, Luis Ortiz	2.50
5	Chipper Jones, Kurt Abbott	17.50
6	Rondell White, Manny Ramirez	15.00
7	Cliff Floyd, Jeffrey Hammonds	3.00
8	Marc Newfield, Nigel Wilson	2.50
9	Salomon Torres, Mark Hutton	2.50

1994 Pinnacle Run Creators

This insert set, exclusive to Pinnacle jumbo packaging, features the top 44 performers of the previous season in the arcane statistic of "runs created." Fronts have an action player photo on which the stadium background has been muted in soft-focus red or blue. The player's last name appears at right in gold foil; the logo, "The Run Creators" is in one of the lower corners. Backs are printed in teal with a color team logo at center, beneath the stats that earned the player's inclusion in the series. The player's runs created are in gold foil above the write-up. Cards are numbered with an "RC" prefix.

		MT
Complete Set (44):		45.00
Common Player:		.75
1	John Olerud	1.00
2	Frank Thomas	4.00
3	Ken Griffey, Jr.	8.00
4	Paul Molitor	1.00
5	Rafael Palmeiro	1.00
6	Roberto Alomar	2.00
7	Juan Gonzalez	4.00
8	Albert Belle	2.50
9	Travis Fryman	.75
10	Rickey Henderson	1.50
11	Tony Phillips	.75
12	Mo Vaughn	1.50
13	Tim Salmon	.75
14	Kenny Lofton	3.00
15	Carlos Baerga	.75
16	Greg Vaughn	.75
17	Jay Buhner	.75
18	Chris Hoiles	.75
19	Mickey Tettleton	.75
20	Kirby Puckett	3.00
21	Danny Tartabull	.75
22	Devon White	.75
23	Barry Bonds	2.50
24	Lenny Dykstra	.75
25	John Kruk	.75
26	Fred McGriff	1.50
27	Gregg Jefferies	.75
28	Mike Piazza	4.00
29	Jeff Blauser	.75
30	Andres Galarraga	.75
31	Darren Daulton	.75
32	Dave Justice	1.50
33	Craig Biggio	.75
34	Mark Grace	1.00
35	Tony Gwynn	3.00
36	Jeff Bagwell	3.00
37	Jay Bell	.75
38	Marquis Grissom	.75
39	Matt Williams	1.00
40	Charlie Hayes	.75
41	Dante Bichette	1.00
42	Bernard Gilkey	.75
43	Brett Butler	.75
44	Rick Wilkins	.75

1994 Pinnacle Team Pinnacle

The double-sided Team Pinnacle insert set features 18 of the top players in the game. Team Pinnacle shows two card fronts, one on each side. They were inserted into 1994 Pinnacle Baseball Series II at a rate of one every 90 packs.

		MT
Complete Set (9):		100.00
Common Player:		5.00
1	Jeff Bagwell, Frank Thomas	20.00
2	Carlos Baerga, Robby Thompson	5.00
3	Matt Williams, Dean Palmer	5.00
4	Cal Ripken, Jr., Jay Bell	25.00
5	Ivan Rodriguez, Mike Piazza	20.00
6	Len Dykstra, Ken Griffey, Jr.	27.50
7	Juan Gonzalez, Barry Bonds	15.00
8	Tim Salmon, Dave Justice	6.00
9	Greg Maddux, Jack McDowell	17.50

1994 Pinnacle Tribute

A hobby-only insert set, found approximately one per 18 foil packs, this nine-card series honors players who reached significant season or career milestones or otherwise had special achievements in 1993. Fronts feature full-bleed action photos. At left is a black strip with "TRIBUTE" in gold foil. A colored strip at bottom has the player name in gold foil and a short description of why he is being feted beneath. The Pinnacle logo is in gold foil at top. The same gold-foil enhancements are found on back, along with a portrait photo. In a black box at bottom are details of the tribute. The Pinnacle optical-variable anti-counterfeiting device is at bottom center. Card numbers are prefixed with "TR".

		MT
Complete Set (18):		60.00
Common Player:		1.50
1	Paul Molitor	3.00
2	Jim Abbott	1.50
3	Dave Winfield	2.00
4	Bo Jackson	1.50
5	Dave Justice	2.00
6	Len Dykstra	1.50
7	Mike Piazza	9.00
8	Barry Bonds	4.00
9	Randy Johnson	2.00
10	Ozzie Smith	3.00
11	Mark Whiten	1.50
12	Greg Maddux	8.00
13	Cal Ripken, Jr.	12.50
14	Frank Thomas	7.50
15	Juan Gonzalez	7.50
16	Roberto Alomar	2.50
17	Ken Griffey, Jr.	15.00
18	Lee Smith	1.50

1994 Pinnacle New Generation

Twenty-five of baseball's hottest rookies and second-year players are featured in this boxed set. Cards are typical Pinnacle quality with full-bleed action photos, UV coating and gold-foil stamping on front and back. A total of 100,000 sets was produced, with a suggested retail price of $9.95.

		MT
Complete Set (25):		8.00
Common Player:		.25
1	Tim Salmon	.50
2	Mike Piazza	2.00
3	Jason Bere	.25
4	Jeffrey Hammonds	.30
5	Aaron Sele	.35
6	Salomon Torres	.25
7	Wil Cordero	.25
8	Allen Watson	.25
9	J.T. Snow	.45
10	Cliff Floyd	.35
10a	Cliff Floyd (overprinted "SAMPLE" card)	2.00
11	Jeff McNeely	.25
12	Butch Huskey	.45
13	J.R. Phillips	.25
14	Bobby Jones	.25
15	Javier Lopez	.50
16	Scott Ruffcorn	.25
17	Manny Ramirez	1.00
18	Carlos Delgado	.30
19	Rondell White	.45
20	Chipper Jones	2.00
21	Billy Ashley	.25
22	Nigel Wilson	.25
23	Jeromy Burnitz	.25
24	Danny Bautista	.25
25	Darrell Whitmore	.25

1994 Pinnacle Power Surge

Twenty-five of the major leagues' heaviest hitters are featured in this boxed set. Cards are typical Pinnacle quality with gold-foil stamping (player's last name at top and Pinnacle logo at bottom) on front, UV coating on both sides and high-tech graphics. Fronts feature game-action photos while backs have smaller portrait and action photos on a marbled background, along with 1993 and career stats and a description of the player's power potential. Cards are numbered with a "PS" prefix in the upper-right on back. A total of 100,000 sets were produced.

		MT
Complete Set (25):		8.00
Common Player:		.25
1	Dave Justice	.50
2	Chris Hoiles	.25
3	Mo Vaughn	.50
4	Tim Salmon	.50
5	J.T. Snow	.35
6	Frank Thomas	1.00
7	Sammy Sosa	1.50
8	Rick Wilkins	.25
9	Robin Ventura	.35
10	Reggie Sanders	.25
11	Albert Belle	.75
12	Carlos Baerga	.25
12a	Carlos Baerga (overprinted "SAMPLE" card)	2.00
13	Manny Ramirez	.75
14	Travis Fryman	.25
15	Gary Sheffield	.45
16	Jeff Bagwell	.75
17	Mike Piazza	1.00
18	Eric Karros	.30
19	Cliff Floyd	.25
20	Mark Whiten	.25
21	Phil Plantier	.25
22	Derek Bell	.30
23	Ken Griffey Jr.	2.00
24	Juan Gonzalez	.75
25	Dean Palmer	.25

1994 Pinnacle The Naturals

The Naturals is a 25-card boxed set issued by Pinnacle. This set puts an action player photo against a textured- foil background. The card backs picture the player on a background of nature photography, including lightning, blue skies and clouds. Pinnacle produced 100,000 sets, which come in a numbered, sealed box with a certificate of authenticity.

		MT
Complete Set (25):		12.00
Common Player:		.25
1	Frank Thomas	1.50
2	Barry Bonds	1.00
3	Ken Griffey, Jr.	2.50
4	Juan Gonzalez	1.25
5	Dave Justice	.50
6	Albert Belle	.75
7	Kenny Lofton	.60
8	Roberto Alomar	.50
9	Tim Salmon	.35
10	Randy Johnson	.50
11	Kirby Puckett	1.00
12	Tony Gwynn	.90
13	Fred McGriff	.40
14	Ryne Sandberg	.90
15	Greg Maddux	1.25
16	Matt Williams	.35
17	Lenny Dykstra	.25
18	Gary Sheffield	.40
18a	Gary Sheffield (overprinted "SAMPLE")	3.00
19	Mike Piazza	1.50
20	Dean Palmer	.25
21	Travis Fryman	.25
22	Carlos Baerga	.25
23	Cal Ripken, Jr.	2.00
24	John Olerud	.35
25	Roger Clemens	.90

1995 Pinnacle Series 1 Samples

This eight-card cello-wrapped sample set was sent to dealers to preview the 1995 Pinnacle Series I cards. The cards are identical to regular-issue Pinnacle cards except they carry a white diagonal "SAMPLE" notation on front and back.

		MT
Complete Set (9):		35.00
Common Player:		3.00
16	Mickey Morandini	3.00
22US	Wil Cordero (Upstart) (card not included in most packs)	10.00
119	Gary Sheffield	4.00
122	Ivan Rodriguez	4.00
132	Alex Rodriguez (Rookie)	10.00
208	Bo Jackson	3.00
223	Jose Rijo	3.00
224	Ryan Klesko	3.00
----	Header card	.15

1995 Pinnacle

The 1995 Pinnacle set was produced in two series of 225 base cards each, plus inserts. Fronts have borderless photos with a large embossed gold foil "wave" at bottom containing the player's last name and team logo. Backs are horizontally formatted and have a portrait photo at left, an action photo at right and a few sentences about the player at center. Stats at the bottom offer previous year, career and career-best numbers. Subsets with the base cards include rookie specials in Series I and II which have a design featuring a green stripe at one side or bottom with the player's name in gold and a special round gold-foil logo. A similar design, with red stripes, is used for Series I cards only featuring Draft Picks. In Series II, a 30-card Swing Men subset has a blue vortex background design and special gold-foil identifier. Basic pack configurations offered 12-card ($2.49) and 15-card ($2.99) counts in both retail and hobby versions, each with some unique inserts.

		MT
Complete Set (450):		30.00
Common Player:		.10
Hobby Wax Box:		45.00
Retail Wax Box:		60.00
Unlisted Stars: .20 to .35		
1	Jeff Bagwell	1.00
2	Roger Clemens	.75
3	Mark Whiten	.10
4	Shawon Dunston	.10
5	Bobby Bonilla	.10
6	Kevin Tapani	.10
7	Eric Karros	.15
8	Cliff Floyd	.10
9	Pat Kelly	.10
10	Jeffrey Hammonds	.10
11	Jeff Conine	.10
12	Fred McGriff	.25
13	Chris Bosio	.10
14	Mike Mussina	.40
15	Danny Bautista	.10
16	Mickey Morandini	.10
17	Chuck Finley	.10
18	Jim Thome	.40
19	Luis Ortiz	.10
20	Walt Weiss	.10
21	Don Mattingly	1.00
22	Bob Hamelin	.10
23	Melido Perez	.10
24	Kevin Mitchell	.10
25	John Smoltz	.25
26	Hector Carrasco	.10
27	Pat Hentgen	.10
28	Derrick May	.10
29	Mike Kingery	.10
30	Chuck Carr	.10
31	Billy Ashley	.10
32	Todd Hundley	.15
33	Luis Gonzalez	.10
34	Marquis Grissom	.10
35	Jeff King	.10
36	Eddie Williams	.10
37	Tom Pagnozzi	.10
38	Chris Hoiles	.10
39	Sandy Alomar	.15
40	Mike Greenwell	.10
41	Lance Johnson	.10
42	Junior Felix	.10
43	Felix Jose	.10
44	Scott Leius	.10
45	Ruben Sierra	.10
46	Kevin Seitzer	.10
47	Wade Boggs	.25
48	Reggie Jefferson	.10
49	Jose Canseco	.30
50	Dave Justice	.20
51	John Smiley	.10
52	Joe Carter	.15
53	Rick Wilkins	.10
54	Ellis Burks	.10
55	Dave Weathers	.10
56	Pedro Astacio	.10
57	Ryan Thompson	.10
58	James Mouton	.10
59	Mel Rojas	.10
60	Orlando Merced	.10
61	Matt Williams	.30
62	Bernard Gilkey	.10
63	J.R. Phillips	.10
64	Lee Smith	.10
65	Jim Edmonds	.15
66	Darrin Jackson	.10
67	Scott Cooper	.10
68	Ron Karkovice	.10
69	Chris Gomez	.10
70	Kevin Appier	.10
71	Bobby Jones	.10
72	Doug Drabek	.10
73	Matt Mieske	.10
74	Sterling Hitchcock	.10
75	John Valentin	.10
76	Reggie Sanders	.10
77	Wally Joyner	.10
78	Turk Wendell	.10
79	Wendell Hayes	.10
80	Bret Barberie	.10
81	Troy Neel	.10
82	Ken Caminiti	.25
83	Milt Thompson	.10
84	Paul Sorrento	.10
85	Trevor Hoffman	.10
86	Jay Bell	.10
87	Mark Portugal	.10
88	Sid Fernandez	.10
89	Charles Nagy	.10
90	Jeff Montgomery	.10
91	Chuck Knoblauch	.20
92	Jeff Frye	.10
93	Tony Gwynn	1.00
94	John Olerud	.15
95	David Nied	.10
96	Chris Hammond	.10
97	Edgar Martinez	.10
98	Kevin Stocker	.10
99	Jeff Fassero	.10
100	Curt Schilling	.15
101	Dave Clark	.10
102	Delino DeShields	.10
103	Leo Gomez	.10
104	Dave Hollins	.10
105	Tim Naehring	.10
106	Otis Nixon	.10
107	Ozzie Guillen	.10
108	Jose Lind	.10
109	Stan Javier	.10
110	Greg Vaughn	.15
111	Chipper Jones	2.00
112	Ed Sprague	.10
113	Mike Macfarlane	.10
114	Steve Finley	.10
115	Ken Hill	.10
116	Carlos Garcia	.10
117	Lou Whitaker	.10
118	Todd Zeile	.10
119	Gary Sheffield	.40
120	Ben McDonald	.10
121	Pete Harnisch	.10
122	Ivan Rodriguez	.60
123	Wilson Alvarez	.10
124	Travis Fryman	.15
125	Pedro Munoz	.10
126	Mark Lemke	.10
127	Jose Valentin	.10
128	Ken Griffey Jr.	3.00
129	Omar Vizquel	.10
130	Milt Cuyler	.10
131	Steve Traschel	.25
132	Alex Rodriguez	2.50
133	Garret Anderson	.15
134	Armando Benitez	.10
135	Shawn Green	.20
136	Jorge Fabregas	.10
137	Orlando Miller	.10
138	Rikkert Faneyte	.10
139	Ismael Valdes	.10
140	Jose Oliva	.10
141	Aaron Small	.10
142	Tim Davis	.10
143	Ricky Bottalacio	.10
144	Mike Matheny	.10
145	Roberto Petagine	.10
146	Fausto Cruz	.10
147	Bryce Florie	.10
148	Jose Lima	.10
149	John Hudek	.10
150	Duane Singleton	.10
151	John Mabry	.10
152	Robert Eenhoorn	.10
153	Jon Lieber	.10
154	Garey Ingram	.10
155	Paul Shuey	.10
156	Mike Lieberthal	.10
157	Steve Dunn	.10
158	Charles Johnson	.15
159	Ernie Young	.10
160	Jose Martinez	.10
161	Kurt Miller	.10
162	Joey Eischen	.10
163	Dave Stevens	.10
164	Brian Hunter	.15
165	Jeff Cirillo	.10
166	Mark Smith	.10
167	*McKay Christensen*	.20
168	C.J. Nitkowski	.10
169	*Antone Williamson*	.50
170	Paul Konerko	2.00
171	*Scott Elarton*	.35
172	Jacob Shumate	.10
173	Terrence Long	.15
174	*Mark Johnson*	.25
175	Ben Grieve	2.00
176	*Jayson Peterson*	.20
177	Checklist	.10
178	Checklist	.10
179	Checklist	.10
180	Checklist	.10
181	Brian Anderson	.15
182	Steve Buechele	.10
183	Mark Clark	.10
184	Cecil Fielder	.15
185	Steve Avery	.10
186	Devon White	.10
187	Craig Shipley	.10
188	Brady Anderson	.15
189	Kenny Lofton	.60
190	Alex Cole	.10
191	Brent Gates	.10
192	Dean Palmer	.10
193	Alex Gonzalez	.15
194	Steve Cooke	.10
195	Ray Lankford	.10
196	Mark McGwire	3.00
197	Marc Newfield	.10
198	Pat Rapp	.10
199	Darren Lewis	.10
200	Carlos Baerga	.10
201	Rickey Henderson	.25
202	Kurt Abbott	.10
203	Kirt Manwaring	.10
204	Cal Ripken Jr.	2.50
205	Darren Daulton	.10
206	Greg Colbrunn	.10
207	Darryl Hamilton	.10
208	Bo Jackson	.15
209	Tony Phillips	.10
210	Geronimo Berroa	.10
211	Rich Becker	.10
212	Tony Tarasco	.10
213	Karl Rhodes	.10
214	Phil Plantier	.10
215	J.T. Snow	.20
216	Mo Vaughn	.50
217	Greg Gagne	.10
218	Rickey Bones	.10
219	Mike Bordick	.10
220	Chad Curtis	.10
221	Royce Clayton	.10
222	Roberto Alomar	.60
223	Jose Rijo	.10
224	Ryan Klesko	.25
225	Mark Langston	.10
226	Frank Thomas	1.50
227	Juan Gonzalez	1.50
228	Ron Gant	.15
229	Javier Lopez	.20
230	Sammy Sosa	2.00
231	Kevin Brown	.15
232	Gary DiSarcina	.10
233	Albert Belle	.75
234	Jay Buhner	.15
235	Pedro Martinez	.15
236	Bob Tewksbury	.10
237	Mike Piazza	2.00
238	Darryl Kile	.10
239	Bryan Harvey	.10
240	Andres Galarraga	.20
241	Jeff Blauser	.10
242	Jeff Kent	.10
243	Bobby Munoz	.10
244	Greg Maddux	2.00
245	Paul O'Neill	.15
246	Lenny Dykstra	.10
247	Todd Van Poppel	.10
248	Bernie Williams	.40
249	Glenallen Hill	.10
250	Duane Ward	.10
251	Dennis Eckersley	.10
252	Pat Mahomes	.10
253	Rusty Greer (photo actually Jeff Frye)	.10
254	Roberto Kelly	.10
255	Randy Myers	.10
256	Scott Ruffcorn	.10
257	Robin Ventura	.15
258	Eduardo Perez	.10
259	Aaron Sele	.10
260	Paul Molitor	.35
261	Juan Guzman	.10
262	Darren Oliver	.10
263	Mike Stanley	.10
264	Tom Glavine	.20
265	Rico Brogna	.10
266	Craig Biggio	.15
267	Darrell Whitmore	.10
268	Jimmy Key	.10
269	Will Clark	.30
270	David Cone	.15
271	Brian Jordan	.15
272	Barry Bonds	.75
273	Danny Tartabull	.10
274	Ramon Martinez	.10
275	Al Martin	.10
276	Fred McGriff (Swing Men)	.25
277	Carlos Delgado (Swing Men)	.40
278	Juan Gonzalez (Swing Men)	.50
279	Shawn Green (Swing Men)	.15
280	Carlos Baerga (Swing Men)	.10
281	Cliff Floyd (Swing Men)	.10
282	Ozzie Smith (Swing Men)	.25
283	Alex Rodriguez (Swing Men)	1.50
284	Kenny Lofton (Swing Men)	.40
285	Dave Justice (Swing Men)	.20
286	Tim Salmon (Swing Men)	.15
287	Manny Ramirez (Swing Men)	1.00
288	Will Clark (Swing Men)	.20
289	Garret Anderson (Swing Men)	.10
290	Billy Ashley (Swing Men)	.10
291	Tony Gwynn (Swing Men)	.50
292	Raul Mondesi (Swing Men)	.25
293	Rafael Palmeiro (Swing Men)	.15
294	Matt Williams (Swing Men)	.10
295	Don Mattingly (Swing Men)	.50
296	Kirby Puckett (Swing Men)	.50
297	Paul Molitor (Swing Men)	.20
298	Albert Belle (Swing Men)	.40
299	Barry Bonds (Swing Men)	.40
300	Mike Piazza (Swing Men)	.75
301	Jeff Bagwell (Swing Men)	.50
302	Frank Thomas (Swing Men)	.75
303	Chipper Jones (Swing Men)	.75
304	Ken Griffey Jr. (Swing Men)	2.00
305	Cal Ripken Jr. (Swing Men)	1.50
306	Eric Anthony	.10
307	Todd Benzinger	.10
308	Jacob Brumfield	.10
309	Wes Chamberlain	.10
310	Tino Martinez	.10
311	Roberto Mejia	.10
312	Jose Offerman	.10
313	David Segui	.10
314	Eric Young	.10
315	Rey Sanchez	.10
316	Raul Mondesi	.50
317	Bret Boone	.10
318	Andre Dawson	.15
319	Brian McRae	.10
320	Dave Nilsson	.10
321	Moises Alou	.15
322	Don Slaught	.10
323	Dave McCarty	.10
324	Mike Huff	.10
325	Rick Aguilera	.10
326	Rod Beck	.10
327	Kenny Rogers	.10
328	Andy Benes	.10
329	Allen Watson	.10
330	Randy Johnson	.35
331	Willie Greene	.10
332	Hal Morris	.10
333	Ozzie Smith	.35
334	Jason Bere	.10
335	Scott Erickson	.10
336	Dante Bichette	.35
337	Willie Banks	.10
338	Eric Davis	.10
339	Rondell White	.20
340	Kirby Puckett	.75
341	Deion Sanders	.20
342	Eddie Murray	.40
343	Mike Harkey	.10
344	Joey Hamilton	.10
345	Roger Salkeld	.10
346	Wil Cordero	.10
347	John Wetteland	.10
348	Geronimo Pena	.10
349	Kirk Gibson	.10
350	Manny Ramirez	1.00
351	William Van Landingham	.10
352	B.J. Surhoff	.10
353	Ken Ryan	.10
354	Terry Steinbach	.10
355	Bret Saberhagen	.10
356	John Jaha	.10
357	Joe Girardi	.10
358	Steve Karsay	.10
359	Alex Fernandez	.15
360	Salomon Torres	.10
361	John Burkett	.10
362	Derek Bell	.10
363	Tom Henke	.10
364	Gregg Jefferies	.10
365	Jack McDowell	.10
366	Andujar Cedeno	.10

367	Dave Winfield	.20
368	Carl Everett	.10
369	Danny Jackson	.10
370	Jeromy Burnitz	.10
371	Mark Grace	.20
372	Larry Walker	.25
373	Bill Swift	.10
374	Dennis Martinez	.10
375	Mickey Tettleton	.10
376	Mel Nieves	.10
377	Cal Eldred	.10
378	Orel Hershiser	.10
379	David Wells	.15
380	Gary Gaetti	.10
381	Tim Raines	.10
382	Barry Larkin	.20
383	Jason Jacome	.10
384	Tim Wallach	.10
385	Robby Thompson	.10
386	Frank Viola	.10
387	Dave Stewart	.10
388	Bip Roberts	.10
389	Ron Darling	.10
390	Carlos Delgado	.25
391	Tim Salmon	.20
392	Alan Trammell	.10
393	Kevin Foster	.10
394	Jim Abbott	.10
395	John Kruk	.10
396	Andy Van Slyke	.10
397	Dave Magadan	.10
398	Rafael Palmeiro	.25
399	Mike Devereaux	.10
400	Benito Santiago	.10
401	Brett Butler	.10
402	John Franco	.10
403	Matt Walbeck	.10
404	Terry Pendleton	.10
405	Chris Sabo	.10
406	Andrew Lorraine	.10
407	Dan Wilson	.10
408	Mike Lansing	.10
409	Ray McDavid	.10
410	Shane Andrews	.10
411	Tom Gordon	.10
412	Chad Ogea	.10
413	James Baldwin	.10
414	Russ Davis	.10
415	Ray Holbert	.10
416	Ray Durham	.15
417	Matt Nokes	.10
418	Rodney Henderson	.10
419	Gabe White	.10
420	Todd Hollandsworth	.10
421	Midre Cummings	.10
422	Harold Baines	.10
423	Troy Percival	.10
424	Joe Vitiello	.10
425	Andy Ashby	.10
426	Michael Tucker	.10
427	Mark Gubicza	.10
428	Jim Bullinger	.10
429	Jose Malave	.10
430	Pete Schourek	.10
431	Bobby Ayala	.10
432	Marvin Freeman	.10
433	Pat Listach	.10
434	Eddie Taubensee	.10
435	Steve Howe	.10
436	Kent Mercker	.10
437	Hector Fajardo	.10
438	Scott Kamieniecki	.10
439	Robb Nen	.10
440	Mike Kelly	.10
441	Tom Candiotti	.10
442	Albie Lopez	.10
443	Jeff Granger	.10
444	Rich Aude	.10
445	Luis Polonia	.10
446	A.L. Checklist (Frank Thomas)	.50
447	A.L. Checklist (Ken Griffey Jr.)	1.00
448	N.L. Checklist (Mike Piazza)	.50
449	N.L. Checklist (Jeff Bagwell)	.40
450	Insert Checklist (Frank Thomas, Ken Griffey Jr., Mike Piazza, Jeff Bagwell)	.50

1995 Pinnacle Artist's Proof

Said to represent the first 1,000 of each card printed, the Artist's Proof chase set is a parallel issue with a counterpart for each of the regular-issue cards. The proofs differ in the use of silver, rather than gold foil for front graphic highlights, and the inclusion of a rectangular silver-foil "ARTIST'S PROOF" logo on front. The AP inserts were reported seeded at an average rate of one per 26 packs.

	MT
Complete Set (450):	1650.
Common Player:	2.00
Stars: 15X	
Young Stars/RCs: 10X	
(See 1995 Pinnacle for checklist and base card values.)	

1995 Pinnacle Museum Collection

Pinnacle's Dufex foil-printing technology on the card fronts differentiates the cards in this parallel insert set from the corresponding cards in the regular issue. Backs have a rectangular "1995 Museum Collection" logo at the lower-left. Museum inserts are found at an average rate of one per four packs. Because of production difficulties, trade cards had to be issued in place of seven of the rookie cards in Series 2. Those redemption cards were valid only through Dec. 31, 1995.

	MT
Complete Set (450):	450.00
Common Player:	.75
Stars: 8X	
Young Stars/RCs: 4X	
(See 1995 Pinnacle for checklist and base card values.)	

1995 Pinnacle E.T.A. '95

This hobby-only chase card set identifies six players who were picked to arrive in the major leagues for a 1995 debut. Both front and back have borderless action photos on which the background has been subdued and posterized. Gold-foil headlines on each side of the card give the player's credentials. These inserts are found on average of once per 24 packs.

		MT
Complete Set (6):		20.00
Common Player:		1.00
1	Ben Grieve	15.00
2	Alex Ochoa	1.50
3	Joe Vitiello	1.00
4	Johnny Damon	6.00
5	Trey Beamon	2.00
6	Brooks Kieschnick	1.50

1995 Pinnacle Gate Attraction

Series II jumbo packs are the exclusive source for this chase set. Printed on metallic foil, the cards have a color photo at top and a second photo at bottom that is shown in gold tones only. A "Gate Attraction" seal is in the lower-left corner. Backs have a large portrait photo on a color-streaked background, plus a few words about the player.

		MT
Complete Set (18):		60.00
Common Player:		1.00
1	Ken Griffey Jr.	12.00
2	Frank Thomas	6.00
3	Cal Ripken Jr.	10.00
4	Jeff Bagwell	5.00
5	Mike Piazza	7.50
6	Barry Bonds	3.00
7	Kirby Puckett	3.50
8	Albert Belle	3.00
9	Tony Gwynn	6.00
10	Raul Mondesi	1.00
11	Will Clark	1.50
12	Don Mattingly	3.50
13	Roger Clemens	5.00
14	Paul Molitor	3.00
15	Matt Williams	1.00
16	Greg Maddux	7.00
17	Kenny Lofton	2.00
18	Cliff Floyd	1.00

1995 Pinnacle New Blood

Both hobby and retail packs of Series II Pinnacle hide this insert set of young stars, at an average rate of one card per 90 packs. A player photo appears in the red and silver foil-printed background, and there is a color action photo in the foreground. Conventionally printed backs feature the same photos, but with their prominence reversed. A few words of text describe the player's star potential.

		MT
Complete Set (9):		55.00
Common Player:		2.00
1	Alex Rodriguez	25.00
2	Shawn Green	7.50
3	Brian Hunter	3.00
4	Garret Anderson	2.00
5	Charles Johnson	5.00
6	Chipper Jones	20.00
7	Carlos Delgado	4.00
8	Billy Ashley	2.00
9	J.R. Phillips	2.00

1995 Pinnacle Performers

Series I jumbos were the only place to find this chase set. Fronts have a deep red background with a golden pyramid at center and a silver apex, all in foil printing. A color player action photo is in the center foreground. The reverse repeats the front photo in the background, in one color, and has a second color photo, along with a few words about the player.

		MT
Complete Set (18):		90.00
Common Player:		2.00
1	Frank Thomas	10.00
2	Albert Belle	6.00
3	Barry Bonds	7.50
4	Juan Gonzalez	8.00
5	Andres Galarraga	2.50
6	Raul Mondesi	2.50
7	Paul Molitor	5.00
8	Tim Salmon	2.00
9	Mike Piazza	15.00
10	Gregg Jefferies	2.00
11	Will Clark	3.00
12	Greg Maddux	12.50
13	Manny Ramirez	8.00
14	Kirby Puckett	7.50
15	Shawn Green	5.00
16	Rafael Palmeiro	3.00
17	Paul O'Neill	2.50
18	Jason Bere	2.00

1995 Pinnacle Red Hot

These Series II inserts are found at an average rate of one per 16 packs and feature top veterans stars. Fronts have a large action photo on right, over a background of foil-printed red and yellow flames. A vertical strip at left of graduated red tones has a player portrait photo and the "RED HOT" flame logo, again printed on foil. Backs are conventionally printed and have a black background with large flaming "RED HOT" letters and a color player photo.

		MT
Complete Set (25):		80.00
Common Player:		1.50
1	Cal Ripken Jr.	12.00
2	Ken Griffey Jr.	15.00
3	Frank Thomas	6.00
4	Jeff Bagwell	6.00
5	Mike Piazza	10.00
6	Barry Bonds	4.00
7	Albert Belle	4.00
8	Tony Gwynn	6.00
9	Kirby Puckett	5.00
10	Don Mattingly	5.00
11	Matt Williams	1.50
12	Greg Maddux	10.00
13	Raul Mondesi	2.00
14	Paul Molitor	3.00
15	Manny Ramirez	5.00
16	Joe Carter	1.50
17	Will Clark	2.00
18	Roger Clemens	5.00
19	Tim Salmon	1.50
20	Dave Justice	1.50
21	Kenny Lofton	3.00
22	Deion Sanders	1.50
23	Roberto Alomar	3.00
24	Cliff Floyd	1.50
25	Carlos Baerga	1.50

1995 Pinnacle Team Pinnacle

This nine-card Series I insert set becomes an 18-card challenge if the collector decides to hunt for both versions of each card. As in the past the Team Pinnacle cards picture National and American League counterparts at each position on different sides of the same card. In 1995 each card is printed with one side in Pinnacle's Dufex foil technology, and the other side conventionally printed. Thus card #1 can be found with Mike Mussina in Dufex and Greg Maddux conventionally printed, or with Maddux in Dufex and Mussina conventional. Team Pinnacle cards are found inserted at an average rate of only one per 90 packs.

		MT
Complete Set (9):		180.00
Common Player:		6.00
1	Mike Mussina, Greg Maddux	25.00
2	Carlos Delgado, Mike Piazza	25.00
3	Frank Thomas, Jeff Bagwell	20.00
4	Roberto Alomar, Craig Biggio	10.00
5	Cal Ripken Jr., Ozzie Smith	30.00
6	Travis Fryman, Matt Williams	6.00
7	Ken Griffey Jr., Barry Bonds	40.00
8	Albert Belle, Dave Justice	10.00
9	Kirby Puckett, Tony Gwynn	20.00

1995 Pinnacle Team Pinnacle Pin Trade Cards

In one of the hobby's first major attempts to cross-promote pin- and card-collecting, Series 2 Pinnacle packs offered a special insert set of cards which could be redeemed for a collector's pin of the same player. Seeded at the rate of one per 48 regular packs and one per 36 jumbo packs, the pin redemption cards were valid until Nov. 15, 1995. Payment of $2 handling fee was required for redemption.

		MT
Complete Set (18):		75.00
Common Player:		2.00
1	Greg Maddux	6.00
2	Mike Mussina	2.00
3	Mike Piazza	6.00
4	Carlos Delgado	2.00
5	Jeff Bagwell	4.00
6	Frank Thomas	5.00
7	Craig Biggio	2.00
8	Roberto Alomar	3.00
9	Ozzie Smith	3.00
10	Cal Ripken Jr.	8.00
11	Matt Williams	3.00
12	Travis Fryman	2.00
13	Barry Bonds	5.00
14	Ken Griffey Jr.	10.00
15	Dave Justice	2.00
16	Albert Belle	4.00
17	Tony Gwynn	5.00
18	Kirby Puckett	4.00

1995 Pinnacle Team Pinnacle Collector Pins

Redemption cards in Series 2 packs could be traded in (until Nov. 15, 1995) for an enameled pin of the player pictured on the trade card. Pins are about 1-3/8" x 1-1/4". A raised relief portrait of the player is at center with his name in pennants above and his team logo at bottom, along with the Pinnacle logo. Backs are gold-tone with a post-and-button style of pinback. The unnumbered pins are listed here in the same sequence as the redemption cards.

		MT
Complete Set (18):		150.00
Common Player:		4.00
(1)	Greg Maddux	12.00
(2)	Mike Mussina	4.00
(3)	Mike Piazza	12.00
(4)	Carlos Delgado	4.00
(5)	Jeff Bagwell	8.00
(6)	Frank Thomas	8.00
(7)	Craig Biggio	4.00
(8)	Roberto Alomar	8.00
(9)	Ozzie Smith	6.00
(10)	Cal Ripken Jr.	16.00
(11)	Matt Williams	6.00
(12)	Travis Fryman	4.00
(13)	Barry Bonds	10.00
(14)	Ken Griffey Jr.	16.00
(15)	Dave Justice	4.00
(16)	Albert Belle	8.00
(17)	Tony Gwynn	10.00
(18)	Kirby Puckett	10.00

1995 Pinnacle Pin-Cards

Virtually nothing is known of this issue except that it is connected in some way to the Series 2 Pinnacle player pin issue. The front features portrait and action photos on a red background with gold-foil graphics. Backs have career highlights, a large color photo and a card number with "PPC" prefix. To date only a single card is known.

15	Dave Justice (Value undetermined)	

1995 Pinnacle Upstarts

Thirty of the most dominant young players in the game were featured in this insert series. Cards are printed with most of the photo's background covered by the legs of a large blue and gold star device, which includes the team logo at its red center. A blue circular "'95 UPSTARTS" logo at bottom-left has the player name in gold. These cards are exclusive to Series I, found at an average rate of one per eight packs.

		MT
Complete Set (30):		35.00
Common Player:		.50
1	Frank Thomas	6.00
2	Roberto Alomar	2.00
3	Mike Piazza	9.00
4	Javier Lopez	.60
5	Albert Belle	4.50
6	Carlos Delgado	.75
7	Rusty Greer	.50
8	Tim Salmon	.75
9	Raul Mondesi	.65
10	Juan Gonzalez	6.00
11	Manny Ramirez	4.50
12	Sammy Sosa	10.00
13	Jeff Kent	.50
14	Melvin Nieves	.50
15	Rondell White	.65
16	Shawn Green	1.50
17	Bernie Williams	1.50
18	Aaron Sele	.50
19	Jason Bere	.50
20	Joey Hamilton	.50
21	Mike Kelly	.50
22	Wil Cordero	.50
23	Moises Alou	.60
24	Roberto Kelly	.50
25	Deion Sanders	1.50
26	Steve Karsay	.50
27	Bret Boone	.50
28	Willie Greene	.50
29	Billy Ashley	.50
30	Brian Anderson	.50

1995 Pinnacle FanFest

Pinnacle's sponsorship of the July 7-11, 1995, All-Star FanFest was marked with the issue of this 30-card set. Cards were distributed in two-card packs at various venues around the All-Star celebration in Arlington, Texas, home of the Texas Rangers. Each card features the FanFest logo at lower-left on front, with the player's name and team logo in a stylized gold-foil baseball diamond diagram at lower-right. A full-bleed action photo comprises the rest of the front. Horizontally formatted backs show a portrait photo of the player before a photo of The Ballpark at Arlington. There are black bands at top and bottom. The FanFast logo is repeated at bottom-center.

		MT
Complete Set (30):		15.00
Common Player:		.50
1	Cal Ripken Jr.	2.50
2	Roger Clemens	1.00
3	Don Mattingly	1.50
4	Albert Belle	.75
5	Kirby Puckett	1.00
6	Cecil Fielder	.50
7	Kevin Appier	.50
8	Will Clark	.60
9	Juan Gonzalez	1.25
10	Ivan Rodriguez	.75
11	Ken Griffey Jr.	3.00
12	Tim Salmon	.60
13	Frank Thomas	1.50
14	Roberto Alomar	.60
15	Rickey Henderson	.75
16	Raul Mondesi	.60
17	Matt Williams	.60
18	Ozzie Smith	.90
19	Deion Sanders	.60
20	Tony Gwynn	1.25
21	Greg Maddux	1.50
22	Sammy Sosa	1.50
23	Mike Piazza	1.50
24	Barry Bonds	1.25
25	Jeff Bagwell	1.25
26	Len Dykstra	.50
27	Rico Brogna	.50
28	Larry Walker	.65
29	Gary Sheffield	.65
30	Wil Cordero	.50

1995 Pinnacle White Hot

Similar in format to the Red Hot inserts, and featuring the same players, the hobby-only White Hot cards are a chase set of a chase set. Seeded one per 36 packs on average (more than twice as scarce as the Red Hots), the White Hot cards have fronts totally printed in the Dufex process, with predominantly blue and white background colors, while the backs are highlighted by blue foil printing in the "WHITE HOT" background lettering on black background.

		MT
Complete Set (25):		200.00
Common Player:		4.00
1	Cal Ripken Jr.	25.00
2	Ken Griffey Jr.	30.00
3	Frank Thomas	15.00
4	Jeff Bagwell	12.00
5	Mike Piazza	20.00
6	Barry Bonds	8.00
7	Albert Belle	8.00
8	Tony Gwynn	15.00
9	Kirby Puckett	10.00
10	Don Mattingly	10.00
11	Matt Williams	4.00
12	Greg Maddux	20.00
13	Raul Mondesi	4.00
14	Paul Molitor	6.00
15	Manny Ramirez	8.00
16	Joe Carter	4.00
17	Will Clark	6.00
18	Roger Clemens	8.00
19	Tim Salmon	4.00
20	Dave Justice	4.00
21	Kenny Lofton	6.00
22	Deion Sanders	6.00
23	Roberto Alomar	6.00
24	Cliff Floyd	4.00
25	Carlos Baerga	4.00

1996 Pinnacle Samples

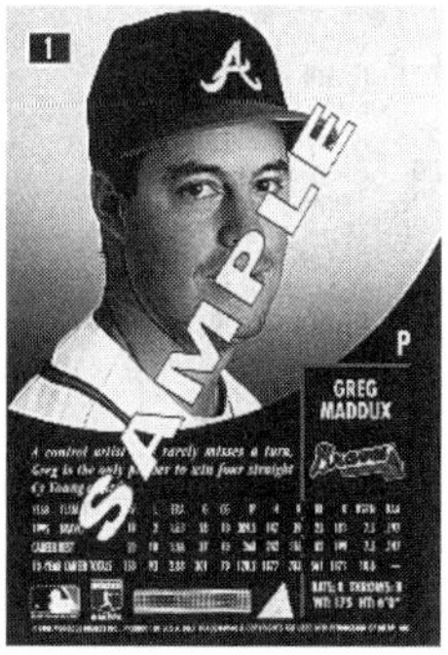

Pinnacle's 1996 issue was premiered with this nine-card sample set. The cards are virtually identical in format to the regular-issue cards, but feature a large white "SAMPLE" printed diagonally on front and back. The cards were sent to dealers and hobby media in a cello pack.

		MT
Complete Set (9):		20.00
Common Player:		3.00
1	Greg Maddux	6.00
2	Bill Pulsipher	3.00
3	Dante Bichette	3.00
4	Mike Piazza	6.00
5	Garret Anderson	3.00
165	Ruben Rivera	3.00
168	Tony Clark	4.00
2	Mo Vaughn (Pinnacle Power)	4.00
---	Header card	.50

Checklists with card numbers in parentheses ( ) indicates the numbers do not appear on the card.

1996 Pinnacle

Pinnacle issued a 399-card regular-issue set with borderless front photos highlighted by prismatic gold-foil graphics in the shape of a triangle at bottom. The player's name is in black in the triangle. Backs have another player photo along with stats and data. Parallel Starburst and Starburst Artist's Proof sets contain only 200 of the cards in the base issue. Series I inserts include a Cal Ripken Jr. "Tribute" card, numbered "1 of 1" (seeded one per 150 packs). The other five Series I inserts are Team Pinnacle, Pinnacle Power, Team Tomorrow, Essence of the Game and First Rate. Series II inserts the Christie Brinkley Collection, Project Stardom, Skylines, Slugfest and Team Spirit. Pinnacle was sold in 10-card hobby and retail foil packs, and 18-card jumbo packs.

		MT
Complete Set (400):		35.00
Common Player:		.10
Unlisted Stars: .20 to .35		
Wax Box:		35.00
1	Greg Maddux	2.00
2	Bill Pulsipher	.10
3	Dante Bichette	.25
4	Mike Piazza	2.00
5	Garret Anderson	.10
6	Steve Finley	.10
7	Andy Benes	.10
8	Chuck Knoblauch	.15
9	Tom Gordon	.10
10	Jeff Bagwell	1.25
11	Wil Cordero	.10
12	John Mabry	.10
13	Jeff Frye	.10
14	Travis Fryman	.15
15	John Wetteland	.10
16	Jason Bates	.10
17	Danny Tartabull	.10
18	Charles Nagy	.10
19	Robin Ventura	.15
20	Reggie Sanders	.10
21	Dave Clark	.10
22	Jaime Navarro	.10
23	Joey Hamilton	.10
24	Al Leiter	.15
25	Deion Sanders	.25
26	Tim Salmon	.20
27	Tino Martinez	.15
28	Mike Greenwell	.10
29	Phil Plantier	.10
30	Bobby Bonilla	.10
31	Kenny Rogers	.10
32	Chili Davis	.10
33	Joe Carter	.15
34	Mike Mussina	.40
35	Matt Mieske	.10
36	Jose Canseco	.30
37	Brad Radke	.10
38	Juan Gonzalez	1.50
39	David Segui	.10
40	Alex Fernandez	.10
41	Jeff Kent	.10
42	Todd Zeile	.10
43	Darryl Strawberry	.10
44	Jose Rijo	.10
45	Ramon Martinez	.10
46	Manny Ramirez	1.00
47	Gregg Jefferies	.10
48	Bryan Rekar	.10
49	Jeff King	.10
50	John Olerud	.15
51	Marc Newfield	.10
52	Charles Johnson	.15
53	Robby Thompson	.10
54	Brian Hunter	.10
55	Mike Blowers	.10
56	Keith Lockhart	.10
57	Ray Lankford	.10

58	Tim Wallach	.10
59	Ivan Rodriguez	.50
60	Ed Sprague	.10
61	Paul Molitor	.30
62	Eric Karros	.10
63	Glenallen Hill	.10
64	Jay Bell	.10
65	Tom Pagnozzi	.10
66	Greg Colbrunn	.10
67	Edgar Martinez	.10
68	Paul Sorrento	.10
69	Kirt Manwaring	.10
70	Pete Schourek	.10
71	Orlando Merced	.10
72	Shawon Dunston	.10
73	Ricky Bottalico	.10
74	Brady Anderson	.15
75	Steve Ontiveros	.10
76	Jim Abbott	.10
77	Carl Everett	.10
78	Mo Vaughn	.75
79	Pedro Martinez	.20
80	Harold Baines	.10
81	Alan Trammell	.10
82	Steve Avery	.10
83	Jeff Cirillo	.10
84	John Valentin	.10
85	Bernie Williams	.50
86	Andre Dawson	.15
87	Dave Winfield	.25
88	B.J. Surhoff	.10
89	Jeff Blauser	.10
90	Barry Larkin	.15
91	Cliff Floyd	.15
92	Sammy Sosa	1.50
93	Andres Galarraga	.15
94	Dave Nilsson	.10
95	James Mouton	.10
96	Marquis Grissom	.10
97	Matt Williams	.25
98	John Jaha	.10
99	Don Mattingly	1.00
100	Tim Naehring	.10
101	Kevin Appier	.10
102	Bobby Higginson	.10
103	Andy Pettitte	.90
104	Ozzie Smith	.40
105	Kenny Lofton	.75
106	Ken Caminiti	.15
107	Walt Weiss	.10
108	Jack McDowell	.10
109	Brian McRae	.10
110	Gary Gaetti	.10
111	Curtis Goodwin	.10
112	Dennis Martinez	.10
113	Omar Vizquel	.10
114	Chipper Jones	2.00
115	Mark Gubicza	.10
116	Ruben Sierra	.10
117	Eddie Murray	.40
118	Chad Curtis	.10
119	Hal Morris	.10
120	Ben McDonald	.10
121	Marty Cordova	.10
122	Ken Griffey Jr.	3.00
123	Gary Sheffield	.20
124	Charlie Hayes	.10
125	Shawn Green	.30
126	Jason Giambi	.15
127	Mark Langston	.10
128	Mark Whiten	.10
129	Greg Vaughn	.15
130	Mark McGwire	3.50
131	Hideo Nomo	.50
132	Eric Karros, Raul Mondesi, Hideo Nomo, Mike Piazza	.50
133	Jason Bere	.10
134	Ken Griffey Jr. (The Naturals)	1.50
135	Frank Thomas (The Naturals)	1.00
136	Cal Ripken Jr. (The Naturals)	1.25
137	Albert Belle (The Naturals)	.40
138	Mike Piazza (The Naturals)	1.00
139	Dante Bichette (The Naturals)	.15
140	Sammy Sosa (The Naturals)	.75
141	Mo Vaughn (The Naturals)	.30
142	Tim Salmon (The Naturals)	.15
143	Reggie Sanders (The Naturals)	.10
144	Cecil Fielder (The Naturals)	.10
145	Jim Edmonds (The Naturals)	.10
146	Rafael Palmeiro (The Naturals)	.10
147	Edgar Martinez (The Naturals)	.10
148	Barry Bonds (The Naturals)	.30
149	Manny Ramirez (The Naturals)	.50
150	Larry Walker (The Naturals)	.15
151	Jeff Bagwell (The Naturals)	.50
152	Ron Gant (The Naturals)	.10
153	Andres Galarraga (The Naturals)	.10
154	Eddie Murray (The Naturals)	.20
155	Kirby Puckett (The Naturals)	.50
156	Will Clark (The Naturals)	.15
157	Don Mattingly (The Naturals)	.60
158	Mark McGwire (The Naturals)	1.50
159	Dean Palmer (The Naturals)	.10
160	Matt Williams (The Naturals)	.15
161	Fred McGriff (The Naturals)	.20
162	Joe Carter (The Naturals)	.10
163	Juan Gonzalez (The Naturals)	.60
164	Alex Ochoa	.10
165	Ruben Rivera	.15
166	Tony Clark	.50
167	Brian Barber	.10
168	Matt Lawton	.10
169	Terrell Wade	.10
170	Johnny Damon	.20
171	Derek Jeter	2.00
172	Phil Nevin	.10
173	Robert Perez	.10
174	C.J. Nitkowski	.10
175	Joe Vitiello	.10
176	Roger Cedeno	.10
177	Ron Coomer	.10
178	Chris Widger	.10
179	Jimmy Haynes	.10
180	Mike Sweeney	.10
181	Howard Battle	.10
182	John Wasdin	.10
183	Jim Pittsley	.10
184	Bob Wolcott	.10
185	LaTroy Hawkins	.10
186	Nigel Wilson	.10
187	Dustin Hermanson	.20
188	Chris Snopek	.10
189	Mariano Rivera	.20
190	Jose Herrera	.10
191	Chris Stynes	.10
192	Larry Thomas	.10
193	David Bell	.10
194	(Frank Thomas) (checklist)	.50
195	(Ken Griffey Jr.) (checklist)	1.50
196	(Cal Ripken Jr.) (checklist)	.75
197	(Jeff Bagwell) (checklist)	.25
198	(Mike Piazza) (checklist)	.45
199	(Barry Bonds) (checklist)	.40
200	(Garrett Anderson, Chipper Jones) (checklist)	.35
201	Frank Thomas	1.50
202	Michael Tucker	.10
203	Kirby Puckett	.75
204	Alex Gonzalez	.10
205	Tony Gwynn	1.00
206	Moises Alou	.10
207	Albert Belle	.75
208	Barry Bonds	.75
209	Fred McGriff	.40
210	Dennis Eckersley	.10
211	Craig Biggio	.20
212	David Cone	.15
213	Will Clark	.25
214	Cal Ripken Jr.	2.50
215	Wade Boggs	.25
216	Pete Schourek	.10
217	Darren Daulton	.10
218	Carlos Baerga	.10
219	Larry Walker	.30
220	Denny Neagle	.10
221	Jim Edmonds	.15
222	Lee Smith	.10
223	Jason Isringhausen	.15
224	Jay Buhner	.15
225	John Olerud	.15
226	Jeff Conine	.10
227	Dean Palmer	.10
228	Jim Abbott	.10
229	Raul Mondesi	.30
230	Tom Glavine	.15
231	Kevin Seitzer	.10
232	Lenny Dykstra	.10
233	Brian Jordan	.10
234	Rondell White	.10
235	Bret Boone	.10
236	Randy Johnson	.35
237	Paul O'Neill	.15
238	Jim Thome	.40
239	Edgardo Alfonzo	.15
240	Terry Pendleton	.10
241	Harold Baines	.10
242	Roberto Alomar	.60
243	Mark Grace	.20
244	Derek Bell	.10
245	Vinny Castilla	.10
246	Cecil Fielder	.15
247	Roger Clemens	.75
248	Orel Hershiser	.10
249	J.T. Snow	.10
250	Rafael Palmeiro	.20
251	Bret Saberhagen	.10
252	Todd Hollandsworth	.10
253	Ryan Klesko	.25
254	Greg Maddux (Hardball Heroes)	1.00
255	Ken Griffey Jr. (Hardball Heroes)	1.50
256	Hideo Nomo (Hardball Heroes)	.25
257	Frank Thomas (Hardball Heroes)	.75
258	Cal Ripken Jr. (Hardball Heroes)	1.25
259	Jeff Bagwell (Hardball Heroes)	.50
260	Barry Bonds (Hardball Heroes)	.40
261	Mo Vaughn (Hardball Heroes)	.25
262	Albert Belle (Hardball Heroes)	.40
263	Sammy Sosa (Hardball Heroes)	.50
264	Reggie Sanders (Hardball Heroes)	.10
265	Mike Piazza (Hardball Heroes)	1.00
266	Chipper Jones (Hardball Heroes)	1.00
267	Tony Gwynn (Hardball Heroes)	.60
268	Kirby Puckett (Hardball Heroes)	.40
269	Wade Boggs (Hardball Heroes)	.15
270	Will Clark (Hardball Heroes)	.15
271	Gary Sheffield (Hardball Heroes)	.15
272	Dante Bichette (Hardball Heroes)	.15
273	Randy Johnson (Hardball Heroes)	.20
274	Matt Williams (Hardball Heroes)	.15
275	Alex Rodriguez (Hardball Heroes)	2.00
276	Tim Salmon (Hardball Heroes)	.20
277	Johnny Damon (Hardball Heroes)	.20
278	Manny Ramirez (Hardball Heroes)	.75
279	Derek Jeter (Hardball Heroes)	1.00
280	Eddie Murray (Hardball Heroes)	.20
281	Ozzie Smith (Hardball Heroes)	.20
282	Garret Anderson (Hardball Heroes)	.10
283	Raul Mondesi (Hardball Heroes)	.20
284	Terry Steinbach	.10
285	Carlos Garcia	.10
286	Dave Justice	.20
287	Eric Anthony	.10
288	Benji Gil	.10
289	Bob Hamelin	.10
290	Dwayne Hosey	.10
291	Andy Pettitte	.75
292	Rod Beck	.10
293	Shane Andrews	.10
294	Julian Tavarez	.10
295	Willie Greene	.10
296	Ismael Valdes	.10
297	Glenallen Hill	.10
298	Troy Percival	.10
299	Ray Durham	.10
300	Jeff Conine (.300 Series)	.10
301.8	Ken Griffey Jr. (.300 Series)	1.50
302	Will Clark (.300 Series)	.20
303	Mike Greenwell (.300 Series)	.10
304.9	Carlos Baerga (.300 Series)	.15
305.3	Paul Molitor (.300 Series)	.20
305.6	Jeff Bagwell (.300 Series)	.50
306	Mark Grace (.300 Series)	.15
307	Don Mattingly (.300 Series)	.60
308	Hal Morris (.300 Series)	.10
309	Butch Huskey	.10
310	Ozzie Guillen	.10
311	Erik Hanson	.10
312	Kenny Lofton (.300 Series)	.40
313	Edgar Martinez (.300 Series)	.10
314	Kurt Abbott	.10
315	John Smoltz	.20
316	Ariel Prieto	.10
317	Mark Carreon	.10
318	Kirby Puckett (.300 Series)	.40
319	Carlos Perez	.10
320	Gary DiSarcina	.10
321	Trevor Hoffman	.15
322	Mike Piazza (.300 Series)	1.00
323	Frank Thomas (.300 Series)	.75
324	Juan Acevedo	.10
325	Bip Roberts	.10
326	Javier Lopez	.15
327	Benito Santiago	.10
328	Mark Lewis	.10
329	Royce Clayton	.10
330	Tom Gordon	.10
331	Ben McDonald	.10
332	Dan Wilson	.10
333	Ron Gant	.15
334	Wade Boggs (.300 Series)	.20
335	Paul Molitor	.25
336	Tony Gwynn (.300 Series)	.60
337	Sean Berry	.10
338	Rickey Henderson	.25
339	Wil Cordero	.10
340	Kent Mercker	.10
341	Kenny Rogers	.10
342	Ryne Sandberg	.75
343	Charlie Hayes	.10
344	Andy Benes	.10
345	Sterling Hitchcock	.10
346	Bernard Gilkey	.10
347	Julio Franco	.10
348	Ken Hill	.10
349	Russ Davis	.10
350	Mike Blowers	.10
351	B.J. Surhoff	.10
352	Lance Johnson	.10
353	Darryl Hamilton	.10
354	Shawon Dunston	.10
355	Rick Aguilera	.10
356	Danny Tartabull	.10
357	Todd Stottlemyre	.10
358	Mike Bordick	.10
359	Jack McDowell	.10
360	Todd Zeile	.10
361	Tino Martinez	.10
362	Greg Gagne	.10
363	Mike Kelly	.10
364	Tim Raines	.15
365	Ernie Young	.10
366	Mike Stanley	.10
367	Wally Joyner	.10
368	Karim Garcia	.40
369	Paul Wilson	.15
370	Sal Fasano	.10
371	Jason Schmidt	.10
372	*Livan Hernandez*	1.00
373	George Arias	.10
374	Steve Gibralter	.10
375	Jermaine Dye	.10
376	Jason Kendall	.15
377	Brooks Kieschnick	.10
378	Jeff Ware	.10
379	Alan Benes	.15
380	Rey Ordonez	.50
381	Jay Powell	.10
382	*Osvaldo Fernandez*	.15
383	*Wilton Guerrero*	.60
384	Eric Owens	.10
385	George Williams	.10
386	Chan Ho Park	.15
387	Jeff Suppan	.10
388	*F.P. Santangelo*	.25
389	Terry Adams	.10
390	Bob Abreu	.15
391	*Quinton McCracken*	.15
392	*Mike Busby*	.10
393	(Cal Ripken Jr.) (checklist)	1.00
394	(Ken Griffey Jr.) (checklist)	1.25
395	(Frank Thomas) (checklist)	.75
396	(Chipper Jones) (checklist)	.60
397	(Greg Maddux) (checklist)	.75
398	(Mike Piazza) (checklist)	.60
399	(Ken Griffey Jr., Frank Thomas, Cal Ripken Jr., Greg Maddux, Chipper Jones, Mike Piazza) (checklist)	.50

1996 Pinnacle Christie Brinkley Collection Promo

To promote its Brinkley-photographed insert cards in Series 2 Pinnacle, the company issued a card of the celebrity photographer. In the same format as the player inserts, the promo card has a gold-foil enhanced borderless glamor photo on front. The back repeats a detail of the front photo and has details of the insert series.

	MT
Christie Brinkley	12.00

1996 Pinnacle Christie Brinkley Collection

Supermodel Christie Brinkley exclusively took photos for these 1996 Pinnacle Series II inserts. The 16 cards capture players from the 1995 World Series participants during a spring training photo session. Cards were seeded one per every 23 hobby packs or 32 retail packs.

		MT
Complete Set (16):		30.00
Common Player:		1.50
1	Greg Maddux	8.00
2	Ryan Klesko	1.50
3	Dave Justice	2.00
4	Tom Glavine	2.00
5	Chipper Jones	8.00
6	Fred McGriff	2.50
7	Javier Lopez	2.00
8	Marquis Grissom	1.50
9	Jason Schmidt	1.50
10	Albert Belle	4.50
11	Manny Ramirez	5.00
12	Carlos Baerga	1.50
13	Sandy Alomar	1.50
14	Jim Thome	2.00
15	Julio Franco	1.50
16	Kenny Lofton	4.00

1996 Pinnacle Essence of the Game

Essence of the Game is an 18-card insert set found only in hobby packs at a one per 23 packs rate in Series 1. Cards are printed on clear plastic with the front photo also appearing in an inverted fashion on back. Micro-etched Dufex printing technology is utilized on the front of the cards.

		MT
Complete Set (18):		90.00
Common Player:		1.50
1	Cal Ripken Jr.	12.00
2	Greg Maddux	8.00
3	Frank Thomas	5.00
4	Matt Williams	2.00
5	Chipper Jones	8.00
6	Reggie Sanders	1.50
7	Ken Griffey Jr.	15.00
8	Kirby Puckett	5.00
9	Hideo Nomo	2.00
10	Mike Piazza	8.00
11	Jeff Bagwell	4.00
12	Mo Vaughn	2.50
13	Albert Belle	4.00
14	Tim Salmon	1.50
15	Don Mattingly	4.00
16	Will Clark	2.00
17	Eddie Murray	2.00
18	Barry Bonds	4.00

1996 Pinnacle First Rate

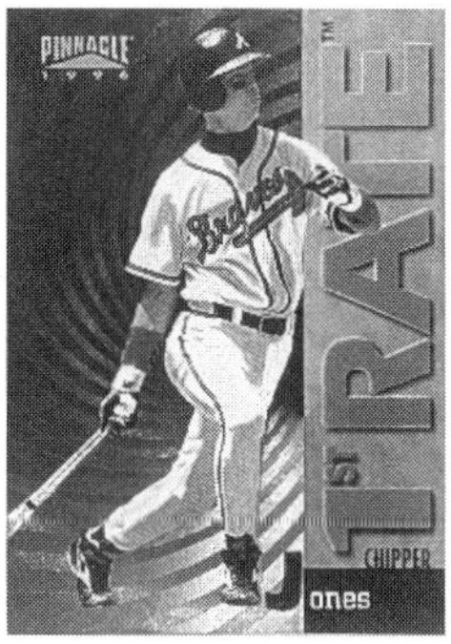

Retail-exclusive First Rate showcases 18 former first round draft picks now in the majors. Printed in Dufex foil throughout, a red swirl pattern covers the left 2/3 of the card front. Backs show the player again, within a large numeral "1". These inserts are found at an average rate of one per 23 packs in Series 1.

		MT
Complete Set (18):		120.00
Common Player:		2.50
1	Ken Griffey Jr.	25.00
2	Frank Thomas	10.00
3	Mo Vaughn	6.00
4	Chipper Jones	15.00
5	Alex Rodriguez	20.00
6	Kirby Puckett	8.00
7	Gary Sheffield	4.00
8	Matt Williams	3.00
9	Barry Bonds	8.00
10	Craig Biggio	2.50
11	Robin Ventura	2.50
12	Michael Tucker	2.50
13	Derek Jeter	15.00
14	Manny Ramirez	8.00
15	Barry Larkin	2.50
16	Shawn Green	5.00
17	Will Clark	4.00
18	Mark McGwire	25.00

1996 Pinnacle Foil Series 2

The 200 cards from Series 2 were paralleled in a special foil edition which was sold at retail outlets only in five-card $2.99 packs. Fronts have a metallic foil background to differentiate them from the regular-issue Series 2 Pinnacle version.

	MT
Complete Set (200):	25.00
Common Player:	.25
Stars: 1.5X	

(See 1996 Pinnacle #201-399 for checklist and base card values.)

1996 Pinnacle Pinnacle Power

Pinnacle Powers inserts are seeded at the rate of one per 47 packs in both hobby and retail Series 1. Twenty different sluggers are featured on a two-layered front. The bottom layer is silver Dufex foil with solid black on top; a color action photo of the player is at center, giving the card a die-cut appearanc

		MT
Complete Set (20):		50.00
Common Player:		1.00
1	Frank Thomas	4.00
2	Mo Vaughn	2.50
2p	Mo Vaughn (promo)	2.00
3	Ken Griffey Jr.	12.50
4	Matt Williams	1.00
5	Barry Bonds	3.00
6	Reggie Sanders	1.00
7	Mike Piazza	7.50
8	Jim Edmonds	1.00
9	Dante Bichette	1.00
10	Sammy Sosa	6.00
11	Jeff Bagwell	5.00
12	Fred McGriff	2.00
13	Albert Belle	3.00
14	Tim Salmon	1.00
15	Joe Carter	1.00
16	Manny Ramirez	3.00
17	Eddie Murray	2.00
18	Cecil Fielder	1.00
19	Larry Walker	2.00
20	Juan Gonzalez	5.00

1996 Pinnacle Project Stardom

These 1996 Pinnacle insert cards feature young players on their way to stardom. The cards, which use Dufex technology, are seeded one per every 35 packs of Series II hobby packs.

		MT
Complete Set (18):		120.00
Common Player:		2.50
1	Paul Wilson	2.50
2	Derek Jeter	25.00
3	Karim Garcia	8.00
4	Johnny Damon	3.00
5	Alex Rodriguez	30.00
6	Chipper Jones	25.00
7	Todd Walker	5.00
8	Bob Abreu	3.00
9	Alan Benes	3.00
10	Richard Hidalgo	3.00
11	Brooks Kieschnick	2.50
12	Garret Anderson	3.00
13	Livan Hernandez	3.00
14	Manny Ramirez	10.00
15	Jermaine Dye	2.50
16	Todd Hollandsworth	3.00
17	Raul Mondesi	5.00
18	Ryan Klesko	3.50

1996 Pinnacle Cal Ripken Tribute

A special Cal Ripken Tribute card was issued in Series 1 Pinnacle packs at a rate of 1:150. Front features an etched metallic foil background, a gold-foil facsimile autograph and a "2,131+ Consecutive Games Played" starburst. Back has a photo of the scoreboard on that historic occasion, and a photo of Ripken being driven around Camden Yards in a red Corvette. The card is numbered "1 of 1", but it is not unique.

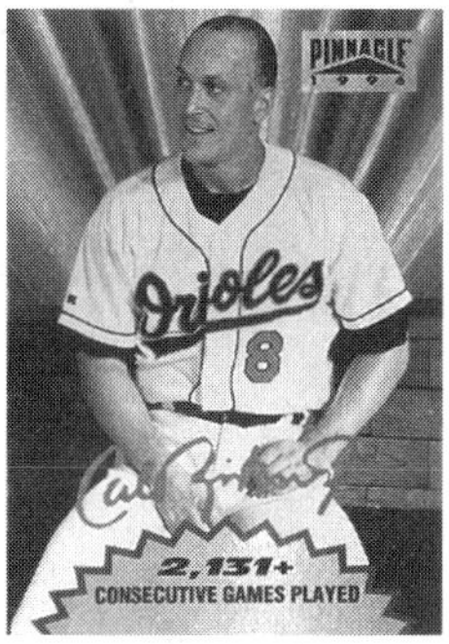

		MT
1 of 1	Cal Ripken Jr.	25.00

1996 Pinnacle Skylines

These 1996 Pinnacle inserts feature cards printed on a clear plastic stock. The cards were seeded one per every 29 Series II magazine packs, and one per 50 retail packs.

		MT
Complete Set (18):		350.00
Common Player:		8.00
1	Ken Griffey Jr.	65.00
2	Frank Thomas	25.00
3	Greg Maddux	30.00
4	Cal Ripken Jr.	50.00
5	Albert Belle	20.00
6	Mo Vaughn	15.00
7	Mike Piazza	35.00
8	Wade Boggs	17.50
9	Will Clark	12.00
10	Barry Bonds	20.00
11	Gary Sheffield	12.00
12	Hideo Nomo	12.00
13	Tony Gwynn	25.00
14	Kirby Puckett	35.00
15	Chipper Jones	35.00
16	Jeff Bagwell	20.00
17	Manny Ramirez	20.00
18	Raul Mondesi	8.00

1996 Pinnacle Slugfest

These 1996 Pinnacle Series II inserts feature 18 of the game's heaviest hitters on all-foil Dufex cards. The cards were seeded one per every 35 retail packs.

		MT
Complete Set (18):		150.00
Common Player:		3.00
1	Frank Thomas	15.00
2	Ken Griffey Jr.	30.00
3	Jeff Bagwell	15.00
4	Barry Bonds	10.00
5	Mo Vaughn	6.00
6	Albert Belle	8.00
7	Mike Piazza	25.00
8	Matt Williams	5.00
9	Dante Bichette	4.00
10	Sammy Sosa	20.00
11	Gary Sheffield	6.00
12	Reggie Sanders	3.00
13	Manny Ramirez	12.50
14	Eddie Murray	5.00
15	Juan Gonzalez	15.00
16	Dean Palmer	3.00
17	Rafael Palmeiro	4.00
18	Cecil Fielder	3.00

1996 Pinnacle Starburst

For 1996 Pinnacle abbreviated its parallel insert set to just half of the cards from the base issue. Only 200 select players are included in the Starburst Dufex-printed parallel set found on average of one per seven hobby packs and once per 10 retail packs. An Artist's Proof version of the Starbursts, a parallel set within a parallel set, are inserted once per 47 (hobby) or 67 (retail) packs. On these super-premium inserts the Artist's Proof logo is repeated throughout the Dufex background.

		MT
Complete Set (200):		400.00
Complete Series 1 (100):		200.00
Complete Series 2 (100):		200.00
Common Player:		.50
Complete Artist's Proof Set (200):		
1200.		
Artist's Proofs: 3X to 4X		
1	Greg Maddux	12.00
2	Bill Pulsipher	.50
3	Dante Bichette	2.50
4	Mike Piazza	12.00
5	Garret Anderson	.50
6	Chuck Knoblauch	.75
7	Jeff Bagwell	5.00
8	Wil Cordero	.50
9	Travis Fryman	.50
10	Reggie Sanders	.50
11	Deion Sanders	2.00
12	Tim Salmon	3.00
13	Tino Martinez	1.00
14	Bobby Bonilla	.50
15	Joe Carter	1.00
16	Mike Mussina	3.00
17	Jose Canseco	3.00
18	Manny Ramirez	5.00
19	Gregg Jefferies	.50
20	Charles Johnson	.50
21	Brian Hunter	.50
22	Ray Lankford	.50
23	Ivan Rodriguez	4.00
24	Paul Molitor	3.00
25	Eric Karros	.50
26	Edgar Martinez	.50
27	Shawon Dunston	.50
28	Mo Vaughn	2.50
29	Pedro Martinez	1.50
30	Marty Cordova	.50
31	Ken Caminiti	1.50
32	Gary Sheffield	1.50
33	Shawn Green	1.50
34	Cliff Floyd	.50
35	Andres Galarraga	1.50
36	Matt Williams	2.00
37	Don Mattingly	6.00
38	Kevin Appier	.50
39	Ozzie Smith	4.00
40	Kenny Lofton	2.50
41	Ken Griffey Jr.	20.00
42	Jack McDowell	.50
43	Gary Gaetti	.50
44	Dennis Martinez	.50
45	Chipper Jones	12.00
46	Eddie Murray	3.00
47	Bernie Williams	2.50
48	Andre Dawson	.75
49	Dave Winfield	.75
50	B.J. Surhoff	.50
51	Barry Larkin	1.00
52	Alan Trammell	.50
53	Sammy Sosa	12.00
54	Hideo Nomo	3.00
55	Mark McGwire	20.00
56	Jay Bell	.50
57	Juan Gonzalez	10.00
58	Chili Davis	.50
59	Robin Ventura	.75
60	John Mabry	.50
61	Ken Griffey Jr. (Naturals)	10.00
62	Frank Thomas (Naturals)	3.00
63	Cal Ripken Jr. (Naturals)	8.00
64	Albert Belle (Naturals)	3.00
65	Mike Piazza (Naturals)	6.00
66	Dante Bichette (Naturals)	1.00
67	Sammy Sosa (Naturals)	5.00
68	Mo Vaughn (Naturals)	1.00
69	Tim Salmon (Naturals)	1.00
70	Reggie Sanders (Naturals)	.50
71	Cecil Fielder (Naturals)	1.00
72	Jim Edmonds (Naturals)	.50
73	Rafael Palmeiro (Naturals)	1.50
74	Edgar Martinez (Naturals)	.50
75	Barry Bonds (Naturals)	3.00
76	Manny Ramirez (Naturals)	3.00
77	Larry Walker (Naturals)	.50
78	Jeff Bagwell (Naturals)	3.00
79	Ron Gant (Naturals)	.50
80	Andres Galarraga (Naturals)	.50
81	Eddie Murray (Naturals)	1.50
82	Kirby Puckett (Naturals)	3.00
83	Will Clark (Naturals)	1.50
84	Don Mattingly (Naturals)	3.00
85	Mark McGwire (Naturals)	15.00
86	Dean Palmer (Naturals)	.50
87	Matt Williams (Naturals)	1.50
88	Fred McGriff (Naturals)	1.50
89	Joe Carter (Naturals)	.50
90	Juan Gonzalez (Naturals)	5.00
91	Alex Ochoa	.50
92	Ruben Rivera	.50
93	Tony Clark	3.00
94	Pete Schourek	.50
95	Terrell Wade	.50
96	Johnny Damon	.75
97	Derek Jeter	12.00
98	Phil Nevin	.50
99	Robert Perez	.50
100	Dustin Hermanson	.50
101	Frank Thomas	6.00
102	Michael Tucker	.50
103	Kirby Puckett	5.00
104	Alex Gonzalez	.50
105	Tony Gwynn	10.00
106	Moises Alou	.50
107	Albert Belle	5.00
108	Barry Bonds	5.00
109	Fred McGriff	2.50
110	Dennis Eckersley	.50
111	Craig Biggio	.75
112	David Cone	.75
113	Will Clark	2.00
114	Cal Ripken Jr.	15.00
115	Wade Boggs	2.50
116	Pete Schourek	.50
117	Darren Daulton	.50
118	Carlos Baerga	.50
119	Larry Walker	2.00
120	Denny Neagle	.50
121	Jim Edmonds	.50
122	Lee Smith	.50
123	Jason Isringhausen	.50
124	Jay Buhner	1.00
125	John Olerud	.75
126	Jeff Conine	.50

127	Dean Palmer	.50
128	Jim Abbott	.50
129	Raul Mondesi	2.00
130	Tom Glavine	.75
131	Kevin Seitzer	.50
132	Lenny Dykstra	.50
133	Brian Jordan	.50
134	Rondell White	.50
135	Bret Boone	.50
136	Randy Johnson	4.00
137	Paul O'Neill	.75
138	Jim Thome	3.00
139	Edgardo Alfonzo	.75
140	Terry Pendleton	.50
141	Harold Baines	.50
142	Roberto Alomar	4.00
143	Mark Grace	1.50
144	Derek Bell	.50
145	Vinny Castilla	.50
146	Cecil Fielder	1.00
147	Roger Clemens	6.00
148	Orel Hershiser	.50
149	J.T. Snow	.50
150	Rafael Palmeiro	1.50
151	Bret Saberhagen	.50
152	Todd Hollandsworth	.50
153	Ryan Klesko	3.00
154	Greg Maddux (Hardball Heroes)	6.00
155	Ken Griffey Jr. (Hardball Heroes)	10.00
156	Hideo Nomo (Hardball Heroes)	2.00
157	Frank Thomas (Hardball Heroes)	3.00
158	Cal Ripken Jr. (Hardball Heroes)	8.00
159	Jeff Bagwell (Hardball Heroes)	3.00
160	Barry Bonds (Hardball Heroes)	3.00
161	Mo Vaughn (Hardball Heroes)	2.50
162	Albert Belle (Hardball Heroes)	3.00
163	Sammy Sosa (Hardball Heroes)	5.00
164	Reggie Sanders (Hardball Heroes)	.50
165	Mike Piazza (Hardball Heroes)	6.00
166	Chipper Jones (Hardball Heroes)	5.00
167	Tony Gwynn (Hardball Heroes)	4.00
168	Kirby Puckett (Hardball Heroes)	3.00
169	Wade Boggs (Hardball Heroes)	1.50
170	Will Clark (Hardball Heroes)	1.50
171	Gary Sheffield (Hardball Heroes)	1.50
172	Dante Bichette (Hardball Heroes)	1.00
173	Randy Johnson (Hardball Heroes)	2.00
174	Matt Williams (Hardball Heroes)	1.00
175	Alex Rodriguez (Hardball Heroes)	8.00
176	Tim Salmon (Hardball Heroes)	1.00
177	Johnny Damon (Hardball Heroes)	.50
178	Manny Ramirez (Hardball Heroes)	3.00
179	Derek Jeter (Hardball Heroes)	6.00
180	Eddie Murray (Hardball Heroes)	2.00
181	Ozzie Smith (Hardball Heroes)	3.00
182	Garret Anderson (Hardball Heroes)	.50
183	Raul Mondesi (Hardball Heroes)	1.00
184	Jeff Conine (.300 Series)	.50
185	Ken Griffey Jr. (.300 Series)	10.00
186	Will Clark (.300 Series)	1.50
187	Mike Greenwell (.300 Series)	.50
188	Carlos Baerga (.300 Series)	.50
189	Paul Molitor (.300 Series)	1.50
190	Jeff Bagwell (.300 Series)	3.00
191	Mark Grace (.300 Series)	.50
192	Don Mattingly (.300 Series)	3.00
193	Hal Morris (.300 Series)	.50
194	Kenny Lofton (.300 Series)	2.00
195	Edgar Martinez (.300 Series)	.50
196	Kirby Puckett (.300 Series)	3.00
197	Mike Piazza (.300 Series)	6.00
198	Frank Thomas (.300 Series)	3.00
199	Wade Boggs (.300 Series)	1.50
200	Tony Gwynn (.300 Series)	4.00

1996 Pinnacle Team Pinnacle

Team Pinnacle inserts offer 18 players in a double-sided nine-card set. Each card can be found with Dufex printing on one side and regular gold-foil printing on the other. Inserted one per 72 packs of Series 1, Team Pinnacle pairs up an American League player and a National Leaguer at the same position on each card.

		MT
Complete Set (9):		100.00
Common Player:		4.00
1	Frank Thomas, Jeff Bagwell	15.00
2	Chuck Knoblauch, Craig Biggio	5.00
3	Jim Thome, Matt Williams	5.00
4	Barry Larkin, Cal Ripken Jr.	20.00
5	Barry Bonds, Tim Salmon	8.00
6	Ken Griffey Jr., Reggie Sanders	25.00
7	Albert Belle, Sammy Sosa	15.00
8	Ivan Rodriguez, Mike Piazza	15.00
9	Greg Maddux, Randy Johnson	15.00

1996 Pinnacle Team Spirit

One in every 72 1996 Pinnacle Series II hobby packs or every 103 retail packs has one of these die-cut insert cards. Each card has a holographic baseball design behind an embossed glossy action photo of the player on a flat black background. Backs are conventionally printed.

		MT
Complete Set (12):		200.00
Common Player:		7.50
1	Greg Maddux	25.00
2	Ken Griffey Jr.	40.00
3	Derek Jeter	25.00
4	Mike Piazza	25.00
5	Cal Ripken Jr.	30.00
6	Frank Thomas	20.00
7	Jeff Bagwell	15.00
8	Mo Vaughn	7.50
9	Albert Belle	10.00
10	Chipper Jones	25.00
11	Johnny Damon	7.50
12	Barry Bonds	10.00

1996 Pinnacle Team Tomorrow

Team Tomorrow showcases 10 young superstars on a horizontal Dufex design. While the player appears twice on the card front, the left side is merely a close-up of the same shot appearing on the right. These inserts are exclusive to Series 1 jumbo packs, found on average at the rate of one per 19 packs.

		MT
Complete Set (10):		50.00
Common Player:		1.50
1	Ruben Rivera	1.50
2	Johnny Damon	2.00
3	Raul Mondesi	2.50
4	Manny Ramirez	9.00
5	Hideo Nomo	4.00
6	Chipper Jones	15.00
7	Garret Anderson	1.50
8	Alex Rodriguez	20.00
9	Derek Jeter	15.00
10	Karim Garcia	4.00

1996 Pinnacle/ Aficionado

Pinnacle's 1996 Aficionado set gives every card its own character; each card is printed as an all-wood card with a maple wood grain. The 200 regular issue cards include 160 cards in sepia-tone, giving each an antique-looking finish. The horizontal card front also has a rainbow holographic foil image of the player featured. His name is in foil in a panel at the bottom. The back has positional comparison statistics that show how each player compares with the league average at that position and the league average at that position in different eras. There are also 60 four-color cards, which include 25 four-color rookie cards, and a 10-card Global Reach subset. This subset, which honors baseball's international flavor, features Aficionado's new heliogram printing process. Artist's Proof parallel cards, seeded one per every 35 packs, were also created. These cards mirror the regular issue and use a unique gold foil stamp on them. There were also three insert sets created: Slick Picks, Rivals and Magic Numbers.

	MT
Complete Set (200):	50.00
Common Player:	.20
Veteran Star Artist's Proofs: 15X	
Young Star Artist's Proofs: 10X	
Wax Box:	50.00

1	Jack McDowell	.20
2	Jay Bell	.20
3	Rafael Palmeiro	.35
4	Wally Joyner	.20
5	Ozzie Smith	.75
6	Mark McGwire	5.00
7	Kevin Seitzer	.20
8	Fred McGriff	.50
9	Roger Clemens	1.50
9s	Roger Clemens (marked "SAMPLE")	5.00
10	Randy Johnson	.75
11	Cecil Fielder	.25
12	David Cone	.35
13	Chili Davis	.20
14	Andres Galarraga	.40
15	Joe Carter	.25
16	Ryne Sandberg	1.25
17	Paul O'Neill	.40
18	Cal Ripken Jr.	4.00
19	Wade Boggs	.50
20	Greg Gagne	.20
21	Edgar Martinez	.20
22	Greg Maddux	3.00
23	Ken Caminiti	.60
24	Kirby Puckett	1.50
25	Craig Biggio	.40
26	Will Clark	.40
27	Ron Gant	.25
28	Eddie Murray	.50
29	Lance Johnson	.20
30	Tony Gwynn	2.50
31	Dante Bichette	.40
32	Darren Daulton	.20
33	Danny Tartabull	.20
34	Jeff King	.20
35	Tom Glavine	.35
36	Rickey Henderson	.40
37	Jose Canseco	.35
38	Barry Larkin	.40
39	Dennis Martinez	.20
40	Ruben Sierra	.20
41	Bobby Bonilla	.30
42	Jeff Conine	.20
43	Lee Smith	.20
44	Charlie Hayes	.20
45	Walt Weiss	.20
46	Jay Buhner	.30
47	Kenny Rogers	.20
48	Paul Molitor	.50
49	Hal Morris	.20
50	Todd Stottlemyre	.20
51	Mike Stanley	.20
52	Mark Grace	.40
53	Lenny Dykstra	.20
54	Andre Dawson	.25
55	Dennis Eckersley	.20
56	Ben McDonald	.20
57	Ray Lankford	.20
58	Mo Vaughn	1.00
59	Frank Thomas	2.50
60	Julio Franco	.20
61	Jim Abbott	.20
62	Greg Vaughn	.25
63	Marquis Grissom	.30
64	Tino Martinez	.30
65	Kevin Appier	.20
66	Matt Williams	.40
67	Sammy Sosa	2.50
68	Larry Walker	.60
69	Ivan Rodriguez	.75
70	Eric Karros	.20
71	Bernie Williams	.60
72	Carlos Baerga	.20
73	Jeff Bagwell	1.50
74	Pete Schourek	.20
75	Ken Griffey Jr.	5.00
76	Bernard Gilkey	.20
77	Albert Belle	1.25
78	Chuck Knoblauch	.40
79	John Smoltz	.30
80	Barry Bonds	1.25
81	Vinny Castilla	.25
82	John Olerud	.30
83	Mike Mussina	1.00
84	Alex Fernandez	.25
85	Shawon Dunston	.20
86	Travis Fryman	.20
87	Moises Alou	.35
88	Dean Palmer	.20
89	Gregg Jefferies	.20
90	Jim Thome	.30
91	Dave Justice	.40
92	B.J. Surhoff	.20
93	Ramon Martinez	.25
94	Gary Sheffield	.60
95	Andy Benes	.20
96	Reggie Sanders	.20
97	Roberto Alomar	1.00
98	Omar Vizquel	.20
99	Juan Gonzalez	2.50
100	Robin Ventura	.25
101	Jason Isringhausen	.20
102	Greg Colbrunn	.20
103	Brian Jordan	.20
104	Shawn Green	.40
105	Brian Hunter	.20
106	Rondell White	.30
107	Ryan Klesko	.30
107s	Ryan Klesko (marked "SAMPLE")	3.00
108	Sterling Hitchcock	.20
109	Manny Ramirez	1.50
110	Bret Boone	.20
111	Michael Tucker	.20
112	Julian Tavarez	.20
113	Benji Gil	.20
114	Kenny Lofton	1.00
115	Mike Kelly	.20
116	Ray Durham	.20
117	Trevor Hoffman	.25
118	Butch Huskey	.20
119	Phil Nevin	.20
120	Pedro Martinez	.40
121	Wil Cordero	.20
122	Tim Salmon	.40
123	Jim Edmonds	.30
124	Mike Piazza	3.00
125	Rico Brogna	.20
126	John Mabry	.20
127	Chipper Jones	3.00
128	Johnny Damon	.20
129	Raul Mondesi	.35
130	Denny Neagle	.20
131	Marc Newfield	.20
132	Hideo Nomo	.75
133	Joe Vitiello	.20
134	Garret Anderson	.20
135	Dave Nilsson	.20
136	Alex Rodriguez	4.00
137	Russ Davis	.20
138	Frank Rodriguez	.20
139	Royce Clayton	.20
140	John Valentin	.20
141	Marty Cordova	.20
142	Alex Gonzalez	.20
143	Carlos Delgado	.50
144	Willie Greene	.20
145	Cliff Floyd	.20
146	Bobby Higginson	.40
147	J.T. Snow	.20
148	Derek Bell	.20
149	Edgardo Alfonzo	.25
150	Charles Johnson	.20
151	Hideo Nomo (Global Reach)	.25
152	Larry Walker (Global Reach)	.30
153	Bob Abreu (Global Reach)	.20
154	Karim Garcia (Global Reach)	.40
155	Dave Nilsson (Global Reach)	.20
156	Chan Ho Park (Global Reach)	.25
157	Dennis Martinez (Global Reach)	.20
158	Sammy Sosa (Global Reach)	1.00
159	Rey Ordonez (Global Reach)	.40
160	Roberto Alomar (Global Reach)	.50
161	George Arias	.20
162	Jason Schmidt	.20
163	Derek Jeter	3.00
164	Chris Snopek	.20
165	Todd Hollandsworth	.20
166	Sal Fasano	.20
167	Jay Powell	.20
168	Paul Wilson	.30
169	Jim Pittsley	.20
170	LaTroy Hawkins	.20
171	Bob Abreu	.30
172	*Mike Grace*	.20
173	Karim Garcia	.75
174	Richard Hidalgo	.20
175	Felipe Crespo	.20
176	Terrell Wade	.20
177	Steve Gibralter	.20
178	Jermaine Dye	.20
179	Alan Benes	.30
180	*Wilton Guerrero*	.50
181	Brooks Kieschnick	.20
182	Roger Cedeno	.20
183	*Osvaldo Fernandez*	.20
184	*Matt Lawton*	.20
185	George Williams	.20
186	Jimmy Haynes	.20
187	*Mike Busby*	.20
188	Chan Ho Park	.40
189	Marc Barcelo	.20
190	Jason Kendall	.20
191	Rey Ordonez	.50
192	Tyler Houston	.20
193	John Wasdin	.20
194	Jeff Suppan	.20
195	Jeff Ware	.20
196	Checklist	.20
197	Checklist	.20
198	Checklist	.20
199	Checklist	.20
200	Checklist	.20

The election of former players to the Hall of Fame does not always have an immediate upward effect on card prices. The hobby market generally has done a good job of predicting those inductions and adjusting values over the course of several years.

1996 Pinnacle/ Aficionado First Pitch Previews

This parallel set differs from the regularly issued version in that there is a "FIRST PITCH / PREVIEW" label printed on the front on the end opposite the heliogram player portrait. Also, whereas on the regular cards, the player portrait is in silver metallic composition, the First Pitch Preview cards have the portrait in gold. These cards were most often obtained by visiting Pinnacle's site on the Internet and answering a trivia question.

		MT
Complete Set (200):		750.00
Common Player:		2.50
	(Star cards valued at 8X-10X regular Aficionado edition.)	

1996 Pinnacle/ Aficionado Magic Numbers Samples

Each of the cards in the Magic Numbers insert set can also be found in a sample version. The promos differ from the issued version in that the player figures are not embossed and there is a large black "SAMPLE" notation on back.

		MT
Complete Set (10):		150.00
Common Player:		6.00
1	Ken Griffey Jr.	30.00
2	Greg Maddux	18.00
3	Frank Thomas	15.00
4	Mo Vaughn	10.00
5	Jeff Bagwell	15.00
6	Chipper Jones	20.00
7	Albert Belle	10.00
8	Cal Ripken Jr.	25.00
9	Matt Williams	9.00
10	Sammy Sosa	17.50

1996 Pinnacle/ Aficionado Magic Numbers

This 1996 Pinnacle Aficionado insert set focuses on 10 of the game's best players by printing them directly on to a wooden card, each of which carries the distinct grain and color of natural wood. The cards, seeded one per every 72 packs, take current players and compare them with other players who have worn the same uniform number. These cards have the most exclusive ratio of the inserts.

		MT
Complete Set (10):		200.00
Common Player:		6.00
1	Ken Griffey Jr.	50.00
2	Greg Maddux	30.00
3	Frank Thomas	20.00
4	Mo Vaughn	10.00
5	Jeff Bagwell	15.00
6	Chipper Jones	30.00
7	Albert Belle	12.00
8	Cal Ripken Jr.	40.00
9	Matt Williams	7.50
10	Sammy Sosa	25.00

1996 Pinnacle/ Aficionado Rivals

These 1996 Pinnacle Aficionado inserts concentrate on the many matchups and rivalries that make baseball fun. Each card uses spot embossing on it. The cards are seeded one per every 24 packs.

		MT
Complete Set (24):		175.00
Common Player:		7.50
1	Ken Griffey Jr., Frank Thomas	20.00
2	Frank Thomas, Cal Ripken Jr.	15.00
3	Cal Ripken Jr., Mo Vaughn	10.00
4	Mo Vaughn, Ken Griffey Jr.	15.00
5	Ken Griffey Jr., Cal Ripken Jr.	25.00
6	Frank Thomas, Mo Vaughn	10.00
7	Cal Ripken Jr., Ken Griffey Jr.	25.00
8	Mo Vaughn, Frank Thomas	10.00
9	Ken Griffey Jr., Mo Vaughn	15.00
10	Frank Thomas, Ken Griffey Jr.	20.00
11	Cal Ripken Jr., Frank Thomas	15.00
12	Mo Vaughn, Cal Ripken Jr.	10.00
13	Mike Piazza, Jeff Bagwell	10.00
14	Jeff Bagwell, Barry Bonds	7.50
15	Jeff Bagwell, Mike Piazza	10.00
16	Tony Gwynn, Mike Piazza	10.00
17	Mike Piazza, Barry Bonds	10.00
18	Jeff Bagwell, Tony Gwynn	7.50
19	Barry Bonds, Mike Piazza	10.00
20	Tony Gwynn, Jeff Bagwell	7.50
21	Mike Piazza, Tony Gwynn	10.00
22	Barry Bonds, Jeff Bagwell	7.50
23	Tony Gwynn, Barry Bonds	7.50
24	Barry Bonds, Tony Gwynn	7.50

1996 Pinnacle/ Aficionado Slick Picks

This 1996 Pinnacle Aficionado insert set pictures 32 of the best players in baseball on cards which use Spectroetch printing. Each card also notes where that player was selected in the annual draft, emphasizing that there are numerous bargains available throughout the amateur draft. The cards were seeded one per every 10 packs, making them the easiest to obtain of the set's insert cards.

		MT
Complete Set (32):		175.00
Common Player:		2.00
1	Mike Piazza	12.00
2	Cal Ripken Jr.	15.00
3	Ken Griffey Jr.	20.00
4	Paul Wilson	2.00
5	Frank Thomas	10.00
6	Mo Vaughn	3.00
7	Barry Bonds	5.00
8	Albert Belle	5.00
9	Jeff Bagwell	8.00
10	Dante Bichette	3.00
11	Hideo Nomo	3.00
12	Raul Mondesi	3.00
13	Manny Ramirez	5.00
14	Greg Maddux	12.00
15	Tony Gwynn	10.00
16	Ryne Sandberg	5.00
17	Reggie Sanders	2.00
18	Derek Jeter	12.00
19	Johnny Damon	2.00
20	Alex Rodriguez	15.00
21	Ryan Klesko	3.00
22	Jim Thome	3.00
23	Kenny Lofton	3.00
24	Tino Martinez	2.00
25	Randy Johnson	4.00
26	Wade Boggs	3.00
27	Juan Gonzalez	10.00
28	Kirby Puckett	8.00
29	Tim Salmon	3.00
30	Chipper Jones	12.00
31	Garret Anderson	2.00
32	Eddie Murray	4.00

1996 Pinnacle FanFest

In conjunction with its title sponsorship of baseball's All-Star FanFest, July 5-9 in Philadelphia, the company produced a 30-card set, distributed in two-card foil packs prior to, and at the show. Card fronts have a negative posterized image of Independence Hall as a backdrop for a player action photo. Textured gold-foil bottom corners hold a team logo and a Liberty Bell silhouette with the player's position. The player name appears in gold foil above the FanFest logo at bottom center. Backs repeat the negative background and have another player photo, a few words about him and all the appropriate logos. The Darren Daulton card is in Sportflix technology as a tribute to the recently retired Phillie fan favorite. Card #31, Steve Carlton, was not distributed in packs. Cards of the Phillie Phanatic team mascot and the city's mayor and several other local dignitaries were produced and given to those persons.

		MT
Complete Set (30, no Carlton):		40.00
Common Player:		1.25
1	Cal Ripken Jr.	3.00
2	Greg Maddux	2.50
3	Ken Griffey Jr.	3.00
4	Frank Thomas	2.00
5	Jeff Bagwell	1.75
6	Hideo Nomo	1.00
7	Tony Gwynn	2.00
8	Albert Belle	1.50
9	Mo Vaughn	1.00
10	Mike Piazza	2.50
11	Dante Bichette	1.00
12	Ryne Sandberg	2.00
13	Wade Boggs	1.75
14	Kirby Puckett	2.00
15	Ozzie Smith	1.75
16	Barry Bonds	1.75
17	Gary Sheffield	1.50
18	Barry Larkin	1.00
19	Kevin Seitzer	1.00
20	Jay Bell	1.00
21	Chipper Jones	2.50
22	Ivan Rodriguez	1.50
23	Cecil Fielder	1.00
24	Manny Ramirez	2.00
25	Randy Johnson	2.00
26	Moises Alou	1.00
27	Mark McGwire	3.00
28	Jason Isringhausen	1.00
29	Joe Carter	1.00
30	Darren Daulton (Sportflix)	1.50
31	Steve Carlton	20.00
---	Benjamin Franklin	10.00
---	Phillie Phanatic (mascot)	10.00
---	Edward G. Rendell (Mayor)	7.50

1996 Pinnacle FanFest Playing Cards

A special version of Pinnacle's FanFest cards was produced for construction of a large "house of cards" at the FanFest site. Following the event, some of the cards made their way into the hobby. Similar in format to the regular cards, the special issue was produced on textured playing-card stock in a 2-1/4" x 3-1/2" format with rounded corners. The playing cards lack the gold-foil found on regular cards and thus the player's name is nowhere to be found. Backs have a large gold and white Pinnacle logo on a black background. Cards are listed here using the numbering found on the regular version; the playing cards are unnumbered.

		MT
Complete Set (29):		925.00
Common Player:		
(1)	Cal Ripken Jr.	75.00
(2)	Greg Maddux	60.00
(3)	Ken Griffey Jr.	75.00
(4)	Frank Thomas	50.00
(5)	Jeff Bagwell	45.00
(6)	Hideo Nomo	25.00
(7)	Tony Gwynn	50.00
(8)	Albert Belle	35.00
(9)	Mo Vaughn	25.00
(10)	Mike Piazza	65.00
(11)	Dante Bichette	25.00
(12)	Ryne Sandberg	50.00
(13)	Wade Boggs	45.00
(14)	Kirby Puckett	50.00
(15)	Ozzie Smith	45.00
(16)	Barry Bonds	45.00
(17)	Gary Sheffield	30.00
(18)	Barry Larkin	25.00
(19)	Kevin Seitzer	25.00
(20)	Jay Bell	25.00
(21)	Chipper Jones	65.00
(22)	Ivan Rodriguez	35.00
(23)	Cecil Fielder	25.00
(24)	Manny Ramirez	50.00
(25)	Randy Johnson	40.00
(26)	Moises Alou	25.00
(27)	Mark McGwire	75.00
(28)	Jason Isringhausen	25.00
(29)	Joe Carter	25.00

1997 Pinnacle

The '97 Pinnacle baseball set consists of 200 base cards. The card fronts consist of the player's name stamped within a foil baseball diamond-shape at the bottom of each card. Card backs contain summaries of the players' 1996 and lifetime statistics. Included within the base set is a 30-card Rookies subset, a 12-card Clout subset and three checklists. Inserts include two parallel sets (Artist's Proof and Museum Collection), Passport to the Majors, Shades, Team Pinnacle, Cardfrontations, and Home/Away. Cards were sold in 10-card packs for $2.49 each.

		MT
Complete Set (200):		20.00
Common Player:		.10
Wax Box:		45.00
1	Cecil Fielder	.15
2	Garret Anderson	.10
3	Charles Nagy	.10
4	Darryl Hamilton	.10
5	Greg Myers	.10
6	Eric Davis	.10
7	Jeff Frye	.10
8	Marquis Grissom	.10
9	Curt Schilling	.15
10	Jeff Fassero	.10
11	Alan Benes	.15
12	Orlando Miller	.10
13	Alex Fernandez	.10
14	Andy Pettitte	.75
15	Andre Dawson	.15
16	Mark Grudzielanek	.10
17	Joe Vitiello	.10
18	Juan Gonzalez	1.25

19	Mark Whiten	.10
20	Lance Johnson	.10
21	Trevor Hoffman	.15
22	Marc Newfield	.10
23	Jim Eisenreich	.10
24	Joe Carter	.15
25	Jose Canseco	.25
26	Bill Swift	.10
27	Ellis Burks	.10
28	Ben McDonald	.10
29	Edgar Martinez	.10
30	Jamie Moyer	.10
31	Chan Ho Park	.15
32	Carlos Delgado	.50
33	Kevin Mitchell	.10
34	Carlos Garcia	.10
35	Darryl Strawberry	.15
36	Jim Thome	.30
37	Jose Offerman	.10
38	Ryan Klesko	.25
39	Ruben Sierra	.10
40	Devon White	.10
41	Brian Jordan	.10
42	Tony Gwynn	1.25
43	Rafael Palmeiro	.20
44	Dante Bichette	.20
45	Scott Stahoviak	.10
46	Roger Cedeno	.10
47	Ivan Rodriguez	.60
48	Bob Abreu	.10
49	Darryl Kile	.10
50	Darren Dreifort	.10
51	Shawon Dunston	.10
52	Mark McGwire	3.50
53	Tim Salmon	.25
54	Gene Schall	.10
55	Roger Clemens	1.00
56	Rondell White	.20
57	Ed Sprague	.10
58	Craig Paquette	.10
59	David Segui	.10
60	Jaime Navarro	.10
61	Tom Glavine	.15
62	Jeff Brantley	.10
63	Kimera Bartee	.10
64	Fernando Vina	.10
65	Eddie Murray	.40
66	Lenny Dykstra	.10
67	Kevin Elster	.10
68	Vinny Castilla	.10
69	Todd Greene	.10
70	Brett Butler	.10
71	Robby Thompson	.10
72	Reggie Jefferson	.10
73	Todd Hundley	.15
74	Jeff King	.10
75	Ernie Young	.10
76	Jeff Bagwell	1.25
77	Dan Wilson	.10
78	Paul Molitor	.35
79	Kevin Seitzer	.10
80	Kevin Brown	.15
81	Ron Gant	.15
82	Dwight Gooden	.10
83	Todd Stottlemyre	.10
84	Ken Caminiti	.20
85	James Baldwin	.10
86	Jermaine Dye	.10
87	Harold Baines	.10
88	Pat Hentgen	.10
89	Frank Rodriguez	.10
90	Mark Johnson	.10
91	Jason Kendall	.10
92	Alex Rodriguez	3.00
93	Alan Trammell	.10
94	Scott Brosius	.10
95	Delino DeShields	.10
96	Chipper Jones	2.00
97	Barry Bonds	.75
98	Brady Anderson	.15
99	Ryne Sandberg	.75
100	Albert Belle	.75
101	Jeff Cirillo	.10
102	Frank Thomas	1.50
103	Mike Piazza	2.00
104	Rickey Henderson	.20
105	Rey Ordonez	.20
106	Mark Grace	.20
107	Terry Steinbach	.10
108	Ray Durham	.10
109	Barry Larkin	.20
110	Tony Clark	.40
111	Bernie Williams	.40
112	John Smoltz	.15
113	Moises Alou	.15
114	Alex Gonzalez	.10
115	Rico Brogna	.10
116	Eric Karros	.10
117	Jeff Conine	.10
118	Todd Hollandsworth	.10
119	Troy Percival	.10
120	Paul Wilson	.10
121	Orel Hershiser	.10
122	Ozzie Smith	.40
123	Dave Hollins	.10
124	Ken Hill	.10
125	Rick Wilkins	.10
126	Scott Servais	.10
127	Fernando Valenzuela	.10
128	Mariano Rivera	.15
129	Mark Loretta	.10
130	Shane Reynolds	.10
131	Darren Oliver	.10
132	Steve Trachsel	.10
133	Darren Bragg	.10
134	Jason Dickson	.35
135	Darren Fletcher	.10
136	Gary Gaetti	.10
137	Joey Cora	.10
138	Terry Pendleton	.10
139	Derek Jeter	1.50
140	Danny Tartabull	.10
141	John Flaherty	.10
142	B.J. Surhoff	.10
143	Mark Sweeney	.10
144	Chad Mottola	.10
145	Andujar Cedeno	.10
146	Tim Belcher	.10
147	Mark Thompson	.10
148	Rafael Bournigal	.10
149	Marty Cordova	.10
150	Osvaldo Fernandez	.10
151	Mike Stanley	.10
152	Ricky Bottalico	.10
153	Donnie Wall	.10
154	Omar Vizquel	.10
155	Mike Mussina	.60
156	Brant Brown	.10
157	F.P. Santangelo	.10
158	Ryan Hancock	.10
159	Jeff D'Amico	.10
160	Luis Castillo	.20
161	Darin Erstad	1.25
162	Ugueth Urbina	.10
163	Andruw Jones	1.50
164	Steve Gibralter	.10
165	Robin Jennings	.10
166	Mike Cameron	.10
167	George Arias	.10
168	Chris Stynes	.10
169	Justin Thompson	.10
170	Jamey Wright	.10
171	Todd Walker	.50
172	Nomar Garciaparra	2.00
173	Jose Paniagua	.10
174	Marvin Benard	.10
175	Rocky Coppinger	.10
176	Quinton McCracken	.10
177	Amaury Telemaco	.10
178	Neifi Perez	.10
179	Todd Greene	.10
180	Jason Thompson	.10
181	Wilton Guerrero	.10
182	Edgar Renteria	.20
183	Billy Wagner	.15
184	Alex Ochoa	.10
185	Billy McMillon	.10
186	Kenny Lofton	.75
187	Andres Galarraga (Clout)	.15
188	Chuck Knoblauch (Clout)	.15
189	Greg Maddux (Clout)	2.00
190	Mo Vaughn (Clout)	.75
191	Cal Ripken Jr. (Clout)	2.50
192	Hideo Nomo (Clout)	.40
193	Ken Griffey Jr. (Clout)	3.50
194	Sammy Sosa (Clout)	1.50
195	Jay Buhner (Clout)	.15
196	Manny Ramirez (Clout)	1.00
197	Matt Williams (Clout)	.25
198	Andruw Jones CL	.75
199	Darin Erstad CL	.50
200	Trey Beamon CL	.10

1997 Pinnacle Artist's Proofs

		MT
Common Bronze (125):		5.00
Bronze Stars: 30X		
Common Silver (50):		10.00
Silver Stars: 45X		
Common Gold:		15.00
Gold Stars: 60X		

(See 1997 Pinnacle for checklist and base card values.)

1997 Pinnacle Museum Collection

Each of the 200 cards in 1997 Pinnacle Series I was also issued in a graphically enhanced Museum Collection parallel set. The Museum cards utilize basically the same design as the regular-issue Pinnacle cards, but the front is printed in the company's Dufex gold-foil technology. On back, a small rectangular logo verifies the card's special status.

		MT
Complete Set (200):		500.00
Common Player:		1.00
Museum Stars: 10X		

(See 1997 Pinnacle for checklist and regular-issue card values.)

1997 Pinnacle Cardfrontations

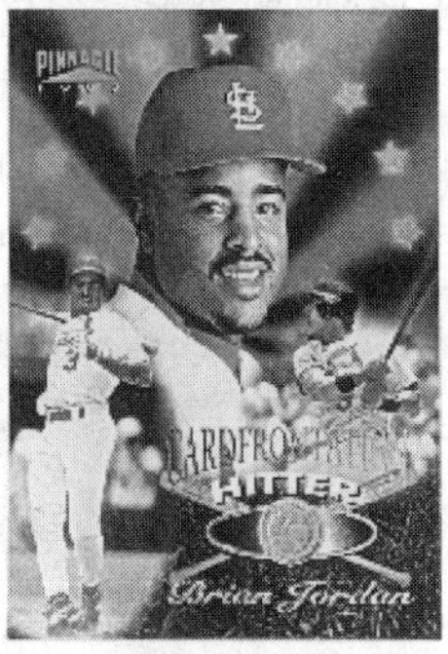

The 20-card, regular-sized, hobby-only set was inserted every 23 packs of 1997 Pinnacle baseball. The card fronts depict a player headshot imaged over a foil rainbow background. The same player is then pictured in action shots with the "Cardfrontation" logo in gold foil in the lower right half. The player's name appears in gold foil below the gold-foil team logo. The card backs depict another player's headshot with a short text describing interaction between the two players. The cards are numbered as "x of 20."

		MT
Complete Set (20):		225.00
Common Player:		4.00
1	Greg Maddux, Mike Piazza	20.00
2	Tom Glavine, Ken Caminiti	4.00
3	Randy Johnson, Cal Ripken Jr.	25.00
4	Kevin Appier, Mark McGwire	35.00
5	Andy Pettitte, Juan Gonzalez	15.00
6	Pat Hentgen, Albert Belle	10.00
7	Hideo Nomo, Chipper Jones	15.00
8	Ismael Valdes, Sammy Sosa	15.00
9	Mike Mussina, Manny Ramirez	12.50
10	David Cone, Jay Buhner	4.00
11	Mark Wohlers, Gary Sheffield	5.00
12	Alan Benes, Barry Bonds	10.00
13	Roger Clemens, Ivan Rodriguez	10.00
14	Mariano Rivera, Ken Griffey Jr.	35.00
15	Dwight Gooden, Frank Thomas	15.00
16	John Wetteland, Darin Erstad	12.50
17	John Smoltz, Brian Jordan	4.00
18	Kevin Brown, Jeff Bagwell	15.00
19	Jack McDowell, Alex Rodriguez	30.00
20	Charles Nagy, Bernie Williams	4.00

1997 Pinnacle Home/Away

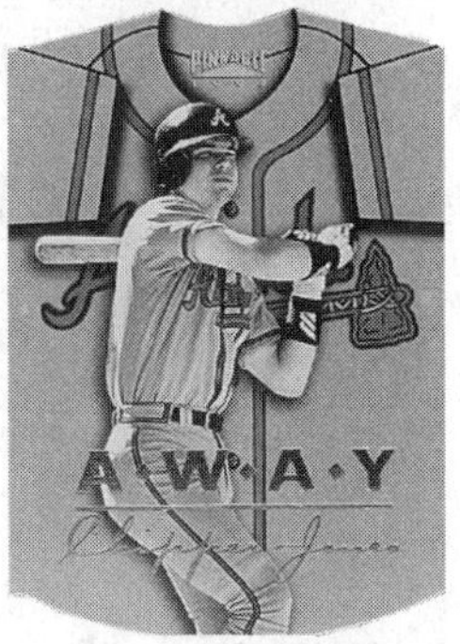

The 24-card, regular-sized, die-cut set was inserted every 33 retail packs. The background on front and back is a facsimile of the player's home or road jersey. A color action photo is on front with gold-foil graphics. Backs have a few words about the player.

		MT
Complete Set (12):		200.00
Common Player:		5.00
1	Chipper Jones	20.00
2	Ken Griffey Jr.	30.00
3	Mike Piazza	20.00
4	Frank Thomas	12.00
5	Jeff Bagwell	12.00
6	Alex Rodriguez	25.00
7	Barry Bonds	10.00
8	Mo Vaughn	8.00
9	Derek Jeter	20.00
10	Mark McGwire	30.00
11	Cal Ripken Jr.	25.00
12	Albert Belle	8.00

1997 Pinnacle Passport to the Majors

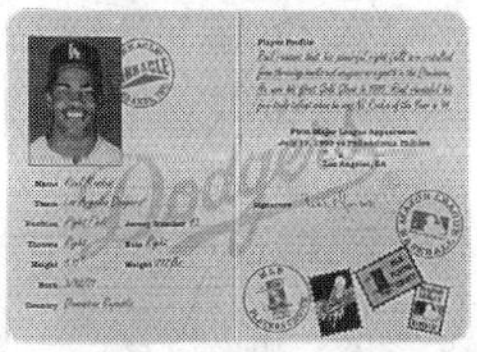

The 25-card, regular-sized set was inserted every 36 packs of 1997 Pinnacle baseball. The cards fold out and resemble a mini passport.

		MT
Complete Set (25):		175.00
Common Player:		3.00
1	Greg Maddux	15.00
1s	Greg Maddux ("SAMPLE" overprint)	10.00
2	Ken Griffey Jr.	25.00
3	Frank Thomas	10.00
4	Cal Ripken Jr.	20.00
5	Mike Piazza	15.00
6	Alex Rodriguez	20.00
7	Mo Vaughn	6.00
8	Chipper Jones	15.00
9	Roberto Alomar	6.00
10	Edgar Martinez	3.00
11	Javier Lopez	4.00
12	Ivan Rodriguez	6.00
13	Juan Gonzalez	12.00
14	Carlos Baerga	3.00
15	Sammy Sosa	15.00
16	Manny Ramirez	8.00
17	Raul Mondesi	4.00
18	Henry Rodriguez	3.00
19	Rafael Palmeiro	3.00
20	Rey Ordonez	5.00
21	Hideo Nomo	4.00
22	Makoto Suzuki	3.00
23	Chan Ho Park	4.00
24	Larry Walker	4.00
25	Ruben Rivera	3.00

1997 Pinnacle Shades

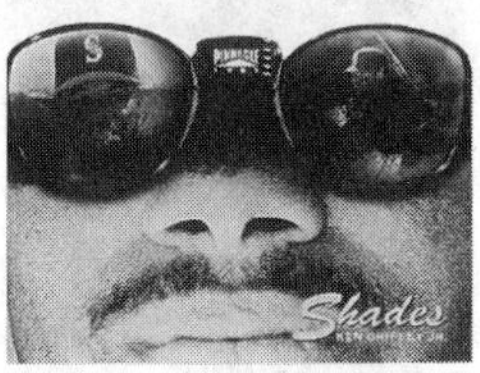

The 10-card, regular-sized set was inserted every 23 retail packs of Pinnacle baseball. The horizontal cards are die-cut at the top of a pair of sunglasses whose lenses contain color portrait and action pictures of the player. The player face beneath the shades is printed on silver foil stock. Backs have a mirror-image of the front photos in the lenses and a baseball diamond in the background.

		MT
Complete Set (10):		75.00
Common Player:		3.00
1	Ken Griffey Jr.	20.00
2	Juan Gonzalez	10.00
3	John Smoltz	3.00
4	Gary Sheffield	3.00
5	Cal Ripken Jr.	15.00
6	Mo Vaughn	3.00
7	Brian Jordan	3.00
8	Mike Piazza	12.00
9	Frank Thomas	10.00
10	Alex Rodriguez	15.00

1997 Pinnacle Team Pinnacle

The 10-card, regular-sized set features top National League players from a position on one side with the best American League players on the other. One side of the card is in Dufex printing and there is actually two versions of each card, as either side can feature the Dufex foil. Team Pinnacle is inserted every 90 packs.

		MT
Complete Set (10):		125.00
Common Player:		6.00
1	Frank Thomas, Jeff Bagwell	20.00
2	Chuck Knoblauch, Eric Young	6.00
3	Ken Caminiti, Jim Thome	7.50
4	Alex Rodriguez, Chipper Jones	25.00
5	Mike Piazza, Ivan Rodriguez	20.00
6	Albert Belle, Barry Bonds	9.00
7	Ken Griffey Jr., Ellis Burks	30.00
8	Juan Gonzalez, Gary Sheffield	15.00
9	John Smoltz, Andy Pettitte	7.50
10	All Players	20.00

The values of some parallel-card issues will have to be calculated based on figures presented in the heading for the regular-issue card set.

1997 New Pinnacle Samples

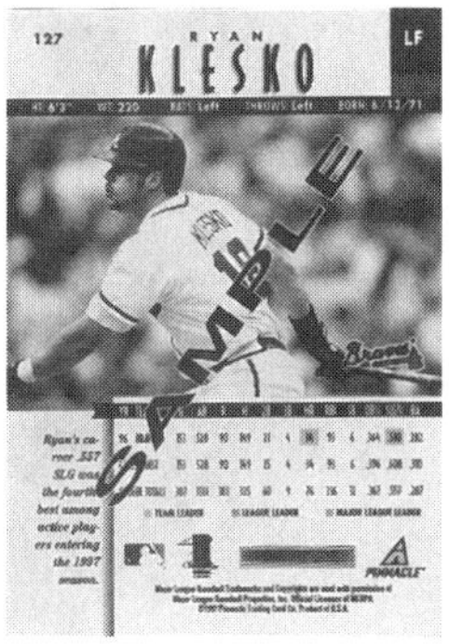

This group of sample cards was sent to dealers to introduce the New Pinnacle brand which took the place of a second series of Pinnacle in 1997. Cards are virtually identical to the issued versions except for the large diagonal black-and-white "SAMPLE" overprint on front and back.

		MT
Complete Set (6):		30.00
Common Player:		5.00
2	Sammy Sosa	10.00
45	Mike Piazza	10.00
57	Jeff Bagwell	5.00
81	Alex Rodriguez	10.00
127	Ryan Klesko	5.00
175	Andruw Jones	5.00

1997 New Pinnacle

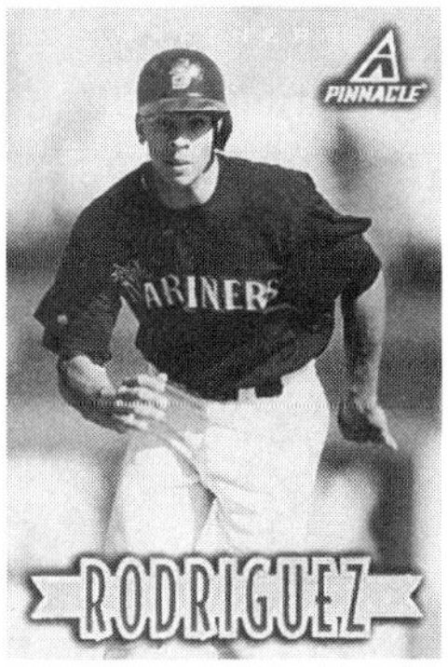

In lieu of a second series of Pinnacle Baseball, the company offered collectors New Pinnacle, a 200-card set sold in 10-card packs for $2.99. Two parallel versions of the 200-card set exist in Museum Collection and Artist's Proof. Other inserts include Press Plates, Spellbound, Keeping the Pace and Interleague Encounter. Collectors who obtained four Press Plates of the same player's card back or front were eligible to win cash prizes.

		MT
Complete Set (200):		25.00
Common Player:		.10
Complete Museum Set (200): 500.00		
Common Museum:		1.50
Museum Stars: 10X		
Common Red Artist's Proof:		5.00
Red Artist's Proof: 15X		
Common Blue Artist's Proof:		15.00
Blue Artist's Proof: 40X		
Common Green Artist's Proof: 30.00		
Green Artist's Proof: 60X		
Wax Box:		45.00
1	Ken Griffey Jr.	3.50
2	Sammy Sosa	2.00
3	Greg Maddux	2.00
4	Matt Williams	.35
5	Jason Isringhausen	.10
6	Gregg Jefferies	.10
7	Chili Davis	.10
8	Paul O'Neill	.15
9	Larry Walker	.35
10	Ellis Burks	.10
11	Cliff Floyd	.10
12	Albert Belle	.75
13	Javier Lopez	.20
14	David Cone	.20
15	Jose Canseco	.30
16	Todd Zeile	.10
17	Bernard Gilkey	.10
18	Andres Galarraga	.20
19	Chris Snopek	.10
20	Tim Salmon	.25
21	Roger Clemens	1.00
22	Reggie Sanders	.10
23	John Jaha	.10
24	Andy Pettitte	.60
25	Kenny Lofton	.60
26	Robb Nen	.10
27	John Wetteland	.10
28	Bobby Bonilla	.10
29	Hideo Nomo	.50
30	Cecil Fielder	.15
31	Garret Anderson	.10
32	Pat Hentgen	.10
33	David Justice	.20
34	Billy Wagner	.15
35	Al Leiter	.15
36	Mark Wohlers	.10
37	Rondell White	.10
38	Charles Johnson	.10
39	Mark Grace	.20
40	Pedro Martinez	.20
41	Tom Goodwin	.10
42	Manny Ramirez	1.00
43	Greg Vaughn	.15
44	Brian Jordan	.10
45	Mike Piazza	2.00
46	Roberto Hernandez	.10
47	Wade Boggs	.20
48	Scott Sanders	.10
49	Alex Gonzalez	.10
50	Kevin Brown	.15
51	Bob Higginson	.10
52	Ken Caminiti	.30
53	Derek Jeter	2.00
54	Carlos Baerga	.10
55	Jay Buhner	.15
56	Tim Naehring	.10
57	Jeff Bagwell	1.25
58	Steve Finley	.10
59	Kevin Appier	.10
60	Jay Bell	.10
61	Ivan Rodriguez	.60
62	Terrell Wade	.10
63	Rusty Greer	.10
64	Juan Guzman	.10
65	Fred McGriff	.30
66	Tino Martinez	.20
67	Ray Lankford	.10
68	Juan Gonzalez	1.25
69	Ron Gant	.10
70	Jack McDowell	.10
71	Tony Gwynn	1.25
72	Joe Carter	.10
73	Wilson Alvarez	.10
74	Jason Giambi	.10
75	Brian Hunter	.10
76	Michael Tucker	.10
77	Andy Benes	.10
78	Brady Anderson	.15
79	Ramon Martinez	.10
80	Troy Percival	.10
81	Alex Rodriguez	3.00
82	Jim Thome	.50
83	Denny Neagle	.10
84	Rafael Palmeiro	.20
85	Jose Valentin	.10
86	Marc Newfield	.10
87	Mariano Rivera	.20
88	Alan Benes	.15
89	Jimmy Key	.10
90	Joe Randa	.10
91	Cal Ripken Jr.	3.00
92	Craig Biggio	.20
93	Dean Palmer	.10
94	Gary Sheffield	.35
95	Ismael Valdez	.10
96	John Valentin	.10
97	Johnny Damon	.10
98	Mo Vaughn	.60
99	Paul Sorrento	.10
100	Randy Johnson	.60
101	Raul Mondesi	.20
102	Roberto Alomar	.60
103	Royce Clayton	.10
104	Mark Grudzielanek	.10
105	Wally Joyner	.10
106	Wil Cordero	.10
107	Will Clark	.25
108	Chuck Knoblauch	.25
109	Derek Bell	.10
110	Henry Rodriguez	.10
111	Edgar Renteria	.10
112	Travis Fryman	.10
113	Eric Young	.10
114	Sandy Alomar Jr.	.15
115	Darin Erstad	1.25
116	Barry Larkin	.10
117	Barry Bonds	.75
118	Frank Thomas	1.50
119	Carlos Delgado	.40
120	Jason Kendall	.10
121	Todd Hollandsworth	.10
122	Jim Edmonds	.10
123	Chipper Jones	2.00
124	Jeff Fassero	.10
125	Deion Sanders	.25
126	Matt Lawton	.10
127	Ryan Klesko	.25
128	Mike Mussina	.60
129	Paul Molitor	.50
130	Dante Bichette	.20
131	Bill Pulsipher	.10
132	Todd Hundley	.20
133	J.T. Snow	.10
134	Chuck Finley	.10
135	Shawn Green	.20
136	Charles Nagy	.10
137	Willie Greene	.10
138	Marty Cordova	.10
139	Eddie Murray	.40
140	Ryne Sandberg	.75
141	Alex Fernandez	.10
142	Mark McGwire	3.50
143	Eric Davis	.10
144	Jermaine Dye	.10
145	Ruben Sierra	.10
146	Damon Buford	.10
147	John Smoltz	.20
148	Alex Ochoa	.10
149	Moises Alou	.15
150	Rico Brogna	.10
151	Terry Steinbach	.10
152	Jeff King	.10
153	Carlos Garcia	.10
154	Tom Glavine	.20
155	Edgar Martinez	.10
156	Kevin Elster	.10
157	Darryl Hamilton	.10
158	Jason Dickson	.20
159	Kevin Orie	.10
160	*Bubba Trammell*	1.00
161	Jose Guillen	1.00
162	Brant Brown	.10
163	Wendell Magee	.10
164	Scott Spiezio	.10
165	Todd Walker	.50
166	*Rod Myers*	.10
167	Damon Mashore	.10
168	Wilton Guerrero	.10
169	Vladimir Guerrero	1.00
170	Nomar Garciaparra	2.00
171	Shannon Stewart	.10
172	Scott Rolen	1.50
173	Bob Abreu	.10
174	*Danny Patterson*	.20
175	Andruw Jones	1.50
176	*Brian Giles*	1.50
177	Dmitri Young	.10
178	Cal Ripken Jr. (East Meets West)	1.25
179	Chuck Knoblauch (East Meets West)	.20
180	Alex Rodriguez (East Meets West)	1.50
181	Andres Galarraga (East Meets West)	.15
182	Pedro Martinez (East Meets West)	.15
183	Brady Anderson (East Meets West)	.10
184	Barry Bonds (East Meets West)	.40
185	Ivan Rodriguez (East Meets West)	.30
186	Gary Sheffield (East Meets West)	.20
187	Denny Neagle (East Meets West)	.10
188	Mark McGwire (Aura)	2.00
189	Ellis Burks (Aura)	.10
190	Alex Rodriguez (Aura)	1.50
191	Mike Piazza (Aura)	1.00
192	Barry Bonds (Aura)	.40
193	Albert Belle (Aura)	.40
194	Chipper Jones (Aura)	1.00
195	Juan Gonzalez (Aura)	.60
196	Brady Anderson (Aura)	.10
197	Frank Thomas (Aura)	.75
198	Checklist (Vladimir Guerrero)	.50
199	Checklist (Todd Walker)	.25
200	Checklist (Scott Rolen)	.60

1997 New Pinnacle Artist's Proof

This 200-card parallel set features a special AP seal and foil treatment and is fractured into three levels of scarcity - Red (125 cards), Blue (50 cards) and Green (25 cards). Cards were inserted at a rate of 1:39 packs. The 200-card parallel set was randomly inserted (about 1:50) in packs of 1997 Pinnacle. Of the 200 cards, 125 were done in bronze foil (common), 50 in silver (uncommon) and 25 gold (rare). "Artist's Proof" is stamped along the lower edge.

	MT
Common Red Artist's Proof:	5.00
Red Artist's Proofs: 15X	
Common Blue Artist's Proof:	15.00
Blue Artist's Proofs: 40X	
Common Green Artist's Proof: 30.00	
Green Artist's Proofs: 60X	

(See 1997 New Pinnacle for checklist and base values.)

1997 New Pinnacle Museum Collection

Dufex printing on gold-foil backgrounds differentiates the Museum Collection parallel of New Pinnacle from the regular-issue cards. Museums were inserted at an average rate of one per nine packs.

	MT
Complete Set (200):	500.00
Common Player:	1.00
Museum Stars: 15X	

(See 1997 New Pinnacle for checklist and base card values.)

1997 New Pinnacle Interleague Encounter

Inserted 1:240 packs, this 10-card set showcases 20 American League and National League rivals with the date of their first interleague matchup on double-sided mirror mylar cards.

		MT
Complete Set (10):		300.00
Common Player:		10.00
1	Albert Belle, Brian Jordan	15.00
2	Andruw Jones, Brady Anderson	25.00
3	Ken Griffey Jr., Tony Gwynn	60.00
4	Cal Ripken Jr., Chipper Jones	50.00
5	Mike Piazza, Ivan Rodriguez	30.00
6	Derek Jeter, Vladimir Guerrero	30.00
7	Greg Maddux, Mo Vaughn	30.00
8	Alex Rodriguez, Hideo Nomo	50.00
9	Juan Gonzalez, Barry Bonds	25.00
10	Frank Thomas, Jeff Bagwell	30.00

1997 New Pinnacle Keeping the Pace

The top sluggers who are considered candidates to break Roger Maris' single-season record of 61 home runs are featured in this 18-card insert set. Cards feature Dot Matrix holographic borders and backgrounds on front. Backs present career stats of an all-time great and project future numbers for the current player. The cards were inserted 1:89 packs.

		MT
Complete Set (18):		500.00
Common Player:		4.00
1	Juan Gonzalez	35.00
2	Greg Maddux	50.00
3	Ivan Rodriguez	20.00
4	Ken Griffey Jr.	75.00
5	Alex Rodriguez	60.00
6	Barry Bonds	20.00
7	Frank Thomas	35.00
8	Chuck Knoblauch	10.00
9	Derek Jeter	50.00
10	Roger Clemens	25.00
11	Kenny Lofton	10.00
12	Tony Gwynn	35.00
13	Troy Percival	4.00
14	Cal Ripken Jr.	60.00
15	Andy Pettitte	10.00
16	Hideo Nomo	10.00
17	Randy Johnson	15.00
18	Mike Piazza	50.00

1997 New Pinnacle Press Plates

Just when collectors thought they had seen every type of pack insert chase card imaginable, New Pinnacle proved them wrong by cutting up and inserting into packs (about one per 1,250) the metal plates used to print the regular cards in the set. There are black, blue, red and yellow plates for the front and back of each card. Rather than touting the collector value of the plates, Pinnacle created a treasure hunt by offering $20,000-35,000 to anybody assembling a complete set of four plates for either the front or back of any card. The $35,000, which would have been awarded for completion prior to Aug. 22, was unclaimed. The amount decreased to $20,000 for any set redeemed by the end of 1997.

(Because of the unique nature of each press plate, no current market value can be quoted.)

1997 New Pinnacle Spellbound

Each of the 50 cards in this insert features a letter of the alphabet as the basic card design. The letters can be used to spell out the names of nine players featured in the set. Cards featured micro-etched foil and are inserted 1:19 packs. Cards of Griffey, Ripken and the Joneses were inserted only in hobby packs; retail packs have cards of Belle, Thomas, Piazza and the Rodriguezes. Values shown are per card; multiply by number of cards to determine a player's set value.

	MT
Complete Set (50):	500.00
1-5AB Albert Belle	5.00
1-6AJ Andruw Jones	8.00
1-4AR Alex Rodriguez	15.00
1-7CJ Chipper Jones	15.00
1-6CR Cal Ripken Jr.	20.00
1-5FT Frank Thomas	10.00
1-5IR Ivan Rodriguez	6.00
1-6KG Ken Griffey Jr.	25.00
1-6MP Mike Piazza	15.00

1997 Pinnacle Certified

This 150-card base features a mirror-like mylar finish and a peel-off protector on each card front. Backs feature the player's 1996 statistics against each opponent. There are four different parallel sets, each with varying degrees of scarcity - Certified Red (1:5), Mirror Red (1:99), Mirror Blue (1:199) and Mirror Gold (1:299). Other inserts include Lasting Impressions, Certified Team, and Certified Gold Team. Cards were sold in six-card packs for a suggested price of $4.99.

		MT
Complete Set (150):		40.00
Common Player:		.15
Common Certified Red:		1.00
Certified Red Stars: 5X		
Common Mirror Red:		4.00
Mirror Red Stars: 20X		
Common Mirror Blue:		8.00
Mirror Blue Stars: 35X		
Common Mirror Gold:		20.00
Mirror Gold Stars: 60X		
Jose Cruz Jr. Redemption:		25.00
Wax Box:		115.00
1	Barry Bonds	1.50
2	Mo Vaughn	1.00
3	Matt Williams	.50
4	Ryne Sandberg	1.50
5	Jeff Bagwell	2.00
6	Alan Benes	.15
7	John Wetteland	.15
8	Fred McGriff	.40
9	Craig Biggio	.25
10	Bernie Williams	1.00
11	Brian L. Hunter	.15
12	Sandy Alomar Jr.	.25
13	Ray Lankford	.15
14	Ryan Klesko	.25
15	Jermaine Dye	.15
16	Andy Benes	.15
17	Albert Belle	1.50
18	Tony Clark	.75
19	Dean Palmer	.15
20	Bernard Gilkey	.15
21	Ken Caminiti	.30
22	Alex Rodriguez	4.00
23	Tim Salmon	.40
24	Larry Walker	.50
25	Barry Larkin	.25
26	Mike Piazza	3.00
27	Brady Anderson	.15
28	Cal Ripken Jr.	4.00
29	Charles Nagy	.15
30	Paul Molitor	.75
31	Darin Erstad	1.50
32	Rey Ordonez	.25
33	Wally Joyner	.15
34	David Cone	.25
35	Sammy Sosa	2.50
36	Dante Bichette	.30
37	Eric Karros	.15
38	Omar Vizquel	.15
39	Roger Clemens	1.50
40	Joe Carter	.15
41	Frank Thomas	2.00
42	Javier Lopez	.20
43	Mike Mussina	1.00
44	Gary Sheffield	.50
45	Tony Gwynn	2.00
46	Jason Kendall	.15
47	Jim Thome	.75
48	Andres Galarraga	.30
49	Mark McGwire	5.00
50	Troy Percival	.15
51	Derek Jeter	3.00
52	Todd Hollandsworth	.15
53	Ken Griffey Jr.	5.00
54	Randy Johnson	.75
55	Pat Hentgen	.15
56	Rusty Greer	.15
57	John Jaha	.15
58	Kenny Lofton	.75
59	Chipper Jones	3.00
60	Robb Nen	.15
61	Rafael Palmeiro	.40
62	Mariano Rivera	.25
63	Hideo Nomo	.75
64	Greg Vaughn	.20
65	Ron Gant	.15
66	Eddie Murray	.40
67	John Smoltz	.30
68	Manny Ramirez	1.50
69	Juan Gonzalez	2.00
70	F.P. Santangelo	.15
71	Moises Alou	.20
72	Alex Ochoa	.15
73	Chuck Knoblauch	.30
74	Raul Mondesi	.30
75	J.T. Snow	.15
76	Rickey Henderson	.30
77	Bobby Bonilla	.15
78	Wade Boggs	.30
79	Ivan Rodriguez	1.50
80	Brian Jordan	.15
81	Al Leiter	.15
82	Jay Buhner	.25
83	Greg Maddux	3.00
84	Edgar Martinez	.15
85	Kevin Brown	.20
86	Eric Young	.15
87	Todd Hundley	.30
88	Ellis Burks	.15
89	Marquis Grissom	.15
90	Jose Canseco	.40
91	Henry Rodriguez	.15
92	Andy Pettitte	.75
93	Mark Grudzielanek	.15
94	Dwight Gooden	.15
95	Roberto Alomar	1.00
96	Paul Wilson	.15
97	Will Clark	.30
98	Rondell White	.15
99	Charles Johnson	.15
100	Jim Edmonds	.15
101	Jason Giambi	.15
102	Billy Wagner	.15
103	Edgar Renteria	.15
104	Johnny Damon	.15
105	Jason Isringhausen	.15
106	Andruw Jones	2.50
107	Jose Guillen	1.00
108	Kevin Orie	.15
109	Brian Giles	.15
110	Danny Patterson	.15
111	Vladimir Guerrero	2.00
112	Scott Rolen	2.00
113	Damon Mashore	.15
114	Nomar Garciaparra	3.00
115	Todd Walker	.75
116	Wilton Guerrero	.15
117	Bob Abreu	.15
118	Brooks Kieschnick	.15
119	Pokey Reese	.15
120	Todd Greene	.15
121	Dmitri Young	.15
122	Raul Casanova	.15
123	Glendon Rusch	.15
124	Jason Dickson	.15
125	Jorge Posada	.15
126	*Rod Myers*	.15
127	*Bubba Trammell*	1.50
128	Scott Spiezio	.15
129	*Hideki Irabu*	3.00
130	Wendell Magee	.15
131	Bartolo Colon	.15
132	Chris Holt	.15
133	Calvin Maduro	.15
134	Ray Montgomery	.15
135	Shannon Stewart	.15
136	Ken Griffey Jr. (Certified Stars)	2.50
137	Vladimir Guerrero (Certified Stars)	.75
138	Roger Clemens (Certified Stars)	.75
139	Mark McGwire (Certified Stars)	2.50
140	Albert Belle (Certified Stars)	.60
141	Derek Jeter (Certified Stars)	1.50
142	Juan Gonzalez (Certified Stars)	1.00
143	Greg Maddux (Certified Stars)	1.50
144	Alex Rodriguez (Certified Stars)	2.00
145	Jeff Bagwell (Certified Stars)	1.00
146	Cal Ripken Jr. (Certified Stars)	2.00
147	Tony Gwynn (Certified Stars)	1.00
148	Frank Thomas (Certified Stars)	1.00
149	Hideo Nomo (Certified Stars)	.40
150	Andruw Jones (Certified Stars)	1.50

1997 Pinnacle Certified Red

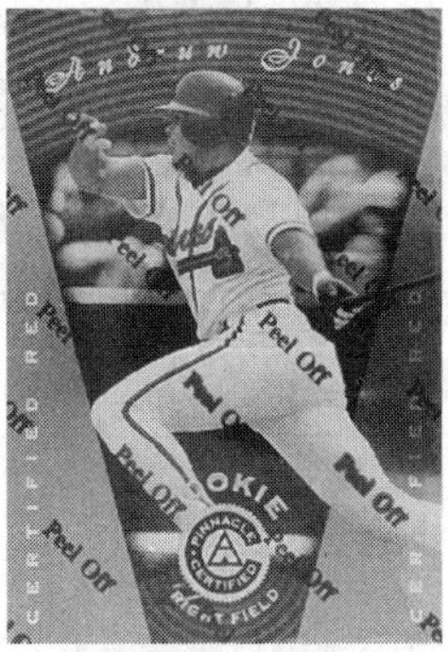

This parallel set features a red tint to the triangular mylar background left and right of the photo on the front. "CERTIFIED RED" is printed vertically on both edges. Backs are identical to regular Certified cards. A peel-off protection coating is on the front of the card. Cards were inserted 1:5 packs.

	MT
Common Certified Red:	1.00
Certified Red Stars: 5X	
(See 1997 Pinnacle Certified for checklist and base values.)	

1997 Pinnacle Certified Mirror Red

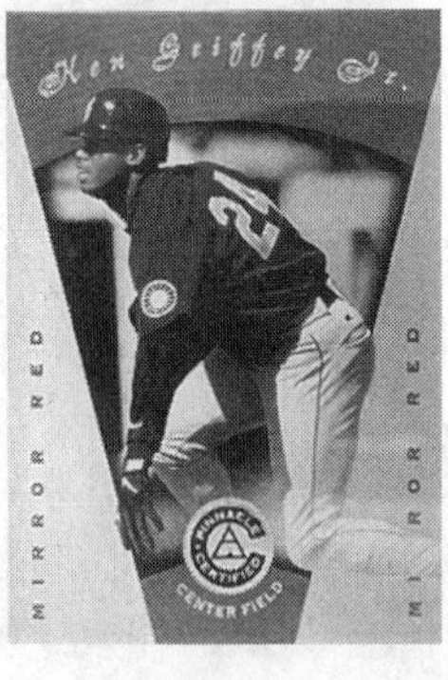

This parallel set features a red design element on the front of each card. Cards were inserted 1:99 packs.

	MT
Common Mirror Red:	4.00
Mirror Red Stars: 20X	
(See 1997 Pinnacle Certified for checklist and base values.)	

1997 Pinnacle Certified Mirror Blue

This parallel set features a blue design element on the front of each card. Cards were inserted 1:199 packs.

	MT
Common Mirror Blue:	8.00
Mirror Blue Stars: 35X	
(See 1997 Pinnacle Certified for checklist and base values.)	

1997 Pinnacle Certified Mirror Gold

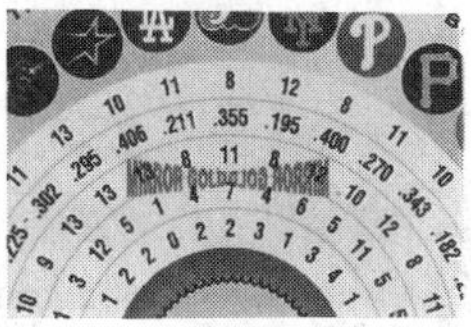

This parallel set features a holographic gold design on the front of each card. Cards were inserted 1:299 packs.

	MT
Common Mirror Gold:	20.00
Mirror Gold Stars: 60X	
(See 1997 Pinnacle Certified for checklist and base values.)	

1997 Pinnacle Certified Mirror Black

The exact nature of these cards is undetermined. They may have been intentionally created and "secretly" seeded in packs as an insert or they may have been test cards which were mistakenly inserted. They are not marked in any fashion. The cards are said to reflect in bright green under direct light. It is commonly believed that each "Mirror Black" card exists in only a single piece, but that has not been verified. Neither is it confirmed that a Mirror Black parallel exists for each of the 151 cards in the base set. Even the most undistinguished player's card can sell for $100 or more due to the scarcity of the type.

	MT
Common Player:	100.00
(Star cards valued at 150-250X base value.)	

1997 Pinnacle Certified Lasting Impression

This 20-card insert features a die-cut design and a mirror mylar finish and pictures some of baseball's top veteran stars. Backs are conventionally printed and include a color portrait photo and a few words about the player. Cards were inserted 1:19 packs.

		MT
Complete Set (20):		110.00
Common Player:		2.00
1	Cal Ripken Jr.	15.00
2	Ken Griffey Jr.	20.00
3	Mo Vaughn	3.00
4	Brian Jordan	2.00
5	Mark McGwire	20.00
6	Chuck Knoblauch	3.00
7	Sammy Sosa	10.00
8	Brady Anderson	2.00
9	Frank Thomas	9.00
10	Tony Gwynn	9.00
11	Roger Clemens	5.00
12	Alex Rodriguez	15.00
13	Paul Molitor	4.00
14	Kenny Lofton	3.00
15	John Smoltz	2.00
16	Roberto Alomar	4.00
17	Randy Johnson	4.00
18	Ryne Sandberg	5.00
19	Manny Ramirez	8.00
20	Mike Mussina	4.00

1997 Pinnacle Certified Team

The top 20 players in the game are honored on cards with frosted silver mylar printing. Cards were inserted 1:19 packs. A parallel version of this set, Certified Gold Team, has a gold mylar design with each card numbered to 500; while a super-premium parallel, Mirror Gold, is numbered to 25.

		MT
Complete Set (20):		150.00
Common Player:		2.00
Gold: 2X		
Mirror Gold: 10X		
1	Frank Thomas	9.00
2	Jeff Bagwell	9.00
3	Derek Jeter	12.50
4	Chipper Jones	12.50
5	Alex Rodriguez	15.00
6	Ken Caminiti	2.00
7	Cal Ripken Jr.	15.00
8	Mo Vaughn	4.00
9	Ivan Rodriguez	5.00
10	Mike Piazza	12.50
11	Juan Gonzalez	10.00
12	Barry Bonds	5.00
13	Ken Griffey Jr.	20.00
14	Andruw Jones	7.50
15	Albert Belle	5.00
16	Gary Sheffield	3.00
17	Andy Pettitte	4.00
18	Hideo Nomo	3.00
19	Greg Maddux	12.50
19s	Greg Maddux (Gold Team "SAMPLE")	5.00
20	John Smoltz	2.00

1997 Totally Certified Samples

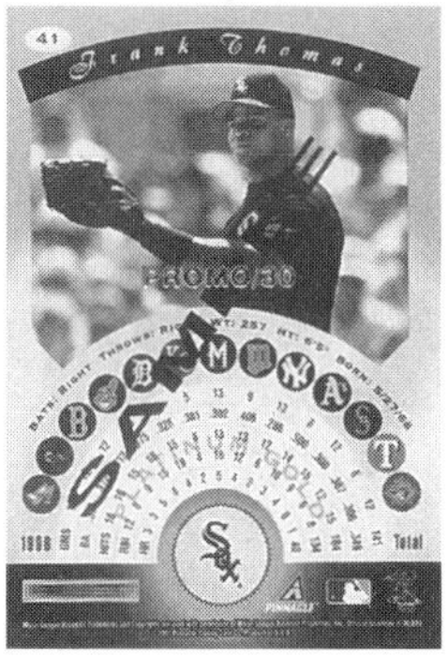

This trio of promo cards previews the high-tech, all-numbered Totally Certified issue. The samples are similar in format to the issued versions except they carry a large, black "SAMPLE" overprint diagonally on front and back. Also, backs have a gold-foil "PROMO" instead of the individual serial number.

		MT
Complete Set (3):		15.00
Common Player:		3.00
18	Tony Clark (Platinum Red)	3.00
39	Roger Clemens (Platinum Blue)	6.00
41	Frank Thomas (Platinum Gold)	5.00

1997 Totally Certified Platinum Red

Totally Certified doesn't have a true base set. Instead, the product consists of three different 150-card parallel sets. Packs consisted of three cards for $6.99 each. The first of three parallels is the Platinum Red set, inserted two per pack, and featuring micro-etched holographic mylar stock with red accents and foil stamping. Each card in the Red set is sequentially-numbered to 3,999.

		MT
Complete Set (150):		250.00
Common Player:		.70
Minor Stars:		1.50
Wax Box:		90.00
1	Barry Bonds	4.00
2	Mo Vaughn	3.00
3	Matt Williams	1.50
4	Ryne Sandberg	4.00
5	Jeff Bagwell	6.00
6	Alan Benes	.75
7	John Wetteland	.75
8	Fred McGriff	1.25
9	Craig Biggio	1.25
10	Bernie Williams	3.00
11	Brian Hunter	.75
12	Sandy Alomar Jr.	1.00
13	Ray Lankford	.75
14	Ryan Klesko	1.50
15	Jermaine Dye	.75
16	Andy Benes	.75
17	Albert Belle	5.00
18	Tony Clark	3.00
19	Dean Palmer	.75
20	Bernard Gilkey	.75
21	Ken Caminiti	2.00
22	Alex Rodriguez	12.50
23	Tim Salmon	1.50
24	Larry Walker	2.50
25	Barry Larkin	1.50
26	Mike Piazza	10.00
27	Brady Anderson	.75
28	Cal Ripken Jr.	12.50
29	Charles Nagy	.75
30	Paul Molitor	3.00
31	Darin Erstad	5.00
32	Rey Ordonez	.75
33	Wally Joyner	.75
34	David Cone	.75
35	Sammy Sosa	7.50
36	Dante Bichette	1.50
37	Eric Karros	.75
38	Omar Vizquel	.75
39	Roger Clemens	6.00
40	Joe Carter	.75
41	Frank Thomas	6.00
42	Javier Lopez	.75
43	Mike Mussina	3.00
44	Gary Sheffield	2.00
45	Tony Gwynn	7.50
46	Jason Kendall	.75
47	Jim Thome	3.00
48	Andres Galarraga	2.00
49	Mark McGwire	15.00
50	Troy Percival	.75
51	Derek Jeter	10.00
52	Todd Hollandsworth	.75
53	Ken Griffey Jr.	15.00
54	Randy Johnson	3.00
55	Pat Hentgen	.75
56	Rusty Greer	.75
57	John Jaha	.75
58	Kenny Lofton	3.00
59	Chipper Jones	10.00
60	Robb Nen	.75
61	Rafael Palmeiro	1.50
62	Mariano Rivera	1.25
63	Hideo Nomo	2.50
64	Greg Vaughn	.75
65	Ron Gant	.75
66	Eddie Murray	2.00
67	John Smoltz	1.50
68	Manny Ramirez	5.00
69	Juan Gonzalez	7.50
70	F.P. Santangelo	.75
71	Moises Alou	1.25
72	Alex Ochoa	.75
73	Chuck Knoblauch	1.50
74	Raul Mondesi	1.50
75	J.T. Snow	.75
76	Rickey Henderson	1.00
77	Bobby Bonilla	1.00
78	Wade Boggs	2.00
79	Ivan Rodriguez	4.00
80	Brian Jordan	.75
81	Al Leiter	.75
82	Jay Buhner	1.00
83	Greg Maddux	10.00
84	Edgar Martinez	.75
85	Kevin Brown	.75
86	Eric Young	.75
87	Todd Hundley	1.25
88	Ellis Burks	.75
89	Marquis Grissom	.75
90	Jose Canseco	1.50
91	Henry Rodriguez	.75
92	Andy Pettitte	3.00
93	Mark Grudzielanek	.75
94	Dwight Gooden	.75
95	Roberto Alomar	3.00
96	Paul Wilson	.75
97	Will Clark	1.50
98	Rondell White	1.25
99	Charles Johnson	.75
100	Jim Edmonds	1.00
101	Jason Giambi	.75
102	Billy Wagner	.75
103	Edgar Renteria	.75
104	Johnny Damon	.75
105	Jason Isringhausen	.75
106	Andruw Jones	7.50
107	Jose Guillen	3.00
108	Kevin Orie	.75
109	Brian Giles	.75
110	Danny Patterson	.75
111	Vladimir Guerrero	5.00
112	Scott Rolen	7.50
113	Damon Mashore	.75
114	Nomar Garciaparra	10.00
115	Todd Walker	2.50
116	Wilton Guerrero	.75
117	Bob Abreu	.75
118	Brooks Kieschnick	.75
119	Pokey Reese	.75
120	Todd Greene	.75
121	Dmitri Young	.75
122	Raul Casanova	.75
123	Glendon Rusch	.75
124	Jason Dickson	.75
125	Jorge Posada	.75
126	Rod Myers	.75
127	Bubba Trammell	1.50
128	Scott Spiezio	.75
129	Hideki Irabu	2.50
130	Wendell Magee	.75
131	Bartolo Colon	.75
132	Chris Holt	.75
133	Calvin Maduro	.75
134	Ray Montgomery	.75
135	Shannon Stewart	.75
136	Ken Griffey Jr. (Certified Stars)	7.50
137	Vladimir Guerrero (Certified Stars)	2.50
138	Roger Clemens (Certified Stars)	3.00
139	Mark McGwire (Certified Stars)	7.50
140	Albert Belle (Certified Stars)	2.50
141	Derek Jeter (Certified Stars)	5.00
142	Juan Gonzalez (Certified Stars)	4.00
143	Greg Maddux (Certified Stars)	4.50
144	Alex Rodriguez (Certified Stars)	6.00
145	Jeff Bagwell (Certified Stars)	3.00
146	Cal Ripken Jr. (Certified Stars)	6.00
147	Tony Gwynn (Certified Stars)	4.00
148	Frank Thomas (Certified Stars)	3.00
149	Hideo Nomo (Certified Stars)	1.00
150	Andruw Jones (Certified Stars)	4.00

1997 Totally Certified Platinum Blue

Featuring blue accents and foil stamping, the Platinum Blue cards are sequentially numbered to 1,999 and inserted one per pack.

	MT
Complete Set (150):	500.00
Common Player:	2.00
Platinum Blue Stars: 2X (See 1997 Totally Certified Platinum Red for checklist and base card values.)	

1997 Totally Certified Platinum Gold

The most difficult to find of the Totally Certified cards, the Platinum Gold versions are sequentially-numbered to 30 per card and inserted 1:79 packs.

	MT
Common Player:	25.00
Platinum Gold Stars: 20X (See 1997 Totally Certified Platinum Red for checklist and base card values.)	

1997 Pinnacle FanFest

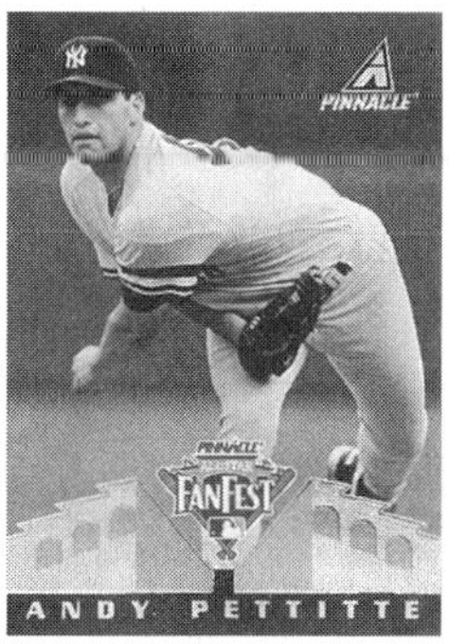

As title sponsor for baseball's All-Star FanFest in Cleveland, July 4-8, 1997, Pinnacle issued a number of special cards including this set which was distributed in three-card cello packs both prior to and during the event. To help promote the event, six of the cards were issued with a schedule back, as well as the regular back design. Fronts have action photos highlighted at bottom by a stadium facade in gold foil. The FanFest logo is at bottom center. Backs feature a player portrait photo within a large star. Also on back are a few stats and personal data, a few words about the player and appropriate logos. Cards are numbered with an "FF" prefix and "of 21" following the number. Card #21 of the host team's Sandy Alomar, Jr., was not issued in packs. A redemption card, which could be traded in at area card shops for the Alomar card, was substituted.

		MT
Complete Set (21):		50.00
Common Player:		1.50
FF1	Frank Thomas	2.50
FF2	Jeff Bagwell	2.25
FF3	Chuck Knoblauch	1.50
FF4	Craig Biggio	1.50
FF5	Alex Rodriguez	3.50
FF6	Chipper Jones	3.00
FF7	Cal Ripken Jr.	4.00
FF8	Ken Caminiti	1.50
FF9	Juan Gonzalez	2.25
FF10	Barry Bonds	2.25
FF11	Ken Griffey Jr.	4.00
FF12	Andruw Jones	1.50
FF13	Manny Ramirez	1.50
FF14	Tony Gwynn	2.25
FF15a	Ivan Rodriguez (schedule back)	10.00
FF15b	Ivan Rodriguez (regular back)	1.50
FF16a	Mike Piazza (schedule back)	15.00
FF16b	Mike Piazza (regular back)	3.00
FF17a	Andy Pettitte (schedule back)	8.00
FF17b	Andy Pettitte (regular back)	1.50
FF18a	Hideo Nomo (schedule back)	8.00
FF18b	Hideo Nomo (regular back)	1.50
FF19a	Roger Clemens (schedule back)	10.00
FF19b	Roger Clemens (regular back)	2.25
FF20a	Greg Maddux (schedule back)	15.00
FF20b	Greg Maddux (regular back)	2.50
FF21	Sandy Alomar Jr.	7.50
----	Sandy Alomar Jr. (trade-in card)	1.50

1997 Pinnacle FanFest Larry Doby

Marking the 50th anniversary of the American League's integration, Pinnacle, title sponsor of baseball's All-Star FanFest, issued a special card of black A.L. pioneer Larry Doby, who debuted in 1947 with the Indians. FanFest and the All-Star Game were held in Cleveland in 1997, with Doby attending many of the functions. In the same format as its FanFest set of current players, the special Doby card has a black-and-white action photo on front, with gold-foil highlights at bottom. Back repeats the front photo within a star and offers some career notes and stats. The Doby card was given away to FanFest volunteer workers and laminated into identification badges for FanFest dealers.

	MT
Larry Doby	15.00

1997 Pinnacle FanFest Personal Cards

Continuing a tradition begun a year earlier, Pinnacle, the title sponsor for baseball's FanFest, produced a series of cards for various local and media celebrities. The cards are in the same format as the FanFest player cards, with color photos on front and gold-foil highlights. Backs have a photo detail within a star design and a few words about the personality, along with stats such as Indians' games attended, popcorn consumer, etc. Cards are numbered with a PC prefix and are difficult to find because their distribution was controlled by the person pictured. Rick Manning was an Indians outfielder from 1975-83. Mike Hegan played in the American League from 1964-77; his father, Jim was a staple behind the plate for the Indians between 1941-57. Six of the cards feature members of the Fox network which televised the 1997 All-Star Game.

		MT
Complete Set (12):		100.00
Common Player:		8.00
PC1	Macie McInnis (Fox)	8.00
PC2	Bill Martin (Fox)	8.00
PC3	Dick Gaddard (Fox)	8.00
PC4	Jack Corrigan (WUAB-TV)	8.00
PC5	Mike Hegan (WUAB-TV)	15.00
PC6	Rick Manning (Sports Channel)	15.00
PC7	John Sanders (Sports Channel)	8.00
PC8	Mayor Michael R. White	10.00
PC9	Wilma Smith (Fox)	8.00
PC10	Tim Taylor (Fox)	8.00
PC11	Robin Swoboda (Fox)	8.00
PC12	Slider (mascot)	8.00

1997 Pinnacle Inside

The first baseball card set to be sold within a sealed tin can, Inside Baseball consisted of a 150-card base set featuring both a color and black-and-white photo of the player on the front of the card. Included in the base set were 20 Rookies' cards and three checklists. Inserts include the Club Edition and Diamond Edition parallel sets, Dueling Dugouts and Fortysomething. In addition, 24 different cans, each featuring a different player, were available. Cans containing one pack of 10 cards were sold for $2.99 each.

		MT
Complete Set (150):		35.00
Common Player:		.10
Club Edition Complete Set (150):		300.00
Common Club Edition:		.75
Club Edition Stars: 5X		
Common Diamond Edition:		5.00
Diamond Edition Stars: 25X		
1	David Cone	.15
2	Sammy Sosa	2.00
3	Joe Carter	.10
4	Juan Gonzalez	2.00
5	Hideo Nomo	.50
6	Moises Alou	.15
7	Marc Newfield	.10
8	Alex Rodriguez	3.00
9	Kimera Bartee	.10
10	Chuck Knoblauch	.25
11	Jason Isringhausen	.10
12	Jermaine Allensworth	.10
13	Frank Thomas	2.00
14	Paul Molitor	.75
15	John Mabry	.10
16	Greg Maddux	2.50
17	Rafael Palmeiro	.20
18	Brian Jordan	.10
19	Ken Griffey Jr.	4.50
20	Brady Anderson	.10
21	Ruben Sierra	.10
22	Travis Fryman	.10
23	Cal Ripken Jr.	3.00
24	Will Clark	.25
25	Todd Hollandsworth	.10
26	Kevin Brown	.15
27	Mike Piazza	2.50
28	Craig Biggio	.20
29	Paul Wilson	.10
30	Andres Galarraga	.20
31	Chipper Jones	2.50
32	Jason Giambi	.10
33	Ernie Young	.10
34	Marty Cordova	.10
35	Albert Belle	1.00
36	Roger Clemens	1.50
37	Ryne Sandberg	1.00
38	Henry Rodriguez	.10
39	Jay Buhner	.15
40	Raul Mondesi	.20
41	Jeff Fassero	.10
42	Edgar Martinez	.10
43	Trey Beamon	.10
44	Mo Vaughn	.75
45	Gary Sheffield	.35
46	Ray Durham	.10
47	Brett Butler	.10
48	Ivan Rodriguez	.75
49	Fred McGriff	.25
50	Dean Palmer	.10
51	Rickey Henderson	.20
52	Andy Pettitte	.75
53	Bobby Bonilla	.10
54	Shawn Green	.20
55	Tino Martinez	.20
56	Tony Gwynn	2.00
57	Tom Glavine	.20
58	Eric Young	.10
59	Kevin Appier	.10
60	Barry Bonds	1.00
61	Wade Boggs	.25
62	Jason Kendall	.10
63	Jeff Bagwell	2.00
64	Jeff Conine	.10
65	Greg Vaughn	.15
66	Eric Karros	.10
67	Manny Ramirez	1.50
68	John Smoltz	.20
69	Terrell Wade	.10
70	John Wetteland	.10
71	Kenny Lofton	.75
72	Jim Thome	.60
73	Bill Pulsipher	.10
74	Darryl Strawberry	.10
75	Roberto Alomar	.75
76	Bobby Higginson	.10
77	James Baldwin	.10
78	Mark McGwire	4.50
79	Jose Canseco	.25
80	Mark Grudzielanek	.10
81	Ryan Klesko	.20
82	Javier Lopez	.15
83	Ken Caminiti	.20
84	Dave Nilsson	.10
85	Tim Salmon	.15
86	Cecil Fielder	.10
87	Derek Jeter	2.50
88	Garret Anderson	.10
89	Dwight Gooden	.10
90	Carlos Delgado	.30
91	Ugueth Urbina	.10
92	Chan Ho Park	.15
93	Eddie Murray	.40
94	Alex Ochoa	.10
95	Rusty Greer	.10
96	Mark Grace	.20
97	Pat Hentgen	.10
98	John Jaha	.10
99	Charles Johnson	.10
100	Jermaine Dye	.10
101	Quinton McCracken	.10
102	Troy Percival	.10
103	Shane Reynolds	.10
104	Rondell White	.10
105	Charles Nagy	.10
106	Alan Benes	.10
107	Tom Goodwin	.10
108	Ron Gant	.10
109	Dan Wilson	.10
110	Darin Erstad	1.50
111	Matt Williams	.25
112	Barry Larkin	.15
113	Mariano Rivera	.15
114	Larry Walker	.40
115	Jim Edmonds	.10
116	Michael Tucker	.10
117	Todd Hundley	.20
118	Alex Fernandez	.10
119	J.T. Snow	.10
120	Ellis Burks	.10
121	Steve Finley	.10
122	Mike Mussina	.60
123	Curtis Pride	.10
124	Derek Bell	.10
125	Dante Bichette	.20
126	Terry Steinbach	.10
127	Randy Johnson	.75
128	Andruw Jones	2.00
129	Vladimir Guerrero	1.50
130	Ruben Rivera	.10
131	Billy Wagner	.15
132	Scott Rolen	2.00
133	Rey Ordonez	.15
134	Karim Garcia	.15
135	George Arias	.10
136	Todd Greene	.10
137	Robin Jennings	.10
138	Raul Casanova	.10
139	Josh Booty	.10
140	Edgar Renteria	.10
141	Chad Mottola	.10
142	Dmitri Young	.10
143	Tony Clark	.60
144	Todd Walker	.75
145	Kevin Brown	.15
146	Nomar Garciaparra	2.50
147	Neifi Perez	.10
148	Derek Jeter, Todd Hollandsworth	.40
149	Pat Hentgen, John Smoltz	.10
150	Juan Gonzalez, Ken Caminiti	.30

1997 Pinnacle Inside Club Edition

A 150-card parallel set featuring a special silver foil design and "CLUB EDITION" notation on back, these cards were inserted 1:7 cans of Inside.

	MT
Complete Club Edition Set (150):	300.00
Common Club Edition:	.75

Stars: 5X
(See 1997 Pinnacle Inside for checklist and base values.)

1997 Pinnacle Inside Diamond Edition

A second parallel set, this time featuring a special die-cut design and gold holographic stamping. Cards were inserted 1:63 packs.

	MT
Common Diamond Edition:	5.00

Stars: 25X
(See 1997 Pinnacle Inside for checklist and base values.)

1997 Pinnacle Inside Cans

In addition to the cards, collectors had the option of collecting the 24 different player cans which are the packs in which the cards were sold. About the size of a can of peas (3" diameter, 4-1/2" tall, the cans feature several color and black-and-white reproductions of the player's Inside card. The package had to be opened with a can opener to access the cards. Values shown are for empty cans which have been opened from the bottom; top-opened cans have little collectible value.

		MT
Complete Set (24):		20.00
Common Can:		.50
Sealed Cans: 2X		
1	Ken Griffey Jr.	2.50
2	Juan Gonzalez	1.25
3	Frank Thomas	1.25
4	Cal Ripken Jr.	2.00
5	Derek Jeter	1.50
6	Andruw Jones	1.50
7	Alex Rodriguez	2.00
8	Mike Piazza	1.50
9	Mo Vaughn	.75
10	Jeff Bagwell	1.00
11	Ken Caminiti	.50
12	Andy Pettitte	.75
13	Barry Bonds	.75
14	Mark McGwire	2.50
15	Ryan Klesko	.50
16	Manny Ramirez	.75
17	Ivan Rodriguez	.50
18	Chipper Jones	1.50
19	Albert Belle	.75
20	Tony Gwynn	1.25
21	Kenny Lofton	.65
22	Greg Maddux	1.25
23	Hideo Nomo	.50
24	John Smoltz	.50

1997 Pinnacle Inside Dueling Dugouts

This 20-card insert set features a veteran player on one side, a rising star on the other, and a spinning wheel that reveals their respective achievements in various statistical categories. Cards were inserted 1:23 packs.

		MT
Complete Set (20):		300.00
Common Player:		5.00
1	Alex Rodriguez, Cal Ripken Jr.	50.00
2	Jeff Bagwell, Ken Caminiti	20.00
3	Barry Bonds, Albert Belle	15.00
4	Mike Piazza, Ivan Rodriguez	25.00
5	Chuck Knoblauch, Roberto Alomar	7.50
6	Ken Griffey Jr., Andruw Jones	50.00
7	Chipper Jones, Jim Thome	25.00
8	Frank Thomas, Mo Vaughn	20.00
9	Fred McGriff, Mark McGwire	45.00
10	Brian Jordan, Tony Gwynn	20.00
11	Barry Larkin, Derek Jeter	20.00
12	Kenny Lofton, Bernie Williams	5.00
13	Juan Gonzalez, Manny Ramirez	20.00
14	Will Clark, Rafael Palmeiro	7.50
15	Greg Maddux, Roger Clemens	20.00
16	John Smoltz, Andy Pettitte	5.00
17	Mariano Rivera, John Wetteland	5.00
18	Hideo Nomo, Mike Mussina	5.00
19	Todd Hollandsworth, Darin Erstad	10.00
20	Vladimir Guerrero, Karim Garcia	10.00

1997 Pinnacle Inside Fortysomething

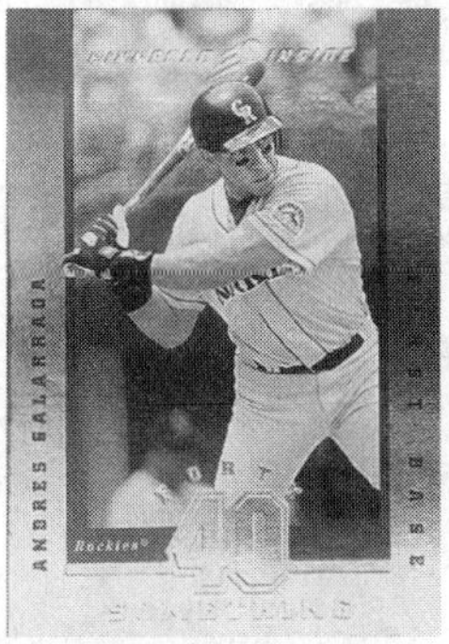

The top home run hitters in the game are pictured in this 16-card set. Cards were inserted 1:47 packs.

		MT
Complete Set (16):		150.00
Common Player:		4.00
1	Juan Gonzalez	20.00
2	Barry Bonds	10.00
3	Ken Caminiti	5.00
4	Mark McGwire	40.00
5	Todd Hundley	4.00
6	Albert Belle	10.00
7	Ellis Burks	4.00
8	Jay Buhner	4.00
9	Brady Anderson	4.00
10	Vinny Castilla	4.00
11	Mo Vaughn	7.50
12	Ken Griffey Jr.	40.00
13	Sammy Sosa	20.00
14	Andres Galarraga	4.00
15	Gary Sheffield	5.00
16	Frank Thomas	20.00

1997 Pinnacle Mint Collection

The 30-card Mint Collection set came in three-card packs that also contained two coins. The cards came in two versions: die-cut and foil. Three foil versions appear with Bronze Act as the common with Silver (1:15) and Gold (1:48) also appearing. The coins that come with each pack arrive in brass, silver and gold and can be matched up with the corresponding player die-cut card. The card fronts feature a player action shot on the left side with a shadowed headshot on the right. On the die-cut versions, the coin-size hole is in the lower right quadrant while the foil team stamp for the common cards is in the same location. The card backs are numbered as "x of 30" and deliver a short text.

		MT
Complete Set (30):		20.00
Common Player:		.25
Bronze Cards: 2X		40.00
Silver Cards: 5X		
Gold Cards: 10X		
Wax Box:		50.00
1	Ken Griffey Jr.	3.50
2	Frank Thomas	1.50
3	Alex Rodriguez	2.50
4	Cal Ripken Jr.	2.50
5	Mo Vaughn	.50
6	Juan Gonzalez	1.25
7	Mike Piazza	2.00
8	Albert Belle	.75
9	Chipper Jones	2.00
10	Andruw Jones	1.50
11	Greg Maddux	1.75
12	Hideo Nomo	.25
13	Jeff Bagwell	1.25
14	Manny Ramirez	1.00
15	Mark McGwire	3.50
16	Derek Jeter	2.00
17	Sammy Sosa	1.50
18	Barry Bonds	.75
19	Chuck Knoblauch	.25
20	Dante Bichette	.25
21	Tony Gwynn	1.25
22	Ken Caminiti	.40
23	Gary Sheffield	.40
24	Tim Salmon	.25
25	Ivan Rodriguez	.50
26	Henry Rodriguez	.25
27	Barry Larkin	.25
28	Ryan Klesko	.40
29	Brian Jordan	.25
30	Jay Buhner	.25

1997 Pinnacle Mint Collection Coins

Two coins from the 30-coin set were included in each three-card pack of 1997 Pinnacle Mint Collection. Brass coins are common while nickel-silver coins were inserted every 20 packs and gold-plated coins were inserted every 48 packs. Redemption cards for solid silver coins were found every 2,300 packs and a redemption card for a solid gold coin was inserted in 47,200 packs. Only one of each 24K gold coin was produced. The front of the coins feature the player's portrait while the backs have a baseball diamond with "Limited Edition, Pinnacle Mint Collection 1997" printed.

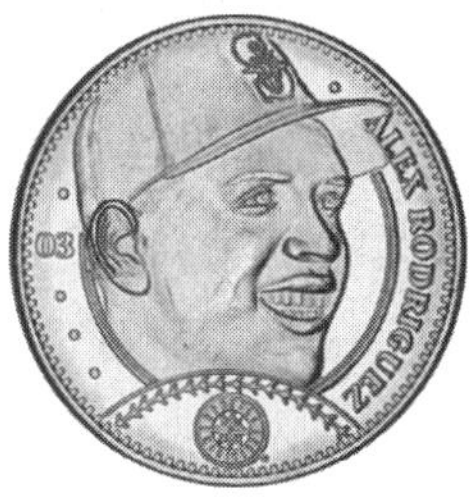

		MT
	Complete Set (30):	50.00
	Common Brass Coin:	.50
	Nickel Coins: 4X	
	Gold Plated Coins: 10X	
	Silver Coins: 200X	
	24K Gold Coins: Value undermined	
1	Ken Griffey Jr.	5.00
2	Frank Thomas	2.00
3	Alex Rodriguez	4.00
4	Cal Ripken Jr.	4.00
5	Mo Vaughn	.75
6	Juan Gonzalez	2.00
7	Mike Piazza	3.00
8	Albert Belle	1.25
9	Chipper Jones	3.00
10	Andruw Jones	2.50
11	Greg Maddux	3.00
12	Hideo Nomo	.50
13	Jeff Bagwell	2.00
14	Manny Ramirez	1.50
15	Mark McGwire	5.00
16	Derek Jeter	3.00
17	Sammy Sosa	2.50
18	Barry Bonds	1.25
19	Chuck Knoblauch	.50
20	Dante Bichette	.75
21	Tony Gwynn	2.00
22	Ken Caminiti	.75
23	Gary Sheffield	.75
24	Tim Salmon	.50
25	Ivan Rodriguez	1.00
26	Henry Rodriguez	.50
27	Barry Larkin	.50
28	Ryan Klesko	.75
29	Brian Jordan	.50
30	Jay Buhner	.50

1997 Pinnacle X-Press

The 150-card set features 115 base cards, a 22-card Rookies subset, 10 Peak Performers and three checklist cards. Each of the regular cards features a horizontal design with two photos of each player on the front of the card and his name across the bottom. There are a number of inserts within this product, including Swing for the Fences (regular player cards as well as base and booster cards that can be used to accumulate points for a sweepstakes), Men of Summer, Far & Away, Melting Pot, Metal Works silver and Metal Works Gold. Cards were sold in eight-card packs for $1.99 each. X-Press Metal Works boxes were also available for $14.99 and contained a regular pack, one metal card and a master deck used to play the Swing for the Fences game.

		MT
	Complete Set (150):	15.00
	Common Player:	.05
	Men of Summer: 8X	
1	Larry Walker	.20
2	Andy Pettitte	.60
3	Matt Williams	.20
4	Juan Gonzalez	1.25
5	Frank Thomas	1.00
6	Kenny Lofton	.60
7	Ken Griffey Jr.	2.50
8	Andres Galarraga	.15
9	Greg Maddux	1.50
10	Hideo Nomo	.25
11	Cecil Fielder	.10
12	Jose Canseco	.15
13	Tony Gwynn	1.25
14	Eddie Murray	.20
15	Alex Rodriguez	2.00
16	Mike Piazza	1.50
17	Ken Hill	.05
18	Chuck Knoblauch	.15
19	Ellis Burks	.05
20	Rafael Palmeiro	.15
21	Vinny Castilla	.05
22	Rusty Greer	.05
23	Chipper Jones	1.50
24	Rey Ordonez	.10
25	Mariano Rivera	.10
26	Garret Anderson	.05
27	Edgar Martinez	.10
28	Dante Bichette	.15
29	Todd Hundley	.15
30	Barry Bonds	.60
31	Barry Larkin	.10
32	Derek Jeter	1.50
33	Marquis Grissom	.10
34	David Justice	.20
35	Ivan Rodriguez	.50
36	Jay Buhner	.10
37	Fred McGriff	.20
38	Brady Anderson	.10
39	Tony Clark	.60
40	Eric Young	.05
41	Charles Nagy	.05
42	Mark McGwire	2.50
43	Paul O'Neill	.15
44	Tino Martinez	.10
45	Ryne Sandberg	.60
46	Bernie Williams	.40
47	Albert Belle	.60
48	Jeff Cirillo	.05
49	Tim Salmon	.15
50	Steve Finley	.05
51	Lance Johnson	.05
52	John Smoltz	.15
53	Javier Lopez	.10
54	Roger Clemens	.60
55	Kevin Appier	.05
56	Ken Caminiti	.20
57	Cal Ripken Jr.	2.00
58	Moises Alou	.15
59	Marty Cordova	.15
60	David Cone	.15
61	Manny Ramirez	.75
62	Ray Durham	.05
63	Jermaine Dye	.05
64	Craig Biggio	.15
65	Will Clark	.20
66	Omar Vizquel	.05
67	Bernard Gilkey	.05
68	Greg Vaughn	.10
69	Wade Boggs	.20
70	Dave Nilsson	.05
71	Mark Grace	.20
72	Dean Palmer	.05
73	Sammy Sosa	1.50
74	Mike Mussina	.50
75	Alex Fernandez	.05
76	Henry Rodriguez	.05
77	Travis Fryman	.05
78	Jeff Bagwell	1.00
79	Pat Hentgen	.05
80	Gary Sheffield	.20
81	Jim Edmonds	.10
82	Darin Erstad	1.00
83	Mark Grudzielanek	.05
84	Jim Thome	.40
85	Bobby Higginson	.15
86	Al Martin	.05
87	Jason Giambi	.05
88	Mo Vaughn	.60
89	Jeff Conine	.05
90	Edgar Renteria	.05
91	Andy Ashby	.05
92	Ryan Klesko	.20
93	John Jaha	.05
94	Paul Molitor	.40
95	Brian Hunter	.05
96	Randy Johnson	.40
97	Joey Hamilton	.05
98	Billy Wagner	.05
99	John Wetteland	.05
100	Jeff Fassero	.05
101	Rondell White	.15
102	Kevin Brown	.15
103	Andy Benes	.10
104	Raul Mondesi	.15
105	Todd Hollandsworth	.05
106	Alex Ochoa	.05
107	Bobby Bonilla	.10
108	Brian Jordan	.05
109	Tom Glavine	.15
110	Ron Gant	.10
111	Jason Kendall	.05
112	Roberto Alomar	.40
113	Troy Percival	.05
114	Michael Tucker	.05
115	Joe Carter	.10
116	Andruw Jones	1.25
117	Nomar Garciaparra	1.50
118	Todd Walker	.20
119	Jose Guillen	.50
120	*Bubba Trammell*	.50
121	Wilton Guerrero	.10
122	Bob Abreu	.05
123	Vladimir Guerrero	.75
124	Dmitri Young	.05
125	Kevin Orie	.05
126	Glendon Rusch	.05
127	Brooks Kieschnick	.05
128	Scott Spiezio	.05
129	*Brian Giles*	.75
130	Jason Dickson	.15
131	Damon Mashore	.05
132	Wendell Magee	.05
133	Matt Morris	.05
134	Scott Rolen	1.25
135	Shannon Stewart	.05
136	*Deivi Cruz*	.25
137	*Hideki Irabu*	1.00
138	Larry Walker (Peak Performers)	.15
139	Ken Griffey Jr. (Peak Performers)	1.00
140	Frank Thomas (Peak Performers)	.50
141	Ivan Rodriguez (Peak Performers)	.20
142	Randy Johnson (Peak Performers)	.20
143	Mark McGwire (Peak Performers)	1.00
144	Tino Martinez (Peak Performers)	.10
145	Tony Clark (Peak Performers)	.25
146	Mike Piazza (Peak Performers)	.60
147	Alex Rodriguez (Peak Performers)	.75
148	Checklist (Roger Clemens)	.25
149	Checklist (Greg Maddux)	.50
150	Checklist (Hideo Nomo)	.20

1997 Pinnacle X-Press Men of Summer

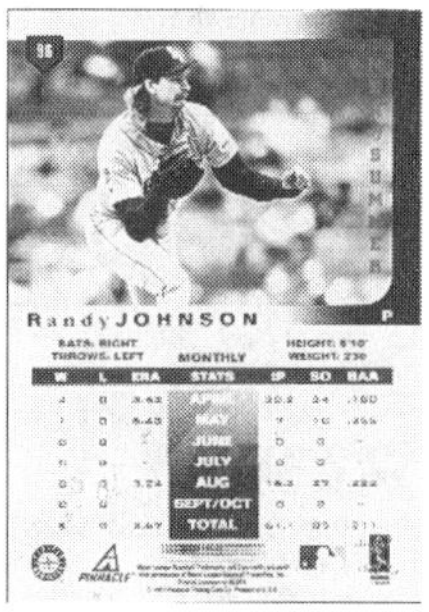

This parallel set of the 150 cards in the base X-Press issue differs in that the fronts are printed on foil backgrounds and the backs have a notation "MEN OF SUMMER" printed in gold vertically at top.

	MT
Complete Set (150):	200.00
Common Player:	.75
(See 1997 Pinnacle X-Press for checklist and base card values.)	

1997 Pinnacle X-Press Far & Away

This 18-card insert highlights the top home run hitters in baseball and is printed with Dufex technology. Cards were inserted 1:19 packs.

		MT
	Complete Set (18):	100.00
	Common Player:	1.50
1	Albert Belle	5.00
2	Mark McGwire	20.00
3	Frank Thomas	10.00
4	Mo Vaughn	5.00
5	Jeff Bagwell	8.00
6	Juan Gonzalez	10.00
7	Mike Piazza	12.00
8	Andruw Jones	10.00
9	Chipper Jones	12.00
10	Gary Sheffield	2.50
11	Sammy Sosa	10.00
12	Darin Erstad	7.00
13	Jay Buhner	1.50
14	Ken Griffey Jr.	20.00
15	Ken Caminiti	1.50
16	Brady Anderson	1.50
17	Manny Ramirez	7.00
18	Alex Rodriguez	15.00

1997 Pinnacle X-Press Melting Pot Samples

		MT
	Complete Set (20):	75.00
	Common Player:	1.00
1	Jose Guillen	2.00
2	Vladimir Guerrero	3.50
3	Andruw Jones	5.00
4	Larry Walker	2.00
5	Manny Ramirez	2.00
6	Ken Griffey Jr.	10.00
7	Alex Rodriguez	7.50
8	Frank Thomas	5.00
9	Juan Gonzalez	5.00
10	Ivan Rodriguez	4.00
11	Hideo Nomo	2.00
12	Rafael Palmeiro	2.00
13	Dave Nilsson	1.00
14	Nomar Garciaparra	6.00
15	Wilton Guerrero	1.00
16	Sammy Sosa	6.00
17	Edgar Renteria	1.00
18	Cal Ripken Jr.	7.50
19	Derek Jeter	6.00
20	Rey Ordonez	1.00

1997 Pinnacle X-Press Melting Pot

This 20-card insert showcases the talents of major leaguers from various countries. Fronts have color player photos on a background which combines shiny silver foil and textured foil in the design of the player's native flag. Backs have another photo and are ink-jet numbered in a white stripe at bottom in an edition of 500 each. Stated insertion rate was one per 288 packs.

		MT
	Complete Set (20):	450.00
	Common Player:	7.50
1	Jose Guillen	15.00
2	Vladimir Guerrero	25.00
3	Andruw Jones	40.00
4	Larry Walker	10.00
5	Manny Ramirez	20.00
6	Ken Griffey Jr.	75.00
7	Alex Rodriguez	60.00
7p	Alex Rodriguez (overprinted "SAMPLE")	5.00
8	Frank Thomas	35.00
9	Juan Gonzalez	35.00
10	Ivan Rodriguez	15.00
11	Hideo Nomo	10.00
12	Rafael Palmeiro	7.50
13	Dave Nilsson	7.50
14	Nomar Garciaparra	40.00
15	Wilton Guerrero	7.50
16	Sammy Sosa	45.00
17	Edgar Renteria	7.50
18	Cal Ripken Jr.	60.00
19	Derek Jeter	45.00
20	Rey Ordonez	7.50

1997 Pinnacle X-Press Metal Works

Each Home Plate Box of X-Press contains one heavy bronze Metal Works "card." The 2-3/8" x 3-1/2" slabs have a player portrait on front. Backs have a few words about the player. Redemption cards for silver-plated parallels were inserted 1:470 packs, while a silver slab was found 1:54 Home Plate Boxes. Silver Metal Works are serially numbered to 400 each. Redemption cards for gold-plated Metal Works cards, numbered in an edition of 200 each, were inserted 1:950 packs or one per 108 Home Plate Boxes.

		MT
	Complete Set (20):	100.00
	Common Player:	2.00
	Silver: 30X	50.00
	Gold: 50X	25.00
1	Ken Griffey Jr.	15.00
2	Frank Thomas	6.00
3	Andruw Jones	3.00
4	Alex Rodriguez	10.00
5	Derek Jeter	7.50
6	Cal Ripken Jr.	10.00
7	Mike Piazza	7.50
8	Chipper Jones	7.50
9	Juan Gonzalez	6.00
10	Greg Maddux	7.50
11	Tony Gwynn	6.00
12	Jeff Bagwell	3.00
13	Albert Belle	3.00
14	Mark McGwire	15.00
15	Nomar Garciaparra	7.50
16	Mo Vaughn	2.00
17	Andy Pettitte	2.00
18	Manny Ramirez	4.00
19	Kenny Lofton	2.00
20	Roger Clemens	4.00

1997 Pinnacle X-Press Swing for the Fences

These inserts allow collectors to play an interactive game based on the number of home runs hit by the home run champions of each league. Player Cards feature 60 different players and were inserted 1:2 packs. Base Cards feature a number between 20-42 printed on them and are found one in every master deck. Booster Cards feature a plus-or-minus point total (i.e. +7, -2) that can be used to add or subtract points to get to the winning home run total. Booster Cards are found 1:2 packs, while Base Cards are found one per master deck. Collectors who accumulated the winning home run totals were eligible to win prizes ranging from autographs to a trip to the 1998 All-Star Game. The unnumbered cards are checklisted here in alphabetical order.

		MT
Complete Set (60):		40.00
Common Player:		.25
(1)	Sandy Alomar Jr.	.50
(2)	Moises Alou	.35
(3)	Brady Anderson	.25
(4)	Jeff Bagwell	1.00
(5)	Derek Bell	.25
(6)	Jay Bell	.25
(7)	Albert Belle	1.00
(8)	Geronimo Berroa	.25
(9)	Dante Bichette	.35
(10)	Barry Bonds	1.00
(11)	Bobby Bonilla	.25
(12)	Jay Buhner	.25
(13)	Ellis Burks	.25
(14)	Ken Caminiti	.50
(15)	Jose Canseco	.75
(16)	Joe Carter	.25
(17)	Vinny Castilla	.25
(18)	Tony Clark	.50
(19)	Carlos Delgado	.50
(20)	Jim Edmonds	.25
(21)	Cecil Fielder	.25
(22)	Andres Galarraga	.50
(23)	Ron Gant	.25
(24)	Bernard Gilkey	.25
(25)	Juan Gonzalez	1.50
(26)	Ken Griffey Jr. (AL WINNER)	10.00
(27)	Vladimir Guerrero	1.50
(28)	Todd Hundley	.25
(29)	John Jaha	.25
(30)	Andruw Jones	2.00
(31)	Chipper Jones	2.50
(32)	David Justice	.50
(33)	Jeff Kent	.25
(34)	Ryan Klesko	.25
(35)	Barry Larkin	.25
(36)	Mike Lieberthal	.25
(37)	Javy Lopez	.25
(38)	Edgar Martinez	.25
(39)	Tino Martinez	.25
(40)	Fred McGriff	.25
(41)	Mark McGwire (AL/ NL WINNER)	10.00
(42)	Raul Mondesi	.25
(43)	Tim Naehring	.25
(44)	Dave Nillson	.25
(45)	Rafael Palmeiro	.50
(46)	Dean Palmer	.25
(47)	Mike Piazza	2.50
(48)	Cal Ripken Jr.	4.00
(49)	Henry Rodriguez	.25
(50)	Tim Salmon	.25
(51)	Gary Sheffield	.45
(52)	Sammy Sosa	2.50
(53)	Terry Steinbach	.25
(54)	Frank Thomas	2.00
(55)	Jim Thome	.25
(56)	Mo Vaughn	.45
(57)	Larry Walker (NL Winner)	3.00
(58)	Rondell White	.25
(59)	Matt Williams	.25
(60)	Todd Zeile	.25

1997 Pinnacle X-Press Swing/Fences Gold

Collectors who correctly matched Swing for the Fences insert game cards of the final 1997 season American and National home run champions with proper point cards equal to the number of home runs each hit could exchange them for a random assortment of 10 upgraded cards featuring gold-foil highlights and a premium card stock. The first 1,000 redemptions received an autographed Andruw Jones gold card. The redemption period ended March 1, 1998.

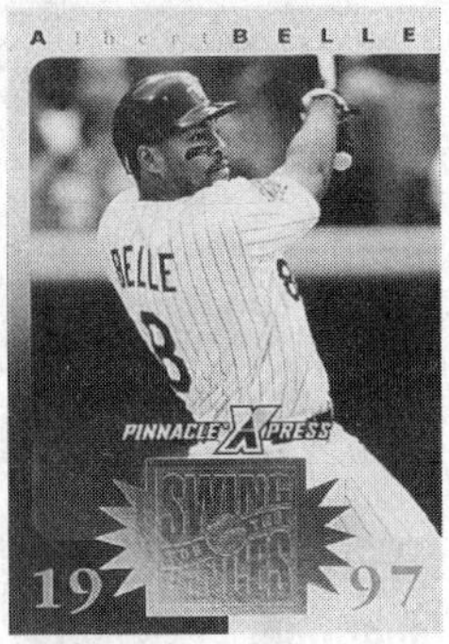

	MT
Complete Set (60):	150.00
Common Player:	1.00
Stars: 4X	
Andruw Jones Autograph:	150.00
(See 1997 Pinnacle X-Press Swing for the Fences for checklist and base values.)	

1998 Pinnacle

Pinnacle Baseball consists of a 200-card base set. The regular cards feature full-bleed photos on front. Three different backs were produced for each card: Home stats, away stats and seasonal stats. The set includes 157 regular cards, 24 Rookies, six Field of Vision, 10 Goin' Jake cards and three checklists. Parallel sets include Artist's Proofs, Press Plates and Museum Collection. Inserts include Epix, Hit it Here, Spellbound and Uncut.

		MT
Complete Set (200):		20.00
Common Player:		.10
1	Tony Gwynn (All-Star)	1.50
2	Pedro Martinez (All-Star)	.25
3	Kenny Lofton (All-Star)	.75
4	Curt Schilling (All-Star)	.15
5	Shawn Estes (All-Star)	.10
6	Tom Glavine (All-Star)	.20
7	Mike Piazza (All-Star)	2.00
8	Ray Lankford (All-Star)	.10
9	Barry Larkin (All-Star)	.20
10	Tony Womack (All-Star)	.10
11	Jeff Blauser (All-Star)	.10
12	Rod Beck (All-Star)	.10
13	Larry Walker (All-Star)	.30
14	Greg Maddux (All-Star)	2.00
15	Mark Grace (All-Star)	.20
16	Ken Caminiti (All-Star)	.20
17	Bobby Jones (All-Star)	.10
18	Chipper Jones (All-Star)	2.00
19	Javier Lopez (All-Star)	.15
20	Moises Alou (All-Star)	.20
21	Royce Clayton (All-Star)	.10
22	Darryl Kile (All-Star)	.10
23	Barry Bonds (All-Star)	.75
24	Steve Finley (All-Star)	.10
25	Andres Galarraga (All-Star)	.25
26	Denny Neagle (All-Star)	.10
27	Todd Hundley (All-Star)	.15
28	Jeff Bagwell	.75
29	Andy Pettitte	.35
30	Darin Erstad	.75
31	Carlos Delgado	.50
32	Matt Williams	.25
33	Will Clark	.20
34	Vinny Castilla	.15
35	Brad Radke	.10
36	John Olerud	.20
37	Andruw Jones	1.00
38	Jason Giambi	.10
39	Scott Rolen	1.00
40	Gary Sheffield	.30
41	Jimmy Key	.10
42	Kevin Appier	.10
43	Wade Boggs	.25
44	Hideo Nomo	.50
45	Manny Ramirez	.75
46	Wilton Guerrero	.10
47	Travis Fryman	.15
48	Chili Davis	.10
49	Jeromy Burnitz	.10
50	Craig Biggio	.20
51	Tim Salmon	.25
52	Jose Cruz Jr.	.15
53	Sammy Sosa	1.50
54	Hideki Irabu	.40
55	Chan Ho Park	.20
56	Robin Ventura	.10
57	Jose Guillen	.30
58	Deion Sanders	.25
59	Jose Canseco	.20
60	Jay Buhner	.15
61	Rafael Palmeiro	.20
62	Vladimir Guerrero	1.00
63	Mark McGwire	4.00
64	Derek Jeter	2.00
65	Bobby Bonilla	.20
66	Raul Mondesi	.20
67	Paul Molitor	.40
68	Joe Carter	.15
69	Marquis Grissom	.10
70	Juan Gonzalez	1.50
71	Kevin Orie	.10
72	Rusty Greer	.10
73	Henry Rodriguez	.10
74	Fernando Tatis	.25
75	John Valentin	.10
76	Matt Morris	.10
77	Ray Durham	.10
78	Geronimo Berroa	.10
79	Scott Brosius	.10
80	Willie Greene	.10
81	Rondell White	.20
82	Doug Drabek	.10
83	Derek Bell	.10
84	Butch Huskey	.10
85	Doug Jones	.10
86	Jeff Kent	.10
87	Jim Edmonds	.10
88	Mark McLemore	.10
89	Todd Zeile	.10
90	Edgardo Alfonzo	.15
91	Carlos Baerga	.10
92	Jorge Fabregas	.10
93	Alan Benes	.15
94	Troy Percival	.10
95	Edgar Renteria	.15
96	Jeff Fassero	.10
97	Reggie Sanders	.10
98	Dean Palmer	.10
99	J.T. Snow	.15
100	Dave Nilsson	.10
101	Dan Wilson	.10
102	Robb Nen	.10
103	Damion Easley	.10
104	Kevin Foster	.10
105	Jose Offerman	.10
106	Steve Cooke	.10
107	Matt Stairs	.10
108	Darryl Hamilton	.10
109	Steve Karsay	.10
110	Gary DiSarcina	.10
111	Dante Bichette	.25
112	Billy Wagner	.15
113	David Segui	.10
114	Bobby Higginson	.10
115	Jeffrey Hammonds	.10
116	Kevin Brown	.20
117	Paul Sorrento	.10
118	Mark Leiter	.10
119	Charles Nagy	.10
120	Danny Patterson	.10
121	Brian McRae	.10
122	Jay Bell	.10
123	Jamie Moyer	.10
124	Carl Everett	.10
125	Greg Colbrunn	.10
126	Jason Kendall	.10
127	Luis Sojo	.10
128	Mike Lieberthal	.10
129	Reggie Jefferson	.10
130	Cal Eldred	.10
131	Orel Hershiser	.10
132	Doug Glanville	.10
133	Willie Blair	.10
134	Neifi Perez	.10
135	Sean Berry	.10
136	Chuck Finley	.10
137	Alex Gonzalez	.10
138	Dennis Eckersley	.15
139	Kenny Rogers	.10
140	Troy O'Leary	.10
141	Roger Bailey	.10
142	Yamil Benitez	.10
143	Wally Joyner	.10
144	Bobby Witt	.10
145	Pete Schourek	.10
146	Terry Steinbach	.10
147	B.J. Surhoff	.10
148	Esteban Loaiza	.10
149	Heathcliff Slocumb	.10
150	Ed Sprague	.10
151	Gregg Jefferies	.10
152	Scott Erickson	.10
153	Jaime Navarro	.10
154	David Wells	.15
155	Alex Fernandez	.10
156	Tim Belcher	.10
157	Mark Grudzielanek	.10
158	Scott Hatteberg	.10
159	Paul Konerko	.25
160	Ben Grieve	1.00
161	Abraham Nunez	.25
162	Shannon Stewart	.10
163	Jaret Wright	1.00
164	Derrek Lee	.10
165	Todd Dunwoody	.15
166	*Steve Woodard*	.25
167	Ryan McGuire	.15
168	Jeremi Gonzalez	.15
169	Mark Kotsay	.50
170	Brett Tomko	.10
171	Bobby Estalella	.15
172	Livan Hernandez	.20
173	Todd Helton	.75
174	Garrett Stephenson	.10
175	Pokey Reese	.10
176	Tony Saunders	.20
177	Antone Williamson	.10
178	Bartolo Colon	.20
179	Karim Garcia	.15
180	Juan Encarnacion	.25
181	Jacob Cruz	.15
182	Alex Rodriguez (Field of Vision)	1.50
183	Cal Ripken Jr., Roberto Alomar (Field of Vision)	1.50
184	Roger Clemens (Field of Vision)	.50
185	Derek Jeter (Field of Vision)	1.00
186	Frank Thomas (Field of Vision)	.75
187	Ken Griffey Jr. (Field of Vision)	1.50
188	Mark McGwire (Goin' Jake)	2.00
189	Tino Martinez (Goin' Jake)	.10
190	Larry Walker (Goin' Jake)	.15
191	Brady Anderson (Goin' Jake)	.10
192	Jeff Bagwell (Goin' Jake)	.50
193	Ken Griffey Jr. (Goin' Jake)	1.50
194	Chipper Jones (Goin' Jake)	1.00
195	Ray Lankford (Goin' Jake)	.10
196	Jim Thome (Goin' Jake)	.20
197	Nomar Garciaparra (Goin' Jake)	1.00
198	Checklist (1997 HR Contest)	.10
199	Checklist (1997 HR Contest Winner)	.10
200	Checklist (Overall View of the Park)	.10
9	Ken Griffey Jr. (All-Star, overprinted "SAMPLE" on back)	4.00
24	Frank Thomas (All-Star, overprinted "SAMPLE" on back)	1.50

1998 Pinnacle Artist's Proofs/ Museums

Artist's Proof is a 100-card partial parallel of the Pinnacle base set. The gold-foil Dufex cards were renumbered and inserted one per 39 packs. The same checklist was used for the Museum Collection which was printed on a silver-foil background with bright gold-foil graphic enhancements and inserted one per nine packs.

		MT
Complete Set (100):		800.00
Common Player:		3.00
Complete Museum Set (100):		400.00
Common Museum:		1.00
Museum Stars: 50%		
1	Tony Gwynn (All-Star)	25.00
2	Pedro Martinez (All-Star)	10.00
3	Kenny Lofton (All-Star)	10.00
4	Curt Schilling (All-Star)	3.00
5	Shawn Estes (All-Star)	3.00
6	Tom Glavine (All-Star)	6.00
7	Mike Piazza (All-Star)	40.00
8	Ray Lankford (All-Star)	3.00
9	Barry Larkin (All-Star)	3.00
10	Tony Womack (All-Star)	3.00
11	Jeff Blauser (All-Star)	3.00
12	Rod Beck (All-Star)	3.00
13	Larry Walker (All-Star)	8.00
14	Greg Maddux (All-Star)	40.00
15	Mark Grace (All-Star)	6.00
16	Ken Caminiti (All-Star)	6.00
17	Bobby Jones (All-Star)	3.00
18	Chipper Jones (All-Star)	40.00
19	Javier Lopez (All-Star)	4.00
20	Moises Alou (All-Star)	4.00
21	Royce Clayton (All-Star)	3.00
22	Darryl Kile (All-Star)	3.00
23	Barry Bonds (All-Star)	15.00
24	Steve Finley (All-Star)	3.00
25	Andres Galarraga (All-Star)	3.00
26	Denny Neagle (All-Star)	3.00
27	Todd Hundley (All-Star)	3.00
28	Jeff Bagwell	25.00
29	Andy Pettitte	10.00
30	Darin Erstad	12.00
31	Carlos Delgado	4.00
32	Matt Williams	4.00
33	Will Clark	5.00
34	Brad Radke	3.00
35	John Olerud	5.00
36	Andruw Jones	20.00
37	Scott Rolen	20.00
38	Gary Sheffield	5.00
39	Jimmy Key	3.00
40	Wade Boggs	5.00
41	Hideo Nomo	10.00
42	Manny Ramirez	15.00
43	Wilton Guerrero	3.00
44	Travis Fryman	3.00
45	Craig Biggio	5.00
46	Tim Salmon	4.00
47	Jose Cruz Jr.	4.00
48	Sammy Sosa	45.00
49	Hideki Irabu	10.00
50	Jose Guillen	6.00
51	Deion Sanders	4.00
52	Jose Canseco	5.00
53	Jay Buhner	3.00
54	Rafael Palmeiro	5.00
55	Vladimir Guerrero	20.00
56	Mark McGwire	60.00
57	Derek Jeter	40.00
58	Bobby Bonilla	3.00
59	Raul Mondesi	5.00
60	Paul Molitor	10.00
61	Joe Carter	3.00
62	Marquis Grissom	3.00
63	Juan Gonzalez	25.00
64	Dante Bichette	4.00
65	Shannon Stewart (Rookie)	3.00

66	Jaret Wright (Rookie)	20.00
67	Derrek Lee (Rookie)	3.00
68	Todd Dunwoody (Rookie)	5.00
69	Steve Woodard (Rookie)	3.00
70	Ryan McGuire (Rookie)	4.00
71	Jeremi Gonzalez (Rookie)	3.00
72	Mark Kotsay (Rookie)	10.00
73	Brett Tomko (Rookie)	3.00
74	Bobby Estalella (Rookie)	5.00
75	Livan Hernandez (Rookie)	5.00
76	Todd Helton (Rookie)	15.00
77	Garrett Stephenson (Rookie)	3.00
78	Pokey Reese (Rookie)	3.00
79	Tony Saunders (Rookie)	5.00
80	Antone Williamson (Rookie)	3.00
81	Bartolo Colon (Rookie)	6.00
82	Karim Garcia (Rookie)	5.00
83	Juan Encarnacion (Rookie)	8.00
84	Jacob Cruz (Rookie)	6.00
85	Alex Rodriguez (Field of Vision)	30.00
86	Cal Ripken Jr., Roberto Alomar (Field of Vision)	25.00
87	Roger Clemens (Field of Vision)	12.00
88	Derek Jeter (Field of Vision)	30.00
89	Frank Thomas (Field of Vision)	15.00
90	Ken Griffey Jr. (Field of Vision)	35.00
91	Mark McGwire (Goin' Jake)	35.00
92	Tino Martinez (Goin' Jake)	3.00
93	Larry Walker (Goin' Jake)	5.00
94	Brady Anderson (Goin' Jake)	3.00
95	Jeff Bagwell (Goin' Jake)	12.00
96	Ken Griffey Jr. (Goin' Jake)	35.00
97	Chipper Jones (Goin' Jake)	20.00
98	Ray Lankford (Goin' Jake)	3.00
99	Jim Thome (Goin' Jake)	3.00
100	Nomar Garciaparra (Goin' Jake)	20.00

1998 Pinnacle Epix

This cross-brand insert was included in Pinnacle, Score, Pinnacle Certified and Zenith. Twenty-four cards were seeded in Pinnacle packs (1:21). The four-tiered set highlights a memorable Game, Season, Moment and Play in a player's career. The dot matrix hologram cards came in three colors: orange, purple and emerald.

		MT
Common Player:		3.00
Purples: 1.5X		
Emeralds: 2.5X		
1	Ken Griffey Jr. G	20.00
2	Juan Gonzalez G	6.00
3	Jeff Bagwell G	5.00
4	Ivan Rodriguez G	8.00
5	Nomar Garciaparra G	12.00
6	Ryne Sandberg G	5.00
7	Frank Thomas S	15.00
8	Derek Jeter S	25.00
9	Tony Gwynn S	20.00
10	Albert Belle S	10.00
11	Scott Rolen S	8.00
12	Barry Larkin S	5.00
13	Alex Rodriguez M	30.00
14	Cal Ripken Jr. M	35.00
15	Chipper Jones M	30.00
16	Roger Clemens M	20.00
17	Mo Vaughn M	10.00
18	Mark McGwire M	60.00
19	Mike Piazza P	8.00
20	Andruw Jones P	3.00
21	Greg Maddux P	8.00
22	Barry Bonds P	5.00
23	Paul Molitor P	4.00
24	Eddie Murray P	3.00

1998 Pinnacle Hit It Here Samples

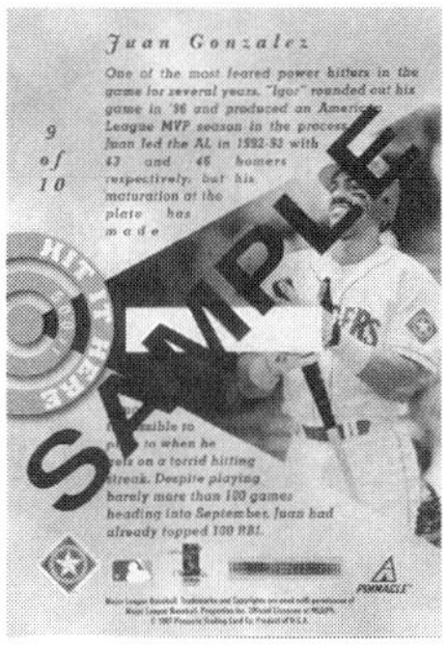

Each of the Hit It Here interactive opening day game cards was also issued in a promo version. Fronts of the promos are identical to the inserts, but backs lack the individual serial number and carry a large black diagonal "SAMPLE" overprint.

		MT
Complete Set (10):		35.00
Common Player:		1.00
1	Larry Walker	2.00
2	Ken Griffey Jr.	10.00
3	Mike Piazza	7.50
4	Frank Thomas	6.00
5	Barry Bonds	4.00
6	Albert Belle	3.00
7	Tino Martinez	1.00
8	Mark McGwire	10.00
9	Juan Gonzalez	4.00
10	Jeff Bagwell	4.00

1998 Pinnacle Hit It Here

Hit it Here is a 10-card insert seeded one per 17 packs. The micro-etched silver foil cards feature a color player photo with a red "Hit it Here" target on the left. Each card has a serial number. If the pictured player hit for the cycle on Opening Day 1998, the collector with the correct serially numbered card would win $1 million.

		MT
Complete Set (10):		40.00
Common Player:		1.00
Inserted 1:17		
1	Larry Walker	2.00
2	Ken Griffey Jr.	10.00
3	Mike Piazza	7.50
4	Frank Thomas	6.00
5	Barry Bonds	3.00
6	Albert Belle	2.50
7	Tino Martinez	1.00
8	Mark McGwire	10.00
9	Juan Gonzalez	4.00
10	Jeff Bagwell	2.50

1998 Pinnacle Spellbound

Spellbound is a 50-card insert seeded one per 17 packs of Pinnacle Baseball. Nine players were featured in the set. The cards featured a photo of the player with a letter from his first or last name in the background. Each player had enough cards to spell either his first or last name.

	MT
Complete Set (50):	350.00
Com. Mark McGwire (1MM-7MM)	20.00
Com. Roger Clemens (1RC-6RC)	8.00
Com. Frank Thomas (1FT-7FT)	7.50
Com. Scott Rolen (1SR-5SR)	5.00
Com. Ken Griffey Jr. (1KG-7KG)	20.00
Com. Larry Walker (1LW-6LW)	5.00
Com. Nomar Garciaparra (39-43)	10.00
Com. Cal Ripken Jr. (1CR-3CR)	12.00
Com. Tony Gwynn (1TG-4TG)	8.00
Inserted 1:17	
(Cards are contiguously numbered "... of 50")	

1998 Pinnacle Inside

Pinnacle Inside Baseball featured cards in a can. The 150 base cards featured full-bleed photos on the front with stats on the right and the player's name and position at the bottom. The Club Edition parallel (1:7) is printed on silver foil board and the Diamond Edition parallel (1:67) is printed on prismatic foil board. Each pack of cards was packaged inside a collectible can. Inserts include Behind the Numbers and Stand Up Guys.

		MT
Complete Set (150):		40.00
Common Player:		.15
Club Editions: 4-8X		
Inserted 1:7		
Diamond Editions: 20-40X		
Inserted 1:67		
1	Darin Erstad	1.00
2	Derek Jeter	2.50
3	Alex Rodriguez	3.00
4	Bobby Higginson	.15
5	Nomar Garciaparra	2.50
6	Kenny Lofton	.60
7	Ivan Rodriguez	1.00
8	Cal Ripken Jr.	3.00
9	Todd Hundley	.15
10	Chipper Jones	2.50
11	Barry Larkin	.30
12	Roberto Alomar	.75
13	Mo Vaughn	.60
14	Sammy Sosa	3.00
15	Sandy Alomar Jr.	.25
16	Albert Belle	.75
17	Scott Rolen	1.50
18	Pokey Reese	.15
19	Ryan Klesko	.25
20	Andres Galarraga	.40
21	Justin Thompson	.25
22	Gary Sheffield	.40
23	David Justice	.40
24	Ken Griffey Jr.	4.50
25	Andruw Jones	2.00
26	Jeff Bagwell	1.50
27	Vladimir Guerrero	1.50
28	Mike Piazza	2.50
29	Chuck Knoblauch	.40
30	Rondell White	.25
31	Greg Maddux	2.50
32	Andy Pettitte	.60
33	Larry Walker	.40
34	Bobby Estalella	.15
35	Frank Thomas	2.00
36	Tony Womack	.15
37	Tony Gwynn	2.00
38	Barry Bonds	1.00
39	Randy Johnson	.75
40	Mark McGwire	4.50
41	Juan Gonzalez	2.00
42	Tim Salmon	.30
43	John Smoltz	.25
44	Rafael Palmeiro	.40
45	Mark Grace	.40
46	Mike Cameron	.25
47	Jim Thome	.40
48	Neifi Perez	.15
49	Kevin Brown	.40
50	Craig Biggio	.40
51	Bernie Williams	.60
52	Hideo Nomo	.50
53	Bob Abreu	.15
54	Edgardo Alfonzo	.20
55	Wade Boggs	.50
56	Jose Guillen	.40
57	Ken Caminiti	.40
58	Paul Molitor	.75
59	Shawn Estes	.15
60	Edgar Martinez	.15
61	Livan Hernandez	.40
62	Ray Lankford	.15
63	Rusty Greer	.15
64	Jim Edmonds	.20
65	Tom Glavine	.25
66	Alan Benes	.15
67	Will Clark	.25
68	Garret Anderson	.15
69	Javier Lopez	.25
70	Mike Mussina	.60
71	Kevin Orie	.15
72	Matt Williams	.40
73	Bobby Bonilla	.15
74	Ruben Rivera	.15
75	Jason Giambi	.15
76	Todd Walker	.40
77	Tino Martinez	.30
78	Matt Morris	.15
79	Fernando Tatis	.25
80	Todd Greene	.15
81	Fred McGriff	.25
82	Brady Anderson	.25
83	Mark Kotsay	.40
84	Raul Mondesi	.40
85	Moises Alou	.25
86	Roger Clemens	1.50
87	Wilton Guerrero	.15
88	Shannon Stewart	.15
89	Chan Ho Park	.25
90	Carlos Delgado	.40
91	Jose Cruz Jr.	.25
92	Shawn Green	.25
93	Robin Ventura	.25
94	Reggie Sanders	.15
95	Orel Hershiser	.15
96	Dante Bichette	.25
97	Charles Johnson	.15
98	Pedro Martinez	.40
99	Mariano Rivera	.40
100	Joe Randa	.15
101	Jeff Kent	.15
102	Jay Buhner	.20
103	Brian Jordan	.15
104	Jason Kendall	.15
105	Scott Spiezio	.15
106	Desi Relaford	.15
107	Bernard Gilkey	.15
108	Manny Ramirez	1.00
109	Tony Clark	.60
110	Eric Young	.15
111	Johnny Damon	.15
112	Glendon Rusch	.15
113	Ben Grieve	1.50
114	Homer Bush	.15
115	Miguel Tejada	1.00
116	Lou Collier	.15
117	Derrek Lee	.15
118	Jacob Cruz	.20
119	Raul Ibanez	.15
120	Ryan McGuire	.15
121	Antone Williamson	.15
122	Abraham Nunez	.15
123	Jeff Abbott	.15
124	Brett Tomko	.15
125	Richie Sexson	.15
126	Todd Helton	1.00
127	Juan Encarnacion	.15
128	Richard Hidalgo	.15
129	Paul Konerko	.75
130	Brad Fullmer	1.00
131	Jeremi Gonzalez	.15
132	Jaret Wright	2.00
133	Derek Jeter (Inside Tips)	1.00
134	Frank Thomas (Inside Tips)	.75
135	Nomar Garciaparra (Inside Tips)	1.00
136	Kenny Lofton (Inside Tips)	.35
137	Jeff Bagwell (Inside Tips)	.75
138	Todd Hundley (Inside Tips)	.15
139	Alex Rodriguez (Inside Tips)	1.00
140	Ken Griffey Jr. (Inside Tips)	2.00
141	Sammy Sosa (Inside Tips)	1.00
142	Greg Maddux (Inside Tips)	1.00
143	Albert Belle (Inside Tips)	.40
144	Cal Ripken Jr. (Inside Tips)	1.50
145	Mark McGwire (Inside Tips)	2.50
146	Chipper Jones (Inside Tips)	1.00
147	Charles Johnson (Inside Tips)	.15
148	Checklist (Ken Griffey Jr.)	1.50
149	Checklist (Jose Cruz Jr.)	.25
150	Checklist (Larry Walker)	.20

1998 Pinnacle Inside Club Edition

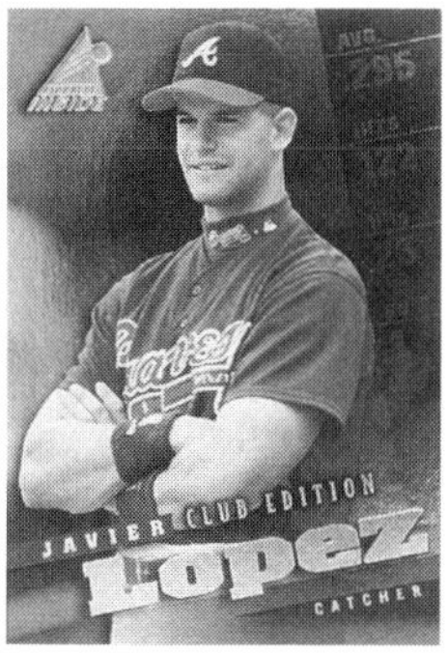

This parallel set is virtually identical to the regular Inside cards, except for the addition of a "CLUB EDITION" notice to the right of the player's first name, and the use of gold foil highlights instead of silver on front.

	MT
Complete Set (150):	400.00
Common Player:	1.00
Club Edition Stars: 4-8X	
Inserted 1:7	
(See 1998 Pinnacle Inside for checklist and base card values.)	

1998 Pinnacle Inside Diamond Edition

Diamond Edition cards paralleled all 150 cards in Pinnacle Inside. The fronts had the insert name and they were printed on a prismatic foil and inserted one per 67 packs.

	MT
Common Card:	4.00
Diamond Edition Stars: 20-40X	

Inserted 1:67
(See 1998 Pinnacle Inside for checklist and base card values.)

1998 Pinnacle Inside Behind the Numbers

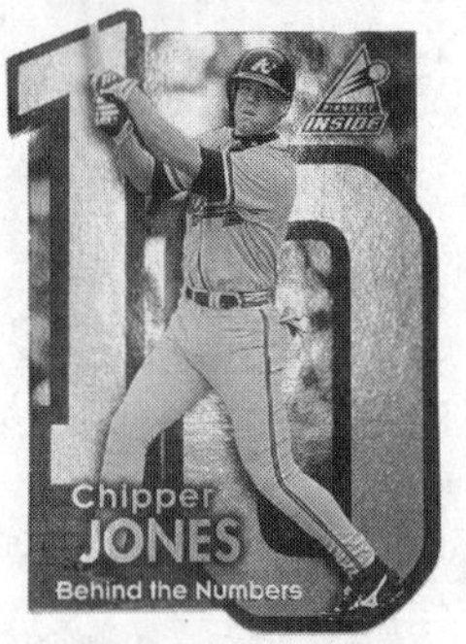

Behind the Numbers is a 20-card insert seeded one per 23 cans. The card front features an action photo printed in front of the player's number. The card is die-cut around the large metallic foil numerals. The back has a portrait photo and text explaining why the player wears that number.

		MT
Complete Set (20):		250.00
Common Player:		4.00
Inserted 1:23		
1	Ken Griffey Jr.	35.00
2	Cal Ripken Jr.	25.00
3	Alex Rodriguez	25.00
4	Jose Cruz Jr.	4.00
5	Mike Piazza	20.00
6	Nomar Garciaparra	20.00
7	Scott Rolen	12.50
8	Andruw Jones	12.50
9	Frank Thomas	15.00
10	Mark McGwire	35.00
11	Ivan Rodriguez	7.50
12	Greg Maddux	20.00
13	Roger Clemens	12.50
14	Derek Jeter	20.00
15	Tony Gwynn	15.00
16	Ben Grieve	7.50
17	Jeff Bagwell	12.50
18	Chipper Jones	20.00
19	Hideo Nomo	6.00
20	Sandy Alomar Jr.	5.00

1998 Pinnacle Inside Cans

Ten-card packs of Pinnacle Inside were packaged in collectible cans. The 24 cans featured a player photo or team logo. Cans were created to honor the Florida Marlins' world championship and the expansion Arizona and Tampa Bay teams. Gold parallel versions of the cans were found one every 47 cans.

		MT
Complete Set (23):		20.00
Common Can:		.40
Sealed Cans:		3.00
Gold Cans: 3X		
1	Ken Griffey Jr.	2.50
2	Frank Thomas	1.50
3	Alex Rodriguez	2.00
4	Andruw Jones	1.25
5	Mike Piazza	1.50
6	Ben Grieve	.75
7	Hideo Nomo	.50
8	Vladimir Guerrero	.60
9	Roger Clemens	1.00
10	Tony Gwynn	1.25
11	Mark McGwire	2.50
12	Cal Ripken Jr.	2.00
13	Jose Cruz Jr.	.40
14	Greg Maddux	1.50
15	Chipper Jones	1.50
16	Derek Jeter	1.50
17	Juan Gonzalez	1.25
18	Nomar Garciaparra (AL ROY)	1.50
19	Scott Rolen (NL ROY)	1.00
20	Florida Marlins World Series Winner	.50
21	Larry Walker (NL MVP)	.50
22	Tampa Bay Devil Rays	.40
23	Arizona Diamondbacks	.40

1998 Pinnacle Inside Stand Up Guys

This 50-card insert was seeded one per can. Each card has a match. The two cards join together in the center to form a stand up collectible featuring four Major League players.

		MT
Complete Set (100):		40.00
Common Player:		.25
Inserted 1:1		
1a	Ken Griffey Jr.	2.00
1b	Cal Ripken Jr.	1.50
1c	Tony Gwynn	1.00
1d	Mike Piazza	1.25
2a	Andruw Jones	.75
2b	Alex Rodriguez	1.50
2c	Scott Rolen	.75
2d	Nomar Garciaparra	1.25
3a	Andruw Jones	.75
3b	Greg Maddux	1.25
3c	Javier Lopez	.25
3d	Chipper Jones	1.25
4a	Jay Buhner	.25
4b	Randy Johnson	.40
4c	Ken Griffey Jr.	2.00
4d	Alex Rodriguez	1.50
5a	Frank Thomas	1.00
5b	Jeff Bagwell	.75
5c	Mark McGwire	2.00
5d	Mo Vaughn	.40
6a	Nomar Garciaparra	1.25
6b	Derek Jeter	1.25
6c	Alex Rodriguez	1.50
6d	Barry Larkin	.25
7a	Mike Piazza	1.25
7b	Ivan Rodriguez	.50
7c	Charles Johnson	.25
7d	Javier Lopez	.25
8a	Cal Ripken Jr.	1.50
8b	Chipper Jones	1.25
8c	Ken Caminiti	.25
8d	Scott Rolen	.75
9a	Jose Cruz Jr.	.25
9b	Vladimir Guerrero	.50
9c	Andruw Jones	.75
9d	Jose Guillen	.25
10a	Larry Walker	.40
10b	Dante Bichette	.25
10c	Ellis Burks	.25
10d	Neifi Perez	.25
11a	Juan Gonzalez	1.00
11b	Sammy Sosa	1.50
11c	Vladimir Guerrero	.50
11d	Manny Ramirez	.50
12a	Greg Maddux	1.25
12b	Roger Clemens	.75
12c	Hideo Nomo	.50
12d	Randy Johnson	.50
13a	Ben Grieve	.50
13b	Paul Konerko	.50
13c	Jose Cruz Jr.	.25
13d	Fernando Tatis	.25
14a	Ryne Sandberg	.50
14b	Chuck Knoblauch	.40
14c	Roberto Alomar	.40
14d	Craig Biggio	.25
15a	Cal Ripken Jr.	1.50
15b	Brady Anderson	.25
15c	Rafael Palmeiro	.25
15d	Roberto Alomar	.40
16a	Darin Erstad	.50
16b	Jim Edmonds	.25
16c	Tim Salmon	.40
16d	Garret Anderson	.25
17a	Mike Piazza	1.25
17b	Hideo Nomo	.40
17c	Raul Mondesi	.25
17d	Eric Karros	.25
18a	Ivan Rodriguez	.50
18b	Juan Gonzalez	1.00
18c	Will Clark	.40
18d	Rusty Greer	.25
19a	Derek Jeter	1.25
19b	Bernie Williams	.35
19c	Tino Martinez	.30
19d	Andy Pettitte	.40
20a	Kenny Lofton	.40
20b	Ken Griffey Jr.	2.00
20c	Brady Anderson	.25
20d	Bernie Williams	.35
21a	Paul Molitor	.40
21b	Eddie Murray	.35
21c	Ryne Sandberg	.50
21d	Rickey Henderson	.35
22a	Tony Clark	.40
22b	Frank Thomas	1.00
22c	Jeff Bagwell	.75
22d	Mark McGwire	2.00
23a	Manny Ramirez	.50
23b	Jim Thome	.40
23c	David Justice	.25
23d	Sandy Alomar Jr.	.25
24a	Barry Bonds	.50
24b	Albert Belle	.50
24c	Jeff Bagwell	.75
24d	Dante Bichette	.25
25a	Ken Griffey Jr.	2.00
25b	Frank Thomas	1.00
25c	Alex Rodriguez	1.50
25d	Andruw Jones	.75

1998 Pinnacle Mint Collection

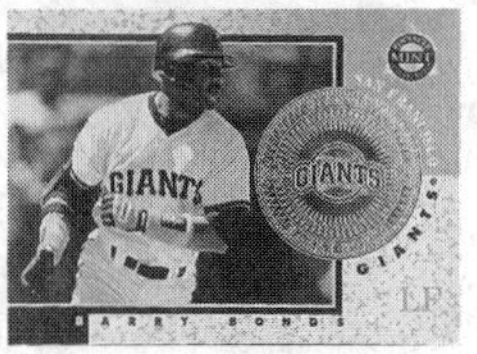

Mint Collection consists of 30 cards and 30 matching coins with numerous parallels of each. The cards come in four different versions. The base card features a player photo on the left with a circular bronze foil team logo on the right. The base cards were inserted one per hobby pack and two per retail pack. Die-cut versions removed the team logo and were inserted two per hobby and one per retail packs. Silver Mint Team (1:15 hobby, 1:23 retail) and Gold Mint Team (1:47 hobby, 1:71 retail) parallels were printed on silver foil and gold foil board, respectively.

		MT
Complete Set (30):		20.00
Common Die-Cut:		.25
Bronze: 1.5X		
Inserted 1:1 H		
Silver: 8X		
Inserted 1:15 H		
Gold: 12X		
Inserted 1:47 H		
Wax Box:		80.00
1	Jeff Bagwell	1.00
2	Albert Belle	.75
3	Barry Bonds	.75
4	Tony Clark	.50
5	Roger Clemens	1.00
6	Juan Gonzalez	1.25
7	Ken Griffey Jr.	2.50
8	Tony Gwynn	1.25
9	Derek Jeter	1.50
10	Randy Johnson	.40
11	Chipper Jones	1.50
12	Greg Maddux	1.50
13	Tino Martinez	.25
14	Mark McGwire	2.50
15	Hideo Nomo	.50
16	Andy Pettitte	.35
17	Mike Piazza	1.50
18	Cal Ripken Jr.	2.00
19	Alex Rodriguez	2.00
20	Ivan Rodriguez	.75
21	Sammy Sosa	1.50
22	Frank Thomas	1.25
23	Mo Vaughn	.40
24	Larry Walker	.40
25	Jose Cruz Jr.	.25
26	Nomar Garciaparra	1.50
27	Vladimir Guerrero	.75
28	Livan Hernandez	.25
29	Andruw Jones	1.25
30	Scott Rolen	1.00

1998 Pinnacle Mint Collection Coins

Two base coins were included in each pack of Mint Collection. The coins feature the player's image, name and number on the front along with his team's name and logo. The back has the Mint Collection logo. Seven parallels were included: Nickel-Silver (1:41), Bronze Proof (numbered to 500), Silver Proof (numbered to 250), Gold Proof (numbered to 100), Gold-Plated (1:199), Solid Silver (1:288 hobby, 1:960 retail) and Solid Gold by redemption (1-of-1).

		MT
Complete Set (30):		60.00
Common Brass Coin:		.50
Nickel: 6X		
Inserted 1:41		
Silver: 25X		
Inserted 1:288 H, 1:960 R		
Gold Plated: 20X		
Inserted 1:199		
1	Jeff Bagwell	2.50
2	Albert Belle	1.50
3	Barry Bonds	1.50
4	Tony Clark	1.00
5	Roger Clemens	2.50
6	Juan Gonzalez	3.00
7	Ken Griffey Jr.	6.00
8	Tony Gwynn	3.00
9	Derek Jeter	4.00
10	Randy Johnson	1.00
11	Chipper Jones	4.00
12	Greg Maddux	4.00
13	Tino Martinez	1.00
14	Mark McGwire	6.00
15	Hideo Nomo	1.00
16	Andy Pettitte	1.00
17	Mike Piazza	4.00
18	Cal Ripken Jr.	5.00
19	Alex Rodriguez	4.00
20	Ivan Rodriguez	1.50
21	Sammy Sosa	3.00
22	Frank Thomas	2.50
23	Mo Vaughn	1.50
24	Larry Walker	1.00
25	Jose Cruz Jr.	.75
26	Nomar Garciaparra	4.00
27	Vladimir Guerrero	1.50
28	Livan Hernandez	.75
29	Andruw Jones	3.00
30	Scott Rolen	2.50

1998 Pinnacle Mint Collection Proof Coins

Special serially numbered editions of three versions of the Mint Collection coins were issued as random pack inserts. Brass proofs are numbered within an edition of 500. Nickel proofs are numbered to 250. Gold-plated proofs are numbered to 100 each.

	MT
Common Brass Proof:	8.00
Brass Proof Stars: 10X	
Common Nickel Proof:	12.00
Nickel Proof Stars: 15X	
Common Gold-plated Proof:	30.00
Gold-plated Proof Stars: 40X	

(See 1998 Pinnacle Mint Collection Coins for checklist and base coin values.)

1998 Pinnacle Mint Collection Mint Gems

Mint Gems is a six-card insert printed on silver foil board. The cards were inserted 1:31 hobby packs and 1:47 retail. The oversized Mint Gems coins are twice the size of the regular coins. The six coins were inserted 1:31 hobby packs.

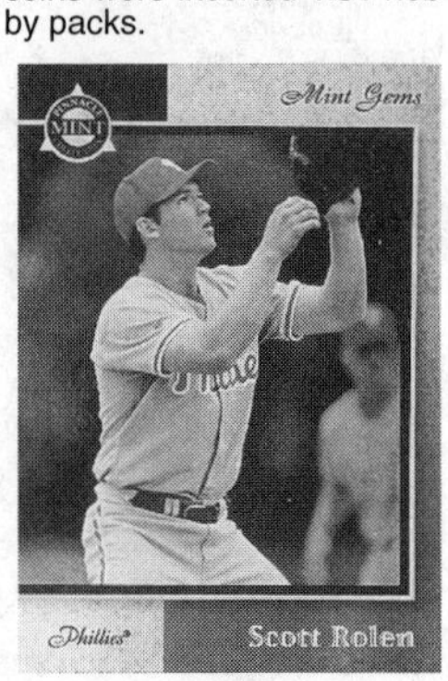

		MT
Complete Set (6):		50.00
Common Player:		4.00
Coins: 1X		
1	Ken Griffey Jr.	20.00
2	Larry Walker	4.00
3	Roger Clemens	8.00
4	Pedro Martinez	4.00
5	Nomar Garciaparra	12.00
6	Scott Rolen	10.00

1998 Pinnacle Performers

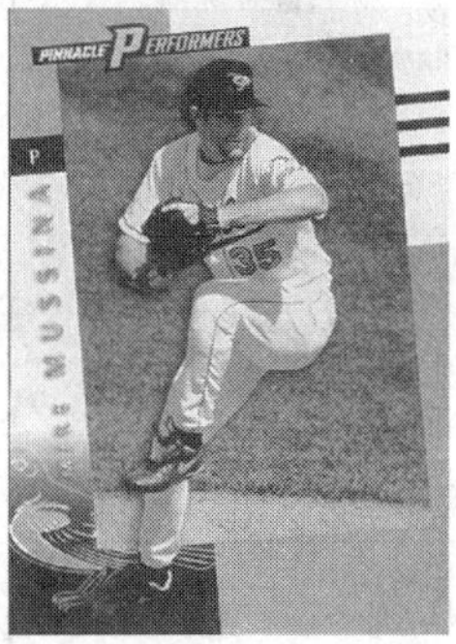

Pinnacle Performers consists of a 150-card base set. The Peak Performers parallel adds silver foil to the base cards and was inserted 1:7. Inserts in the home run-themed product include Big Bang, Launching Pad, Player's Card and Power Trip.

		MT
Complete Set (150):		20.00
Common Player:		.10
Peak Performers: 4-6X		
Inserted 1:7		
1	Ken Griffey Jr.	2.50
2	Frank Thomas	1.50
3	Cal Ripken Jr.	2.00
4	Alex Rodriguez	2.00
5	Greg Maddux	1.50
6	Mike Piazza	1.50
7	Chipper Jones	1.50
8	Tony Gwynn	1.25
9	Derek Jeter	1.50
10	Jeff Bagwell	.75
11	Juan Gonzalez	1.25
12	Nomar Garciaparra	1.50
13	Andruw Jones	.60
14	Hideo Nomo	.25
15	Roger Clemens	.75
16	Mark McGwire	2.50
17	Scott Rolen	.75
18	Vladimir Guerrero	.60
19	Barry Bonds	.60
20	Darin Erstad	.60
21	Albert Belle	.60
22	Kenny Lofton	.45
23	Mo Vaughn	.45
24	Tony Clark	.40
25	Ivan Rodriguez	.60
26	Jose Cruz Jr.	.15
27	Larry Walker	.30
28	Jaret Wright	.60
29	Andy Pettitte	.50
30	Roberto Alomar	.50
31	Randy Johnson	.40
32	Manny Ramirez	.60
33	Paul Molitor	.40
34	Mike Mussina	.50
35	Jim Thome	.40

36	Tino Martinez	.20
37	Gary Sheffield	.25
38	Chuck Knoblauch	.25
39	Bernie Williams	.40
40	Tim Salmon	.20
41	Sammy Sosa	1.50
42	Wade Boggs	.40
43	Will Clark	.35
44	Andres Galarraga	.25
45	Raul Mondesi	.25
46	Rickey Henderson	.20
47	Jose Canseco	.25
48	Pedro Martinez	.50
49	Jay Buhner	.20
50	Ryan Klesko	.25
51	Barry Larkin	.20
52	Charles Johnson	.10
53	Tom Glavine	.20
54	Edgar Martinez	.10
55	Fred McGriff	.20
56	Moises Alou	.20
57	Dante Bichette	.20
58	Jim Edmonds	.20
59	Mark Grace	.25
60	Chan Ho Park	.20
61	Justin Thompson	.10
62	John Smoltz	.20
63	Craig Biggio	.20
64	Ken Caminiti	.20
65	Richard Hidalgo	.10
66	Carlos Delgado	.25
67	David Justice	.25
68	J.T. Snow	.10
69	Jason Giambi	.10
70	Garret Anderson	.10
71	Rondell White	.20
72	Matt Williams	.25
73	Brady Anderson	.10
74	Eric Karros	.15
75	Javier Lopez	.10
76	Pat Hentgen	.10
77	Todd Hundley	.10
78	Ray Lankford	.10
79	Denny Neagle	.10
80	Sandy Alomar Jr.	.20
81	Jason Kendall	.10
82	Omar Vizquel	.10
83	Kevin Brown	.20
84	Kevin Appier	.10
85	Al Martin	.10
86	Rusty Greer	.10
87	Bobby Bonilla	.10
88	Shawn Estes	.10
89	Rafael Palmeiro	.25
90	Edgar Renteria	.10
91	Alan Benes	.10
92	Bobby Higginson	.10
93	Mark Grudzielanek	.10
94	Jose Guillen	.20
95	Neifi Perez	.10
96	Jeff Abbott	.10
97	Todd Walker	.25
98	Eric Young	.10
99	Brett Tomko	.10
100	Mike Cameron	.10
101	Karim Garcia	.10
102	Brian Jordan	.10
103	Jeff Suppan	.10
104	Robin Ventura	.20
105	Henry Rodriguez	.10
106	Shannon Stewart	.10
107	Kevin Orie	.10
108	Bartolo Colon	.20
109	Bob Abreu	.10
110	Vinny Castilla	.20
111	Livan Hernandez	.10
112	Derrek Lee	.10
113	Mark Kotsay	.25
114	Todd Greene	.10
115	Edgardo Alfonzo	.10
116	A.J. Hinch	.40
117	Paul Konerko	.30
118	Todd Helton	.60
119	Miguel Tejada	.30
120	Fernando Tatis	.20
121	Ben Grieve	.75
122	Travis Lee	.50
123	Kerry Wood	.75
124	Eli Marrero	.10
125	David Ortiz	.10
126	Juan Encarnacion	.10
127	Brad Fullmer	.25
128	Richie Sexson	.10
129	Aaron Boone	.10
130	Enrique Wilson	.10
131	Javier Valentin	.10
132	Abraham Nunez	.10
133	Ricky Ledee	.25
134	Carl Pavano	.10
135	Bobby Estalella	.10
136	Homer Bush	.10
137	Brian Rose	.10
138	Ken Griffey Jr. (Far and Away)	1.25
139	Frank Thomas (Far and Away)	.50
140	Cal Ripken Jr. (Far and Away)	1.00
141	Alex Rodriguez (Far and Away)	.75
142	Greg Maddux (Far and Away)	.75
143	Chipper Jones (Far and Away)	.75
144	Mike Piazza (Far and Away)	.75
145	Tony Gwynn (Far and Away)	.60
146	Derek Jeter (Far and Away)	.60
147	Jeff Bagwell (Far and Away)	.40
148	Checklist (Hideo Nomo)	.10
149	Checklist (Roger Clemens)	.40
150	Checklist (Greg Maddux)	.60

1998 Pinnacle Performers Big Bang

This 20-card insert features top power hitters. The micro-etched cards are sequentially numbered to 2,500. Each player has a Seasonal Outburst parallel, with a red overlay and numbered to that player's best seasonal home run total.

		MT
Complete Set (20):		175.00
Common Player:		4.00
Production 2,500 sets		
1	Ken Griffey Jr.	25.00
2	Frank Thomas	12.00
3	Mike Piazza	15.00
4	Chipper Jones	15.00
5	Alex Rodriguez	18.00
6	Nomar Garciaparra	15.00
7	Jeff Bagwell	10.00
8	Cal Ripken Jr.	18.00
9	Albert Belle	6.00
10	Mark McGwire	25.00
10s	Mark McGwire (SAMPLE overprint on back)	15.00
11	Juan Gonzalez	12.00
12	Larry Walker	4.00
13	Tino Martinez	4.00
14	Jim Thome	4.00
15	Manny Ramirez	8.00
16	Barry Bonds	6.00
17	Mo Vaughn	4.00
18	Jose Cruz Jr.	4.00
19	Tony Clark	5.00
20	Andruw Jones	6.00

1998 Pinnacle Performers Big Bang Season Outburst

Season Outburst parallels the Big Bang insert. The cards have a red overlay and are sequentially numbered to each player's season-high home run total.

		MT
Common Player:		25.00
#'d to player's 1997 home run total		
1	Ken Griffey Jr. (56)	175.00
2	Frank Thomas (35)	60.00
3	Mike Piazza (40)	100.00
4	Chipper Jones (21)	200.00
5	Alex Rodriguez (23)	220.00
6	Nomar Garciaparra (30)	125.00
7	Jeff Bagwell (43)	40.00
8	Cal Ripken Jr. (17)	300.00
9	Albert Belle (30)	40.00
10	Mark McGwire (58)	250.00
11	Juan Gonzalez (42)	60.00
12	Larry Walker (49)	30.00
13	Tino Martinez (44)	30.00
14	Jim Thome (40)	30.00
15	Manny Ramirez (26)	80.00
16	Barry Bonds (40)	50.00
17	Mo Vaughn (35)	40.00
18	Jose Cruz Jr. (26)	25.00
19	Tony Clark (32)	25.00
20	Andruw Jones (18)	75.00

1998 Pinnacle Performers Launching Pad

Launching Pad is a 20-card insert seeded one per nine packs. It features top sluggers on foil-on-foil cards with an outer space background.

		MT
Complete Set (20):		75.00
Common Player:		1.50
Inserted 1:9		
1	Ben Grieve	3.00
2	Ken Griffey Jr.	12.00
3	Derek Jeter	6.00
4	Frank Thomas	5.00
5	Travis Lee	2.00
6	Vladimir Guerrero	2.50
7	Tony Gwynn	5.00
8	Jose Cruz Jr.	1.50
9	Cal Ripken Jr.	8.00
10	Chipper Jones	6.00
11	Scott Rolen	3.00
12	Andruw Jones	2.50
13	Ivan Rodriguez	2.50
14	Todd Helton	2.50
15	Nomar Garciaparra	6.00
16	Mark McGwire	12.00
17	Gary Sheffield	1.50
18	Bernie Williams	2.00
19	Alex Rodriguez	8.00
20	Mike Piazza	6.00

1998 Pinnacle Performers Power Trip

This 10-card insert was seeded 1:21. Printed on silver foil, each card is sequentially-numbered to 10,000. Card backs have details about one of the player's power-hitting highlights of the previous season.

		MT
Complete Set (10):		55.00
Common Player:		3.00
Production 10,000 sets		
1	Frank Thomas	4.00
2	Alex Rodriguez	7.50
3	Nomar Garciaparra	6.00
4	Jeff Bagwell	3.00
5	Cal Ripken Jr.	7.50
6	Mike Piazza	6.00
7	Chipper Jones	6.00
8	Ken Griffey Jr.	10.00
9	Mark McGwire	10.00
10	Juan Gonzalez	4.00

1998 Pinnacle Performers Peak Performers

This 150-card parallel set is printed on silver foil vs. the white cardboard stock used on regular-issue cards. The parallel set name is printed down the right side in gold letters and they were seeded one per seven packs.

	MT
Complete Set (150):	150.00
Common Player:	.50
Peak Performers Stars: 4-6X	
Inserted 1:7	
(See 1998 Pinnacle Performers for checklist and base card values.)	

1998 Pinnacle Performers Swing for the Fences

Pinnacle Performers included the "Swing for the Fences" sweepstakes. Fifty players were featured on cards with numbers on an all-red background. Fifty Home Run Points cards were also inserted, with each card featuring a point total on the front. Collectors who found the player cards of the AL and NL home run leaders, as well as enough point cards to match each of their season totals, were eligible to win prizes. A player or point card was inserted in each pack.

		MT
Complete Set (50):		25.00
Common Player:		.25
Inserted 1:1		
1	Brady Anderson	.25
2	Albert Belle	.75
3	Jay Buhner	.35
4	Jose Canseco	.45
5	Tony Clark	.60
6	Jose Cruz Jr.	.60
7	Jim Edmonds	.25
8	Cecil Fielder	.25
9	Travis Fryman	.25
10	Nomar Garciaparra	2.00
11	Juan Gonzalez	1.50
12	Ken Griffey Jr.	3.50
13	David Justice	.40
14	Travis Lee	1.25
15	Edgar Martinez	.25
16	Tino Martinez	.35
17	Rafael Palmeiro	.40
18	Manny Ramirez	.75
19	Cal Ripken Jr.	2.50
20	Alex Rodriguez	2.50
21	Tim Salmon	.35
22	Frank Thomas	2.00
23	Jim Thome	.45
24	Mo Vaughn	.45
25	Bernie Williams	.45
26	Fred McGriff	.30
27	Jeff Bagwell	1.00
28	Dante Bichette	.40
29	Barry Bonds	.75
30	Ellis Burks	.25
31	Ken Caminiti	.25
32	Vinny Castilla	.25
33	Andres Galarraga	.40
34	Vladimir Guerrero	.75
35	Todd Helton	.60
36	Todd Hundley	.25
37	Andruw Jones	.75
38	Chipper Jones	2.00
39	Eric Karros	.25
40	Ryan Klesko	.35
41	Ray Lankford	.25
42	Mark McGwire	3.50
43	Raul Mondesi	.30
44	Mike Piazza	2.00
45	Scott Rolen	.90
46	Gary Sheffield	.40
47	Sammy Sosa	1.50
48	Larry Walker	.50
49	Matt Williams	.40
50	WILDCARD	.25

1998 Pinnacle Power Packs Supers

Two dozen regular and subset (Goin' Jake, Field of Vision) cards from Pinnacle are paralleled in this super-size (3-1/2" x 5") version which was included along with 21 regular cards in a $5.99 "Power Pack". Other than being four times the size of the regular card, these supers differ only in their numbering which specifies "x of 24" on back.

		MT
Complete Set (24):		20.00
Common Player:		.50
1	Alex Rodriguez (Field of Vision)	2.50
2	Cal Ripken Jr., Roberto Alomar (Field of Vision)	2.00
3	Roger Clemens (Field of Vision)	1.00
4	Derek Jeter (Field of Vision)	2.00
5	Frank Thomas (Field of Vision)	1.50
5s	Frank Thomas (FoV, "SAMPLE" overprint on back)	2.00
6	Ken Griffey Jr. (Field of Vision)	3.00
7	Mark McGwire (Goin' Jake)	3.00
8	Tino Martinez (Goin' Jake)	.50
9	Larry Walker (Goin' Jake)	.75
10	Brady Anderson (Goin' Jake)	.50
11	Jeff Bagwell (Goin' Jake)	1.00
12	Ken Griffey Jr. (Goin' Jake)	3.00
13	Chipper Jones (Goin' Jake)	2.00
14	Ray Lankford (Goin' Jake)	.50
15	Jim Thome (Goin' Jake)	.50
16	Nomar Garciaparra (Goin' Jake)	2.00
17	Mike Piazza	2.00
18	Andruw Jones	1.00
19	Greg Maddux	1.50
20	Tony Gwynn	1.00
21	Larry Walker	.75
22	Jeff Bagwell	1.00
23	Chipper Jones	2.00
24	Scott Rolen	.75

1998 Pinnacle Plus

Pinnacle Plus consists of a 200-card base set. Five subsets are included: Field of Vision, Naturals, All-Stars, Devil Rays and Diamondbacks. Artist's Proof is a 60-card partial parallel of the base set, inserted 1:35 packs. Gold Artist's Proof cards are numbered to 100 and Mirror Artist's Proofs are 1-of-1 inserts. Inserts include Lasting Memories, Yardwork, A Piece of the Game, All-Star Epix, Team Pinnacle, Gold Team Pinnacle, Pinnabilia and Certified Souvenir.

		MT
Complete Set (200):		25.00
Common Player:		.10
Nolan Ryan Auto. Baseball (1,000)		85.00
1	Roberto Alomar (All-star)	.50
2	Sandy Alomar Jr. (All-star)	.15
3	Brady Anderson (All-star)	.10
4	Albert Belle (All-star)	.75
5	Jeff Cirillo (All-star)	.10
6	Roger Clemens (All-star)	1.00
7	David Cone (All-star)	.20
8	Nomar Garciaparra (All-star)	2.00
9	Ken Griffey Jr. (All-star)	3.00
10	Jason Dickson (All-star)	.10
11	Edgar Martinez (All-star)	.10
12	Tino Martinez (All-star)	.25
13	Randy Johnson (All-star)	.50
14	Mark McGwire (All-star)	3.00
15	David Justice (All-star)	.25
16	Mike Mussina (All-star)	.50
17	Chuck Knoblauch (All-star)	.30
18	Joey Cora (All-star)	.10
19	Pat Hentgen (All-star)	.10
20	Randy Myers (All-star)	.10
21	Cal Ripken Jr. (All-star)	2.50
22	Mariano Rivera (All-star)	.20
23	Jose Rosado (All-star)	.10
24	Frank Thomas (All-star)	1.00
25	Alex Rodriguez (All-star)	2.50
26	Justin Thompson (All-star)	.10
27	Ivan Rodriguez (All-star)	.75
28	Bernie Williams All-star)	.40
29	Pedro Martinez	.50
30	Tony Clark	.40
31	Garret Anderson	.10
32	Travis Fryman	.10
33	Mike Piazza	2.00
33s	Mike Piazza ("SAMPLE" overprint on back)	3.00
34	Carl Pavano	.10
35	*Kevin Millwood*	2.50
36	Miguel Tejada	.25
37	Willie Blair	.10
38	Devon White	.10
39	Andres Galarraga	.30
40	Barry Larkin	.20
41	Al Leiter	.15
42	Moises Alou	.20
43	Eric Young	.10
44	John Jaha	.10
45	Bernard Gilkey	.10
46	Freddy Garcia	.10
47	Ruben Rivera	.10
48	Robb Nen	.10
49	Ray Lankford	.10
50	Kenny Lofton	.60
51	Joe Carter	.10
52	Jason McDonald	.10
53	Quinton McCracken	.10
54	Kerry Wood	.75
55	Mike Lansing	.10
56	Chipper Jones	2.00
57	Barry Bonds	.75
58	Brad Fullmer	.25
59	Jeff Bagwell	1.00
60	Rondell White	.20
61	Geronimo Berroa	.10
62	*Magglio Ordonez*	1.00
63	Dwight Gooden	.10
64	Brian Hunter	.10
65	Todd Walker	.20
66	*Frank Catalanotto*	.20
67	Tony Saunders	.10
68	Travis Lee	.75
69	Michael Tucker	.10
70	Reggie Sanders	.10
71	Derrek Lee	.10
72	Larry Walker	.25
72s	Larry Walker ("SAMPLE" overprint on back)	2.50
73	Marquis Grissom	.10
74	Craig Biggio	.20
75	Kevin Brown	.20
76	J.T. Snow	.10
77	Eric Davis	.10
78	Jeff Abbott	.10
79	Jermaine Dye	.10
80	Otis Nixon	.10
81	Curt Schilling	.20
82	Enrique Wilson	.10
83	Tony Gwynn	1.50
84	Orlando Cabrera	.10
85	Ramon Martinez	.10
86	Greg Vaughn	.20
87	Alan Benes	.10
88	Dennis Eckersley	.10
89	Jim Thome	.40
90	Juan Encarnacion	.25
91	Jeff King	.10
92	Shannon Stewart	.10
93	Roberto Hernandez	.10
94	Raul Ibanez	.10
95	Darryl Kile	.10
96	Charles Johnson	.10
97	Rich Becker	.10
98	Hal Morris	.10
99	Ismael Valdes	.10
100	Orel Hershiser	.10
101	Mo Vaughn	.60
102	Aaron Boone	.10
103	Jeff Conine	.10
104	Paul O'Neill	.25
105	Tom Candiotti	.10
106	Wilson Alvarez	.10
107	Mike Stanley	.10
108	Carlos Delgado	.40
109	Tony Batista	.10
110	Dante Bichette	.25
111	Henry Rodriguez	.10
112	Karim Garcia	.15
113	Shane Reynolds	.10
114	Ken Caminiti	.20
115	Jose Silva	.10
116	Juan Gonzalez	1.50
117	Brian Jordan	.10
118	Jim Leyritz	.10
119	Manny Ramirez	1.00
120	Fred McGriff	.20
121	Brooks Kieschnick	.10
122	Sean Casey	.25
123	John Smoltz	.20
124	Rusty Greer	.10
125	Cecil Fielder	.10
126	Mike Cameron	.20
127	Reggie Jefferson	.10
128	Bobby Higginson	.10
129	Kevin Appier	.10
130	Robin Ventura	.15
131	Ben Grieve	1.00
132	Wade Boggs	.40
133	Jose Cruz Jr.	.15
134	Jeff Suppan	.10
135	Vinny Castilla	.20
136	Sammy Sosa	2.00
137	Mark Wohlers	.10
138	Jay Bell	.10
139	Brett Tomko	.10
140	Gary Sheffield	.25
141	Tim Salmon	.25
142	Jaret Wright	.75
143	Kenny Rogers	.10
144	Brian Anderson	.10
145	Darrin Fletcher	.10
146	John Flaherty	.10
147	Dmitri Young	.10
148	Andruw Jones	.75
149	Matt Williams	.25
150	Bobby Bonilla	.10
151	Mike Hampton	.10
152	Al Martin	.10
153	Mark Grudzielanek	.10
154	Dave Nilsson	.10
155	Roger Cedeno	.10
156	Greg Maddux	2.00
157	Mark Kotsay	.40
158	Steve Finley	.10
159	Wilson Delgado	.10
160	Ron Gant	.10
161	Jim Edmonds	.10
162	Jeff Blauser	.10
163	Dave Burba	.10
164	Pedro Astacio	.10
165	Livan Hernandez	.10
166	Neifi Perez	.10
167	Ryan Klesko	.15
168	Fernando Tatis	.10
169	Richard Hidalgo	.10
170	Carlos Perez	.10
171	Bob Abreu	.10
172	Francisco Cordova	.10
173	Todd Helton	.40
174	Doug Glanville	.10
175	Brian Rose	.10
176	Yamil Benitez	.10
177	Darin Erstad	.75
178	Scott Rolen	.75
179	John Wetteland	.10
180	Paul Sorrento	.10
181	Walt Weiss	.10
182	Vladimir Guerrero	.75
183	Ken Griffey Jr. (The Naturals)	1.50
184	Alex Rodriguez (The Naturals)	1.25
185	Cal Ripken Jr. (The Naturals)	1.25
186	Frank Thomas (The Naturals)	.50
187	Chipper Jones (The Naturals)	.75
188	Hideo Nomo (The Naturals)	.30
189	Nomar Garciaparra (The Naturals)	1.00
190	Mike Piazza (The Naturals)	1.00
191	Greg Maddux (The Naturals)	1.00
192	Tony Gwynn (The Naturals)	.75
193	Mark McGwire (The Naturals)	1.50
194	Roger Clemens (The Naturals)	.50
195	Mike Piazza (Field of Vision)	1.00
196	Mark McGwire (Field of Vision)	1.50
197	Chipper Jones (Field of Vision)	.75
198	Larry Walker (Field of Vision)	.20
199	Hideo Nomo (Field of Vision)	.30
200	Barry Bonds (Field of Vision)	.40

1998 Pinnacle Plus Artist's Proofs

Artist's Proofs is a 60-card partial parallel of the Pinnacle Plus base set. The dot matrix hologram cards were inserted 1:35. Gold Artist's Proofs added a gold finish and are sequentially numbered to 100. Mirror Artist's Proofs are a "1-of-1" insert.

		MT
Complete Set (60):		550.00
Common Player:		2.50
Inserted 1:35		
Golds: 25-40X		
Production 100 sets		
1	Roberto Alomar (All-Star)	12.00
2	Albert Belle (All-Star)	15.00
3	Roger Clemens (All-Star)	25.00
4	Nomar Garciaparra (All-Star)	40.00
5	Ken Griffey Jr. (All-Star)	60.00
6	Tino Martinez (All-Star)	6.00
7	Randy Johnson (All-Star)	10.00
8	Mark McGwire (All-Star)	60.00
9	David Justice (All-Star)	4.00
10	Chuck Knoblauch (All-Star)	5.00
11	Cal Ripken Jr. (All-Star)	50.00
12	Frank Thomas (All-Star)	35.00
13	Alex Rodriguez (All-Star)	50.00
14	Ivan Rodriguez (All-Star)	15.00
15	Bernie Williams (All-Star)	10.00
16	Pedro Martinez	10.00
17	Tony Clark	10.00
18	Mike Piazza	40.00
19	Miguel Tejada	5.00
20	Andres Galarraga	5.00
21	Barry Larkin	3.50
22	Kenny Lofton	10.00
23	Chipper Jones	40.00
24	Barry Bonds	15.00
25	Brad Fullmer	4.00
26	Jeff Bagwell	20.00
27	Todd Walker	4.00
28	Travis Lee	12.00
29	Larry Walker	5.00
30	Craig Biggio	3.50
31	Tony Gwynn	30.00
32	Jim Thome	4.00
33	Juan Encarnacion	4.00
34	Mo Vaughn	10.00
35	Karim Garcia	4.00
36	Ken Caminiti	4.00
37	Juan Gonzalez	30.00
38	Manny Ramirez	15.00
39	Fred McGriff	4.00
40	Rusty Greer	2.50
41	Bobby Higginson	2.50
42	Ben Grieve	12.00
43	Wade Boggs	5.00
44	Jose Cruz Jr.	3.00
45	Sammy Sosa	40.00
46	Gary Sheffield	4.00
47	Tim Salmon	3.50
48	Jaret Wright	12.00
49	Andruw Jones	15.00
50	Matt Williams	4.00
51	Greg Maddux	35.00
52	Jim Edmonds	2.50
53	Livan Hernandez	2.50
54	Neifi Perez	2.50
55	Fernando Tatis	3.00
56	Richard Hidalgo	2.50
57	Todd Helton	12.00
58	Darin Erstad	15.00
59	Scott Rolen	15.00
60	Vladimir Guerrero	18.00

1998 Pinnacle Plus All-Star Epix

The All-Star Epix insert is part of the cross-brand Epix set. This 12-card set honors the All-Star Game achievements of baseball's stars on cards with dot matrix holograms. All-Star Epix was seeded 1:21.

		MT
Complete Set (12):		175.00
Common Player:		4.00
Purples: 1.5X		
Emeralds: 2.5X		
Overall Odds 1:21		
13	Alex Rodriguez	30.00
14	Cal Ripken Jr.	30.00
15	Chipper Jones	20.00
16	Roger Clemens	15.00
17	Mo Vaughn	6.00
18	Mark McGwire	40.00
19	Mike Piazza	20.00
20	Andruw Jones	12.00
21	Greg Maddux	15.00
22	Barry Bonds	10.00
23	Paul Molitor	9.00
24	Hideo Nomo	4.00

1998 Pinnacle Plus A Piece of the Game

Inserted 1:17 hoby packs (1:19 retail), this 10-card insert features baseball's top players on micro-etched foil cards.

		MT
Complete Set (10):		75.00
Common Player:		3.00
Inserted 1:19		
1	Ken Griffey Jr.	15.00
2	Frank Thomas	6.00
3	Alex Rodriguez	10.00
4	Chipper Jones	8.00
5	Cal Ripken Jr.	10.00
6	Mike Piazza	8.00
7	Greg Maddux	7.50
8	Juan Gonzalez	7.50
9	Nomar Garciaparra	8.00
10	Larry Walker	3.00

1998 Pinnacle Plus Lasting Memories

Lasting Memories is a 30-card insert seeded 1:5. Printed on foil board, the cards feature a player photo with a sky background.

		MT
Complete Set (30):		40.00
Common Player:		.50
Inserted 1:5		
1	Nomar Garciaparra	3.00
2	Ken Griffey Jr.	6.00
3	Livan Hernandez	.50
4	Hideo Nomo	.50
5	Ben Grieve	1.50
6	Scott Rolen	1.50
7	Roger Clemens	2.00
8	Cal Ripken Jr.	4.00
9	Mo Vaughn	1.00
10	Frank Thomas	2.00
11	Mark McGwire	6.00
12	Barry Larkin	.50
13	Matt Williams	.50
14	Jose Cruz Jr.	.50
15	Andruw Jones	1.25
16	Mike Piazza	3.00
17	Jeff Bagwell	1.50
18	Chipper Jones	3.00
19	Juan Gonzalez	2.50
20	Kenny Lofton	1.00
21	Greg Maddux	3.00
22	Ivan Rodriguez	1.25
23	Alex Rodriguez	4.00
24	Derek Jeter	3.00
25	Albert Belle	1.25
26	Barry Bonds	1.25
27	Larry Walker	.75
28	Sammy Sosa	4.00
29	Tony Gwynn	2.50
30	Randy Johnson	1.00

Player names in *Italic* type indicate a rookie card.

1998 Pinnacle Plus Team Pinnacle

Team Pinnacle is a 15-card, double-sided insert. Printed on mirror-mylar, the cards were inserted 1:71. The hobby-only Gold Team Pinnacle parallel was inserted 1:199 packs.

		MT
Complete Set (15):		300.00
Common Player:		10.00
Inserted 1:71		
Golds: 1.5-2X		
Inserted 1:199		
1	Mike Piazza, Ivan Rodriguez	30.00
2	Mark McGwire, Mo Vaughn	60.00
3	Roberto Alomar, Craig Biggio	10.00
4	Alex Rodriguez, Barry Larkin	35.00
5	Cal Ripken Jr., Chipper Jones	40.00
6	Ken Griffey Jr., Larry Walker	60.00
7	Juan Gonzalez, Tony Gwynn	25.00
8	Albert Belle, Barry Bonds	12.00
9	Kenny Lofton, Andruw Jones	12.00
10	Tino Martinez, Jeff Bagwell	15.00
11	Frank Thomas, Andres Galarraga	20.00
12	Roger Clemens, Greg Maddux	30.00
13	Pedro Martinez, Hideo Nomo	10.00
14	Nomar Garciaparra, Scott Rolen	30.00
15	Ben Grieve, Paul Konerko	15.00

1998 Pinnacle Plus Yardwork

Yardwork is a 15-card insert seeded one per 19 packs. It features the top home run hitters in Major League Baseball.

		MT
Complete Set (15):		30.00
Common Player:		.75
Inserted 1:9		
1	Mo Vaughn	1.00
2	Frank Thomas	3.00
3	Albert Belle	1.50
4	Nomar Garciaparra	4.00
5	Tony Clark	1.00
6	Tino Martinez	.75
7	Ken Griffey Jr.	6.00
8	Juan Gonzalez	3.00
9	Sammy Sosa	4.00
10	Jose Cruz Jr.	.75
11	Jeff Bagwell	2.00
12	Mike Piazza	4.00
13	Larry Walker	.75
14	Mark McGwire	6.00
15	Barry Bonds	1.50

1998 Pinnacle Snapshots

One of Pinnacle's last issues was a team-oriented presentation of large-format (4" x 6") cards called Snapshots. Like their namesake, the focus on this issue is on candid photos rather than posed portraits or game-action pictures. The cards are printed on thin high-gloss cardboard stock resembling photo paper. Fronts, many of them horizontally formatted, are borderless and have no graphic enhancement. Backs are lightly printed with Pinnacle and licensor logos and a card number expressed "x of 18". The player's name is nowhere to be found.

MT

(See individual teams for checklists and values.)

1998 Pinnacle Snapshots Angels

		MT
Complete Set (18):		6.00
Common Player:		.25
1	Jason Dickson	.35
2	Gary DiSarcina	.25
3	Garret Anderson	.35
4	Shigetosi Hasegawa	.35
5	Ken Hill	.25
6	Todd Greene	.35
7	Tim Salmon	.50
8	Jim Edmonds	.50
9	Garret Anderson	.35
10	Dave Hollins	.25
11	Todd Greene	.35
12	Troy Percival	.25
13	Gary DiSarcina	.25
14	Cecil Fielder	.35
15	Darin Erstad	1.00
16	Chuck Finley	.35
17	Jim Edmonds	.50
18	Jason Dickson	.35

1998 Pinnacle Snapshots Braves

		MT
Complete Set (18):		10.00
Common Player:		.25
1	Ryan Klesko	.45
2	Walt Weiss	.25
3	Tom Glavine	.50
4	Randall Simon	.25
5	John Smoltz	.50
6	Chipper Jones	2.00
7	Javier Lopez	.75
8	Greg Maddux	2.00
9	Andruw Jones	1.50
10	Michael Tucker	.25
11	Andres Galarraga	.45
12	Andres Galarraga	.45
13	Greg Maddux	2.00
14	Wes Helms	.50
15	Bruce Chen	.35
16	Denny Neagle	.25
17	Mark Wohlers	.25
18	Kevin Millwood	1.00

1998 Pinnacle Snapshots Cardinals

		MT
Complete Set (18):		9.00
Common Player:		.25
1	Alan Benes	.35
2	Ron Gant	.45
3	Donovan Osborne	.25
4	Eli Marrero	.25
5	Mark McGwire	3.00
6	Delino DeShields	.25
7	Tom Pagnozzi	.25
8	Delino DeShields	.25
9	Mark McGwire	3.00
10	Royce Clayton	.25
11	Brian Jordan	.50
12	Ray Lankford	.50
13	Brian Jordan	.50
14	Matt Morris	.35
15	John Mabry	.25
16	Luis Ordaz	.25
17	Ron Gant	.50
18	Todd Stottlemyre	.25

1998 Pinnacle Snapshots Cubs

		MT
Complete Set (18):		9.00
Common Player:		.25
1	Mark Grace	1.00
2	Manny Alexander	.25
3	Jeremi Gonzalez	.35
4	Brant Brown	.50
5	Mark Grace	1.00
6	Lance Johnson	.25
7	Mark Clark	.35
8	Kevin Foster	.25
9	Brant Brown	.50
10	Kevin Foster	.25
11	Kevin Tapani	.25
12	Sammy Sosa	2.50
13	Sammy Sosa	2.50
14	Pat Cline	.35
15	Kevin Orie	.25
16	Steve Trachsel	.35
17	Lance Johnson	.25
18	Robin Jennings	.25

1998 Pinnacle Snapshots Devil Rays

		MT
Complete Set (18):		6.00
Common Player:		.25
1	Kevin Stocker	.25
2	Paul Sorrento	.25
3	John Flaherty	.25
4	Wade Boggs	1.50
5	Rich Butler	.25
6	Wilson Alvarez	.25
7	Bubba Trammell	.50
8	David Martinez	.25
9	Brooks Kieschnick	.25
10	Tony Saunders	.25
11	Esteban Yan	.25
12	Quinton McCracken	.25
13	Albie Lopez	.25
14	Roberto Hernandez	.35
15	Fred McGriff	.75
16	Bubba Trammell	.50
17	Brooks Kieschnick	.25
18	Fred McGriff	.75

1998 Pinnacle Snapshots Diamondbacks

		MT
Complete Set (18):		6.50
Common Player:		.25
1	Travis Lee	1.00
2	Matt Williams	.75
3	Jay Bell	.45
4	Devon White	.35
5	Andy Benes	.35
6	Tony Batista	.25
7	Jay Bell	.45
8	Edwin Diaz	.25
9	Devon White	.35
10	Bob Wolcott	.25
11	Karim Garcia	.75
12	Yamil Benitez	.25
13	Jorge Fabregas	.25
14	Jeff Suppan	.25
15	Ben Ford	.25
16	Brian Anderson	.50
17	Travis Lee	1.00
18	Matt Williams	.75

1998 Pinnacle Snapshots Dodgers

		MT
Complete Set (18):		8.00
Common Player:		.25
1	Mike Piazza	2.00
2	Eric Karros	.45
3	Raul Mondesi	.60
4	Wilton Guerrero	.25
5	Darren Dreifort	.25
6	Roger Cedeno	.35
7	Todd Zeile	.25
8	Paul Konerko	.50
9	Todd Hollandsworth	.25
10	Ismael Valdes	.25
11	Hideo Nomo	.75
12	Ramon Martinez	.45
13	Chan Ho Park	.75
14	Eric Young	.35
15	Dennis Reyes	.25
16	Eric Karros	.45
17	Mike Piazza	2.00
18	Raul Mondesi	.60

1998 Pinnacle Snapshots Indians

		MT
Complete Set (18):		7.00
Common Player:		.25
1	Manny Ramirez	1.00
2	Travis Fryman	.35
3	Jaret Wright	1.00
4	Brian Giles	.45
5	Bartolo Colon	.45
6	Kenny Lofton	.75
7	David Justice	.75
8	Brian Giles	.45
9	Sandy Alomar Jr.	.50
10	Jose Mesa	.25
11	Jim Thome	.50
12	Sandy Alomar Jr.	.50
13	Omar Vizquel	.35
14	Geronimo Berroa	.25
15	John Smiley	.25
16	Chad Ogea	.25
17	Charles Nagy	.40
18	Enrique Wilson	.35

1998 Pinnacle Snapshots Mariners

		MT
Complete Set (18):		10.00
Common Player:		.25
1	Alex Rodriguez	2.00
2	Jay Buhner	.35
3	Russ Davis	.25
4	Joey Cora	.25
5	Joey Cora	.25
6	Jay Buhner	.35
7	Ken Griffey Jr.	3.00
8	Raul Ibanez	.45
9	Rich Amaral	.25
10	Shane Monahan	.25
11	Alex Rodriguez	2.00
12	Dan Wilson	.25
13	Bob Wells	.25
14	Randy Johnson	1.00
15	Randy Johnson	1.00
16	Jeff Fassero	.25
17	Ken Cloude	.25
18	Edgar Martinez	.25

1998 Pinnacle Snapshots Mets

		MT
Complete Set (18):		6.00
Common Player:		.25
1	Rey Ordonez	.75
2	Todd Hundley	.40
3	Preston Wilson	.40
4	Rich Becker	.25
5	Bernard Gilkey	.25
6	Rey Ordonez	.75
7	Butch Huskey	.35
8	Carlos Baerga	.25
9	Edgardo Alfonzo	.75
10	Bill Pulsipher	.25
11	John Franco	.25
12	Todd Pratt	.25
13	Brian McRae	.25
14	Bobby Jones	.25
15	John Olerud	.60
16	Todd Hundley	.40
17	Jay Payton	.25
18	Paul Wilson	.25

1998 Pinnacle Snapshots Orioles

		MT
Complete Set (18):		9.00
Common Player:		.25
1	Cal Ripken Jr.	2.50
2	Rocky Coppinger	.25
3	Eric Davis	.35
4	Chris Hoiles	.25
5	Mike Mussina	.75
6	Joe Carter	.75
7	Rafael Palmeiro	.75
8	B.J. Surhoff	.35
9	Jimmy Key	.25
10	Scott Erickson	.35
11	Armando Benitez	.25
12	Roberto Alomar	.75
13	Cal Ripken Jr.	2.50
14	Mike Bordick	.25
15	Roberto Alomar	.75
16	Jeffrey Hammonds	.25
17	Rafael Palmeiro	.75
18	Brady Anderson	.40

1998 Pinnacle Snapshots Rangers

		MT
Complete Set (18):		6.00
Common Player:		.25
1	Ivan Rodriguez	.75
2	Fernando Tatis	.45
3	Danny Patterson	.25
4	Will Clark	.50
5	Kevin Elster	.25
6	Rusty Greer	.25
7	Darren Oliver	.25
8	John Burkett	.25
9	Tom Goodwin	.25
10	Roberto Kelly	.25
11	Aaron Sele	.25
12	Rick Helling	.25
13	Mark McLemore	.25
14	Lee Stevens	.25
15	John Wetteland	.25
16	Will Clark	.50
17	Juan Gonzalez	1.50
18	Roger Pavlik	.25

1998 Pinnacle Snapshots Red Sox

		MT
Complete Set (18):		6.50
Common Player:		.25
1	Tim Naehring	.25
2	Brian Rose	.25
3	Darren Bragg	.25
4	Pedro Martinez	.75
5	Mo Vaughn	.75
6	Jim Leyritz	.25
7	Troy O'Leary	.25
8	Mo Vaughn	.75
9	Nomar Garciaparra	2.00
10	Michael Coleman	.25
11	Tom Gordon	.25
12	Tim Naehring	.25
13	Nomar Garciaparra	2.00
14	John Valentin	.35
15	Steve Avery	.25
16	Damon Buford	.35
17	Troy O'Leary	.25
18	Bret Saberhagen	.35

1998 Pinnacle Snapshots Rockies

		MT
Complete Set (18):		6.00
Common Player:		.25
1	Larry Walker	.75
2	Pedro Astacio	.25
3	Jamey Wright	.25
4	Darryl Kile	.25
5	Kirt Manwaring	.25
6	Todd Helton	1.00
7	Mike Lansing	.25
8	Neifi Perez	.35
9	Dante Bichette	.75
10	Derrick Gibson	.50
11	Neifi Perez	.35
12	Darryl Kile	.25
13	Larry Walker	.75
14	Roger Bailey	.25
15	Ellis Burks	.35
16	Dante Bichette	.75
17	Derrick Gibson	.50
18	Ellis Burks	.35

1998 Pinnacle Snapshots Yankees

		MT
Complete Set (18):		10.00
Common Player:		.25
1	Andy Pettitte	.60
2	Darryl Strawberry	.40
3	Joe Girardi	.25
4	Derek Jeter	2.00
5	Andy Pettitte	.60
6	Tim Raines	.35
7	Mariano Rivera	.40
8	Tino Martinez	.35
9	Derek Jeter	2.00
10	Hideki Irabu	.75
11	Tino Martinez	.35
12	David Cone	.40
13	Bernie Williams	.50
14	David Cone	.40
15	Bernie Williams	.50
16	Chuck Knoblauch	.35
17	Paul O'Neill	.35
18	David Wells	.35

1998 Pinnacle All-Star FanFest John Elway

The quarterback of the World's Champion Denver Broncos was featured on a card harkening back to his minor league baseball playing days. During the July, 1998, All-Star FanFest in Denver, Pinnacle sold a special card of Elway, with proceeds benefitting the city's schools. Initial cost was $2 per card. Front has a black-and-white posed action photo with blue and white pinstriped backgrounds. Back has a ghosted photo of Elway in his Broncos uniform and provides details of his baseball career.

	MT
John Elway	3.00

1998 Team Pinnacle Baseball

With each $30 membership in Pinnacle's collectors' club, "Team Pinnacle," the member received a litho tin box with 10 each special baseball, football and hockey cards, and a pack of unnumbered promo cards. In standard 2-1/2" x 3-1/2", cards have game-action photos on front, bordered in a dominant team color and enhanced with a gold-foil Team Pinnacle logo at bottom. Backs have portrait photos, a few personal details, career highlights and the player's uniform number ghosted in the background.

		MT
Complete Set (10):		10.00
Common Player:		1.00
B1	Ken Griffey Jr.	3.00
B2	Frank Thomas	1.50
B3	Cal Ripken Jr.	2.50
B4	Alex Rodriguez	2.50
B5	Mike Piazza	2.00
B6	Derek Jeter	1.50
B7	Greg Maddux	1.25
B8	Chipper Jones	1.50
B9	Mark McGwire	3.00
B10	Juan Gonzalez	1.00
---	Cal Ripken Jr. (unmarked sample)	2.50

1998 Pinnacle Uncut

Advertised as the "BIGGEST CARD EVER!" these 13-3/8" x 18-5/8" cards are approximately 30 times larger than standard cards. Sold in individual cello bags with a suggested retail price of around $10, the cards are super-size replicas of the same players' cards found in the Field of Vision subset in regular 1998 Pinnacle. The giant cards have an etched metallic foil front not found on the regular cards. They are packaged with a die-cut cardboard backing which tends to bruise the edges or chip off small patches of ink.

		MT
Complete Set (6):		50.00
Common Card:		10.00
182	Alex Rodriguez	10.00
183	Cal Ripken Jr., Roberto Alomar	8.00
184	Roger Clemens	8.00
185	Derek Jeter	10.00
186	Frank Thomas	8.00
186p	Frank Thomas ("SAMPLE" on back)	10.00
187	Ken Griffey Jr.	12.00

1996 Pitch Publications

These collectors' issue art cards feature black-and-white portraits of Hall of Fame players in a 4" x 6" format. Backs have a list of teams player for and career major league stats. The unnumbered cards are checklisted here in alphabetical order.

		MT
Complete Set (12):		12.00
Common Player:		1.50
(1)	Frank Baker	1.50
(2)	Frank Chance	1.50
(3)	Fred Clarke	1.50
(4)	Eddie Collins	1.50
(5)	Sam Crawford	1.50
(6)	Johnny Evers	1.50
(7)	Willie Keeler	1.50
(8)	Nap Lajoie	1.50
(9)	Rube Marquard	1.50
(10)	Eddie Plank	1.50
(11)	Joe Tinker	1.50
(12)	Rube Waddell	1.50

1992 Pittsburgh Brewing Co. Roberto Clemente Tribute

Apparently given away in conjunction with an in-stadium promotion, this perforated pair of cards pays tribute to Roberto Clemente. The 7" square panel has a pair of two-part cards. Each side has a 3-1/2" x 5-1/2" picture portion at top and a 1-1/2" tab at bottom, perforated for easy separation. The left side has a portrait of the Pirate great with his first name; at right is his last name and an action picture. Back of the portrait card has career stats; back of the action card has career highlights. The sponsor logo is on back of each tab along with a quotation and copyright information.

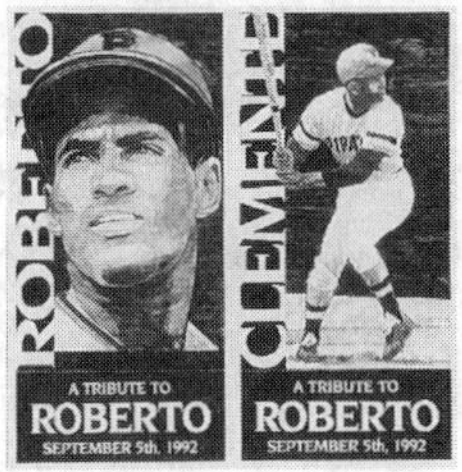

		MT
Complete Panel:		18.00
Complete Set (2):		15.00
#21	Roberto (portrait)	
#21	Clemente (action)	

1984 Pittsburgh Pirates Promotional Dates Cards

This 27-card set advertises the various Pirates promotional game dates. Each 3-3/8" x 5-1/4" card features a player portrait with facsimile autograph. In the white border at bottom are the player's name, position and uniform number. Black-and-white backs advertise upcoming home games at which premium items will be given away, fireworks displays held, etc. The set was sold by mail from the team.

		MT
Complete Set (27):		25.00
Common Player:		1.00
2	Jim Morrison	1.00
3	Johnny Ray	1.00
4	Dale Berra	1.00
5	Bill Madlock	1.50
6	Tony Pena	1.25
7	Chuck Tanner	1.00
12	Brian Harper	1.00
14	Milt May	1.00
16	Lee Mazzilli	1.00
17	Lee Lacy	1.00
19	Rod Scurry	1.00
22	Lee Tunnell	1.00
24	John Tudor	1.00
25	Jose DeLeon	1.00
26	Amos Otis	1.00
27	Kent Tekulve	1.00
29	Rick Rhoden	1.00
30	Jason Thompson	1.00
36	Marvell Wynne	1.00
37	Rafael Belliard	1.00
38	Manny Sarmiento	1.00
43	Don Robinson	1.00
45	John Candelaria	1.00
47	Cecilio Guante	1.00
49	Larry McWilliams	1.00
50	Hedi Vargas	1.00
51	Doug Frobel	1.00

1985 Pittsburgh Pirates Promotional Dates Cards

Again in 1985 the Pirates produced and sold via a mail-in offer a set of postcard-size advertising cards, which were also distributed at Three Rivers Stadium. The 3-3/8" x 5-1/4" cards feature on front player portraits and facsimile autographs. In the white bottom border are the player's name, position and uniform number. Backs are printed in black-and-white and contain an ad for an upcoming game at which promotional items were to be given away, fireworks displayed, etc. The Kent Tekulve card was withdrawn early in the distribution cycle when he was traded to the Phillies.

		MT
Complete Set (23) (no Tekulve):		20.00
Complete Set (24) (w/ Tekulve):		25.00
Common Player:		1.00
2	Jim Morrison	1.00
3	Johnny Ray	1.00
5	Bill Madlock	1.25
6	Tony Pena	1.00
7	Chuck Tanner	1.00
10	Tim Foli	1.00
12	Bill Almon	1.00
13	Steve Kemp	1.00
15	George Hendrick	1.00
16	Lee Mazzilli	1.00
19	Rod Scurry	1.00
22	Lee Tunnell	1.00
25	Jose DeLeon	1.00
26	Junior Ortiz	1.00
27	Kent Tekulve	6.00
28	Sixto Lezcano	1.00
29	Rick Rhoden	1.00
30	Jason Thompson	1.00
34	Mike Bielecki	1.00
36	Marvell Wynne	1.00
37	Rafael Belliard	1.00
43	Don Robinson	1.00
45	John Candelaria	1.00
49	Larry McWilliams	1.00

1985 Pittsburgh Pirates Yearbook Cards

This 18-card set was issued on two nine-card perforated panels inserted into the Bucs' 1985 yearbook. Individual cards measure 2-1/2" x 3-1/2" and feature color photos surrounded by black and gold borders. The player's name, position and uniform number are printed in a white panel at bottom. Backs are in black-and-white and offer complete major and minor league stats, along with the logos of sponsors Cameron/Coca-Cola.

		MT
Complete Set (18):		10.00
Common Player:		.50
2	Jim Morrison	.50
3	Johnny Ray	.50
5	Bill Madlock	.60
6	Tony Pena	.60
7	Chuck Tanner	.50
10	Tim Foli	.50
13	Steve Kemp	.50
15	George Hendrick	.50
25	Jose DeLeon	.50
27	Kent Tekulve	.50
28	Sixto Lezcano	.50
29	Rick Rhoden	.50
30	Jason Thompson	.50
36	Marvell Wynne	.50
43	Don Robinson	.50
45	John Candelaria	.50
49	Larry McWilliams	.50
51	Doug Frobel	.50

1987 Pittsburgh Pirates team issue

These large-format (5" x 7-1/2") black-and-white cards were provided to players and staff for use in answering fan requests for pictures and autographs. The cards have portrait photos with white borders. In the wide bottom border are the player's name and position. Backs are blank. The unnumbered cards are listed alphabetically. Complete sets were not available from the team.

		MT
Complete Set (29):		35.00
Common Player:		1.00
(1)	Rafael Belliard	1.00
(2)	Barry Bonds	6.00
(3)	Bobby Bonilla	3.00
(4)	Sid Bream	1.00
(5)	John Cangelosi	1.00
(6)	Mike Diaz	1.00
(7)	Rich Donnelly	1.00
(8)	Doug Drabek	1.25
(9)	Logan Easley	1.00
(10)	Brian Fisher	1.00
(11)	Barry Jones	1.00
(12)	Bob Kipper	1.00
(13)	Gene Lamont	1.00
(14)	Mike La Valliere	1.00
(15)	Jim Leyland	1.50
(16)	Milt May	1.00
(17)	Ray Miller	1.00
(18)	Jim Morrison	1.00
(19)	Joe Orsulak	1.00
(20)	Junior Ortiz	1.00
(21)	Bob Patterson	1.00
(22)	Johnny Ray	1.00
(23)	Rick Reuschel	1.00
(24)	R.J. Reynolds	1.00
(25)	Don Robinson	1.00
(26)	Tommy Sandt	1.00
(27)	John Smiley	1.00
(28)	Andy Van Slyke	1.50
(29)	Bob Walk	1.00

1988 Pittsburgh Pirates Photocards

These postcard-size (3-1/2" x 5") color cards were provided to players and staff for use in answering fan requests for pictures and autographs. Backs are blank. The unnumbered cards are listed alphabetically. Complete sets were not available from the team.

		MT
Complete Set (33):		25.00
Common Player:		1.00
(1)	Rafael Belliard	1.00
(2)	Barry Bonds	5.00
(3)	Bobby Bonilla	2.50
(4)	Sid Bream	1.00
(5)	John Cangelosi	1.00
(6)	Darnell Coles	1.00
(7)	Mike Diaz	1.00
(8)	Rich Donnelly	1.00
(9)	Doug Drabek	1.50
(10)	Mike Dunn	1.00
(11)	Felix Fermin	1.00
(12)	Brian Fisher	1.00
(13)	Lanny Frattare (broadcaster)	1.00
(14)	Jim Gott	1.00
(15)	Barry Jones	1.00
(16)	Bob Kipper	1.00
(17)	Gene Lamont	1.00
(18)	Mike La Valliere	1.00
(19)	Jim Leyland	1.50
(20)	Jose Lind	1.00
(21)	Milt May	1.00
(22)	Ray Miller	1.00
(23)	Randy Milligan	1.00
(24)	Junior Ortiz	1.00
(25)	Al Pedrique	1.00
(26)	R.J. Reynolds	1.00
(27)	Jeff Robinson	1.00
(28)	Jim Rooker (broadcaster)	1.00
(29)	Tommy Sandt	1.00
(30)	John Smiley	1.00
(31)	Andy Van Slyke	1.50
(32)	Bob Walk	1.00
(33)	Pirate Parrot (mascot)	1.00

1988 Pittsburgh Pirates Schedule Cards

This series of Pirates photocards features on its back a schedule of the team's 1988 home games. Fronts of the 3-1/2" x 5-1/2" cards have color portrait photos with team logo and player name in the wide white border at bottom. Besides the schedule, backs have a few bits of personal data and a uniform number. The set is checklisted here in alphabetical order and may not be complete as shown.

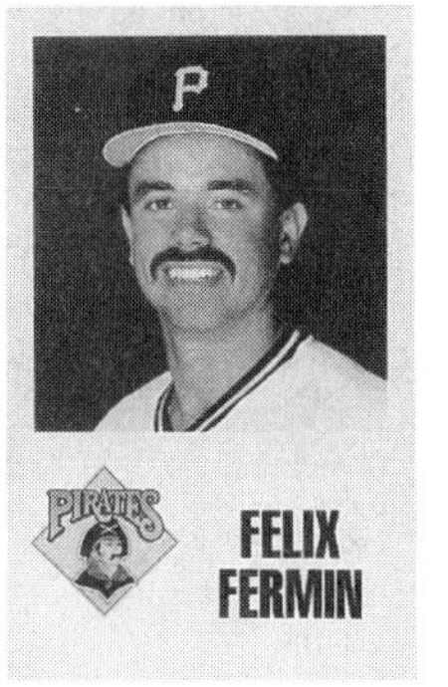

		MT
Complete Set (23):		15.00
Common Player:		.75
(1)	Pirate Parrot (mascot)	.75
(2)	(Rafael Belliard)	.75
(3)	Barry Bonds	6.00
(4)	Sid Bream	.75
(5)	Bobby Bonilla	2.50
(6)	John Cangelosi	.75
(7)	Darnell Coles	.75
(8)	Mike Dion	.75
(9)	Rich Donnelly	.75
(10)	Doug Drabek	.90
(11)	Mike Dunn	.75
(12)	Felix Fermin	.75
(13)	Brian Fisher	.75
(14)	Lanny Frattare (announcer)	.75
(15)	Jim Gott	.75
(16)	Mike LaValliere	.75
(17)	Jim Leyland	.75
(18)	Jose Lind	.75
(19)	Al Pedrique	.75
(20)	R.J. Reynolds	.75
(21)	Jeff Robinson	.75
(22)	Jim Rooker	.75
(23)	Andy Van Slyke	1.00

1989 Pittsburgh Pirates team issue

These large-format (3-1/2" x 5-1/2") color cards were provided to players and staff for use in answering fan requests for pictures and autographs. The cards have portrait photos with a black frame line and white borders. In the wide white bottom border are the player's name in black and gold and a color team logo. Backs are blank. The unnumbered cards are listed alphabetically. Complete sets were not available from the team.

		MT
Complete Set (38):		40.00
Common Player:		1.00
(1)	Barry Bonds	5.00
(2)	Bobby Bonilla	3.00
(3)	Sid Bream	1.00
(4)	Rafael Belliard	1.00
(5)	Dann Billardello	1.00
(6)	John Cangelosi	1.00
(7)	Benny Distefano	1.00
(8)	Rich Donnelly	1.00
(9)	Doug Drabek	1.50
(10)	Logan Easley	1.00
(11)	Brian Fisher	1.00
(12)	Miguel Garcia	1.00
(13)	Jim Gott	1.00
(14)	Neal Heaton	1.00
(15)	Bruce Kimm	1.00
(16)	Jeff King	2.00
(17)	Bob Kipper	1.00
(18)	Randy Kramer	1.00
(19)	Bill Landrum	1.00
(20)	Gene Lamont	1.00
(21)	Mike La Valliere	1.00
(22)	Jim Leyland	2.00
(23)	Jose Lind	1.00
(24)	Morris Madden	1.00
(25)	Scott Medvin	1.00
(26)	Ray Miller	1.00
(27)	Junior Ortiz	1.00
(28)	Tom Prince	1.00
(29)	Rey Quinones	1.00
(30)	Gary Redus	1.00
(31)	R.J. Reynolds	1.00
(32)	Jeff Robinson	1.00
(33)	Tommy Sandt	1.00
(34)	John Smiley	1.00
(35)	Dorn Taylor	1.00
(36)	Andy Van Slyke	2.00
(37)	Bob Walk	1.00
(38)	Glenn Wilson	1.00

1995 Pittsburgh Pirates team issue

Produced for player and staff use, these cards were not sold as team sets. Fronts of the 3-1/2" x 5-3/4" thin cardboard cards have player photos surrounded by team-color borders of yellow and black. The team name is in red script at top, while the player name is at bottom in black within a yellow box. Backs are black and white, have a few biographical details and a large team logo. The cards are checklisted here according to the uniform numbers on back. Some of the cards are identical to those produced in 1994 with Quintex or Nationwide Insurance ads on back.

		MT
Complete Set (40):		18.00
Common Player:		.50
3	Jay Bell	.75
5	Jacob Brumfield	.60
6	Orlando Merced	.60
7	Jeff King	.75
10	Jim Leyland	.50
11	Don Slaught	.60
13	Carlos Garcia	.60
14	Mark Parent	.50
15	Denny Neagle	.50
16	Nelson Liriano	.50
18	Bill Virdon	.50
19	Dan Plesac	.50
22	Freddy Garcia	.50
25	Steve Pegues	.50
26	Steve Cooke	.50
28	Al Martin	.60
31	Ray Miller	.50
32	Dan Miceli	.50
34	Esteban Loaiza	.75
35	Dave Clark	.50
36	Mark Johnson	.50
37	Tommy Sandt	.50
38	Jim Gott	.50
39	Milt May	.50
41	Jason Christiansen	.50
43	Paul Wagner	.50
44	Rick White	.50
45	Rich Donnelly	.50
47	Jon Lieber	.50
48	Rich Aude	.50
53	Jeff McCurry	.50
54	Spin Williams	.50
60	Steve Parris	.50
62	Mike Dyer	.50
---	Steve Blass (announcer)	.50
---	Greg Brown (announcer)	.50
---	Lanny Frattare (announcer)	.50
---	Bob Walk (announcer)	.50
---	Pirate Parrot (mascot)	.50
---	Three Rivers Stadium	.75

1997 Pittsburgh Post-Gazette Jason Kendall

This variation of the 1996 Pittsburgh Pirates photocard series carries on back the advertising of the city's daily newspaper, instead of that of Advance Auto Parts, which sponsored the 1996 team set. The facsimile autographed 3-1/2" x 5-3/4" color card (black-and-white back) also showcases the newly adopted (1997) team logo. Cards were inserted into polybagged copies of the newspaper given to fans in attendance at the preseason PiratesFest.

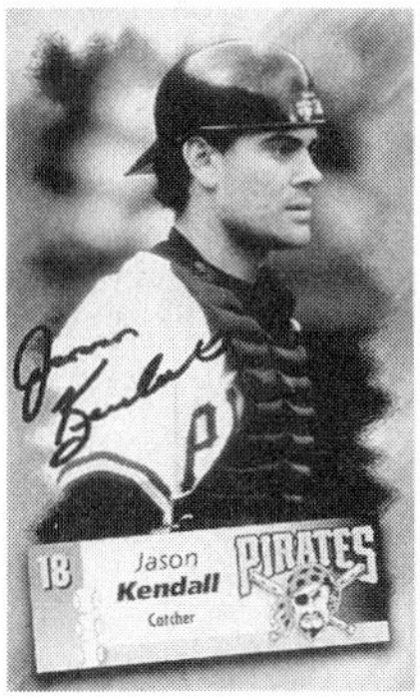

	MT
Jason Kendall	6.00

1998 Pittsburgh Post-Gazette Pirates

A special edition of the Pittsburgh Post-Gazette distributed at Pirates Fan Fest included a trio of cards; others were distributed during the season. The 3-1/2" x 5-3/4" cards have color action photos on front with wide black borders. The player's name and position are at bottom with the team logo in the lower-right. Horizontal backs repeat the logo, offer a few vital statistics and the player's 1997 record. The cards are listed here alphabetically.

		MT
Complete Set (7):		12.00
(1)	Francisco Cordova	2.00
(2)	Jose Guillen	2.00
(3)	Jason Kendall	4.00
(4)	Rich Loiselle	2.00
(5)	Jason Schmidt	2.00
(6)	Tony Womack	2.00
(7)	Kevin Young	2.50

1999 Pittsburgh Post-Gazette Pirates

Virtually identical in format to the 1998 issue, the 1999 photocards have the team logo on front in the upper-left corner and have 1998 stats on back. Distribution method is unsure and it is likely this alphabetized checklist is not complete.

		MT
Complete Set (7):		15.00
Common Player:		2.00
(1)	Brian Giles	4.00
(2)	Jason Kendall	3.00
(3)	Pat Meares	2.00
(4)	Warren Morris	2.00
(5)	Jason Schmidt	2.00
(6)	Ed Sprague	2.00
(7)	Kevin Young	2.50

1984 Pizza Hut Place Mats

Popular players from the Atlanta Braves and Chicago White Sox were featured on a series of placemats issued regionally by the pizza chain. In 17" x 11" format and printed on heavy paper, the mats each picture a pair of players painted in a portrait and two action poses. Fronts are bordered in team colors, have full major and minor league stats for the pictured players and logos of the teams, players' union, Pizza Hut and flagship TV station. Backs are printed in red, blue and black and feature the team's 1984 schedule.

		MT
Complete Set (8):		18.00
Common Placemat:		3.00
	Atlanta Braves team set:	12.00
(1)	Bruce Benedict, Steve Bedrosian	3.00
(2)	Chris Chambliss, Bob Horner	3.00
(3)	Glenn Hubbard, Rafael Ramirez	3.00
(4)	Craig McMurtry, Dale Murphy	4.50
	Chicago White Sox team set:	12.00
(1)	Harold Baines, LaMarr Hoyt	3.00
(2)	Floyd Bannister, Carlton Fisk	4.50
(3)	Julio Cruz, Greg Luzinski	3.00
(4)	Richard Dotson, Ron Kittle	3.00

1996 Pizza Hut

In conjunction with a foam bat/ball promotion, Pizza Hut issued a small set of small cards (2-1/2" x 2-1/4") featuring players involved in the endorsement. The player portrait photos on the cards are devoid of cap logos and surrounded by a rainbow border. Player names are in yellow with a nickname in red. A choking hazard warning is in black-and-white on bottom. Backs are printed in red and black and have career summaries, logos and copyright notice. The unnumbered cards are checklisted here alphabetically.

		MT
Complete Set (4):		8.00
Common Card:		1.50
(1)	Jeff Bagwell (thumper), Orel Hershiser (bulldawg)	1.50
(2)	David Cone (controller), Mike Piazza (crusher)	2.00
(3)	Ken Griffey Jr. (junior), Greg Maddux (surgeon)	4.00
(4)	Randy Johnson (big unit), Mo Vaughn (hit dog)	1.50

1991 Playball U.S.A. Will Clark

Playball U.S.A. was the licensed entity owned by Ed Broder who produced many collectors issues in the 1970s and 1980s, both before and after it became a "crime" against MLB and the players' union. The Playball U.S.A. issues are a confusing array of single-player sets and promo cards all issued 1991-92. Glossy fronts feature color photos in several different styles: Borderless, with color stripe at bottom, or with color stripes top and bottom. Backs are generally horizontal in format and include team and MLB logos and card numbers which begin with a "91-" prefix.

		MT
Common Card:		.25
91-3	Will Clark (promo)	.25
91-21	Will Clark (left-side pose)	.25
91-22	Will Clark (throwing)	.25
91-23	Will Clark (going to bat)	.25
91-24	Will Clark (portrait)	.25
91-25	Will Clark (batting)	.25
91-39	Will Clark (batting)	.25
91-40	Will Clark (left-side view)	.25
91-41	Will Clark (batting)	.25
91-42	Will Clark (portrait, sunglasses)	.25
91-43	Will Clark (running)	.25
------	Will Clark (unnumbered promo)	.25

1991 Playball U.S.A. Ken Griffey, Jr.

Playball U.S.A. was the licensed entity owned by Ed Broder who produced many collectors issues in the 1970s and 1980s, both before and after it became a "crime" against MLB and the players' union. The Playball U.S.A. issues are a confusing array of single-player sets and promo cards all issued 1991-92. Glossy fronts feature color photos in several different styles: Borderless, with color stripe at bottom, or with color stripes top and bottom. Backs are generally horizontal in format and include team and MLB logos and card numbers which begin with a "91-" prefix.

		MT
Common Card:		.50
1	Ken Griffey Jr. (promo)	.50
11	Ken Griffey Jr. (batting)	.50
12	Ken Griffey Jr.	.50
13	Ken Griffey Jr.	.50
14	Ken Griffey Jr.	.50
15	Ken Griffey Jr.	.50
16	Ken Griffey Jr.	.50

17 Ken Griffey Jr. (fielding) .50
18 Ken Griffey Jr. .50
19 Ken Griffey Jr. .50
20 Ken Griffey Jr. .50
32 Ken Griffey Jr. (in batting cage) .50
33 Ken Griffey Jr. (running) .50
34 Ken Griffey Jr. (batting) .50
35 Ken Griffey Jr. (batting) .50
36 Ken Griffey Jr. (batting follow-through) .50
37 Ken Griffey Jr. (holding bat) .50
38 Ken Griffey Jr. (profile) .50
49 Ken Griffey Jr. (promo) .50
50 Ken Griffey Jr. (promo) .50
61 Ken Griffey Jr. (batting) .50
61p Ken Griffey Jr. (gray-back promo card) .50
62 Ken Griffey Jr. (batting cage) .50
63 Ken Griffey Jr. (bat on shoulder) .50
64 Ken Griffey Jr. (standing) .50
65 Ken Griffey Jr. (on deck) .50
66 Ken Griffey Jr. (portrait w/jacket) .50
69 Ken Griffey Jr. (swinging bat, black/gold borders promo) .50
70 Ken Griffey Jr. (sliding, black/gold borders promo) .50
71 Ken Griffey Jr. (promo card) .50
72 Ken Griffey Jr. (on base, black/gold borders promo) .50

1991 Playball U.S.A. Don Mattingly

Playball U.S.A. was the licensed entity owned by Ed Broder who produced many collectors issues in the 1970s and 1980s, both before and after it became a "crime" against MLB and the players' union. The Playball U.S.A. issues are a confusing array of single-player sets and promo cards all issued 1991-92. Glossy fronts feature color photos in several different styles: Borderless, with color stripe at bottom, or with color stripes top and bottom. Backs are generally horizontal in format and include team and MLB logos and card numbers which begin with a "91-" prefix.

		MT
	Common Card:	.50
2	Don Mattingly (promo)	.50
26	Don Mattingly (looking over shoulder)	.50
27	Don Mattingly (going to bat)	.50
28	Don Mattingly (at bat)	.50
29	Don Mattingly (in blue jersey)	.50
30	Don Mattingly (throwing)	.50
44	Don Mattingly (batting)	.50
45	Don Mattingly (pose w/helmet)	.50
46	Don Mattingly (blue practice jersey)	.50
47	Don Mattingly (going to bat)	.50
48	Don Mattingly (watching batted ball)	.50
51	GOLD-FOIL BORDERS Don Mattingly (promo)	.50
------	Don Mattingly (unnumbered promo)	.50
	GOLD-FOIL BORDERS	
G-4	Don Mattingly	2.00
G-5	Don Mattingly	2.00

1991 Playball U.S.A. Darryl Strawberry

Playball U.S.A. was the licensed entity owned by Ed Broder who produced many collectors issues in the 1970s and 1980s, both before and after it became a "crime" against MLB and the players' union. The Playball U.S.A. issues are a confusing array of single-player sets and promo cards all issued 1991-92. Glossy fronts feature color photos in several different styles: Borderless, with color stripe at bottom, or with color stripes top and bottom. Backs are generally horizontal in format and include team and MLB logos and card numbers which begin with a "91-" prefix.

		MT
	Common Card:	.25
7	Darryl Strawberry (promo)	.25
31	Darryl Strawberry (promo)	.25
53	Darryl Strawberry (bat on shoulder)	.25
54	Darryl Strawberry (batting)	.25
55	Darryl Strawberry (batting)	.25
56	Darryl Strawberry (batting cage)	.25
57	Darryl Strawberry (holding bat)	.25
58	Darryl Strawberry (batting)	.25
60	Darryl Strawberry (bat on shoulder)	.25
60p	Darryl Strawberry (promo card)	.25

1992 Playball U.S.A. Ken Griffey Jr.

These unnumbered cards feature color action photos of Junior surrounded by prismatic metallic foil borders. Backs are horizontal and have player and manufacturer identification.

		MT
	Complete Set (4):	6.00
	Common Card:	1.50
(1)	Ken Griffey Jr. (bat in hand)	1.50
(2)	Ken Griffey Jr. (beginning swing)	1.50
(3)	Ken Griffey Jr. (follow-through)	1.50
(4)	Ken Griffey Jr. (running)	1.50

1985 Polaroid/ J.C. Penney Indians

While the Cleveland Indians continued its four-year tradition of baseball card promotional game issues in 1985, the sponsor changed from Wheaties to Polaroid/ J.C. Penney. The set features 30 player cards, a manager card and a group card of the coaching staff. Though produced in the "safety set" format - slightly oversize (2-13/16" by 4-1/8") with wide white borders - the Indians cards carry no safety message. Backs, once again numbered by uniform number, contain major and minor league stats.

		MT
	Complete Set (32):	9.00
	Common Player:	.25
2	Brett Butler	.50
4	Tony Bernazard	.25
8	Carmen Castillo	.25
10	Pat Tabler	.25
12	Benny Ayala	.25
13	Ernie Camacho	.25
14	Julio Franco	.50
16	Jerry Willard	.25
18	Pat Corrales	.25
20	Otis Nixon	.35
21	Mike Hargrove	.25
22	Mike Fischlin	.25
23	Chris Bando	.25
24	George Vukovich	.25
26	Brook Jacoby	.25
27	Mel Hall	.25
28	Bert Blyleven	.50
29	Andre Thornton	.30
30	Joe Carter	2.00
32	Rick Behenna	.25
33	Roy Smith	.25
35	Jerry Reed	.25
36	Jamie Easterly	.25
38	Dave Von Ohlen	.25
41	Rich Thompson	.25
43	Bryan Clark	.25
44	Neal Heaton	.25
48	Vern Ruhle	.25
49	Jeff Barkley	.25
50	Ramon Romero	.25
54	Tom Waddell	.25
---	Coaches (Bobby Bonds, Johnny Goryl, Don McMahon, Ed Napolean, Dennis Sommers)	.25

1983 Post Super Sugar Crisp Team Cards

This series of team history cards was packaged inside boxes of Post Super Sugar Crisp cereal. The 2-7/8" x 3-1/2" cards are printed on thin cardboard. Fronts have a background of a baseball field with a large color team logo at center. At bottom are the cereal and MLB logos. Backs are printed in red with a short team history.

	MT
Complete Set (26):	40.00
Team logo card	2.00

1990 Post Cereal

Post Cereal returned in 1990 with a 30-card set. The card fronts feature borders in white, red and blue, with the post logo in the upper left and the Major League Baseball logo in the upper right. Below the full-color shot of the player is his name in red. Backs of the cards show complete major league statistics; underneath is a facsimile autograph. The player photos do not display team logos. Cards were included three per box, inside Alpha-Bits cereal. Considered a difficult set to complete, the insert offer was only available for a limited time. An uncut sheet version of the set was also offered in a run of 5,000 serially numbered pieces.

		MT
	Complete Set (30):	6.00
	Common Player:	.15
	Uncut Sheet:	30.00
1	Don Mattingly	.50
2	Roger Clemens	.40
3	Kirby Puckett	.40
4	George Brett	.45
5	Tony Gwynn	.50
6	Ozzie Smith	.40
7	Will Clark	.25
8	Orel Hershiser	.15
9	Ryne Sandberg	.40
10	Darryl Strawberry	.20
11	Nolan Ryan	1.00
12	Mark McGwire	2.00
13	Jim Abbott	.15
14	Bo Jackson	.20
15	Kevin Mitchell	.15
16	Jose Canseco	.35
17	Wade Boggs	.35
18	Dale Murphy	.20
19	Mark Grace	.30
20	Mike Scott	.15
21	Cal Ripken, Jr.	1.00
22	Pedro Guerrero	.15
23	Ken Griffey, Jr.	2.00
24	Eric Davis	.15
25	Rickey Henderson	.25
26	Robin Yount	.35
27	Von Hayes	.15
28	Alan Trammell	.15
29	Dwight Gooden	.20
30	Joe Carter	.15

1991 Post Cereal

These superstar trading cards were inserted in Post Honeycomb, Super Golden Crisp, Cocoa Pebbles, Fruity Pebbles, Alpha-Bits and Marshmallow Alpha-Bits children's cereals. The complete set features 30 cards of baseball's top players. The cards were produced by Mike Schechter Associates, Inc. and are authorized by The Major League Baseball Players Association. The card fronts feature a player photo, the Post logo and the MLBPA logo. The flip sides feature statistics and a facsimile autograph.

		MT
	Complete Set (30):	6.00
	Common Player:	.20
1	Dave Justice	.35
2	Mark McGwire	2.00
3	Will Clark	.25
4	Jose Canseco	.35
5	Vince Coleman	.20
6	Sandy Alomar, Jr.	.25
7	Darryl Strawberry	.20
8	Len Dykstra	.20
9	Gregg Jefferies	.20
10	Tony Gwynn	.50
11	Ken Griffey, Jr.	2.50
12	Roger Clemens	.40
13	Chris Sabo	.20
14	Bobby Bonilla	.20
15	Gary Sheffield	.25
16	Ryne Sandberg	.40
17	Nolan Ryan	1.00
18	Barry Larkin	.20
19	Cal Ripken, Jr.	1.00
20	Jim Abbott	.20
21	Barry Bonds	.45
22	Mark Grace	.35
23	Cecil Fielder	.20
24	Kevin Mitchell	.20
25	Todd Zeile	.20
26	George Brett	.50
27	Rickey Henderson	.25
28	Kirby Puckett	.40
29	Don Mattingly	.50
30	Kevin Maas	.20

1991 Post Cereal - Canadian

SÉRIE DES ÉTOILES 1991 SUPER STAR SERIES
Post
BENITO SANTIAGO
SAN DIEGO PADRES DE SAN DIEGO

Specially-marked Post cereal boxes sold in Canada included one of 30 cards from a 1991 Super Star series of cards that featured 14 National League and 16 American League players. The cards are bilingual, and include player statistics and biographical information on the backs. The major league logos are airbrushed from the player's caps and uniforms. American Leaguer's cards have blue stripes above and below the photo on front and as a back border color; National Leaguers are in red.

		MT
	Complete Set (30):	18.00
	Common Player:	.50
1	Delino DeShields	.50
2	Tim Wallach	.50
3	Andres Galarraga	.75
4	Dave Magadan	.50
5	Barry Bonds	1.00
6	Len Dykstra	.50
7	Andre Dawson	.50
8	Ozzie Smith	.75
9	Will Clark	.65
10	Chris Sabo	.50
11	Eddie Murray	.75
12	Dave Justice	.60
13	Benito Santiago	.50
14	Glenn Davis	.50
15	Kelly Gruber	.50
16	Dave Stieb	.50
17	John Olerud	.60
18	Roger Clemens	.75
19	Cecil Fielder	.50

20	Kevin Maas	.50
21	Robin Yount	.75
22	Cal Ripken, Jr.	3.00
23	Sandy Alomar	.60
24	Rickey Henderson	.65
25	Bobby Thigpen	.50
26	Ken Griffey, Jr.	4.00
27	Nolan Ryan	3.00
28	Dave Winfield	.65
29	George Brett	1.00
30	Kirby Puckett	1.00

1992 Post Cereal

The addition of a back photo is notable on Post's 1992 30-card set. Again packaged at the rate of three cards in specially marked boxes, a complete set was available via a mail-in offer. Front photos had a blue strip at top with the Post logo at upper-left. A red stripe at bottom has the player's name and the logo of the Major League Baseball Player's Association. The absence of a Major League Baseball logo, and the airbrushing of uniform logos on all photos identifies this set as the work of Mike Schechter Associates. Backs have a small photo at left, bordered in red. At right are biographical details, career stats and a facsimile autograph. The cards of 1991 Rookies of the Year Jeff Bagwell and Chuck Knoblauch are designated with a "Rookie Star" banner over the front photo.

		MT
Complete Set (30):		4.00
Common Player:		.25
1	Jeff Bagwell	.65
2	Ryne Sandberg	.60
3	Don Mattingly	.50
4	Wally Joyner	.25
5	Dwight Gooden	.30
6	Chuck Knoblauch	.30
7	Kirby Puckett	.45
8	Ozzie Smith	.50
9	Cal Ripken, Jr.	1.00
10	Darryl Strawberry	.30
11	George Brett	.60
12	Joe Carter	.30
13	Cecil Fielder	.25
14	Will Clark	.35
15	Barry Bonds	.60
16	Roger Clemens	.45
17	Paul Molitor	.40
18	Scott Erickson	.25
19	Wade Boggs	.40
20	Ken Griffey, Jr.	1.50
21	Bobby Bonilla	.30
22	Terry Pendleton	.25
23	Barry Larkin	.25
24	Frank Thomas	.75
25	Jose Canseco	.35
26	Tony Gwynn	.65
27	Nolan Ryan	1.00
28	Howard Johnson	.25
29	Dave Justice	.30
30	Danny Tartabull	.25

1992 Post Cereal - Canadian

For the second year in a row Post Cereal of Canada issued a set of cards, this time 18 cards that were inserted in cereal boxes. The 1992 cards have a player photo on front (with airbrushed cap) and information on the reverse in both English and French. The back of the card also contains an action photo, which has a pop-up tab which when opened stands up, revealing a statistical base.

		MT
Complete Set (18):		15.00
Common Player:		.50
1	Dennis Martinez	.50
2	Benito Santiago	.50
3	Will Clark	.75
4	Ryne Sandberg	1.50
5	Tim Wallach	.50
6	Ozzie Smith	.90
7	Darryl Strawberry	.60
8	Brett Butler	.50
9	Barry Bonds	1.50
10	Roger Clemens	1.00
11	Sandy Alomar	.60
12	Cecil Fielder	.50
13	Roberto Alomar	.75
14	Kelly Gruber	.50
15	Cal Ripken, Jr.	4.00
16	Jose Canseco	.75
17	Kirby Puckett	1.50
18	Rickey Henderson	.60

1993 Post Cereal

Post Cereal issued a 30-card set in 1993 of many of the top players in the game. The Post Cereal Collectors Series features a black border which runs along the bottom and the right side of the card, with the Post symbol located in the top right-hand corner and the player's name, team and position along the bottom. Team logos have been air-brushed from the uniforms. Backs have a black background, a color player portrait photo, personal data, a career summary, 1992 and career stats, and a red strip with a white facsimile autograph.

		MT
Complete Set (30):		5.00
Common Player:		.25
1	Dave Fleming	.25
2	Will Clark	.50
3	Kirby Puckett	.85
4	Roger Clemens	.75
5	Fred McGriff	.40
6	Eric Karros	.25
7	Ken Griffey, Jr.	2.00
8	Tony Gwynn	.75
9	Cal Ripken, Jr.	1.00
10	Cecil Fielder	.25
11	Gary Sheffield	.30
12	Don Mattingly	.85
13	Ryne Sandberg	.60
14	Frank Thomas	1.00
15	Barry Bonds	.90
16	Paul Molitor	.50
17	Terry Pendleton	.25
18	Darren Daulton	.25
19	Mark McGwire	2.00
20	Nolan Ryan	1.00
21	Tom Glavine	.30
22	Roberto Alomar	.40
23	Juan Gonzalez	.75
24	Bobby Bonilla	.30
25	George Brett	.80
26	Ozzie Smith	.60
27	Andy Van Slyke	.25
28	Barry Larkin	.25
29	John Kruk	.25
30	Robin Yount	.50

1993 Post Cereal - Canadian

For the third consecutive year, Post Canada produced a set of cards of Major League players. The 1993 set of 18 cards features a two-sided card with one side containing a special pop-up feature, much the same as their 1992 offering. There are 18 black-bordered and gold-lettered cards in the set. The cards were available in specially-marked boxes of cereal.

		MT
Complete Set (18):		15.00
Common Player:		.50
1	Pat Borders	.50
2	Juan Guzman	.50
3	Roger Clemens	1.00
4	Joe Carter	.50
5	Roberto Alomar	.75
6	Robin Yount	.75
7	Cal Ripken, Jr.	3.00
8	Kirby Puckett	1.50
9	Ken Griffey, Jr.	4.00
10	Darren Daulton	.50
11	Andy Van Slyke	.50
12	Bobby Bonilla	.50
13	Larry Walker	.65
14	Ryne Sandberg	1.00
15	Barry Larkin	.50
16	Gary Sheffield	.60
17	Ozzie Smith	.75
18	Terry Pendleton	.50

1994 Post Cereal

Post Cereal, makers of several popular, relatively large sets in the 1960s, returned to the baseball card arena in 1990, this time issuing smaller sets that concentrate on the top players in the game. In 1994, that meant a 30-card set that was issued three cards at a time in cellophane packages in Post cereals.

		MT
Complete Set (30):		4.00
Common Player:		.25
1	Mike Piazza	.75
2	Don Mattingly	.60
3	Juan Gonzalez	.65
4	Kirby Puckett	.65
5	Gary Sheffield	.35
6	David Justice	.35
7	Jack McDowell	.25
8	Mo Vaughn	.35
9	Darren Daulton	.25
10	Bobby Bonilla	.25
11	Barry Bonds	.55
12	Barry Larkin	.25
13	Tony Gwynn	.65
14	Mark Grace	.35
15	Ken Griffey, Jr.	1.00
16	Tom Glavine	.25
17	Cecil Fielder	.25
18	Roberto Alomar	.35
19	Mark Whiten	.25
20	Lenny Dykstra	.25
21	Frank Thomas	.80
22	Will Clark	.35
23	Andres Galarraga	.25
24	John Olerud	.25
25	Cal Ripken, Jr.	.80
26	Tim Salmon	.25
27	Albert Belle	.50
28	Gregg Jefferies	.25
29	Jeff Bagwell	.55
30	Orlando Merced	.25

1994 Post Cereal - Canadian

The emphasis was on Expos and Blue Jays players in the 1994 Post cereal cards issued in Canada. Several of the cards featured gold-foil stamping on the fronts. Like all contemporary Post cards, the uniform logos were airbrushed from the photos due to lack of licensing from Major League Baseball.

		MT
Complete Set (18):		12.00
Common Player:		.25
1	Joe Carter	1.00
2	Paul Molitor	.60
3	Roberto Alomar	.65
4	John Olerud	.25
5	Dave Stewart	.25
6	Juan Guzman	.25
7	Pat Borders	.25
8	Larry Walker	.60
9	Moises Alou	.35
10	Ken Griffey, Jr.	2.50
11	Barry Bonds	.75
12	Frank Thomas	1.50
13	Cal Ripken, Jr.	2.00
14	Mike Piazza	1.25
15	Juan Gonzalez	.75
16	Lenny Dykstra	.25
17	David Justice	.40
18	Kirby Puckett	.65

1995 Post Cereal

The 1995 Post Collector Series differs dramatically in format from the company's recent cereal-box insert issues. Each card measures 5" x 3-1/2" and is vertically scored at center to allow it to be folded. When folded, the front has a player action photo against a blue marbled background. On back is another photo, with career stats and highlights and a yellow facsimile autograph. In the center of the folded piece is a large game-action photo. All pictures have had the team logos removed for lack of a license by MLB. The cards are licensed by the players' association. Complete sets of the '95 Post cards were available in a special cardboard display folder. Large quantities of the set made their way into dealer hands by 1998, and the value plummeted.

		MT
Complete Set (18):		5.00
Common Player:		.15
1	Wade Boggs	.25
2	Jeff Bagwell	.40
3	Greg Maddux	.50
4	Ken Griffey Jr.	1.50
5	Roberto Alomar	.25
6	Kirby Puckett	.30
7	Tony Gwynn	.45
8	Cal Ripken Jr.	1.00
9	Matt Williams	.20
10	Dave Justice	.20
11	Barry Bonds	.35
12	Mike Piazza	.50
13	Albert Belle	.25
14	Frank Thomas	.75
15	Len Dykstra	.15
16	Will Clark	.20

1995 Post Cereal - Canadian

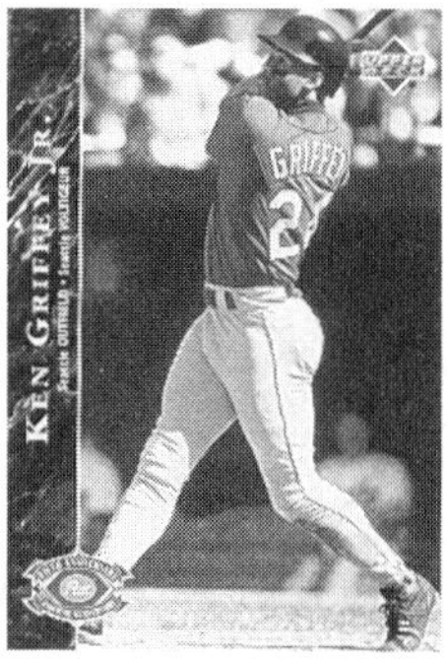

Post cereals celebrated its fifth anniversary of baseball card production for the Canadian market by switching providers to Upper Deck, and issuing a high-quality album to house the 18-card set. Cards feature color action photos that are borderless at top, bottom and right. At left is a vertical black marbled panel with the player's name, team and position. An Upper Deck logo is at top-right; a Post anniversary logo at lower-left. Because the cards are licensed by the Major League Players Association, but not Major League Baseball, team logos have been airbrushed from photos. Backs have another player photo plus bi-lingual biographical data, career highlights and stats for the previous five seasons and lifetime. A ghost image of the front photo appears under the typography. As might be expected, the set's roster is especially rich in Expos and Blue Jays players.

		MT
Complete Set (18):		18.00
Common Player:		.50
Album:		6.00
1	Ken Griffey Jr.	4.00
2	Roberto Alomar	.75
3	Paul Molitor	1.00
4	Devon White	.50
5	Moises Alou	.70
6	Ken Hill	.50
7	Paul O'Neill	.50
8	Joe Carter	.50
9	Kirby Puckett	1.00
10	Jimmy Key	.50
11	Frank Thomas	3.00
12	David Cone	.50
13	Tony Gwynn	1.50
14	Matt Williams	.60
15	Jeff Bagwell	1.50
16	Greg Maddux	2.00
17	Barry Bonds	1.00
18	Cal Ripken Jr.	3.50

1985 P.R.E. Pete Rose Set

This 120-card set traces the career of Pete Rose through the 1985 season, following his quest for baseball's all-time hit record. Cards feature many photos used on earlier Topps cards. Each card, and the box in which they were sold, says the set was "Designed by Topps Chewing Gum Inc." The set was distributed within the hobby by Renata Galasso and the copyright-holder is identified as "P.R.E." (Pete Rose Enterprises?). Besides the Topps photos, the cards include a number of original paintings by Ron Lewis, a few family-album type photos and some game-action shots of career highlights. Backs of the first three cards offer complete minor and major league stats through 1985. Cards #4-90 have a question and answer format on back and the final 30 cards in the set have a puzzle-back depicting many of Rose's Topps cards in full color. Single cards from the set are seldom offered in the market. A borderless version of card #1 was issued in ab=n edition of 1,000, all cards being autographed.

		MT
Complete Set (120):		9.00
Single Card:		.25
1-120	Pete Rose	
1a	Pete Rose (autographed promo card)	300.00

1998 Premier Concepts Premier Replays

Large, clear motion technology is featured on these plaques. The 7" x 5" image area is set in an 8" x 6-1/2" black plastic frame, which can be rested on an easel included in the suggested $6 retail package. When the angle of view is changed, the player or players go into action and the name (s) alternate with licensors' logos along the bottom. The unnumbered plaques are listed here alphabetically.

		MT
Complete Set (18):		100.00
Common Player:		6.00
	SINGLE-PLAYER PLAQUES	
(1)	Jeff Bagwell	6.00
(2)	Barry Bonds	6.00
(3)	Nomar Garciaparra	6.00
(4)	Ken Griffey Jr. (batting)	7.50
(5)	Ken Griffey Jr. (fielding)	7.50
(6)	Tony Gwynn	6.00
(7)	Chipper Jones	7.00
(8)	Mike Piazza	7.00
(9)	Cal Ripken Jr.	7.00
(10)	Alex Rodriguez	7.00
(11)	Frank Thomas	7.00
(12)	Larry Walker	6.00
	DUAL-PLAYER PLAQUES	
(1)	Sandy Alomar, Omar Vizquel	6.00
(2)	Brady Anderson, Mike Mussina	6.00
(3)	Juan Gonzalez, Ivan Rodriguez	6.00
(4)	Livan Hernandez, Charles Johnson	6.00
(5)	Derek Jeter, Andy Pettitte	6.00
(6)	David Justice, Jim Thome	6.00
(7)	Ray Lankford, Mark McGwire	7.00
(8)	Tino Martinez, Bernie Williams	6.00

1995 Premier Mint Gold Signature Cards

Some of baseball's top stars of the present and past are honored in this series of 22-karat gold embossed cards. A color player photo with a gold facsimile autograph superimposed is wed to the embossed background which includes baseball designs, biographical data and career stats and highlights. Each card is serial numbered within an edition of 25,000 and comes boxed with a like-numbered certificate of authenticity.

		MT
Complete Set (4):		160.00
Common Player:		40.00
(1)	Roberto Clemente	40.00
(2)	Ken Griffey Jr.	40.00
(3)	Cal Ripken Jr.	40.00
(4)	Nolan Ryan	40.00

1990s Pro Athletes Outreach Folders

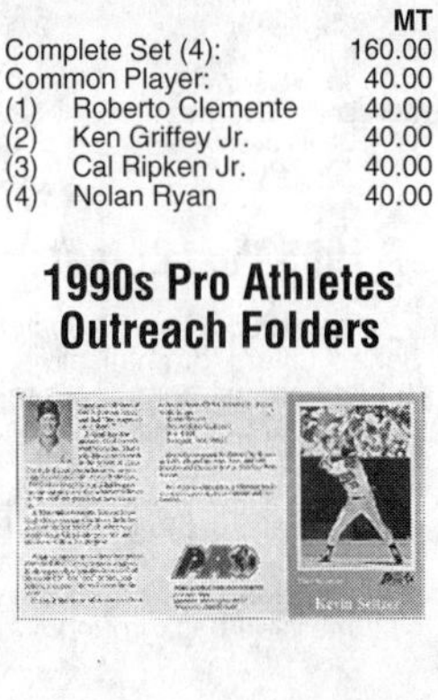

Testifying to their Christian beliefs, a number of professional athletes are featured in an on-going series of folders. Several formats are seen, including double- and triple-folders. When folded, the pieces are the same size as current sportscards, 2-1/2" x 3-1/2". Fronts have color player photos, inside pages have a personal message and the back page has details for contacting the PAO group. It is likely this list is not complete.

	MT
Blas Minor (Mets)	2.00
Kevin Seitzer (Royals)	2.00

1999 ProCom Champion Phone Cards

This series of $10 phone cards is printed on a styrene 4" x 7-1/4" plastic carrier from which it can be removed via the die-cutting around the approximately 2-1/2" x 3-1/2" central area. Fronts have action photos with player identification, facsimile autograph, team, licensor and issuer logos. Backs have instructions for use of the card and a dot-matrix card number. Two poses each exist for several of the players in the series. The unnumbered cards are listed here in alphabetical order. Cards phone use expired in Dec., 2000.

		MT
Complete Set (18):		175.00
Common Player:		10.00
(1)	Roberto Alomar	10.00
(2)	Roger Clemens	10.00
(3)	Luis Gonzalez	10.00
(4)	Mark Grace	10.00
(5)	Ken Griffey Jr.	10.00
(6)	Ken Griffey Jr.	10.00
(7)	Derek Jeter	10.00
(8)	Derek Jeter	10.00
(9)	Randy Johnson	10.00
(10)	Pedro Martinez	10.00
(11)	Pedro Martinez	10.00
(12)	Mark McGwire	10.00
(13)	Mark McGwire	10.00
(14)	Manny Ramirez	10.00
(15)	Manny Ramirez	10.00
(16)	Sammy Sosa	10.00
(17)	Sammy Sosa	10.00
(18)	Frank Thomas	10.00

1992 Pro File National Convention Promos

To promote its collectors' magazine at the 1992 National Sports Collectors Convention in Atlanta, Pro File issued this set of collectors' cards. Fronts of the standard-size cards have a color photo in a central oval on a prismatic foil background. A strip at top announces "Premier Edition," while a blue ribbon at bottom carries "Pro File". Backs have a large color logo of the Atlanta National, advertising for Profiles in Sports magazine and promotional card status notices. The players are identified nowhere on the cards.

		MT
Complete Set (12):		6.00
Common Player:		.25
1	Frank Thomas (white jersey)	1.00
2	Mark McGwire	2.00
3	David Justice	.35
4	Brien Taylor (portrait)	.25
5	Cal Ripken Jr. (portrait)	1.00
6	Frank Thomas (black jersey)	1.00
7	Ivan Rodriguez	.50
8	Deion Sanders	.35
9	Nolan Ryan	1.00
10	Mickey Mantle	2.00
11	Brien Taylor (w/trophy)	.25
12	Cal Ripken Jr. (batting)	1.00

1992 Pro Line Portraits Team NFL

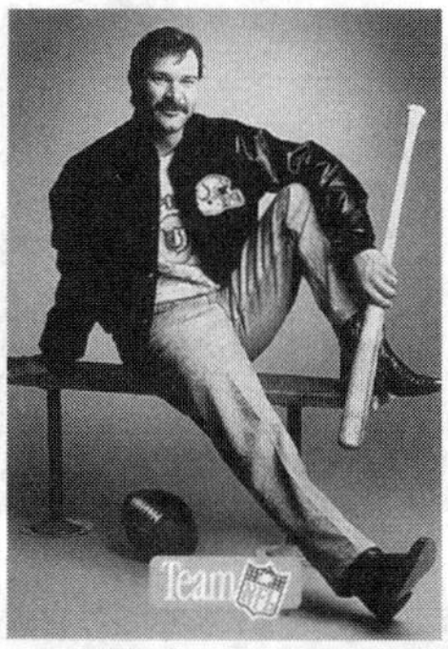

One of five celebrity cards inserted into the 1992 Pro Line Portraits football card issue was Yankees first baseman Don Mattingly, who is pictured on the card in licensed apparel of the Indianapolis Colts. The card back has a quote from Mattingly about his high school football career and his choice of pro baseball.

		MT
3	Don Mattingly	3.00

1996 Pro Magnets

Large team logos on silver metallic foil are the background for the action player photos in this set of card-like magnets. At right is a color strip with the team nickname printed vertically. The player name is in gold foil. Backs of the 2-1/8" x 3-3/8" magnets are, of course, blank.

		MT
Complete Set (94):		27.50
Common Player:		.25
1	Fred McGriff	.50
2	Ryan Klesko	.50
3	David Justice	.50
4	Greg Maddux	.90
5	Jamie Navarro	.25
6	Shawon Dunston	.25
7	Brian McRae	.25
8	Barry Larkin	.25
9	Reggie Sanders	.25
10	Benito Santiago	.25
11	Dante Bichette	.25
12	Vinny Castilla	.25
13	Andres Galarraga	.35
14	Larry Walker	.50
15	Gary Sheffield	.50
16	Jeff Conine	.25
17	Terry Pendleton	.25
18	Jeff Bagwell	1.00
19	Doug Drabek	.25
20	Shane Reynolds	.25
21	Mike Piazza	2.50
22	Delino DeShields	.25
23	Hideo Nomo	.65
24	Wil Cordero	.25
25	Pedro Martinez	1.00
26	Todd Hundley	.25
27	Jose Vizcaino	.25
28	Jim Eisenreich	.25
29	Gregg Jefferies	.25
30	Darren Daulton	.25
31	Orlando Merced	.25
32	Carlos Garcia	.25
33	Jay Bell	.25
34	Brian Jordan	.25
35	Ray Lankford	.25
36	Tom Pagnozzi	.25
37	Ozzie Smith	1.00
38	Tony Gwynn	1.00
39	Andujar Cedeno	.25
40	Andy Ashby	.25
41	Matt Williams	.50
42	Barry Bonds	1.50
43	Deion Sanders	.50
44	Cal Ripken Jr.	3.00
45	Bobby Bonilla	.25
46	Mike Mussina	.35
47	Rafael Palmeiro	.45
48	Mo Vaughn	.50
49	Jose Canseco	.75
50	Mike Greenwell	.25
51	Tim Salmon	.25
52	J.T. Snow	.25
53	Brian Anderson	.25
54	Frank Thomas	2.50
55	Ozzie Guillen	.25
56	Robin Ventura	.25
57	Ron Karkovice	.25
58	Kenny Lofton	.40
59	Albert Belle	1.00
60	Eddie Murray	1.00
61	Manny Ramirez	1.00
62	Charles Nagy	.25
63	Travis Fryman	.25
64	Alan Trammell	.50
65	Cecil Fielder	.25
66	Jon Nunnally	.25
67	Kevin Appier	.25
68	Kevin Seitzer	.25
69	Pat Listach	.25
70	John Jaha	.25
71	Chuck Knoblauch	.35
72	Kirby Puckett	1.00
73	Marty Cordova	.25
74	Wade Boggs	1.00
75	Jimmy Key	.25
76	Paul O'Neill	.25
77	David Cone	.35
78	Mark McGwire	3.00
79	Terry Steinbach	.25
80	Danny Tartabull	.25
81	Randy Johnson	1.00
82	Ken Griffey Jr.	4.00
83	Jay Buhner	.25
84	Edgar Martinez	.25
85	Alex Rodriguez	3.00
86	Will Clark	.45
87	Juan Gonzalez	1.00
88	Ivan Rodriguez	.50
89	Benji Gil	.25
90	Roberto Alomar	.35
91	Pat Hentgen	.25
92	Joe Carter	.25

93	John Olerud	.25
94	Carlos Delgado	.25

1996 Pro Magnets All-Stars

Sets of American and National League All-Star magnets were produced by Chris Martin Enterprises. The 2-1/8" x 3-3/8" magnets were sold in 10-player league sets with a league logo magnet and a header magnet. Player magnets have a color action photo on a black-and-gold background of the appropriate league's logo. The league logo appears in color in the lower-left corner, while the Philadelphia All-Star Game logo and those of the licensors appear at lower-right. The player name appears in silver vertically up one side, and issuer's logo is at top-right. Magnets are numbered in the lower-left corner, except Ken Griffey, Jr., which has no number. Production was reportedly 1,000 sets.

		MT
Complete Set (24):		50.00
Common Player:		2.00
	American League team set:	30.00
---	All-Star Game logo	1.00
---	American League logo	1.00
01	Brady Anderson	3.00
02	Jose Canseco	4.00
(03)	Ken Griffey Jr.	9.00
04	Kenny Lofton	3.00
05	Cal Ripken Jr.	8.00
06	Frank Thomas	7.50
07	Ivan Rodriguez	5.00
08	Mo Vaughn	2.00
09	Albert Belle	3.00
10	Alex Rodriguez	7.50
	National League team set:	30.00
---	All-Star Game logo	1.00
---	National League logo	1.00
11	Hideo Nomo	3.00
12	Greg Maddux	6.00
13	Jeff Bagwell	5.00
14	Barry Bonds	5.00
15	Ryan Klesko	3.00
16	Mike Piazza	6.00
17	Dave Justice	3.00
18	Dante Bichette	3.00
19	Barry Larkin	2.00
20	Tony Gwynn	5.00

1994 Pro Mint

These embossed 22 karat gold cards were produced in an edition of 50,000 each, with each card being serially numbered on the back. Because the cards are licensed only by the players' association and not Major League baseball, player pictures do not include uniform logos. Backs have a few vital statistics, a ballpark diagram and career highlights. Each card was also produced in a "Diamond Series" edition of 25,000, featuring a small (5 pt.) sparkler embedded on the card front.

		MT
Complete Set (11):		250.00
Common Player:		17.50
Diamond Series: Value 3X regular edition		
(1)	Jeff Bagwell	17.50
(2)	Barry Bonds	17.50
(3)	George Brett	17.50
(4)	Roger Clemens	17.50
(5)	Ken Griffey, Jr.	17.50
(6)	Mike Piazza	17.50
(7)	Kirby Puckett	17.50
(8)	Babe Ruth	17.50
(9)	Nolan Ryan	24.00
(10)	Nolan Ryan (double card, yellow/white gold)	35.00
(11)	Frank Thomas	17.50

1995 Pro Mint

Pro Mint continued its line of 22-karat gold-plated cards into 1995. The 2-1/2" x 3-1/2" cards feature embossed player pictures on front in generic uniforms (due to lack of a license from Major League Baseball). Backs have a ballpark diagram with a few vital stats and career highlights, along with a serial number from an announced edition of 50,000 of each card. Card numbers are in the upper-right corner.

		MT
Complete Set (7):		120.00
Common Player:		17.50
(1)	Albert Belle	17.50
(2)	Greg Maddux	17.50
(3)	Don Mattingly	17.50
(4)	Hideo Nomo	17.50
(5)	Cal Ripken Jr.	17.50
(6)	Deion Sanders	17.50
(7)	Ozzie Smith	17.50

1996 Pro Mint

Production of the basic 22-karat gold embossed version Pro Mint cards was dropped to 25,000 for the 1996 issues. Another 10,000 cards were made with a 5-pt. diamond embedded in the card front. The 2-1/2" x 3-1/2" cards feature players in generic uniforms as the issue is licensed only by the individual players, and not Major League Baseball, which controls the rights to uniform logos.

		MT
Complete Set, Gold (3):		45.00
Complete Set, Diamond (3):		90.00
Common Player, Gold:		17.50
Common Player, Diamond:		45.00
(1g)	Mark McGwire (gold)	17.50
(1d)	Mark McGwire (diamond)	45.00
(2g)	Ryne Sandberg (gold)	20.00
(2d)	Ryne Sandberg (diamond)	45.00
(3g)	Mo Vaughn (gold)	20.00
(3d)	Mo Vaughn (diamond)	45.00

1996 Pro Mint Diamond Edition

A specially marked promo version of old and new Pro Mint cards was created in an edition of 1,000 each. Besides the 22K gold embossed front and back, each card has a 5-pt. diamond embedded in the card front. The 2-1/2" x 3-1/2" cards feature players in generic uniforms as the issue is licensed only by the individual players, and not Major League Baseball, which controls the rights to uniform logos.

		MT
Complete Set (10):		600.00
Common Player:		60.00
(1)	Barry Bonds	60.00
(2)	George Brett	60.00
(3)	Ken Griffey Jr.	75.00
(4)	Tony Gwynn	60.00
(5)	Don Mattingly	60.00
(6)	Mike Piazza	65.00
(7)	Kirby Puckett	60.00
(8)	Nolan Ryan	70.00
(9)	Ozzie Smith	60.00
(10)	Frank Thomas	70.00

1986 Provigo Expos

This 28-card set was issued in three-card panels of 7-1/2" x 3-3/8". Each card measures 2-1/2" x 3-3/8", and each panel includes two players and an advertising card. Panels are perforated to allow for separation, if desired. Card fronts have high quality game-action color photos with the player's name, uniform number and Expos and Provigo logos. Card backs include biographical information in both French and English and list the card's number within the set. There are 24 player, one manager and two coaches cards, along with a card of the Expos mascot, Youppi.

		MT
Complete Panel Set:		10.00
Complete Singles Set:		4.00
Common Panel:		.35
Common Single Player:		.15
Panel 1		.35
1	Hubie Brooks	.15
2	Dann Bilardello	.15
----	Checklist	.03
Panel 2		.35
3	Buck Rodgers	.15
4	Andy McGaffigan	.15
----	Album Offer	.03
Panel 3		.35
5	Mitch Webster	.15
6	Jim Wohlford	.15
----	Album Offer	.03
Panel 4		2.00
7	Tim Raines	.65
8	Jay Tibbs	.15
----	Album Offer	.03
Panel 5		2.00
9	Andre Dawson	1.00
10	Andres Galarraga	1.00
----	Album Offer	.03
Panel 6		.60
11	Tim Wallach	.25
12	Dan Schatzeder	.15
----	Checklist	.03
Panel 7		.50
13	Jeff Reardon	.25
14	Expos' Coaching Staff (Larry Bearnarth, Joe Kerrigan, Bobby Winkles)	.15
----	Album Offer	.03
Panel 8		.35
15	Jason Thompson	.15
16	Bert Roberge	.15
----	$1 Expos Ticket Coupon	.03
Panel 9		.35
17	Al Newman	.15
18	Tim Burke	.15
----	Album Offer	.03
Panel 10		.35
19	Bryn Smith	.15
20	Wayne Krenchicki	.15
----	Album Offer	.03
Panel 11		.35
21	Joe Hesketh	.15
22	Herman Winningham	.15
----	Album Offer	.03
Panel 12		.35
23	Vance Law	.15
24	Floyd Youmans	.15
----	Album Offer	.03
Panel 13		.35
25	Jeff Parrett	.15
26	Mike Fitzgerald	.15
----	Album Offer	.03
Panel 14		.35
27	Youppi (mascot)	.15
28	Expos' Coaching Staff (Ron Hansen, Ken Macha, Rick Renick)	.15
----	Album Offer	.03

1986 Provigo Expos Posters

This Provigo issue is much scarcer than the smaller card panels issued the same year. These posters measure about 9" x 14-7/8". A large (9" x 12-1/2") player portrait is separated from a bottom coupon panel. Backs are blank and can be found in red, white or blue. The player pictures have facsimile autographs and a white strip at bottom with identification, uniform number, team and sponsor logos and card number. Values shown are for complete poster/coupon combinations.

		MT
Complete Set (12):		25.00
Common Player:		2.00
1	Tim Raines	5.00
2	Bryn Smith	2.00
3	Hubie Brooks	2.50
4	Buck Rodgers	2.00
5	Mitch Webster	2.00
6	Joe Hesketh	2.00
7	Mike Fitzgerald	2.00
8	Andy McGaffigan	2.00
9	Andre Dawson	7.50
10	Tim Wallach	3.00
11	Jeff Reardon	2.50
12	Vance Law	2.00

1994 PruCare N.Y. Mets

Top names on the 1994 Mets are featured in this issue sponsored by PruCare, a division of Prudential Insurance, whose logo appears on front and back. Cards were issued in a nine-card panel, perforated for easy separation. Individual cards are 2-1/2" x 3-1/2". Fronts have color action photos surrounded by team-color frames and white borders. Backs are printed in orange and blue with personal data, 1993 stats and highlights and career major league stats. The unnumbered cards are checklisted here in alphabetical order.

		MT
Complete Sheet:		7.50
Complete Set (9):		5.00
Common Player:		.50
(1)	Bobby Bonilla	.75
(2)	Jeromy Burnitz	.65
(3)	John Franco	.50
(4)	Dwight Gooden	.60
(5)	Bud Harrelson	.50
(6)	Jeff Kent	.65
(7)	Kevin McReynolds	.50
(8)	Ryan Thompson	.50
(9)	Mookie Wilson	.50

1990 Publications Int'l Hottest Players Stickers

Established major league stars are featured in this set of large format (4-1/8" x 5-7/16") blank-back stickers. The stickers are printed four per sheet and were sold with a 36-page album for mounting. The album has player data, stats and highlights for each of the stars. Stickers have color action photos with a white frame at center. There is a red stripe at top of the frame and a blue stripe at bottom, which contains the player name. The unnumbered stickers are checklisted here in alphabetical order.

		MT
Complete Set, w/Album (56):		4.00
Common Player:		.05
(1)	George Bell	.05
(2)	Wade Boggs	.15
(3)	Bobby Bonilla	.10
(4)	Jose Canseco	.20
(5)	Joe Carter	.05
(6)	Will Clark	.20
(7)	Roger Clemens	.25
(8)	Alvin Davis	.05
(9)	Eric Davis	.05
(10)	Glenn Davis	.05
(11)	Mark Davis	.05
(12)	Carlton Fisk	.20
(13)	John Franco	.05
(14)	Gary Gaetti	.05
(15)	Andres Galarraga	.05
(16)	Dwight Gooden	.10
(17)	Mark Grace	.20
(18)	Pedro Guerrero	.05
(19)	Tony Gwynn	.35
(20)	Rickey Henderson	.15
(21)	Orel Hershiser	.05
(22)	Bo Jackson	.05
(23)	Ricky Jordan	.05
(24)	Wally Joyner	.05
(25)	Don Mattingly	.35
(26)	Fred McGriff	.10
(27)	Kevin Mitchell	.05
(28)	Paul Molitor	.25
(29)	Dale Murphy	.10
(30)	Eddie Murray	.15
(31)	Kirby Puckett	.40
(32)	Tim Raines	.05
(33)	Harold Reynolds	.05
(34)	Cal Ripken Jr.	.50
(35)	Nolan Ryan	.50
(36)	Bret Saberhagen	.05
(37)	Ryne Sandberg	.35
(38)	Steve Sax	.05
(39)	Mike Scott	.05
(40)	Ruben Sierra	.05
(41)	Ozzie Smith	.20
(42)	John Smoltz	.05
(43)	Darryl Strawberry	.05
(44)	Greg Swindell	.05
(45)	Mickey Tettleton	.05
(46)	Alan Trammell	.05
(47)	Andy Van Slyke	.05
(48)	Lou Whitaker	.05
(49)	Devon White	.05
(50)	Robin Yount	.25
(51)	Dodger Stadium	.05
(52)	Jack Murphy Stadium	.05
(53)	Shea Stadium	.05
(54)	Three Rivers Stadium	.05
(55)	Tiger Stadium	.05
(56)	Yankee Stadium	.05

1990 Publications Int'l Hottest Rookies Stickers

This set of large-format (4-1/8" x 5-7/16") stickers features the rookie crop of 1990 along with other young players who were not technically rookies in 1990. The stickers were sold four per sheet in complete sets which included a 36-page color album to mount the stamps. The album pages have personal data, career stats and highlights about each player. On the stickers, each action photo has a central frame in white with a blue stripe at top and a red stripe at bottom bearing the player name. Backs are, of course, blank. The set is checklisted here alphabetically.

		MT
Complete Set, w/Album (56):		4.00
Common Player:		.05
(1)	Jim Abbott	.05
(2)	Sandy Alomar	.15
(3)	Kent Anderson	.05
(4)	Eric Anthony	.05
(5)	Jeff Ballard	.05
(6)	Joey Belle	.50
(7)	Andy Benes	.10
(8)	Lance Blankenship	.05
(9)	Jeff Brantley	.05
(10)	Cris Carpenter	.05
(11)	Mark Carreon	.05
(12)	Dennis Cook	.05
(13)	Scott Coolbaugh	.05
(14)	Luis de los Santos	.05
(15)	Junior Felix	.05
(16)	Mark Gardner	.05
(17)	German Gonzalez	.05
(18)	Tom Gordon	.05
(19)	Ken Griffey Jr.	1.00
(20)	Marquis Grissom	.10
(21)	Charlie Hayes	.05
(22)	Gregg Jefferies	.15
(23)	Randy Johnson	.25
(24)	Felix Jose	.05
(25)	Jeff King	.05
(26)	Randy Kramer	.05
(27)	Derek Lilliquist	.05
(28)	Greg Litton	.05
(29)	Kelly Mann	.05
(30)	Ramon Martinez	.10
(31)	Luis Medina	.05
(32)	Hal Morris	.10
(33)	Joe Oliver	.05
(34)	Gregg Olson	.05
(35)	Dean Palmer	.10
(36)	Carlos Quintana	.05
(37)	Kevin Ritz	.05
(38)	Deion Sanders	.25
(39)	Scott Scudder	.05
(40)	Steve Searcy	.05
(41)	Gary Sheffield	.25
(42)	Dwight Smith	.05
(43)	Sam Sosa	.75
(44)	Greg Vaughn	.10
(45)	Robin Ventura	.10
(46)	Jerome Walton	.05
(47)	Dave West	.05
(48)	John Wetteland	.05
(49)	Eric Yelding	.05
(50)	Todd Zeile	.05
(51)	Dodger Stadium	.05
(52)	Jack Murphy Stadium	.05
(53)	Shea Stadium	.05
(54)	Three Rivers Stadium	.05
(55)	Tiger Stadium	.05
(56)	Yankee Stadium	.05

Q

1986 Quaker Oats

The Quaker Company, in conjunction with Topps, produced this 33-card set of current baseball stars for packaging in groups of three in Chewy Granola Bars packages. The cards are noted as the "1st Annual Collectors Edition." They are numbered and measure 2-1/2" x 3-1/2". Card fronts feature full-color player photos with the product name at the top and the player name, team and position below the photo. The complete set was offered via mail order by the Quaker Company.

		MT
Complete Set (33):		6.00
Common Player:		.15
1	Willie McGee	.15
2	Dwight Gooden	.20
3	Vince Coleman	.15
4	Gary Carter	.25
5	Jack Clark	.15
6	Steve Garvey	.25
7	Tony Gwynn	.85
8	Dale Murphy	.35
9	Dave Parker	.15
10	Tim Raines	.20
11	Pete Rose	1.00
12	Nolan Ryan	2.00
13	Ryne Sandberg	.80
14	Mike Schmidt	.80
15	Ozzie Smith	.50
16	Darryl Strawberry	.20
17	Fernando Valenzuela	.20
18	Don Mattingly	.90
19	Bret Saberhagen	.15
20	Ozzie Guillen	.15
21	Bert Blyleven	.15
22	Wade Boggs	.50
23	George Brett	.80
24	Darrell Evans	.15
25	Rickey Henderson	.35
26	Reggie Jackson	.40
27	Eddie Murray	.40
28	Phil Niekro	.25
29	Dan Quisenberry	.15
30	Jim Rice	.15
31	Cal Ripken, Jr.	2.00
32	Tom Seaver	.50
33	Dave Winfield	.35
----	Offer Card	.03

1993 Quintex Pittsbugh Pirates

(See 1993 Nationwide/Quintex Pirates for checklist and values.)

1994 Quintex Pittsburgh Pirates

(See Nationwide/Quintex Pirates for checklist, values.)

Many modern-section card sets are listed under the manufacturer which produced them, rather than the sponsor, such as 1990 Score McDonald's, found under 1990 Score.

R

1997 R & N China Co. Keeper Series

R & N China Co. produces licensed porcelain versions of baseball cards for sale to collectors. The Keepers Series is an edition of star players' Topps rookie cards done on a platinum-plated porcelain blank which measures 2-1/2" x 3-1/2" and has rounded corners. The Keepers were marketed by Hobby Editions in a heavy plastic holder and leather-look and felt display box. Each Keepers card comes with a numbered certificate of authenticity specifying the card's place from an edition of 500. The number is also inked on the back of the card. A scratch-off ticket with each card gave buyer's the opportunity to win a porcelain version of one of Mickey Mantle's Topps cards. Original retail price for the Keeper Series cards was about $30.

		MT
Complete Set (7):		200.00
Common Player:		30.00
(1)	Ken Griffey Jr. (1989 #41T)	30.00
(2)	Derek Jeter (1993 #98)	30.00
(3)	Andruw Jones (1997 #455)	30.00
(4)	Kirby Puckett (1985 #536)	30.00
(5)	Cal Ripken Jr. (1982 #98T)	30.00
(6)	Jackie Robinson (1952 #312)	30.00
(7)	Frank Thomas (1990 #414)	30.00

1997 R & N China Co. Vintage Keeper Series

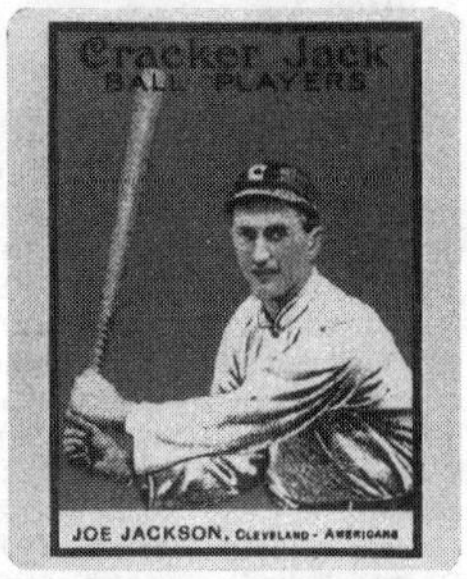

Top stars from the 1914 Cracker Jack set were produced by R & N China Co., and marketed by Hobby Editions as Vintage Keepers. Fronts and backs are authentically recreated on a round-cornered 2-3/8" x 2-7/8" platinum-plated porcelain blank. Each of the Vintage Keepers cards is numbered on back from within an edition of 150. The porcelain collectors issues are sold in a leather-look and velvet box with a numbered certificate of authenticity and a scratch-off card for a chance to win one of 120 T-206 Honus Wagner porcelain replicas. Issue price was about $30.

		MT
Complete Set (8):		225.00
Common Player:		30.00
30	Ty Cobb	30.00
37	Grover Alexander	30.00
57	Walter Johnson	30.00
65	Tris Speaker	30.00
66	Nap Lajoie	30.00
68	Honus Wagner	30.00
88	Christy Mathewson	30.00
103	Joe Jackson	30.00

1993 Rainbow Foods Dave Winfield

Dave Winfield's return to Minnesota where he excelled in college sports was marked by the "Homecoming Collection," tracing the future Hall of Famer's career. Standard-size 2-1/2" x 3-1/2" cards have black-and-white or color photos on front and back. Each side also sports a special logo idetifying the issue. Rainbow's logo appears on front, while that of a major food brand such as Kraft or Oscar Meyer appear on back, along with information about Winfield's career. Cards were sold in five-card packs with four blue-bordered cards and one gold-bordered parallel card.

		MT
Complete Set, Blue (10):		10.00
Common Player, Blue:		1.50
Gold: 2X-3X		
1	Dave Winfield (University of Minnesota Outfielder)	1.50
2	Dave Winfield (University of Minnesota Pitcher)	1.50
3	Dave Winfield (University of Minnesota Basketball Star)	1.50
4	Dave Winfield (San Diego Padres 1973-1980)	1.50
5	Dave Winfield (N.Y. Yankees 1981-1990)	1.50
6	Dave Winfield (California Angels 1990-1991)	1.50
7	Dave Winfield (Toronto Blue Jays 1992)	1.50
8	Dave Winfield (Minnesota Twins 1993-)	1.50
9	Dave Winfield (7-time Gold Glove Winner)	1.50
10	Dave Winfield (Pride of Minnesota)	1.50

1989 Rainier Farms Super Stars Discs

This set is one of the scarcer late-1980s disc issues produced by Michael Schechter Associates for various local businesses. The bakery began distribution of the discs by placing them directly in the cello wrapper with a loaf of bread. This resulted in those cards being severely grease stained and often creased. It also resulted in problems with public health officials who halted the distribution. Since the bakery could not economically and sanitarily package the cards they dropped the promotion and sold the remainder cards into the hobby. Discs measure 2-3/4" in diameter and have a color player photo (with team logos airbrushed away) at center with a white border. A Rainier Farms Homestyle logo is at top in red and black. Backs are printed in dark blue and feature a few stats, biographical details and a card number.

		MT
Complete Set (20):		40.00
Common Player:		1.50
1	Wally Joyner	1.50
2	Wade Boggs	4.00
3	Ozzie Smith	3.50
4	Don Mattingly	6.00
5	Jose Canseco	4.00
6	Tony Gwynn	4.50
7	Eric Davis	1.50
8	Kirby Puckett	4.50
9	Kevin Seitzer	1.50
10	Darryl Strawberry	1.50
11	Gregg Jefferies	1.50
12	Mark Grace	2.50
13	Matt Nokes	1.50
14	Mark McGwire	10.00
15	Bobby Bonilla	1.50
16	Roger Clemens	4.00
17	Frank Viola	1.50
18	Orel Hershiser	1.50
19	Dave Cone	1.50
20	Kirk Gibson	1.50

1984 Ralston Purina

This set, produced in conjunction with Topps, has 33 of the game's top players. Photos on the 2-1/2" x 3-1/2" cards are all close-up poses. Topps' logo appears only on the card fronts, and the backs are completely different from Topps' regular issue of 1984. Card backs feature a checkerboard look, coinciding with the well-known Ralston Purina logo. Cards are numbered 1-33, with odd numbers for American Leaguers and even numbered cards for National Leaguers. Four cards were packed in boxes of Cookie Crisp and Donkey Kong Junior brand cereals, and the complete set was available via a mail-in offer in panel form.

		MT
Complete Set, Singles (33):		7.00
Complete Set, Panel		5.00
Common Player:		.15
1	Eddie Murray	.40
2	Ozzie Smith	.45
3	Ted Simmons	.15
4	Pete Rose	1.00
5	Greg Luzinski	.15
6	Andre Dawson	.25
7	Dave Winfield	.45
8	Tom Seaver	.50
9	Jim Rice	.25
10	Fernando Valenzuela	.15
11	Wade Boggs	.70
12	Dale Murphy	.25
13	George Brett	.90
14	Nolan Ryan	2.00
15	Rickey Henderson	.45
16	Steve Carlton	.40
17	Rod Carew	.40
18	Steve Garvey	.25
19	Reggie Jackson	.40
20	Dave Concepcion	.15
21	Robin Yount	.75
22	Mike Schmidt	.90
23	Jim Palmer	.40
24	Bruce Sutter	.15
25	Dan Quisenberry	.15
26	Bill Madlock	.15
27	Cecil Cooper	.15
28	Gary Carter	.25
29	Fred Lynn	.15
30	Pedro Guerrero	.15
31	Ron Guidry	.15
32	Keith Hernandez	.15
33	Carlton Fisk	.40

1987 Ralston Purina

The Ralston Purina Company, in conjunction with Mike Schechter Associates, issued a 15-card set in specially marked boxes of Cookie Crisp and Honey Graham Chex cereal. Three different cards, wrapped in cellophane, were inserted in each box. The card fronts contain a full-color photo with the team insignia airbrushed away. Above the photo are two yellow crossed bats and a star, with the player's uniform number inside the star. The card backs are grey with red printing and contain the set name, card number, player's name, personal information and career major league statistics. As part of the Ralston Purina promotion, the company advertised an uncut sheet of cards which was available by finding an "instant-winner" game card or sending $1 plus two non-winning cards. Cards on the uncut sheet are identical in design to the single cards, save the omission of the words "1987 Collectors Edition" in the upper right corner. A complete uncut sheet in Mint condition is valued at $10.

		MT
Complete Set (15):		15.00
Common Player:		1.00
1	Nolan Ryan	3.00
2	Steve Garvey	1.00
3	Wade Boggs	1.50
4	Dave Winfield	1.25
5	Don Mattingly	2.00
6	Don Sutton	1.00
7	Dave Parker	1.00
8	Eddie Murray	1.00
9	Gary Carter	1.00
10	Roger Clemens	1.50
11	Fernando Valenzuela	1.00
12	Cal Ripken Jr.	3.00
13	Ozzie Smith	1.50
14	Mike Schmidt	1.50
15	Ryne Sandberg	1.50

1987 Ralston Purina Collectors' Sheet

		MT
Complete Panel Set:		10.00
Complete Singles Set (15):		3.50
Common Single Player:		.15
1	Nolan Ryan	.90
2	Steve Garvey	.20
3	Wade Boggs	.40
4	Dave Winfield	.40
5	Don Mattingly	.75
6	Don Sutton	.15
7	Dave Parker	.15
8	Eddie Murray	.30
9	Gary Carter	.15
10	Roger Clemens	.45
11	Fernando Valenzuela	.15
12	Cal Ripken Jr.	.90
13	Ozzie Smith	.40
14	Mike Schmidt	.50
15	Ryne Sandberg	.50

1989 Ralston Purina

The Ralston Purina Co., in conjunction with Mike Schechter Associates, issued a 12-card "Superstars" set in 1989. As part of a late-spring and early-summer promotion, the standard-size cards were inserted, two per box, in specially-marked boxes of Crisp Crunch, Honey Nut O's, Fruit Rings and Frosted Flakes in most parts of the country. Ads on cereal boxes also offered complete sets through a mail-in offer. The fronts of the cards feature full-color player photos flanked by stars in all four corners. "Super Stars" appears at the top; the player's name and position are at the bottom. The backs include player stats and data, the card number and copyright line. Team logos have been removed from the photos.

		MT
Complete Set (12):		6.00
Common Player:		.50
1	Ozzie Smith	1.00
2	Andre Dawson	.50
3	Darryl Strawberry	.50
4	Mike Schmidt	1.25
5	Orel Hershiser	.50
6	Tim Raines	.50
7	Roger Clemens	1.50
8	Kirby Puckett	2.00
9	George Brett	2.00
10	Alan Trammell	.50
11	Don Mattingly	2.00
12	Jose Canseco	1.25

1983 Rawlings Activewear Cards

Though the statistics on the back of these cards would point to a 1982 issue date, the wax wrapper in which they distributed with a piece of gum at sporting goods trade shows carries a 1983 date. The cards are printed with black-and-white portrait photos on front, and red graphics in the standard 2-1/2" x 3-1/2" format. Backs are printed in red and white. Featured on back are stats, personal data, career highlights and an ad for Rawlings Activewear. Cards are numbered according to players' uniform numbers.

		MT
Complete Set (3):		60.00
Common Player:		15.00
20	Bucky Dent	15.00
30	Willie Randolph	15.00
41	Tom Seaver	35.00

1983 Rawlings Activewear Hang Tags

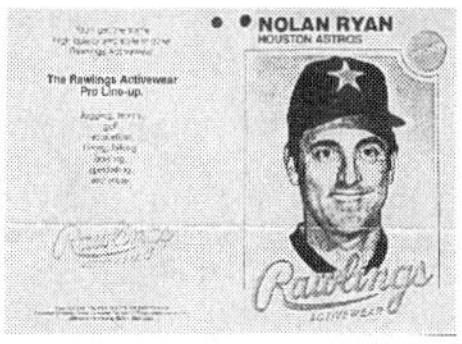

Rawlings took the concept of hang-tag cards to its line of sports clothing endorsed by Major Legue ballplayers. The cards are 2-3/4" x 3-3/4" (folded). Fronts have a color portrait photo (cap logos removed), player identification and a large Rawlings logo. Inside is a color photo of the player in leisure wear, some words of endorsement, a facsimile autograph and career data. A hole is punched in the upper-left corner to facilitate attaching the card to the clothing with which it was sold. Cards can be found with regular or glossy finish.

		MT
Complete Set (3):		125.00
Common Player:		4.00
		4.00
(1)	Bucky Dent	4.00
(2)	Willie Randolph	4.00
(3)	Nolan Ryan	125.00

1984 Rawlings Glove Hang Tags

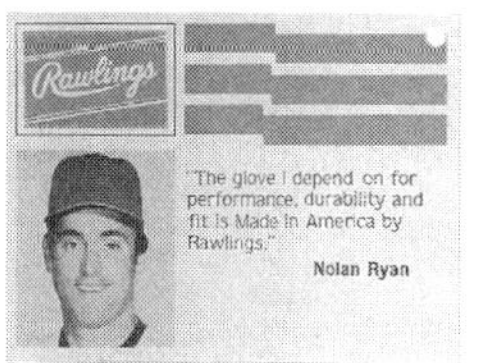

These player endorsement cards were issued attached to baseball gloves in retail outlets. The horizontal cards measure about 4" x 3". Fronts are printed in black, white and red. A player portrait photo (cap logos removed) is at left; a few words of praise for the glove are at right. A large Rawlings logo is at top. Backs are in red, white and blue and repreat the Rawlings logo. Within an outline map of the U.S.A. is printed "American-Made / For America's Best".

		MT
Complete Set (5):		65.00
Common Player:		6.00
(1)	Keith Hernandez	6.00
(2)	Lance Parrish	6.00
(3)	Cal Ripken, Jr.	24.00
(4)	Nolan Ryan	30.00
(5)	Ozzie Smith	12.00

1995 Rawlings Collector Cards

This series of hang tags is labeled "Collector Cards." Like predecessor issue, there is a hole punched at top to allow the card to be attached to baseball gloves in retail outlets. Cards measure about 2-1/2" x 3-3/4" and have color action photos on front. The player's name is vertically at top left. At bottom is a Rawlings logo and "ADVISORY STAFF" designation, along with the player's position. Colorful backs have career highlights and personal data.

		MT
Complete Set (3):		30.00
(1)	Steve Avery	4.00
(2)	Ken Griffey Jr.	15.00
(3)	Nolan Ryan	15.00
---	Ken Griffey Jr. poster offer hang tag	3.00
---	Ken Griffey Jr. mail-in poster	15.00

1990 Real Milk Mike Henneman

"Get in the Game" urges the headline on each of the cards in this collection featuring then-star Tiger relief pitcher Mike Henneman. The 2-1/2" x 3-1/2" cards have red, white and blue borders with a color photo at center. Backs are in red, black and white with Henneman's stats or career highlights. The set was available as a mail-in premium.

		MT
Complete Set (8):		6.00
Common Card:		.25
1	Mike Henneman (drinking milk)	2.00
2	Mike Henneman (pitching)	2.00
3	Mike Henneman (in jacket)	2.00
4	Mike Henneman (rubbing up ball)	2.00
5	Milk carton	.25
6	Hand holding carton	.25
--	Title card	.25

--	Tiger Clubhouse membership card	.25

1982 Red Lobster Cubs

This 28-card set was co-sponsored by the team and a seafood restaurant chain for distribution at a 1982 Cubs promotional game. Card fronts are unbordered color photos, with player name, number, position and a superimposed facsimile autograph. The set includes 25 players on the 2-1/4" x 3-1/2" cards, along with a card for manager Lee Elia, an unnumbered card for the coaching staff and a team picture. Card backs have complete player statistics and a Red Lobster ad. Production was reported to be 15,000 sets.

		MT
	Complete Set (28):	30.00
	Common Player:	.50
1	Larry Bowa	.50
4	Lee Elia	.50
6	Keith Moreland	.50
7	Jody Davis	.50
10	Leon Durham	.50
15	Junior Kennedy	.50
17	Bump Wills	.50
18	Scot Thompson	.50
21	Jay Johnstone	.50
22	Bill Buckner	.50
23	Ryne Sandberg	24.00
24	Jerry Morales	.50
25	Gary Woods	.50
28	Steve Henderson	.50
29	Bob Molinaro	.50
31	Fergie Jenkins	4.00
33	Al Ripley	.50
34	Randy Martz	.50
36	Mike Proly	.50
37	Ken Kravec	.50
38	Willie Hernandez	.50
39	Bill Campbell	.50
41	Dick Tidrow	.50
46	Lee Smith	3.00
47	Doug Bird	.50
48	Dickie Noles	.50
---	Team Photo	.50
---	Coaching Staff (Billy Connors, Tom Harmon, Gordy MacKenzie, John Vukovich, Billy Williams)	.50

1987-91 Regent Glove Hang Tags

Several different front and back designs are found on these series of player endorsement hang tags attached to baseball gloves at retail outlets. Most are approximately 1-3/4" x 2-3/4". Fronts have color action photos (uniform and cap logos removed). Backs have information about the advisory staff and Regent gloves. Year of issue can be determined by back color.

		MT
	Complete Set (15):	80.00
	Common Player:	4.00
	1984-86 (brown, no UPC)	
(1)	Bob Bailor	4.00
(2)	Doug DeCinces	4.00
(3)	George Foster	5.00
(4)	Rick Miller	4.00
	1987-88 (brown, w/ UPC)	
(1)	Bob Bailor (photo is Jeff Leonard)	4.00
(2)	Doug DeCinces	4.00
(3)	George Foster	5.00
(4)	Dennis Leonard	4.00
(5)	Jeff Leonard	4.00
(6)	Candy Maldonado	4.00
(7)	Rick Miller (photo is Jeff Leonard)	4.00
(8)	Mookie Wilson	4.00
(9)	Joel Youngblood	4.00
	1989 (yellow)	
(1)	Dwight Evans	6.00
(2)	Al Leiter	5.00
(3)	Jeff Leonard	4.00
(4)	Candy Maldonado	4.00
(5)	Mookie Wilson	4.00
	1990 (blue)	
(1)	Dwight Evans	6.00
(2)	Al Leiter	5.00
(3)	Darryl Strawberry	6.00
	1991 (green)	
(1)	Jeff Ballard	4.00
(2)	Darryl Strawberry	6.00

1991 Retort Negro League Legends, Series 1

One of the most extensive collectors' issues featuring former Negro League players was issued over a two-year period by Robert Retort Enterprises. Sold only in a boxed set with accompanying history book, the premiere issue featured 65 individual players, plus game-action and team photos. Fronts of the 3-1/2" x 5-1/2" cards feature sepia photos with a sepia border. Player identification is in the bottom border. Postcard style backs specify the teams on which the player appeared, have a card number and a serial number from within the edition of 10,000 sets.

		MT
	Complete Set (100):	45.00
	Common Player:	.50
1	Otha Bailey	.50
2	Harry Barnes	.50
3	Gene Benson	.50
4	Bill Beverly	.50
5	Charlie Biot	.50
6	Bob Boyd	.65
7	Allen Bryant	.50
8	Marlin Carter	.50
9	Bill Cash	.50
10	Jim Cohen	.50
11	Elliott Coleman	.50
12	Johnnie Cowan	.50
13	Jimmie Crutchfield	.65
14	Saul Davis	.50
15	Piper Davis	.65
16	Leon Day	2.00
17	Lou Dials	.75
18	Mahlon Duckett	.50
19	Felix Evans	.50
20	Rudy Fernandez	.50
21	Joe Fillmore	.50
22	George Giles	.50
23	Louis Gillis	.50
24	Stanley Glenn	.50
25	Willie Grace	.50
26	Wiley Griggs	.50
27	Albert Haywood	.50
28	Jimmy Hill	.50
29	Cowan Hyde	.50
30	Monte Irvin	1.50
31	Sam Jethroe	1.00
32	Connie Johnson	.65
33	Josh Johnson	.50
34	Clinton Jones	.50
35	Larry Kimbrough	.50
36	Clarence King	.50
37	Jim LaMarque	.50
38	Buck Leonard	2.00
39	Max Manning	.50
40	Verdell Mathis	.50
41	Nath McClinic	.50
42	Clinton McCord	.50
43	Clyde McNeal	.50
44	John Miles	.50
45	Buck O'Neil	2.00
46	Frank Pearson	.50
47	Art Pennington	.75
48	Nathan Peoples	.50
49	Andy Porter	.50
50	Ted Radcliffe	1.00
51	Chico Renfroe	.50
52	Bobby Robinson	.50
53	Tommy Sampson	.50
54	Joe Scott	.50
55	Joe Burt Scott	.50
56	Herb Simpson	.50
57	Lonnie Summers	.50
58	Alfred Surratt	.50
59	Bob Thurman	.50
60	Harold Tinker	.50
61	Quincy Trouppe	.75
62	Edsall Walker	.50
63	Al Wilmore	.50
64	Artie Wilson	.75
65	Jim Zapp	.50
66	Grays vs. Stars 1937	.50
67	Grays vs. Eagles 1943	.50
68	Homestead Grays 1944	.50
69	Grays vs. Cuban Stars 1944	.50
70	Grays vs. Cubans 1944	.50
71	Grays vs. Eagles 1945	.50
72	Eagles Pitching Staff 1941	.50
73	Buckeyes Infield 1945	.50
74	Homestead Grays 1948	.50
75	Chicago Murderers Row 1943	.50
76	Indianapolis Clowns 1945	.50
77	East All-Stars 1937	.50
78	East All-Stars 1938	.50
79	East All-Stars 1939	.50
80	East All-Stars 1948	.50
81	West All-Stars 1948	.50
82	Homestead Grays 1931	.50
83	Homestead Grays 1938	.50
84	Pittsburgh Crawfords 1936	.50
85	Kansas City Monarchs 1934	.50
86	Kansas City Monarchs 1949	.50
87	Chicago American Giants 1941	.50
88	Chicago American Giants 1947	.50
89	Memphis Red Sox 1940	.50
90	Memphis Red Sox 1946	.50
91	Birmingham Black Barons 1946	.50
92	Birmingham Black Barons 1948	.50
93	Birmingham Black Barons 1950	.50
94	Harlem Globetrotters 1948	.50
95	Cleveland Buckeyes 1947	.50
96	Philadelphia Stars 1944	.50
97	Newark Eagles 1939	.50
98	Baltimore Elite Giants 1949	.50
99	Indianapolis Clowns 1943	.50
100	Cincinnati Tigers 1937	.50

1993 Retort Negro League Legends, Series 2

One of the most extensive collectors' issues featuring former Negro League players was issued over a two-year period by Robert Retort Enterprises. Sold only in a boxed set, the Series 2 issue features 41 individual players, plus game-action and team photos. Fronts of the 3-1/2" x 5-1/2" cards feature sepia photos with a white border. Player identification is in the bottom border, which also has space for autographing. Postcard style backs specify the teams on which the player appeared, have a card number and a serial number from within the edition of 10,000 sets.

		MT
	Complete Set (100):	40.00
	Common Player:	.50
1	Frank Barnes	.50
2	John Bissant	.50
3	Garnett Blair	.50
4	Jim "Fireball" Bolden	.50
5	Luther Branham	.50
6	Sherwood Brewer	.50
7	Jimmy Dean	.50
8	Frank Duncan, Jr.	.50
9	Wilmer Fields	.50
10	Harold Gordon	.50
11	Bill Greason	.50
12	Acie Griggs	.50
13	Napoleon Gulley	.75
14	Ray Haggins	.50
15	Wilmer Harris	.50
16	Bob Harvey	.50
17	Jehosie Heard	.65
18	Gordon Hopkins	.50
19	Herman Horn	.50
20	James Ivory	.50
21	Henry Kimbro	.75
22	Milford Laurent	.50
23	Ernest Long	.50
24	Frank Marsh	.50
25	Francis Matthews	.50
26	Jim McCurine	.50
27	John Mitchell	.50
28	Lee Moody	.50
29	Rogers Pierre	.50
30	Nathaniel Pollard	.50
31	Merle Porter	.50
32	William Powell	.50
33	Ulysses Redd	.50
34	Harry Rhodes	.50
35	DeWitt Smallwood	.50
36	Joseph Spencer	.50
37	Riley Stewart	.50
38	Earl Taborn	.50
39	Ron Teasley	.50
40	Joe Wiley	.50
41	Buck Leonard	2.00
42	Grays vs. Giants 1945	.50
43	Grays vs. Monarchs 1945	.50
44	Homestead Grays 1948	.50
45	Pittsburgh Crawfords 1928	.50
46	Pittsburgh Crawfords 1935	.50
47	Kansas City Monarchs 1942	.50
48	Buck O'Neil, William Dismukes	.50
49	Chicago American Giants 1942	.50
50	Nashville Elite Giants 1935	.50
51	Baltimore Elite Giants 1941	.50
52	Birmingham Black Barons 1948	.50
53	Birmingham Black Barons 1959	.50
54	Memphis Red Sox 1954	.50
55	Indianapolis ABCs 1923	.50
56	Harlem Globetrotters 1948	.50
57	Harlem Globetrotters 1948	.50
58	Bismarck Barons 1955	.50
59	Culican 1952	.50
60	Santurce 1947	.50
61	Pittsburgh Crawfords 1928	.50
62	Pittsburgh Crawfords 1932	.50
63	Pittsburgh Crawfords 1935	.50
64	Homestead Grays 1937	.50
65	Homestead Grays 1938	.50
66	Homestead Grays 1940	.50
67	Homestead Grays 1945	.50
68	Homestead Grays 1948	.50
69	Kansas City Monarchs 1932	.50
70	Kansas City Monarchs 1934	.50
71	Kansas City Monarchs 1941	.50
72	Kansas City Monarchs 1946	.50
73	Chicago American Giants 1950	.50
74	Memphis Red Sox 1949	.50
75	Birmingham Black Barons 1946	.50
76	Birmingham Black Barons 1948	.50
77	Birmingham Black Barons 1951	.50
78	Birmingham Black Barons 1954	.50
79	St. Louis Stars 1931	.50
80	Newark Dodgers 1935	.50
81	Brooklyn Eagles 1935	.50
82	Newark Eagles 1946	.50
83	Philadelphia Stars 1939	.50
84	Philadelphia Stars 1946	.50
85	Philadelphia Stars 1949	.50
86	Nashville Elite Giants 1935	.50
87	Baltimore Elite Giants 1939	.50
88	Baltimore Elite Giants 1949	.50
89	Cleveland Buckeyes 1947	.50
90	Cincinnati Tigers 1936	.50
91	Miami Ethiopian Clowns 1940	.50
92	Indianapolis Clowns 1944	.50
93	Indianapolis Clowns 1948	.50
94	New York Cubans 1943	.50
95	Harlem Globetrotters 1948	.50
96	House of David 1938	.50
97	E.T. Community 1926	.50
98	Bismarck Giants 1935	.50
99	American All-Stars 1945	.50
100	New York Stars 1949	.50

1988 Revco

This super-glossy boxed set of 33 standard-size cards was produced by Topps for exclusive distribution by Revco stores east of the Mississippi River. Card fronts feature a large blue Revco logo in the upper-left corner opposite a yellow and black boxed "Topps League Leader" label. Player photos are framed in black and orange with a diagonal player identification banner in the lower-right corner. Backs are horizontal, printed in red and black on white stock and include the player name, biographical data, batting/pitching stats and a brief career summary.

		MT
	Complete Set (33):	5.00
	Common Player:	.10
1	Tony Gwynn	.60
2	Andre Dawson	.15
3	Vince Coleman	.10
4	Jack Clark	.10
5	Tim Raines	.15
6	Tim Wallach	.10
7	Juan Samuel	.10
8	Nolan Ryan	1.00
9	Rick Sutcliffe	.10
10	Kent Tekulve	.10
11	Steve Bedrosian	.10
12	Orel Hershiser	.15
13	Rick Rueschel	.10
14	Fernando Valenzuela	.10
15	Bob Welch	.10
16	Wade Boggs	.50
17	Mark McGwire	2.00
18	George Bell	.10
19	Harold Reynolds	.10
20	Paul Molitor	.50
21	Kirby Puckett	.75
22	Kevin Seitzer	.10
23	Brian Downing	.10
24	Dwight Evans	.10
25	Willie Wilson	.10
26	Danny Tartabull	.10

27	Jimmy Key	.10
28	Roger Clemens	.75
29	Dave Stewart	.10
30	Mark Eichhorn	.10
31	Tom Henke	.10
32	Charlie Hough	.10
33	Mark Langston	.10

1985-86 RGI

Renata Galasso Inc.
(See listings under
Renata Galasso)

1988 Rite Aid

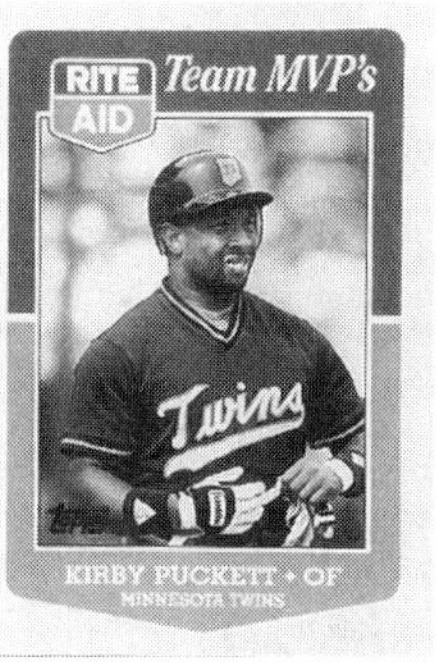

This premiere edition was produced by Topps for distribution by Rite Aid discount drug stores in the Eastern U.S. The boxed set includes 33 standard-size full-color cards with at least one card for each major league team. Four cards in the set highlight MVPs from the 1987 season. Card fronts have white borders and carry a yellow "Team MVP's" header above the player photo which is bordered in red and blue. A large Rite Aid logo appears upper-left; the player's name appears bottom center. The numbered card backs are black on blue and white card stock in a horizontal layout containing the player name, biography and statistics.

		MT
Complete Set (33):		4.50
Common Player:		.10
1	Dale Murphy	.15
2	Andre Dawson	.15
3	Eric Davis	.10
4	Mike Scott	.10
5	Pedro Guerrero	.10
6	Tim Raines	.15
7	Darryl Strawberry	.15
8	Mike Schmidt	.75
9	Mike Dunne	.10
10	Jack Clark	.10
11	Tony Gwynn	.75
12	Will Clark	.45
13	Cal Ripken, Jr.	1.50
14	Wade Boggs	.60
15	Wally Joyner	.10
16	Harold Baines	.10
17	Joe Carter	.10
18	Alan Trammell	.10
19	Kevin Seitzer	.10
20	Paul Molitor	.50
21	Kirby Puckett	.75
22	Don Mattingly	.75
23	Mark McGwire	2.00
24	Alvin Davis	.10
25	Ruben Sierra	.10
26	George Bell	.10
27	Jack Morris	.10
28	Jeff Reardon	.10
29	John Tudor	.10
30	Rick Rueschel	.10
31	Gary Gaetti	.10
32	Jeffrey Leonard	.10
33	Frank Viola	.10

1998 Rocky Mountain News All-Star Poster

Commemorating the first All-Star Game in Denver, the June 30 edition of the Rocky Mountain News contained an 11" x 14" glossy poster featuring the starting line-ups of the teams; the A.L. on one side, the N.L. on the other. The posters were also given away at the newspaper's booth at FanFest.

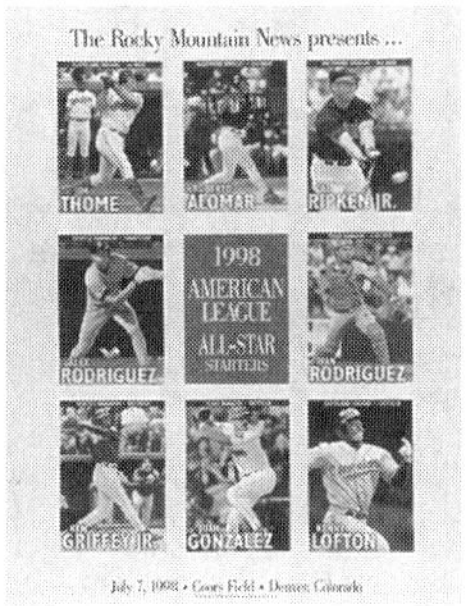

		MT
Poster:		12.00
	AMERICAN LEAGUE	
(1)	Roberto Alomar	
(2)	Juan Gonzalez	
(3)	Ken Griffey Jr.	
(4)	Kenny Lofton	
(5)	Cal Ripken Jr.	
(6)	Alex Rodriguez	
(7)	Ivan Rodriguez	
(8)	Jim Thome	
	NATIONAL LEAGUE	
(9)	Craig Biggio	
(10)	Barry Bonds	
(11)	Tony Gwynn	
(12)	Chipper Jones	
(13)	Mark McGwire	
(14)	Mike Piazza	
(15)	Larry Walker	
(16)	Walt Weiss	

1982 Roy Rogers N.Y. Yankees Lids

Members of the N.Y. Yankees (although in uniform which have the logos removed) are featured on these soft drink lids given away at Roy Rogers restaurants in the metropolitan area. Lids are 3-9/16" in diameter with a red plastic ring around a cardboard disc. At the center of the disc is a black-and-white player portrait photo. Player data appears in colored panels at the sides and in the white center section at bottom. The unnumbered lids are checklisted here in alphabetical order.

		MT
Complete Set:		40.00
Common Player:		3.00
(1)	Rick Cerone	3.00
(2)	Goose Gossage	4.50
(3)	Ken Griffey	4.50
(4)	Ron Guidry	3.00
(5)	Steve Kemp	3.00
(6)	Jerry Mumphrey	3.00
(7)	Graig Nettles	3.00
(8)	Lou Piniella	4.00
(9)	Willie Randolph	3.00
(10)	Andre Robertson	3.00
(11)	Roy Smalley	3.00
(12)	Dave Winfield	8.00

1993 Rolaids Cubs Relief Pitchers

The Chicago Cubs issued a four-card All-Time Cubs Relief Pitchers set as a giveaway at the Sept. 4, 1993 game at Wrigley Field The four were selected by Cubs fans in a ballot conducted by Rolaids. The standard-sized cards have white borders with a color photo at center. Backs include the player's name, years he pitched for the Cubs, the Rolaids logo and an explanation of the card set's purpose.

		MT
Complete Set (4):		4.50
Common Player:		1.00
(1)	Randy Myers	1.00
(2)	Lee Smith	1.50
(3)	Bruce Sutter	1.00
(4)	Mitch Williams	1.00

1983 Pete Rose Price Guide Insert Card

A pocket price guide book which carried the Hit King's name, cover portrait and endorsement had a large-format (about 4" x 5-1/4") bound into each copy. The front is a borderless action photo of Rose, with a facsimile autograph. On back personal data, career highlights and stats.

	MT
Pete Rose	8.00

S

1983 San Diego Padres Photocards

This set of player photocards challenges the collector in that the pictured player is not identified anywhere on the card. Fronts of the 3-1/2" x 5-1/2" cards have borderless color poses with no extraneous graphics. Backs are blank. The unnumbered cards are checklisted here in alphabetical order.

		MT
Complete Set (32):		60.00
Common Player:		2.00
(1)	Kurt Bevacqua	2.00
(2)	Juan Bonilla	2.00
(3)	Greg Booker	2.00
(4)	Nate Colbert	2.00
(5)	Luis DeLeon	2.00
(6)	Dave Dravecky	3.00
(7)	Tim Flannery	2.00
(8)	Steve Garvey	5.00
(9)	Tony Gwynn	15.00
(10)	Ruppert Jones	2.00
(11)	Terry Kennedy	2.00
(12)	Jack Krol	2.00
(13)	Sixto Lezcano	2.00
(14)	Tim Lollar	2.00
(15)	Gary Lucas	2.00
(16)	Jack McKeon (gm)	2.00
(17)	Kevin McReynolds	2.00
(18)	Sid Monge	2.00
(19)	John Montefusco	2.00
(20)	Mario Ramirez	2.00
(21)	Gene Richards	2.00
(22)	Luis Salazar	2.00
(23)	Norm Sherry	2.00
(24)	Eric Show	2.00
(25)	Elias Sosa	2.00
(26)	Mark Thurmond	2.00
(27)	Bobby Tolan	2.00
(28)	Jerry Turner	2.00
(29)	Ozzie Virgil	2.00
(30)	Ed Whitson	2.00
(31)	Alan Wiggins	2.00
(32)	Dick Williams	2.50

1984 San Diego Padres Fire Safety

This set of 28 full-color 2-1/2" x 3-1/2" cards pictures Padres players, coaches, broadcasters and the Famous Chicken each posing with Smokey the Bear. Smokey's portrait and logo of the California and U.S. Forest Services are printed in the bottom border. Backs offer brief player information and a fire prevention tip. The cards were given away at a home game.

		MT
Complete Set (28):		8.00
Common Player:		.25
1	Garry Templeton	.25
2	Alan Wiggins	.25
4	Luis Salazar	.25
6	Steve Garvey	1.50
7	Kurt Bevacqua	.25
10	Doug Gwosdz	.25
11	Tim Flannery	.25
16	Terry Kennedy	.25
18	Kevin McReynolds	.35
19	Tony Gwynn	5.00
20	Bobby Brown	.25
30	Eric Show	.25
31	Ed Whitson	.25
35	Luis DeLeon	.25
38	Mark Thurmond	.25
42	Sid Monge	.25
43	Dave Dravecky	.35
48	Tim Lollar	.25
---	Smokey Logo Card	.25
---	The Chicken (mascot)	.25
---	Dave Campbell (broadcaster)	.25
---	Jerry Coleman (broadcaster)	.25
---	Harry Dunlop	.25
---	Harold (Doug) Harvey (umpire)	.25
---	Jack Krol (coach)	.25
---	Jack McKeon (vice president)	.25
---	Norm Sherry (coach)	.25
---	Ozzie Virgil (coach)	.25
---	Dick Williams (manager)	.25

1985-86 San Diego Padres Postcards

You really have to know your Pads to collect this set of 3-1/2" x 5" color player postcards as the team members are identified nowhere on the cards. Fronts have borderless chest-to-cap posed portraits of the players against a light brown background. Backs have only a vertical center dividing line and "PLACE / STAMP / HERE" box. The unnumbered cards are checklisted here alphabetically.

		MT
Complete Set (41):		80.00
Common Player:		3.00
(1)	Sandy Alomar	5.00
(2)	Kurt Bevacqua	3.00
(3)	Bruce Bochy	3.00
(4)	Greg Booker	3.00
(5)	Steve Boros	3.00
(6)	Bobby Brown	3.00
(7)	Al Bumbry	3.00
(8)	Galen Cisco	3.00
(9)	Jerry Davis	3.00
(10)	Luis DeLeon	3.00
(11)	Dave Dravecky	4.00
(12)	Harry Dunlop	3.00
(13)	Tim Flannery	3.00
(14)	Steve Garvey	6.00
(15)	Goose Gossage	4.00
(16)	Tony Gwynn	15.00
(17)	Andy Hawkins	3.00
(18)	LaMarr Hoyt	3.00
(19)	Dane Iorg	3.00
(20)	Deacon Jones	3.00
(21)	Terry Kennedy	3.00
(22)	Jack Krol	3.00
(23)	John Kruk	4.00
(24)	Craig Lefferts	3.00
(25)	Carmelo Martinez	3.00
(26)	Lance McCullers	3.00
(27)	Jack McKeon	3.00
(28)	Kevin McReynolds	4.00
(29)	Graig Nettles	5.00
(30)	Mario Ramirez	3.00
(31)	Bip Roberts	4.00
(32)	Jerry Royster	3.00
(33)	Eric Show	3.00
(34)	Tim Stoddard	3.00
(35)	Garry Templeton	4.00
(36)	Mark Thurmond	3.00
(37)	Ozzie Virgil	3.00
(38)	Gene Walter	3.00
(39)	Dick Williams	3.00
(40)	Ed Wojna	3.00
(41)	Marvell Wynne	3.00

Player names in *Italic* type indicate a rookie card.

1986-87 San Diego Padres Fire Safety Flip Books

Differing from the contemporary fire safety issues of its time, the 1986-87 Padres promotional effort took the form of 24-page flip books, rather than cards. About 3-1/2" x 2-1/2", the multi-page black-and-white books offered photographic playing tips when the pictures were rapidly thumbed. When turned over, the books showed Smokey in action preventing forest fires. The 1987 books, McCullers and Santiago, are slightly larger, at about 4-1/2" x 2-3/4".

		MT
Complete Set (5):		32.00
Common Player:		4.00
(1)	Dave Dravecky	4.00
(2)	Tim Flannery	4.00
(3)	Tony Gwynn	15.00
(4)	Lance McCullers	4.00
(5)	Benito Santiago	5.00

1988 San Diego Padres Fire Safety

This oversized (3" x 5") set was produced in conjunction with the U.S. Forest Service as a fire prevention campaign promotion. A full-color player photo, framed by a thin white line, fills the card face. The player number, position and Smokey Bear logo appear at lower-right. Backs are printed in horizontal postcard format, with player info and a Smokey Bear cartoon on the left half of the card back. The set was available for purchase at the Padres Gift Shop. Cards of Candy Sierra and Larry Bowa were not released by the Padres and are quite rare. The complete set price does not include the two rare cards.

		MT
Complete Set (31):		15.00
Common Player:		.30
(1)	Shawn Abner	.30
(2)	Roberto Alomar	3.00
(3)	Sandy Alomar	1.00
(4)	Greg Booker	.30
(5)	Larry Bowa	8.00
(6)	Chris Brown	.30
(7)	Mark Davis	.30
(8)	Pat Dobson	.30
(9)	Tim Flannery	.30
(10)	Mark Grant	.30
(11)	Tony Gwynn	4.00
(12)	Andy Hawkins	.30
(13)	Stan Jefferson	.30
(14)	Jimmy Jones	.30
(15)	John Kruk	.35
(16)	Dave Leiper	.30
(17)	Shane Mack	.30
(18)	Carmelo Martinez	.30
(19)	Lance McCullers	.30
(20)	Keith Moreland	.30
(21)	Eric Nolte	.30
(22)	Amos Otis	.30
(23)	Mark Parent	.30
(24)	Randy Ready	.30
(25)	Greg Riddoch	.30
(26)	Benito Santiago	.45
(27)	Eric Show	.30
(28)	Candy Sierra	8.00
(29)	Denny Sommers	.30
(30)	Garry Templeton	.30
(31)	Dickie Thon	.30
(32)	Ed Whitson	.30
(33)	Marvell Wynne	.30

1989 San Diego Padres Magazine/ S.D. Sports inserts

During the course of the 1989 season, a 24-card set sponsored by a local baseball card dealer was offered to collectors as an insert to the team's official game program, "Padres Magazine." The cards were offered in six panels of four cards. Each panel included a former Padres star and a career highlight. To complete the set, at least six copies of the $1.50 program had to be purchased. The 2-1/2" x 3-1/2" cards have color portrait photos on front. Backs have player identification and a career stats line, along with trivia about the player.

		MT
Complete Set (24):		15.00
Common Player:		.50
1	Jack McKeon	.50
2	Sandy Alomar Jr.	.75
3	Tony Gwynn	4.00
4	Willie McCovey	1.50
5	John Kruk	.60
6	Jack Clark	.60
7	Eric Show	.50
8	Rollie Fingers	1.50
9	The Alomars (Sandy Alomar, Roberto Alomar, Sandy Alomar Jr.)	.65
10	Carmelo Martinez	.50
11	Benito Santiago	.60
12	Nate Colbert	.50
13	Mark Davis	.50
14	Roberto Alomar	2.50
15	Tim Flannery	.50
16	Randy Jones	.50
17	Dennis Rasmussen	.50
18	Greg Harris	.50
19	Garry Templeton	.60
20	Steve Garvey	1.50
21	Bruce Hurst	.60
22	Ed Whitson	.50
23	Chris James	.50
24	Gaylord Perry	1.50

1989 San Diego Padres Postcards

Players, coaches and executives are included in this team-issued set. Cards are in 3-3/4" x 5-3/4" size with borderless color photos on front. A white pinstripe, player name and position are printed on the photo. Postcard-style backs have player biographical data. The unnumbered cards are checklisted here in alphabetical order.

		MT
Complete Set (36):		35.00
Common Player:		1.00
(1)	Shawn Abner	1.00
(2)	Roberto Alomar	4.00
(3)	Sandy Alomar Jr.	3.00
(4)	Sandy Alomar Sr.	1.00
(5)	Jack Clark	2.00
(6)	Jerald Clark	1.00
(7)	Pat Clements	1.00
(8)	Mark Davis	1.00
(9)	Pat Dobson	1.00
(10)	Tim Flannery	1.00
(11)	Mark Grant	1.00
(12)	Gary Green	1.00
(13)	Tony Gwynn	5.00
(14)	Greg Harris	1.00
(15)	Bruce Hurst	1.00
(16)	Chris James	1.00
(17)	Dave Leiper	1.00
(18)	Carmelo Martinez	1.00
(19)	Jack McKeon (gm)	1.00
(20)	Rob Nelson	1.00
(21)	Amos Otis	1.00
(22)	Mike Pagliarulo	1.00
(23)	Mark Parent	1.00
(24)	Dennis Rasmussen	1.00
(25)	Greg Riddoch	1.00
(26)	Bip Roberts	1.50
(27)	Luis Salazar	1.00
(28)	Benito Santiago	2.00
(29)	Eric Show	1.00
(30)	Don Schulze	1.00
(31)	Tony Siegle (vp)	1.00
(32)	Denny Sommers	1.00
(33)	Garry Templeton	1.00
(34)	Fred Tolliver	1.00
(35)	Ed Whitson	1.00
(36)	Marvell Wynne	1.00

1990 San Diego Padres Magazine/ Unocal inserts

The first 24 cards in this set, sponsored by area Unocal service stations, were found in four-card panels bound into various issues of Padres Magazine, the team's official program. Sheets measure about 5" x 9" and the individual perforated cards are about 2-1/2" x 3-1/2". A coupon attached to the sheets could be redeemed at participating gas stations for cards #25-27. Fronts have color action photos with team logo at top and sponsor logo at lower-right. Black-and-white backs have player data, a line of career stats and highlights of his time with the Padres.

		MT
Complete Set (27):		15.00
Common Player:		.50
1	Tony Gwynn	3.00
2	Benito Santiago	.75
3	Mike Pagliarulo	.50
4	Dennis Rasmussen	.50
5	Eric Show	.50
6	Darrin Jackson	.50
7	Mark Parent	.50
8	Jerry Coleman, Rick Monday (announcers)	.50
9	Andy Benes	1.00
10	Roberto Alomar	2.50
11	Craig Lefferts	.50
12	Ed Whitson	.50
13	Calvin Schiraldi	.50
14	Garry Templeton	.60
15	Tony Gwynn	3.00
16	Bob Chandler, Ted Leitner (announcers)	.50
17	Fred Lynn	.65
18	Jack Clark	.65
19	Mike Dunne	.50
20	Mark Grant	.50
21	Benito Santiago	.75
22	Sandy Alomar Sr., Pat Dobson, Amos Otis, Greg Riddoch, Denny Sommers	.50
23	Bruce Hurst	.50
24	Greg Harris	.50
25	Jack McKeon	1.00
26	Bip Roberts	2.00
27	Joe Carter	4.00

1991 San Diego Padres Magazine/ Rally's inserts

The first 27 cards of this set were issued as 5" x 8" perforated panels stapled into issues of "Padres Magazine." Due to substitutions dictated by player moves during the season (which also created Short-Printed cards) it would have been necessary to purchase six of the $2 programs to get the 27-card basic set. The final three cards were only available at Rally's restaurants with a coupon attached to the magazine panels. Single cards measure about 2-1/2" x 3-1/2". Fronts have color portrait photos on a diamond background. Player name and position are in an orange banner at bottom. Team and sponsor logos appear in the upper corners on a dark blue background. Backs are in black-and-white with player identification, a line of career stats and highlights of his tenure in San Diego.

		MT
Complete Set (30):		30.00
Common Player:		.50
1	Greg Riddoch	.50
2	Dennis Rasmussen	.50
3	Thomas Howard	.50
4	Tom Lampkin	.50
5	Bruce Hurst	.60
6	Darrin Jackson	.50
7	Jerald Clark	.50
8	Shawn Abner	.50
9	Bip Roberts	.60
10	Marty Barrett	.50
11	Jim Vatcher	.50
12	Greg Gross	.50
13	Greg Harris	.50
14	Ed Whitson	.50
15a	Calvin Schiraldi (SP)	2.00
15b	Jerald Clark	.50
16	Rich Rodriguez	.50
17	Larry Andersen	.50
18	Andy Benes	2.00
19a	Wes Gardner (SP)	2.00
19b	Bruce Hurst	.60
20	Paul Faries	.50
21	Craig Lefferts	.50
22	Tony Gwynn	8.00
23a	Jim Presley	.50
23b	Bip Roberts	.60
24	Fred McGriff	1.50
25	Gaylord Perry	2.00
26	Benito Santiago	1.50
27	Tony Fernandez	1.50

1992 San Diego Padres Fire Safety

The Padres issued a Smokey the Bear postcard set, sponsored by the U.S. Forest Service. Backs contain the usual fire safety messages, but they are also translated into Spanish. Fronts have full-bleed color photos with the player's name and position in orange in a dark blue box at bottom-center. A color Smokey logo appears in one of the upper corners. The unnumbered cards are checklisted here alphabetically.

		MT
Complete Set (36):		15.00
Common Player:		.25
(1)	Larry Andersen	.25
(2)	Oscar Azocar	.25
(3)	Andy Benes	.80
(4)	Dan Bilardello	.25
(5)	Jerald Clark	.25
(6)	Pat Clements	.25
(7)	Dave Eiland	.25
(8)	Tony Fernandez	.25
(9)	Tony Gwynn	4.00
(10)	Gene Harris	.25
(11)	Greg Harris	.25
(12)	Jeremy Hernandez	.25
(13)	Bruce Hurst	.25
(14)	Darrin Jackson	.50
(15)	Tom Lampkin	.25
(16)	Bruce Kimm	.25
(17)	Craig Lefferts	.25
(18)	Mike Maddux	.25
(19)	Fred McGriff	3.00
(20)	Jose Melendez	.25
(21)	Randy Myers, Craig Shipley	.35
(22)	Gary Pettis	.25
(23)	Rob Picciolo	.25
(24)	Merv Rettenmund	.25
(25)	Greg Riddoch	.25
(26)	Mike Roarke	.25
(27)	Rich Rodriguez	.25
(28)	Benito Santiago	.35
(29)	Frank Seminara	.25
(30)	Gary Sheffield	2.00
(32)	Jim Snyder	.25
(33)	Dave Staton	.25
(34)	Kurt Stillwell	.25
(35)	Tim Teufel	.25
(36)	Kevin Ward	.25

1992 San Diego Padres Police

Anti-drug messages are featured on this safety set. The 2-1/2" x 3-1/2" cards have color action photos on front with wide white borders. Backs are horizontally formatted and feature a few player biographical notes, the D.A.R.E. logo and safety message. Unnumbered cards are checklisted here in alphabetical order. Cards #28-30 in this checklist were not distributed with the rest of the set and are scarcer.

		MT
Complete Set (30):		18.00
Common Player:		.50
(1)	Oscar Azocar	.50
(2)	Andy Benes	1.00
(3)	Jerald Clark	.50
(4)	Jim Deshaies	.50
(5)	Dave Eiland	.50
(6)	Tony Fernandez	.75
(7)	Tony Gwynn	5.00
(8)	Greg W. Harris	.50
(9)	Bruce Hurst	.50
(10)	Darrin Jackson	.50
(11)	Tom Lampkin	.50
(12)	Fred McGriff	2.50
(13)	Merv Rettenmund	.50
(14)	Greg Riddoch	.50
(15)	Benito Santiago	.60
(16)	Frank Seminara	.50
(17)	Gary Sheffield	1.50
(18)	Craig Shipley	.50
(19)	Phil Stephenson	.50
(20)	Kurt Stillwell	.50
(21)	Tim Teufel	.50
(22)	Dan Walters	.50
(23)	Kevin Ward	.50
(24)	Padres relievers (Larry Andersen, Mike Maddux, Jose Melendez, Rich Rodriguez, Tim Scott)	.50
(25)	Coaches (Bruce Kimm, Rob Picciolo, Merv Rettenmund, Mike Roarke, Jim Snyder)	.50
(26)	Bluepper (mascot)	.50
(27)	Jack Murphy Stadium	.50
(28)	Craig Lefferts	1.00
(29)	Rob Picciolo	1.00
(30)	Fred McGriff, Tony Fernandez, Gary Sheffield, Tony Gwynn	2.00

1981 San Diego Sports Collectors Association

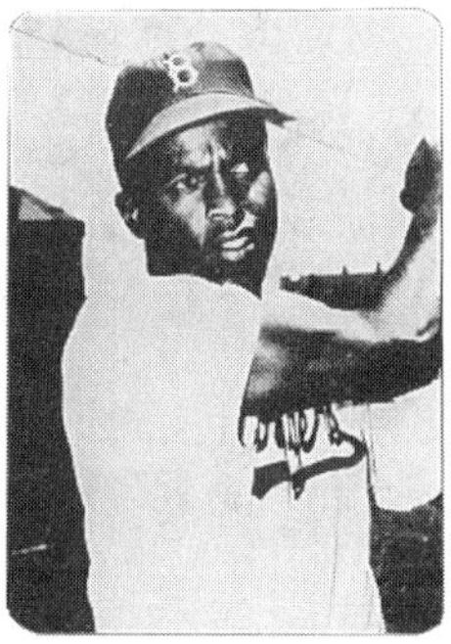

To promote the first large sports card and memorabilia show in San Diego, sponsors issued this set of round-cornered, 2-1/2" x 3-1/2" black-and-white cards. It was reported that 30,000 of the cards were printed, many of them being distributed to youngsters in the area. Fronts have borderless player photos, backs are basically an ad for the show. Cards were good for a 50-cent admission discount and complete sets were available at the show.

		MT
	Complete Set (20):	50.00
	Common Card:	1.00
1	Gary Butcher	1.00
2	Hank Aaron	4.00
3	Duke Snider	2.00
4	Al Kaline	2.00
5	Vic Power	1.00
6	Jackie Robinson	4.00
7	Carl Erskine	1.00
8	Ted Williams	4.00
9	Ted Williams	4.00
10	Mickey Mantle	12.00
11	Mickey Mantle	12.00
12	Mickey Mantle, Willie Mays	6.00
13	Mickey Mantle, Stan Musial	6.00
14	Joe DiMaggio	4.00
15	Roger Maris	2.00
16	Roger Maris	2.00
17	Lou Gehrig	4.00
18	Bill Dickey, Lou Gehrig	2.00
19	Joe Cronin, Bill Dickey, Joe DiMaggio, Lou Gehrig	1.00
20	Gary Butcher	1.00

1991 San Francisco Examiner A's

Evidently issued over the course of the season by the Bay Area daily newspaper, these large-format (8-3/8" x 10-7/8") cards are printed on light cardboard pre-punched for a three-ring binder. Color photos on the fronts are surrounded by team colors of green and yellow. The newspaper's logo appears in black at the top. Backs are in black-and-white with a portrait photo of the player, biographical data, major league stats and career highlights. The unnumbered cards are checklisted here alphabetically.

		MT
	Complete Set (15):	45.00
	Common Player:	2.00
(1)	Harold Baines	2.50
(2)	Jose Canseco	5.00
(3)	Dennis Eckersley	2.50
(4)	Mike Gallego	2.00
(5)	Dave Henderson	2.00
(6)	Rickey Henderson	4.50
(7)	Rick Honeycutt	2.00
(8)	Mark McGwire	12.00
(9)	Mike Moore	2.00
(10)	Gene Nelson	2.00
(11)	Eric Show	2.00
(12)	Terry Steinbach	2.00
(13)	Dave Stewart	2.50
(14)	Walt Weiss	2.00
(15)	Bob Welch	2.00

1991 San Francisco Examiner Giants

Evidently issued over the course of the season by the Bay Area daily newspaper, these large-format (8-3/8" x 10-7/8") cards are printed on light cardboard pre-punched for a three-ring binder. Color photos on the fronts are surrounded by team-color borders of orange and black on a gray background. The newspaper's logo appears in black at the top. Backs are in black-and-white with a portrait photo of the player, biographical data, major league stats and career highlights. The unnumbered cards are checklisted here alphabetically.

		MT
	Complete Set (16):	37.50
	Common Player:	2.00
(1)	Kevin Bass	2.00
(2)	Mike Benjamin	2.00
(3)	Bud Black	2.00
(4)	Jeff Brantley	2.00
(5)	John Burkett	2.00
(6)	Will Clark	6.00
(7)	Steve Decker	2.00
(8)	Scott Garrelts	2.00
(9)	Mike LaCoss	2.00
(10)	Willie McGee	3.00
(11)	Kevin Mitchell	2.00
(12)	Dave Righetti	2.00
(13)	Don Robinson	2.00
(14)	Robby Thompson	2.00
(15)	Jose Uribe	2.00
(16)	Matt Williams	4.00

1995 S.F. Examiner Negro Leagues Souvenir Sheet

To honor the 75th anniversary of the founding of the Negro Leagues, the S.F. Examiner and the S.F. Giants issued this souvenir sheet picturing a dozen Hall of Famers from the storied black leagues. The sheet measures 14-1/4" x 11-1/4", if cut from the sheets, individual cards measure 2-1/4" x 4". Cards have sepia player photos (generally images which have been used on collectors issues many times in the past) and a colored anniversary logo at bottom. Backs have an extensive career summary and the sponsors' logos.

		MT
	Complete Sheet:	15.00
(1)	Cool Papa Bell	
(2)	Oscar Charleston	
(3)	Ray Dandridge	
(4)	Leon Day	
(5)	Martin Dihigo	
(6)	Andrew "Rube" Foster	
(7)	Josh Gibson	
(8)	Monte Irvin	
(9)	Judy Johnson	
(10)	Walter "Buck" Leonard	
(11)	Pop Lloyd	
(12)	Leroy "Satchel" Paige	

1979 San Francisco Giants Police

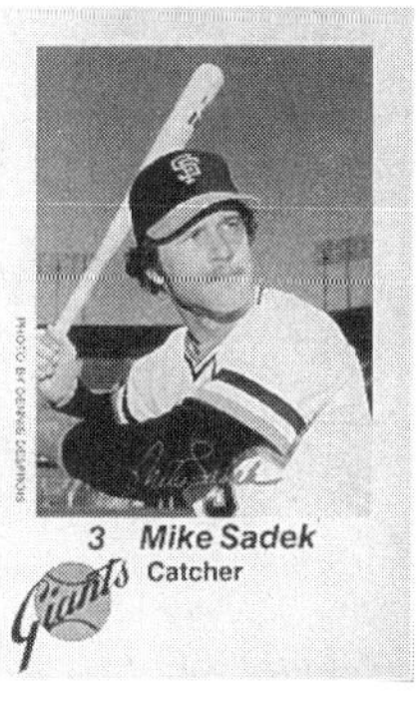

Each of the full-color cards measures 2-5/8" x 4-1/8" and is numbered by player uniform number. The set includes players and coaches. The player's name, position and facsimile autograph are on front, along with the Giants logo. Backs have a "Tip from the Giants" and sponsor logos for the Giants and radio station KNBR, all printed in orange and black. Half of the set was distributed at a ballpark promotion, while the other cards were available from police agencies in several San Francisco Bay area counties.

		NM
	Complete Set (29):	15.00
	Common Player:	.50
1	Dave Bristol	.50
2	Marc Hill	.50
3	Mike Sadek	.50
5	Tom Haller	.50
6	Joe Altobelli	.50
8	Larry Shepard	.50
9	Heity Cruz	.50
10	Johnnie LeMaster	.50
12	Jim Davenport	.50
14	Vida Blue	.75
15	Mike Ivie	.50
16	Roger Metzger	.50
17	Randy Moffitt	.50
18	Bill Madlock	.60
21	Rob Andrews	.50
22	Jack Clark	.75
25	Dave Roberts	.50
26	John Montefusco	.50
28	Ed Halicki	.50
30	John Tamargo	.50
31	Larry Herndon	.50
36	Bill North	.50
39	Bob Knepper	.50
40	John Curtis	.50
41	Darrell Evans	.75
43	Tom Griffin	.50
44	Willie McCovey	5.00
46	Gary Lavelle	.50
49	Max Venable	.50

1980 San Francisco Giants Police

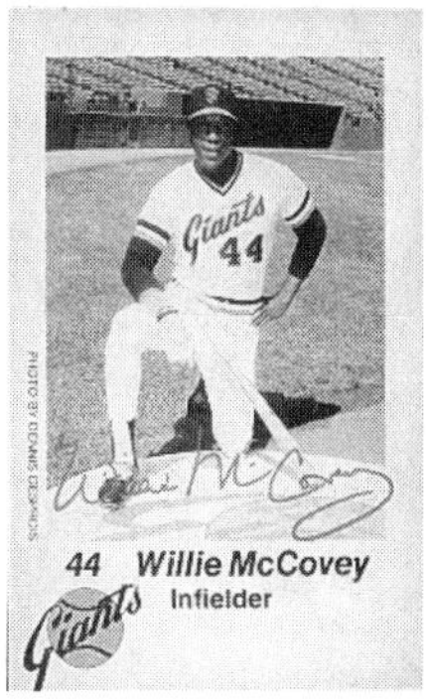

The 1980 Giants police set is virtually identical in format to its 1979 forerunner, with radio station KNBR and the San Francisco Police Department once again co-sponsors. The 2-5/8" x 4-1/8" cards feature full-color photos and facsimile autographs. Backs are in the team's orange and black colors. The set includes players and coaches, with each card numbered by uniform number. As in 1979, half the cards were distributed at a stadium promotion, with the remainder available only from police officers.

		NM
	Complete Set (31):	10.00
	Common Player:	.30
1	Dave Bristol	.30
2	Marc Hill	.30
3	Mike Sadek	.30
5	Jim Lefebvre	.30
6	Rennie Stennett	.30
7	Milt May	.30
8	Vern Benson	.30
9	Jim Wohlford	.30
10	Johnnie LeMaster	.30
12	Jim Davenport	.30
14	Vida Blue	.50
15	Mike Ivie	.30
16	Roger Metzger	.30
17	Randy Moffitt	.30
19	Al Holland	.30
20	Joe Strain	.30
22	Jack Clark	.60
26	John Montefusco	.30
28	Ed Halicki	.30
31	Larry Herndon	.30
32	Ed Whitson	.30
36	Bill North	.30
38	Greg Minton	.30
39	Bob Knepper	.30
41	Darrell Evans	.60
42	John Van Ornum	.30
43	Tom Griffin	.30
44	Willie McCovey	4.00
45	Terry Whitfield	.30
46	Gary Lavelle	.30
47	Don McMahon	.30

1983 San Francisco Giants Postcards

The first club-issued color player postcard set by the Giants was this collaborative effort by photographer Dennis Desprois and producer Barry Colla. The 3-1/2" x 5-1/2" cards have high-gloss borderless fronts which feature only a posed player photo; no graphics. Backs are in black-and-white with player ID at upper-left, credits at lower-left and postcard indicia at right. A card number appears beneath the stamp box. Cards were sold only as complete sets in a white paper window envelope for $6. Production is said to have been limited to 3,000 sets.

		MT
	Complete Set (28):	24.00
	Common Player:	1.50
383	Frank Robinson	5.00
482	Candlestick Park	2.00
483	Joe Pettini	1.50
583	Champ Summers	1.50
683	Milt May	1.50
783	Coaches (Tom McCraw, Herm Starrette, Danny Ozark, Don Buford, John Van Ornum)	1.50
883	Max Venable	1.50
983	Fred Breining	1.50
1083	Gary Lavelle	1.50
1183	Darrell Evans	2.50
1283	Mike Krukow	1.50
1383	Joel Youngblood	1.50
1483	Greg Minton	1.50
1583	Tom O'Malley	1.50
1683	Jim Barr	1.50
1783	Not issued	
1883	Johnnie LeMaster	1.50
1983	Mike Chris	1.50
2083	Chili Davis	2.50
2183	Andy McGaffigan	1.50
2283	Atlee Hammaker	1.50
2383	Jeff Leonard	1.50
2483	Mark Calvert	1.50
2583	Jack Clark	2.50
2683	Bob Brenly	1.50
2783	Bill Laskey	1.50
2883	Duane Kuiper	1.50
2983	Dave Bergman	1.50
3083	Renie Martin	1.50

1984 San Francisco Giants Postcards

For a second year Giants photographer Dennis Desprois and producer Barry Colla collaborated on a color player postcard set to be issued by the team. The format was basically unchanged from the previous year. Cards are 3-1/2" x 5-1/2" with high-gloss fronts that have only a posed player photo, unencumbered with name or other graphics. Backs are in black-and-white with postcard indicia at right (a card number is printed under the stamp box), and player ID and credits at left. The cards were sold only as a complete set.

		MT
	Complete Set (31):	24.00
	Common Player:	1.50
184	Frank Robinson	5.00
284	Don Buford	1.50
384	Tom McCraw	1.50
484	Danny Ozark	1.50
584	Herm Starrette	1.50
684	John Van Ornum	1.50
784	Al Oliver	2.50

884	Dusty Baker	3.00
984	John Rabb	1.50
1084	Steve Nicosia	1.50
1184	Joel Youngblood	1.50
1284	Manny Trillo	1.50
1384	John LeMaster	1.50
1484	Mark Davis	1.50
1584	Atlee Hammaker	1.50
1684	Bob Brenly	1.50
1784	Fran Mullins	1.50
1884	Renie Martin	1.50
1984	Duane Kuiper	1.50
2084	Bill Laskey	1.50
2184	Jack Clark	2.50
2284	Gene Richards	1.50
2384	Jeff Leonard	1.50
2484	Randy Lerch	1.50
2584	Chili Davis	2.50
2684	Jeff Robinson	1.50
2784	Greg Minton	1.50
2884	Mike Krukow	1.50
2984	Scot Thompson	1.50
3084	Gary Lavelle	1.50
3184	Frank Williams	1.50

1985 San Francisco Giants Postcards

The Giants continued their run of quality team-issued postcards into 1985 with another set featuring (according to the credits on back) the players in posed color photos by Dennis Desprois and production by Barry Colla. Once again the 3-1/2" x 5-1/2" cards have borderless color photos on front with no other graphic elements and a high-gloss finish. Backs are in black-and-white with postcard indicia at right and player ID at top left. A card number appears beneath the stamp box. The cards were sold as sets in a white paper window envelope with team logo.

		MT
Complete Set (31):		24.00
Common Player:		1.50
3285	Rocky Bridges	1.50
3385	Chuck Hiller	1.50
3485	Tom McCraw	1.50
3585	Bob Miller	1.50
3685	Jack Mull	1.50
3785	Bob Brenly	1.50
3885	Johnnie LeMaster	1.50
3985	Greg Minton	1.50
4085	Atlee Hammaker	1.50
4185	Chili Davis	2.50
4285	Jim Gott	1.50
4385	Chris Brown	1.50
4485	Bill Laskey	1.50
4585	Scot Thompson	1.50
4685	Mark Davis	1.50
4785	Dave LaPoint	1.50
4885	Frank Williams	1.50
4985	Jose Uribe	1.50
5085	Jeff Leonard	1.50
5185	Manny Trillo	1.50
5285	Mike Krukow	1.50
5385	Dan Gladden	2.00
5485	Vida Blue	2.00
5585	David Green	1.50
5685	Joel Youngblood	1.50
5785	Doug Gwosdz	1.50
5885	Scott Garrelts	1.50
5985	Rob Deer	2.00
6085	Dave Rajsich	1.50
6185	Brad Wellman	1.50
6285	Jim Davenport	1.50

1986 San Francisco Giants Postcards

Team photographer Dennis Desprois did an excellent job of capturing the '86 Giants is this team-issued player postcard set. Fronts are borderless color poses with no player identification. On the postcard backs there are boxes for address and stamp, credits for photography and printing, and player name. The unnumbered cards are checklisted here alphabetically.

		MT
Complete Set (30):		30.00
Common Player:		1.50
(1)	Mike Aldrete	1.50
(2)	Juan Berenguer	1.50
(3)	Vida Blue	2.00
(4)	Bob Brenly	1.50
(5)	Chris Brown	1.50
(6)	Will Clark	4.00
(7)	Roger Craig	1.50
(8)	Chili Davis	2.00
(9)	Mark Davis	1.50
(10)	Bill Fahey	1.50
(11)	Scott Garrelts	1.50
(12)	Dan Gladden	1.50
(13)	Jim Gott	1.50
(14)	Atlee Hammaker	1.50
(15)	Mike Krukow	1.50
(16)	Bill Laskey	1.50
(17)	Jeffrey Leonard	1.50
(18)	Bob Lillis	1.50
(19)	Candy Maldonado	1.50
(20)	Roger Mason	1.50
(21)	Willie Mays, Willie McCovey	8.00
(22)	Gordon MacKenzie	1.50
(23)	Bob Melvin	1.50
(24)	Greg Minton	1.50
(25)	Jose Morales	1.50
(26)	Jeff Robinson	1.50
(27)	Norm Sherry	1.50
(28)	Rob Thompson	1.50
(29)	Jose Uribe	1.50
(30)	Brad Wellman	1.50

1987 San Francisco Giants Postcards

The postcard back on this team-issue set differs from that of the previous year. The lines for writing the address are not boxed and there is no team logo in the stamp box. The postcards were again photographed by Dennis Desprois, but production was by Woodford Publishing. Card fronts have borderless color photos with no identification. The unnumbered cards are checklisted here alphabetically.

		MT
Complete Set (36):		30.00
Common Player:		1.50
(1)	Mike Aldrete	1.50
(2)	Randy Bockus	1.50
(3)	Bob Brenly	1.50
(4)	Chris Brown	1.50
(5)	Will Clark	6.00
(6)	Keith Comstock	1.50
(7)	Roger Craig	1.50
(8)	Chili Davis	2.00
(9)	Mark Davis	1.50
(10)	Kelly Downs	1.50
(11)	Bill Fahey	1.50
(12)	Scott Garrelts	1.50
(13)	Jim Gott	1.50
(14)	Atlee Hammaker	1.50
(15)	Mike Krukow	1.50
(16)	Mike LaCoss	1.50
(17)	Jeffrey Leonard	1.50
(18)	Bob Lillis	1.50
(19)	Gordy MacKenzie	1.50
(20)	Candy Maldonado	1.50
(21)	Willie Mays	8.00
(22)	Willie McCovey	5.00
(23)	Bob Melvin	1.50
(24)	Eddie Milner	1.50
(25)	Jose Morales	1.50
(26)	Jon Perlman	1.50
(27)	Jeff Robinson	1.50
(28)	Norm Sherry	1.50
(29)	Chris Speier	1.50
(30)	Harry Spilman	1.50
(31)	Robby Thompson	1.50
(32)	Jose Uribe	1.50
(33)	Mark Wasinger	1.50
(34)	Matt Williams	5.00
(35)	Joel Youngblood	1.50
(36)	Don Zimmer	1.50

1988 San Francisco Giants Postcards

This team-issued set of 3-1/2" x 5-1/2" postcards features on front borderless color poses or action shots by team photographer Dennis Desprois. Backs are in black-and-white with standard postcard indicia, the player's name and photo/production credits. Sets were originally sold for about $9 in a printed envelope. The unnumbered cards are checklisted here in alphabetical order. Only the player selection and pose differentiate this set from that of the previous year.

		MT
Complete Set (35)		30.00
Common Player:		1.00
(1)	Mike Aldrete	1.00
(2)	Dusty Baker	1.50
(3)	Bob Brenly	1.00
(4)	Brett Butler	1.50
(5)	Will Clark	3.00
(6)	Roger Craig	1.00
(7)	Kelly Downs	1.00
(8)	Dave Dravecky	1.00
(9)	Bill Fahey	1.00
(10)	Scott Garrelts	1.00
(11)	Atlee Hammaker	1.00
(12)	Mike Krukow	1.00
(13)	Mike LaCoss	1.00
(14)	Craig Lefferts	1.00
(15)	Jeffrey Leonard	1.00
(16)	Bob Lillis	1.00
(17)	Gordon MacKenzie	1.00
(18)	Candy Maldonado	1.00
(19)	Willie Mays	7.50
(20)	Willie McCovey	4.00
(21)	Bob Melvin	1.00
(22)	Kevin Mitchell	1.00
(23)	Jose Morales	1.00
(24)	Joe Price	1.00
(25)	Rick Reuschel	1.00
(26)	Don Robinson	1.00
(27)	Norm Sherry	1.00
(28)	Chris Speier	1.00
(29)	Harry Spilman	1.00
(30)	Robby Thompson	1.00
(31)	Jose Uribe	1.00
(32)	Mark Wasinger	1.00
(33)	Joel Youngblood	1.00
(34)	Candlestick Park	2.00
(35)	Giants 1987 N.L. West Championship Logo	1.00

1990 San Francisco Giants Postcards

The N.L. Champion S.F. Giants are featured in this set of 3-1/2" x 5-1/2" color player postcards. Only the envelope in which the cards were sold carries the 1990 date. Cards have borderless action poses on front, with the player's name, position and uniform number in black-and-white at bottom. Standard postcard style backs have a team logo at top-left, and a photography credit to either Roy Garibaldi or Martha Jane Stanton at bottom-left. The checklist is arranged here by uniform number.

		MT
Complete Set (34):		12.00
Common Player:		.50
1	Ernest Riles	.50
2	Brett Butler	.65
5	Bob Lillis	.50
6	Robby Thompson	.50
7	Kevin Mitchell	.50
8	Gary Carter	.75
9	Matt Williams	1.00
10	Dave Anderson	.50
12	Dusty Baker	.60
13	Greg Litton	.50
16	Terry Kennedy	.50
17	Kevin Bass	.50
18	Bill Bathe	.50
20	Wendell Kim	.50
22	Will Clark	2.00
23	Jose Uribe	.50
26	Mike Kingery	.50
[illegible]	Mike LaCoss	.50
30	Mark Thurmond	.50
31	Don Robinson	.50
32	Rick Parker	.50
33	John Burkett	.60
34	Norm Sherry	.50
37	Kelly Downs	.50
38	Roger Craig	.50
40	Steve Bedrosian	.50
42	Bill Fahey	.50
45	Francisco Oliveras	.50
46	Trevor Wilson	.60
48	Rick Reuschel	.50
49	Jeff Brantley	.50
50	Scott Garrelts	.50
55	Randy O'Neal	.50
---	Candlestick Park	.75

1989 SCD Baseball Card Price Guide Pocket Price Guides

Between its premiere issue of April, 1988, and the Sept., 1989, issue, SCD's monthly price guide magazine issued a gatefold player poster in each issue. Beginning with the Oct., 1989, issue, panels of five (later six) repli-cards were stapled into the magazine in place of the posters. The 1989 repli-card series depicts contemporary players in the design of the 1964 Topps. Backs are in black-and-white with a photo of the player's rookie card and market advice pertaining to the player.

		MT
Complete Set (15):		12.00
Common Player:		.50
1	Mark McGwire	3.00
2	Bo Jackson	.50
3	Ken Griffey	3.00
4	Kevin Mitchell	.50
5	Ryne Sandberg	.75
6	Will Clark	.65
7	Gregg Jefferies	.50
8	Gary Sheffield	.50
9	Fred McGriff	.50
10	Don Mattingly	2.00
11	Jim Abbott	.50
12	Mitch Williams	.50
13	Glenn Davis	.50
14	Ruben Sierra	.50
15	Robin Yount	.75

1990 SCD Baseball Card Price Guide Pocket Price Guides

For its first full year of inserting repli-cards in each issue, SCD Baseball Card Price Guide Monthly magazine rendered the game's stars and hot rookies in the style of 1957 Topps cards. Black, white and red backs have a photo of one of the player's other cards, personal data, current values of selected cards and market advice. Cards were printed on panels of five stapled into each month's issue.

		MT
Complete Set (60):		50.00
Common Player:		.50
1	Darryl Strawberry	.50
2	Wade Boggs	.75
3	Roger Clemens	1.00
4	Paul Molitor	.75
5	Craig Biggio	.50
6	Ruben Sierra	.50
7	Sandy Alomar Jr.	.50
8	Rickey Henderson	.75
9	Mark Langston	.50
10	Dwight Evans	.50
11	Ben McDonald	.50
12	Bo Jackson	.50
13	Don Mattingly	2.00
14	Todd Zeile	.50
15	Mike Greenwell	.50
16	Eric Anthony	.50
17	Dennis Eckersley	.50
18	Greg Vaughn	.50
19	Kevin Mitchell	.50
20	Ryne Sandberg	1.00
21	Will Clark	.75
22	Robin Yount	.75
23	Kirby Puckett	1.00
24	Andy Benes	.65
25	Wally Joyner	.50

26	Ozzie Smith	1.00
27	John Olerud	.50
28	Devon White	.50
29	Alan Trammell	.50
30	Bobby Bonilla	.50
31	Jose Canseco	.65
32	Fred McGriff	.50
33	Mark Grace	.65
34	Ricky Jordan	.50
35	George Brett	1.00
36	Eric Davis	.50
37	Tony Gwynn	1.50
38	Cal Ripken Jr.	2.50
39	Bret Saberhagen	.50
40	Howard Johnson	.50
41	Jerome Walton	.50
42	Mark McGwire	3.00
43	A.L. East Power Hitters (Mike Greenwell, Don Mattingly)	.75
44	Ken Griffey Jr.	3.00
45	Texas' Top Twirlers (Nolan Ryan, Mike Scott)	1.50
46	Barry Larkin	.50
47	Delino DeShields	.50
48	Roberto Alomar	.50
49	Frank Viola	.50
50	Kelly Gruber	.50
51	Michael Jordan	12.00
52	Glenn Davis	.50
53	Marquis Grissom	.50
54	Joe Carter	.50
55	Gregg Jefferies	.50
56	Gary Sheffield	.50
57	Cecil Fielder	.50
58	Matt Williams	.50
59	Ramon Martinez	.50
60	Len Dykstra	.50

1991 SCD Baseball Card Price Guide Pocket Price Guides

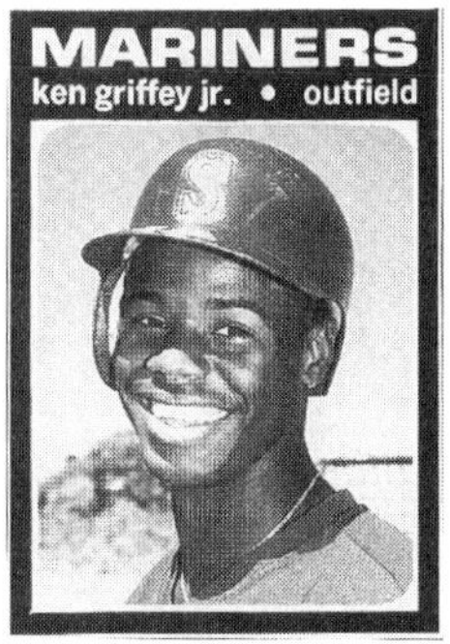

In its third year of including insert cards with each issue, the Price Guide chose the classic 1971 Topps design to showcase the game's top stars and hot rookies. The first five cards have red backgrounds on their backs, the rest are deep green. Backs have a black-and-white photo of one of the player's other cards, along with selected card value data. Also presented are some personal data and the editors' thoughts on each player's future market value.

		MT
Complete Set (60):		40.00
Common Player:		.50
1	Ryne Sandberg	.75
2	Bobby Thigpen	.50
3	Rickey Henderson	.75
4	Dwight Gooden	.50
5	Kevin Maas	.50
6	Ron Gant	.50
7	Frank Thomas	2.50
8	Doug Drabek	.50
9	Bobby Bonilla	.50
10	Sandy Alomar Jr.	.50
11	Bob Welch	.50
12	Joe Carter	.50
13	Cecil Fielder	.50
14	Dave Justice	.50
15	Barry Bonds	.75
16	Barry Larkin	.50
17	Ramon Martinez	.50
18	Ben McDonald	.50
19	Roger Clemens	1.00
20	Jose Canseco	.75
21	Will Clark	.75
22	Jeff Conine	.50
23	Chris Sabo	.50
24	Alan Trammell	.50
25	Howard Johnson	.50
26	Dale Murphy	.50
27	Gregg Jefferies	.50
28	Bo Jackson	.50
29	Craig Biggio	.50
30	Delino DeShields	.50
31	Rafael Palmeiro	.50
32	Robin Yount	.75
33	Mark McGwire	3.00
34	Kevin Mitchell	.50
35	George Brett	.75
36	Tim Wallach	.50
37	Andre Dawson	.50
38	Kirby Puckett	1.00
39	Matt Williams	.50
40	Wade Boggs	.75
41	Dave Winfield	.65
42	Don Mattingly	2.00
43	Carlton Fisk	.65
44	Dave Stewart	.50
45	Ken Griffey Jr.	3.00
46	Ruben Sierra	.50
47	George Bell	.50
48	Cal Ripken	2.50
49	Ellis Burks	.50
50	Roberto Alomar	.50
51	Tim Raines	.50
52	Mike Greenwell	.50
53	Benito Santiago	.50
54	Tom Glavine	.50
55	Scott Erickson	.50
56	Chuck Finley	.50
57	Julio Franco	.50
58	Paul Molitor	.75
59	Todd Van Poppel	.50
60	Mo Vaughn	.50

1992 BB Card Price Guide/Sports Card Price Guide

New collector focus on other team sports resulted in SCD's Baseball Card Price Guide Monthly changing its name to Sports Card Price Guide Monthly with its May, 1992, issue. The title change was also reflected in the annual series of repli-cards stapled into each issue. For the first time football, basketball and hockey players joined the baseball stars. That change was effective with card #21. The '92 series utilized the design of Topps' 1974 baseball cards. Backs are printed in black, white and green and, as in previous years, include a photo of one of the player's cards along with selective current values and a market forecast. Only the set's baseball players are listed here.

		MT
Complete (Baseball) Set (56):		36.00
Common Player:		.50
1	Will Clark	.65
2	Albert Belle	1.00
3	Luis Gonzalez	.50
4	Ramon Martinez	.50
5	Frank Thomas	2.50
6	Travis Fryman	.50
7	Carlton Fisk	.75
8	Bo Jackson	.50
9	Chuck Knoblauch	.50
10	Ron Gant	.50
11	Jose Canseco	.65
12	Roger Clemens	1.00
13	Darren Lewis	.50
14	Kirby Puckett	1.00
15	Tom Glavine	.50
16	Royce Clayton	.50
18	Ozzie Smith	1.00
20	Robin Ventura	.50
21	Derek Bell	.50
23	Ryne Sandberg	.75
25	Andy Van Slyke	.50
26	Jim Abbott	.50
27	Ken Griffey Jr.	3.00
30	Jeff Bagwell	.75
32	Dwight Gooden	.50
33	Ruben Sierra	.50
35	David Justice	.50
36	Wade Boggs	1.00
38	Barry Larkin	.50
39	Felix Jose	.50
40	Howard Johnson	.50
42	Fred McGriff	.50
44	Todd Van Poppel	.50
46	Brien Taylor	.50
48	Cal Ripken Jr.	2.50
50	Dave Winfield	.75
52	Juan Gonzalez	.75
53	Reggie Sanders	.50
57	Gary Sheffield	.50
58	Roberto Alomar	.50
59	Barry Bonds	.75
60	Tom Glavine	.50
62	Kenny Lofton	.50
63	Joe Carter	.50
66	Paul Molitor	.75
67	Phil Plantier	.50
69	Mark McGwire	3.00
70	Nolan Ryan	2.50
72	Darryl Strawberry	.50
73	Pat Listach	.50
74	Dennis Eckersley	.50
75	Bobby Bonilla	.50
78	Delino DeShields	.50
80	Doug Drabek	.50
81	Deion Sanders	.65
84	Darren Daulton	.50

1993 Sports Card Pocket Price Guide

The final year of production of an annual repli-card insert set for the SCD price guide magazine combined stars and hot rookies from all four major team sports. Cards were produced in the style of Topps' 1973 football issue, with varying colored striped pennants down the left side of the front. Backs are printed in black, white and green (#1-8) and black, white and red (#9-96), and include a cartoon trivia question along with price guide and player data. The repli-cards were printed on sheets of eight stapled into the magazine's monthly issues. Only the baseball players are listed here.

		MT
Complete (Baseball) Set (49):		32.00
Common Player:		.50
1	Tyler Green	.50
3	Ozzie Smith	1.00
5	Fred McGriff	.50
7	Marquis Grissom	.50
13	John Smoltz	.50
16	Ruben Sierra	.50
19	Roberto Alomar	.50
20	Gary Sheffield	.50
23	Carlos Baerga	.50
24	Robin Ventura	.50
25	Nigel Wilson	.60
26	David Nied	.50
27	Cal Ripken Jr.	3.00
28	Albert Belle	.75
34	Larry Walker	.50
37	Eric Karros	.50
38	Dwight Gooden	.50
39	Nolan Ryan	3.00
40	Juan Gonzalez	.75
41	Robin Yount	.75
44	Darryl Strawberry	.50
45	George Brett	1.00
46	Ray Lankford	.50
47	Kirby Puckett	1.00
48	David Justice	.50
49	Travis Fryman	.50
50	Eddie Murray	.75
51	Tony Gwynn	.75
52	Jack McDowell	.50
57	Ryne Sandberg	1.00
58	Deion Sanders	.75
61	Frank Thomas	2.50
62	Carlton Fisk	.65
65	Tim Salmon	.50
66	Jeff Conine	.50
67	Benito Santiago	.50
68	Mike Piazza	2.00
71	Gregg Jefferies	.50
76	Joe Carter	.50
77	Rickey Henderson	.65
80	Barry Larkin	.50
82	Juan Gonzalez	.75
83	Gary Sheffield	.50
84	Will Clark	.65
89	Mark Grace	.65
90	Cliff Floyd	.50
91	Bobby Bonds Jr.	.50
92	Barry Bonds	.75
94	Matt Williams	.50

1989 Schafer's Bakery Super Stars Discs

(See 1989 Holsum for checklist and value information. Distributed in Michigan.)

1986 Schnucks Milk St. Louis Cardinals

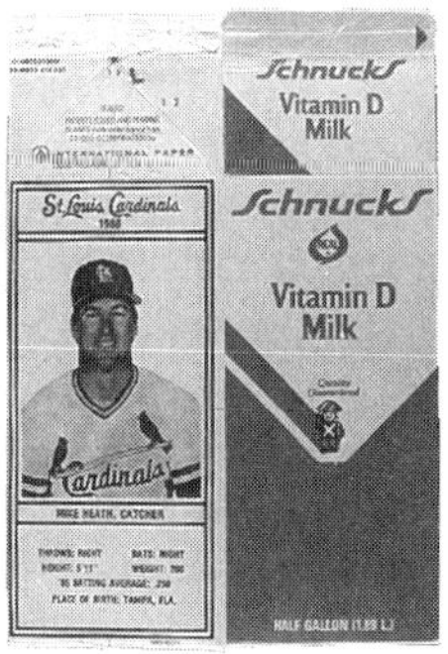

These milk carton panels were sold by Schnucks supermarkets in the St. Louis and southwestern Illinois areas. The 3-3/4" x 7-1/2" blank-backed panels feature black-and-white photos of 24 different St. Louis players along with personal information and 1985 playing statistics. A mascot and schedule card were also included in the set.

		MT
Complete Set (26):		30.00
Common Player:		1.00
(1)	Jack Clark	1.50
(2)	Vince Coleman	2.00
(3)	Tim Conroy	1.00
(4)	Danny Cox	1.00
(5)	Ken Dayley	1.00
(6)	Bob Forsch	1.00
(7)	Mike Heath	1.00
(8)	Tom Herr	1.00
(9)	Rick Horton	1.00
(10)	Clint Hurdle	1.00
(11)	Kurt Kepshire	1.00
(12)	Jeff Lahti	1.00
(13)	Tito Landrum	1.00
(14)	Mike Lavalliere	1.00
(15)	Tom Lawless	1.00
(16)	Willie McGee	3.00
(17)	Jose Oquendo	1.00
(18)	Rick Ownbey	1.00
(19)	Terry Pendleton	3.00
(20)	Pat Perry	1.00
(21)	Ozzie Smith	8.00
(22)	John Tudor	1.00
(23)	Andy Van Slyke	2.00
(24)	Todd Worrell	1.00
(25)	Fred Bird (mascot) (mascot)	1.00
(26)	1986 Cardinals Schedule	.50

1987 Schnucks St. Louis Cardinals

Sponsored by Schnucks food stores, and distributed at more than 50 locations around St. Louis, the company is not mentioned anywhere on these photos. The set of 6" x 9" photocards depicts the players without caps or other visible uniform logos in color photos against a plain blue backdrop. A facsimile autograph appears in the lower-left corner, with a Players' Association logo at upper-left. Backs are blank. The unnumbered cards are checklisted here alphabetically.

		MT
Complete Set (16):		12.00
Common Player:		.50
(1)	Jack Clark	.50
(2)	Vince Coleman	.75
(3)	Danny Cox	.50
(4)	Curt Ford	.50
(5)	Bob Forsch	.50
(6)	Tom Herr	.50
(7)	Whitey Herzog	.50
(8)	Ricky Horton	.50
(9)	Greg Mathews	.50
(10)	Willie McGee	.75
(11)	Jose Oquendo	.50
(12)	Tony Pena	.50
(13)	Terry Pendleton	.75
(14)	Ozzie Smith	4.00
(15)	John Tudor	.50
(16)	Todd Worrell	.50

1996 Schwebel's Stars Discs

Distributed in loaves of bread in the Youngstown, Ohio, area, the players in this disc set lean heavily towards Cleveland Indians. The 2-3/4" diameter discs were inserted into a special pocket in the bread wrapper to keep them from contact with the bread. Fronts have a purple-to-red graduated color scheme around the border, with a player photo at center. Uniform logos have been removed from the photos because the discs are licensed only by the players' union; they are a product of Mike Schechter Assoc. Backs are printed in purple with 1995 and career stats along with appropriate logos. A die-cut poster into which the discs could be inserted for display was also available.

		MT
Complete Set (20):		32.00
Common Player:		1.50
1	Jim Thome	1.50
2	Orel Hershiser	1.50
3	Greg Maddux	3.00
4	Charles Nagy	1.50
5	Omar Vizquel	1.50
6	Manny Ramirez	1.50
7	Dennis Martinez	1.50
8	Eddie Murray	2.00

9	Albert Belle	2.00
10	Fred McGriff	1.50
11	Jack McDowell	1.50
12	Kenny Lofton	1.50
13	Cal Ripken Jr.	3.50
14	Jose Mesa	1.50
15	Randy Johnson	1.50
16	Ken Griffey Jr.	4.00
17	Carlos Baerga	1.50
18	Frank Thomas	3.50
19	Sandy Alomar Jr.	1.50
20	Barry Bonds	2.50

1988 Score Promo Cards

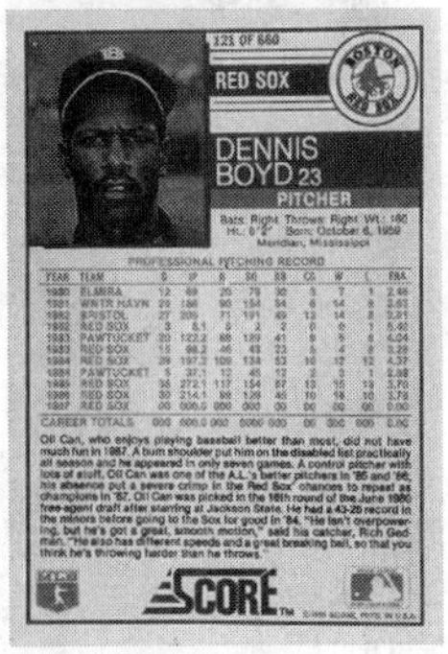

While these Score promotional sample cards carry a 1988 copyright date on back, they were actually released to hobby dealers late in 1987. They can be easily differentiated from regular-issue 1988 cards by the use of zeros in the stats lines on back for 1987 and career figures. Most of the promos are otherwise identical to the issued versions of the same players. These were among the first promo cards to be widely distributed within the hobby.

		MT
Complete Set (6):		30.00
Common Player:		5.00
30	Mark Langston	7.50
48	Tony Pena	5.00
71	Keith Moreland	5.00
72	Barry Larkin	10.00
121	Dennis Boyd	5.00
149	Denny Walling	5.00

1988 Score

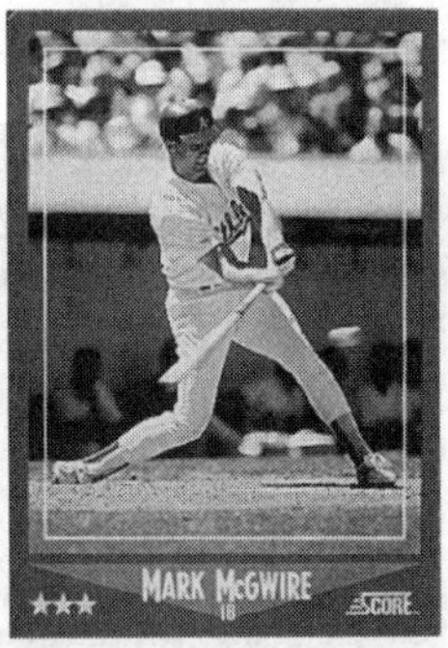

A fifth member joined the group of nationally distributed baseball cards in 1988. Titled "Score," the cards are characterized by extremely sharp color photography and printing. Card backs are full-color also and carry a player portrait along with a brief biography, player data and statistics. The 660 cards in the set are standard 2-1/2" x 3-1/2" format. The fronts come with one of six different border colors which are equally divided at 110 cards per color. The Score set was produced by Major League Marketing, the same company that marketed the "triple-action" Sportflics card sets.

		MT
Complete Set (660):		15.00
Common Player:		.05
Wax Box:		10.00
1	Don Mattingly	.50
2	Wade Boggs	.25
3	Tim Raines	.10
4	Andre Dawson	.15
5	Mark McGwire	1.50
6	Kevin Seitzer	.05
7	Wally Joyner	.10
8	Jesse Barfield	.05
9	Pedro Guerrero	.05
10	Eric Davis	.10
11	George Brett	.35
12	Ozzie Smith	.25
13	Rickey Henderson	.20
14	Jim Rice	.10
15	*Matt Nokes*	.05
16	Mike Schmidt	.40
17	Dave Parker	.10
18	Eddie Murray	.20
19	Andres Galarraga	.10
20	Tony Fernandez	.05
21	Kevin McReynolds	.05
22	B.J. Surhoff	.10
23	Pat Tabler	.05
24	Kirby Puckett	.45
25	Benny Santiago	.05
26	Ryne Sandberg	.40
27	Kelly Downs	.05
28	Jose Cruz	.05
29	Pete O'Brien	.05
30	Mark Langston	.05
31	Lee Smith	.05
32	Juan Samuel	.05
33	Kevin Bass	.05
34	R.J. Reynolds	.05
35	Steve Sax	.05
36	John Kruk	.05
37	Alan Trammell	.10
38	Chris Bosio	.05
39	Brook Jacoby	.05
40	Willie McGee	.05
41	Dave Magadan	.05
42	Fred Lynn	.05
43	Kent Hrbek	.10
44	Brian Downing	.05
45	Jose Canseco	.25
46	Jim Presley	.05
47	Mike Stanley	.05
48	Tony Pena	.05
49	David Cone	.15
50	Rick Sutcliffe	.05
51	Doug Drabek	.05
52	Bill Doran	.05
53	Mike Scioscia	.05
54	Candy Maldonado	.05
55	Dave Winfield	.20
56	Lou Whitaker	.05
57	Tom Henke	.05
58	Ken Gerhart	.05
59	Glenn Braggs	.05
60	Julio Franco	.05
61	Charlie Leibrandt	.05
62	Gary Gaetti	.05
63	Bob Boone	.05
64	*Luis Polonia*	.10
65	Dwight Evans	.05
66	Phil Bradley	.05
67	Mike Boddicker	.05
68	Vince Coleman	.05
69	Howard Johnson	.05
70	Tim Wallach	.05
71	Keith Moreland	.05
72	Barry Larkin	.15
73	Alan Ashby	.10
74	Rick Rhoden	.05
75	Darrell Evans	.10
76	Dave Stieb	.05
77	Dan Plesac	.05
78	Will Clark	.25
79	Frank White	.05
80	Joe Carter	.10
81	Mike Witt	.05
82	Terry Steinbach	.05
83	Alvin Davis	.05
84	Tom Herr	.05
85	Vance Law	.05
86	Kal Daniels	.05
87	Rick Honeycutt	.05
88	Alfredo Griffin	.05
89	Bret Saberhagen	.10
90	Bert Blyleven	.05
91	Jeff Reardon	.05
92	Cory Snyder	.05
93	Greg Walker	.05
94	*Joe Magrane*	.10
95	Rob Deer	.05
96	Ray Knight	.05
97	Casey Candaele	.05
98	John Cerutti	.05
99	Buddy Bell	.05
100	Jack Clark	.05
101	Eric Bell	.05
102	Willie Wilson	.10
103	Dave Schmidt	.05
104	Dennis Eckersley	.10
105	Don Sutton	.15
106	Danny Tartabull	.05
107	Fred McGriff	.25
108	*Les Straker*	.05
109	Lloyd Moseby	.05
110	Roger Clemens	.35
111	Glenn Hubbard	.05
112	*Ken Williams*	.05
113	Ruben Sierra	.05
114	Stan Jefferson	.05
115	Milt Thompson	.05
116	Bobby Bonilla	.10
117	Wayne Tolleson	.05
118	Matt Williams	.20
119	Chet Lemon	.05
120	Dale Sveum	.05
121	Dennis Boyd	.05
122	Brett Butler	.05
123	Terry Kennedy	.05
124	Jack Howell	.05
125	Curt Young	.05
126a	Dale Valle (first name incorrect)	.25
126b	Dave Valle (correct spelling)	.05
127	Curt Wilkerson	.05
128	Tim Teufel	.05
129	Ozzie Virgil	.05
130	Brian Fisher	.05
131	Lance Parrish	.05
132	Tom Browning	.05
133a	Larry Anderson (incorrect spelling)	.25
133b	Larry Andersen (correct spelling)	.05
134a	Bob Brenley (incorrect spelling)	.25
134b	Bob Brenly (correct spelling)	.05
135	Mike Marshall	.05
136	Gerald Perry	.05
137	Bobby Meacham	.05
138	Larry Herndon	.05
139	*Fred Manrique*	.05
140	Charlie Hough	.05
141	Ron Darling	.05
142	Herm Winningham	.05
143	Mike Diaz	.05
144	*Mike Jackson*	.05
145	Denny Walling	.05
146	Rob Thompson	.05
147	Franklin Stubbs	.05
148	Albert Hall	.05
149	Bobby Witt	.05
150	Lance McCullers	.05
151	Scott Bradley	.05
152	Mark McLemore	.05
153	Tim Laudner	.05
154	Greg Swindell	.05
155	Marty Barrett	.05
156	Mike Heath	.05
157	Gary Ward	.05
158a	Lee Mazilli (incorrect spelling)	.25
158b	Lee Mazzilli (correct spelling)	.05
159	Tom Foley	.05
160	Robin Yount	.30
161	Steve Bedrosian	.05
162	Bob Walk	.05
163	Nick Esasky	.05
164	*Ken Caminiti*	.75
165	Jose Uribe	.05
166	Dave Anderson	.05
167	Ed Whitson	.05
168	Ernie Whitt	.05
169	Cecil Cooper	.05
170	Mike Pagliarulo	.05
171	Pat Sheridan	.05
172	Chris Bando	.05
173	Lee Lacy	.05
174	Steve Lombardozzi	.05
175	Mike Greenwell	.05
176	Greg Minton	.05
177	Moose Haas	.05
178	Mike Kingery	.05
179	Greg Harris	.05
180	Bo Jackson	.20
181	Carmelo Martinez	.05
182	Alex Trevino	.05
183	Ron Oester	.05
184	Danny Darwin	.05
185	Mike Krukow	.05
186	Rafael Palmeiro	.20
187	Tim Burke	.05
188	Roger McDowell	.05
189	Garry Templeton	.05
190	Terry Pendleton	.05
191	Larry Parrish	.05
192	Rey Quinones	.05
193	Joaquin Andujar	.05
194	Tom Brunansky	.05
195	Donnie Moore	.05
196	Dan Pasqua	.05
197	Jim Gantner	.05
198	Mark Eichhorn	.05
199	John Grubb	.05
200	*Bill Ripken*	.05
201	*Sam Horn*	.05
202	Todd Worrell	.05
203	Terry Leach	.05
204	Garth Iorg	.05
205	Brian Dayett	.05
206	Bo Diaz	.05
207	Craig Reynolds	.05
208	Brian Holton	.05
209	Marvelle Wynne (Marvell)	.05
210	Dave Concepcion	.05
211	Mike Davis	.05
212	Devon White	.10
213	Mickey Brantley	.05
214	Greg Gagne	.05
215	Oddibe McDowell	.05
216	Jimmy Key	.05
217	Dave Bergman	.05
218	Calvin Schiraldi	.05
219	Larry Sheets	.05
220	Mike Easler	.05
221	Kurt Stillwell	.05
222	*Chuck Jackson*	.05
223	Dave Martinez	.05
224	Tim Leary	.05
225	Steve Garvey	.15
226	Greg Mathews	.05
227	Doug Sisk	.05
228	Dave Henderson	.05
229	Jimmy Dwyer	.05
230	Larry Owen	.05
231	Andre Thornton	.05
232	Mark Salas	.05
233	Tom Brookens	.05
234	Greg Brock	.05
235	Rance Mulliniks	.05
236	Bob Brower	.05
237	Joe Niekro	.05
238	Scott Bankhead	.05
239	Doug DeCinces	.05
240	Tommy John	.10
241	Rich Gedman	.05
242	Ted Power	.05
243	*Dave Meads*	.05
244	Jim Sundberg	.05
245	Ken Oberkfell	.05
246	Jimmy Jones	.05
247	Ken Landreaux	.05
248	Jose Oquendo	.05
249	*John Mitchell*	.05
250	Don Baylor	.10
251	Scott Fletcher	.05
252	Al Newman	.05
253	Carney Lansford	.05
254	Johnny Ray	.05
255	Gary Pettis	.05
256	Ken Phelps	.05
257	Rick Leach	.05
258	Tim Stoddard	.05
259	Ed Romero	.05
260	Sid Bream	.05
261a	Tom Neidenfuer (incorrect spelling)	.25
261b	Tom Niedenfuer (correct spelling)	.05
262	Rick Dempsey	.05
263	Lonnie Smith	.05
264	Bob Forsch	.05
265	Barry Bonds	.50
266	Willie Randolph	.05
267	Mike Ramsey	.05
268	Don Slaught	.05
269	Mickey Tettleton	.05
270	Jerry Reuss	.05
271	Marc Sullivan	.05
272	Jim Morrison	.05
273	Steve Balboni	.05
274	Dick Schofield	.05
275	John Tudor	.05
276	*Gene Larkin*	.05
277	Harold Reynolds	.05
278	Jerry Browne	.05
279	Willie Upshaw	.05
280	Ted Higuera	.05
281	Terry McGriff	.05
282	Terry Puhl	.05
283	*Mark Wasinger*	.05
284	Luis Salazar	.05
285	Ted Simmons	.05
286	John Shelby	.05
287	*John Smiley*	.15
288	Curt Ford	.05
289	Steve Crawford	.05
290	Dan Quisenberry	.05
291	Alan Wiggins	.05
292	Randy Bush	.05
293	John Candelaria	.05
294	Tony Phillips	.05
295	Mike Morgan	.05
296	Bill Wegman	.05
297a	Terry Franconia (incorrect spelling)	.25
297b	Terry Francona (correct spelling)	.05
298	Mickey Hatcher	.05
299	Andres Thomas	.05
300	Bob Stanley	.05
301	*Alfredo Pedrique*	.05
302	Jim Lindeman	.05
303	Wally Backman	.05
304	Paul O'Neill	.15
305	Hubie Brooks	.05
306	Steve Buechele	.05
307	Bobby Thigpen	.05
308	George Hendrick	.05
309	John Moses	.05
310	Ron Guidry	.10
311	Bill Schroeder	.05
312	*Jose Nunez*	.05
313	Bud Black	.05
314	Joe Sambito	.05
315	Scott McGregor	.05
316	Rafael Santana	.05
317	Frank Williams	.05
318	Mike Fitzgerald	.05
319	Rick Mahler	.05
320	Jim Gott	.05
321	Mariano Duncan	.05
322	Jose Guzman	.05
323	Lee Guetterman	.05
324	Dan Gladden	.05
325	Gary Carter	.10
326	Tracy Jones	.05
327	Floyd Youmans	.05
328	Bill Dawley	.05
329	*Paul Noce*	.05
330	Angel Salazar	.05
331	Goose Gossage	.10
332	George Frazier	.05
333	Ruppert Jones	.05
334	Billy Jo Robidoux	.05
335	Mike Scott	.05
336	Randy Myers	.05
337	Bob Sebra	.05
338	Eric Show	.05
339	Mitch Williams	.05
340	Paul Molitor	.30
341	Gus Polidor	.05
342	Steve Trout	.05
343	Jerry Don Gleaton	.05
344	Bob Knepper	.05
345	Mitch Webster	.05
346	John Morris	.05
347	Andy Hawkins	.05
348	Dave Leiper	.05
349	Ernest Riles	.05
350	Dwight Gooden	.15
351	Dave Righetti	.05
352	Pat Dodson	.05
353	John Habyan	.05
354	Jim Deshaies	.05
355	Butch Wynegar	.05
356	Bryn Smith	.05
357	Matt Young	.05
358	*Tom Pagnozzi*	.05
359	Floyd Rayford	.05
360	Darryl Strawberry	.10
361	Sal Butera	.05
362	Domingo Ramos	.05
363	Chris Brown	.05
364	Jose Gonzalez	.05
365	Dave Smith	.05
366	Andy McGaffigan	.05
367	Stan Javier	.05
368	Henry Cotto	.05
369	Mike Birkbeck	.05
370	Len Dykstra	.05
371	Dave Collins	.05
372	Spike Owen	.05
373	Geno Petralli	.05
374	Ron Karkovice	.05
375	Shane Rawley	.05
376	*DeWayne Buice*	.05
377	*Bill Pecota*	.05
378	Leon Durham	.05
379	Ed Olwine	.05
380	Bruce Hurst	.05
381	Bob McClure	.05
382	Mark Thurmond	.05
383	Buddy Biancalana	.05
384	Tim Conroy	.05
385	Tony Gwynn	.30
386	Greg Gross	.05
387	*Barry Lyons*	.05
388	Mike Felder	.05
389	Pat Clements	.05
390	Ken Griffey	.10
391	Mark Davis	.05
392	Jose Rijo	.05
393	Mike Young	.05
394	Willie Fraser	.05
395	Dion James	.05
396	*Steve Shields*	.05
397	Randy St. Claire	.05
398	Danny Jackson	.05
399	Cecil Fielder	.10
400	Keith Hernandez	.05
401	Don Carman	.05
402	*Chuck Crim*	.05
403	Rob Woodward	.05
404	Junior Ortiz	.05
405	Glenn Wilson	.05
406	Ken Howell	.05
407	Jeff Kunkel	.05
408	Jeff Reed	.05
409	Chris James	.05
410	Zane Smith	.05
411	Ken Dixon	.05
412	Ricky Horton	.05
413	Frank DiPino	.05
414	*Shane Mack*	.10
415	Danny Cox	.05
416	Andy Van Slyke	.05
417	Danny Heep	.05
418	John Cangelosi	.05
419a	John Christiansen (incorrect spelling)	.25
419b	John Christensen (correct spelling)	.05
420	*Joey Cora*	.10
421	Mike LaValliere	.05
422	Kelly Gruber	.05
423	Bruce Benedict	.05
424	Len Matuszek	.05
425	Kent Tekulve	.05
426	Rafael Ramirez	.05
427	Mike Flanagan	.05
428	Mike Gallego	.05
429	Juan Castillo	.05
430	Neal Heaton	.05
431	Phil Garner	.05
432	*Mike Dunne*	.05
433	Wallace Johnson	.05
434	Jack O'Connor	.05
435	Steve Jeltz	.05
436	*Donnell Nixon*	.05
437	Jack Lazorko	.05
438	*Keith Comstock*	.05
439	Jeff Robinson	.05
440	Graig Nettles	.10

441	Mel Hall	.05
442	*Gerald Young*	.05
443	Gary Redus	.05
444	Charlie Moore	.05
445	Bill Madlock	.05
446	Mark Clear	.05
447	Greg Booker	.05
448	Rick Schu	.05
449	Ron Kittle	.05
450	Dale Murphy	.10
451	Bob Dernier	.05
452	Dale Mohorcic	.05
453	Rafael Belliard	.05
454	Charlie Puleo	.05
455	Dwayne Murphy	.05
456	Jim Eisenreich	.05
457	David Palmer	.05
458	Dave Stewart	.10
459	Pascual Perez	.05
460	Glenn Davis	.05
461	Dan Petry	.05
462	Jim Winn	.05
463	Darrell Miller	.05
464	Mike Moore	.05
465	Mike LaCoss	.05
466	Steve Farr	.05
467	Jerry Mumphrey	.05
468	Kevin Gross	.05
469	Bruce Bochy	.05
470	Orel Hershiser	.10
471	Eric King	.05
472	*Ellis Burks*	.30
473	Darren Daulton	.05
474	Mookie Wilson	.05
475	Frank Viola	.05
476	Ron Robinson	.05
477	Bob Melvin	.05
478	Jeff Musselman	.05
479	Charlie Kerfeld	.05
480	Richard Dotson	.05
481	Kevin Mitchell	.05
482	Gary Roenicke	.05
483	Tim Flannery	.05
484	Rich Yett	.05
485	Pete Incaviglia	.05
486	Rick Cerone	.05
487	Tony Armas	.05
488	Jerry Reed	.05
489	Davey Lopes	.05
490	Frank Tanana	.05
491	Mike Loynd	.05
492	Bruce Ruffin	.05
493	Chris Speier	.05
494	Tom Hume	.05
495	Jesse Orosco	.05
496	*Robby Wine, Jr.*	.05
497	*Jeff Montgomery*	.20
498	Jeff Dedmon	.05
499	Luis Aguayo	.05
500	Reggie Jackson (1968-75)	.20
501	Reggie Jackson (1976)	.20
502	Reggie Jackson (1977-81)	.20
503	Reggie Jackson (1982-86)	.20
504	Reggie Jackson (1987)	.20
505	Billy Hatcher	.05
506	Ed Lynch	.05
507	Willie Hernandez	.05
508	Jose DeLeon	.05
509	Joel Youngblood	.05
510	Bob Welch	.05
511	Steve Ontiveros	.05
512	Randy Ready	.05
513	Juan Nieves	.05
514	Jeff Russell	.05
515	Von Hayes	.05
516	Mark Gubicza	.05
517	Ken Dayley	.05
518	Don Aase	.05
519	Rick Reuschel	.05
520	*Mike Henneman*	.15
521	Rick Aguilera	.05
522	Jay Howell	.05
523	Ed Correa	.05
524	Manny Trillo	.05
525	Kirk Gibson	.05
526	*Wally Ritchie*	.05
527	Al Nipper	.05
528	Atlee Hammaker	.05
529	Shawon Dunston	.05
530	Jim Clancy	.05
531	Tom Paciorek	.05
532	Joel Skinner	.05
533	Scott Garrelts	.05
534	Tom O'Malley	.05
535	John Franco	.05
536	*Paul Kilgus*	.05
537	Darrell Porter	.05
538	Walt Terrell	.05
539	*Bill Long*	.05
540	George Bell	.05
541	Jeff Sellers	.05
542	*Joe Boever*	.05
543	Steve Howe	.05
544	Scott Sanderson	.05
545	Jack Morris	.10
546	*Todd Benzinger*	.10
547	Steve Henderson	.05
548	Eddie Milner	.05
549	*Jeff Robinson*	.05
550	Cal Ripken, Jr.	.60
551	Jody Davis	.05
552	Kirk McCaskill	.05
553	Craig Lefferts	.05
554	Darnell Coles	.05
555	Phil Niekro	.25
556	Mike Aldrete	.05
557	Pat Perry	.05
558	Juan Agosto	.05
559	Rob Murphy	.05
560	Dennis Rasmussen	.05
561	Manny Lee	.05
562	*Jeff Blauser*	.10
563	Bob Ojeda	.05
564	Dave Dravecky	.05
565	Gene Garber	.05
566	Ron Roenicke	.05
567	*Tommy Hinzo*	.05
568	*Eric Nolte*	.05
569	Ed Hearn	.05
570	*Mark Davidson*	.05
571	*Jim Walewander*	.05
572	Donnie Hill	.05
573	Jamie Moyer	.05
574	Ken Schrom	.05
575	Nolan Ryan	.60
576	Jim Acker	.05
577	Jamie Quirk	.05
578	*Jay Aldrich*	.05
579	Claudell Washington	.05
580	Jeff Leonard	.05
581	Carmen Castillo	.05
582	Daryl Boston	.05
583	*Jeff DeWillis*	.05
584	*John Marzano*	.05
585	Bill Gullickson	.05
586	Andy Allanson	.05
587	Lee Tunnell	.05
588	Gene Nelson	.05
589	Dave LaPoint	.05
590	Harold Baines	.10
591	Bill Buckner	.05
592	Carlton Fisk	.15
593	Rick Manning	.05
594	*Doug Jones*	.10
595	Tom Candiotti	.05
596	Steve Lake	.05
597	*Jose Lind*	.10
598	*Ross Jones*	.05
599	Gary Matthews	.05
600	Fernando Valenzuela	.10
601	Dennis Martinez	.10
602	*Les Lancaster*	.10
603	Ozzie Guillen	.05
604	Tony Bernazard	.05
605	Chili Davis	.10
606	Roy Smalley	.05
607	Ivan Calderon	.05
608	Jay Tibbs	.05
609	Guy Hoffman	.05
610	Doyle Alexander	.05
611	Mike Bielecki	.05
612	*Shawn Hillegas*	.05
613	Keith Atherton	.05
614	Eric Plunk	.05
615	Sid Fernandez	.05
616	Dennis Lamp	.05
617	Dave Engle	.05
618	Harry Spilman	.05
619	Don Robinson	.05
620	*John Farrell*	.05
621	*Nelson Liriano*	.05
622	Floyd Bannister	.05
623	*Randy Milligan*	.10
624	*Kevin Elster*	.10
625	*Jody Reed*	.15
626	*Shawn Abner*	.05
627	*Kirt Manwaring*	.10
628	*Pete Stanicek*	.05
629	*Rob Ducey*	.05
630	Steve Kiefer	.05
631	*Gary Thurman*	.05
632	*Darrel Akerfelds*	.05
633	Dave Clark	.05
634	*Roberto Kelly*	.15
635	*Keith Hughes*	.05
636	*John Davis*	.05
637	*Mike Devereaux*	.10
638	*Tom Glavine*	.75
639	*Keith Miller*	.05
640	*Chris Gwynn*	.05
641	*Tim Crews*	.05
642	*Mackey Sasser*	.05
643	*Vicente Palacios*	.05
644	Kevin Romine	.05
645	*Gregg Jefferies*	.25
646	*Jeff Treadway*	.05
647	*Ron Gant*	.25
648	Rookie Sluggers (Mark McGwire, Matt Nokes)	.75
649	Speed and Power (Tim Raines, Eric Davis)	.10
650	Game Breakers (Jack Clark, Don Mattingly)	.20
651	Super Shortstops (Tony Fernandez, Cal Ripken, Jr., Alan Trammell)	.25
652	Vince Coleman (Highlight)	.05
653	Kirby Puckett (Highlight)	.30
654	Benito Santiago (Highlight)	.05
655	Juan Nieves (Highlight)	.05
656	Steve Bedrosian (Highlight)	.05
657	Mike Schmidt (Highlight)	.20
658	Don Mattingly (Highlight)	.30
659	Mark McGwire (Highlight)	.75
660	Paul Molitor (Highlight)	.15

1988 Score Glossy

With production of a reported 5,000 sets, there is a significant premium attached to the glossy version of Score's debut baseball card issue. The specially packaged collector's edition features cards with a high-gloss front finish and was sold only as a complete set.

	MT
Complete Set (660):	200.00
Common Player:	.50
Stars: 15X	
(See 1988 Score for checklist and base card values.)	

1988 Score Box Panels

This 18-card set, produced by Major League Marketing and manufactured by Optigraphics, is the premiere box-bottom set issued under the Score trademark. The set features 1987 major league All-star players in full-color action poses, framed by a white border. A "1987 All-Star" banner (red or purple) curves above an orange player name block beneath the player photo. Card backs are printed in red, blue, gold and black and carry the card number, player name and position and league logo. Six colorful "Great Moments in Baseball" trivia cards are also included in this set.

		MT
Complete Panel Set:		8.00
Complete Singles Set (18):		3.00
Common Panel:		1.50
Common Single Player:		.15
Panel 1		1.50
1	Terry Kennedy	.15
3	Willie Randolph	.15
15	Eric Davis	.25
Panel 2		3.50
3	Don Mattingly	.75
5	Cal Ripken, Jr.	2.00
11	Jack Clark	.15
Panel 3		1.75
4	Wade Boggs	.60
9	Bret Saberhagen	.20
12	Ryne Sandberg	.60
Panel 4		1.75
6	George Bell	.15
13	Mike Schmidt	.65
18	Mike Scott	.15
Panel 5		1.75
7	Rickey Henderson	.50
16	Andre Dawson	.25
17	Darryl Strawberry	.20
Panel 6		2.50
8	Dave Winfield	.40
10	Gary Carter	.20
14	Ozzie Smith	.50

1988 Score Traded/Rookie

This 110-card set featuring rookies and traded veterans is similar in design to the 1988 Score set, except for a change in border color. Individual standard-size player cards (2-1/2" x 3-1/2") feature a bright orange border framing action photos highlighted by a thin white outline. The player name (in white) is centered in the bottom margin, flanked by three yellow stars lower left and a yellow Score logo lower right. The backs carry full-color player portraits on a cream-colored background, plus team name and logo, personal information and a purple stats chart that lists year-by-year and major league totals. A brief player profile follows the stats chart and, on some cards, information is included about the player's trade or acquisition. The boxed update set also includes 10 Magic Motion 3-D trivia cards. The cards are numbered with a "T" suffix.

		MT
Complete Set (110):		50.00
Common Player:		.20
1	Jack Clark	.20
2	Danny Jackson	.20
3	Brett Butler	.20
4	Kurt Stillwell	.20
5	Tom Brunansky	.20
6	Dennis Lamp	.20
7	Jose DeLeon	.20
8	Tom Herr	.20
9	Keith Moreland	.20
10	Kirk Gibson	.25
11	Bud Black	.20
12	Rafael Ramirez	.20
13	Luis Salazar	.20
14	Goose Gossage	.25
15	Bob Welch	.20
16	Vance Law	.20
17	Ray Knight	.20
18	Dan Quisenberry	.20
19	Don Slaught	.20
20	Lee Smith	.25
21	Rick Cerone	.20
22	Pat Tabler	.20
23	Larry McWilliams	.20
24	Rick Horton	.20
25	Graig Nettles	.20
26	Dan Petry	.20
27	Jose Rijo	.20
28	Chili Davis	.25
29	Dickie Thon	.20
30	Mackey Sasser	.20
31	Mickey Tettleton	.20
32	Rick Dempsey	.20
33	Ron Hassey	.20
34	Phil Bradley	.20
35	Jay Howell	.20
36	Bill Buckner	.20
37	Alfredo Griffin	.20
38	Gary Pettis	.20
39	Calvin Schiraldi	.20
40	John Candelaria	.20
41	Joe Orsulak	.20
42	Willie Upshaw	.20
43	Herm Winningham	.20
44	Ron Kittle	.20
45	Bob Dernier	.20
46	Steve Balboni	.20
47	Steve Shields	.20
48	Henry Cotto	.20
49	Dave Henderson	.20
50	Dave Parker	.25
51	Mike Young	.20
52	Mark Salas	.20
53	Mike Davis	.20
54	Rafael Santana	.20
55	Don Baylor	.35
56	Dan Pasqua	.20
57	Ernest Riles	.20
58	Glenn Hubbard	.20
59	Mike Smithson	.20
60	Richard Dotson	.20
61	Jerry Reuss	.20
62	Mike Jackson	.20
63	Floyd Bannister	.20
64	Jesse Orosco	.20
65	Larry Parrish	.20
66	Jeff Bittiger	.20
67	Ray Hayward	.20
68	Ricky Jordan	.20
69	Tommy Gregg	.20
70	*Brady Anderson*	5.00
71	Jeff Montgomery	.25
72	Darryl Hamilton	1.00
73	Cecil Espy	.20
74	Greg Briley	.20
75	Joey Meyer	.20
76	Mike Macfarlane	.25
77	Oswald Peraza	.20
78	Jack Armstrong	.20
79	Don Heinkel	.20
80	*Mark Grace*	10.00
81	Steve Curry	.20
82	Damon Berryhill	.20
83	Steve Ellsworth	.20
84	Pete Smith	.20
85	*Jack McDowell*	2.50
86	Rob Dibble	.25
87	Bryan Harvey	.25
88	John Dopson	.25
89	Dave Gallagher	.20
90	Todd Stottlemyre	2.00
91	Mike Schooler	.20
92	Don Gordon	.20
93	Sil Campusano	.20
94	Jeff Pico	.20
95	*Jay Buhner*	4.00
96	Nelson Santovenia	.20
97	Al Leiter	2.50
98	Luis Alicea	.25
99	Pat Borders	.50
100	Chris Sabo	.25
101	Tim Belcher	.25
102	Walt Weiss	.40
103	*Craig Biggio*	15.00
104	Don August	.20
105	*Roberto Alomar*	20.00
106	Todd Burns	.20
107	John Costello	.20
108	Melido Perez	.25
109	Darrin Jackson	.50
110	Orestes Destrade	.20

1988 Score Traded/Rookie Glossy

Among the scarcest of the major card companies' high-gloss collector's editions of the late 1980s is the 1988 Score Rookie/Traded issue. Production of the regular-finish set was limited in itself and the glossy version is more so, adding a significant premium value.

	MT
Complete Set (110):	250.00
Common Player:	.50
Stars: 3X	
(See 1988 Score Traded/Rookie for checklist and base card values.)	

1988 Score Young Superstar Series 1

This 40-card set of 2-1/2" x 3-1/2" cards is divided into five separate 8-card subsets. Similar to the company's regular issue, these cards are distinguished by excellent full-color photography on both front and back. The glossy player photos are centered on a white background and framed by a vivid blue and green border. A player name banner beneath the photo includes the name, position and uniform number. The card backs feature color player portraits beneath a hot pink player name/Score logo banner. Hot pink also frames the personal stats (in green), career stats (in black) and career biography (in blue). The backs also include quotes from well-known baseball authorities discussing player performance. This set was distributed via a write-in offer printed on 1988 Score 17-card package wrappers.

		MT
Complete Set (40):		7.00
Common Player:		.10
1	Mark McGwire	3.00
2	Benito Santiago	.10
3	Sam Horn	.10
4	Chris Bosio	.10
5	Matt Nokes	.10
6	Ken Williams	.10
7	Dion James	.10
8	B.J. Surhoff	.15
9	Joe Margrane	.10
10	Kevin Seitzer	.10
11	Stanley Jefferson	.10
12	Devon White	.30
13	Nelson Liriano	.10
14	Chris James	.10
15	Mike Henneman	.10
16	Terry Steinbach	.20
17	John Kruk	.10
18	Matt Williams	.75
19	Kelly Downs	.10
20	Bill Ripken	.10
21	Ozzie Guillen	.10
22	Luis Polonia	.10
23	Dave Magadan	.10
24	Mike Greenwell	.10
25	Will Clark	.75
26	Mike Dunne	.10
27	Wally Joyner	.50
28	Robby Thompson	.10
29	Ken Caminiti	.25
30	Jose Canseco	1.00
31	Todd Benzinger	.10
32	Pete Incaviglia	.10
33	John Farrell	.10
34	Casey Candaele	.10
35	Mike Aldrete	.10
36	Ruben Sierra	.10
37	Ellis Burks	.15
38	Tracy Jones	.10
39	Kal Daniels	.10
40	Cory Snyder	.10

1988 Score Young Superstar Series 2

This set of 40 standard-size cards and five Magic trivia cards is part of a double series issued by Score. Each series is divided into five smaller sets of eight baseball cards and one trivia card. The design on both series is similar, except for border color. Series I has blue and green borders. Series II has red and blue borders framing full-color player photos. Backs carry color portrait photos and stats in a variety of colors. Young Superstar series were offered via a write-in offer on '88 Score wrappers. For each 8-card subset, collectors were instructed to send two Score wrappers and $1. Complete sets were offered by a number of hobby dealers nationwide.

		MT
Complete Set (40):		7.00
Common Player:		.10
1	Don Mattingly	1.50
2	Glenn Braggs	.10
3	Dwight Gooden	.15
4	Jose Lind	.10
5	Danny Tartabull	.10
6	Tony Fernandez	.10
7	Julio Franco	.10
8	Andres Galarraga	.25
9	Bobby Bonilla	.15
10	Eric Davis	.15
11	Gerald Young	.10
12	Barry Bonds	2.00
13	Jerry Browne	.10
14	Jeff Blauser	.10
15	Mickey Brantley	.10
16	Floyd Youmans	.10
17	Bret Saberhagen	.25
18	Shawon Dunston	.15
19	Len Dykstra	.10
20	Darryl Strawberry	.20
21	Rick Aguilera	.10
22	Ivan Calderon	.10
23	Roger Clemens	1.00
24	Vince Coleman	.10
25	Gary Thurman	.10
26	Jeff Treadway	.10
27	Oddibe McDowell	.10
28	Fred McGriff	.50
29	Mark McLemore	.10
30	Jeff Musselman	.10
31	Mitch Williams	.10
32	Dan Plesac	.10
33	Juan Nieves	.10
34	Barry Larkin	.30
35	Greg Mathews	.10
36	Shane Mack	.10
37	Scott Bankhead	.10
38	Eric Bell	.10
39	Greg Swindell	.10
40	Kevin Elster	.10

1989 Score

This set of 660 cards plus 56 Magic Motion trivia cards is the second annual basic issue from Score. Full-color player photos highlight 651 individual players and 9 season highlights, including the first Wrigley Field night game. Action photos are framed by thin brightly colored borders (green, cyan blue, purple, orange, red, royal blue) with a baseball diamond logo/player name beneath the photo. Full-color player close-ups (1-5/16" x 1-5/8") are printed on the pastel-colored backs, along with personal information, stats and career highlights. The cards measure 2-1/2" x 3-1/2".

		MT
Complete Set (660):		10.00
Common Player:		.05
Wax Box:		9.00
1	Jose Canseco	.25
2	Andre Dawson	.10
3	Mark McGwire	1.50
4	Benny Santiago	.05
5	Rick Reuschel	.05
6	Fred McGriff	.20
7	Kal Daniels	.05
8	Gary Gaetti	.05
9	Ellis Burks	.10
10	Darryl Strawberry	.15
11	Julio Franco	.05
12	Lloyd Moseby	.05
13	*Jeff Pico*	.05
14	Johnny Ray	.05
15	Cal Ripken, Jr.	.60
16	Dick Schofield	.05
17	Mel Hall	.05
18	Bill Ripken	.05
19	Brook Jacoby	.05
20	Kirby Puckett	.35
21	Bill Doran	.05
22	Pete O'Brien	.05
23	Matt Nokes	.05
24	Brian Fisher	.05
25	Jack Clark	.05
26	Gary Pettis	.05
27	Dave Valle	.05
28	Willie Wilson	.05
29	Curt Young	.05
30	Dale Murphy	.10
31	Barry Larkin	.15
32	Dave Stewart	.10
33	Mike LaValliere	.05
34	Glenn Hubbard	.05
35	Ryne Sandberg	.25
36	Tony Pena	.05
37	Greg Walker	.05
38	Von Hayes	.05
39	Kevin Mitchell	.05
40	Tim Raines	.10
41	Keith Hernandez	.05
42	Keith Moreland	.05
43	Ruben Sierra	.05
44	Chet Lemon	.05
45	Willie Randolph	.05
46	Andy Allanson	.05
47	Candy Maldonado	.05
48	Sid Bream	.05
49	Denny Walling	.05
50	Dave Winfield	.15
51	Alvin Davis	.05
52	Cory Snyder	.05
53	Hubie Brooks	.05
54	Chili Davis	.05
55	Kevin Seitzer	.05
56	Jose Uribe	.05
57	Tony Fernandez	.05
58	Tim Teufel	.05
59	Oddibe McDowell	.05
60	Les Lancaster	.05
61	Billy Hatcher	.05
62	Dan Gladden	.05
63	Marty Barrett	.05
64	Nick Esasky	.05
65	Wally Joyner	.10
66	Mike Greenwell	.05
67	Ken Williams	.05
68	Bob Horner	.05
69	Steve Sax	.05
70	Rickey Henderson	.20
71	Mitch Webster	.05
72	Rob Deer	.05
73	Jim Presley	.05
74	Albert Hall	.05
75a	George Brett ("At age 33 ...")	1.00
75b	George Brett ("At age 35 ...")	.30
76	Brian Downing	.05
77	Dave Martinez	.05
78	Scott Fletcher	.05
79	Phil Bradley	.05
80	Ozzie Smith	.25
81	Larry Sheets	.05
82	Mike Aldrete	.05
83	Darnell Coles	.05
84	Len Dykstra	.05
85	Jim Rice	.10
86	Jeff Treadway	.05
87	Jose Lind	.05
88	Willie McGee	.05
89	Mickey Brantley	.05
90	Tony Gwynn	.40
91	R.J. Reynolds	.05
92	Milt Thompson	.05
93	Kevin McReynolds	.05
94	Eddie Murray	.25
95	Lance Parrish	.05
96	Ron Kittle	.05
97	Gerald Young	.05
98	Ernie Whitt	.05
99	Jeff Reed	.05
100	Don Mattingly	.40
101	Gerald Perry	.05
102	Vance Law	.05
103	John Shelby	.05
104	*Chris Sabo*	.15
105	Danny Tartabull	.05
106	Glenn Wilson	.05
107	Mark Davidson	.05
108	Dave Parker	.10
109	Eric Davis	.10
110	Alan Trammell	.10
111	Ozzie Virgil	.05
112	Frank Tanana	.05
113	Rafael Ramirez	.05
114	Dennis Martinez	.10
115	Jose DeLeon	.05
116	Bob Ojeda	.05
117	Doug Drabek	.05
118	Andy Hawkins	.05
119	Greg Maddux	.50
120	Cecil Fielder (reversed negative)	.20
121	Mike Scioscia	.05
122	Dan Petry	.05
123	Terry Kennedy	.05
124	Kelly Downs	.05
125	Greg Gross	.05
126	Fred Lynn	.05
127	Barry Bonds	.50
128	Harold Baines	.10
129	Doyle Alexander	.05
130	Kevin Elster	.05
131	Mike Heath	.05
132	Teddy Higuera	.05
133	Charlie Leibrandt	.05
134	Tim Laudner	.05
135a	Ray Knight (photo reversed)	.40
135b	Ray Knight (correct photo)	.05
136	Howard Johnson	.05
137	Terry Pendleton	.05
138	Andy McGaffigan	.05
139	Ken Oberkfell	.05
140	Butch Wynegar	.05
141	Rob Murphy	.05
142	*Rich Renteria*	.05
143	Jose Guzman	.05
144	Andres Galarraga	.15
145	Rick Horton	.05
146	Frank DiPino	.05
147	Glenn Braggs	.05
148	John Kruk	.05
149	Mike Schmidt	.30
150	Lee Smith	.05
151	Robin Yount	.25
152	Mark Eichhorn	.05
153	DeWayne Buice	.05
154	B.J. Surhoff	.05
155	Vince Coleman	.05
156	Tony Phillips	.05
157	Willie Fraser	.05
158	Lance McCullers	.05
159	Greg Gagne	.05
160	Jesse Barfield	.05
161	Mark Langston	.05
162	Kurt Stillwell	.05
163	Dion James	.05
164	Glenn Davis	.05
165	Walt Weiss	.05
166	Dave Concepcion	.05
167	Alfredo Griffin	.05
168	*Don Heinkel*	.05
169	Luis Rivera	.05
170	Shane Rawley	.05
171	Darrell Evans	.10
172	Robby Thompson	.05
173	Jody Davis	.05
174	Andy Van Slyke	.05
175	Wade Boggs	.25
176	Garry Templeton	.05
177	Gary Redus	.05
178	Craig Lefferts	.05
179	Carney Lansford	.05
180	Ron Darling	.05
181	Kirk McCaskill	.05
182	Tony Armas	.05
183	Steve Farr	.05
184	Tom Brunansky	.05
185	*Bryan Harvey*	.10
186	Mike Marshall	.05
187	Bo Diaz	.05
188	Willie Upshaw	.05
189	Mike Pagliarulo	.05
190	Mike Krukow	.05
191	Tommy Herr	.05
192	Jim Pankovits	.05
193	Dwight Evans	.05
194	Kelly Gruber	.05
195	Bobby Bonilla	.10
196	Wallace Johnson	.05
197	Dave Stieb	.05
198	*Pat Borders*	.25
199	Rafael Palmeiro	.20
200	Dwight Gooden	.10
201	Pete Incaviglia	.05
202	Chris James	.05
203	Marvell Wynne	.05
204	Pat Sheridan	.05
205	Don Baylor	.10
206	Paul O'Neill	.15
207	Pete Smith	.05
208	Mark McLemore	.05
209	Henry Cotto	.05
210	Kirk Gibson	.05
211	Claudell Washington	.05
212	Randy Bush	.05
213	Joe Carter	.10
214	Bill Buckner	.05
215	Bert Blyleven	.05
216	Brett Butler	.05
217	Lee Mazzilli	.05
218	Spike Owen	.05
219	Bill Swift	.05
220	Tim Wallach	.05
221	David Cone	.15
222	Don Carman	.05
223	Rich Gossage	.10
224	Bob Walk	.05
225	Dave Righetti	.05
226	Kevin Bass	.05
227	Kevin Gross	.05
228	Tim Burke	.05
229	Rick Mahler	.05
230	Lou Whitaker	.05
231	*Luis Alicea*	.10
232	Roberto Alomar	.30
233	Bob Boone	.05
234	Dickie Thon	.05
235	Shawon Dunston	.05
236	Pete Stanicek	.05
237	Craig Biggio	.15
238	Dennis Boyd	.05
239	Tom Candiotti	.05
240	Gary Carter	.10
241	Mike Stanley	.05
242	Ken Phelps	.05
243	Chris Bosio	.05
244	Les Straker	.05
245	Dave Smith	.05
246	John Candelaria	.05
247	Joe Orsulak	.05
248	Storm Davis	.05
249	Floyd Bannister	.05
250	Jack Morris	.05
251	Bret Saberhagen	.10
252	Tom Niedenfuer	.05
253	Neal Heaton	.05
254	Eric Show	.05
255	Juan Samuel	.05
256	Dale Sveum	.05
257	Jim Gott	.05
258	Scott Garrelts	.05
259	Larry McWilliams	.05
260	Steve Bedrosian	.05
261	Jack Howell	.05
262	Jay Tibbs	.05
263	Jamie Moyer	.05
264	Doug Sisk	.05
265	Todd Worrell	.05
266	John Farrell	.05
267	Dave Collins	.05
268	Sid Fernandez	.05
269	Tom Brookens	.05
270	Shane Mack	.05
271	Paul Kilgus	.05
272	Chuck Crim	.05
273	Bob Knepper	.05
274	Mike Moore	.05
275	Guillermo Hernandez	.05
276	Dennis Eckersley	.10
277	Graig Nettles	.05
278	Rich Dotson	.05
279	Larry Herndon	.05
280	Gene Larkin	.05
281	Roger McDowell	.05
282	Greg Swindell	.05
283	Juan Agosto	.05
284	Jeff Robinson	.05
285	Mike Dunne	.05
286	Greg Mathews	.05
287	Kent Tekulve	.05
288	Jerry Mumphrey	.05
289	Jack McDowell	.10
290	Frank Viola	.05
291	Mark Gubicza	.05
292	Dave Schmidt	.05
293	Mike Henneman	.05
294	Jimmy Jones	.05
295	Charlie Hough	.05
296	Rafael Santana	.05
297	Chris Speier	.05
298	Mike Witt	.05
299	Pascual Perez	.05
300	Nolan Ryan	.60
301	Mitch Williams	.05
302	Mookie Wilson	.05
303	Mackey Sasser	.05
304	John Cerutti	.05
305	Jeff Reardon	.05
306	Randy Myers	.05
307	Greg Brock	.05
308	Bob Welch	.05
309	Jeff Robinson	.05
310	Harold Reynolds	.05
311	Jim Walewander	.05
312	Dave Magadan	.05
313	Jim Gantner	.05
314	Walt Terrell	.05
315	Wally Backman	.05
316	Luis Salazar	.05
317	Rick Rhoden	.05
318	Tom Henke	.05
319	*Mike Macfarlane*	.15
320	Dan Plesac	.05
321	Calvin Schiraldi	.05
322	Stan Javier	.05
323	Devon White	.10
324	Scott Bradley	.05
325	Bruce Hurst	.05
326	Manny Lee	.05
327	Rick Aguilera	.05
328	Bruce Ruffin	.05
329	Ed Whitson	.05
330	Bo Jackson	.15
331	Ivan Calderon	.05
332	Mickey Hatcher	.05
333	Barry Jones	.05
334	Ron Hassey	.05
335	Bill Wegman	.05
336	Damon Berryhill	.05
337	Steve Ontiveros	.05
338	Dan Pasqua	.05
339	Bill Pecota	.05
340	Greg Cadaret	.05
341	Scott Bankhead	.05
342	Ron Guidry	.10
343	Danny Heep	.05
344	Bob Brower	.05
345	Rich Gedman	.05
346	*Nelson Santovenia*	.05
347	George Bell	.05
348	Ted Power	.05
349	Mark Grant	.05
350a	Roger Clemens (778 wins)	2.00
350b	Roger Clemens (78 wins)	.30
351	Bill Long	.05
352	Jay Bell	.05
353	Steve Balboni	.05
354	Bob Kipper	.05
355	Steve Jeltz	.05
356	Jesse Orosco	.05
357	Bob Dernier	.05
358	Mickey Tettleton	.05
359	Duane Ward	.05
360	Darrin Jackson	.05
361	Rey Quinones	.05

362	Mark Grace	.20
363	Steve Lake	.05
364	Pat Perry	.05
365	Terry Steinbach	.05
366	Alan Ashby	.10
367	Jeff Montgomery	.05
368	Steve Buechele	.05
369	Chris Brown	.05
370	Orel Hershiser	.10
371	Todd Benzinger	.05
372	Ron Gant	.15
373	Paul Assenmacher	.05
374	Joey Meyer	.05
375	Neil Allen	.05
376	Mike Davis	.05
377	Jeff Parrett	.05
378	Jay Howell	.05
379	Rafael Belliard	.05
380	Luis Polonia	.05
381	Keith Atherton	.05
382	Kent Hrbek	.10
383	Bob Stanley	.05
384	Dave LaPoint	.05
385	Rance Mulliniks	.05
386	Melido Perez	.05
387	Doug Jones	.05
388	Steve Lyons	.05
389	Alejandro Pena	.05
390	Frank White	.05
391	Pat Tabler	.05
392	Eric Plunk	.05
393	Mike Maddux	.05
394	Allan Anderson	.05
395	Bob Brenly	.05
396	Rick Cerone	.05
397	Scott Terry	.05
398	Mike Jackson	.05
399	Bobby Thigpen	.05
400	Don Sutton	.10
401	Cecil Espy	.05
402	Junior Ortiz	.05
403	Mike Smithson	.05
404	Bud Black	.05
405	Tom Foley	.05
406	Andres Thomas	.05
407	Rick Sutcliffe	.05
408	Brian Harper	.05
409	John Smiley	.05
410	Juan Nieves	.05
411	Shawn Abner	.05
412	Wes Gardner	.05
413	Darren Daulton	.05
414	Juan Berenguer	.05
415	Charles Hudson	.05
416	Rick Honeycutt	.05
417	Greg Booker	.05
418	Tim Belcher	.05
419	Don August	.05
420	Dale Mohorcic	.05
421	Steve Lombardozzi	.05
422	Atlee Hammaker	.05
423	Jerry Don Gleaton	.05
424	Scott Bailes	.05
425	Bruce Sutter	.05
426	Randy Ready	.05
427	Jerry Reed	.05
428	Bryn Smith	.05
429	Tim Leary	.05
430	Mark Clear	.05
431	Terry Leach	.05
432	John Moses	.05
433	Ozzie Guillen	.05
434	Gene Nelson	.05
435	Gary Ward	.05
436	Luis Aguayo	.05
437	Fernando Valenzuela	.05
438	Jeff Russell	.05
439	Cecilio Guante	.05
440	Don Robinson	.05
441	Rick Anderson	.05
442	Tom Glavine	.25
443	Daryl Boston	.05
444	Joe Price	.05
445	Stewart Cliburn	.05
446	Manny Trillo	.05
447	Joel Skinner	.05
448	Charlie Puleo	.05
449	Carlton Fisk	.10
450	Will Clark	.25
451	Otis Nixon	.05
452	Rick Schu	.05
453	Todd Stottlemyre	.10
454	Tim Birtsas	.05
455	*Dave Gallagher*	.05
456	Barry Lyons	.05
457	Fred Manrique	.05
458	Ernest Riles	.05
459	*Doug Jennings*	.05
460	Joe Magrane	.05
461	Jamie Quirk	.05
462	*Jack Armstrong*	.05
463	Bobby Witt	.05
464	Keith Miller	.05
465	*Todd Burns*	.05
466	*John Dopson*	.05
467	Rich Yett	.05
468	Craig Reynolds	.05
469	Dave Bergman	.05
470	Rex Hudler	.05
471	Eric King	.05
472	Joaquin Andujar	.05
473	*Sil Campusano*	.05
474	Terry Mulholland	.05
475	Mike Flanagan	.05
476	Greg Harris	.05
477	Tommy John	.10
478	Dave Anderson	.05
479	Fred Toliver	.05

480	Jimmy Key	.05
481	Donell Nixon	.05
482	Mark Portugal	.05
483	Tom Pagnozzi	.05
484	Jeff Kunkel	.05
485	Frank Williams	.05
486	Jody Reed	.05
487	Roberto Kelly	.05
488	Shawn Hillegas	.05
489	Jerry Reuss	.05
490	Mark Davis	.05
491	Jeff Sellers	.05
492	Zane Smith	.05
493	Al Newman	.05
494	Mike Young	.05
495	Larry Parrish	.05
496	Herm Winningham	.05
497	Carmen Castillo	.05
498	Joe Hesketh	.05
499	Darrell Miller	.05
500	Mike LaCoss	.05
501	Charlie Lea	.05
502	Bruce Benedict	.05
503	Chuck Finley	.05
504	Brad Wellman	.05
505	Tim Crews	.05
506	Ken Gerhart	.05
507a	Brian Holton (Born: 1/25/65, Denver)	.15
507b	Brian Holton (Born: 11/29/59, McKeesport)	.05
508	Dennis Lamp	.05
509	Bobby Meacham	.05
510	Tracy Jones	.05
511	Mike Fitzgerald	.05
512	*Jeff Bittiger*	.05
513	Tim Flannery	.05
514	Ray Hayward	.05
515	Dave Leiper	.05
516	Rod Scurry	.05
517	Carmelo Martinez	.05
518	Curtis Wilkerson	.05
519	Stan Jefferson	.05
520	Dan Quisenberry	.05
521	Lloyd McClendon	.05
522	Steve Trout	.05
523	Larry Andersen	.05
524	Don Aase	.05
525	Bob Forsch	.05
526	Geno Petralli	.05
527	Angel Salazar	.05
528	*Mike Schooler*	.05
529	Jose Oquendo	.05
530	Jay Buhner	.15
531	Tom Bolton	.05
532	Al Nipper	.05
533	Dave Henderson	.05
534	*John Costello*	.05
535	Donnie Moore	.05
536	Mike Laga	.05
537	Mike Gallego	.05
538	Jim Clancy	.05
539	Joel Youngblood	.05
540	Rick Leach	.05
541	Kevin Romine	.05
542	Mark Salas	.05
543	Greg Minton	.05
544	Dave Palmer	.05
545	Dwayne Murphy	.05
546	Jim Deshaies	.05
547	Don Gordon	.05
548	*Ricky Jordan*	.10
549	Mike Boddicker	.05
550	Mike Scott	.05
551	Jeff Ballard	.05
552a	Jose Rijo (uniform number #24 on card back)	.15
552b	Jose Rijo (uniform number #27 on card back)	.10
553	Danny Darwin	.05
554	Tom Browning	.05
555	Danny Jackson	.05
556	Rick Dempsey	.05
557	Jeffrey Leonard	.05
558	Jeff Musselman	.05
559	Ron Robinson	.05
560	John Tudor	.05
561	Don Slaught	.05
562	Dennis Rasmussen	.05
563	Brady Anderson	.15
564	Pedro Guerrero	.05
565	Paul Molitor	.25
566	*Terry Clark*	.05
567	Terry Puhl	.05
568	Mike Campbell	.05
569	Paul Mirabella	.05
570	Jeff Hamilton	.05
571	*Oswald Peraza*	.05
572	Bob McClure	.05
573	*Jose Bautista*	.10
574	Alex Trevino	.05
575	John Franco	.05
576	*Mark Parent*	.05
577	Nelson Liriano	.05
578	Steve Shields	.05
579	Odell Jones	.05
580	Al Leiter	.10
581	Dave Stapleton	.05
582	1988 World Series (Jose Canseco, Kirk Gibson, Orel Hershiser, Dave Stewart)	.10
583	Donnie Hill	.05

584	Chuck Jackson	.05
585	Rene Gonzales	.05
586	Tracy Woodson	.05
587	Jim Adduci	.05
588	Mario Soto	.05
589	Jeff Blauser	.05
590	Jim Traber	.05
591	Jon Perlman	.05
592	Mark Williamson	.05
593	Dave Meads	.05
594	Jim Eisenreich	.05
595	*Paul Gibson*	.05
596	Mike Birkbeck	.05
597	Terry Francona	.05
598	Paul Zuvella	.05
599	Franklin Stubbs	.05
600	Gregg Jefferies	.10
601	John Cangelosi	.05
602	Mike Sharperson	.05
603	Mike Diaz	.05
604	*Gary Varsho*	.05
605	*Terry Blocker*	.05
606	Charlie O'Brien	.05
607	Jim Eppard	.05
608	John Davis	.05
609	Ken Griffey, Sr.	.10
610	Buddy Bell	.05
611	Ted Simmons	.05
612	Matt Williams	.25
613	Danny Cox	.05
614	Al Pedrique	.05
615	Ron Oester	.05
616	John Smoltz	.20
617	Bob Melvin	.05
618	*Rob Dibble*	.15
619	Kirt Manwaring	.05
620	Felix Fermin	.05
621	*Doug Dascenzo*	.05
622	*Bill Brennan*	.05
623	*Carlos Quintana*	.05
624	*Mike Harkey*	.05
625	*Gary Sheffield*	.75
626	*Tom Prince*	.05
627	*Steve Searcy*	.05
628	*Charlie Hayes*	.25
629	*Felix Jose*	.05
630	*Sandy Alomar*	.75
631	*Derek Lilliquist*	.05
632	Geronimo Berroa	.05
633	*Luis Medina*	.05
634	*Tom Gordon*	.15
635	*Ramon Martinez*	.50
636	*Craig Worthington*	.05
637	Edgar Martinez	.15
638	*Chad Krueter*	.05
639	*Ron Jones*	.05
640	*Van Snider*	.05
641	*Lance Blankenship*	.10
642	*Dwight Smith*	.05
643	*Cameron Drew*	.05
644	*Jerald Clark*	.10
645	*Randy Johnson*	1.50
646	*Norm Charlton*	.10
647	Todd Frohwirth	.05
648	*Luis de los Santos*	.05
649	*Tim Jones*	.05
650	*Dave West*	.10
651	*Bob Milacki*	.10
652	1988 Highlight (Wrigley Field)	.05
653	1988 Highlight (Orel Hershiser)	.10
654a	1988 Highlight (Wade Boggs) ("...sixth consecutive seaason..." on back)	2.00
654b	1988 Highlight (Wade Boggs) ("season" corrected)	.10
655	1988 Highlight (Jose Canseco)	.15
656	1988 Highlight (Doug Jones)	.05
657	1988 Highlight (Rickey Henderson)	.10
658	1988 Highlight (Tom Browning)	.05
659	1988 Highlight (Mike Greenwell)	.05
660	1988 Highlight (Joe Morgan) (A.L. Win Streak)	.05

1989 Scoremasters Promo Folder

To introduce its boxed set of fine-art baseball cards, Score produced this tri-fold brochure. The 17-1/8" x 8-3/4" piece is printed on glossy stock and pictures five of the paintings to be used in the card set. The sixth panel gives details on the card set.

	MT
Brochure: Ellis Burks, Vince Coleman, Carlton Fisk, Cal Ripken Jr., Darryl Strawberry	15.00

1989 Scoremasters

This unique 42-card boxed set from Score was reproduced from original artwork done by New York artist Jeffrey Rubin. The paintings are reproduced on a standard-size, white, glossy stock, and the set includes the top stars of the game, plus selected rookies.

		MT
Complete Set (42):		6.00
Common Player:		.10
1	Bo Jackson	.25
2	Jerome Walton	.10
3	Cal Ripken, Jr.	1.50
4	Mike Scott	.10
5	Nolan Ryan	1.50
6	Don Mattingly	.75
7	Tom Gordon	.10
8	Jack Morris	.10
9	Carlton Fisk	.25
10	Will Clark	.30
11	George Brett	.75
12	Kevin Mitchell	.10
13	Mark Langston	.10
14	Dave Stewart	.10
15	Dale Murphy	.15
16	Gary Gaetti	.10
17	Wade Boggs	.25
18	Eric Davis	.15
19	Kirby Puckett	.50
20	Roger Clemens	.50
21	Orel Hershiser	.15
22	Mark Grace	.25
23	Ryne Sandberg	.50
24	Barry Larkin	.20
25	Ellis Burks	.10
26	Dwight Gooden	.20
27	Ozzie Smith	.40
28	Andre Dawson	.15
29	Julio Franco	.10
30	Ken Griffey, Jr.	3.00
31	Ruben Sierra	.10
32	Mark McGwire	3.00
33	Andres Galarraga	.20
34	Joe Carter	.10
35	Vince Coleman	.10
36	Mike Greenwell	.10
37	Tony Gwynn	.50
38	Andy Van Slyke	.10
39	Gregg Jefferies	.15
40	Jose Canseco	.30
41	Dave Winfield	.30
42	Darryl Strawberry	.15

1989 Score Rising Stars

Similar in design to the Score Superstar set, this 100-card set showcased a host of rookies. Full-color action photos are surrounded by a bright blue border with a green inner highlight line. Backs display a full-color player portrait above his name and career highlights. The card number and player's rookie year are featured to the right. A "Rising Star" headline highlights the top border. The Score "Rising Star" set was marketed as a combination with a related magazine: "1988-89 Baseball's 100 Hottest Rookies". The set also includes six Magic Motion baseball trivia cards featuring "Rookies to Remember." The magazine/card sets were available at a select group of retailers.

		MT
Complete Set (100):		10.00
Common Player:		.07
1	Gregg Jefferies	.30
2	Vicente Palacios	.10
3	Cameron Drew	.10
4	Doug Dascenzo	.10
5	Luis Medina	.10
6	Craig Worthington	.10
7	Rob Ducey	.10
8	Hal Morris	.10
9	Bill Brennan	.10
10	Gary Sheffield	.75
11	Mike Devereaux	.10
12	Hensley Meulens	.10
13	Carlos Quintana	.10
14	Todd Frohwirth	.10
15	Scott Lusader	.10
16	Mark Carreon	.15
17	Torey Lovullo	.10
18	Randy Velarde	.10
19	Billy Bean	.10
20	Lance Blankenship	.10
21	Chris Gwynn	.10
22	Felix Jose	.10
23	Derek Lilliquist	.10
24	Gary Thurman	.10
25	Ron Jones	.10
26	Dave Justice	.75
27	Johnny Paredes	.10
28	Tim Jones	.10
29	Jose Gonzalez	.10
30	Geronimo Berroa	.10
31	Trevor Wilson	.10
32	Morris Madden	.10
33	Lance Johnson	.10
34	Marvin Freeman	.10
35	Jose Cecena	.10
36	Jim Corsi	.10
37	Rolando Roomes	.10
38	Scott Medvin	.10
39	Charlie Hayes	.10
40	Edgar Martinez	.10
41	Van Snider	.10
42	John Fishel	.10
43	Bruce Fields	.10
44	Darryl Hamilton	.15
45	Tom Prince	.10
46	Kirt Manwaring	.10
47	Steve Searcy	.10
48	Mike Harkey	.10
49	German Gonzalez	.10
50	Tony Perezchica	.10
51	Chad Kreuter	.10
52	Luis de los Santos	.10
53	Steve Curry	.10
54	Greg Bailey	.10
55	Ramon Martinez	.50
56	Ron Tingley	.10
57	Randy Kramer	.10
58	Alex Madrid	.10
59	Kevin Reimer	.10
60	Dave Otto	.10
61	Ken Patterson	.10
62	Keith Miller	.10
63	Randy Johnson	.75
64	Dwight Smith	.10
65	Eric Yelding	.10
66	Bob Geren	.10
67	Shane Turner	.10
68	Tom Gordon	.10
69	Jeff Huson	.10
70	Marty Brown	.10
71	Nelson Santovenia	.10
72	Roberto Alomar	1.00
73	Mike Schooler	.10
74	Pete Smith	.10
75	John Costello	.10
76	Chris Sabo	.10
77	Damon Berryhill	.10
78	Mark Grace	.60
79	Melido Perez	.10

80 Al Leiter .15
81 Todd Stottlemyre .10
82 Mackey Sasser .10
83 Don August .10
84 Jeff Treadway .10
85 Jody Reed .10
86 Mike Campbell .10
87 Ron Gant .60
88 Ricky Jordan .10
89 Terry Clark .10
90 Roberto Kelly .10
91 Pat Borders .10
92 Bryan Harvey .10
93 Joey Meyer .10
94 Tim Belcher .10
95 Walt Weiss .10
96 Dave Gallagher .10
97 Mike Macfarlane .10
98 Craig Biggio .65
99 Jack Armstrong .10
100 Todd Burns .10

1989 Score Superstars

This 100-card set features full-color action photos of baseball's superstars, and six Magic Motion "Rookies to Remember" baseball trivia cards. Card fronts have a bright red border with a blue line inside highlighting the photo. The player ID is displayed in overlapping triangles of white, green, and yellow. The flip side features a full-color player close-up directly beneath a bright red "Superstar" headline. The set was marketed along with the magazine "1989 Baseball's 100 Hottest Players," at select retailers.

MT
Complete Set (100): 8.00
Common Player: .06
1 Jose Canseco .50
2 David Cone .10
3 Dave Winfield .40
4 George Brett .75
5 Frank Viola .05
6 Cory Snyder .05
7 Alan Trammell .10
8 Dwight Evans .05
9 Tim Leary .05
10 Don Mattingly .90
11 Kirby Puckett .75
12 Carney Lansford .05
13 Dennis Martinez .10
14 Kent Hrbek .10
15 Doc Gooden .10
16 Dennis Eckersley .10
17 Kevin Seitzer .05
18 Lee Smith .10
19 Danny Tartabull .05
20 Gerald Perry .05
21 Gary Gaetti .05
22 Rick Reuschel .05
23 Keith Hernandez .05
24 Jeff Reardon .05
25 Mark McGwire 1.50
26 Juan Samuel .05
27 Jack Clark .05
28 Robin Yount .50
29 Steve Bedrosian .05
30 Kirk Gibson .05
31 Barry Bonds .75
32 Dan Plesac .05
33 Steve Sax .05
34 Jeff Robinson .05
35 Orel Hershiser .10
36 Julio Franco .05
37 Dave Righetti .05
38 Bob Knepper .05
39 Carlton Fisk .15
40 Tony Gwynn .60
41 Doug Jones .05
42 Bobby Bonilla .10
43 Ellis Burks .10
44 Pedro Guerrero .05
45 Rickey Henderson .30
46 Glenn Davis .05
47 Benny Santiago .05
48 Greg Maddux 1.00
49 Teddy Higuera .05
50 Darryl Strawberry .15
51 Ozzie Guillen .05
52 Barry Larkin .10
53 Tony Fernandez .05
54 Ryne Sandberg .75
55 Joe Carter .10
56 Rafael Palmeiro .25
57 Paul Molitor .50
58 Eric Davis .10
59 Mike Henneman .05
60 Mike Scott .05
61 Tom Browning .05
62 Mark Davis .05
63 Tom Henke .05
64 Nolan Ryan 1.25
65 Fred McGriff .30
66 Dale Murphy .15
67 Mark Langston .05
68 Bobby Thigpen .05
69 Mark Gubicza .05
70 Mike Greenwell .05
71 Ron Darling .05
72 Gerald Young .05
73 Wally Joyner .10
74 Andres Galarraga .20
75 Danny Jackson .05
76 Mike Schmidt .75
77 Cal Ripken, Jr. 1.25
78 Alvin Davis .05
79 Bruce Hurst .05
80 Andre Dawson .15
81 Bob Boone .05
82 Harold Reynolds .05
83 Eddie Murray .30
84 Robby Thompson .05
85 Will Clark .45
86 Vince Coleman .05
87 Doug Drabek .05
88 Ozzie Smith .40
89 Bob Welch .05
90 Roger Clemens .65
91 George Bell .05
92 Andy Van Slyke .05
93 Willie McGee .05
94 Todd Worrell .05
95 Tim Raines .10
96 Kevin McReynolds .05
97 John Franco .05
98 Jim Gott .05
99 Johnny Ray .05
100 Wade Boggs .50

1989 Score Traded

Score issued its second consecutive traded set in 1989 to supplement and update its regular set. The 110-card traded set features the same basic card design as the regular 1989 Score set. The set consists of rookies and traded players pictured with correct teams. The set was sold by hobby dealers in a special box that included an assortment of "Magic Motion" trivia cards. Cards are numbered with a "T" suffix.

MT
Complete Set (110): 50.00
Common Player: .06
1 Rafael Palmeiro .35
2 Nolan Ryan 2.00
3 Jack Clark .10
4 Dave LaPoint .10
5 Mike Moore .10
6 Pete O'Brien .10
7 Jeffrey Leonard .10
8 Rob Murphy .10
9 Tom Herr .10
10 Claudell Washington .10
11 Mike Pagliarulo .10
12 Steve Lake .10
13 Spike Owen .10
14 Andy Hawkins .10
15 Todd Benzinger .10
16 Mookie Wilson .10
17 Bert Blyleven .10
18 Jeff Treadway .10
19 Bruce Hurst .10
20 Steve Sax .10
21 Juan Samuel .10
22 Jesse Barfield .10
23 Carmelo Castillo .10
24 Terry Leach .10
25 Mark Langston .10
26 Eric King .10
27 Steve Balboni .10
28 Len Dykstra .10
29 Keith Moreland .10
30 Terry Kennedy .10
31 Eddie Murray .20
32 Mitch Williams .10
33 Jeff Parrett .10
34 Wally Backman .10
35 Julio Franco .10
36 Lance Parrish .10
37 Nick Esasky .10
38 Luis Polonia .10
39 Kevin Gross .10
40 John Dopson .10
41 Willie Randolph .10
42 Jim Clancy .10
43 Tracy Jones .10
44 Phil Bradley .10
45 Milt Thompson .10
46 Chris James .10
47 Scott Fletcher .10
48 Kal Daniels .10
49 Steve Bedrosian .10
50 Rickey Henderson .20
51 Dion James .10
52 Tim Leary .10
53 Roger McDowell .10
54 Mel Hall .10
55 Dickie Thon .10
56 Zane Smith .10
57 Danny Heep .10
58 Bob McClure .10
59 Brian Holton .10
60 Randy Ready .10
61 Bob Melvin .10
62 Harold Baines .15
63 Lance McCullers .10
64 Jody Davis .10
65 Darrell Evans .15
66 Joel Youngblood .10
67 Frank Viola .10
68 Mike Aldrete .10
69 Greg Cadaret .10
70 John Kruk .10
71 Pat Sheridan .10
72 Oddibe McDowell .10
73 Tom Brookens .10
74 Bob Boone .10
75 Walt Terrell .10
76 Joel Skinner .10
77 Randy Johnson 1.00
78 Felix Fermin .10
79 Rick Mahler .10
80 Rich Dotson .10
81 Cris Carpenter .10
82 Bill Spiers .10
83 Junior Felix .10
84 Joe Girardi .15
85 Jerome Walton .10
86 Greg Litton .10
87 Greg Harris .10
88 Jim Abbott .15
89 Kevin Brown .50
90 John Wetteland .15
91 Gary Wayne .10
92 Rich Monteleone .10
93 Bob Geren .10
94 Clay Parker .10
95 Steve Finley .25
96 Gregg Olson .10
97 Ken Patterson .10
98 *Ken Hill* .25
99 Scott Scudder .10
100 *Ken Griffey, Jr.* 40.00
101 Jeff Brantley .10
102 Donn Pall .10
103 Carlos Martinez .10
104 Joe Oliver .10
105 Omar Vizquel .20
106 *Albert Belle* 10.00
107 Kenny Rogers .15
108 Mark Carreon .15
109 Rolando Roomes .10
110 Pete Harnisch .25

1989 Score Yankees

This team set was sponsored by National Westminster Bank and produced by Score as an in-stadium promotion in 1989; distributed to fans attending the July 29 game at Yankee Stadium. The standard-size cards include a full-color player photo with a line drawing of the famous Yankee Stadium facade running along the top of the card. The player's name, "New York Yankees" and position appear below the photo. A second full-color photo is included on the back of the card, along with stats, data and a brief player profile. The set includes a special Thurman Munson commemorative card.

MT
Complete Set (33): 15.00
Common Player: .30
1 Don Mattingly 2.50
2 Steve Sax .30
3 Alvaro Espinoza .30
4 Luis Polonia .30
5 Jesse Barfield .30
6 Dave Righetti .30
7 Dave Winfield 2.00
8 John Candelaria .30
9 Wayne Tolleson .30
10 Ken Phelps .30
11 Rafael Santana .30
12 Don Slaught .30
13 Mike Pagliarulo .30
14 Lance McCullers .30
15 Dave LaPoint .30
16 Dale Mohorcic .30
17 Steve Balboni .30
18 Roberto Kelly .45
19 Andy Hawkins .30
20 Mel Hall .30
21 Tom Brookens .30
22 Deion Sanders 2.00
23 Richard Dotson .30
24 Lee Guetterman .30
25 Bob Geren .30
26 Jimmy Jones .30
27 Chuck Cary .30
28 Ron Guidry .60
29 Hal Morris .45
30 Clay Parker .30
31 Dallas Green .30
32 Thurman Munson 2.00
33 Sponsor card .30

1989 Score Young Superstars Series 1

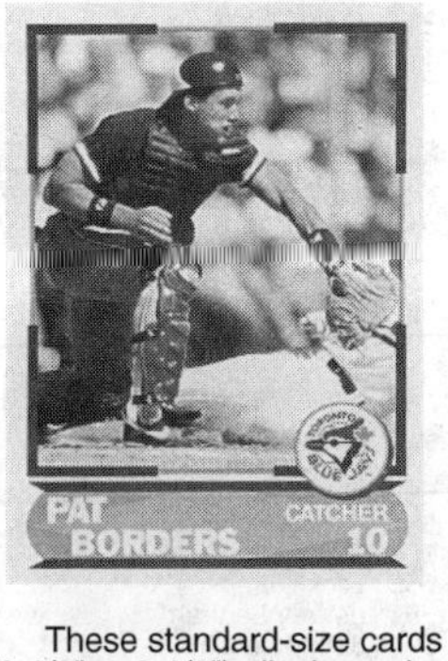

These standard-size cards (2-1/2" x 3-1/2") display color action photos with a high-gloss finish. Fronts feature a red and blue border surrounding the photo with the team logo in the lower right. A red band beneath the photo provides the setting for the player ID including name, position, and uniform number. Backs feature a red "Young Superstar" headline above a portrait photo. Above the headline appears the player's personal information and statistics in orange and black. To the right photo a condensed scouting report and career hightlights are revealed. The card number and related logos appear on the bottom portion. Five trivia cards featuring "A Year to Remember" accompanied the series. Each trivia card relates to a highlight from the past 56 years. This set was distributed via a write-in offer with Score card wrappers.

MT
Complete Set (42): 5.00
Common Player: .10
1 Gregg Jefferies .25
2 Jody Reed .10
3 Mark Grace .50
4 Dave Gallagher .10
5 Bo Jackson .25
6 Jay Buhner .15
7 Melido Perez .10
8 Bobby Witt .10
9 David Cone .15
10 Chris Sabo .10
11 Pat Borders .10
12 Mark Grant .10
13 Mike Macfarlane .10
14 Mike Jackson .10
15 Ricky Jordan .10
16 Ron Gant .30
17 Al Leiter .15
18 Jeff Parrett .10
19 Pete Smith .10
20 Walt Weiss .10
21 Doug Drabek .10
22 Kirt Manwaring .10
23 Keith Miller .10
24 Damon Berryhill .10
25 Gary Sheffield .40
26 Brady Anderson .15
27 Mitch Williams .10
28 Roberto Alomar .50
29 Bobby Thigpen .10
30 Bryan Harvey .10
31 Jose Rijo .10
32 Dave West .10
33 Joey Meyer .10
34 Allan Anderson .10
35 Rafael Palmeiro .35
36 Tim Belcher .10
37 John Smiley .10
38 Mackey Sasser .10
39 Greg Maddux 1.00
40 Ramon Martinez .20
41 Randy Myers .10
42 Scott Bankhead .10

1989 Score Young Superstars Series 2

Score followed up with a second series of Young Superstars in 1989. The second series also included 42 cards and featured the same design as the first series. The set was also distributed via a write-in offer with Score card wrappers.

MT
Complete Set (42): 6.00
Common Player: .10
1 Sandy Alomar .35
2 Tom Gordon .10
3 Ron Jones .10
4 Todd Burns .10
5 Paul O'Neill .20
6 Gene Larkin .10
7 Eric King .10
8 Jeff Robinson .10
9 Bill Wegman .10
10 Cecil Espy .10
11 Jose Guzman .10
12 Kelly Gruber .10
13 Duane Ward .10
14 Mark Gubicza .10
15 Norm Charlton .10
16 Jose Oquendo .10
17 Geronimo Berroa .10
18 Ken Griffey Jr. 5.00
19 Lance McCullers .10
20 Todd Stottlemyre .10
21 Craig Worthington .10
22 Mike Devereaux .10
23 Tom Glavine .20
24 Dale Sveum .10
25 Roberto Kelly .10
26 Luis Medina .10
27 Steve Searcy .10

28	Don August	.10
29	Shawn Hillegas	.10
30	Mike Campbell	.10
31	Mike Harkey	.10
32	Randy Johnson	.45
33	Craig Biggio	.35
34	Mike Schooler	.10
35	Andres Thomas	.10
36	Jerome Walton	.10
37	Cris Carpenter	.10
38	Kevin Mitchell	.10
39	Eddie Williams	.10
40	Chad Kreuter	.10
41	Danny Jackson	.10
42	Kurt Stillwell	.10

1990 Score Promos

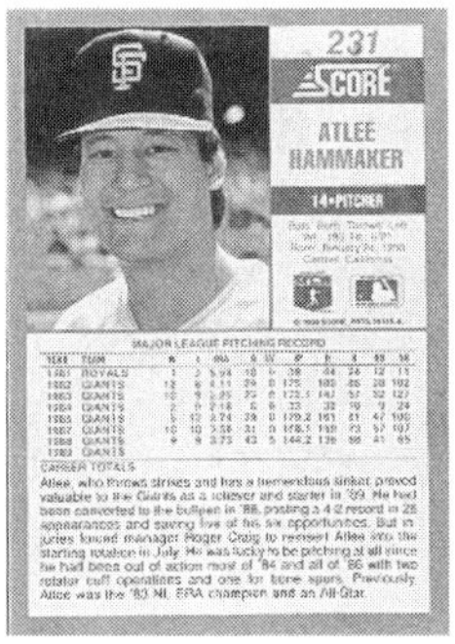

To preview its 1990 baseball cards, Score pre-released the first 110 cards (#221-330) from its red-bordered series as samples. Subtle differences exist on most cards between the samples and the issued version; most easily spotted is that the samples have no statistics on the 1989 season or career lines. Many cards have different versions of the career highlight write-ups on the back, as well. A handful of the sample cards were widely distributed to dealers and the hobby press, while others from the sheet were released more sparingly, creating inequities in the number of each card available. As few as two examples are known of some of the superstar cards, making them extremely expensive among the single-player specialists.

		MT
Common Player:		25.00
221	Steve Buechele	25.00
222	Jesse Barfield	25.00
223	Juan Berenguer	25.00
224	Andy McGaffigan	25.00
225	Pete Smith	25.00
226	Mike Witt	25.00
227	Jay Howell	25.00
228	Scott Bradley	25.00
229	Jerome Walton	25.00
230	Greg Swindell	25.00
231	Atlee Hammaker	25.00
232	Mike Devereaux	25.00
233	Ken Hill	25.00
234	Craig Worthington	25.00
235	Scott Terry	25.00
236	Brett Butler	25.00
237	Doyle Alexander	25.00
238	Dave Anderson	25.00
239	Bob Milacki	25.00
240	Dwight Smith	25.00
241	Otis Nixon	25.00
242	Pat Tabler	25.00
243	Derek Lilliquist	25.00
244	Danny Tartabull	25.00
245	Wade Boggs	300.00
246	Scott Garrelts	25.00
247	Spike Owen	25.00
248	Norm Charlton	25.00
249	Gerald Perry	25.00
250	Nolan Ryan	950.00
251	Kevin Gross	25.00
252	Randy Milligan	25.00
253	Mike LaCoss	25.00
254	Dave Bergman	25.00
255	Tony Gwynn	350.00
256	Felix Fermin	25.00
257	Greg W. Harris	25.00
258	Junior Felix	25.00
259	Mark Davis	25.00
260	Vince Coleman	25.00
261	Paul Gibson	25.00
262	Mitch Williams	25.00
263	Jeff Russell	25.00
264	Omar Vizquel	25.00
265	Andre Dawson	65.00
266	Storm Davis	25.00
267	Guillermo Hernandez	25.00
268	Mike Felder	25.00
269	Tom Candiotti	25.00
270	Bruce Hurst	25.00
271	Fred McGriff	35.00
272	Glenn Davis	25.00
273	John Franco	25.00
274	Rich Yett	25.00
275	Craig Biggio	45.00
276	Gene Larkin	25.00
277	Rob Dibble	25.00
278	Randy Bush	25.00
279	Kevin Bass	25.00
280	Bo Jackson	45.00
281	Wally Backman	25.00
282	Larry Andersen	25.00
283	Chris Bosio	25.00
284	Juan Agosto	25.00
285	Ozzie Smith	350.00
286	George Bell	25.00
287	Rex Hudler	25.00
288	Pat Borders	25.00
289	Danny Jackson	25.00
290	Carlton Fisk	90.00
291	Tracy Jones	25.00
292	Allan Anderson	25.00
293	Johnny Ray	25.00
294	Lee Guetterman	25.00
295	Paul O'Neill	35.00
296	Carney Lansford	25.00
297	Tom Brookens	25.00
298	Claudell Washington	25.00
299	Hubie Brooks	25.00
300	Will Clark	250.00
301	Kenny Rogers	25.00
302	Darrell Evans	25.00
303	Greg Briley	25.00
304	Donn Pall	25.00
305	Teddy Higuera	25.00
306	Dan Pasqua	25.00
307	Dave Winfield	100.00
308	Dennis Powell	25.00
309	Jose DeLeon	25.00
310	Roger Clemens	300.00
311	Melido Perez	25.00
312	Devon White	25.00
313	Dwight Gooden	30.00
314	Carlos Martinez	25.00
315	Dennis Eckersley	35.00
316	Clay Parker	25.00
317	Rick Honeycutt	25.00
318	Tim Laudner	25.00
319	Joe Carter	30.00
320	Robin Yount	150.00
321	Felix Jose	25.00
322	Mickey Tettleton	25.00
323	Mike Gallego	25.00
324	Edgar Martinez	30.00
325	Dave Henderson	25.00
326	Chili Davis	25.00
327	Steve Balboni	25.00
328	Jody Davis	25.00
329	Shawn Hillegas	25.00
330	Jim Abbott	30.00

1990 Score

The regular Score set increased to 704 cards in 1990. Included were a series of cards picturing first-round draft picks, an expanded subset of rookie cards, four World Series specials, five Highlight cards, and a 13-card "Dream Team" series featuring the game's top players pictured on old tobacco-style cards. For the first time in a Score set, team logos are displayed on the card fronts Card backs include a full-color portrait photo with player data. A one-paragraph write-up of each player was again provided by former Sports Illustrated editor Les Woodcock. The Score set was again distributed with "Magic Motion" trivia cards, this year using "Baseball's Most Valuable Players" as its theme.

		MT
Complete Set (704):		15.00
Common Player:		.05
Wax Box:		17.50
1	Don Mattingly	.30
2	Cal Ripken, Jr.	.60
3	Dwight Evans	.05
4	Barry Bonds	.40
5	Kevin McReynolds	.05
6	Ozzie Guillen	.05
7	Terry Kennedy	.05
8	Bryan Harvey	.05
9	Alan Trammell	.10
10	Cory Snyder	.05
11	Jody Reed	.05
12	Roberto Alomar	.30
13	Pedro Guerrero	.05
14	Gary Redus	.05
15	Marty Barrett	.05
16	Ricky Jordan	.05
17	Joe Magrane	.05
18	Sid Fernandez	.05
19	Rich Dotson	.05
20	Jack Clark	.05
21	Bob Walk	.05
22	Ron Karkovice	.05
23	Lenny Harris	.05
24	Phil Bradley	.05
25	Andres Galarraga	.15
26	Brian Downing	.05
27	Dave Martinez	.05
28	Eric King	.05
29	Barry Lyons	.05
30	Dave Schmidt	.05
31	Mike Boddicker	.05
32	Tom Foley	.05
33	Brady Anderson	.10
34	Jim Presley	.05
35	Lance Parrish	.05
36	Von Hayes	.05
37	Lee Smith	.05
38	Herm Winningham	.05
39	Alejandro Pena	.05
40	Mike Scott	.05
41	Joe Orsulak	.05
42	Rafael Ramirez	.05
43	Gerald Young	.05
44	Dick Schofield	.05
45	Dave Smith	.05
46	Dave Magadan	.05
47	Dennis Martinez	.05
48	Greg Minton	.05
49	Milt Thompson	.05
50	Orel Hershiser	.10
51	Bip Roberts	.05
52	Jerry Browne	.05
53	Bob Ojeda	.05
54	Fernando Valenzuela	.05
55	Matt Nokes	.05
56	Brook Jacoby	.05
57	Frank Tanana	.05
58	Scott Fletcher	.05
59	Ron Oester	.05
60	Bob Boone	.05
61	Dan Gladden	.05
62	Darnell Coles	.05
63	Gregg Olson	.05
64	Todd Burns	.05
65	Todd Benzinger	.05
66	Dale Murphy	.15
67	Mike Flanagan	.05
68	Jose Oquendo	.05
69	Cecil Espy	.05
70	Chris Sabo	.05
71	Shane Rawley	.05
72	Tom Brunansky	.05
73	Vance Law	.05
74	B.J. Surhoff	.05
75	Lou Whitaker	.05
76	Ken Caminiti	.20
77	Nelson Liriano	.05
78	Tommy Gregg	.05
79	Don Slaught	.05
80	Eddie Murray	.25
81	Joe Boever	.05
82	Charlie Leibrandt	.05
83	Jose Lind	.05
84	Tony Phillips	.05
85	Mitch Webster	.05
86	Dan Plesac	.05
87	Rick Mahler	.05
88	Steve Lyons	.05
89	Tony Fernandez	.05
90	Ryne Sandberg	.30
91	Nick Esasky	.05
92	Luis Salazar	.05
93	Pete Incaviglia	.05
94	Ivan Calderon	.05
95	Jeff Treadway	.05
96	Kurt Stillwell	.05
97	Gary Sheffield	.25
98	Jeffrey Leonard	.05
99	Andres Thomas	.05
100	Roberto Kelly	.10
101	Alvaro Espinoza	.05
102	Greg Gagne	.05
103	John Farrell	.05
104	Willie Wilson	.05
105	Glenn Braggs	.05
106	Chet Lemon	.05
107	Jamie Moyer	.05
108	Chuck Crim	.05
109	Dave Valle	.05
110	Walt Weiss	.05
111	Larry Sheets	.05
112	Don Robinson	.05
113	Danny Heep	.05
114	Carmelo Martinez	.05
115	Dave Gallagher	.05
116	Mike LaValliere	.05
117	Bob McClure	.05
118	Rene Gonzales	.05
119	Mark Parent	.05
120	Wally Joyner	.10
121	Mark Gubicza	.05
122	Tony Pena	.05
123	Carmen Castillo	.05
124	Howard Johnson	.05
125	Steve Sax	.05
126	Tim Belcher	.05
127	Tim Burke	.05
128	Al Newman	.05
129	Dennis Rasmussen	.05
130	Doug Jones	.05
131	Fred Lynn	.05
132	Jeff Hamilton	.05
133	German Gonzalez	.05
134	John Morris	.05
135	Dave Parker	.10
136	Gary Pettis	.05
137	Dennis Boyd	.05
138	Candy Maldonado	.05
139	Rick Cerone	.05
140	George Brett	.30
141	Dave Clark	.05
142	Dickie Thon	.05
143	Junior Ortiz	.05
144	Don August	.05
145	Gary Gaetti	.05
146	Kirt Manwaring	.05
147	Jeff Reed	.05
148	Jose Alvarez	.05
149	Mike Schooler	.05
150	Mark Grace	.25
151	Geronimo Berroa	.05
152	Barry Jones	.05
153	Geno Petralli	.05
154	Jim Deshaies	.05
155	Barry Larkin	.15
156	Alfredo Griffin	.05
157	Tom Henke	.05
158	Mike Jeffcoat	.05
159	Bob Welch	.05
160	Julio Franco	.05
161	Henry Cotto	.05
162	Terry Steinbach	.05
163	Damon Berryhill	.05
164	Tim Crews	.05
165	Tom Browning	.05
166	Frd Manrique	.05
167	Harold Reynolds	.05
168a	Ron Hassey (uniform #27 on back)	.05
168b	Ron Hassey (uniform #24 on back)	.50
169	Shawon Dunston	.05
170	Bobby Bonilla	.10
171	Tom Herr	.05
172	Mike Heath	.05
173	Rich Gedman	.05
174	Bill Ripken	.05
175	Pete O'Brien	.05
176a	Lloyd McClendon (uniform number 1 on back)	1.00
176b	Lloyd McClendon (uniform number 10 on back)	.05
177	Brian Holton	.05
178	Jeff Blauser	.05
179	Jim Eisenreich	.05
180	Bert Blyleven	.05
181	Rob Murphy	.05
182	Bill Doran	.05
183	Curt Ford	.05
184	Mike Henneman	.05
185	Eric Davis	.10
186	Lance McCullers	.05
187	*Steve Davis*	.05
188	Bill Wegman	.05
189	Brian Harper	.05
190	Mike Moore	.05
191	Dale Mohorcic	.05
192	Tim Wallach	.05
193	Keith Hernandez	.05
194	Dave Righetti	.05
195a	Bret Saberhagen ("joke" on card back)	.25
195b	Bret Saberhagen ("joker" on card back)	.30
196	Paul Kilgus	.05
197	Bud Black	.05
198	Juan Samuel	.05
199	Kevin Seitzer	.05
200	Darryl Strawberry	.10
201	Dave Stoib	.05
202	Charlie Hough	.05
203	Jack Morris	.05
204	Rance Mulliniks	.05
205	Alvin Davis	.05
206	Jack Howell	.05
207	Ken Patterson	.05
208	Terry Pendleton	.05
209	Craig Lefferts	.05
210	Kevin Brown	.05
211	Dan Petry	.05
212	Dave Leiper	.05
213	Daryl Boston	.05
214	Kevin Hickey	.05
215	Mike Krukow	.05
216	Terry Francona	.05
217	Kirk McCaskill	.05
218	Scott Bailes	.05
219	Bob Forsch	.05
220	Mike Aldrete	.05
221	Steve Buechele	.05
222	Jesse Barfield	.05
223	Juan Berenguer	.05
224	Andy McGaffigan	.05
225	Pete Smith	.05
226	Mike Witt	.05
227	Jay Howell	.05
228	Scott Bradley	.05
229	*Jerome Walton*	.10
230	Greg Swindell	.05
231	Atlee Hammaker	.05
232a	Mike Devereaux (RF)	.05
232b	Mike Devereaux (CF)	.10
233	Ken Hill	.15
234	Craig Worthington	.05
235	Scott Terry	.05
236	Brett Butler	.05
237	Doyle Alexander	.05
238	Dave Anderson	.05
239	Bob Milacki	.05
240	Dwight Smith	.05
241	Otis Nixon	.05
242	Pat Tabler	.05
243	Derek Lilliquist	.05
244	Danny Tartabull	.05
245	Wade Boggs	.30
246	Scott Garrelts	.05
247	Spike Owen	.05
248	Norm Charlton	.05
249	Gerald Perry	.05
250	Nolan Ryan	.60
251	Kevin Gross	.05
252	Randy Milligan	.05
253	Mike LaCoss	.05
254	Dave Bergman	.05
255	Tony Gwynn	.30
256	Felix Fermin	.05
257	Greg Harris	.05
258	*Junior Felix*	.10
259	Mark Davis	.05
260	Vince Coleman	.05
261	Paul Gibson	.05
262	Mitch Williams	.05
263	Jeff Russell	.05
264	*Omar Vizquel*	.25
265	Andre Dawson	.15
266	Storm Davis	.05
267	Guillermo Hernandez	.05
268	Mike Felder	.05
269	Tom Candiotti	.05
270	Bruce Hurst	.05
271	Fred McGriff	.25
272	Glenn Davis	.05
273	John Franco	.05
274	Rich Yett	.05
275	Craig Biggio	.20
276	Gene Larkin	.05
277	Rob Dibble	.05
278	Randy Bush	.05
279	Kevin Bass	.05
280a	Bo Jackson ("Watham" on back)	.15
280b	Bo Jackson ("Wathan" on back)	1.00
281	Wally Backman	.05
282	Larry Andersen	.05
283	Chris Bosio	.05
284	Juan Agosto	.05
285	Ozzie Smith	.30
286	George Bell	.05
287	Rex Hudler	.05
288	Pat Borders	.05
289	Danny Jackson	.05
290	Carlton Fisk	.15
291	Tracy Jones	.05
292	Allan Anderson	.05
293	Johnny Ray	.05
294	Lee Guetterman	.05
295	Paul O'Neill	.15
296	Carney Lansford	.05
297	Tom Brookens	.05
298	Claudell Washington	.05
299	Hubie Brooks	.05
300	Will Clark	.25
301	*Kenny Rogers*	.20
302	Darrell Evans	.10
303	Greg Briley	.05
304	Donn Pall	.05
305	Teddy Higuera	.05
306	Dan Pasqua	.05
307	Dave Winfield	.25
308	Dennis Powell	.05
309	Jose DeLeon	.05
310	Roger Clemens	.35
311	Melido Perez	.05
312	Devon White	.10
313	Dwight Gooden	.10
314	*Carlos Martinez*	.10
315	Dennis Eckersley	.05
316	Clay Parker	.05
317	Rick Honeycutt	.05
318	Tim Laudner	.05
319	Joe Carter	.10
320	Robin Yount	.30
321	Felix Jose	.05
322	Mickey Tettleton	.05
323	Mike Gallego	.05
324	Edgar Martinez	.05
325	Dave Henderson	.05
326	Chili Davis	.05
327	Steve Balboni	.05
328	Jody Davis	.05
329	Shawn Hillegas	.05
330	Jim Abbott	.10
331	John Dopson	.05

332	Mark Williamson	.05
333	Jeff Robinson	.05
334	John Smiley	.05
335	Bobby Thigpen	.05
336	Garry Templeton	.05
337	Marvell Wynne	.05
338a	Ken Griffey, Sr. (uniform #25 on card back)	.25
338b	Ken Griffey, Sr. (uniform #30 on card back)	3.00
339	*Steve Finley*	.25
340	Ellis Burks	.10
341	Frank Williams	.05
342	Mike Morgan	.05
343	Kevin Mitchell	.05
344	Joel Youngblood	.05
345	Mike Greenwell	.05
346	Glenn Wilson	.05
347	John Costello	.05
348	Wes Gardner	.05
349	Jeff Ballard	.05
350	Mark Thurmond	.05
351	Randy Myers	.05
352	Shawn Abner	.05
353	Jesse Orosco	.05
354	Greg Walker	.05
355	Pete Harnisch	.10
356	Steve Farr	.05
357	Dave LaPoint	.05
358	Willie Fraser	.05
359	Mickey Hatcher	.05
360	Rickey Henderson	.25
361	Mike Fitzgerald	.05
362	Bill Schroeder	.05
363	Mark Carreon	.05
364	Ron Jones	.05
365	Jeff Montgomery	.05
366	Bill Krueger	.05
367	John Cangelosi	.05
368	Jose Gonzalez	.05
369	*Greg Hibbard*	.10
370	John Smoltz	.15
371	*Jeff Brantley*	.10
372	Frank White	.05
373	Ed Whitson	.05
374	Willie McGee	.05
375	Jose Canseco	.25
376	Randy Ready	.05
377	Don Aase	.05
378	Tony Armas	.05
379	Steve Bedrosian	.05
380	Chuck Finley	.05
381	Kent Hrbek	.10
382	Jim Gantner	.05
383	Mel Hall	.05
384	Mike Marshall	.05
385	Mark McGwire	2.00
386	Wayne Tolleson	.05
387	Brian Holton	.05
388	*John Wetteland*	.20
389	Darren Daulton	.05
390	Rob Deer	.05
391	John Moses	.05
392	Todd Worrell	.05
393	Chuck Cary	.05
394	Stan Javier	.05
395	Willie Randolph	.05
396	Bill Buckner	.05
397	Robby Thompson	.05
398	Mike Scioscia	.05
399	Lonnie Smith	.05
400	Kirby Puckett	.30
401	Mark Langston	.05
402	Danny Darwin	.05
403	Greg Maddux	.60
404	Lloyd Moseby	.05
405	Rafael Palmeiro	.20
406	Chad Kreuter	.05
407	Jimmy Key	.05
408	Tim Birtsas	.05
409	Tim Raines	.10
410	Dave Stewart	.10
411	*Eric Yelding*	.15
412	*Kent Anderson*	.05
413	Les Lancaster	.05
414	Rick Dempsey	.05
415	Randy Johnson	.35
416	Gary Carter	.10
417	Rolando Roomes	.05
418	Dan Schatzeder	.05
419	Bryn Smith	.05
420	Ruben Sierra	.05
421	Steve Jeltz	.05
422	Ken Oberkfell	.05
423	Sid Bream	.05
424	Jim Clancy	.05
425	Kelly Gruber	.05
426	Rick Leach	.05
427	Len Dykstra	.05
428	Jeff Pico	.05
429	John Cerutti	.05
430	David Cone	.15
431	Jeff Kunkel	.05
432	Luis Aquino	.05
433	Ernie Whitt	.05
434	Bo Diaz	.05
435	Steve Lake	.05
436	Pat Perry	.05
437	Mike Davis	.05
438	Cecilio Guante	.05
439	Duane Ward	.05
440	Andy Van Slyke	.05
441	Gene Nelson	.05
442	Luis Polonia	.05
443	Kevin Elster	.05
444	Keith Moreland	.05
445	Roger McDowell	.05
446	Ron Darling	.05
447	Ernest Riles	.05
448	Mookie Wilson	.05
449a	*Bill Spiers* (66 missing for year of birth)	1.25
449b	*Bill Spiers* (1966 for birth year)	.15
450	Rick Sutcliffe	.05
451	Nelson Santovenia	.05
452	Andy Allanson	.05
453	Bob Melvin	.05
454	Benny Santiago	.05
455	Jose Uribe	.05
456	Bill Landrum	.05
457	Bobby Witt	.05
458	Kevin Romine	.05
459	Lee Mazzilli	.05
460	Paul Molitor	.30
461	Ramon Martinez	.15
462	Frank DiPino	.05
463	Walt Terrell	.05
464	*Bob Geren*	.05
465	Rick Reuchel	.05
466	Mark Grant	.05
467	John Kruk	.05
468	Gregg Jefferies	.15
469	R.J. Reynolds	.05
470	Harold Baines	.05
471	Dennis Lamp	.05
472	Tom Gordon	.05
473	Terry Puhl	.05
474	Curtis Wilkerson	.05
475	Dan Quisenberry	.05
476	Oddibe McDowell	.05
477a	Zane Smith (Career ERA 3.93)	1.50
477b	Zane Smith	.05
478	Franklin Stubbs	.05
479	Wallace Johnson	.05
480	Jay Tibbs	.05
481	Tom Glavine	.15
482	Manny Lee	.05
483	Joe Hesketh	.05
484	Mike Bielecki	.05
485	Greg Brock	.05
486	Pascual Perez	.05
487	Kirk Gibson	.05
488	Scott Sanderson	.05
489	Domingo Ramos	.05
490	Kal Daniels	.05
491a	David Wells (reversed negative on back photo)	3.00
491b	David Wells (corrected)	.10
492	Jerry Reed	.05
493	Eric Show	.05
494	Mike Pagliarulo	.05
495	Ron Robinson	.05
496	Brad Komminsk	.05
497	*Greg Litton*	.05
498	Chris James	.05
499	Luis Quinones	.05
500	Frank Viola	.05
501	Tim Teufel	.05
502	Terry Leach	.05
503	Matt Williams	.25
504	Tim Leary	.05
505	Doug Drabek	.05
506	Mariano Duncan	.05
507	Charlie Hayes	.05
508	Albert Belle	.75
509	Pat Sheridan	.05
510	Mackey Sasser	.05
511	Jose Rijo	.05
512	Mike Smithson	.05
513	Gary Ward	.05
514	Dion James	.05
515	Jim Gott	.05
516	Drew Hall	.05
517	Doug Bair	.05
518	*Scott Scudder*	.10
519	Rick Aguilera	.05
520	Rafael Belliard	.05
521	Jay Buhner	.10
522	Jeff Reardon	.05
523	Steve Rosenberg	.05
524	Randy Velarde	.05
525	Jeff Musselman	.05
526	Bill Long	.05
527	*Gary Wayne*	.05
528	*Dave Johnson*	.05
529	Ron Kittle	.05
530	Erik Hanson	.05
531	Steve Wilson	.05
532	Joey Meyer	.05
533	Curt Young	.05
534	Kelly Downs	.05
535	Joe Girardi	.05
536	Lance Blankenship	.05
537	Greg Mathews	.05
538	Donell Nixon	.05
539	Mark Knudson	.05
540	*Jeff Wetherby*	.05
541	Darrin Jackson	.05
542	Terry Mulholland	.05
543	Eric Hetzel	.05
544	*Rick Reed*	.05
545	Dennis Cook	.05
546	Mike Jackson	.05
547	Brian Fisher	.05
548	*Gene Harris*	.05
549	Jeff King	.10
550	Dave Dravecky (Salute)	.10
551	Randy Kutcher	.05
552	Mark Portugal	.05
553	*Jim Corsi*	.05
554	Todd Stottlemyre	.05
555	Scott Bankhead	.05
556	Ken Dayley	.05
557	*Rick Wrona*	.15
558	*Sammy Sosa*	5.00
559	Keith Miller	.05
560	Ken Griffey, Jr.	2.00
561a	Ryne Sandberg (Highlight, 3B on front)	10.00
561b	Ryne Sandberg (Highlight, no position)	.25
562	Billy Hatcher	.05
563	Jay Bell	.05
564	*Jack Daugherty*	.05
565	*Rich Monteleone*	.05
566	Bo Jackson (All-Star MVP)	.25
567	*Tony Fossas*	.05
568	*Roy Smith*	.05
569	*Jaime Navarro*	.10
570	Lance Johnson	.05
571	*Mike Dyer*	.05
572	*Kevin Ritz*	.10
573	Dave West	.05
574	*Gary Mielke*	.05
575	Scott Lusader	.05
576	*Joe Oliver*	.10
577	Sandy Alomar, Jr.	.15
578	Andy Benes	.15
579	Tim Jones	.05
580	*Randy McCament*	.05
581	Curt Schilling	.10
582	*John Orton*	.05
583a	*Milt Cuyler* (998 games)	2.00
583b	*Milt Cuyler* (98 games)	.10
584	*Eric Anthony*	.25
585	*Greg Vaughn*	.30
586	Deion Sanders	.20
587	Jose DeJesus	.05
588	*Chip Hale*	.10
589	*John Olerud*	.50
590	*Steve Olin*	.10
591	*Marquis Grissom*	.40
592	*Moises Alou*	.45
593	Mark Lemke	.05
594	*Dean Palmer*	.30
595	Robin Ventura	.35
596	Tino Martinez	.10
597	*Mike Huff*	.05
598	*Scott Hemond*	.10
599	*Wally Whitehurst*	.10
600	*Todd Zeile*	.15
601	Glenallen Hill	.10
602	Hal Morris	.10
603	Juan Bell	.05
604	*Bobby Rose*	.05
605	*Matt Merullo*	.10
606	*Kevin Maas*	.05
607	*Randy Nosek*	.05
608a	*Billy Bates* ("12 triples" mentioned in second-last line ine)	.05
608b	Billy Bates (triples not mentioned)	.50
609	*Mike Stanton*	.10
610	*Goose Gozzo*	.10
611	*Charles Nagy*	.40
612	*Scott Coolbaugh*	.05
613	*Jose Vizcaino*	.25
614	*Greg Smith*	.05
615	*Jeff Huson*	.10
616	*Mickey Weston*	.05
617	*John Pawlowski*	.05
618a	*Joe Skalski* (uniform #27 on card back)	.15
618b	*Joe Skalski* (uniform #67 on card back)	2.00
619	*Bernie Williams*	1.50
620	*Shawn Holman*	.05
621	*Gary Eave*	.05
622	*Darrin Fletcher*	.15
623	*Pat Combs*	.10
624	*Mike Blowers*	.10
625	Kevin Appier	.05
626	*Pat Austin*	.05
627	*Kelly Mann*	.05
628	*Matt Kinzer*	.05
629	*Chris Hammond*	.15
630	*Dean Wilkins*	.10
631	*Larry Walker*	1.00
632	*Blaine Beatty*	.10
633a	Tom Barrett (uniform #29 on card back)	.10
633b	Tom Barrett (uniform #14 on card back)	2.00
634	*Stan Belinda*	.10
635	*Tex Smith*	.05
636	*Hensley Meulens*	.10
637	*Juan Gonzalez*	3.00
638	*Lenny Webster*	.10
639	*Mark Gardner*	.10
640	*Tommy Greene*	.25
641	*Mike Hartley*	.05
642	*Phil Stephenson*	.05
643	*Kevin Mmahat*	.10
644	*Ed Whited*	.10
645	*Delino DeShields*	.25
646	Kevin Blankenship	.10
647	*Paul Sorrento*	.20
648	*Mike Roesler*	.10
649	*Jason Grimsley*	.10
650	*Dave Justice*	.50
651	*Scott Cooper*	.10
652	Dave Eiland	.05
653	*Mike Munoz*	.05
654	*Jeff Fischer*	.05
655	*Terry Jorgenson*	.05
656	*George Canale*	.05
657	*Brian DuBois*	.05
658	Carlos Quintana	.05
659	Luis de los Santos	.05
660	Jerald Clark	.05
661	*Donald Harris* (1st Round Pick)	.10
662	*Paul Coleman* (1st Round Pick)	.20
663	*Frank Thomas* (1st Round Pick)	4.50
664	*Brent Mayne* (1st Round Pick)	.10
665	*Eddie Zosky* (1st Round Pick)	.10
666	*Steve Hosey* (1st Round Pick)	.25
667	*Scott Bryant* (1st Round Pick)	.10
668	*Tom Goodwin* (1st Round Pick)	.10
669	*Cal Eldred* (1st Round Pick)	.25
670	*Earl Cunningham* (1st Round Pick)	.10
671	*Alan Zinter* (1st Round Pick)	.15
672	*Chuck Knoblauch* (1st Round Pick)	.50
672 (a)	Chuck Knoblauch (3,000 autographed cards with a special hologram on back were inserted into 1992 rack	50.00
673	*Kyle Abbott* (1st Round Pick)	.10
674	*Roger Salkeld* (1st Round Pick)	.15
675	*Mo Vaughn* (1st Round Pick)	2.00
676	*Kiki Jones* (1st Round Pick)	.10
677	*Tyler Houston* (1st Round Pick)	.10
678	*Jeff Jackson* (1st Round Pick)	.10
679	*Greg Gohr* (1st Round Pick)	.10
680	*Ben McDonald* (1st Round Pick)	.25
681	*Greg Blosser* (1st Round Pick)	.15
682	*Willie Green* (Greene) 1st Round Pick)	.15
683	Wade Boggs (Dream Team)	.15
684	Will Clark (Dream Team)	.20
685	Tony Gwynn (Dream Team)	.25
686	Rickey Henderson (Dream Team)	.15
687	Bo Jackson (Dream Team)	.15
688	Mark Langston (Dream Team)	.10
689	Barry Larkin (Dream Team)	.15
690	Kirby Puckett (Dream Team)	.25
691	Ryne Sandberg (Dream Team)	.25
692	Mike Scott (Dream Team)	.10
693	Terry Steinbach (Dream Team)	.10
694	Bobby Thigpen (Dream Team)	.05
695	Mitch Williams (Dream Team)	.10
696	Nolan Ryan (Highlight)	.45
697	Bo Jackson (FB/BB)	1.00
698	Rickey Henderson (ALCS MVP)	.15
699	Will Clark (NLCS MVP)	.15
700	World Series Games 1-2	.10
701	Lights Out: Candlestick	.15
702	World Series Game 3	.10
703	World Series Wrap-up	.20
704	Wade Boggs (Highlight)	.10

1990 Score Rookie Dream Team

This 10-card "Rookie Dream Team" set, in the same format as those found in the regular-issue 1990 Score, was available only in factory sets for the hobby trade. Factory sets for general retail outlets did not include these cards, nor were they available in Score packs. Cards carry a "B" prefix to their numbers.

		MT
Complete Set (10):		4.00
Common Player:		.25
1	A. Bartlett Giamatti	.25
2	Pat Combs	.25
3	Todd Zeile	.30
4	Luis de los Santos	.25
5	Mark Lemke	.25
6	Robin Ventura	1.50
7	Jeff Huson	.25
8	Greg Vaughn	.40
9	Marquis Grissom	1.50
10	Eric Anthony	.25

1990 Score Rising Stars

For the second consecutive year Score produced a 100-card "Rising" Stars" set. The 1990 issue was made available as a boxed set and also marketed with a related magazine like the 1989 issue. Magic Motion trivia cards featuring past MVP's accompany the card set. The cards feature full-color action photos on the front and portrait photos on the back.

		MT
Complete Set (100):		9.00
Common Player:		.10
1	Tom Gordon	.10
2	Jerome Walton	.10
3	Ken Griffey, Jr.	5.00
4	Dwight Smith	.10
5	Jim Abbott	.10
6	Todd Zeile	.20
7	Donn Pall	.10
8	Rick Reed	.10
9	Joey Belle	.50
10	Gregg Jefferies	.20
11	Kevin Ritz	.10
12	Charlie Hayes	.10
13	Kevin Appier	.10
14	Jeff Huson	.10
15	Gary Wayne	.10
16	Eric Yelding	.10
17	Clay Parker	.10
18	Junior Felix	.10
19	Derek Lilliquist	.10
20	Gary Sheffield	.25
21	Craig Worthington	.10
22	Jeff Brantley	.10
23	Eric Hetzel	.10
24	Greg Harris	.10
25	John Wetteland	.10
26	Joe Oliver	.10
27	Kevin Maas	.10
28	Kevin Brown	.10
29	Mike Stanton	.10
30	Greg Vaughn	.20
31	Ron Jones	.10
32	Gregg Olson	.10
33	Joe Girardi	.10

34 Ken Hill .10
35 Sammy Sosa 1.50
36 Geronimo Berroa .10
37 Omar Vizquel .15
38 Dean Palmer .10
39 John Olerud .25
40 Deion Sanders .40
41 Randy Kramer .10
42 Scott Lusader .10
43 Dave Johnson .10
44 Jeff Wetherby .10
45 Eric Anthony .10
46 Kenny Rogers .10
47 Matt Winters .10
48 Goose Gozzo .10
49 Carlos Quintana .10
50 Bob Geren .10
51 Chad Kreuter .10
52 Randy Johnson .50
53 Hensley Meulens .10
54 Gene Harris .10
55 Bill Spiers .10
56 Kelly Mann .10
57 Tom McCarthy .10
58 Steve Finley .15
59 Ramon Martinez .25
60 Greg Briley .10
61 Jack Daugherty .10
62 Tim Jones .10
63 Doug Strange .10
64 John Orton .10
65 Scott Scudder .10
66 Mark Gardner (photo on back actually Steve Frey) .10
67 Mark Carreon .10
68 Bob Milacki .10
69 Andy Benes .10
70 Carlos Martinez .10
71 Jeff King .15
72 Brad Arnsberg .10
73 Rick Wrona .10
74 Cris Carpenter .10
75 Dennis Cook .10
76 Pete Harnisch .10
77 Greg Hibbard .10
78 Ed Whited .10
79 Scott Coolbaugh .10
80 Billy Bates .10
81 German Gonzalez .10
82 Lance Blankenship .10
83 Lenny Harris .10
84 Milt Cuyler .10
85 Erik Hanson .10
86 Kent Anderson .10
87 Hal Morris .10
88 Mike Brumley .10
89 Ken Patterson .10
90 Mike Devereaux .10
91 Greg Litton .10
92 Rolando Roomes .10
93 Ben McDonald .10
94 Curt Schilling .20
95 Jose DeJesus .10
96 Robin Ventura .25
97 Steve Searcy .10
98 Chip Hale .10
99 Marquis Grissom .40
100 Luis de los Santos .10

1990 Score Superstars

The game's top 100 players are featured in this set. The card fronts feature full-color action photos and are similar in style to the past Score Superstar set. The set was marketed as a boxed set and with a special magazine devoted to baseball's 100 hottest players. Each set includes a series of Magic Motion cards honoring past MVP winners. The player cards measure 2-1/2" x 3-1/2".

	MT
Complete Set (100):	8.00
Common Player:	.08

1 Kirby Puckett .60
2 Steve Sax .08
3 Tony Gwynn .50
4 Willie Randolph .08
5 Jose Canseco .50
6 Ozzie Smith .45
7 Rick Reuschel .08
8 Bill Doran .08
9 Mickey Tettleton .08
10 Don Mattingly .90
11 Greg Swindell .08
12 Bert Blyleven .08
13 Dave Stewart .10
14 Andres Galarraga .20
15 Darryl Strawberry .15
16 Ellis Burks .12
17 Paul O'Neill .12
18 Bruce Hurst .08
19 Dave Smith .08
20 Carney Lansford .08
21 Robby Thompson .08
22 Gary Gaetti .08
23 Jeff Russell .08
24 Chuck Finley .08
25 Mark McGwire 1.50
26 Alvin Davis .08
27 George Bell .08
28 Cory Snyder .08
29 Keith Hernandez .08
30 Will Clark .40
31 Steve Bedrosian .08
32 Ryne Sandberg .60
33 Tom Browning .08
34 Tim Burke .08
35 John Smoltz .12
36 Phil Bradley .08
37 Bobby Bonilla .10
38 Kirk McCaskill .08
39 Dave Righetti .08
40 Bo Jackson .25
41 Alan Trammell .12
42 Mike Moore .08
43 Harold Reynolds .08
44 Nolan Ryan 1.00
45 Fred McGriff .25
46 Brian Downing .08
47 Brett Butler .08
48 Mike Scioscia .08
49 John Franco .08
50 Kevin Mitchell .08
51 Mark Davis .08
52 Glenn Davis .08
53 Barry Bonds .75
54 Dwight Evans .08
55 Terry Steinbach .08
56 Dave Gallagher .08
57 Roberto Kelly .08
58 Rafael Palmeiro .20
59 Joe Carter .12
60 Mark Grace .25
61 Pedro Guerrero .08
62 Von Hayes .08
63 Benny Santiago .10
64 Dale Murphy .15
65 John Smiley .08
66 Cal Ripken, Jr. 1.00
67 Mike Greenwell .08
68 Devon White .08
69 Ed Whitson .08
70 Carlton Fisk .15
71 Lou Whitaker .08
72 Danny Tartabull .08
73 Vince Coleman .08
74 Andre Dawson .15
75 Tim Raines .10
76 George Brett .60
77 Tom Herr .08
78 Andy Van Slyke .08
79 Roger Clemens .45
80 Wade Boggs .40
81 Wally Joyner .10
82 Lonnie Smith .08
83 Howard Johnson .08
84 Julio Franco .08
85 Ruben Sierra .08
86 Dan Plesac .08
87 Bobby Thigpen .08
88 Kevin Seitzer .08
89 Dave Steib .08
90 Rickey Henderson .30
91 Jeffrey Leonard .08
92 Robin Yount .30
93 Mitch Williams .08
94 Orel Hershiser .12
95 Eric Davis .10
96 Mark Langston .08
97 Mike Scott .08
98 Paul Molitor .35
99 Dwight Gooden .10
100 Kevin Bass .08

1990 Score Traded

This 110-card set features players with new teams as well as 1990 Major League rookies. The cards feature full-color action photos framed in yellow with an orange border. The player's ID appears in green below the photo. The team logo is displayed next to the player's name. The card backs feature posed player photos and follow the style of the regular 1990 Score issue. The cards are numbered 1T-110T. Young hockey phenom Eric Lindros is featured trying out for the Toronto Blue Jays.

	MT
Complete Set (110):	5.00
Common Player:	.05

1 Dave Winfield .25
2 Kevin Bass .05
3 Nick Esasky .05
4 Mitch Webster .05
5 Pascual Perez .05
6 Gary Pettis .05
7 Tony Pena .05
8 Candy Maldonado .05
9 Cecil Fielder .10
10 Carmelo Martinez .05
11 Mark Langston .05
12 Dave Parker .15
13 Don Slaught .05
14 Tony Phillips .05
15 John Franco .05
16 Randy Myers .05
17 Jeff Reardon .05
18 Sandy Alomar, Jr. .25
19 Joe Carter .15
20 Fred Lynn .05
21 Storm Davis .05
22 Craig Lefferts .05
23 Pete O'Brien .05
24 Dennis Boyd .05
25 Lloyd Moseby .05
26 Mark Davis .05
27 Tim Leary .05
28 Gerald Perry .05
29 Don Aase .05
30 Ernie Whitt .05
31 Dale Murphy .25
32 Alejandro Pena .05
33 Juan Samuel .05
34 Hubie Brooks .05
35 Gary Carter .10
36 Jim Presley .05
37 Wally Backman .05
38 Matt Nokes .05
39 Dan Petry .05
40 Franklin Stubbs .05
41 Jeff Huson .05
42 Billy Hatcher .05
43 Terry Leach .05
44 Phil Bradley .05
45 Claudell Washington .05
46 Luis Polonia .05
47 Daryl Boston .05
48 Lee Smith .05
49 Tom Brunansky .05
50 Mike Witt .05
51 Willie Randolph .05
52 Stan Javier .05
53 Brad Komminsk .05
54 John Candelaria .05
55 Bryn Smith .05
56 Glenn Braggs .05
57 Keith Hernandez .05
58 Ken Oberkfell .05
59 Steve Jeltz .05
60 Chris James .05
61 Scott Sanderson .05
62 Bill Long .05
63 Rick Cerone .05
64 Scott Bailes .05
65 Larry Sheets .05
66 Junior Ortiz .05
67 Francisco Cabrera .05
68 Gary DiSarcina .10
69 Greg Olson .05
70 Beau Allred .05
71 Oscar Azocar .05
72 Kent Mercker .10
73 John Burkett .10
74 *Carlos Baerga* .35
75 Dave Hollins .35
76 *Todd Hundley* .75
77 Rick Parker .05
78 Steve Cummings .05
79 Bill Sampen .05
80 Jerry Kutzler .05
81 Derek Bell .30
82 Kevin Tapani .20
83 Jim Leyritz .10
84 *Ray Lankford* .75
85 Wayne Edwards .05
86 Frank Thomas 3.00
87 Tim Naehring .05
88 Willie Blair .10
89 Alan Mills .10
90 Scott Radinsky .10
91 Howard Farmer .05
92 Julio Machado .05
93 Rafael Valdez .05
94 Shawn Boskie .10
95 David Segui .20
96 Chris Hoiles .10
97 D.J. Dozier .05
98 Hector Villanueva .05
99 Eric Gunderson .05
100 *Eric Lindros* 1.50
101 Dave Otto .05
102 Dana Kiecker .05
103 Tim Drummond .05
104 Mickey Pina .05
105 Craig Grebeck .10
106 *Bernard Gilkey* .40
107 Tim Layana .05
108 Scott Chiamparino .05
109 Steve Avery .05
110 Terry Shumpert .05

1990 Score Young Superstars Set 1

For the third consecutive year, Score produced Young Superstars boxed sets. The 1990 versions contain 42 player cards plus five Magic-Motion trivia cards. The cards are similar to previous Young Superstar sets, with action photography on the front and a glossy finish. Card backs have a color portrait, major league statistics and scouting reports. Besides the boxed set, cards from Set I were inserted into rack packs.

	MT
Complete Set (42):	5.00
Common Player:	.15

1 Bo Jackson .25
2 Dwight Smith .15
3 Joey Belle .50
4 Gregg Olson .15
5 Jim Abbott .25
6 Felix Fermin .15
7 Brian Holman .15
8 Clay Parker .15
9 Junior Felix .15
10 Joe Oliver .15
11 Steve Finley .15
12 Greg Briley .15
13 Greg Vaughn .20
14 Bill Spiers .15
15 Eric Yelding .15
16 Jose Gonzalez .15
17 Mark Carreon .15
18 Greg Harris .15
19 Felix Jose .15
20 Bob Milacki .15
21 Kenny Rogers .15
22 Rolando Roomes .15
23 Bip Roberts .15
24 Jeff Brantley .15
25 Jeff Ballard .15
26 John Dopson .15
27 Ken Patterson .15
28 Omar Vizquel .25
29 Kevin Brown .15
30 Derek Lilliquist .15
31 David Wells .25
32 Ken Hill .15
33 Greg Litton .15
34 Rob Ducey .15
35 Carlos Martinez .15
36 John Smoltz .45
37 Lenny Harris .15
38 Charlie Hayes .15
39 Tommy Gregg .15
40 John Wetteland .15
41 Jeff Huson .15
42 Eric Anthony .15

Player names in *Italic* type indicate a rookie card.

1990 Score Young Superstars Set 2

Available only as a boxed set via a mail-order offer, Set II of 1990 Score Young Superstars is identical in format to Set I, with the exception that the graphic elements on the front of Set II cards are in red and green, while in Set I they are in blue and magenta.

	MT
Complete Set (42):	25.00
Common Player:	.15

1 Todd Zeile .25
2 Ben McDonald .15
3 Delino DeShields .20
4 Pat Combs .15
5 John Olerud .40
6 Marquis Grissom .50
7 Mike Stanton .15
8 Robin Ventura .60
9 Larry Walker .50
10 Dante Bichette .50
11 Jack Armstrong .15
12 Jay Bell .15
13 Andy Benes .25
14 Joey Cora .15
15 Rob Dibble .15
16 Jeff King .15
17 Jeff Hamilton .15
18 Erik Hanson .15
19 Pete Harnisch .15
20 Greg Hibbard .15
21 Stan Javier .15
22 Mark Lemke .15
23 Steve Olin .15
24 Tommy Greene .15
25 Sammy Sosa 24.00
26 Gary Wayne .15
27 Deion Sanders .60
28 Steve Wilson .15
29 Joe Girardi .15
30 John Orton .15
31 Kevin Tapani .15
32 Carlos Baerga .20
33 Glenallen Hill .15
34 Mike Blowers .15
35 Dave Hollins .20
36 Lance Blankenship .15
37 Hal Morris .15
38 Lance Johnson .15
39 Chris Gwynn .15
40 Doug Dascenzo .15
41 Jerald Clark .15
42 Carlos Quintana .15

1990 Score Yankees

For a second year, National Westminster Bank sponsored a Score-produced team set as a stadium promotion. The set features color player photos on front and back and is graphically enhanced by the team's traditional pinstripe motif. A tribute card to former Yankees infielder and manager Billy Martin, who was killed the previous Christmas, is included in the set.

		MT
Complete Set (32):		9.00
Common Player:		.25
1	Stump Merrill	.25
2	Don Mattingly	2.00
3	Steve Sax	.25
4	Alvaro Espinoza	.25
5	Jesse Barfield	.25
6	Roberto Kelly	.25
7	Mel Hall	.25
8	Claudell Washington	.25
9	Bob Geren	.25
10	Jim Leyritz	.40
11	Pascual Perez	.25
12	Dave LaPoint	.25
13	Tim Leary	.25
14	Mike Witt	.25
15	Chuck Cary	.25
16	Dave Righetti	.25
17	Lee Guetterman	.25
18	Andy Hawkins	.25
19	Greg Cadaret	.25
20	Eric Plunk	.25
21	Jimmy Jones	.25
22	Deion Sanders	1.50
23	Jeff Robinson	.25
24	Matt Nokes	.25
25	Steve Balboni	.25
26	Wayne Tolleson	.25
27	Randy Velarde	.25
28	Rick Cerone	.25
29	Alan Mills	.25
30	Billy Martin	.35
31	Yankee Stadium	.25
32	All-Time Yankee Records	.25

1990 Score/Sportflics 11th National Nolan Ryan

This two-fronted card is a unique souvenir given to those who participated in a special 1990 convention tour of the Optigraphics card manufacturing plant in Dallas. The card features Nolan Ryan on two of the company's best-known products, Score on one side, Sportflics on the other. Each side is similar to Ryan's regularly issued card in those sets, but carries logos or typography related to the 11th Annual National Sports Collectors Convention, held in nearby Arlington. Only 600 of the cards were reported produced.

	MT
Nolan Ryan	450.00

1991 Score Promos

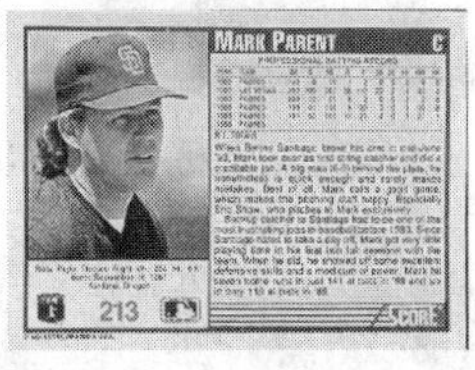

To preview its 1991 baseball cards Score pre-released the 110 cards from its teal-bordered series (cards #111-220) as samples. The main difference on most cards between the samples and the issued version is that the samples have no statistics on the 1990 season or career lines. Many cards have different career highlight write-ups on back, as well. A handful of the sample cards were widely distributed to dealers and the hobby press, while others from the sheet were released more sparingly. As few as two specimens are known of some superstar cards, driving up their prices among single-player specialty collectors.

		MT
Common Player:		25.00
111	Juan Berenguer	25.00
112	Mike Heath	25.00
113	Scott Bradley	25.00
114	Jack Morris	25.00
115	Barry Jones	25.00
116	Kevin Romine	25.00
117	Garry Templeton	25.00
118	Scott Sanderson	25.00
119	Roberto Kelly	25.00
120	George Brett	250.00
121	Oddibe McDowell	25.00
122	Jim Acker	25.00
123	Bill Swift	25.00
124	Eric King	25.00
125	Jay Buhner	35.00
126	Matt Young	25.00
127	Alvaro Espinoza	25.00
128	Greg Hibbard	25.00
129	Jeff M. Robinson	25.00
130	Mike Greenwell	25.00
131	Dion James	25.00
132	Donn Pall	25.00
133	Lloyd Moseby	25.00
134	Randy Velarde	25.00
135	Allan Anderson	25.00
136	Mark Davis	25.00
137	Eric Davis	35.00
138	Phil Stephenson	25.00
139	Felix Fermin	25.00
140	Pedro Guerrero	25.00
141	Charlie Hough	25.00
142	Mike Henneman	25.00
143	Jeff Montgomery	25.00
144	Lenny Harris	25.00
145	Bruce Hurst	25.00
146	Eric Anthony	25.00
147	Paul Assenmacher	25.00
148	Jesse Barfield	25.00
149	Carlos Quintana	25.00
150	Dave Stewart	30.00
151	Roy Smith	25.00
152	Paul Gibson	25.00
153	Mickey Hatcher	25.00
154	Jim Eisenreich	25.00
155	Kenny Rogers	25.00
156	Dave Schmidt	25.00
157	Lance Johnson	25.00
158	Dave West	25.00
159	Steve Balboni	25.00
160	Jeff Brantley	25.00
161	Craig Biggio	75.00
162	Brook Jacoby	25.00
163	Dan Gladden	25.00
164	Jeff Reardon	25.00
165	Mark Carreon	25.00
166	Mel Hall	25.00
167	Gary Mielke	25.00
168	Cecil Fielder	45.00
169	Darrin Jackson	25.00
170	Rick Aguilera	25.00
171	Walt Weiss	25.00
172	Steve Farr	25.00
173	Jody Reed	25.00
174	Mike Jeffcoat	25.00
175	Mark Grace	150.00
176	Larry Sheets	25.00
177	Bill Gullickson	25.00
178	Chris Gwynn	25.00
179	Melido Perez	25.00
180	Sid Fernandez	25.00
181	Tim Burke	25.00
182	Gary Pettis	25.00
183	Rob Murphy	25.00
184	Craig Lefferts	25.00
185	Howard Johnson	25.00
186	Ken Caminiti	45.00
187	Tim Belcher	25.00
188	Greg Cadaret	25.00
189	Matt Williams	150.00
190	Dave Magadan	25.00
191	Geno Petralli	25.00
192	Jeff D. Robinson	25.00
193	Jim Deshaies	25.00
194	Willie Randolph	25.00
195	George Bell	25.00
196	Hubie Brooks	25.00
197	Tom Gordon	25.00
198	Mike Fitzgerald	25.00
199	Mike Pagliarulo	25.00
200	Kirby Puckett	250.00
201	Shawon Dunston	25.00
202	Dennis Boyd	25.00
203	Junior Felix	25.00
204	Alejandro Pena	25.00
205	Pete Smith	25.00
206	Tom Glavine	60.00
207	Luis Salazar	25.00
208	John Smoltz	45.00
209	Doug Dascenzo	25.00
210	Tim Wallach	25.00
211	Greg Gagne	25.00
212	Mark Gubicza	25.00
213	Mark Parent	25.00
214	Ken Oberkfell	25.00
215	Gary Carter	50.00
216	Rafael Palmeiro	100.00
217	Tom Niedenfuer	25.00
218	Dave LaPoint	25.00
219	Jeff Treadway	25.00
220	Mitch Williams	25.00

1991 Score

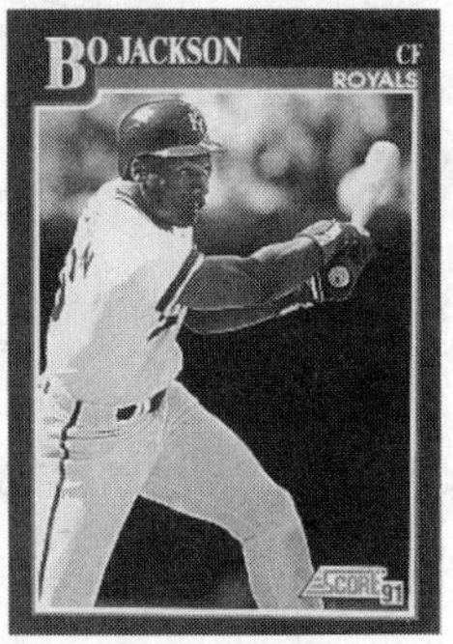

Score introduced a two series format in 1991. The first series includes cards 1-441. Score cards once again feature multiple border colors within the set, several subsets (Master Blaster, K-Man, Highlights and Riflemen), full-color action photos on the front and portraits on the flip side. Score eliminated display of the player's uniform number on the 1991 cards. Black-and-white Dream Team cards, plus Prospects and #1 Draft Picks highlight the 1991 set. The second series was released in February of 1991.

		MT
Complete Set (893):		10.00
Common Player:		.05
Wax Box:		10.00
1	Jose Canseco	.35
2	Ken Griffey, Jr.	1.50
3	Ryne Sandberg	.25
4	Nolan Ryan	.75
5	Bo Jackson	.15
6	Bret Saberhagen	.10
7	Will Clark	.20
8	Ellis Burks	.10
9	Joe Carter	.10
10	Rickey Henderson	.25
11	Ozzie Guillen	.05
12	Wade Boggs	.25
13	Jerome Walton	.05
14	John Franco	.05
15	Ricky Jordan	.05
16	Wally Backman	.05
17	Rob Dibble	.05
18	Glenn Braggs	.05
19	Cory Snyder	.05
20	Kal Daniels	.05
21	Mark Langston	.05
22	Kevin Gross	.05
23	Don Mattingly	.30
24	Dave Righetti	.05
25	Roberto Alomar	.30
26	Robby Thompson	.05
27	Jack McDowell	.05
28	Bip Roberts	.05
29	Jay Howell	.05
30	Dave Steib	.05
31	Johnny Ray	.05
32	Steve Sax	.05
33	Terry Mulholland	.05
34	Lee Guetterman	.05
35	Tim Raines	.10
36	Scott Fletcher	.05
37	Lance Parrish	.05
38	Tony Phillips	.05
39	Todd Stottlemyre	.05
40	Alan Trammell	.10
41	Todd Burns	.05
42	Mookie Wilson	.05
43	Chris Bosio	.05
44	Jeffrey Leonard	.05
45	Doug Jones	.05
46	Mike Scott	.05
47	Andy Hawkins	.05
48	Harold Reynolds	.05
49	Paul Molitor	.20
50	John Farrell	.05
51	Danny Darwin	.05
52	Jeff Blauser	.05
53	John Tudor	.05
54	Milt Thompson	.05
55	Dave Justice	.30
56	*Greg Olson*	.05
57	*Willie Blair*	.10
58	*Rick Parker*	.10
59	*Shawn Boskie*	.15
60	Kevin Tapani	.05
61	Dave Hollins	.10
62	*Scott Radinsky*	.10
63	Francisco Cabrera	.05
64	*Tim Layana*	.10
65	*Jim Leyritz*	.15
66	Wayne Edwards	.05
67	Lee Stevens	.10
68	*Bill Sampen*	.10
69	*Craig Grebeck*	.10
70	John Burkett	.10
71	*Hector Villanueva*	.05
72	*Oscar Azocar*	.05
73	*Alan Mills*	.15
74	Carlos Baerga	.10
75	Charles Nagy	.10
76	Tim Drummond	.05
77	*Dana Kiecker*	.05
78	*Tom Edens*	.05
79	Kent Mercker	.05
80	Steve Avery	.05
81	Lee Smith	.05
82	Dave Martinez	.05
83	Dave Winfield	.15
84	Bill Spiers	.05
85	Dan Pasqua	.05
86	Randy Milligan	.05
87	Tracy Jones	.05
88	Greg Myers	.05
89	Keith Hernandez	.05
90	Todd Benzinger	.05
91	Mike Jackson	.05
92	Mike Stanley	.05
93	Candy Maldonado	.05
94	John Kruk	.05
95	Cal Ripken, Jr.	.75
96	Willie Fraser	.05
97	Mike Felder	.05
98	Bill Landrum	.05
99	Chuck Crim	.05
100	Chuck Finley	.05
101	Kirt Manwaring	.05
102	Jaime Navarro	.05
103	Dickie Thon	.05
104	Brian Downing	.05
105	Jim Abbott	.10
106	Tom Brookens	.05
107	Darryl Hamilton	.05
108	Bryan Harvey	.05
109	Greg Harris	.05
110	Greg Swindell	.05
111	Juan Berenguer	.05
112	Mike Heath	.05
113	Scott Bradley	.05
114	Jack Morris	.05
115	Barry Jones	.05
116	Kevin Romine	.05
117	Garry Templeton	.05
118	Scott Sanderson	.05
119	Roberto Kelly	.05
120	George Brett	.30
121	Oddibe McDowell	.05
122	Jim Acker	.05
123	Bill Swift	.05
124	Eric King	.05
125	Jay Buhner	.10
126	Matt Young	.05
127	Alvaro Espinoza	.05
128	Greg Hibbard	.05
129	Jeff Robinson	.05
130	Mike Greenwell	.05
131	Dion James	.05
132	Donn Pall	.05
133	Lloyd Moseby	.05
134	Randy Velarde	.05
135	Allan Anderson	.05
136	Mark Davis	.05
137	Eric Davis	.10
138	Phil Stephenson	.05
139	Felix Fermin	.05
140	Pedro Guerrero	.05
141	Charlie Hough	.05
142	Mike Henneman	.05
143	Jeff Montgomery	.05
144	Lenny Harris	.05
145	Bruce Hurst	.05
146	Eric Anthony	.05
147	Paul Assenmacher	.05
148	Jesse Barfield	.05
149	Carlos Quintana	.05
150	Dave Stewart	.10
151	Roy Smith	.05
152	Paul Gibson	.05
153	Mickey Hatcher	.05
154	Jim Eisenreich	.05
155	Kenny Rogers	.05
156	Dave Schmidt	.05
157	Lance Johnson	.05
158	Dave West	.05
159	Steve Balboni	.05
160	Jeff Brantley	.05
161	Craig Biggio	.20
162	Brook Jacoby	.05
163	Dan Gladden	.05
164	Jeff Reardon	.05
165	Mark Carreon	.05
166	Mel Hall	.05
167	Gary Mielke	.05
168	Cecil Fielder	.10
169	Darrin Jackson	.05
170	Rick Aguilera	.05
171	Walt Weiss	.05
172	Steve Farr	.05
173	Jody Reed	.05
174	Mike Jeffcoat	.05
175	Mark Grace	.15
176	Larry Sheets	.05
177	Bill Gullickson	.05
178	Chris Gwynn	.05
179	Melido Perez	.05
180	Sid Fernandez	.05
181	Tim Burke	.05
182	Gary Pettis	.05
183	Rob Murphy	.05
184	Craig Lefferts	.05
185	Howard Johnson	.05
186	Ken Caminiti	.15
187	Tim Belcher	.05
188	Greg Cadaret	.05
189	Matt Williams	.20
190	Dave Magadan	.05
191	Geno Petralli	.05
192	Jeff Robinson	.05
193	Jim Deshaies	.05
194	Willie Randolph	.05
195	George Bell	.05
196	Hubie Brooks	.05
197	Tom Gordon	.05
198	Mike Fitzgerald	.05
199	Mike Pagliarulo	.05
200	Kirby Puckett	.25
201	Shawon Dunston	.05
202	Dennis Boyd	.05
203	Junior Felix	.05
204	Alejandro Pena	.05
205	Pete Smith	.05
206	Tom Glavine	.10
207	Luis Salazar	.05
208	John Smoltz	.15
209	Doug Dascenzo	.05
210	Tim Wallach	.05
211	Greg Gagne	.05
212	Mark Gubicza	.05
213	Mark Parent	.05
214	Ken Oberkfell	.05
215	Gary Carter	.10
216	Rafael Palmeiro	.10
217	Tom Niedenfuer	.05
218	Dave LaPoint	.05
219	Jeff Treadway	.05
220	Mitch Williams	.05
221	Jose DeLeon	.05
222	Mike LaValliere	.05
223	Darrel Akerfelds	.05
224	Kent Anderson	.05
225	Dwight Evans	.05
226	Gary Redus	.05
227	Paul O'Neill	.15
228	Marty Barrett	.05
229	Tom Browning	.05
230	Terry Pendleton	.05
231	Jack Armstrong	.05
232	Mike Boddicker	.05
233	Neal Heaton	.05
234	Marquis Grissom	.10
235	Bert Blyleven	.05
236	Curt Young	.05
237	Don Carman	.05
238	Charlie Hayes	.05
239	Mark Knudson	.05
240	Todd Zeile	.10
241	Larry Walker	.25
242	Jerald Clark	.05
243	Jeff Ballard	.05
244	Jeff King	.05
245	Tom Brunansky	.05
246	Darren Daulton	.05
247	Scott Terry	.05
248	Rob Deer	.05
249	Brady Anderson	.10
250	Len Dykstra	.05
251	Greg Harris	.05
252	Mike Hartley	.05
253	Joey Cora	.05
254	Ivan Calderon	.05
255	Ted Power	.05
256	Sammy Sosa	.75
257	Steve Buechele	.05
258	Mike Devereaux	.05
259	Brad Komminsk	.05
260	Teddy Higuera	.05
261	Shawn Abner	.05
262	Dave Valle	.05
263	Jeff Huson	.05
264	Edgar Martinez	.05
265	Carlton Fisk	.10
266	Steve Finley	.05
267	John Wetteland	.10
268	Kevin Appier	.05
269	Steve Lyons	.05
270	Mickey Tettleton	.05
271	Luis Rivera	.05
272	Steve Jeltz	.05
273	R.J. Reynolds	.05
274	Carlos Martinez	.05
275	Dan Plesac	.05
276	Mike Morgan	.05
277	Jeff Russell	.05
278	Pete Incaviglia	.05
279	Kevin Seitzer	.05
280	Bobby Thigpen	.05
281	Stan Javier	.05
282	Henry Cotto	.05
283	Gary Wayne	.05

284	Shane Mack	.05
285	Brian Holman	.05
286	Gerald Perry	.05
287	Steve Crawford	.05
288	Nelson Liriano	.05
289	Don Aase	.05
290	Randy Johnson	.25
291	Harold Baines	.05
292	Kent Hrbek	.05
293	Les Lancaster	.05
294	Jeff Musselman	.05
295	Kurt Stillwell	.05
296	Stan Belinda	.05
297	Lou Whitaker	.05
298	Glenn Wilson	.05
299	Omar Vizquel	.10
300	Ramon Martinez	.10
301	Dwight Smith	.05
302	Tim Crews	.05
303	Lance Blankenship	.05
304	Sid Bream	.05
305	Rafael Ramirez	.05
306	Steve Wilson	.05
307	Mackey Sasser	.05
308	Franklin Stubbs	.05
309	Jack Daugherty	.05
310	Eddie Murray	.20
311	Bob Welch	.05
312	Brian Harper	.05
313	Lance McCullers	.05
314	Dave Smith	.05
315	Bobby Bonilla	.10
316	Jerry Don Gleaton	.05
317	Greg Maddux	.75
318	Keith Miller	.05
319	Mark Portugal	.05
320	Robin Ventura	.15
321	Bob Ojeda	.05
322	Mike Harkey	.05
323	Jay Bell	.05
324	Mark McGwire	1.50
325	Gary Gaetti	.05
326	Jeff Pico	.05
327	Kevin McReynolds	.05
328	Frank Tanana	.05
329	Eric Yelding	.05
330	Barry Bonds	.40
331	*Brian McRae*	.20
332	*Pedro Munoz*	.10
333	*Daryl Irvine*	.10
334	Chris Hoiles	.05
335	*Thomas Howard*	.10
336	*Jeff Schulz*	.05
337	Jeff Manto	.05
338	Beau Allred	.05
339	*Mike Bordick*	.15
340	Todd Hundley	.10
341	*Jim Vatcher*	.05
342	Luis Sojo	.05
343	*Jose Offerman*	.15
344	*Pete Coachman*	.10
345	Mike Benjamin	.05
346	*Ozzie Canseco*	.05
347	Tim McIntosh	.05
348	*Phil Plantier*	.10
349	*Terry Shumpert*	.05
350	Darren Lewis	.10
351	*David Walsh*	.05
352	*Scott Chiamparino*	.05
353	*Julio Valera*	.10
354	*Anthony Telford*	.10
355	Kevin Wickander	.05
356	*Tim Naehring*	.05
357	*Jim Poole*	.05
358	*Mark Whiten*	.10
359	*Terry Wells*	.05
360	*Rafael Valdez*	.05
361	*Mel Stottlemyre*	.05
362	*David Segui*	.10
363	Paul Abbott	.05
364	*Steve Howard*	.05
365	*Karl Rhodes*	.10
366	*Rafael Novoa*	.10
367	*Joe Grahe*	.10
368	*Darren Reed*	.15
369	Jeff McKnight	.05
370	Scott Leius	.10
371	*Mark Dewey*	.05
372	*Mark Lee*	.05
373	*Rosario Rodriguez*	.05
374	Chuck McElroy	.05
375	*Mike Bell*	.05
376	Mickey Morandini	.05
377	*Bill Haselman*	.05
378	*Dave Pavlas*	.05
379	Derrick May	.05
380	*Jeromy Burnitz* (1st Draft Pick)	.25
381	*Donald Peters* (1st Draft Pick)	.10
382	*Alex Fernandez* (1st Draft Pick)	.25
383	*Mike Mussina* (1st Draft Pick)	1.25
384	*Daniel Smith* (1st Draft Pick)	.10
385	*Lance Dickson* (1st Draft Pick)	.15
386	*Carl Everett* (1st Draft Pick)	.20
387	*Thomas Nevers* (1st Draft Pick)	.15
388	*Adam Hyzdu* (1st Draft Pick)	.15
389	*Todd Van Poppel* (1st Draft Pick)	.10
390	*Rondell White* (1st Draft Pick)	.50
391	*Marc Newfield* (1st Draft Pick)	.10
392	Julio Franco (AS)	.05
393	Wade Boggs (AS)	.10
394	Ozzie Guillen (AS)	.05
395	Cecil Fielder (AS)	.10
396	Ken Griffey, Jr. (AS)	.50
397	Rickey Henderson (AS)	.15
398	Jose Canseco (AS)	.10
399	Roger Clemens (AS)	.15
400	Sandy Alomar,Jr. (AS)	.10
401	Bobby Thigpen (AS)	.05
402	Bobby Bonilla (Master Blaster)	.05
403	Eric Davis (Master Blaster)	.10
404	Fred McGriff (Master Blaster)	.10
405	Glenn Davis (Master Blaster)	.05
406	Kevin Mitchell (Master Blaster)	.05
407	Rob Dibble (K-Man)	.05
408	Ramon Martinez (K-Man)	.10
409	David Cone (K-Man)	.10
410	Bobby Witt (K-Man)	.05
411	Mark Langston (K-Man)	.05
412	Bo Jackson (Rifleman)	.15
413	Shawon Dunston (Rifleman)	.05
414	Jesse Barfield (Rifleman)	.05
415	Ken Caminiti (Rifleman)	.10
416	Benito Santiago (Rifleman)	.05
417	Nolan Ryan (Highlight)	.35
418	Bobby Thigpen (HL)	.05
419	Ramon Martinez (HL)	.05
420	Bo Jackson (HL)	.15
421	Carlton Fisk (HL)	.10
422	Jimmy Key	.05
423	Junior Noboa	.05
424	Al Newman	.05
425	Pat Borders	.05
426	Von Hayes	.05
427	Tim Teufel	.05
428	Eric Plunk	.05
429	John Moses	.05
430	Mike Witt	.05
431	Otis Nixon	.05
432	Tony Fernandez	.05
433	Rance Mulliniks	.05
434	Dan Petry	.05
435	Bob Geren	.05
436	Steve Frey	.05
437	Jamie Moyer	.05
438	Junior Ortiz	.05
439	Tom O'Malley	.05
440	Pat Combs	.05
441	Jose Canseco (Dream Team)	.30
442	Alfredo Griffin	.05
443	Andres Galarraga	.10
444	Bryn Smith	.05
445	Andre Dawson	.10
446	Juan Samuel	.05
447	Mike Aldrete	.05
448	Ron Gant	.10
449	Fernando Valenzuela	.05
450	Vince Coleman	.05
451	Kevin Mitchell	.05
452	Spike Owen	.05
453	Mike Bielecki	.05
454	Dennis Martinez	.05
455	Brett Butler	.05
456	Ron Darling	.05
457	Dennis Rasmussen	.05
458	Ken Howell	.05
459	Steve Bedrosian	.05
460	Frank Viola	.05
461	Jose Lind	.05
462	Chris Sabo	.05
463	Dante Bichette	.10
464	Rick Mahler	.05
465	John Smiley	.05
466	Devon White	.10
467	John Orton	.05
468	Mike Stanton	.05
469	Billy Hatcher	.05
470	Wally Joyner	.10
471	Gene Larkin	.05
472	Doug Drabek	.05
473	Gary Sheffield	.10
474	David Wells	.10
475	Andy Van Slyke	.05
476	Mike Gallego	.05
477	B.J. Surhoff	.05
478	Gene Nelson	.05
479	Mariano Duncan	.05
480	Fred McGriff	.20
481	Jerry Browne	.05
482	Alvin Davis	.05
483	Bill Wegman	.05
484	Dave Parker	.10
485	Dennis Eckersley	.10
486	Erik Hanson	.05
487	Bill Ripken	.05
488	Tom Candiotti	.05
489	Mike Schooler	.05
490	Gregg Olson	.05
491	Chris James	.05
492	Pete Harnisch	.05
493	Julio Franco	.05
494	Greg Briley	.05
495	Ruben Sierra	.05
496	Steve Olin	.05
497	Mike Fetters	.05
498	Mark Williamson	.05
499	Bob Tewksbury	.05
500	Tony Gwynn	.30
501	Randy Myers	.05
502	Keith Comstock	.05
503	Craig Worthington	.05
504	Mark Eichhorn	.05
505	Barry Larkin	.10
506	Dave Johnson	.05
507	Bobby Witt	.05
508	Joe Orsulak	.05
509	Pete O'Brien	.05
510	Brad Arnsberg	.05
511	Storm Davis	.05
512	Bob Milacki	.05
513	Bill Pecota	.05
514	Glenallen Hill	.05
515	Danny Tartabull	.05
516	Mike Moore	.05
517	Ron Robinson	.05
518	Mark Gardner	.05
519	Rick Wrona	.05
520	Mike Scioscia	.05
521	Frank Wills	.05
522	Greg Brock	.05
523	Jack Clark	.05
524	Bruce Ruffin	.05
525	Robin Yount	.25
526	Tom Foley	.05
527	Pat Perry	.05
528	Greg Vaughn	.10
529	Wally Whitehurst	.05
530	Norm Charlton	.05
531	Marvell Wynne	.05
532	Jim Gantner	.05
533	Greg Litton	.05
534	Manny Lee	.05
535	Scott Bailes	.05
536	Charlie Leibrandt	.05
537	Roger McDowell	.05
538	Andy Benes	.10
539	Rick Honeycutt	.05
540	Dwight Gooden	.10
541	Scott Garrelts	.05
542	Dave Clark	.05
543	Lonnie Smith	.05
544	Rick Reuschel	.05
545	Delino DeShields	.05
546	Mike Sharperson	.05
547	Mike Kingery	.05
548	Terry Kennedy	.05
549	David Cone	.15
550	Orel Hershiser	.10
551	Matt Nokes	.05
552	Eddie Williams	.05
553	Frank DiPino	.05
554	Fred Lynn	.05
555	Alex Cole	.05
556	Terry Leach	.05
557	Chet Lemon	.05
558	Paul Mirabella	.05
559	Bill Long	.05
560	Phil Bradley	.05
561	Duane Ward	.05
562	Dave Bergman	.05
563	Eric Show	.05
564	Xavier Hernandez	.05
565	Jeff Parrett	.05
566	Chuck Cary	.05
567	Ken Hill	.05
568	Bob Welch	.05
569	John Mitchell	.05
570	Travis Fryman	.10
571	Derek Lilliquist	.05
572	Steve Lake	.05
573	*John Barfield*	.05
574	Randy Bush	.05
575	Joe Magrane	.05
576	Edgar Diaz	.05
577	Casy Candaele	.05
578	Jesse Orosco	.05
579	Tom Henke	.05
580	Rick Cerone	.05
581	Drew Hall	.05
582	Tony Castillo	.05
583	Jimmy Jones	.05
584	Rick Reed	.05
585	Joe Girardi	.05
586	*Jeff Gray*	.05
587	Luis Polonia	.05
588	Joe Klink	.05
589	Rex Hudler	.05
590	Kirk McCaskill	.05
591	Juan Agosto	.05
592	Wes Gardner	.05
593	*Rich Rodriguez*	.05
594	Mitch Webster	.05
595	Kelly Gruber	.05
596	Dale Mohorcic	.05
597	Willie McGee	.05
598	Bill Krueger	.05
599	Bob Walk	.05
600	Kevin Maas	.05
601	Danny Jackson	.05
602	Craig McMurtry	.05
603	Curtis Wilkerson	.05
604	Adam Peterson	.05
605	Sam Horn	.05
606	Tommy Gregg	.05
607	Ken Dayley	.05
608	Carmelo Castillo	.05
609	John Shelby	.05
610	Don Slaught	.05
611	Calvin Schiraldi	.05
612	Dennis Lamp	.05
613	Andres Thomas	.05
614	Jose Gonzales	.05
615	Randy Ready	.05
616	Kevin Bass	.05
617	Mike Marshall	.05
618	Daryl Boston	.05
619	Andy McGaffigan	.05
620	Joe Oliver	.05
621	Jim Gott	.05
622	Jose Oquendo	.05
623	Jose DeJesus	.05
624	Mike Brumley	.05
625	John Olerud	.25
626	Ernest Riles	.05
627	Gene Harris	.05
628	Jose Uribe	.05
629	Darnell Coles	.05
630	Carney Lansford	.05
631	Tim Leary	.05
632	Tim Hulett	.05
633	Kevin Elster	.05
634	Tony Fossas	.05
635	Francisco Oliveras	.05
636	Bob Patterson	.05
637	Gary Ward	.05
638	Rene Gonzales	.05
639	Don Robinson	.05
640	Darryl Strawberry	.10
641	Dave Anderson	.05
642	Scott Scudder	.05
643	*Reggie Harris*	.10
644	Dave Henderson	.05
645	Ben McDonald	.05
646	Bob Kipper	.05
647	Hal Morris	.05
648	Tim Birtsas	.05
649	Steve Searcy	.05
650	Dale Murphy	.15
651	Ron Oester	.05
652	Mike LaCoss	.05
653	Ron Jones	.05
654	Kelly Downs	.05
655	Roger Clemens	.35
656	Herm Winningham	.05
657	Trevor Wilson	.05
658	Jose Rijo	.05
659	Dann Bilardello	.05
660	Gregg Jefferies	.15
661	Doug Drabek (All-Star)	.05
662	Randy Myers (AS)	.05
663	Benito Santiago (AS)	.05
664	Will Clark (AS)	.15
665	Ryne Sandberg (AS)	.15
666	Barry Larkin (AS)	.10
667	Matt Williams (AS)	.05
668	Barry Bonds (AS)	.20
669	Eric Davis	.10
670	Bobby Bonilla (AS)	.05
671	*Chipper Jones* (1st Draft Pick)	3.00
672	*Eric Christopherson* (1st Draft Pick)	.10
673	*Robbie Beckett* (1st Draft Pick)	.25
674	*Shane Andrews* (1st Draft Pick)	.45
675	*Steve Karsay* (1st Draft Pick)	.25
676	*Aaron Holbert* (1st Draft Pick)	.10
677	*Donovan Osborne* (1st Draft Pick)	.10
678	*Todd Ritchie* (1st Draft Pick)	.15
679	*Ron Walden* (1st Draft Pick)	.10
680	*Tim Costo* (1st Draft Pick)	.20
681	*Dan Wilson* (1st Draft Pick)	.15
682	*Kurt Miller* (1st Draft Pick)	.15
683	*Mike Lieberthal* (1st Draft Pick)	.25
684	Roger Clemens (K-Man)	.15
685	Dwight Gooden (K-Man)	.10
686	Nolan Ryan (K-Man)	.30
687	Frank Viola (K-Man)	.05
688	Erik Hanson (K-Man)	.05
689	Matt Williams (Master Blaster)	.05
690	Jose Canseco (Master Blaster)	.10
691	Darryl Strawberry (Master Blaster)	.10
692	Bo Jackson (Master Blaster)	.10
693	Cecil Fielder (Master Blaster)	.05
694	Sandy Alomar, Jr. (Rifleman)	.10
695	Cory Snyder (Rifleman)	.05
696	Eric Davis (Rifleman)	.05
697	Ken Griffey, Jr. (Rifleman)	.50
698	Andy Van Slyke (Rifleman)	.05
699	Mark Langston, Mike Witt (No-hitter)	.05
700	Randy Johnson (No-hitter)	.15
701	Nolan Ryan (No-hitter)	.30
702	Dave Stewart (No-hitter)	.05
703	Fernando Valenzuela (No-hitter)	.05
704	Andy Hawkins (No-hitter)	.05
705	Melido Perez (No-hitter)	.05
706	Terry Mulholland (No-hitter)	.05
707	Dave Stieb (No-hitter)	.05
708	*Brian Barnes*	.05
709	*Bernard Gilkey*	.20
710	*Steve Decker*	.10
711	*Paul Faries*	.10
712	*Paul Marak*	.10
713	*Wes Chamberlain*	.10
714	*Kevin Belcher*	.10
715	Dan Boone	.05
716	*Steve Adkins*	.10
717	*Geronimo Pena*	.10
718	*Howard Farmer*	.10
719	*Mark Leonard*	.05
720	Tom Lampkin	.05
721	*Mike Gardiner*	.10
722	*Jeff Conine*	.40
723	*Efrain Valdez*	.05
724	Chuck Malone	.05
725	*Leo Gomez*	.10
726	*Paul McClellan*	.05
727	*Mark Leiter*	.05
728	*Rich DeLucia*	.15
729	Mel Rojas	.05
730	*Hector Wagner*	.05
731	*Ray Lankford*	.25
732	*Turner Ward*	.10
733	*Gerald Alexander*	.05
734	*Scott Anderson*	.05
735	Tony Perezchica	.05
736	Jimmy Kremers	.05
737	American Flag	.25
738	*Mike York*	.05
739	Mike Hochford	.05
740	Scott Aldred	.05
741	*Rico Brogna*	.15
742	*Dave Burba*	.10
743	*Ray Stephens*	.05
744	*Eric Gunderson*	.10
745	*Troy Afenir*	.05
746	Jeff Shaw	.10
747	*Orlando Merced*	.15
748	*Omar Oliveras*	.05
749	Jerry Kutzler	.05
750	Mo Vaughn	.30
751	*Matt Stark*	.05
752	*Randy Hennis*	.05
753	*Andujar Cedeno*	.10
754	Kelvin Torve	.05
755	Joe Kraemer	.05
756	*Phil Clark*	.05
757	*Ed Vosberg*	.05
758	*Mike Perez*	.10
759	*Scott Lewis*	.10
760	*Steve Chitren*	.10
761	*Ray Young*	.05
762	*Andres Santana*	.05
763	*Rodney McCray*	.05
764	*Sean Berry*	.10
765	Brent Mayne	.05
766	*Mike Simms*	.05
767	*Glenn Sutko*	.05
768	Gary Disarcina	.05
769	George Brett (HL)	.20
770	Cecil Fielder (HL)	.05
771	Jim Presley	.05
772	John Dopson	.05
773	Bo Jackson (Breaker)	.10
774	Brent Knackert	.05
775	Bill Doran	.05
776	Dick Schofield	.05
777	Nelson Santovenia	.05
778	Mark Guthrie	.05
779	Mark Lemke	.05
780	Terry Steinbach	.05
781	Tom Bolton	.05
782	*Randy Tomlin*	.10
783	Jeff Kunkel	.05
784	Felix Jose	.05
785	Rick Sutcliffe	.05
786	John Cerutti	.05
787	Jose Vizcaino	.05
788	Curt Schilling	.10
789	Ed Whitson	.05
790	Tony Pena	.05
791	John Candelaria	.05
792	Carmelo Martinez	.05
793	Sandy Alomar, Jr.	.15
794	*Jim Neidlinger*	.05
795	Red's October (Barry Larkin, Chris Sabo)	.10
796	Paul Sorrento	.05
797	Tom Pagnozzi	.05
798	Tino Martinez	.10
799	Scott Ruskin	.05
800	Kirk Gibson	.05
801	Walt Terrell	.05
802	John Russell	.05
803	Chili Davis	.05
804	Chris Nabholz	.05
805	Juan Gonzalez	.60
806	Ron Hassey	.05
807	Todd Worrell	.05
808	Tommy Greene	.05
809	Joel Skinner	.05
810	Benito Santiago	.05
811	Pat Tabler	.05

812	*Scott Erickson*	.10
813	Moises Alou	.20
814	Dale Sveum	.05
815	Ryne Sandberg (Man of the Year)	.20
816	Rick Dempsey	.05
817	Scott Bankhead	.05
818	Jason Grimsley	.05
819	Doug Jennings	.05
820	Tom Herr	.05
821	Rob Ducey	.05
822	Luis Quinones	.05
823	Greg Minton	.05
824	Mark Grant	.05
825	Ozzie Smith	.20
826	Dave Eiland	.05
827	Danny Heep	.05
828	Hensley Meulens	.05
829	Charlie O'Brien	.05
830	Glenn Davis	.05
831	John Marzano	.05
832	Steve Ontiveros	.05
833	Ron Karkovice	.05
834	Jerry Goff	.05
835	Ken Griffey, Sr.	.10
836	Kevin Reimer	.05
837	Randy Kutcher	.05
838	Mike Blowers	.05
839	Mike Macfarlane	.05
840	Frank Thomas	.75
841	Ken Griffey Sr., Ken Griffey Jr.	.50
842	Jack Howell	.05
843	Mauro Gozzo	.05
844	Gerald Young	.05
845	Zane Smith	.05
846	Kevin Brown	.05
847	Sil Campusano	.05
848	Larry Andersen	.05
849	Cal Ripken, Jr. (Franchise)	.15
850	Roger Clemens (Franchise)	.15
851	Sandy Alomar, Jr. (Franchise)	.05
852	Alan Trammell (Franchise)	.05
853	George Brett (Franchise)	.15
854	Robin Yount (Franchise)	.10
855	Kirby Puckett (Franchise)	.10
856	Don Mattingly (Franchise)	.10
857	Rickey Henderson (Franchise)	.10
858	Ken Griffey, Jr. (Franchise)	.50
859	Ruben Sierra (Franchise)	.05
860	John Olerud (Franchise)	.20
861	Dave Justice (Franchise)	.15
862	Ryne Sandberg (Franchise)	.15
863	Eric Davis (Franchise)	.05
864	Darryl Strawberry (Franchise)	.05
865	Tim Wallach (Franchise)	.05
866	Dwight Gooden (Franchise)	.05
867	Len Dykstra (Franchise)	.05
868	Barry Bonds (Franchise)	.25
869	Todd Zeile (Franchise)	.05
870	Benito Santiago (Franchise)	.05
871	Will Clark (Franchise)	.10
872	Craig Biggio (Franchise)	.05
873	Wally Joyner (Franchise)	.05
874	Frank Thomas (Franchise)	.45
875	Rickey Henderson (MVP)	.10
876	Barry Bonds (MVP)	.25
877	Bob Welch (Cy Young)	.05
878	Doug Drabek (Cy Young)	.05
879	Sandy Alomar, Jr. (ROY)	.10
880	Dave Justice (ROY)	.25
881	Damon Berryhill	.05
882	Frank Viola (Dream Team)	.05
883	Dave Stewart (Dream Team)	.10
884	Doug Jones (Dream Team)	.05
885	Randy Myers (Dream Team)	.05
886	Will Clark (Dream Team)	.20
887	Roberto Alomar (Dream Team)	.25
888	Barry Larkin (Dream Team)	.10
889	Wade Boggs (Dream Team)	.20
890	Rickey Henderson (Dream Team)	.15
891	Kirby Puckett (Dream Team)	.40
892	Ken Griffey, Jr. (Dream Team)	.75
893	Benito Santiago (Dream Team)	.10

1991 Score Cooperstown

This seven-card set was included as an insert in every factory set. The card fronts are white, with an oval-vignetted player portrait. The backs have green borders surrounding a yellow background which contains a summary of the player's career.

		MT
Complete Set (7):		7.50
Common Player:		.50
B1	Wade Boggs	1.00
B2	Barry Larkin	.50
B3	Ken Griffey, Jr.	5.00
B4	Rickey Henderson	.50
B5	George Brett	2.00
B6	Will Clark	.50
B7	Nolan Ryan	4.00

1991 Score Hot Rookies

These standard-size cards were inserted one per every 100-card 1991 Score blister pack. Action photos with white borders are featured on the front, and "Hot Rookie" is written in yellow at the top. The background is shaded from yellow to orange. The backs are numbered and each has a color mug shot and a career summary.

		MT
Complete Set (10):		18.00
Common Player:		.50
1	Dave Justice	2.00
2	Kevin Maas	.50
3	Hal Morris	.75
4	Frank Thomas	4.00
5	Jeff Conine	1.00
6	Sandy Alomar Jr.	1.00
7	Ray Lankford	.75
8	Steve Decker	.50
9	Juan Gonzalez	4.00
10	Jose Offerman	.50

1991 Score Blue Jays

Sold as a special boxed issue including 40 player cards and five trivia cards, this set features the 1991 Blue Jays and their hosting of the 1991 All-Star Game. Cards carry a super-glossy front finish that features a player action photo in a home plate-shaped frame at center. Around the photo are blue and white border designs with the player's name and position at top, and Score and Blue Jays logos at bottom. Backs repeat the blue and white motif with a color player portrait, biographical notes, stats and career summary.

		MT
Complete Set (40):		15.00
Common Player:		.25
1	Joe Carter	.50
2	Tom Henke	.25
3	Jimmy Key	.25
4	Al Leiter	.40
5	Dave Steib	.35
6	Todd Stottlemyre	.35
7	Mike Timlin	.25
8	Duane Ward	.25
9	David Wells	.75
10	Frank Wills	.25
11	Pat Borders	.25
12	Greg Myers	.25
13	Roberto Alomar	3.00
14	Rene Gonzalez	.25
15	Kelly Gruber	.25
16	Manny Lee	.25
17	Rance Mulliniks	.25
18	John Olerud	1.00
19	Pat Tabler	.25
20	Derek Bell	.45
21	Jim Acker	.25
22	Rob Ducey	.25
23	Devon White	.45
24	Mookie Wilson	.35
25	Juan Guzman	.25
26	Ed Sprague	.25
27	Ken Dayley	.25
28	Tom Candiotti	.25
29	Candy Maldonado	.25
30	Eddie Zosky	.25
31	Steve Karsay	.25
32	Bob MacDonald	.25
33	Ray Giannelli	.25
34	Jerry Schunk	.25
35	Dave Weathers	.25
36	Cito Gaston	.25
37	Joe Carter (All-Star)	.45
38	Jimmy Key (All-Star)	.25
39	Roberto Alomar (All-Star)	1.50
40	1991 All-Star Game	.25

1991 Score FanFest/ National

Two versions of this 10-card set were produced for distribution at the All-Star FanFest and the National Sports Collectors Convention. The appropriate venue is listed in a red stripe on back under the player career summary. Fronts have a color action photo against a background of pale green with blue ballplayer silhouettes and yellow baseballs. Backs repeat the player figure and baseball motif on a white background. A trapezoid at center has a player portrait photo, color team logo, biographical details and career highlights. At present neither version of these cards carries a premium over the other.

		MT
Complete Set (10):		6.00
Common Player:		.50
1	Ray Lankford	1.00
2	Steve Decker	.50
3	Gary Scott	.50
4	Hensley Meulens	.50
5	Tim Naehring	.50
6	Mark Whiten	.50
7	Ed Sprague	.50
8	Charles Nagy	.75
9	Terry Shumpert	.50
10	Chuck Knoblauch	2.00

1991 Score "Life and Times of Nolan Ryan"

This four-card career highlights set was distributed with a series of four collector magazines. Cards feature color photos with Score and Texas Rangers logos in separate corners. A red stripe above the photo, or to its left, names the highlight; a blue stripe above or to the left of that has his name and position. Horizontally formatted backs have another color photo and a paragraph about the milestone.

		MT
Complete Set:		20.00
Common Player:		6.00
1	5,000th Career Strikeout (Nolan Ryan)	6.00
2	6th Career No-Hitter (Nolan Ryan)	6.00
3	300th Career Victory (Nolan Ryan)	6.00
4	7th Career No-Hitter (Nolan Ryan)	6.00

1991 Score Mickey Mantle

This special set recalls Mickey Mantle's career as a Yankee. Card fronts are glossy and have red and white borders. The card's caption appears at the bottom in a blue stripe. The backs have a photo and a summary of the caption, plus the card number and serial number. Dealers and media members received the sets, which were limited to 5,000, in a wax-pack wrapper. A total of 2,500 of the cards were numbered and autographed.

		MT
Complete Set (7):		250.00
Common Card:		50.00
Autographed Card:		500.00
1	The Rookie	50.00
2	Triple Crown	50.00
3	World Series	50.00
4	Going, Going, Gone	50.00
5	Speed and Grace	50.00
6	A True Yankee	50.00
7	Twilight	50.00

1991 Score Rising Stars

Marketed along with 1990-91 "Baseball's Hottest Rookies" magazine, this 100-card set features top rookies and young players. The cards are similar in design to the Score Superstar set. The magazine/card sets were available to a select group of retailers.

		MT
Complete Set (100):		7.50
Common Player:		.10
1	Sandy Alomar,Jr.	.15
2	Tom Edens	.10
3	Terry Shumpert	.10
4	Shawn Boskie	.10
5	Steve Avery	.10
6	Deion Sanders	.35
7	John Burkett	.20
8	Stan Belinda	.10
9	Thomas Howard	.10
10	Wayne Edwards	.10
11	Rick Parker	.10
12	Randy Veres	.10
13	Alex Cole	.10
14	Scott Chaimparino	.10
15	Greg Olson	.10
16	Jose DeJesus	.10
17	Mike Blowers	.10
18	Jeff Huson	.10
19	Willie Blair	.10
20	Howard Farmer	.10
21	Larry Walker	.45
22	Scott Hemond	.10
23	Mel Stottlemyre	.10
24	Mark Whiten	.10
25	Jeff Schulz	.10
26	Gary Disarcina	.10
27	George Canale	.10
28	Dean Palmer	.20
29	Jim Leyritz	.20
30	Carlos Baerga	.15
31	Rafael Valdez	.10
32	Derek Bell	.20
33	Francisco Cabrera	.10
34	Chris Hoiles	.10
35	Craig Grebeck	.10
36	Scott Coolbaugh	.10
37	Kevin Wickander	.10
38	Marquis Grissom	.25
39	Chip Hale	.10
40	Kevin Maas	.10
41	Juan Gonzalez	1.50
42	Eric Anthony	.10
43	Luis Sojo	.10
44	Paul Sorrento	.10
45	Dave Justice	.90
46	Oscar Azocar	.10
47	Charles Nagy	.15
48	Robin Ventura	.35
49	Reggie Harris	.10
50	Ben McDonald	.10
51	Hector Villanueva	.10
52	Kevin Tapani	.10

53	Brian Bohanon	.10
54	Tim Layana	.10
55	Delino DeShields	.10
56	Beau Allred	.10
57	Eric Gunderson	.10
58	Kent Mercker	.10
59	Juan Bell	.10
60	Glenallen Hill	.10
61	David Segui	.10
62	Alan Mills	.10
63	Mike Harkey	.10
64	Bill Sampen	.10
65	Greg Vaughn	.20
66	Alex Fernandez	.35
67	Mike Hartley	.10
68	Travis Fryman	.15
69	Dave Rohde	.10
70	Tom Lampkin	.10
71	Mark Gardner	.10
72	Pat Combs	.10
73	Kevin Appier	.10
74	Mike Fetters	.10
75	Greg Myers	.10
76	Steve Searcy	.10
77	Tim Naehring	.10
78	Frank Thomas	1.50
79	Todd Hundley	.15
80	Ed Vosburg	.10
81	Todd Zeile	.20
82	Lee Stevens	.10
83	Scott Radinsky	.10
84	Hensley Meulens	.10
85	Brian DuBois	.10
86	Steve Olin	.10
87	Julio Machado	.10
88	Jose Vizcaino	.10
89	Mark Lemke	.10
90	Felix Jose	.10
91	Wally Whitehurst	.10
92	Dana Kiecker	.10
93	Mike Munoz	.10
94	Adam Peterson	.10
95	Tim Drummond	.10
96	Dave Hollins	.15
97	Craig Wilson	.10
98	Hal Morris	.15
99	Jose Offerman	.10
100	John Olerud	.40

1991 Score Rookies

This 40-card boxed set did not receive much attention in the hobby world, but features some of the top young players of 1991. The card fronts feature full-color action photos with a "Rookies" banner along the side border. The backs feature statistics and a player profile. This set was available through hobby dealers and is Score's first release of its kind.

		MT
Complete Set (40):		5.00
Common Player:		.10
1	Mel Rojas	.10
2	Ray Lankford	.25
3	Scott Aldred	.10
4	Turner Ward	.10
5	Omar Olivares	.10
6	Mo Vaughn	1.00
7	Phil Clark	.10
8	Brent Mayne	.10
9	Scott Lewis	.10
10	Brian Barnes	.10
11	Bernard Gilkey	.25
12	Steve Decker	.10
13	Paul Marak	.10
14	Wes Chamberlain	.10
15	Kevin Belcher	.10
16	Steve Adkins	.10
17	Geronimo Pena	.10
18	Mark Leonard	.10
19	Jeff Conine	.25
20	Leo Gomez	.10
21	Chuck Malone	.10
22	Beau Allred	.10
23	Todd Hundley	.25
24	Lance Dickson	.15
25	Mike Benjamin	.10
26	Jose Offerman	.15
27	Terry Shumpert	.10
28	Darren Lewis	.25
29	Scott Chiamparino	.10
30	Tim Naehring	.10
31	David Segui	.10
32	Karl Rhodes	.10
33	Mickey Morandini	.15
34	Chuck McElroy	.10
35	Tim McIntosh	.10
36	Derrick May	.10
37	Rich DeLucia	.10
38	Tino Martinez	.35
39	Hensley Meulens	.10
40	Andujar Cedeno	.10

1991 Score Superstars

This 100-card set features full-color action photos on the card fronts and posed shots on the flip sides. The set was marketed along with the magazine "1991 Baseball's Hottest Players". The cards feature red, white, and blue borders. The backs contain brief career highlights. The magazine/card set combo was available to select retailers.

		MT
Complete Set (100):		5.00
Common Player:		.10
1	Jose Canseco	.25
2	Bo Jackson	.25
3	Wade Boggs	.25
4	Will Clark	.30
5	Ken Griffey, Jr.	2.00
6	Doug Drabek	.10
7	Kirby Puckett	.50
8	Joe Orsulak	.10
9	Eric Davis	.15
10	Rickey Henderson	.30
11	Lenny Dykstra	.10
12	Ruben Sierra	.10
13	Paul Molitor	.45
14	Ron Gant	.15
15	Ozzie Guillen	.10
16	Ramon Martinez	.15
17	Edgar Martinez	.10
18	Ozzie Smith	.45
19	Charlie Hayes	.10
20	Barry Larkin	.15
21	Cal Ripken, Jr.	1.00
22	Andy Van Slyke	.10
23	Don Mattingly	.50
24	Dave Stewart	.10
25	Nolan Ryan	1.00
26	Barry Bonds	.50
27	Gregg Olson	.10
28	Chris Sabo	.10
29	John Franco	.10
30	Gary Sheffield	.25
31	Jeff Treadway	.10
32	Tom Browning	.10
33	Jose Lind	.10
34	Dave Magadan	.10
35	Dale Murphy	.15
36	Tom Candiotti	.10
37	Willie McGee	.10
38	Robin Yount	.45
39	Mark McGwire	2.00
40	George Bell	.10
41	Carlton Fisk	.15
42	Bobby Bonilla	.10
43	Randy Milligan	.10
44	Dave Parker	.15
45	Shawon Dunston	.10
46	Brian Harper	.10
47	John Tudor	.10
48	Ellis Burks	.10
49	Bob Welch	.10
50	Roger Clemens	.45
51	Mike Henneman	.10
52	Eddie Murray	.40
53	Kal Daniels	.10
54	Doug Jones	.10
55	Craig Biggio	.20
56	Rafael Palmeiro	.15
57	Wally Joyner	.15
58	Tim Wallach	.10
59	Bret Saberhagen	.10
60	Ryne Sandberg	.40
61	Benito Santiago	.10
62	Darryl Strawberry	.15
63	Alan Trammell	.10
64	Kelly Gruber	.10
65	Dwight Gooden	.15
66	Dave Winfield	.25
67	Rick Aguilera	.10
68	Dave Righetti	.10
69	Jim Abbott	.10
70	Frank Viola	.10
71	Fred McGriff	.15
72	Steve Sax	.10
73	Dennis Eckersley	.10
74	Cory Snyder	.10
75	Mackey Sasser	.10
76	Candy Maldonado	.10
77	Matt Williams	.20
78	Kent Hrbek	.10
79	Randy Myers	.10
80	Gregg Jefferies	.15
81	Joe Carter	.10
82	Mike Greenwell	.10
83	Jack Armstrong	.10
84	Julio Franco	.10
85	George Brett	.65
86	Howard Johnson	.10
87	Andre Dawson	.15
88	Cecil Fielder	.10
89	Tim Raines	.15
90	Chuck Finley	.10
91	Mark Grace	.20
92	Brook Jacoby	.10
93	Dave Steib	.10
94	Tony Gwynn	.45
95	Bobby Thigpen	.10
96	Roberto Kelly	.10
97	Kevin Seitzer	.10
98	Kevin Mitchell	.10
99	Dwight Evans	.10
100	Roberto Alomar	.30

1991 Score Traded

This 110-card set features players with new teams as well as 1991 Major League rookies. The cards are designed in the same style as the regular 1991 Score issue. The cards once again feature a "T" designation along with the card number. The complete set was sold at hobby shops in a special box.

		MT
Complete Set (110):		5.00
Common Player:		.05
1	Bo Jackson	.15
2	Mike Flanagan	.05
3	Pete Incaviglia	.05
4	Jack Clark	.05
5	Hubie Brooks	.05
6	Ivan Calderon	.05
7	Glenn Davis	.05
8	Wally Backman	.05
9	Dave Smith	.05
10	Tim Raines	.15
11	Joe Carter	.10
12	Sid Bream	.05
13	George Bell	.05
14	Steve Bedrosian	.05
15	Willie Wilson	.05
16	Darryl Strawberry	.10
17	Danny Jackson	.05
18	Kirk Gibson	.05
19	Willie McGee	.05
20	Junior Felix	.05
21	Steve Farr	.05
22	Pat Tabler	.05
23	Brett Butler	.05
24	Danny Darwin	.05
25	Mickey Tettleton	.05
26	Gary Carter	.10
27	Mitch Williams	.05
28	Candy Maldonado	.05
29	Otis Nixon	.05
30	Brian Downing	.05
31	Tom Candiotti	.05
32	John Candelaria	.05
33	Rob Murphy	.05
34	Deion Sanders	.25
35	Willie Randolph	.05
36	Pete Harnisch	.05
37	Dante Bichette	.10
38	Garry Templeton	.05
39	Gary Gaetti	.05
40	John Cerutti	.05
41	Rick Cerone	.05
42	Mike Pagliarulo	.05
43	Ron Hassey	.05
44	Roberto Alomar	.30
45	Mike Boddicker	.05
46	Bud Black	.05
47	Rob Deer	.05
48	Devon White	.10
49	Luis Sojo	.05
50	Terry Pendleton	.05
51	Kevin Gross	.05
52	Mike Huff	.05
53	Dave Righetti	.05
54	Matt Young	.05
55	Ernest Riles	.05
56	Bill Gullickson	.05
57	Vince Coleman	.05
58	Fred McGriff	.15
59	Franklin Stubbs	.05
60	Eric King	.05
61	Cory Snyder	.05
62	Dwight Evans	.05
63	Gerald Perry	.05
64	Eric Show	.05
65	Shawn Hillegas	.05
66	Tony Fernandez	.05
67	Tim Teufel	.05
68	Mitch Webster	.05
69	Mike Heath	.05
70	Chili Davis	.05
71	Larry Andersen	.05
72	Gary Varsho	.05
73	Juan Berenguer	.05
74	Jack Morris	.05
75	Barry Jones	.05
76	Rafael Belliard	.05
77	Steve Buechele	.05
78	Scott Sanderson	.05
79	Bob Ojeda	.05
80	Curt Schilling	.10
81	Brian Drahman	.05
82	*Ivan Rodriguez*	3.00
83	David Howard	.05
84	Heath Slocumb	.05
85	Mike Timlin	.05
86	Darryl Kile	.10
87	Pete Schourek	.10
88	Bruce Walton	.05
89	Al Osuna	.05
90	Gary Scott	.05
91	Doug Simons	.05
92	Chris Jones	.05
93	Chuck Knoblauch	.50
94	Dana Allison	.05
95	Erik Pappas	.05
96	*Jeff Bagwell*	3.00
97	Kirk Dressendorfer	.05
98	Freddie Benavides	.05
99	*Luis Gonzalez*	.50
100	Wade Taylor	.05
101	Ed Sprague	.05
102	Bob Scanlan	.05
103	Rick Wilkins	.05
104	Chris Donnels	.05
105	Joe Slusarski	.05
106	Mark Lewis	.10
107	Pat Kelly	.05
108	John Briscoe	.05
109	Luis Lopez	.05
110	Jeff Johnson	.05

1992 Score/Pinnacle Promo Panels

Score debuted both its base-brand (Score) and premium-brand (Pinnacle) sets at one time in 1992 with this issue of four-card panels. Each panel measures 1/16" short each way of 5" x 7" and features Score cards in the upper-left and lower-right, with Pinnacle samples at upper-right and lower-left. Backs have a very light gray overprint, "FOR PROMOTIONAL PURPOSES ONLY NOT FOR RESALE". Cards cut from the panels would be otherwise indistinguishable from the issued versions. Panels are checklisted here alphabetically according to the lowest-numbered Score player. S prefix to the card number indicates Score, P is for Pinnacle. The prefixes do not appear on the cards.

		MT
Complete Set (25):		150.00
Common Panel:		3.00
(1)	S2 Nolan Ryan, S13 Lonnie Smith, P7 Willie McGee, P18 Terry Pendleton	35.00
(2)	S3 Will Clark, S12 Mark Langston, P8 Paul Molitor, P17 Devon White	7.50
(3)	S4 Dave Justice, S19 Mark Carreon, P1 Frank Thomas, P16 Dave Henderson	6.00
(4)	S5 Dave Henderson, S15 Roberto Alomar, P10 Ryne Sandberg, P20 Kirby Puckett	15.00
(5)	S9 Darryl Strawberry, S14 Jeff Montgomery, P6 Ozzie Smith, P11 Kevin Seitzer	7.50
(6)	S22 Chuck Crim, S33 Jimmy Jones, P27 Jay Buhner, P38 Robin Yount	7.50
(7)	S23 Don Mattingly, S32 Dave Winfield, P28 Matt Williams, P37 George Bell	10.00
(8)	S24 Dickie Thon, S39 Gary Gaetti, P21 Orel Hershiser, P36 Wes Chamberlain	3.00
(9)	S25 Ron Gant, S35 Andres Galarraga, P30 Alex Fernandez, P40 Bruce Hurst	3.00
(10)	S29 Melido Perez, S34 Kevin Gross, P26 Ellis Burks, P31 Albert Belle	4.50
(11)	S42 Rick Aguilera, S53 Doug Jones, P47 Bill Doran, P58 Ivan Calderon	3.00
(12)	S43 Mike Gallego, S52 Todd Zeile, P48 Jerald Clark, P57 Lenny Harris	3.00
(13)	S44 Eric Davis, S59 Randy Ready, P41 Harold Baines, P56 Walt Weiss	3.00
(14)	S45 George Bell, S55 Rafael Palmeiro, P50 Nolan Ryan, P60 George Brett	45.00
(15)	S49 David Wells, S54 Bob Walk, P46 Chili Davis, P51 Phil Plantier	4.50
(16)	S62 Jack McDowell, S73 Juan Samuel, P67 Dave Hollins, P78 John Olerud	4.50
(17)	S63 Jim Acker, S72 Carlton Fisk, P68 Kent Hrbek, P77 Dennis Martinez	4.50
(18)	S64 Jay Buhner, S79 Kirk McCaskill, P61 Gregg Olson, P76 Terry Steinbach	3.00
(19)	S65 Travis Fryman, S75 Andre Dawson, P70 Jeff Bagwell, P80 Darryl Strawberry	4.50
(20)	S69 Ken Caminiti, S74 Todd Stottlemyre, P66 Alex Cole, P71 Jim Gantner	3.00
(21)	S82 Alex Fernandez, S93 Shawn Hillegas, P87 Bill Gullickson, P90 Jose Guzman	3.00
(22)	S83 Ivan Calderon, S92 Ozzie Guillen, P88 Bernard Gilkey, P97 Omar Vizquel	3.00
(23)	S84 Brent Mayne, S99 Tom Bolton, P81 Gary Gaetti, P96 Doug Drabek	3.00
(24)	S85 Jody Reed, S95 Vince Coleman, P90 Kevin Maas, P100 Dave Justice	3.00

(25) S89 Hensley Meulens, S94 Chili Davis, P86 David Howard, P91 Mark Lewis 3.00

1992 Score Promos

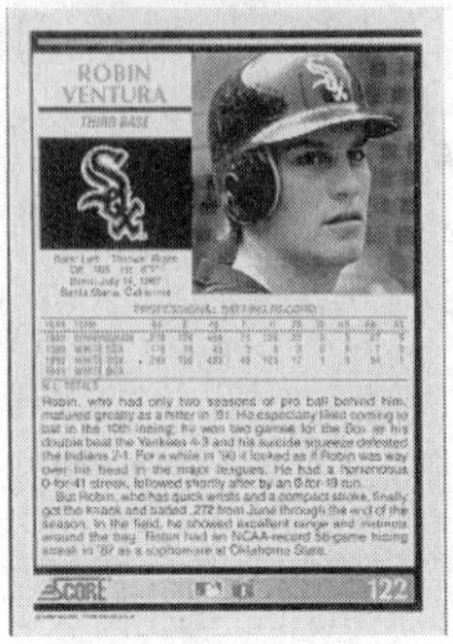

The six known Score promo cards differ from the issued versions in 1992 only in the lack of 1991 and career stats on the back and changes in the career summaries on some of the cards. The promos of Sandberg and Mack were distributed at a St. Louis baseball card show in November, 1991, and are somewhat scarcer than the others.

		MT
Complete Set (6):		66.00
Common Player:		6.00
1	Ken Griffey Jr.	24.00
4	Dave Justice	12.00
122	Robin Ventura	8.00
200	Ryne Sandberg	18.00
241	Steve Avery	6.00
284	Shane Mack	6.00

1992 Score

Score used a two series format for the second consecutive year in 1992. Cards 1-442 are featured in the first series. Fronts feature full-color game action photos. Backs feature color head shots of the players, team logo and career stats on a vertical layout. Several subsets are included in 1992, including a five-card Joe DiMaggio set. DiMaggio autographed cards were also inserted into random packs. Cards 736-772 can be found with or without a "Rookie Prospects" banner on the card front.

		MT
Complete Set (893):		15.00
Common Player:		.05
C. Knoblauch Auto/3,000		50.00
Series 1 or 2 Wax Box:		10.00
1	Ken Griffey, Jr.	1.50
2	Nolan Ryan	.90
3	Will Clark	.25
4	Dave Justice	.20
5	Dave Henderson	.05
6	Bret Saberhagen	.10
7	Fred McGriff	.15
8	Erik Hanson	.05
9	Darryl Strawberry	.10
10	Dwight Gooden	.10

11	Juan Gonzalez	.60
12	Mark Langston	.05
13	Lonnie Smith	.05
14	Jeff Montgomery	.05
15	Roberto Alomar	.25
16	Delino DeShields	.05
17	Steve Bedrosian	.05
18	Terry Pendleton	.05
19	Mark Carreon	.05
20	Mark McGwire	1.50
21	Roger Clemens	.25
22	Chuck Crim	.05
23	Don Mattingly	.50
24	Dickie Thon	.05
25	Ron Gant	.10
26	Milt Cuyler	.05
27	Mike Macfarlane	.05
28	Dan Gladden	.05
29	Melido Perez	.05
30	Willie Randolph	.05
31	Albert Belle	.30
32	Dave Winfield	.15
33	Jimmy Jones	.05
34	Kevin Gross	.05
35	Andres Galarraga	.10
36	Mike Devereaux	.05
37	Chris Bosio	.05
38	Mike LaValliere	.05
39	Gary Gaetti	.05
40	Felix Jose	.05
41	Alvaro Espinoza	.05
42	Rick Aguilera	.05
43	Mike Gallego	.05
44	Eric Davis	.10
45	George Bell	.05
46	Tom Brunansky	.05
47	Steve Farr	.05
48	Duane Ward	.05
49	David Wells	.10
50	Cecil Fielder	.10
51	Walt Weiss	.05
52	Todd Zeile	.10
53	Doug Jones	.05
54	Bob Walk	.05
55	Rafael Palmeiro	.10
56	Rob Deer	.05
57	Paul O'Neill	.15
58	Jeff Reardon	.05
59	Randy Ready	.05
60	Scott Erickson	.05
61	Paul Molitor	.25
62	Jack McDowell	.05
63	Jim Acker	.05
64	Jay Buhner	.10
65	Travis Fryman	.10
66	Marquis Grissom	.10
67	Mike Harkey	.05
68	Luis Polonia	.05
69	Ken Caminiti	.20
70	Chris Sabo	.05
71	Gregg Olson	.05
72	Carlton Fisk	.10
73	Juan Samuel	.05
74	Todd Stottlemyre	.05
75	Andre Dawson	.10
76	Alvin Davis	.05
77	Bill Doran	.05
78	B.J. Surhoff	.05
79	Kirk McCaskill	.05
80	Dale Murphy	.15
81	Jose DeLeon	.05
82	Alex Fernandez	.20
83	Ivan Calderon	.05
84	Brent Mayne	.05
85	Jody Reed	.05
86	Randy Tomlin	.05
87	Randy Milligan	.05
88	Pascual Perez	.05
89	Hensley Meulens	.05
90	Joe Carter	.10
91	Mike Moore	.05
92	Ozzie Guillen	.05
93	Shawn Hillegas	.05
94	Chili Davis	.05
95	Vince Coleman	.05
96	Jimmy Key	.05
97	Billy Ripken	.05
98	Dave Smith	.05
99	Tom Bolton	.05
100	Barry Larkin	.10
101	Kenny Rogers	.05
102	Mike Boddicker	.05
103	Kevin Elster	.05
104	Ken Hill	.05
105	Charlie Leibrandt	.05
106	Pat Combs	.05
107	Hubie Brooks	.05
108	Julio Franco	.05
109	Vicente Palacios	.05
110	Kal Daniels	.05
111	Bruce Hurst	.05
112	Willie McGee	.05
113	Ted Power	.05
114	Milt Thompson	.05
115	Doug Drabek	.05
116	Rafael Belliard	.05
117	Scott Garrelts	.05
118	Terry Mulholland	.05
119	Jay Howell	.05
120	Danny Jackson	.05
121	Scott Ruskin	.05
122	Robin Ventura	.15
123	Bip Roberts	.05
124	Jeff Russell	.05
125	Hal Morris	.05
126	Teddy Higuera	.05
127	Luis Sojo	.05
128	Carlos Baerga	.10
129	Jeff Ballard	.05
130	Tom Gordon	.05
131	Sid Bream	.05
132	Rance Mulliniks	.05
133	Andy Benes	.10
134	Mickey Tettleton	.05
135	Rich DeLucia	.05
136	Tom Pagnozzi	.05
137	Harold Baines	.05
138	Danny Darwin	.05
139	Kevin Bass	.05
140	Chris Nabholz	.05
141	Pete O'Brien	.05
142	Jeff Treadway	.05
143	Mickey Morandini	.05
144	Eric King	.05
145	Danny Tartabull	.05
146	Lance Johnson	.05
147	Casey Candaele	.05
148	Felix Fermin	.05
149	Rich Rodriguez	.05
150	Dwight Evans	.05
151	Joe Klink	.05
152	Kevin Reimer	.05
153	Orlando Merced	.05
154	Mel Hall	.05
155	Randy Myers	.05
156	Greg Harris	.05
157	Jeff Brantley	.05
158	Jim Eisenreich	.05
159	Luis Rivera	.05
160	Cris Carpenter	.05
161	Bruce Ruffin	.05
162	Omar Vizquel	.10
163	Gerald Alexander	.05
164	Mark Guthrie	.05
165	Scott Lewis	.05
166	Bill Sampen	.05
167	Dave Anderson	.05
168	Kevin McReynolds	.05
169	Jose Vizcaino	.05
170	Bob Geren	.05
171	Mike Morgan	.05
172	Jim Gott	.05
173	Mike Pagliarulo	.05
174	Mike Jeffcoat	.05
175	Craig Lefferts	.05
176	Steve Finley	.05
177	Wally Backman	.05
178	Kent Mercker	.05
179	John Cerutti	.05
180	Jay Bell	.05
181	Dale Sveum	.05
182	Greg Gagne	.05
183	Donnie Hill	.05
184	Rex Hudler	.05
185	Pat Kelly	.05
186	Jeff Robinson	.05
187	Jeff Gray	.05
188	Jerry Willard	.05
189	Carlos Quintana	.05
190	Dennis Eckersley	.05
191	Kelly Downs	.05
192	Gregg Jefferies	.10
193	Darrin Fletcher	.05
194	Mike Jackson	.05
195	Eddie Murray	.20
196	Billy Landrum	.05
197	Eric Yelding	.05
198	Devon White	.10
199	Larry Walker	.15
200	Ryne Sandberg	.25
201	Dave Magadan	.05
202	Steve Chitren	.05
203	Scott Fletcher	.05
204	Dwayne Henry	.05
205	Scott Coolbaugh	.05
206	Tracy Jones	.05
207	Von Hayes	.05
208	Bob Melvin	.05
209	Scott Scudder	.05
210	Luis Gonzalez	.10
211	Scott Sanderson	.05
212	*Chris Donnels*	.05
213	*Heath Slocumb*	.05
214	Mike Timlin	.05
215	Brian Harper	.05
216	Juan Berenguer	.05
217	Mike Henneman	.05
218	Bill Spiers	.05
219	Scott Terry	.05
220	Frank Viola	.05
221	Mark Eichhorn	.05
222	Ernest Riles	.05
223	Ray Lankford	.10
224	Pete Harnisch	.05
225	Bobby Bonilla	.10
226	Mike Scioscia	.05
227	Joel Skinner	.05
228	Brian Holman	.05
229	Gilberto Reyes	.05
230	Matt Williams	.20
231	Jaime Navarro	.05
232	Jose Rijo	.05
233	Atlee Hammaker	.05
234	Tim Teufel	.05
235	John Kruk	.05
236	Kurt Stillwell	.05
237	Dan Pasqua	.05
238	Tim Crews	.05
239	Dave Gallagher	.05
240	Leo Gomez	.05
241	Steve Avery	.05
242	Bill Gullickson	.05
243	Mark Portugal	.05
244	Lee Guetterman	.05
245	Benny Santiago	.05
246	Jim Gantner	.05
247	Robby Thompson	.05
248	Terry Shumpert	.05
249	*Mike Bell*	.05
250	Harold Reynolds	.05
251	Mike Felder	.05
252	Bill Pecota	.05
253	Bill Krueger	.05
254	Alfredo Griffin	.05
255	Lou Whitaker	.05
256	Roy Smith	.05
257	Jerald Clark	.05
258	Sammy Sosa	.75
259	Tim Naehring	.05
260	Dave Righetti	.05
261	Paul Gibson	.05
262	Chris James	.05
263	Larry Andersen	.05
264	Storm Davis	.05
265	Jose Lind	.05
266	Greg Hibbard	.05
267	Norm Charlton	.05
268	Paul Kilgus	.05
269	Greg Maddux	.75
270	Ellis Burks	.10
271	Frank Tanana	.05
272	Gene Larkin	.05
273	Ron Hassey	.05
274	Jeff Robinson	.05
275	Steve Howe	.05
276	Daryl Boston	.05
277	Mark Lee	.05
278	*Jose Segura*	.05
279	Lance Blankenship	.05
280	Don Slaught	.05
281	Russ Swan	.05
282	Bob Tewksbury	.05
283	Geno Petralli	.05
284	Shane Mack	.05
285	Bob Scanlan	.05
286	Tim Leary	.05
287	John Smoltz	.10
288	Pat Borders	.05
289	Mark Davidson	.05
290	Sam Horn	.05
291	Lenny Harris	.05
292	Franklin Stubbs	.05
293	Thomas Howard	.05
294	Steve Lyons	.05
295	Francisco Oliveras	.05
296	Terry Leach	.05
297	Barry Jones	.05
298	Lance Parrish	.05
299	Wally Whitehurst	.05
300	Bob Welch	.05
301	Charlie Hayes	.05
302	Charlie Hough	.05
303	Gary Redus	.05
304	Scott Bradley	.05
305	Jose Oquendo	.05
306	Pete Incaviglia	.05
307	Marvin Freeman	.05
308	Gary Pettis	.05
309	Joe Slusarski	.05
310	Kevin Seitzer	.05
311	Jeff Reed	.05
312	Pat Tabler	.05
313	Mike Maddux	.05
314	Bob Milacki	.05
315	Eric Anthony	.05
316	Dante Bichette	.15
317	Steve Decker	.05
318	Jack Clark	.05
319	Doug Dascenzo	.05
320	Scott Leius	.10
321	Jim Lindeman	.05
322	Bryan Harvey	.05
323	Spike Owen	.05
324	Roberto Kelly	.05
325	Stan Belinda	.05
326	Joey Cora	.05
327	Jeff Innis	.05
328	Willie Wilson	.05
329	Juan Agosto	.05
330	Charles Nagy	.10
331	Scott Bailes	.05
332	*Pete Schourek*	.10
333	Mike Flanagan	.05
334	Omar Olivares	.05
335	Dennis Lamp	.05
336	Tommy Greene	.05
337	Randy Velarde	.05
338	Tom Lampkin	.05
339	John Russell	.05
340	Bob Kipper	.05
341	Todd Burns	.05
342	Ron Jones	.05
343	Dave Valle	.05
344	Mike Heath	.05
345	John Olerud	.25
346	Gerald Young	.05
347	Ken Patterson	.05
348	Les Lancaster	.05
349	Steve Crawford	.05
350	John Candelaria	.05
351	Mike Aldrete	.05
352	Mariano Duncan	.05
353	Julio Machado	.05
354	Ken Williams	.05
355	Walt Terrell	.05
356	Mitch Williams	.05
357	Al Newman	.05
358	Bud Black	.05
359	Joe Hesketh	.05
360	Paul Assenmacher	.05
361	Bo Jackson	.10
362	Jeff Blauser	.05
363	Mike Brumley	.05
364	Jim Deshaies	.05
365	Brady Anderson	.10
366	Chuck McElroy	.05
367	Matt Merullo	.05
368	Tim Belcher	.05
369	Luis Aquino	.05
370	Joe Oliver	.05
371	Greg Swindell	.05
372	Lee Stevens	.05
373	Mark Knudson	.05
374	Bill Wegman	.05
375	Jerry Don Gleaton	.05
376	Pedro Guerrero	.05
377	Randy Bush	.05
378	Greg Harris	.05
379	Eric Plunk	.05
380	Jose DeJesus	.05
381	Bobby Witt	.05
382	Curtis Wilkerson	.05
383	Gene Nelson	.05
384	Wes Chamberlain	.05
385	Tom Henke	.05
386	Mark Lemke	.05
387	Greg Briley	.05
388	Rafael Ramirez	.05
389	Tony Fossas	.05
390	Henry Cotto	.05
391	Tim Hulett	.05
392	Dean Palmer	.05
393	Glenn Braggs	.05
394	Mark Salas	.05
395	*Rusty Meacham*	.10
396	*Andy Ashby*	.25
397	*Jose Melendez*	.05
398	*Warren Newson*	.10
399	*Frank Castillo*	.10
400	*Chito Martinez*	.05
401	Bernie Williams	.20
402	Derek Bell	.10
403	*Javier Ortiz*	.05
404	*Tim Sherrill*	.10
405	*Rob MacDonald*	.05
406	Phil Plantier	.05
407	Troy Afenir	.05
408	*Gino Minutelli*	.05
409	*Reggie Jefferson*	.10
410	*Mike Remlinger*	.10
411	*Carlos Rodriguez*	.10
412	*Joe Redfield*	.05
413	Alonzo Powell	.05
414	*Scott Livingstone*	.10
415	*Scott Kamieniecki*	.10
416	*Tim Spehr*	.10
417	*Brian Hunter*	.10
418	*Ced Landrum*	.05
419	*Bret Barberie*	.10
420	Kevin Morton	.05
421	*Doug Henry*	.10
422	*Doug Piatt*	.15
423	*Pat Rice*	.10
424	Juan Guzman	.05
425	Nolan Ryan (No-Hit)	.30
426	Tommy Greene (No-Hit)	.10
427	Bob Milacki, Mike Flanagan, Mark Williamson, Gregg Olson (No-Hit)	.10
428	Wilson Alvarez (No-Hit)	.10
429	Otis Nixon (Highlight)	.05
430	Rickey Henderson (Highlight)	.10
431	Cecil Fielder (All-Star)	.05
432	Julio Franco (AS)	.05
433	Cal Ripken, Jr. (AS)	.25
434	Wade Boggs (AS)	.10
435	Joe Carter (AS)	.05
436	Ken Griffey, Jr. (AS)	.60
437	Ruben Sierra (AS)	.05
438	Scott Erickson (AS)	.05
439	Tom Henke (AS)	.05
440	Terry Steinbach (AS)	.05
441	Rickey Henderson (Dream Team)	.10
442	Ryne Sandberg (Dream Team)	.25
443	Otis Nixon	.05
444	Scott Radinsky	.05
445	Mark Grace	.15
446	Tony Pena	.05
447	Billy Hatcher	.05
448	Glenallen Hill	.05
449	Chris Gwynn	.05
450	Tom Glavine	.10
451	John Habyan	.05
452	Al Osuna	.05
453	Tony Phillips	.05
454	Greg Cadaret	.05
455	Rob Dibble	.05
456	Rick Honeycutt	.05
457	Jerome Walton	.05
458	Mookie Wilson	.05
459	Mark Gubicza	.05
460	Craig Biggio	.20
461	Dave Cochrane	.05
462	Keith Miller	.05
463	Alex Cole	.05
464	Pete Smith	.05
465	Brett Butler	.05
466	Jeff Huson	.05
467	Steve Lake	.05
468	Lloyd Moseby	.05
469	Tim McIntosh	.05
470	Dennis Martinez	.05
471	Greg Myers	.05
472	Mackey Sasser	.05
473	Junior Ortiz	.05

474 Greg Olson .05
475 Steve Sax .05
476 Ricky Jordan .05
477 Max Venable .05
478 Brian McRae .05
479 Doug Simons .05
480 Rickey Henderson .15
481 Gary Varsho .05
482 Carl Willis .05
483 *Rick Wilkins* .10
484 Donn Pall .05
485 Edgar Martinez .05
486 Tom Foley .05
487 Mark Williamson .05
488 Jack Armstrong .05
489 Gary Carter .10
490 Ruben Sierra .05
491 Gerald Perry .05
492 Rob Murphy .05
493 Zane Smith .05
494 *Darryl Kile* .10
495 Kelly Gruber .05
496 Jerry Browne .05
497 Darryl Hamilton .05
498 Mike Stanton .05
499 Mark Leonard .05
500 Jose Canseco .15
501 Dave Martinez .05
502 Jose Guzman .05
503 Terry Kennedy .05
504 *Ed Sprague* .10
505 Frank Thomas .75
506 Darren Daulton .05
507 Kevin Tapani .05
508 Luis Salazar .05
509 Paul Faries .05
510 Sandy Alomar, Jr. .15
511 Jeff King .05
512 Gary Thurman .05
513 Chris Hammond .05
514 *Pedro Munoz* .10
515 Alan Trammell .10
516 Geronimo Pena .05
517 Rodney McCray .05
518 Manny Lee .05
519 Junior Felix .05
520 Kirk Gibson .05
521 Darrin Jackson .05
522 John Burkett .05
523 Jeff Johnson .05
524 Jim Corsi .05
525 Robin Yount .25
526 Jamie Quirk .05
527 Bob Ojeda .05
528 Mark Lewis .05
529 Bryn Smith .05
530 Kent Hrbek .05
531 Dennis Boyd .05
532 Ron Karkovice .05
533 Don August .05
534 Todd Frohwirth .05
535 Wally Joyner .10
536 Dennis Rasmussen .05
537 Andy Allanson .05
538 Rich Gossage .05
539 John Marzano .05
540 Cal Ripken, Jr. 1.00
541 Bill Swift .05
542 Kevin Appier .05
543 Dave Bergman .05
544 Bernard Gilkey .10
545 Mike Greenwell .05
546 Jose Uribe .05
547 Jesse Orosco .05
548 Bob Patterson .05
549 Mike Stanley .05
550 Howard Johnson .05
551 Joe Orsulak .05
552 Dick Schofield .05
553 Dave Hollins .05
554 David Segui .05
555 Barry Bonds .40
556 Mo Vaughn .25
557 Craig Wilson .05
558 Bobby Rose .05
559 Rod Nichols .05
560 Len Dykstra .05
561 Craig Grebeck .05
562 Darren Lewis .10
563 Todd Benzinger .05
564 Ed Whitson .05
565 Jesse Barfield .05
566 Lloyd McClendon .05
567 Dan Plesac .05
568 Danny Cox .05
569 Skeeter Barnes .05
570 Bobby Thigpen .05
571 Deion Sanders .10
572 Chuck Knoblauch .10
573 Matt Nokes .05
574 Herm Winningham .05
575 Tom Candiotti .05
576 Jeff Bagwell .50
577 Brook Jacoby .05
578 Chico Walker .05
579 Brian Downing .05
580 Dave Stewart .05
581 Francisco Cabrera .05
582 Rene Gonzales .05
583 Stan Javier .05
584 Randy Johnson .25
585 Chuck Finley .05
586 Mark Gardner .05
587 Mark Whiten .05
588 Garry Templeton .05
589 Gary Sheffield .15
590 Ozzie Smith .25
591 Candy Maldonado .05
592 Mike Sharperson .05
593 Carlos Martinez .05
594 Scott Bankhead .05
595 Tim Wallach .05
596 Tino Martinez .10
597 Roger McDowell .05
598 Cory Snyder .05
599 Andujar Cedeno .05
600 Kirby Puckett .30
601 Rick Parker .05
602 Todd Hundley .10
603 Greg Litton .05
604 Dave Johnson .05
605 John Franco .05
606 Mike Fetters .05
607 Luis Alicea .05
608 Trevor Wilson .05
609 Rob Ducey .05
610 Ramon Martinez .10
611 Dave Burba .05
612 Dwight Smith .05
613 Kevin Maas .05
614 John Costello .05
615 Glenn Davis .05
616 Shawn Abner .05
617 Scott Hemond .05
618 Tom Prince .05
619 Wally Ritchie .05
620 Jim Abbott .05
621 Charlie O'Brien .05
622 Jack Daugherty .05
623 Tommy Gregg .05
624 Jeff Shaw .05
625 Tony Gwynn .35
626 Mark Leiter .05
627 Jim Clancy .05
628 Tim Layana .05
629 Jeff Schaefer .05
630 Lee Smith .05
631 Wade Taylor .05
632 Mike Simms .05
633 Terry Steinbach .05
634 Shawon Dunston .05
635 Tim Raines .10
636 Kirt Manwaring .05
637 Warren Cromartie .05
638 Luis Quinones .05
639 Greg Vaughn .10
640 Kevin Mitchell .05
641 Chris Hoiles .05
642 Tom Browning .05
643 Mitch Webster .05
644 Steve Olin .05
645 Tony Fernandez .05
646 Juan Bell .05
647 Joe Boever .05
648 Carney Lansford .05
649 Mike Benjamin .05
650 George Brett .25
651 Tim Burke .05
652 Jack Morris .05
653 Orel Hershiser .10
654 Mike Schooler .05
655 Andy Van Slyke .05
656 Dave Stieb .05
657 Dave Clark .05
658 Ben McDonald .05
659 John Smiley .05
660 Wade Boggs .20
661 Eric Bullock .05
662 Eric Show .05
663 Lenny Webster .05
664 Mike Huff .05
665 Rick Sutcliffe .05
666 Jeff Manto .05
667 Mike Fitzgerald .05
668 Matt Young .05
669 Dave West .05
670 Mike Hartley .05
671 Curt Schilling .10
672 Brian Bohanon .05
673 Cecil Espy .05
674 Joe Grahe .05
675 Sid Fernandez .05
676 Edwin Nunez .05
677 Hector Villanueva .05
678 Sean Berry .05
679 Dave Eiland .05
680 David Cone .10
681 Mike Bordick .05
682 Tony Castillo .05
683 John Barfield .05
684 Jeff Hamilton .05
685 Ken Dayley .05
686 Carmelo Martinez .05
687 Mike Capel .05
688 Scott Chiamparino .05
689 Rich Gedman .05
690 Rich Monteleone .05
691 Alejandro Pena .05
692 Oscar Azocar .05
693 Jim Poole .05
694 Mike Gardiner .05
695 Steve Buechele .05
696 Rudy Seanez .05
697 Paul Abbott .05
698 Steve Searcy .05
699 Jose Offerman .05
700 Ivan Rodriguez .30
701 Joe Girardi .05
702 Tony Perezchica .05
703 Paul McClellan .05
704 *David Howard* .10
705 Dan Petry .05
706 Jack Howell .05
707 Jose Mesa .05
708 Randy St. Claire .05
709 Kevin Brown .05
710 Ron Darling .05
711 Jason Grimsley .05
712 John Orton .05
713 Shawn Boskie .05
714 Pat Clements .05
715 Brian Barnes .05
716 *Luis Lopez* .05
717 Bob McClure .05
718 Mark Davis .05
719 Dann Billardello .05
720 Tom Edens .05
721 Willie Fraser .05
722 Curt Young .05
723 Neal Heaton .05
724 Craig Worthington .05
725 Mel Rojas .05
726 Daryl Irvine .05
727 Roger Mason .05
728 Kirk Dressendorfer .05
729 Scott Aldred .05
730 Willie Blair .05
731 Allan Anderson .05
732 Dana Kiecker .05
733 Jose Gonzalez .05
734 Brian Drahman .05
735 Brad Komminsk .05
736 *Arthur Rhodes* .10
737 *Terry Mathews* .05
738 *Jeff Fassero* .05
739 *Mike Magnante* .05
740 *Kip Gross* .05
741 *Jim Hunter* .05
742 *Jose Mota* .05
743 Joe Bitker .05
744 *Tim Mauser* .05
745 *Ramon Garcia* .05
746 *Rod Beck* .25
747 *Jim Austin* .05
748 *Keith Mitchell* .05
749 *Wayne Rosenthal* .05
750 *Bryan Hickerson* .05
751 *Bruce Egloff* .05
752 *John Wehner* .05
753 Darren Holmes .05
754 Dave Hansen .05
755 Mike Mussina .25
756 *Anthony Young* .05
757 Ron Tingley .05
758 *Ricky Bones* .05
759 *Mark Wohlers* .10
760 Wilson Alvarez .10
761 *Harvey Pulliam* .05
762 *Ryan Bowen* .10
763 Terry Bross .05
764 *Joel Johnston* .05
765 *Terry McDaniel* .05
766 *Esteban Beltre* .05
767 *Rob Maurer* .05
768 Ted Wood .05
769 *Mo Sanford* .10
770 *Jeff Carter* .05
771 *Gil Heredia* .10
772 Monty Fariss .05
773 Will Clark (AS) .10
774 Ryne Sandberg (AS) .15
775 Barry Larkin (AS) .10
776 Howard Johnson (AS) .05
777 Barry Bonds (AS) .25
778 Brett Butler (AS) .05
779 Tony Gwynn (AS) .15
780 Ramon Martinez (AS) .05
781 Lee Smith (AS) .05
782 Mike Scioscia (AS) .05
783 Dennis Martinez (Highlight) .05
784 Dennis Martinez (No-Hit) .05
785 Mark Gardner (No-Hit) .05
786 Bret Saberhagen (No-Hit) .05
787 Kent Mercker, Mark Wohlers, Alejandro Pena (No-Hit) .05
788 Cal Ripken (MVP) .25
789 Terry Pendleton (MVP) .05
790 Roger Clemens (CY) .15
791 Tom Glavine (CY) .05
792 Chuck Knoblauch (ROY) .10
793 Jeff Bagwell (ROY) .25
794 Cal Ripken, Jr. (Man of the Year) .25
795 David Cone (Highlight) .05
796 Kirby Puckett (Highlight) .15
797 Steve Avery (Highlight) .05
798 Jack Morris (Highlight) .05
799 *Allen Watson* .25
800 *Manny Ramirez* 4.00
801 *Cliff Floyd* .40
802 *Al Shirley* .05
803 *Brian Barber* .05
804 *Jon Farrell* .05
805 *Brent Gates* .25
806 *Scott Ruffcorn* .20
807 *Tyrone Hill* .10
808 *Benji Gil* .10
809 *Aaron Sele* .30
810 *Tyler Green* .25
811 Chris Jones .05
812 Steve Wilson .05
813 *Cliff Young* .10
814 *Don Wakamatsu* .05
815 *Mike Humphreys* .05
816 *Scott Servais* .05
817 *Rico Rossy* .05
818 *John Ramos* .05
819 Rob Mallicoat .05
820 *Milt Hill* .10
821 Carlos Carcia .05
822 Stan Royer .10
823 *Jeff Plympton* .10
824 *Braulio Castillo* .10
825 *David Haas* .05
826 *Luis Mercedes* .10
827 Eric Karros .15
828 *Shawn Hare* .10
829 Reggie Sanders .10
830 Tom Goodwin .05
831 *Dan Gakeler* .05
832 *Stacy Jones* .05
833 *Kim Batiste* .05
834 Cal Eldred .05
835 *Chris George* .05
836 *Wayne Housie* .05
837 *Mike Ignasiak* .05
838 *Josias Manzanillo* .05
839 *Jim Olander* .05
840 *Gary Cooper* .05
841 Royce Clayton .05
842 Hector Fajardo .05
843 Blaine Beatty .05
844 *Jorge Pedre* .05
845 Kenny Lofton .30
846 Scott Brosius .15
847 *Chris Cron* .05
848 Denis Boucher .05
849 Kyle Abbott .10
850 Bob Zupcic .05
851 *Rheal Cormier* .15
852 *Jim Lewis* .05
853 Anthony Telford .05
854 *Cliff Brantley* .05
855 *Kevin Campbell* .05
856 *Craig Shipley* .05
857 Chuck Carr .05
858 *Tony Eusebio* .10
859 Jim Thome .25
860 *Vinny Castilla* 1.00
861 Dann Howitt .05
862 *Kevin Ward* .05
863 *Steve Wapnick* .05
864 Rod Brewer .05
865 Todd Van Poppel .10
866 *Jose Hernandez* .05
867 *Amalio Carreno* .05
868 *Calvin Jones* .05
869 *Jeff Gardner* .05
870 *Jarvis Brown* .05
871 *Eddie Taubensee* .10
872 *Andy Mota* .10
873 Chris Haney (Front photo actually Scott Ruskin) .05
874 Roberto Hernandez .10
875 *Laddie Renfroe* .05
876 Scott Cooper .05
877 *Armando Reynoso* .05
878 Ty Cobb (Memorabilia) .30
879 Babe Ruth (Memorabilia) .40
880 Honus Wagner (Memorabilia) .20
881 Lou Gehrig (Memorabilia) .30
882 Satchel Paige (Memorabilia) .20
883 Will Clark (Dream Team) .20
884 Cal Ripken, Jr. (Dream Team) .35
885 Wade Boggs (Dream Team) .20
886 Kirby Puckett (Dream Team) .30
887 Tony Gwynn (Dream Team) .30
888 Craig Biggio (Dream Team) .10
889 Scott Erickson (Dream Team) .05
890 Tom Glavine (Dream Team) .15
891 Rob Dibble (Dream Team) .05
892 Mitch Williams (Dream Team) .05
893 Frank Thomas (Dream Team) .50

1992 Score Joe DiMaggio

Colorized vintage photos are featured on the front and back of each of five Joe DiMaggio tribute cards which were issued as random inserts in 1992 Score Series 1 packs. A limited number (1,800) of each card were autographed. Curiously, the cards carry a 1993 copyright date.

		MT
	Complete Set (5):	100.00
	Common Card:	25.00
	Autographed Card:	300.00
1	Joe DiMaggio (The Minors)	25.00
2	Joe DiMaggio (The Rookie)	25.00
3	Joe DiMaggio (The MVP)	25.00
4	Joe DiMaggio (The Streak)	25.00
5	Joe DiMaggio (The Legend)	25.00

1992 Score Factory Inserts

Available exclusively in factory sets these 17 cards are divided into four subsets commemorating the 1991 World Series, potential Hall of Famers, the career of Joe DiMaggio and Carl Yastrzemski's 1967 Triple Crown season. Cards carry a "B" prefix to the card number.

		MT
	Complete Set (17):	7.50
	Common World Series (1-7):	.15
	Common Cooperstown (8-11):	.70
	Common DiMaggio (12-14):	.35
	Common Yastrzemski (15-17):	.20
1	World Series Game 1 (Greg Gagne)	.15
2	World Series Game 2 (Scott Leius)	.15
3	World Series Game 3 (David Justice, Brian Harper)	.15
4	World Series Game 4 (Lonnie Smith, Brian Harper)	.15
5	World Series Game 5 (David Justice)	.30
6	World Series Game 6 (Kirby Puckett)	.60
7	World Series Game 7 (Gene Larkin)	.15
8	Carlton Fisk (Cooperstown)	.45
9	Ozzie Smith (Cooperstown)	.75
10	Dave Winfield (Cooperstown)	.75
11	Robin Yount (Cooperstown)	.75
12	Joe DiMaggio (The Hard Hitter)	.75
13	Joe DiMaggio (The Stylish Fielder)	.75
14	Joe DiMaggio (The Champion Player)	.75
15	Carl Yastrzemski (The Impossible Dream)	.20

16	Carl Yastrzemski (The Triple Crown)	.20
17	Carl Yastrzemski (The World Series)	.20

1992 Score The Franchise

This four-card set, in both autographed and unautographed form, was a random insert in various premium packaging of Score's 1992 Series II cards. Each of the four cards was produced in an edition of 150,000, with 2,000 of each player's card being autographed and 500 of the triple-player card carrying the autographs of all three superstars.

		MT
Complete Set (4):		30.00
Common Player:		6.00
Musial Autograph:		150.00
Mantle Autograph:		400.00
Yastrzemski Autograph:		100.00
Triple Autograph:		1000.
1	Stan Musial	8.00
2	Mickey Mantle	12.00
3	Carl Yastrzemski	6.00
4	Stan Musial, Mickey Mantle, Carl Yastrzemski	9.00

1992 Score Hot Rookies

This 10-card rookie issue was produced as an insert in special blister packs of 1992 Score cards sold at retail outlets. Action photos on front and portraits on back are set against white backgrounds with orange highlights. Cards are standard 2-1/2" x 3-1/2".

		MT
Complete Set (10):		10.00
Common Player:		.70
1	Cal Eldred	.50
2	Royce Clayton	1.00
3	Kenny Lofton	5.00
4	Todd Van Poppel	.50
5	Scott Cooper	.50
6	Todd Hundley	1.50
7	Tino Martinez	2.00
8	Anthony Telford	.50
9	Derek Bell	1.50
10	Reggie Jefferson	.50

1992 Score Impact Players

Jumbo packs of 1992 Score Series I and II cards contained five of these special inserts labeled "90's Impact Players". Front action photos contrast with portrait photos on the backs, which are color-coded by team. Cards #1-45 were packaged with Series I, cards #46-90 were included in Series II packs.

		MT
Complete Set (90):		20.00
Common Player:		.10
1	Chuck Knoblauch	.25
2	Jeff Bagwell	1.00
3	Juan Guzman	.10
4	Milt Cuyler	.10
5	Ivan Rodriguez	.60
6	Rich DeLucia	.10
7	Orlando Merced	.10
8	Ray Lankford	.20
9	Brian Hunter	.10
10	Roberto Alomar	.60
11	Wes Chamberlain	.10
12	Steve Avery	.10
13	Scott Erickson	.10
14	Jim Abbott	.15
15	Mark Whiten	.10
16	Leo Gomez	.10
17	Doug Henry	.10
18	Brent Mayne	.10
19	Charles Nagy	.15
20	Phil Plantier	.10
21	Mo Vaughn	.60
22	Craig Biggio	.20
23	Derek Bell	.20
24	Royce Clayton	.15
25	Gary Cooper	.10
26	Scott Cooper	.10
27	Juan Gonzalez	1.00
28	Ken Griffey, Jr.	3.00
29	Larry Walker	.45
30	John Smoltz	.20
31	Todd Hundley	.15
32	Kenny Lofton	.60
33	Andy Mota	.10
34	Todd Zeile	.10
35	Arthur Rhodes	.10
36	Jim Thome	.25
37	Todd Van Poppel	.10
38	Mark Wohlers	.10
39	Anthony Young	.10
40	Sandy Alomar Jr.	.15
41	John Olerud	.25
42	Robin Ventura	.25
43	Frank Thomas	1.00
44	Dave Justice	.50
45	Hal Morris	.10
46	Ruben Sierra	.10
47	Travis Fryman	.10
48	Mike Mussina	.20
49	Tom Glavine	.15
50	Barry Larkin	.20
51	Will Clark	.30
52	Jose Canseco	.45
53	Bo Jackson	.25
54	Dwight Gooden	.15
55	Barry Bonds	1.00
56	Fred McGriff	.40
57	Roger Clemens	.75
58	Benito Santiago	.10
59	Darryl Strawberry	.15
60	Cecil Fielder	.15
61	John Franco	.10
62	Matt Williams	.25
63	Marquis Grissom	.15
64	Danny Tartabull	.10
65	Ron Gant	.20
66	Paul O'Neill	.15
67	Devon White	.10
68	Rafael Palmeiro	.25
69	Tom Gordon	.10
70	Shawon Dunston	.10
71	Rob Dibble	.10
72	Eddie Zosky	.10
73	Jack McDowell	.10
74	Len Dykstra	.10
75	Ramon Martinez	.15
76	Reggie Sanders	.20
77	Greg Maddux	1.50
78	Ellis Burks	.20
79	John Smiley	.10
80	Roberto Kelly	.10
81	Ben McDonald	.10
82	Mark Lewis	.10
83	Jose Rijo	.10
84	Ozzie Guillen	.10
85	Lance Dickson	.10
86	Kim Batiste	.10
87	Gregg Olson	.10
88	Andy Benes	.15
89	Cal Eldred	.10
90	David Cone	.15

1992 Score Procter & Gamble

In 1992 Score and Procter and Gamble combined to produce an 18-card All-Star set, reportedly two million cards making 101,000 sets offered to collectors originally for $1.49 along with proof of purchase from P & G products. Card fronts feature a color player action photo set against a background of blue star and pink-to-purple diagonal stripes (American Leaguers) or red star and green stripes (National Leaguers). Back designs include a color player portrait photo at upper-right, with personal data, career stats and highlights. Appropriate logos and card number complete the design, which is bordered in color striping similar to the front background.

		MT
Complete Set (18):		6.00
Common Player:		.20
1	Sandy Alomar Jr.	.25
2	Mark McGwire	1.50
3	Roberto Alomar	.40
4	Wade Boggs	.40
5	Cal Ripken, Jr.	1.00
6	Kirby Puckett	.50
7	Ken Griffey, Jr.	1.50
8	Jose Canseco	.40
9	Kevin Brown	.25
10	Benito Santiago	.20
11	Fred McGriff	.30
12	Ryne Sandberg	.50
13	Terry Pendleton	.20
14	Ozzie Smith	.40
15	Barry Bonds	.65
16	Tony Gwynn	.50
17	Andy Van Slyke	.20
18	Tom Glavine	.25

1992 Score Rising Stars

Sold in a blister pack with a book and a handful of "Magic Motion" trivia cards this 100-card set features baseball's top young players. Backs have a player portrait, a career summary and team, league and card company logos.

		MT
Complete Set (100):		5.00
Common Player:		.05
1	Milt Cuyler	.05
2	David Howard	.05
3	Brian Hunter	.05
4	Darryl Kile	.05
5	Pat Kelly	.05
6	Luis Gonzalez	.10
7	Mike Benjamin	.05
8	Eric Anthony	.05
9	Moises Alou	.15
10	Darren Lewis	.05
11	Chuck Knoblauch	.15
12	Geronimo Pena	.05
13	Jeff Plympton	.05
14	Bret Barberie	.05
15	Chris Haney	.05
16	Rick Wilkins	.05
17	Julio Valera	.05
18	Joe Slusarski	.05
19	Jose Melendez	.05
20	Pete Schourek	.05
21	Jeff Conine	.10
22	Paul Faries	.05
23	Scott Kamieniecki	.05
24	Bernard Gilkey	.10
25	Wes Chamberlain	.05
26	Charles Nagy	.10
27	Juan Guzman	.05
28	Heath Slocumb	.05
29	Eddie Taubensee	.05
30	Cedric Landrum	.05
31	Jose Offerman	.05
32	Andres Santana	.05
33	David Segui	.05
34	Bernie Williams	.40
35	Jeff Bagwell	.75
36	Kevin Morton	.05
37	Kirk Dressendorfer	.05
38	Mike Fetters	.05
39	Darren Holmes	.05
40	Jeff Johnson	.05
41	Scott Aldred	.05
42	Kevin Ward	.05
43	Ray Lankford	.10
44	Terry Shumpert	.05
45	Wade Taylor	.05
46	Rob MacDonald	.05
47	Jose Mota	.05
48	Reggie Harris	.05
49	Mike Remlinger	.05
50	Mark Lewis	.05
51	Tino Martinez	.15
52	Ed Sprague	.05
53	Freddie Benavides	.05
54	Rich DeLucia	.05
55	Brian Drahman	.05
56	Steve Decker	.05
57	Scott Livingstone	.05
58	Mike Timlin	.05
59	Bob Scanlan	.05
60	Dean Palmer	.05
61	Frank Castillo	.05
62	Mark Leonard	.05
63	Chuck McElroy	.05
64	Derek Bell	.20
65	Andujar Cedeno	.05
66	Leo Gomez	.05
67	Rusty Meacham	.05
68	Dann Howitt	.05
69	Chris Jones	.05
70	Dave Cochrane	.05
71	Carlos Martinez	.05
72	Hensley Meulens	.05
73	Rich Reed	.05
74	Pedro Munoz	.05
75	Orlando Merced	.05
76	Chito Martinez	.05
77	Ivan Rodriguez	.35
78	Brian Barnes	.05
79	Chris Donnels	.05
80	Todd Hundley	.20
81	Gary Scott	.05
82	John Wehner	.05
83	Al Osuna	.05
84	Luis Lopez	.05
85	Brent Mayne	.05
86	Phil Plantier	.05
87	Joe Bitker	.05
88	Scott Cooper	.05
89	Chris Hammond	.05
90	Tim Sherrill	.05
91	Doug Simons	.05
92	Kip Gross	.05
93	Tim McIntosh	.05
94	Larry Casian	.05
95	Mike Dalton	.05
96	Lance Dickson	.05
97	Joe Grahe	.05
98	Glenn Sutko	.05
99	Gerald Alexander	.05
100	Mo Vaughn	.50

1992 Score Rookie & Traded

This 110-card set features traded players, free agents and top rookies from 1992. The cards are styled after the regular 1992 Score cards. Cards 80-110 feature the rookies. The set was released as a boxed set and was available only through hobby dealers.

		MT
Complete Set (110):		15.00
Common Player:		.05
1	Gary Sheffield	.30
2	Kevin Seitzer	.05
3	Danny Tartabull	.05
4	Steve Sax	.05
5	Bobby Bonilla	.05
6	Frank Viola	.05
7	Dave Winfield	.45
8	Rick Sutcliffe	.05
9	Jose Canseco	.65
10	Greg Swindell	.05
11	Eddie Murray	.40
12	Randy Myers	.05
13	Wally Joyner	.10
14	Kenny Lofton	3.00
15	Jack Morris	.05
16	Charlie Hayes	.05
17	Pete Incaviglia	.05
18	Kevin Mitchell	.05
19	Kurt Stillwell	.05
20	Bret Saberhagen	.10
21	Steve Buechele	.05
22	John Smiley	.05
23	Sammy Sosa	4.00
24	George Bell	.05
25	Curt Schilling	.10
26	Dick Schofield	.05
27	David Cone	.10
28	Dan Gladden	.05
29	Kirk McCaskill	.05
30	Mike Gallego	.05
31	Kevin McReynolds	.05
32	Bill Swift	.05
33	Dave Martinez	.05
34	Storm Davis	.05
35	Willie Randolph	.05
36	Melido Perez	.05
37	Mark Carreon	.05
38	Doug Jones	.05
39	Gregg Jefferies	.20
40	Mike Jackson	.05
41	Dickie Thon	.05
42	Eric King	.05
43	Herm Winningham	.05
44	Derek Lilliquist	.05
45	Dave Anderson	.05
46	Jeff Reardon	.05
47	Scott Bankhead	.05
48	Cory Snyder	.05
49	Al Newman	.05
50	Keith Miller	.05
51	Dave Burba	.05
52	Bill Pecota	.05
53	Chuck Crim	.05
54	Mariano Duncan	.05
55	Dave Gallagher	.05
56	Chris Gwynn	.05
57	Scott Ruskin	.05
58	Jack Armstrong	.05
59	Gary Carter	.10
60	Andres Galarraga	.30
61	Ken Hill	.05
62	Eric Davis	.10
63	Ruben Sierra	.05
64	Darrin Fletcher	.05
65	Tim Belcher	.05
66	Mike Morgan	.05
67	Scott Scudder	.05
68	Tom Candiotti	.05
69	Hubie Brooks	.05
70	Kal Daniels	.05
71	Bruce Ruffin	.05
72	Billy Hatcher	.05
73	Bob Melvin	.05
74	Lee Guetterman	.05
75	Rene Gonzales	.05
76	Kevin Bass	.05
77	Tom Bolton	.05
78	John Wetteland	.05
79	Bip Roberts	.05
80	Pat Listach	.05
81	John Doherty	.05
82	Sam Militello	.05
83	*Brian Jordan*	1.50
84	Jeff Kent	.60
85	Dave Fleming	.10
86	Jeff Tackett	.05
87	*Chad Curtis*	.50
88	Eric Fox	.05
89	Denny Neagle	.05
90	Donovan Osborne	.05
91	Carlos Hernandez	.05
92	Tim Wakefield	.10
93	Tim Salmon	5.00
94	Dave Nilsson	.10
95	Mike Perez	.05
96	Pat Hentgen	.10
97	Frank Seminara	.05
98	Ruben Amaro, Jr.	.10
99	Archi Cianfrocco	.05
100	Andy Stankiewicz	.05
101	Jim Bullinger	.10
102	Pat Mahomes	.10
103	Hipolito Pichardo	.05
104	Bret Boone	.50
105	John Vander Wal	.10
106	Vince Horsman	.05
107	James Austin	.05

108	Brian Williams	.05
109	Dan Walters	.05
110	Wil Cordero	.75

1992 Score Rookies

A selection of 40 1992 rookie players is featured in this boxed set. Fronts have green borders with a red and white "1992 ROOKIE" notation printed vertically to the left of a color action photo. Backs repeat the notation on a graduated blue background with a player color portrait photo at top, biographical details and a career summary at center and appropriate logos at bottom.

		MT
Complete Set (40):		6.00
Common Player:		.10
1	Todd Van Poppel	.10
2	Kyle Abbott	.15
3	Derek Bell	.35
4	Jim Thome	.30
5	Mark Wohlers	.10
6	Todd Hundley	.30
7	Arthur Rhodes	.10
8	John Ramos	.10
9	Chris George	.10
10	Kenny Lofton	2.00
11	Ted Wood	.10
12	Royce Clayton	.25
13	Scott Cooper	.10
14	Anthony Young	.10
15	Joel Johnston	.10
16	Andy Mota	.10
17	Lenny Webster	.10
18	Andy Ashby	.15
19	Jose Mota	.10
20	Tim McIntosh	.10
21	Terry Bross	.10
22	Harvey Pulliam	.10
23	Hector Fajardo	.10
24	Esteban Beltre	.10
25	Gary DiSarcina	.15
26	Mike Humphreys	.10
27	Jarvis Brown	.10
28	Gary Cooper	.10
29	Chris Donnels	.10
30	Monty Fariss	.10
31	Eric Karros	.65
32	Braulio Castillo	.10
33	Cal Eldred	.15
34	Tom Goodwin	.10
35	Reggie Sanders	.50
36	Scott Servais	.15
37	Kim Batiste	.10
38	Eric Wedge	.10
39	Willie Banks	.10
40	Mo Sanford	.10

1992 Score Superstars

Available in a blister pack with a book and six "Magic Motion" trivia cards, this 100-card set spotlights the games top veteran stars.

		MT
Complete Set (100):		5.00
Common Player:		.05
1	Ken Griffey, Jr.	1.50
2	Scott Erickson	.05
3	John Smiley	.05
4	Rick Aguilera	.05
5	Jeff Reardon	.05
6	Chuck Finley	.05
7	Kirby Puckett	.75
8	Paul Molitor	.45
9	Dave Winfield	.45
10	Mike Greenwell	.05
11	Bret Saberhagen	.10
12	Pete Harnisch	.05
13	Ozzie Guillen	.05
14	Hal Morris	.05
15	Tom Glavine	.15
16	David Cone	.10
17	Edgar Martinez	.05
18	Willie McGee	.05
19	Jim Abbott	.10
20	Mark Grace	.25
21	George Brett	.60
22	Jack McDowell	.05
23	Don Mattingly	.75
24	Will Clark	.35
25	Dwight Gooden	.15
26	Barry Bonds	.75
27	Rafael Palmeiro	.20
28	Lee Smith	.10
29	Wally Joyner	.15
30	Wade Boggs	.45
31	Tom Henke	.05
32	Mark Langston	.05
33	Robin Ventura	.15
34	Steve Avery	.05
35	Joe Carter	.10
36	Benito Santiago	.05
37	Dave Stieb	.05
38	Julio Franco	.05
39	Albert Belle	.30
40	Dale Murphy	.15
41	Rob Dibble	.05
42	Dave Justice	.30
43	Jose Rijo	.05
44	Eric Davis	.10
45	Terry Pendleton	.05
46	Kevin Maas	.05
47	Ozzie Smith	.35
48	Andre Dawson	.15
49	Sandy Alomar, Jr.	.15
50	Nolan Ryan	.90
51	Frank Thomas	.75
52	Craig Biggio	.15
53	Doug Drabek	.05
54	Bobby Thigpen	.05
55	Darryl Strawberry	.15
56	Dennis Eckersley	.05
57	John Franco	.05
58	Paul O'Neill	.15
59	Scott Sanderson	.05
60	Dave Stewart	.05
61	Ivan Calderon	.05
62	Frank Viola	.05
63	Mark McGwire	1.50
64	Kelly Gruber	.05
65	Fred McGriff	.30
66	Cecil Fielder	.10
67	Jose Canseco	.50
68	Howard Johnson	.05
69	Juan Gonzalez	.75
70	Tim Wallach	.05
71	John Olerud	.15
72	Carlton Fisk	.15
73	Otis Nixon	.05
74	Roger Clemens	.60
75	Ramon Martinez	.15
76	Ron Gant	.15
77	Barry Larkin	.15
78	Eddie Murray	.30
79	Vince Coleman	.05
80	Bobby Bonilla	.05
81	Tony Gwynn	.50
82	Roberto Alomar	.30
83	Ellis Burks	.10
84	Robin Yount	.35
85	Ryne Sandberg	.60
86	Len Dykstra	.05
87	Ruben Sierra	.05
88	George Bell	.05
89	Cal Ripken, Jr.	1.00
90	Danny Tartabull	.05
91	Gregg Olson	.05
92	Dave Henderson	.05
93	Kevin Mitchell	.05
94	Ben McDonald	.05
95	Matt Williams	.15
96	Roberto Kelly	.05
97	Dennis Martinez	.05
98	Kent Hrbek	.05
99	Felix Jose	.05
100	Rickey Henderson	.35

1993 Score

Score's 1993 cards have white borders surrounding color action photographs. The player's name is at the bottom of the card, while his team's name and position appears on the left side in a color band. Backs have color portraits, statistics and text. Subsets feature rookies, award winners, draft picks, highlights, World Series highlights, all-star caricatures, dream team players, and the Man of the Year (Kirby Puckett). Insert sets include: Boys of Summer, the Franchise and Stat Leaders, which feature Select's card design.

		MT
Complete Set (660):		30.00
Common Player:		.05
Wax Box:		18.00
1	Ken Griffey, Jr.	2.00
2	Gary Sheffield	.20
3	Frank Thomas	1.00
4	Ryne Sandberg	.40
5	Larry Walker	.20
6	Cal Ripken, Jr.	1.50
7	Roger Clemens	.75
8	Bobby Bonilla	.05
9	Carlos Baerga	.10
10	Darren Daulton	.05
11	Travis Fryman	.10
12	Andy Van Slyke	.05
13	Jose Canseco	.20
14	Roberto Alomar	.35
15	Tom Glavine	.10
16	Barry Larkin	.15
17	Gregg Jefferies	.10
18	Craig Biggio	.15
19	Shane Mack	.05
20	Brett Butler	.05
21	Dennis Eckersley	.05
22	Will Clark	.20
23	Don Mattingly	.50
24	Tony Gwynn	.75
25	Ivan Rodriguez	.30
26	Shawon Dunston	.05
27	Mike Mussina	.25
28	Marquis Grissom	.10
29	Charles Nagy	.10
30	Len Dykstra	.05
31	Cecil Fielder	.10
32	Jay Bell	.05
33	B.J. Surhoff	.05
34	Bob Tewksbury	.05
35	Danny Tartabull	.05
36	Terry Pendleton	.05
37	Jack Morris	.05
38	Hal Morris	.05
39	Luis Polonia	.05
40	Ken Caminiti	.15
41	Robin Ventura	.15
42	Darryl Strawberry	.10
43	Wally Joyner	.10
44	Fred McGriff	.15
45	Kevin Tapani	.05
46	Matt Williams	.15
47	Robin Yount	.25
48	Ken Hill	.05
49	Edgar Martinez	.05
50	Mark Grace	.15
51	Juan Gonzalez	.75
52	Curt Schilling	.10
53	Dwight Gooden	.10
54	Chris Hoiles	.05
55	Frank Viola	.05
56	Ray Lankford	.10
57	George Brett	.40
58	Kenny Lofton	.50
59	Nolan Ryan	1.25
60	Mickey Tettleton	.05
61	John Smoltz	.10
62	Howard Johnson	.05
63	Eric Karros	.10
64	Rick Aguilera	.05
65	Steve Finley	.05
66	Mark Langston	.05
67	Bill Swift	.05
68	John Olerud	.15
69	Kevin McReynolds	.05
70	Jack McDowell	.05
71	Rickey Henderson	.20
72	Brian Harper	.05
73	Mike Morgan	.05
74	Rafael Palmeiro	.15
75	Dennis Martinez	.05
76	Tino Martinez	.10
77	Eddie Murray	.20
78	Ellis Burks	.10
79	John Kruk	.05
80	Gregg Olson	.05
81	Bernard Gilkey	.10
82	Milt Cuyler	.05
83	Mike LaValliere	.05
84	Albert Belle	.40
85	Bip Roberts	.05
86	Melido Perez	.05
87	Otis Nixon	.05
88	Bill Spiers	.05
89	Jeff Bagwell	.75
90	Orel Hershiser	.10
91	Andy Benes	.10
92	Devon White	.10
93	Willie McGee	.05
94	Ozzie Guillen	.05
95	Ivan Calderon	.05
96	Keith Miller	.05
97	Steve Buechele	.05
98	Kent Hrbek	.05
99	Dave Hollins	.05
100	Mike Bordick	.05
101	Randy Tomlin	.05
102	Omar Vizquel	.05
103	Lee Smith	.10
104	Leo Gomez	.05
105	Jose Rijo	.05
106	Mark Whiten	.05
107	Dave Justice	.15
108	Eddie Taubensee	.05
109	Lance Johnson	.05
110	Felix Jose	.05
111	Mike Harkey	.05
112	Randy Milligan	.05
113	Anthony Young	.05
114	Rico Brogna	.05
115	Bret Saberhagen	.05
116	Sandy Alomar, Jr.	.10
117	Terry Mulholland	.05
118	Darryl Hamilton	.05
119	Todd Zeile	.10
120	Bernie Williams	.35
121	Zane Smith	.05
122	Derek Bell	.10
123	Deion Sanders	.15
124	Luis Sojo	.05
125	Joe Oliver	.05
126	Craig Grebeck	.05
127	Andujar Cedeno	.05
128	Brian McRae	.05
129	Jose Offerman	.05
130	Pedro Munoz	.05
131	Bud Black	.05
132	Mo Vaughn	.25
133	Bruce Hurst	.05
134	Dave Henderson	.05
135	Tom Pagnozzi	.05
136	Erik Hanson	.05
137	Orlando Merced	.05
138	Dean Palmer	.05
139	John Franco	.05
140	Brady Anderson	.10
141	Ricky Jordan	.05
142	Jeff Blauser	.05
143	Sammy Sosa	1.25
144	Bob Walk	.05
145	Delino DeShields	.05
146	Kevin Brown	.10
147	Mark Lemke	.05
148	Chuck Knoblauch	.20
149	Chris Sabo	.05
150	Bobby Witt	.05
151	Luis Gonzalez	.10
152	Ron Karkovice	.05
153	Jeff Brantley	.05
154	Kevin Appier	.05
155	Darrin Jackson	.05
156	Kelly Gruber	.05
157	Royce Clayton	.05
158	Chuck Finley	.05
159	Jeff King	.05
160	Greg Vaughn	.10
161	Geronimo Pena	.05
162	Steve Farr	.05
163	Jose Oquendo	.05
164	Mark Lewis	.05
165	John Wetteland	.05
166	Mike Henneman	.05
167	Todd Hundley	.10
168	Wes Chamberlain	.05
169	Steve Avery	.05
170	Mike Devereaux	.05
171	Reggie Sanders	.10
172	Jay Buhner	.10
173	Eric Anthony	.05
174	John Burkett	.05
175	Tom Candiotti	.05
176	Phil Plantier	.05
177	Doug Henry	.05
178	Scott Leius	.05
179	Kirt Manwaring	.05
180	Jeff Parrett	.05
181	Don Slaught	.05
182	Scott Radinsky	.05
183	Luis Alicea	.05
184	Tom Gordon	.05
185	Rick Wilkins	.05
186	Todd Stottlemyre	.05
187	Moises Alou	.15
188	Joe Grahe	.05
189	Jeff Kent	.05
190	Bill Wegman	.05
191	Kim Batiste	.05
192	Matt Nokes	.05
193	Mark Wohlers	.05
194	Paul Sorrento	.05
195	Chris Hammond	.05
196	Scott Livingstone	.05
197	Doug Jones	.05
198	Scott Cooper	.05
199	Ramon Martinez	.10
200	Dave Valle	.05
201	Mariano Duncan	.05
202	Ben McDonald	.05
203	Darren Lewis	.05
204	Kenny Rogers	.05
205	Manuel Lee	.05
206	Scott Erickson	.05
207	Dan Gladden	.05
208	Bob Welch	.05
209	Greg Olson	.05
210	Dan Pasqua	.05
211	Tim Wallach	.05
212	Jeff Montgomery	.05
213	Derrick May	.05
214	Ed Sprague	.05
215	David Haas	.05
216	Darrin Fletcher	.05
217	Brian Jordan	.10
218	Jaime Navarro	.05
219	Randy Velarde	.05
220	Ron Gant	.10
221	Paul Quantrill	.05
222	Damion Easley	.05
223	Charlie Hough	.05
224	*Brad Brink*	.05
225	*Barry Manual*	.05
226	*Kevin Koslofski*	.05
227	*Ryan Thompson*	.10
228	*Mike Munoz*	.05
229	*Dan Wilson*	.10
230	*Peter Hoy*	.05
231	*Pedro Astacio*	.20
232	*Matt Stairs*	.15
233	*Jeff Reboulet*	.15
234	*Manny Alexander*	.10
235	*Willie Banks*	.05
236	*John Jaha*	.15
237	*Scooter Tucker*	.05
238	*Russ Springer*	.05
239	*Paul Miller*	.05
240	*Dan Peltier*	.05
241	*Ozzie Canseco*	.05
242	*Ben Rivera*	.05
243	*John Valentin*	.20
244	Henry Rodriguez	.10
245	*Derek Parks*	.10
246	*Carlos Garcia*	.10
247	*Tim Pugh*	.10
248	*Melvin Nieves*	.10
249	*Rich Amaral*	.05
250	*Willie Greene*	.15
251	*Tim Scott*	.05
252	*Dave Silvestri*	.10
253	*Rob Mallicoat*	.05
254	*Donald Harris*	.10
255	*Craig Colbert*	.05
256	Jose Guzman	.05
257	*Domingo Martinez*	.05
258	*William Suero*	.05
259	*Juan Guerrero*	.05
260	*J.T. Snow*	.50
261	Tony Pena	.05
262	*Tim Fortugno*	.05
263	*Tom Marsh*	.05
264	*Kurt Knudsen*	.05
265	*Tim Costo*	.10
266	*Steve Shifflett*	.05
267	*Billy Ashley*	.10
268	Jerry Nielsen	.05
269	*Pete Young*	.05
270	*Johnny Guzman*	.05
271	*Greg Colbrunn*	.10
272	Jeff Nelson	.05
273	*Kevin Young*	.10
274	Jeff Frye	.05
275	*J.T. Bruett*	.05
276	*Todd Pratt*	.05
277	*Mike Butcher*	.05
278	*John Flaherty*	.10
279	*John Patterson*	.10
280	*Eric Hillman*	.05
281	*Bien Figueros*	.05
282	*Shane Reynolds*	.10
283	*Rich Rowland*	.05
284	*Steve Foster*	.05
285	*Dave Mlicki*	.05
286	Mike Piazza	1.00
287	*Mike Trombley*	.10
288	*Jim Pena*	.05
289	*Bob Ayrault*	.05
290	*Henry Mercedes*	.10
291	Bob Wickman	.05
292	*Jacob Brumfield*	.05
293	*David Hulse*	.10
294	Ryan Klesko	.25
295	Doug Linton	.05
296	Steve Cooke	.05
297	Eddie Zosky	.05
298	*Gerald Williams*	.10
299	*Jonathan Hurst*	.10
300	*Larry Carter*	.05
301	*William Pennyfeather*	.05
302	*Cesar Hernandez*	.05
303	*Steve Hosey*	.10
304	*Blas Minor*	.10
305	*Jeff Grotewold*	.10
306	*Bernardo Brito*	.05
307	*Rafael Bournigal*	.10
308	*Jeff Branson*	.10
309	*Tom Quinlan*	.05
310	*Pat Gomez*	.10
311	*Sterling Hitchcock*	.10
312	Kent Bottenfield	.05
313	Alan Trammell	.10
314	*Cris Colon*	.05
315	*Paul Wagner*	.05
316	*Matt Maysey*	.05
317	Mike Stanton	.05
318	*Rick Trlicek*	.05
319	*Kevin Rogers*	.10
320	*Mark Clark*	.10
321	Pedro Martinez	.20
322	*Al Martin*	.15
323	Mike Macfarlane	.05
324	*Rey Sanchez*	.10
325	*Roger Pavlik*	.05
326	Troy Neel	.10
327	*Kerry Woodson*	.05
328	*Wayne Kirby*	.10
329	*Ken Ryan*	.15
330	*Jesse Levis*	.05
331	James Austin	.05
332	Dan Walters	.05
333	Brian Williams	.05
334	Wil Cordero	.10
335	Bret Boone	.10

336	Hipolito Pichardo	.05
337	Pat Mahomes	.05
338	Andy Stankiewicz	.05
339	Jim Bullinger	.05
340	Archi Cianfrocco	.05
341	Ruben Amaro, Jr.	.05
342	Frank Seminara	.05
343	Pat Hentgen	.05
344	Dave Nilsson	.05
345	Mike Perez	.05
346	Tim Salmon	.25
347	*Tim Wakefield*	.15
348	Carlos Hernandez	.05
349	Donovan Osborne	.05
350	Denny Naegle	.05
351	Sam Militello	.05
352	Eric Fox	.05
353	John Doherty	.05
354	Chad Curtis	.05
355	Jeff Tackett	.05
356	Dave Fleming	.05
357	Pat Listach	.05
358	Kevin Wickander	.05
359	John VanderWal	.05
360	Arthur Rhodes	.05
361	Bob Scanlan	.05
362	Bob Zupcic	.05
363	Mel Rojas	.05
364	Jim Thome	.25
365	Bill Pecota	.05
366	Mark Carreon	.05
367	Mitch Williams	.05
368	Cal Eldred	.05
369	Stan Belinda	.05
370	Pat Kelly	.05
371	Pheal Cormier	.05
372	Juan Guzman	.05
373	Damon Berryhill	.05
374	Gary DiSarcina	.05
375	Norm Charlton	.05
376	Roberto Hernandez	.05
377	Scott Kamieniecki	.05
378	Rusty Meacham	.05
379	Kurt Stillwell	.05
380	Lloyd McClendon	.05
381	Mark Leonard	.05
382	Jerry Browne	.05
383	Glenn Davis	.05
384	Randy Johnson	.35
385	Mike Greenwell	.05
386	Scott Chiamparino	.05
387	George Bell	.05
388	Steve Olin	.05
389	Chuck McElroy	.05
390	Mark Gardner	.05
391	Rod Beck	.05
392	Dennis Rasmussen	.05
393	Charlie Leibrandt	.05
394	Julio Franco	.05
395	Pete Harnisch	.05
396	Sid Bream	.05
397	Milt Thompson	.05
398	Glenallen Hill	.05
399	Chico Walker	.05
400	Alex Cole	.05
401	Trevor Wilson	.05
402	Jeff Conine	.10
403	Kyle Abbott	.05
404	Tom Browning	.05
405	Jerald Clark	.05
406	Vince Horsman	.05
407	Kevin Mitchell	.05
408	Pete Smith	.05
409	Jeff Innis	.05
410	Mike Timlin	.05
411	Charlie Hayes	.05
412	Alex Fernandez	.10
413	Jeff Russell	.05
414	Jody Reed	.05
415	Mickey Morandini	.05
416	Darnell Coles	.05
417	Xavier Hernandez	.05
418	Steve Sax	.05
419	Joe Girardi	.05
420	Mike Fetters	.05
421	Danny Jackson	.05
422	Jim Gott	.05
423	Tim Belcher	.05
424	Jose Mesa	.05
425	Junior Felix	.05
426	Thomas Howard	.05
427	Julio Valera	.05
428	Dante Bichette	.25
429	Mike Sharperson	.05
430	Darryl Kile	.05
431	Lonnie Smith	.05
432	Monty Fariss	.05
433	Reggie Jefferson	.05
434	Bob McClure	.05
435	Craig Lefferts	.05
436	Duane Ward	.05
437	Shawn Abner	.05
438	Roberto Kelly	.05
439	Paul O'Neill	.15
440	Alan Mills	.05
441	Roger Mason	.05
442	Gary Pettis	.05
443	Steve Lake	.05
444	Gene Larkin	.05
445	Larry Anderson	.05
446	Doug Dascenzo	.05
447	Daryl Boston	.05
448	John Candelaria	.05
449	Storm Davis	.05
450	Tom Edens	.05
451	Mike Maddux	.05
452	Tim Naehring	.05
453	John Orton	.05
454	Joey Cora	.05
455	Chuck Crim	.05
456	Dan Plesac	.05
457	Mike Bielecki	.05
458	*Terry Jorgensen*	.05
459	John Habyan	.05
460	Pete O'Brien	.05
461	Jeff Treadway	.05
462	Frank Castillo	.05
463	Jimmy Jones	.05
464	Tommy Greene	.05
465	Tracy Woodson	.05
466	Rich Rodriguez	.05
467	Joe Hesketh	.05
468	Greg Myers	.05
469	Kirk McCaskill	.05
470	Ricky Bones	.05
471	Lenny Webster	.05
472	Francisco Cabrera	.05
473	Turner Ward	.05
474	Dwayne Henry	.05
475	Al Osuna	.05
476	Craig Wilson	.05
477	Chris Nabholz	.05
478	Rafael Belliard	.05
479	Terry Leach	.05
480	Tim Teufel	.05
481	Dennis Eckersley (Award Winner)	.05
482	Barry Bonds (Award Winner)	.20
483	Dennis Eckersley (Award Winner)	.05
484	Greg Maddux (Award Winner)	.50
485	Pat Listach (ROY)	.05
486	Eric Karros (ROY)	.15
487	*Jamie Arnold*	.10
488	B.J. Wallace	.10
489	*Derek Jeter*	10.00
490	*Jason Kendall*	1.00
491	Rick Helling	.05
492	*Derek Wallace*	.15
493	*Sean Lowe*	.10
494	*Shannon Stewart*	.35
495	*Benji Grigsby*	.15
496	*Todd Steverson*	.15
497	*Dan Serafini*	.15
498	Michael Tucker	.10
499	Chris Roberts (Draft Pick)	.10
500	*Pete Janicki* (Draft Pick)	.10
501	*Jeff Schmidt*	.10
502	Edgar Martinez (All-Star)	.05
503	Omar Vizquel (AS)	.05
504	Ken Griffey, Jr. (AS)	1.00
505	Kirby Puckett (AS)	.25
506	Joe Carter (AS)	.05
507	Ivan Rodriguez (AS)	.15
508	Jack Morris (AS)	.05
509	Dennis Eckersley (AS)	.05
510	Frank Thomas (AS)	.50
511	Roberto Alomar (AS)	.15
512	Mickey Morandini (Highlight)	.05
513	Dennis Eckersley (Highlight)	.05
514	Jeff Reardon (Highlight)	.05
515	Danny Tartabull (Highlight)	.05
516	Bip Roberts (Highlight)	.05
517	George Brett (Highlight)	.20
518	Robin Yount (Highlight)	.15
519	Kevin Gross (Highlight)	.05
520	Ed Sprague (World Series Highlight)	.05
521	Dave Winfield (World Series Highlight)	.10
522	Ozzie Smith (AS)	.15
523	Barry Bonds (AS)	.15
524	Andy Van Slyke (AS)	.05
525	Tony Gwynn (AS)	.25
526	Darren Daulton (AS)	.05
527	Greg Maddux (AS)	.50
528	Fred McGriff (AS)	.05
529	Lee Smith (AS)	.05
530	Ryne Sandberg (AS)	.25
531	Gary Sheffield (AS)	.15
532	Ozzie Smith (Dream Team)	.15
533	Kirby Puckett (Dream Team)	.25
534	Gary Sheffield (Dream Team)	.15
535	Andy Van Slyke (Dream Team)	.05
536	Ken Griffey, Jr. (Dream Team)	1.00
537	Ivan Rodriguez (Dream Team)	.10
538	Charles Nagy (Dream Team)	.05
539	Tom Glavine (Dream Team)	.10
540	Dennis Eckersley (Dream Team)	.05
541	Frank Thomas (Dream Team)	.50
542	Roberto Alomar (Dream Team)	.15
543	Sean Barry	.05
544	Mike Schooler	.05
545	Chuck Carr	.05
546	Lenny Harris	.05
547	Gary Scott	.05
548	Derek Lilliquist	.05
549	Brian Hunter	.05
550	Kirby Puckett (MOY)	.25
551	Jim Eisenreich	.05
552	Andre Dawson	.10
553	David Nied	.05
554	Spike Owen	.05
555	Greg Gagne	.05
556	Sid Fernandez	.05
557	Mark McGwire	2.00
558	Bryan Harvey	.05
559	Harold Reynolds	.05
560	Barry Bonds	.55
561	*Eric Wedge*	.05
562	Ozzie Smith	.35
563	Rick Sutcliffe	.05
564	Jeff Reardon	.05
565	*Alex Arias*	.05
566	Greg Swindell	.05
567	Brook Jacoby	.05
568	Pete Incaviglia	.05
569	*Butch Henry*	.10
570	Eric Davis	.10
571	Kevin Seitzer	.05
572	Tony Fernandez	.05
573	*Steve Reed*	.10
574	Cory Snyder	.05
575	Joe Carter	.10
576	Greg Maddux	1.00
577	Bert Blyleven	.05
578	Kevin Bass	.05
579	Carlton Fisk	.10
580	Doug Drabek	.05
581	Mark Gubicza	.05
582	Bobby Thigpen	.05
583	Chili Davis	.05
584	Scott Bankhead	.05
585	Harold Baines	.05
586	*Eric Young*	.20
587	Lance Parrish	.05
588	Juan Bell	.05
589	Bob Ojeda	.05
590	Joe Orsulak	.05
591	Benito Santiago	.05
592	Wade Boggs	.30
593	Robby Thompson	.05
594	Erik Plunk	.05
595	Hensley Meulens	.05
596	Lou Whitaker	.05
597	Dale Murphy	.10
598	Paul Molitor	.35
599	Greg W. Harris	.05
600	Darren Holmes	.05
601	Dave Martinez	.05
602	Tom Henke	.05
603	Mike Benjamin	.05
604	Rene Gonzales	.05
605	Roger McDowell	.05
606	Kirby Puckett	.75
607	Randy Myers	.05
608	Ruben Sierra	.05
609	Wilson Alvarez	.05
610	Dave Segui	.05
611	Juan Samuel	.05
612	Tom Brunansky	.05
613	Willie Randolph	.05
614	Tony Phillips	.05
615	Candy Maldonado	.05
616	Chris Bosio	.05
617	Bret Barberie	.05
618	Scott Sanderson	.05
619	Ron Darling	.05
620	Dave Winfield	.15
621	Mike Felder	.05
622	Greg Hibbard	.05
623	Mike Scioscia	.05
624	John Smiley	.05
625	Alejandro Pena	.05
626	Terry Steinbach	.05
627	Freddie Benavides	.05
628	Kevin Reimer	.05
629	Braulio Castillo	.05
630	Dave Stieb	.05
631	Dave Magadan	.05
632	Scott Fletcher	.05
633	Cris Carpenter	.05
634	Kevin Maas	.05
635	Todd Worrell	.05
636	Rob Deer	.05
637	Dwight Smith	.05
638	Chito Martinez	.05
639	Jimmy Key	.05
640	Greg Harris	.05
641	Mike Moore	.05
642	Pat Borders	.05
643	Bill Gullickson	.05
644	Gary Gaetti	.05
645	David Howard	.05
646	Jim Abbott	.05
647	Willie Wilson	.05
648	David Wells	.10
649	Andres Galarraga	.10
650	Vince Coleman	.05
651	Rob Dibble	.05
652	Frank Tanana	.05
653	Steve Decker	.05
654	David Cone	.10
655	Jack Armstrong	.05
656	Dave Stewart	.05
657	Billy Hatcher	.05
658	Tim Raines	.10
659	Walt Weiss	.05
660	Jose Lind	.05

1993 Score Boys of Summer

These cards were available as inserts only in Score 35-card Super Packs, about one in every four packs. Borderless fronts have a color action photo of the player superimposed over the sun. The player's name is in black script in a green strip at bottom, along with a subset logo. On back is a player portrait, again with the sun as a background. Subset, company, team and major league logos are in color on the right, and there is a short career summary on the green background at bottom.

		MT
Complete Set (30):		50.00
Common Player:		.75
1	Billy Ashley	.75
2	Tim Salmon	6.00
3	Pedro Martinez	10.00
4	Luis Mercedes	.75
5	Mike Piazza	30.00
6	Troy Neel	1.00
7	Melvin Nieves	.75
8	Ryan Klesko	2.00
9	Ryan Thompson	1.00
10	Kevin Young	.75
11	Gerald Williams	1.50
12	Willie Greene	1.50
13	John Patterson	.75
14	Carlos Garcia	1.50
15	Eddie Zosky	.75
16	Sean Berry	1.00
17	Rico Brogna	1.00
18	Larry Carter	.75
19	Bobby Ayala	.75
20	Alan Embree	.75
21	Donald Harris	.75
22	Sterling Hitchcock	1.00
23	David Nied	.75
24	Henry Mercedes	.75
25	Ozzie Canseco	.75
26	David Hulse	.75
27	Al Martin	1.00
28	Dan Wilson	1.00
29	Paul Miller	.75
30	Rich Rowland	.75

1993 Score The Franchise

These glossy inserts have full-bleed color action photos against a darkened background so that the player stands out. Cards could be found in 16-card packs only; odds of finding one are 1 in every 24 packs. The fronts have gold-foil highlights.

		MT
Complete Set (28):		100.00
Common Player:		1.00
1	Cal Ripken, Jr.	25.00
2	Roger Clemens	10.00
3	Mark Langston	1.00
4	Frank Thomas	15.00
5	Carlos Baerga	1.00
6	Cecil Fielder	1.00
7	Gregg Jefferies	1.00
8	Robin Yount	7.50
9	Kirby Puckett	12.00
10	Don Mattingly	12.00
11	Dennis Eckersley	1.00
12	Ken Griffey, Jr.	30.00
13	Juan Gonzalez	12.00
14	Roberto Alomar	5.00
15	Terry Pendleton	1.00
16	Ryne Sandberg	7.50
17	Barry Larkin	3.00
18	Jeff Bagwell	12.00
19	Brett Butler	1.00
20	Larry Walker	4.00
21	Bobby Bonilla	1.00
22	Darren Daulton	1.00
23	Andy Van Slyke	1.00
24	Ray Lankford	1.00
25	Gary Sheffield	4.00
26	Will Clark	2.00
27	Bryan Harvey	1.00
28	David Nied	1.00

1993 Score Gold Dream Team

This 11-player insert set consists of the same players in the regular set's Dream Team subset, except the cards are gold-foil stamped. There is an unnumbered header card in the set, which was available only via a mail-in offer.

		MT
Complete Set (12):		6.00
Common Player:		.25
1	Ozzie Smith	.75
2	Kirby Puckett	1.25
3	Gary Sheffield	.50
4	Andy Van Slyke	.25
5	Ken Griffey, Jr.	2.50
6	Ivan Rodriguez	.50
7	Charles Nagy	.25
8	Tom Glavine	.40
9	Dennis Eckersley	.40
10	Frank Thomas	1.50
11	Roberto Alomar	.50
---	Header card	.05

1993 Score Procter & Gamble Rookies

This set was available via a mail-in offer in the summer of 1993. Ten proofs of purchase were required along with a small amount of cash for postage. Fronts feature a player action photo in a diamond at center with the name, position and team logo in a home plate device at the bottom of the photo. At bottom center is a color photo of the player's home stadium, flanked by silver-foil stripes on a dark green background. Above the player photo are gold-foil Score and P&G logos on a dark green background. A center bar in gold foil has the word "ROOKIE" in green. Backs have a small player portrait photo at top against a dark green background. His name and position are in white at left and personal data at right. At center is a large color photo of the player's hometeam skyline, with the city name in gold type in a green stripe below. At bottom are complete major and minor league stats, MLB and MLBPA logos and the card number.

		MT
Complete Set (10):		5.00
Common Player:		.50
1	Wil Cordero	.50
2	Pedro Martinez	2.00
3	Bret Boone	1.00
4	Melvin Nieves	.50
5	Ryan Klesko	1.00
6	Ryan Thompson	.50
7	Kevin Young	.50
8	Willie Greene	.50
9	Eric Wedge	.50
10	David Nied	.50

1993 Score "The Naturals" Souvenir Sheet

Given away in conjunction with Score's appearance at major 1993 card shows, this souvenir sheet presents three each cards of the company's Score, Select and Pinnacle lines. The sheet is 8-1/2" x 11" and printed on heavy glossy paper. The front has a woodgrain background, the color card reproductions, brand and licensors' logos. At top each sheet is serially numbered from within an edition of 100,000. The back is blank. Player cards reproduced on the sheet are listed alphabetically here.

	MT
Souvenir Sheet:	10.00
Roberto Alomar (Score)	
Carlos Baerga (Pinnacle)	
Will Clark (Score)	
Roger Clemens (Score)	
Juan Gonzalez (Select)	
Bo Jackson (Pinnacle)	
Eric Karros (Pinnacle)	
John Olerud (Select)	
Nolan Ryan (Select)	

1994 Score Samples

Regular and Gold Rush versions of the first eight cards in the 1994 Score set were produced in a special promo version to familiarize buyers with the new issue. Cards have all zeroes in place of the 1993 stats and are overprinted on front and back with a diagonal black "SAMPLE". The samples were distributed in 11-card cello packs containing eight regular sample cards, one of the Gold Rush samples, a Barry Larkin Dream Team promo card and a header.

		MT
Complete Set (18):		120.00
Common Player:		1.50
1	Barry Bonds	4.50
1	Barry Bonds (Gold Rush)	15.00
2	John Olerud	2.00
2	John Olerud (Gold Rush)	6.00
3	Ken Griffey Jr.	7.50
3	Ken Griffey Jr. (Gold Rush)	35.00
4	Jeff Bagwell	4.00
4	Jeff Bagwell (Gold Rush)	15.00
5	John Burkett	1.50
5	John Burkett (Gold Rush)	5.00
6	Jack McDowell	1.50
6	Jack McDowell (Gold Rush)	5.00
7	Albert Belle	2.50
7	Albert Belle (Gold Rush)	7.50
8	Andres Galarraga	1.50
8	Andres Galarraga (Gold Rush)	6.00
5	Barry Larkin (Dream Team)	4.50
--	Hobby Header Card	.03
--	Retail Header Card	.03

1994 Score

Score's 1994 set, with a new design and UV coating, was issued in two series of 330 cards each. The cards, which use more action photos than before, have dark blue borders with the player's name in a team color-coded strip at the bottom. A special Gold Rush card, done for each card in the set, is included in every pack. Series I includes American League checklists, which are printed on the backs of cards depicting panoramic views of each team's ballpark. Series II has the National League team checklists. Insert sets include Dream Team players, and National (Series I packs) and American League Gold Stars (Series II packs), which use the Gold Rush process and appear once every 18 packs.

		MT
Complete Set (660):		20.00
Common Player:		.05
Gold Rush: 3X		
Series 1 or 2 Wax Box:		30.00
1	Barry Bonds	.35
2	John Olerud	.15
3	Ken Griffey, Jr.	1.25
4	Jeff Bagwell	.50
5	John Burkett	.05
6	Jack McDowell	.05
7	Albert Belle	.20
8	Andres Galarraga	.10
9	Mike Mussina	.15
10	Will Clark	.15
11	Travis Fryman	.10
12	Tony Gwynn	.30
13	Robin Yount	.20
14	Dave Magadan	.05
15	Paul O'Neill	.10
16	Ray Lankford	.10
17	Damion Easley	.05
18	Andy Van Slyke	.05
19	Brian McRae	.05
20	Ryne Sandberg	.25
21	Kirby Puckett	.35
22	Dwight Gooden	.10
23	Don Mattingly	.65
24	Kevin Mitchell	.05
25	Roger Clemens	.35
26	Eric Karros	.10
27	Juan Gonzalez	.35
28	John Kruk	.05
29	Gregg Jefferies	.05
30	Tom Glavine	.10
31	Ivan Rodriguez	.25
32	Jay Bell	.05
33	Randy Johnson	.15
34	Darren Daulton	.05
35	Rickey Henderson	.20
36	Eddie Murray	.15
37	Brian Harper	.05
38	Delino DeShields	.05
39	Jose Lind	.05
40	Benito Santiago	.05
41	Frank Thomas	.75
42	Mark Grace	.15
43	Roberto Alomar	.25
44	Andy Benes	.05
45	Luis Polonia	.05
46	Brett Butler	.05
47	Terry Steinbach	.05
48	Craig Biggio	.15
49	Greg Vaughn	.10
50	Charlie Hayes	.05
51	Mickey Tettleton	.05
52	Jose Rijo	.05
53	Carlos Baerga	.10
54	Jeff Blauser	.05
55	Leo Gomez	.05
56	Bob Tewksbury	.05
57	Mo Vaughn	.20
58	Orlando Merced	.05
59	Tino Martinez	.10
60	Len Dykstra	.05
61	Jose Canseco	.15
62	Tony Fernandez	.05
63	Donovan Osborne	.05
64	Ken Hill	.05
65	Kent Hrbek	.05
66	Bryan Harvey	.05
67	Wally Joyner	.05
68	Derrick May	.05
69	Lance Johnson	.05
70	Willie McGee	.05
71	Mark Langston	.05
72	Terry Pendleton	.05
73	Joe Carter	.10
74	Barry Larkin	.10
75	Jimmy Key	.05
76	Joe Girardi	.05
77	B.J. Surhoff	.05
78	Pete Harnisch	.05
79	Lou Whitaker	.05
80	Cory Snyder	.05
81	Kenny Lofton	.25
82	Fred McGriff	.15
83	Mike Greenwell	.05
84	Mike Perez	.05
85	Cal Ripken, Jr.	1.00
86	Don Slaught	.05
87	Omar Vizquel	.05
88	Curt Schilling	.10
89	Chuck Knoblauch	.10
90	Moises Alou	.10
91	Greg Gagne	.05
92	Bret Saberhagen	.05
93	Ozzie Guillen	.05
94	Matt Williams	.10
95	Chad Curtis	.05
96	Mike Harkey	.05
97	Devon White	.10
98	Walt Weiss	.05
99	Kevin Brown	.10
100	Gary Sheffield	.10
101	Wade Boggs	.20
102	Orel Hershiser	.10
103	Tony Phillips	.05
104	Andujar Cedeno	.05
105	Bill Spiers	.05
106	Otis Nixon	.05
107	Felix Fermin	.05
108	Bip Roberts	.05
109	Dennis Eckersley	.05
110	Dante Bichette	.15
111	Ben McDonald	.05
112	Jim Poole	.05
113	John Dopson	.05
114	Rob Dibble	.05
115	Jeff Treadway	.05
116	Ricky Jordan	.05
117	Mike Henneman	.05
118	Willie Blair	.05
119	Doug Henry	.05
120	Gerald Perry	.05
121	Greg Myers	.05
122	John Franco	.05
123	Roger Mason	.05
124	Chris Hammond	.05
125	Hubie Brooks	.05
126	Kent Mercker	.05
127	Jim Abbott	.05
128	Kevin Bass	.05
129	Rick Aguilera	.05
130	Mitch Webster	.05
131	Eric Plunk	.05
132	Mark Carreon	.05
133	Dave Stewart	.05
134	Willie Wilson	.05
135	Dave Fleming	.05
136	Jeff Tackett	.05
137	Geno Petralli	.05
138	Gene Harris	.05
139	Scott Bankhead	.05
140	Trevor Wilson	.05
141	Alvaro Espinoza	.05
142	Ryan Bowen	.05
143	Mike Moore	.05
144	Bill Pecota	.05
145	Jaime Navarro	.05
146	Jack Daugherty	.05
147	Bob Wickman	.05
148	Chris Jones	.05
149	Todd Stottlemyre	.05
150	Brian Williams	.05
151	Chuck Finley	.05
152	Lenny Harris	.05
153	Alex Fernandez	.10
154	Candy Maldonado	.05
155	Jeff Montgomery	.05
156	David West	.05
157	Mark Williamson	.05
158	Milt Thompson	.05
159	Ron Darling	.05
160	Stan Belinda	.05
161	Henry Cotto	.05
162	Mel Rojas	.05
163	Doug Strange	.05
164	Rene Arocha (1993 Rookie)	.10
165	Tim Hulett	.05
166	Steve Avery	.05
167	Jim Thome	.10
168	Tom Browning	.05
169	Mario Diaz	.05
170	Steve Reed (1993 Rookie)	.05
171	Scott Livingstone	.05
172	Chris Donnels	.05
173	John Jaha	.05
174	Carlos Hernandez	.05
175	Dion James	.05
176	Bud Black	.05
177	Tony Castillo	.05
178	Jose Guzman	.05
179	Torey Lovullo	.05
180	John Vander Wal	.05
181	Mike LaValliere	.05
182	Sid Fernandez	.05
183	Brent Mayne	.05
184	Terry Mulholland	.05
185	Willie Banks	.05
186	Steve Cooke (1993 Rookie)	.05
187	Brent Gates (1993 Rookie)	.10
188	Erik Pappas (1993 Rookie)	.10
189	Bill Haselman (1993 Rookie)	.05
190	Fernando Valenzuela	.05
191	Gary Redus	.05
192	Danny Darwin	.05
193	Mark Portugal	.05
194	Derek Lilliquist	.05
195	Charlie O'Brien	.05
196	Matt Nokes	.05
197	Danny Sheaffer	.05
198	Bill Gullickson	.05
199	Alex Arias (1993 Rookie)	.10
200	Mike Fetters	.05
201	Brian Jordan	.10
202	Joe Grahe	.05
203	Tom Candiotti	.05
204	Jeremy Stanton	.05
205	Mike Stanton	.05
206	David Howard	.05
207	Darren Holmes	.05
208	Rick Honeycutt	.05
209	Danny Jackson	.05
210	Rich Amaral (1993 Rookie)	.05
211	Blas Minor (1993 Rookie)	.10
212	Kenny Rogers	.05
213	Jim Leyritz	.05
214	Mike Morgan	.05
215	Dan Gladden	.05
216	Randy Velarde	.05
217	Mitch Williams	.05
218	Hipolito Pichardo	.05
219	Dave Burba	.05
220	Wilson Alvarez	.05
221	Bob Zupcic	.05
222	Francisco Cabrera	.05
223	Julio Valera	.05
224	Paul Assenmacher	.05
225	Jeff Branson	.05
226	Todd Frohwirth	.05
227	Armando Reynoso	.05
228	Rich Rowland (1993 Rookie)	.05
229	Freddie Benavides	.05
230	Wayne Kirby (1993 Rookie)	.05
231	Darryl Kile	.05
232	Skeeter Barnes	.05
233	Ramon Martinez	.10
234	Tom Gordon	.05
235	Dave Gallagher	.05
236	Ricky Bones	.05
237	Larry Andersen	.05
238	Pat Meares (1993 Rookie)	.05
239	Zane Smith	.05
240	Tim Leary	.05
241	Phil Clark	.05
242	Danny Cox	.05
243	Mike Jackson	.05
244	Mike Gallego	.05
245	Lee Smith	.05
246	Todd Jones (1993 Rookie)	.05
247	Steve Bedrosian	.05
248	Troy Neel	.10
249	Jose Bautista	.05
250	Steve Frey	.05
251	Jeff Reardon	.05
252	Stan Javier	.05
253	Mo Sanford (1993 Rookie)	.05
254	Steve Sax	.05
255	Luis Aquino	.05
256	Domingo Jean (1993 Rookie)	.05
257	Scott Servais	.05
258	Brad Pennington (1993 Rookie)	.05
259	Dave Hansen	.05
260	Goose Gossage	.05
261	Jeff Fassero	.05
262	Junior Ortiz	.05
263	Anthony Young	.05
264	Chris Bosio	.05
265	Ruben Amaro, Jr.	.05
266	Mark Eichhorn	.05
267	Dave Clark	.05
268	Gary Thurman	.05
269	Les Lancaster	.05
270	Jamie Moyer	.05
271	Ricky Gutierrez (1993 Rookie)	.10
272	Greg Harris	.05
273	Mike Benjamin	.05
274	Gene Nelson	.05
275	Damon Berryhill	.05
276	Scott Radinsky	.05
277	Mike Aldrete	.05
278	Jerry DiPoto (1993 Rookie)	.05
279	Chris Haney	.05
280	Richie Lewis (1993 Rookie)	.05
281	Jarvis Brown	.05
282	Juan Bell	.05
283	Joe Klink	.05
284	Graeme Lloyd (1993 Rookie)	.05
285	Casey Candaele	.05
286	Bob MacDonald	.05
287	Mike Sharperson	.05
288	Gene Larkin	.05
289	Brian Barnes	.05
290	David McCarty (1993 Rookie)	.10
291	Jeff Innis	.05
292	Bob Patterson	.05
293	Ben Rivera	.05
294	John Habyan	.05
295	Rich Rodriguez	.05
296	Edwin Nunez	.05
297	Rod Brewer	.05
298	Mike Timlin	.05
299	Jesse Orosco	.05
300	Gary Gaetti	.05
301	Todd Benzinger	.05
302	Jeff Nelson	.05
303	Rafael Belliard	.05
304	Matt Whiteside	.05
305	Vinny Castilla	.10
306	Matt Turner	.05
307	Eduardo Perez	.05
308	Joel Johnston	.05
309	Chris Gomez	.05
310	Pat Rapp	.05
311	Jim Tatum	.05
312	Kirk Rueter	.05
313	John Flaherty	.05
314	Tom Kramer	.05
315	Mark Whiten (Highlights)	.05
316	Chris Bosio (Highlights)	.05
317	Orioles Checklist	.05
318	Red Sox Checklist	.05
319	Angels Checklist	.05
320	White Sox Checklist	.05
321	Indians Checklist	.05
322	Tigers Checklist	.05
323	Royals Checklist	.05
324	Brewers Checklist	.05
325	Twins Checklist	.05

326	Yankees Checklist	.05
327	Athletics Checklist	.05
328	Mariners Checklist	.05
329	Rangers Checklist	.05
330	Blue Jays Checklist	.05
331	Frank Viola	.05
332	Ron Gant	.10
333	Charles Nagy	.10
334	Roberto Kelly	.05
335	Brady Anderson	.10
336	Alex Cole	.05
337	Alan Trammell	.10
338	Derek Bell	.10
339	Bernie Williams	.25
340	Jose Offerman	.05
341	Bill Wegman	.05
342	Ken Caminiti	.15
343	Pat Borders	.05
344	Kirt Manwaring	.05
345	Chili Davis	.05
346	Steve Buechele	.05
347	Robin Ventura	.15
348	Teddy Higuera	.05
349	Jerry Browne	.05
350	Scott Kamieniecki	.05
351	Kevin Tapani	.05
352	Marquis Grissom	.05
353	Jay Buhner	.05
354	Dave Hollins	.05
355	Dan Wilson	.05
356	Bob Walk	.05
357	Chris Hoiles	.05
358	Todd Zeile	.05
359	Kevin Appier	.05
360	Chris Sabo	.05
361	David Segui	.05
362	Jerald Clark	.05
363	Tony Pena	.05
364	Steve Finley	.05
365	Roger Pavlik	.05
366	John Smoltz	.10
367	Scott Fletcher	.05
368	Jody Reed	.05
369	David Wells	.10
370	Jose Vizcaino	.05
371	Pat Listach	.05
372	Orestes Destrade	.05
373	Danny Tartabull	.05
374	Greg W. Harris	.05
375	Juan Guzman	.05
376	Larry Walker	.10
377	Gary DiSarcina	.05
378	Bobby Bonilla	.05
379	Tim Raines	.10
380	Tommy Greene	.05
381	Chris Gwynn	.05
382	Jeff King	.05
383	Shane Mack	.05
384	Ozzie Smith	.20
385	*Eddie Zambrano*	.05
386	Mike Devereaux	.05
387	Erik Hanson	.05
388	Scott Cooper	.05
389	Dean Palmer	.05
390	John Wetteland	.05
391	Reggie Jefferson	.05
392	Mark Lemke	.05
393	Cecil Fielder	.05
394	Reggie Sanders	.10
395	Darryl Hamilton	.05
396	Daryl Boston	.05
397	Pat Kelly	.05
398	Joe Orsulak	.05
399	Ed Sprague	.05
400	Eric Anthony	.05
401	Scott Sanderson	.05
402	Jim Gott	.05
403	Ron Karkovice	.05
404	Phil Plantier	.05
405	David Cone	.10
406	Robby Thompson	.05
407	Dave Winfield	.15
408	Dwight Smith	.05
409	Ruben Sierra	.05
410	Jack Armstrong	.05
411	Mike Felder	.05
412	Wil Cordero	.05
413	Julio Franco	.05
414	Howard Johnson	.05
415	Mark McLemore	.05
416	Pete Incaviglia	.05
417	John Valentin	.05
418	Tim Wakefield	.05
419	Jose Mesa	.05
420	Bernard Gilkey	.10
421	Kirk Gibson	.05
422	Dave Justice	.10
423	Tom Brunansky	.05
424	John Smiley	.05
425	Kevin Maas	.05
426	Doug Drabek	.05
427	Paul Molitor	.20
428	Darryl Strawberry	.10
429	Tim Naehring	.05
430	Bill Swift	.05
431	Ellis Burks	.05
432	Greg Hibbard	.05
433	Felix Jose	.05
434	Bret Barberie	.05
435	Pedro Munoz	.05
436	Darrin Fletcher	.05
437	Bobby Witt	.05
438	Wes Chamberlain	.05
439	Mackey Sasser	.05
440	Mark Whiten	.05
441	Harold Reynolds	.05
442	Greg Olson	.05
443	Billy Hatcher	.05
444	Joe Oliver	.05
445	Sandy Alomar Jr.	.10
446	Tim Wallach	.05
447	Karl Rhodes	.05
448	Royce Clayton	.05
449	Cal Eldred	.05
450	Rick Wilkins	.05
451	Mike Stanley	.05
452	Charlie Hough	.05
453	Jack Morris	.05
454	*Jon Ratliff*	.05
455	Rene Gonzales	.05
456	Eddie Taubensee	.05
457	Roberto Hernandez	.05
458	Todd Hundley	.10
459	Mike MacFarlane	.05
460	Mickey Morandini	.05
461	Scott Erickson	.05
462	Lonnie Smith	.05
463	Dave Henderson	.05
464	Ryan Klesko	.10
465	Edgar Martinez	.05
466	Tom Pagnozzi	.05
467	Charlie Leibrandt	.05
468	*Brian Anderson*	.10
469	Harold Baines	.05
470	Tim Belcher	.05
471	Andre Dawson	.10
472	Eric Young	.05
473	Paul Sorrento	.05
474	Luis Gonzalez	.10
475	Rob Deer	.05
476	Mike Piazza	.75
477	Kevin Reimer	.05
478	Jeff Gardner	.05
479	Melido Perez	.05
480	Darren Lewis	.05
481	Duane Ward	.05
482	Rey Sanchez	.05
483	Mark Lewis	.05
484	Jeff Conine	.05
485	Joey Cora	.05
486	*Trot Nixon*	.35
487	Kevin McReynolds	.05
488	Mike Lansing	.05
489	Mike Pagliarulo	.05
490	Mariano Duncan	.05
491	Mike Bordick	.05
492	Kevin Young	.05
493	Dave Valle	.05
494	*Wayne Gomes*	.10
495	Rafael Palmeiro	.15
496	Deion Sanders	.15
497	Rick Sutcliffe	.05
498	Randy Milligan	.05
499	Carlos Quintana	.05
500	Chris Turner	.05
501	Thomas Howard	.05
502	Greg Swindell	.05
503	Chad Kreuter	.05
504	Eric Davis	.05
505	Dickie Thon	.05
506	*Matt Drews*	.10
507	Spike Owen	.05
508	Rod Beck	.05
509	Pat Hentgen	.05
510	Sammy Sosa	.75
511	J.T. Snow	.05
512	Chuck Carr	.05
513	Bo Jackson	.10
514	Dennis Martinez	.05
515	Phil Hiatt	.05
516	Jeff Kent	.05
517	*Brooks Kieschnick*	.20
518	*Kirk Presley*	.15
519	Kevin Seitzer	.05
520	Carlos Garcia	.05
521	Mike Blowers	.05
522	Luis Alicea	.05
523	David Hulse	.05
524	Greg Maddux	.75
525	Gregg Olson	.05
526	Hal Morris	.05
527	Daron Kirkreit	.05
528	David Nied	.05
529	Jeff Russell	.05
530	Kevin Gross	.05
531	John Doherty	.05
532	*Matt Brunson*	.10
533	Dave Nilsson	.05
534	Randy Myers	.05
535	Steve Farr	.05
536	*Billy Wagner*	.20
537	Darnell Coles	.05
538	Frank Tanana	.05
539	Tim Salmon	.10
540	Kim Batiste	.05
541	George Bell	.05
542	Tom Henke	.05
543	Sam Horn	.05
544	Doug Jones	.05
545	Scott Leius	.05
546	Al Martin	.05
547	Bob Welch	.05
548	*Scott Christman*	.05
549	Norm Charlton	.05
550	Mark McGwire	1.25
551	Greg McMichael	.05
552	Tim Costo	.05
553	Rodney Bolton	.05
554	Pedro Martinez	.10
555	Marc Valdes	.05
556	Darrell Whitmore	.05
557	Tim Bogar	.05
558	Steve Karsay	.05
559	Danny Bautista	.05
560	Jeffrey Hammonds	.10
561	Aaron Sele	.05
562	Russ Springer	.05
563	Jason Bere	.05
564	Billy Brewer	.05
565	Sterling Hitchcock	.05
566	Bobby Munoz	.05
567	Craig Paquette	.05
568	Bret Boone	.05
569	Dan Peltier	.05
570	Jeromy Burnitz	.05
571	*John Wasdin*	.10
572	Chipper Jones	.75
573	*Jamey Wright*	.10
574	Jeff Granger	.05
575	*Jay Powell*	.10
576	Ryan Thompson	.05
577	Lou Frazier	.05
578	Paul Wagner	.05
579	Brad Ausmus	.05
580	Jack Voigt	.05
581	Kevin Rogers	.05
582	Damon Buford	.10
583	Paul Quantrill	.05
584	Marc Newfield	.05
585	*Derrek Lee*	.35
586	Shane Reynolds	.05
587	Cliff Floyd	.10
588	Jeff Schwarz	.05
589	*Ross Powell*	.05
590	Gerald Williams	.05
591	Mike Trombley	.05
592	Ken Ryan	.05
593	John O'Donoghue	.05
594	Rod Correia	.05
595	Darrell Sherman	.05
596	Steve Scarsone	.05
597	Sherman Obando	.05
598	Kurt Abbott	.05
599	Dave Telgheder	.05
600	Rick Trlicek	.05
601	Carl Everett	.10
602	Luis Ortiz	.05
603	*Larry Luebbers*	.05
604	Kevin Roberson	.05
605	Butch Huskey	.10
606	Benji Gil	.05
607	Todd Van Poppel	.05
608	Mark Hutton	.05
609	Chip Hale	.05
610	Matt Maysey	.05
611	Scott Ruffcorn	.05
612	Hilly Hathaway	.05
613	Allen Watson	.05
614	Carlos Delgado	.15
615	Roberto Mejia	.05
616	Turk Wendell	.05
617	Tony Tarasco	.05
618	Raul Mondesi	.25
619	Kevin Stocker	.10
620	Javier Lopez	.15
621	*Keith Kessinger*	.10
622	Bob Hamelin	.05
623	John Roper	.05
624	Len Dykstra (World Series)	.05
625	Joe Carter (World Series)	.05
626	Jim Abbott (Highlight)	.05
627	Lee Smith (Highlight)	.05
628	Ken Griffey, Jr. (HL)	.75
629	Dave Winfield (Highlight)	.05
630	Darryl Kile (Highlight)	.05
631	Frank Thomas (MVP)	.45
632	Barry Bonds (MVP)	.15
633	Jack McDowell (Cy Young)	.05
634	Greg Maddux (Cy Young)	.50
635	Tim Salmon (ROY)	.10
636	Mike Piazza (ROY)	.50
637	*Brian Turang*	.10
638	Rondell White	.15
639	Nigel Wilson	.05
640	*Torii Hunter*	.10
641	Salomon Torres	.05
642	Kevin Higgins	.05
643	Eric Wedge	.05
644	Roger Salkeld	.05
645	Manny Ramirez	.60
646	Jeff McNeely	.05
647	Braves Checklist	.05
648	Cubs Checklist	.05
649	Reds Checklist	.05
650	Rockies Checklist	.05
651	Marlins Checklist	.05
652	Astros Checklist	.05
653	Dodgers Checklist	.05
654	Expos Checklist	.05
655	Mets Checklist	.05
656	Phillies Checklist	.05
657	Pirates Checklist	.05
658	Cardinals Checklist	.05
659	Padres Checklist	.05
660	Giants Checklist	.05

1994 Score Gold Rush

Opting to include one insert card in each pack of its 1994 product, Score created a "Gold Rush" version of each card in its regular set. Gold Rush cards are basically the same as their counterparts with a few enhancements. Card fronts are printed on foil with a gold border and a Score Gold Rush logo in one of the upper corners. The background of the photo has been metalized, allowing the color player portion to stand out in sharp contrast. Backs are identical to the regular cards except for the appearance of a large Gold Rush logo under the typography.

	MT
Complete Set (660):	150.00
Common Player:	.25
Stars: 3X	

(See 1994 Score for checklist and base card values.)

1994 Score Boys of Summer

A heavy emphasis on rookies and recent rookies is noted in this 1994 Score insert set. Released in two series, cards #1-30 with Score's Series I and #31-60 packaged with Series II, card fronts feature a color action photo on which the background has been rendered in a blurred watercolor effect. A hot-color aura separates the player from the background. The player's name appears vertically in gold foil. Backs have backgrounds in reds and orange with a portrait-style player photo on one side and a large "Boys of Summer" logo on the other. A short description of the player's talents appears at center.

		MT
Complete Set (60):		65.00
Common Player:		.50
1	Jeff Conine	1.00
2	Aaron Sele	.75
3	Kevin Stocker	.50
4	Pat Meares	.50
5	Jeromy Burnitz	1.00
6	Mike Piazza	10.00
7	Allen Watson	.50
8	Jeffrey Hammonds	.75
9	Kevin Roberson	.50
10	Hilly Hathaway	.50
11	Kirk Reuter	.50
12	Eduardo Perez	.50
13	Ricky Gutierrez	.50
14	Domingo Jean	.50
15	David Nied	.50
16	Wayne Kirby	.50
17	Mike Lansing	1.00
18	Jason Bere	.50
19	Brent Gates	1.00
20	Javier Lopez	3.00
21	Greg McMichael	.50
22	David Hulse	.50
23	Roberto Mejia	.50
24	Tim Salmon	2.50
25	Rene Arocha	.50
26	Bret Boone	1.00
27	David McCarty	.50
28	Todd Van Poppel	.50
29	Lance Painter	.50
30	Erik Pappas	.50
31	Chuck Carr	.50
32	Mark Hutton	.50
33	Jeff McNeely	.50
34	Willie Greene	.50
35	Nigel Wilson	.50
36	Rondell White	2.50
37	Brian Turang	.50
38	Manny Ramirez	9.00
39	Salomon Torres	.50
40	Melvin Nieves	.50
41	Ryan Klesko	1.00
42	Keith Kessinger	.50
43	Eric Wedge	.50
44	Bob Hamelin	.50
45	Carlos Delgado	1.50
46	Marc Newfield	.50
47	Raul Mondesi	5.00
48	Tim Costo	.50
49	Pedro Martinez	2.50
50	Steve Karsay	.75
51	Danny Bautista	.50
52	Butch Huskey	1.00
53	Kurt Abbott	.75
54	Darrell Sherman	.50
55	Damon Buford	1.00
56	Ross Powell	.50
57	Darrell Whitmore	.50
58	Chipper Jones	10.00
59	Jeff Granger	.50
60	Cliff Floyd	1.00

1994 Score The Cycle

Leaders in the previous season's production of singles, doubles, triples and home runs are featured in this insert set which was packaged with Series II Score. Player action photos pop out of a circle at center and are surrounded by dark blue borders. "The Cycle" in printed in green at top. The player's name is in gold foil at bottom, printed over an infield diagram in a green strip. The stat which earned the player inclusion in the set is in gold foil at bottom right. On back are the rankings for the statistical category. Cards are numbered with a "TC" prefix.

		MT
Complete Set (20):		275.00
Common Player:		5.00
1	Brett Butler	6.00
2	Kenny Lofton	25.00
3	Paul Molitor	12.00
4	Carlos Baerga	6.00
5	Gregg Jefferies, Tony Phillips	5.00
6	John Olerud	6.00
7	Charlie Hayes	5.00
8	Len Dykstra	5.00
9	Dante Bichette	8.00
10	Devon White	5.00
11	Lance Johnson	5.00
12	Joey Cora, Steve Finley	5.00
13	Tony Fernandez	5.00
14	David Hulse, Brett Butler	5.00
15	Jay Bell, Brian McRae, Mickey Morandini	5.00
16	Juan Gonzalez, Barry Bonds	20.00
17	Ken Griffey, Jr.	65.00
18	Frank Thomas	25.00
19	Dave Justice	12.00
20	Matt Williams, Albert Belle	12.00

1994 Score Dream Team

Score's 1994 "Dream Team," one top player at each position, was featured in a 10-card insert set. The stars were decked out in vintage uniforms and equipment for the photos. Green and black bars at top and bottom frame the photo, and all printing on the front is in gold foil. Backs have a white background with green highlights. A color player portrait photo is featured, along with a brief justification for the player's selection to the squad. Cards are UV coated on both sides. Stated odds of finding a Dream Team insert were given as one per 72 packs.

		MT
Complete Set (10):		85.00
Common Player:		4.00
1	Mike Mussina	8.00
2	Tom Glavine	6.00
3	Don Mattingly	25.00
4	Carlos Baerga	4.00
5	Barry Larkin	7.50
6	Matt Williams	7.50
7	Juan Gonzalez	25.00
8	Andy Van Slyke	4.00
9	Larry Walker	7.50
10	Mike Stanley	4.00

1994 Score Gold Stars

Limited to inclusion in hobby packs, Score's 60-card "Gold Stars" insert set features 30 National League players, found in Series I packs, and 30 American Leaguers inserted with Series II. Stated odds of finding a Gold Stars card were listed on the wrapper as one in 18 packs. A notation on the cards' back indicates that no more than 6,500 sets of Gold Stars were produced. The high-tech cards feature a color player action photo, the full-bleed background of which has been converted to metallic tones. Backs have a graduated gold background with a portrait-style color player photo.

		MT
Complete Set (60):		215.00
Common Player:		1.00
1	Barry Bonds	10.00
2	Orlando Merced	1.00
3	Mark Grace	3.00
4	Darren Daulton	1.00
5	Jeff Blauser	1.00
6	Deion Sanders	3.00
7	John Kruk	1.00
8	Jeff Bagwell	15.00
9	Gregg Jefferies	1.00
10	Matt Williams	3.00
11	Andres Galarraga	3.00
12	Jay Bell	1.00
13	Mike Piazza	20.00
14	Ron Gant	1.00
15	Barry Larkin	2.50
16	Tom Glavine	2.00
17	Len Dykstra	1.00
18	Fred McGriff	2.00
19	Andy Van Slyke	1.00
20	Gary Sheffield	2.50
21	John Burkett	1.00
22	Dante Bichette	4.00
23	Tony Gwynn	15.00
24	Dave Justice	2.00
25	Marquis Grissom	1.50
26	Bobby Bonilla	1.00
27	Larry Walker	4.00
28	Brett Butler	1.00
29	Robby Thompson	1.00
30	Jeff Conine	1.00
31	Joe Carter	1.00
32	Ken Griffey, Jr.	30.00
33	Juan Gonzalez	15.00
34	Rickey Henderson	2.00
35	Bo Jackson	1.50
36	Cal Ripken, Jr.	25.00
37	John Olerud	2.00
38	Carlos Baerga	1.00
39	Jack McDowell	1.00
40	Cecil Fielder	1.00
41	Kenny Lofton	6.00
42	Roberto Alomar	6.00
43	Randy Johnson	5.00
44	Tim Salmon	4.00
45	Frank Thomas	15.00
46	Albert Belle	8.00
47	Greg Vaughn	1.50
48	Travis Fryman	1.00
49	Don Mattingly	8.00
50	Wade Boggs	4.00
51	Mo Vaughn	6.00
52	Kirby Puckett	8.00
53	Devon White	1.00
54	Tony Phillips	1.00
55	Brian Harper	1.00
56	Chad Curtis	1.00
57	Paul Molitor	6.00
58	Ivan Rodriguez	8.00
59	Rafael Palmeiro	3.00
60	Brian McRae	1.00

1994 Score Cal Ripken, Jr.

Although the cards themselves do not indicate it, this issue was co-sponsored by Burger King and Coke, and distributed in BK restaurants in the Baltimore-Washington area. Cards were available in three-card packs for 25 cents with the purchase of a Coke product. Each pack contains two regular cards and a gold card. Each of the nine cards could be found in a regular and gold version. Cards feature color photos with a semi-circular black border at top or left. "Score '94" appears in orange in one of the upper corners, along with an Orioles logo. Cal Ripken, Jr.'s name appears at the bottom. On the gold premium version, there is a gold-foil circle around the Orioles logo and Ripken's name appears in gold, rather than white. Backs have a smaller color photo, again meeting at a semi-circular edge with the black border at left and bottom. In the black are another Score logo, a card number, an Orioles logo, a headline and a few career details and/or stats. Cards are UV coated on each side. Several hundred of the cards were personally autographed by Ripken and distributed in a drawing.

		MT
Complete Set (9):		6.00
Complete Set, Gold (9):		14.00
Common Player:		1.00
Common Card, Gold:		2.50
Autographed Card:		300.00
1	Double Honors	.25
1a	Double Honors (gold)	.75
2	Perennial All-Star	.25
2a	Perennial All-Star (gold)	.75
3	Peerless Power	.25
3a	Peerless Power (gold)	.75
4	Fitness Fan	.25
4a	Fitness Fan (gold)	.75
5	Prime Concerns	.25
5a	Prime Concerns (gold)	.75
6	Home Run Club	.25
6a	Home Run Club (gold)	.75
7	The Iron Man	.25
7a	The Iron Man (gold)	.75
8	Heavy Hitter	.25
8a	Heavy Hitter (gold)	.75
9	Gold Glover	.25
9a	Gold Glover (gold)	.75

1994 Score Rookie/Traded Samples

To introduce the various types of cards which would be included in the 1994 Score Rookie/Traded set, the company produced this sample set. Cards are virtually identical to the issued versions except for the overprint "SAMPLE" running diagonally on front and back. The Rafael Palmeiro "Changing Places" sample card does not feature the red foil logo found on issued cards.

		MT
Complete Set (11):		20.00
Common Player:		2.00
1RT	Lee Smith	1.00
2CP	Rafael Palmeiro (Changing Places)	2.00
2RT	Will Clark	4.00
2SU	Manny Ramirez (Super Rookie)	5.00
3RT	Bo Jackson (Gold Rush)	2.00
4RT	Ellis Burks	1.00
5RT	Eddie Murray	4.00
6RT	Delino DeShields	1.00
102RT	Carlos Delgado	2.00
---	September Call-Up Winner Card	1.00
---	Hobby header card	1.00
---	Retail header card	1.00

1994 Score Rookie/Traded

Score Rookie & Traded completed the 1994 Score baseball issue with a 165-card update set. These were available in both retail and hobby packs. Score issued Super Rookies and Changing Places insert sets, as well as a Traded Redemption card and a parallel Gold Rush set. Basic cards features red front borders. Team logos are in a bottom corner in a gold polygon. One of the upper corners contains a green polygon with a gold Score logo. Most cards #71-163 feature a square multi-colored "Rookie '94" logo in a lower corner. Backs of all cards have a purple background. Traded players' card backs are vertical and contain two additional photos. Backs of the rookie cards are horizontal and feature a portrait photo at left. The "Rookie '94" logo is repeated in the upper-right corner. This is in reverse of the card fronts, on which traded players have a single photo and rookie cards have both portrait and action photos.

		MT
Complete Set (165):		8.00
Common Player:		.05
Wax Box:		25.00
1	Will Clark	.25
2	Lee Smith	.05
3	Bo Jackson	.15
4	Ellis Burks	.10
5	Eddie Murray	.20
6	Delino DeShields	.05
7	Erik Hanson	.05
8	Rafael Palmeiro	.25
9	Luis Polonia	.05
10	Omar Vizquel	.10
11	Kurt Abbott	.05
12	Vince Coleman	.05
13	Rickey Henderson	.40
14	Terry Mulholland	.05
15	Greg Hibbard	.05
16	Walt Weiss	.05
17	Chris Sabo	.05
18	Dave Henderson	.05
19	Rick Sutcliffe	.05
20	Harold Reynolds	.05
21	Jack Morris	.05
22	Dan Wilson	.05
23	Dave Magadan	.05
24	Dennis Martinez	.05
25	Wes Chamberlain	.05
26	Otis Nixon	.05
27	Eric Anthony	.05
28	Randy Milligan	.05
29	Julio Franco	.05
30	Kevin McReynolds	.05
31	Anthony Young	.05
32	Brian Harper	.05
33	Lenny Harris	.05
34	Eddie Taubensee	.05
35	David Segui	.05
36	Stan Javier	.05
37	Felix Fermin	.05
38	Darrin Jackson	.05
39	Tony Fernandez	.05
40	Jose Vizcaino	.05
41	Willie Banks	.05
42	Brian Hunter	.05
43	Reggie Jefferson	.05
44	Junior Felix	.05
45	Jack Armstrong	.05
46	Bip Roberts	.05
47	Jerry Browne	.05
48	Marvin Freeman	.05
49	Jody Reed	.05
50	Alex Cole	.05
51	Sid Fernandez	.05
52	Pete Smith	.05
53	Xavier Hernandez	.05
54	Scott Sanderson	.05
55	Turner Ward	.05
56	Rex Hudler	.05
57	Deion Sanders	.25
58	Sid Bream	.05
59	Tony Pena	.05
60	Bret Boone	.05
61	Bobby Ayala	.05
62	Pedro Martinez	.15
63	Howard Johnson	.05
64	Mark Portugal	.05
65	Roberto Kelly	.05
66	Spike Owen	.05
67	Jeff Treadway	.05
68	Mike Harkey	.05
69	Doug Jones	.05
70	Steve Farr	.05
71	Billy Taylor	.05
72	Manny Ramirez	1.50
73	Bob Hamelin	.05
74	Steve Karsay	.05
75	Ryan Klesko	.25
76	Cliff Floyd	.10
77	Jeffrey Hammonds	.10
78	Javier Lopez	.20
79	Roger Salkeld	.05
80	Hector Carrasco	.05
81	Gerald Williams	.05
82	Raul Mondesi	.75
83	Sterling Hitchcock	.05
84	Danny Bautista	.05
85	Chris Turner	.05
86	Shane Reynolds	.05
87	Rondell White	.20
88	Salomon Torres	.05
89	Turk Wendell	.05
90	Tony Tarasco	.05
91	Shawn Green	.25
92	Greg Colbrunn	.05
93	Eddie Zambrano	.05
94	Rich Becker	.05
95	Chris Gomez	.05
96	John Patterson	.05
97	Derek Parks	.05
98	Rich Rowland	.05
99	James Mouton	.10
100	Tim Hyers	.10
101	Jose Valentin	.05
102	Carlos Delgado	.25
103	Robert Eenhoorn	.05
104	John Hudek	.10
105	Domingo Cedeno	.05
106	Denny Hocking	.10
107	Greg Pirkl	.05
108	Mark Smith	.05
109	Paul Shuey	.05
110	Jorge Fabregas	.05
111	Rikkert Faneyte	.05
112	Rob Butler	.05
113	Darren Oliver	.05
114	Troy O'Leary	.05
115	Scott Brow	.05
116	Tony Eusebio	.05
117	Carlos Reyes	.05
118	J.R. Phillips	.05
119	Alex Diaz	.05
120	Charles Johnson	.15
121	Nate Minchey	.05
122	Scott Sanders	.05
123	Daryl Boston	.05
124	Joey Hamilton	.30
125	Brian Anderson	.25
126	Dan Miceli	.05
127	Tom Brunansky	.05
128	Dave Staton	.05
129	Mike Oquist	.05
130	John Mabry	.15
131	Norberto Martin	.05
132	Hector Fajardo	.05
133	Mark Hutton	.05
134	Fernando Vina	.05
135	Lee Tinsley	.05
136	Chan Ho Park	.50
137	Paul Spoljaric	.05
138	Matias Carrillo	.05
139	Mark Kiefer	.05
140	Stan Royer	.05
141	Bryan Eversgerd	.05
143	Joe Hall	.05
144	Johnny Ruffin	.05
145	Alex Gonzalez	.25
146	Keith Lockhart	.05
147	Tom Marsh	.05
148	Tony Longmire	.05
149	Keith Mitchell	.05
150	Melvin Nieves	.05
151	Kelly Stinnett	.15
152	Miguel Jimenez	.05
153	Jeff Juden	.05
154	Matt Walbeck	.05
155	Marc Newfield	.05
156	Matt Mieske	.05
157	Marcus Moore	.05
158	Jose Lima	2.50
159	Mike Kelly	.05
160	Jim Edmonds	.30
161	Steve Trachsel	.25
162	Greg Blosser	.05
163	Mark Acre	.10
164	AL Checklist	.05
165	NL Checklist	.05

1994 Score Rookie/Traded Gold Rush

Each pack of Score Rookie and Traded cards included one Gold Rush parallel version of one of the set's cards. The insert cards feature fronts that are printed directly on gold foil and include a Gold Rush logo in an upper corner.

	MT
Complete Set (165):	45.00
Common Player:	.25
Stars: 2X	

(See 1994 Score Rookie/Traded for checklist and base card values.)

1994 Score Rookie/Traded Changing Places

Changing Places documented the relocation of 10 veteran superstars. Cards were inserted into one of every 36 retail or hobby packs. Fronts have a color photo of the player in his new uniform and are enhanced with red foil. Backs have a montage of color and black-and-white photos and a few words about the trade.

		MT
Complete Set (10):		20.00
Common Player:		1.00
1	Will Clark	4.00
2	Rafael Palmeiro	4.00
3	Roberto Kelly	1.00
4	Bo Jackson	2.00
5	Otis Nixon	1.00
6	Rickey Henderson	4.00
7	Ellis Burks	1.00
8	Lee Smith	1.00
9	Delino DeShields	1.00
10	Deion Sanders	4.00

1994 Score Rookie/Traded Redemption Card

The Score Rookie and Traded Redemption card was inserted at a rate of one every 240 packs. It gave collectors a chance to mail in for the best rookie in the annual September call-up: Alex Rodriguez

	MT
September Call-Up redemption card (expired)	12.00
Alex Rodriguez	600.00

1994 Score Rookie/Traded Super Rookies

Super Rookies is an 18-card set honoring baseball's brightest young stars. Super Rookies appear only in hobby packs at a rate of one every 36 packs. Fronts are printed on foil, with a multi-colored border. Backs feature another photo, most of which is rendered in single-color blocks, along with a few words about the player and a large Super Rookie logo. Cards are numbered with an SU prefix.

		MT
Complete Set (18):		50.00
Common Player:		1.50
1	Carlos Delgado	3.00
2	Manny Ramirez	15.00
3	Ryan Klesko	3.00
4	Raul Mondesi	8.00
5	Bob Hamelin	1.50
6	Steve Karsay	1.50
7	Jeffrey Hammonds	2.00
8	Cliff Floyd	2.00
9	Kurt Abbott	2.00
10	Marc Newfield	1.50
11	Javier Lopez	5.00
12	Rich Becker	1.50
13	Greg Pirkl	1.50
14	Rondell White	4.00
15	James Mouton	1.50
16	Tony Tarasco	1.50
17	Brian Anderson	2.00
18	Jim Edmonds	6.00

1995 Score Samples

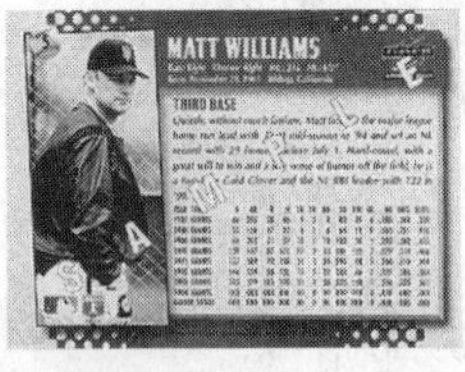

This cello-wrapped 10-card sample set of 1995 Score cards was sent to dealers to preview the issue. Cards are identical to the regular-issue versions except they have a diagonal white "SAMPLE" printed on front and back.

		MT
Complete Set (10):		30.00
Common Player:		2.00
2	Roberto Alomar	3.00
4	Jose Canseco	4.00
5	Matt Williams	3.00
5HG	Cal Ripken, Jr. (Hall of Gold)	10.00
8DP	McKay Christensen ('94 Draft Pick)	1.00
221	Jeff Bagwell	5.00
223	Albert Belle	4.00
224	Chuck Carr	1.00
288	Jorge Fabreges (Rookie)	2.50
	Header card	.50

1995 Score

Score 1995 Baseball is composed of 605 cards, issued in two series; the first comprising 330 cards, the second, 275. Basic cards have photos placed on a dirt-like background with a green strip running up each side. The player's name, position, and team logo is given in white letters on a blue strip across the bottom. Backs resemble the fronts, except with a smaller, portrait photo of the player, which leaves room for statistics and biographical information. Score had a parallel set of Gold Rush cards, along with several other series of inserts. Eleven players in Series II can be found in two team variations as the result of a redemption program for updated cards.

		MT
Complete Set (605):		24.00
Common Player:		.05
Series 1 or 2 Wax Box:		27.00
Gold Rush: 3X		
Platinums: 6X		
1	Frank Thomas	1.25
2	Roberto Alomar	.40
3	Cal Ripken, Jr.	2.00
4	Jose Canseco	.25
5	Matt Williams	.25
6	Esteban Beltre	.05
7	Domingo Cedeno	.05
8	John Valentin	.05
9	Glenallen Hill	.05
10	Rafael Belliard	.05
11	Randy Myers	.05
12	Mo Vaughn	.40
13	Hector Carrasco	.05
14	Chili Davis	.05
15	Dante Bichette	.25
16	Darren Jackson	.05
17	Mike Piazza	1.25
18	Junior Felix	.05
19	Moises Alou	.10
20	Mark Gubicza	.05
21	Bret Saberhagen	.05
22	Len Dykstra	.05
23	Steve Howe	.05
24	Mark Dewey	.05
25	Brian Harper	.05
26	Ozzie Smith	.30
27	Scott Erickson	.05
28	Tony Gwynn	.75
29	Bob Welch	.05
30	Barry Bonds	.50
31	Leo Gomez	.05
32	Greg Maddux	1.25
33	Mike Greenwell	.05
34	Sammy Sosa	1.25
35	Darnell Coles	.05
36	Tommy Greene	.05
37	Will Clark	.20
38	Steve Ontiveros	.05
39	Stan Javier	.05
40	Bip Roberts	.05
41	Paul O'Neill	.10
42	Bill Haselman	.05
43	Shane Mack	.05
44	Orlando Merced	.05
45	Kevin Seitzer	.05
46	Trevor Hoffman	.10
47	Greg Gagne	.05
48	Jeff Kent	.05
49	Tony Phillips	.05
50	Ken Hill	.05
51	Carlos Baerga	.10
52	Henry Rodriguez	.05
53	Scott Sanderson	.05
54	Jeff Conine	.05
55	Chris Turner	.05
56	Ken Caminiti	.15
57	Harold Baines	.05
58	Charlie Hayes	.05
59	Roberto Kelly	.05
60	John Olerud	.15
61	Tim Davis	.05
62	Rich Rowland	.05
63	Rey Sanchez	.05
64	Junior Ortiz	.05
65	Ricky Gutierrez	.05
66	Rex Hudler	.05
67	Johnny Ruffin	.05
68	Jay Buhner	.10
69	Tom Pagnozzi	.05
70	Julio Franco	.05
71	Eric Young	.05
72	Mike Bordick	.05
73	Don Slaught	.05
74	Goose Gossage	.05
75	Lonnie Smith	.05
76	Jimmy Key	.05
77	Dave Hollins	.05
78	Mickey Tettleton	.05
79	Luis Gonzalez	.10
80	Dave Winfield	.15
81	Ryan Thompson	.05
82	Felix Jose	.05
83	Rusty Meacham	.05
84	Darryl Hamilton	.05
85	John Wetteland	.05
86	Tom Brunansky	.05
87	Mark Lemke	.05
88	Spike Owen	.05
89	Shawon Dunston	.05
90	Wilson Alvarez	.05
91	Lee Smith	.05
92	Scott Kamieniecki	.05
93	Jacob Brumfield	.05
94	Kirk Gibson	.05
95	Joe Girardi	.05
96	Mike Macfarlane	.05
97	Greg Colbrunn	.05
98	Ricky Bones	.05
99	Delino DeShields	.05
100	Pat Meares	.05
101	Jeff Fassero	.05
102	Jim Leyritz	.05
103	Gary Redus	.05
104	Terry Steinbach	.05
105	Kevin McReynolds	.05
106	Felix Fermin	.05
107	Danny Jackson	.05
108	Chris James	.05
109	Jeff King	.05
110	Pat Hentgen	.05
111	Gerald Perry	.05
112	Tim Raines	.10
113	Eddie Williams	.05
114	Jamie Moyer	.05
115	Bud Black	.05
116	Chris Gomez	.05
117	Luis Lopez	.05
118	Roger Clemens	.50
119	Javier Lopez	.20
120	Dave Nilsson	.05
121	Karl Rhodes	.05
122	Rick Aguilera	.05
123	Tony Fernandez	.05
124	Bernie Williams	.40
125	James Mouton	.05
126	Mark Langston	.05
127	Mike Lansing	.05
128	Tino Martinez	.10
129	Joe Orsulak	.05
130	David Hulse	.05
131	Pete Incaviglia	.05
132	Mark Clark	.05
133	Tony Eusebio	.05
134	Chuck Finley	.05
135	Lou Frazier	.05
136	Craig Grebeck	.05
137	Kelly Stinnett	.05
138	Paul Shuey	.05
139	David Nied	.05
140	Billy Brewer	.05
141	Dave Weathers	.05
142	Scott Leius	.05
143	Brian Jordan	.10
144	Melido Perez	.05
145	Tony Tarasco	.05
146	Dan Wilson	.05
147	Rondell White	.20
148	Mike Henneman	.05
149	Brian Johnson	.10
150	Tom Henke	.05
151	John Patterson	.05
152	Bobby Witt	.05
153	Eddie Taubensee	.05
154	Pat Borders	.05
155	Ramon Martinez	.10
156	Mike Kingery	.05
157	Zane Smith	.05
158	Benito Santiago	.05
159	Matias Carrillo	.05
160	Scott Brosius	.05
161	Dave Clark	.05
162	Mark McLemore	.05
163	Curt Schilling	.10
164	J.T. Snow	.10
165	Rod Beck	.05
166	Scott Fletcher	.05
167	Bob Tewksbury	.05
168	Mike LaValliere	.05
169	Dave Hansen	.05
170	Pedro Martinez	.10
171	Kirk Rueter	.05
172	Jose Lind	.05
173	Luis Alicea	.05
174	Mike Moore	.05
175	Andy Ashby	.10
176	Jody Reed	.05
177	Darryl Kile	.05
178	Carl Willis	.05
179	Jeromy Burnitz	.10
180	Mike Gallego	.05
181	*W. Van Landingham*	.10
182	Sid Fernandez	.05
183	Kim Batiste	.05
184	Greg Myers	.05
185	Steve Avery	.05
186	Steve Farr	.05
187	Robb Nen	.05
188	Dan Pasqua	.05
189	Bruce Ruffin	.05
190	Jose Valentin	.05
191	Willie Banks	.05
192	Mike Aldrete	.05
193	Randy Milligan	.05
194	Steve Karsay	.10
195	Mike Stanley	.05
196	Jose Mesa	.05
197	Tom Browning	.05
198	John Vander Wal	.05
199	Kevin Brown	.10
200	Mike Oquist	.05
201	Greg Swindell	.05
202	Eddie Zambrano	.05
203	Joe Boever	.05
204	Gary Varsho	.05
205	Chris Gwynn	.05
206	David Howard	.05
207	Jerome Walton	.05
208	Danny Darwin	.05
209	Darryl Strawberry	.10
210	Todd Van Poppel	.05
211	Scott Livingstone	.05
212	Dave Fleming	.05
213	Todd Worrell	.05
214	Carlos Delgado	.25
215	Bill Pecota	.05
216	Jim Lindeman	.05
217	Rick White	.05
218	Jose Oquendo	.05
219	Tony Castillo	.05
220	Fernando Vina	.05
221	Jeff Bagwell	.60
222	Randy Johnson	.25
223	Albert Belle	.50
224	Chuck Carr	.05
225	Mark Leiter	.05
226	Hal Morris	.05
227	Robin Ventura	.15
228	Mike Munoz	.05
229	Jim Thome	.20
230	Mario Diaz	.05
231	John Doherty	.05
232	Bobby Jones	.05
233	Raul Mondesi	.35
234	Ricky Jordan	.05
235	John Jaha	.05
236	Carlos Garcia	.05
237	Kirby Puckett	.75
238	Orel Hershiser	.10
239	Don Mattingly	.75
240	Sid Bream	.05
241	Brent Gates	.05
242	Tony Longmire	.05
243	Robby Thompson	.05
244	Rick Sutcliffe	.05
245	Dean Palmer	.05
246	Marquis Grissom	.05
247	Paul Molitor	.30
248	Mark Carreon	.05
249	Jack Voight	.05
250	Greg McMichael	.05
251	Damon Berryhill	.05
252	Brian Dorsett	.05
253	Jim Edmonds	.15
254	Barry Larkin	.15
255	Jack McDowell	.05
256	Wally Joyner	.10
257	Eddie Murray	.25
258	Lenny Webster	.05
259	Milt Cuyler	.05
260	Todd Benzinger	.05
261	Vince Coleman	.05
262	Todd Stottlemyre	.05
263	Turner Ward	.05
264	Ray Lankford	.10
265	Matt Walbeck	.05
266	Deion Sanders	.15
267	Gerald Williams	.05
268	Jim Gott	.05
269	Jeff Frye	.05
270	Jose Rijo	.05
271	Dave Justice	.15
272	Ismael Valdes	.10
273	Ben McDonald	.05
274	Darren Lewis	.05
275	Graeme Lloyd	.05
276	Luis Ortiz	.05
277	Julian Tavarez	.05
278	Mark Dalesandro	.05
279	Brett Merriman	.05
280	Ricky Bottalico	.05
281	Robert Eenhoorn	.05
282	Rikkert Faneyte	.05
283	Mike Kelly	.05
284	Mark Smith	.05
285	Turk Wendell	.05
286	Greg Blosser	.05
287	Garey Ingram	.05
288	Jorge Fabregas	.05

289 Blaise Ilsley .05
290 Joe Hall .05
291 Orlando Miller .05
292 Jose Lima .10
293 Greg O'Halloran .05
294 Mark Kiefer .05
295 Jose Oliva .05
296 Rich Becker .05
297 Brian Hunter .10
298 Dave Silvestri .05
299 *Armando Benitez* .15
300 Darren Dreifort .05
301 John Mabry .05
302 Greg Pirkl .05
303 J.R. Phillips .05
304 Shawn Green .20
305 Roberto Petagine .05
306 Keith Lockhart .05
307 Jonathon Hurst .05
308 Paul Spoljaric .05
309 Mike Lieberthal .10
310 Garret Anderson .10
311 John Johnston .05
312 Alex Rodriguez 2.00
313 Kent Mercker .05
314 John Valentin .05
315 Kenny Rogers .05
316 Fred McGriff .20
317 Atlanta Braves, Baltimore Orioles .05
318 Chicago Cubs, Boston Red Sox .05
319 Cincinnati Reds, California Angels .05
320 Colorado Rockies, Chicago White Sox .05
321 Cleveland Indians, Florida Marlins .05
322 Houston Astros, Detroit Tigers .05
323 Los Angels Dodgers, Kansas City Royals .05
324 Montreal Expos, Milwaukee Brewers .05
325 New York Mets, Minnesota Twins .05
326 Philadelphia Phillies, New York Yankees .05
327 Pittsburgh Pirates, Oakland Athletics .05
328 San Diego Padres, Seattle Mariners .05
329 San Francisco Giants, Texas Rangers .05
330 St. Louis Cardinals, Toronto Blue Jays .05
331 Pedro Munoz .05
332 Ryan Klesko .20
333a Andre Dawson (Red Sox) .15
333b Andre Dawson (Marlins) .40
334 Derrick May .05
335 Aaron Sele .05
336 Kevin Mitchell .05
337 Steve Traschel .10
338 Andres Galarraga .10
339a Terry Pendleton (Braves) .05
339b Terry Pendleton (Marlins) .15
340 Gary Sheffield .30
341 Travis Fryman .05
342 Bo Jackson .10
343 Gary Gaetti .05
344a Brett Butler (Dodgers) .10
344b Brett Butler (Mets) .25
345 B. J. Surhoff .05
346a Larry Walker (Expos) .25
346b Larry Walker (Rockies) .50
347 Kevin Tapani .05
348 Rick Wilkins .05
349 Wade Boggs .20
350 Mariano Duncan .05
351 Ruben Sierra .05
352a Andy Van Slyke (Pirates) .05
352b Andy Van Slyke (Orioles) .25
353 Reggie Jefferson .05
354 Gregg Jefferies .10
355 Tim Naehring .05
356 John Roper .05
357 Joe Carter .10
358 Kurt Abbott .05
359 Lenny Harris .05
360 Lance Johnson .05
361 Brian Anderson .10
362 Jim Eisenreich .05
363 Jerry Browne .05
364 Mark Grace .15
365 Devon White .10
366 Reggie Sanders .10
367 Ivan Rodriguez .35
368 Kirt Manwaring .05
369 Pat Kelly .05
370 Ellis Burks .10
371 Charles Nagy .10
372 Kevin Bass .05
373 Lou Whitaker .05
374 Rene Arocha .05
375 Derrick Parks .05
376 Mark Whiten .05
377 Mark McGwire 2.50
378 Doug Drabek .05
379 Greg Vaughn .10
380 Al Martin .05
381 Ron Darling .05
382 Tim Wallach .05
383 Alan Trammell .10
384 Randy Velarde .05
385 Chris Sabo .05
386 Wil Cordero .05
387 Darrin Fletcher .05
388 David Segui .05
389 Steve Buechele .05
390 Otis Nixon .05
391 Jeff Brantley .05
392a Chad Curtis (Angels) .05
392b Chad Curtis (Tigers) .25
393 Cal Eldred .05
394 Jason Bere .05
395 Bret Barberie .05
396 Paul Sorrento .05
397 Steve Finley .05
398 Cecil Fielder .10
399 Eric Karros .10
400 Jeff Montgomery .05
401 Cliff Floyd .10
402 Matt Mieske .05
403 Brian Hunter .05
404 Alex Cole .05
405 Kevin Stocker .05
406 Eric Davis .10
407 Marvin Freeman .05
408 Dennis Eckersley .05
409 Todd Zeile .10
410 Keith Mitchell .05
411 Andy Benes .05
412 Juan Bell .05
413 Royce Clayton .05
414 Ed Sprague .05
415 Mike Mussina .25
416 Todd Hundley .15
417 Pat Listach .05
418 Joe Oliver .05
419 Rafael Palmeiro .15
420 Tim Salmon .15
421 Brady Anderson .10
422 Kenny Lofton .40
423 Craig Biggio .15
424 Bobby Bonilla .05
425 Kenny Rogers .05
426 Derek Bell .05
427a Scott Cooper (Red Sox) .05
427b Scott Cooper (Cardinals) .25
428 Ozzie Guillen .05
429 Omar Vizquel .05
430 Phil Plantier .05
431 Chuck Knoblauch .10
432 Darren Daulton .05
433 Bob Hamelin .05
434 Tom Glavine .15
435 Walt Weiss .05
436 Jose Vizcaino .05
437 Ken Griffey Jr. 2.50
438 Jay Bell .05
439 Juan Gonzalez 1.00
440 Jeff Blauser .05
441 Rickey Henderson .20
442 Bobby Ayala .05
443a David Cone (Royals) .10
443b David Cone (Blue Jays) .50
444 Pedro Martinez .05
445 Manny Ramirez .75
446 Mark Portugal .05
447 Damion Easley .05
448 Gary DiSarcina .05
449 Roberto Hernandez .05
450 Jeffrey Hammonds .10
451 Jeff Treadway .05
452a Jim Abbott (Yankees) .10
452b Jim Abbott (White Sox) .25
453 Carlos Rodriguez .05
454 Joey Cora .05
455 Bret Boone .05
456 Danny Tartabull .05
457 John Franco .05
458 Roger Salkeld .05
459 Fred McGriff .30
460 Pedro Astacio .05
461 Jon Lieber .05
462 Luis Polonia .05
463 Geronimo Pena .05
464 Tom Gordon .05
465 Brad Ausmus .05
466 Willie McGee .05
467 Doug Jones .05
468 John Smoltz .15
469 Troy Neel .05
470 Luis Sojo .05
471 John Smiley .05
472 Rafael Bournigal .05
473 Billy Taylor .05
474 Juan Guzman .05
475 Dave Magadan .05
476 Mike Devereaux .05
477 Andujar Cedeno .05
478 Edgar Martinez .05
479 Troy Neel .05
480 Allen Watson .05
481 Ron Karkovice .05
482 Joey Hamilton .05
483 Vinny Castilla .10
484 Kevin Gross .05
485 Bernard Gilkey .10
486 John Burkett .05
487 Matt Nokes .05
488 Mel Rojas .05
489 Craig Shipley .05
490 Chip Hale .05
491 Bill Swift .05
492 Pat Rapp .05
493a Brian McRae (Royals) .05
493b Brian McRae (Cubs) .35
494 Mickey Morandini .05
495 Tony Pena .05
496 Danny Bautista .05
497 Armando Reynoso .05
498 Ken Ryan .05
499 Billy Ripken .05
500 Pat Mahomes .05
501 Mark Acre .05
502 Geronimo Berroa .05
503 Norberto Martin .05
504 Chad Kreuter .05
505 Howard Johnson .05
506 Eric Anthony .05
507 Mark Wohlers .05
508 Scott Sanders .05
509 Pete Harnisch .05
510 Wes Chamberlain .05
511 Tom Candiotti .05
512 Albie Lopez .05
513 Denny Neagle .05
514 Sean Berry .05
515 Billy Hatcher .05
516 Todd Jones .05
517 Wayne Kirby .05
518 Butch Henry .05
519 Sandy Alomar Jr. .10
520 Kevin Appier .05
521 Robert Mejia .05
522 Steve Cooke .05
523 Terry Shumpert .05
524 Mike Jackson .05
525 Kent Mercker .05
526 David Wells .10
527 Juan Samuel .05
528 Salomon Torres .05
529 Duane Ward .05
530a Rob Dibble (Reds) .05
530b Rob Dibble (White Sox) .25
531 Mike Blowers .05
532 Mark Eichhorn .05
533 Alex Diaz .05
534 Dan Miceli .05
535 Jeff Branson .05
536 Dave Stevens .05
537 Charlie O'Brien .05
538 Shane Reynolds .05
539 Rich Amaral .05
540 Rusty Greer .05
541 Alex Arias .05
542 Eric Plunk .05
543 John Hudek .05
544 Kirk McCaskill .05
545 Jeff Reboulet .05
546 Sterling Hitchcock .05
547 Warren Newson .05
548 Bryan Harvey .05
549 Mike Huff .05
550 Lance Parrish .05
551 Ken Griffey Jr. (Hitters Inc.) 1.00
552 Matt Williams (Hitters Inc.) .15
553 Roberto Alomar (Hitters Inc.) .20
554 Jeff Bagwell (Hitters Inc.) .35
555 Dave Justice (Hitters Inc.) .10
556 Cal Ripken Jr. (Hitters Inc.) 1.00
557 Albert Belle (Hitters Inc.) .20
558 Mike Piazza (Hitters Inc.) .50
559 Kirby Puckett (Hitters Inc.) .40
560 Wade Boggs (Hitters Inc.) .15
561 Tony Gwynn (Hitters Inc.) .40
562 Barry Bonds (Hitters Inc.) .25
563 Mo Vaughn (Hitters Inc.) .20
564 Don Mattingly (Hitters Inc.) .50
565 Carlos Baerga (Hitters Inc.) .05
566 Paul Molitor (Hitters Inc.) .20
567 Raul Mondesi (Hitters Inc.) .15
568 Manny Ramirez (Hitters Inc.) .40
569 Alex Rodriguez (Hitters Inc.) 1.00
570 Will Clark (Hitters Inc.) .15
571 Frank Thomas (Hitters Inc.) .50
572 Moises Alou (Hitters Inc.) .05
573 Jeff Conine (Hitters Inc.) .05
574 Joe Ausanio .05
575 Charles Johnson .10
576 Ernie Young .05
577 Jeff Granger .05
578 Robert Perez .05
579 Melvin Nieves .05
580 Gar Finnvold .05
581 Duane Singleton .05
582 Chan Ho Park .15
583 Fausto Cruz .05
584 Dave Staton .05
585 Denny Hocking .05
586 Nate Minchey .05
587 Marc Newfield .05
588 Jayhawk Owens .05
589 Darren Bragg .05
590 Kevin King .05
591 Kurt Miller .05
592 Aaron Small .05
593 Troy O'Leary .05
594 Phil Stidham .05
595 Steve Dunn .05
596 Cory Bailey .10
597 Alex Gonzalez .10
598 Jim Bowie .05
599 Jeff Cirillo .10
600 Mark Hutton .05
601 Russ Davis .05
602 Team Checklist .05
603 Team Checklist .05
604 Team Checklist .05
605 Team Checklist .05
---- "You Trade 'em" redemption card (Expired Dec. 31, 1995) .50

1995 Score Gold Rush

Besides being collectible in their own right, the gold-foil printed parallel versions of the Score regular-issue cards could be collected into team sets and exchanged with a trade card for platinum versions. The deadline for redemption of Series I was July 1, 1995; Oct. 1, 1995, for Series II. Gold Rush cards were found either one or two per pack, depending on pack card count. Gold Rush versions exist for each card in the Score set and have fronts that are identical to the regular cards except they are printed on foil and have gold borders. Backs of the Gold Rush cards have a small rectangular "GOLD RUSH" logo overprinted.

	MT
Complete Set (605):	100.00
Common Player:	.25
Gold Rush Stars: 3X	

(See 1995 Score for checklist and base card values.)

1995 Score Platinum Redemption Team Sets

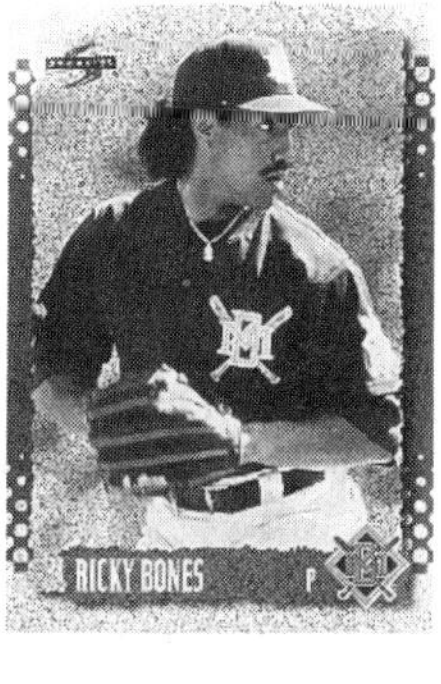

This top of the line parallel set was only available by exchanging a complete Series 1 or Series 2 Gold Rush team set, along with a redemption card. Production of the Platinum sets was limited to 4,950 of each team in each series. Using the same photos and format as the regular issue and Gold Rush cards, the Platinum parallels have card fronts printed on silver prismatic foil. Backs are identical to the regular versions. Platinum series team sets were sent to collectors in specially printed plastic cases with a certificate of authenticity.

	MT
Complete Set (587):	300.00
Complete Series 1 (316):	200.00
Complete Series 2 (271)	100.00
Common Player:	.50
Platinum Stars: 6X	

(See 1995 Score for checklist and base card values.)

1995 Score Ad Prize Cards

In a series of ads in hobby and public media, Score offered a pair of special cards as prizes in a mail-in offer. Cards feature the same basic design as 1995 Score, but are printed on platinum foil on front. Backs are conventionally printed with a portrait photo and a few words about the player.

	MT
Complete Set (2):	50.00
Common Player:	15.00
AD1 Alex Rodriguez	35.00
AD2 Ivan Rodriguez	15.00

1995 Score Airmail

Young ballplayers with a propensity for hitting the long ball are featured in this insert set found only in Series II jumbo packs. Cards have a player batting action photo set in sky-and-clouds background. A gold-foil stamp in the upper-left corner identifies the series. Backs have a background photo of sunset and dark clouds, with a player portrait photo in the foreground. A few stats and sentences describe the player's power hitting potential. Cards have an AM prefix to the number. Stated odds for insertion rate are an average of one Airmail chase card per 24 packs.

		MT
Complete Set (18):		50.00
Common Player:		1.00
1	Bob Hamelin	1.00
2	John Mabry	1.00
3	Marc Newfield	1.00
4	Jose Oliva	1.00
5	Charles Johnson	3.00
6	Russ Davis	1.00
7	Ernie Young	1.00
8	Billy Ashley	1.00
9	Ryan Klesko	3.00
10	J.R. Phillips	1.00
11	Cliff Floyd	3.00
12	Carlos Delgado	4.00
13	Melvin Nieves	1.00
14	Raul Mondesi	5.00
15	Manny Ramirez	12.00
16	Mike Kelly	1.00
17	Alex Rodriguez	25.00
18	Rusty Greer	2.00

1995 Score Double Gold Champions

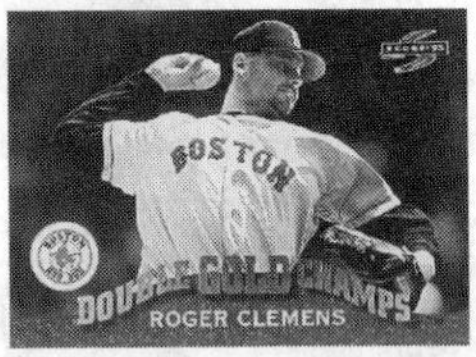

A dozen veteran players, who have won at least two of the game's top awards are designated as "Double Gold Champs," in this Series II hobby insert set. Fronts have horizontal action photos at top, with a speckled red border at bottom. Vertical backs have a portrait photo and a list of the major awards won by the player. Cards have a GC prefix to the number. These chase cards were reportedly inserted at an average rate of one per 36.

		MT
Complete Set (11):		85.00
Common Player:		3.00
1	Frank Thomas	15.00
2	Ken Griffey Jr.	20.00
3	Barry Bonds	7.50
4	Tony Gwynn	10.00
5	Don Mattingly	8.00
6	Greg Maddux	12.00
7	Roger Clemens	8.00
8	Kenny Lofton	6.00
9	Jeff Bagwell	8.00
10	Matt Williams	3.00
11	Kirby Puckett	8.00

1995 Score Draft Picks

These cards were randomly included in 1995 Score hobby packs at a rate of one per every 36 packs. The cards showcase 18 of baseball's potential superstars and document their professional beginnings. The card front has the player's team logo and name in the lower-right corner. " '94 Draft Pick" appears in the upper-right corner. The front also has a mug shot and an action shot of the player. The card back has a portrait and career summary and is numbered with a DP prefix.

		MT
Complete Set (18):		30.00
Common Player:		1.00
1	McKay Christensen	1.00
2	Brett Wagner	1.00
3	Paul Wilson	2.00
4	C.J. Nitkowski	1.00
5	Josh Booty	2.50
6	Antone Williamson	1.00
7	Paul Konerko	8.00
8	Scott Elarton	3.00
9	Jacob Shumate	1.00
10	Terrence Long	1.00
11	Mark Johnson	1.00
12	Ben Grieve	10.00
13	Doug Million	1.00
14	Jayson Peterson	1.00
15	Dustin Hermanson	3.00
16	Matt Smith	1.00
17	Kevin Witt	1.00
18	Brian Buchanon	1.00

1995 Score Dream Team Gold

The Major Leagues' top players at each position are featured in this Series I insert set. Fronts are printed entirely on rainbow holographic foil and feature a large and a small player action photo. Backs have a single-color version of one of the front photos as well as a color portrait photo in a circle at center, all in conventional printing technology. Card numbers have a DG prefix.

		MT
Complete Set (12):		120.00
Common Player:		2.00
1	Frank Thomas	17.50
2	Roberto Alomar	6.00
3	Cal Ripken Jr.	25.00
4	Matt Williams	4.00
5	Mike Piazza	20.00
6	Albert Belle	8.00
7	Ken Griffey Jr.	30.00
8	Tony Gwynn	15.00
9	Paul Molitor	7.50
10	Jimmy Key	2.00
11	Greg Maddux	17.50
12	Lee Smith	2.00

1995 Score Hall of Gold

Hall of Gold inserts picture 110 of the top players on gold foil cards. Each card front has the Hall of Gold logo in an upper corner, plus a color action photo of the player, and his name and team logo at the bottom. The card back is numbered using an "HG" prefix and includes another color photo of the player, his team's name, his position, and a career summary. Cards were inserted one per every six regular 1995 Score packs and one per every two jumbo packs. Updated versions of five traded players were issued in Series II, available only via mail-in offer with a trade card found randomly inserted in packs.

		MT
Complete Set (110):		80.00
Common Player:		.20
1	Ken Griffey Jr.	8.00
2	Matt Williams	.40
3	Roberto Alomar	1.50
4	Jeff Bagwell	3.00
5	Dave Justice	.40
6	Cal Ripken Jr.	6.50
7	Randy Johnson	.50
8	Barry Larkin	.40
9	Albert Belle	2.50
10	Mike Piazza	5.00
11	Kirby Puckett	2.50
12	Moises Alou	.25
13	Jose Canseco	.60
14	Tony Gwynn	3.00
15	Roger Clemens	3.00
16	Barry Bonds	2.50
17	Mo Vaughn	1.50
18	Greg Maddux	4.50
19	Dante Bichette	.60
20	Will Clark	.60
21	Len Dykstra	.20
22	Don Mattingly	2.50
23	Carlos Baerga	.20
24	Ozzie Smith	.75
25	Paul Molitor	.75
26	Paul O'Neill	.25
27	Deion Sanders	.80
28	Jeff Conine	.20
29	John Olerud	.25
30	Jose Rijo	.20
31	Sammy Sosa	4.00
32	Robin Ventura	.25
33	Raul Mondesi	.80
34	Eddie Murray	.60
35	Marquis Grissom	.20
36	Darryl Strawberry	.20
37	Dave Nilsson	.20
38	Manny Ramirez	3.00
39	Delino DeShields	.20
40	Lee Smith	.20
41	Alex Rodriguez	6.50
42	Julio Franco	.20
43	Bret Saberhagen	.20
44	Ken Hill	.20
45	Roberto Kelly	.20
46	Hal Morris	.20
47	Jimmy Key	.20
48	Terry Steinbach	.20
49	Mickey Tettleton	.20
50	Tony Phillips	.20
51	Carlos Garcia	.20
52	Jim Edmonds	.40
53	Rod Beck	.20
54	Shane Mack	.20
55	Ken Caminiti	.30
56	Frank Thomas	4.00
57	Kenny Lofton	1.50
58	Jack McDowell	.20
59	Jason Bere	.20
60	Joe Carter	.20
61	Gary Sheffield	.40
62	Andres Galarraga	.25
63	Gregg Jefferies	.20
64	Bobby Bonilla	.20
65	Tom Glavine	.25
66	John Smoltz	.30
67	Fred McGriff	.50
68	Craig Biggio	.30
69	Reggie Sanders	.20
70	Kevin Mitchell	.20
71a	Larry Walker (Expos)	.50
71b	Larry Walker (Rockies)	2.00
72	Carlos Delgado	.30
73	Andujar Cedeno	.20
74	Ivan Rodriguez	.60
75	Ryan Klesko	.40
76a	John Kruk (Phillies)	.20
76b	John Kruk (White Sox)	.60
77a	Brian McRae (Royals)	.20
77b	Brian McRae (Cubs)	.60
78	Tim Salmon	.40
79	Travis Fryman	.20
80	Chuck Knoblauch	.25
81	Jay Bell	.20
82	Cecil Fielder	.25
83	Cliff Floyd	.20
84	Ruben Sierra	.20
85	Mike Mussina	1.00
86	Mark Grace	.45
87	Dennis Eckersley	.20
88	Dennis Martinez	.20
89	Rafael Palmeiro	.25
90	Ben McDonald	.20
91	Dave Hollins	.20
92	Steve Avery	.20
93a	David Cone (Royals)	.25
93b	David Cone (Blue Jays)	.60
94	Darren Daulton	.20
95	Bret Boone	.20
96	Wade Boggs	.50
97	Doug Drabek	.20
98	Derek Bell	.20
99	Jim Thome	.60
100	Chili Davis	.20
101	Jeffrey Hammonds	.20
102	Rickey Henderson	.30
103	Brett Butler	.20
104	Tim Wallach	.20
105	Wil Cordero	.20
106	Mark Whiten	.20
107	Bob Hamelin	.20
108	Rondell White	.25
109	Devon White	.20
110a	Tony Tarasco (Braves)	.20
110b	Tony Tarasco (Expos)	.45
----	Redemption trade card (Expired Dec. 31, 1995)	.25

1995 Score Rookie Dream Team

These Series II inserts feature a dozen of 1995's best rookie prospects. Fronts are printed on a silver-foil background. The words "ROOKIE DREAM TEAM" are formed of sky-and-cloud images within the letters. Horizontal backs repeat the motif and include another player photo in a vignette at center. Card numbers have an RDT prefix.

		MT
Complete Set (12):		45.00
Common Player:		1.00
1	J.R. Phillips	1.00
2	Alex Gonzalez	4.00
3	Alex Rodriguez	25.00
4	Jose Oliva	1.00
5	Charles Johnson	3.00
6	Shawn Green	5.00
7	Brian Hunter	3.00
8	Garret Anderson	3.00
9	Julian Tavarez	1.00
10	Jose Lima	5.00
11	Armando Benitez	1.50
12	Ricky Bottalico	2.50

1995 Score Rookie Greatness

This single-card insert set is the toughest pull among the 1995 Score chase cards. Honoring slugging Braves star Ryan Klesko, the card is inserted at the rate of one per 720 retail packs. An even scarcer autographed version of the card in an edition of just over 6,000 was also created for insertion into hobby packs.

		MT
Complete Set (2):		45.00
RG1	Ryan Klesko	12.50
SG1	Ryan Klesko (autographed)	37.00

1995 Score Score Rules

Series I jumbo packs were the only sources for "Score Rules" insert set of rookie and veteran stars. A color player photo at left has a team logo toward the bottom, beneath which is a gold-foil "tie tack" device with the league initials and position. At top-right is a baseball which appears to be dripping orange and green goop down the card. The player's last name is presented vertically with a sepia photo of the player within the letters. Backs repeat the green baseball and ooze motif, with three progressive color proof versions of the sepia front photo and a few sentences about the star. Cards are numbered with an "SR" prefix.

		MT
Complete Set (30):		100.00
Common Player:		1.50
1	Ken Griffey, Jr.	20.00
2	Frank Thomas	10.00
3	Mike Piazza	12.00
4	Jeff Bagwell	10.00
5	Alex Rodriguez	15.00
6	Albert Belle	5.00
7	Matt Williams	2.00
8	Roberto Alomar	3.00
9	Barry Bonds	6.00
10	Raul Mondesi	3.00
11	Jose Canseco	2.50
12	Kirby Puckett	8.00
13	Fred McGriff	2.50
14	Kenny Lofton	4.00
15	Greg Maddux	12.00
16	Juan Gonzalez	10.00
17	Cliff Floyd	1.50
18	Cal Ripken, Jr.	15.00
19	Will Clark	2.50
20	Tim Salmon	2.50
21	Paul O'Neill	1.50
22	Jason Bere	1.50
23	Tony Gwynn	10.00
24	Manny Ramirez	6.00
25	Don Mattingly	9.00
26	Dave Justice	2.00
27	Javier Lopez	1.50
28	Ryan Klesko	2.00
29	Carlos Delgado	2.00
30	Mike Mussina	3.00

1995 Score Score Rules Supers

While colorful in the standard size, the Score Rules super-size cards found in special collectors kits are positively garish. The 7-1/2" x 10-1/2" cards are virtually identical to the Series 1 inserts, except that on back is a box with a serial number identifying the card from among an edition of 3,000. The Score Rules supers were available only in a collectors kit sold at large retail chains and came packaged with 26 Series 1 and 2 foil packs, a three-ring binder and 10 plastic sheets with a suggested retail price of around $25.

		MT
Complete Set (30):		500.00
Common Player:		8.00
1	Ken Griffey, Jr.	60.00
2	Frank Thomas	30.00
3	Mike Piazza	35.00
4	Jeff Bagwell	25.00
5	Alex Rodriguez	50.00
6	Albert Belle	20.00
7	Matt Williams	8.00
8	Roberto Alomar	8.00
9	Barry Bonds	25.00
10	Raul Mondesi	8.00
11	Jose Canseco	12.00
12	Kirby Puckett	25.00
13	Fred McGriff	8.00
14	Kenny Lofton	8.00
15	Greg Maddux	35.00
16	Juan Gonzalez	20.00
17	Cliff Floyd	8.00
18	Cal Ripken, Jr.	50.00
19	Will Clark	8.00
20	Tim Salmon	6.00
21	Paul O'Neill	6.00
22	Jason Bere	6.00
23	Tony Gwynn	25.00
24	Manny Ramirez	12.00
25	Don Mattingly	25.00
26	Dave Justice	6.00
27	Javier Lopez	6.00
28	Ryan Klesko	6.00
29	Carlos Delgado	6.00
30	Mike Mussina	6.00

1996 Score Samples

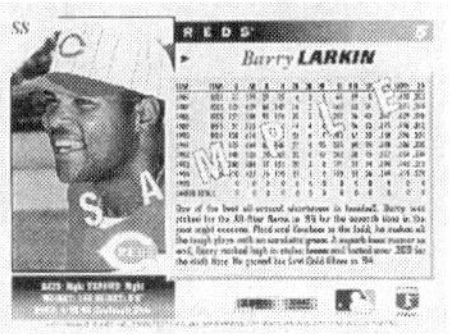

Score premiered its 1996 base brand offering with a cello pack of nine cards, including one of its new Dugout Collection inserts. The samples are virtually identical to the issued versions except that all 1995 and career stats are stated as zeros and the word "SAMPLE" is printed in white letters diagonally across front and back. Each of the cards can be found as a Dugout Collection version, making them eight times scarcer than the other samples.

		MT
Complete Set (16):		80.00
Common Player:		3.00
3	Ryan Klesko	3.00
3	Ryan Klesko (Dugout Collection)	6.00
4	Jim Edmonds	3.00
4	Jim Edmonds (Dugout Collection)	6.00
5	Barry Larkin	3.00
5	Barry Larkin (Dugout Collection)	6.00
6	Jim Thome	3.00
6	Jim Thome (Dugout Collection)	8.00
7	Raul Mondesi	4.00
7	Raul Mondesi (Dugout Collection)	12.00
110	Derek Bell	3.00
110	Derek Bell (Dugout Collection)	6.00
240	Derek Jeter	9.00
240	Derek Jeter (Dugout Collection)	25.00
241	Michael Tucker	3.00
241	Michael Tucker (Dugout Collection)	6.00

1996 Score

Large, irregularly shaped action photos are featured on the fronts of the basic cards in the 1996 Score issue. Backs feature a portrait photo (in most cases) at left and a full slate of major and minor league stats at right, along with a few words about the player. Slightly different design details and a "ROOKIE" headline identify that subset within the regular issue. A wide variety of insert cards was produced, most of them exclusive to one type of packaging.

		MT
Complete Set (510):		24.00
Complete Series 1 (275):		13.50
Complete Series 2 (235):		11.00
Common Player:		.05
Unlisted Stars: .20 to .30		
Series 1 or 2 Wax Box:		30.00
1	Will Clark	.20
2	Rich Becker	.05
3	Ryan Klesko	.20
4	Jim Edmonds	.10
5	Barry Larkin	.15
6	Jim Thome	.20
7	Raul Mondesi	.20
8	Don Mattingly	.60
9	Jeff Conine	.10
10	Rickey Henderson	.20
11	Chad Curtis	.05
12	Darren Daulton	.05
13	Larry Walker	.20
14	Carlos Garcia	.05
15	Carlos Baerga	.05
16	Tony Gwynn	.60
17	Jon Nunally	.05
18	Deion Sanders	.20
19	Mark Grace	.20
20	Alex Rodriguez	1.50
21	Frank Thomas	.75
22	Brian Jordan	.10
23	J.T. Snow	.10
24	Shawn Green	.15
25	Tim Wakefield	.05
26	Curtis Goodwin	.05
27	John Smoltz	.10
28	Devon White	.10
29	Brian Hunter	.10
30	Rusty Greer	.05
31	Rafael Palmeiro	.10
32	Bernard Gilkey	.10
33	John Valentin	.05
34	Randy Johnson	.20
35	Garret Anderson	.10
36	Rikkert Faneyte	.05
37	Ray Durham	.05
38	Bip Roberts	.05
39	Jaime Navarro	.05
40	Mark Johnson	.05
41	Darren Lewis	.05
42	Tyler Green	.05
43	Bill Pulsipher	.05
44	Jason Giambi	.10
45	Kevin Ritz	.05
46	Jack McDowell	.05
47	Felipe Lira	.05
48	Rico Brogna	.05
49	Terry Pendleton	.05
50	Rondell White	.10
51	Andre Dawson	.10
52	Kirby Puckett	.60
53	Wally Joyner	.10
54	B.J. Surhoff	.05
55	Chan Ho Park	.10
56	Greg Vaughn	.10
57	Roberto Alomar	.30
58	Dave Justice	.10
59	Kevin Seitzer	.05
60	Cal Ripken Jr.	1.50
61	Ozzie Smith	.20
62	Mo Vaughn	.45
63	Ricky Bones	.05
64	Gary DiSarcina	.05
65	Matt Williams	.20
66	Wilson Alvarez	.05
67	Lenny Dykstra	.05
68	Brian McRae	.05
69	Todd Stottlemyre	.05
70	Bret Boone	.05
71	Sterling Hitchcock	.05
72	Albert Belle	.40
73	Todd Hundley	.10
74	Vinny Castilla	.10
75	Moises Alou	.10
76	Cecil Fielder	.10
77	Brad Radke	.05
78	Quilvio Veras	.05
79	Eddie Murray	.25
80	James Mouton	.05
81	Pat Listach	.05
82	Mark Gubicza	.05
83	Dave Winfield	.15
84	Fred McGriff	.25
85	Darryl Hamilton	.05
86	Jeffrey Hammonds	.05
87	Pedro Munoz	.05
88	Craig Biggio	.15
89	Cliff Floyd	.05
90	Tim Naehring	.05
91	Brett Butler	.05
92	Kevin Foster	.05
93	Patrick Kelly	.05
94	John Smiley	.05
95	Terry Steinbach	.05
96	Orel Hershiser	.10
97	Darrin Fletcher	.05
98	Walt Weiss	.05
99	John Wetteland	.05
100	Alan Trammell	.10
101	Steve Avery	.05
102	Tony Eusebio	.05
103	Sandy Alomar	.10
104	Joe Girardi	.05
105	Rick Aguilera	.05
106	Tony Tarasco	.05
107	Chris Hammond	.05
108	Mike McFarlane	.05
109	Doug Drabek	.05
110	Derek Bell	.05
111	Ed Sprague	.05
112	Todd Hollandsworth	.05
113	Otis Nixon	.05
114	Keith Lockhart	.05
115	Donovan Osborne	.05
116	Dave Magadan	.05
117	Edgar Martinez	.05
118	Chuck Carr	.05
119	J.R. Phillips	.05
120	Sean Bergman	.05
121	Andujar Cedeno	.05
122	Eric Young	.10
123	Al Martin	.05
124	Ken Hill	.05
125	Jim Eisenreich	.05
126	Benito Santiago	.05
127	Ariel Prieto	.05
128	Jim Bullinger	.05
129	Russ Davis	.05
130	Jim Abbott	.05
131	Jason Isringhausen	.10
132	Carlos Perez	.05
133	David Segui	.05
134	Troy O'Leary	.05
135	Pat Meares	.05
136	Chris Hoiles	.05
137	Ismael Valdes	.10
138	Jose Oliva	.05
139	Carlos Delgado	.20
140	Tom Goodwin	.05
141	Bob Tewksbury	.05
142	Chris Gomez	.05
143	Jose Oquendo	.05
144	Mark Lewis	.05
145	Salomon Torres	.05
146	Luis Gonzalez	.10
147	Mark Carreon	.05
148	Lance Johnson	.05
149	Melvin Nieves	.05
150	Lee Smith	.05
151	Jacob Brumfield	.05
152	Armando Benitez	.05
153	Curt Shilling	.10
154	Javier Lopez	.10
155	Frank Rodriguez	.05
156	Alex Gonzalez	.10
157	Todd Worrell	.05
158	Benji Gil	.05
159	Greg Gagne	.05
160	Tom Henke	.05
161	Randy Myers	.05
162	Joey Cora	.05
163	Scott Ruffcorn	.05
164	William VanLandingham	.05
165	Tony Phillips	.05
166	Eddie Williams	.05
167	Bobby Bonilla	.05
168	Denny Neagle	.05
169	Troy Percival	.05
170	Billy Ashley	.05
171	Andy Van Slyke	.05
172	Jose Offerman	.05
173	Mark Parent	.05
174	Edgardo Alfonzo	.10
175	Trevor Hoffman	.10
176	David Cone	.10
177	Dan Wilson	.05
178	Steve Ontiveros	.05
179	Dean Palmer	.05
180	Mike Kelly	.05
181	Jim Leyritz	.05
182	Ron Karkovice	.05
183	Kevin Brown	.10
184	*Jose Valentin*	.05
185	Jorge Fabregas	.05
186	Jose Mesa	.05
187	Brent Mayne	.05
188	Carl Everett	.05
189	Paul Sorrento	.05
190	Pete Shourek	.05
191	Scott Kamieniecki	.05
192	Roberto Hernandez	.05
193	Randy Johnson (Radar Rating)	.05
194	Greg Maddux (Radar Rating)	.45
195	Hideo Nomo (Radar Rating)	.15
196	David Cone (Radar Rating)	.05
197	Mike Mussina (Radar Rating)	.10
198	Andy Benes (Radar Rating)	.05
199	Kevin Appier (Radar Rating)	.05
200	John Smoltz (Radar Rating)	.05
201	John Wetteland (Radar Rating)	.05
202	Mark Wohlers (Radar Rating)	.05
203	Stan Belinda	.05
204	Brian Anderson	.05
205	Mike Devereaux	.05
206	Mark Wohlers	.05
207	Omar Vizquel	.05
208	Jose Rijo	.05
209	Willie Blair	.05
210	Jamie Moyer	.05
211	Craig Shipley	.05
212	Shane Reynolds	.05
213	Chad Fonville	.05
214	Jose Vizcaino	.05
215	Sid Fernandez	.05
216	Andy Ashby	.10
217	Frank Castillo	.05
218	Kevin Tapani	.05
219	Kent Mercker	.05
220	Karim Garcia	.25
221	Chris Snopek	.05
222	Tim Unroe	.05
223	Johnny Damon	.10
224	LaTroy Hawkins	.10
225	Mariano Rivera	.15
226	Jose Alberro	.05
227	Angel Martinez	.05
228	Jason Schmidt	.05
229	Tony Clark	.30
230	Kevin Jordan	.05
231	Mark Thompson	.05
232	Jim Dougherty	.05
233	Roger Cedeno	.10
234	Ugueth Urbina	.10
235	Ricky Otero	.05
236	Mark Smith	.05
237	Brian Barber	.05
238	Marc Kroon	.05
239	Joe Rosselli	.05
240	Derek Jeter	1.25
241	Michael Tucker	.05
242	*Joe Borowski*	.05
243	Joe Vitiello	.05
244	Orlando Palmeiro	.05
245	James Baldwin	.05
246	Alan Embree	.05
247	Shannon Penn	.05
248	Chris Stynes	.05
249	Oscar Munoz	.05
250	Jose Herrera	.05
251	Scott Sullivan	.05
252	Reggie Williams	.05
253	Mark Grudzielanek	.05
254	Kevin Jordan	.05
255	Terry Bradshaw	.05
256	*F.P. Santangelo*	.05
257	Doug Johns	.05
258	George Williams	.05
259	Larry Thomas	.05
260	Rudy Pemberton	.05
261	Jim Pittsley	.05
262	Les Norman	.05
263	Ruben Rivera	.10
264	*Cesar Devarez*	.05
265	Greg Zaun	.05
266	Eric Owens	.05
267	John Frascatore	.05
268	Shannon Stewart	.05
269	Checklist	.05
270	Checklist	.05
271	Checklist	.05
272	Checklist	.05
273	Checklist	.05
274	Checklist	.05
275	Checklist	.05
276	Greg Maddux	1.25
277	Pedro Martinez	.10
278	Bobby Higginson	.05
279	Ray Lankford	.10
280	Shawon Dunston	.05
281	Gary Sheffield	.20
282	Ken Griffey Jr.	2.50
283	Paul Molitor	.20
284	Kevin Appier	.05
285	Chuck Knoblauch	.10
286	Alex Fernandez	.10
287	Steve Finley	.05
288	Jeff Blauser	.05
289	Charles Johnson	.10
290	John Franco	.05
291	Mark Langston	.05
292	Bret Saberhagen	.05
293	John Mabry	.05
294	Ramon Martinez	.10
295	Mike Blowers	.05
296	Paul O'Neill	.10
297	Dave Nilsson	.05
298	Dante Bichette	.10
299	Marty Cordova	.10
300	Jay Bell	.05
301	Mike Mussina	.25
302	Ivan Rodriguez	.30
303	Jose Canseco	.20
304	Jeff Bagwell	.60
305	Manny Ramirez	.60
306	Dennis Martinez	.05
307	Charlie Hayes	.05
308	Joe Carter	.10
309	Travis Fryman	.05
310	Mark McGwire	2.50
311	Reggie Sanders	.10
312	Julian Tavarez	.05
313	Jeff Montgomery	.05
314	Andy Benes	.05
315	John Jaha	.05
316	Jeff Kent	.05
317	Mike Piazza	1.25
318	Erik Hanson	.05
319	Kenny Rogers	.05
320	Hideo Nomo	.30
321	Gregg Jefferies	.10
322	Chipper Jones	1.25
323	Jay Buhner	.10
324	Dennis Eckersley	.05
325	Kenny Lofton	.30
326	Robin Ventura	.15
327	Tom Glavine	.10
328	Tim Salmon	.10
329	Andres Galarraga	.10
330	Hal Morris	.05
331	Brady Anderson	.10
332	Chili Davis	.05
333	Roger Clemens	.60
334	Marquis Grissom	.10
335	Jeff (Mike) Greenwell	.05
336	Sammy Sosa	1.25
337	Ron Gant	.10
338	Ken Caminiti	.15
339	Danny Tartabull	.05
340	Barry Bonds	.40
341	Ben McDonald	.05
342	Ruben Sierra	.05
343	Bernie Williams	.30
344	Wil Cordero	.05
345	Wade Boggs	.20
346	Gary Gaetti	.05
347	Greg Colbrunn	.05
348	Juan Gonzalez	.75
349	Marc Newfield	.05
350	Charles Nagy	.10
351	Robby Thompson	.05
352	Roberto Petagine	.05
353	Darryl Strawberry	.10
354	Tino Martinez	.10
355	Eric Karros	.10
356	Cal Ripken Jr.	.75
357	Cecil Fielder	.10
358	Kirby Puckett	.25
359	Jim Edmonds	.10
360	Matt Williams	.10
361	Alex Rodriguez	.75
362	Barry Larkin	.10
363	Rafael Palmeiro	.10
364	David Cone	.10
365	Roberto Alomar	.20
366	Eddie Murray	.10
367	Randy Johnson	.10
368	Ryan Klesko	.10
369	Raul Mondesi	.15
370	Mo Vaughn	.25
371	Will Clark	.10
372	Carlos Baerga	.10
373	Frank Thomas	.40
374	Larry Walker	.10
375	Garret Anderson	.10
376	Edgar Martinez	.05
377	Don Mattingly	.30
378	Tony Gwynn	.30
379	Albert Belle	.20
380	Jason Isringhausen	.10
381	Ruben Rivera	.10
382	Johnny Damon	.10
383	Karim Garcia	.15
384	Derek Jeter	.60
385	David Justice	.10
386	Royce Clayton	.05
387	Mark Whiten	.05
388	Mickey Tettleton	.05
389	Steve Trachsel	.05
390	Danny Bautista	.05
391	Midre Cummings	.05
392	Scott Leius	.05
393	Manny Alexander	.05
394	Brent Gates	.05
395	Rey Sanchez	.05
396	Andy Pettitte	.45
397	Jeff Cirillo	.05
398	Kurt Abbott	.05
399	Lee Tinsley	.05
400	Paul Assenmacher	.05
401	Scott Erickson	.05

402	Todd Zeile	.05
403	Tom Pagnozzi	.05
404	Ozzie Guillen	.05
405	Jeff Frye	.05
406	Kirt Manwaring	.05
407	Chad Ogea	.05
408	Harold Baines	.05
409	Jason Bere	.05
410	Chuck Finley	.05
411	Jeff Fassero	.05
412	Joey Hamilton	.05
413	John Olerud	.15
414	Kevin Stocker	.05
415	Eric Anthony	.05
416	Aaron Sele	.05
417	Chris Bosio	.05
418	Michael Mimbs	.05
419	Orlando Miller	.05
420	Stan Javier	.05
421	Matt Mieske	.05
422	Jason Bates	.05
423	Orlando Merced	.05
424	John Flaherty	.05
425	Reggie Jefferson	.05
426	Scott Stahoviak	.05
427	John Burkett	.05
428	Rod Beck	.05
429	Bill Swift	.05
430	Scott Cooper	.05
431	Mel Rojas	.05
432	Todd Van Poppel	.05
433	Bobby Jones	.05
434	Mike Harkey	.05
435	Sean Berry	.05
436	Glenallen Hill	.05
437	Ryan Thompson	.05
438	Luis Alicea	.05
439	Esteban Loaiza	.10
440	Jeff Reboulet	.05
441	Vince Coleman	.05
442	Ellis Burks	.10
443	Allen Battle	.05
444	Jimmy Key	.05
445	Ricky Bottalico	.05
446	Delino DeShields	.05
447	Albie Lopez	.05
448	Mark Petkovsek	.05
449	Tim Raines	.10
450	Bryan Harvey	.05
451	Pat Hentgen	.05
452	Tim Laker	.05
453	Tom Gordon	.05
454	Phil Plantier	.05
455	Ernie Young	.05
456	Pete Harnisch	.05
457	Roberto Kelly	.05
458	Mark Portugal	.05
459	Mark Leiter	.05
460	Tony Pena	.05
461	Roger Pavlik	.05
462	Jeff King	.05
463	Bryan Rekar	.05
464	Al Leiter	.10
465	Phil Nevin	.05
466	Jose Lima	.10
467	Mike Stanley	.05
468	David McCarty	.05
469	Herb Perry	.05
470	Geronimo Berroa	.05
471	David Wells	.10
472	Vaughn Eshelman	.05
473	Greg Swindell	.05
474	Steve Sparks	.05
475	Luis Sojo	.05
476	Derrick May	.05
477	Joe Oliver	.05
478	Alex Arias	.05
479	Brad Ausmus	.05
480	Gabe White	.05
481	Pat Rapp	.05
482	Damon Buford	.10
483	Turk Wendell	.05
484	Jeff Brantley	.05
485	Curtis Leskanic	.05
486	Robb Nen	.05
487	Lou Whitaker	.05
488	Melido Perez	.05
489	Luis Polonia	.05
490	Scott Brosius	.05
491	Robert Perez	.05
492	*Mike Sweeney*	.05
493	Mark Loretta	.05
494	Alex Ochoa	.05
495	*Matt Lawton*	.05
496	Shawn Estes	.05
497	John Wasdin	.05
498	Marc Kroon	.05
499	Chris Snopek	.05
500	Jeff Suppan	.05
501	Terrell Wade	.05
502	*Marvin Benard*	.05
503	Chris Widger	.05
504	Quinton McCracken	.05
505	Bob Wolcott	.05
506	C.J. Nitkowski	.05
507	Aaron Ledesma	.05
508	Scott Hatteberg	.05
509	Jimmy Haynes	.05
510	Howard Battle	.05

1996 Score All-Stars

An exclusive insert found only in 20-card Series 2 jumbo packs at an average rate of one per nine packs, these inserts feature the game's top stars printed in a rainbow holographic-foil technology.

		MT
Complete Set (20):		60.00
Common Player:		.75
1	Frank Thomas	5.00
2	Albert Belle	3.00
3	Ken Griffey Jr.	12.00
4	Cal Ripken Jr.	9.00
5	Mo Vaughn	2.00
6	Matt Williams	1.50
7	Barry Bonds	3.00
8	Dante Bichette	.75
9	Tony Gwynn	5.00
10	Greg Maddux	7.50
11	Randy Johnson	2.00
12	Hideo Nomo	1.50
13	Tim Salmon	1.50
14	Jeff Bagwell	4.00
15	Edgar Martinez	.75
16	Reggie Sanders	.75
17	Larry Walker	1.50
18	Chipper Jones	7.50
19	Manny Ramirez	3.00
20	Eddie Murray	1.50

1996 Score Big Bats

Gold foil printing highlights cards of 20 of the game's top hitters found in this retail-packaging exclusive insert set. Stated odds of picking a Big Bats card are one in 31 packs.

		MT
Complete Set (20):		100.00
Common Player:		2.00
1	Cal Ripken Jr.	15.00
2	Ken Griffey Jr.	20.00
3	Frank Thomas	10.00
4	Jeff Bagwell	7.50
5	Mike Piazza	12.00
6	Barry Bonds	6.00
7	Matt Williams	2.50
8	Raul Mondesi	2.50
9	Tony Gwynn	7.50
10	Albert Belle	5.00
11	Manny Ramirez	6.00
12	Carlos Baerga	2.00
13	Mo Vaughn	4.00
14	Derek Bell	2.00
15	Larry Walker	2.50
16	Kenny Lofton	4.00
17	Edgar Martinez	2.00
18	Reggie Sanders	2.00
19	Eddie Murray	3.00
20	Chipper Jones	12.00

1996 Score Diamond Aces

Thirty of the top veterans and young stars are included in this jumbo-only insert set, seeded at a rate of one per eight packs.

		MT
Complete Set (30):		125.00
Common Player:		2.50
1	Hideo Nomo	4.00
2	Brian Hunter	2.50
3	Ray Durham	2.50
4	Frank Thomas	15.00
5	Cal Ripken Jr.	25.00
6	Barry Bonds	8.00
7	Greg Maddux	20.00
8	Chipper Jones	20.00
9	Raul Mondesi	3.00
10	Mike Piazza	20.00
11	Derek Jeter	20.00
12	Bill Pulsipher	2.50
13	Larry Walker	3.00
14	Ken Griffey Jr.	30.00
15	Alex Rodriguez	25.00
16	Manny Ramirez	12.00
17	Mo Vaughn	4.00
18	Reggie Sanders	2.50
19	Derek Bell	2.50
20	Jim Edmonds	2.50
21	Albert Belle	8.00
22	Eddie Murray	4.00
23	Tony Gwynn	10.00
24	Jeff Bagwell	10.00
25	Carlos Baerga	2.50
26	Matt Williams	3.00
27	Garret Anderson	2.50
28	Todd Hollandsworth	2.50
29	Johnny Damon	3.00
30	Tim Salmon	3.00

1996 Score Dream Team

The hottest player at each position is honored in the Dream Team insert set. Once again featured on holographic foil printing technology, the cards are found in all types of Score packaging at a rate of once per 72 packs.

		MT
Complete Set (9):		100.00
Common Player:		4.00
1	Cal Ripken Jr.	20.00
2	Frank Thomas	10.00
3	Carlos Baerga	4.00
4	Matt Williams	5.00
5	Mike Piazza	15.00
6	Barry Bonds	7.00
7	Ken Griffey Jr.	25.00
8	Manny Ramirez	7.00
9	Greg Maddux	15.00

1996 Score Dugout Collection

The concept of a partial parallel set, including the stars and rookies but not the journeymen and bench warmers, was initiated with Score's "Dugout Collection," with fewer than half of the cards from the regular series chosen for inclusion. The white borders of the regular cards are replaced with copper-foil and background printing is also done on foil in this special version. On back is a special "Dugout Collection '96" logo. Advertised insertion rate of the copper-version cards is one per three packs.

		MT
Complete Set (220):		75.00
Complete Series 1 (1-110):		40.00
Complete Series 2 (1-110)		40.00
Common Player:		.25
Artist's Proofs: 4X		
	SERIES 1	
1	(Will Clark)	.60
2	(Rich Becker)	.25
3	(Ryan Klesko)	.35
4	(Jim Edmonds)	.35
5	(Barry Larkin)	.30
6	(Jim Thome)	.40
7	(Raul Mondesi)	.40
8	(Don Mattingly)	.75
9	(Jeff Conine)	.25
10	(Rickey Henderson)	.35
11	(Chad Curtis)	.25
12	(Darren Daulton)	.25
13	(Larry Walker)	.40
14	(Carlos Baerga)	.25
15	(Tony Gwynn)	1.50
16	(Jon Nunnally)	.25
17	(Deion Sanders)	.35
18	(Mark Grace)	.40
19	(Alex Rodriguez)	4.00
20	(Frank Thomas)	2.00
21	(Brian Jordan)	.25
22	(J.T. Snow)	.30
23	(Shawn Green)	.40
24	(Tim Wakefield)	.25
25	(Curtis Goodwin)	.25
26	(John Smoltz)	.30
27	(Devon White)	.25
28	(Brian Hunter)	.25
29	(Rusty Greer)	.25
30	(Rafael Palmeiro)	.35
31	(Bernard Gilkey)	.25
32	(John Valentin)	.25
33	(Randy Johnson)	.45
34	(Garret Anderson)	.25
35	(Ray Durham)	.25
36	(Bip Roberts)	.25
37	(Tyler Green)	.25
38	(Bill Pulsipher)	.25
39	(Jason Giambi)	.25
40	(Jack McDowell)	.25
41	(Rico Brogna)	.25
42	(Terry Pendleton)	.25
43	(Rondell White)	.35
44	(Andre Dawson)	.35
45	(Kirby Puckett)	1.50
46	(Wally Joyner)	.25
47	(B.J. Surhoff)	.25
48	(Randy Velarde)	.25
49	(Greg Vaughn)	.30
50	(Roberto Alomar)	.50
51	(David Justice)	.40
52	(Cal Ripken Jr.)	4.00
53	(Ozzie Smith)	1.25
54	(Mo Vaughn)	.60
55	(Gary DiSarcina)	.25
56	(Matt Williams)	.40
57	(Lenny Dykstra)	.25
58	(Bret Boone)	.25
59	(Albert Belle)	1.50
60	(Vinny Castilla)	.30
61	(Moises Alou)	.25
62	(Cecil Fielder)	.25
63	(Brad Radke)	.25
64	(Quilvio Veras)	.25
65	(Eddie Murray)	.40
66	(Dave Winfield)	.40
67	(Fred McGriff)	.35
68	(Craig Biggio)	.35
69	(Cliff Floyd)	.25
70	(Tim Naehring)	.25
71	(John Wetteland)	.25
72	(Alan Trammell)	.35
73	(Steve Avery)	.25
74	(Rick Aguilera)	.25
75	(Derek Bell)	.25
76	(Todd Hollandsworth)	.25
77	(Edgar Martinez)	.25
78	(Mark Lemke)	.25
79	(Ariel Prieto)	.25
80	(Russ Davis)	.25
81	(Jim Abbott)	.25
82	(Jason Isringhausen)	.25
83	(Carlos Perez)	.25
84	(David Segui)	.25
85	(Troy O'Leary)	.25
86	(Ismael Valdes)	.25
87	(Carlos Delgado)	.30
88	(Lee Smith)	.25
89	(Javy Lopez)	.30
90	(Frank Rodriguez)	.25
91	(Alex Gonzalez)	.30
92	(Benji Gil)	.25
93	(Greg Gagne)	.25
94	(Randy Myers)	.25
95	(Bobby Bonilla)	.25
96	(Billy Ashley)	.25
97	(Andy Van Slyke)	.25
98	(Edgardo Alfonzo)	.30
99	(David Cone)	.30
100	(Dean Palmer)	.25
101	(Jose Mesa)	.25
102	(Karim Garcia)	.50
103	(Johnny Damon)	.35
104	(LaTroy Hawkins)	.25
105	(Mark Smith)	.25
106	(Derek Jeter)	4.00
107	(Michael Tucker)	.25
108	(Joe Vitiello)	.25
109	(Ruben Rivera)	.25
110	(Greg Zaun)	.25
	SERIES 2	
1	Greg Maddux	2.50
2	Pedro Martinez	.35
3	Bobby Higginson	.35
4	Ray Lankford	.25
5	Shawon Dunston	.25
6	Gary Sheffield	.60
7	Ken Griffey Jr.	5.00
8	Paul Molitor	1.25
9	Kevin Appier	.25
10	Chuck Knoblauch	.45
11	Alex Fernandez	.30
12	Steve Finley	.25
13	Jeff Blauser	.25
14	Charles Johnson	.35
15	John Franco	.25
16	Mark Langston	.25
17	Bret Saberhagen	.35
18	John Mabry	.25
19	Ramon Martinez	.30
20	Mike Blowers	.25
21	Paul O'Neill	.30
22	Dave Nilsson	.25
23	Dante Bichette	.40
24	Marty Cordova	.25
25	Jay Bell	.25
26	Mike Mussina	.35
27	Ivan Rodriguez	.40
28	Jose Canseco	.40
29	Jeff Bagwell	.75
30	Manny Ramirez	.60
31	Dennis Martinez	.25
32	Charlie Hayes	.25
33	Joe Carter	.05
34	Travis Fryman	.25
35	Mark McGwire	5.00
36	Reggie Sanders	.25
37	Julian Tavarez	.25
38	Jeff Montgomery	.25
39	Andy Benes	.25
40	John Jaha	.25
41	Jeff Kent	.25
42	Mike Piazza	2.50
43	Erik Hanson	.25
44	Kenny Rogers	.25
45	Hideo Nomo	1.00
46	Gregg Jefferies	.25
47	Chipper Jones	2.50
48	Jay Buhner	.35
49	Dennis Eckersley	.25
50	Kenny Lofton	.35
51	Robin Ventura	.30
52	Tom Glavine	.30
53	Tim Salmon	.35
54	Andres Galarraga	.30
55	Hal Morris	.25
56	Brady Anderson	.30
57	Chili Davis	.25
58	Roger Clemens	.65
59	Marquis Grissom	.30
60	Mike Greenwell	.25
61	Sammy Sosa	2.00
62	Ron Gant	.25
63	Ken Caminiti	.30
64	Danny Tartabull	.25
65	Barry Bonds	1.50
66	Ben McDonald	.25
67	Ruben Sierra	.25
68	Bernie Williams	.45
69	Wil Cordero	.25
70	Wade Boggs	.45
71	Gary Gaetti	.25
72	Greg Colbrunn	.25
73	Juan Gonzalez	.75
74	Marc Newfield	.25
75	Charles Nagy	.25
76	Robby Thompson	.25

77	Roberto Petagine	.25
78	Darryl Strawberry	.35
79	Tino Martinez	.25
80	Eric Karros	.25
81	Cal Ripken Jr. (Star Struck)	3.00
82	Cecil Fielder (Star Struck)	.25
83	Kirby Puckett (Star Struck)	1.00
84	Jim Edmonds (Star Struck)	.25
85	Matt Williams (Star Struck)	.25
86	Alex Rodriguez (Star Struck)	3.00
87	Barry Larkin (Star Struck)	.25
88	Rafael Palmeiro (Star Struck)	.25
89	David Cone (Star Struck)	.25
90	Roberto Alomar (Star Struck)	.35
91	Eddie Murray (Star Struck)	.30
92	Randy Johnson (Star Struck)	.35
93	Ryan Klesko (Star Struck)	.30
94	Raul Mondesi (Star Struck)	.30
95	Mo Vaughn (Star Struck)	.60
96	Will Clark (Star Struck)	.30
97	Carlos Baerga (Star Struck)	.25
98	Frank Thomas (Star Struck)	2.00
99	Larry Walker (Star Struck)	.30
100	Garret Anderson (Star Struck)	.25
101	Edgar Martinez (Star Struck)	.25
102	Don Mattingly (Star Struck)	.75
103	Tony Gwynn (Star Struck)	.75
104	Albert Belle (Star Struck)	1.50
105	Jason Isringhausen (Star Struck)	.25
106	Ruben Rivera (Star Struck)	.25
107	Johnny Damon (Star Struck)	.25
108	Karim Garcia (Star Struck)	.35
109	Derek Jeter (Star Struck)	2.50
110	David Justice (Star Struck)	.35

1996 Score Dugout Collection Artist's Proofs

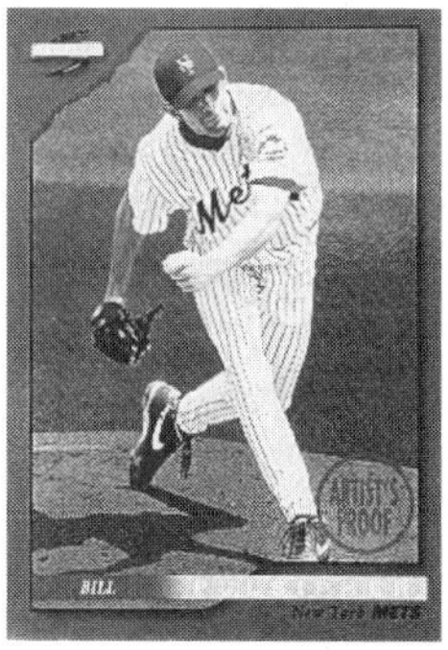

A parallel set within a parallel set, the Artist's Proof logo added to the copper-foil design of the Dugout Collection cards raises the odds of finding one to just once in 36 packs.

	MT
Complete Set (220):	600.00
Common Player:	1.50
Artist's Proof Stars: 4X	
(See 1996 Score Dugout Collection for checklist and base card values.)	

1996 Score Future Franchise

Future Franchise is the most difficult insert to pull from packs of Series 2, at the rate of once per 72 packs, on average. Sixteen young stars are showcased on holographic gold-foil printing in the set.

		MT
Complete Set (16):		110.00
Common Player:		3.00
1	Jason Isringhausen	3.00
2	Chipper Jones	25.00
3	Derek Jeter	25.00
4	Alex Rodriguez	35.00
5	Alex Ochoa	3.00
6	Manny Ramirez	15.00
7	Johnny Damon	4.00
8	Ruben Rivera	3.00
9	Karim Garcia	7.50
10	Garret Anderson	3.00
11	Marty Cordova	3.00
12	Bill Pulsipher	3.00
13	Hideo Nomo	6.00
14	Marc Newfield	3.00
15	Charles Johnson	4.00
16	Raul Mondesi	5.00

1996 Score Gold Stars

Appearing once in every 15 packs of Series 2, Gold Stars are labeled with a stamp in the upper-left corner. The set contains 30 top current stars printed on gold-foil and seeded at the average rate of one per 15 packs.

		MT
Complete Set (30):		50.00
Common Player:		.75
1	Ken Griffey Jr.	9.00
2	Frank Thomas	5.00
3	Reggie Sanders	.75
4	Tim Salmon	1.00
5	Mike Piazza	6.00
6	Tony Gwynn	4.00
7	Gary Sheffield	1.00
8	Matt Williams	1.00
9	Bernie Williams	1.00
10	Jason Isringhausen	.75
11	Albert Belle	2.50
12	Chipper Jones	6.00
13	Edgar Martinez	.75
14	Barry Larkin	1.00
15	Barry Bonds	2.50
16	Jeff Bagwell	4.00
17	Greg Maddux	6.00
18	Mo Vaughn	2.00
19	Ryan Klesko	1.00
20	Sammy Sosa	6.00
21	Darren Daulton	.75
22	Ivan Rodriguez	1.50
23	Dante Bichette	1.00
24	Hideo Nomo	1.00
25	Cal Ripken Jr.	7.50
26	Rafael Palmeiro	1.00
27	Larry Walker	1.00
28	Carlos Baerga	.75
29	Randy Johnson	1.50
30	Manny Ramirez	4.00

1996 Score Numbers Game

Some of the 1995 season's most impressive statistical accomplishments are featured in this chase set. Cards are enhanced with gold foil and found in all types of Score packs at an average rate of one per 15 packs.

		MT
Complete Set (30):		60.00
Common Player:		.75
1	Cal Ripken Jr.	8.00
2	Frank Thomas	5.00
3	Ken Griffey Jr.	10.00
4	Mike Piazza	6.00
5	Barry Bonds	2.50
6	Greg Maddux	6.00
7	Jeff Bagwell	4.00
8	Derek Bell	.75
9	Tony Gwynn	4.00
10	Hideo Nomo	1.00
11	Raul Mondesi	1.25
12	Manny Ramirez	4.00
13	Albert Belle	2.50
14	Matt Williams	1.00
15	Jim Edmonds	.75
16	Edgar Martinez	.75
17	Mo Vaughn	2.00
18	Reggie Sanders	.75
19	Chipper Jones	6.00
20	Larry Walker	1.00
21	Juan Gonzalez	5.00
22	Kenny Lofton	2.00
23	Don Mattingly	4.00
24	Ivan Rodriguez	1.50
25	Randy Johnson	2.00
26	Derek Jeter	6.00
27	J.T. Snow	.75
28	Will Clark	1.00
29	Rafael Palmeiro	1.00
30	Alex Rodriguez	8.00

1996 Score Power Pace

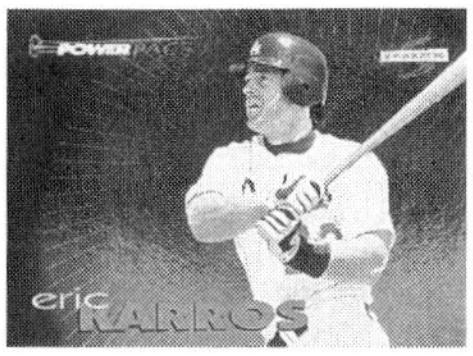

Power Pace is exclusive to retail packs in Series 2, where they are found on average every 31 packs. Eighteen top power hitters are featured in this issue in a gold-foil design.

		MT
Complete Set (18):		60.00
Common Player:		1.50
1	Mark McGwire	17.50
2	Albert Belle	4.00
3	Jay Buhner	1.50
4	Frank Thomas	7.50
5	Matt Williams	2.00
6	Gary Sheffield	2.00
7	Mike Piazza	12.50
8	Larry Walker	2.00
9	Mo Vaughn	3.00
10	Rafael Palmeiro	2.00
11	Dante Bichette	2.00
12	Ken Griffey Jr.	17.50
13	Barry Bonds	4.00
14	Manny Ramirez	6.00
15	Sammy Sosa	10.00
16	Tim Salmon	2.00
17	Dave Justice	1.50
18	Eric Karros	1.50

1996 Score Reflexions

Appearing only in hobby packs this insert set pairs 20 veteran stars with 20 up-and-coming players in a foil-printed format. Odds of finding a Reflexions insert are stated as one per 31 packs.

		MT
Complete Set (20):		100.00
Common Player:		1.50
1	Cal Ripken Jr., Chipper Jones	20.00
2	Ken Griffey Jr., Alex Rodriguez	25.00
3	Frank Thomas, Mo Vaughn	10.00
4	Kenny Lofton, Brian Hunter	3.00
5	Don Mattingly, J.T. Snow	4.00
6	Manny Ramirez, Raul Mondesi	7.50
7	Tony Gwynn, Garret Anderson	5.00
8	Roberto Alomar, Carlos Baerga	3.00
9	Andre Dawson, Larry Walker	2.00
10	Barry Larkin, Derek Jeter	10.00
11	Barry Bonds, Reggie Sanders	4.00
12	Mike Piazza, Albert Belle	10.00
13	Wade Boggs, Edgar Martinez	1.50
14	David Cone, John Smoltz	1.50
15	Will Clark, Jeff Bagwell	5.00
16	Mark McGwire, Cecil Fielder	20.00
17	Greg Maddux, Mike Mussina	10.00
18	Randy Johnson, Hideo Nomo	2.50
19	Jim Thome, Dean Palmer	1.50
20	Chuck Knoblauch, Craig Biggio	2.00

1996 Score Cal Ripken Tribute

The toughest pick among the 1996 Score inserts is this special card marking Cal Ripken's 2,131st consecutive game. The insertion rate is one per 300 packs hobby and retail, one per 150 jumbo packs.

	MT
2131 Cal Ripken Jr. (Tribute)	16.00

1996 Score Titantic Taters

One of the more creative names in the 1996 insert lineup, Titanic Taters are found one in every 31 packs of Series 2 hobby. Gold-foil fronts feature 18 of the game's heaviest hitters.

		MT
Complete Set (18):		80.00
Common Player:		2.00
1	Albert Belle	5.00
2	Frank Thomas	10.00
3	Mo Vaughn	4.00
4	Ken Griffey Jr.	20.00
5	Matt Williams	2.50
6	Mark McGwire	20.00
7	Dante Bichette	2.50
8	Tim Salmon	2.50
9	Jeff Bagwell	7.50
10	Rafael Palmeiro	2.50
11	Mike Piazza	15.00
12	Cecil Fielder	2.00
13	Larry Walker	2.50
14	Sammy Sosa	12.00
15	Manny Ramirez	7.50
16	Gary Sheffield	2.50
17	Barry Bonds	5.00
18	Jay Buhner	2.00

1997 Score

A total of 551 cards make up the base set, with 330 cards sold in Series I and 221 making up Series II. The basic card design features a color action photo surrounded by a white border. The player's name is above the photo, with the team name underneath. Backs feature text and statistics against a white background with the image of the team logo ghosted into the background. Two parallel insert sets - Artist's Proof and Showcase Series - were part of each series. Other inserts in Series I were Pitcher Perfect, The Franchise, The Glowing Franchise, Titanic Taters (retail exclusive), Stellar Season (magazine packs only), and The Highlight Zone (hobby exclusive). Series II inserts were Blastmasters, Heart of the Order and Stand and Deliver. Cards were sold in 10-card packs for 99 cents each.

		MT
Complete Set (551):		35.00
Complete Series 1 Set (330):		20.00
Complete Series 2 Set (221):		15.00
Common Player:		.05
Wax Box:		30.00
1	Jeff Bagwell	.75
2	Mickey Tettleton	.05
3	Johnny Damon	.15
4	Jeff Conine	.05
5	Bernie Williams	.40
6	Will Clark	.20
7	Ryan Klesko	.25

8	Cecil Fielder	.10
9	Paul Wilson	.05
10	Gregg Jefferies	.05
11	Chili Davis	.05
12	Albert Belle	.50
13	Ken Hill	.05
14	Cliff Floyd	.05
15	Jaime Navarro	.05
16	Ismael Valdes	.05
17	Jeff King	.05
18	Chris Bosio	.05
19	Reggie Sanders	.05
20	Darren Daulton	.05
21	Ken Caminiti	.15
22	Mike Piazza	1.25
23	Chad Mottola	.05
24	Darin Erstad	.75
25	Dante Bichette	.15
26	Frank Thomas	1.00
27	Ben McDonald	.05
28	Raul Casanova	.05
29	Kevin Ritz	.05
30	Garret Anderson	.05
31	Jason Kendall	.05
32	Billy Wagner	.10
33	David Justice	.10
34	Marty Cordova	.05
35	Derek Jeter	1.25
36	Trevor Hoffman	.10
37	Geronimo Berroa	.05
38	Walt Weiss	.05
39	Kirt Manwaring	.05
40	Alex Gonzalez	.10
41	Sean Berry	.05
42	Kevin Appier	.05
43	Rusty Greer	.05
44	Pete Incaviglia	.05
45	Rafael Palmeiro	.10
46	Eddie Murray	.30
47	Moises Alou	.10
48	Mark Lewis	.05
49	Hal Morris	.05
50	Edgar Renteria	.25
51	Rickey Henderson	.20
52	Pat Listach	.05
53	John Wasdin	.05
54	James Baldwin	.05
55	Brian Jordan	.05
56	Edgar Martinez	.05
57	Wil Cordero	.05
58	Danny Tartabull	.05
59	Keith Lockhart	.05
60	Rico Brogna	.05
61	Ricky Bottalico	.05
62	Terry Pendleton	.05
63	Bret Boone	.05
64	Charlie Hayes	.05
65	Marc Newfield	.05
66	Sterling Hitchcock	.05
67	Roberto Alomar	.50
68	John Jaha	.05
69	Greg Colbrunn	.05
70	Sal Fasano	.05
71	Brooks Kieschnick	.05
72	Pedro Martinez	.10
73	Kevin Elster	.05
74	Ellis Burks	.05
75	Chuck Finley	.05
76	John Olerud	.10
77	Jay Bell	.05
78	Allen Watson	.05
79	Darryl Strawberry	.05
80	Orlando Miller	.05
81	Jose Herrera	.05
82	Andy Pettitte	.40
83	Juan Guzman	.05
84	Alan Benes	.05
85	Jack McDowell	.05
86	Ugueth Urbina	.05
87	Rocky Coppinger	.05
88	Jeff Cirillo	.05
89	Tom Glavine	.15
90	Robby Thompson	.05
91	Barry Bonds	.50
92	Carlos Delgado	.25
93	Mo Vaughn	.50
94	Ryne Sandberg	.40
95	Alex Rodriguez	2.00
96	Brady Anderson	.10
97	Scott Brosius	.05
98	Dennis Eckersley	.05
99	Brian McRae	.05
100	Rey Ordonez	.25
101	John Valentin	.05
102	Brett Butler	.05
103	Eric Karros	.10
104	Harold Baines	.05
105	Javier Lopez	.15
106	Alan Trammell	.05
107	Jim Thome	.25
108	Frank Rodriguez	.05
109	Bernard Gilkey	.05
110	Reggie Jefferson	.05
111	Scott Stahoviak	.05
112	Steve Gibralter	.05
113	Todd Hollandsworth	.05
114	Ruben Rivera	.10
115	Dennis Martinez	.05
116	Mariano Rivera	.25
117	John Smoltz	.20
118	John Mabry	.05
119	Tom Gordon	.05
120	Alex Ochoa	.05
121	Jamey Wright	.05
122	Dave Nilsson	.05
123	Bobby Bonilla	.05
124	Al Leiter	.10
125	Rick Aguilera	.05
126	Jeff Brantley	.05
127	Kevin Brown	.10
128	George Arias	.05
129	Darren Oliver	.05
130	Bill Pulsipher	.05
131	Roberto Hernandez	.05
132	Delino DeShields	.05
133	Mark Grudzielanek	.05
134	John Wetteland	.05
135	Carlos Baerga	.05
136	Paul Sorrento	.05
137	Leo Gomez	.05
138	Andy Ashby	.05
139	Julio Franco	.05
140	Brian Hunter	.05
141	Jermaine Dye	.10
142	Tony Clark	.40
143	Ruben Sierra	.05
144	Donovan Osborne	.05
145	Mark McLemore	.05
146	Terry Steinbach	.05
147	Bob Wells	.05
148	Chan Ho Park	.10
149	Tim Salmon	.15
150	Paul O'Neill	.10
151	Cal Ripken Jr.	2.00
152	Wally Joyner	.05
153	Omar Vizquel	.05
154	Mike Mussina	.40
155	Andres Galarraga	.15
156	Ken Griffey Jr.	3.00
157	Kenny Lofton	.50
158	Ray Durham	.05
159	Hideo Nomo	.25
160	Ozzie Guillen	.05
161	Roger Pavlik	.05
162	Manny Ramirez	.60
163	Mark Lemke	.05
164	Mike Stanley	.05
165	Chuck Knoblauch	.10
166	Kimera Bartee	.05
167	Wade Boggs	.20
168	Jay Buhner	.10
169	Eric Young	.05
170	Jose Canseco	.20
171	Dwight Gooden	.05
172	Fred McGriff	.20
173	Sandy Alomar Jr.	.10
174	Andy Benes	.05
175	Dean Palmer	.05
176	Larry Walker	.25
177	Charles Nagy	.10
178	David Cone	.10
179	Mark Grace	.15
180	Robin Ventura	.10
181	Roger Clemens	.60
182	Bobby Witt	.05
183	Vinny Castilla	.10
184	Gary Sheffield	.15
185	Dan Wilson	.05
186	Roger Cedeno	.05
187	Mark McGwire	3.00
188	Darren Bragg	.05
189	Quinton McCracken	.05
190	Randy Myers	.05
191	Jeromy Burnitz	.05
192	Randy Johnson	.25
193	Chipper Jones	1.25
194	Greg Vaughn	.10
195	Travis Fryman	.05
196	Tim Naehring	.05
197	B.J. Surhoff	.05
198	Juan Gonzalez	.75
199	Terrell Wade	.05
200	Jeff Frye	.05
201	Joey Cora	.05
202	Raul Mondesi	.15
203	Ivan Rodriguez	.50
204	Armando Reynoso	.05
205	Jeffrey Hammonds	.05
206	Darren Dreifort	.05
207	Kevin Seitzer	.05
208	Tino Martinez	.25
209	Jim Bruske	.05
210	Jeff Suppan	.05
211	Mark Carreon	.05
212	Wilson Alvarez	.05
213	John Burkett	.05
214	Tony Phillips	.05
215	Greg Maddux	1.25
216	Mark Whiten	.05
217	Curtis Pride	.05
218	Lyle Mouton	.05
219	Todd Hundley	.10
220	Greg Gagne	.05
221	Rich Amaral	.05
222	Tom Goodwin	.05
223	Chris Hoiles	.05
224	Jayhawk Owens	.05
225	Kenny Rogers	.05
226	Mike Greenwell	.05
227	Mark Wohlers	.05
228	Henry Rodriguez	.05
229	Robert Perez	.05
230	Jeff Kent	.05
231	Darryl Hamilton	.05
232	Alex Fernandez	.10
233	Ron Karkovice	.05
234	Jimmy Haynes	.05
235	Craig Biggio	.15
236	Ray Lankford	.05
237	Lance Johnson	.05
238	Matt Williams	.20
239	Chad Curtis	.05
240	Mark Thompson	.05
241	Jason Giambi	.05
242	Barry Larkin	.15
243	Paul Molitor	.25
244	Sammy Sosa	1.00
245	Kevin Tapani	.05
246	Marquis Grissom	.05
247	Joe Carter	.10
248	Ramon Martinez	.10
249	Tony Gwynn	.75
250	Andy Fox	.05
251	Troy O'Leary	.05
252	Warren Newson	.05
253	Troy Percival	.05
254	Jamie Moyer	.05
255	Danny Graves	.05
256	David Wells	.10
257	Todd Zeile	.05
258	Raul Ibanez	.05
259	Tyler Houston	.05
260	LaTroy Hawkins	.05
261	Joey Hamilton	.05
262	Mike Sweeney	.05
263	Brant Brown	.05
264	Pat Hentgen	.05
265	Mark Johnson	.05
266	Robb Nen	.05
267	Justin Thompson	.05
268	Ron Gant	.05
269	Jeff D'Amico	.05
270	Shawn Estes	.05
271	Derek Bell	.05
272	Fernando Valenzuela	.05
273	Luis Castillo	.10
274	Ray Montgomery	.05
275	Ed Sprague	.05
276	F.P. Santangelo	.05
277	Todd Greene	.05
278	Butch Huskey	.05
279	Steve Finley	.05
280	Eric Davis	.05
281	Shawn Green	.10
282	Al Martin	.05
283	Michael Tucker	.05
284	Shane Reynolds	.05
285	Matt Mieske	.05
286	Jose Rosado	.05
287	Mark Langston	.05
288	Ralph Milliard	.05
289	Mike Lansing	.05
290	Scott Servais	.05
291	Royce Clayton	.05
292	Mike Grace	.05
293	James Mouton	.05
294	Charles Johnson	.05
295	Gary Gaetti	.05
296	Kevin Mitchell	.05
297	Carlos Garcia	.05
298	Desi Relaford	.05
299	Jason Thompson	.05
300	Osvaldo Fernandez	.05
301	Fernando Vina	.05
302	Jose Offerman	.05
303	Yamil Benitez	.05
304	J.T. Snow	.05
305	Rafael Bournigal	.05
306	Jason Isringhausen	.05
307	Bob Higginson	.05
308	*Nerio Rodriguez*	.15
309	*Brian Giles*	.75
310	Andruw Jones	1.00
311	Billy McMillon	.05
312	Arquimedez Pozo	.05
313	Jermaine Allensworth	.05
314	Luis Andujar	.05
315	Angel Echevarria	.05
316	Karim Garcia	.30
317	Trey Beamon	.05
318	Makoto Suzuki	.05
319	Robin Jennings	.05
320	Dmitri Young	.05
321	*Damon Mashore*	.05
322	Wendell Magee	.05
323	*Dax Jones*	.05
324	Todd Walker	.40
325	Marvin Benard	.05
326	*Brian Raabe*	.05
327	Marcus Jensen	.05
328	Checklist	.05
329	Checklist	.05
330	Checklist	.05
331	Norm Charlton	.05
332	Bruce Ruffin	.05
333	John Wetteland	.05
334	Marquis Grissom	.05
335	Sterling Hitchcock	.05
336	John Olerud	.10
337	David Wells	.10
338	Chili Davis	.05
339	Mark Lewis	.05
340	Kenny Lofton	.50
341	Alex Fernandez	.10
342	Ruben Sierra	.05
343	Delino DeShields	.05
344	John Wasdin	.05
345	Dennis Martinez	.05
346	Kevin Elster	.05
347	Bobby Bonilla	.05
348	Jaime Navarro	.05
349	Chad Curtis	.05
350	Terry Steinbach	.05
351	Ariel Prieto	.05
352	Jeff Kent	.05
353	Carlos Garcia	.05
354	Mark Whiten	.05
355	Todd Zelle	.05
356	Eric Davis	.05
357	Greg Colbrunn	.05
358	Moises Alou	.10
359	Allen Watson	.05
360	Jose Canseco	.20
361	Matt Williams	.25
362	Jeff King	.05
363	Darryl Hamilton	.05
364	Mark Clark	.05
365	J.T. Snow	.05
366	Kevin Mitchell	.05
367	Orlando Miller	.05
368	Rico Brogna	.05
369	Mike James	.05
370	Brad Ausmus	.05
371	Darryl Kile	.05
372	Edgardo Alfonzo	.10
373	Julian Tavarez	.05
374	Darren Lewis	.05
375	Steve Karsay	.05
376	Lee Stevens	.05
377	Albie Lopez	.05
378	Orel Hershiser	.05
379	Lee Smith	.05
380	Rick Helling	.05
381	Carlos Perez	.05
382	Tony Tarasco	.05
383	Melvin Nieves	.05
384	Benji Gil	.05
385	Devon White	.05
386	Armando Benitez	.05
387	Bill Swift	.05
388	John Smiley	.05
389	Midre Cummings	.05
390	Tim Belcher	.05
391	Tim Raines	.05
392	Todd Worrell	.05
393	Quilvio Veras	.05
394	Matt Lawton	.05
395	Aaron Sele	.05
396	Bip Roberts	.05
397	Denny Neagle	.05
398	Tyler Green	.05
399	Hipolito Pichardo	.05
400	Scott Erickson	.05
401	Bobby Jones	.05
402	Jim Edmonds	.05
403	Chad Ogea	.05
404	Cal Eldred	.05
405	Pat Listach	.05
406	Todd Stottlemyre	.05
407	Phil Nevin	.05
408	Otis Nixon	.05
409	Billy Ashley	.05
410	Jimmy Key	.05
411	Mike Timlin	.05
412	Joe Vitiello	.05
413	Rondell White	.10
414	Jeff Fassero	.05
415	Rex Hudler	.05
416	Curt Schilling	.10
417	Rich Becker	.05
418	William VanLandingham	.05
419	Chris Snopek	.05
420	David Segui	.05
421	Eddie Murray	.25
422	Shane Andrews	.05
423	Gary DiSarcina	.05
424	Brian Hunter	.05
425	Willie Greene	.05
426	Felipe Crespo	.05
427	Jason Bates	.05
428	Albert Belle	.50
429	Rey Sanchez	.05
430	Roger Clemens	.75
431	Deion Sanders	.20
432	Ernie Young	.05
433	Jay Bell	.05
434	Jeff Blauser	.05
435	Lenny Dykstra	.05
436	Chuck Carr	.05
437	Russ Davis	.05
438	Carl Everett	.05
439	Damion Easley	.05
440	Pat Kelly	.05
441	Pat Rapp	.05
442	David Justice	.15
443	Graeme Lloyd	.05
444	Damon Buford	.05
445	Jose Valentin	.05
446	Jason Schmidt	.05
447	Dave Martinez	.05
448	Danny Tartabull	.05
449	Jose Vizcaino	.05
450	Steve Avery	.05
451	Mike Devereaux	.05
452	Jim Eisenreich	.05
453	Mark Leiter	.05
454	Roberto Kelly	.05
455	Benito Santiago	.05
456	Steve Trachsel	.05
457	Gerald Williams	.05
458	Pete Schourek	.05
459	Esteban Loaiza	.05
460	Mel Rojas	.05
461	Tim Wakefield	.05
462	Tony Fernandez	.05
463	Doug Drabek	.05
464	Joe Girardi	.05
465	Mike Bordick	.05
466	Jim Leyritz	.05
467	Erik Hanson	.05
468	Michael Tucker	.05
469	*Tony Womack*	.25
470	Doug Glanville	.05
471	Rudy Pemberton	.05
472	Keith Lockhart	.05
473	Nomar Garciaparra	1.25
474	Scott Rolen	.75
475	Jason Dickson	.15
476	Glendon Rusch	.05
477	Todd Walker	.40
478	Dmitri Young	.05
479	*Rod Myers*	.05
480	Wilton Guerrero	.10
481	Jorge Posada	.05
482	Brant Brown	.05
483	*Bubba Trammell*	.50
484	Jose Guillen	.50
485	Scott Spiezio	.05
486	Bob Abreu	.05
487	Chris Holt	.05
488	*Deivi Cruz*	.25
489	Vladimir Guerrero	.60
490	Julio Santana	.05
491	Ray Montgomery	.05
492	Kevin Orie	.05
493	Todd Hundley (Goin' Yard)	.10
494	Tim Salmon (Goin' Yard)	.15
495	Albert Belle (Goin' Yard)	.25
496	Manny Ramirez (Goin' Yard)	.30
497	Rafael Palmeiro (Goin' Yard)	.10
498	Juan Gonzalez (Goin' Yard)	.40
499	Ken Griffey Jr. (Goin' Yard)	1.50
500	Andruw Jones (Goin' Yard)	.50
501	Mike Piazza (Goin' Yard)	.60
502	Jeff Bagwell (Goin' Yard)	.40
503	Bernie Williams (Goin' Yard)	.20
504	Barry Bonds (Goin' Yard)	.25
505	Ken Caminiti (Goin' Yard)	.10
506	Darin Erstad (Goin' Yard)	.50
507	Alex Rodriguez (Goin' Yard)	1.00
508	Frank Thomas (Goin' Yard)	.50
509	Chipper Jones (Goin' Yard)	.60
510	Mo Vaughn (Goin' Yard)	.25
511	Mark McGwire (Goin' Yard)	1.50
512	Fred McGriff (Goin' Yard)	.15
513	Jay Buhner (Goin' Yard)	.05
514	Jim Thome (Goin' Yard)	.15
515	Gary Sheffield (Goin' Yard)	.15
516	Dean Palmer (Goin' Yard)	.05
517	Henry Rodriguez (Goin' Yard)	.05
518	Andy Pettitte (Rock & Fire)	.25
519	Mike Mussina (Rock & Fire)	.20
520	Greg Maddux (Rock & Fire)	.60
521	John Smoltz (Rock & Fire)	.10
522	Hideo Nomo (Rock & Fire)	.15
523	Troy Percival (Rock & Fire)	.05
524	John Wetteland (Rock & Fire)	.05
525	Roger Clemens (Rock & Fire)	.25
526	Charles Nagy (Rock & Fire)	.05
527	Mariano Rivera (Rock & Fire)	.10
528	Tom Glavine (Rock & Fire)	.10
529	Randy Johnson (Rock & Fire)	.20
530	Jason Isringhausen (Rock & Fire)	.05
531	Alex Fernandez (Rock & Fire)	.05
532	Kevin Brown (Rock & Fire)	.05
533	Chuck Knoblauch (True Grit)	.10
534	Rusty Greer (True Grit)	.05
535	Tony Gwynn (True Grit)	.40
536	Ryan Klesko (True Grit)	.20
537	Ryne Sandberg (True Grit)	.25
538	Barry Larkin (True Grit)	.10
539	Will Clark (True Grit)	.10
540	Kenny Lofton (True Grit)	.25
541	Paul Molitor (True Grit)	.15
542	Roberto Alomar (True Grit)	.20
543	Rey Ordonez (True Grit)	.05
544	Jason Giambi (True Grit)	.05
545	Derek Jeter (True Grit)	.60

546	Cal Ripken Jr. (True Grit)	.75
547	Ivan Rodriguez (True Grit)	.20
548	Checklist (Ken Griffey Jr.)	.75
549	Checklist (Frank Thomas)	.40
550	Checklist (Mike Piazza)	.50
551a	*Hideki Irabu* (SP) (English on back; factory sets/retail packs)	1.00
551b	*Hideki Irabu* (SP) (Japanese back; Hobby Reserve packs)	1.00

1997 Score Artist's Proofs

Specially marked Artist's Proof cards were random inserts in Series 1 and 2 retail packs.

	MT
Complete Set (551):	1600.
Complete Series 1 (330)	900.00
Complete Series 2 (221)	700.00
Common Player:	1.50
Artist's Proof Stars: 15X	
(See 1997 Score for checklist and base card values.)	

1997 Score Hobby Reserve

This is a hobby-only parallel version of Score Series 2, similar in concept to the Series 1 Premium Stock. Cards are identical to the regular Series 2 cards except for the addition of a gold Hobby Reserve foil seal on front.

	MT
Complete Set (221):	30.00
Common Player:	.10
Hobby Reserve Stars: 1.5X	
(See 1997 Score #331-551 for checklist and base card values.)	

1997 Score Premium Stock

This is an upscale version of Score's regular Series 1 1997 issue, designated for hobby sales only. The cards are basically the same as the regular issue, except for the use of gray borders on front and an embossed gold-foil "Premium Stock" logo.

	MT
Complete Set (330):	30.00
Common Player:	.10
Premium Stock Stars: 1,5X	
(See 1997 Score #1-330 for checklist and base card values.)	

1997 Score Reserve Collection

This was a hobby-only parallel version of Score Series 2, Cards are similar to regular Series 2 Score except for the use of a textured ray-like silver-foil background on front and a Reserve Collection underprint on back. Cards are numbered with an "HR" prefix. Average insertion rate was one per 11 packs.

	MT
Complete Set (221):	450.00
Common Player:	2.00
Reserve Collection Stars: 10X	
(See 1997 Score #331-551 for checklist and base card values.)	

1997 Score Showcase

A silver metallic-foil background distinguishes the cards in this parallel set, inserted at a rate of about one per seven packs of both hobby and retail.

	MT
Complete Set (551):	450.00
Common Player:	.50
Showcase Stars: 4X	
(See 1997 Score for checklist and base card values.)	

1997 Score Showcase Artist's Proofs

This is a parallel of the Showcase parallel set covering all 551 cards of the base '97 Score set. The Artist's Proofs cards carry over the silver foil background of the Showcase cards on front with a rainbow-wave effect, and are marked with a round red "ARTIST'S PROOF" logo.

	MT
Complete Set (330):	1500.
Common Player:	2.00
Showcase Artist's Proof Stars: 15X	
(See 1997 Score for checklist and base card values.)	

1997 Score Blast Masters

This 18-card set was inserted into every 35 Series II retail packs and every 23 hobby packs. The set displays the top power hitters in the game over a prismatic gold foil background. The word "Blast" is printed across the top, while "Master" is printed across the bottom, both in red. Backs are predominantly black with a color player photo at center.

		MT
Complete Set (18):		95.00
Common Player:		1.50
1	Mo Vaughn	4.00
2	Mark McGwire	20.00
3	Juan Gonzalez	7.50
4	Albert Belle	4.50
5	Barry Bonds	4.50
6	Ken Griffey Jr.	20.00
7	Andruw Jones	7.50
8	Chipper Jones	12.50
9	Mike Piazza	12.50
10	Jeff Bagwell	7.50
11	Dante Bichette	1.50
12	Alex Rodriguez	15.00
13	Gary Sheffield	2.00
14	Ken Caminiti	1.50
15	Sammy Sosa	12.50
16	Vladimir Guerrero	6.00
17	Brian Jordan	1.50
18	Tim Salmon	2.00

1997 Score The Franchise Samples

Each of the cards in Score's "The Franchise" chase set can also be found in a sample card version. The promos are identical to the regularly issued Franchise cards except for the large black "SAMPLE" overprint diagonally on front and back.

		MT
Complete Set (9):		95.00
Common Player:		3.00
1	Ken Griffey Jr.	25.00
2	John Smoltz	3.00
3	Cal Ripken Jr.	20.00
4	Chipper Jones	15.00
5	Mike Piazza	15.00
6	Albert Belle	8.00
7	Frank Thomas	10.00
8	Sammy Sosa	12.00
9	Roberto Alomar	6.00

1997 Score The Franchise

There were two versions made for these 1997 Score Series 1 inserts - regular and The Glowing Franchise, which has glow-in-the-dark highlights. The regular version is seeded one per 72 packs; glow-in-the-dark cards are seeded one per 240 packs.

		MT
Complete Set (9):		95.00
Common Player:		3.00
Glowing: 5X		
1	Ken Griffey Jr.	25.00
2	John Smoltz	3.00
3	Cal Ripken Jr.	20.00
4	Chipper Jones	15.00
5	Mike Piazza	15.00
6	Albert Belle	8.00
7	Frank Thomas	10.00
8	Sammy Sosa	12.50
9	Roberto Alomar	6.00

1997 Score Heart of the Order

This 36-card set was distributed in Series II retail and hobby packs, with cards 1-18 in retail (one per 23 packs) and cards 19-36 in hobby (one per 15). The cards are printed in a horizontal format, with some of the top hitters in the game included in the insert. Fronts are highlighted in red metallic foil. Backs have a color portrait photo and a few words about the player.

		MT
Complete Set (36):		100.00
Complete Retail Set (1-18):		60.00
Complete Hobby Set (19-36):		40.00
Common Player:		1.00
1	Ivan Rodriguez	2.50
2	Will Clark	1.25
3	Juan Gonzalez	6.00
4	Frank Thomas	6.00
5	Albert Belle	3.00
6	Robin Ventura	1.25
7	Alex Rodriguez	9.00
8	Ken Griffey Jr.	12.00
9	Jay Buhner	1.00
10	Roberto Alomar	2.50
11	Rafael Palmeiro	1.25
12	Cal Ripken Jr.	9.00
13	Manny Ramirez	5.00
14	Matt Williams	1.50
15	Jim Thome	2.00
16	Derek Jeter	7.50
17	Wade Boggs	1.50
18	Bernie Williams	2.00
19	Chipper Jones	7.50
20	Andruw Jones	5.00
21	Ryan Klesko	1.00
22	Wilton Guerrero	1.00
23	Mike Piazza	7.50
24	Raul Mondesi	1.50
25	Tony Gwynn	6.00
26	Ken Caminiti	1.25
27	Greg Vaughn	1.00
28	Brian Jordan	1.00
29	Ron Gant	1.00
30	Dmitri Young	1.00
31	Darin Erstad	4.50
32	Jim Edmonds	1.00
33	Tim Salmon	1.25
34	Chuck Knoblauch	1.25
35	Paul Molitor	2.50
36	Todd Walker	3.00

1997 Score Highlight Zone

Exclusive to 1997 Score Series I hobby packs are these Highlight Zone inserts, seeded one per every 35 packs. Within the 18-card set, card numbers 1-9 are in regular hobby packs, while numbers 10-18 are found only in premium stock packs.

		MT
Complete Set (18):		120.00
Common Player:		2.00
1	Frank Thomas	10.00
2	Ken Griffey Jr.	20.00
3	Mo Vaughn	4.00
4	Albert Belle	5.00
5	Mike Piazza	12.00
6	Barry Bonds	5.00
7	Greg Maddux	12.00
8	Sammy Sosa	12.00
9	Jeff Bagwell	8.00
10	Alex Rodriguez	15.00
11	Chipper Jones	12.00
12	Brady Anderson	2.00
13	Ozzie Smith	5.00
14	Edgar Martinez	2.00
15	Cal Ripken Jr.	15.00
16	Ryan Klesko	2.00
17	Randy Johnson	5.00
18	Eddie Murray	4.00

1997 Score Pitcher Perfect

Seattle Mariners' star pitcher and accomplished photographer Randy Johnson makes his picks for the top talent in this 1997 Score Series I insert set. Fronts have player photos with a gold-foil filmstrip graphic at bottom featuring player names and a portrait of The Big Unit. Backs have additional color photos in a filmstrip design and a few words about the player.

		MT
Complete Set (15):		70.00
Common Player:		1.50
1	Cal Ripken Jr.	12.00
2	Alex Rodriguez	12.00
3	Cal Ripken Jr., Alex Rodriguez	12.00
4	Edgar Martinez	1.50
5	Ivan Rodriguez	4.00
6	Mark McGwire	15.00
7	Tim Salmon	2.00
8	Chili Davis	1.50
9	Joe Carter	2.00
10	Frank Thomas	6.00
11	Will Clark	2.00
12	Mo Vaughn	3.00
13	Wade Boggs	4.00
14	Ken Griffey Jr.	15.00
15	Randy Johnson	2.00

1997 Score Stand & Deliver

This 24-card insert was printed on a silver foil background, with the series name and team logo in gold foil across the bottom. Cards were found in Series II packs one per 71 retail, one per 41 hobby. Card numbers 21-24 (Florida Marlins) were designated as the winning group, meaning the first 225 collectors that mailed in the complete four card set received a gold upgrade version of the set framed in glass.

		MT
Complete Set (24):		325.00
Common Player:		3.00
1	Andruw Jones	20.00
2	Greg Maddux	30.00
3	Chipper Jones	30.00
4	John Smoltz	4.00
5	Ken Griffey Jr.	50.00
6	Alex Rodriguez	40.00
7	Jay Buhner	3.00
8	Randy Johnson	12.00
9	Derek Jeter	30.00
10	Andy Pettitte	10.00
11	Bernie Williams	10.00
12	Mariano Rivera	3.00
13	Mike Piazza	30.00
14	Hideo Nomo	10.00
15	Raul Mondesi	5.00
16	Todd Hollandsworth	3.00
17	Manny Ramirez	15.00
18	Jim Thome	8.00
19	David Justice	5.00
20	Matt Williams	8.00
21	Juan Gonzalez	25.00
22	Jeff Bagwell	20.00
23	Cal Ripken Jr.	40.00
24	Frank Thomas	20.00

1997 Score Stellar Season

These 1997 Score Series I inserts were seeded one per every 17 magazine packs.

		MT
Complete Set (18):		90.00
Common Player:		2.00
1	Juan Gonzalez	9.00
2	Chuck Knoblauch	3.00
3	Jeff Bagwell	7.50
4	John Smoltz	3.00
5	Mark McGwire	20.00
6	Ken Griffey Jr.	20.00
7	Frank Thomas	9.00
8	Alex Rodriguez	15.00
9	Mike Piazza	12.00
10	Albert Belle	5.00
11	Roberto Alomar	4.00
12	Sammy Sosa	12.00
13	Mo Vaughn	3.00
14	Brady Anderson	2.00
15	Henry Rodriguez	2.00
16	Eric Young	2.00
17	Gary Sheffield	2.00
18	Ryan Klesko	2.00

1997 Score Titanic Taters

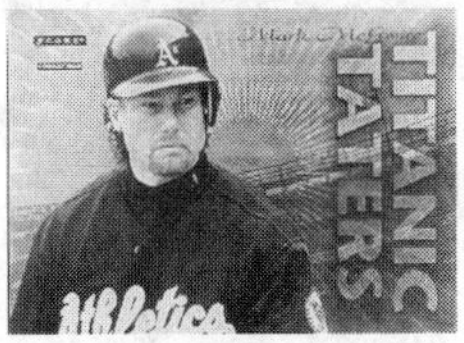

Some of the game's most powerful hitters are featured on these 1997 Score Series I inserts. The cards were seeded one per every 35 retail packs.

		MT
Complete Set (18):		120.00
Common Player:		3.00
1	Mark McGwire	25.00
2	Mike Piazza	15.00
3	Ken Griffey Jr.	25.00
4	Juan Gonzalez	12.00
5	Frank Thomas	10.00
6	Albert Belle	6.00
7	Sammy Sosa	15.00
8	Jeff Bagwell	10.00
9	Todd Hundley	3.00
10	Ryan Klesko	3.00
11	Brady Anderson	3.00
12	Mo Vaughn	5.00
13	Jay Buhner	3.00
14	Greg Vaughn	3.00
15	Barry Bonds	6.00
16	Gary Sheffield	4.00
17	Alex Rodriguez	20.00
18	Cecil Fielder	3.00

1997 Score Team Collection

Team sets consisting of 15 players each were produced for 10 different teams. Each card is similar in design to the regular 1997 Score set except for a special foil stamping at the bottom of the card that corresponds with team colors. In a parallel "Platinum" version, seeded one per six packs, the background and team foil on front are replaced with silver prismatic foil. A top of the line parallel set, "Premier" utilizes gold foil highlights on fronts and is found one per 31 packs. Team Collection was sold in five-card, single-team packs with a suggested retail price of about $1.29. It was reported that 100 cases of each team were issued.

		MT
Complete Set (150):		60.00
Common Player:		.25
Platinums: 4X		
Premiers: 15X		
Braves Wax Box:		80.00
Orioles Wax Box:		70.00
Red Sox Wax Box:		60.00
White Sox Wax Box:		70.00
Indians Wax Box:		70.00
Rockies Wax Box:		55.00
Dodgers Wax Box:		70.00
Yankees Wax Box:		75.00
Mariners Wax Box:		120.00
Rangers Wax Box:		60.00
	Atlanta Braves	8.00
1	Ryan Klesko	.25
2	David Justice	.35
3	Terry Pendleton	.25
4	Tom Glavine	.35
5	Javier Lopez	.35
6	John Smoltz	.35
7	Jermaine Dye	.30
8	Mark Lemke	.25
9	Fred McGriff	.40
10	Chipper Jones	2.50
11	Terrell Wade	.25
12	Greg Maddux	2.50
13	Mark Wohlers	.25
14	Marquis Grissom	.25
15	Andruw Jones	2.00
	Baltimore Orioles	5.00
1	Rafael Palmeiro	.35
2	Eddie Murray	.50
3	Roberto Alomar	1.00
4	Rocky Coppinger	.25
5	Brady Anderson	.35
6	Bobby Bonilla	.25
7	Cal Ripken Jr.	3.00
8	Mike Mussina	.50
9	Nerio Rodriguez	.25
10	Randy Myers	.25
11	B.J. Surhoff	.25
12	Jeffrey Hammonds	.25
13	Chris Hoiles	.25
14	Jimmy Haynes	.25
15	David Wells	.25
	Boston Red Sox	4.00
1	Wil Cordero	.25
2	Mo Vaughn	1.00
3	John Valentin	.25
4	Reggie Jefferson	.25
5	Tom Gordon	.25
6	Mike Stanley	.25
7	Jose Canseco	.40
8	Roger Clemens	.75
9	Darren Bragg	.25
10	Jeff Frye	.25
11	Jeff Suppan	.25
12	Mike Greenwell	.25
13	Arquimedez Pozo	.25
14	Tim Naehring	.25
15	Troy O'Leary	.25
	Chicago White Sox	6.00
1	Frank Thomas	2.00
2	James Baldwin	.25
3	Danny Tartabull	.25
4	Jeff Darwin	.25
5	Harold Baines	.25
6	Roberto Hernandez	.25
7	Ray Durham	.25
8	Robin Ventura	.30
9	Wilson Alvarez	.25
10	Lyle Mouton	.25
11	Alex Fernandez	.30
12	Ron Karkovice	.25
13	Kevin Tapani	.25
14	Tony Phillips	.25
15	Mike Cameron	.25
	Cleveland Indians	6.00
1	Albert Belle	1.50
2	Jack McDowell	.25
3	Jim Thome	.60
4	Dennis Martinez	.25
5	Julio Franco	.25
6	Omar Vizquel	.25
7	Kenny Lofton	1.00
8	Manny Ramirez	1.50
9	Sandy Alomar Jr.	.30
10	Charles Nagy	.25
11	Kevin Seitzer	.25
12	Mark Carreon	.25
13	Jeff Kent	.25
14	Danny Graves	.25
15	Brian Giles	.25
	Colorado Rockies	4.00
1	Dante Bichette	.40
2	Kevin Ritz	.25
3	Walt Weiss	.25
4	Ellis Burks	.25
5	Jamey Wright	.25
6	Andres Galarraga	.35
7	Eric Young	.25
8	Larry Walker	.50
9	Vinny Castilla	.25
10	Quinton McCracken	.25
11	Armando Reynoso	.25
12	Jayhawk Owens	.25
13	Mark Thompson	.25
14	John Burke	.25
15	Bruce Ruffin	.25
	Los Angeles Dodgers	6.00
1	Ismael Valdez	.25
2	Mike Piazza	2.50
3	Todd Hollandsworth	.25
4	Delino DeShields	.25
5	Chan Ho Park	.30
6	Roger Cedeno	.25
7	Raul Mondesi	.40
8	Darren Dreifort	.25
9	Jim Bruske	.25
10	Greg Gagne	.25
11	Chad Curtis	.25
12	Ramon Martinez	.25
13	Brett Butler	.25
14	Eric Karros	.25
15	Hideo Nomo	.50
	New York Yankees	6.00
1	Bernie Williams	.75
2	Cecil Fielder	.25
3	Derek Jeter	2.50
4	Darryl Strawberry	.25
5	Andy Pettitte	1.00
6	Ruben Rivera	.30
7	Mariano Rivera	.40
8	John Wetteland	.25
9	Paul O'Neill	.30
10	Wade Boggs	.50
11	Dwight Gooden	.25
12	David Cone	.35
13	Tino Martinez	.25
14	Kenny Rogers	.25
15	Andy Fox	.25
	Seattle Mariners	12.00
1	Chris Bosio	.25
2	Edgar Martinez	.25
3	Alex Rodriguez	3.00
4	Paul Sorrento	.25
5	Bob Wells	.25
6	Ken Griffey Jr.	4.00
7	Jay Buhner	.30
8	Dan Wilson	.25
9	Randy Johnson	.40
10	Joey Cora	.25
11	Mark Whiten	.25
12	Rich Amaral	.25
13	Raul Ibanez	.25
14	Jamie Moyer	.25
15	Makoto Suzuki	.25
	Texas Rangers	5.00
1	Mickey Tettleton	.25
2	Will Clark	.40
3	Ken Hill	.25
4	Rusty Greer	.25
5	Kevin Elster	.25
6	Darren Oliver	.25
7	Mark McLemore	.25
8	Roger Pavlik	.25
9	Dean Palmer	.25
10	Bobby Witt	.25
11	Juan Gonzalez	2.00
12	Ivan Rodriguez	.50
13	Darryl Hamilton	.25
14	John Burkett	.25
15	Warren Newson	.25

1997 Score Team Collection Platinum Team

Team sets consisting of 15 players each were produced for 10 different teams. Each card is similar in design to the regular 1997 Score set except for a special foil stamping at the bottom of the card that corresponds with team colors. In a parallel "Platinum" version, seeded one per six packs, the background and team foil on front are replaced with silver prismatic foil. Backs are overprinted in gold script, "Platinum Team." Team Collection was sold in five-card, single-team packs with a suggested retail price of about $1.29. It was reported that 100 cases of each team were issued.

	MT
Complete Set (150):	250.00
Common Player:	2.00
Platinum Stars: 4X	

(See 1997 Score Team Collection for checklists and base card values.)

1997 Score Team Collection Premier Club

Team sets consisting of 15 players each were produced for 10 different teams. Each card is similar in design to the regular 1997 Score set except for a special foil stamping at the bottom of the card that corresponds with team colors. In a top of the line parallel "Premier Club" version, seeded one per 31 packs, the background and team foil on front are replaced with gold prismatic foil, and backs are overprinted "Premier Club" in gold script. Team Collection was sold in five-card, single-team packs with a suggested retail price of about $1.29. It was reported that 100 cases of each team were issued.

	MT
Complete Set (150):	900.00
Common Player:	6.00
Premier Club Stars: 15X	

(See 1997 Score Team Collection for checklists and base card values.)

1997 Score Andruw Jones Goin' Yard

This special card was a blister-pack topper on Series 2 jumbo retail packs. Jones' home run swing is featured on front with a background of the distances of his blasts. Back has details on Series 2 inserts and the Stand and Deliver promotion.

	MT
Andruw Jones	2.00

1998 Score Samples

Half a dozen top stars were picked to introduce 1998 Score in this series of promo cards. Cards are virtually identical to the issued version except for the large black overprinted "SAMPLE" on back and the use of zeroes to replace 1997 stats.

		MT
Complete Set (6):		15.00
Common Player:		2.00
10	Alex Rodriguez	3.00
24	Mike Piazza	2.50
34	Ken Griffey Jr.	4.00
43	Cal Ripken Jr.	3.00
51	Chipper Jones	2.50
60	Carlos Delgado	2.00

1998 Score

The cards in the 270-card base set feature a color photo inside a black and white border. The player's name is printed in the left border. The entire base set is paralleled in the silver-foil Showcase Series (1:5). The Artist's Proof partial parallel gives a prismatic foil treatment to 165 base cards and was seeded 1:23. Inserts included All-Stars, Complete Players and Epix.

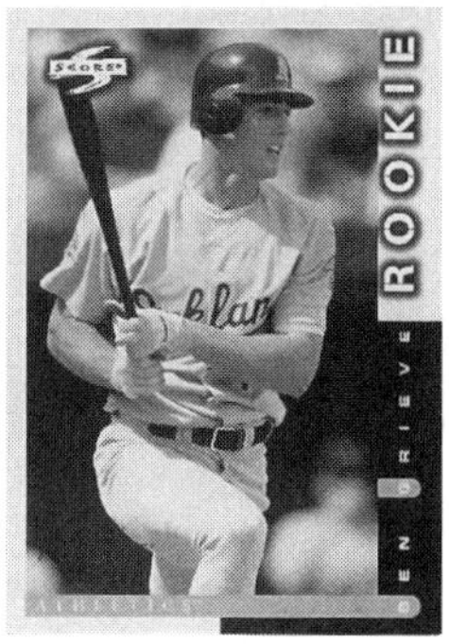

MT
Complete Set (270): 25.00
Common Player: .05
Showcases: 3X
Artist's Proofs: 12X
Wax Box: 32.00
1 Andruw Jones 1.00
2 Dan Wilson .05
3 Hideo Nomo .25
4 Chuck Carr .05
5 Barry Bonds .50
6 Jack McDowell .05
7 Albert Belle .50
8 Francisco Cordova .05
9 Greg Maddux 1.25
10 Alex Rodriguez 1.75
11 Steve Avery .05
12 Chuck McElroy .05
13 Larry Walker .20
14 Hideki Irabu .50
15 Roberto Alomar .40
16 Neifi Perez .05
17 Jim Thome .30
18 Rickey Henderson .20
19 Andres Galarraga .20
20 Jeff Fassero .05
21 Kevin Young .05
22 Derek Jeter 1.25
23 Andy Benes .05
24 Mike Piazza 1.25
25 Todd Stottlemyre .05
26 Michael Tucker .05
27 Denny Neagle .05
28 Javier Lopez .10
29 Aaron Sele .05
30 Ryan Klesko .10
31 Dennis Eckersley .05
32 Quinton McCracken .05
33 Brian Anderson .05
34 Ken Griffey Jr. 2.50
35 Shawn Estes .05
36 Tim Wakefield .05
37 Jimmy Key .05
38 Jeff Bagwell .75
39 Edgardo Alfonzo .10
40 Mike Cameron .05
41 Mark McGwire 2.50
42 Tino Martinez .15
43 Cal Ripken Jr. 1.75
44 Curtis Goodwin .05
45 Bobby Ayala .05
46 Sandy Alomar Jr. .10
47 Bobby Jones .05
48 Omar Vizquel .05
49 Roger Clemens .75
50 Tony Gwynn 1.00
51 Chipper Jones 1.25
52 Ron Coomer .05
53 Dmitri Young .05
54 Brian Giles .05
55 Steve Finley .05
56 David Cone .10
57 Andy Pettitte .40
58 Wilton Guerrero .05
59 Deion Sanders .15
60 Carlos Delgado .25
61 Jason Giambi .05
62 Ozzie Guillen .05
63 Jay Bell .05
64 Barry Larkin .15
65 Sammy Sosa 1.00
66 Bernie Williams .40
67 Terry Steinbach .05
68 Scott Rolen 1.00
69 Melvin Nieves .05
70 Craig Biggio .15
71 Todd Greene .05
72 Greg Gagne .05
73 Shigetosi Hasegawa .05
74 Mark McLemore .05
75 Darren Bragg .05
76 Brett Butler .05
77 Ron Gant .05
78 Mike Difelice .05
79 Charles Nagy .05
80 Scott Hatteberg .05
81 Brady Anderson .15
82 Jay Buhner .10
83 Todd Hollandsworth .05
84 Geronimo Berroa .05
85 Jeff Suppan .05
86 Pedro Martinez .25
87 Roger Cedeno .05
88 Ivan Rodriguez .50
89 Jaime Navarro .05
90 Chris Hoiles .05
91 Nomar Garciaparra 1.25
92 Rafael Palmeiro .15
93 Darin Erstad .75
94 Kenny Lofton .40
95 Mike Timlin .05
96 Chris Clemons .05
97 Vinny Castilla .10
98 Charlie Hayes .05
99 Lyle Mouton .05
100 Jason Dickson .05
101 Justin Thompson .05
102 Pat Kelly .05
103 Chan Ho Park .05
104 Ray Lankford .05
105 Frank Thomas 1.00
106 Jermaine Allensworth .05
107 Doug Drabek .05
108 Todd Hundley .15
109 Carl Everett .05
110 Edgar Martinez .05
111 Robin Ventura .10
112 John Wetteland .05
113 Mariano Rivera .15
114 Jose Rosado .05
115 Ken Caminiti .15
116 Paul O'Neill .15
117 Tim Salmon .20
118 Eduardo Perez .05
119 Mike Jackson .05
120 John Smoltz .10
121 Brant Brown .05
122 John Mabry .05
123 Chuck Knoblauch .20
124 Reggie Sanders .05
125 Ken Hill .05
126 Mike Mussina .40
127 Chad Curtis .05
128 Todd Worrell .05
129 Chris Widger .05
130 Damon Mashore .05
131 Kevin Brown .10
132 Bip Roberts .05
133 Tim Naehring .05
134 Dave Martinez .05
135 Jeff Blauser .05
136 David Justice .20
137 Dave Hollins .05
138 Pat Hentgen .05
139 Darren Daulton .05
140 Ramon Martinez .05
141 Raul Casanova .05
142 Tom Glavine .15
143 J.T. Snow .05
144 Tony Graffanino .05
145 Randy Johnson .35
146 Orlando Merced .05
147 Jeff Juden .05
148 Darryl Kile .05
149 Ray Durham .05
150 Alex Fernandez .05
151 Joey Cora .05
152 Royce Clayton .05
153 Randy Myers .05
154 Charles Johnson .05
155 Alan Benes .05
156 Mike Bordick .05
157 Heathcliff Slocumb .05
158 Roger Bailey .05
159 Reggie Jefferson .05
160 Ricky Bottalico .05
161 Scott Erickson .05
162 Matt Williams .20
163 Robb Nen .05
164 Matt Stairs .05
165 Ismael Valdes .05
166 Lee Stevens .05
167 Gary DiSarcina .05
168 Brad Radke .05
169 Mike Lansing .05
170 Armando Benitez .05
171 Mike James .05
172 Russ Davis .05
173 Lance Johnson .05
174 Joey Hamilton .05
175 John Valentin .05
176 David Segui .05
177 David Wells .05
178 Delino DeShields .05
179 Eric Karros .10
180 Jim Leyritz .05
181 Raul Mondesi .15
182 Travis Fryman .05
183 Todd Zeile .05
184 Brian Jordan .05
185 Rey Ordonez .10
186 Jim Edmonds .05
187 Terrell Wade .05
188 Marquis Grissom .10
189 Chris Snopek .05
190 Shane Reynolds .05
191 Jeff Frye .05
192 Paul Sorrento .05
193 James Baldwin .05
194 Brian McRae .05
195 Fred McGriff .15
196 Troy Percival .05
197 Rich Amaral .05
198 Juan Guzman .05
199 Cecil Fielder .05
200 Willie Blair .05
201 Chili Davis .05
202 Gary Gaetti .05
203 B.J. Surhoff .05
204 Steve Cooke .05
205 Chuck Finley .05
206 Jeff Kent .05
207 Ben McDonald .05
208 Jeffrey Hammonds .05
209 Tom Goodwin .05
210 Billy Ashley .05
211 Wil Cordero .05
212 Shawon Dunston .05
213 Tony Phillips .05
214 Jamie Moyer .05
215 John Jaha .05
216 Troy O'Leary .05
217 Brad Ausmus .05
218 Garret Anderson .05
219 Wilson Alvarez .05
220 Kent Mercker .05
221 Wade Boggs .25
222 Mark Wohlers .05
223 Kevin Appier .05
224 Tony Fernandez .05
225 Ugueth Urbina .05
226 Gregg Jefferies .05
227 Mo Vaughn .40
228 Arthur Rhodes .05
229 Jorge Fabregas .05
230 Mark Gardner .05
231 Shane Mack .05
232 Jorge Posada .05
233 Jose Cruz Jr. .15
234 Paul Konerko .60
235 Derrek Lee .05
236 *Steve Woodard* .15
237 Todd Dunwoody .10
238 Fernando Tatis .20
239 Jacob Cruz .10
240 *Pokey Reese* .25
241 Mark Kotsay .30
242 Matt Morris .05
243 *Antone Williamson* .05
244 Ben Grieve .60
245 Ryan McGuire .05
246 *Lou Collier* .05
247 Shannon Stewart .05
248 *Brett Tomko* .05
249 Bobby Estalella .05
250 *Livan Hernandez* .15
251 Todd Helton .40
252 Jaret Wright .75
253 Darryl Hamilton (Interleague Moments) .05
254 Stan Javier (Interleague Moments) .05
255 Glenallen Hill (Interleague Moments) .05
256 Mark Gardner (Interleague Moments) .05
257 Cal Ripken Jr. (Interleague Moments) .75
258 Mike Mussina (Interleague Moments) .20
259 Mike Piazza (Interleague Moments) .60
260 Sammy Sosa (Interleague Moments) .50
261 Todd Hundley (Interleague Moments) .05
262 Eric Karros (Interleague Moments) .05
263 Denny Neagle (Interleague Moments) .05
264 Jeromy Burnitz (Interleague Moments) .05
265 Greg Maddux (Interleague Moments) .60
266 Tony Clark (Interleague Moments) .20
267 Vladimir Guerrero (Interleague Moments) .40
268 Checklist .05
269 Checklist .05
270 Checklist .05

1998 Score Artist's Proofs

This partial parallel reprinted 160 of the 270 cards in Score Baseball on a foil background with an Artist's Proof logo on the front. The cards were renumbered within the 160-card set and inserted one per 35 packs. Cards have a "PP" prefix to the number on back.

MT
Complete Set (160): 400.00
Common Player: 1.50
Inserted 1:35
1 Andruw Jones 7.50
2 Dan Wilson 2.50
3 Hideo Nomo 6.00
4 Neifi Perez 2.50
5 Jim Thome 5.00
6 Jeff Fassero 2.50
7 Derek Jeter 15.00
8 Andy Benes 2.50
9 Michael Tucker 2.50
10 Ryan Klesko 2.50
11 Dennis Eckersley 2.50
12 Jimmy Key 2.50
13 Edgardo Alfonzo 3.00
14 Mike Cameron 2.50
15 Omar Vizquel 2.50
16 Ron Coomer 2.50
17 Dmitri Young 2.50
18 Brian Giles 2.50
19 Steve Finley 2.50
20 Andy Pettitte 4.00
21 Wilton Guerrero 2.50
22 Deion Sanders 3.00
23 Carlos Delgado 6.00
24 Jason Giambi 2.50
25 David Cone 3.50
26 Jay Bell 2.50
27 Sammy Sosa 12.50
28 Barry Larkin 2.50
29 Scott Rolen 7.50
30 Todd Greene 2.50
31 Bernie Williams 4.00
32 Brett Butler 2.50
33 Ron Gant 2.50
34 Brady Anderson 2.50
35 Craig Biggio 3.50
36 Charles Nagy 2.50
37 Jay Buhner 2.50
38 Geronimo Berroa 2.50
39 Jeff Suppan 2.50
40 Rafael Palmeiro 4.00
41 Darin Erstad 7.50
42 Mike Timlin 2.50
43 Vinny Castilla 2.50
44 Carl Everett 2.50
45 Robin Ventura 3.00
46 John Wetteland 2.50
47 Paul O'Neill 3.00
48 Tim Salmon 2.50
49 Mike Jackson 2.50
50 John Smoltz 2.50
51 Brant Brown 2.50
52 Reggie Sanders 2.50
53 Ken Hill 2.50
54 Todd Worrell 2.50
55 Bip Roberts 2.50
56 Tim Naehring 2.50
57 Darren Daulton 2.50
58 Ramon Martinez 4.00
59 Raul Casanova 2.50
60 J.T. Snow 2.50
61 Jeff Juden 2.50
62 Royce Clayton 2.50
63 Charles Johnson 2.50
64 Alan Benes 2.50
65 Reggie Jefferson 2.50
66 Ricky Bottalico 2.50
67 Scott Erickson 2.50
68 Matt Williams 2.50
69 Robb Nen 2.50
70 Matt Stairs 2.50
71 Ismael Valdes 2.50
72 Brad Radke 2.50
73 Armando Benitez 2.50
74 Russ Davis 2.50
75 Lance Johnson 2.50
76 Joey Hamilton 2.50
77 John Valentin 2.50
78 David Segui 2.50
79 David Wells 2.50
80 Eric Karros 2.50
81 Raul Mondesi 4.00
82 Travis Fryman 2.50
83 Todd Zeile 2.50
84 Brian Jordan 2.50
85 Rey Ordonez 2.50
86 Jim Edmonds 2.50
87 Marquis Grissom 2.50
88 Shane Reynolds 2.50
89 Paul Sorrento 2.50
90 Brian McRae 2.50
91 Fred McGriff 3.50
92 Troy Percival 2.50
93 Juan Guzman 2.50
94 Cecil Fielder 2.50
95 Chili Davis 2.50
96 B.J. Surhoff 2.50
97 Chuck Finley 2.50
98 Jeff Kent 2.50
99 Ben McDonald 2.50
100 Jeffrey Hammonds 2.50
101 Tom Goodwin 2.50
102 Wil Cordero 2.50
103 Tony Phillips 2.50
104 John Jaha 2.50
105 Garret Anderson 2.50
106 Wilson Alvarez 2.50
107 Wade Boggs 7.50
108 Mark Wohlers 2.50
109 Kevin Appier 2.50
110 Mo Vaughn 4.00
111 Ray Durham 2.50
112 Alex Fernandez 2.50
113 Barry Bonds 10.00
114 Albert Belle 8.00
115 Greg Maddux 10.00
116 Alex Rodriguez 20.00
117 Larry Walker 4.00
118 Roberto Alomar 6.00
119 Andres Galarraga 2.50
120 Mike Piazza 12.50
121 Denny Neagle 2.50
122 Javier Lopez 2.50
123 Ken Griffey Jr. 25.00
124 Shawn Estes 4.00
125 Jeff Bagwell 10.00
126 Mark McGwire 25.00
127 Tino Martinez 2.50
128 Cal Ripken Jr. 20.00
129 Sandy Alomar Jr. 3.00
130 Bobby Jones 2.50
131 Roger Clemens 10.00
132 Tony Gwynn 10.00
133 Chipper Jones 15.00
134 Orlando Merced 2.50
135 Todd Stottlemyre 2.50
136 Delino DeShields 2.50
137 Pedro Martinez 4.00
138 Ivan Rodriguez 6.00
139 Nomar Garciaparra 12.50
140 Kenny Lofton 3.00
141 Jason Dickson 2.50
142 Justin Thompson 2.50
143 Ray Lankford 2.50
144 Frank Thomas 10.00
145 Todd Hundley 2.50
146 Edgar Martinez 2.50
147 Mariano Rivera 3.00
148 Jose Rosado 2.50
149 Ken Caminiti 3.50
150 Chuck Knoblauch 3.00
151 Mike Mussina 3.00
152 Kevin Brown 3.00
153 Jeff Blauser 2.50
154 David Justice 3.00
155 Pat Hentgen 2.50
156 Tom Glavine 3.00
157 Randy Johnson 4.00
158 Darryl Kile 2.50
159 Joey Cora 2.50
160 Randy Myers 2.50

1998 Score All Score Team

For its 10th anniversary Score selected an all-star team and issued this insert set. Cards have player action photos on a silver-foil background with an anniversary logo at bottom. Backs have a portrait photo and a career summary. The cards were inserted one per 35 packs.

MT
Complete Set (20): 100.00
Common Player: 2.00
Inserted 1:35
1 Mike Piazza 12.00
2 Ivan Rodriguez 5.00
3 Frank Thomas 8.00
4 Mark McGwire 20.00
5 Ryne Sandberg 4.00
6 Roberto Alomar 4.00
7 Cal Ripken Jr. 15.00
8 Barry Larkin 2.00
9 Paul Molitor 3.00
10 Travis Fryman 2.00
11 Kirby Puckett 5.00
12 Tony Gwynn 10.00
13 Ken Griffey Jr. 20.00
14 Juan Gonzalez 7.00
15 Barry Bonds 5.00
16 Andruw Jones 4.00
17 Roger Clemens 8.00
18 Randy Johnson 3.00
19 Greg Maddux 10.00
20 Dennis Eckersley 2.00

Player names in *Italic* type indicate a rookie card.

1998 Score All Score Team Andruw Jones Autograph

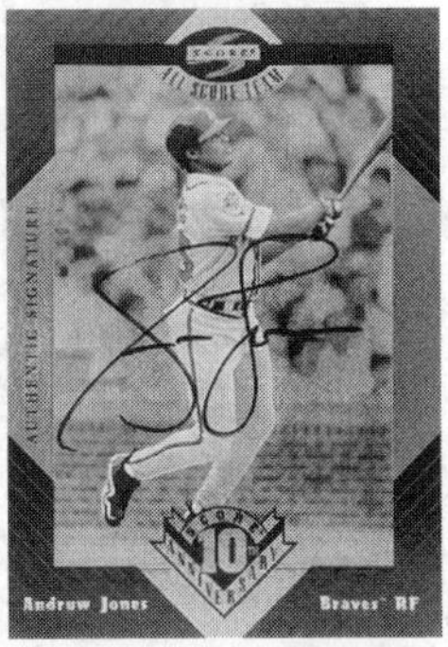

This special version of Jones' All Score Team was a prize in a random hobby-shop drawing. Instead of the silver foil seen on regular All Score Team inserts, this version has a gold-foil background and an "AUTHENTIC SIGNATURE" notation at right-center. Only 500 of the cards were produced.

		MT
16	Andruw Jones	80.00

1998 Score Complete Players

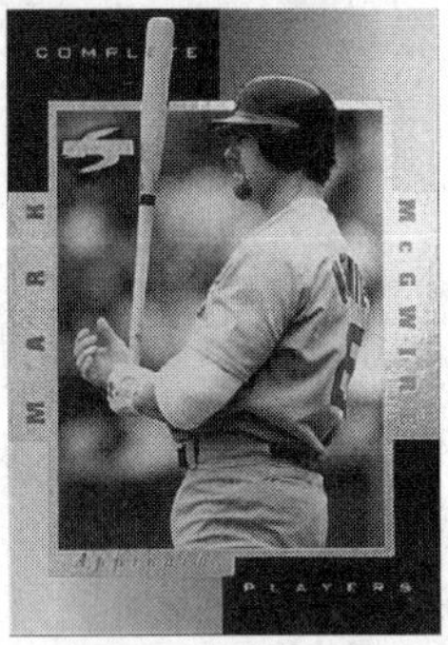

Complete Players is a 30-card insert featuring 10 players who can do it all. Each player had three cards displaying their variety of skills. The cards feature holographic foil highlights on fronts. Backs form a three-piece vertical picture of the player. Values shown are for each of the three cards (A, B, C) per player. The cards were inserted about one per 23 packs. Cards can be found with either gold or silver holographic foil.

		MT
Complete Set (30):		150.00
Common Player:		1.50
Inserted 1:23		
1	Ken Griffey Jr.	12.50
2	Mark McGwire	12.50
3	Derek Jeter	8.00
4	Cal Ripken Jr.	10.00
5	Mike Piazza	8.00
6	Darin Erstad	3.00
7	Frank Thomas	7.50
8	Andruw Jones	6.00
9	Nomar Garciaparra	8.00
10	Manny Ramirez	4.00

1998 Score Epix

Epix is a cross-brand insert, with 24 cards appearing in Score. The cards are printed on 20-point stock with dot matrix hologram technology. The cards honor the top Play, Game, Season and Moment in a players career and come in Orange, Purple and Emerald versions. Game cards were inserted 1:141, Plays 1:171, Seasons 1:437 and Moments 1:757.

		MT
Common Card:		3.00
Purple: 1.5X		
Emeralds: 2.5X		
1	Ken Griffey Jr. P	15.00
2	Juan Gonzalez P	5.00
3	Jeff Bagwell P	3.00
4	Ivan Rodriguez P	3.00
5	Nomar Garciaparra P	10.00
6	Ryne Sandberg P	3.00
7	Frank Thomas G	8.00
8	Derek Jeter G	15.00
9	Tony Gwynn G	12.00
10	Albert Belle G	5.00
11	Scott Rolen G	6.00
12	Barry Larkin G	3.00
13	Alex Rodriguez S	40.00
14	Cal Ripken Jr. S	40.00
15	Chipper Jones S	30.00
16	Roger Clemens S	25.00
17	Mo Vaughn S	8.00
18	Mark McGwire S	60.00
19	Mike Piazza M	50.00
20	Andruw Jones M	15.00
21	Greg Maddux M	45.00
22	Barry Bonds M	20.00
23	Paul Molitor M	15.00
24	Eddie Murray M	15.00

1998 Score First Pitch

These inserts were a 1:11 pack find in Score's All-Star edition. Fronts have portrait photos printed in the center of textured foil background of red and silver. The basic design is repeated on back, with career highlights and team logo instead of a photo.

		MT
Complete Set (20):		60.00
Common Player:		1.00
Inserted 1:11 All-Star Edition		
1	Ken Griffey Jr.	9.00
2	Frank Thomas	4.00
3	Alex Rodriguez	7.00
4	Cal Ripken Jr.	7.00
5	Chipper Jones	5.00
6	Juan Gonzalez	4.00
7	Derek Jeter	5.00
8	Mike Piazza	5.00
9	Andruw Jones	2.50
10	Nomar Garciaparra	5.00
11	Barry Bonds	2.50
12	Jeff Bagwell	3.00
13	Scott Rolen	3.00
14	Hideo Nomo	1.00
15	Roger Clemens	3.00
16	Mark McGwire	9.00
17	Greg Maddux	5.00
18	Albert Belle	2.00
19	Ivan Rodriguez	2.00
20	Mo Vaughn	1.00

1998 Score Loaded Lineup

This insert series was packaged on average of one card per 45 packs of Score's All-Star edition. Fronts have action photos printed on a copper and silver textured metallic-foil background. Backs have a portrait photo, career highlights, the Loaded Lineup batting order and stats for the player's best season. Cards have an "LL" prefix to their number.

		MT
Complete Set (10):		60.00
Common Player:		2.50
Inserted 1:45 All-Star Edition		
LL1	Chuck Knoblauch	2.50
LL2	Tony Gwynn	8.00
LL3	Frank Thomas	8.00
LL4	Ken Griffey Jr.	15.00
LL5	Mike Piazza	10.00
LL6	Barry Bonds	4.00
LL7	Cal Ripken Jr.	12.00
LL8	Paul Molitor	3.00
LL9	Nomar Garciaparra	10.00
LL10	Greg Maddux	10.00

1998 Score New Season

		MT
Complete Set (15):		60.00
Common Player:		2.00
Inserted 1:23 All-Star Edition		
NS1	Kenny Lofton	3.00
NS2	Nomar Garciaparra	8.00
NS3	Todd Helton	2.50
NS4	Miguel Tejada	2.00
NS5	Jaret Wright	4.00
NS6	Alex Rodriguez	10.00
NS7	Vladimir Guerrero	4.00
NS8	Ken Griffey Jr.	12.00
NS9	Ben Grieve	4.00
NS10	Travis Lee	3.00
NS11	Jose Cruz Jr.	2.00
NS12	Paul Konerko	2.00
NS13	Frank Thomas	7.00
NS14	Chipper Jones	8.00
NS15	Cal Ripken Jr.	10.00

1998 Score Showcase Series

This partial parallel reprinted 160 of the 270 cards in Score Baseball on silver foil. They were marked on the back and renumbered within the 160-card set. Showcase parallels were inserted one per seven packs. All Showcase Series cards except #1 have a "PP" prefix to the number.

		MT
Complete Set (160):		150.00
Common Player:		.50
Inserted 1:7		
1	Andruw Jones	1.50
2	Dan Wilson	.50
3	Hideo Nomo	1.00
4	Neifi Perez	.50
5	Jim Thome	2.00
6	Jeff Fassero	.50
7	Derek Jeter	5.00
8	Andy Benes	.50
9	Michael Tucker	.50
10	Ryan Klesko	.60
11	Dennis Eckersley	.50
12	Jimmy Key	.50
13	Edgardo Alfonzo	.60
14	Mike Cameron	.50
15	Omar Vizquel	.50
16	Ron Coomer	.50
17	Dmitri Young	.50
18	Brian Giles	.50
19	Steve Finley	.50
20	Andy Pettitte	.90
21	Wilton Guerrero	.50
22	Deion Sanders	.75
23	Carlos Delgado	.75
24	Jason Giambi	.50
25	David Cone	.60
26	Jay Bell	.50
27	Sammy Sosa	4.00
28	Barry Larkin	.90
29	Scott Rolen	1.50
30	Todd Greene	.50
31	Bernie Williams	.75
32	Brett Butler	.50
33	Ron Gant	.50
34	Brady Anderson	.50
35	Craig Biggio	.75
36	Charles Nagy	.50
37	Jay Buhner	.50
38	Geronimo Berroa	.50
39	Jeff Suppan	.50
40	Rafael Palmeiro	1.00
41	Darin Erstad	2.00
42	Mike Timlin	.50
43	Vinny Castilla	.50
44	Carl Everett	.50
45	Robin Ventura	.75
46	John Wetteland	.50
47	Paul O'Neill	.60
48	Tim Salmon	.60
49	Mike Jackson	.50
50	John Smoltz	.50
51	Brant Brown	.50
52	Reggie Sanders	.50
53	Ken Hill	.50
54	Todd Worrell	.50
55	Bip Roberts	.50
56	Tim Naehring	.50
57	Darren Daulton	.50
58	Ramon Martinez	.75
59	Raul Casanova	.50
60	J.T. Snow	.50
61	Jeff Juden	.50
62	Royce Clayton	.50
63	Charles Johnson	.50
64	Alan Benes	.50
65	Reggie Jefferson	.50
66	Ricky Bottalico	.50
67	Scott Erickson	.50
68	Matt Williams	.75
69	Robb Nen	.50
70	Matt Stairs	.50
71	Ismael Valdes	.50
72	Brad Radke	.50
73	Armando Benitez	.50
74	Russ Davis	.50
75	Lance Johnson	.50
76	Joey Hamilton	.50
77	John Valentin	.50
78	David Segui	.50
79	David Wells	.60
80	Eric Karros	.60
81	Raul Mondesi	.75
82	Travis Fryman	.50
83	Todd Zeile	.60
84	Brian Jordan	.60
85	Rey Ordonez	.50
86	Jim Edmonds	.50
87	Marquis Grissom	.50
88	Shane Reynolds	.50
89	Paul Sorrento	.50
90	Brian McRae	.50
91	Fred McGriff	.75
92	Troy Percival	.50
93	Juan Guzman	.50
94	Cecil Fielder	.50
95	Chili Davis	.50
96	B.J. Surhoff	.50
97	Chuck Finley	.50
98	Jeff Kent	.50
99	Ben McDonald	.50
100	Jeffrey Hammonds	.50
101	Tom Goodwin	.50
102	Wil Cordero	.50
103	Tony Phillips	.50
104	John Jaha	.50
105	Garret Anderson	.50
106	Wilson Alvarez	.50
107	Wade Boggs	2.00
108	Mark Wohlers	.50
109	Kevin Appier	.50
110	Mo Vaughn	1.00
111	Ray Durham	.50
112	Alex Fernandez	.50
113	Barry Bonds	4.00
114	Albert Belle	4.00
115	Greg Maddux	4.00
116	Alex Rodriguez	6.00
117	Larry Walker	1.50
118	Roberto Alomar	1.25
119	Andres Galarraga	.60
120	Mike Piazza	5.00
121	Denny Neagle	.50
122	Javier Lopez	.50
123	Ken Griffey Jr.	7.50
124	Shawn Estes	.50
125	Jeff Bagwell	3.00
126	Mark McGwire	7.50
127	Tino Martinez	.60
128	Cal Ripken Jr.	6.00
129	Sandy Alomar Jr.	.60
130	Bobby Jones	.50
131	Roger Clemens	2.00
132	Tony Gwynn	2.00
133	Chipper Jones	4.00
134	Orlando Merced	.50
135	Todd Stottlemyre	.50
136	Delino DeShields	.50
137	Pedro Martinez	.90
138	Ivan Rodriguez	1.25
139	Nomar Garciaparra	5.00
140	Kenny Lofton	.75
141	Jason Dickson	.50
142	Justin Thompson	.50
143	Ray Lankford	.50
144	Frank Thomas	3.00
145	Todd Hundley	.50
146	Edgar Martinez	.50
147	Mariano Rivera	.50
148	Jose Rosado	.50
149	Ken Caminiti	.75
150	Chuck Knoblauch	.75
151	Mike Mussina	.75
152	Kevin Brown	.75
153	Jeff Blauser	.50
154	David Justice	1.00
155	Pat Hentgen	.50
156	Tom Glavine	.60
157	Randy Johnson	1.00
158	Darryl Kile	.50
159	Joey Cora	.50
160	Randy Myers	.50

1998 Score Rookie & Traded

Score Rookie/Traded consists of a 270-card base set. The base cards have a white and gray border with the player's name on the left. The Showcase Series parallels 110 base cards and was inserted 1:7. Artist's Proofs is a 50-card partial parallel done on prismatic foil and inserted 1:35. Inserts included All-Star Epix, Complete Players and Star Gazing.

		MT
Complete Set (270):		25.00
Common SP (1-50):		.25
Common Player (51-270):		.10
Paul Konerko Auto. (500):		25.00
Wax Box:		28.00
1	Tony Clark	.40
2	Juan Gonzalez	1.50
3	Frank Thomas	1.25
4	Greg Maddux	2.00
5	Barry Larkin	.30
6	Derek Jeter	2.00
7	Randy Johnson	.50
8	Roger Clemens	1.00
9	Tony Gwynn	1.50
10	Barry Bonds	.75
11	Jim Edmonds	.25
12	Bernie Williams	.40
13	Ken Griffey Jr.	3.00
14	Tim Salmon	.40
15	Mo Vaughn	.60
16	David Justice	.40
17	Jose Cruz Jr.	.25
18	Andruw Jones	.75
19	Sammy Sosa	1.25
20	Jeff Bagwell	1.00
21	Scott Rolen	1.00
22	Darin Erstad	.75
23	Andy Pettitte	.40
24	Mike Mussina	.40
25	Mark McGwire	3.00
26	Hideo Nomo	.40
27	Chipper Jones	2.00
28	Cal Ripken Jr.	2.50
29	Chuck Knoblauch	.40
30	Alex Rodriguez	2.50
31	Jim Thome	.50
32	Mike Piazza	2.00
33	Ivan Rodriguez	.75
34	Roberto Alomar	.50

35	Nomar Garciaparra	2.00
36	Albert Belle	.75
37	Vladimir Guerrero	.75
38	Raul Mondesi	.25
39	Larry Walker	.40
40	Manny Ramirez	.75
41	Tino Martinez	.40
42	Craig Biggio	.35
43	Jay Buhner	.40
44	Kenny Lofton	.60
45	Pedro Martinez	.60
46	Edgar Martinez	.25
47	Gary Sheffield	.30
48	Jose Guillen	.25
49	Ken Caminiti	.35
50	Bobby Higginson	.25
51	Alan Benes	.10
52	Shawn Green	.15
53	Ron Coomer	.10
54	Charles Nagy	.10
55	Steve Karsay	.10
56	Matt Morris	.10
57	Bobby Jones	.10
58	Jason Kendall	.10
59	Jeff Conine	.10
60	Joe Girardi	.10
61	Mark Kotsay	.30
62	Eric Karros	.15
63	Bartolo Colon	.15
64	Mariano Rivera	.20
65	Alex Gonzalez	.15
66	Scott Spiezio	.10
67	Luis Castillo	.10
68	Joey Cora	.10
69	Mark McLemore	.10
70	Reggie Jefferson	.10
71	Lance Johnson	.10
72	Damian Jackson	.10
73	Jeff D'Amico	.10
74	David Ortiz	.10
75	J.T. Snow	.10
76	Todd Hundley	.15
77	Billy Wagner	.15
78	Vinny Castilla	.20
79	Ismael Valdes	.10
80	Neifi Perez	.10
81	Derek Bell	.10
82	Ryan Klesko	.25
83	Rey Ordonez	.15
84	Carlos Garcia	.10
85	Curt Schilling	.20
86	Robin Ventura	.20
87	Pat Hentgen	.10
88	Glendon Rusch	.10
89	Hideki Irabu	.40
90	Antone Williamson	.10
91	Denny Neagle	.10
92	Kevin Orie	.10
93	Reggie Sanders	.10
94	Brady Anderson	.10
95	Andy Benes	.10
96	John Valentin	.10
97	Bobby Bonilla	.10
98	Walt Weiss	.10
99	Robin Jennings	.10
100	Marty Cordova	.10
101	Brad Ausmus	.10
102	Brian Rose	.10
103	Calvin Maduro	.10
104	Raul Casanova	.10
105	Jeff King	.10
106	Sandy Alomar	.20
107	Tim Naehring	.10
108	Mike Cameron	.10
109	Omar Vizquel	.10
110	Brad Radke	.10
111	Jeff Fassero	.10
112	Deivi Cruz	.10
113	Dave Hollins	.10
114	Dean Palmer	.10
115	Esteban Loaiza	.10
116	Brian Giles	.10
117	Steve Finley	.10
118	Jose Canseco	.25
119	Al Martin	.10
120	Eric Young	.10
121	Curtis Goodwin	.10
122	Ellis Burks	.10
123	Mike Hampton	.10
124	Lou Collier	.10
125	John Olerud	.20
126	Ramon Martinez	.10
127	Todd Dunwoody	.10
128	Jermaine Allensworth	.10
129	Eduardo Perez	.10
130	Dante Bichette	.25
131	Edgar Renteria	.10
132	Bob Abreu	.10
133	Rondell White	.20
134	Michael Coleman	.10
135	Jason Giambi	.10
136	Brant Brown	.10
137	Michael Tucker	.10
138	Dave Nilsson	.10
139	Benito Santiago	.10
140	Ray Durham	.10
141	Jeff Kent	.10
142	Matt Stairs	.10
143	Kevin Young	.10
144	Eric Davis	.10
145	John Wetteland	.10
146	Esteban Yan	.10
147	Wilton Guerrero	.10
148	Moises Alou	.20
149	Edgardo Alfonzo	.15
150	Andy Ashby	.10
151	Todd Walker	.20
152	Jermaine Dye	.10
153	Brian Hunter	.10
154	Shawn Estes	.10
155	Bernard Gilkey	.10
156	Tony Womack	.10
157	John Smoltz	.20
158	Delino DeShields	.10
159	Jacob Cruz	.10
160	Javier Valentin	.10
161	Chris Hoiles	.10
162	Garret Anderson	.10
163	Dan Wilson	.10
164	Paul O'Neill	.20
165	Matt Williams	.25
166	Travis Fryman	.10
167	Javier Lopez	.10
168	Ray Lankford	.10
169	Bobby Estalella	.10
170	Henry Rodriguez	.10
171	Quinton McCracken	.10
172	Jaret Wright	.50
173	Darryl Kile	.10
174	Wade Boggs	.30
175	Orel Hershiser	.10
176	B.J. Surhoff	.10
177	Fernando Tatis	.20
178	Carlos Delgado	.25
179	Jorge Fabregas	.10
180	Tony Saunders	.10
181	Devon White	.10
182	Dmitri Young	.10
183	Ryan McGuire	.10
184	Mark Bellhorn	.10
185	Joe Carter	.15
186	Kevin Stocker	.10
187	Mike Lansing	.10
188	Jason Dickson	.10
189	Charles Johnson	.10
190	Will Clark	.25
191	Shannon Stewart	.10
192	Johnny Damon	.10
193	Todd Greene	.10
194	Carlos Baerga	.10
195	David Cone	.20
196	Pokey Reese	.10
197	Livan Hernandez	.10
198	Tom Glavine	.20
199	Geronimo Berroa	.10
200	Darryl Hamilton	.10
201	Terry Steinbach	.10
202	Robb Nen	.10
203	Ron Gant	.10
204	Rafael Palmeiro	.25
205	Rickey Henderson	.20
206	Justin Thompson	.10
207	Jeff Suppan	.10
208	Kevin Brown	.20
209	Jimmy Key	.10
210	Brian Jordan	.10
211	Aaron Sele	.10
212	Fred McGriff	.20
213	Jay Bell	.10
214	Andres Galarraga	.20
215	Mark Grace	.25
216	Brett Tomko	.10
217	Francisco Cordova	.10
218	Rusty Greer	.10
219	Bubba Trammell	.10
220	Derrek Lee	.10
221	Brian Anderson	.10
222	Mark Grudzielanek	.10
223	Marquis Grissom	.10
224	Gary DiSarcina	.10
225	Jim Leyritz	.10
226	Jeffrey Hammonds	.10
227	Karim Garcia	.15
228	Chan Ho Park	.30
229	Brooks Kieschnick	.10
230	Trey Beamon	.10
231	Kevin Appier	.10
232	Wally Joyner	.10
233	Richie Sexson	.10
234	*Frank Catalanotto*	.20
235	Rafael Medina	.10
236	Travis Lee	.60
237	Eli Marrero	.10
238	Carl Pavano	.20
239	Enrique Wilson	.10
240	Richard Hidalgo	.10
241	Todd Helton	.50
242	Ben Grieve	.75
243	Mario Valdez	.10
244	*Magglio Ordonez*	.75
245	Juan Encarnacion	.10
246	Russell Branyan	.10
247	Sean Casey	.25
248	Abraham Nunez	.10
249	Brad Fullmer	.25
250	Paul Konerko	.25
251	Miquel Tejada	.30
252	*Mike Lowell*	.30
253	Ken Griffey Jr. (Spring Training)	1.00
254	Frank Thomas (Spring Training)	.60
255	Alex Rodriguez (Spring Training)	.75
256	Jose Cruz Jr. (Spring Training)	.10
257	Jeff Bagwell (Spring Training)	.30
258	Chipper Jones (Spring Training)	.60
259	Mo Vaughn (Spring Training)	.20
260	Nomar Garciaparra (Spring Training)	.60
261	Jim Thome (Spring Training)	.20
262	Derek Jeter (Spring Training)	.60
263	Mike Piazza (Spring Training)	.60
264	Tony Gwynn (Spring Training)	.50
265	Scott Rolen (Spring Training)	.30
266	Andruw Jones (Spring Training)	.25
267	Cal Ripken Jr. (Spring Training)	.75
268	Checklist (Ken Griffey Jr.)	.75
269	Checklist (Cal Ripken Jr.)	.60
270	Checklist (Jose Cruz Jr.)	.10

1998 Score Rookie & Traded Artist's Proofs

This partial parallel reprints 160 (the same cards as the Showcase Series) of the 270 cards in Score Rookie & Traded. The cards are printed on a foil surface and feature an Artist's Proof logo on front. The cards were renumbered within the 160-card set and inserted one per 35 packs.

	MT
Complete Set (160):	600.00
Common Player:	1.50
Artist's Proof Stars: 10X	
(See 1998 Score Rookie & Traded Showcase for checklist and base card values.)	

1998 Score Rookie & Traded Artist's Proofs 1 of 1

Printed on primatic gold metallic foil background and featuring a gold "001/001 One of One" seal on front, these were random inserts in hobby packs.

	MT
Common Player:	100.00
(See 1998 Score Rookie & Traded Showcase Series for checklist.)	

1998 Score Rookie & Traded All-Star Epix

All-Star Epix is a 12-card insert seeded 1:61. The cards honor the top All-Star Game moments of 12 star players. The dot matrix hologram cards were printed in orange, purple and emerald versions.

		MT
Complete Set (12):		475.00
Common Player:		15.00
Purples: 2X		
Emeralds: 4X		
1	Ken Griffey Jr.	100.00
2	Juan Gonzalez	50.00
3	Jeff Bagwell	30.00
4	Ivan Rodriguez	25.00
5	Nomar Garciaparra	60.00
6	Ryne Sandberg	25.00
7	Frank Thomas	50.00
8	Derek Jeter	60.00
9	Tony Gwynn	50.00
10	Albert Belle	25.00
11	Scott Rolen	30.00
12	Barry Larkin	15.00

1998 Score Rookie & Traded Complete Player Samples

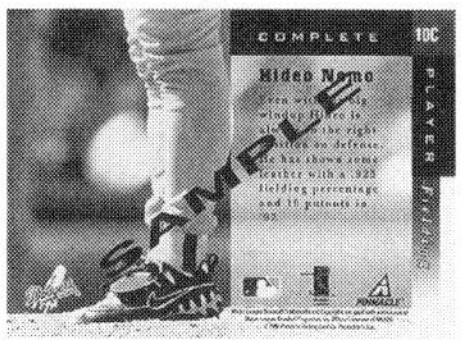

Each of the cards in the Complete Players trios can be found with a sample overprint. The cards were issued to preview the series. Values shown are for each of the cards (A, B and C) which comprise a player set.

		MT
Complete Set (30):		75.00
Common Player:		2.00
1	Ken Griffey Jr.	6.00
2	Larry Walker	2.00
3	Alex Rodriguez	4.00
4	Jose Cruz Jr.	2.00
5	Jeff Bagwell	3.00
6	Greg Maddux	3.00
7	Ivan Rodriguez	2.00
8	Roger Clemens	3.00
9	Chipper Jones	3.00
10	Hideo Nomo	2.00

1998 Score Rookie & Traded Complete Players

Complete Players is a 30-card insert seeded one per 11 packs. The set highlights 10 players who can do it all on the field. Each player has three cards showcasing one of their talents. The cards feature holographic foil stamping. Values shown are for each card (A, B and C) in the player set trios.

		MT
Complete Set (30):		90.00
Common Player:		1.50
Inserted 1:11		
1	Ken Griffey Jr.	9.00
2	Larry Walker	1.50
3	Alex Rodriguez	7.00
4	Jose Cruz	1.50
5	Jeff Bagwell	3.00
6	Greg Maddux	5.00
7	Ivan Rodriguez	2.50
8	Roger Clemens	3.00
9	Chipper Jones	5.00
10	Hideo Nomo	1.50

1998 Score Rookie & Traded Showcase Series

The Showcase Series is a partial parallel reprint of 160 of the 270 cards in Rookie & Traded. The cards are printed on a foil surface, marked on the back and renumbered (with a "PP" prefix) within the 160-card set. Showcase parallels were inserted one per seven packs.

		MT
Complete Set (160):		125.00
Common Player:		.75
1	Tony Clark	1.50
2	Juan Gonzalez	4.50
3	Frank Thomas	5.00
4	Greg Maddux	6.00
5	Barry Larkin	1.00
6	Derek Jeter	6.00
7	Randy Johnson	1.50
8	Roger Clemens	3.50
9	Tony Gwynn	4.50
10	Barry Bonds	2.50
11	Jim Edmonds	.75
12	Bernie Williams	1.50
13	Ken Griffey Jr.	9.00
14	Tim Salmon	1.00
15	Mo Vaughn	1.50
16	David Justice	1.50
17	Jose Cruz Jr.	.75
18	Andruw Jones	2.50
19	Sammy Sosa	5.00
20	Jeff Bagwell	3.50
21	Scott Rolen	3.00
22	Darin Erstad	2.00
23	Andy Pettitte	1.00
24	Mike Mussina	1.50
25	Mark McGwire	9.00
26	Hideo Nomo	1.50
27	Chipper Jones	6.00
28	Cal Ripken Jr.	7.50
29	Chuck Knoblauch	1.50
30	Alex Rodriguez	7.50
31	Jim Thome	1.50
32	Mike Piazza	6.00
33	Ivan Rodriquez	2.50
34	Roberto Alomar	2.00
35	Nomar Garciaparra	6.00
36	Albert Belle	2.00
37	Vladimir Guerrero	2.00
38	Raul Mondesi	1.00
39	Larry Walker	1.50
40	Manny Ramirez	3.00
41	Tino Martinez	1.00
42	Craig Biggio	1.00
43	Jay Buhner	.75
44	Kenny Lofton	1.00
45	Pedro Martinez	2.00
46	Edgar Martinez	.75
47	Gary Sheffield	.75
48	Jose Guillen	.75
49	Ken Caminiti	1.00
50	Bobby Higginson	1.00
51	Alan Benes	.75
52	Shawn Green	1.50
53	Matt Morris	.75
54	Jason Kendall	1.00
55	Mark Kotsay	.75
56	Bartolo Colon	1.00
57	Damian Jackson	.75
58	David Ortiz	.75
59	J.T. Snow	.75
60	Todd Hundley	.75
61	Neifi Perez	.75
62	Ryan Klesko	1.00
63	Robin Ventura	1.00
64	Pat Hentgen	.75
65	Antone Williamson	.75
66	Kevin Orie	.75
67	Brady Anderson	.75
68	Bobby Bonilla	.75
69	Brian Rose	.75
70	Sandy Alomar Jr.	1.00
71	Mike Cameron	.75
72	Omar Vizquel	.75
73	Steve Finley	.75
74	Jose Canseco	1.50
75	Al Martin	.75
76	Eric Young	.75
77	Ellis Burks	.75
78	Todd Dunwoody	.75
79	Dante Bichette	.75
80	Edgar Renteria	.75
81	Bobby Abreu	.75
82	Rondell White	.75
83	Michael Coleman	.75
84	Jason Giambi	.75
85	Wilton Guerrero	.75
86	Moises Alou	1.00
87	Todd Walker	.75
88	Shawn Estes	.75
89	John Smoltz	1.00
90	Jacob Cruz	.75
91	Javier Valentin	.75
92	Garret Anderson	.75
93	Paul O'Neill	1.00
94	Matt Williams	1.50
95	Travis Fryman	.75
96	Javier Lopez	1.00
97	Ray Lankford	.75
98	Bobby Estalella	.75
99	Jaret Wright	1.50
100	Wade Boggs	1.50
101	Fernando Tatis	1.00
102	Carlos Delgado	1.50
103	Joe Carter	.75
104	Jason Dickson	.75
105	Charles Johnson	.75
106	Will Clark	1.50

107	Shannon Stewart	.75
108	Todd Greene	.75
109	Pokey Reese	.75
110	Livan Hernandez	.75
111	Tom Glavine	1.00
112	Rafael Palmeiro	1.25
113	Justin Thompson	.75
114	Jeff Suppan	.75
115	Kevin Brown	1.50
116	Brian Jordan	.75
117	Fred McGriff	1.00
118	Andres Galarraga	.75
119	Mark Grace	1.50
120	Rusty Greer	.75
121	Bubba Trammell	.75
122	Derrek Lee	.75
123	Brian Anderson	.75
124	Karim Garcia	.75
125	Chan Ho Park	.75
126	Richie Sexson	.75
127	Frank Catalanotto	.75
128	Rafael Medina	.75
129	Travis Lee	1.00
130	Eli Marrero	.75
131	Carl Pavano	.75
132	Enrique Wilson	.75
133	Richard Hidalgo	.75
134	Todd Helton	.75
135	Ben Grieve	1.00
136	Mario Valdez	.75
137	Magglio Ordonez	.75
138	Juan Encarnacion	.75
139	Russell Branyan	.75
140	Sean Casey	1.25
141	Abraham Nunez	.75
142	Brad Fullmer	1.00
143	Paul Konerko	1.00
144	Miguel Tejada	1.00
145	Mike Lowell	.75
146	Ken Griffey Jr. (Spring Training)	3.00
147	Frank Thomas (Spring Training)	1.00
148	Alex Rodriguez (Spring Training)	2.00
149	Jose Cruz Jr. (Spring Training)	.75
150	Jeff Bagwell (Spring Training)	1.50
151	Chipper Jones (Spring Training)	2.00
152	Mo Vaughn (Spring Training)	1.00
153	Nomar Garciaparra (Spring Training)	1.50
154	Jim Thome (Spring Training)	.75
155	Derek Jeter (Spring Training)	2.00
156	Mike Piazza (Spring Training)	2.00
157	Tony Gwynn (Spring Training)	2.00
158	Scott Rolen (Spring Training)	1.50
159	Andruw Jones (Spring Training)	1.00
160	Cal Ripken Jr. (Spring Training)	2.50

1998 Score Rookie & Traded Star Gazing

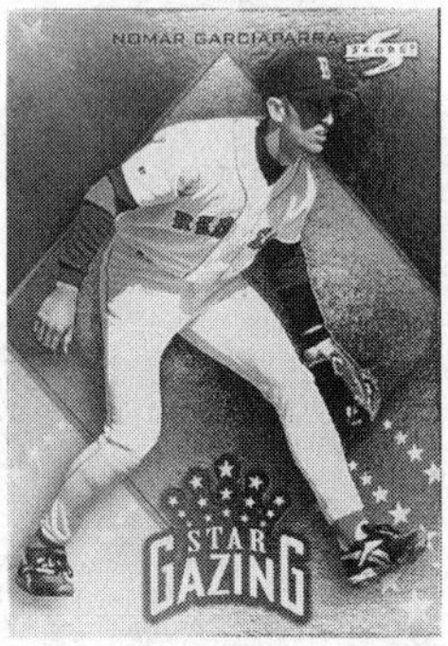

Printed on micro-etched foil board, Star Gazing features 20 top players and was seeded 1:35.

		MT
Complete Set (20):		150.00
Common Player:		3.00
Inserted 1:35		
1	Ken Griffey Jr.	20.00
2	Frank Thomas	10.00
3	Chipper Jones	12.00
4	Mark McGwire	20.00
5	Cal Ripken Jr.	15.00
6	Mike Piazza	12.00
7	Nomar Garciaparra	12.00
8	Derek Jeter	15.00
9	Juan Gonzalez	10.00
10	Vladimir Guerrero	5.00
11	Alex Rodriguez	15.00
12	Tony Gwynn	10.00
13	Andruw Jones	5.00
14	Scott Rolen	7.00
15	Jose Cruz	3.00
16	Mo Vaughn	3.00
17	Bernie Williams	4.00
18	Greg Maddux	12.00
19	Tony Clark	3.00
20	Ben Grieve	6.00

1998 Score Andruw Jones Icon Order Card

This special card was the pack-topper on retail 27-card blister packs of 1998 Score. The front is identical to the regular Jones card in the set but the back carries an ad for Pinnacle's Icon card display mail-in offer.

	MT
Andruw Jones	2.00

1996-97 Score Board All Sport PPF

Stars and prospects, Past, Present and Future (PPF), in the four major team sports are featured in this two series set whose issue spanned late 1996 and early 1997. Borderless action photos and gold-foil graphic highlights are featured on front. Another photo, stats and personal data can be found on back. Only the baseball players from the 200-card set are listed here. A gold parallel edition was also issued.

		MT
Common Player:		.10
21	Ryan Minor	.25
60	Rey Ordonez	.15
61	Todd Greene	.10
62	Jermaine Dye	.15
63	Karim Garcia	.25
64	Todd Walker	.15
65	Calvin Reese	.10
66	Roger Cedeno	.15
67	Ben Davis	.10
68	Chad Hermansen	.20
69	Vladimir Guerrero	.50
70	Billy Wagner	.25
94	Barry Bonds	.25
95	Vladimir Guerrero	.50
96	Livan Hernandez	.15
160	Barry Bonds	.25
161	Jay Payton	.10
162	Jose Cruz Jr.	.25
163	Richard Hidalgo	.10
164	Bartolo Colon	.15
165	Matt Drews	.10
166	Kerry Wood	.20
167	Ben Grieve	.35
168	Wes Helms	.10
169	Livan Hernandez	.15
196	Todd Walker	.15
197	Rey Ordonez	.15
198	Todd Greene	.10

1996-97 Score Board All Sport PPF Retro

Current and potential stars in the format of classic sports cards are featured in this Series 2 insert found at an announced rate of one per 35 packs. Only a single baseball player is included among the 10 cards in the set.

		MT
R10	Rey Ordonez	4.00

1996-97 Score Board All Sport PPF Revivals

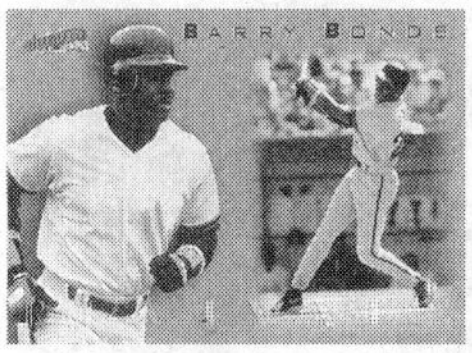

Current and potential stars in the format of classic sports cards are featured in this Series 1 insert found at an announced rate of one per 35 packs. Only a single baseball player is included among the 10 cards in the set.

		MT
REV10	Barry Bonds	1.50

1997 Score Board Mickey Mantle Shoe Box Collection

Yet another collectors' issue of Mickey Mantle cards, the Score Board "Shoe Box Collection" offered packs containing two of the 75 Mantle cards or seven-card insert set, along with a genuine - usually a low-grade common - Topps card from 1951-69. Several designs of Mantle cards are featured in the set, including color photos as well as blue-and-white duotones. Five of the cards are printed with gold-foil backgrounds and die-cut. Cards #51-69 are short-printed at a ratio of about 1-to-3 with cards #1-50. Suggested retail price was $6.50 per pack.

		MT
Complete Set (75):		50.00
Common Card:		.75
1	Summary Of The Legend (foil die-cut)	7.00
1p	Summary of the Legend (promo card)	11.00
2	Triple Crown 1956	.75
3	MVP 1956	.75
4	MVP 1957	.75
5	MVP 1962	.75
6	Uniform #6 (foil die-cut)	7.00
6p	Uniform #6 (promo card)	11.00
7	Uniform #7 (foil die-cut)	7.00
7p	Uniform #7 (promo card)	11.00
8	Gold Glove Winner	.75
9	17-time All-Star	.75
10	4-time HR Champion	.75
11	World Series Records	.75
12	The Dirty Dozen (post-seasons)	.75
13	World Champion-1951	.75
14	World Champion-1952	.75
15	World Champion-1953	.75
16	World Champion-1956	.75
17	World Champion-1958	.75
18	World Champion-1961	.75
19	World Champion-1962	.75
20	Replacing A Legend	.75
21	Casey On Mantle	.75
22	Mickey & The Media	.75
23	Family Man	.75
24	Fan Favorite	.75
25	Playing Injured	.75
26	Clubhouse Leader	.75
27	Team Leader	.75
28	M & M Boys	.75
29	Legendary Friendships	.75
30	Time Out	.75
31	Mantle Is Born	.75
32	Mutt Mantle	.75
33	Growing Up	.75
34	5-tool player-Arm	.75
35	5-tool player-Defense	.75
36	5-tool player-Average	.75
37	5-tool player-Speed	.75
38	5-tool player-Power	.75
39	First Homer	.75
40	100th Homer	.75
41	200th Homer	.75
42	300th Homer	.75
43	400th Homer	.75
44	500th Homer	.75
45	536 Career Homers	.75
46	Yankee Stadium Blasts	.75
47	Switch-hit Home Runs	.75
48	565-ft. Home Run	.75
49	Signs 1st Pro Contract	.75
50	Mickey In The Minors	.75
51	1951 Trading Card	1.50
52	1952 Trading Card	1.50
53	1953 Trading Card	1.50
54	1954 Trading Card	1.50
55	1955 Trading Card	1.50
56A	1956 Trading Card	1.50
56B	1956 Trading Card	1.50
57	1957 Trading Card	1.50
58	1958 Trading Card	1.50
59	1959 Trading Card	1.50
60	1960 Trading Card	1.50
61	1961 Trading Card	1.50
62	1962 Trading Card	1.50
63	1963 Trading Card	1.50
64	1964 Trading Card	1.50
65	1965 Trading Card	1.50
66	1966 Trading Card	1.50
67	1967 Trading Card	1.50
68	1968 Trading Card	1.50
69	1969 Trading Card	1.50
70	Number Retired By Yankees (foil die-cut)	7.00
70p	Number Retired By Yankees (promo card)	11.00
71	Mickey Mantle Day (1965)	.75
72	Mickey Mantle Day (1969)	.75
73	Life After Baseball	.75
74	Hall Of Fame Induction (foil die-cut)	7.00
74p	Hall of Fame Induction (promo card)	11.00

1997 Score Board Mickey Mantle Shoe Box Inserts

A set of seven insert cards, found on average of one per 16 packs, was part of the Mickey Mantle Shoe Box Collection. The inserts have a photo of Mantle on front, with blue metallic foil highlights. Contest rules on the back specify that the first seven persons to redeem a complete set of the seven insert cards will win a $7,000 Mantle phone card. All others redeeming the set of seven prior to July 7, 1998, received a $700 Mantle phone card. The #7 insert card was short-printed to limit the number of phone card winners.

		MT
Complete Set (7):		300.00
Common Card:		25.00
$700 Phone Card:		475.00
$7,000 Phone Card:		3500.
1	Mickey Mantle Insert #1	25.00
2	Mickey Mantle Insert #2	25.00
3	Mickey Mantle Insert #3	25.00
4	Mickey Mantle Insert #4	25.00
5	Mickey Mantle Insert #5	50.00
6	Mickey Mantle Insert #6	25.00
7	Mickey Mantle Insert #7 (short-print)	175.00

1997 Score Board Players Club

Seven baseball players are among the cards in this multi-sport issue. Card fronts feature borderless action photos from which uniform logos have been removed. The player's name and the city in which he plays are in gold-foil in a baseball strip at bottom. Backs have another photo, biographical data and stats, including projected 1998 figures. Only the baseball players in the set are listed here.

		MT
Complete Set (70):		8.00
Common Player:		.05
3	Barry Bonds	.50
7	Jose Cruz Jr.	.25
17	Matt Drews	.25
27	Wes Helms	.25
37	Richard Hidalgo	.25
48	Jay Payton	.25
69	Kerry Wood	.50

1997 Score Board Players Club #1 Die-Cuts

Former #1 draft picks from all four major sports are included in this insert set. Highlighted in gold foil, cards are die-cut into the shape of a numeral 1. Backs have biographical information and stats. Cards are numbered with a "D" prefix. Only the baseball players are listed here.

		MT
Complete Set (20):		75.00
Common Player:		2.00
D10	Jose Cruz Jr.	2.00
D11	Barry Bonds	5.00

1997 Score Board Talk N' Sports

Insert phone cards with talk time worth up to $1,000, along with trivia contests to win memorabilia were among the incentives to purchase this four-sport issue. The base card set features 50 stars and prospects, all of whom are also found, along with a few other superstars, in the inserts. Fronts of the base cards have action photos on which uniform logos have been airbrushed away. Backs have a couple more photos, some player bio and stats. Only the baseball players from the set are listed here.

		MT
Complete Set (50):		5.00
Common Player:		.05
40	Barry Bonds	.25
41	Jay Payton	.05
42	Todd Walker	.10
43	Jose Cruz Jr.	.15
44	Kerry Wood	.50
45	Wes Helms	.10

Checklists with card numbers in parentheses ( ) indicates the numbers do not appear on the card.

1997 Score Board Talk N' Sports Essentials

See-through plastic and action photos are combined on this 1:20 pack insert. Only a single baseball player is included among the four-sport stars and prospects.

		MT
Complete Set (10):		75.00
Common Player:		5.00
E3	Barry Bonds	7.50

1997 Score Board Talk N' Sports $1 Phone Cards

These phone cards were a one-per-pack insert and paralleled the base set. Phone time expired on July 31, 1998. Only the baseball players are listed.

		MT
Complete Set (50):		50.00
Common Player:		.50
40	Barry Bonds	1.00
41	Jay Payton	.50
42	Todd Walker	.50
43	Jose Cruz Jr.	.75
44	Kerry Wood	2.00
45	Wes Helms	.75

1997 Score Board Talk N' Sports $10 Phone Cards

These phone/trivia cards were inserted at a 1:12 pack ratio and individually serial numbered within an edition of 3,960 each. Each card allowed the holder to use either $10 worth of calling time or to call into a trivia contest which offered autographed bats of top stars as prizes. The cards expired on May 20, 1998. Only one baseball player was included.

		MT
Complete Set (10):		90.00
Common Player:		10.00
6	Cal Ripken Jr.	15.00

1997 Score Board Talk N' Sports $20 Phone Cards

These phone cards were inserted at a 1:36 pack ratio and individually serial numbered within an edition of 1,440 each. Each card allowed the holder to use $20 worth of calling time either regularly or on a special sports score hot line. The cards expired on July 31, 1998. Only two baseball players were included.

		MT
Complete Set (10):		125.00
Common Player:		12.50
3	Barry Bonds	15.00
4	Cal Ripken Jr.	25.00

1997 Score Board Talk N' Sports $50 Phone Card

The 50th anniversary of Jackie Robinson's major league debut was marked with this special insert phone card. Only 499 serially numbered cards were produced, inserted at a rate of one per 200 packs. The phone time expired July 31, 1998.

	MT
Jackie Robinson	35.00

1997 Score Board Talk N' Sports $1,000 Phone Cards

Only 10 serially numbered cards of each of five sports stars were produced in this high-value insert card, found on average of one per 11,000 packs. The phone time expired on July 31, 1998.

		MT
Complete Set (5):		1200.
Common Player:		300.00
1	Cal Ripken Jr.	350.00

1997 Score Board Visions Signings

Stars and prospects from all four major team sports are included in this issue. Fronts have borderless action photos with professional logos removed as necessary to meet licensing regulations. Front graphics feature holographic foil highlights. Backs have another photo along with stats, personal data and career notes. Cards were sold in five-card packs, each of which contained either an autographed card or an insert card. Only the seven baseball players from the 50-card set are listed here.

		MT
Common Player:		.25
Gold Parallel: 2-4X		
1	Barry Bonds	.50
5	Jose Cruz Jr.	.25
6	Ben Grieve	1.00
7	Kerry Wood	1.00
44	Wes Helms	.50
45	Richard Hidalgo	.50
46	Jay Payton	.25

1997 Score Board Visions Signings Autographs

Each five-card pack of Score Board Vision Signings contained either an authentically autographed card or an insert card. Only the baseball players from the 63 autographed cards in the multi-sports set of stars and prospects are listed here.

		MT
Common Player:		6.00
9	Jose Cruz Jr.	15.00
20	Ben Grieve	45.00
21	Vladimir Guerrero	45.00
26	Wes Helms	9.00
27	Richard Hidalgo	9.00
34	Jason Kendall	12.00
44	Jay Payton	6.00
62	Paul Wilson	6.00
63	Kerry Wood	45.00

1997 Score Board Visions Signings Artistry

These specially printed cards were a one-in-six packs insert (regular version; 1:18 autographed) in five-card Visions Signings packs. Only a single baseball player is represented among the 20 cards in the set.

		MT
1	Jose Cruz Jr.	5.00
1	Jose Cruz Jr. (autographed)	25.00

1998 Score Board Autographed Collection

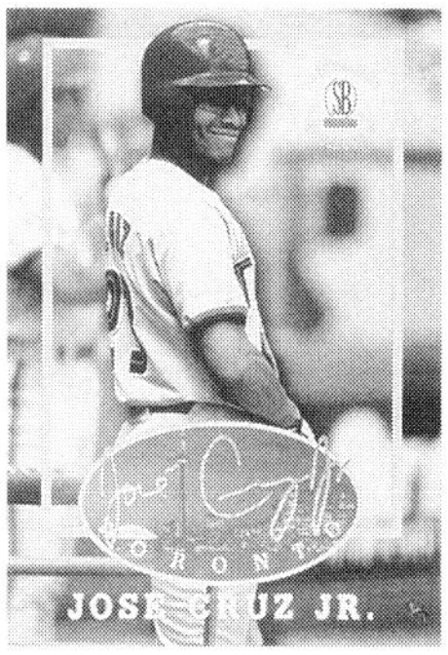

A handful of baseball players are among the four-sport stars and prospects in this set. Luring collectors was the presence of autographed cards at the rate of one per 4-1/2 packs, Blue Ribbon serially numbered autographs and memorabilia redemption cards (many of which became worthless when Score Board went bankrupt shortly after the set was issued). Because the cards are licensed only by the players, and not leagues, there are no uniform logos on the photos, nor mention of team names, only cities. Only the baseball players are listed here.

		MT
Complete Set (50):		9.00
Common Player:		.05
3	J.D. Drew	3.00
11	Matt White	.25
12	Jay Payton	.25
23	Brandon Larson	.50
28	Jose Cruz Jr.	.50
49	Adrian Beltre	2.00

1998 Score Board Autographed Collection Autographs

Authentically autographed cards were inserted in this issue at the rate of about four per 18-pack box. Cards have a round player photo at center with the signature in a white oval below. Backs have a congratulatory message. Only the baseball players among the four-sport stars and prospects are listed here. Cards are unnumbered.

	MT
Complete Set (23):	200.00
Common Player:	5.00
Ben Grieve	50.00
Wes Helms	12.50

1998 Score Board Autographed Collection Blue Ribbon

These one-per-box inserts are similar in format to the autographed cards, but have a blue ribbon beneath the player photo on which the signature has been penned. Each card is individually serial numbered from within editions which vary from fewer than 100 to nearly 2,000. Only one baseball player was among the four-sport stars and prospects.

	MT
Jose Cruz Jr. (1,600)	35.00

1998 Score Board Autographed Collection Sports City USA

Players whose teams share a common city are featured in this insert series, found on average one per nine packs. A parallel version, embossed "Strongbox" was issued in special $125 television-offer packages of Autographed Collection. The parallels are individually serial numbered to 600. Only cards with baseball players are listed here.

		MT
Complete Set (15):		50.00
Common Card:		3.00
Embossed: 2-4X		
SC3	Richard Hidalgo (Olajuwan, Drexler)	5.00
SC4	Kerry Wood (Pippen, Autry)	7.50

SC6	Adrian Beltre (Bryant)	10.00
SC7	J.D. Drew (Thomas, Staley)	9.00
SC12	Wes Helms (Hanspard, Gray)	3.00
SC14	Jay Payton (Barber, Van Horn)	5.00
SC15	Matt Drews (Westbrook, Pollard)	3.00

1998 Score Board Autographed Collection Strongbox

As part of a special $125 television offer, a parallel version of Score Board's Autographed Collection was offered featuring special inserts, autographs and memorabilia. The parallel cards are marked with an embossed "Strongbox" logo.

		MT
Complete Set (50):		10.00
Common Player:		.10
3	J.D. Drew	4.50
11	Matt White	.40
12	Jay Payton	.50
23	Brandon Larson	.75
28	Jose Cruz Jr.	.75
49	Adrian Beltre	.75

1981 Seattle Mariners Police

These 2-5/8" x 4-1/8" cards were co-sponsored by the Washington State Crime Prevention Assoc., Coca-Cola, Kiawanis and Ernst Home Centers. There are 16 players featured in this full-color set with each card numbered in the lower left of the card back. Card fronts list player name and position and have a team logo. Card backs are printed in blue and red and offer a "Tip from the Mariners" along with the four sponsor logos.

		MT
Complete Set (16):		4.00
Common Player:		.25
1	Jeff Burroughs	.25
2	Floyd Bannister	.25
3	Glenn Abbott	.25
4	Jim Anderson	.25
5	Danny Meyer	.25
6	Dave Edler	.25
7	Julio Cruz	.25
8	Kenny Clay	.25
9	Lenny Randle	.25
10	Mike Parrott	.25
11	Tom Paciorek	.25
12	Jerry Narron	.25
13	Richie Zisk	.25
14	Maury Wills	.50
15	Joe Simpson	.25
16	Shane Rawley	.25

1982 Seattle Mariners Postcards

This set of player postcards was available through the team. Fronts are in black-and-white with asemi-gloss surface and a player portrait photo. Backs are also in black-and-white. The cards measure 3-3/4" x 5-1/2". The unnumbered cards are checklisted here in alphabetical order.

		MT
Complete Set (30):		12.00
Common Player:		.50
(1)	Brian Allard	.50
(2)	Rick Auerbach	.50
(3)	Floyd Bannister	.65
(4)	Bruce Bochte	.50
(5)	Thad Bosley	.50
(6)	Bobby Brown	.50
(7)	Bud Bulling	.50
(8)	Terry Bulling	.50
(9)	Jeff Burroughs	.75
(10)	Manny Castillo	.50
(11)	Bryan Clark	.50
(12)	Ken Clay	.50
(13)	Al Cowens	.50
(14)	Julio Cruz	.75
(15)	Todd Cruz	.50
(16)	Tommy Davis	.75
(17)	Dick Drago	.50
(18)	Dave Duncan	.50
(19)	Jim Essian	.50
(20)	Jerry Don Gleaton	.50
(21)	Dave Henderson	.65
(22)	Jim Maler	.50
(23)	Jerry Narron	.50
(24)	Tom Paciorek	.50
(25)	Vada Pinson	1.25
(26)	Lenny Randle	.50
(27)	Paul Serna	.50
(28)	Mike Stanton	.50
(29)	Steve Stroughter	.50
(30)	Ken Wilson	.50

1993 Select Promos

Zeroes in the stats lines on the back of the card distinguish the promo cards for Score's premiere issue of its Select brand name. The promo cards were distributed to introduce dealers and collectors to the new mid-range set.

		MT
Complete Set (5):		40.00
Common Player:		2.50
22	Robin Yount	15.00
24	Don Mattingly	20.00
26	Sandy Alomar Jr.	5.00
41	Gary Sheffield	10.00
75	John Smiley	2.50

1993 Select Dufex Proofs

To test the Dufex textured foil printing technology which was used on its Stars, Rookies and Triple Crown insert sets, Select produced a very limited number of blank-back proof cards.

Select Rookies: 15X
Select Stars: 20X
Select Triple Crown: 20X
(See 1993 Select Rookies, Stars and Triple Crown for checklist and base card values.)

1993 Select

This 400-card set from Score is designed for the mid-priced card market. The card fronts feature green borders on two sides of the card with the photo filling the remaining portion of the card front. The backs feature an additional photo, player information and statistics. Cards numbered 271-360 are devoted to rookies and draft picks.

		MT
Complete Set (405):		20.00
Common Player:		.05
Wax Box:		30.00
1	Barry Bonds	.75
2	Ken Griffey, Jr.	3.00
3	Will Clark	.25
4	Kirby Puckett	1.00
5	Tony Gwynn	1.00
6	Frank Thomas	2.00
7	Tom Glavine	.15
8	Roberto Alomar	.60
9	Andre Dawson	.15
10	Ron Darling	.05
11	Bobby Bonilla	.10
12	Danny Tartabull	.05
13	Darren Daulton	.05
14	Roger Clemens	1.00
15	Ozzie Smith	.50
16	Mark McGwire	3.00
17	Terry Pendleton	.05
18	Cal Ripken, Jr.	2.50
19	Fred McGriff	.20
20	Cecil Fielder	.10
21	Darryl Strawberry	.10
22	Robin Yount	.75
23	Barry Larkin	.15
24	Don Mattingly	.75
25	Craig Biggio	.20
26	Sandy Alomar Jr.	.15
27	Larry Walker	.30
28	Junior Felix	.05
29	Eddie Murray	.20
30	Robin Ventura	.15
31	Greg Maddux	2.00
32	Dave Winfield	.15
33	John Kruk	.05
34	Wally Joyner	.05
35	Andy Van Slyke	.05
36	Chuck Knoblauch	.20
37	Tom Pagnozzi	.05
38	Dennis Eckersley	.05
39	Dave Justice	.20
40	Juan Gonzalez	1.50
41	Gary Sheffield	.35
42	Paul Molitor	.75
43	Delino DeShields	.05
44	Travis Fryman	.10
45	Hal Morris	.05
46	Gregg Olson	.05
47	Ken Caminiti	.20
48	Wade Boggs	.25
49	Orel Hershiser	.10
50	Albert Belle	.75
51	Bill Swift	.05
52	Mark Langston	.05
53	Joe Girardi	.05
54	Keith Miller	.05
55	Gary Carter	.10
56	Brady Anderson	.10
57	Dwight Gooden	.10
58	Julio Franco	.05
59	Len Dykstra	.05
60	Mickey Tettleton	.05
61	Randy Tomlin	.05
62	B.J. Surhoff	.05
63	Todd Zeile	.05
64	Roberto Kelly	.05
65	Rob Dibble	.05
66	Leo Gomez	.05
67	Doug Jones	.05
68	Ellis Burks	.10
69	Mike Scioscia	.05
70	Charles Nagy	.10
71	Cory Snyder	.05
72	Devon White	.10
73	Mark Grace	.20
74	Luis Polonia	.05
75	John Smiley	.05
76	Carlton Fisk	.15
77	Luis Sojo	.05
78	George Brett	.75
79	Mitch Williams	.05
80	Kent Hrbek	.05
81	Jay Bell	.05
82	Edgar Martinez	.05
83	Lee Smith	.05
84	Deion Sanders	.15
85	Bill Gullickson	.05
86	Paul O'Neill	.15
87	Kevin Seitzer	.05
88	Steve Finley	.10
89	Mel Hall	.05
90	Nolan Ryan	2.00
91	Eric Davis	.10
92	Mike Mussina	.50
93	Tony Fernandez	.05
94	Frank Viola	.05
95	Matt Williams	.25
96	Joe Carter	.10
97	Ryne Sandberg	.75
98	Jim Abbott	.05
99	Marquis Grissom	.10
100	George Bell	.05
101	Howard Johnson	.05
102	Kevin Appier	.05
103	Dale Murphy	.10
104	Shane Mack	.05
105	Jose Lind	.05
106	Rickey Henderson	.20
107	Bob Tewksbury	.05
108	Kevin Mitchell	.05
109	Steve Avery	.05
110	Candy Maldonado	.05
111	Bip Roberts	.05
112	Lou Whitaker	.05
113	Jeff Bagwell	1.00
114	Dante Bichette	.25
115	Brett Butler	.05
116	Melido Perez	.05
117	Andy Benes	.10
118	Randy Johnson	.40
119	Willie McGee	.05
120	Jody Reed	.05
121	Shawon Dunston	.05
122	Carlos Baerga	.10
123	Bret Saberhagen	.10
124	John Olerud	.20
125	Ivan Calderon	.05
126	Bryan Harvey	.05
127	Terry Mulholland	.05
128	Ozzie Guillen	.05
129	Steve Buechele	.05
130	Kevin Tapani	.05
131	Felix Jose	.05
132	Terry Steinbach	.05
133	Ron Gant	.10
134	Harold Reynolds	.05
135	Chris Sabo	.05
136	Ivan Rodriguez	.60
137	Eric Anthony	.05
138	Mike Henneman	.05
139	Robby Thompson	.05
140	Scott Fletcher	.05
141	Bruce Hurst	.05
142	Kevin Maas	.05
143	Tom Candiotti	.05
144	Chris Hoiles	.05
145	Mike Morgan	.05
146	Mark Whiten	.05
147	Dennis Martinez	.05
148	Tony Pena	.05
149	Dave Magadan	.05
150	Mark Lewis	.05
151	Mariano Duncan	.05
152	Gregg Jefferies	.05
153	Doug Drabek	.05
154	Brian Harper	.05
155	Ray Lankford	.10
156	Carney Lansford	.05
157	Mike Sharperson	.05
158	Jack Morris	.05
159	Otis Nixon	.05
160	Steve Sax	.05
161	Mark Lemke	.05
162	Rafael Palmeiro	.20
163	Jose Rijo	.05
164	Omar Vizquel	.05
165	Sammy Sosa	1.50
166	Milt Cuyler	.05
167	John Franco	.05
168	Darryl Hamilton	.05
169	Ken Hill	.05
170	Mike Devereaux	.05
171	Don Slaught	.05
172	Steve Farr	.05
173	Bernard Gilkey	.10
174	Mike Fetters	.05
175	Vince Coleman	.05
176	Kevin McReynolds	.05
177	John Smoltz	.15
178	Greg Gagne	.05
179	Greg Swindell	.05
180	Juan Guzman	.05
181	Kal Daniels	.05
182	Rick Sutcliffe	.05
183	Orlando Merced	.05
184	Bill Wegman	.05
185	Mark Gardner	.05
186	Rob Deer	.05
187	Dave Hollins	.05
188	Jack Clark	.05
189	Brian Hunter	.05
190	Tim Wallach	.05
191	Tim Belcher	.05
192	Walt Weiss	.05
193	Kurt Stillwell	.05
194	Charlie Hayes	.05
195	Willie Randolph	.05
196	Jack McDowell	.05
197	Jose Offerman	.05
198	Chuck Finley	.05
199	Darrin Jackson	.05
200	Kelly Gruber	.05
201	John Wetteland	.05
202	Jay Buhner	.10
203	Mike LaValliere	.05
204	Kevin Brown	.10
205	Luis Gonzalez	.10
206	Rick Aguilera	.05
207	Norm Charlton	.05
208	Mike Bordick	.05
209	Charlie Leibrandt	.05
210	Tom Brunansky	.05
211	Tom Henke	.05
212	Randy Milligan	.05
213	Ramon Martinez	.10
214	Mo Vaughn	.60
215	Randy Myers	.05
216	Greg Hibbard	.05
217	Wes Chamberlain	.05
218	Tony Phillips	.05
219	Pete Harnisch	.05
220	Mike Gallego	.05
221	Bud Black	.05
222	Greg Vaughn	.10
223	Milt Thompson	.05
224	Ben McDonald	.05
225	Billy Hatcher	.05
226	Paul Sorrento	.05
227	Mark Gubicza	.05
228	Mike Greenwell	.05
229	Curt Schilling	.10
230	Alan Trammell	.10
231	Zane Smith	.05
232	Bobby Thigpen	.05
233	Greg Olson	.05
234	Joe Orsulak	.05
235	Joe Oliver	.05
236	Tim Raines	.10
237	Juan Samuel	.05
238	Chili Davis	.05
239	Spike Owen	.05
240	Dave Stewart	.05
241	Jim Eisenreich	.05
242	Phil Plantier	.05
243	Sid Fernandez	.05
244	Dan Gladden	.05
245	Mickey Morandini	.05
246	Tino Martinez	.15
247	Kirt Manwaring	.05
248	Dean Palmer	.05
249	Tom Browning	.05
250	Brian McRae	.05
251	Scott Leius	.05
252	Bert Blyleven	.05
253	Scott Erickson	.05
254	Bob Welch	.05
255	Pat Kelly	.05
256	Felix Fermin	.05
257	Harold Baines	.10
258	Duane Ward	.05
259	Bill Spiers	.05
260	Jaime Navarro	.05
261	Scott Sanderson	.05
262	Gary Gaetti	.05
263	Bob Ojeda	.05
264	Jeff Montgomery	.05
265	Scott Bankhead	.05
266	Lance Johnson	.05
267	Rafael Belliard	.05
268	Kevin Reimer	.05
269	Benito Santiago	.05
270	Mike Moore	.05
271	Dave Fleming	.05
272	Moises Alou	.15
273	Pat Listach	.05
274	Reggie Sanders	.10
275	Kenny Lofton	.60
276	Donovan Osborne	.05
277	Rusty Meacham	.05
278	Eric Karros	.15
279	Andy Stankiewicz	.05
280	Brian Jordan	.10
281	Gary DiSarcina	.05
282	Mark Wohlers	.05
283	Dave Nilsson	.05
284	Anthony Young	.05
285	Jim Bullinger	.05
286	Derek Bell	.10
287	Brian Williams	.10
288	Julio Valera	.05
289	Dan Walters	.05
290	Chad Curtis	.05
291	Michael Tucker	.05
292	Bob Zupcic	.05

293	Todd Hundley	.20
294	Jeff Tackett	.05
295	Greg Colbrunn	.05
296	Cal Eldred	.05
297	Chris Roberts	.05
298	John Doherty	.05
299	Denny Neagle	.05
300	Arthur Rhodes	.05
301	Mark Clark	.05
302	Scott Cooper	.05
303	*Jamie Arnold*	.10
304	Jim Thome	.25
305	Frank Seminara	.05
306	Kurt Knudsen	.05
307	Tim Wakefield	.05
308	John Jaha	.05
309	Pat Hentgen	.05
310	B.J. Wallace	.05
311	Roberto Hernandez	.05
312	Hipolito Pichardo	.05
313	Eric Fox	.05
314	Willie Banks	.05
315	Sam Militello	.05
316	Vince Horsman	.05
317	Carlos Hernandez	.05
318	Jeff Kent	.15
319	Mike Perez	.05
320	Scott Livingstone	.05
321	Jeff Conine	.10
322	James Austin	.05
323	John Vander Wal	.05
324	Pat Mahomes	.05
325	Pedro Astacio	.10
326	Bret Boone	.10
327	Matt Stairs	.10
328	Damion Easley	.10
329	Ben Rivera	.05
330	Reggie Jefferson	.10
331	Luis Mercedes	.05
332	Kyle Abbott	.10
333	Eddie Taubensee	.05
334	Tim McIntosh	.05
335	Phil Clark	.05
336	Wil Cordero	.10
337	Russ Springer	.05
338	Craig Colbert	.05
339	Tim Salmon	.50
340	Braulio Castillo	.05
341	Donald Harris	.05
342	Eric Young	.10
343	Bob Wickman	.05
344	John Valentin	.10
345	Dan Wilson	.05
346	Steve Hosey	.10
347	Mike Piazza	2.00
348	Willie Greene	.10
349	Tom Goodwin	.05
350	Eric Hillman	.05
351	*Steve Reed*	.10
352	*Dan Serafini*	.15
353	*Todd Steverson*	.15
354	Benji Grigsby	.05
355	*Shannon Stewart*	.75
356	Sean Lowe	.10
357	Derek Wallace	.10
358	Rick Helling	.05
359	*Jason Kendall*	2.00
360	*Derek Jeter*	8.00
361	David Cone	.15
362	Jeff Reardon	.05
363	Bobby Witt	.05
364	Jose Canseco	.25
365	Jeff Russell	.05
366	Ruben Sierra	.05
367	Alan Mills	.05
368	Matt Nokes	.05
369	Pat Borders	.05
370	Pedro Munoz	.05
371	Danny Jackson	.05
372	Geronimo Pena	.05
373	Craig Lefferts	.05
374	Joe Grahe	.05
375	Roger McDowell	.05
376	Jimmy Key	.05
377	Steve Olin	.05
378	Glenn Davis	.05
379	Rene Gonzales	.05
380	Manuel Lee	.05
381	Ron Karkovice	.05
382	Sid Bream	.05
383	Gerald Williams	.05
384	Lenny Harris	.05
385	*J.T. Snow*	.75
386	Dave Stieb	.05
387	Kirk McCaskill	.05
388	Lance Parrish	.05
389	Craig Greback	.05
390	Rick Wilkins	.05
391	Manny Alexander	.05
392	Mike Schooler	.05
393	Bernie Williams	.40
394	Kevin Koslofski	.05
395	Willie Wilson	.05
396	Jeff Parrett	.05
397	Mike Harkey	.05
398	Frank Tanana	.05
399	Doug Henry	.05
400	Royce Clayton	.05
401	Eric Wedge	.05
402	Derrick May	.05
403	Carlos Garcia	.05
404	Henry Rodriguez	.10
405	Ryan Klesko	.15

1993 Select Aces

Cards from this set feature 24 of the top pitchers from 1992 and were included one per every 27-card Super Pack. The fronts have a picture of the player in action against an Ace card background. Backs have text and a portrait in the middle of a card suit for an Ace.

		MT
Complete Set (24):		50.00
Common Player:		1.50
1	Roger Clemens	12.50
2	Tom Glavine	4.00
3	Jack McDowell	1.50
4	Greg Maddux	15.00
5	Jack Morris	1.50
6	Dennis Martinez	1.50
7	Kevin Brown	4.00
8	Dwight Gooden	2.00
9	Kevin Appier	1.50
10	Mike Morgan	1.50
11	Juan Guzman	1.50
12	Charles Nagy	2.00
13	John Smiley	1.50
14	Ken Hill	1.50
15	Bob Tewksbury	1.50
16	Doug Drabek	1.50
17	John Smoltz	4.00
18	Greg Swindell	1.50
19	Bruce Hurst	1.50
20	Mike Mussina	8.00
21	Cal Eldred	1.50
22	Melido Perez	1.50
23	Dave Fleming	1.50
24	Kevin Tapani	1.50

1993 Select Rookies

Top newcomers in 1992 are featured in this 21-card insert set. Cards were randomly inserted in 15-card hobby packs. The fronts, printed on metallic foil, have a Score Select Rookies logo on the front. The backs have text and a player portrait.

		MT
Complete Set (21):		45.00
Common Player:		1.00
1	Pat Listach	1.00
2	Moises Alou	2.50
3	Reggie Sanders	2.00
4	Kenny Lofton	20.00
5	Eric Karros	2.00
6	Brian Williams	1.00
7	Donovan Osborne	1.00
8	Sam Militello	1.00
9	Chad Curtis	1.50
10	Bob Zupcic	1.00
11	Tim Salmon	12.50
12	Jeff Conine	2.50
13	Pedro Astacio	1.50
14	Arthur Rhodes	1.00
15	Cal Eldred	1.00
16	Tim Wakefield	1.00
17	Andy Stankiewicz	1.00
18	Wil Cordero	1.50
19	Todd Hundley	5.00
20	Dave Fleming	1.00
21	Bret Boone	1.50

1993 Select Stars

The top 24 players from 1992 are featured in this insert set. Cards were randomly inserted in 15-card retail packs. Fronts are printed on metallic foil.

		MT
Complete Set (24):		75.00
Common Player:		1.00
Minor Stars:		2.00
1	Fred McGriff	1.50
2	Ryne Sandberg	5.00
3	Ozzie Smith	5.00
4	Gary Sheffield	2.00
5	Darren Daulton	1.00
6	Andy Van Slyke	1.00
7	Barry Bonds	6.00
8	Tony Gwynn	10.00
9	Greg Maddux	12.50
10	Tom Glavine	1.50
11	John Franco	1.00
12	Lee Smith	1.00
13	Cecil Fielder	1.00
14	Roberto Alomar	3.50
15	Cal Ripken, Jr.	15.00
16	Edgar Martinez	1.00
17	Ivan Rodriguez	4.00
18	Kirby Puckett	9.00
19	Ken Griffey, Jr.	20.00
20	Joe Carter	1.00
21	Roger Clemens	9.00
22	Dave Fleming	1.00
22s	Dave Fleming (blank-back sample card)	5.00
23	Paul Molitor	4.50
24	Dennis Eckersley	1.00

1993 Select Stat Leaders

This 90-card set features 1992 American League and National League leaders in various statistical categories. Each card front indicates the league and the category in which the player finished at or near the top. The backs have a list of the leaders; the pictured player's name is in larger type size. Cards were inserted one per foil pack.

		MT
Complete Set (90):		10.00
Common Player:		.10
1	Edgar Martinez	.10
2	Kirby Puckett	.50
3	Frank Thomas	.50
4	Gary Sheffield	.20
5	Andy Van Slyke	.10
6	John Kruk	.10
7	Kirby Puckett	.50
8	Carlos Baerga	.10
9	Paul Molitor	.25
10	Andy Van Slyke, Terry Pendleton	.10
11	Ryne Sandberg	.40
12	Mark Grace	.20
13	Frank Thomas	.50
14	Don Mattingly	.50
15	Ken Griffey, Jr.	1.00
16	Andy Van Slyke	.10
17	Mariano Duncan, Jerald Clark, Ray Lankford	.10
18	Marquis Grissom, Terry Pendleton	.10
19	Lance Johnson	.10
20	Mike Devereaux	.10
21	Brady Anderson	.15
22	Deion Sanders	.20
23	Steve Finley	.10
24	Andy Van Slyke	.10
25	Juan Gonzalez	.40
26	Mark McGwire	.75
27	Cecil Fielder	.10
28	Fred McGriff	.20
29	Barry Bonds	.40
30	Gary Sheffield	.20
31	Cecil Fielder	.10
32	Joe Carter	.10
33	Frank Thomas	.50
34	Darren Daulton	.10
35	Terry Pendleton	.10
36	Fred McGriff	.20
37	Tony Phillips	.10
38	Frank Thomas	.50
39	Roberto Alomar	.25
40	Barry Bonds	.40
41	Dave Hollins	.10
42	Andy Van Slyke	.10
43	Mark McGwire	.75
44	Edgar Martinez	.10
45	Frank Thomas	.50
46	Barry Bonds	.40
47	Gary Sheffield	.20
48	Fred McGriff	.20
49	Frank Thomas	.50
50	Danny Tartabull	.10
51	Roberto Alomar	.25
52	Barry Bonds	.40
53	John Kruk	.10
54	Brett Butler	.10
55	Kenny Lofton	.30
56	Pat Listach	.10
57	Brady Anderson	.15
58	Marquis Grissom	.15
59	Delino DeShields	.10
60	Steve Finley, Bip Roberts	.10
61	Jack McDowell	.10
62	Kevin Brown	.15
63	Melido Perez	.10
64	Terry Mulholland	.10
65	Curt Schilling	.15
66	John Smoltz, Doug Drabek, Greg Maddux	.35
67	Dennis Eckersley	.10
68	Rick Aguilera	.10
69	Jeff Montgomery	.10
70	Lee Smith	.10
71	Randy Myers	.10
72	John Wetteland	.10
73	Randy Johnson	.25
74	Melido Perez	.10
75	Roger Clemens	.40
76	John Smoltz	.15
77	David Cone	.15
78	Greg Maddux	.60
79	Roger Clemens	.40
80	Kevin Appier	.10
81	Mike Mussina	.30
82	Bill Swift	.10
83	Bob Tewksbury	.10
84	Greg Maddux	.60
85	Kevin Brown	.15
86	Jack McDowell	.10
87	Roger Clemens	.40
88	Tom Glavine	.15
89	Ken Hill, Bob Tewksbury	.10
90	Dennis Martinez, Mike Morgan	.10

1993 Select Triple Crown

This three-card set commemorates the Triple Crown seasons of Hall of Famers Mickey Mantle, Frank Robinson and Carl Yastrzemski. Cards were randomly inserted in 15-card hobby packs. Card fronts have a green metallic-look textured border, with the player's name at top in gold, and "Triple Crown" in gold at bottom. There are other silver and green highlights around the photo, which feature the player set against a metallized background. Dark green backs have a player photo and information on his Triple Crown season.

		MT
Complete Set (3):		60.00
Common Player:		12.50
1	Mickey Mantle	45.00
2	Frank Robinson	12.50
3	Carl Yastrzemski	12.50

1993 Select Rookie/Traded

Production of this 150-card set was limited to 1,950 numbered cases. Several future Hall of Famers and six dozen top rookies are featured in the set. Cards were available in packs rather than collated sets and include randomly inserted FX cards, which feature Nolan Ryan (two per 24-box case), Tim Salmon and Mike Piazza (one per 576 packs) and All-Star Rookie Team members (one per 58 packs).

		MT
Complete Set (150):		15.00
Common Player:		.15
Wax Box:		55.00
1	Rickey Henderson	.30
2	Rob Deer	.15
3	Tim Belcher	.15
4	Gary Sheffield	.40
5	Fred McGriff	.30
6	Mark Whiten	.15
7	Jeff Russell	.15
8	Harold Baines	.15
9	Dave Winfield	.30
10	Ellis Burks	.15
11	Andre Dawson	.20
12	Gregg Jefferies	.15
13	Jimmy Key	.15
14	Harold Reynolds	.15
15	Tom Henke	.15
16	Paul Molitor	.75
17	Wade Boggs	.35
18	David Cone	.30
19	Tony Fernandez	.15
20	Roberto Kelly	.15
21	Paul O'Neill	.20
22	Jose Lind	.15
23	Barry Bonds	2.50
24	Dave Stewart	.15
25	Randy Myers	.15
26	Benito Santiago	.15
27	Tim Wallach	.15
28	Greg Gagne	.15
29	Kevin Mitchell	.15
30	Jim Abbott	.15
31	Lee Smith	.15
32	*Bobby Munoz*	.20
33	*Mo Sanford*	.25
34	John Roper	.15
35	*David Hulse*	.20
36	Pedro Martinez	2.00

37	*Chuck Carr*	.15
38	*Armando Reynoso*	.25
39	Ryan Thompson	.25
40	*Carlos Garcia*	.20
41	Matt Whiteside	.15
42	Benji Gil	.15
43	*Rodney Bolton*	.15
44	J.T. Snow	.50
45	David McCarty	.15
46	*Paul Quantrill*	.15
47	Al Martin	.15
48	Lance Painter	.15
49	*Lou Frazier*	.15
50	Eduardo Perez	.15
51	Kevin Young	.15
52	Mike Trombley	.15
53	*Sterling Hitchcock*	.35
54	*Tim Bogar*	.25
55	*Hilly Hathaway*	.25
56	*Wayne Kirby*	.15
57	*Craig Paquette*	.15
58	Bret Boone	.25
59	*Greg McMichael*	.20
60	*Mike Lansing*	.35
61	Brent Gates	.25
62	Rene Arocha	.20
63	Ricky Gutierrez	.25
64	*Kevin Rogers*	.20
65	*Ken Ryan*	.25
66	Phil Hiatt	.15
67	*Pat Meares*	.25
68	Troy Neel	.20
69	Steve Cooke	.15
70	*Sherman Obando*	.15
71	*Blas Minor*	.15
72	*Angel Miranda*	.15
73	*Tom Kramer*	.20
74	*Chip Hale*	.20
75	*Brad Pennington*	.25
76	*Graeme Lloyd*	.15
77	*Darrell Whitmore*	.20
78	David Nied	.15
79	Todd Van Poppel	.15
80	*Chris Gomez*	.25
81	Jason Bere	.15
82	Jeffrey Hammonds	.25
83	*Brad Ausmus*	.20
84	Kevin Stocker	.15
85	Jeromy Burnitz	.25
86	Aaron Sele	.25
87	*Roberto Mejia*	.15
88	*Kirk Rueter*	.25
89	*Kevin Roberson*	.25
90	*Allen Watson*	.35
91	Charlie Leibrandt	.15
92	Eric Davis	.15
93	Jody Reed	.15
94	Danny Jackson	.15
95	Gary Gaetti	.15
96	Norm Charlton	.15
97	Doug Drabek	.15
98	Scott Fletcher	.15
99	Greg Swindell	.15
100	John Smiley	.15
101	Kevin Reimer	.15
102	Andres Galarraga	.20
103	Greg Hibbard	.15
104	Chris Hammond	.15
105	Darnell Coles	.15
106	Mike Felder	.15
107	Jose Guzman	.15
108	Chris Bosio	.15
109	Spike Owen	.15
110	Felix Jose	.15
111	Cory Snyder	.15
112	Craig Lefferts	.15
113	David Wells	.20
114	Pete Incaviglia	.15
115	Mike Pagliarulo	.15
116	Dave Magadan	.15
117	Charlie Hough	.15
118	Ivan Calderon	.15
119	Manuel Lee	.15
120	Bob Patterson	.15
121	Bob Ojeda	.15
122	Scott Bankhead	.15
123	Greg Maddux	4.00
124	Chili Davis	.15
125	Milt Thompson	.15
126	Dave Martinez	.15
127	Frank Tanana	.15
128	Phil Plantier	.15
129	Juan Samuel	.15
130	Eric Young	.25
131	Joe Orsulak	.15
132	Derek Bell	.15
133	Darrin Jackson	.15
134	Tom Brunansky	.15
135	Jeff Reardon	.15
136	*Kevin Higgins*	.15
137	*Joel Johnston*	.15
138	*Rick Trlicek*	.15
139	*Richie Lewis*	.25
140	*Jeff Gardner*	.20
141	*Jack Voigt*	.15
142	*Rod Correia*	.15
143	*Billy Brewer*	.15
144	*Terry Jorgensen*	.15
145	*Rich Amaral*	.15
146	*Sean Berry*	.30
147	*Dan Peltier*	.20
148	*Paul Wagner*	.35
149	*Damon Buford*	.75
150	Wil Cordero	.15

Player names in *Italic* type indicate a rookie card.

1993 Select Rookie/Traded All-Star Rookies

These cards were randomly inserted into the Score Select Rookie/Traded packs, making them among the scarcest of the year's many "chase" cards. Card fronts feature metallic foil printing. Backs have a few words about the player. Stated odds of finding an All-Star Rookie Team insert card are one per 58 packs.

		MT
Complete Set (10):		100.00
Common Player:		3.00
1	Jeff Conine	5.00
2	Brent Gates	3.00
3	Mike Lansing	5.00
4	Kevin Stocker	4.00
5	Mike Piazza	75.00
6	Jeffrey Hammonds	4.00
7	David Hulse	3.00
8	Tim Salmon	20.00
9	Rene Arocha	3.00
10	Greg McMichael	3.00

1993 Select Rookie/Traded Inserts

Three cards honoring the 1993 Rookies of the Year and retiring superstar Nolan Ryan were issued as random inserts in the Select Rookie/Traded packs. Cards are printed with metallic foil front backgrounds. Stated odds of finding a Piazza or Salmon card are about one per 24-box case; Ryan cards are found on average two per case.

		MT
Complete Set (3):		150.00
Common Player:		25.00
1NR	Nolan Ryan	75.00
1ROY	Tim Salmon	20.00
2ROY	Mike Piazza	75.00

1994 Select Promos

To introduce its 1994 offering to dealers and collectors, Score Select created an eight-card promo set. Cards are identical in format to regular-issue cards with the exception of the word "SAMPLE" overprinted diagonally on front and back. The promos included five of the regular-run cards, a Rookie Prospect card and one each of its Rookie Surge '94 and Crown Contenders insert sets. The promos were cello-packaged with a header card describing the set and chase cards.

		MT
Complete Set (8):		25.00
Common Player:		2.00
3	Paul Molitor	4.00
17	Kirby Puckett	6.00
19	Randy Johnson	4.00
24	John Kruk	2.00
51	Jose Lind	2.00
197	Ryan Klesko (Rookie Prospect)	4.00
1CC	Lenny Dykstra (Crown Contenders)	3.00
1RS	Cliff Floyd (Rookie Surge '94)	5.00
----	Header card	.10

1994 Select

Both series of this premium brand from the Score/Pinnacle lineup offered 210 regular cards for a combined 420 cards, and seven insert sets. The announced press runs for Series I and II was 4,950 20-box cases. Cards have a horizontal format with a color action photo at right and a second action photo at left done in a single team color-coded hue. The player's last name is dropped out of a vertical gold-foil strip between the two photos, with his first name in white at top-center. Backs are vertically oriented with yet another color action photo at center. In a vertical bar at right, matching the color-coding on front and printed over the photo are 1993 and career stats, a "Select Stat," and a few sentences about the player. The appropriate logos and Pinnacle's optical-variable counterfeiting device are at bottom-center. Thirty of the final 33 cards in the first series are a "1994 Rookie Prospect" subset, so noted in a special gold-foil logo on front.

		MT
Complete Set (420):		25.00
Complete Series 1 (210):		15.00
Complete Series 2 (210):		10.00
Common Player:		.10
Series 1 Wax Box:		30.00
Series 2 Wax Box:		20.00
1	Ken Griffey, Jr.	3.50
2	Greg Maddux	2.00
3	Paul Molitor	.65
4	Mike Piazza	2.00
5	Jay Bell	.10
6	Frank Thomas	1.00
7	Barry Larkin	.20
8	Paul O'Neill	.15
9	Darren Daulton	.10
10	Mike Greenwell	.10
11	Chuck Carr	.10
12	Joe Carter	.15
13	Lance Johnson	.10
14	Jeff Blauser	.10
15	Chris Hoiles	.10
16	Rick Wilkins	.10
17	Kirby Puckett	1.00
18	Larry Walker	.35
19	Randy Johnson	.40
20	Bernard Gilkey	.10
21	Devon White	.15
22	Randy Myers	.10
23	Don Mattingly	1.00
24	John Kruk	.10
25	Ozzie Guillen	.10
26	Jeff Conine	.10
27	Mike Macfarlane	.10
28	Dave Hollins	.10
29	Chuck Knoblauch	.15
30	Ozzie Smith	.60
31	Harold Baines	.10
32	Ryne Sandberg	.65
33	Ron Karkovice	.10
34	Terry Pendleton	.10
35	Wally Joyner	.10
36	Mike Mussina	.40
37	Felix Jose	.10
38	Derrick May	.10
39	Scott Cooper	.10
40	Jose Rijo	.10
41	Robin Ventura	.20
42	Charlie Hayes	.10
43	Jimmy Key	.10
44	Eric Karros	.10
45	Ruben Sierra	.10
46	Ryan Thompson	.10
47	Brian McRae	.10
48	Pat Hentgen	.10
49	John Valentin	.10
50	Al Martin	.10
51	Jose Lind	.10
52	Kevin Stocker	.10
53	Mike Gallego	.10
54	Dwight Gooden	.15
55	Brady Anderson	.15
56	Jeff King	.10
57	Mark McGwire	3.50
58	Sammy Sosa	1.50
59	Ryan Bowen	.10
60	Mark Lemke	.10
61	Roger Clemens	1.00
62	Brian Jordan	.10
63	Andres Galarraga	.15
64	Kevin Appier	.10
65	Don Slaught	.10
66	Mike Blowers	.10
67	Wes Chamberlain	.10
68	Troy Neel	.10
69	John Wetteland	.10
70	Joe Girardi	.10
71	Reggie Sanders	.10
72	Edgar Martinez	.10
73	Todd Hundley	.15
74	Pat Borders	.10
75	Roberto Mejia	.10
76	David Cone	.15
77	Tony Gwynn	.75
78	Jim Abbott	.10
79	Jay Buhner	.10
80	Mark McLemore	.10
81	Wil Cordero	.10
82	Pedro Astacio	.10
83	Bob Tewksbury	.10
84	Dave Winfield	.25
85	Jeff Kent	.10
86	Todd Van Poppel	.10
87	Steve Avery	.10
88	Mike Lansing	.10
89	Len Dykstra	.10
90	Jose Guzman	.10
91	Brian Hunter	.10
92	Tim Raines	.15
93	Andre Dawson	.15
94	Joe Orsulak	.10
95	Ricky Jordan	.10
96	Billy Hatcher	.10
97	Jack McDowell	.10
98	Tom Pagnozzi	.10
99	Darryl Strawberry	.15
100	Mike Stanley	.10
101	Bret Saberhagen	.10
102	Willie Greene	.10
103	Bryan Harvey	.10
104	Tim Bogar	.10
105	Jack Voight	.10
106	Brad Ausmus	.10
107	Ramon Martinez	.10
108	Mike Perez	.10
109	Jeff Montgomery	.10
110	Danny Darwin	.10
111	Wilson Alvarez	.10
112	Kevin Mitchell	.10
113	David Nied	.10
114	Rich Amaral	.10
115	Stan Javier	.10
116	Mo Vaughn	.50
117	Ben McDonald	.10
118	Tom Gordon	.10
119	Carlos Garcia	.10
120	Phil Plantier	.10
121	Mike Morgan	.10
122	Pat Meares	.10
123	Kevin Young	.10
124	Jeff Fassero	.10
125	Gene Harris	.10
126	Bob Welch	.10
127	Walt Weiss	.10
128	Bobby Witt	.10
129	Andy Van Slyke	.10
130	Steve Cooke	.10
131	Mike Devereaux	.10
132	Joey Cora	.10
133	Bret Barberie	.10
134	Orel Hershiser	.10
135	Ed Sprague	.10
136	Shawon Dunston	.10
137	Alex Arias	.10
138	Archi Cianfrocco	.10
139	Tim Wallach	.10
140	Bernie Williams	.50
141	Karl Rhodes	.10
142	Pat Kelly	.10
143	Dave Magadan	.10
144	Kevin Tapani	.10
145	Eric Young	.10
146	Derek Bell	.10
147	Dante Bichette	.35
148	Geronimo Pena	.10
149	Joe Oliver	.10
150	Orestes Destrade	.10
151	Tim Naehring	.10
152	Ray Lankford	.10
153	Phil Clark	.10
154	David McCarty	.10
155	Tommy Greene	.10
156	Wade Boggs	.50
157	Kevin Gross	.10
158	Hal Morris	.10
159	Moises Alou	.15
160	Rick Aguilera	.10
161	Curt Schilling	.15
162	Chip Hale	.10
163	Tino Martinez	.15
164	Mark Whiten	.10
165	Dave Stewart	.10
166	Steve Buechele	.10
167	Bobby Jones	.25
168	Darrin Fletcher	.10
169	John Smiley	.10
170	Cory Snyder	.10
171	Scott Erickson	.10
172	Kirk Rueter	.10
173	Dave Fleming	.10
174	John Smoltz	.20
175	Ricky Gutierrez	.10
176	Mike Bordick	.10
177	*Chan Ho Park*	.35
178	Alex Gonzalez	.25
179	Steve Karsay	.15
180	Jeffrey Hammonds	.10
181	Manny Ramirez	1.00
182	Salomon Torres	.10
183	Raul Mondesi	.30
184	James Mouton	.10
185	Cliff Floyd	.15
186	Danny Bautista	.10
187	*Kurt Abbott*	.35
188	Javier Lopez	.15
189	John Patterson	.10
190	Greg Blosser	.10
191	Bob Hamelin	.10
192	Tony Eusebio	.10
193	Carlos Delgado	.40
194	Chris Gomez	.10
195	Kelly Stinnett	.10
196	Shane Reynolds	.10
197	Ryan Klesko	.25
198	Jim Edmonds	.25
199	James Hurst	.10
200	Dave Staton	.10
201	Rondell White	.30
202	Keith Mitchell	.10
203	Darren Oliver	.10
204	Mike Matheny	.10
205	Chris Turner	.10
206	Matt Mieske	.10
207	N.L. team checklist	.10
208	N.L. team checklist	.10
209	A.L. team checklist	.10
210	A.L. team checklist	.10
211	Barry Bonds	.75
212	Juan Gonzalez	1.00
213	Jim Eisenreich	.10
214	Ivan Rodriguez	.50
215	Tony Phillips	.10
216	John Jaha	.10
217	Lee Smith	.10
218	Bip Roberts	.10
219	Dave Hansen	.10
220	Pat Listach	.10
221	Willie McGee	.10
222	Damion Easley	.10
223	Dean Palmer	.10
224	Mike Moore	.10
225	Brian Harper	.10
226	Gary DiSarcina	.10
227	Delino DeShields	.10
228	Otis Nixon	.10
229	Roberto Alomar	.65
230	Mark Grace	.30
231	Kenny Lofton	.50
232	Gregg Jefferies	.10
233	Cecil Fielder	.10
234	Jeff Bagwell	1.00
235	Albert Belle	.65
236	Dave Justice	.35
237	Tom Henke	.10
238	Bobby Bonilla	.10
239	John Olerud	.15
240	Robby Thompson	.10

241	Dave Valle	.10
242	Marquis Grissom	.15
243	Greg Swindell	.10
244	Todd Zeile	.10
245	Dennis Eckersley	.10
246	Jose Offerman	.10
247	Greg McMichael	.10
248	Tim Belcher	.10
249	Cal Ripken, Jr.	2.50
250	Tom Glavine	.15
251	Luis Polonia	.10
252	Bill Swift	.10
253	Juan Guzman	.10
254	Rickey Henderson	.25
255	Terry Mulholland	.10
256	Gary Sheffield	.15
257	Terry Steinbach	.10
258	Brett Butler	.10
259	Jason Bere	.10
260	Doug Strange	.10
261	Kent Hrbek	.10
262	Graeme Lloyd	.10
263	Lou Frazier	.10
264	Charles Nagy	.10
265	Bret Boone	.10
266	Kirk Gibson	.10
267	Kevin Brown	.15
269	Matt Williams	.35
270	Greg Gagne	.10
271	Mariano Duncan	.10
272	Jeff Russell	.10
273	Eric Davis	.10
274	Shane Mack	.10
275	Jose Vizcaino	.10
276	Jose Canseco	.35
277	Roberto Hernandez	.10
278	Royce Clayton	.10
279	Carlos Baerga	.10
280	Pete Incaviglia	.10
281	Brent Gates	.10
282	Jeromy Burnitz	.10
283	Chili Davis	.10
284	Pete Harnisch	.10
285	Alan Trammell	.10
286	Eric Anthony	.10
287	Ellis Burks	.10
288	Julio Franco	.10
289	Jack Morris	.10
290	Erik Hanson	.10
291	Chuck Finley	.10
292	Reggie Jefferson	.10
293	Kevin McReynolds	.10
294	Greg Hibbard	.10
295	Travis Fryman	.10
296	Craig Biggio	.20
297	Kenny Rogers	.10
298	Dave Henderson	.10
299	Jim Thome	.30
300	Rene Arocha	.10
301	Pedro Munoz	.10
302	David Hulse	.10
303	Greg Vaughn	.15
304	Darren Lewis	.10
305	Deion Sanders	.25
306	Danny Tartabull	.10
307	Darryl Hamilton	.10
308	Andujar Cedeno	.10
309	Tim Salmon	.30
310	Tony Fernandez	.10
311	Alex Fernandez	.10
312	Roberto Kelly	.10
313	Harold Reynolds	.10
314	Chris Sabo	.10
315	Howard Johnson	.10
316	Mark Portugal	.10
317	Rafael Palmeiro	.25
318	Pete Smith	.10
319	Will Clark	.30
320	Henry Rodriguez	.10
321	Omar Vizquel	.10
322	David Segui	.10
323	Lou Whitaker	.10
324	Felix Fermin	.10
325	Spike Owen	.10
326	Darryl Kile	.10
327	Chad Kreuter	.10
328	Rod Beck	.10
329	Eddie Murray	.40
330	B.J. Surhoff	.10
331	Mickey Tettleton	.10
332	Pedro Martinez	.20
333	Roger Pavlik	.10
334	Eddie Taubensee	.10
335	John Doherty	.10
336	Jody Reed	.10
337	Aaron Sele	.10
338	Leo Gomez	.10
339	Dave Nilsson	.10
340	Rob Dibble	.10
341	John Burkett	.10
342	Wayne Kirby	.10
343	Dan Wilson	.10
344	Armando Reynoso	.10
345	Chad Curtis	.10
346	Dennis Martinez	.10
347	Cal Eldred	.10
348	Luis Gonzalez	.10
349	Doug Drabek	.10
350	Jim Leyritz	.10
351	Mark Langston	.10
352	Darrin Jackson	.10
353	Sid Fernandez	.10
354	Benito Santiago	.10
355	Kevin Seitzer	.10
356	Bo Jackson	.20
357	David Wells	.15
358	Paul Sorrento	.10
359	Ken Caminiti	.15
360	Eduardo Perez	.10
361	Orlando Merced	.10
362	Steve Finley	.10
363	Andy Benes	.10
364	Manuel Lee	.10
365	Todd Benzinger	.10
366	Sandy Alomar Jr.	.15
367	Rex Hudler	.10
368	Mike Henneman	.10
369	Vince Coleman	.10
370	Kirt Manwaring	.10
371	Ken Hill	.10
372	Glenallen Hill	.10
373	Sean Berry	.10
374	Geronimo Berroa	.10
375	Duane Ward	.10
376	Allen Watson	.10
377	Marc Newfield	.10
378	Dan Miceli	.10
379	Denny Hocking	.10
380	Mark Kiefer	.10
381	Tony Tarasco	.10
382	Tony Longmire	.10
383	*Brian Anderson*	.25
384	Fernando Vina	.10
385	Hector Carrasco	.10
386	Mike Kelly	.10
387	Greg Colbrunn	.10
388	Roger Salkeld	.10
389	Steve Trachsel	.15
390	Rich Becker	.10
391	*Billy Taylor*	.10
392	Rich Rowland	.10
393	Carl Everett	.10
394	Johnny Ruffin	.10
395	*Keith Lockhart*	.10
396	J.R. Phillips	.10
397	Sterling Hitchcock	.10
398	Jorge Fabregas	.10
399	Jeff Granger	.10
400	*Eddie Zambrano*	.10
401	*Rikkert Faneyte*	.10
402	Gerald Williams	.10
403	Joey Hamilton	.10
404	*Joe Hall*	.10
405	*John Hudek*	.15
406	Roberto Petagine	.10
407	Charles Johnson	.15
408	Mark Smith	.10
409	Jeff Juden	.10
410	*Carlos Pulido*	.10
411	Paul Shuey	.10
412	Rob Butler	.10
413	Mark Acre	.10
414	Greg Pirkl	.10
415	Melvin Nieves	.10
416	*Tim Hyers*	.10
417	N.L. checklist	.10
418	N.L. checklist	.10
419	A.L. checklist	.10
420	A.L. checklist	.10

1994 Select Crown Contenders

Candidates for the major baseball annual awards are featured in this subset. Horizontal-format cards have a color player photo printed on a holographic foil background. Backs are vertically oriented with a player portrait photo and justification for the player's inclusion in the set. Cards are numbered with a "CC" prefix and feature a special optical-variable anti-counterfeiting device at bottom-center. According to stated odds of one card on average in every 24 packs it has been estimated that fewer than 12,000 of each Crown Contenders card was produced.

		MT
Complete Set (10):		75.00
Common Player:		1.50
1	Len Dykstra	1.50
2	Greg Maddux	15.00
3	Roger Clemens	6.00
4	Randy Johnson	4.00
5	Frank Thomas	10.00
6	Barry Bonds	5.00
7	Juan Gonzalez	9.00
8	John Olerud	3.00
9	Mike Piazza	15.00
10	Ken Griffey, Jr.	20.00

1994 Select MVP

Paul Molitor was the 1994 Select MVP and is featured in this one card set. Molitor is pictured in front of three distinct foil designs across the rest of the card.

		MT
MVP1	Paul Molitor	10.00

1994 Select Rookie of the Year

Carlos Delgado was the 1994 Select Rookie of the Year. Delgado is pictured on top of a glowing foil background with his initials in large capital letters in the background and Rookie of the Year printed across the bottom.

		MT
RY1	Carlos Delgado	5.00

1994 Select Rookie Surge

Each series of 1994 Score Select offered a chase card set of nine top rookies. Fronts feature action photos set against a rainbow-colored metallic foil background. Backs have a portrait photo and a few words about the player. Cards are numbered with an "RS" prefix and were inserted at an average rate of one per 48 packs.

		MT
Complete Set (18):		75.00
Complete Series 1 (9):		30.00
Complete Series 2 (9):		45.00
Common Player:		1.50
1	Cliff Floyd	3.00
2	Bob Hamelin	1.50
3	Ryan Klesko	3.00
4	Carlos Delgado	8.00
5	Jeffrey Hammonds	1.50
6	Rondell White	5.00
7	Salomon Torres	1.50
8	Steve Karsay	2.00
9	Javier Lopez	8.00
10	Manny Ramirez	30.00
11	Tony Tarasco	1.50
12	Kurt Abbott	2.00
13	Chan Ho Park	10.00
14	Rich Becker	1.50
15	James Mouton	1.50
16	Alex Gonzalez	5.00
17	Raul Mondesi	10.00
18	Steve Trachsel	2.50

1994 Select Salute

With odds of finding one of these cards stated at one per 360 packs, it is estimated that only about 4,000 of each of this two-card chase set were produced.

		MT
Complete Set (2):		45.00
1	Cal Ripken, Jr.	40.00
2	Dave Winfield	5.00

1994 Select Skills

Select Skills is a 10-card insert that was randomly inserted into every 24 packs. Ten specific skills were designated and matched with the player whom, in the opinion of Select officials, demonstrated that particular skill the best in baseball. Each card is printed on a foil background with the player name running along the lower right side of the card and the skill that they are being featured for along the bottom.

		MT
Complete Set (10):		50.00
Common Player:		3.00
1	Randy Johnson	5.00
2	Barry Larkin	4.00
3	Len Dykstra	3.00
4	Kenny Lofton	6.00
5	Juan Gonzalez	12.00
6	Barry Bonds	9.00
7	Marquis Grissom	3.00
8	Ivan Rodriguez	7.00
9	Larry Walker	4.00
10	Travis Fryman	3.00

1995 Select Samples

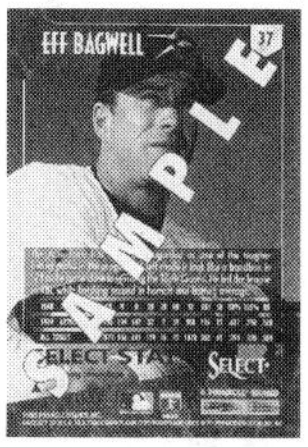

Pinnacle's hobby-only Select brand issue for 1995 was previewed with this four-card cello-packed sample set. Three player cards are in the basic format of the regular-issue Select cards, except they have a large white "SAMPLE" printed diagonally across the front and back. The fourth card in the sample pack is a header card advertising the features of the issue.

		MT
Complete Set (4):		20.00
Common Player:		5.00
34	Roberto Alomar	5.00
37	Jeff Bagwell	9.00
241	Alex Rodriguez	12.00
--	Header card	.15

1995 Select

The 250 regular-issue cards in Pinnacle's mid-price brand baseball set feature three basic formats. Veteran players' cards are presented in a horizontal design which features an action photo at left. At right is a portrait in a trapezoidal gold-foil frame set against a team color-coordinated marbled background. The team logo beneath the portrait and the player's name below that are printed in gold foil. Backs feature a black-and-white photo with a few career highlights, 1994 and Major League cumulative stats, and a "Select Stat" printed in red. The colored marble effect is carried over from the front. The Select Rookie cards which are grouped toward the end of the set are vertical in format and feature a borderless player photo with a gold-foil band at bottom which includes the player name and team logo, along with waves of gold emanating from the logo. Backs have a small, narrow color photo at left, with a large sepia version of the same photo ghosted at center and overprinted with a career summary. At bottom are 1994 and career stats. Ending the set are a series of "Show Time" cards of top prospects. Cards feature large gold-foil "Show Time" and team logos at bottom, with a facsimile autograph printed above. The player photo is shown as if at a curtain raising, with spotlight effects behind. Backs repeat the curtain and spotlight motif and feature another player photo, with autograph above. Production of this hobby-only product was stated as 4,950 cases, which translates to about 110,000 of each regular-issue card. A special card (#251) of Hideo Nomo was added to the set later. It was not issued in foil packs, but distributed to dealers who had purchased Select cases.

		MT
Complete Set (251):		15.00
Common Player:		.10
Artist's Proofs: 25X		
Wax Box:		40.00
1	Cal Ripken Jr.	2.50
2	Robin Ventura	.15
3	Al Martin	.10
4	Jeff Frye	.10
5	Darryl Strawberry	.15
6	Chan Ho Park	.15
7	Steve Avery	.10
8	Bret Boone	.10
9	Danny Tartabull	.10
10	Dante Bichette	.25
11	Rondell White	.20
12	Dave McCarty	.10
13	Bernard Gilkey	.10
14	Mark McGwire	3.00
15	Ruben Sierra	.10
16	Wade Boggs	.40
17	Mike Piazza	2.00
18	Jeffrey Hammonds	.10
19	Mike Mussina	.35
20	Darryl Kile	.10
21	Greg Maddux	2.00
22	Frank Thomas	1.00
23	Kevin Appier	.10
24	Jay Bell	.10
25	Kirk Gibson	.10
26	Pat Hentgen	.10
27	Joey Hamilton	.10
28	Bernie Williams	.40
29	Aaron Sele	.10
30	Delino DeShields	.10
31	Danny Bautista	.10
32	Jim Thome	.35
33	Rikkert Faneyte	.10
34	Roberto Alomar	.60
35	Paul Molitor	.50
36	Allen Watson	.10
37	Jeff Bagwell	1.00
38	Jay Buhner	.15
39	Marquis Grissom	.10
40	Jim Edmonds	.20
41	Ryan Klesko	.25
42	Fred McGriff	.30
43	Tony Tarasco	.10
44	Darren Daulton	.10
45	Marc Newfield	.10
46	Barry Bonds	.75
47	Bobby Bonilla	.10
48	Greg Pirkl	.10
49	Steve Karsay	.10
50	Bob Hamelin	.10
51	Javier Lopez	.15
52	Barry Larkin	.20
53	Kevin Young	.10
54	Sterling Hitchcock	.10
55	Tom Glavine	.15
56	Carlos Delgado	.40
57	Darren Oliver	.10
58	Cliff Floyd	.15
59	Tim Salmon	.20
60	Albert Belle	.65
61	Salomon Torres	.10
62	Gary Sheffield	.40
63	Ivan Rodriguez	.60
64	Charles Nagy	.10
65	Eduardo Perez	.10
66	Terry Steinbach	.10
67	Dave Justice	.20
68	Jason Bere	.10
69	Dave Nilsson	.10
70	Brian Anderson	.10
71	Billy Ashley	.10
72	Roger Clemens	.75
73	Jimmy Key	.10
74	Wally Joyner	.10
75	Andy Benes	.10
76	Ray Lankford	.10
77	Jeff Kent	.10
78	Moises Alou	.15
79	Kirby Puckett	1.00
80	Joe Carter	.15
81	Manny Ramirez	.75
82	J.R. Phillips	.10
83	Matt Mieske	.10
84	John Olerud	.15
85	Andres Galarraga	.15
86	Juan Gonzalez	1.00
87	Pedro Martinez	.15
88	Dean Palmer	.10
89	Ken Griffey Jr.	3.00
90	Brian Jordan	.15
91	Hal Morris	.10
92	Lenny Dykstra	.10
93	Wil Cordero	.10
94	Tony Gwynn	1.00
95	Alex Gonzalez	.15
96	Cecil Fielder	.10
97	Mo Vaughn	.55
98	John Valentin	.10
99	Will Clark	.25
100	Geronimo Pena	.10
101	Don Mattingly	1.00
102	Charles Johnson	.15
103	Raul Mondesi	.35
104	Reggie Sanders	.10
105	Royce Clayton	.10
106	Reggie Jefferson	.10
107	Craig Biggio	.20
108	Jack McDowell	.10
109	James Mouton	.10
110	Mike Greenwell	.10
111	David Cone	.15
112	Matt Williams	.25
113	Garret Anderson	.10
114	Carlos Garcia	.10
115	Alex Fernandez	.10
116	Deion Sanders	.25
117	Chili Davis	.10
118	Mike Kelly	.10
119	Jeff Conine	.10
120	Kenny Lofton	.55
121	Rafael Palmeiro	.20
122	Chuck Knoblauch	.15
123	Ozzie Smith	.50
124	Carlos Baerga	.10
125	Brett Butler	.10
126	Sammy Sosa	1.50
127	Ellis Burks	.10
128	Bret Saberhagen	.10
129	Doug Drabek	.10
130	Dennis Martinez	.10
131	Paul O'Neill	.15
132	Travis Fryman	.10
133	Brent Gates	.10
134	Rickey Henderson	.40
135	Randy Johnson	.40
136	Mark Langston	.10
137	Greg Colbrunn	.10
138	Jose Rijo	.10
139	Bryan Harvey	.10
140	Dennis Eckersley	.10
141	Ron Gant	.10
142	Carl Everett	.10
143	Jeff Granger	.10
144	Ben McDonald	.10
145	Kurt Abbott	.10
146	Jim Abbott	.10
147	Jason Jacome	.10
148	Rico Brogna	.10
149	Cal Eldred	.10
150	Rich Becker	.10
151	Pete Harnisch	.10
152	Roberto Petagine	.10
153	Jacob Brumfield	.10
154	Todd Hundley	.15
155	Roger Cedeno	.10
156	Harold Baines	.10
157	Steve Dunn	.10
158	Tim Belk	.10
159	Marty Cardova	.10
160	Russ Davis	.10
161	Jose Malave	.10
162	Brian Hunter	.10
163	Andy Pettitte	.60
164	Brooks Kieschnick	.10
165	Midre Cummings	.10
166	Frank Rodriguez	.10
167	Chad Mottola	.10
168	Brian Barber	.10
169	Tim Unroe	.10
170	Shane Andrews	.10
171	Kevin Flora	.10
172	Ray Durham	.20
173	Chipper Jones	2.00
174	Butch Huskey	.10
175	Ray McDavid	.10
176	Jeff Cirillo	.10
177	Terry Pendleton	.10
178	Scott Ruffcorn	.10
179	Ray Holbert	.10
180	Joe Randa	.10
181	Jose Oliva	.10
182	Andy Van Slyke	.10
183	Albie Lopez	.10
184	Chad Curtis	.10
185	Ozzie Guillen	.10
186	Chad Ogea	.10
187	Dan Wilson	.10
188	Tony Fernandez	.10
189	John Smoltz	.25
190	Willie Greene	.10
191	Darren Lewis	.10
192	Orlando Miller	.10
193	Kurt Miller	.10
194	Andrew Lorraine	.10
195	Ernie Young	.10
196	Jimmy Haynes	.10
197	*Raul Casanova*	.20
198	Joe Vitiello	.10
199	Brad Woodall	.10
200	Juan Acevedo	.10
201	Michael Tucker	.10
202	Shawn Green	.25
203	Alex Rodriguez	2.50
204	Julian Tavarez	.10
205	Jose Lima	.10
206	Wilson Alvarez	.10
207	Rich Aude	.10
208	Armando Benitez	.10
209	Dwayne Hosey	.10
210	Gabe White	.10
211	Joey Eischen	.10
212	Bill Pulsipher	.10
213	Robby Thompson	.10
214	Toby Borland	.10
215	Rusty Greer	.10
216	Fausto Cruz	.10
217	Luis Ortiz	.10
218	Duane Singleton	.10
219	Troy Percival	.10
220	Gregg Jefferies	.10
221	Mark Grace	.25
222	Mickey Tettleton	.10
223	Phil Plantier	.10
224	Larry Walker	.25
225	Ken Caminiti	.20
226	Dave Winfield	.35
227	Brady Anderson	.10
228	Kevin Brown	.15
229	Andujar Cedeno	.10
230	Roberto Kelly	.10
231	Jose Canseco	.35
231	(Scott Ruffcorn) (Showtime)	.10
232	Billy Ashley (Showtime)	.10
234	J.R. Phillips (Showtime)	.10
235	Chipper Jones (Showtime)	.75
236	Charles Johnson (Showtime)	.10
237	Midre Cummings (Showtime)	.10
238	Brian Hunter (Showtime)	.10
239	Garret Anderson (Showtime)	.10
240	Shawn Green (Showtime)	.20
241	Alex Rodriguez (Showtime)	1.50
242	Checklist #1 (Frank Thomas)	.75
243	Checklist #2 (Ken Griffey Jr.)	1.25
244	Checklist #3 (Albert Belle)	.30
245	Checklist #4 (Cal Ripken Jr.)	1.00
246	Checklist #5 (Barry Bonds)	.35
247	Checklist #6 (Raul Mondesi)	.20
248	Checklist #7 (Mike Piazza)	.60
249	Checklist #8 (Jeff Bagwell)	.50
250	Checklist #9 (Jeff Bagwell, Frank Thomas, Ken Griffey Jr., Mike Piazza)	.40
251	Hideo Nomo	2.00

1995 Select Artist's Proofs

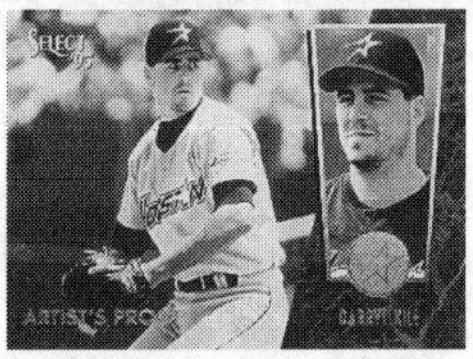

Among the scarcest and most valuable of 1995's baseball card inserts are the Select Artist's Proof parallel set. While an AP card is found on average once per 24 packs, the limited print run of the basic Select set means that only about 475 of each of the 250 regular-issue cards in the Select set were made in this edition. The AP inserts have a gold-foil "ARTIST'S PROOF" line at bottom, and other gold-foil highlights are embossed, rather than merely stamped on, as on regular Select cards.

	MT
Complete Set (250):	1200.
Common Player:	2.00
Artist's Proof Stars: 25X	
(See 1995 Select for checklist and base card values.)	

1995 Select Big Sticks

With fronts printed in what Pinnacle describes as "holographic Gold Rush technology," the Big Sticks chase card issue offers a dozen of the game's big hitters in action photos superimposed over their team logo. Conventionally printed backs have another player photo, along with a summary of career highlights and description of the player's power potential. Stated odds of pulling a Big Sticks chase card are one per 48 packs, on average. Cards are numbered with a "BS" prefix.

		MT
Complete Set (12):		100.00
Common Player:		4.00
1	Frank Thomas	12.00
2	Ken Griffey Jr.	25.00
3	Cal Ripken Jr.	20.00
4	Mike Piazza	15.00
5	Don Mattingly	10.00
6	Will Clark	4.00
7	Tony Gwynn	12.00
8	Jeff Bagwell	10.00
9	Barry Bonds	6.00
10	Paul Molitor	5.00
11	Matt Williams	4.00
12	Albert Belle	5.00

1995 Select Can't Miss

A mix of rookies and sophomore standouts, along with a few players of slightly longer service are presented in this chase set. Cards feature color player action photos printed on a metallic red background, with their last name in gold foil at lower-left. An umpire on the "Can't Miss" logo is at upper-left. Backs repeat the logo, have a tall, narrow player photo, a few biographical details and a paragraph of career summary. Cards are numbered with a "CM" prefix.

		MT
Complete Set (12):		60.00
Common Player:		2.00
1	Cliff Floyd	3.00
2	Ryan Klesko	3.00
3	Charles Johnson	3.00
4	Raul Mondesi	4.00
5	Manny Ramirez	8.00
6	Billy Ashley	2.00
7	Alex Gonzalez	3.00
8	Carlos Delgado	4.00
9	Garret Anderson	2.00
10	Alex Rodriguez	30.00
11	Chipper Jones	20.00
12	Shawn Green	4.00

1995 Select Sure Shots

Ten of Select's picks for future stardom are featured in this chase set, the toughest find of any of the 1995 Select inserts, at an average rate of one per 90 packs. Card fronts feature player action photos set against a gold "Dufex" foil printed background with a Sure Shots logo vertically at left. Backs have a blue background with a few words about the player and a portrait photo at left. Cards are numbered with a "SS" prefix.

		MT
Complete Set (10):		60.00
Common Player:		2.00
1	Ben Grieve	30.00
2	Kevin Witt	2.00
3	Mark Farris	2.00
4	Paul Konerko	20.00
5	Dustin Hermanson	10.00
6	Ramon Castro	2.00
7	McKay Christensen	2.00
8	Brian Buchanan	3.00
9	Paul Wilson	3.00
10	Terrence Long	2.00

1995 Select Certified Samples

Pinnacle's hobby-only Select brand issue for 1995 was previewed with this four-card cello-packed sample set. Three player cards are in the basic format of the regular issue Select cards, except they have a large which "SAMPLE" printed diagonally across the front and back. The fourth card in the sample pack is a header card advertising the features of the issue.

		MT
Complete Set (8):		27.00
Common Player:		3.00
2	Reggie Sanders	3.00
10	Mo Vaughn	4.50
39	Mike Piazza	7.50
50	Mark McGwire	9.00
75	Roberto Alomar	5.00
89	Larry Walker	4.50
110	Ray Durham	3.00
3 of 12	Cal Ripken Jr. (Gold Team)	12.00

1995 Select Certified

The concepts of hobby-only distribution and limited production which were the hallmarks of Pinnacle's Select brand were carried a step further with the post-season release of Select Certified baseball. Printed on double-thick cardboard stock, card fronts feature all metallic-foil printing protected by a double laminated gloss coat. Backs have key player stats against each team in the league. The final 44 cards in the set are distinguished with a special Rookie logo and with gold added to the silver foil in the photo background.

		MT
Complete Set (135):		40.00
Common Player:		.20
Mirror Gold Stars: 10X		
Wax Box:		80.00
1	Barry Bonds	1.00
2	Reggie Sanders	.20
3	Terry Steinbach	.20
4	Eduardo Perez	.20
5	Frank Thomas	2.00
6	Wil Cordero	.20
7	John Olerud	.40
8	Deion Sanders	.40
9	Mike Mussina	.75
10	Mo Vaughn	.75
11	Will Clark	.50
12	Chili Davis	.20
13	Jimmy Key	.20
14	Eddie Murray	.50
15	Bernard Gilkey	.20
16	David Cone	.35
17	Tim Salmon	.40
18	(Not issued, see #2131)	
19	Steve Ontiveros	.20
20	Andres Galarraga	.40
21	Don Mattingly	1.25
22	Kevin Appier	.20
23	Paul Molitor	.75
24	Edgar Martinez	.20
25	Andy Benes	.20
26	Rafael Palmeiro	.40
27	Barry Larkin	.35
28	Gary Sheffield	.75
29	Wally Joyner	.20
30	Wade Boggs	.50
31	Rico Brogna	.20
32	Eddie Murray (Murray Tribute)	.75
33	Kirby Puckett	1.50
34	Bobby Bonilla	.20
35	Hal Morris	.20
36	Moises Alou	.30
37	Javier Lopez	.30
38	Chuck Knoblauch	.40
39	Mike Piazza	3.00
40	Travis Fryman	.20
41	Rickey Henderson	.50
42	Jim Thome	.60
43	Carlos Baerga	.20
44	Dean Palmer	.20
45	Kirk Gibson	.20
46	Bret Saberhagen	.20
47	Cecil Fielder	.20
48	Manny Ramirez	1.50
49	Derek Bell	.20
50	Mark McGwire	5.00
51	Jim Edmonds	.35
52	Robin Ventura	.30
53	Ryan Klesko	.40
54	Jeff Bagwell	1.50
55	Ozzie Smith	.75
56	Albert Belle	1.00
57	Darren Daulton	.20
58	Jeff Conine	.20
59	Greg Maddux	2.50
60	Lenny Dykstra	.20
61	Randy Johnson	.75
62	Fred McGriff	.40
63	Ray Lankford	.20
64	Dave Justice	.40
65	Paul O'Neill	.40
66	Tony Gwynn	2.00
67	Matt Williams	.50
68	Dante Bichette	.40
69	Craig Biggio	.40
70	Ken Griffey Jr.	5.00
71	J.T. Snow	.20
72	Cal Ripken Jr.	4.00
73	Jay Bell	.20
74	Joe Carter	.35
75	Roberto Alomar	.75
76	Benji Gil	.20
77	Ivan Rodriguez	1.00
78	Raul Mondesi	.50
79	Cliff Floyd	.25
80	Eric Karros, Mike Piazza, Raul Mondesi (Dodger Dynasty)	.75
81	Royce Clayton	.20
82	Billy Ashley	.20
83	Joey Hamilton	.20
84	Sammy Sosa	2.50
85	Jason Bere	.20
86	Dennis Martinez	.20
87	Greg Vaughn	.25
88	Roger Clemens	1.50
89	Larry Walker	.50
90	Mark Grace	.50
91	Kenny Lofton	.75
92	*Carlos Perez*	.40
93	Roger Cedeno	.20
94	Scott Ruffcorn	.20
95	Jim Pittsley	.20
96	Andy Pettitte	.75
97	James Baldwin	.20
98	*Hideo Nomo*	3.00
99	Ismael Valdes	.20
100	Armando Benitez	.20
101	Jose Malave	.20
102	*Bobby Higginson*	1.50
103	LaTroy Hawkins	.35
104	Russ Davis	.20
105	Shawn Green	.35
106	Joe Vitiello	.20
107	Chipper Jones	3.00
108	Shane Andrews	.20
109	Jose Oliva	.20
110	Ray Durham	.35
111	Jon Nunnally	.20
112	Alex Gonzalez	.40
113	Vaughn Eshelman	.20
114	Marty Cordova	.20
115	*Mark Grudzielanek*	.75
116	Brian Hunter	.20
117	Charles Johnson	.40
118	Alex Rodriguez	4.00
119	David Bell	.20
120	Todd Hollandsworth	.20
121	Joe Randa	.20
122	Derek Jeter	3.00
123	Frank Rodriguez	.20
124	Curtis Goodwin	.20
125	Bill Pulsipher	.20
126	John Mabry	.20
127	Julian Tavarez	.20
128	Edgardo Alfonzo	.25
129	Orlando Miller	.20
130	Juan Acevedo	.20
131	Jeff Cirillo	.20
132	Roberto Petagine	.20
133	Antonio Osuna	.20
134	Michael Tucker	.20
135	Garret Anderson	.20
2131	Cal Ripken Jr. (Consecutive Game Record)	4.00

1995 Select Certified Mirror Gold

Inserted at an average rate of one per nine packs, this parallel set is a gold-foil version of the regular Select Certified set. Backs have a "MIRROR GOLD" notation at bottom.

	MT
Complete Set (135):	750.00
Common Player:	2.00
Mirror Gold Stars: 9X	
(See 1995 Select Certified for checklist and base card values.)	

1995 Select Certified Checklists

The seven checklists issued with Select Certified are not numbered as part of the set. They are found one per foil pack and are printed on much thinner card stock than the regular-issue cards.

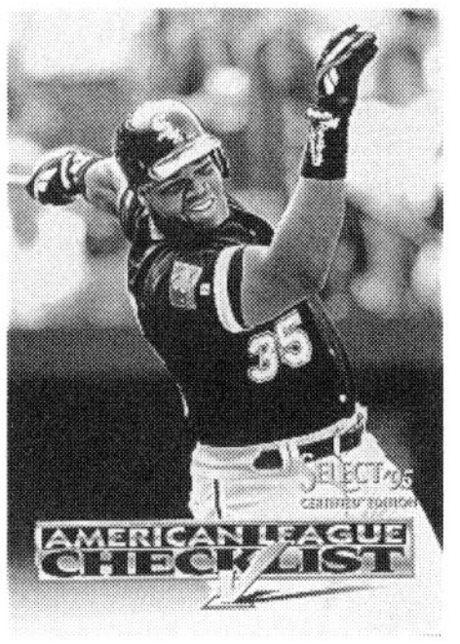

		MT
Complete Set (7):		2.00
Common Player:		.35
1	Ken Griffey Jr. (A.L., #3-41)	.75
2	Frank Thomas (A.L., #42-95)	.50
3	Cal Ripken Jr. (A.L., #96-135)	.60
4	Jeff Bagwell (N.L., #1-58)	.40
5	Mike Piazza (N.L., #59-92)	.50
6	Barry Bonds (N.L., #93-133)	.40
7	Manny Ramirez, Raul Mondesi (Chase cards)	.40

1995 Select Certified Future

A striking new all-metal, brushed-foil printing technology was used in the production of this chase set of 10 rookie players with "unlimited future potential." Stated odds of finding a Certified Future insert card were one in 19 packs.

		MT
Complete Set (10):		60.00
Common Player:		2.50
1	Chipper Jones	15.00
2	Curtis Goodwin	2.50
3	Hideo Nomo	4.50
4	Shawn Green	6.50
5	Ray Durham	3.00
6	Todd Hollandsworth	2.50
7	Brian Hunter	3.00
8	Carlos Delgado	9.00
9	Michael Tucker	2.50
10	Alex Rodriguez	25.00

1995 Select Certified Gold Team

A dozen of the top position players in the league were selected for appearance in this insert set. Cards are printed in a special double-sided, all-gold Dufex technology. An action photo is featured on the front, a portrait on back. Odds of picking a Gold Team card were stated as one in 41 packs.

		MT
Complete Set (12):		220.00
Common Player:		8.00
1	Ken Griffey Jr.	50.00
2	Frank Thomas	25.00
3	Cal Ripken Jr.	40.00
4	Jeff Bagwell	20.00
5	Mike Piazza	30.00
6	Barry Bonds	12.00
7	Matt Williams	8.00
8	Don Mattingly	20.00
9	Will Clark	8.00
10	Tony Gwynn	25.00
11	Kirby Puckett	25.00
12	Jose Canseco	8.00

1995 Select Certified Potential Unlimited

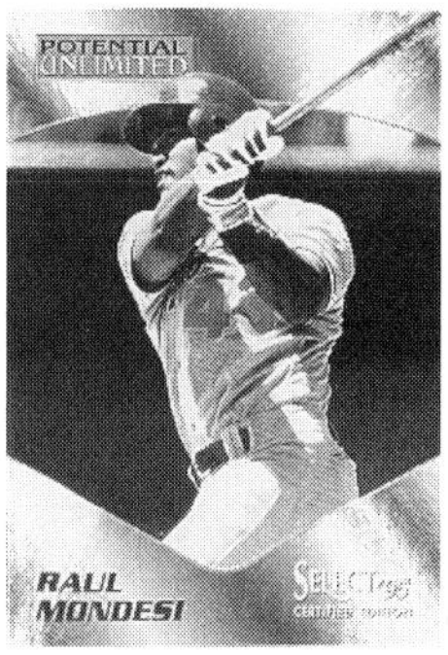

Dufex printing with textured foil highlights and transparent inks is featured in this chase set which was produced in an edition of no more the 1,975 sets, as witnessed by the numbering on card backs. Approximate odds of finding a Potential Unlimited card are one per 29 packs. A super-scarce edition of 903 cards each featuring "micro-etch" foil printing technology was issued at the rate of one per 70 packs.

		MT
Complete Set (20):		200.00
Common Player:		5.00
Comp. Numbered 903 Set		300.00
903's: 1.5X		
1	Cliff Floyd	6.00
2	Manny Ramirez	25.00
3	Raul Mondesi	8.00
4	Scott Ruffcorn	5.00
5	Billy Ashley	5.00
6	Alex Gonzalez	7.50
7	Midre Cummings	5.00
8	Charles Johnson	6.00
9	Garret Anderson	5.00
10	Hideo Nomo	15.00
11	Chipper Jones	35.00
12	Curtis Goodwin	5.00
13	Frank Rodriguez	5.00
14	Shawn Green	10.00
15	Ray Durham	5.00
16	Todd Hollandsworth	5.00
17	Brian Hunter	5.00
18	Carlos Delgado	8.00
19	Michael Tucker	5.00
20	Alex Rodriguez	60.00

1996 Select

Select's 1996 baseball set has 200 cards in it, including 35 rookies, five checklists and 10 Lineup Leaders subset cards. All 200 cards are also reprinted as part of an Artist's Proof parallel set, using a holographic Artist's Proof logo. Cards were seeded one per every 35 packs; there were approximately 435 sets produced. Three insert sets were also created: Claim to Fame, En Fuego and Team Nucleus.

		MT
Complete Set (200):		15.00
Common Player:		.10
Artist's Proofs: 20X		
Wax Box:		40.00
1	Wade Boggs	.30
2	Shawn Green	.20
3	Andres Galarraga	.15
4	Bill Pulsipher	.10
5	Chuck Knoblauch	.10
6	Ken Griffey Jr.	3.00
7	Greg Maddux	1.50
8	Manny Ramirez	1.00
9	Ivan Rodriguez	.50
10	Tim Salmon	.25
11	Frank Thomas	1.00
12	Jeff Bagwell	1.00
13	Travis Fryman	.15
14	Kenny Lofton	.75
15	Matt Williams	.25
16	Jay Bell	.10
17	Ken Caminiti	.15
18	Ray Lankford	.10
19	Cal Ripken Jr.	2.50
20	Roger Clemens	.60
21	Carlos Baerga	.10
22	Mike Piazza	2.00
23	Gregg Jefferies	.10
24	Reggie Sanders	.10
25	Rondell White	.15
26	Sammy Sosa	1.50
27	Kevin Appier	.10
28	Kevin Seitzer	.10
29	Gary Sheffield	.15
30	Mike Mussina	.40
31	Mark McGwire	3.00
32	Barry Larkin	.20
33	Marc Newfield	.10
34	Ismael Valdes	.10
35	Marty Cordova	.10
36	Albert Belle	.75
37	Johnny Damon	.25
38	Garret Anderson	.10
39	Cecil Fielder	.15
40	John Mabry	.10
41	Chipper Jones	2.00
42	Omar Vizquel	.10
43	Jose Rijo	.10
44	Charles Johnson	.10
45	Alex Rodriquez	2.50
46	Rico Brogna	.10
47	Joe Carter	.15
48	Mo Vaughn	.75
49	Moises Alou	.15
50	Raul Mondesi	.30
51	Robin Ventura	.20
52	Jim Thome	.40
53	Dave Justice	.20
54	Jeff King	.10
55	Brian Hunter	.15
56	Juan Gonzalez	1.00
57	John Olerud	.15
58	Rafael Palmeiro	.20
59	Tony Gwynn	1.00
60	Eddie Murray	.35
61	Jason Isringhausen	.25
62	Dante Bichette	.20
63	Randy Johnson	.35
64	Kirby Puckett	1.00
65	Jim Edmonds	.15
66	David Cone	.15
67	Ozzie Smith	.30
68	Fred McGriff	.35
69	Darren Daulton	.10
70	Edgar Martinez	.10
71	J.T. Snow	.10
72	Butch Huskey	.10
73	Hideo Nomo	.40
74	Pedro Martinez	.20
75	Bobby Bonilla	.10
76	Jeff Conine	.10
77	Ryan Klesko	.20
78	Bernie Williams	.35
79	Andre Dawson	.15
80	Trevor Hoffman	.15
81	Mark Grace	.20
82	Benji Gil	.10
83	Eric Karros	.10
84	Pete Schourek	.10
85	Edgardo Alfonzo	.15
86	Jay Buhner	.15

87	Vinny Castilla	.10
88	Bret Boone	.10
89	Ray Durham	.10
90	Brian Jordan	.10
91	Jose Canseco	.25
92	Paul O'Neill	.15
93	Chili Davis	.10
94	Tom Glavine	.15
95	Julian Tavarez	.10
96	Derek Bell	.10
97	Will Clark	.25
98	Larry Walker	.25
99	Denny Neagle	.10
100	Alex Fernandez	.10
101	Barry Bonds	.60
102	Ben McDonald	.10
103	Andy Pettitte	.75
104	Tino Martinez	.10
105	Sterling Hitchcock	.10
106	Royce Clayton	.10
107	Jim Abbott	.10
108	Rickey Henderson	.25
109	Ramon Martinez	.10
110	Paul Molitor	.35
111	Dennis Eckersley	.10
112	Alex Gonzalez	.10
113	Marquis Grissom	.10
114	Greg Vaughn	.15
115	Lance Johnson	.10
116	Todd Stottlemyre	.10
117	Jack McDowell	.10
118	Ruben Sierra	.10
119	Brady Anderson	.15
120	Julio Franco	.10
121	Brooks Kieshnick	.10
122	Roberto Alomar	.50
123	Greg Gagne	.10
124	Wally Joyner	.10
125	John Smoltz	.20
126	John Valentin	.10
127	Russ Davis	.10
128	Joe Vitiello	.10
129	Shawon Dunston	.10
130	Frank Rodriguez	.10
131	Charlie Hayes	.10
132	Andy Benes	.10
133	B.J. Surhoff	.10
134	Dave Nilsson	.10
135	Carlos Delgado	.40
136	Walt Weiss	.10
137	Mike Stanley	.10
138	Greg Colbrunn	.10
139	Mike Kelly	.10
140	Ryne Sandberg	.50
141	Lee Smith	.10
142	Dennis Martinez	.10
143	Bernard Gilkey	.10
144	Lenny Dykstra	.10
145	Danny Tartabull	.10
146	Dean Palmer	.10
147	Craig Biggio	.20
148	Juan Acevedo	.10
149	Michael Tucker	.10
150	Bobby Higginson	.15
151	Ken Griffey Jr. (Line Up Leaders)	1.25
152	Frank Thomas (Line Up Leaders)	.50
153	Cal Ripken Jr. (Line Up Leaders)	1.00
154	Albert Belle (Line Up Leaders)	.40
155	Mike Piazza (Line Up Leaders)	.60
156	Barry Bonds (Line Up Leaders)	.25
157	Sammy Sosa (Line Up Leaders)	.75
158	Mo Vaughn (Line Up Leaders)	.25
159	Greg Maddux (Line Up Leaders)	.75
160	Jeff Bagwell (Line Up Leaders)	.50
161	Derek Jeter	2.00
162	Paul Wilson	.10
163	Chris Snopek	.10
164	Jason Schmidt	.10
165	Jimmy Haynes	.10
166	George Arias	.10
167	Steve Gibralter	.10
168	Bob Wolcott	.10
169	Jason Kendall	.10
170	Greg Zaun	.10
171	Quinton McCracken	.10
172	Alan Benes	.15
173	Rey Ordonez	.40
174	Ugueth Urbina	.10
175	*Osvaldo Fernandez*	.20
176	Marc Barcelo	.10
177	Sal Fasano	.10
178	*Mike Grace*	.10
179	Chan Ho Park	.15
180	Robert Perez	.10
181	Todd Hollandsworth	.10
182	*Wilton Guerrero*	.60
183	John Wasdin	.10
184	Jim Pittsley	.10
185	LaTroy Hawkins	.10
186	Jay Powell	.10
187	Felipe Crespo	.10
188	Jermaine Dye	.15
189	Bob Abreu	.10
190	*Matt Luke*	.15
191	Richard Hidalgo	.10
192	Karim Garcia	.35
193	Tavo Alvarez	.10
194	*Andy Fox*	.10
195	Terrell Wade	.10
196	Frank Thomas (checklist)	.40
197	Ken Griffey Jr. (checklist)	1.00
198	Greg Maddux (checklist)	.60
199	Mike Piazza (checklist)	.50
200	Cal Ripken Jr. (checklist)	.75

1996 Select Artist's Proofs

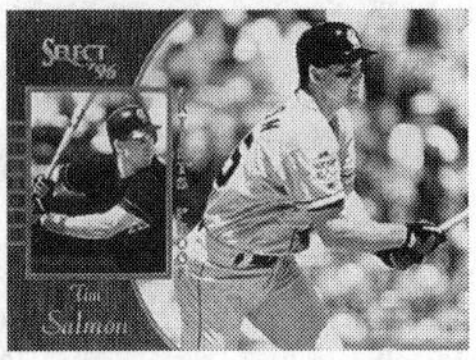

Approximately once per 35 packs, a card from this parallel chase set is encountered among 1996 Select. Reported production was 435 sets. The Artist's Proof cards are distinguished by a holographic logo testifying to their status on the front of the card.

	MT
Complete Set (200):	1200.
Common Player:	2.00
Artist's Proof Stars: 20X	
(See 1996 Select for checklist and base card values.)	

1996 Select Claim to Fame

Twenty different stars are featured on these 1996 Select insert cards. Each card is numbered "1 of 2100" and uses an external die-cut design. The cards were seeded one per every 72 packs.

		MT
Complete Set (20):		250.00
Common Player:		3.00
1	Cal Ripken Jr.	30.00
2	Greg Maddux	25.00
3	Ken Griffey Jr.	40.00
4	Frank Thomas	20.00
5	Mo Vaughn	6.00
6	Albert Belle	10.00
7	Jeff Bagwell	15.00
8	Sammy Sosa	25.00
8s	Sammy Sosa (overprinted "SAMPLE")	15.00
9	Reggie Sanders	3.00
10	Hideo Nomo	6.00
11	Chipper Jones	25.00
12	Mike Piazza	25.00
13	Matt Williams	5.00
14	Tony Gwynn	20.00
15	Johnny Damon	3.00
16	Dante Bichette	3.00
17	Kirby Puckett	10.00
18	Barry Bonds	10.00
19	Randy Johnson	8.00
20	Eddie Murray	4.00

1996 Select En Fuego

ESPN announcer Dan Patrick is featured on his own card in this set, inspired by his Sportscenter catch phrase "en fuego," which means "on fire." Patrick's teammate, Keith Olberman, wrote the card backs. The 25 cards, printed on all-foil Dufex stock, are seeded one per every 48 packs of 1996 Select baseball.

		MT
Complete Set (25):		180.00
Common Player:		3.00
1	Ken Griffey Jr.	25.00
2	Frank Thomas	12.00
3	Cal Ripken Jr.	20.00
4	Greg Maddux	15.00
5	Jeff Bagwell	8.00
6	Barry Bonds	6.00
7	Mo Vaughn	4.00
8	Albert Belle	6.00
9	Sammy Sosa	15.00
10	Reggie Sanders	3.00
11	Mike Piazza	15.00
12	Chipper Jones	15.00
13	Tony Gwynn	12.00
14	Kirby Puckett	6.00
15	Wade Boggs	4.00
16	Dan Patrick	3.00
17	Gary Sheffield	3.00
18	Dante Bichette	4.00
19	Randy Johnson	5.00
20	Matt Williams	3.00
21	Alex Rodriguez	20.00
22	Tim Salmon	3.00
23	Johnny Damon	3.00
24	Manny Ramirez	8.00
25	Hideo Nomo	4.00

1996 Select Team Nucleus

This 1996 Select insert set pays tribute to the three top players from each Major League Baseball team; each card features the three teammates on it. The cards are printed on a clear plastic, utilizing a holographic micro-etched design. They are seeded one per every 18 packs.

		MT
Complete Set (28):		80.00
Common Player:		2.00
1	Albert Belle, Manny Ramirez, Carlos Baerga	6.00
2	Ray Lankford, Brian Jordan, Ozzie Smith	4.00
3	Jay Bell, Jeff King, Denny Neagle	2.00
4	Dante Bichette, Andres Galarraga, Larry Walker	3.00
5	Mark McGwire, Mike Bordick, Terry Steinbach	10.00
6	Bernie Williams, Wade Boggs, David Cone	5.00
7	Joe Carter, Alex Gonzalez, Shawn Green	3.00
8	Roger Clemens, Mo Vaughn, Jose Canseco	5.00
9	Ken Griffey Jr., Edgar Martinez, Randy Johnson	15.00
10	Gregg Jefferies, Darren Daulton, Lenny Dykstra	2.00
11	Mike Piazza, Raul Mondesi, Hideo Nomo	9.00
12	Greg Maddux, Chipper Jones, Ryan Klesko	9.00
13	Cecil Fielder, Travis Fryman, Phil Nevin	2.00
14	Ivan Rodriguez, Will Clark, Juan Gonzalez	5.00
15	Ryne Sandberg, Sammy Sosa, Mark Grace	10.00
16	Gary Sheffield, Charles Johnson, Andre Dawson	3.00
17	Johnny Damon, Michael Tucker, Kevin Appier	2.00
18	Barry Bonds, Matt Williams, Rod Beck	3.00
19	Kirby Puckett, Chuck Knoblauch, Marty Cordova	3.00
20	Cal Ripken Jr., Bobby Bonilla, Mike Mussina	9.00
21	Jason Isringhausen, Bill Pulsipher, Rico Brogna	2.50
22	Tony Gwynn, Ken Caminiti, Marc Newfield	5.00
23	Tim Salmon, Garret Anderson, Jim Edmonds	2.50
24	Moises Alou, Rondell White, Cliff Floyd	2.50
25	Barry Larkin, Reggie Sanders, Bret Boone	2.00
26	Jeff Bagwell, Craig Biggio, Derek Bell	7.50
27	Frank Thomas, Robin Ventura, Alex Fernandez	6.00
28	John Jaha, Greg Vaughn, Kevin Seitzer	2.00

1996 Select Certified

This hobby-exclusive set has 144 cards in its regular issue, plus six parallel versions and two insert sets. The parallel sets are: Certified Red (one per five packs), Certified Blue (one per 50), Artist's Proofs (one per 12), Mirror Red (one per 100), Mirror Blue (one per 200), and Mirror Gold (one per 300). Breaking down the numbers, there are 1,800 Certified Red sets, 180 Certified Blue, 500 Artist's Proofs, 90 Mirror Red 45 Mirror Blue and 30 Mirror Gold sets. The insert sets are Interleague Preview cards and Select Few. Cards #135-144 are a "Pastime Power" subset.

		MT
Complete Set (144):		40.00
Common Player:		.20
Unlisted Stars: .40 to .60		
Comp. Certified Red Set (144):		500.00
Common Red:		1.00
Reds: 2.5X		
Artist's Proofs: 10X		
Blues: 25X		
Wax Box:		200.00
1	Frank Thomas	2.00
2	Tino Martinez	.35
3	Gary Sheffield	.75
4	Kenny Lofton	.75
5	Joe Carter	.25
6	Alex Rodriguez	4.00
7	Chipper Jones	3.00
8	Roger Clemens	1.50
9	Jay Bell	.20
10	Eddie Murray	.50
11	Will Clark	.50
12	Mike Mussina	.75
13	Hideo Nomo	.75
14	Andres Galarraga	.35
15	Marc Newfield	.20
16	Jason Isringhausen	.20
17	Randy Johnson	.75
18	Chuck Knoblauch	.40
19	J.T. Snow	.20
20	Mark McGwire	5.00
21	Tony Gwynn	2.00
22	Albert Belle	1.50
23	Gregg Jefferies	.20
24	Reggie Sanders	.20
25	Bernie Williams	.75
26	Ray Lankford	.20
27	Johnny Damon	.20
28	Ryne Sandberg	1.25
29	Rondell White	.40
30	Mike Piazza	3.00
31	Barry Bonds	1.25
32	Greg Maddux	3.00
33	Craig Biggio	.35
34	John Valentin	.20
35	Ivan Rodriguez	1.25
36	Rico Brogna	.20
37	Tim Salmon	.35
38	Sterling Hitchcock	.20
39	Charles Johnson	.20
40	Travis Fryman	.20
41	Barry Larkin	.35
42	Tom Glavine	.40
43	Marty Cordova	.20
44	Shawn Green	.35
45	Ben McDonald	.20
46	Robin Ventura	.30
47	Ken Griffey Jr.	5.00
48	Orlando Merced	.20
49	Paul O'Neill	.40
50	Ozzie Smith	1.00
51	Manny Ramirez	1.50
52	Ismael Valdes	.20
53	Cal Ripken Jr.	4.00
54	Jeff Bagwell	2.00
55	Greg Vaughn	.25
56	Juan Gonzalez	2.00
57	Raul Mondesi	.40
58	Carlos Baerga	.20
59	Sammy Sosa	2.50
60	Mike Kelly	.20
61	Edgar Martinez	.20
62	Kirby Puckett	1.00
63	Cecil Fielder	.25
64	David Cone	.30
65	Moises Alou	.35
66	Fred McGriff	.40
67	Mo Vaughn	.75
68	Edgardo Alfonzo	.25
69	Jim Thome	.75
70	Rickey Henderson	.40
71	Dante Bichette	.40
72	Lenny Dykstra	.20
73	Benji Gil	.20
74	Wade Boggs	.50
75	Jim Edmonds	.20
76	Michael Tucker	.20
77	Carlos Delgado	.75
78	Butch Huskey	.20
79	Billy Ashley	.20
80	Dean Palmer	.20
81	Paul Molitor	.50
82	Ryan Klesko	.35
83	Brian Hunter	.20
84	Jay Buhner	.25
85	Larry Walker	.60
86	Mike Bordick	.20
87	Matt Williams	.40
88	Jack McDowell	.20
89	Hal Morris	.20
90	Brian Jordan	.20
91	Andy Pettitte	.75
92	Melvin Nieves	.20
93	Pedro Martinez	.40
94	Mark Grace	.40
95	Garret Anderson	.20
96	Andre Dawson	.30
97	Ray Durham	.20
98	Jose Canseco	.50
99	Roberto Alomar	1.00
100	Derek Jeter	3.00
101	Alan Benes	.20
102	Karim Garcia	.60
103	*Robin Jennings*	.20
104	Bob Abreu	.20
105	Sal Fasano (Card front has Livan Hernandez' name)	.20
106	Steve Gibralter	.20
107	Jermaine Dye	.20
108	Jason Kendall	.20
109	*Mike Grace*	.20
110	Jason Schmidt	.20
111	Paul Wilson	.20
112	Rey Ordonez	.75
113	*Wilton Guerrero*	1.00
114	Brooks Kieschnick	.20
115	George Arias	.20
116	*Osvaldo Fernandez*	.20
117	Todd Hollandsworth	.20
118	John Wasdin	.20
119	Eric Owens	.20
120	Chan Ho Park	.25

121 Mark Loretta .20
122 Richard Hidalgo .20
123 Jeff Suppan .20
124 Jim Pittsley .20
125 LaTroy Hawkins .20
126 Chris Snopek .20
127 Justin Thompson .20
128 Jay Powell .20
129 Alex Ochoa .20
130 Felipe Crespo .20
131 *Matt Lawton* .20
132 Jimmy Haynes .20
133 Terrell Wade .20
134 Ruben Rivera .25
135 Frank Thomas (Pastime Power) 1.00
136 Ken Griffey Jr. (Pastime Power) 3.00
137 Greg Maddux (Pastime Power) 2.00
138 Mike Piazza (Pastime Power) 2.00
139 Cal Ripken Jr. (Pastime Power) 2.50
140 Albert Belle (Pastime Power) 1.00
141 Mo Vaughn (Pastime Power) .75
142 Chipper Jones (Pastime Power) 2.00
143 Hideo Nomo (Pastime Power) .40
144 Ryan Klesko (Pastime Power) .25

1996 Select Certified Artist's Proofs

Only 500 cards each of this parallel issue were produced, seeded one in every dozen packs. The cards are identical to the regular-issue Select Certified except for the presence on front of a prismatic gold Artist's Proof logo.

MT
Complete Set (144): 1000.
Common Player: 2.00
Artist's Proof Stars: 10X
(See 1996 Select Certified for checklist and base card values.)

1996 Select Certified Red, Blue

These 1996 Select Certified insert cards were the most common of the parallel cards issued; they were seeded one per five packs. There were 1,800 Certified Red sets produced, with the number of Certified Blue sets at 180. Cards are essentially the same as regular-issue Select Certified except for the color of the foil background on front.

MT
Complete Set, Red (144): 500.00
Common Player, Red: 1.00
Red Stars: 2.5X
Complete Set, Blue (144): 3000.
Common Player, Blue: 5.00
Blue Stars: 25X
(See 1996 Select Certified for checklist and base card values.)

1996 Select Certified Mirror Parallels

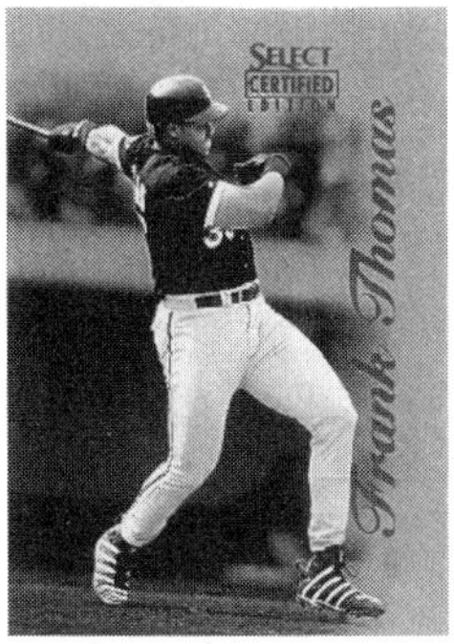

These 1996 Select Certified inserts are the scarcest of the set. Only 30 Mirror Gold sets were made, with 60 Mirror Blue sets and 90 Mirror Red. Due to the improbability of completing the collection, no complete set price is given.

MT
Mirror Gold (144):
Common Player, Gold: 75.00
Mirror Blue: (144): 35-40% of Gold
Common Player, Blue: 35.00
Mirror Red (144): 20-25% of Gold
Common Player, Red: 20.00
1 Frank Thomas 1000.
2 Tino Martinez 350.00
3 Gary Sheffield 200.00
4 Kenny Lofton 400.00
5 Joe Carter 150.00
6 Alex Rodriguez 1200.
7 Chipper Jones 1200.
8 Roger Clemens 800.00
9 Jay Bell 75.00
10 Eddie Murray 200.00
11 Will Clark 300.00
12 Mike Mussina 400.00
13 Hideo Nomo 200.00
14 Andres Galarraga 250.00
15 Marc Newfield 75.00
16 Jason Isringhausen 75.00
17 Randy Johnson 400.00
18 Chuck Knoblauch 300.00
19 J.T. Snow 75.00
20 Mark McGwire 2000.
21 Tony Gwynn 1000.
22 Albert Belle 500.00
23 Gregg Jefferies 75.00
24 Reggie Sanders 75.00
25 Bernie Williams 400.00
26 Ray Lankford 125.00
27 Johnny Damon 100.00
28 Ryne Sandberg 500.00
29 Rondell White 150.00
30 Mike Piazza 1200.
31 Barry Bonds 500.00
32 Greg Maddux 1200.
33 Craig Biggio 300.00
34 John Valentin 75.00
35 Ivan Rodriguez 500.00
36 Rico Brogna 100.00
37 Tim Salmon 200.00
38 Sterling Hitchcock 75.00
39 Charles Johnson 125.00
40 Travis Fryman 150.00
41 Barry Larkin 150.00
42 Tom Glavine 200.00
43 Marty Cordova 75.00
44 Shawn Green 75.00
45 Ben McDonald 75.00
46 Robin Ventura 150.00
47 Ken Griffey Jr. 2000.
48 Orlando Merced 75.00
49 Paul O'Neill 150.00
50 Ozzie Smith 400.00
51 Manny Ramirez 500.00
52 Ismael Valdes 100.00
53 Cal Ripken Jr. 1400.
54 Jeff Bagwell 500.00
55 Greg Vaughn 125.00
56 Juan Gonzalez 1000.
57 Raul Mondesi 200.00
58 Carlos Baerga 75.00
59 Sammy Sosa 800.00
60 Mike Kelly 75.00
61 Edgar Martinez 75.00
62 Kirby Puckett 500.00
63 Cecil Fielder 150.00
64 David Cone 100.00
65 Moises Alou 150.00
66 Fred McGriff 150.00
67 Mo Vaughn 500.00
68 Edgardo Alfonzo 100.00
59 Jim Thome 300.00
70 Rickey Henderson 150.00
71 Dante Bichette 200.00
72 Lenny Dykstra 75.00
73 Benji Gil 75.00
74 Wade Boggs 300.00
75 Jim Edmonds 200.00
76 Michael Tucker 75.00
77 Carlos Delgado 125.00
78 Butch Huskey 75.00
79 Billy Ashley 75.00
80 Dean Palmer 125.00
81 Paul Molitor 400.00
82 Ryan Klesko 150.00
83 Brian Hunter 100.00
84 Jay Buhner 200.00
85 Larry Walker 300.00
86 Mike Bordick 75.00
87 Matt Williams 200.00
88 Jack McDowell 75.00
89 Hal Morris 75.00
90 Brian Jordan 75.00
91 Andy Pettitte 250.00
92 Melvin Nieves 75.00
93 Pedro Martinez 400.00
94 Mark Grace 200.00
95 Garret Anderson 100.00
96 Andre Dawson 150.00
97 Ray Durham 75.00
98 Jose Canseco 250.00
99 Roberto Alomar 400.00
100 Derek Jeter 1200.
101 Alan Benes 75.00
102 Karim Garcia 75.00
103 Robin Jennings 75.00
104 Bob Abreu 75.00
105 Livan Hernandez (photo actually Sal Fasano) 75.00
106 Steve Gibralter 75.00
107 Jermaine Dye 75.00
108 Jason Kendall 75.00
109 Mike Grace 75.00
110 Jason Schmidt 75.00
111 Paul Wilson 75.00
112 Rey Ordonez 100.00
113 Wilton Guerrero 100.00
114 Brooks Kieschnick 75.00
115 George Arias 75.00
116 Osvaldo Fernandez 75.00
117 Todd Hollandsworth 75.00
118 John Wasdin 75.00
119 Eric Owens 75.00
120 Chan Ho Park 150.00
121 Mark Loretta 75.00
122 Richard Hidalgo 125.00
123 Jeff Suppan 75.00
124 Jim Pittsley 75.00
125 LaTroy Hawkins 75.00
126 Chris Snopek 75.00
127 Justin Thompson 100.00
128 Jay Powell 75.00
129 Alex Ochoa 125.00
130 Felipe Crespo 75.00
131 Matt Lawton 75.00
132 Jimmy Haynes 75.00
133 Terrell Wade 75.00
134 Ruben Rivera 75.00
135 Frank Thomas (Pastime Power) 600.00
136 Ken Griffey Jr. (Pastime Power) 1500.
137 Greg Maddux (Pastime Power) 700.00
138 Mike Piazza (Pastime Power) 700.00
139 Cal Ripken Jr. (Pastime Power) 1000.
140 Albert Belle (Pastime Power) 250.00
141 Mo Vaughn (Pastime Power) 200.00
142 Chipper Jones (Pastime Power) 500.00
143 Hideo Nomo (Pastime Power) 75.00
144 Ryan Klesko (Pastime Power) 100.00

1996 Select Certified Interleague Preview Samples

These samples preview the "Interleague Preview" insert set and were sent to hobby dealers. They differ from the issued version only in the overprinted "SAMPLE" on front and back.

MT
Complete Set (25): 125.00
Common Player: 2.50
1 Ken Griffey Jr., Hideo Nomo 12.00
2 Greg Maddux, Mo Vaughn 7.50
3 Frank Thomas, Sammy Sosa 10.00
4 Mike Piazza, Jim Edmonds 7.50
5 Ryan Klesko, Roger Clemens 7.50
6 Derek Jeter, Rey Ordonez 7.50
7 Johnny Damon, Ray Lankford 2.50
8 Manny Ramirez, Reggie Sanders 3.50
9 Barry Bonds, Jay Buhner 3.50
10 Jason Isringhausen, Wade Boggs 3.00
11 David Cone, Chipper Jones 7.50
12 Jeff Bagwell, Will Clark 4.50
13 Tony Gwynn, Randy Johnson 6.00
14 Cal Ripken Jr., Tom Glavine 10.00
15 Kirby Puckett, Alan Benes 4.50
16 Gary Sheffield, Mike Mussina 3.00
17 Raul Mondesi, Tim Salmon 3.50
18 Rondell White, Carlos Delgado 2.50
19 Cecil Fielder, Ryne Sandberg 6.00
20 Kenny Lofton, Brian Hunter 2.50
21 Paul Wilson, Paul O'Neill 2.50
22 Ismael Valdes, Edgar Martinez 2.50
23 Matt Williams, Mark McGwire 12.00
24 Albert Belle, Barry Larkin 4.00
25 Brady Anderson, Marquis Grissom 2.50

1996 Select Certified Interleague Preview

These 1996 Select Certified insert cards feature 21 prospective matchups from when interleague play begins. The cards were seeded one per every 42 packs.

MT
Complete Set (25): 125.00
Common Player: 3.00
1 Ken Griffey Jr., Hideo Nomo 15.00
2 Greg Maddux, Mo Vaughn 10.00
3 Frank Thomas, Sammy Sosa 12.00
4 Mike Piazza, Jim Edmonds 10.00
5 Ryan Klesko, Roger Clemens 6.00
6 Derek Jeter, Rey Ordonez 10.00
7 Johnny Damon, Ray Lankford 3.00
8 Manny Ramirez, Reggie Sanders 5.00
9 Barry Bonds, Jay Buhner 4.00
10 Jason Isringhausen, Wade Boggs 3.00
11 David Cone, Chipper Jones 10.00
12 Jeff Bagwell, Will Clark 4.00
13 Tony Gwynn, Randy Johnson 7.50
14 Cal Ripken Jr., Tom Glavine 12.50
15 Kirby Puckett, Alan Benes 4.00
16 Gary Sheffield, Mike Mussina 3.00
17 Raul Mondesi, Tim Salmon 3.00
18 Rondell White, Carlos Delgado 3.00
19 Cecil Fielder, Ryne Sandberg 4.00
20 Kenny Lofton, Brian Hunter 3.00
21 Paul Wilson, Paul O'Neill 3.00
22 Ismael Valdes, Edgar Martinez 3.00
23 Matt Williams, Mark McGwire 15.00
24 Albert Belle, Barry Larkin 4.00
25 Brady Anderson, Marquis Grissom 3.00

1996 Select Certified Select Few

Eighteen top players are featured on these 1996 Select Certified inserts, which utilize holographic technology with a dot matrix hologram. Cards were seeded one per every 60 packs.

MT
Complete Set (18): 190.00
Common Player: 4.00
1 Sammy Sosa 20.00
2 Derek Jeter 20.00
3 Ken Griffey Jr. 30.00
4 Albert Belle 8.00
5 Cal Ripken Jr. 25.00
6 Greg Maddux 20.00
7 Frank Thomas 15.00
8 Mo Vaughn 6.00
9 Chipper Jones 20.00
10 Mike Piazza 20.00
11 Ryan Klesko 4.00
12 Hideo Nomo 6.00
13 Alan Benes 4.00
14 Manny Ramirez 10.00
15 Gary Sheffield 6.00
16 Barry Bonds 8.00
17 Matt Williams 4.00
18 Johnny Damon 4.00

The election of former players to the Hall of Fame does not always have an immediate upward effect on card prices. The hobby market generally has done a good job of predicting those inductions and adjusting values over the course of several years.

1997 Select Samples

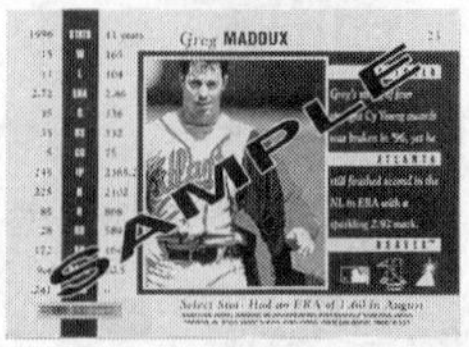

The 1997 edition of Select was previewed with the issue of several regular-issue cards carrying a large black "SAMPLE" overprint on front and back. The Rodriguez sample, untrimmed and larger than standard size, was not distributed in the cello packs with the other three cards.

		MT
Complete Set (4):		30.00
Common Player:		5.00
3	Tony Gwynn	5.00
23	Greg Maddux	5.00
47	Ken Griffey Jr.	9.00
53	Alex Rodriguez	12.00

1997 Select

The Series 1 base set is made up of 150 cards printed on a thick 16-point stock. Each card features a distinctive silver-foil treatment and either red (100 cards) or blue (50 cards) foil accent. Blue-foiled cards were short-printed at a ratio of 1:2 compared to the red-foil cards. Blue-foil cards are indicated with a (B) in the checklist. Subsets include 40 Rookies, eight Super Stars and two checklists. Inserts include two parallel sets, (Artist's Proof and Registered Gold), Tools of the Trade, Mirror Blue Tools of the Trade, and Rookie Revolution. The cards were sold only at hobby shops in six-card packs for $2.99 each. A high-number series was issued with each card bearing a "Select Company" notation.

		MT
Complete Set (200):		80.00
Complete Series 1 (150):		50.00
Common Red Player:		.10
Common Blue Player:		.25
Registered Golds: 4X		
Artist's Proofs: 20X		
Complete High Series (50):		
Common High Series:		.25
Wax Box:		35.00
1	Juan Gonzalez (B)	3.00
2	Mo Vaughn (B)	1.00
3	Tony Gwynn	1.50
4	Manny Ramirez (B)	1.50
5	Jose Canseco	.60
6	David Cone	.15
7	Chan Ho Park	.15
8	Frank Thomas (B)	1.50
9	Todd Hollandsworth	.10
10	Marty Cordova	.10
11	Gary Sheffield (B)	.50
12	John Smoltz (B)	.75
13	Mark Grudzielanek	.10
14	Sammy Sosa (B)	3.00
15	Paul Molitor	.40
16	Kevin Brown	.15
17	Albert Belle (B)	1.50
18	Eric Young	.15
19	John Wetteland	.10
20	Ryan Klesko (B)	.60
21	Joe Carter	.15
22	Alex Ochoa	.10
23	Greg Maddux (B)	4.00
24	Roger Clemens (B)	3.00
25	Ivan Rodriguez (B)	1.50
26	Barry Bonds (B)	1.50
27	Kenny Lofton (B)	1.00
28	Javy Lopez	.25
29	Hideo Nomo (B)	1.50
30	Rusty Greer	.10
31	Rafael Palmeiro	.30
32	Mike Piazza (B)	4.00
33	Ryne Sandberg	.75
34	Wade Boggs	.75
35	Jim Thome (B)	.75
36	Ken Caminiti (B)	.75
37	Mark Grace	.30
38	Brian Jordan (B)	.25
39	Craig Biggio	.30
40	Henry Rodriguez	.10
41	Dean Palmer	.10
42	Jason Kendall	.15
43	Bill Pulsipher	.10
44	Tim Salmon (B)	.75
45	Marc Newfield	.10
46	Pat Hentgen	.10
47	Ken Griffey Jr. (B)	6.00
48	Paul Wilson	.10
49	Jay Buhner (B)	.25
50	Rickey Henderson	.75
51	Jeff Bagwell (B)	1.50
52	Cecil Fielder	.15
53	Alex Rodriguez (B)	4.00
54	John Jaha	.10
55	Brady Anderson (B)	.15
56	Andres Galarraga	.60
57	Raul Mondesi	.30
58	Andy Pettitte	.40
59	Roberto Alomar (B)	1.25
60	Derek Jeter (B)	4.00
61	Charles Johnson	.15
62	Travis Fryman	.15
63	Chipper Jones (B)	3.00
64	Edgar Martinez	.10
65	Bobby Bonilla	.10
66	Greg Vaughn	.15
67	Bobby Higginson	.15
68	Garret Anderson	.10
69	Chuck Knoblauch (B)	1.25
70	Jermaine Dye	.10
71	Cal Ripken Jr. (B)	5.00
72	Jason Giambi	.15
73	Trey Beamon	.10
74	Shawn Green	.30
75	Mark McGwire (B)	6.00
76	Carlos Delgado	.20
77	Jason Isringhausen	.10
78	Randy Johnson (B)	1.25
79	Troy Percival (B)	.25
80	Ron Gant	.10
81	Ellis Burks	.10
82	Mike Mussina (B)	1.25
83	Todd Hundley	.15
84	Jim Edmonds	.15
85	Charles Nagy	.15
86	Dante Bichette (B)	.60
87	Mariano Rivera	.15
88	Matt Williams (B)	.60
89	Rondell White	.15
90	Steve Finley	.10
91	Alex Fernandez	.15
92	Barry Larkin	.20
93	Tom Goodwin	.10
94	Will Clark	.50
95	Michael Tucker	.10
96	Derek Bell	.10
97	Larry Walker	.40
98	Alan Benes	.10
99	Tom Glavine	.15
100	Darin Erstad (B)	2.00
101	Andruw Jones (B)	2.00
102	Scott Rolen	1.50
103	Todd Walker (B)	1.25
104	Dmitri Young	.10
105	Vladimir Guerrero (B)	2.50
106	Nomar Garciaparra	2.00
107	*Danny Patterson*	.10
108	Karim Garcia	.20
109	Todd Greene	.10
110	Ruben Rivera	.15
111	Raul Casanova	.10
112	Mike Cameron	.10
113	Bartolo Colon	.15
114	*Rod Myers*	.10
115	Todd Dunn	.10
116	Torii Hunter	.10
117	Jason Dickson	.20
118	*Gene Kingsale*	.20
119	Rafael Medina	.10
120	Raul Ibanez	.10
121	*Bobby Henley*	.20
122	Scott Spiezio	.10
123	*Bobby Smith*	.20
124	J.J. Johnson	.10
125	*Bubba Trammell*	1.00
126	Jeff Abbott	.10
127	Neifi Perez	.10
128	Derrek Lee	.10
129	*Kevin Brown*	.20
130	Mendy Lopez	.10
131	Kevin Orie	.10
132	Ryan Jones	.10
133	Juan Encarnacion	.40
134	Jose Guillen (B)	1.25
135	Greg Norton	.10
136	Richie Sexson	.15
137	Jay Payton	.10
138	Bob Abreu	.10
139	*Ronnie Belliard*	.25
140	Wilton Guerrero (B)	.25
141	Alex Rodriguez (Select Stars) (B)	2.00
142	Juan Gonzalez (Select Stars) (B)	1.50
143	Ken Caminiti (Select Stars) (B)	.50
144	Frank Thomas (Select Stars) (B)	1.50
145	Ken Griffey Jr. (Select Stars) (B)	3.00
146	John Smoltz (Select Stars) (B)	.50
147	Mike Piazza (Select Stars) (B)	2.00
148	Derek Jeter (Select Stars) (B)	2.00
149	Frank Thomas (checklist)	.75
150	Ken Griffey Jr. (checklist)	1.50
151	*Jose Cruz Jr.*	1.50
152	Moises Alou	1.50
153	*Hideki Irabu*	1.00
154	Glendon Rusch	.25
155	Ron Coomer	.25
156	*Jeremi Gonzalez*	.50
157	*Fernando Tatis*	4.00
158	John Olerud	.75
159	Rickey Henderson	.75
160	Shannon Stewart	.50
161	Kevin Polcovich	.25
162	Jose Rosado	.25
163	Ray Lankford	.25
164	David Justice	.75
165	*Mark Kotsay*	.60
166	*Deivi Cruz*	.25
167	Billy Wagner	.45
168	Jacob Cruz	.50
169	Matt Morris	.35
170	Brian Banks	.25
171	Brett Tomko	.25
172	Todd Helton	1.00
173	Eric Young	.35
174	Bernie Williams	1.00
175	Jeff Fassero	.25
176	Ryan McGuire	.35
177	Darryl Kile	.25
178	*Kelvim Escobar*	.50
179	Dave Nilsson	.25
180	Geronimo Berroa	.25
181	Livan Hernandez	.35
182	*Tony Womack*	.40
183	Deion Sanders	.40
184	Jeff Kent	.25
185	Brian Hunter	.25
186	Jose Malave	.25
187	*Steve Woodard*	.50
188	Brad Radke	.50
189	Todd Dunwoody	.75
190	Joey Hamilton	.25
191	Denny Naegle	.25
192	Bobby Jones	.25
193	Tony Clark	1.50
194	*Jaret Wright*	3.00
195	Matt Stairs	.50
196	Francisco Cordova	.25
197	Justin Thompson	.25
198	Pokey Reese	.50
199	Garrett Stephenson	.25
200	Carl Everett	.25

1997 Select Artist's Proofs

Featuring a holographic foil background and special Artist's Proof logo on front, this parallel of the 150-card Series 1 Select was a random pack insert at an average pull rate of 1:71 for reds and 1:355 for blues.

	MT
Complete Set (150):	3000.
Common Red:	4.00
Common Blue:	10.00
Artist's Proof Stars: 20X	
(See 1997 Select #1-150 for checklist and base card values.)	

1997 Select Company

Select Company was intended to be a one-per-pack parallel found in '97 high series. The cards have the front background photo replaced with textured silver metallic foil and "Select Company" printed vertically at right-center. While all high-number (151-200) cards have the "Select Company" notation erroneously printed on front, only those cards with silver-foil backgrounds are true parallels.

	MT
Complete Set (200):	150.00
Common Player:	.50
Red Stars: 3X	
Blue Stars: 1.5X	
High-Series Stars: 1.5X	
(See 1997 Select for checklist and base card values.)	

1997 Select Registered Gold

This parallel insert set, like the regular issue, can be found with 100 red-foil and 50 blue-foil enhanced cards. They differ from the regular issue in the use of gold foil instead of silver on the right side of the front. Also, the inserts have "Registered Gold" printed vertically on the right side of the photo. Backs are identical to the regular issue. Red-foil Registered Gold cards are found on average of once every 11 packs; blue-foiled cards are a 1-in-47 pick.

	MT
Complete Set (150):	600.00
Common Red Gold:	1.00
Common Blue Gold:	2.00
(See 1997 Select #1-150 for checklist and base card values.)	

1997 Select Autographs

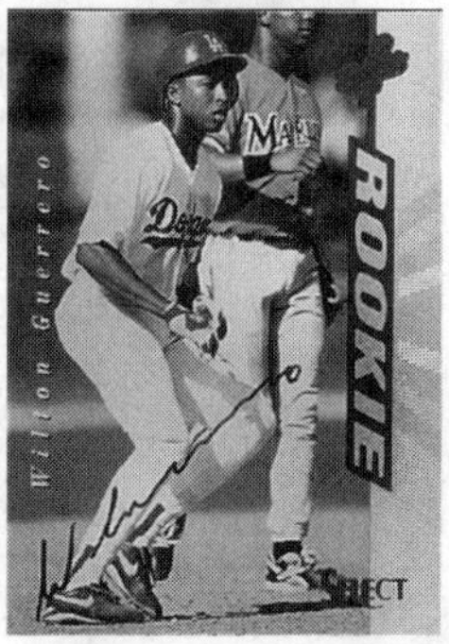

Four top candidates for the 1997 Rookie of the Year Award - Wilton Guerrero, Jose Guillen, Andruw Jones and Todd Walker - each signed a limited number of their Select Rookie cards. Jones signed 2,500 cards while each of the other players signed 3,000 each.

		MT
Complete Set (4):		50.00
Common Autograph:		8.00
AU1	Wilton Guerrero	8.00
AU2	Jose Guillen	10.00
AU3	Andruw Jones	30.00
AU4	Todd Walker	10.00

1997 Select Rookie Revolution

This 20-card insert highlights some of the top young stars in the game. Cards feature a silver micro-etched mylar design on front. Backs are sequentially numbered and contain a few words about the player. Odds of finding a card are 1:56 packs.

		MT
Complete Set (20):		50.00
Common Player:		1.00
1	Andruw Jones	7.50
2	Derek Jeter	12.50
3	Todd Hollandsworth	1.00
4	Edgar Renteria	2.50
5	Jason Kendall	4.00
6	Rey Ordonez	5.00
7	F.P. Santangelo	1.50
8	Jermaine Dye	1.50
9	Alex Ochoa	1.50
10	Vladimir Guerrero	10.00
11	Dmitri Young	1.00
12	Todd Walker	3.00
13	Scott Rolen	7.50
14	Nomar Garciaparra	12.50
15	Ruben Rivera	1.50
16	Darin Erstad	6.00
17	Todd Greene	1.50
18	Mariano Rivera	6.00
19	Trey Beamon	1.00
20	Karim Garcia	2.00

1997 Select Tools of the Trade

A 25-card insert featuring a double-front design salutes a top veteran player on one side and a promising youngster on the other. Cards feature a silver-foil card stock with gold-foil stamping. Cards were inserted 1:9 packs. A parallel to this set - Blue Mirror Tools of the Trade - features blue-foil stock with an insert ratio of 1:240 packs.

		MT
Complete Set (25):		125.00
Common Player:		2.00
Mirror Blues: 4X		
1	Ken Griffey Jr., Andruw Jones	15.00
2	Greg Maddux, Andy Pettitte	8.00
3	Cal Ripken Jr., Chipper Jones	10.00
4	Mike Piazza, Jason Kendall	8.00
5	Albert Belle, Karim Garcia	5.00
6	Mo Vaughn, Dmitri Young	3.00
7	Juan Gonzalez, Vladimir Guerrero	6.00
8	Tony Gwynn, Jermaine Dye	6.00
9	Barry Bonds, Alex Ochoa	4.00
10	Jeff Bagwell, Jason Giambi	4.00
11	Kenny Lofton, Darin Erstad	5.00
12	Gary Sheffield, Manny Ramirez	4.00
13	Tim Salmon, Todd Hollandsworth	2.00
14	Sammy Sosa, Ruben Rivera	8.00
15	Paul Molitor, George Arias	3.00
16	Jim Thome, Todd Walker	2.00
17	Wade Boggs, Scott Rolen	6.00
18	Ryne Sandberg, Chuck Knoblauch	4.00
19	Mark McGwire, Frank Thomas	15.00
20	Ivan Rodriguez, Charles Johnson	4.00
21	Brian Jordan, Trey Beamon	2.00
22	Roger Clemens, Troy Percival	5.00
23	John Smoltz, Mike Mussina	3.00
24	Alex Rodriguez, Rey Ordonez	9.00
25	Derek Jeter, Nomar Garciaparra	10.00

1998 Select Selected Samples

Intended as a 1:23 pack insert for a set which was never released due to Pinnacle's closing, Selected exists only as sample cards. Fronts have color action photos on bright metallic-foil backgrounds with a large "S". Backs have a smaller version of the front photo along with career highlights and a large overprinted "SAMPLE".

		MT
Complete Set (10):		45.00
Common Player:		4.00
1	Vladimir Guerrero	6.00
2	Nomar Garciaparra	8.00
3	Ben Grieve	6.00
4	Travis Lee	6.00
5	Jose Cruz Jr.	4.00
6	Alex Rodriguez	8.00
7	Todd Helton	4.00
8	Derek Jeter	8.00
9	Scott Rolen	6.00
10	Jaret Wright	5.00

1992 Sentry Robin Yount

At the Sept. 25, 1992, Brewers home game, the first 25,000 fans through the turnstile received a four-card set commemorating Robin Yount's 3,000th career hit. The 2-1/2" x 3-1/2" cards feature on front a gold-foil framed action photo set against a purple marbled border. Backs have a write-up about the career milestone hit and include the grocery store logo at bottom. The cards are unnumbered and were issued in a heavy paper wrapper.

		MT
Complete Set (4):		20.00
Common Card:		5.00
(1)	Hit #1, April 12, 1974 (Robin Yount)	5.00
(2)	Hit #1,000, Aug. 16, 1980 (Robin Yount)	5.00
(3)	Hit #2,000, Sept. 6, 1986 (Robin Yount)	5.00
(4)	Hit #3,000, Sept. 9, 1992 (Robin Yount)	5.00

1993 Sentry Brewers Memorable Moments

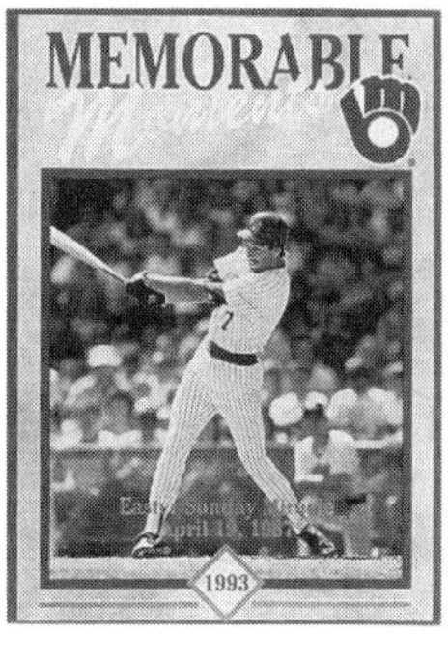

Fans at a special Brewer home game were given this set of team highlight cards. Fronts have a color photo of the highlight with a brief description and date printed in gold foil. The photo is framed in dark blue, which is also used for the border of the card. The territory between the photo and broder is printed in light blue and includes at top the Brewers logo and "Memorable Moments" headline. Backs have a description of the action shown on front, and the sponsor's logo. Cards are numbered according to player uniform number printed on back.

		MT
Complete Set (4):		8.00
Common Card:		1.00
4	Paul Molitor	3.00
7	Dale Sveum	1.00
19	Robin Yount	4.00
20	Juan Nieves	1.00

1993 Sentry Milwaukee Brewers

This set of a dozen coupon/card combos was distributed at Milwaukee area Sentry grocery stores during the 1993 season. A new card was issued every week or two between April 27 and Sept. 28. Each piece measures 12-1/2" x 7" and has a 5" x 7" Brewer player photo attached to six perforated coupons, each of which has a postage stamp-size Brewer photo at lower-right. Backs are blank. Cards #11 and 12 were never officially issued and have blank coupons.

		MT
Complete Set (12):		12.00
Common Player:		.60
1	Pat Listach	.60
2	Tom Brunansky	.60
3	B.J. Surhoff	1.00
4	Kevin Reimer	.50
5	Darryl Hamilton	.75
6	Greg Vaughn	.75
7	Robin Yount	5.00
8	Phil Garner	.60
9	Bill Spiers	.60
10	Dave Nilsson	.60
11	Bill Wegman	1.00
12	Cal Eldred	1.00

1994 Sentry Brewer Highlights

This eight-card set featuring highlights from Brewers history was issued in the team's 25th anniversary season. Sponsored by Sentry Foods, the cards were available on a one-per-week basis, attached to an 8-1/2" x 11" sheet of coupons, from May through August. (The last two cards were never officially issued due to the strike.) In standard 2-1/2" x 3-1/2", cards feature wide violet borders highlighted by green and gold geometric shapes. The team's 25th anniversary logo is at top-left, with the featured highlight at upper-right in gold. The player's name appears in white in a black ribbon beneath the color photo. Backs describe the highlight and are printed in blue and black. There is no sponsor's logo or card number.

Cards are checklisted here alphabetically.

		MT
Complete Set (8):		14.00
Common Player:		1.00
(1)	Hank Aaron (Final Home Run)	5.00
(2)	Rollie Fingers (Cy Young/MVP Season)	1.50
(3)	Pat Listach (Rookie of the Year)	1.00
(4)	Paul Molitor (39-game Hitting Streak)	3.00
(5)	Juan Nieves (No-hitter)	1.00
(6)	Don Sutton (3,000th Strikeout)	1.00
(7)	Robin Yount (3,000 Hit)	4.00
(8)	Triumphant Trio (Jim Gantner, Paul Molitor, Robin Yount)	2.50

1983 7-11 Slurpee Coins

This first production of player coins by 7-Eleven stores was distributed only in the Los Angeles area. The test promotion, which awarded a coin to every purchaser of a large Slurpee drink, must have proved successful, as it was expanded nationally in subsequent years. Six California Angels and six Los Angeles Dodgers are included in the full-color set, with Angels players in red backgrounds and the Dodgers in blue. The 1-3/4" diameter plastic coins feature both an action and a portrait photo of the player, which can be alternately seen by moving the coin slightly from side to side. The 12 coin backs are numbered and include brief statistics and the company logo.

		MT
Complete Set (12):		8.00
Common Player:		.50
1	Rod Carew	2.50
2	Steve Sax	.50
3	Fred Lynn	.50
4	Pedro Guerrero	.50
5	Reggie Jackson	2.50
6	Dusty Baker	.50
7	Doug DeCinces	.50
8	Fernando Valenzuela	.60
9	Tommy John	.60
10	Rick Monday	.50
11	Bobby Grich	.50
12	Greg Brock	.50

1984 7-11 Slurpee Coins Central Region

The 7-Eleven/Slurpee coins were distributed nationally in 1984 with 60 different players in three regional issues of 24 pieces each. Coins of Brett, Dawson, Murphy, Murray, Schmidt and Yount were common to all three regions. The 1-3/4" diameter plastic coins feature an action and a portrait photo on front which change when the viewing angle is altered. Statistics and coin numbers are found on the backs, along with the 7-Eleven logo.

		MT
Complete Set (24):		22.00
Common Player:		.50
1	Andre Dawson	1.00
2	Robin Yount	2.50
3	Dale Murphy	1.25
4	Mike Schmidt	3.00
5	George Brett	3.00
6	Eddie Murray	2.00
7	Bruce Sutter	.50
8	Cecil Cooper	.50
9	Willie McGee	.65
10	Mike Hargrove	.50
11	Kent Hrbek	.55
12	Carlton Fisk	1.00
13	Mario Soto	.50
14	Lonnie Smith	.50
15	Gary Carter	.90
16	Lou Whitaker	.50
17	Ron Kittle	.50
18	Paul Molitor	2.00
19	Ozzie Smith	2.00
20	Fergie Jenkins	1.00
21	Ted Simmons	.50
22	Pete Rose	3.00
23	LaMarr Hoyt	.50
24	Dan Quisenberry	.50

1984 7-11 Slurpee Coins Eastern Region

		MT
Complete Set (24):		25.00
Common Player:		.50
1	Andre Dawson	.90
2	Robin Yount	2.50
3	Dale Murphy	1.25
4	Mike Schmidt	3.00
5	George Brett	3.00
6	Eddie Murray	2.00
7	Dave Winfield	2.00
8	Tom Seaver	2.00
9	Mike Boddicker	.50
10	Wade Boggs	2.00
11	Bill Madlock	.50
12	Steve Carlton	1.25
13	Dave Stieb	.50
14	Cal Ripken, Jr.	6.00
15	Jim Rice	.50
16	Ron Guidry	.50
17	Darryl Strawberry	.75
18	Tony Pena	.50
19	John Denny	.50
20	Tim Raines	.60
21	Rick Dempsey	.50
22	Rich Gossage	.50
23	Gary Matthews	.50
24	Keith Hernandez	.50

1984 7-11 Slurpee Coins Western Region

		MT
Complete Set (24):		25.00
Common Player:		.50
1	Andre Dawson	.90
2	Robin Yount	2.50
3	Dale Murphy	1.25
4	Mike Schmidt	3.00
5	George Brett	3.00
6	Eddie Murray	2.00
7	Steve Garvey	1.00
8	Rod Carew	2.00
9	Fernando Valenzuela	.65
10	Bob Horner	.50
11	Buddy Bell	.50
12	Reggie Jackson	2.00
13	Nolan Ryan	5.00
14	Pedro Guerrero	.50
15	Atlee Hammaker	.50
16	Fred Lynn	.50
17	Terry Kennedy	.50
18	Dusty Baker	.50
19	Jose Cruz	.50
20	Steve Rogers	.50
21	Rickey Henderson	1.50
22	Steve Sax	.50
23	Dickie Thon	.50
24	Matt Young	.50

1984 7-11 Slurpee Jumbo Coin

Dale Murphy, the MVP of the National League in 1983 was featured on a jumbo-format (4-1/2" diameter) "3D" disc distributed by 7-11 stores in conjunction with their Slurpee fountain drink. Like the smaller Slurpee coins, the photos on the disc change as the viewing angle is changed.

		MT
	Dale Murphy	20.00

1985 7-11 Slurpee Coins Eastern Region

In 1985, the "Slurpee Disc" promotion was further expanded to a total of 94 full-color coins. The formats were very similar to the previous two years, but there were six different regional sets. Five of these regional series contain 16 coins, with a Detroit series totaling 14. The other five regions are: East, West, Great Lakes, Central and Southeast. The coins are again 1-1/4" in diameter, printed on plastic with double-image photos. All coins are numbered. No player appears in all regions. although several are in two or more.

		MT
Complete Set (16):		18.00
Common Player:		.50
1	Eddie Murray	1.50
2	George Brett	2.00
3	Steve Carlton	1.50
4	Jim Rice	.50
5	Dave Winfield	1.50
6	Mike Boddicker	.50
7	Wade Boggs	1.50
8	Dwight Evans	.50
9	Dwight Gooden	.75
10	Keith Hernandez	.50
11	Bill Madlock	.50
12	Don Mattingly	3.00
13	Dave Righetti	.50
14	Cal Ripken, Jr.	5.00
15	Juan Samuel	.50
16	Mike Schmidt	2.50

1985 7-11 Slurpee Coins Great Lakes Region

		MT
Complete Set (16):		15.00
Common Player:		.50
1	Willie Hernandez	.50
2	George Brett	2.00
3	Dave Winfield	1.50
4	Eddie Murray	1.25
5	Bruce Sutter	.50
6	Harold Baines	.50
7	Bert Blyleven	.50
8	Leon Durham	.50
9	Chet Lemon	.50
10	Pete Rose	2.50
11	Ryne Sandberg	2.00
12	Tom Seaver	2.00
13	Mario Soto	.50
14	Rick Sutcliffe	.50
15	Alan Trammell	.60
16	Robin Yount	2.00

1985 7-11 Slurpee Coins Southeastern Region

		MT
Complete Set (16):		15.00
Common Player:		.50
1	Dale Murphy	1.25
2	Steve Carlton	1.50
3	Nolan Ryan	4.00
4	Bruce Sutter	.50
5	Dave Winfield	1.50
6	Steve Bedrosian	.50
7	Andre Dawson	.90
8	Kirk Gibson	.50
9	Fred Lynn	.50
10	Gary Matthews	.50
11	Phil Niekro	1.00
12	Tim Raines	.60
13	Darryl Strawberry	.75
14	Dave Stieb	.50
15	Willie Upshaw	.50
16	Lou Whitaker	.50

1985 7-11 Slurpee Coins Southwest/ Central Region

		MT
Complete Set (16):		16.00
Common Player:		.50
1	Nolan Ryan	4.00
2	George Brett	2.50
3	Dave Winfield	1.50
4	Mike Schmidt	2.50
5	Bruce Sutter	.50
6	Joaquin Andujar	.50
7	Willie Hernandez	.50
8	Wade Boggs	1.50
9	Gary Carter	.90
10	Jose Cruz	.50
11	Kent Hrbek	.60
12	Reggie Jackson	2.00
13	Lance Parrish	.50
14	Terry Puhl	.50
15	Dan Quisenberry	.50
16	Ozzie Smith	1.50

1985 7-11 Slurpee Coins Tigers

		MT
Complete Set (14):		10.00
Common Player:		.60
1	Sparky Anderson	1.00
2	Darrell Evans	.60
3	Kirk Gibson	.60
4	Willie Hernandez	.60
5	Larry Herndon	.60
6	Chet Lemon	.60
7	Aurelio Lopez	.60
8	Jack Morris	.75
9	Lance Parrish	.75
10	Dan Petry	.60
11	Dave Rozema	.60
12	Alan Trammell	1.50
13	Lou Whitaker	.90
14	Milt Wilcox	.60

1985 7-11 Slurpee Coins Western Region

		MT
Complete Set (16):		15.00
Common Player:		.50
1	Mike Schmidt	3.00
2	Jim Rice	.50
3	Dale Murphy	1.25
4	Eddie Murray	1.50
5	Dave Winfield	1.50
6	Rod Carew	1.50
7	Alvin Davis	.50
8	Steve Garvey	1.00
9	Rich Gossage	.50
10	Pedro Guerrero	.50
11	Tony Gwynn	2.50
12	Rickey Henderson	1.00
13	Reggie Jackson	1.50
14	Jeff Leonard	.50
15	Alejandro Pena	.50
16	Fernando Valenzuela	.60

1985 7-11 Slurpee Jumbo Coins

World Series MVP Alan Trammell and Yankees slugger Dave Winfield were featured on jumbo-format (4-1/2" diameter) "3D" discs distributed by 7-11 stores in conjunction with their Slurpee fountain drink. Like the smaller Slurpee coins, the photos on the disc change as the viewing angle is changed.

		MT
Complete Set (2):		15.00
(1)	Alan Trammell	6.00
(2)	Dave Winfield	9.00

1985 7-11 Slurpee Test Coins

These 3-D "Magic Motion" coins are identical to the regional issues in all aspects except size. These test coins are 2-1/4" diameter, an inch bigger than the issued versions.

		MT
Complete Set (3):		4.00
Common Player:		.50
4	Mike Schmidt	2.50
5	Bruce Sutter	.50
5	Dave Winfield	1.50

1985 7-11 Twins

The Minnesota Twins, in co-operation with 7-Eleven and the Fire Marshall's Association, issued this set of 13 baseball fire safety cards. The card fronts feature full-color pictures of Twins players. A fire safety tip and short player history appear on the back. The cards were given out at all 7-Eleven stores in the state and at the Twins June 3 baseball game. Each fan received one baseball card with a poster which told how to collect the other cards in the set. Twelve cards feature players and the 13th card has an artist's rendering of Twins players on the front and a checklist of the set on the back. A group of 50,000 cards was distributed to fifth graders throughout the state by the fire departments.

		MT
Complete Set (13):		10.00
Common Player:		.25
1	Kirby Puckett	8.00
2	Frank Viola	.25
3	Mickey Hatcher	.25
4	Kent Hrbek	.75
5	John Butcher	.25
6	Roy Smalley	.25
7	Tom Brunansky	.25
8	Ron Davis	.25
9	Gary Gaetti	.50
10	Tim Teufel	.25
11	Mike Smithson	.25
12	Tim Laudner	.25
---	Checklist	.10

1986 7-11 Slurpee Coins Eastern Region

This marked the fourth year of production for these coins, issued with the purchase of a large Slurpee drink at 7-Eleven stores. Once again, there are different regional issues, with 16 coins issued for four different regions in 1986. The 1-3/4" diameter plastic coins each feature three different players' pictures, which can be seen alternately by tilting from side to side. Eight of the coins are the same in every region. Each coin is numbered on the back, along with brief player information.

		MT
Complete Set (16):		10.00
Common Coin:		.50
1	Dwight Gooden	.75
2	Batting Champs (Wade Boggs, George Brett, Pete Rose)	2.00
3	MVP's (Keith Hernandez, Don Mattingly, Cal Ripken, Jr.)	2.50
4	Slugging Champs (Harold Baines, Pedro Guerrero, Dave Parker)	.50
5	Home Run Champs (Dale Murphy, Jim Rice, Mike Schmidt)	2.00
6	Cy Young Winners (Ron Guidry, Bret Saberhagen, Fernando Valenzuela)	.50
7	Bullpen Aces (Rich Gossage, Dan Quisenberry, Bruce Sutter)	.50
8	Strikeout Kings (Steve Carlton, Nolan Ryan, Tom Seaver)	2.50
9	1985 Rookies (Steve Lyons, Rick Schu, Larry Sheets)	.50
10	Bullpen Aces (Jeff Reardon, Dave Righetti, Bob Stanley)	.50
11	Power Hitters (George Bell, Darryl Strawberry, Dave Winfield)	.75
12	Base Stealers (Rickey Henderson, Tim Raines, Juan Samuel)	.75
13	Home Run Hitters (Andre Dawson, Dwight Evans, Eddie Murray)	.75
14	Ace Pitchers (Mike Boddicker, Ron Darling, Dave Stieb)	.50
15	1985 Bullpen Rookies (Tim Burke, Brian Fisher, Roger McDowell)	.50
16	Sluggers (Jesse Barfield, Gary Carter, Fred Lynn)	.50

1986 7-11 Slurpee Coins Mideastern Region

		MT
Complete Set (16):		11.00
Common Coin:		.50
1	Dwight Gooden	.75
2	Batting Champs (Wade Boggs, George Brett, Pete Rose)	2.00
3	MVP's (Keith Hernandez, Don Mattingly, Cal Ripken)	2.50
4	Slugging Champs (Harold Baines, Pedro Guerrero, Dave Parker)	.50
5	Home Run Champs (Dale Murphy, Jim Rice, Mike Schmidt)	2.00
6	Cy Young Winners (Ron Guidry, Bret Saberhagen, Fernando Valenzuela)	.50
7	Bullpen Aces (Rich Gossage, Dan Quisenberry, Bruce Sutter)	.50
8	Strikeout Kings (Steve Carlton, Nolan Ryan, Tom Seaver)	2.50
9	MVP's (Willie Hernandez, Ryne Sandberg, Robin Yount)	2.00
10	Ace Pitchers (Bert Blyleven, Jack Morris, Rick Sutcliffe)	.50
11	Bullpen Aces (Rollie Fingers, Bob James, Lee Smith)	.50
12	All-Star Catchers (Carlton Fisk, Lance Parrish, Tony Pena)	.50
13	1985 Rookies (Shawon Dunston, Ozzie Guillen, Ernest Riles)	.50
14	Star Outfielders (Brett Butler, Chet Lemon, Willie Wilson)	.50
15	Home Run Hitters (Tom Brunansky, Cecil Cooper, Darrell Evans)	.50
16	Big Hitters (Kirk Gibson, Paul Molitor, Greg Walker)	.50

1986 7-11 Slurpee Coins Midwestern Region

		MT
Complete Set (16)		10.00
Common Coin:		.50
1	Dwight Gooden	.75
2	Batting Champs (Wade Boggs, George Brett, Pete Rose)	2.00
3	MVP's (Keith Hernandez, Don Mattingly, Cal Ripken, Jr.)	2.50
4	Slugging Champs (Harold Baines, Pedro Guerrero, Dave Parker)	.50
5	Home Run Champs (Dale Murphy, Jim Rice, Mike Schmidt)	2.00
6	Cy Young Winners (Ron Guidry, Bret Saberhagen, Fernando Valenzuela)	.50
7	Bullpen Aces (Rich Gossage, Dan Quisenberry, Bruce Sutter)	.50
8	Strikeout Kings (Steve Carlton, Nolan Ryan, Tom Seaver)	2.50
9	1985 Rookies (Vince Coleman, Glenn Davis, Oddibe McDowell)	.50
10	Gold Glovers (Buddy Bell, Ozzie Smith, Lou Whitaker)	.50
11	Ace Pitchers (Mike Scott, Mario Soto, John Tudor)	.50
12	Bullpen Aces (Jeff Lahti, Ted Power, Dave Smith)	.50
13	Big Hitters (Jack Clark, Jose Cruz, Bob Horner)	.50

14	Star Second Basemen (Bill Doran, Tommy Herr, Ron Oester)	.50
15	1985 Rookie Pitchers (Tom Browning, Joe Hesketh, Todd Worrell)	.50
16	Top Switch-Hitters (Willie McGee, Jerry Mumphrey, Pete Rose)	.75

1986 7-11 Slurpee Coins Western Region

		MT
Complete Set (16):		11.00
Common Coin:		.50
1	Dwight Gooden	.75
2	Batting Champs (Wade Boggs, George Brett, Pete Rose)	2.00
3	MVP's (Keith Hernandez, Don Mattingly, Cal Ripken, Jr.)	2.50
4	Slugging Champs (Harold Baines, Pedro Guerrero, Dave Parker)	.50
5	Home Run Champs (Dale Murphy, Jim Rice, Mike Schmidt)	2.00
6	Cy Young Winners (Ron Guidry, Bret Saberhagen, Fernando Valenzuela)	.50
7	Bullpen Aces (Rich Gossage, Dan Quisenberry, Bruce Sutter)	.50
8	Strikeout Kings (Steve Carlton, Nolan Ryan, Tom Seaver)	2.50
9	Home Run Champs (Reggie Jackson, Dave Kingman, Gorman Thomas)	1.00
10	Batting Champs (Rod Carew, Tony Gwynn, Carney Lansford)	1.50
11	Sluggers (Phil Bradley, Mike Marshall, Graig Nettles)	.50
12	Ace Pitchers (Andy Hawkins, Orel Hershiser, Mike Witt)	.50
13	1985 Rookies (Chris Brown, Ivan Calderon, Mariano Duncan)	.50
14	Big Hitters (Steve Garvey, Bill Madlock, Jim Presley)	.50
15	Bullpen Aces (Jay Howell, Donnie Moore, Ed Nunez)	.50
16	1985 Bullpen Rookies (Karl Best, Stewart Cliburn, Steve Ontiveros)	.50

1986 7-11 Slurpee Jumbo Coin

Three of the game's top stars were featured on a jumbo-format (4-1/2" diameter) "3D" disc distributed by 7-11 stores in conjunction with their Slurpee fountain drink. Like the smaller Slurpee coins, the photos on the disc change as the viewing angle is changed.

	MT
Wade Boggs, George Brett, Pete Rose	10.00

1987 7-11 Slurpee Coins Eastern Region

Continuing with a tradition started in 1983, 7-Eleven stores offered a free "Super Star Sports Coin" with the purchase of a Slurpee drink. Five different regional sets of Slurpee coins were issued for 1987, a total of 75 coins. Each coin measures 1-3/4" in diameter and features a multiple image effect which allows three different pictures to be seen, depending on how the coin is tilted. The coin reverses contain career records and personal player information.

		MT
Complete Set (15):		10.00
Common Player:		.50
1	Gary Carter	.75
2	Don Baylor	.50
3	Rickey Henderson	1.00
4	Lenny Dykstra	.50
5	Wade Boggs	1.00
6	Mike Pagliarulo	.50
7	Dwight Gooden	.60
8	Roger Clemens	1.50
9	Dave Righetti	.50
10	Keith Hernandez	.50
11	Pat Dodson	.50
12	Don Mattingly	2.00
13	Darryl Strawberry	.60
14	Jim Rice	.50
15	Dave Winfield	1.00

1987 7-11 Slurpee Coins Great Lakes Region

		MT
Complete Set (16):		9.00
Common Player:		.50
1	Harold Baines	.50
2	Jody Davis	.50
3	John Cangelosi	.50
4	Shawon Dunston	.50
5	Dave Cochrane	.50
6	Leon Durham	.50
7	Carlton Fisk	1.00
8	Dennis Eckersley	.75
9	Ozzie Guillen	.50
10	Gary Matthews	.50
11	Ron Karkovice	.50
12	Keith Moreland	.50
13	Bobby Thigpen	.50
14	Ryne Sandberg	2.00
15	Greg Walker	.50
16	Lee Smith	.50

1987 7-11 Slurpee Coins Mideastern Region

		MT
Complete Set (16):		14.00
Common Player:		.50
1	Gary Carter	.65
2	Marty Barrett	.50
3	Jody Davis	.50
4	Don Aase	.50
5	Lenny Dykstra	.50
6	Wade Boggs	1.50
7	Keith Moreland	.50
8	Mike Boddicker	.50
9	Dwight Gooden	.60
10	Roger Clemens	2.00
11	Ryne Sandberg	2.00
12	Eddie Murray	1.00
13	Keith Hernandez	.50
14	Jim Rice	.50
15	Lee Smith	.50
16	Cal Ripken, Jr.	5.00

1987 7-11 Slurpee Tigers Coins

		MT
Complete Set (12):		6.50
Common Player:		.50
1	Darnell Coles	.50
2	Darrell Evans	.50
3	Kirk Gibson	.60
4	Willie Hernandez	.50
5	Larry Herndon	.50
6	Chet Lemon	.50
7	Dwight Lowry	.50
8	Jack Morris	.60
9	Dan Petry	.50
10	Frank Tanana	.50
11	Alan Trammell	1.00
12	Lou Whitaker	.65

1987 7-11 Slurpee Coins Western Region

		MT
Complete Set (16):		8.00
Common Player:		.50
1	Doug DeCinces	.50
2	Mariano Duncan	.50
3	Wally Joyner	.65
4	Pedro Guerrero	.50
5	Kirk McCaskill	.50
6	Orel Hershiser	.65
7	Gary Pettis	.50
8	Mike Marshall	.50
9	Dick Schofield	.50
10	Steve Sax	.50
11	Don Sutton	.75
12	Mike Scioscia	.50
13	Devon White	.60
14	Franklin Stubbs	.50
15	Mike Witt	.50
16	Fernando Valenzuela	.65

1991 7-11 Slurpee Coins Atlantic Region

After a three-year hiatus, "3-D" magic-motion coins returned to 7-11 stores in the form of regional sets produced by Score under the name Superstar Sports Coins and given away with the purchase of Slurpee fountain drinks. In the familiar 1-3/4" diameter, the discs have alternating portrait and action images on the front with the player name at top, the team at bottom, the uniform number at left and position at right. Each regional set has a different border color. Backs have 7-11 and Score logos along with career stats and a short career summary. The 120 coins in the sets feature 81 different major leaguers.

		MT
Complete Set (15):		11.00
Common Player:		.25
1	Glenn Davis	.25
2	Dwight Evans	.25
3	Leo Gomez	.25
4	Ken Griffey Jr.	3.00
5	Rickey Henderson	.75
6	Jose Canseco	.75
7	Dave Justice	.50
8	Ben McDonald	.25
9	Randy Milligan	.25
10	Gregg Olson	.25
11	Kirby Puckett	1.50
12	Bill Ripken	.25
13	Cal Ripken Jr.	2.50
14	Nolan Ryan	2.50
15	David Segui	.25

1991 7-11 Slurpee Coins Florida Region

		MT
Complete Set (15):		13.00
Common Player:		.25
1	Barry Bonds	2.00
2	George Brett	2.00
3	Roger Clemens	2.00
4	Glenn Davis	.25
5	Alex Fernandez	.35
6	Cecil Fielder	.25
7	Ken Griffey Jr.	3.00
8	Dwight Gooden	.35
9	Dave Justice	.50
10	Barry Larkin	.35
11	Ramon Martinez	.50
12	Jose Offerman	.25
13	Kirby Puckett	2.00
14	Nolan Ryan	2.50
15	Terry Schumpert	.25

1991 7-11 Slurpee Coins Metro Northeast Region

		MT
Complete Set (15):		9.00
Common Player:		.25
1	Wade Boggs	1.00
2	Barry Bonds	1.50
3	Roger Clemens	1.50
4	Len Dykstra	.25
5	Dwight Gooden	.35
6	Ken Griffey Jr.	3.00
7	Rickey Henderson	.75
8	Gregg Jefferies	.35
9	Roberto Kelly	.25
10	Kevin Maas	.25
11	Don Mattingly	2.00
12	Mickey Morandini	.25
13	Dale Murphy	.40
14	Darryl Strawberry	.35
15	Frank Viola	.25

1991 7-11 Slurpee Coins Midwest

		MT
Complete Set (15):		10.00
Common Player:		.25
1	George Brett	1.50
2	Andre Dawson	.40
3	Cecil Fielder	.40
4	Carlton Fisk	.75
5	Travis Fryman	.25
6	Mark Grace	.75
7	Ken Griffey Jr.	3.00
8	Ozzie Guillen	.25
9	Alex Fernandez	.25
10	Ray Lankford	.25
11	Ryne Sandberg	1.00
12	Ozzie Smith	1.00
13	Bobby Thigpen	.25
14	Frank Thomas	2.00
15	Alan Trammell	.40

1991 7-11 Slurpee Coins Northern California Region

		MT
Complete Set (15):		10.00
Common Player:		.25
1	John Burkett	.25
2	Jose Canseco	.75
3	Will Clark	.65
4	Steve Decker	.25
5	Dennis Eckersley	.25
6	Ken Griffey Jr.	3.00
7	Rickey Henderson	.75
8	Nolan Ryan	2.50
9	Mark McGwire	3.00
10	Kevin Mitchell	.25
11	Terry Steinbach	.25
12	Dave Stewart	.25
13	Todd Van Poppel	.25
14	Bob Welch	.25
15	Matt Williams	.40

1991 7-11 Slurpee Coins Northwest Region

		MT
Complete Set (15):		9.00
Common Player:		.25
1	George Brett	.75
2	Jose Canseco	.75
3	Alvin Davis	.25
4	Ken Griffey Jr., Ken Griffey Sr.	1.50
5	Ken Griffey Jr.	3.00
6	Erik Hanson	.25
7	Rickey Henderson	.75
8	Ryne Sandberg	.75
9	Randy Johnson	.35
10	Dave Justice	.60
11	Edgar Martinez	.25
12	Tino Martinez	.25
13	Harold Reynolds	.25
14	Nolan Ryan	2.50
15	Mike Schooler	.25

1991 7-11 Slurpee Coins Southern California Region

		MT
Complete Set (15):		10.00
Common Player:		.25
1	Jim Abbott	.30
2	Jose Canseco	.75
3	Ken Griffey Jr.	3.00
4	Tony Gwynn	2.00
5	Orel Hershiser	.25
6	Eric Davis	.25
7	Wally Joyner	.30
8	Ramon Martinez	.35
9	Fred McGriff	.50
10	Eddie Murray	.90
11	Jose Offerman	.25
12	Nolan Ryan	2.50
13	Benito Santiago	.25
14	Darryl Strawberry	.30
15	Fernando Valenzuela	.30

1991 7-11 Slurpee Coins Texas Region

		MT
Complete Set (15):		11.00
Common Player:		.25
1	Craig Biggio	.45
2	Barry Bonds	1.50
3	Jose Canseco	.75
4	Roger Clemens	1.25
5	Glenn Davis	.25
6	Julio Franco	.25
7	Juan Gonzalez	1.00
8	Ken Griffey Jr.	3.00
9	Mike Scott	.25
10	Rafael Palmeiro	.65
11	Nolan Ryan	2.50
12	Ryne Sandberg	.75
13	Ruben Sierra	.25
14	Todd Van Poppel	.25
15	Bobby Witt	.25

1992 7-11 Slurpee Superstar Action Coins

Score baseball 3-D coins returned to 7-11 stores on a very limited basis in 1992. A 26-piece set of the plastic coins (one for each major league team) was produced by Score in the familiar 1-3/4" diameter format. The coins feature a maroon border on which is printed in white the player's name, team, position and uniform number. At center is a 1-1/4" circle with "flasher" portrait and action photos of the player. Backs have a black border with the player name in yellow at the top, a few career stats, 7-11 and Score logos and a coin number in a pale yellow center circle. At bottom in green is "Superstar Action Coin".

		MT
Complete Set (26):		25.00
Common Player:		.50
1	Dwight Gooden	.65
2	Don Mattingly	2.00
3	Roger Clemens	1.00
4	Ivan Calderon	.50
5	Roberto Alomar	1.50
6	Sandy Alomar, Jr.	.65
7	Andy Van Slyke	.50
8	Lenny Dykstra	.50
9	Cal Ripken, Jr.	2.50
10	Dave Justice	.75
11	Nolan Ryan	2.50
12	Craig Biggio	.65
13	Barry Larkin	.65
14	Ozzie Smith	1.00
15	Ryne Sandberg	1.50
16	Frank Thomas	2.50
17	Robin Yount	1.00
18	Kirby Puckett	1.50
19	Cecil Fielder	.60
20	Will Clark	.75
21	Jose Canseco	.65
22	Jim Abbott	.65
23	Tony Gwynn	2.00
24	Darryl Strawberry	.65
25	George Brett	1.50
26	Ken Griffey, Jr.	3.00

1996 7-11/Classic Phone Cards

Taking advantage of a short-lived hobby craze, Classic produced this line of baseball player phone cards which were sold through 7-11 convenience stores. The $6 cards offered 15 minutes of long-distance phone service. Cards are printed in the standard 2-1/8" x 3-3/8" round-cornered format on thick plastic. Fronts have action photos with team, 7-11 and Classic logos, along with a facsimile autograph, player name vertically at left and a card number. Backs are in black-and-white with directions for the card's use. Cards were issued four per month, June-August.

		MT
Complete Set (12):		40.00
Common Player:		2.00
1	Cal Ripken Jr.	5.00
2	Frank Thomas	4.00
3	Hideo Nomo	4.00
4	Jeff Conine	2.00
5	Ken Griffey Jr.	6.00
6	Greg Maddux	4.00
7	Wade Boggs	3.00
8	Ivan Rodriguez	4.00
9	Barry Bonds	4.00
10	Kirby Puckett	3.50
11	Mo Vaughn	2.00
12	Tony Gwynn	4.00

1997 7-11/Classic Phone Cards

Taking advantage of a short-lived hobby craze, 7-11 stores produced this line of baseball player phone cards. Cards are printed in the standard 2-1/8" x 3-3/8" round-cornered format on thick plastic. Fronts have action photos with team and 7-11 logos, along with player name at right. A strip at bottom has the card number. Backs are in black-and-white with directions for the card's use. Cards were sold during June-July.

		MT
Complete Set (12):		75.00
Common Player:		3.00
1	Cal Ripken Jr.	10.00
2	Ken Griffey Jr.	12.50
3	Mike Piazza	7.50
4	Derek Jeter	6.00
5	Frank Thomas	9.00
6	Alex Rodriguez	10.00
7	Mark McGwire	12.50
8	Tony Gwynn	7.50
9	Chipper Jones	7.50
10	Gary Sheffield	3.00
11	Barry Bonds	4.50
12	Juan Gonzalez	6.00

1997 7-11 Colorado Rockies

Two of the Rockies most popular players are featured in this set of motionvision cards sold in the Denver area with 12-packs of Coca-Cola products at 7-Eleven stores. The 4" x 3" horizontal cards have excellent "moving" images of the players batting and sliding. The team and Coke logos are at top and the player's name in purple at bottom. Cards are borderless and have rounded corners. Backs have a color 7-Eleven logo and information about the purchase of the cards. The manufacturer's name, World Holographics of Los Angeles, is at bottom.

		MT
Complete Set (4):		8.00
Common Player:		2.00
(1)	Dante Bichette (batting)	2.00
(2)	Dante Bichette (sliding)	2.00
(3)	Ellis Burks (batting)	2.00
(4)	Ellis Burks (sliding)	2.00

1981 7-Up

These 5-1/2" x 8-1/2" color photocards may have been part of a series. Fronts have a borderless photo, a facsimile autograph and, at lower-right, a 7-Up logo and slogan. Back is printed in black, red and green on white and features a career summary through the 1980 season, and a large version of the soda logo.

		MT
(1)	George Brett	15.00
(2)	Mike Schmidt	12.00

1984 7-Up Cubs

The Chicago Cubs and 7-Up issued this 28-card set featuring full-color game-action photos on a 2-1/4" x 3-1/2" borderless front. The backs have the player's stats and personal information. This was the third consecutive year the Cubs issued this type of set as a giveaway at a "Baseball Card Day" promotional game.

		MT
Complete Set (28):		12.00
Common Player:		.25
1	Larry Bowa	.25
6	Keith Moreland	.25
7	Jody Davis	.25
10	Leon Durham	.25
11	Ron Cey	.35
15	Ron Hassey	.25
18	Richie Hebner	.25
19	Dave Owen	.25
20	Bob Dernier	.25
21	Jay Johnstone	.25
23	Ryne Sandberg	4.00
24	Scott Sanderson	.25
25	Gary Woods	.25
27	Thad Bosley	.25
28	Henry Cotto	.25
34	Steve Trout	.25
36	Gary Matthews	.25
39	George Frazier	.25
40	Rick Sutcliffe	.25
41	Warren Brusstar	.25
42	Rich Bordi	.25
43	Dennis Eckersley	1.00
44	Dick Ruthven	.25
46	Lee Smith	.75
47	Rick Reuschel	.25
49	Tim Stoddard	.25
---	Jim Frey	.25
---	Cubs Coaches (Ruben Amaro, Billy Connors, Johnny Oates, John Vukovich, Don Zimmer)	.25

1985 7-Up Cubs

This was the second year a Chicago Cubs card set was released with 7-Up as the sponsor. The set has 28 unnumbered cards in the standard 2-1/2" x 3-1/2" size. They were distributed to fans attending the Cubs game on August 14 at Wrigley Field. They feature full-color game-action photos of the players. Card backs contain the player's professional stats.

		MT
Complete Set (28):		8.00
Common Player:		.25
1	Larry Bowa	.25
6	Keith Moreland	.25
7	Jody Davis	.25
10	Leon Durham	.25
11	Ron Cey	.35
15	Davey Lopes	.25
16	Steve Lake	.25
18	Richie Hebner	.25
20	Bob Dernier	.25
21	Scott Sanderson	.25
22	Billy Hatcher	.25
23	Ryne Sandberg	3.00
24	Brian Dayett	.25
25	Gary Woods	.25
27	Thad Bosley	.25
28	Chris Speier	.25
31	Ray Fontenot	.25
34	Steve Trout	.25
36	Gary Matthews	.25
39	George Frazier	.25
40	Rick Sutcliffe	.25
41	Warren Brusstar	.25
42	Lary Sorensen	.25
43	Dennis Eckersley	.75
44	Dick Ruthven	.25
46	Lee Smith	.75
---	Jim Frey	.25
---	Coaching Staff (Ruben Amaro, Billy Connors, Johnny Oates, John Vukovich, Don Zimmer)	.25

1992 Silver Star Hologram Promo Cards

To promote its forthcoming 3-D hologram cards, Silver Star issued these coventionally printed promo cards, though the line-up on the promo cards differs from the list of holographic cards actually issued. The promos are in 2-1/2" x 3-1/2" format with color player photos and black borders on front. Backs have holographic foil printing on a black background. The unnumbered cards are checklisted here in alphabetical order.

		MT
Complete Set (6):		6.00
Common Player:		.50
(1)	Barry Bonds	.75
(2)	Will Clark	.50
(3)	Roger Clemens	.50
(4)	Ken Griffey Jr.	2.00
(5)	Darryl Strawberry	.50
(6)	Frank Thomas	1.25

1992 Silver Star Holograms

This collectors' issue consists of seven player hologram cards and accompanying "Authentickets" plus a hologram header card depicting the Gold Glove Award. The Gold Glove card has a black back on which is printed a serial number in gold foil. The player holograms are standard 2-1/2" x 3-1/2". The player's name is featured in the upper-left corner, with "Silver Star Holograms" in the upper-right. Some holograms have a card title (Non-Stop shortstop, Pride of Texas, etc.) in the lower-right corner. Backs are printed in team colors and feature a player portrait photo and some 1991 stats and season highlights. The player's position and uniform number are in the upper corners. The 5-3/8" x 2-1/16" Authenticket sold with each hologram contains a serial number, player photo, 1991 season highlights and a black panel at left with "Silver Star" in silver prismatic foil. This piece is blank-backed. The checklist is presented here by uniform number. Values given are for player hologram/Authenticket combinations. Holograms alone are worth about half the values shown; unaccompanied Authentickets have little collector value.

		MT
Complete Set (8):		10.00
Common Player:		1.00
8	Cal Ripken, Jr.	2.50
21	Roger Clemens	1.00
22	Will Clark	1.00
23	Dave Justice	1.00
24	Rickey Henderson	1.00
34	Nolan Ryan	2.00
44	Darryl Strawberry	1.00
----	Rawlings Gold Glove Award	1.00

Player names in *Italic* type indicate a rookie card.

1992 Silver Star Dodger Stadium Hologram

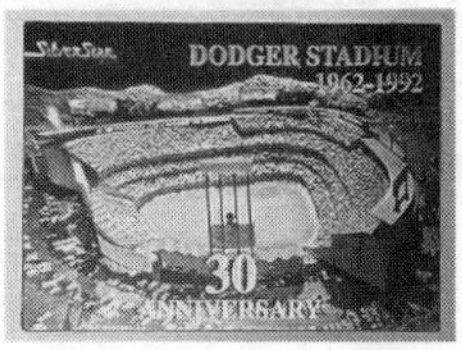

In honor of the 30th anniversary of Dodger Stadium, part of the limited edition of 100,000 of these cards was given to fans attending the May 2, 1992 game there. The 3-1/2" x 2-1/2" card has a holographic view of the stadium on front and a conventionally printed color photo on back.

	MT
Dodger Stadium hologram	3.00

1995 Skin Bracer

This three-card set was included in several packagings of Mennen skin care products for men. Three sepia-toned 3-1/2" x 2-1/2" cards feature great moments in post-season play. Fronts are trimmed in gold ink and feature the player's name in a green box. Backs are printed in black, green and gold and describe the highlight. Logos of the sponsor and Major League Baseball Players Alumni Association are also included on back. A related offer allowed collectors to purchase autographed 8" x 10" photos of the events for $7.99 each via a coupon.

		MT
Complete Set (3):		9.00
Common Player:		3.00
(1)	The Perfect Game (Don Larsen)	3.00
(2)	The Series Ender (Bill Mazeroski)	3.00
(3)	The Shot Heard 'Round the World (Bobby Thomson)	3.00

1995 SkyBox E-Motion Promo

To introduce its new super-premium baseball card line, SkyBox debuted a Cal Ripken promo card at the 1995 National Sports Collectors Convention. The card is virtually identical to Ripken's card in the regular issue, except for diagonal overprinting on each side which reads, "Promotional Sample".

		MT
8	Cal Ripken Jr. (Class)	4.00

1995 SkyBox E-Motion

This is a super-premium debut issue from the newly merged Fleer/SkyBox company. Printed on double-thick cardboard, card fronts have borderless photos marred by the presence of four gold-foil "viewfinder" corner marks. The player's last name and team are printed in gold foil near the bottom. On each card there is a large silver-foil word printed in block letters; either a nickname or an emotion or attribute associated with the player. Backs have two more player photos, 1994 and career stats and a few biographical bits. Eight-cards packs were issued with a suggested retail price of $4.99.

		MT
Complete Set (200):		40.00
Common Player:		.15
Wax Box:		80.00
1	Brady Anderson	.25
2	Kevin Brown	.20
3	Curtis Goodwin	.15
4	Jeffrey Hammonds	.15
5	Ben McDonald	.15
6	Mike Mussina	.75
7	Rafael Palmeiro	.25
8	Cal Ripken Jr.	3.00
9	Jose Canseco	.40
10	Roger Clemens	1.50
11	Vaughn Eshelman	.15
12	Mike Greenwell	.15
13	Erik Hanson	.15
14	Tim Naehring	.15
15	Aaron Sele	.15
16	John Valentin	.15
17	Mo Vaughn	.75
18	Chili Davis	.15
19	Gary DiSarcina	.15
20	Chuck Finley	.15
21	Tim Salmon	.30
22	Lee Smith	.15
23	J.T. Snow	.15
24	Jim Abbott	.15
25	Jason Bere	.15
26	Ray Durham	.15
27	Ozzie Guillen	.15
28	Tim Raines	.15
29	Frank Thomas	1.50
30	Robin Ventura	.25
31	Carlos Baerga	.15
32	Albert Belle	1.00
33	Orel Hershiser	.15
34	Kenny Lofton	.75
35	Dennis Martinez	.15
36	Eddie Murray	.60
37	Manny Ramirez	1.00
38	Julian Tavarez	.15
39	Jim Thome	.50
40	Dave Winfield	.30
41	Chad Curtis	.15
42	Cecil Fielder	.15
43	Travis Fryman	.15
44	Kirk Gibson	.15
45	*Bob Higginson*	1.50
46	Alan Trammell	.15
47	Lou Whitaker	.15
48	Kevin Appier	.15
49	Gary Gaetti	.15
50	Jeff Montgomery	.15
51	Jon Nunnally	.15
52	Ricky Bones	.15
53	Cal Eldred	.15
54	Joe Oliver	.15
55	Kevin Seitzer	.15
56	Marty Cordova	.15
57	Chuck Knoblauch	.25
58	Kirby Puckett	1.50
59	Wade Boggs	.50
60	Derek Jeter	2.00
61	Jimmy Key	.15
62	Don Mattingly	1.50
63	Jack McDowell	.15
64	Paul O'Neill	.20
65	Andy Pettitte	.75
66	Ruben Rivera	.50
67	Mike Stanley	.15
68	John Wetteland	.15
69	Geronimo Berroa	.15
70	Dennis Eckersley	.15
71	Rickey Henderson	.30
72	Mark McGwire	4.00
73	Steve Ontiveros	.15
74	Ruben Sierra	.15
75	Terry Steinbach	.15
76	Jay Buhner	.20
77	Ken Griffey Jr.	4.00
78	Randy Johnson	.60
79	Edgar Martinez	.15
80	Tino Martinez	.20
81	Marc Newfield	.15
82	Alex Rodriguez	3.00
83	Will Clark	.40
84	Benji Gil	.15
85	Juan Gonzalez	1.50
86	Rusty Greer	.15
87	Dean Palmer	.15
88	Ivan Rodriguez	.75
89	Kenny Rogers	.15
90	Roberto Alomar	.75
91	Joe Carter	.15
92	David Cone	.25
93	Alex Gonzalez	.15
94	Shawn Green	.25
95	Pat Hentgen	.15
96	Paul Molitor	.40
97	John Olerud	.20
98	Devon White	.15
99	Steve Avery	.15
100	Tom Glavine	.25
101	Marquis Grissom	.15
102	Chipper Jones	2.00
103	Dave Justice	.25
104	Ryan Klesko	.35
105	Javier Lopez	.25
106	Greg Maddux	2.00
107	Fred McGriff	.40
108	John Smoltz	.30
109	Shawon Dunston	.15
110	Mark Grace	.25
111	Brian McRae	.15
112	Randy Myers	.15
113	Sammy Sosa	2.00
114	Steve Trachsel	.15
115	Bret Boone	.15
116	Ron Gant	.25
117	Barry Larkin	.25
118	Deion Sanders	.25
119	Reggie Sanders	.15
120	Pete Schourek	.15
121	John Smiley	.15
122	Jason Bates	.15
123	Dante Bichette	.50
124	Vinny Castilla	.15
125	Andres Galarraga	.25
126	Larry Walker	.40
127	Greg Colbrunn	.15
128	Jeff Conine	.15
129	Andre Dawson	.20
130	Chris Hammond	.15
131	Charles Johnson	.15
132	Gary Sheffield	.60
133	Quilvio Veras	.15
134	Jeff Bagwell	1.25
135	Derek Bell	.15
136	Craig Biggio	.25
137	Jim Dougherty	.15
138	John Hudek	.15
139	Orlando Miller	.15
140	Phil Plantier	.15
141	Eric Karros	.20
142	Ramon Martinez	.15
143	Raul Mondesi	.50
144	*Hideo Nomo*	2.00
145	Mike Piazza	2.00
146	Ismael Valdes	.15
147	Todd Worrell	.15
148	Moises Alou	.15
149	*Yamil Benitez*	.15
150	Wil Cordero	.15
151	Jeff Fassero	.15
152	Cliff Floyd	.15
153	Pedro Martinez	.40
154	*Carlos Perez*	.25
155	Tony Tarasco	.15
156	Rondell White	.15
157	Edgardo Alfonzo	.15
158	Bobby Bonilla	.15
159	Rico Brogna	.15
160	Bobby Jones	.15
161	Bill Pulsipher	.15
162	Bret Saberhagen	.15
163	Ricky Bottalico	.15
164	Darren Daulton	.15
165	Lenny Dykstra	.15
166	Charlie Hayes	.15
167	Dave Hollins	.15
168	Gregg Jefferies	.15
169	*Michael Mimbs*	.40
170	Curt Schilling	.15
171	Heathcliff Slocumb	.15
172	Jay Bell	.15
173	*Micah Franklin*	.15
174	*Mark Johnson*	.40
175	Jeff King	.15
176	Al Martin	.15
177	Dan Miceli	.15
178	Denny Neagle	.15
179	Bernard Gilkey	.15
180	Ken Hill	.15
181	Brian Jordan	.20
182	Ray Lankford	.15
183	Ozzie Smith	.75
184	Andy Benes	.15
185	Ken Caminiti	.25
186	Steve Finley	.15
187	Tony Gwynn	1.50
188	Joey Hamilton	.20
189	Melvin Nieves	.15
190	Scott Sanders	.15
191	Rod Beck	.15
192	Barry Bonds	.75
193	Royce Clayton	.15
194	Glenallen Hill	.15
195	Darren Lewis	.15
196	Mark Portugal	.15
197	Matt Williams	.40
198	Checklist	.05
199	Checklist	.05
200	Checklist	.05

1995 SkyBox E-Motion Cal Ripken Jr. Timeless

A white background with a clockface and gold-foil "TIMELESS" logo are the standard elements of this insert tribute to Cal Ripken, Jr. Each card front features a large color photo and a smaller sepia photo contemporary to some phase of his career. The first 10 cards in the set chronicle Ripken's career through 1994. A special mail-in offer provided five more cards featuring highlights of his 1995 season.

		MT
Complete Set (15):		60.00
Common Player:		5.00
1	High School Pitcher	5.00
2	Role Model	5.00
3	Rookie of the Year	5.00
4	1st MVP Season	5.00
5	95 Consecutive Errorless Games	5.00
6	All-Star MVP	5.00
7	Conditioning	5.00
8	Shortstop HR Record	5.00
9	Literacy Work	5.00
10	2000th Consecutive Game	5.00
11	All-Star Selection	5.00
12	Record-tying Game	5.00
13	Record-breaking Game	5.00
14	2,153 and Counting	5.00
15	Birthday	5.00

1995 SkyBox E-Motion Masters

Ten of the game's top veterans are featured in this chase card set. A large close-up photo in a single team-related color in the background, with a color action photo in the foreground. Backs have a borderless color photo and a top to bottom color bar with some good words about the player. The Masters inserts are found at an average rate of one per eight packs.

		MT
Complete Set (10):		50.00
Common Player:		2.50
1	Barry Bonds	4.00
2	Juan Gonzalez	6.00
3	Ken Griffey Jr.	15.00
4	Tony Gwynn	6.00
5	Kenny Lofton	3.00
6	Greg Maddux	10.00
7	Raul Mondesi	3.00
8	Cal Ripken Jr.	12.00
9	Frank Thomas	6.00
10	Matt Williams	3.00

1995 SkyBox E-Motion N-Tense

A colored wave-pattern printed on metallic foil is the background for the action photo of one of baseball's top sluggers in this chase card set. A huge rainbow prismatic foil "N" appears in an upper corner. The player's name and team are at lower-right in gold foil. Backs are conventionally printed and repeat the front's patterned background, with another color player photo and a shaded box with a few career highlights.

		MT
Complete Set (12):		130.00
Common Player:		4.00
1	Jeff Bagwell	12.00
2	Albert Belle	10.00
3	Barry Bonds	10.00
4	Cecil Fielder	3.00
5	Ron Gant	3.00
6	Ken Griffey Jr.	35.00
7	Mark McGwire	35.00
8	Mike Piazza	25.00
9	Manny Ramirez	12.00
10	Frank Thomas	15.00
11	Mo Vaughn	6.00
12	Matt Williams	6.00

1995 SkyBox E-Motion Rookies

A bold colored background with outline white letters repeating the word "ROOKIE" is the frame for the central action photo in this insert series. The top of the photo is vignetted with a white circle that has the player's name in gold at left, and his team in white at right. Backs repeat the front background and include a player portrait photo and a few sentences about his potential. Rookie inserts are found at an average rate of one per five packs.

		MT
Complete Set (10):		24.00
Common Player:		1.00
1	Edgardo Alfonzo	2.00
2	Jason Bates	1.00
3	Marty Cordova	1.00
4	Ray Durham	1.50
5	Alex Gonzalez	2.00
6	Shawn Green	4.00
7	Charles Johnson	2.00
8	Chipper Jones	6.00
9	Hideo Nomo	4.00
10	Alex Rodriguez	8.00

1996 SkyBox E-Motion XL

Each card in SkyBox's 1996 E-Motion XL Baseball arrives on two layers of stock - a die-cut matte frame over a UV-coated card. The frames come in three colors - blue, green and maroon (but each player has only one color version). The 300-card set also includes four insert sets: Legion of Boom, D-Fense, N-Tense and Rare Breed.

		MT
Complete Set (300):		70.00
Common Player:		.20
Unlisted Stars: .30 to .50		
Wax Box:		65.00
1	Roberto Alomar	1.50
2	Brady Anderson	.30
3	Bobby Bonilla	.20
4	Jeffrey Hammonds	.20
5	Chris Hoiles	.20
6	Mike Mussina	1.00
7	Randy Myers	.20
8	Rafael Palmeiro	.40
9	Cal Ripken Jr.	5.00
10	B.J. Surhoff	.20
11	Jose Canseco	.50
12	Roger Clemens	2.00
13	Wil Cordero	.20
14	Mike Greenwell	.20
15	Dwayne Hosey	.20
16	Tim Naehring	.20
17	Troy O'Leary	.20
18	Mike Stanley	.20
19	John Valentin	.20
20	Mo Vaughn	1.00
21	Jim Abbott	.20

22	Garret Anderson	.20
23	George Arias	.20
24	Chili Davis	.20
25	Jim Edmonds	.30
26	Chuck Finley	.20
27	Todd Greene	.20
28	Mark Langston	.20
29	Troy Percival	.20
30	Tim Salmon	.40
31	Lee Smith	.20
32	J.T. Snow	.20
33	Harold Baines	.20
34	Jason Bere	.20
35	Ray Durham	.20
36	Alex Fernandez	.20
37	Ozzie Guillen	.20
38	Darren Lewis	.20
39	Lyle Mouton	.20
40	Tony Phillips	.20
41	Danny Tartabull	.20
42	Frank Thomas	2.50
43	Robin Ventura	.25
44	Sandy Alomar	.25
45	Carlos Baerga	.20
46	Albert Belle	1.50
47	Julio Franco	.20
48	Orel Hershiser	.20
49	Kenny Lofton	1.00
50	Dennis Martinez	.20
51	Jack McDowell	.20
52	Jose Mesa	.20
53	Eddie Murray	.75
54	Charles Nagy	.20
55	Manny Ramirez	2.00
55p	Manny Ramirez (overprinted "PROMOTIONAL SAMPLE")	3.00
56	Jim Thome	1.00
57	Omar Vizquel	.20
58	Chad Curtis	.20
59	Cecil Fielder	.20
60	Travis Fryman	.20
61	Chris Gomez	.20
62	Felipe Lira	.20
63	Alan Trammell	.20
64	Kevin Appier	.20
65	Johnny Damon	.50
66	Tom Goodwin	.20
67	Mark Gubicza	.20
68	Jeff Montgomery	.20
69	Jon Nunnally	.20
70	Bip Roberts	.20
71	Ricky Bones	.20
72	Chuck Carr	.20
73	John Jaha	.20
74	Ben McDonald	.20
75	Matt Mieske	.20
76	Dave Nilsson	.20
77	Kevin Seitzer	.20
78	Greg Vaughn	.20
79	Rick Aguilera	.20
80	Marty Cordova	.20
81	Roberto Kelly	.20
82	Chuck Knoblauch	.25
83	Pat Meares	.20
84	Paul Molitor	1.00
85	Kirby Puckett	2.00
86	Brad Radke	.20
87	Wade Boggs	.50
88	David Cone	.35
89	Dwight Gooden	.20
90	Derek Jeter	3.50
91	Tino Martinez	.30
92	Paul O'Neill	.25
93	Andy Pettitte	1.00
94	Tim Raines	.20
95	Ruben Rivera	.60
96	Kenny Rogers	.20
97	Ruben Sierra	.20
98	John Wetteland	.20
99	Bernie Williams	1.00
100	Allen Battle	.20
101	Geronimo Berroa	.20
102	Brent Gates	.20
103	Doug Johns	.20
104	Mark McGwire	7.00
105	Pedro Munoz	.20
106	Ariel Prieto	.20
107	Terry Steinbach	.20
108	Todd Van Poppel	.20
109	Chris Bosio	.20
110	Jay Buhner	.30
111	Joey Cora	.20
112	Russ Davis	.20
113	Ken Griffey Jr.	7.00
114	Sterling Hitchcock	.20
115	Randy Johnson	1.25
116	Edgar Martinez	.20
117	Alex Rodriguez	5.00
118	Paul Sorrento	.20
119	Dan Wilson	.20
120	Will Clark	.50
121	Juan Gonzalez	3.00
122	Rusty Greer	.20
123	Kevin Gross	.20
124	Ken Hill	.20
125	Dean Palmer	.20
126	Roger Pavlik	.20
127	Ivan Rodriguez	1.50
128	Mickey Tettleton	.20
129	Joe Carter	.30
130	Carlos Delgado	.75
131	Alex Gonzalez	.20
132	Shawn Green	.30
133	Erik Hanson	.20
134	Pat Hentgen	.20
135	Otis Nixon	.20
136	John Olerud	.30
137	Ed Sprague	.20
138	Steve Avery	.20
139	Jermaine Dye	.30
140	Tom Glavine	.40
141	Marquis Grissom	.20
142	Chipper Jones	3.50
143	David Justice	.40
144	Ryan Klesko	.35
145	Javier Lopez	.35
146	Greg Maddux	3.50
147	Fred McGriff	.75
148	Jason Schmidt	.20
149	John Smoltz	.75
150	Mark Wohlers	.20
151	Jim Bullinger	.20
152	Frank Castillo	.20
153	Kevin Foster	.20
154	Luis Gonzalez	.20
155	Mark Grace	.40
156	Brian McRae	.20
157	Jaime Navarro	.20
158	Rey Sanchez	.20
159	Ryne Sandberg	2.00
160	Sammy Sosa	3.00
161	Bret Boone	.20
162	Jeff Brantley	.20
163	Vince Coleman	.20
164	Steve Gibralter	.20
165	Curtis Goodwin	.20
166	Barry Larkin	.35
167	Hal Morris	.20
168	Mark Portugal	.20
169	Reggie Sanders	.20
170	Pete Schourek	.20
171	John Smiley	.20
172	Jason Bates	.20
173	Dante Bichette	.40
174	Ellis Burks	.20
175	Vinny Castilla	.20
176	Andres Galarraga	.40
177	Kevin Ritz	.20
178	Bill Swift	.20
179	Larry Walker	.40
180	Walt Weiss	.20
181	Eric Young	.20
182	Kurt Abbott	.20
183	Kevin Brown	.30
184	John Burkett	.20
185	Greg Colbrunn	.20
186	Jeff Conine	.20
187	Chris Hammond	.20
188	Charles Johnson	.20
189	Terry Pendleton	.20
190	Pat Rapp	.20
191	Gary Sheffield	1.00
192	Quilvio Veras	.20
193	Devon White	.20
194	Jeff Bagwell	2.50
195	Derek Bell	.20
196	Sean Berry	.20
197	Craig Biggio	.30
198	Doug Drabek	.20
199	Tony Eusebio	.20
200	Mike Hampton	.20
201	Brian Hunter	.30
202	Derrick May	.20
203	Orlando Miller	.20
204	Shane Reynolds	.20
205	Mike Blowers	.20
206	Tom Candiotti	.20
207	Delino DeShields	.20
208	Greg Gagne	.20
209	Karim Garcia	.75
210	Todd Hollandsworth	.20
211	Eric Karros	.20
212	Ramon Martinez	.20
213	Raul Mondesi	.40
214	Hideo Nomo	1.00
215	Mike Piazza	3.50
216	Ismael Valdes	.20
217	Todd Worrell	.20
218	Moises Alou	.20
219	Yamil Benitez	.20
220	Jeff Fassero	.20
221	Darrin Fletcher	.20
222	Cliff Floyd	.20
223	Pedro Martinez	.40
224	Carlos Perez	.20
225	Mel Rojas	.20
226	David Segui	.20
227	Rondell White	.20
228	Rico Brogna	.20
229	Carl Everett	.20
230	John Franco	.20
231	Bernard Gilkey	.20
232	Todd Hundley	.20
233	Jason Isringhausen	.30
234	Lance Johnson	.20
235	Bobby Jones	.20
236	Jeff Kent	.20
237	Rey Ordonez	.75
238	Bill Pulsipher	.20
239	Jose Vizcaino	.20
240	Paul Wilson	.35
241	Ricky Bottalico	.20
242	Darren Daulton	.20
243	Lenny Dykstra	.20
244	Jim Eisenreich	.20
245	Sid Fernandez	.20
246	Gregg Jefferies	.20
247	Mickey Morandini	.20
248	Benito Santiago	.20
249	Curt Schilling	.20
250	Mark Whiten	.20
251	Todd Zeile	.20
252	Jay Bell	.20
253	Carlos Garcia	.20
254	Charlie Hayes	.20
255	Jason Kendall	.20
256	Jeff King	.20
257	Al Martin	.20
258	Orlando Merced	.20
259	Dan Miceli	.20
260	Denny Neagle	.20
261	Alan Benes	.30
262	Andy Benes	.20
263	Royce Clayton	.20
264	Dennis Eckersley	.20
265	Gary Gaetti	.20
266	Ron Gant	.30
267	Brian Jordan	.20
268	Ray Lankford	.20
269	John Mabry	.20
270	Tom Pagnozzi	.20
271	Ozzie Smith	1.00
272	Todd Stottlemyre	.20
273	Andy Ashby	.20
274	Brad Ausmus	.20
275	Ken Caminiti	.40
276	Steve Finley	.20
277	Tony Gwynn	2.00
278	Joey Hamilton	.20
279	Rickey Henderson	.35
280	Trevor Hoffman	.25
281	Wally Joyner	.20
282	Jody Reed	.20
283	Bob Tewksbury	.20
284	Fernando Valenzuela	.20
285	Rod Beck	.20
286	Barry Bonds	1.50
287	Mark Carreon	.20
288	Shawon Dunston	.20
289	*Osvaldo Fernandez*	.30
290	Glenallen Hill	.20
291	Stan Javier	.20
292	Mark Leiter	.20
293	Kirt Manwaring	.20
294	Robby Thompson	.20
295	William VanLandingham	.20
296	Allen Watson	.20
297	Matt Williams	.50
298	Checklist	.10
299	Checklist	.10
300	Checklist	.10

1996 SkyBox E-Motion XL D-Fense

Ten top defensive players are featured on these 1996 SkyBox E-Motion XL insert cards. The cards were seeded at a rate of one per every four packs.

		MT
Complete Set (10):		20.00
Common Player:		.75
1	Roberto Alomar	1.00
2	Barry Bonds	2.00
3	Mark Grace	.75
4	Ken Griffey Jr.	7.50
5	Kenny Lofton	.75
6	Greg Maddux	4.00
7	Raul Mondesi	.75
8	Cal Ripken Jr.	5.00
9	Ivan Rodriguez	1.50
10	Matt Williams	.75

Player names in *Italic* type indicate a rookie card.

1996 SkyBox E-Motion XL Legion of Boom

The top power hitters in baseball are featured on these 1996 SkyBox E-Motion XL insert cards. The cards, exclusive to hobby packs at a ratio of one per every 36 packs, have translucent card backs.

		MT
Complete Set (12):		200.00
Common Player:		6.00
1	Albert Belle	15.00
2	Barry Bonds	15.00
3	Juan Gonzalez	25.00
4	Ken Griffey Jr.	50.00
5	Mark McGwire	50.00
6	Mike Piazza	30.00
7	Manny Ramirez	20.00
8	Tim Salmon	10.00
9	Sammy Sosa	30.00
10	Frank Thomas	15.00
11	Mo Vaughn	10.00
12	Matt Williams	10.00

1996 SkyBox E-Motion XL N-Tense

Ten top clutch performers are featured on these 1996 SkyBox E-Motion XL insert cards. The cards, which use an N-shaped die-cut design, were included one per every 12 packs.

		MT
Complete Set (10):		60.00
Common Player:		2.00
1	Albert Belle	3.50
2	Barry Bonds	4.50
3	Jose Canseco	2.50
4	Ken Griffey Jr.	15.00
5	Tony Gwynn	6.00
6	Randy Johnson	3.50
7	Greg Maddux	9.00
8	Cal Ripken Jr.	12.00
9	Frank Thomas	6.00
10	Matt Williams	2.00

1996 SkyBox E-Motion XL Rare Breed

These 1996 E-Motion XL inserts are the most difficult to find; they are seeded one per every 100 packs. The cards showcase top young stars on 3-D lenticular design, similar to the Hot Numbers in Fleer Flair basketball.

		MT
Complete Set (10):		110.00
Common Player:		5.00
1	Garret Anderson	6.00
2	Marty Cordova	6.00
3	Brian Hunter	6.00
4	Jason Isringhausen	6.00
5	Charles Johnson	6.00
6	Chipper Jones	40.00
7	Raul Mondesi	7.50
8	Hideo Nomo	12.00
9	Manny Ramirez	25.00
10	Rondell White	6.00

1997 SkyBox E-X2000 Sample

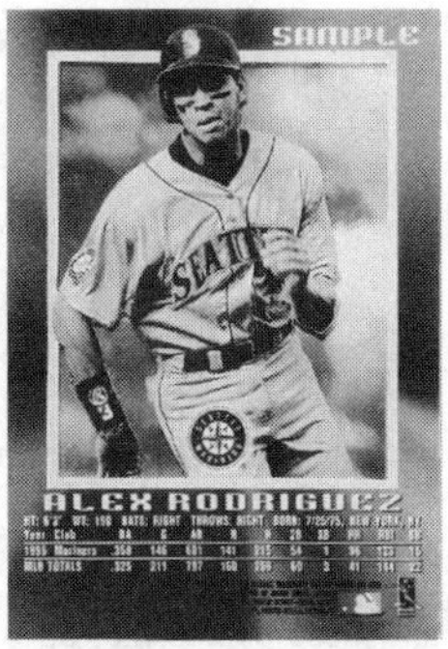

To introduce its innovative high-tech premium brand, SkyBox released this promo card. It is identical in format to the issued version, except it carries a "SAMPLE" notation instead of a card number on back.

	MT
Alex Rodriguez	10.00

1997 SkyBox E-X2000

The premiere issue of E-X2000 consists of 100 base cards designed with "Sky-View" technology, utilizing a die-cut holofoil border and the player silhouetted in front of a transparent "window" featuring a variety of sky patterns. Inserts include two sequentially-numbered parallel sets - Credentials (1:50 packs) and Essential Credentials (1:200 packs) - as well as Emerald Autograph Exchange Cards, A Cut Above, Hall of Nothing, and Star Date. Cards were sold in two-card packs for $3.99 each.

	MT
Complete Set (100):	80.00
Common Player:	.50
Credentials Stars: 6X	
Essential Credentials: 15X	
Wax Box:	85.00

1	Jim Edmonds	.50
2	Darin Erstad	4.00
3	Eddie Murray	2.00
4	Roberto Alomar	2.00
5	Brady Anderson	.50
6	Mike Mussina	1.50
7	Rafael Palmeiro	1.50
8	Cal Ripken Jr.	8.00
9	Steve Avery	.50
10	Nomar Garciaparra	6.00
11	Mo Vaughn	1.50
12	Albert Belle	2.50
13	Mike Cameron	.50
14	Ray Durham	.50
15	Frank Thomas	6.00
16	Robin Ventura	.75
17	Manny Ramirez	4.50
18	Jim Thome	1.00
19	Matt Williams	1.50
20	Tony Clark	1.50
21	Travis Fryman	.50
22	Bob Higginson	.50
23	Kevin Appier	.50
24	Johnny Damon	.50
25	Jermaine Dye	.50
26	Jeff Cirillo	.50
27	Ben McDonald	.50
28	Chuck Knoblauch	1.00
29	Paul Molitor	2.00
30	Todd Walker	2.00
31	Wade Boggs	2.00
32	Cecil Fielder	.75
33	Derek Jeter	6.00
34	Andy Pettitte	1.50
35	Ruben Rivera	.50
36	Bernie Williams	1.50
37	Jose Canseco	2.00
38	Mark McGwire	10.00
39	Jay Buhner	.75
40	Ken Griffey Jr.	10.00
41	Randy Johnson	2.00
42	Edgar Martinez	.50
43	Alex Rodriguez	8.00
44	Dan Wilson	.50
45	Will Clark	1.50
46	Juan Gonzalez	5.00
47	Ivan Rodriguez	2.50
48	Joe Carter	.50
49	Roger Clemens	3.00
50	Juan Guzman	.50
51	Pat Hentgen	.50
52	Tom Glavine	1.50
53	Andruw Jones	5.00
54	Chipper Jones	6.00
55	Ryan Klesko	.50
56	Kenny Lofton	1.50
57	Greg Maddux	6.00
58	Fred McGriff	1.50
59	John Smoltz	1.25
60	Mark Wohlers	.50
61	Mark Grace	2.00
62	Ryne Sandberg	2.50
63	Sammy Sosa	6.00
64	Barry Larkin	1.00
65	Deion Sanders	1.00
66	Reggie Sanders	.50
67	Dante Bichette	1.50
68	Ellis Burks	.50
69	Andres Galarraga	1.50
70	Moises Alou	.50
71	Kevin Brown	.50
72	Cliff Floyd	.50
73	Edgar Renteria	.50
74	Gary Sheffield	1.50
75	Bob Abreu	.50
76	Jeff Bagwell	4.00
77	Craig Biggio	1.50
78	Todd Hollandsworth	.50
79	Eric Karros	.50
80	Raul Mondesi	1.50
81	Hideo Nomo	1.50
82	Mike Piazza	6.00
83	Vladimir Guerrero	3.00
84	Henry Rodriguez	.50
85	Todd Hundley	1.50
86	Rey Ordonez	.50
87	Alex Ochoa	.50
88	Gregg Jefferies	.50
89	Scott Rolen	5.00
90	Jermaine Allensworth	.50
91	Jason Kendall	.50
92	Ken Caminiti	1.50
93	Tony Gwynn	5.00
94	Rickey Henderson	1.00
95	Barry Bonds	2.50
96	J.T. Snow	.50
97	Dennis Eckersley	.50
98	Ron Gant	.50
99	Brian Jordan	.50
100	Ray Lankford	.50

1997 SkyBox E-X2000 Credentials

This parallel set features different colored foils from the base cards, as well as different images on the "window." Cards are sequentially numbered on back within an issue of 299. Cards were inserted 1:50 packs.

	MT
Common Player:	4.00
Credentials Stars: 6X	
(See E-X2000 for checklist, base card values)	

1997 SkyBox E-X2000 Essential Credentials

A sequentially-numbered parallel set, found one per 200 packs, and limited to 99 total sets.

	MT
Common Player:	8.00
Essential Credentials Stars: 15X	
(See 1997 SkyBox E-X2000 for checklist and base card values.)	

1997 SkyBox E-X2000 A Cut Above

Some of the game's elite players are featured in this 1:288 pack insert that features a die-cut design resembling a saw blade. Printed on silver-foil stock, the player's name and Cut Above logo are embossed on front. On back is another color photo and a few words about the player.

		MT
Complete Set (10):		100.00
Common Player:		4.00
1	Frank Thomas	12.50
2	Ken Griffey Jr.	30.00
3	Alex Rodriguez	20.00
4	Albert Belle	7.50
5	Juan Gonzalez	10.00
6	Mark McGwire	30.00
7	Mo Vaughn	4.00
8	Manny Ramirez	9.00
9	Barry Bonds	7.50
10	Fred McGriff	4.00

1997 SkyBox E-X2000 Emerald Autograph Redemptions

Inserted 1:480 packs, these cards could be exchanged by mail prior to May 1, 1998, for autographed cards or memorabilia from one of six major leaguers.

		MT
Complete Set (6):		80.00
Common Player:		4.00
(1)	Darin Erstad	20.00
(2)	Todd Hollandsworth	6.00
(3)	Alex Ochoa	4.00
(4)	Alex Rodriguez	50.00
(5)	Scott Rolen	25.00
(6)	Todd Walker	6.00

1997 SkyBox E-X2000 Emerald Autographs

These authentically autographed versions of the players' E-X2000 cards were available (until May 1, 1998) by a mail-in exchange of redemption cards. The autographed cards are authenticated by the presence of an embossed SkyBox logo seal.

		MT
Complete Set (6):		400.00
Common Player:		16.00
2	Darin Erstad	80.00
30	Todd Walker	40.00
43	Alex Rodriguez	200.00
78	Todd Hollandsworth	20.00
86	Alex Ochoa	16.00
89	Scott Rolen	100.00

1997 SkyBox E-X2000 Hall or Nothing

This 20-card insert, featuring players who are candidates for the Hall of Fame, utilizes a die-cut design on plastic stock. Stately architectural details and brush bronze highlights frame the player picture on front. The player silhouette on back contains career information. Cards were inserted 1:20 packs.

		MT
Complete Set (20):		150.00
Common Player:		2.00
1	Frank Thomas	10.00
2	Ken Griffey Jr.	25.00
3	Eddie Murray	3.00
4	Cal Ripken Jr.	17.50
5	Ryne Sandberg	5.00
6	Wade Boggs	4.00
7	Roger Clemens	7.50
8	Tony Gwynn	10.00
9	Alex Rodriguez	17.50
10	Mark McGwire	25.00
11	Barry Bonds	6.50
12	Greg Maddux	12.00
13	Juan Gonzalez	6.50
14	Albert Belle	3.00
15	Mike Piazza	12.50
16	Jeff Bagwell	6.00
17	Dennis Eckersley	2.00
18	Mo Vaughn	2.00
19	Roberto Alomar	3.00
20	Kenny Lofton	2.00

1997 SkyBox E-X2000 Star Date 2000

A 15-card set highlighting young stars that are likely to be the game's top players in the year 2000. Cards were inserted 1:9 packs.

		MT
Complete Set (15):		40.00
Common Player:		1.50
1	Alex Rodriguez	10.00
2	Andruw Jones	4.50
3	Andy Pettitte	2.00
4	Brooks Kieschnick	1.50
5	Chipper Jones	7.50
6	Darin Erstad	4.00
7	Derek Jeter	7.50
8	Jason Kendall	3.00
9	Jermaine Dye	1.50
10	Neifi Perez	1.50
11	Scott Rolen	4.50
12	Todd Hollandsworth	1.50
13	Todd Walker	2.00
14	Tony Clark	3.00
15	Vladimir Guerrero	6.00

1997 SkyBox E-X2000 Alex Rodriguez Jumbo

This 8" x 10" version of A-Rod's SkyBox E-X2000 card was given to dealers who ordered case quantities of the new product. The card is identical in design to the standard-sized issued version, but is numbered on back from within an edition of 3,000.

	MT
Alex Rodriguez	30.00

1998 SkyBox E-X2001 Sample

To preview its high-tech E-X2001 brand for 1998, SkyBox issued this sample card of A-Rod. Similar in format to the issued version, it is numbered "SAMPLE" on back and has a "PROMOTIONAL SAMPLE" overprint on back.

	MT
Alex Rodriguez	4.50

1998 SkyBox E-X2001

This super-premium set featured 100 players on a layered, die-cuct design utilizing mirror-image silhouetted photography and etched holofoil treatment over a clear, 20-point plastic card.

		MT
Complete Set (100):		90.00
Common Player:		.50
Unlisted Stars: 1.50 to 2.00		
Kerry Wood Exchange:		15.00
Wax Box:		100.00
1	Alex Rodriguez	8.00
2	Barry Bonds	2.50
3	Greg Maddux	6.00
4	Roger Clemens	4.00
5	Juan Gonzalez	5.00
6	Chipper Jones	6.00
7	Derek Jeter	6.00
8	Frank Thomas	5.00
9	Cal Ripken Jr.	8.00
10	Ken Griffey Jr.	10.00
11	Mark McGwire	10.00
12	Hideo Nomo	1.00
13	Tony Gwynn	5.00
14	Ivan Rodriguez	2.50
15	Mike Piazza	6.00
16	Roberto Alomar	2.00
17	Jeff Bagwell	4.00
18	Andruw Jones	2.50
19	Albert Belle	2.00
20	Mo Vaughn	1.50
21	Kenny Lofton	1.50
22	Gary Sheffield	.50
23	Tony Clark	1.50
24	Mike Mussina	2.00
25	Barry Larkin	.50
26	Moises Alou	.50
27	Brady Anderson	.50
28	Andy Pettitte	1.50
29	Sammy Sosa	6.00
30	Raul Mondesi	.50
31	Andres Galarraga	1.00
32	Chuck Knoblauch	1.00
33	Jim Thome	1.50
34	Craig Biggio	.50
35	Jay Buhner	.50
36	Rafael Palmeiro	.50
37	Curt Schilling	.50
38	Tino Martinez	1.00
39	Pedro Martinez	1.50
40	Jose Canseco	1.00
41	Jeff Cirillo	.50
42	Dean Palmer	.50
43	Tim Salmon	1.50
44	Jason Giambi	.50
45	Bobby Higginson	.50
46	Jim Edmonds	.50
47	David Justice	1.00
48	John Olerud	.50
49	Ray Lankford	.50
50	Al Martin	.50
51	Mike Lieberthal	.50
52	Henry Rodriguez	.50
53	Edgar Renteria	.50
54	Eric Karros	.50
55	Marquis Grissom	.50
56	Wilson Alvarez	.50
57	Darryl Kile	.50
58	Jeff King	.50
59	Shawn Estes	.50
60	Tony Womack	.50
61	Willie Greene	.50
62	Ken Caminiti	1.00
63	Vinny Castilla	.50
64	Mark Grace	1.00
65	Ryan Klesko	.75
66	Robin Ventura	.50
67	Todd Hundley	.50
68	Travis Fryman	.50
69	Edgar Martinez	.50
70	Matt Williams	1.00
71	Paul Molitor	1.50
72	Kevin Brown	.50
73	Randy Johnson	1.50
74	Bernie Williams	1.50

75	Manny Ramirez	2.50
76	Fred McGriff	.50
77	Tom Glavine	.50
78	Carlos Delgado	.50
79	Larry Walker	1.00
80	Hideki Irabu	1.50
81	Ryan McGuire	.50
82	Justin Thompson	.50
83	Kevin Orie	.50
84	Jon Nunnally	.50
85	Mark Kotsay	2.00
86	Todd Walker	.50
87	Jason Dickson	.50
88	Fernando Tatis	.50
89	Karim Garcia	.50
90	Ricky Ledee	1.50
91	Paul Konerko	1.50
92	Jaret Wright	3.00
93	Darin Erstad	2.50
94	Livan Hernandez	.75
95	Nomar Garciaparra	6.00
96	Jose Cruz Jr.	1.00
97	Scott Rolen	3.00
98	Ben Grieve	3.00
99	Vladimir Guerrero	3.00
100	Travis Lee	2.50

1998 SkyBox E-X2001 Essential Credentials Future

Essential Credentials Future, along with Essential Credentials Now, paralleled all 100 cards in the base set. Production varied depending on the card number, with the exact production number of each player determined by subtracting his card number from 101. Number issued for each card is shown in parentheses. Because of rarity, the value of cards #93-100 cannot be determined.

		MT
	Common Player:	15.00
1	Alex Rodriguez (100)	135.00
2	Barry Bonds (99)	50.00
3	Greg Maddux (98)	125.00
4	Roger Clemens (97)	75.00
5	Juan Gonzalez (96)	60.00
6	Chipper Jones (95)	125.00
7	Derek Jeter (94)	125.00
8	Frank Thomas (93)	75.00
9	Cal Ripken Jr. (92)	150.00
10	Ken Griffey Jr. (91)	200.00
11	Mark McGwire (90)	200.00
12	Hideo Nomo (89)	25.00
13	Tony Gwynn (88)	90.00
14	Ivan Rodriguez (87)	60.00
15	Mike Piazza (86)	130.00
16	Roberto Alomar (85)	40.00
17	Jeff Bagwell (84)	60.00
18	Andruw Jones (83)	45.00
19	Albert Belle (82)	40.00
20	Mo Vaughn (81)	40.00
21	Kenny Lofton (80)	40.00
22	Gary Sheffield (79)	25.00
23	Tony Clark (78)	25.00
24	Mike Mussina (77)	40.00
25	Barry Larkin (76)	30.00
26	Moises Alou (75)	30.00
27	Brady Anderson (74)	25.00
28	Andy Pettitte (73)	40.00
29	Sammy Sosa (72)	140.00
30	Raul Mondesi (71)	25.00
31	Andres Galarraga (70)	25.00
32	Chuck Knoblauch (69)	35.00
33	Jim Thome (68)	45.00
34	Craig Biggio (67)	50.00
35	Jay Buhner (66)	25.00
36	Rafael Palmeiro (65)	40.00
37	Curt Schilling (64)	30.00
38	Tino Martinez (63)	30.00
39	Pedro Martinez (62)	100.00
40	Jose Canseco (61)	50.00
41	Jeff Cirillo (60)	20.00
42	Dean Palmer (59)	20.00
43	Tim Salmon (58)	50.00
44	Jason Giambi (57)	30.00
45	Bobby Higginson (56)	30.00
46	Jim Edmonds (55)	30.00
47	David Justice (54)	35.00
48	John Olerud (53)	40.00
49	Ray Lankford (52)	20.00
50	Al Martin (51)	20.00
51	Mike Lieberthal (50)	25.00
52	Henry Rodriguez (49)	15.00
53	Edgar Renteria (48)	25.00
54	Eric Karros (47)	20.00
55	Marquis Grissom (46)	20.00
56	Wilson Alvarez (45)	15.00
57	Darryl Kile (44)	10.00
58	Jeff King (43)	10.00
59	Shawn Estes (42)	15.00
60	Tony Womack (41)	15.00
61	Willie Greene (40)	15.00
62	Ken Caminiti (39)	60.00
63	Vinny Castilla (38)	50.00
64	Mark Grace (37)	75.00
65	Ryan Klesko (36)	45.00
66	Robin Ventura (35)	50.00
67	Todd Hundley (34)	35.00
68	Travis Fryman (33)	35.00
69	Edgar Martinez (32)	30.00
70	Matt Williams (31)	45.00
71	Paul Molitor (30)	80.00
72	Kevin Brown (29)	50.00
73	Randy Johnson (28)	75.00
74	Bernie Williams (27)	65.00
75	Manny Ramirez (26)	125.00
76	Fred McGriff (25)	50.00
77	Tom Glavine (24)	50.00
78	Carlos Delgado (23)	75.00
79	Larry Walker (22)	75.00
80	Hideki Irabu (21)	50.00
81	Ryan McGuire (20)	30.00
82	Justin Thompson (19)	30.00
83	Kevin Orie (18)	30.00
84	Jon Nunnally (17)	30.00
85	Mark Kotsay (16)	40.00
86	Todd Walker (15)	50.00
87	Jason Dickson (14)	30.00
88	Fernando Tatis (13)	50.00
89	Karim Garcia (12)	50.00
90	Ricky Ledee (11)	50.00
91	Paul Konerko (10)	50.00
92	Jaret Wright (9)	65.00
93	Darin Erstad (8)	100.00
94	Livan Hernandez (7)	75.00
95	Nomar Garciaparra (6)	300.00
96	Jose Cruz (5)	75.00
97	Scott Rolen (4)	250.00
98	Ben Grieve (3)	250.00
99	Vladimir Guerrero (2)	350.00
100	Travis Lee (1)	200.00

1998 SkyBox E-X2001 Essential Credentials Now

Essential Credentials Now parallels all 100 cards in the E-X2001 base set. Production for each card was limited to that player's card number, as shown in parentheses. Values for cards #1-15 are not valued due to rarity.

		MT
	Common Player:	15.00
1	Alex Rodriguez (1)	1500.
2	Barry Bonds (2)	900.00
3	Greg Maddux (3)	450.00
4	Roger Clemens (4)	300.00
5	Juan Gonzalez (5)	300.00
6	Chipper Jones (6)	250.00
7	Derek Jeter (7)	350.00
8	Frank Thomas (8)	250.00
9	Cal Ripken Jr. (9)	450.00
10	Ken Griffey Jr. (10)	650.00
11	Mark McGwire (11)	600.00
12	Hideo Nomo (12)	125.00
13	Tony Gwynn (13)	150.00
14	Ivan Rodriguez (14)	125.00
15	Mike Piazza (15)	150.00
16	Roberto Alomar (16)	90.00
17	Jeff Bagwell (17)	125.00
18	Andruw Jones (18)	100.00
19	Albert Belle (19)	90.00
20	Mo Vaughn (20)	90.00
21	Kenny Lofton (21)	75.00
22	Gary Sheffield (22)	75.00
23	Tony Clark (23)	50.00
24	Mike Mussina (24)	75.00
25	Barry Larkin (25)	50.00
26	Moises Alou (26)	40.00
27	Brady Anderson (27)	40.00
28	Andy Pettitte (28)	50.00
29	Sammy Sosa (29)	250.00
30	Raul Mondesi (30)	40.00
31	Andres Galarraga (31)	50.00
32	Chuck Knoblauch (32)	50.00
33	Jim Thome (33)	50.00
34	Craig Biggio (34)	60.00
35	Jay Buhner (35)	30.00
36	Rafael Palmeiro (36)	45.00
37	Curt Schilling (37)	25.00
38	Tino Martinez (38)	40.00
39	Pedro Martinez (39)	100.00
40	Jose Canseco (40)	60.00
41	Jeff Cirillo (41)	20.00
42	Dean Palmer (42)	20.00
43	Tim Salmon (43)	30.00
44	Jason Giambi (44)	25.00
45	Bobby Higginson (45)	25.00
46	Jim Edmonds (46)	25.00
47	David Justice (47)	35.00
48	John Olerud (48)	35.00
49	Ray Lankford (49)	20.00
50	Al Martin (50)	10.00
51	Mike Lieberthal (51)	20.00
52	Henry Rodriguez (52)	10.00
53	Edgar Renteria (53)	15.00
54	Eric Karros (54)	15.00
55	Marquis Grissom (55)	15.00
56	Wilson Alvarez (56)	10.00
57	Darryl Kile (57)	10.00
58	Jeff King (58)	10.00
59	Shawn Estes (59)	10.00
60	Tony Womack (60)	10.00
61	Willie Greene (61)	10.00
62	Ken Caminiti (62)	25.00
63	Vinny Castilla (63)	20.00
64	Mark Grace (64)	25.00
65	Ryan Klesko (65)	15.00
66	Robin Ventura (66)	30.00
67	Todd Hundley (67)	15.00
68	Travis Fryman (68)	15.00
69	Edgar Martinez (69)	12.50
70	Matt Williams (70)	20.00
71	Paul Molitor (71)	40.00
72	Kevin Brown (72)	25.00
73	Randy Johnson (73)	40.00
74	Bernie Williams (74)	40.00
75	Manny Ramirez (75)	50.00
76	Fred McGriff (76)	25.00
77	Tom Glavine (77)	25.00
78	Carlos Delgado (78)	25.00
79	Larry Walker (79)	40.00
80	Hideki Irabu (80)	15.00
81	Ryan McGuire (81)	10.00
82	Justin Thompson (82)	10.00
83	Kevin Orie (83)	10.00
84	Jon Nunnally (84)	10.00
85	Mark Kotsay (85)	15.00
86	Todd Walker (86)	15.00
87	Jason Dickson (87)	10.00
88	Fernando Tatis (88)	30.00
89	Karim Garcia (89)	15.00
90	Ricky Ledee (90)	20.00
91	Paul Konerko (91)	30.00
92	Jaret Wright (92)	30.00
93	Darin Erstad (93)	40.00
94	Livan Hernandez (94)	15.00
95	Nomar Garciaparra (95)	150.00
96	Jose Cruz Jr. (96)	25.00
97	Scott Rolen (97)	60.00
98	Ben Grieve (98)	40.00
99	Vladimir Guerrero (99)	50.00
100	Travis Lee (100)	25.00

1998 SkyBox E-X2001 Cheap Seat Treats

This 20-card die-cut insert arrived in the shape of a stadium seat. Inserted at one per 24 packs, Cheap Seat Treats included some of the top home run hitters and were numbered with a "CS" prefix.

		MT
	Complete Set (20):	160.00
	Common Player:	3.00
	Inserted 1:24	
1	Frank Thomas	10.00
2	Ken Griffey Jr.	30.00
3	Mark McGwire	30.00
4	Tino Martinez	3.00
5	Larry Walker	6.00
6	Juan Gonzalez	10.00
7	Mike Piazza	20.00
8	Jeff Bagwell	8.00
9	Tony Clark	5.00
10	Albert Belle	4.00
11	Andres Galarraga	4.00
12	Jim Thome	5.00
13	Mo Vaughn	3.00
14	Barry Bonds	8.00
15	Vladimir Guerrero	8.00
16	Scott Rolen	8.00
17	Travis Lee	5.00
18	David Justice	3.00
19	Jose Cruz Jr.	3.00
20	Andruw Jones	5.00

1998 SkyBox E-X2001 Destination: Cooperstown

Destination: Cooperstown captured a mixture of rising young stars and top veterans on die-cut cards that were inserted one per 720 packs. This insert included 15 players and was numbered with a "DC" prefix.

		MT
	Complete Set (15):	1200.
	Common Player:	15.00
	Inserted 1:720	
1	Alex Rodriguez	150.00
2	Frank Thomas	75.00
3	Cal Ripken Jr.	150.00
4	Roger Clemens	75.00
5	Greg Maddux	125.00
6	Chipper Jones	125.00
7	Ken Griffey Jr.	200.00
8	Mark McGwire	200.00
9	Tony Gwynn	100.00
10	Mike Piazza	125.00
11	Jeff Bagwell	60.00
12	Jose Cruz Jr.	15.00
13	Derek Jeter	125.00
14	Hideo Nomo	20.00
15	Ivan Rodriguez	50.00

1998 SkyBox E-X2001 Signature 2001

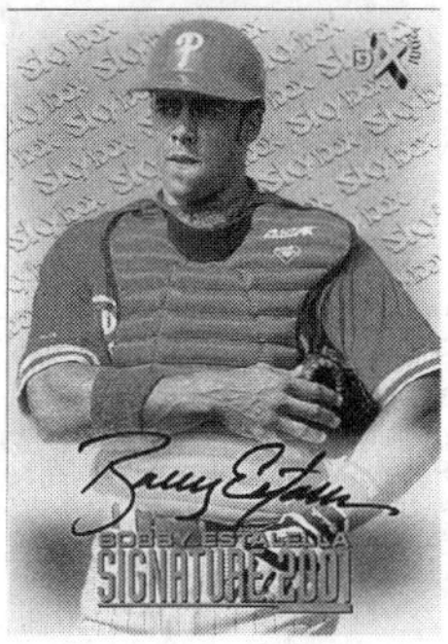

Seventeen top young and future stars signed cards for Signature 2001 inserts in E-X2001. The cards featured the player over a blue and white, sky-like background, with an embossed SkyBox seal of authenticity. Backs were horizontal and also included a Certificate of Authenticity. These cards were unnumbered and inserted one per 60 packs.

		MT
	Complete Set (17):	450.00
	Common Player:	10.00
	Inserted 1:60	
1	Ricky Ledee	20.00
2	Derrick Gibson	15.00
3	Mark Kotsay	25.00
4	Kevin Millwood	50.00
5	Brad Fullmer	25.00
6	Todd Walker	20.00
7	Ben Grieve	40.00
8	Tony Clark	20.00
9	Jaret Wright	25.00
10	Randall Simon	10.00
11	Paul Konerko	20.00
12	Todd Helton	30.00
13	David Ortiz	10.00
14	Alex Gonzalez	15.00
15	Bobby Estalella	10.00
16	Alex Rodriguez	150.00
17	Mike Lowell	10.00

1998 SkyBox E-X2001 Star Date 2001

Star Date 2001 displays 15 of the top rising stars on an acetate space/planet background with gold-foil printing on front. This insert was seeded one per 12 packs and was numbered with a "SD" suffix.

		MT
	Complete Set (15):	30.00
	Common Player:	1.00
	Inserted 1:12	
1	Travis Lee	5.00
2	Jose Cruz Jr.	1.50
3	Paul Konerko	2.00
4	Bobby Estalella	1.00
5	Magglio Ordonez	3.00
6	Juan Encarnacion	1.00
7	Richard Hidalgo	1.00
8	Abraham Nunez	1.00
9	Sean Casey	3.00
10	Todd Helton	2.50
11	Brad Fullmer	2.00
12	Ben Grieve	7.50
13	Livan Hernandez	1.00
14	Jaret Wright	6.00
15	Todd Dunwoody	1.00

1998 SkyBox E-X2001 Kerry Wood

In an effort to get rookie pitching phenom Kerry Wood into its E-X2001 set, SkyBox created a cardboard, rather than plastic, trade card and inserted it at a rate of one per 50 packs. The trade card could be exchanged by mail for a plastic version.

		MT
	Complete Set (2):	10.00
---	Kerry Wood (cardboard trade card)	8.00
101	Kerry Wood (plastic redemption card)	5.00

1998 SkyBox Dugout Axcess

Dugout Axcess was a 150-card set that attempted to provide collectors with an inside look at baseball. The cards were printed on "playing card" quality stock and used unique information and photography. The product arrived in 12-card packs with an Inside Axcess parallel set that was individually numbered to 50 sets. Six different inserts sets were available, including Double Header, Frequent Flyers, Dishwashers, Superheroes, Gronks and Autograph Redemptions.

		MT
Complete Set (150):		15.00
Common Player:		.10
Inside Axcess Stars: 60-75X		
Production 50 sets		
Wax Box:		45.00
1	Travis Lee	.75
2	Matt Williams	.25
3	Andy Benes	.10
4	Chipper Jones	1.50
5	Ryan Klesko	.25
6	Greg Maddux	1.50
7	Sammy Sosa	1.50
8	Henry Rodriguez	.10
9	Mark Grace	.25
10	Barry Larkin	.20
11	Bret Boone	.10
12	Reggie Sanders	.10
13	Vinny Castilla	.10
14	Larry Walker	.30
15	Darryl Kile	.10
16	Charles Johnson	.10
17	Edgar Renteria	.10
18	Gary Sheffield	.30
19	Jeff Bagwell	.75
20	Craig Biggio	.20
21	Moises Alou	.20
22	Mike Piazza	1.50
23	Hideo Nomo	.20
24	Raul Mondesi	.20
25	John Jaha	.10
26	Jeff Cirillo	.10
27	Jeromy Burnitz	.10
28	Mark Grudzielanek	.10
29	Vladimir Guerrero	.60
30	Rondell White	.20
31	Edgardo Alfonzo	.10
32	Rey Ordonez	.10
33	Bernard Gilkey	.10
34	Scott Rolen	.75
35	Curt Schilling	.20
36	Ricky Bottalico	.10
37	Tony Womack	.10
38	Al Martin	.10
39	Jason Kendall	.10
40	Ron Gant	.10
41	Mark McGwire	2.50
42	Ray Lankford	.10
43	Tony Gwynn	1.25
44	Ken Caminiti	.20
45	Kevin Brown	.10
46	Barry Bonds	.60
47	J.T. Snow	.10
48	Shawn Estes	.10
49	Jim Edmonds	.10
50	Tim Salmon	.20
51	Jason Dickson	.10
52	Cal Ripken Jr.	2.00
53	Mike Mussina	.50
54	Roberto Alomar	.50
55	Mo Vaughn	.45
56	Pedro Martinez	.50
57	Nomar Garciaparra	1.50
58	Albert Belle	.60
59	Frank Thomas	1.25
60	Robin Ventura	.20
61	Jim Thome	.40
62	Sandy Alomar Jr.	.20
63	Jaret Wright	.75
64	Bobby Higginson	.10
65	Tony Clark	.30
66	Justin Thompson	.10
67	Dean Palmer	.10
68	Kevin Appier	.10
69	Johnny Damon	.10
70	Paul Molitor	.45
71	Marty Cordova	.10
72	Brad Radke	.10
73	Derek Jeter	1.50
74	Bernie Williams	.40
75	Andy Pettitte	.40
76	Matt Stairs	.10
77	Ben Grieve	.75
78	Jason Giambi	.10
79	Randy Johnson	.40
80	Ken Griffey Jr.	2.50
81	Alex Rodriguez	2.00
82	Fred McGriff	.20
83	Wade Boggs	.25
84	Wilson Alvarez	.10
85	Juan Gonzalez	1.25
86	Ivan Rodriguez	.60
87	Fernando Tatis	.20
88	Roger Clemens	.75
89	Jose Cruz Jr.	.50
90	Shawn Green	.15
91	Jeff Suppan (Little Dawgs)	.10
92	Eli Marrero (Little Dawgs)	.10
93	*Mike Lowell* (Little Dawgs)	.30
94	Ben Grieve (Little Dawgs)	.50
95	Cliff Politte (Little Dawgs)	.10
96	*Rolando Arrojo* (Little Dawgs)	.40
97	Mike Caruso (Little Dawgs)	.10
98	Miguel Tejada (Little Dawgs)	.20
99	Rod Myers (Little Dawgs)	.10
100	Juan Encarnacion (Little Dawgs)	.10
101	Enrique Wilson (Little Dawgs)	.10
102	Brian Giles (Little Dawgs)	.10
103	*Magglio Ordonez* (Little Dawgs)	.75
104	Brian Rose (Little Dawgs)	.10
105	*Ryan Jackson* (Little Dawgs)	.25
106	Mark Kotsay (Little Dawgs)	.30
107	Desi Relaford (Little Dawgs)	.10
108	A.J. Hinch (Little Dawgs)	.10
109	Eric Milton (Little Dawgs)	.10
110	Ricky Ledee (Little Dawgs)	.25
111	Karim Garcia (Little Dawgs)	.10
112	Derrek Lee (Little Dawgs)	.10
113	Brad Fullmer (Little Dawgs)	.20
114	Travis Lee (Little Dawgs)	.50
115	Greg Norton (Little Dawgs)	.10
116	Rich Butler (Little Dawgs)	.10
117	*Masato Yoshii* (Little Dawgs)	.40
118	Paul Konerko (Little Dawgs)	.25
119	Richard Hidalgo (Little Dawgs)	.10
120	Todd Helton (Little Dawgs)	.40
121	Nomar Garciaparra (7th Inning Sketch)	.75
122	Scott Rolen (7th Inning Sketch)	.40
123	Cal Ripken Jr. (7th Inning Sketch)	1.00
124	Derek Jeter (7th Inning Sketch)	.60
125	Mike Piazza (7th Inning Sketch)	.75
126	Tony Gwynn (7th Inning Sketch)	.60
127	Mark McGwire (7th Inning Sketch)	1.50
128	Kenny Lofton (7th Inning Sketch)	.30
129	Greg Maddux (7th Inning Sketch)	.75
130	Jeff Bagwell (7th Inning Sketch)	.40
131	Randy Johnson (7th Inning Sketch)	.25
132	Alex Rodriguez (7th Inning Sketch)	1.00
133	Mo Vaughn (Name Plates)	.30
134	Chipper Jones (Name Plates)	.75
135	Juan Gonzalez (Name Plates)	.60
136	Tony Clark (Name Plates)	.20
137	Fred McGriff (Name Plates)	.10
138	Roger Clemens (Name Plates)	.40
139	Ken Griffey Jr. (Name Plates)	1.25
140	Ivan Rodriguez (Name Plates)	.30
141	Vinny Castilla (Trivia Card)	.10
142	Livan Hernandez (Trivia Card)	.10
143	Jose Cruz Jr. (Trivia Card)	.25
144	Andruw Jones (Trivia Card)	.30
145	Rafael Palmeiro (Trivia Card)	.20
146	Chuck Knoblauch (Trivia Card)	.10
147	Jay Buhner (Trivia Card)	.10
148	Andres Galarraga (Trivia Card)	.10
149	Frank Thomas (Trivia Card)	.60
150	Todd Hundley (Trivia Card)	.10

1998 SkyBox Dugout Axcess Autograph Redemption Cards

These scarce - one per 96 packs - inserts were redeemable (until March 31, 1999) for autographed baseballs or gloves from more than a dozen established stars and promising youngsters. Because the cards do not picture the player involved, having a generic photo of a person's arm signing an autograph, the exchange cards don't have tremendous collector value now that the redemption period has expired. The autographed balls and gloves would be valued according to supply and demand in the memorabilia marketplace.

		MT
Complete Set (15):		75.00
Common Card:		3.00
(1)	Jay Buhner (Ball)	3.00
(2)	Roger Clemens (Ball)	5.00
(3)	Jose Cruz Jr. (Ball)	4.50
(4)	Darin Erstad (Glove)	12.50
(5)	Nomar Garciaparra (Ball)	6.00
(6)	Tony Gwynn (Ball)	5.00
(7)	Roberto Hernandez (Ball)	3.00
(8)	Todd Hollandsworth (Glove)	10.00
(9)	Greg Maddux (Ball)	6.00
(10)	Alex Ochoa (Glove)	10.00
(11)	Alex Rodriguez (Ball)	7.50
(12)	Scott Rolen (Glove)	12.50
(13)	Scott Rolen (Ball)	5.00
(14)	Todd Walker (Glove)	12.50
(15)	Tony Womack (Ball)	3.00

1998 SkyBox Dugout Axcess Dishwashers

This 10-card set was a tribute to the game's best pitchers who "clean the home plate of opposing batters." Cards were inserted one per eight packs.

		MT
Complete Set (10):		6.00
Common Player:		.25
Inserted 1:8		
D1	Greg Maddux	3.00
D2	Kevin Brown	.50
D3	Pedro Martinez	1.00
D4	Randy Johnson	1.00
D5	Curt Schilling	.40
D6	John Smoltz	.50
D7	Darryl Kile	.25
D8	Roger Clemens	2.00
D9	Andy Pettitte	.75
D10	Mike Mussina	.75

1998 SkyBox Dugout Axcess Double Header

Double Header featured 20 players on cards that doubled as game pieces. The game instructions were on the card and required two dice to play. These were inserted at a rate of two per pack.

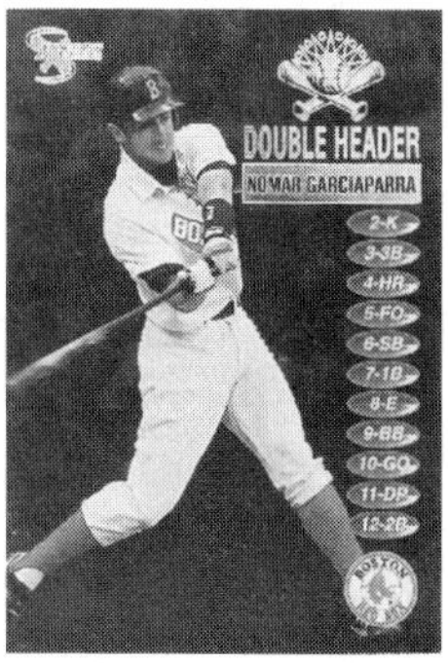

		MT
Complete Set (20):		5.00
Common Player:		.20
Inserted 2:1		
DH1	Jeff Bagwell	.30
DH2	Albert Belle	.25
DH3	Barry Bonds	.25
DH4	Derek Jeter	.60
DH5	Tony Clark	.20
DH6	Nomar Garciaparra	.60
DH7	Juan Gonzalez	.50
DH8	Ken Griffey Jr.	1.00
DH9	Chipper Jones	.60
DH10	Kenny Lofton	.20
DH11	Mark McGwire	1.00
DH12	Mo Vaughn	.20
DH13	Mike Piazza	.60
DH14	Cal Ripken Jr.	.75
DH15	Ivan Rodriguez	.25
DH16	Scott Rolen	.30
DH17	Frank Thomas	.50
DH18	Tony Gwynn	.50
DH19	Travis Lee	.40
DH20	Jose Cruz Jr.	.20

1998 SkyBox Dugout Axcess Frequent Flyers

The game's top 10 base stealers were included in Frequent Flyers. This insert was designed to look like airline frequent flyer cards and was inserted one per four packs. Fronts have player action photos on a metallic-foil background of a cloudy sky. Backs have a portrait photo and a few words about the player's base-stealing ability. Cards are numbered with an "FF" prefix.

		MT
Complete Set (10):		3.00
Common Player:		.25
Inserted 1:4		
FF1	Brian Hunter	.25
FF2	Kenny Lofton	.50
FF3	Chuck Knoblauch	.40
FF4	Tony Womack	.25
FF5	Marquis Grissom	.25
FF6	Craig Biggio	.35
FF7	Barry Bonds	.75
FF8	Tom Goodwin	.25
FF9	Delino DeShields	.25
FF10	Eric Young	.25

1998 SkyBox Dugout Axcess Gronks

Gronks featured 10 of the top home run hitters and was a hobby exclusive insert. The name of the insert originated from shortstop Greg Gagne, and the cards were inserted in one per 72 packs.

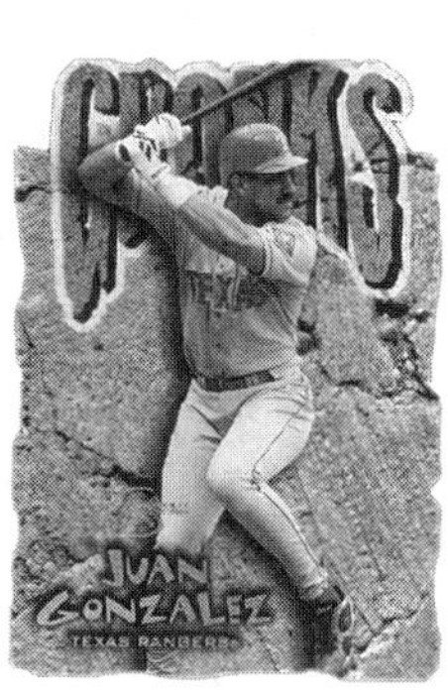

		MT
Complete Set (10):		100.00
Common Player:		5.00
Inserted 1:72		
G1	Jeff Bagwell	12.50
G2	Albert Belle	7.50
G3	Juan Gonzalez	15.00
G4	Ken Griffey Jr.	30.00
G5	Mark McGwire	30.00
G6	Mike Piazza	20.00
G7	Frank Thomas	15.00
G8	Mo Vaughn	5.00
G9	Ken Caminiti	7.50
G10	Tony Clark	5.00

1998 SkyBox Dugout Axcess Inside Axcess

This 150-card parallel set was sequentially numbered to 50 sets, with each card containing a stamped logo on the front and serial numbering on the back.

	MT
Common Player:	10.00
Inside Axcess Stars: 60-75X	
(See 1998 SkyBox Dugout Access for checklist and base card values.)	

1998 SkyBox Dugout Axcess SuperHeroes

SuperHeroes combined 10 top superstars with the Marvel Comics superhero with whom they share a common trait in this 10-card insert set. Cards were inserted at a rate of one per 20 packs.

		MT
Complete Set (10):		50.00
Common Player:		2.00
Inserted 1:20		
SH1	Barry Bonds	4.00
SH2	Andres Galarraga	2.00
SH3	Ken Griffey Jr.	15.00
SH4	Chipper Jones	10.00
SH5	Andruw Jones	4.00
SH6	Hideo Nomo	2.00
SH7	Cal Ripken Jr.	12.00
SH8	Alex Rodriguez	12.00
SH9	Frank Thomas	6.00
SH10	Mo Vaughn	2.00

Player names in *Italic* type indicate a rookie card.

1998 SkyBox SportsFest

As part of its participation at SportsFest in Philadelphia in May, 1998, SkyBox issued a special card of hometown hero Scott Rolen. The card was available only as a wrapper redemption at the show and was limited to 5,000. Front has an action photo of Rolen on a colorful background with the team and show logos at bottom. Back has a portrait photo and stats.

		MT
SF1	Scott Rolen	6.00

1999 SkyBox E-X Century

The 120-card base set features a clear plastic stock with the player name, logo and position stamped in holographic foil. Card backs have the featured player's vital information along with his '98 statistics and his major league totals. Cards 91-120 are part of a prospects subset and are short-printed seeded 1:2 packs. Three-card packs have a SRP of $5.99.

		MT
Complete Set (120):		125.00
Common Player:		.40
Common SP (91-120):		1.00
Inserted 1:2		
Wax Box:		75.00
1	Scott Rolen	2.50
2	Nomar Garciaparra	4.50
3	Mike Piazza	4.50
4	Tony Gwynn	4.00
5	Sammy Sosa	4.50
6	Alex Rodriguez	6.00
7	Vladimir Guerrero	2.50
8	Chipper Jones	4.50
9	Derek Jeter	4.50
10	Kerry Wood	1.00
11	Juan Gonzalez	3.50
12	Frank Thomas	2.50
13	Mo Vaughn	1.00
14	Greg Maddux	4.50
15	Jeff Bagwell	2.50
16	Mark McGwire	7.50
17	Ken Griffey Jr.	7.50
18	Roger Clemens	2.50
19	Cal Ripken Jr.	6.00
20	Travis Lee	1.50
21	Todd Helton	1.50
22	Darin Erstad	2.00
23	Pedro Martinez	1.50
24	Barry Bonds	2.00
25	Andruw Jones	1.50
26	Larry Walker	1.25
27	Albert Belle	2.00
28	Ivan Rodriguez	2.00
29	Magglio Ordonez	.40
30	Andres Galarraga	.75
31	Mike Mussina	1.25
32	Randy Johnson	1.50
33	Tom Glavine	.60
34	Barry Larkin	.50
35	Jim Thome	.75
36	Gary Sheffield	.50
37	Bernie Williams	1.25
38	Carlos Delgado	.60
39	Rafael Palmeiro	.60
40	Edgar Renteria	.40
41	Brad Fullmer	.40
42	David Wells	.40
43	Dante Bichette	.75
44	Jaret Wright	.75
45	Ricky Ledee	.40
46	Ray Lankford	.40
47	Mark Grace	.60
48	Jeff Cirillo	.40
49	Rondell White	.40
50	Jeromy Burnitz	.40
51	Sean Casey	.60
52	Rolando Arrojo	.40
53	Jason Giambi	.40
54	John Olerud	.50
55	Will Clark	.75
56	Raul Mondesi	.60
57	Scott Brosius	.40
58	Bartolo Colon	.40
59	Steve Finley	.40
60	Javy Lopez	.40
61	Tim Salmon	.50
62	Roberto Alomar	1.25
63	Vinny Castilla	.40
64	Craig Biggio	1.25
65	Jose Guillen	.40
66	Greg Vaughn	.40
67	Jose Canseco	1.00
68	Shawn Green	.50
69	Curt Schilling	.50
70	Orlando Hernandez	1.50
71	Jose Cruz Jr.	.60
72	Alex Gonzalez	.40
73	Tino Martinez	.50
74	Todd Hundley	.40
75	Brian Giles	.40
76	Cliff Floyd	.40
77	Paul O'Neill	.60
78	Ken Caminiti	.60
79	Ron Gant	.40
80	Juan Encarnacion	.60
81	Ben Grieve	2.00
82	Brian Jordan	.40
83	Rickey Henderson	.60
84	Tony Clark	.75
85	Shannon Stewart	.40
86	Robin Ventura	.50
87	Todd Walker	.40
88	Kevin Brown	.60
89	Moises Alou	.50
90	Manny Ramirez	2.50
91	Gabe Alvarez	1.25
92	Jeremy Giambi	1.50
93	Adrian Beltre	2.50
94	George Lombard	1.50
95	Ryan Minor	1.50
96	Kevin Witt	1.25
97	*Scott Hunter*	1.25
98	Carlos Guillen	1.25
99	Derrick Gibson	1.25
100	Trot Nixon	1.25
101	Troy Glaus	7.50
102	Armando Rios	1.50
103	Preston Wilson	1.25
104	*Pat Burrell*	15.00
105	J.D. Drew	5.00
106	Bruce Chen	1.50
107	Matt Clement	1.00
108	Carlos Beltran	4.50
109	Carlos Febles	2.00
110	Rob Fick	1.00
111	Russell Branyan	1.50
112	*Roosevelt Brown*	2.50
113	Corey Koskie	1.25
114	Mario Encarnacion	2.00
115	*Peter Tucci*	1.25
116	Eric Chavez	4.00
117	Gabe Kapler	6.00
118	Marlon Anderson	2.00
119	*A.J. Burnett*	3.50
120	Ryan Bradley	1.25
---	Checklist 1-96	.10
---	Checklist 97-120/ Inserts	.10

1999 SkyBox E-X Century Essential Credentials Future

A glossy silver design replaces the clear plastic portions seen on the base cards. Production varied depending on the card number, with the exact production number of each player determined by subtracting his card number from 121. Quantity issued is listed in parentheses. Cards #114-120 are not priced due to rarity.

		MT
Common Player:		15.00
1	Scott Rolen (120)	75.00
2	Nomar Garciaparra (119)	125.00
3	Mike Piazza (118)	125.00
4	Tony Gwynn (117)	100.00
5	Sammy Sosa (116)	125.00
6	Alex Rodriguez (115)	140.00
7	Vladimir Guerrero (114)	60.00
8	Chipper Jones (113)	125.00
9	Derek Jeter (112)	125.00
10	Kerry Wood (111)	50.00
11	Juan Gonzalez (110)	75.00
12	Frank Thomas (109)	75.00
13	Mo Vaughn (108)	50.00
14	Greg Maddux (107)	100.00
15	Jeff Bagwell (106)	60.00
16	Mark McGwire (105)	200.00
17	Ken Griffey Jr. (104)	200.00
18	Roger Clemens (103)	75.00
19	Cal Ripken Jr. (102)	140.00
20	Travis Lee (101)	30.00
21	Todd Helton (100)	40.00
22	Darin Erstad (99)	30.00
23	Pedro Martinez (98)	60.00
24	Barry Bonds (97)	60.00
25	Andruw Jones (96)	40.00
26	Larry Walker (95)	40.00
27	Albert Belle (94)	40.00
28	Ivan Rodriguez (93)	40.00
29	Magglio Ordonez (92)	40.00
30	Andres Galarraga (91)	30.00
31	Mike Mussina (90)	60.00
32	Randy Johnson (89)	60.00
33	Tom Glavine (88)	30.00
34	Barry Larkin (87)	25.00
35	Jim Thome (86)	30.00
36	Gary Sheffield (85)	30.00
37	Bernie Williams (84)	50.00
38	Carlos Delgado (83)	40.00
39	Rafael Palmeiro (82)	40.00
40	Edgar Renteria (81)	15.00
41	Brad Fullmer (80)	15.00
42	David Wells (79)	15.00
43	Dante Bichette (78)	30.00
44	Jaret Wright (77)	25.00
45	Ricky Ledee (76)	20.00
46	Ray Lankford (75)	10.00
47	Mark Grace (74)	30.00
48	Jeff Cirillo (73)	10.00
49	Rondell White (72)	15.00
50	Jeromy Burnitz (71)	10.00
51	Sean Casey (70)	50.00
52	Rolando Arrojo (69)	15.00
53	Jason Giambi (68)	15.00
54	John Olerud (67)	30.00
55	Will Clark (66)	50.00
56	Raul Mondesi (65)	30.00
57	Scott Brosius (64)	15.00
58	Bartolo Colon (63)	25.00
59	Steve Finley (62)	15.00
60	Javy Lopez (61)	25.00
61	Tim Salmon (60)	30.00
62	Roberto Alomar (59)	75.00
63	Vinny Castilla (58)	25.00
64	Craig Biggio (57)	60.00
65	Jose Guillen (56)	20.00
66	Greg Vaughn (55)	20.00
67	Jose Canseco (54)	70.00
68	Shawn Green (53)	30.00
69	Curt Schilling (52)	25.00
70	Orlando Hernandez (51)	75.00
71	Jose Cruz Jr. (50)	25.00
72	Alex Gonzalez (49)	20.00
73	Tino Martinez (48)	40.00
74	Todd Hundley (47)	20.00
75	Brian Giles (46)	20.00
76	Cliff Floyd (45)	20.00
77	Paul O'Neill (44)	35.00
78	Ken Caminiti (43)	40.00
79	Ron Gant (42)	30.00
80	Juan Encarnacion (41)	40.00
81	Ben Grieve (40)	70.00
82	Brian Jordan (39)	20.00
83	Rickey Henderson (38)	40.00
84	Tony Clark (37)	40.00
85	Shannon Stewart (36)	20.00
86	Robin Ventura (35)	30.00
87	Todd Walker (34)	25.00
88	Kevin Brown (33)	40.00
89	Moises Alou (32)	35.00
90	Manny Ramirez (31)	125.00
91	Gabe Alvarez (30)	25.00
92	Jeremy Giambi (29)	25.00
93	Adrian Beltre (28)	40.00
94	George Lombard (27)	35.00
95	Ryan Minor (26)	40.00
96	Kevin Witt (25)	25.00
97	Scott Hunter (24)	25.00
98	Carlos Guillen (23)	25.00
99	Derrick Gibson (22)	35.00
100	Trot Nixon (21)	25.00
101	Troy Glaus (20)	125.00
102	Armando Rios (19)	30.00
103	Preston Wilson (18)	40.00
104	Pat Burrell (17)	300.00
105	J.D. Drew (16)	100.00
106	Bruce Chen (15)	40.00
107	Matt Clement (14)	40.00
108	Carlos Beltran (13)	125.00
109	Carlos Febles (12)	40.00
110	Rob Fick (11)	40.00
111	Russell Branyan (10)	60.00
112	Roosevelt Brown (9)	100.00
113	Corey Koskie (8)	40.00
114	Mario Encarnacion (7)	60.00
115	Peter Tucci (6)	75.00
116	Eric Chavez (5)	125.00
117	Gabe Kapler (4)	125.00
118	Marlon Anderson (3)	150.00
119	A.J. Burnett (2)	150.00
120	Ryan Bradley (1)	200.00

1999 SkyBox E-X Century Essential Credentials Now

Like Future, this is a parallel of the base set, with production of each card limited to that player's card number. These cards have a glossy gold look. Cards #1-9 are not priced due to rarity.

		MT
Common Player:		15.00
1	Scott Rolen (1)	600.00
2	Nomar Garciaparra (2)	300.00
3	Mike Piazza (3)	300.00
4	Tony Gwynn (4)	250.00
5	Sammy Sosa (5)	450.00
6	Alex Rodriguez (6)	400.00
7	Vladimir Guerrero (7)	200.00
8	Chipper Jones (8)	300.00
9	Derek Jeter (9)	300.00
10	Kerry Wood (10)	170.00
11	Juan Gonzalez (11)	250.00
12	Frank Thomas (12)	250.00
13	Mo Vaughn (13)	100.00
14	Greg Maddux (14)	200.00
15	Jeff Bagwell (15)	175.00
16	Mark McGwire (16)	800.00
17	Ken Griffey Jr. (17)	800.00
18	Roger Clemens (18)	200.00
19	Cal Ripken Jr. (19)	500.00
20	Travis Lee (20)	60.00
21	Todd Helton (21)	80.00
22	Darin Erstad (22)	60.00
23	Pedro Martinez (23)	80.00
24	Barry Bonds (24)	150.00
25	Andruw Jones (25)	120.00
26	Larry Walker (26)	80.00
27	Albert Belle (27)	120.00
28	Ivan Rodriguez (28)	100.00
29	Magglio Ordonez (29)	50.00
30	Andres Galarraga (30)	60.00
31	Mike Mussina (31)	90.00
32	Randy Johnson (32)	100.00
33	Tom Glavine (33)	40.00
34	Barry Larkin (34)	30.00
35	Jim Thome (35)	40.00
36	Gary Sheffield (36)	30.00
37	Bernie Williams (37)	75.00
38	Carlos Delgado (38)	50.00
39	Rafael Palmeiro (39)	60.00
40	Edgar Renteria (40)	25.00
41	Brad Fullmer (41)	20.00
42	David Wells (42)	20.00
43	Dante Bichette (43)	40.00
44	Jaret Wright (44)	25.00
45	Ricky Ledee (45)	20.00
46	Ray Lankford (46)	15.00
47	Mark Grace (47)	40.00
48	Jeff Cirillo (48)	15.00
49	Rondell White (49)	25.00
50	Jeromy Burnitz (50)	15.00
51	Sean Casey (51)	50.00
52	Rolando Arrojo (52)	15.00
53	Jason Giambi (53)	15.00
54	John Olerud (54)	25.00
55	Will Clark (55)	50.00
56	Raul Mondesi (56)	40.00
57	Scott Brosius (57)	15.00
58	Bartolo Colon (58)	20.00
59	Steve Finley (59)	15.00
60	Javy Lopez (60)	20.00
61	Tim Salmon (61)	20.00
62	Roberto Alomar (62)	75.00
63	Vinny Castilla (63)	20.00
64	Craig Biggio (64)	50.00
65	Jose Guillen (65)	15.00
66	Greg Vaughn (66)	15.00
67	Jose Canseco (67)	60.00
68	Shawn Green (68)	25.00
69	Curt Schilling (69)	20.00
70	Orlando Hernandez (70)	40.00
71	Jose Cruz Jr. (71)	15.00
72	Alex Gonzalez (72)	15.00
73	Tino Martinez (73)	20.00
74	Todd Hundley (74)	20.00
75	Brian Giles (75)	15.00
76	Cliff Floyd (76)	15.00
77	Paul O'Neill (77)	25.00
78	Ken Caminiti (78)	30.00
79	Ron Gant (79)	15.00
80	Juan Encarnacion (80)	20.00
81	Ben Grieve (81)	20.00
82	Brian Jordan (82)	15.00
83	Rickey Henderson (83)	30.00
84	Tony Clark (84)	40.00
85	Shannon Stewart (85)	15.00
86	Robin Ventura (86)	20.00
87	Todd Walker (87)	20.00
88	Kevin Brown (88)	30.00
89	Moises Alou (89)	20.00
90	Manny Ramirez (90)	60.00
91	Gabe Alvarez (91)	15.00
92	Jeremy Giambi (92)	15.00
93	Adrian Beltre (93)	25.00
94	George Lombard (94)	20.00
95	Ryan Minor (95)	25.00
96	Kevin Witt (96)	15.00
97	Scott Hunter (97)	15.00
98	Carlos Guillen (98)	15.00
99	Derrick Gibson (99)	20.00
100	Trot Nixon (100)	15.00
101	Troy Glaus (101)	40.00
102	Armando Rios (102)	15.00
103	Preston Wilson (103)	20.00
104	Pat Burrell (104)	125.00
105	J.D. Drew (105)	40.00
106	Bruce Chen (106)	15.00
107	Matt Clement (107)	15.00
108	Carlos Beltran (108)	40.00
109	Carlos Febles (109)	25.00
110	Rob Fick (110)	15.00
111	Russell Branyan (111)	20.00
112	Roosevelt Brown (112)	25.00
113	Corey Koskie (113)	15.00
114	Mario Encarnacion (114)	20.00
115	Peter Tucci (115)	15.00
116	Eric Chavez (116)	30.00
117	Gabe Kapler (117)	40.00
118	Marlon Anderson (118)	15.00
119	A.J. Burnett (119)	30.00
120	Ryan Bradley (120)	15.00

1999 SkyBox E-X Century Authen-Kicks

Authen-Kicks is a game-used insert that embeds game-worn shoe swatches from the featured player. Each is done in a horizontal format and is sequentially numbered. The number of swatch cards differs from player to player, and is indicated here in parentheses. Autographed versions of two colors of J.D. Drew shoes were also produced.

		MT
Complete Set (9):		700.00
Common Player:		50.00
(1)	J.D. Drew (160)	125.00
(1ab)	J.D. Drew (autographed black) (8)	600.00

(1ar)	J.D. Drew (autographed red) (8)	600.00
(2)	Travis Lee (175)	75.00
(3)	Kevin Millwood (160)	75.00
(4)	Bruce Chen (205)	50.00
(5)	Troy Glaus (205)	120.00
(6)	Todd Helton (205)	75.00
(7)	Ricky Ledee (180)	60.00
(8)	Scott Rolen (205)	150.00
(9)	Jeremy Giambi (205)	50.00

1999 SkyBox E-X Century E-X Quisite

15 of baseball's top young players are showcased, with a black background and interior die-cutting around the player image. These are seeded 1:18 packs.

		MT
Complete Set (15):		50.00
Common Player:		2.00
Inserted 1:18		
1	Troy Glaus	7.50
2	J.D. Drew	6.00
3	Pat Burrell	20.00
4	Russell Branyan	2.00
5	Kerry Wood	3.00
6	Eric Chavez	6.00
7	Ben Grieve	2.00
8	Gabe Kapler	7.50
9	Adrian Beltre	4.00
10	Todd Helton	5.00
11	Roosevelt Brown	4.00
12	Marlon Anderson	2.00
13	Jeremy Giambi	4.00
14	Magglio Ordonez	2.50
15	Travis Lee	6.00

1999 SkyBox E-X Century Favorites for Fenway

This 20-card set pays tribute to one of baseball's favorite ballparks, Fenway Park the venue for the 1999 All-Star Game. These have a photo of the featured player with an image of Fenway Park in the background on a horizontal format. These are seeded 1:36 packs.

		MT
Complete Set (20):		325.00
Common Player:		5.00
Inserted 1:36		
1	Mo Vaughn	5.00
2	Nomar Garciaparra	25.00
3	Frank Thomas	20.00
4	Ken Griffey Jr.	40.00
5	Roger Clemens	15.00
6	Alex Rodriguez	30.00
7	Derek Jeter	25.00
8	Juan Gonzalez	20.00
9	Cal Ripken Jr.	30.00
10	Ivan Rodriguez	8.00
11	J.D. Drew	8.00
12	Barry Bonds	10.00
13	Tony Gwynn	20.00
14	Vladimir Guerrero	12.00
15	Chipper Jones	25.00
16	Kerry Wood	8.00
17	Mike Piazza	25.00
18	Sammy Sosa	25.00
19	Scott Rolen	12.00
20	Mark McGwire	40.00

1999 SkyBox E-X Century Milestones of the Century

This 10-card set spotlights the top statistical performances from the 1998 season, sequentially numbered to that performance in a multi-layered design.

		MT
Complete Set (10):		1350.
Common Player:		15.00
Numbered to featured milestone		
1	Kerry Wood (20)	75.00
2	Mark McGwire (70)	300.00
3	Sammy Sosa (66)	150.00
4	Ken Griffey Jr. (350)	75.00
5	Roger Clemens (98)	100.00
6	Cal Ripken Jr. (17)	500.00
7	Alex Rodriguez (40)	200.00
8	Barry Bonds (400)	15.00
9	N.Y. Yankees (114)	100.00
10	Travis Lee (98)	50.00

1999 SkyBox Molten Metal

Distributed exclusively to the hobby, the 150-card set consists of three subsets: Metal Smiths, Heavy Metal and Supernatural. Metal Smiths (1-100) show baseball's top players, Heavy Metal (101-130) focus on power hitters and Supernatural (131-150) focus on rookies. Base cards feature silver foil stamping on a 24-point stock with holofoil and wet-laminate overlays. Molten Metal was released in six-card packs with a SRP of $4.99. A special version of the issue was sold only at the 20th Nat'l Sports Collectors Convention in Atlanta, July 19-24. The show version includes autograph redemption cards for show guests and a die-cut series of 30 current and former Braves favorites. Each of the show version cards has a small National Convention logo printed on back; they currently carry no premium.

		MT
Complete Set (150):		120.00
Common Metalsmiths (1-100):		.25
Inserted 4:1		
Common Heavy Metal (101-130):		.40
Inserted 1:1		
Common Supernatural (131-150):		1.00
Inserted 1:2		
Wax Box:		65.00
1	Larry Walker	1.00
2	Jose Canseco	1.00
3	Brian Jordan	.25
4	Rafael Palmeiro	.75
5	Edgar Renteria	.25
6	Dante Bichette	.50
7	Mark Kotsay	.25
8	Denny Neagle	.25
9	Ellis Burks	.25
10	Paul O'Neill	.35
11	Miguel Tejada	.40
12	Ken Caminiti	.35
13	David Cone	.35
14	Jason Kendall	.35
15	Ruben Rivera	.25
16	Todd Walker	.25
17	Bobby Higginson	.25
18	Derrek Lee	.25
19	Rondell White	.35
20	Pedro J. Martinez	1.25
21	Jeff Kent	.25
22	Randy Johnson	1.00
23	Matt Williams	.50
24	Sean Casey	.40
25	Eric Davis	.25
26	Ryan Klesko	.25
27	Curt Schilling	.35
28	Geoff Jenkins	.25
29	Armand Abreu	.25
30	Vinny Castilla	.35
31	Will Clark	.75
32	Ray Durham	.25
33	Ray Lankford	.25
34	Richie Sexson	.25
35	Derrick Gibson	.25
36	Mark Grace	.50
37	Greg Vaughn	.25
38	Bartolo Colon	.25
39	Steve Finley	.25
40	Chuck Knoblauch	.50
41	Ricky Ledee	.25
42	John Smoltz	.25
43	Moises Alou	.40
44	Jim Edmonds	.25
45	Cliff Floyd	.25
46	Javy Lopez	.25
47	Jim Thome	.50
48	J.T. Snow	.25
49	Sandy Alomar Jr.	.25
50	Andy Pettitte	.35
51	Juan Encarnacion	.25
52	Travis Fryman	.25
53	Eli Marrero	.25
54	Jeff Cirillo	.25
55	Brady Anderson	.25
56	Jose Cruz Jr.	.40
57	Edgar Martinez	.25
58	Garret Anderson	.25
59	Paul Konerko	.25
60	Eric Milton	.25
61	Jason Giambi	.25
62	Tom Glavine	.35
63	Justin Thompson	.25
64	Brad Fullmer	.25
65	Marquis Grissom	.25
66	Fernando Tatis	.35
67	Carlos Beltran	1.50
68	Charles Johnson	.25
69	Raul Mondesi	.40
70	Richard Hildalgo	.25
71	Barry Larkin	.35
72	David Wells	.25
73	Jay Buhner	.25
74	Matt Clement	.25
75	Eric Karros	.25
76	Carl Pavano	.25
77	Mariano Rivera	.40
78	Livan Hernandez	.25
79	A.J. Hinch	.25
80	Tino Martinez	.40
81	Rusty Greer	.25
82	Jose Guillen	.25
83	Robin Ventura	.40
84	Kevin Brown	.40
85	Chan Ho Park	.25
86	John Olerud	.40
87	Johnny Damon	.25
88	Todd Hundley	.25
89	Fred McGriff	.40
90	Wade Boggs	.75
91	Mike Cameron	.25
92	Gary Sheffield	.35
93	Rickey Henderson	.40
94	Pat Hentgen	.25
95	Omar Vizquel	.25
96	Craig Biggio	.60
97	Mike Caruso	.25
98	Neifi Perez	.25
99	Mike Mussina	.75
100	Carlos Delgado	.50
101	Andruw Jones (Heavy Metal)	1.50
102	*Pat Burrell* (Heavy Metal)	10.00
103	Orlando Hernandez (Heavy Metal)	1.50
104	Darin Erstad (Heavy Metal)	1.25
105	Roberto Alomar (Heavy Metal)	1.00
106	Tim Salmon (Heavy Metal)	.75
107	Albert Belle (Heavy Metal)	1.50
108	*Chad Allen* (Heavy Metal)	1.50
109	Travis Lee (Heavy Metal)	1.50
110	*Jesse Garcia* (Heavy Metal)	1.00
111	Tony Clark (Heavy Metal)	.50
112	Ivan Rodriguez (Heavy Metal)	1.50
113	Troy Glaus (Heavy Metal)	1.50
114	*A.J. Burnett* (Heavy Metal)	3.00
115	David Justice (Heavy Metal)	.50
116	Adrian Beltre (Heavy Metal)	.75
117	Eric Chavez (Heavy Metal)	.75
118	Kenny Lofton (Heavy Metal)	1.00
119	Michael Barrett (Heavy Metal)	.75
120	*Jeff Weaver* (Heavy Metal)	4.00
121	Manny Ramirez (Heavy Metal)	2.00
122	Barry Bonds (Heavy Metal)	1.50
123	Bernie Williams (Heavy Metal)	.75
124	*Freddy Garcia* (Heavy Metal)	6.00
125	*Scott Hunter* (Heavy Metal)	1.00
126	Jeremy Giambi (Heavy Metal)	.40
127	*Masao Kida* (Heavy Metal)	1.00
128	Todd Helton (Heavy Metal)	1.00
129	Mike Figga (Heavy Metal)	.40
130	Mo Vaughn (Heavy Metal)	.75
131	J.D. Drew (Supernaturals)	2.50
132	Cal Ripken Jr. (Supernaturals)	6.00
133	Ken Griffey Jr. (Supernaturals)	8.00
134	Mark McGwire (Supernaturals)	8.00
135	Nomar Garciaparra (Supernaturals)	6.00
136	Greg Maddux (Supernaturals)	6.00
137	Mike Piazza (Supernaturals)	6.00
138	Alex Rodriguez (Supernaturals)	8.00
139	Frank Thomas (Supernaturals)	5.00
140	Juan Gonzalez (Supernaturals)	5.00
141	Tony Gwynn (Supernaturals)	5.00
142	Derek Jeter (Supernaturals)	6.00
143	Chipper Jones (Supernaturals)	6.00
144	Scott Rolen (Supernaturals)	3.00
145	Sammy Sosa (Supernaturals)	5.00
146	Kerry Wood (Supernaturals)	2.00
147	Roger Clemens (Supernaturals)	3.00
148	Jeff Bagwell (Supernaturals)	2.00
149	Vladimir Guerrero (Supernaturals)	3.00
150	Ben Grieve (Supernaturals)	1.00

1999 SkyBox Molten Metal Fusion

Fusion is a 50-card partial parallel that is paralleled three times: Fusion, Sterling Fusion and Titanium Fusion. The three parallels consist of the two subsets Heavy Metal and Supernatural. Fusion Heavy Metals (1-30) are seeded 1:12 packs and Supernatural Fusions are seeded 1:24 packs. Fusions are laser die-cut with additional silver-foil stamping. Sterling Fusions are limited to 500 numbered sets with each card laser die-cut on a blue background with blue foil stamping. Titanium Fusions are limited to 50 sequentially numbered sets with gold background and enhanced with gold foil highlights.

		MT
Complete Set (50):		500.00
Common Heavy Metal (1-30):		2.00
Inserted 1:12		
Common Supernatural (31-50):		5.00
Inserted 1:24		
Sterling (1-30): 2X		
Sterling (31-50): 1.5X		
Production 500 sets		
Titanium (1-30): 8X		
Titanium (31-50): 6X		
Production 50 sets		
1	Andruw Jones	5.00
2	Pat Burrell	25.00
3	Orlando Hernandez	5.00
4	Darin Erstad	5.00
5	Roberto Alomar	4.00
6	Tim Salmon	3.00
7	Albert Belle	4.00
8	Chad Allen	2.00
9	Travis Lee	4.00
10	Jesse Garcia	2.00
11	Tony Clark	2.00
12	Ivan Rodriguez	4.00
13	Troy Glaus	6.00
14	A.J. Burnett	5.00
15	David Justice	2.00
16	Adrian Beltre	3.00
17	Eric Chavez	3.00
18	Kenny Lofton	2.00
19	Michael Barrett	2.00
20	Jeff Weaver	6.00
21	Manny Ramirez	8.00
22	Barry Bonds	6.00
23	Bernie Williams	4.00
24	Freddy Garcia	15.00
25	Scott Hunter	2.00
26	Jeremy Giambi	2.00
27	Masao Kida	2.00
28	Todd Helton	5.00
29	Mike Figga	2.00
30	Mo Vaughn	2.00
31	J.D. Drew	8.00
32	Cal Ripken Jr.	30.00
33	Ken Griffey Jr.	40.00
34	Mark McGwire	40.00
35	Nomar Garciaparra	25.00
36	Greg Maddux	25.00
37	Mike Piazza	25.00
38	Alex Rodriguez	30.00
39	Frank Thomas	20.00
40	Juan Gonzalez	20.00
41	Tony Gwynn	20.00
42	Derek Jeter	25.00
43	Chipper Jones	25.00
44	Scott Rolen	10.00
45	Sammy Sosa	25.00
46	Kerry Wood	6.00
47	Roger Clemens	15.00
48	Jeff Bagwell	10.00
49	Vladimir Guerrero	15.00
50	Ben Grieve	5.00

1999 SkyBox Molten Metal Fusion - Sterling

Sterling Fusions are limited to 500 numbered sets with each card laser die-cut on a blue background with blue foil graphic highlights. A special version of the issue was sold only at the 20th Nat'l Sports Collectors Convention in Atlanta, July 19-24. Each of the show-version cards has a small National Convention logo printed on back; they currently carry no premium.

	MT
Complete Set (50):	750.00
Common Player:	4.00
Sterling Stars: 1.5X	

(See 1999 Molten Metal Fusion for checklist and base card values.)

1999 SkyBox Molten Metal Fusion - Titanium

Titanium Fusions are limited to 50 sequentially numbered sets with gold background and enhanced with gold foil highlights. A special version of the issue was sold only at the 20th Nat'l Sports Collectors Convention in Atlanta, July 19-24. Each of the show-version cards has a small National Convention logo printed on back; they currently carry no premium.

	MT
Common Player:	15.00
Titanium Stars: 6X	

(See 1999 SkyBox Molten Metal Fusion for checklist and base card values.)

1999 SkyBox Molten Metal Oh Atlanta!

This 30-card set features players who are either current or former Atlanta Braves like Chipper Jones and Dave Justice. These inserts are seeded one per pack and was produced in conjunction with the 20th annual National Sports Collectors Convention in Atlanta.

		MT
	Complete Set (30):	50.00
	Common Player:	1.00
	Inserted 1:1	
1	Kenny Lofton	3.00
2	Kevin Millwood	6.00
3	Bret Boone	1.00
4	Otis Nixon	1.00
5	Vinny Castilla	1.00
6	Brian Jordan	1.00
7	Chipper Jones	15.00
8	Dave Justice	3.00
9	Micah Bowie	1.00
10	Fred McGriff	2.00
11	Ron Gant	1.00
12	Andruw Jones	6.00
13	Kent Mercker	1.00
14	Greg McMichael	1.00
15	Steve Avery	1.00
16	Marquis Grissom	1.00
17	Jason Schmidt	1.00
18	Ryan Klesko	1.50
19	Charlie O'Brien	1.00
20	Terry Pendleton	1.00
21	Denny Neagle	1.00
22	Greg Maddux	15.00
23	Tom Glavine	2.00
24	Javy Lopez	1.50
25	John Rocker	1.50
26	Walt Weiss	1.00
27	John Smoltz	1.50
28	Michael Tucker	1.00
29	Odalis Perez	1.00
30	Andres Galarraga	2.00

1999 SkyBox Molten Metal Xplosion

This is a 150-card parallel set, which is seeeded 1:2 packs. These are made of actual metal that have added etching and some foil stamping.

	MT
Complete Set (150):	500.00
Common Player:	1.00
Metalsmith Stars (1-100): 5X	
Heavy Metal Stars (101-130): 4X	
Supernatural Stars (131-150): 3X	
Inserted 1:2	

(See 1999 SkyBox Molten Metal for checklist and base card values.)

1999 SkyBox Premium

The base set consists of 300 cards, base cards feature full bleed fronts with gold-foil stamped player and team names. Card backs have complete year-by-year stats along with a close-up photo. The Rookie subset (223-272) also have a short-printed parallel version as well. Different photos are used but they have the same card number and card back. The short-print versions are seeded 1:8 packs and have an action photo front while the non-seeded cards have a close-up photo.

		MT
	Complete Set (300):	30.00
	Complete Set w/sp's (350):	200.00
	Common Player:	.15
	Common SP (223-272):	1.50
	SPs inserted 1:8	
	Star Rubies: 50x to 90x	
	Production 50 sets	
	SP Star Rubies: 10x to 20x	
	Production 15 sets	
	Wax Box:	60.00
1	Alex Rodriguez	3.00
2	Sidney Ponson	.15
3	Shawn Green	.25
4	Dan Wilson	.15
5	Rolando Arrojo	.15
6	Roberto Alomar	.50
7	Matt Anderson	.15
8	David Segui	.15
9	Alex Gonzalez	.15
10	Edgar Renteria	.15
11	Benito Santiago	.15
12	Todd Stottlemyre	.15
13	Rico Brogna	.15
14	Troy Glaus	.75
15	Al Leiter	.15
16	Pedro J. Martinez	1.00
17	Paul O'Neill	.25
18	Manny Ramirez	1.00
19	Scott Rolen	.75
20	Curt Schilling	.25
21	Bobby Abreu	.15
22	Robb Nen	.15
23	Andy Pettitte	.40
24	John Wetteland	.15
25	Bobby Bonilla	.15
26	Darin Erstad	.60
27	Shawn Estes	.15
28	John Franco	.15
29	Nomar Garciaparra	2.00
30	Rick Helling	.15
31	David Justice	.25
32	Chuck Knoblauch	.25
33	Quinton McCracken	.15
34	Kenny Rogers	.15
35	Brian Giles	.15
36	Armando Benitez	.15
37	Trevor Hoffman	.15
38	Charles Johnson	.15
39	Travis Lee	.50
40	Tom Glavine	.25
41	Rondell White	.25
42	Orlando Hernandez	.40
43	Mickey Morandini	.15
44	Darryl Kile	.15
45	Greg Vaughn	.25
46	Gregg Jefferies	.15
47	Mark McGwire	4.00
48	Kerry Wood	.40
49	Jeromy Burnitz	.15
50	Ron Gant	.15
51	Vinny Castilla	.15
52	Doug Glanville	.15
53	Juan Guzman	.15
54	Dustin Hermanson	.15
55	Jose Hernandez	.15
56	Bob Higginson	.15
57	A.J. Hinch	.15
58	Randy Johnson	.50
59	Eli Marrero	.15
60	Rafael Palmeiro	.50
61	Carl Pavano	.15
62	Brett Tomko	.15
63	Jose Guillen	.15
64	Mike Lieberthal	.15
65	Jim Abbott	.15
66	Dante Bichette	.25
67	Jeff Cirillo	.15
68	Eric Davis	.20
69	Delino DeShields	.15
70	Steve Finley	.15
71	Mark Grace	.25
72	Jason Kendall	.25
73	Jeff Kent	.15
74	Desi Relaford	.15
75	Ivan Rodriguez	.75
76	Shannon Stewart	.15
77	Geoff Jenkins	.15
78	Ben Grieve	.60
79	Cliff Floyd	.15
80	Jason Giambi	.15
81	Rod Beck	.15
82	Derek Bell	.15
83	Will Clark	.40
84	David Dellucci	.15
85	Joey Hamilton	.15
86	Livan Hernandez	.15
87	Barry Larkin	.20
88	Matt Mantei	.15
89	Dean Palmer	.15
90	Chan Ho Park	.25
91	Jim Thome	.40
92	Miguel Tejada	.15
93	Justin Thompson	.15
94	David Wells	.15
95	Bernie Williams	.50
96	Jeff Bagwell	.75
97	Derrek Lee	.15
98	Devon White	.15
99	Jeff Shaw	.15
100	Brad Radke	.15
101	Mark Grudzielanek	.15
102	Javy Lopez	.25
103	Mike Sirotka	.15
104	Robin Ventura	.25
105	Andy Ashby	.15
106	Juan Gonzalez	1.50
107	Albert Belle	.75
108	Andy Benes	.15
109	Jay Buhner	.15
110	Ken Caminiti	.25
111	Roger Clemens	1.25
112	Mike Hampton	.15
113	Pete Harnisch	.15
114	Mike Piazza	2.00
115	J.T. Snow	.15
116	John Olerud	.25
117	Tony Womack	.15
118	Todd Zeile	.15
119	Tony Gwynn	1.50
120	Brady Anderson	.15
121	Sean Casey	.50
122	Jose Cruz Jr.	.25
123	Carlos Delgado	.50
124	Edgar Martinez	.15
125	Jose Mesa	.15
126	Shane Reynolds	.25
127	John Valentin	.15
128	Mo Vaughn	.50
129	Kevin Young	.15
130	Jay Bell	.15
131	Aaron Boone	.15
132	John Smoltz	.15
133	Mike Stanley	.15
134	Bret Saberhagen	.15
135	Tim Salmon	.25
136	Mariano Rivera	.25
137	Ken Griffey Jr.	4.00
138	Jose Offerman	.15
139	Troy Percival	.15
140	Greg Maddux	2.00
141	Frank Thomas	1.50
142	Steve Avery	.15
143	Kevin Millwood	.40
144	Sammy Sosa	2.00
145	Larry Walker	.60
146	Matt Williams	.30
147	Mike Caruso	.15
148	Todd Helton	.60
149	Andruw Jones	.50
150	Ray Lankford	.15
151	Craig Biggio	.40
152	Ugueth Urbina	.15
153	Wade Boggs	.40
154	Derek Jeter	2.00
155	Wally Joyner	.15
156	Mike Mussina	.50
157	Gregg Olson	.15
158	Henry Rodriguez	.15
159	Reggie Sanders	.15
160	Fernando Tatis	.40
161	Dmitri Young	.15
162	Rick Aguilera	.15
163	Marty Cordova	.15
164	Johnny Damon	.15
165	Ray Durham	.15
166	Brad Fullmer	.15
167	Chipper Jones	2.00
168	Bobby Smith	.15
169	Omar Vizquel	.15
170	Todd Hundley	.15
171	David Cone	.25
172	Royce Clayton	.15
173	Ryan Klesko	.15
174	Jeff Montgomery	.15
175	Magglio Ordonez	.25
176	Billy Wagner	.15
177	Masato Yoshii	.15
178	Jason Christiansen	.15
179	Chuck Finley	.15
180	Tom Gordon	.15
181	Wilton Guerrero	.15
182	Rickey Henderson	.25
183	Sterling Hitchcock	.15
184	Kenny Lofton	.50
185	Tino Martinez	.20
186	Fred McGriff	.30
187	Matt Stairs	.15
188	Neifi Perez	.15
189	Bob Wickman	.15
190	Barry Bonds	.75
191	Jose Canseco	.50
192	Damion Easley	.15
193	Jim Edmonds	.15
194	Juan Encarnacion	.25
195	Travis Fryman	.25
196	Tom Goodwin	.15
197	Rusty Greer	.15
198	Roberto Hernandez	.15
199	B.J. Surhoff	.15
200	Scott Brosius	.15
201	Brian Jordan	.15
202	Paul Konerko	.25
203	Ismael Valdes	.15
204	Eric Milton	.15
205	Adrian Beltre	.40
206	Tony Clark	.40
207	Bartolo Colon	.15
208	Cal Ripken Jr.	3.00
209	Moises Alou	.25
210	Wilson Alvarez	.15
211	Kevin Brown	.25
212	Orlando Cabrera	.15
213	Vladimir Guerrero	1.00
214	Jose Rosado	.15
215	Raul Mondesi	.25
216	Dave Nilsson	.15
217	Carlos Perez	.15
218	Jason Schmidt	.15
219	Richie Sexson	.25
220	Gary Sheffield	.25
221	Fernando Vina	.15
222	Todd Walker	.15
223	*Scott Sauerbeck*	.25
223	*Scott Sauerbeck (sp)*	1.50
224	*Pascual Matos*	.50
224	*Pascual Matos (sp)*	2.50
225	*Kyle Farnsworth*	.25
225	*Kyle Farnsworth (sp)*	1.50
226	*Freddy Garcia*	5.00
226	*Freddy Garcia (sp)*	15.00
227	*David Lundquist*	.25
227	*David Lundquist (sp)*	1.50
228	*Jolbert Cabrera*	.25
228	*Jolbert Cabrera (sp)*	1.50
229	*Dan Perkins*	.25
229	*Dan Perkins (sp)*	1.50
230	Warren Morris	.15
230	Warren Morris (sp)	2.00
231	Carlos Febles	.75
231	Carlos Febles (sp)	3.00
232	*Brett Hinchliffe*	.25
232	*Brett Hinchliffe (sp)*	1.50
233	*Jason Phillips*	.25
233	*Jason Phillips (sp)*	1.50
234	*Glen Barker*	.25
234	*Glen Barker (sp)*	1.50
235	*Jose Macias*	.50
235	*Jose Macias (sp)*	2.50
236	*Joe Mays*	.40
236	*Joe Mays (sp)*	2.00
237	*Chad Allen*	.25
237	*Chad Allen (sp)*	1.50
238	*Miguel Del Toro*	.25
238	*Miguel Del Toro (sp)*	1.50
239	Chris Singleton	.75
239	Chris Singleton (sp)	4.00
240	*Jesse Garcia*	.25
240	*Jesse Garcia (sp)*	1.50
241	Kris Benson	.25
241	Kris Benson (sp)	2.00
242	*Clay Bellinger*	.40
242	*Clay Bellinger (sp)*	2.00
243	Scott Williamson	.15
243	Scott Williamson (sp)	1.50
244	*Masao Kida*	.50
244	*Masao Kida (sp)*	2.50
245	*Guillermo Garcia*	.25
245	*Guillermo Garcia (sp)*	1.50
246	*A.J. Burnett*	2.00
246	*A.J. Burnett (sp)*	6.00
247	*Bo Porter*	.25
247	*Bo Porter (sp)*	1.50
248	*Pat Burrell*	5.00
248	*Pat Burrell (sp)*	15.00
249	Carlos Lee	.25
249	Carlos Lee (sp)	3.00
250	*Jeff Weaver*	2.50
250	*Jeff Weaver (sp)*	8.00
251	Ruben Mateo	.50
251	Ruben Mateo (sp)	2.00
252	J.D. Drew	1.50
252	J.D. Drew (sp)	10.00
253	Jeremy Giambi	.25
253	Jeremy Giambi (sp)	1.50
254	*Gary Bennett*	.25
254	*Gary Bennett (sp)*	1.50
255	*Edwards Guzman*	.25
255	*Edwards Guzman (sp)*	1.50
256	Ramon Martinez	.15
256	Ramon Martinez (sp)	1.50
257	*Giomar Guevara*	.40
257	*Giomar Guevara (sp)*	2.50
258	*Joe McEwing*	1.50
258	*Joe McEwing (sp)*	5.00
259	*Tom Davey*	.25
259	*Tom Davey (sp)*	1.50
260	Gabe Kapler	.75
260	Gabe Kapler (sp)	3.00
261	*Ryan Rupe*	.25
261	*Ryan Rupe (sp)*	1.50
262	*Kelly Dransfeldt*	.50
262	*Kelly Dransfeldt (sp)*	2.50
263	Michael Barrett	.15
263	Michael Barrett (sp)	1.50
264	Eric Chavez	.50
264	Eric Chavez (sp)	3.00
265	*Orber Moreno*	.25
265	*Orber Moreno (sp)*	1.50
266	Marlon Anderson	.15
266	Marlon Anderson (sp)	2.00
267	Carlos Beltran	2.00
267	Carlos Beltran (sp)	6.00
268	Doug Mientkiewicz	.50
268	Doug Mientkiewicz (sp)	2.00
269	Roy Halladay	.50
269	Roy Halladay (sp)	2.00
270	Torii Hunter	.25
270	Torii Hunter (sp)	1.50
271	Stan Spencer	.15
271	Stan Spencer (sp)	1.50
272	Alex Gonzalez	.15
272	Alex Gonzalez (sp)	1.50
273	Mark McGwire (Spring Fling)	2.00
274	Scott Rolen (Spring Fling)	.40
275	Jeff Bagwell (Spring Fling)	.40
276	Derek Jeter (Spring Fling)	1.00
277	Tony Gwynn (Spring Fling)	.75
278	Frank Thomas (Spring Fling)	.50
279	Sammy Sosa (Spring Fling)	1.00
280	Nomar Garciaparra (Spring Fling)	1.00
281	Cal Ripken Jr. (Spring Fling)	1.25
282	Albert Belle (Spring Fling)	.40
283	Kerry Wood (Spring Fling)	.25
284	Greg Maddux (Spring Fling)	1.00
285	Barry Bonds (Spring Fling)	.40
286	Juan Gonzalez (Spring Fling)	.75
287	Ken Griffey Jr. (Spring Fling)	1.50
288	Alex Rodriguez (Spring Fling)	1.50
289	Ben Grieve (Spring Fling)	.30
290	Travis Lee (Spring Fling)	.25
291	Mo Vaughn (Spring Fling)	.30
292	Mike Piazza (Spring Fling)	1.00
293	Roger Clemens (Spring Fling)	.60
294	J.D. Drew (Spring Fling)	.50
295	Randy Johnson (Spring Fling)	.25
296	Chipper Jones (Spring Fling)	1.00

297	Vladimir Guerrero (Spring Fling)	.50
298	Checklist (Nomar Garciaparra)	.75
299	Checklist (Ken Griffey Jr.)	1.00
300	Checklist (Mark McGwire)	1.00

1999 SkyBox Premium Star Rubies

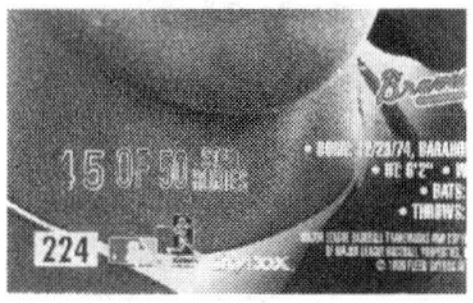

Star Rubies are a parallel of the base set and are limited to 50 sequentially numbered sets. SP Rookie parallels are limited to 15 numbered sets. Rubies feature a complete prism foil front with red-foil stamping.

Star Rubies: 50x to 90x
Production 50 sets
SP Star Rubies: 10x to 20x
Production 15 sets
(See 1999 SkyBox Premium for checklist and base card values.)

1999 SkyBox Premium Autographics

This 54-card autographed set feature an embossed Sky-Box Seal of Authenticity stamp and are seeded 1:68 packs. Cards are commonly found signed in black ink. Blue-ink versions, serially numbered to 50 each, were also produced.

	MT
Common Player:	10.00
Inserted 1:68	
Blue Ink: 2X	
Production 50 sets	
Roberto Alomar	30.00
Paul Bako	10.00
Michael Barrett	20.00
Kris Benson	10.00
Micah Bowie	10.00
Roosevelt Brown	15.00
A.J. Burnett	25.00
Pat Burrell	75.00
Ken Caminiti	25.00
Royce Clayton	10.00
Edgard Clemente	10.00
Bartolo Colon	20.00
J.D. Drew	40.00
Damion Easley	10.00
Derrin Ebert	10.00
Mario Encarnacion	15.00
Juan Encarnacion	15.00
Troy Glaus	25.00
Tom Glavine	30.00
Juan Gonzalez	125.00
Shawn Green	40.00
Wilton Guerrero	10.00
Jose Guillen	10.00
Tony Gwynn	150.00
Mark Harriger	10.00
Bobby Higginson	15.00
Todd Hollandsworth	10.00
Scott Hunter	10.00
Gabe Kapler	25.00
Scott Karl	10.00
Mike Kinkade	10.00
Ray Lankford	10.00
Barry Larkin	25.00
Matt Lawton	10.00
Ricky Ledee	15.00
Travis Lee	25.00
Eli Marrero	10.00
Ruben Mateo	25.00
Joe McEwing	25.00
Doug Mientkiewicz	10.00
Russ Ortiz	10.00
Jim Parque	10.00
Robert Person	10.00
Alex Rodriguez	150.00
Scott Rolen	40.00
Benj Sampson	10.00
Luis Saturria	10.00
Curt Schilling	25.00
David Segui	10.00
Fernando Tatis	25.00
Peter Tucci	10.00
Javier Vasquez	10.00
Robin Ventura	25.00
Autographics checklist	.10

1999 SkyBox Premium Diamond Debuts

This 15-card set features the best rookies of 1999 on a silver rainbow holo-foil card stock. These are seeded 1:49 packs. Card backs are numbered with a "DD" suffix.

		MT
Complete Set (15):		80.00
Common Player:		4.00
Inserted 1:49		
1	Eric Chavez	7.50
2	Kyle Farnsworth	4.00
3	Ryan Rupe	4.00
4	Jeremy Giambi	4.00
5	Marlon Anderson	4.00
6	J.D. Drew	15.00
7	Carlos Febles	5.00
8	Joe McEwing	6.00
9	Jeff Weaver	15.00
10	Alex Gonzalez	4.00
11	Chad Allen	4.00
12	Michael Barrett	6.00
13	Gabe Kapler	7.50
14	Carlos Lee	6.00
15	Edwards Guzman	4.00

1999 SkyBox Premium Intimidation Nation

This 15-card set highlights the top performers in baseball and features gold rainbow holo-foil stamping. These are limited to 99 sequentially numbered sets. Card backs are numbered with a "IN" suffix.

		MT
Complete Set (15):		1000.
Common Player:		25.00
Production 99 sets		
1	Cal Ripken Jr.	135.00
2	Tony Gwynn	75.00
3	Nomar Garciaparra	100.00
4	Frank Thomas	75.00
5	Mike Piazza	100.00
6	Mark McGwire	175.00
7	Scott Rolen	40.00
8	Chipper Jones	100.00
9	Greg Maddux	100.00
10	Ken Griffey Jr.	175.00
11	Juan Gonzalez	75.00
12	Derek Jeter	100.00
13	J.D. Drew	35.00
14	Roger Clemens	60.00
15	Alex Rodriguez	135.00

1999 SkyBox Premium Live Bats

This 15-card set spotlights baseball's top hitters and feature red foil stamping. Card backs are numbered with a "LB" suffix and are seeded 1:7 packs.

		MT
Complete Set (15):		25.00
Common Player:		.50
Inserted 1:7		
1	Juan Gonzalez	1.75
2	Mark McGwire	4.00
3	Jeff Bagwell	1.00
4	Frank Thomas	1.75
5	Mike Piazza	2.50
6	Nomar Garciaparra	2.50
7	Alex Rodriguez	3.00
8	Scott Rolen	.75
9	Travis Lee	.50
10	Tony Gwynn	1.75
11	Derek Jeter	2.50
12	Ben Grieve	.50
13	Chipper Jones	2.50
14	Ken Griffey Jr.	4.00
15	Cal Ripken Jr.	3.00

1999 SkyBox Premium Show Business

This 15-card set features some of the best players in the "show" on double foil-stamped card fronts. Card backs are numbered with a "SB" suffix and are seeded 1:70 packs.

		MT
Complete Set (15):		300.00
Common Player:		6.00
Inserted 1:70		
1	Mark McGwire	45.00
2	Tony Gwynn	20.00
3	Nomar Garciaparra	25.00
4	Juan Gonzalez	20.00
5	Roger Clemens	15.00
6	Chipper Jones	25.00
7	Cal Ripken Jr.	30.00
8	Alex Rodriguez	30.00
9	Orlando Hernandez	6.00
10	Greg Maddux	25.00
11	Mike Piazza	25.00
12	Frank Thomas	15.00
13	Ken Griffey Jr.	45.00
14	Scott Rolen	9.00
15	Derek Jeter	25.00

1999 SkyBox Premium Soul of The Game

This 15-card set features rainbow foil stamping and the name Soul of the Game prominently stamped, covering the entire card behind the player photo. Card backs are numbered with a "SG" suffix and are seeded 1:14 packs.

		MT
Complete Set (15):		55.00
Common Player:		2.00
Inserted 1:14		
1	Alex Rodriguez	6.00
2	Vladimir Guerrero	2.50
3	Chipper Jones	4.50
4	Derek Jeter	4.50
5	Tony Gwynn	3.50
6	Scott Rolen	2.00
7	Juan Gonzalez	3.50
8	Mark McGwire	9.00
9	Ken Griffey Jr.	9.00
10	Jeff Bagwell	2.50
11	Cal Ripken Jr.	6.00
12	Frank Thomas	3.50
13	Mike Piazza	4.50
14	Nomar Garciaparra	4.50
15	Sammy Sosa	4.50

1999 SkyBox Thunder

Skybox Thunder consists of a 300-card base set with three parallels and six inserts. The base set is inserted at varying odds. In hobby packs, regular-player cards #'s 1-140 come 4-5 per pack; veteran stars on cards #'s 141-240 come 2 per pack; and super-stars on cards #'s 241-300 are seeded one per pack. For re-tail packs the odds were: #'s 1-141 (3-4 per pack); #'s 141-240 (2 per pack); and #'s 241-300 (1 per pack). The parallel sets include Rave (# to 150 sets) and Super Rave (# to 25), which are both hobby ex-clusive. The Rant parallel set is retail exclusive (1:2). The in-serts are Unlea shed (1:6), www.batterz.com (1:18), In Depth (1:24), Hip-No-Tiz ed (1:36), Turbo-Charged (1:72), and Dial "1" (1:300).

		MT
Complete Set (300):		35.00
Common Player (1-140):		.10
Common Player (141-240):		.15
Common Player (241-300):		.25
Raves (1-140): 30x to 50x		
Raves (141-240): 15x to 30x		
Raves (241-300): 15x to 25x		
Production 150 sets		
SuperRaves (1-140): 100x to 200x		
SuperRaves (141-240): 50x to 120x		
SuperRaves (241-300): 40x to 90x		
Production 25 sets		
Wax Box:		35.00
1	John Smoltz	.20
2	Garret Anderson	.10
3	Matt Williams	.25
4	Daryle Ward	.10
5	Andy Ashby	.10
6	Miguel Tejada	.20
7	Dmitri Young	.10
8	Roberto Alomar	.50
9	Kevin Brown	.20
10	Eric Young	.10
11	Odalis Perez	.10
12	Preston Wilson	.15
13	Jeff Abbott	.10
14	Bret Boone	.10
15	Mendy Lopez	.10
16	B.J. Surhoff	.10
17	Steve Woodard	.10
18	Ron Coomer	.10
19	Rondell White	.20
20	Edgardo Alfonzo	.15
21	Kevin Millwood	.60
22	Jose Canseco	.40
23	Blake Stein	.10
24	Quilvio Veras	.10
25	Chuck Knoblauch	.40
26	David Segui	.10
27	Eric Davis	.10
28	Francisco Cordova	.10
29	Randy Winn	.10
30	Will Clark	.30
31	Billy Wagner	.15
32	Kevin Witt	.10
33	Jim Edmonds	.20
34	Todd Stottlemyre	.10
35	Shane Andrews	.10
36	Michael Tucker	.10
37	Sandy Alomar Jr.	.10
38	Neifi Perez	.10
39	Jaret Wright	.25
40	Devon White	.10
41	Edgar Renteria	.10
42	Shane Reynolds	.10
43	Jeff King	.10
44	Darren Dreifort	.10
45	Fernando Vina	.10
46	Marty Cordova	.10
47	Ugueth Urbina	.10
48	Bobby Bonilla	.20
49	Omar Vizquel	.10
50	Tom Gordon	.10
51	Ryan Christenson	.10
52	Aaron Boone	.10
53	Jamie Moyer	.10
54	Brian Giles	.10
55	Kevin Tapani	.10
56	Scott Brosius	.10
57	Ellis Burks	.10
58	Al Leiter	.10
59	Royce Clayton	.10
60	Chris Carpenter	.10
61	Bubba Trammell	.10
62	Tom Glavine	.20
63	Shannon Stewart	.10
64	Todd Zeile	.10
65	J.T. Snow	.10
66	Matt Clement	.10
67	Matt Stairs	.10
68	Ismael Valdes	.10
69	Todd Walker	.10
70	Jose Lima	.10
71	Mike Caruso	.10
72	Brett Tomko	.10
73	Mike Lansing	.10
74	Justin Thompson	.10
75	Damion Easley	.10
76	Derrek Lee	.10
77	Derek Bell	.10
78	Brady Anderson	.10
79	Charles Johnson	.10
80	Rafael Roque	.10
81	Corey Koskie	.10
82	Fernando Seguignol	.50
83	Jay Tessmer	.10
84	Jason Giambi	.10
85	Mike Lieberthal	.10
86	Jose Guillen	.10
87	Jim Leyritz	.10
88	Shawn Estes	.10
89	Ray Lankford	.10
90	Paul Sorrento	.10
91	Javy Lopez	.20
92	John Wetteland	.10
93	Sean Casey	.15
94	Chuck Finley	.10
95	Trot Nixon	.10
96	Ray Durham	.10
97	Reggie Sanders	.10
98	Bartolo Colon	.10
99	Henry Rodriguez	.10
100	Rolando Arrojo	.10
101	Geoff Jenkins	.10
102	Darryl Kile	.10
103	Mark Kotsay	.10
104	Craig Biggio	.40
105	Omar Daal	.10
106	Carlos Febles	.10
107	Eric Karros	.10
108	Matt Lawton	.10
109	Carl Pavano	.10
110	Brian McRae	.10
111	Mariano Rivera	.20
112	Jay Buhner	.15
113	Doug Glanville	.10
114	Jason Kendall	.10
115	Wally Joyner	.10
116	Jeff Kent	.10
117	Shane Monahan	.10
118	Eli Marrero	.10
119	Bobby Smith	.10
120	Shawn Green	.15
121	Kirk Rueter	.10
122	Tom Goodwin	.10
123	Andy Benes	.10
124	Ed Sprague	.10
125	Mike Mussina	.50
126	Jose Offerman	.10
127	Mickey Morandini	.10
128	Paul Konerko	.25
129	Denny Neagle	.10
130	Travis Fryman	.10
131	John Rocker	.10
132	Rob Fick	.10
133	Livan Hernandez	.10
134	Ken Caminiti	.20
135	Johnny Damon	.10
136	Jeff Kubenka	.10
137	Marquis Grissom	.10
138	Doug Mientkiewicz	.10
139	Dustin Hermanson	.25
140	Carl Everett	.10
141	Hideo Nomo	.20
142	Jorge Posada	.15
143	Rickey Henderson	.25
144	Robb Nen	.15
145	Ron Gant	.25
146	Aramis Ramirez	.25
147	Trevor Hoffman	.15
148	Bill Mueller	.15
149	Edgar Martinez	.15
150	Fred McGriff	.30
151	Rusty Greer	.15
152	Tom Evans	.15
153	Todd Greene	.15

154 Jay Bell .15
155 Mike Lowell .25
156 Orlando Cabrera .15
157 Troy O'Leary .15
158 Jose Hernandez .15
159 Magglio Ordonez .25
160 Barry Larkin .30
161 David Justice .30
162 Derrick Gibson .15
163 Luis Gonzalez .15
164 Alex Gonzalez .15
165 Scott Elarton .15
166 Dermal Brown .15
167 Eric Milton .15
168 Raul Mondesi .40
169 Jeff Cirillo .15
170 Benj Sampson .15
171 John Olerud .25
172 Andy Pettitte .40
173 A.J. Hinch .15
174 Rico Brogna .15
175 Jason Schmidt .15
176 Dean Palmer .25
177 Matt Morris .15
178 Quinton McCracken .15
179 Rick Helling .15
180 Walt Weiss .15
181 Troy Percival .15
182 Tony Batista .15
183 Brian Jordan .15
184 Jerry Hairston .15
185 Bret Saberhagen .15
186 Mark Grace .30
187 Brian Simmons .15
188 Pete Harnisch .15
189 Kenny Lofton .75
190 Vinny Castilla .25
191 Bobby Higginson .15
192 Joey Hamilton .15
193 Cliff Floyd .15
194 Andres Galarraga .40
195 Chan Ho Park .40
196 Jeromy Burnitz .15
197 David Ortiz .15
198 Wilton Guerrero .15
199 Rey Ordonez .15
200 Paul O'Neill .30
201 Kenny Rogers .15
202 Marlon Anderson .15
203 Tony Womack .15
204 Robin Ventura .25
205 Russ Ortiz .15
206 Mike Frank .15
207 Fernando Tatis .15
208 Miguel Cairo .15
209 Ivan Rodriguez 1.00
210 Carlos Delgado .30
211 Tim Salmon .30
212 Brian Anderson .15
213 Ryan Klesko .20
214 Scott Erickson .15
215 Mike Stanley .15
216 Brant Brown .15
217 Rod Beck .15
218 *Guillermo Garcia* .15
219 David Wells .15
220 Dante Bichette .40
221 Armando Benitez .15
222 Todd Dunwoody .15
223 Kelvim Escobar .15
224 Richard Hidalgo .15
225 Angel Pena .15
226 Ronnie Belliard .15
227 Brad Radke .15
228 Brad Fullmer .30
229 Jay Payton .15
230 Tino Martinez .30
231 Scott Spiezio .15
232 Bobby Abreu .15
233 John Valentin .15
234 Kevin Young .15
235 Steve Finley .15
236 David Cone .30
237 Armando Rios .15
238 Russ Davis .15
239 Wade Boggs .45
240 Aaron Sele .15
241 Jose Cruz Jr. .50
242 George Lombard .25
243 Todd Helton .75
244 Andruw Jones 1.25
245 Troy Glaus 1.25
246 Manny Ramirez 2.00
247 Ben Grieve 1.25
247p Ben Grieve ("PROMOTIONAL SAMPLE") 3.00
248 Richie Sexson .25
249 Juan Encarnacion .50
250 Randy Johnson .75
251 Gary Sheffield .35
252 Rafael Palmeiro .50
253 Roy Halladay .40
254 Mike Piazza 3.00
255 Tony Gwynn 2.50
256 Juan Gonzalez 2.50
257 Jeremy Giambi .25
258 Ben Davis .25
259 Russ Branyon .25
260 Pedro Martinez 1.00
261 Frank Thomas 2.50
262 Calvin Pickering .25
263 Chipper Jones 3.00
264 Ryan Minor .25
265 Roger Clemens 2.00
266 Sammy Sosa 3.00
267 Mo Vaughn .75
268 Carlos Beltran .25
269 Jim Thome .75
270 Mark McGwire 6.00
271 Travis Lee .60
272 Darin Erstad 1.25
273 Derek Jeter 3.00
274 Greg Maddux 3.00
275 Ricky Ledee .50
276 Alex Rodriguez 4.50
277 Vladimir Guerrero 2.00
278 Greg Vaughn .35
279 Scott Rolen 1.25
280 Carlos Guillen .25
281 Jeff Bagwell 1.25
282 Bruce Chen .25
283 Tony Clark .75
284 Albert Belle 1.25
285 Cal Ripken Jr. 4.50
286 Barry Bonds 1.25
287 Curt Schilling .35
288 Eric Chavez 1.00
289 Larry Walker .75
290 Orlando Hernandez 1.50
291 Moises Alou .40
292 Ken Griffey Jr. 6.00
293 Kerry Wood .75
294 Nomar Garciaparra 3.00
295 Gabe Kapler 1.25
296 Bernie Williams .75
297 Matt Anderson .25
298 Adrian Beltre .50
299 J.D. Drew 1.00
300 Ryan Bradley .25
--- Checklist 1-230
--- Checklist 231-300 and inserts
--- Video Game Sweepstakes form (Derek Jeter)

1999 SkyBox Thunder Dial "1"

Designed to look like a mobile phone, this insert set featured 10 cards of long distance hitters. The set consisted of black plastic cards with rounded corners, and were seeded one card per every 300 packs.

		MT
Complete Set (10):		425.00
Common Player:		15.00
Inserted 1:300		
1D	Nomar Garciaparra	50.00
2D	Juan Gonzalez	40.00
3D	Ken Griffey Jr.	90.00
4D	Chipper Jones	50.00
5D	Mark McGwire	90.00
6D	Mike Piazza	50.00
7D	Manny Ramirez	30.00
8D	Alex Rodriguez	75.00
9D	Sammy Sosa	50.00
10D	Mo Vaughn	15.00

1999 SkyBox Thunder Hip-No-Tized

This insert set consisted of 15 cards, featuring both hitters and pitchers. The cards were seeded one card in every 36 packs, and consist of mesmerizing patterned holo-foil stamping.

		MT
Complete Set (15):		150.00
Common Player:		3.00
Inserted 1:36		
1H	J.D. Drew	5.00
2H	Nomar Garciaparra	12.00
3H	Juan Gonzalez	10.00
4H	Ken Griffey Jr.	25.00
5H	Derek Jeter	12.00
6H	Randy Johnson	4.00
7H	Chipper Jones	12.00
8H	Mark McGwire	25.00
9H	Mike Piazza	12.00
10H	Cal Ripken Jr.	17.50
11H	Alex Rodriguez	17.50
12H	Sammy Sosa	12.00
13H	Frank Thomas	10.00
14H	Jim Thome	3.00
15H	Kerry Wood	5.00

1999 SkyBox Thunder In Depth

This insert set consists of 10 cards, featuring baseball's elite players. The cards are highlighted with gold rainbow holo-foil and gold metallic ink. The insertion rate for this insert was one card in every 24 packs.

		MT
Complete Set (10):		60.00
Common Player:		2.50
Inserted 1:240		
1ID	Albert Belle	3.00
2ID	Barry Bonds	4.00
3ID	Roger Clemens	6.00
4ID	Juan Gonzalez	8.00
5ID	Ken Griffey Jr.	15.00
6ID	Mark McGwire	15.00
7ID	Mike Piazza	10.00
8ID	Sammy Sosa	10.00
9ID	Mo Vaughn	2.50
10ID	Kerry Wood	4.00

1999 SkyBox Thunder Turbo Charged

This 10-card insert set consisted of the top home run hitters. The players were featured on plastic see-through cards with rainbow holofoil. One card was included in every 72 packs.

		MT
Complete Set (10):		120.00
Common Player:		5.00
Inserted 1:72		
1TC	Jose Canseco	5.00
2TC	Juan Gonzalez	12.00
3TC	Ken Griffey Jr.	25.00
4TC	Vladimir Guerrero	10.00
5TC	Mark McGwire	25.00
6TC	Mike Piazza	15.00
7TC	Manny Ramirez	10.00
8TC	Alex Rodriguez	20.00
9TC	Sammy Sosa	15.00
10TC	Mo Vaughn	5.00

1999 SkyBox Thunder Unleashed

This insert set contained 15 cards designed to resemble a cereal box. The players featured included the best young talent in baseball. The cards were silver-foil stamped, and offered facsimile signatures of each player. One card was included with every six packs.

		MT
Complete Set (15):		20.00
Common Player:		.75
Inserted 1:6		
1U	Carlos Beltran	1.50
2U	Adrian Beltre	1.25
3U	Eric Chavez	2.00
4U	J.D. Drew	3.00
5U	Juan Encarnacion	1.00
6U	Jeremy Giambi	1.00
7U	Troy Glaus	1.25
8U	Ben Grieve	1.00
9U	Todd Helton	2.00
10U	Orlando Hernandez	3.00
11U	Gabe Kapler	3.00
12U	Travis Lee	1.50
13U	Calvin Pickering	.75
14U	Richie Sexson	.75
15U	Kerry Wood	1.00

1999 SkyBox Thunder www.Batterz.com

www.batterz.com is a 10 card insert set that was seeded one card per every 18 packs. The game's best hitters are in their own home site in this computer-inspired set.

		MT
Complete Set (10):		50.00
Common Player:		1.00
Inserted 1:18		
1WB	J.D. Drew	2.50
2WB	Nomar Garciaparra	6.00
3WB	Ken Griffey Jr.	10.00
4WB	Tony Gwynn	4.00
5WB	Derek Jeter	6.00
6WB	Mark McGwire	10.00
7WB	Alex Rodriguez	8.00
8WB	Scott Rolen	2.00
9WB	Sammy Sosa	5.00
10WB	Bernie Williams	1.00

1999 SkyBox Thunder Rant

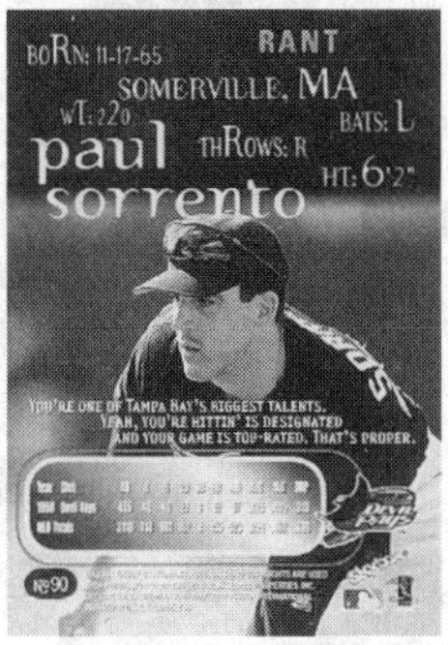

A retail-only parallel of the 300-card base set, Rant substitutes purple metallic foil highlights for the regular-issue's silver on front, and a has a "RANT" notation at upper-right on back, also in purple. The stated insertion rate for the parallel is one per two retail packs.

	MT
Complete Set (300):	250.00
Common Player:	.25
Rant Stars: 5X	

(See 1999 SkyBox Thunder for checklist and base card values.)

2000 SkyBox Dominion

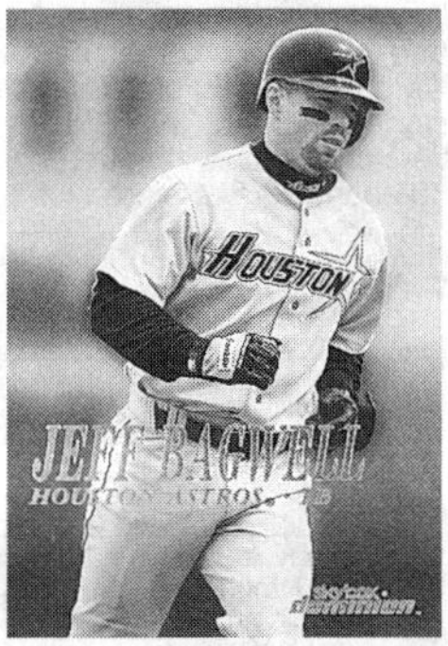

		MT
Complete Set (300):		35.00
Common Player:		.10
1	Mark McGwire, Ken Griffey Jr. (League Leaders)	.75
2	Mark McGwire, Manny Ramirez (League Leaders)	.50
3	Larry Walker, Nomar Garciaparra (League Leaders)	.25
4	Tony Womack, Brian Hunter (League Leaders)	.10
5	Mike Hampton, Pedro Martinez (League Leaders)	.25
6	Randy Johnson, Pedro Martinez (League Leaders)	.25
7	Randy Johnson, Pedro Martinez (League Leaders)	.25
8	Ugueth Urbina, Mariano Rivera (League Leaders)	.10
9	Vinny Castilla (Highlights)	.10
10	Orioles host Cuban National Team (Highlights)	.10
11	Jose Canseco (Highlights)	.25

12	Fernando Tatis (Highlights)	.10
13	Robin Ventura (Highlights)	.10
14	Roger Clemens (Highlights)	.40
15	Jose Jimenez (Highlights)	.10
16	David Cone (Highlights)	.10
17	Mark McGwire (Highlights)	.75
18	Cal Ripken Jr. (Highlights)	.50
19	Tony Gwynn (Highlights)	.25
20	Wade Boggs (Highlights)	.10
21	Ivan Rodriguez (Highlights)	.25
22	Chuck Finley (Highlights)	.10
23	Eric Milton (Highlights)	.10
24	Adrian Beltre (Highlights)	.10
25	Brad Radke	.10
26	Derek Bell	.10
27	Garret Anderson	.10
28	Ivan Rodriguez	.50
29	Jeff Kent	.10
30	Jeremy Giambi	.10
31	John Franco	.10
32	Jose Hernandez	.10
33	Jose Offerman	.10
34	Jose Rosado	.10
35	Kevin Appier	.10
36	Kris Benson	.10
37	Mark McGwire	2.00
38	Matt Williams	.25
39	Paul O'Neill	.20
40	Rickey Henderson	.25
41	Todd Greene	.10
42	Russ Ortiz	.10
43	Sean Casey	.25
44	Tony Womack	.10
45	Troy O'Leary	.10
46	Ugueth Urbina	.10
47	Tom Glavine	.20
48	Mike Mussina	.40
49	Carlos Febles	.10
50	Jon Lieber	.10
51	Juan Gonzalez	.50
52	Matt Clement	.10
53	Moises Alou	.10
54	Ray Durham	.10
55	Robb Nen	.10
56	Tino Martinez	.25
57	Troy Glaus	.20
58	Curt Schilling	.15
59	Mike Sweeney	.10
60	Steve Finley	.10
61	Roger Cedeno	.10
62	Bobby Jones	.10
63	John Smoltz	.15
64	Darin Erstad	.20
65	Carlos Delgado	.25
66	Ray Lankford	.10
67	Todd Stottlemyre	.10
68	Andy Ashby	.10
69	Bobby Abreu	.10
70	Chuck Finley	.10
71	Damion Easley	.10
72	Dustin Hermanson	.10
73	Frank Thomas	.60
74	Kevin Brown	.15
75	Kevin Millwood	.20
76	Mark Grace	.15
77	Matt Stairs	.10
78	Mike Hampton	.10
79	Omar Vizquel	.10
80	Preston Wilson	.10
81	Robin Ventura	.15
82	Todd Helton	.20
83	Tony Clark	.20
84	Al Leiter	.15
85	Alex Fernandez	.10
86	Bernie Williams	.40
87	Edgar Martinez	.15
88	Edgar Renteria	.10
89	Fred McGriff	.20
90	Jermaine Dye	.10
91	Joe McEwing	.10
92	John Halama	.10
93	Lee Stevens	.10
94	Matt Lawton	.10
95	Mike Piazza	1.25
96	Pete Harnisch	.10
97	Scott Karl	.10
98	Tony Fernandez	.10
99	Sammy Sosa	1.25
100	Bobby Higginson	.10
101	Tony Gwynn	1.00
102	J.D. Drew	.50
103	Roberto Hernandez	.20
104	Rondell White	.15
105	David Nilsson	.10
106	Shane Reynolds	.15
107	Jaret Wright	.10
108	Jeff Bagwell	.50
109	Jay Bell	.10
110	Kevin Tapani	.10
111	Michael Barrett	.10
112	Neifi Perez	.10
113	Pat Hentgen	.10
114	Roger Clemens	.75
115	Travis Fryman	.15
116	Aaron Sele	.10
117	Eric Davis	.15
118	Trevor Hoffman	.10
119	Chris Singleton	.10
120	Ryan Klesko	.15
121	Scott Rolen	.50
122	Jorge Posada	.15
123	Abraham Nunez	.10
124	Alex Gonzalez	.10
125	B.J. Surhoff	.10
126	Barry Bonds	.50
127	Billy Koch	.10
128	Billy Wagner	.10
129	Brad Ausmus	.10
130	Bret Boone	.10
131	Cal Ripken Jr.	1.25
132	Chad Allen	.10
133	Chris Carpenter	.10
134	Craig Biggio	.25
135	Dante Bichette	.15
136	Dean Palmer	.10
137	Derek Jeter	1.25
138	Ellis Burks	.10
139	Freddy Garcia	.10
140	Gabe Kapler	.10
141	Greg Maddux	1.00
142	Greg Vaughn	.25
143	Jason Kendall	.15
144	Jim Parque	.10
145	John Valentin	.10
146	Jose Vidro	.10
147	Ken Griffey Jr.	2.00
148	Kenny Lofton	.40
149	Kenny Rogers	.10
150	Kent Bottenfield	.10
151	Chuck Knoblauch	.20
152	Larry Walker	.40
153	Manny Ramirez	.50
154	Mickey Morandini	.10
155	Mike Cameron	.10
156	Mike Lieberthal	.10
157	Mo Vaughn	.40
158	Randy Johnson	.40
159	Rey Ordonez	.10
160	Roberto Alomar	.40
161	Scott Williamson	.10
162	Shawn Estes	.10
163	Tim Wakefield	.10
164	Tony Batista	.10
165	Will Clark	.25
166	Wade Boggs	.25
167	David Cone	.15
168	Doug Glanville	.10
169	Jeff Cirillo	.10
170	John Jaha	.10
171	Mariano Rivera	.20
172	Tom Gordon	.10
173	Wally Joyner	.10
174	Alex Gonzalez	.10
175	Andruw Jones	.25
176	Barry Larkin	.25
177	Bartolo Colon	.10
178	Brian Giles	.10
179	Carlos Lee	.10
180	Darren Dreifort	.10
181	Eric Chavez	.10
182	Henry Rodriguez	.10
183	Ismael Valdes	.10
184	Jason Giambi	.10
185	John Wetteland	.10
186	Juan Encarnacion	.10
187	Luis Gonzalez	.10
188	Reggie Sanders	.10
189	Richard Hidalgo	.10
190	Ryan Rupe	.10
191	Sean Berry	.10
192	Rick Helling	.10
193	Randy Wolf	.10
194	Cliff Floyd	.10
195	Jose Lima	.10
196	Chipper Jones	1.00
197	Charles Johnson	.10
198	Nomar Garciaparra	1.25
199	Magglio Ordonez	.20
200	Shawn Green	.40
201	Travis Lee	.15
202	Jose Canseco	.40
203	Fernando Tatis	.10
204	Bruce Aven	.10
205	Johnny Damon	.10
206	Gary Sheffield	.20
207	Ken Caminiti	.15
208	Ben Grieve	.20
209	Sidney Ponson	.10
210	Vinny Castilla	.10
211	Alex Rodriguez	1.25
212	Chris Widger	.10
213	Carl Pavano	.10
214	J.T. Snow	.10
215	Jim Thome	.25
216	Kevin Young	.10
217	Mike Sirotka	.10
218	Rafael Palmeiro	.25
219	Rico Brogna	.10
220	Todd Walker	.10
221	Todd Zelle	.10
222	Brian Rose	.10
223	Chris Fussell	.10
224	Corey Koskie	.10
225	Rich Aurilla	.10
226	Geoff Jenkins	.10
227	Pedro Martinez	.50
228	Todd Hundley	.10
229	Brian Jordan	.10
230	Cristian Guzman	.10
231	Raul Mondesi	.15
232	Tim Hudson	.10
233	Albert Belle	.40
234	Andy Pettitte	.20
235	Brady Anderson	.15
236	Brian Bohannon	.10
237	Carlos Beltran	.15
238	Doug Mientkiewicz	.10
239	Jason Schmidt	.10
240	Jeff Zimmerman	.10
241	John Olerud	.20
242	Paul Byrd	.10
243	Vladimir Guerrero	.60
244	Warren Morris	.10
245	Eric Karros	.10
246	Jeff Weaver	.10
247	Jeromy Burnitz	.10
248	David Bell	.10
249	Rusty Greer	.10
250	Kevin Stocker	.10
251	Shea Hillenbrand (Prospect)	.20
252	Alfonso Soriano (Prospect)	1.50
253	Micah Bowie (Prospect)	.20
254	Gary Matthews Jr. (Prospect)	.20
255	Lance Berkman (Prospect)	.20
256	Pat Burrell (Prospect)	1.50
257	Ruben Mateo (Prospect)	.25
258	Kip Wells (Prospect)	.25
259	Wilton Veras (Prospect)	.50
260	Ben Davis (Prospect)	.20
261	Eric Munson (Prospect)	.40
262	Ramon Hernandez (Prospect)	.20
263	Tony Armas, Jr. (Prospect)	.25
264	Erubiel Durazo (Prospect)	.25
265	Chad Meyers (Prospect)	.25
266	Rick Ankiel (Prospect)	4.00
267	Ramon Ortiz (Prospect)	.25
268	Adam Kennedy (Prospect)	.20
269	Vernon Wells (Prospect)	.20
270	Chad Hermansen (Prospect)	.20
271	Norm Hutchins, Trent Durrington (Prospects)	.25
272	Gabe Molina, B.J. Ryan (Prospects)	.25
273	Juan Pena, *Tomokazu Ohka* (Prospects)	.25
274	Pat Daneker, Aaron Myette (Prospects)	.25
275	Jason Rakers, Russell Branyan (Prospects)	.25
276	Beiker Graterol, Dave Borkowski (Prospects)	.25
277	Mark Quinn, Dan Reichert (Prospects)	.50
278	Mark Redman, Jacque Jones (Prospects)	.25
279	Ed Yarnall, Wily Pena (Prospects)	1.00
280	Chad Harville, Brett Laxton (Prospects)	.25
281	Aaron Scheffer, Gil Meche (Prospects)	.25
282	Jim Morris, Dan Wheeler (Prospects)	.25
283	Danny Kolb, Kelly Dransfeldt (Prospects)	.25
284	Peter Munro, Casey Blake (Prospects)	.25
285	Rob Ryan, Byung-Hyun Kim (Prospects)	.25
286	Derrin Ebert, Pascual Matos (Prospects)	.50
287	Richard Barker, Kyle Farnsworth (Prospects)	.25
288	Jason LaRue, Travis Dawkins (Prospects)	.50
289	Chris Sexton, Edgard Clemente (Prospects)	.25
290	Amaury Garcia, A.J. Burnett (Prospects)	.50
291	Carlos Hernandez, Daryle Ward (Prospects)	.50
292	Eric Gagne, Jeff Williams (Prospects)	.25
293	Kyle Peterson, Kevin Barker (Prospects)	.25
294	Fernando Seguignol, Guillermo Mota (Prospects)	.25
295	Melvin Mora, Octavio Dotel (Prospects)	.25
296	Anthony Shumaker, Cliff Politte (Prospects)	.25
297	Yamid Haad, Jimmy Anderson (Prospects)	.25
298	Rick Heiserman, Chad Hutchinson (Prospects)	.25
299	Mike Darr, Wiki Gonzalez (Prospects)	.25
300	Joe Nathan, Calvin Murray (Prospects)	.25

2000 SkyBox Dominion Autographics

		MT
Common Player:		15.00
Inserted 1:144		
1	Rick Ankiel	75.00
2	Peter Bergeron	15.00
3	Wade Boggs	100.00
4	Barry Bonds	80.00
5	Pat Burrell	75.00
6	Miguel Cairo	15.00
7	Mike Cameron	15.00
8	Ben Davis	15.00
9	Russ Davis	15.00
10	Einar Diaz	15.00
11	Scott Elarton	15.00
12	Jeremy Giambi	20.00
13	Todd Greene	15.00
14	Vladimir Guerrero	150.00
15	Tony Gwynn	125.00
16	Bobby Howry	15.00
17	Tim Hudson	20.00
18	Randy Johnson	60.00
19	Andruw Jones	40.00
20	Jacque Jones	15.00
21	Jason LaRue	15.00
22	Matt Lawton	15.00
23	Greg Maddux	200.00
24	Pedro Martinez	100.00
25	Pokey Reese	15.00
26	Alex Rodriguez	200.00
27	Ryan Rupe	15.00
28	J.T. Snow	15.00
29	Jose Vidro	15.00
30	Tony Womack	15.00
31	Ed Yarnall	20.00
32	Kevin Young	20.00

2000 SkyBox Dominion Double Play

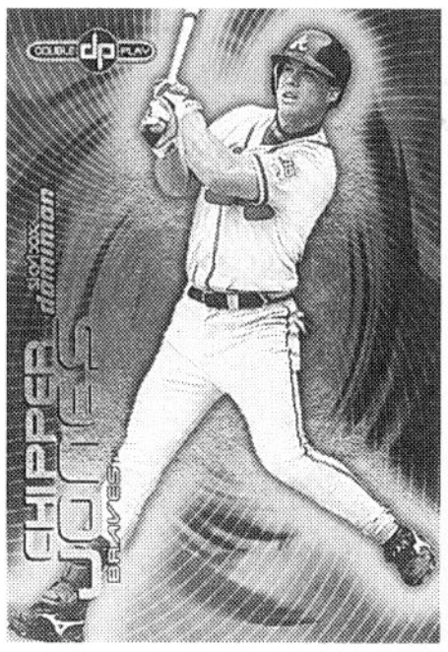

		MT
Complete Set (10):		25.00
Common Player:		1.50
Inserted 1:9		
Plus: 2x-4x		
Inserted 1:90		
WarpTek: 12x to 20x		
Inserted 1:900		
1	Nomar Garciaparra	4.00
2	Pedro Martinez	1.50
3	Chipper Jones	3.00
4	Mark McGwire	6.00
5	Cal Ripken Jr.	4.00
6	Roger Clemens	2.00
7	Juan Gonzalez	1.50
8	Tony Gwynn	3.00
9	Sammy Sosa	4.00
10	Mike Piazza	4.00

2000 SkyBox Dominion Eye on October

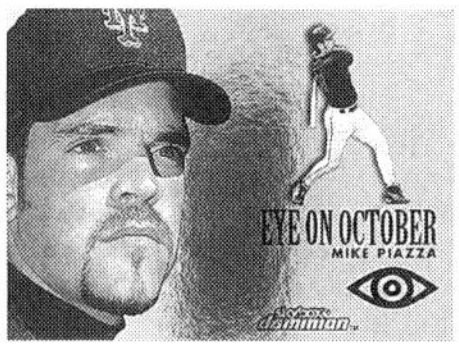

		MT
Complete Set (15):		75.00
Common Player:		2.00
Inserted 1:24		
Plus: 2x to 5x		
Inserted 1:240		
1	Ken Griffey Jr.	12.00
2	Mark McGwire	12.00
3	Derek Jeter	8.00
4	Juan Gonzalez	3.00
5	Chipper Jones	6.00
6	Sammy Sosa	8.00
7	Greg Maddux	6.00
8	Frank Thomas	3.00
9	Nomar Garciaparra	8.00
10	Shawn Green	2.00
11	Cal Ripken Jr.	8.00
12	Manny Ramirez	3.00
13	Scott Rolen	3.00
14	Mike Piazza	8.00
15	Alex Rodriguez	8.00

2000 SkyBox Dominion Hats Off

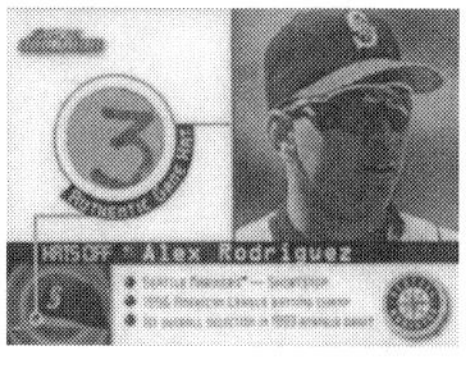

		MT
Common Player:		40.00
Inserted 1:468 H		
1	Wade Boggs	100.00
2	Barry Bonds	120.00
3	J.D. Drew	80.00
4	Shawn Green	100.00
5	Vladimir Guerrero	100.00
6	Randy Johnson	80.00
7	Andruw Jones	80.00
8	Greg Maddux	150.00
9	Pedro Martinez	125.00
10	Mike Mussina	80.00
11	Rafael Palmeiro	60.00
12	Alex Rodriguez	200.00
13	Scott Rolen	80.00
14	Tim Salmon	40.00
15	Robin Ventura	50.00

2000 SkyBox Dominion Milestones

		MT
Complete Set (6):		450.00
Common Player:		50.00
Inserted 1:1,999		
1	Mark McGwire	150.00
2	Roger Clemens	75.00
3	Tony Gwynn	75.00
4	Wade Boggs	40.00
5	Cal Ripken Jr.	120.00
6	Jose Canseco	60.00

2000 SkyBox Dominion New Era

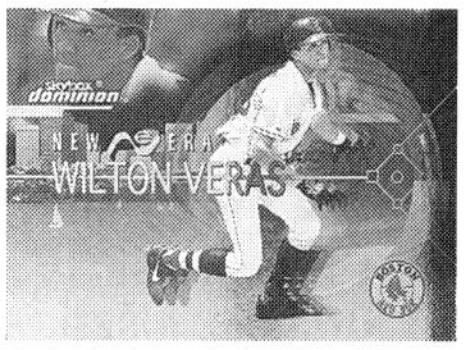

		MT
Complete Set (20):		15.00
Common Player:		.50
Inserted 1:3		
Plus: 2x to 4x		
Inserted 1:30		
WarpTek: 5x to 10x		
Inserted 1:300		
1	Pat Burrell	2.00
2	Ruben Mateo	.50
3	Wilton Veras	.50
4	Eric Munson	.75
5	Jeff Weaver	.75
6	Tim Hudson	.75
7	Carlos Beltran	.75
8	Chris Singleton	.50
9	Lance Berkman	.50
10	Freddy Garcia	1.00
11	Erubiel Durazo	.75
12	Randy Wolf	.50
13	Shea Hillenbrand	.50
14	Kip Wells	.50
15	Alfonso Soriano	2.00
16	Rick Ankiel	5.00
17	Ramon Ortiz	.50
18	Adam Kennedy	.50
19	Vernon Wells	.50
20	Chad Hermansen	.50

1999 Slammin' Sammy's

Randomly packaged in boxes of Slammin' Sammy's breakfast cereal sold regionally in the Chicago area by Famous Fixins of New York were an edition of 1,000 cards commemorating Sammy Sosa's 66 home runs during the 1998 season.

	MT
Sammy Sosa	12.00

1992 Snyder's Bread Washington Sports Heroes

This set was sponsored by Snyder's, a Northwest baker, and produced by Little Sun, which had earlier done a number of amateur baseball card sets. Two baseball players are included in the set: Ryne Sandberg (in a high school football jersey) and John Olerud (pitching for WSU). Cards picture the athletes against a pine tree border photo. Backs are printed in blue and yellow on white and feature a summary of the athlete's days in Washington.

		MT
Complete Set (8):		8.00
Common Player:		.50
1	Ryne Sandberg	6.00
2	Mark Rypien (football)	2.50
3	Doug Christie (basketball)	1.00
4	Leila Wagner	.50
5	The Mahre Brothers (Phil Mahre, Steve Mahre) (skiing)	.50
6	John Olerud	4.00
7	Lou Whittaker (mountain climber)	.50
8	Dana Hall (football)	1.00

1989 Socko Orel Hershiser

This set of pitching tips cards was issued by Socko beverages, but the sponsor's name does not appear on the cards. In 2-1/2" x 3-1/2" format, the cards have dark blue borders on front with a color action photo of the pitcher at center. Hershiser's Dodger uniform logos have been air-brushed off the photos. The cards are unnumbered.

		MT
Complete Set (7):		6.00
Common Card:		1.00
(1)	Orel Hershiser (Backing Up the Catcher)	1.00
(2)	Orel Hershiser (Barehanding the Ball)	1.00
(3)	Orel Hershiser (Pitching From the Stretch)	1.00
(4)	Orel Hershiser (The Follow-Through)	1.00
(5)	Orel Hershiser (The Grip)	1.00
(6)	Orel Hershiser (The Kick)	1.00
(7)	Orel Hershiser (The Release)	1.00

1995 Sonic/Coke Heroes of Baseball

In a promotion with the Sonic chain of Southern drive-in restaurants, Upper Deck issued a 20-card set of baseball greats. Cards featured vintage sepia photos on the front, with player biographies and stats on the back. The Coca-Cola and Sonic logos also appear on back.

		MT
Complete Set (20):		10.00
Common Player:		.50
1	Whitey Ford	.60
2	Cy Young	.50
3	Babe Ruth	2.00
4	Lou Gehrig	1.00
5	Mike Schmidt	.75
6	Nolan Ryan	2.00
7	Robin Yount	.60
8	Gary Carter	.50
9	Tom Seaver	.60
10	Reggie Jackson	.60
11	Bob Gibson	.50
12	Gil Hodges	.60
13	Monte Irvin	.50
14	Minnie Minoso	.50
15	Willie Stargell	.50
16	Al Kaline	.50
17	Joe Jackson	1.00
18	Walter Johnson	.50
19	Ty Cobb	.65
20	Satchel Paige	.75

1995 Sonic/Pepsi Baseball Greats

While some Sonic drive-in restaurants (basically a Southern chain) featured a baseball card promotion using Upper Deck cards with a Coca-Cola logo on back, other drive-ins in the chain featured a 12-card set sponsored by Pepsi. Cards have a red border on front and a color photo of a player on which team logos have been airbrushed away. Backs have career data and the Pepsi logo, along with that of the Major League Baseball Players Alumni, and are printed in red and blue. The cards were issued in three-card cello packs with a meal purchase. The unnumbered cards are checklisted here in alphabetical order.

		MT
Complete Set (12):		3.50
Common Player:		.15
(1)	Bert Campaneris	.15
(2)	George Foster	.15
(3)	Steve Garvey	.60
(4)	Fergie Jenkins	.40
(5)	Tommy John	.25
(6)	Harmon Killebrew	.75
(7)	Sparky Lyle	.15
(8)	Fred Lynn	.25
(9)	Joe Morgan	.40
(10)	Graig Nettles	.15
(11)	Warren Spahn	.75
(12)	Maury Wills	.25

1987 Sonshine Industries 19th Century Baseball

There is no indication of the origins of this collectors issue on the cards themselves. Fronts feature black-and-white reproductions of vintage woodcuts of the players with an ornate orange framework. Backs of the 2-1/2" x 3-1/2" cards are printed in black on blue-gray with lengthy biographical information. The unnumbered cards are checklisted here in alphabetical order.

		MT
Complete Set:		24.00
Common Player:		1.50
(1)	A.C. Anson	2.00
(2)	Cap Anson	2.00
(3)	D. Brouthers	1.50
(4)	Alexander Cartwright	1.50
(5)	Alexander Cartwright	1.50
(6)	L.N. David	1.50
(7)	Wes Fisler	1.50
(8)	F.E. Goldsmith	1.50
(9)	T.J. Keefe	1.50
(10)	M.J. Kelly	2.00
(11)	Robert T. Mathews	1.50
(12)	Wm. McLean	1.50
(13)	C.A. McVey	1.50
(14)	James Mutrie	1.50
(15)	Lipman Pike	1.50
(16)	John J. Smith	1.50
(17)	A.G. Spalding	1.50
(18)	M. Welch	1.50
(19)	N.E. Young	1.50
(20)	Going to the game	1.50

1995 Southwestern Bell Stan Musial Phonecards

The career of St. Louis Cardinal Hall of Famer Stan Musial is chronicled in this set of phonecards. In standard 2-1/2" x 3-3/8" round-cornered plastic format, the cards picture Musial in black-and-white and color photos on front, with a logo dating and describing the photo. Cards were issued in denominations of $10, $15 and $25 and could be purchased singly, in groups of three or as a complete set. An album autographed by Musial and containing a matched-number set of the cards was also available.

		MT
Complete Set (10):		160.00
Complete Set W/Album:		160.00
Common Card:		10.00
1	The Rookie (Stan Musial)	25.00
2	The Man (Stan Musial)	15.00
3	The Swing (Stan Musial)	10.00
4	Greatest Day (Stan Musial)	15.00
5	3,000th Hit (Stan Musial)	25.00
6	Accomplishments (Stan Musial)	10.00
7	Hall of Fame (Stan Musial)	25.00
8	Living Legend (Stan Musial)	10.00
9	Saturday Evening Post (Stan Musial)	15.00
10	Major League Tryout (Stan Musial)	10.00

1993 SP

Upper Deck's first super-premium baseball card issue features 290 cards in the single-series set; 252 are individual player cards, while the remainder includes a Premier Prospects subset featuring top prospects (20 cards), 18 All-Stars and a Platinum Power insert set of 20 top home run hitters. Cards, which were available in 12-card foil packs, feature borderless color photos and UV coating on the front, plus a special logo using lenticular printing. Foil is also used intricately in the design. Backs have a large color photo and statistics. Cards are numbered and color-coded by team.

		MT
Complete Set (290):		125.00
Common Player:		.15
Wax Box:		150.00
1	Roberto Alomar	1.50
2	Wade Boggs	.60
3	Joe Carter	.20
4	Ken Griffey, Jr.	12.00
5	Mark Langston	.15
6	John Olerud	.50
7	Kirby Puckett	4.00
8	Cal Ripken, Jr.	8.00
9	Ivan Rodriguez	2.50
10	Barry Bonds	2.50
11	Darren Daulton	.15
12	Marquis Grissom	.20
13	Dave Justice	.40
14	John Kruk	.15
15	Barry Larkin	.60
16	Terry Mulholland	.15
17	Ryne Sandberg	2.50
18	Gary Sheffield	.40
19	Chad Curtis	.20
20	Chili Davis	.15
21	Gary DiSarcina	.15
22	Damion Easley	.15
23	Chuck Finley	.15
24	Luis Polonia	.15
25	Tim Salmon	1.50
26	*J.T. Snow*	1.00
27	Russ Springer	.15
28	Jeff Bagwell	5.00
29	Craig Biggio	.40
30	Ken Caminiti	.40
31	Andujar Cedeno	.15
32	Doug Drabek	.15
33	Steve Finley	.15
34	Luis Gonzalez	.15
35	Pete Harnisch	.15
36	Darryl Kile	.15
37	Mike Bordick	.15
38	Dennis Eckersley	.15
39	Brent Gates	.15
40	Rickey Henderson	.40
41	Mark McGwire	12.00
42	Craig Paquette	.15
43	Ruben Sierra	.15
44	Terry Steinbach	.15
45	Todd Van Poppel	.15
46	Pat Borders	.15
47	Tony Fernandez	.15
48	Juan Guzman	.15
49	Pat Hentgen	.15
50	Paul Molitor	2.00
51	Jack Morris	.15
52	Ed Sprague	.15
53	Duane Ward	.15
54	Devon White	.20
55	Steve Avery	.15
56	Jeff Blauser	.15
57	Ron Gant	.20
58	Tom Glavine	.40
59	Greg Maddux	6.00
60	Fred McGriff	.40
61	Terry Pendleton	.15
62	Deion Sanders	1.00
63	John Smoltz	.40
64	Cal Eldred	.15
65	Darryl Hamilton	.15
66	John Jaha	.15
67	Pat Listach	.15
68	Jaime Navarro	.15
69	Kevin Reimer	.15
70	B.J. Surhoff	.15
71	Greg Vaughn	.20
72	Robin Yount	1.50
73	*Rene Arocha*	.25
74	Bernard Gilkey	.15
75	Gregg Jefferies	.15
76	Ray Lankford	.15
77	Tom Pagnozzi	.15
78	Lee Smith	.15
79	Ozzie Smith	2.00
80	Bob Tewksbury	.15
81	Mark Whiten	.15
82	Steve Buechele	.15
83	Mark Grace	.35
84	Jose Guzman	.15
85	Derrick May	.15
86	Mike Morgan	.15
87	Randy Myers	.15
88	*Kevin Roberson*	.40
89	Sammy Sosa	5.00
90	Rick Wilkins	.15
91	Brett Butler	.15
92	Eric Davis	.15
93	Orel Hershiser	.20
94	Eric Karros	.20
95	Ramon Martinez	.20
96	Raul Mondesi	1.25
97	Jose Offerman	.15
98	Mike Piazza	6.00
99	Darryl Strawberry	.25
100	Moises Alou	.25
101	Wil Cordero	.15
102	Delino DeShields	.15
103	Darrin Fletcher	.15
104	Ken Hill	.15
105	*Mike Lansing*	.40
106	Dennis Martinez	.15
107	Larry Walker	.75
108	John Wetteland	.15
109	Rod Beck	.15
110	John Burkett	.15
111	Will Clark	.75
112	Royce Clayton	.15
113	Darren Lewis	.15
114	Willie McGee	.15
115	Bill Swift	.15
116	Robby Thompson	.15
117	Matt Williams	.60

118	Sandy Alomar Jr.	.25
119	Carlos Baerga	.15
120	Albert Belle	2.50
121	Reggie Jefferson	.15
122	Kenny Lofton	1.50
123	Wayne Kirby	.15
124	Carlos Martinez	.15
125	Charles Nagy	.15
126	Paul Sorrento	.15
127	Rich Amaral	.15
128	Jay Buhner	.20
129	Norm Charlton	.15
130	Dave Fleming	.15
131	Erik Hanson	.15
132	Randy Johnson	1.50
133	Edgar Martinez	.15
134	Tino Martinez	.45
135	Omar Vizquel	.15
136	Bret Barberie	.15
137	Chuck Carr	.15
138	Jeff Conine	.15
139	Orestes Destrade	.15
140	Chris Hammond	.15
141	Bryan Harvey	.15
142	Benito Santiago	.15
143	Walt Weiss	.15
144	*Darrell Whitmore*	.15
145	*Tim Bolger*	.15
146	Bobby Bonilla	.20
147	Jeromy Burnitz	.15
148	Vince Coleman	.15
149	Dwight Gooden	.20
150	Todd Hundley	.50
151	Howard Johnson	.15
152	Eddie Murray	.75
153	Bret Saberhagen	.15
154	Brady Anderson	.25
155	Mike Devereaux	.15
156	Jeffrey Hammonds	.20
157	Chris Hoiles	.15
158	Ben McDonald	.15
159	Mark McLemore	.15
160	Mike Mussina	1.50
161	Gregg Olson	.15
162	David Segui	.15
163	Derek Bell	.15
164	Andy Benes	.25
165	Archi Cianfrocco	.15
166	Ricky Gutierrez	.15
167	Tony Gwynn	3.00
168	Gene Harris	.15
169	Trevor Hoffman	.20
170	*Ray McDavid*	.20
171	Phil Plantier	.15
172	Mariano Duncan	.15
173	Len Dykstra	.15
174	Tommy Greene	.15
175	Dave Hollins	.15
176	Pete Incaviglia	.15
177	Mickey Morandini	.15
178	Curt Schilling	.30
179	Kevin Stocker	.15
180	Mitch Williams	.15
181	Stan Belinda	.15
182	Jay Bell	.15
183	Steve Cooke	.15
184	Carlos Garcia	.15
185	Jeff King	.15
186	Orlando Merced	.15
187	Don Slaught	.15
188	Andy Van Slyke	.15
189	Kevin Young	.15
190	Kevin Brown	.35
191	Jose Canseco	.75
192	Julio Franco	.15
193	Benji Gil	.15
194	Juan Gonzalez	2.50
195	Tom Henke	.15
196	Rafael Palmeiro	.50
197	Dean Palmer	.15
198	Nolan Ryan	8.00
199	Roger Clemens	3.00
200	Scott Cooper	.15
201	Andre Dawson	.20
202	Mike Greenwell	.15
203	Carlos Quintana	.15
204	Jeff Russell	.15
205	Aaron Sele	.20
206	Mo Vaughn	1.50
207	Frank Viola	.15
208	Rob Dibble	.15
209	Roberto Kelly	.15
210	Kevin Mitchell	.15
211	Hal Morris	.15
212	Joe Oliver	.15
213	Jose Rijo	.15
214	Bip Roberts	.15
215	Chris Sabo	.15
216	Reggie Sanders	.15
217	Dante Bichette	.50
218	Jerald Clark	.15
219	Alex Cole	.15
220	Andres Galarraga	.40
221	Joe Girardi	.15
222	Charlie Hayes	.15
223	*Robert Mejia*	.15
224	Armando Reynoso	.15
225	Eric Young	.15
226	Kevin Appier	.15
227	George Brett	3.00
228	David Cone	.30
229	Phil Hiatt	.15
230	Felix Jose	.15
231	Wally Joyner	.15
232	Mike Macfarlane	.15
233	Brian McRae	.15
234	Jeff Montgomery	.15
235	Rob Deer	.15
236	Cecil Fielder	.20
237	Travis Fryman	.15
238	Mike Henneman	.15
239	Tony Phillips	.15
240	Mickey Tettleton	.15
241	Alan Trammell	.20
242	David Wells	.20
243	Lou Whitaker	.15
244	Rick Aguilera	.15
245	Scott Erickson	.15
246	Brian Harper	.15
247	Kent Hrbek	.15
248	Chuck Knoblauch	.40
249	Shane Mack	.15
250	David McCarty	.15
251	Pedro Munoz	.15
252	Dave Winfield	.35
253	Alex Fernandez	.30
254	Ozzie Guillen	.15
255	Bo Jackson	.25
256	Lance Johnson	.15
257	Ron Karkovice	.15
258	Jack McDowell	.15
259	Tim Raines	.15
260	Frank Thomas	5.00
261	Robin Ventura	.35
262	Jim Abbott	.15
263	Steve Farr	.15
264	Jimmy Key	.15
265	Don Mattingly	2.50
266	Paul O'Neill	.30
267	Mike Stanley	.15
268	Danny Tartabull	.15
269	Bob Wickman	.15
270	Bernie Williams	1.25
271	Jason Bere	.15
272	*Roger Cedeno*	.75
273	*Johnny Damon*	2.00
274	*Russ Davis*	.45
275	Carlos Delgado	1.50
276	Carl Everett	.25
277	Cliff Floyd	.60
278	Alex Gonzalez	1.50
279	*Derek Jeter*	100.00
280	Chipper Jones	10.00
281	Javier Lopez	.75
282	*Chad Mottola*	.40
283	Marc Newfield	.15
284	Eduardo Perez	.15
285	Manny Ramirez	10.00
286	*Todd Steverson*	.40
287	Michael Tucker	.15
288	Allen Watson	.15
289	Rondell White	.75
290	Dmitri Young	.15

1993 SP Platinum Power

This 20-card insert set features 20 of the game's top home run hitters. The top of each insert card features a special die cut treatment. Backs are numbered with a PP prefix.

		MT
Complete Set (20):		100.00
Common Player:		2.00
1	Albert Belle	5.00
2	Barry Bonds	6.00
3	Joe Carter	2.00
4	Will Clark	4.50
5	Darren Daulton	2.00
6	Cecil Fielder	2.00
7	Ron Gant	2.50
8	Juan Gonzalez	10.00
9	Ken Griffey, Jr.	25.00
10	Dave Hollins	2.00
11	Dave Justice	3.00
12	Fred McGriff	3.00
13	Mark McGwire	20.00
14	Dean Palmer	2.00
15	Mike Piazza	15.00
16	Tim Salmon	3.00
17	Ryne Sandberg	6.00
18	Gary Sheffield	3.00
19	Frank Thomas	10.00
20	Matt Williams	3.00

1993 SP Jumbos

These jumbo-size (8-1/2" x 11") versions of the players' 1993 SP cards were sold through Upper Deck Authenticated. Each player's jumbo card was produced in a limited edition of 1,000, except for Frank Thomas, whose jumbo card was an edition of 1,993. The jumbos were sold in heavy plastic screwdown holders.

		MT
Complete Set (5):		75.00
Common Player:		25.00
10	Barry Bonds	15.00
58	Tom Glavine	12.50
173	Lenny Dykstra	10.00
199	Roger Clemens	20.00
260	Frank Thomas	20.00

1994 SP Promo

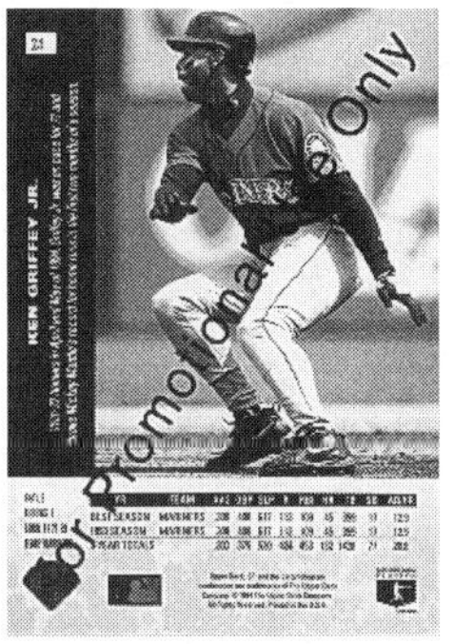

Virtually identical to the issued version of Ken Griffey, Jr.'s card in the regular SP set (#105) this differs in the card number on the back (#24) and the inclusion on front and back of the notice, "For Promotional Use Only".

		MT
24	Ken Griffey Jr.	8.00

1994 SP

The second edition of Upper Deck's top-shelf SP brand features each card with a front background printed on metallic foil; the first 20 cards in the set, a series of "Prospects," have front backgrounds of textured metallic foil. Backs are printed with standard processes and include a color player photo a few stats and typical copyright notice and logos. Each foil pack contains one card featuring a special die-cut treatment at top.

		MT
Complete Set (200):		100.00
Common Player:		.15
Wax Box:		275.00
1	*Mike Bell*	.50
2	D.J. Boston	.15
3	Johnny Damon	.40
4	*Brad Fullmer*	3.00
5	Joey Hamilton	.50
6	Todd Hollandsworth	.50
7	Brian Hunter	.50
8	*LaTroy Hawkins*	1.00
9	*Brooks Kieschnick*	1.50
10	*Derrek Lee*	2.00
11	*Trot Nixon*	1.00
12	Alex Ochoa	.15
13	*Chan Ho Park*	3.00
14	*Kirk Presley*	.50
15	*Alex Rodriguez*	90.00
16	*Jose Silva*	.30
17	*Terrell Wade*	.50
18	*Billy Wagner*	3.00
19	*Glenn Williams*	1.00
20	Preston Wilson	.25
21	Brian Anderson	.20
22	Chad Curtis	.15
23	Chili Davis	.15
24	Bo Jackson	.25
25	Mark Langston	.15
26	Tim Salmon	.40
27	Jeff Bagwell	2.00
28	Craig Biggio	.30
29	Ken Caminiti	.40
30	Doug Drabek	.15
31	John Hudek	.15
32	Greg Swindell	.15
33	Brent Gates	.15
34	Rickey Henderson	.40
35	Steve Karsay	.15
36	Mark McGwire	5.00
37	Ruben Sierra	.15
38	Terry Steinbach	.15
39	Roberto Alomar	1.00
40	Joe Carter	.15
41	Carlos Delgado	.75
42	Alex Gonzalez	.25
43	Juan Guzman	.15
44	Paul Molitor	.75
45	John Olerud	.25
46	Devon White	.20
47	Steve Avery	.15
48	Jeff Blauser	.15
49	Tom Glavine	.30
50	Dave Justice	.25
51	Roberto Kelly	.15
52	Ryan Klesko	.65
53	Javier Lopez	.30
54	Greg Maddux	2.50
55	Fred McGriff	.35
56	Ricky Bones	.15
57	Cal Eldred	.15
58	Brian Harper	.15
59	Pat Listach	.15
60	B.J. Surhoff	.15
61	Greg Vaughn	.20
62	Bernard Gilkey	.15
63	Gregg Jefferies	.15
64	Ray Lankford	.15
65	Ozzie Smith	.75
66	Bob Tewksbury	.15
67	Mark Whiten	.15
68	Todd Zeile	.15
69	Mark Grace	.30
70	Randy Myers	.15
71	Ryne Sandberg	1.00
72	Sammy Sosa	2.50
73	Steve Trachsel	.20
74	Rick Wilkins	.15
75	Brett Butler	.15
76	Delino DeShields	.15
77	Orel Hershiser	.15
78	Eric Karros	.20
79	Raul Mondesi	.60
80	Mike Piazza	2.50
81	Tim Wallach	.15
82	Moises Alou	.25
83	Cliff Floyd	.15
84	Marquis Grissom	.15
85	Pedro Martinez	.50
86	Larry Walker	.40
87	John Wetteland	.15
88	Rondell White	.35
89	Rod Beck	.15
90	Barry Bonds	1.25
91	John Burkett	.15
92	Royce Clayton	.15
93	Billy Swift	.15
94	Robby Thompson	.15
95	Matt Williams	.40
96	Carlos Baerga	.15
97	Albert Belle	1.00
98	Kenny Lofton	.75
99	Dennis Martinez	.15
100	Eddie Murray	.50
101	Manny Ramirez	1.50
102	Eric Anthony	.15
103	Chris Bosio	.15
104	Jay Buhner	.15
105	Ken Griffey, Jr.	5.00
106	Randy Johnson	.50
107	Edgar Martinez	.15
108	Chuck Carr	.15
109	Jeff Conine	.15
110	Carl Everett	.15
111	Chris Hammond	.15
112	Bryan Harvey	.15
113	Charles Johnson	.20
114	Gary Sheffield	.50
115	Bobby Bonilla	.20
116	Dwight Gooden	.20
117	Todd Hundley	.25
118	Bobby Jones	.20
119	Jeff Kent	.15
120	Bret Saberhagen	.15
121	Jeffrey Hammonds	.15
122	Chris Hoiles	.15
123	Ben McDonald	.15
124	Mike Mussina	1.00
125	Rafael Palmeiro	.35
126	Cal Ripken, Jr.	4.00
127	Lee Smith	.15
128	Derek Bell	.15
129	Andy Benes	.20
130	Tony Gwynn	1.50
131	Trevor Hoffman	.20
132	Phil Plantier	.15
133	Bip Roberts	.15
134	Darren Daulton	.15
135	Len Dykstra	.15
136	Dave Hollins	.15
137	Danny Jackson	.15
138	John Kruk	.15
139	Kevin Stocker	.15
140	Jay Bell	.15
141	Carlos Garcia	.15
142	Jeff King	.15
143	Orlando Merced	.15
144	Andy Van Slyke	.15
145	Paul Wagner	.15
146	Jose Canseco	.40
147	Will Clark	.40
148	Juan Gonzalez	2.00
149	Rick Helling	.15
150	Dean Palmer	.15
151	Ivan Rodriguez	1.00
152	Roger Clemens	1.50
153	Scott Cooper	.15
154	Andre Dawson	.20
155	Mike Greenwell	.15
156	Aaron Sele	.20
157	Mo Vaughn	.75
158	Bret Boone	.15
159	Barry Larkin	.20
160	Kevin Mitchell	.15
161	Jose Rijo	.15
162	Deion Sanders	.25
163	Reggie Sanders	.20
164	Dante Bichette	.40
165	Ellis Burks	.20
166	Andres Galarraga	.30
167	Charlie Hayes	.15
168	David Nied	.15
169	Walt Weiss	.15
170	Kevin Appier	.15
171	David Cone	.20
172	Jeff Granger	.20
173	Felix Jose	.15
174	Wally Joyner	.15
175	Brian McRae	.15
176	Cecil Fielder	.20
177	Travis Fryman	.15
178	Mike Henneman	.15
179	Tony Phillips	.15
180	Mickey Tettleton	.15
181	Alan Trammell	.15
182	Rick Aguilera	.15
183	Rich Becker	.15
184	Scott Erickson	.15
185	Chuck Knoblauch	.25
186	Kirby Puckett	1.50
187	Dave Winfield	.30
188	Wilson Alvarez	.15
189	Jason Bere	.15
190	Alex Fernandez	.20
191	Julio Franco	.15
192	Jack McDowell	.15
193	Frank Thomas	2.00
194	Robin Ventura	.20
195	Jim Abbott	.15
196	Wade Boggs	.35
197	Jimmy Key	.15
198	Don Mattingly	2.00
199	Paul O'Neill	.20
200	Danny Tartabull	.15

1994 SP Die-Cut

Upper Deck SP Die-cuts are a 200-card parallel set inserted at the rate of one per foil pack. Each card has a die-cut top instead of the flat-top found on regular SP cards. Die-cuts also have a silver-foil Upper Deck hologram logo on back, in contrast to the gold-tone hologram found on regular SP; this is an effort to prevent fraudulent replication by any crook with a pair of scissors.

	MT
Complete Set (200):	150.00
Common Player:	.25

(Star cards valued at 1.5-3X corresponding cards in regular SP issue)

1994 SP Holoview Blue

Holoview F/X Blue is a 38-card set utilizing Holoview printing technology, which features 200 frames of video to produce a true, three-dimensional image on the bottom third of each card. The hologram is bordered in blue and there is a blue stripe running down the right side of the card. Backs are done with a blue background and feature a player photo over top of bold letters reading "HoloView FX". This insert could be found in one per five packs of SP baseball.

		MT
Complete Set (38):		150.00
Common Player:		1.50
1	Roberto Alomar	7.50
2	Kevin Appier	1.50
3	Jeff Bagwell	10.00
4	Jose Canseco	4.00
5	Roger Clemens	10.00
6	Carlos Delgado	2.50
7	Cecil Fielder	3.00
8	Cliff Floyd	1.50
9	Travis Fryman	1.50
10	Andres Galarraga	3.00
11	Juan Gonzalez	12.00
12	Ken Griffey, Jr.	30.00
13	Tony Gwynn	10.00
14	Jeffrey Hammonds	1.50
15	Bo Jackson	2.50
16	Michael Jordan	30.00
17	Dave Justice	4.00
18	Steve Karsay	1.50
19	Jeff Kent	1.50
20	Brooks Kieschnick	2.00
21	Ryan Klesko	5.00
22	John Kruk	1.50
23	Barry Larkin	2.00
24	Pat Listach	1.50
25	Don Mattingly	12.00
26	Mark McGwire	30.00
27	Raul Mondesi	4.00
28	Trot Nixon	2.00
29	Mike Piazza	15.00
30	Kirby Puckett	9.00
31	Manny Ramirez	10.00
32	Cal Ripken, Jr.	20.00
33	Alex Rodriguez	45.00
34	Tim Salmon	3.00
35	Gary Sheffield	3.00
36	Ozzie Smith	6.00
37	Sammy Sosa	20.00
38	Andy Van Slyke	1.50

1994 SP Holoview Red

HoloView F/X Red is a parallel set to the Blue insert. Once again, this 38-card set utilizes Holoview printing technology. However, these cards have a red border surrounding the hologram and along the right side, as well as a red background on the back and a large "SPECIAL FX" under the player photo. Holoview red cards also have die-cut tops. Red cards are much scarcer than blue; the red being inserted once per 75 packs of SP baseball.

		MT
Complete Set (38):		1000.
Common Player:		4.50
1	Roberto Alomar	15.00
2	Kevin Appier	4.50
3	Jeff Bagwell	35.00
4	Jose Canseco	12.00
5	Roger Clemens	40.00
6	Carlos Delgado	7.50
7	Cecil Fielder	6.00
8	Cliff Floyd	4.50
9	Travis Fryman	4.50
10	Andres Galarraga	6.00
11	Juan Gonzalez	45.00
12	Ken Griffey, Jr.	100.00
13	Tony Gwynn	45.00
14	Jeffrey Hammonds	4.50
15	Bo Jackson	6.00
16	Michael Jordan	150.00
17	Dave Justice	9.00
18	Steve Karsay	4.50
19	Jeff Kent	4.50
20	Brooks Kieschnick	6.00
21	Ryan Klesko	9.00
22	John Kruk	4.50
23	Barry Larkin	6.00
24	Pat Listach	4.50
25	Don Mattingly	25.00
26	Mark McGwire	100.00
27	Raul Mondesi	15.00
28	Trot Nixon	6.00
29	Mike Piazza	60.00
30	Kirby Puckett	25.00
31	Manny Ramirez	35.00
32	Cal Ripken, Jr.	75.00
33	Alex Rodriguez	200.00
34	Tim Salmon	9.00
35	Gary Sheffield	15.00
36	Ozzie Smith	25.00
37	Sammy Sosa	50.00
38	Andy Van Slyke	4.50

1995 SP

Foil highlights and die-cut specialty cards are once again featured in Upper Deck's premium-brand SP baseball card issue. The 207-card set opens with four die-cut tribute cards, followed by 20 Premier Prospect die-cuts printed on metallic foil backgrounds with copper-foil highlights. Three checklists follow, also die-cut. The regular player cards in the set are arranged in team-alphabetical order within league. Card fronts feature photos which are borderless at top, bottom and right. On the left is a gold-highlighted metallic foil border of blue for N.L., red for A.L. Backs have a large photo at top, with a few stats and career highlights at bottom, along with a gold infield-shaped hologram. The SP insert program consists of a "SuperbaFoil" parallel set, in which each card's normal foil highlights are replaced with silver foil; a 48-card Special F/X set utilizing holographic portraits, and, a 20-card Platinum Power set. The hobby-only SP was issued in eight-card foil packs with a $3.99 suggested retail price.

		MT
Complete Set (207):		40.00
Common Player:		.15
Wax Box:		55.00
1	Cal Ripken Jr. (Salute)	3.00
2	Nolan Ryan (Salute)	2.00
3	George Brett (Salute)	1.00
4	Mike Schmidt (Salute)	.75
5	Dustin Hermanson (Premier Prospects)	.25
6	Antonio Osuna (Premier Prospects)	.25
7	*Mark Grudzielanek* (Premier Prospects)	.75
8	Ray Durham (Premier Prospects)	.35
9	Ugueth Urbina (Premier Prospects)	.25
10	Ruben Rivera (Premier Prospects)	1.50
11	Curtis Goodwin (Premier Prospects)	.15
12	Jimmy Hurst (Premier Prospects)	.15
13	Jose Malave (Premier Prospects)	.15
14	*Hideo Nomo* (Premier Prospects)	2.00
15	Juan Acevedo (Premier Prospects)	.15
16	Tony Clark (Premier Prospects)	1.50
17	Jim Pittsley (Premier Prospects)	.15
18	*Freddy Garcia* (Premier Prospects)	.50
19	*Carlos Perez* (Premier Prospects)	.25
20	*Raul Casanova* (Premier Prospects)	.50
21	Quilvio Veras (Premier Prospects)	.25
22	Edgardo Alfonzo (Premier Prospects)	.50
23	Marty Cordova (Premier Prospects)	.25
24	C.J. Nitkowski (Premier Prospects)	.25
25	Checklist 1-69 (Wade Boggs)	.25
26	Checklist 70-138 (Dave Winfield)	.25
27	Checklist 139-207 (Eddie Murray)	.50
28	Dave Justice	.30
29	Marquis Grissom	.15
30	Fred McGriff	.50
31	Greg Maddux	2.50
32	Tom Glavine	.30
33	Steve Avery	.15
34	Chipper Jones	2.50
35	Sammy Sosa	2.50
36	Jaime Navarro	.15
37	Randy Myers	.15
38	Mark Grace	.30
39	Todd Zeile	.15
40	Brian McRae	.15
41	Reggie Sanders	.15
42	Ron Gant	.15
43	Deion Sanders	.25
44	Barry Larkin	.25
45	Bret Boone	.15
46	Jose Rijo	.15
47	Jason Bates	.15
48	Andres Galarraga	.40
49	Bill Swift	.15
50	Larry Walker	.40
51	Vinny Castilla	.15
52	Dante Bichette	.40
53	Jeff Conine	.15
54	John Burkett	.15
55	Gary Sheffield	.40
56	Andre Dawson	.25
57	Terry Pendleton	.15
58	Charles Johnson	.20
59	Brian L. Hunter	.20
60	Jeff Bagwell	1.25
61	Craig Biggio	.35
62	Phil Nevin	.15
63	Doug Drabek	.15
64	Derek Bell	.15
65	Raul Mondesi	.50
66	Eric Karros	.15
67	Roger Cedeno	.15
68	Delino DeShields	.15
69	Ramon Martinez	.15
70	Mike Piazza	2.00
71	Billy Ashley	.15
72	Jeff Fassero	.15
73	Shane Andrews	.15
74	Wil Cordero	.15
75	Tony Tarasco	.15
76	Rondell White	.25
77	Pedro Martinez	.25
78	Moises Alou	.20
79	Rico Brogna	.15
80	Bobby Bonilla	.20
81	Jeff Kent	.15
82	Brett Butler	.15
83	Bobby Jones	.15
84	Bill Pulsipher	.15
85	Bret Saberhagen	.15
86	Gregg Jefferies	.15
87	Lenny Dykstra	.15
88	Dave Hollins	.15
89	Charlie Hayes	.15
90	Darren Daulton	.15
91	Curt Schilling	.25
92	Heathcliff Slocumb	.15
93	Carlos Garcia	.15
94	Denny Neagle	.15
95	Jay Bell	.15
96	Orlando Merced	.15
97	Dave Clark	.15
98	Bernard Gilkey	.15
99	Scott Cooper	.15
100	Ozzie Smith	.75
100	Ken Griffey Jr. (promo card)	6.00
101	Tom Henke	.15
102	Ken Hill	.15
103	Brian Jordan	.15
104	Ray Lankford	.15
105	Tony Gwynn	1.25
106	Andy Benes	.15
107	Ken Caminiti	.35
108	Steve Finley	.15
109	Joey Hamilton	.20
110	Bip Roberts	.15
111	Eddie Williams	.15
112	Rod Beck	.15
113	Matt Williams	.40
114	Glenallen Hill	.15
115	Barry Bonds	1.00
116	Robby Thompson	.15
117	Mark Portugal	.15
118	Brady Anderson	.30
119	Mike Mussina	.60
120	Rafael Palmeiro	.30
121	Chris Hoiles	.15
122	Harold Baines	.15
123	Jeffrey Hammonds	.15
124	Tim Naehring	.15
125	Mo Vaughn	.60
126	Mike Macfarlane	.15
127	Roger Clemens	1.00
128	John Valentin	.15
129	Aaron Sele	.15
130	Jose Canseco	.40
131	J.T. Snow	.20
132	Mark Langston	.15
133	Chili Davis	.15
134	Chuck Finley	.15
135	Tim Salmon	.25
136	Tony Phillips	.15
137	Jason Bere	.15
138	Robin Ventura	.25
139	Tim Raines	.20
140a	Frank Thomas (5-yr. BA .326)	1.50
140b	Frank Thomas (5-yr. BA .303)	4.00
141	Alex Fernandez	.20
142	Jim Abbott	.15
143	Wilson Alvarez	.15
144	Carlos Baerga	.15
145	Albert Belle	.75
146	Jim Thome	.40
147	Dennis Martinez	.15
148	Eddie Murray	.60
149	Dave Winfield	.35
150	Kenny Lofton	.60
151	Manny Ramirez	1.00
152	Chad Curtis	.15
153	Lou Whitaker	.15
154	Alan Trammell	.15
155	Cecil Fielder	.20
156	Kirk Gibson	.15
157	Michael Tucker	.15
158	Jon Nunnally	.15
159	Wally Joyner	.15
160	Kevin Appier	.15
161	Jeff Montgomery	.15
162	Greg Gagne	.15
163	Ricky Bones	.15
164	Cal Eldred	.15
165	Greg Vaughn	.20
166	Kevin Seitzer	.15
167	Jose Valentin	.15
168	Joe Oliver	.15
169	Rick Aguilera	.15
170	Kirby Puckett	1.50
171	Scott Stahoviak	.15
172	Kevin Tapani	.15
173	Chuck Knoblauch	.25
174	Rich Becker	.15
175	Don Mattingly	1.50
176	Jack McDowell	.15
177	Jimmy Key	.15
178	Paul O'Neill	.20
179	John Wetteland	.15
180	Wade Boggs	.50
181	Derek Jeter	3.00
182	Rickey Henderson	.35
183	Terry Steinbach	.15
184	Ruben Sierra	.15
185	Mark McGwire	4.00
186	Todd Stottlemyre	.15
187	Dennis Eckersley	.15
188	Alex Rodriguez	3.00
189	Randy Johnson	.50
190	Ken Griffey Jr.	4.00
190a	Ken Griffey Jr. (certified autograph)	200.00
191	Tino Martinez	.20
192	Jay Buhner	.20
193	Edgar Martinez	.15
194	Mickey Tettleton	.15
195	Juan Gonzalez	1.75
196	Benji Gil	.15
197	Dean Palmer	.15
198	Ivan Rodriguez	.75
199	Kenny Rogers	.15
200	Will Clark	.40
201	Roberto Alomar	.75
202	David Cone	.25
203	Paul Molitor	.75
204	Shawn Green	.25
205	Joe Carter	.20
206	Alex Gonzalez	.20
207	Pat Hentgen	.15

1995 SP SuperbaFoil

This chase set parallels the 207 regular cards in the SP issue. Cards were found at the rate of one per eight-card foil pack. SuperbaFoil cards feature a silver-rainbow metallic foil in place of the gold, copper, red or blue foil highlights on regular-issue SP cards. On back, the SuperbaFoil inserts have a silver hologram instead of the gold version found on standard cards.

	MT
Complete Set (207):	80.00
Common Player:	.25
SuperbaFoil Stars: 2X	

(See 1995 SP for checklist and base values.)

1995 SP Platinum Power

This die-cut insert set features the game's top power hitters in color action photos set against a background of two-toned gold rays emanating from the SP logo at lower-right. Player name, team and position are printed in white in a black band at bottom. Backs repeat the golden ray effect in the background and have a color photo at center. Career and 1994 stats are presented. An infield-shaped gold foil hologram is at lower-right. Cards have a "PP" prefix. Stated odds of finding one of the 20 Platinum Power inserts are one per five packs.

		MT
	Complete Set (20):	20.00
	Common Player:	.50
1	Jeff Bagwell	2.00
2	Barry Bonds	1.50
3	Ron Gant	.50
4	Fred McGriff	.75
5	Raul Mondesi	.75
6	Mike Piazza	3.00
7	Larry Walker	.75
8	Matt Williams	.75
9	Albert Belle	1.00
10	Cecil Fielder	.50
11	Juan Gonzalez	2.00
12	Ken Griffey Jr.	5.00
13	Mark McGwire	5.00
14	Eddie Murray	1.00
15	Manny Ramirez	2.00
16	Cal Ripken Jr.	4.00
17	Tim Salmon	.60
18	Frank Thomas	3.00
19	Jim Thome	.60
20	Mo Vaughn	.75

1995 SP Special F/X

By far the preferred pick of the '95 SP insert program is the Special F/X set of 48. The cards have a color action photo on front, printed on a metallic foil background. A 3/4" square holographic portrait is printed on the front. Backs are printed in standard technology and include another photo and a few stats and career highlights. Stated odds of finding a Special F/X card are 1 per 75 packs, or about one per two boxes.

		MT
	Complete Set (48):	425.00
	Common Player:	3.00
1	Jose Canseco	5.00
2	Roger Clemens	20.00
3	Mo Vaughn	10.00
4	Tim Salmon	4.00
5	Chuck Finley	3.00
6	Robin Ventura	4.00
7	Jason Bere	3.00
8	Carlos Baerga	3.00
9	Albert Belle	10.00
10	Kenny Lofton	10.00
11	Manny Ramirez	15.00
12	Jeff Montgomery	3.00
13	Kirby Puckett	12.50
14	Wade Boggs	7.50
15	Don Mattingly	12.50
16	Cal Ripken Jr.	40.00
17	Ruben Sierra	3.00
18	Ken Griffey Jr.	45.00
19	Randy Johnson	9.00
20	Alex Rodriguez	40.00
21	Will Clark	5.00
22	Juan Gonzalez	25.00
23	Roberto Alomar	7.50
24	Joe Carter	3.00
25	Alex Gonzalez	4.00
26	Paul Molitor	7.50
27	Ryan Klesko	4.00
28	Fred McGriff	4.00
29	Greg Maddux	30.00
30	Sammy Sosa	30.00
31	Bret Boone	3.00
32	Barry Larkin	4.00
33	Reggie Sanders	3.00
34	Dante Bichette	4.00
35	Andres Galarraga	5.00
36	Charles Johnson	3.00
37	Gary Sheffield	4.00
38	Jeff Bagwell	20.00
39	Craig Biggio	4.50
40	Eric Karros	3.00
41	Billy Ashley	3.00
42	Raul Mondesi	4.00
43	Mike Piazza	30.00
44	Rondell White	3.00
45	Bret Saberhagen	3.00
46	Tony Gwynn	25.00
47	Melvin Nieves	3.00
48	Matt Williams	4.00

1995 SP Griffey Gold Signature

A specially autographed version of Griffey's card from 1995 SP was made available from Upper Deck Authenticated. These cards are signed and numbered in gold ink from within an edition of 1,000.

		MT
190	Ken Griffey Jr.	125.00

1995 SP/ Championship

Championship was a version of Upper Deck's popular SP line designed for sale in retail outlets. The first 20 cards in the set are a "Diamond in the Rough" subset featuring hot rookies printed on textured metallic foil background. Regular player cards are arranged by team within league, alphabetically by city name. Each team set is led off with a "Pro Files" card of a star player; those card backs feature team season and post-season results. Each of the regular player cards has a borderless action photo on front, highlighted with a gold-foil SP Championship logo. The team name is in a blue-foil oval on National Leaguers' cards; red on American Leaguers. Backs have a portrait photo, a few stats and career highlights. Situated between the N.L. and A.L. cards in the checklist are a subset of 15 October Legends. A parallel set of cards with die-cut tops was inserted into the six-card foil packs at the rate of one per pack. A special card honoring Cal Ripken Jr.'s consecutive-game record was issued as a super-scarce insert.

		MT
	Complete Set (200):	40.00
	Common Player:	.15
	Wax Box:	90.00
1	*Hideo Nomo* (Diamonds in the Rough)	2.00
2	Roger Cedeno (Diamonds in the Rough)	.25
3	Curtis Goodwin (Diamonds in the Rough)	.15
4	Jon Nunnally (Diamonds in the Rough)	.15
5	Bill Pulsipher (Diamonds in the Rough)	.25
6	C.J. Nitkowski (Diamonds in the Rough)	.15
7	Dustin Hermanson (Diamonds in the Rough)	.15
8	Marty Cordova (Diamonds in the Rough)	.25
9	Ruben Rivera (Diamonds in the Rough)	.75
10	*Ariel Prieto* (Diamonds in the Rough)	.25
11	Edgardo Alfonzo (Diamonds in the Rough)	.30
12	Ray Durham (Diamonds in the Rough)	.25
13	Quilvio Veras (Diamonds in the Rough)	.25
14	Ugueth Urbina (Diamonds in the Rough)	.25
15	*Carlos Perez* (Diamonds in the Rough)	.20
16	*Glenn Dishman* (Diamonds in the Rough)	.25
17	Jeff Suppan (Diamonds in the Rough)	.20
18	Jason Bates (Diamonds in the Rough)	.15
19	Jason Isringhausen (Diamonds in the Rough)	.50
20	Derek Jeter (Diamonds in the Rough)	3.00
21	Fred McGriff (Major League ProFiles)	.40
22	Marquis Grissom	.15
23	Fred McGriff	.50
24	Tom Glavine	.25
25	Greg Maddux	2.00
26	Chipper Jones	2.00
27	Sammy Sosa (Major League ProFiles)	1.50
28	Randy Myers	.15
29	Mark Grace	.25
30	Sammy Sosa	2.50
31	Todd Zeile	.15
32	Brian McRae	.15
33	Ron Gant (Major League ProFiles)	.15
34	Reggie Sanders	.15
35	Ron Gant	.20
36	Barry Larkin	.30
37	Bret Boone	.15
38	John Smiley	.15
39	Larry Walker (Major League ProFiles)	.25
40	Andres Galarraga	.25
41	Bill Swift	.15
42	Larry Walker	.35
43	Vinny Castilla	.15
44	Dante Bichette	.50
45	Jeff Conine (Major League ProFiles)	.15
46	Charles Johnson	.15
47	Gary Sheffield	.30
48	Andre Dawson	.20
49	Jeff Conine	.15
50	Jeff Bagwell (Major League ProFiles)	.40
51	Phil Nevin	.15
52	Craig Biggio	.25
53	Brian L. Hunter	.20
54	Doug Drabek	.15
55	Jeff Bagwell	1.25
56	Derek Bell	.15
57	Mike Piazza (Major League ProFiles)	.60
58	Raul Mondesi	.40
59	Eric Karros	.20
60	Mike Piazza	2.00
61	Ramon Martinez	.20
62	Billy Ashley	.15
63	Rondell White (Major League ProFiles)	.20
64	Jeff Fassero	.15
65	Moises Alou	.20
66	Tony Tarasco	.15
67	Rondell White	.20
68	Pedro Martinez	.25
69	Bobby Jones (Major League ProFiles)	.15
70	Bobby Bonilla	.20
71	Bobby Jones	.15
72	Bret Saberhagen	.15
73	Darren Daulton (Major League ProFiles)	.15
74	Darren Daulton	.15
75	Gregg Jefferies	.15
76	Tyler Green	.15
77	Heathcliff Slocumb	.15
78	Lenny Dykstra	.15
79	Jay Bell (Major League ProFiles)	.15
80	Denny Neagle	.15
81	Orlando Merced	.15
82	Jay Bell	.15
83	Ozzie Smith (Major League ProFiles)	.30
84	Ken Hill	.15
85	Ozzie Smith	.50
86	Bernard Gilkey	.15
87	Ray Lankford	.15
88	Tony Gwynn (Major League ProFiles)	.50
89	Ken Caminiti	.25
90	Tony Gwynn	1.25
91	Joey Hamilton	.15
92	Bip Roberts	.15
93	Deion Sanders (Major League ProFiles)	.25
94	Glenallen Hill	.15
95	Matt Williams	.30
96	Barry Bonds	.75
97	Rod Beck	.15
98	Eddie Murray (Checklist)	.25
99	Cal Ripken Jr. (Checklist)	1.50
100	Roberto Alomar (October Legends)	.40
101	George Brett (October Legends)	.75
102	Joe Carter (Ocober Legends)	.20
103	Will Clark (October Legends)	.25
104	Dennis Eckersley (October Legends)	.15
105	Whitey Ford (October Legends)	.40
106	Steve Garvey (October Legends)	.15
107	Kirk Gibson (October Legends)	.15
108	Orel Hershiser (October Legends)	.15
109	Reggie Jackson (October Legends)	.50
110	Paul Molitor (October Legends)	.25
111	Kirby Puckett (October Legends)	.75
112	Mike Schmidt (October Legends)	.50
113	Dave Stewart (October Legends)	.15
114	Alan Trammell (October Legends)	.15
115	Cal Ripken Jr. (Major League ProFiles)	1.50
116	Brady Anderson	.20
117	Mike Mussina	.50
118	Rafael Palmeiro	.25
119	Chris Hoiles	.15
120	Cal Ripken Jr.	2.50
121	Mo Vaughn (Major League ProFiles)	.35
122	Roger Clemens	.75
123	Tim Naehring	.15
124	John Valentin	.15
125	Mo Vaughn	.60
126	Tim Wakefield	.15
127	Jose Canseco	.35
128	Rick Aguilera	.15
129	Chili Davis (Major League ProFiles)	.15
130	Lee Smith	.15
131	Jim Edmonds	.30
132	Chuck Finley	.15
133	Chili Davis	.15
134	J.T. Snow	.15
135	Tim Salmon	.30
136	Frank Thomas (Major League ProFiles)	.75
137	Jason Bere	.15
138	Robin Ventura	.25
139	Tim Raines	.20
140	Frank Thomas	1.50
141	Alex Fernandez	.20
142	Eddie Murray (Major League ProFiles)	.25
143	Carlos Baerga	.15
144	Eddie Murray	.40
145	Albert Belle	.75
146	Jim Thome	.30
147	Dennis Martinez	.15
148	Dave Winfield	.25
149	Kenny Lofton	.60
150	Manny Ramirez	.75
151	Cecil Fielder (Major League ProFiles)	.20
152	Lou Whitaker	.15
153	Alan Trammell	.15
154	Kirk Gibson	.15
155	Cecil Fielder	.20
156	*Bobby Higginson*	1.50
157	Kevin Appier (Major League ProFiles)	.15
158	Wally Joyner	.15
159	Jeff Montgomery	.15
160	Kevin Appier	.15
161	Gary Gaetti	.15
162	Greg Gagne	.15
163	Ricky Bones (Major League ProFiles)	.15
164	Greg Vaughn	.20
165	Kevin Seitzer	.15
166	Ricky Bones	.15
167	Kirby Puckett (Major League ProFiles)	.40
168	Pedro Munoz	.15
169	Chuck Knoblauch	.25
170	Kirby Puckett	1.00
171	Don Mattingly (Major League ProFiles)	.50
172	Wade Boggs	.40
173	Paul O'Neill	.20
174	John Wetteland	.15
175	Don Mattingly	1.00
176	Jack McDowell	.15
177	Mark McGwire (Major League ProFiles)	2.00
178	Rickey Henderson	.30
179	Terry Steinbach	.15
180	Ruben Sierra	.15
181	Mark McGwire	3.00
182	Dennis Eckersley	.15
183	Ken Griffey Jr. (Major League ProFiles)	1.50
184	Alex Rodriguez	2.50
185	Ken Griffey Jr.	3.00
186	Randy Johnson	.60
187	Jay Buhner	.15
188	Edgar Martinez	.15
100	Will Clark (Major League ProFiles)	.25
190	Juan Gonzalez	1.25
191	Benji Gil	.15
192	Ivan Rodriguez	.60
193	Kenny Rogers	.15
194	Will Clark	.30
195	Paul Molitor (Major League ProFiles)	.25
196	Roberto Alomar	.60
197	David Cone	.20
198	Paul Molitor	.50
199	Shawn Green	.25
200	Joe Carter	.20
CR1	Cal Ripken Jr. (2,131 games tribute)	15.00
CR1	Cal Ripken Jr. die-cut	50.00

1995 SP/ Championship Die-Cuts

Each of the 200 cards in the regular SP championship issue, plus the 20 insert cards, can also be found in a parallel chase card set with die-cut tops. One die-cut card was found in each six-card foil pack, making them five times scarcer than the regular cards. To prevent regular cards from being fraudulently cut, factory-issue die-cuts have the Upper Deck hologram on back in silver tone, rather than the gold holograms found on regular cards.

	MT
Complete Set (200):	90.00
Common Player:	.25
Die-Cut Stars: 2X	
(See 1995 SP/ Championship for checklist and base values.)	

1995 SP/ Championship Classic Performances

Vintage action photos are featured in this chase set marking great post-season performances of modern times. The cards have a wide red strip at top with "CLASSIC PERFORMANCES" in gold-foil; the player's name, team and the SP Championship embossed logo at bottom are also in gold. Backs have a portrait photo and description of the highlight along with stats from that series. Regular Classic Performances cards are found at a stated rate of one per 15 foil packs, with die-cut versions in every 75 packs, on average. The die-cuts have silver UD holograms on back as opposed to the gold hologram found on regular versions of the chase cards.

		MT
Complete Set (10):		40.00
Common Player:		2.50
Complete Die-Cut Set (10):		175.00
Common Die-Cuts:		10.00
CP1	Reggie Jackson (Game 6 of '77 WS)	3.00
CP1	Reggie Jackson (die-cut)	12.00
CP2	Nolan Ryan (Game 3 of '69 WS)	20.00
CP2	Nolan Ryan (die-cut)	75.00
CP3	Kirk Gibson (Game 1 of '88 WS)	2.50
CP3	Kirk Gibson (die-cut)	10.00
CP4	Joe Carter (Game 6 of '93 WS)	2.50
CP4	Joe Carter (die-cut)	10.00
CP5	George Brett (Game 3 of '80 ALCS)	6.00
CP5	George Brett (die-cut)	25.00
CP6	Roberto Alomar (Game 4 of '92 ALCS)	4.00
CP6	Roberto Alomar (die-cut)	16.00
CP7	Ozzie Smith (Game 5 of '85 NLCS)	4.00
CP7	Ozzie Smith (die-cut)	16.00
CP8	Kirby Puckett (Game 6 of '91 WS)	6.00
CP8	Kirby Puckett (die-cut)	24.00
CP9	Bret Saberhagen (Game 7 of '85 WS)	2.50
CP9	Bret Saberhagen (die-cut)	10.00
CP10	Steve Garvey (Game 4 of '84 NLCS)	2.50
CP10	Steve Garvey (die-cut)	10.00

1995 SP/ Championship Destination: Fall Classic

Colored foil background printing and copper-foil graphic highlights are featured on this insert set picturing players who, for the most part, had yet to make a post-season appearance prior to 1995's expanded playoffs. Found at a stated average rate of one per 40 foil packs, the cards have short career summaries and another photo on back. A die-cut version of the cards was also issued, with a silver UD hologram on back rather than the gold found on the standard chase cards. The die-cut Fall Classic cards were inserted at a rate of one per 75 packs.

		MT
Complete Set (9):		80.00
Common Player:		4.00
Complete Die-Cut Set (9):		200.00
Common Die-Cut:		10.00
1	Ken Griffey Jr.	25.00
1	Ken Griffey Jr. (die-cut)	60.00
2	Frank Thomas	10.00
2	Frank Thomas (die-cut)	25.00
3	Albert Belle	6.00
3	Albert Belle (die-cut)	15.00
4	Mike Piazza	15.00
4	Mike Piazza (die-cut)	40.00
5	Don Mattingly	10.00
5	Don Mattingly (die-cut)	25.00
6	Hideo Nomo	6.00
6	Hideo Nomo (die-cut)	15.00
7	Greg Maddux	15.00
7	Greg Maddux (die-cut)	40.00
8	Fred McGriff	4.00
8	Fred McGriff (die-cut)	10.00
9	Barry Bonds	8.00
9	Barry Bonds (die-cut)	20.00

1996 SP FanFest Promos

To introduce its SP product, Upper Deck prepared an eight-card promo set for distribution at the All-Star FanFest in Philadelphia. The promos are identical in format to the issued versions except for the presence of a bright silver-foil FanFest logo in the lower-left corner of each card's front. The cards lack the overprint which has become standard on promo cards in the recent years.

		MT
Complete Set (8):		50.00
Common Player:		3.00
1	Ken Griffey Jr.	12.00
2	Frank Thomas	6.00
3	Albert Belle	4.00
4	Mo Vaughn	3.00
5	Barry Bonds	7.50
6	Mike Piazza	8.00
7	Matt Williams	3.00
8	Sammy Sosa	7.50

1996 SP

This 188-card set, distributed through hobby-only channels, features tremendous photography, including two photos on the front, and six insert sets. The inserts sets are Heroes, Marquee Matchups Blue and Die-Cut Marquee Matchups Red, Holoview Special F/X Blue and Die-Cut Holoview Special F/X Red, and the continuation of the Cal Ripken Collection.

		MT
Complete Set (188):		40.00
Common Player:		.15
Unlisted Stars: .30 to .50		
Wax Box:		60.00
1	Rey Ordonez (Premier Prospects)	.50
2	George Arias (Premier Prospects)	.15
3	*Osvaldo Fernandez* (Premier Prospects)	.30
4	*Darin Erstad* (Premier Prospects)	8.00
5	Paul Wilson (Premier Prospects)	.30
6	Richard Hidalgo (Premier Prospects)	.15
7	Bob Wolcott (Premier Prospects)	.15
8	Jimmy Haynes (Premier Prospects)	.15
9	Edgar Renteria (Premier Prospects)	.35
10	Alan Benes (Premier Prospects)	.30
11	Chris Snopek (Premier Prospects)	.15
12	Billy Wagner (Premier Prospects)	.45
13	*Mike Grace* (Premier Prospects)	.20
14	Todd Greene (Premier Prospects)	.15
15	Karim Garcia (Premier Prospects)	.75
16	John Wasdin (Premier Prospects)	.15
17	Jason Kendall (Premier Prospects)	.25
18	Bob Abreu (Premier Prospects)	.40
19	Jermaine Dye (Premier Prospects)	.25
20	Jason Schmidt (Premier Prospects)	.15
21	Javy Lopez	.20
22	Ryan Klesko	.45
23	Tom Glavine	.25
24	John Smoltz	.30
25	Greg Maddux	2.50
26	Chipper Jones	2.50
27	Fred McGriff	.40
28	David Justice	.20
29	Roberto Alomar	.75
30	Cal Ripken Jr.	3.00
31	Jeffrey Hammonds	.15
32	Bobby Bonilla	.15
33	Mike Mussina	.75
34	Randy Myers	.15
35	Rafael Palmeiro	.25
36	Brady Anderson	.25
37	Tim Naehring	.15
38	Jose Canseco	.40
39	Roger Clemens	2.00
40	Mo Vaughn	.60
41	*Jose Valentin*	.20
42	Kevin Mitchell	.15
43	Chili Davis	.15
44	Garret Anderson	.15
45	Tim Salmon	.30
46	Chuck Finley	.15
47	Mark Langston	.15
48	Jim Abbott	.15
49	J.T. Snow	.15
50	Jim Edmonds	.25
51	Sammy Sosa	2.50
52	Brian McRae	.15
53	Ryne Sandberg	1.25
54	Mark Grace	.30
55	Jaime Navarro	.15
56	Harold Baines	.15
57	Robin Ventura	.20
58	Tony Phillips	.15
59	Alex Fernandez	.25
60	Frank Thomas	2.00
61	Ray Durham	.15
62	Bret Boone	.15
63	Barry Larkin	.30
64	Pete Schourek	.15
65	Reggie Sanders	.15
66	John Smiley	.15
67	Carlos Baerga	.15
68	Jim Thome	.60
69	Eddie Murray	.60
70	Albert Belle	1.00
71	Dennis Martinez	.15
72	Jack McDowell	.15
73	Kenny Lofton	.60
74	Manny Ramirez	1.50
75	Dante Bichette	.35
76	Vinny Castilla	.15
77	Andres Galarraga	.35
78	Walt Weiss	.15
79	Ellis Burks	.15
80	Larry Walker	.40
81	Cecil Fielder	.20
82	Melvin Nieves	.15
83	Travis Fryman	.15
84	Chad Curtis	.15
85	Alan Trammell	.15
86	Gary Sheffield	.50
87	Charles Johnson	.15
88	Andre Dawson	.20
89	Jeff Conine	.15
90	Greg Colbrunn	.15
91	Derek Bell	.15
92	Brian Hunter	.15
93	Doug Drabek	.15
94	Craig Biggio	.25
95	Jeff Bagwell	1.50
96	Kevin Appier	.15
97	Jeff Montgomery	.15
98	Michael Tucker	.15
99	Bip Roberts	.15
100	Johnny Damon	.20
101	Eric Karros	.15
102	Raul Mondesi	.40
103	Ramon Martinez	.15
104	Ismael Valdes	.15
105	Mike Piazza	2.50
106	Hideo Nomo	.50
107	Chan Ho Park	.20
108	Ben McDonald	.15
109	Kevin Seitzer	.15
110	Greg Vaughn	.20
111	Jose Valentin	.15
112	Rick Aguilera	.15
113	Marty Cordova	.15
114	Brad Radke	.15
115	Kirby Puckett	1.50
116	Chuck Knoblauch	.25
117	Paul Molitor	.50
118	Pedro Martinez	.25
119	Mike Lansing	.15
120	Rondell White	.15
121	Moises Alou	.20
122	Mark Grudzielanek	.15
123	Jeff Fassero	.15
124	Rico Brogna	.15
125	Jason Isringhausen	.15
126	Jeff Kent	.15
127	Bernard Gilkey	.15
128	Todd Hundley	.25
129	David Cone	.25
130	Andy Pettitte	.75
131	Wade Boggs	.35
132	Paul O'Neill	.25
133	Ruben Sierra	.15
134	John Wetteland	.15
135	Derek Jeter	2.50
136	Geronimo Pena	.15
137	Terry Steinbach	.15
138	Ariel Prieto	.15
139	Scott Brosius	.15
140	Mark McGwire	4.00
141	Lenny Dykstra	.15
142	Todd Zeile	.15
143	Benito Santiago	.15
144	Mickey Morandini	.15
145	Gregg Jefferies	.15
146	Denny Neagle	.15
147	Orlando Merced	.15
148	Charlie Hayes	.15
149	Carlos Garcia	.15
150	Jay Bell	.15
151	Ray Lankford	.15
152	Alan Benes	.20
153	Dennis Eckersley	.15
154	Gary Gaetti	.15
155	Ozzie Smith	.75
156	Ron Gant	.20
157	Brian Jordan	.15
158	Ken Caminiti	.40
159	Rickey Henderson	.25
160	Tony Gwynn	1.50
161	Wally Joyner	.15
162	Andy Ashby	.15
163	Steve Finley	.15
164	Glenallen Hill	.15
165	Matt Williams	.30
166	Barry Bonds	1.00
167	William VanLandingham	.15
168	Rod Beck	.15
169	Randy Johnson	.50
170	Ken Griffey Jr.	4.00
170p	Ken Griffey Jr. (unmarked promo; bio on back says, ". . . against Cleveland" as opposed to ". . . against the	15.00
171	Alex Rodriguez	3.00
172	Edgar Martinez	.15
173	Jay Buhner	.15
174	Russ Davis	.15
175	Juan Gonzalez	2.00
176	Mickey Tettleton	.15
177	Will Clark	.40
178	Ken Hill	.15
179	Dean Palmer	.15
180	Ivan Rodriguez	.60
181	Carlos Delgado	.40
182	Alex Gonzalez	.20
183	Shawn Green	.25
184	Erik Hanson	.15
185	Joe Carter	.20
186	Checklist (Hideo Nomo)	.25
187	Checklist (Cal Ripken Jr.)	1.50
188	Checklist (Ken Griffey Jr.)	2.00

1996 SP Baseball Heroes

This 1996 insert set is a continuation of the series which began in 1990. These cards, numbered 81-90, feature nine of today's top stars, plus a Ken Griffey Jr. header card (#81). The cards were seeded one per every 96 packs.

		MT
Complete Set (10):		275.00
Common Player:		8.00
81	Ken Griffey Jr. Header	40.00
82	Frank Thomas	25.00
83	Albert Belle	10.00
84	Barry Bonds	15.00
85	Chipper Jones	40.00
86	Hideo Nomo	8.00
87	Mike Piazza	40.00
88	Manny Ramirez	15.00
89	Greg Maddux	35.00
90	Ken Griffey Jr.	60.00

1996 SP Marquee Matchups Blue

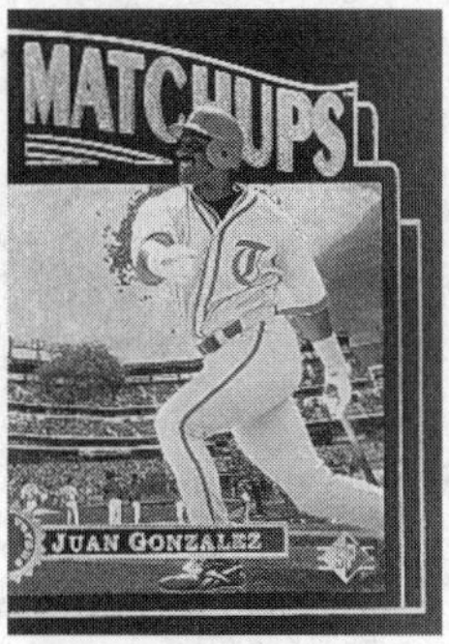

This 20-card Upper Deck SP insert set contains cards that allow collectors to match up the game's top players against each other, such as Greg Maddux against Cal Ripken Jr. The design and stadiums in the background match together when the two cards are next to each other. Blue versions are seeded one per every five packs. Red versions, with die-cut tops but otherwise identical to the blue, are found on average of once in 61 packs. Cards are numbered with a "MM" prefix.

		MT
Complete Set (20):		50.00
Common Player:		1.00
Complete Die-Cut Set:		200.00
Die-Cuts: 10X		
1	Ken Griffey Jr.	8.00
2	Hideo Nomo	1.50
3	Derek Jeter	5.00
4	Rey Ordonez	1.50
5	Tim Salmon	1.00
6	Mike Piazza	5.00
7	Mark McGwire	8.00
8	Barry Bonds	2.00
9	Cal Ripken Jr.	6.00
10	Greg Maddux	5.00
11	Albert Belle	2.00
12	Barry Larkin	1.00
13	Jeff Bagwell	4.00
14	Juan Gonzalez	4.00
15	Frank Thomas	3.00
16	Sammy Sosa	5.00
17	Mike Mussina	1.00
18	Chipper Jones	5.00
19	Roger Clemens	2.00
20	Fred McGriff	1.50

1996 SP Marquee Matchups Red

A parallel set to the blue Marquee Matchups, the red cards are found on average of one per 61 packs. Besides the red background printing, this version is distinguished from the more common blue version by the die-cutting around the top. Cards are numbered with a "MM" prefix.

		MT
Complete Set (20):		200.00
Common Player:		3.00
1	Ken Griffey Jr.	35.00
2	Hideo Nomo	5.00
3	Derek Jeter	20.00
4	Rey Ordonez	5.00
5	Tim Salmon	4.00
6	Mike Piazza	20.00
7	Mark McGwire	35.00
8	Barry Bonds	8.00
9	Cal Ripken Jr.	25.00
10	Greg Maddux	20.00
11	Albert Belle	4.00
12	Barry Larkin	4.00
13	Jeff Bagwell	8.00
14	Juan Gonzalez	15.00
15	Frank Thomas	15.00
16	Sammy Sosa	20.00
17	Mike Mussina	6.00
18	Chipper Jones	20.00
19	Roger Clemens	10.00
20	Fred McGriff	4.00

1996 SP Ripken Collection

The last five cards of the Cal Ripken Jr. Collection, which began in Collector's Choice Series I, are featured in this Upper Deck SP product. These five cards, numbered 18-22, cover Ripken's early days, including his 1982 Rookie of the Year Award, his Major League debut, and photos of him playing third base. Ripken Collection inserts are found one per every 45 packs.

		MT
Complete Set (5):		40.00
Common Ripken:		8.00
18	Cal Ripken Jr.	8.00
19	Cal Ripken Jr.	8.00
20	Cal Ripken Jr.	8.00
21	Cal Ripken Jr.	8.00
22	Cal Ripken Jr.	8.00

1996 SP SpecialFX

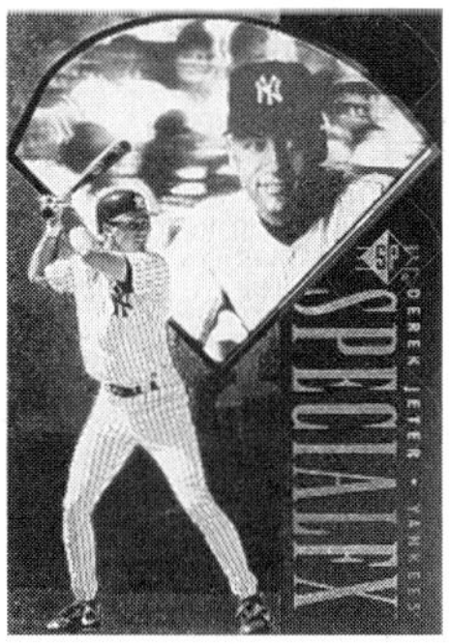

These 48 cards capture Upper Deck Holoview technology. Blue versions were seeded one per every five packs of 1996 Upper Deck SP baseball.

		MT
Complete Set (48):		120.00
Common Player:		1.50
1	Greg Maddux	7.50
2	Eric Karros	1.50
3	Mike Piazza	7.50
4	Raul Mondesi	1.75
5	Hideo Nomo	1.75
6	Jim Edmonds	1.50
7	Jason Isringhausen	1.50
8	Jay Buhner	1.50
9	Barry Larkin	1.50
10	Ken Griffey Jr.	12.00
11	Gary Sheffield	1.50
12	Craig Biggio	2.00
13	Paul Wilson	1.50
14	Rondell White	1.50
15	Chipper Jones	7.50
16	Kirby Puckett	3.50
17	Ron Gant	1.50
18	Wade Boggs	3.00
19	Fred McGriff	1.50
20	Cal Ripken Jr.	9.00
21	Jason Kendall	1.50
22	Johnny Damon	1.50
23	Kenny Lofton	2.00
24	Roberto Alomar	2.50
25	Barry Bonds	3.00
26	Dante Bichette	1.50
27	Mark McGwire	12.00
28	Rafael Palmeiro	2.00
29	Juan Gonzalez	5.00
30	Albert Belle	2.50
31	Randy Johnson	2.50
32	Jose Canseco	1.75
33	Sammy Sosa	6.00
34	Eddie Murray	2.00
35	Frank Thomas	5.00
36	Tom Glavine	1.50
37	Matt Williams	1.75
38	Roger Clemens	3.00
39	Paul Molitor	2.50
40	Tony Gwynn	6.00
41	Mo Vaughn	2.00
42	Tim Salmon	1.50
43	Manny Ramirez	3.00
44	Jeff Bagwell	5.00
45	Edgar Martinez	1.50
46	Rey Ordonez	1.50
47	Osvaldo Fernandez	1.50
48	Livan Hernandez	1.50

1996 SP SpecialFX Red

These 1996 Upper Deck SP red die-cut cards use Upper Deck's Holoview technology. They are scarcer than the blue versions; these being seeded one per every 75 packs.

		MT
Complete Set (48):		800.00
Common Player:		8.00
1	Greg Maddux	60.00
2	Eric Karros	8.00
3	Mike Piazza	60.00
4	Raul Mondesi	12.50
5	Hideo Nomo	15.00
6	Jim Edmonds	8.00
7	Jason Isringhausen	8.00
8	Jay Buhner	8.00
9	Barry Larkin	8.00
10	Ken Griffey Jr.	100.00
11	Gary Sheffield	10.00
12	Craig Biggio	10.00
13	Paul Wilson	8.00
14	Rondell White	8.00
15	Chipper Jones	60.00
16	Kirby Puckett	40.00
17	Ron Gant	8.00
18	Wade Boggs	10.00
19	Fred McGriff	10.00
20	Cal Ripken Jr.	80.00
21	Jason Kendall	8.00
22	Johnny Damon	8.00
23	Kenny Lofton	20.00
24	Roberto Alomar	20.00
25	Barry Bonds	25.00
26	Dante Bichette	10.00
27	Mark McGwire	100.00
28	Rafael Palmeiro	15.00
29	Juan Gonzalez	45.00
30	Albert Belle	25.00
31	Randy Johnson	20.00
32	Jose Canseco	15.00
33	Sammy Sosa	60.00
34	Eddie Murray	15.00
35	Frank Thomas	40.00
36	Tom Glavine	8.00
37	Matt Williams	12.50
38	Roger Clemens	25.00
39	Paul Molitor	20.00
40	Tony Gwynn	40.00
41	Mo Vaughn	20.00
42	Tim Salmon	10.00
43	Manny Ramirez	25.00
44	Jeff Bagwell	40.00
45	Edgar Martinez	8.00
46	Rey Ordonez	8.00
47	Osvaldo Fernandez	8.00
48	Livan Hernandez	8.00

1996 SPx

Upper Deck's 1996 SPX set has 60 players in it, which are each paralleled as a Gold version (one per every seven packs). Base cards feature a new look with a different perimeter die-cut design from those used in the past for basketball and football sets. A 10-card insert set, Bound for Glory, was also produced. Tribute cards were also made for Ken Griffey Jr. and Mike Piazza, with scarcer autographed versions also produced for each player.

		MT
Complete Set (60):		90.00
Common Player:		1.00
Complete Gold Set (60):		300.00
Golds: 2.5X		
Ken Griffey Jr. Autograph:		300.00
Mike Piazza Autograph:		200.00
Unlisted Stars: 1.50 to 2.00		
Wax Box:		65.00
1	Greg Maddux	6.00
2	Chipper Jones	6.00
3	Fred McGriff	1.50
4	Tom Glavine	1.00
5	Cal Ripken Jr.	8.00
6	Roberto Alomar	2.00
7	Rafael Palmeiro	1.50
8	Jose Canseco	1.50
9	Roger Clemens	4.00
10	Mo Vaughn	1.50
11	Jim Edmonds	1.00
12	Tim Salmon	1.00
13	Sammy Sosa	5.00
14	Ryne Sandberg	2.50
15	Mark Grace	1.00
16	Frank Thomas	5.00
17	Barry Larkin	1.00
18	Kenny Lofton	1.50
19	Albert Belle	2.50
20	Eddie Murray	1.50
21	Manny Ramirez	4.00
22	Dante Bichette	1.50
23	Larry Walker	1.50
24	Vinny Castilla	1.00
25	Andres Galarraga	1.50
26	Cecil Fielder	1.00
27	Gary Sheffield	1.50
28	Craig Biggio	1.00
29	Jeff Bagwell	3.00
30	Derek Bell	1.00
31	Johnny Damon	1.00
32	Eric Karros	1.00
33	Mike Piazza	6.00
34	Raul Mondesi	1.50
35	Hideo Nomo	1.50
36	Kirby Puckett	3.00
37	Paul Molitor	2.00
38	Marty Cordova	1.00
39	Rondell White	1.00
40	Jason Isringhausen	1.00
41	Paul Wilson	1.00
42	Rey Ordonez	1.00
43	Derek Jeter	6.00
44	Wade Boggs	2.00
45	Mark McGwire	12.00
46	Jason Kendall	1.00
47	Ron Gant	1.00
48	Ozzie Smith	2.00
49	Tony Gwynn	5.00
50	Ken Caminiti	1.50
51	Barry Bonds	2.50
52	Matt Williams	1.50
53	*Osvaldo Fernandez*	1.00
54	Jay Buhner	1.00
55	Ken Griffey Jr.	12.00
55p	Ken Griffey Jr. (overprinted "For Promotional Use Only")	15.00
56	Randy Johnson	2.00
57	Alex Rodriguez	8.00
58	Juan Gonzalez	5.00
59	Joe Carter	1.00
60	Carlos Delgado	1.50

1996 SPx Bound for Glory

Some of baseball's best players are highlighted on these 1996 Upper Deck SPX insert cards. The cards were seeded one per every 24 packs. Fronts of the die-cut cards feature a color photograph on a background of silver-foil holographic portrait and action photos. Backs have another portrait photo, stats, career highlights and logos.

		MT
Complete Set (10):		100.00
Common Player:		6.00
1	Ken Griffey Jr.	25.00
2	Frank Thomas	12.50
3	Barry Bonds	8.00
4	Cal Ripken Jr.	20.00
5	Greg Maddux	15.00
6	Chipper Jones	15.00
7	Roberto Alomar	6.00
8	Manny Ramirez	10.00
9	Tony Gwynn	12.50
10	Mike Piazza	15.00

1996 SPx Ken Griffey Jr. Commemorative

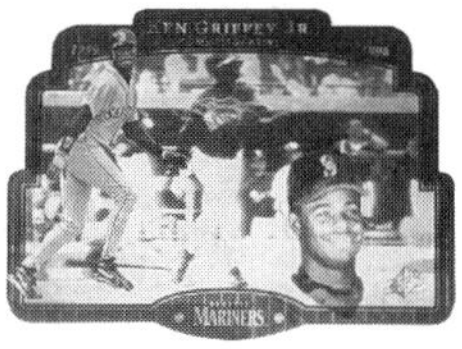

Seattle Mariners' star Ken Griffey Jr. has this tribute card in Upper Deck's 1996 SPX set. The card was seeded one per every 75 packs. Autographed versions were also produced; these cards were seeded one per every 2,000 packs.

		MT
		20.00
KG1	Ken Griffey Jr.	15.00
KG1	Ken Griffey Jr. (autographed)	300.00

1996 SPx Mike Piazza Tribute

Los Angeles Dodgers' star catcher Mike Piazza is featured on this 1996 Upper Deck SPX insert card. Normal versions of the card are found one per every 95 packs, making it scarcer than the Ken Griffey Jr. inserts. Autographed Piazza cards are seeded one per every 2,000 packs.

		MT
		10.00
MP1	Mike Piazza	9.00
MP1	Mike Piazza (autographed)	200.00

1997 SP Sample

To preview its SP brand for 1997, Upper Deck issued a sample card of Ken Griffey, Jr. Similar in format to the issued cards, the promo bears card number 1 and is overprinted "SAMPLE" on back.

		MT
1	Ken Griffey Jr.	6.00

1997 SP

The fifth anniversary edition of SP Baseball features 184 regular cards sold in eight-card packs for $4.39. Card fronts feature the player's name in gold foil-stamping at bottom. Team name and position are vertically at one edge. Backs have two more photos along with "Best Year" and career stats. Inserts include Marquee Matchups, Special FX, Inside Info, Baseball Heroes, Game Film, SPx Force, and Autographed Vintage SP Cards.

		MT
Complete Set (184):		40.00
Common Player:		.15
Wax Box:		100.00
1	Andruw Jones (Great Futures)	2.00
2	Kevin Orie (Great Futures)	.15
3	Nomar Garciaparra (Great Futures)	2.50
4	Jose Guillen (Great Futures)	1.50
5	Todd Walker (Great Futures)	1.00
6	Derrick Gibson (Great Futures)	.50
7	Aaron Boone (Great Futures)	.25
8	Bartolo Colon (Great Futures)	.45
9	Derrek Lee (Great Futures)	.25
10	Vladimir Guerrero (Great Futures)	2.00
11	Wilton Guerrero (Great Futures)	.15
12	Luis Castillo (Great Futures)	.15
13	Jason Dickson (Great Futures)	.15
14	*Bubba Trammell* (Great Futures)	1.50
15	*Jose Cruz Jr.* (Great Futures)	1.00
16	Eddie Murray	.50
17	Darin Erstad	1.50
18	Garret Anderson	.15
19	Jim Edmonds	.15
20	Tim Salmon	.40
21	Chuck Finley	.15
22	John Smoltz	.30
23	Greg Maddux	2.50
24	Kenny Lofton	.60
25	Chipper Jones	2.50
26	Ryan Klesko	.40
27	Javier Lopez	.15
28	Fred McGriff	.40
29	Roberto Alomar	.75
30	Rafael Palmeiro	.30
31	Mike Mussina	.75
32	Brady Anderson	.15
33	Rocky Coppinger	.15
34	Cal Ripken Jr.	4.00
35	Mo Vaughn	.60
36	Steve Avery	.15
37	Tom Gordon	.15
38	Tim Naehring	.15
39	Troy O'Leary	.15
40	Sammy Sosa	2.50
41	Brian McRae	.15
42	Mel Rojas	.15
43	Ryne Sandberg	1.00
44	Mark Grace	.30
45	Albert Belle	1.00
46	Robin Ventura	.20
47	Roberto Hernandez	.15
48	Ray Durham	.15
49	Harold Baines	.15
50	Frank Thomas	2.00
51	Bret Boone	.15
52	Reggie Sanders	.15
53	Deion Sanders	.25
54	Hal Morris	.15
55	Barry Larkin	.25
56	Jim Thome	.60
57	Marquis Grissom	.15
58	David Justice	.50
59	Charles Nagy	.15
60	Manny Ramirez	1.50
61	Matt Williams	.35
62	Jack McDowell	.15
63	Vinny Castilla	.15
64	Dante Bichette	.25
65	Andres Galarraga	.25
66	Ellis Burks	.15
67	Larry Walker	.50
68	Eric Young	.15
69	Brian L. Hunter	.15
70	Travis Fryman	.15
71	Tony Clark	1.00
72	Bobby Higginson	.15
73	Melvin Nieves	.15
74	Jeff Conine	.15
75	Gary Sheffield	.50
76	Moises Alou	.15
77	Edgar Renteria	.15
78	Alex Fernandez	.15
79	Charles Johnson	.15
80	Bobby Bonilla	.15
81	Darryl Kile	.15
82	Derek Bell	.15
83	Shane Reynolds	.15
84	Craig Biggio	.35
85	Jeff Bagwell	2.00
86	Billy Wagner	.15
87	Chili Davis	.15
88	Kevin Appier	.15
89	Jay Bell	.15
90	Johnny Damon	.15
91	Jeff King	.15
92	Hideo Nomo	.50
93	Todd Hollandsworth	.15
94	Eric Karros	.15
95	Mike Piazza	2.50
96	Ramon Martinez	.15
97	Todd Worrell	.15
98	Raul Mondesi	.40
99	Dave Nilsson	.15
100	John Jaha	.15
101	Jose Valentin	.15
102	Jeff Cirillo	.15
103	Jeff D'Amico	.15
104	Ben McDonald	.15
105	Paul Molitor	.50
106	Rich Becker	.15
107	Frank Rodriguez	.15
108	Marty Cordova	.15
109	Terry Steinbach	.15
110	Chuck Knoblauch	.30
111	Mark Grudzielanek	.15
112	Mike Lansing	.15
113	Pedro Martinez	.30
114	Henry Rodriguez	.15
115	Rondell White	.15
116	Rey Ordonez	.15
117	Carlos Baerga	.15
118	Lance Johnson	.15
119	Bernard Gilkey	.15
120	Todd Hundley	.30
121	John Franco	.15
122	Bernie Williams	.60
123	David Cone	.30
124	Cecil Fielder	.20
125	Derek Jeter	3.00
126	Tino Martinez	.25
127	Mariano Rivera	.25
128	Andy Pettitte	.60
129	Wade Boggs	.50
130	Mark McGwire	5.00
131	Jose Canseco	.40
132	Geronimo Berroa	.15
133	Jason Giambi	.15
134	Ernie Young	.15
135	Scott Rolen	1.50
136	Ricky Bottalico	.15
137	Curt Schilling	.15
138	Gregg Jefferies	.15
139	Mickey Morandini	.15
140	Jason Kendall	.15
141	Kevin Elster	.15
142	Al Martin	.15
143	Joe Randa	.15
144	Jason Schmidt	.15
145	Ray Lankford	.15
146	Brian Jordan	.15
147	Andy Benes	.15
148	Alan Benes	.20
149	Gary Gaetti	.15
150	Ron Gant	.15
151	Dennis Eckersley	.15
152	Rickey Henderson	.25
153	Joey Hamilton	.20
154	Ken Caminiti	.40
155	Tony Gwynn	2.00
156	Steve Finley	.15
157	Trevor Hoffman	.15
158	Greg Vaughn	.15
159	J.T. Snow	.15
160	Barry Bonds	1.00
161	Glenallen Hill	.15
162	William VanLandingham	.15
163	Jeff Kent	.15
164	Jay Buhner	.15
165	Ken Griffey Jr.	5.00
166	Alex Rodriguez	4.00
167	Randy Johnson	.75
168	Edgar Martinez	.15
169	Dan Wilson	.15
170	Ivan Rodriguez	.75
171	Roger Pavlik	.15
172	Will Clark	.30
173	Dean Palmer	.15
174	Rusty Greer	.15
175	Juan Gonzalez	2.00
176	John Wetteland	.15
177	Joe Carter	.15
178	Ed Sprague	.15
179	Carlos Delgado	.50
180	Roger Clemens	1.00
181	Juan Guzman	.15
182	Pat Hentgen	.15
183	Ken Griffey Jr.	4.00
184	*Hideki Irabu*	2.00

1997 SP Autographed Inserts

To celebrate the fifth anniversary of its premium SP brand, Upper Deck went into the hobby market to buy nearly 3,000 previous years' cards for a special insert program in 1997 SP packs. Various SP cards from 1993-96 issues and inserts were autographed by star players and a numbered holographic seal added on back. The number of each particular card signed ranged widely from fewer than 10 to more than 100. Numbers in parentheses in the checklist are the quantity reported signed for that card. All cards were inserted into foil packs except those of Mo Vaughn, which were a mail-in redemption.

		MT
Common Autograph:		25.00
	1993 SP	
4	Ken Griffey Jr. (16)	2000.
28	Jeff Bagwell (7)	25.00
167	Tony Gwynn (17)	600.00
280	Chipper Jones (34)	400.00
	1993 SP Platinum Power	
PP9	Ken Griffey Jr. (5)	2000.
	1994 SP	
6	Todd Hollandsworth (167)	25.00
15	Alex Rodriguez (94)	500.00
105	Ken Griffey Jr. (103)	800.00
114	Gary Sheffield (130)	50.00
130	Tony Gwynn (367)	125.00
	1994 SP Holoview Blue	
13	Tony Gwynn (31)	400.00
	1994 SP Holoview Red	
35	Gary Sheffield (4)	100.00
	1995 SP	
34	Chipper Jones (60)	300.00
60	Jeff Bagwell (173)	100.00
75	Gary Sheffield (221)	30.00
105	Tony Gwynn (64)	300.00
188	Alex Rodriguez (63)	400.00
190	Ken Griffey Jr. (38)	1000.
195	Jay Buhner (57)	50.00
	1996 SP	
1	Rey Ordonez (111)	30.00
18	Gary Sheffield (58)	60.00
26	Chipper Jones (102)	250.00
40	Mo Vaughn (250)	50.00
95	Jeff Bagwell (292)	100.00
160	Tony Gwynn (20)	500.00
170	Ken Griffey Jr. (312)	400.00
171	Alex Rodriguez (73)	400.00
173	Jay Buhner (79)	40.00
	1996 SP Marquee Matchups	
MM13	Jeff Bagwell (23)	300.00
MM4	Rey Ordonez (40)	75.00
	1996 SP Special F/X	
8	Jay Buhner (27)	75.00

1997 SP Game Film

A 10-card insert utilizing pieces of actual game footage to highlight the top stars in the game. Only 500 of each card were available. Cards are numbered with a "GF" prefix.

		MT
Complete Set (10):		375.00
Common Player:		12.50
1	Alex Rodriguez	60.00
2	Frank Thomas	30.00
3	Andruw Jones	20.00
4	Cal Ripken Jr.	60.00
5	Mike Piazza	45.00
6	Derek Jeter	40.00
7	Mark McGwire	75.00
8	Chipper Jones	45.00
9	Barry Bonds	20.00
10	Ken Griffey Jr.	75.00

1997 SP Griffey Baseball Heroes

First started in 1990, this single-player insert continues with a salute to Ken Griffey Jr. Each card in the set is numbered to 2,000.

		MT
Complete Set (10):		150.00
Common Griffey Jr.:		20.00
91	Ken Griffey Jr.	20.00
92	Ken Griffey Jr.	20.00
93	Ken Griffey Jr.	20.00
94	Ken Griffey Jr.	20.00
95	Ken Griffey Jr.	20.00
96	Ken Griffey Jr.	20.00
97	Ken Griffey Jr.	20.00
98	Ken Griffey Jr.	20.00
99	Ken Griffey Jr.	20.00
100	Ken Griffey Jr.	20.00

1997 SP Inside Info

Each of the 25 cards in this insert feature a pull-out panel describing the player's major accomplishments. Both front and back are printed on metallic-foil stock. Cards were inserted one per box.

		MT
Complete Set (25):		250.00
Common Player:		4.00
1	Ken Griffey Jr.	35.00
2	Mark McGwire	35.00
3	Kenny Lofton	6.00
4	Paul Molitor	8.00
5	Frank Thomas	12.00
6	Greg Maddux	20.00
7	Mo Vaughn	6.00
8	Cal Ripken Jr.	25.00
9	Jeff Bagwell	12.00
10	Alex Rodriguez	25.00
11	John Smoltz	4.00
12	Manny Ramirez	8.00
13	Sammy Sosa	20.00
14	Vladimir Guerrero	10.00
15	Albert Belle	6.00
16	Mike Piazza	20.00
17	Derek Jeter	20.00
18	Scott Rolen	12.00
19	Tony Gwynn	12.00
20	Barry Bonds	7.50
21	Ken Caminiti	4.00
22	Chipper Jones	20.00
23	Juan Gonzalez	15.00
24	Roger Clemens	9.00
25	Andruw Jones	15.00

1997 SP Marquee Matchups

A 20-card die-cut set designed to highlight top interleague matchups. When the matching cards are put together, a third player is highlighted in the background. Cards were inserted 1:5 packs.

		MT
Complete Set (30):		50.00
Common Player:		1.00
MM1	Ken Griffey Jr.	9.00
MM2	Andres Galarraga	1.50
MM2	Juan Gonzalez	5.00
MM3	Barry Bonds	2.50
MM4	Mark McGwire	9.00
MM4	Jose Canseco	1.50
MM5	Mike Piazza	5.00
MM6	Tim Salmon	1.50
MM6	Hideo Nomo	1.50
MM7	Tony Gwynn	4.00
MM8	Alex Rodriguez	6.00
MM8	Ken Caminiti	1.00
MM9	Chipper Jones	5.00
MM10	Derek Jeter	5.00
MM10	Andruw Jones	2.50
MM11	Manny Ramirez	2.50
MM12	Jeff Bagwell	3.00
MM12	Matt Williams	1.50
MM13	Greg Maddux	5.00
MM14	Cal Ripken Jr.	6.00
MM14	Brady Anderson	1.00
MM15	Mo Vaughn	1.00
MM16	Gary Sheffield	1.00
MM16	Vladimir Guerrero	3.00
MM17	Jim Thome	1.00
MM18	Barry Larkin	1.00
MM18	Deion Sanders	1.00
MM19	Frank Thomas	4.00
MM20	Sammy Sosa	6.00
MM20	Albert Belle	2.00

1997 SP Special FX

Color 3-D motion portraits are front and center on these cards that also feature a die-cut design. The rest of the front includes color action photos printed on silver-foil stock that also features a die-cut design. Backs have another color photo. The Alex Rodriguez card features the 1996 die-cut design since it was not available in the '96 set and is numbered 49 of 49. Cards were inserted 1:9 packs.

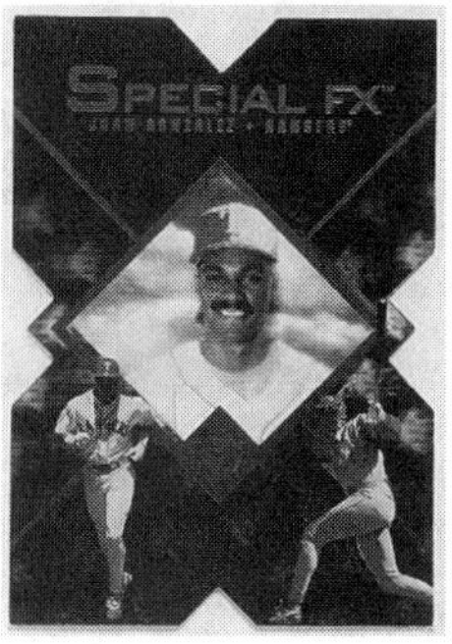

		MT
Complete Set (48):		250.00
Common Player:		3.00
1	Ken Griffey Jr.	25.00
2	Frank Thomas	12.00
3	Barry Bonds	6.00
4	Albert Belle	5.00
5	Mike Piazza	15.00
6	Greg Maddux	15.00
7	Chipper Jones	15.00
8	Cal Ripken Jr.	20.00
9	Jeff Bagwell	10.00
10	Alex Rodriguez	20.00
11	Mark McGwire	25.00
12	Kenny Lofton	4.00
13	Juan Gonzalez	12.00
14	Mo Vaughn	4.00
15	John Smoltz	3.00
16	Derek Jeter	15.00
17	Tony Gwynn	12.00
18	Ivan Rodriguez	5.00
19	Barry Larkin	3.00
20	Sammy Sosa	15.00
21	Mike Mussina	4.00
22	Gary Sheffield	3.50
23	Brady Anderson	3.00
24	Roger Clemens	8.00
25	Ken Caminiti	3.00
26	Roberto Alomar	4.50
27	Hideo Nomo	4.00
28	Bernie Williams	3.50
29	Todd Hundley	3.00
30	Manny Ramirez	8.00
31	Eric Karros	3.00
32	Tim Salmon	3.50
33	Jay Buhner	3.00
34	Andy Pettitte	3.50
35	Jim Thome	3.00
36	Ryne Sandberg	6.00
37	Matt Williams	4.00
38	Ryan Klesko	3.00
39	Jose Canseco	4.00
40	Paul Molitor	4.00
41	Eddie Murray	4.00
42	Darin Erstad	8.00
43	Todd Walker	5.00
44	Wade Boggs	4.00
45	Andruw Jones	10.00
46	Scott Rolen	12.00
47	Vladimir Guerrero	8.00
48	not issued	
49	Alex Rodriguez	20.00

1997 SP SPx Force

Each of the 10 cards in this set feature four different players. Cards are individually numbered to 500. In addition, a number of players signed 100 versions of their SPx Force cards that are also randomly inserted into packs.

		MT
Complete Set (10):		500.00
Common Player:		30.00
1	Ken Griffey Jr., Jay Buhner, Andres Galarraga, Dante Bichette	90.00
2	Albert Belle, Brady Anderson, Mark McGwire, Cecil Fielder	50.00
3	Mo Vaughn, Ken Caminiti, Frank Thomas, Jeff Bagwell	40.00
4	Gary Sheffield, Sammy Sosa, Barry Bonds, Jose Canseco	35.00
5	Greg Maddux, Roger Clemens, John Smoltz, Randy Johnson	60.00
6	Alex Rodriguez, Derek Jeter, Chipper Jones, Rey Ordonez	100.00
7	Todd Hollandsworth, Mike Piazza, Raul Mondesi, Hideo Nomo	30.00
8	Juan Gonzalez, Manny Ramirez, Roberto Alomar, Ivan Rodriguez	50.00
9	Tony Gwynn, Wade Boggs, Eddie Murray, Paul Molitor	45.00
10	Andruw Jones, Vladimir Guerrero, Todd Walker, Scott Rolen	75.00

1997 SP SPx Force Autographs

Ten players signed cards for this insert, which was serially numbered to 100. The cards were randomly seeded in packs except the Mo Vaughn card which was available by redemption.

		MT
Complete Set (10):		1500.
Common Player:		125.00
1	Ken Griffey Jr.	600.00
2	Albert Belle	100.00
3	Mo Vaughn	75.00
4	Gary Sheffield	50.00
5	Greg Maddux	300.00
6	Alex Rodriguez	400.00
7	Todd Hollandsworth	50.00
8	Roberto Alomar	100.00
9	Tony Gwynn	250.00
10	Andruw Jones	150.00

1997 SPx

Fifty cards, each featuring a perimeter die-cut design and a 3-D holoview photo, make up the SPx base set. Five different parallel sets - Steel (1:1 pack), Bronze (1:1), Silver (1:1), Gold (1:17) and Grand Finale (50 per card) - are found as inserts, as are Cornerstones of the Game, Bound for Glory and Bound for Glory Signature cards. Packs contain three cards and carried a suggested retail price of $5.99.

		MT
Complete Set (50):		60.00
Common Player:		.50
Steel: 2X		
Bronze: 2X		
Silver: 3X		
Gold: 5X		
Wax box:		100.00
1	Eddie Murray	1.25
2	Darin Erstad	3.00
3	Tim Salmon	1.00
4	Andruw Jones	3.00
5	Chipper Jones	4.00
6	John Smoltz	.50
7	Greg Maddux	4.00
8	Kenny Lofton	1.00
9	Roberto Alomar	1.25
10	Rafael Palmeiro	.50
11	Brady Anderson	.50
12	Cal Ripken Jr.	5.00
13	Nomar Garciaparra	3.00
14	Mo Vaughn	1.00
15	Ryne Sandberg	1.50
16	Sammy Sosa	4.00
17	Frank Thomas	3.00
18	Albert Belle	1.25
19	Barry Larkin	.50
20	Deion Sanders	.50
21	Manny Ramirez	2.00
22	Jim Thome	1.25
23	Dante Bichette	.50
24	Andres Galarraga	.50
25	Larry Walker	1.00
26	Gary Sheffield	1.00
27	Jeff Bagwell	2.50
28	Raul Mondesi	.50
29	Hideo Nomo	1.00
30	Mike Piazza	4.00
31	Paul Molitor	1.00
32	Todd Walker	1.00
33	Vladimir Guerrero	2.00
34	Todd Hundley	.50
35	Andy Pettitte	1.00
36	Derek Jeter	4.00
37	Jose Canseco	.50
38	Mark McGwire	7.50
39	Scott Rolen	2.50
40	Ron Gant	.50
41	Ken Caminiti	.50
42	Tony Gwynn	3.00
43	Barry Bonds	1.50
44	Jay Buhner	.50
45	Ken Griffey Jr.	7.50
45s	Ken Griffey Jr. (overprinted SAMPLE on back)	6.00
46	Alex Rodriguez	6.00
47	*Jose Cruz Jr.*	1.00
48	Juan Gonzalez	3.00
49	Ivan Rodriguez	1.25
50	Roger Clemens	2.00

1997 SPx Bound for Glory

A 20-card insert utilizing Holoview technology and sequentially numbered to 1,500 per card. Five players (Andruw Jones, Gary Sheffield, Alex Rodriguez, Ken Griffey Jr. and Jeff Bagwell) signed versions of their cards as part of the Bound For Glory Supreme Signatures set.

		MT
Complete Set (20):		450.00
Common Player:		10.00
1	Andruw Jones	20.00
2	Chipper Jones	40.00
3	Greg Maddux	40.00
4	Kenny Lofton	10.00
5	Cal Ripken Jr.	50.00
6	Mo Vaughn	10.00
7	Frank Thomas	30.00
8	Albert Belle	12.50
9	Manny Ramirez	15.00
10	Gary Sheffield	10.00
11	Jeff Bagwell	25.00
12	Mike Piazza	40.00
13	Derek Jeter	40.00
14	Mark McGwire	60.00
15	Tony Gwynn	30.00
16	Ken Caminiti	10.00
17	Barry Bonds	20.00
18	Alex Rodriguez	50.00
19	Ken Griffey Jr.	60.00
20	Juan Gonzalez	30.00

1997 SPx Bound for Glory Supreme Signatures

This five-card set featured autographs from the players and was sequentially numbered to 250.

		MT
Complete Set (5):		1000.
Common Player:		60.00
1	Jeff Bagwell	200.00
2	Ken Griffey Jr.	450.00
3	Andruw Jones	150.00
4	Alex Rodriguez	350.00
5	Gary Sheffield	60.00

The election of former players to the Hall of Fame does not always have an immediate upward effect on card prices. The hobby market generally has done a good job of predicting those inductions and adjusting values over the course of several years.

1997 SPx Cornerstones of the Game

A 20-card insert utilizing a double-front design highlighting 40 of the top players in the game. Each card is sequentially numbered to 500.

		MT
Complete Set (10):		300.00
Common Player:		20.00
1	Ken Griffey Jr., Barry Bonds	60.00
2	Frank Thomas, Albert Belle	20.00
3	Chipper Jones, Greg Maddux	40.00
4	Tony Gwynn, Paul Molitor	25.00
5	Andruw Jones, Vladimir Guerrero	25.00
6	Jeff Bagwell, Ryne Sandberg	20.00
7	Mike Piazza, Ivan Rodriguez	35.00
8	Cal Ripken Jr., Eddie Murray	40.00
9	Mo Vaughn, Mark McGwire	50.00
10	Alex Rodriguez, Derek Jeter	50.00

1998 SP Authentic Sample

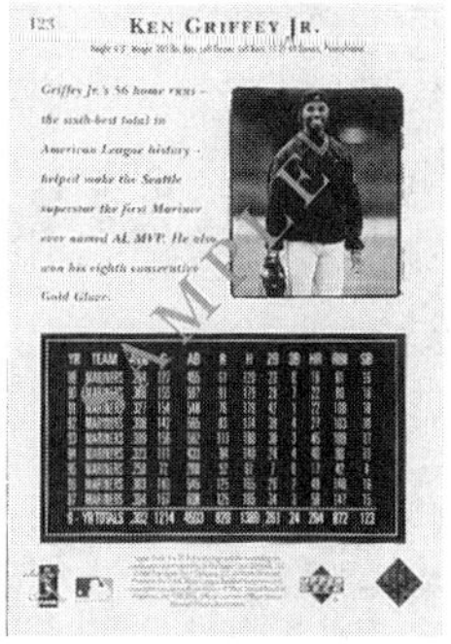

This card of Upper Deck spokesman Ken Griffey, Jr., was issued to preview the new SP Authentic line. Design is similar to the issued version but the sample displays different photos, a different the card number and the word "SAMPLE" printed in large letters on back.

	MT
Ken Griffey Jr.	6.00

1998 SP Authentic

The SP Authentic base set consists of 198 cards, including the 30-card Future Watch subset and one checklist card. The base cards have a color photo inside a thick white border. Inserts include Chirography, Sheer Dominance and SP Authentics.

		MT
Complete Set (198):		50.00
Common Player:		.25
Wax Box:		110.00
1	Travis Lee (Future Watch)	1.50
2	Mike Caruso (Future Watch)	.40
3	Kerry Wood (Future Watch)	1.00
4	Mark Kotsay (Future Watch)	.50
5	*Magglio Ordonez* (Future Watch)	5.00
6	Scott Elarton (Future Watch)	.25
7	Carl Pavano (Future Watch)	.25
8	A.J. Hinch (Future Watch)	.25
9	*Rolando Arrojo* (Future Watch)	.75
10	Ben Grieve (Future Watch)	1.50
11	Gabe Alvarez (Future Watch)	.25
12	*Mike Kinkade* (Future Watch)	1.50
13	Bruce Chen (Future Watch)	.25
14	Juan Encarnacion (Future Watch)	.40
15	Todd Helton (Future Watch)	1.25
16	Aaron Boone (Future Watch)	.25
17	Sean Casey (Future Watch)	.50
18	Ramon Hernandez (Future Watch)	.25
19	Daryle Ward (Future Watch)	.25
20	Paul Konerko (Future Watch)	.50
21	David Ortiz (Future Watch)	.25
22	Derrek Lee (Future Watch)	.25
23	Brad Fullmer (Future Watch)	.40
24	Javier Vazquez (Future Watch)	.25
25	Miguel Tejada (Future Watch)	1.00
26	David Dellucci (Future Watch)	.25
27	Alex Gonzalez (Future Watch)	.25
28	Matt Clement (Future Watch)	.25
29	Eric Milton (Future Watch)	.25
30	Russell Branyan (Future Watch)	.25
31	Chuck Finley	.25
32	Jim Edmonds	.25
33	Darren Erstad	1.25
34	Jason Dickson	.25
35	Tim Salmon	.40
36	Cecil Fielder	.25
37	Todd Greene	.25
38	Andy Benes	.25
39	Jay Bell	.25
40	Matt Williams	.50
41	Brian Anderson	.25
42	Karim Garcia	.40
43	Javy Lopez	.25
44	Tom Glavine	.50
45	Greg Maddux	3.00
46	Andruw Jones	1.25
47	Chipper Jones	3.00
48	Ryan Klesko	.30
49	John Smoltz	.40
50	Andres Galarraga	.50
51	Rafael Palmeiro	.50
52	Mike Mussina	1.00
53	Roberto Alomar	1.00
54	Joe Carter	.25
55	Cal Ripken Jr.	4.00
56	Brady Anderson	.25
57	Mo Vaughn	1.00
58	John Valentin	.25
59	Dennis Eckersley	.25
60	Nomar Garciaparra	3.00
61	Pedro J. Martinez	1.00
62	Jeff Blauser	.25
63	Kevin Orie	.25
64	Henry Rodriguez	.25
65	Mark Grace	.50
66	Albert Belle	1.25
67	Mike Cameron	.25
68	Robin Ventura	.25
69	Frank Thomas	2.50
70	Barry Larkin	.30
71	Brett Tomko	.25
72	Willie Greene	.25
73	Reggie Sanders	.25
74	Sandy Alomar Jr.	.40
75	Kenny Lofton	1.00
76	Jaret Wright	1.25
77	David Justice	.25
78	Omar Vizquel	.25
79	Manny Ramirez	1.50
80	Jim Thome	.60
81	Travis Fryman	.25
82	Neifi Perez	.25
83	Mike Lansing	.25

84	Vinny Castilla	.25
85	Larry Walker	.75
86	Dante Bichette	.40
87	Darryl Kile	.25
88	Justin Thompson	.25
89	Damion Easley	.25
90	Tony Clark	.75
91	Bobby Higginson	.25
92	Brian L. Hunter	.25
93	Edgar Renteria	.25
94	Craig Counsell	.25
95	Mike Piazza	3.00
96	Livan Hernandez	.25
97	Todd Zeile	.25
98	Richard Hidalgo	.25
99	Moises Alou	.40
100	Jeff Bagwell	1.50
101	Mike Hampton	.25
102	Craig Biggio	.50
103	Dean Palmer	.25
104	Tim Belcher	.25
105	Jeff King	.25
106	Jeff Conine	.25
107	Johnny Damon	.25
108	Hideo Nomo	.60
109	Raul Mondesi	.40
110	Gary Sheffield	.60
111	Ramon Martinez	.25
112	Chan Ho Park	.50
113	Eric Young	.25
114	Charles Johnson	.25
115	Eric Karros	.25
116	Bobby Bonilla	.25
117	Jeromy Burnitz	.25
118	Carl Eldred	.25
119	Jeff D'Amico	.25
120	Marquis Grissom	.25
121	Dave Nilsson	.25
122	Brad Radke	.25
123	Marty Cordova	.25
124	Ron Coomer	.25
125	Paul Molitor	1.00
126	Todd Walker	.50
127	Rondell White	.40
128	Mark Grudzielanek	.25
129	Carlos Perez	.25
130	Vladimir Guerrero	1.25
131	Dustin Hermanson	.25
132	Butch Huskey	.25
133	John Franco	.25
134	Rey Ordonez	.25
135	Todd Hundley	.25
136	Edgardo Alfonzo	.25
137	Bobby Jones	.25
138	John Olerud	.40
139	Chili Davis	.25
140	Tino Martinez	.40
141	Andy Pettitte	.60
142	Chuck Knoblauch	.40
143	Bernie Williams	1.00
144	David Cone	.40
145	Derek Jeter	3.00
146	Paul O'Neill	.40
147	Rickey Henderson	.50
148	Jason Giambi	.25
149	Kenny Rogers	.25
150	Scott Rolen	1.50
151	Curt Schilling	.40
152	Ricky Bottalico	.25
153	Mike Lieberthal	.25
154	Francisco Cordova	.25
155	Jose Guillen	.50
156	Jason Schmidt	.25
157	Jason Kendall	.25
158	Kevin Young	.25
159	Delino DeShields	.25
160	Mark McGwire	5.00
161	Ray Lankford	.25
162	Brian Jordan	.25
163	Ron Gant	.25
164	Todd Stottlemyre	.25
165	Ken Caminiti	.40
166	Kevin Brown	.40
167	Trevor Hoffman	.25
168	Steve Finley	.25
169	Wally Joyner	.25
170	Tony Gwynn	2.50
171	Shawn Estes	.25
172	J.T. Snow	.25
173	Jeff Kent	.25
174	Robb Nen	.25
175	Barry Bonds	1.25
176	Randy Johnson	1.00
177	Edgar Martinez	.25
178	Jay Buhner	.25
179	Alex Rodriguez	4.00
180	Ken Griffey Jr.	5.00
181	Ken Cloude	.25
182	Wade Boggs	.60
183	Tony Saunders	.25
184	Wilson Alvarez	.25
185	Fred McGriff	.40
186	Roberto Hernandez	.25
187	Kevin Stocker	.25
188	Fernando Tatis	.40
189	Will Clark	.50
190	Juan Gonzalez	2.50
191	Rusty Greer	.25
192	Ivan Rodriguez	1.25
193	Jose Canseco	.50
194	Carlos Delgado	.50
195	Roger Clemens	1.75
196	Pat Hentgen	.25
197	Randy Myers	.25
198	Checklist (Ken Griffey Jr.)	2.00

1998 SP Authentic Chirography

Chirography is a 30-card insert seeded one per 25 packs. The featured player signed his cards in the white border at the bottom.

		MT
Complete Set (30):		1600.
Common Card:		15.00
Inserted 1:25		
RA	Roberto Alomar	75.00
RB	Russell Branyan	15.00
SC	Sean Casey	30.00
TC	Tony Clark	30.00
RC	Roger Clemens	175.00
JC	Jose Cruz Jr.	15.00
DE	Darin Erstad	60.00
NG	Nomar Garciaparra	150.00
BG	Ben Grieve	60.00
KG	Ken Griffey Jr.	350.00
VG	Vladimir Guerrero	80.00
TG	Tony Gwynn	125.00
TH	Todd Helton	50.00
LH	Livan Hernandez	30.00
CJ	Charles Johnson	25.00
AJ	Andruw Jones	60.00
CHIP	Chipper Jones	120.00
PK	Paul Konerko	30.00
MK	Mark Kotsay	30.00
RL	Ray Lankford	25.00
TL	Travis Lee	50.00
PM	Paul Molitor	75.00
MM	Mike Mussina	60.00
AR	Alex Rodriguez	180.00
IR	Ivan Rodriguez	75.00
SR	Scott Rolen	60.00
DL	Gary Sheffield	35.00
MT	Miguel Tejada	40.00
JW	Jaret Wright	40.00
MV	Mo Vaughn	60.00

1998 SP Authentic Ken Griffey Jr. 300th HR Redemption

This 5" x 7" version of Ken Griffey Jr.'s SP Authentic card was issued as a redemption for one of the 1000 Trade Cards which were foil-pack inserts.

		MT
KG300	Ken Griffey Jr.	30.00

1998 SP Authentic Jersey Swatch

These 5" x 7" redemption cards were issued in exchange for Trade Cards found as random foil-packs inserts. Fronts have a player action photo on a white background. Backs have a congratulatory message of authenticity. Sandwiched between in a swatch of that player's uniform jersey. The large-format jersey cards were available in limited editions which are listed in parentheses, though all might not have been redeemed prior to the Aug. 1, 1999, cut-off date.

		MT
Complete Set (6):		1000.
Common Player:		50.00
(1)	Jay Buhner (125)	50.00
(2)	Ken Griffey Jr. (125)	450.00
(3)	Tony Gwynn (415)	125.00
(4)	Greg Maddux (125)	200.00
(5)	Alex Rodriguez (125)	300.00
(6)	Gary Sheffield (125)	75.00

1998 SP Authentic Trade Cards

Cards which could be traded (prior to the Aug. 1, 1999 cut-off) for special cards and autographed memorabilia were inserted into SP Authentic foil packs at an announced rate of one per 291 packs. Trade cards have a white background on front with a color player action photo and the name of the redemption item. Backs gives details for redemption. In some cases, because of their insertation-rate rarity, the cards are worth more than the redemption items. The unnumbered cards are listed here alphabetically.

		MT
Common Card:		20.00
(1)	Roberto Alomar (autographed ball 100)	30.00
(2)	Albert Belle (autographed ball 100)	30.00
(3)	Jay Buhner (jersey card 125)	20.00
(4)	Ken Griffey Jr. (autographed glove 30)	350.00
(5)	Ken Griffey Jr. (autographed jersey 30)	350.00
(6)	Ken Griffey Jr. (jersey card 125)	150.00
(7)	Ken Griffey Jr. (standee 200)	75.00
(8)	Ken Griffey Jr. (300th HR card 1000)	25.00
(9)	Tony Gwynn (jersey card 415)	25.00
(10)	Brian Jordan (autographed ball 50)	25.00
(11)	Greg Maddux (jersey card 125)	50.00
(12)	Raul Mondesi (autographed ball 100)	25.00
(13)	Alex Rodriguez (jersey card 125)	60.00
(14)	Gary Sheffield (jersey card 125)	20.00
(15)	Robin Ventura (autographed ball)	25.00

1998 SP Authentic Sheer Dominance

Sheer Dominance is a 42-card insert. The base set is inserted one per three packs. The Sheer Dominance Gold parallel is sequentially numbered to 2,000 and the Titanium parallel is numbered to 100. The cards feature a player photo inside a white border. The background color corresponds to the level of the insert.

	MT
Complete Set (42):	120.00
Common Player:	1.00
Inserted 1:3	
Gold: 4X	
Production 2,000 sets	
Titanium: 25X	
Production 100 sets	

SD1	Ken Griffey Jr.	12.00
SD2	Rickey Henderson	1.50
SD3	Jaret Wright	3.00
SD4	Craig Biggio	1.50
SD5	Travis Lee	2.50
SD6	Kenny Lofton	1.50
SD7	Raul Mondesi	1.50
SD8	Cal Ripken Jr.	10.00
SD9	Matt Williams	1.50
SD10	Mark McGwire	12.00
SD11	Alex Rodriguez	10.00
SD12	Fred McGriff	1.00
SD13	Scott Rolen	4.00
SD14	Paul Molitor	2.50
SD15	Nomar Garciaparra	8.00
SD16	Vladimir Guerrero	3.00
SD17	Andruw Jones	3.00
SD18	Manny Ramirez	5.00
SD19	Tony Gwynn	6.00
SD20	Barry Bonds	3.00
SD21	Ben Grieve	4.00
SD22	Ivan Rodriguez	3.00
SD23	Jose Cruz Jr.	1.00
SD24	Pedro J. Martinez	2.50
SD25	Chipper Jones	8.00
SD26	Albert Belle	2.50
SD27	Todd Helton	3.00
SD28	Paul Konerko	1.50
SD29	Sammy Sosa	6.00
SD30	Frank Thomas	6.00
SD31	Greg Maddux	8.00
SD32	Randy Johnson	2.50
SD33	Larry Walker	2.00
SD34	Roberto Alomar	2.50
SD35	Roger Clemens	5.00
SD36	Mo Vaughn	1.50
SD37	Jim Thome	1.50
SD38	Jeff Bagwell	4.00
SD39	Tino Martinez	1.00
SD40	Mike Piazza	8.00
SD41	Derek Jeter	8.00
SD42	Juan Gonzalez	6.00

1998 SP Authentic Sheer Dominance Gold

Identical in format and using the same photos as the Silver version, the scarcer Sheer Dominance Gold card differs on front in its use of a gold-metallic foil background within the white border. Backs of the gold version are individually serial numbered within an edition of 2,000 each.

	MT
Complete Set (42):	500.00
Common Player:	3.00
Gold Stars: 6X (Star and rookie cards valued at 3X Silver version.)	

1998 SP Authentic Sheer Dominance Titanium

Sheer Dominance Titanium is a parallel of the 42-card Sheer Dominance insert. The cards are numbered to 100 and have a gray background with "Titanium" printed across it.

	MT
Common Player:	20.00
Titanium Stars: 25X (See 1998 SP Authentic Sheer Dominance for checklist and base card values.)	

1998 SPx Finite

SPx Finite is an all-sequentially numbered set issued in two 180-card series. The Series 1 base set consists of five subsets: 90 regular cards (numbered to 9,000), 30 Star Focus (7,000), 30 Youth Movement (5,000), 20 Power Explosion (4,000) and 10 Heroes of the Game (2,000). The set is paralleled in the Radiance and Spectrum sets. Radiance regular cards are numbered to 4,500, Star Focus to 3,500, Youth Movement to 2,500, Power Explosion to 1,000 and Heroes of the Game to 100. Spectrum regular cards are numbered to 2,250, Star Focus to 1,750, Youth Movement to 1,250, Power Explosion to 50 and Heroes of the Game to 1. The Series 2 base set has 90 regular cards (numbered to 9,000), 30 Power Passion (7,000), 30 Youth Movement (5,000), 20 Tradewinds (4,000) and 10 Cornerstones of the Game (2,000). Series 2 also has Radiance and Spectrum parallels. Radiance regular cards are numbered to 4,500, Power Passion to 3,500, Youth Movement to 2,500, Tradewinds to 1,000 and Cornerstones of the Game to 100. Spectrum regular cards are numbered to 2,250, Power Passion to 1,750, Youth Movement to 1,250, Tradewinds to 50 and Cornerstones of the Game to 1. The only insert is Home Run Hysteria.

		MT
Complete Set (360):		2000.
Common Youth Movement (#1-30, 181-210):		1.00
Radiance Youth Movement (2,500): 2x		
Spectrum Youth Movement (1,250): 4x		
Common Power Explosion (#31-50):		3.00
Radiance Power Explosion (1,000): 4x		
Common Regular Card (#51-140, 241-330):		1.00
Radiance Regular Card (4,500): 2x		
Spectrum Regular Card (2,250): 4x		
Common Star Focus (#141-170):		1.50
Radiance Star Focus (3,500): 2x		
Spectrum Star Focus (1,750): 4x		
Common Heroes of the Game (#171-180):		12.00
Common Power Passion (#211-240):		1.50
Radiance Power Passion (3,500) 2x		
Spectrum Power Passion (1,750) 4x		
Common Tradewinds (#331-350):		2.50
Radiance Tradewinds (1,000) 4x		
Common Cornerstones (#351-360):		12.00
Wax Box:		95.00
1	Nomar Garciaparra (Youth Movement)	15.00
2	Miguel Tejada (Youth Movement)	2.50
3	Mike Cameron (Youth Movement)	1.00
4	Ken Cloude (Youth Movement)	2.00
5	Jaret Wright (Youth Movement)	10.00
6	Mark Kotsay (Youth Movement)	2.50
7	Craig Counsell (Youth Movement)	1.00

8 Jose Guillen (Youth Movement) 2.00
9 Neifi Perez (Youth Movement) 1.00
10 Jose Cruz Jr. (Youth Movement) 1.00
11 Brett Tomko (Youth Movement) 1.00
12 Matt Morris (Youth Movement) 1.50
13 Justin Thompson (Youth Movement) 1.00
14 Jeremi Gonzalez (Youth Movement) 1.00
15 Scott Rolen (Youth Movement) 10.00
16 Vladimir Guerrero (Youth Movement) 6.00
17 Brad Fullmer (Youth Movement) 2.50
18 Brian Giles (Youth Movement) 1.00
19 Todd Dunwoody (Youth Movement) 1.00
20 Ben Grieve (Youth Movement) 8.00
21 Juan Encarnacion (Youth Movement) 1.00
22 Aaron Boone (Youth Movement) 1.00
23 Richie Sexson (Youth Movement) 1.00
24 Richard Hidalgo (Youth Movement) 1.00
25 Andruw Jones (Youth Movement) 6.00
26 Todd Helton (Youth Movement) 6.00
27 Paul Konerko (Youth Movement) 3.00
28 Dante Powell (Youth Movement) 1.00
29 Elieser Marrero (Youth Movement) 1.00
30 Derek Jeter (Youth Movement) 15.00
31 Mike Piazza (Power Explosion) 15.00
32 Tony Clark (Power Explosion) 4.00
33 Larry Walker (Power Explosion) 3.00
34 Jim Thome (Power Explosion) 4.00
35 Juan Gonzalez (Power Explosion) 12.00
36 Jeff Bagwell (Power Explosion) 10.00
37 Jay Buhner (Power Explosion) 3.00
38 Tim Salmon (Power Explosion) 3.00
39 Albert Belle (Power Explosion) 6.00
40 Mark McGwire (Power Explosion) 12.00
41 Sammy Sosa (Power Explosion) 8.00
42 Mo Vaughn (Power Explosion) 6.00
43 Manny Ramirez (Power Explosion) 8.00
44 Tino Martinez (Power Explosion) 3.00
45 Frank Thomas (Power Explosion) 10.00
46 Nomar Garciaparra (Power Explosion) 15.00
47 Alex Rodriguez (Power Explosion) 15.00
48 Chipper Jones (Power Explosion) 15.00
49 Barry Bonds (Power Explosion) 6.00
50 Ken Griffey Jr. (Power Explosion) 25.00
51 Jason Dickson 1.00
52 Jim Edmonds 1.50
53 Darin Erstad 4.00
54 Tim Salmon 2.00
55 Chipper Jones 10.00
56 Ryan Klesko 2.00
57 Tom Glavine 1.50
58 Denny Neagle 1.00
59 John Smoltz 1.00
60 Javy Lopez 1.00
61 Roberto Alomar 3.00
62 Rafael Palmeiro 1.50
63 Mike Mussina 4.00
64 Cal Ripken Jr. 12.00
65 Mo Vaughn 4.00
66 Tim Naehring 1.00
67 John Valentin 1.00
68 Mark Grace 2.00
69 Kevin Orie 1.00
70 Sammy Sosa 6.00
71 Albert Belle 4.00
72 Frank Thomas 6.00
73 Robin Ventura 1.50
74 David Justice 2.00
75 Kenny Lofton 4.00
76 Omar Vizquel 1.00
77 Manny Ramirez 5.00
78 Jim Thome 2.50
79 Dante Bichette 2.00
80 Larry Walker 2.00
81 Vinny Castilla 1.50
82 Ellis Burks 1.00
83 Bobby Higginson 1.00
84 Brian L. Hunter 1.00
85 Tony Clark 2.50
86 Mike Hampton 1.00
87 Jeff Bagwell 6.00
88 Craig Biggio 2.00
89 Derek Bell 1.00
90 Mike Piazza 10.00
91 Ramon Martinez 1.00
92 Raul Mondesi 2.00
93 Hideo Nomo 2.00
94 Eric Karros 1.50
95 Paul Molitor 3.00
96 Marty Cordova 1.00
97 Brad Radke 1.00
98 Mark Grudzielanek 1.00
99 Carlos Perez 1.00
100 Rondell White 1.50
101 Todd Hundley 1.00
102 Edgardo Alfonzo 1.00
103 John Franco 1.00
104 John Olerud 1.50
105 Tino Martinez 2.00
106 David Cone 1.50
107 Paul O'Neill 1.50
108 Andy Pettitte 2.50
109 Bernie Williams 3.00
110 Rickey Henderson 1.50
111 Jason Giambi 1.00
112 Matt Stairs 1.00
113 Gregg Jefferies 1.00
114 Rico Brogna 1.00
115 Curt Schilling 1.50
116 Jason Schmidt 1.00
117 Jose Guillen 2.00
118 Kevin Young 1.00
119 Ray Lankford 1.00
120 Mark McGwire 8.00
121 Delino DeShields 1.00
122 Ken Caminiti 2.00
123 Tony Gwynn 8.00
124 Trevor Hoffman 1.00
125 Barry Bonds 4.00
126 Jeff Kent 1.00
127 Shawn Estes 1.00
128 J.T. Snow 1.00
129 Jay Buhner 2.00
130 Ken Griffey Jr. 15.00
131 Dan Wilson 1.00
132 Edgar Martinez 1.00
133 Alex Rodriguez 10.00
134 Rusty Greer 1.00
135 Juan Gonzalez 8.00
136 Fernando Tatis 1.00
137 Ivan Rodriguez 4.00
138 Carlos Delgado 1.50
139 Pat Hentgen 1.00
140 Roger Clemens 6.00
141 Chipper Jones (Star Focus) 12.00
142 Greg Maddux (Star Focus) 12.00
143 Rafael Palmeiro (Star Focus) 2.00
144 Mike Mussina (Star Focus) 4.00
145 Cal Ripken Jr. (Star Focus) 14.00
146 Nomar Garciaparra (Star Focus) 12.00
147 Mo Vaughn (Star Focus) 5.00
148 Sammy Sosa (Star Focus) 6.00
149 Albert Belle (Star Focus) 5.00
150 Frank Thomas (Star Focus) 6.00
151 Jim Thome (Star Focus) 4.00
152 Kenny Lofton (Star Focus) 5.00
153 Manny Ramirez (Star Focus) 6.00
154 Larry Walker (Star Focus) 2.50
155 Jeff Bagwell (Star Focus) 8.00
156 Craig Biggio (Star Focus) 1.50
157 Mike Piazza (Star Focus) 12.00
158 Paul Molitor (Star Focus) 4.00
159 Derek Jeter (Star Focus) 10.00
160 Tino Martinez (Star Focus) 2.50
161 Curt Schilling (Star Focus) 1.50
162 Mark McGwire (Star Focus) 10.00
163 Tony Gwynn (Star Focus) 10.00
164 Barry Bonds (Star Focus) 5.00
165 Ken Griffey Jr. (Star Focus) 18.00
166 Randy Johnson (Star Focus) 3.00
167 Alex Rodriguez (Star Focus) 12.00
168 Juan Gonzalez (Star Focus) 10.00
169 Ivan Rodriguez (Star Focus) 5.00
170 Roger Clemens (Star Focus) 8.00
171 Greg Maddux (Heroes of the Game) 30.00
172 Cal Ripken Jr. (Heroes of the Game) 40.00
173 Frank Thomas (Heroes of the Game) 20.00
174 Jeff Bagwell (Heroes of the Game) 20.00
175 Mike Piazza (Heroes of the Game) 30.00
176 Mark McGwire (Heroes of the Game) 25.00
177 Barry Bonds (Heroes of the Game) 12.00
178 Ken Griffey Jr. (Heroes of the Game) 50.00
179 Alex Rodriguez (Heroes of the Game) 40.00
180 Roger Clemens (Heroes of the Game) 20.00
181 Mike Caruso 1.00
182 David Ortiz 2.00
183 Gabe Alvarez 1.00
184 Gary Matthews Jr. 1.00
185 Kerry Wood 10.00
186 Carl Pavano 1.00
187 Alex Gonzalez 1.00
188 Masato Yoshii 2.00
189 Larry Sutton 1.00
190 Russell Branyan 1.00
191 Bruce Chen 1.00
192 Rolando Arrojo 2.50
193 Ryan Christenson 1.00
194 Cliff Politte 1.00
195 A.J. Hinch 1.00
196 Kevin Witt 1.00
197 Daryle Ward 1.00
198 Corey Koskie 1.00
199 Mike Lowell 1.00
200 Travis Lee 6.00
201 Kevin Millwood 3.00
202 Robert Smith 1.00
203 *Magglio Ordonez* 10.00
204 Eric Milton 1.00
205 Geoff Jenkins 1.00
206 Rich Butler 1.00
207 *Mike Kinkade* 1.00
208 Braden Looper 1.00
209 Matt Clement 1.00
210 Derrek Lee 1.00
211 Randy Johnson 3.00
212 John Smoltz 1.50
213 Roger Clemens 5.00
214 Curt Schilling 2.00
215 Pedro J. Martinez 4.00
216 Vinny Castilla 1.00
217 Jose Cruz Jr. 1.50
218 Jim Thome 2.50
219 Alex Rodriguez 10.00
220 Frank Thomas 5.00
221 Tim Salmon 2.00
222 Larry Walker 2.50
223 Albert Belle 4.00
224 Manny Ramirez 5.00
225 Mark McGwire 15.00
226 Mo Vaughn 4.00
227 Andres Galarraga 2.00
228 Scott Rolen 4.00
229 Travis Lee 4.00
230 Mike Piazza 10.00
231 Nomar Garciaparra 10.00
232 Andruw Jones 4.00
233 Barry Bonds 4.00
234 Jeff Bagwell 5.00
235 Juan Gonzalez 8.00
236 Tino Martinez 2.00
237 Vladimir Guerrero 4.00
238 Rafael Palmeiro 2.00
239 Russell Branyan 1.00
240 Ken Griffey Jr. 15.00
241 Cecil Fielder 1.00
242 Chuck Finley 1.00
243 Jay Bell 1.00
244 Andy Benes 1.00
245 Matt Williams 1.50
246 Brian Anderson 1.00
247 David Dellucci 1.00
248 Andres Galarraga 2.00
249 Andruw Jones 2.50
250 Greg Maddux 6.00
251 Brady Anderson 1.00
252 Joe Carter 1.00
253 Eric Davis 1.00
254 Pedro J. Martinez 2.50
255 Nomar Garciaparra 6.00
256 Dennis Eckersley 1.00
257 Henry Rodriguez 1.00
258 Jeff Blauser 1.00
259 Jaime Navarro 1.00
260 Ray Durham 1.00
261 Chris Stynes 1.00
262 Willie Greene 1.00
263 Reggie Sanders 1.00
264 Bret Boone 1.00
265 Barry Larkin 1.50
266 Travis Fryman 1.00
267 Charles Nagy 1.00
268 Sandy Alomar Jr. 1.00
269 Darryl Kile 1.00
270 Mike Lansing 1.00
271 Pedro Astacio 1.00
272 Damion Easley 1.00
273 Joe Randa 1.00
274 Luis Gonzalez 1.00
275 Mike Piazza 6.00
276 Todd Zeile 1.00
277 Edgar Renteria 1.00
278 Livan Hernandez 1.00
279 Cliff Floyd 1.00
280 Moises Alou 1.50
281 Billy Wagner 1.00
282 Jeff King 1.00
283 Hal Morris 1.00
284 Johnny Damon 1.00
285 Dean Palmer 1.00
286 Tim Belcher 1.00
287 Eric Young 1.00
288 Bobby Bonilla 1.00
289 Gary Sheffield 1.50
290 Chan Ho Park 1.50
291 Charles Johnson 1.00
292 Jeff Cirillo 1.00
293 Jeromy Burnitz 1.00
294 Jose Valentin 1.00
295 Marquis Grissom 1.00
296 Todd Walker 1.00
297 Terry Steinbach 1.00
298 Rick Aguilera 1.00
299 Vladimir Guerrero 2.50
300 Rey Ordonez 1.00
301 Butch Huskey 1.00
302 Bernard Gilkey 1.00
303 Mariano Rivera 1.50
304 Chuck Knoblauch 1.50
305 Derek Jeter 5.00
306 Ricky Bottalico 1.00
307 Bob Abreu 1.00
308 Scott Rolen 3.00
309 Al Martin 1.00
310 Jason Kendall 1.00
311 Brian Jordan 1.00
312 Ron Gant 1.00
313 Todd Stottlemyre 1.00
314 Greg Vaughn 1.00
315 J. Kevin Brown 1.00
316 Wally Joyner 1.00
317 Robb Nen 1.00
318 Orel Hershiser 1.00
319 Russ Davis 1.00
320 Randy Johnson 2.00
321 Quinton McCracken 1.00
322 Tony Saunders 1.00
323 Wilson Alvarez 1.00
324 Wade Boggs 1.50
325 Fred McGriff 1.50
326 Lee Stevens 1.00
327 John Wetteland 1.00
328 Jose Canseco 1.50
329 Randy Myers 1.00
330 Jose Cruz Jr. 2.00
331 Matt Williams 3.00
332 Andres Galarraga 4.00
333 Walt Weiss 2.50
334 Joe Carter 2.50
335 Pedro J. Martinez 5.00
336 Henry Rodriguez 2.50
337 Travis Fryman 2.50
338 Darryl Kile 2.50
339 Mike Lansing 2.50
340 Mike Piazza 12.00
341 Moises Alou 3.00
342 Charles Johnson 2.50
343 Chuck Knoblauch 4.00
344 Rickey Henderson 2.50
345 J. Kevin Brown 3.00
346 Orel Hershiser 2.50
347 Wade Boggs 3.00
348 Fred McGriff 3.00
349 Jose Canseco 3.00
350 Gary Sheffield 3.00
351 Travis Lee 8.00
352 Nomar Garciaparra 25.00
353 Frank Thomas 15.00
354 Cal Ripken Jr. 30.00
355 Mark McGwire 45.00
356 Mike Piazza 25.00
357 Alex Rodriguez 30.00
358 Barry Bonds 10.00
359 Tony Gwynn 20.00
360 Ken Griffey Jr. 45.00

1998 SPx Finite Spectrum Power Explosion

Spectrum Power Explosion is a parallel of the 20-card subset in Series One. The horizontal cards have two images of the player and are numbered to 50.

	MT
Common Player:	40.00
Semistars:	75.00
Production 50 sets	
31 Mike Piazza	200.00
32 Tony Clark	40.00
33 Larry Walker	60.00
34 Jim Thome	30.00
35 Juan Gonzalez	200.00
36 Jeff Bagwell	75.00
37 Jay Buhner	30.00
38 Tim Salmon	30.00
39 Albert Belle	50.00
40 Mark McGwire	300.00
41 Sammy Sosa	200.00
42 Mo Vaughn	40.00
43 Manny Ramirez	75.00
44 Tino Martinez	40.00
45 Frank Thomas	100.00
46 Nomar Garciaparra	200.00
47 Alex Rodriguez	250.00
48 Chipper Jones	200.00
49 Barry Bonds	75.00
50 Ken Griffey Jr.	300.00

1998 SPx Finite Radiance Heroes of the Game

Radiance Heroes of the Game is a parallel of the 10-card subset. The cards have a horizontal layout and are numbered to 100.

	MT
Common Player:	40.00
Production 100 sets	
171 Greg Maddux	90.00
172 Cal Ripken Jr.	140.00
173 Frank Thomas	60.00
174 Jeff Bagwell	50.00
175 Mike Piazza	100.00
176 Mark McGwire	175.00
177 Barry Bonds	40.00
178 Ken Griffey Jr.	175.00
179 Alex Rodriguez	140.00
180 Roger Clemens	60.00

1998 SPx Finite Spectrum Tradewinds

Spectrum Tradewinds is a parallel of the 20-card subset in Series Two. The horizontal cards have two images of the player and are numbered to 50.

	MT
Common Player (50 sets):	30.00
331 Matt Williams	45.00
332 Andres Galarraga	50.00
333 Walt Weiss	30.00
334 Joe Carter	40.00
335 Pedro J. Martinez	100.00
336 Henry Rodriguez	30.00
337 Travis Fryman	30.00
338 Darryl Kile	30.00
339 Mike Lansing	30.00
340 Mike Piazza	200.00
341 Moises Alou	40.00
342 Charles Johnson	30.00
343 Chuck Knoblauch	45.00
344 Rickey Henderson	60.00
345 Kevin Brown	40.00
346 Orel Hershiser	30.00
347 Wade Boggs	60.00
348 Fred McGriff	60.00
349 Jose Canseco	75.00
350 Gary Sheffield	40.00

Checklists with card numbers in parentheses ( ) indicates the numbers do not appear on the card.

1998 SPx Finite Radiance Cornerstones

Radiance Cornerstones of the Game is a parallel of the 10-card subset. The cards have two images of the player on the front and are numbered to 100.

		MT
Common Player (100 sets):		15.00
351	Travis Lee	20.00
352	Nomar Garciaparra	100.00
353	Frank Thomas	75.00
354	Cal Ripken Jr.	140.00
355	Mark McGwire	175.00
356	Mike Piazza	100.00
357	Alex Rodriguez	140.00
358	Barry Bonds	40.00
359	Tony Gwynn	75.00
360	Ken Griffey Jr.	175.00

1998 SPx Finite Home Run Hysteria

Home Run Hysteria is a 10-card insert in SPx Finite Series Two. The cards were sequentially numbered to 62.

		MT
Complete Set (10):		900.00
Common Player:		75.00
Production 62 sets		
HR1	Ken Griffey Jr.	250.00
HR2	Mark McGwire	250.00
HR3	Sammy Sosa	175.00
HR4	Albert Belle	60.00
HR5	Alex Rodriguez	175.00
HR6	Greg Vaughn	40.00
HR7	Andres Galarraga	50.00
HR8	Vinny Castilla	40.00
HR9	Juan Gonzalez	75.00
HR10	Chipper Jones	150.00

1999 SP Authentic Sample

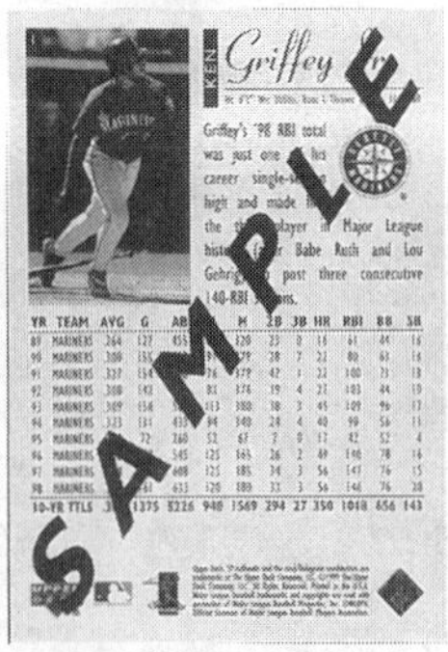

UD spokesman Ken Griffey Jr. is featured on the promo card for '99 SP Authentic. In the same format as the issued version, the sample card has different photos on front and back, a different season summary on back and a large, black "SAMPLE" overprint on back.

		MT
1	Ken Griffey Jr.	6.00

1999 SP Authentic

SP Authentic Baseball was a 135-card set that sold in packs of 5 cards for $4.99 per pack. The set included a 30-card Future Watch subset and a 15-card Season to Remember subset. Both subsets were shorted-printed, with each card sequentially numbered to 2,700. The insert lineup included Ernie Banks 500 Club 'Piece of History' Bat cards. Each card features a piece of a Ernie Banks game-used bat. Only 350 of the cards were produced. Fourteen more of the cards were produced and autographed by Ernie Banks. Other insert sets included SP Chirography, The Home Run Chronicles, Epic Figures, Reflections, and SP Authentics.

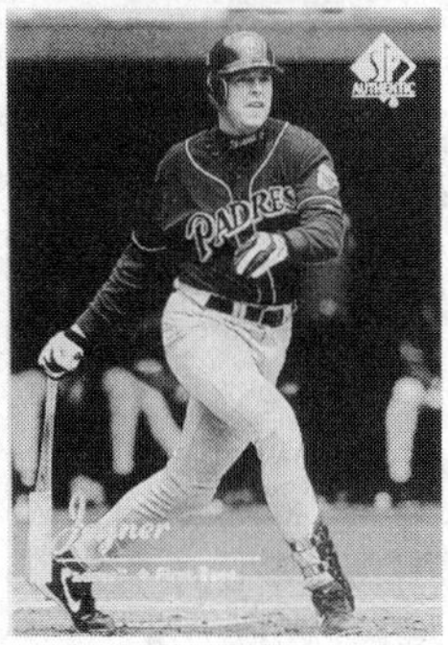

		MT
Complete Set (135):		450.00
Common Player (1-90):		.25
Common Future Watch (91-120):		4.00
Production 2,700 sets		
Common Season to Remember (121-135):		4.00
Production 2,700 sets		
Wax Box:		140.00
1	Mo Vaughn	.75
2	Jim Edmonds	.25
3	Darin Erstad	1.25
4	Travis Lee	1.00
5	Matt Williams	.50
6	Randy Johnson	.75
7	Chipper Jones	3.00
8	Greg Maddux	3.00
9	Andruw Jones	1.25
10	Andres Galarraga	.75
11	Tom Glavine	.50
12	Cal Ripken Jr.	4.00
13	Brady Anderson	.25
14	Albert Belle	1.25
15	Nomar Garciaparra	3.00
16	Donnie Sadler	.25
17	Pedro Martinez	1.00
18	Sammy Sosa	3.00
19	Kerry Wood	.50
20	Mark Grace	.50
21	Mike Caruso	.25
22	Frank Thomas	2.00
23	Paul Konerko	.50
24	Sean Casey	.35
25	Barry Larkin	.35
26	Kenny Lofton	.75
27	Manny Ramirez	1.50
28	Jim Thome	.75
29	Bartolo Colon	.25
30	Jaret Wright	.50
31	Larry Walker	.75
32	Todd Helton	1.00
33	Tony Clark	.75
34	Dean Palmer	.25
35	Mark Kotsay	.25
36	Cliff Floyd	.25
37	Ken Caminiti	.50
38	Craig Biggio	.75
39	Jeff Bagwell	1.25
40	Moises Alou	.40
41	Johnny Damon	.25
42	Larry Sutton	.25
43	Kevin Brown	.35
44	Gary Sheffield	.35
45	Raul Mondesi	.35
46	Jeromy Burnitz	.25
47	Jeff Cirillo	.25
48	Todd Walker	.50
49	David Ortiz	.25
50	Brad Radtke	.25
51	Vladimir Guerrero	1.50
52	Rondell White	.35
53	Brad Fullmer	.50
54	Mike Piazza	3.00
55	Robin Ventura	.40
56	John Olerud	.40
57	Derek Jeter	3.00
58	Tino Martinez	.60
59	Bernie Williams	.75
60	Roger Clemens	2.00
61	Ben Grieve	1.25
62	Miguel Tejada	.35
63	A.J. Hinch	.25
64	Scott Rolen	1.25
65	Curt Schilling	.35
66	Doug Glanville	.25
67	Aramis Ramirez	.25
68	Tony Womack	.25
69	Jason Kendall	.25
70	Tony Gwynn	2.50
71	Wally Joyner	.25
72	Greg Vaughn	.35
73	Barry Bonds	1.25
74	Ellis Burks	.25
75	Jeff Kent	.25
76	Ken Griffey Jr.	5.00
77	Alex Rodriguez	3.50
78	Edgar Martinez	.25
79	Mark McGwire	6.00
80	Eli Marrero	.25
81	Matt Morris	.25
82	Rolando Arrojo	.25
83	Quinton McCracken	.25
84	Jose Canseco	.75
85	Ivan Rodriguez	1.25
86	Juan Gonzalez	2.50
87	Royce Clayton	.25
88	Shawn Green	.35
89	Jose Cruz Jr.	.25
90	Carlos Delgado	.40
91	Troy Glaus (Future Watch)	15.00
92	George Lombard (Future Watch)	4.00
93	Ryan Minor (Future Watch)	8.00
94	Calvin Pickering (Future Watch)	4.00
95	Jin Ho Cho (Future Watch)	12.50
96	Russ Branyon (Future Watch)	4.00
97	Derrick Gibson (Future Watch)	6.00
98	Gabe Kapler (Future Watch)	20.00
99	Matt Anderson (Future Watch)	6.00
100	Preston Wilson (Future Watch)	5.00
101	Alex Gonzalez (Future Watch)	6.00
102	Carlos Beltran (Future Watch)	6.00
103	Dee Brown (Future Watch)	4.00
104	Jeremy Giambi (Future Watch)	10.00
105	Angel Pena (Future Watch)	10.00
106	Geoff Jenkins (Future Watch)	4.00
107	Corey Koskie (Future Watch)	6.00
108	A.J. Pierzynski (Future Watch)	4.00
109	Michael Barrett (Future Watch)	8.00
110	Fernando Seguignol (Future Watch)	10.00
111	Mike Kinkade (Future Watch)	4.00
112	Ricky Ledee (Future Watch)	10.00
113	Mike Lowell (Future Watch)	6.00
114	Eric Chavez (Future Watch)	15.00
115	Matt Clement (Future Watch)	8.00
116	Shane Monahan (Future Watch)	8.00
117	J.D. Drew (Future Watch)	20.00
118	Bubba Trammell (Future Watch)	4.00
119	Kevin Witt (Future Watch)	6.00
120	Roy Halladay (Future Watch)	10.00
121	Mark McGwire (Season to Remember)	40.00
122	Mark McGwire, Sammy Sosa (Season to Remember)	30.00
123	Sammy Sosa (Season to Remember)	20.00
124	Ken Griffey Jr. (Season to Remember)	40.00
125	Cal Ripken Jr. (Season to Remember)	25.00
126	Juan Gonzalez (Season to Remember)	15.00
127	Kerry Wood (Season to Remember)	6.00
128	Trevor Hoffman (Season to Remember)	4.00
129	Barry Bonds (Season to Remember)	8.00
130	Alex Rodriguez (Season to Remember)	25.00
131	Ben Grieve (Season to Remember)	8.00
132	Tom Glavine (Season to Remember)	5.00
133	David Wells (Season to Remember)	4.00
134	Mike Piazza (Season to Remember)	20.00
135	Scott Brosius (Season to Remember)	4.00

1999 SP Authentic Chirography

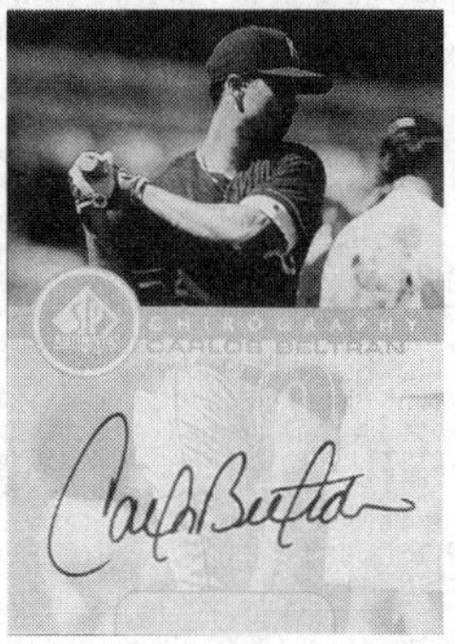

Baseball's top players and future stars are included in this 39-card autograph insert set. The set was split into Level 1 and Level 2 versions. Level cards are not numbered, and were inserted one card per 24 packs. Level 2 cards are sequentially numbered to the featured player's jersey number.

		MT
Complete Set (39):		1850.
Common Player:		15.00
Inserted 1:24		
EC	Eric Chavez	40.00
GK	Gabe Kapler	75.00
GMj	Gary Matthews Jr.	25.00
CP	Calvin Pickering	25.00
CK	Corey Koskie	25.00
SM	Shane Monahan	20.00
RH	Richard Hidalgo	20.00
MK	Mike Kinkade	25.00
CB	Carlos Beltran	25.00
AG	Alex Gonzalez	25.00
BC	Bruce Chen	20.00
MA	Matt Anderson	20.00
RM	Ryan Minor	25.00
RL	Ricky Ledee	35.00
RR	Ruben Rivera	20.00
BF	Brad Fullmer	30.00
RB	Russ Branyon	20.00
ML	Mike Lowell	20.00
JG	Jeremy Giambi	50.00
GL	George Lombard	20.00
KW	Kevin Witt	25.00
TW	Todd Walker	25.00
SR	Scott Rolen	75.00
KW	Kerry Wood	50.00
BG	Ben Grieve	50.00
JR	Ken Griffey Jr.	300.00
CJ	Chipper Jones	150.00
IR	Ivan Rodriguez	75.00
TGl	Troy Glaus	75.00
TL	Travis Lee	50.00
VG	Vladimir Guerrero	65.00
GV	Greg Vaughn	20.00
JT	Jim Thome	25.00
JD	J.D. Drew	50.00
TH	Todd Helton	40.00
GM	Greg Maddux	200.00
NG	Nomar Garciaparra	175.00
TG	Tony Gwynn	125.00
CR	Cal Ripken Jr.	250.00

1999 SP Authentic Chirography Gold

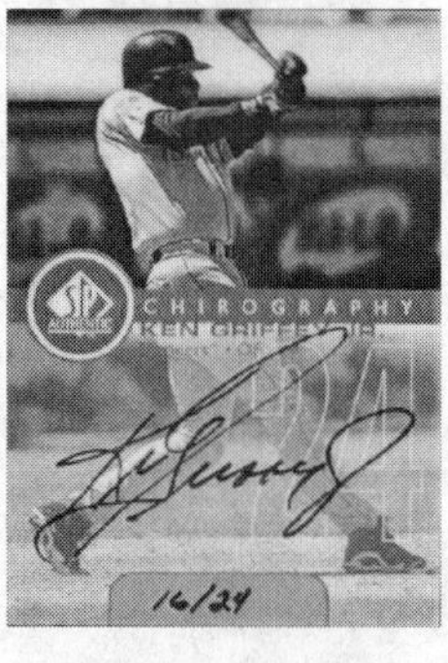

These Chirography parallels and can be identified by the gold tint on the card front and their sequential numbering; each featured player signed to his jersey number.

		MT
Common Player:		20.00
Inserted 1:24		
EC	Eric Chavez (30)	90.00
GK	Gabe Kapler (51)	40.00
GMj	Gary Matthews Jr. (68)	15.00
CP	Calvin Pickering (6)	150.00
CK	Corey Koskie (47)	25.00
SM	Shane Monahan (12)	60.00
RH	Richard Hidalgo (15)	75.00
MK	Mike Kinkade (33)	40.00
CB	Carlos Beltran (36)	125.00
AG	Alex Gonzalez (22)	50.00
BC	Bruce Chen (48)	45.00
MA	Matt Anderson (14)	50.00
RM	Ryan Minor (10)	150.00
RL	Ricky Ledee (38)	60.00
RR	Ruben Rivera (28)	40.00
BF	Brad Fullmer (20)	60.00
RB	Russ Branyon (66)	30.00
ML	Mike Lowell (60)	25.00
JG	Jeremy Giambi (15)	100.00
GL	George Lombard (26)	60.00
KW	Kevin Witt (6)	150.00
TW	Todd Walker (12)	100.00
SR	Scott Rolen (17)	250.00
KW	Kerry Wood (34)	60.00
BG	Ben Grieve (14)	125.00
JR	Ken Griffey Jr. (24)	1100.
CJ	Chipper Jones (10)	400.00
IR	Ivan Rodriguez (7)	250.00
TGl	Troy Glaus (14)	75.00
TL	Travis Lee (16)	75.00
VG	Vladimir Guerrero (27)	125.00
GV	Greg Vaughn (23)	40.00
JT	Jim Thome (25)	100.00
JD	J.D. Drew (8)	300.00
TH	Todd Helton (17)	160.00
GM	Greg Maddux (31)	400.00
NG	Nomar Garciaparra (5)	750.00
TG	Tony Gwynn (19)	500.00
CR	Cal Ripken Jr. (8)	1500.

1999 SP Authentic Epic Figures

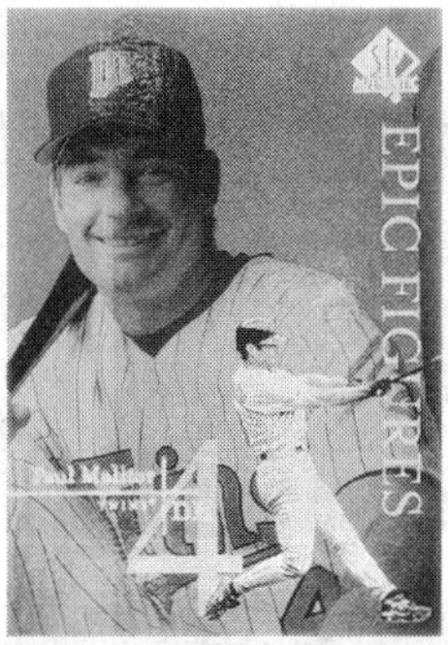

This 30-card set highlights baseball's biggest talents, including Mark McGwire and Derek Jeter. The card fronts have two photos, with the larger photo done with a shadow look in the background. Fronts also feature a holographic look, while the card backs feature the player's career highlights. These are seeded one per seven packs.

		MT
Complete Set (30):		150.00
Common Player:		1.50
Inserted 1:7		
E01	Mo Vaughn	2.00
E02	Travis Lee	3.00
E03	Andres Galarraga	2.00
E04	Andruw Jones	5.00
E05	Chipper Jones	12.00
E06	Greg Maddux	12.00
E07	Cal Ripken Jr.	15.00
E08	Nomar Garciaparra	12.00
E09	Sammy Sosa	12.00
E10	Frank Thomas	10.00
E11	Kerry Wood	8.00
E12	Kenny Lofton	2.00
E13	Manny Ramirez	8.00
E14	Larry Walker	3.00
E15	Jeff Bagwell	5.00
E16	Paul Molitor	4.00
E17	Vladimir Guerrero	6.00
E18	Derek Jeter	12.00

E19	Tino Martinez	1.50
E20	Mike Piazza	12.00
E21	Ben Grieve	2.00
E22	Scott Rolen	4.00
E23	Mark McGwire	25.00
E24	Tony Gwynn	10.00
E25	Barry Bonds	5.00
E26	Ken Griffey Jr.	25.00
E27	Alex Rodriguez	15.00
E28	J.D. Drew	4.00
E29	Juan Gonzalez	10.00
E30	Kevin Brown	1.50

1999 SP Authentic Home Run Chronicles

This two-tiered 70-card set focuses on the amazing seasons of McGwire, Sosa and Griffey Jr. Other players help round out the 70-card set, but special emphasis has been placed on the trio. These are seeded one per pack. A die-cut version also exists, with each card serially numbered to 70.

	MT
Complete Set (70):	140.00
Common Player:	.50
HR01Mark McGwire	10.00
HR02Sammy Sosa	2.00
HR03Ken Griffey Jr.	3.00
HR04Mark McGwire	4.00
HR05Mark McGwire	4.00
HR06Albert Belle	.75
HR07Jose Canseco	.50
HR08Juan Gonzalez	1.50
HR09Manny Ramirez	1.00
HR10Rafael Palmeiro	.50
HR11Mo Vaughn	.50
HR12Carlos Delgado	.50
HR13Nomar Garciaparra	2.00
HR14Barry Bonds	.75
HR15Alex Rodriguez	2.00
HR16Tony Clark	.50
HR17Jim Thome	.50
HR18Edgar Martinez	.50
HR19Frank Thomas	2.00
HR20Greg Vaughn	.50
HR21Vinny Castilla	.50
HR22Andres Galarraga	.50
HR23Moises Alou	.50
HR24Jeromy Burnitz	.50
HR25Vladimir Guerrero	1.00
HR26Jeff Bagwell	.75
HR27Chipper Jones	1.50
HR28Javier Lopez	.50
HR29Mike Piazza	2.00
HR30Andruw Jones	.75
HR31Henry Rodriguez	.50
HR32Jeff Kent	.50
HR33Ray Lankford	.50
HR34Scott Rolen	.75
HR35Raul Mondesi	.50
HR36Ken Caminiti	.50
HR37J.D. Drew	1.50
HR38Troy Glaus	1.00
HR39Gabe Kapler	1.00
HR40Alex Rodriguez	2.00
HR41Ken Griffey Jr.	3.00
HR42Sammy Sosa	2.00
HR43Mark McGwire	4.00
HR44Sammy Sosa	2.00
HR45Mark McGwire	4.00
HR46Vinny Castilla	.50
HR47Sammy Sosa	2.00
HR48Mark McGwire	4.00
HR49Sammy Sosa	2.00
HR50Greg Vaughn	.50
HR51Sammy Sosa	2.00
HR52Mark McGwire	4.00
HR53Sammy Sosa	2.00
HR54Mark McGwire	4.00
HR55Sammy Sosa	2.00
HR56Ken Griffey Jr.	3.00
HR57Sammy Sosa	2.00
HR58Mark McGwire	4.00
HR59Sammy Sosa	2.00
HR60Mark McGwire	4.00
HR61Mark McGwire	10.00
HR62Mark McGwire	12.00
HR63Mark McGwire	4.00
HR64Mark McGwire	4.00
HR65Mark McGwire	4.00
HR66Sammy Sosa	10.00
HR67Mark McGwire	4.00
HR68Mark McGwire	4.00
HR69Mark McGwire	4.00
HR70Mark McGwire	20.00

1999 SP Authentic Home Run Chronicles Die-Cuts

Each of the 70 cards in the Home Run Chronicles insert set was also issued in a die-cut version. The die-cuts share the basic front and back design of the regular HR Chronicle cards but have portions of the upper-left and lower-right cut away. On back, each of the die-cuts features an ink-jetted serial number from within an edition of 70.

	MT
Complete Die-Cut Set (70):	1750.
HR Chronicle Die-Cuts: 15X	
(See 1999 SP Authentics Home Run Chronicles for checklist, base values.)	

1999 SP Authentic Reflections

Dot Matrix technology is utilized to provide a unique look at 30 of the best players in the game. Card fronts are horizontal with two small and one large photo. These are seeded 1:23 packs.

		MT
Complete Set (30):		375.00
Common Player:		2.50
Inserted 1:23		
R01	Mo Vaughn	2.50
R02	Travis Lee	5.00
R03	Andres Galarraga	3.50
R04	Andruw Jones	6.00
R05	Chipper Jones	15.00
R06	Greg Maddux	15.00
R07	Cal Ripken Jr.	20.00
R08	Nomar Garciaparra	15.00
R09	Sammy Sosa	15.00
R10	Frank Thomas	12.00
R11	Kerry Wood	6.00
R12	Kenny Lofton	2.50
R13	Manny Ramirez	7.50
R14	Larry Walker	3.50
R15	Jeff Bagwell	6.00
R16	Paul Molitor	5.00
R17	Vladimir Guerrero	6.00
R18	Derek Jeter	15.00
R19	Tino Martinez	2.50
R20	Mike Piazza	15.00
R21	Ben Grieve	5.00
R22	Scott Rolen	6.00
R23	Mark McGwire	25.00
R24	Tony Gwynn	12.00
R25	Barry Bonds	6.00
R26	Ken Griffey Jr.	25.00
R27	Alex Rodriguez	20.00
R28	J.D. Drew	6.00
R29	Juan Gonzalez	12.00
R30	Roger Clemens	9.00

1999 SP Authentic SP Authentics

These 1:864 pack inserts are redemption cards that could be redeemed for special pieces of memorabilia from either Ken Griffey Jr. or Mark McGwire. The redemption period ended March 1, 2000. Because of rarity any surviving unredeemed McGwire home run-game autographed tickets cannot be valued.

		MT
Complete Set (8):		600.00
Common Card:		25.00
(1)	Ken Griffey Jr. (autographed baseball) (75)	150.00
(2)	Ken Griffey Jr. (glove) (200)	50.00
(3)	Ken Griffey Jr. (home run cel card) (346)	25.00
(4)	Ken Griffey Jr. (autographed jersey) (25)	300.00
(5)	Ken Griffey Jr. (autographed mini-helmet) (75)	150.00
(6)	Ken Griffey Jr. (Sports Illustrated Cover) (200)	25.00
(7)	Ken Griffey Jr. (autographed SI cover) (75)	150.00
(8)	Ken Griffey Jr. (standee) (300)	25.00
(9)	Mark McGwire (autographed 62HR ticket) (1)	
(10)	Mark McGwire (autographed 70HR ticket) (3)	

1999 SP Authentic 500 Club Piece of History

These cards feature a piece of game-used bat once swung by Ernie Banks. Approximately 350 cards exist. An autographed version of this card also exists, only 14 were produced.

		MT
		225.00
EB	Ernie Banks	250.00
EB	Ernie Banks (autographed) (14)	400.00

1999 SP Signature Edition

		MT
Complete Set (180):		180.00
Common Player:		.50
Wax Box:		280.00
1	Nomar Garciaparra	5.00
2	Ken Griffey Jr.	8.00
3	J.D. Drew	2.50
4	Alex Rodriguez	6.00
5	Juan Gonzalez	2.00
6	Mo Vaughn	1.00
7	Greg Maddux	5.00
8	Chipper Jones	5.00
9	Frank Thomas	2.00
10	Vladimir Guerrero	3.00
11	Mike Piazza	5.00
12	Eric Chavez	.75
13	Tony Gwynn	4.00
14	Orlando Hernandez	1.50
15	Pat Burrell	15.00
16	Darin Erstad	1.50
17	Greg Vaughn	.75
18	Russ Branyan	.50
19	Gabe Kapler	1.50
20	Craig Biggio	1.50
21	Troy Glaus	2.00
22	Pedro J. Martinez	1.00
23	Carlos Beltran	2.00
24	Derrek Lee	.50
25	Manny Ramirez	2.50
26	Shea Hillenbrand	2.00
27	Carlos Lee	.50
28	Angel Pena	.50
29	Rafael Roque	1.00
30	Octavio Dotel	.50
31	Jeromy Burnitz	.50
32	Jeremy Giambi	.50
33	Andruw Jones	1.50
34	Todd Helton	1.50
35	Scott Rolen	2.00
36	Jason Kendall	.50
37	Trevor Hoffman	.50
38	Barry Bonds	2.00
39	Ivan Rodriguez	2.00
40	Roy Halladay	.50
41	Rickey Henderson	1.00
42	Ryan Minor	.75
43	Brian Jordan	.50
44	Alex Gonzalez	.50
45	Raul Mondesi	.75
46	Corey Koskie	.50
47	Paul O'Neill	.75
48	Todd Walker	.50
49	Carlos Febles	1.00
50	Travis Fryman	.50
51	Albert Belle	2.00
52	Travis Lee	1.00
53	Bruce Chen	.50
54	Reggie Taylor	.50
55	Jerry Hairston Jr.	.50
56	Carlos Guillen	.50
57	Michael Barrett	.75
58	Jason Conti	.50
59	Joe Lawrence	.50
60	Jeff Cirillo	.50
61	Juan Melo	.50
62	Chad Hermansen	.50
63	Ruben Mateo	1.50
64	Ben Davis	.50
65	Mike Caruso	.50
66	Jason Giambi	.50
67	Jose Canseco	1.00
68	Chad Hutchinson	5.00
69	Mitch Meluskey	.50
70	Adrian Beltre	1.50
71	Mark Kotsay	.50
72	Juan Encarnacion	.50
73	Dermal Brown	.50
74	Kevin Witt	.50
75	Vinny Castilla	.50
76	Aramis Ramirez	.50
77	Marlon Anderson	.50
78	Mike Kinkade	.50
79	Kevin Barker	.50
80	Ron Belliard	.50
81	Chris Haas	.50
82	Bob Henley	.50
83	Fernando Seguignol	.50
84	Damon Minor	.50
85	A.J. Burnett	.50
86	Calvin Pickering	.50
87	Mike Darr	.50
88	Cesar King	.50
89	Rob Bell	.50
90	Derrick Gibson	.50
91	Ober Moreno	1.50
92	Robert Fick	.50
93	Doug Mientkiewicz	1.50
94	A.J. Pierzynski	.50
95	Orlando Palmeiro	.50
96	Sidney Ponson	.50
97	Ivanon Coffie	.50
98	Juan Pena	1.00
99	Mark Karchner	1.50
100	Carlos Castillo	.50
101	Bryan Ward	1.00
102	Mario Valdez	.50
103	Billy Wagner	.50
104	Miguel Tejada	.75
105	Jose Cruz Jr.	.50
106	George Lombard	.50
107	Geoff Jenkins	.50
108	Ray Lankford	.50
109	Todd Stottlemyre	.50
110	Mike Lowell	.50
111	Matt Clement	.50
112	Scott Brosius	.50
113	Preston Wilson	.50
114	Bartolo Colon	.50
115	Rolando Arrojo	.50
116	Jose Guillen	.50
117	Ron Gant	.50
118	Ricky Ledee	.60
119	Carlos Delgado	1.50
120	Abraham Nunez	.50
121	John Olerud	1.00
122	Chan Ho Park	.75
123	Brad Radke	.50
124	Al Leiter	.50
125	Gary Matthews Jr.	.50
126	F.P. Santangelo	.50
127	Brad Fullmer	.50
128	Matt Anderson	.50
129	A.J. Hinch	.50
130	Sterling Hitchcock	.50
131	Edgar Martinez	.50
132	Fernando Tatis	1.00
133	Bobby Smith	.50
134	Paul Konerko	.75
135	Sean Casey	1.00
136	Donnie Sadler	.50
137	Denny Neagle	.50
138	Sandy Alomar	.50
139	Mariano Rivera	.75
140	Emil Brown	.50
141	J.T. Snow	.50
142	Eli Marrero	.50
143	Rusty Greer	.50
144	Johnny Damon	.50
145	Damion Easley	.50
146	Eric Milton	.50
147	Rico Brogna	.50
148	Ray Durham	.50
149	Wally Joyner	.50
150	Royce Clayton	.50
151	David Ortiz	.50
152	Wade Boggs	1.25
153	Ugueth Urbina	.50
154	Richard Hidalgo	.50
155	Bobby Abreu	.50
156	Robb Nen	.50
157	David Segui	.50
158	Sean Berry	.50
159	Kevin Tapani	.50
160	Jason Varitek	.50
161	Fernando Vina	.50
162	Jim Leyritz	.50
163	Enrique Wilson	.50
164	Jim Parque	.50
165	Doug Glanville	.50
166	Jesus Sanchez	.50
167	Nolan Ryan	6.00
168	Robin Yount	2.00
169	Stan Musial	4.00
170	Tom Seaver	2.00
171	Mike Schmidt	2.50
172	Willie Stargell	1.00
173	Rollie Fingers	.75
174	Willie McCovey	.75
175	Harmon Killebrew	1.00
176	Eddie Mathews	1.00
177	Reggie Jackson	2.50
178	Frank Robinson	2.00
179	Ken Griffey Sr.	.50
180	Eddie Murray	1.50

1999 SP Signature Edition Autographs

Authentically autographed cards of nearly 100 current stars, top prospects and Hall of Famers were featured as one-per-pack inserts in SP Signature Edition. Some players did not return their signed cards in time for pack inclusion and had to be obtained by returning an exchange card prior to the May 12, 2000, deadline.

		MT
Common Player:		8.00
Inserted 1:1		
BA	Bobby Abreu	10.00
SA	Sandy Alomar	10.00
MA	Marlon Anderson	8.00
KB	Kevin Barker	8.00
MB	Michael Barrett	15.00
RoB	Rob Bell	8.00
AB	Albert Belle	40.00
RBe	Ron Belliard	8.00
CBe	Carlos Beltran	35.00
ABe	Adrian Beltre	15.00
BB	Barry Bonds	90.00
RB	Russ Branyan	8.00
SB	Scott Brosius	8.00
DB	Dermal Brown	8.00
EB	Emil Brown	8.00
AJB	A.J. Burnett (exchange card)	15.00
AJB	A.J. Burnett (autographed)	20.00
PB	Pat Burrell	75.00
JoC	Jose Canseco	125.00
MC	Mike Caruso	8.00
SC	Sean Casey (exchange card)	25.00
SC	Sean Casey (autographed)	35.00
VC	Vinny Castilla (exchange card)	10.00
VC	Vinny Castilla (autographed)	15.00
CC	Carlos Castillo	8.00
EC	Eric Chavez	20.00
BC	Bruce Chen	12.00
JCi	Jeff Cirillo	8.00
RC	Royce Clayton	8.00
MCl	Matt Clement	8.00
IC	Ivanon Coffie	8.00
BCo	Bartolo Colon (exchange card)	12.00
BCo	Bartolo Colon (autographed)	15.00
JC	Jason Conti	8.00
JDa	Johnny Damon	12.00
BD	Ben Davis	8.00
CD	Carlos Delgado	25.00
OD	Octavio Dotel	12.00
JD	J.D. Drew	45.00
RD	Ray Durham	8.00
DEa	Damion Easley	8.00
JE	Juan Encarnacion	12.00
DE	Darin Erstad	25.00
CF	Carlos Febles	20.00
Rob	Robert Fick	8.00

RoI	Rollie Fingers	20.00
BF	Brad Fullmer	15.00
RGa	Ron Gant	15.00
NG	Nomar Garciaparra	200.00
JaG	Jason Giambi	15.00
DG	Derrick Gibson	8.00
DGl	Doug Glanville	8.00
TGl	Troy Glaus	20.00
AG	Alex Gonzalez	8.00
RGr	Rusty Greer	8.00
Jr.	Ken Griffey Jr.	350.00
Sr.	Ken Griffey Sr.	20.00
VG	Vladimir Guerrero	50.00
JG	Jose Guillen	12.00
TG	Tony Gwynn	80.00
CHa	Chris Haas	8.00
JHj	Jerry Hairston Jr.	8.00
RH	Roy Halladay	12.00
THe	Todd Helton	25.00
BH	Bob Henley	8.00
ED	Orlando Hernandez	40.00
CH	Chad Hermansen	15.00
ShH	Shea Hillenbrand	8.00
StH	Sterling Hitchcock	8.00
THo	Trevor Hoffman	12.00
CHu	Chad Hutchinson	25.00
RJ	Reggie Jackson	175.00
GJ	Geoff Jenkins	15.00
AJ	Andruw Jones	35.00
CJ	Chipper Jones	100.00
WJ	Wally Joyner	15.00
GK	Gabe Kapler	30.00
MKa	Mark Karchner	8.00
JK	Jason Kendall	15.00
HK	Harmon Killebrew	40.00
CKi	Cesar King	8.00
MKi	Mike Kinkade	8.00
PK	Paul Konerko	12.00
CK	Corey Koskie	12.00
MK	Mark Kotsay	12.00
RL	Ray Lankford	15.00
JLa	Joe Lawrence	8.00
CL	Carlos Lee	20.00
DL	Derrek Lee	8.00
AL	Al Leiter	12.00
JLe	Jim Leyritz	8.00
GL	George Lombard	8.00
GM	Greg Maddux	150.00
Eli	Eli Marrero	8.00
EM	Edgar Martinez	10.00
PM	Pedro J. Martinez (exchange card)	75.00
PM	Pedro J. Martinez (autographed)	120.00
RMa	Ruben Mateo (exchange card)	20.00
RMa	Ruben Mateo (autographed)	30.00
EMa	Eddie Mathews	50.00
GMj	Gary Matthews Jr.	12.00
WMc	Willie McCovey	40.00
JM	Juan Melo	8.00
MMe	Mitch Meluskey	8.00
DoM	Doug Mientkiewicz	8.00
EMi	Eric Milton	8.00
DaM	Damon Minor	8.00
RM	Ryan Minor	8.00
EMu	Eddie Murray	60.00
SM	Stan Musial	120.00
RN	Robb Nen	8.00
AN	Abraham Nunez	8.00
JO	John Olerud	20.00
PO	Paul O'Neill	20.00
DO	David Ortiz	8.00
OP	Orlando Palmeiro	8.00
JP	Jim Parque	8.00
AP	Angel Pena	8.00
MP	Mike Piazza (exchange card)	100.00
MP	Mike Piazza (autographed)	175.00
CP	Calvin Pickering	12.00
AJP	A.J. Pierzynski	8.00
SP	Sidney Ponson	8.00
BR	Brad Radke	8.00
ARa	Aramis Ramirez	8.00
MR	Manny Ramirez	60.00
MRi	Mariano Rivera	20.00
FR	Frank Robinson	50.00
AR	Alex Rodriguez	200.00
PG	Ivan Rodriguez	60.00
SR	Scott Rolen (exchange card)	40.00
SR	Scott Rolen (autographed)	50.00
RR	Rafael Roque	8.00
NR	Nolan Ryan	275.00
DS	Donnie Sadler	8.00
JS	Jesus Sanchez	8.00
MS	Mike Schmidt	125.00
TSe	Tom Seaver	90.00
DSe	David Segui	8.00
FS	Fernando Seguignol	8.00
BS	Bobby Smith	8.00
JT	J.T. Snow (exchange card)	10.00
JT	J.T. Snow (autographed)	12.00
POP	Willie Stargell (exchange card)	40.00
POP	Willie Stargell (autographed)	50.00
TSt	Todd Stottlemyre	12.00
FTa	Fernando Tatis	15.00
RT	Reggie Taylor	8.00
MT	Miguel Tejada	25.00
FT	Frank Thomas	80.00
MV	Mario Valdez	8.00
JV	Jason Varitek	8.00
GV	Greg Vaughn	15.00
MO	Mo Vaughn	30.00
FV	Fernando Vina	12.00
BWa	Billy Wagner	12.00
TW	Todd Walker	12.00
BW	Bryan Ward	8.00
EW	Enrique Wilson	8.00
KW	Kevin Witt	8.00
RY	Robin Yount	75.00

1999 SP Signature Edition Autographs Gold

This parallel edition of the Signature Series Autographs features special gold graphic highlights on front and cards serially numbered within an edition of 50 each (except A.J. Burnett). Cards of 11 in the checklist), while cards of several others had to be in the checklist, while cards of several others had to be obtained by sending in an exchange card, valid through May 12, 2000.

		MT
	Common Player:	15.00
BA	Bobby Abreu	15.00
SA	Sandy Alomar	15.00
MA	Marlon Anderson	15.00
KB	Kevin Barker	15.00
MB	Michael Barrett	30.00
RoB	Rob Bell	15.00
AB	Albert Belle	80.00
RBe	Ron Belliard	15.00
CBe	Carlos Beltran	70.00
ABe	Adrian Beltre	30.00
CB	Craig Biggio (unsigned)	25.00
BB	Barry Bonds	180.00
RB	Russ Branyan	15.00
SB	Scott Brosius	15.00
DB	Dermal Brown	15.00
EB	Emil Brown	15.00
AJB	A.J. Burnett (exchange card)	30.00
AJB	A.J. Burnett (autographed edition of 20)	40.00
JB	Jeromy Burnitz (unsigned)	15.00
PB	Pat Burrell	150.00
JoC	Jose Canseco	120.00
MC	Mike Caruso	15.00
SC	Sean Casey	70.00
VC	Vinny Castilla (exchange card)	20.00
VC	Vinny Castilla (autographed)	30.00
CC	Carlos Castillo	15.00
EC	Eric Chavez	40.00
BC	Bruce Chen	24.00
JCi	Jeff Cirillo	15.00
RC	Royce Clayton	15.00
MCl	Matt Clement	15.00
IC	Ivanon Coffie	15.00
BCo	Bartolo Colon	30.00
JC	Jason Conti	15.00
JDa	Johnny Damon	15.00
MD	Mike Darr (unsigned)	15.00
BD	Ben Davis	15.00
CD	Carlos Delgado	30.00
OD	Octavio Dotel	24.00
JD	J.D. Drew	90.00
RD	Ray Durham	15.00
DEa	Damion Easley	15.00
JE	Juan Encarnacion	20.00
DE	Darin Erstad	50.00
CF	Carlos Febles	40.00
Rob	Robert Fick	15.00
RoI	Rollie Fingers	40.00
TF	Travis Fryman (unsigned)	15.00
BF	Brad Fullmer	30.00
RGa	Ron Gant	30.00
NG	Nomar Garciaparra	400.00
JaG	Jason Giambi	30.00
JeG	Jeremy Giambi (unsigned)	15.00
DG	Derrick Gibson	15.00
DGl	Doug Glanville	15.00
TGl	Troy Glaus	40.00
AG	Alex Gonzalez	15.00
JG	Juan Gonzalez (unsigned)	75.00
RGr	Rusty Greer	15.00
Jr.	Ken Griffey Jr.	800.00
Sr.	Ken Griffey Sr.	40.00
VG	Vladimir Guerrero	90.00
JG	Jose Guillen (unsigned)	15.00
TG	Tony Gwynn	150.00
CHa	Chris Haas	15.00
JHj	Jerry Hairston Jr.	15.00
RH	Roy Halladay	24.00
THe	Todd Helton	50.00
RH	Rickey Henderson (unsigned)	40.00
BH	Bob Henley	15.00
ED	Orlando Hernandez	80.00
CH	Chad Hermansen	30.00
ShH	Shea Hillenbrand	15.00
StH	Sterling Hitchcock	15.00
THo	Trevor Hoffman	24.00
CHu	Chad Hutchinson	50.00
RJ	Reggie Jackson	300.00
GJ	Geoff Jenkins	30.00
AJ	Andruw Jones	70.00
CJ	Chipper Jones	250.00
BJ	Brian Jordan (unsigned)	25.00
WJ	Wally Joyner	30.00
GK	Gabe Kapler	60.00
MKa	Mark Karchner	15.00
JK	Jason Kendall	30.00
HK	Harmon Killebrew	80.00
CKi	Cesar King	15.00
MKi	Mike Kinkade	15.00
PK	Paul Konerko	24.00
CK	Corey Koskie	24.00
MK	Mark Kotsay	24.00
RL	Ray Lankford	30.00
JLa	Joe Lawrence	15.00
CL	Carlos Lee	40.00
DL	Derrek Lee	15.00
TL	Travis Lee (unsigned)	20.00
AL	Al Leiter	24.00
JLe	Jim Leyritz	15.00
GL	George Lombard	15.00
GM	Greg Maddux	300.00
Eli	Eli Marrero	15.00
EM	Edgar Martinez	20.00
PM	Pedro Martinez (exchange card)	200.00
PM	Pedro Martinez (autographed)	250.00
RMa	Ruben Mateo (exchange card)	60.00
RMa	Ruben Mateo (autographed)	75.00
EMa	Eddie Mathews	100.00
GMj	Gary Matthews Jr.	24.00
WMc	Willie McCovey	80.00
JM	Juan Melo	15.00
MMe	Mitch Meluskey	15.00
DoM	Doug Mientkiewicz	15.00
EMi	Eric Milton	15.00
DaM	Damon Minor	15.00
RM	Ryan Minor	15.00
EMu	Eddie Murray	120.00
SM	Stan Musial	240.00
RN	Robb Nen	15.00
AN	Abraham Nunez	15.00
JO	John Olerud	40.00
PO	Paul O'Neill	40.00
DO	David Ortiz	15.00
OP	Orlando Palmeiro	15.00
JP	Jim Parque	15.00
AP	Angel Pena	15.00
MP	Mike Piazza (exchange card)	300.00
MP	Mike Piazza (autographed)	400.00
CP	Calvin Pickering	24.00
AJP	A.J. Pierzynski	15.00
SP	Sidney Ponson	15.00
BR	Brad Radke	15.00
ARa	Aramis Ramirez	15.00
MR	Manny Ramirez	120.00
MRi	Mariano Rivera	40.00
FR	Frank Robinson	100.00
AR	Alex Rodriguez	400.00
PG	Ivan Rodriguez	120.00
SR	Scott Rolen (exchange card)	90.00
SR	Scott Rolen (autographed)	100.00
RR	Rafael Roque	15.00
NR	Nolan Ryan	550.00
DS	Donnie Sadler	15.00
JS	Jesus Sanchez	15.00
MS	Mike Schmidt	300.00
TSe	Tom Seaver	180.00
DSe	David Segui	15.00
FS	Fernando Seguignol	15.00
BS	Bobby Smith	15.00
JT	J.T. Snow	15.00
POP	Willie Stargell	100.00
TSt	Todd Stottlemyre	15.00
FTa	Fernando Tatis	30.00
RT	Reggie Taylor	15.00
MT	Miguel Tejada	50.00
FT	Frank Thomas	240.00
MV	Mario Valdez	15.00
JV	Jason Varitek	15.00
GV	Greg Vaughn	15.00
MO	Mo Vaughn	50.00
FV	Fernando Vina	24.00
BWa	Billy Wagner	24.00
TW	Todd Walker	24.00
BW	Bryan Ward	15.00
EW	Enrique Wilson	15.00
KW	Kevin Witt	15.00
RY	Robin Yount	150.00

1999 SP Signature Edition Legendary Cuts

Each of the cards in this one-of-one insert series is unique, thus catalog values are impossible to assign.

Roy	Roy Campanella
XX	Jimmie Foxx
LG	Lefty Grove
W	Walter Johnson
MO	Mel Ott
Mel1	Mel Ott
Mel2	Mel Ott
BR	Babe Ruth
CY	Cy Young

1999 SP Signature Edition Piece of History

		MT
MO	Mel Ott (350)	250.00

1999 SPx

Formerly SPx Finite, this super-premium product showcases 80 of baseball's veteran players on regular cards and a 40-card rookie subset, which are serially numbered to 1,999. Two top rookies, J.D. Drew and Gabe Kapler autographed all 1,999 of their rookie subset cards. There are two parallels, SPx Radiance and SPx Spectrum. Radiance are serially numbered to 100 with Drew and Kapler signing all 100 of their cards. They are exclusive to Finite Radiance Hot Packs. Spectrums are limited to only one set and available only in Finite Spectrum Hot Packs. Packs consist of three cards with a S.R.P. of $5.99.

		MT
	Complete Set (120):	575.00
	Common Player:	.50
	Common SPx Rookie (81-120):	4.00
	Production 1,999 sets	
	Wax Box:	75.00
1	Mark McGwire #61	6.00
2	Mark McGwire #62	8.00
3	Mark McGwire #63	5.00
4	Mark McGwire #64	5.00
5	Mark McGwire #65	5.00
6	Mark McGwire #66	5.00
7	Mark McGwire #67	5.00
8	Mark McGwire #68	5.00
9	Mark McGwire #69	5.00
10	Mark McGwire #70	15.00
11	Mo Vaughn	1.50
12	Darin Erstad	2.50
13	Travis Lee	2.00
14	Randy Johnson	2.00
15	Matt Williams	1.25
16	Chipper Jones	6.00
17	Greg Maddux	6.00
18	Andruw Jones	2.50
19	Andres Galarraga	1.50
20	Cal Ripken Jr.	8.00
21	Albert Belle	2.50
22	Mike Mussina	2.00
23	Nomar Garciaparra	6.00
24	Pedro Martinez	2.00
25	John Valentin	.50
26	Kerry Wood	2.50
27	Sammy Sosa	6.00
28	Mark Grace	1.25
29	Frank Thomas	5.00
30	Mike Caruso	.50
31	Barry Larkin	.75
32	Sean Casey	1.00
33	Jim Thome	1.50
34	Kenny Lofton	1.50
35	Manny Ramirez	3.00
36	Larry Walker	1.50
37	Todd Helton	2.00
38	Vinny Castilla	.50
39	Tony Clark	1.50
40	Derrek Lee	.50
41	Mark Kotsay	.50
42	Jeff Bagwell	2.50
43	Craig Biggio	1.50
44	Moises Alou	.50
45	Larry Sutton	.50
46	Johnny Damon	.50
47	Gary Sheffield	.50
48	Raul Mondesi	1.00
49	Jeromy Burnitz	.50
50	Todd Walker	.75
51	David Ortiz	.50
52	Vladimir Guerrero	3.00
53	Rondell White	.50
54	Mike Piazza	6.00
55	Derek Jeter	6.00
56	Tino Martinez	1.00
57	David Wells	.50
58	Ben Grieve	2.00
59	A.J. Hinch	.50
60	Scott Rolen	2.50
61	Doug Glanville	.50
62	Aramis Ramirez	.50
63	Jose Guillen	.50
64	Tony Gwynn	5.00
65	Greg Vaughn	.50
66	Ruben Rivera	.50
67	Barry Bonds	2.50
68	J.T. Snow	.50
69	Alex Rodriguez	8.00
70	Ken Griffey Jr.	10.00
71	Jay Buhner	.50
72	Mark McGwire	12.00
73	Fernando Tatis	.50
74	Quinton McCracken	.50
75	Wade Boggs	1.50
76	Ivan Rodriguez	2.50
77	Juan Gonzalez	5.00
78	Rafael Palmeiro	1.50
79	Jose Cruz Jr.	.50
80	Carlos Delgado	1.00
81	Troy Glaus	15.00
82	Vladimir Nunez	4.00
83	George Lombard	8.00
84	Bruce Chen	6.00
85	Ryan Minor	15.00
86	Calvin Pickering	6.00
87	Jin Ho Cho	6.00
88	Russ Branyon	6.00
89	Derrick Gibson	5.00
90	Gabe Kapler (autographed)	75.00
91	Matt Anderson	8.00
92	Robert Fick	4.00
93	Juan Encarnacion	8.00
94	Preston Wilson	8.00
95	Alex Gonzalez	8.00
96	Carlos Beltran	12.00
97	Jeremy Giambi	15.00
98	Dee Brown	4.00
99	Adrian Beltre	10.00
100	Alex Cora	4.00
101	Angel Pena	8.00
102	Geoff Jenkins	6.00
103	Ronnie Belliard	6.00
104	Corey Koskie	6.00
105	A.J. Pierzynski	6.00
106	Michael Barrett	12.00
107	Fernando Seguignol	12.00
108	Mike Kinkade	10.00
109	Mike Lowell	8.00
110	Ricky Ledee	8.00
111	Eric Chavez	15.00
112	Abraham Nunez	6.00
113	Matt Clement	10.00
114	Ben Davis	6.00
115	Mike Darr	8.00
116	Ramon Martinez	8.00
117	Carlos Guillen	10.00
118	Shane Monahan	6.00
119	J.D. Drew (autographed)	50.00
120	Kevin Witt	6.00

Player names in *Italic* type indicate a rookie card.

1999 SPx Dominance

This 20-card set showcases the most dominant MLB superstars, including Derek Jeter and Alex Rodriguez. These are seeded 1:17 packs and numbered with a FB prefix.

		MT
Complete Set (20):		200.00
Common Player:		4.00
Inserted 1:17		
1	Chipper Jones	20.00
2	Greg Maddux	20.00
3	Cal Ripken Jr.	25.00
4	Nomar Garciaparra	20.00
5	Mo Vaughn	4.00
6	Sammy Sosa	20.00
7	Albert Belle	6.00
8	Frank Thomas	15.00
9	Jim Thome	4.00
10	Jeff Bagwell	8.00
11	Vladimir Guerrero	10.00
12	Mike Piazza	20.00
13	Derek Jeter	20.00
14	Tony Gwynn	15.00
15	Barry Bonds	8.00
16	Ken Griffey Jr.	30.00
17	Alex Rodriguez	25.00
18	Mark McGwire	30.00
19	J.D. Drew	5.00
20	Juan Gonzalez	15.00

1999 SPx Power Explosion

This 30-card set salutes the top power hitters in the game today, including Mark McGwire and Sammy Sosa. These are seeded 1:3 packs, and numbered with a PE prefix.

		MT
Complete Set (30):		60.00
Common Player:		.60
Inserted 1:3		
1	Troy Glaus	1.50
2	Mo Vaughn	1.00
3	Travis Lee	1.25
4	Chipper Jones	3.50
5	Andres Galarraga	1.00
6	Brady Anderson	.60
7	Albert Belle	1.50
8	Nomar Garciaparra	3.50
9	Sammy Sosa	3.50
10	Frank Thomas	2.50
11	Jim Thome	.60
12	Manny Ramirez	2.00
13	Larry Walker	1.25
14	Tony Clark	1.25
15	Jeff Bagwell	1.50
16	Moises Alou	.60
17	Ken Caminiti	.60
18	Vladimir Guerrero	1.75
19	Mike Piazza	3.50
20	Tino Martinez	.60
21	Ben Grieve	1.25
22	Scott Rolen	1.50
23	Greg Vaughn	.60
24	Barry Bonds	1.50
25	Ken Griffey Jr.	6.00
26	Alex Rodriguez	4.50
27	Mark McGwire	6.00
28	J.D. Drew	2.00
29	Juan Gonzalez	3.00
30	Ivan Rodriguez	1.25

1999 SPx Premier Stars

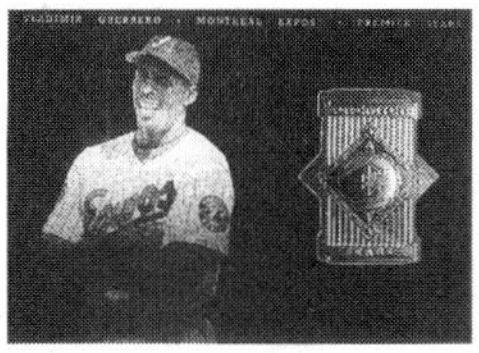

This 30-card set captures baseball's most dominant players, including Randy Johnson and Ken Griffey Jr. Featured on a rainbow-foil design, these are seeded 1:17 packs and numbered with a PS prefix.

		MT
Complete Set (30):		350.00
Common Player:		3.00
Inserted 1:17		
1	Mark McGwire	35.00
2	Sammy Sosa	20.00
3	Frank Thomas	15.00
4	J.D. Drew	6.00
5	Kerry Wood	8.00
6	Moises Alou	3.00
7	Kenny Lofton	3.00
8	Jeff Bagwell	8.00
9	Tony Clark	6.00
10	Roberto Alomar	6.00
11	Cal Ripken Jr.	25.00
12	Derek Jeter	20.00
13	Mike Piazza	20.00
14	Jose Cruz Jr.	3.00
15	Chipper Jones	20.00
16	Nomar Garciaparra	20.00
17	Greg Maddux	20.00
18	Scott Rolen	8.00
19	Vladimir Guerrero	10.00
20	Albert Belle	5.00
21	Ken Griffey Jr.	35.00
22	Alex Rodriguez	25.00
23	Ben Grieve	6.00
24	Juan Gonzalez	15.00
25	Barry Bonds	8.00
26	Larry Walker	6.00
27	Tony Gwynn	15.00
28	Randy Johnson	6.00
29	Travis Lee	6.00
30	Mo Vaughn	3.00

1999 SPx Star Focus

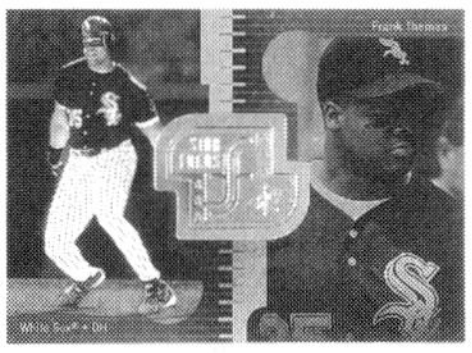

This 30-card set focuses on the 30 brightest stars in the game. These are seeded 1:8 packs and numbered with a SF prefix.

		MT
Complete Set (30):		150.00
Common Player:		2.00
Inserted 1:8		
1	Chipper Jones	10.00
2	Greg Maddux	10.00
3	Cal Ripken Jr.	12.50
4	Nomar Garciaparra	10.00
5	Mo Vaughn	2.00
6	Sammy Sosa	10.00
7	Albert Belle	4.00
8	Frank Thomas	8.00
9	Jim Thome	2.00
10	Kenny Lofton	2.00
11	Manny Ramirez	6.00
12	Larry Walker	3.00
13	Jeff Bagwell	4.00
14	Craig Biggio	3.00
15	Randy Johnson	3.00
16	Vladimir Guerrero	5.00
17	Mike Piazza	10.00
18	Derek Jeter	10.00
19	Tino Martinez	2.00
20	Bernie Williams	2.00
21	Curt Schilling	2.00
22	Tony Gwynn	8.00
23	Barry Bonds	4.00
24	Ken Griffey Jr.	15.00
25	Alex Rodriguez	12.50
26	Mark McGwire	15.00
27	J.D. Drew	5.00
28	Juan Gonzalez	8.00
29	Ivan Rodriguez	3.00
30	Ben Grieve	3.00

1999 SPx Winning Materials

This eight-card set includes a piece of the featured player's game-worn jersey and game-used bat on each card. These are seeded 1:251 packs.

		MT
Complete Set (8):		1300.
Common Player:		100.00
Inserted 1:251		
VC	Vinny Castilla	100.00
JD	J.D. Drew	125.00
JR	Ken Griffey Jr.	500.00
VG	Vladimir Guerrero	175.00
TG	Tony Gwynn	225.00
TH	Todd Helton	125.00
TL	Travis Lee	125.00
IR	Ivan Rodriguez	150.00

1999 SPx 500 Club Piece of History

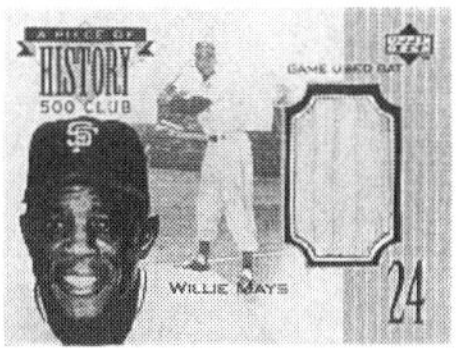

Each of these approximately 350 cards include a piece of game-used Louisville Slugger once swung by Wilie Mays. Mays also signed 24 of his Piece of History cards.

		MT
WM	Willie Mays (350)	350.00
WM	Willie Mays (autographed) (24)	500.00

1993 Spectrum Diamond Club Promo Set

Ten Hall of Famers are featured in this promo card set. Fronts of the 2-1/2" x 3-1/2" cards have borderless player action or posed photos. The issuer's logo, player's name and striping are printed in gold. Backs have a color ghost-image photo of the player along with personal data and career summary. A box near the bottom indicates the set's serial number from within an edition of 10,000.

		MT
Complete Set (10):		2.00
Common Player:		.25
1	Carl Yastrzemski	.40
2	Johnny Bench (numbered promo)	.25
--	Johnny Bench ("For Promotional Use Only" on back)	.25
3	Al Kaline	.25
4	Ernie Banks	.50
5	Catfish Hunter	.25
6	Rod Carew	.25
7	Mike Schmidt	.50
8	Harmon Killebrew	.25
9	Frank Robinson	.40
10	Rollie Fingers	.25

1993 Spectrum Diamond Club Red Sox

This collectors' issue features five stars of the Boston Red Sox from the 1940s-1970s. Fronts have action photos on which uniform logos are eliminated. A pinstripe around the photo, the issuer's logo and player name are printed in gold. Size is standard 2-1/2" x 3-1/2". Horizontal backs have a color Fenway Park photo ghosted in the background. Player career highlights and stats are overprinted.

		MT
Complete Set (5):		1.00
Common Player:		.25
1	Carl Yastrzemski	.50
2	Bobby Doerr	.25
3	Dwight Evans	.25
4	Fred Lynn	.25
5	Luis Tiant	.25

1993 Spectrum Legends of Baseball

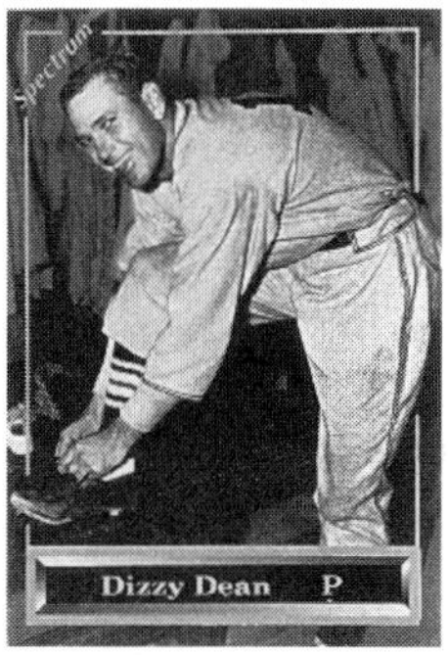

This collectors edition of 10 of baseball greatest players was issued in two versions, with and without a gold facsimile autograph on the cards' fronts. The gold-signature cards were limited to an edition of 5,000 numbered cards of each player. Fronts have black-and-white photos with gold-foil graphic highlights. Backs have another photo subdued in the background with career history and stats and personal data overprinted in black. Copyright information is at bottom. Cards were issued in two series of five each and are checklisted here alphabetically.

		MT
Complete Set:		7.50
Complete Set, Gold-signature:		150.00
Common Player:		.50
Common Player, Gold-signature:		10.00
(1)	Grover Alexander	.50
(1g)	Grover Alexander (gold-signature)	10.00
(2)	Ty Cobb	.75
(2g)	Ty Cobb (gold-signature)	15.00
(3)	Dizzy Dean	.50
(3g)	Dizzy Dean (gold-signature)	10.00
(4)	Lou Gehrig	1.00
(4g)	Lou Gehrig (gold-signature)	20.00
(5)	Rogers Hornsby	.50
(5g)	Rogers Hornsby (gold-signature)	10.00
(6)	Satchel Paige	.75
(6g)	Satchel Paige (gold-signature)	15.00
(7)	Babe Ruth	2.00
(7g)	Babe Ruth (gold-signature)	40.00
(8)	Casey Stengel	.50
(8g)	Casey Stengel (gold-signature)	10.00
(9)	Honus Wagner	.75
(9g)	Honus Wagner (gold-signature)	15.00
(10)	Cy Young	.50
(10g)	Cy Young (gold-signature)	10.00

1993 Spectrum Nolan Ryan 23K

A "pure gold" background on front offsets the color action photo of Ryan in action (team logos have been removed for licensing reasons). Backs of the 2-1/2" x 3-1/2" cards have career highlights and stats.

		MT
Complete Set (3):		6.00
Common Card:		2.00
1	Nolan Ryan	2.00
2	Nolan Ryan	2.00
3	Nolan Ryan	2.00

1994 Spectrum 1969 Miracle Mets

The 1969 Miracle Mets card set, produced by Spectrum Holdings Group of Birmingham, Mich. was part of what the company called "an integrated memorabilia program, with the 1969 Mets card set as the centerpiece." The 70-card set measures the standard 2-1/2" x 3-1/2", complete with UV coating on both sides and gold foil on the fronts, was sold complete at $24.95, and limited to 25,000 sets. A total of

750 numbered sets were signed by all 25 living players, including Hall of Famer Tom Seaver and future Cooperstown resident Nolan Ryan.

		MT
	Complete Set (69):	25.00
	Common Player:	.25
1	Commemorative Card	.25
2	Team Photo	.25
3	Tom Seaver	3.00
4	Jerry Koosman	.45
5	Tommie Agee	.25
6	Bud Harrelson	.25
7	Nolan Ryan	7.50
8	Jerry Grote	.25
9	Ron Swoboda	.25
10	Donn Clendenon	.25
11	Art Shamsky	.25
12	Tug McGraw	.35
13	Ed Kranepool	.35
14	Cleon Jones	.35
15	Ron Taylor	.25
16	Gary Gentry	.25
17	Ken Boswell	.25
18	Ed Charles	.25
19	J.C. Martin	.25
20	Al Weis	.25
21	Jack DiLauro	.25
22	Duffy Dyer	.25
23	Wayne Garrett	.25
24	Jim McAndrew	.25
25	Rod Gaspar	.25
26	Don Cardwell	.25
27	Bob Pfeil	.25
28	Cal Koonce	.25
29	Gil Hodges	2.00
30	Yogi Berra	2.50
31	Joe Pignatano	.25
32	Rube Walker	.25
33	Eddie Yost	.25
34	First-ever Met Game	.25
35	Opening Day 1969	.25
36	Kranepool Breaks Home Run Record	.25
37	Koosman Sets Club Strikeout Record	.25
38	Mets Trade for Clendenon	.25
39	Koosman's 23 Scoreless Innings	.25
40	Mets Begin 7-Game Winning Streak	.25
41	Mets vs. Division Leading Cubs	.25
42	Seaver's Near Perfect Game	.25
43	Mets Trail by 3-1/2	.25
44	All-Star Break	.25
45	All-Star Game	.25
46	Mets Sweep Atlanta	.25
47	Mets Sweep Padres	.25
48	Mets Defeat Cubs, Koosman Strikes Out 1	.25
49	Mets Defeat Cubs 1/2 Game Back	.25
50	First Place!	.25
51	Mets Continue Nine Game Winning Streak	.25
52	Seaver Earns 22nd Victory	.25
53	Mets Win, Carlton Strikes Out 19	.25
54	Koosman Pitches 15th Complete Game	.25
55	Eastern Division Champs!	.25
56	100th Victory	.25
57	Final Game, Mets Prepare for Braves	.25
58	N.L. Championship Series, Game 1	.25
59	N.L. Championship Series, Game 2	.25
60	N.L. Championship Series, Game 3	.25
61	World Series, Game 1	.25
62	World Series, Game 2	.25
63	World Series, Game 3	.25
64	World Series, Game 4	.25
65	World Series, Game 5	.25
66	World Champions	.25
67	World Champions	.25
68	World Champions	.25
69	World Champions	.25
----	Checklist	.25

1986 Sportflics Prototype Cards

This six-card set was apparently produced as a prototype as part of the licensing process. Similar in format to the 1986 Sportflics issue the cards have stats through the 1984 season. The prototype cards are much rarer than the promo cards. The Schmidt, Sutter and Winfield cards are standard 2-1/2" x 3-1/2" in size while the DiMaggio card is 1-5/16" square and the MLB logo card is 1-3/4" x 2".

		MT
	Complete Set (6):	125.00
	Common Player:	5.00
(1)	Joe DiMaggio (black-and-white)	25.00
(2)	Mike Schmidt	30.00
(3)	Bruce Sutter	5.00
(4)	Dave Winfield (biographical back)	50.00
(5)	Dave Winfield (statistical back)	35.00
(6)	Major League Baseball Logo	3.00

1986 Sportflics Promo Cards

Though they carry stats only through 1984, and have a 1986 copyright date, these promo cards were issued late in 1985 to preview the "Triple Action Sportflics" concept. They were the first really widely distributed promo cards. Each of the promo cards differs slightly from the issued version. The RBI Sluggers card in the issued set, for instance, was #126 and pictured Gary Carter, George Foster and Al Oliver. In the regular set, Pete Rose's card was #50 while Tom Seaver was #25. The regular-issue 1986 Sportflics cards, of course, include complete 1985 stats on back. Promo cards were distributed in three-card cello packs.

		MT
	Complete Set (3):	60.00
	Common Player:	20.00
1	RBI Sluggers (Dale Murphy, Jim Rice, Mike Schmidt)	20.00
43	Pete Rose	25.00
45	Tom Seaver	20.00

1986 Sportflics

The premiere issue from Sportflics was distributed nationally by Amurol Division of Wrigley Gum Company. These high quality, three-phase "Magic Motion" cards depict three different photos per card, with each visible separately as the card is tilted. The 1986 issue features 200 full-color baseball cards plus 133 trivia cards. The cards come in the standard 2-1/2" x 3-1/2" size with the backs containing player stats and personal information. There are three different types of picture cards: 1) Tri-Star cards - 50 cards feature three players on one card; 2) Big Six cards - 10 cards which have six players in special categories; and 3) the Big Twelve card of 12 World Series players from the Kansas City Royals. The trivia cards are 1-3/4" x 2" and do not have player photos.

		MT
	Complete Set (200):	10.00
	Common Player:	.10
1	George Brett	2.00
2	Don Mattingly	3.00
3	Wade Boggs	1.25
4	Eddie Murray	1.00
5	Dale Murphy	.65
6	Rickey Henderson	.65
7	Harold Baines	.15
8	Cal Ripken, Jr.	5.00
9	Orel Hershiser	.15
10	Bret Saberhagen	.15
11	Tim Raines	.15
12	Fernando Valenzuela	.15
13	Tony Gwynn	1.50
14	Pedro Guerrero	.10
15	Keith Hernandez	.10
16	Ernest Riles	.10
17	Jim Rice	.15
18	Ron Guidry	.10
19	Willie McGee	.15
20	Ryne Sandberg	1.50
21	Kirk Gibson	.10
22	Ozzie Guillen	.10
23	Dave Parker	.10
24	Vince Coleman	.10
25	Tom Seaver	.75
26	Brett Butler	.10
27	Steve Carlton	.65
28	Gary Carter	.25
29	Cecil Cooper	.10
30	Jose Cruz	.10
31	Alvin Davis	.10
32	Dwight Evans	.10
33	Julio Franco	.10
34	Damaso Garcia	.10
35	Steve Garvey	.40
36	Kent Hrbek	.10
37	Reggie Jackson	.75
38	Fred Lynn	.10
39	Paul Molitor	.75
40	Jim Presley	.10
41	Dave Righetti	.10
42a	Robin Yount (Yankees logo on back)	150.00
42b	Robin Yount (Brewers logo)	1.25
43	Nolan Ryan	5.00
44	Mike Schmidt	1.25
45	Lee Smith	.10
46	Rick Sutcliffe	.10
47	Bruce Sutter	.10
48	Lou Whitaker	.10
49	Dave Winfield	.65
50	Pete Rose	3.00
51	N.L. MVPs (Steve Garvey, Pete Rose, Ryne Sandberg)	.75
52	Slugging Stars (Harold Baines, George Brett, Jim Rice)	.35
53	No-Hitters (Phil Niekro, Jerry Reuss, Mike Witt)	.25
54	Big Hitters (Don Mattingly, Cal Ripken, Jr., Robin Yount)	2.00
55	Bullpen Aces (Goose Gossage, Dan Quisenberry, Lee Smith)	.10
56	Rookies of the Year (Pete Rose, Steve Sax, Darryl Strawberry)	1.00
57	A.L. MVPs (Don Baylor, Reggie Jackson, Cal Ripken, Jr.)	.50
58	Repeat Batting Champs (Bill Madlock, Dave Parker, Pete Rose)	.45
59	Cy Young Winners (Mike Flanagan, Ron Guidry, LaMarr Hoyt)	.10
60	Double Award Winners (Tom Seaver, Rick Sutcliffe, Fernando Valenzuela)	.20
61	Home Run Champs (Tony Armas, Reggie Jackson, Jim Rice)	.25
62	N.L. MVPs (Keith Hernandez, Dale Murphy, Mike Schmidt)	.40
63	A.L. MVPs (George Brett, Fred Lynn, Robin Yount)	.30
64	Comeback Players (Bert Blyleven, John Denny, Jerry Koosman)	.10
65	Cy Young Relievers (Rollie Fingers, Willie Hernandez, Bruce Sutter)	.10
66	Rookies of the Year (Andre Dawson, Bob Horner, Gary Matthews)	.20
67	Rookies of the Year (Carlton Fisk, Ron Kittle, Tom Seaver)	.20
68	Home Run Champs (George Foster, Dave Kingman, Mike Schmidt)	.25
69	Double Award Winners (Rod Carew, Cal Ripken, Jr., Pete Rose)	2.00
70	Cy Young Winners (Steve Carlton, Tom Seaver, Rick Sutcliffe)	.25
71	Top Sluggers (Reggie Jackson, Fred Lynn, Robin Yount)	.40
72	Rookies of the Year (Dave Righetti, Rick Sutcliffe, Fernando Valenzuela)	.10
73	Rookies of the Year (Fred Lynn, Eddie Murray, Cal Ripken, Jr.)	.50
74	Rookies of the Year (Rod Carew, Alvin Davis, Lou Whitaker)	.20
75	Batting Champs (Wade Boggs, Carney Lansford, Don Mattingly)	1.00
76	Jesse Barfield	.10
77	Phil Bradley	.10
78	Chris Brown	.10
79	Tom Browning	.10
80	Tom Brunansky	.10
81	Bill Buckner	.10
82	Chili Davis	.10
83	Mike Davis	.10
84	Rich Gedman	.10
85	Willie Hernandez	.10
86	Ron Kittle	.10
87	Lee Lacy	.10
88	Bill Madlock	.10
89	Mike Marshall	.10
90	Keith Moreland	.10
91	Graig Nettles	.10
92	Lance Parrish	.10
93	Kirby Puckett	2.50
94	Juan Samuel	.10
95	Steve Sax	.10
96	Dave Stieb	.10
97	Darryl Strawberry	.25
98	Willie Upshaw	.10
99	Frank Viola	.10
100	Dwight Gooden	.25
101	Joaquin Andujar	.10
102	George Bell	.10
103	Bert Blyleven	.10
104	Mike Boddicker	.10
105	Britt Burns	.10
106	Rod Carew	.65
107	Jack Clark	.10
108	Danny Cox	.10
109	Ron Darling	.10
110	Andre Dawson	.25
111	Leon Durham	.10
112	Tony Fernandez	.10
113	Tom Herr	.10
114	Teddy Higuera	.10
115	Bob Horner	.10
116	Dave Kingman	.10
117	Jack Morris	.10
118	Dan Quisenberry	.10
119	Jeff Reardon	.10
120	Bryn Smith	.10
121	Ozzie Smith	.75
122	John Tudor	.10
123	Tim Wallach	.10
124	Willie Wilson	.10
125	Carlton Fisk	.25
126	RBI Sluggers (Gary Carter, George Foster, Al Oliver)	.10
127	Run Scorers (Keith Hernandez, Tim Raines, Ryne Sandberg)	.25
128	Run Scorers (Paul Molitor, Cal Ripken, Jr., Willie Wilson)	.50
129	No-Hitters (John Candelaria, Dennis Eckersley, Bob Forsch)	.10
130	World Series MVPs (Ron Cey, Rollie Fingers, Pete Rose)	.35
131	All-Star Game MVPs (Dave Concepcion, George Foster, Bill Madlock)	.10
132	Cy Young Winners (Vida Blue, John Denny, Fernando Valenzuela)	.10
133	Comeback Players (Doyle Alexander, Joaquin Andujar, Richard Dotson)	.10
134	Big Winners (John Denny, Tom Seaver, Rick Sutcliffe)	.10
135	Veteran Pitchers (Phil Niekro, Tom Seaver, Don Sutton)	.25
136	Rookies of the Year (Vince Coleman, Dwight Gooden, Alfredo Griffin)	.40
137	All-Star Game MVPs (Gary Carter, Steve Garvey, Fred Lynn)	.20
138	Veteran Hitters (Tony Perez, Pete Rose, Rusty Staub)	.50
139	Power Hitters (George Foster, Jim Rice, Mike Schmidt)	.30
140	Batting Champs (Bill Buckner, Tony Gwynn, Al Oliver)	.35
141	No-Hitters (Jack Morris, Dave Righetti, Nolan Ryan)	.50
142	No-Hitters (Vida Blue, Bert Blyleven, Tom Seaver)	.10
143	Strikeout Kings (Dwight Gooden, Nolan Ryan, Fernando Valenzuela)	1.25
144	Base Stealers (Dave Lopes, Tim Raines, Willie Wilson)	.10
145	RBI Sluggers (Tony Armas, Cecil Cooper, Eddie Murray)	.15
146	A.L. MVPs (Rod Carew, Rollie Fingers, Jim Rice)	.15
147	World Series MVPs (Rick Dempsey, Reggie Jackson, Alan Trammell)	.25
148	World Series MVPs (Pedro Guerrero, Darrell Porter, Mike Schmidt)	.20
149	ERA Leaders (Mike Boddicker, Ron Guidry, Rick Sutcliffe)	.10
150	Comeback Players (Reggie Jackson, Dave Kingman, Fred Lynn)	.20
151	Buddy Bell	.10
152	Dennis Boyd	.10
153	Dave Concepcion	.10
154	Brian Downing	.10
155	Shawon Dunston	.10
156	John Franco	.10
157	Scott Garrelts	.10
158	Bob James	.10
159	Charlie Leibrandt	.10
160	Oddibe McDowell	.10
161	Roger McDowell	.10
162	Mike Moore	.10
163	Phil Niekro	.50
164	Al Oliver	.10

165	Tony Pena	.10
166	Ted Power	.10
167	Mike Scioscia	.10
168	Mario Soto	.10
169	Bob Stanley	.10
170	Garry Templeton	.10
171	Andre Thornton	.10
172	Alan Trammell	.20
173	Doug DeCinces	.10
174	Greg Walker	.10
175	Don Sutton	.45
176	1985 Award Winners (Vince Coleman, Dwight Gooden, Ozzie Guillen, Don Mattingly, Willie McGee, Bret Saberhagen)	.75
177	1985 Hot Rookies (Stewart Cliburn, Brian Fisher, Joe Hesketh, Joe Orsulak, Mark Salas, Larry Sheets)	.10
178a	Future Stars (Jose Canseco, Mark Funderburk, Mike Greenwell, Steve Lombardozzi, Billy Joe Robidoux, Danny Tartabull)	4.50
178b	Future Stars (Jose Canseco, Mike Greenwell, Steve Lombardozzi, Billy Jo Robidoux, Danny Tartabull, Jim Wilson)	60.00
179	Gold Glove (George Brett, Ron Guidry, Keith Hernandez, Don Mattingly, Willie McGee, Dale Murphy)	1.00
180	.300 (Wade Boggs, George Brett, Rod Carew, Cecil Cooper, Don Mattingly, Willie Wilson)	1.00
181	.300 (Pedro Guerrero, Tony Gwynn, Keith Hernandez, Bill Madlock, Dave Parker, Pete Rose)	.75
182	1985 Milestones (Rod Carew, Phil Niekro, Pete Rose, Nolan Ryan, Tom Seaver, Matt Tallman)	1.50
183	1985 Triple Crown (Wade Boggs, Darrell Evans, Don Mattingly, Willie McGee, Dale Murphy, Dave Parker)	1.00
184	1985 HL (Wade Boggs, Dwight Gooden, Rickey Henderson, Don Mattingly, Willie McGee, John Tudor)	1.00
185	1985 20-Game Winners (Joaquin Andujar, Tom Browning, Dwight Gooden, Ron Guidry, Bret Saberhagen, John Tudor)	.35
186	World Series Champs (Steve Balboni, George Brett, Dane Iorg, Danny Jackson, Charlie Leibrandt, Darryl Motley, Dan Quisenberry, Bret Saberhagen, Lonnie Smith, Jim Sundberg, Frank White, Willie Wilson)	.40
187	Hubie Brooks	.10
188	Glenn Davis	.10
189	Darrell Evans	.10
190	Rich Gossage	.10
191	Andy Hawkins	.10
192	Jay Howell	.10
193	LaMarr Hoyt	.10
194	Davey Lopes	.10
195	Mike Scott	.10
196	Ted Simmons	.10
197	Gary Ward	.10
198	Bob Welch	.10
199	Mike Young	.10
200	Buddy Biancalana	.10

1986 Sportflics Decade Greats Sample Cards

To promote its Decade Greats set of current and former cards, Sportflics issued this two-card promo set. Card fronts are identical to the issued versions. Backs are printed in blue on white: "DECADE GREATS / SAMPLE CARD". The players are not identified on the cards.

		MT
Complete Set (2):		7.50
(1)	Dwight Gooden	4.00
(2)	Mel Ott	4.00

1986 Sportflics Decade Greats

This set, produced by Sportflics, features outstanding players, by position, from the 1930s to the 1980s by decades. The card fronts are printed in sepia-toned photos or full-color with the Sportflics three-phase "Magic Motion" animation. The complete set contains 75 cards with 59 single player cards and 16 multi-player cards. Biographies appear on the card backs which are printed in full-color and color-coded by decade. The set was distributed only through hobby dealers and is in the popular 2-1/2" x 3-1/2" size.

		MT
Complete Set (75):		15.00
Common Player:		.15
1	Babe Ruth	3.00
2	Jimmie Foxx	.40
3	Lefty Grove	.30
4	Hank Greenberg	.35
5	Al Simmons	.15
6	Carl Hubbell	.30
7	Joe Cronin	.25
8	Mel Ott	.30
9	Lefty Gomez	.30
10	Lou Gehrig	1.50
11	Pie Traynor	.15
12	Charlie Gehringer	.30
13	Catchers (Mickey Cochrane, Bill Dickey, Gabby Hartnett)	.30
14	Pitchers (Dizzy Dean, Paul Derringer, Red Ruffing)	.30
15	Outfielders (Earl Averill, Joe Medwick, Paul Waner)	.15
16	Bob Feller	.60
17	Lou Boudreau	.15
18	Enos Slaughter	.25
19	Hal Newhouser	.15
20	Joe DiMaggio	1.50
21	Pee Wee Reese	.40
22	Phil Rizzuto	.30
23	Ernie Lombardi	.15
24	Infielders (Joe Cronin, George Kell, Johnny Mize)	.15
25	Ted Williams	2.00
26	Mickey Mantle	4.00
27	Warren Spahn	.30
28	Jackie Robinson	2.00
29	Ernie Banks	.30
30	Stan Musial	1.00
31	Yogi Berra	.60
32	Duke Snider	.75
33	Roy Campanella	.75
34	Eddie Mathews	.30
35	Ralph Kiner	.25
36	Early Wynn	.15
37	Double Play Duo (Luis Aparicio, Nellie Fox)	.50
38	First Basemen (Gil Hodges, Ted Kluszewski, Mickey Vernon)	.35
40	Henry Aaron	1.00
41	Frank Robinson	.30
42	Bob Gibson	.30
43	Roberto Clemente	3.00
44	Whitey Ford	.40
45	Brooks Robinson	.50
46	Juan Marichal	.25
47	Carl Yastrzemski	.60
48	First Basemen (Orlando Cepeda, Harmon Killebrew, Willie McCovey)	.30
49	Catchers (Bill Freehan, Elston Howard, Joe Torre)	.15
50	Willie Mays	1.00
51	Outfielders (Al Kaline, Tony Oliva, Billy Williams)	.30
52	Tom Seaver	.50
53	Reggie Jackson	.75
54	Steve Carlton	.40
55	Mike Schmidt	.75
56	Joe Morgan	.25
57	Jim Rice	.20
58	Jim Palmer	.30
59	Lou Brock	.30
60	Pete Rose	1.50
61	Steve Garvey	.40
62	Catchers (Carlton Fisk, Thurman Munson, Ted Simmons)	.25
63	Pitchers (Vida Blue, Catfish Hunter, Nolan Ryan)	.30
64	George Brett	.75
65	Don Mattingly	1.25
66	Fernando Valenzuela	.20
67	Dale Murphy	.65
68	Wade Boggs	.75
69	Rickey Henderson	.65
70	Eddie Murray	.60
71	Ron Guidry	.25
72	Catchers (Gary Carter, Lance Parrish, Tony Pena)	.25
73	Infielders (Cal Ripken, Jr., Lou Whitaker, Robin Yount)	.75
74	Outfielders (Pedro Guerrero, Tim Raines, Dave Winfield)	.30
75	Dwight Gooden	.30

1986 Sportflics Rookies

The 1986 Rookies set offers 50 cards and features 47 individual rookie players. In addition, there are two Tri-Star cards; one highlights former Rookies of the Year and the other features three prominent players. There is one "Big Six" card featuring six superstars. The full-color photos on the 2-1/2" x 3-1/2" cards use Sportflics three-phase "Magic Motion" animation. The set was packaged in a collector box which also contained 34 trivia cards that measure 1-3/4" x 2". The set was distributed only by hobby dealers.

		MT
Complete Set (50):		8.00
Common Player:		.10
1	John Kruk	.10
2	Edwin Correa	.10
3	Pete Incaviglia	.10
4	Dale Sveum	.10
5	Juan Nieves	.10
6	Will Clark	1.50
7	Wally Joyner	.75
8	Lance McCullers	.10
9	Scott Bailes	.10
10	Dan Plesac	.10
11	Jose Canseco	2.00
12	Bobby Witt	.10
13	Barry Bonds	4.00
14	Andres Thomas	.10
15	Jim Deshaies	.10
16	Ruben Sierra	.10
17	Steve Lombardozzi	.10
18	Cory Snyder	.10
19	Reggie Williams	.10
20	Mitch Williams	.10
21	Glenn Braggs	.10
22	Danny Tartabull	.10
23	Charlie Kerfeld	.10
24	Paul Assenmacher	.10
25	Robby Thompson	.10
26	Bobby Bonilla	.25
27	Andres Galarraga	.40
28	Billy Jo Robidoux	.10
29	Bruce Ruffin	.10
30	Greg Swindell	.10
31	John Cangelosi	.10
32	Jim Traber	.10
33	Russ Morman	.10
34	Barry Larkin	.30
35	Todd Worrell	.10
36	John Cerutti	.10
37	Mike Kingery	.10
38	Mark Eichhorn	.10
39	Scott Bankhead	.10
40	Bo Jackson	.30
41	Greg Mathews	.10
42	Eric King	.10
43	Kal Daniels	.10
44	Calvin Schiraldi	.10
45	Mickey Brantley	.10
46	Outstanding Rookie Seasons (Fred Lynn, Willie Mays, Pete Rose)	.60
47	Outstanding Rookie Seasons (Dwight Gooden, Tom Seaver, Fernando Valenzuela)	.25
48	Outstanding Rookie Seasons (Eddie Murray, Dave Righetti, Cal Ripken, Jr., Steve Sax, Darryl Strawberry)	.50
49	Kevin Mitchell	.10
50	Mike Diaz	.10

1986 Sportflics Dwight Gooden Discs

As the viewing angle changes on these 3-D simulated motion plastic discs, three different pictures of "Dr. K" can be seen, two action and one portrait. The discs are found in two diameters, 2-1/4" and 4-1/2". Fronts have team-color borders of blue with orange lettering. Backs are blank.

		MT
Complete Set:		
(1)	Dwight Gooden (2-1/4")	1.50
(2)	Dwight Gooden (4-1/2")	3.00

1986 Sportflics Jumbo Discs

A portrait and two action pictures of the players are featured in these large-format (4-1/2" diameter) "Magic Motion" discs. Fronts have the player's name below the photos, with a title above. Backs are printed in purple, red, black and white. Discs were available for $5 each with a paper coupon found in Sportflics packs.

		MT
Complete Set (5):		18.00
Common Player:		3.00
	DISCS	
(1)	Wade Boggs	4.00
(2)	Roger Clemens	5.00
(3)	Wally Joyner	3.00
(4)	Mickey Mantle	8.00
(5)	Don Mattingly	4.00
	COUPONS	
(1)	Wade Boggs	.50
(2)	Roger Clemens	1.00
(3)	Wally Joyner	.50
(4)	Mickey Mantle	2.00
(5)	Don Mattingly	1.00

1987 Sportflics

In its second year in the national market, Sportflics' basic issue was again a 200-card set of 2-1/2" x 3-1/2" "Magic Motion" cards, which offer three different photos on the same card, each visible in turn as the card is moved from top to bottom or side to side. Besides single-player cards, the '87 Sportflics set includes several three- and six-player cards, though not as many as in the 1986 set. The card backs feature a small player portrait photo on the single-player cards, an innovation for 1987.

		MT
Complete Set (200):		10.00
Common Player:		.10
1	Don Mattingly	1.00
2	Wade Boggs	1.00
3	Dale Murphy	.50
4	Rickey Henderson	.50
5	George Brett	1.00
6	Eddie Murray	.75
7	Kirby Puckett	1.00

8	Ryne Sandberg	1.00
9	Cal Ripken, Jr.	4.00
10	Roger Clemens	1.00
11	Ted Higuera	.10
12	Steve Sax	.10
13	Chris Brown	.10
14	Jesse Barfield	.10
15	Kent Hrbek	.10
16	Robin Yount	1.00
17	Glenn Davis	.10
18	Hubie Brooks	.10
19	Mike Scott	.10
20	Darryl Strawberry	.25
21	Alvin Davis	.10
22	Eric Davis	.10
23	Danny Tartabull	.10
24a	Cory Snyder (Pat Tabler photo on back)	2.00
24b	Cory Snyder (Pat Tabler photo on back) (facing front, 1/4 swing on front)	2.00
24c	Cory Snyder (Snyder photo on back) (facing to side)	1.00
25	Pete Rose	1.00
26	Wally Joyner	.25
27	Pedro Guerrero	.10
28	Tom Seaver	.75
29	Bob Knepper	.10
30	Mike Schmidt	1.00
31	Tony Gwynn	1.00
32	Don Slaught	.10
33	Todd Worrell	.10
34	Tim Raines	.15
35	Dave Parker	.10
36	Bob Ojeda	.10
37	Pete Incaviglia	.10
38	Bruce Hurst	.10
39	Bobby Witt	.10
40	Steve Garvey	.35
41	Dave Winfield	.75
42	Jose Cruz	.10
43	Orel Hershiser	.10
44	Reggie Jackson	1.00
45	Chili Davis	.10
46	Robby Thompson	.10
47	Dennis Boyd	.10
48	Kirk Gibson	.10
49	Fred Lynn	.10
50	Gary Carter	.25
51	George Bell	.10
52	Pete O'Brien	.10
53	Ron Darling	.10
54	Paul Molitor	.75
55	Mike Pagliarulo	.10
56	Mike Boddicker	.10
57	Dave Righetti	.10
58	Len Dykstra	.15
59	Mike Witt	.10
60	Tony Bernazard	.10
61	John Kruk	.10
62	Mike Krukow	.10
63	Sid Fernandez	.10
64	Gary Gaetti	.10
65	Vince Coleman	.10
66	Pat Tabler	.10
67	Mike Scioscia	.10
68	Scott Garrelts	.10
69	Brett Butler	.10
70	Bill Buckner	.10
71a	Dennis Rasmussen (John Montefusco photo on back)	.25
71b	Dennis Rasmussen (Rasmussen photo on back)	.10
72	Tim Wallach	.10
73	Bob Horner	.10
74	Willie McGee	.10
75	A.L. First Basemen (Wally Joyner, Don Mattingly, Eddie Murray)	.50
76	Jesse Orosco	.10
77	N.L. Relief Pitchers (Jeff Reardon, Dave Smith, Todd Worrell)	.10
78	Candy Maldonado	.10
79	N.L. Shortstops (Hubie Brooks, Shawon Dunston, Ozzie Smith)	.15
80	A.L. Left Fielders (George Bell, Jose Canseco, Jim Rice)	.25
81	Bert Blyleven	.10
82	Mike Marshall	.10
83	Ron Guidry	.10
84	Julio Franco	.10
85	Willie Wilson	.10
86	Lee Lacy	.10
87	Jack Morris	.10
88	Ray Knight	.10
89	Phil Bradley	.10
90	Jose Canseco	.75
91	Gary Ward	.10
92	Mike Easler	.10
93	Tony Pena	.10
94	Dave Smith	.10
95	Will Clark	.75
96	Lloyd Moseby	.10
97	Jim Rice	.10
98	Shawon Dunston	.10
99	Don Sutton	.45
100	Dwight Gooden	.15
101	Lance Parrish	.10
102	Mark Langston	.10
103	Floyd Youmans	.10
104	Lee Smith	.10
105	Willie Hernandez	.10
106	Doug DeCinces	.10
107	Ken Schrom	.10
108	Don Carman	.10
109	Brook Jacoby	.10
110	Steve Bedrosian	.10
111	A.L. Pitchers (Roger Clemens, Teddy Higuera, Jack Morris)	.25
112	A.L. Second Basemen (Marty Barrett, Tony Bernazard, Lou Whitaker)	.10
113	A.L. Shortstops (Tony Fernandez, Scott Fletcher, Cal Ripken, Jr.)	.25
114	A.L. Third Basemen (Wade Boggs, George Brett, Gary Gaetti)	.25
115	N.L. Third Basemen (Chris Brown, Mike Schmidt, Tim Wallach)	.20
116	N.L. Second Basemen (Bill Doran, Johnny Ray, Ryne Sandberg)	.15
117	N.L. Right Fielders (Kevin Bass, Tony Gwynn, Dave Parker)	.15
118	Hot Rookie Prospects (David Clark, Pat Dodson, Ty Gainey, Phil Lombardi, Benito Santiago), *(Terry*	.55
119	1986 Season Highlights (Dave Righetti, Mike Scott, Fernando Valenzuela)	.10
120	N.L. Pitchers (Dwight Gooden, Mike Scott, Fernando Valenzuela)	.10
121	Johnny Ray	.10
122	Keith Moreland	.10
123	Juan Samuel	.10
124	Wally Backman	.10
125	Nolan Ryan	4.00
126	Greg Harris	.10
127	Kirk McCaskill	.10
128	Dwight Evans	.10
129	Rick Rhoden	.10
130	Bill Madlock	.10
131	Oddibe McDowell	.10
132	Darrell Evans	.10
133	Keith Hernandez	.10
134	Tom Brunansky	.10
135	Kevin McReynolds	.10
136	Scott Fletcher	.10
137	Lou Whitaker	.10
138	Carney Lansford	.10
139	Andre Dawson	.25
140	Carlton Fisk	.25
141	Buddy Bell	.10
142	Ozzie Smith	.75
143	Dan Pasqua	.10
144	Kevin Mitchell	.10
145	Bret Saberhagen	.10
146	Charlie Kerfeld	.10
147	Phil Niekro	.45
148	John Candelaria	.10
149	Rich Gedman	.10
150	Fernando Valenzuela	.10
151	N.L. Catchers (Gary Carter, Tony Pena, Mike Scioscia)	.10
152	N.L. Left Fielders (Vince Coleman, Jose Cruz, Tim Raines)	.10
153	A.L. Right Fielders (Harold Baines, Jesse Barfield, Dave Winfield)	.10
154	A.L. Catchers (Rich Gedman, Lance Parrish, Don Slaught)	.10
155	N.L. Center Fielders (Kevin McReynolds, Dale Murphy, Eric Davis)	.15
156	'86 Highlights (Jim Deshaies, Mike Schmidt, Don Sutton)	.10
157	A.L. Speedburners (John Cangelosi, Rickey Henderson, Gary Pettis)	.10
158	Hot Rookie Prospects (Randy Asadoor, Casey Candaele, Dave Cochrane, Rafael Palmeiro, Tim Pyznarski),	.75
159	The Best of the Best (Roger Clemens, Dwight Gooden, Rickey Henderson, Don Mattingly, Dale Murphy, Eddie Murray)	1.00
160	Roger McDowell	.10
161	Brian Downing	.10
162	Bill Doran	.10
163	Don Baylor	.10
164	Alfredo Griffin	.10
165	Don Aase	.10
166	Glenn Wilson	.10
167	Dan Quisenberry	.10
168	Frank White	.10
169	Cecil Cooper	.10
170	Jody Davis	.10
171	Harold Baines	.10
172	Rob Deer	.10
173	John Tudor	.10
174	Larry Parrish	.10
175	Kevin Bass	.10
176	Joe Carter	.10
177	Mitch Webster	.10
178	Dave Kingman	.10
179	Jim Presley	.10
180	Mel Hall	.10
181	Shane Rawley	.10
182	Marty Barrett	.10
183	Damaso Garcia	.10
184	Bobby Grich	.10
185	Leon Durham	.10
186	Ozzie Guillen	.10
187	Tony Fernandez	.10
188	Alan Trammell	.10
189	Jim Clancy	.10
190	Bo Jackson	.35
191	Bob Forsch	.10
192	John Franco	.10
193	Von Hayes	.10
194	A.L. Relief Pitchers (Don Aase, Mark Eichhorn, Dave Righetti)	.10
195	N.L. First Basemen (Will Clark, Glenn Davis, Keith Hernandez)	.20
196	'86 Highlights (Roger Clemens, Joe Cowley, Bob Horner)	.15
197	The Best of the Best (Wade Boggs, George Brett, Hubie Brooks, Tony Gwynn, Tim Raines, Ryne Sandberg)	.80
198	A.L. Center Fielders (Rickey Henderson, Fred Lynn, Kirby Puckett)	.50
199	N.L. Speedburners (Vince Coleman, Tim Raines, Eric Davis)	.10
200	Steve Carlton	.45

1987 Sportflics Rookie Prospects

The Rookie Prospects set consists of 10 cards in standard 2-1/2" x 3-1/2" size. The card fronts feature Sportflics' "Magic Motion" process. Card backs contain a player photo plus a short biography and player personal and statistical information. The set was offered in two separately wrapped mylar packs of five cards to hobby dealers purchasing cases of Sportflics' Team Preview set. Twenty-four packs of "Rookie Prospects" cards were included with each case.

		MT
Complete Set (10):		6.00
Common Player:		.50
1	Terry Steinbach	.50
2	Rafael Palmeiro	2.00
3	Dave Magadan	.50
4	Marvin Freeman	.50
5	Brick Smith	.50
6	B.J. Surhoff	.60
7	John Smiley	.50
8	Alonzo Powell	.50
9	Benny Santiago	.50
10	Devon White	.75

1987 Sportflics Rookies

The Rookies set was issued in two series of 25 cards. The first was released in July with the second series following in October. The cards, which are the standard 2-1/2" x 3-1/2", feature Sportflics' special "Magic Motion" process. The card fronts contain a full-color photo and present three different pictures, depending on how the card is held. The backs also contain a full-color photo along with player statistics and a biography.

		MT
Complete Set (50):		15.00
Common Player:		.20
1	Eric Bell	.20
2	Chris Bosio	.20
3	Bob Brower	.20
4	Jerry Browne	.20
5	Ellis Burks	.45
6	Casey Candaele	.20
7	Ken Gerhart	.20
8	Mike Greenwell	.20
9	Stan Jefferson	.20
10	Dave Magadan	.20
11	Joe Magrane	.20
12	Fred McGriff	3.00
13	Mark McGwire	12.00
14	Mark McLemore	.25
15	Jeff Musselman	.20
16	Matt Nokes	.20
17	Paul O'Neill	.90
18	Luis Polonia	.20
19	Benny Santiago	.25
20	Kevin Seitzer	.20
21	John Smiley	.20
22	Terry Steinbach	.25
23	B.J. Surhoff	.25
24	Devon White	.60
25	Matt Williams	3.00
26	DeWayne Buice	.20
27	Willie Fraser	.20
28	Bill Ripken	.20
29	Mike Henneman	.20
30	Shawn Hillegas	.20
31	Shane Mack	.20
32	Rafael Palmeiro	2.50
33	Mike Jackson	.20
34	Gene Larkin	.20
35	Jimmy Jones	.20
36	Gerald Young	.10
37	Ken Caminiti	.75
38	Sam Horn	.20
39	David Cone	.75
40	Mike Dunne	.20
41	Ken Williams	.20
42	John Morris	.20
43	Jim Lindeman	.20
44	Mike Stanley	.20
45	Les Straker	.20
46	Jeff Robinson	.20
47	Todd Benzinger	.20
48	Jeff Blauser	.20
49	John Marzano	.20
50	Keith Miller	.20

1987 Sportflics Rookie Discs

The 1987 Sportflics Rookie Discs set consists of seven discs which measure 4" in diameter. The front of the discs offer three "Magic Motion" photos in full color, encompassed by a blue border. The disc backs are printed in color and include the team logo, player statistics, biography and the disc number. The set was issued with Cooperstown Timeless Trivia Cards.

		MT
Complete Set (7):		10.00
Common Player:		1.00
1	Casey Candaele	1.00
2	Mark McGwire	6.00
3	Kevin Seitzer	1.00
4	Joe Magrane	1.00
5	Benito Santiago	1.00
6	Dave Magadan	1.00
7	Devon White	2.00

1987 Sportflics Superstar Discs

Released in three series of six discs, the Superstar Disc set features the special "Magic Motion" process. Each disc, which measures 4-1/2" in diameter, contains three different player photos, depending which way it is tilted. A red border, containing 11 stars, the player's name and uniform number, surrounds the photo. The backs have a turquoise border which carries the words "Superstar Disc Collector Series." The backs also include the team logo, player statistics, biography and the disc number. The discs were issued with 18 1-3/4" x 2-1/2" Cooperstown Timeless Trivia Cards.

		MT
Complete Set (18):		27.50
Common Player:		1.00
1	Jose Canseco	1.50
2	Mike Scott	1.00
3	Ryne Sandberg	2.00
4	Mike Schmidt	2.50
5	Dale Murphy	1.50
6	Fernando Valenzuela	1.00
7	Tony Gwynn	2.00
8	Cal Ripken, Jr.	5.00
9	Gary Carter	1.00
10	Cory Snyder	1.00
11	Kirby Puckett	2.50
12	George Brett	2.50
13	Keith Hernandez	1.00
14	Rickey Henderson	1.50
15	Tim Raines	1.00
16	Bo Jackson	1.50
17	Pete Rose	2.50
18	Eric Davis	1.00

1987 Sportflics Team Previews

The 1987 Sportflics Team Preview set appeared to be a good idea, but never caught on with collectors. The intent of the set is to provide a pre-season look at each of the 26 major league clubs. The card backs contain three categories of the team preview: Outlook, Newcomers to Watch and Summary. Using the "Magic Motion" process, 12 different players are featured on the card fronts. Four of the different player photos can be made visible at once. The cards, which measure 2-1/2" x 3-1/2", were issued with team logo/trivia cards in a specially designed box.

		MT
	Complete Set (26):	7.00
	Common Team:	.50
1	Texas Rangers (Scott Fletcher, Greg Harris, Charlie Hough, Pete Incaviglia, Mike Loynd, Oddibe McDowell, Pete O'Brien, Larry Parrish, Ruben Sierra, Don Slaught, Mitch Williams, Bobby Witt)	.50
2	New York Mets (Wally Backman, Gary Carter, Ron Darling, Lenny Dykstra, Sid Fernandez, Dwight Gooden, Keith Hernandez, Dave Magadan, Kevin McReynolds, Randy Myers, Bob Ojeda, Darryl Strawberry)	.50
3	Cleveland Indians (Tony Bernazard, Brett Butler, Tom Candiotti, Joe Carter, Julio Franco, Mel Hall, Brook Jacoby, Phil Niekro, Ken Schrom, Cory Snyder, Greg Swindell, Pat Tabler)	.50
4	Cincinnati Reds (Buddy Bell, Tom Browning, Kal Daniels, John Franco, Bill Gullickson, Tracy Jones, Barry Larkin, Rob Murphy, Paul O'Neill, Dave Parker, Pete Rose, Eric Davis)	.50
5	Toronto Blue Jays (Jesse Barfield, George Bell, John Cerutti, Mark Eichhorn, Tony Fernandez, Tom Henke, Glenallen Hill, Jimmy Key, Fred McGriff, Lloyd Moseby, Dave Stieb, Willie Upshaw)	.50
6	Philadelphia Phillies (Steve Bedrosian, Don Carman, Marvin Freeman, Kevin Gross, Von Hayes, Shane Rawley, Bruce Ruffin, Mike Schmidt, Kent Tekulve, Milt Thompson, Glenn Wilson)	.50
7	New York Yankees (Rickey Henderson, Phil Lombardi, Don Mattingly, Mike Pagliarulo, Dan Pasqua, Willie Randolph, Dennis Rasmussen, Rick Rhoden, Dave Righetti, Joel Skinner, Bob Tewksbury, Dave Winfield)	1.00
8	Houston Astros (Kevin Bass, Jose Cruz, Glenn Davis, Jim Deshaies, Bill Doran, Ty Gainey, Charlie Kerfeld, Bob Knepper, Nolan Ryan, Mike Scott, Dave Smith, Robby Wine)	1.00
9	Boston Red Sox (Marty Barrett, Don Baylor, Wade Boggs, Dennis Boyd, Roger Clemens, Pat Dodson, Dwight Evans, Mike Greenweld, Dave Henderson, Bruce Hurst, Jim Rice, Calvin Schiraldi)	.50
10	San Francisco Giants (Bob Brenly, Chris Brown, Will Clark, Chili Davis, Kelly Downs, Scott Garrelts, Mark Grant, Mike Krukow, Jeff Leonard, Candy Maldonado, Terry Mulholland, Robby Thompson)	.50
11	California Angels (John Candelaria, Doug DeCinces, Brian Downing, Ruppert Jones, Wally Joyner, Kirk McCaskill, Darrell Miller, Donnie Moore, Gary Pettis, Don Sutton, Devon White, Mike Witt)	.50
12	St. Louis Cardinals (Jack Clark, Vince Coleman, Danny Cox, Bob Forsch, Tom Herr, Joe Magrane, Willie McGee, Terry Pendleton, Ozzie Smith, John Tudor, Andy Van Slyke, Todd Worrell)	.50
13	Kansas City Royals (George Brett, Mark Gubicza, Bo Jackson, Charlie Leibrandt, Hal McRae, Dan Quisenberry, Bret Saberhagen, Kevin Seitzer, Lonnie Smith, Danny Tartabull, Frank White, Willie Wilson)	.65
14	Los Angeles Dodgers (Ralph Bryant, Mariano Duncan, Jose Gonzalez, Pedro Guerrero, Orel Hershiser, Mike Marshall, Steve Sax, Mike Scioscia, Mike Sciosccia, Franklin Stubbs, Fernando Valenzuela, Reggie Williams, Matt Young)	.50
15	Detroit Tigers (Darnell Coles, Darrell Evans, Kirk Gibson, Willie Hernandez, Eric King, Chet Lemon, Dwight Lowry, Jack Morris, Dan Petry, Frank Tanana, Alan Trammell, Lou Whitaker)	.50
16	San Diego Padres (Randy Asadoor, Steve Garvey, Tony Gwynn, Andy Hawkins, Jim Jones, John Kruk, Craig Lefferts, Shane Mack, Lance McCullers, Kevin Mitchell, Benny Santiago, Ed Wojna)	.50
17	Minnesota Twins (Bert Blyleven, Tom Brunansky, Gary Gaetti, Greg Gagne, Kent Hrbek, Joe Klink, Steve Lombardozzi, Kirby Puckett, Jeff Reardon, Mark Salas, Roy Smalley, Frank Viola)	.50
18	Pittsburgh Pirates (Barry Bonds, Bobby Bonilla, Sid Bream, Mike Diaz, Brian Fisher, Jim Morrison, Joe Orsulak, Bob Patterson, Tony Pena, Johnny Ray, R.J. Reynolds, John Smiley)	.60
19	Milwaukee Brewers (Glenn Braggs, Rob Deer, Teddy Higuera, Paul Molitor, Juan Nieves, Dan Plesac, Tim Pyznarski, Ernest Riles, Billy Jo Robidoux, B.J. Surhoff, Dale Sveum, Robin Yount)	.50
20	Montreal Expos (Hubie Brooks, Tim Burke, Casey Candaele, Dave Collins, Mike Fitzgerald, Andres Galarraga, Billy Moore, Alonzo Powell, Randy St. Claire, Tim Wallach, Mitch Webster, Floyd Youmans)	.50
21	Baltimore Orioles (Don Aase, Eric Bell, Mike Boddicker, Ken Gerhardt, Terry Kennedy, Ray Knight, Lee Lacy, Fred Lynn, Eddie Murray, Cal Ripken, Jr., Larry Sheets, Jim Traber)	1.00
22	Chicago Cubs (Jody Davis, Shawon Dunston, Leon Durham, Dennis Eckersley, Greg Maddux, Dave Martinez, Keith Mooreland, Jerry Mumphrey, Rafael Palmeiro, Ryne Sandberg, Scott Sanderson, Lee Smith)	.50
23	Oakland Athletics (Jose Canseco, Mike Davis, Alfredo Griffin, Reggie Jackson, Carney Lansford, Mark McGwire, Dwayne Murphy, Rob Nelson, Tony Phillips, Jose Rijo, Terry Steinbach, Curt Young)	3.00
24	Atlanta Braves (Paul Assenmacher, Gene Garber, Tom Glavine, Ken Griffey, Glenn Hubbard, Dion James, Rick Mahler, Dale Murphy, Ken Oberkfell, David Palmer, Zane Smith, Andres Thomas)	.50
25	Seattle Mariners (Scott Bankhead, Phil Bradley, Scott Bradley, Mickey Brantley, Alvin Davis, Steve Fireovid, Mark Langston, Mike Moore, Donell Nixon, Ken Phelps, Jim Presley, Dave Valle)	.50
26	Chicago White Sox (Harold Baines, John Cangelosi, Dave Cochrane, Joe Cowley, Carlton Fisk, Ozzie Guillen, Ron Hassy, Bob James, Ron Karkovice, Russ Mormon, Bobby Thigpen, Greg Walker)	.50

1988 Sportflics

The design of the 1988 Sportflics set differs greatly from the previous two years. Besides increasing the number of cards in the set to 225, Sportflics included the player name, team and uniform number on the card front. The triple-action color photos are surrounded by a red border. The backs are re-designed, also. Full-color action photos, plus extensive statistics and informative biographies are utilized. Three highlights cards and three rookie prospects card are included in the set. The cards are the standard 2-1/2" x 3-1/2".

		MT
	Complete Set (225):	20.00
	Common Player:	.10
1	Don Mattingly	1.00
2	Tim Raines	.15
3	Andre Dawson	.25
4	George Bell	.10
5	Joe Carter	.10
6	Matt Nokes	.10
7	Dave Winfield	.75
8	Kirby Puckett	1.00
9	Will Clark	.75
10	Eric Davis	.15
11	Rickey Henderson	.65
12	Ryne Sandberg	1.00
13	Jesse Barfield	.10
14	Ozzie Guillen	.10
15	Bret Saberhagen	.12
16	Tony Gwynn	1.50
17	Kevin Seitzer	.10
18	Jack Clark	.10
19	Danny Tartabull	.10
20	Ted Higuera	.10
21	Charlie Leibrandt, Jr.	.10
22	Benny Santiago	.10
23	Fred Lynn	.10
24	Rob Thompson	.10
25	Alan Trammell	.10
26	Tony Fernandez	.10
27	Rick Sutcliffe	.10
28	Gary Carter	.20
29	Cory Snyder	.10
30	Lou Whitaker	.10
31	Keith Hernandez	.10
32	Mike Witt	.10
33	Harold Baines	.10
34	Robin Yount	1.50
35	Mike Schmidt	1.00
36	Dion James	.10
37	Tom Candiotti	.10
38	Tracy Jones	.10
39	Nolan Ryan	2.50
40	Fernando Valenzuela	.10
41	Vance Law	.10
42	Roger McDowell	.10
43	Carlton Fisk	.20
44	Scott Garrelts	.10
45	Lee Guetterman	.10
46	Mark Langston	.10
47	Willie Randolph	.10
48	Bill Doran	.10
49	Larry Parrish	.10
50	Wade Boggs	.65
51	Shane Rawley	.10
52	Alvin Davis	.10
53	Jeff Reardon	.10
54	Jim Presley	.10
55	Kevin Bass	.10
56	Kevin McReynolds	.10
57	B.J. Surhoff	.10
58	Julio Franco	.10
59	Eddie Murray	.40
60	Jody Davis	.10
61	Todd Worrell	.10
62	Von Hayes	.10
63	Billy Hatcher	.10
64	John Kruk	.10
65	Tom Henke	.10
66	Mike Scott	.10
67	Vince Coleman	.10
68	Ozzie Smith	.75
69	Ken Williams	.10
70	Steve Bedrosian	.10
71	Luis Polonia	.10
72	Brook Jacoby	.10
73	Ron Darling	.10
74	Lloyd Moseby	.10
75	Wally Joyner	.10
76	Dan Quisenberry	.10
77	Scott Fletcher	.10
78	Kirk McCaskill	.10
79	Paul Molitor	1.00
80	Mike Aldrete	.10
81	Neal Heaton	.10
82	Jeffrey Leonard	.10
83	Dave Magadan	.10
84	Danny Cox	.10
85	Lance McCullers	.10
86	Jay Howell	.10
87	Charlie Hough	.10
88	Gene Garber	.10
89	Jesse Orosco	.10
90	Don Robinson	.10
91	Willie McGee	.10
92	Bert Blyleven	.10
93	Phil Bradley	.10
94	Terry Kennedy	.10
95	Kent Hrbek	.10
96	Juan Samuel	.10
97	Pedro Guerrero	.10
98	Sid Bream	.10
99	Devon White	.10
100	Mark McGwire	3.00
101	Dave Parker	.10
102	Glenn Davis	.10
103	Greg Walker	.10
104	Rick Rhoden	.10
105	Mitch Webster	.10
106	Lenny Dykstra	.10
107	Gene Larkin	.10
108	Floyd Youmans	.10
109	Andy Van Slyke	.10
110	Mike Scioscia	.10
111	Kirk Gibson	.10
112	Kal Daniels	.10
113	Ruben Sierra	.10
114	Sam Horn	.10
115	Ray Knight	.10
116	Jimmy Key	.10
117	Bo Diaz	.10
118	Mike Greenwell	.10
119	Barry Bonds	1.50
120	Reggie Jackson	.75
121	Mike Pagliarulo	.10
122	Tommy John	.10
123	Bill Madlock	.10
124	Ken Caminiti	.30
125	Gary Ward	.10
126	Candy Maldonado	.10
127	Harold Reynolds	.10
128	Joe Magrane	.10
129	Mike Henneman	.10
130	Jim Gantner	.10
131	Bobby Bonilla	.10
132	John Farrell	.10
133	Frank Tanana	.10
134	Zane Smith	.10
135	Dave Righetti	.10
136	Rick Reuschel	.10
137	Dwight Evans	.10
138	Howard Johnson	.10
139	Terry Leach	.10
140	Casey Candaele	.10
141	Tom Herr	.10
142	Tony Pena	.10
143	Lance Parrish	.10
144	Ellis Burks	.15
145	Pete O'Brien	.10
146	Mike Boddicker	.10
147	Buddy Bell	.10
148	Bo Jackson	.35
149	Frank White	.10
150	George Brett	1.50
151	Tim Wallach	.10
152	Cal Ripken, Jr.	2.50
153	Brett Butler	.10
154	Gary Gaetti	.10
155	Darryl Strawberry	.20
156	Alfredo Griffin	.10
157	Marty Barrett	.10
158	Jim Rice	.10
159	Terry Pendleton	.10
160	Orel Hershiser	.10
161	Larry Sheets	.10
162	Dave Stewart	.10
163	Shawon Dunston	.10
164	Keith Moreland	.10
165	Ken Oberkfell	.10
166	Ivan Calderon	.10
167	Bob Welch	.10
168	Fred McGriff	.50
169	Pete Incaviglia	.10
170	Dale Murphy	.25
171	Mike Dunne	.10
172	Chili Davis	.10
173	Milt Thompson	.10
174	Terry Steinbach	.10
175	Oddibe McDowell	.10
176	Jack Morris	.10
177	Sid Fernandez	.10
178	Ken Griffey	.10
179	Lee Smith	.10
180	1987 Highlights (Juan Nieves, Kirby Puckett, Mike Schmidt)	.25
181	Brian Downing	.10
182	Andres Galarraga	.25

183	Rob Deer	.10
184	Greg Brock	.10
185	Doug DeCinces	.10
186	Johnny Ray	.10
187	Hubie Brooks	.10
188	Darrell Evans	.10
189	Mel Hall	.10
190	Jim Deshaies	.10
191	Dan Plesac	.10
192	Willie Wilson	.10
193	Mike LaValliere	.10
194	Tom Brunansky	.10
195	John Franco	.10
196	Frank Viola	.10
197	Bruce Hurst	.10
198	John Tudor	.10
199	Bob Forsch	.10
200	Dwight Gooden	.15
201	Jose Canseco	.75
202	Carney Lansford	.10
203	Kelly Downs	.10
204	Glenn Wilson	.10
205	Pat Tabler	.10
206	Mike Davis	.10
207	Roger Clemens	1.00
208	Dave Smith	.10
209	Curt Young	.10
210	Mark Eichhorn	.10
211	Juan Nieves	.10
212	Bob Boone	.10
213	Don Sutton	.25
214	Willie Upshaw	.10
215	Jim Clancy	.10
216	Bill Ripken	.10
217	Ozzie Virgil	.10
218	Dave Concepcion	.10
219	Alan Ashby	.10
220	Mike Marshall	.10
221	'87 Highlights (Vince Coleman, Mark McGwire, Paul Molitor)	2.00
222	'87 Highlights (Steve Bedrosian, Don Mattingly, Benito Santiago)	.40
223	Hot Rookie Prospects (Shawn Abner), *(Jay Buhner*, Gary Thurman)	.25
224	Hot Rookie Prospects (Tim Crews, John Davis, Vincente Palacios)	.10
225	Hot Rookie Prospects (Keith Miller, Jody Reed, Jeff Treadway)	.10

1988 Sportflics Gamewinners

This set of 25 standard-size cards (2-1/2" x 3-1/2"), featuring star players in the Sportflics patented 3-D Magic Motion design, was issued by Weiser Card Co. of Plainsboro, N.J., for use as a youth organizational fundraiser. (Weiser's president was former Yankees outfielder Bobby Murcer.) A limited number of sets was produced for test marketing in the Northwestern U.S., with plans for a 1989 set to be marketed nationwide. A green-and-yellow Gamewinners logo banner spans the upper border of the cards face, with a matching player name (with uniform number and position) below the full-color triple photo. The card backs carry large full-color player photos along with stats, personal information and career highlights.

		MT
Complete Set (25):		9.00
Common Player:		.20
1	Don Mattingly	1.50
2	Mark McGwire	3.00
3	Wade Boggs	.65
4	Will Clark	.50
5	Eric Davis	.25
6	Willie Randolph	.20
7	Dave Winfield	.65
8	Rickey Henderson	.60
9	Dwight Gooden	.30
10	Benny Santiago	.20
11	Keith Hernandez	.20
12	Juan Samuel	.20
13	Kevin Seitzer	.20
14	Gary Carter	.30
15	Darryl Strawberry	.30
16	Rick Rhoden	.20
17	Howard Johnson	.20
18	Matt Nokes	.20
19	Dave Righetti	.20
20	Roger Clemens	1.50
21	Mike Schmidt	1.00
22	Kevin McReynolds	.20
23	Mike Pagliarulo	.20
24	Kevin Elster	.20
25	Jack Clark	.20

1989 Sportflics

This basic issue includes 225 standard-size player cards (2-1/2" x 3-1/2") and 153 trivia cards, all featuring the patented Magic Motion design. A 5-card sub-set of "Tri-Star" cards features a mix of veterans and rookies. The card fronts feature a white outer border and double color inner border in one of six color schemes. The inner border color changes when the card is tilted and the bottom border carries a double stripe of colors. The player name appears in the top border, player position and uniform number appear, alternately, in the bottom border. The card backs contain crisp 1-7/8" by 1-3/4" player action shots, along with personal information, stats and career highlights. "The Unforgettables" trivia cards in this set salute members of the Hall of Fame.

		MT
Complete Set (225):		20.00
Common Player:		.10
1	Jose Canseco	.60
2	Wally Joyner	.20
3	Roger Clemens	.75
4	Greg Swindell	.10
5	Jack Morris	.10
6	Mickey Brantley	.10
7	Jim Presley	.10
8	Pete O'Brien	.10
9	Jesse Barfield	.10
10	Frank Viola	.10
11	Kevin Bass	.10
12	Glenn Wilson	.10
13	Chris Sabo	.10
14	Fred McGriff	.50
15	Mark Grace	.25
16	Devon White	.10
17	Juan Samuel	.10
18	Lou Whitaker	.10
19	Greg Walker	.10
20	Roberto Alomar	.50
21	Mike Schmidt	.75
22	Benny Santiago	.10
23	Dave Stewart	.10
24	Dave Winfield	.40
25	George Bell	.10
26	Jack Clark	.10
27	Doug Drabek	.10
28	Ron Gant	.15
29	Glenn Braggs	.10
30	Rafael Palmeiro	.25
31	Brett Butler	.10
32	Ron Darling	.10
33	Alvin Davis	.10
34	Bob Walk	.10
35	Dave Stieb	.10
36	Orel Hershiser	.10
37	John Farrell	.10
38	Doug Jones	.10
39	Kelly Downs	.10
40	Bob Boone	.10
41	Gary Sheffield	.60
42	Doug Dascenzo	.10
43	Chad Krueter	.10
44	Ricky Jordan	.10
45	Dave West	.10
46	Danny Tartabull	.10
47	Teddy Higuera	.10
48	Gary Gaetti	.10
49	Dave Parker	.10
50	Don Mattingly	1.00
51	David Cone	.10
52	Kal Daniels	.10
53	Carney Lansford	.10
54	Mike Marshall	.10
55	Kevin Seitzer	.10
56	Mike Henneman	.10
57	Bill Doran	.10
58	Steve Sax	.10
59	Lance Parrish	.10
60	Keith Hernandez	.10
61	Jose Uribe	.10
62	Jose Lind	.10
63	Steve Bedrosian	.10
64	George Brett	.75
65	Kirk Gibson	.10
66	Cal Ripken, Jr.	2.00
67	Mitch Webster	.10
68	Fred Lynn	.10
69	Eric Davis	.10
70	Bo Jackson	.50
71	Kevin Elster	.10
72	Rick Reuschel	.10
73	Tim Burke	.10
74	Mark Davis	.10
75	Claudell Washington	.10
76	Lance McCullers	.10
77	Mike Moore	.10
78	Robby Thompson	.10
79	Roger McDowell	.10
80	Danny Jackson	.10
81	Tim Leary	.10
82	Bobby Witt	.10
83	Jim Gott	.10
84	Andy Hawkins	.10
85	Ozzie Guillen	.10
86	John Tudor	.10
87	Todd Burns	.10
88	Dave Gallagher	.10
89	Jay Buhner	.10
90	Gregg Jefferies	.25
91	Bob Welch	.10
92	Charlie Hough	.10
93	Tony Fernandez	.10
94	Ozzie Virgil	.10
95	Andre Dawson	.25
96	Hubie Brooks	.10
97	Kevin McReynolds	.10
98	Mike LaValliere	.10
99	Terry Pendleton	.10
100	Wade Boggs	.75
101	Dennis Eckersley	.10
102	Mark Gubicza	.10
103	Frank Tanana	.10
104	Joe Carter	.10
105	Ozzie Smith	.40
106	Dennis Martinez	.10
107	Jeff Treadway	.10
108	Greg Maddux	1.00
109	Bret Saberhagen	.10
110	Dale Murphy	.25
111	Rob Deer	.10
112	Pete Incaviglia	.10
113	Vince Coleman	.10
114	Tim Wallach	.10
115	Nolan Ryan	2.00
116	Walt Weiss	.10
117	Brian Downing	.10
118	Melido Perez	.10
119	Terry Steinbach	.10
120	Mike Scott	.10
121	Tim Belcher	.10
122	Mike Boddicker	.10
123	Len Dykstra	.10
124	Fernando Valenzuela	.10
125	Gerald Young	.10
126	Tom Henke	.10
127	Dave Henderson	.10
128	Dan Plesac	.10
129	Chili Davis	.10
130	Bryan Harvey	.10
131	Don August	.10
132	Mike Harkey	.10
133	Luis Polonia	.10
134	Craig Worthington	.10
135	Joey Meyer	.10
136	Barry Larkin	.20
137	Glenn Davis	.10
138	Mike Scioscia	.10
139	Andres Galarraga	.20
140	Doc Gooden	.15
141	Keith Moreland	.10
142	Kevin Mitchell	.10
143	Mike Greenwell	.10
144	Mel Hall	.10
145	Rickey Henderson	.35
146	Barry Bonds	1.00
147	Eddie Murray	.40
148	Lee Smith	.10
149	Julio Franco	.10
150	Tim Raines	.10
151	Mitch Williams	.10
152	Tim Laudner	.10
153	Mike Pagliarulo	.10
154	Floyd Bannister	.10
155	Gary Carter	.25
156	Kirby Puckett	.75
157	Harold Baines	.10
158	Dave Righetti	.10
159	Mark Langston	.10
160	Tony Gwynn	.75
161	Tom Brunansky	.10
162	Vance Law	.10
163	Kelly Gruber	.10
164	Gerald Perry	.10
165	Harold Reynolds	.10
166	Andy Van Slyke	.10
167	Jimmy Key	.10
168	Jeff Reardon	.10
169	Milt Thompson	.10
170	Will Clark	.65
171	Chet Lemon	.10
172	Pat Tabler	.10
173	Jim Rice	.10
174	Billy Hatcher	.10
175	Bruce Hurst	.10
176	John Franco	.10
177	Van Snider	.10
178	Ron Jones	.10
179	Jerald Clark	.10
180	Tom Browning	.10
181	Von Hayes	.10
182	Bobby Bonilla	.10
183	Todd Worrell	.10
184	John Kruk	.10
185	Scott Fletcher	.10
186	Willie Wilson	.10
187	Jody Davis	.10
188	Kent Hrbek	.10
189	Ruben Sierra	.10
190	Shawon Dunston	.10
191	Ellis Burks	.15
192	Brook Jacoby	.10
193	Jeff Robinson	.10
194	Rich Dotson	.10
195	Johnny Ray	.10
196	Cory Snyder	.10
197	Mike Witt	.10
198	Marty Barrett	.10
199	Robin Yount	.75
200	Mark McGwire	2.50
201	Ryne Sandberg	.75
202	John Candelaria	.10
203	Matt Nokes	.10
204	Dwight Evans	.10
205	Darryl Strawberry	.25
206	Willie McGee	.10
207	Bobby Thigpen	.10
208	B.J. Surhoff	.10
209	Paul Molitor	.40
210	Jody Reed	.10
211	Doyle Alexander	.10
212	Dennis Rasmussen	.10
213	Kevin Gross	.10
214	Kirk McCaskill	.10
215	Alan Trammell	.10
216	Damon Berryhill	.10
217	Rick Sutcliffe	.10
218	Don Slaught	.10
219	Carlton Fisk	.25
220	Allan Anderson	.10
221	'88 Highlights (Wade Boggs, Jose Canseco, Mike Greenwell)	.50
222	'88 Highlights (Tom Browning, Dennis Eckersley, Orel Hershiser)	.10
223	Hot Rookie Prospects (Sandy Alomar, Gregg Jefferies, Gary Sheffield)	1.00
224	Hot Rookie Prospects (Randy Johnson, Ramon Martinez, Bob Milacki)	2.00
225	Hot Rookie Prospects (Geronimo Berroa, Cameron Drew, Ron Jones)	.10

1990 Sportflics

The Sportflics set for 1990 again contains 225 cards. The cards feature the unique "Magic Motion" effect which displays either of two different photos depending on how the card is tilted. (Previous years' sets had used three photos per card.) The two-photo "Magic Motion" sequence is designed to depict sequential game-action, showing a batter following through on his swing, a pitcher completing his motion, etc. Sportflics also added a moving red and yellow "marquee" border on the cards to complement the animation effect. The player's name, which appears below the animation, remains stationary. The set includes 19 special rookie cards. The backs contain a color player photo, team logo, player information and stats. The cards were distributed in non-transparent mylar packs with small MVP trivia cards.

		MT
Complete Set (225):		18.00
Common Player:		.10
1	Kevin Mitchell	.10
2	Wade Boggs	.75
3	Cory Snyder	.10
4	Paul O'Neill	.20
5	Will Clark	.50
6	Tony Fernandez	.10
7	Ken Griffey, Jr.	3.00
8	Nolan Ryan	2.00
9	Rafael Palmeiro	.25
10	Jesse Barfield	.10
11	Kirby Puckett	.75
12	Steve Sax	.10
13	Fred McGriff	.40
14	Gregg Jefferies	.20
15	Mark Grace	.25
16	Devon White	.10
17	Juan Samuel	.10
18	Robin Yount	.75
19	Glenn Davis	.10
20	Jeffrey Leonard	.10
21	Chili Davis	.10
22	Craig Biggio	.25
23	Jose Canseco	.60
24	Derek Lilliquist	.10
25	Chris Bosio	.10
26	Dave Steib	.10
27	Bobby Thigpen	.10
28	Jack Clark	.10
29	Kevin Ritz	.10
30	Tom Gordon	.10
31	Bryan Harvey	.10
32	Jim Deshaies	.10
33	Terry Steinbach	.10
34	Tom Glavine	.15
35	Bob Welch	.10
36	Charlie Hayes	.10
37	Jeff Reardon	.10
38	Joe Orsulak	.10
39	Scott Garrelts	.10
40	Bob Boone	.10
41	Scott Bankhead	.10
42	Tom Henke	.10
43	Greg Briley	.10
44	Teddy Higuera	.10
45	Pat Borders	.10
46	Kevin Seitzer	.10
47	Bruce Hurst	.10
48	Ozzie Guillen	.10
49	Wally Joyner	.15
50	Mike Greenwell	.10
51	Gary Gaetti	.10
52	Gary Sheffield	.40
53	Dennis Martinez	.10
54	Ryne Sandberg	.60
55	Mike Scott	.10
56	Todd Benzinger	.10
57	Kelly Gruber	.10
58	Jose Lind	.10
59	Allan Anderson	.10
60	Robby Thompson	.10
61	John Smoltz	.15
62	Mark Davis	.10
63	Tom Herr	.10
64	Randy Johnson	.45
65	Lonnie Smith	.10
66	Pedro Guerrero	.10
67	Jerome Walton	.10
68	Ramon Martinez	.10
69	Tim Raines	.10
70	Matt Williams	.40
71	Joe Oliver	.10
72	Nick Esasky	.10
73	Kevin Brown	.15
74	Walt Weiss	.10
75	Roger McDowell	.10
76	Jose DeLeon	.10
77	Brian Downing	.10
78	Jay Howell	.10
79	Jose Uribe	.10
80	Ellis Burks	.15
81	Sammy Sosa	2.50
82	Johnny Ray	.10
83	Danny Darwin	.10
84	Carney Lansford	.10
85	Jose Oquendo	.10
86	John Cerutti	.10
87	Dave Winfield	.40
88	Dave Righetti	.10
89	Danny Jackson	.10
90	Andy Benes	.20
91	Tom Browning	.10
92	Pete O'Brien	.10
93	Roberto Alomar	.50
94	Bret Saberhagen	.10
95	Phil Bradley	.10
96	Doug Jones	.10
97	Eric Davis	.10
98	Tony Gwynn	1.00
99	Jim Abbott	.10
100	Cal Ripken, Jr.	2.00
101	Andy Van Slyke	.10

102 Dan Plesac .10
103 Lou Whitaker .10
104 Steve Bedrosian .10
105 Dave Gallagher .10
106 Keith Hernandez .10
107 Duane Ward .10
108 Andre Dawson .15
109 Howard Johnson .10
110 Mark Langston .10
111 Jerry Browne .10
112 Alvin Davis .10
113 Sid Fernandez .10
114 Mike Devereaux .10
115 Benny Santiago .10
116 Bip Roberts .10
117 Craig Worthington .10
118 Kevin Elster .10
119 Harold Reynolds .10
120 Joe Carter .10
121 Brian Harper .10
122 Frank Viola .10
123 Jeff Ballard .10
124 John Kruk .10
125 Harold Baines .10
126 Tom Candiotti .10
127 Kevin McReynolds .10
128 Mookie Wilson .10
129 Danny Tartabull .10
130 Craig Lefferts .10
131 Jose DeJesus .10
132 John Orton .10
133 Curt Schilling .10
134 Marquis Grissom .10
135 Greg Vaughn .10
136 Brett Butler .10
137 Rob Deer .10
138 John Franco .10
139 Keith Moreland .10
140 Dave Smith .10
141 Mark McGwire 3.00
142 Vince Coleman .10
143 Barry Bonds .75
144 Mike Henneman .10
145 Doc Gooden .15
146 Darryl Strawberry .15
147 Von Hayes .10
148 Andres Galarraga .15
149 Roger Clemens .75
150 Don Mattingly 1.00
151 Joe Magrane .10
152 Dwight Smith .10
153 Ricky Jordan .10
154 Alan Trammell .10
155 Brook Jacoby .10
156 Lenny Dykstra .10
157 Mike LaValliere .10
158 Julio Franco .10
159 Joey Belle .75
160 Barry Larkin .20
161 Rick Reuschel .10
162 Nelson Santovenia .10
163 Mike Scioscia .10
164 Damon Berryhill .10
165 Todd Worrell .10
166 Jim Eisenreich .10
167 Ivan Calderon .10
168 Goose Gozzo .10
169 Kirk McCaskill .10
170 Dennis Eckersley .10
171 Mickey Tettleton .10
172 Chuck Finley .10
173 Dave Magadan .10
174 Terry Pendleton .10
175 Willie Randolph .10
176 Jeff Huson .10
177 Todd Zeile .10
178 Steve Olin .10
179 Eric Anthony .10
180 Scott Coolbaugh .10
181 Rick Sutcliffe .10
182 Tim Wallach .10
183 Paul Molitor .75
184 Roberto Kelly .10
185 Mike Moore .10
186 Junior Felix .10
187 Mike Schooler .10
188 Ruben Sierra .10
189 Dale Murphy .20
190 Dan Gladden .10
191 John Smiley .10
192 Jeff Russell .10
193 Bert Blyleven .10
194 Dave Stewart .10
195 Bobby Bonilla .10
196 Mitch Williams .10
197 Orel Hershiser .10
198 Kevin Bass .10
199 Tim Burke .10
200 Bo Jackson .40
201 David Cone .10
202 Gary Pettis .10
203 Kent Hrbek .10
204 Carlton Fisk .15
205 Bob Geren .10
206 Bill Spiers .10
207 Oddibe McDowell .10
208 Rickey Henderson .40
209 Ken Caminiti .15
210 Devon White .10
211 Greg Maddux 1.00
212 Ed Whitson .10
213 Carlos Martinez .10
214 George Brett .75
215 Gregg Olson .10
216 Kenny Rogers .10
217 Dwight Evans .10
218 Pat Tabler .10
219 Jeff Treadway .10
220 Scott Fletcher .10
221 Deion Sanders .40
222 Robin Ventura .15
223 Chip Hale .10
224 Tommy Greene .10
225 Dean Palmer .10

1994 Sportflics 2000 Promos

To reintroduce its "Magic Motion" baseball cards to the hobby (last produced by Score in 1990), Pinnacle Brands produced a three-card promo set which it sent to dealers along with a header card explaining the issue. In the same format as the regular issue, though some different photos were used, the promos feature on front what Sportflics calls "state-of-the-art lenticular technology" to create an action effect when the card is moved. Backs are produced by standard printing techniques and are gold-foil highlighted and UV-coated. Each of the promo cards has a large black "SAMPLE" overprinted diagonally across front and back.

		MT
Complete Set (4):		12.00
Common Player:		4.00
1	Lenny Dykstra	1.00
7	Javy Lopez (Shakers)	4.00
193	Greg Maddux (Starflics)	10.00
	Header card	.40
7	Javy Lopez (Shakers)	16.00
----	Header card	.40

1994 Sportflics 2000

The concept of "Magic Motion" baseball cards returned to the hobby in 1994 after a three-year hiatus. Pinnacle Brands refined its "state-of-the-art lenticular technology" to produce cards which show alternating pictures when viewed from different angles on the basic cards, and to create a striking 3-D effect on its "Starflics" A.L. and N.L. all-star team subset. Backs use conventional printing techniques and are UV-coated and gold-foil highlighted, featuring a player photo and recent stats. Cards were sold in eight-card foil packs with a suggested retail price of $2.49.

		MT
Complete Set (193):		20.00
Common Player:		.10
Wax Box:		30.00
1	Len Dykstra	.10
2	Mike Stanley	.10
3	Alex Fernandez	.10
4	Mark McGuire (McGwire)	3.00
5	Eric Karros	.10
6	Dave Justice	.15
7	Jeff Bagwell	.75
8	Darren Lewis	.10
9	David McCarty	.10
10	Albert Belle	.60
11	Ben McDonald	.10
12	Joe Carter	.10
13	Benito Santiago	.10
14	Rob Dibble	.10
15	Roger Clemens	.60
16	Travis Fryman	.10
17	Doug Drabek	.10
18	Jay Buhner	.10
19	Orlando Merced	.10
20	Ryan Klesko	.40
21	Chuck Finley	.10
22	Dante Bichette	.30
23	Wally Joyner	.10
24	Robin Yount	.60
25	Tony Gwynn	.75
26	Allen Watson	.10
27	Rick Wilkins	.10
28	Gary Sheffield	.30
29	John Burkett	.10
30	Randy Johnson	.30
31	Roberto Alomar	.50
32	Fred McGriff	.30
33	Ozzie Guillen	.10
34	Jimmy Key	.10
35	Juan Gonzalez	1.00
36	Wil Cordero	.10
37	Aaron Sele	.10
38	Mark Langston	.10
39	David Cone	.10
40	John Jaha	.10
41	Ozzie Smith	.60
42	Kirby Puckett	1.00
43	Kenny Lofton	.45
44	Mike Mussina	.30
45	Ryne Sandberg	.75
46	Robby Thompson	.10
47	Bryan Harvey	.10
48	Marquis Grissom	.10
49	Bobby Bonilla	.10
50	Dennis Eckersley	.10
51	Curt Schilling	.10
52	Andy Benes	.10
53	Greg Maddux	2.00
54	Bill Swift	.10
55	Andres Galarraga	.20
56	Tony Phillips	.10
57	Darryl Hamilton	.10
58	Duane Ward	.10
59	Bernie Williams	.30
60	Steve Avery	.10
61	Eduardo Perez	.10
62	Jeff Conine	.10
63	Dave Winfield	.25
64	Phil Plantier	.10
65	Ray Lankford	.10
66	Robin Ventura	.10
67	Mike Piazza	2.00
68	Jason Bere	.10
69	Cal Ripken, Jr.	2.50
70	Frank Thomas	1.50
71	Carlos Baerga	.10
72	Darryl Kile	.10
73	Ruben Sierra	.10
74	Gregg Jefferies	.10
75	John Olerud	.10
76	Andy Van Slyke	.10
77	Larry Walker	.30
78	Cecil Fielder	.10
79	Andre Dawson	.15
80	Tom Glavine	.20
81	Sammy Sosa	1.00
82	Charlie Hayes	.10
83	Chuck Knoblauch	.15
84	Kevin Appier	.10
85	Dean Palmer	.10
86	Royce Clayton	.10
87	Moises Alou	.10
88	Ivan Rodriguez	.60
89	Tim Salmon	.35
90	Ron Gant	.10
91	Barry Bonds	.75
92	Jack McDowell	.10
93	Alan Trammell	.10
94	Dwight Gooden	.10
95	Jay Bell	.10
96	Devon White	.10
97	Wilson Alvarez	.10
98	Jim Thome	.20
99	Ramon Martinez	.10
100	Kent Hrbek	.10
101	John Kruk	.10
102	Wade Boggs	.45
103	Greg Vaughn	.10
104	Tom Henke	.10
105	Brian Jordan	.10
106	Paul Molitor	.45
107	Cal Eldred	.10
108	Deion Sanders	.30
109	Barry Larkin	.20
110	Mike Greenwell	.10
111	Jeff Blauser	.10
112	Jose Rijo	.10
113	Pete Harnisch	.10
114	Chris Hoiles	.10
115	Edgar Martinez	.10
116	Juan Guzman	.10
117	Todd Zeile	.10
118	Danny Tartabull	.10
119	Chad Curtis	.10
120	Mark Grace	.25
121	J.T. Snow	.10
122	Mo Vaughn	.45
123	Lance Johnson	.10
124	Eric Davis	.10
125	Orel Hershiser	.10
126	Kevin Mitchell	.10
127	Don Mattingly	1.00
128	Darren Daulton	.10
129	Rod Beck	.10
130	Charles Nagy	.10
131	Mickey Tettleton	.10
132	Kevin Brown	.10
133	Pat Hentgen	.10
134	Terry Mulholland	.10
135	Steve Finley	.10
136	John Smoltz	.15
137	Frank Viola	.10
138	Jim Abbott	.10
139	Matt Williams	.25
140	Bernard Gilkey	.10
141	Jose Canseco	.40
142	Mark Whiten	.10
143	Ken Griffey, Jr.	3.00
144	Rafael Palmeiro	.20
145	Dave Hollins	.10
146	Will Clark	.25
147	Paul O'Neill	.10
148	Bobby Jones	.10
149	Butch Huskey	.15
150	Jeffrey Hammonds	.10
151	Manny Ramirez	.75
152	Bob Hamelin	.10
153	Kurt Abbott	.10
154	Scott Stahoviak	.10
155	Steve Hosey	.10
156	Salomon Torres	.10
157	Sterling Hitchcock	.10
158	Nigel Wilson	.10
159	Luis Lopez	.10
160	Chipper Jones	2.00
161	Norberto Martin	.10
162	Raul Mondesi	.45
163	Steve Karsay	.10
164	J.R. Phillips	.10
165	Marc Newfield	.10
166	Mark Hutton	.10
167	Curtis Pride	.10
168	Carl Everett	.10
169	Scott Ruffcorn	.10
170	Turk Wendell	.10
171	Jeff McNeely	.10
172	Javier Lopez	.25
173	Cliff Floyd	.10
174	Rondell White	.20
175	Scott Lydy	.10
176	Frank Thomas	.75
177	Roberto Alomar	.40
178	Travis Fryman	.10
179	Cal Ripken, Jr.	1.25
180	Chris Hoiles	.10
181	Ken Griffey, Jr.	1.50
182	Juan Gonzalez	.60
183	Joe Carter	.10
184	Jack McDowell	.10
185	Fred McGriff	.25
186	Robby Thompson	.10
187	Matt Williams	.20
188	Jay Bell	.10
189	Mike Piazza	1.00
190	Barry Bonds	.50
191	Len Dykstra	.10
192	Dave Justice	.20
193	Greg Maddux	1.00

1994 Sportflics 2000 Commemoratives

A pair of extra-rare commemorative chase cards was produced for the Sportflics 2000 set honoring Canada's veteran superstar Paul Molitor and its hottest rookie, Cliff Floyd. Cards, utilizing Magic Motion technology to alternate card-front pictures when the viewing angle changes, were inserted on average once in every 360 packs.

		MT
Complete Set (2):		12.50
1	Paul Molitor	10.00
2	Cliff Floyd	3.75

Player names in *Italic* type indicate a rookie card.

1994 Sportflics 2000 Movers

A dozen top veteran ballplayers were featured in the "Movers" insert set produced for inclusion in retail packaging of Sportflics 2000. The inserts feature the same Magic Motion features as the regular cards, showing different images on the card front when the card is viewed from different angles. The UV-coated, gold-foil highlighted backs are printed conventionally. A special "Movers" logo is found on both front and back. Stated odds of finding a Movers card are one in 24 packs.

		MT
Complete Set (12):		40.00
Common Player:		2.00
1	Gregg Jefferies	2.00
2	Ryne Sandberg	6.00
3	Cecil Fielder	2.00
4	Kirby Puckett	8.00
5	Tony Gwynn	8.00
6	Andres Galarraga	2.00
7	Sammy Sosa	12.00
8	Rickey Henderson	2.50
9	Don Mattingly	10.00
10	Joe Carter	2.00
11	Carlos Baerga	2.00
12	Len Dykstra	2.00

1994 Sportflics 2000 Shakers

Hobby packs are the exclusive source for this 12-card insert set of top rookies, found on average once every 24 packs. The chase cards utilize the Sportflics Magic Motion technology to create two different images on the card front when the card is viewed from different angles. Backs are printed conventionally but feature UV-coating and gold-foil highlights. The "Shakers" logo appears on both front and back.

		MT
Complete Set (12):		60.00
Common Player:		2.00
1	Kenny Lofton	6.00
2	Tim Salmon	3.00
3	Jeff Bagwell	12.00
4	Jason Bere	2.00
5	Salomon Torres	2.00
6	Rondell White	3.00
7	Javier Lopez	3.00

7s	Javier Lopez (overprinted "SAMPLE")	5.00
8	Dean Palmer	2.00
9	Jim Thome	3.00
10	J.T. Snow	2.50
11	Mike Piazza	15.00
12	Manny Ramirez	10.00

1994 Sportflics 2000 Rookie/Traded Promos

This nine-card set was issued to promote the Sportflics Rookie/Traded update set which was released as a hobby-only product. Cards are virtually identical to the corresponding cards in the R/T set except for the overprinted "SAMPLE" in white on front and back.

		MT
Complete Set (9):		8.00
Common Player:		1.00
1	Will Clark	2.50
14	Bret Boone	1.00
20	Ellis Burks	1.00
25	Deion Sanders	1.50
62	Chris Turner	1.00
82	Tony Tarasco	1.00
102	Rich Becker	1.00
GG1	Gary Sheffield (Going, Going, Gone)	2.00
---	Header card	.20

1994 Sportflics 2000 Rookie/Traded

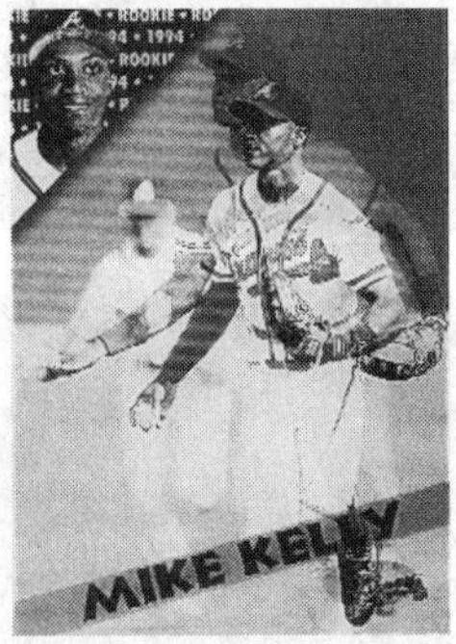

Each of the 150 regular cards in the Sportflics 2000 Rookie & Traded issue was also produced in a parallel chase card set designated on front with a black and gold "Artist's Proof" logo. Stated odds of finding an AP card were one per 24 packs. Fewer than 1,000 or each AP card were reportedly produced.

		MT
Complete Set (150):		25.00
Common Player:		.25
Wax Box:		60.00
1	Will Clark	1.00
2	Sid Fernandez	.25
3	Joe Magrane	.25
4	Pete Smith	.25
5	Roberto Kelly	.25
6	Delino DeShields	.25
7	Brian Harper	.25
8	Darrin Jackson	.25
9	Omar Vizquel	.30
10	Luis Polonia	.25
11	Reggie Jefferson	.25
12	Geronimo Berroa	.25
13	Mike Harkey	.25
14	Bret Boone	.30
15	Dave Henderson	.25
16	Pedro Martinez	.60
17	Jose Vizcaino	.25
18	Xavier Hernandez	.25
19	Eddie Taubensee	.25
20	Ellis Burks	.30
21	Turner Ward	.25
22	Terry Mulholland	.25
23	Howard Johnson	.25
24	Vince Coleman	.25
25	Deion Sanders	1.50
26	Rafael Palmeiro	.75
27	Dave Weathers	.25
28	Kent Mercker	.25
29	Gregg Olson	.25
30	Cory Bailey	.25
31	Brian Hunter	1.50
32	Garey Ingram	.25
33	Daniel Smith	.25
34	Denny Hocking	.25
35	Charles Johnson	1.50
36	Otis Nixon	.25
37	Hector Fajardo	.25
38	Lee Smith	.25
39	Phil Stidham	.25
40	Melvin Nieves	.25
41	Julio Franco	.25
42	Greg Gohr	.25
43	Steve Dunn	.25
44	Tony Fernandez	.25
45	Toby Borland	.25
46	Paul Shuey	.25
47	Shawn Hare	.25
48	Shawn Green	2.00
49	*Julian Tavarez*	.25
50	Ernie Young	.50
51	Chris Sabo	.25
52	Greg O'Halloran	.25
53	Donnie Elliott	.25
54	Jim Converse	.25
55	Ray Holbert	.25
56	Keith Lockhart	.25
57	Tony Longmire	.25
58	Jorge Fabregas	.25
59	Ravelo Manzanillo	.25
60	Marcus Moore	.25
61	Carlos Rodriguez	.25
62	Mark Portugal	.25
63	Yorkis Perez	.25
64	Dan Miceli	.25
65	Chris Turner	.25
66	Mike Oquist	.25
67	Tom Quinlan	.25
68	Matt Walbeck	.25
69	Dave Staton	.25
70	*Bill Van Landingham*	.25
71	Dave Stevens	.25
72	Domingo Cedeno	.25
73	Alex Diaz	.25
74	Darren Bragg	.30
75	James Hurst	.25
76	Alex Gonzalez	.60
77	Steve Dreyer	.25
78	Robert Eenhoorn	.25
79	Derek Parks	.25
80	Jose Valentin	.25
81	Wes Chamberlain	.25
82	Tony Tarasco	.25
83	Steve Trachsel	.40
84	Willie Banks	.25
85	Rob Butler	.25
86	Miguel Jimenez	.25
87	Gerald Williams	.25
88	Aaron Small	.25
89	Matt Mieske	.25
90	Tim Hyers	.25
91	Eddie Murray	.75
92	Dennis Martinez	.25
93	Tony Eusebio	.25
94	*Brian Anderson*	1.00
95	Blaise Ilsley	.25
96	Johnny Ruffin	.25
97	Carlos Reyes	.25
98	Greg Pirkl	.25
99	Jack Morris	.25
100	John Mabry	.50
101	Mike Kelly	.25
102	Rich Becker	.25
103	Chris Gomez	.25
104	Jim Edmonds	1.50
105	Rich Rowland	.25
106	Damon Buford	.25
107	Mark Kiefer	.25
108	Matias Carrillo	.25
109	James Mouton	.25
110	Kelly Stinnett	.25
111	Billy Ashley	.25
112	*Fausto Cruz*	.35
113	Roberto Petagine	.25
114	Joe Hall	.25
115	*Brian Johnson*	.40
116	Kevin Jarvis	.25
117	Tim Davis	.25
118	John Patterson	.25
119	Stan Royer	.25
120	Jeff Juden	.25
121	Bryan Eversgerd	.25
122	*Chan Ho Park*	1.50
123	Shane Reynolds	.25
124	Danny Bautista	.25
125	Rikkert Faneyte	.25
126	Carlos Pulido	.25
127	Mike Matheny	.25
128	Hector Carrasco	.25
129	Eddie Zambrano	.25
130	Lee Tinsley	.25
131	Roger Salkeld	.25
132	Carlos Delgado	.75
133	Troy O'Leary	.25
134	Keith Mitchell	.25
135	Lance Painter	.25
136	Nate Minchey	.25
137	Eric Anthony	.25
138	Rafael Bournigal	.25
139	Joey Hamilton	1.50
140	Bobby Munoz	.25
141	Rex Hudler	.25
142	Alex Cole	.25
143	Stan Javier	.25
144	Jose Oliva	.25
145	Tom Brunansky	.25
146	Greg Colbrunn	.25
147	Luis Lopez	.25
148	*Alex Rodriguez*	15.00
149	Darryl Strawberry	.35
150	Bo Jackson	.40

1994 Sportflics 2000 Rookie/Traded Artist's Proof

Each of the 150 regular cards in the Sportflics 2000 Rookie & Traded issue was also produced in a parallel chase set designated on front with a black and gold "Artist's Proof" logo. Stated odds of finding an AP card were one per 24 packs. Fewer than 1,000 of each AP card were reportedly produced.

	MT
Complete Set (150):	750.00
Common Player:	3.00
Stars: 30X	
(Star cards valued at 15X-20X corresponding cards in regular issue)	

1994 Sportflics 2000 Rookie/Traded Going, Going, Gone

A dozen of the game's top home run hitters are featured in this insert set. On front, simulated 3-D action photos depict the player's swing for the fences. Backs have a portrait photo and information about the player's home run prowess. A crossed bats and "Going, Going Gone" logo appear on both front and back. Cards are numbered with a "GG" prefix. Stated odds of finding one of these inserts were once in 18 packs.

		MT
Complete Set (12):		40.00
Common Player:		1.50
1	Gary Sheffield	2.50
2	Matt Williams	2.00
3	Juan Gonzalez	6.00
4	Ken Griffey Jr.	15.00
5	Mike Piazza	8.00
6	Frank Thomas	6.00
7	Tim Salmon	1.50
8	Barry Bonds	5.00
9	Fred McGriff	2.50
10	Cecil Fielder	1.50
11	Albert Belle	3.50
12	Joe Carter	1.50

1994 Sportflics 2000 Rookie/Traded Rookies of the Year

Sportflics' choices for Rookies of the Year were featured on this one-card insert set. Ryan Klesko (National League) and Manny Ramirez (American League) are shown on the card when viewed from different angles. Sportflics batted .000 in their guesses, however, as Raul Mondesi and Bob Hamelin were the actual R.O.Y. selections. This card was inserted at the average rate of once per 360 packs.

		MT
Complete Set (1):		
RO1	Ryan Klesko, Manny Ramirez	10.00

1994 Sportflics 2000 Rookie/Traded 3-D Rookies

Eighteen of 1994's premier rookies are featured in this insert set. Combining a 3-D look and Sportflics' "Magic Motion" technology, the horizontal-format Starflics rookie cards present a striking appearance. Backs feature a full-bleed color photo overprinted with gold foil. A notice on back gives the production run of the chase cards as "No more than 5,000 sets." Stated odds of finding a Starflics Rookie card were given as one per 36 packs. Cards are numbered with a "TR" prefix.

		MT
Complete Set (18):		100.00
Common Player:		3.00
1	John Hudek	3.00
2	Manny Ramirez	20.00
3	Jeffrey Hammonds	3.00
4	Carlos Delgado	6.00
5	Javier Lopez	10.00
6	Alex Gonzalez	4.00
7	Raul Mondesi	10.00
8	Bob Hamelin	3.00
9	Ryan Klesko	4.00
10	Brian Anderson	3.00
11	Alex Rodriguez	40.00
12	Cliff Floyd	3.00
13	Chan Ho Park	7.50
14	Steve Karsay	3.00
15	Rondell White	5.00
16	Shawn Green	6.00
17	Rich Becker	3.00
18	Charles Johnson	5.00

1994 Sportflics FanFest All-Stars

An American and a National League player at each position share the fronts of these "Magic Motion" cards. Cards were available by redeeming coupons acquired at various locations around the Pittsburgh All-Star FanFest celebration in July, 1994. Action photos of the players alternate on the fronts of the cards when the viewing angle is changed. The N.L. player's name appears at upper-left; the A.L. All-Star at lower-right. Backs have portrait photos of the players and a few stats and comments. The players' names, teams, position and card number are printed in gold foil, along with the notation "1 of 10,000". Cards are numbered with an "AS" prefix.

		MT
Complete Set (9):		55.00
Common Card:		4.00
1	Fred McGriff, Frank Thomas	6.00
2	Ryne Sandberg, Roberto Alomar	6.00
3	Matt Williams, Travis Fryman	4.00
4	Ozzie Smith, Cal Ripken Jr.	10.00
5	Mike Piazza, Ivan Rodriguez	9.00
6	Barry Bonds, Juan Gonzalez	8.00
7	Len Dykstra, Ken Griffey Jr.	12.00
8	Gary Sheffield, Kirby Puckett	6.00
9	Greg Maddux, Mike Mussina	6.00

1995 Sportflix Samples

This nine-card promo pack was sent to Pinnacle's dealer network to introduce its re-vamped (new logo, spelling) magic-motion card set for 1995. The sample cards are identical in format to the regular-issue Sportflix cards except that a large white "SAMPLE" is printed diagonally on front and back of the promos.

		MT
Complete Set (9):		35.00
Common Player:		3.00
3	Fred McGriff	3.00
20	Frank Thomas	6.00
105	Manny Ramirez	5.00
122	Cal Ripken Jr.	9.00
128	Roberto Alomar	3.00
152	Russ Davis (Rookie)	3.00
162	Chipper Jones (Rookie)	7.50
DE2	Matt Williams (Detonators)	3.00
----	Advertising Card	.15

1995 Sportflix

With only 170 cards in the set, only the biggest stars and hottest rookies (25 of them in a specially designed subset) are included in this simulated 3-D issue. Fronts feature two borderless action photos which are alternately visible as the card's viewing angle is changed. Backs are conventionally printed and have a portrait photo, a few career stats and a couple of sentences about the player. The basic packaging options for '95 Sportflix were five- and eight card foils at $1.89 and $2.99, respectively.

		MT
Complete Set (170):		20.00
Common Player:		.15
Complete Artist's Proof Set (170):		600.00
Artist's Proofs: 15X		
Wax Box:		30.00
1	Ken Griffey Jr.	3.00
2	Jeffrey Hammonds	.15
3	Fred McGriff	.25
4	Rickey Henderson	.35
5	Derrick May	.15
6	Robin Ventura	.25
7	Royce Clayton	.15
8	Paul Molitor	.45
9	Charlie Hayes	.15
10	David Nied	.15
11	Ellis Burks	.15
12	Bernard Gilkey	.15
13	Don Mattingly	.75
14	Albert Belle	.45
15	Doug Drabek	.15
16	Tony Gwynn	.75
17	Delino DeShields	.15
18	Bobby Bonilla	.15
19	Cliff Floyd	.15
20	Frank Thomas	1.00
21	Raul Mondesi	.40
22	Dave Nilsson	.15
23	Todd Zeile	.15
24	Bernie Williams	.45
25	Kirby Puckett	.75
26	David Cone	.20
27	Darren Daulton	.15
28	Marquis Grissom	.15
29	Randy Johnson	.40
30	Jeff Kent	.15
31	Orlando Merced	.15
32	Dave Justice	.25
33	Ivan Rodriguez	.50
34	Kirk Gibson	.15
35	Alex Fernandez	.15
36	Rick Wilkins	.15
37	Andy Benes	.15
38	Bret Saberhagen	.15
39	Billy Ashley	.15
40	Jose Rijo	.15
41	Matt Williams	.40
42	Lenny Dykstra	.15
43	Jay Bell	.15
44	Reggie Jefferson	.15
45	Greg Maddux	1.50
46	Gary Sheffield	.40
47	Bret Boone	.15
48	Jeff Bagwell	1.00
49	Ben McDonald	.15
50	Eric Karros	.15
51	Roger Clemens	.75
52	Sammy Sosa	1.00
53	Barry Bonds	.60
54	Joey Hamilton	.20
55	Brian Jordan	.15
56	Wil Cordero	.15
57	Aaron Sele	.15
58	Paul O'Neill	.20
59	Carlos Garcia	.15
60	Mike Mussina	.40
61	John Olerud	.20
62	Kevin Appier	.15
63	Matt Mieske	.15
64	Carlos Baerga	.15
65	Ryan Klesko	.25
66	Jimmy Key	.15
67	James Mouton	.15
68	Tim Salmon	.20
69	Hal Morris	.15
70	Albie Lopez	.15
71	Dave Hollins	.15
72	Greg Colbrunn	.15
73	Juan Gonzalez	1.00
74	Wally Joyner	.15
75	Bob Hamelin	.15
76	Brady Anderson	.20
77	Deion Sanders	.25
78	Javier Lopez	.15
79	Brian McRae	.15
80	Craig Biggio	.25
81	Kenny Lofton	.40
82	Cecil Fielder	.15
83	Mike Piazza	1.50
84	Rafael Palmeiro	.30
85	Jim Thomo	.40
86	Ruben Sierra	.15
87	Mark Langston	.15
88	John Valentin	.15
89	Shawon Dunston	.15
90	Travis Fryman	.15
91	Chuck Knoblauch	.30
92	Dean Palmer	.15
93	Robby Thompson	.15
94	Barry Larkin	.20
95	Darren Lewis	.15
96	Andres Galarraga	.25
97	Tony Phillips	.15
98	Mo Vaughn	.40
99	Pedro Martinez	.30
100	Chad Curtis	.15
101	Brent Gates	.15
102	Pat Hentgen	.15
103	Rico Brogna	.15
104	Carlos Delgado	.40
105	Manny Ramirez	.75
106	Mike Greenwell	.15
107	Wade Boggs	.35
108	Ozzie Smith	.45
109	Rusty Greer	.15
110	Willie Greene	.15
111	Chili Davis	.15
112	Reggie Sanders	.15
113	Roberto Kelly	.15
114	Tom Glavine	.25
115	Moises Alou	.25
116	Dennis Eckersley	.15
117	Danny Tartabull	.15
118	Jeff Conine	.15
119	Will Clark	.25
120	Joe Carter	.15
121	Mark McGwire	3.00
122	Cal Ripken Jr.	2.50
123	Danny Jackson	.15
124	Phil Plantier	.15
125	Dante Bichette	.25
126	Jack McDowell	.15
127	Jose Canseco	.35
128	Roberto Alomar	.50
129	Rondell White	.25
130	Ray Lankford	.15
131	Ryan Thompson	.15
132	Ken Caminiti	.25
133	Gregg Jefferies	.15
134	Omar Vizquel	.15
135	Mark Grace	.25
136	Derek Bell	.15
137	Mickey Tettleton	.15
138	Wilson Alvarez	.15
139	Larry Walker	.25
140	Bo Jackson	.20
141	Alex Rodriguez	2.50
142	Orlando Miller	.15
143	Shawn Green	.20
144	Steve Dunn	.15
145	Midre Cummings	.15
146	Chan Ho Park	.25
147	Jose Oliva	.15
148	Armando Benitez	.15
149	J.R. Phillips	.15
150	Charles Johnson	.25
151	Garret Anderson	.20
152	Russ Davis	.15
153	Brian Hunter	.15
154	Ernie Young	.15
155	Marc Newfield	.15
156	Greg Pirkl	.15
157	Scott Ruffcorn	.15
158	Rikkert Faneyte	.15
159	Duane Singleton	.15
160	Gabe White	.15
161	Alex Gonzalez	.15
162	Chipper Jones	1.50
163	Mike Kelly	.15
164	Kurt Miller	.15
165	Roberto Petagine	.15
166	Checklist (Jeff Bagwell)	.25
167	Checklist (Mike Piazza)	.40
168	Checklist (Ken Griffey Jr.)	1.00
169	Checklist (Frank Thomas)	.50
170	Checklist (Barry Bonds, Cal Ripken Jr.)	.75

1995 Sportflix Artist's Proofs

Each of the 170 cards in the regular Sportflix set can be found with a special tombstone shaped black-and-gold "Artist's Proof" seal designating it as one of a parallel edition of 700 cards each. Cards are otherwise identical to the regular-issue version. AP cards were inserted at an average rate of one per 36 packs.

	MT
Complete Set (170):	600.00
Common Player:	1.00
Stars: 15X	
(See 1995 Sportflix for checklist and base card values.)	

1995 Sportflix Double Take

A see-through plastic background and A.L. and N.L. stars at the same position sharing the card with their shadows marks this chase set as the top of the line for '95 Sportflix. Found at an average rate of one per 48 packs, the Double Take inserts represent a new level in "magic motion" card technology.

		MT
Complete Set (12):		65.00
Common Player:		2.00
1	Frank Thomas, Jeff Bagwell	6.00
2	Will Clark, Fred McGriff	3.00
3	Roberto Alomar, Jeff Kent	4.00
4	Wade Boggs, Matt Williams	3.00
5	Cal Ripken Jr., Ozzie Smith	12.00
6	Alex Rodriguez, Wil Cordero	9.00
7	Carlos Delgado, Mike Piazza	7.50
8	Kenny Lofton, Dave Justice	4.00
9	Ken Griffey Jr., Barry Bonds	15.00
10	Albert Belle, Raul Mondesi	4.00
11	Kirby Puckett, Tony Gwynn	6.00
12	Jimmy Key, Greg Maddux	6.00

1995 Sportflix ProMotion

Twelve of baseball's biggest stars morph into team logos on a bright team-color background in this chase series. Backs have a portrait photo and a few words about the players. The ProMotion inserts are a one per 18 pack pick in jumbo packs only.

		MT
Complete Set (12):		90.00
Common Player:		2.50
1	Ken Griffey Jr.	18.00
2	Frank Thomas	7.00
3	Cal Ripken Jr.	14.00
4	Jeff Bagwell	6.00
5	Mike Piazza	9.00
6	Matt Williams	3.00
7	Albert Belle	5.00
8	Jose Canseco	4.00
9	Don Mattingly	7.00
10	Barry Bonds	6.00
11	Will Clark	4.00
12	Kirby Puckett	7.00

1995 Sportflix 3D Detonators

With the players up on a pedestal and fireworks in the background, this chase set lives up to its name, "Detonators." The cards feature a deep 3-D look on front. Backs have a close-up photo of the player in the pedestal's column. Detonator cards are pulled at an average rate of one per 16 packs.

		MT
Complete Set (9):		25.00
Common Player:		1.50
1	Jeff Bagwell	4.00
2	Matt Williams	2.00
3	Ken Griffey Jr.	10.00
4	Frank Thomas	5.00
5	Mike Piazza	6.00
6	Barry Bonds	4.00
7	Albert Belle	3.00
8	Cliff Floyd	1.50
9	Juan Gonzalez	3.00

1995 Sportflix 3D Hammer Team

Sledge hammers flying in formation through a cloud-studded sky are the background for this insert set featuring the game's heavy hitters. Backs have a portrait photo and a few words about the player's power hitting prowess. Hammer Team cards are picked on an average of once per four packs.

		MT
Complete Set (18):		20.00
Common Player:		.50
1	Ken Griffey Jr.	4.00
2	Frank Thomas	1.75
3	Jeff Bagwell	1.50
4	Mike Piazza	2.00
5	Cal Ripken Jr.	3.00
6	Albert Belle	1.00
7	Barry Bonds	1.50
8	Don Mattingly	1.75
9	Will Clark	.75
10	Tony Gwynn	1.50
11	Matt Williams	1.00
12	Kirby Puckett	1.50
13	Manny Ramirez	1.50
14	Fred McGriff	.75
15	Juan Gonzalez	1.00
16	Kenny Lofton	.75
17	Raul Mondesi	.75
18	Tim Salmon	.60

1995 Sportflix/UC3 Samples

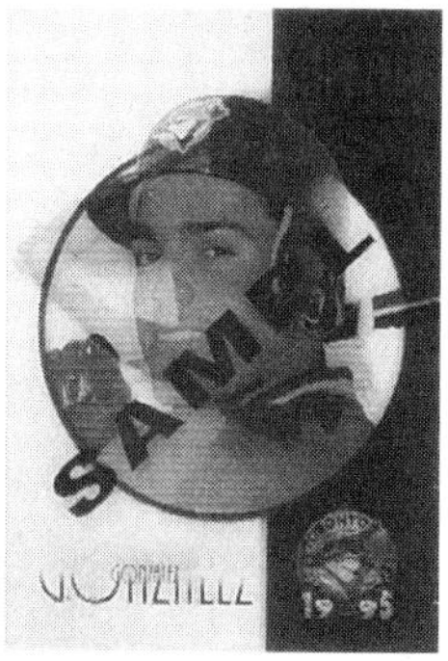

To introduce the new technology it was bringing to the insert cards in the Sportflix UC3 issue, the company sent a sample of the Clear Shots insert, along with a header card describing the entire UC3 issue, to card dealers and the media in June, 1995. A large, black, "SAMPLE" is overprinted diagonally on the front. A similarly marked Fred McGriff previewed the set's regular cards.

		MT
Complete Set (3):		12.00
3	Fred McGriff	4.00
CS8	Cliff Floyd	5.00
CS10	Alex Gonzalez	5.00
--	Header card	.05

1995 Sportflix/UC3

Using advanced technology to create a premium 3-D card brand and inserts, the UC3 set offers three distinctly different card formats in the regular 147-card set, plus a parallel set and three insert sets. All cards have borderless fronts and feature a heavy ribbed plastic top layer. The first 95 cards in the set are veteran players in a horizontal format. A central player action photo is flanked at left by a large gold glove (National Leaguers) or baseball (A.L.), and at right by a blue and green vista from which flies one (N.L.) or three (A.L.) baseballs. The player's name and team are in red in the upper-left, the UC3 logo at lower-left. Backs have another color photo and a few stats set against a background of the team logo in team color. Cards #96-122 are a vertical-format Rookie subset. Player photos are set against a purple and green vista with a large bat, ball and glove behind the player. His name is at upper-right; team logo at lower-right. Horizontal backs are similar to the other cards. The final 25 cards of the set are a subset titled, "In-Depth." These vertically formatted cards feature eye-popping graphics on front in which the main player photo almost jumps from the background. The only graphics are the player's name at left and the UC3 logo at upper-left. The backs have a player portrait photo at top, bathed in golden rays. A team logo is at center and an outer space design at bottom. There is a short paragraph describing the player at right.

		MT
Complete Set (147):		20.00
Common Player:		.10
Complete Artist's Proofs Set (147):		900.00
Wax Box:		60.00
1	Frank Thomas	1.50
2	Wil Cordero	.10
3	John Olerud	.15
4	Deion Sanders	.20
5	Mike Mussina	.40
6	Mo Vaughn	.40
7	Will Clark	.25
8	Chili Davis	.10
9	Jimmy Key	.10
10	John Valentin	.10
11	Tony Tarasco	.10
12	Alan Trammell	.10
13	David Cone	.10
14	Tim Salmon	.20
15	Danny Tartabull	.10
16	Aaron Sele	.10
17	Alex Fernandez	.10
18	Barry Bonds	.75
19	Andres Galarraga	.15
20	Don Mattingly	1.00
21	Kevin Appier	.10
22	Paul Molitor	.40
23	Omar Vizquel	.10
24	Andy Benes	.10
25	Rafael Palmeiro	.25
26	Barry Larkin	.15
27	Bernie Williams	.25
28	Gary Sheffield	.25
29	Wally Joyner	.15
30	Wade Boggs	.40
31	Rico Brogna	.10
32	Ken Caminiti	.15
33	Kirby Puckett	.75
34	Bobby Bonilla	.10
35	Hal Morris	.10
36	Moises Alou	.10
37	Jim Thome	.25
38	Chuck Knoblauch	.10
39	Mike Piazza	2.00
40	Travis Fryman	.10
41	Rickey Henderson	.35
42	Jack McDowell	.10
43	Carlos Baerga	.10
44	Gregg Jeffries	.10
45	Kirk Gibson	.10
46	Bret Saberhagen	.10
47	Cecil Fielder	.10
48	Manny Ramirez	.75
49	Marquis Grissom	.10
50	Dave Winfield	.15
51	Mark McGwire	3.00
52	Dennis Eckersley	.10
53	Robin Ventura	.15
54	Ryan Klesko	.40
55	Jeff Bagwell	1.00
56	Ozzie Smith	.40
57	Brian McRae	.10
58	Albert Belle	.60
59	Darren Daulton	.10
60	Jose Canseco	.35
61	Greg Maddux	2.00
62	Ben McDonald	.10
63	Lenny Dykstra	.10
64	Randy Johnson	.30
65	Fred McGriff	.35
66	Ray Lankford	.10
67	Dave Justice	.20
68	Paul O'Neill	.10
69	Tony Gwynn	.80
70	Matt Williams	.25
71	Dante Bichette	.30
72	Craig Biggio	.25
73	Ken Griffey Jr.	3.00
74	Juan Gonzalez	1.50
75	Cal Ripken Jr.	2.50
76	Jay Bell	.10
77	Joe Carter	.10
78	Roberto Alomar	.60
79	Mark Langston	.10
80	Dave Hollins	.10
81	Tom Glavine	.15
82	Ivan Rodriguez	.30
83	Mark Whiten	.10
84	Raul Mondesi	.40
85	Kenny Lofton	.40
86	Ruben Sierra	.10
87	Mark Grace	.20
88	Royce Clayton	.10
89	Billy Ashley	.10
90	Larry Walker	.30
91	Sammy Sosa	1.00
92	Jason Bere	.10
93	Bob Hamelin	.10
94	Greg Vaughn	.10
95	Roger Clemens	.65
96	Scott Ruffcorn	.10
97	*Hideo Nomo*	1.50
98	Michael Tucker	.10
99	J.R. Phillips	.10
100	Roberto Petagine	.10
101	Chipper Jones	2.00
102	Armando Benitez	.10
103	Orlando Miller	.10
104	Carlos Delgado	.40
105	Jeff Cirillo	.10
106	Shawn Green	.20
107	Joe Rando	.10
108	Vaughn Eshelman	.10
109	Frank Rodriguez	.10
110	Russ Davis	.10
111	Todd Hollandsworth	.10
112	Mark Grudzielanek	.10
113	Jose Oliva	.10
114	Ray Durham	.15
115	Alex Rodriguez	2.50
116	Alex Gonzalez	.10
117	Midre Cummings	.10
118	Marty Cordova	.10
119	John Mabry	.10
120	Jason Jacome	.10
121	Joe Vitiello	.10
122	Charles Johnson	.10
123	Cal Ripken Jr. (In Depth)	1.25
124	Ken Griffey Jr. (In Depth)	1.50
125	Frank Thomas (In Depth)	.75
126	Mike Piazza (In Depth)	.50
127	Matt Williams (In Depth)	.15
128	Barry Bonds (In Depth)	.40
129	Greg Maddux (In Depth)	1.00
130	Randy Johnson (In Depth)	.15
131	Albert Belle (In Depth)	.35
132	Will Clark (In Depth)	.15
133	Tony Gwynn (In Depth)	.40
134	Manny Ramirez (In Depth)	.40
135	Raul Mondesi (In Depth)	.15
136	Mo Vaughn (In Depth)	.15
137	Mark McGwire (In Depth)	1.50
138	Kirby Puckett (In Depth)	.40
139	Don Mattingly (In Depth)	.50
140	Carlos Baerga (In Depth)	.10
141	Roger Clemens (In Depth)	.35
142	Fred McGriff (In Depth)	.15
143	Kenny Lofton (In Depth)	.35
144	Jeff Bagwell (In Depth)	.40
145	Larry Walker (In Depth)	.15
146	Joe Carter (In Depth)	.10
147	Rafael Palmeiro (In Depth)	.15

1995 Sportflix/UC3 Artist's Proof

This chase set parallels the 147 regular cards in the UC3 set with a version on which a round, gold "ARTIST'S PROOF" seal is printed on the front of the card. The AP cards are found on the average of one per box (36 packs).

	MT
Complete Set (147):	900.00
Common Player:	2.00
Stars: 15X	

(See 1995 Sportflix UC3 for checklist and base card values.)

1995 Sportflix/UC3 Clear Shots

Seeded at the rate of about one per 24 packs, the 12 cards in this chase set feature top rookies in a technologically advanced format. The left two-thirds of the card are clear plastic, the right third is blue (American League) or red-purple (N.L.). At center is a circle which features the player photos, portrait and action, depending on the viewing angle. Also changing with the viewpoint are the words "CLEAR" and "SHOT" at top-right, and team and UC3 logos at bottom-right. The player's last name is in black at lower-left and appears to change size as the card is moved. Backs have a gray strip vertically at left with the card number, manufacturer and licensor logos and copyright information. Card numbers have a "CS" prefix.

		MT
Complete Set (12):		50.00
Common Player:		2.00
1	Alex Rodriguez	25.00
2	Shawn Green	4.50
3	Hideo Nomo	6.00
4	Charles Johnson	3.00
5	Orlando Miller	1.00
6	Billy Ashley	1.00
7	Carlos Delgado	3.00
8	Cliff Floyd	3.00
9	Chipper Jones	15.00
10	Alex Gonzalez	2.00
11	J.R. Phillips	1.00
12	Michael Tucker	1.00

1995 Sportflix/UC3 Cyclone Squad

The most commonly encountered (one per four packs, on average) of the UC3 chase cards are the 20-card Cyclone Squad, featuring the game's top batsmen. Cards have a player in a batting pose set against a dark copper background with two golden pinwheels behind him which appear to spin when the card is moved. Horizontal backs have a green toned photo of the player in his follow-through swing, with shock waves radiating from the lower-left corner. Cards have a CS prefix.

		MT
Complete Set (20):		15.00
Common Player:		.40
1	Frank Thomas	1.50
2	Ken Griffey Jr.	4.00
3	Jeff Bagwell	1.50
4	Cal Ripken Jr.	3.00
5	Barry Bonds	1.00
6	Mike Piazza	2.00
7	Matt Williams	.50
8	Kirby Puckett	1.50
9	Jose Canseco	.75
10	Will Clark	.50
11	Don Mattingly	1.50
12	Albert Belle	.75
13	Tony Gwynn	1.50
14	Raul Mondesi	.40
15	Bobby Bonilla	.40
16	Rafael Palmeiro	.50
17	Fred McGriff	.50
18	Tim Salmon	.40
19	Kenny Lofton	.75
20	Joe Carter	.40

1995 Sportflix/UC3 In Motion

Found on an average of once per 18 packs, the cards in this chase set feature maximim motion. When the card is held almost vertically a small eight-piece jigsaw puzzle photo of the player is visible against a light blue background. As the card is moved toward a horizontal postion, the pieces appear to become large and move together until the picture fills most of the card. The player's name is in orange at lower-left, with manufacturer's logos at top. Horizontal backs have a green background, two color player photos and a few words of career highlights. The In Motion card numbers are preceded by an "IM" prefix.

		MT
Complete Set (10):		25.00
Common Player:		.75
1	Cal Ripken Jr.	5.00
2	Ken Griffey Jr.	6.00
3	Frank Thomas	2.50
4	Mike Piazza	4.00
5	Barry Bonds	2.00
6	Matt Williams	.75
7	Kirby Puckett	2.00
8	Greg Maddux	4.00
9	Don Mattingly	2.00
10	Will Clark	.75

1996 Sportflix

Distributed in only retail locations, this 1996 Sportflix set has 144 cards, including 24-card UC3 and 21-card Rookies subsets. The set also has a parallel set, Artist's Proof; these cards are seeded one per every 48 packs. Four insert sets were also produced: Double Take, Hit Parade, Power Surge and ProMotion.

		MT
Complete Set (144):		25.00
Common Player:		.10
1	Wade Boggs	.25
2	Tim Salmon	.20
3	Will Clark	.35
4	Dante Bichette	.25
5	Barry Bonds	.75
6	Kirby Puckett	1.00
7	Albert Belle	.60
8	Greg Maddux	2.00
9	Tony Gwynn	1.00
10	Mike Piazza	1.50
11	Ivan Rodriguez	.15
12	Marty Cordova	.15
13	Frank Thomas	1.00
14	Raul Mondesi	.35
15	Johnny Damon	.40
16	Mark McGwire	3.00
17	Lenny Dykstra	.10
18	Ken Griffey Jr.	3.00
19	Chipper Jones	1.50
20	Alex Rodriguez	2.50
21	Jeff Bagwell	1.00
22	Jim Edmonds	.15
23	Edgar Martinez	.10
24	David Cone	.10
25	Tom Glavine	.15
26	Eddie Murray	.25
27	Paul Molitor	.30
28	Ryan Klesko	.40
29	Rafael Palmeiro	.20
30	Manny Ramirez	.75
31	Mo Vaughn	.45
32	Rico Brogna	.10
33	Marc Newfield	.10
34	J.T. Snow	.10
35	Reggie Sanders	.10

36 Fred McGriff .40
37 Craig Biggio .20
38 Jeff King .10
39 Kenny Lofton .45
40 Gary Gaetti .10
41 Eric Karros .10
42 Jason Isringhausen .15
43 B.J. Surhoff .10
44 Michael Tucker .10
45 Gary Sheffield .20
46 Chili Davis .10
47 Bobby Bonilla .10
48 Hideo Nomo .50
49 Ray Durham .10
50 Phil Nevin .10
51 Randy Johnson .40
52 Bill Pulsipher .10
53 Ozzie Smith .40
54 Cal Ripken Jr. 2.50
55 Cecil Fielder .10
56 Matt Williams .30
57 Sammy Sosa 1.50
58 Roger Clemens .40
59 Brian Hunter .10
60 Barry Larkin .20
61 Charles Johnson .10
62 Dave Justice .20
63 Garret Anderson .10
64 Rondell White .10
65 Derek Bell .10
66 Andres Galarraga .15
67 Moises Alou .10
68 Travis Fryman .10
69 Pedro Martinez .20
70 Carlos Baerga .10
71 John Valentin .10
72 Larry Walker .20
73 Roberto Alomar .60
74 Mike Mussina .50
75 Kevin Appier .10
76 Bernie Williams .20
77 Ray Lankford .10
78 Gregg Jefferies .10
79 Robin Ventura .10
80 Kenny Rogers .10
81 Paul O'Neill .10
82 Mark Grace .20
83 Deion Sanders .25
84 Tino Martinez .10
85 Joe Carter .10
86 Pete Schourek .10
87 Jack McDowell .10
88 John Mabry .10
89 Darren Daulton .10
90 Jim Thome .25
91 Jay Buhner .10
92 Jay Bell .10
93 Kevin Seitzer .10
94 Jose Canseco .35
95 Juan Gonzalez 1.25
96 Jeff Conine .10
97 Chipper Jones .75
98 Ken Griffey Jr. 1.50
99 Frank Thomas .50
100 Cal Ripken Jr. 1.50
101 Albert Belle .50
102 Mike Piazza .75
103 Dante Bichette .15
104 Sammy Sosa .75
105 Mo Vaughn .25
106 Tim Salmon .20
107 Reggie Sanders .10
108 Gary Sheffield .10
109 Ruben Rivera .25
110 Rafael Palmeiro .15
111 Edgar Martinez .10
112 Barry Bonds .40
113 Manny Ramirez .40
114 Larry Walker .15
115 Jeff Bagwell .50
116 Matt Williams .20
117 Mark McGwire 2.00
118 Johnny Damon .25
119 Eddie Murray .20
120 Jay Buhner .10
121 Tim Unroe .10
122 Todd Hollandsworth .10
123 Tony Clark .40
124 Roger Cedeno .20
125 Jim Pittsley .10
126 Ruben Rivera .40
127 Bob Wolcott .10
128 Chan Ho Park .15
129 Chris Snopek .15
130 Alex Ochoa .10
131 Yamil Benitez .10
132 Jimmy Haynes .10
133 Dustin Hermanson .10
134 Shawn Estes .10
135 Howard Battle .10
136 *Matt Lawton* .10
137 Terrell Wade .10
138 Jason Schmidt .10
139 Derek Jeter 1.50
140 Shannon Stewart .10
141 Chris Stynes .10
142 Ken Griffey Jr. CL 1.50
143 Greg Maddux CL 1.00
144 Ripken Jr. CL 1.25

1996 Sportflix Artist's Proofs

Artist's Proof parallels to 1996 Sportflix are a 1:48 find and are distinctively marked with an AP seal on front.

MT
Complete Set (144): 1000.
Common Player: 2.50
AP Stars: 15X
(See 1996 Sportflix for checklist and base card values.)

1996 Sportflix Double Take

These 1996 Sportflix insert cards each feature two players who are tops at a particular position. The cards were seeded one per every 22 packs.

MT
Complete Set (12): 100.00
Common Player: 4.00
1 Barry Larkin, Cal Ripken Jr. 15.00
2 Roberto Alomar, Craig Biggio 4.00
3 Chipper Jones, Matt Williams 9.00
4 Ken Griffey Jr., Ruben Rivera 20.00
5 Greg Maddux, Hideo Nomo 9.00
6 Frank Thomas, Mo Vaughn 7.50
7 Mike Piazza, Ivan Rodriguez 9.00
8 Albert Belle, Barry Bonds 4.00
9 Alex Rodriguez, Derek Jeter 15.00
10 Kirby Puckett, Tony Gwynn 7.50
11 Manny Ramirez, Sammy Sosa 12.00
12 Jeff Bagwell, Rico Brogna 4.00

1996 Sportflix Hit Parade

Sixteen of baseball's most productive hitters are featured in full-motion animation on these 1996 Sportflix inserts. The cards were seeded one per every 35 packs.

MT
Complete Set (16): 60.00
Common Player: 1.50
1 Ken Griffey Jr. 10.00
2 Cal Ripken Jr. 9.00
3 Frank Thomas 5.00
4 Mike Piazza 7.00
5 Mo Vaughn 2.00
6 Albert Belle 2.50
7 Jeff Bagwell 4.00
8 Matt Williams 1.50
9 Sammy Sosa 5.00
9p Sammy Sosa (overprinted "SAMPLE") 8.00
10 Kirby Puckett 5.00
11 Dante Bichette 1.50
12 Gary Sheffield 2.00
13 Tony Gwynn 4.00
14 Wade Boggs 2.50
15 Chipper Jones 7.00
16 Barry Bonds 5.00

1996 Sportflix Power Surge

This 1996 Sportflix insert set showcases 24 sluggers on a clear 3-D parallel rendition of the UC3 subset in the main issue. These cards are seeded one per every 35 packs.

MT
Complete Set (25): 90.00
Common Player: 1.50
1 Chipper Jones 10.00
2 Ken Griffey Jr. 17.50
3 Frank Thomas 6.00
4 Cal Ripken Jr. 15.00
5 Albert Belle 5.00
6 Mike Piazza 10.00
7 Dante Bichette 2.00
8 Sammy Sosa 8.00
9 Mo Vaughn 1.50
10 Tim Salmon 1.50
11 Reggie Sanders 1.50
12 Gary Sheffield 1.50
13 Ruben Rivera 1.50
14 Rafael Palmeiro 2.00
15 Edgar Martinez 1.50
16 Barry Bonds 6.00
17 Manny Ramirez 5.00
18 Larry Walker 2.00
19 Jeff Bagwell 6.00
20 Matt Williams 1.50
21 Mark McGwire 17.50
22 Johnny Damon 2.00
23 Eddie Murray 2.00
24 Jay Buhner 1.50
25 Kirby Puckett 6.00

1996 Sportflix ProMotion

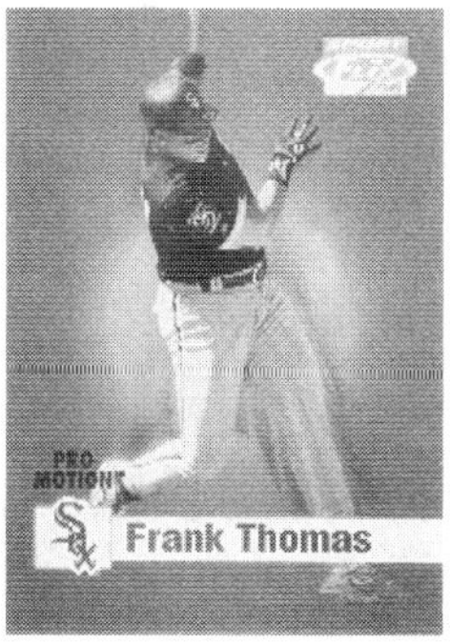

These 1996 Sportflix inserts were seeded one per every 17 packs. The cards' "morphing" technology turns baseball equipment, such as bats, balls and gloves, into 20 of the top veteran superstars using multi-phase animation.

MT
Complete Set (20): 60.00
Common Player: .50
1 Cal Ripken Jr. 8.00
2 Greg Maddux 6.00
3 Mo Vaughn 1.00
4 Albert Belle 3.00
5 Mike Piazza 6.00
6 Ken Griffey Jr. 10.00
7 Frank Thomas 5.00
8 Jeff Bagwell 4.00
9 Hideo Nomo 2.00
10 Chipper Jones 6.00
11 Tony Gwynn 4.00
12 Don Mattingly 5.00
13 Dante Bichette 1.00
14 Matt Williams 1.00
15 Manny Ramirez 3.00
16 Barry Bonds 4.00
17 Reggie Sanders .50
18 Tim Salmon .75
19 Ruben Rivera .75
20 Garret Anderson .50

1996 Sportflix Rookie Supers

Eight of the young players included in the Sportflix Rookies subset are featured in an enlarged version which was issued one per retail box. The cards measure 3" x 5" and are numbered "X of 8," on back, but are otherwise identical to the smaller version.

MT
Complete Set (8): 35.00
Common player: 4.00
1 Jason Schmidt 4.00
2 Chris Snopek 4.00
3 Tony Clark 6.00
4 Todd Hollandsworth 4.00
5 Alex Ochoa 4.00
6 Derek Jeter 15.00
7 Howard Battle 4.00
8 Bob Wolcott 4.00

1981 Sporting News Conlon Collection

This set of 100 cards was sold directly into the hobby by The Sporting News in a slipcover case for $50. The blank-backed cards measure 4"x5" and feature a sepi-toned photo surrounded by a 1/4" white border. The photos were the first of several uses on baseball cards of TSN's archives of ballplayer photos taken by Charles Martin Conlon between 1915-1935. The paper's logo appears at the top of the card. At bottom are the player's or players' names (s), team at the time the photo was taken, and position or positions played for the season indicated. A card number appears at lower-right.

MT
Complete Set (100): 100.00
Common Player: 1.00
1 Ty Cobb 10.00
2 Hughie Jennings 1.00
3 Miller Huggins 1.00
4 Babe Ruth 13.00
5 Lou Gehrig 10.00
6 John McGraw 1.00
7 Bill Terry 1.00
8 Stan Baumgartner 1.00
9 Christy Mathewson 5.00
10 Grover Alexander 2.00
11 Tony Lazzeri 1.00
12 Frank Chance, Joe Tinker 2.00
13 Johnny Evers 1.00
14 Tris Speaker 2.00
15 Harry Hooper 1.00
16 Duffy Lewis 1.00
17 Joe Wood 1.00
18 Hugh Duffy 1.00
19 Rogers Hornsby 5.00
20 Earl Averill 1.00
21 Dizzy Dean 2.00
22 Daffy Dean 1.00
23 Frankie Frisch 2.00
24 Pepper Martin 1.00
25 Blondie Ryan 1.00
26 Hank Gowdy 1.00
27 Fred Merkle 1.00
28 Ernie Lombardi 1.00
29 Greasy Neale 1.00
30 Morris Badgro 1.00
31 Jim Thorpe 7.50
32 Roy Johnson 1.00
33 Bob Johnson 1.00
34 Mule Solters 1.00
35 Specs Toporcer 1.00
36 Jackie Hayes 1.00
37 Walter Johnson 5.00
38 Lefty Grove 1.00
39 Eddie Collins 1.00
40 Buck Weaver 4.00
41 Cozy Dolan 1.00
42 Emil Meusel 1.00
43 Bob Meusel 1.00
44 Lefty Gomez 1.00
45 Rube Marquard 1.00
46 Jeff Tesreau 1.00
47 Joe Heving 1.00
48 John Heving 1.00
49 Rick Ferrell 1.00
50 Wes Ferrell 1.00
51 Bill Wambsganss 1.00
52 Ben Chapman 1.00
53 Joe Sewell 1.00
54 Luke Sewell 1.00
55 Odell Hale 1.00
56 Sammy Hale 1.00
57 Earle Mack 1.00
58 Connie Mack 1.00
59 Rube Walberg 1.00
60 Mule Haas 1.00
61 Paul Waner 1.00
62 Lloyd Waner 1.00
63 Pie Traynor 1.00
64 Honus Wagner 2.00
65 Joe Cronin 1.00
66 Joe Harris 1.00
67 Dave Harris 1.00
68 Bucky Harris 1.00
69 Alex Gaston 1.00
70 Milt Gaston 1.00
71 Casey Stengel 2.00
72 Amos Rusie 1.00
73 Mickey Welch 1.00
74 Roger Bresnaham 1.00
75 Jesse Burkett 1.00
76 Harry Heilmann 1.00
77 Heinie Manush 1.00
78 Charlie Gehringer 1.00
79 Hank Greenberg 2.00
80 Jimmie Foxx 4.00
81 Al Simmons 1.00
82 Eddie Plank 1.00
83 George Sisler 1.00
84 Joe Medwick 1.00
85 Mel Ott 1.00
86 Hack Wilson 1.00
87 Jimmy Wilson 1.00
88 Chuck Klein 1.00
89 Gabby Hartnett 1.00
90 Henie Groh 1.00
91 Ping Bodie 1.00
92 Ted Lyons 1.00
93 Jack Quinn 1.00
94 Oscar Roettger 1.00
95 Wally Roettger 1.00
96 Bubbles Hargrave 1.00
97 Pinky Hargrave 1.00
98 Sam Crawford 1.00
99 Gee Walker 1.00
100 Homer Summa 1.00

1983 Sporting News Conlon Collection

This set was issued to mark the 50th anniversary of the first All-Star game in 1933. Besides the American and National League players who made up those teams, the set includes a group of all-stars from the Negro Leagues. The oversize (4-1/2" x 6-1/8") cards were sold only as complete sets. The cards feature sepia player photos on front, with a facsimile autograph and appropriate commemorative labeling. Black-and-white backs feature 1933 stats, an anecdote about the player, and the logos of appropriate parties in the set's marketing. The major leaguers' photos were the work of Charles M. Conlon, while the Black ballplayers' pictures were garnered from a variety of sources.

MT
Complete Set (60): 24.00
Common Player: .25
1 Jimmie Foxx .50
2 Heinie Manush .25
3 Lou Gehrig 2.50
4 Al Simmons .25
5 Charlie Gehringer .35
6 Luke Appling .25
7 Mickey Cochrane .25
8 Joe Kuhel .25
9 Bill Dickey .40
10 Pinky Higgins .25
11 Roy Johnson .25

12 Ben Chapman .25
13 Johnny Hodapp .25
14 Joe Cronin .35
15 Evar Swanson .25
16 Earl Averill .25
17 Babe Ruth 4.00
18 Tony Lazzeri .40
19 Alvin Crowder .25
20 Lefty Grove .25
21 Earl Whitehill .25
22 Lefty Gomez .25
23 Mel Harder .25
24 Tommy Bridges .25
25 Chuck Klein .25
26 Spud Davis .25
27 Riggs Stephenson .25
28 Tony Piet .25
29 Bill Terry .35
30 Wes Schulmerich .25
31 Pepper Martin .25
32 Arky Vaughan .25
33 Wally Berger .25
34 Rip Collins .25
35 Fred Lindstrom .25
36 Chick Fullis .25
37 Paul Waner .25
38 Johnny Frederick .25
39 Joe Medwick .25
40 Pie Traynor .25
41 Frank Frisch .35
42 Chick Hafey .25
43 Carl Hubbell .35
44 Guy Bush .25
45 Dizzy Dean .40
46 Hal Schumacher .25
47 Larry French .25
48 Lon Warneke .25
49 Cool Papa Bell .35
50 Oscar Charleston .35
51 Josh Gibson .50
52 Satchel Paige 1.00
53 Dave Malarcher .35
54 Pop Lloyd .35
55 Rube Foster .35
56 Buck Leonard .45
57 Smoky Joe Williams .45
58 Willie Wells .45
59 Judy Johnson .35
60 Martin DiHigo .35

1984 Sporting News Conlon Collection

This 60-card set, mostly Hall of Famers, was produced in conjunction with the Smithsonian Institution's "Baseball Immortals" photo exhibition of the work of Charles Martin Conlon. The oversize (4-1/4" x 6-1/8") cards have sepia-toned photos on front; backs are printed in black-and-white. The issue was initially sold only as a complete set.

MT
Complete Set (60): 25.00
Common Player: .25
1 Grover Cleveland Alexander .50
2 Chief Bender .25
3 Fred Clarke .25
4 Ty Cobb 1.00
5 Ty Cobb 1.00
6 Ty Cobb 1.00
7 Ty Cobb 1.00
8 Mickey Cochrane .25
9 Jack Coombs .25
10 Charles & Margie Conlon .25
11 Charles Conlon .25
12 Joe Cronin .25
13 Dizzy Dean .50
14 Leo Durocher .25
15 Jimmie Foxx .40
16 The Gashouse Gang (Frank Frisch, Mike Gonzalez, Buzzy Wares) .25
17 Lou Gehrig 1.00
18 Lou Gehrig 1.00
19 Lou Gehrig 1.00
20 Lou Gehrig 1.00
21 Charlie Gehringer .25
22 Lefty Gomez .25
23 Lefty Grove .25
24 Bucky Harris .25
25 Harry Heilmann .25
26 Rogers Hornsby .50
27 Waite Hoyt .25
28 Carl Hubbell .25
29 Miller Huggins .25
30 Walter Johnson .50
31 Bill Klem .25
32 Connie Mack .25
33 Heinie Manush .25
34 Rube Marquard .25
35 Pepper Martin .25
36 Christy Mathewson .50
37 Christy Mathewson .50
38 Christy Mathewson .50
39 Joe McCarthy .25
40 John McGraw .25
41 Fred Merkle .25
42 Mel Ott .25
43 Roger Peckinpaugh .25
44 Herb Pennock .25
45 Babe Ruth 1.50
46 Babe Ruth 1.50
47 Babe Ruth 1.50
48 Babe Ruth 1.50
49 Babe Ruth 1.50
50 Babe Ruth 1.50
51 Al Simmons .25
52 Tris Speaker .50
53 Casey Stengel .40
54 Bill Terry .25
55 Pie Traynor .25
56 Rube Waddell .25
57 Honus Wagner .75
58 Lloyd Waner, Paul Waner .25
59 Paul Waner .25
60 Hack Wilson .25

1991 Sports Cards Inserts

One of the many card publications which sprang up in the early 1990s was this monthly titled, "Allen Kaye's Sports Cards News & Price Guides". Among its features were three different series of card inserts. The largest was the four-sport series which was inserted at the rate of 18 cards per issue. Cards were printed in sheets of nine on bright silver foil. Backs are in red and black and feature a career summary and copyright information, along with photo credits and card number. Only the baseball player cards are checklisted here.

MT
Complete (Baseball) Set (17): 11.00
Common Player: .25
1 Nolan Ryan 2.00
3 Roger Clemens .75
5 Eric Lindros .75
7 John Olerud .40
10 Nolan Ryan 2.00
12 Ryne Sandberg .75
15 Jose Canseco .50
17 Wade Boggs .50
20 Cal Ripken Jr. 2.50
22 Scott Erickson .25
24 Cecil Fielder .25
25 Darryl Strawberry .40
27 Kevin Maas .25
28 Ramon Martinez .25
30 Cal Ripken Jr. 2.50
32 Tom Glavine .25
35 Bobby Bonilla, Will Clark .25

Player names in *Italic* type indicate a rookie card.

1991-92 Sports Cards Old Time Tobacco Cards

Through the course of its 11-issue run between Oct.-Nov., 1991 and Oct., 1992, "Allen Kaye's Sports Cards News & Price Guides" magazine issued this collectors issue as part of a cardboard sheet inserted into each magazine. Five of the cards were printed around the top and side of a larger portrait card. Instructions in the early issues said to cut out the smaller cards to 1-1/2" x 2-5/8" size. After the 5th issue, the cards were printed with outside lines to guide cutting. The cards feature sepia photos and graphics with backs printed in red and black.

MT
Complete Set (55): 12.00
Common Card: .25
1 Babe Ruth 1.00
2 Lou Gehrig .50
3 Ty Cobb .50
4 Walter Johnson .40
5 Rogers Hornsby .40
6 Cy Young .40
7 Nap Lajoie .25
8 Christy Mathewson .40
9 Tris Speaker .25
10 Honus Wagner .40
11 John McGraw .25
12 Connie Mack .25
13 Joe Cronin .25
14 Mickey Cochrane .25
15 Grover Alexander .25
16 Joe Jackson .75
17 Jimmie Foxx .25
18 Pie Traynor .25
19 Lefty Grove .25
20 Carl Hubbell .25
21 Dizzy Dean .40
22 Mel Ott .25
23 Hank Greenberg .40
24 Bill Dickey .25
25 Frankie Frisch .25
26 Jim Thorpe .50
27 Bill Terry .25
28 Gabby Hartnett .25
29 Luke Appling .25
30 Charlie Gehringer .25
31 Rube Foster .25
32 Martin Dihigo .25
33 Buck Leonard .25
34 Oscar Charleston .25
35 Pop Lloyd .25
36 Cool Papa Bell .25
37 Ray Dandridge .25
38 Lou Dials .25
39 Judy Johnson .25
40 Josh Gibson .40
41 Satchel Paige .50
42 Monte Irvin .25
43 Roy Campanella .40
44 Larry Doby .40
45 Jackie Robinson .50
46 Babe Ruth (All-Star Pitcher) .50
47 Babe Ruth (Bambino Sold To Yanks) .50
48 Babe Ruth (Slugging Superstar) .50
49 Babe Ruth (1921 Subway Series) .50
50 Babe Ruth (AL MVP) .50
51 Babe Ruth (Ruth Rebounds In 1926) .50
52 Babe Ruth (The Babe Hits 60 HRs) .50
53 Babe Ruth (Best Team In History) (w/ Lou Gehrig) .50
54 Babe Ruth (The Called Shot) .50
55 Babe Ruth (The Makings Of The Man) .50

1991-92 Sports Cards Portrait Cards

One of the features of "Allen Kaye's Sports Cards News & Price Guides" magazine was the pair of large-format (5-1/4" x 8-1/4") "Portrait" cards in each issue. One of the cards appeared on the cover and the other was inserted on an inside page on a cardboard sheet with five smaller cards. The cards featured a portrait and a couple of action pictures by artist Clifford Spohn. The player's name appears in large type at top, with team-color graphics around. Backs have a dotted line to indicate cutting dimensions and include a black-and-white photo, career highlights and summary. Beginning with Issue #9 (Aug., 1992) the front design was changed to include just one action picture along with the portrait, with the name now appearing in a banner at top. The numbering sequence was reset at that point. Only the baseball players are included in this checklist.

MT
Complete (Baseball) Set (14): 27.50
Common Card: .50
1 Nolan Ryan 5.00
3 Pete Rose 3.00
7 Cal Ripken Jr. 5.00
9 Bobby Bonilla .50
11 Frank Thomas 5.00
12 Jose Canseco 1.50
13 Roger Clemens 1.50
15 Ken Griffey Jr. 6.00
16 Mickey Mantle 6.00
1 Ryne Sandberg 2.00
2 Hank Aaron 3.00
3 Will Clark 1.00
4 Joe DiMaggio 4.00
5 Dave Justice 1.00

1992 Sports Cards Inserts

As "Allen Kaye's Sports Cards News & Price Guides" magazine continued into 1992, the design of the 18 insert cards which appeared in each issue was slightly changed, with each of the nine-card sheets being printed on bright gold-foil instead of 1991's silver. The border around the color player photo was also changed from red to purple. Backs continued to provide career information in red and black. Only the baseball players from the set are included in this checklist.

MT
Complete (Baseball) Set (90): 29.00
Common Player: .25
2 Chuck Knoblauch .45
4 Juan Gonzalez .40
6 Reggie Sanders .25
8 Phil Plantier .25
9 Kirby Puckett .75
11 Steve Avery .25
14 Frank Thomas 2.50
16 Ivan Rodriguez .35
18 Andujar Cedeno .25
20 Ozzie Smith .40
23 Jim Abbott .25
24 Tino Martinez .25
27 Robin Ventura .25
30 Robin Yount .40
32 Andy Van Slyke .25
33 Barry Bonds .50
35 Jeff Bagwell .40
39 Ryan Klesko .30
41 Todd Van Poppel .25
42 Terry Pendleton .25
43 Mark Langston .25
47 Royce Clayton .25
49 Derek Bell .25
51 Ken Griffey Jr. 3.00
52 Pat Kelly .25
54 Fred McGriff .35
56 Don Mattingly .60
58 Ron Gant .25
59 Barry Larkin .35
60 Andre Dawson .35
63 Andujar Cedeno .25
64 Roberto Alomar .50
65 Will Clark .30
69 Mark Grace .40
71 Ruben Sierra .25
73 Howard Johnson .25
75 Alan Trammell .25
77 Roger Clemens .50
84 Ramon Martinez .25
85 Benito Santiago .25
86 Dave Justice .35
89 Scott Erickson .25
90 George Brett .60
93 Vince Coleman .25
94 Jose Canseco .40
95 Mark McGwire 3.00
99 Jim Thome .25
100 Ryne Sandberg .50
104 Bo Jackson .35
106 Jack Morris .25
107 Sandy Alomar Jr. .25
109 Birth Of A Legend (Nolan Ryan) .75
110 Ryans's World Series Save (Nolan Ryan) .75
111 Nolan Joins The Angels (Nolan Ryan) .75
112 Ryan Throws 4 No-Hitters (Nolan Ryan) .75
113 Nolan Returns Home (Nolan Ryan) .75
114 Ryan Sets Strikeout Mark (Nolan Ryan) .75
115 Nolan Signs With Texas (Nolan Ryan) .75
116 Ryan Hurls 7th No-Hitter (Nolan Ryan) .75
117 Remarkable Nolan Ryan (Nolan Ryan) .75
122 Brien Taylor .25
128 Eric Karros .25
129 Lee Smith .25
130 Todd Hundley .25
131 Danny Tartabull .25
132 Shawn Green .45
137 Tony Gwynn .50
138 Dean Palmer .25
139 Dave McCarty .25
141 Matt Williams .35
143 Raul Mondesi .40
145 Johnny Bench (World Series Heroes) .50
146 Brooks Robinson (World Series Heroes) .40
147 Roberto Clemente (World Series Heroes) 2.00
148 Don Drysdale (World Series Heroes) .25
149 Mickey Mantle (World Series Heroes) 4.00
150 Sandy Koufax (World Series Heroes) 1.50
151 Eddie Mathews (World Series Heroes) .25

152	Al Kaline (World Series Heroes)	.40
153	Mike Schmidt (World Series Heroes)	.50
154	Lou Brock (World Series Heroes)	.25
155	Reggie Jackson (World Series Heroes)	.40
156	George Brett (World Series Heroes)	.50
157	Willie McCovey (World Series Heroes)	.25
158	Hank Aaron (World Series Heroes)	.75
159	Willie Mays (World Series Heroes)	.75
160	Warren Spahn (World Series Heroes)	.25
161	Duke Snider (World Series Heroes)	.40
162	Frank Robinson (World Series Heroes)	.35

1986 Sportsco Living Legends

This collectors issue, though labeled Series 1 on back, does not appear to have been followed up with any additional cards. In 2-1/2" x 3-1/2" format with broadly rounded corners, the color photos on card fronts are enhanced with a glossy coating. Backs are in black-and-white with the official title, "The Living Legends" at top and player identification at center. A copyright line appears at bottom with a series and card number.

		MT
Complete Set (6):		6.00
Common Player:		.50
1	Mickey Mantle	5.00
2	Whitey Ford	1.00
3	Ernie Banks	1.00
4	Al Kaline	1.00
5	Frank Robinson	1.00
6	Al Kaline, Harmon Killebrew, Warren Spahn, Hoyt Wilhelm	.50

1986 Sportsco N.Y. Mets

This collectors issue is officially titled, "The Incredible Boys from New York," as printed on the back. The cards are in the standard 2-1/2" x 3-1/2" format with broadly rounded corners. The color photos on front are enhanced by a glossy finish. Backs are in black-and-white with the player's name and position, a copyright notice and card number.

		MT
Complete Set (6):		6.00
Common Player:		.50
1	Dwight Gooden	2.00
2	Darryl Strawberry	2.00
3	Gary Carter	.75
4	Kevin Mitchell	.50
5	Keith Hernandez	.75
6	Ray Knight	.50

Player names in *Italic* type indicate a rookie card.

1984 Sports Design Products Doug West

The art of Doug West is featured in portrait and action pictures on each card in this collectors set. The player art is on a blue background. In the white border at bottom a red box displays the player name and position in white. The producer's logo is in black at bottom-right. Backs are printed in red and blue on white with personal data, career summary and stats. Production was reported as 5,000 sets, including 250 uncut sheets. Issue price was about $10.

		MT
Complete Set (24):		24.00
Common Player:		.50
1	Jackie Robinson	1.00
2	Luis Aparicio	.50
3	Roberto Clemente	3.50
4	Mickey Mantle	5.00
5	Joe DiMaggio	3.00
6	Tony Stargell	.50
7	Brooks Robinson	.60
8	Ty Cobb	1.50
9	Don Drysdale	.50
10	Bob Feller	.50
11	Stan Musial	1.00
12	Al Kaline	.50
13	Willie Mays	1.75
14	Willie McCovey	.50
15	Thurman Munson	.75
16	Charlie Gehringer	.50
17	Eddie Mathews	.50
18	Carl Yastrzemski	.50
19	Warren Spahn	.50
20	Ted Williams	2.00
21	Ernie Banks	.60
22	Roy Campanella	.75
23	Harmon Killebrew	.50
24	Duke Snider	.75

1985 Sports Design Products Doug West

The art of Doug West is featured in portrait and action pictures on each card in this collectors' set. In the white border at bottom a blue box displays the player name and position in white. The producer's logo is in black at bottom-right. Backs are printed in red and blue on white with personal data, career summary and stats. Cards are numbered sequentially from the previous year's issue. Besides 5,000 complete sets (issued at $8), 250 uncut sheets were also sold.

		MT
Complete Set (24):		10.00
Common Player:		.25
25	Lou Gehrig	1.00
26	Hoyt Wilhelm	.25
27	Enos Slaughter	.25
28	Lou Brock	.25
29	Mickey Cochrane	.25
30	Gil Hodges	.50
31	Yogi Berra	.50
32	Carl Hubbell	.25
33	Hank Greenberg	.50
34	Casey Stengel	.40
35	Pee Wee Reese	.35
36	Ralph Kiner	.25
37	Satchel Paige	.50
38	Richie Ashburn	.35
39	Connie Mack	.25
40	Dick Groat	.25
41	Tony Oliva	.25
42	Honus Wagner	.40
43	Denny McLain	.25
44	Johnny Mize	.25
45	Bob Lemon	.25
46	Fergie Jenkins	.25
47	Babe Ruth	2.00
48	Ted Kluszewski	.35

1986 Sports Design Products J.D. McCarthy

This collectors issue (actually produced in 1985 but carrying a 1986 copyright) combines the classic 1969 Topps design with the color photos of baseball's premier photographer of the 1960s, J.D. McCarthy. Cards are checklisted here alphabetically.

		MT
Complete Set (24):		12.00
Common Player:		.50
(1)	Hank Aaron	2.00
(2)	Felipe Alou	.50
(3)	Walter Alston	.50
(4)	Ernie Banks	.60
(5)	Ernie Banks, Gil Hodges	.50
(6)	Lou Brock	.50
(7)	Jim Bunning	.50
(8)	Roberto Clemente	4.00
(9)	Joe DiMaggio	4.00
(10)	Whitey Ford	.75
(11)	Sandy Koufax	1.50
(12)	Mickey Mantle	6.00
(13)	Juan Marichal	.50
(14)	Roger Maris	2.00
(15)	Eddie Mathews	.50
(16)	Willie Mays	2.00
(17)	J.D. McCarthy, Ted Williams	.50
(18)	Robin Roberts	.50
(19)	Brooks Robinson	.60
(20)	Duke Snider	.60
(21)	Willie Stargell	.50
(22)	Casey Stengel	.50
(23)	Billy Williams	.50
(24)	Carl Yastrzemski	.50

1991 Sports Educational Workbook

By inserting nine-card sheets into what they termed an educational workbook, the producers of these collectors cards sought to get around the licensing requirements - it didn't work. Each $7.95 workbook contains two pages on cardboard stock featuring color action photos bordered in gold foil. Backs are printed in black and blue on white and feature recent stats. A print run of 50,000 copies was announced, with extra card sets being made available for $15.

		MT
Complete Set (18):		5.50
Common Player:		.25
1	Will Clark	.25
2	Ryne Sandberg	.50
3	Roger Clemens	.40
4	Ken Griffey Jr.	1.25
5	Frank Thomas	1.00
6	Nolan Ryan	1.00
7	Dwight Gooden	.35
8	Cal Ripkin Jr. (Ripken)	1.00
9	Wade Boggs	.45
10	Darryl Strawberry	.25
11	Dave Justice	.25
12	George Brett	.35
13	Jose Canseco	.35
14	Bo Jackson	.25
15	Rickey Henderson	.25
16	Cecil Fielder	.25
17	"Pudge" Rodriguez	.35
18	Todd Van Poppel	.25

1989-91 Sports Illustrated For Kids

Beginning with its January, 1989, issue and continuing for three years, the magazine "Sports Illustrated For Kids" produced a set of sportscards featuring many professional and amateur stars in more than a dozen sports. Generally issued in a nine-card panel, cards were perforated so they could be removed from the magazine and seperated from each other. A variety of designs and formats were used in that period. Only the pro baseball cards from the series are checklisted here.

		MT
Complete (Baseball) Set (60):		95.00
Common Player:		.50
5	Orel Hershiser	.50
11	Jose Canseco	1.50
20	Darryl Strawberry	1.50
31	Mike Greenwell	.50
33	Tony Gwynn	2.50
35	Frank Viola	.50
37	Don Mattingly	4.00
43	Ozzie Smith	2.50
46	Rickey Henderson	1.50
48	Chris Sabo	.50
52	Andre Dawson	.75
56	Alan Trammell	.50
60	Roger Clemens	2.50
63	Andres Galarraga	.75
64	John Franco	.50
69	Cal Ripken Jr.	5.00
70	Will Clark	1.50
75	Bo Jackson	.75
81	Nolan Ryan	5.00
90	Mike Schmidt	3.50
112	Kevin Mitchell	.50
121	Ryne Sandberg	2.50
127	Robin Yount	2.50
133	Dave Stewart	.50
140	Eric Davis	.75
144	Mike Scott	.50
146	Mark McGwire	6.00
151	Dwight Gooden	1.50
158	Ken Griffey Jr.	6.00
162	George Brett	3.00
165	Ruben Sierra	.50
167	Kirby Puckett	3.50
171	Carlton Fisk	.75
172	Fred McGriff	.50
176	Wade Boggs	1.50
178	Tim Raines	.50
181	Bobby Bonilla	.50
189	Kelly Gruber	.50
197	Dennis Eckersley	.50
205	Cecil Fielder	.50
212	Jackie Robinson	4.00
216	Babe Ruth	5.00
229	Barry Bonds	3.50
240	Jose Rijo	.50
248	Sandy Alomar Jr.	.65
251	Ron Gant	.50
259	David Justice	.65
261	Bob Welch	.50
266	Doug Drabek	.50
268	Rafael Palmeiro	.65
271	Paul Molitor	2.00
275	Bobby Thigpen	.50
279	Edgar Martinez	.50
282	Dave Winfield	2.00
283	Mark Grace	1.50
288	Dwight Evans	.50
289	Dave Henderson	.50
294	Lee Smith	.50
303	Ramon Martinez	.50
321	Ty Cobb	1.00

1992-2000 Sports Illustrated For Kids

A new series, with cards numbered consecutively from #1, of magazine insert cards was begun with SI For Kids' in its January, 1992, issue. Like the earlier series, cards are 2-1/2" x 3-1/2" inches and most often found as a nine-card panel, with each card perforated for removal from the magazine and separation from the other cards. As before, the cards feature a number of different designs, formats and back treatments. Backs usually include a few personal details and a trivia question. Only the cards of pro baseball players are checklisted here.

		MT
Complete (Baseball) Set (150):		165.00
Common Player:		.25
24	Terry Pendleton	.25
29	Kirby Puckett	2.00
36	Roger Clemens	2.00
40	Tom Glavine	.50
45	Frank Thomas	5.00
50	Jim Abbott	.35
54	Roberto Alomar	.75
64	Matt Williams	.55
68	Bobby Bonilla	.25
72	Chuck Finley	.25
75	Danny Tartabull	.25
81	Jack Morris	.25
86	Will Clark	1.50
108	Lou Gehrig	2.00
121	Juan Gonzalez	2.00
132	Cal Ripken Jr.	5.00
136	Jack McDowell	.25
144	Marquis Grissom	.25
145	Andy Van Slyke	.25
152	Dennis Eckersley	.25
157	Barry Bonds	2.50
162	Greg Maddux	3.00
168	Nolan Ryan	5.00
170	Dave Winfield	1.50
173	Ken Griffey Jr.	6.00
178	Wade Boggs	1.00
185	Kirk Gibson	.25
187	Albert Belle	.75
190	John Burkett	.25
196	John Kruk	.25
199	Randy Johnson	.75
204	Lou Whitaker	.25
212	Yogi Berra	.50
236	Lenny Dykstra	.25
244	Carlos Baerga	.25

254	Joe Carter	.25
266	Chuck Carr	.25
268	Julie Croteau (Colorado Silver Bullets)	.25
270	Michael Jordan	6.00
274	Andres Galarraga	.75
278	Jeff Bagwell	1.00
281	John Olerud	.65
288	Tony Gwynn	2.50
292	Gregg Jefferies	.25
297	Mo Vaughn	.50
298	Moises Alou	.60
305	Jimmy Key	.25
311	Mike Mussina	.75
313	Mike Piazza	3.00
320	Stan Musial	1.50
327	Matt Williams	.55
343	Frank Thomas (boyhood photo)	4.00
349	Michael Jordan (boyhood photo)	4.00
359	Kenny Lofton	.50
362	Raul Mondesi	.50
381	David Cone	.50
386	Brady Anderson	.50
390	Eric Karros	.25
391	Paul O'Neill	.50
398	Eddie Murray	1.50
402	Barry Larkin	.25
407	Edgar Martinez	.25
412	Mark McGwire	6.00
416	Albert Belle (cartoon)	.65
430	Mark Grace	.75
433	Chuck Knoblauch	.35
447	Chipper Jones	3.00
451	Tom Glavine (boyhood photo)	.25
455	Cal Ripken Jr. (boyhood photo)	4.00
462	Jeff Conine	.25
470	Hideo Nomo	.75
475	Bernie Williams	.50
478	Craig Biggio	.75
485	Jose Mesa	.25
497	Roberto Alomar	.75
503	John Smoltz	.45
505	Henry Rodriguez	.25
513	Rey Ordonez	.50
516	Ellis Burks	.25
518	Ivan Rodriguez	.75
543	Alex Rodriguez	5.00
553	Mo Vaughn	.50
561	Andy Pettitte	.50
562	Barry Bonds	2.50
582	Andruw Jones	3.00
		.50
570	Randy Johnson (April Fool card as L.A. Laker)	1.00
572	Ken Griffey Jr. (April Fool card as Orlando Magic)	4.00
588	Brian Jordan	.25
589	Derek Jeter	2.00
596	Juan Gonzalez	2.00
598	Andres Galarraga	.50
608	Mark McGwire	6.00
611	Pat Hentgen	.25
627	Cal Ripken Jr. (cartoon as Tin Man)	4.50
634	Sandy Alomar Jr.	.65
641	Brady Anderson	.50
652	Jeff Bagwell	1.00
669	Larry Walker	.50
673	Roger Clemens	.75
685	Frank Thomas	2.00
693	Denny Neagle	.25
695	Tony Gwynn	.75
697	Mike Piazza	2.00
703	Kenny Lofton	.25
708	Moises Alou	.25
712	Dante Bichette	.35
720	John Wetteland	.25
721	Curt Schilling	.25
725	Nomar Garciaparra	1.50
734	Ken Griffey Jr. (cartoon as The Cat in the Hat)	2.00
737	Greg Maddux (cartoon as Encyclopedia Brown)	.50
743	Sammy Sosa	3.00
749	David Wells	.25
	Mark McGwire (The Best of 1998)	3.00
758	Pedro Martinez	.75
768	Ila Borders	.25
770	David Cone	.25
784	Mike Piazza (April Fool's - hockey player)	.50
790	Mark McGwire (April Fool's - Chicago Cub)	3.00
795	Craig Biggio	.75
796	Tom Glavine	.25
802	Alex Rodriguez	.75
804	Trevor Hoffman	.25
813	Rickey Henderson	.50
815	Mo Vaughn	.25
817	Vinny Castilla	.25
820	John Smoltz	.25
825	Jose Canseco	.35
831	Matt Williams	.25
833	Derek Jeter	2.00
840	Ivan Rodriguez (as Darth Vader)	.35
841	Roger Clemens (as lion)	.25
846	Ken Caminiti (as ghoul)	.25
849	Roberto Alomar	.35
No#	Greg Maddux (Fall/ Winter 1999)	.25
No#	Ken Griffey Jr. (Fall/ Winter 1999)	3.00
856	Randy Johnson	.25
866	Babe Ruth	2.00
869	Mickey Mantle	5.00
870	Jackie Robinson	2.00
882	Mark McGwire (kid photo)	1.00
884	Mariano Rivera	.25
892	Billy the Marlin (mascot)	.25
896	The Phillie Phanatic (mascot)	.25
901	Kevin Millwood	.25
906	Manny Ramirez	.35
910	Bernie Williams	.25
914	Larry Walker	.25

1996-98 Sports Illustrated For Kids Legends

Unlike the nine-card panels which appear in every issue of SI For Kids, the Legends series appear sporadically as a four-card panel honoring the past greats of many sports. While designs vary from issue to issue, the format of the cards has remained a consistent 2-9/16" x 4". Only the baseball players are listed here.

		MT
Complete (Baseball) Set (7):		9.00
Common Player:		.25
45	Sadaharu Oh	1.00
52	Willie Mays	2.00
66	Mike Schmidt	1.50
	APRIL, 1998	
(1)	Mickey Mantle	3.00
(2)	Bob Feller	.50
(3)	Lou Brock	.50
(4)	Honus Wagner	.50

1999 SI for Kids 10th Anniversary Sheet

Saluting Sports Illustrated for Kids on its 10th anniversary, Major League Baseball, the players' association and the four card licensees created a special eight-card insert sheet which appears in the magazine's July, 1999, issue. The sheet consists of nine 2-1/2" x 3-1/2" cards printed on thin cardboard and perforated for easy separation. The Fleer and Upper Deck cards are very similar to those companies' regular 1999 issues, except for the absence of foil printing and UV coating. The Topps and Pacific offerings are new designs. All player cards feature action photos on front along with card company and SI for Kids logos. Backs have another photo plus stats, biographical data and copyright notice.

		MT
Complete Sheet:		6.00
Complete Set (9):		4.00
Common Player:		.50
7	J.D. Drew (Fleer Tradition)	.75
49	Cal Ripken Jr. (Upper Deck)	.75
205	Ken Griffey Jr. (Upper Deck)	1.00
266	Sammy Sosa (SkyBox Thunder)	.50
---	Roger Clemens (Topps)	.50
---	Tony Gwynn (Pacific)	.50
---	Mark McGwire (Pacific)	1.00
---	Mike Piazza (Topps)	.50
---	Sponsors' card	.50

1997 Sports Illustrated

Fleer teamed up with Sports Illustrated to produce a 180-card World Series Fever set. The regular set is divided into six different subsets: 96 Player Cards, 27 Fresh Faces, 18 Inside Baseball, 18 SIber Vision, 12 covers and 9 Newsmakers. Inserts included the Extra Edition parallel set, Great Shots, Cooperstown Collection and Autographed Mini-Cover Redemption Cards. Cards were sold in six-card packs for $1.99 each.

		MT
Complete Set (180):		40.00
Common Player:		.10
Wax Box:		40.00
1	Bob Abreu (Fresh Faces)	.20
2	Jaime Bluma (Fresh Faces)	.10
3	Emil Brown (Fresh Faces)	.10
4	Jose Cruz, Jr. (Fresh Faces)	.50
5	Jason Dickson (Fresh Faces)	.15
6	Nomar Garciaparra (Fresh Faces)	2.50
7	Todd Greene (Fresh Faces)	.20
8	Vladimir Guerrero (Fresh Faces)	1.50
9	Wilton Guerrero (Fresh Faces)	.10
10	Jose Guillen (Fresh Faces)	1.00
11	Hideki Irabu (Fresh Faces)	1.00
12	Russ Johnson (Fresh Faces)	.10
13	Andruw Jones (Fresh Faces)	2.00
14	Damon Mashore (Fresh Faces)	.10
15	Jason McDonald (Fresh Faces)	.10
16	Ryan McGuire (Fresh Faces)	.10
17	Matt Morris (Fresh Faces)	.10
18	Kevin Orie (Fresh Faces)	.10
19	Dante Powell (Fresh Faces)	.10
20	Pokey Reese (Fresh Faces)	.15
21	Joe Roa (Fresh Faces)	.10
22	Scott Rolen (Fresh Faces)	2.00
23	Glendon Rusch (Fresh Faces)	.10
24	Scott Spiezio (Fresh Faces)	.10
25	Bubba Trammell (Fresh Faces)	1.00
26	Todd Walker (Fresh Faces)	.75
27	Jamey Wright (Fresh Faces)	.10
28	Ken Griffey Jr. (Season Highlights)	2.00
29	Tino Martinez (Season Highlights)	.10
30	Roger Clemens (Season Highlights)	.50
31	Hideki Irabu (Season Highlights)	.75
32	Kevin Brown (Season Highlights)	.10
33	Chipper Jones, Cal Ripken Jr. (Season Highlights)	1.25
34	Sandy Alomar (Season Highlights)	.10
35	Ken Caminiti (Season Highlights)	.20
36	Randy Johnson (Season Highlights)	.40
37	Andy Ashby (Inside Baseball)	.10
38	Jay Buhner (Inside Baseball)	.10
39	Joe Carter (Inside Baseball)	.10
40	Darren Daulton (Inside Baseball)	.10
41	Jeff Fassero (Inside Baseball)	.10
42	Andres Galarraga (Inside Baseball)	.10
43	Rusty Greer (Inside Baseball)	.10
44	Marquis Grissom (Inside Baseball)	.10
45	Joey Hamilton (Inside Baseball)	.10
46	Jimmy Key (Inside Baseball)	.10
47	Ryan Klesko (Inside Baseball)	.25
48	Eddie Murray (Inside Baseball)	.40
49	Charles Nagy (Inside Baseball)	.10
50	Dave Nilsson (Inside Baseball)	.10
51	Ricardo Rincon (Inside Baseball)	.10
52	Billy Wagner (Inside Baseball)	.10
53	Dan Wilson (Inside Baseball)	.10
54	Dmitri Young (Inside Baseball)	.10
55	Roberto Alomar (S.I.BER Vision)	.60
56	Sandy Alomar Jr. (S.I.BER Vision)	.10
57	Scott Brosius (S.I.BER Vision)	.10
58	Tony Clark (S.I.BER Vision)	.50
59	Carlos Delgado (S.I.BER Vision)	.25
60	Jermaine Dye (S.I.BER Vision)	.10
61	Darin Erstad (S.I.BER Vision)	2.00
62	Derek Jeter (S.I.BER Vision)	1.50
63	Jason Kendall (S.I.BER Vision)	.10
64	Hideo Nomo (S.I.BER Vision)	.25
65	Rey Ordonez (S.I.BER Vision)	.10
66	Andy Pettitte (S.I.BER Vision)	.50
67	Manny Ramirez (S.I.BER Vision)	.60
68	Edgar Renteria (S.I.BER Vision)	.10
69	Shane Reynolds (S.I.BER Vision)	.10
70	Alex Rodriguez (S.I.BER Vision)	1.50
71	Ivan Rodriguez (S.I.BER Vision)	.40
72	Jose Rosado (S.I.BER Vision)	.10
73	John Smoltz	.20
74	Tom Glavine	.20
75	Greg Maddux	2.50
76	Chipper Jones	2.50
77	Kenny Lofton	.50
78	Fred McGriff	.30
79	Kevin Brown	.10
80	Alex Fernandez	.10
81	Al Leiter	.10
82	Bobby Bonilla	.10
83	Gary Sheffield	.30
84	Moises Alou	.20
85	Henry Rodriguez	.10
86	Mark Grudzielanek	.10
87	Pedro Martinez	.25
88	Todd Hundley	.20
89	Bernard Gilkey	.10
90	Bobby Jones	.10
91	Curt Schilling	.10
92	Ricky Bottalico	.10
93	Mike Lieberthal	.10
94	Sammy Sosa	2.00
95	Ryne Sandberg	1.00
96	Mark Grace	.35
97	Deion Sanders	.20
98	Reggie Sanders	.10
99	Barry Larkin	.20
100	Craig Biggio	.20
101	Jeff Bagwell	1.50
102	Derek Bell	.10
103	Brian Jordan	.10
104	Ray Lankford	.10
105	Ron Gant	.10
106	Al Martin	.10
107	Kevin Elster	.10
108	Jermaine Allensworth	.10
109	Vinny Castilla	.10
110	Dante Bichette	.20
111	Larry Walker	.30
112	Mike Piazza	2.50
113	Eric Karros	.10
114	Todd Hollandsworth	.10
115	Raul Mondesi	.25
116	Hideo Nomo	.50
117	Ramon Martinez	.10
118	Ken Caminiti	.25
119	Tony Gwynn	2.00
120	Steve Finley	.10
121	Barry Bonds	1.00
122	J.T. Snow	.10
123	Rod Beck	.10
124	Cal Ripken Jr.	3.00
125	Mike Mussina	.60
126	Brady Anderson	.10
127	Bernie Williams	.75
128	Derek Jeter	3.00
129	Tino Martinez	.15
130	Andy Pettitte	.75
131	David Cone	.20
132	Mariano Rivera	.20
133	Roger Clemens	1.50
134	Pat Hentgen	.10
135	Juan Guzman	.10
136	Bob Higginson	.10
137	Tony Clark	1.00
138	Travis Fryman	.10
139	Mo Vaughn	.50
140	Tim Naehring	.10
141	John Valentin	.10
142	Matt Williams	.25
143	David Justice	.30
144	Jim Thome	.60
145	Chuck Knoblauch	.25
146	Paul Molitor	.40
147	Marty Cordova	.10
148	Frank Thomas	1.50
149	Albert Belle	.75
150	Robin Ventura	.10
151	John Jaha	.10
152	Jeff Cirillo	.10
153	Jose Valentin	.10
154	Jay Bell	.10
155	Jeff King	.10
156	Kevin Appier	.10
157	Ken Griffey Jr.	4.00
158	Alex Rodriguez	3.00
158p	Alex Rodriguez (overprinted "PROMOTIONAL SAMPLE")	3.00
159	Randy Johnson	.60
160	Juan Gonzalez	2.00
161	Will Clark	.25
162	Dean Palmer	.10
163	Tim Salmon	.15
164	Jim Edmonds	.10
165	Jim Leyritz	.10
166	Jose Canseco	.30
167	Jason Giambi	.10
168	Mark McGwire	4.00
169	Barry Bonds	1.00
170	Alex Rodriguez	1.50
171	Roger Clemens	.75
172	Ken Griffey Jr.	2.00
173	Greg Maddux	1.25
174	Mike Piazza	1.25
175	Will Clark, Mark McGwire	2.00
176	Hideo Nomo	.25
177	Cal Ripken Jr.	1.50
178	Ken Griffey Jr., Frank Thomas	.75
179	Alex Rodriguez, Derek Jeter	1.50
180	John Wetteland	.10

1997 Sports Illustrated Extra Edition

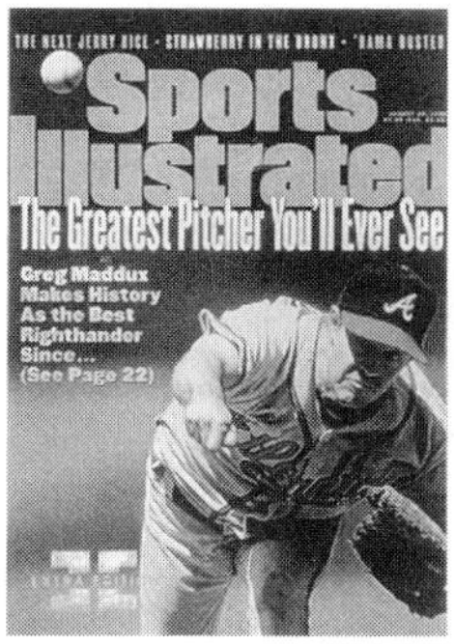

Each of the regular cards in the premiere Fleer SI issue is also found in a parallel set designated on front in gold holographic foil as "Extra Edition". Backs of the cards carry a serial number from within a production of 500 of each card.

	MT
Complete Set (180):	1200.
Common Player:	2.50
Extra Edition Stars: 15X (See 1997 Sports Illustrated for checklist and base card values.)	

1997 Sports Illustrated Autographed Mini-Covers

Six different players autographed 250 magazine mini-covers that were available through randomly seeded redemption cards. The players who autographed cards were Hank Aaron, Willie Mays, Frank Robinson, Kirby Puckett, Cal Ripken Jr., and Alex Rodriguez.

	MT
Complete Set (6):	800.00
Common Player:	60.00
Alex Rodriguez	200.00
Cal Ripken Jr.	250.00
Kirby Puckett	125.00
Willie Mays	150.00
Frank Robinson	60.00
Hank Aaron	150.00

1997 Sports Illustrated Box Topper

This special version of A-Rod's card was packaged one per box of foil packs. It was intended to be inserted into die-cuts on the box to create a sample display for the new issue. The card measures 2-1/2" x 4-1/16". The back is in black-and-white with instructions on how to insert the card into the box.

	MT
Alex Rodriguez	6.00

1997 Sports Illustrated Cooperstown Collection

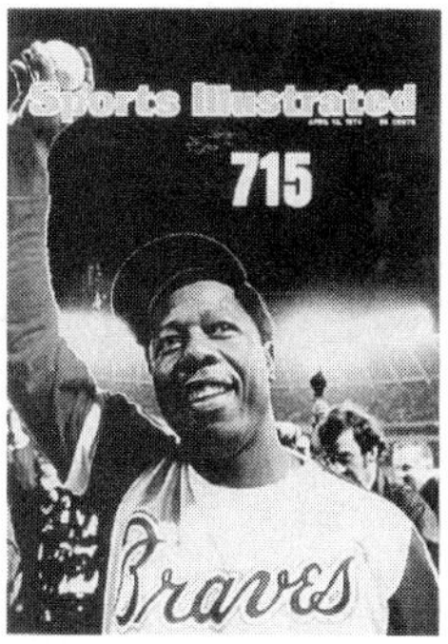

This 12-card insert (found 1:12 packs) lets collectors relive classic SI baseball covers with a description of each issue on the back.

		MT
	Complete Set (12):	60.00
	Common Player:	5.00
1	Hank Aaron	15.00
2	Yogi Berra	8.00
3	Lou Brock	5.00
4	Rod Carew	5.00
5	Juan Marichal	5.00
6	Al Kaline	5.00
7	Joe Morgan	5.00
8	Brooks Robinson	10.00
9	Willie Stargell	5.00
10	Kirby Puckett	12.00
11	Willie Mays	15.00
12	Frank Robinson	8.00

1997 Sports Illustrated Great Shots

A 25-card insert, found one per pack, designed to highlight Sports Illustrated's classic photography. Each card in the set folds out to a 5" x 7" format to showcase a larger photo.

		MT
	Complete Set (25):	5.00
	Common Player:	.10
(1)	Roberto Alomar	.20
(2)	Andy Ashby	.10
(3)	Albert Belle	.25
(4)	Barry Bonds	.25
(5)	Jay Buhner	.10
(6)	Vinny Castilla, Andres Galarraga	.10
(7)	Darren Daulton	.10
(8)	Juan Gonzalez	.40
(9)	Ken Griffey Jr.	1.00
(10)	Derek Jeter	.60
(11)	Randy Johnson	.15
(12)	Chipper Jones	.60
(13)	Eric Karros	.10
(14)	Ryan Klesko	.15
(15)	Kenny Lofton	.20
(16)	Greg Maddux	.45
(17)	Mark McGwire	1.00
(18)	Mike Piazza	.60
(19)	Cal Ripken Jr.	.75
(20)	Alex Rodriguez	.75
(21)	Ryne Sandberg	.35
(22)	Deion Sanders	.15
(23)	John Smoltz	.10
(24)	Frank Thomas	.50
(25)	Mo Vaughn	.20

1998 Sports Illustrated Promo

This sample card was issued to preview the 1998 Sports Illustrated set presented by Fleer. The card is in the same format as the regular issue, but has a different card number and is overprinted "PROMOTIONAL SAMPLE" on front and back.

		MT
8	Cal Ripken Jr.	5.00

1998 Sports Illustrated

The second of three Sports Illustrated releases of 1998 from Fleer contained 200 cards and featured exclusive Sports Illustrated photography and commentary. Cards arrived in six-card packs and carried a Sports Illustrated logo in a top corner. The set included a Travis Lee One to Watch cards (#201) that was inserted just before going to press. Subsets included: Baseball's Best (129-148), One to Watch (149-176), and '97 in Review (177-200). Inserts sets include: Extra Edition and First Edition parallels, Autographs, Covers, Editor's Choice and Opening Day Mini Posters.

		MT
	Complete Set (201):	40.00
	Common Player:	.10
	Wax Box:	42.00
1	Edgardo Alfonzo	.10
2	Roberto Alomar	.50
3	Sandy Alomar	.10
4	Moises Alou	.20
5	Brady Anderson	.20
6	Garret Anderson	.10
7	Kevin Appier	.10
8	Jeff Bagwell	1.00
9	Jay Bell	.10
10	Albert Belle	.75
11	Dante Bichette	.25
12	Craig Biggio	.20
13	Barry Bonds	.75
14	Bobby Bonilla	.10
15	Kevin Brown	.20
16	Jay Buhner	.10
17	Ellis Burks	.10
18	Mike Cameron	.20
19	Ken Caminiti	.20
20	Jose Canseco	.25
21	Joe Carter	.10
22	Vinny Castilla	.10
23	Jeff Cirillo	.10
24	Tony Clark	.50
25	Will Clark	.25
26	Roger Clemens	1.00
27	David Cone	.20
28	Jose Cruz Jr.	.20
29	Carlos Delgado	.25
30	Jason Dickson	.10
31	Dennis Eckersley	.10
32	Jim Edmonds	.20
33	Scott Erickson	.10
34	Darin Erstad	.75
35	Shawn Estes	.10
36	Jeff Fassero	.10
37	Alex Fernandez	.10
38	Chuck Finley	.10
39	Steve Finley	.10
40	Travis Fryman	.10
41	Andres Galarraga	.25
42	Ron Gant	.20
43	Nomar Garciaparra	1.50
44	Jason Giambi	.10
45	Tom Glavine	.20
46	Juan Gonzalez	1.50
47	Mark Grace	.25
48	Willie Green	.10
49	Rusty Greer	.10
50	Ben Grieve	1.00
51	Ken Griffey Jr.	4.00
52	Mark Grudzielanek	.10
53	Vladimir Guerrero	1.00
54	Juan Guzman	.10
55	Tony Gwynn	1.50
56	Joey Hamilton	.10
57	Rickey Henderson	.25
58	Pat Hentgen	.10
59	Livan Hernandez	.10
60	Bobby Higginson	.10
61	Todd Hundley	.20
62	Hideki Irabu	.25
63	John Jaha	.10
64	Derek Jeter	2.00
65	Charles Johnson	.10
66	Randy Johnson	.50
67	Andruw Jones	.75
68	Bobby Jones	.10
69	Chipper Jones	2.00
70	Brian Jordan	.10
71	David Justice	.25
72	Eric Karros	.10
73	Jeff Kent	.10
74	Jimmy Key	.10
75	Darryl Kile	.10
76	Jeff King	.10
77	Ryan Klesko	.20
78	Chuck Knoblauch	.25
79	Ray Lankford	.10
80	Barry Larkin	.20
81	Kenny Lofton	.45
82	Greg Maddux	2.00
83	Al Martin	.10
84	Edgar Martinez	.10
85	Pedro Martinez	.25
86	Tino Martinez	.20
87	Mark McGwire	4.00
88	Paul Molitor	.50
89	Raul Mondesi	.25
90	Jamie Moyer	.10
91	Mike Mussina	.60
92	Tim Naehring	.10
93	Charles Nagy	.10
94	Denny Neagle	.10
95	Dave Nilsson	.10
96	Hideo Nomo	.50
97	Rey Ordonez	.10
98	Dean Palmer	.10
99	Rafael Palmeiro	.20
100	Andy Pettitte	.50
101	Mike Piazza	2.00
102	Brad Radke	.10
103	Manny Ramirez	.75
104	Edgar Renteria	.10
105	Cal Ripken Jr.	2.50
106	Alex Rodriguez	3.00
106p	Alex Rodriguez ("PROMOTIONAL SAMPLE")	3.00
107	Henry Rodriguez	.10
108	Ivan Rodriguez	.75
109	Scott Rolen	1.00
110	Tim Salmon	.25
111	Curt Schilling	.25
112	Gary Sheffield	.25
113	John Smoltz	.20
114	J.T. Snow	.10
115	Sammy Sosa	2.00
116	Matt Stairs	.10
117	Shannon Stewart	.10
118	Frank Thomas	1.00
119	Jim Thome	.40
120	Justin Thompson	.20
121	Mo Vaughn	.45
122	Robin Ventura	.20
123	Larry Walker	.40
124	Rondell White	.20
125	Bernie Williams	.60
126	Matt Williams	.25
127	Tony Womack	.10
128	Jaret Wright	1.75
129	Edgar Renteria (Baseball's Best)	.10
130	Kenny Lofton (Baseball's Best)	.40
131	Tony Gwynn (Baseball's Best)	.75
132	Mark McGwire (Baseball's Best)	2.00
133	Craig Biggio (Baseball's Best)	.10
134	Charles Johnson (Baseball's Best)	.10
135	J.T. Snow (Baseball's Best)	.10
136	Ken Caminiti (Baseball's Best)	.10
137	Vladimir Guerrero (Baseball's Best)	.40
138	Jim Edmonds (Baseball's Best)	.10
139	Randy Johnson (Baseball's Best)	.25
140	Darryl Kile (Baseball's Best)	.10
141	John Smoltz (Baseball's Best)	.10
142	Greg Maddux (Baseball's Best)	1.00
143	Andy Pettitte (Baseball's Best)	.25
144	Ken Griffey Jr. (Baseball's Best)	1.50
145	Mike Piazza (Baseball's Best)	1.00
146	Todd Greene (Baseball's Best)	.10
147	Vinny Castilla (Baseball's Best)	.10
148	Derek Jeter (Baseball's Best)	1.00
149	Robert Machado (One to Watch)	.10
150	Mike Gulan (One to Watch)	.10
151	Randall Simon (One to Watch)	.20
152	Michael Coleman (One to Watch)	.10
153	Brian Rose (One to Watch)	.25
154	*Scott Eyre* (One to Watch)	.25
155	*Magglio Ordonez* (One to Watch)	1.00
156	Todd Helton (One to Watch)	.75
157	Juan Encarnacion (One to Watch)	.10
158	Mark Kotsay (One to Watch)	.50
159	Josh Booty (One to Watch)	.10
160	*Melvin Rosario* (One to Watch)	.25
161	Shane Halter (One to Watch)	.10
162	Paul Konerko (One to Watch)	1.00
163	*Henry Blanco* (One to Watch)	.20
164	Antone Williamson (One to Watch)	.10
165	Brad Fullmer (One to Watch)	.20
166	Ricky Ledee (One to Watch)	.50
167	Ben Grieve (One to Watch)	.60
168	*Frank Catalanotto* (One to Watch)	.20
169	Bobby Estalella (One to Watch)	.10
170	Dennis Reyes (One to Watch)	.10
171	Kevin Polcovich (One to Watch)	.10
172	Jacob Cruz (One to Watch)	.10
173	Ken Cloude (One to Watch)	.10
174	Eli Marrero (One to Watch)	.10
175	Fernando Tatis (One to Watch)	.10
176	Tom Evans (One to Watch)	.10
177	Everett, Garciaparra (97 in Review)	.75
178	Eric Davis (97 in Review)	.10
179	Roger Clemens (97 in Review)	.50
180	Butler, Murray (97 in Review)	.10
181	Frank Thomas (97 in Review)	.75
182	Curt Schilling (97 in Review)	.10
183	Jeff Bagwell (97 in Review)	.50
184	McGwire, Griffey (97 in Review)	1.50
185	Kevin Brown (97 in Review)	.10
186	Cordova, Rincon (97 in Review)	.10
187	Charles Johnson (97 in Review)	.10
188	Hideki Irabu (97 in Review)	.20
189	Tony Gwynn (97 in Review)	.75
190	Sandy Alomar (97 in Review)	.10
191	Ken Griffey Jr. (97 in Review)	1.50

192 Larry Walker (97 in Review) .20
193 Roger Clemens (97 in Review) .50
194 Pedro Martinez (97 in Review) .20
195 Nomar Garciaparra (97 in Review) .75
196 Scott Rolen (97 in Review) .50
197 Brian Anderson (97 in Review) .10
198 Tony Saunders (97 in Review) .10
199 Fla. Celebration (97 in Review) .10
200 Livan Hernandez (97 in Review) .10
201 Travis Lee (One to Watch) (SP) 2.00

1998 Sports Illustrated Extra Edition

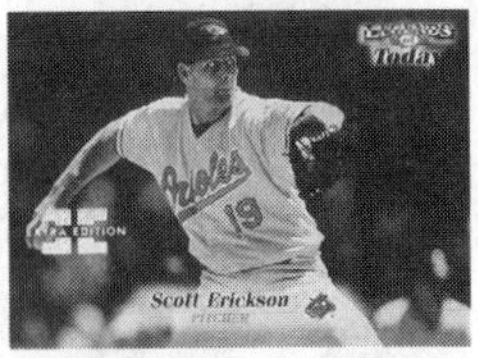

Extra Edition is a 201-card parallel set that includes a holofoil stamp on the front and sequential numbering to 250 on the back. There is also a First Edition version of these that was identical on the front, but contains the text "The Only 1 of 1 First Edition" in purple lettering on the card back.

	MT
Common Player:	4.00
Extra Edition Stars: 20X (See 1998 Sports Illustrated for checklist and base card values.)	

1998 Sports Illustrated Autographs

This six-card insert featured autographs of players with the following production: Brock 500, Cruz Jr. 250, Fingers 500, Grieve 250, Konerko 250 and Robinson 500. The Konerko and Greive cards were available through redemptions until Nov. 1, 1999.

	MT
Complete Set (6):	400.00
Common Player:	30.00
Lou Brock (500)	75.00
Jose Cruz Jr. (250)	30.00
Rollie Fingers (500)	20.00
Ben Grieve (exchange card) (250)	45.00
Ben Grieve (signed card)	90.00
Paul Konerko (exchange card) (250)	20.00
Paul Konerko (signed card)	40.00
Brooks Robinson (250)	75.00

1998 Sports Illustrated Covers

This 10-card insert set pictures actual Sports Illustrated covers on trading cards. The cards are numbered with a "C" prefix and inserted one per nine packs.

		MT
Complete Set (10):		30.00
Common Player:		2.00
Inserted 1:9		
1	Griffey, Piazza	7.00
2	Derek Jeter	5.00
3	Ken Griffey Jr.	8.00
4	Cal Ripken Jr.	6.00
5	Manny Ramirez	3.50
6	Jay Buhner	2.00
7	Matt Williams	2.00
8	Randy Johnson	2.00
9	Deion Sanders	2.00
10	Jose Canseco	2.00

1998 Sports Illustrated Editor's Choice

Editor's Choice includes 10 top players in 1998 as profiled by the editors of Sports Illustrated. Cards are numbered with an "EC" prefix and seeded one per 24 packs.

		MT
Complete Set (10):		100.00
Common Player:		4.00
Inserted 1:24		
1	Ken Griffey Jr.	20.00
2	Alex Rodriguez	15.00
3	Frank Thomas	10.00
4	Mark McGwire	20.00
5	Greg Maddux	12.00
6	Derek Jeter	12.00
7	Cal Ripken Jr.	15.00
8	Nomar Garciaparra	12.00
9	Jeff Bagwell	8.00
10	Jose Cruz Jr.	4.00

1998 Sports Illustrated Mini-Posters

Thirty 5" x 7" mini-posters were available at a rate of one per pack. The posters took the top player or two from each team and added their 1998 schedule. Backs were blank so the cards are numbered on the front with an "OD" prefix.

		MT
Complete Set (30):		8.00
Common Player:		.15
Inserted 1:1		
1	Tim Salmon	.25
2	Travis Lee	.40
3	John Smoltz, Greg Maddux	.75
4	Cal Ripken Jr.	1.50
5	Nomar Garciaparra	.75
6	Sammy Sosa	.50
7	Frank Thomas	.75
8	Barry Larkin	.15
9	David Justice	.15
10	Larry Walker	.25
11	Tony Clark	.40
12	Livan Hernandez	.15
13	Jeff Bagwell	.60
14	Kevin Appier	.15
15	Mike Piazza	1.00
16	Fernando Vina	.15
17	Chuck Knoblauch	.25
18	Vladimir Guerrero	.40
19	Rey Ordonez	.15
20	Bernie Williams	.30
21	Matt Stairs	.15
22	Curt Schilling	.15
23	Tony Womack	.15
24	Mark McGwire	2.00
25	Tony Gwynn	.75
26	Barry Bonds	.50
27	Ken Griffey Jr.	2.00
28	Fred McGriff	.25
29	Juan Gonzalez, Alex Rodriguez	.75
30	Roger Clemens	.75

1998 Sports Illustrated Then & Now

Then and Now was the first of three Sports Illustrated Baseball releases in 1998. It contained 150 cards and sold in six-card packs, with five cards and a mini-poster. Fronts carried photos of active and retired players, as well as rookies. There was only one subset - A Place in History (37-53) - and it compared statistics between current players and retired greats. The product arrived with an Extra Edition parallel set, Art of the Game, Autograph Redemptions, Covers and Great Shots inserts. There was also an Alex Rodriguez checklist/ mini-poster seeded every 12th pack.

		MT
Complete Set (150):		25.00
Common Player:		.10
Extra Edition Stars: 15X		
Production 500 sets		
Wax Box:		45.00
1	Luis Aparicio (Legends of the Game)	.10
2	Richie Ashburn (Legends of the Game)	.10
3	Ernie Banks (Legends of the Game)	.75
4	Yogi Berra (Legends of the Game)	.75
5	Lou Boudreau (Legends of the Game)	.10
6	Lou Brock (Legends of the Game)	.25
7	Jim Bunning (Legends of the Game)	.10
8	Rod Carew (Legends of the Game)	.25
9	Bob Feller (Legends of the Game)	.25
10	Rollie Fingers (Legends of the Game)	.10
11	Bob Gibson (Legends of the Game)	.50
12	Fergie Jenkins (Legends of the Game)	.10
13	Al Kaline (Legends of the Game)	.25
14	George Kell (Legends of the Game)	.10
15	Harmon Killebrew (Legends of the Game)	.50
16	Ralph Kiner (Legends of the Game)	.10
17	Tommy Lasorda (Legends of the Game)	.10
18	Juan Marichal (Legends of the Game)	.10
19	Eddie Mathews (Legends of the Game)	.40
20	Willie Mays (Legends of the Game)	1.50
21	Willie McCovey (Legends of the Game)	.10
22	Joe Morgan (Legends of the Game)	.10
23	Gaylord Perry (Legends of the Game)	.10
24	Kirby Puckett (Legends of the Game)	1.00
25	Pee Wee Reese (Legends of the Game)	.10
26	Phil Rizzuto (Legends of the Game)	.25
27	Robin Roberts (Legends of the Game)	.10
28	Brooks Robinson (Legends of the Game)	.75
29	Frank Robinson (Legends of the Game)	.50
30	Red Schoendienst (Legends of the Game)	.10
31	Enos Slaughter (Legends of the Game)	.10
32	Warren Spahn (Legends of the Game)	.50
33	Willie Stargell (Legends of the Game)	.20
34	Earl Weaver (Legends of the Game)	.10
35	Billy Williams (Legends of the Game)	.20
36	Early Wynn (Legends of the Game)	.10
37	Rickey Henderson (A Place in History)	.15
38	Greg Maddux (A Place in History)	1.50
39	Mike Mussina (A Place in History)	.50
40	Cal Ripken Jr. (A Place in History)	2.00
41	Albert Belle (A Place in History)	.60
42	Frank Thomas (A Place in History)	1.50
43	Jeff Bagwell (A Place in History)	.75
44	Paul Molitor (A Place in History)	.45
45	Chuck Knoblauch (A Place in History)	.25
46	Todd Hundley (A Place in History)	.10
47	Bernie Williams (A Place in History)	.40
48	Tony Gwynn (A Place in History)	1.00
49	Barry Bonds (A Place in History)	.60
50	Ken Griffey Jr. (A Place in History)	2.50
51	Randy Johnson (A Place in History)	.50
52	Mark McGwire (A Place in History)	2.50
53	Roger Clemens (A Place in History)	.75
54	Jose Cruz Jr. (A Place in History)	.25
55	Roberto Alomar (Legends of Today)	.50
56	Sandy Alomar (Legends of Today)	.10
57	Brady Anderson (Legends of Today)	.10
58	Kevin Appier (Legends of Today)	.10
59	Jeff Bagwell (Legends of Today)	.75
60	Albert Belle (Legends of Today)	.60
61	Dante Bichette (Legends of Today)	.20
62	Craig Biggio (Legends of Today)	.25
63	Barry Bonds (Legends of Today)	.60
64	Kevin Brown (Legends of Today)	.10
65	Jay Buhner (Legends of Today)	.10
66	Ellis Burks (Legends of Today)	.10
67	Ken Caminiti (Legends of Today)	.25
68	Jose Canseco (Legends of Today)	.25
69	Joe Carter (Legends of Today)	.10
70	Vinny Castilla (Legends of Today)	.10
71	Tony Clark (Legends of Today)	.40
72	Roger Clemens (Legends of Today)	.75
73	David Cone (Legends of Today)	.20
74	Jose Cruz Jr. (Legends of Today)	.25
75	Jason Dickson (Legends of Today)	.10
76	Jim Edmonds (Legends of Today)	.10
77	Scott Erickson (Legends of Today)	.10
78	Darin Erstad (Legends of Today)	.60
79	Alex Fernandez (Legends of Today)	.10
80	Steve Finley (Legends of Today)	.10
81	Travis Fryman (Legends of Today)	.10
82	Andres Galarraga (Legends of Today)	.25
83	Nomar Garciaparra (Legends of Today)	1.50
84	Tom Glavine (Legends of Today)	.20
85	Juan Gonzalez (Legends of Today)	1.00
86	Mark Grace (Legends of Today)	.25
87	Willie Greene (Legends of Today)	.10
88	Ken Griffey Jr. (Legends of Today)	2.50
89	Vladimir Guerrero (Legends of Today)	1.00
90	Tony Gwynn (Legends of Today)	1.00
91	Livan Hernandez (Legends of Today)	.10
92	Bobby Higginson (Legends of Today)	.10
93	Derek Jeter (Legends of Today)	1.50
94	Charles Johnson (Legends of Today)	.10
95	Randy Johnson (Legends of Today)	.40
96	Andruw Jones (Legends of Today)	1.00
97	Chipper Jones (Legends of Today)	1.50
98	David Justice (Legends of Today)	.25
99	Eric Karros (Legends of Today)	.10
100	Jason Kendall (Legends of Today)	.10
101	Jimmy Key (Legends of Today)	.10
102	Darryl Kile (Legends of Today)	.10
103	Chuck Knoblauch (Legends of Today)	.25
104	Ray Lankford (Legends of Today)	.10
105	Barry Larkin (Legends of Today)	.15
106	Kenny Lofton (Legends of Today)	.45
107	Greg Maddux (Legends of Today)	1.50
108	Al Martin (Legends of Today)	.10
109	Edgar Martinez (Legends of Today)	.10
110	Pedro Martinez (Legends of Today)	.25
111	Ramon Martinez (Legends of Today)	.10
112	Tino Martinez (Legends of Today)	.15
113	Mark McGwire (Legends of Today)	2.50
114	Raul Mondesi (Legends of Today)	.25
115	Matt Morris (Legends of Today)	.10
116	Charles Nagy (Legends of Today)	.10
117	Denny Neagle (Legends of Today)	.10
118	Hideo Nomo (Legends of Today)	.50
119	Dean Palmer (Legends of Today)	.10
120	Andy Pettitte (Legends of Today)	.50
121	Mike Piazza (Legends of Today)	1.50

122	Manny Ramirez (Legends of Today)	.75
123	Edgar Renteria (Legends of Today)	.10
124	Cal Ripken Jr. (Legends of Today)	2.00
125	Alex Rodriguez (Legends of Today)	2.00
126	Henry Rodriguez (Legends of Today)	.10
127	Ivan Rodriguez (Legends of Today)	.60
128	Scott Rolen (Legends of Today)	1.00
129	Tim Salmon (Legends of Today)	.15
130	Curt Schilling (Legends of Today)	.10
131	Gary Sheffield (Legends of Today)	.20
132	John Smoltz (Legends of Today)	.20
133	Sammy Sosa (Legends of Today)	2.00
134	Frank Thomas (Legends of Today)	1.50
135	Jim Thome (Legends of Today)	.50
136	Mo Vaughn (Legends of Today)	.45
137	Robin Ventura (Legends of Today)	.10
138	Larry Walker (Legends of Today)	.25
139	Bernie Williams (Legends of Today)	.40
140	Matt Williams (Legends of Today)	.25
141	Jaret Wright (Legends of Today)	1.00
142	Michael Coleman (Legends of the Future)	.10
143	Juan Encarnacion (Legends of the Future)	.20
144	Brad Fullmer (Legends of the Future)	.25
145	Ben Grieve (Legends of the Future)	1.00
146	Todd Helton (Legends of the Future)	.75
147	Paul Konerko (Legends of the Future)	.75
148	Derrek Lee (Legends of the Future)	.20
149	*Magglio Ordonez* (Legends of the Future)	1.00
150	Enrique Wilson (Legends of the Future)	.10

1998 Sports Illustrated Then & Now Extra Edition

This 150-card set paralleled the base set and was distinguished by an "Extra Edition" foil stamp on the front. There were 500 sets of Extra Edition and the cards were individually numbered on the back.

	MT
Common Extra Edition:	2.00
Extra Edition Stars: 15X	
Production 500 sets	
(See 1998 Sports Illustrated Then & Now for checklist and base card values.)	

1998 Sports Illustrated Then & Now Art of the Game

Art of the Game was an eight-card insert featuring reproductions of original artwork of current and retired baseball stars done by eight popular sports artists. Cards are numbered with a "AG" prefix and inserted one per nine packs.

		MT
Complete Set (8):		22.00
Common Player:		1.50
Inserted 1:9		
1	It's Gone	5.00
2	Alex Rodriguez	5.00
3	Mike Piazza	4.00
4	Brooks Robinson	2.50
5	David Justice (All-Star)	2.00
6	Cal Ripken Jr.	5.00
7	The Prospect and the Prospector	1.50
8	Barry Bonds	2.50

1998 Sports Illustrated Then & Now Autographs

Six autograph redemption cards were randomly inserted into packs of Then & Now and could be exchanged prior to Nov. 1, 1999. The signed cards were produced in the following quantities: Clemens 250, Gibson 500, Gwynn 250, Killebrew 500, Mays 250 and Rolen 250. Four of the six cards use the same fronts as the Covers insert; Gibson and Rolen cards each feature unique card fronts.

	MT
Complete Set (6):	600.00
Common Autograph:	70.00
Redemption Cards: 25%	
Bob Gibson (500)	40.00
Tony Gwynn (250)	150.00
Roger Clemens (250)	200.00
Scott Rolen (250)	125.00
Willie Mays (250)	200.00
Harmon Killebrew (500)	40.00

1998 Sports Illustrated Then & Now Covers

This 12-card insert features color shots of six actual Sports Illustrated covers, including six current players and six retired players. The cards are numbered with a "C" prefix and were seeded one per 18 packs.

		MT
Complete Set (12):		75.00
Common Player:		4.00
Inserted 1:18		
1	Lou Brock (10/16/67)	4.00
2	Kirby Puckett (4/6/92)	8.00
3	Harmon Killebrew (4/8/63 - inside)	4.00
4	Eddie Mathews (8/16/54)	10.00
5	Willie Mays (5/22/72)	10.00
6	Frank Robinson (10/6/69)	6.00
7	Cal Ripken Jr. (9/11/95)	12.00
8	Roger Clemens (5/12/86)	8.00
9	Ken Griffey Jr. (10/16/95)	15.00
10	Mark McGwire (6/1/92)	15.00
11	Tony Gwynn (7/28/97)	8.00
12	Ivan Rodriguez (8/11/97)	5.00

1998 Sports Illustrated Then & Now Great Shots!

This 25-card set featured 5" x 7" fold-out mini-posters using Sports Illustrated photos. Great Shots were inserted one per pack and contained a mix of retired and current players.

		MT
Complete Set (25):		5.00
Common Player:		.10
Inserted 1:1		
1	Ken Griffey Jr.	1.50
2	Frank Thomas	.50
3	Alex Rodriguez	.75
4	Andruw Jones	.40
5	Chipper Jones	.60
6	Cal Ripken Jr.	.75
7	Mark McGwire	1.50
8	Derek Jeter	.60
9	Greg Maddux	.60
10	Jeff Bagwell	.40
11	Mike Piazza	.60
12	Scott Rolen	.40
13	Nomar Garciaparra	.60
14	Jose Cruz Jr.	.10
15	Charles Johnson	.10
16	Fergie Jenkins	.10
17	Lou Brock	.10
18	Bob Gibson	.10
19	Harmon Killebrew	.10
20	Juan Marichal	.10
21	Brooks Robinson	.25
22	Rod Carew	.20
23	Yogi Berra	.25
24	Willie Mays	.50
25	Kirby Puckett	.50

1998 Sports Illustrated Then & Now Road to Cooperstown

Road to Cooperstown features 10 current players who are having Hall of Fame careers. The insert name is printed across the back in bold, gold letters. Cards are numbered with a "RC" prefix and were inserted one per 24 packs.

		MT
Complete Set (10):		80.00
Common Player:		3.00
Inserted 1:24		
1	Barry Bonds	5.00
2	Roger Clemens	8.00
3	Ken Griffey Jr.	20.00
4	Tony Gwynn	10.00
5	Rickey Henderson	3.00
6	Greg Maddux	12.00
7	Paul Molitor	4.00
8	Mike Piazza	12.00
9	Cal Ripken Jr.	15.00
10	Frank Thomas	10.00

1998 Sports Illustrated World Series Fever

The third and final Sports Illustrated release of 1998 contained 150 cards and focused on the World Series while recapping memorable moments from the season. The set also included many stars of tomorrow, like Kerry Wood, Orlando Hernandez, Ben Grieve and Travis Lee. Once again, all the photos were taken from Sports Illustrated archives. The set has two subsets - 10 Magnificent Moments and 20 Cover Collection. The set is paralleled twice in Extra and First Edition parallel sets, and has three insert sets - MVP Collection, Reggie Jackson's Picks and Autumn Excellence.

		MT
Complete Set (150):		40.00
Common Player:		.10
Wax Box:		42.00
1	Mickey Mantle (Covers)	3.00
2	1957 World Series Preview (Covers)	.20
3	1958 World Series Preview (Covers)	.20
4	1959 World Series Preview (Covers)	.20
5	1962 World Series (Covers)	.20
6	Lou Brock (Covers)	.30
7	Brooks Robinson (Covers)	.75
8	Frank Robinson (Covers)	.50
9	1974 World Series (Covers)	.20
10	Reggie Jackson (Covers)	.50
11	1985 World Series (Covers)	.20
12	1987 World Series (Covers)	.20
13	Orel Hershiser (Covers)	.10
14	Rickey Henderson (Covers)	.10
15	1991 World Series (Covers)	.20
16	1992 World Series (Covers)	.10
17	Joe Carter (Covers)	.10
18	1995 World Series (Covers)	.20
19	1996 World Series (Covers)	.40
20	Edgar Renteria (Covers)	.10
21	Bill Mazeroski (Magnificent Moments)	.10
22	Joe Carter (Magnificent Moments)	.10
23	Carlton Fisk (Magnificent Moments)	.10
24	Bucky Dent (Magnificent Moments)	.10
25	Mookie Wilson (Magnificent Moments)	.10
26	Enos Slaughter (Magnificent Moments)	.10
27	Mickey Lolich (Magnificent Moments)	.10
28	Bobby Richardson (Magnificent Moments)	.10
29	Kirk Gibson (Magnificent Moments)	.10
30	Edgar Renteria (Magnificent Moments)	.10
31	Albert Belle	.60
32	Kevin Brown	.10
33	Brian Rose	.10
34	Ron Gant	.15
35	Jeromy Burnitz	.10
36	Andres Galarraga	.40
37	Jim Edmonds	.10
38	Jose Cruz Jr.	.20
39	Mark Grudzielanek	.10
40	Shawn Estes	.10
41	Mark Grace	.25
42	Nomar Garciaparra	2.00
43	Juan Gonzalez	1.50
44	Tom Glavine	.20
45	Brady Anderson	.10
46	Tony Clark	.50
47	Jeff Cirillo	.10
48	Dante Bichette	.25
49	Ben Grieve	1.00
50	Ken Griffey Jr.	3.00
51	Edgardo Alfonzo	.10
52	Roger Clemens	1.00
53	Pat Hentgen	.10
54	Todd Helton	.75
55	Andy Benes	.10
56	Tony Gwynn	1.50
57	Andruw Jones	.75
58	Bobby Higginson	.10
59	Bobby Jones	.10
60	Darryl Kile	.10
61	Chan Ho Park	.25
62	Charles Johnson	.10
63	Rusty Greer	.10
64	Travis Fryman	.10
65	Derek Jeter	2.00
66	Jay Buhner	.10
67	Chuck Knoblauch	.40
68	David Justice	.40
69	Brian Hunter	.10
70	Eric Karros	.10
71	Edgar Martinez	.10
72	Chipper Jones	2.00
73	Barry Larkin	.15
74	Mike Lansing	.10
75	Craig Biggio	.25
76	Al Martin	.10
77	Barry Bonds	.75
78	Randy Johnson	.50
79	Ryan Klesko	.25
80	Mark McGwire	3.00
81	Fred McGriff	.25
82	Javy Lopez	.10
83	Kenny Lofton	.50
84	Sandy Alomar Jr.	.10
85	Matt Morris	.10
86	Paul Konerko	.25
87	Ray Lankford	.10
88	Kerry Wood	.75
89	Roberto Alomar	.50
90	Greg Maddux	2.00
91	Travis Lee	.75
92	Moises Alou	.25
93	Dean Palmer	.10
94	Hideo Nomo	.40
95	Ken Caminiti	.20
96	Pedro Martinez	.75
97	Raul Mondesi	.25
98	Denny Neagle	.10
99	Tino Martinez	.30
100	Mike Mussina	.00
101	Kevin Appier	.10
102	Vinny Castilla	.20
103	Jeff Bagwell	1.00
104	Paul O'Neill	.20
105	Rey Ordonez	.10
106	Vladimir Guerrero	1.00
107	Rafael Palmeiro	.25
108	Alex Rodriguez	2.50
109	Andy Pettitte	.50
110	Carl Pavano	.20
111	Henry Rodriguez	.10
112	Gary Sheffield	.25
113	Curt Schilling	.20
114	John Smoltz	.20
115	Reggie Sanders	.10
116	Scott Rolen	1.00

117	Mike Piazza	2.00
118	Manny Ramirez	1.00
119	Cal Ripken Jr.	2.50
120	Brad Radke	.10
121	Tim Salmon	.30
122	Brett Tomko	.10
123	Robin Ventura	.10
124	Mo Vaughn	.50
125	A.J. Hinch	.10
126	Derrek Lee	.10
127	*Orlando Hernandez*	3.00
128	Aramis Ramirez	.50
129	Frank Thomas	1.50
130	J.T. Snow	.10
131	*Magglio Ordonez*	.75
132	Bobby Bonilla	.10
133	Marquis Grissom	.10
134	Jim Thome	.40
135	Justin Thompson	.10
136	Matt Williams	.30
137	Matt Stairs	.10
138	Wade Boggs	.40
139	Chuck Finley	.10
140	Jaret Wright	.75
141	Ivan Rodriguez	.75
142	Brad Fullmer	.25
143	Bernie Williams	.40
144	Jason Giambi	.10
145	Larry Walker	.40
146	Tony Womack	.10
147	Sammy Sosa	2.00
148	Rondell White	.20
149	Todd Stottlemyre	.10
150	Shane Reynolds	.10

1998 Sports Illustrated WS Fever Extra Edition

Extra Edition parallels the entire 150-card base set and is identified by a gold foil stamp on the card front and sequential numbering to 98 sets on the back. World Series Fever also includes one-of-one parallel versions called First Edition. These have the same fronts, but are numbered 1 of 1 on back.

	MT
Common Player:	5.00
Stars: 30X	
Production 98 sets	
(See 1998 Sports Illustrated World Series Fever for checklist and base values.)	

1998 Sports Illustrated WS Fever Autumn Excellence

Autumn Excellence honors players with the most select World Series records. The 10-card set was seeded one per 24 packs, while rarer Gold versions were seeded one per 240 packs.

		MT
Complete Set (10):		60.00
Common Player:		2.00
Inserted 1:24		
Golds: 4X		
Inserted 1:240		
AE1	Willie Mays	7.50
AE2	Kirby Puckett	6.00
AE3	Babe Ruth	20.00
AE4	Reggie Jackson	5.00
AE5	Whitey Ford	2.00
AE6	Lou Brock	2.00
AE7	Mickey Mantle	15.00
AE8	Yogi Berra	5.00
AE9	Bob Gibson	4.00
AE10	Don Larsen	4.00

1998 Sports Illustrated WS Fever Reggie Jackson Picks

Reggie Jackson's Picks contains top players that Jackson believes have what it takes to perform on center stage in the World Series. Fronts have a shot of the player with his name in the background, and a head shot of Reggie Jackson in the bottom right corner. These were numbered with a "RP" prefix and inserted one per 12 packs.

		MT
Complete Set (15):		70.00
Common Player:		1.50
Inserted 1:12		
1	Paul O'Neill	1.50
2	Barry Bonds	3.00
3	Ken Griffey Jr.	12.50
4	Juan Gonzalez	6.00
5	Greg Maddux	7.50
6	Mike Piazza	7.50
7	Larry Walker	2.00
8	Mo Vaughn	1.50
9	Roger Clemens	4.00
10	John Smoltz	1.50
11	Alex Rodriguez	9.00
12	Frank Thomas	5.00
13	Mark McGwire	12.50
14	Jeff Bagwell	4.00
15	Randy Johnson	2.50

1998 Sports Illustrated WS Fever MVP Collection

This 10-card insert set features select MVPs from the World Series. Card fronts contain a shot of the player over a white border with the year in black letters and the insert and player's name in blue foil. MVP Collection inserts were seeded one per four packs and numbered with a "MC" prefix.

		MT
Complete Set (10):		7.50
Common Player:		.75
Inserted 1:4		
1	Frank Robinson	1.50
2	Brooks Robinson	2.00
3	Willie Stargell	.75
4	Bret Saberhagen	.75
5	Rollie Fingers	.75
6	Orel Hershiser	.75
7	Paul Molitor	2.00
8	Tom Glavine	.75
9	John Wetteland	.75
10	Livan Hernandez	.75

1999 Sports Illustrated

The Sports Illustrated Baseball by Fleer set consists of a 180-card base set. The base set is composed of 107 player cards, and four subsets. They include Team 2000, Postseason Review, Award Winners, and Season Highlights. Cards come in six-card packs with an SRP of $1.99. The set also includes five insert sets, along with hobby exclusive autographed J.D. Drew cards numbered to 250. The insert sets include: Headliners (1:4), Ones to Watch (1:12), Fabulous 40's (1:20), Fabulous 40's Extra (hobby exclusive), and The Dominators (1:90 and 1:180).

		MT
Complete Set (180):		30.00
Common Player:		.10
Wax Box:		40.00
1	Yankees (Postseason Review)	.25
2	Scott Brosius (Postseason Review)	.10
3	David Wells (Postseason Review)	.10
4	Sterling Hitchcock (Postseason Review)	.10
5	David Justice (Postseason Review)	.25
6	David Cone (Postseason Review)	.20
7	Greg Maddux (Postseason Review)	1.00
8	Jim Leyritz (Postseason Review)	.10
9	Gary Gaetti (Postseason Review)	.10
10	Mark McGwire (Award Winners)	1.50
11	Sammy Sosa (Award Winners)	1.00
12	Larry Walker (Award Winners)	.25
13	Tony Womack (Award Winners)	.10
14	Tom Glavine (Award Winners)	.10
15	Curt Schilling (Award Winners)	.10
16	Greg Maddux (Award Winners)	1.00
17	Trevor Hoffman (Award Winners)	.10
18	Kerry Wood (Award Winners)	.50
19	Tom Glavine (Award Winners)	.10
20	Sammy Sosa (Award Winners)	1.00
21	Travis Lee (Season Highlights)	.30
22	Roberto Alomar (Season Highlights)	.25
23	Roger Clemens (Season Highlights)	.75
24	Barry Bonds (Season Highlights)	.40
25	Paul Molitor (Season Highlights)	.30
26	Todd Stottlemyre (Season Highlights)	.10
27	Chris Hoiles (Season Highlights)	.10
28	Albert Belle (Season Highlights)	.40
29	Tony Clark (Season Highlights)	.25
30	Kerry Wood (Season Highlights)	.50
31	David Wells (Season Highlights)	.10
32	Dennis Eckersley (Season Highlights)	.10
33	Mark McGwire (Season Highlights)	1.50
34	Cal Ripken Jr. (Season Highlights)	1.25
35	Ken Griffey Jr. (Season Highlights)	1.50
36	Alex Rodriguez (Season Highlights)	1.25
37	Craig Biggio (Season Highlights)	.20
38	Sammy Sosa (Season Highlights)	1.00
39	Dennis Martinez (Season Highlights)	.10
40	Curt Schilling (Season Highlights)	.20
41	Orlando Hernandez (Season Highlights)	.50
42	Troy Glaus, *Ben Molina*, Todd Greene ("Team" 2000)	.50
43	Mitch Meluskey, Daryle Ward, Mike Grzanich ("Team" 2000)	.15
44	Eric Chavez, Mike Neill, *Steve Connelly* ("Team" 2000)	.50
45	Roy Halladay, Tom Evans, Kevin Witt ("Team" 2000)	.25
46	George Lombard, Adam Butler, Bruce Chen ("Team" 2000)	.10
47	Ronnie Belliard, Valerio de los Santos, *Rafael Roque* ("Team" 2000)	.25
48	J.D. Drew, Placido Polanco, *Mark Little* ("Team" 2000)	1.00
49	Jason Maxwell, *Jose Nieves*, Jeremi Gonzalez ("Team" 2000)	.20
50	Scott McClain, Kerry Robinson, *Mike Duvall* ("Team" 2000)	.25
51	Ben Ford, *Bryan Corey*, Danny Klassen ("Team" 2000)	.25
52	Angel Pena, Jeff Kubenka, Paul LoDuca ("Team" 2000)	.10
53	Kirk Bullinger, Fernando Seguignol, Tim Young ("Team" 2000)	.10
54	Ramon Martinez, Wilson Delgado, Armando Rios ("Team" 2000)	.10
55	Russ Branyon, *Jolbert Cabrera*, Jason Rakers ("Team" 2000)	.20
56	*Carlos Guillen*, *David Holdridge*, *Giomar Guevara* ("Team" 2000)	.25
57	Alex Gonzalez, Joe Fontenot, Preston Wilson ("Team" 2000)	.25
58	Mike Kinkade, Jay Payton, Masato Yoshii ("Team" 2000)	.10
59	Willis Otanez, Ryan Minor, Calvin Pickering ("Team" 2000)	.20
60	Ben Davis, Matt Clement, Stan Spencer ("Team" 2000)	.10
61	Marlon Anderson, Mike Welch, *Gary Bennett* ("Team" 2000)	.25
62	Abraham Nunez, *Sean Lawrence*, Aramis Ramirez ("Team" 2000)	.10
63	Jonathan Johnson, *Rob Sasser*, *Scott Sheldon* ("Team" 2000)	.25
64	*Keith Glauber*, *Guillermo Garcia*, Eddie Priest ("Team" 2000)	.25
65	Brian Barkley, Jin Ho Cho, Donnie Sadler ("Team" 2000)	.15
66	Derrick Gibson, Mark Strittmatter, *Edgard Clemente* ("Team" 2000)	.15
67	Jeremy Giambi, Dermal Brown, *Chris Hatcher* ("Team" 2000)	.25
68	*Rob Fick*, Gabe Kapler, Marino Santana ("Team" 2000)	.75
69	Corey Koskie, A.J. Pierzynski, Benj Sampson ("Team" 2000)	.20
70	Brian Simmons, Mark Johnson, Craig Wilson ("Team" 2000)	.10
71	Ryan Bradley, Mike Lowell, Jay Tessmer ("Team" 2000)	.10
72	Ben Grieve	.75
73	Shawn Green	.20
74	Rafael Palmeiro	.25
75	Juan Gonzalez	1.50
76	Mike Piazza	2.00
77	Devon White	.10
78	Jim Thome	.30
79	Barry Larkin	.15
80	Scott Rolen	.75
81	Raul Mondesi	.25
82	Jason Giambi	.10
83	Jose Canseco	.40
84	Tony Gwynn	1.50
85	Cal Ripken Jr.	2.50
86	Andy Pettitte	.30
87	Carlos Delgado	.25
88	Jeff Cirillo	.10
89	Bret Saberhagen	.10
90	John Olerud	.20
91	Ron Coomer	.10
92	Todd Helton	.60
93	Ray Lankford	.10
94	Tim Salmon	.25
95	Fred McGriff	.20
96	Matt Stairs	.10
97	Ken Griffey Jr.	3.00
98	Chipper Jones	2.00
99	Mark Grace	.20
100	Ivan Rodriguez	.75
101	Jeromy Burnitz	.10
102	Kenny Rogers	.10
103	Kevin Millwood	.40
104	Vinny Castilla	.20
105	Jim Edmonds	.15
106	Craig Biggio	.40
107	Andres Galarraga	.40
108	Sammy Sosa	2.00
109	Juan Encarnacion	.25
110	Larry Walker	.50
111	John Smoltz	.20
112	Randy Johnson	.50
113	Bobby Higginson	.10
114	Albert Belle	.75
115	Jaret Wright	.40
116	Edgar Renteria	.10
117	Andruw Jones	.75
118	Barry Bonds	.75
119	Rondell White	.20
120	Jamie Moyer	.10
121	Darin Erstad	.75
122	Al Leiter	.20
123	Mark McGwire	3.00
124	Mo Vaughn	.50
125	Livan Hernandez	.10
126	Jason Kendall	.10
127	Frank Thomas	.75
128	Denny Neagle	.10
129	Johnny Damon	.10
130	Derek Bell	.10
131	Jeff Kent	.10
132	Tony Womack	.10
133	Trevor Hoffman	.10
134	Gary Sheffield	.25
135	Tino Martinez	.20
136	Travis Fryman	.10
137	Rolando Arrojo	.20
138	Dante Bichette	.25
139	Nomar Garciaparra	2.00
140	Moises Alou	.20
141	Chuck Knoblauch	.40
142	Robin Ventura	.10
143	Scott Erickson	.10
144	David Cone	.20
145	Greg Vaughn	.20
146	Wade Boggs	.35
147	Mike Mussina	.50
148	Tony Clark	.20
149	Alex Rodriguez	2.50
150	Javy Lopez	.20
151	Bartolo Colon	.10
152	Derek Jeter	2.00
153	Greg Maddux	2.00
154	Kevin Brown	.20
155	Curt Schilling	.20
156	Jeff King	.10
157	Bernie Williams	.50
158	Roberto Alomar	.50
159	Travis Lee	.60
160	Kerry Wood	.75
160p	Kerry Wood ("PROMOTIONAL SAMPLE")	1.00
161	Jeff Bagwell	.75
162	Roger Clemens	1.00
163	Matt Williams	.20

164	Chan Ho Park	.25
165	Damion Easley	.10
166	Manny Ramirez	1.00
167	Quinton McCracken	.10
168	Todd Walker	.25
169	Eric Karros	.20
170	Will Clark	.40
171	Edgar Martinez	.10
172	Cliff Floyd	.10
173	Vladimir Guerrero	1.00
174	Tom Glavine	.25
175	Pedro Martinez	.50
176	Chuck Finley	.10
177	Dean Palmer	.10
178	Omar Vizquel	.10
179	Checklist	.10
180	Checklist	.10

1999 Sports Illustrated Diamond Dominators

This 10-card insert set features five hitters and five pitchers on embossed cards. The hitters are seeded 1 in every 180 packs, while the pitchers are seeded 1 in every 90 packs.

		MT
Complete Set (10):		325.00
Common Player:		7.50
Pitchers inserted 1:90		
Hitters inserted 1:180		
1DD	Kerry Wood	10.00
2DD	Roger Clemens	20.00
3DD	Randy Johnson	7.50
4DD	Greg Maddux	30.00
5DD	Pedro Martinez	7.50
6DD	Ken Griffey Jr.	75.00
7DD	Sammy Sosa	55.00
8DD	Nomar Garciaparra	45.00
9DD	Mark McGwire	75.00
10DD	Alex Rodriguez	55.00

1999 Sports Illustrated Fabulous 40s

This 13-card insert set consists of the players that hit 40 or more homers during the 1998 season. The cards are sculpture embossed and foil-stamped, with the player's home run total also on the card. One card comes with every 20 packs.

		MT
Complete Set (13):		75.00
Common Player:		2.50
Inserted 1:20		
1FF	Mark McGwire	20.00
2FF	Sammy Sosa	12.00
3FF	Ken Griffey Jr.	20.00
4FF	Greg Vaughn	2.50
5FF	Albert Belle	4.50
6FF	Jose Canseco	4.50
7FF	Vinny Castilla	2.50
8FF	Juan Gonzalez	9.00
9FF	Manny Ramirez	7.50
10FF	Andres Galarraga	3.00
11FF	Rafael Palmeiro	3.00
12FF	Alex Rodriguez	15.00
13FF	Mo Vaughn	3.00

1999 Sports Illustrated Fabulous 40s Extra

The insert set parallels the 13 cards in the Fabulous 40s insert set. The cards are hobby exclusive, and contained silver pattern holofoil. Each players cards are hand- numbered to the total number of home runs he hit in 1998.

		MT
Common Player:		30.00
Numbered to amount of HRs		
1FF	Mark McGwire (70)	250.00
2FF	Sammy Sosa (66)	150.00
3FF	Ken Griffey Jr. (56)	250.00
4FF	Greg Vaughn (50)	30.00
5FF	Albert Belle (49)	50.00
6FF	Jose Canseco (46)	60.00
7FF	Vinny Castilla (46)	30.00
8FF	Juan Gonzalez (45)	100.00
9FF	Manny Ramirez (45)	100.00
10FF	Andres Galarraga (44)	40.00
11FF	Rafael Palmeiro (43)	40.00
12FF	Alex Rodriguez (42)	150.00
13FF	Mo Vaughn (40)	50.00

1999 Sports Illustrated Headliners

Headliners is a 25-card insert set that features silver foil stamped, team-color coded cards. One card comes with every four packs.

		MT
Complete Set (25):		45.00
Common Player:		.75
Inserted 1:4		
1H	Vladimir Guerrero	1.75
2H	Randy Johnson	.75
3H	Mo Vaughn	.75
4H	Chipper Jones	3.00
5H	Jeff Bagwell	1.25
6H	Juan Gonzalez	2.50
7H	Mark McGwire	5.00
8H	Cal Ripken Jr.	3.50
9H	Frank Thomas	1.50
10H	Manny Ramirez	1.70
11H	Ken Griffey Jr.	5.00
12H	Scott Rolen	1.25
13H	Alex Rodriguez	3.50
14H	Barry Bonds	1.25
15H	Roger Clemens	1.75
16H	Darin Erstad	1.25
17H	Nomar Garciaparra	3.00
18H	Mike Piazza	3.00
19H	Greg Maddux	0.00
20H	Ivan Rodriguez	1.25
21H	Derek Jeter	3.00
22H	Sammy Sosa	3.00
23H	Andruw Jones	1.25
24H	Pedro Martinez	.75
25H	Kerry Wood	1.00

1999 Sports Illustrated Ones To Watch

This 15-card insert set features the game's top rookies and young stars. The cards have 100%-foil background, and are team-color coded. One card was inserted in every 12 packs.

		MT
Complete Set (15):		20.00
Common Player:		.75
Inserted 1:12		
1OW	J.D. Drew	4.00
2OW	Marlon Anderson	.75
3OW	Roy Halladay	1.50
4OW	Ben Grieve	2.00
5OW	Todd Helton	1.50
6OW	Gabe Kapler	3.00
7OW	Troy Glaus	2.00
8OW	Ben Davis	.75
9OW	Eric Chavez	2.50
10OW	Richie Sexson	.75
11OW	Fernando Seguignol	1.50
12OW	Kerry Wood	2.00
13OW	Bobby Smith	.75
14OW	Ryan Minor	.75
15OW	Jeremy Giambi	1.25
	J.D. Drew Auto. (250)	50.00

1999 Sports Illustrated Greats of the Game

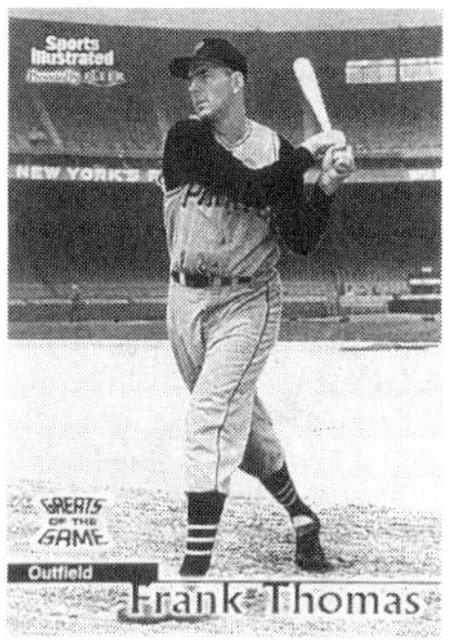

The 90-card base set includes many legendary major-leaguers including Babe Ruth and Cy Young. Card fronts feature a full bleed photo with the player name across the bottom and Greats of the Game printed on the bottom left portion of the card. Card backs have the player's vital information, along with career statistics and a few career highlights. Seven-card packs were issued with a SRP of $15.

		MT
Complete Set (90):		60.00
Common Player:		.25
Wax Box:		260.00
1	Jimmie Foxx	1.00
2	Red Schoendienst	.25
3	Babe Ruth	5.00
4	Lou Gehrig	4.00
5	Mel Ott	1.00
6	Stan Musial	2.00
7	Mickey Mantle	5.00
8	Carl Yastrzemski	1.50
9	Enos Slaughter	.25
10	Andre Dawson	.25
11	Luis Aparicio	.75
12	Ferguson Jenkins	1.00
13	Christy Mathewson	1.50
14	Ernie Banks	1.50
15	Johnny Podres	.25
16	George Foster	.25
17	Jerry Koosman	.25
18	Curt Simmons	.25
19	Bob Feller	1.00
20	Frank Robinson	1.00
21	Gary Carter	.25
22	Frank Thomas	.25
23	Bill Lee	.25
24	Willie Mays	3.00
25	Tommie Agee	.25
26	Boog Powell	.25
27	Jimmy Wynn	.25
28	Sparky Lyle	.25
29	Bo Belinsky	.25
30	Maury Wills	.25
31	Bill Buckner	.25
32	Steve Carlton	1.00
33	Harmon Killebrew	1.00
34	Nolan Ryan	4.00
35	Randy Jones	.25
36	Robin Roberts	.25
37	Al Oliver	.25
38	Rico Petrocelli	.25
39	Dave Parker	.25
40	Eddie Mathews	1.00
41	Earl Weaver	.25
42	Jackie Robinson	4.00
43	Lou Brock	1.00
44	Reggie Jackson	2.00
45	Bob Gibson	1.00
46	Jeff Burroughs	.25
47	Jim Bouton	.25
48	Bob Forsch	.25
49	Ron Guidry	.25
50	Ty Cobb	3.00
51	Roy White	.25
52	Joe Rudi	.25
53	Moose Skowron	.25
54	Goose Gossage	.25
55	Ed Kranepool	.25
56	Paul Blair	.25
57	Kent Hrbek	.25
58	Orlando Cepeda	.75
59	Buck O'Neil	.50
60	Al Kaline	1.00
61	Vida Blue	.25
62	Sam McDowell	.25
63	Jesse Barfield	.25
64	Dave Kingman	.25
65	Ron Santo	.25
66	Steve Garvey	.25
67	Gaylord Perry	.25
68	Darrell Evans	.25
69	Rollie Fingers	.25
70	Walter Johnson	1.00
71	Al Hrabosky	.25
72	Mickey Rivers	.25
73	Mike Torrez	.25
74	Hank Bauer	.25
75	Tug McGraw	.25
76	David Clyde	.25
77	Jim Lonborg	.25
78	Clete Boyer	.25
79	Harry Walker	.25
80	Cy Young	1.50
81	Bud Harrelson	.25
82	Paul Splittorff	.25
83	Bert Campaneris	.25
84	Joe Niekro	.25
85	Bob Horner	.25
86	Jerry Royster	.25
87	Tommy John	.25
88	Mark Fidrych	.25
89	Dick Williams	.25
90	Graig Nettles	.25

1999 Sports Illustrated Greats/Game Autographs

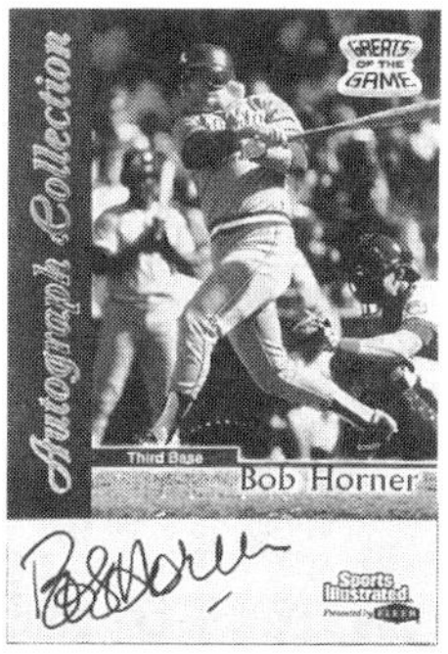

Each Greats of the Game pack has one autograph from the 80 card autograph checklist. Each card is autographed on the white portion on the bottom of the card, and is stamped "seal of authenticity". Card backs certify the autograph is authentic and "has been embossed with the Fleer Mark of Authenticity." The unnumbered cards are checklisted here in alphabetical order.

		MT
Common Player:		8.00
Inserted 1:1		
(1)	Tommie Agee	8.00
(2)	Luis Aparicio	15.00
(3)	Ernie Banks	45.00
(4)	Jesse Barfield	8.00
(5)	Hank Bauer	12.00
(6)	Bo Belinsky	10.00
(7)	Paul Blair	8.00
(8)	Vida Blue	15.00
(9)	Jim Bouton	10.00
(10)	Clete Boyer	8.00
(11)	Lou Brock	25.00
(12)	Bill Buckner	10.00
(13)	Jeff Burroughs	8.00
(14)	Bert Campaneris	8.00
(15)	Steve Carlton	60.00
(16)	Gary Carter	15.00
(17)	Orlando Cepeda	15.00
(18)	David Clyde	8.00
(19)	Andre Dawson	15.00
(20)	Darrell Evans	8.00
(21)	Bob Feller	30.00
(22)	Mark Fidrych	10.00
(23)	Rollie Fingers	15.00
(24)	Bob Forsch	8.00
(25)	George Foster	8.00
(26)	Steve Garvey	15.00
(27)	Bob Gibson	30.00
(28)	Goose Gossage	8.00
(29)	Ron Guidry	8.00
(30)	Bud Harrelson	8.00
(31)	Bob Horner	8.00
(32)	Al Hrabosky	8.00
(33)	Kent Hrbek	8.00
(34a)	Reggie Jackson	150.00
(34b)	Reggie Jackson ("Mr. October")	350.00
(34c)	Reggie Jackson ("HoF 83")	
(35)	Ferguson Jenkins	15.00
(36)	Tommy John	8.00
(37)	Randy Jones	8.00
(38)	Al Kaline	35.00
(39)	Harmon Killebrew	35.00
(40)	Dave Kingman	10.00
(41)	Jerry Koosman	8.00
(42)	Ed Kranepool	8.00
(43)	Bill Lee	8.00
(44)	Jim Lonborg	8.00
(45)	Sparky Lyle	8.00
(46)	Eddie Mathews	35.00
(47)	Willie Mays	200.00
(48)	Sam McDowell	8.00
(49)	Tug McGraw	8.00
(50)	Stan Musial	180.00
(51)	Graig Nettles	10.00
(52)	Joe Niekro	8.00
(53)	Buck O'Neil	15.00
(54)	Al Oliver	8.00
(55)	Dave Parker	8.00
(56)	Gaylord Perry	8.00
(57)	Rico Petrocelli	8.00
(58)	Johnny Podres	10.00
(59)	Boog Powell	8.00
(60)	Mickey Rivers	8.00
(61)	Robin Roberts	10.00
(62)	Frank Robinson	40.00
(63)	Jerry Royster	8.00
(64)	Joe Rudi	8.00
(65)	Nolan Ryan	250.00
(66)	Ron Santo	8.00
(67)	Red Schoendienst	8.00
(68)	Curt Simmons	8.00
(69)	Moose Skowron	8.00
(70)	Enos Slaughter	8.00
(71)	Paul Splittorff	8.00
(72)	Frank Thomas	8.00
(73)	Mike Torrez	8.00
(74)	Harry Walker	8.00
(75)	Earl Weaver	8.00
(76)	Roy White	8.00
(77)	Dick Williams	8.00
(78)	Maury Wills	15.00
(79)	Jimmy Wynn	8.00
(80)	Carl Yastrzemski	100.00

1999 Sports Illustrated Greats/Game Cover Collection

Each pack features one of the 50 chosen baseball covers from the Sports Illustrated archives. Card fronts are a reprint of the actual cover, while the backs give a brief description of the cover article and date of the magazine cover. Each card is numbered with a "C" suffix.

		MT
Complete Set (50):		45.00
Common Player:		.25
Inserted 1:1		
1	Johnny Podres	.35
2	Mickey Mantle	6.00
3	Stan Musial	1.50
4	Eddie Mathews	1.00
5	Frank Thomas	.25
6	Willie Mays	3.00
7	Red Schoendienst	.25
8	Luis Aparicio	.25
9	Mickey Mantle	6.00
10	Al Kaline	1.00
11	Maury Wills	.25
12	Sam McDowell	.25
13	Harry Walker	.25
14	Carl Yastrzemski	1.00
15	Carl Yastrzemski	1.00
16	Lou Brock	1.00
17	Ron Santo	.25
18	Reggie Jackson	1.50
19	Frank Robinson	1.00
20	Jerry Koosman	.25
21	Bud Harrelson	.25
22	Vida Blue	.50
23	Ferguson Jenkins	.50
24	Sparky Lyle	.25
25	Steve Carlton	1.00
26	Bert Campaneris	.25
27	Jimmy Wynn	.25
28	Steve Garvey	.25
29	Nolan Ryan	4.00
30	Randy Jones	.25
31	Reggie Jackson	1.50
32	Joe Rudi	.25
33	Reggie Jackson	1.50
34	Dave Parker	.25
35	Mark Fidrych	.25
36	Earl Weaver	.25
37	Nolan Ryan	4.00
38	Steve Carlton	1.00
39	Reggie Jackson	1.50
40	Rollie Fingers	.50
41	Gary Carter	.25
42	Graig Nettles	.25
43	Gaylord Perry	.25
44	Kent Hrbek	.25
45	Gary Carter	.25
46	Steve Garvey	.25
47	Steve Carlton	1.00
48	Nolan Ryan	4.00
49	Nolan Ryan	4.00
50	Mickey Mantle	6.00

1999 Sports Illustrated Greats/Game Record Breakers

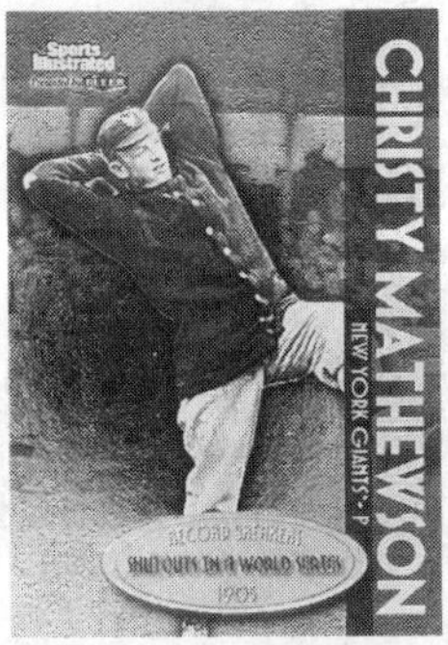

This 10-card set spotlights the top record breakers in the past century from Christy Mathewson to Nolan Ryan. Card fronts are full foiled with a oblong stamp on the bottom portion detailing the player's respective record. Card backs are numbered with a "RB" suffix and gives more detail on the featured player's record. These are seeded 1:12 packs. A Gold parallel is also randomly seeded 1:120 packs and have gold holo-foil.

		MT
Complete Set (10):		120.00
Common Player:		5.00
Inserted 1:12		
Golds: 4X		
Inserted 1:120		
1	Mickey Mantle	25.00
2	Stan Musial	10.00
3	Babe Ruth	25.00
4	Christy Mathewson	5.00
5	Cy Young	5.00
6	Nolan Ryan	20.00
7	Jackie Robinson	20.00
8	Lou Gehrig	20.00
9	Ty Cobb	10.00
10	Walter Johnson	5.00

1982 Sportschannel N.Y. Mets Photo Album

This stadium promotional giveaway features 28 pages of Mets player and staff portrait photos. The album and each inside page measures about 8" square. The cover features the team logo and is printed in blue and orange. On the back cover, in red and blue, is the logo of Sportschannel, the Mets cable TV carrier. Interior pages are printed only on one side, allowing them to be removed (they are perforated at the left edge) and displayed. Player portraits are bordered in white. In the upper-right corner is the uniform number in orange; at lower-left is a white panel with a facsimile autograph, also in orange.

		MT
Complete Album:		20.00
1	Mookie Wilson	
4	Bob Bailor	
5	Mike Howard	
6	Wally Backman	
7	Hubie Brooks	
10	Rusty Staub	
11	Tom Veryzer	
12	John Stearns	
13	Neil Allen	
15	George Foster	
17	Ellis Valentine	
19	Ron Gardenhire	
20/23	Rick Ownbey, Brian Giles	
21	Gary Rajsich	
22	Mike Jorgensen	
25	Charlie Puleo	
26	Dave Kingman	
27	Craig Swan	
30	Mike Scott	
31	George Bamberger	
32	Tom Hausman	
33	Pete Falcone	
35	Randy Jones	
36	Ed Lynch	
40	Pat Zachry	
42	Ron Hodges	
47	Jesse Orosco	
	Coaches (Jim Frey, Bud Harrelson, Frank Howard, Bill Monbouquette)	

1992 Sports Legends

This series of old-time greats' cards is in the format of a greeting card. The 9-1/4" x 6-3/4" cards are folded once vertically at center to create a 4-5/8" x 6-3/4" card. For most players in the series, the front features portrait and action paintings of the player, framed in white with a red border. The back of the folded card is printed in black and blue and offers lifetime stats and biographical data.

		MT
Complete Set (10):		12.00
Common Player:		1.00
1	Ty Cobb	2.00
2	Honus Wagner	2.00
3	Babe Ruth	3.00
4	Lou Gehrig	2.00
5	Jimmie Foxx	1.00
6	Cy Young	1.00
7	Christy Mathewson	1.00
8	Jackie Robinson	2.00
9	Roberto Clemente	2.50
10	Connie Mack	1.00

1992 Sports Report

Yet another attempt to circumvent licensing requirements by wrapping a magazine around sheets of collectors cards, Sports Report issued an 18-card four-sport set with its "Prototype Issue," dated June, 1992. Fifteen thousand copies were reportedly produced. Cards were printed nine to an 8-1/2" x 11" sheet. If cut from the sheet, individual cards would measure the standard 2-1/2" x 3-1/2". Fronts feature color photos with the player name and "SR" logo in gold foil. Backs are in black-and-white with career highlights.

		MT
Complete Magazine:		4.00
Common Player:		.25
1	Christian Laettner	.25
2	Cal Ripken Jr.	.75
3	Deion Sanders	.25
4	Roger Clemens	.35
5	Jose Canseco	.25
6	Shaquille O'Neal	.45
7	Barry Bonds	.35
8	Michael Jordan	.75
9	Will Clark	.25
10	Cecil Fielder	.25
11	Harold Miner	.25
12	Jimmy Jackson	.25
13	Frank Thomas	.50
14	Roberto Alomar	.25
15	Mark McGwire	.75
16	Brett Hull	.25
17	Ryne Sandberg	.40
18	Ken Griffey Jr.	1.00

1991 Sports Shots Portfolios

After three years of producing cardboard portfolios with enlarged versions of Topps cards on front and back, Sports Shots created an original design for 1991. Fronts of the 9-1/2" x 11-3/4" folders have a color action photo of the player, with name and team identification. In the background is a collage of baseballs with facsimile autographs of the players in the series. Backs are similar in design to the fronts except the photo is a portrait. The pocketed folders had a suggested retail price at issue of $1.29. The unnumbered pieces are checklisted here alphabetically.

		MT
Complete Set (27):		65.00
Common Player:		2.00
(1)	Wade Boggs	3.00
(2)	Barry Bonds	3.00
(3)	George Brett	3.00
(4)	Jose Canseco	3.00
(5)	Roger Clemens	3.00
(6)	Andre Dawson	2.00
(7)	Doug Drabek	2.00
(8)	Cecil Fielder	2.00
(9)	Dwight Gooden	2.50
(10)	Ken Griffey Jr.	6.00
(11)	Tony Gwynn	4.00
(12)	Rickey Henderson	2.00
(13)	Barry Larkin	2.00
(14)	Don Mattingly	4.00
(15)	Mark McGwire	5.00
(16)	Kevin Mitchell	2.00
(17)	Eddie Murray	3.00
(18)	Kirby Puckett	4.00
(19)	Cal Ripken Jr.	5.00
(20)	Nolan Ryan	5.00
(21)	Chris Sabo	2.00
(22)	Ryne Sandberg	3.00
(23)	Dave Stewart	2.00
(24)	Darryl Strawberry	2.00
(25)	Bobby Thigpen	2.00
(26)	Frank Viola	2.00
(27)	Lou Whitaker	2.00

1997 Sports Specialties Matt Williams

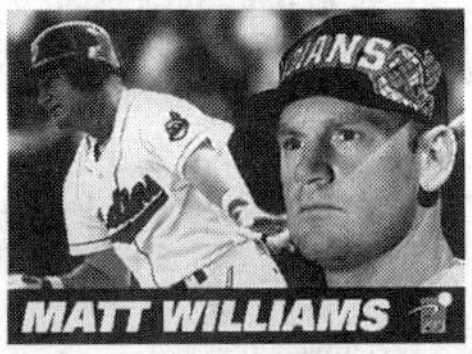

This card was produced as a give-away at the All-Star FanFest to promote a new line of team logo baseball caps. The 7" x 5" card has a color portrait and black-and-white action photo on front. The back advertises the "Matt's new grid cap" can be purchased at all 13 Indians team shop locations and has a scorecard for the All-Star Game.

	MT
Matt Williams	1.00

1981 Spot-bilt George Brett

This one-card set was released in both 1981 and 1982 (see stats on back to differentiate) in boxes of turf baseball shoes, for which Brett served on the athletic advisory staff. Cards are standard 2-1/2" x 3-1/2". Despite the card number 5 on the back, there are no other players in the series. Brett wore uniform #5.

		MT
5	George Brett	5.00

1986 Springhill Papers

An obscure "old-timers" issue, this five-card set was available through a mail-in offer advertising in printing trade publications in 1986. The four player cards, and a header card which advertises the company's paper stock, are printed on thin cardboard and measure 2-3/4" x 4-1/8". Card fronts have a blue-and-white duo-tone portrait of the player set in a 1-3/4" red circle. The player's name and position are in white above and below the portrait. A light blue pinstriped background behind the circle is framed by an orange diamond, which in turn is surrounded by a blue background. Two of the four orange circles in the corners have logos of the paper brand and its parent company - International Paper. Backs have a black border, blue interior and player biographical data and career stats printed in black. The set was packaged in a white paper envelope with logos similar to the header card.

		MT
Complete Set (5):		5.00
Common Player:		2.00
(1)	Grover Alexander	2.00
(2)	John McGraw	2.00
(3)	Honus Wagner	2.00
(4)	Cy Young	2.00
(5)	Header card	.05

1996 Springwater Ken Griffey, Jr.

This set of cards was apparently distributed as a cello pack with cookie and confectionary treats from an Ohio firm. Standard 2-1/2" x 3-1/2" cards have photos on front and back in three different designs. All photos are devoid of Mariners team logos as the issue was not licensed by Major League Baseball, only by Griffey. Besides the photos on back, there are stats and career highlights.

		MT
Complete Set (4):		12.00
Common Card:		2.00
24	Ken Griffey, Jr. (batting)	2.00
---	Ken Griffey, Jr. (fielding)	2.00
---	Ken Griffey, Jr. (on base)	2.00
---	Ken Griffey Jr. (Grand Slam)	6.00

1981 Squirt

These cards, issued in conjunction with Topps, were issued as two-card panels in eight-pack cartons of the soft drink. Individual cards measure the standard 2-1/2" x 3-1/2", while the vertical panels measure 2-1/2" x 10-1/2", with a promotional card reading "Free Topps 1981 Baseball Cards" attached. The promotional card is blank-backed, while the player card backs are similar to Topps' regular issue, though re-numbered for inclusion in this 33-card set. Most of the game's top players are included. There are only 22 different two-card panels, as card numbers 1-11 appear in two different bottom panel combinations. Card fronts feature a color player portrait photo within a baseball design, team and position designation, and the Squirt logo.

		MT
Complete Panel Set (22):		30.00
Complete Singles Set (33):		17.00
Common Panel:		.50
Common Single Player:		.15
Panel (1)		4.00
1	George Brett	2.00
12	Garry Templeton	.15
Panel (2)		4.00
1	George Brett	2.00
23	Jerry Mumphrey	.15
Panel (3)		.50
2	George Foster	.25
13	Rick Burleson	.15
Panel (4)		.50
2	George Foster	.25
24	Tony Armas	.15
Panel (5)		.50
3	Ben Oglivie	.15
14	Dave Kingman	.15
Panel (6)		.50
3	Ben Oglivie	.15
25	Fred Lynn	.15
Panel (7)		2.00
4	Steve Garvey	.50
15	Eddie Murray	.75
Panel (8)		1.00
4	Steve Garvey	.50
26	Ron LeFlore	.15
Panel (9)		2.00
5	Reggie Jackson	.75
16	Don Sutton	.50
Panel (10)		1.75
5	Reggie Jackson	.75
27	Steve Kemp	.15
Panel (11)		.50
6	Bill Buckner	.15
17	Dusty Baker	.15
Panel (12)		1.75
6	Bill Buckner	.15
28	Rickey Henderson	.75
Panel (13)		.50
7	Jim Rice	.25
18	Jack Clark	.15
Panel (14)		.50
7	Jim Rice	.25
29	John Castino	.15
Panel (15)		3.00
8	Mike Schmidt	1.00
19	Dave Winfield	.75
Panel (16)		2.00
8	Mike Schmidt	1.00
30	Cecil Cooper	.15
Panel (17)		3.00
9	Rod Carew	.75
20	Johnny Bench	1.00
Panel (18)		1.50
9	Rod Carew	.75
31	Bruce Bochte	.15
Panel (19)		.75
10	Dave Parker	.25
21	Lee Mazzilli	.15
Panel (20)		1.00
10	Dave Parker	.25
32	Joe Charboneau	.25
Panel (21)		4.00
11	Pete Rose	2.00
22	Al Oliver	.15
Panel (22)		4.00
11	Pete Rose	2.00
33	Chet Lemon	.15

1982 Squirt

This set was again prepared in conjunction with Topps, but the 1982 Squirt cards are completely different from Topps' regular issue. Only 22 players are included in the full-color set, with the 2-1/2" x 3-1/2" player cards available on one- or two-player panels. Card panels come in four variations, with free grocery contest and scratch-off game cards taking one or two of the positions on the three-card panels. Card backs are numbered and list player statistics.

		MT
Complete Set (22):		13.50
Common Player:		.25
1	Cecil Cooper	.25
2	Jerry Remy	.25
3	George Brett	2.00
4	Alan Trammell	.30
5	Reggie Jackson	1.75
6	Kirk Gibson	.25
7	Dave Winfield	1.25
8	Carlton Fisk	1.00
9	Ron Guidry	.25
10	Dennis Leonard	.25
11	Rollie Fingers	1.00
12	Pete Rose	3.25
13	Phil Garner	.25
14	Mike Schmidt	1.75
15	Dave Concepcion	.25
16	George Hendrick	.25
17	Andre Dawson	.50
18	George Foster	.25
19	Gary Carter	.50
20	Fernando Valenzuela	.30
21	Tom Seaver	1.75
22	Bruce Sutter	.25

1985-88 SSK Glove Hang Tags

Sasaki Sports of Japan produced two types of player endorsement cards for its line of baseball gloves in the late 1980s. There were hang tag cards with holes punched in a top corner for attachment to the glove in retail outlets, and unpunched, authentically autographed cards which were available from the company. Cards measure about 3-1/2" x 5" and feature color photos on front. Some are blank-backed, others have career information or stats.

		MT
Complete Set (11):		90.00
Common Player:		6.00
	1985	
(1)	Alan Trammell (red SSK logo)	7.50
	1986	
(1)	Alan Trammell (white logo, info back)	7.50
	1987	
(1)	Jack Morris (hang tag, blank back)	6.00
(2)	Jack Morris (hang tag, stat back)	7.50
(3)	Jack Morris (unpunched, autographed)	12.00
(4)	Don Sutton (hang tag)	10.00
(5)	Don Sutton (unpunched, autographed)	24.00
(6)	Garry Templeton (hang tag)	6.00
(7)	Garry Templeton (unpunched, autographed)	10.00
(8)	Alan Trammell (hang tag)	7.50
(9)	Alan Trammell (unpunched, autographed)	15.00

1996 St. Louis Browns Historical Society

This collectors issue honoring the 1944 American League Champion St. Louis Browns was issued in conjunction with a reunion of that team in 1996, sponsored by the St. Louis Browns Historical Society. Every player on the '44 team is included in the set, representing the first-ever baseball card for some of them. Fronts of the 2-5/8" x 3-3/4" cards feature color portraits by artist Ronnie Joyner. Shades of brown form the border. Backs are also printed in brown tones and include a cartoon, 1944 season and World Series stats, lifetime stats, personal data, a career summary and part of a team "Timeline" of the 1944 season. It was reported 2,500 sets were issued at $10 retail.

		MT
Complete Set (36):		10.00
Common Player:		.50
1	Team logo card	.50
2	Don Gutteridge	.50
3	Milt Byrnes	.50
4	Al Hollingsworth	.50
5	Willis Hudlin	.50
6	Sig Jakucki	.50
7	Nelson Potter	.50
8	Len Schulte	.50
9	Vern Stephens	.50
10	Frank Demaree	.50
11	Al Zarilla	.50
12	Bob Muncrief	.50
13	Steve Sundra	.50
14	Jack Kramer	.50
15	Lefty West	.50
16	Denny Galehouse	.50
17	Luke Sewell	.50
18	Joe Schultz	.50
19	George McQuinn	.50
20	Ellis Clary	.50
21	Babe Martin	.50
22	Red Hayworth	.50
23	Frank Mancuso	.50
24	Tex Shirley	.50
25	Mike Chartak	.50
26	Mark Christman	.50
27	Tom Hafey	.50
28	Tom Turner	.50
29	Floyd Baker	.50
30	Mike Kreevich	.50
31	George Caster	.50
32	Gene Moore	.50
33	Chet Laabs	.50
34	Sam Zoldak	.50
35	Hal Epps	.50
36	Team composite/ checklist card	.50

1984 St. Louis Cardinals Photocards

These 3-1/4" x 5-1/2" black-and-white photo cards feature portraits of the players and staff. White borders surround the photos on front, with a facsimile autograph and a union printers' label appearing in the wide bottom border. Backs are blank. The unnumbered photocards are checklisted here in alphabetical order.

		MT
Complete Set (32):		35.00
Common Player:		1.00
(1)	Neil Allen	1.00
(2)	Joaquin Andujar	1.00
(3)	Steve Braun	1.00
(4)	Glenn Brummer	1.00
(5)	Ralph Citarella	1.00
(6)	Dan Cox	1.00
(7)	Bob Forsch	1.00
(8)	David Green	1.00
(9)	George Hendrick	1.50
(10)	Tom Herr	1.50
(11)	Whitey Herzog	1.50
(12)	Rick Horton	1.00
(13)	Art Howe	1.00
(14)	Mike Jorgensen	1.00
(15)	Jeff Lahti	1.00
(16)	Tito Landrum	1.00
(17)	Hal Lanier	1.00
(18)	Dave LaPoint	1.00
(19)	Nick Levya	1.00
(20)	Bill Lyons	1.00
(21)	Willie McGee	2.00
(22)	Darrell Porter	1.00
(23)	Dave Ricketts	1.00
(24)	Mike Roarke	1.00
(25)	Dave Rucker	1.00
(26)	Mark Salas	1.00
(27)	Red Schoendienst	2.00
(28)	Lonnie Smith	1.00
(29)	Ozzie Smith	6.00
(30)	Bruce Sutter	1.50
(31)	Andy Van Slyke	1.50
(32)	Dave Von Ohlen	1.00

1985 St. Louis Cardinals Photocards

Only the player selection differentiates the 1985 team-issue photocards from those of 1983-86. The 3-1/4" x 5-1/2" black-and-white photo cards feature portrait photos of the players and staff. White borders surround the photos on front, with a facsimile autograph and a union printers' label appearing in the wide bottom border. Backs are blank. The unnumbered photocards are checklisted here in alphabetical order.

		MT
Complete Set (33):		24.00
Common Player:		1.00
(1)	Neil Allen	1.00
(2)	Joaquin Andujar	1.00
(3)	Steve Braun	1.00
(4)	Bill Campbell	1.00
(5)	Jack Clark	1.50
(6)	Vince Coleman	1.50
(7)	Danny Cox	1.00
(8)	Ken Dayley	1.00
(9)	Ivan DeJesus	1.00
(10)	Bob Forsch	1.00
(11)	Brian Harper	1.00
(12)	Andy Hassler	1.00
(13)	Tommy Herr	1.25
(14)	Whitey Herzog	1.25
(15)	Ricky Horton	1.00
(16)	Mike Jorgensen	1.00
(17)	Kurt Kepshire	1.00
(18)	Hal Lanier	1.00
(19)	Jeff Lahti	1.00
(20)	Tito Landrum	1.00
(21)	Tom Lawless	1.00
(22)	Johnny Lewis	1.00
(23)	Nick Leyva	1.00
(24)	Willie McGee	2.00
(25)	Tom Nieto	1.00
(26)	Terry Pendleton	1.50
(27)	Darrell Porter	1.00
(28)	Dave Ricketts	1.00
(29)	Mike Roarke	1.00
(30)	Red Schoendienst	1.50
(31)	Ozzie Smith	5.00
(32)	John Tudor	1.00
(33)	Andy Van Slyke	1.50

1986 St. Louis Cardinals Photocards

The shape of the union logo in the lower-left corner

distinguishes the 1986 version of these team-issued cards from the nearly identical issues of 1987-88. The logo of the Graphic Arts International Union on the 1986 cards is a vertical oval. The cards are printed in a 3-1/4" x 5-1/2" back-and-white format on thin semi-gloss cardboard. Portrait photos are surrounded with white borders and the player's facsimile autograph appears in the wide bottom border. Backs are blank. The unnumbered cards are checklisted here in alphabetical order.

		MT
Complete Set (33):		24.00
Common Player:		1.00
(1)	Greg Bargar	1.00
(2)	Ray Burris	1.00
(3)	Jack Clark	1.50
(4)	Vince Coleman	1.50
(5)	Tim Conroy	1.00
(6)	Dan Cox	1.00
(7)	Ken Dayley	1.00
(8)	Bob Forsch	1.00
(9)	Richard Hacker	1.00
(10)	Mike Heath	1.00
(11)	Tom Herr	1.25
(12)	Whitey Herzog	1.25
(13)	Rick Horton	1.00
(14)	Clint Hurdle	1.00
(15)	Jeff Lahti	1.00
(16)	Tito Landrum	1.00
(17)	Mike La Valliere	1.00
(18)	Tom Lawless	1.00
(19)	Johnny Lewis	1.00
(20)	Nick Leyva	1.00
(21)	Greg Mathews	1.00
(22)	Willie McGee	2.00
(23)	Jose Oquendo	1.00
(24)	Rick Ownbey	1.00
(25)	Terry Pendleton	1.50
(26)	Pat Perry	1.00
(27)	Dave Ricketts	1.00
(28)	Mike Roarke	1.00
(29)	Red Schoendienst	2.50
(30)	Ozzie Smith	5.00
(31)	John Tudor	1.00
(32)	Andy Van Slyke	1.50
(33)	Todd Worrell	1.00

1987 St. Louis Cardinals Fire Safety

Approximately 25,000 fans in attendance at Busch Stadium on Aug. 24 received this set produced by the U.S. Forestry Service. The cards measure 4" x 6". Fronts feature a full-color photo set inside an oval frame. Only the player's last name appears on front. Backs carry the player's name, position and personal data plus a Smokey Bear cartoon fire prevention message.

		MT
Complete Set (25):		6.00
Common Player:		.25
1	Ray Soff	.25
2	Todd Worrell	.25
3	John Tudor	.25
4	Pat Perry	.25
5	Rick Horton	.25
6	Dan Cox	.25
7	Bob Forsch	.25
8	Greg Mathews	.25
9	Bill Dawley	.25
10	Steve Lake	.25
11	Tony Pena	.25
12	Tom Pagnozzi	.25
13	Jack Clark	.25
14	Jim Lindeman	.25
15	Mike Laga	.25
16	Terry Pendleton	.30
17	Ozzie Smith	2.50
18	Jose Oquendo	.25
19	Tom Lawless	.25
20	Tom Herr	.25
21	Curt Ford	.25
22	Willie McGee	.50
23	Tito Landrum	.25
24	Vince Coleman	.30
25	Whitey Herzog	.25

1987 St. Louis Cardinals Photocards

The shape of the union logo in the lower-left corner distinguishes the 1987 version of these team-issued cards from the nearly identical issues of 1983-86. The logo of the printers' union on the 1987 cards is a horizontal oval. The cards are printed in the same 3-1/4" x 5-1/2" back-and-white format on thin semi-gloss cardboard. Portrait photos are surrounded with white borders and the player's facsimile autograph appears in the wide bottom border. Backs are blank. The unnumbered cards are checklisted here in alphabetical order.

		MT
Complete Set (33):		20.00
Common Player:		1.00
(1)	Rod Booker	1.00
(2)	Jack Clark	1.50
(3)	Vince Coleman	1.50
(4)	Tim Conroy	1.00
(5)	Dan Cox	1.00
(6)	Ken Dayley	1.00
(7)	Bill Dawley	1.00
(8)	Curt Ford	1.00
(9)	Bob Forsch	1.00
(10)	Richard Hacker	1.00
(11)	Tom Herr	1.25
(12)	Whitey Herzog	1.25
(13)	Ricky Horton	1.00
(14)	Steve Lake	1.00
(15)	Tito Landrum	1.00
(16)	Tom Lawless	1.00
(17)	Johnny Lewis	1.00
(18)	Nick Leyva	1.00
(19)	Jim Lindeman	1.00
(20)	Joe Magrane	1.00
(21)	Willie McGee	2.00
(22)	John Morris	1.00
(23)	Jose Oquendo	1.00
(24)	Tony Pena	1.25
(25)	Terry Pendleton	1.50
(26)	Pat Perry	1.00
(27)	Dave Ricketts	1.00
(28)	Mike Roarke	1.00
(29)	Red Schoendienst	2.00
(30)	Ozzie Smith	5.00
(31)	John Tudor	1.00
(32)	Lee Tunnell	1.00
(33)	Todd Worrell	1.00

1987 St. Louis Cardinals Player Photos

(See 1987 Schnucks St. Louis Cardinals)

1988 St. Louis Cardinals Fire Safety

This set of oversized (3" x 5") cards features full-color action photos that fill the entire front. A thin white line frames the player photo. The player name, team logo and Smokey Bear picture logo are printed in the lower-right corner. Black-and-white backs contain player information and a Smokey Bear fire prevention cartoon. The sets were distributed to young St. Louis fans as part of a U.S. Forest Service fire prevention campaign. The National Association of State Foresters co-sponsored this set.

		MT
Complete Set (25):		5.00
Common Player:		.25
1	Whitey Herzog	.25
2	Danny Cox	.25
3	Ken Dayley	.25
4	Jose DeLeon	.25
5	Bob Forsch	.25
6	Joe Magrane	.25
7	Greg Mathews	.25
8	Scott Terry	.25
9	John Tudor	.25
10	Todd Worrell	.25
11	Steve Lake	.25
12	Tom Pagnozzi	.25
13	Tony Pena	.25
14	Bob Horner	.25
15	Tom Lawless	.25
16	Jose Oquendo	.25
17	Terry Pendleton	.25
18	Ozzie Smith	1.50
19	Vince Coleman	.25
20	Curt Ford	.25
21	Willie McGee	.45
22	Larry McWilliams	.25
23	Steve Peters	.25
24	Luis Alicea	.25
25	Tom Brunansky	.25

1988 St. Louis Cardinals Photocards

Other than player selection, there is nothing to distinguish the 1988 version of these team-issued cards from the nearly identical issue of 1987. The logo of the printers' union on the cards is a horizontal oval. The cards are printed in the same 3-1/4" x 5-1/2" back-and-white format on thin semi-gloss cardboard. Portrait photos are surrounded with white borders and the player's facsimile autograph appears in the wide bottom border. Backs are blank. The unnumbered cards are checklisted here in alphabetical order.

		MT
Complete Set (36):		24.00
Common Player:		1.00
(1)	Luis Alicea	1.25
(2)	Tom Brunansky	1.25
(3)	Vince Coleman	1.50
(4)	Dan Cox	1.00
(5)	Ken Dayley	1.00
(6)	Jose DeLeon	1.00
(7)	Curt Ford	1.00
(8)	Bob Forsch	1.00
(9)	Richard Hacker	1.00
(10)	Whitey Herzog	1.25
(11)	Bob Horner	1.25
(12)	Michael Joyce	1.00
(13)	Steve Lake	1.00
(14)	Tom Lawless	1.00
(15)	Johnny Lewis	1.00
(16)	Nick Leyva	1.00
(17)	Jim Lindeman	1.00
(18)	Joe Magrane	1.00
(19)	Greg Mathews	1.00
(20)	Willie McGee	2.00
(21)	Larry McWilliams	1.00
(22)	John Morris	1.00
(23)	Randy O'Neal	1.00
(24)	Jose Oquendo	1.00
(25)	Tom Pagnozzi	1.00
(26)	Tony Pena	1.25
(27)	Terry Pendleton	1.50
(28)	Steve Peters	1.00
(29)	Dave Ricketts	1.00
(30)	Mike Roarke	1.00
(31)	Red Schoendienst	2.00
(32)	Ozzie Smith	5.00
(33)	Scott Terry	1.00
(34)	John Tudor	1.00
(35)	Duane Walker	1.00
(36)	Todd Worrell	1.00

1989 St. Louis Cardinals Fire Safety

This set featuring action player photos was issued by the U.S. Forest Service to promote fire safety. The cards measure 4" x 6" and include the player's name, team logo and a small picture of Smokey Bear beneath the player photo.

		MT
Complete Set (25):		6.00
Common Player:		.25
(1)	Tom Brunansky	.25
(2)	Cris Carpenter	.25
(3)	Vince Coleman	.25
(4)	John Costello	.25
(5)	Ken Dayley	.25
(6)	Jose DeLeon	.25
(7)	Frank DiPino	.25
(8)	Whitey Herzog	.25
(9)	Ken Hill	.35
(10)	Pedro Guerrero	.25
(11)	Tim Jones	.25
(12)	Jim Lindeman	.25
(13)	Joe Magrane	.25
(14)	Willie McGee	.40
(15)	John Morris	.25
(16)	Jose Oquendo	.25
(17)	Tom Pagnozzi	.25
(18)	Tony Pena	.25
(19)	Terry Pendleton	.25
(20)	Dan Quisenberry	.25
(21)	Ozzie Smith	1.50
(22)	Scott Terry	.25
(23)	Milt Thompson	.25
(24)	Denny Walling	.25
(25)	Todd Worrell	.25

1989 St. Louis Cardinals Photocards

The 1989 version of these team-issued cards can be distinguished from those of earlier years by the absence of a printers' union logo in the lower-left corner. The cards are printed in the same 3-1/4" x 5-1/2" back-and-white format on thin semi-gloss cardboard. Portrait photos are surrounded with white borders and the player's facsimile autograph appears in the wide bottom border. Backs are blank. The unnumbered cards are checklisted here in alphabetical order.

		MT
Complete Set (34):		20.00
Common Player:		1.00
(1)	Tom Brunansky	1.00
(2)	Cris Carpenter	1.00
(3)	Vince Coleman	1.50
(4)	John Costello	1.00
(5)	Dan Cox	1.00
(6)	Ken Dayley	1.00
(7)	Jose DeLeon	1.00
(8)	Frank DiPino	1.00
(9)	Pedro Guerrero	1.50
(10)	Rich Hacker	1.00
(11)	Whitey Herzog	1.50
(12)	Ken Hill	1.00
(13)	Tim Jones	1.00
(14)	Johnny Lewis	1.00
(15)	Jim Lindeman	1.00
(16)	Joe Magrane	1.00
(17)	Greg Mathews	1.00
(18)	Willie McGee	2.00
(19)	John Morris	1.00
(20)	Jose Oquendo	1.00
(21)	Tom Pagnozzi	1.00
(22)	Tony Pena	1.00
(23)	Terry Pendleton	1.50
(24)	Ted Power	1.00
(25)	Dan Quisenberry	1.00
(26)	Dave Ricketts	1.00
(27)	Jim Riggleman	1.00
(28)	Mike Roarke	1.00
(29)	Red Schoendienst	1.50
(30)	Ozzie Smith	4.00
(31)	Scott Terry	1.00
(32)	Milt Thompson	1.00
(33)	Denny Walling	1.00
(34)	Todd Worrell	1.00

1989 St. Louis Cardinals team issue

These black-and-white glossy photos of players and staff were available to fans and collectors for $5 per set. The cards measure 3-1/4" x 5-1/2" and have portrait photos bordered in white with a facsimile autograph in the wide bottom border. Backs are blank. The unnumbered cards are checklisted here alphabetically.

		MT
Complete Set (34):		20.00
Common Player:		1.00
(1)	Tom Brunansky	1.00
(2)	Cris Carpenter	1.00
(3)	Vince Coleman	1.50
(4)	John Costello	1.00
(5)	Dan Cox	1.00
(6)	Ken Dayley	1.00
(7)	Jose DeLeon	1.00
(8)	Frank DiPino	1.00
(9)	Pedro Guerrero	1.50
(10)	Rich Hacker	1.00
(11)	Whitey Herzog	1.50
(12)	Ken Hill	1.00
(13)	Tim Jones	1.00
(14)	Johnny Lewis	1.00
(15)	Jim Lindeman	1.00
(16)	Joe Magrane	1.00
(17)	Greg Mathews	1.00
(18)	Willie McGee	2.00
(19)	John Morris	1.00
(20)	Jose Oquendo	1.00

(21)	Tom Pagnozzi	1.00
(22)	Tony Pena	1.00
(23)	Terry Pendleton	1.50
(24)	Ted Power	1.00
(25)	Dan Quisenberry	1.00
(26)	Dave Ricketts	1.00
(27)	Jim Riggleman	1.00
(28)	Mike Roarke	1.00
(29)	Red Schoendienst	1.50
(30)	Ozzie Smith	4.00
(31)	Scott Terry	1.00
(32)	Milt Thompson	1.00
(33)	Denny Walling	1.00
(34)	Todd Worrell	1.00

1990 St. Louis Cardinals Fire Safety

Player photos dominate the fronts of this large-format (3" x 5") set sponsored by the U.S. Forest Service. Backs have a cartoon fire safety tip plus a few stats and personal data. The unnumbered cards are checklisted here in alphabetical order.

		MT
Complete Set (27):		9.00
Common Player:		.25
(1)	Vince Coleman	.25
(2)	Dave Collins	.25
(3)	Danny Cox	.25
(4)	Ken Dayley	.25
(5)	Frank DiPino	.25
(6)	Jose DeLeon	.25
(7)	Pedro Guerrero	.25
(8)	Whitey Herzog	.25
(9)	Rick Horton	.25
(10)	Rex Hudler	.25
(11)	Tim Jones	.25
(12)	Joe Magrane	.25
(13)	Greg Mathews	.25
(14)	Willie McGee	.40
(15)	John Morris	.25
(16)	Tom Niedenfuer	.25
(17)	Jose Oquendo	.25
(18)	Tom Pagnozzi	.25
(19)	Terry Pendleton	.25
(20)	Bryn Smith	.25
(21)	Lee Smith	.60
(22)	Ozzie Smith	3.00
(23)	Scott Terry	.25
(24)	Milt Thompson	.25
(25)	John Tudor	.25
(26)	Denny Walling	.25
(27)	Todd Zeile	.50

1991 St. Louis Cardinals Police

Color action photos are featured prominently on these large-format (2-5/8" x 4-1/16") cards. In the white border at bottom, the team name is printed in red, with the player name and uniform number printed in black. Backs feature a large cartoon safety message, career stats, some biographical data and the logos of the set's sponsors, Kansas City Life Insurance and the Greater St. Louis Law Enforcement Agencies. Backs are printed in red on white.

		MT
Complete Set (24):		5.00
Common Player:		.15
1	Ozzie Smith	.75
7	Geronimo Pena	.15
9	Joe Torre	.45
10	Rex Hudler	.15
11	Jose Oquendo	.15
12	Craig Wilson	.15
16	Ray Lankford	.40
19	Tom Pagnozzi	.15
21	Gerald Perry	.15
23	Bernard Gilkey	.25
25	Milt Thompson	.15
27	Todd Zeile	.20
28	Pedro Guerrero	.15
29	Rich Gedman	.15
34	Felix Jose	.15
35	Frank DiPino	.15
36	Bryn Smith	.15
37	Scott Terry	.15
38	Todd Worrell	.15
39	Bob Tewksbury	.15
43	Ken Hill	.15
47	Lee Smith	.25
48	Jose DeLeon	.15
49	Juan Agosto	.15

1992 St. Louis Cardinals Police

The Cardinals were the subject of this set given out at Busch Stadium on April 25. Sponsored by Kansas City Life Insurance and distributed by Greater St. Louis law enforcement agencies, the cards are 2-1/2" x 4", and contain a special logo on the front which commemorates the team's 100th anniversary.

		MT
Complete Set (27):		5.00
Common Player:		.25
1	Ozzie Smith	1.00
7	Geronimo Pena	.25
9	Joe Torre	.40
10	Rex Hudler	.25
11	Jose Oquendo	.25
12	Craig Wilson	.25
16	Ray Lankford	.50
19	Tom Pagnozzi	.25
21	Gerald Perry	.25
23	Bernard Gilkey	.35
25	Milt Thompson	.25
26	Omar Olivares	.25
27	Todd Zeile	.30
28	Pedro Guerrero	.25
29	Rich Gedman	.25
32	Joe Magrane	.25
34	Felix Jose	.25
36	Bryn Smith	.25
37	Scott Terry	.25
38	Todd Worrell	.25
39	Bob Tewksbury	.25
41	Andres Galarraga	.60
44	Cris Carpenter	.25
47	Lee Smith	.30
48	Jose DeLeon	.25
49	Juan Agosto	.25
---	Checklist	.25

1993 St. Louis Cardinals Police

This Cardinals/Kansas City Life police set features 2-5/8" x 4" cards with a blue border and "Cardinals" printed in red at top. The team logo appears in the lower-left corner, while the player's name, position and number appear lower-right. Backs are printed in red on a white background with the player's biography and statistics listed above a safety message.

		MT
Complete Set (25):		4.00
Common Player:		.25
1	Ozzie Smith	.75
3	Brian Jordan	.50
5	Stan Royer	.30
9	Joe Torre	.40
11	Jose Oquendo	.25
16	Ray Lankford	.35
18	Luis Alicea	.25
19	Tom Pagnozzi	.25
21	Geronimo Pena	.25
23	Bernard Gilkey	.30
25	Gregg Jefferies	.30
26	Rob Murphy	.25
27	Todd Zeile	.30
28	Gerald Perry	.25
29	Hector Villanueva	.25
31	Donovan Osborne	.25
33	Rod Brewer	.25
39	Bob Tewksbury	.25
42	Mike Perez	.25
43	Rene Arocha	.25
46	Ozzie Canseco	.30
47	Lee Smith	.30
52	Rheal Cormier	.25
54	Tracy Woodson	.25
---	Checklist	.25

1994 St. Louis Cardinals Police

An emphasis on border graphics marks the perennial Cardinals safety set for 1994. The 2-5/8" x 4" cards have a cream colored border. Near the left edge is a vertical red stripe with a team logo at top. Above the color photo at center is the team name.The player name and position are at lower-left. A baseball zooms out of the photo at lower-right carrying the uniform number. Backs are printed in red on white and feature a large cartoon safety message at center. Career stats and biographical data are at top. At bottom are sponsors' logos for the Kansas City Life Insurance Co., and Greater St. Louis Law Enforcement Agencies.

		MT
Complete Set (26):		5.00
Common Player:		.15
1	Ozzie Smith	.65
3	Brian Jordan	.35
5	Stan Royer	.25
9	Joe Torre	.35
11	Jose Oquendo	.15
12	Erik Pappas	.15
16	Ray Lankford	.30
18	Luis Alicea	.15
19	Tom Pagnozzi	.15
21	Geronimo Pena	.15
22	Mark Whiten	.15
23	Bernard Gilkey	.25
25	Gregg Jefferies	.25
26	Omar Olivares	.15
27	Todd Zeile	.20
28	Gerald Perry	.15
34	Tom Urbani	.15
36	Paul Kilgus	.15
38	Allen Watson	.15
39	Bob Tewksbury	.15
40	Rick Sutcliffe	.15
42	Mike Perez	.15
43	Rene Arocha	.15
46	Rob Murphy	.15
48	Rich Batchelor	.15
52	Rheal Cormier	.15

1995 St. Louis Cardinals Police

In 1995, the Cardinals safety set was sponsored by Kansas City Life Insurance Co., and distributed by law enforcement agencies in the greater St. Louis area. The cards measure about 2-5/8" x 4" and feature action photos on front. The team name is scripted at bottom and the player's last name and "1995" are vertically at right. Backs have a few vital data, a career stats line, a safety message and sponsor's logo. Cards are listed here in alphabetical order.

		MT
Complete Set (12):		8.00
Common Player:		.50
(1)	Rene Arocha	.50
(2)	Scott Cooper	.50
(3)	Tripp Cromer	.50
(4)	Bernard Gilkey	.75
(5)	Tom Henke	.50
(6)	Ken Hill	.50
(7)	Danny Jackson	.50
(8)	Brian Jordan	.75
(9)	Ray Lankford	.75
(10)	Jose Oquendo	.50
(11)	Tom Pagnozzi	.50
(12)	Ozzie Smith	2.00

1996 St. Louis Cardinals Police

Once again for 1996, the Cardinals safety set was sponsored by Kansas City Life Insurance Co., and distributed by law enforcement agencies in the greater St. Louis area. The cards measure about 2-5/8" x 4" and feature action photos on front. The team name is vertically in a ghosted strip at left. At bottom, beneath a "torn" photo edge are the player's last name, uniform number and the team logo. Backs have a few vital data, a career stats line, a safety message and sponsor's logo.

		MT
Complete Set (26):		8.00
Common Player:		.25
1	Ozzie Smith	1.00
3	Brian Jordan	.45
5	Ron Gant	.35
8	Gary Gaetti	.25
10	Tony LaRussa	.30
12	Royce Clayton	.30
16	Ray Lankford	.35
19	Tom Pagnozzi	.25
22	Mike Gallego	.25
23	Mark Sweeney	.35
24	Tom Urbani	.25
29	Danny Jackson	.25
30	Todd Stottlemyre	.30
31	Donovan Osborne	.25
32	Rick Honeycutt	.25
33	T.J. Mathews	.25
36	Mike Morgan	.25
38	Pat Borders	.25
40	Andy Benes	.45
41	Alan Benes	.40
43	Dennis Eckersley	.50
46	Mark Petkovsek	.25
47	John Mabry	.35
48	Tony Fossas	.25
51	Willie McGee	.35
---	Fredbird/checklist (mascot)	.25

1998 St. Louis Cardinals Police

Similar in format to those used in the preceding years, this safety issue is printed on a 2-1/4" x 4" format. Fronts have color action photos surrounded by busy borders in predominantly yellow and green. A blue strip at bottom has player name and uniform number and team logo. Backs are in red-and-white with a few biographical details and stats, a cartoon baseball figure, safety message and sponsors' credits. Cards are checklisted here by uniform number.

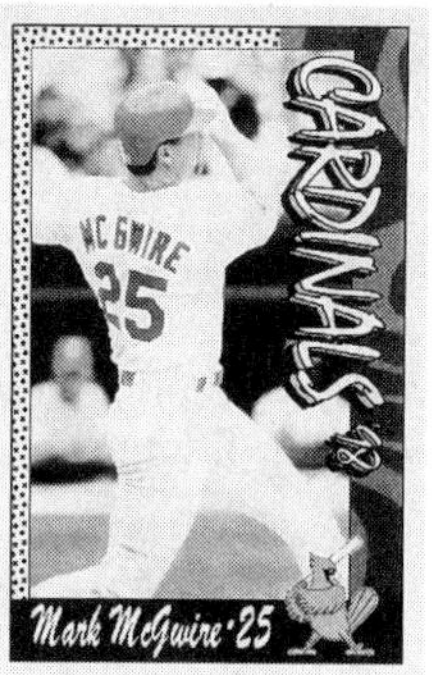

		MT
Complete Set (26):		14.00
Common Player:		.25
3	Brian Jordan	.50
5	Ron Gant	.50
7	Delino DeShields	.25
8	Gary Gaetti	.25
10	Tony LaRussa	.35
11	Royce Clayton	.25
13	David Howard	.25
16	Ray Lankford	.45
19	Tom Pagnozzi	.25
25	Mark McGwire	8.00
26	Eli Marrero	.65
28	Lance Painter	.25
30	Todd Stottlemyre	.25
35	Matt Morris	.50
37	Kent Bottenfield	.25
38	Manny Aybar	.45
41	Alan Benes	.25
43	Kent Mercker	.25
44	Jeff Brantley	.25
46	Mark Petkovsek	.25
47	John Mabry	.25
49	Tom Lampkin	.25
50	John Frascatore	.25
51	Willie McGee	.25
57	Curtis King	.25
	Fredbird (mascot)	.25

1985 St. Louis News K.C. Royals

These "cards" are actually cutouts published in various issues of the St. Louis News. The pictures are 2-1/2" x 4-1/2" with dotted line borders for cutting. Fronts have black-and-white portrait photos at center with the team name in a banner above. Player information is printed below. Any printing on back is not germiane to the cards. The unnumbered cards are listed here in alphabetical order. The Royals were the Cadinals' opponent in the 1985 World Series.

		MT
Complete Set (25):		25.00
Common Player:		1.00

(1)	Steve Balboni	1.00
(2)	Joe Beckwith	1.00
(3)	Buddy Biancalana	1.00
(4)	Bud Black	1.00
(5)	George Brett	6.00
(6)	Onix Concepcion	1.00
(7)	Steve Farr	1.00
(8)	Mark Gubicza	1.50
(9)	Dane Iorg	1.00
(10)	Danny Jackson	1.00
(11)	Lynn Jones	1.00
(12)	Charlie Leibrandt	1.00
(13)	Hal McRae	1.50
(14)	Darryl Motley	1.00
(15)	Jorge Orta	1.00
(16)	Greg Pryor	1.00
(17)	Jamie Quirk	1.00
(18)	Dan Quisenberry	1.50
(19)	Bret Saberhagen	2.00
(20)	Pat Sheridan	1.00
(21)	Lonnie Smith	1.00
(22)	Jim Sundberg	1.00
(23)	John Wathan	1.00
(24)	Frank White	1.50
(25)	Willie Wilson	1.50

1985 St. Louis News L.A. Dodgers

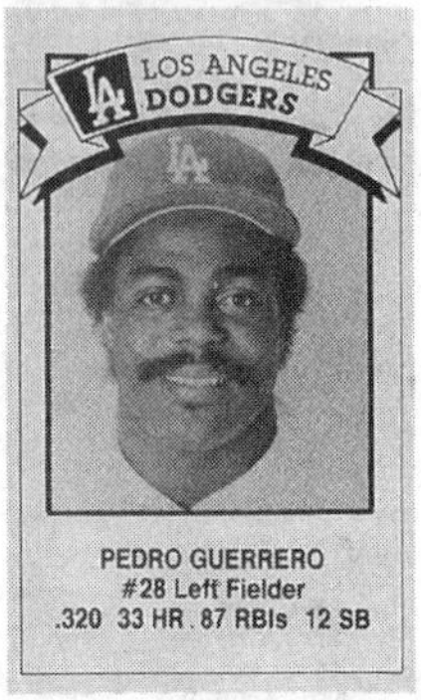

These "cards" are actually cutouts published in various issues of the St. Louis News. The pictures are 2-1/2" x 4-1/2" with dotted line borders for cutting. Fronts have black-and-white portrait photos at center with the team name in a banner above. Player information is printed below. Any printing on back is not germaine to the cards. The unnumbered cards are listed here in alphabetical order. The Dodgers were the Cardinals' opponent in the NLCS.

		MT
Complete Set (25):		21.00
Common Player:		1.00
(1)	Dave Anderson	1.00
(2)	Bob Bailor	1.00
(3)	Greg Brock	1.00
(4)	Enos Cabell	1.00
(5)	Bobby Castillo	1.00
(6)	Carlos Diaz	1.00
(7)	Mariano Duncan	1.50
(8)	Pedro Guerrero	1.00
(9)	Orel Hershiser	2.00
(10)	Rick Honeycutt	1.00
(11)	Ken Howell	1.00
(12)	Jay Johnstone	1.00
(13)	Ken Landreaux	1.00
(14)	Bill Madlock	1.50
(15)	Candy Maldonado	1.00
(16)	Mike Marshall	1.00
(17)	Len Matuszek	1.00
(18)	Tom Neidenfuer	1.00
(19)	Jerry Reuss	1.00
(20)	Steve Sax	1.00
(21)	Mike Scioscia	1.00
(22)	Fernando Valenzuela	1.50
(23)	Bob Welch	1.00
(24)	Terry Whitfield	1.00
(25)	Steve Yeager	1.00

1985 St. Louis News St. Louis Cardinals (b/w)

These "cards" are actually cutouts published in various issues of the St. Louis News. The pictures are 2-1/2" x 4-1/2" with dotted line borders for cutting. Fronts have black-and-white portrait photos at center with the team name in a banner above. Player information is printed below. Any printing on back is not germaine to the cards. The unnumbered cards are listed here in alphabetical order.

		MT
Complete Set (24):		24.00
Common Player:		1.00
(1)	Joaquin Andujar	1.00
(2)	Steve Braun	1.00
(3)	Bill Campbell	1.00
(4)	Cesar Cedeno	1.00
(5)	Jack Clark	1.50
(6)	Vince Coleman	1.50
(7)	Danny Cox	1.00
(8)	Ken Dayley	1.00
(9)	Ivan DeJesus	1.00
(10)	Bob Forsch	1.00
(11)	Brian Harper	1.00
(12)	Tommy Herr	1.00
(13)	Rick Horton	1.00
(14)	Mike Jorgensen	1.00
(15)	Jeff Lahti	1.00
(16)	Tito Landrum	1.00
(17)	Willie McGee	1.50
(18)	Tom Nieto	1.00
(19)	Terry Pendleton	1.25
(20)	Darrell Porter	1.00
(21)	Ozzie Smith	4.00
(22)	John Tudor	1.00
(23)	Andy Van Slyke	1.50
(24)	Todd Worrell, Kurt Kepshire	1.00

1985 St. Louis News St. Louis Cardinals (color)

These "cards" are actually cutouts published in various issues of the St. Louis News. The pictures are 2-1/2" x 4". Fronts have color portrait photos at center with the team name in a banner above. Player information is printed below and includes stats from the 1985 regular season, league championships and World Series. Any printing on back is not germaine to the cards. The unnumbered cards are listed here in alphabetical order.

		MT
Complete Set (25):		35.00
Common Player:		1.50
(1)	Joaquin Andujar	1.50
(2)	Steve Braun	1.50
(3)	Bill Campbell	1.50
(4)	Cesar Cedeno	1.50
(5)	Jack Clark	2.50
(6)	Vince Coleman	2.50
(7)	Danny Cox	1.50
(8)	Ken Dayley	1.50
(9)	Ivan DeJesus	1.50
(10)	Bob Forsch	1.50
(11)	Brian Harper	1.50
(12)	Tommy Herr	1.50
(13)	Rick Horton	1.50
(14)	Mike Jorgensen	1.50
(15)	Jeff Lahti	1.50
(16)	Tito Landrum	1.50
(17)	Tom Lawless	1.50
(18)	Willie McGee	2.00
(19)	Tom Nieto	1.50
(20)	Terry Pendleton	2.00
(21)	Darrell Porter	1.50
(22)	Ozzie Smith	8.00
(23)	John Tudor	1.50
(24)	Andy Van Slyke	2.00
(25)	Todd Worrell	1.50

1991 Stadium Club Promos

Topps' response to the upscale Leaf baseball card issue was a new brand labeled Stadium Club. To introduce the premium cards, a set of 50 promo cards was produced with single cards distributed to employees and candy companies. Production has been reported in the area of 600 of each card. The promos differ from the issued cards on front in that there are four horizontal gold-foil stripes on the promos, instead of three. The back of each promo card is identical, showing a 1986 Topps Traded Jose Canseco card. The unnumbered cards are checklisted here in alphabetical order.

		MT
Complete Set (50):		1000.
Common Player:		10.00
(1)	Allan Anderson	10.00
(2)	Steve Balboni	10.00
(3)	Jeff Ballard	10.00
(4)	Jesse Barfield	10.00
(5)	Andy Benes	15.00
(6)	Bobby Bonilla	10.00
(7)	Chris Bosio	10.00
(8)	Daryl Boston	10.00
(9)	Chuck Cary	10.00
(10)	Pat Combs	10.00
(11)	Delino DeShields	10.00
(12)	Shawon Dunston	10.00
(13)	Alvaro Espinoza	10.00
(14)	Sid Fernandez	10.00
(15)	Bob Geren	10.00
(16)	Brian Holman	10.00
(17)	Jay Howell	10.00
(18)	Stan Javier	10.00
(19)	Dave Johnson	10.00
(20)	Howard Johnson	10.00
(21)	Kevin Maas	10.00
(22)	Shane Mack	10.00
(23)	Joe Magrane	10.00
(24)	Denny Martinez	10.00
(25)	Don Mattingly	200.00
(26)	Ben McDonald	10.00
(27)	Eddie Murray	125.00
(28)	Matt Nokes	10.00
(29)	Greg Olson	10.00
(30)	Gregg Olson	10.00
(31)	Jose Oquendo	10.00
(32)	Tony Phillips	10.00
(33)	Rafael Ramirez	10.00
(34)	Dennis Rasmussen	10.00
(35)	Billy Ripken	10.00
(36)	Nolan Ryan	500.00
(37)	Bill Sampen	10.00
(38)	Steve Sax	10.00
(39)	Mike Scioscia	10.00
(40)	David Segui	10.00
(41)	Zane Smith	10.00
(42)	B.J. Surhoff	10.00
(43)	Bobby Thigpen	10.00
(44)	Alan Trammell	15.00
(45)	Fernando Valenzuela	12.50
(46)	Andy Van Slyke	10.00
(47)	Hector Villanueva	10.00
(48)	Larry Walker	40.00
(49)	Walt Weiss	10.00
(50)	Bob Welch	10.00

1991 Stadium Club

One of the most popular sets of 1991, this 600-card issue was released in two 300-card series. The cards were available in foil packs only. No factory sets were available. The cards feature borderless high gloss photos on the front and a player evaluation and card photo on the back. Stadium Club cards were considered scarce in many areas, this driving up the price per pack. A special Stadium Club membership package was made available for $29.95 with 10 proof of purchase seals from wrappers.

		MT
Complete Set (600):		80.00
Complete Series 1 (300):		50.00
Complete Series 2 (300):		30.00
Common Player:		.20
Series 1 Wax Box:		110.00
Series 2 Wax Box:		60.00
1	Dave Stewart	.20
2	Wally Joyner	.30
3	Shawon Dunston	.20
4	Darren Daulton	.20
5	Will Clark	.75
6	Sammy Sosa	6.00
7	Dan Plesac	.20
8	Marquis Grissom	.30
9	Erik Hanson	.20
10	Geno Petralli	.20
11	Jose Rijo	.20
12	Carlos Quintana	.20
13	Junior Ortiz	.20
14	Bob Walk	.20
15	Mike Macfarlane	.20
16	Eric Yelding	.20
17	Bryn Smith	.20
18	Bip Roberts	.20
19	Mike Scioscia	.20
20	Mark Williamson	.20
21	Don Mattingly	2.00
22	John Franco	.20
23	Chet Lemon	.20
24	Tom Henke	.20
25	Jerry Browne	.20
26	Dave Justice	1.00
27	Mark Langston	.20
28	Damon Berryhill	.20
29	Kevin Bass	.20
30	Scott Fletcher	.20
31	Moises Alou	.40
32	Dave Valle	.20
33	Jody Reed	.20
34	Dave West	.20
35	Kevin McReynolds	.20
36	Pat Combs	.20
37	Eric Davis	.20
38	Bret Saberhagen	.25
39	Stan Javier	.20
40	Chuck Cary	.20
41	Tony Phillips	.20
42	Lee Smith	.20
43	Tim Teufel	.20
44	Lance Dickson	.20
45	Greg Litton	.20
46	Teddy Higuera	.20
47	Edgar Martinez	.20
48	Steve Avery	.20
49	Walt Weiss	.20
50	David Segui	.20
51	Andy Benes	.35
52	Karl Rhodes	.20
53	Neal Heaton	.20
54	Dan Gladden	.20
55	Luis Rivera	.20
56	Kevin Brown	.20
57	Frank Thomas	5.00
58	Terry Mulholland	.20
59	Dick Schofield	.20
60	Ron Darling	.20
61	Sandy Alomar, Jr.	.30
62	Dave Stieb	.20
63	Alan Trammell	.30
64	Matt Nokes	.20
65	Lenny Harris	.20
66	Milt Thompson	.20
67	Storm Davis	.20
68	Joe Oliver	.20
69	Andres Galarraga	.45
70	Ozzie Guillen	.20
71	Ken Howell	.20
72	Garry Templeton	.20
73	Derrick May	.20
74	Xavier Hernandez	.20
75	Dave Parker	.25
76	Rick Aguilera	.20
77	Robby Thompson	.20
78	Pete Incaviglia	.20
79	Bob Welch	.20
80	Randy Milligan	.20
81	Chuck Finley	.20
82	Alvin Davis	.20
83	Tim Naehring	.20
84	Jay Bell	.20
85	Joe Magrane	.20
86	Howard Johnson	.20
87	Jack McDowell	.20
88	Kevin Seitzer	.20
89	Bruce Ruffin	.20
90	Fernando Valenzuela	.25
91	Terry Kennedy	.20
92	Barry Larkin	.45
93	Larry Walker	.75
94	Luis Salazar	.20
95	Gary Sheffield	.60
96	Bobby Witt	.20
97	Lonnie Smith	.20
98	Bryan Harvey	.20
99	Mookie Wilson	.20
100	Dwight Gooden	.25
101	Lou Whitaker	.20
102	Ron Karkovice	.20
103	Jesse Barfield	.20
104	Jose DeJesus	.20
105	Benito Santiago	.20
106	Brian Holman	.20
107	Rafael Ramirez	.20
108	Ellis Burks	.30
109	Mike Bielecki	.20
110	Kirby Puckett	2.00
111	Terry Shumpert	.20
112	Chuck Crim	.20
113	Todd Benzinger	.20
114	Brian Barnes	.20
115	Carlos Baerga	.20
116	Kal Daniels	.20
117	Dave Johnson	.20
118	Andy Van Slyke	.20
119	John Burkett	.20
120	Rickey Henderson	.50
121	Tim Jones	.20
122	Daryl Irvine	.20
123	Ruben Sierra	.20
124	Jim Abbott	.20
125	Daryl Boston	.20
126	Greg Maddux	4.00
127	Von Hayes	.20
128	Mike Fitzgerald	.20
129	Wayne Edwards	.20
130	Greg Briley	.20
131	Rob Dibble	.20
132	Gene Larkin	.20
133	David Wells	.25
134	Steve Balboni	.20
135	Greg Vaughn	.25
136	Mark Davis	.20
137	Dave Rohde	.20
138	Eric Show	.20
139	Bobby Bonilla	.20
140	Dana Kiecker	.20
141	Gary Pettis	.20
142	Dennis Boyd	.20
143	Mike Benjamin	.20
144	Luis Polonia	.20
145	Doug Jones	.20
146	Al Newman	.20
147	Alex Fernandez	.40
148	Bill Doran	.20
149	Kevin Elster	.20
150	Len Dykstra	.20
151	Mike Gallego	.20
152	Tim Belcher	.20
153	Jay Buhner	.20
154	Ozzie Smith	1.00
155	Jose Canseco	.75
156	Gregg Olson	.20
157	Charlie O'Brien	.20
158	Frank Tanana	.20
159	George Brett	2.00
160	Jeff Huson	.20
161	Kevin Tapani	.20
162	Jerome Walton	.20
163	Charlie Hayes	.20
164	Chris Bosio	.20
165	Chris Sabo	.20
166	Lance Parrish	.20
167	Don Robinson	.20
168	Manuel Lee	.20
169	Dennis Rasmussen	.20
170	Wade Boggs	1.50
171	Bob Geren	.20
172	Mackey Sasser	.20
173	Julio Franco	.20
174	Otis Nixon	.20
175	Bert Blyleven	.20
176	Craig Biggio	.75
177	Eddie Murray	.60

178	Randy Tomlin	.20
179	Tino Martinez	.35
180	Carlton Fisk	.80
181	Dwight Smith	.20
182	Scott Garrelts	.20
183	Jim Gantner	.20
184	Dickie Thon	.20
185	John Farrell	.20
186	Cecil Fielder	.20
187	Glenn Braggs	.20
188	Allan Anderson	.20
189	Kurt Stillwell	.20
190	Jose Oquendo	.20
191	Joe Orsulak	.20
192	Ricky Jordan	.20
193	Kelly Downs	.20
194	Delino DeShields	.20
195	Omar Vizquel	.20
196	Mark Carreon	.20
197	Mike Harkey	.20
198	Jack Howell	.20
199	Lance Johnson	.20
200	Nolan Ryan	6.00
201	John Marzano	.20
202	Doug Drabek	.20
203	Mark Lemke	.20
204	Steve Sax	.20
205	Greg Harris	.20
206	B.J. Surhoff	.20
207	Todd Burns	.20
208	Jose Gonzalez	.20
209	Mike Scott	.20
210	Dave Magadan	.20
211	Dante Bichette	.75
212	Trevor Wilson	.20
213	Hector Villanueva	.20
214	Dan Pasqua	.20
215	Greg Colbrunn	.20
216	Mike Jeffcoat	.20
217	Harold Reynolds	.20
218	Paul O'Neill	.35
219	Mark Guthrie	.20
220	Barry Bonds	1.50
221	Jimmy Key	.20
222	Billy Ripken	.20
223	Tom Pagnozzi	.20
224	Bo Jackson	.40
225	Sid Fernandez	.20
226	Mike Marshall	.20
227	John Kruk	.20
228	Mike Fetters	.20
229	Eric Anthony	.20
230	Ryne Sandberg	1.50
231	Carney Lansford	.20
232	Melido Perez	.20
233	Jose Lind	.20
234	Darryl Hamilton	.20
235	Tom Browning	.20
236	Spike Owen	.20
237	Juan Gonzalez	5.00
238	Felix Fermin	.20
239	Keith Miller	.20
240	Mark Gubicza	.20
241	Kent Anderson	.20
242	Alvaro Espinoza	.20
243	Dale Murphy	.40
244	Orel Hershiser	.30
245	Paul Molitor	1.25
246	Eddie Whitson	.20
247	Joe Girardi	.20
248	Kent Hrbek	.25
249	Bill Sampen	.20
250	Kevin Mitchell	.20
251	Mariano Duncan	.20
252	Scott Bradley	.20
253	Mike Greenwell	.20
254	Tom Gordon	.20
255	Todd Zeile	.25
256	Bobby Thigpen	.20
257	Gregg Jefferies	.30
258	Kenny Rogers	.20
259	Shane Mack	.20
260	Zane Smith	.20
261	Mitch Williams	.20
262	Jim DeShaies	.20
263	Dave Winfield	.50
264	Ben McDonald	.20
265	Randy Ready	.20
266	Pat Borders	.20
267	Jose Uribe	.20
268	Derek Lilliquist	.20
269	Greg Brock	.20
270	Ken Griffey, Jr.	8.00
271	Jeff Gray	.20
272	Danny Tartabull	.20
273	Dennis Martinez	.20
274	Robin Ventura	.35
275	Randy Myers	.20
276	Jack Daugherty	.20
277	Greg Gagne	.20
278	Jay Howell	.20
279	Mike LaValliere	.20
280	Rex Hudler	.20
281	Mike Simms	.20
282	Kevin Maas	.20
283	Jeff Ballard	.20
284	Dave Henderson	.20
285	Pete O'Brien	.20
286	Brook Jacoby	.20
287	Mike Henneman	.20
288	Greg Olson	.20
289	Greg Myers	.20
290	Mark Grace	.40
291	Shawn Abner	.20
292	Frank Viola	.20
293	Lee Stevens	.20
294	Jason Grimsley	.20
295	Matt Williams	.40
296	Ron Robinson	.20
297	Tom Brunansky	.20
298	Checklist	.20
299	Checklist	.20
300	Checklist	.20
301	Darryl Strawberry	.40
302	Bud Black	.20
303	Harold Baines	.25
304	Roberto Alomar	1.00
305	Norm Charlton	.20
306	Gary Thurman	.20
307	Mike Felder	.20
308	Tony Gwynn	3.00
309	Roger Clemens	3.00
310	Andre Dawson	.40
311	Scott Radinsky	.20
312	Bob Melvin	.20
313	Kirk McCaskill	.20
314	Pedro Guerrero	.20
315	Walt Terrell	.20
316	Sam Horn	.20
317	*Wes Chamberlain*	.20
318	*Pedro Munoz*	.20
319	Roberto Kelly	.20
320	Mark Portugal	.20
321	Tim McIntosh	.20
322	Jesse Orosco	.20
323	Gary Green	.20
324	Greg Harris	.20
325	Hubie Brooks	.20
326	Chris Nabholz	.20
327	Terry Pendleton	.20
328	Eric King	.20
329	Chili Davis	.20
330	Anthony Telford	.20
331	Kelly Gruber	.20
332	Dennis Eckersley	.20
333	Mel Hall	.20
334	Bob Kipper	.20
335	Willie McGee	.20
336	Steve Olin	.20
337	Steve Buechele	.20
338	Scott Leius	.20
339	Hal Morris	.20
340	Jose Offerman	.25
341	Kent Mercker	.20
342	Ken Griffey	.20
343	Pete Harnisch	.20
344	Kirk Gibson	.20
345	Dave Smith	.20
346	Dave Martinez	.20
347	Atlee Hammaker	.20
348	Brian Downing	.20
349	Todd Hundley	.35
350	Candy Maldonado	.20
351	Dwight Evans	.20
352	Steve Searcy	.20
353	Gary Gaetti	.20
354	Jeff Reardon	.20
355	Travis Fryman	.30
356	Dave Righetti	.20
357	Fred McGriff	.60
358	Don Slaught	.20
359	Gene Nelson	.20
360	Billy Spiers	.20
361	Lee Guetterman	.20
362	Darren Lewis	.20
363	Duane Ward	.20
364	Lloyd Moseby	.20
365	John Smoltz	.60
366	Felix Jose	.20
367	David Cone	.30
368	Wally Backman	.20
369	Jeff Montgomery	.20
370	Rich Garces	.20
371	Billy Hatcher	.20
372	Bill Swift	.20
373	Jim Eisenreich	.20
374	Rob Ducey	.20
375	Tim Crews	.20
376	Steve Finley	.20
377	Jeff Blauser	.20
378	Willie Wilson	.20
379	Gerald Perry	.20
380	Jose Mesa	.20
381	Pat Kelly	.20
382	Matt Merullo	.20
383	Ivan Calderon	.20
384	Scott Chiamparino	.20
385	Lloyd McClendon	.20
386	Dave Bergman	.20
387	Ed Sprague	.20
388	*Jeff Bagwell*	10.00
389	Brett Butler	.20
390	Larry Andersen	.20
391	Glenn Davis	.20
392	Alex Cole (photo is Otis Nixon)	.20
393	Mike Heath	.20
394	Danny Darwin	.20
395	Steve Lake	.20
396	Tim Layana	.20
397	Terry Leach	.20
398	Bill Wegman	.20
399	Mark McGwire	8.00
400	Mike Boddicker	.20
401	Steve Howe	.20
402	Bernard Gilkey	.20
403	Thomas Howard	.20
404	Rafael Belliard	.20
405	Tom Candiotti	.20
406	Rene Gonzalez	.20
407	Chuck McElroy	.20
408	Paul Sorrento	.20
409	Randy Johnson	1.00
410	Brady Anderson	.30
411	Dennis Cook	.20
412	Mickey Tettleton	.20
413	Mike Stanton	.20
414	Ken Oberkfell	.20
415	Rick Honeycutt	.20
416	Nelson Santovenia	.20
417	Bob Tewksbury	.20
418	Brent Mayne	.20
419	Steve Farr	.20
420	Phil Stephenson	.20
421	Jeff Russell	.20
422	Chris James	.20
423	Tim Leary	.20
424	Gary Carter	.30
425	Glenallen Hill	.20
426	Matt Young	.20
427	Sid Bream	.20
428	Greg Swindell	.20
429	Scott Aldred	.20
430	Cal Ripken, Jr.	6.00
431	Bill Landrum	.20
432	Ernie Riles	.20
433	Danny Jackson	.20
434	Casey Candaele	.20
435	Ken Hill	.20
436	Jaime Navarro	.20
437	Lance Blankenship	.20
438	Randy Velarde	.20
439	Frank DiPino	.20
440	Carl Nichols	.20
441	Jeff Robinson	.20
442	Deion Sanders	.45
443	Vincente Palacios	.20
444	Devon White	.25
445	John Cerutti	.20
446	Tracy Jones	.20
447	Jack Morris	.20
448	Mitch Webster	.20
449	Bob Ojeda	.20
450	Oscar Azocar	.20
451	Luis Aquino	.20
452	Mark Whiten	.20
453	Stan Belinda	.20
454	Ron Gant	.30
455	Jose DeLeon	.20
456	Mark Salas	.20
457	Junior Felix	.20
458	Wally Whitehurst	.20
459	*Phil Plantier*	.35
460	Juan Berenguer	.20
461	Franklin Stubbs	.20
462	Joe Boever	.20
463	Tim Wallach	.20
464	Mike Moore	.20
465	Albert Belle	1.50
466	Mike Witt	.20
467	Craig Worthington	.20
468	Jerald Clark	.20
469	Scott Terry	.20
470	Milt Cuyler	.20
471	John Smiley	.20
472	Charles Nagy	.25
473	Alan Mills	.20
474	John Russell	.20
475	Bruce Hurst	.20
476	Andujar Cedeno	.20
477	Dave Eiland	.20
478	*Brian McRae*	.75
479	Mike LaCoss	.20
480	Chris Gwynn	.20
481	Jamie Moyer	.20
482	John Olerud	.30
483	Efrain Valdez	.20
484	Sil Campusano	.20
485	Pascual Perez	.20
486	Gary Redus	.20
487	Andy Hawkins	.20
488	Cory Snyder	.20
489	Chris Hoiles	.20
490	Ron Hassey	.20
491	Gary Wayne	.20
492	Mark Lewis	.20
493	Scott Coolbaugh	.20
494	Gerald Young	.20
495	Juan Samuel	.20
496	Willie Fraser	.20
497	Jeff Treadway	.20
498	Vince Coleman	.20
499	Cris Carpenter	.20
500	Jack Clark	.20
501	Kevin Appier	.20
502	Rafael Palmeiro	.50
503	Hensley Meulens	.20
504	George Bell	.20
505	Tony Pena	.20
506	Roger McDowell	.20
507	Luis Sojo	.20
508	Mike Schooler	.20
509	Robin Yount	1.50
510	Jack Armstrong	.20
511	Rick Cerone	.20
512	Curt Wilkerson	.20
513	Joe Carter	.20
514	Tim Burke	.20
515	Tony Fernandez	.20
516	Ramon Martinez	.25
517	Tim Hulett	.20
518	Terry Steinbach	.20
519	Pete Smith	.20
520	Ken Caminiti	.30
521	Shawn Boskie	.20
522	Mike Pagliarulo	.20
523	Tim Raines	.30
524	Alfredo Griffin	.20
525	Henry Cotto	.20
526	Mike Stanley	.20
527	Charlie Leibrandt	.20
528	Jeff King	.20
529	Eric Plunk	.20
530	Tom Lampkin	.20
531	Steve Bedrosian	.20
532	Tom Herr	.20
533	Craig Lefferts	.20
534	Jeff Reed	.20
535	Mickey Morandini	.20
536	Greg Cadaret	.20
537	Ray Lankford	.30
538	John Candelaria	.20
539	Rob Deer	.20
540	Brad Arnsberg	.20
541	Mike Sharperson	.20
542	Jeff Robinson	.20
543	Mo Vaughn	2.00
544	Jeff Parrett	.20
545	Willie Randolph	.20
546	Herm Winningham	.20
547	Jeff Innis	.20
548	Chuck Knoblauch	2.00
549	Tommy Greene	.20
550	Jeff Hamilton	.20
551	Barry Jones	.20
552	Ken Dayley	.20
553	Rick Dempsey	.20
554	Greg Smith	.20
555	Mike Devereaux	.20
556	Keith Comstock	.20
557	Paul Faries	.20
558	Tom Glavine	.60
559	Craig Grebeck	.20
560	Scott Erickson	.20
561	Joel Skinner	.20
562	Mike Morgan	.20
563	Dave Gallagher	.20
564	Todd Stottlemyre	.20
565	Rich Rodriguez	.20
566	*Craig Wilson*	.20
567	Jeff Brantley	.20
568	Scott Kamieniecki	.20
569	Steve Decker	.20
570	Juan Agosto	.20
571	Tommy Gregg	.20
572	Kevin Wickander	.20
573	Jamie Quirk	.20
574	Jerry Don Gleaton	.20
575	Chris Hammond	.20
576	*Luis Gonzalez*	.60
577	Russ Swan	.20
578	*Jeff Conine*	2.00
579	Charlie Hough	.20
580	Jeff Kunkel	.20
581	Darrel Akerfelds	.20
582	Jeff Manto	.20
583	Alejandro Pena	.20
584	Mark Davidson	.20
585	Bob MacDonald	.20
586	Paul Assenmacher	.20
587	Dan Wilson	.20
588	Tom Bolton	.20
589	Brian Harper	.20
590	John Habyan	.20
591	John Orton	.20
592	Mark Gardner	.20
593	Turner Ward	.20
594	Bob Patterson	.20
595	Edwin Nunez	.20
596	Gary Scott	.20
597	Scott Bankhead	.20
598	Checklist	.20
599	Checklist	.20
600	Checklist	.20

1991 Stadium Club Charter Members

Charter members of Topps Stadium Club received a package which included a 50-card multi-sport set unavailable in any other fashion. Cards were similar in format to S.C. regular issues, with full-bleed photos on front, UV coating and gold-foil highlights. This special edition has a gold foil "Charter Member" notation at the bottom of each card front. Backs have a simulated newspaper page describing a career highlight. The cards are unnumbered and the checklist here includes only the baseball cards from the set.

		MT
Complete Set (32):		15.00
Common Player:		.25
(1)	Sandy Alomar, Jr.	.35
(2)	George Brett	1.50
(3)	Barry Bonds	1.50
(4)	Ellis Burks	.25
(5)	Eric Davis	.25
(6)	Delino DeShields	.25
(7)	Doug Drabek	.25
(8)	Cecil Fielder	.25
(9)	Carlton Fisk	.35
(10)	Ken Griffey, Jr., Ken Griffey, Sr.	2.00
(11)	Billy Hatcher	.25
(12)	Andy Hawkins	.25
(13)	Rickey Henderson (A.L. MVP)	.50
(14)	Rickey Henderson (A.L. base-stealing leader)	.50
(15)	Randy Johnson	.50
(16)	Dave Justice	.75
(17)	Mark Langston, Mike Witt	.25
(18)	Kevin Maas	.25
(19)	Ramon Martinez	.25
(20)	Willie McGee	.25
(21)	Terry Mulholland	.25
(22)	Jose Offerman	.25
(23)	Melido Perez	.25
(24)	Nolan Ryan (no-hitter)	2.50
(25)	Nolan Ryan (300th win)	2.50
(26)	Ryne Sandberg	1.00
(27)	Dave Stewart	.25
(28)	Dave Stieb	.25
(29)	Bobby Thigpen	.25
(30)	Fernando Valenzuela	.25
(31)	Frank Viola	.25
(32)	Bob Welch	.25

1991 Stadium Club Members Only

Each member of Topps Stadium Club during 1991 received three packages of multi-sport cards bearing a special design and stamped "Members Only" in gold foil on the front. Cards followed the basic Stadium Club format of full-bleed action photos on front. Backs have a facsimile newspaper page - the "Stadium Club Herald" - which gives details of a career highlight. Cards are unnumbered and the baseball-only checklist here is arranged alphabetically.

		MT
Complete Set (30):		12.00
Common Player:		.25
(1)	A.L. Home Run Leaders (Jose Canseco, Cecil Fielder)	.40
(2)	Wilson Alvarez	.25
(3)	Andy Ashby	.25
(4)	Jeff Bagwell	4.00
(5)	Braves no-hitter (Kent Mercker, Mark Wohlers, Alejandro Pena)	.25
(6)	Roger Clemens	1.00
(7)	David Cone	.35
(8)	Carlton Fisk	.35
(9)	Julio Franco	.25
(10)	Tom Glavine	.35
(11)	Tommy Greene	.25
(12)	Pete Harnisch	.25
(13)	Rickey Henderson (all-time theft leader)	.40

(14) Rickey Henderson (11th time A.L. theft leader) .40
(15) Howard Johnson .25
(16) Chuck Knoblauch 1.50
(17) Ray Lankford .25
(18) Denny Martinez .25
(19) Paul Molitor .50
(20) Jack Morris .25
(21) Orioles No-Hitter (Bob Milacki, Mike Flanagan, Mark Williamson, Gregg Olson, Chris Hoiles) .25
(22) Terry Pendleton (N.L. leading hitter) .25
(23) Terry Pendleton (MVP) .25
(24) Jeff Reardon .25
(25) Cal Ripken, Jr. 2.00
(26) Nolan Ryan (7th no-hitter) 2.00
(27) Nolan Ryan (22nd 100-K season) 2.00
(28) Bret Saberhagen .35
(29) Robby Thompson .25
(30) Dave Winfield .50

1991 Stadium Club Nolan Ryan Bronze

One of the premiums included with charter membership in the Topps Stadium Club was a bronze replica of the Nolan Ryan card from the Charter Member's card set. The replica measures 2-1/2" x 3-1/2" and reproduces both front and back of the Ryan card on a 10-oz. metal slab.

	MT
Nolan Ryan (bronze)	15.00

1992 Stadium Club

This 900-card set was released in three 100-card series. Like the 1991 issue, the cards feature borderless high-gloss photos on the front. The flip sides feature the player's first Topps card and a player evaluation. Topps released updated cards in the third series for traded player and free agents. Several players appear on two cards. Special Members Choice cards are included in the set. Series III features special inserts of the last three number one draft picks: Phil Nevin, Brien Taylor and Chipper Jones.

		MT
	Complete Set (900):	60.00
	Common Player:	.10
	Series 1,2,3 Wax Box:	28.00
1	Cal Ripken, Jr.	4.00
2	Eric Yelding	.10
3	Geno Petralli	.10
4	Wally Backman	.10
5	Milt Cuyler	.10
6	Kevin Bass	.10
7	Dante Bichette	.30
8	Ray Lankford	.10
9	Mel Hall	.10
10	Joe Carter	.10
11	Juan Samuel	.10
12	Jeff Montgomery	.10
13	Glenn Braggs	.10
14	Henry Cotto	.10
15	Deion Sanders	.30
16	Dick Schofield	.10
17	David Cone	.15
18	Chili Davis	.10
19	Tom Foley	.10
20	Ozzie Guillen	.10
21	Luis Salazar	.10
22	Terry Steinbach	.10
23	Chris James	.10
24	Jeff King	.10
25	Carlos Quintana	.10
26	Mike Maddux	.10
27	Tommy Greene	.10
28	Jeff Russell	.10
29	Steve Finley	.10
30	Mike Flanagan	.10
31	Darren Lewis	.10
32	Mark Lee	.10
33	Willie Fraser	.10
34	Mike Henneman	.10
35	Kevin Maas	.10
36	Dave Hansen	.10
37	Erik Hanson	.10
38	Bill Doran	.10
39	Mike Boddicker	.10
40	Vince Coleman	.10
41	Devon White	.15
42	Mark Gardner	.10
43	Scott Lewis	.10
44	Juan Berenguer	.10
45	Carney Lansford	.10
46	Curt Wilkerson	.10
47	Shane Mack	.10
48	Bip Roberts	.10
49	Greg Harris	.10
50	Ryne Sandberg	.50
51	Mark Whiten	.10
52	Jack McDowell	.10
53	Jimmy Jones	.10
54	Steve Lake	.10
55	Bud Black	.10
56	Dave Valle	.10
57	Kevin Reimer	.10
58	Rich Gedman	.10
59	Travis Fryman	.10
60	Steve Avery	.10
61	Francisco de la Rosa	.10
62	Scott Hemond	.10
63	Hal Morris	.10
64	Hensley Meulens	.10
65	Frank Castillo	.10
66	Gene Larkin	.10
67	Jose DeLeon	.10
68	Al Osuna	.10
69	Dave Cochrane	.10
70	Robin Ventura	.25
71	John Cerutti	.10
72	Kevin Gross	.10
73	Ivan Calderon	.10
74	Mike Macfarlane	.10
75	Stan Belinda	.10
76	Shawn Hillegas	.10
77	Pat Borders	.10
78	Jim Vatcher	.10
79	Bobby Rose	.10
80	Roger Clemens	.75
81	Craig Worthington	.10
82	Jeff Treadway	.10
83	Jamie Quirk	.10
84	Randy Bush	.10
85	Anthony Young	.10
86	Trevor Wilson	.10
87	Jaime Navarro	.10
88	Les Lancaster	.10
89	Pat Kelly	.10
90	Alvin Davis	.10
91	Larry Andersen	.10
92	Rob Deer	.10
93	Mike Sharperson	.10
94	Lance Parrish	.10
95	Cecil Espy	.10
96	Tim Spehr	.10
97	Dave Stieb	.10
98	Terry Mulholland	.10
99	Dennis Boyd	.10
100	Barry Larkin	.15
101	Ryan Bowen	.10
102	Felix Fermin	.10
103	Luis Alicea	.10
104	Tim Hulett	.10
105	Rafael Belliard	.10
106	Mike Gallego	.10
107	Dave Righetti	.10
108	Jeff Schaefer	.10
109	Ricky Bones	.10
110	Scott Erickson	.10
111	Matt Nokes	.10
112	Bob Scanlan	.10
113	Tom Candiotti	.10
114	Sean Berry	.10
115	Kevin Morton	.10
116	Scott Fletcher	.10
117	B.J. Surhoff	.10
118	Dave Magadan	.10
119	Bill Gullickson	.10
120	Marquis Grissom	.10
121	Lenny Harris	.10
122	Wally Joyner	.15
123	Kevin Brown	.10
124	Braulio Castillo	.10
125	Eric King	.10
126	Mark Portugal	.10
127	Calvin Jones	.10
128	Mike Heath	.10
129	Todd Van Poppel	.10
130	Benny Santiago	.10
131	Gary Thurman	.10
132	Joe Girardi	.10
133	Dave Eiland	.10
134	Orlando Merced	.10
135	Joe Orsulak	.10
136	John Burkett	.10
137	Ken Dayley	.10
138	Ken Hill	.10
139	Walt Terrell	.10
140	Mike Scioscia	.10
141	Junior Felix	.10
142	Ken Caminiti	.20
143	Carlos Baerga	.10
144	Tony Fossas	.10
145	Craig Grebeck	.10
146	Scott Bradley	.10
147	Kent Mercker	.10
148	Derrick May	.10
149	Jerald Clark	.10
150	George Brett	.75
151	Luis Quinones	.10
152	Mike Pagliarulo	.10
153	Jose Guzman	.10
154	Charlie O'Brien	.10
155	Darren Holmes	.10
156	Joe Boever	.10
157	Rich Monteleone	.10
158	Reggie Harris	.10
159	Roberto Alomar	.60
160	Robby Thompson	.10
161	Chris Hoiles	.10
162	Tom Pagnozzi	.10
163	Omar Vizquel	.10
164	John Candelaria	.10
165	Terry Shumpert	.10
166	Andy Mota	.10
167	Scott Bailes	.10
168	Jeff Blauser	.10
169	Steve Olin	.10
170	Doug Drabek	.10
171	Dave Bergman	.10
172	Eddie Whitson	.10
173	Gilberto Reyes	.10
174	Mark Grace	.20
175	Paul O'Neill	.15
176	Greg Cadaret	.10
177	Mark Williamson	.10
178	Casey Candaele	.10
179	Candy Maldonado	.10
180	Lee Smith	.10
181	Harold Reynolds	.10
182	Dave Justice	.20
183	Lenny Webster	.10
184	Donn Pall	.10
185	Gerald Alexander	.10
186	Jack Clark	.10
187	Stan Javier	.10
188	Ricky Jordan	.10
189	Franklin Stubbs	.10
190	Dennis Eckersley	.10
191	Danny Tartabull	.10
192	Pete O'Brien	.10
193	Mark Lewis	.10
194	Mike Felder	.10
195	Mickey Tettleton	.10
196	Dwight Smith	.10
197	Shawn Abner	.10
198	Jim Leyritz	.10
199	Mike Devereaux	.10
200	Craig Biggio	.25
201	Kevin Elster	.10
202	Rance Mulliniks	.10
203	Tony Fernandez	.10
204	Allan Anderson	.10
205	Herm Winningham	.10
206	Tim Jones	.10
207	Ramon Martinez	.15
208	Teddy Higuera	.10
209	John Kruk	.10
210	Jim Abbott	.10
211	Dean Palmer	.10
212	Mark Davis	.10
213	Jay Buhner	.10
214	Jesse Barfield	.10
215	Kevin Mitchell	.10
216	Mike LaValliere	.10
217	Mark Wohlers	.10
218	Dave Henderson	.10
219	Dave Smith	.10
220	Albert Belle	.75
221	Spike Owen	.10
222	Jeff Gray	.10
223	Paul Gibson	.10
224	Bobby Thigpen	.10
225	Mike Mussina	.60
226	Darrin Jackson	.10
227	Luis Gonzalez	.15
228	Greg Briley	.10
229	Brent Mayne	.10
230	Paul Molitor	.50
231	Al Leiter	.15
232	Andy Van Slyke	.10
233	Ron Tingley	.10
234	Bernard Gilkey	.10
235	Kent Hrbek	.10
236	Eric Karros	.10
237	Randy Velarde	.10
238	Andy Allanson	.10
239	Willie McGee	.10
240	Juan Gonzalez	1.00
241	Karl Rhodes	.10
242	Luis Mercedes	.10
243	Billy Swift	.10
244	Tommy Gregg	.10
245	David Howard	.10
246	Dave Hollins	.10
247	Kip Gross	.10
248	Walt Weiss	.10
249	Mackey Sasser	.10
250	Cecil Fielder	.10
251	Jerry Browne	.10
252	Doug Dascenzo	.10
253	Darryl Hamilton	.10
254	Dann Bilardello	.10
255	Luis Rivera	.10
256	Larry Walker	.40
257	Ron Karkovice	.10
258	Bob Tewksbury	.10
259	Jimmy Key	.10
260	Bernie Williams	.60
261	Gary Wayne	.10
262	Mike Simms	.10
263	John Orton	.10
264	Marvin Freeman	.10
265	Mike Jeffcoat	.10
266	Roger Mason	.10
267	Edgar Martinez	.10
268	Henry Rodriguez	.10
269	Sam Horn	.10
270	Brian McRae	.10
271	Kirt Manwaring	.10
272	Mike Bordick	.10
273	Chris Sabo	.10
274	Jim Olander	.10
275	Greg Harris	.10
276	Dan Gakeler	.10
277	Bill Sampen	.10
278	Joel Skinner	.10
279	Curt Schilling	.15
280	Dale Murphy	.25
281	Lee Stevens	.10
282	Lonnie Smith	.10
283	Manuel Lee	.10
284	Shawn Boskie	.10
285	Kevin Seitzer	.10
286	Stan Royer	.10
287	John Dopson	.10
288	Scott Bullett	.10
289	Ken Patterson	.10
290	Todd Hundley	.15
291	Tim Leary	.10
292	Brett Butler	.10
293	Gregg Olson	.10
294	Jeff Brantley	.10
295	Brian Holman	.10
296	Brian Harper	.10
297	Brian Bohanon	.10
298	Checklist 1-100	.10
299	Checklist 101-200	.10
300	Checklist 201-300	.10
301	Frank Thomas	2.00
302	Lloyd McClendon	.10
303	Brady Anderson	.15
304	Julio Valera	.10
305	Mike Aldrete	.10
306	Joe Oliver	.10
307	Todd Stottlemyre	.10
308	Rey Sanchez	.10
309	Gary Sheffield	.25
310	Andujar Cedeno	.10
311	Kenny Rogers	.10
312	Bruce Hurst	.10
313	Mike Schooler	.10
314	Mike Benjamin	.10
315	Chuck Finley	.10
316	Mark Lemke	.10
317	Scott Livingstone	.10
318	Chris Nabholz	.10
319	Mike Humphreys	.10
320	Pedro Guerrero	.10
321	Willie Banks	.10
322	Tom Goodwin	.10
323	Hector Wagner	.10
324	Wally Ritchie	.10
325	Mo Vaughn	.60
326	Joe Klink	.10
327	Cal Eldred	.10
328	Daryl Boston	.10
329	Mike Huff	.10
330	Jeff Bagwell	1.50
331	Bob Milacki	.10
332	Tom Prince	.10
333	Pat Tabler	.10
334	Ced Landrum	.10
335	Reggie Jefferson	.10
336	Mo Sanford	.10
337	Kevin Ritz	.10
338	Gerald Perry	.10
339	Jeff Hamilton	.10
340	Tim Wallach	.10
341	Jeff Huson	.10
342	Jose Melendez	.10
343	Willie Wilson	.10
344	Mike Stanton	.10
345	Joel Johnston	.10
346	Lee Guetterman	.10
347	Francisco Olivares	.10
348	Dave Burba	.10
349	Tim Crews	.10
350	Scott Leius	.10
351	Danny Cox	.10
352	Wayne Housie	.10
353	Chris Donnels	.10
354	Chris George	.10
355	Gerald Young	.10
356	Roberto Hernandez	.10
357	Neal Heaton	.10
358	Todd Frohwirth	.10
359	Jose Vizcaino	.10
360	Jim Thome	.60
361	Craig Wilson	.10
362	Dave Haas	.10
363	Billy Hatcher	.10
364	John Barfield	.10
365	Luis Aquino	.10
366	Charlie Leibrandt	.10
367	Howard Farmer	.10
368	Bryn Smith	.10
369	Mickey Morandini	.10
370	Jose Canseco (Members Choice, should have been #597)	.50
371	Jose Uribe	.10
372	Bob MacDonald	.10
373	Luis Sojo	.10
374	Craig Shipley	.10
375	Scott Bankhead	.10
376	Greg Gagne	.10
377	Scott Cooper	.10
378	Jose Offerman	.10
379	Billy Spiers	.10
380	John Smiley	.10
381	Jeff Carter	.10
382	Heathcliff Slocumb	.10
383	Jeff Tackett	.10
384	John Kiely	.10
385	John Vander Wal	.10
386	Omar Olivares	.10
387	Ruben Sierra	.10
388	Tom Gordon	.10
389	Charles Nagy	.10
390	Dave Stewart	.10
391	Pete Harnisch	.10
392	Tim Burke	.10
393	Roberto Kelly	.10
394	Freddie Benavides	.10
395	Tom Glavine	.20
396	Wes Chamberlain	.10
397	Eric Gunderson	.10
398	Dave West	.10
399	Ellis Burks	.10
400	Ken Griffey, Jr.	5.00
401	Thomas Howard	.10
402	Juan Guzman	.10
403	Mitch Webster	.10
404	Matt Merullo	.10
405	Steve Buechele	.10
406	Danny Jackson	.10
407	Felix Jose	.10
408	Doug Piatt	.10
409	Jim Eisenreich	.10
410	Bryan Harvey	.10
411	Jim Austin	.10
412	Jim Poole	.10
413	Glenallen Hill	.10
414	Gene Nelson	.10
415	Ivan Rodriguez	.75
416	Frank Tanana	.10
417	Steve Decker	.10
418	Jason Grimsley	.10
419	Tim Layana	.10
420	Don Mattingly	1.25
421	Jerome Walton	.10
422	Rob Ducey	.10
423	Andy Benes	.15
424	John Marzano	.10
425	Gene Harris	.10
426	Tim Raines	.15
427	Bret Barberie	.10
428	Harvey Pulliam	.10
429	Cris Carpenter	.10
430	Howard Johnson	.10
431	Orel Hershiser	.15
432	Brian Hunter	.10
433	Kevin Tapani	.10
434	Rick Reed	.10
435	Ron Witmeyer	.10
436	Gary Gaetti	.10
437	Alex Cole	.10
438	Chito Martinez	.10
439	Greg Litton	.10
440	Julio Franco	.10
441	Mike Munoz	.10
442	Erik Pappas	.10
443	Pat Combs	.10
444	Lance Johnson	.10
445	Ed Sprague	.10
446	Mike Greenwell	.10
447	Milt Thompson	.10
448	Mike Magnante	.10
449	Chris Haney	.10
450	Robin Yount	1.00
451	Rafael Ramirez	.10
452	Gino Minutelli	.10
453	Tom Lampkin	.10
454	Tony Perezchica	.10
455	Dwight Gooden	.15
456	Mark Guthrie	.10
457	Jay Howell	.10
458	Gary DiSarcina	.10
459	John Smoltz	.15
460	Will Clark	.50
461	Dave Otto	.10
462	Rob Maurer	.10
463	Dwight Evans	.10
464	Tom Brunansky	.10
465	*Shawn Hare*	.10

466	Geronimo Pena	.10
467	Alex Fernandez	.15
468	Greg Myers	.10
469	Jeff Fassero	.10
470	Len Dykstra	.10
471	Jeff Johnson	.10
472	Russ Swan	.10
473	Archie Corbin	.10
474	Chuck McElroy	.10
475	Mark McGwire	5.00
476	Wally Whitehurst	.10
477	Tim McIntosh	.10
478	Sid Bream	.10
479	Jeff Juden	.10
480	Carlton Fisk	.15
481	Jeff Plympton	.10
482	Carlos Martinez	.10
483	Jim Gott	.10
484	Bob McClure	.10
485	Tim Teufel	.10
486	Vicente Palacios	.10
487	Jeff Reed	.10
488	Tony Phillips	.10
489	Mel Rojas	.10
490	Ben McDonald	.10
491	Andres Santana	.10
492	Chris Beasley	.10
493	Mike Timlin	.10
494	Brian Downing	.10
495	Kirk Gibson	.10
496	Scott Sanderson	.10
497	Nick Esasky	.10
498	*Johnny Guzman*	.10
499	Mitch Williams	.10
500	Kirby Puckett	1.00
501	Mike Harkey	.10
502	Jim Gantner	.10
503	Bruce Egloff	.10
504	Josias Manzanillo	.10
505	Delino DeShields	.10
506	Rheal Cormier	.10
507	Jay Bell	.10
508	Rich Rowland	.10
509	Scott Servais	.10
510	Terry Pendleton	.10
511	Rich DeLucia	.10
512	Warren Newson	.10
513	Paul Faries	.10
514	Kal Daniels	.10
515	Jarvis Brown	.10
516	Rafael Palmeiro	.25
517	Kelly Downs	.10
518	Steve Chitren	.10
519	Moises Alou	.20
520	Wade Boggs	.40
521	Pete Schourek	.10
522	Scott Terry	.10
523	Kevin Appier	.10
524	Gary Redus	.10
525	George Bell	.10
526	Jeff Kaiser	.10
527	Alvaro Espinoza	.10
528	Luis Polonia	.10
529	Darren Daulton	.10
530	Norm Charlton	.10
531	John Olerud	.20
532	Dan Plesac	.10
533	Billy Ripken	.10
534	Rod Nichols	.10
535	Joey Cora	.10
536	Harold Baines	.10
537	Bob Ojeda	.10
538	Mark Leonard	.10
539	Danny Darwin	.10
540	Shawon Dunston	.10
541	Pedro Munoz	.10
542	Mark Gubicza	.10
543	Kevin Baez	.10
544	Todd Zeile	.15
545	Don Slaught	.10
546	Tony Eusebio	.10
547	Alonzo Powell	.10
548	Gary Pettis	.10
549	Brian Barnes	.10
550	Lou Whitaker	.10
551	Keith Mitchell	.10
552	Oscar Azocar	.10
553	Stu Cole	.10
554	Steve Wapnick	.10
555	Derek Bell	.15
556	Luis Lopez	.10
557	Anthony Telford	.10
558	Tim Mauser	.10
559	Glenn Sutko	.10
560	Darryl Strawberry	.15
561	Tom Bolton	.10
562	Cliff Young	.10
563	Bruce Walton	.10
564	Chico Walker	.10
565	John Franco	.10
566	Paul McClellan	.10
567	Paul Abbott	.10
568	Gary Varsho	.10
569	Carlos Maldonado	.10
570	Kelly Gruber	.10
571	Jose Oquendo	.10
572	Steve Frey	.10
573	Tino Martinez	.15
574	Bill Haselman	.10
575	Eric Anthony	.10
576	John Habyan	.10
577	Jeffrey McNeely	.10
578	Chris Bosio	.10
579	Joe Grahe	.10
580	Fred McGriff	.40
581	Rick Honeycutt	.10
582	Matt Williams	.60
583	Cliff Brantley	.10
584	Rob Dibble	.10
585	Skeeter Barnes	.10
586	Greg Hibbard	.10
587	Randy Milligan	.10
588	Checklist 301-400	.10
589	Checklist 401-500	.10
590	Checklist 501-600	.10
591	Frank Thomas (Members Choice)	1.00
592	Dave Justice (Members Choice)	.20
593	Roger Clemens (Members Choice)	.40
594	Steve Avery (Members Choice)	.10
595	Cal Ripken, Jr. (Members Choice)	2.00
596	Barry Larkin (Members Choice)	.15
597	Not issued (See #370)	
598	Will Clark (Members Choice)	.30
599	Cecil Fielder (Members Choice)	.10
600	Ryne Sandberg (Members Choice)	.40
601	Chuck Knoblauch (Members Choice)	.20
602	Dwight Gooden (Members Choice)	.15
603	Ken Griffey, Jr. (Members Choice)	2.50
604	Barry Bonds (Members Choice)	.45
605	Nolan Ryan (Members Choice)	1.50
606	Jeff Bagwell (Members Choice)	1.00
607	Robin Yount (Members Choice)	.50
608	Bobby Bonilla (Members Choice)	.10
609	George Brett (Members Choice)	.50
610	Howard Johnson (Members Choice)	.10
611	Esteban Beltre	.10
612	Mike Christopher	.10
613	Troy Afenir	.10
614	Mariano Duncan	.10
615	Doug Henry	.10
616	Doug Jones	.10
617	Alvin Davis	.10
618	Craig Lefferts	.10
619	Kevin McReynolds	.10
620	Barry Bonds	.75
621	Turner Ward	.10
622	Joe Magrane	.10
623	Mark Parent	.10
624	Tom Browning	.10
625	John Smiley	.10
626	Steve Wilson	.10
627	Mike Gallego	.10
628	Sammy Sosa	1.50
629	Rico Rossy	.10
630	Royce Clayton	.10
631	Clay Parker	.10
632	Pete Smith	.10
633	Jeff McKnight	.10
634	Jack Daugherty	.10
635	Steve Sax	.10
636	Joe Hesketh	.10
637	Vince Horsman	.10
638	Eric King	.10
639	Joe Boever	.10
640	Jack Morris	.10
641	Arthur Rhodes	.10
642	Bob Melvin	.10
643	Rick Wilkins	.10
644	Scott Scudder	.10
645	Bip Roberts	.10
646	Julio Valera	.10
647	Kevin Campbell	.10
648	Steve Searcy	.10
649	Scott Kamieniecki	.10
650	Kurt Stillwell	.10
651	Bob Welch	.10
652	Andres Galarraga	.15
653	Mike Jackson	.10
654	Bo Jackson	.15
655	Sid Fernandez	.10
656	Mike Bielecki	.10
657	Jeff Reardon	.10
658	Wayne Rosenthal	.10
659	Eric Bullock	.10
660	Eric Davis	.10
661	Randy Tomlin	.10
662	Tom Edens	.10
663	Rob Murphy	.10
664	Leo Gomez	.10
665	Greg Maddux	2.00
666	Greg Vaughn	.15
667	Wade Taylor	.10
668	Brad Arnsberg	.10
669	Mike Moore	.10
670	Mark Langston	.10
671	Barry Jones	.10
672	Bill Landrum	.10
673	Greg Swindell	.10
674	Wayne Edwards	.10
675	Greg Olson	.10
676	*Bill Pulsipher*	.60
677	Bobby Witt	.10
678	Mark Carreon	.10
679	Patrick Lennon	.10
680	Ozzie Smith	.50
681	John Briscoe	.10
682	Matt Young	.10
683	Jeff Conine	.15
684	Phil Stephenson	.10
685	Ron Darling	.10
686	Bryan Hickerson	.10
687	Dale Sveum	.10
688	Kirk McCaskill	.10
689	Rich Amaral	.10
690	Danny Tartabull	.10
691	Donald Harris	.10
692	Doug Davis	.10
693	John Farrell	.10
694	Paul Gibson	.10
695	Kenny Lofton	1.00
696	Mike Fetters	.10
697	Rosario Rodriguez	.10
698	Chris Jones	.10
699	Jeff Manto	.10
700	Rick Sutcliffe	.10
701	Scott Bankhead	.10
702	Donnie Hill	.10
703	Todd Worrell	.10
704	Rene Gonzales	.10
705	Rick Cerone	.10
706	Tony Pena	.10
707	Paul Sorrento	.10
708	Gary Scott	.10
709	Junior Noboa	.10
710	Wally Joyner	.15
711	Charlie Hayes	.10
712	Rich Rodriguez	.10
713	Rudy Seanez	.10
714	Jim Bullinger	.10
715	Jeff Robinson	.10
716	Jeff Branson	.10
717	Andy Ashby	.15
718	Dave Burba	.10
719	Rich Gossage	.10
720	Randy Johnson	.50
721	David Wells	.15
722	Paul Kilgus	.10
723	Dave Martinez	.10
724	Denny Neagle	.10
725	Andy Stankiewicz	.10
726	Rick Aguilera	.10
727	Junior Ortiz	.10
728	Storm Davis	.10
729	Don Robinson	.10
730	Ron Gant	.15
731	Paul Assenmacher	.10
732	Mark Gardiner	.10
733	Milt Hill	.10
734	Jeremy Hernandez	.10
735	Ken Hill	.10
736	Xavier Hernandez	.10
737	Gregg Jefferies	.15
738	Dick Schofield	.10
739	Ron Robinson	.10
740	Sandy Alomar	.15
741	Mike Stanley	.10
742	Butch Henry	.10
743	Floyd Bannister	.10
744	Brian Drahman	.10
745	Dave Winfield	.50
746	Bob Walk	.10
747	Chris James	.10
748	Don Prybylinski	.10
749	Dennis Rasmussen	.10
750	Rickey Henderson	.35
751	Chris Hammond	.10
752	Bob Kipper	.10
753	Dave Rohde	.10
754	Hubie Brooks	.10
755	Bret Saberhagen	.15
756	Jeff Robinson	.10
757	*Pat Listach*	.10
758	Bill Wegman	.10
759	John Wetteland	.10
760	Phil Plantier	.10
761	Wilson Alvarez	.10
762	Scott Aldred	.10
763	*Armando Reynoso*	.15
764	Todd Benzinger	.10
765	Kevin Mitchell	.10
766	Gary Sheffield	.25
767	Allan Anderson	.10
768	Rusty Meacham	.10
769	Rick Parker	.10
770	Nolan Ryan	3.00
771	Jeff Ballard	.10
772	Cory Snyder	.10
773	Denis Boucher	.10
774	Jose Gonzales	.10
775	Juan Guerrero	.10
776	Ed Nunez	.10
777	Scott Ruskin	.10
778	Terry Leach	.10
779	Carl Willis	.10
780	Bobby Bonilla	.10
781	Duane Ward	.10
782	Joe Slusarski	.10
783	David Segui	.10
784	Kirk Gibson	.10
785	Frank Viola	.10
786	Keith Miller	.10
787	Mike Morgan	.10
788	Kim Batiste	.10
789	Sergio Valdez	.10
790	Eddie Taubensee	.10
791	Jack Armstrong	.10
792	Scott Fletcher	.10
793	Steve Farr	.10
794	Dan Pasqua	.10
795	Eddie Murray	.25
796	John Morris	.10
797	Francisco Cabrera	.10
798	Mike Perez	.10
799	Ted Wood	.10
800	Jose Rijo	.10
801	Danny Gladden	.10
802	Arci Cianfrocco	.10
803	Monty Fariss	.10
804	Roger McDowell	.10
805	Randy Myers	.10
806	Kirk Dressendorfer	.10
807	Zane Smith	.10
808	Glenn Davis	.10
809	Torey Lovullo	.10
810	Andre Dawson	.15
811	Bill Pecota	.10
812	Ted Power	.10
813	Willie Blair	.10
814	Dave Fleming	.10
815	Chris Gwynn	.10
816	Jody Reed	.10
817	Mark Dewey	.10
818	Kyle Abbott	.10
819	Tom Henke	.10
820	Kevin Seitzer	.10
821	Al Newman	.10
822	Tim Sherrill	.10
823	Chuck Crim	.10
824	Darren Reed	.10
825	Tony Gwynn	.75
826	Steve Foster	.10
827	Steve Howe	.10
828	Brook Jacoby	.10
829	Rodney McCray	.10
830	Chuck Knoblauch	.15
831	John Wehner	.10
832	Scott Garrelts	.10
833	Alejandro Pena	.10
834	Jeff Parrett	.10
835	Juan Bell	.10
836	Lance Dickson	.10
837	Darryl Kile	.10
838	Efrain Valdez	.10
839	*Bob Zupcic*	.10
840	George Bell	.10
841	Dave Gallagher	.10
842	Tim Belcher	.10
843	Jeff Shaw	.10
844	Mike Fitzgerald	.10
845	Gary Carter	.15
846	John Russell	.10
847	*Eric Hillman*	.15
848	Mike Witt	.10
849	Curt Wilkerson	.10
850	Alan Trammell	.15
851	Rex Hudler	.10
852	*Michael Walkden*	.10
853	Kevin Ward	.10
854	Tim Naehring	.10
855	Bill Swift	.10
856	Damon Berryhill	.10
857	Mark Eichhorn	.10
858	Hector Villanueva	.10
859	Jose Lind	.10
860	Denny Martinez	.10
861	Bill Krueger	.10
862	Mike Kingery	.10
863	Jeff Innis	.10
864	Derek Lilliquist	.10
865	Reggie Sanders	.15
866	Ramon Garcia	.10
867	Bruce Ruffin	.10
868	Dickie Thon	.10
869	Melido Perez	.10
870	Ruben Amaro	.10
871	Alan Mills	.10
872	Matt Sinatro	.10
873	Eddie Zosky	.10
874	Pete Incaviglia	.10
875	Tom Candiotti	.10
876	Bob Patterson	.10
877	Neal Heaton	.10
878	*Terrel Hansen*	.10
879	Dave Eiland	.10
880	Von Hayes	.10
881	Tim Scott	.10
882	Otis Nixon	.10
883	Herm Winningham	.10
884	Dion James	.10
885	Dave Wainhouse	.10
886	Frank DiPino	.10
887	Dennis Cook	.10
888	Jose Mesa	.10
889	Mark Leiter	.10
890	Willie Randolph	.10
891	Craig Colbert	.10
892	Dwayne Henry	.10
893	Jim Lindeman	.10
894	Charlie Hough	.10
895	Gil Heredia	.10
896	Scott Chiamparino	.10
897	Lance Blankenship	.10
898	Checklist 601-700	.10
899	Checklist 701-800	.10
900	Checklist 801-900	.10

1992 Stadium Club East Coast National

In conjunction with its appearance at the August, 1992, East Coast National card show, Topps distributed 22,000 five-card cello packs of its 1992 Stadium Club series bearing a special gold-foil show commemorative overprint. The cards are in all other respects identical to regular issue '92 S.C. Only 100 cards from Series III can be found with the overprint. Production of each card thus totals 1,100.

		MT
Complete Set (100):		300.00
Common Player:		5.00
601	Chuck Knoblauch (Members Choice)	15.00
602	Dwight Gooden (Members Choice)	10.00
603	Ken Griffey, Jr. (Members Choice)	75.00
604	Barry Bonds (Members Choice)	30.00
605	Nolan Ryan (Members Choice)	75.00
606	Jeff Bagwell (Members Choice)	30.00
607	Robin Yount (Members Choice)	25.00
608	Bobby Bonilla (Members Choice)	5.00
609	George Brett (Members Choice)	45.00
610	Howard Johnson (Members Choice)	5.00
611	Esteban Beltre	5.00
612	Mike Christopher	5.00
613	Troy Afenir	5.00
619	Kevin McReynolds	5.00
620	Barry Bonds	40.00
622	Joe Magrane	5.00
623	Mark Parent	5.00
626	Steve Wilson	5.00
629	Rico Rossy	5.00
631	Clay Parker	5.00
633	Jeff McKnight	5.00
637	Vince Horsman	5.00
638	Eric King	5.00
639	Joe Boever	5.00
641	Arthur Rhodes	5.00
647	Kevin Campbell	5.00
653	Mike Jackson	5.00
661	Randy Tomlin	5.00
665	Greg Maddux	50.00
668	Brad Arnsberg	5.00
671	Barry Jones	5.00
672	Bill Landrum	5.00
673	Greg Swindell	5.00
676	Bill Pulsipher	5.00
679	Patrick Lennon	5.00
681	John Briscoe	5.00
684	Phil Stephenson	5.00
685	Ron Darling	5.00
686	Bryan Hickerson	5.00
688	Kirk McCaskill	5.00
689	Rich Amaral	5.00
692	Doug Davis	5.00
693	John Farrell	5.00
700	Rick Sutcliffe	5.00
704	Rene Gonzalez	5.00
713	Rudy Seanez	5.00
714	Jim Bullinger	5.00
716	Jeff Branson	5.00
717	Andy Ashby	5.00
725	Andy Stankiewicz	5.00
733	Milt Hill	5.00
739	Ron Robinson	5.00
742	Butch Henry	5.00
747	Chris James	5.00
749	Dennis Rasmussen	5.00
753	Dave Rohde	5.00
757	Pat Listach	5.00
758	Bill Wegman	5.00
763	Armando Reynoso	5.00
765	Kevin Mitchell	5.00
766	Gary Sheffield	15.00
769	Rick Parker	5.00
771	Jeff Ballard	5.00
772	Cory Snyder	5.00
774	Jose Gonzalez	5.00
775	Juan Guerrero	5.00
776	Edwin Nunez	5.00
778	Terry Leach	5.00
782	Joe Slusarski	5.00
784	Kirk Gibson	5.00
788	Kim Batiste	5.00
802	Arci Cianfrocco	5.00
806	Kirk Dressendorfer	5.00
807	Zane Smith	5.00
814	Dave Fleming	5.00
815	Chris Gwynn	5.00

817	Mark Dewey	5.00
819	Tom Henke	5.00
822	Tim Sherrill	5.00
826	Steve Foster	5.00
831	John Wehner	5.00
832	Scott Garrelts	5.00
840	George Bell	5.00
841	Dave Gallagher	5.00
846	John Russell	5.00
847	Eric Hillman	5.00
852	Michael Walkden	5.00
855	Bill Swift	5.00
864	Derek Lilliquist	5.00
876	Bob Patterson	5.00
878	Terrel Hansen	5.00
881	Tim Scott	5.00
886	Frank DiPino	5.00
891	Craig Colbert	5.00
892	Dwayne Henry	5.00
893	Jim Lindeman	5.00
895	Gil Heredia	5.00
898	Checklist 601-700	.50
899	Checklist 701-800	.50
900	Checklist 801-900	.50

1992 Stadium Club National Convention

To promote its Stadium Club baseball card brand to dealers, Topps distributed sample cards during the National Sports Collectors Convention in Atlanta, Ga. The sample cards are regular-issue S.C. cards which have received a gold-foil overprint of the 1992 National logo. Only 100 cards from the third series can be found with the overprint. Only 5,000 4-card packs were distributed, thus only 200 of each card were made.

		MT
Complete Set (100):		1325.
Common Player:		10.00
616	Doug Jones	10.00
617	Alvin Davis	10.00
618	Craig Lefferts	10.00
621	Turner Ward	10.00
625	John Smiley	10.00
627	Mike Gallego	10.00
630	Royce Clayton	10.00
634	Jack Daugherty	10.00
635	Steve Sax	10.00
636	Joe Hesketh	10.00
643	Rick Wilkins	10.00
644	Scott Scudder	10.00
645	Bip Roberts	10.00
650	Kurt Stillwell	10.00
652	Andres Galarraga	20.00
657	Jeff Reardon	10.00
660	Eric Davis	12.50
662	Tom Edens	10.00
675	Greg Olson	10.00
678	Mark Carreon	10.00
680	Ozzie Smith	85.00
682	Matt Young	10.00
690	Danny Tartabull	10.00
691	Donald Harris	10.00
695	Kenny Lofton	40.00
697	Rosario Rodriguez	10.00
701	Scott Bankhead	10.00
705	Rick Cerone	10.00
706	Tony Pena	10.00
709	Junior Noboa	10.00
710	Wally Joyner	15.00
711	Charlie Hayes	10.00
712	Rich Rodriguez	10.00
721	David Wells	12.50
723	Dave Martinez	10.00
726	Rick Aguilera	10.00
727	Junior Ortiz	10.00
729	Don Robinson	10.00
730	Ron Gant	12.50
731	Paul Assenmacher	10.00
732	Mark Gardiner	10.00
735	Ken Hill	10.00
736	Xavier Hernandez	10.00
737	Gregg Jefferies	15.00
740	Sandy Alomar, Jr.	15.00
741	Mike Stanley	10.00
744	Brian Drahman	10.00
746	Bob Walk	10.00
751	Chris Hammond	10.00
759	John Wetteland	10.00
760	Phil Plantier	10.00
761	Wilson Alvarez	10.00
773	Denis Boucher	10.00
777	Scott Ruskin	10.00
779	Carl Willis	10.00
783	David Segui	10.00
786	Keith Miller	10.00
790	Eddie Taubensee	10.00
791	Jack Armstrong	10.00
792	Scott Fletcher	10.00
793	Steve Farr	10.00
794	Dan Pasqua	10.00
797	Francisco Cabrera	10.00
798	Mike Perez	10.00
801	Danny Gladden	10.00
803	Monty Fariss	10.00
804	Roger McDowell	10.00
805	Randy Myers	10.00
808	Glenn Davis	10.00
809	Torey Lovullo	10.00
816	Jody Reed	10.00
825	Tony Gwynn	85.00
827	Steve Howe	10.00
828	Brook Jacoby	10.00
829	Rodney McCray	10.00
830	Chuck Knoblauch	25.00
835	Juan Bell	10.00
836	Lance Dickson	10.00
837	Darryl Kile	10.00
842	Tim Belcher	10.00
843	Jeff Shaw	10.00
844	Mike Fitzgerald	10.00
845	Gary Carter	15.00
850	Alan Trammell	15.00
851	Rex Hudler	10.00
856	Damon Berryhill	10.00
857	Mark Eichhorn	10.00
858	Hector Villanueva	10.00
860	Denny Martinez	10.00
865	Reggie Sanders	12.50
869	Melido Perez	10.00
874	Pete Incaviglia	10.00
875	Tom Candiotti	10.00
877	Neal Heaton	10.00
879	Dave Eiland	10.00
882	Otis Nixon	10.00
883	Herm Winningham	10.00
884	Dion James	10.00
887	Dennis Cook	10.00
894	Charlie Hough	10.00

1992 Stadium Club First Draft Picks

Issued as inserts with Stadium Club Series III, this three-card set features the No. 1 draft picks of 1990-92. Fronts have a full-bleed photo with S.C. logo and player name in the lower-right corner. At bottom-left in a red strip is a gold-foil stamping, "#1 Draft Pick of the '90's". An orange circle at upper-right has the year the player was the No. 1 choice. The basic red-and-black back has a color photo, a few biographical and draft details and a gold facsimile autograph among other gold-foil highlights.

		MT
Complete Set (3):		12.00
Common Player:		1.00
1	Chipper Jones	10.00
2	Brien Taylor	1.00
3	Phil Nevin	1.00

1992 Stadium Club Master Photos

Uncropped versions of the photos which appear on regular Stadium Club cards are featured on these large-format (5" x 7") cards. The photos are set against a white background and trimmed with holographic foil. Backs are blank and the cards are unnumbered. Members of Topps' Stadium Club received a Master Photo in their members' packs for 1992. The cards were also available as inserts in special boxes of Stadium Club cards sold at Wal-Mart stores.

		MT
Complete Set (15):		45.00
Common Player:		1.00
(1)	Wade Boggs	3.00
(2)	Barry Bonds	4.00
(3)	Jose Canseco	3.00
(4)	Will Clark	2.50
(5)	Cecil Fielder	1.00
(6)	Dwight Gooden	2.00
(7)	Ken Griffey, Jr.	9.00
(8)	Rickey Henderson	2.00
(9)	Lance Johnson	1.00
(10)	Cal Ripken, Jr.	7.50
(11)	Nolan Ryan	7.50
(12)	Deion Sanders	2.50
(13)	Darryl Strawberry	2.00
(14)	Danny Tartabull	1.00
(15)	Frank Thomas	6.00

1992 Stadium Club Members Only

A multi-sport set of 50 cards was sent in four installments to members of Topps' Stadium Club as part of their 1992 benefits package. Cards are similar in format to regular. Stadium Club cards, 2-1/2" x 3-1/2", UV coated on front. Fronts have a special gold foil "Members Only" logo on front. Backs have a stadium scoreboard design with details of a career highlight. The unnumbered cards (baseball only) are checklisted here alphabetically.

		MT
Complete Set (36):		24.00
Common Player:		.25
(1)	Carlos Baerga	.25
(2)	Wade Boggs	1.00
(3)	Barry Bonds	1.00
(4)	Bret Boone	.25
(5)	Pat Borders	.25
(6)	George Brett	1.50
(7)	George Brett (3,000 hits)	1.50
(8)	Jim Bullinger	.25
(9)	Gary Carter	.35
(10)	Andujar Cedeno	.25
(11)	Roger Clemens, Matt Young	.35
(12)	Dennis Eckersley (Cy Young Award)	.25
(13)	Dennis Eckersley (MVP)	.25
(14)	Dave Eiland	.25
(15)	Dwight Gooden, Gary Sheffield	.35
(16)	Ken Griffey Jr.	3.00
(17)	Kevin Gross	.25
(18)	Bo Jackson	.50
(19)	Eric Karros	.25
(20)	Pat Listach	.25
(21)	Greg Maddux	2.00
(22)	Fred McGriff, Gary Sheffield	.50
(23)	Mickey Morandini	.25
(24)	Jack Morris	.25
(25)	Eddie Murray	.75
(26)	Eddie Murray	.75
(27)	Bip Roberts	.25
(28)	Nolan Ryan (27 seasons)	2.50
(29)	Nolan Ryan (1993 finale)	2.50
(30)	Lee Smith	.25
(31)	Ozzie Smith (2,000 hits)	.75
(32)	Ozzie Smith (7,000 assists)	.75
(33)	Ozzie Smith (stolen base record)	.75
(34)	Bobby Thigpen	.25
(35)	Dave Winfield	.65
(36)	Robin Yount	.75

1992 Stadium Club Special Edition (SkyDome)

This 200-card special Stadium Club set from Topps was uniquely packaged in a plastic replica of the Toronto SkyDome, the home of the 1991 All-Star Game. Featured in the set are members of Team USA, All-Stars, draft picks, top prospects and high cards from the World Series between the Twins and Braves. The cards are styled much like the regular Stadium Club cards. Some cards have been found with incorrect gold-foil identifiers as well as the correct version.

		MT
Complete Set (200):		30.00
Common Player:		.10
1	*Terry Adams*	.10
2	Tommy Adams	.10
3	Rick Aguilera	.10
4	Ron Allen	.10
5	Roberto Alomar (All-Star)	.50
6	Sandy Alomar	.20
7	Greg Anthony	.10
8	James Austin	.10
9	Steve Avery	.10
10	Harold Baines	.10
11	*Brian Barber*	.15
12	Jon Barnes	.10
13	George Bell	.10
14	Doug Bennett	.10
15	Sean Bergman	.10
16	Craig Biggio	.10
17	Bill Bliss	.30
18	Wade Boggs (AS)	.30
19	Bobby Bonilla (AS)	.10
20	Russell Brock	.10
21	Tarrik Brock	.10
22	Tom Browning	.10
23	Brett Butler	.10
24	Ivan Calderon	.10
25	Joe Carter	.10
26	Joe Caruso	.10
27	Dan Cholowsky	.10
28	Will Clark (AS)	.20
29	Roger Clemens (AS)	.40
30	Shawn Curran	.10
31	Chris Curtis	.10
32	Chili Davis	.10
33	Andre Dawson	.15
34	Joe DeBerry	.10
35	John Dettmer	.10
36	Rob Dibble	.10
37	*John Donati*	.10
38	Dave Doorneweerd	.10
39	Darren Dreifort	.10
40	Mike Durant	.10
41	Chris Durkin	.10
42	Dennis Eckersley	.10
43	*Brian Edmondson*	.10
44	*Vaughn Eshelman*	.25
45	*Shawn Estes*	1.00
46	*Jorge Fabregas*	.15
47	Jon Farrell	.10
48	Cecil Fielder (AS)	.10
49	Carlton Fisk	.15
50	Tim Flannelly	.10
51	*Cliff Floyd*	.50
52	Julio Franco	.10
53	Greg Gagne	.10
54	*Chris Gambs*	.10
55	Ron Gant	.15
56	Brent Gates	.15
57	Dwayne Gerald	.10
58	Jason Giambi	.60
59	*Benji Gil*	.20
60	Mark Gipner	.10
61	Danny Gladden	.10
62	Tom Glavine	.20
63	Jimmy Gonzalez	.10
64	Jeff Granger	.10
65	Dan Grapenthien	.10
66	Dennis Gray	.10
67	*Shawn Green*	20.00
68	Tyler Green	.15
69	Todd Greene	1.00
70	Ken Griffey, Jr. (AS)	2.50
71	Kelly Gruber	.10
72	Ozzie Guillen	.10
73	Tony Gwynn (AS)	.50
74	Shane Halter	.10
75	Jeffrey Hammonds	.15
76	Larry Hanlon	.10
77	Pete Harnisch	.10
78	Mike Harrison	.10
79	Bryan Harvey	.10
80	Scott Hatteberg	.15
81	Rick Helling	.10
82	Dave Henderson	.10
83	Rickey Henderson (AS)	.25
84	Tyrone Hill	.10
85	*Todd Hollandsworth*	1.00
86	Brian Holliday	.10
87	Terry Horn	.10
88	Jeff Hostetler	.10
89	Kent Hrbek	.10
90	Mark Hubbard	.10
91	Charles Johnson	1.00
92	Howard Johnson	.10
93	Todd Johnson	.10
94	*Bobby Jones*	.75
95	Dan Jones	.10
96	Felix Jose	.10
97	Dave Justice	.30
98	Jimmy Key	.10
99	*Marc Kroom*	.10
100	John Kruk	.10
101	Mark Langston	.10
102	Barry Larkin	.20
103	Mike LaValliere	.10
104a	Scott Leius (1991 N.L. All-Star - error)	.10
104b	Scott Leius (1991 World Series - correct)	.10
105	Mark Lemke	.10
106	Donnie Leshnock	.10
107	Jimmy Lewis	.10
108	Shawn Livesy	.10
109	Ryan Long	.10
110	Trevor Mallory	.10
111	Denny Martinez	.10
112	Justin Mashore	.10
113	Jason McDonald	.10
114	Jack McDowell	.10
115	Tom McKinnon	.10
116	Billy McKinnon	.10
117	*Buck McNabb*	.10
118	Jim Mecir	.10
119	Dan Melendez	.10
120	*Shawn Miller*	.10
121	Trever Miller	.15
122	Paul Molitor	.40
123	Vincent Moore	.10
124	Mike Morgan	.10
125	Jack Morris (World Series)	.10
126	Jack Morris (All-Star)	.10
127	Sean Mulligan	.10
128	Eddie Murray	.30
129	Mike Neill	.10
130	Phil Nevin	.10
131	Mark O'Brien	.10
132	*Alex Ochoa*	.25
133	*Chad Ogea*	.20
134	Greg Olson	.10
135	Paul O'Neill	.15
136	Jared Osentowski	.10
137	Mike Pagliarulo	.10
138	Rafael Palmeiro	.20
139	Rodney Pedraza	.10
140	Tony Phillips	.10
141	*Scott Pisciotta*	.10
142	Chris Pritchett	.10
143	Jason Pruitt	.10
144a	Kirby Puckett (1991 N.L. All-Star - error)	.75
144b	Kirby Puckett (1991 World Series - correct)	.75

145 Kirby Puckett (AS) .75
146 *Manny Ramirez* 20.00
147 Eddie Ramos .10
148 Mark Ratekin .10
149 Jeff Reardon .10
150 Sean Rees .10
151 *Calvin Reese* .40
152 *Desmond Relaford* .20
153 Eric Richardson .10
154 Cal Ripken, Jr. (AS) 2.00
155 Chris Roberts .15
156 Mike Robertson .10
157 Steve Rodriguez .10
158 Mike Rossiter .10
159 Scott Ruffcorn .10
160a Chris Sabo (1991 World Series - error) .10
160b Chris Sabo (1991 N.L. All-Star - correct) .10
161 Juan Samuel .10
162 Ryne Sandberg (AS) .50
163 Scott Sanderson .10
164 Benito Santiago .10
165 *Gene Schall* .10
166 Chad Schoenvogel .10
167 *Chris Seelbach* .10
168 *Aaron Sele* 1.00
169 Basil Shabazz .10
170 *Al Shirley* .10
171 Paul Shuey .10
172 Ruben Sierra .10
173 John Smiley .10
174 Lee Smith .10
175 Ozzie Smith .30
176 Tim Smith .10
177 Zane Smith .10
178 John Smoltz .15
179 Scott Stahoviak .10
180 Kennie Steenstra .10
181 Kevin Stocker .10
182 *Chris Stynes* .10
183 Danny Tartabull .10
184 Brien Taylor .10
185 Todd Taylor .10
186 Larry Thomas .10
187a *Ozzie Timmons* .10
187b David Tuttle (should be #188) .10
188 Not issued
189 Andy Van Slyke .10
190a Frank Viola (1991 World Series - error) .10
190b Frank Viola (1991 N.L. All-Star - correct) .10
191 Michael Walkden .10
192 Jeff Ware .10
193 *Allen Watson* .15
194 Steve Whitaker .10
195a Jerry Willard (1991 Draft Pick - error) .10
195b Jerry Willard (1991 World Series - correct) .10
196 Craig Wilson .10
197 Chris Wimmer .15
198 *Steve Wojciechowski* .10
199 Joel Wolfe .10
200 Ivan Zweig .10

1993 Stadium Club Promotional Postcard

Produced by Topps for use by its dealers in promoting sales of Series II and III Stadium Club, this 7" x 5" postcard has a color front picturing SC cards of three players from the then-new Colorado Rockies and Florida Marlins. The back has the SC and team logos, a message from Topps and the address of a dealer from whom the cards could be reserved.

MT

Alex Cole, Benny Santiago, Walt Weiss 3.00

1993 Stadium Club

Topps' premium set for 1993 was issued in three series, two 300-card series and a final series of 150. Boxes contained 24 packs this year, compared to 36 in the past. Packs had 14 cards and an insert card. Each box had a 5" x 7" Master Photo card.

	MT
Complete Set (750):	60.00
Complete Series 1 (300):	20.00
Complete Series 2 (300):	30.00
Complete Series 3 (150):	10.00
Common Player:	.10
Series 1,2,3 Wax Box:	28.00

1 Pat Borders .10
2 Greg Maddux 2.50
3 Daryl Boston .10
4 Bob Ayrault .10
5 Tony Phillips .10
6 Damion Easley .10
7 Kip Gross .10
8 Jim Thome .40
9 Tim Belcher .10
10 Gary Wayne .10
11 Sam Militello .10
12 Mike Magnante .10
13 Tim Wakefield .10
14 Tim Hulett .10
15 Rheal Cormier .10
16 Juan Guerrero .10
17 Rich Gossage .10
18 Tim Laker .10
19 Darrin Jackson .10
20 Jack Clark .10
21 Roberto Hernandez .10
22 Dean Palmer .10
23 Harold Reynolds .10
24 Dan Plesac .10
25 Brent Mayne .10
26 Pat Hentgen .10
27 Luis Sojo .10
28 Ron Gant .15
29 Paul Gibson .10
30 Bip Roberts .10
31 Mickey Tettleton .10
32 Randy Velarde .10
33 Brian McRae .10
34 Wes Chamberlain .10
35 Wayne Kirby .10
36 Rey Sanchez .10
37 Jesse Orosco .10
38 Mike Stanton .10
39 Royce Clayton .10
40 Cal Ripken, Jr. 2.50
41 John Dopson .10
42 Gene Larkin .10
43 Tim Raines .15
44 Randy Myers .10
45 Clay Parker .10
46 Mike Scioscia .10
47 Pete Incaviglia .10
48 Todd Van Poppel .10
49 Ray Lankford .15
50 Eddie Murray .30
51 Barry Bonds .75
52 Gary Thurman .10
53 Bob Wickman .10
54 Joey Cora .10
55 Kenny Rogers .10
56 Mike Devereaux .10
57 Kevin Seitzer .10
58 Rafael Belliard .10
59 David Wells .15
60 Mark Clark .10
61 Carlos Baerga .10
62 Scott Brosius .10
63 Jeff Grotewold .10
64 Rick Wrona .10
65 Kurt Knudsen .10
66 Lloyd McClendon .10
67 Omar Vizquel .10
68 Jose Vizcaino .10
69 Rob Ducey .10
70 Casey Candaele .10
71 Ramon Martinez .15
72 Todd Hundley .20
73 John Marzano .10
74 Derek Parks .10
75 Jack McDowell .10
76 Tim Scott .10
77 Mike Mussina .40
78 Delino DeShields .10
79 Chris Bosio .10
80 Mike Bordick .10
81 Rod Beck .10
82 Ted Power .10
83 John Kruk .10
84 Steve Shifflett .10
85 Danny Tartabull .10
86 Mike Greenwell .10
87 Jose Melendez .10
88 Craig Wilson .10
89 Melvin Nieves .10
90 Ed Sprague .10
91 Willie McGee .10
92 Joe Orsulak .10
93 Jeff King .10
94 Dan Pasqua .10
95 Brian Harper .10
96 Joe Oliver .10
97 Shane Turner .10
98 Lenny Harris .10
99 Jeff Parrett .10
100 Luis Polonia .10
101 Kent Bottenfield .10
102 Albert Belle .75
103 Mike Maddux .10
104 Randy Tomlin .10
105 Andy Stankiewicz .10
106 Rico Rossy .10
107 Joe Hesketh .10
108 Dennis Powell .10
109 Derrick May .10
110 Pete Harnisch .10
111 Kent Mercker .10
112 Scott Fletcher .10
113 Rex Hudler .10
114 Chico Walker .10
115 Rafael Palmeiro .20
116 Mark Leiter .10
117 Pedro Munoz .10
118 Jim Bullinger .10
119 Ivan Calderon .10
120 Mike Timlin .10
121 Rene Gonzales .10
122 Greg Vaughn .15
123 Mike Flanagan .10
124 Mike Hartley .10
125 Jeff Montgomery .10
126 Mike Gallego .10
127 Don Slaught .10
128 Charlie O'Brien .10
129 Jose Offerman .10
130 Mark Wohlers .10
131 Eric Fox .10
132 Doug Strange .10
133 Jeff Frye .10
134 Wade Boggs .40
135 Lou Whitaker .10
136 Craig Grebeck .10
137 Rich Rodriguez .10
138 Jay Bell .10
139 Felix Fermin .10
140 Denny Martinez .10
141 Eric Anthony .10
142 Roberto Alomar .50
143 Darren Lewis .10
144 Mike Blowers .10
145 Scott Bankhead .10
146 Jeff Reboulet .10
147 Frank Viola .10
148 Bill Pecota .10
149 Carlos Hernandez .10
150 Bobby Witt .10
151 Sid Bream .10
152 Todd Zeile .10
153 Dennis Cook .10
154 Brian Bohanon .10
155 Pat Kelly .10
156 Milt Cuyler .10
157 Juan Bell .10
158 Randy Milligan .10
159 Mark Gardner .10
160 Pat Tabler .10
161 Jeff Reardon .10
162 Ken Patterson .10
163 Bobby Bonilla .10
164 Tony Pena .10
165 Greg Swindell .10
166 Kirk McCaskill .10
167 Doug Drabek .10
168 Franklin Stubbs .10
169 Ron Tingley .10
170 Willie Banks .10
171 Sergio Valdez .10
172 Mark Lemke .10
173 Robin Yount .60
174 Storm Davis .10
175 Dan Walters .10
176 Steve Farr .10
177 Curt Wilkerson .10
178 Luis Alicea .10
179 Russ Swan .10
180 Mitch Williams .10
181 Wilson Alvarez .10
182 Carl Willis .10
183 Craig Biggio .25
184 Sean Berry .10
185 Trevor Wilson .10
186 Jeff Tackett .10
187 Ellis Burks .10
188 Jeff Branson .10
189 Matt Nokes .10
190 John Smiley .10
191 Danny Gladden .10
192 Mike Boddicker .10
193 Roger Pavlik .10
194 Paul Sorrento .10
195 Vince Coleman .10
196 Gary DiSarcina .10
197 Rafael Bournigal .10
198 Mike Schooler .10
199 Scott Ruskin .10
200 Frank Thomas 1.50
201 Kyle Abbott .10
202 Mike Perez .10
203 Andre Dawson .15
204 Bill Swift .10
205 Alejandro Pena .10
206 Dave Winfield .40
207 Andujar Cedeno .10
208 Terry Steinbach .10
209 Chris Hammond .10
210 Todd Burns .10
211 Hipolito Pichardo .10
212 John Kiely .10
213 Tim Teufel .10
214 Lee Guetterman .10
215 Geronimo Pena .10
216 Brett Butler .10
217 Bryan Hickerson .10
218 Rick Trlicek .10
219 Lee Stevens .10
220 Roger Clemens 1.00
221 Carlton Fisk .15
222 Chili Davis .10
223 Walt Terrell .10
224 Jim Eisenreich .10
225 Ricky Bones .10
226 Henry Rodriguez .10
227 Ken Hill .10
228 Rick Wilkins .10
229 Ricky Jordan .10
230 Bernard Gilkey .10
231 Tim Fortugno .10
232 Geno Petralli .10
233 Jose Rijo .10
234 Jim Leyritz .10
235 Kevin Campbell .10
236 Al Osuna .10
237 Pete Smith .10
238 Pete Schourek .10
239 Moises Alou .20
240 Donn Pall .10
241 Denny Neagle .10
242 Dan Peltier .10
243 Scott Scudder .10
244 Juan Guzman .10
245 Dave Burba .10
246 Rick Sutcliffe .10
247 Tony Fossas .10
248 Mike Munoz .10
249 Tim Salmon .30
250 Rob Murphy .10
251 Roger McDowell .10
252 Lance Parrish .10
253 Cliff Brantley .10
254 Scott Leius .10
255 Carlos Martinez .10
256 Vince Horsman .10
257 Oscar Azocar .10
258 Craig Shipley .10
259 Ben McDonald .10
260 Jeff Brantley .10
261 Damon Berryhill .10
262 Joe Grahe .10
263 Dave Hansen .10
264 Rich Amaral .10
265 *Tim Pugh* .20
266 Dion James .10
267 Frank Tanana .10
268 Stan Belinda .10
269 Jeff Kent .10
270 Bruce Ruffin .10
271 Xavier Hernandez .10
272 Darrin Fletcher .10
273 Tino Martinez .10
274 Benny Santiago .10
275 Scott Radinsky .10
276 Mariano Duncan .10
277 Kenny Lofton .50
278 Dwight Smith .10
279 Joe Carter .10
280 Tim Jones .10
281 Jeff Huson .10
282 Phil Plantier .10
283 Kirby Puckett 1.00
284 Johnny Guzman .10
285 Mike Morgan .10
286 Chris Sabo .10
287 Matt Williams .30
288 Checklist 1-100 .10
289 Checklist 101-200 .10
290 Checklist 201-300 .10
291 Dennis Eckersley (Members Choice) .10
292 Eric Karros (Members Choice) .10
293 Pat Listach (Members Choice) .10
294 Andy Van Slyke (Members Choice) .10
295 Robin Ventura (Members Choice) .10
296 Tom Glavine (Members Choice) .10
297 Juan Gonzalez (Members Choice) .50
298 Travis Fryman (Members Choice) .10
299 Larry Walker (Members Choice) .20
300 Gary Sheffield (Members Choice) .20
301 Chuck Finley .10
302 Luis Gonzalez .10
303 Darryl Hamilton .10
304 Bien Figueroa .10
305 Ron Darling .10
306 Jonathan Hurst .10
307 Mike Sharperson .10
308 Mike Christopher .10
309 Marvin Freeman .10
310 Jay Buhner .10
311 Butch Henry .10
312 Greg Harris .10
313 Darren Daulton .10
314 Chuck Knoblauch .25
315 Greg Harris .10
316 John Franco .10
317 John Wehner .10
318 Donald Harris .10
319 Benny Santiago .10
320 Larry Walker .30
321 Randy Knorr .10
322 *Ramon D. Martinez* .10
323 Mike Stanley .10
324 Bill Wegman .10
325 Tom Candiotti .10
326 Glenn Davis .10
327 Chuck Crim .10
328 Scott Livingstone .10
329 Eddie Taubensee .10
330 George Bell .10
331 Edgar Martinez .10
332 Paul Assenmacher .10
333 Steve Hosey .10
334 Mo Vaughn .50
335 Bret Saberhagen .10
336 Mike Trombley .10
337 Mark Lewis .10
338 Terry Pendleton .10
339 Dave Hollins .10
340 Jeff Conine .15
341 Bob Tewksbury .10
342 Billy Ashley .10
343 Zane Smith .10
344 John Wetteland .10
345 Chris Hoiles .10
346 Frank Castillo .10
347 Bruce Hurst .10
348 Kevin McReynolds .10
349 Dave Henderson .10
350 Ryan Bowen .10
351 Sid Fernandez .10
352 Mark Whiten .10
353 Nolan Ryan 2.50
354 Rick Aguilera .10
355 Mark Langston .10
356 Jack Morris .10
357 Rob Deer .10
358 Dave Fleming .10
359 Lance Johnson .10
360 Joe Millette .10
361 Wil Cordero .10
362 Chito Martinez .10
363 Scott Servais .10
364 Bernie Williams .60
365 Pedro Martinez .40
366 Ryne Sandberg .60
367 Brad Ausmus .10
368 Scott Cooper .10
369 Rob Dibble .10
370 Walt Weiss .10
371 Mark Davis .10
372 Orlando Merced .10
373 Mike Jackson .10
374 Kevin Appier .10
375 Esteban Beltre .10
376 Joe Slusarski .10
377 William Suero .10
378 Pete O'Brien .10
379 Alan Embree .10
380 Lenny Webster .10
381 Eric Davis .10
382 Duane Ward .10
383 John Habyan .10
384 Jeff Bagwell 1.00
385 Ruben Amaro .10
386 Julio Valera .10
387 Robin Ventura .25
388 Archi Cianfrocco .10
389 Skeeter Barnes .10
390 Tim Costo .10
391 Luis Mercedes .10
392 Jeremy Hernandez .10
393 Shawon Dunston .10
394 Andy Van Slyke .10
395 Kevin Maas .10
396 Kevin Brown .10
397 J.T. Bruett .10
398 Darryl Strawberry .10
399 Tom Pagnozzi .10
400 Sandy Alomar .15
401 Keith Miller .10
402 Rich DeLucia .10
403 Shawn Abner .10
404 Howard Johnson .10
405 Mike Benjamin .10
406 *Roberto Mejia* .15
407 Mike Butcher .10
408 Deion Sanders .20
409 Todd Stottlemyre .10
410 Scott Kamieniecki .10
411 Doug Jones .10
412 John Burkett .10
413 Lance Blankenship .10
414 Jeff Parrett .10
415 Barry Larkin .15
416 Alan Trammell .10
417 Mark Kiefer .10
418 Gregg Olson .10
419 Mark Grace .25
420 Shane Mack .10
421 Bob Walk .10
422 Curt Schilling .15
423 Erik Hanson .10
424 George Brett .60
425 Reggie Jefferson .10

426	Mark Portugal	.10
427	Ron Karkovice	.10
428	Matt Young	.10
429	Troy Neel	.10
430	Hector Fajardo	.10
431	Dave Righetti	.10
432	Pat Listach	.10
433	Jeff Innis	.10
434	Bob MacDonald	.10
435	Brian Jordan	.10
436	Jeff Blauser	.10
437	*Mike Myers*	.10
438	Frank Seminara	.10
439	Rusty Meacham	.10
440	Greg Briley	.10
441	Derek Lilliquist	.10
442	John Vander Wal	.10
443	Scott Erickson	.10
444	Bob Scanlan	.10
445	Todd Frohwirth	.10
446	Tom Goodwin	.10
447	William Pennyfeather	.10
448	Travis Fryman	.15
449	Mickey Morandini	.10
450	Greg Olson	.10
451	Trevor Hoffman	.15
452	Dave Magadan	.10
453	Shawn Jeter	.10
454	Andres Galarraga	.25
455	Ted Wood	.10
456	Freddie Benavides	.10
457	Junior Felix	.10
458	Alex Cole	.10
459	John Orton	.10
460	Eddie Zosky	.10
461	Dennis Eckersley	.10
462	Lee Smith	.10
463	John Smoltz	.20
464	Ken Caminiti	.15
465	Melido Perez	.15
466	Tom Marsh	.10
467	Jeff Nelson	.10
468	Jesse Levis	.10
469	Chris Nabholz	.10
470	Mike Mcfarlane	.10
471	Reggie Sanders	.15
472	Chuck McElroy	.10
473	Kevin Gross	.10
474	*Matt Whiteside*	.15
475	Cal Eldred	.10
476	Dave Gallagher	.10
477	Len Dykstra	.10
478	Mark McGwire	3.00
479	David Segui	.10
480	Mike Henneman	.10
481	Bret Barberie	.10
482	Steve Sax	.10
483	Dave Valle	.10
484	Danny Darwin	.10
485	Devon White	.10
486	Eric Plunk	.10
487	Jim Gott	.10
488	Scooter Tucker	.10
489	Omar Oliveres	.10
490	Greg Myers	.10
491	Brian Hunter	.10
492	Kevin Tapani	.10
493	Rich Monteleone	.10
494	Steve Buechele	.10
495	Bo Jackson	.20
496	Mike LaValliere	.10
497	Mark Leonard	.10
498	Daryl Boston	.10
499	Jose Canseco	.25
500	Brian Barnes	.10
501	Randy Johnson	.50
502	Tim McIntosh	.10
503	Cecil Fielder	.10
504	Derek Bell	.15
505	Kevin Koslofski	.10
506	Darren Holmes	.10
507	Brady Anderson	.15
508	John Valentin	.15
509	Jerry Browne	.10
510	Fred McGriff	.25
511	Pedro Astacio	.10
512	Gary Gaetti	.10
513	*John Burke*	.10
514	Dwight Gooden	.15
515	Thomas Howard	.10
516	*Darrell Whitmore*	.20
517	Ozzie Guillen	.10
518	Darryl Kile	.10
519	Rich Rowland	.10
520	Carlos Delgado	.60
521	Doug Henry	.10
522	Greg Colbrunn	.10
523	Tom Gordon	.10
524	Ivan Rodriguez	.75
525	Kent Hrbek	.10
526	Eric Young	.10
527	Rod Brewer	.10
528	Eric Karros	.10
529	Marquis Grissom	.10
530	Rico Brogna	.10
531	Sammy Sosa	1.50
532	Bret Boone	.10
533	Luis Rivera	.10
534	Hal Morris	.10
535	Monty Fariss	.10
536	Leo Gomez	.10
537	Wally Joyner	.15
538	Tony Gwynn	1.00
539	Mike Williams	.10
540	Juan Gonzalez	1.00
541	Ryan Klesko	.50
542	Ryan Thompson	.15
543	Chad Curtis	.15
544	Orel Hershiser	.10
545	Carlos Garcia	.10
546	Bob Welch	.10
547	Vinny Castilla	.15
548	Ozzie Smith	.60
549	Luis Salazar	.10
550	Mark Guthrie	.10
551	Charles Nagy	.10
552	Alex Fernandez	.15
553	Mel Rojas	.10
554	Orestes Destrade	.10
555	Mark Gubicza	.10
556	Steve Finley	.10
557	Don Mattingly	1.00
558	Rickey Henderson	.40
559	Tommy Greene	.10
560	Arthur Rhodes	.10
561	Alfredo Griffin	.10
562	Will Clark	.25
563	Bob Zupcic	.10
564	Chuck Carr	.10
565	Henry Cotto	.10
566	Billy Spiers	.10
567	Jack Armstrong	.10
568	Kurt Stillwell	.10
569	David McCarty	.10
570	Joe Vitiello	.10
571	Gerald Williams	.10
572	Dale Murphy	.20
573	Scott Aldred	.10
574	Bill Gullickson	.10
575	Bobby Thigpen	.10
576	Glenallen Hill	.10
577	Dwayne Henry	.10
578	Calvin Jones	.10
579	Al Martin	.15
580	Ruben Sierra	.10
581	Andy Benes	.10
582	Anthony Young	.10
583	Shawn Boskie	.10
584	*Scott Pose*	.15
585	Mike Piazza	2.50
586	Donovan Osborne	.10
587	James Austin	.10
588	Checklist 301-400	.10
589	Checklist 401-500	.10
590	Checklist 501-600	.10
591	Ken Griffey, Jr. (Members Choice)	2.00
592	Ivan Rodriguez (Members Choice)	.40
593	Carlos Baerga (Members Choice)	.10
594	Fred McGriff (Members Choice)	.20
595	Mark McGwire (Members Choice)	2.00
596	Roberto Alomar (Members Choice)	.40
597	Kirby Puckett (Members Choice)	.40
598	Marquis Grissom (Members Choice)	.10
599	John Smoltz (Members Choice)	.10
600	Ryne Sandberg (Members Choice)	.40
601	Wade Boggs	.40
602	Jeff Reardon	.10
603	Billy Ripken	.10
604	Bryan Harvey	.10
605	Carlos Quintana	.10
606	Greg Hibbard	.10
607	Ellis Burks	.10
608	Greg Swindell	.10
609	Dave Winfield	.30
610	Charlie Hough	.10
611	Chili Davis	.10
612	Jody Reed	.10
613	Mark Williamson	.10
614	Phil Plantier	.10
615	Jim Abbott	.10
616	Dante Bichette	.35
617	Mark Eichhorn	.10
618	Gary Sheffield	.25
619	*Richie Lewis*	.10
620	Joe Girardi	.10
621	Jaime Navarro	.10
622	Willie Wilson	.10
623	Scott Fletcher	.10
624	Bud Black	.10
625	Tom Brunansky	.10
626	Steve Avery	.10
627	Paul Molitor	.60
628	Gregg Jefferies	.15
629	Dave Stewart	.10
630	Javier Lopez	.35
631	Greg Gagne	.10
632	Bobby Kelly	.10
633	Mike Fetters	.10
634	Ozzie Canseco	.10
635	Jeff Russell	.10
636	Pete Incaviglia	.10
637	Tom Henke	.10
638	Chipper Jones	1.50
639	Jimmy Key	.10
640	Dave Martinez	.10
641	Dave Stieb	.10
642	Milt Thompson	.10
643	Alan Mills	.10
644	Tony Fernandez	.10
645	Randy Bush	.10
646	Joe Magrane	.10
647	Ivan Calderon	.10
648	Jose Guzman	.10
649	John Olerud	.25
650	Tom Glavine	.20
651	Julio Franco	.10
652	Armando Reynoso	.10
653	Felix Jose	.10
654	Ben Rivera	.10
655	Andre Dawson	.20
656	Mike Harkey	.10
657	Kevin Seitzer	.10
658	Lonnie Smith	.10
659	Norm Charlton	.10
660	Dave Justice	.40
661	Fernando Valenzuela	.10
662	Dan Wilson	.10
663	Mark Gardner	.10
664	Doug Dascenzo	.10
665	Greg Maddux	2.50
666	Harold Baines	.10
667	Randy Myers	.10
668	Harold Reynolds	.10
669	Candy Maldonado	.10
670	Al Leiter	.15
671	Jerald Clark	.10
672	Doug Drabek	.10
673	Kirk Gibson	.10
674	*Steve Reed*	.10
675	Mike Felder	.10
676	Ricky Gutierrez	.10
677	Spike Owen	.10
678	Otis Nixon	.10
679	Scott Sanderson	.10
680	Mark Carreon	.10
681	Troy Percival	.10
682	Kevin Stocker	.10
683	*Jim Converse*	.10
684	Barry Bonds	.75
685	Greg Gohr	.10
686	Tim Wallach	.10
687	Matt Mieske	.10
688	Robby Thompson	.10
689	Brien Taylor	.10
690	Kirt Manwaring	.10
691	*Mike Lansing*	.25
692	Steve Decker	.10
693	Mike Moore	.10
694	Kevin Mitchell	.10
695	Phil Hiatt	.10
696	*Tony Tarasco*	.10
697	Benji Gil	.10
698	Jeff Juden	.10
699	Kevin Reimer	.10
700	Andy Ashby	.15
701	John Jaha	.15
702	*Tim Bogar*	.20
703	David Cone	.15
704	Willie Greene	.15
705	*David Hulse*	.15
706	Cris Carpenter	.10
707	Ken Griffey, Jr.	3.00
708	Steve Bedrosian	.10
709	Dave Nilsson	.10
710	Paul Wagner	.10
711	B.J. Surhoff	.10
712	*Rene Arocha*	.15
713	Manny Lee	.10
714	Brian Williams	.10
715	*Sherman Obando*	.15
716	Terry Mulholland	.10
717	Paul O'Neill	.20
718	David Nied	.10
719	*J.T. Snow*	.75
720	Nigel Wilson	.10
721	Mike Bielecki	.10
722	Kevin Young	.10
723	Charlie Leibrandt	.10
724	Frank Bolick	.10
725	*Jon Shave*	.15
726	Steve Cooke	.10
727	*Domingo Martinez*	.15
728	Todd Worrell	.10
729	Jose Lind	.10
730	*Jim Tatum*	.10
731	Mike Hampton	.10
732	Mike Draper	.10
733	Henry Mercedes	.15
734	*John Johnstone*	.15
735	Mitch Webster	.10
736	Russ Springer	.10
737	Rob Natal	.10
738	Steve Howe	.10
739	*Darrell Sherman*	.15
740	Pat Mahomes	.10
741	Alex Arias	.10
742	Damon Buford	.15
743	Charlie Hayes	.10
744	Guillermo Velasquez	.10
745	Checklist 601-750	.10
746	Frank Thomas (Members Choice)	1.00
747	Barry Bonds (Members Choice)	.35
748	Roger Clemens (Members Choice)	.50
749	Joe Carter (Members Choice)	.10
750	Greg Maddux (Members Choice)	1.00

1993 Stadium Club 1st Day Production

Inserted at the rate of about one per box, with an estimated production of 2,000 apiece, 1st Day Production cards are a parallel of 1993 TSC on which an embossed silver holographic foil logo has been added. Because of the considerably higher value of the 1st Day parallels, collectors should be aware that fakes can be created by cutting the logo off a common player's card and attaching it to a superstar card.

	MT
Complete Set (750):	1600.
Complete Series 1 (1-300)	600.00
Complete Series 2 (301-600):	700.00
Complete Series 3 (601-750):	400.00
Common Player:	1.00
1st Day Stars: 15X	
(See 1993 Stadium Club for checklist and base card values.)	

1993 Stadium Club I Inserts

Four bonus cards were produced as special inserts in Series I Stadium Club packs. Two of the full-bleed, gold-foil enhanced cards honor Robin Yount and George Brett for achieving the 3,000-hit mark, while the other two commemorate the first picks in the 1993 expansion draft by the Colorado Rockies (David Nied) and Marlins (Nigel Wilson).

		MT
Complete Set (4):		5.00
Common Player:		.75
1	Robin Yount (3,000 hits)	2.00
2	George Brett (3,000 hits)	3.00
3	David Nied (#1 pick)	.75
4	Nigel Wilson (#1 pick)	.75

1993 Stadium Club II Inserts

Cross-town and regional rivals were featured in this four-card insert set found, on average, one per 24 packs of Series II Stadium Club. Each of the two-faced cards is typical S.C. quality with gold-foil stamping and UV coating front and back.

		MT
Complete Set (4):		10.00
Common Card:		2.00
1	Pacific Terrific (Will Clark, Mark McGwire)	3.50
2	Broadway Stars (Dwight Gooden, Don Mattingly)	2.00
3	Second City Sluggers (Ryne Sandberg, Frank Thomas)	3.00
4	Pacific Terrific (Ken Griffey, Jr., Darryl Strawberry)	3.50

1993 Stadium Club III Inserts

Team "firsts" - first game, first pitch, first batter, etc. - for the 1993 expansion Florida Marlins and Colorado Rockies are featured on this pair of inserts found in Series III Stadium Club packs. Fronts featured game-action photos with the player's name in gold foil. On back is a stadium scene with the team first overprinted in black. At top the team name and Stadium Club logo are in gold foil.

		MT
Complete Set (2):		1.00
Common Player:		.50
1	David Nied	.50
2	Charlie Hough	.50

1993 Stadium Club Master Photos

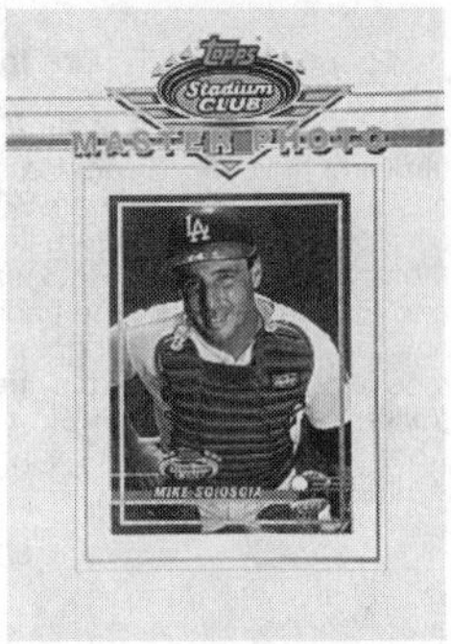

Each box of 1993 Stadium Club packs included one Master Photo premium insert. Prize cards good for three Master Photos in a mail-in offer were also included in each of the three series. The 5" x 7"

Master Photos feature wide white borders and a large Stadium Club logo at top, highlighted by prismatic foil. The same foil is used as a border for a larger-format version of the player's regular S.C. card at the center of the Master Photo. A "Members Only" version of each of the 1993 Master Photos was available as a premium with the purchase of a Members Only Stadium Club set. The Members Only Master Photos have a gold-foil seal in the upper-right corner.

		MT
Complete Set (30):		25.00
Common Player:		.25
Series I		
(1)	Carlos Baerga	.25
(2)	Delino DeShields	.25
(3)	Brian McRae	.25
(4)	Sam Militello	.25
(5)	Joe Oliver	.25
(6)	Kirby Puckett	2.00
Series II		
(13)	George Brett	2.00
(14)	Jose Canseco	.75
(15)	Will Clark	.75
(16)	Travis Fryman	.25
(17)	Dwight Gooden	.50
(18)	Mark Grace	.75
Series III		
(25)	Barry Bonds	2.00
(26)	Ken Griffey, Jr.	5.00
(27)	Greg Maddux	3.00
(28)	David Nied	.25
(29)	J.T. Snow	.50
(30)	Brien Taylor	.25

1993 Stadium Club Members Only

A special version of the Topps' 1993 Stadium Club set was made available exclusively to members of the company's Stadium Club program. The set is a parallel of the regular-issue SC set (plus insert) on which a gold-foil "Members Only" shield logo has been added to the card front. In all other respects the cards are identical to the regular SC issue. Production was a reported 12,000 sets.

	MT
Complete Set (750):	450.00
Common Player:	1.00
Members Only Stars: 12X	
(See 1993 Stadium Club for checklist and base card values.)	

1993 Stadium Club Members Only Baseball

As a benefit of membership in Topps' Stadium Club, each member received a 59-card set in four separate shipments. The cards featured highlights of the 1993 baseball, hockey, football and basketball seasons. Besides the 28 baseball player cards checklisted here there were nine football cards, six hockey cards and 16 basketball cards. Each sport's cards came separately in a heat-sealed cello wrap in a special box. Cards were typical S.C. quality, featuring full-bleed action photos on the front, with the Stadium Club logo and player name enhanced with gold-foil stamping and a gold-foil "Members Only" notice beneath the player's name. Backs feature a parti-color background with a colorized, stylized player figure at right. At left is the story of the player's season or career highlight. The cards are unnumbered and are checklisted alphabetically.

		MT
Complete Set (28):		24.00
Common Player:		.25
(1)	Jim Abbott	.25
(2)	Barry Bonds	2.00
(3)	Chris Bosio	.25
(4)	George Brett	2.00
(5)	Jay Buhner	.25
(6)	Joe Carter (3 HR in game 5th time)	.25
(7)	Joe Carter (World Series-winning HR)	.25
(8)	Carlton Fisk	.60
(9)	Travis Fryman	.25
(10)	Mark Grace	.75
(11)	Ken Griffey, Jr.	4.00
(12)	Darryl Kile	.25
(13)	Darren Lewis	.25
(14)	Greg Maddux	2.50
(15)	Jack McDowell	.25
(16)	Paul Molitor	.75
(17)	Eddie Murray	.65
(18)	Mike Piazza (Rookie catcher HR record)	2.00
(19)	Mike Piazza (N.L. Rookie of the Year)	2.00
(20)	Kirby Puckett	2.00
(21)	Jeff Reardon	.25
(22)	Tim Salmon	.50
(23)	Curt Schilling	.25
(24)	Lee Smith	.25
(25)	Dave Stewart	.25
(26)	Frank Thomas	2.50
(27)	Mark Whiten	.25
(28)	Dave Winfield	.75

1993 Stadium Club Special (Murphy)

Though the packaging and the cards themselves identify this 200-card set as a 1992 issue, it was not released until 1993 and is thought of by the hobby at large as a 1993 set. The set is sold in a plastic replica of Jack Murphy Stadium in San Diego, venue for the 1993 All-Star Game. Fifty-six of the cards feature players from that contest and are so identified by a line of gold-foil on the card front and an All-Star logo on back. Twenty-five members of the 1992 Team U.S.A. Olympic baseball squad are also included in the set, with appropriate logos and notations front and back. There are 19 cards depicting action and stars of the the 1992 League Championships and World Series. The other 100 cards in the set are 1992 draft picks. All cards have the same basic format as the regular-issue 1992 Topps Stadium Club cards, full-bleed photos on front and back, UV coating on both sides and gold-foil highlights on front. Besides the 200 standard-size cards, the Special Edition set included a dozen "Master Photos", 5" x 7" white-bordered premium cards.

		MT
Complete Set (200):		120.00
Common Player:		.10
1	Dave Winfield	.20
2	Juan Guzman	.10
3	Tony Gwynn	2.00
4	Chris Roberts	.20
5	Benny Santiago	.10
6	Sherard Clinkscales	.10
7	*Jonathan Nunnally*	.40
8	Chuck Knoblauch	.30
9	*Bob Wolcott*	.10
10	Steve Rodriguez	.10
11	*Mark Williams*	.10
12	*Danny Clyburn*	.15
13	Darren Dreifort	.15
14	Andy Van Slyke	.10
15	Wade Boggs	.45
16	Scott Patton	.10
17	Gary Sheffield	.25
18	Ron Villone	.10
19	Roberto Alomar	.50
20	Marc Valdes	.10
21	Daron Kirkreit	.10
22	Jeff Granger	.15
23	Levon Largusa	.10
24	Jimmy Key	.10
25	Kevin Pearson	.10
26	Michael Moore	.10
27	*Preston Wilson*	8.00
28	Kirby Puckett	1.00
29	*Tim Crabtree*	.15
30	Bip Roberts	.10
31	Kelly Gruber	.10
32	Tony Fernandez	.10
33	Jason Angel	.10
34	Calvin Murray	.10
35	Chad McConnell	.15
36	Jason Moler	.10
37	Mark Lemke	.10
38	Tom Knauss	.10
39	Larry Mitchell	.10
40	Doug Mirabelli	.10
41	Everett Stull II	.10
42	Chris Wimmer	.10
43	*Dan Serafini*	.10
44	Ryne Sandberg	.60
45	Steve Lyons	.10
46	Ryan Freeburg	.10
47	Ruben Sierra	.10
48	David Mysel	.10
49	Joe Hamilton	.15
50	Steve Rodriguez	.10
51	Tim Wakefield	.10
52	Scott Gentile	.10
53	Doug Jones	.10
54	Willie Brown	.10
55	*Chad Mottola*	.20
56	Ken Griffey, Jr.	6.00
57	Jon Lieber	.10
58	Denny Martinez	.10
59	Joe Petcka	.10
60	Benji Simonton	.10
61	Brett Backlund	.10
62	Damon Berryhill	.10
63	Juan Guzman	.10
64	Doug Hecker	.10
65	Jamie Arnold	.10
66	Bob Tewksbury	.10
67	Tim Leger	.10
68	Todd Etler	.10
69	Lloyd McClendon	.10
70	Kurt Ehmann	.10
71	Rick Magdaleno	.10
72	Tom Pagnozzi	.10
73	Jeffrey Hammonds	.15
74	Joe Carter	.10
75	Chris Holt	.10
76	Charles Johnson	.60
77	Bob Walk	.10
78	Fred McGriff	.20
79	Tom Evans	.10
80	Scott Klingenbeck	.10
81	Chad McConnell	.15
82	Chris Eddy	.10
83	Phil Nevin	.10
84	John Kruk	.10
85	Tony Sheffield	.10
86	John Smoltz	.20
87	Trevor Humphry	.10
88	Charles Nagy	.15
89	Sean Runyan	.10
90	Mike Gulan	.10
91	Darren Daulton	.10
92	Otis Nixon	.10
93	Nomar Garciaparra	40.00
94	Larry Walker	.35
95	Hut Smith	.10
96	Rick Helling	.10
97	Roger Clemens	1.50
98	Ron Gant	.15
99	Kenny Felder	.10
100	Steve Murphy	.10
101	Mike Smith	.10
102	Terry Pendleton	.10
103	Tim Davis	.10
104	Jeff Patzke	.10
105	Craig Wilson	.10
106	Tom Glavine	.20
107	Mark Langston	.10
108	Mark Thompson	.10
109	*Eric Owens*	.10
110	Keith Johnson	.10
111	Robin Ventura	.20
112	Ed Sprague	.10
113	*Jeff Schmidt*	.10
114	Don Wengert	.10
115	Craig Biggio	.20
116	Kenny Carlyle	.10
117	*Derek Jeter*	60.00
118	Manuel Lee	.10
119	Jeff Haas	.10
120	Roger Bailey	.10
121	Sean Lowe	.10
122	Rick Aguilera	.10
123	Sandy Alomar	.20
124	Derek Wallace	.10
125	B.J. Wallace	.10
126	Greg Maddux	2.00
127	Tim Moore	.10
128	Lee Smith	.10
129	Todd Steverson	.15
130	Chris Widger	.15
131	Paul Molitor	.60
132	Chris Smith	.10
133	*Chris Gomez*	.20
134	Jimmy Baron	.10
135	John Smoltz	.15
136	Pat Borders	.10
137	Donnie Leshnock	.10
138	Gus Gandarillos	.10
139	Will Clark	.25
140	*Ryan Luzinski*	.10
141	Cal Ripken, Jr.	3.00
142	B.J. Wallace	.10
143	*Trey Beamon*	.40
144	Norm Charlton	.10
145	Mike Mussina	.35
146	Billy Owens	.10
147	Ozzie Smith	.60
148	*Jason Kendall*	8.00
149	*Mike Matthews*	.10
150	David Spykstra	.10
151	Benji Grigsby	.10
152	Sean Smith	.10
153	Mark McGwire	6.00
154	David Cone	.20
155	*Shon Walker*	.15
156	Jason McDowell	.10
157	Jack McDowell	.10
158	Paxton Briley	.10
159	Edgar Martinez	.10
160	Brian Sackinsky	.10
161	Barry Bonds	.75
162	Roberto Kelly	.10
163	Jeff Alkire	.10
164	Mike Sharperson	.10
165	Jamie Taylor	.10
166	John Saffer	.10
167	Jerry Browne	.10
168	Travis Fryman	.10
169	Brady Anderson	.15
170	Chris Roberts	.20
171	Lloyd Peever	.10
172	Francisco Cabrera	.10
173	Ramiro Martinez	.10
174	Jeff Alkire	.10
175	Ivan Rodriguez	.60
176	Kevin Brown	.15
177	Chad Roper	.10
178	Rod Henderson	.10
179	Dennis Eckersley	.10
180	*Shannon Stewart*	8.00
181	DeShawn Warren	.10
182	Lonnie Smith	.10
183	Willie Adams	.10
184	Jeff Montgomery	.10
185	Damon Hollins	.10
186	Byron Matthews	.10
187	Harold Baines	.10
188	Rick Greene	.10
189	Carlos Baerga	.10
190	Brandon Cromer	.10
191	Roberto Alomar	.50
192	Rich Ireland	.10
193	Steve Montgomery	.10
194	Brant Brown	1.50
195	Ritchie Moody	.10
196	Michael Tucker	.10
197	*Jason Varitek*	.75
198	David Manning	.10
199	Marquis Riley	.10
200	Jason Giambi	.25

1993 Stadium Club Special Master Photos

Each 1993 Stadium Club Special (Jack Murphy Stadium) set included 12 Master Photos replicating cards from the set. There were nine All-Stars, two '92 rookies and a Team USA player among the Master Photos. Gold-tone prismatic foil highlights the 5" x 7" cards, decorating the large logo at top and separating the card photo from the wide white border. Backs have Stadium Club and MLB logos and copyright information printed in black. The unnumbered cards are checklisted here in alphabetical order.

		MT
Complete Set (12):		5.00
Common Player:		.25
(1)	Sandy Alomar	.35
(2)	Tom Glavine	.35
(3)	Ken Griffey, Jr.	3.00
(4)	Tony Gwynn	1.50
(5)	Chuck Knoblauch	.60
(6)	Chad Mottola	.25
(7)	Kirby Puckett	2.00
(8)	Chris Roberts	.40
(9)	Ryne Sandberg	1.50
(10)	Gary Sheffield	.75
(11)	Larry Walker	.75
(12)	Preston Wilson	.75

1993 Stadium Club Team Sets

This special edition of Stadium Club cards consists of 16 separate team sets of 30 cards each. Each blister-packed team set was priced around $6 and sold exclusively at Wal-Mart. Fronts of the UV coated cards have a player photo that is is borderless at the top, bottom and left. At right is a green stripe, at top of which is a partial baseball design and some other striping in gold-foil. Backs are basically green, with a light blue box at lower-right containing personal information and stats, along with the S.C. logo. A player photo is at upper-left, with his name superimposed on a bat. Cards are checklisted here within team set.

		MT
Complete Set (480):		80.00
Common Player:		.10
ATLANTA BRAVES		
	Team set:	8.00
1	Tom Glavine	.25
2	Bill Pecota	.10
3	David Justice	.50
4	Mark Lemke	.10
5	Jeff Blauser	.10
6	Ron Gant	.40
7	Greg Olson	.10
8	Francisco Cabrera	.10
9	Chipper Jones	2.00
10	Steve Avery	.10
11	Kent Mercker	.10
12	John Smoltz	.25
13	Pete Smith	.10
14	Damon Berryhill	.10
15	Sid Bream	.10
16	Otis Nixon	.10
17	Mike Stanton	.10
18	Greg Maddux	2.00
19	Jay Howell	.10
20	Rafael Belliard	.10
21	Terry Pendleton	.10
22	Deion Sanders	.50
23	Brian Hunter	.10
24	Marvin Freeman	.10
25	Mark Wohlers	.10
26	Ryan Klesko	.75
27	Javy Lopez	.50
28	Melvin Nieves	.10
29	Tony Tarasco	.10
30	Ramon Caraballo	.10
CHICAGO CUBS		
	Team set:	5.00
1	Ryne Sandberg	1.50
2	Greg Hibbard	.10
4	Candy Maldonado	.10
5	Willie Wilson	.15
6	Dan Plesac	.10
7	Steve Buechele	.10
8	Mark Grace	.90
9	Shawon Dunston	.15
10	Steve Lake	.10
11	Dwight Smith	.10
12	Derrick May	.10
13	Paul Assenmacher	.10
14	Mike Harkey	.10
15	Lance Dickson	.15
16	Randy Myers	.15
17	Mike Morgan	.10
18	Chuck McElroy	.10
19	Jose Guzman	.10
20	Jose Vizcaino	.10
21	Frank Castillo	.10
22	Bob Scanlon	.10
23	Rick Wilkins	.15
24	Rey Sanchez	.10
25	Phil Dauphin	.10
26	Jim Bullinger	.10
27	Jessie Hollins	.10
28	Matt Walbeck	.10
29	Fernando Ramsey	.10
30	Jose Bautista	.10
CALIFORNIA ANGELS		
	Team set:	4.00
1	J.T. Snow	.50
2	Chuck Crim	.10
3	Chili Davis	.15
4	Mark Langston	.25
5	Ron Tingley	.10
6	Eduardo Perez	.10
7	Scott Sanderson	.10
8	Jorge Fabregas	.15
9	Troy Percival	.15
10	Rod Carreia	.10
11	Greg Myers	.10
12	Steve Frey	.10
13	Tim Salmon	1.00
14	Scott Lewis	.10
15	Rene Gonzales	.10
16	Chuck Finley	.15
17	John Orton	.10
18	Joe Grahe	.10
19	Luis Polonia	.10
20	John Farrell	.10
21	Damion Easley	.15
22	Gene Nelson	.10
23	Chad Curtis	.45
24	Russ Springer	.15
25	De Shawn Warren	.10
26	Darryl Scott	.10
27	Gary DiSarcina	.15
28	Jerry Nielson	.10
29	Torey Lovullo	.10
30	Julio Valera	.10
CHICAGO WHITE SOX		
	Team set:	5.00
1	Frank Thomas	1.50
2	Bo Jackson	.40
3	Rod Bolton	.10
4	Dave Stieb	.10
5	Tim Raines	.20
6	Joey Cora	.10
7	Warren Newson	.10
8	Roberto Hernandez	.15
9	Brandon Wilson	.10
10	Wilson Alvarez	.15
11	Dan Pasqua	.10
12	Ozzie Guillen	.10
13	Robin Ventura	.60
14	Craig Grebeck	.10
15	Lance Johnson	.15
16	Carlton Fisk	.50
17	Ron Karkovice	.10
18	Jack McDowell	.10
19	Scott Radinsky	.10
20	Bobby Thigpen	.10
21	Donn Pall	.10
22	George Bell	.10
23	Alex Fernandez	.50
24	Mike Huff	.10
25	Jason Bere	.10
26	Johnny Ruffin	.10
27	Ellis Burks	.25
28	Kirk McCaskill	.10
29	Terry Leach	.10
30	Shawn Gilbert	.10
COLORADO ROCKIES		
	Team set:	3.50
1	David Nied	.10
2	Quinton McCracken	.15
3	Charlie Hayes	.10
4	Bryn Smith	.10
5	Dante Bichette	.60
6	Alex Cole	.10
7	Scott Aldred	.10
8	Roberto Mejia	.10
9	Jeff Parrett	.10
10	Joe Girardi	.15
11	Andres Galarraga	.50
12	Daryl Boston	.10
13	Jerald Clark	.10
14	Gerald Young	.10
15	Bruce Ruffin	.10
16	Rudy Seanez	.10
17	Darren Holmes	.15
18	Andy Ashby	.25
19	Chris Jones	.10
20	Mark Thompson	.10
21	Freddie Benavides	.10
22	Eric Wedge	.10
23	Vinny Castilla	.45
24	Butch Henry	.10
25	Jim Tatum	.10
26	Steve Reed	.10
27	Eric Young	.10
28	Danny Sheaffer	.10
29	Roger Bailey	.10
30	Brad Ausmus	.10
FLORIDA MARLINS		
	Team set:	3.50
1	Nigel Wilson	.10
2	Bryan Harvey	.10
3	Bob McClure	.10
4	Alex Arias	.10
5	Walt Weiss	.15
6	Charlie Hough	.15
7	Scott Chiamparino	.10
8	Junior Felix	.10
9	Jack Armstrong	.10
10	Dave Magadan	.10
11	Cris Carpenter	.10
12	Benny Santiago	.15
13	Jeff Conine	.45
14	Jerry Don Gleaton	.10
15	Steve Decker	.10
16	Ryan Bowen	.20
17	Ramon Martinez	.10
18	Bret Barberie	.15
19	Monty Fariss	.10
20	Trevor Hoffman	.50
21	Scott Pose	.10
22	Mike Myers	.10
23	Geronimo Berroa	.10
24	Darrell Whitmore	.10
25	Chuck Carr	.10
26	Dave Weathers	.10
27	Matt Turner	.10
28	Jose Martinez	.10
29	Orestes Destrade	.10
30	Carl Everett	.25
HOUSTON ASTROS		
	Team set:	5.00
1	Doug Drabek	.10
2	Eddie Taubensee	.10
3	James Mouton	.10
4	Ken Caminiti	.35
5	Chris James	.10
6	Jeff Juden	.10
7	Eric Anthony	.15
8	Jeff Bagwell	.90
9	Greg Swindell	.10
10	Steve Finley	.25
11	Al Osuna	.10
12	Gary Mota	.10
13	Scott Servais	.10
14	Craig Biggio	.50
15	Doug James	.10
16	Rob Mallicoat	.10
17	Darryl Kile	.15
18	Kevin Bass	.10
19	Pete Harnisch	.20
20	Andujar Cedeno	.10
21	Brian Hunter	.40
22	Brian Williams	.10
23	Chris Donnels	.10
24	Xavier Hernandez	.15
25	Todd Jones	.10
26	Luis Gonzalez	.25
27	Rick Parker	.10
28	Casey Candaele	.10
29	Tony Eusebio	.10
30	Mark Portugal	.10
KANSAS CITY ROYALS		
	Team set:	4.00
1	George Brett	1.50
2	Mike MacFarlane	.15
3	Tom Gordon	.20
4	Wally Joyner	.30
5	Kevin Appier	.15
6	Phil Hiatt	.10
7	Keith Miller	.10
8	Hipolito Pichardo	.10
9	Chris Gwynn	.10
10	Jose Lind	.10
11	Mark Gubicza	.15
12	Dennis Rasmussen	.10
13	Mike Magnante	.10
14	Joe Vitiello	.15
15	Kevin McReynolds	.10
16	Greg Gagne	.15
17	David Cone	.40
18	Brent Mayne	.10
19	Jeff Montgomery	.15
20	Joe Randa	.10
21	Felix Jose	.10
22	Bill Sampen	.10
23	Curt Wilkerson	.10
24	Mark Gardner	.10
25	Brian McRae	.15
26	Hubie Brooks	.10
27	Chris Eddy	.10
28	Harvey Pulliam	.10
29	Rusty Meacham	.10
30	Danny Miceli	.10
LOS ANGELES DODGERS		
	Team set:	6.00
1	Darryl Strawberry	.50
2	Pedro Martinez	1.00
3	Jody Reed	.10
4	Carlos Hernandez	.10
5	Kevin Gross	.10
6	Mike Piazza	2.50
7	Jim Gott	.10
8	Eric Karros	.25
9	Mike Sharperson	.10
10	Ramon Martinez	.25
11	Tim Wallach	.10
12	Pedro Astacio	.10
13	Lenny Harris	.10
14	Brett Butler	.25
15	Raul Mondesi	1.00
16	Todd Worrell	.10
17	Jose Offerman	.10
18	Mitch Webster	.10
19	Tom Candiotti	.10
20	Eric Davis	.15
21	Michael Moore	.10
22	Billy Ashley	.15
23	Orel Hershiser	.25
24	Roger Cedeno	.25
25	Roger McDowell	.10
26	Mike James	.10
27	Steve Wilson	.10
28	Todd Hollandsworth	.25
29	Cory Snyder	.10
30	Todd Williams	.10
NEW YORK YANKEES		
	Team set:	5.00
1	Don Mattingly	1.50
2	Jim Abbott	.25
3	Matt Nokes	.10
4	Danny Tartabull	.10
5	Wade Boggs	1.00
6	Melido Perez	.10
7	Steve Farr	.10
8	Kevin Maas	.10
9	Randy Velarde	.10
10	Mike Humphreys	.10
11	Mike Gallego	.10
12	Mike Stanley	.10
13	Jimmy Key	.10
14	Paul O'Neill	.35
15	Spike Owen	.10
16	Pat Kelly	.10
17	Sterling Hitchcock	.15
18	Mike Witt	.10
19	Scott Kamieniecki	.10
20	John Habyan	.10
21	Bernie Williams	.75
22	Brien Taylor	.15
23	Rich Monteleone	.10
24	Mark Hutton	.10
25	Robert Eenhoorn	.10
26	Gerald Williams	.15
27	Sam Militello	.10
28	Bob Wickman	.10
29	Andy Stankiewicz	.10
30	Domingo Jean	.10
OAKLAND A'S		
	Team set:	4.50
1	Dennis Eckersley	.35
2	Lance Blankenship	.10
3	Mike Mohler	.10
4	Jerry Browne	.10
5	Kevin Seitzer	.10
6	Storm Davis	.10
7	Mark McGwire	3.00
8	Rickey Henderson	.75
9	Terry Steinbach	.10
10	Ruben Sierra	.10
11	Dave Henderson	.10
12	Bob Welch	.10
13	Rick Honeycutt	.10
14	Ron Darling	.10
15	Joe Boever	.10
16	Bobby Witt	.10
17	Izzy Molina	.10
18	Mike Bordick	.10
19	Brent Gates	.20
20	Shawn Hillegas	.10
21	Scott Hammond	.10
22	Todd Van Poppel	.10
23	Johnny Guzman	.10
24	Scott Lydy	.10
25	Scott Baker	.10
26	Todd Revenig	.10
27	Scott Brosius	.15
28	Troy Neel	.10
29	Dale Sveum	.10
30	Mike Neill	.10
PHILADELPHIA PHILLIES		
	Team set:	3.00
1	Darren Daulton	.10
2	Larry Anderson	.10
3	Kyle Abbott	.15
4	Chad McConnell	.10
5	Danny Jackson	.10
6	Kevin Stocker	.10
7	Jim Eisenreich	.10
8	Mickey Morandini	.15
9	Bob Ayrault	.10
10	Doug Lindsey	.10
11	Dave Hollins	.15
12	Dave West	.10
13	Wes Chamberlain	.10
14	Curt Schilling	.40
15	Len Dykstra	.15
16	Trevor Humphry	.10
17	Terry Mulholland	.15
18	Gene Schall	.10
19	Mike Lieberthal	.30
20	Ben Rivera	.10
21	Mariano Duncan	.10
22	Pete Incaviglia	.10
23	Ron Blazier	.10
24	Jeff Jackson	.10
25	Jose DeLeon	.10
26	Ron Lockett	.10
27	Tommy Greene	.15
28	Milt Thompson	.10
29	Mitch Williams	.10
30	John Kruk	.15
ST. LOUIS CARDINALS		
	Team set:	4.50
1	Ozzie Smith	1.00
2	Rene Arocha	.15
3	Bernard Gilkey	.25
4	Jose Oquendo	.10
5	Mike Perez	.10
6	Tom Pagnozzi	.10
7	Rod Brewer	.10
8	Joe Magrane	.10
9	Todd Zeile	.25
10	Bob Tewksbury	.10
11	Darrel Deak	.10
12	Gregg Jefferies	.40
13	Lee Smith	.15
14	Ozzie Canseco	.10
15	Tom Urbani	.10
16	Donovan Osborne	.10
17	Ray Lankford	.25
18	Rheal Cormier	.10
19	Allen Watson	.15
20	Geronimo Pena	.10
21	Rob Murphy	.10
22	Tracy Woodson	.10
23	Basil Shabazz	.10
24	Omar Olivares	.10
25	Brian Jordan	.25
26	Les Lancaster	.10
27	Sean Lowe	.10
28	Hector Villanueva	.10
29	Brian Barber	.10
30	Aaron Holbert	.10
SAN FRANCISCO GIANTS		
	Team set:	5.00
1	Barry Bonds	1.50
2	Dave Righetti	.10
3	Matt Williams	.50
4	Royce Clayton	.15
5	Salomon Torres	.10
6	Kirt Manwaring	.10
7	J.R. Phillips	.15
8	Kevin Rogers	.10
9	Will Clark	.85
10	John Burkett	.25
11	Willie McGee	.15
12	Rod Beck	.15
13	Jeff Reed	.10
14	Jeff Brantley	.10
15	Steve Hosey	.10
16	Chris Hancock	.10
17	Adell Davenport	.10
18	Mike Jackson	.10
19	Dave Martinez	.10
20	Bill Swift	.10
21	Steve Scarsone	.10
22	Trevor Wilson	.15
23	Mark Carreon	.10
24	Bud Black	.10
25	Darren Lewis	.25
26	Dan Carlson	.10
27	Craig Colbert	.10
28	Greg Brummet	.10
29	Bryan Hickerson	.10
30	Robby Thompson	.10
SEATTLE MARINERS		
	Team set:	6.00
1	Ken Griffey Jr.	2.50
2	Desi Relaford	.15
3	Dave Weinhouse	.10
4	Rich Amaral	.10
5	Brian Deak	.10
6	Bret Boone	.35
7	Bill Haselman	.10
8	Dave Fleming	.10
9	Fernando Vina	.10
10	Greg Litton	.10
11	Mackey Sasser	.10
12	Lee Tinsley	.10
13	Norm Charlton	.10
14	Russ Swan	.10
15	Brian Holman	.10
16	Randy Johnson	.50
17	Erik Hanson	.10
18	Tino Martinez	.35
19	Marc Newfield	.10
20	Dave Valle	.10
21	John Cummings	.10
22	Mike Hampton	.10
23	Jay Buhner	.25
24	Edgar Martinez	.20
25	Omar Vizquel	.25
26	Pete O'Brien	.10
27	Brian Turang	.10
28	Chris Bosio	.10
29	Mike Felder	.10
30	Shawn Estes	.10
TEXAS RANGERS		
	Team set:	6.50
1	Nolan Ryan	2.00
2	Ritchie Moody	.10
3	Matt Whiteside	.10
4	David Hulse	.10
5	Roger Pavlik	.10
6	Dan Smith	.10
7	Donald Harris	.10
8	Butch Davis	.10
9	Benji Gil	.10
10	Ivan Rodriguez	.75
11	Dean Palmer	.15
12	Jeff Huson	.10
13	Rob Mauer	.10
14	Gary Redus	.10
15	Doug Dascenzo	.10
16	Charlie Liebrandt	.10
17	Tom Henke	.10
18	Manuel Lee	.10
19	Kenny Rogers	.15
20	Kevin Brown	.30
21	Juan Gonzalez	1.50
22	Geno Petralli	.10
23	John Russell	.10
24	Robb Nen	.10
25	Julio Franco	.10
26	Rafael Palmeiro	.45
27	Todd Burns	.10
28	Jose Canseco	.75
29	Billy Ripken	.10
30	Dan Peltier	.10

1993 Stadium Club Ultra Pro

Special packages of plastic sheets and sleeves carrying the "Topps Stadium Club UltraPro" brand name included one of 10 special Stadium Club cards of Barry Bonds, Bobby Bonds and/or Willie Mays. Cards are typical UV coated, gold-foil quality, but because the cards were not licensed by Major League Baseball, team logos were removed from the photos.

		MT
Complete Set (10):		10.00
Common Card:		1.00
1	Barry Bonds, Willie Mays, Bobby Bonds	1.00
2	Willie Mays	2.00
3	Bobby Bonds	1.00
4	Barry Bonds	1.00
5	Barry Bonds, Bobby Bonds	1.00
6	Willie Mays	2.00
7	Barry Bonds (business suit)	1.00
8	Willie Mays, Bobby Bonds	1.00
9	Willie Mays	2.00
10	Barry Bonds (tuxedo)	1.00

1994 Stadium Club Pre-production

These sample cards introducing the 1994 Stadium Club set differ from their regular-issue counterparts only in the inclusion of a line of type vertically on the back-right, "Pre-Production Sample."

	MT
Complete Set (9):	7.00
Common Player:	.50
6 Al Martin	.50
15 Junior Ortiz	.50
36 Tim Salmon	1.50
56 Jerry Spradlin	.50
122 Tom Pagnozzi	.50
123 Ron Gant	.75
125 Dennis Eckersley	.75
135 Jose Lind	.50
238 Barry Bonds	3.00

1994 Stadium Club

Issued in three series to a total of 720 cards, Topps' mid-price brand features a hip look and a wide range of insert specials. The regular cards feature a borderless photo with the player's name presented in a unique typewriter/label maker style at bottom. The player's last name and Topps Stadium Club logo at top are in red foil. Backs feature another player photo, some personal data and a headlined career summary. Various stats and skills rankings complete the data. Subsets within the issue include cards annotated with Major League debut dates, 1993 awards won, home run club cards, cards featuring two or three players, and Final Tribute cards for George Brett and Nolan Ryan.

	MT
Complete Set (720):	50.00
Common Player:	.10
Series 1,2,3 Wax Box:	20.00

1 Robin Yount .75
2 Rick Wilkins .10
3 Steve Scarsone .10
4 Gary Sheffield .40
5 George Brett .75
6 Al Martin .10
7 Joe Oliver .10
8 Stan Belinda .10
9 Donny Hocking .10
10 Roberto Alomar .60
11 Luis Polonia .10
12 Scott Hemond .10
13 Joey Reed .10
14 Mel Rojas .10
15 Junior Ortiz .10
16 Harold Baines .10
17 Brad Pennington .10
18 Jay Bell .10
19 Tom Henke .10
20 Jeff Branson .10
21 Roberto Mejia .10
22 Pedro Munoz .10
23 Matt Nokes .10
24 Jack McDowell .10
25 Cecil Fielder .10
26 Tony Fossas .10
27 Jim Eisenreich .10
28 Anthony Young .10
29 Chuck Carr .10
30 Jeff Treadway .10
31 Chris Nabholz .10
32 Tom Candiotti .10
33 Mike Maddux .10
34 Nolan Ryan 2.50
35 Luis Gonzalez .15
36 Tim Salmon .45
37 Mark Whiten .10
38 Roger McDowell .10
39 Royce Clayton .10
40 Troy Neel .10
41 Mike Harkey .10
42 Darrin Fletcher .10
43 Wayne Kirby .10
44 Rich Amaral .10
45 Robb Nen .10
46 Tim Teufel .10
47 Steve Cooke .10
48 Jeff McNeely .10
49 Jeff Montgomery .10
50 Skeeter Barnes .10
51 Scott Stahoviak .10
52 Pat Kelly .10
53 Brady Anderson .20
54 Mariano Duncan .10
55 Brian Bohanon .10
56 Jerry Spradlin .10
57 Ron Karkovice .10
58 Jeff Gardner .10
59 Bobby Bonilla .10
60 Tino Martinez .15
61 Todd Benzinger .10
62 *Steve Trachsel* .35
63 Brian Jordan .15
64 Steve Bedrosian .10
65 Brent Gates .10
66 Shawn Green .20
67 Sean Berry .10
68 Joe Klink .10
69 Fernando Valenzuela .10
70 Andy Tomberlin .10
71 Tony Pena .10
72 Eric Young .10
73 Chris Gomez .10
74 Paul O'Neill .15
75 Ricky Gutierrez .10
76 Brad Holman .10
77 Lance Painter .10
78 Mike Butcher .10
79 Sid Bream .10
80 Sammy Sosa 1.50
81 Felix Fermin .10
82 Todd Hundley .20
83 Kevin Higgins .10
84 Todd Pratt .10
85 Ken Griffey, Jr. 3.50
86 John O'Donoghue .10
87 Rick Renteria .10
88 John Burkett .10
89 Jose Vizcaino .10
90 Kevin Seitzer .10
91 Bobby Witt .10
92 Chris Turner .10
93 Omar Vizquel .10
94 Dave Justice .25
95 David Segui .10
96 Dave Hollins .10
97 Doug Strange .10
98 Jerald Clark .10
99 Mike Moore .10
100 Joey Cora .10
101 Scott Kamieniecki .10
102 Andy Benes .10
103 Chris Bosio .10
104 Rey Sanchez .10
105 John Jaha .10
106 Otis Nixon .10
107 Rickey Henderson .40
108 Jeff Bagwell 1.00
109 Gregg Jefferies .15
110 Topps Trios (Roberto Alomar, Paul Molitor, John Olerud) .25
111 Topps Trios (Ron Gant, David Justice, Fred McGriff) .25
112 Topps Trios (Juan Gonzalez, Rafael Palmeiro, Dean Palmer) .25
113 Greg Swindell .10
114 Bill Hasleman .10
115 Phil Plantier .10
116 Ivan Rodriguez .75
117 Kevin Tapani .10
118 Mike LaValliere .10
119 Tim Costo .10
120 Mickey Morandini .10
121 Brett Butler .10
122 Tom Pagnozzi .10
123 Ron Gant .15
124 Damion Easley .10
125 Dennis Eckersley .10
126 Matt Mieske .10
127 Cliff Floyd .10
128 *Julian Tavarez* .10
129 Arthur Rhodes .10
130 Dave West .10
131 Tim Naehring .10
132 Freddie Benavides .10
133 Paul Assenmacher .10
134 David McCarty .10
135 Jose Lind .10
136 Reggie Sanders .15
137 Don Slaught .10
138 Andujar Cedeno .10
139 Rob Deer .10
140 Mike Piazza 2.00
141 Moises Alou .15
142 Tom Foley .10
143 Benny Santiago .10
144 Sandy Alomar .15
145 Carlos Hernandez .10
146 Luis Alicea .10
147 Tom Lampkin .10
148 Ryan Klesko .40
149 Juan Guzman .10
150 Scott Servais .10
151 Tony Gwynn 1.00
152 Tim Wakefield .10
153 David Nied .10
154 Chris Haney .10
155 Danny Bautista .10
156 Randy Velarde .10
157 Darrin Jackson .10
158 *J.R. Phillips* .20
159 Greg Gagne .10
160 Luis Aquino .10
161 John Vander Wal .10
162 Randy Myers .10
163 Ted Power .10
164 Scott Brosius .10
165 Len Dykstra .10
166 Jacob Brumfield .10
167 Bo Jackson .20
168 Eddie Taubensee .10
169 Carlos Baerga .10
170 Tim Bogar .10
171 Jose Canseco .35
172 Greg Blosser .10
173 Chili Davis .10
174 Randy Knorr .10
175 Mike Perez .10
176 Henry Rodriguez .10
177 *Brian Turang* .15
178 Roger Pavlik .10
179 Aaron Sele .15
180 Tale of 2 Players (Fred McGriff, Gary Sheffield) .20
181 Tale of 2 Players (J.T. Snow, Tim Salmon) .20
182 Roberto Hernandez .10
183 Jeff Reboulet .10
184 John Doherty .10
185 Danny Sheaffer .10
186 Bip Roberts .10
187 Denny Martinez .10
188 Darryl Hamilton .10
189 Eduardo Perez .10
190 Pete Harnisch .10
191 Rick Gossage .10
192 Mickey Tettleton .10
193 Lenny Webster .10
194 Lance Johnson .10
195 Don Mattingly 1.00
196 Gregg Olson .10
197 Mark Gubicza .10
198 Scott Fletcher .10
199 Jon Shave .10
200 Tim Mauser .10
201 Jeromy Burnitz .10
202 Rob Dibble .10
203 Will Clark .40
204 Steve Buechele .10
205 Brian Williams .10
206 Carlos Garcia .10
207 Mark Clark .10
208 Rafael Palmeiro .15
209 Eric Davis .10
210 Pat Meares .10
211 Chuck Finley .10
212 Jason Bere .10
213 Gary DiSarcina .10
214 Tony Fernandez .10
215 B.J. Surhoff .10
216 Lee Guetterman .10
217 Tim Wallach .10
218 Kirt Manwaring .10
219 Albert Belle .75
220 Dwight Gooden .15
221 Archi Cianfrocco .10
222 Terry Mulholland .10
223 Hipolito Pichardo .10
224 Kent Hrbek .10
225 Criag Grebeck .10
226 Todd Jones .10
227 Mike Bordick .10
228 John Olerud .15
229 Jeff Blauser .10
230 Alex Arias .10
231 Bernard Gilkey .10
232 Denny Neagle .10
233 *Pedro Borbon* .10
234 Dick Schofield .10
235 Matias Carrillo .10
236 Juan Bell .10
237 Mike Hampton .10
238 Barry Bonds .75
239 Cris Carpenter .10
240 Eric Karros .15
241 Greg McMichael .10
242 Pat Hentgen .10
243 Tim Pugh .10
244 Vinny Castilla .10
245 Charlie Hough .10
246 Bobby Munoz .10
247 Kevin Baez .10
248 Todd Frohwirth .10
249 Charlie Hayes .10
250 Mike Macfarlane .10
251 Danny Darwin .10
252 Ben Rivera .10
253 Dave Henderson .10
254 Steve Avery .10
255 Tim Belcher .10
256 Dan Plesac .10
257 Jim Thome .40
258 Albert Belle (35+ HR Hitter) .30
259 Barry Bonds (35+ HR Hitter) .35
260 Ron Gant (35+ HR Hitter) .10
261 Juan Gonzalez (35+ HR Hitter) .50
262 Ken Griffey, Jr. (35+ HR Hitter) 1.50
263 Dave Justice (35+ HR Hitter) .20
264 Fred McGriff (35+ HR Hitter) .20
265 Rafael Palmeiro (35+ HR Hitter) .10
266 Mike Piazza (35+ HR Hitter) .75
267 Frank Thomas (35+ HR Hitter) 1.00
268 Matt Williams (35+ HR Hitter) .10
269a Checklist 1-135 .10
269b Checklist 271-408 .10
270a Checklist 136-270 .10
270b Checklist 409-540 .10
271 Mike Stanley .10
272 Tony Tarasco .10
273 Teddy Higuera .10
274 Ryan Thompson .10
275 Rick Aguilera .10
276 Ramon Martinez .15
277 Orlando Merced .10
278 Guillermo Velasquez .10
279 Mark Hutton .10
280 Larry Walker .25
281 Kevin Gross .10
282 Jose Offerman .10
283 Jim Leyritz .10
284 Jamie Moyer .10
285 Frank Thomas 2.00
286 Derek Bell .10
287 Derrick May .10
288 Dave Winfield .30
289 Curt Schilling .10
290 Carlos Quintana .10
291 Bob Natal .10
292 David Cone .15
293 Al Osuna .10
294 Bob Hamelin .10
295 Chad Curtis .10
296 Danny Jackson .10
297 Bob Welch .10
298 Felix Jose .10
299 Jay Buhner .10
300 Joe Carter .10
301 Kenny Lofton .45
302 *Kirk Rueter* .15
303 Kim Batiste .10
304 Mike Morgan .10
305 Pat Borders .10
306 Rene Arocha .10
307 Ruben Sierra .10
308 Steve Finley .10
309 Travis Fryman .10
310 Zane Smith .10
311 Willie Wilson .10
312 Trevor Hoffman .15
313 Terry Pendleton .10
314 Salomon Torres .10
315 Robin Ventura .15
316 Randy Tomlin .10
317 Dave Stewart .10
318 Mike Benjamin .10
319 Matt Turner .10
320 Manny Ramirez 1.00
321 Kevin Young .10
322 Ken Caminiti .25
323 Joe Girardi .10
324 Jeff McKnight .10
325 Gene Harris .10
326 Devon White .10
327 Darryl Kile .10
328 Craig Paquette .10
329 Cal Eldred .10
330 Bill Swift .10
331 Alan Trammell .10
332 Armando Reynoso .10
333 Brent Mayne .10
334 Chris Donnels .10
335 Darryl Strawberry .15
336 Dean Palmer .10
337 Frank Castillo .10
338 Jeff King .10
339 John Franco .10
340 Kevin Appier .10
341 Lance Blankenship .10
342 Mark McLemore .10
343 Pedro Astacio .10
344 Rich Batchelor .10
345 Ryan Bowen .10
346 Terry Steinbach .10
347 Troy O'Leary .10
348 Willie Blair .10
349 Wade Boggs .35
350 Tim Raines .15
351 Scott Livingstone .10
352 Rod Carreia .10
353 Ray Lankford .15
354 Pat Listach .10
355 Milt Thompson .10
356 Miguel Jimenez .10
357 Marc Newfield .10
358 Mark McGwire 3.50
359 Kirby Puckett .75
360 Kent Mercker .10
361 John Kruk .10
362 Jeff Kent .10
363 Hal Morris .10
364 Edgar Martinez .10
365 Dave Magadan .10
366 Dante Bichette .25
367 Chris Hammond .10
368 Bret Saberhagen .10
369 Billy Ripken .10
370 Bill Gullickson .10
371 Andre Dawson .15
372 Bobby Kelly .10
373 Cal Ripken, Jr. 2.50
374 Craig Biggio .25
375 Dan Pasqua .10
376 Dave Nilsson .10
377 Duane Ward .10
378 Greg Vaughn .15
379 Jeff Fassero .10
380 Jerry Dipoto .10
381 John Patterson .10
382 Kevin Brown .10
383 Kevin Roberson .10
384 Joe Orsulak .10
385 Hilly Hathaway .10
386 Mike Greenwell .10
387 Orestes Destrade .10
388 Mike Gallego .10
389 Ozzie Guillen .10
390 Raul Mondesi .75
391 Scott Lydy .10
392 Tom Urbani .10
393 Wil Cordero .10
394 Tony Longmire .10
395 Todd Zeile .10
396 Scott Cooper .10
397 Ryne Sandberg .60
398 Ricky Bones .10
399 Phil Clark .10
400 Orel Hershiser .15
401 Mike Henneman .10
402 Mark Lemke .10
403 Mark Grace .25
404 Ken Ryan .10
405 John Smoltz .20
406 Jeff Conine .10
407 Greg Harris .10
408 Doug Drabek .10
409 Dave Fleming .10
410 Danny Tartabull .10
411 Chad Kreuter .10
412 Brad Ausmus .10
413 Ben McDonald .10
414 Barry Larkin .15
415 Bret Barberie .10
416 Chuck Knoblauch .20
417 Ozzie Smith .45
418 Ed Sprague .10
419 Matt Williams .25
420 Jeremy Hernandez .10
421 Jose Bautista .10
422 Kevin Mitchell .10
423 Manuel Lee .10
424 Mike Devereaux .10
425 Omar Olivares .10
426 Rafael Belliard .10
427 Richie Lewis .10
428 Ron Darling .10
429 Shane Mack .10
430 Tim Hulett .10
431 Wally Joyner .15
432 Wes Chamberlain .10
433 Tom Browning .10
434 Scott Radinsky .10
435 Rondell White .25
436 Rod Beck .10
437 Rheal Cormier .10
438 Randy Johnson .40
439 Pete Schourek .10
440 Mo Vaughn .45
441 Mike Timlin .10
442 Mark Langston .10
443 Lou Whitaker .10
444 Kevin Stocker .10
445 Ken Hill .10
446 John Wetteland .10
447 J.T. Snow .15
448 Erik Pappas .10
449 David Hulse .10
450 Darren Daulton .10
451 Chris Hoiles .10
452 Bryan Harvey .10
453 Darren Lewis .10
454 Andres Galarraga .20
455 Joe Hesketh .10
456 Jose Valentin .10
457 Dan Peltier .10
458 Joe Boever .10
459 Kevin Rogers .10
460 Craig Shipley .10
461 Alvaro Espinoza .10
462 Wilson Alvarez .10
463 Cory Snyder .10
464 Candy Maldonado .10
465 Blas Minor .10
466 Rod Bolton .10
467 Kenny Rogers .10
468 Greg Myers .10
469 Jimmy Key .10
470 Tony Castillo .10
471 Mike Stanton .10
472 Deion Sanders .25
473 Tito Navarro .10
474 Mike Gardiner .10

475	Steve Reed	.10
476	John Roper	.10
477	Mike Trombley	.10
478	Charles Nagy	.10
479	Larry Casian	.10
480	Eric Hillman	.10
481	Bill Wertz	.10
482	Jeff Schwarz	.10
483	John Valentin	.10
484	Carl Willis	.10
485	Gary Gaetti	.10
486	Bill Pecota	.10
487	John Smiley	.10
488	Mike Mussina	.40
489	*Mike Ignasiak*	.15
490	Billy Brewer	.10
491	Jack Voigt	.10
492	Mike Munoz	.10
493	Lee Tinsley	.10
494	Bob Wickman	.10
495	Roger Salkeld	.10
496	Thomas Howard	.10
497	Mark Davis	.10
498	Dave Clark	.10
499	Turk Wendell	.10
500	Rafael Bournigal	.10
501	Chip Hale	.10
502	Matt Whiteside	.10
503	Brian Koelling	.10
504	Jeff Reed	.10
505	Paul Wagner	.10
506	Torey Lovullo	.10
507	Curtis Leskanic	.10
508	Derek Lilliquist	.10
509	Joe Magrane	.10
510	Mackey Sasser	.10
511	Lloyd McClendon	.10
512	*Jayhawk Owens*	.15
513	*Woody Williams*	.15
514	Gary Redus	.10
515	Tim Spehr	.10
516	Jim Abbott	.10
517	Lou Frazier	.10
518	Erik Plantenberg	.10
519	Tim Worrell	.10
520	Brian McRae	.10
521	*Chan Ho Park*	2.00
522	Mark Wohlers	.10
523	Geronimo Pena	.10
524	Andy Ashby	.10
525	Tale of 2 Players (Tim Raines, Andre Dawson)	.10
526	Tale of 2 Players (Paul Molitor, Dave Winfield)	.35
527	Joe Carter (RBI Leader)	.10
528	Frank Thomas (HR Leader)	1.00
529	Ken Griffey, Jr. (TB Leader)	1.50
530	Dave Justice (HR Leader)	.10
531	Gregg Jefferies (AVG Leader)	.10
532	Barry Bonds (HR Leader)	.35
533	John Kruk (Quick Start)	.10
534	Roger Clemens (Quick Start)	.20
535	Cecil Fielder (Quick Start)	.10
536	Ruben Sierra (Quick Start)	.10
537	Tony Gwynn (Quick Start)	.40
538	Tom Glavine (Quick Start)	.10
539	Not issued, see #269	
540	Not issued, see #270	
541	Ozzie Smith (Career Leader)	.25
542	Eddie Murray (Career Leader)	.25
543a	Lee Smith (Career Leader)	.10
543b	Lonnie Smith (should be #643)	.10
544	Greg Maddux	2.00
545	Denis Boucher	.10
546	Mark Gardner	.10
547	Bo Jackson	.15
548	Eric Anthony	.10
549	Delino DeShields	.10
550	Turner Ward	.10
551	Scott Sanderson	.10
552	Hector Carrasco	.10
553	Tony Phillips	.10
554	Melido Perez	.10
555	Mike Felder	.10
556	Jack Morris	.10
557	Rafael Palmeiro	.20
558	Shane Reynolds	.10
559	Pete Incaviglia	.10
560	Greg Harris	.10
561	Matt Walbeck	.10
562	Todd Van Poppel	.10
563	Todd Stottlemyre	.10
564	Ricky Bones	.10
565	Mike Jackson	.10
566	Kevin McReynolds	.10
567	Melvin Nieves	.10
568	Juan Gonzalez	1.00
569	Frank Viola	.10
570	Vince Coleman	.10
571	*Brian Anderson*	.20
572	Omar Vizquel	.10
573	Bernie Williams	.50
574	Tom Glavine	.20
575	Mitch Williams	.10
576	Shawon Dunston	.10
577	Mike Lansing	.10
578	Greg Pirkl	.10
579	Sid Fernandez	.10
580	Doug Jones	.10
581	Walt Weiss	.10
582	Tim Belcher	.10
583	Alex Fernandez	.10
584	Alex Cole	.10
585	Greg Cadaret	.10
586	Bob Tewksbury	.10
587	Dave Hansen	.10
588	*Kurt Abbott*	.25
589	*Rick White*	.15
590	Kevin Bass	.10
591	Geronimo Berroa	.10
592	Jaime Navarro	.10
593	Steve Farr	.10
594	Jack Armstrong	.10
595	Steve Howe	.10
596	Jose Rijo	.10
597	Otis Nixon	.10
598	Robby Thompson	.10
599	Kelly Stinnett	.10
600	Carlos Delgado	.50
601	*Brian Johnson*	.15
602	Gregg Olson	.10
603	Jim Edmonds	.20
604	Mike Blowers	.10
605	Lee Smith	.10
606	Pat Rapp	.10
607	Mike Magnante	.10
608	Karl Rhodes	.10
609	Jeff Juden	.10
610	Rusty Meacham	.10
611	Pedro Martinez	.25
612	Todd Worrell	.10
613	Stan Javier	.10
614	Mike Hampton	.10
615	Jose Guzman	.10
616	Xavier Hernandez	.10
617	David Wells	.10
618	John Habyan	.10
619	Chris Nabholz	.10
620	Bobby Jones	.15
621	Chris James	.10
622	Ellis Burks	.15
623	Erik Hanson	.10
624	Pat Meares	.10
625	Harold Reynolds	.10
626	Bob Hamelin (Rookie Rocker)	.10
627	Manny Ramirez (Rookie Rocker)	.50
628	Ryan Klesko (Rookie Rocker)	.25
629	Carlos Delgado (Rookie Rocker)	.25
630	Javier Lopez (Rookie Rocker)	.20
631	Steve Karsay (Rookie Rocket)	.15
632	Rick Helling (Rookie Rocket)	.10
633	Steve Trachsel (Rookie Rocket)	.15
634	Hector Carrasco (Rookie Rocket)	.10
635	Andy Stankiewicz	.10
636	Paul Sorrento	.10
637	Scott Erickson	.10
638	Chipper Jones	2.00
639	Luis Polonia	.10
640	Howard Johnson	.10
641	John Dopson	.10
642	Jody Reed	.10
643	Not issued, see #543	
644	Mark Portugal	.10
645	Paul Molitor	.50
646	Paul Assenmacher	.10
647	Hubie Brooks	.10
648	Gary Wayne	.10
649	Sean Berry	.10
650	Roger Clemens	.50
651	Brian Hunter	.10
652	Wally Whitehurst	.10
653	Allen Watson	.10
654	Rickey Henderson	.35
655	Sid Bream	.10
656	Dan Wilson	.10
657	Ricky Jordan	.10
658	Sterling Hitchcock	.10
659	Darrin Jackson	.10
660	Junior Felix	.10
661	Tom Brunansky	.10
662	Jose Vizcaino	.10
663	Mark Leiter	.10
664	Gil Heredia	.10
665	Fred McGriff	.30
666	Will Clark	.30
667	Al Leiter	.10
668	James Mouton	.10
669	Billy Bean	.10
670	Scott Leius	.10
671	Bret Boone	.10
672	Darren Holmes	.10
673	Dave Weathers	.10
674	Eddie Murray	.50
675	Felix Fermin	.10
676	Chris Sabo	.10
677	Billy Spiers	.10
678	Aaron Sele	.10
679	Juan Samuel	.10
680	Julio Franco	.10
681	Heathcliff Slocumb	.10
682	Denny Martinez	.10
683	Jerry Browne	.10
684	*Pedro A. Martinez*	.10
685	Rex Hudler	.10
686	Willie McGee	.10
687	Andy Van Slyke	.10
688	Pat Mahomes	.10
689	Dave Henderson	.10
690	Tony Eusebio	.10
691	Rick Sutcliffe	.10
692	Willie Banks	.10
693	Alan Mills	.10
694	Jeff Treadway	.10
695	Alex Gonzalez	.25
696	David Segui	.10
697	Rick Helling	.10
698	Bip Roberts	.10
699	*Jeff Cirillo*	.15
700	Terry Mulholland	.10
701	Marvin Freeman	.10
702	Jason Bere	.10
703	Javier Lopez	.25
704	Greg Hibbard	.10
705	Tommy Greene	.10
706	Marquis Grissom	.10
707	Brian Harper	.10
708	Steve Karsay	.10
709	Jeff Brantley	.10
710	Jeff Russell	.10
711	Bryan Hickerson	.10
712	*Jim Pittsley*	.20
713	Bobby Ayala	.10
714	John Smoltz (Fantastic Finisher)	.20
715	Jose Rijo (Fantastic Finisher)	.10
716	Greg Maddux (Fantastic Finisher)	1.00
717	Matt Williams (Fantastic Finisher)	.25
718	Frank Thomas (Fantastic Finisher)	1.00
719	Ryne Sandberg (Fantastic Finisher)	.40
720	Checklist	.10

1994 Stadium Club Golden Rainbow

Found at the rate of one per pack, Stadium Club "Golden Rainbow" cards were issued for each of the 720 cards in the regular set. These inserts are distinguished by the use of gold prismatic foil highlights for the S.C. logo and box with the player's last name, instead of the red foil found on regular S.C. cards.

	MT
Complete Set (720):	150.00
Common Player:	.50
Stars: 3X	
(See 1994 Stadium Club for checklist and base card values.)	

1994 Stadium Club 1st Day Production

A special silver-foil embossment designating "1st Day Issue" was placed on fewer than 2,000 of each of the 720 regular cards in the '94 Stadium Club set. Inserted at the rate of one per 24 foil packs and one per 15 jumbo packs, the cards are otherwise identical to the regular TSC cards.

	MT
Complete Set (720):	2000.
Common Player:	2.00
Stars: 15x	
(See 1994 Stadium Club for checklist and base card values.)	

1994 Stadium Club Dugout Dirt

Cartoons of some of baseball's top stars are featured on the backs of this 12-card insert set. Fronts are virtually identical in format to regular S.C. cards, except the logo and box with the player's last name are in gold-foil, rather than red. Stated odds of finding a Dugout Dirt insert card were one per six packs, on average. Cards can also be found with a gold "Members Only" seal on front.

		MT
Complete Set (12):		12.00
Common Player:		.25
1	Mike Piazza (Catch of the Day)	2.00
2	Dave Winfield (The Road to 3,000)	.50
3	John Kruk (From Coal Mine to Gold Mine)	.25
4	Cal Ripken, Jr. (On Track)	3.00
5	Jack McDowell (Chin Music)	.25
6	Barry Bonds (The Bonds Market)	1.00
7	Ken Griffey, Jr. (Gold Gloves/All-Star)	4.00
8	Tim Salmon (The Salmon Run)	.35
9	Frank Thomas (Big Hurt)	2.00
10	Jeff Kent (Super Kent)	.25
11	Randy Johnson (High Heat)	.50
12	Darren Daulton (Daulton's Gym)	.25

1994 Stadium Club Finest

This insert set was included only in Series III packs of Topps Stadium Club, at the rate of one card per six packs, on average. Cards utilize Topps Finest technology and feature a player action photo on front, set against a red-and-gold sunburst background. Backs have a player portrait photo, a few stats and appropriate logos. Cards can also be found with a "Members Only" logo on front.

		MT
Complete Set (10):		25.00
Common Player:		1.00
1	Jeff Bagwell	2.50
2	Albert Belle	2.00
3	Barry Bonds	2.50
4	Juan Gonzalez	4.00
5	Ken Griffey, Jr.	10.00
6	Marquis Grissom	1.00
7	David Justice	1.00
8	Mike Piazza	5.00
9	Tim Salmon	1.50
10	Frank Thomas	4.00

1994 Stadium Club Finest Jumbo

Found only as a one per tub insert in special Wal-Mart repackaging of baseball packs, these 5" x 7" versions of the Series III Stadium Club inserts are identical to the smaller version. Cards utilize Topps Finest technology and feature a player action photo on front, set against a red-and-gold sunburst background. Backs have a player portrait photo, a few stats and appropriate logos.

		MT
Complete Set (10):		125.00
Common Player:		10.00
1	Jeff Bagwell	15.00
2	Albert Belle	12.00
3	Barry Bonds	15.00
4	Juan Gonzalez	15.00
5	Ken Griffey, Jr.	30.00
6	Marquis Grissom	10.00
7	David Justice	12.00
8	Mike Piazza	25.00
9	Tim Salmon	10.00
10	Frank Thomas	15.00

1994 Stadium Club Super Teams

With its football card issue the previous year, Topps Stadium Club debuted the idea of an insert card set whose value rose and fell with the on-field performance of each team.

Super Team cards were issued for each of the 28 major league teams and inserted at the rate of one per 24 regular packs and one per 15 jumbo packs. At the end of the 1995 season (the promotion was carried over when the 1994 season was ended prematurely by the players' strike), persons holding Super Team cards of the divisions winners, league champions and World Champions could redeem the cards for prizes. Division winning team cards could be redeemed for a set of 10 S.C. cards of that team with a special division winner embossed logo. League champion cards could be redeemed for a set of 10 Master Photos of the team with a special league logo embossed. Persons with a Super Team card of the eventual World Series champion could trade the card in for a complete set of Stadium Club cards embossed with a World's Champion logo. Each of the Super Team cards features a small group of players on the front with the Super Team Card and S.C. logos in gold foil, and the team name in prismatic foil. Backs contain redemption rules. A version of the Super Team cards was distributed with "Members Only" sets containing such an indicia on front and team roster on back.

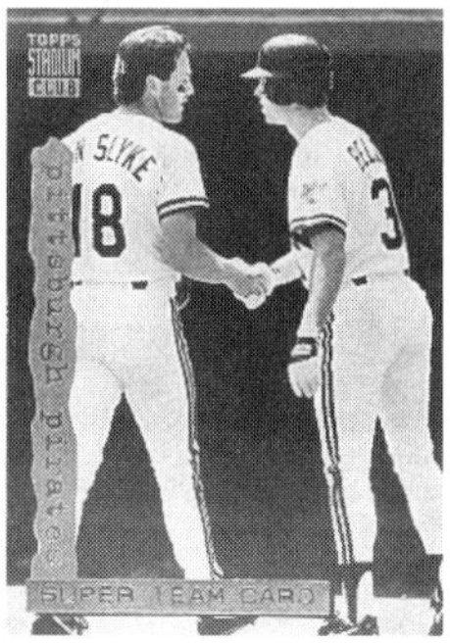

		MT
Complete Set (28):		50.00
Common Team:		1.50
Expired Jan. 31, 1996		
1	Atlanta Braves	10.00
2	Chicago Cubs	1.50
3	Cincinnati Reds	2.50
4	Colorado Rockies	2.00
5	Florida Marlins	1.50
6	Houston Astros	2.00
7	Los Angeles Dodgers	3.00
8	Montreal Expos	2.00
9	New York Mets	1.50
10	Philadelphia Phillies	1.50
11	Pittsburgh Pirates	1.50
12	St. Louis Cardinals	1.50
13	San Diego Padres	1.50
14	San Francisco Giants	2.50
15	Baltimore Orioles	2.50
16	Boston Red Sox	2.00
17	California Angels	1.50
18	Chicago White Sox	3.00
19	Cleveland Indians	4.00
20	Detroit Tigers	1.50
21	Kansas City Royals	2.00
22	Milwaukee Brewers	1.50
23	Minnesota Twins	2.00
24	New York Yankees	2.00
25	Oakland Athletics	2.00
26	Seattle Mariners	4.00
27	Texas Rangers	2.00
28	Toronto Blue Jays	2.00

1994 Stadium Club Members Only

This special gold-seal embossed version of the 1994 Topps Stadium Club set was available by a mail-in offer to club members for $230. The set includes all regular Stadium Club cards from Series I, II and III, along with the Dugout Dirt, Finest, and Super Teams insert cards. The Super Team cards, which were not eligible for the contest, have team rosters on back, rather than contest rules. All other cards are identical to the regular-issue S.C. cards except for the present of the 1/2" round gold-foil "Members Only" seal beneath or alongside of the red-foil Topps Stadium Club logo on front. There are two different checklists each numbered 269 and 270. Only 5,000 sets were produced.

	MT
Complete Set (770):	300.00
Common Player:	.50
Stars: 8X	
(See 1994 Stadium Club for checklist and base card values.)	

1994 Stadium Club Members Only Baseball

Available for purchase by Topps Stadium Club members as a 50-card boxed set (football and basketball sets were also available), this issue features top stars, performances and career highlights from the 1993 season. Cards feature borderless action photos on front with the Topps logo and player's last name in gold-foil. Backs are horizontal and feature a black background on which the player's achievement is detailed in blue and gold. A second player photo appears on the card back. Cards #46-50 were produced in the Topps Finest-style foil-printing technology.

		MT
Complete Set (50):		28.00
Common Player:		.25
1	Juan Gonzalez	1.50
2	Tom Henke	.25
3	John Kruk	.25
4	Paul Molitor	1.00
5	Dave Justice	.45
6	Rafael Palmeiro	.40
7	John Smoltz	.35
8	Matt Williams	.40
9	John Olerud	.40
10	Mark Grace	.40
11	Joe Carter	.25
12	Wilson Alvarez	.25
13	Lenny Dykstra	.25
14	Kevin Appier	.25
15	Andres Galarraga	.30
16	Mark Langston	.25
17	Ken Griffey, Jr.	4.00
18	Albert Belle	.75
19	Gregg Jefferies	.35
20	Duane Ward	.25
21	Jack McDowell	.25
22	Randy Johnson	.50
23	Tom Glavine	.35
24	Barry Bonds	1.50
25	Chuck Carr	.25
26	Ron Gant	.30
27	Kenny Lofton	.50
28	Mike Piazza	2.00
29	Frank Thomas	2.00
30	Fred McGriff	.45
31	Bryan Harvey	.25
32	John Burkett	.25
33	Roberto Alomar	.45
34	Cecil Fielder	.25
35	Marquis Grissom	.35
36	Randy Myers	.25
37	Tony Phillips	.25
38	Rickey Henderson	.40
39	Luis Polonia	.25
40	Jose Rijo	.25
41	Jeff Montgomery	.25
42	Greg Maddux	2.00
43	Tony Gwynn	1.50
44	Rod Beck	.25
45	Carlos Baerga	.25
46	Wil Cordero	.25
47	Tim Salmon	.50
48	Mike Lansing	.25
49	J.T. Snow	.40
50	Jeff Conine	.35

1994 Stadium Club Superstar Sampler

A small, round black-and-white "Topps Superstar Sampler" logo printed on the back is all that distinguishes these cards from regular-issue S.C. cards. This version of 45 of the top stars from the Stadium Club set was issued only in three-card cello packs inserted into 1994 Topps retail factory sets. The packs also contained the same player's cards from the Bowman and Finest sets, similarly marked.

		MT
Complete Set (45):		200.00
Common Player:		2.50
4	Gary Sheffield	3.50
10	Roberto Alomar	5.00
24	Jack McDowell	2.50
25	Cecil Fielder	2.50
36	Tim Salmon	3.00
59	Bobby Bonilla	2.50
85	Ken Griffey Jr.	25.00
94	Dave Justice	3.50
108	Jeff Bagwell	8.00
109	Gregg Jefferies	3.00
127	Cliff Floyd	2.50
140	Mike Piazza	15.00
151	Tony Gwynn	7.50
165	Len Dykstra	2.50
169	Carlos Baerga	2.50
171	Jose Canseco	6.00
195	Don Mattingly	10.00
203	Will Clark	3.50
208	Rafael Palmeiro	3.50
219	Albert Belle	5.00
228	John Olerud	3.00
238	Barry Bonds	10.00
280	Larry Walker	3.50
285	Frank Thomas	15.00
300	Joe Carter	2.50
320	Manny Ramirez	6.00
359	Kirby Puckett	7.50
373	Cal Ripken Jr.	20.00
[illegible]	Raul Mondesi	3.50
397	Ryne Sandberg	10.00
403	Mark Grace	4.50
414	Barry Larkin	3.00
419	Matt Williams	3.00
438	Randy Johnson	3.50
440	Mo Vaughn	3.00
450	Darren Daulton	2.50
454	Andres Galarraga	3.00
544	Greg Maddux	15.00
568	Juan Gonzalez	7.50
574	Tom Glavine	3.00
645	Paul Molitor	4.50
650	Roger Clemens	6.00
665	Fred McGriff	3.50
687	Andy Van Slyke	2.50
706	Marquis Grissom	2.50

1994 Stadium Club Draft Picks

Produced well after the end of the strike-truncated 1994 baseball season, this set was largely ignored by the hobby at the time of issue. The full-bleed card fronts feature up-close and personal poses of 1994's top draft picks in major league uniforms, giving the hobby a good first look at tomorrow's stars. A home plate design in an upper corner has "Draft '94 Pick" in gold-foil. The player's name is printed in gold foil down one of the sides. Backs are horizontally arranged and have a parti-colored background that includes standard scouting report phrases. There is another color portrait of the player at one end with his name and position printed above. At the opposite end are the team by which the player was drafted, a few biographical details, some amateur and pro career highlights and a box detailing how the team's other recent draft picks at that round have fared.

		MT
Complete Set (90):		22.00
Common Player:		.25
1	Jacob Shumate	.30
2	C.J. Nitkowski	.40
3	Doug Million	.25
4	Matt Smith	.35
5	Kevin Lovinger	.25
6	Alberto Castillo	.25
7	Mike Russell	.25
8	Dan Lock	.25
9	Tom Szimanski	.25
10	Aaron Boone	.45
11	Jayson Peterson	.25
12	Mark Johnson	.40
13	Cade Gaspar	.25
14	George Lombard	.75
15	Russ Johnson	.40
16	Travis Miller	.35
17	Jay Payton	.75
18	Brian Buchanan	.35
19	Jacob Cruz	.75
20	Gary Rath	.25
21	Ramon Castro	.25
22	Tommy Davis	.25
23	Tony Terry	.25
24	Jerry Whittaker	.25
25	Mike Darr	.50
26	Doug Webb	.25
27	Jason Camilli	.25
28	Brad Rigby	.25
29	Ryan Nye	.25
30	Carl Dale	.25
31	Andy Taulbee	.25
32	Trey Moore	.25
33	John Crowther	.25
34	Joe Giuliano	.25
35	Brian Rose	.25
36	Paul Failla	.25
37	Brian Meadows	.25
38	Oscar Robles	.25
39	Mike Metcalff	.25
40	Larry Barnes	.25
41	Paul Ottavinia	.25
42	Chris McBride	.25
43	Ricky Stone	.25
44	Billy Blythe	.25
45	Eddie Priest	.25
46	Scott Forster	.25
47	Eric Pickett	.25
48	Matt Beaumont	.25
49	Darrell Nicolas	.25
50	Mike Hampton	.25
51	Paul O'Malley	.25
52	Steve Shoemaker	.25
53	Jason Sikes	.25
54	Bryan Farson	.25
55	Yates Hall	.25
56	Troy Brohawn	.25
57	Dan Hower	.25
58	Clay Caruthers	.25
59	Pepe McNeal	.25
60	Ray Ricken	.25
61	Scott Shores	.25
62	Eddie Brooks	.25
63	Dave Kauflin	.25
64	David Meyer	.25
65	Geoff Blum	.25
66	Roy Marsh	.25
67	Ryan Beeney	.25
68	Derek Dukart	.25
69	Nomar Garciaparra	7.00
70	Jason Kelley	.25
71	Jesse Ibarra	.25
72	Bucky Buckles	.25
73	Mark Little	.25
74	Heath Murray	.25
75	Greg Morris	.25
76	Mike Halperin	.25
77	Wes Helms	.65
78	Ray Brown	.25
79	Kevin Brown	.65
80	Paul Konerko	1.00
81	Mike Thurman	.25
82	Paul Wilson	.65
83	Terrence Long	.50
84	Ben Grieve	2.00
85	Mark Farris	.25
86	Bret Wagner	.25
87	Dustin Hermanson	.60
88	Kevin Witt	.25
89	Corey Pointer	.25
90	Tim Grieve	.30

1994 Stadium Club Draft Picks First Day Issue

Identical to the regular-issue S.C. Draft Picks cards except for a silver-foil First Day Issue logo on front, this parallel set was found on the average of one card per six packs of S.C. Draft Picks.

	MT
Complete Set (90):	150.00
Common Player:	1.50
Stars: 6X	
(See 1994 Stadium Club Draft Picks for checklist and base card values.)	

1994 Team Stadium Club

Only 12 of the 28 major league teams are included in this special issue marketed in both team-set blister packs and foil packs at Wal-Mart stores around the country. Card fronts feature a player action photo bordered in the lower-right corner by a dark green mottled effect. The player's name, team and "Team Stadium Club" logo are in gold foil. Backs have a second player photo set against a background in mottled shades of green. There are a few stats and player biographical details.

		MT
Complete Set (360):		65.00
Common Player:		.15
1	Barry Bonds	2.00
2	Royce Clayton	.15
3	Kirt Manwaring	.15
4	J.R. Phillips	.15
5	Robby Thompson	.15
6	Willie McGee	.20
7	Steve Hosey	.15
8	Dave Burba	.15
9	Steve Scarsone	.15
10	Salomon Torres	.15
11	Bryan Hickerson	.15
12	Mike Benjamin	.15
13	Mark Carreon	.15
14	Rich Monteleone	.15
15	Dave Martinez	.15
16	Bill Swift	.15
17	Jeff Reed	.15
18	John Patterson	.15
19	Darren Lewis	.15
20	Mark Portugal	.15
21	Trevor Wilson	.15
22	Matt Williams	.60
23	Kevin Rogers	.15
24	Luis Mercedes	.15
25	Mike Jackson	.15
26	Steve Frey	.15
27	Tony Menendez	.15
28	John Burkett	.15
29	Todd Benzinger	.15
30	Rod Beck	.15
31	Greg Maddux	2.50
32	Steve Avery	.15
33	Milt Hill	.15
34	Charlie O'Brien	.15
35	John Smoltz	.30
36	Jarvis Brown	.15
37	Dave Gallagher	.15
38	Ryan Klesko	.40
39	Kent Mercker	.15
40	Terry Pendleton	.15
41	Ron Gant	.40
42	Pedro Borbon	.15
43	Steve Bedrosian	.15
44	Ramon Caraballo	.15
45	Tyler Houston	.15
46	Mark Lemke	.15
47	Fred McGriff	.75
48	Jose Oliva	.15
49	David Justice	1.00
50	Chipper Jones	3.00
51	Tony Tarasco	.15
52	Javy Lopez	.50
53	Mark Wohlers	.15
54	Deion Sanders	.60
55	Greg McMichael	.15
56	Tom Glavine	.25
57	Bill Pecota	.15
58	Mike Stanton	.15
59	Rafael Belliard	.15
60	Jeff Blauser	.15
61	Bryan Harvey	.15
62	Bret Barberie	.15
63	Rick Renteria	.15
64	Chris Hammond	.15
65	Pat Rapp	.15
66	Nigel Wilson	.15
67	Gary Sheffield	.75
68	Jerry Browne	.15
69	Charlie Hough	.15
70	Orestes Destrade	.15
71	Mario Diaz	.15
72	Ryan Bowen	.15
73	Carl Everett	.20
74	Richie Lewis	.15
75	Bob Natal	.15
76	Rich Rodriguez	.15
77	Darrell Whitmore	.15
78	Matt Turner	.15
79	Benny Santiago	.15
80	Robb Nen	.15
81	Dave Magadan	.15
82	Brian Drahman	.15
83	Mark Gardner	.15
84	Chuck Carr	.15
85	Alex Arias	.15
86	Kurt Abbott	.15
87	Joe Klink	.15
88	Jeff Mutis	.15
89	Dave Weathers	.15
90	Jeff Conine	.50
91	Andres Galarraga	.50
92	Vinny Castilla	.25
93	Roberto Mejia	.15
94	Darrell Sherman	.15
95	Mike Harkey	.15
96	Danny Sheaffer	.15
97	Pedro Castellano	.15
98	Walt Weiss	.15
99	Greg Harris	.15
100	Jayhawk Owens	.15
101	Bruce Ruffin	.15
102	Mike Munoz	.15
103	Armando Reynoso	.15
104	Eric Young	.15
105	Dante Bichette	.60
106	Marvin Freeman	.15
107	Joe Girardi	.20
108	Kent Bottenfield	.15
109	Howard Johnson	.15
110	Nelson Liriano	.15
111	David Nied	.15
112	Steve Reed	.15
113	Eric Wedge	.15
114	Charlie Hayes	.15
115	Ellis Burks	.20
116	Willie Blair	.15
117	Darren Holmes	.15
118	Curtis Leskanic	.15
119	Lance Painter	.15
120	Jim Tatum	.15
121	Frank Thomas	2.00
122	Jack McDowell	.15
123	Ron Karkovice	.15
124	Mike LaValliere	.15
125	Scott Radinsky	.15
126	Robin Ventura	.50
127	Scott Ruffcorn	.15
128	Steve Sax	.15
129	Roberto Hernandez	.15
130	Jose DeLeon	.15
131	Rod Bolton	.15
132	Wilson Alvarez	.15
133	Craig Grebeck	.15
134	Lance Johnson	.15
135	Kirk McCaskill	.15
136	Tim Raines	.25
137	Jeff Schwarz	.15
138	Warren Newson	.15
139	Norberto Martin	.15
140	Mike Huff	.15
141	Ozzie Guillen	.15
142	Alex Fernandez	.25
143	Joey Cora	.15
144	Jason Bere	.15
145	James Baldwin	.15
146	Esteban Beltre	.15
147	Julio Franco	.15
148	Matt Merullo	.15
149	Dan Pasqua	.15
150	Darrin Jackson	.15
151	Joe Carter	.15
152	Danny Cox	.15
153	Roberto Alomar	1.00
154	Woody Williams	.15
155	Duane Ward	.15
156	Ed Sprague	.15
157	Domingo Martinez	.15
158	Pat Hentgen	.15
159	Shawn Green	.35
160	Dick Schofield	.15
161	Paul Molitor	1.00
162	Darnell Coles	.15
163	Willie Canate	.15
164	Domingo Cedeno	.15
165	Pat Borders	.15
166	Greg Cadaret	.15
167	Tony Castillo	.15
168	Carlos Delgado	.50
169	Scott Brow	.15
170	Juan Guzman	.15
171	Al Leiter	.20
172	John Olerud	.30
173	Todd Stottlemyre	.25
174	Devon White	.25
175	Paul Spoljaric	.15
176	Randy Knorr	.15
177	Huck Flener	.15
178	Rob Butler	.15
179	Dave Stewart	.15
180	Mike Timlin	.15
181	Don Mattingly	2.00
182	Mark Hutton	.15
183	Mike Gallego	.15
184	Jim Abbott	.20
185	Paul Gibson	.15
186	Scott Kamieniecki	.15
187	Sam Horn	.15
188	Melido Perez	.15
189	Randy Velarde	.15
190	Gerald Williams	.20
191	Dave Silvestri	.15
192	Jim Leyritz	.15
193	Steve Howe	.15
194	Russ Davis	.15
195	Paul Assenmacher	.15
196	Pat Kelly	.15
197	Mike Stanley	.15
198	Bernie Williams	.75
199	Paul O'Neill	.30
200	Donn Pall	.15
201	Xavier Hernandez	.15
202	James Austin	.15
203	Sterling Hitchcock	.15
204	Wade Boggs	1.50
205	Jimmy Key	.15
206	Matt Nokes	.15
207	Terry Mulholland	.15
208	Luis Polonia	.15
209	Danny Tartabull	.15
210	Bob Wickman	.15
211	Len Dykstra	.15
212	Kim Batiste	.15
213	Tony Longmire	.15
214	Bobby Munoz	.15
215	Pete Incaviglia	.15
216	Doug Jones	.15
217	Mariano Duncan	.15
218	Jeff Juden	.15
219	Milt Thompson	.15
220	Dave West	.15
221	Roger Mason	.15
222	Tommy Greene	.15
223	Larry Andersen	.15
224	Jim Eisenreich	.15
225	Dave Hollins	.20
226	John Kruk	.15
227	Todd Pratt	.15
228	Ricky Jordan	.15
229	Curt Schilling	.20
230	Mike Williams	.15
231	Heathcliff Slocumb	.15
232	Ben Rivera	.15
233	Mike Lieberthal	.25
234	Mickey Morandini	.15
235	Danny Jackson	.15
236	Kevin Foster	.15
237	Darren Daulton	.15
238	Wes Chamberlain	.15
239	Tyler Green	.25
240	Kevin Stocker	.15
241	Juan Gonzalez	2.00
242	Rick Honeycutt	.15
243	Bruce Hurst	.15
244	Steve Dreyer	.15
245	Brian Bohanon	.15
246	Benji Gil	.15
247	Jon Shave	.15
248	Manuel Lee	.15
249	Donald Harris	.15
250	Jose Canseco	1.00
251	David Hulse	.15
252	Kenny Rogers	.15
253	Jeff Huson	.15
254	Dan Peltier	.15
255	Mike Scioscia	.15
256	Jack Armstrong	.15
257	Rob Ducey	.15
258	Will Clark	1.00
259	Cris Carpenter	.15
260	Kevin Brown	.35
261	Jeff Frye	.15
262	Jay Howell	.15
263	Roger Pavlik	.15
264	Gary Redus	.15
265	Ivan Rodriguez	.75
266	Matt Whiteside	.15
267	Doug Strange	.15
268	Billy Ripken	.15
269	Dean Palmer	.15
270	Tom Henke	.15
271	Cal Ripken Jr.	5.00
272	Mark McLemore	.15
273	Sid Fernandez	.15
274	Sherman Obando	.15
275	Paul Carey	.15
276	Mike Oquist	.15
277	Alan Mills	.15
278	Harold Baines	.20
279	Mike Mussina	.35
280	Arthur Rhodes	.15
281	Kevin McGehee	.15
282	Mark Eichhorn	.15
283	Damon Buford	.15
284	Ben McDonald	.15
285	David Segui	.15
286	Brad Pennington	.15
287	Jamie Moyer	.15
288	Chris Hoiles	.15
289	Mike Cook	.15
290	Brady Anderson	.30
291	Chris Sabo	.15
292	Jack Voigt	.15
293	Jim Poole	.15
294	Jeff Tackett	.15
295	Rafael Palmeiro	.60
296	Alex Ochoa	.25
297	John O'Donoghue	.15
298	Tim Hulett	.15
299	Mike Devereaux	.15
300	Manny Alexander	.15
301	Ozzie Smith	1.00
302	Omar Olivares	.15
303	Rheal Cormier	.15
304	Donovan Osborne	.15
305	Mark Whiten	.15
306	Todd Zeile	.25
307	Geronimo Pena	.15
308	Brian Jordan	.20
309	Luis Alicea	.15
310	Ray Lankford	.20
311	Stan Royer	.15
312	Bob Tewksbury	.15
313	Jose Oquendo	.15
314	Steve Dixon	.15
315	Rene Arocha	.15
316	Bernard Gilkey	.20
317	Gregg Jefferies	.35
318	Rob Murphy	.15
319	Tom Pagnozzi	.15
320	Mike Perez	.15
321	Tom Urbani	.15
322	Allen Watson	.15
323	Erik Pappas	.15
324	Paul Kilgus	.15
325	John Habyan	.15
326	Rod Brewer	.15
327	Rich Batchelor	.15
328	Tripp Cromer	.15
329	Gerald Perry	.15
330	Les Lancaster	.15
331	Ryne Sandberg	1.50
332	Derrick May	.15
333	Steve Buechele	.15
334	Willie Banks	.15
335	Larry Luebbers	.15
336	Tommy Shields	.15
337	Eric Yelding	.15
338	Rey Sanchez	.15
339	Mark Grace	.30
340	Jose Bautista	.15
341	Frank Castillo	.15
342	Jose Guzman	.15
343	Rafael Novoa	.15
344	Karl Rhodes	.15
345	Steve Trachsel	.20
346	Rick Wilkins	.15
347	Sammy Sosa	2.50
348	Kevin Roberson	.15
349	Mark Parent	.15
350	Randy Myers	.15
351	Glenallen Hill	.15
352	Lance Dickson	.15
353	Shawn Boskie	.15
354	Shawon Dunston	.15
355	Dan Plesac	.15
356	Jose Vizcaino	.15
357	Willie Wilson	.15
358	Turk Wendell	.15
359	Mike Morgan	.15
360	Jim Bullinger	.15

1994 Team Stadium Club 1st Day Issue

Each of the cards in the Stadium Club Team Series can be found with a speial embossed silver-foil "1st Day Issue" seal on front. Cards are otherwise identical to the regular issue.

	MT
Complete Set (360):	600.00
Common Player:	1.00
Stars: 8X	

(See 1994 Team Stadium Club for checklist and base card values.)

1994 Team Stadium Club Finest

One player from each of the 12 teams in the Stadium Club Team Series issue was printed in a chromium-metallic technology reminiscent of Topps Finest cards. These special cards are labeled "Team Stadium Club Finest." Other than the printing, the cards are in the same format as the rest of the issue.

		MT
Complete Set (12):		45.00
Common Player:		2.00
1	Roberto Alomar	2.50
2	Barry Bonds	5.00
3	Len Dykstra	2.00
4	Andres Galarraga	2.00
5	Juan Gonzalez	5.00
6	Dave Justice	3.00
7	Don Mattingly	4.00
8	Cal Ripken Jr.	7.50
9	Ryne Sandberg	4.00
10	Gary Sheffield	2.00
11	Ozzie Smith	4.00
12	Frank Thomas	4.00

1995 Stadium Club

Topps' upscale brand was issued for 1995 in three series of, respectively, 270, 225 and 135 cards. Fronts have borderless color photos with a gold-foil device at bottom holding the team logo. Also in gold are the player's name at bottom and the Stadium Club logo at top. Backs have another player photo at left with a pair of computer-enhanced close-ups above it. At right are bar graphs detailing the player's '94 stats and his skills rankings. A number of specially designed subsets - "Best Seat in the House, Cover Story, MLB Debut," etc., are spread throughout the issue, which also includes a full slate of chase cards depending on the series and packaging.

		MT
Complete Set (630):		55.00
Complete Series 1 (270):		20.00
Complete Series 2 (225):		20.00
Complete High Series (135):		15.00
Common Player:		.10
Series 1 or 2 Wax Box:		40.00
Series 3 Wax Box:		45.00
1	Cal Ripken Jr.	2.50
2	Bo Jackson	.15
3	Bryan Harvey	.10
4	Curt Schilling	.15
5	Bruce Ruffin	.10
6	Travis Fryman	.10
7	Jim Abbott	.10
8	David McCarty	.10
9	Gary Gaetti	.10
10	Roger Clemens	.75
11	Carlos Garcia	.10
12	Lee Smith	.10
13	Bobby Ayala	.10
14	Charles Nagy	.15
15	Lou Frazier	.10
16	Rene Arocha	.10
17	Carlos Delgado	.40
18	Steve Finley	.10
19	Ryan Klesko	.40
20	Cal Eldred	.10
21	Rey Sanchez	.10
22	Ken Hill	.10
23	Benny Santiago	.10
24	Julian Tavarez	.10
25	Jose Vizcaino	.10
26	Andy Benes	.10
27	Mariano Duncan	.10
28	Checklist A	.10
29	Shawon Dunston	.10
30	Rafael Palmeiro	.15
31	Dean Palmer	.10
32	Andres Galarraga	.15
33	Joey Cora	.10
34	Mickey Tettleton	.10
35	Barry Larkin	.15
36	Carlos Baerga	.10
37	Orel Hershiser	.15
38	Jody Reed	.10
39	Paul Molitor	.40
40	Jim Edmonds	.15
41	Bob Tewksbury	.10
42	John Patterson	.10
43	Ray McDavid	.10
44	Zane Smith	.10
45	Bret Saberhagen	.10
46	Greg Maddux	1.00
47	Frank Thomas	1.00
48	Carlos Baerga	.10

49	Billy Spiers	.10
50	Stan Javier	.10
51	Rex Hudler	.10
52	Denny Hocking	.10
53	Todd Worrell	.10
54	Mark Clark	.10
55	Hipilito Pichardo	.10
56	Bob Wickman	.10
57	Raul Mondesi	.50
58	Steve Cooke	.10
59	Rod Beck	.10
60	Tim Davis	.10
61	Jeff Kent	.10
62	John Valentin	.10
63	Alex Arias	.10
64	Steve Reed	.10
65	Ozzie Smith	.40
66	Terry Pendleton	.10
67	Kenny Rogers	.10
68	Vince Coleman	.10
69	Tom Pagnozzi	.10
70	Roberto Alomar	.75
71	Darrin Jackson	.10
72	Dennis Eckersley	.10
73	Jay Buhner	.10
74	Darren Lewis	.10
75	Dave Weathers	.10
76	Matt Walbeck	.10
77	Brad Ausmus	.10
78	Danny Bautista	.10
79	Bob Hamelin	.10
80	Steve Traschel	.20
81	Ken Ryan	.10
82	Chris Turner	.10
83	David Segui	.10
84	Ben McDonald	.10
85	Wade Boggs	.35
86	John Vander Wal	.10
87	Sandy Alomar	.15
88	Ron Karkovice	.10
89	Doug Jones	.10
90	Gary Sheffield	.25
91	Ken Caminiti	.15
92	Chris Bosio	.10
93	Kevin Tapani	.10
94	Walt Weiss	.10
95	Erik Hanson	.10
96	Ruben Sierra	.10
97	Nomar Garciaparra	2.50
98	Terrence Long	.10
99	Jacob Shumate	.10
100	Paul Wilson	.15
101	Kevin Witt	.10
102	Paul Konerko	2.50
103	Ben Grieve	3.00
104	*Mark Johnson*	.25
105	*Cade Gaspar*	.10
106	Mark Farris	.10
107	Dustin Hermanson	.15
108	*Scott Elarton*	.35
109	Doug Million	.10
110	Matt Smith	.10
111	*Brian Buchanan*	.20
112	*Jayson Peterson*	.20
113	Bret Wagner	.10
114	C.J. Nitkowski	.15
115	*Ramon Castro*	.15
116	Rafael Bournigal	.10
117	Jeff Fassero	.10
118	Bobby Bonilla	.10
119	Ricky Gutierrez	.10
120	Roger Pavlik	.10
121	Mike Greenwell	.10
122	Deion Sanders	.20
123	Charlie Hayes	.10
124	Paul O'Neill	.15
125	Jay Bell	.10
126	Royce Clayton	.10
127	Willie Banks	.10
128	Mark Wohlers	.10
129	Todd Jones	.10
130	Todd Stottlemyre	.10
131	Will Clark	.30
132	Wilson Alvarez	.10
133	Chili Davis	.10
134	Dave Burba	.10
135	Chris Hoiles	.10
136	Jeff Blauser	.10
137	Jeff Reboulet	.10
138	Bret Saberhagen	.10
139	Kirk Rueter	.10
140	Dave Nilsson	.10
141	Pat Borders	.10
142	Ron Darling	.10
143	Derek Bell	.10
144	Dave Hollins	.10
145	Juan Gonzalez	1.25
146	Andre Dawson	.15
147	Jim Thome	.15
148	Larry Walker	.20
149	Mike Piazza	1.75
150	Mike Perez	.10
151	Steve Avery	.10
152	Dan Wilson	.10
153	Andy Van Slyke	.10
154	Junior Felix	.10
155	Jack McDowell	.10
156	Danny Tartabull	.10
157	Willie Blair	.10
158	William Van Landingham	.10
159	Robb Nen	.10
160	Lee Tinsley	.10
161	Ismael Valdes	.10
162	Juan Guzman	.10
163	Scott Servais	.10
164	Cliff Floyd	.15
165	Allen Watson	.10
166	Eddie Taubensee	.10
167	Scott Hemond	.10
168	Jeff Tackett	.10
169	Chad Curtis	.10
170	Rico Brogna	.10
171	Luis Polonia	.10
172	Checklist B	.10
173	Lance Johnson	.10
174	Sammy Sosa	1.50
175	Mike MacFarlane	.10
176	Darryl Hamilton	.10
177	Rick Aguilera	.10
178	Dave West	.10
179	Mike Gallego	.10
180	Marc Newfield	.10
181	Steve Buechele	.10
182	David Wells	.10
183	Tom Glavine	.15
184	Joe Girardi	.10
185	Craig Biggio	.25
186	Eddie Murray	.25
187	Kevin Gross	.10
188	Sid Fernandez	.10
189	John Franco	.10
190	Bernard Gilkey	.15
191	Matt Williams	.35
192	Darrin Fletcher	.10
193	Jeff Conine	.10
194	Ed Sprague	.10
195	Eduardo Perez	.10
196	Scott Livingstone	.10
197	Ivan Rodriguez	.75
198	Orlando Merced	.10
199	Ricky Bones	.10
200	Javier Lopez	.20
201	Miguel Jimenez	.10
202	Terry McGriff	.10
203	Mike Lieberthal	.15
204	David Cone	.15
205	Todd Hundley	.15
206	Ozzie Guillen	.10
207	Alex Cole	.10
208	Tony Phillips	.10
209	Jim Eisenreich	.10
210	Greg Vaughn	.15
211	Barry Larkin	.15
212	Don Mattingly	.50
213	Mark Grace	.15
214	Jose Canseco	.35
215	Joe Carter	.10
216	David Cone	.15
217	Sandy Alomar	.15
218	Al Martin	.10
219	Roberto Kelly	.10
220	Paul Sorrento	.10
221	Tony Fernandez	.10
222	Stan Belinda	.10
223	Mike Stanley	.10
224	Doug Drabek	.10
225	Todd Van Poppel	.10
226	Matt Mieske	.10
227	Tino Martinez	.15
228	Andy Ashby	.10
229	Midre Cummings	.10
230	Jeff Frye	.10
231	Hal Morris	.10
232	Jose Lind	.10
233	Shawn Green	.20
234	Rafael Belliard	.10
235	Randy Myers	.10
236	Frank Thomas	1.50
237	Darren Daulton	.10
238	Sammy Sosa	.75
239	Cal Ripken Jr.	2.00
240	Jeff Bagwell	.60
241	Ken Griffey Jr.	3.00
242	Brett Butler	.10
243	Derrick May	.10
244	Pat Listach	.10
245	Mike Bordick	.10
246	Mark Langston	.10
247	Randy Velarde	.10
248	Julio Franco	.10
249	Chuck Knoblauch	.15
250	Bill Gullickson	.10
251	Dave Henderson	.10
252	Bret Boone	.10
253	Al Martin	.10
254	Armando Benitez	.10
255	Wil Cordero	.10
256	Al Leiter	.10
257	Luis Gonzalez	.10
258	Charlie O'Brien	.10
259	Tim Wallach	.10
260	Scott Sanders	.10
261	Tom Henke	.10
262	Otis Nixon	.10
263	Darren Daulton	.10
264	Manny Ramirez	1.00
265	Bret Barberie	.10
266	Mel Rojas	.10
267	John Burkett	.10
268	Brady Anderson	.20
269	John Roper	.10
270	Shane Reynolds	.10
271	Barry Bonds	.75
272	Alex Fernandez	.10
273	Brian McRae	.10
274	Todd Zeile	.10
275	Greg Swindell	.10
276	Johnny Ruffin	.10
277	Troy Neel	.10
278	Eric Karros	.10
279	John Hudek	.10
280	Thomas Howard	.10
281	Joe Carter	.10
282	Mike Devereaux	.10
283	Butch Henry	.10
284	Reggie Jefferson	.10
285	Mark Lemke	.10
286	Jeff Montgomery	.10
287	Ryan Thompson	.10
288	Paul Shuey	.10
289	Mark McGwire	3.00
290	Bernie Williams	.50
291	Mickey Morandini	.10
292	Scott Leius	.10
293	David Hulse	.10
294	Greg Gagne	.10
295	Moises Alou	.15
296	Geronimo Berroa	.10
297	Eddie Zambrano	.10
298	Alan Trammell	.15
299	Don Slaught	.10
300	Jose Rijo	.10
301	Joe Ausanio	.10
302	Tim Raines	.10
303	Melido Perez	.10
304	Kent Mercker	.10
305	James Mouton	.10
306	Luis Lopez	.10
307	Mike Kingery	.10
308	Willie Greene	.10
309	Cecil Fielder	.10
310	Scott Kamieniecki	.10
311	Mike Greenwell (Best Seat in the House)	.10
312	Bobby Bonilla (Best Seat in the House)	.10
313	Andres Galarraga (Best Seat in the House)	.10
314	Cal Ripken Jr. (Best Seat in the House)	1.25
315	Matt Williams (Best Seat in the House)	.25
316	Tom Pagnozzi (Best Seat in the House)	.10
317	Len Dykstra (Best Seat in the House)	.10
318	Frank Thomas (Best Seat in the House)	.75
319	Kirby Puckett (Best Seat in the House)	.75
320	Mike Piazza (Best Seat in the House)	.75
321	Jason Jacome	.10
322	Brian Hunter	.10
323	Brent Gates	.10
324	Jim Converse	.10
325	Damion Easley	.10
326	Dante Bichette	.15
327	Kurt Abbott	.10
328	Scott Cooper	.10
329	Mike Henneman	.10
330	Orlando Miller	.10
331	John Kruk	.10
332	Jose Oliva	.10
333	Reggie Sanders	.10
334	Omar Vizquel	.10
335	Devon White	.10
336	Mike Morgan	.10
337	J.R. Phillips	.10
338	Gary DiSarcina	.10
339	Joey Hamilton	.15
340	Randy Johnson	.40
341	Jim Leyritz	.10
342	Bobby Jones	.10
343	Jaime Navarro	.10
344	Bip Roberts	.10
345	Steve Karsay	.10
346	Kevin Stocker	.10
347	Jose Canseco	.30
348	Bill Wegman	.10
349	Rondell White	.20
350	Mo Vaughn	.45
351	Joe Orsulak	.10
352	Pat Meares	.10
353	Albie Lopez	.10
354	Edgar Martinez	.10
355	Brian Jordan	.10
356	Tommy Greene	.10
357	Chuck Carr	.10
358	Pedro Astacio	.10
359	Russ Davis	.10
360	Chris Hammond	.10
361	Gregg Jefferies	.10
362	Shane Mack	.10
363	Fred McGriff	.30
364	Pat Rapp	.10
365	Bill Swift	.10
366	Checklist	.10
367	Robin Ventura	.15
368	Bobby Witt	.10
369	Karl Rhodes	.10
370	Eddie Williams	.10
371	John Jaha	.10
372	Steve Howe	.10
373	Leo Gomez	.10
374	Hector Fajardo	.10
375	Jeff Bagwell	.75
376	Mark Acre	.10
377	Wayne Kirby	.10
378	Mark Portugal	.10
379	Jesus Tavarez	.10
380	Jim Lindeman	.10
381	Don Mattingly	1.00
382	Trevor Hoffman	.15
383	Chris Gomez	.10
384	Garret Anderson	.10
385	Bobby Munoz	.10
386	Jon Lieber	.10
387	Rick Helling	.10
388	Marvin Freeman	.10
389	Juan Castillo	.10
390	Jeff Cirillo	.10
391	Sean Berry	.10
392	Hector Carrasco	.10
393	Mark Grace	.20
394	Pat Kelly	.10
395	Tim Naehring	.10
396	Greg Pirkl	.10
397	John Smoltz	.15
398	Robby Thompson	.10
399	Rick White	.10
400	Frank Thomas	1.50
401	Jeff Conine Cover Story)	.10
402	Jose Valentin (Cover Story)	.10
403	Carlos Baerga (Cover Story)	.10
404	Rick Aguilera (Cover Story)	.10
405	Wilson Alvarez (Cover Story)	.10
406	Juan Gonzalez (Cover Story)	.50
407	Barry Larkin (Cover Story)	.10
408	Ken Hill (Cover Story)	.10
409	Chuck Carr (Cover Story)	.10
410	Tim Raines (Cover Story)	.10
411	Bryan Eversgerd	.10
412	Phil Plantier	.10
413	Josias Manzanillo	.10
414	Roberto Kelly	.10
415	Rickey Henderson	.30
416	John Smiley	.10
417	Kevin Brown	.10
418	Jimmy Key	.10
419	Wally Joyner	.15
420	Roberto Hernandez	.10
421	Felix Fermin	.10
422	Checklist	.10
423	Greg Vaughn	.15
424	Ray Lankford	.15
425	Greg Maddux	2.00
426	Mike Mussina	.40
427	Geronimo Pena	.10
428	David Nied	.10
429	Scott Erickson	.10
430	Kevin Mitchell	.10
431	Mike Lansing	.10
432	Brian Anderson	.15
433	Jeff King	.10
434	Ramon Martinez	.15
435	Kevin Seitzer	.10
436	Salomon Torres	.10
437	Brian Hunter	.10
438	Melvin Nieves	.10
439	Mike Kelly	.10
440	Marquis Grissom	.10
441	Chuck Finley	.10
442	Len Dykstra	.10
443	Ellis Burks	.10
444	Harold Baines	.10
445	Kevin Appier	.10
446	Dave Justice	.20
447	Darryl Kile	.10
448	John Olerud	.15
449	Greg McMichael	.10
450	Kirby Puckett	1.00
451	Jose Valentin	.10
452	Rick Wilkins	.10
453	Arthur Rhodes	.10
454	Pat Hentgen	.10
455	Tom Gordon	.10
456	Tom Candiotti	.10
457	Jason Bere	.10
458	Wes Chamberlain	.10
459	Greg Colbrunn	.10
460	John Doherty	.10
461	Kevin Foster	.10
462	Mark Whiten	.10
463	Terry Steinbach	.10
464	Aaron Sele	.15
465	Kirt Manwaring	.10
466	Darren Hall	.10
467	Delino DeShields	.10
468	Andujar Cedeno	.10
469	Billy Ashley	.10
470	Kenny Lofton	.50
471	Pedro Munoz	.10
472	John Wetteland	.10
473	Tim Salmon	.20
474	Denny Neagle	.10
475	Tony Gwynn	1.00
476	Vinny Castilla	.10
477	Steve Dreyer	.10
478	Jeff Shaw	.10
479	Chad Ogea	.10
480	Scott Ruffcorn	.10
481	Lou Whitaker	.10
482	J.T. Snow	.10
483	Rich Rowland	.10
484	Dennis Martinez	.10
485	Pedro Martinez	.35
486	Rusty Greer	.10
487	Dave Fleming	.10
488	John Dettmer	.10
489	Albert Belle	.75
490	Ravelo Manzanillo	.10
491	Henry Rodriguez	.10
492	Andrew Lorraine	.15
493	Dwayne Hosey	.10
494	Mike Blowers	.10
495	Turner Ward	.10
496	Fred McGriff (Extreme Corps)	.20
497	Sammy Sosa (Extreme Corps)	.75
498	Barry Larkin (Extreme Corps)	.10
499	Andres Galarraga (Extreme Corps)	.10
500	Gary Sheffield (Extreme Corps)	.10
501	Jeff Bagwell (Extreme Corps)	.40
502	Mike Piazza (Extreme Corps)	.60
503	Moises Alou (Extreme Corps)	.10
504	Bobby Bonilla (Extreme Corps)	.10
505	Darren Daulton (Extreme Corps)	.10
506	Jeff King (Extreme Corps)	.10
507	Ray Lankford (Extreme Corps)	.10
508	Tony Gwynn (Extreme Corps)	.50
509	Barry Bonds (Extreme Corps)	.35
510	Cal Ripken Jr. (Extreme Corps)	1.25
511	Mo Vaughn (Extreme Corps)	.30
512	Tim Salmon (Extreme Corps)	.10
513	Frank Thomas (Extreme Corps)	.75
514	Albert Belle (Extreme Corps)	.40
515	Cecil Fielder (Extreme Corps)	.10
516	Kevin Appier (Extreme Corps)	.10
517	Greg Vaughn (Extreme Corps)	.10
518	Kirby Puckett (Extreme Corps)	.50
519	Paul O'Neill (Extreme Corps)	.10
520	Ruben Sierra (Extreme Corps)	.10
521	Ken Griffey Jr. (Extreme Corps)	1.25
522	Will Clark (Extreme Corps)	.25
523	Joe Carter (Extreme Corps)	.10
524	Antonio Osuna	.10
525	Glenallen Hill	.10
526	Alex Gonzalez	.10
527	Dave Stewart	.10
528	Ron Gant	.15
529	Jason Bates	.10
530	Mike Macfarlane	.10
531	Esteban Loaiza	.15
532	Joe Randa	.10
533	Dave Winfield	.25
534	Danny Darwin	.10
535	Pete Harnisch	.10
536	Joey Cora	.10
537	Jaime Navarro	.10
538	Marty Cordova	.15
539	Andujar Cedeno	.10
540	Mickey Tettleton	.10
541	Andy Van Slyke	.10
542	*Carlos Perez*	.20
543	Chipper Jones	2.00
544	Tony Fernandez	.10
545	Tom Henke	.10
546	Pat Borders	.10
547	Chad Curtis	.10
548	Ray Durham	.15
549	Joe Oliver	.10
550	Jose Mesa	.10
551	Steve Finley	.10
552	Otis Nixon	.10
553	Jacob Brumfield	.10
554	Bill Swift	.10
555	Quilvio Veras	.10
556	*Hideo Nomo*	3.00
557	Joe Vitiello	.10
558	Mike Perez	.10
559	Charlie Hayes	.10
560	*Brad Radke*	.20
561	Darren Bragg	.10
562	Orel Hershiser	.15
563	Edgardo Alfonzo	.15
564	Doug Jones	.10
565	Andy Pettitte	.75
566	Benito Santiago	.10
567	John Burkett	.10
568	Brad Clontz	.10
569	Jim Abbott	.10
570	Joe Rosselli	.10
571	*Mark Grudzielanek*	.75
572	Dustin Hermanson	.10
573	Benji Gil	.10
574	Mark Whiten	.10
575	Mike Ignasiak	.10
576	Kevin Ritz	.10
577	Paul Quantrill	.10
578	Andre Dawson	.15
579	Jerald Clark	.10
580	Frank Rodriguez	.10
581	Mark Kiefer	.10
582	Trevor Wilson	.10
583	*Gary Wilson*	.10
584	Andy Stankiewicz	.10
585	Felipe Lira	.10
586	*Mike Mimbs*	.15
587	Jon Nunnally	.10
588	*Tomas Perez*	.15
589	Checklist	.10

590	Todd Hollandsworth	.15
591	Roberto Petagine	.10
592	Mariano Rivera	.10
593	Mark McLemore	.10
594	Bobby Witt	.10
595	Jose Offerman	.10
596	Jason Christiansen	.10
597	Jeff Manto	.10
598	Jim Dougherty	.10
599	Juan Acevedo	.10
600	Troy O'Leary	.10
601	Ron Villone	.10
602	Tripp Cromer	.10
603	Steve Scarsone	.10
604	Lance Parrish	.10
605	Ozzie Timmons	.10
606	Ray Holbert	.10
607	Tony Phillips	.10
608	Phil Plantier	.10
609	Shane Andrews	.10
610	Heathcliff Slocumb	.10
611	*Bobby Higginson*	1.50
612	Bob Tewksbury	.10
613	Terry Pendleton	.10
614	Scott Cooper (Trans-Action)	.10
615	John Wetteland (Trans-Action)	.10
616	Ken Hill (Trans-Action)	.10
617	Marquis Grissom (Trans-Action)	.10
618	Larry Walker (Trans-Action)	.25
619	Derek Bell (Trans-Action)	.10
620	David Cone (Trans-Action)	.10
621	Ken Caminiti (Trans-Action)	.10
622	Jack McDowell (Trans-Action)	.10
623	Vaughn Eshelman (Trans-Action)	.10
624	Brian McRae (Trans-Action)	.10
625	Gregg Jefferies (Trans-Action)	.10
626	Kevin Brown (Trans-Action)	.10
627	Lee Smith (Trans-Action)	.10
628	Tony Tarasco (Trans-Action)	.10
629	Brett Butler (Trans-Action)	.10
630	Jose Canseco (Trans-Action)	.35

1995 Stadium Club 1st Day Pre-production

Stadium Club 1st Day Pre-production cards were randomly packed into one every 36 packs of Topps Series I baseball. The set of nine cards is only found in hobby packs.

		MT
Complete Set (9):		34.00
Common Player:		3.00
29	Shawon Dunston	2.00
39	Paul Molitor	7.50
79	Bob Hamelin	2.00
96	Ruben Sierra	2.00
131	Will Clark	4.00
149	Mike Piazza	12.00
153	Andy Van Slyke	2.00
166	Jeff Tackett	2.00
197	Ivan Rodriguez	6.00

1995 Stadium Club 1st Day Issue

Series II hobby packs of Topps baseball featured a chase set of Stadium Club 1st Day Issue cards, #1-270. The FDI cards have a small gold embossed seal on front. Cards were seeded on an average of one per six packs. Ten FDI cards were also randomly inserted in each Factory set.

	MT
Complete Set (270):	225.00
Common Player:	.50
Stars: 10X	

(See 1995 Stadium Club #1-270 for checklist and base card values.)

1995 Stadium Club Clear Cut

Among the most technically advanced of 1995's insert cards is the Clear Cut chase set found in Series I and II packs. Cards feature a color player action photo printed on see-through plastic. There is a rainbow-hued trapezoid behind the player with an overall background tinted in blue, green and gold. The player's name is in white in a vertical blue bar at right. Backs have a few stats and data in a blue bar vertically at left. Each of the cards can also be found in a version with the round Members Only seal embossed into the plastic at lower left.

		MT
Complete Set (28):		80.00
Common Player:		1.00
1	Mike Piazza	8.00
2	Ruben Sierra	1.00
3	Tony Gwynn	6.50
4	Frank Thomas	8.00
5	Fred McGriff	2.50
6	Rafael Palmeiro	2.00
7	Bobby Bonilla	1.00
8	Chili Davis	1.00
9	Hal Morris	1.00
10	Jose Canseco	2.00
11	Jay Bell	1.00
12	Kirby Puckett	6.50
13	Gary Sheffield	2.00
14	Bob Hamelin	1.00
15	Jeff Bagwell	6.50
16	Albert Belle	4.50
17	Sammy Sosa	12.00
18	Ken Griffey Jr.	15.00
19	Todd Zeile	1.00
20	Mo Vaughn	1.50
21	Moises Alou	1.25
22	Paul O'Neill	1.50
23	Andres Galarraga	1.25
24	Greg Vaughn	1.00
25	Len Dykstra	1.00
26	Joe Carter	1.00
27	Barry Bonds	4.50
28	Cecil Fielder	1.00

1995 Stadium Club Crunch Time

Series I rack packs were the exclusive provenance of these cards featuring baseball's top run creators. Fronts are printed on rainbow prismatic foil. The central color action photo is repeated as an enlarged background photo, along with a team logo. At bottom in gold foil are the player name and Crunch Time logo. Backs have a positive and a negative image of the same photo as background to a pie chart and stats relative to the player's runs-created stats.

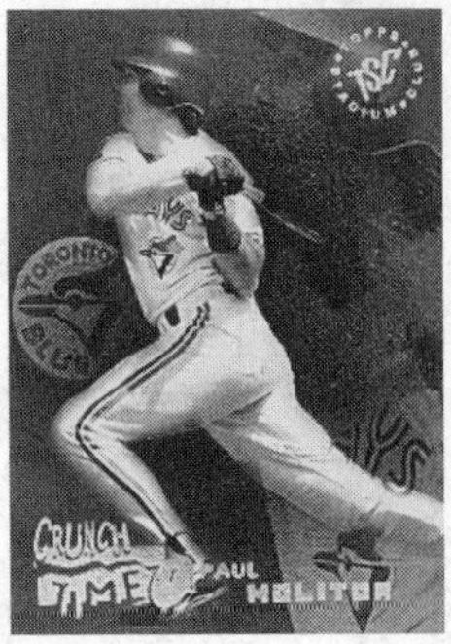

		MT
Complete Set (20):		30.00
Common Player:		1.00
1	Jeff Bagwell	2.50
2	Kirby Puckett	3.00
3	Frank Thomas	4.00
4	Albert Belle	2.00
5	Julio Franco	1.00
6	Jose Canseco	1.50
7	Paul Molitor	2.00
8	Joe Carter	1.00
9	Ken Griffey Jr.	8.00
10	Larry Walker	1.50
11	Dante Bichette	1.50
12	Carlos Baerga	1.00
13	Fred McGriff	1.50
14	Ruben Sierra	1.00
15	Will Clark	1.50
16	Moises Alou	1.00
17	Rafael Palmeiro	1.50
18	Travis Fryman	1.00
19	Barry Bonds	2.50
20	Cal Ripken Jr.	6.00

1995 Stadium Club Crystal Ball

Multi-colored swirls around a clear central circle with the player's photo, all printed on foil, are the front design for this Series III insert. Backs have a portrait photo in a floating crystal ball image at one side. At the other end are year-by-year minor league stats and a few words about each of the player's seasons. This insert was also produced in an edition of 4,000 bearing a gold-foil "Members Only" seal, sold in complete Stadium Club Members Only factory sets.

		MT
Complete Set (15):		55.00
Common Player:		2.00
1	Chipper Jones	16.00
2	Dustin Hermanson	2.00
3	Ray Durham	3.00
4	Phil Nevin	2.00
5	Billy Ashley	2.00
6	Shawn Green	6.00
7	Jason Bates	2.00
8	Benji Gil	2.00
9	Marty Cordova	4.00
10	Quilvio Veras	2.00
11	Mark Grudzielanek	4.00
12	Ruben Rivera	4.00
13	Bill Pulsipher	2.00
14	Derek Jeter	20.00
15	LaTroy Hawkins	2.00

1995 Stadium Club Power Zone

The performance in several parks around the league is chronicled on the back of these Series III inserts. Fronts are printed on foil and feature a player swinging into an exploding asteroid. His name is printed vertically down one side in prismatic glitter foil. Backs also have a portrait photo and a baseball with a weird red and green vapor trail. A special edition of 4,000 each of these inserts was included with the purchase of Stadium Club Members Only factory sets; those cards have an embossed gold-foil seal on front.

		MT
Complete Set (12):		55.00
Common Player:		1.50
1	Jeff Bagwell	6.00
2	Albert Belle	5.00
3	Barry Bonds	5.00
4	Joe Carter	1.50
5	Cecil Fielder	1.50
6	Andres Galarraga	1.50
7	Ken Griffey Jr.	15.00
8	Paul Molitor	3.00
9	Fred McGriff	2.00
10	Rafael Palmeiro	1.50
11	Frank Thomas	6.00
12	Matt Williams	1.50

1995 Stadium Club Ring Leaders

With a background that looks like an explosion at a jewelry factory, these cards feature players who have won championship, All-Star or other award rings. Fronts are foil-printed with a player action photo on a background of flying rings and stars, and, - for some reason - an attacking eagle. Backs repeat the background motif, have a player portrait in an oval frame at top-left, photos of some of his rings and a list of rings won. Cards were random inserts in both Series I and II; complete sets could also be won in Stadium Club's phone card insert contest. A version with the Members Only gold seal was also issued for each.

		MT
Complete Set (40):		165.00
Common Player:		1.25
1	Jeff Bagwell	9.00
2	Mark McGwire	20.00
3	Ozzie Smith	5.00
4	Paul Molitor	5.00
5	Darryl Strawberry	1.50
6	Eddie Murray	3.00
7	Tony Gwynn	9.00
8	Jose Canseco	3.00
9	Howard Johnson	1.25
10	Andre Dawson	1.25
11	Matt Williams	2.00
12	Tim Raines	1.25
13	Fred McGriff	2.00
14	Ken Griffey Jr.	20.00
15	Gary Sheffield	2.00
16	Dennis Eckersley	1.25
17	Kevin Mitchell	1.25
18	Will Clark	1.75
19	Darren Daulton	1.25
20	Paul O'Neill	1.50
21	Julio Franco	1.25
22	Albert Belle	6.00
23	Juan Gonzalez	12.00
24	Kirby Puckett	9.00
25	Joe Carter	1.25
26	Frank Thomas	10.00
27	Cal Ripken Jr.	17.50
28	John Olerud	2.00
29	Ruben Sierra	1.25
30	Barry Bonds	5.00
31	Cecil Fielder	1.25
32	Roger Clemens	5.00
33	Don Mattingly	12.00
34	Terry Pendleton	1.25
35	Rickey Henderson	2.50
36	Dave Winfield	2.50
37	Edgar Martinez	1.25
38	Wade Boggs	3.00
39	Willie McGee	1.25
40	Andres Galarraga	1.25

1995 Stadium Club Ring Leaders Phone Cards

An interactive contest carrying through the "Ring Leaders" insert card set theme featured randomly inserted phone cards picturing All-Star Game players' rings. The 2-1/8" x 3/-3/8" plastic cards could be found in regular, silver and gold editions. By using the card for a long distance call, the holder could determine if it was a further winner. Regular card winners received a set of Stadium Club Ring Leaders insert cards. Winners on a silver card received a complete set of the 13 different phone cards in all three versions. Gold card winners received the genuine All-Star ring pictured on the card. Approximately 217,000 phone cards were inserted in the program; odds of finding a regular card were about one per 40 packs; silver, one per 237 packs, and, gold, one per 2,955 packs. Cards picturing the 1988 and 1989 All-Star rings were not issued. Phone cards with the number panel on back scratched off are worth 40-60% of values quoted.

		MT
Complete Set, Regular:		20.00
Complete Set, Silver:		65.00
Complete Set, Gold:		175.00
Common Card, Regular:		2.00
Common Card, Silver:		7.00
Common Card, Gold:		15.00
(1)	1980 All-Star Game, Los Angeles	2.00
(1s)	1980 All-Star Game, Los Angeles (silver)	7.00
(1g)	1980 All-Star Game, Los Angeles (gold)	15.00
(2)	1981 All-Star Game, Cleveland	2.00
(2s)	1981 All-Star Game, Cleveland (silver)	7.00
(2g)	1981 All-Star Game, Cleveland (gold)	15.00
(3)	1982 All-Star Game, Montreal	2.00
(3s)	1982 All-Star Game, Montreal (silver)	7.00
(3g)	1982 All-Star Game, Montreal (gold)	15.00
(4)	1983 All-Star Game, Chicago A.L.	2.00
(4s)	1983 All-Star Game, Chicago A.L. (silver)	7.00
(4g)	1983 All-Star Game, Chicago A.L. (gold)	15.00
(5)	1984 All-Star Game, San Francisco	2.00
(5s)	1984 All-Star Game, San Francisco (silver)	7.00

(5g)	1984 All-Star Game, San Francisco (gold)	15.00
(6)	1985 All-Star Game, Minneapolis	2.00
(6s)	1985 All-Star Game, Minneapolis (silver)	7.00
(6g)	1985 All-Star Game, Minneapolis (gold)	15.00
(7)	1986 All-Star Game, Houston	2.00
(7s)	1986 All-Star Game, Houston (silver)	7.00
(7g)	1986 All-Star Game, Houston (gold)	15.00
(8)	1987 All-Star Game, Oakland	2.00
(8s)	1987 All-Star Game, Oakland (silver)	7.00
(8g)	1987 All-Star Game, Oakland (gold)	15.00
(9)	1990 All-Star Game, Chicago N.L.	2.00
(9s)	1990 All-Star Game Chicago N.L. (silver)	7.00
(9g)	1990 All-Star Game, Chicago N.L. (gold)	15.00
(10)	1991 All-Star Game, Toronto	2.00
(10s)	1991 All-Star Game, Toronto (silver)	7.00
(10g)	1991 All-Star Game, Toronto (gold)	15.00
(11)	1992 All-Star Game, San Diego	2.00
(11s)	1992 All-Star Game, San Diego (silver)	7.00
(11g)	1992 All-Star Game, San Diego (gold)	15.00
(12)	1993 All-Star Game, Baltimore	2.00
(12s)	1993 All-Star Game, Baltimore (silver)	7.00
(12g)	1993 All-Star Game, Baltimore (gold)	15.00
(13)	1994 All-Star Game, Pittsburgh	2.00
(13s)	1994 All-Star Game, Pittsburgh (silver)	7.00
(13g)	1994 All-Star Game, Pittsburgh (gold)	15.00

1995 Stadium Club Super Skills

These random hobby pack inserts in both Series I and II are printed on rainbow prismatic foil which features as a background an enlarged version of the front photo. The S.C. and Super Skills logos are printed in gold foil in opposite corners, while the player's name is in blue at bottom-right. Backs repeat the enlarged background image of a close-up foreground photo, while a few choice words about the player's particular specialties are in white at left. Each card can also be found in a version featuring the Members Only gold-foil seal on front.

		MT
Complete Set (20):		55.00
Complete Series 1 (9):		25.00
Complete Series 2 (11):		30.00
Common Player:		1.50
1	Roberto Alomar	5.00
2	Barry Bonds	7.50
3	Jay Buhner	2.00
4	Chuck Carr	1.50
5	Don Mattingly	10.00
6	Raul Mondesi	3.00
7	Tim Salmon	2.00
8	Deion Sanders	2.50
9	Devon White	1.50
10	Mark Whiten	1.50
11	Ken Griffey Jr.	25.00
12	Marquis Grissom	2.00
13	Paul O'Neill	2.00
14	Kenny Lofton	3.00
15	Larry Walker	2.50
16	Scott Cooper	1.50
17	Barry Larkin	2.00
18	Matt Williams	2.00
19	John Wetteland	1.50
20	Randy Johnson	2.50

1995 Stadium Club Virtual Reality

A partial parallel set found one per foil pack, two per rack pack, these cards share the basic front and back with the corresponding card in the regular S.C. issue. On front, however, is a "Virtual Reality" seal around the team logo at bottom (gold foil in Series I, silver-foil in Series II). Backs differ in that instead of actual 1994 season stats, they present a bar graph of computer projected stats representing full 162-game season instead of the strike-shortened reality. Each of these inserts can also be found in a version bearing the round gold- (Series I) or silver-foil (Series II) Members Only seal on the front.

		MT
Complete Set (270):		80.00
Complete Series I (135):		40.00
Complete Series II (135):		40.00
Common Player:		.25
1	Cal Ripken Jr.	7.50
2	Travis Fryman	.25
3	Jim Abbott	.25
4	Gary Gaetti	.25
5	Roger Clemens	2.00
6	Carlos Garcia	.25
7	Lee Smith	.25
8	Bobby Ayala	.25
9	Charles Nagy	.25
10	Rene Arocha	.25
11	Carlos Delgado	.75
12	Steve Finley	.25
13	Ryan Klesko	.50
14	Cal Eldred	.25
15	Rey Sanchez	.25
16	Ken Hill	.25
17	Jose Vizcaino	.25
18	Andy Benes	.25
19	Shawon Dunston	.25
20	Rafael Palmeiro	.50
21	Dean Palmer	.25
22	Joey Cora	.25
23	Mickey Tettleton	.25
24	Barry Larkin	.35
25	Carlos Baerga	.25
26	Orel Hershiser	.25
27	Jody Reed	.25
28	Paul Molitor	1.50
29	Jim Edmonds	.25
30	Bob Tewksbury	.25
31	Ray McDavid	.25
32	Stan Javier	.25
33	Todd Worrell	.25
34	Bob Wickman	.25
35	Raul Mondesi	1.00
36	Rod Beck	.25
37	Jeff Kent	.25
38	John Valentin	.25
39	Ozzie Smith	1.50
40	Terry Pendleton	.25
41	Kenny Rogers	.25
42	Vince Coleman	.25
43	Roberto Alomar	1.50
44	Darrin Jackson	.25
45	Dennis Eckersley	.25
46	Jay Buhner	.25
47	Dave Weathers	.25
48	Danny Bautista	.25
49	Bob Hamelin	.25
50	Steve Trachsel	.25
51	Ben McDonald	.25
52	Wade Boggs	.75
53	Sandy Alomar	.30
54	Ron Karkovice	.25
55	Doug Jones	.25
56	Gary Sheffield	1.00
57	Ken Caminiti	.75
58	Kevin Tapani	.25
59	Ruben Sierra	.25
60	Bobby Bonilla	.25
61	Deion Sanders	1.00
62	Charlie Hayes	.25
63	Paul O'Neill	.30
64	Jay Bell	.25
65	Todd Jones	.25
66	Todd Stottlemyre	.25
67	Will Clark	1.00
68	Wilson Alvarez	.25
69	Chili Davis	.25
70	Chris Hoiles	.25
71	Bret Saberhagen	.25
72	Dave Nilsson	.25
73	Derek Bell	.25
74	Juan Gonzalez	2.50
75	Andre Dawson	.35
76	Jim Thome	.60
77	Larry Walker	.60
78	Mike Piazza	5.00
79	Dan Wilson	.25
80	Junior Felix	.25
81	Jack McDowell	.25
82	Danny Tartabull	.25
83	William Van Landingham	.25
84	Robb Nen	.25
85	Ismael Valdes	.25
86	Juan Guzman	.25
87	Cliff Floyd	.25
88	Rico Brogna	.25
89	Luis Polonia	.25
90	Lance Johnson	.25
91	Sammy Sosa	5.00
92	Dave West	.25
93	Tom Glavine	.35
94	Joe Girardi	.25
95	Craig Biggio	.35
96	Eddie Murray	.75
97	Kevin Gross	.25
98	John Franco	.25
99	Matt Williams	.75
100	Darrin Fletcher	.25
101	Jeff Conine	.25
102	Ed Sprague	.25
103	Ivan Rodriguez	1.50
104	Orlando Merced	.25
105	Ricky Bones	.25
106	David Cone	.40
107	Todd Hundley	.40
108	Alex Cole	.25
109	Tony Phillips	.25
110	Jim Eisenreich	.25
111	Paul Sorrento	.25
112	Mike Stanley	.25
113	Doug Drabek	.25
114	Matt Mieske	.25
115	Tino Martinez	.30
116	Midre Cummings	.25
117	Hal Morris	.25
118	Shawn Green	.35
119	Randy Myers	.25
120	Ken Griffey Jr.	10.00
121	Brett Butler	.25
122	Julio Franco	.25
123	Chuck Knoblauch	.50
124	Bret Boone	.25
125	Wil Cordero	.25
126	Luis Gonzalez	.25
127	Tim Wallach	.25
128	Scott Sanders	.25
129	Tom Henke	.25
130	Otis Nixon	.25
131	Darren Daulton	.25
132	Manny Ramirez	2.00
133	Bret Barberie	.25
134	Brady Anderson	.35
135	Shane Reynolds	.25
136	Barry Bonds	2.00
137	Alex Fernandez	.25
138	Brian McRae	.25
139	Todd Zeile	.25
140	Greg Swindell	.25
141	Troy Neel	.25
142	Eric Karros	.25
143	John Hudek	.25
144	Joe Carter	.25
145	Mike Devereaux	.25
146	Butch Henry	.25
147	Mark Lemke	.25
148	Jeff Montgomery	.25
149	Ryan Thompson	.25
150	Bernie Williams	.75
151	Scott Leius	.25
152	Greg Gagne	.25
153	Moises Alou	.25
154	Geronimo Berroa	.25
155	Alan Trammell	.25
156	Don Slaught	.25
157	Jose Rijo	.25
158	Tim Raines	.25
159	Melido Perez	.25
160	Kent Mercker	.25
161	James Mouton	.25
162	Luis Lopez	.25
163	Mike Kingery	.25
164	Cecil Fielder	.25
165	Scott Kamieniecki	.25
166	Brent Gates	.25
167	Jason Jacome	.25
168	Dante Bichette	.75
169	Kurt Abbott	.25
170	Mike Henneman	.25
171	John Kruk	.25
172	Jose Oliva	.25
173	Reggie Sanders	.35
174	Omar Vizquel	.25
175	Devon White	.25
176	Mark McGwire	10.00
177	Gary DiSarcina	.25
178	Joey Hamilton	.25
179	Randy Johnson	1.00
180	Jim Leyritz	.25
181	Bobby Jones	.25
182	Bip Roberts	.25
183	Jose Canseco	.75
184	Mo Vaughn	1.00
185	Edgar Martinez	.25
186	Tommy Greene	.25
187	Chuck Carr	.25
188	Pedro Astacio	.25
189	Shane Mack	.25
190	Fred McGriff	.75
191	Pat Rapp	.25
192	Bill Swift	.25
193	Robin Ventura	.35
194	Bobby Witt	.25
195	Steve Howe	.25
196	Leo Gomez	.25
197	Hector Fajardo	.25
198	Jeff Bagwell	2.50
199	Rondell White	.40
200	Don Mattingly	2.50
201	Trevor Hoffman	.25
202	Chris Gomez	.25
203	Bobby Munoz	.25
204	Marvin Freeman	.25
205	Sean Berry	.25
206	Mark Grace	.40
207	Pat Kelly	.25
208	Eddie Williams	.25
209	Frank Thomas	4.00
210	Bryan Eversgerd	.25
211	Phil Plantier	.25
212	Roberto Kelly	.25
213	Rickey Henderson	.50
214	John Smiley	.25
215	Kevin Brown	.30
216	Jimmy Key	.25
217	Wally Joyner	.25
218	Roberto Hernandez	.25
219	Felix Fermin	.25
220	Greg Vaughn	.25
221	Ray Lankford	.30
222	Greg Maddux	5.00
223	Mike Mussina	1.00
224	David Nied	.25
225	Scott Erickson	.25
226	Kevin Mitchell	.25
227	Brian Anderson	.25
228	Jeff King	.25
229	Ramon Martinez	.25
230	Kevin Seitzer	.25
231	Marquis Grissom	.25
232	Chuck Finley	.25
233	Len Dykstra	.25
234	Ellis Burks	.25
235	Harold Baines	.25
236	Kevin Appier	.25
237	Dave Justice	.40
238	Darryl Kile	.25
239	John Olerud	.35
240	Greg McMichael	.25
241	Kirby Puckett	2.00
242	Jose Valentin	.25
243	Rick Wilkins	.25
244	Pat Hentgen	.25
245	Tom Gordon	.25
246	Tom Candiotti	.25
247	Jason Bere	.25
248	Wes Chamberlain	.25
249	Jeff Cirillo	.25
250	Kevin Foster	.25
251	Mark Whiten	.25
252	Terry Steinbach	.25
253	Aaron Sele	.25
254	Kirt Manwaring	.25
255	Delino DeShields	.25
256	Andujar Cedeno	.25
257	Kenny Lofton	1.00
258	John Wetteland	.25
259	Tim Salmon	.40
260	Denny Neagle	.25
261	Tony Gwynn	2.50
262	Lou Whitaker	.25
263	J.T. Snow	.25
264	Dennis Martinez	.25
265	Pedro Martinez	.40
266	Rusty Greer	.25
267	Dave Fleming	.25
268	John Dettmer	.25
269	Albert Belle	1.50
270	Henry Rodriguez	.25

1995 Stadium Club VR Extremist

A huge silver-blue metallic baseball separates the player from the background of the photo in this Series II insert found only in rack packs. A blue sky and clouds provides the front border. The player rises out of the clouds in a back photo in the foreground of which are some pie-in-the-sky stats. The metallic baseball is also repeated on the back, with the player's name in orange script on the sweet spot. Each card was also issued in the Members Only boxed set in a version with a round silver-foil Members Only seal on front. Cards are numbered with a "VRE" prefix.

		MT
Complete Set (10):		80.00
Common Player:		2.00
1	Barry Bonds	8.00
2	Ken Griffey Jr.	30.00
3	Jeff Bagwell	8.00
4	Albert Belle	6.00
5	Frank Thomas	12.00
6	Tony Gwynn	10.00
7	Kenny Lofton	4.00
8	Deion Sanders	4.00
9	Ken Hill	2.00
10	Jimmy Key	2.00

1995 Stadium Club Super Team Division Winners

Persons who saved 1994 Topps Stadium Club Super Team cards for the 1995 divisional winners in Major League Baseball's new playoff format were able to redeem them for a set of 10 SC cards of that team's players with a special gold-foil division series logo on front. The cards are otherwise identical to the regular-issue '95 SC versions. Included in the cello-wrapped team set was a Super Team card with the gold logo on front and a white "REDEEMED" across the back.

		MT
Complete Set (66):		40.00
Common Player:		.15
	Atlanta Braves team set	9.50
1	Atlanta Braves Super Team	.30
19	Ryan Klesko	.90
128	Mark Wohlers	.15
151	Steve Avery	.15
183	Tom Glavine	.30
200	Javy Lopez	.60
393	Fred McGriff	1.25
397	John Smoltz	.45
425	Greg Maddux	3.50
446	David Justice	1.25
543	Chipper Jones	3.50
	Boston Red Sox team set	4.50
16	Boston Red Sox Super Team	.30
10	Roger Clemens	2.00
62	John Valentin	.15
121	Mike Greenwell	.15
160	Lee Tinsley	.15
347	Jose Canseco	.90
350	Mo Vaughn	1.00
395	Tim Naehring	.15

464 Aaron Sele .15
530 Mike MacFarlane .15
600 Troy O'Leary .15
Cincinnati Red team set 2.50
3 Cincinnati Reds Super Team .30
35 Barry Larkin .50
231 Hal Morris .15
252 Bret Boone .15
280 Thomas Howard .15
300 Jose Rijo .15
333 Reggie Sanders .45
392 Hector Carrasco .15
416 John Smiley .15
528 Ron Gant .45
566 Benito Santiago .15
Cleveland Indians team set 9.50
19 Cleveland Indians Super Team .30
36 Carlos Baerga .15
147 Jim Thome .45
186 Eddie Murray 2.00
264 Manny Ramirez 1.50
334 Omar Vizquel .25
470 Kenny Lofton 1.00
484 Dennis Martinez .15
489 Albert Belle 1.75
550 Jose Mesa .15
562 Orel Hershiser .45
Los Angeles Dodgers team set 6.00
7 Los Angeles Dodgers Super Team .30
57 Raul Mondesi .90
149 Mike Piazza 3.50
161 Ismael Valdez .15
242 Brett Butler .15
259 Tim Wallach .15
278 Eric Karros .20
434 Ramon Martinez .25
456 Tom Candiotti .15
467 Delino DeShields .15
556 Hideo Nomo 1.75
Seattle Mariners team set 9.00
26 Seattle Mariners Super Team .30
73 Jay Buhner .15
92 Chris Bosio .15
152 Dan Wilson .15
227 Tino Martinez .35
241 Ken Griffey Jr. 7.50
340 Randy Johnson 1.50
354 Edgar Martinez .15
421 Felix Fermin .15
494 Mike Blowers .15
536 Joey Cora .15

1995 Stadium Club League Champion Master Photos

Persons who held onto Braves and Indians Super Team insert cards from the 1994 Stadium Club issue could redeem them following the 1995 season for special Master Photos team sets of the League Champions. Each team set included 10 player cards and a Super Team card with special gold-foil League Champion logos on the fronts. The player cards are in 5" x 7" format with the player's 1995 SC card in the center of a blue background. Backs are in black-and-white with a card number and appropriate logos and copyright. The Super Team card is 2-1/2" x 3-1/2" with a white "REDEEMED" notice overprinted on back.

	MT
Complete Set (22):	25.00
Common Player:	.45

Atlanta Braves team set 15.00
1 Steve Avery .45
2 Tom Glavine .60
3 Chipper Jones 5.00
4 David Justice 1.50
5 Ryan Klesko 1.25
6 Javy Lopez 1.25
7 Greg Maddux 5.00
8 Fred McGriff 1.50
9 John Smoltz 1.25
10 Mark Wohlers .45
1 Atlanta Braves Super Team .45
Cleveland Indians team set 12.50
11 Carlos Baerga .45
12 Albert Belle 3.50
13 Orel Hershiser .60
14 Kenny Lofton 2.50
15 Dennis Martinez .45
16 Jose Mesa .45
17 Eddie Murray 2.50
18 Manny Ramirez 3.50
19 Jim Thome 1.25
20 Omar Vizquel .60
19 Cleveland Indians Super Team .45

1995 Stadium Club World Series Winners

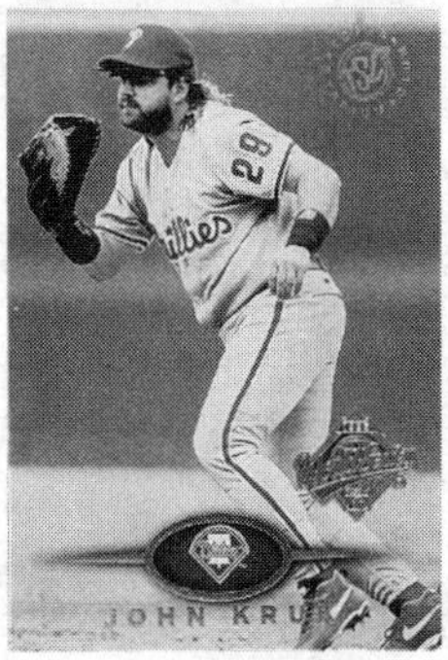

Persons who redeemed a 1994 Stadium Club Atlanta Braves Super Team insert following the Tribe's 1995 World Series victory received a set of 1995 Stadium Club cards, each of which bears a gold-foil World's Series logo on front. The cards are otherwise identical to the regular-issue SC cards.

	MT
Complete Set (630):	150.00
Common Player:	.25

Stars: 4X
(See 1995 Stadium Club for checklist and base card values.)

1995 Stadium Club Members Only

A special version of all of the regular cards from Stadium Club Series I-III, as well as many of the insert sets was offered to members of Topps' Stadium Club. Virtually identical to the regular S.C. cards, the specially boxed set differs in the presence on each card front of an embossed round 1/2" gold-foil "Members Only" seal. Even the plastic Clear Cut inserts have the members' seal embossed directly into the plastic. The edition was limited to 4,000 sets.

	MT
Complete Set (630):	250.00
Common Player:	.25

Stars: 15X
Inserts: 50-100%
(See 1995 Stadium Club for checklist and base card values.)

1995 Stadium Club Members Only Baseball

This boxed set was sold exclusively through the newsletter for Topps Stadium Club members. Cards feature noteworthy performances and achievements of the 1994 baseball season. Borderless card fronts have a player action photo on which the background has been quartered in colors of blue, green, orange and magenta. The Members Only logo, and player name and position are presented in gold foil. Backs have another player photo at left and a description of the highlight printed in white on a blue background at right. Both front and back of each card are UV coated. The final five cards in the set are printed in Topps Finest technology and feature the company's choice of the top rookies of 1994.

	MT
Complete Set (50):	15.00
Common Player:	.10

1 Moises Alou .15
2 Jeff Bagwell .75
3 Albert Belle .35
4 Andy Benes .10
5 Dante Bichette .15
6 Craig Biggio .20
7 Wade Boggs .40
8 Barry Bonds .75
9 Brett Butler .10
10 Jose Canseco .50
11 Joe Carter .10
12 Vince Coleman .10
13 Jeff Conine .15
14 Cecil Fielder .10
15 John Franco .10
16 Julio Franco .10
17 Travis Fryman .10
18 Andres Galarraga .15
19 Ken Griffey Jr. 3.00
20 Marquis Grissom .10
21 Tony Gwynn .75
22 Ken Hill .10
23 Randy Johnson .25
24 Lance Johnson .10
25 Jimmy Key .10
26 Chuck Knoblauch .15
27 Ray Lankford .15
28 Darren Lewis .10
29 Kenny Lofton .25
30 Greg Maddux 1.00
31 Fred McGriff .20
32 Kevin Mitchell .10
33 Paul Molitor .50
34 Hal Morris .10
35 Paul O'Neill .15
36 Rafael Palmeiro .20
37 Tony Phillips .10
38 Mike Piazza 1.00
39 Kirby Puckett .75
40 Cal Ripken Jr. 2.00
41 Deion Sanders .15
42 Lee Smith .10
43 Frank Thomas 1.00
44 Larry Walker .35
45 Matt Williams .25
46 Manny Ramirez (Rookie Picks) 2.00
47 Joey Hamilton (Rookie Picks) 1.00
48 Raul Mondesi (Rookie Picks) 1.50
49 Bob Hamelin (Rookie Picks) .15
50 Ryan Klesko (Rookie Picks) 1.50

1996 Stadium Club

Consisting of 450 cards in a pair of 225-card series, Stadium Club continued Topps' 1996 tribute to Mickey Mantle with 19 Retrospective inserts. Cards feature full-bleed photos with gold-foil graphic highlights. Backs offer a TSC Skills Matrix along with another player photo, some biographical data and stats. Team TSC is the only subset with 45 cards each in Series 1 and 2. Stadium Club was issued in retail and hobby packs, with inserts found at differing ratios in each type of packaging.

	MT
Complete Set (450):	60.00
Common Player:	.10
Series 1 or 2 Wax Box:	40.00

1 Hideo Nomo (Extreme Player) .50
2 Paul Molitor .40
3 Garret Anderson (Extreme Player) .15
4 Jose Mesa (Extreme Player) .10
5 Vinny Castilla (Extreme Player) .15
6 Mike Mussina (Extreme Player) .40
7 Ray Durham (Extreme Player) .10
8 Jack McDowell (Extreme Player) .10
9 Juan Gonzalez (EP) 1.50
10 Chipper Jones (Extreme Player) 2.50
11 Deion Sanders (Extreme Player) .25
12 Rondell White (Extreme Player) .15
13 Tom Henke (Extreme Player) .10
14 Derek Bell (Extreme Player) .10
15 Randy Myers (Extreme Player) .10
16 Randy Johnson (Extreme Player) .40
17 Len Dykstra (Extreme Player) .10
18 Bill Pulsipher (Extreme Player) .10
19 Greg Colbrunn .10
20 David Wells .15
21 Chad Curtis (Extreme Player) .10
22 Roberto Hernandez (Extreme Player) .10
23 Kirby Puckett (Extreme Player) 1.00
24 Joe Vitiello .10
25 Roger Clemens (Extreme Player) 1.00
26 Al Martin .10
27 Chad Ogea .10
28 David Segui .10
29 Joey Hamilton .10
30 Dan Wilson .10
31 Chad Fonville (Extreme Player) .15
32 Bernard Gilkey (Extreme Player) .15
33 Kevin Seitzer .10
34 Shawn Green (Extreme Player) .25
35 Rick Aguilera (Extreme Player) .10
36 Gary DiSarcina .10
37 Jaime Navarro .10
38 Doug Jones .10
39 Brent Gates .10
40 Dean Palmer (Extreme Player) .10
41 Pat Rapp .10
42 Tony Clark .50
43 Bill Swift .10
44 Randy Velarde .10
45 Matt Williams (Extreme Player) .30
46 John Mabry .10
47 Mike Fetters .10
48 Orlando Miller .10
49 Tom Glavine (Extreme Player) .15
50 Delino DeShields (Extreme Player) .10
51 Scott Erickson .10
52 Andy Van Slyke .10
53 Jim Bullinger .10
54 Lyle Mouton .10
55 Bret Saberhagen .10
56 Benito Santiago (Extreme Player) .10
57 Dan Miceli .10
58 Carl Everett .10
59 Rod Beck (Extreme Player) .10
60 Phil Nevin .10
61 Jason Giambi .20
62 Paul Menhart .10
63 Eric Karros (Extreme Player) .15
64 Allen Watson .10
65 Jeff Cirillo .10
66 Lee Smith (Extreme Player) .10
67 Sean Berry .10
68 Luis Sojo .10
69 Jeff Montgomery (Extreme Player) .10
70 Todd Hundley (Extreme Player) .20
71 John Burkett .10
72 Mark Gubicza .10
73 Don Mattingly (Extreme Player) 1.00
74 Jeff Brantley .10
75 Matt Walbeck .10
76 Steve Parris .10
77 Ken Caminiti (Extreme Player) .40
78 Kirt Manwaring .10
79 Greg Vaughn .10
80 Pedro Martinez (Extreme Player) .30
81 Benji Gil .10
82 Heathcliff Slocumb (Extreme Player) .10
83 Joe Girardi (Extreme Player) .10
84 Sean Bergman .10
85 Matt Karchner .10
86 Butch Huskey .10
87 Mike Morgan .10
88 Todd Worrell (Extreme Player) .10
89 Mike Bordick .10
90 Bip Roberts (Extreme Player) .10
91 Mike Hampton .10
92 Troy O'Leary .10
93 Wally Joyner .10
94 Dave Stevens .10
95 Cecil Fielder (Extreme Player) .15
96 Wade Boggs (Extreme Player) .20
97 Hal Morris .10
98 Mickey Tettleton (Extreme Player) .10
99 Jeff Kent (Extreme Player) .10
100 Denny Martinez .10
101 Luis Gonzalez (Extreme Player) .15
102 John Jaha .10
103 Javy Lopez (Extreme Player) .20
104 Mark McGwire (Extreme Player) 4.00
105 Ken Griffey Jr. (EP) 4.00
106 Darren Daulton (Extreme Player) .10
107 Bryan Rekar .10
108 Mike Macfarlane (Extreme Player) .10
109 Gary Gaetti (Extreme Player) .10
110 Shane Reynolds (Extreme Player) .10
111 Pat Meares .10
112 Jason Schmidt .10
113 Otis Nixon .10
114 John Franco (Extreme Player) .10
115 Marc Newfield .10
116 Andy Benes (Extreme Player) .10
117 Ozzie Guillen .10
118 Brian Jordan (Extreme Player) .15
119 Terry Pendleton (Extreme Player) .10

120 Chuck Finley (Extreme Player) .10
121 Scott Stahoviak .10
122 Sid Fernandez .10
123 Derek Jeter (Extreme Player) 2.50
124 John Smiley (Extreme Player) .10
125 David Bell .10
126 Brett Butler (Extreme Player) .10
127 Doug Drabek (Extreme Player) .10
128 J.T. Snow (Extreme Player) .10
129 Joe Carter (Extreme Player) .15
130 Dennis Eckersley (Extreme Player) .10
131 Marty Cordova (Extreme Player) .20
132 Greg Maddux (Extreme Player) 2.50
133 Tom Goodwin .10
134 Andy Ashby .10
135 Paul Sorrento (Extreme Player) .10
136 Ricky Bones .10
137 Shawon Dunston (Extreme Player) .15
138 Moises Alou (Extreme Player) .15
139 Mickey Morandini .10
140 Ramon Martinez (Extreme Player) .15
141 Royce Clayton (Extreme Player) .10
142 Brad Ausmus .10
143 Kenny Rogers (Extreme Player) .10
144 Tim Naehring (Extreme Player) .10
145 Chris Gomez (Extreme Player) .10
146 Bobby Bonilla (Extreme Player) .10
147 Wilson Alvarez .10
148 Johnny Damon (Extreme Player) .20
149 Pat Hentgen .10
150 Andres Galarraga (Extreme Player) .20
151 David Cone (Extreme Player) .15
152 Lance Johnson (Extreme Player) .10
153 Carlos Garcia .10
154 Doug Johns .10
155 Midre Cummings .10
156 Steve Sparks .10
157 *Sandy Martinez* .10
158 William Van Landingham .10
159 Dave Justice (Extreme Player) .20
160 Mark Grace (Extreme Player) .15
161 Robb Nen (Extreme Player) .10
162 Mike Greenwell (Extreme Player) .10
163 Brad Radke .10
164 Edgardo Alfonzo .15
165 Mark Leiter .10
166 Walt Weiss .10
167 Mel Rojas (Extreme Player) .10
168 Bret Boone (Extreme Player) .10
169 Ricky Bottalico .10
170 Bobby Higginson .10
171 Trevor Hoffman .15
172 Jay Bell (Extreme Player) .10
173 Gabe White .10
174 Curtis Goodwin .10
175 Tyler Green .10
176 Roberto Alomar (Extreme Player) .75
177 Sterling Hitchcock .10
178 Ryan Klesko (Extreme Player) .25
179 *Donne Wall* .10
180 Brian McRae .10
181 Will Clark (Team TSC) .20
182 Frank Thomas (Team TSC) 1.50
183 Jeff Bagwell (Team TSC) 1.50
184 Mo Vaughn (Team TSC) .75
185 Tino Martinez (Team TSC) .15
186 Craig Biggio (Team TSC) .15
187 Chuck Knoblauch (Team TSC) .25
188 Carlos Baerga (Team TSC) .15
189 Quilvio Veras (Team TSC) .10
190 Luis Alicea (Team TSC) .10
191 Jim Thome (Team TSC) .30
192 Mike Blowers (Team TSC) .10
193 Robin Ventura (Team TSC) .15
194 Jeff King (Team TSC) .10
195 Tony Phillips (Team TSC) .10
196 John Valentin (Team TSC) .10
197 Barry Larkin (Team TSC) .20
198 Cal Ripken Jr. (Team TSC) 3.00
199 Omar Vizquel (Team TSC) .10
200 Kurt Abbott (Team TSC) .10
201 Albert Belle (Team TSC) 1.25
202 Barry Bonds (Team TSC) .75
203 Ron Gant (Team TSC) .10
204 Dante Bichette (Team TSC) .25
205 Jeff Conine (Team TSC) .10
206 Jim Edmonds (Team TSC) .15
207 Stan Javier (Team TSC) .10
208 Kenny Lofton (Team TSC) .75
209 Ray Lankford (Team TSC) .15
210 Bernie Williams (Team TSC) .60
211 Jay Buhner (Team TSC) .15
212 Paul O'Neill (Team TSC) .10
213 Tim Salmon (Team TSC) .25
214 Reggie Sanders (Team TSC) .10
215 Manny Ramirez (Team TSC) .75
216 Mike Piazza (Team TSC) 2.50
217 Mike Stanley (Team TSC) .10
218 Tony Eusebio (Team TSC) .10
219 Chris Hoiles (Team TSC) .10
220 Ron Karkovice (Team TSC) .10
221 Edgar Martinez (Team TSC) .10
222 Chili Davis (Team TSC) .10
223 Jose Canseco (Team TSC) .35
224 Eddie Murray (Team TSC) .40
225 Geronimo Berroa (Team TSC) .10
226 Chipper Jones (Team TSC) 2.50
227 Garret Anderson (Team TSC) .20
228 Marty Cordova (Team TSC) .20
229 Jon Nunnally (Team TSC) .10
230 Brian Hunter (Team TSC) .10
231 Shawn Green (Team TSC) .15
232 Ray Durham (Team TSC) .10
233 Alex Gonzalez (Team TSC) .10
234 Bobby Higginson (Team TSC) .15
235 Randy Johnson (Team TSC) .40
236 Al Leiter (Team TSC) .10
237 Tom Glavine (Team TSC) .15
238 Kenny Rogers (Team TSC) .10
239 Mike Hampton (Team TSC) .10
240 David Wells (Team TSC) .10
241 Jim Abbott (Team TSC) .10
242 Denny Neagle (Team TSC) .10
243 Wilson Alvarez (Team TSC) .10
244 John Smiley (Team TSC) .10
245 Greg Maddux (Team TSC) 2.50
246 Andy Ashby (Team TSC) .10
247 Hideo Nomo (Team TSC) .50
248 Pat Rapp (Team TSC) .10
249 Tim Wakefield (Team TSC) .10
250 John Smoltz (Team TSC) .25
251 Joey Hamilton (Team TSC) .10
252 Frank Castillo (Team TSC) .10
253 Denny Martinez (Team TSC) .10
254 Jaime Navarro (Team TSC) .10
255 Karim Garcia (Team TSC) .40
256 Bob Abreu (Team TSC) .30
257 Butch Huskey (Team TSC) .15
258 Ruben Rivera (Team TSC) .40
259 Johnny Damon (Team TSC) .15
260 Derek Jeter (Team TSC) 2.50
261 Dennis Eckersley (Team TSC) .10
262 Jose Mesa (Team TSC) .10
263 Tom Henke (Team TSC) .10
264 Rick Aguilera (Team TSC) .10
265 Randy Myers (Team TSC) .10
266 John Franco (Team TSC) .10
267 Jeff Brantley (Team TSC) .10
268 John Wetteland (Team TSC) .10
269 Mark Wohlers (Team TSC) .10
270 Rod Beck (Team TSC) .10
271 Barry Larkin .20
272 Paul O'Neill .15
273 Bobby Jones .10
274 Will Clark .25
275 Steve Avery .10
276 Jim Edmonds .20
277 John Olerud .15
278 Carlos Perez .10
279 Chris Hoiles .10
280 Jeff Conine .10
281 Jim Eisenreich .10
282 Jason Jacome .10
283 Ray Lankford .15
284 John Wasdin .10
285 Frank Thomas 1.50
286 Jason Isringhausen .15
287 Glenallen Hill .10
288 Esteban Loaiza .15
289 Bernie Williams .60
290 Curtis Leskanic .10
291 Scott Cooper .10
292 Curt Schilling .10
293 Eddie Murray .50
294 Rick Krivda .10
295 Domingo Cedeno .10
296 Jeff Fassero .10
297 Albert Belle .75
298 Craig Biggio .20
299 Fernando Vina .10
300 Edgar Martinez .10
301 Tony Gwynn 1.00
302 Felipe Lira .10
303 Mo Vaughn .75
304 Alex Fernandez .15
305 Keith Lockhart .10
306 Roger Pavlik .10
307 Lee Tinsley .10
308 Omar Vizquel .10
309 Scott Servais .10
310 Danny Tartabull .10
311 Chili Davis .10
312 Cal Eldred .10
313 Roger Cedeno .15
314 Chris Hammond .10
315 Rusty Greer .10
316 Brady Anderson .20
317 Ron Villone .10
318 Mark Carreon .10
319 Larry Walker .30
320 Pete Harnisch .10
321 Robin Ventura .15
322 Tim Belcher .10
323 Tony Tarasco .10
324 Juan Guzman .10
325 Kenny Lofton .75
326 Kevin Foster .10
327 Wil Cordero .10
328 Troy Percival .10
329 Turk Wendell .10
330 Thomas Howard .10
331 Carlos Baerga .10
332 B.J. Surhoff .10
333 Jay Buhner .10
334 Andujar Cedeno .10
335 Jeff King .10
336 Dante Bichette .25
337 Alan Trammell .15
338 Scott Leius .10
339 Chris Snopek .10
340 Roger Bailey .10
341 Jacob Brumfield .10
342 Jose Canseco .35
343 Rafael Palmeiro .25
344 Quilvio Veras .10
345 Darrin Fletcher .10
346 Carlos Delgado .50
347 Tony Eusebio .10
348 Ismael Valdes .10
349 Terry Steinbach .10
350 Orel Hershiser .10
351 Kurt Abbott .10
352 Jody Reed .10
353 David Howard .10
354 Ruben Sierra .10
355 John Ericks .10
356 Buck Showalter .10
357 Jim Thome .40
358 Geronimo Berroa .10
359 Robby Thompson .10
360 Jose Vizcaino .10
361 Jeff Frye .10
362 Kevin Appier .10
363 Pat Kelly .10
364 Ron Gant .15
365 Luis Alicea .10
366 Armando Benitez .10
367 Rico Brogna .10
368 Manny Ramirez 1.00
369 Mike Lansing .10
370 Sammy Sosa 2.00
371 Don Wengert .10
372 Dave Nilsson .10
373 Sandy Alomar .15
374 Joey Cora .10
375 Larry Thomas .10
376 John Valentin .10
377 Kevin Ritz .10
378 Steve Finley .10
379 Frank Rodriguez .10
380 Ivan Rodriguez .60
381 Alex Ochoa .10
382 Mark Lemke .10
383 Scott Brosius .10
384 James Mouton .10
385 Mark Langston .10
386 Ed Sprague .10
387 Joe Oliver .10
388 Steve Ontiveros .10
389 Rey Sanchez .10
390 Mike Henneman .10
391 *Jose Valentin* .10
392 Tom Candiotti .10
393 Damon Buford .10
394 Erik Hanson .10
395 Mark Smith .10
396 Pete Schourek .10
397 John Flaherty .10
398 Dave Martinez .10
399 Tommy Greene .10
400 Gary Sheffield .40
401 Glenn Dishman .10
402 Barry Bonds .60
403 Tom Pagnozzi .10
404 Todd Stottlemyre .10
405 Tim Salmon .25
406 John Hudek .10
407 Fred McGriff .30
408 Orlando Merced .10
409 Brian Barber .10
410 Ryan Thompson .10
411 Mariano Rivera .25
412 Eric Young .10
413 Chris Bosio .10
414 Chuck Knoblauch .20
415 Jamie Moyer .10
416 Chan Ho Park .15
417 Mark Portugal .10
418 Tim Raines .10
419 Antonio Osuna .10
420 Todd Zeile .10
421 Steve Wojciechowski .10
422 Marquis Grissom .15
423 Norm Charlton .10
424 Cal Ripken Jr. 3.00
425 Gregg Jefferies .15
426 Mike Stanton .10
427 Tony Fernandez .10
428 Jose Rijo .10
429 Jeff Bagwell 1.00
430 Raul Mondesi .30
431 Travis Fryman .10
432 Ron Karkovice .10
433 Alan Benes .15
434 Tony Phillips .10
435 Reggie Sanders .15
436 Andy Pettitte .75
437 *Matt Lawton* .10
438 Jeff Blauser .10
439 Michael Tucker .10
440 Mark Loretta .10
441 Charlie Hayes .10
442 Mike Piazza 2.50
443 Shane Andrews .10
444 Jeff Suppan .10
445 Steve Rodriguez .10
446 Mike Matheny .10
447 Trenidad Hubbard .10
448 Denny Hocking .10
449 Mark Grudzielanek .10
450 Joe Randa .10

1996 Stadium Club Mickey Mantle "Cereal Box" Set

This factory-set version of TSC was packaged in boxes which resembled single-serving cereal boxes. The cards are identical to the regular TSC version except for the use of silver-foil, rather than gold-foil, highlights on front.

	MT
Complete Set (450):	60.00
Common Player:	.10

(See 1996 Stadium Club for checklist and values.)

Player names in *Italic* type indicate a rookie card.

1996 Stadium Club Extreme Player

A special interactive version of 179 players' cards in 1996 Stadium Club was issued as an insert set across Series 1 and 2. Specially stamped with an "Extreme Player" logo in bronze (1 per 12 packs average), silver (1:24) or gold (1:48), the cards have backs which detail a contest by which the player's on-field performance was used to rank each by position. At season's end, cards of the winning players at each position could be redeemed for special prizes.

		MT
Complete Bronze Set (179):		200.00
Common Bronze:		.50
Silvers: 1.5X		
Golds: 3X		
1	(Hideo Nomo)	6.00
3	Garret Anderson	1.00
4	Jose Mesa	.50
5	Vinny Castilla	.50
6	Mike Mussina	3.00
7	Ray Durham	.50
8	Jack McDowell	.50
9	Juan Gonzalez	8.00
10	Chipper Jones	15.00
11	Deion Sanders	2.00
12	Rondell White	.50
13	Tom Henke	.50
14	Derek Bell	.50
15	Randy Myers	.50
16	Randy Johnson	4.00
17	Len Dykstra	.50
18	Bill Pulsipher	.50
21	Chad Curtis	.50
22	Roberto Hernandez	.50
23	Kirby Puckett	7.00
25	Roger Clemens	4.00
31	Chad Fonville	.50
32	Bernard Gilkey	1.00
34	Shawn Green	1.00
35	Rick Aguilera	.50
40	Dean Palmer	.50
45	Matt Williams	1.50
49	Tom Glavine	2.00
50	Delino DeShields	.50
56	Benito Santiago	.50
59	Rod Beck	.50
63	Eric Karros	.50
66	Lee Smith	.50
69	Jeff Montgomery	.50
70	Todd Hundley	2.00
73	Don Mattingly	8.00
77	Ken Caminiti	1.50
80	Pedro Martinez	1.50
82	Heathcliff Slocumb	.50
83	Joe Girardi	.50
88	Todd Worrell	.50
90	Bip Roberts	.50
95	Cecil Fielder	.50
96	Wade Boggs	4.00
98	Mickey Tettleton	.50
99	Jeff Kent	.50
101	Luis Gonzalez	.50
103	Javier Lopez	1.50
104	Mark McGwire	25.00
105	Ken Griffey Jr.	25.00
106	Darren Daulton	.50
108	Mike Macfarlane	.50
109	Gary Gaetti	.50
110	Shane Reynolds	.50
114	John Franco	.50
116	Andy Benes	.50
118	Brian Jordan	.50
119	Terry Pendleton	.50
120	Chuck Finley	.50
123	Derek Jeter	15.00
124	John Smiley	.50
126	Brett Butler	.50
127	Doug Drabek	.50
128	J.T. Snow	.50
129	Joe Carter	.50
130	Dennis Eckersley	.50
131	Marty Cordova	.50
132	Greg Maddux	15.00
135	Paul Sorrento	.50

137	Shawon Dunston	.50
138	Moises Alou	.50
140	Ramon Martinez	.50
141	Royce Clayton	.50
143	Kenny Rogers	.50
144	Tim Naehring	.50
145	Chris Gomez	.50
146	Bobby Bonilla	.50
148	Johnny Damon	1.50
150	Andres Galarraga	.75
151	David Cone	1.50
152	Lance Johnson	.50
159	Dave Justice	2.00
160	Mark Grace	2.50
161	Robb Nen	.50
162	Mike Greenwell	.50
167	Mel Rojas	.50
168	Bret Boone	.50
172	Jay Bell	.50
176	Roberto Alomar	6.00
178	Ryan Klesko	3.00
271	Barry Larkin	1.00
272	Paul O'Neill	.75
274	Will Clark	2.50
275	Steve Avery	.50
276	Jim Edmonds	1.00
277	John Olerud	2.00
279	Chris Hoiles	.50
280	Jeff Conine	.50
283	Ray Lankford	.50
285	Frank Thomas	12.50
286	Jason Isringhausen	.50
287	Glenallen Hill	.50
289	Bernie Williams	2.00
290	Eddie Murray	1.50
296	Jeff Fassero	.50
297	Albert Belle	6.00
298	Craig Biggio	1.00
300	Edgar Martinez	.50
301	Tony Gwynn	10.00
303	Mo Vaughn	1.50
304	Alex Fernandez	.50
308	Omar Vizquel	.50
310	Danny Tartabull	.50
316	Brady Anderson	1.00
319	Larry Walker	1.50
321	Robin Ventura	.75
325	Kenny Lofton	1.50
327	Wil Cordero	.50
328	Troy Percival	1.00
331	Carlos Baerga	.50
333	Jay Buhner	.50
335	Jeff King	.50
336	Dante Bichette	1.50
337	Alan Trammell	.50
342	Jose Canseco	2.00
343	Rafael Palmeiro	1.00
344	Quilvio Veras	.50
345	Darrin Fletcher	.50
347	Tony Eusebio	.50
348	Ismael Valdes	.50
349	Terry Steinbach	.50
350	Orel Hershiser	.50
351	Kurt Abbott	.50
354	Ruben Sierra	.50
357	Jim Thome	1.50
358	Geronimo Berroa	.50
359	Robby Thompson	.50
360	Jose Vizcaino	.50
362	Kevin Appier	.50
364	Ron Gant	.50
367	Rico Brogna	.50
368	Manny Ramirez	7.50
370	Sammy Sosa	15.00
373	Sandy Alomar	.75
378	Steve Finley	.50
380	Ivan Rodriguez	1.25
382	Mark Lemke	.50
385	Mark Langston	.50
386	Ed Sprague	.50
388	Steve Ontiveros	.50
392	Tom Candiotti	.50
394	Erik Hanson	.50
396	Pete Schourek	.50
400	Gary Sheffield	1.50
402	Barry Bonds	8.00
403	Tom Pagnozzi	.50
404	Todd Stottlemyre	.50
405	Tim Salmon	1.50
407	Fred McGriff	2.00
408	Orlando Merced	.50
412	Eric Young	.50
414	Chuck Knoblauch	2.00
417	Mark Portugal	.50
418	Tim Raines	.50
420	Todd Zeile	.50
422	Marquis Grissom	.50
423	Norm Charlton	.50
424	Cal Ripken Jr.	20.00
425	Gregg Jefferies	.50
428	Jose Rijo	.50
429	Jeff Bagwell	8.00
430	Raul Mondesi	2.00
431	Travis Fryman	.50
434	Tony Phillips	.50
435	Reggie Sanders	.50
436	Andy Pettitte	3.00
438	Jeff Blauser	.50
441	Charlie Hayes	.50
442	Mike Piazza	15.00

1996 Stadium Club Extreme Player - Bronze Winner

Ten-card sets of these special bronze-foil highlighted cards were the prize for those who redeemed bronze statistical winners' cards from the Stadium Club Extreme Player interactive series. Backs have statistical ratings pertinent to the game and scoring rules. Cards have an "EW" prefix to the number. The same photos and back design were used in different technologies in the bronze, silver and gold winners cards.

		MT
Complete Set (10):		20.00
Common Player:		1.00
1	Greg Maddux	4.00
2	Mike Piazza	4.00
3	Andres Galarraga	1.00
4	Chuck Knoblauch	1.00
5	Ken Caminiti	1.00
6	Barry Larkin	1.00
7	Barry Bonds	2.00
8	Ken Griffey Jr.	8.00
9	Gary Sheffield	1.00
10	Todd Worrell	1.00

1996 Stadium Club Extreme Player - Silver Winner

Ten-card sets of these Finest technology cards were the prize for those who redeemed statistical winners' cards from the Stadium Club Extreme Player interactive series. Backs have statistical ratings pertinent to the game and scoring rules. Cards have an "EW" prefix to the number.

		MT
Complete Set (10):		60.00
Common Player:		2.50
1	Greg Maddux	15.00
2	Mike Piazza	20.00
3	Andres Galarraga	2.50
4	Chuck Knoblauch	2.50
5	Ken Caminiti	2.50
6	Barry Larkin	2.50
7	Barry Bonds	7.00
8	Ken Griffey Jr.	25.00
9	Gary Sheffield	2.50
10	Todd Worrell	2.50

1996 Stadium Club Extreme Player - Gold Winner

One of these large (2-3/4" x 3-3/4"), heavy, acrylic-coated bronze refractor cards was the prize for those who redeemed the same player's gold statistical winners' card from the Stadium Club Extreme Player interactive series. Backs have statistical ratings pertinent to the game and scoring rules. Cards have an "EW" prefix to the number. The same photos and back design were used in different technologies in the bronze, silver and gold winners cards.

		MT
Complete Set (10):		250.00
Common Player:		10.00
1	Greg Maddux	50.00
2	Mike Piazza	65.00
3	Andres Galarraga	10.00
4	Chuck Knoblauch	10.00
5	Ken Caminiti	10.00
6	Barry Larkin	10.00
7	Barry Bonds	25.00
8	Ken Griffey Jr.	100.00
9	Gary Sheffield	10.00
10	Todd Worrell	10.00

1996 Stadium Club Bash & Burn

Inserted in one per 24 retail packs and one per 48 hobby packs of Series II, Bash & Burn includes 10 players on double-fronted cards. Both sides are foil-etched with the Bash side highlighting home runs and runs batted in for 1995 and career, and the Burn side featured stolen base and runs scored leaders for 1995 and career. Cards are numbered with a "B&B" prefix.

		MT
Complete Set (10):		30.00
Common Player:		1.00
1	Sammy Sosa	15.00
2	Barry Bonds	6.00
3	Reggie Sanders	3.00
4	Craig Biggio	2.50
5	Raul Mondesi	3.00
6	Ron Gant	1.00
7	Ray Lankford	1.00
8	Glenallen Hill	1.00
9	Chad Curtis	1.00
10	John Valentin	1.00

1996 Stadium Club Mickey Mantle Retrospective

Following the success of the Mantle reprints in Topps baseball, Stadium Club produced a series of 19 Mickey Mantle Retrospective inserts; nine black-and-white cards in Series 1 and 10 color cards in Series 2. The cards chronicle Mantle's career and provide insights from baseball contemporaries. Throughout both series, the Mantle cards are found on an average of once per 24 Series 1 packs and once per 12 Series 2 packs. Cards are numbered with an "MM" prefix.

		MT
Complete Set (19):		150.00
Complete Series 1 (9):		100.00
Complete Series 2 (10):		50.00
Common Series 1:		12.00
Common Series 2:		7.50
1	Mickey Mantle (1950, minor league)	12.00
2	Mickey Mantle (1951)	12.00
3	Mickey Mantle (1951)	12.00
4	Mickey Mantle (1953)	12.00
5	Mickey Mantle (1954) (w/ Yogi Berra)	12.00
6	Mickey Mantle (1956)	12.00
7	Mickey Mantle (1957)	12.00
8	Mickey Mantle (1958) (w/ Casey Stengel)	12.00
9	Mickey Mantle (1959)	12.00
10	Mickey Mantle (1960) (w/ Elston Howard)	7.50
11	Mickey Mantle (1961)	7.50
12	Mickey Mantle (1961) (w/ Roger Maris)	12.00
13	Mickey Mantle (1962)	7.50
14	Mickey Mantle (1963)	7.50
15	Mickey Mantle (1964)	7.50
16	Mickey Mantle	7.50
17	Mickey Mantle (1968)	7.50
18	Mickey Mantle (1969)	7.50
19	Mickey Mantle (In Memoriam)	7.50

1996 Stadium Club Mega Heroes

Ten heroes players are matched with a comic book-style illustration depicting their nickname in the Mega Heroes insert set. Printed on foilboard in a defraction technology, the cards are found, on average, once per 48 Series I hobby packs and twice as often in retail packs.

		MT
Complete Set (10):		40.00
Common Player:		2.00
1	Frank Thomas	7.50
2	Ken Griffey Jr.	15.00
3	Hideo Nomo	4.50
4	Ozzie Smith	5.00
5	Will Clark	2.50
6	Jack McDowell	2.00
7	Andres Galarraga	2.00
8	Roger Clemens	6.00
9	Deion Sanders	3.00
10	Mo Vaughn	4.00

1996 Stadium Club Metalists

Eight players who have won two or more major awards in their careers are featured in this Series II insert. Cards are printed on foilboard and feature intricate laser-cut designs that depict the player's face. Metalist inserts are found one per 96 retail and one per 48 hobby packs, on average. Cards are numbered with a "M" prefix.

		MT
Complete Set (8):		45.00
Common Player:		1.50
1	Jeff Bagwell	6.00
2	Barry Bonds	6.00
3	Jose Canseco	2.50
4	Roger Clemens	4.50
5	Dennis Eckersley	1.50
6	Greg Maddux	12.00
7	Cal Ripken Jr.	15.00
8	Frank Thomas	7.50

1996 Stadium Club Midsummer Matchups

These inserts salute 1995 National League and American League All-Stars on back-to-back etched-foil cards. Players are matched by position in the 10-card set. Average insertion rate is one per 48 hobby packs and one per 24 retail packs in Series I. Cards are numbered with a "M" prefix.

		MT
Complete Set (10):		60.00
Common Player:		2.50
1	Hideo Nomo, Randy Johnson	4.00
2	Mike Piazza, Ivan Rodriguez	12.00
3	Fred McGriff, Frank Thomas	7.50
4	Craig Biggio, Carlos Baerga	2.50
5	Vinny Castilla, Wade Boggs	3.00
6	Barry Larkin, Cal Ripken Jr.	15.00
7	Barry Bonds, Albert Belle	6.00
8	Len Dykstra, Kenny Lofton	2.50
9	Tony Gwynn, Kirby Puckett	7.00
10	Ron Gant, Edgar Martinez	2.50

1996 Stadium Club Power Packed

Topps' Power Matrix technology is used to showcase 15 of the biggest, strongest players in this Series II insert set. Card backs feature a diagram of the player's home park with baseball graphics measuring this home runs during the 1995 season. The inserts are a one in 48 packs pick, on average, both hobby and retail. Cards are numbered with a "PP" prefix.

		MT
Complete Set (15):		85.00
Common Player:		3.00
1	Albert Belle	6.00
2	Mark McGwire	20.00
3	Jose Canseco	4.00
4	Mike Piazza	15.00
5	Ron Gant	3.00
6	Ken Griffey Jr.	20.00
7	Mo Vaughn	3.00
8	Cecil Fielder	3.00
9	Tim Salmon	3.00
10	Frank Thomas	7.50
11	Juan Gonzalez	10.00
12	Andres Galarraga	3.00
13	Fred McGriff	4.00
14	Jay Buhner	3.00
15	Dante Bichette	3.00

1996 Stadium Club Power Streak

The best power hitters in baseball are featured in Power Matrix technology on these Series I inserts. Average insertion rate is one per 24 hobby and 48 retail packs. Cards are numbered with a "PS" prefix.

		MT
Complete Set (15):		60.00
Common Player:		2.25
1	Randy Johnson	4.00
2	Hideo Nomo	4.00
3	Albert Belle	4.00
4	Dante Bichette	3.00
5	Jay Buhner	2.25
6	Frank Thomas	6.00
7	Mark McGwire	20.00
8	Rafael Palmeiro	3.00
9	Mo Vaughn	3.00
10	Sammy Sosa	10.00
11	Larry Walker	3.00
12	Gary Gaetti	2.25
13	Tim Salmon	2.50
14	Barry Bonds	5.00
15	Jim Edmonds	3.00

1996 Stadium Club Prime Cuts

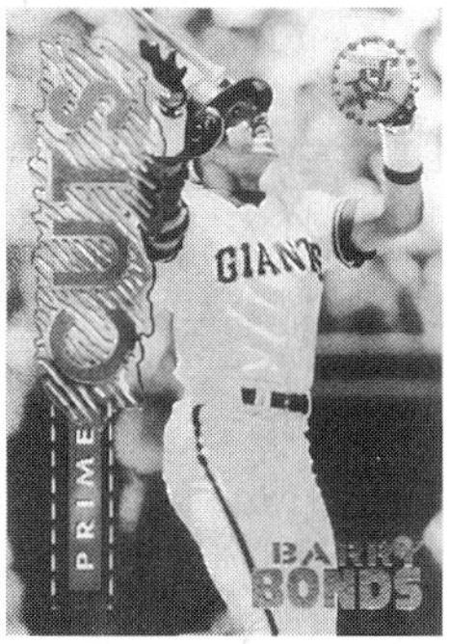

The purest swings in baseball are the focus on these laser-cut, defraction-foil inserts found in Series 1 packs at an average rate of one per 36 hobby and 72 retail packs. Cards are numbered with a "PC" prefix.

		MT
Complete Set (8):		60.00
Common Player:		3.00
1	Albert Belle	5.00
2	Barry Bonds	6.00
3	Ken Griffey Jr.	25.00
4	Tony Gwynn	10.00
5	Edgar Martinez	3.00
6	Rafael Palmeiro	4.00
7	Mike Piazza	15.00
8	Frank Thomas	8.00

1996 Stadium Club TSC Awards

TSC Awards insert cards allowed Topps' experts to honor best performances, newcomer, comeback, etc. The cards are found in Series II packs at an average rate of one per 24 retail and 48 hobby packs.

		MT
Complete Set (10):		40.00
Common Player:		1.00
1	Cal Ripken Jr.	10.00
2	Albert Belle	4.50
3	Tom Glavine	1.50
4	Jeff Conine	1.50
5	Ken Griffey Jr.	15.00
6	Hideo Nomo	2.50
7	Greg Maddux	7.50
8	Chipper Jones	7.50
9	Randy Johnson	3.00
10	Jose Mesa	1.00

1996 Stadium Club Members Only

For the fourth year Topps offered a special edition of its high-end Stadium Club issue to members of its mail-order family. Each of the regular and insert cards was stamped with a gold- or silver-foil "MEMBERS ONLY" seal. The '96 edition was the scarcest ever produced, with only 750 sets offered at $200. Single "Members Only" cards paralleling the regular-issue Stadium Club cards sell for a premium while the M.O. versions of the inserts usually sell at par or even a discount from the issued cards.

	MT
Complete Set (660):	400.00
Common Player:	1.00
Stars: 12X	
Inserts: 50-100%	
(See 1996 Topps Stadium Club for checklists and base card values.)	

1996 Stadium Club Members Only Baseball

This 50-card boxed set was offered to members of Topps Stadium Club at about $15 retail. The first 45 cards in the set represent Topps' choice of 1995's top players in each league. The final five cards, printed in Topps Finest technology, honor hot rookies. The basic cards feature borderless action photos on which the background has been posterized and darkened to make the color photo stand out in the foreground. A gold-foil strip at bottom has the player name and position; a "Members Only" logo is in gold foil in an upper corner. Horizontal backs once again have much of the photo background darkened with a close-up photo at right and a few sentences about the player at left. "Member's Choice" Finest rookie cards have a stylized baseball diamond in red tones as background to the action photos. Backs have a large red-shaded baseball with player write-up at bottom and - honest - a pea-green portrait photo at upper-left. Each of the Finest cards has a peel-off protective layer on front.

		MT
Complete Set (50):		24.00
Common Player:		.25
1	Carlos Baerga	.25
2	Derek Bell	.25
3	Albert Belle	1.00
4	Dante Bichette	.25
5	Craig Biggio	.35
6	Wade Boggs	1.00
7	Barry Bonds	1.00
8	Jay Buhner	.25
9	Vinny Castilla	.25
10	Jeff Conine	.25
11	Jim Edmonds	.25
12	Steve Finley	.25
13	Andres Galarraga	.25
14	Mark Grace	.35
15	Tony Gwynn	1.00
16	Lance Johnson	.25
17	Randy Johnson	.40
18	Eric Karros	.25
19	Chuck Knoblauch	.35
20	Barry Larkin	.25
21	Kenny Lofton	.30
22	Greg Maddux	1.50
23	Edgar Martinez	.25
24	Tino Martinez	.30
25	Mark McGwire	2.00
26	Brian McRae	.25
27	Jose Mesa	.25
28	Eddie Murray	.50
29	Mike Mussina	.35
30	Randy Myers	.25
31	Hideo Nomo	1.00
32	Rafael Palmeiro	.35
33	Tony Phillips	.25
34	Mike Piazza	1.50
35	Kirby Puckett	1.00
36	Manny Ramirez	.75
37	Tim Salmon	.30
38	Reggie Sanders	.25
39	Sammy Sosa	1.50
40	Frank Thomas	1.50
41	Jim Thome	.30
42	John Valentin	.25
43	Mo Vaughn	.30
44	Quilvio Veras	.25
45	Larry Walker	.35
46	Hideo Nomo (Finest)	5.00
47	Marty Cordova (Finest)	1.50
48	Chipper Jones (Finest)	8.00
49	Garret Anderson (Finest)	1.50
50	Andy Pettitte (Finest)	4.00

1997 Stadium Club

Stadium Club totalled 390 cards in 1997, issued in two Series of 195 cards each. In Series 1 (Feb.), cards #181-195 are a rookie subset called TSC 2000. In Series 2 (April), cards #376-390 form a subset called Stadium Slugger. Each of these subsets was short-printed and inserted about one per two packs. TSC is printed on an improved 20-point stock with Topps' Super Color process.

		MT
Complete Set (390):		80.00
Common Player:		.10
Wax Box:		50.00
1	Chipper Jones	2.00
2	Gary Sheffield	.40
3	Kenny Lofton	.60
4	Brian Jordan	.10
5	Mark McGwire	4.00
6	Charles Nagy	.10
7	Tim Salmon	.20
8	Cal Ripken Jr.	2.50
9	Jeff Conine	.10
10	Paul Molitor	.40
11	Mariano Rivera	.20
12	Pedro Martinez	.15
13	Jeff Bagwell	1.25
14	Bobby Bonilla	.10
15	Barry Bonds	.75
16	Ryan Klesko	.40
17	Barry Larkin	.20
18	Jim Thome	.30
19	Jay Buhner	.10
20	Juan Gonzalez	1.50
21	Mike Mussina	.30
22	Kevin Appier	.10
23	Eric Karros	.10
24	Steve Finley	.10
25	Ed Sprague	.10
26	Bernard Gilkey	.10
27	Tony Phillips	.10
28	Henry Rodriguez	.10
29	John Smoltz	.20
30	Dante Bichette	.20
31	Mike Piazza	2.00
32	Paul O'Neill	.15
33	Billy Wagner	.15
34	Reggie Sanders	.10
35	John Jaha	.10
36	Eddie Murray	.40
37	Eric Young	.10
38	Roberto Hernandez	.10
39	Pat Hentgen	.10
40	Sammy Sosa	1.50
41	Todd Hundley	.10
42	Mo Vaughn	.60
43	Robin Ventura	.15
44	Mark Grudzielanek	.10
45	Shane Reynolds	.10
46	Andy Pettitte	.75
47	Fred McGriff	.25
48	Rey Ordonez	.20
49	Will Clark	.25
50	Ken Griffey Jr.	3.00
51	Todd Worrell	.10
52	Rusty Greer	.10
53	Mark Grace	.20
54	Tom Glavine	.20
55	Derek Jeter	2.00
56	Rafael Palmeiro	.15
57	Bernie Williams	.60
58	Marty Cordova	.10
59	Andres Galarraga	.15
60	Ken Caminiti	.35
61	Garret Anderson	.10
62	Denny Martinez	.10
63	Mike Greenwell	.10
64	David Segui	.10
65	Julio Franco	.10
66	Rickey Henderson	.25
67	Ozzie Guillen	.10
68	Pete Harnisch	.10
69	Chan Ho Park	.20
70	Harold Baines	.10
71	Mark Clark	.10
72	Steve Avery	.10
73	Brian Hunter	.10
74	Pedro Astacio	.10
75	Jack McDowell	.10
76	Gregg Jefferies	.10
77	Jason Kendall	.10
78	Todd Walker	.75
79	B.J. Surhoff	.10
80	Moises Alou	.20
81	Fernando Vina	.10
82	Darryl Strawberry	.10
83	Jose Rosado	.10
84	Chris Gomez	.10
85	Chili Davis	.10
86	Alan Benes	.10
87	Todd Hollandsworth	.10
88	Jose Vizcaino	.10
89	Edgardo Alfonzo	.15
90	Ruben Rivera	.20
91	Donovan Osborne	.10
92	Doug Glanville	.10
93	Gary DiSarcina	.10
94	Brooks Kieschnick	.10
95	Bobby Jones	.10
96	Raul Casanova	.10
97	Jermaine Allensworth	.10
98	Kenny Rogers	.10
99	Mark McLemore	.10
100	Jeff Fassero	.10
101	Sandy Alomar	.15
102	Chuck Finley	.10
103	Eric Owens	.10
104	Billy McMillon	.10
105	Dwight Gooden	.10
106	Sterling Hitchcock	.10
107	Doug Drabek	.10
108	Paul Wilson	.10
109	Chris Snopek	.10
110	Al Leiter	.10
111	Bob Tewksbury	.10
112	Todd Greene	.10
113	Jose Valentin	.10
114	Delino DeShields	.10
115	Mike Bordick	.10
116	Pat Meares	.10
117	Mariano Duncan	.10
118	Steve Trachsel	.10
119	Luis Castillo	.25
120	Andy Benes	.10
121	Donne Wall	.10
122	Alex Gonzalez	.10
123	Dan Wilson	.10
124	Omar Vizquel	.10
125	Devon White	.10
126	Darryl Hamilton	.10
127	Orlando Merced	.10
128	Royce Clayton	.10
129	William VanLandingham	.10
130	Terry Steinbach	.10
131	Jeff Blauser	.10
132	Jeff Cirillo	.10
133	Roger Pavlik	.10
134	Danny Tartabull	.10
135	Jeff Montgomery	.10
136	Bobby Higginson	.10
137	Mike Grace	.10

138	Kevin Elster	.10
139	*Brian Giles*	1.50
140	Rod Beck	.10
141	Ismael Valdes	.10
142	Scott Brosius	.10
143	Mike Fetters	.10
144	Gary Gaetti	.10
145	Mike Lansing	.10
146	Glenallen Hill	.10
147	Shawn Green	.20
148	Mel Rojas	.10
149	Joey Cora	.10
150	John Smiley	.10
151	Marvin Benard	.10
152	Curt Schilling	.10
153	Dave Nilsson	.10
154	Edgar Renteria	.20
155	Joey Hamilton	.10
156	Carlos Garcia	.10
157	Nomar Garciaparra	2.00
158	Kevin Ritz	.10
159	Keith Lockhart	.10
160	Justin Thompson	.10
161	Terry Adams	.10
162	Jamey Wright	.10
163	Otis Nixon	.10
164	Michael Tucker	.10
165	Mike Stanley	.10
166	Ben McDonald	.10
167	John Mabry	.10
168	Troy O'Leary	.10
169	Mel Nieves	.10
170	Bret Boone	.10
171	Mike Timlin	.10
172	Scott Rolen	1.50
173	Reggie Jefferson	.10
174	Neifi Perez	.10
175	Brian McRae	.10
176	Tom Goodwin	.10
177	Aaron Sele	.10
178	Benny Santiago	.10
179	Frank Rodriguez	.10
180	Eric Davis	.10
181	Andruw Jones (TSC 2000)	4.00
182	Todd Walker (TSC 2000)	1.50
183	Wes Helms (TSC 2000)	1.00
184	*Nelson Figueroa* (TSC 2000)	.75
185	Vladimir Guerrero (TSC 2000)	4.00
186	Billy McMillon (TSC 2000)	.40
187	Todd Helton (TSC 2000)	2.00
188	Nomar Garciaparra (TSC 2000)	4.00
189	Katsuhiro Maeda (TSC 2000)	1.00
190	Russell Branyan (TSC 2000)	.75
191	Glendon Rusch (TSC 2000)	.25
192	Bartolo Colon (TSC 2000)	.50
193	Scott Rolen (TSC 2000)	3.00
194	Angel Echevarria (TSC 2000)	.15
195	Bob Abreu (TSC 2000)	.25
196	Greg Maddux	2.00
197	Joe Carter	.10
198	Alex Ochoa	.10
199	Ellis Burks	.10
200	Ivan Rodriguez	.60
201	Marquis Grissom	.10
202	Trevor Hoffman	.15
203	Matt Williams	.25
204	Carlos Delgado	.50
205	Ramon Martinez	.10
206	Chuck Knoblauch	.20
207	Juan Guzman	.10
208	Derek Bell	.10
209	Roger Clemens	1.00
210	Vladimir Guerrero	1.00
211	Cecil Fielder	.10
212	Hideo Nomo	.50
213	Frank Thomas	1.00
214	Greg Vaughn	.10
215	Javy Lopez	.20
216	Raul Mondesi	.25
217	Wade Boggs	.30
218	Carlos Baerga	.10
219	Tony Gwynn	1.25
220	Tino Martinez	.15
221	Vinny Castilla	.20
222	Lance Johnson	.10
223	David Justice	.25
224	Rondell White	.20
225	Dean Palmer	.10
226	Jim Edmonds	.10
227	Albert Belle	.75
228	Alex Fernandez	.20
229	Ryne Sandberg	.75
230	Jose Mesa	.10
231	David Cone	.20
232	Troy Percival	.10
233	Edgar Martinez	.10
234	Jose Canseco	.25
235	Kevin Brown	.10
236	Ray Lankford	.10
237	Karim Garcia	.20
238	J.T. Snow	.10
239	Dennis Eckersley	.10
240	Roberto Alomar	.60
241	John Valentin	.10
242	Ron Gant	.15
243	Geronimo Berroa	.10
244	Manny Ramirez	1.00
245	Travis Fryman	.10
246	Denny Neagle	.10
247	Randy Johnson	.60
248	Darin Erstad	1.25
249	Mark Wohlers	.10
250	Ken Hill	.10
251	Larry Walker	.35
252	Craig Biggio	.20
253	Brady Anderson	.10
254	John Wetteland	.10
255	Andruw Jones	2.50
256	Turk Wendell	.10
257	Jason Isringhausen	.10
258	Jaime Navarro	.10
259	Sean Berry	.10
260	Albie Lopez	.10
261	Jay Bell	.10
262	Bobby Witt	.10
263	Tony Clark	.50
264	Tim Wakefield	.10
265	Brad Radke	.10
266	Tim Belcher	.10
267	Mark Lewis	.10
268	Roger Cedeno	.10
269	Tim Naehring	.10
270	Kevin Tapani	.10
271	Joe Randa	.10
272	Randy Myers	.10
273	Dave Burba	.10
274a	Mike Sweeney	.10
274b	Tom Pagnozzi (should be #374)	.10
275	Danny Graves	.10
276	Chad Mottola	.10
277	Ruben Sierra	.10
278	Norm Charlton	.10
279	Scott Servais	.10
280	Jacob Cruz	.10
281	Mike Macfarlane	.10
282	Rich Becker	.10
283	Shannon Stewart	.10
284	Gerald Williams	.10
285	Jody Reed	.10
286	Jeff D'Amico	.10
287	Walt Weiss	.10
288	Jim Leyritz	.10
289	Francisco Cordova	.15
290	F.P. Santangelo	.10
291	Scott Erickson	.10
292	Hal Morris	.10
293	Ray Durham	.10
294	Andy Ashby	.10
295	Darryl Kile	.10
296	Jose Paniagua	.10
297	Mickey Tettleton	.10
298	Joe Girardi	.10
299	Rocky Coppinger	.10
300	Bob Abreu	.10
301	John Olerud	.15
302	Paul Shuey	.10
303	Jeff Brantley	.10
304	Bob Wells	.10
305	Kevin Seitzer	.10
306	Shawon Dunston	.10
307	Jose Herrera	.10
308	Butch Huskey	.10
309	Jose Offerman	.10
310	Rick Aguilera	.10
311	Greg Gagne	.10
312	John Burkett	.10
313	Mark Thompson	.10
314	Alvaro Espinoza	.10
315	Todd Stottlemyre	.10
316	Al Martin	.10
317	James Baldwin	.10
318	Cal Eldred	.10
319	Sid Fernandez	.10
320	Mickey Morandini	.10
321	Robb Nen	.10
322	Mark Lemke	.10
323	Pete Schourek	.10
324	Marcus Jensen	.10
325	Rich Aurilia	.10
326	Jeff King	.10
327	Scott Stahoviak	.10
328	Ricky Otero	.10
329	Antonio Osuna	.10
330	Chris Hoiles	.10
331	Luis Gonzalez	.10
332	Wil Cordero	.10
333	Johnny Damon	.10
334	Mark Langston	.10
335	Orlando Miller	.10
336	Jason Giambi	.10
337	Damian Jackson	.10
338	David Wells	.10
339	Bip Roberts	.10
340	Matt Ruebel	.10
341	Tom Candiotti	.10
342	Wally Joyner	.10
343	Jimmy Key	.10
344	Tony Batista	.10
345	Paul Sorrento	.10
346	Ron Karkovice	.10
347	Wilson Alvarez	.10
348	John Flaherty	.10
349	Rey Sanchez	.10
350	John Vander Wal	.10
351a	Jermaine Dye	.15
351b	Brant Brown (should be #361)	.25
352	Mike Hampton	.10
353	Greg Colbrunn	.10
354	Heathcliff Slocumb	.10
355	Ricky Bottalico	.10
356	Marty Janzen	.10
357	Orel Hershiser	.10
358	Rex Hudler	.10
359	Amaury Telemaco	.10
360	Darrin Fletcher	.10
361	Not issued - see #351	
362	Russ Davis	.10
363	Allen Watson	.10
364	Mike Lieberthal	.10
365	Dave Stevens	.10
366	Jay Powell	.10
367	Tony Fossas	.10
368	Bob Wolcott	.10
369	Mark Loretta	.10
370	Shawn Estes	.10
371	Sandy Martinez	.10
372	Wendell Magee Jr.	.10
373	John Franco	.10
374	Not issued - see #274	
375	Willie Adams	.10
376	Chipper Jones (Stadium Sluggers)	4.00
377	Mo Vaughn (Stadium Sluggers)	2.00
378	Frank Thomas (Stadium Sluggers)	1.50
379	Albert Belle (Stadium Sluggers)	1.50
380	Andres Galarraga (Stadium Sluggers)	.25
381	Gary Sheffield (Stadium Sluggers)	.25
382	Jeff Bagwell (Stadium Sluggers)	2.50
383	Mike Piazza (Stadium Sluggers)	4.00
384	Mark McGwire (Stadium Sluggers)	8.00
385	Ken Griffey Jr. (Stadium Sluggers)	6.00
386	Barry Bonds (Stadium Sluggers)	1.50
387	Juan Gonzalez (Stadium Sluggers)	3.00
388	Brady Anderson (Stadium Sluggers)	.20
389	Ken Caminiti (Stadium Sluggers)	.25
390	Jay Buhner (Stadium Sluggers)	.15

1997 Stadium Club Co-Signers

Each Series of Stadium Club included five different Co-Signers, with an insertion ratio of one per 168 hobby packs. These double-sided cards featured authentic autographs from each star, one per side.

		MT
Complete Set (10):		400.00
Common Card:		15.00
CO1	Andy Pettitte, Derek Jeter	150.00
CO2	Paul Wilson, Todd Hundley	15.00
CO3	Jermaine Dye, Mark Wohlers	15.00
CO4	Scott Rolen, Gregg Jefferies	75.00
CO5	Todd Hollandsworth, Jason Kendall	20.00
CO6	Alan Benes, Robin Ventura	25.00
CO7	Eric Karros, Raul Mondesi	35.00
CO8	Rey Ordonez, Nomar Garciaparra	125.00
CO9	Rondell White, Marty Cordova	20.00
CO10	Tony Gwynn, Karim Garcia	100.00

1997 Stadium Club Firebrand Redemption

Because of production problems with its "Laser-Etched Wood" technology, Stadium Club was unable to package the Firebrand insert cards with the rest of the issue. Instead, a redemption card was substituted. The redemption card pictures the Firebrand card on its horizontal front; the back has details for exchanging the redemption card for the actual wood-printed, die-cut version. The exchange offer ended Sept. 30, 1997.

		MT
Complete Set (12):		85.00
Common Player:		3.00
F1	Jeff Bagwell	8.00
F2	Albert Belle	4.00
F3	Barry Bonds	5.00
F4	Andres Galarraga	3.00
F5	Ken Griffey Jr.	15.00
F6	Brady Anderson	3.00
F7	Mark McGwire	15.00
F8	Chipper Jones	12.50
F9	Frank Thomas	10.00
F10	Mike Piazza	12.50
F11	Mo Vaughn	3.00
F12	Juan Gonzalez	10.00

1997 Stadium Club Firebrand

This 12-card insert was found only in packs sold at retail chains. Cards were inserted 1:36 packs. The hortizontal format cards are printed on thin wood stock, die-cut at top. Fronts are trimmed in gold foil. Cards are numbered with a "F" prefix.

		MT
Complete Set (12):		125.00
Common Player:		4.00
1	Jeff Bagwell	12.00
2	Albert Belle	6.00
3	Barry Bonds	8.00
4	Andres Galarraga	4.00
5	Ken Griffey Jr.	30.00
6	Brady Anderson	4.00
7	Mark McGwire	30.00
8	Chipper Jones	20.00
9	Frank Thomas	12.00
10	Mike Piazza	20.00
11	Mo Vaughn	4.00
12	Juan Gonzalez	15.00

1997 Stadium Club Instavision

Instavision features holographic cards with exciting moments from the 1996 playoffs and World Series. Inserted one per 24 hobby packs and one per 36 retail packs, these cards are printed on a horizontal, plastic card. Cards carry an "I" prefix, with the first 10 found in Series I and the final 12 in Series II.

		MT
Complete Set (22):		50.00
Complete Series 1 Set (10):		20.00
Complete Series 2 Set (12):		30.00
Common Player:		1.50
11	Eddie Murray	2.00
12	Paul Molitor	4.00
13	Todd Hundley	2.00
14	Roger Clemens	5.00
15	Barry Bonds	4.00
16	Mark McGwire	12.50
17	Brady Anderson	1.50
18	Barry Larkin	2.50
19	Ken Caminiti	2.50
110	Hideo Nomo	3.00
111	Bernie Williams	2.00
112	Juan Gonzalez	6.00
113	Andy Pettitte	4.00
114	Albert Belle	3.00
115	John Smoltz	2.00
116	Brian Jordan	1.50
117	Derek Jeter	7.50
118	Ken Caminiti	2.00
119	John Wetteland	1.50
120	Brady Anderson	1.50
121	Andruw Jones	5.00
122	Jim Leyritz	1.50

1997 Stadium Club Millenium

Millennium was a 40-card insert that was released with 20 cards in Series I and Series II. The set featured 40 top prospects and rookies on a silver foil, holographic front, with a Future Forecast section on the back. Cards carried an "M" prefix and were numbered consecutively M1-M40. Millennium inserts were found every 24 hobby packs and every 36 retail packs.

		MT
Complete Set (40):		190.00
Complete Series 1 Set (20):		90.00
Complete Series 2 Set (20):		100.00
Common Player:		2.00
1	Derek Jeter	25.00
2	Mark Grudzielanek	2.00
3	Jacob Cruz	3.00
4	Ray Durham	2.00
5	Tony Clark	8.00
6	Chipper Jones	25.00
7	Luis Castillo	2.00
8	Carlos Delgado	6.00
9	Brant Brown	2.00
10	Jason Kendall	2.00
11	Alan Benes	3.00
12	Rey Ordonez	4.00
13	Justin Thompson	3.00
14	Jermaine Allensworth	2.00
15	Brian Hunter	2.00
16	Marty Cordova	2.00
17	Edgar Renteria	4.00
18	Karim Garcia	5.00
19	Todd Greene	2.00
20	Paul Wilson	2.00
21	Andruw Jones	20.00
22	Todd Walker	8.00
23	Alex Ochoa	2.00
24	Bartolo Colon	5.00
25	Wendell Magee Jr.	3.00
26	Jose Rosado	2.00
27	Katsuhiro Maeda	2.00
28	Bob Abreu	5.00
29	Brooks Kieschnick	2.00
30	Derrick Gibson	3.00
31	Mike Sweeney	2.00
32	Jeff D'Amico	2.00
33	Chad Mottola	2.00
34	Chris Snopek	2.00
35	Jaime Bluma	2.00
36	Vladimir Guerrero	12.00

37	Nomar Garciaparra	24.00
38	Scott Rolen	15.00
39	Dmitri Young	2.00
40	Neifi Perez	2.00

1997 Stadium Club Patent Leather

Patent Leather featured 13 of the top gloves in baseball on a leather, die-cut card. The cards carry a "PL" prefix and are inerted one per 36 retail packs.

		MT
Complete Set (13):		100.00
Common Player:		5.00
1	Ivan Rodriguez	8.00
2	Ken Caminiti	6.00
3	Barry Bonds	10.00
4	Ken Griffey Jr.	35.00
5	Greg Maddux	20.00
6	Craig Biggio	7.00
7	Andres Galarraga	5.00
8	Kenny Lofton	6.00
9	Barry Larkin	5.00
10	Mark Grace	6.00
11	Rey Ordonez	6.00
12	Roberto Alomar	8.00
13	Derek Jeter	20.00

1997 Stadium Club Pure Gold

Pure Gold featured 20 of the top players in baseball on gold, embossed foil cards. Cards carry a "PG" prefix and were inserted every 72 hobby packs and every 108 retail packs. The first 10 cards were in Series I packs, while the final 10 cards are exclusive to Series II.

		MT
Complete Set (20):		350.00
Complete Series 1 Set (10):		150.00
Complete Series 2 Set (10):		200.00
Common Player:		3.00
1	Brady Anderson	8.00
2	Albert Belle	15.00
3	Dante Bichette	8.00
4	Barry Bonds	20.00
5	Jay Buhner	8.00
6	Tony Gwynn	30.00
7	Chipper Jones	40.00
8	Mark McGwire	65.00
9	Gary Sheffield	8.00
10	Frank Thomas	25.00
11	Juan Gonzalez	30.00
12	Ken Caminiti	8.00
13	Kenny Lofton	8.00
14	Jeff Bagwell	30.00
15	Ken Griffey Jr.	65.00
16	Cal Ripken Jr.	50.00
17	Mo Vaughn	8.00
18	Mike Piazza	40.00
19	Derek Jeter	40.00
20	Andres Galarraga	8.00

1997 Stadium Club TSC Matrix

TSC Matrix consists of 120 cards from Series I and II reprinted with Power Matrix technology. In each Series, 60 of the 190 cards were selected for inclusion in TSC Matrix and inserted every 12 hobby packs and every 18 retail packs. Each insert carries the TSC Matrix logo in a top corner of the card.

		MT
Complete Set (120):		400.00
Common Player:		1.00
1	Chipper Jones	25.00
2	Gary Sheffield	3.00
3	Kenny Lofton	6.00
4	Brian Jordan	1.00
5	Mark McGwire	40.00
6	Charles Nagy	1.00
7	Tim Salmon	1.50
8	Cal Ripken Jr.	30.00
9	Jeff Conine	1.00
10	Paul Molitor	5.00
11	Mariano Rivera	2.00
12	Pedro Martinez	1.00
13	Jeff Bagwell	15.00
14	Bobby Bonilla	1.00
15	Barry Bonds	8.00
16	Ryan Klesko	1.50
17	Barry Larkin	1.00
18	Jim Thome	3.00
19	Jay Buhner	1.00
20	Juan Gonzalez	15.00
21	Mike Mussina	4.00
22	Kevin Appier	1.00
23	Eric Karros	1.00
24	Steve Finley	1.00
25	Ed Sprague	1.00
26	Bernard Gilkey	1.00
27	Tony Phillips	1.00
28	Henry Rodriguez	1.00
29	John Smoltz	2.00
30	Dante Bichette	2.00
31	Mike Piazza	25.00
32	Paul O'Neill	1.50
33	Billy Wagner	1.50
34	Reggie Sanders	1.00
35	John Jaha	1.00
36	Eddie Murray	4.00
37	Eric Young	1.00
38	Roberto Hernandez	1.00
39	Pat Hentgen	1.00
40	Sammy Sosa	20.00
41	Todd Hundley	1.00
42	Mo Vaughn	6.00
43	Robin Ventura	1.00
44	Mark Grudzielanek	1.00
45	Shane Reynolds	1.00
46	Andy Pettitte	6.00
47	Fred McGriff	2.50
48	Rey Ordonez	2.00
49	Will Clark	2.50
50	Ken Griffey Jr.	40.00
51	Todd Worrell	1.00
52	Rusty Greer	1.00
53	Mark Grace	2.50
54	Tom Glavine	1.50
55	Derek Jeter	25.00
56	Rafael Palmeiro	2.00
57	Bernie Williams	6.00
58	Marty Cordova	1.00
59	Andres Galarraga	2.00
60	Ken Caminiti	3.00
196	Greg Maddux	25.00
197	Joe Carter	1.00
198	Alex Ochoa	1.00
199	Ellis Burks	1.00
200	Ivan Rodriguez	8.00
201	Marquis Grissom	1.00
202	Trevor Hoffman	1.00
203	Matt Williams	2.00
204	Carlos Delgado	3.00
205	Ramon Martinez	1.00
206	Chuck Knoblauch	2.00
207	Juan Guzman	1.00
208	Derek Bell	1.00
209	Roger Clemens	10.00
210	Vladimir Guerrero	12.00
211	Cecil Fielder	1.00
212	Hideo Nomo	6.00
213	Frank Thomas	20.00
214	Greg Vaughn	1.00
215	Javy Lopez	2.00
216	Raul Mondesi	2.00
217	Wade Boggs	3.50
218	Carlos Baerga	1.00
219	Tony Gwynn	15.00
220	Tino Martinez	2.00
221	Vinny Castilla	1.00
222	Lance Johnson	1.00
223	David Justice	2.00
224	Rondell White	1.00
225	Dean Palmer	1.00
226	Jim Edmonds	1.00
227	Albert Belle	10.00
228	Alex Fernandez	2.00
229	Ryne Sandberg	12.00
230	Jose Mesa	1.00
231	David Cone	2.00
232	Troy Percival	1.00
233	Edgar Martinez	1.00
234	Jose Canseco	3.00
235	Kevin Brown	1.00
236	Ray Lankford	1.00
237	Karim Garcia	4.00
238	J.T. Snow	1.00
239	Dennis Eckersley	1.00
240	Roberto Alomar	8.00
241	John Valentin	1.00
242	Ron Gant	1.00
243	Geronimo Berroa	1.00
244	Manny Ramirez	12.00
245	Travis Fryman	1.00
246	Denny Neagle	1.00
247	Randy Johnson	6.00
248	Darin Erstad	12.00
249	Mark Wohlers	1.00
250	Ken Hill	1.00
251	Larry Walker	2.00
252	Craig Biggio	2.00
253	Brady Anderson	1.50
254	John Wetteland	1.00
255	Andruw Jones	15.00

1997 Stadium Club Members Only

Production was reported at just 750 complete sets of these specially marked Stadium Club cards and inserts. Sold only as complete sets through Topps' Stadium Club program, each card differs from the regular-issue TSC version only in the presence of a subdued "MEMBERS ONLY" repeated all across the cards' backs. Star players' cards sell for a significant premium over regular-issue TSC version; inserts, depending on the scarcity of the regular version, usually sell for a significant discount in the Members Only version.

	MT
Complete Set:	300.00
Common Player:	1.00
Stars: 12X	
Inserts: 50-100%	

(See 1997 Topps Stadium Club and inserts for checklists and base card values.)

> Checklists with card numbers in parentheses ( ) indicates the numbers do not appear on the card.

1997 Stadium Club Members Only Baseball

This boxed set was available only to members of Topps, Stadium Club for a price of $15, which included a year's membership in the club. Fronts feature action photos with a 2-1/2" circle behind the player, a gold-foil Members Only seal and the player's name, also in gold-foil. Backs feature another photo and a career summary on a red background which has the Members Only seal in a repeating pattern. Cards #51-55 are rookie stars and are printed in Topps Finest technologies.

		MT
Complete Set (55):		15.00
Common Player:		.25
1	Brady Anderson	.25
2	Carlos Baerga	.25
3	Jeff Bagwell	.60
4	Albert Belle	.40
5	Dante Bichette	.30
6	Craig Biggio	.35
7	Wade Boggs	.50
8	Barry Bonds	.75
9	Jay Buhner	.25
10	Ellis Burks	.25
11	Ken Caminiti	.30
12	Jose Canseco	.40
13	Joe Carter	.25
14	Roger Clemens	.50
15	Jeff Conine	.25
16	Andres Galarraga	.25
17	Ron Gant	.25
18	Juan Gonzalez	.65
19	Mark Grace	.35
20	Ken Griffey Jr.	3.00
21	Tony Gwynn	1.00
22	Pat Hentgen	.25
23	Todd Hollandsworth	.25
24	Todd Hundley	.30
25	Derek Jeter	1.50
26	Randy Johnson	.35
27	Chipper Jones	1.50
28	Ryan Klesko	.30
29	Chuck Knoblauch	.30
30	Barry Larkin	.25
31	Kenny Lofton	.30
32	Greg Maddux	1.00
33	Mark McGwire	3.00
34	Paul Molitor	.45
35	Raul Mondesi	.35
36	Hideo Nomo	.30
37	Rafael Palmeiro	.35
38	Mike Piazza	1.50
39	Manny Ramirez	.50
40	Cal Ripken Jr.	2.00
41	Ivan Rodriguez	.40
42	Tim Salmon	.25
43	Gary Sheffield	.25
44	John Smoltz	.25
45	Sammy Sosa	1.00
46	Frank Thomas	1.50
47	Jim Thome	.25
48	Mo Vaughn	.30
49	Bernie Williams	.35
50	Matt Williams	.30
51	Darin Erstad (Finest)	2.00
52	Vladimir Guerrero (Finest)	3.00
53	Andruw Jones (Finest)	3.00
54	Scott Rolen (Finest)	2.00
55	Todd Walker (Finest)	2.00

1998 Stadium Club

Stadium Club was issued in two separate series for 1998, with 200 odd-numbered cards in Series I and 200 even- numbered cards in Series II. Retail packs contained six cards and an SRP of $2, hobby packs contained nine cards and an SRP of $3 and HTA packs contained 15 cards and an SRP of $5. Three subets were included in the set, with Future Stars (361-379) and Draft Picks (381-399) both being odd-numbered and Traded (356-400) being even- numbered. Inserts in Series I include: First Day Issue parallels (retail), One of a Kind parallels (hobby), Printing Plates parallels (HTA), Bowman Previews, Co-Signers (hobby), In the Wings, Never Compromise, and Triumvirates (retail). Inserts in Series II include: First Day Issue parallels (retail), One of a Kind parallels (hobby), Printing Plates parallels (HTA), Bowman Prospect Previews, Co-Signers (hobby), Playing with Passion, Royal Court and Triumvirates (retail).

		MT
Complete Set (400):		75.00
Complete Series 1 (200):		40.00
Complete Series 2 (200):		35.00
Common Player:		.10
Wax Box:		65.00
1	Chipper Jones	2.00
2	Frank Thomas	1.50
3	Vladimir Guerrero	1.00
4	Ellis Burks	.10
5	John Franco	.10
6	Paul Molitor	.60
7	Rusty Greer	.10
8	Todd Hundley	.10
9	Brett Tomko	.10
10	Eric Karros	.15
11	Mike Cameron	.10
12	Jim Edmonds	.10
13	Bernie Williams	.50
14	Denny Neagle	.10
15	Jason Dickson	.10
16	Sammy Sosa	2.00
17	Brian Jordan	.10
18	Jose Vidro	.10
19	Scott Spiezio	.10
20	Jay Buhner	.15
21	Jim Thome	.40
22	Sandy Alomar	.20
23	Devon White	.10
24	Roberto Alomar	.60
25	John Flaherty	.10
26	John Wetteland	.10
27	Willie Greene	.10
28	Gregg Jefferies	.10
29	Johnny Damon	.10
30	Barry Larkin	.20
31	Chuck Knoblauch	.25
32	Mo Vaughn	.50
33	Tony Clark	.40
34	Marty Cordova	.10
35	Vinny Castilla	.10
36	Jeff King	.10
37	Reggie Jefferson	.10
38	Mariano Rivera	.20
39	Jermaine Allensworth	.10
40	Livan Hernandez	.10
41	Heathcliff Slocumb	.10
42	Jacob Cruz	.10
43	Barry Bonds	.75
44	Dave Magadan	.10
45	Chan Ho Park	.15
46	Jeremi Gonzalez	.10
47	Jeff Cirillo	.10
48	Delino DeShields	.10
49	Craig Biggio	.25
50	Benito Santiago	.10
51	Mark Clark	.10
52	Fernando Vina	.10
53	F.P. Santangelo	.10
54	Pep Harris	.25
55	Edgar Renteria	.10

56	Jeff Bagwell	1.50
57	Jimmy Key	.10
58	Bartolo Colon	.10
59	Curt Schilling	.20
60	Steve Finley	.10
61	Andy Ashby	.10
62	John Burkett	.10
63	Orel Hershiser	.10
64	Pokey Reese	.10
65	Scott Servais	.10
66	Todd Jones	.10
67	Javy Lopez	.20
68	Robin Ventura	.20
69	Miguel Tejada	.50
70	Raul Casanova	.10
71	Reggie Sanders	.10
72	Edgardo Alfonzo	.10
73	Dean Palmer	.10
74	Todd Stottlemyre	.10
75	David Wells	.10
76	Troy Percival	.10
77	Albert Belle	.60
78	Pat Hentgen	.10
79	Brian Hunter	.10
80	Richard Hidalgo	.10
81	Darren Oliver	.10
82	Mark Wohlers	.10
83	Cal Ripken Jr.	3.00
84	Hideo Nomo	.50
85	Derrek Lee	.15
86	Stan Javier	.10
87	Rey Ordonez	.10
88	Randy Johnson	.60
89	Jeff Kent	.10
90	Brian McRae	.10
91	Manny Ramirez	.75
92	Trevor Hoffman	.10
93	Doug Glanville	.10
94	Todd Walker	.20
95	Andy Benes	.10
96	Jason Schmidt	.10
97	Mike Matheny	.10
98	Tim Naehring	.10
99	Jeff Blauser	.10
100	Jose Rosado	.10
101	Roger Clemens	1.00
102	Pedro Astacio	.10
103	Mark Bellhorn	.10
104	Paul O'Neill	.20
105	Darin Erstad	.75
106	Mike Lieberthal	.10
107	Wilson Alvarez	.10
108	Mike Mussina	.60
109	George Williams	.10
110	Cliff Floyd	.10
111	Shawn Estes	.10
112	Mark Grudzielanek	.10
113	Tony Gwynn	1.50
114	Alan Benes	.15
115	Terry Steinbach	.10
116	Greg Maddux	2.00
117	Andy Pettitte	.50
118	Dave Nilsson	.10
119	Deivi Cruz	.10
120	Carlos Delgado	.50
121	Scott Hatteberg	.10
122	John Olerud	.20
123	Moises Alou	.20
124	Garret Anderson	.10
125	Royce Clayton	.10
126	Dante Powell	.10
127	Tom Glavine	.20
128	Gary DiSarcina	.10
129	Terry Adams	.10
130	Raul Mondesi	.30
131	Dan Wilson	.10
132	Al Martin	.10
133	Mickey Morandini	.10
134	Rafael Palmeiro	.25
135	Juan Encarnacion	.25
136	Jim Pittsley	.10
137	*Magglio Ordonez*	1.50
138	Will Clark	.30
139	Todd Helton	1.00
140	Kelvim Escobar	.10
141	Esteban Loaiza	.10
142	John Jaha	.10
143	Jeff Fassero	.10
144	Harold Baines	.10
145	Butch Huskey	.10
146	Pat Meares	.10
147	Brian Giles	.10
148	Ramiro Mendoza	.10
149	John Smoltz	.20
150	Felix Martinez	.10
151	Jose Valentin	.10
152	Brad Rigby	.10
153	Ed Sprague	.10
154	Mike Hampton	.10
155	Mike Lansing	.10
156	Ray Lankford	.10
157	Bobby Bonilla	.10
158	Bill Mueller	.10
159	Jeffrey Hammonds	.10
160	Charles Nagy	.10
161	Rich Loiselle	.10
162	Al Leiter	.10
163	Larry Walker	.25
164	Chris Hoiles	.10
165	Jeff Montgomery	.10
166	Francisco Cordova	.10
167	James Baldwin	.10
168	Mark McLemore	.10
169	Kevin Appier	.10
170	Jamey Wright	.10
171	Nomar Garciaparra	2.00
172	Matt Franco	.10
173	Armando Benitez	.10
174	Jeromy Burnitz	.10
175	Ismael Valdes	.10
176	Lance Johnson	.10
177	Paul Sorrento	.10
178	Rondell White	.20
179	Kevin Elster	.10
180	Jason Giambi	.10
181	Carlos Baerga	.10
182	Russ Davis	.10
183	Ryan McGuire	.10
184	Eric Young	.10
185	Ron Gant	.10
186	Manny Alexander	.10
187	Scott Karl	.10
188	Brady Anderson	.10
189	Randall Simon	.10
190	Tim Belcher	.10
191	Jaret Wright	1.00
192	Dante Bichette	.25
193	John Valentin	.10
194	Darren Bragg	.10
195	Mike Sweeney	.10
196	Craig Counsell	.10
197	Jaime Navarro	.10
198	Todd Dunn	.10
199	Ken Griffey Jr.	4.00
200	Juan Gonzalez	1.50
201	Billy Wagner	.10
202	Tino Martinez	.10
203	Mark McGwire	4.00
204	Jeff D'Amico	.10
205	Rico Brogna	.10
206	Todd Hollandsworth	.10
207	Chad Curtis	.10
208	Tom Goodwin	.10
209	Neifi Perez	.10
210	Derek Bell	.10
211	Quilvio Veras	.10
212	Greg Vaughn	.10
213	Roberto Hernandez	.10
214	Arthur Rhodes	.10
215	Cal Eldred	.10
216	Bill Taylor	.10
217	Todd Greene	.10
218	Mario Valdez	.10
219	Ricky Bottalico	.10
220	Frank Rodriguez	.10
221	Rich Becker	.10
222	Roberto Duran	.10
223	Ivan Rodriguez	.75
224	Mike Jackson	.10
225	Deion Sanders	.20
226	Tony Womack	.10
227	Mark Kotsay	.50
228	Steve Trachsel	.10
229	Ryan Klesko	.20
230	Ken Cloude	.25
231	Luis Gonzalez	.10
232	Gary Gaetti	.10
233	Michael Tucker	.10
234	Shawn Green	.15
235	Ariel Prieto	.10
236	Kirt Manwaring	.10
237	Omar Vizquel	.10
238	Matt Beech	.10
239	Justin Thompson	.20
240	Bret Boone	.10
241	Derek Jeter	2.00
242	Ken Caminiti	.25
243	Jay Bell	.10
244	Kevin Tapani	.10
245	Jason Kendall	.10
246	Jose Guillen	.20
247	Mike Bordick	.10
248	Dustin Hermanson	.10
249	Darrin Fletcher	.10
250	Dave Hollins	.10
251	Ramon Martinez	.20
252	Hideki Irabu	.50
253	Mark Grace	.25
254	Jason Isringhausen	.10
255	Jose Cruz Jr.	.20
256	Brian Johnson	.10
257	Brad Ausmus	.10
258	Andruw Jones	.75
259	Doug Jones	.10
260	Jeff Shaw	.10
261	Chuck Finley	.10
262	Gary Sheffield	.30
263	David Segui	.10
264	John Smiley	.10
265	Tim Salmon	.20
266	J.T. Snow Jr.	.10
267	Alex Fernandez	.10
268	Matt Stairs	.10
269	B.J. Surhoff	.10
270	Keith Foulke	.10
271	Edgar Martinez	.10
272	Shannon Stewart	.10
273	Eduardo Perez	.10
274	Wally Joyner	.10
275	Kevin Young	.10
276	Eli Marrero	.10
277	Brad Radke	.10
278	Jamie Moyer	.10
279	Joe Girardi	.10
280	Troy O'Leary	.10
281	Aaron Sele	.10
282	Jose Offerman	.10
283	Scott Erickson	.10
284	Sean Berry	.10
285	Shigetosi Hasegawa	.10
286	Felix Heredia	.10
287	Willie McGee	.10
288	Alex Rodriguez	3.00
289	Ugueth Urbina	.10
290	Jon Lieber	.10
291	Fernando Tatis	.10
292	Chris Stynes	.10
293	Bernard Gilkey	.10
294	Joey Hamilton	.10
295	Matt Karchner	.10
296	Paul Wilson	.10
297	Mel Nieves	.10
298	*Kevin Millwood*	4.00
299	Quinton McCracken	.10
300	Jerry DiPoto	.10
301	Jermaine Dye	.10
302	Travis Lee	.75
303	Ron Coomer	.10
304	Matt Williams	.25
305	Bobby Higginson	.10
306	Jorge Fabregas	.10
307	Hal Morris	.10
308	Jay Bell	.10
309	Joe Randa	.10
310	Andy Benes	.10
311	Sterling Hitchcock	.10
312	Jeff Suppan	.10
313	Shane Reynolds	.10
314	Willie Blair	.10
315	Scott Rolen	1.50
316	Wilson Alvarez	.10
317	David Justice	.25
318	Fred McGriff	.25
319	Bobby Jones	.10
320	Wade Boggs	.40
321	Tim Wakefield	.10
322	Tony Saunders	.10
323	David Cone	.20
324	Roberto Hernandez	.10
325	Jose Canseco	.30
326	Kevin Stocker	.10
327	Gerald Williams	.10
328	Quinton McCracken	.10
329	Mark Gardner	.10
330	Ben Grieve (Prime Rookie)	1.50
331	Kevin Brown	.20
332	*Mike Lowell* (Prime Rookie)	.40
333	Jed Hansen	.10
334	Abraham Nunez (Prime Rookie)	.25
335	John Thomson	.10
336	Derrek Lee (Prime Rookie)	.10
337	Mike Piazza	2.00
338	Brad Fullmer (Prime Rookie)	.10
339	Ray Durham	.10
340	Kerry Wood (Prime Rookie)	.75
341	*Kevin Polcovich*	.10
342	Russ Johnson (Prime Rookie)	.10
343	Darryl Hamilton	.10
344	David Ortiz (Prime Rookie)	.40
345	Kevin Orie	.10
346	Sean Casey (Prime Rookie)	.50
347	Juan Guzman	.10
348	Ruben Rivera (Prime Rookie)	.10
349	Rick Aguilera	.10
350	Bobby Estalella (Prime Rookie)	.10
351	Bobby Witt	.10
352	Paul Konerko (Prime Rookie)	.50
353	Matt Morris	.10
354	Carl Pavano (Prime Rookie)	.20
355	Todd Zeile	.10
356	Kevin Brown (Transaction)	.10
357	Alex Gonzalez	.10
358	Chuck Knoblauch (Transaction)	.40
359	Joey Cora	.10
360	Mike Lansing (Transaction)	.10
361	Adrian Beltre (Future Stars)	1.50
362	Dennis Eckersley (Transaction)	.10
363	A.J. Hinch (Future Stars)	1.50
364	Kenny Lofton (Transaction)	.50
365	Alex Gonzalez (Future Stars)	.10
366	Henry Rodriguez (Transaction)	.10
367	*Mike Stoner* (Future Stars)	2.00
368	Darryl Kile (Transaction)	.10
369	Carl Pavano (Future Stars)	.50
370	Walt Weiss (Transaction)	.10
371	Kris Benson (Future Stars)	.75
372	Cecil Fielder (Transaction)	.10
373	Dermal Brown (Future Stars)	1.50
374	Rod Beck (Transaction)	.10
375	Eric Milton (Future Stars)	1.00
376	Travis Fryman (Transaction)	.10
377	Preston Wilson (Future Stars)	.10
378	Chili Davis (Transaction)	.10
379	Travis Lee (Future Stars)	1.50
380	Jim Leyritz (Transaction)	.10
381	Vernon Wells (Draft Picks)	1.50
382	Joe Carter (Transaction)	.10
383	J.J. Davis (Draft Picks)	1.00
384	Marquis Grissom (Transaction)	.10
385	*Mike Cuddyer* (Draft Picks)	1.50
386	Rickey Henderson (Transaction)	.15
387	*Chris Enochs* (Draft Picks)	1.00
388	Andres Galarraga (Transaction)	.40
389	Jason Dellaero (Draft Picks)	.20
390	Robb Nen (Transaction)	.10
391	Mark Mangum (Draft Picks)	.10
392	Jeff Blauser (Transaction)	.10
393	Adam Kennedy (Draft Picks)	.20
394	Bob Abreu (Transaction)	.10
395	*Jack Cust* (Draft Picks)	1.00
396	Jose Vizcaino (Transaction)	.10
397	Jon Garland (Draft Picks)	.50
398	Pedro Martinez (Transaction)	.40
399	Aaron Akin (Draft Picks)	.10
400	Jeff Conine (Transaction)	.10

1998 Stadium Club First Day Issue

	MT
Common Player:	5.00
Stars: 30X	
Production 200 sets	
(See 1998 Stadium Club for checklist and base card values.)	

1998 Stadium Club One of a Kind

This hobby-only parallel set includes all 400 cards from Series 1 and 2 printed on a silver mirrorboard stock. Cards are sequentially numbered to 150 and inserted one per 21 Series 1 packs and one per 24 Series 2 packs.

	MT
Common Player:	5.00
Stars: 40X	
Production 150 sets	
(See 1998 Stadium Club for checklist and base card values.)	

1998 Stadium Club Bowman Preview

This Series I insert gave collectors a sneak peak at Bowman's 50th anniversary set, with 10 top veterans displayed on the 1998 Bowman design. The cards were inserted one per 12 packs and numbered with a "BP" prefix.

		MT
Complete Set (10):		40.00
Common Player:		1.00
Inserted 1:12		
BP1	Nomar Garciaparra	6.50
BP2	Scott Rolen	4.50
BP3	Ken Griffey Jr.	10.00
BP4	Frank Thomas	5.00
BP5	Larry Walker	1.25
BP6	Mike Piazza	6.50
BP7	Chipper Jones	6.50
BP8	Tino Martinez	1.00
BP9	Mark McGwire	10.00
BP10	Barry Bonds	3.00

1998 Stadium Club Bowman Prospect Preview

Bowman Prospect Previews were inserted into Series II retail and hobby packs at a rate of one per 12 and HTA packs at one per four. The 10-card insert previews the upcoming 1998 Bowman set and includes top prospects that are expected to make an impact in 1998.

		MT
Complete Set (10):		15.00
Common Player:		1.00
Inserted 1:12		
BP1	Ben Grieve	4.00
BP2	Brad Fullmer	1.50
BP3	Ryan Anderson	5.00
BP4	Mark Kotsay	1.50
BP5	Bobby Estalella	1.25
BP6	Juan Encarnacion	1.50
BP7	Todd Helton	3.00
BP8	Mike Lowell	1.00
BP9	A.J. Hinch	1.25
BP10	Richard Hidalgo	1.00

1998 Stadium Club Co-Signers

Co-Signers were inserted into both Series 1 and 2 hobby and HTA packs. The complete set is 36 cards and contains two top players on one side along with both autographs. They were available in three levels of scarcity: Series 1 Group A 1:4,372 hobby and 1:2,623 HTA; Series 1 Group B 1:1,457 hobby and HTA 1:874; Series 1 Group C 1:121 hobby and 1:73 HTA; Series 2 Group A 1:4,702 hobby and 1:2,821 HTA; Series 2 Group B 1:1,567 hobby and 1:940 HTA, Series 2 Group C 1:1,131 hobby and 1:78 HTA.

	MT
Common Player:	25.00
Group A 1:4,372	
Group B 1:1,457	
Group C 1:121	
CS1 Nomar Garciaparra, Scott Rolen (A)	700.00
CS2 Nomar Garciaparra, Derek Jeter (B)	250.00
CS3 Nomar Garciaparra, Eric Karros (C)	100.00
CS4 Scott Rolen, Derek Jeter (C)	150.00
CS5 Scott Rolen, Eric Karros (B)	150.00
CS6 Derek Jeter, Eric Karros (A)	500.00
CS7 Travis Lee, Jose Cruz Jr. (B)	40.00
CS8 Travis Lee, Mark Kotsay (C)	25.00
CS9 Travis Lee, Paul Konerko (A)	75.00
CS10Jose Cruz Jr., Mark Kotsay (A)	50.00
CS11Jose Cruz Jr., Paul Konerko (C)	25.00
CS12Mark Kotsay, Paul Konerko (B)	60.00
CS13Tony Gwynn, Larry Walker (A)	500.00
CS14Tony Gwynn, Mark Grudzielanek (C)	100.00
CS15Tony Gwynn, Andres Galarraga (B)	150.00
CS16Larry Walker, Mark Grudzielanek (B)	75.00
CS17Larry Walker, Andres Galarraga (C)	100.00
CS18Mark Grudzielanek, Andres Galarraga (A)	50.00
CS19Sandy Alomar, Roberto Alomar (A)	400.00
CS20Sandy Alomar, Andy Pettitte (C)	40.00
CS21Sandy Alomar, Tino Martinez (B)	75.00
CS22Roberto Alomar, Andy Pettitte (B)	125.00
CS23Roberto Alomar, Tino Martinez (C)	60.00
CS24Andy Pettitte, Tino Martinez (A)	150.00
CS25Tony Clark, Todd Hundley (A)	100.00
CS26Tony Clark, Tim Salmon (B)	75.00
CS27Tony Clark, Robin Ventura (C)	50.00
CS28Todd Hundley, Tim Salmon (C)	50.00
CS29Todd Hundley, Robin Ventura (B)	50.00
CS30Tim Salmon, Robin Ventura (A)	100.00
CS31Roger Clemens, Randy Johnson (B)	225.00
CS32Roger Clemens, Jaret Wright (A)	400.00
CS33Roger Clemens, Matt Morris (C)	100.00
CS34Randy Johnson, Jaret Wright (C)	80.00
CS35Randy Johnson, Matt Morris (A)	150.00
CS36Jaret Wright, Matt Morris (B)	75.00

1998 Stadium Club In the Wings

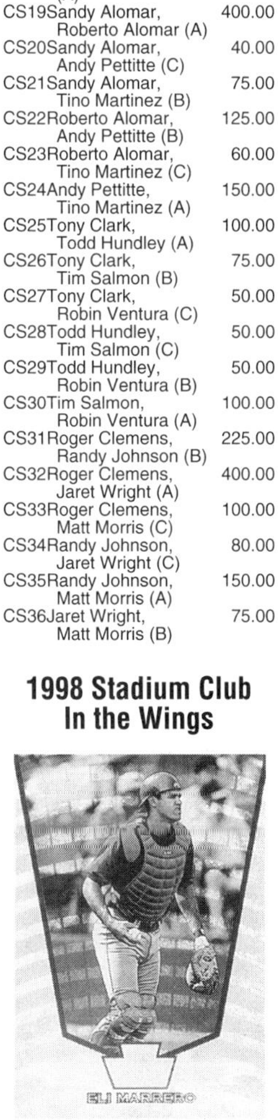

In the Wings was a Series I insert found every 36 packs. It included 15 future stars on uniluster technology.

	MT
Complete Set (15):	45.00
Common Player:	1.50
Inserted 1:36	
W1 Juan Encarnacion	2.50
W2 Brad Fullmer	3.00
W3 Ben Grieve	10.00
W4 Todd Helton	7.50
W5 Richard Hidalgo	1.50
W6 Russ Johnson	1.50
W7 Paul Konerko	7.50
W8 Mark Kotsay	4.00
W9 Derrek Lee	3.00
W10 Travis Lee	6.00
W11 Eli Marrero	1.50
W12 David Ortiz	1.50
W13 Randall Simon	2.00
W14 Shannon Stewart	2.00
W15 Fernando Tatis	3.00

1998 Stadium Club Never Compromise

Never Compromise was a 20-card insert found in packs of Series I. Cards were inserted one per 12 packs and numbered with a "NC" prefix.

	MT
Complete Set (20):	100.00
Common Player:	1.00
Inserted 1:12	
NC1 Cal Ripken Jr.	15.00
NC2 Ivan Rodriguez	5.00
NC3 Ken Griffey Jr.	20.00
NC4 Frank Thomas	10.00
NC5 Tony Gwynn	10.00
NC6 Mike Piazza	12.00
NC7 Randy Johnson	3.00
NC8 Greg Maddux	12.00
NC9 Roger Clemens	8.00
NC10Derek Jeter	12.00
NC11Chipper Jones	12.00
NC12Barry Bonds	5.00
NC13Larry Walker	2.00
NC14Jeff Bagwell	8.00
NC15Barry Larkin	1.00
NC16Ken Caminiti	1.00
NC17Mark McGwire	20.00
NC18Manny Ramirez	5.00
NC19Tim Salmon	1.00
NC20Paul Molitor	3.00

1998 Stadium Club Playing with Passion

This Series II insert displayed 10 players with a strong desire to win. The cards were inserted one per 12 packs and numbered with a "P" prefix.

	MT
Complete Set (10):	30.00
Common Player:	1.00
Inserted 1:12	
P1 Bernie Williams	1.00
P2 Jim Edmonds	1.00
P3 Chipper Jones	4.00
P4 Cal Ripken Jr.	5.00
P5 Craig Biggio	1.00
P6 Juan Gonzalez	3.25
P7 Alex Rodriguez	5.00
P8 Tino Martinez	1.00
P9 Mike Piazza	4.00
P10 Ken Griffey Jr.	7.00

1998 Stadium Club Royal Court

Fifteen players were showcased on uniluster technology for this Series II insert. The set is broken up into 10 Kings (veterans) and five Princes (rookies) and inserted one per 36 packs.

	MT
Complete Set (15):	180.00
Common Player:	3.00
Inserted 1:36	
RC1 Ken Griffey Jr.	30.00
RC2 Frank Thomas	15.00
RC3 Mike Piazza	20.00
RC4 Chipper Jones	20.00
RC5 Mark McGwire	30.00
RC6 Cal Ripken Jr.	25.00
RC7 Jeff Bagwell	12.00
RC8 Barry Bonds	8.00
RC9 Juan Gonzalez	15.00
RC10Alex Rodriguez	25.00
RC11Travis Lee	6.00
RC12Paul Konerko	3.00
RC13Todd Helton	5.00
RC14Ben Grieve	8.00
RC15Mark Kotsay	3.00

1998 Stadium Club Screen Plays Sound Chips

One of the packs in each Home Team Advantage box of TSC "Odd Series" cards contained this special "card" commemorating the home run hit by Cal Ripken Jr. in his historic 2,131st game on Sept. 6, 1995. The item is 3-1/2" x 2-1/2" x 3/8" deep. Glued to the top is a magic motion card showing Ripken hitting the blast. When a corner of the card is squeezed, a sound chip replays the radio call of the home run by Jon Miller and President Bill Clinton. The top of the package opens to reveal a newspaper-like presentation with a picture of Ripken, details of his home run and the technology used to produce the item.

	MT
SC1 Cal Ripken Jr.	12.50

1998 Stadium Club Triumvirate

Triumvirates were included in both series of Stadium Club and were available only in retail packs. Series 1 has 24 players, with three players from eight different teams, while Series 2 has 30 players, with three players from 10 different positions. The cards are all die-cut and fit together to form three-card panels. Three different versions of each card were available - Luminous (regular) versions were seeded one per 48 packs, Luminescent versions were seeded one per 192 packs and Illuminator versions were seeded one per 384 packs.

	MT
Complete Set (54):	700.00
Complete Series 1 (24):	300.00
Complete Series 2 (30):	400.00
Common Player:	4.00
Luminous 1:48	
Luminescents 1:192: 2X	
Illuminators 1:384: 4X	
T1a Chipper Jones	30.00
T1b Andruw Jones	20.00
T1c Kenny Lofton	8.00
T2a Derek Jeter	30.00
T2b Bernie Williams	8.00
T2c Tino Martinez	4.00
T3a Jay Buhner	4.00
T3b Edgar Martinez	4.00
T3c Ken Griffey Jr.	50.00
T4a Albert Belle	12.00
T4b Robin Ventura	5.00
T4c Frank Thomas	25.00
T5a Brady Anderson	4.00
T5b Cal Ripken Jr.	40.00
T5c Rafael Palmeiro	6.00
T6a Mike Piazza	30.00
T6b Raul Mondesi	6.00
T6c Eric Karros	4.00
T7a Vinny Castilla	4.00
T7b Andres Galarraga	6.00
T7c Larry Walker	6.00
T8a Jim Thome	6.00
T8b Manny Ramirez	10.00
T8c David Justice	6.00
T9a Mike Mussina	10.00
T9b Greg Maddux	30.00
T9c Randy Johnson	10.00
T10a Mike Piazza	30.00
T10b Sandy Alomar	4.00
T10c Ivan Rodriguez	12.00
T11a Mark McGwire	50.00
T11b Tino Martinez	4.00
T11c Frank Thomas	25.00
T12a Roberto Alomar	10.00
T12b Chuck Knoblauch	8.00
T12c Craig Biggio	5.00
T13a Cal Ripken Jr.	40.00
T13b Chipper Jones	30.00
T13c Ken Caminiti	4.00
T14a Derek Jeter	30.00
T14b Nomar Garciaparra	30.00
T14c Alex Rodriguez	40.00
T15a Barry Bonds	12.00
T15b David Justice	6.00
T15c Albert Belle	12.00
T16a Bernie Williams	8.00
T16b Ken Griffey Jr.	50.00
T16c Ray Lankford	4.00
T17a Tim Salmon	4.00
T17b Larry Walker	6.00
T17c Tony Gwynn	25.00
T18a Paul Molitor	10.00
T18b Edgar Martinez	4.00
T18c Juan Gonzalez	25.00

1999 Stadium Club

Released in two series with Series 1 170-cards and Series 2 185-cards. Base cards feature a full bleed design on 20-pt. stock with an embossed holographic logo. Draft Pick and Prospect subset cards are short-printed, seeded in every three packs. Card backs have 1998 statistics and personal information. Hobby packs consist of six cards with a S.R.P. of $2.

	MT
Complete Set (355):	115.00
Complete Series 1 Set (170):	65.00
Complete Series 2 Set (185):	55.00
Common Player:	.15
Common Prospect (141-148):	1.50
Inserted 1:3	
Common Draft Pick (149-160):	1.50
Inserted 1:3	
Common SP (311-335, 346-355):	1.00
Common SP (336-345):	2.00
Series 1 H Wax Box:	40.00
Series 2 H Wax Box:	35.00
1 Alex Rodriguez	2.50
2 Chipper Jones	2.00
3 Rusty Greer	.15
4 Jim Edmonds	.20
5 Ron Gant	.15
6 Kevin Polcovich	.15
7 Darryl Strawberry	.25
8 Bill Mueller	.15
9 Vinny Castilla	.15
10 Wade Boggs	.40
11 Jose Lima	.15
12 Darren Dreifort	.15
13 Jay Bell	.15
14 Ben Grieve	.75
15 Shawn Green	.25
16 Andres Galarraga	.60
17 Bartolo Colon	.15
18 Francisco Cordova	.15
19 Paul O'Neill	.30
20 Trevor Hoffman	.15
21 Darren Oliver	.15
22 John Franco	.15
23 Eli Marrero	.15
24 Roberto Hernandez	.15
25 Craig Biggio	.30
26 Brad Fullmer	.25
27 Scott Erickson	.15
28 Tom Gordon	.15
29 Brian Hunter	.15
30 Raul Mondesi	.25
31 Rick Reed	.15
32 Jose Canseco	.40
33 Robb Nen	.15
34 Turner Ward	.15
35 Bret Boone	.15
36 Jose Offerman	.15
37 Matt Lawton	.15
38 David Wells	.15
39 Bob Abreu	.15
40 Jeromy Burnitz	.15
41 Deivi Cruz	.15
42 Mike Cameron	.15
43 Rico Brogna	.15
44 Dmitri Young	.15
45 Chuck Knoblauch	.30

46	Johnny Damon	.15
47	Brian Meadows	.15
48	Jeremi Gonzalez	.15
49	Gary DiSarcina	.15
50	Frank Thomas	1.50
51	F.P. Santangelo	.15
52	Tom Candiotti	.15
53	Shane Reynolds	.15
54	Rod Beck	.15
55	Rey Ordonez	.15
56	Todd Helton	.75
57	Mickey Morandini	.15
58	Jorge Posada	.15
59	Mike Mussina	.50
60	Bobby Bonilla	.15
61	David Segui	.15
62	Brian McRae	.15
63	Fred McGriff	.25
64	Brett Tomko	.15
65	Derek Jeter	2.00
66	Sammy Sosa	2.50
67	Kenny Rogers	.15
68	Dave Nilsson	.15
69	Eric Young	.15
70	Mark McGwire	3.00
71	Kenny Lofton	.45
72	Tom Glavine	.20
73	Joey Hamilton	.15
74	John Valentin	.15
75	Mariano Rivera	.25
76	Ray Durham	.15
77	Tony Clark	.50
78	Livan Hernandez	.15
79	Rickey Henderson	.30
80	Vladimir Guerrero	1.00
81	J.T. Snow Jr.	.15
82	Juan Guzman	.15
83	Darryl Hamilton	.15
84	Matt Anderson	.25
85	Travis Lee	.75
86	Joe Randa	.15
87	Dave Dellucci	.15
88	Moises Alou	.20
89	Alex Gonzalez	.15
90	Tony Womack	.15
91	Neifi Perez	.15
92	Travis Fryman	.15
93	Masato Yoshii	.15
94	Woody Williams	.15
95	Ray Lankford	.15
96	Roger Clemens	1.00
97	Dustin Hermanson	.15
98	Joe Carter	.15
99	Jason Schmidt	.15
100	Greg Maddux	2.00
101	Kevin Tapani	.15
102	Charles Johnson	.15
103	Derrek Lee	.15
104	Pete Harnisch	.15
105	Dante Bichette	.40
106	Scott Brosius	.15
107	Mike Caruso	.15
108	Eddie Taubensee	.15
109	Jeff Fassero	.15
110	Marquis Grissom	.15
111	Jose Hernandez	.15
112	Chan Ho Park	.25
113	Wally Joyner	.15
114	Bobby Estalella	.15
115	Pedro Martinez	.50
116	Shawn Estes	.15
117	Walt Weiss	.15
118	John Mabry	.15
119	Brian Johnson	.15
120	Jim Thome	.35
121	Bill Spiers	.15
122	John Olerud	.25
123	Jeff King	.15
124	Tim Belcher	.15
125	John Wetteland	.15
126	Tony Gwynn	1.50
127	Brady Anderson	.15
128	Randy Winn	.15
129	Devon White	.15
130	Eric Karros	.15
131	Kevin Millwood	.40
132	Andy Benes	.15
133	Andy Ashby	.15
134	Ron Comer	.15
135	Juan Gonzalez	1.50
136	Randy Johnson	.50
137	Aaron Sele	.15
138	Edgardo Alfonzo	.15
139	B.J. Surhoff	.15
140	Jose Vizcaino	.15
141	*Chad Moeller* (Prospect)	2.00
142	*Mike Zwicka* (Prospect)	1.50
143	Angel Pena (Prospect)	3.00
144	*Nick Johnson* (Prospect)	8.00
145	*Giuseppe Chiaramonte* (Prospect)	2.50
146	*Kit Pellow* (Prospect)	2.50
147	*Clayton Andrews* (Prospect)	2.00
148	*Jerry Hairston Jr.* (Prospect)	3.00
149	*Jason Tyner* (Draft Pick)	1.50
150	*Chip Ambres* (Draft Pick)	2.00
151	*Pat Burrell* (Draft Pick)	12.00
152	*Josh McKinley* (Draft Pick)	2.00
153	*Choo Freeman* (Draft Pick)	3.00
154	*Rick Elder* (Draft Pick)	3.00
155	*Eric Valent* (Draft Pick)	4.00
156	*Jeff Winchester* (Draft Pick)	2.00
157	*Mike Nannini* (Draft Pick)	2.00
158	*Mamon Tucker* (Draft Pick)	2.00
159	*Nate Bump* (Draft Pick)	1.50
160	*Andy Brown* (Draft Pick)	1.50
161	Troy Glaus (Future Star)	1.00
162	Adrian Beltre (Future Star)	.40
163	Mitch Meluskey (Future Star)	1.00
164	Alex Gonzalez (Future Star)	.20
165	George Lombard (Future Star)	.20
166	Eric Chavez (Future Star)	.50
167	Ruben Mateo (Future Star)	.75
168	Calvin Pickering (Future Star)	.20
169	Gabe Kapler (Future Star)	1.50
170	Bruce Chen (Future Star)	.15
171	Darin Erstad	.75
172	Sandy Alomar	.25
173	Miguel Cairo	.15
174	Jason Kendall	.25
175	Cal Ripken Jr.	2.50
176	Darryl Kile	.15
177	David Cone	.25
178	Mike Sweeney	.15
179	Royce Clayton	.15
180	Curt Schilling	.30
181	Barry Larkin	.30
182	Eric Milton	.15
183	Ellis Burks	.15
184	A.J. Hinch	.15
185	Garret Anderson	.15
186	Sean Bergman	.15
187	Shannon Stewart	.15
188	Bernard Gilkey	.15
189	Jeff Blauser	.15
190	Andruw Jones	.75
191	Omar Daal	.15
192	Jeff Kent	.15
193	Mark Kotsay	.15
194	Dave Burba	.15
195	Bobby Higginson	.15
196	Hideki Irabu	.30
197	Jamie Moyer	.15
198	Doug Glanville	.15
199	Quinton McCracken	.15
200	Ken Griffey Jr.	3.00
201	Mike Lieberthal	.15
202	Carl Everett	.15
203	Omar Vizquel	.15
204	Mike Lansing	.15
205	Manny Ramirez	1.50
206	Ryan Klesko	.25
207	Jeff Montgomery	.15
208	Chad Curtis	.15
209	Rick Helling	.15
210	Justin Thompson	.15
211	Tom Goodwin	.15
212	Todd Dunwoody	.15
213	Kevin Young	.15
214	Tony Saunders	.15
215	Gary Sheffield	.25
216	Jaret Wright	.15
217	Quilvio Veras	.15
218	Marty Cordova	.15
219	Tino Martinez	.40
220	Scott Rolen	.75
221	Fernando Tatis	.15
222	Damion Easley	.15
223	Aramis Ramirez	.15
224	Brad Radke	.15
225	Nomar Garciaparra	2.00
226	Magglio Ordonez	.15
227	Andy Pettitte	.40
228	David Ortiz	.15
229	Todd Jones	.15
230	Larry Walker	.50
231	Tim Wakefield	.15
232	Jose Guillen	.15
233	Gregg Olson	.15
234	Ricky Gutierrez	.15
235	Todd Walker	.25
236	Abraham Nunez	.15
237	Sean Casey	.40
238	Greg Norton	.15
239	Bret Saberhagen	.15
240	Bernie Williams	.45
241	Tim Salmon	.30
242	Jason Giambi	.15
243	Fernando Vina	.15
244	Darrin Fletcher	.15
245	Greg Vaughn	.30
246	Dennis Reyes	.15
247	Hideo Nomo	.25
248	Reggie Sanders	.15
249	Mike Hampton	.15
250	Kerry Wood	.75
251	Ismael Valdes	.15
252	Pat Hentgen	.15
253	Scott Spiezio	.15
254	Chuck Finley	.15
255	Troy Glaus	.15
256	Bobby Jones	.15
257	Wayne Gomes	.15
258	Rondell White	.25
259	Todd Zeile	.15
260	Matt Williams	.30
261	Henry Rodriguez	.25
262	Matt Stairs	.15
263	Jose Valentin	.15
264	David Justice	.40
265	Javy Lopez	.25
266	Matt Morris	.15
267	Steve Trachsel	.15
268	Edgar Martinez	.15
269	Al Martin	.15
270	Ivan Rodriguez	.75
271	Carlos Delgado	.40
272	Mark Grace	.35
273	Ugueth Urbina	.15
274	Jay Buhner	.15
275	Mike Piazza	2.00
276	Rick Aguilera	.15
277	Javier Valentin	.15
278	Brian Anderson	.15
279	Cliff Floyd	.15
280	Barry Bonds	.75
281	Troy O'Leary	.15
282	Seth Greisinger	.15
283	Mark Grudzielanek	.15
284	Jose Cruz Jr.	.25
285	Jeff Bagwell	.75
286	John Smoltz	.25
287	Jeff Cirillo	.15
288	Richie Sexson	.15
289	Charles Nagy	.15
290	Pedro Martinez	.50
291	Juan Encarnacion	.25
292	Phil Nevin	.15
293	Terry Steinbach	.15
294	Miguel Tejada	.25
295	Dan Wilson	.15
296	Chris Peters	.15
297	Brian Moehler	.15
298	Jason Christiansen	.15
299	Kelly Stinnett	.15
300	Dwight Gooden	.25
301	Randy Velarde	.15
302	Kirt Manwaring	.15
303	Jeff Abbott	.15
304	Dave Hollins	.15
305	Kerry Ligtenberg	.15
306	Aaron Boone	.15
307	Carlos Hernandez	.15
308	Mike DiFelice	.15
309	Brian Meadows	.15
310	Tim Bogar	.15
311	Greg Vaughn (Transaction)	1.00
312	Brant Brown (Transaction)	1.00
313	Steve Finley (Transaction)	1.00
314	Bret Boone (Transaction)	1.00
315	Albert Belle (Transaction)	1.50
316	Robin Ventura (Transaction)	1.00
317	Eric Davis (Transaction)	1.00
318	Todd Hundley (Transaction)	1.00
319	Jose Offerman (Transaction)	1.00
320	Kevin Brown (Transaction)	1.50
321	Denny Neagle (Transaction)	1.00
322	Brian Jordan (Transaction)	1.00
323	Brian Giles (Transaction)	1.00
324	Bobby Bonilla (Transaction)	1.00
325	Roberto Alomar (Transaction)	1.50
326	Ken Caminiti (Transaction)	1.25
327	Todd Stottlemyre (Transaction)	1.00
328	Randy Johnson (Transaction)	1.50
329	Luis Gonzalez (Transaction)	1.00
330	Rafael Palmeiro (Transaction)	1.50
331	Devon White (Transaction)	1.00
332	Will Clark (Transaction)	1.50
333	Dean Palmer (Transaction)	1.00
334	Gregg Jefferies (Transaction)	1.00
335	Mo Vaughn (Transaction)	1.25
336	*Brad Lidge* (Draft Pick)	2.00
337	*Chris George* (Draft Pick)	2.00
338	*Austin Kearns* (Draft Pick)	3.00
339	*Matt Belisle* (Draft Pick)	2.00
340	*Nate Cornejo* (Draft Pick)	2.00
341	*Matt Holiday* (Draft Pick)	3.00
342	*J.M. Gold* (Draft Pick)	2.00
343	*Matt Roney* (Draft Pick)	2.00
344	*Seth Etherton* (Draft Pick)	2.50
345	*Adam Everett* (Draft Pick)	4.00
346	Marlon Anderson (Future Star)	1.00
347	Ron Belliard (Future Star)	1.00
348	Fernando Seguignol (Future Star)	1.50
349	Michael Barrett (Future Star)	1.00
350	Dernell Stenson (Future Star)	2.00
351	Ryan Anderson (Future Star)	2.50
352	Ramon Hernandez (Future Star)	1.00
353	Jeremy Giambi (Future Star)	1.50
354	Ricky Ledee (Future Star)	1.00
355	Carlos Lee (Future Star)	1.50

1999 Stadium Club First Day Issue

A parallel of the 355-card set inserted exclusively in retail packs, Series I (1-170) are serially numbered to 170 at a rate of 1:75 packs. Series 2 (171-355) are serially numbered to 200 and inserted at a rate of 1:60 packs.

	MT
Common Player:	3.00
Stars: 15X	
SP Stars: 4X	

(See 1999 Stadium Club for checklist and base card values.)

1999 Stadium Club One of a Kind

This insert set parallels the 355-card base set. Cards feature a mirrorboard look and are serially numbered to 150. Inserted exclusively in hobby packs, insertion rate for Series 1 is 1:53 and Series 2 is 1:48 packs.

Stars: 15X
SP Stars: 4X
(See 1999 Stadium Club for checklist and base card values.)

1999 Stadium Club Autographs

This 10-card autographed set was issued in Series 1 and 2 with five players signing in each series. Available exclusively in retail chains, Series 1 autographs were seeded 1:1,107 packs, while Series 2 were inserted in every 877 packs. Each autograph is marked with the Topps Certified Autograph Issue stamp. Card numbers have an "SCA" prefix.

		MT
Complete Set (10):		600.00
Complete Series 1 (5):		350.00
Complete Series 2 (5):		250.00
Common Player:		25.00
Inserted 1:1,107		
1	Alex Rodriguez	150.00
2	Chipper Jones	100.00
3	Barry Bonds	50.00
4	Tino Martinez	25.00
5	Ben Grieve	45.00
6	Juan Gonzalez	80.00
7	Vladimir Guerrero	60.00
8	Albert Belle	45.00
9	Kerry Wood	40.00
10	Todd Helton	45.00

1999 Stadium Club Chrome

This 40-card set was inserted in series 1 and 2 packs, with 1-20 in first series packs and 21-40 in Series 2. Chrome appropriately utilizes chromium technology. The insertion rate is 1:24 packs with Refractor parallel versions also seeded 1:96 packs. Card numbers have an "SCC" prefix.

		MT
Complete Set (40):		125.00
Complete Series 1 (20):		65.00
Complete Series 2 (20):		65.00
Common Player:		1.00
Inserted 1:24		
Refractors: 2X		
Inserted 1:96		
1	Nomar Garciaparra	6.00
2	Kerry Wood	2.50
3	Jeff Bagwell	4.00
4	Ivan Rodriguez	2.50
5	Albert Belle	2.00
6	Gary Sheffield	1.00
7	Andruw Jones	2.50
8	Kevin Brown	1.00
9	David Cone	1.00
10	Darin Erstad	2.50
11	Manny Ramirez	4.00
12	Larry Walker	2.00
13	Mike Piazza	6.00
14	Ken Caminiti	1.00
15	Pedro Martinez	2.00
16	Greg Vaughn	1.00
17	Barry Bonds	2.50
18	Mo Vaughn	1.00
19	Bernie Williams	1.50
20	Ken Griffey Jr.	10.00
21	Alex Rodriguez	7.50
22	Chipper Jones	6.00
23	Ben Grieve	2.50
24	Frank Thomas	4.00
25	Derek Jeter	6.00
26	Sammy Sosa	6.00
27	Mark McGwire	10.00
28	Vladimir Guerrero	3.00
29	Greg Maddux	6.00
30	Juan Gonzalez	5.00
31	Troy Glaus	2.50
32	Adrian Beltre	2.00
33	Mitch Meluskey	1.00

34	Alex Gonzalez	1.00
35	George Lombard	2.00
36	Eric Chavez	3.00
37	Ruben Mateo	2.50
38	Calvin Pickering	1.00
39	Gabe Kapler	2.50
40	Bruce Chen	1.00

1999 Stadium Club Co-Signers

Co-Signers feature two autographs on each card and also for the first time includes one level of four autographs per card. Co-Signers are grouped into categories A, B, C and D. Group A Co-Signers are autographed by four players, while B-D are signed by two players. Insertion odds are as follows: Group D, 1:254; C, 1:3,014; B, 1:9,043; A, 1:45,213. Each card features the Topps Certified Autograph Issue stamp.

	MT
Common Group A:	
Inserted 1:18,085	
Common Group B:	50.00
Inserted 1:9043	
Common Group C:	25.00
Inserted 1:3014	
Common Group D:	15.00
Inserted 1:254	
CS1 Ben Grieve, Richie Sexson (D)	50.00
CS2 Todd Helton, Troy Glaus (D)	60.00
CS3 Alex Rodriguez, Scott Rolen (D)	200.00
CS4 Derek Jeter, Chipper Jones (D)	200.00
CS5 Cliff Floyd, Eli Marrero (D)	15.00
CS6 Jay Buhner, Kevin Young (D)	15.00
CS7 Ben Grieve, Troy Glaus (C)	50.00
CS8 Todd Helton, Richie Sexson (C)	50.00
CS9 Alex Rodriguez, Chipper Jones (C)	300.00
CS10Derek Jeter, Scott Rolen (C)	200.00
CS11Cliff Floyd, Kevin Young (C)	25.00
CS12Jay Buhner, Eli Marrero (B)	50.00
CS13Ben Grieve, Todd Helton (B)	150.00
CS14Richie Sexson, Troy Glaus (B)	100.00
CS15Alex Rodriguez, Derek Jeter (B)	450.00
CS16Chipper Jones, Scott Rolen (B)	250.00
CS17Cliff Floyd, Jay Buhner (B)	50.00
CS18Eli Marrero, Kevin Young (B)	50.00
CS19Ben Grieve, Todd Helton, Richie Sexson, Troy Glaus (A)	300.00
CS20Alex Rodriguez, Derek Jeter, Chipper Jones, Scott Rolen (A)	2500.
CS21Cliff Floyd, Jay Buhner, Eli Marrero, Kevin Young (A)	150.00
CS22Edgardo Alfonzo, Jose Guillen (D)	45.00
CS23Mike Lowell, Ricardo Rincon (D)	25.00
CS24Juan Gonzalez, Vinny Castilla (D)	100.00
CS25Moises Alou, Roger Clemens (D)	75.00
CS26Scott Spezio, Tony Womack (D)	15.00
CS27Fernando Vina, Quilvio Veras (D)	15.00
CS28Edgardo Alfonzo, Ricardo Rincon (C)	30.00
CS29Jose Guillen, Mike Lowell (C)	30.00
CS30Juan Gonzalez, Moises Alou (C)	150.00
CS31Roger Clemens, Vinny Castilla (C)	150.00
CS32Scott Spezio, Fernando Vina (C)	25.00
CS33Tony Womack, Quilvio Veras (B)	50.00
CS34Edgardo Alfonzo, Mike Lowell (B)	60.00
CS35Jose Guillen, Ricardo Rincon (B)	60.00
CS36Juan Gonzalez, Roger Clemens (B)	300.00
CS37Moises Alou, Vinny Castilla (B)	75.00
CS38Scott Spezio, Quilvio Veras (B)	50.00
CS39Tony Womack, Fernando Vina (B)	50.00
CS40Edgardo Alfonzo, Jose Guillen, Mike Lowell, Ricardo Rincon (A)	200.00
CS41Juan Gonzalez, Moises Alou, Roger Clemens, Vinny Castilla (A)	1500.
CS42Scott Spezio, Tony Womack, Fernando Vina, Quilvio Veras (A)	200.00

1999 Stadium Club Never Compromise

Topps selected players who bring hard work and devotion to the field every game are highlighted, including Cal Ripken Jr. The first 10 cards in the set are inserted in series I packs while the remaining 10 are seeded in series II at a rate of 1:12 packs.

	MT
Complete Set (20):	65.00
Complete Series 1 (10):	40.00
Complete Series 2 (10):	25.00
Common Player:	1.50
Inserted 1:12	
NC1 Mark McGwire	9.00
NC2 Sammy Sosa	7.50
NC3 Ken Griffey Jr.	9.00
NC4 Greg Maddux	6.00
NC5 Barry Bonds	2.00
NC6 Alex Rodriguez	7.50
NC7 Darin Erstad	2.00
NC8 Roger Clemens	4.00
NC9 Nomar Garciaparra	6.00
NC10Derek Jeter	6.00
NC11Cal Ripken Jr.	7.50
NC12Mike Piazza	6.00
NC13Greg Vaughn	1.50
NC14Andres Galarraga	1.50
NC15Vinny Castilla	1.50
NC16Jeff Bagwell	2.00
NC17Chipper Jones	6.00
NC18Eric Chavez	2.00
NC19Orlando Hernandez	2.00
NC20Troy Glaus	2.50

1999 Stadium Club Photography

The photos used on some of Stadium's Club Series 1 cards was available as a special issue in the format of a framed 11" x 14" color photo. The borderless action photos could be ordered from a form found in TSC packs. With a $4 shipping charge, the initial cost per picture was $23.99. The numbers here are as given on the order form.

	MT
Complete Set (10):	240.00
Common Player:	24.00
1 Alex Rodriguez	24.00
65 Derek Jeter	24.00
66 Sammy Sosa	24.00
135 Juan Gonzalez	24.00
NC1 Mark McGwire	24.00
NC3 Ken Griffey Jr.	24.00
SCA5Ben Grieve	24.00
SCC1Nomar Garciaparra	24.00
SCC2Kerry Wood	24.00
SCC13 Mike Piazza	24.00

1999 Stadium Club Triumvirate

Three of these inserts "fuse" together to form a set of three cards, forming a Triumvirate. 48 players, 24 from each series, are available in three different technologies, Luminous, Luminescent and Illuminator. The insert ratio is as follows: Luminous (1:36), Luminescent (1:144) and Illuminator (1:288).

	MT
Complete Set (48):	350.00
Complete Series 1 (24):	165.00
Complete Series 2 (24):	185.00
Common Player:	3.00
Inserted 1:36	
Luminescents: 2X	
Inserted 1:144	
Illuminators: 4X	
Inserted 1:288	
T1A Greg Vaughn	3.00
T1B Ken Caminiti	3.00
T1C Tony Gwynn	12.50
T2A Andruw Jones	6.50
T2B Chipper Jones	15.00
T2C Andres Galarraga	4.50
T3A Jay Buhner	3.00
T3B Ken Griffey Jr.	25.00
T3C Alex Rodriguez	17.50
T4A Derek Jeter	15.00
T4B Tino Martinez	3.00
T4C Bernie Williams	4.50
T5A Brian Jordan	3.00
T5B Ray Lankford	3.00
T5C Mark McGwire	25.00
T6A Jeff Bagwell	8.00
T6B Craig Biggio	5.00
T6C Randy Johnson	5.00
T7A Nomar Garciaparra	15.00
T7B Pedro Martinez	5.00
T7C Mo Vaughn	4.00
T8A Mark Grace	5.00
T8B Sammy Sosa	15.00
T8C Kerry Wood	4.50
T9A Alex Rodriguez	17.50
T9B Nomar Garciaparra	15.00
T9C Derek Jeter	15.00
T10ATodd Helton	6.50
T10BTravis Lee	5.00
T10CPat Burrell	12.50
T11AGreg Maddux	15.00
T11BKerry Wood	4.50
T11CTom Glavine	3.00
T12AChipper Jones	15.00
T12BVinny Castilla	3.00
T12CScott Rolen	6.50
T13AJuan Gonzalez	12.50
T13BKen Griffey Jr.	25.00
T13CBen Grieve	6.50
T14ASammy Sosa	15.00
T14BVladimir Guerrero	8.00
T14CBarry Bonds	8.00
T15AFrank Thomas	10.00
T15BJim Thome	4.00
T15CTino Martinez	3.00
T16AMark McGwire	25.00
T16BAndres Galarraga	4.50
T16CJeff Bagwell	8.00

1999 Stadium Club Video Replay

Utilizing lenticular technology, these inserts capture highlights, such as McGwire's 70th home run, from the '98 season. By tilting the card, successive images show the selected highlight almost come to life. Video Replays are inserted in series II packs at a rate of 1:12.

	MT
Complete Set (5):	20.00
Common Player:	2.00
Inserted 1:12	
VR1 Mark McGwire	7.50
VR2 Sammy Sosa	5.00
VR3 Ken Griffey Jr.	7.50
VR4 Kerry Wood	2.00
VR5 Alex Rodriguez	5.00

2000 Stadium Club

Released in one series, the base set consists of 250 cards, embossed and printed on 20-pt. stock with silver holo foil stamping. Card backs have a small photo, with the player's vital information and 1999 season statistical breakdown. The 20-card Draft Pick subset (#231-250) are shortprinted, seeded 1:5 packs.

		MT
Complete Set (250):		200.00
Common Player:		.15
Common SP (201-250):		2.00
Inserted 1:5		
Wax Box:		45.00
1	Nomar Garciaparra	2.00
2	Brian Jordan	.15
3	Mark Grace	.25
4	Jeromy Burnitz	.15
5	Shane Reynolds	.15
6	Alex Gonzalez	.15
7	Jose Offerman	.15
8	Orlando Hernandez	.15
9	Mike Caruso	.15
10	Tony Clark	.40
11	Sean Casey	.50
12	Johnny Damon	.15
13	Dante Bichette	.25
14	Kevin Young	.15
15	Juan Gonzalez	.75
16	Chipper Jones	1.50
17	Quilvio Veras	.15
18	Trevor Hoffman	.15
19	Roger Cedeno	.15
20	Ellis Burks	.15
21	Richie Sexson	.15
22	Gary Sheffield	.25
23	Delino DeShields	.15
24	Wade Boggs	.40
25	Ray Lankford	.15
26	Kevin Appier	.15
27	Roy Halladay	.15
28	Harold Baines	.15
29	Todd Zeile	.15
30	Barry Larkin	.40
31	Ron Coomer	.15
32	Jorge Posada	.25
33	Magglio Ordonez	.25
34	Brian Giles	.15
35	Jeff Kent	.15
36	Henry Rodriguez	.15
37	Fred McGriff	.25
38	Shawn Green	.50
39	Derek Bell	.15
40	Ben Grieve	.30
41	Dave Nilsson	.15
42	Mo Vaughn	.50
43	Rondell White	.25
44	Doug Glanville	.15
45	Paul O'Neill	.25
46	Carlos Lee	.15
47	Vinny Castilla	.20
48	Mike Sweeney	.15
49	Rico Brogna	.15
50	Alex Rodriguez	2.00
51	Luis Castillo	.15
52	Kevin Brown	.25
53	Jose Vidro	.15
54	John Smoltz	.15
55	Garret Anderson	.15
56	Matt Stairs	.15
57	Omar Vizquel	.15
58	Tom Goodwin	.15
59	Scott Brosius	.15
60	Robin Ventura	.25
61	B.J. Surhoff	.15
62	Andy Ashby	.15
63	Chris Widger	.15
64	Tim Hudson	.40
65	Javy Lopez	.15
66	Tim Salmon	.25
67	Warren Morris	.15
68	John Wetteland	.15
69	Gabe Kapler	.25
70	Bernie Williams	.50
71	Rickey Henderson	.40
72	Andruw Jones	.50
73	Eric Young	.15
74	Bob Abreu	.15
75	David Cone	.25
76	Rusty Greer	.15
77	Ron Belliard	.15
78	Troy Glaus	.40
79	Mike Hampton	.15
80	Miguel Tejada	.15
81	Jeff Cirillo	.15
82	Todd Hundley	.15
83	Roberto Alomar	.50
84	Charles Johnson	.15
85	Rafael Palmeiro	.40
86	Doug Mientkiewicz	.15
87	Mariano Rivera	.25
88	Neifi Perez	.15
89	Jermaine Dye	.15
90	Ivan Rodriguez	.75
91	Jay Buhner	.15
92	Pokey Reese	.15
93	John Olerud	.25
94	Brady Anderson	.20
95	Manny Ramirez	.75
96	Keith Osik	.15
97	Mickey Morandini	.15
98	Matt Williams	.40
99	Eric Karros	.25
100	Ken Griffey Jr.	3.00
101	Bret Boone	.15
102	Ryan Klesko	.15
103	Craig Biggio	.40
104	John Jaha	.15
105	Vladimir Guerrero	1.00
106	Devon White	.15
107	Tony Womack	.15
108	Marvin Benard	.15
109	Kenny Lofton	.40
110	Preston Wilson	.15
111	Al Leiter	.25
112	Reggie Sanders	.15
113	Scott Williamson	.15
114	Deivi Cruz	.15
115	Carlos Beltran	.30
116	Ray Durham	.15
117	Ricky Ledee	.15
118	Torii Hunter	.15
119	John Valentin	.15
120	Scott Rolen	.75
121	Jason Kendall	.25
122	Dave Martinez	.15
123	Jim Thome	.40
124	David Bell	.15
125	Jose Canseco	.75
126	Jose Lima	.15
127	Carl Everett	.15
128	Kevin Millwood	.25
129	Bill Spiers	.15
130	Omar Daal	.15
131	Miguel Cairo	.15
132	Mark Grudzielanek	.15
133	David Justice	.25
134	Russ Ortiz	.15
135	Mike Piazza	2.00
136	Brian Meadows	.15
137	Tony Gwynn	1.50
138	Cal Ripken Jr.	2.00
139	Kris Benson	.15
140	Larry Walker	.50
141	Cristian Guzman	.15
142	Tino Martinez	.25
143	Chris Singleton	.15
144	Lee Stevens	.15
145	Rey Ordonez	.15
146	Russ Davis	.15
147	J.T. Snow Jr.	.15
148	Luis Gonzalez	.15
149	Marquis Grissom	.15
150	Greg Maddux	1.50
151	Fernando Tatis	.25
152	Jason Giambi	.15
153	Carlos Delgado	.50
154	Joe McEwing	.15
155	Raul Mondesi	.25
156	Rich Aurilia	.15
157	Alex Fernandez	.15
158	Albert Belle	.60
159	Pat Meares	.15
160	Mike Lieberthal	.15

161	Mike Cameron	.15
162	Juan Encarnacion	.15
163	Chuck Knoblauch	.30
164	Pedro Martinez	.75
165	Randy Johnson	.50
166	Shannon Stewart	.15
167	Jeff Bagwell	.75
168	Edgar Renteria	.15
169	Barry Bonds	.75
170	Steve Finley	.15
171	Brian Hunter	.15
172	Tom Glavine	.25
173	Mark Kotsay	.15
174	Tony Fernandez	.15
175	Sammy Sosa	2.00
176	Geoff Jenkins	.15
177	Adrian Beltre	.15
178	Jay Bell	.15
179	Mike Bordick	.15
180	Ed Sprague	.15
181	Dave Roberts	.15
182	Greg Vaughn	.25
183	Brian Daubach	.15
184	Damion Easley	.15
185	Carlos Febles	.15
186	Kevin Tapani	.15
187	Frank Thomas	.75
188	Roger Clemens	1.00
189	Mike Benjamin	.15
190	Curt Schilling	.25
191	Edgardo Alfonzo	.25
192	Mike Mussina	.50
193	Todd Helton	.30
194	Todd Jones	.15
195	Dean Palmer	.15
196	John Flaherty	.15
197	Derek Jeter	2.00
198	Todd Walker	.15
199	Brad Ausmus	.15
200	Mark McGwire	3.00
201	Erubiel Durazo (Future Stars)	4.00
202	Nick Johnson (Future Stars)	6.00
203	Ruben Mateo (Future Stars)	4.00
204	Lance Berkman (Future Stars)	3.00
205	Pat Burrell (Future Stars)	8.00
206	Pablo Ozuna (Future Stars)	2.00
207	Roosevelt Brown (Future Stars)	3.00
208	Alfonso Soriano (Future Stars)	8.00
209	A.J. Burnett (Future Stars)	4.00
210	Rafael Furcal (Future Stars)	5.00
211	Scott Morgan (Future Stars)	2.00
212	Adam Piatt (Future Stars)	4.00
213	Dee Brown (Future Stars)	3.00
214	Corey Patterson (Future Stars)	15.00
215	Mickey Lopez (Future Stars)	2.00
216	Rob Ryan (Future Stars)	2.00
217	Sean Burroughs (Future Stars)	6.00
218	Jack Cust (Future Stars)	3.00
219	John Patterson (Future Stars)	4.00
220	Kit Pellow (Future Stars)	2.00
221	Chad Hermansen (Future Stars)	3.00
222	Daryle Ward (Future Stars)	3.00
223	Jayson Werth (Future Stars)	4.00
224	Jason Standridge (Future Stars)	2.00
225	Mark Mulder (Future Stars)	4.00
226	Peter Bergeron (Future Stars)	3.00
227	Willi Mo Pena (Future Stars)	6.00
228	Aramis Ramirez (Future Stars)	2.00
229	*John Sneed* (Future Stars)	5.00
230	Wilton Veras (Future Stars)	3.00
231	Josh Hamilton (Draft Picks)	10.00
232	Eric Munson (Draft Picks)	10.00
233	*Bobby Bradley* (Draft Picks)	3.00
234	*Larry Bigbie* (Draft Picks)	3.00
235	*B.J. Garbe* (Draft Picks)	6.00
236	*Brett Myers* (Draft Picks)	4.00
237	*Jason Stumm* (Draft Picks)	7.00
238	*Corey Myers* (Draft Picks)	4.00
239	*Ryan Christianson* (Draft Picks)	4.00
240	David Walling (Draft Picks)	3.00
241	Josh Girdley (Draft Picks)	2.00
242	Omar Ortiz (Draft Picks)	2.00
243	Jason Jennings (Draft Picks)	3.00
244	*Kyle Snyder* (Draft Picks)	3.00
245	Jay Gehrke (Draft Picks)	2.00
246	*Mike Paradis* (Draft Picks)	3.00
247	*Chance Caple* (Draft Picks)	4.00
248	*Ben Christiansen* (Draft Picks)	5.00
249	*Brad Baker* (Draft Picks)	5.00
250	*Rick Asadoorian* (Draft Picks)	12.00

2000 Stadium Club First Day Issue

Identifiable by the "First Day Issue" stamp, this retail exclusive parallel set is limited to 150 sequentially numbered sets.

Stars: 20x-30x
Short-prints: 3x-5x
Production 150 sets R
(See 2000 Stadium Club for checklist and base card values.)

2000 Stadium Club One of a Kind

This 250-card set is a parallel to the base set, is hobby exclusive and limited to 150 serially numbered sets.

Stars: 20x-30x
Short-prints: 3x-5x
Production 150 sets H
(See 2000 Stadium Club for checklist and base card values.)

2000 Stadium Club Bats of Brilliance

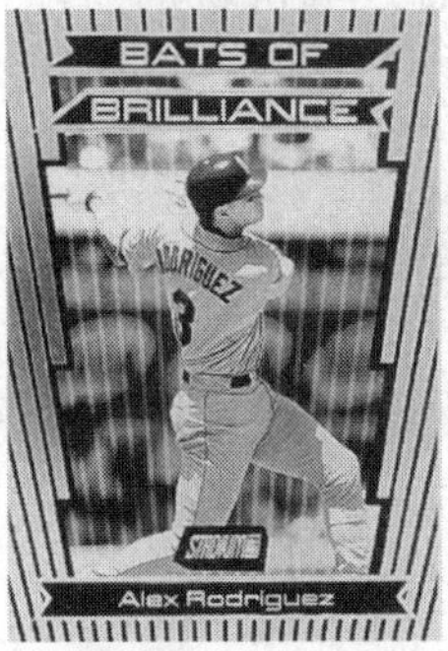

This insert set focused on 10 of baseball's top hitters. Card fronts have a silver foil border over a black backdrop. Backs highlight the player's statistics from 1999 and his career statistics. They are numbered with a "BB" prefix and are seeded 1:12 packs. A die-cut parallel is also randomly seeded 1:60 packs.

		MT
Complete Set (10):		30.00
Common Player:		1.50
Inserted 1:12		
1	Mark McGwire	6.00
2	Sammy Sosa	4.00
3	Jose Canseco	1.50
4	Jeff Bagwell	1.50
5	Ken Griffey Jr.	6.00
6	Nomar Garciaparra	4.00
7	Mike Piazza	4.00
8	Alex Rodriguez	4.00
9	Vladimir Guerrero	2.00
10	Chipper Jones	3.00

2000 Stadium Club Capture The Action

This 20-card set is divided into 3 categories: Rookies, Stars and Legends. These were seeded 1:12 packs and have the insert head, player name and logo stamped in silver foil. They are numbered with a "CA" prefix on the backs. A hobby exclusive parallel version is also available. They are serially numbered to 100 and features a replica of the actual photo slide used to create the card and is viewable from both sides.

		MT
Complete Set (20):		80.00
Common Player:		1.50
Inserted 1:12		
Game View Stars: 8x-15x		
Yng stars: 3x-6x		
Production 100 sets H		
1	Josh Hamilton	8.00
2	Pat Burrell	6.00
3	Erubiel Durazo	5.00
4	Alfonso Soriano	6.00
5	A.J. Burnett	1.50
6	Alex Rodriguez	6.00
7	Sean Casey	1.50
8	Derek Jeter	6.00
9	Vladimir Guerrero	3.00
10	Nomar Garciaparra	6.00
11	Mike Piazza	6.00
12	Ken Griffey Jr.	10.00
13	Sammy Sosa	6.00
14	Juan Gonzalez	2.50
15	Mark McGwire	10.00
16	Ivan Rodriguez	2.50
17	Barry Bonds	2.50
18	Wade Boggs	1.50
19	Tony Gwynn	5.00
20	Cal Ripken Jr.	8.00

2000 Stadium Club Co-Signers

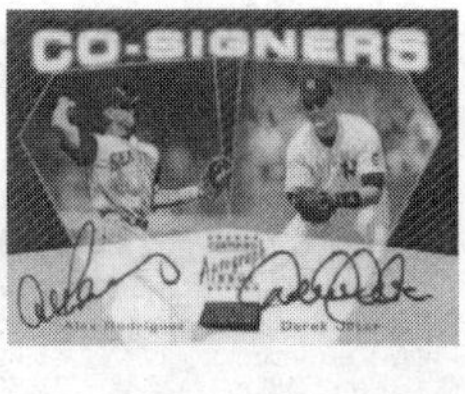

This 15-card hobby exclusive set features two signatures on the card front, with the Topps "Certified Autograph Issue" stamp as well as the Topps 3M sticker to ensure its authenticity. The cards are divided into three groupings with the following odds: Group A - 1:10,184; Group B - 1:5,092; and Group C - 1:508.

		MT
Common Player:		40.00
Group A 1:10,184		
Group B 1:5,092		
Group C 1:508		
1	Alex Rodriguez, Derek Jeter	800.00
2	Derek Jeter, Omar Vizquel	250.00
3	Alex Rodriguez, Rey Ordonez	250.00
4	Derek Jeter, Rey Ordonez	250.00
5	Omar Vizquel, Alex Rodriguez	250.00
6	Rey Ordonez, Omar Vizquel	50.00
7	Wade Boggs, Robin Ventura	80.00
8	Randy Johnson, Mike Mussina	120.00
9	Pat Burrell, Magglio Ordonez	60.00
10	Chad Hermansen, Pat Burrell	60.00
11	Maggio Ordonez, Chad Hermansen	40.00
12	Josh Hamilton, Corey Myers	60.00
13	B.J. Garbe, Josh Hamilton	80.00
14	Corey Myers, B.J. Garbe	60.00
15	Tino Martinez, Fred McGriff	50.00

2000 Stadium Club Lone Star Signatures

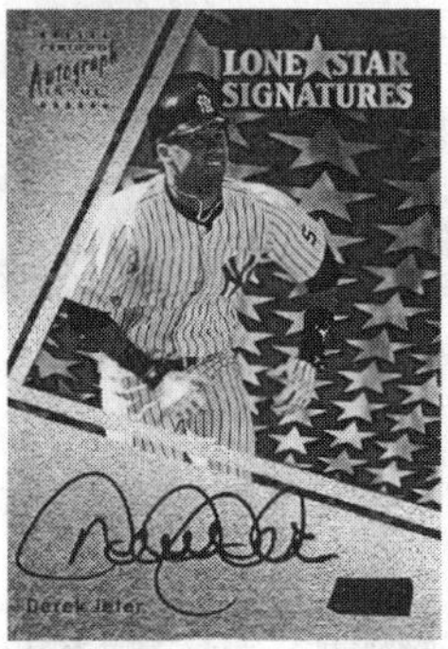

This 16-card autographed set features the Topps "Certified Autograph Issue" stamp to verify its authenticity. The cards are divided into four groupings with the following odds: Group 1, 1:1,979 hobby; Group 2, 1:2,374 hobby; Group 3, 1:1,979; and Group 4, 1:424 hobby.

		MT
Common Player:		20.00
Group 1 1:1,979		
Group 2 1:2,374		
Group 3 1:1,979		
Group 4 1:424		
1	Derek Jeter	250.00
2	Alex Rodriguez	250.00
3	Wade Boggs	75.00
4	Robin Ventura	40.00
5	Randy Johnson	60.00
6	Mike Mussina	60.00
7	Tino Martinez	40.00
8	Fred McGriff	30.00
9	Omar Vizquel	30.00
10	Rey Ordonez	30.00
11	Pat Burrell	50.00
12	Chad Hermansen	20.00
13	Magglio Ordonez	20.00
14	Josh Hamilton	60.00
15	Corey Myers	30.00
16	B.J. Garbe	50.00

2000 Stadium Club Onyx Extreme

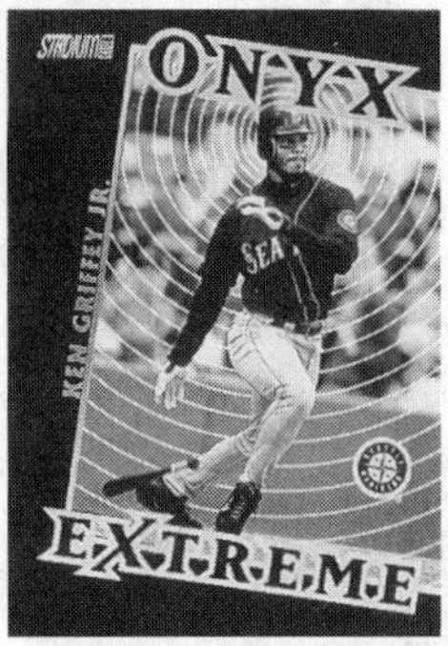

This 10-card set features black styrene technology with silver foil stamping and are seeded 1:12 packs. A die-cut parallel is also randomly inserted 1:60 hobby packs.

		MT
Complete Set (10):		20.00
Common Player:		1.00
Inserted 1:12		
Die-cuts: 2x-3x		
Inserted 1:60		
1	Ken Griffey Jr.	6.00
2	Derek Jeter	4.00
3	Vladimir Guerrero	2.00
4	Nomar Garciaparra	4.00
5	Barry Bonds	1.50
6	Alex Rodriguez	4.00
7	Sammy Sosa	4.00
8	Ivan Rodriguez	1.50
9	Larry Walker	1.00
10	Andruw Jones	1.00

2000 Stadium Club Scenes

Available only in hobby and Home Team Advantage boxes, these broaden the view of the featured player and have a format sized 2 1/2" x 4 11/16". These are boxtoppers, seeded one per box.

		MT
Complete Set (9):		30.00
Common Player:		1.00
Inserted 1:box		
1	Mark McGwire	6.00
2	Alex Rodriguez	4.00
3	Cal Ripken Jr.	5.00
4	Sammy Sosa	4.00
5	Derek Jeter	4.00
6	Ken Griffey Jr.	6.00
7	Raul Mondesi	1.00
8	Chipper Jones	3.00
9	Nomar Garciaparra	4.00

2000 Stadium Club Souvenirs

These memorabilia inserts feature die-cut technology that incorporates an actual piece of a game-used uniform. Each card back contains the Topps 3M sticker to ensure its authenticity. The insert rate is 2:339 hobby packs and 2:136 HTA packs.

		MT
Complete Set (3):		160.00
Common Player:		40.00
Inserted 2:339		
1	Wade Boggs	100.00
2	Randy Johnson	50.00
3	Robin Ventura	40.00

2000 Stadium Club 3 X 3

Ten groups of three top-notch players are arranged by position on three different laser-cut technologies. The three players can be "fused" together to form one oversize card. The three versions are luminous (1:18), luminescent (1:72) and illuminator (1:144).

		MT
Complete Set (30):		120.00
Common Player:		1.50
Inserted 1:18		
Luminescent: 2x		
Inserted 1:72		
Illuminator: 3x-4x		
Inserted 1:144		
1A	Randy Johnson	3.00
1B	Pedro Martinez	4.00
1C	Greg Maddux	8.00
2A	Mike Piazza	10.00
2B	Ivan Rodriguez	4.00
2C	Mike Lieberthal	1.50
3A	Mark McGwire	15.00
3B	Jeff Bagwell	4.00
3C	Sean Casey	2.00
4A	Craig Biggio	2.00
4B	Roberto Alomar	2.50
4C	Jay Bell	1.50
5A	Chipper Jones	8.00
5B	Matt Williams	2.00
5C	Robin Ventura	2.00
6A	Alex Rodriguez	10.00
6B	Derek Jeter	10.00
6C	Nomar Garciaparra	10.00
7A	Barry Bonds	4.00
7B	Luis Gonzalez	1.50
7C	Dante Bichette	1.50
8A	Ken Griffey Jr.	15.00
8B	Bernie Williams	3.00
8C	Andruw Jones	3.00
9A	Manny Ramirez	4.00
9B	Sammy Sosa	10.00
9C	Juan Gonzalez	4.00
10A	Jose Canseco	4.00
10B	Frank Thomas	4.00
10C	Rafael Palmeiro	2.50

1983 Star '83

Star's first baseball card issue was a 15-card tribute to Mike Schmidt, subtitled "Ten Years of Excellence". On the cards' fronts, Schmidt is shown in various posed and game-action photos, surrounded by a red border. Backs tell his story in words and numbers. The cards are the standard 2-1/2" x 3-1/2" and were sold only as complete sets through hobby dealers. Single cards are not listed because the sets are seldom broken for individual card sales.

	MT
Complete Set:	30.00
1-15 Mike Schmidt	

1984 Star '84

Star broadened the selection of its single-player collectors' issues in 1984 and adopted a new design which it used with little variation for several years. Most cards were issued in panels of three, perforated for easy separation. Each set has posed and game-action photos surrounded by colorful borders. Team logos are in a circle at lower-left; "Star '84" is in an inset at the photo's upper-right. Backs within a set feature stats, career highlights personal information and, sometimes, puzzle pieces.

	MT
Complete Set (144):	55.00
1-24 George Brett	20.00
1-24 Steve Carlton	12.00
1-36 Steve Garvey	7.50
1-36 Darryl Strawberry	10.00
1-24 Carl Yastrzemski (not issued in panels)	12.00

1985 Star '85

Star maintained the basic format of 1984 for its sole single-player issue of 1985. The 36-card set of Reggie Jackson has portrait and action photos surrounded by colorful borders. The logo of the A's, Orioles or Yankees appears in a circle at lower-left on front, with a "Star '85" logo at upper-right. Backs have a mix of stats, personal data and career highlights. Cards were issued in a dozen three-card panels, perforated between the cards.

	MT
Complete Set (36):	
1-36 Reggie Jackson	12.50

1986 Star Promos

Several of the 1986 Star single-player series were introduced with the issue of a promo cards, different on their backs, but otherwise similar in appearance to the regular cards.

		MT
Complete Set (7):		110.00
Common Player:		5.00
(1)	Rod Carew (ad back)	7.50
(2)	Don Mattingly (white card) (blank back)	10.00
(3)	Don Mattingly (yellow sticker) (blank back)	15.00
(4)	Dale Murphy (ad back)	7.50
(5)	Jim Rice (blank back)	5.00
(6)	Nolan Ryan (ad back)	50.00
(7)	Tom Seaver (name on back)	10.00

1986 Star '86

The basic format of previous years' issues was retained for Star's single-player sets of 1986. Player poses and game-action photos are presented on the front, bordered in a bright color usually associated with the player's team. In standard 2-1/2" x 3-1/2" size, the cards have a circle at lower-left with the player's name - first only or first and last. At top-right, infringing on the photo is the notation, "Star '86". Backs have stats, career highlights, personal data or puzzle pieces. Most sets were issued in three-card perforated panels. Some of the player sets can also be found in a glossy edition and/or a blank-back sticker version. Single cards are seldom offered and are not listed here.

	MT
1-24 Wade Boggs	9.00
1-24 Wade Boggs (glossy set)	25.00
(1-24)Wade Boggs (sticker set)	5.00
1-15 Jose Canseco (not issued in panels)	10.00
1-15 Jose Canseco (glossy set)	25.00
(1-15)Jose Canseco (sticker set)	5.00
1-24 Rod Carew	7.50
1-15 Wally Joyner (not issued in panels)	6.00
1-15 Wally Joyner (glossy set)	15.00
(1-15)Wally Joyner (sticker set)	5.00
1-24 Don Mattingly	10.00
1-24 Don Mattingly (glossy set)	50.00
(1-24)Don Mattingly (sticker set)	6.00
1-24 Dale Murphy	7.50
1-20 Jim Rice (four-card panels)	6.00
1-20 Jim Rice (glossy set)	10.00
(1-20)Jim Rice (sticker set)	5.00
1-24 Nolan Ryan	35.00
1-24 Tom Seaver	12.00

1987 Star Promos

Most of Star's single-player sets issued for 1987 were preceded by the issue of blank-backed promo cards in a nearly identical format to the issued version.

		MT
Complete Set (6):		42.50
Common Player:		5.00
(1)	Steve Carlton	10.00
(2)	Gary Carter	7.50
(3)	Roger Clemens	12.00
(4)	Keith Hernandez	5.00
(5)	Tim Raines	5.00
(6)	Fernando Valenzuela	5.00

1987 Star '87

The single-player sets issued by Star in 1987 retain the basic format used since 1984. Standard size (2-1/2" x 3-1/2") cards were printed singly, rather than in panels, but the design remained virtually unchanged. Posed and action photos are surrounded by a colorful border which protrudes into the photo at upper-right with the logo "Star '87". At lower-left is a circle with the player's first name, or, in the case of Fernando Valenzuela, the team logo. Backs have stats, personal data or career highlights. Sets were also issued in a limited glossy version and/or as blank-back stickers. Single cards are usually not sold, so are not listed here.

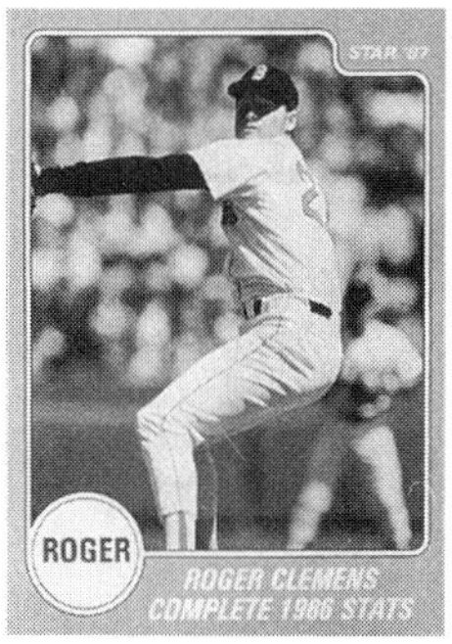

	MT
	35.00
(1-5) Wade Boggs, Jose Canseco (unnumbered)	7.50
(1-5) Wade Boggs, Jose Canseco (glossy set) (unnumbered)	12.00
1-14 Steve Carlton (glossy version only)	10.00
1-14 Gary Carter	7.50
1-14 Gary Carter (glossy set)	15.00
(1-10)Gary Carter (sticker set) (different photos)	5.00
1-12 Roger Clemens	9.00
1-12 Roger Clemens (glossy set)	15.00
(1-5) Roger Clemens (Update) (unnumbered)	5.00
(1-5) Roger Clemens (Update, glossy) (unnumbered)	20.00
1-13 Keith Hernandez	6.00
1-13 Keith Hernandez (glossy set)	12.00
(1-6) Don Mattingly (unnumbered, five blank-back cards, one w/ 1986 stats)	7.00
(1-6) Don Mattingly (glossy) (unnumbered, five cards blank-back, one w/ 1986 stats)	45.00
1-12 Tim Raines	6.00
1-12 Tim Raines (glossy set)	12.00
1-13 Fernando Valenzuela	6.00
1-13 Fernando Valenzuela (glossy set)	12.00
(1-10)Fernando Valenzuela (sticker set) (different photos)	5.00

1988-89 Star Promos

The lengthy series of 11-card sets issued by Star in 1988-89 in the company's "new" format included one promo card for nearly every player's set. The promos are blank-backed but otherwise similar in design to the regular cards.

		MT
Complete Set (40):		
Common Player:		4.00
(1)	Alomar Brothers (Roberto Alomar)	4.00
(2)	Sandy Alomar Jr. (Alomar Brothers)	4.00
(3)	Sandy Alomar Jr.	4.00
(4)	Wade Boggs	6.00
(5)	Jose Canseco (blue borders)	7.50
(6)	Jose Canseco (yellow borders)	7.50
(7)	Jose Canseco (Bay Bombers Series)	9.00
(8)	Will Clark (purple/yellow)	8.00
(9)	Will Clark (Clark/Mitchell set, gold borders)	4.00
(10)	Will Clark (Bay Bombers Series)	7.50
(11)	David Cone	4.00
(12)	Dwight Gooden	4.00
(13)	Tom Gordon	4.00
(14)	Mark Grace	7.50
(15)	Mike Greenwell (blue borders)	4.00
(16)	Mike Greenwell (pink borders)	4.00
(17)	Ken Griffey Jr. (white-back set, blue/white borders)	10.00
(18)	Ken Griffey Jr. (yellow-back set, yellow borders)	25.00
(19)	Orel Hershiser	4.00
(20)	Sam Horn	4.00
(21)	Bo Jackson	5.00
(22)	Gregg Jefferies (blue-border set, orange borders)	4.00
(23)	Gregg Jefferies (orange-border set, dark blue borders, misspelled Greg)	4.00
(24)	Gregg Jefferies (pink-border set, light blue borders, misspelled Greg)	4.00
(25)	Ricky Jordan	4.00
(26)	Don Mattingly	10.00
(27)	Kevin McReynolds	4.00
(28)	Kevin Mitchell (Clark/Mitchell set, gold borders)	4.00
(29)	Kevin Mitchell (orange borders)	4.00
(30)	Matt Nokes (yellow borders, glossy)	4.00
(31)	Kirby Puckett	12.00
(32)	Nolan Ryan	10.00
(33)	Benito Santiago	4.00
(34)	Gary Sheffield	4.00
(35)	Darryl Strawberry (blue-border set, pink borders)	4.00
(36)	Darryl Strawberry (purple-border set, orange borders)	4.00
(37)	Alan Trammell	4.00
(38)	Robin Ventura	4.00
(39)	Jerome Walton (regular set, borders in two shades of blue)	4.00
(40)	Jerome Walton (glossy set, solid blue borders, portrait)	4.00

1988-89 Star

Late in 1988 Star introduced a new format for its single-player card sets which it carried forward into 1989. Sets were standardized at 11 cards in the 2-1/2" x 3-1/2" format. Fronts feature posed and game-action photos which are bordered by graduating shades of a particular color, or two different colors, going from dark at top to light at bottom, or vice versa. (The first Gregg Jefferies set is an exception, having the same shade of blue on all borders.) Backs may be printed in any of a variety of colors on white, yellow, pink or green backgrounds. Stats, personal data, career highlights and team logos are found on back. Sets may carry either a 1988 or 1989 copyright date. Because the sets are seldom broken up for singles sales, individual cards are not listed here. The number of player sets for which glossy versions were issued is uncertain. Existing glossy sets should retail for 2X-5X the regular version, depending on player popularity.

		MT
Common Player Set:		4.00
1-11	Alomar Brothers (Roberto Alomar, Sandy Alomar Jr.)	4.00
1-11	Sandy Alomar Jr.	5.00
1-11	Bay Bombers Series (Jose Canseco) (solid green borders)	8.00
1-11	Bay Bombers Series (Will Clark) (solid orange borders)	8.00
1-11	Wade Boggs (solid red borders)	8.00
1-11	Jose Canseco (error set - "Conseco")	40.00
1-11	Jose Canseco (correct, dark green borders, white name)	8.00
1-11	Jose Canseco (correct, light green borders, green name)	8.00
1-11	Will Clark	8.00
1-11	Will Clark, Kevin Mitchell	4.00
1-11	David Cone	4.00
1-11	Dwight Gooden	4.00
1-11	Tom Gordon	4.00
1-11	Mark Grace (solid orange borders)	5.00
1-11	Mike Greenwell (purple borders)	4.00
1-11	Mike Greenwell (red borders)	4.00
1-11	Ken Griffey Jr. (white backs)	10.00
1-11	Ken Griffey Jr. (yellow backs, different photos)	25.00
1-11	Orel Hershiser	4.00
1-11	Sam Horn (solid blue borders)	4.00
1-11	Bo Jackson	4.00
1-11	Gregg Jefferies (blue borders)	4.00
1-11	Gregg Jefferies (orange borders)	4.00
1-11	Gregg Jefferies (pink borders)	4.00
1-11	Ron Jones	4.00
1-11	Ricky Jordan	4.00
1-11	Kevin McReynolds	4.00
1-11	Kevin Mitchell	4.00
1-11	Matt Nokes (3,500 sets, each bag serial numbered)	4.00
1-11	Kirby Puckett	12.00
---	Pete Rose (blank-back, Reds)	30.00
1-11	Nolan Ryan	25.00
1-11	Benito Santiago	4.00
1-11	Gary Sheffield	5.00
1-11	Darryl Strawberry (blue borders)	4.00
1-11	Darryl Strawberry (purple borders)	4.00
1-11	Alan Trammell (#4 misspelled Trammel)	4.00
1-11	Robin Ventura	5.00
1-11	Jerome Walton	4.00
1-11	Jerome Walton (glossy, borders one shade of blue)	5.00

1988-92 Star Ad Cards

These cards were distributed to give dealers and collectors basic information about Star's baseball issues. Fronts look like contemporary Star cards, but most (not all) have the notation "Ad Card" beneath the city name at lower-right. Backs have an advertising message with general information except for Horn and Jefferies, whose ads are specific to ordering those player sets. Some cards exist in both regular and glossy finish. Except for the 1992s, the Ad Cards are undated and some of the dates on this possibly incomplete checklist are only best estimates. The unnumbered cards are checklisted here alphabetically.

		MT
Complete Set (43):		
Common Player:		5.00
(1)	Sandy Alomar Jr. (1989) (regular gray)	5.00
(1g)	Sandy Alomar Jr. (1989) (glossy gray)	5.00
(2)	Steve Avery (1992) (plastic red/blue)	5.00
(3)	Jeff Bagwell (1992) (plastic orange/green)	5.00
(4)	Wade Boggs (1989) (regular pink)	7.50
(5)	Bobby Bonilla (1991) (regular purple)	5.00
(5g)	Bobby Bonilla (1991) (glossy purple)	5.00
(6)	Will Clark (1988) (regular green)	5.00
(6g)	Will Clark (1988) (glossy green)	5.00
(7)	Roger Clemens (1988) (regular)	7.50
(8)	Eric Davis (1989) (glossy red)	5.00
(9)	Ken Griffey Jr. (1989) (regular purple)	10.00
(10)	Ken Griffey Jr. (1990) (regular green)	10.00
(10g)	Ken Griffey Jr. (1990) (glossy green)	10.00
(11)	Rickey Henderson (1991) (regular green/yellow)	5.00
(11g)	Rickey Henderson (1991) (glossy green/yellow)	5.00
(12)	Keith Hernandez (1989) (regular orange)	5.00
(13)	Orel Hershiser (1989) (regular purple)	5.00
(14)	Sam Horn (1988) (regular purple)	5.00
(15)	Bo Jackson (1990) (regular blue)	5.00
(16)	Bo Jackson (1992) (regular green)	5.00
(17)	Gregg Jefferies (1988) (regular blue)	5.00
(18)	Howard Johnson (1990) (regular orange)	5.00
(19)	David Justice (1992) (plastic blue/yellow)	5.00
(20)	Eric Karros (1992) (glossy white)	5.00
(21)	Barry Larkin (1990) (regular red))	5.00
(22)	Kevin Maas (1990) (regular white)	5.00
(23)	Don Mattingly (1988) (regular green)	10.00
(24)	Don Mattingly (1989) (regular blue)	10.00
(25)	Don Mattingly (1989) (regular gray)	10.00
(26)	Kevin Mitchell (1990) (regular white/black)	5.00
(27)	Phil Plantier (1992) (plastic blue/purple)	5.00
(28)	Kirby Puckett (1989) (regular red)	20.00
(29)	Kirby Puckett (1992) (plastic purple/blue)	10.00
(30)	Cal Ripken Jr. (1992) (regular black/orange)	10.00
(31)	Reggie Sanders (1992) (glossy white)	5.00
(32)	Benito Santiago (1990) (regular purple)	5.00
(33)	Mike Scott (1989) (regular green)	5.00
(34)	Darryl Strawberry (1991) (regular red)	5.00
(35g)	Frank Thomas (1991) (glossy blue/red)	10.00
(35p)	Frank Thomas (1991) (plastic blue/red)	10.00
(36)	Frank Thomas (1992) (plastic red/yellow)	10.00
(37)	Alan Trammell (1989) (glossy blue)	5.00
(38)	Robin Ventura (1990) (glossy gold)	10.00
(39)	Jerome Walton (1990) (regular blue/red)	5.00

1988-89 Star Gold Edition

This 180-card set was released from late 1988 into 1989 (though all cards bear 1988 copyright date) in a format matching the regular-issue player sets of the 1988-89 issue. Eighteen single-player sets of 10 cards each are included. The high quality photographs on front feature a special gold embossing. The cards devoted to each player are noted by number in the corresponding listings. Single cards are not checklisted because the issue is usually sold only as complete single-player sets. Fifteen hundred of each set were produced, plus 300 black-bordered, blank-back "promo" cards of each player.

	MT
Complete Set (180):	175.00
Common Player Set (10):	5.00
Complete Promo Set:	300.00
Common Promo Card:	10.00
Gregg Jefferies (#1-10)	6.00
Gregg Jefferies (promo card)	25.00
Sam Horn (#11-20)	5.00
Sam Horn (promo card)	15.00
Don Mattingly (#21-30)	25.00
Don Mattingly (promo card)	35.00
Matt Nokes (#31-40)	5.00
Matt Nokes (promo card)	15.00
Darryl Strawberry (#41-50)	8.00
Darryl Strawberry (promo card)	10.00
Will Clark (#51-60)	12.00
Will Clark (promo card)	15.00
Wade Boggs (#61-70)	15.00
Wade Boggs (promo card)	20.00
Mark Grace (#71-80)	12.00
Mark Grace (promo card)	15.00
Bo Jackson (#81-90)	9.00
Bo Jackson (promo card)	15.00
Jose Canseco (#91-100)	15.00
Jose Canseco (promo card)	20.00
Eric Davis (#101-110)	6.00
Eric Davis (promo card)	10.00
Orel Hershiser (#110-119; card #120 misnumbered #110)	6.00
Orel Hershiser (promo card)	10.00
Mike Greenwell (#121-130)	5.00
Mike Greenwell (promo card)	10.00
Dave Winfield (#131-140)	12.00
Dave Winfield (promo card)	20.00
Alan Trammell (#141-150)	10.00
Alan Trammell (promo card)	15.00
Roger Clemens (#151-160)	15.00
Roger Clemens (promo card)	25.00
Kirby Puckett (#161-170)	15.00
Kirby Puckett (promo card)	25.00
Kevin Seitzer (#171-180)	5.00
Kevin Seitzer (promo card)	10.00

1988-89 Star Nova Edition

With production limited to just 500 sets and 40 promo cards of each player, these are the most limited of the regular Star issues of 1989. Cards follow the format of the regular-issue Star single-player sets of the 1988-89 issue. Each of the 9-card player sets is listed here in alphabetical order. Single cards are not listed because complete player sets are seldom broken for individual card sales. The Nova promo cards have blue borders at the top and red at bottom. Cards #109-117 were not issued. Ryne Sandberg cards #154-161 have his name misspelled Sanberg on front and back.

	MT
Complete Set (153):	600.00
Common Player Set (10):	20.00
Complete Promo Card Set (17):	2000.
Common Promo Card:	50.00
Mike Greenwell (#1-9)	20.00
Mike Greenwell (promo card)	50.00
Darryl Strawberry (#10-18)	20.00
Darryl Strawberry (promo card)	50.00
Don Mattingly (#19-27)	75.00
Don Mattingly (promo card)	250.00
Eric Davis (#28-36)	20.00
Eric Davis (promo)	50.00
Jose Canseco (#37-45)	50.00
Jose Canseco (promo card)	150.00
Sandy Alomar Jr. (#46-54)	20.00
Sandy Alomar Jr. (promo card)	50.00
Kirby Puckett (#55-63)	60.00
Kirby Puckett (promo card)	200.00
Orel Hershiser (#64-72)	20.00
Orel Hershiser (promo card)	50.00
Wade Boggs (#73-81)	50.00
Wade Boggs (promo card)	150.00
Rickey Henderson (#82-90)	25.00
Rickey Henderson (promo card)	60.00
Will Clark (#91-99)	30.00
Will Clark (promo card)	100.00
Bo Jackson (#100-108)	25.00
Bo Jackson (promo card)	90.00
Ken Griffey Jr. (#118-126)	100.00
Ken Griffey Jr. (promo card)	250.00
Mike Schmidt (#127-135)	75.00
Mike Schmidt (promo card)	175.00
Gary Sheffield (#136-144)	25.00
Gary Sheffield (promo card)	60.00
Cal Ripken Jr. (#145-153)	90.00
Cal Ripken Jr. (promo card)	250.00
Ryne Sandberg (#154-162)	50.00
Ryne Sandberg (promo card)	125.00

1988 Star Platinum Edition

Twelve single-player sets make up the 1988 Star Platinum series. Ten cards were devoted to each player. While the cards were sold as individual player sets, they were numbered continguously. Fronts feature color photos with various colorful borders (by player), highlighted in silver foil. No single card prices are quoted because the cards are usually sold only as complete player sets. One thousand sets of each player were issued, along with 200 gold-bordered promo cards per player.

	MT
Complete Set (120):	150.00
Common Player Set (10):	10.00
Complete Promo Set (12):	300.00
Common Promo Player:	15.00
Don Mattingly (#1-10)	50.00
Don Mattingly (promo card)	80.00
Dwight Gooden (#11-20)	10.00
Dwight Gooden (promo card)	20.00
Roger Clemens (#21-30)	20.00
Roger Clemens (promo card)	25.00
Mike Schmidt (#31-40)	25.00
Mike Schmidt (promo card)	30.00
Wade Boggs (#41-50)	20.00
Wade Boggs (promo card)	25.00
Mark McGwire (#51-60)	45.00
Mark McGwire (promo card)	40.00
Andre Dawson (#61-70)	12.00
Andre Dawson (promo card)	20.00

Jose Canseco (#71-80)	20.00
Jose Canseco (promo card)	30.00
Eric Davis (#81-90)	10.00
Eric Davis (promo card)	15.00
George Brett (#91-100)	25.00
George Brett (promo card) (throwing)	30.00
Darryl Strawberry (#101-110)	10.00
Darryl Strawberry (promo card) (blue uniform)	15.00
Dale Murphy (#111-120)	10.00
Dale Murphy (promo card)	15.00

1988-89 Star Silver Edition

This 90-card issue features 10 single-player sets. Only Only 2,000 serial numbered sets were printed (plus 400 "promo" cards of each player, featuring black borders fading to white at the middle). Single-card values are not quoted because the player sets are seldom broken for individual card sales. Cards follow the format of the regular-issue 1988-89 Star player sets.

	MT
Complete Set (90):	150.00
Common Player Set:	5.00
Complete Promo Card Set (10):	200.00
Common Promo Card:	10.00
Ken Griffey Jr. (#1-9)	60.00
Ken Griffey Jr. (promo card)	30.00
Wade Boggs (#10-18)	15.00
Wade Boggs (promo card)	20.00
Ricky Jordan (#19-27)	5.00
Ricky Jordan (promo card)	10.00
Mike Greenwell (#28-36)	5.00
Mike Greenwell (promo card)	10.00
Sandy Alomar Jr. (#37-45)	10.00
Sandy Alomar Jr. (promo card)	15.00
Mike Schmidt (#46-54)	20.00
Mike Schmidt (promo card)	25.00
Gary Sheffield (#55-63)	10.00
Gary Sheffield (promo card)	10.00
Will Clark (#64-72)	10.00
Will Clark (promo card)	15.00
Ron Jones (#73-81)	5.00
Ron Jones (promo card)	10.00
Kirby Puckett (#82-90)	20.00
Kirby Puckett (promo card)	25.00

1988 Star '88 Promos

Most of the Star '88 single- and dual-player card sets also had a promo card issued; blank-backed but otherwise nearly identical to the regular cards.

	MT
Complete Set (23):	195.00
Common Player:	3.00
(1) George Bell	5.00
(2) Wade Boggs	8.00
(3) Wade Boggs, Tony Gwynn	7.50
(4) Gary Carter	6.00
(5) Will Clark	8.00
(6) Roger Clemens, Dwight Gooden	6.00
(7) Eric Davis	3.00
(8) Andre Dawson	7.50
(9) Dwight Gooden	6.00
(10) Tony Gwynn	7.50
(11) Bo Jackson	10.00
(12) Don Mattingly	10.00
(13) Don Mattingly, Mike Schmidt	15.00
(14) Mark McGwire (yellow-border set, green-border promo)	15.00
(15) Mark McGwire (aqua-border set, yellow-border promo)	17.50
(16) Mark McGwire (green-border set, white-border promo)	17.50
(17) Eddie Murray	10.00
(18) Cal Ripken Jr.	20.00
(19) Mike Schmidt	10.00
(20) Mike Scott	5.00
(21) Kevin Seitzer	5.00
(22) Cory Snyder	3.00
(23) Dave Winfield	5.00

1988 Star '88

For the fifth straight year Star utilized the same basic format for its single-player card sets of 1988. Fronts have player posed and game-action photos surrounded by a brightly colored border. Pushing into the top-right of the photo is a "Star '88" logo. A circle at the lower-left contains the player name or logo. Backs have stats, personal data, career highlights or a checklist. Single cards are not listed here because sets are seldom broken. Each player set was also issued in a more limited glossy edition, which generally sells for about twice the price of the regular issue.

	MT
Common Player Set:	5.00
1-11 George Bell	5.00
(1-10)George Bell (sticker set)	4.00
1-11 Wade Boggs	8.00
1-11 Wade Boggs, Tony Gwynn	7.50
1-11 Gary Carter	6.00
1-11 Will Clark	8.00
1-11 Roger Clemens, Dwight Gooden	6.00
1-12 Eric Davis	5.00
1-11 Eric Davis, Mark McGwire	15.00
1-11 Andre Dawson	7.50
1-12 Dwight Gooden	6.00
1-11 Tony Gwynn	12.00
1-16 Bo Jackson (set includes four blank-back cards as Auburn football player)	10.00
1-11 Don Mattingly (card #3 exists with fielding or batting pose)	10.00
1-11 Don Mattingly, Mike Schmidt	15.00
1-12 Mark McGwire (yellow borders)	20.00
1-11 Mark McGwire (aqua borders)	15.00
1-11 Mark McGwire (green borders)	15.00
1-12 Eddie Murray (glossy version only)	10.00
1-12 Cal Ripken Jr.	20.00
1-12 Mike Schmidt (glossy version only)	10.00
1-11 Mike Scott	5.00
1-11 Kevin Seitzer	5.00
1-11 Cory Snyder	5.00
(1-8) Cory Snyder (sticker set)	4.00
1-12 Dave Winfield	9.00
(1-10)Dave Winfield (sticker set)	5.00

1989-90 Star Rookies

Two-card "sets" of each of 12 promising players were produced in an edition of 10,000 each as an exclusive for a New York comic book dealer. Cards have player photos on front with a few stats on back. Cards #1-12 have borders of red and gold and backs printed in red and tan. The 1990 cards, #13-24, are bordered in purple and yellow with backs printed in purple on yellow. All cards have 1989 copyright dates. contemporary Star sets, no glossy or promo cards were made.

	MT
Complete Set (24):	10.00
Common Player:	.25
1 Eric Anthony	.25
2 Eric Anthony	.25
3 Mark Lewis	.50
4 Mark Lewis	.50
5 Pete Rose, Jr.	1.00
6 Pete Rose, Jr.	1.00
7 Robin Ventura	.75
8 Robin Ventura	.75
9 Beau Allred	.25
10 Beau Allred	.25
11 Pat Combs	.25
12 Pat Combs	.25
13 Deion Sanders	1.00
14 Deion Sanders	1.00
15 Bob Hamelin	.25
16 Bob Hamelin	.25
17 Andy Benes	.50
18 Andy Benes	.50
19 Bam Bam Muelens	.25
20 Bam Bam Meulens	.25
21 Trey McCoy	.25
22 Trey McCoy	.25
23 Sandy Alomar Jr.	.50
24 Sandy Alomar Jr.	.50

1990-91 Star Promos

Most of the 1990-91 series of Star player sets feature a promo card in the same format. They are blank-backed and have the word "Promo" on front beneath the city name. Regular and glossy promos exist for most cards.

	MT
Complete Set (43):	275.00
Common Player:	5.00
(1) Jim Abbott	5.00
(2) Andy Benes	5.00
(3) Barry Bonds	7.50
(4) Bobby Bonilla	5.00
(5) Jose Canseco (blue borders, from purple set)	5.00
(6) Jose Canseco (orange borders, from yellow set)	5.00
(7) Jose Canseco (green borders, from yellow set)	5.00
(8) Will Clark (black borders)	5.00
(9) Will Clark (purple)	5.00
(10) Will Clark (orange, from Clark/Grace set)	5.00
(11) Mark Davis	5.00
(12) Cecil Fielder (purple, from blue set)	5.00
(13) Cecil Fielder (yellow glossy, from blue set)	50.00
(14) Ken Griffey Jr. (purple, from blue set)	6.00
(15) Ken Griffey Jr. (blue on yellow, from blue set)	6.00
(16) Ken Griffey Jr. (red, batting with "S" on helmet, from yellow set)	6.00
(17) Ken Griffey Jr. (red, no "S" on helmet, from aqua Jr./Sr. set)	6.00
(18) Ken Griffey Jr. (red on yellow, from red Jr./Sr. set)	6.00
(19) Ken Griffey Sr. (blue, from aqua set)	5.00
(20) Ken Griffey Sr. (yellow, from red set)	5.00
(21) Rickey Henderson (blue, 1990)	5.00
(22) Rickey Henderson (green, running, 1990)	5.00
(23) Rickey Henderson (green, batting, 1991)	5.00
(24) Bo Jackson (running)	5.00
(25) Bo Jackson (portrait)	5.00
(26) Bo Jackson (Diamond Terror, yellow)	5.00
(27) David Justice	5.00
(28) Barry Larkin	5.00
(29) Kevin Maas	5.00
(30) Ben McDonald	5.00
(31) Kevin Mitchell	5.00
(32) Gregg Olson	5.00
(33) Cal Ripken Jr.	7.50
(34) Nolan Ryan (blue, from Rangers set)	20.00
(35) Nolan Ryan (yellow, from all-team set)	10.00
(36) Bret Saberhagen	5.00
(37) Ryne Sandberg	5.00
(38) Darryl Strawberry	5.00
(39) Frank Thomas	5.00
(40) Jerome Walton	5.00
(41) Matt Williams	5.00
(42) Robin Yount (brown on yellow, from Mitchell/Yount set)	5.00
(43) Robin Yount (blue on yellow)	5.00

1990-91 Star

Issued as single-player sets over the two-year span these sets maintain a design continuity despite the fact some have a 1990 copyright line on back and some have a 1991 date. Fronts of all cards have posed and game-action photos which are bordered in a single bright color, by player. That border color is darkest at top and bottom and fades to white at the center. Backs are printed in one of several colors on white cardboard and feature personal data, stats, career highlights, checklists and team logos. Single cards are not listed because sets are seldom broken for individual card sales. Glossy versions are known for most, but not all, player sets.

	MT
Common Player Set:	5.00
1-11 Jim Abbott	5.00
1-11 Andy Benes	5.00
1-11 Barry Bonds (error, cards #2-11 say "Bobby Bonds")	40.00
1-11 Barry Bonds (corrected)	5.00
1-11 Bobby Bonilla	5.00
1-11 Jose Canseco (purple borders)	4.00
1-11 Jose Canseco (yellow borders)	5.00
1-11 Will Clark	5.00
1-11 Will Clark, Mark Grace	5.00
1-11 Cecil Fielder (blue borders)	5.00
1-11 Cecil Fielder (orange borders)	5.00
1-11 Ken Griffey Jr. (blue borders)	9.00
1-11 Ken Griffey Jr. (yellow borders)	9.00
1-11 Ken Griffey Jr., Ken Griffey Sr. (aqua borders)	4.00
1-11 Ken Griffey Jr., Ken Griffey Sr. (red borders)	4.00
1-11 Rickey Henderson (1990)	5.00
1-11 Rickey Henderson (1991)	5.00
1-11 Bo Jackson	5.00
1-11 Bo Jackson, Barry Larkin (Diamond Terror)	5.00
1 Howard Johnson (autographed card numbered to 400)	10.00
1-11 Dave Justice	5.00
1-11 Dave Justice, Kevin Maas	5.00
1-11 Barry Larkin	5.00
1-11 Kevin Maas	5.00
1-11 Ben McDonald	5.00
1-11 Kevin Mitchell, Robin Yount	5.00
1-11 Cal Ripken Jr.	10.00
1-11 Nolan Ryan (Card #1 pitching, all Rangers photos)	20.00
1-11 Nolan Ryan (Card #1 portrait, all four teams)	20.00
1-11 Bret Saberhagen, Mark Davis	5.00
1-11 Ryne Sandberg	6.00
1-11 Darryl Strawberry	5.00
1-11 Frank Thomas	10.00
1-11 Jerome Walton, Gregg Olson	5.00
1-11 Matt Williams	5.00
1-11 Robin Yount	7.50

1990-93 Star "Career Stats"

These unnumbered cards are not part of any Star sets. They share a common design of two-color graduated borders on front, with color photos both front and back. The words "Career Stats" are prominently displayed on both front and back. Some players were sold in both autographed and unautographed versions, while some are known only in one version or the other.

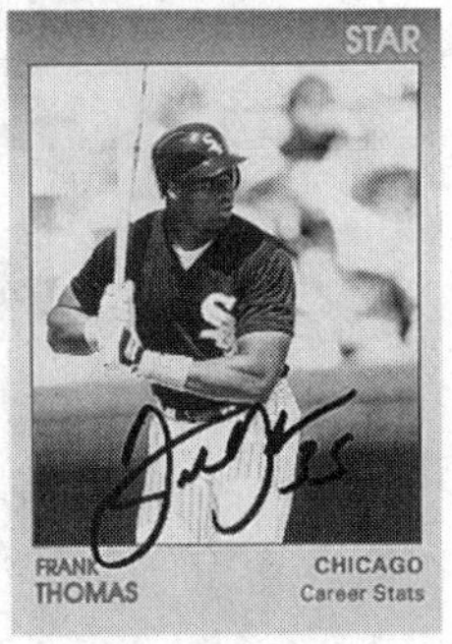

	MT
Complete Set (26):	225.00
Common Player:	5.00
(1) Ken Griffey Jr. (1990)	15.00
(2) Barry Bonds (1991)	5.00
(2a) Barry Bonds (1991) (autographed)	20.00
(3) Bobby Bonilla (1991)	5.00
(4) Scott Erickson (1991)	5.00
(4a) Scott Erickson (1991) (autographed)	10.00
(5) Chuck Knoblauch (1991)	5.00
(5a) Chuck Knoblauch (1991) (autographed)	10.00
(6) Frank Thomas (1991)	10.00
(6a) Frank Thomas (1991) (autographed)	30.00
(6g) Frank Thomas (1991) (glossy)	10.00
(7) Matt Williams (1991)	5.00
(7a) Matt Williams (1991) (autographed)	10.00
(8) Jeff Bagwell (1992)	5.00
(9a) Pat Kelly (1992) (autographed)	10.00
(10a) Mark Lewis (1992) (autographed)	10.00
(11a) John Olerud (1992) (autographed)	10.00
(12) Jim Abbott (1993)	5.00
(12a) Jim Abbott (1993) (autographed)	10.00
(13) Bret Barberie (1993)	5.00
(13a) Bret Barberie (1993) (autographed)	10.00
(14) Andy Benes (1993)	5.00
(14a) Andy Benes (1993) (autographed)	10.00
(15) Rickey Henderson (1993)	5.00
(16a) Eric Karros (1993) (autographed)	10.00
(17) Ryan Klesko (1993)	5.00
(18) Kevin Mass (1993) (Maas)	5.00
(19) Dean Palmer (1993)	5.00

1990-91 Star Gold Edition

Only 1,500 of each 9-card, single-player set was produced in Star's 1990-91 Gold Edition. Single cards are not listed or priced because the issue is almost exclusively traded in complete player sets. Cards were numbered contiguously as noted in the alphabetical checklist presented here. Suggested retail price at issue was $15-20 per set. An edition of 300 gray-bordered promo cards was issued for each player.

	MT
Complete Set (180):	225.00
Common Nine-card Player Set:	8.00
Complete Promo Card Set (20):	350.00
Common Promo Card:	10.00
(1) Wade Boggs (#136-144)	15.00
(1)_ Wade Boggs (promo card)	17.50
(2) Bobby Bonilla (#145-153)	9.00
(2) Bobby Bonilla (promo card)	12.50
(3) Jose Canseco (#19-27)	12.50
(3) Jose Canseco (promo card)	17.50
(4) Will Clark (#64-72)	15.00
(4) Will Clark (promo card)	20.00
(5) Dwight Gooden (#109-117)	8.00
(5) Dwight Gooden (promo card)	12.50
(6) Mark Grace (#154-162)	12.00
(6) Mark Grace (promo card)	15.00
(7) Ken Griffey Jr. (#10-18)	25.00
(7) Ken Griffey Jr. (promo card)	50.00
(8) Rickey Henderson (#82-90)	9.00
(8) Rickey Henderson (promo card)	12.50
(9) Bo Jackson (#1-9)	9.00
(9) Bo Jackson (promo card)	12.50
(10) Howard Johnson (#163-171)	8.00
(10) Howard Johnson (promo card)	10.00
(11) David Justice (#118-126)	12.00
(11) David Justice (promo card)	12.50
(12) Barry Larkin (#91-99)	9.00
(12) Barry Larkin (promo card)	12.50
(13) Kevin Maas (#127-135)	8.00
(13) Kevin Maas (promo card)	10.00
(14) Don Mattingly (#100-108)	17.50
(14) Don Mattingly (promo card)	30.00
(15) Kirby Puckett (#55-63)	17.50
(15) Kirby Puckett (promo card)	30.00
(16) Tim Raines (#37-45)	8.00
(16) Tim Raines (promo card)	12.50
(17) Cal Ripken Jr. (#73-81)	25.00
(17) Cal Ripken Jr. (promo card)	50.00
(18) Ryne Sandberg (#46-54)	15.00
(18) Ryne Sandberg (promo card)	20.00
(19) Darryl Strawberry (#172-180)	8.00
(19) Darryl Strawberry (promo card)	12.50
(20) Robin Ventura (#28-36)	10.00
(20) Robin Ventura (promo card)	12.50

1990-91 Star Nova Edition

With just 500 of each nine-card single-player set produced, the Nova Edition was Star's top of the line in 1990. Player sets are listed alphabetically. Single cards are not listed because sets are seldom broken. Each set is also represented by an issue of 100 promo cards, featuring black borders at top and yellow at bottom.

	MT
Complete Set (180):	560.00
Common Nine-card Player Set:	15.00
Complete Promo Set (20):	750.00
Common Promo Card:	20.00
(1) Wade Boggs (#28-36)	25.00
(1) Wade Boggs (promo card)	35.00
(2) Jose Canseco (#55-63)	25.00
(2) Jose Canseco (promo card)	35.00
(3) Joe Carter (#118-126)	15.00
(3) Joe Carter (promo card)	20.00
(4) Will Clark (#46-54)	20.00
(4) Will Clark (promo card)	30.00
(5) Roger Clemens (#109-117)	45.00
(5) Roger Clemens (promo card)	45.00
(6) Glenn Davis (#127-135)	15.00
(6) Glenn Davis (promo card)	20.00
(7) Len Dykstra (#163-171)	15.00
(7) Len Dykstra (promo card)	20.00
(8) Cecil Fielder (#154-162)	15.00
(8) Cecil Fielder (promo card)	30.00
(9) Ken Griffey Jr. (#172-180)	75.00
(9) Ken Griffey Jr. (promo card)	100.00
(10) Rickey Henderson (#73-81)	20.00
(10) Rickey Henderson (promo card)	30.00
(11) Bo Jackson (#64-72)	15.00
(11) Bo Jackson (promo card)	25.00
(12) Howard Johnson (#37-45)	15.00
(12) Howard Johnson (promo card)	20.00
(13) Barry Larkin (#100-108)	15.00
(13) Barry Larkin (promo card)	30.00
(14) Don Mattingly (#1-9)	45.00
(14) Don Mattingly (promo card)	60.00
(15) Kevin Mitchell (#145-153)	15.00
(15) Kevin Mitchell (promo card)	20.00
(16) Nolan Ryan (#19-27)	60.00
(16) Nolan Ryan (promo card)	125.00
(17) Ryne Sandberg (#136-144)	25.00
(17) Ryne Sandberg (promo card)	35.00
(18) Dave Stewart (#91-99)	15.00
(18) Dave Stewart (promo card)	20.00
(19) Darryl Strawberry (#82-90)	15.00
(19) Darryl Strawberry (promo card)	20.00
(20) Robin Yount (#10-18)	25.00
(20) Robin Yount (promo card)	45.00

1990-91 Star Platinum Edition

The stars in Star's Platinum Edition were featured in nine-card sets with production of 1,000 each (plus 200 black-bordered promo cards of each player). Suggested retail price at the time of issue was about $20. The player sets are checklisted here in alphabetical order. Single cards are not listed because the sets are almost never broken up. Cards are numbered contiguously as noted in the alphabetical checklisted.

	MT
Complete Set (200):	275.00
Common Nine-player Set:	8.00
Complete Promo Set (21):	350.00
Common Promo Card:	10.00
(1) Jim Abbott (#19-27)	8.00
(1) Jim Abbott (promo card)	8.00
(2) Wade Boggs (#145-153)	20.00
(2) Wade Boggs (promo card)	25.00
(3) Jose Canseco (#91-99)	20.00
(3) Jose Canseco (promo card)	25.00
(4) Will Clark (#1-9)	20.00
(4) Will Clark (promo card)	25.00
(5) Roger Clemens (#46-54)	25.00
(5) Roger Clemens (promo card)	30.00
(6) Eric Davis (#55-63)	8.00
(6) Eric Davis (promo card)	8.00
(7) Dwight Gooden (#82-90)	8.00
(7) Dwight Gooden (promo card)	8.00
(8) Mark Grace (#172-180) (#172 says "Silver Series")	15.00
(8) Mark Grace (promo card)	20.00
(9) Mike Greenwell (#64-72)	8.00
(9) Mike Greenwell (promo card)	8.00
(10) Ken Griffey Jr. (#100-108)	30.00
(10) Ken Griffey Jr. (promo card)	40.00
(11) Tony Gwynn (#28-36)	25.00
(11) Tony Gwynn (promo card)	30.00
(12) Bo Jackson (#136-144)	8.00
(12) Bo Jackson (promo card)	8.00
(13) Howard Johnson (#109-117)	8.00
(13) Howard Johnson (promo card)	8.00
(14) Don Mattingly (#73-81)	25.00
(14) Don Mattingly (promo card)	30.00
(15) Kevin Mitchell (#10-18)	8.00
(15) Kevin Mitchell (promo card, batting)	8.00
(16) Kevin Mitchell (#154-162)	8.00
(16) Kevin Mitchell (promo card, running)	8.00
(17) Kirby Puckett (#37-45)	25.00
(17) Kirby Puckett (promo card)	30.00
(18) Ryne Sandberg (#163-171)	15.00
(18) Ryne Sandberg (promo card)	20.00
(19) Darryl Strawberry (#118-126)	8.00
(19) Darryl Strawberry (promo card)	15.00
(20) Matt Williams (#127-135)	8.00
(20) Matt Williams (promo card)	

1990-91 Star Silver Edition

Many of 1990's biggest stars are represented in nine-card single-player sets within Star Co.'s Silver Edition. Production of each silver-foil trimmed set was limited to 2,000. Because single cards are seldom offered, only complete player sets are priced. Cards are numbered contiguously as noted in the alphabetical checklist presented here. Retail price at issue was $10-15. Each player is also represented by an issue of 400 black-bordered promo cards.

	MT
Complete Set (180):	150.00
Common Player Set (9):	6.00
Complete Promo Set:	175.00
Common Promo Card:	6.00
(1) Jim Abbott (#1-9)	6.00
(1) Jim Abbott (promo card)	6.00
(2) Sandy Alomar Jr. (#55-63)	8.00
(2) Sandy Alomar Jr. (promo card)	10.00
(3) Andy Benes (#19-27)	6.00
(3) Andy Benes (promo card)	6.00
(4) Barry Bonds (#172-180)	10.00
(4) Barry Bonds (promo card)	10.00
(5) Bobby Bonilla (#154-162)	8.00
(5) Bobby Bonilla (promo card)	10.00
(6) Jose Canseco (#127-135)	10.00
(6) Jose Canseco (promo card)	15.00
(7) Will Clark (#73-81)	10.00
(7) Will Clark (promo card)	15.00
(8) Delino DeShields (#145-153)	6.00
(8) Delino DeShields (promo card)	6.00
(9) Tom Gordon (#37-45)	6.00
(9) Tom Gordon (promo card)	6.00
(10) Mark Grace (#10-18)	10.00
(10) Mark Grace (promo card)	10.00
(11) Ken Griffey Jr. (#91-99)	24.00
(11) Ken Griffey Jr. (promo card)	30.00
(12) Mike Harkey (#163-171)	6.00
(12) Mike Harkey (promo card)	6.00
(13) Wally Joyner (#28-36)	9.00
(13) Wally Joyner (promo card)	10.00
(14) David Justice (#118-126)	10.00
(14) David Justice (promo card)	10.00
(15) Kevin Maas (#109-117)	6.00
(15) Kevin Maas (promo card)	6.00
(16) Don Mattingly (#136-144)	15.00
(16) Don Mattingly (promo card)	25.00
(17) Ben McDonald (#100-108)	6.00
(17) Ben McDonald (promo card)	6.00
(18) Benito Santiago (#64-72)	6.00
(18) Benito Santiago (promo card)	6.00
(19) Alan Trammell (#46-54) (all cards misspelled "Allan")	10.00
(19) Alan Trammell (promo card)	10.00
(20) Jerome Walton (#82-90)	6.00
(20) Jerome Walton (promo card)	6.00

1990 Star Sophomore Stars

This special six-card set was distributed only at the 1990 Arlington 11th National Sports Collectors Convention. The set came polybagged with a DC comic book in exchange for a donation to the Arthritis Foundation. The 2-1/2" x 3-1/2" cards feature a border that changes from dark blue at the top to red at the bottom. Backs are printed in blue-on-white and include team and MLB logos along with major and minor league career stats.

	MT
Complete Set (6):	22.00
Common Player:	.50

1	Ken Griffey, Jr. (batting cage)	10.00
2	Ken Griffey, Jr. (sitting)	10.00
3	Gary Sheffield (portrait)	2.00
4	Gary Sheffield (batting)	2.00
5	Jerome Walton (portrait)	.50
6	Jerome Walton (batting)	.50

1991 Star

A common design is again shared by the single-player card sets released by Star for 1991. Cards feature posed and action photos on front with borders that graduate from one color at top to another at bottom (yellow to blue; green to gray, etc.). The player name is at left beneath the photo, his city at right and the card name beneath that. Backs are printed in one of several colors on white stock and feature personal data, stats, career highlights, checklist or team logo. Each set was also produced in a high-gloss version, which carries a 4X-5X premium today. Single cards are not listed here because player sets are seldom broken for individual card sales. All promo cards except Clemens have a solid-color border.

		MT
	Complete Set (88):	55.00
	Common Player Set:	5.00
	Complete Promo Set (6):	45.00
	Common Promo Card:	5.00
1-11	Roger Clemens	6.00
	Roger Clemens (promo card)	6.00
1-11	Rickey Henderson	5.00
1-11	Bo Jackson	5.00
	Bo Jackson (promo card)	5.00
1-11	Pat Kelly (glossy version only)	5.00
	Pat Kelly (promo card)	5.00
1-11	Cal Ripken Jr.	10.00
	Cal Ripken Jr. (promo card)	10.00
1-11	Nolan Ryan	15.00
	Nolan Ryan (promo card)	15.00
1-11	Darryl Strawberry	5.00
1-11	Frank Thomas (glossy version only)	10.00
	Frank Thomas (promo card)	10.00

1991 Star All-Stars

This Star issue is comprised of 500 sets and 100 promo cards of each player. (Except Jackson who has 200). The checklist is arranged alphabetically.

		MT
	Complete Set (126):	325.00
	Common Player Set:	20.00
	Complete Promo Set (14):	360.00
	Common Promo Card:	20.00
(1)	Wade Boggs (#109-117)	25.00
(1)	Wade Boggs (promo card)	30.00
(2)	Jose Canseco (#37-45)	25.00
(2)	Jose Canseco (promo card)	25.00
(3)	Roger Clemens (#64-72)	25.00
(3)	Roger Clemens (promo card)	25.00
(4)	Lenny Dykstra (#91-99)	20.00
(4)	Lenny Dykstra (promo card)	20.00
(5)	Cecil Fielder (#118-126)	20.00
(6)	Cecil Fielder (promo card)	20.00
(6)	Dwight Gooden (#82-90)	20.00
(6)	Dwight Gooden (promo card)	20.00
(7)	Ken Griffey Jr. (#1-9)	30.00
(7)	Ken Griffey Jr. (promo card)	35.00
(8)	Rickey Henderson (#19-27)	25.00
(8)	Rickey Henderson (promo card)	25.00
(9)	Bo Jackson (#46-54)	20.00
(9)	Bo Jackson (promo card)	20.00
(10)	Don Mattingly (#73-81)	30.00
(10)	Don Mattingly (promo card)	40.00
(11)	Kirby Puckett (#100-108)	30.00
(11)	Kirby Puckett (promo card)	40.00
(12)	Cal Ripken Jr. (#55-63)	30.00
(12p)	Cal Ripken Jr. (#55-63) (plastic test issue)	30.00
(12)	Cal Ripken Jr. (promo card)	40.00
(12p)	Cal Ripken Jr. (promo card) (plastic)	40.00
(13)	Nolan Ryan (#10-18)	30.00
(13)	Nolan Ryan (promo card)	35.00
(14)	Ryne Sandberg (#28-36)	25.00
(14)	Ryne Sandberg (promo card)	25.00

1991 Star Diamond Series

Production of these nine-card, single-player sets was limited to 2,000 of each (plus 400 promo cards each), with a suggested retail price at issue of $25. Players in the edition are listed here in alphabetical order. Cards are numbered contiguously throughout the issue, as noted in the alpha-order listings here. Single cards are not priced because the sets are seldom broken up.

		MT
	Complete Set (126):	200.00
	Common Player Set:	10.00
	Complete Promo Set:	250.00
	Common Promo Card:	10.00
(1)	Barry Bonds (#10-18)	15.00
(1)	Barry Bonds (promo card)	20.00
(2)	Bobby Bonilla (#46-54)	10.00
(2)	Bobby Bonilla (promo card)	10.00
(3)	Jose Canseco (#37-45)	15.00
(3)	Jose Canseco (promo card)	20.00
(4)	Roger Clemens (#64-72)	15.00
(4)	Roger Clemens (promo card)	20.00
(5)	Cecil Fielder (#118-126)	10.00
(5)	Cecil Fielder (promo card)	15.00
(6)	Ken Griffey Jr. (#55-63)	20.00
(6)	Ken Griffey Jr. (promo card)	25.00
(7)	Tony Gwynn (#100-108)	15.00
(7)	Tony Gwynn (promo card)	20.00
(8)	Bo Jackson (#1-9)	10.00
(8)	Bo Jackson (promo card)	15.00
(9)	Don Mattingly (#19-27)	20.00
(9)	Don Mattingly (promo card)	25.00
(10)	Kirby Puckett (#82-90)	20.00
(10)	Kirby Puckett (promo card)	25.00
(11)	Cal Ripken Jr. (#28-36)	20.00
(11)	Cal Ripken Jr. (promo card)	25.00
(12)	Nolan Ryan (#109-117)	20.00
(12)	Nolan Ryan (promo card)	25.00
(13)	Darryl Strawberry (#73-81)	10.00
(13)	Darryl Strawberry (promo card)	10.00
(14)	Frank Thomas (#91-99)	20.00
(14)	Frank Thomas (promo card)	25.00

1991 Star The Future

A few players who had not yet been included among the flood of 1991 Star issues joined the others in this post-season issue. Production was put at 1,000 nine-card sets per player, plus 200 promo cards of each. Players are listed here in alphabetical order. Individual cards are not listed because the sets are usually never sold as singles.

		MT
	Complete Set (90):	125.00
	Common Player Set:	10.00
	Complete Promo Set (10):	135.00
	Common Promo Card:	10.00
(1)	Jeff Bagwell (#28-36)	20.00
(1)	Jeff Bagwell (promo card)	25.00
(2)	Albert Belle (#55-63)	15.00
(2)	Albert Belle (promo card)	20.00
(3)	Scott Erickson (#82-90)	10.00
(3)	Scott Erickson (promo card)	10.00
(4)	Juan Gonzalez (#1-9)	15.00
(4)	Juan Gonzalez (promo card)	15.00
(5)	Pat Kelly (#10-18)	10.00
(5)	Pat Kelly (promo card)	10.00
(6)	Mark Lewis (#73-81)	10.00
(6)	Mark Lewis (promo card)	10.00
(7)	Ramon Martinez (#46-54)	10.00
(7)	Ramon Martinez (promo card)	10.00
(8)	Brian McRae (#64-72)	10.00
(8)	Brian McRae (promo card)	10.00
(9)	Frank Thomas (#37-45)	25.00
(9)	Frank Thomas (promo card)	30.00
(10)	Mo Vaughn (#19-27)	12.00
(10)	Mo Vaughn (promo card)	14.00

1991 Star Gold Edition

Only 1,500 of each nine-card, single-player set was produced - along with 300 promo cards of each player - in Star's 1991 Gold Edition. Cards are numbered contiguously throughout the issue, as noted in the alphabetical checklist shown here. Single cards are not listed or priced because the issue is almost exclusively traded in complete-player sets.

		MT
	Complete Set (144):	200.00
	Common Player Set:	10.00
	Complete Promo Set (16):	250.00
	Common Promo Card:	15.00
(1)	Albert Belle (#118-126)	12.00
(1)	Albert Belle (promo card)	15.00
(2)	Barry Bonds (#73-81)	12.00
(2)	Barry Bonds (promo card)	15.00
(3)	Bobby Bonilla (#127-135)	10.00
(3)	Bobby Bonilla (promo card)	15.00
(4)	Jose Canseco (#55-63)	15.00
(4)	Jose Canseco (promo card)	20.00
(5)	Will Clark (#28-36)	12.00
(5)	Will Clark (promo card)	15.00
(6)	Roger Clemens (#64-72)	15.00
(6)	Roger Clemens (promo card)	25.00
(7)	Ken Griffey Jr. (#19-27)	25.00
(7)	Ken Griffey Jr. (promo card)	30.00
(8)	Bo Jackson (#37-45)	10.00
(8)	Bo Jackson (promo card)	15.00
(9)	David Justice (#82-90)	10.00
(9)	David Justice (promo card)	15.00
(10)	Don Mattingly (#91-99)	25.00
(10)	Don Mattingly (promo card)	30.00
(11)	Fred McGriff (#136-144)	10.00
(11)	Fred McGriff (promo card)	15.00
(12)	Kirby Puckett (#1-9)	25.00
(12)	Kirby Puckett (promo card)	30.00
(13)	Nolan Ryan (#109-117)	25.00
(13)	Nolan Ryan (promo card)	30.00
(14)	Ryne Sandberg (#10-18)	15.00
(14)	Ryne Sandberg (promo card)	20.00
(15)	Darryl Strawberry (#46-54)	10.00
(15)	Darryl Strawberry (promo card)	15.00
(16)	Frank Thomas (#100-108)	20.00
(16)	Frank Thomas (promo card)	25.00

1991 Star Home Run Series

With a suggested retail price at issue of $25 or so, and an edition limit of 1,500 each of the single-player, nine-card sets (plus 300 promo cards of each player), these are among the scarcer of the 1991 Star issues. Numbers on individual player cards run contiguously throughout the issue and are noted in the alphabetical checklist. Because sets are seldom available as singles, individual cards are not listed here.

		MT
	Complete Set (126):	200.00
	Common Player Set:	10.00
	Complete Promo Set (14):	250.00
	Common Promo Card:	10.00
(1)	Wade Boggs (#91-99)	15.00
(1)	Wade Boggs (promo card)	20.00
(2)	Barry Bonds (#64-72)	12.00
(2)	Barry Bonds (promo card)	15.00
(3)	Bobby Bonilla (#10-18)	10.00
(3)	Bobby Bonilla (promo card)	10.00
(4)	Jose Canseco (#1-9)	15.00
(4)	Jose Canseco (promo card)	20.00
(5)	Ken Griffey Jr. (#37-45)	25.00
(5)	Ken Griffey Jr. (promo card)	30.00
(6)	Dwight Gooden (#73-81)	10.00
(6)	Dwight Gooden (promo card)	10.00
(7)	Rickey Henderson (#19-27)	12.00
(7)	Rickey Henderson (promo card)	15.00
(8)	Bo Jackson (#82-90)	10.00
(8)	Bo Jackson (promo card)	10.00
(9)	Don Mattingly (#46-54)	25.00
(9)	Don Mattingly (promo card)	30.00
(10)	Cal Ripken Jr. (#109-117)	25.00
(10)	Cal Ripken Jr. (promo card)	30.00
(11)	Nolan Ryan (#55-63)	25.00
(11)	Nolan Ryan (promo card)	35.00
(12)	Ryne Sandberg (#100-108)	15.00
(12)	Ryne Sandberg (promo card)	20.00
(13)	Darryl Strawberry (#28-36)	10.00
(13)	Darryl Strawberry (promo card)	10.00
(14)	Frank Thomas (#118-126)	20.00
(14)	Frank Thomas (promo card)	25.00

1991 Star Millennium Edition

As the name suggests, production of each of these nine-card, single-player sets was pegged at 1,000 (plus 200 promo cards of each player). Suggested retail price at issue was about $30. Cards are numbered contiguously throughout the issue, as noted in the alphabetical checklist (part of each Ripken and Gooden set are misnumbered). Individual cards are not listed or priced because the sets are almost never broken down for singles sales.

	MT
Complete Set (126):	260.00
Common Player Set:	10.00
Complete Promo Set (14):	280.00
Common Promo Card:	10.00
(1) Wade Boggs (#55-63)	20.00
(1) Wade Boggs (promo card)	25.00
(2) Will Clark (#46-54)	15.00
(2) Will Clark (promo card)	15.00
(3) Cecil Fielder (#109-117)	15.00
(3) Cecil Fielder (promo card)	15.00
(4) Dwight Gooden (#10-14, 78-81)	15.00
(4) Dwight Gooden (promo card)	15.00
(5) Ken Griffey Jr. (#91-99)	25.00
(5) Ken Griffey Jr. (promo card)	30.00
(6) Howard Johnson (#64-72)	10.00
(6) Howard Johnson (promo card)	10.00
(7) Dave Justice (#100-108)	15.00
(7) David Justice (promo card)	15.00
(8) Kevin Maas (#82-90)	10.00
(8) Kevin Maas (promo card)	10.00
(9) Don Mattingly (#37-45)	25.00
(9) Don Mattingly (promo card)	30.00
(10) Kirby Puckett (#19-27)	25.00
(10) Kirby Puckett (promo card)	30.00
(11) Cal Ripken Jr. (#15-18, 73-77)	20.00
(11) Cal Ripken Jr. (promo card)	30.00
(12) Ryne Sandberg (#28-36)	20.00
(12) Ryne Sandberg (promo card)	20.00
(13) Frank Thomas (#118-126)	20.00
(13) Frank Thomas (promo card)	25.00
(14) Robin Yount (#1-9)	25.00
(14) Robin Yount (promo card)	25.00

1991 Star Nova Edition

Production of these nine-card, single-player sets was limited to 500 of each (plus 100 promo cards of each player). Sets are checklisted here in alphabetical order. Individual cards are numbered contiguously throughout the issue, as noted. Single cards are not priced because sets are seldom broken up for sale of individual cards.

	MT
Complete Set (144):	425.00
Common Player Set:	15.00
Complete Promo Set (16):	500.00
Common Promo Card:	15.00
(1) Wade Boggs (#82-90)	35.00
(1) Wade Boggs (promo card)	50.00
(2) Jose Canseco (#55-63)	30.00
(2) Jose Canseco (promo card)	40.00
(3) Vince Coleman (#127-135)	15.00
(3) Vince Coleman (promo card)	15.00
(4) Cecil Fielder (#136-144)	20.00
(4) Cecil Fielder (promo card)	20.00
(5) Dwight Gooden (#10-18)	20.00
(5) Dwight Gooden (promo card)	20.00
(6) Ken Griffey Jr. (#91-99)	50.00
(6) Ken Griffey Jr. (promo card)	50.00
(7) Tony Gwynn (#100-108)	30.00
(7) Tony Gwynn (promo card)	40.00
(8) Rickey Henderson (#1-9)	20.00
(8) Rickey Henderson (promo card)	20.00
(9) Bo Jackson (#28-36)	20.00
(9) Bo Jackson (promo card)	20.00
(10) Howard Johnson (#118-126)	15.00
(10) Howard Johnson (promo card)	15.00
(11) Don Mattingly (#64-72)	50.00
(11) Don Mattingly (promo card)	50.00
(12) Kirby Puckett (#109-117)	50.00
(12) Kirby Puckett (promo card)	50.00
(13) Cal Ripken Jr. (#46-54)	50.00
(13) Cal Ripken Jr. (promo card)	50.00
(14) Nolan Ryan (#19-27)	50.00
(14) Nolan Ryan (promo card)	75.00
(15) Ryne Sandberg (#73-81)	30.00
(15) Ryne Sandberg (promo card)	40.00
(16) Darryl Strawberry (#37-45)	20.00
(16) Darryl Strawberry (promo card)	20.00

1991 Star Cal Ripken Promo Set

This unusual Star set has five solid orange-bordered cards of Ripken. Unlike the other Star promo cards, which are blank-backed, the backs of these glossy-finish cards says "1 of 1,000 Promo Sets," and include stats and other information.

	MT
1-5 Cal Ripken Jr.	25.00

1991 Star Rookie Guild Prototypes

Labeled as "Prototype" cards, these unnumbered blank-back cards can be found in a confusing variety of regular, glossy and plastic finish for the six players in the Rookie Guild set. Only those cards confirmed to exist are listed here.

	MT
Complete Set, Regular (3):	25.00
Complete Set, Glossy (3):	30.00
Complete Set, Plastic (4):	45.00
(1g) Jeff Bagwell (glossy)	8.00
(1p) Jeff Bagwell (plastic)	10.00
(2) Albert Belle	10.00
(3g) Juan Gonzalez (glossy)	8.00
(3p) Juan Gonzalez (plastic)	10.00
(4a) Chris Knoblauch (Chuck)	10.00
(4bp) Chuck Knoblauch (plastic)	10.00
(5) Mark Lewis	5.00
(6g) Frank Thomas (glossy)	15.00
(6p) Frank Thomas (plastic)	15.00

1991 Star Rookie Guild Promos

A confusing variety of regular, glossy and plastic finish promo cards were issued in different combinations for the six players in Star's 1991 Rookie Guild issue. The blank-back, unnumbered cards are checklisted here in alphabetical order. Only those cards confirmed to have been issued are listed.

	MT
Complete Promo Set, Regular (3):	25.00
Complete Promo Set, Glossy (6):	80.00
Complete Promo Set, Plastic (4):	50.00
(1g) Jeff Bagwell (glossy)	8.00
(1p) Jeff Bagwell (plastic)	10.00
(2) Albert Belle	10.00
(2g) Albert Belle (glossy)	20.00
(3g) Juan Gonzalez (glossy)	8.00
(3p) Juan Gonzalez (plastic)	10.00
(4a) Chris Knoblauch (Chuck)	10.00
(4ag) Chris Knoblauch (Chuck) (glossy)	20.00
(4bp) Chuck Knoblauch (plastic)	12.00
(5) Mark Lewis	5.00
(5g) Mark Lewis (glossy)	10.00
(6g) Frank Thomas (glossy)	15.00
(6p) Frank Thomas (plastic)	20.00

1991 Star Rookie Guild

Late in the 1991 baseball season, Star introduced yet another series of single-player card sets. The emphasis was on young stars in 11-card sets. Most player sets were produced in some combination of regular and glossy finish, or glossy and plastic finish. Each player was also represented with some combination of 1,000 each promotional (border other than white) and prototype cards and 50 glossy and/or plastic promo cards. Single cards are not listed because sets are seldom broken for individual card sales. Complete set prices do not include the scarce "Chris" Knoblauch variation.

	MT
Complete Set, Regular (22):	11.00
Complete Set, Glossy (66):	60.00
Complete Set, Plastic (33):	75.00
(1) Albert Belle (#1-11)	6.00
(1g) Albert Belle (glossy)	20.00
(2a) Chris Knoblauch (Chuck)	50.00
(2ag) Chris Knoblauch (Chuck) (glossy)	20.00
(2bg) Chuck Knoblauch (#12-22) (glossy only)	6.00
(3) Mark Lewis (#23-33)	5.00
(3g) Mark Lewis (glossy)	15.00
(4g) Frank Thomas (#33-44) (glossy)	10.00
(4p) Frank Thomas (plastic)	30.00
(5g) Juan Gonzalez (#45-55) (glossy)	6.00
(5p) Juan Gonzalez (plastic)	25.00
(6g) Jeff Bagwell (#56-66) (glossy)	6.00
(6p) Jeff Bagwell (plastic)	25.00

1991 Star Platinum Edition

These nine-card, single-player sets were produced in an edition of 1,000 each (plus 200 promo cards per player). Sets are checklisted here alphabetically, with individual card numbers shown for each player. Single cards are not listed because the sets are seldom offered as singles.

	MT
Complete Set (108):	250.00
Common Player Set:	10.00
Complete Promo Set (14):	325.00
Common Promo Card:	15.00
(1) Wade Boggs (#109-117)	20.00
(1) Wade Boggs (promo card)	25.00
(2) Barry Bonds (#28-36)	15.00
(2) Barry Bonds (promo card)	15.00
(3) Bobby Bonilla (#73-81)	10.00
(3) Bobby Bonilla (promo card)	10.00
(4) Jose Canseco (#19-27)	20.00
(4) Jose Canseco (promo card)	25.00
(5) Will Clark (#118-126)	15.00
(5) Will Clark (promo card)	15.00
(6) Roger Clemens (#10-18)	20.00
(6) Roger Clemens (promo card)	30.00
(7) Mark Grace (#1-9)	15.00
(7) Mark Grace (promo card)	15.00
(8) Ken Griffey Jr. (#55-63)	30.00
(8) Ken Griffey Jr. (promo card)	50.00
(9) Rickey Henderson (#46-54)	15.00
(9) Rickey Henderson (promo card)	15.00
(10) Kevin Maas (#37-45)	10.00
(10) Kevin Maas (promo card)	15.00
(11) Don Mattingly (#82-90)	25.00
(11) Don Mattingly (promo card)	35.00
(12) Cal Ripken Jr. (#91-99)	20.00
(12) Cal Ripken Jr. (promo card)	35.00
(13) Nolan Ryan (#64-72)	15.00
(13) Nolan Ryan (promo card)	30.00
(14) Frank Thomas (#100-108)	20.00
(14) Frank Thomas (promo card)	25.00

1991 Star Silver Edition

Two thousand of each nine-card player set was produced in Star's silver-enhanced set, along with 400 promo cards of each player. Players are listed here in alphabetical order. Individual cards are not listed because the sets are seldom offered as singles.

	MT
Complete Set (126):	175.00
Common Player Set:	10.00
Complete Promo Set (15):	200.00
Common Promo Card:	10.00
(1) Wade Boggs (#10-18)	15.00
(1) Wade Boggs (promo card)	10.00
(2) Bobby Bonilla (#37-45)	10.00
(2) Bobby Bonilla (promo card)	10.00
(3) Jose Canseco (#109-117)	15.00
(3) Jose Canseco (promo card)	15.00
(4) Vince Coleman (#1-9)	10.00
(4) Vince Coleman (promo card)	10.00
(5) Dwight Gooden (#73-81)	10.00
(5) Dwight Gooden (promo card)	10.00
(6) Ken Griffey Jr. (#91-99)	25.00
(6) Ken Griffey Jr. (promo card)	30.00
(7) Tony Gwynn (#46-54)	15.00
(7) Tony Gwynn (promo card)	20.00
(8) Rickey Henderson (#82-90)	12.00
(8) Rickey Henderson (promo card)	15.00
(9) Bo Jackson (#100-108)	8.00
(9) Bo Jackson (promo card)	10.00
(10) Kevin Maas (#28-36)	10.00
(10) Kevin Maas (promo card)	10.00
(11) Don Mattingly (#19-27)	25.00
(11) Don Mattingly (promo card)	30.00
(12) Nolan Ryan (#55-63)	25.00
(12) Nolan Ryan (promo card)	30.00
(13) Ryne Sandberg (#64-72)	15.00
(13) Ryne Sandberg (promo card)	15.00
(14) Frank Thomas (#118-126)	20.00
(14) Frank Thomas (promo card)	20.00
(15) Albert Belle (promo card only, produced in error)	15.00

1991 Star Stellar Edition

The same players who appear in other Star sets for 1991 are repackaged into this edition of 500 sets of each player. One hundred promo cards of each player were also issued.

	MT
Complete Set (126):	340.00
Common Player Set:	20.00
Complete Promo Set (14):	340.00
Common Promo Card:	20.00
(1) Bobby Bonilla (#55-63)	20.00
(1) Bobby Bonilla (promo card)	20.00
(2) Will Clark (#37-45)	25.00
(2) Will Clark (promo card)	25.00
(3) Roger Clemens (#10-18)	25.00
(3) Roger Clemens (promo card)	25.00
(4) Vince Coleman (#73-81)	20.00
(4) Vince Coleman (promo card)	20.00
(5) Ken Griffey Jr. (#1-9)	30.00
(5) Ken Griffey Jr. (promo card)	35.00
(6) Tony Gwynn (#46-54)	25.00
(6) Tony Gwynn (promo card)	25.00
(7) Rickey Henderson (#118-126)	25.00
(7) Rickey Henderson (promo card)	25.00

(8) Howard Johnson (#100-108)	20.00
(8) Rickey Henderson (promo card)	20.00
(9) Don Mattingly (#109-117)	35.00
(9) Don Mattingly (promo card)	35.00
(10) Kirby Puckett (#64-72)	30.00
(10) Kirby Puckett (promo card)	35.00
(11) Cal Ripken Jr. (#82-90)	35.00
(11) Cal Ripken Jr. (promo card)	35.00
(12) Nolan Ryan (#19-27)	30.00
(12) Nolan Ryan (promo card)	30.00
(13) Ryne Sandberg (#91-99)	25.00
(13) Ryne Sandberg (promo card)	25.00
(14) Robin Yount (#28-36)	30.00
(14) Robin Yount (promo card)	30.00

1991 Star '92

Though labeled "Star '92" on front, these single-player 11-card sets were produced in 1991. Fronts feature borders which fade from one color at top to gray at the bottom. The photos at center are a mix of poses and game-action shots. Backs have a small color portrait photo - the same on all cards within a set - at upper-left. Stats, personal data, highlights, checklists and team logos are printed in color on yellow cardboard. The cards carry a 1991 copyright line at bottom center. Each set can be found in a glossy version, which carries a premium of 2X.

	MT
Complete Set (22):	10.00
Common Player Set:	5.00
Complete Promo Set (2):	10.00
Common Promo Card:	5.00
1-11 Scott Erickson	3.00
Scott Erickson (promo card)	5.00
1-11 Todd Van Poppel	3.00
Todd Van Poppel (promo card)	5.00

1992 Star Gold Edition

The 12 players in Star's 1992 Gold Edition are represented in an issue of 750 sets each, plus 150 promo cards. The checklist is arranged alphabetically. Single cards are not listed because sets are not often broken up for individual card sales.

	MT
Complete Set (108):	230.00
Common Player Set:	15.00
Complete Promo Set (12):	280.00
Common Promo Card:	20.00
(1) Steve Avery (#91-99)	15.00
(1) Steve Avery (promo card)	20.00
(2) Jose Canseco (#19-27)	20.00
(2) Jose Canseco (promo card)	25.00
(3) Will Clark (#28-36)	20.00
(3) Will Clark (promo card)	25.00
(4) Ken Griffey Jr. (#82-90)	30.00
(4) Ken Griffey Jr. (promo card)	35.00
(5) Bo Jackson (#46-54)	15.00
(5) Bo Jackson (promo card)	20.00
(6) David Justice (#10-18)	15.00
(6) David Justice (promo card)	20.00
(7) Don Mattingly (#1-9)	25.00
(7) Don Mattingly (promo card)	30.00
(8) Cal Ripken Jr. (#64-72)	30.00
(8) Cal Ripken Jr. (promo card)	35.00
(9) Nolan Ryan (#37-45)	30.00
(9) Nolan Ryan (promo card)	35.00
(10) Ryne Sandberg (#55-63)	20.00
(10) Ryne Sandberg (promo card)	25.00
(11) Darryl Strawberry (#100-108)	15.00
(11) Darryl Strawberry (promo card)	20.00
(12) Frank Thomas (#73-81)	25.00
(12) Frank Thomas (promo card)	30.00

1992 Star The Kid

This five-card set was reportedly produced in an edition of 1,000 to be sold along with Star's porcelain statue of Ken Griffey, Jr. No promo cards or glossy version were issued.

	MT
Complete Set (5):	
1-5 Ken Griffey Jr.	25.00

1992 Star Millennium Edition

Star's Millenium Edition for 1992 included an issue of 750 sets and 150 promo cards for each of 12 players, listed alphabetically in the checklist here. Single cards are not listed because player sets are seldom broken for individual card sales.

	MT
Complete Set (108):	265.00
Common Player Set:	15.00
Complete Promo Set (12):	315.00
Common Promo Card:	20.00
(1) Wade Boggs (#100-108)	25.00
(1) Wade Boggs (promo card)	30.00
(2) Jose Canseco (#10-18)	25.00
(2) Jose Canseco (promo card)	30.00
(3) Roger Clemens (#28-36)	25.00
(3) Roger Clemens (promo card)	30.00
(4) Ken Griffey Jr. (#1-9)	35.00
(4) Ken Griffey Jr. (promo card)	35.00
(5) Bo Jackson (#82-90)	15.00
(5) Bo Jackson (promo card)	20.00
(6) David Justice (#73-81)	15.00
(6) David Justice (promo card)	20.00
(7) Don Mattingly (#37-45)	30.00
(7) Don Mattingly (promo card)	40.00
(8) Kirby Puckett (#91-99)	30.00
(8) Kirby Puckett (promo card)	40.00
(9) Cal Ripken Jr. (#19-27)	35.00
(9) Cal Ripken Jr. (promo card)	35.00
(10) Nolan Ryan (#55-63)	35.00
(10) Nolan Ryan (promo card)	35.00
(11) Ryne Sandberg (#46-54)	25.00
(11) Ryne Sandberg (promo card)	30.00
(12) Frank Thomas (#64-72)	30.00
(12) Frank Thomas (promo card)	35.00

1992 Star Nova Edition

These nine-card, single-player sets were limited to an edition of 500 for each player, plus 100 promo cards. Numbering errors occurred on the Avery and Strawberry cards. The former were supposed to be numbered 10-18; the latter 64-72

	MT
Complete Set (108):	330.00
Common Player Set:	20.00
Complete Promo Set:	350.00
Common Promo Card:	20.00
(1) Nolan Ryan (#1-9)	40.00
(1) Nolan Ryan (promo card)	40.00
(2) Steve Avery (#10-14, 69-72)	20.00
(2) Steve Avery (promo card)	20.00
(3) Frank Thomas (#19-27)	30.00
(3) Frank Thomas (promo card)	40.00
(4) Don Mattingly (#28-36)	40.00
(4) Don Mattingly (promo card)	50.00
(5) Ken Griffey Jr. (#37-45)	40.00
(5) Ken Griffey Jr. (promo card)	40.00
(6) David Justice (#46-54)	20.00
(6) David Justice (promo card)	20.00
(7) Ryne Sandberg (#55-63)	30.00
(7) Ryne Sandberg (promo card)	30.00
(8) Darryl Strawberry (#64-68, 15-18)	20.00
(8) Darryl Strawberry (promo card)	20.00
(9) Cal Ripken Jr. (#73-81)	40.00
(9) Cal Ripken Jr. (promo card)	40.00
(10) Bo Jackson (#82-90)	20.00
(10) Bo Jackson (promo card)	20.00
(11) Jose Canseco (#91-99)	30.00
(11) Jose Canseco (promo card)	30.00
(12) Roger Clemens (#100-108)	30.00
(12) Roger Clemens (promo card)	40.00

1992 Star Platinum Edition

A dozen established stars are featured in the '92 Star Platinum issue, each in nine-card sets, contiguously numbered. One thousand sets of each player were issued, along with 200 promo cards. The cards are listed here in alphabetical order. Single cards are not listed because the player sets are not often broken up for individual sales.

	MT
Complete Set (108):	225.00
Common Player Set:	15.00
Complete Promo Set (12):	265.00
Common Promo Card:	15.00
(1) Jeff Bagwell (#55-63)	20.00
(1) Jeff Bagwell (promo card)	25.00
(2) Jose Canseco (#73-81)	20.00
(2) Jose Canseco (promo card)	25.00
(3) Will Clark (#100-108)	20.00
(3) Will Clark (promo card)	25.00
(4) Roger Clemens (#91-99)	20.00
(4) Roger Clemens (promo card)	25.00
(5) Ken Griffey Jr. (#37-45)	25.00
(5) Ken Griffey Jr. (promo card)	30.00
(6) Bo Jackson (#28-36)	15.00
(6) Bo Jackson (promo card)	15.00
(7) David Justice (#10-18)	15.00
(7) David Justice (promo card)	15.00
(8) Don Mattingly (#64-72)	25.00
(8) Don Mattingly (promo card)	30.00
(9) Cal Ripken Jr. (#46-54)	25.00
(9) Cal Ripken Jr. (promo card)	30.00
(10) Nolan Ryan (#82-90)	25.00
(10) Nolan Ryan (promo card)	30.00
(11) Ryne Sandberg (#1-9)	20.00
(11) Ryne Sandberg (promo card)	25.00
(12) Frank Thomas (#19-27)	25.00
(12) Frank Thomas (promo card)	30.00

1992 Star Rookie Guild

Each of the four players in the '92 Rookie Guild issue is represented by an 11-card set, a promo card and a gold preview card. The first 10 cards in each player's set have blue borders, while the last card has white borders. Cards are seldom available as singles since the sets are rarely broken up.

	MT
Complete Set (44):	20.00
Complete Promo Set:	24.00
Complete Preview Set:	60.00
1-11 Reggie Sanders	5.00
Reggie Sanders (promo card)	6.00
Reggie Sanders (gold preview)	15.00
12-22 Phil Plantier	5.00
Phil Plantier (promo card)	6.00
Phil Plantier (gold preview)	15.00
23-33 Dean Palmer	5.00
Dean Palmer (promo card)	6.00
Dean Palmer (gold preview)	15.00
34-44 Eric Karros	7.50
Eric Karros (promo card)	10.00
Eric Karros (gold preview)	20.00
Eric Karros (ad card)	10.00

1992 Star Silver Edition

Nearly the same line-up as found in other special edition Star nine-card player sets is found in the silver version. Announced production was 1,000 sets of each player along with 200 promo cards. The cards are listed here in alphabetical order. Single cards are not listed because the player sets are not often broken up for individual sales.

	MT
Complete Set (108):	175.00
Common Player Set:	10.00
Complete Promo Set (12):	215.00
Common Promo Card:	10.00
(1) Jeff Bagwell (#46-54)	15.00
(1) Jeff Bagwell (promo card)	20.00
(2) Jose Canseco (#64-72)	15.00
(2) Jose Canseco (promo card)	20.00
(3) Will Clark (#1-9)	15.00
(3) Will Clark (promo card)	20.00
(4) Ken Griffey Jr. (#28-36)	20.00
(4) Ken Griffey Jr. (promo card)	25.00
(5) Bo Jackson (#37-45)	10.00
(5) Bo Jackson (promo card)	10.00
(6) David Justice (#19-27)	10.00
(6) David Justice (promo card)	10.00
(7) Don Mattingly (#100-108)	20.00
(7) Don Mattingly (promo card)	25.00
(8) Cal Ripken Jr. (#82-90)	20.00
(8) Cal Ripken Jr. (promo card)	25.00
(9) Nolan Ryan (#73-81)	20.00
(9) Nolan Ryan (promo card)	25.00
(10) Ryne Sandberg (#10-18)	15.00
(10) Ryne Sandberg (promo card)	20.00
(11) Darryl Strawberry (#91-99)	10.00
(11) Darryl Strawberry (promo card)	10.00
(12) Frank Thomas (#55-63)	20.00
(12) Frank Thomas (promo card)	25.00

1992 Star Stellar Edition

Among the scarcer of Star's 1992 single-player, nine-card sets, the Stellar Edition was produced in an issue of 500 sets and 100 promo cards of each player, contiguously numbered. The cards are listed here in alphabetical order. Single cards are not listed because the player sets are not often broken up for individual sales.

	MT
Complete Set (108):	275.00
Common Player Set:	20.00
Complete Promo Set (12):	325.00
Common Promo Card:	20.00
(1) Jeff Bagwell (#19-27)	25.00
(1) Jeff Bagwell (promo card)	30.00
(2) Jose Canseco (#100-108)	25.00
(2) Jose Canseco (promo card)	30.00
(3) Will Clark (#37-45)	25.00
(3) Will Clark (promo card)	30.00
(4) Roger Clemens (#10-18)	25.00
(4) Roger Clemens (promo card)	30.00
(5) Ken Griffey Jr. (#55-63)	30.00
(5) Ken Griffey Jr. (promo card)	35.00
(6) Bo Jackson (#73-81)	20.00
(6) Bo Jackson (promo card)	20.00
(7) David Justice (#64-72)	20.00
(7) David Justice (promo card)	20.00
(8) Don Mattingly (#91-99)	30.00
(8) Don Mattingly (promo card)	35.00
(9) Cal Ripken Jr. (#46-54)	30.00
(9) Cal Ripken Jr. (promo card)	35.00
(10) Nolan Ryan (#82-90)	30.00
(10) Nolan Ryan (promo card)	35.00
(11) Ryne Sandberg (#28-36)	25.00
(11) Ryne Sandberg (promo card)	30.00
(12) Frank Thomas (#1-9)	30.00
(12) Frank Thomas (promo card)	35.00

1992 Star '92

Utilizing a design introduced the previous year, the Star '92 single-player card sets produced in 1992 are printed on cardboard laminated with thin high-gloss plastic surfaces front and back. Each player's cards are bordered with a single bright color at top which fades to gray at bottom. Photos are a mix of poses and game-action shots. Backs have a yellow background with a small color portrait (the same throughout the player's set) at upper-left. Stats, personal data, career highlights, checklist or team logo are printed in colored ink. The cards carry a 1992 copyright date and each set has a large capital letter in the lower-right corner. It is not known whether sets were issued for the letters missing in the checklist below, though prototype cards are known for some. Production was reported as 4,000 of each player set and 800 of each promo and prototype card. Only confirmed cards are listed. Single cards are not listed because sets are seldom broken for individual card sales.

		MT
	Common Player Set:	5.00
	Common Promo Card:	10.00
	Common Prototype Card:	10.00
A1-11	Jeff Bagwell	5.00
	Jeff Bagwell (promo card)	10.00
	Jeff Bagwell (prototype)	20.00
B1-11	Albert Belle	5.00
	Albert Belle (promo)	20.00
C1-11	Ron Gant	5.00
	Ron Gant (promo card)	10.00
	Ron Gant (prototype)	10.00
D1-11	Bo Jackson	5.00
	Bo Jackson (promo card)	10.00
	Bo Jackson (prototype)	10.00
E1-11	Dave Justice	5.00
	David Justice (promo card)	10.00
	David Justice (prototype)	10.00
F1-11	Chuck Knoblauch	5.00
	Chuck Knoblauch (promo card)	10.00
	Chuck Knoblauch (prototype)	10.00
G1-11	Kirby Puckett	10.00
	Kirby Puckett (promo card)	25.00
	Kirby Puckett (prototype)	25.00
H1-11	Ryne Sandberg	8.00
	Ryne Sandberg (promo)	20.00
	Ryne Sandberg (prototype)	15.00
I1-11	Steve Avery	5.00
	Steve Avery (promo)	10.00
	Steve Avery (prototype)	10.00
J1-11	Phil Plantier	5.00
	Phil Plantier (promo)	10.00
K	Wade Boggs (prototype)	15.00
M1-11	Will Clark	20.00
	Will Clark (promo card)	15.00
N1-11	Ken Griffey Jr.	30.00
	Ken Griffey Jr. (promo card)	25.00
	Ken Griffey Jr. (prototype)	25.00
O	Cal Ripken Jr. (prototype)	30.00
P	Nolan Ryan (prototype, regular finish)	25.00
	Nolan Ryan (plastic prototype)	35.00
R	Frank Thomas (prototype)	25.00
S	Bobby Bonilla (prototype)	10.00
T	Kevin Mitchell (prototype)	10.00
U1-11	Danny Tartabull	5.00
	Danny Tartabull (promo card)	10.00
V1-11	Dean Palmer	5.00
	Dean Palmer (promo)	10.00
	Dean Palmer (prototype)	10.00

1995 Star Cal Ripken, Jr.

A major design fault apparently prevented this issue from being widely circulated. Each of the 80 cards in the boxed set has an extraneous comma between "Cal" and "Ripken". That fatal flaw aside, the set does a creditable job of detailing Ripken's major league career through his record 2,131st consecutive game in 1995. Glossy card fronts have color photos at center with orange and brown graphic highlights. Each card has him identified as "Cal, Ripken, Jr." at bottom, below which there is a card title. Backs have a baseball at center with career highlights, stats, personal information or trivia. The name error is repeated in orange script at bottom. The set was fully licensed by Ripken and Major League Baseball.

	MT
Complete Boxed Set (80):	20.00
Common Card:	.50
1-80 Cal Ripken Jr.	

1987 Starline Posters

Several dozen baseball player and team posters were produced by Starline in 1987 as part of a multi-sport issue. The 2' x 3' posters have large color action photos surrounded by team color borders with the player's name at top. Licensor logos appear in the bottom-right border. Backs are blank. Posters originially retailed for about $6.50.

		MT
	Complete Set (52):	150.00
	Common Player:	5.00
(1)	Wally Backman	5.00
(2)	Wade Boggs	8.00
(3)	George Brett	9.00
(4)	Jose Canseco	7.50
(5)	Gary Carter	5.00
(6)	Jack Clark	5.00
(7)	Will Clark	7.50
(8)	Roger Clemens	8.00
(9)	Ron Darling	5.00
(10)	Andre Dawson	5.00
(11)	Eric Davis	5.00
(12)	Lenny Dykstra	5.00
(13)	Dwight Gooden	5.00
(14)	Rickey Henderson	7.50
(15)	Keith Hernandez	5.00
(16)	Pete Incaviglia	5.00
(17)	Bo Jackson	7.50
(18)	Wally Joyner	5.00
(19)	Don Mattingly	9.00
(20)	Mark McGwire	12.00
(21)	Dale Murphy	7.50
(22)	Eddie Murray	7.50
(23)	Kirby Puckett	7.50
(24)	Jim Rice	5.00
(25)	Dave Righetti	5.00
(26)	Cal Ripken Jr.	10.00
(27)	Bret Saberhagen	5.00
(28)	Ryne Sandberg	7.50
(29)	Mike Schmidt	9.00
(30)	Cory Snyder	5.00
(31)	Darryl Strawberry	5.00
(32)	Fernando Valenzuela	5.00
(33)	Dave Winfield	5.00
(34)	A.L. Superstars	5.00
(35)	N.L. Superstars	5.00
(36)	California Angels	5.00
(37)	Houston Astros	5.00
(38)	Toronto Blue Jays	5.00
(39)	Atlanta Braves	5.00
(40)	St. Louis Cardinals	5.00
(41)	Chicago Cubs	5.00
(42)	L.A. Dodgers	5.00
(43)	S.F. Giants	5.00
(44)	Cleveland Indians	5.00
(45)	N.Y. Mets	5.00
(46)	Balitmore Orioles	5.00
(47)	Philadelphia Phils	5.00
(48)	Cincinnati Reds	5.00
(49)	Boston Red Sox	5.00
(50)	Detroit Tigers	5.00
(51)	Minnesota Twins	5.00
(52)	N.Y. Yankees	5.00

1989 Starline Prototypes

Prior to its first major baseball card issue, Starline produced five variations of a prototype issue. The seven-card sets feature game-action photos on the front, surrounded by colorful borders and with a combination of up to three logos in the bottom border. Cards were produced with just the Starline logo, with the Starline and Coca-Cola logos and with the card company and soft drink logos in conjunction with those of McDonald's, 7-11 or Dominos pizza. Backs repeat the logos at bottom, along with that of Major League Baseball. At top is a color player photo, along with biographical data, complete major and minor league stats and career highlights. The unnumbered cards are checklisted here alphabetically.

		MT
	Complete Set (7):	175.00
	Common Player:	25.00
(1)	Eric Davis	25.00
(2)	Mark Grace	35.00
(3)	Tony Gwynn	45.00
(4)	Gregg Jefferies	25.00
(5)	Don Mattingly	40.00
(6)	Mark McGwire	50.00
(7)	Darryl Strawberry	25.00

1990 Starline

Five-card cello packs of this Coca-Cola sponsored issue were given away with the purchase of dinner and a soft drink at Long John Silver fish restaurants. Cards feature game-action photos on front, bordered in team colors. Backs repeat the team-color scheme and feature a portrait photo along with major league stats and career highlights. Most of the players had two or more cards in the 40-card issue. A header card in each pack offered a 2' x 3' poster of one of 18 players in set for $3.99.

		MT
	Complete Set (40):	6.00
	Common Player:	.25
1	Don Mattingly	.75
2	Mark Grace	.60
3	Eric Davis	.30
4	Tony Gwynn	.75
5	Bobby Bonilla	.25
6	Wade Boggs	.60
7	Frank Viola	.25
8	Ruben Sierra	.25
9	Mark McGwire	1.50
10	Alan Trammell	.30
11	Mark McGwire	1.50
12	Gregg Jefferies	.25
13	Nolan Ryan	1.00
14	John Smoltz	.40
15	Glenn Davis	.25
16	Mark Grace	.60
17	Wade Boggs	.60
18	Frank Viola	.25
19	Bret Saberhagen	.25
20	Chris Sabo	.25
21	Darryl Strawberry	.35
22	Wade Boggs	.60
23	Tim Raines	.35
24	Alan Trammell	.30
25	Chris Sabo	.25
26	Nolan Ryan	1.00
27	Mark McGwire	1.50
28	Don Mattingly	.75
29	Tony Gwynn	.75
30	Glenn Davis	.25
31	Bobby Bonilla	.25
32	Gregg Jefferies	.25
33	Ruben Sierra	.25
34	John Smoltz	.40
35	Don Mattingly	.75
36	Bret Saberhagen	.25
37	Darryl Strawberry	.35
38	Eric Davis	.30
39	Tim Raines	.35
40	Mark Grace	.60
---	Header card/poster offer	.10

1991 Starline Prototypes

These sample cards were produced for submission to baseball licensing authorities for approval, and to prospective sponsors. Only 60 of each card were reported produced. Card fronts have color action photos and a team logo set against a black background. The player's name appears in white and red at top and along the side. Backs have a smaller player photo at upper-right. All of the prototypes have back stats and biography of Nolan Ryan, with a gray diagonal "PROTOTYPE" across them. The Starline, MLB and Players' Associations logo appear across the bottom.

		MT
	Complete Set (5):	125.00
	Common Player:	25.00
(1)	George Bell	25.00
(2)	Bobby Bonilla	25.00
(3)	Roger Clemens	50.00
(4)	Tim Raines	25.00
(5)	Darryl Strawberry	25.00

1983 Starliner Stickers

This is an unauthorized collector issue based on 16 of the cards issued by Dexter Press in 1967 as Coca-Cola premiums. In July, 1983, a Midwestern card dealer produced these stickers by reprinting the 5-1/2" x 7" Dexter Press cards in 2-7/16" x 3-1/4" format and eliminating the white border. The stickers can be found with either white ("Mactac Starliner") or tan ("Touchdown Splitless") paper on back. By the early 1990's, the story of the true origins of these stickers had been largely forgotten within the hobby and some dealers were charging between $10-50 apiece for them. The unnumbered stickers are checklisted here in alphabetical order. Production of the white-back stickers was reported at 2,000 sets, with Mantle and Rose double printed.

		MT
	Complete Set (16):	80.00
	Common Card:	5.00
(1)	Hank Aaron	7.50
(2)	Ernie Banks	6.00
(3)	Roberto Clemente	12.00
(4)	Rocky Colavito	5.00
(5)	Al Kaline	5.00
(6)	Harmon Killebrew	5.00
(7)	Mickey Mantle (DP)	15.00
(8)	Willie Mays	7.50
(9)	Willie McCovey	5.00
(10)	Joe Morgan	5.00
(11)	Jim Palmer	5.00
(12)	Brooks Robinson	5.00
(13)	Frank Robinson	5.00
(14)	Pete Rose (DP)	7.50
(15)	Willie Stargell	5.00
(16)	Carl Yastrzemski	6.00

1991 Starshots Player Pins

This set of "Official Sports Celebrity Badge" pin-backs was distributed in retail locations in Southern California. Production was reported to be 4,700 of each. The 2-1/2" pins are attached to a cardboard backing which can be folded to create a display easel for the pin, providing stats and career summary at a glance. The approximately 2-3/4" x 5-1/4" pieces were sold in blister packs at a suggested retail of $1.99. Values shown are for complete, unfolded pin-and-easel pairs.

		MT
Complete Set (54):		135.00
Common Player:		3.50
101	Jim Abbott	3.50
102	Eric Davis	3.50
103	Sandy Alomar Jr.	3.50
104	Glenn Davis	3.50
105	Andre Dawson	3.50
106	Wade Boggs	5.00
107	Bobby Bonilla	3.50
108	Barry Bonds	6.00
109	George Brett	7.50
110	Jose Canseco	4.50
111	Will Clark	4.50
112	Roger Clemens	6.00
113	Kelly Gruber	3.50
114	Delino DeShields	3.50
115	Lenny Dykstra	3.50
116	Shawon Dunston	3.50
117	Doug Drabek	3.50
118	Cecil Fielder	3.50
119	Carlton Fisk	6.00
120	Ron Gant	3.50
121	Dwight Gooden	3.50
122	Ken Griffey Jr.	15.00
123	Tony Gwynn	7.50
124	Rickey Henderson	4.50
125	Orel Hershiser	3.50
126	Wally Joyner	3.50
127	David Justice	4.00
128	Kevin McReynolds	3.50
129	Barry Larkin	3.50
130	Eddie Murray	4.50
131	Bret Saberhagen	3.50
132	Don Mattingly	7.50
133	Dave Steib	3.50
134	Mark McGwire	15.00
135	Paul Molitor	4.50
136	Dave Parker	3.50
137	Kirby Puckett	6.00
138	Dave Winfield	4.50
139	Cal Ripken Jr.	12.50
140	Billy Ripken	3.50
141	Nolan Ryan	12.50
142	Chris Sabo	3.50
143	Benito Santiago	3.50
144	Ryne Sandberg	6.00
145	Steve Sax	3.50
146	Mike Scioscia	3.50
147	Kevin Mitchell	3.50
148	Ruben Sierra	3.50
149	Ozzie Smith	5.00
150	Darryl Strawberry	3.50
151	Alan Trammell	3.50
152	Tim Wallach	3.50
153	Bob Welch	3.50
154	Matt Williams	3.50

1988 Starting Lineup Talking Baseball

Measuring 2-5/8" x 3", these cards were part of the Starting Lineup Talking Baseball game produced by Kenner Parker Toys Inc. The electronic game, with a computer memory and keyboard to respond to a particular baseball game situation, retailed for more than $100. However, several hobby dealers sold the cards separately from the game. The set includes seven instruction cards that do not picture players.

		MT
Complete Set (40):		60.00
Common Player:		.75
11a	Terry Kennedy	.75
11b	Gary Carter	1.50
12a	Carlton Fisk	2.00
12b	Steve Sax	.75
13a	Eddie Murray	2.00
13b	Jack Clark	.75
14a	Don Mattingly	5.00
14b	Keith Hernandez	.75
15a	Willie Randolph	.75
15b	Buddy Bell	.75
16a	Cal Ripken	8.00
16b	Ryne Sandberg	2.00
17a	Lou Whitaker	.75
17b	Ozzie Smith	2.00
18a	Wade Boggs	2.00
18b	Dale Murphy	1.50
19a	George Brett	4.50
19b	Mike Schmidt	3.00
20a	Alan Trammell	.90
20b	Eric Davis	.90
21a	Kirby Puckett	4.00
21b	Tony Gwynn	5.00
22a	George Bell	.75
22b	Darryl Strawberry	1.00
23a	Rickey Henderson	2.00
23b	Tim Raines	1.00
24a	Dave Winfield	2.00
24b	Andre Dawson	1.00
25a	Jack Morris	.75
25b	Mike Scott	.75
26a	Robin Yount	3.00
26b	Jody Davis	.75
27a	Roger Clemens	3.00
27b	Todd Worrell	.75
28a	Bret Saberhagen	.75
28b	Fernando Valenzuela	.75
29a	Dave Righetti	.75
29b	Dwight Gooden	.90
30a	Dan Quisenberry	.75
30b	Nolan Ryan	7.50

1988 Starting Lineup Talking Baseball Team Sets

Similar in format to the cards issued with the Parker Brothers game, these accessory cards could be purchased in groups of three team sets. The team-set cards share the format (2-5/8" x 3") and design of the boxed-set cards, but differ in that the player portraits are presented as colored drawings rather than photos. Because the issue was licensed only by the players' union, and not MLB, the caps have no team logos. Backs are in black-and-white. Each team set has 20 player cards (the Indians have only 19) plus a batting order/checklist card. Several players appear in more than one set as a result of trades. The cards are checklisted here alphabetically within team.

		MT
Complete Set (545):		275.00
Common Player:		.50
	Atlanta Braves team set:	15.00
(1)	Jim Acker	.50
(2)	Paul Assenmacher	.50
(3)	Jeff Blauser	.50
(4)	Jeff Dedmon	.50
(5)	Ron Gant	.50
(6)	Tom Glavine	2.50
(7)	Ken Griffey	.50
(8)	Albert Hall	.50
(9)	Glenn Hubbard	.50
(10)	Dion James	.50
(11)	Rick Mahler	.50
(12)	Dale Murphy	3.00
(13)	Ken Oberkfell	.50
(14)	Gerald Perry	.50
(15)	Gary Roenicke	.50
(16)	Paul Runge	.50
(17)	Ted Simmons	.50
(18)	Pete Smith	.50
(19)	Andres Thomas	.50
(20)	Ozzie Virgil	.50
(21)	Batting order/ checklist	.50
	Baltimore Orioles team set:	37.00
(1)	Eric Bell	.50
(2)	Mike Boddicker	.50
(3)	Jim Dwyer	.50
(4)	Ken Gerhart	.50
(5)	Rene Gonzalez	.50
(6)	Terry Kennedy	.50
(7)	Ray Knight	.50
(8)	Lee Lacy	.50
(9)	Fred Lynn	.50
(10)	Eddie Murray	3.00
(11)	Tom Niedenfuer	.50
(12)	Billy Ripkin (Ripken)	.50
(13)	Cal Ripken Jr.	27.00
(14)	Dave Schmidt	.50
(15)	Larry Sheets	.50
(16)	Pete Stanicek	.50
(17)	Mark Thurmond	.50
(18)	Ron Washington	.50
(19)	Mark Williamson	.50
(20)	Mike Young	.50
(21)	Batting order/ checklist	.50
	Boston Red Sox team set:	15.00
(1)	Marty Barrett	.50
(2)	Todd Benzinger	.50
(3)	Wade Boggs	6.00
(4)	Dennis Boyd	.50
(5)	Ellis Burks	.50
(6)	Roger Clemens	7.50
(7)	Dwight Evans	.50
(8)	Wes Gardner	.50
(9)	Rich Gedman	.50
(10)	Mike Greenwell	.50
(11)	Sam Horn	.50
(12)	Bruce Hurst	.50
(13)	John Marzano	.50
(14)	Spike Owen	.50
(15)	Jody Reed	.50
(16)	Jim Rice	.75
(17)	Ed Romero	.50
(18)	Kevin Romine	.50
(19)	Lee Smith	.50
(20)	Bob Stanley	.50
(21)	Batting order/ checklist	.50
	California Angels team set:	7.50
(1)	(Tony Armas)	.50
(2)	Bob Boone	.50
(3)	Bill Buckner	.50
(4)	DeWayne Buice	.50
(5)	Brian Downing	.50
(6)	Chuck Finley	.50
(7)	Willie Fraser	.50
(8)	George Hendrick	.50
(9)	Jack Howell	.50
(10)	Ruppert Jones	.50
(11)	Wally Joyner	.65
(12)	Kirk McCaskill	.50
(13)	Mark McLemore	.50
(14)	Darrell Miller	.50
(15)	Greg Minton	.50
(16)	Gary Pettis	.50
(17)	Johnny Ray	.50
(18)	Dick Schofield	.50
(19)	Devon White	.60
(20)	Mike Witt	.50
(21)	Batting order/ checklist	.50
	Chicago Cubs team set:	13.50
(1)	Jody Davis	.50
(2)	Andre Dawson	1.00
(3)	Bob Dernier	.50
(4)	Frank DiPino	.50
(5)	Shawon Dunston	.50
(6)	Leon Durham	.50
(7)	Dave Martinez	.50
(8)	Keith Moreland	.50
(9)	Jamie Moyer	.50
(10)	Jerry Mumphrey	.50
(11)	Paul Noce	.50
(12)	Rafael Palmeiro	.75
(13)	Luis Quinones	.50
(14)	Ryne Sandberg	6.00
(15)	Scott Sanderson	.50
(16)	Calvin Schiraldi	.50
(17)	Lee Smith	.50
(18)	Jim Sundberg	.50
(19)	Rick Sutcliffe	.50
(20)	Manny Trillo	.50
(21)	Batting order/ checklist	.50
	Chicago White Sox team set:	7.50
(1)	Harold Baines	.60
(2)	Floyd Bannister	.50
(3)	Daryl Boston	.50
(4)	Ivan Calderon	.50
(5)	Jose DeLeon	.50
(6)	Rich Dotson	.50
(7)	Carlton Fisk	2.50
(8)	Ozzie Guillen	.50
(9)	Jerry Hairston	.50
(10)	Donnie Hill	.50
(11)	Dave LaPoint	.50
(12)	Steve Lyons	.50
(13)	Fred Manrique	.50
(14)	Dan Pasqua	.50
(15)	Gary Redus	.50
(16)	Mark Salas	.50
(17)	Ray Searage	.50
(18)	Bobby Thigpen	.50
(19)	Greg Walker	.50
(20)	Ken Williams	.50
(21)	Batting order/ checklist	.50
	Cincinnati Reds team set:	9.00
(1)	Buddy Bell	.50
(2)	Tom Browning	.50
(3)	Dave Collins	.50
(4)	Dave Concepcion	.50
(5)	Kal Daniels	.50
(6)	Eric Davis	.65
(7)	Bo Diaz	.50
(8)	Nick Esasky	.50
(9)	John Franco	.50
(10)	Terry Francona	.50
(11)	Tracy Jones	.50
(12)	Barry Larkin	1.00
(13)	Rob Murphy	.50
(14)	Paul O'Neill	.60
(15)	Dave Parker	.50
(16)	Ted Power	.50
(17)	Dennis Rasmussen	.50
(18)	Kurt Stillwell	.50
(19)	Jeff Treadway	.50
(20)	Frank Williams	.50
(21)	Batting order/ checklist	.50
	Cleveland Indians team set:	9.00
(1)	Andy Allanson	.50
(2)	Scott Bailes	.50
(3)	Chris Bando	.50
(4)	Jay Bell	.50
(5)	Brett Butler	.60
(6)	Tom Candiotti	.50
(7)	Joe Carter	.50
(8)	Carmen Castillo	.50
(9)	Dave Clark	.50
(10)	John Farrell	.50
(11)	Julio Franco	.50
(12)	Mel Hall	.50
(13)	Tom Hinzo	.50
(14)	Brook Jacoby	.50
(15)	Doug Jones	.50
(16)	Junior Noboa	.50
(17)	Ken Schrom	.50
(18)	Cory Snyder	.50
(19)	Pat Tabler	.50
(20)	Batting order/ checklist	.50
	Detroit Tigers team set:	9.00
(1)	(Doyle Alexander)	.50
(2)	Dave Bergman	.50
(3)	Tom Brookens	.50
(4)	Darrell Evans	.65
(5)	Kirk Gibson	.50
(6)	Mike Heath	.50
(7)	Mike Henneman	.50
(8)	Willie Hernandez	.50
(9)	Larry Herndon	.50
(10)	Eric King	.50
(11)	Ray Knight	.50
(12)	Chet Lemon	.50
(13)	Bill Madlock	.50
(14)	Jack Morris	.50
(15)	Jim Morrison	.50
(16)	Matt Nokes	.50
(17)	Pat Sheridan	.50
(18)	Frank Tanana	.50
(19)	Alan Trammell	.75
(20)	Lou Whitaker	.50
(21)	Batting order/ checklist	.50
	Houston Astros team set:	30.00
(1)	Juan Agosto	.50
(2)	Larry Anderson	.50
(3)	Alan Ashby	.50
(4)	Kevin Bass	.50
(5)	Ken Caminiti	1.00
(6)	Jose Cruz	.50
(7)	Danny Darwin	.50
(8)	Glenn Davis	.50
(9)	Bill Doran	.50
(10)	Billy Hatcher	.50
(11)	Jim Pankovitz	.50
(12)	Terry Puhl	.50
(13)	Rafael Ramirez	.50
(14)	Craig Reynolds	.50
(15)	Nolan Ryan	27.00
(16)	Mike Scott	.50
(17)	Dave Smith	.50
(18)	Marc Sullivan	.50
(19)	Dennis Walling	.50
(20)	Eric Young	.50
(21)	Batting order/ checklist	.50
	Kansas City Royals team set:	24.00
(1)	Steve Balboni	.50
(2)	George Brett	18.00
(3)	Jim Eisenreich	.50
(4)	Gene Garber	.50
(5)	Jerry Don Gleaton	.50
(6)	Mark Gubicza	.50
(7)	Bo Jackson	1.50
(8)	Charlie Leibrandt	.50
(9)	Mike Macfarlane	.50
(10)	Larry Owen	.50
(11)	Bill Pecota	.50
(12)	Jamie Quirk	.50
(13)	Dan Quisenberry	.50
(14)	Bret Saberhagen	.60
(15)	Kevin Seitzer	.50
(16)	Kurt Stillwell	.50
(17)	Danny Tartabull	.50
(18)	Gary Thurman	.50
(19)	Frank White	.50
(20)	Willie Wilson	.60
(21)	Batting order/ checklist	.50
	Los Angeles Dodgers team set:	9.00
(1)	Dave Anderson	.50
(2)	Mike Davis	.50
(3)	Mariano Duncan	.50
(4)	Kirk Gibson	.50
(5)	Alfredo Griffin	.50
(6)	Pedro Guerrero	.50
(7)	Mickey Hatcher	.50
(8)	Orel Hershiser	.60
(9)	Glenn Hoffman	.50
(10)	Brian Holton	.50
(11)	Mike Marshall	.50
(12)	Jesse Orosco	.50
(13)	Alejandro Pena	.50
(14)	Steve Sax	.50
(15)	Mike Scioscia	.50
(16)	John Shelby	.50
(17)	Franklin Stubbs	.50
(18)	Don Sutton	1.50
(19)	Alex Trevino	.50
(20)	Fernando Valenzuela	.50
(21)	Batting order/ checklist	.50
	Milwaukee Brewers team set:	9.00
(1)	Chris Bosio	.50
(2)	Glenn Braggs	.50
(3)	Greg Brock	.50
(4)	Juan Castillo	.50
(5)	Chuck Crim	.50
(6)	Rob Deer	.50
(7)	Mike Felder	.50
(8)	Jim Gantner	.50
(9)	Teddy Higuera	.50
(10)	Steve Kiefer	.50
(11)	Paul Molitor	5.00
(12)	Juan Nieves	.50
(13)	Dan Plesac	.50
(14)	Ernie Riles	.50
(15)	Billy Jo Robidoux	.50
(16)	Bill Schroeder	.50
(17)	B.J. Surhoff	.50
(18)	Dale Sveum	.50
(19)	Bill Wegman	.50
(20)	Robin Yount	6.00
(21)	Batting order/ checklist	.50
	Minnesota Twins team set:	9.00
(1)	Don Baylor	.60
(2)	Juan Berenguer	.50
(3)	Bert Blyleven	.50
(4)	Tom Brunansky	.50
(5)	Randy Bush	.50
(6)	Mark Davidson	.50
(7)	Gary Gaetti	.50
(8)	Greg Gagne	.50
(9)	Dan Gladden	.50
(10)	Kent Hrbek	.50
(11)	Gene Larkin	.50
(12)	Tim Laudner	.50
(13)	Steve Lombardozzi	.50
(14)	Al Newman	.50
(15)	Kirby Puckett	7.50
(16)	Jeff Reardon	.50
(17)	Dan Schatzeder	.50
(18)	Roy Smalley	.50
(19)	Les Straker	.50
(20)	Frank Viola	.50
(21)	Batting order/ checklist	.50
	Montreal Expos team set:	7.50
(1)	Hubie Brooks	.50
(2)	Tim Burke	.50
(3)	Casey Candaele	.50
(4)	Mike Fitzgerald	.50
(5)	Tom Foley	.50
(6)	Andres Galarraga	.75
(7)	Neal Heaton	.50
(8)	Randy Johnson	4.00
(9)	Vance Law	.50
(10)	Bob McClure	.50
(11)	Andy McGaffigan	.50
(12)	Dennis Powell	.50
(13)	Tim Raines	1.00
(14)	Jeff Reed	.50
(15)	Luis Rivera	.50
(16)	Bryn Smith	.50
(17)	Tim Wallach	.50
(18)	Mitch Webster	.50
(19)	Herm Winningham	.50
(20)	Floyd Youmans	.50
(21)	Batting order/ checklist	.50

New York Mets team issue: 15.00
(1) Bill Almon .50
(2) Wally Backman .50
(3) Gary Carter 1.00
(4) David Cone .60
(5) Ron Darling .50
(6) Lenny Dykstra .50
(7) Sid Fernandez .50
(8) Dwight Gooden .75
(9) Keith Hernandez .50
(10) Howard Johnson .50
(11) Barry Lyons .50
(12) Dave Magadan .50
(13) Lee Mazzilli .50
(14) Roger McDowell .50
(15) Kevin McReynolds .50
(16) Jesse Orosco .50
(17) Rafael Santana .50
(18) Darryl Strawberry 1.50
(19) Tim Teufel .50
(20) Mookie Wilson .50
(21) Batting order/checklist .50

New York Yankees team set: 30.00
(1) Rick Cerone .50
(2) Jack Clark .50
(3) Pat Clements .50
(4) Mike Easler .50
(5) Ron Guidry .50
(6) Rickey Henderson 3.00
(7) Tommy John .50
(8) Don Mattingly 7.50
(9) Bobby Meacham .50
(10) Mike Pagliarulo .50
(11) Willie Randolph .50
(12) Rick Rhoden .50
(13) Dave Righetti .50
(14) Jerry Royster .50
(15) Don Slaught .50
(16) Tim Stoddard .50
(17) Wayne Tolleson .50
(18) Gary Ward .50
(19) Claudell Washington .50
(20) Dave Winfield 3.00
(21) Batting order/checklist .50

Oakland A's team set: 37.00
(1) Tony Bernazard .50
(2) Jose Canseco 4.50
(3) Mike Davis .50
(4) Dennis Eckersley .60
(5) Mike Gallego .50
(6) Alfredo Griffin .50
(7) Rickey Henderson 3.00
(8) Reggie Jackson 6.00
(9) Carney Lansford .50
(10) Mark McGwire 30.00
(11) Gene Nelson .50
(12) Steve Ontiveros .50
(13) Dave Parker .50
(14) Tony Phillips .50
(15) Luis Polonia .50
(16) Terry Steinbach .50
(17) Dave Stewart .50
(18) Mickey Tettleton .50
(19) Bob Welch .50
(20) Curt Young .50
(21) Batting order/checklist .50

Philadelphia Phillies team set: 9.00
(1) Luis Aguayo .50
(2) Steve Bedrosian .50
(3) Phil Bradley .50
(4) Jeff Calhoun .50
(5) Don Carman .50
(6) Darren Daulton .50
(7) Bob Dernier .50
(8) Greg Gross .50
(9) Von Hayes .50
(10) Chris James .50
(11) Steve Jeltz .50
(12) Lance Parrish .50
(13) Shane Rawley .50
(14) Bruce Ruffin .50
(15) Juan Samuel .50
(16) Mike Schmidt 6.00
(17) Rick Schu .50
(18) Kent Tekulve .50
(19) Milt Thompson .50
(20) Glenn Wilson .50
(21) Batting order/checklist .50

Pittsburgh Pirates team set: 13.50
(1) Rafael Belliard .50
(2) Barry Bonds 6.00
(3) Bobby Bonilla .50
(4) Sid Bream .50
(5) John Cangelosi .50
(6) Darnell Coles .50
(7) Mike Diaz .50
(8) Doug Drabek .50
(9) Mike Dunne .50
(10) Felix Fermin .50
(11) Brian Fisher .50
(12) Jim Gott .50
(13) Mike LaValliere .50
(14) Jose Lind .50
(15) Junior Ortiz .50
(16) Al Pedrique .50
(17) R.J. Reynolds .50
(18) Jeff Robinson .50
(19) John Smiley .50
(20) Andy Van Slyke .50
(21) Batting order/checklist .50

San Diego Padres team set: 15.00
(1) Shawn Abner .50
(2) Roberto Alomar 5.00
(3) Bobby Brown .50
(4) Joey Cora .50
(5) Mark Davis .50
(6) Tim Flannery .50
(7) Goose Gossage .50
(8) Mark Grant .50
(9) Tony Gwynn 6.00
(10) Stan Jefferson .50
(11) John Kruk .50
(12) Shane Mack .50
(13) Carmelo Martinez .50
(14) Lance McCullers .50
(15) Randy Ready .50
(16) Benito Santiago .50
(17) Eric Show .50
(18) Garry Templeton .50
(19) Ed Whitson .50
(20) Marvell Wynne .50
(21) Batting order/checklist .50

San Francisco Giants team set: 15.00
(1) Mike Aldrete .50
(2) Bob Brenly .50
(3) Brett Butler .50
(4) Will Clark 3.00
(5) Chili Davis .50
(6) Dave Dravecky .50
(7) Scott Garrelts .50
(8) Atlee Hammaker .50
(9) Craig Lefferts .50
(10) Jeffrey Leonard .50
(11) Candy Maldonado .50
(12) Bob Melvin .50
(13) Kevin Mitchell .50
(14) Rick Reuschel .50
(15) Don Robinson .50
(16) Chris Speier .50
(17) Chris Spielman .50
(18) Robby Thompson .50
(19) Jose Uribe .50
(20) Matt Williams 2.00
(21) Batting order/checklist .50

Seattle Mariners team set: 9.00
(1) Phil Bradley .50
(2) Scott Bradley .50
(3) Mickey Brantley .50
(4) Mike Campbell .50
(5) Henry Cotto .50
(6) Alvin Davis .50
(7) Mike Kingery .50
(8) Mark Langston .50
(9) Mike Moore .50
(10) John Moses .50
(11) Donell Nixon .50
(12) Ed Nunez .50
(13) Ken Phelps .50
(14) Jim Presley .50
(15) Rey Quinones .50
(16) Jerry Reed .50
(17) Harold Reynolds .50
(18) Dave Valle .50
(19) Bill Wilkinson .50
(20) Glenn Wilson .50
(21) Batting order/checklist .50

St. Louis Cardinals team set: 12.00
(1) Greg Booker .50
(2) Jack Clark .50
(3) Vince Coleman .50
(4) Danny Cox .50
(5) Ken Dayley .50
(6) Curt Ford .50
(7) Tom Herr .50
(8) Bob Horner .50
(9) Ricky Horton .50
(10) Lance Johnson .50
(11) Steve Lake .50
(12) Jim Lindeman .50
(13) Greg Mathews .50
(14) Willie McGee .50
(15) Jose Oquendo .50
(16) Tony Pena .50
(17) Terry Pendleton .50
(18) Ozzie Smith 5.00
(19) John Tudor .50
(20) Todd Worrell .50
(21) Batting order/checklist .50

Texas Rangers team set: 9.00
(1) Jerry Browne .50
(2) Bob Brower .50
(3) Steve Buechele .50
(4) Scott Fletcher .50
(5) Juan Guzman .50
(6) Charlie Hough .50
(7) Pete Incaviglia .50
(8) Oddibe McDowell .50
(9) Dale Mohorcic .50
(10) Pete O'Brien .50
(11) Tom O'Malley .50
(12) Larry Parrish .50
(13) Geno Petralli .50
(14) Jeff Russell .50
(15) Ruben Sierra .50
(16) Don Slaught .50
(17) Mike Stanley .50
(18) Curt Wilkerson .50
(19) Mitch Williams .50
(20) Bobby Witt .50
(21) Batting order/checklist .50

Toronto Blue Jays team set: 15.00
(1) Jesse Barfield .50
(2) George Bell .50
(3) Juan Beniquez .50
(4) Jim Clancy .50
(5) Mark Eichhorn .50
(6) Tony Fernandez .50
(7) Cecil Fielder .50
(8) Tom Henke .50
(9) Garth Iorg .50
(10) Jimmy Key .50
(11) Rick Leach .50
(12) Manny Lee .50
(13) Nelson Liriano .50
(14) Fred McGriff 3.00
(15) Lloyd Moseby .50
(16) Rance Mulliniks .50
(17) Jeff Musselman .50
(18) Dave Steib .50
(19) Willie Upshaw .50
(20) Ernie Whitt .50
(21) Batting order/checklist .50

1988 Starting Lineup Baseball

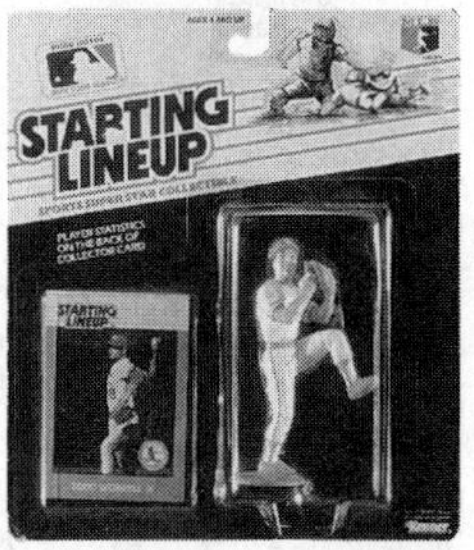

This massive three-sport set was distributed in conjunction with Kenner's Starting Lineup sports figurines, one card per statue. Cards were not sold separately. Baseball, football and basketball stars were included in the lineup of full-color figurines, with 123 figure/card combinations devoted to baseball. Individual major league team assortments include one to seven players per team. The figurines are mildly reminiscent of the 1950s Hartland Statues, but Kenner's version features smaller (4" to 6") figures and a more extensive catalog which includes athletes other than baseball players. The Starting Lineup cards feature action photos framed in red and white, with the "Starting Lineup" logo in the upper-left corner and the player's name printed along the bottom border. Colorful team logos are superimposed in the lower-right corner of the photo. Card backs were printed in blue and contain major league stats, a few biographical details, a facsimile autograph and the major league and Kenner logos. Values shown are for unopened package of both statue and card for the 123 baseball players in the set. Loose figures will bring up to 40% of the listed values, while single cards sell for about 15% of the quoted figures. Several players which were included in the checklist printed on the package were never produced.

MT
Complete Set (124): 3000.
Common Piece: 15.00
Collector Stand: 75.00
Autographed Baseball: 80.00
(1) Alan Ashby 18.00
(2) Harold Baines 15.00
(3) Kevin Bass 12.00
(4) Steve Bedrosian 15.00
(5) Buddy Bell 20.00
(6) George Bell 15.00
(7) Mike Boddicker 20.00
(8) Wade Boggs 35.00
(9) Barry Bonds 80.00
(10) Bobby Bonilla 20.00
(11) Sid Bream 12.00
(12) George Brett 80.00
(13) Chris Brown 10.00
(14) Tom Brunansky 22.00
(15) Ellis Burks 40.00
(16) Jose Canseco 40.00
(17) Gary Carter 20.00
(18) Joe Carter 30.00
(19) Jack Clark 17.00
(20) Will Clark 25.00
(21) Roger Clemens 80.00
(22) Vince Coleman 10.00
(23) Kal Daniels 15.00
(24) Alvin Davis 12.00
(25) Eric Davis 10.00
(26) Glenn Davis 12.00
(27) Jody Davis 14.00
(28) Andre Dawson 20.00
(29) Rob Deer 16.00
(30) Brian Downing 12.00
(31) Mike Dunne 10.00
(32) Shawon Dunston 15.00
(33) Leon Durham 14.00
(34) Len Dykstra 10.00
(35) Dwight Evans 20.00
(36) Carlton Fisk 65.00
(37) John Franco 16.00
(38) Julio Franco 18.00
(39) Gary Gaetti 15.00
(40) Dwight Gooden 12.00
(41) Ken Griffey, Sr. 25.00
(42) Pedro Guerrero 10.00
(43) Ozzie Guillen 17.00
(44) Tony Gwynn 200.00
(45) Mel Hall 12.00
(46) Billy Hatcher 14.00
(47) Von Hayes 15.00
(48) Rickey Henderson 20.00
(49) Keith Hernandez 15.00
(50) Willie Hernandez 14.00
(51) Tom Herr 12.00
(52) Ted Higuera 15.00
(53) Charlie Hough 18.00
(54) Kent Hrbek 15.00
(55) Pete Incaviglia 18.00
(56) Howard Johnson 14.00
(57) Wally Joyner 12.00
(58) Terry Kennedy 15.00
(59) John Kruk 20.00
(60) Mark Langston 30.00
(61) Carney Lansford 20.00
(62) Jeffrey Leonard 15.00
(63) Fred Lynn 20.00
(64) Candy Maldonado 10.00
(65) Mike Marshall 14.00
(66) Don Mattingly 25.00
(67) Willie McGee 16.00
(68) Mark McGwire 225.00
(69) Kevin McReynolds 15.00
(70) Paul Molitor 65.00
(71) Donnie Moore 20.00
(72) Jack Morris 24.00
(73) Dale Murphy 14.00
(74) Eddie Murray 75.00
(75) Matt Nokes 12.00
(76) Pete O'Brien 12.00
(77) Ken Oberkfell 12.00
(78) Dave Parker 25.00
(79) Larry Parrish 12.00
(80) Ken Phelps 12.00
(81) Jim Presley 12.00
(82) Kirby Puckett 75.00
(83) Dan Quisenberry 16.00
(84) Tim Raines 14.00
(85) Willie Randolph 14.00
(86) Shane Rawley 12.00
(87) Jeff Reardon 25.00
(88) Gary Redus 12.00
(89) Rick Reuschel 12.00
(90) Jim Rice 24.00
(91) Dave Righetti 15.00
(92) Cal Ripken, Jr. 300.00
(93) Pete Rose 75.00
(94) Nolan Ryan 300.00
(95) Bret Saberhagen 20.00
(96) Juan Samuel 20.00
(97) Ryne Sandberg 70.00
(98) Benito Santiago 20.00
(99) Steve Sax 13.00
(100) Mike Schmidt 70.00
(101) Mike Scott 10.00
(102) Kevin Seitzer 14.00
(103) Ruben Sierra 25.00
(104) Ozzie Smith 75.00
(105) Zane Smith 12.00
(106) Cory Snyder 12.00
(107) Darryl Strawberry 10.00
(108) Franklin Stubbs 12.00
(109) B.J. Surhoff 20.00
(110) Rick Sutcliffe 17.00
(111) Pat Tabler 12.00
(112) Danny Tartabull 17.00
(113) Alan Trammell 20.00
(114) Fernando Valenzuela 10.00
(115) Andy Van Slyke 20.00
(116) Frank Viola 18.00
(117) Ozzie Virgil 12.00
(118) Greg Walker 12.00
(119) Lou Whitaker 24.00
(120) Devon White 30.00
(121) Dave Winfield 40.00
(122) Mike Witt 12.00
(123) Todd Worrell 18.00
(124) Robin Yount 80.00

1988 Starting Lineup Unissued

Largely because of player transactions which would have resulted in players being issued in outdated uniforms, nine cards of projected debut-year SLUs exist without accompanying statues (except prototypes). These unissued cards are often found as part of uncut sheets which made their way into the hobby by various means. The cards are in the same format as those packaged with the first SLUs, having red and white borders on front and blue-printed backs. The unissued cards are listed here in alphabetical order.

MT
Complete Set (9): 600.00
Common Player: 60.00
(1) Phil Bradley (Mariners) 60.00
(2) Chili Davis (Giants) 90.00
(3) Mike Davis (A's) 60.00
(4) Kirk Gibson (Padres) 120.00
(5) Goose Gossage (Padres) 120.00
(6) Ray Knight (Orioles) 75.00
(7) Lee Smith (Cubs) 120.00
(8) Bob Welch (Dodgers) 75.00
(9) Glenn Wilson (Phillies) 60.00

1989 Starting Lineup Baseball

Kenner returned in 1989 with another set of sports figurines and accompanying trading cards. As in the previous year, the figurines were sold individually in a blister pack with one card packaged with each figure. No cards were sold separately. The 1989 cards have a green border with the "Starting Lineup" logo in the upper-left; "1989 Edition" and the player's name and uniform number appear at bottom. Backs are identical in format to the previous year. Values listed here are for complete, unopened packages of figure and card. Values are based on relative scarcity, resulting in some minor stars and common players being priced higher than superstars, whose cards and figures were produced in much greater numbers. Loose figures generally sell for up to 40% of the package value, with single cards bringing about 15%.

MT
Complete Set (168): 4500.
Common Piece: 12.00
Counter Display: 300.00
(1) *Roberto Alomar* 450.00
(2) *Brady Anderson* 150.00
(3) Harold Baines 15.00
(4) *Marty Barrett* 14.00
(5) Kevin Bass 15.00
(6) Steve Bedrosian 12.00
(7) George Bell 12.00
(8) *Damon Berryhill* 12.00
(9) Wade Boggs 30.00
(10) Barry Bonds 80.00
(11) Bobby Bonilla 16.00
(12) *Phil Bradley* 22.00
(13) *Glenn Braggs* 12.00

(14)	*Mickey Brantley*	12.00
(15)	George Brett	75.00
(16)	*Tom Brookens*	12.00
(17)	Tom Brunansky	12.00
(18)	*Steve Buechele*	18.00
(19)	Ellis Burks	25.00
(20)	*Brett Butler*	20.00
(21)	*Ivan Calderon*	10.00
(22)	Jose Canseco	30.00
(23)	Gary Carter	18.00
(24)	Joe Carter	20.00
(25)	Will Clark	22.00
(26)	Roger Clemens	60.00
(27)	Vince Coleman	10.00
(28)	*David Cone*	60.00
(29)	Kal Daniels	12.00
(30)	Alvin Davis	15.00
(31)	*Chili Davis*	140.00
(32)	Eric Davis	10.00
(33)	Glenn Davis	10.00
(34)	*Mark Davis*	30.00
(35)	Andre Dawson	20.00
(36)	Rob Deer	10.00
(37)	*Bo Diaz*	14.00
(38)	*Bill Doran*	20.00
(39)	*Doug Drabek*	30.00
(40)	Shawon Dunston	15.00
(41)	Len Dykstra	30.00
(42)	*Dennis Eckersley*	90.00
(43)	*Kevin Elster*	12.00
(44)	*Scott Fletcher*	12.00
(45)	John Franco	12.00
(46)	Gary Gaetti	12.00
(47)	*Ron Gant*	175.00
(48)	*Kirk Gibson*	15.00
(49)	*Dan Gladden*	14.00
(50)	Dwight Gooden	10.00
(51)	*Mark Grace*	42.00
(52)	*Mike Greenwell*	10.00
(53)	*Mark Gubicza*	10.00
(54)	Pedro Guerrero	10.00
(55)	Ozzie Guillen	24.00
(56)	Tony Gwynn	500.00
(57)	*Albert Hall*	14.00
(58)	Mel Hall	12.00
(59)	Billy Hatcher	10.00
(60)	Von Hayes	12.00
(61)	Rickey Henderson	20.00
(62)	*Mike Henneman*	10.00
(63)	Keith Hernandez	12.00
(64)	*Orel Hershiser*	20.00
(65)	Ted Higuera	20.00
(66)	*Jack Howell*	100.00
(67)	Kent Hrbek	14.00
(68)	Pete Incaviglia	12.00
(69)	*Bo Jackson*	25.00
(70)	*Danny Jackson*	14.00
(71)	*Brook Jacoby*	10.00
(72)	*Chris James*	12.00
(73)	*Dion James*	15.00
(74)	*Gregg Jefferies*	32.00
(75)	*Doug Jones*	18.00
(76)	Wally Joyner	14.00
(77)	John Kruk	30.00
(78)	Mark Langston	20.00
(79)	Carney Lansford	20.00
(80)	*Barry Larkin*	75.00
(81)	*Tim Laudner*	15.00
(82)	*Mike LaValliere*	10.00
(83)	*Al Leiter*	16.00
(84)	*Chet Lemon*	14.00
(85)	*Jose Lind*	20.00
(86)	*Greg Maddux*	375.00
(87)	Candy Maldonado	12.00
(88)	Mike Marshall	10.00
(89)	Don Mattingly	27.00
(90)	Willie McGee	25.00
(91)	Mark McGwire	160.00
(92)	Kevin McReynolds	18.00
(93)	*Kevin Mitchell*	20.00
(94)	Paul Molitor	35.00
(95)	Jack Morris	20.00
(96)	Dale Murphy	15.00
(97)	*Randy Myers*	18.00
(98)	Matt Nokes	10.00
(99)	*Mike Pagliarulo*	10.00
(100)	Dave Parker	25.00
(101)	*Dan Pasqua*	15.00
(102)	*Tony Pena*	18.00
(103)	*Terry Pendleton*	25.00
(104)	*Melido Perez*	30.00
(105)	*Gerald Perry*	16.00
(106)	*Dan Plesac*	10.00
(107)	Kirby Puckett	60.00
(108)	*Rey Quinones*	18.00
(109)	Tim Raines	11.00
(110)	*Johnny Ray*	120.00
(111)	Jeff Reardon	30.00
(112)	*Harold Reynolds*	25.00
(113)	Jim Rice	16.00
(114)	Dave Righetti	16.00
(115)	Cal Ripken, Jr.	400.00
(116)	*Jeff Russell*	18.00
(117)	Bret Saberhagen	16.00
(118)	*Chris Sabo*	20.00
(119)	*Luis Salazar*	15.00
(120)	Juan Samuel	10.00
(121)	Ryne Sandberg	50.00
(122)	Benito Santiago	25.00
(123)	Mike Schmidt	60.00
(124)	*Dick Schofield*	120.00
(125)	*Mike Scioscia*	40.00
(126)	Mike Scott	10.00
(127)	Kevin Seitzer	12.00
(128)	*Larry Sheets*	12.00
(129)	*John Shelby*	10.00
(130)	Ruben Sierra	30.00
(131)	*Don Slaught*	12.00
(132)	*Dave Smith*	10.00
(133)	*Lee Smith*	70.00
(134)	Ozzie Smith	50.00
(135)	Zane Smith	12.00
(136)	Cory Snyder	12.00
(137)	*Pete Stanicek*	15.00
(138)	*Terry Steinbach*	18.00
(139)	*Dave Stewart*	25.00
(140)	*Kurt Stillwell*	12.00
(141)	Darryl Strawberry	10.00
(142)	B.J. Surhoff	18.00
(143)	Rick Sutcliffe	16.00
(144)	*Bruce Sutter*	30.00
(145)	*Greg Swindell*	20.00
(146)	Pat Tabler	13.00
(147)	Danny Tartabull	12.00
(148)	*Bobby Thigpen*	45.00
(149)	*Milt Thompson*	15.00
(150)	*Robby Thompson*	15.00
(151)	Alan Trammell	18.00
(152)	*Jeff Treadway*	40.00
(153)	*Jose Uribe*	12.00
(154)	Fernando Valenzuela	14.00
(155)	Andy Van Slyke	16.00
(156)	Frank Viola	10.00
(157)	*Bob Walk*	12.00
(158)	Greg Walker	18.00
(159)	*Walt Weiss*	30.00
(160)	*Bob Welch*	20.00
(161)	Lou Whitaker	25.00
(162)	Devon White	140.00
(163)	Dave Winfield	30.00
(164)	Mike Witt	120.00
(165)	Todd Worrell	14.00
(166)	*Marvell Wynne*	32.00
(167)	*Gerald Young*	12.00
(168)	Robin Yount	80.00

1989 Starting Lineup Baseball Greats

The "Baseball Greats" series of figurines and trading cards was an addition to the Kenner "Starting Lineup" series for 1989. The series features baseball greats of the past, and were packaged two figurines and two collector cards per package. The collector cards that accompany the figures feature an original action photo of the player done in a sepia-tone to enhance the historic nature of the set. The Starting Lineup logo and "Baseball Greats" heading appear at the top of the card. The player's name and a descriptive nickname, such as "Sultan of Swat" appear below the photo. The backs of the cards carry a blue-and- white color scheme and include career stats. The values listed below are for unopened packages with both figures and both cards.

		MT
Complete Set (10):		400.00
Set Price Includes Ruth/Gehrig Gray/White Version Only.		
(1)	Hank Aaron, Eddie Mathews	50.00
(2)	Ernie Banks, Billy Williams	40.00
(3)	Johnny Bench, Pete Rose	60.00
(4)	Roberto Clemente, Willie Stargell	55.00
(5)	Don Drysdale, Reggie Jackson	60.00
(6)	Mickey Mantle, Joe DiMaggio	90.00
(7)	Willie Mays, Willie McCovey	45.00
(8)	Stan Musial, Bob Gibson	40.00
(9a)	Babe Ruth gray, Lou Gehrig white	45.00
(9b)	Babe Ruth white, Lou Gehrig gray	40.00
(9c)	Babe Ruth white, Lou Gehrig white	60.00
(10)	Carl Yastrzemski, Hank Aaron	75.00

1990 Starting Lineup Baseball

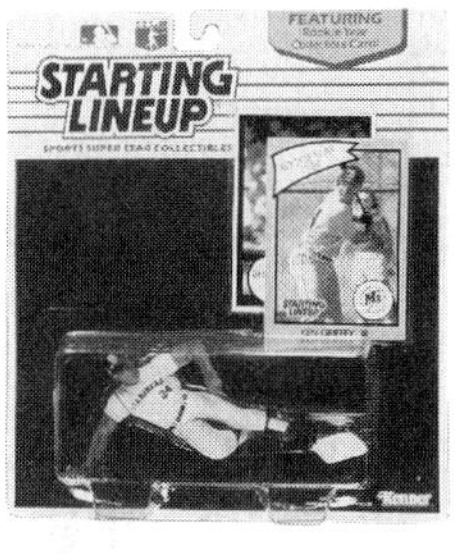

Kenner introduced special bonus rookie year cards with its regular card/statue package in 1990. The cards follow designs much like the Kenner cards of 1988 and 1989. The values are based on relative scarcity. Esasky, Backman and Pettis Kenners were pulled when the players switched teams, thus making them rare. Five variations of figures are included in the 1990 set. Prices listed are for unopened package of statue and card. Statues alone bring up to 40% of the package value, with loose cards worth 10-15%.

		MT
Complete Set (85):		1600.
Common Piece:		12.00
(1)	*Allan Anderson*	12.00
(4)	*Wally Backman*	25.00
(5)	*Jeff Ballard*	12.00
(6)	*Jesse Barfield*	10.00
(7)	Steve Bedrosian	10.00
(8)	*Todd Benzinger*	14.00
(9)	Damon Berryhill	12.00
(10)	Wade Boggs	24.00
(11)	Barry Bonds	60.00
(12)	Bobby Bonilla	15.00
(13)	*Chris Bosio*	15.00
(14)	Ellis Burks	15.00
(15)	Jose Canseco	28.00
(17a)	Will Clark batting (bat held in one hand)	15.00
(17b)	Will Clark power (swinging)	15.00
(18)	Roger Clemens	50.00
(19)	Vince Coleman	10.00
(20)	*Ron Darling*	20.00
(21)	Eric Davis	12.00
(22)	Andre Dawson	18.00
(23)	*Rob Dibble*	16.00
(24)	Len Dykstra	25.00
(25)	Dennis Eckersley	60.00
(26)	*Nick Esasky*	24.00
(27)	Gary Gaetti	12.00
(28)	*Andres Galarraga*	35.00
(29)	Kirk Gibson	10.00
(30)	Dwight Gooden	12.00
(31a)	Mark Grace batting (standing at bat)	18.00
(31b)	Mark Grace power (swinging)	22.00
(32)	Mike Greenwell	10.00
(33a)	*Ken Griffey, Jr.* (sliding)	135.00
(34)	Pedro Guerrero	10.00
(35)	*Von Hayes*	10.00
(36)	*Dave Henderson*	13.00
(37)	Rickey Henderson	15.00
(38)	Tom Herr	10.00
(39)	Orel Hershiser	18.00
(40)	Kent Hrbek	10.00
(42)	Gregg Jefferies	15.00
(43)	Howard Johnson	10.00
(44)	*Ricky Jordan*	10.00
(45)	*Roberto Kelly*	15.00
(46)	Barry Larkin	50.00
(47)	Greg Maddux	100.00
(48)	*Joe Magrane*	10.00
(49a)	Don Mattingly (bat in one hand)	20.00
(49b)	Don Mattingly power (swinging)	24.00
(51)	*Fred McGriff*	40.00
(52)	Mark McGwire	100.00
(53)	Kevin McReynolds	10.00
(54)	Kevin Mitchell	12.00
(55)	Paul Molitor	30.00
(56)	Eddie Murray	150.00
(57)	Matt Nokes	15.00
(58)	*Paul O'Neill*	35.00
(59)	*Jose Oquendo*	15.00
(60)	*Gary Pettis*	20.00
(61)	Kirby Puckett	40.00
(62)	Willie Randolph	10.00
(63)	*Jody Reed*	15.00
(64)	Rick Reuschel	10.00
(65)	Dave Righetti	15.00
(66)	Cal Ripken, Jr.	175.00
(67)	Nolan Ryan	60.00
(68)	Chris Sabo	12.00
(69)	Juan Samuel	12.00
(70)	Ryne Sandberg	35.00
(71)	Steve Sax	10.00
(72)	Mike Scott	10.00
(73)	*Gary Sheffield*	35.00
(74)	*John Smiley*	13.00
(75)	Ozzie Smith	40.00
(76)	Dave Stewart	15.00
(77a)	Darryl Strawberry batting (standing at bat)	10.00
(77b)	Darryl Strawberry (fielding)	10.00
(78)	Rick Sutcliffe	14.00
(79)	*Mickey Tettleton*	16.00
(80)	Alan Trammell	14.00
(81)	Andy Van Slyke	20.00
(82)	Frank Viola	12.00
(84)	Lou Whitaker	15.00
(85)	*Mitch Williams*	15.00
(86)	Dave Winfield	45.00
(87)	Robin Yount	70.00

1990 Starting Lineup Baseball Extended

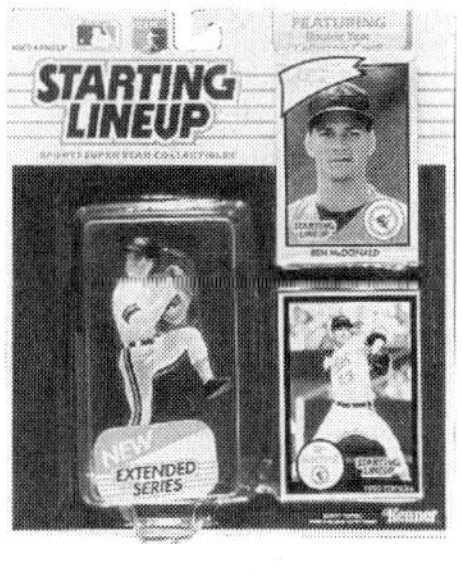

The seven-piece addition to the 92-figure base baseball set was Kenner's first extended set issued. The Ken Griffey Jr. jumping figure heads the set. The blister card package comes with two cards and as with all Starting Lineup sets, must be kept in unopened condition to maintain its top value.

		MT
Complete Set (7):		200.00
(1)	*Jim Abbott*	15.00
(2)	*Sandy Alomar*	15.00
(3)	Joe Carter	25.00
(4)	Ken Griffey Jr. Jump	145.00
(5)	Bo Jackson	10.00
(6)	*Ben McDonald*	15.00
(7)	*Jerome Walton*	10.00

1991 Starting Lineup Baseball

Kenner continued its Starting Lineup with 54 baseball figures for 1991. A bonus with the 1991 card and figure was an aluminum collector coin depicting the player. The 1991 cards featured a yellow border. Players are listed here alphabetically. Values are based on demand and relative scarcity for complete statue/card/coin unopened packages. Loose statues sell for up to 40% of unopened packages; single cards bring about 15% of the package value.

		MT
Complete Set (46):		400.00
Common Piece:		10.00
Send Away Card Poster:		15.00
(1)	Jim Abbott	10.00
(2)	Sandy Alomar, Jr.	16.00
(3)	*Jack Armstrong*	12.00
(5)	Barry Bonds	30.00
(6)	Bobby Bonilla	14.00
(7)	*Tom Browning*	20.00
(8)	Jose Canseco	15.00
(9)	Will Clark	16.00
(11)	Eric Davis	8.00
(13)	Andre Dawson	10.00
(14)	*Delino DeShields*	10.00
(15)	Doug Drabek	14.00
(16)	Shawon Dunston	12.00
(17)	Len Dykstra	14.00
(18)	*Cecil Fielder*	15.00
(19)	John Franco	10.00
(20)	Dwight Gooden	9.00
(21)	Mark Grace	12.00
(22a)	Ken Griffey, Jr. batting (batting)	40.00
(24)	*Kelly Gruber*	10.00
(25)	Ozzie Guillen	12.00
(26)	Rickey Henderson	12.00
(28)	Bo Jackson royals (Royals)	10.00
(29)	Gregg Jefferies	13.00
(30)	Howard Johnson	10.00
(32)	Roberto Kelly	10.00
(33)	Barry Larkin	20.00
(34)	*Kevin Maas*	9.00
(35)	*Dave Magadan*	9.00
(36)	*Ramon Martinez*	20.00
(37)	Don Mattingly	18.00
(38)	Ben McDonald	10.00
(39)	Mark McGwire	65.00
(40)	Kevin Mitchell	10.00
(41)	Kirby Puckett	25.00
(42)	Nolan Ryan	40.00
(44)	Chris Sabo	8.00
(45)	Ryne Sandberg	30.00
(46)	Benito Santiago	12.00
(47)	Steve Sax	12.00
(48)	Dave Stewart	13.00
(50)	Darryl Strawberry mets (Mets)	10.00
(51)	Alan Trammell	14.00
(52)	Frank Viola	10.00
(53)	*Matt Williams*	36.00
(54)	*Todd Zeile*	14.00

1991 Starting Lineup Baseball Extended

The 1991 10-figure "update" release included both Ken Griffey Jr. and Sr., as well as Nolan Ryan, Bo Jackson and Dave Justice. Ken Griffey Jr. was included in the 55-player base set in a batting pose, but his extended figure depicts the Mariners' star in a running pose. Values are for unopened packages. Statues along sell for up to 40% of values quoted; single cards can bring up to 15%.

		MT
Complete Set (10):		175.00
(1)	George Bell	10.00
(2)	Vince Coleman	10.00
(3)	Glenn Davis	10.00
(4)	Ken Griffey Jr. Run.	50.00
(5)	Ken Griffey Sr.	20.00
(6)	Bo Jackson W.S.	15.00
(7)	*David Justice*	30.00
(8)	Tim Raines	13.00
(9)	Nolan Ryan	45.00
(10)	Darryl Strawberry L.A.	10.00

1991 Starting Lineup Headline Collection

The debut Headline set features seven stars on base stands that have an attached sports page headline. The seven-figure set incudes Nolan Ryan, Ken Griffey Jr. and Rickey Henderson. The Headline Collection figures were not sold with cards.

		MT
Complete Set (7):		200.00
(1)	Jose Canseco	20.00
(2)	Will Clark	20.00

(3)	Ken Griffey Jr.	60.00
(4)	Rickey Henderson	25.00
(5)	Bo Jackson	12.00
(6)	Don Mattingly	42.00
(7)	Nolan Ryan	60.00

1992 Starting Lineup Baseball

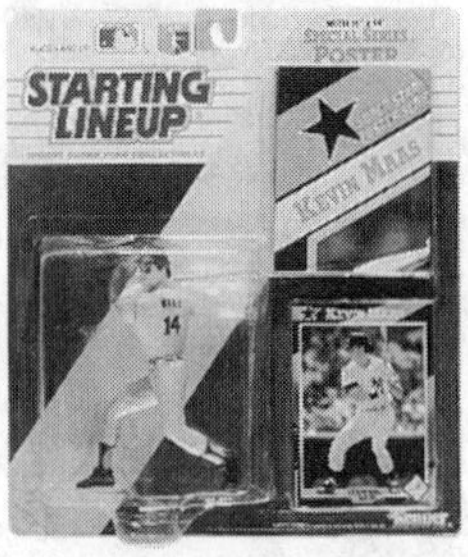

Kenner reduced its figurine/card set to 37 subjects in 1992. Besides the action figure and a baseball card, the package includes an 11" x 14" poster of the player. The players are listed here alphabetically. Values are based on demand and relative scarcity for complete unopened statue/card/poster packages. Opened packages can command prices of up to 40% for the statue, 15% for card and poster.

		MT
Complete Set (37):		400.00
Common Piece:		10.00
Give Away Poster:		15.00
(1)	Roberto Alomar	15.00
(3)	George Bell	10.00
(4)	*Albert Belle*	20.00
(5)	*Craig Biggio*	20.00
(6)	Barry Bonds	20.00
(8)	Ivan Calderon	8.00
(9)	Jose Canseco	15.00
(10)	Will Clark	15.00
(11)	Roger Clemens	32.00
(13)	Rob Dibble	8.00
(14)	*Scott Erickson*	10.00
(15)	Cecil Fielder	10.00
(16)	*Chuck Finley*	8.00
(17)	*Tom Glavine*	30.00
(18)	*Juan Gonzalez*	40.00
(19a)	Ken Griffey, Jr. regular (Regular)	40.00
(19b)	Ken Griffey, Jr. spring (Spring Training)	40.00
(20)	Tony Gwynn	35.00
(21)	Dave Henderson	7.00
(22)	Rickey Henderson	10.00
(23a)	Bo Jackson regular (Regular)	9.00
(23b)	Bo Jackson spring (Spring Training)	10.00
(24)	Howard Johnson	10.00
(25)	*Felix Jose*	12.00
(26)	Dave Justice	15.00
(27)	Kevin Maas	8.00
(28)	Ramon Martinez	8.00
(29)	Fred McGriff	16.00
(30)	*Brian McRae*	9.00
(32)	Cal Ripken, Jr.	75.00
(33)	Nolan Ryan	35.00
(35)	Chris Sabo	8.00
(36)	Ryne Sandberg	18.00
(38)	Ruben Sierra	14.00
(39)	Darryl Strawberry	10.00
(41b)	*Frank Thomas fielding* (fielding)	25.00
(43)	Matt Williams	15.00

1992 Starting Lineup Baseball Extended

The 1992 Extended baseball includes the rookie figure of Steve Avery and second pose of Frank Thomas, whose rookie figure appeared in the 1992 46-player set. Also, Hall of Fame pitcher Tom Seaver was included in his Mets' uniform.

		MT
Complete Set (9):		175.00
(1)	*Steve Avery*	14.00
(2)	Bobby Bonilla	10.00
(3)	Eric Davis	8.00
(4)	Kirby Puckett	15.00
(5)	Bret Saberhagen	8.00
(6)	*Tom Seaver*	24.00
(7)	Danny Tartabull	10.00
(8)	*Frank Thomas Bat.*	34.00
(9)	*Todd Van Poppel*	10.00

1992 Starting Lineup Headline Collection

The 1992 seven-piece Headline set includes Nolan Ryan, Ken Griffey Jr. and George Brett's final Starting Lineup.

		MT
Complete Set (7):		150.00
(1)	George Brett	40.00
(2)	Cecil Fielder	15.00
(3)	Ken Griffey Jr.	40.00
(4)	Rickey Henderson	15.00
(5)	Bo Jackson	10.00
(6)	Nolan Ryan	50.00
(7)	Ryne Sandberg	32.00

1993 Starting Lineup Baseball

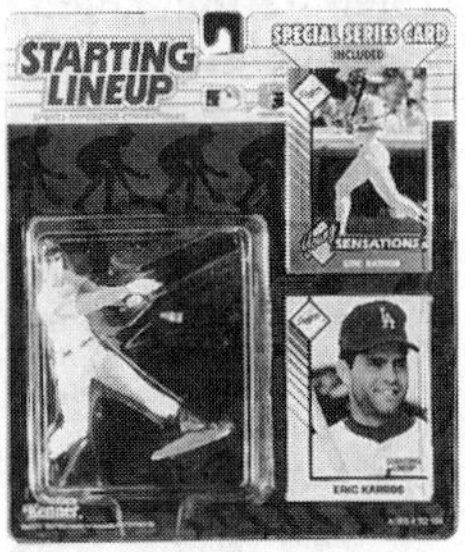

In its sixth year, the roster of these popular little figurines continued with 43 players in 45 collectible poses. As before, the moveable figures were blister-packed with two baseball cards. The "regular" card features a player portrait with a wide white border at left and bottom, highlighted by color stripes. At top-left is a color team logo. Back is the same format used since 1988. Each 1993 figure also includes a "Special Series" card on which the player action photo is bordered in color with white accent stripes. The theme of the "Special Series" is printed at bottom, above the player's name. On back, printed in blue is a short career summary of the player, along with logos of the toy company and Major League Baseball. Values of complete, unopened statue/cards packages listed alphabetically here are based on relative scarcity as well as demand. Loose figures will bring up to 40% of the values shown; single cards usually sell at about 15%.

		MT
Complete Set (38):		450.00
Common Piece:		10.00
(1)	Roberto Alomar	10.00
(2)	*Carlos Baerga*	10.00
(3)	*Jeff Bagwell*	35.00
(4a)	Barry Bonds Pirates (Pirates)	15.00
(5)	*Kevin Brown*	15.00
(6)	Jose Canseco	16.00
(7)	Will Clark	8.00
(8)	Roger Clemens	28.00
(9)	David Cone	10.00
(11)	*Travis Fryman*	15.00
(12)	Tom Glavine	25.00
(13)	Juan Gonzalez	20.00
(14)	Ken Griffey, Jr.	35.00
(15)	*Marquis Grissom*	10.00
(16)	*Juan Guzman*	8.00
(18)	*Eric Karros*	12.00
(19)	Roberto Kelly	6.00
(20)	John Kruk	12.00
(21)	*Ray Lankford*	12.00
(22)	Barry Larkin	15.00
(24)	*Shane Mack*	6.00
(25)	*Jack McDowell*	9.00
(26)	Fred McGriff	15.00
(27)	Mark McGwire	65.00
(28)	*Mike Mussina*	30.00
(30)	*Dean Palmer*	10.00
(31)	Terry Pendleton	6.00
(32)	Kirby Puckett	15.00
(33)	Cal Ripken, Jr.	40.00
(34)	*Bip Roberts*	9.00
(35)	Nolan Ryan	40.00
(37)	Ryne Sandberg	15.00
(39)	Gary Sheffield	10.00
(40)	*John Smoltz*	45.00
(41)	Frank Thomas	12.00
(42)	Andy Van Slyke	6.00
(43)	*Robin Ventura*	15.00
(44)	*Larry Walker*	32.00

1993 Starting Lineup Baseball Extended

Kenner's 1993 Extended baseball, a seven-piece release, included Nolan Ryan's retirement figure. The Greg Maddux figure, complete with a Braves' uniform, was Kenner's first Maddux piece since 1990.

		MT
Complete Set (7):		375.00
(1)	Barry Bonds (Giants)	15.00
(2)	Carlton Fisk	20.00
(3)	Bo Jackson	10.00
(4)	Greg Maddux	140.00
(5)	*David Nied*	10.00
(6)	Nolan Ryan (retired)	150.00
(7)	Benito Santiago	10.00

1993 Starting Lineup Baseball Stadium Stars

The 1993 Stadium Stars release was Kenner's debut of its figures adorning player stadiums. The six-piece set includes Ken Griffey Jr., Roger Clemens, Nolan Ryan and Frank Thomas.

		MT
Complete Set (6):		175.00
1	Roger Clemens	40.00
2	Cecil Fielder	20.00
3	Ken Griffey Jr.	40.00
4	Nolan Ryan	60.00
5	Ryne Sandberg	30.00
6	Frank Thomas	32.00

1993 Starting Lineup Headline Collection

The eight-player release was Kenner's final Headline issue and included a Cal Ripken Jr. figurine which describes his run at Lou Gehrig's consecutve game streak.

		MT
Complete Set (8):		180.00
1	Jim Abbott	14.00
2	Roberto Alomar	15.00
3	Tom Glavine	20.00
4	Mark McGwire	70.00
5	Cal Ripken	50.00
6	Nolan Ryan	50.00
7	Deion Sanders	20.00
8	Frank Thomas	20.00

1994 Starting Lineup Baseball

Many new players were added to Kenner's Starting Lineup for 1994. As in previous years, a blister pack containing a baseball card and a poseable plastic figure comprise the basic collectible unit. Cards have a player photo on a red background with white border. A team logo is in a purple stripe at top, while the player's name is in a yellow stripe at bottom. On back, personal data and complete career stats are printed in blue. Prices listed here are for complete, unopened statue/card packages. SLU values are determined by relative scarcity (not all figures are produced in similar quantities) as well as player popularity. Suggested retail price at issue was about $6. Loose statues are now selling for up to 40% of the total package value; cards will bring about 15%.

		MT
Complete Set (57):		450.00
Common Piece:		10.00
(1)	*Kevin Appier*	10.00
(2)	Steve Avery	10.00
(3)	Carlos Baerga	8.00
(4)	Jeff Bagwell	15.00
(5)	*Derek Bell*	12.00
(6)	*Jay Bell*	14.00
(7)	Albert Belle	10.00
(8)	Wade Boggs	8.00
(9)	Barry Bonds	10.00
(10)	*John Burkett*	7.00
(11)	Joe Carter	7.00
(12)	Roger Clemens	24.00
(13)	David Cone	10.00
(14)	*Chad Curtis*	10.00
(15)	*Darren Daulton*	8.00
(16)	Delino DeShields	8.00
(17)	*Alex Fernandez*	12.00
(18)	Cecil Fielder	8.00
(19)	Andres Galarraga	8.00
(21)	Mark Grace	8.00
(22)	*Tommy Greene*	8.00
(23)	Ken Griffey, Jr.	30.00
(24)	*Brian Harper*	8.00
(25)	*Bryan Harvey*	8.00
(26)	*Charlie Hayes*	8.00
(27)	*Chris Hoiles*	8.00
(28)	*Dave Hollins*	8.00
(29)	Gregg Jefferies	7.00
(30)	*Randy Johnson*	35.00
(31)	David Justice	10.00
(32)	Eric Karros	8.00
(33)	*Jimmy Key*	15.00
(34)	*Darryl Kile*	10.00
(35)	*Chuck Knoblauch*	16.00
(36)	Mark Langston	8.00
(38)	Don Mattingly	10.00
(39)	*Orlando Merced*	8.00
(40)	Paul Molitor	10.00
(41)	Mike Mussina	10.00
(42)	*John Olerud*	12.00
(43)	*Tony Phillips*	10.00
(44)	*Mike Piazza*	60.00
(45)	*Jose Rijo*	8.00
(46)	Cal Ripken, Jr.	40.00
(47)	*Ivan Rodriguez*	25.00
(48)	*Tim Salmon*	12.00
(49)	Ryne Sandberg	15.00
(50)	*Curt Schilling*	15.00
(51)	Gary Sheffield	7.00
(52)	*J.T. Snow*	12.00
(53)	Frank Thomas	15.00
(54)	Robby Thompson	7.00
(55)	*Greg Vaughn*	15.00
(56)	*Mo Vaughn*	18.00
(57)	Robin Ventura	7.00
(58)	Matt Williams	10.00
(59)	Dave Winfield	10.00

1994 Starting Lineup Baseball Extended

This eight-figure set includes the first SLUs of Steve Carlton and Rafael Palmeiro. Each figure comes packaged with a standard-size trading card of the player.

		MT
Complete Set (8):		150.00
(1)	*Steve Carlton*	15.00
(2)	Will Clark	12.00
(3)	Lenny Dykstra	12.00
(4)	Juan Gonzalez	20.00
(5)	*Kenny Lofton*	45.00
(6)	Fred McGriff	15.00
(7)	*Rafael Palmeiro*	15.00
(8)	Gary Sheffield power	12.00

1994 Starting Lineup Baseball Stadium Stars

The 1994 Stadium Stars features eight players atop their respective stadiums. The key figure in the set is Bo Jackson, although Deion Sanders' figure is gaining.

		MT
Complete Set (8):		200.00
(1)	Barry Bonds	20.00
(2)	Will Clark	18.00
(3)	Dennis Eckersley	18.00
(4)	Tom Glavine	25.00
(5)	Juan Gonzalez	25.00
(6)	Bo Jackson	50.00
(7)	Kirby Puckett	20.00
(8)	Deion Sanders	40.00

1994 Starting Lineup Cooperstown Collection

Kenner's 1994 Cooperstown set contained eight Hall of Famers including Lou Gehrig, Willie Mays, Cy Young and Babe Ruth. Jackie Robinson was also included in the set, in two versions: #42 and the ultra-rare error piece, #44.

		MT
Complete Set (8):		130.00
(1)	Ty Cobb	14.00
(2)	Lou Gehrig	14.00
(3)	Reggie Jackson	30.00
(4)	Willie Mays	16.00
(5a)	Jackie Robinson (42) (correct)	14.00
(5b)	Jackie Robinson (44) (error)	350.00
(6)	Babe Ruth	14.00
(7)	Honus Wagner	30.00
(8)	Cy Young	14.00

Checklists with card numbers in parentheses ( ) indicates the numbers do not appear on the card.

1995 Starting Lineup Baseball

A player action photo in a large circle with the left, right and bottom truncated at the edge is featured on the card inserted in 1995 SLU packaging. The player's name appears in white at the top, with a team logo in color at upper-left. Backs are printed in blue on white and feature full major league stats, a bit of biography and all appropriate logos. Prices quoted here are for complete sealed packages of card and statue. Loose statues will sell for up to 40% of the values shown; single cards can bring 15% of the total-package price.

		MT
Complete Set (58):		500.00
Common Piece:		10.00
(1)	Jim Abbott	10.00
(2)	*Moises Alou*	15.00
(3)	Carlos Baerga	8.00
(4)	Jeff Bagwell	14.00
(5)	Albert Belle	10.00
(6)	*Geronimo Berroa*	10.00
(7)	*Dante Bichette*	14.00
(8)	Barry Bonds	12.00
(9)	*Jay Buhner*	14.00
(10)	Jose Canseco	12.00
(11)	*Chuck Carr*	10.00
(12)	Joe Carter	8.00
(13)	*Andujar Cedeno*	10.00
(14)	Will Clark	8.00
(15)	Roger Clemens	20.00
(16)	*Jeff Conine*	10.00
(17)	*Scott Cooper*	10.00
(18)	Darren Daulton	10.00
(19)	*Carlos Delgado*	18.00
(20)	Cecil Fielder	8.00
(21)	*Cliff Floyd*	10.00
(22)	Julio Franco	8.00
(23)	Juan Gonzalez	10.00
(24)	Ken Griffey, Jr.	30.00
(25)	Tony Gwynn	20.00
(26)	*Bob Hamelin*	10.00
(27)	*Jeffrey Hammonds*	12.00
(28)	Randy Johnson	16.00
(29)	*Jeff Kent*	10.00
(30)	*Jeff King*	10.00
(31)	*Ryan Klesko*	20.00
(32)	Chuck Knoblauch	10.00
(33)	John Kruk	10.00
(34)	Ray Lankford	8.00
(35)	Barry Larkin	12.00
(36)	*Javier Lopez*	25.00
(37)	*Al Martin*	10.00
(38)	Brian McRae	8.00
(39)	Paul Molitor	8.00
(40)	*Raul Mondesi*	25.00
(41)	Mike Mussina	8.00
(42)	*Troy Neel*	10.00
(43)	*Dave Nilsson*	12.00
(44)	John Olerud	8.00
(45)	Paul O'Neill	10.00
(46)	Mike Piazza	25.00
(47)	Kirby Puckett	10.00
(48)	Cal Ripken, Jr.	35.00
(49)	Tim Salmon	10.00
(50)	Deion Sanders	12.00
(51)	*Reggie Sanders*	10.00
(52)	*Sammy Sosa*	90.00
(53)	Mickey Tettleton	12.00
(54)	Frank Thomas	12.00
(55)	Andy Van Slyke	10.00
(56)	Mo Vaughn	10.00
(57)	*Rich Wilkins*	10.00
(58)	Matt Williams	10.00

1995 Starting Lineup Baseball Extended

Thanks to the Alex Rodriguez rookie piece, this nine-player set is extremely popular. Other key pieces are Kenny Lofton's second SLU, Mike Piazza's third SLU and Cal Ripken Jr.'s streak piece.

	MT
Complete Set (9):	300.00
Jose Canseco	12.00
Rusty Greer	16.00
Kenny Lofton	40.00
Tom Pagnozzi	10.00
Mike Piazza hitting	30.00
Manny Ramirez	75.00
Cal Ripken Jr.	70.00
Alex Rodriguez	125.00
Mike Schmidt	15.00

1995 Starting Lineup Baseball Stadium Stars

The 1995 Stadium Stars 10-piece set is led by Randy Johnson, Ken Griffey Jr. and Greg Maddux.

		MT
Complete Set (9):		250.00
(1)	Darren Daulton	20.00
(2)	Lenny Dykstra	20.00
(3)	Ken Griffey Jr.	35.00
(4)	Randy Johnson	65.00
(5)	Dave Justice	20.00
(6)	Greg Maddux	60.00
(7)	Mark McGwire	62.00
(8)	Frank Thomas	20.00
(9)	Mo Vaughn	20.00

1995 Starting Lineup Cooperstown Collection

Kenner continued its line-up of action figures of former baseball stars with this series in 1995. Packaged with each plastic statue is a baseball card depicting the player in a contemporary photo. The words "Cooperstown Collection" are prominently printed in gold in the blue background above the photo's ornate frame. Backs are printed in blue on white and contain complete career stats and a few personal details, plus appropriate licensors' logos and rights notices.

		MT
Complete Set (10):		125.00
(1)	Rod Carew	10.00
(2)	Dizzy Dean	10.00
(3)	Don Drysdale	10.00
(4)	Bob Feller	10.00
(5)	Whitey Ford	10.00
(6)	Bob Gibson	10.00
(7)	Harmon Killebrew	18.00
(8)	Eddie Mathews	15.00
(9)	Satchel Paige	10.00
(10)	Babe Ruth	15.00

1996 Starting Lineup Baseball

The 1996 base set features 69 players and includes the first pieces of Wil Cordero, Hideo Nomo, Ken Caminiti, Derek Jeter and Edgar Martinez. Chipper Jones' rookie piece, though, is the hottest rookie release of the set.

		MT
Complete Set (52):		550.00
(1)	Roberto Alomar	10.00
(2a)	Jeff Bagwell blk (black bat)	10.00
(2b)	Jeff Bagwell tan (tan bat)	15.00
(3)	Albert Belle	10.00
(4)	Craig Biggio	10.00
(5)	Barry Bonds	10.00
(6)	*Ricky Bones*	8.00
(7)	*Rico Brogna*	10.00
(8)	*Ken Caminiti*	15.00
(9)	*Vinny Castilla*	16.00
(10)	Will Clark	8.00
(11)	David Cone	10.00
(12)	Wil Cordero	10.00
(13)	*Marty Cordova*	12.00
(14)	Shawon Dunston	8.00
(15)	Lenny Dykstra	8.00
(16)	*Jim Edmonds*	12.00
(17)	*Jim Eisenreich*	8.00
(18)	Gary Gaetti	8.00
(19)	Ron Gant	8.00
(20)	Ken Griffey Jr.	20.00
(21)	Marquis Grissom	12.00
(22)	Ozzie Guillen	8.00
(23)	*Brian Hunter*	10.00
(24)	*Derek Jeter*	80.00
(25)	*Charles Johnson*	12.00
(26)	*Chipper Jones*	155.00
(27)	Greg Maddux	40.00
(28)	*Jeff Manto*	10.00
(29)	*Edgar Martinez*	15.00
(30)	Fred McGriff	8.00
(31)	Mark McGwire	35.00
(32)	Raul Mondesi	10.00
(33)	Eddie Murray	12.00
(34a)	*Hideo Nomo gray* (gray)	15.00
(34b)	*Hideo Nomo white* (white)	15.00
(35)	Paul O'Neil	8.00
(36)	Mike Piazza	18.00
(37)	Kirby Puckett	10.00
(38)	Cal Ripken Jr. (fielding)	32.00
(39)	Cal Ripken Jr. (sliding)	32.00
(40)	Ivan Rodriguez	10.00
(41)	Deion Sanders	8.00
(42)	Ozzie Smith	12.00
(43)	Sammy Sosa	35.00
(44)	Terry Steinbach	8.00
(45)	Frank Thomas	12.00
(46)	*Jim Thome*	25.00
(47)	*Ryan Thompson*	8.00
(48)	*John Valentin*	10.00
(49)	Mo Vaughn	8.00
(50)	Larry Walker	15.00
(51)	*Rondell White*	10.00
(52)	Matt Williams	8.00

1996 Starting Lineup Baseball Extended

The 16-player release was Kenner's largest Extended issue to date and included Ken Griffey Jr. and Don Mattingly in the new standing pose.

		MT
Complete Set (16):		220.00
(1)	Moises Alou	12.00
(2)	*Garret Anderson*	12.00
(3)	Carlos Baerga	10.00
(4)	Dante Bichette	12.00
(5)	Joe Carter	10.00
(6)	Jeff Conine	10.00
(7)	Chad Curtis	10.00
(8)	Juan Gonzalez	20.00
(9)	Ken Griffey Jr.	55.00
(10)	Dave Justice	15.00
(11)	Eric Karros	10.00
(12)	Barry Larkin	15.00
(13)	Don Mattingly	18.00
(14)	*Hal Morris*	8.00
(15)	Denny Neagle	18.00
(16)	Rafael Palmeiro	12.00

1996 Starting Lineup Baseball Stadium Stars

The 11-figure release featured top contemporary players atop their respective home stadiums, except for Mike Piazza, Cal Ripken Jr. and Albert Belle who appear on Philadelphia's Veterans Stadium, site of the 1996 All-Star Game.

		MT
Complete Set (11):		275.00
(1)	Albert Belle	20.00
(2)	Jay Buhner	25.00
(3)	Jose Canseco	20.00
(4)	Darren Daulton	20.00
(5)	Mark Grace	20.00
(6)	Chuck Knoblauch	20.00
(7)	Javy Lopez	35.00
(8)	Mike Piazza	35.00
(9)	Cal Ripken Jr.	55.00
(10)	Robin Ventura	20.00
(11)	Matt Williams	20.00

1996 Starting Lineup Cooperstown Collection

The 10-piece release is led by the Hank Aaron and Jackie Robinson pieces. The Robinson SLU is Kenner's second attempt at his Cooperstown issue. In 1994, Kenner inadvertently made some Robinsons with #44, not his #42.

		MT
Complete Set (10):		125.00
Set price does not include the Ashburn.		
(1)	Hank Aaron	20.00
(2)	Grover Alexander	10.00
(3)	Richie Ashburn (produced for sale exclusively at a Philadelphia-area retail chain)	20.00
(4)	Roberto Clemente	16.00
(5)	Jimmie Foxx	15.00
(6)	Hank Greenberg	10.00
(7)	Rogers Hornsby	15.00
(8)	Joe Morgan	10.00
(9)	Mel Ott	10.00
(10)	Robin Roberts	15.00
(11)	Jackie Robinson	18.00

1996 Starting Lineup Cooperstown 12" Figures

The 12-inch set featured two Babe Ruths: Boston Red Sox and New York Yankees. The Red Sox figure was available through Kay-Bee toy stores. The Honus Wagner piece was sold through Toys R Us.

		MT
Complete Set (6):		130.00
(1)	Ty Cobb	15.00
(2)	Lou Gehrig	15.00
(3)	Babe Ruth (Red Sox)	15.00
(4)	Babe Ruth (Yankees)	15.00
(5)	Honus Wagner	15.00
(6)	Cy Young	15.00

1997 Starting Lineup Baseball

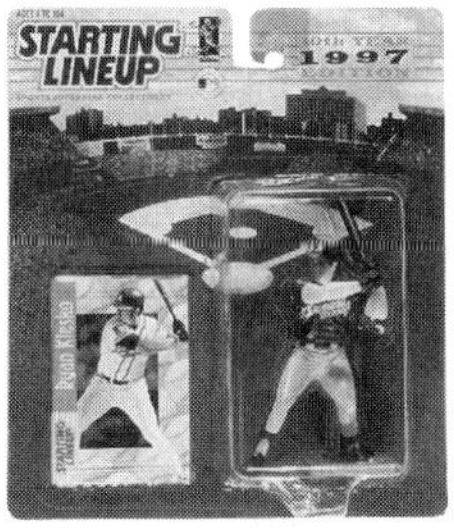

The 1997 release features the rookies of Scott Brosius, Johnny Damon, Steve Finley, Todd Hundley, Jason Isringhausen, John Jaha, Jason Kendall, Tino Martinez, Brian McRae, Jose Mesa, Rey Ordonez, Chan Ho Park, Henry Rodriguez, Ismael Valdes and Bernie Williams.

		MT
Complete Set (48):		700.00
(1)	Roberto Alomar	10.00
(2)	Brady Anderson	12.00
(3)	Jeff Bagwell	10.00
(4)	Derek Bell	8.00
(5)	Albert Belle	12.00
(6)	Dante Bichette	10.00
(7)	Barry Bonds	12.00
(8)	*Scott Brosius*	10.00
(9)	Ellis Burks	12.00
(10)	Roger Clemens	20.00
(11)	*Johnny Damon*	10.00
(12)	*Steve Finley*	10.00
(13)	Tom Glavine	15.00
(14)	Rusty Greer	8.00
(15)	Ken Griffey Jr.	20.00
(16)	*Todd Hundley*	12.00
(17)	*Jason Isringhausen*	10.00
(18)	*John Jaha*	10.00
(19)	Randy Johnson	15.00
(20)	Chipper Jones	35.00
(21)	*Brian Jordan*	16.00
(22)	Wally Joyner	8.00
(23)	*Jason Kendall*	14.00
(24)	Ryan Klesko	15.00
(25)	Javier Lopez	14.00
(26)	*Tino Martinez*	30.00
(27)	Brian McRae	8.00
(28)	*Jose Mesa*	10.00
(29)	Paul Molitor	10.00
(30)	Raul Mondesi	10.00
(31)	Hideo Nomo	12.00
(32)	*Rey Ordonez*	18.00
(33)	*Chan Ho Park*	15.00
(34)	Mike Piazza	12.00
(35)	Manny Ramirez	15.00
(36)	Cal Ripken Jr	16.00
(37)	Alex Rodriguez	20.00
(38)	*Henry Rodriguez*	12.00
(39)	Ivan Rodriguez	12.00
(40)	Ryne Sandberg	10.00
(41)	Reggie Sanders	8.00
(42)	John Smoltz	18.00
(43)	J.T. Snow	12.00
(44)	Frank Thomas	12.00
(45)	*Ismael Valdes*	15.00
(46)	Devon White	10.00

(47)	*Bernie Williams*	20.00
(48)	Matt Williams	10.00

1997 Starting Lineup Baseball Extended

This 14-figure set includes the first figures of Tony Clark, Andruw Jones and Andy Pettitte. Each figure comes with a standard-size trading card of the player.

	MT
Complete Set (14):	200.00
Albert Belle	10.00
Ricky Bottalico	10.00
Ken Caminiti	10.00
Tony Clark	18.00
Roger Clemens	18.00
Dennis Eckersley	10.00
Derek Jeter	25.00
Andruw Jones	25.00
Mark McGwire	30.00
Mike Mussina	10.00
Andy Pettitte	20.00
Alex Rodriguez	15.00
Deion Sanders	10.00
Matt Williams	10.00

1997 Starting Lineup Baseball Freeze Frames

This six-figure set was exclusive to Toys R Us stores. The set was packaged in two case assortments.

		MT
Complete Set (6):		200.00
(1)	Dante Bichette	15.00
(2)	Juan Gonzalez	15.00
(3)	Ken Griffey Jr.	35.00
(4)	Chipper Jones	35.00
(5)	Mike Piazza	20.00
(6)	Frank Thomas	20.00

1997 Starting Lineup Baseball Microverse

This was the first release of the Microverse line. The four 1" figures were packaged in the Swinging Stars assortment. The second assortment, Living Legends, was never released.

	MT
Complete Set (1):	12.00
Bonds, Griffey, Piazza, Thomas	12.00

1997 Starting Lineup Baseball 12" Figures

This four-figure set features current stars in Kenner's 12" format. A 12" Jackie Robinson piece was created as a Target retail special.

		MT
Complete Set (4):		150.00
(1)	Ken Griffey Jr.	35.00
(2)	Greg Maddux	25.00
(3)	Mike Piazza	25.00
(4)	Cal Ripken Jr.	25.00

1997 Starting Lineup Classic Doubles

The first series of Classic Doubles featured 10 pairs of players featured on regular SLUs. Each set came with a standard-size trading card for each player.

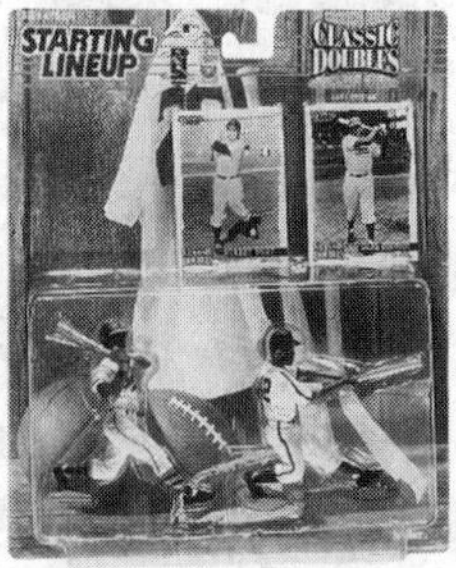

		MT
Complete Set (10):		275.00
(1)	Hank Aaron, Jackie Robinson	15.00
(2)	Barry Bonds, Bobby Bonds	15.00
(3)	Don Drysdale, Hideo Nomo	15.00
(4)	Ken Griffey Sr., Ken Griffey Jr.	25.00
(5)	Randy Johnson, Nolan Ryan	30.00
(6)	Greg Maddux, Cy Young	60.00
(7)	Mickey Mantle, Roger Maris	30.00
(8)	Roger Maris, Mark McGwire	65.00
(9)	Cal Ripken Jr., Brooks Robinson	25.00
(10)	Babe Ruth, Frank Thomas	25.00

1997 Starting Lineup Cooperstown Collection

The 10-figure Cooperstown Collection set featured baseball players who are members of the Hall of Fame. The set includes the first woman baseball player to have an SLU, Dottie Kamenshek. Each figure is packaged with a standard-size trading card of the player.

		MT
Complete Set (11):		125.00
(1)	Johnny Bench	10.00
(2)	Rollie Fingers	10.00
(3)	Josh Gibson	10.00
(4)	Walter Johnson	12.00
(5)	Dotty Kamenshek	10.00
(6)	Mickey Mantle	20.00
(7)	Brooks Robinson	15.00
(8)	Jackie Robinson	75.00
(9)	Duke Snider	10.00
(10)	Hoyt Wilhelm	10.00
(11)	Carl Yastrzemski	10.00

1997 Starting Lineup Cooperstown Stadium Stars

This seven-figure set features Hall of Fame players. Each player is standing on top of a replica of his home stadium.

		MT
Complete Set (7):		175.00
		25.00
(1)	Hank Aaron	20.00
(2)	Fergie Jenkins	20.00
(3)	Al Kaline	20.00
(4)	Mickey Mantle	35.00
(5)	Babe Ruth	25.00
(6)	Mike Schmidt	20.00
(7)	Carl Yastrzemski	20.00

1997 Starting Lineup Nolan Ryan Minor League

	MT
Nolan Ryan	25.00

1998 Starting Lineup Baseball

The figures in this 39-piece set are packaged with a standard-size trading card. The set includes first figures of Nomar Garciaparra, Darin Erstad and Mariano Rivera.

	MT
Complete Set (40):	450.00
Albert Belle	8.00
Craig Biggio	10.00
Barry Bonds	10.00
Kevin Brown	10.00
Jose Canseco	12.00
Will Clark	8.00
Darin Erstad	14.00
Andres Galarraga	8.00
Nomar Garciaparra	65.00
Tom Glavine	15.00
Juan Gonzalez	10.00
Mark Grace	10.00
Mark Grace Special	25.00
Ken Griffey Jr.	20.00
Mark Grudzielanek	10.00
Tony Gwynn	12.00
Bobby Higginson	10.00
Glenallen Hill	8.00
Derek Jeter	18.00
Chipper Jones	22.00
David Justice	10.00
Chuck Knoblauch	12.00
Ray Lankford	8.00
Barry Larkin	10.00
Mickey Morandini	10.00
Marc Newfield	8.00
Hideo Nomo	10.00
Rafael Palmeiro	10.00
Mike Piazza	15.00
Cal Ripken Jr.	15.00
Mariano Rivera	25.00
Alex Rodriguez	15.00
Deion Sanders	12.00
Gary Sheffield	10.00
Ed Sprague	10.00
Frank Thomas	12.00
Jim Thome	10.00
Mo Vaughn	10.00
Larry Walker	12.00
Bernie Williams	10.00

1998 Starting Lineup Baseball Extended

This 14-figure set features the first SLUs of Scott Rolen and Hideki Irabu as well as the first piece portraying Mark McGwire in a St. Louis Cardinals' uniform. Each piece comes with a standard-size trading card.

	MT
Complete Set (14):	300.00
Sandy Alomar	8.00
Moises Alou	12.00
Jay Bell	10.00
Jim Edmonds	12.00
Ken Griffey Jr.	18.00
Hideki Irabu	15.00
Greg Maddux	20.00
Fred McGriff	10.00
Mark McGwire	100.00
Dean Palmer	8.00
Scott Rolen	35.00
Sammy Sosa	90.00
Larry Walker	12.00
Tony Womack	15.00

1998 Starting Lineup Baseball Classic Doubles

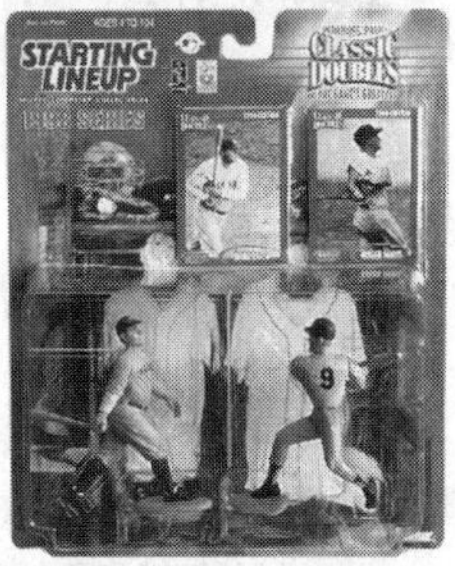

This set consists of 10 pairs of figures. Five of the sets feature legendary players and the other five portray current stars. Each set comes with two trading cards, one for each player.

	MT
Complete Set (10):	200.00
Albert Belle, Frank Thomas	20.00
Johnny Bench, Joe Morgan	20.00
Yogi Berra, Thurman Munson	20.00
Jose Canseco, Mark McGwire	35.00
Reggie Jackson, Catfish Hunter	20.00
Derek Jeter, Rey Ordonez	24.00
Mike Piazza, Ivan Rodriguez	24.00
Alex Rodriguez, Ken Griffey Jr.	25.00
Babe Ruth, Roger Maris	25.00
Nolan Ryan, Walter Johnson	25.00

1998 Starting Lineup Baseball Freeze Frame

	MT
Complete Set (6):	140.00
Jeff Bagwell	20.00
Barry Bonds	20.00
Derek Jeter	25.00
Greg Maddux	25.00
Cal Ripken	25.00
Alex Rodriguez	25.00

1998 Starting Lineup Baseball Stadium Stars

This seven-figure set featured star players standing on top of a replica of their home stadium.

	MT
Complete Set (7):	150.00
Albert Belle	20.00
Ken Griffey Jr.	24.00
Mike Piazza	25.00
Cal Ripken Jr.	24.00
Ivan Rodriguez	25.00
John Smoltz	20.00
Bernie Williams	20.00

1998 Starting Lineup Baseball 12" Figures

	MT
Complete Set (4):	100.00
Derek Jeter	25.00
Chipper Jones	25.00
Hideo Nomo	25.00
Alex Rodriguez	25.00

1998 Starting Lineup Cooperstown Collection

This 11-figure set features Hall of Fame players. The standard-size SLUs come with a trading card of the player.

	MT
Complete Set (11):	100.00
Yogi Berra	8.00
Lou Brock	10.00
Roy Campanella	8.00
Roberto Clemente	12.00
Buck Leonard	8.00
Phil Niekro	8.00
Jim Palmer	10.00
Frank Robinson	8.00
Tom Seaver	8.00
Warren Spahn	10.00
Tris Speaker	15.00

1999 Starting Lineup Baseball

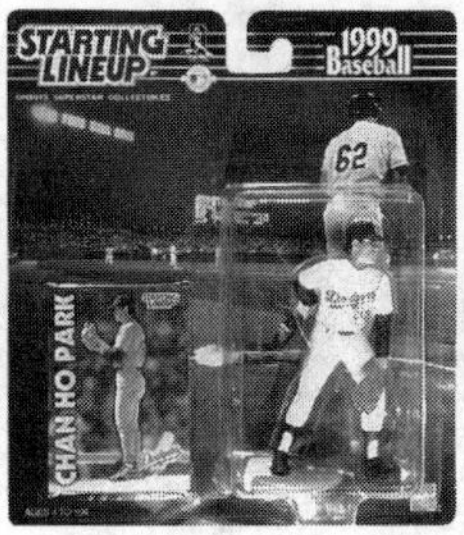

	MT
Complete Set (39):	525.00
Common Player:	12.00
Edgardo Alfonzo	20.00
Wilson Alvarez	10.00
Jeff Bagwell	10.00
Vinny Castilla	12.00
Tony Clark	10.00
Roger Clemens	14.00
David Cone	12.00
Jose Cruz Jr.	18.00

Darin Erstad	12.00
Nomar Garciaparra	18.00
Juan Gonzalez	10.00
Ken Griffey Jr.	15.00
Vladimir Guerrero	45.00
Jose Guillen	10.00
Tony Gwynn	12.00
Livan Hernandez	14.00
Derek Jeter	12.00
Randy Johnson	14.00
Chipper Jones	15.00
Travis Lee	15.00
Kenny Lofton	10.00
Mark McGwire	20.00
Pedro Martinez	45.00
Tino Martinez	12.00
Denny Neagle	10.00
Chan Ho Park	12.00
Mike Piazza	15.00
Brad Radke	10.00
Manny Ramirez	10.00
Edgar Renteria	12.00
Cal Ripken Jr.	15.00
Scott Rolen	15.00
Scott Rolen	15.00
Alex Rodriguez	12.00
Ivan Rodriguez	10.00
Sammy Sosa	20.00
Omar Vizquel	20.00
Larry Walker	14.00
Kerry Wood	18.00

1999 Starting Lineup Baseball Extended

	MT
Complete Set (10):	175.00
Kevin Brown	10.00
Sean Casey	40.00
J.D. Drew	25.00
Nomar Garciaparra	15.00
Ben Grieve	15.00
Greg Maddux	12.00
Mo Vaughn	10.00
Dave Wells	10.00
Bernie Williams	10.00
Jaret Wright	12.00

1999 Starting Lineup Baseball One-on-One

	MT
Complete Set (5):	100.00
Sandy Alomar, Ken Griffey Jr.	35.00
Nomar Garciaparra, Jim Edmonds	25.00
Chipper Jones, Larry Walker	28.00
Jason Kendall, Rey Ordonez	25.00
Cal Ripken Jr., Kenny Lofton	30.00

1999 Starting Lineup Baseball Stadium Stars

	MT
Complete Set (7):	160.00
Roger Clemens	25.00
Nomar Garciaparra	25.00
Derek Jeter	25.00
Chipper Jones	25.00
Kenny Lofton	25.00
Mark McGwire	35.00
Alex Rodriguez	25.00

1999 Starting Lineupe Baseball Wal-Mart Exclusives

	MT
Complete Set (8):	180.00
Mark McGwire Reg.	18.00
Sammy Sosa Reg.	18.00
Mark McGwire Stad. Star	35.00
Sammy Sosa Stad. Star	35.00
Mark McGwire Sports Star	20.00
Sammy Sosa Sports Star	20.00
Mark McGwire CD, Roger Maris CD	25.00
Sammy Sosa CD, Roger Maris CD	25.00

1999 Starting Lineup Baseball 12" Figures

	MT
Complete Set (6):	150.00
Common Player:	
Roger Clemens	25.00
Nomar Garciaparra	25.00
Ken Griffey Jr.	25.00
Tony Gwynn	25.00
Mark McGwire	40.00
Sammy Sosa	25.00

1999 Starting Lineup Classic Doubles

For its 1999 Classic Doubles series, Hasbro used the theme "From the Minors to the Majors". Each 10" x 12" blister-pack contains two figures and two baseball cards; one depicting the player with his '99 major league team, and the other with one of his minor league teams. Values shown are for complete, unopened packages.

		MT
Complete Set (10):		175.00
Common Player:		10.00
(1)	Sandy Alomar	20.00
(2)	Darin Erstad	18.00
(3)	Nomar Garciaparra	24.00
(4)	Ken Griffey Jr.	30.00
(5)	Derek Jeter	24.00
(6)	Javy Lopez	20.00
(7)	Greg Maddux	25.00
(8)	Mark McGwire	35.00
(9)	Raul Mondesi	20.00
(10)	Alex Rodriguez	25.00

1999 Starting Lineup Cooperstown Collection

	MT
Complete Set (7):	80.00
Common Player:	
George Brett	16.00
Pepper Davis	10.00
Bob Gibson	10.00
Juan Marichal	10.00
Nolan Ryan	20.00
Earl Weaver	12.00
Ted Williams	16.00

1996 Stouffer's Legends of Baseball

To promote its French bread frozen pizza, this Nestle's subsidiary issued a series of five three-dimensional cards featuring current and future Hall of Famers. The 2-1/2" x 3-1/2" cards have a die-cut action photo on front connected to a tab at the card top. When the tab is pulled, the player figure stands up. The back of the card has another player photo and a few career highlights. Because the promotion was licensed only by individuals, and not Major League Baseball, uniform and cap logos have been air-brushed off the photos.

		MT
Complete Set (6):		2.00
Common Player:		.50
1	Yogi Berra	1.00
2	Gary Carter	.50
3	Don Drysdale	1.00
4	Bob Feller	1.00
5	Willie Stargell	.75

1985 Straw Hat Pizza California Angels

The 25th anniversary of the Los Angeles/California Angels expansion team was marked with a set of posters issued by the Straw Hat Pizza restaurants in Southern California. The 11" x 16" posters are printed on thin, textured cardboard and feature color portrait paintings of Angels stars with commemorative dates, logos and a facsimile autograph. Beneath the picture are logos of the pizza chain and a local radio station. Coupons at bottom offer discounts on a pizza and a chance to enter a drawing to win the original paintings on which the posters were based. The blank-backed, unnumbered posters are checklisted here alphabetically.

		MT
Complete Set (13):		85.00
Common Player:		5.00
(1)	Gene Autry	7.50
(2)	Don Baylor	5.00
(3)	Bo Belinsky	7.50
(4)	Rod Carew	10.00
(5)	Dean Chance	5.00
(6)	Jim Fregosi	5.00
(7)	Bobby Grich, Bobby Knoop	5.00
(8)	Reggie Jackson	10.00
(9)	Alex Johnson	5.00
(10)	Ted Kluszewski, Albie Pearson	7.50
(11)	Nolan Ryan	30.00
(12)	Frank Tanana	5.00
(13)	Mike Witt	5.00

1983 Stuart Expos

This set of Montreal Expos players and coaches was issued by a Montreal area baking company for inclusion in packages of snack cakes. The 30 cards feature full-color player photos, with the player name, number and team logo also on the card fronts. The backs list brief player biographies in both English and French. Twenty-five players are pictured on the 2-1/2" x 3-1/2" cards.

		MT
Complete Set (30):		9.00
Common Player:		.40
1	Bill Virdon	.40
2	Woodie Fryman	.40
3	Vern Rapp	.40
4	Andre Dawson	3.00
5	Jeff Reardon	.40
6	Al Oliver	.50
7	Doug Flynn	.40
8	Gary Carter	3.00
9	Tim Raines	2.25
10	Steve Rogers	.40
11	Billy DeMars	.40
12	Tim Wallach	.50
13	Galen Cisco	.40
14	Terry Francona	.40
15	Bill Gullickson	.40
16	Ray Burris	.40
17	Scott Sanderson	.40
18	Warren Cromartie	.40
19	Jerry White	.40
20	Bobby Ramos	.40
21	Jim Wolhford	.40
22	Dan Schatzeder	.40
23	Charlie Lea	.40
24	Bryan Little	.40
25	Mel Wright	.40
26	Tim Blackwell	.40
27	Chris Speier	.40
28	Randy Lerch	.40
29	Bryn Smith	.40
30	Brad Mills	.40

1984 Stuart Expos

For the second year in a row, Stuart Cakes issued a full-color card set of the Montreal Expos. The 2-1/2" x 3-1/2" cards again list the player name and number along with the team and company logos on the card fronts. The backs are bilingual with biographical information in both English and French. The 40-card set was issued in two series. Card numbers 21-40, issued late in the summer, are more difficult to find than the first 20 cards. The 40 cards include players, the manager, coaches and team mascot.

		MT
Complete Set (40):		12.00
Common Player (1-20):		.25
Common Player (21-40):		.50
1	Youppi! (mascot)	.25
2	Bill Virdon	.25
3	Billy DeMars	.25
4	Galen Cisco	.25
5	Russ Nixon	.25
6	Felipe Alou	.65
7	Dan Schatzeder	.25
8	Charlie Lea	.25
9	Bobby Ramos	.25
10	Bob James	.25
11	Andre Dawson	2.00
12	Gary Lucas	.25
13	Jeff Reardon	.35
14	Tim Wallach	.35
15	Gary Carter	2.00
16	Bill Gullickson	.25
17	Pete Rose	6.00
18	Terry Francona	.25
19	Steve Rogers	.25
20	Tim Raines	1.25
21	Bryn Smith	.25
22	Greg Harris	.50
23	David Palmer	.50
24	Jim Wohlford	.50
25	Miguel Dilone	.50
26	Mike Stenhouse	.50
27	Chris Speier	.50
28	Derrel Thomas	.50
29	Doug Flynn	.50
30	Bryan Little	.50
31	Argenis Salazar	.50
32	Mike Fuentes	.50
33	Joe Kerrigan	.50
34	Andy McGaffigan	.50
35	Fred Breining	.50
36	Expos 1983 All-Stars (Gary Carter, Andre Dawson, Tim Raines, Steve Rogers)	.75
37	Co-Players Of The Year (Andre Dawson, Tim Raines)	.75
38	Expos' Coaching Staff (Felipe Alou, Galen Cisco, Billy DeMars, Joe Kerrigan, Russ Nixon, Bill Virdon)	.50
39	Team Photo	.50
40	Checklist	.10

1987 Stuart

Twenty-eight four-part folding panels make up the 1987 Stuart Super Stars set, which was issued only in Canada. Three player cards and a sweepstakes entry form card comprise each panel. All 26 major league teams are included with the Montreal Expos and Toronto Blue Jays being represented twice. The cards, which are full color and measure 2-1/2" x 3-1/2", are written in both English and French. The card backs contain the player's previous year's statistics. All team insignias have been airbrushed away.

		MT
Complete Panel Set (28):		45.00
Complete Singles Set (84):		20.00
Common Panel:		.75
Common Single Player:		.10
Panel (New York Mets)		1.25
1a	Gary Carter	.25
1b	Keith Hernandez	.10
1c	Darryl Strawberry	.25
Panel (Atlanta Braves)		1.25
2a	Bruce Benedict	.10
2b	Ken Griffey	.15
2c	Dale Murphy	.30
Panel (Chicago Cubs)		1.00
3a	Jody Davis	.10
3b	Andre Dawson	.25
3c	Leon Durham	.10
Panel (Cincinnati Reds)		1.00
4a	Buddy Bell	.10
4b	Eric Davis	.15
4c	Dave Parker	.15
Panel (Houston Astros)		3.50
5a	Glenn Davis	.10
5b	Nolan Ryan	1.50
5c	Mike Scott	.10
Panel (Los Angeles Dodgers)		.75
6a	Pedro Guerrero	.10
6b	Mike Marshall	.10
6c	Fernando Valenzuela	.15
Panel (Montreal Expos)		1.00
7a	Tim Raines	.25
7b	Tim Wallach	.10
7c	Mitch Webster	.10
Panel (Montreal Expos)		.75
8a	Hubie Brooks	.10
8b	Bryn Smith	.10
8c	Floyd Youmans	.10
Panel (Philadelphia Phillies)		2.50
9a	Shane Rawley	.10
9b	Juan Samuel	.10
9c	Mike Schmidt	1.00
Panel (Pittsburgh Pirates)		.75
10a	Jim Morrison	.10
10b	Johnny Ray	.10
10c	R.J. Reynolds	.10
Panel (St. Louis Cardinals)		1.50
11a	Jack Clark	.10
11b	Vince Coleman	.10

11c	Ozzie Smith	.50
	Panel (San Diego Padres)	2.00
12a	Steve Garvey	.25
12b	Tony Gwynn	.60
12c	John Kruk	.10
	Panel (San Francisco Giants)	.75
13a	Chili Davis	.15
13b	Jeffrey Leonard	.10
13c	Robbie Thompson	.10
	Panel (Baltimore Orioles)	5.00
14a	Fred Lynn	.10
14b	Eddie Murray	.75
14c	Cal Ripken, Jr.	2.00
	Panel (Boston Red Sox)	3.25
15a	Don Baylor	.15
15b	Wade Boggs	.75
15c	Roger Clemens	.90
	Panel (California Angels)	.80
16a	Doug DeCinces	.10
16b	Wally Joyner	.15
16c	Mike Witt	.10
	Panel (Chicago White Sox)	1.50
17a	Harold Baines	.15
17b	Carlton Fisk	.50
17c	Ozzie Guillen	.10
	Panel (Cleveland Indians)	.75
18a	Joe Carter	.15
18b	Julio Franco	.10
18c	Pat Tabler	.10
	Panel (Detroit Tigers)	.75
19a	Kirk Gibson	.10
19b	Jack Morris	.10
19c	Alan Trammell	.15
	Panel (Kansas City Royals)	2.50
20a	George Brett	1.00
20b	Bret Saberhagen	.15
20c	Willie Wilson	.10
	Panel (Milwaukee Brewers)	3.00
21a	Cecil Cooper	.10
21b	Paul Molitor	.75
21c	Robin Yount	1.00
	Panel (Minnesota Twins)	1.50
22a	Tom Brunansky	.10
22b	Kent Hrbek	.15
22c	Kirby Puckett	.75
	Panel (New York Yankees)	5.00
23a	Rickey Henderson	.60
23b	Don Mattingly	1.00
23c	Dave Winfield	.75
	Panel (Oakland A's)	2.00
24a	Jose Canseco	.65
24b	Alfredo Griffin	.10
24c	Carney Lansford	.10
	Panel (Seattle Mariners)	.75
25a	Phil Bradley	.10
25b	Alvin Davis	.10
25c	Mark Langston	.15
	Panel (Texas Rangers)	.75
26a	Pete Incaviglia	.10
26b	Pete O'Brien	.10
26c	Larry Parrish	.10
	Panel (Toronto Blue Jays)	.75
27a	Jesse Barfield	.10
27b	George Bell	.10
27c	Tony Fernandez	.10
	Panel (Toronto Blue Jays)	.75
28a	Lloyd Moseby	.10
28b	Dave Stieb	.10
28c	Ernie Whitt	.10

1991 Studio Preview

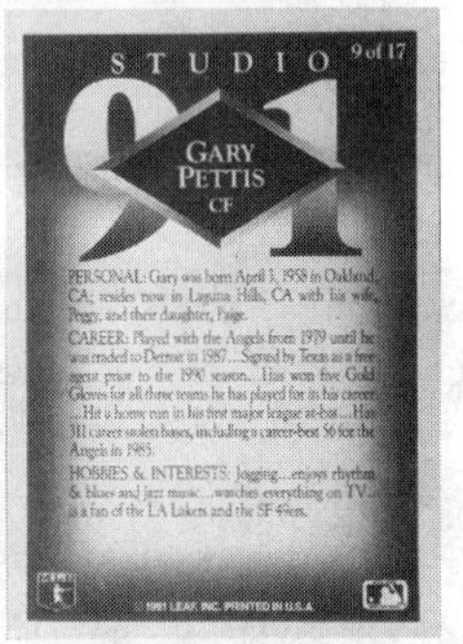

Each 1991 Donruss set packaged for the retail trade included a pack of four cards previewing the debut Studio set. The cards are in the same format as the regular set, 2-1/2" x 3-1/2" with evocative black-and-white photos bordered in maroon on front, and a biographical write-up on the back.

		MT
	Complete Set (18):	75.00
	Common Player:	3.00
1	Juan Bell	3.00
2	Roger Clemens	15.00
3	Dave Parker	3.00
4	Tim Raines	4.50
5	Kevin Seitzer	3.00
6	Teddy Higuera	3.00
7	Bernie Williams	8.00
8	Harold Baines	4.50
9	Gary Pettis	3.00
10	Dave Justice	8.00
11	Eric Davis	4.00
12	Andujar Cedeno	3.00
13	Tom Foley	3.00
14	Dwight Gooden	6.00
15	Doug Drabek	3.00
16	Steve Decker	3.00
17	Joe Torre	4.50
18	Header card	.50

1991 Studio

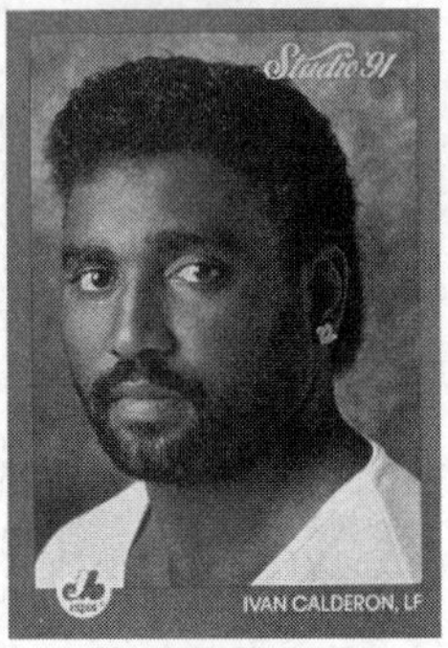

Donruss introduced this 264-card set in 1991. The cards feature maroon borders surrounding black and white posed player photos. The card backs are printed in black and white and feature personal data, career highlights, hobbies and interests and the player's hero. The cards were released in foil packs only and feature a special Rod Carew puzzle.

		MT
	Complete Set (264):	15.00
	Common Player:	.10
	Wax Box:	27.00
1	Glenn Davis	.10
2	Dwight Evans	.10
3	Leo Gomez	.10
4	Chris Hoiles	.10
5	Sam Horn	.10
6	Ben McDonald	.10
7	Randy Milligan	.10
8	Gregg Olson	.10
9	Cal Ripken, Jr.	2.00
10	David Segui	.10
11	Wade Boggs	.50
12	Ellis Burks	.10
13	Jack Clark	.10
14	Roger Clemens	.75
15	Mike Greenwell	.10
16	Tim Naehring	.10
17	Tony Pena	.10
18	*Phil Plantier*	.10
19	Jeff Reardon	.10
20	Mo Vaughn	.75
21	Jimmy Reese	.15
22	Jim Abbott	.10
23	Bert Blyleven	.10
24	Chuck Finley	.10
25	Gary Gaetti	.10
26	Wally Joyner	.15
27	Mark Langston	.10
28	Kirk McCaskill	.10
29	Lance Parrish	.10
30	Dave Winfield	.40
31	Alex Fernandez	.15
32	Carlton Fisk	.35
33	Scott Fletcher	.10
34	Greg Hibbard	.10
35	Charlie Hough	.10
36	Jack McDowell	.10
37	Tim Raines	.15
38	Sammy Sosa	2.00
39	Bobby Thigpen	.10
40	Frank Thomas	2.00
41	Sandy Alomar	.15
42	John Farrell	.10
43	Glenallen Hill	.10
44	Brook Jacoby	.10
45	Chris James	.10
46	Doug Jones	.10
47	Eric King	.10
48	Mark Lewis	.10
49	Greg Swindell	.10
50	Mark Whiten	.10
51	Milt Cuyler	.10
52	Rob Deer	.10
53	Cecil Fielder	.10
54	Travis Fryman	.10
55	Bill Gullickson	.10
56	Lloyd Moseby	.10
57	Frank Tanana	.10
58	Mickey Tettleton	.10
59	Alan Trammell	.20
60	Lou Whitaker	.10
61	Mike Boddicker	.10
62	George Brett	.50
63	Jeff Conine	.25
64	Warren Cromartie	.10
65	Storm Davis	.10
66	Kirk Gibson	.10
67	Mark Gubicza	.10
68	*Brian McRae*	.40
69	Bret Saberhagen	.15
70	Kurt Stillwell	.10
71	Tim McIntosh	.10
72	Candy Maldonado	.10
73	Paul Molitor	.50
74	Willie Randolph	.10
75	Ron Robinson	.10
76	Gary Sheffield	.25
77	Franklin Stubbs	.10
78	B.J. Surhoff	.10
79	Greg Vaughn	.15
80	Robin Yount	.50
81	Rick Aguilera	.10
82	Steve Bedrosian	.10
83	Scott Erickson	.10
84	Greg Gagne	.10
85	Dan Gladden	.10
86	Brian Harper	.10
87	Kent Hrbek	.10
88	Shane Mack	.10
89	Jack Morris	.10
90	Kirby Puckett	.60
91	Jesse Barfield	.10
92	Steve Farr	.10
93	Steve Howe	.10
94	Roberto Kelly	.10
95	Tim Leary	.10
96	Kevin Maas	.10
97	Don Mattingly	.75
98	Hensley Meulens	.10
99	Scott Sanderson	.10
100	Steve Sax	.10
101	Jose Canseco	.35
102	Dennis Eckersley	.10
103	Dave Henderson	.10
104	Rickey Henderson	.40
105	Rick Honeycutt	.10
106	Mark McGwire	4.00
107	Dave Stewart	.10
108	Eric Show	.10
109	*Todd Van Poppel*	.10
110	Bob Welch	.10
111	Alvin Davis	.10
112	Ken Griffey, Jr.	4.00
113	Ken Griffey, Sr.	.10
114	Erik Hanson	.10
115	Brian Holman	.10
116	Randy Johnson	.45
117	Edgar Martinez	.10
118	Tino Martinez	.20
119	Harold Reynolds	.10
120	David Valle	.10
121	Kevin Belcher	.10
122	Scott Chiamparino	.10
123	Julio Franco	.10
124	Juan Gonzalez	1.50
125	Rich Gossage	.10
126	Jeff Kunkel	.10
127	Rafael Palmeiro	.25
128	Nolan Ryan	2.00
129	Ruben Sierra	.10
130	Bobby Witt	.10
131	Roberto Alomar	.50
132	Tom Candiotti	.10
133	Joe Carter	.10
134	Ken Dayley	.10
135	Kelly Gruber	.10
136	John Olerud	.20
137	Dave Stieb	.10
138	Turner Ward	.10
139	Devon White	.15
140	Mookie Wilson	.10
141	Steve Avery	.10
142	Sid Bream	.10
143	Nick Esasky	.10
144	Ron Gant	.15
145	Tom Glavine	.25
146	Dave Justice	.25
147	Kelly Mann	.10
148	Terry Pendleton	.10
149	John Smoltz	.20
150	Jeff Treadway	.10
151	George Bell	.10
152	Shawn Boskie	.10
153	Andre Dawson	.15
154	Lance Dickson	.10
155	Shawon Dunston	.10
156	Joe Girardi	.10
157	Mark Grace	.25
158	Ryne Sandberg	.50
159	Gary Scott	.10
160	Dave Smith	.10
161	Tom Browning	.10
162	Eric Davis	.15
163	Rob Dibble	.10
164	Mariano Duncan	.10
165	Chris Hammond	.10
166	Billy Hatcher	.10
167	Barry Larkin	.20
168	Hal Morris	.15
169	Paul O'Neill	.15
170	Chris Sabo	.10
171	Eric Anthony	.10
172	*Jeff Bagwell*	4.00
173	Craig Biggio	.25
174	Ken Caminitti	.25
175	Jim Deshaies	.10
176	Steve Finley	.10
177	Pete Harnisch	.10
178	Darryl Kile	.15
179	Curt Schilling	.15
180	Mike Scott	.10
181	Brett Butler	.10
182	Gary Carter	.15
183	Orel Hershiser	.15
184	Ramon Martinez	.15
185	Eddie Murray	.40
186	Jose Offerman	.10
187	Bob Ojeda	.10
188	Juan Samuel	.10
189	Mike Scioscia	.10
190	Darryl Strawberry	.15
191	Moises Alou	.15
192	Brian Barnes	.10
193	Oil Can Boyd	.10
194	Ivan Calderon	.10
195	Delino DeShields	.10
196	Mike Fitzgerald	.10
197	Andres Galarraga	.20
198	Marquis Grissom	.15
199	Bill Sampen	.10
200	Tim Wallach	.10
201	Daryl Boston	.10
202	Vince Coleman	.10
203	John Franco	.10
204	Dwight Gooden	.15
205	Tom Herr	.10
206	Gregg Jefferies	.10
207	Howard Johnson	.10
208	Dave Magadan	.10
209	Kevin McReynolds	.10
210	Frank Viola	.10
211	Wes Chamberlain	.10
212	Darren Daulton	.10
213	Len Dykstra	.10
214	Charlie Hayes	.10
215	Ricky Jordan	.10
216	Steve Lake	.10
217	Roger McDowell	.10
218	Mickey Morandini	.10
219	Terry Mulholland	.10
220	Dale Murphy	.25
221	Jay Bell	.10
222	Barry Bonds	.75
223	Bobby Bonilla	.15
224	Doug Drabek	.10
225	Bill Landrum	.10
226	Mike LaValliere	.10
227	Jose Lind	.10
228	Don Slaught	.10
229	John Smiley	.10
230	Andy Van Slyke	.10
231	Bernard Gilkey	.15
232	Pedro Guerrero	.10
233	Rex Hudler	.10
234	Ray Lankford	.15
235	Joe Magrane	.10
236	Jose Oquendo	.10
237	Lee Smith	.10
238	Ozzie Smith	.50
239	Milt Thompson	.10
240	Todd Zeile	.10
241	Larry Andersen	.10
242	Andy Benes	.15
243	Paul Faries	.10
244	Tony Fernandez	.10
245	Tony Gwynn	.75
246	Atlee Hammaker	.10
247	Fred McGriff	.30
248	Bip Roberts	.10
249	Benito Santiago	.10
250	Ed Whitson	.10
251	Dave Anderson	.10
252	Mike Benjamin	.10
253	John Burkett	.10
254	Will Clark	.35
255	Scott Garrelts	.10
256	Willie McGee	.10
257	Kevin Mitchell	.10
258	Dave Righetti	.10
259	Matt Williams	.25
260	Black & Decker (Bud Black, Steve Decker)	.20
261	Checklist	.05
262	Checklist	.05
263	Checklist	.05
264	Checklist	.05

1992 Studio Preview

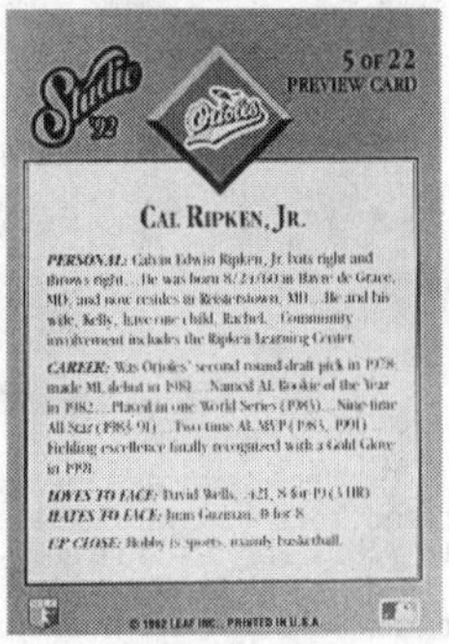

To introduce its 1992 Studio brand, Leaf produced 22 preview cards in format virtually identical to the issued versions of the same cards. The only differences are the appearance of the word "PREVIEW" in the lower-right corner of the card front, in place of the player's position, and the number "X of 22 / Preview Card" on the back where regular cards have the card number in the upper-right corner. The cards were distributed on a very limited basis to members of the Donruss dealers' network.

		MT
	Complete Set (22):	1050.
	Common Player:	25.00
1	Ruben Sierra	25.00
2	Kirby Puckett	75.00
3	Ryne Sandberg	55.00
4	John Kruk	25.00
5	Cal Ripken, Jr.	90.00
6	Robin Yount	65.00
7	Dwight Gooden	30.00
8	David Justice	45.00
9	Don Mattingly	75.00
10	Wally Joyner	25.00
11	Will Clark	45.00
12	Rob Dibble	25.00
13	Roberto Alomar	35.00
14	Wade Boggs	55.00
15	Barry Bonds	65.00
16	Jeff Bagwell	60.00
17	Mark McGwire	100.00
18	Frank Thomas	60.00
19	Brett Butler	25.00
20	Ozzie Smith	60.00
21	Jim Abbott	25.00
22	Tony Gwynn	75.00

1992 Studio

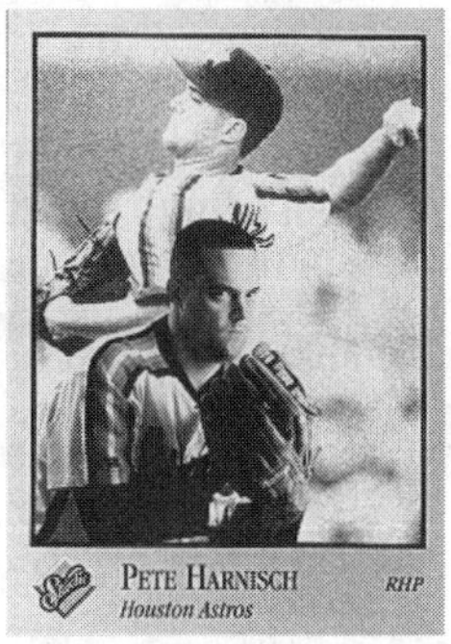

Donruss introduced the Studio line in 1991 and released another 264-card set entitled Leaf Studio for 1992. The cards feature a color player closeup with a large, rough-textured black-and-white photo of the player in the background. Tan borders surround the photos. The cards were only released in foil packs. Special Heritage insert cards featuring top players in vintage uniforms could be found in foil and jumbo packs.

		MT
	Complete Set (264):	15.00
	Common Player:	.05
	Wax Box:	22.00
1	Steve Avery	.05
2	Sid Bream	.05
3	Ron Gant	.10
4	Tom Glavine	.15
5	Dave Justice	.25
6	Mark Lemke	.05
7	Greg Olson	.05
8	Terry Pendleton	.05
9	Deion Sanders	.30
10	John Smoltz	.15
11	Doug Dascenzo	.05
12	Andre Dawson	.15
13	Joe Girardi	.05
14	Mark Grace	.25
15	Greg Maddux	1.50
16	Chuck McElroy	.05
17	Mike Morgan	.05
18	Ryne Sandberg	.50
19	Gary Scott	.05
20	Sammy Sosa	1.50
21	Norm Charlton	.05
22	Rob Dibble	.05
23	Barry Larkin	.15
24	Hal Morris	.05
25	Paul O'Neill	.15
26	Jose Rijo	.05
27	Bip Roberts	.05
28	Chris Sabo	.05
29	Reggie Sanders	.20

30	Greg Swindell	.05
31	Jeff Bagwell	1.00
32	Craig Biggio	.20
33	Ken Caminiti	.20
34	Andujar Cedeno	.05
35	Steve Finley	.05
36	Pete Harnisch	.05
37	Butch Henry	.05
38	Doug Jones	.05
39	Darryl Kile	.05
40	Eddie Taubensee	.05
41	Brett Butler	.05
42	Tom Candiotti	.05
43	Eric Davis	.10
44	Orel Hershiser	.10
45	Eric Karros	.10
46	Ramon Martinez	.15
47	Jose Offerman	.05
48	Mike Scioscia	.05
49	Mike Sharperson	.05
50	Darryl Strawberry	.15
51	Bret Barbarie	.05
52	Ivan Calderon	.05
53	Gary Carter	.15
54	Delino DeShields	.05
55	Marquis Grissom	.10
56	Ken Hill	.05
57	Dennis Martinez	.05
58	Spike Owen	.05
59	Larry Walker	.25
60	Tim Wallach	.05
61	Bobby Bonilla	.10
62	Tim Burke	.05
63	Vince Coleman	.05
64	John Franco	.05
65	Dwight Gooden	.10
66	Todd Hundley	.15
67	Howard Johnson	.05
68	Eddie Murray	.35
69	Bret Saberhagen	.10
70	Anthony Young	.05
71	Kim Batiste	.05
72	Wes Chamberlain	.05
73	Darren Daulton	.05
74	Mariano Duncan	.05
75	Len Dykstra	.05
76	John Kruk	.05
77	Mickey Morandini	.05
78	Terry Mulholland	.05
79	Dale Murphy	.25
80	Mitch Williams	.05
81	Jay Bell	.05
82	Barry Bonds	.60
83	Steve Buechele	.05
84	Doug Drabek	.05
85	Mike LaValliere	.05
86	Jose Lind	.05
87	Denny Neagle	.05
88	Randy Tomlin	.05
89	Andy Van Slyke	.05
90	Gary Varsho	.05
91	Pedro Guerrero	.05
92	Rex Hudler	.05
93	Brian Jordan	.10
94	Felix Jose	.05
95	Donovan Osborne	.05
96	Tom Pagnozzi	.05
97	Lee Smith	.05
98	Ozzie Smith	.40
99	Todd Worrell	.05
100	Todd Zeile	.10
101	Andy Benes	.10
102	Jerald Clark	.05
103	Tony Fernandez	.05
104	Tony Gwynn	.75
105	Greg Harris	.05
106	Fred McGriff	.30
107	Benito Santiago	.05
108	Gary Sheffield	.25
109	Kurt Stillwell	.05
110	Tim Teufel	.05
111	Kevin Bass	.05
112	Jeff Brantley	.05
113	John Burkett	.05
114	Will Clark	.25
115	Royce Clayton	.05
116	Mike Jackson	.05
117	Darren Lewis	.05
118	Bill Swift	.05
119	Robby Thompson	.05
120	Matt Williams	.20
121	Brady Anderson	.20
122	Glenn Davis	.05
123	Mike Devereaux	.05
124	Chris Hoiles	.05
125	Sam Horn	.05
126	Ben McDonald	.05
127	Mike Mussina	.30
128	Gregg Olson	.05
129	Cal Ripken, Jr.	2.00
130	Rick Sutcliffe	.05
131	Wade Boggs	.40
132	Roger Clemens	.65
133	Greg Harris	.05
134	Tim Naehring	.05
135	Tony Pena	.05
136	Phil Plantier	.05
137	Jeff Reardon	.05
138	Jody Reed	.05
139	Mo Vaughn	.40
140	Frank Viola	.05
141	Jim Abbott	.05
142	Hubie Brooks	.05
143	*Chad Curtis*	.20
144	Gary DiSarcina	.05
145	Chuck Finley	.05
146	Bryan Harvey	.05
147	Von Hayes	.05
148	Mark Langston	.10
149	Lance Parrish	.05
150	Lee Stevens	.05
151	George Bell	.05
152	Alex Fernandez	.10
153	Greg Hibbard	.05
154	Lance Johnson	.05
155	Kirk McCaskill	.05
156	Tim Raines	.10
157	Steve Sax	.05
158	Bobby Thigpen	.05
159	Frank Thomas	1.50
160	Robin Ventura	.25
161	Sandy Alomar, Jr.	.15
162	Jack Armstrong	.05
163	Carlos Baerga	.05
164	Albert Belle	.50
165	Alex Cole	.05
166	Glenallen Hill	.05
167	Mark Lewis	.05
168	Kenny Lofton	.40
169	Paul Sorrento	.05
170	Mark Whiten	.05
171	Milt Cuyler (color photo actually Lou Whitaker)	.05
172	Rob Deer	.05
173	Cecil Fielder	.10
174	Travis Fryman	.10
175	Mike Henneman	.05
176	Tony Phillips	.05
177	Frank Tanana	.05
178	Mickey Tettleton	.05
179	Alan Trammell	.10
180	Lou Whitaker	.05
181	George Brett	.65
182	Tom Gordon	.05
183	Mark Gubicza	.05
184	Gregg Jefferies	.10
185	Wally Joyner	.10
186	Brent Mayne	.05
187	Brian McRae	.10
188	Kevin McReynolds	.05
189	Keith Miller	.05
190	Jeff Montgomery	.05
191	Dante Bichette	.20
192	Ricky Bones	.05
193	Scott Fletcher	.05
194	Paul Molitor	.50
195	Jaime Navarro	.05
196	Franklin Stubbs	.05
197	B.J. Surhoff	.05
198	Greg Vaughn	.10
199	Bill Wegman	.05
200	Robin Yount	.50
201	Rick Aguilera	.05
202	Scott Erickson	.05
203	Greg Gagne	.05
204	Brian Harper	.05
205	Kent Hrbek	.05
206	Scott Leius	.05
207	Shane Mack	.05
208	Pat Mahomes	.05
209	Kirby Puckett	.65
210	John Smiley	.05
211	Mike Gallego	.05
212	Charlie Hayes	.05
213	Pat Kelly	.05
214	Roberto Kelly	.05
215	Kevin Maas	.05
216	Don Mattingly	.75
217	Matt Nokes	.05
218	Melido Perez	.05
219	Scott Sanderson	.05
220	Danny Tartabull	.05
221	Harold Baines	.10
222	Jose Canseco	.35
223	Dennis Eckersley	.05
224	Dave Henderson	.05
225	Carney Lansford	.05
226	Mark McGwire	3.00
227	Mike Moore	.05
228	Randy Ready	.05
229	Terry Steinbach	.05
230	Dave Stewart	.05
231	Jay Buhner	.05
232	Ken Griffey, Jr.	3.00
233	Erik Hanson	.05
234	Randy Johnson	.25
235	Edgar Martinez	.05
236	Tino Martinez	.15
237	Kevin Mitchell	.05
238	Pete O'Brien	.05
239	Harold Reynolds	.05
240	David Valle	.05
241	Julio Franco	.05
242	Juan Gonzalez	.65
243	Jose Guzman	.05
244	Rafael Palmeiro	.25
245	Dean Palmer	.05
246	Ivan Rodriguez	.50
247	Jeff Russell	.05
248	Nolan Ryan	1.50
249	Ruben Sierra	.05
250	Dickie Thon	.05
251	Roberto Alomar	.40
252	Derek Bell	.15
253	Pat Borders	.05
254	Joe Carter	.10
255	Kelly Gruber	.05
256	Juan Guzman	.05
257	Jack Morris	.05
258	John Olerud	.20
259	Devon White	.15
260	Dave Winfield	.40
261	Checklist	.05
262	Checklist	.05
263	Checklist	.05
264	History card	.05

1992 Studio Heritage

Superstars of 1992 were photographed in vintage-style uniforms in this 14-card insert set found in packages of Studio's 1992 issue. Cards #1-8 could be found in standard foil packs while #9-14 were inserted in Studio jumbos. Cards featured a sepia-tone photo bordered in turquoise and highlighted with copper foil. Cards carry a "BC" prefix to the card number on back.

		MT
Complete Set (14):		22.00
Common Player:		1.00
1	Ryne Sandberg	1.50
2	Carlton Fisk	1.00
3	Wade Boggs	1.50
4	Jose Canseco	1.50
5	Don Mattingly	3.00
6	Darryl Strawberry	1.00
7	Cal Ripken, Jr.	5.00
8	Will Clark	1.00
9	Andre Dawson	1.00
10	Andy Van Slyke	1.00
11	Paul Molitor	1.50
12	Jeff Bagwell	2.00
13	Darren Daulton	1.00
14	Kirby Puckett	3.00

1993 Studio

This 220-card set features full-bleed photos. The player's portrait appears against one of several backgrounds featuring his team's uniform. His signature and the Studio logo are printed in gold foil. Backs have an extreme closeup partial portrait of the player and insights into his personality.

		MT
Complete Set (220):		20.00
Common Player:		.10
Wax Box:		28.00
1	Dennis Eckersley	.10
2	Chad Curtis	.10
3	Eric Anthony	.10
4	Roberto Alomar	.50
5	Steve Avery	.10
6	Cal Eldred	.10
7	Bernard Gilkey	.10
8	Steve Buechele	.10
9	Brett Butler	.10
10	Terry Mulholland	.10
11	Moises Alou	.15
12	Barry Bonds	.75
13	Sandy Alomar Jr.	.15
14	Chris Bosio	.10
15	Scott Sanderson	.10
16	Bobby Bonilla	.10
17	Brady Anderson	.15
18	Derek Bell	.10
19	Wes Chamberlain	.10
20	Jay Bell	.10
21	Kevin Brown	.15
22	Roger Clemens	1.00
23	Roberto Kelly	.10
24	Dante Bichette	.20
25	George Brett	.75
26	Rob Deer	.10
27	Brian Harper	.10
28	George Bell	.10
29	Jim Abbott	.10
30	Dave Henderson	.10
31	Wade Boggs	.35
32	Chili Davis	.10
33	Ellis Burks	.10
34	Jeff Bagwell	1.00
35	Kent Hrbek	.10
36	Pat Borders	.10
37	Cecil Fielder	.10
38	Sid Bream	.10
39	Greg Gagne	.10
40	Darryl Hamilton	.10
41	Jerald Clark	.10
42	Mark Grace	.20
43	Barry Larkin	.15
44	John Burkett	.10
45	Scott Cooper	.10
46	*Mike Lansing*	.25
47	Jose Canseco	.25
48	Will Clark	.25
49	Carlos Garcia	.10
50	Carlos Baerga	.10
51	Darren Daulton	.10
52	Jay Buhner	.10
53	Andy Benes	.10
54	Jeff Conine	.10
55	Mike Devereaux	.10
56	Vince Coleman	.10
57	Terry Steinbach	.10
58	*J.T. Snow*	.75
59	Greg Swindell	.10
60	Devon White	.10
61	John Smoltz	.15
62	Todd Zeile	.10
63	Rick Wilkins	.10
64	Tim Wallach	.10
65	John Wetteland	.10
66	Matt Williams	.30
67	Paul Sorrento	.10
68	David Valle	.10
69	Walt Weiss	.10
70	John Franco	.10
71	Nolan Ryan	2.50
72	Frank Viola	.10
73	Chris Sabo	.10
74	David Nied	.10
75	Kevin McReynolds	.10
76	Lou Whitaker	.10
77	Dave Winfield	.30
78	Robin Ventura	.15
79	Spike Owen	.10
80	Cal Ripken, Jr.	2.50
81	Dan Walter	.10
82	Mitch Williams	.10
83	Tim Wakefield	.10
84	Rickey Henderson	.30
85	Gary DiSarcina	.10
86	Craig Biggio	.20
87	Joe Carter	.10
88	Ron Gant	.15
89	John Jaha	.10
90	Gregg Jefferies	.10
91	Jose Guzman	.10
92	Eric Karros	.10
93	Wil Cordero	.10
94	Royce Clayton	.10
95	Albert Belle	.60
96	Ken Griffey, Jr.	3.00
97	Orestes Destrade	.10
98	Tony Fernandez	.10
99	Leo Gomez	.10
100	Tony Gwynn	1.00
101	Len Dykstra	.10
102	Jeff King	.10
103	Julio Franco	.10
104	Andre Dawson	.15
105	Randy Milligan	.10
106	Alex Cole	.10
107	Phil Hiatt	.10
108	Travis Fryman	.10
109	Chuck Knoblauch	.15
110	Bo Jackson	.15
111	Pat Kelly	.10
112	Bret Saberhagen	.10
113	Ruben Sierra	.10
114	Tim Salmon	.30
115	Doug Jones	.10
116	Ed Sprague	.10
117	Terry Pendleton	.10
118	Robin Yount	.50
119	Mark Whiten	.10
120	Checklist	.10
121	Sammy Sosa	1.50
122	Darryl Strawberry	.15
123	Larry Walker	.25
124	Robby Thompson	.10
125	Carlos Martinez	.10
126	Edgar Martinez	.10
127	Benito Santiago	.10
128	Howard Johnson	.10
129	Harold Reynolds	.10
130	Craig Shipley	.10
131	Curt Schilling	.10
132	Andy Van Slyke	.10
133	Ivan Rodriguez	.50
134	Mo Vaughn	.50
135	Bip Roberts	.10
136	Charlie Hayes	.10
137	Brian McRae	.10
138	Mickey Tettleton	.10
139	Frank Thomas	1.50
140	Paul O'Neill	.15
141	Mark McGwire	3.00
142	Damion Easley	.10
143	Ken Caminiti	.20
144	Juan Guzman	.10
145	Tom Glavine	.15
146	Pat Listach	.10
147	Lee Smith	.10
148	Derrick May	.10
149	Ramon Martinez	.10
150	Delino DeShields	.10
151	Kirt Manwaring	.10
152	Reggie Jefferson	.10
153	Randy Johnson	.40
154	Dave Magadan	.10
155	Dwight Gooden	.15
156	Chris Hoiles	.10
157	Fred McGriff	.20
158	Dave Hollins	.10
159	Al Martin	.10
160	Juan Gonzalez	1.00
161	Mike Greenwell	.10
162	Kevin Mitchell	.10
163	Andres Galarraga	.20
164	Wally Joyner	.15
165	Kirk Gibson	.10
166	Pedro Munoz	.10
167	Ozzie Guillen	.10
168	Jimmy Key	.10
169	Kevin Seitzer	.10
170	Luis Polonia	.10
171	Luis Gonzalez	.10
172	Paul Molitor	.50
173	Dave Justice	.20
174	B.J. Surhoff	.10
175	Ray Lankford	.10
176	Ryne Sandberg	.50
177	Jody Reed	.10
178	Marquis Grissom	.10
179	Willie McGee	.10
180	Kenny Lofton	.50
181	Junior Felix	.10
182	Jose Offerman	.10
183	John Kruk	.10
184	Orlando Merced	.10
185	Rafael Palmeiro	.25
186	Billy Hatcher	.10
187	Joe Oliver	.10
188	Joe Girardi	.10
189	Jose Lind	.10
190	Harold Baines	.10
191	Mike Pagliarulo	.10
192	Lance Johnson	.10
193	Don Mattingly	1.00
194	Doug Drabek	.10
195	John Olerud	.20
196	Greg Maddux	2.00
197	Greg Vaughn	.15
198	Tom Pagnozzi	.10
199	Willie Wilson	.10
200	Jack McDowell	.10
201	Mike Piazza	2.00
202	Mike Mussina	.40
203	Charles Nagy	.10
204	Tino Martinez	.15
205	Charlie Hough	.10
206	Todd Hundley	.20
207	Gary Sheffield	.20
208	Mickey Morandini	.10
209	Don Slaught	.10
210	Dean Palmer	.10
211	Jose Rijo	.10
212	Vinny Castilla	.10
213	Tony Phillips	.10
214	Kirby Puckett	75.00
215	Tim Raines	.15
216	Otis Nixon	.10
217	Ozzie Smith	.50
218	Jose Vizcaino	.10
220	Checklist	.10

1993 Studio Heritage

All types of 1993 Leaf Studio packs were candidates for having one of 12 Heritage cards inserted in them. The fronts feature the player posing in an old-time uniform, framed in turquiose with copper highlights. The backs have a mug shot surrounded by an ornate frame and describe the uniform on the front. Team trivia is also included.

		MT
Complete Set (12):		20.00
Common Player:		1.00
1	George Brett	4.00
2	Juan Gonzalez	5.00
3	Roger Clemens	3.00
4	Mark McGwire	12.00
5	Mark Grace	1.50
6	Ozzie Smith	2.50
7	Barry Larkin	1.00
8	Frank Thomas	5.00
9	Carlos Baerga	1.00
10	Eric Karros	1.00
11	J.T. Snow	1.00
12	John Kruk	1.00

1993 Studio Silhouettes

These insert cards were randomly included in jumbo packs only. The card fronts feature a ghosted image of the player against an action silhouette on a gray background. The player's name is in bronze foil at bottom. Backs have a player action photo and description of career highlights.

		MT
Complete Set (10):		25.00
Common Player:		1.00
1	Frank Thomas	4.00
2	Barry Bonds	2.50
3	Jeff Bagwell	4.00
4	Juan Gonzalez	3.00
5	Travis Fryman	1.00
6	J.T. Snow	1.00
7	John Kruk	1.00
8	Jeff Blauser	1.00
9	Mike Piazza	6.00
10	Nolan Ryan	7.50

1993 Studio Superstars on Canvas

Ten players are featured on these insert cards, which were available in hobby and retail packs. The cards show player portraits which mix photography and artwork.

		MT
Complete Set (10):		25.00
Common Player:		1.00
1	Ken Griffey, Jr.	12.00
2	Jose Canseco	1.50
3	Mark McGwire	12.00
4	Mike Mussina	2.00
5	Joe Carter	1.00
6	Frank Thomas	6.00
7	Darren Daulton	1.00
8	Mark Grace	1.50
9	Andres Galarraga	1.00
10	Barry Bonds	3.00

1993 Studio Frank Thomas

This five-card set is devoted to Frank Thomas. Cards were randomly included in all types of 1993 Leaf Studio packs. Topics covered on the cards include Thomas' childhood, his baseball memories, his family, his performance and being a role model.

		MT
Complete Set (5):		20.00
Common Player:		4.00
1	Childhood	4.00
2	Baseball Memories	4.00
3	Importance of Family	4.00
4	Performance	4.00
5	On Being a Role Model	4.00

1994 Studio Promotional Samples

To introduce its "locker-room look" issue for 1994 Leaf's Studio brand produced this three-star sample set and distributed it to its hobby dealer network. The cards are basically the same as the regular-issue cards of those players except for the addition of a "Promotional Sample" overprinted diagonally on front and back. The "Up Close" biographies on the cards' backs are different between the promos and the regular cards and there is a slight difference in front photo cropping on the Gonzalez card.

		MT
Complete Set (3):		15.00
Common Player:		4.00
83	Barry Bonds	5.00
154	Juan Gonzalez	4.00
209	Frank Thomas	5.00

Player names in *Italic* type indicate a rookie card.

1994 Studio

Studio baseball from Donruss returned in mid-August, 1994, with a three-time MVP spokesman, several jazzy and short-printed inserts subsets and a reduced overall production figure that represents a sharp drop from 1993. Barry Bonds is the MVP whose mug adorns Studio counter boxes and advertisements. According to Donruss officials, production was limited to 8,000 cases of 20 boxes each, which represents a 35 percent decrease from 1993 and works out to about 315,000 of each card. Only 2,000 cases were earmarked for retail distribution and no jumbo packs were produced. Studio 1994 features 220 cards issued in one series, once again with close-up personal portraits of the top stars in the game. Each card is foil-stamped with a borderless design and UV coating front and back. The front of the card features the player in the foreground with his locker in the background. As in the previous three Studio offerings, the backs of the cards contain personal information about the players.

		MT
Complete Set (220):		15.00
Common Player:		.10
Wax Box:		25.00
1	Dennis Eckersley	.10
2	Brent Gates	.10
3	Rickey Henderson	.35
4	Mark McGwire	3.00
5	Troy Neel	.10
6	Ruben Sierra	.10
7	Terry Steinbach	.10
8	Chad Curtis	.10
9	Chili Davis	.10
10	Gary DiSarcina	.10
11	Damion Easley	.10
12	Bo Jackson	.25
13	Mark Langston	.10
14	Eduardo Perez	.10
15	Tim Salmon	.20
16	Jeff Bagwell	1.00
17	Craig Biggio	.25
18	Ken Caminiti	.20
19	Andujar Cedeno	.10
20	Doug Drabek	.10
21	Steve Finley	.10
22	Luis Gonzalez	.10
23	Darryl Kile	.10
24	Roberto Alomar	.75
25	Pat Borders	.10
26	Joe Carter	.10
27	Carlos Delgado	.40
28	Pat Hentgen	.10
29	Paul Molitor	.50
30	John Olerud	.15
31	Ed Sprague	.10
32	Devon White	.10
33	Steve Avery	.10
34	Tom Glavine	.15
35	David Justice	.20
36	Roberto Kelly	.10
37	Ryan Klesko	.20
38	Javier Lopez	.10
39	Greg Maddux	1.50
40	Fred McGriff	.25
41	Terry Pendleton	.10
42	Ricky Bones	.10
43	Darryl Hamilton	.10
44	Brian Harper	.10
45	John Jaha	.10
46	Dave Nilsson	.10
47	Kevin Seitzer	.10
48	Greg Vaughn	.15
49	Turner Ward	.10
50	Bernard Gilkey	.10
51	Gregg Jefferies	.10
52	Ray Lankford	.10
53	Tom Pagnozzi	.10
54	Ozzie Smith	.50
55	Bob Tewksbury	.10
56	Mark Whiten	.10
57	Todd Zeile	.10
58	Steve Buechele	.10
59	Shawon Dunston	.10
60	Mark Grace	.25
61	Derrick May	.10
62	Tuffy Rhodes	.10
63	Ryne Sandberg	.60
64	Sammy Sosa	1.50
65	Rick Wilkins	.10
66	Brett Butler	.10
67	Delino DeShields	.10
68	Orel Hershiser	.10
69	Eric Karros	.10
70	Raul Mondesi	.35
71	Jose Offerman	.10
72	Mike Piazza	1.50
73	Tim Wallach	.10
74	Moises Alou	.15
75	Sean Berry	.10
76	Wil Cordero	.10
77	Cliff Floyd	.10
78	Marquis Grissom	.10
79	Ken Hill	.10
80	Larry Walker	.25
81	John Wetteland	.10
82	Rod Beck	.10
83	Barry Bonds	.75
84	Royce Clayton	.10
85	Darren Lewis	.10
86	Willie McGee	.10
87	Bill Swift	.10
88	Robby Thompson	.10
89	Matt Williams	.20
90	Sandy Alomar Jr.	.15
91	Carlos Baerga	.10
92	Albert Belle	.60
93	Kenny Lofton	.45
94	Eddie Murray	.30
95	Manny Ramirez	.75
96	Paul Sorrento	.10
97	Jim Thome	.20
98	Rich Amaral	.10
99	Eric Anthony	.10
100	Jay Buhner	.10
101	Ken Griffey, Jr.	3.00
102	Randy Johnson	.25
103	Edgar Martinez	.10
104	Tino Martinez	.20
105	*Kurt Abbott*	.15
106	Bret Barberie	.10
107	Chuck Carr	.10
108	Jeff Conine	.10
109	Chris Hammond	.10
110	Bryan Harvey	.10
111	Benito Santiago	.10
112	Gary Sheffield	.35
113	Bobby Bonilla	.10
114	Dwight Gooden	.15
115	Todd Hundley	.10
116	Bobby Jones	.10
117	Jeff Kent	.10
118	Kevin McReynolds	.10
119	Bret Saberhagen	.10
120	Ryan Thompson	.10
121	Harold Baines	.10
122	Mike Devereaux	.10
123	Jeffrey Hammonds	.10
124	Ben McDonald	.10
125	Mike Mussina	.25
126	Rafael Palmeiro	.25
127	Cal Ripken, Jr.	2.50
128	Lee Smith	.10
129	Brad Ausmus	.10
130	Derek Bell	.10
131	Andy Benes	.10
132	Tony Gwynn	.75
133	Trevor Hoffman	.10
134	Scott Livingstone	.10
135	Phil Plantier	.10
136	Darren Daulton	.10
137	Mariano Duncan	.10
138	Len Dykstra	.10
139	Dave Hollins	.10
140	Pete Incaviglia	.10
141	Danny Jackson	.10
142	John Kruk	.10
143	Kevin Stocker	.10
144	Jay Bell	.10
145	Carlos Garcia	.10
146	Jeff King	.10
147	Al Martin	.10
148	Orlando Merced	.10
149	Don Slaught	.10
150	Andy Van Slyke	.10
151	Kevin Brown	.15
152	Jose Canseco	.35
153	Will Clark	.25
154	Juan Gonzalez	1.00
155	David Hulse	.10
156	Dean Palmer	.10
157	Ivan Rodriguez	.50
158	Kenny Rogers	.10
159	Roger Clemens	1.00
160	Scott Cooper	.10
161	Andre Dawson	.15
162	Mike Greenwell	.10
163	Otis Nixon	.10
164	Aaron Sele	.10
165	John Valentin	.10
166	Mo Vaughn	.45
167	Bret Boone	.10
168	Barry Larkin	.20
169	Kevin Mitchell	.10
170	Hal Morris	.10
171	Jose Rijo	.10
172	Deion Sanders	.20
173	Reggie Sanders	.10
174	John Smiley	.10
175	Dante Bichette	.30
176	Ellis Burks	.10
177	Andres Galarraga	.15
178	Joe Girardi	.10
179	Charlie Hayes	.10
180	Roberto Mejia	.10
181	Walt Weiss	.10
182	David Cone	.15
183	Gary Gaetti	.10
184	Greg Gagne	.10
185	Felix Jose	.10
186	Wally Joyner	.10
187	Mike Macfarlane	.10
188	Brian McRae	.10
189	Eric Davis	.10
190	Cecil Fielder	.10
191	Travis Fryman	.10
192	Tony Phillips	.10
193	Mickey Tettleton	.10
194	Alan Trammell	.10
195	Lou Whitaker	.10
196	Kent Hrbek	.10
197	Chuck Knoblauch	.15
198	Shane Mack	.10
199	Pat Meares	.10
200	Kirby Puckett	.75
201	Matt Walbeck	.10
202	Dave Winfield	.25
203	Wilson Alvarez	.10
204	Alex Fernandez	.10
205	Julio Franco	.10
206	Ozzie Guillen	.10
207	Jack McDowell	.10
208	Tim Raines	.10
209	Frank Thomas	1.50
210	Robin Ventura	.15
211	Jim Abbott	.10
212	Wade Boggs	.35
213	Pat Kelly	.10
214	Jimmy Key	.10
215	Don Mattingly	1.00
216	Paul O'Neill	.15
217	Mike Stanley	.10
218	Danny Tartabull	.10
219	Checklist	.10
220	Checklist	.10

1994 Studio Editor's Choice

Printed in similitude to a strip of color slide film, each of the cards in this insert set feature a complete player photo at center, with partial "frames" at top and bottom. Printed on acetate, the back of the card shows a reversed image of the front. Stated odds of finding an Editor's Choice insert card are about one per box of 36 packs.

		MT
Complete Set (8):		35.00
Common Player:		1.00
1	Barry Bonds	5.00
2	Frank Thomas	6.00
3	Ken Griffey, Jr.	15.00
4	Andres Galarraga	1.00
5	Juan Gonzalez	5.00
6	Tim Salmon	2.00
7	Paul O'Neill	1.00
8	Mike Piazza	8.00

1994 Studio Heritage

Besides picturing today's players in vintage uniforms, the 1994 Studio Heritage inserts have the player portraits set against sepia-toned photos of old ballparks. Fronts are enhanced by copper-foil logos and by a round device at upper-left containing the player's name, team and year represented. Backs have a second color player photo and a short write-up about the team represented. Unlike the other cards in the set, the Heritage cards are printed on a porous cardboard stock to enhance the image of antiquity. Stated odds of finding a Heritage Collection insert card are one in nine packs.

		MT
Complete Set (8):		15.00
Common Player:		1.00
1	Barry Bonds	2.50
2	Frank Thomas	4.00
3	Joe Carter	1.00
4	Don Mattingly	3.00
5	Ryne Sandberg	2.50
6	Javier Lopez	1.50
7	Gregg Jefferies	1.00
8	Mike Mussina	1.50

1994 Studio Silver Stars

Each of the 10 players in this insert set was produced in an edition of 10,000 cards. Printed on acetate, fronts feature action photos set against a clear plastic background with a silver-foil seal at bottom. Within the player silhouette on back, a second photo is printed. The back also features a black-and-white version of the seal, including the card's unique serial number. Stated odds of picking a Silver Series Star are one per 60 packs, on average.

		MT
Complete Set (10):		80.00
Common Player:		4.00
1	Tony Gwynn	8.00
2	Barry Bonds	5.00
3	Frank Thomas	8.00
4	Ken Griffey, Jr.	20.00
5	Joe Carter	4.00
6	Mike Piazza	15.00
7	Cal Ripken, Jr.	15.00
8	Greg Maddux	12.00
9	Juan Gonzalez	8.00
10	Don Mattingly	8.00

Player names in *Italic* type indicate a rookie card.

1994 Studio Gold Stars

The scarcest of the 1994 Studio chase cards, only 5,000 cards of each of the 10 players were produced. Printed on acetate, fronts feature an action photo set against a clear plastic background. At bottom is a large gold-foil seal. Backs have another player photo, within the silhouette of the front photo, and a black-and-white version of the seal, including the card's unique serial number. According to the series wrapper, odds of finding a Gold Series Star card are one in 120 packs.

		MT
Complete Set (10):		300.00
Common Player:		10.00
1	Tony Gwynn	25.00
2	Barry Bonds	20.00
3	Frank Thomas	25.00
4	Ken Griffey, Jr.	70.00
5	Joe Carter	10.00
6	Mike Piazza	40.00
7	Cal Ripken, Jr.	60.00
8	Greg Maddux	40.00
9	Juan Gonzalez	25.00
10	Don Mattingly	25.00

1995 Studio

Known since its inception as a brand name for its innovative design, Studio did not disappoint in 1995, unveiling a baseball card with a credit card look. In horizontal format the cards feature embossed stats and data on front, plus a team logo hologram. Backs have a color player photo, facsimile autograph and simulated magnetic data strip to carry through the credit card impression.

		MT
Complete Set (200):		40.00
Common Player:		.10
Wax Box:		48.00
1	Frank Thomas	1.50
2	Jeff Bagwell	1.00
3	Don Mattingly	1.50
4	Mike Piazza	2.00
5	Ken Griffey Jr.	4.00
6	Greg Maddux	2.00
7	Barry Bonds	.75
8	Cal Ripken Jr.	2.50
9	Jose Canseco	.35
10	Paul Molitor	.50
11	Kenny Lofton	.50
12	Will Clark	.30
13	Tim Salmon	.25
14	Joe Carter	.10
15	Albert Belle	.60
16	Roger Clemens	1.00
17	Roberto Alomar	.60
18	Alex Rodriguez	3.00
19	Raul Mondesi	.40
20	Deion Sanders	.25
21	Juan Gonzalez	1.50
22	Kirby Puckett	1.00
23	Fred McGriff	.30
24	Matt Williams	.25
25	Tony Gwynn	.75
26	Cliff Floyd	.10
27	Travis Fryman	.10
28	Shawn Green	.15
29	Mike Mussina	.35
30	Bob Hamelin	.10
31	Dave Justice	.20
32	Manny Ramirez	1.00
33	David Cone	.15
34	Marquis Grissom	.10
35	Moises Alou	.15
36	Carlos Baerga	.10
37	Barry Larkin	.20
38	Robin Ventura	.15
39	Mo Vaughn	.50
40	Jeffrey Hammonds	.10
41	Ozzie Smith	.50
42	Andres Galarraga	.15
43	Carlos Delgado	.50
44	Lenny Dykstra	.10
45	Cecil Fielder	.10
46	Wade Boggs	.35
47	Gregg Jefferies	.10
48	Randy Johnson	.30
49	Rafael Palmeiro	.20
50	Craig Biggio	.20
51	Steve Avery	.10
52	Ricky Bottalico	.10
53	Chris Gomez	.10
54	Carlos Garcia	.10
55	Brian Anderson	.10
56	Wilson Alvarez	.10
57	Roberto Kelly	.10
58	Larry Walker	.25
59	Dean Palmer	.10
60	Rick Aguilera	.10
61	Javy Lopez	.10
62	Shawon Dunston	.10
63	William Van Landingham	.10
64	Jeff Kent	.10
65	David McCarty	.10
66	Armando Benitez	.10
67	Brett Butler	.10
68	Bernard Gilkey	.10
69	Joey Hamilton	.10
70	Chad Curtis	.10
71	Dante Bichette	.25
72	Chuck Carr	.10
73	Pedro Martinez	.15
74	Ramon Martinez	.10
75	Rondell White	.15
76	Alex Fernandez	.10
77	Dennis Martinez	.10
78	Sammy Sosa	1.50
79	Bernie Williams	.35
80	Lou Whitaker	.10
81	Kurt Abbott	.10
82	Tino Martinez	.15
83	Willie Greene	.10
84	Garret Anderson	.15
85	Jose Rijo	.10
86	Jeff Montgomery	.10
87	Mark Langston	.10
88	Reggie Sanders	.10
89	Rusty Greer	.10
90	Delino DeShields	.10
91	Jason Bere	.10
92	Lee Smith	.10
93	Devon White	.10
94	John Wetteland	.10
95	Luis Gonzalez	.10
96	Greg Vaughn	.10
97	Lance Johnson	.10
98	Alan Trammell	.10
99	Bret Saberhagen	.10
100	Jack McDowell	.10
101	Trevor Hoffman	.10
102	Dave Nilsson	.10
103	Bryan Harvey	.10
104	Chuck Knoblauch	.20
105	Bobby Bonilla	.10
106	Hal Morris	.10
107	Mark Whiten	.10
108	Phil Plantier	.10
109	Ryan Klesko	.20
110	Greg Gagne	.10
111	Ruben Sierra	.10
112	J.R. Phillips	.10
113	Terry Steinbach	.10
114	Jay Buhner	.10
115	Ken Caminiti	.25
116	Gary DiSarcina	.10
117	Ivan Rodriguez	.50
118	Bip Roberts	.10
119	Jay Bell	.10
120	Ken Hill	.10
121	Mike Greenwell	.10
122	Rick Wilkins	.10
123	Rickey Henderson	.30
124	Dave Hollins	.10
125	Terry Pendleton	.10
126	Rich Becker	.10
127	Billy Ashley	.10
128	Derek Bell	.10
129	Dennis Eckersley	.10
130	Andujar Cedeno	.10
131	John Jaha	.10
132	Chuck Finley	.10
133	Steve Finley	.10
134	Danny Tartabull	.10
135	Jeff Conine	.10
136	Jon Lieber	.10
137	Jim Abbott	.10
138	Steve Traschel	.10
139	Bret Boone	.10
140	Charles Johnson	.10
141	Mark McGwire	4.00
142	Eddie Murray	.40
143	Doug Drabek	.10
144	Steve Cooke	.10
145	Kevin Seitzer	.10
146	Rod Beck	.10
147	Eric Karros	.10
148	Tim Raines	.15
149	Joe Girardi	.10
150	Aaron Sele	.10
151	Robby Thompson	.10
152	Chan Ho Park	.15
153	Ellis Burks	.10
154	Brian McRae	.10
155	Jimmy Key	.10
156	Rico Brogna	.10
157	Ozzie Guillen	.10
158	Chili Davis	.10
159	Darren Daulton	.10
160	Chipper Jones	2.00
161	Walt Weiss	.10
162	Paul O'Neill	.15
163	Al Martin	.10
164	John Valentin	.10
165	Tim Wallach	.10
166	Scott Erickson	.10
167	Ryan Thompson	.10
168	Todd Zeile	.10
169	Scott Cooper	.10
170	Matt Mieske	.10
171	Allen Watson	.10
172	Brian Hunter	.10
173	Kevin Stocker	.10
174	Cal Eldred	.10
175	Tony Phillips	.10
176	Ben McDonald	.10
177	Mark Grace	.20
178	Midre Cummings	.10
179	Orlando Merced	.10
180	Jeff King	.10
181	Gary Sheffield	.40
182	Tom Glavine	.20
183	Edgar Martinez	.10
184	Steve Karsay	.10
185	Pat Listach	.10
186	Wil Cordero	.10
187	Brady Anderson	.15
188	Bobby Jones	.10
189	Andy Benes	.10
190	Ray Lankford	.10
191	John Doherty	.10
192	Wally Joyner	.15
193	Jim Thome	.20
194	Royce Clayton	.10
195	John Olerud	.15
196	Steve Buechele	.10
197	Harold Baines	.10
198	Geronimo Berroa	.10
199	Checklist	.10
200	Checklist	.10

1995 Studio Gold

The chase cards in 1995 Studio are plastic versions of some of the regular cards. The round-cornered plastic format of the inserts gives them an even greater similitude to credit cards. The first 50 numbers in the regular set are reproduced in a parallel Studio Gold plastic version, found one per pack, except for those packs which have a platinum card.

		MT
Complete Set (50):		30.00
Common Player:		.25
1	Frank Thomas	1.50
2	Jeff Bagwell	1.50
3	Don Mattingly	1.50
4	Mike Piazza	2.00
5	Ken Griffey Jr.	4.00
6	Greg Maddux	2.00
7	Barry Bonds	1.00
8	Cal Ripken Jr.	3.00
9	Jose Canseco	.50
10	Paul Molitor	1.00
11	Kenny Lofton	.75
12	Will Clark	.50
13	Tim Salmon	.35
14	Joe Carter	.25
15	Albert Belle	.75
16	Roger Clemens	1.50
17	Roberto Alomar	.75
18	Alex Rodriguez	3.00
19	Raul Mondesi	.50
20	Deion Sanders	.40
21	Juan Gonzalez	1.50
22	Kirby Puckett	1.50
23	Fred McGriff	.40
24	Matt Williams	.35
25	Tony Gwynn	1.50
26	Cliff Floyd	.25
27	Travis Fryman	.25
28	Shawn Green	.35
29	Mike Mussina	.60
30	Bob Hamelin	.25
31	Dave Justice	.50
32	Manny Ramirez	.75
33	David Cone	.25
34	Marquis Grissom	.25
35	Moises Alou	.25
36	Carlos Baerga	.25
37	Barry Larkin	.30
38	Robin Ventura	.30
39	Mo Vaughn	.60
40	Jeffrey Hammonds	.25
41	Ozzie Smith	1.00
42	Andres Galarraga	.35
43	Carlos Delgado	.50
44	Lenny Dykstra	.25
45	Cecil Fielder	.25
46	Wade Boggs	.50
47	Gregg Jefferies	.25
48	Randy Johnson	.50
49	Rafael Palmeiro	.40
50	Craig Biggio	.35

1995 Studio Platinum

Found at the rate of one per 10 packs, Studio Platinum cards are silver-toned plastic versions of the first 25 cards from the regular set.

		MT
Complete Set (25):		100.00
Common Player:		1.50
1	Frank Thomas	6.00
2	Jeff Bagwell	6.00
3	Don Mattingly	5.00
4	Mike Piazza	8.00
5	Ken Griffey Jr.	15.00
6	Greg Maddux	8.00
7	Barry Bonds	4.00
8	Cal Ripken Jr.	12.00
9	Jose Canseco	2.00
10	Paul Molitor	4.00
11	Kenny Lofton	2.00
12	Will Clark	1.50
13	Tim Salmon	1.50
14	Joe Carter	1.50
15	Albert Belle	3.00
16	Roger Clemens	5.00
17	Roberto Alomar	2.00
18	Alex Rodriguez	12.00
19	Raul Mondesi	1.50
20	Deion Sanders	1.50
21	Juan Gonzalez	6.00
22	Kirby Puckett	5.00
23	Fred McGriff	1.50
24	Matt Williams	1.50
25	Tony Gwynn	6.00

1996 Studio

The 1996 Studio set is the first Donruss product to be released under the Pinnacle Brands flagship. The 150-card set has three parallel sets - Bronze Press Proofs (2,000 sets), Silver Press Proofs (found only in magazine packs, 100 sets), and Gold Press Proofs (500 sets). Three insert sets were also made - Hit Parade, Masterstrokes and Stained Glass Stars.

		MT
Complete Set (150):		15.00
Common Player:		.10
Wax Box:		45.00
1	Cal Ripken Jr.	2.50
2	Alex Gonzalez	.10
3	Roger Cedeno	.15
4	Todd Hollandsworth	.10
5	Gregg Jefferies	.10
6	Ryne Sandberg	.75
7	Eric Karros	.10
8	Jeff Conine	.10
9	Rafael Palmeiro	.25
10	Bip Roberts	.10
11	Roger Clemens	1.00
12	Tom Glavine	.20
13	Jason Giambi	.15
14	Rey Ordonez	.40
15	Chan Ho Park	.15
16	Vinny Castilla	.10
17	Butch Huskey	.10
18	Greg Maddux	2.00
19	Bernard Gilkey	.10
20	Marquis Grissom	.10
21	Chuck Knoblauch	.20
22	Ozzie Smith	.75
23	Garret Anderson	.10
24	J.T. Snow	.10
25	John Valentin	.10
26	Barry Larkin	.20
27	Bobby Bonilla	.10
28	Todd Zeile	.10
29	Roberto Alomar	.65
30	Ramon Martinez	.10
31	Jeff King	.10
32	Dennis Eckersley	.10
33	Derek Jeter	2.00
34	Edgar Martinez	.10
35	Geronimo Berroa	.10
36	Hal Morris	.10
37	Troy Percival	.10
38	Jason Isringhausen	.15
39	Greg Vaughn	.10
40	Robin Ventura	.15
41	Craig Biggio	.20
42	Will Clark	.30
43	Sammy Sosa	1.50
44	Bernie Williams	.40
45	Kenny Lofton	.45
46	Wade Boggs	.30
47	Javy Lopez	.15
48	Reggie Sanders	.10
49	Jeff Bagwell	1.25
50	Fred McGriff	.35
51	Charles Johnson	.10
52	Darren Daulton	.10
53	Jose Canseco	.35
54	Cecil Fielder	.10
55	Raul Mondesi	.30
56	Tim Salmon	.25
57	Carlos Delgado	.50
58	David Cone	.15
59	Tim Raines	.10
60	Lyle Mouton	.10
61	Wally Joyner	.10
62	Bret Boone	.10
63	Hideo Nomo	.50
64	Gary Sheffield	.30
65	Alex Rodriguez	3.00
66	Russ Davis	.10
67	Checklist	.10
68	Marty Cordova	.10
69	Ruben Sierra	.10
70	Jose Mesa	.10
71	Matt Williams	.30
72	Chipper Jones	2.00
73	Randy Johnson	.40
74	Kirby Puckett	1.00
75	Jim Edmonds	.10
76	Barry Bonds	.75
77	David Segui	.10
78	Larry Walker	.30
79	Jason Kendall	.10
80	Mike Piazza	2.00
81	Brian Hunter	.10
82	Julio Franco	.10
83	Jay Bell	.10
84	Kevin Seitzer	.10
85	John Smoltz	.20
86	Joe Carter	.10
87	Ray Durham	.10
88	Carlos Baerga	.10
89	Ron Gant	.10
90	Orlando Merced	.10
91	Lee Smith	.10
92	Pedro Martinez	.15
93	Frank Thomas	1.50
94	Al Martin	.10
95	Chad Curtis	.10
96	Eddie Murray	.40
97	Rusty Greer	.10
98	Jay Buhner	.10
99	Rico Brogna	.10
100	Todd Hundley	.15
101	Moises Alou	.10
102	Chili Davis	.10
103	Ismael Valdes	.10
104	Mo Vaughn	.45
105	Juan Gonzalez	1.25
106	Mark Grudzielanek	.10
107	Derek Bell	.10
108	Shawn Green	.15
109	David Justice	.20
110	Paul O'Neill	.15
111	Kevin Appier	.10
112	Ray Lankford	.10
113	Travis Fryman	.10
114	Manny Ramirez	1.00
115	Brooks Kieschnick	.10
116	Ken Griffey Jr.	4.00
117	Jeffrey Hammonds	.10
118	Mark McGwire	4.00
119	Denny Neagle	.10
120	Quilvio Veras	.10
121	Alan Benes	.10
122	Rondell White	.10
123	*Osvaldo Fernandez*	.20
124	Andres Galarraga	.20
125	Johnny Damon	.20
126	Lenny Dykstra	.10
127	Jason Schmidt	.10
128	Mike Mussina	.50
129	Ken Caminiti	.25
130	Michael Tucker	.10
131	LaTroy Hawkins	.10
132	Checklist	.10
133	Delino DeShields	.10
134	Dave Nilsson	.10
135	Jack McDowell	.10
136	Joey Hamilton	.10
137	Dante Bichette	.20
138	Paul Molitor	.40
139	Ivan Rodriguez	.50
140	Mark Grace	.25
141	Paul Wilson	.20
142	Orel Hershiser	.10
143	Albert Belle	.60
144	Tino Martinez	.15
145	Tony Gwynn	1.00
146	George Arias	.10
147	Brian Jordan	.15
148	Brian McRae	.10
149	Rickey Henderson	.25
150	Ryan Klesko	.20

1996 Studio Press Proofs

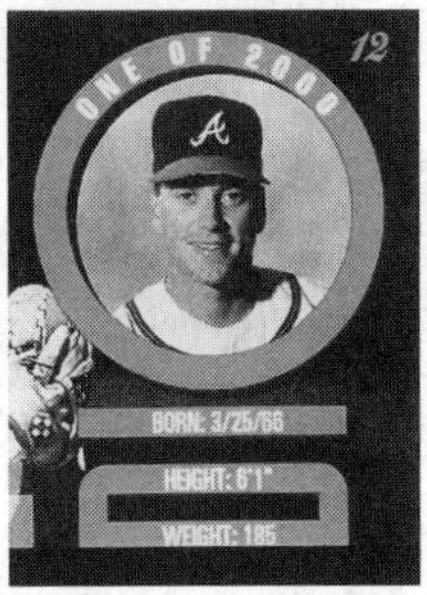

The basic 150-card 1996 Studio set was also produced in three parallel press proof versions. Each is basically identical to the regular-issue cards except for appropriately colored foil highlights on front and a notation of edition size in the circle around the portrait photo on back. Bronze press proofs were issued in an edition of 2,000 each and were inserted at an average rate of one per six packs. Gold press proofs were an edition of 500 with an average insertion rate of one per 24 packs. The silver press proofs were inserted only into magazine packs and limited to just 100 cards of each.

	MT
Complete Set, Bronze (150):	400.00
Common Player, Bronze:	.75
Bronze Stars: 8X	
Complete Set, Gold (150):	1200.
Common Player, Gold:	3.00
Gold Rookies, Stars: 30X	
Common Player, Silver:	7.50
Silver Rookies, Stars: 60X	

(See 1996 Studio for checklist, base card values)

1996 Studio Hit Parade

These die-cut inserts resemble an album with half of the record pulled out of the sleeve. Hit Parade cards, which feature top long ball hitters, were seeded one per every 36 packs. The cards were individually numbered up to 7,500. Each card can also be found in a sample version which has a "XXXX/5000" serial number on back.

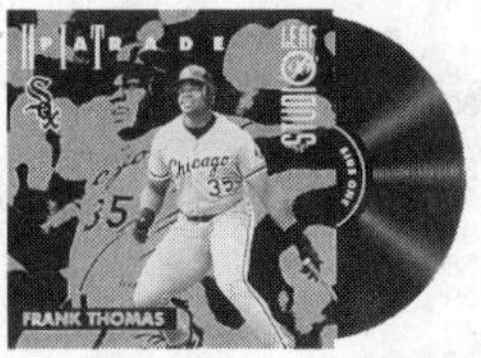

		MT
Complete Set (10):		80.00
Common Player:		4.00
1	Tony Gwynn	10.00
2	Ken Griffey Jr.	25.00
3	Frank Thomas	10.00
4	Jeff Bagwell	8.00
5	Kirby Puckett	6.00
6	Mike Piazza	18.00
7	Barry Bonds	6.00
8	Albert Belle	5.00
9	Tim Salmon	4.00
10	Mo Vaughn	4.00

1996 Studio Masterstrokes Samples

Each of the Masterstrokes insert cards can also be found in a sample edition which was distributed one card at a time to hobby dealers. They differ from the issued version only in appearance of a sample notation.

		MT
Complete Set (8):		65.00
Common Player:		5.00
1	Tony Gwynn	7.50
2	Mike Piazza	9.00
3	Jeff Bagwell	6.00
4	Manny Ramirez	6.00
5	Cal Ripken Jr.	10.00
6	Frank Thomas	6.00
7	Ken Griffey Jr.	12.50
8	Greg Maddux	7.50

1996 Studio Masterstrokes

Only 5,000 each of these 1996 Studio insert cards were made. The cards simulate oil painting detail on an embossed canvas-feel front. Backs are glossy and individually serial numbered. They are found on average of once per 70 packs. Sample versions of each card overprinted as such on the back and numbered "PROMO/5000" are also known.

		MT
Complete Set (8):		100.00
Common Player:		5.00
1	Tony Gwynn	9.00
2	Mike Piazza	15.00
3	Jeff Bagwell	8.00
4	Manny Ramirez	8.00
5	Cal Ripken Jr.	20.00
6	Frank Thomas	8.00
7	Ken Griffey Jr.	25.00
8	Greg Maddux	12.50

1996 Studio Stained Glass Stars

Twelve superstars are featured on these clear, die-cut plastic cards which resemble stained glass windows. These 1996 Studio inserts were seeded one per every 30 packs.

		MT
Complete Set (12):		90.00
Common Player:		4.00
1	Cal Ripken Jr.	12.50
2	Ken Griffey Jr.	15.00
3	Frank Thomas	7.50
4	Greg Maddux	10.00
5	Chipper Jones	10.00
6	Mike Piazza	10.00
7	Albert Belle	3.00
8	Jeff Bagwell	9.00
9	Hideo Nomo	3.00
10	Barry Bonds	4.00
11	Manny Ramirez	8.00
12	Kenny Lofton	3.00

1997 Studio

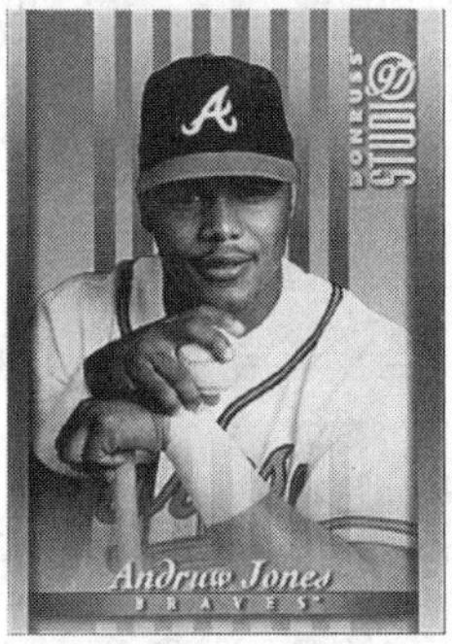

Innovations in both product and packaging marked the seventh annual issue of Donruss' Studio brand. As in the past, the 165 cards in the base set rely on high-quality front photos to bring out the players' personalities. For '97, the photos are set against a background of variously shaded gray horizontal stripes. Backs have a second player photo, often an action shot, along with a short career summary. The "pack" for '97 Studio is something totally new to the hobby. An 8-1/2" x 12" cardboard envelope, complete with a zip strip opener in the style of an express-mail envelope, contains a cello pack of five standard-size cards plus either an 8" x 10" Studio Portrait card or an 8" x 10" version of the Master Strokes insert. Suggested retail price at issue was $2.49 per pack. Regular-size Master Strokes cards are one of several insert series which includes silver and gold press proofs and die-cut plastic Hard Hats.

		MT
Complete Set (165):		40.00
Common Player:		.10
Wax Box:		45.00
1	Frank Thomas	1.50
2	Gary Sheffield	.25
3	Jason Isringhausen	.10
4	Ron Gant	.10
5	Andy Pettitte	.65
6	Todd Hollandsworth	.10
7	Troy Percival	.10
8	Mark McGwire	4.00
9	Barry Larkin	.20
10	Ken Caminiti	.20
11	Paul Molitor	.50
12	Travis Fryman	.10
13	Kevin Brown	.15
14	Robin Ventura	.15
15	Andres Galarraga	.20
16	Ken Griffey Jr.	4.00
17	Roger Clemens	1.00
18	Alan Benes	.10
19	David Justice	.25
20	Damon Buford	.10
21	Mike Piazza	2.00
22	Ray Durham	.10
23	Billy Wagner	.10
24	Dean Palmer	.10
25	David Cone	.20
26	Ruben Sierra	.10
27	Henry Rodriguez	.10
28	Ray Lankford	.10
29	Jamey Wright	.10
30	Brady Anderson	.15
31	Tino Martinez	.20
32	Manny Ramirez	1.00
33	Jeff Conine	.10
34	Dante Bichette	.20
35	Jose Canseco	.30
36	Mo Vaughn	.50
37	Sammy Sosa	1.50
38	Mark Grudzielanek	.10
39	Mike Mussina	.60
40	Bill Pulsipher	.10
41	Ryne Sandberg	.75
42	Rickey Henderson	.25
43	Alex Rodriguez	3.00
44	Eddie Murray	.40
45	Ernie Young	.10
46	Joey Hamilton	.10
47	Wade Boggs	.35
48	Rusty Greer	.10
49	Carlos Delgado	.50
50	Ellis Burks	.10
51	Cal Ripken Jr.	3.00
52	Alex Fernandez	.10
53	Wally Joyner	.10
54	James Baldwin	.10
55	Juan Gonzalez	1.25
56	John Smoltz	.15
57	Omar Vizquel	.10
58	Shane Reynolds	.10
59	Barry Bonds	.75
60	Jason Kendall	.10
61	Marty Cordova	.10
62	Charles Johnson	.10
63	John Jaha	.10
64	Chan Ho Park	.15
65	Jermaine Allensworth	.10
66	Mark Grace	.20
67	Tim Salmon	.15
68	Edgar Martinez	.10
69	Marquis Grissom	.10
70	Craig Biggio	.20
71	Bobby Higginson	.10
72	Kevin Seitzer	.10
73	Hideo Nomo	.50
74	Dennis Eckersley	.10
75	Bobby Bonilla	.10
76	Dwight Gooden	.10
77	Jeff Cirillo	.10
78	Brian McRae	.10
79	Chipper Jones	2.00
80	Jeff Fassero	.10
81	Fred McGriff	.25
82	Garret Anderson	.10
83	Eric Karros	.10
84	Derek Bell	.10
85	Kenny Lofton	.50
86	John Mabry	.10
87	Pat Hentgen	.10
88	Greg Maddux	2.00
89	Jason Giambi	.10
90	Al Martin	.10
91	Derek Jeter	2.00
92	Rey Ordonez	.15
93	Will Clark	.25
94	Kevin Appier	.10
95	Roberto Alomar	.50
96	Joe Carter	.10
97	Bernie Williams	.50
98	Albert Belle	.60
99	Greg Vaughn	.10
100	Tony Clark	.50
101	Matt Williams	.25
102	Jeff Bagwell	1.25
103	Reggie Sanders	.10
104	Mariano Rivera	.20
105	Larry Walker	.35
106	Shawn Green	.15
107	Alex Ochoa	.10
108	Ivan Rodriguez	.60
109	Eric Young	.10
110	Javier Lopez	.10
111	Brian Hunter	.10
112	Raul Mondesi	.25
113	Randy Johnson	.60
114	Tony Phillips	.10
115	Carlos Garcia	.10
116	Moises Alou	.15
117	Paul O'Neill	.15

118 Jim Thome .30
119 Jermaine Dye .10
120 Wilson Alvarez .10
121 Rondell White .10
122 Michael Tucker .10
123 Mike Lansing .10
124 Tony Gwynn 1.25
125 Ryan Klesko .15
126 Jim Edmonds .10
127 Chuck Knoblauch .20
128 Rafael Palmeiro .20
129 Jay Buhner .10
130 Tom Glavine .20
131 Julio Franco .10
132 Cecil Fielder .10
133 Paul Wilson .10
134 Deion Sanders .20
135 Alex Gonzalez .10
136 Charles Nagy .10
137 Andy Ashby .10
138 Edgar Renteria .10
139 Pedro Martinez .20
140 Brian Jordan .10
141 Todd Hundley .20
142 Marc Newfield .10
143 Darryl Strawberry .10
144 Dan Wilson .10
145 *Brian Giles* 1.50
146 Bartolo Colon .10
147 Shannon Stewart .10
148 Scott Spiezio .10
149 Andruw Jones 1.50
150 Karim Garcia .10
151 Vladimir Guerrero 1.00
152 George Arias .10
153 Brooks Kieschnick .10
154 Todd Walker .50
155 Scott Rolen 1.50
156 Todd Greene .10
157 Dmitri Young .10
158 Ruben Rivera .10
159 Trey Beamon .10
160 Nomar Garciaparra 2.00
161 Bob Abreu .15
162 Darin Erstad 1.25
163 Ken Griffey Jr. (checklist) 1.00
164 Frank Thomas (checklist) .50
165 Alex Rodriguez (checklist) .75

1997 Studio Press Proofs

Each of the 165 cards in the base set of '97 Studio was also produced in a pair of Press Proof versions as random pack inserts. Fronts of the Press Proofs have either silver or gold holographic foil replacing the silver foil graphics found on regular cards, as well as foil strips down each side. Backs are identical to the regular issue. The silver Press Proofs were issued in an edition of 1,500 of each player; the golds are limited to 500 of each.

MT
Complete Set, Silver (165): 450.00
Common Player, Silver: 1.50
Silver Stars: 8X
Complete Set, Gold (165): 1600.
Common Player, Gold: 4.00
Gold Stars: 20X
(Silver stars valued at 8-15X regular cards; gold at 15-40X.)

1997 Studio Hard Hats

Die-cut plastic is used to represent a player's batting helmet in this set of '97 Studio inserts. A player action photo appears in the foreground with his name and other graphic elements in silver foil. Backs feature a small portrait photo, short career summary and a serial number from within the edition of 5,000 of each card.

MT
Complete Set (24): 160.00
Common Player: 2.00
1 Ivan Rodriguez 6.00
2 Albert Belle 5.00
3 Ken Griffey Jr. 25.00
4 Chuck Knoblauch 4.00
5 Frank Thomas 12.00
6 Cal Ripken Jr. 20.00
7 Todd Walker 4.00
8 Alex Rodriguez 20.00
9 Jim Thome 3.00
10 Mike Piazza 15.00
11 Barry Larkin 3.00
12 Chipper Jones 15.00
13 Derek Jeter 15.00
14 Jermaine Dye 2.00
15 Jason Giambi 2.00
16 Tim Salmon 4.00
17 Brady Anderson 2.00
18 Rondell White 2.00
19 Bernie Williams 4.00
20 Juan Gonzalez 12.00
21 Karim Garcia 4.00
22 Scott Rolen 8.00
23 Darin Erstad 6.00
24 Brian Jordan 2.00

1997 Studio Master Strokes

The look and feel of a painting on canvas is the effect presented by '97 Studio's Master Strokes inserts. Card fronts feature unique player action art and are highlighted by gold-foil graphics. Each card has a facsimile autograph on front. UV-coated backs are team-color coordinated and have a few sentences about the player. Gold-foil serial numbering identifies the card from an edition of 2,000 of each player.

MT
Complete Set (24): 450.00
Common Player: 7.50
1 Derek Jeter 25.00
2 Jeff Bagwell 15.00
3 Ken Griffey Jr. 50.00
4 Barry Bonds 12.50
5 Frank Thomas 15.00
6 Andy Pettitte 10.00
7 Mo Vaughn 7.50
8 Alex Rodriguez 35.00
9 Andruw Jones 12.50
10 Kenny Lofton 7.50
11 Cal Ripken Jr. 35.00
12 Greg Maddux 20.00
13 Manny Ramirez 15.00
14 Mike Piazza 25.00
14p Mike Piazza (promo) 7.50
15 Vladimir Guerrero 12.50
16 Albert Belle 10.00
17 Chipper Jones 25.00
18 Hideo Nomo 7.50
19 Sammy Sosa 20.00
20 Tony Gwynn 17.50
21 Gary Sheffield 7.50
22 Mark McGwire 50.00
23 Juan Gonzalez 17.50
24 Paul Molitor 10.00

1997 Studio Master Strokes 8x10

The look and feel of a painting on canvas is the effect presented by the 8" x 10" version of '97 Studio's Master Strokes inserts. Card fronts feature unique player action art and are highlighted by gold-foil graphics. Each card has a facsimile autograph on front. UV-coated backs are team-color coordinated and have a few sentences about the player. Gold-foil serial numbering identifies the card from an edition of 5,000 of each player - making the super-size version more than twice as common as the 2-1/2" x 3-1/2" version.

MT
Complete Set (24): 220.00
Common Player: 4.00
1 Derek Jeter 15.00
2 Jeff Bagwell 10.00
3 Ken Griffey Jr. 25.00
4 Barry Bonds 6.00
5 Frank Thomas 10.00
6 Andy Pettitte 5.00
7 Mo Vaughn 4.00
8 Alex Rodriguez 20.00
9 Andruw Jones 12.00
10 Kenny Lofton 4.00
11 Cal Ripken Jr. 20.00
12 Greg Maddux 15.00
13 Manny Ramirez 9.00
14 Mike Piazza 15.00
15 Vladimir Guerrero 8.00
16 Albert Belle 5.00
17 Chipper Jones 15.00
18 Hideo Nomo 4.00
19 Sammy Sosa 15.00
20 Tony Gwynn 10.00
21 Gary Sheffield 4.00
22 Mark McGwire 25.00
23 Juan Gonzalez 10.00
24 Paul Molitor 6.00

1997 Studio Portraits

Perhaps the most innovative feature of '97 Studio is the 8" x 10" Portrait cards which come one per pack (except when a pack contains a Master Strokes 8x10). Virtually identical to the player's regular-size Studio card, the jumbo version has the word "PORTRAIT" in black beneath the team name on front. Backs have different card numbers than the same player's card in the regular set. The Portrait cards are produced with a special UV coating on front to facilitate autographing. Pre-autographed cards of three youngsters in the series were included as random pack inserts.

MT
Complete Set (24): 25.00
Common Player: .50
1 Ken Griffey Jr. 4.00
1s Frank Thomas (overprinted "SAMPLE") .50
2 Frank Thomas 1.50
3 Alex Rodriguez 3.00
4 Andruw Jones 1.50
5 Cal Ripken Jr. 3.00
6 Greg Maddux 2.00
7 Mike Piazza 2.00
8 Chipper Jones 2.00
9 Albert Belle 1.00
10 Derek Jeter 2.00
11 Juan Gonzalez 1.00
12 Todd Walker .75
12a Todd Walker (autographed edition of 1,250) 40.00
13 Mark McGwire 4.00
14 Barry Bonds .75
15 Jeff Bagwell 1.00
16 Manny Ramirez 1.00
17 Kenny Lofton .50
18 Mo Vaughn .50
19 Hideo Nomo .50
20 Tony Gwynn 1.00
21 Vladimir Guerrero 1.50
21a Vladimir Guerrero (autographed edition of 500) 100.00
22 Gary Sheffield .50
23 Ryne Sandberg .75
24 Scott Rolen 1.25
24a Scott Rolen (autographed edition of 1,000) 75.00

1997 Studio Portrait Collection

In a departure from traditional sportscard marketing, the 1997 Studio program offered a pair of specially framed editions directly to consumers. The offer was made in a color brochure found in about half the packs advertising the "Portrait Collection." The offer includes one standard-size card and an 8" x 10" Portrait or Master card similar to those in the regular issue. These cards differ from the regular issue in that they are trimmed in platinum holographic foil, individually hand-numbered and signed by the photographer. The cards were sold framed with a metal plaque, also numbered, attesting to the limited-edition status. The framed Studio Portrait piece was produced in an edition of 500 of each player; the Master Strokes piece was limited to 100 for each player on the checklist. The former was issued at $159; the latter at $299.

MT
Complete Set, Studio Portrait (24): 3800.
Complete Set, Master Strokes (24): 7000.
Common Plaque, Studio Portrait: 160.00
Common Plaque, Master Strokes: 300.00
P1 Ken Griffey Jr. 160.00
P2 Frank Thomas 160.00
P3 Alex Rodriguez 160.00
P4 Andruw Jones 160.00
P5 Cal Ripken Jr. 160.00
P6 Greg Maddux 160.00
P7 Mike Piazza 160.00
P8 Chipper Jones 160.00
P9 Albert Belle 160.00
P10 Derek Jeter 160.00
P11 Juan Gonzalez 160.00
P12 Todd Walker 160.00
P13 Mark McGwire 160.00
P14 Barry Bonds 160.00
P15 Jeff Bagwell 160.00
P16 Manny 160.00
P17 Kenny Lofton 160.00
P18 Mo Vaughn 160.00
P19 Hideo Nomo 160.00
P20 Tony Gwynn 160.00
P21 Vladimir Guerrero 160.00
P22 Gary Sheffield 160.00
P23 Ryne Sandberg 160.00
P24 Scott Rolen 160.00
M1 Derek Jeter 300.00
M2 Jeff Bagwell 300.00
M3 Ken Griffey Jr. 300.00
M4 Barry Bonds 300.00
M5 Frank Thomas 300.00
M6 Andy Pettitte 300.00
M7 Mo Vaughn 300.00
M8 Alex Rodriguez 300.00
M9 Andruw Jones 300.00
M10 Kenny Lofton 300.00
M11 Cal Ripken Jr. 300.00
M12 Greg Maddux 300.00
M13 Manny Ramirez 300.00
M14 Mike Piazza 300.00
M15 Vladimir Guerrero 300.00
M16 Albert Belle 300.00
M17 Chipper Jones 300.00
M18 Hideo Nomo 300.00
M19 Sammy Sosa 300.00
M20 Tony Gwynn 300.00
M21 Gary Sheffield 300.00
M22 Mark McGwire 300.00
M23 Juan Gonzalez 300.00
M24 Paul Molitor 300.00

1998 Studio

The Donruss Studio base set consists of 220 regular-sized cards and 36 8-x-10 portraits. The base cards feature a posed photo with an action shot in the background, surrounded by a white border. Silver Studio Proofs (numbered to 1,000) and Gold Studio Proofs (300) parallel the regular-size base set. Inserts included Freeze Frame, Hit Parade and Masterstrokes.

MT
Complete Set (220): 35.00
Common Player: .15
Wax Box: 50.00
1 Tony Clark .40
2 Jose Cruz Jr. .20
3 Ivan Rodriguez .75
4 Mo Vaughn .50
5 Kenny Lofton .50
6 Will Clark .25
7 Barry Larkin .20
8 Jay Bell .15
9 Kevin Young .15
10 Francisco Cordova .15
11 Justin Thompson .15
12 Paul Molitor .50
13 Jeff Bagwell 1.25
14 Jose Canseco .35
15 Scott Rolen 1.00
16 Wilton Guerrero .15
17 Shannon Stewart .15
18 Hideki Irabu .50
19 Michael Tucker .15
20 Joe Carter .15
21 Gabe Alvarez .15
22 Ricky Ledee .40
23 Karim Garcia .20
24 Eli Marrero .15
25 Scott Elarton .15
26 Mario Valdez .15
27 Ben Grieve 1.00
28 Paul Konerko .40
29 *Esteban Yan* .20
30 Esteban Loaiza .15
31 Delino DeShields .15
32 Bernie Williams .40
33 Joe Randa .15
34 Randy Johnson .50
35 Brett Tomko .15
36 *Todd Erdos* .20
37 Bobby Higginson .15
38 Jason Kendall .15

39	Ray Lankford	.15
40	Mark Grace	.30
41	Andy Pettitte	.40
42	Alex Rodriguez	2.50
43	Hideo Nomo	.40
44	Sammy Sosa	2.00
45	J.T. Snow	.15
46	Jason Varitek	.25
47	Vinny Castilla	.15
48	Neifi Perez	.15
49	Todd Walker	.15
50	Mike Cameron	.15
51	Jeffrey Hammonds	.15
52	Deivi Cruz	.15
53	Brian Hunter	.15
54	Al Martin	.15
55	Ron Coomer	.15
56	Chan Ho Park	.15
57	Pedro Martinez	.40
58	Darin Erstad	.75
59	Albert Belle	.60
60	Nomar Garciaparra	2.00
61	Tony Gwynn	1.50
62	Mike Piazza	2.00
63	Todd Helton	.75
64	David Ortiz	.30
65	Todd Dunwoody	.15
66	Orlando Cabrera	.15
67	Ken Cloude	.15
68	Andy Benes	.15
69	Mariano Rivera	.25
70	Cecil Fielder	.15
71	Brian Jordan	.15
72	Darryl Kile	.15
73	Reggie Jefferson	.15
74	Shawn Estes	.15
75	Bobby Bonilla	.15
76	Denny Neagle	.15
77	Robin Ventura	.25
78	Omar Vizquel	.15
79	Craig Biggio	.30
80	Moises Alou	.25
81	Garret Anderson	.15
82	Eric Karros	.15
83	Dante Bichette	.30
84	Charles Johnson	.15
85	Rusty Greer	.15
86	Travis Fryman	.15
87	Fernando Tatis	.25
88	Wilson Alvarez	.15
89	Carl Pavano	.15
90	Brian Rose	.15
91	Geoff Jenkins	.15
92	*Magglio Ordonez*	1.50
93	David Segui	.15
94	David Cone	.25
95	John Smoltz	.20
96	Jim Thome	.30
97	Gary Sheffield	.40
98	Barry Bonds	.75
99	Andres Galarraga	.40
100	Brad Fullmer	.40
101	Bobby Estalella	.15
102	Enrique Wilson	.15
103	*Frank Catalanotto*	.20
104	*Mike Lowell*	.40
105	Kevin Orie	.15
106	Matt Morris	.20
107	Pokey Reese	.15
108	Shawn Green	.20
109	Tony Womack	.15
110	Ken Caminiti	.25
111	Roberto Alomar	.50
112	Ken Griffey Jr.	3.00
113	Cal Ripken Jr.	2.50
114	Lou Collier	.15
115	Larry Walker	.40
116	Fred McGriff	.30
117	Jim Edmonds	.20
118	Edgar Martinez	.15
119	Matt Williams	.30
120	Ismael Valdes	.15
121	Bartolo Colon	.20
122	Jeff Cirillo	.15
123	*Steve Woodard*	.25
124	*Kevin Millwood*	4.00
125	Derrick Gibson	.15
126	Jacob Cruz	.15
127	Russell Branyan	.15
128	Sean Casey	.40
129	Derrek Lee	.15
130	Paul O'Neill	.25
131	Brad Radke	.15
132	Kevin Appier	.15
133	John Olerud	.25
134	Alan Benes	.15
135	Todd Greene	.15
136	*Carlos Mendoza*	.35
137	Wade Boggs	.40
138	Jose Guillen	.25
139	Tino Martinez	.30
140	Aaron Boone	.15
141	Abraham Nunez	.15
142	Preston Wilson	.15
143	Randall Simon	.20
144	Dennis Reyes	.15
145	Mark Kotsay	.30
146	Richard Hidalgo	.15
147	Travis Lee	.60
148	*Hanley Frias*	.15
149	Ruben Rivera	.15
150	Rafael Medina	.15
151	Dave Nilsson	.15
152	Curt Schilling	.25
153	Brady Anderson	.15
154	Carlos Delgado	.50
155	Jason Giambi	.15
156	Pat Hentgen	.15
157	Tom Glavine	.25
158	Ryan Klesko	.20
159	Chipper Jones	2.00
160	Juan Gonzalez	1.50
161	Mark McGwire	3.00
162	Vladimir Guerrero	1.00
163	Derek Jeter	2.00
164	Manny Ramirez	1.00
165	Mike Mussina	.60
166	Rafael Palmeiro	.30
167	Henry Rodriguez	.15
168	Jeff Suppan	.15
169	Eric Milton	.15
170	Scott Spiezio	.15
171	Wilson Delgado	.15
172	Bubba Trammell	.15
173	Ellis Burks	.15
174	Jason Dickson	.15
175	Butch Huskey	.15
176	Edgardo Alfonzo	.15
177	Eric Young	.15
178	Marquis Grissom	.15
179	Lance Johnson	.15
180	Kevin Brown	.25
181	Sandy Alomar Jr.	.25
182	Todd Hundley	.15
183	Rondell White	.20
184	Javier Lopez	.20
185	Damian Jackson	.15
186	Raul Mondesi	.40
187	Rickey Henderson	.35
188	David Justice	.40
189	Jay Buhner	.15
190	Jaret Wright	1.00
191	Miguel Tejada	.40
192	Ron Wright	.15
193	Livan Hernandez	.15
194	A.J. Hinch	.50
195	Richie Sexson	.15
196	Bob Abreu	.15
197	Luis Castillo	.15
198	Michael Coleman	.15
199	Greg Maddux	2.00
200	Frank Thomas	1.50
201	Andruw Jones	.75
202	Roger Clemens	1.25
203	Tim Salmon	.30
204	Chuck Knoblauch	.40
205	Wes Helms	.15
206	Juan Encarnacion	.15
207	Russ Davis	.15
208	John Valentin	.15
209	Tony Saunders	.15
210	Mike Sweeney	.15
211	Steve Finley	.15
212	*David Dellucci*	.50
213	Edgar Renteria	.15
214	Jeremi Gonzalez	.15
215	Checklist (Jeff Bagwell)	.60
216	Checklist (Mike Piazza)	1.00
217	Checklist (Greg Maddux)	1.00
218	Checklist (Cal Ripken Jr.)	1.25
219	Checklist (Frank Thomas)	.75
220	Checklist (Ken Griffey Jr.)	1.50

1998 Studio Silver Proofs

This parallel set includes all 220 cards in Studio baseball. Cards are identified by a silver holographic strip around the borders. Silver versions are limited to 1,000 sets.

	MT
Complete Set (220):	850.00
Common Player:	1.50
Silver Stars: 8X	

(See 1998 Studio for checklist, base card values.)

Player names in *Italic* type indicate a rookie card.

1998 Studio Gold Proofs

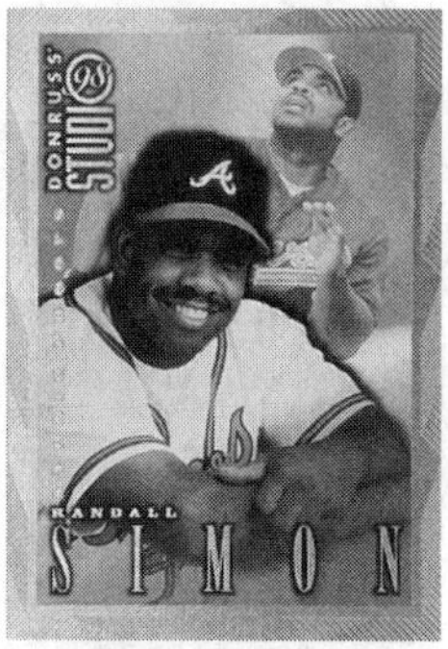

Gold proofs is a parallel of the 220-card base set. Card fronts feature gold holo-foil highlights. Backs are sequentially numbered to 300 each.

	MT
Complete Set (220):	2500.
Common Player:	4.00
Stars: 25X	

(See 1998 Studio for checklist and base card values.)

1998 Studio Autographs

Three top rookies signed a number of 8x10s for this product. Lee signed 500 while the other two autographed 1,000 each.

		MT
1	Travis Lee (500)	60.00
2	Todd Helton (1000)	40.00
3	Ben Grieve (1000)	40.00

1998 Studio Freeze Frame

Freeze Frame is a 30-card insert sequentially numbered to 5,000. The cards are designed to look like a piece of film with a color action photo. The first 500 of each card are die-cut.

		MT
Complete Set (30):		245.00
Common Player:		3.00
Production 4,500 sets		
Die-Cuts: 8X		
Production 500 sets		
1	Ken Griffey Jr.	20.00
2	Derek Jeter	15.00
3	Ben Grieve	6.00
4	Cal Ripken Jr.	17.50
5	Alex Rodriguez	17.50
6	Greg Maddux	15.00
7	David Justice	4.50
8	Mike Piazza	15.00
9	Chipper Jones	15.00
10	Randy Johnson	4.50
11	Jeff Bagwell	9.00
12	Nomar Garciaparra	15.00
13	Andruw Jones	6.00
14	Frank Thomas	9.00
15	Scott Rolen	6.00
16	Barry Bonds	6.00
17	Kenny Lofton	4.00
18	Ivan Rodriguez	5.00
19	Chuck Knoblauch	4.00
20	Jose Cruz Jr.	3.00
21	Bernie Williams	4.00
22	Tony Gwynn	12.00
23	Juan Gonzalez	12.00
24	Gary Sheffield	3.00
25	Roger Clemens	7.50
26	Travis Lee	4.50
27	Brad Fullmer	6.00
28	Tim Salmon	3.00
29	Raul Mondesi	3.00
30	Roberto Alomar	4.00

1998 Studio Hit Parade

These 20 cards are printed on micro-etched foil board. This set honors baseball's top hitters and is sequentially numbered to 5,000.

		MT
Complete Set (20):		140.00
Common Player:		4.00
Production 5,000 sets		
1	Tony Gwynn	12.00
2	Larry Walker	4.00
3	Mike Piazza	15.00
4	Frank Thomas	10.00
5	Manny Ramirez	9.00
6	Ken Griffey Jr.	25.00
7	Todd Helton	6.00
8	Vladimir Guerrero	6.00
9	Albert Belle	5.00
10	Jeff Bagwell	10.00
11	Juan Gonzalez	12.00
12	Jim Thome	4.00
13	Scott Rolen	8.00
14	Tino Martinez	4.00
15	Mark McGwire	25.00
16	Barry Bonds	6.00
17	Tony Clark	4.00
18	Mo Vaughn	4.00
19	Darin Erstad	6.00
20	Paul Konerko	4.00

1998 Studio Masterstrokes

Printed on a canvas-like material, these 20 cards are numbered to 1,000.

		MT
Complete Set (20):		650.00
Common Player:		10.00
Production 1,000 sets		
1	Travis Lee	20.00
2	Kenny Lofton	10.00
3	Mo Vaughn	10.00
4	Ivan Rodriguez	15.00
5	Roger Clemens	30.00
6	Mark McGwire	75.00
7	Hideo Nomo	10.00
8	Andruw Jones	20.00
9	Nomar Garciaparra	50.00
10	Juan Gonzalez	40.00
11	Jeff Bagwell	25.00
12	Derek Jeter	50.00
13	Tony Gwynn	40.00
14	Chipper Jones	50.00
15	Mike Piazza	50.00
16	Greg Maddux	50.00
17	Alex Rodriguez	60.00
18	Cal Ripken Jr.	60.00
19	Frank Thomas	25.00
20	Ken Griffey Jr.	75.00

1998 Studio Sony MLB 99

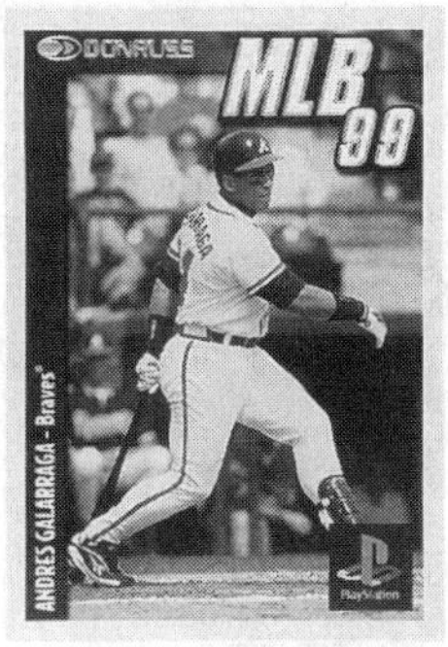

Twenty Sony MLB '99 sweepstakes cards were inserted one per two Studio packs. The fronts feature a color action shot and the backs have sweepstakes rules and a MLB '99 tip.

		MT
Complete Set (20):		10.00
Common Player:		.25
1	Cal Ripken Jr.	2.00
2	Nomar Garciaparra	1.50
3	Barry Bonds	.60
4	Mike Mussina	.50
5	Pedro Martinez	.40
6	Derek Jeter	1.50
7	Andruw Jones	.60
8	Kenny Lofton	.40
9	Gary Sheffield	.25
10	Raul Mondesi	.25
11	Jeff Bagwell	.75
12	Tim Salmon	.25
13	Tom Glavine	.25
14	Ben Grieve	.75
15	Matt Williams	.25
16	Juan Gonzalez	1.25
17	Mark McGwire	3.00
18	Bernie Williams	.40
19	Andres Galarraga	.25
20	Jose Cruz Jr.	.25

1998 Studio 8x10 Portraits Samples

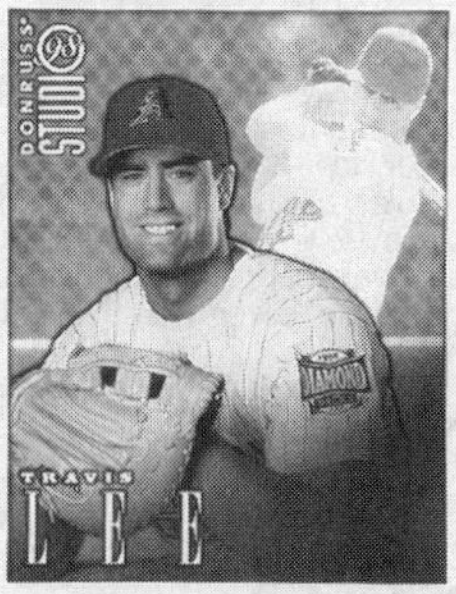

Sample versions of the 8x10 cards which would be found in '98 Studio packs were also issued. They are identical in format to the issued cards, with UV coating and silver-foil graphics on fronts. Backs have a large black "SAMPLE" overprinted diagonally.

		MT
Common Player:		3.00
001	Travis Lee	2.00
002	Todd Helton	3.00

1998 Studio 8x10 Portraits

One Studio 8-x-10 was included in each pack. The cards were blown-up versions of the regular-size base cards, which were inserted seven per pack. The large portraits are paralleled in the Gold Proofs set, which adds gold holo-foil to the cards. Gold Proofs are numbered to 300.

		MT
Complete Set (36):		40.00
Common Player:		.50
Inserted 1:1		
1	Travis Lee	1.50
2	Todd Helton	1.25
3	Ben Grieve	1.50
4	Paul Konerko	.75
5	Jeff Bagwell	2.00
6	Derek Jeter	3.00
7	Ivan Rodriguez	1.50
8	Cal Ripken Jr.	4.00
9	Mike Piazza	3.00
10	Chipper Jones	3.00
11	Frank Thomas	2.50
12	Tony Gwynn	2.50
13	Nomar Garciaparra	3.00
14	Juan Gonzalez	2.50
15	Greg Maddux	3.00
16	Hideo Nomo	.75
17	Scott Rolen	1.50
18	Barry Bonds	1.50
19	Ken Griffey Jr.	5.00
20	Alex Rodriguez	4.00
21	Roger Clemens	2.00
22	Mark McGwire	5.00
23	Jose Cruz Jr.	.50
24	Andruw Jones	1.50
25	Tino Martinez	.50
26	Mo Vaughn	.75
27	Vladimir Guerrero	1.50
28	Tony Clark	1.00
29	Andy Pettitte	1.00
30	Jaret Wright	1.50
31	Paul Molitor	1.00
32	Darin Erstad	1.50
33	Larry Walker	.50
34	Chuck Knoblauch	.50
35	Barry Larkin	.50
36	Kenny Lofton	.75

1998 Studio 8x10 Portraits Gold Proof

This parallel of the 8x10 base set adds gold holo-foil treatments to the 36 cards, which are sequentially numbered to 300 and randomly inserted in packs.

	MT
Complete Set (36):	600.00
Common Player:	8.00
Stars: 20X	

(See 1998 Studio 8X10 Portraits for checklist and base card values.)

1995 Summit Samples

Nine-card cello packs of Summit cards, including "Big Bang" inserts, were released to dealers to debut the new Score brand. Cards are specially marked as promotional samples.

		MT
Complete Set (9):		25.00
Common Player:		2.50
10	Barry Larkin	2.50
11	Albert Belle	3.00
79	Cal Ripken Jr.	9.00
80	David Cone	2.50
125	Alex Gonzalez (Rookie)	3.00
130	Charles Johnson (Rookie)	3.00
BB12	Jose Canseco (Big Bang)	6.00
BB17	Fred McGriff (Big Bang)	3.00
---	Information card	.25

1995 Summit

A late-season release, Summit introduced the Score label to a premium brand card. Printed on extra heavy cardboard stock and UV coated on both sides the veteran player cards (#1-111) feature horizontal or vertical action photos with the player's name and team logo printed in gold-foil on front. Backs have a player portrait photo along with his 1994 stats in monthly charted form. The rookie cards subset (#112-173) have a large black "ROOKIE" on top-front while the back has a short career summary instead of stats. Other subsets include "BAT SPEED" (#174-188), honoring top hitters, and "SPECIAL DELIVERY" (#189-193), featuring top pitchers. Each are designated on front with special gold-foil logos. Seven checklists close out the regular 200-card set. The Summit issued featured a four-tiered chase card program, including a parallel "Nth Degree" set. Summit was a hobby-only issue sold in 7-card foil packs.

		MT
Complete Set (200):		20.00
Common Player:		.10
Wax Box:		40.00
1	Ken Griffey Jr.	3.00
2	Alex Fernandez	.15
3	Fred McGriff	.35
4	Ben McDonald	.10
5	Rafael Palmeiro	.15
6	Tony Gwynn	1.00
7	Jim Thome	.30
8	Ken Hill	.10
9	Barry Bonds	.75
10	Barry Larkin	.20
11	Albert Belle	.60
12	Billy Ashley	.10
13	Matt Williams	.25
14	Andy Benes	.10
15	Midre Cummings	.10
16	J.R. Phillips	.10
17	Edgar Martinez	.10
18	Manny Ramirez	.75
19	Jose Canseco	.35
20	Chili Davis	.10
21	Don Mattingly	1.00
22	Bernie Williams	.40
23	Tom Glavine	.20
24	Robin Ventura	.15
25	Jeff Conine	.10
26	Mark Grace	.20
27	Mark McGwire	3.00
28	Carlos Delgado	.50
29	Greg Colbrunn	.10
30	Greg Maddux	2.00
31	Craig Biggio	.25
32	Kirby Puckett	1.00
33	Derek Bell	.10
34	Lenny Dykstra	.10
35	Tim Salmon	.20
36	Deion Sanders	.20
37	Moises Alou	.15
38	Ray Lankford	.10
39	Willie Greene	.10
40	Ozzie Smith	.50
41	Roger Clemens	.75
42	Andres Galarraga	.20
43	Gary Sheffield	.30
44	Sammy Sosa	1.50
45	Larry Walker	.30
46	Kevin Appier	.10
47	Raul Mondesi	.30
48	Kenny Lofton	.50
49	Darryl Hamilton	.10
50	Roberto Alomar	.60
51	Hal Morris	.10
52	Cliff Floyd	.10
53	Brent Gates	.10
54	Rickey Henderson	.35
55	John Olerud	.15
56	Gregg Jefferies	.10
57	Cecil Fielder	.10
58	Paul Molitor	.50
59	Bret Boone	.10
60	Greg Vaughn	.10
61	Wally Joyner	.15
62	Jeffrey Hammonds	.10
63	James Mouton	.10
64	Omar Vizquel	.10
65	Wade Boggs	.35
66	Terry Steinbach	.10
67	Wil Cordero	.10
68	Joey Hamilton	.10
69	Rico Brogna	.10
70	Darren Daulton	.10
71	Chuck Knoblauch	.20
72	Bob Hamelin	.10
73	Carl Everett	.10
74	Joe Carter	.10
75	Dave Winfield	.35
76	Bobby Bonilla	.10
77	Paul O'Neill	.15
78	Javier Lopez	.15
79	Cal Ripken Jr.	2.50
80	David Cone	.15
81	Bernard Gilkey	.10
82	Ivan Rodriguez	.50
83	Dean Palmer	.10
84	Jason Bere	.10
85	Will Clark	.25
86	Scott Cooper	.10
87	Royce Clayton	.10
88	Mike Piazza	2.00
89	Ryan Klesko	.30
90	Juan Gonzalez	1.50
91	Travis Fryman	.10
92	Frank Thomas	1.50
93	Eduardo Perez	.10
94	Mo Vaughn	.50
95	Jay Bell	.10
96	Jeff Bagwell	1.00
97	Randy Johnson	.35
98	Jimmy Key	.10
99	Dennis Eckersley	.10
100	Carlos Baerga	.10
101	Eddie Murray	.35
102	Mike Mussina	.40
103	Brian Anderson	.10
104	Jeff Cirillo	.10
105	Dante Bichette	.25
106	Bret Saberhagen	.10
107	Jeff Kent	.10
108	Ruben Sierra	.10
109	Kirk Gibson	.10
110	Reggie Sanders	.15
111	Dave Justice	.20
112	Benji Gil	.10
113	Vaughn Eshelman	.10
114	*Carlos Perez*	.20
115	Chipper Jones	2.00
116	Shane Andrews	.10
117	Orlando Miller	.10
118	Scott Ruffcorn	.10
119	Jose Oliva	.10
120	Joe Vitiello	.10
121	Jon Nunnally	.10
122	Garret Anderson	.15
123	Curtis Goodwin	.10
124	*Mark Grudzielanek*	.35
125	Alex Gonzalez	.15
126	David Bell	.10
127	Dustin Hermanson	.10
128	Dave Nilsson	.10
129	Wilson Heredia	.10
130	Charles Johnson	.15
131	Frank Rodriguez	.10
132	Alex Ochoa	.10
133	Alex Rodriguez	2.50
134	*Bobby Higginson*	1.50
135	Edgardo Alfonzo	.15
136	Armando Benitez	.10
137	Rich Aude	.10
138	Tim Naehring	.10
139	Joe Randa	.10
140	Quilvio Veras	.10
141	*Hideo Nomo*	2.00
142	Ray Holbert	.10
143	Michael Tucker	.10
144	Chad Mottola	.10
145	John Valentin	.10
146	James Baldwin	.10
147	Esteban Loaiza	.10
148	Marty Cordova	.15
149	*Juan Acevedo*	.10
150	*Tim Unroe*	.10
151	Brad Clontz	.10
152	Steve Rodriguez	.10
153	Rudy Pemberton	.10
154	Ozzie Timmons	.10
155	Ricky Otero	.10
156	Allen Battle	.10
157	Joe Roselli	.10
158	Roberto Petagine	.10
159	Todd Hollandsworth	.10
160	Shannon Penn	.10
161	Antonio Osuna	.10
162	Russ Davis	.10
163	Jason Giambi	.10
164	Terry Bradshaw	.10
165	Ray Durham	.10
166	Todd Steverson	.10
167	Tim Belk	.10
168	Andy Pettitte	.60
169	Roger Cedeno	.10
170	Jose Parra	.10
171	Scott Sullivan	.10
172	LaTroy Hawkins	.10
173	Jeff McCurry	.10
174	Ken Griffey Jr. (Bat Speed)	1.50
175	Frank Thomas (Bat Speed)	.75
176	Cal Ripken Jr. (Bat Speed)	1.25
177	Jeff Bagwell (Bat Speed)	.50
178	Mike Piazza (Bat Speed)	.60
179	Barry Bonds (Bat Speed)	.35
180	Matt Williams (Bat Speed)	.20
181	Don Mattingly (Bat Speed)	.50
182	Will Clark (Bat Speed)	.20
183	Tony Gwynn (Bat Speed)	.40
184	Kirby Puckett (Bat Speed)	.50
185	Jose Canseco (Bat Speed)	.20
186	Paul Molitor (Bat Speed)	.25
187	Albert Belle (Bat Speed)	.40
188	Joe Carter (Bat Speed)	.10
189	Greg Maddux (Special Delivery)	1.00
190	Roger Clemens (Special Delivery)	.40
191	David Cone (Special Delivery)	.10
192	Mike Mussina (Special Delivery)	.20
193	Randy Johnson (Special Delivery)	.15
194	Checklist (Frank Thomas)	.50
195	Checklist (Ken Griffey Jr.)	.75
196	Checklist (Cal Ripken Jr.)	.60
197	Checklist (Jeff Bagwell)	.30
198	Checklist (Mike Piazza)	.40
199	Checklist (Barry Bonds)	.25
200	Checklist (Mo Vaughn, Matt Williams)	.20

1995 Summit Big Bang

The game's top sluggers are featured in this insert set. The front is printed on prismatic metallic foil, a process which Score calls "Spectroetch," with large and small action photos. Backs are conventionally printed and have a large photo with a career highlight printed beneath. The toughest of the Summit chase cards, these are found on the average of once every two boxes (72 packs). Cards are numbered with a "BB" prefix.

		MT
Complete Set (20):		250.00
Common Player:		3.00
1	Ken Griffey Jr.	50.00
2	Frank Thomas	20.00
3	Cal Ripken Jr.	40.00
4	Jeff Bagwell	20.00
5	Mike Piazza	30.00
6	Barry Bonds	12.00
7	Matt Williams	4.00
8	Don Mattingly	15.00
9	Will Clark	4.00
10	Tony Gwynn	25.00
11	Kirby Puckett	20.00
12	Jose Canseco	6.00
13	Paul Molitor	10.00
14	Albert Belle	10.00
15	Joe Carter	3.00
16	Rafael Palmeiro	4.00
17	Fred McGriff	4.00
18	Dave Justice	3.00
19	Tim Salmon	3.00
20	Mo Vaughn	3.00

1995 Summit New Age

Printed on metallic foil in a horizontal format, the New Age inserts were seeded at a rate of about one per 18 packs. Red and silver colors predominate on front, while the backs are printed in standard technology and feature a second photo and a short career summary of the players who were generally in their second or third Major League season in 1995.

		MT
Complete Set (15):		50.00
Common Player:		1.00
1	Cliff Floyd	1.00
2	Manny Ramirez	10.00
3	Raul Mondesi	5.00
4	Alex Rodriguez	30.00
5	Billy Ashley	1.00
6	Alex Gonzalez	2.00
7	Michael Tucker	1.00
8	Charles Johnson	3.00
9	Carlos Delgado	5.00
10	Benji Gil	1.00
11	Chipper Jones	25.00
12	Todd Hollandsworth	1.50
13	Frank Rodriguez	1.00
14	Shawn Green	5.00
15	Ray Durham	2.00

1995 Summit Nth Degree

	MT
Complete Set (200):	400.00
Common Player:	1.00
Stars: 8X	

(See 1995 Summit for checklist, base card values.)

1995 Summit 21 Club

Metallic foil printing on front and back distinguishes this set of chase cards. A large red-foil "21 / CLUB" logo on each side identifies the theme of this set as players who professed to be that age during the 1955 baseball season. The players are pictured in action pose on front and a portrait on back. On average the

21 Club cards are seeded one per box (36 packs). Cards are numbered with a "TC" prefix.

		MT
Complete Set (9):		30.00
Common Player:		3.00
1	Bob Abreu	6.00
2	Pokey Reese	4.00
3	Edgardo Alfonzo	6.00
4	Jim Pittsley	3.00
5	Ruben Rivera	4.00
6	Chan Ho Park	8.00
7	Julian Tavarez	3.00
8	Ismael Valdes	4.00
9	Dmitri Young	3.00

1996 Summit

Pinnacle's 1996 Summit baseball has 200 cards, including 35 rookies, four checklists and 10 Deja Vu subset cards. Each card is also reprinted in three parallel versions - Above and Beyond (one per seven packs), Artist's Proofs (one in 36) and a retail-only silver foil-bordered version. Above and Beyond cards use an all-prismatic foil design; Artist's Proof cards have holographic foil stamping. Five insert sets were produced: Big Bang; Mirage (a parallel set to Big Bang); Hitters, Inc.; Ballparks; and Positions (found one per every 50 magazine packs).

		MT
Complete Set (200):		20.00
Common Player:		.10
Wax Box:		40.00
1	Mike Piazza	2.00
2	Matt Williams	.30
3	Tino Martinez	.20
4	Reggie Sanders	.10
5	Ray Durham	.10
6	Brad Radke	.10
7	Jeff Bagwell	1.25
8	Ron Gant	.15
9	Lance Johnson	.10
10	Kevin Seitzer	.10
11	Dante Bichette	.25
12	Ivan Rodriguez	.60
13	Jim Abbott	.10
14	Greg Colbrunn	.10
15	Rondell White	.10
16	Shawn Green	.20
17	Gregg Jefferies	.10
18	Omar Vizquel	.10
19	Cal Ripken Jr.	3.00
20	Mark McGwire	4.00
21	Wally Joyner	.10
22	Chili Davis	.10
23	Jose Canseco	.35
24	Royce Clayton	.10
25	Jay Bell	.10
26	Travis Fryman	.10
27	Jeff King	.10
28	Todd Hundley	.20
29	Joe Vitiello	.10
30	Russ Davis	.10
31	Mo Vaughn	.50
32	Raul Mondesi	.30
33	Ray Lankford	.10
34	Mike Stanley	.10
35	B.J. Surhoff	.10
36	Greg Vaughn	.10
37	Todd Stottlemyre	.10
38	Carlos Delgado	.40
39	Kenny Lofton	.50
40	Hideo Nomo	.60
41	Sterling Hitchcock	.10
42	Pete Schourek	.10
43	Edgardo Alfonzo	.15
44	Ken Hill	.10
45	Ken Caminiti	.25
46	Bobby Higginson	.15
47	Michael Tucker	.10
48	David Cone	.20
49	Cecil Fielder	.10
50	Brian Hunter	.10
51	Charles Johnson	.10
52	Bobby Bonilla	.10
53	Eddie Murray	.40
54	Kenny Rogers	.10
55	Jim Edmonds	.15
56	Trevor Hoffman	.10
57	Kevin Mitchell	.10
58	Ruben Sierra	.10
59	Benji Gil	.10
60	Juan Gonzalez	1.50
61	Larry Walker	.40
62	Jack McDowell	.10
63	Shawon Dunston	.10
64	Andy Benes	.10
65	Jay Buhner	.10
66	Rickey Henderson	.25
67	Alex Gonzalez	.10
68	Mike Kelly	.10
69	Fred McGriff	.35
70	Ryne Sandberg	.75
71	Ernie Young	.10
72	Kevin Appier	.10
73	Moises Alou	.10
74	John Jaha	.10
75	J.T. Snow	.10
76	Jim Thome	.20
77	Kirby Puckett	1.00
78	Hal Morris	.10
79	Robin Ventura	.15
80	Ben McDonald	.10
81	Tim Salmon	.20
82	Albert Belle	.75
83	Marquis Grissom	.10
84	Alex Rodriguez	3.00
85	Manny Ramirez	1.00
86	Ken Griffey Jr.	4.00
87	Sammy Sosa	1.50
88	Frank Thomas	1.00
89	Lee Smith	.10
90	Marty Cordova	.15
91	Greg Maddux	2.00
92	Lenny Dykstra	.10
93	Butch Huskey	.10
94	Garret Anderson	.10
95	Mike Bordick	.10
96	Dave Justice	.20
97	Chad Curtis	.10
98	Carlos Baerga	.10
99	Jason Isringhausen	.10
100	Gary Sheffield	.30
101	Roger Clemens	1.25
102	Ozzie Smith	.50
103	Ramon Martinez	.10
104	Paul O'Neill	.15
105	Will Clark	.25
106	Tom Glavine	.15
107	Barry Bonds	.75
108	Barry Larkin	.20
109	Derek Bell	.10
110	Randy Johnson	.40
111	Jeff Conine	.10
112	John Mabry	.10
113	Julian Tavarez	.10
114	Gary DiSarcina	.10
115	Andres Galarraga	.20
116	Marc Newfield	.10
117	Frank Rodriguez	.10
118	Brady Anderson	.15
119	Mike Mussina	.40
120	Orlando Merced	.10
121	Melvin Nieves	.10
122	Brian Jordan	.15
123	Rafael Palmeiro	.20
124	Johnny Damon	.15
125	Wil Cordero	.10
126	Chipper Jones	2.00
127	Eric Karros	.10
128	Darren Daulton	.10
129	Vinny Castilla	.10
130	Joe Carter	.10
131	Bernie Williams	.50
132	Bernard Gilkey	.10
133	Bret Boone	.10
134	Tony Gwynn	1.25
135	Dave Nilsson	.10
136	Ryan Klesko	.20
137	Paul Molitor	.40
138	John Olerud	.15
139	Craig Biggio	.20
140	John Valentin	.10
141	Chuck Knoblauch	.20
142	Edgar Martinez	.10
143	Rico Brogna	.10
144	Dean Palmer	.10
145	Mark Grace	.25
146	Roberto Alomar	.75
147	Alex Fernandez	.15
148	Andre Dawson	.10
149	Wade Boggs	.35
150	Mark Lewis	.10
151	Gary Gaetti	.10
152	Paul Wilson, Roger Clemens (Deja Vu)	.30
153	Rey Ordonez, Ozzie Smith (Deja Vu)	.50
154	Derek Jeter, Cal Ripken Jr. (Deja Vu)	1.00
155	Alan Benes, Andy Benes (Deja Vu)	.10
156	Jason Kendall, Mike Piazza (Deja Vu)	.75
157	Ryan Klesko, Frank Thomas (Deja Vu)	.50
158	Johnny Damon, Ken Griffey Jr. (Deja Vu)	1.00
159	Karim Garcia, Sammy Sosa (Deja Vu)	1.00
160	Raul Mondesi, Tim Salmon (Deja Vu)	.20
161	Chipper Jones, Matt Williams (Deja Vu)	.75
162	Rey Ordonez	.40
163	Bob Wolcott	.10
164	Brooks Kieschnick	.10
165	Steve Gibralter	.10
166	Bob Abreu	.20
167	Greg Zaun	.10
168	Tavo Alvarez	.10
169	Sal Fasano	.10
170	George Arias	.10
171	Derek Jeter	2.00
172	*Livan Hernandez*	2.00
173	Alan Benes	.15
174	George Williams	.10
175	John Wasdin	.10
176	Chan Ho Park	.15
177	Paul Wilson	.20
178	Jeff Suppan	.20
179	Quinton McCracken	.10
180	*Wilton Guerrero*	.75
181	Eric Owens	.10
182	Felipe Crespo	.10
183	LaTroy Hawkins	.10
184	Jason Schmidt	.10
185	Terrell Wade	.10
186	*Mike Grace*	.30
187	Chris Snopek	.10
188	Jason Kendall	.20
189	Todd Hollandsworth	.15
190	Jim Pittsley	.10
191	Jermaine Dye	.15
192	*Mike Busby*	.10
193	Richard Hidalgo	.10
194	Tyler Houston	.10
195	Jimmy Haynes	.10
196	Karim Garcia	.40
197	Ken Griffey Jr. (Checklist)	2.00
198	Frank Thomas (Checklist)	.50
199	Greg Maddux (Checklist)	1.00
200	Cal Ripken Jr. (Checklist)	1.50

1996 Summit Above & Beyond

These 200 insert cards parallel Pinnacle's 1996 Summit set, using all-prismatic foil for each card. The cards were seeded one per every four packs.

	MT
Complete Set (200):	400.00
Common Player:	1.00
Stars: 8X	

(See 1996 Summit for checklist, base card values.)

1996 Summit Artist's Proof

Holographic-foil highlights and an "ARTIST'S PROOF" notation on the front photo distinguish the cards in this parallel edition. The AP cards are found once per 36 packs.

	MT
Complete Set (200):	1500.
Common Player:	2.50
Stars: 25X	

(See 1996 Summit for checklist, base card values.)

1996 Summit Foil

This parallel issue was an exclusive in Summit retail packaging. The black borders of the regular Summit versions have been replaced on these cards by silver foil.

	MT
Complete Set (200):	50.00
Common Player:	.25
Stars: 2X	

(See 1996 Summit for checklist and base card values.)

1996 Summit Ballparks

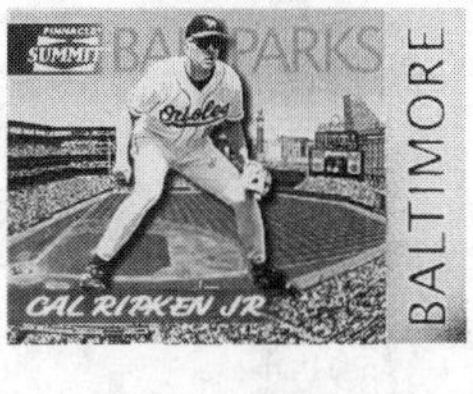

These 18 cards feature images of players superimposed over their respective teams' ballparks. The cards were seeded one per every 18 packs of 1996 Pinnacle Summit baseball.

		MT
Complete Set (18):		125.00
Common Player:		2.50
1	Cal Ripken Jr.	15.00
2	Albert Belle	6.00
3	Dante Bichette	2.50
4	Mo Vaughn	2.50
5	Ken Griffey Jr.	20.00
6	Derek Jeter	12.50
7	Juan Gonzalez	10.00
8	Greg Maddux	12.50
9	Frank Thomas	10.00
10	Ryne Sandberg	6.00
11	Mike Piazza	12.50
12	Johnny Damon	4.00
13	Barry Bonds	6.00
14	Jeff Bagwell	9.00
15	Paul Wilson	2.50
16	Tim Salmon	2.50
17	Kirby Puckett	8.00
18	Tony Gwynn	9.00

1996 Summit Big Bang

Sixteen of the biggest hitters are featured on these 1996 Pinnacle Summit insert cards. The cards, seeded one per every 72 packs, use Spectroetched backgrounds with foil highlights.

		MT
Complete Set (16):		500.00
Common Player:		10.00
Mirages: 1X		
1	Frank Thomas	50.00
2	Ken Griffey Jr.	120.00
3	Albert Belle	20.00
4	Mo Vaughn	10.00
5	Barry Bonds	30.00
6	Cal Ripken Jr.	90.00
7	Jeff Bagwell	35.00
8	Mike Piazza	75.00
9	Ryan Klesko	10.00
10	Manny Ramirez	30.00
11	Tim Salmon	10.00
12	Dante Bichette	10.00
13	Sammy Sosa	60.00
14	Raul Mondesi	10.00
15	Chipper Jones	75.00
16	Garret Anderson	10.00

1996 Summit Big Bang Mirage

These 18 cards form a parallel version to Pinnacle's Big Bang inserts. The cards, found one per every 72 packs, use an all-new technology that creates a floating background behind the player's image. By holding the card in direct sunlight or an incandescent bulb, a collector can see three dimensions and a floating baseball that seems to levitate in the background. Mirage cards are serially numbered in an edition of 600 each.

		MT
Complete Set (16):		500.00
Common Player:		10.00
1	Frank Thomas	50.00
2	Ken Griffey Jr.	120.00
3	Albert Belle	20.00
4	Mo Vaughn	10.00
5	Barry Bonds	30.00

6	Cal Ripken Jr.	90.00
7	Jeff Bagwell	35.00
8	Mike Piazza	75.00
9	Ryan Klesko	10.00
10	Manny Ramirez	30.00
11	Tim Salmon	10.00
12	Dante Bichette	10.00
13	Sammy Sosa	60.00
14	Raul Mondesi	10.00
15	Chipper Jones	75.00
16	Garret Anderson	10.00

1996 Summit Hitters, Inc.

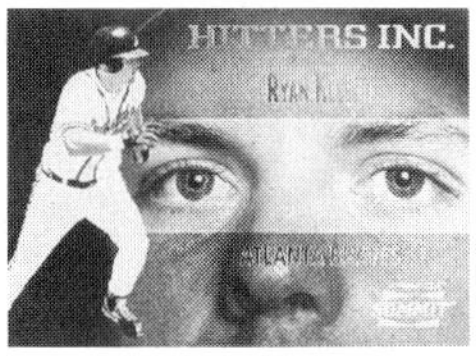

This 1996 Pinnacle Summit set honors 16 top hitters. The cards, seeded one per every 36 packs, puts an embossed highlight on an enlarged photo of the player's eyes.

		MT
Complete Set (16):		200.00
Common Player:		5.00
1	Tony Gwynn	15.00
2	Mo Vaughn	5.00
3	Tim Salmon	5.00
4	Ken Griffey Jr.	40.00
5	Sammy Sosa	25.00
6	Frank Thomas	15.00
7	Wade Boggs	10.00
8	Albert Belle	10.00
9	Cal Ripken Jr.	30.00
10	Manny Ramirez	12.00
11	Ryan Klesko	5.00
11p	Ryan Klesko (overprinted "SAMPLE")	4.50
12	Dante Bichette	5.00
13	Mike Piazza	25.00
14	Chipper Jones	25.00
15	Ryne Sandberg	10.00
16	Matt Williams	5.00

1996 Summit Positions

This insert issue features top players at each position. It is an exclusive magazine pack find, seeded about one per 50 packs. Fronts have action photos of three top players at the position on a baseball infield background at top. Close-ups of those photo appear at bottom, separated by a gold-foil strip. Backs have narrow action photos of each player, a few stats and a serial number from within an edition of 1,500 each.

		MT
Complete Set (9):		225.00
Common Card:		12.00
1	Jeff Bagwell, Mo Vaughn, Frank Thomas (First Base)	15.00
2	Roberto Alomar, Craig Biggio, Chuck Knoblauch (Second Base)	12.00
3	Matt Williams, Jim Thome, Chipper Jones (Third Base)	20.00
4	Barry Larkin, Cal Ripken Jr., Alex Rodriguez (Short Stop)	50.00
5	Mike Piazza, Ivan Rodriguez, Charles Johnson (Catcher)	30.00
6	Hideo Nomo, Greg Maddux, Randy Johnson (Pitcher)	20.00
7	Barry Bonds, Albert Belle, Ryan Klesko (Left Field)	15.00
8	Johnny Damon, Jim Edmonds, Ken Griffey Jr. (Center Field)	40.00
9	Manny Ramirez, Gary Sheffield, Sammy Sosa (Right Field)	35.00

1987 Sun Foods Milwaukee Brewers

Though they are nowhere identified on the cards, Sun Foods was the sponsor of this team set, issuing four cards per week. Measuring 6" x 9", the cards were licensed only by the players' association and so do not feature team uniform logos. Bare-headed players are photographed against a blue background with a black facsimile autograph at bottom. An MLBPA logo appears in the upper-left. Backs are blank. The unnumbered cards are checklisted here in alphabetical order.

		MT
Complete Set (16):		15.00
Common Player:		.50
(1)	Glenn Braggs	.50
(2)	Greg Brock	.50
(3)	Mark Clear	.50
(4)	Cecil Cooper	.75
(5)	Rob Deer	.50
(6)	Jim Gantner	.50
(7)	Ted Higuera	.50
(8)	Paul Molitor	4.00
(9)	Juan Nieves	.50
(10)	Dan Plesac	.50
(11)	Billy Jo Robidoux	.50
(12)	Bill Schroeder	.50
(13)	B.J. Surhoff	.75
(14)	Dale Sveum	.50
(15)	Bill Wegman	.50
(16)	Robin Yount	5.00

1995 Superare Reprint Super Gloves Baseball Greats

A group of Rawlings premium cards of the early 1960s was reprinted in 2-1/2" x 3-1/2" format in this collectors issue. The central posed color photos of the players (each prominently displaying his Rawlings glove) are surrounded with a black border. A black facsimile autograph appears on front. Backs are in black-and-white. Players are listed alphabetically in this checklist.

		MT
Complete Set (8):		10.00
Common Player:		.50
(1)	Ken Boyer	.50
(2)	Tommy Davis	.50
(3)	Dick Groat	.50
(4)	Mickey Mantle	6.00
(5)	Brooks Robinson	1.00
(6)	Warren Spahn	.75
(7)	Tom Tresh	.50
(8)	Billy Williams	.75

1989 Super Bubble "Major League"

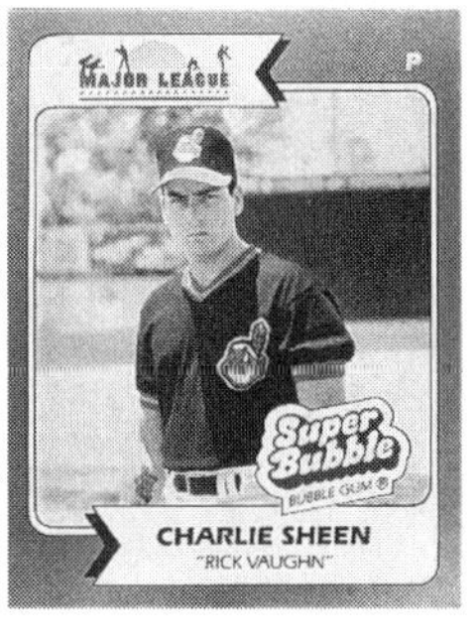

"Super Bubble" gum is the fictitious sponsor of this set of cards issued to promote the movie, "Major League." How the cards were distributed is unknown. They are blank-backed and measure a non-standard 2-3/4" x 3-1/2" with posed color photos of the actors in costume. The actor's name and character portrayed are in a yellow banner in the blue border at bottom. Photos on the cards aren't terrific, with several underexposed faces, etc. No card was issued of one of the movie's bigger stars, Corbin Bernsen.

		MT
Complete Set (10):		200.00
Common Card:		15.00
(1)	Tom Berenger (Jake Taylor)	25.00
(2)	James Gammon (Lou Brown)	15.00
(3)	Dennis Haysbert (Pedro Cerrano)	15.00
(4)	Andy Romano (Pepper Leach)	15.00
(5)	Chelcie Ross (Steve Harris)	15.00
(6)	Charlie Sheen (Rick Vaughn)	50.00
(7)	Wesley Snipes (Willie Mays Hayes)	50.00
(8)	Steve Yeager (Duke Temple)	25.00
(9)	Charlie Sheen, Dennis Haysbert, Tom Berenger, Wesley Snipes	15.00
(10)	Andy Romano, James Gammon, Steve Yeager	15.00
(11)	Andy Romano, James Gammon, Steve Yeager	15.00

1994 SuperSlam

An innovative issued felled by the 1994 baseball strike, SuperSlams are a 5-1/2" x 7-1/2" tent-fold display card. Front and back have a gridded silver metallic background. At center on front is a 3-3/4" x 5-1/4" color photo on which is superimposed a 3-D action pose of the player. Backs have extensive "This is my life" biographical information about extensive biographical information about the player, the player, personalizing him for the reader. The cards are skip-numbered in the upper-right corner. Promo cards of Jack McDowell were issued with either silver or gold background. Cards were sold for $7.95 apiece with reported production between 2,000 and 50,000, depending on player.

		MT
Complete Set (18):		100.00
Common Player:		6.00
(3)	Greg Maddux	9.00
(4)	Fred McGriff	6.00
(5)	Moises Alou	6.00
(19)	Roberto Alomar	6.00
(27)	Cal Ripken Jr.	10.00
(28)	Roger Clemens	7.50
(40)	Mike Piazza	9.00
(42)	Barry Bonds	7.50
(47)	Tony Gwynn	7.50
(53)	Rickey Henderson	6.00
(58)	Tim Salmon	6.00
(60)	Ken Griffey Jr.	12.00
(65)	Juan Gonzalez	7.50
(67)	Jeff Bagwell	7.50
(83)	Albert Belle	6.00
(84)	Kenny Lofton	6.00
(90)	Kirby Puckett	6.00
(95)	Frank Thomas	7.50
(P1)	Jack McDowell (gold)	6.00
(P2)	Jack McDowell (silver)	6.00

1987 Super Stars Discs

Produced by Mike Schecter Associates, the Super Stars disc set was released as part of a promotion for various brands of iced tea mixes in many parts of the country. Among the brands participating in the promotion were Acme, Alpha Beta, Bustelo, Key, King Kullen, Lady Lee, Our Own and Weis. The discs were issued in three-part folding panels with each disc measuring 2-1/2" in diameter. Fronts feature a full-color photo to inside a bright yellow border. Two player discs were included in each panel along with a coupon disc offering either an uncut press sheet of the set or a facsimile autographed ball. Because the series was licensed only by the players' union, and not MLB, cap logos were removed.

		MT
Complete Panel Set (10):		8.00
Complete Singles Set (20):		4.00
Common Panel:		.25
Common Single Player:		.05
	Panel (1)	1.25
1	Wade Boggs	.40
9	Roger Clemens	.35
	Panel (2)	.25
2	Ellis Burks	.05
8	Kevin Seitzer	.05
	Panel (3)	1.00
3	Don Mattingly	.50
13	Dave Magadan	.05
	Panel (4)	2.00
4	Mark McGwire	1.00
10	Will Clark	.30
	Panel (5)	.25
5	Matt Nokes	.05
11	Vince Coleman	.05
	Panel (6)	1.25
6	Kirby Puckett	.45
12	Eric Davis	.10
	Panel (7)	.25
7	Billy Ripken	.05
18	Steve Bedrosian	.05
	Panel (8)	1.25
14	Dale Murphy	.25
16	Mike Schmidt	.35
	Panel (9)	.50
15	Benito Santiago	.05
20	Fernando Valenzuela	.10
	Panel (10)	1.00
17	Darryl Strawberry	.15
19	Dwight Gooden	.15

1988 Super Stars Discs

The "Second Annual Collector's Edition" of Super Stars discs is similar to the 1987 issue. A set of 20 discs (2-1/2" diameter) featuring full-color player photos was inserted in specially marked cannisters of iced tea and fruit drinks. Each triple-fold insert consists of two player discs and one redemption card. Player discs are bright blue, yellow, red and green with a diamond design framing the player portrait. The player name appears upper left, the set logo appears upper right. Personalized disc series were issued for Tetley, Weis, Key Food and A&P supermarkets (untitled series were also sold at Lucky, Skaggs, Alpha Beta, Acme King Kullen, Laneco and Krasdale stores). The series name (i.e. Weis Winners) is printed below the player photo. Backs are in red with a few personal data and stats. Because the discs are licensed only through the players' union, cap logos have been airbrushed off the photos.

		MT
Complete Panel Set (10):		7.00
Complete Singles Set (20):		3.50
Common Panel:		.25
Common Single Player:		.05
	Panel (1)	.90
1	Wade Boggs	.35
2	Ellis Burks	.05
	Panel (2)	3.00
3	Don Mattingly	.50
4	Mark McGwire	1.00
	Panel (3)	1.00
5	Matt Nokes	.05
6	Kirby Puckett	.50
	Panel (4)	.25
7	Billy Ripken	.05
8	Kevin Seitzer	.05
	Panel (5)	1.50
9	Roger Clemens	.45
10	Will Clark	.30
	Panel (6)	.30
11	Vince Coleman	.05
12	Eric Davis	.10
	Panel (7)	.60
13	Dave Magadan	.05
14	Dale Murphy	.25
	Panel (8)	1.00
15	Benito Santiago	.05
16	Mike Schmidt	.50
	Panel (9)	.30
17	Darryl Strawberry	.10
18	Steve Bedrosian	.05
	Panel (10)	.40
19	Dwight Gooden	.10
20	Fernando Valenzuela	.05

Player names in *Italic* type indicate a rookie card.

1989 Super Stars Discs

The third annual series of Super Stars perforated disc folders again offered two players and an offer for a a facsimile autographed baseball or an uncut sheet of discs. The 2-3/4" diameter discs have a yellow border with a red star at center. A player portrait photo is in the star. Backs are printed in black and have a few previous season stats and biographical bits. As in previous years, the discs were produced by Michael Schechter Associates, which does business only with the players' union, precluding the use of MLB logos on the player photos.

		MT
Complete Panel Set (10):		9.00
Complete Singles Set (20):		5.00
Common Panel:		.25
Common Player:		.05
	Panel (1)	1.00
1	Don Mattingly	.50
2	David Cone	.10
	Panel (2)	2.50
3	Mark McGwire	1.00
4	Will Clark	.20
	Panel (3)	.50
5	Darryl Strawberry	.10
6	Dwight Gooden	.10
	Panel (4)	1.75
7	Wade Boggs	.45
8	Roger Clemens	.45
	Panel (5)	.25
9	Benito Santiago	.05
10	Orel Hershiser	.05
	Panel (6)	1.25
11	Eric Davis	.10
	Panel (7)	1.00
13	Dave Winfield	.30
14	Andre Dawson	.10
	Panel (8)	2.00
15	Steve Bedrosian	.05
16	Cal Ripken Jr.	.90
	Panel (9)	.75
17	Andy Van Slyke	.05
18	Jose Canseco	.25
	Panel (10)	.25
19	Jose Oquendo	.05
20	Dale Murphy	.10

1990 Super Stars Discs

In its fourth annual edition the Super Stars discs continued the three-piece perforated folder format. Each panel consists of two player discs and a disc offering a 1990-1991 calendar at the center of an uncut sheet of the discs. Discs have a red border with a player portrait photo in the center of a tombstone-shaped yellow frame. A few 1989 stats and biographical notes are printed in black on the back. Because the discs are licensed only by the players' union, and not Major League Baseball, the player photos have had team logos excised.

		MT
Complete Panel Set (10):		10.00
Complete Set, Singles (20):		6.00
Common Panel:		.25
Common Player:		.05
	Panel (1)	.60
1	Will Clark	.25
2	Howard Johnson	.05
	Panel (2)	.75
3	Chris Sabo	.05
4	Jose Canseco	.30
	Panel (3)	.25
5	Bo Jackson	.10
6	Kevin Mitchell	.05
	Panel (4)	4.50
7	Wade Boggs	.45
8	Ken Griffey Jr.	2.00
	Panel (5)	.25
9	George Bell	.05
10	Dwight Gooden	.10
	Panel (6)	.90
11	Bobby Bonilla	.10
12	Ryne Sandberg	.35
	Panel (7)	1.50
13	Kirby Puckett	.75
14	Don Mattingly	.75
	Panel (8)	2.00
15	Mark McGwire	1.00
16	Frank Viola	.05
	Panel (9)	.25
17	Bret Saberhagen	.10
18	Mike Greenwell	.05
	Panel (10)	2.00
19	Steve Sax	.05
20	Nolan Ryan	1.00

1983 Super Star Sports Coins

These 1-1/4" diameter plastic coins are the prototypes for what would become the lengthy annual issues of 7-Eleven Slurpee issues. They were evidently prepared to showcase the concept to potential national sponsors. Each coin pictures Rod Carew at center with a wide red border containing his name, team and uniform number. Backs repeat the wide red border, imprinted with "Super Star Sports Coins Collector Series". In the white center are Carews personal data, stats, coin number, date, and, at top, the logo of the potential sponsor.

		MT
Complete Set (8):		65.00
Single Coin:		10.00
(1)	Burger King (Rod Carew)	10.00
(2)	Coca-Cola (Rod Carew)	12.50
(3)	General Mills (Rod Carew)	10.00
(4)	Kellogg's (Rod Carew)	10.00
(5)	Kentucky Fried Chicken (Rod Carew)	10.00
(6)	McDonald's (Rod Carew)	12.50
(7)	Pepsi Cola (Rod Carew)	10.00
(8)	Wendy's (Rod Carew)	10.00

1994 System 4 Toronto Blue Jays Postcards

Commemorating the team's consecutive World Championships of 1992 and 1993 is this set of color postcards. The cards were sold as a complete set in a colorful folder. Measuring 4" x 6", most cards feature game-action photos, though there are also some posed portraits and a few non-player cards. Fronts are borderless with no graphics. Backs are in black-and-white with standard postcard markings. At top-left is the player identification. Licensing and issuer data is at lower-left. At center is a bar code which includes a unique identification number as shown in this checklist.

		MT
Complete Set (12):		12.00
Common Player:		.50
68201	Joe Carter	.50
68301	John Olerud	1.00
68401	Roberto Alomar	2.00
68501	Paul Molitor	2.50
68601	Carlos Delgado	.75
68701	Pat Borders	.50
68801	Juan Guzman	.50
69001	Devon White	.60
69101	Ed Sprague	.50
69501	World Championship Trophies	.50
69601	World Championship Rings	.50
69701	World Championship team logo	.50

T

1988 T & M Sports Umpires

The first umpires to be featured on baseball cards since the 1955 Bowman set are the arbitrators included in this boxed set issued T & M and licensed by the umps' union. Cards have posed photos framed in red (American League) green (National League) with a black border on front. The correct league logo is in a lower corner. The umpire's uniform number and name are in white at bottom. The back has a blue background with personal data, career summary, service record and card number, along with licensor logos.

		MT
Complete Set (64):		12.00
Common Card:		.15
1	Doug Harvey	.15
2	Lee Weyer	.15
3	Billy Williams	.15
4	John Kibler	.15
5	Bob Engel	.15
6	Harry Wendelstedt	.15
7	Larry Barnett	.15
8	Don Denkinger	.15
9	Dave Phillips	.15
10	Larry McCoy	.15
11	Bruce Froemming	.15
12	John McSherry	.15
13	Jim Evans	.15
14	Frank Pulli	.15
15	Joe Brinkman	.15
16	Terry Tata	.15
17	Paul Runge	.15
18	Dutch Rennert	.15
19	Nick Bremigan	.15
20	Jim McKean	.15
21	Terry Cooney	.15
22	Rich Garcia	.15
23	Dale Ford	.15
24	Al Clark	.15
25	Greg Kosc	.15
26	Jim Quick	.15
27	Ed Montague	.15
28	Jerry Crawford	.15
29	Steve Palermo	.15
30	Durwood Merrill	.15
31	Ken Kaiser	.15
32	Vic Voltaggio	.15
33	Mike Reilly	.15
34	Eric Gregg	.15
35	Ted Hendry	.15
36	Joe West	.15
37	Dave Pallone	.15
38	Fred Brocklander	.15
39	John Shulock	.15
40	Derryl Cousins	.15
41	Charlie Williams	.15
42	Rocky Roe	.15
43	Randy Marsh	.15
44	Bob Davidson	.15
45	Drew Coble	.15
46	Tim McClelland	.15
47	Dan Morrison	.15
48	Rick Reed	.15
49	Steve Rippley	.15
50	John Hirschbeck	.15
51	Mark Johnson	.15
52	Gerry Davis	.15
53	Dana DeMuth	.15
54	Larry Young	.15
55	Tim Welke	.15
56	Greg Bonin	.15
57	Tom Hallion	.15
58	Dale Scott	.15
59	Tim Tschida	.15
60	Dick Stello	.15
61	1987 All-Star Game (Derryl Cousins, Bob Davidson, Don Denkinger, Dick Stello, Vic Voltaggio, Joe West)	.15
62	1987 World Series (Ken Kaiser, Greg Kosc, John McSherry, Dave Phillips, Terry Tata, Lee Weyer)	.15
63	Jocko Conlan	.30
64	Checklist	.15

1989 T & M Sports Senior League

The 120-card 1989-90 T&M Sports Senior League set featured a full-color photo of the player on the front on a borderless card. A red stripe separates the photo from the black bottom with the player's name, team logo and position. The cards were printed on heavy, white cardboard stock and sold as a boxed set. The backs have a red border across the top and bio and career notes, along with a summary of the player's career. Included in the set are eight static-cling puzzle pieces which, when put together, show a drawing of a prominent player from each team.

		MT
Complete Set (120):		4.00
Common Player:		.05
1	Curt Flood (Commissioner)	.10
2	Willie Aikens	.05
3	Gary Allenson	.05
4	Stan Bahnsen	.05
5	Alan Bannister	.05
6	Juan Beniquez	.05
7	Jim Bibby	.05
8	Paul Blair	.05
9	Vida Blue	.10
10	Bobby Bonds	.15
11	Pedro Borbon	.05
12	Clete Boyer	.05
13	Gates Brown	.05
14	Al Bumbry	.05
15	Sal Butera	.05
16	Bert Campaneris	.10
17	Bill Campbell	.05
18	Bernie Carbo	.05
19	Dave Cash	.05
20	Cesar Cedeno	.05
21	Gene Clines	.05
22	Dave Collins	.05
23	Cecil Cooper	.05
24	Doug Corbett	.05
25	Al Cowens	.05
26	Jose Cruz	.05
27	Mike Cuellar	.10
28	Pat Dobson	.05
29	Dick Drago	.05
30	Dan Driessen	.05
31	Jamie Easterly	.05
32	Juan Eichelberger	.05
33	Dock Ellis	.05
34	Ed Figueroa	.05
35	Rollie Fingers	.50
36	George Foster	.15
37	Oscar Gamble	.05
38	Wayne Garland	.05
39	Wayne Garrett	.05
40	Ross Grimsley	.05
41	Jerry Grote	.05
42	Johnny Grubb	.05
43	Mario Guerrero	.05
44	Toby Harrah	.05
45	Steve Henderson	.05
46	George Hendrick	.05
47	Butch Hobson	.05
48	Roy Howell	.05
49	Al Hrabosky	.05
50	Clint Hurdle	.05
51	Garth Iorg	.05
52	Tim Ireland	.05
53	Grant Jackson	.05
54	Ron Jackson	.05
55	Ferguson Jenkins	.50
56	Odell Jones	.05
57	Mike Kekich	.05
58	Steve Kemp	.05
59	Dave Kingman	.10
60	Bruce Kison	.05
61	Lee Lacy	.05
62	Rafael Landestoy	.05
63	Ken Landreaux	.05
64	Tito Landrum	.05
65	Dave LaRoche	.05
66	Bill Lee	.05
67	Ron LeFlore	.05
68	Dennis Leonard	.05
69	Bill Madlock	.10
70	Mickey Mahler	.05
71	Rick Manning	.05
72	Tippy Martinez	.05
73	Jon Matlack	.05
74	Bake McBride	.05
75	Steve McCarty	.05
76	Hal McRae	.10
77	Dan Meyer	.05
78	Felix Millan	.05
79	Paul Mirabella	.05
80	Omar Moreno	.05
81	Jim Morrison	.05
82	Graig Nettles	.05
83	Al Oliver	.10
84	Amos Otis	.05
85	Tom Paciorek	.05
86	Lowell Plamer	.05
87	Pat Putnam	.05
88	Lenny Randle	.05
89	Ken Reitz	.05
90	Gene Richards	.05
91	Mickey Rivers	.05
92	Leon Roberts	.05
93	Joe Sambito	.05
94	Rodney Scott	.05
95	Bob Shirley	.05
96	Jim Slaton	.05
97	Elias Sosa	.05
98	Fred Stanley	.05

99	Bill Stein	.05
100	Rennie Stennett	.05
101	Sammy Stewart	.05
102	Tim Stoddard	.05
103	Champ Summers	.05
104	Derrell Thomas	.05
105	Luis Tiant	.10
106	Bobby Tolan	.05
107	Bill Travers	.05
108	Ton Underwood	.05
109	Rick Waits	.05
110	Ron Washington	.05
111	U.L. Washington	.05
112	Earl Weaver	.25
113	Jerry White	.05
114	Milt Wilcox	.05
115	Dick Williams	.05
116	Walt Williams	.05
117	Rick Wise	.05
118	Favorite Suns (Luis Tiant, Cesar Cedeno)	.05
119	Home Run Legends (George Foster, Bobby Bonds)	.05
120	Sunshine Skippers (Earl Weaver, Dick Williams)	.25

1989 T & M Sports Umpires

A second edition of umpires' cards from T & M was also sold as a boxed set. Fronts of the 2-1/2" x 3-1/2" cards have color photos which are borderless at top and sides. At bottom is a strip with the ump's name and uniform number at right and league logo at left. Backs have personal data and a career summary, along with logos of MLB and the Umpires' Association.

		MT
Complete Set:		8.00
Common Card:		.15
1	Doug Harvey	.25
2	John Kibler	.15
3	Bob Engel	.15
4	Harry Wendelstedt	.15
5	Larry Barnett	.15
6	Don Denkinger	.15
7	Dave Phillips	.15
8	Larry McCoy	.15
9	Bruce Froemming	.15
10	John McSherry	.20
11	Jim Evans	.15
12	Frank Pulli	.15
13	Joe Brinkman	.15
14	Terry Tata	.15
15	Nick Bremigan	.15
16	Jim McKean	.15
17	Paul Runge	.15
18	Dutch Rennert	.15
19	Terry Cooney	.15
20	Rich Garcia	.15
21	Dale Ford	.15
22	Al Clark	.15
23	Greg Kosc	.15
24	Jim Quick	.15
25	Ed Montague	.15
26	Jerry Crawford	.15
27	Steve Palermo	.35
28	Durwood Merrill	.15
29	Ken Kaiser	.20
30	Vic Voltaggio	.15
31	Mike Reilly	.15
32	Eric Gregg	.25
33	Ted Hendry	.15
34	Joe West	.15
35	Dave Pallone	.25
36	Fred Brocklander	.15
37	John Shulock	.15
38	Derryl Cousins	.15
39	Charlie Williams	.15
40	Rocky Roe	.15
41	Randy Marsh	.15
42	Bob Davidson	.15
43	Drew Coble	.15
44	Tim McClelland	.15
45	Dan Morrison	.15
46	Rick Reed	.15
47	Steve Rippley	.15
48	John Hirschbeck	.15
49	Mark Johnson	.15
50	Gerry Davis	.15
51	Dana DeMuth	.15
52	Larry Young	.15
53	Tim Welke	.15
54	Greg Bonin	.15
55	Tom Hallion	.15
56	Dale Scott	.15
57	Tim Tschida	.15
58	Gary Darling	.15
59	Mark Hirschbeck	.15
60	All-Star Crew	.15
61	World Series Crew	.15
62	Lee Weyer	.15
63	Tom Connolly, Bill Klem	.25

1990 T & M Sports Umpires

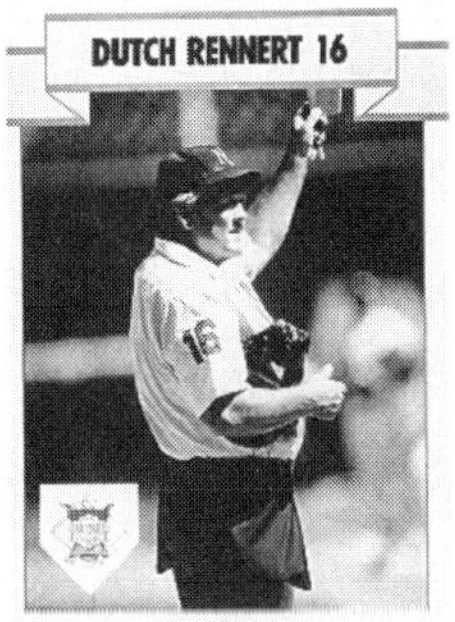

Puzzle piece inserts and a send-away premium card offer are featured in the 1990 umpires set. Card fronts have action photos of the arbitrators with league insignia in a home plate-shaped frame in a lower corner. Above the photo, the umpire's name and uniform number are printed in a banner. Backs have biographical data, a baseball rules trivia question and the logos of MLB and the Major League Umpires Association. Card #71, Hall of Fame umpire Al Barlick, was only available by sending in the four puzzle pieces overprinted with the National League logo.

		MT
Complete Set (70, no Barlick):		6.00
Common Card:		.10
1	Doug Harvey	.10
2	John Kibler	.10
3	Bob Engel	.10
4	Harry Wendelstedt	.10
5	Larry Barnett	.10
6	Don Denkinger	.10
7	Dave Phillips	.10
8	Larry McCoy	.10
9	Bruce Froemming	.10
10	John McSherry	.10
11	Jim Evans	.10
12	Frank Pulli	.10
13	Joe Brinkman	.10
14	Terry Tata	.10
15	Jim McKean	.10
16	Dutch Rennert	.10
17	Paul Runge	.10
18	Terry Cooney	.10
19	Rich Garcia	.10
20	Dale Ford	.10
21	Al Clark	.10
22	Greg Kosc	.10
23	Jim Quick	.10
24	Eddie Montague	.10
25	Jerry Crawford	.10
26	Steve Palermo	.10
27	Durwood Merrill	.10
28	Ken Kaiser	.10
29	Vic Voltaggio	.10
30	Mike Reilly	.10
31	Eric Gregg	.10
32	Ted Hendry	.10
33	Joe West	.10
34	Fred Brocklander	.10
35	John Shulock	.10
36	Derryl Cousins	.10
37	Charlie Williams	.10
38	Rocky Roe	.10
39	Randy Marsh	.10
40	Bob Davidson	.10
41	Drew Coble	.10
42	Tim McClelland	.10
43	Dan Morrison	.10
44	Rick Reed	.10
45	Steve Rippley	.10
46	John Hirschbeck	.10
47	Mark Johnson	.10
48	Gerry Davis	.10
49	Dana DeMuth	.10
50	Larry Young	.10
51	Tim Welke	.10
52	Greg Bonin	.10
53	Tom Hallion	.10
54	Dale Scott	.10
55	Tim Tschida	.10
56	Gary Darling	.10
57	Mark Hirschbeck	.10
58	Jerry Layne	.10
59	Jim Joyce	.10
60	Bill Hohn	.10
61	All-Star Game	.10
62	World Series	.10
63	Nick Bremigan	.10
64	The Runges (Ed Runge, Paul Runge)	.10
65	A. Bartlett Giamatti	.10
66	Puzzle Piece #1	.10
66a	Puzzle Piece #1 (w/ N.L. logo on back)	.10
67	Puzzle Piece #2	.10
67a	Puzzle Piece #3 (N.L. logo)	.10
68	Puzzle Piece #3	.10
68a	Puzzle Piece #3 (N.L. logo)	.10
69	Puzzle Piece #4	.10
69a	Puzzle piece #4 (N.L. logo)	.10
70	Checklist	.05
71	Al Barlick	4.00

1994 Taco Bell Jack Clark Rookie Cards

This cross-sport collectible offers two Jack Clark "rookie" cards, a reproduction of his 1976 Topps baseball card and an original card from his debut season as a drag racer. Sponsored and distributed by Taco Bell in the Houston area, the cards are perforated to separate them from a 10" x 7" color photo of Clark's fire-breathing Taco Bell rail. Overall the sheet measures 12-1/2" x 7". The back has several more photos and a capsule history of Clark's baseball career, along with details of his new sports interest. The Topps card is labeled "Reprinted in 1994 with permission".

	MT
Complete Sheet: Jack Clark	4.00

1993 Taco Time Griffey 24

These six unnumbered cards were distributed by Taco Time restaurants in the Northwest. The 2-1/2" x 3-1/2" cards have photos of Griffey on brightly colored backgrounds with gold-foil striped borders. Gold or red metallic foil on front has the Taco Time logo with "GRIFFEY 24" in one corner. Some cards mention that they are one of 24,000. The Griffey photos have had team logos removed. Backs (except for the photo on the All-Star MVP card) have career highlights, stats, personal data or playing and safety tips.

		MT
Complete Set (6):		10.00
Common Card:		2.00
(1)	Ken Griffey Jr. (All-Star MVP)	2.00
(2)	Ken Griffey Jr. (batting)	2.00
(3)	Ken Griffey Jr. (portrait)	2.00
(4)	Ken Griffey Jr. (running)	2.00
(5)	Ken Griffey Jr. (sliding)	2.00
(6)	Ken Griffey Jr. (throwing)	2.00

1994 Taco Time Ken Griffey Jr. Promos

This two-card set was issued to cash in on the promo card bandwagon and features a pair of 11-card Taco Time set with a "Promotional Sample" overprint on back. Otherwise the 3" x 5" cards are identical to the issued versions.

		MT
Complete Set (2):		10.00
Common Card:		5.00
(1)	Ken Griffey Jr. (diving for ball)	6.00
(2)	Ken Griffey Jr. (Mariners group picture)	5.00

1994 Taco Time Ken Griffey, Jr.

Western Washington collectors had the chance in the summer of 1994 to get a Ken Griffey collector cup and an individually foil-wrapped card, courtesy of Alrak, which has printed Griffey Jr. cards for several years, and Taco Time. The card series is limited to 50,000 sets, with 11 different 3-1/2" x 5" cards available. The cards are numbered 1-6 and SP1-SP5. They depict the artwork of Larry Weber, highlighted by UV coating and silver foil accents. Additionally, 5,000 of each card were randomly inserted with gold foil accents. In conjunction with Taco Time's in-store promotion, the Mariners randomly distributed 25,000 of the cards to fans attending the June 24 game against the White Sox.

		MT
Complete Set (11):		20.00
Common Card:		1.50
Gold Version: 2-3X		
1	1990 1st Gold Glove (Ken Griffey Jr.)	1.50
2	Ken Griffey Jr. 1993 (Ken Griffey Jr.)	1.50
3	1993 AL Defensive Player (Ken Griffey Jr.)	1.50
4	1992 All-Star MVP (Ken Griffey Jr.)	1.50
5	1994 All-Star (Ken Griffey Jr.)	1.50
6	Mariners Care (Ken Griffey Jr.)	1.50
SP1	Ken Griffey Jr. (1993 A.L. Defensive Record)	3.00
SP2	Ken Griffey Jr. (1993 HR Streak)	3.00
SP3	Ken Griffey Jr. (100th Home Run)	3.00
SP4	Ken Griffey Jr. (1993 Off the Wall)	3.00
SP5	Ken Griffey Jr. (1989 Major League Debut)	3.00

1988 Tara Toys Superstar Collectible Plaques

This series of player plaques was sold singly (at about 50 cents retail) and in selected team packs. Each was enclosed in a blister pack which features the checklist on back. Plaques measure 7-1/4" x 7-1/2" and are printed on thick cardboard. Fronts have a baseball diamond background with a large baseball design on which is printed the player photo. A bat at lower-right has a facsimile autograph and his name and team are listed above home plate. Backs are black. The plaques can be displayed by hanging them from a hole at top center, or using a folding easel included with the pack. The unnumbered plaques are listed here alphabetically. As is sometimes the case, late production changes and the creation of the team assortments may have resulted in the addition or deletion of some players from the printed checklist.

		MT
Complete Set (60):		225.00
Common Player:		3.00
(1)	Harold Baines	3.00
(2)	Steve Bedrosian	3.00
(3)	George Bell	3.00
(4)	Wade Boggs	6.00
(5)	Bobby Bonilla	3.00
(6)	George Brett	12.00
(7)	Jose Canseco	6.00
(8)	Will Clark	6.00
(9)	Roger Clemens	12.00
(10)	Vince Coleman	3.00
(11)	Eric Davis	3.00
(12)	Andre Dawson	3.00
(13)	Bo Diaz	3.00
(14)	Dennis Eckersley	3.00

(15)	Carlton Fisk	5.00
(16)	Kirk Gibson	3.00
(17)	Dwight Gooden	4.00
(18)	Mike Greenwell	3.00
(19)	Tony Gwynn	10.00
(20)	Rickey Henderson	6.00
(21)	Keith Hernandez	3.00
(22)	Orel Hershiser	3.50
(23)	Pete Incaviglia	3.00
(24)	Wally Joyner	3.00
(25)	Mark Langston	3.00
(26)	Candy Maldonado	3.00
(27)	Don Mattingly	15.00
(28)	Mark McGwire	25.00
(29)	Paul Molitor	6.00
(30)	Jack Morris	3.00
(31)	Dale Murphy	6.00
(32)	Kirby Puckett	10.00
(33)	Tim Raines	4.00
(34)	Cal Ripken Jr.	20.00
(35)	Nolan Ryan	24.00
(36)	Chris Sabo	3.00
(37)	Ryne Sandberg	7.50
(38)	Benny Santiago	3.00
(39)	Mike Schmidt	9.00
(40)	Mike Scott	3.00
(41)	Kevin Seitzer	3.00
(42)	Ozzie Smith	9.00
(43)	Cory Snyder	3.00
(44)	Darryl Strawberry	4.00
(45)	Alan Trammell	3.50
(46)	Fernando Valenzuela	3.00
(47)	Andy Van Slyke	3.00
(48)	Frank Viola	3.00
(49)	Dave Winfield	5.00

1990 Target Dodgers

Virtually every player who appeared in the uniform of the Brooklyn/Los Angeles Dodgers between 1890-1990 was included in this 1,100-card issue. Quality of the photo varies wildly from sharp to barely identifiable. Cards measure 2-1/16" x 3" and are perforated on two, three or four sides, depending where they were positioned on the 15-card perforated sheets in which the cards were distributed at various Dodgers home games. Player photos are in dark blue and white, bordered in speckled blue. Name and position appear in black in a light blue banner at top. At lower-left is the Dodgers 100th anniversary logo, with the Target stores logo at lower-right. On back the player's name and position reappear at top, with the logos below and the card number in a banner at bottom. Cards were numbered roughly alphabetically, though many are out of order. Some cards have duplicated numbers and there were some numbers skipped in the issue. All back printing is in blue on white. Career major league stats and the years in which the player was with the Dodgers are also noted on back.

		MT
Complete Set (1,103):		100.00
Common Player:		.10
1	Bert Abbey	.10
2	Cal Abrams	.10
3	Hank Aguirre	.10
4	Eddie Ainsmith	.10
5	Ed Albosta	.10
6	Luis Alcaraz	.10
7	Doyle Alexander	.10
8	Dick Allen	.25
9	Frank Allen	.10
10	Johnny Allen	.10
11	Mel Almada	.20
12	Walter Alston	.20
13	Ed Amelung	.10
14	Sandy Amoros	.15
15	Dave Anderson	.10
16	Ferrell Anderson	.10
17	John Anderson	.10
18	Stan Andrews	.10
19	Bill Antonello	.10
20	Jimmy Archer	.10
21	Bob Aspromonte	.10
22	Rick Auerbach	.10
23	Charlie Babb	.10
24	Johnny Babich	.10
25	Bob Bailey	.10
26	Bob Bailor	.10
27	Dusty Baker	.15
28	Tom Baker	.10
29	Dave Bancroft	.10
30	Dan Bankhead	.10
31	Jack Banta	.10
32	Jim Barbieri	.10
33	Red Barkley	.10
34	Jesse Barnes	.10
35	Rex Barney	.10
36	Billy Barnie	.10
37	Bob Barrett	.10
38	Jim Baxes	.10
39	Billy Bean	.10
40	Boom Boom Beck	.10
41	Joe Beckwith	.10
42	Hank Behrman	.10
43	Mark Belanger	.10
44	Wayne Belardi	.10
45	Tim Belcher	.10
46	George Bell	.10
47	Ray Benge	.10
48	Moe Berg	.75
49	Bill Bergen	.10
50	Ray Berres	.10
51	Don Bessent	.10
52	Steve Bilko	.10
53	Jack Billingham	.10
54	Babe Birrer	.10
55	Del Bissonette	.10
56	Joe Black	.15
57	Lu Blue	.10
58	George Boehler	.10
59	Sammy Bohne	.10
60	John Boiling	.10
61	Ike Boone	.10
62	Frenchy Bordagaray	.10
63	Ken Boyer	.15
64	Buzz Boyle	.10
65	Mark Bradley	.10
66	Bobby Bragan	.10
67	Ralph Branca	.15
68	Ed Brandt	.10
69	Sid Bream	.10
70	Marv Breeding	.10
71	Tom Brennan	.10
72	William Brennan	.10
73	Rube Bressler	.10
74	Ken Brett	.10
75	Jim Brewer	.10
76	Tony Brewer	.10
77	Rocky Bridges	.10
78	Greg Brock	.10
79	Dan Brouthers	.10
80	Eddie Brown	.10
81	Elmer Brown	.10
82	Lindsay Brown	.10
83	Lloyd Brown	.10
84	Mace Brown	.10
85	Tommy Brown	.10
86	Pete Browning	.10
87	Ralph Bryant	.10
88	Jim Bucher	.10
89	Bill Buckner	.15
90	Jim Bunning	.15
91	Jack Burdock	.10
92	Glenn Burke	.10
93	Buster Burrell	.10
94	Larry Burright	.10
95	Doc Bushong	.10
96	Max Butcher	.10
97	Johnny Butler	.10
98	Enos Cabell	.10
99	Leon Cadore	.10
100	Bruce Caldwell	.10
101	Dick Calmus	.10
102	Dolf Camilli	.10
103	Doug Camilli	.10
104	Roy Campanella	2.00
105	Al Campanis	.10
106	Jim Campanis	.10
107A	Leo Callahan	.10
107B	Gilly Campbell	.10
108	Jimmy Canavan	.10
109	Chris Cannizzaro	.10
110	Guy Cantrell	.10
111	Ben Cantwell	.10
112	Andy Carey	.10
113	Max Carey	.10
114	Tex Carleton	.10
115	Ownie Carroll	.10
116	Bob Caruthers	.10
117	Doc Casey	.10
118	Hugh Casey	.10
119	Bobby Castillo	.10
120	Cesar Cedeno	.10
121	Ron Cey	.15
122	Ed Chandler	.10
123	Ben Chapman	.10
124	Larry Cheney	.10
125	Bob Chipman	.10
126	Chuck Churn	.10
127	Gino Cimoli	.10
128	Moose Clabaugh	.10
129	Bud Clancy	.10
130	Bob Clark	.10
131	Watty Clark	.10
132	Alta Cohen	.10
133	Rocky Colavito	.60
134	Jackie Collum	.10
135	Chuck Connors	.75
136	Jack Coombs	.10
137	Johnny Cooney	.10
138	Tommy Corcoran	.10
139	Pop Corkhill	.10
140	John Corriden	.10
141	Pete Coscarart	.10
142	Wes Covington	.10
143	Billy Cox	.10
144	Roger Craig	.15
145	Not issued	
146	Willie Crawford	.10
147	Tim Crews	.10
148	John Cronin	.10
149	Lave Cross	.10
150	Bill Crouch	.10
151	Don Crow	.10
152	Henry Cruz	.10
153	Tony Cuccinello	.10
154	Roy Cullenbine	.10
155	George Culver	.10
156	Nick Cullop	.10
157	George Cutshaw	.10
158	Kiki Cuyler	.10
159	Bill Dahlen	.10
160	Babe Dahlgren	.10
161	Jack Dalton	.10
162	Tom Daly	.10
163	Cliff Dapper	.10
164	Bob Darnell	.10
165	Bobby Darwin	.10
166	Jake Daubert	.10
167	Vic Davalillo	.10
168	Curt Davis	.10
169	Mike Davis	.10
170	Ron Davis	.10
171	Tommy Davis	.15
172	Willie Davis	.15
173	Pea Ridge Day	.10
174	Tommy Dean	.10
175	Hank DeBerry	.10
176	Art Decatur	.10
177	Raoul Dedeaux	.10
178	Ivan DeJesus	.10
179	Don Demeter	.10
180	Gene DeMontreville	.10
181	Rick Dempsey	.10
182	Eddie Dent	.10
183	Mike Devereaux	.10
184	Carlos Diaz	.10
185	Dick Dietz	.10
186	Pop Dillon	.10
187	Bill Doak	.10
188	John Dobbs	.10
189	George Dockins	.10
190	Cozy Dolan	.10
191	Patsy Donovan	.10
192	Wild Bill Donovan	.10
193	Mickey Doolan	.10
194	Jack Doscher	.10
195	Phil Douglas	.10
196	Snooks Dowd	.10
197	Al Downing	.10
198	Red Downs	.10
199	Jack Doyle	.10
200	Solly Drake	.10
201	Tom Drake	.10
202	Chuck Dressen	.10
203	Don Drysdale	.75
204	Clise Dudley	.10
205	Mariano Duncan	.10
206	Jack Dunn	.10
207	Bull Durham	.10
208	Leo Durocher	.20
209	Billy Earle	.10
210	George Earnshaw	.10
211	Ox Eckhardt	.10
212	Bruce Edwards	.10
213	Hank Edwards	.10
214	Dick W. Egan	.10
215	Harry Eisenstat	.10
216	Kid Elberfeld	.10
217	Jumbo Elliot	.10
218	Don Elston	.10
219	Gil English	.10
220	Johnny Enzmann	.10
221	Al Epperly	.10
222	Carl Erskine	.15
223	Tex Erwin	.10
224	Cecil Espy	.10
225	Chuck Essegian	.10
226	Dude Esterbrook	.10
227	Red Evans	.10
228	Bunny Fabrique	.10
229	Jim Fairey	.10
230	Ron Fairly	.15
231	George Fallon	.10
232	Turk Farrell	.10
233	Duke Farrel	.10
234	Jim Faulkner	.10
235	Alex Ferguson	.10
236	Joe Ferguson	.10
237	Chico Fernandez	.10
238	Sid Fernandez	.10
239	Al Ferrara	.10
240	Wes Ferrell	.10
241	Lou Fette	.10
242	Chick Fewster	.10
243	Jack Fimple	.10
244	Neal "Mickey" Finn	.10
245	Bob Fisher	.10
246	Freddie Fitzsimmons	.10
247	Tim Flood	.10
248	Jake Flowers	.10
249	Hod Ford	.10
250	Terry Forster	.10
251	Alan Foster	.10
252	Jack Fournier	.10
253	Dave Foutz	.10
254	Art Fowler	.10
255	Fred Frankhouse	.10
256	Herman Franks	.10
257	Johnny Frederick	.10
258	Larry French	.10
259	Lonny Frey	.10
260	Pepe Frias	.10
261	Charlie Fuchs	.10
262	Carl Furillo	.35
263	Len Gabrielson	.10
264	Augie Galan	.10
265	Joe Gallagher	.10
266	Phil Gallivan	.10
267	Balvino Galvez	.10
268	Mike Garman	.10
269	Phil Garner	.10
270	Steve Garvey	.25
271	Ned Garvin	.10
272	Hank Gastright	.10
273	Sid Gautreaux	.10
274	Jim Gentile	.10
275	Greek George	.10
276	Ben Geraghty	.10
277	Gus Getz	.10
278	Bob Giallombardo	.10
279	Kirk Gibson	.15
280	Charlie Gilbert	.10
281	Jim Gilliam	.15
282	Al Gionfriddo	.10
283	Tony Giuliani	.10
284	Al Glossop	.10
285	John Gochnaur	.10
286	Jim Golden	.10
287	Dave Goltz	.10
288	Jose Gonzalez	.10
289	Johnny Gooch	.10
290	Ed Goodson	.10
291	Bill Grabarkewitz	.10
292	Jack Graham	.10
293	Mudcat Grant	.10
294	Dick Gray	.10
295	Kent Greenfield	.10
296	Hal Gregg	.10
297	Alfredo Griffin	.10
298	Mike Griffin	.10
299	Derrell Griffith	.10
300	Tommy Griffith	.10
301	Burleigh Grimes	.10
302	Lee Grissom	.10
303	Jerry Grote	.10
304	Pedro Guerrero	.15
305	Brad Gulden	.10
306	Ad Gumbert	.10
307	Chris Gwynn	.10
308	Bert Haas	.10
309	John Hale	.10
310	Tom Haller	.10
311	Bill Hallman	.10
312	Jeff Hamilton	.10
313	Luke Hamlin	.10
314	Ned Hanlon	.10
315	Gerald Hannahs	.10
316	Charlie Hargreaves	.10
317	Tim Harkness	.10
318	Harry Harper	.10
319	Joe Harris	.10
320	Lenny Harris	.10
321	Bill F. Hart	.10
322	Buddy Hassett	.10
323	Mickey Hatcher	.10
324	Joe Hatten	.10
325	Phil Haugstad	.10
326	Brad Havens	.10
327	Ray Hayworth	.10
328	Ed Head	.10
329	Danny Heep	.10
330	Fred Heimach	.10
331	Harvey Hendrick	.10
332	Weldon Henley	.10
333	Butch Henline	.10
334	Dutch Henry	.10
335	Roy Henshaw	.10
336	Babe Herman	.15
337	Billy Herman	.15
338	Gene Hermanski	.10
339	Enzo Hernandez	.10
340	Art Herring	.10
341	Orel Hershiser	.15
342	Dave J. Hickman	.10
343	Jim Hickman	.10
344	Kirby Higbe	.10
345	Andy High	.10
346	George Hildebrand	.10
347	Hunkey Hines	.10
348	Don Hoak	.10
349	Oris Hockett	.10
350	Gil Hodges	1.00
351	Glenn Hoffman	.10
352	Al Hollingsworth	.10
353	Tommy Holmes	.10
354	Brian Holton	.10
355	Rick Honeycutt	.10
356	Burt Hooton	.10
357	Gail Hopkins	.10
358	Johnny Hopp	.10
359	Charlie Hough	.15
360	Frank Howard	.15
361	Steve Howe	.15
362	Dixie Howell	.10
363	Harry Howell	.10
364	Jay Howell	.10
365	Ken Howell	.10
366	Waite Hoyt	.10
367	Johnny Hudson	.10
368	Jim J. Hughes	.10
369	Jim R. Hughes	.10
370	Mickey Hughes	.10
371	John Hummel	.10
372	Ron Hunt	.10
373	Willard Hunter	.10
374	Ira Hutchinson	.10
375	Tom Hutton	.10
376	Charlie Irwin	.10
377	Fred Jacklitsch	.10
378	Randy Jackson	.10
379	Merwin Jacobson	.10
380	Cleo James	.10
381	Hal Janvrin	.10
382	Roy Jarvis	.10
383	George Jeffcoat	.10
384	Jack Jenkins	.10
385	Hughie Jennings	.10
386	Tommy John	.15
387	Lou Johnson	.10
388	Fred Ivy Johnston	.10
389	Jimmy Johnston	.10
390	Jay Johnstone	.15
391	Fielder Jones	.10
392	Oscar Jones	.10
393	Tim Jordan	.10
394	Spider Jorgensen	.10
395	Von Joshua	.10
396	Bill Joyce	.10
397	Joe Judge	.10
398	Alex Kampouris	.10
399	Willie Keeler	.10
400	Mike Kekich	.10
401	John Kelleher	.10
402	Frank Kellert	.10
403	Joe Kelley	.10
404	George Kelly	.10
405	Bob Kennedy	.10
406	Brickyard Kennedy	.10
407	John Kennedy	.10
408	Not issued	
409	Newt Kimball	.10
410	Clyde King	.10
411	Enos Kirkpatrick	.10
412	Frank Kitson	.10
413	Johnny Klippstein	.10
414	Elmer Klumpp	.10
415	Len Koenecke	.10
416	Ed Konetchy	.10
417	Andy Kosco	.10
418	Sandy Koufax	4.00
419	Ernie Koy	.10
420	Charlie Kress	.10
421	Bill Krueger	.10
422	Ernie Krueger	.10
423	Clem Labine	.15
424	Candy LaChance	.10
425	Lee Lacy	.10
426	Lerrin LaGrow	.10
427	Bill Lamar	.10
428	Wayne LaMaster	.10
429	Ray Lamb	.10
430	Rafael Landestoy	.10
431	Ken Landreaux	.10
432	Tito Landrum	.10
433	Norm Larker	.15
434	Lyn Lary	.10
435	Tom Lasorda	.20
436	Cookie Lavagetto	.10
437	Rudy Law	.10
438	Tony Lazzeri	.10
439	Tim Leary	.10
440	Bob Lee	.10
441	Hall Lee	.10
442	Leron Lee	.10
443	Jim Lefebvre	.10
444	Ken Lehman	.10
445	Don LeJohn	.10
446	Steve Lembo	.10
447	Ed Lennox	.10
448	Dutch Leonard	.10
449	Jeffery Leonard	.10
450	Not issued	
451	Dennis Lewallyn	.10
452	Bob Lillis	.10
453	Jim Lindsey	.10
454	Fred Lindstrom	.10
455	Billy Loes	.10
456	Bob Logan	.10
457	Bill Lohrman	.10
458	Not issued	
459	Vic Lombardi	.10
460	Davey Lopes	.15
461	Al Lopez	.10
462	Ray Lucas	.10
463	Not issued	
464	Harry Lumley	.10
465	Don Lund	.10
466	Dolf Luque	.10
467	Jim Lyttle	.10
468	Max Macon	.10
469	Bill Madlock	.15
470	Lee Magee	.10
471	Sal Maglie	.10
472	George Magoon	.10
473	Duster Mails	.10
474	Candy Maldonado	.10
475	Tony Malinosky	.10
476	Lew Malone	.10
477	Al Mamaux	.10
478	Gus Mancuso	.10
479	Charlie Manuel	.10
480	Heinie Manush	.10

481	Rabbit Maranville	.10
482	Juan Marichal	.20
483	Rube Marquard	.10
484	Bill Marriott	.10
485	Buck Marrow	.10
486	Mike A. Marshall	.10
487	Mike G. Marshall	.10
488	Morrie Martin	.10
489	Ramon Martinez	.20
490	Teddy Martinez	.10
491	Earl Mattingly	.10
492	Len Matuszek	.10
493	Gene Mauch	.10
494	Al Maul	.10
495	Carmen Mauro	.10
496	Alvin McBean	.10
497	Bill McCarren	.10
498	Jack McCarthy	.10
499	Tommy McCarthy	.10
500	Lew McCarty	.10
501	Mike J. McCormick	.10
502	Judge McCreedie	.10
503	Tom McCreery	.10
504	Danny McDevitt	.10
505	Chappie McFarland	.10
506	Joe McGinnity	.10
507	Bob McGraw	.10
508	Deacon McGuire	.10
509	Bill McGunnigle	.10
510	Harry McIntyre	.10
511	Cal McLish	.10
512	Ken McMullen	.10
513	Dough McWeeny	.10
514	Joe Medwick	.10
515	Rube Melton	.10
516	Fred Merkle	.10
517	Orlando Mercado	.10
518	Andy Messersmith	.10
519	Irish Meusel	.10
520	Benny Meyer	.10
521	Russ Meyer	.10
522	Chief Meyers	.10
523	Gene Michael	.10
524	Pete Mikkelsen	.10
525	Eddie Miksis	.10
526	Johnny Miljus	.10
527	Bob Miller	.10
528	Larry Miller	.10
529	Otto Miller	.10
530	Ralph Miller	.10
531	Walt Miller	.10
532	Wally Millies	.10
533	Bob Milliken	.10
534	Buster Mills	.10
535	Paul Minner	.10
536	Bobby Mitchell	.10
537	Clarence Mitchell	.10
538	Dale Mitchell	.10
539	Fred Mitchell	.10
540	Johnny Mitchell	.10
541	Joe Moeller	.10
542	Rick Monday	.10
543	Wally Moon	.10
544	Cy Moore	.10
545	Dee Moore	.10
546	Eddie Moore	.10
547	Gene Moore	.10
548	Randy Moore	.10
549	Ray Moore	.10
550	Jose Morales	.10
551	Bobby Morgan	.10
552	Eddie Morgan	.10
553	Mike Morgan	.10
554	Johnny Morrison	.10
555	Walt Moryn	.10
556	Ray Moss	.10
557	Manny Mota	.15
558	Joe Mulvey	.10
559	Van Lingle Mungo	.10
560	Les Munns	.10
561	Mike Munoz	.10
562	Simmy Murch	.10
563	Eddie Murray	.25
564	Hy Myers	.10
565	Sam Nahem	.10
566	Earl Naylor	.10
567	Charlie Neal	.10
568	Ron Negray	.10
569	Bernie Neis	.10
570	Rocky Nelson	.10
571	Dick Nen	.10
572	Don Newcombe	.20
573	Bobo Newsom	.10
574	Doc Newton	.10
575	Tom Niedenfuer	.10
576	Otho Nitcholas	.10
577	Al Nixon	.10
578	Jerry Nops	.10
579	Irv Noren	.10
580	Fred Norman	.10
581	Bill North	.10
582	Johnny Oates	.10
583	Bob O'Brien	.10
584	John O'Brien	.10
585	Lefty O'Doul	.10
586	Joe Oeschger	.10
587	Al Oliver	.10
588	Nate Oliver	.10
589	Luis Olmo	.10
590	Ivy Olson	.10
591	Mickey O'Neil	.10
592	Joe Orengo	.10
593	Jesse Orosco	.10
594	Frank O'Rourke	.10
595	Jorge Orta	.10
596	Phil Ortega	.10
597	Claude Osteen	.10
598	Fritz Ostermueller	.10
599	Mickey Owen	.10
600	Tom Paciorek	.10
601	Don Padgett	.10
602	Andy Pafko	.10
603	Erv Palica	.10
604	Ed Palmquist	.10
605	Wes Parker	.10
606	Jay Partridge	.10
607	Camilo Pascual	.10
608	Kevin Pasley	.10
609	Dave Patterson	.10
610	Harley Payne	.15
611	Johnny Peacock	.10
612	Hal Peck	.10
613	Stu Pederson	.10
614	Alejandro Pena	.10
615	Jose Pena	.10
616	Jack Perconte	.10
617	Charlie Perkins	.10
618	Ron Perranoski	.10
619	Jim Peterson	.10
620	Jesse Petty	.10
621	Jeff Pfeffer	.10
622	Babe Phelps	.10
623	Val Picinich	.10
624	Joe Pignatano	.10
625	George Pinckney	.10
626	Ed Pipgras	.10
627	Bud Podbielan	.10
628	Johnny Podres	.15
629	Boots Poffenberger	.10
630	Nick Polly	.10
631	Paul Popovich	.10
632	Bill Posedel	.10
633	Boog Powell	.10
634	Dennis Powell	.10
635	Paul Ray Powell	.10
636	Ted Power	.10
637	Tot Pressnell	.10
638	John Purdin	.10
639	Jack Quinn	.10
640	Marv Rackley	.10
641	Jack Radtke	.10
642	Pat Ragan	.10
643	Ed Rakow	.10
644	Bob Ramazzotti	.10
645	Willie Ramsdell	.10
646	Mike James Ramsey	.10
647	Mike Jeffery Ramsey	.10
648	Willie Randolph	.10
649	Doug Rau	.10
650	Lance Rautzhan	.10
651	Howie Reed	.10
652	Pee Wee Reese	2.00
653	Phil Regan	.10
654	Bill Reidy	.10
655	Bobby Reis	.10
656	Pete Reiser	.15
657	Rip Repulski	.10
658	Ed Reulbach	.10
659	Jerry Reuss	.10
660	R.J. Reynolds	.10
661	Billy Rhiel	.10
662	Rick Rhoden	.10
663	Paul Richards	.10
664	Danny Richardson	.10
665	Pete Richert	.10
666	Harry Riconda	.10
667	Joe Riggert	.10
668	Lew Riggs	.10
669	Jimmy Ripple	.10
670	Lou Ritter	.10
671	German Rivera	.10
672	Johnny Rizzo	.10
673	Jim Roberts	.10
674	Earl Robinson	.10
675	Frank Robinson	.50
676	Jackie Robinson	4.00
677A	Wilbert Robinson	.10
678	Rich Rodas	.10
678B	Sergio Robles	.10
679	Ellie Rodriguez	.10
680	Preacher Roe	.15
681	Ed Roebuck	.10
682	Ron Roenicke	.10
683	Oscar Roettger	.10
684	Lee Rogers	.10
685	Packy Rogers	.10
686	Stan Rojek	.10
687	Vicente Romo	.10
688	Johnny Roseboro	.15
689	Goody Rosen	.10
690	Don Ross	.10
691	Ken Rowe	.10
692	Schoolboy Rowe	.10
693	Luther Roy	.10
694	Jerry Royster	.10
695	Nap Rucker	.10
696	Dutch Ruether	.10
697	Bill Russell	.15
698	Jim Russell	.10
699	John Russell	.10
700	Johnny Rutherford	.10
701	John Ryan	.10
702	Rosy Ryan	.10
703	Mike Sandlock	.10
704	Ted Savage	.10
705	Dave Sax	.10
706	Steve Sax	.15
707	Bill Sayles	.10
708	Bill Schardt	.10
709	Johnny Schmitz	.10
710	Dick Schofield	.10
711	Howie Schultz	.10
712	Ferdie Schupp	.10
713	Mike Scioscia	.15
714	Dick Scott	.10
715	Tom Seats	.10
716	Jimmy Sebring	.10
717	Larry See	.10
718	Dave Sells	.10
719	Greg Shanahan	.10
720	Mike Sharperson	.10
721	Joe Shaute	.10
722	Merv Shea	.10
723	Jimmy Sheckard	.10
724	Jack Sheehan	.10
725	John Shelby	.10
726	Vince Sherlock	.10
727	Larry Sherry	.15
728	Norm Sherry	.15
729	Bill Shindle	.10
730	Craig Shipley	.10
731	Bart Shirley	.10
732	Steve Shirley	.10
733	Burt Shotton	.10
734	George Shuba	.10
735	Dick Siebert	.10
736	Joe Simpson	.10
737	Duke Sims	.10
738	Bill Singer	.10
739	Fred Sington	.10
740	Ted Sizemore	.10
741	Frank Skaff	.10
742	Bill Skowron	.20
743	Gordon Slade	.10
744	Dwain Lefty Sloat	.10
745	Charley Smith	.10
746	Dick Smith	.10
747	George Smith	.10
748	Germany Smith	.10
749	Jack Smith	.10
750	Reggie Smith	.15
751	Sherry Smith	.10
752	Harry Smythe	.10
753	Duke Snider	2.00
754	Eddie Solomon	.10
755	Elias Sosa	.10
756	Daryl Spencer	.10
757	Roy Spencer	.10
758	Karl Spooner	.10
759	Eddie Stack	.10
760	Tuck Stainback	.10
761	George Stallings	.10
762	Jerry Standaert	.10
763	Don Stanhouse	.10
764	Eddie Stanky	.10
765	Dolly Stark	.10
766	Jigger Statz	.10
767	Casey Stengel	.20
768	Jerry Stephenson	.10
769	Ed Stevens	.10
770	Dave Stewart	.15
771	Stuffy Stewart	.10
772	Bob Stinson	.10
773	Milt Stock	.10
774	Harry Stovey	.10
775	Mike Strahler	.10
776	Sammy Strang	.10
777	Elmer Stricklett	.10
778	Joe Stripp	.10
779	Dick Stuart	.10
780	Franklin Stubbs	.10
781	Bill Sudakis	.10
782	Clyde Sukeforth	.10
783	Billy Sullivan	.10
784	Tom Sunkel	.10
785	Rick Sutcliffe	.10
786	Don Sutton	.40
787	Bill Swift	.10
788	Vito Tamulis	.10
789	Danny Taylor	.10
790	Harry Taylor	.10
791	Zack Taylor	.10
792	Not issued	
793	Chuck Templeton	.10
794	Wayne Terwilliger	.10
795	Derrel Thomas	.10
796	Fay Thomas	.10
797	Gary Thomasson	.10
798	Don Thompson	.10
799	Fresco Thompson	.10
800	Tim Thompson	.10
801	Hank Thormahlen	.10
802	Sloppy Thurston	.10
803	Cotton Tierney	.10
804	Al Todd	.10
805	Bert Tooley	.10
806	Jeff Torborg	.10
807	Dick Tracewski	.10
808	Nick Tremark	.10
809	Alex Trevino	.10
810	Tommy Tucker	.10
811	John Tudor	.10
812	Mike Vail	.10
813	Rene Valdes (Valdez)	.10
814	Bobby Valentine	.10
815	Fernando Valenzuela	.15
816	Elmer Valo	.10
817	Dazzy Vance	.15
818	Sandy Vance	.10
819	Chris Van Cuyk	.10
820	Ed VandeBerg	.10
821	Arky Vaughan	.10
822	Zoilo Versalles	.10
823	Joe Vosmik	.10
824	Ben Wade	.10
825	Dixie Walker	.10
826	Rube Walker	.10
827	Stan Wall	.10
828	Lee Walls	.10
829	Danny Walton	.10
830	Lloyd Waner	.10
831	Paul Waner	.10
832	Chuck Ward	.10
833	John Monte Ward	.10
834	Preston Ward	.10
835	Jack Warner	.10
836	Tommy Warren	.10
837	Carl Warwick	.10
838	Jimmy Wasdell	.10
839	Ron Washington	.10
840	George Watkins	.10
841	Hank Webb	.10
842	Les Webber	.10
843	Gary Weiss	.10
844	Bob Welch	.15
845	Brad Wellman	.10
846	John Werhas	.15
847	Max West	.10
848	Gus Weyhing	.10
849	Mack Wheat	.10
850	Zack Wheat	.10
851	Ed Wheeler	.10
852	Larry White	.10
853	Myron White	.10
854	Terry Whitfield	.10
855	Dick Whitman	.10
856	Possum Whitted	.10
857	Kemp Wicker	.10
858	Hoyt Wilhelm	.15
859	Kaiser Wilhelm	.10
860	Nick Willhite	.10
861	Dick Williams	.15
862	Reggie Williams	.10
863	Stan Williams	.10
864	Woody Williams	.10
865	Maury Wills	.15
866	Hack Wilson	.15
867	Robert Wilson	.10
868	Gordon Windhorn	.10
869	Jim Winford	.10
870	Lave Winham	.10
871	Tom Winsett	.10
872	Hank Winston	.10
873	Whitey Witt	.10
874	Pete Wojey	.10
875	Tracy Woodson	.10
876	Clarence Wright	.10
877	Glenn Wright	.10
878	Ricky Wright	.10
879	Whit Wyatt	.10
880	Jimmy Wynn	.10
881	Joe Yeager	.10
882	Steve Yeager	.10
883	Matt Young	.10
884	Tom Zachary	.10
885	Pat Zachry	.10
886	Geoff Zahn	.10
887	Don Zimmer	.15
888	Morrie Aderholt	.10
889	Raleigh Aitchison	.10
890	Whitey Alperman	.10
891	Orlando Alvarez	.10
892	Pat Ankeman	.10
893	Ed Appleton	.10
894	Doug Baird	.10
895	Lady Baldwin	.10
896	Win Ballou	.10
897	Bob Barr	.10
898	Boyd Bartley	.10
899	Eddie Basinski	.10
900	Erve Beck	.10
901	Ralph Birkofer	.10
902	Not issued	
903	Joe Bradshaw	.10
904	Bruce Brubaker	.10
905	Oyster Burns	.10
906	John Butler	.10
907	Not issued	
908	Kid Carsey	.10
909	Pete Cassidy	.10
910	Tom Catterson	.10
911	Glenn Chapman	.10
912	Paul Chervinko	.10
913	George Cisar	.10
914	Wally Clement	.10
915	Bill Collins	.10
916	Chuck Corgan	.10
917	Dick Cox	.10
918	George Crable	.10
919	Sam Crane	.10
920	Cliff Curtis	.10
921	Fats Dantonio	.10
922	Con Daily	.10
923	Jud Daley	.10
924	Jake Daniel	.10
925	Kal Daniels	.10
926	Dan Daub	.10
927	Lindsay Deal	.10
928	Artie Dede	.10
929	Pat Deisel	.10
930	Bert Delmas	.10
931	Rube Dessau	.10
932	Leo Dickerman	.10
933	John Douglas	.10
934	Red Downey	.10
935	Carl Doyle	.10
936	John Duffie	.10
937	Dick Durning	.10
938	Red Durrett	.10
939	Mal Eason	.10
940	Charlie Ebbetts	.15
941	Rube Ehardt	.10
942	Rowdy Elliot	.10
943	Bones Ely	.10
944	Woody English	.10
945	Roy Evans	.10
946	Gus Felix	.10
947	Bill Fischer	.10
948	Jeff Fischer	.10
949	Chauncey Fisher	.10
950	Tom Fitzsimmons	.10
951	Darrin Fletcher	.10
952	Wes Flowers	.10
953	Howard Freigau	.10
954	Nig Fuller	.10
955	John Gaddy	.10
956	Welcome Gaston	.10
957	Frank Gatins	.10
958	Pete Gilbert	.10
959	Wally Wilbert	.10
960	Carden Gillenwater	.10
961	Roy Gleason	.10
962	Harvey Green	.10
963	Nelson Greene	.10
964	John Grim	.10
965	Dan Griner	.10
967	Bill Hall	.10
968	Johnny Hall	.10
969	Not issued	
970	Pat Hanifin	.10
971	Bill Harris	.10
972	Bill W. Hart	.10
973	Chris Hartje	.10
974	Mike Hartley	.10
975	Gil Hatfield	.10
976	Chris Haughey	.10
977	Hugh Hearne	.10
978	Mike Hechinger	.10
979	Jake Hehl	.10
980	Bob Higgins	.10
981	Still Bill Hill	.10
982	Shawn Hillegas	.10
983	Wally Hood	.10
984	Lefty Hopper	.10
985	Ricky Horton	.10
986	Ed Householder	.10
987	Bill Hubbell	.10
988	Al Humphrey	.10
989	Bernie Hungling	.10
990	George Hunter	.10
991	Pat Hurley	.10
992	Joe Hutcheson	.10
993	Roy Hutson	.10
994	Bert Inks	.10
995	Dutch Jordan	.10
996	Not issued	
997	Frank Kane	.10
998	Chet Kohn	.10
999	Maury Kent	.10
1000	Tom Kinslow	.10
1001	Fred Kipp	.10
1002	Joe Klugman	.10
1003	Elmer Knetzer	.10
1004	Barney Koch	.10
1005	Jim Korwan	.10
1006	Joe Koukalik	.10
1007	Lou Koupal	.10
1008	Joe Kustus	.10
1009	Frank Lamanske	.10
1010	Tacks Latimer	.10
1011	Bill Leard	.10
1012	Phil Lewis	.10
1013	Mickey Livingston	.10
1014	Dick Loftus	.10
1015	Charlie Loudenslager	.10
1016	Tom Lovett	.10
1017	Charlie Malay	.10
1018	Mal Mallett	.10
1019	Ralph Mauriello	.10
1020	Bill McCabe	.10
1021	Gene McCann	.10
1022	Mike McCormick	.10
1023	Terry McDermott	.10
1024	John McDougal	.10
1025	Pryor McElveen	.10
1026	Dan McGann	.10
1027	Pat McGlothin	.10
1028	Doc McJames	.10
1029	Kit McKenna	.10
1030	Sadie McMahon	.10
1031	Not issued	
1032	Tommy McMillan	.10
1033	Glenn Mickens	.10
1034	Don Miles	.10
1035	Hack Miller	.10
1036	John Miller	.10
1037	Lemmie Miller	.10
1038	George Mohart	.10
1039	Gary Moore	.10
1040	Herbie Moran	.10
1041	Earl Mossor	.10
1042	Glen Moulder	.10
1043	Billy Mullen	.10
1045	Curly Onis	.10
1046	Tiny Osbourne	.10
1047	Jim Pastorius	.10
1048	Art Parks	.10
1049	Chink Outen	.10
1050	Jimmy Pattison	.10
1051	Norman Pitt	.10
1052	Doc Reisling	.10
1053	Gilberto Reyes	.10
1054	Not issued	
1055	Lou Rochelli	.10
1056	Jim Romano	.10
1057	Max Rosenfeld	.10
1058	Andy Rush	.10
1059	Jack Ryan	.10
1060	Jack Savage	.10
1061	Not issued	
1062	Ray Schmandt	.10
1063	Henry Schmidt	.10
1064	Charlie Schmutz	.10
1065	Joe Schultz	.10
1066	Ray Searage	.10
1067	Elmer Sexauer	.10
1068	George Sharrott	.10
1069	Tommy Sheehan	.10
1071	George Shoch	.10
1072	Broadway Aleck Smith	.10

1073	Hap Smith	.10
1074	Red Smith	.10
1075	Tony Smith	.10
1076	Gene Snyder	.10
1077	Denny Sothern	.10
1078	Bill Steele	.10
1080	Farmer Steelman	.10
1081	Dutch Stryker	.10
1082	Tommy Tatum	.10
1084	Adonis Terry	.10
1085	Ray Thomas	.10
1086	George Treadway	.10
1087	Overton Tremper	.10
1088	Ty Tyson	.10
1089	Rube Vickers	.10
1090	Jose Vizcaino	.10
1091	Bull Wagner	.10
1092	Butts Wagner	.10
1093	Rube Ward	.10
1094	John Wetteland	.10
1095	Eddie Wilson	.10
1096	Tex Wilson	.10
1097	Zeke Wrigley	.10
1098	Not issued	
1099	Rube Yarrison	.10
1100	Earl Yingling	.10
1101	Chink Zachary	.10
1102	Lefty Davis	.10
1103	Bob Hall	.10
1104	Darby O'Brien	.10
1105	Larry LeJeune	.10
1144	Hub Northen	.10

1982 Tastykake Phillies

Tastykake's initial sponsorship resulted in this black-and-white, blank-backed set in approximate postcard size (3-1/4" x 5-1/2"). Most, but not all, of the cards have the Tastykake name on front beneath the player's name. The unnumbered cards are checklisted here alphabetically.

		MT
Complete Set (35):		12.00
Common Player:		.50
(1)	Luis Aguayo	.50
(2)	Porfi Altamirano	.50
(3)	Dave Bristol	.50
(4)	Warren Brusstar	.50
(5)	Marty Bystrom	.50
(6)	Steve Carlton	2.00
(7)	Larry Christenson	.50
(8)	Pat Corrales	.50
(9)	Dick Davis	.50
(10)	Mark Davis	.50
(11)	Ivan DeJesus	.60
(12)	Bob Dernier	.50
(13)	Bo Diaz	.50
(14)	Ed Farmer	.50
(15)	Greg Gross	.50
(16)	Deron Johnson	.50
(17)	Mike Krukow	.50
(18)	Sparky Lyle	.75
(19)	Garry Maddox	.60
(20)	Gary Matthews	.60
(21)	Len Matuszek	.50
(22)	Tug McGraw	.75
(23)	Sid Monge	.50
(24)	Claude Osteen	.50
(25)	Ron Reed	.50
(26)	Dave Roberts	.50
(27)	Pete Rose	4.00
(28)	Dick Ruthven	.50
(29)	Mike Ryan	.50
(30)	Mike Schmidt	3.00
(31)	Manny Trillo	.50
(32)	Del Unser	.50
(33)	Ozzie Virgil	.50
(34)	George Vukovich	.50
(35)	Bobby Wine	.50

1983 Tastykake Phillies

In 1983 for the first time the Phillies produced a full-color postcard-size (3-1/2" x 5-1/4") set, sponsored by Tastykake, whose advertising appears on the back, along with an inspirational message. On some cards a "Dear Fan" note has been added. The unnumbered cards are checklisted here alphabetically.

		MT
Complete Set (32):		16.00
Common Player:		.25
(1)	Luis Aguayo	.25
(2)	Joe Amalfitano	.25
(3)	Marty Bystrom	.25
(4)	Steve Carlton	2.00
(5)	Larry Christenson	.25
(6)	Pat Corrales	.25
(7)	Ivan DeJesus	.25
(8)	John Denny	.25
(9)	Bob Dernier	.25
(10)	Bo Diaz	.25
(11)	Ed Farmer	.25
(12)	Greg Gross	.25
(13)	Von Hayes	.25
(14)	Al Holland	.25
(15)	Garry Maddox	.25
(16)	Gary Matthews	.35
(17)	Tug McGraw	.35
(18)	Larry Milbourne	.25
(19)	Bob Molinaro	.25
(20a)	Sid Monge ("Quitters never win ...")	.25
(20b)	Sid Monge ("Dear Fan:")	.25
(21)	Joe Morgan	1.50
(22)	Tony Perez	1.00
(23)	Ron Reed	.25
(24)	Dave Roberts	.25
(25a)	Bill Robinson ("Stay in school ...")	.25
(25b)	Bill Robinson ("Dear Fan:")	.25
(26a)	Pete Rose ("A good education ...")	4.00
(26b)	Pete Rose ("Dear Fan:")	4.00
(27)	Dick Ruthven	.25
(28)	Mike Schmidt	3.00
(29)	Ozzie Virgil	.25
(30)	Phils coaches	.25
(31a)	Phillie Phanatic ("Tell your parents ...")	.25
(31b)	Phillie Phanatic ("Dear Fan:")	.25
(32)	Vet Stadium	.25

1984 Tastykake Phillies

This set was issued as a promotion by Tastykake in 1984 and was distributed as a complete set to fans attending the April 21 game at Veterans Stadium. The large (3-1/2" x 5-1/4") full-color cards have a white border surrounding the photo with "Phillies" at the top and the player's name at the bottom. A 1984 Phillies copyright line appears in the lower-left corner. The backs display facsimile autographs, a brief inspirational message and the Tastykake and Phillies logos. The set includes special cards featuring the club's broadcasters, manager and coaches, a team photo, logo/checklist card and two action photos of Mike Schmidt and Steve Carlton, labeled "Future Hall of Famers".

		MT
Complete Set (47):		8.00
Common Player:		.20
(1)	Luis Aguayo	.20
(2)	Larry Andersen	.20
(3)	Dave Bristol	.20
(4)	Marty Bystrom	.20
(5)	Bill Campbell	.20
(6)	Steve Carlton	2.00
(7)	Future Hall of Famer (Steve Carlton)	1.50
(8)	Don Carman	.20
(9)	Tim Corcoran	.20
(10)	Darren Daulton	.50
(11)	Ivan DeJesus	.20
(12)	John Denny	.20
(13)	Bo Diaz	.20
(14)	John Felske	.20
(15)	Steve Fireovid	.20
(16)	Kiko Garcia	.20
(17)	Tony Ghelfi	.20
(18)	Greg Gross	.20
(19)	Kevin Gross	.20
(20)	Von Hayes	.25
(21)	Al Holland	.20
(22)	Charles Hudson	.20
(23)	Steve Jeltz	.20
(24)	Deron Johnson	.20
(25)	Jerry Koosman	.25
(26)	Joe Lefebvre	.20
(27)	Sixto Lezcano	.20
(28)	Garry Maddox	.20
(29)	Len Matuszek	.25
(30)	Tug McGraw	.40
(31)	Claude Osteen	.20
(32)	Paul Owens	.20
(33)	John Russell	.20
(34)	Mike Ryan	.20
(35)	Juan Samuel	.25
(36)	Mike Schmidt	4.00
(37)	Future Hall of Famer (Mike Schmidt)	3.00
(38)	Jeff Stone	.20
(39)	Ozzie Virgil	.20
(40)	Dave Wehrmeister	.20
(41)	Glenn Wilson	.20
(42)	John Wockenfuss	.20
(43)	Phillie Phanatic	.20
(44)	Phillies Broadcasters (Richie Ashburn, Harry Kalas, Andy Musser, Chris Wheeler)	.50
(45)	Veterans Stadium	.20
(46)	Team Photo	.25
(47)	Checklist	.20

1985 Tastykake Phillies

This regional set of Phillies cards, sponsored by Tastykake, was given away at a stadium promotion on April 21st at Philadelphia's Veterans Stadium. The 47 full-color cards measure a large 3" x 5" and are numbered according to the player's uniform number. In addition to player's from the 1985 Phillies roster, the set includes the manager, coaches, group photos, and cards of 14 promising minor leaguers in the club's farm system. The full-color cards are printed on a white, glossy stock and surrrounded by a white border. The player's uniform number, name and position appear below, with a 1985 Phillies copyright in the lower right corner. The backs of the cards display the Phillies and Tastykake logos at the top and bottom respectively, with player information in the center.

		MT
Complete Set (48):		9.00
Common Player:		.20
(1)	Checklist	.10
(2)	John Felske	.20
(3)	Dave Bristol	.20
(4)	Lee Elia	.20
(5)	Claude Osteen	.20
(6)	Mike Ryan	.20
(7)	Del Unser	.20
(8)	Phillies Coaching Staff (Dave Bristol, Lee Elia, John Felske, Hank King, Claude Osteen, Mike Ryan, Del	.20
(9)	Phillies Pitchers (Larry Andersen, Bill Campbell, Steve Carlton, Don Carman, John Denny, Kevin Gross), Al Holland, Charles Hudson, (Jerry Koosman, Shane Rawley, Pat Zachry)	.20
(10)	Phillies Catchers (Darren Daulton, Bo Diaz, Ozzie Virgil)	.20
(11)	Phillies Infielders (Luis Aguayo, Ivan De Jesus, Steve Jeltz, John Russell, Juan Samuel, Mike	.50
(12)	Phillies Outfielders (Tim Corcoran, Greg Gross, Von Hayes, Jeff Stone, Glenn Wilson)	.20
(13)	Larry Andersen	.20
(14)	Steve Carlton	1.50
(15)	Don Carman	.20
(16)	John Denny	.20
(17)	Tony Ghelfi	.20
(18)	Kevin Gross	.20
(19)	Al Holland	.20
(20)	Charles Hudson	.20
(21)	Jerry Koosman	.25
(22)	Shane Rawley	.20
(23)	Pat Zachry	.20
(24)	Darren Daulton	.40
(25)	Bo Diaz	.20
(26)	Ozzie Virgil	.20
(27)	John Wockenfuss	.20
(28)	Luis Aguayo	.20
(29)	Kiko Garcia	.20
(30)	Steve Jeltz	.20
(31)	John Russell	.20
(32)	Juan Samuel	.20
(33)	Mike Schmidt	3.50
(34)	Tim Corcoran	.20
(35)	Greg Gross	.20
(36)	Von Hayes	.20
(37)	Joe Lefebvre	.20
(38)	Garry Maddox	.20
(39)	Jeff Stone	.20
(40)	Glenn Wilson	.20
(41)	Future Phillies (Ramon Caraballo, Mike Diaz)	.20
(42)	Future Phillies (Rodger Cole, Mike Maddux)	.20
(43)	Future Phillies (Chris James, Rick Schu)	.20
(44)	Future Phillies (Ken Jackson, Francisco Melendez)	.20
(45)	Future Phillies (Rocky Childress, Randy Salava)	.20
(46)	Future Phillies (Ralph Citarella, Rich Surhoff)	.20
(47)	Team Photo	.25

1986 Tastykake Phillies

The 1986 Tastykake Phillies set consists of 49 cards that measure 3-1/2" x 5-1/4" in size. The cards were given away at the Phillies' annual baseball card day promotion. The card fronts feature a full-color photo along with the player's name, uniform number and position. The card backs are printed in red and black and carry a brief player biography. Five cards commemorating past Phillies' pennants were included in the set.

		MT
Complete Set (49):		7.00
Common Player:		.15
2	Jim Davenport	.15
3	Claude Osteen	.15
4	Lee Elia	.15
5	Mike Ryan	.15
6	John Russell	.15
7	John Felske	.15
8	Juan Samuel	.15
9	Von Hayes	.15
10	Darren Daulton	.25
11	Tom Foley	.15
12	Glenn Wilson	.15
14	Jeff Stone	.15
15	Rick Schu	.15
16	Luis Aguayo	.15
20	Mike Schmidt	3.50
21	Greg Gross	.15
22	Gary Redus	.15
23	Joe Lefebvre	.15
24	Milt Thompson	.25
25	Del Unser	.15
26	Chris James	.15
27	Kent Tekulve	.15
28	Shane Rawley	.15
29	Ronn Reynolds	.15
30	Steve Jeltz	.15
31	Garry Maddox	.15
32	Steve Carlton	1.50
33	Dave Shipanoff	.15
35	Randy Lerch	.15
36	Robin Roberts	1.50
39	Dave Rucker	.15
40	Steve Bedrosian	.15
41	Tom Hume	.15
42	Don Carman	.15
43	Fred Toliver	.15
46	Kevin Gross	.15
47	Larry Andersen	.15
48	Dave Stewart	.50
49	Charles Hudson	.15
50	Rocky Childress	.15
---	Future Phillies (Ramon Caraballo, Joe Cipolloni)	.15
---	Future Phillies (Arturo Gonzalez, Mike Maddux)	.15
---	Future Phillies (Ricky Jordan, Francisco Melendez)	.25
---	Future Phillies (Randy Day, Kevin Ward)	.15
---	The 1915 Phillies	.15
---	The 1950 Phillies	.15
---	The 1980 Phillies	.15
---	The 1983 Phillies	.15
---	June 11, 1985 - A Night To Remember	.15

1987 Tastykake Phillies

A 46-card set featuring the Philadelphia Phillies and sponsored by Tastykake was given out to fans present at Veterans Stadium for the Phillies' April 12th baseball card day promotion. The cards measure 3-1/2" x 5-1/4" with fronts that feature a full-color player photo framed with a white border. The player's number, name and position appear below the photo. Card backs are printed in red and black and contain a brief biography. The set was available for $4 via a mail-in offer to the Phillies ball club.

		MT
	Complete Set (51):	12.00
	Common Player:	.15
4	Lee Elia	.15
6	John Russell	.15
7	John Felske	.15
8	Juan Samuel	.15
9	Von Hayes	.15
10	Darren Daulton	.25
11	Greg Legg	.15
12	Glenn Wilson	.15
13	Lance Parrish	.25
14	Jeff Stone	.15
15	Rick Schu	.15
16	Luis Aguayo	.15
17	Ron Roenicke	.15
18	Chris James	.15
19	Keith Hughes	.15
20	Mike Schmidt	3.00
21	Greg Gross	.15
23	Joe Cipolloni	.15
24	Milt Thompson	.15
27	Kent Tekulve	.15
28	Shane Rawley	.15
29	Ronn Reynolds	.15
30	Steve Jeltz	.15
31	Jeff Calhoun	.15
33	Mike Jackson	.15
34	Mike Easler	.15
35	Dan Schatzeder	.15
37	Ken Dowell	.15
38a	Jim Olander	.15
38b	Wally Ritchie	.15
39a	Joe Cowley	.15
39b	Bob Scanlan	.15
40	Steve Bedrosian	.15
41	Tom Hume	.15
42	Don Carman	.15
43	Freddie Toliver	.15
44	Mike Maddux	.15
45	Greg Jelks	.15
46	Kevin Gross	.15
47	Bruce Ruffin	.20
48	Marvin Freeman	.15
49	Len Watts	.15
50	Tom Newell	.15
51	Ken Jackson	.15
52	Todd Frohwirth	.20
58	Doug Bair	.15
---	Shawn Burton	.15
---	Rick Lundblade	.15
---	Jeff Kaye	.15
---	Darren Loy	.15
---	Phillies Coaches (Jim Davenport, Lee Elia, Claude Osteen, Mike Ryan, Del Unser)	.15
---	Phillie Phanatic	.15
---	Team Photo	.25

1988 Tastykake Phillies

This 39-card set was co-produced by Tastykake and the Phillies. The semi-glossy oversize cards, 4-7/8" x 6-1/4", feature full-color action photos with white borders. The coaching staff, young player prospects, the team mascot and a full team photo are included in the set. The card backs carry personal data and career stats in black letters, with the Phillies and Tastykake logos in red. Card numbers correspond to player uniform numbers. The cards were available upon request from individual players and were not made available as a set. Nine cards (#'s 4, 6, 7, 11, 15 Gutierrez, 16 Bowa, 17, 33 and Broadcasters) were added later in the year. These cards have blank backs.

		MT
	Complete Set (39):	10.00
	Common Player:	.15
4a	Lee Elia (vertical format)	.15
4b	Lee Elia (horizontal format)	.15
6	John Russell	.15
7	John Vukovich	.15
8	Juan Samuel	.15
9	Von Hayes	.15
10	Darren Daulton	.20
11	Keith Miller	.15
13	Lance Parrish	.20
15a	Bill Almon	.15
15b	Jackie Gutierrez	.15
16a	Luis Aguayo	.15
16b	Larry Bowa	.15
17	Ricky Jordan	.15
18	Chris James	.15
19	Mike Young	.15
20	Mike Schmidt	2.00
21	Greg Gross	.15
22	Bob Dernier	.15
24	Milt Thompson	.15
27	Kent Tekulve	.15
28	Shane Rawley	.15
29	Phil Bradley	.15
30	Steve Jeltz	.15
31	Jeff Calhoun	.15
33	Greg Harris	.15
38	Wally Ritchie	.15
40	Steve Bedrosian	.15
42	Don Carman	.15
44	Mike Maddux	.15
45	David Palmer	.15
46	Kevin Gross	.15
47	Bruce Ruffin	.15
52	Todd Frohwirth	.15
---	Coaching Staff (Dave Bristol, Claude Osteen, Mike Ryan, Tony Taylor, Del Unser, John Vukovich)	.15
---	Phillies Prospects (Tom Barrett, Brad Brink, Steve Deangelis, Ron Jones, Keith Miller, Brad Moore),	.25
---	Phillie Phanatic	.15
---	Team Photo	.25
---	Broadcasters (Richie Ashburn, Harry Kalas, Garry Maddox, Andy Musser, Chris Wheeler)	.25

1989 Tastykake Phillies

These oversize (approximately 4" x 6") cards feature very nice borderless action photos of the Philadelphia Phillies. The 36-card set was sponsored by Tastykake (whose logo appears on the bottom of the card backs) and was given to fans attending the May 13 Phillies game as a stadium promotion. The backs include player information and complete stats.

		MT
	Complete Set (37):	10.00
	Common Player:	.15
2	Larry Bowa	.15
3	Darold Knowles	.15
4a	Lenny Dykstra	.30
4b	Denis Menke	.15
5	Mike Ryan	.15
6	Dwayne Murphy	.15
7	John Vuckovich	.15
8a	Juan Samuel	.15
8b	Charlie Hayes	.25
9	Von Hayes	.15
10	Darren Daulton	.20
11	John Kruk	.30
12	Tony Taylor	.15
13	Roger McDowell	.25
15	Floyd Youmans	.15
16	Nick Leyva	.15
17	Ricky Jordan	.15
18	Jim Adduci (Update Card)	.25
19	Tom Nieto	.15
20	Mike Schmidt	2.00
21	Dickie Thon	.15
22	Bob Dernier	.15
23	Randy Ready (Update Card)	.25
24	Curt Ford	.15
25	Steve Lake	.15
26a	Chris James	.15
26b	Ron Jones	.15
27	Randy O'Neal	.15
28	Tom Herr	.15
30	Steve Jeltz	.15
31	Mark Ryal	.15
33	Greg Harris	.15
34	Alex Madrid	.15
35	Eric Bullock (Update Card)	.25
39	Dennis Cook (Update Card)	.25
40	Steve Bedrosian	.15
41	Steve Ontiveros	.15
42	Don Carman	.15
43	Ken Howell	.15
44	Mike Maddux	.15
45	Terry Mulholland (Update Card)	.45
46	Larry McWilliams	.15
47	Bruce Ruffin	.15
49	Jeff Parrett	.15
52	Todd Frohwirth	.15
---	Sponsor card	.15

1989 Taystee Kansas City Royals

The 1989 Royals are featured on this set of discs distributed by a K.C. area bakery. The 2-3/4" discs have color player photos at center. The team logo has been airbrushed off the caps because the issue was licensed only by the players, and not by Major League Baseball. In the white border is the issuer's logo in red at top, player identification at bottom in a yellow banner and "AL STARS" in blue stars at each side. Backs are printed in blue with player data, 1988 stats and copyright information.

		MT
	Complete Set (12):	18.00
	Common Player:	1.00
1	George Brett	8.00
2	Kevin Seitzer	1.00
3	Pat Tabler	1.00
4	Danny Tartabull	1.00
5	Willie Wilson	1.50
6	Bo Jackson	2.00
7	Frank White	1.00
8	Kurt Stillwell	1.00
9	Mark Gubicza	1.25
10	Charlie Leibrandt	1.00
11	Bret Saberhagen	2.00
12	Steve Farr	1.00

1981 TCMA The 1960's, Series 2

A second series of cards depicting major and minor league players of the 1960s was produced by TCMA in 1981. The cards continued in the same 2-1/2" x 3-1/2" format as the earlier series. Fronts are unadorned color photos, backs have player identification, data and career summary printed in green on white. The numbering of the cards continues at #294, where the first series concluded.

		MT
	Complete Set (189):	55.00
	Common Player:	.25
294	Fritzie Brickell	.25
295	Craig Anderson	.25
296	Cliff Cook	.25
297	Pumpsie Green	.25
298	Choo Choo Coleman	.25
299	Don Buford	.25
300	Sparky Anderson	.35
301	John Anderson	.25
302	Ted Beard	.25
303	Mickey Mantle, Roger Maris	5.00
304	Gene Freese	.25
305	Don Wilkinson	.25
306	Walter Alston	.35
307	George Bamberger	.25
308	Nelson Briles	.25
309	Dave Baldwin	.25
310	Bob Bailey	.25
311	Paul Blair	.25
312	Ken Boswell	.25
313	Sam Bowens	.25
314	Ray Barker	.25
315	Tommie Agee, Gil Hodges	.25
316	Elmer Valo	.25
317	Ken Walters	.25
318	Joel Horlen	.25
319	Not issued	
320	Charlie Maxwell	.25
321	Joe Foy	.25
322	Tommie Agee, Cleon Jones, Ron Swoboda	.25
323	Paul Foytack	.25
324	Ron Fairly	.25
325	Wilbur Wood	.25
326	Not issued	
327	Felix Mantilla	.25
328a	Ed Bouchee	.25
328b	Don Wilson	.25
329	Sandy Valdespino	.25
330	Al Ferrera	.25
331	Jose Tartabull	.25
332	Dick Kenworthy	.25
333	Don Pavletich	.25
334	Jim Fairey	.25
335	Rico Petrocelli	.25
336	Gary Roggenburk	.25
337	Rick Reichardt	.25
338	Ken McMullen	.25
339	Dooley Womack	.25
340	Joe Moock	.25
341	Lou Brock	.40
342	Hector Torres	.25
343	Ted Savage	.25
344	Hobie Landrith	.25
345	Ed Lopat	.25
346	Mel Nelson	.25
347	Mickey Lolich	.30
348	Al Lopez	.35
349	Frederico Olivo	.25
350	Bob Moose	.25
351	Bill McCool	.25
352	Ernie Bowman	.25
353	Tom McCraw	.25
354	Sam Mele	.25
355	Len Boehmer	.25
356	Hank Aaron	3.00
357	Ron Hunt	.25
358	Luis Aparicio	.40
359	Gene Mauch	.25
360	Barry Moore	.25
361	John Buzhardt	.25
362	Spring Training (St. Louis Cardinals)	.25
363	Duke Snider	.50
364	Billy Martin	.35
365	Wes Parker	.25
366	Dick Stuart	.25
367	Glenn Beckert	.25
368	Ollie Brown	.25
369	Stan Bahnsen	.25
370	Lee Bales	.25
371	Johnny Keane	.25
372	Wally Moon	.25
373	Larry Miller	.25
374	Fred Newman	.25
375	John Orsino	.25
376	Joe Pactwa	.25
377	John O'Donoghue	.25
378	Jim Ollom	.25
379	Ray Oyler	.25
380	Ron Nischwitz	.25
381	Ron Paul	.25
382	Yogi Berra, John Blanchard, Roger Maris	.35
383	Jim McKnight	.25
384	Gene Michael	.25
385	Dave May	.25
386	Tim McCarver	.30
387	Larry Mason	.25
388	Don Hoak	.25
389	Nate Oliver	.25
390	Phil Ortega	.25
391	Billy Madden	.25
392	John Miller	.25
393	Danny Murtaugh	.25
394	Nelson Mathews	.25
395	Red Schoendienst	.30
396	Roger Nelson	.25
397	Tom Matchick	.25
398	Donnie Musgraves	.25
399	Chet Trail	.25
400	Fracis Peters	.25
401	Tony Pierce	.25
402	Billy Williams	.40
403	Dave Boswell	.25
404	Ray Washburn	.25
405	Al Worthington	.25
406	Jesus Alou	.25
407	Yogi Berra, Gil Hodges, Joe Pignatano, Eddie Yost	.35
408	Wally Bunker	.25
409	Jim Brenneman	.25
410	Bobby Bragan	.25
411	Cal McLish	.25
412	Curt Blefary	.25
413	Jim Bethke	.25
414	Infield 1964 (St. Louis Cardinals)	.25
415	Richie Allen	.35
416	Larry Brown	.25
417	Mike Andrews	.25
418	Don Mossi	.25
419	J.C. Martin	.25
420	Dick Rusteck	.25
421	Elly Rodriguez	.25
422	Casey Stengel	.40
423	Gil Hodges, Ed Vargo	.25
424	Johnny Briggs	.25
425	Bud Harrelson, Al Weis	.25
426	Doc Edwards	.25
427	Joe Hague	.25
428	Lee Elia	.25
429	Billy Moran	.25
430	Not issued	
431	Pete Mikkelsen	.25
432a	Al Moran (should be #430)	.25
432b	Aurelio Monteagudo	.25
433	Ken MacKenzie	.25
434	Dick Egan	.25
435	Al McBean	.25
436	Mike Ferraro	.25
437	Gary Wagner	.25
438	Jerry Grote, J.C. Martin	.25
439	Ted Kluszewski	.35
440	Jerry Johnson	.25
441	Ross Moschitto	.25
442	Zoilo Versalles	.25
443	Dennis Ribant	.25
444	Ted Williams	3.00
445	Steve Whitaker	.25
446	Frank Bertaina	.25
447	Bo Belinsky	.35
448	Joe Moeller	.25
449	Don Shaw, Ron Taylor	.25
450	Al Downing, Whitey Ford, Fritz Peterson, Mel Stottlemyre	.35
451	Jack Tracy	.25
452	Tony Curry	.25
453	Roy White	.25
454	Jim Bunning	.40
455	Ralph Houk	.25
456	Bobby Shantz	.25
457	Bill Rigney	.25
458	Roger Repoz	.25
459	Robin Roberts, Bob Turley	.25

460	Gordon Richardson	.25
461	Dick Tracewski	.25
462	Thad Tillotson	.25
463	Larry Osborne	.25
464	Larry Burright	.25
465	Alan Foster	.25
466	Ron Taylor	.25
467	Fred Talbot	.25
468	Bob Miller	.25
469	Frank Tepedino	.25
470	Danny Frisella	.25
471	Cecil Perkins	.25
472	Danny Napoleon	.25
473	John Upham	.25
474	Yogi Berra, Elston Howard, Mickey Mantle, Roger Maris, Bill Skowron	2.00
475	Al Weis	.25
476	Rich Beck	.25
477	Clete Boyer, Tony Kubek, Joe Pepitone, Bobby Richardson	.50
478	Jack Fisher	.25
479	Archie Moore	.25
480	Roger Craig	.25
481	Frank Crosetti, Mike Hegan, Ralph Houk, Wally Moses	.25
482	Roger Craig, Gil Hodges, Clem Labine, Cookie Lavagetto	.25

1981 TCMA 1962 San Francisco Giants

The National League Champions for 1962 are featured in this collector's edition card set. The 2-1/2" x 3-1/2" cards have orange borders on front, around black-and-white player photos. Backs are in black-and-white with personal data, career information and 1982 stats.

		MT
Complete Set (36):		48.00
Common Player:		1.00
1	Alvin Dark	1.00
2	Whitey Lockman	1.00
3	Larry Jansen	1.00
4	Wes Westrum	1.00
5	Ed Bailey	1.00
6	Tom Haller	1.00
7	Harvey Kuenn	1.00
8	Willie Mays	16.00
9	Felipe Alou	1.50
10	Orlando Cepeda	3.00
11	Chuck Hiller	1.00
12	Jose Pagan	1.00
13	Jim Davenport	1.00
14	Willie McCovey	3.00
15	Matty Alou	1.00
16	Manny Mota	1.50
17	Ernie Bowman	1.00
18	Carl Boles	1.00
19	John Orsino	1.00
20	Joe Pignatano	1.00
21	Gaylord Perry	2.00
22	Jim Duffalo	1.00
23	Dick LeMay	1.00
24	Bob Garibaldi	1.00
25	Bobby Bolin	1.00
26	Don Larsen	1.25
27	Mike McCormick	1.00
28	Stu Miller	1.00
29	Jack Sanford	1.00
30	Billy O'Dell	1.00
31	Juan Marichal	2.00
32	Billy Pierce	1.00
33	Dick Phillips	1.00
34	Cap Peterson	1.00
35	Bob Nieman	1.00

Player names in *Italic* type indicate a rookie card.

1981 TCMA 1959 Chicago White Sox

The A.L. Champion Chicago White Sox are featured in this collectors' issue. The 2-1/2" x 3-1/2" cards have black-and-white player photos with dark blue borders. Backs are in black-and-white with a few bits of player data, career information, 1959 and lifetime stats, along with a TCMA copyright line.

		MT
Complete Set (45):		48.00
Common Player:		1.00
1	Earl Torgeson	1.00
2	Nellie Fox	5.00
3	Luis Aparicio	5.00
4	Bubba Phillips	1.00
5	Jim McAnany	1.00
6	Jim Landis	1.00
7	Al Smith	1.00
8	Sherman Lollar	1.00
9	Billy Goodman	1.00
10	Jim Rivera	1.00
11	Sammy Esposito	1.00
12	Norm Cash	1.50
13	Johnny Romano	1.00
14	Johnny Callison	1.00
15	Harry Simpson	1.00
16	Ted Kluszewski	3.00
17	Del Ennis	1.00
18	Earl Battey	1.00
19	Larry Doby	4.00
20	Ron Jackson	1.00
21	Ray Boone	1.00
22	Lou Skizas	1.00
23	Joe Hicks	1.00
24	Don Mueller	1.00
25	J.C. Martin	1.00
26	Cam Carreon	1.00
27	Early Wynn	3.00
28	Bob Shaw	1.00
29	Billy Pierce	1.50
30	Turk Lown	1.00
31	Dick Donovan	1.00
32	Gerry Staley	1.00
33	Barry Latman	1.00
34	Ray Moore	1.00
35	Rudy Arias	1.00
36	Joe Stanka	1.00
37	Ken McBride	1.00
38	Don Rudolph	1.00
39	Claude Raymond	1.00
40	Gary Peters	1.00
41	Al Lopez	1.50
42	Don Gutteridge	1.00
43	Ray Berres	1.00
44	Tony Cuccinello	1.00
45	John Cooney	1.00

1982 TCMA Baseball's Greatest Hitters

Baseball's hit kings of the past are featured in this collectors set. Fronts of the 2-1/2" x 3-1/2" cards have a color or black-and-white photo surroiunded by a colored frame. Backs are in black-and-white with a career summary, lifetime stats and Major League Baseball licensee logo.

		MT
Complete Set (45):		12.50
Common Player:		.25
1	Ted Williams	1.00
2	Stan Musial	1.00
3	Joe DiMaggio	2.00
4	Roberto Clemente	2.00
5	Jackie Robinson	.75
6	Willie Mays	1.00
7	Lou Brock	.25
8	Al Kaline	.25
9	Richie Ashburn	.25
10	Tony Oliva	.25
11	Harvey Kuenn	.25
12	Mickey Vernon	.25
13	Tommy Davis	.25
14	Ty Cobb	.50
15	Rogers Hornsby	.25
16	Joe Jackson	1.00
17	Willie Keeler	.25
18	Tris Speaker	.25
19	Babe Ruth	2.50
20	Harry Heilmann	.25
21	Bill Terry	.25
22	George Sisler	.25
23	Lou Gehrig	1.50
24	Nap Lajoie	.25
25	Riggs Stephenson	.25
26	Al Simmons	.25
27	Cap Anson	.25
28	Paul Waner	.25
29	Eddie Collins	.25
30	Heinie Manush	.25
31	Honus Wagner	.40
32	Earle Combs	.25
33	Sam Rice	.25
34	Charlie Gehringer	.25
35	Chick Hafey	.25
36	Zack Wheat	.25
37	Frank Frisch	.25
38	Bill Dickey	.25
39	Ernie Lombardi	.25
40	Joe Cronin	.25
41	Lefty O'Doul	.25
42	Luke Appling	.25
43	Ferris Fain	.25
44	Arky Vaughan	.25
45	Joe Medwick	.25

1982 TCMA Baseball's Greatest Pitchers

The best pitchers who were no longer active are featured in this collectors issue. Color or black-and-white photos are presented at center of the 2-1/2" x 3-1/2" cards, with a colored frame surrounding the title, name and position. Backs are printed in dark blue and have a career summary and lifetime stats.

		MT
Complete Set (45):		12.50
Common Player:		.25
1	Bob Feller	.35
2	Bob Lemon	.25
3	Whitey Ford	.50
4	Joe Page	.25
5	Wilbur Wood	.25
6	Robin Roberts	.25
7	Warren Spahn	.25
8	Sandy Koufax	1.00
9	Juan Marichal	.25
10	Don Newcombe	.25
11	Hoyt Wilhelm	.25
12	Roy Face	.25
13	Allie Reynolds	.25
14	Don Drysdale	.25
15	Bob Gibson	.25
16	Cy Young	.25
17	Walter Johnson	.25
18	Grover Alexander	.25
19	Jack Chesbro	.25
20	Lefty Gomez	.25
21	Wes Ferrell	.25
22	Hal Newhouser	.25
23	Early Wynn	.25
24	Denny McLain	.35
25	Catfish Hunter	.25
26	Jim Lonborg	.25
27	Frank Lary	.25
28	Red Ruffing	.25
29	Lefty Grove	.25
30	Herb Pennock	.25
31	Satchel Paige	.75
32	Iron Man McGinnity	.25
33	Christy Mathewson	.50
34	Mordecai Brown	.25
35	Eppa Rixey	.25
36	Dizzy Dean	.40
37	Carl Hubbell	.25
38	Dazzy Vance	.25
39	Jim Bunning	.25
40	Smoky Joe Wood	.25
41	Freddie Fitzsimmons	.25
42	Rube Waddell	.25
43	Addie Joss	.25
44	Burleigh Grimes	.25
45	Chief Bender	.25

1982 TCMA Baseball's Greatest Sluggers

The heaviest hitters in baseball history are featured in this collectors issue. The 2-1/2" x 3-1/2" cards have color or black-and-white photos on front framed in red or green and bordered in white. Backs have a few personal data, career stats and career summary along with a logo indicating licensing by Major League Baseball, all in black-and-white.

		MT
Complete Set (45):		13.00
Common Player:		.25
1	Harmon Killebrew	.25
2	Roger Maris	1.50
3	Mickey Mantle	3.00
4	Hank Aaron	1.00
5	Ralph Kiner	.25
6	Willie McCovey	.25
7	Eddie Mathews	.25
8	Ernie Banks	.25
9	Duke Snider	.25
10	Frank Howard	.25
11	Ted Kluszewski	.25
12	Frank Robinson	.25
13	Billy Williams	.25
14	Gil Hodges	.25
15	Yogi Berra	.25
16	Richie Allen	.25
17	Joe Adcock	.25
18	Babe Ruth	2.50
19	Lou Gehrig	2.00
20	Jimmie Foxx	.25
21	Rogers Hornsby	.25
22	Ted Williams	1.00
23	Hack Wilson	.25
24	Al Simmons	.25
25	John Mize	.25
26	Chuck Klein	.25
27	Hank Greenberg	.25
28	Babe Herman	.25
29	Norm Cash	.25
30	Rudy York	.25
31	Gavvy Cravath	.25
32	Mel Ott	.25
33	Orlando Cepeda	.25
34	Dolf Camilli	.25
35	Frank Baker	.25
36	Larry Doby	.25
37	Jim Gentile	.25
38	Harry Davis	.25
39	Rocco Colavito	.25
40	Cy Williams	.25
41	Roy Sievers	.25
42	Boog Powell	.25
43	Willie Mays	1.00
44	Joe DiMaggio	2.00
45	Earl Averill	.25

1982 TCMA "1952" Bowman

A find of player paintings evidently intended for use in Bowman's 1952 baseball card set allowed TCMA to produce this collectors issue of 15 Bowman "high numbers that never were." The 2-1/8" x 3-1/8" cards approximate the size of the originals. Fronts have only the color picture with a white border around; the facsimile signatures found on original 1952 Bowmans are not present. Backs have layout and style similar to the 1952 cards, along with a 1982 TCMA copyright. The issue was numbered consecutively from #253, beginning where the original issue ended.

		MT
Complete Set (15):		12.00
Common Player:		1.00
253	Bob Kennedy	1.00
254	Barney McCosky	1.00
255	Chris Van Cuyk	1.00
256	Morrie Martin	1.00
257	Jim Wilson	1.00
258	Bob Thorpe	1.00
259	Bill Henry	1.00
260	Bob Addis	1.00
261	Terry Moore	1.00
262	Joe Dobson	1.00
263	Jack Merson	1.00
264	Virgil Trucks	1.00
265	Johnny Hopp	1.00
266	Cookie Lavagetto	1.00
267	George Shuba	1.00

1983 TCMA All-Time Athletics

This was one of several early 1980s collectors issues from TCMA depicting an All-Time team. The 2-1/2" x 3-1/2" cards have black-and-white photos on front with red graphics. Backs are printed in blue and offer personal data, a career summary and lifetime stats.

		MT
Complete Set (12):		12.00
Common Player:		.75
1	Jimmie Foxx	1.50
2	Eddie Collins	1.25
3	Frank Baker	1.25
4	Jack Barry	.75
5	Al Simmons	1.25
6	Mule Haas	.75
7	Bing Miller	.75
8	Mickey Cochrane	1.25
9	Chief Bender	1.25
10	Lefty Grove	1.25
11	John Wyatt	.75
12	Connie Mack	1.25

1983 TCMA All-Time Cardinals

A picked team of Cardinal greats through the 1970s is featured on this collectors' issue. The 2-1/2" x 3-1/2" cards have black-and-white photos on front, with the set title printed in red in the white bottom border. Backs have player data and a career summary printed in purple on gray or blue on white.

		MT
Complete Set (12):		18.00
Common Player:		1.00
1	Jim Bottomley	1.00
2	Rogers Hornsby	1.25
3	Ken Boyer	1.50
4	Marty Marion	1.00
5	Ducky Medwick	1.00
6	Chick Hafey	1.00
7	Stan Musial	6.00
8	Tim McCarver	1.25
9	Robert "Bob" Gibson	1.50
10	Harry Brecheen	1.00
11	Alpha Brazle	1.00
12	Red Schoendienst	1.25

1983 TCMA 1942 Play Ball

Between 1983-85, TCMA produced eight sets of collectors' cards resurrecting the Play Ball brand name which had been active in the field from 1939-41. The TCMA sets attempt to replicate the style and substance of the earlier Play Ball cards as if the company had continued production through World War II and the end of the 1940s. The "1942" set features sepia-toned photos on front, with black graphics. Backs are printed on gray stock in blue ink. Size approximates the original Play Balls at 2-1/2" x 3-1/4".

		MT
Complete Set (45):		30.00
Common Player:		1.50
1	Joe Gordon	1.50
2	Joe DiMaggio	6.50
3	Bill Dickey	2.00
4	Joe McCarthy	1.50
5	Tex Hughson	1.50
6	Ted Williams	5.00
7	Walt Judnich	1.50
8	Vern Stephens	1.50
9	Denny Galehouse	1.50
10	Lou Boudreau	1.50
11	Ken Keltner	1.50
12	Jim Bagby	1.50
13	Rudy York	1.50
14	Barney McCosky	1.50
15	Schoolboy Rowe	1.50
16	Luke Appling	1.50
17	Taft Wright	1.50
18	Ted Lyons	1.50
19	Mickey Vernon	1.50
20	George Case	1.50
21	Bobo Newsom	1.50
22	Bob Johnson	1.50
23	Buddy Blair	1.50
24	Pete Suder	1.50
25	Terry Moore	1.50
26	Stan Musial	5.00
27	Marty Marion	1.50
28	Pee Wee Reese	3.50
29	Arky Vaughan	1.50
30	Larry French	1.50
31	Johnny Mize	2.00
32	Mel Ott	2.00
33	Willard Marshall	1.50
34	Carl Hubbell	2.00
35	Frank McCormick	1.50
36	Linus Frey	1.50
37	Bob Elliott	1.50
38	Vince DiMaggio	1.50
39	Al Lopez	1.50
40	Stan Hack	1.50
41	Lou Novikoff	1.50
42	Casey Stengel	2.00
43	Tommy Holmes	1.50
44	Ron Northey	1.50
45	Rube Melton	1.50

1983 TCMA 1943 Play Ball

Between 1983-85, TCMA produced eight sets of collectors cards resurrecting the Play Ball brand name which had been active in the field from 1939-41. The TCMA sets attempt to replicate the style and substance of the earlier Play Ball cards as if the company had continued production through World War II and the end of the 1940s. The "1943" set features sepia-toned photos on front, with black graphics. Backs are printed on gray stock in purple ink. Size approximates the original Play Balls at 2-1/2" x 3-1/4".

		MT
Complete Set (45):		30.00
Common Player:		1.50
1	Spud Chandler	1.50
2	Frank Crosetti	1.50
3	Johnny Lindell	1.50
4	Emil "Dutch" Leonard	1.50
5	Stan Spence	1.50
6	Ray Mack	1.50
7	Hank Edwards	1.50
8	Al Smith	1.50
9	Mike Tresh	1.50
10	Don Kolloway	1.50
11	Orval Grove	1.50
12	Doc Cramer	1.50
13	Pinky Higgins	1.50
14	Dick Wakefield	1.50
15	Harland Clift (Harlond)	1.50
16	Chet Laabs	1.50
17	George McQuinn	1.50
18	Tony Lupien	1.50
19	Oscar Judd	1.50
20	Roy Partee	1.50
21	Lum Harris	1.50
22	Roger Wolf	1.50
23	Dick Siebert	1.50
24	Walker Cooper	1.50
25	Mort Cooper	1.50
26	Whitey Kurowski	1.50
27	Eddie Miller	1.50
28	Elmer Riddle	1.50
29	Bucky Walters	1.50
30	Whitlow Wyatt	1.50
31	Dolf Camilli	1.50
32	Elbie Fletcher	1.50
33	Frank Gustine	1.50
34	Rip Sewell	1.50
35	Phil Cavarretta	1.50
36	Bill "Swish" Nicholson	1.50
37	Peanuts Lowrey	1.50
38	Phil Masi	1.50
39	Al Javery	1.50
40	Jim Tobin	1.50
41	Glen Stewart	1.50
42	Mickey Livingston	1.50
43	Ace Adams	1.50
44	Joe Medwick	2.50
45	Sid Gordon	1.50

1983 TCMA 1944 Play Ball

Between 1983-85, TCMA produced eight sets of collectors cards resurrecting the Play Ball brand name which had been active in the field from 1939-41. The TCMA sets attempt to replicate the style and substance of the earlier Play Ball cards as if the company had continued production through World War II and the end of the 1940s. The "1944" set features black-and-white photos on front, with blue graphics. Backs are printed on gray stock in black ink. Size approximates the original Play Balls at 2-1/2" x 3-1/4".

		MT
Complete Set (45):		30.00
Common Player:		1.50
1	Don Gutteridge	1.50
2	Mark Christman	1.50
3	Mike Kreevich	1.50
4	Jimmy Outlaw	1.50
5	Paul Richards	1.50
6	Hal Newhouser	2.50
7	Bud Metheny	1.50
8	Mike Garbark	1.50
9	Hersh Martin	1.50
10	Bob Johnson	1.50
11	Mike Ryba	1.50
12	Oris Hockett	1.50
13	Ed Klieman	1.50
14	Ford Garrison	1.50
15	Irv Hall	1.50
16	Ed Busch	1.50
17	Ralph Hogdin	1.50
18	Thurman Tucker	1.50
19	Bill Dietrich	1.50
20	Rick Ferrell	2.00
21	John Sullivan	1.50
22	Mickey Haefner	1.50
23	Ray Sanders	1.50
24	Johnny Hopp	1.50
25	Ted Wilks	1.50
26	John Barrett	1.50
27	Jim Russell	1.50
28	Nick Strincevich	1.50
29	Eric Tipton	1.50
30	Jim Konstanty	1.50
31	Gee Walker	1.50
32	Dom Dellessandro	1.50
33	Bob Chipman	1.50
34	Hank Wyse	1.50
35	Phil Weintraub	1.50
36	George Hausmann	1.50
37	Bill Voiselle	1.50
38	Whitey Wietelmann	1.50
39	Clyde Kluttz	1.50
40	Connie Ryan	1.50
41	Eddie Stanky	1.50
42	Augie Galan	1.50
43	Mickey Owen	1.50
44	Charlie Schanz	1.50
45	Bob Finley	1.50

1983 TCMA 1945 Play Ball

Between 1983-85, TCMA produced eight sets of collectors cards resurrecting the Play Ball brand name which had been active in the field from 1939-41. The TCMA sets attempt to replicate the style and substance of the earlier Play Ball cards as if the company had continued production through World War II and the end of the 1940s. The "1945" set features black-and-white photos on front, with blue graphics. Backs are printed on gray stock in black ink. Size approximates the original Play Balls at 2-1/2" x 3-1/4".

		MT
Complete Set (45):		30.00
Common Player:		1.50
1	Eddie Mayo	1.50
2	Dizzy Trout	1.50
3	Roy Cullenbine	1.50
4	Joe Kuhel	1.50
5	George Binks	1.50
6	Roger Wolff	1.50
7	Gene Moore	1.50
8	Frank Mancuso	1.50
9	Bob Muncrief	1.50
10	Tuck Stainback	1.50
11	Bill Bevens	1.50
12	Snuffy Stirnweiss	1.50
13	Don Ross	1.50
14	Felix Mackiewicz	1.50
15	Jeff Heath	1.50
16	John Dickshot	1.50
17	Ed Lopat	2.00
18	Skeeter Newsom (Newsome)	1.50
19	Eddie Lake	1.50
20	John Lazor	1.50
21	Hal Peck	1.50
22	Al Brancato	1.50
23	Paul Derringer	1.50
24	Stan Hack	1.50
25	Len Merullo	1.50
26	Emil Verban	1.50
27	Ken O'Dea	1.50
28	Red Barrett	1.50
29	Eddie Basinski	1.50
30	Dixie Walker	1.50
31	Goody Rosen	1.50
32	Preacher Roe	1.50
33	Pete Coscarat	1.50
34	Frankie Frisch	2.50
35	Napoleon Reyes	1.50
36	Dan Gardella	1.50
37	Buddy Kerr	1.50
38	Dick Culler	1.50
39	Tommy Holmes	1.50
40	Al Libke	1.50
41	Howie Fox	1.50
42	Johnny Riddle	1.50
43	Andy Seminick	1.50
44	Andy Karl	1.50
45	Rene Monteguedo	1.50

1984 TCMA 1946 Play Ball

Between 1983-85, TCMA produced eight sets of collectors cards resurrecting the Play Ball brand name which had been active in the field from 1939-41. The TCMA sets attempt to replicate the style and substance of the earlier Play Ball cards as if the company had continued production through World War II and the end of the 1940s. The "1946" set features black-and-white photos on front, with green graphics. Backs are printed on white stock in black ink. Size approximates the originals at 2-1/2" x 3-1/4".

		MT
Complete Set (45):		45.00
Common Player:		1.50
1	Dom DiMaggio	2.00
2	Boo Ferriss	1.50
3	Johnny Pesky	1.50
4	Hank Greenberg	3.00
5	George Kell	1.50
6	Virgil Trucks	1.50
7	Phil Rizzuto	2.50
8	Charlie Keller	2.00
9	Tommy Henrich	2.00
10	Cecil Travis	1.50
11	Al Evans	1.50
12	Buddy Lewis	1.50
13	Edgar Smith	1.50
14	Dario Lodigiani	1.50
15	Earl Caldwell	1.50
16	Jim Hegan	1.50
17	Bob Feller	2.50
18	John Berardino	2.00
19	Jack Kramer	1.50
20	John Lucadello	1.50
21	Hank Majeski	1.50
22	Elmer Valo	1.50
23	Buddy Rosar	1.50
24	Red Schoendienst	2.00
25	Dick Sisler	1.50
26	John Beazley	1.50
27	Vic Lombardi	1.50
28	Dick Whitman	1.50
29	Carl Furillo	2.50
30	Bill Jurges	1.50
31	Marv Rickert	1.50
32	Clyde McCullough	1.50
33	Johnny Hopp	1.50
34	Mort Cooper	1.50
35	Johnny Sain	2.00
36	Del Ennis	1.50
37	Roy Hughes	1.50
38	Bert Haas	1.50
39	Grady Hatton	1.50
40	Ed Bahr	1.50
41	Billy Cox	1.50
42	Lee Handley	1.50
43	Bill Rigney	1.50
44	Babe Young	1.50
45	Buddy Blattner	1.50

1985 TCMA 1947 Play Ball

Between 1983-85, TCMA produced eight sets of collectors cards resurrecting the Play Ball brand name which had been active in the field from 1939-41. The TCMA sets attempt to replicate the style and substance of the earlier Play Ball cards as if the company had continued production through World War II and the end of the 1940s. The "1947" set features black-and-white photos on front, with green graphics. Backs are printed on white stock in black ink. Size approximates the originals at 2-1/2" x 3-1/4".

		MT
Complete Set (45):		26.00
Common Player:		1.00
1	Hal Wagner	1.00
2	Jake Jones	1.00
3	Bobby Doerr	1.00
4	Fred Hutchinson	1.00
5	Bob Swift	1.00
6	Pat Mullin	1.00
7	Joe Page	1.00
8	Allie Reynolds	1.00
9	Billy Johnson	1.00
10	Early Wynn	1.00
11	Eddie Yost	1.00
12	Floyd Baker	1.00
13	Dave Philley	1.00
14	George Dickey	1.00
15	Dale Mitchell	1.00
16	Bob Lemon	1.00
17	Jerry Witte	1.00
18	Paul Lehner	1.00
19	Sam Zoldak	1.00
20	Sam Chapman	1.00
21	Eddie Joost	1.00
22	Ferris Fain	1.00
23	Erv Dusak	1.00
24	Joe Garagiola	1.00

25	Vernal "Nippy" Jones	1.00
26	Bobby Bragan	1.00
27	Jackie Robinson	6.00
28	Spider Jorgensen	1.00
29	Bob Scheffing	1.00
30	Johnny Schmitz	1.00
31	Doyle Lade	1.00
32	Earl Torgeson	1.00
33	Warren Spahn	1.00
34	Walt Lanfranconi	1.00
35	Johnny Wyrostek	1.00
36	Oscar Judd	1.00
37	Ewell Blackwell	1.00
38	Ed Lukon	1.00
39	Benny Zientara	1.00
40	Gene Woodling	1.00
41	Ernie Bonham	1.00
42	Hank Greenberg	3.00
43	Bobby Thomson	1.00
44	Jack "Lucky" Lohrke	1.00
45	Dave Koslo	1.00

1985 TCMA 1948 Play Ball

Between 1983-85, TCMA produced eight sets of collectors cards resurrecting the Play Ball brand name which had been active in the field from 1939-41. The TCMA sets attempt to replicate the style and substance of the earlier Play Ball cards as if the company had continued production through World War II and the end of the 1940s. The "1948" set features black-and-white photos on front, with red graphics. Backs are printed on white stock in black ink. Size approximates the originals at 2-1/2" x 3-1/4".

		MT
Complete Set (45):		35.00
Common Player:		1.00
1	Murry Dickson	1.00
2	Enos Slaughter	1.50
3	Don Lang	1.00
4	Joe Hatten	1.00
5	Gil Hodges	2.00
6	Gene Hermanski	1.00
7	Eddie Waitkus	1.00
8	Jess Dobernic	1.00
9	Andy Pafko	1.00
10	Vern Bickford	1.00
11	Mike McCormick	1.00
12	Harry Walker	1.00
13	Putsy Caballero	1.00
14	Hubert "Dutch" Leonard	1.00
15	Frankie Baumholtz	1.00
16	Ted Kluszewski	1.50
17	Virgil Stallcup	1.00
18	Bob Chesnes	1.00
19	Ted Beard	1.00
20	Wes Westrum	1.00
21	Clint Hartung	1.00
22	Whitey Lockman	1.00
23	Billy Goodman	1.00
24	Jack Kramer	1.00
25	Mel Parnell	1.00
26	George Vico	1.00
27	Walter "Hoot" Evers	1.00
28	Vic Wertz	1.00
29	Yogi Berra	2.00
30	Joe DiMaggio	8.00
31	Tommy Byrne	1.00
32	Al Kozar	1.00
33	Jake Early	1.00
34	Gil Coan	1.00
35	Pat Seerey	1.00
36	Ralph Hodgin	1.00
37	Allie Clark	1.00
38	Gene Bearden	1.00
39	Steve Gromek	1.00
40	Al Zarilla	1.00
41	Fred Sanford	1.00
42	Les Moss	1.00
43	Don White	1.00
44	Carl Scheib	1.00
45	Lou Brissie	1.00

1985 TCMA 1949 Play Ball

Between 1983-85, TCMA produced eight sets of collectors cards resurrecting the Play Ball brand name which had been active in the field from 1939-41. The TCMA sets attempt to replicate the style and substance of the earlier Play Ball cards as if the company had continued production through World War II and the end of the 1940s. The "1949" set features black-and-white photos on front, with red graphics. Backs are printed on white stock in black ink. Size approximates the originals at 2-1/2" x 3-1/4".

		MT
Complete Set (45):		40.00
Common Player:		1.00
1	Al Brazle	1.00
2	Harry Brecheen	1.00
3	Howie Pollett	1.00
4	Cal Abrams	1.00
5	Ralph Branca	1.00
6	Duke Snider	2.50
7	Charlie Grimm	1.00
8	Clarence Maddern	1.00
9	Hal Jeffcoat	1.00
10	Johnny Antonelli	1.00
11	Alvin Dark	1.00
12	Nelson Potter	1.00
13	Granny Hamner	1.00
14	Willie Jones	1.00
15	Robin Roberts	1.50
16	Lloyd Merriman	1.00
17	Bobby Adams	1.00
18	Herman Wehmeier	1.00
19	Ralph Kiner	1.00
20	Dino Restelli	1.00
21	Larry Jansen	1.00
22	Sheldon Jones	1.00
23	Red Webb	1.00
24	Vern Stephens	1.00
25	Tex Hughson	1.00
26	Ellis Kinder	1.00
27	Neil Berry	1.00
28	Johnny Groth	1.00
29	Art Houtteman	1.00
30	Hank Bauer	1.00
31	Vic Raschi	1.00
32	Bobby Brown	1.00
33	Joe Haynes	1.00
34	Eddie Robinson	1.00
35	Sam Dente	1.00
36	Herb Adams	1.00
37	Don Wheeler	1.00
38	Randy Gumpert	1.00
39	Ray Boone	1.00
40	Larry Doby	1.50
41	Jack Graham	1.00
42	Bob Dillinger	1.00
43	Dick Kokos	1.00
44	Wally Moses	1.00
45	Mike Guerra	1.00

1985 TCMA Home Run Champs

This polybagged set of 2-1/2" x 3-1/2" cards is formatted on two perforated strips. Fronts have color photos while backs detail the player's slugging prowess. The header cards presents the history of the award. The unnumbered cards are listed here alphabetically.

		MT
Complete Set (10):		10.00
Common Player:		.50
(1)	Hank Aaron	2.50
(2)	Orlando Cepeda	1.00
(3)	Joe DiMaggio	3.00
(4)	Larry Doby	1.00
(5)	Ralph Kiner	1.00
(6)	Eddie Mathews	1.00
(7)	Willie McCovey	1.00
(8)	Al Rosen	.50
(9)	Duke Snider	1.00
(10)	Ted Williams	2.00

1985 TCMA Most Valuable Players - N.L.

This polybagged set of 2-1/2" x 3-1/2" cards is formatted on two perforated strips. Fronts have color photos while backs detail the player's MVP season (s). The header card presents the history of the award. The unnumbered cards are listed here alphabetically.

		MT
Complete Set (10):		10.00
Common Player:		.50
(1)	Ernie Banks	1.00
(2)	Johnny Bench	1.00
(3)	Roy Campanella	1.00
(4)	Roberto Clemente	3.00
(5)	Dick Groat	.50
(6)	Willie Mays	2.00
(7)	Stan Musial	1.50
(8)	Frank Robinson	1.00
(9)	Willie Stargell	.75
(10)	Maury Wills	.50

1985 TCMA N.Y. Mets Postcards

A certain sameness of poses, generally belt-to-cap, marks the cards in this color player postcard issue produced by TCMA for team issue. The 3-1/2" x 5-1/2" cards have borderless color photos with a glossy finish and no extraneous graphics. Backs have a large, light blue team logo at left, with player ID at top and a line of 1984 stats at bottom. A TCMA copyright line is vertically at center. The postcard indicia at right includes a card number at the bottom of the stamp box; the number is preceded by an "NYM85-" prefix.

		MT
Complete Set (40):		30.00
Common Player:		1.00
1	Davey Johnson	1.50
2	Vern Hoscheit	1.00
3	Bill Robinson	1.00
4	Mel Stottlemyre	1.50
5	Bobby Valentine	1.00
6	Bruce Berenyi	1.00
7	Jeff Bettendorf	1.00
8	Ron Darling	1.00
9	Sid Fernandez	1.00
10	Brent Gaff	1.00
11	Wes Gardner	1.00
12	Dwight Gooden	4.00
13	Tom Gorman	1.00
14	Ed Lynch	1.00
15	Jesse Orosco	1.00
16	Calvin Schiraldi	1.00
17	Doug Sisk	1.00
18	Gary Carter	2.00
19	John Gibbons	1.00
20	Ronn Reynolds	1.00
21	Wally Backman	1.00
22	Kelvin Chapman	1.00
23	Ron Gardenhire	1.00
24	Keith Hernandez	2.00
25	Howard Johnson	1.50
26	Ray Knight	1.50
27	Kevin Mitchell	2.00
28	Terry Blocker	1.00
29	Rafael Santana	1.00
30	Billy Beane	1.00
31	John Christensen	1.00
32	Len Dykstra	2.50
33	George Foster	2.00
34	Danny Heep	1.00
35	Darryl Strawberry	4.00
36	Mookie Wilson	1.50
37	Jeff Bittiger	1.00
38	Clint Hurdle	1.00
39	Laschelle Tarver	1.00
40	Roger McDowell	1.00

1985 TCMA N.Y. Yankees Postcards

In 1985-86, TCMA produced color player postcard sets for the two New York teams. The 1985 Yankees set is 3-1/2" x 5-1/2" with borderless color poses on front. Backs have a light blue Yankees logo at left. Player identification and data is at top-left with 1984 stats at bottom. A TCMA copyright lines is vertically at center. Cards are numbered in the stamp box NYY85-1 through NYY85-40.

		MT
Complete Set (40):		25.00
Common Player:		1.00
1	Yogi Berra	3.00
2	Mark Connor	1.00
3	Stump Merrill	1.00
4	Gene Michael	1.00
5	Lou Piniella	1.50
6	Jeff Torborg	1.00
7	Mike Armstrong	1.00
8	Rich Bordi	1.00
9	Clay Christensen	1.00
10	Joe Cowley	1.00
11	Jim Deshaies	1.00
12	Ron Guidry	1.50
13	John Montefusco	1.00
14	Dale Murray	1.00
15	Phil Niekro	2.50
16	Alfonso Pulido	1.00
17	Dennis Rasmussen	1.00
18	Dave Righetti	1.00
19	Bob Shirley	1.00
20	Ed Whitson	1.00
21	Scott Bradley	1.00
22	Ron Hassey	1.00
23	Butch Wynegar	1.00
24	Dale Berra	1.00
25	Billy Sample	1.00
26	Rex Hudler	1.00
27	Don Mattingly	6.00
28	Bobby Meacham	1.00
29	Mike Pagliarulo	1.00
30	Willie Randolph	1.50
31	Andre Robertson	1.00
32	Henry Cotto	1.00
33	Don Baylor	2.00
34	Ken Griffey	1.00
35	Rickey Henderson	4.00
36	Vic Mata	1.00
37	Omar Moreno	1.00
38	Dan Pasqua	1.00
39	Dave Winfield	4.00
40	Brian Fisher	1.00

1985 TCMA Rookies of the Year

This polybagged set of 2-1/2" x 3-1/2" cards is formatted on two perforated strips. Fronts have color photos while backs detail the player's ROY season. The header card presents the history of the award. The unnumbered cards are listed here alphabetically.

		MT
Complete Set (10):		8.00
Common Player:		.50
(1)	Tommy Agee	.50
(2)	Luis Aparicio	1.00
(3)	Frank Howard	.75
(4)	Harvey Kuenn	.75
(5)	Thurman Munson	1.00
(6)	Don Newcombe	.75
(7)	Tony Oliva	.50
(8)	Jackie Robinson	3.00
(9)	Herb Score	.50
(10)	Billy Williams	1.00

1986 TCMA All Time Teams

Similar to TCMA sets of 1980-83, these sets feature 11 all-time great players and a manager from each team. In standard 2-1/2" x 3-1/2" format, most of the cards utilize black-and-white player photos, though some more recent stars are pictured in color. Several decorative borders, varying by team, surround the front photos. On most team sets there is an "All Time" designation at top, with the player name and (usually) position at bottom. Backs are fairly uniform, printed in blue, and offering a few biographical details and career highlights. Besides hobby sales, these old-timers' sets were also sold in several major retails chains, originally priced at about $4.

(Team sets listed individually)

1986 TCMA All Time Angels

	MT
Complete Set (12):	7.00
Common Player:	.50
1-ANGRod Carew	2.00
2-ANGSandy Alomar	.50
3-ANGJim Fregosi	.50
4-ANGDave Chalk	.50
5-ANGLeon Wagner	.50
6-ANGAlbie Pearson	.50
7-ANGRick Reichardt	.50
8-ANGBob Rodgers	.50
9-ANGDean Chance	.50
10-ANGClyde Wright	.50
11-ANGBob Lee	.50
12-ANGBill Rigney	.50

1986 TCMA All Time Astros

	MT
Complete Set (12):	7.00
Common Player:	.50
1-ASTBob Watson	.50
2-ASTJoe Morgan	1.75
3-ASTRoger Metzger	.50
4-ASTDoug Rader	.50
5-ASTJimmy Wynn	.70
6-ASTCesar Cedeno	.70
7-ASTRusty Staub	.70
8-ASTJohnny Edwards	.50
9-ASTJ.R. Richard	.80
10-ASTDave Roberts	.50
11-ASTFred Gladding	.50
12-ASTBill Virdon	.50

1986 TCMA All Time Blue Jays

	MT
Complete Set (12):	6.00
Common Player:	.50
1-BLUJohn Mayberry	.50
2-BLUBob Bailor	.50
3-BLULuis Gomez	.50
4-BLURoy Howell	.50
5-BLUOtto Velez	.50
6-BLURick Bosetti	.50
7-BLUAl Woods	.50
8-BLURick Cerone	.50
9-BLUDave Lemanczyk	.50
10-BLUTom Underwood	.50
11-BLUJoey McLaughlin	.50
12-BLUBobby Cox	.75

1986 TCMA All Time Boston/ Milwaukee Braves

		MT
Complete Set (12):		12.00
Common Player:		.50
1B	Joe Adcock	.70
2B	Felix Millan	.50
3B	Rabbit Maranville	.50
4B	Eddie Mathews	2.00
5B	Hank Aaron	6.00
6B	Wally Berger	.50
7B	Tommy Holmes	.50
8B	Del Crandall	.50
9B	Warren Spahn	2.00
10B	Charles "Kid" Nichols	.50
11B	Cecil Upshaw	.50
12B	Fred Haney	.50

1986 TCMA All Time Brewers

	MT
Complete Set (12):	7.00
Common Player:	.50
1-BREGeorge Scott	.75
2-BREPedro Garcia	.50
3-BRETim Johnson	.50
4-BREDon Money	.50
5-BRESixto Lezcano	.50
6-BREJohn Briggs	.50
7-BREDave May	.50
8-BREDarrell Porter	.50
9-BREJim Colborn	.50
10-BREMike Caldwell	.50
11-BRERollie Fingers	1.50
12-BREHarvey Kuenn	.50

1986 TCMA All Time Expos

	MT
Complete Set (12):	6.00
Common Player:	.50
1-EXPRon Fairly	.50
2-EXPDave Cash	.50
3-EXPTim Foley	.50
4-EXPBob Bailey	.50
5-EXPKen Singleton	.75
6-EXPEllis Valentine	.50
7-EXPRusty Staub	.75
8-EXPJohn Bateman	.50
9-EXPSteve Rogers	.50
10-EXPWoodie Fryman	.50
11-EXPMike Marshall	.50
12-EXPJim Fanning	.50

1986 TCMA All Time Indians

	MT
Complete Set (12):	15.00
Common Player:	.50
1-INDHal Trosky	.50
2-INDNap Lajoie	.60
3-INDLou Boudreau	.60
4-INDAl Rosen	.50
5-INDJoe Jackson	10.00
6-INDTris Speaker	1.00
7-INDLarry Doby	1.25
8-INDJim Hegan	.50
9-INDCy Young	1.00
10-INDSam McDowell	.60
11-INDRay Narleski	.50
12-INDAl Lopez	.50

1986 TCMA All Time Mariners

	MT
Complete Set (12):	6.00
Common Player:	.50
1-MARPat Putnam	.50
2-MARLarry Milbourne	.50
3-MARTodd Cruz	.50
4-MARBill Stein	.50
5-MARLeon Roberts	.50
6-MARLeroy Stanton	.50
7-MARDan Meyer	.50
8-MARBob Stinson	.50
9-MARGlenn Abbott	.50
10-MARJohn Montague	.50
11-MARBryan Clark	.50
12-MARRene Lachemann	.50

1986 TCMA All Time Mets

		MT
Complete Set (12):		10.00
Common Player:		
1M	Ed Kranepool	1.25
2M	Ron Hunt	1.25
3M	Bud Harrelson	1.25
4M	Wayne Garrett	1.25
5M	Cleon Jones	1.25
6M	Tommie Agee	1.25
7M	Rusty Staub	1.25
8M	Jerry Grote	1.25
9M	Gary Gentry	1.25
10M	Jerry Koosman	1.25
11M	Tug McGraw	1.25
12M	Gil Hodges	2.50

1986 TCMA All Time Oakland A's

	MT
Complete Set (12):	8.00
Common Player:	.50
1-ATHGene Tenace	.50
2-ATHDick Green	.50
3-ATHBert Campaneris	.75
4-ATHSal Bando	.50
5-ATHJoe Rudi	.75
6-ATHRick Monday	.50
7-ATHBill North	.50
8-ATHDave Duncan	.50
9-ATHJim "Catfish" Hunter	1.50
10-ATHKen Holtzman	.50
11-ATHRollie Fingers	1.50
12-ATHAlvin Dark	.50

1986 TCMA All Time Orioles

		MT
Complete Set (12):		15.00
Common Player:		.50
1BA	Hoyt Wilhelm	.75
2BA	Hank Bauer	.50
3BA	Jim Palmer	2.00
4BA	Dave McNally	.50
5BA	Paul Blair	.50
6BA	Gus Triandos	.50
7BA	Frank Robinson	3.00
8BA	Ken Singleton	.50
9BA	Luis Aparicio	2.50
10BA	Brooks Robinson	4.00
11BA	John "Boog" Powell	1.00
12BA	Dave Johnson	.50

1986 TCMA All Time Padres

	MT
Complete Set (12):	7.00
Common Player:	.50
1-PADNate Colbert	.50
2-PADTito Fuentes	.50
3-PADEnzo Hernandez	.50
4-PADDave Roberts	.50
5-PADGene Richards	.50
6-PADOllie Brown	.50
7-PADClarence Gaston	.70
8-PADFred Kendall	.50
9-PADGaylord Perry	1.50
10-PADRandy Jones	.50
11-PADRollie Fingers	1.50
12-PADPreston Gomez	.50

Player names in *Italic* type indicate a rookie card.

1986 TCMA All Time Phillies

		MT
Complete Set (12):		15.00
Common Player:		.50
1PP	Chuck Klein	1.00
2PP	Richie Ashburn	4.00
3PP	Del Ennis	.50
4PP	Spud Davis	.50
5PP	Grover Alexander	1.00
6PP	Chris Short	.50
7PP	Jim Konstanty	.50
8PP	Danny Ozark	.50
9PP	Larry Bowa	.50
10PP	Richie Allen	1.50
11PP	Don Hurst	.50
12PP	Tony Taylor	.50

1986 TCMA All Time Pirates

	MT
Complete Set (12):	15.00
Common Player:	.50
1-PIRWillie Stargell	2.50
2-PIRBill Mazeroski	2.50
3-PIRHonus Wagner	2.50
4-PIRPie Traynor	.50
5-PIRRalph Kiner	.80
6-PIRPaul Waner	.50
7-PIRRoberto Clemente	5.00
8-PIRManny Sanguillen	.50
9-PIRVic Willis	.75
10-PIRWilbur Cooper	.50
11-PIRRoy Face	.50
12-PIRDanny Murtaugh	.50

1986 TCMA All Time Rangers

	MT
Complete Set (12):	7.00
Common Player:	.50
1-RANGaylord Perry	2.00
2-RANJon Matlack	.50
3-RANJim Kern	.50
4-RANBilly Hunter	.50
5-RANMike Hargrove	.70
6-RANBump Wills	.50
7-RANToby Harrah	.70
8-RANLenny Randle	.50
9-RANAl Oliver	.90
10-RANMickey Rivers	.50
11-RANJeff Burroughs	.50
12-RANDick Billings	.50

1986 TCMA All Time Reds

		MT
Complete Set (12):		10.00
Common Player:		.50
1CR	Clay Carroll	.50
2CR	Bill McKechnie	.50
3CR	Paul Derringer	.50
4CR	Eppa Rixey	.50
5CR	Frank Robinson	2.50
6CR	Vada Pinson	1.00
7CR	Leo Cardenas	.50
8CR	Heinie Groh	.50
9CR	Ted Kluszewski	2.00
10CR	Joe Morgan	1.50
11CR	Edd Roush	.50
12CR	Johnny Bench	3.00

1986 TCMA All Time Red Sox

	MT
Complete Set (12):	16.00
Common Player:	.50
1BRSSammy White	.50
2BRSLefty Grove	.50
3BRSCy Young	1.00
4BRSJimmie Foxx	.90
5BRSBobby Doerr	.50
6BRSJoe Cronin	.50
7BRSFrank Malzone	.50
8BRSTed Williams	6.00
9BRSCarl Yastrzemski	4.00
10BRSTris Speaker	.90
11BRSDick Radatz	.50
12BRSDick Williams	.50

1986 TCMA All Time Royals

	MT
Complete Set (12):	6.00
Common Player:	.50
1-ROYJohn Mayberry	.50
2-ROYCookie Rojas	.50
3-ROYFred Patek	.50
4-ROYPaul Schall	.50
5-ROYLou Piniella	.90
6-ROYAmos Otis	.50
7-ROYTom Poquette	.50
8-ROYEd Kirkpatrick	.50
9-ROYSteve Busby	.50
10-ROYPaul Splittorff	.50
11-ROYMark Littell	.50
12-ROYJim Frey	.50

1986 TCMA All Time Twins

	MT
Complete Set (12):	10.00
Common Player:	.50
1-TWIHarmon Killebrew	2.50
2-TWIRod Carew	4.00
3-TWIZoilo Versalles	.50
4-TWICesar Tovar	.50
5-TWIBob Allison	.50
6-TWILarry Hisle	.50
7-TWITony Oliva	.50
8-TWIEarl Battey	.50
9-TWIJim Perry	.50
10-TWIJim Kaat	.80
11-TWIAllan Worthington	.50
12-TWISam Mele	.50

1986 TCMA N.Y. Mets Postcards

For a second, and final, year TCMA produced a set of color player postcards for the Mets. The 3-1/2" x 5-1/2" cards have borderless player poses on their glossy fronts; there are no other graphic elements. Backs have a large, light blue team 25th anniversary logo at left, with player ID above and a line of 1985 stats below. There is a TCMA copyright line vertically at center. Among the postcard indicia at right, a card number prefixed with "NYM86-" appears within the stamp box. Cards were sold only as complete sets, for $7.95.

		MT
Complete Set (40):		30.00
Common Player:		1.00
1	Rick Aguilera	1.00
2	Bruce Berenyi	1.00
3	Ron Darling	1.00
4	Sid Fernandez	1.00
5	Dwight Gooden	2.50
6	Tom Gorman	1.00
7	Ed Lynch	1.00
8	Roger McDowell	1.00
9	Randy Myers	1.50
10	Bob Ojeda	1.00
11	Jesse Orosco	1.00
12	Doug Sisk	1.00
13	Gary Carter	2.00
14	John Gibbons	1.00
15	Barry Lyons	1.00
16	Wally Backman	1.00
17	Ron Gardenhire	1.00
18	Keith Hernandez	1.50
19	Howard Johnson	1.50
20	Ray Knight	1.50
21	Kevin Mitchell	1.50
22	Rafael Santana	1.00
23	Tim Teufel	1.00
24	Lenny Dykstra	1.50
25	George Foster	1.50
26	Danny Heep	1.00
27	Mel Stottlemyre	1.50
28	Darryl Strawberry	3.00
29	Mookie Wilson	1.50
31	Randy Nieman	1.00
32	Ed Hearn	1.00
33	Stan Jefferson	1.00
34	Bill Robinson	1.00
35	Shawn Abner	1.00
36	Terry Blocker	1.00
37	Davey Johnson	1.50
38	Bud Harrelson	1.50
39	Vern Hoscheit	1.00
40	Greg Pavlick	1.00
43	Tim Corcoran	1.00

1986 TCMA N.Y. Yankees Postcards

For a second consecutive year TCMA produced a set of color player postcards for team issue. Similar in format to the 1985 cards, the 1986 version is in 3-1/2" x 5-1/2" format. Fronts have borderless color poses with no other graphics and a high-gloss finish. Backs have a Yankee logo in light blue at left and (usually) a line of 1985 stats at lower-left. Player ID is at upper left. A TCMA copyright line is vertically at center. Among the postcard indicia at right is a card number within the stamp box; cards are skip-numbered with an "NYY86-" prefix; there are two #18. The cards were sold only as complete sets, for $7.95.

		MT
Complete Set (40):		30.00
Common Player:		1.00
1	Tommy John	2.00
2	Brad Arnsburg (Arnsberg)	1.00
3	Al Holland (Al)	1.00
4	Mike Armstrong	1.00
5	Marty Bystrom	1.00
6	Doug Drabek	1.50
7	Brian Fisher	1.00
8	Stump Merrill	1.00
9	Ron Guidry	1.50
10	Joe Niekro	1.50
12	Dennis Rasmussen	1.00
13	Dave Righetti	1.00
14	Rod Scurry	1.00
15	Bob Shirley	1.00
16	Bob Tewksbury	1.00
17	Ed Whitson	1.00
18a	Britt Burns	1.00
18b	Gene Michael	1.00
19	Butch Wynegar	1.00
20	Ron Hassey	1.00
21	Dale Berra	1.00
22	Jeff Torborg	1.00
23	Mike Fischlin	1.00
24	Don Mattingly	6.00
25	Bobby Meacham	1.00
26	Mike Pagliarulo	1.00
27	Willie Randolph	1.50
28	Andre Robertson	1.00
29	Roy White	1.50
31	Henry Cotto	1.00
32	Ken Griffey	1.00
33	Rickey Henderson	4.00
34	Vic Mata	1.00

35	Dan Pasqua	1.00
36	Dave Winfield	4.00
37	Gary Roenicke	1.00
38	Lou Piniella	1.50
39	Joe Altobelli	1.00
40	Sammy Ellis	1.00
45	Mike Easler	1.00

1986 TCMA Premium Autographs

This three-card set was made available with the purchase of other items from TCMA. The 2-1/2" x 3-1/2" cards have a glossy front finish and each card is personally autographed by the player depicted. Backs have a message about card collecting from the player and 1985 stats, along with TCMA advertising.

		MT
Complete Set (3):		175.00
Common Player:		45.00
(1)	Gary Carter	45.00
(2)	Tony Gwynn	90.00
(3)	Bret Saberhagen	45.00

1986 TCMA Simon's Super Stars

The paintings of sports artist Robert Stephen Simon are reproduced in an unusually sized (2-13/16" x 3-1/2") card issue marketed to collectors. Fronts have color pictures with no extraneous graphics, bordered in white. Backs, printed in blue and white, have biographical and career information.

		MT
Complete Set (50):		20.00
Common Player:		.50
1	Carl Erskine	.50
2	Babe Ruth, Henry Aaron	1.50
3	Ted Williams	1.50
4	Mickey Mantle	2.00
5	Gil Hodges	.75
6	Roberto Clemente	1.50
7	Mickey Mantle	2.00
8	Walter Johnson	.50
9	N.Y. Yankees stars	1.50
10	Carl Yastrzemski, Ted Williams	1.50
11	Mickey Mantle	2.00
12	Harmon Killebrew	.50
13	Warren Spahn	.50
14	Ralph Kiner, Babe Ruth	1.00
15	Bob Gibson	.50
16	Pee Wee Reese	.50
17	Billy Martin	.50
18	Joe DiMaggio, Mickey Mantle	2.00
19	Phil Rizzuto	.50
20	Sandy Koufax	1.00
21	Jackie Robinson	1.00
22	Don Drysdale	.50
23	Mickey Mantle	2.00
24	Mickey Mantle	2.00
25	Joe DiMaggio	1.50
26	Robin Roberts	.50
27	Lou Brock	.50
28	Lou Gehrig	1.50
29	Willie Mays	1.00
30	Brooks Robinson	.50
31	Thurman Munson	.50
32	Roger Maris	1.00
33	Jim Palmer	.50
34	Stan Musial	.75
35	Roy Campanella	.50
36	Joe Pepitone	.50
37	Ebbetts Field	.50
38	Honus Wagner	.50
39	Yogi Berra	.50
40	Eddie Mathews	.50
41	Carl Yastrzemski	.50
42	Babe Ruth	1.50
43	Babe Ruth	1.50
44	Pete Reiser	.50
45	Don Larsen	.50
46	Ernie Banks	.50
47	Casey Stengel	.50
48	Jackie Robinson	1.00
49	Duke Snider	.50
50	Checklist (Duke Snider)	.50

1987 TCMA All Time N.Y. Yankees

Essentially a reprint of its 1980 team set, this TCMA collectors issue can be distinguished by the presence on back of a Major League Baseball logo. The earlier set has a TCMA date line on back. Fronts of the 2-1/2" x 3-1/2" cards have black-and-white player photos with an ornate blue frame and white border. Backs are in black-and-white and include the All Time team roster.

		MT
Complete Set (12):		33.00
Common Player:		.35
1	Lou Gehrig	7.00
2	Tony Lazzeri	.50
3	Red Rolfe	.40
4	Phil Rizzuto	1.25
5	Babe Ruth	7.50
6	Mickey Mantle	9.00
7	Joe DiMaggio	7.00
8	Bill Dickey	.70
9	Red Ruffing	.40
10	Whitey Ford	1.25
11	Johnny Murphy	.40
12	Casey Stengel	.60

1987 TCMA Baseball's Greatest Teams

Ten of the greatest lineups in baseball history are featured in this collectors' series. Each of the nine-card team sets features a different front design while backs share a common format offering player biographical details. The earlier teams picture players in black-and-white photos, while the later sets have color photos. Original issue price was about $1 per set, retail.

		MT
Complete Set (90):		90.00
Common Team Set (9):		6.00
Common Player:		.50
	1907 Chicago Cubs team set	6.00
1	Harry Steinfeldt	.50
2	Three-Finger Brown	.50
3	Ed Reulbach	.50
4	Johnny Kling	.50
5	Orvie Overall	.50
6	Joe Tinker	1.00
7	Wildfire Schulte	.50
8	Frank Chance	1.00
9	Johnny Evers	1.00
	1927 N.Y. Yankees team set	24.00
1	Miller Huggins	.50
2	Herb Pennock	.50
3	Tony Lazzeri	.50
4	Waite Hoyt	.50
5	Wilcy Moore	.50
6	Earle Combs	.50
7	Bob Meusel	.50
8	Lou Gehrig	8.00
9	Babe Ruth	12.00
	1934 St. Louis Cardinals team set	6.00
1	Dizzy Dean	2.00
2	Daffy Dean	.75
3	Pepper Martin	.50
4	Rip Collins	.50
5	Frank Frisch	.50
6	Leo Durocher	.50
7	Ducky Medwick	.50
8	Tex Carleton	.50
9	Spud Davis	.50
	1946 Boston Red Sox team set	10.00
1	Joe Cronin	.50
2	Rudy York	.50
3	Bobby Doerr	.50
4	Johnny Pesky	.50
5	Dom DiMaggio	.75
6	Ted Williams	6.00
7	Boo Ferriss	.50
8	Tex Hughson	.50
9	Mickey Harris	.50
	1950 Philadelphia Phillies team set	6.00
1	Eddie Sawyer	.50
2	Curt Simmons	.50
3	Jim Konstanty	.50
4	Eddie Waitkus	.50
5	Granny Hamner	.50
6	Del Ennis	.50
7	Richie Ashburn	.75
8	Dick Sisler	.50
9	Robin Roberts	.75
	1955 Brooklyn Dodgers team set	10.00
1	Duke Snider, Walt Alston	1.00
2	Roy Campanella	2.00
3	Jackie Robinson	4.00
4	Carl Furillo	.75
5	Gil Hodges	1.00
6	Pee Wee Reese, Jim Gilliam	1.00
7	Don Newcombe	.75
8	Ed Roebuck, Clem Labine	.50
9	Carl Erskine	.50
	1957 Milwaukee Braves team set	10.00
1	Hank Aaron	6.00
2	Eddie Mathews	.75
3	Bob Hazle	.50
4	Johnny Logan	.50
5	Red Schoendienst	.50
6	Wes Covington	.50
7	Lew Burdette	.50
8	Warren Spahn	.75
9	Bob Buhl	.50
	1960 Pittsburgh Pirates team set	10.00
1	Dick Stuart	.50
2	Bill Mazeroski	.75
3	Dick Groat	.50
4	Roberto Clemente	7.50
5	Bob Skinner	.50
6	Smokey Burgess	.50
7	Roy Face	.50
8	Bob Friend	.50
9	Vernon Law	.50
	1961 N.Y. Yankees team set	30.00
1	Bill Skowron	.75
2	Mickey Mantle	15.00
3	Bobby Richardson	.50
4	Tony Kubek	.50
5	Elston Howard	.50
6	Yogi Berra	3.00
7	Whitey Ford	3.00
8	Roger Maris	6.00
9	Ralph Houk	.50
	1969 N.Y. Mets team set	6.00
1	Ed Kranepool	.50
2	Bud Harrelson	.50
3	Cleon Jones, Tommie Agee, Ron Swoboda	.50
4	Jerry Koosman	.50
5	Gary Gentry	.50
6	Tug McGraw	.50
7	Ron Taylor	.50
8	Jerry Grote	.50
9	Ken Boswell	.50

1996 George Teague Celebrity Softball Challenge

Participants in a July 8, 1995, charity softball game at Appleton, Wis., between celebrity teams are featured in this card set which was given to fans at the 1996 game on July 13. The Green Bay Packers defensive back captained the "Teague's League" of area sports and media stars while singer Michael Bolton piloted "Bolton's Bombers," featuring several top softball stars. Cards feature game-action color photos bordered in blue or green, and several special cards describing the game's charitable aspect to benefit the Rebecca Fund and Michael Bolton Foundation.

		MT
Complete Set (34):		12.00
Common Card:		.05
	BOLTON'S BOMBERS	
2	Mugs Cain	.05
5	Pat McCollum	.05
7 (a)	Michael Bolton (full-body pose)	1.00
7 (b)	Michael Bolton (close-up)	1.00
8	Johnny Dodd	.05
9	Richie Vaughn	.05
11	Bucky Ford	.05
12	Phil Higgins	.25
14	Kim Turner	.25
15	Gary Whitefield	.05
21	Mike Bolen	.25
30	Donnie Slye	.05
30A	Rebecca Slye	.05
57	Louis Levin	.05
69	Bobby Olah	.25
---	1995 Bolton Bombers team photo	.05
	TEAGUE'S LEAGUE	
6	Sal Bando	.25
11	Ty Detmer	.50
13	Quinn Teague	.05
19	Robin Yount	6.00
22	Lenny McGill	.50
25	Jimmy Slye	.05
31	George Teague	.50
64	John Jurkovic	.50
87	Robert Brooks	1.00
89	Mark Chmura	.50
94	Dan Jansen	.50
101	Murphy in the Morning	.05
---	1995 Teague's League team photo	.05
---	Closing Remarks for ESPN2	.05
---	The Michael Bolton Foundation	.05
---	Rebecca Fund	.05
---	Rebecca Showcase Event	.05
---	1995 Check Presentation $166,000	.05

1996 Team Metal Ken Griffey Jr.

CUI, the parent firm of the company which produces Metallic Images sports and non-sports cards, created this set of metal cards for sale in large retail chains. The four cards come packaged in a lithographed steel box about the size and shape of a Band-aid tin. The 2-5/8" x 3-9/16" cards have a blue and teal background with a color game-action photo at center. Backs have rolled metal edges and share a photo at left. A few sentences about the player are printed at right. Logos and copyright data are at bottom. Issue price of the four-card set was just under $10.

		MT
Complete Set (4):		10.00
Common Card:		2.50
1	Ken Griffey Jr. (home run trot)	2.50
2	Ken Griffey Jr. (sliding)	2.50
3	Ken Griffey Jr. (batting follow-through)	2.50
4	Ken Griffey Jr. (batting follow-through)	2.50

1996 Team Metal Cal Ripken, Jr.

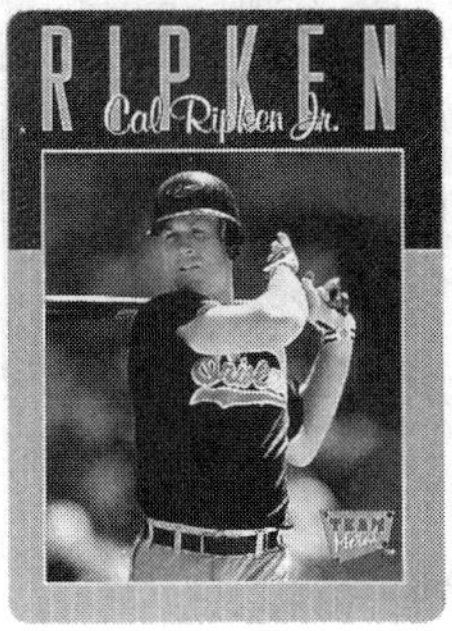

CUI, the parent firm of the company which produces Metallic Impressions sports and non-sports cards, created this set of metal cards for sale in large retail chains. The four cards come packaged in a lithographed steel box about the size and shape of a Band-aid tin. The 2-5/8" x 3-9/16" cards have a green and orange background with a color game-action photo at center. Backs have rolled metal edges and share a photo at left. A few sentences about the player are printed at right. Logos and copyright data are at bottom. Issue price of the four-card set was just under $10.

		MT
Complete Set (4):		10.00
Common Card:		2.50
1	Cal Ripken Jr. (batting, black jersey)	2.50
2	Cal Ripken Jr. (batting follow-through)	2.50
3	Cal Ripken Jr. (fielding)	2.50
4	Cal Ripken Jr. (batting, white jersey)	2.50

1996 Team Out! Game

This baseball card game is sold as a boxed set containing 37 of the 91 different player cards, plus an assortment of 23 of the 10 cartoon "action" cards used to play the game. Cards are 2-1/4" x 3-1/2" with rounded corners and glossy surfaces. Backs have a close-up photo of a baseball with product and licensor logos and copyright information. Fronts of the player photo cards are bordered in black; the cartoon action cards have red or blue borders. The unnumbered cards are checklisted here in alphabetical order.

		MT
Complete Set (101):		80.00
Common Player:		.25
(1)	Roberto Alomar	2.50
(2)	Brady Anderson	.50
(3)	Kevin Appier	.25
(4)	Carlos Baerga	.25
(5)	Jeff Bagwell	4.00
(6)	Albert Belle	3.00
(7)	Dante Bichette	.50
(8)	Craig Biggio	.75
(9)	Wade Boggs	3.00
(10)	Barry Bonds	5.00
(11)	Kevin Brown	.35
(12)	Jay Buhner	.25
(13)	Ellis Burks	.25
(14)	Ken Caminiti	.25
(15)	Joe Carter	.25
(16)	Vinny Castilla	.25
(17)	Jeff Cirillo	.25
(18)	Will Clark	.75
(19)	Jeff Conine	.25
(20)	Joey Cora	.25
(21)	Marty Cordova	.25
(22)	Eric Davis	.25
(23)	Ray Durham	.25
(24)	Jim Edmonds	.25
(25)	Cecil Fielder	.25
(26)	Travis Fryman	.25
(27)	Jason Giambi	.25
(28)	Bernard Gilkey	.25
(29)	Tom Glavine	.25
(30)	Juan Gonzalez	5.00
(31)	Mark Grace	.75
(32)	Ken Griffey Jr.	6.00
(33)	Marquis Grissom	.25
(34)	Mark Grudzielanek	.25
(35)	Ozzie Guillen	.25
(36)	Tony Gwynn	4.00
(37)	Bobby Higginson	.25
(38)	Todd Hundley	.25
(39)	Derek Jeter	5.00
(40)	Lance Johnson	.25
(41)	Randy Johnson	.40
(42)	Chipper Jones	5.50
(43)	Brian Jordan	.25
(44)	Wally Joyner	.25
(45)	Jason Kendall	.25
(46)	Chuck Knoblauch	.25
(47)	Ray Lankford	.25
(48)	Mike Lansing	.25
(49)	Barry Larkin	.25
(50)	Kenny Lofton	.50
(51)	Javier Lopez	.25
(52)	Mike MacFarlane	.25
(53)	Greg Maddux	5.00
(54)	Al Martin	.25
(55)	Brian McRae	.25
(56)	Mark McGwire	6.00
(57)	Raul Mondesi	.50
(58)	Denny Neagle	.25
(59)	Hideo Nomo	1.00
(60)	John Olerud	.40
(61)	Rey Ordonez	.25
(62)	Troy Percival	.25
(63)	Mike Piazza	5.50
(64)	Andy Pettitte	.25
(65)	Manny Ramirez	.45
(66)	Cal Ripken Jr.	5.75
(67)	Alex Rodriguez	5.75
(68)	Ivan Rodriguez	.60
(69)	Ryne Sandberg	1.50
(70)	Tim Salmon	.25
(71)	Benito Santiago	.25
(72)	Kevin Seitzer	.25
(73)	Scott Servais	.25
(74)	Gary Sheffield	.50
(75)	Ozzie Smith	1.50
(76)	John Smoltz	.25
(77)	Sammy Sosa	4.00
(78)	Mike Stanley	.25
(79)	Terry Steinbach	.25
(80)	Frank Thomas	5.00
(81)	Steve Trachsel	.25
(82)	Jose Valentin	.25
(83)	Mo Vaughn	1.00
(84)	Jose Vizcaino	.25
(85)	Robin Ventura	.25
(86)	Larry Walker	.40
(87)	Walt Weiss	.25
(88)	Bernie Williams	.50
(89)	Matt Williams	.40
(90)	Eric Young	.25
(91)	Todd Zeile	.25
(92)	Double Play (Roberto Alomar) (cartoon)	.25
(93)	Free Agent Acquisition (Barry Bonds) (cartoon)	.25
(94)	No Trade - Infield (Mark McGwire, Ozzie Smith, Mo Vaughn) (cartoon)	1.00
(95)	No Trade - Outfield (Albert Belle, Raul Mondesi) (cartoon)	.25
(96)	Out! (Mike Piazza, Matt Williams) (cartoon)	.40
(97)	Pitcher Bombed (cartoon)	.11
(98)	Pitcher Stays (Greg Maddux) (cartoon)	.25
(99)	Safe! (Frank Thomas) (cartoon)	.25
(100)	Trade - Infield (Cal Ripken Jr., Alex Rodriguez) (cartoon)	.50
(101)	Trade - Outfield (Ken Griffey Jr., Sammy Sosa) (cartoon)	.40

1988 Tetley Tea Discs

The Tetley iced tea discs are virtually identical in format to the 1988 Baseball Super Stars discs, but are labeled "FIRST ANNUAL COLLECTORS' EDITION", rather than Second and appear to have slight differences in the player pairs which make up each folder. Values for these can be extrapolated by combining the values of individual discs shown under the 1988 Baseball Super Stars listing.

(See 1988 Super Stars Discs for checklist and price guide.)

1989 Tetley Tea Discs

Issued in two-player folders which also contained a disc offering autographed baseballs and uncut sheets of discs, this set was identified as Tetley iced tea's "Second Annual Collectors' Edition." The 2-5/8" diameter discs have a bright yellow background with a red star at center framing the player's portrait photo. Uniform logos have been airbrushed off the player photos. A blue stripe beneath the photo contains the Tetley logo in white. The player's name and team are printed at bottom. Backs are printed in black-and-white and repeat the star design at center, with a few bits of personal data and the player's 1988 stats. The three-panel folders were distributed in canisters of iced tea mix in the East.

		MT
Complete Set, Panels (10):		10.00
Complete Set, Singles (20):		6.00
Common Panel:		.60
Common Player:		.15
Panel 1-2		1.00
1	Don Mattingly	.50
2	David Cone	.20
Panel 3-4		4.00
3	Mark McGwire	2.00
4	Will Clark	.30
Panel 5-6		.75
5	Darryl Strawberry	.30
6	Dwight Gooden	.20
Panel 7-8		1.25
7	Wade Boggs	.40
8	Roger Clemens	.60
Panel 9-10		.80
9	Benito Santiago	.15
10	Orel Hershiser	.25
Panel 11-12		1.25
11	Eric Davis	.15
12	Kirby Puckett	.75
Panel 13-14		.90
13	Dave Winfield	.40
14	Andre Dawson	.20
Panel 15-16		2.00
15	Steve Bedrosian	.15
16	Cal Ripken, Jr.	1.00
Panel 17-18		1.00
17	Andy Van Slyke	.15
18	Jose Canseco	.40
Panel 19-20		.60
19	Jose Oquendo	.15
20	Dale Murphy	.25

1990 Tetley Tea Discs

(See 1990 Super Stars Discs for checklist and values.)

1986 Texas Gold Ice Cream Reds

One of the last regional baseball card sets produced during the 1986 season was a 28-card team set sponsored by a Cincinnati-area ice cream company and given to fans attending the Sept. 19 game. Photos on the 2-1/2" x 3-1/2" cards are game-action shots, and include three different cards of playing manager Pete Rose. The set is also notable for the inclusion of first cards of some of the Reds' young prospects.

		MT
Complete Set (28):		15.00
Common Player:		.25
6	Bo Diaz	.25
9	Max Venable	.25
11	Kurt Stillwell	.25
12	Nick Esasky	.25
13	Dave Concepcion	.25
14a	Pete Rose (commemorative)	3.00
14b	Pete Rose (infield)	3.00
14c	Pete Rose (manager)	3.00
16	Ron Oester	.25
20	Eddie Milner	.25
22	Sal Butera	.25
24	Tony Perez	1.00
25	Buddy Bell	.35
28	Kal Daniels	.25
29	Tracy Jones	.25
31	John Franco	.40
32	Tom Browning	.25
33	Ron Robinson	.25
34	Bill Gullickson	.25
36	Mario Soto	.25
39	Dave Parker	.50
40	John Denny	.25
44	Eric Davis	.60
45	Chris Welsh	.25
48	Ted Power	.25
49	Joe Price	.25
---	Reds coaches (Scott Breeden, Billy Demars, Tommy Helms, Bruce Kimm, Jim Lett, George Scherger)	.25
---	Logo/Coupon card	.10

1987 Texas Rangers Fire Safety

Co-sponsored by the team, U.S. and Texas Forest Services, the set was given out to fans at special promotions at Arlington Stadium. Cards measure 4-1/4" x 6" and feature color action photos. Backs contain brief player personal information along with a Smokey the Bear wildfire prevention message. Cards of Mike Mason and Tom Paciorek were withdrawn from the sets given out by the Rangers and are quite scarce.

		MT
Complete Set (32):		45.00
Common Player:		.30
1	Charlie Hough	.35
2	Greg Harris	.30
3	Jose Guzman	.30
4	Mike Mason	20.00
5	Dale Mohorcic	.30
6	Bobby Witt	.45
7	Mitch Williams	.40
8	Geno Petralli	.30
9	Don Slaught	.30
10	Darrell Porter	.30
11	Steve Beuchele	.30
12	Pete O'Brien	.30
13	Scott Fletcher	.30
14	Tom Paciorek	20.00
15	Pete Incaviglia	.40
16	Oddibe McDowell	.30
17	Ruben Sierra	.75
18	Larry Parrish	.30
19	Bobby Valentine	.30
20	Tom House	.30
21	Tom Robson	.30
22	Edwin Correa	.30
23	Mike Stanley	.30
24	Joe Ferguson	.30
25	Art Howe	.30
26	Bob Brower	.30
27	Mike Loynd	.30
28	Curtis Wilkerson	.30
29	Tim Foli	.30
30	Dave Oliver	.30
31	Jerry Browne	.30
32	Jeff Russell	.30

1988 Texas Rangers Fire Safety

This oversized (3-1/2" x 5") set was distributed to Rangers' fans at Smokey Bear Game Day on Aug. 7. Fronts feature full-color action photos framed in an oval blue and red border on a white background. A nameplate above the photo identifies the player and a "Wildfire Prevention" logo is printed beneath the photo. Rangers (left) and Smokey (right) logos fill the upper corners of the card face. The card backs are black-and-white and include player info, U.S. and Texas Forest Service logos, and fire prevention tips.

		MT
Complete Set (21):		5.00
Common Player:		.30
1	Tom O'Malley	.30
2	Pete O'Brien	.30
3	Geno Petralli	.30
4	Pete Incaviglia	.30
5	Oddibe McDowell	.30
6	Dale Mohorcic	.30
7	Bobby Witt	.45
8	Bobby Valentine	.30
9	Ruben Sierra	.35
10	Scott Fletcher	.30
11	Mike Stanley	.30
12	Steve Buechele	.30
13	Charlie Hough	.35
14	Larry Parrish	.30
15	Jerry Browne	.30
16	Bob Brower	.30
17	Jeff Russell	.30
18	Edwin Correa	.30
19	Mitch Williams	.35
20	Jose Guzman	.30
21	Curtis Wilkerson	.30

1989 Texas Rangers Fire Safety

Given away at a Rangers home game in 1989, this large-format (4-1/4" x 6") set features player portrait photos within an oval frame on a white border. The team logo is at upper-left; Smokey the Bear at upper-right. Backs have minimal biographical data and stats and a cartoon fire prevention tip. The unnumbered cards are checklisted here alphabetically.

		MT
Complete Set (34):		15.00
Common Player:		.25
(1)	Darrel Akerfelds	.25
(2)	Brad Arnsberg	.25
(3)	Buddy Bell	.25
(4)	Kevin Brown	1.50
(5)	Steve Buechele	.25
(6)	Dick Egan	.25
(7)	Cecil Espy	.25
(8)	Scott Fletcher	.25

(9)	Julio Franco	.45
(10)	Cecilio Guante	.25
(11)	Jose Guzman	.25
(12)	Drew Hall	.25
(13)	Toby Harrah	.30
(14)	Charlie Hough	.35
(15)	Tom House	.25
(16)	Pete Incaviglia	.30
(17)	Chad Kreuter	.25
(18)	Jeff Kunkel	.25
(19)	Rick Leach	.25
(20)	Davey Lopes	.30
(21)	Craig McMurtry	.25
(22)	Jamie Moyer	.25
(23)	Dave Oliver	.25
(24)	Rafael Palmeiro	2.50
(25)	Geno Petralli	.25
(26)	Tom Robson	.25
(27)	Kenny Rogers	.35
(28)	Jeff Russell	.25
(29)	Nolan Ryan	6.00
(30)	Ruben Sierra	.30
(31)	Mike Stanley	.25
(32)	Jim Sundberg	.25
(33)	Bobby Valentine	.25
(34)	Bobby Witt	.35

1984 The Natural Roy Hobbs

Bernard Malamud's fictional New York Knights outfielder Roy Hobbs appears on this collectors' card as portrayed by Robert Redford in the movie "The Natural". In the style of a 1940 Play Ball card, this 2-1/2" x 3-1/8" card has a color portrait photo on front, highlighted with blue graphics. The back is blank.

	MT
Roy Hobbs (Robert Redford)	20.00

1992 The Perfect Game Ken Griffey Jr.

This collectors issue traces the career of Griffey Jr. through the 1991 season. Standard-size cards feature pencil artwork by Anthony Douglas. Borders are black and typography is gold foil. At the top of each card is "The Natural Progression". Backs have career summary and the producer's logo. Card #3 in each set carries on back a certificate of authenticity serially numbered from within an edition of 10,000 sets.

		MT
	Complete Set (9):	15.00
	Common Card:	2.00
1	Ken Griffey Jr.	2.00
2	Ken Griffey Jr. (Moeller High)	2.00
3	Ken Griffey Jr. (Bellingham Mariners)	2.00
4	Ken Griffey Jr. (San Bernadino Spirit)	2.00
5	Ken Griffey Jr. (Vermont Mariners)	2.00
6	Ken Griffey Jr. (The Seattle Rookie)	2.00
7	Ken Griffey Jr. (All Stap/MVP)	2.00
8	Ken Griffey Jr. (Gold Glove)	2.00
9	Ken Griffey Jr. (Father and Son)	2.00

1983 Thorn Apple Valley Cubs

This set of 27 cards was issued in conjuction with a "Baseball Card Day" promotion at Wrigley Field in 1983. Thorn Apple Valley was the meat company which produced the hot dogs sold at the ballpark. The cards feature borderless color photos with the player's name, uniform number (also the card's number in the checklist) and an abbreviation for their position. Card backs feature annual statistics. Of the 27 cards, which measure 2-1/4" x 3-1/2", 25 feature players, one is a team card, and one features the manager and coaches.

		MT
	Complete Set (27):	35.00
	Common Player:	.50
1	Larry Bowa	.50
6	Keith Moreland	.50
7	Jody Davis	.50
10	Leon Durham	.50
11	Ron Cey	.50
16	Steve Lake	.50
20	Thad Bosley	.50
21	Jay Johnstone	.50
22	Bill Buckner	1.00
23	Ryne Sandberg	17.50
24	Jerry Morales	.50
25	Gary Woods	.50
27	Mel Hall	.50
29	Tom Veryzer	.50
30	Chuck Rainey	.50
31	Fergie Jenkins	3.50
32	Craig Lefferts	.50
33	Joe Carter	6.00
34	Steve Trout	.50
36	Mike Proly	.50
39	Bill Campbell	.50
41	Warren Brusstar	.50
44	Dick Ruthven	.50
46	Lee Smith	2.50
48	Dickie Noles	.50
---	Coaching Staff (Ruben Amaro, Billy Connors, Duffy Dyer, Lee Elia, Fred Koenig, John Vukovich)	.50
---	Team Photo	.50

1994 Times Orange County California Angels

These player pictures were a give-away, possibly inserted into issues of the Orange County edition of the L.A. Times newspaper which were sold at Anaheim Stadium. In 7-1/2" x 8-3/4" format, the pictures feature borderless color action photos on front, with the player's last name in large white letters, a team logo and a "Collector Series" logo with picture number. Backs have complete player stats, some personal data and the team's 1994 schedule. Team and sponsor logos also appear on back.

		MT
	Complete Set (26):	24.00
	Common Player:	1.00
1	Chili Davis	1.50
2	Chad Curtis	1.00
3	John Dopson	1.00
4	Gary DiSarcina	1.00
5	Jim Edmonds	2.00
6	Joe Grahe	1.00
7	Bo Jackson	2.50
8	Joe Magrane	1.00
9	Phil Leftwich	1.00
10	Bill Sampen	1.00
11	Chuck Finley	1.50
12	Dwight Smith	1.00
13	Mark Leiter	1.00
14	Mark Langston	1.50
15	Mike Butcher	1.00
16	Rex Hudler	1.00
17	Craig Lefferts	1.00
18	Damion Easley	1.00
19	Greg Myers	1.00
20	Chris Turner	1.00
21	Tim Salmon	3.00
22	Harold Reynolds	1.00
23	Bob Patterson	1.00
24	Spike Owen	1.00
25	Eduardo Perez	1.00
26	Marcel Lacheman	1.00

1994 Tombstone Pizza

Score produced a special 30-card set which could be obtained by eating a lot of frozen pizzas (one card per pizza) or by sending in a dollar and five proofs of purchase. Titled "'94 Tombstone Super-Pro Series," the cards are black-bordered and UV coated on front and back. Because the set is licensed only by the players' union and not by Major League Baseball, the uniform logos on the front action photos and back portraits have been airbrushed away. Cards feature the Tombstone logo on both front and back. Backs have recent and career stats, a facsimile autograph and a card number.

		MT
	Complete Set (30):	17.50
	Common Player:	.50
1	Jeff Bagwell	1.00
2	Jay Bell	.50
3	Barry Bonds	1.25
4	Bobby Bonilla	.60
5	Andres Galarraga	.60
6	Mark Grace	.75
7	Marquis Grissom	.50
8	Tony Gwynn	1.00
9	Bryan Harvey	.50
10	Gregg Jefferies	.50
11	David Justice	.75
12	John Kruk	.50
13	Barry Larkin	.50
14	Greg Maddux	1.50
15	Mike Piazza	1.50
16	Jim Abbott	.50
17	Albert Belle	1.00
18	Cecil Fielder	.50
19	Juan Gonzalez	1.50
20	Mike Greenwell	.50
21	Ken Griffey, Jr.	2.50
22	Jack McDowell	.50
23	Jeff Montgomery	.50
24	John Olerud	.60
25	Kirby Puckett	1.00
26	Cal Ripken, Jr.	2.00
27	Tim Salmon	.60
28	Ruben Sierra	.50
29	Frank Thomas	1.50
30	Robin Yount	1.50

1995 Tombstone Pizza

Tombstone's second annual baseball card issue was available either singly in frozen pizza packages, or as a 30-card boxed set via a mail-in offer. Cards feature action player photos on front and portrait photos on back; both have had uniform logos airbrushed for lack of a MLB license. There is a graduated red to black border on each side. On front at lower-right are the player and team name and the Tombstone logo. Backs have biographical data, recent stats and career highlights. At bottom is a card number and the players' association logo.

		MT
	Complete Set (30):	17.50
	Common Player:	.50
1	Frank Thomas	2.50
2	David Cone	.50
3	Bob Hamelin	.50
4	Jeff Bagwell	1.50
5	Greg Maddux	2.00
6	Raul Mondesi	1.00
7	Chili Davis	.50
8	Cecil Fielder	.50
9	Ken Griffey Jr.	4.00
10	Jimmy Key	.50
11	Kenny Lofton	1.00
12	Paul Molitor	1.50
13	Kirby Puckett	1.50
14	Cal Ripken Jr.	3.50
15	Ivan Rodriguez	1.50
16	Kevin Seitzer	.50
17	Ruben Sierra	.50
18	Mo Vaughn	1.00
19	Moises Alou	.55
20	Barry Bonds	1.50
21	Jeff Conine	.50
22	Lenny Dykstra	.50
23	Andres Galarraga	.50
24	Tony Gwynn	1.50
25	Barry Larkin	.50
26	Fred McGriff	.75
27	Orlando Merced	.50
28	Bret Saberhagen	.50
29	Ozzie Smith	1.25
30	Sammy Sosa	2.50

1981 Topps

This is another 726-card set of 2-1/2" x 3-1/2" cards from Topps. The cards have the usual color photo with all cards from the same team sharing the same color borders. Player names appear under the photo with team and position on a baseball cap at lower-left. The Topps logo returned in a small baseball in the lower-right. Card backs include the usual stats along with a headline and a cartoon if there was room. Specialty cards include previous season record-breakers, highlights of the playoffs and World Series, along with the final appearance of team cards. Eleven cards on each of the six press sheets were double-printed.

		MT
	Complete Set (726):	50.00
	Common Player:	.10
	Wax Box:	90.00
1	Batting Leaders (George Brett, Bill Buckner)	.75
2	Home Run Leaders (Reggie Jackson, Ben Oglivie, Mike Schmidt)	.75
3	RBI Leaders (Cecil Cooper, Mike Schmidt)	.30
4	Stolen Base Leaders (Rickey Henderson, Ron LeFlore)	.50
5	Victory Leaders (Steve Carlton, Steve Stone)	.15
6	Strikeout Leaders (Len Barker, Steve Carlton)	.15
7	ERA Leaders (Rudy May, Don Sutton)	.10
8	Leading Firemen (Rollie Fingers, Tom Hume, Dan Quisenberry)	.10
9	Pete LaCock (DP)	.10
10	Mike Flanagan	.10
11	Jim Wohlford (DP)	.10
12	Mark Clear	.10
13	*Joe Charboneau*	.25
14	*John Tudor*	.20
15	Larry Parrish	.10
16	Ron Davis	.10
17	Cliff Johnson	.10
18	Glenn Adams	.10
19	Jim Clancy	.10
20	Jeff Burroughs	.10
21	Ron Oester	.10
22	Danny Darwin	.10
23	Alex Trevino	.10
24	Don Stanhouse	.10
25	Sixto Lezcano	.10
26	U.L. Washington	.10
27	Champ Summers (DP)	.10
28	Enrique Romo	.10
29	Gene Tenace	.10
30	Jack Clark	.10
31	Checklist 1-121 (DP)	.10
32	Ken Oberkfell	.10
33	Rick Honeycutt	.10
34	Aurelio Rodriguez	.10
35	Mitchell Page	.10
36	Ed Farmer	.10
37	Gary Roenicke	.10
38	Win Remmerswaal	.10
39	Tom Veryzer	.10
40	Tug McGraw	.10
41	Rangers Future Stars (Bob Babcock, John Butcher, Jerry Don Gleaton)	.10
42	Jerry White (DP)	.10
43	Jose Morales	.10
44	Larry McWilliams	.10
45	Enos Cabell	.10
46	Rick Bosetti	.10
47	Ken Brett	.10

48	Dave Skaggs	.10
49	Bob Shirley	.10
50	Dave Lopes	.10
51	Bill Robinson (DP)	.10
52	Hector Cruz	.10
53	Kevin Saucier	.10
54	Ivan DeJesus	.10
55	Mike Norris	.10
56	Buck Martinez	.10
57	Dave Roberts	.10
58	Joel Youngblood	.10
59	Dan Petry	.10
60	Willie Randolph	.10
61	Butch Wynegar	.10
62	Joe Pettini	.10
63	Steve Renko (DP)	.10
64	Brian Asselstine	.10
65	Scott McGregor	.10
66	Royals Future Stars (Manny Castillo, Tim Ireland, Mike Jones)	.10
67	Ken Kravec	.10
68	Matt Alexander (DP)	.10
69	Ed Halicki	.10
70	Al Oliver (DP)	.10
71	Hal Dues	.10
72	Barry Evans (DP)	.10
73	Doug Bair	.10
74	Mike Hargrove	.10
75	Reggie Smith	.10
76	Mario Mendoza	.10
77	Mike Barlow	.10
78	Steve Dillard	.10
79	Bruce Robbins	.10
80	Rusty Staub	.15
81	Dave Stapleton	.10
82	Astros Future Stars (Danny Heep, Alan Knicely, Bobby Sprowl) (DP)	.10
83	Mike Proly	.10
84	Johnnie LeMaster	.10
85	Mike Caldwell	.10
86	Wayne Gross	.10
87	Rick Camp	.10
88	Joe Lefebvre	.10
89	Darrell Jackson	.10
90	Bake McBride	.10
91	Tim Stoddard (DP)	.10
92	Mike Easler	.10
93	Ed Glynn (DP)	.10
94	Harry Spilman (DP)	.10
95	Jim Sundberg	.10
96	A's Future Stars (Dave Beard, *Ernie Camacho*, Pat Dempsey)	.10
97	Chris Speier	.10
98	Clint Hurdle	.10
99	Eric Wilkins	.10
100	Rod Carew	2.00
101	Benny Ayala	.10
102	Dave Tobik	.10
103	Jerry Martin	.10
104	Terry Forster	.10
105	Jose Cruz	.15
106	Don Money	.10
107	Rich Wortham	.10
108	Bruce Benedict	.10
109	Mike Scott	.10
110	Carl Yastrzemski	2.00
111	Greg Minton	.10
112	White Sox Future Stars (Rusty Kuntz, Fran Mullins, Leo Sutherland)	.10
113	Mike Phillips	.10
114	Tom Underwood	.10
115	Roy Smalley	.10
116	Joe Simpson	.10
117	Pete Falcone	.10
118	Kurt Bevacqua	.10
119	Tippy Martinez	.10
120	Larry Bowa	.10
121	Larry Harlow	.10
122	John Denny	.10
123	Al Cowens	.10
124	Jerry Garvin	.10
125	Andre Dawson	.90
126	*Charlie Leibrandt*	.40
127	Rudy Law	.10
128	Gary Allenson (DP)	.10
129	Art Howe	.10
130	Larry Gura	.10
131	*Keith Moreland*	.20
132	Tommy Boggs	.10
133	Jeff Cox	.10
134	Steve Mura	.10
135	Gorman Thomas	.10
136	Doug Capilla	.10
137	Hosken Powell	.10
138	*Rich Dotson* (DP)	.20
139	Oscar Gamble	.10
140	Bob Forsch	.10
141	Miguel Dilone	.10
142	Jackson Todd	.10
143	Dan Meyer	.10
144	Allen Ripley	.10
145	Mickey Rivers	.10
146	Bobby Castillo	.10
147	Dale Berra	.10
148	Randy Niemann	.10
149	Joe Nolan	.10
150	Mark Fidrych	.15
151	Claudell Washington (DP)	.10
152	John Urrea	.10
153	Tom Poquette	.10
154	Rick Langford	.10
155	Chris Chambliss	.10
156	Bob McClure	.10
157	John Wathan	.10
158	Fergie Jenkins	.90
159	Brian Doyle	.10
160	Garry Maddox	.10
161	Dan Graham	.10
162	Doug Corbett	.10
163	Billy Almon	.10
164	*Lamarr Hoyt (LaMarr)*	.15
165	Tony Scott	.10
166	Floyd Bannister	.10
167	Terry Whitfield	.10
168	Don Robinson (DP)	.10
169	John Mayberry	.10
170	Ross Grimsley	.10
171	Gene Richards	.10
172	Gary Woods	.10
173	Bump Wills	.10
174	Doug Rau	.10
175	Dave Collins	.10
176	Mike Krukow	.10
177	Rick Peters	.10
178	Jim Essian (DP)	.10
179	Rudy May	.10
180	Pete Rose	3.00
181	Elias Sosa	.10
182	Bob Grich	.10
183	Dick Davis (DP)	.10
184	Jim Dwyer	.10
185	Dennis Leonard	.10
186	Wayne Nordhagen	.10
187	Mike Parrott	.10
188	Doug DeCinces	.10
189	Craig Swan	.10
190	Cesar Cedeno	.10
191	Rick Sutcliffe	.10
192	Braves Future Stars (*Terry Harper*, Ed Miller, *Rafael Ramirez*)	.10
193	Pete Vuckovich	.10
194	*Rod Scurry*	.10
195	Rich Murray	.10
196	Duffy Dyer	.10
197	Jim Kern	.10
198	Jerry Dybzinski	.10
199	Chuck Rainey	.10
200	George Foster	.15
201	Johnny Bench (Record Breaker)	.45
202	Steve Carlton (Record Breaker)	.35
203	Bill Gullickson (Record Breaker)	.10
204	Ron LeFlore, Rodney Scott (Record Breaker)	.10
205	Pete Rose (Record Breaker)	1.50
206	Mike Schmidt (Record Breaker)	1.00
207	Ozzie Smith (Record Breaker)	1.00
208	Willie Wilson (Record Breaker)	.10
209	Dickie Thon (DP)	.10
210	Jim Palmer	1.50
211	Derrel Thomas	.10
212	Steve Nicosia	.10
213	*Al Holland*	.10
214	Angels Future Stars (Ralph Botting, Jim Dorsey, John Harris)	.10
215	Larry Hisle	.10
216	John Henry Johnson	.10
217	Rich Hebner	.10
218	Paul Splittorff	.10
219	Ken Landreaux	.10
220	Tom Seaver	2.00
221	Bob Davis	.10
222	Jorge Orta	.10
223	Roy Lee Jackson	.10
224	Pat Zachry	.10
225	Ruppert Jones	.10
226	Manny Sanguillen (DP)	.10
227	Fred Martinez	.10
228	Tom Paciorek	.10
229	Rollie Fingers	.90
230	George Hendrick	.10
231	Joe Beckwith	.10
232	Mickey Klutts	.10
233	Skip Lockwood	.10
234	Lou Whitaker	.20
235	Scott Sanderson	.10
236	Mike Ivie	.10
237	Charlie Moore	.10
238	Willie Hernandez	.10
239	Rick Miller (DP)	.10
240	Nolan Ryan	12.00
241	Checklist 122-242 (DP)	.10
242	Chet Lemon	.10
243	Sal Butera	.10
244	Cardinals Future Stars (*Tito Landrum*, Al Olmsted, Andy Rincon)	.10
245	Ed Figueroa	.10
246	Ed Ott (DP)	.10
247	Glenn Hubbard (DP)	.10
248	Joey McLaughlin	.10
249	Larry Cox	.10
250	Ron Guidry	.20
251	Tom Brookens	.10
252	Victor Cruz	.10
253	Dave Bergman	.10
254	Ozzie Smith	7.50
255	Mark Littell	.10
256	Bombo Rivera	.10
257	Rennie Stennett	.10
258	*Joe Price*	.10
259	Mets Future Stars (Juan Berenguer, *Hubie Brooks, Mookie Wilson*)	.75
260	Ron Cey	.15
261	Rickey Henderson	7.00
262	Sammy Stewart	.10
263	Brian Downing	.10
264	Jim Norris	.10
265	John Candelaria	.10
266	Tom Herr	.10
267	Stan Bahnsen	.10
268	Jerry Royster	.10
269	Ken Forsch	.10
270	Greg Luzinski	.10
271	Bill Castro	.10
272	Bruce Kimm	.10
273	Stan Papi	.10
274	Craig Chamberlain	.10
275	Dwight Evans	.10
276	Dan Spillner	.10
277	Alfredo Griffin	.10
278	Rick Sofield	.10
279	Bob Knepper	.10
280	Ken Griffey	.10
281	Fred Stanley	.10
282	Mariners Future Stars (Rick Anderson, Greg Biercevicz, Rodney Craig)	.10
283	Billy Sample	.10
284	Brian Kingman	.10
285	Jerry Turner	.10
286	Dave Frost	.10
287	Lenn Sakata	.10
288	Bob Clark	.10
289	Mickey Hatcher	.10
290	Bob Boone (DP)	.10
291	Aurelio Lopez	.10
292	Mike Squires	.10
293	*Charlie Lea*	.15
294	Mike Tyson (DP)	.10
295	Hal McRae	.10
296	Bill Nahorodny (DP)	.10
297	Bob Bailor	.10
298	Buddy Solomon	.10
299	Elliott Maddox	.10
300	Paul Molitor	5.00
301	Matt Keough	.10
302	Dodgers Future Stars (*Jack Perconte, Mike Scioscia, Fernando Valenzuela*)	2.00
303	Johnny Oates	.10
304	John Castino	.10
305	Ken Clay	.10
306	Juan Beniquez (DP)	.10
307	Gene Garber	.10
308	Rick Manning	.10
309	*Luis Salazar*	.10
310	Vida Blue (DP)	.10
311	Freddie Patek	.10
312	Rick Rhoden	.10
313	Luis Pujols	.10
314	Rich Dauer	.10
315	*Kirk Gibson*	3.00
316	Craig Minetto	.10
317	Lonnie Smith	.10
318	Steve Yeager	.10
319	Rowland Office	.10
320	Tom Burgmeier	.10
321	*Leon Durham*	.15
322	Neil Allen	.10
323	Jim Morrison (DP)	.10
324	Mike Willis	.10
325	Ray Knight	.10
326	Biff Pocoroba	.10
327	Moose Haas	.10
328	Twins Future Stars (*Dave Engle*, Greg Johnston, Gary Ward)	.15
329	Joaquin Andujar	.10
330	Frank White	.10
331	Dennis Lamp	.10
332	Lee Lacy (DP)	.10
333	Sid Monge	.10
334	Dane Iorg	.10
335	Rick Cerone	.10
336	Eddie Whitson	.10
337	Lynn Jones	.10
338	Checklist 243-363	.10
339	John Ellis	.10
340	Bruce Kison	.10
341	Dwayne Murphy	.10
342	Eric Rasmussen (DP)	.10
343	Frank Taveras	.10
344	Byron McLaughlin	.10
345	Warren Cromartie	.10
346	Larry Christenson (DP)	.10
347	*Harold Baines*	8.00
348	Bob Sykes	.10
349	Glenn Hoffman	.10
350	J.R. Richard	.15
351	Otto Velez	.10
352	Dick Tidrow (DP)	.10
353	Terry Kennedy	.10
354	Mario Soto	.10
355	Bob Horner	.10
356	Padres Future Stars (George Stablein, Craig Stimac, Tom Tellmann)	.10
357	Jim Slaton	.10
358	Mark Wagner	.10
359	Tom Hausman	.10
360	Willie Wilson	.15
361	Joe Strain	.10
362	Bo Diaz	.10
363	Geoff Zahn	.10
364	*Mike Davis*	.10
365	Graig Nettles (DP)	.15
366	Mike Ramsey	.10
367	Denny Martinez	.10
368	Leon Roberts	.10
369	Frank Tanana	.10
370	Dave Winfield	4.00
371	Charlie Hough	.10
372	Jay Johnstone	.10
373	Pat Underwood	.10
374	Tom Hutton	.10
375	Dave Concepcion	.10
376	Ron Reed	.10
377	Jerry Morales	.10
378	Dave Rader	.10
379	Lary Sorensen	.10
380	Willie Stargell	1.00
381	Cubs Future Stars (Carlos Lezcano, Steve Macko, Randy Martz)	.10
382	*Paul Mirabella*	.10
383	Eric Soderholm (DP)	.10
384	Mike Sadek	.10
385	Joe Sambito	.10
386	Dave Edwards	.10
387	Phil Niekro	.90
388	Andre Thornton	.10
389	Marty Pattin	.10
390	Cesar Geronimo	.10
391	Dave Lemanczyk (DP)	.10
392	Lance Parrish	.10
393	Broderick Perkins	.10
394	Woodie Fryman	.10
395	Scot Thompson	.10
396	Bill Campbell	.10
397	Julio Cruz	.10
398	Ross Baumgarten	.10
399	Orioles Future Stars (*Mike Boddicker*, Mark Corey, *Floyd Rayford*)	.20
400	Reggie Jackson	2.00
401	A.L. Championships (Royals Sweep Yankees)	.75
402	N.L. Championships (Phillies Squeak Past Astros)	.35
403	World Series (Phillies Beat Royals In 6)	.25
404	World Series Summary (Phillies Win First World Series)	.25
405	Nino Espinosa	.10
406	Dickie Noles	.10
407	Ernie Whitt	.10
408	Fernando Arroyo	.10
409	Larry Herndon	.10
410	Bert Campaneris	.10
411	Terry Puhl	.10
412	*Britt Burns*	.10
413	Tony Bernazard	.10
414	John Pacella (DP)	.10
415	Ben Oglivie	.10
416	Gary Alexander	.10
417	Dan Schatzeder	.10
418	Bobby Brown	.10
419	Tom Hume	.10
420	Keith Hernandez	.10
421	Bob Stanley	.10
422	Dan Ford	.10
423	Shane Rawley	.10
424	Yankees Future Stars (Tim Lollar, Bruce Robinson, Dennis Werth)	.10
425	Al Bumbry	.10
426	Warren Brusstar	.10
427	John D'Acquisto	.10
428	John Stearns	.10
429	Mick Kelleher	.10
430	Jim Bibby	.10
431	Dave Roberts	.10
432	Len Barker	.10
433	Rance Mulliniks	.10
434	Roger Erickson	.10
435	Jim Spencer	.10
436	Gary Lucas	.10
437	Mike Heath (DP)	.10
438	John Montefusco	.10
439	Denny Walling	.10
440	Jerry Reuss	.10
441	Ken Reitz	.10
442	Ron Pruitt	.10
443	Jim Beattie (DP)	.10
444	Garth Iorg	.10
445	Ellis Valentine	.10
446	Checklist 364-484	.10
447	Junior Kennedy (DP)	.10
448	Tim Corcoran	.10
449	Paul Mitchell	.10
450	Dave Kingman (DP)	.10
451	Indians Future Stars (Chris Bando, Tom Brennan, Sandy Wihtol)	.10
452	Renie Martin	.10
453	Rob Wilfong (DP)	.10
454	Andy Hassler	.10
455	Rick Burleson	.10
456	*Jeff Reardon*	1.50
457	Mike Lum	.10
458	Randy Jones	.10
459	Greg Gross	.10
460	Rich Gossage	.10
461	Dave McKay	.10
462	Jack Brohamer	.10
463	Milt May	.10
464	Adrian Devine	.10
465	Bill Russell	.10
466	Bob Molinaro	.10
467	Dave Stieb	.15
468	Johnny Wockenfuss	.10
469	Jeff Leonard	.10
470	Manny Trillo	.10
471	Mike Vail	.10
472	Dyar Miller (DP)	.10
473	Jose Cardenal	.10
474	Mike LaCoss	.10
475	Buddy Bell	.10
476	Jerry Koosman	.10
477	Luis Gomez	.10
478	Juan Eichelberger	.10
479	Expos Future Stars (*Bobby Pate, Tim Raines, Roberto Ramos*)	4.00
480	Carlton Fisk	.90
481	Bob Lacey (DP)	.10
482	Jim Gantner	.10
483	Mike Griffin	.10
484	Max Venable (DP)	.10
485	Garry Templeton	.10
486	Marc Hill	.10
487	Dewey Robinson	.10
488	*Damaso Garcia*	.10
489	John Littlefield (photo actually Mark Riggins)	.10
490	Eddie Murray	5.00
491	Gordy Pladson	.10
492	Barry Foote	.10
493	Dan Quisenberry	.10
494	*Bob Walk*	.20
495	Dusty Baker	.15
496	Paul Dade	.10
497	Fred Norman	.10
498	Pat Putnam	.10
499	Frank Pastore	.10
500	Jim Rice	.25
501	Tim Foli (DP)	.10
502	Giants Future Stars (Chris Bourjos, Al Hargesheimer, Mike Rowland)	.10
503	Steve McCatty	.10
504	Dale Murphy	.90
505	Jason Thompson	.10
506	Phil Huffman	.10
507	Jamie Quirk	.10
508	Rob Dressler	.10
509	Pete Mackanin	.10
510	Lee Mazzilli	.10
511	Wayne Garland	.10
512	Gary Thomasson	.10
513	Frank LaCorte	.10
514	George Riley	.10
515	Robin Yount	4.00
516	Doug Bird	.10
517	Richie Zisk	.10
518	Grant Jackson	.10
519	John Tamargo (DP)	.10
520	Steve Stone	.10
521	Sam Mejias	.10
522	Mike Colbern	.10
523	John Fulgham	.10
524	Willie Aikens	.10
525	Mike Torrez	.10
526	Phillies Future Stars (Marty Bystrom, Jay Loviglio, Jim Wright)	.10
527	Danny Goodwin	.10
528	Gary Matthews	.10
529	Dave LaRoche	.10
530	Steve Garvey	.75
531	John Curtis	.10
532	Bill Stein	.10
533	Jesus Figueroa	.10
534	*Dave Smith*	.15
535	Omar Moreno	.10
536	Bob Owchinko (DP)	.10
537	Ron Hodges	.10
538	Tom Griffin	.10
539	Rodney Scott	.10
540	Mike Schmidt (DP)	4.00
541	Steve Swisher	.10
542	Larry Bradford (DP)	.10
543	Terry Crowley	.10
544	Rich Gale	.10
545	Johnny Grubb	.10
546	Paul Moskau	.10
547	Mario Guerrero	.10
548	Dave Goltz	.10
549	Jerry Remy	.10
550	Tommy John	.20
551	Pirates Future Stars (*Vance Law, Tony Pena, Pascual Perez*)	.75
552	Steve Trout	.10
553	Tim Blackwell	.10
554	Bert Blyleven	.10
555	Cecil Cooper	.10
556	Jerry Mumphrey	.10
557	Chris Knapp	.10
558	Barry Bonnell	.10
559	Willie Montanez	.10

560 Joe Morgan .90
561 Dennis Littlejohn .10
562 Checklist 485-605 .10
563 Jim Kaat .25
564 Ron Hassey (DP) .10
565 Burt Hooton .10
566 Del Unser .10
567 Mark Bomback .10
568 Dave Revering .10
569 Al Williams (DP) .10
570 Ken Singleton .10
571 Todd Cruz .10
572 Jack Morris .25
573 Phil Garner .10
574 Bill Caudill .10
575 Tony Perez .30
576 Reggie Cleveland .10
577 Blue Jays Future Stars (Luis Leal, Brian Milner, *Ken Schrom*) .10
578 *Bill Gullickson* .20
579 Tim Flannery .10
580 Don Baylor .15
581 Roy Howell .10
582 Gaylord Perry .90
583 Larry Milbourne .10
584 Randy Lerch .10
585 Amos Otis .10
586 Silvio Martinez .10
587 Jeff Newman .10
588 Gary Lavelle .10
589 Lamar Johnson .10
590 Bruce Sutter .10
591 John Lowenstein .10
592 Steve Comer .10
593 Steve Kemp .10
594 Preston Hanna (DP) .10
595 Butch Hobson .10
596 Jerry Augustine .10
597 Rafael Landestoy .10
598 George Vukovich (DP) .10
599 Dennis Kinney .10
600 Johnny Bench 3.00
601 Don Aase .10
602 Bobby Murcer .10
603 John Verhoeven .10
604 Rob Picciolo .10
605 Don Sutton .90
606 Reds Future Stars (Bruce Berenyi, Geoff Combe, Paul Householder) (DP) .10
607 Dave Palmer .10
608 Greg Pryor .10
609 Lynn McGlothen .10
610 Darrell Porter .10
611 Rick Matula (DP) .10
612 Duane Kuiper .10
613 Jim Anderson .10
614 Dave Rozema .10
615 Rick Dempsey .10
616 Rick Wise .10
617 Craig Reynolds .10
618 John Milner .10
619 Steve Henderson .10
620 Dennis Eckersley .50
621 Tom Donohue .10
622 Randy Moffitt .10
623 Sal Bando .10
624 Bob Welch .10
625 Bill Buckner .15
626 Tigers Future Stars (Dave Steffen, Jerry Ujdur, Roger Weaver) .10
627 Luis Tiant .10
628 Vic Correll .10
629 Tony Armas .10
630 Steve Carlton 2.00
631 Ron Jackson .10
632 Alan Bannister .10
633 Bill Lee .10
634 Doug Flynn .10
635 Bobby Bonds .10
636 Al Hrabosky .10
637 Jerry Narron .10
638 Checklist 606 .10
639 Carney Lansford .10
640 Dave Parker .50
641 Mark Belanger .10
642 Vern Ruhle .10
643 *Lloyd Moseby* .20
644 Ramon Aviles (DP) .10
645 Rick Reuschel .10
646 Marvis Foley .10
647 Dick Drago .10
648 Darrell Evans .15
649 Manny Sarmiento .10
650 Bucky Dent .10
651 Pedro Guerrero .10
652 John Montague .10
653 Bill Fahey .10
654 Ray Burris .10
655 Dan Driessen .10
656 Jon Matlack .10
657 Mike Cubbage (DP) .10
658 Milt Wilcox .10
659 Brewers Future Stars (John Flinn, Ed Romero, Ned Yost) .10
660 Gary Carter .75
661 Orioles Team (Earl Weaver) .25
662 Red Sox Team (Ralph Houk) .15
663 Angels Team (Jim Fregosi) .10
664 White Sox Team (Tony LaRussa) .25
665 Indians Team (Dave Garcia) .10
666 Tigers Team (Sparky Anderson) .30
667 Royals Team (Jim Frey) .10
668 Brewers Team (Bob Rodgers) .10
669 Twins Team (John Goryl) .10
670 Yankees Team (Gene Michael) .25
671 A's Team (Billy Martin) .25
672 Mariners Team (Maury Wills) .15
673 Rangers Team (Don Zimmer) .15
674 Blue Jays Team (Bobby Mattick) .10
675 Braves Team (Bobby Cox) .25
676 Cubs Team (Joe Amalfitano) .15
677 Reds Team (John McNamara) .10
678 Astros Team (Bill Virdon) .10
679 Dodgers Team (Tom Lasorda) .40
680 Expos Team (Dick Williams) .15
681 Mets Team (Joe Torre) .25
682 Phillies Team (Dallas Green) .25
683 Pirates Team (Chuck Tanner) .15
684 Cardinals Team (Whitey Herzog) .25
685 Padres Team (Frank Howard) .15
686 Giants Team (Dave Bristol) .10
687 Jeff Jones .10
688 Kiko Garcia .10
689 Red Sox Future Stars (*Bruce Hurst*, Keith MacWhorter, *Reid Nichols*) .60
690 Bob Watson .10
691 Dick Ruthven .10
692 Lenny Randle .10
693 *Steve Howe* .20
694 Bud Harrelson (DP) .10
695 Kent Tekulve .10
696 Alan Ashby .10
697 Rick Waits .10
698 Mike Jorgensen .10
699 Glenn Abbott .10
700 George Brett 6.00
701 Joe Rudi .10
702 George Medich .10
703 Alvis Woods .10
704 Bill Travers (DP) .10
705 Ted Simmons .10
706 Dave Ford .10
707 Dave Cash .10
708 Doyle Alexander .10
709 Alan Trammell (DP) .50
710 Ron LeFlore (DP) .10
711 Joe Ferguson .10
712 Bill Bonham .10
713 Bill North .10
714 Pete Redfern .10
715 Bill Madlock .10
716 Glenn Borgmann .10
717 Jim Barr (DP) .10
718 Larry Biittner .10
719 Sparky Lyle .10
720 Fred Lynn .10
721 Toby Harrah .10
722 Joe Niekro .10
723 Bruce Bochte .10
724 Lou Piniella .10
725 Steve Rogers .10
726 Rick Monday .10

1981 Topps Traded

The 132 cards in this extension set are numbered from 727 to 858, technically making them a high-numbered series of the regular Topps set. The set was not packaged in gum packs, but rather placed in a specially designed red box and sold through baseball card dealers only. While many complained about the method, the fact remains, even at higher prices, the set has done well for its owners as it features not only mid-season trades, but also single-player rookie cards of some of the hottest prospects. The cards measure 2-1/2" x 3-1/2".

MT
Complete Set (132): 30.00
Common Player: .20
727 Danny Ainge 6.00
728 Doyle Alexander .20
729 Gary Alexander .20
730 Billy Almon .20
731 Joaquin Andujar .20
732 Bob Bailor .20
733 Juan Beniquez .20
734 Dave Bergman .20
735 Tony Bernazard .20
736 Larry Biittner .20
737 Doug Bird .20
738 Bert Blyleven .30
739 Mark Bomback .20
740 Bobby Bonds .25
741 Rick Bosetti .20
742 Hubie Brooks .35
743 Rick Burleson .20
744 Ray Burris .20
745 Jeff Burroughs .20
746 Enos Cabell .20
747 Ken Clay .20
748 Mark Clear .20
749 Larry Cox .20
750 Hector Cruz .20
751 Victor Cruz .20
752 Mike Cubbage .20
753 Dick Davis .20
754 Brian Doyle .20
755 Dick Drago .20
756 Leon Durham .20
757 Jim Dwyer .20
758 Dave Edwards .20
759 Jim Essian .20
760 Bill Fahey .20
761 Rollie Fingers 2.50
762 Carlton Fisk 7.50
763 Barry Foote .20
764 Ken Forsch .20
765 Kiko Garcia .20
766 Cesar Geronimo .20
767 Gary Gray .20
768 Mickey Hatcher .20
769 Steve Henderson .20
770 Marc Hill .20
771 Butch Hobson .20
772 Rick Honeycutt .20
773 Roy Howell .20
774 Mike Ivie .20
775 Roy Lee Jackson .20
776 Cliff Johnson .20
777 Randy Jones .20
778 Ruppert Jones .20
779 Mick Kelleher .20
780 Terry Kennedy .20
781 Dave Kingman .20
782 Bob Knepper .20
783 Ken Kravec .20
784 Bob Lacey .20
785 Dennis Lamp .20
786 Rafael Landestoy .20
787 Ken Landreaux .20
788 Carney Lansford .20
789 Dave LaRoche .20
790 Joe Lefebvre .20
791 Ron LeFlore .20
792 Randy Lerch .20
793 Sixto Lezcano .20
794 John Littlefield .20
795 Mike Lum .20
796 Greg Luzinski .50
797 Fred Lynn .20
798 Jerry Martin .20
799 Buck Martinez .20
800 Gary Matthews .20
801 Mario Mendoza .20
802 Larry Milbourne .20
803 Rick Miller .20
804 John Montefusco .20
805 Jerry Morales .20
806 Jose Morales .20
807 Joe Morgan 3.00
808 Jerry Mumphrey .20
809 Gene Nelson .20
810 Ed Ott .20
811 Bob Owchinko .20
812 Gaylord Perry 2.50
813 Mike Phillips .20
814 Darrell Porter .20
815 Mike Proly .20
816 Tim Raines 12.00
817 Lenny Randle .20
818 Doug Rau .20
819 Jeff Reardon 1.00
820 Ken Reitz .20
821 Steve Renko .20
822 Rick Reuschel .20
823 Dave Revering .20
824 Dave Roberts .20
825 Leon Roberts .20
826 Joe Rudi .20
827 Kevin Saucier .20
828 Tony Scott .20
829 Bob Shirley .20
830 Ted Simmons .20
831 Lary Sorensen .20
832 Jim Spencer .20
833 Harry Spilman .20
834 Fred Stanley .20
835 Rusty Staub .45
836 Bill Stein .20
837 Joe Strain .20
838 Bruce Sutter .20
839 Don Sutton 2.50
840 Steve Swisher .20
841 Frank Tanana .20
842 Gene Tenace .20
843 Jason Thompson .20
844 Dickie Thon .20
845 Bill Travers .20
846 Tom Underwood .20
847 John Urrea .20
848 Mike Vail .20
849 Ellis Valentine .20
850 Fernando Valenzuela 2.00
851 Pete Vuckovich .20
852 Mark Wagner .20
853 Bob Walk .20
854 Claudell Washington .20
855 Dave Winfield 12.00
856 Geoff Zahn .20
857 Richie Zisk .20
858 Checklist 727-858 .10

1981 Topps Team Card Sheet

Via a special mail-in offer, uncut sheets of team cards from the 1981 Topps issue were made available to collectors.

MT
Team card sheet 20.00

1981 Topps Home Team 5x7 Photos

Once again testing the popularity of large cards, Topps issued 4-7/8" x 6-7/8" cards in two different sets. The Home Team cards feature a large color photo, facsimile autograph and white border on the front. Backs have the player's name, team, position and a checklist at the bottom. The 102 cards were sold in limited areas corresponding to the teams' geographic home. It was also possible to order the whole set by mail. Eleven teams are involved in the issue, with the number of players from each team ranging from 6 to 12. Although it is an attractive set featuring many stars, ready availability and many collectors' aversion to large cards keep prices relatively low today.

MT
Complete Set (102): 24.00
Common Player: .25
(1) Dusty Baker .30
(2) Don Baylor .40
(3) Rick Burleson .25
(4) Rod Carew 1.00
(5) Ron Cey .25
(6) Steve Garvey .75
(7) Bobby Grich .25
(8) Butch Hobson .25
(9) Burt Hooton .25
(10) Steve Howe .25
(11) Dave Lopes .25
(12) Fred Lynn .25
(13) Rick Monday .25
(14) Jerry Reuss .25
(15) Bill Russell .25
(16) Reggie Smith .25
(17) Bob Welch .25
(18) Steve Yeager .25
(19) Buddy Bell .25
(20) Cesar Cedeno .25
(21) Jose Cruz .25
(22) Art Howe .25
(23) Jon Matlack .25
(24) Al Oliver .25
(25) Terry Puhl .25
(26) Mickey Rivers .25
(27) Nolan Ryan 4.00
(28) Jim Sundberg .25
(29) Don Sutton .90
(30) Bump Wills .25
(31) Tim Blackwell .25
(32) Bill Buckner .25
(33) Britt Burns .25
(34) Ivan DeJesus .25
(35) Rich Dotson .25
(36) Leon Durham .25
(37) Ed Farmer .25
(38) Lamar Johnson .25
(39) Dave Kingman .30
(40) Mike Krukow .25
(41) Ron LeFlore .25
(42) Chet Lemon .25
(43) Bob Molinaro .25
(44) Jim Morrison .25
(45) Wayne Nordhagen .25
(46) Ken Reitz .25
(47) Rick Reuschel .25
(48) Mike Tyson .25
(49) Neil Allen .25
(50) Rick Cerone .25
(51) Bucky Dent .25
(52) Doug Flynn .25
(53) Rich Gossage .50
(54) Ron Guidry .30
(55) Reggie Jackson 1.00
(56) Tommy John .50
(57) Ruppert Jones .25
(58) Rudy May .25
(59) Lee Mazzilli .25
(60) Graig Nettles .25
(61) Willie Randolph .25
(62) Rusty Staub .35
(63) Frank Taveras .25
(64) Alex Trevino .25
(65) Bob Watson .25
(66) Dave Winfield 1.00
(67) Bob Boone .40
(68) Larry Bowa .25
(69) Steve Carlton 1.00
(70) Greg Luzinski .25
(71) Garry Maddox .25
(72) Bake McBride .25
(73) Tug McGraw .25
(74) Pete Rose 2.00
(75) Dick Ruthven .25
(76) Mike Schmidt 1.50
(77) Manny Trillo .25
(78) Del Unser .25
(79) Tom Burgmeier .25
(80) Dennis Eckersley .60
(81) Dwight Evans .25
(82) Carlton Fisk .75
(83) Glenn Hoffman .25
(84) Carney Lansford .25
(85) Tony Perez .30
(86) Jim Rice .35
(87) Bob Stanley .25
(88) Dave Stapleton .25
(89) Frank Tanana .25
(90) Carl Yastrzemski 1.00
(91) Johnny Bench 1.00
(92) Dave Collins .25
(93) Dave Concepcion .25
(94) Dan Driessen .25
(95) George Foster .25
(96) Ken Griffey .25
(97) Tom Hume .25
(98) Ray Knight .25
(99) Joe Nolan .25
(100) Ron Oester .25
(101) Tom Seaver 1.00
(102) Mario Soto .25

1981 Topps National 5x7 Photos

This set is the other half of Topps' efforts with large cards in 1981. Measuring 4-7/8" x 6-7/8", the National photo issue was limited to 15 cards. They were sold in areas not covered by the Home Team sets and feature ten cards which carry the same photos as found in the Home Team set, but with no checklist on the backs. Five cards are unique to the National set: George Brett, Cecil Cooper, Jim Palmer, Dave Parker and Ted Simmons. With their wide distribution and a limited demand, there are currently plenty of these cards to meet the demand, thus keeping prices fairly low.

		MT
	Complete Set (15):	4.00
	Common Player:	.15
(1)	Buddy Bell	.15
(2)	Johnny Bench	.45
(3)	George Brett	.75
(4)	Rod Carew	.45
(5)	Cecil Cooper	.15
(6)	Steve Garvey	.35
(7)	Rich Gossage	.20
(8)	Reggie Jackson	.45
(9)	Jim Palmer	.45
(10)	Dave Parker	.15
(11)	Jim Rice	.20
(12)	Pete Rose	1.00
(13)	Mike Schmidt	.75
(14)	Tom Seaver	.45
(15)	Ted Simmons	.15

1981 Topps Mets Magic Memories

Celebrating 20 years of N.Y. Mets baseball, the team issued a set of "Magic Memories" cards. Topps produced 20,000 each of the 6-7/8" x 4-7/8" cards. The cards were individually cello wrapped. Cards #1-2 were distributed at the team's Aug. 27 game; cards #3-4 at the Sept. 22 contest. The first card is a sepia team photo of the 1962 Mets. Cards #2-3 are color team photos from 1969 and 1973. The team photo cards have player stats on back. The fourth card depicts four of the Mets managers on front, with biographies on back.

		MT
	Complete Set (4):	12.00
	Common Player:	3.00
1	1962 Mets team photo	3.00
2	1969 Mets team photo	3.00
3	1973 Mets team photo	3.00
4	New York Mets managers (Casey Stengel, Gil Hodges, Yogi Berra, Joe Torre)	6.00

1981 Topps Scratchoffs

Sold as a separate issue with bubble gum, this 108-card set was issued in three-card panels that measure 3-1/4" x 5-1/4". Each individual card measures 1-13/16" x 3-1/4" and contains a small player photo alongside a series of black dots designed to be scratched off as part of a baseball game. Cards of National League players have a green backgrounds, while American League players have a red background. While there are 108 different players in the set, there are 144 possible panel combinations. An intact panel of three cards is valued approximately 20-25 percent more the sum of the individual cards.

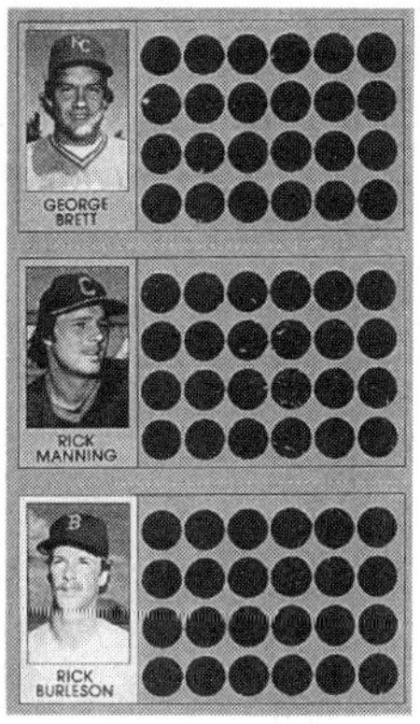

		MT
	Complete Set (108):	7.50
	Common Player:	.15
1	George Brett	.45
2	Cecil Cooper	.15
3	Reggie Jackson	.25
4	Al Oliver	.15
5	Fred Lynn	.15
6	Tony Armas	.15
7	Ben Oglivie	.15
8	Tony Perez	.20
9	Eddie Murray	.25
10	Robin Yount	.25
11	Steve Kemp	.15
12	Joe Charboneau	.20
13	Jim Rice	.20
14	Lance Parrish	.15
15	John Mayberry	.15
16	Richie Zisk	.15
17	Ken Singleton	.15
18	Rod Carew	.25
19	Rick Manning	.15
20	Willie Wilson	.15
21	Buddy Bell	.15
22	Dave Revering	.15
23	Tom Paciorek	.15
24	Champ Summers	.15
25	Carney Lansford	.15
26	Lamar Johnson	.15
27	Willie Aikens	.15
28	Rick Cerone	.15
29	Al Bumbry	.15
30	Bruce Bochte	.15
31	Mickey Rivers	.15
32	Mike Hargrove	.15
33	John Castino	.15
34	Chet Lemon	.15
35	Paul Molitor	.25
36	Willie Randolph	.15
37	Rick Burleson	.15
38	Alan Trammell	.15
39	Rickey Henderson	.25
40	Dan Meyer	.15
41	Ken Landreaux	.15
42	Damaso Garcia	.15
43	Roy Smalley	.15
44	Otto Velez	.15
45	Sixto Lezcano	.15
46	Toby Harrah	.15
47	Frank White	.15
48	Dave Stapleton	.15
49	Steve Stone	.15
50	Jim Palmer	.25
51	Larry Gura	.15
52	Tommy John	.15
53	Mike Norris	.15
54	Ed Farmer	.15
55	Bill Buckner	.15
56	Steve Garvey	.20
57	Reggie Smith	.15
58	Bake McBride	.15
59	Dave Parker	.15
60	Mike Schmidt	.45
61	Bob Horner	.15
62	Pete Rose	.50
63	Ted Simmons	.15
64	Johnny Bench	.25
65	George Foster	.15
66	Gary Carter	.20
67	Keith Hernandez	.15
68	Ozzie Smith	.25
69	Dave Kingman	.15
70	Jack Clark	.15
71	Dusty Baker	.15
72	Dale Murphy	.20
73	Ron Cey	.15
74	Greg Luzinski	.15
75	Lee Mazzilli	.15
76	Gary Matthews	.15
77	Cesar Cedeno	.15
78	Warren Cromartie	.15
79	Steve Henderson	.15
80	Ellis Valentine	.15
81	Mike Easler	.15
82	Garry Templeton	.15
83	Jose Cruz	.15
84	Dave Collins	.15
85	George Hendrick	.15
86	Gene Richards	.15
87	Terry Whitfield	.15
88	Terry Puhl	.15
89	Larry Parrish	.15
90	Andre Dawson	.20
91	Ken Griffey	.15
92	Dave Lopes	.15
93	Doug Flynn	.15
94	Ivan DeJesus	.15
95	Dave Concepcion	.15
96	John Stearns	.15
97	Jerry Mumphrey	.15
98	Jerry Martin	.15
99	Art Howe	.15
100	Omar Moreno	.15
101	Ken Reitz	.15
102	Phil Garner	.15
103	Jerry Reuss	.15
104	Steve Carlton	.25
105	Jim Bibby	.15
106	Steve Rogers	.15
107	Tom Seaver	.30
108	Vida Blue	.15

1981 Topps Stickers

The 262 stickers in this full-color set measure 1-15/16" x 2-9/16" and are numbered on both the front and back. They were produced for Topps by the Panini Company of Italy. The set includes a series of "All-Star" stickers printed on silver or gold "foil". An album to house the stickers was also available.

		MT
	Complete Set (262):	15.00
	Common Player:	.05
	Sticker Album:	2.00
1	Steve Stone	.05
2	Tommy John, Mike Norris	.05
3	Rudy May	.05
4	Mike Norris	.05
5	Len Barker	.05
6	Mike Norris	.05
7	Dan Quisenberry	.05
8	Rich Gossage	.10
9	George Brett	.25
10	Cecil Cooper	.05
11	Reggie Jackson, Ben Oglivie	.10
12	Gorman Thomas	.05
13	Cecil Cooper	.05
14	George Brett, Ben Oglivie	.10
15	Rickey Henderson	.25
16	Willie Wilson	.05
17	Bill Buckner	.05
18	Keith Hernandez	.05
19	Mike Schmidt	.25
20	Bob Horner	.05
21	Mike Schmidt	.25
22	George Hendrick	.05
23	Ron LeFlore	.05
24	Omar Moreno	.05
25	Steve Carlton	.20
26	Joe Niekro	.05
27	Don Sutton	.15
28	Steve Carlton	.20
29	Steve Carlton	.20
30	Nolan Ryan	.50
31	Rollie Fingers, Tom Hume	.05
32	Bruce Sutter	.05
33	Ken Singleton	.05
34	Eddie Murray	.20
35	Al Bumbry	.05
36	Rich Dauer	.05
37	Scott McGregor	.05
38	Rick Dempsey	.05
39	Jim Palmer	.20
40	Steve Stone	.05
41	Jim Rice	.10
42	Fred Lynn	.05
43	Carney Lansford	.05
44	Tony Perez	.10
45	Carl Yastrzemski	.30
46	Carlton Fisk	.10
47	Dave Stapleton	.05
48	Dennis Eckersley	.05
49	Rod Carew	.20
50	Brian Downing	.05
51	Don Baylor	.05
52	Rick Burleson	.05
53	Bobby Grich	.05
54	Butch Hobson	.05
55	Andy Hassler	.05
56	Frank Tanana	.05
57	Chet Lemon	.05
58	Lamar Johnson	.05
59	Wayne Nordhagen	.05
60	Jim Morrison	.05
61	Bob Molinaro	.05
62	Rich Dotson	.05
63	Britt Burns	.05
64	Ed Farmer	.05
65	Toby Harrah	.05
66	Joe Charboneau	.10
67	Miguel Dilone	.05
68	Mike Hargrove	.05
69	Rick Manning	.05
70	Andre Thornton	.05
71	Ron Hassey	.05
72	Len Barker	.05
73	Lance Parrish	.05
74	Steve Kemp	.05
75	Alan Trammell	.05
76	Champ Summers	.05
77	Rick Peters	.05
78	Kirk Gibson	.05
79	Johnny Wockenfuss	.05
80	Jack Morris	.05
81	Willie Wilson	.05
82	George Brett	.25
83	Frank White	.05
84	Willie Aikens	.05
85	Clint Hurdle	.05
86	Hal McRae	.05
87	Dennis Leonard	.05
88	Larry Gura	.05
89	American League Pennant Winner (Kansas City Royals Team)	.05
90	American League Pennant Winner (Kansas City Royals Team)	.05
91	Paul Molitor	.20
92	Ben Oglivie	.05
93	Cecil Cooper	.05
94	Ted Simmons	.05
95	Robin Yount	.25
96	Gorman Thomas	.05
97	Mike Caldwell	.05
98	Moose Haas	.05
99	John Castino	.05
100	Roy Smalley	.05
101	Ken Landreaux	.05
102	Butch Wynegar	.05
103	Ron Jackson	.05
104	Jerry Koosman	.05
105	Roger Erickson	.05
106	Doug Corbett	.05
107	Reggie Jackson	.25
108	Willie Randolph	.05
109	Rick Cerone	.05
110	Bucky Dent	.05
111	Dave Winfield	.20
112	Ron Guidry	.10
113	Rich Gossage	.10
114	Tommy John	.10
115	Rickey Henderson	.25
116	Tony Armas	.05
117	Dave Revering	.05
118	Wayne Gross	.05
119	Dwayne Murphy	.05
120	Jeff Newman	.05
121	Rick Langford	.05
122	Mike Norris	.05
123	Bruce Bochte	.05
124	Tom Paciorek	.05
125	Dan Meyer	.05
126	Julio Cruz	.05
127	Richie Zisk	.05
128	Floyd Bannister	.05
129	Shane Rawley	.05
130	Buddy Bell	.05
131	Al Oliver	.05
132	Mickey Rivers	.05
133	Jim Sundberg	.05
134	Bump Wills	.05
135	Jon Matlack	.05
136	Danny Darwin	.05
137	Damaso Garcia	.05
138	Otto Velez	.05
139	John Mayberry	.05
140	Alfredo Griffin	.05
141	Alvis Woods	.05
142	Dave Stieb	.05
143	Jim Clancy	.05
144	Gary Matthews	.05
145	Bob Horner	.05
146	Dale Murphy	.15
147	Chris Chambliss	.05
148	Phil Niekro	.15
149	Glenn Hubbard	.05
150	Rick Camp	.05
151	Dave Kingman	.05
152	Bill Caudill	.05
153	Bill Buckner	.05
154	Barry Foote	.05
155	Mike Tyson	.05
156	Ivan DeJesus	.05
157	Rick Reuschel	.05
158	Ken Reitz	.05
159	George Foster	.05
160	Johnny Bench	.25
161	Dave Concepcion	.05
162	Dave Collins	.05
163	Ken Griffey	.05
164	Dan Driessen	.05
165	Tom Seaver	.20
166	Tom Hume	.05
167	Cesar Cedeno	.05
168	Rafael Landestoy	.05
169	Jose Cruz	.05
170	Art Howe	.05
171	Terry Puhl	.05
172	Joe Sambito	.05
173	Nolan Ryan	.50
174	Joe Niekro	.05
175	Dave Lopes	.05
176	Steve Garvey	.15
177	Ron Cey	.05
178	Reggie Smith	.05
179	Bill Russell	.05
180	Burt Hooton	.05
181	Jerry Reuss	.05
182	Dusty Baker	.05
183	Larry Parrish	.05
184	Gary Carter	.15
185	Rodney Scott	.05
186	Ellis Valentine	.05
187	Andre Dawson	.15
188	Warren Cromartie	.05
189	Chris Speier	.05
190	Steve Rogers	.05
191	Lee Mazzilli	.05
192	Doug Flynn	.05
193	Steve Henderson	.05
194	John Stearns	.05
195	Joel Youngblood	.05
196	Frank Taveras	.05
197	Pat Zachry	.05
198	Neil Allen	.05
199	Mike Schmidt	.25
200	Pete Rose	.40
201	Larry Bowa	.05
202	Bake McBride	.05
203	Bob Boone	.05
204	Garry Maddox	.05
205	Tug McGraw	.05
206	Steve Carlton	.20
207	National League Pennant Winner (Philadelphia Phillies Team)	.05
208	National League Pennant Winner (Philadelphia Phillies Team)	.05
209	Phil Garner	.05
210	Dave Parker	.05
211	Omar Moreno	.05
212	Mike Easler	.05
213	Bill Madlock	.05
214	Ed Ott	.05
215	Willie Stargell	.20
216	Jim Bibby	.05
217	Garry Templeton	.05
218	Sixto Lezcano	.05
219	Keith Hernandez	.05
220	George Hendrick	.05
221	Bruce Sutter	.05
222	Ken Oberkfell	.05
223	Tony Scott	.05
224	Darrell Porter	.05
225	Gene Richards	.05
226	Broderick Perkins	.05
227	Jerry Mumphrey	.05
228	Luis Salazar	.05
229	Jerry Turner	.05
230	Ozzie Smith	.20
231	John Curtis	.05
232	Rick Wise	.05
233	Terry Whitfield	.05
234	Jack Clark	.05
235	Darrell Evans	.10
236	Larry Herndon	.05
237	Milt May	.05
238	Greg Minton	.05
239	Vida Blue	.05
240	Eddie Whitson	.05
241	Cecil Cooper	.05
242	Willie Randolph	.05
243	George Brett	.25
244	Robin Yount	.25
245	Reggie Jackson	.30
246	Al Oliver	.05
247	Willie Wilson	.05
248	Rick Cerone	.05
249	Steve Stone	.05
250	Tommy John	.10
251	Rich Gossage	.10
252	Steve Garvey	.15
253	Phil Garner	.05
254	Mike Schmidt	.25
255	Garry Templeton	.05

256 George Hendrick .05
257 Dave Parker .05
258 Cesar Cedeno .05
259 Gary Carter .15
260 Jim Bibby .05
261 Steve Carlton .25
262 Tug McGraw .05

1981 Topps Thirst Break Comics

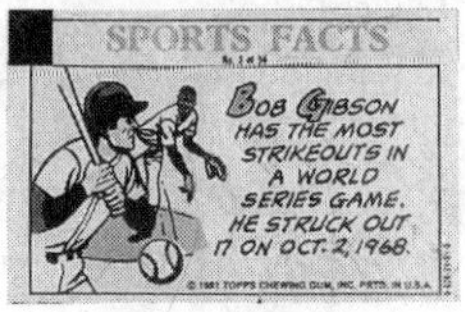

These 2-1/2" x 1-5/8" wax paper comics were the wrappers for Thirst Break Gum, a Topps test issue distributed to parts of Ohio and Pennsylvania. Each orange foil pack contained five comics (labeled as "Sport Facts") which were folded and wrapped around five soft gum pieces. A total of 56 different comics were produced, 20 of which were baseball players. The great majority of comics found today are slightly wrinkled and stained by the gum, but are usually considered to be in Near Mint condition.

MT
Complete (Baseball) Set (20):
Common Player: 2.50
1 Shortest Game 2.50
2 Lefty Gomez 2.50
3 Bob Gibson 2.50
4 Hoyt Wilhelm 2.50
5 Babe Ruth 10.00
6 Toby Harrah 2.50
7 Carl Hubbell 2.50
8 Harvey Haddix 2.50
9 Steve Carlton 2.50
10 Nolan Ryan, Tom Seaver, Steve Carlton 9.00
11 Lou Brock 2.50
12 Mickey Mantle 12.00
13 Tom Seaver 6.00
14 Don Drysdale 2.50
15 Billy Williams 2.50
20 Christy Mathewson 2.50
21 Hank Aaron 9.00
22 Ron Blomberg 2.50
23 Joe Nuxhall 2.50
24 Reggie Jackson 6.00

1982 Topps

At 792 cards, this was the largest issue produced up to that time, eliminating the need for double-printed cards. The 2-1/2" x 3-1/2" cards feature a front color photo with a pair of stripes down the left side. Under the player's photo are found his name, team and position. A facsimile autograph runs across the front of the picture. Specialty cards include great performances of the previous season, All-Stars, statistical leaders and "In Action" cards (indicated by "IA" in listings below). Managers and hitting/pitching leaders have cards, while rookies are shown as "Future Stars" on group cards.

MT
Complete Set (792): 100.00
Common Player: .10
Wax Box: 225.00
1 Steve Carlton (1981 Highlight) .25
2 Ron Davis (1981 Highlight) .10
3 Tim Raines (1981 Highlight) .15
4 Pete Rose (1981 Highlight) .75
5 Nolan Ryan (1981 Highlight) 3.00
6 Fernando Valenzuela (1981 Highlight) .10
7 Scott Sanderson .10
8 Rich Dauer .10
9 Ron Guidry .15
10 Ron Guidry (In Action) .10
11 Gary Alexander .10
12 Moose Haas .10
13 Lamar Johnson .10
14 Steve Howe .10
15 Ellis Valentine .10
16 Steve Comer .10
17 Darrell Evans .15
18 Fernando Arroyo .10
19 Ernie Whitt .10
20 Garry Maddox .10
21 Orioles Future Stars (*Bob Bonner*, *Cal Ripken, Jr.*, *Jeff Schneider*) 60.00
22 Jim Beattie .10
23 Willie Hernandez .10
24 Dave Frost .10
25 Jerry Remy .10
26 Jorge Orta .10
27 Tom Herr .10
28 John Urrea .10
29 Dwayne Murphy .10
30 Tom Seaver 1.50
31 Tom Seaver (In Action) 1.00
32 Gene Garber .10
33 Jerry Morales .10
34 Joe Sambito .10
35 Willie Aikens .10
36 Rangers Batting/Pitching Leaders (George Medich, Al Oliver) .10
37 Dan Graham .10
38 Charlie Lea .10
39 Lou Whitaker .20
40 Dave Parker .20
41 Dave Parker (In Action) .10
42 Rick Sofield .10
43 Mike Cubbage .10
44 Britt Burns .10
45 Rick Cerone .10
46 Jerry Augustine .10
47 Jeff Leonard .10
48 Bobby Castillo .10
49 Alvis Woods .10
50 Buddy Bell .10
51 Chicago Cubs Future Stars (*Jay Howell*, *Carlos Lezcano*, *Ty Waller*) .40
52 Larry Andersen .10
53 Greg Gross .10
54 Ron Hassey .10
55 Rick Burleson .10
56 Mark Littell .10
57 Craig Reynolds .10
58 John D'Acquisto .10
59 *Rich Gedman* .10
60 Tony Armas .10
61 Tommy Boggs .10
62 Mike Tyson .10
63 Mario Soto .10
64 Lynn Jones .10
65 Terry Kennedy .10
66 Astros Batting/Pitching Leaders (Art Howe, Nolan Ryan) .75
67 Rich Gale .10
68 Roy Howell .10
69 Al Williams .10
70 Tim Raines 1.00
71 Roy Lee Jackson .10
72 Rick Auerbach .10
73 Buddy Solomon .10
74 Bob Clark .10
75 Tommy John .30
76 Greg Pryor .10
77 Miguel Dilone .10
78 George Medich .10
79 Bob Bailor .10
80 Jim Palmer 1.00
81 Jim Palmer (In Action) .30
82 Bob Welch .10
83 Yankees Future Stars (*Steve Balboni*, *Andy McGaffigan*, *Andre Robertson*) .15
84 Rennie Stennett .10
85 Lynn McGlothen .10
86 Dane Iorg .10
87 Matt Keough .10
88 Biff Pocoroba .10
89 Steve Henderson .10
90 Nolan Ryan 12.00
91 Carney Lansford .10
92 Brad Havens .10
93 Larry Hisle .10
94 Andy Hassler .10
95 Ozzie Smith 3.00
96 Royals Batting/Pitching Leaders (George Brett, Larry Gura) .35
97 Paul Moskau .10
98 Terry Bulling .10
99 Barry Bonnell .10
100 Mike Schmidt 3.00
101 Mike Schmidt (In Action) 1.25
102 Dan Briggs .10
103 Bob Lacey .10
104 Rance Mulliniks .10
105 Kirk Gibson .20
106 Enrique Romo .10
107 Wayne Krenchicki .10
108 Bob Sykes .10
109 Dave Revering .10
110 Carlton Fisk 1.00
111 Carlton Fisk (In Action) .65
112 Billy Sample .10
113 Steve McCatty .10
114 Ken Landreaux .10
115 Gaylord Perry .60
116 Jim Wohlford .10
117 Rawly Eastwick .10
118 Expos Future Stars (*Terry Francona*, *Brad Mills*, *Bryn Smith*) .20
119 Joe Pittman .10
120 Gary Lucas .10
121 Ed Lynch .10
122 Jamie Easterly .10
123 Danny Goodwin .10
124 Reid Nichols .10
125 Danny Ainge 1.00
126 Braves Batting/Pitching Leaders (Rick Mahler, Claudell Washington) .10
127 Lonnie Smith .10
128 Frank Pastore .10
129 Checklist 1-132 .10
130 Julio Cruz .10
131 Stan Bahnsen .10
132 Lee May .10
133 Pat Underwood .10
134 Dan Ford .10
135 Andy Rincon .10
136 Lenn Sakata .10
137 George Cappuzzello .10
138 Tony Pena .10
139 Jeff Jones .10
140 Ron LeFlore .10
141 Indians Future Stars (Chris Bando, Tom Brennan, *Von Hayes*) .20
142 Dave LaRoche .10
143 Mookie Wilson .10
144 Fred Breining .10
145 Bob Horner .10
146 Mike Griffin .10
147 Denny Walling .10
148 Mickey Klutts .10
149 Pat Putnam .10
150 Ted Simmons .10
151 Dave Edwards .10
152 Ramon Aviles .10
153 Roger Erickson .10
154 Dennis Werth .10
155 Otto Velez .10
156 A's Batting/Pitching Leaders (Rickey Henderson, Steve McCatty) .15
157 Steve Crawford .10
158 Brian Downing .10
159 Larry Biittner .10
160 Luis Tiant .10
161 Batting Leaders (Carney Lansford, Bill Madlock) .10
162 Home Run Leaders (Tony Armas, Dwight Evans, Bobby Grich, Eddie Murray, Mike Schmidt) .25
163 RBI Leaders (Eddie Murray, Mike Schmidt) .50
164 Stolen Base Leaders (Rickey Henderson, Tim Raines) .50
165 Victory Leaders (Denny Martinez, Steve McCatty, Jack Morris, Tom Seaver, Pete Vuckovich) .20
166 Strikeout Leaders (Len Barker, Fernando Valenzuela) .10
167 ERA Leaders (Steve McCatty, Nolan Ryan) 1.50
168 Leading Relievers (Rollie Fingers, Bruce Sutter) .20
169 Charlie Leibrandt .10
170 Jim Bibby .10
171 Giants Future Stars (*Bob Brenly*, *Chili Davis*, *Bob Tufts*) 3.00
172 Bill Gullickson .10
173 Jamie Quirk .10
174 Dave Ford .10
175 Jerry Mumphrey .10
176 Dewey Robinson .10
177 John Ellis .10
178 Dyar Miller .10
179 Steve Garvey .75
180 Steve Garvey (In Action) .30
181 Silvio Martinez .10
182 Larry Herndon .10
183 Mike Proly .10
184 Mick Kelleher .10
185 Phil Niekro 1.00
186 Cardinals Batting/Pitching Leaders (Bob Forsch, Keith Hernandez) .10
187 Jeff Newman .10
188 Randy Martz .10
189 Glenn Hoffman .10
190 J.R. Richard .15
191 *Tim Wallach* 2.50
192 Broderick Perkins .10
193 Darrell Jackson .10
194 Mike Vail .10
195 Paul Molitor 4.00
196 Willie Upshaw .10
197 Shane Rawley .10
198 Chris Speier .10
199 Don Aase .10
200 George Brett 5.00
201 George Brett (In Action) 2.50
202 Rick Manning .10
203 Blue Jays Future Stars (*Jesse Barfield*, Brian Milner, Boomer Wells) .50
204 Gary Roenicke .10
205 Neil Allen .10
206 Tony Bernazard .10
207 Rod Scurry .10
208 Bobby Murcer .10
209 Gary Lavelle .10
210 Keith Hernandez .10
211 Dan Petry .10
212 Mario Mendoza .10
213 *Dave Stewart* 4.00
214 Brian Asselstine .10
215 Mike Krukow .10
216 White Sox Batting/Pitching Leaders (Dennis Lamp, Chet Lemon) .10
217 Bo McLaughlin .10
218 Dave Roberts .10
219 John Curtis .10
220 Manny Trillo .10
221 Jim Slaton .10
222 Butch Wynegar .10
223 Lloyd Moseby .10
224 Bruce Bochte .10
225 Mike Torrez .10
226 Checklist 133-264 .10
227 Ray Burris .10
228 Sam Mejias .10
229 Geoff Zahn .10
230 Willie Wilson .10
231 Phillies Future Stars (*Mark Davis*, *Bob Dernier*, *Ozzie Virgil*) .20
232 Terry Crowley .10
233 Duane Kuiper .10
234 Ron Hodges .10
235 Mike Easler .10
236 John Martin .10
237 Rusty Kuntz .10
238 Kevin Saucier .10
239 Jon Matlack .10
240 Bucky Dent .10
241 Bucky Dent (In Action) .10
242 Milt May .10
243 Bob Owchinko .10
244 Rufino Linares .10
245 Ken Reitz .10
246 Mets Batting/Pitching Leaders (Hubie Brooks, Mike Scott) .10
247 Pedro Guerrero .10
248 Frank LaCorte .10
249 Tim Flannery .10
250 Tug McGraw .10
251 Fred Lynn .10
252 Fred Lynn (In Action) .10
253 Chuck Baker .10
254 *George Bell* 1.00
255 Tony Perez .25
256 Tony Perez (In Action) .10
257 Larry Harlow .10
258 Bo Diaz .10
259 Rodney Scott .10
260 Bruce Sutter .10
261 Tigers Future Stars (Howard Bailey, Marty Castillo, Dave Rucker) .10
262 Doug Bair .10
263 Victor Cruz .10
264 Dan Quisenberry .10
265 Al Bumbry .10
266 Rick Leach .10
267 Kurt Bevacqua .10
268 Rickey Keeton .10
269 Jim Essian .10
270 Rusty Staub .15
271 Larry Bradford .10
272 Bump Wills .10
273 Doug Bird .10
274 *Bob Ojeda* .60
275 Bob Watson .10
276 Angels Batting/Pitching Leaders (Rod Carew, Ken Forsch) .25
277 Terry Puhl .10
278 John Littlefield .10
279 Bill Russell .10
280 Ben Oglivie .10
281 John Verhoeven .10
282 Ken Macha .10
283 Brian Allard .10
284 Bob Grich .10
285 Sparky Lyle .10
286 Bill Fahey .10
287 Alan Bannister .10
288 Garry Templeton .10
289 Bob Stanley .10
290 Ken Singleton .10
291 Pirates Future Stars (Vance Law, Bob Long, *Johnny Ray*) .15
292 Dave Palmer .10
293 Rob Picciolo .10
294 Mike LaCoss .10
295 Jason Thompson .10
296 Bob Walk .10
297 Clint Hurdle .10
298 Danny Darwin .10
299 Steve Trout .10
300 Reggie Jackson 3.00
301 Reggie Jackson (In Action) 1.50
302 Doug Flynn .10
303 Bill Caudill .10
304 Johnnie LeMaster .10
305 Don Sutton .65
306 Don Sutton (In Action) .20
307 Randy Bass .10
308 Charlie Moore .10
309 Pete Redfern .10
310 Mike Hargrove .10
311 Dodgers Batting/Pitching Leaders (Dusty Baker, Burt Hooton) .10
312 Lenny Randle .10
313 John Harris .10
314 Buck Martinez .10
315 Burt Hooton .10
316 Steve Braun .10
317 Dick Ruthven .10
318 Mike Heath .10
319 Dave Rozema .10
320 Chris Chambliss .10
321 Chris Chambliss (In Action) .10
322 Garry Hancock .10
323 Bill Lee .10
324 Steve Dillard .10
325 Jose Cruz .10
326 Pete Falcone .10
327 Joe Nolan .10
328 Ed Farmer .10
329 U.L. Washington .10
330 Rick Wise .10
331 Benny Ayala .10
332 Don Robinson .10
333 Brewers Future Stars (*Frank DiPino*, Marshall Edwards, Chuck Porter) .10
334 Aurelio Rodriguez .10
335 Jim Sundberg .10
336 Mariners Batting/Pitching Leaders (Glenn Abbott, Tom Paciorek) .10
337 Pete Rose (All-Star) 1.25
338 Dave Lopes (All-Star) .10
339 Mike Schmidt (All-Star) 1.00
340 Dave Concepcion (All-Star) .10
341 Andre Dawson (All-Star) .25
342a George Foster (All-Star no autograph) 2.50
342b George Foster (All-Star autograph on front) .15
343 Dave Parker (All-Star) .10
344 Gary Carter (All-Star) .15
345 Fernando Valenzuela (All-Star) .10
346 Tom Seaver (All-Star) .75
347 Bruce Sutter (All-Star) .10
348 Derrel Thomas .10

349 George Frazier .10
350 Thad Bosley .10
351 Reds Future Stars (Scott Brown, Geoff Combe, Paul Householder) .10
352 Dick Davis .10
353 Jack O'Connor .10
354 Roberto Ramos .10
355 Dwight Evans .10
356 Denny Lewallyn .10
357 Butch Hobson .10
358 Mike Parrott .10
359 Jim Dwyer .10
360 Len Barker .10
361 Rafael Landestoy .10
362 Jim Wright .10
363 Bob Molinaro .10
364 Doyle Alexander .10
365 Bill Madlock .10
366 Padres Batting/ Pitching Leaders (Juan Eichelberger, Luis Salazar) .10
367 Jim Kaat .20
368 Alex Trevino .10
369 Champ Summers .10
370 Mike Norris .10
371 Jerry Don Gleaton .10
372 Luis Gomez .10
373 *Gene Nelson* .10
374 Tim Blackwell .10
375 Dusty Baker .15
376 Chris Welsh .10
377 Kiko Garcia .10
378 Mike Caldwell .10
379 Rob Wilfong .10
380 Dave Stieb .10
381 Red Sox Future Stars (Bruce Hurst, Dave Schmidt, Julio Valdez) .25
382 Joe Simpson .10
383a Pascual Perez (no position on front) 8.00
383b Pascual Perez ("Pitcher" on front) .10
384 Keith Moreland .10
385 Ken Forsch .10
386 Jerry White .10
387 Tom Veryzer .10
388 Joe Rudi .10
389 George Vukovich .10
390 Eddie Murray 4.00
391 Dave Tobik .10
392 Rick Bosetti .10
393 Al Hrabosky .10
394 Checklist 265-396 .10
395 Omar Moreno .10
396 Twins Batting/ Pitching Leaders (Fernando Arroyo, John Castino) .10
397 Ken Brett .10
398 Mike Squires .10
399 Pat Zachry .10
400 Johnny Bench 1.50
401 Johnny Bench (In Action) .40
402 Bill Stein .10
403 Jim Tracy .10
404 Dickie Thon .10
405 Rick Reuschel .10
406 Al Holland .10
407 Danny Boone .10
408 Ed Romero .10
409 Don Cooper .10
410 Ron Cey .10
411 Ron Cey (In Action) .10
412 Luis Leal .10
413 Dan Meyer .10
414 Elias Sosa .10
415 Don Baylor .15
416 Marty Bystrom .10
417 Pat Kelly .10
418 Rangers Future Stars (John Butcher, Bobby Johnson, *Dave Schmidt*) .10
419 Steve Stone .15
420 George Hendrick .10
421 Mark Clear .10
422 Cliff Johnson .10
423 Stan Papi .10
424 Bruce Benedict .10
425 John Candelaria .10
426 Orioles Batting/ Pitching Leaders (Eddie Murray, Sammy Stewart) .25
427 Ron Oester .10
428 Lamarr Hoyt (LaMarr) .10
429 John Wathan .10
430 Vida Blue .10
431 Vida Blue (In Action) .10
432 Mike Scott .10
433 Alan Ashby .10
434 Joe Lefebvre .10
435 Robin Yount 3.50
436 Joe Strain .10
437 Juan Berenguer .10
438 Pete Mackanin .10
439 *Dave Righetti* .90
440 Jeff Burroughs .10
441 Astros Future Stars (Danny Heep, Billy Smith, Bobby Sprowl) .10
442 Bruce Kison .10
443 Mark Wagner .10
444 Terry Forster .10
445 Larry Parrish .10
446 Wayne Garland .10
447 Darrell Porter .10
448 Darrell Porter (In Action) .10
449 *Luis Aguayo* .10
450 Jack Morris .10
451 Ed Miller .10
452 *Lee Smith* 8.00
453 Art Howe .10
454 Rick Langford .10
455 Tom Burgmeier .10
456 Cubs Batting & Pitching Ldrs. (Bill Buckner, Randy Martz) .10
457 Tim Stoddard .10
458 Willie Montanez .10
459 Bruce Berenyi .10
460 Jack Clark .10
461 Rich Dotson .10
462 Dave Chalk .10
463 Jim Kern .10
464 Juan Bonilla .10
465 Lee Mazzilli .10
466 Randy Lerch .10
467 Mickey Hatcher .10
468 Floyd Bannister .10
469 Ed Ott .10
470 John Mayberry .10
471 Royals Future Stars (*Atlee Hammaker*, Mike Jones, Darryl Motley) .15
472 Oscar Gamble .10
473 Mike Stanton .10
474 Ken Oberkfell .10
475 Alan Trammell .45
476 Brian Kingman .10
477 Steve Yeager .10
478 Ray Searage .10
479 Rowland Office .10
480 Steve Carlton 1.00
481 Steve Carlton (In Action) .40
482 Glenn Hubbard .10
483 Gary Woods .10
484 Ivan DeJesus .10
485 Kent Tekulve .10
486 Yankees Batting & Pitching Ldrs. (Tommy John, Jerry Mumphrey) .10
487 Bob McClure .10
488 Ron Jackson .10
489 Rick Dempsey .10
490 Dennis Eckersley .20
491 Checklist 397-528 .10
492 Joe Price .10
493 Chet Lemon .10
494 Hubie Brooks .10
495 Dennis Leonard .10
496 Johnny Grubb .10
497 Jim Anderson .10
498 Dave Bergman .10
499 Paul Mirabella .10
500 Rod Carew 1.00
501 Rod Carew (In Action) .40
502 Braves Future Stars (*Steve Bedrosian*, *Brett Butler*, Larry Owen) 2.00
503 Julio Gonzalez .10
504 Rick Peters .10
505 Graig Nettles .10
506 Graig Nettles (In Action) .10
507 Terry Harper .10
508 *Jody Davis* .15
509 Harry Spilman .10
510 Fernando Valenzuela .20
511 Ruppert Jones .10
512 Jerry Dybzinski .10
513 Rick Rhoden .10
514 Joe Ferguson .10
515 Larry Bowa .10
516 Larry Bowa (In Action) .10
517 Mark Brouhard .10
518 Garth Iorg .10
519 Glenn Adams .10
520 Mike Flanagan .10
521 Billy Almon .10
522 Chuck Rainey .10
523 Gary Gray .10
524 Tom Hausman .10
525 Ray Knight .10
526 Expos Batting & Pitching Ldrs. (Warren Cromartie, Bill Gullickson) .10
527 John Henry Johnson .10
528 Matt Alexander .10
529 Allen Ripley .10
530 Dickie Noles .10
531 A's Future Stars (Rich Bordi, Mark Budaska, Kelvin Moore) .10
532 Toby Harrah .10
533 Joaquin Andujar .10
534 Dave McKay .10
535 Lance Parrish .10
536 Rafael Ramirez .10
537 Doug Capilla .10
538 Lou Piniella .10
539 Vern Ruhle .10
540 Andre Dawson .80
541 Barry Evans .10
542 Ned Yost .10
543 Bill Robinson .10
544 Larry Christenson .10
545 Reggie Smith .10
546 Reggie Smith (In Action) .10
547 Rod Carew (All-Star) .25
548 Willie Randolph (All-Star) .10
549 George Brett (All-Star) 1.50
550 Bucky Dent (All-Star) .10
551 Reggie Jackson (All-Star) .80
552 Ken Singleton (All-Star) .10
553 Dave Winfield (All-Star) .60
554 Carlton Fisk (All-Star) .20
555 Scott McGregor (All-Star) .10
556 Jack Morris (All-Star) .10
557 Rich Gossage (All-Star) .10
558 John Tudor .10
559 Indians Batting & Pitching Ldrs. (Bert Blyleven, Mike Hargrove) .10
560 Doug Corbett .10
561 Cardinals Future Stars (Glenn Brummer, Luis DeLeon, Gene Roof) .10
562 Mike O'Berry .10
563 Ross Baumgarten .10
564 Doug DeCinces .10
565 Jackson Todd .10
566 Mike Jorgensen .10
567 Bob Babcock .10
568 Joe Pettini .10
569 Willie Randolph .10
570 Willie Randolph (In Action) .10
571 Glenn Abbott .10
572 Juan Beniquez .10
573 Rick Waits .10
574 Mike Ramsey .10
575 Al Cowens .10
576 Giants Batting & Pitching Ldrs. (Vida Blue, Milt May) .10
577 Rick Monday .10
578 Shooty Babitt .10
579 *Rick Mahler* .10
580 Bobby Bonds .10
581 Ron Reed .10
582 Luis Pujols .10
583 Tippy Martinez .10
584 Hosken Powell .10
585 Rollie Fingers .40
586 Rollie Fingers (In Action) .15
587 Tim Lollar .10
588 Dale Berra .10
589 Dave Stapleton .10
590 Al Oliver .10
591 Al Oliver (In Action) .10
592 Craig Swan .10
593 Billy Smith .10
594 Renie Martin .10
595 Dave Collins .10
596 Damaso Garcia .10
597 Wayne Nordhagen .10
598 Bob Galasso .10
599 White Sox Future Stars (Jay Loviglio, Reggie Patterson, Leo Sutherland) .10
600 Dave Winfield 2.50
601 Sid Monge .10
602 Freddie Patek .10
603 Rich Hebner .10
604 Orlando Sanchez .10
605 Steve Rogers .10
606 Blue Jays Batting & Pitching Ldrs. (John Mayberry, Dave Stieb) .10
607 Leon Durham .10
608 Jerry Royster .10
609 Rick Sutcliffe .10
610 Rickey Henderson 3.50
611 Joe Niekro .10
612 Gary Ward .10
613 Jim Gantner .10
614 Juan Eichelberger .10
615 Bob Boone .10
616 Bob Boone (In Action) .10
617 Scott McGregor .10
618 Tim Foli .10
619 Bill Campbell .10
620 Ken Griffey .10
621 Ken Griffey (In Action) .10
622 Dennis Lamp .10
623 Mets Future Stars (Ron Gardenhire, *Terry Leach, Tim Leary*) .20
624 Fergie Jenkins .65
625 Hal McRae .10
626 Randy Jones .10
627 Enos Cabell .10
628 Bill Travers .10
629 Johnny Wockenfuss .10
630 Joe Charboneau .10
631 Gene Tenace .10
632 Bryan Clark .10
633 Mitchell Page .10
634 Checklist 529-660 .10
635 Ron Davis .10
636 Phillies Batting & Pitching Ldrs. (Steve Carlton, Pete Rose) .50
637 Rick Camp .10
638 John Milner .10
639 Ken Kravec .10
640 Cesar Cedeno .10
641 Steve Mura .10
642 Mike Scioscia .10
643 Pete Vuckovich .10
644 John Castino .10
645 Frank White .10
646 Frank White (In Action) .10
647 Warren Brusstar .10
648 Jose Morales .10
649 Ken Clay .10
650 Carl Yastrzemski 1.50
651 Carl Yastrzemski (In Action) .60
652 Steve Nicosia .10
653 Angels Future Stars (*Tom Brunansky, Luis Sanchez, Daryl Sconiers*) .40
654 Jim Morrison .10
655 Joel Youngblood .10
656 Eddie Whitson .10
657 Tom Poquette .10
658 Tito Landrum .10
659 Fred Martinez .10
660 Dave Concepcion .10
661 Dave Concepcion (In Action) .10
662 Luis Salazar .10
663 Hector Cruz .10
664 Dan Spillner .10
665 Jim Clancy .10
666 Tigers Batting & Pitching Ldrs. (Steve Kemp, Dan Petry) .10
667 Jeff Reardon .50
668 Dale Murphy 1.25
669 Larry Milbourne .10
670 Steve Kemp .10
671 Mike Davis .10
672 Bob Knepper .10
673 Keith Drumright .10
674 Dave Goltz .10
675 Cecil Cooper .10
676 Sal Butera .10
677 Alfredo Griffin .10
678 Tom Paciorek .10
679 Sammy Stewart .10
680 Gary Matthews .10
681 Dodgers Future Stars (*Mike Marshall, Ron Roenicke, Steve Sax*) .75
682 Jesse Jefferson .10
683 Phil Garner .10
684 Harold Baines .30
685 Bert Blyleven .10
686 Gary Allenson .10
687 Greg Minton .10
688 Leon Roberts .10
689 Lary Sorensen .10
690 Dave Kingman .10
691 Dan Schatzeder .10
692 Wayne Gross .10
693 Cesar Geronimo .10
694 Dave Wehrmeister .10
695 Warren Cromartie .10
696 Pirates Batting & Pitching Ldrs. (Bill Madlock, Buddy Solomon) .10
697 John Montefusco .10
698 Tony Scott .10
699 Dick Tidrow .10
700 George Foster .10
701 George Foster (In Action) .10
702 Steve Renko .10
703 Brewers Batting & Pitching Ldrs. (Cecil Cooper, Pete Vuckovich) .10
704 Mickey Rivers .10
705 Mickey Rivers (In Action) .10
706 Barry Foote .10
707 Mark Bomback .10
708 Gene Richards .10
709 Don Money .10
710 Jerry Reuss .10
711 Mariners Future Stars (*Dave Edler*), (*Dave Henderson, Reggie Walton*) .50
712 Denny Martinez .10
713 Del Unser .10
714 Jerry Koosman .10
715 Willie Stargell .80
716 Willie Stargell (In Action) .30
717 Rick Miller .10
718 Charlie Hough .10
719 Jerry Narron .10
720 Greg Luzinski .15
721 Greg Luzinski (In Action) .10
722 Jerry Martin .10
723 Junior Kennedy .10
724 Dave Rosello .10
725 Amos Otis .10
726 Amos Otis (In Action) .10
727 Sixto Lezcano .10
728 Aurelio Lopez .10
729 Jim Spencer .10
730 Gary Carter .75
731 Padres Future Stars (Mike Armstrong, Doug Gwosdz, Fred Kuhaulua) .10
732 Mike Lum .10
733 Larry McWilliams .10
734 Mike Ivie .10
735 Rudy May .10
736 Jerry Turner .10
737 Reggie Cleveland .10
738 Dave Engle .10
739 Joey McLaughlin .10
740 Dave Lopes .10
741 Dave Lopes (In Action) .10
742 Dick Drago .10
743 John Stearns .10
744 *Mike Witt* .50
745 Bake McBride .10
746 Andre Thornton .10
747 John Lowenstein .10
748 Marc Hill .10
749 Bob Shirley .10
750 Jim Rice .15
751 Rick Honeycutt .10
752 Lee Lacy .10
753 Tom Brookens .10
754 Joe Morgan .75
755 Joe Morgan (In Action) .20
756 Reds Batting & Pitching Ldrs. (Ken Griffey, Tom Seaver) .30
757 Tom Underwood .10
758 Claudell Washington .10
759 Paul Splittorff .10
760 Bill Buckner .10
761 Dave Smith .10
762 Mike Phillips .10
763 Tom Hume .10
764 Steve Swisher .10
765 Gorman Thomas .10
766 Twins Future Stars (*Lenny Faedo*), (*Kent Hrbek*), (*Tim Laudner*) 2.00
767 Roy Smalley .10
768 Jerry Garvin .10
769 Richie Zisk .10
770 Rich Gossage .15
771 Rich Gossage (In Action) .10
772 Bert Campaneris .10
773 John Denny .10
774 Jay Johnstone .10
775 Bob Forsch .10
776 Mark Belanger .10
777 Tom Griffin .10
778 Kevin Hickey .10
779 Grant Jackson .10
780 Pete Rose 3.00
781 Pete Rose (In Action) 1.50
782 Frank Taveras .10
783 *Greg Harris* .15
784 Milt Wilcox .10
785 Dan Driessen .10
786 Red Sox Batting & Pitching Ldrs. (Carney Lansford, Mike Torrez) .10
787 Fred Stanley .10
788 Woodie Fryman .10
789 Checklist 661-792 .10
790 Larry Gura .10
791 Bobby Brown .10
792 Frank Tanana .10

1982 Topps "Blackless"

Whether through faulty pre-production work or the simple fact that the black ink well may have run dry during printing, exactly half of the 1982 Topps cards can be found in a "blackless" version. All cards on the set's A, B and C press sheets can be found blackless while none of the D, E, or F cards are known to exhibit this variation. On regular player's cards the lack of black printing is most obvious in the absence of the facsimile autograph on front. The thin black pinstripe around the player photo is also missing on those cards. On cards in which the position was supposed to be printed in black, it will be missing on these variations. All-Star cards affected by this error will be missing the player's name. It is estimated fewer than 100 of each "blackless" card were released. Originally cards from the A and B sheets were found in metro New York, while the C cards turned up most often in the Midwest.

		MT
Complete Set (396):		2500.
Common Player:		3.00
8	Rich Dauer	3.00
9	Ron Guidry	5.00
10	Ron Guidry (In Action)	3.00
11	Gary Alexander	3.00
12	Moose Haas	3.00
13	Lamar Johnson	3.00
14	Steve Howe	3.00
17	Darrell Evans	5.00
18	Fernando Arroyo	3.00
20	Garry Maddox	3.00
24	Dave Frost	3.00
26	Jorge Orta	3.00
28	John Urrea	3.00
31	Tom Seaver (In Action)	25.00
35	Willie Aikens	3.00
37	Dan Graham	3.00
38	Charlie Lea	3.00
39	Lou Whitaker	5.00
40	Dave Parker	4.00
42	Rick Sofield	3.00
48	Bobby Castillo	3.00
49	Alvis Woods	3.00
50	Buddy Bell	3.00
52	Larry Andersen	3.00
54	Ron Hassey	3.00
55	Rick Burleson	3.00
60	Tony Armas	3.00
64	Lynn Jones	3.00
65	Terry Kennedy	3.00
67	Rich Gale	3.00
68	Roy Howell	3.00
70	Tim Raines	7.50
71	Roy Lee Jackson	3.00
72	Rick Auerbach	3.00
73	Buddy Solomon	3.00
74	Bob Clark	3.00
77	Miguel Dilone	3.00
78	George Medich	3.00
80	Jim Palmer	50.00
81	Jim Palmer (In Action)	15.00
84	Rennie Stennett	3.00
87	Matt Keough	3.00
88	Biff Pocoroba	3.00
89	Steve Henderson	3.00
90	Nolan Ryan	250.00
91	Carney Lansford	3.00
92	Brad Havens	3.00
94	Andy Hassler	3.00
95	Ozzie Smith	90.00
98	Terry Bulling	3.00
99	Barry Bonnell	3.00
100	Mike Schmidt	100.00
101	Mike Schmidt (In Action)	50.00
105	Kirk Gibson	10.00
107	Wayne Krenchicki	3.00
109	Dave Revering	3.00
110	Carlton Fisk	40.00
111	Carlton Fisk (In Action)	12.00
112	Billy Sample	3.00
113	Steve McCatty	3.00
114	Ken Landreaux	3.00
115	Gaylord Perry	40.00
116	Jim Wohlford	3.00
117	Rawly Eastwick	3.00
119	Joe Pittman	3.00
120	Gary Lucas	3.00
122	Jamie Easterley	3.00
123	Danny Goodwin	3.00
125	Danny Ainge	25.00
127	Lonnie Smith	3.00
128	Frank Pastore	3.00
130	Julio Cruz	3.00
131	Stan Bahnsen	3.00
132	Lee May	3.00
134	Dan Ford	3.00
135	Andy Rincon	3.00
136	Lenn Sakata	3.00
137	George Cappuzzello	3.00
138	Tony Pena	3.00
140	Ron LeFlore	3.00
143	Mookie Wilson	3.00
147	Denny Walling	3.00
150	Ted Simmons	3.00
155	Otto Velez	3.00
157	Steve Crawford	3.00
158	Brian Downing	3.00
159	Larry Biittner	3.00
160	Luis Tiant	3.50
170	Jim Bibby	3.00
172	Bill Gullickson	3.00
173	Jamie Quirk	3.00
174	Dave Ford	3.00
175	Jerry Mumphrey	3.00
177	John Ellis	3.00
178	Dyar Miller	3.00
179	Steve Garvey	30.00
181	Silvio Martinez	3.00
183	Mike Proly	3.00
185	Phil Niekro	35.00
189	Glenn Hoffman	3.00
190	J.R. Richard	4.00
192	Broderick Perkins	3.00
198	Chris Speier	3.00
200	George Brett	90.00
201	George Brett (In Action)	45.00
204	Gary Roenicke	3.00
209	Gary Lavelle	3.00
210	Keith Hernandez	4.00
211	Dan Petry	3.00
212	Mario Mendoza	3.00
215	Mike Krukow	3.00
220	Manny Trillo	3.00
221	Jim Slaton	3.00
222	Butch Wynegar	3.00
223	Lloyd Moseby	3.00
224	Bruce Bochte	3.00
225	Mike Torrez	3.00
228	Sam Mejias	3.00
230	Willie Wilson	3.00
232	Terry Crowley	3.00
233	Duane Kuiper	3.00
234	Ron Hodges	3.00
235	Mike Easler	3.00
237	Rusty Kuntz	3.00
238	Kevin Saucier	3.00
239	Jon Matlack	3.00
240	Bucky Dent	3.00
241	Bucky Dent (In Action)	3.00
245	Ken Reitz	3.00
247	Pedro Guerrero	3.00
251	Fred Lynn	4.00
255	Tony Perez	9.00
256	Tony Perez (In Action)	3.00
257	Larry Harlow	3.00
258	Bo Diaz	3.00
259	Rodney Scott	3.00
260	Bruce Sutter	3.00
262	Doug Bair	3.00
264	Dan Quisenberry	3.00
265	Al Bumbry	3.00
267	Kurt Bevacqua	3.00
270	Rusty Staub	5.00
272	Bump Wills	3.00
275	Bob Watson	3.00
278	John Littlefield	3.00
280	Ben Oglivie	3.00
281	John Verhoeven	3.00
282	Ken Macha	3.00
283	Brian Allard	3.00
285	Sparky Lyle	3.00
287	Alan Bannister	3.00
288	Garry Templeton	3.00
289	Bob Stanley	3.00
290	Ken Singleton	3.00
297	Clint Hurdle	3.00
299	Steve Trout	3.00
300	Reggie Jackson	75.00
302	Doug Flynn	3.00
305	Don Sutton	40.00
307	Randy Bass	3.00
308	Charlie Moore	3.00
310	Mike Hargrove	3.00
312	Lenny Randle	3.00
313	John Harris	3.00
315	Burt Hooton	3.00
317	Dick Ruthven	3.00
323	Bill Lee	3.00
324	Steve Dillard	3.00
325	Jose Cruz	3.00
328	Ed Farmer	3.00
329	U.L. Washington	3.00
330	Rick Wise	3.00
332	Don Robinson	3.00
334	Aurelio Rodriguez	3.00
335	Jim Sundberg	3.00
339	Mike Schmidt (All-Star)	50.00
340	Dave Concepcion (All-Star)	3.00
341	Andre Dawson (All-Star)	15.00
342	George Foster (All-Star)	3.00
343	Dave Parker (All-Star)	4.00
344	Gary Carter (All-Star)	7.50
345	Fernando Valenzuela (All-Star)	3.50
349	George Frazier	3.00
352	Dick Davis	3.00
354	Roberto Ramos	3.00
355	Dwight Evans	3.50
357	Butch Hobson	3.00
359	Jim Dwyer	3.00
360	Len Barker	3.00
363	Bob Molinaro	3.00
365	Bill Madlock	3.50
370	Mike Norris	3.00
380	Dave Stieb	4.00
382	Joe Simpson	3.00
385	Ken Forsch	3.00
387	Tom Veryzer	3.00
388	Joe Rudi	3.00
390	Eddie Murray	40.00
397	Ken Brett	3.00
398	Mike Squires	3.00
399	Pat Zachry	3.00
400	Johnny Bench	65.00
406	Al Holland	3.00
409	Don Cooper	3.00
412	Luis Leal	3.00
413	Dan Meyer	3.00
415	Don Baylor	5.00
417	Pat Kelly	3.00
419	Steve Stone	3.00
420	George Hendrick	3.00
421	Mark Clear	3.00
422	Cliff Johnson	3.00
423	Stan Papi	3.00
424	Bruce Benedict	3.00
425	John Candelaria	3.00
430	Vida Blue	4.00
440	Jeff Burroughs	3.00
442	Bruce Kison	3.00
443	Mark Wagner	3.00
445	Larry Parrish	3.00
446	Wayne Garland	3.00
448	Darrell Porter (In Action)	3.00
450	Jack Morris	4.00
451	Ed Miller	3.00
459	Bruce Berenyi	3.00
460	Jack Clark	4.00
461	Rich Dotson	3.00
462	Dave Chalk	3.00
463	Jim Kern	3.00
464	Juan Bonilla	3.00
465	Lee Mazzilli	3.00
467	Mickey Hatcher	3.00
468	Floyd Bannister	3.00
472	Oscar Gamble	3.00
475	Alan Trammell	12.50
476	Brian Kingman	3.00
477	Steve Yeager	3.00
480	Steve Carlton	50.00
481	Steve Carlton (In Action)	15.00
484	Ivan DeJesus	3.00
490	Dennis Eckersley	7.50
492	Joe Price	3.00
493	Chet Lemon	3.00
494	Hubie Brooks	3.00
495	Dennis Leonard	3.00
496	Johnny Grubb	3.00
498	Dave Bergman	3.00
499	Paul Mirabella	3.00
500	Rod Carew	55.00
501	Rod Carew (In Action)	15.00
503	Julio Gonzalez	3.00
507	Terry Harper	3.00
510	Fernando Valenzuela	10.00
511	Ruppert Jones	3.00
512	Jerry Dybzinski	3.00
515	Larry Bowa	3.00
518	Garth Iorg	3.00
519	Glenn Adams	3.00
520	Mike Flanagan	3.00
521	Bill Almon	3.00
523	Gary Gray	3.00
524	Tom Hausman	3.00
532	Toby Harrah	3.00
534	Dave McKay	3.00
536	Rafael Ramirez	3.00
540	Andre Dawson	35.00
541	Barry Evans	3.00
542	Ned Yost	3.00
543	Bill Robinson	3.00
547	Rod Carew (All-Star)	15.00
548	Willie Randolph (All-Star)	3.00
549	George Brett (All-Star)	25.00
550	Bucky Dent (All-Star)	3.00
551	Reggie Jackson (All-Star)	20.00
552	Ken Singleton (All-Star)	3.00
553	Dave Winfield (All-Star)	15.00
554	Carlton Fisk (All-Star)	7.50
555	Scott McGregor (All-Star)	3.00
556	Jack Morris (All-Star)	3.00
557	Rich Gossage (All-Star)	3.00
560	Doug Corbett	3.00
563	Ross Baumgarten	3.00
564	Doug DeCinces	3.00
565	Jackson Todd	3.00
567	Bob Babcock	3.00
568	Joe Pettini	3.00
569	Willie Randolph	3.00
573	Rick Waits	3.00
574	Mike Ramsey	3.00
575	Al Cowens	3.00
579	Rick Mahler	3.00
580	Bobby Bonds	3.50
581	Ron Reed	3.00
582	Luis Pujols	3.00
585	Rollie Fingers	40.00
588	Dale Berra	3.00
590	Al Oliver	4.00
594	Renie Martin	3.00
600	Dave Winfield	60.00
601	Sid Monge	3.00
602	Freddie Patek	3.00
603	Richie Hebner	3.00
608	Jerry Royster	3.00
610	Rickey Henderson	40.00
611	Joe Niekro	3.00
612	Gary Ward	3.00
613	Jim Gantner	3.00
615	Bob Boone	4.00
616	Bob Boone (In Action)	4.00
622	Dennis Lamp	3.00
624	Fergie Jenkins	40.00
625	Hal McRae	3.00
626	Randy Jones	3.00
627	Enos Cabell	3.00
629	Johnny Wockenfuss	3.00
630	Joe Charboneau	4.00
632	Bryan Clark	3.00
635	Ron Davis	3.00
637	Rick Camp	3.00
640	Cesar Cedeno	3.00
645	Frank White	3.00
646	Frank White (In Action)	3.00
648	Jose Morales	3.00
649	Ken Clay	3.00
654	Jim Morrison	3.00
655	Joel Youngblood	3.00
656	Eddie Whitson	3.00
661	Dave Concepcion (In Action)	3.00
663	Hector Cruz	3.00
664	Dan Spillner	3.00
665	Jim Clancy	3.00
668	Dale Murphy	45.00
669	Larry Milbourne	3.00
670	Steve Kemp	3.00
672	Bob Knepper	3.00
675	Cecil Cooper	3.00
677	Alfredo Griffin	3.00
678	Tom Paciorek	3.00
684	Harold Baines	7.50
685	Bert Blyleven	4.00
686	Gary Allenson	3.00
690	Dave Kingman	3.50
691	Dan Schatzeder	3.00
694	Dave Wehrmeister	3.00
695	Warren Cromartie	3.00
700	George Foster	4.00
702	Steve Renko	3.00
704	Mickey Rivers	3.00
705	Mickey Rivers (In Action)	3.00
706	Barry Foote	3.00
707	Mark Bomback	3.00
708	Gene Richards	3.00
710	Jerry Reuss	3.00
713	Del Unser	3.00
715	Willie Stargell	45.00
716	Willie Stargell (In Action)	20.00
718	Charlie Hough	3.00
720	Greg Luzinski	3.50
721	Greg Luzinski (In Action)	3.00
722	Jerry Martin	3.00
724	Dave Rosello	3.00
725	Amos Otis	3.00
730	Gary Carter	25.00
735	Rudy May	3.00
737	Reggie Cleveland	3.00
738	Dave Engle	3.00
739	Joey McLaughlin	3.00
740	Dave Lopes	3.50
741	Dave Lopes (In Action)	3.00
742	Dick Drago	3.00
743	John Stearns	3.00
745	Bake McBride	3.00
747	John Lowenstein	3.00
748	Marc Hill	3.00
751	Rick Honeycutt	3.00
753	Tom Brookens	3.00
754	Joe Morgan	40.00
757	Tom Underwood	3.00
760	Bill Buckner	4.00
761	Dave Smith	3.00
764	Steve Swisher	3.00
765	Gorman Thomas	3.00
767	Roy Smalley	3.00
768	Jerry Garvin	3.00
769	Richie Zisk	3.00
771	Rich Gossage (In Action)	3.00
775	Bob Forsch	3.00
776	Mark Belanger	3.00
777	Tom Griffin	3.00
778	Kevin Hickey	3.00
780	Pete Rose	125.00
781	Pete Rose (In Action)	75.00
782	Frank Taveras	3.00
784	Milt Wilcox	3.00
788	Woodie Fryman	3.00
790	Larry Gura	3.00
792	Frank Tanana	

1982 Topps Traded

Topps released its second straight 132-card Traded set in September of 1982. Again, the 2-1/2" x 3-1/2" cards feature not only players who had been traded during the season, but also promising rookies who were given their first individual cards. The cards follow the basic design of the regular issues, but have their backs printed in red rather than the regular-issue green. As in 1981, the cards were not available in normal retail outlets and could only be purchased through regular baseball card dealers. Unlike the previous year, the cards are numbered 1-132 with the letter "T" following the number.

		MT
Complete Set (132):		250.00
Common Player:		.20
1T	Doyle Alexander	.20
2T	Jesse Barfield	.20
3T	Ross Baumgarten	.20
4T	Steve Bedrosian	.20
5T	Mark Belanger	.20
6T	Kurt Bevacqua	.20
7T	Tim Blackwell	.20
8T	Vida Blue	.20
9T	Bob Boone	.30
10T	Larry Bowa	.20
11T	Dan Briggs	.20
12T	Bobby Brown	.20
13T	Tom Brunansky	.20
14T	Jeff Burroughs	.20
15T	Enos Cabell	.20
16T	Bill Campbell	.20
17T	Bobby Castillo	.20
18T	Bill Caudill	.20
19T	Cesar Cedeno	.20
20T	Dave Collins	.20
21T	Doug Corbett	.20
22T	Al Cowens	.20
23T	Chili Davis	1.00
24T	Dick Davis	.20
25T	Ron Davis	.20
26T	Doug DeCinces	.20
27T	Ivan DeJesus	.20
28T	Bob Dernier	.20
29T	Bo Diaz	.20
30T	Roger Erickson	.20
31T	Jim Essian	.20
32T	Ed Farmer	.20
33T	Doug Flynn	.20
34T	Tim Foli	.20
35T	Dan Ford	.20
36T	George Foster	.20
37T	Dave Frost	.20
38T	Rich Gale	.20
39T	Ron Gardenhire	.20
40T	Ken Griffey	.25
41T	Greg Harris	.20
42T	Von Hayes	.20
43T	Larry Herndon	.20
44T	Kent Hrbek	4.00
45T	Mike Ivie	.20
46T	Grant Jackson	.20
47T	Reggie Jackson	12.00
48T	Ron Jackson	.20
49T	Fergie Jenkins	2.50
50T	Lamar Johnson	.20
51T	Randy Johnson	.20
52T	Jay Johnstone	.20
53T	Mick Kelleher	.20
54T	Steve Kemp	.20
55T	Junior Kennedy	.20
56T	Jim Kern	.20
57T	Ray Knight	.20
58T	Wayne Krenchicki	.20
59T	Mike Krukow	.20
60T	Duane Kuiper	.20
61T	Mike LaCoss	.20
62T	Chet Lemon	.20
63T	Sixto Lezcano	.20
64T	Dave Lopes	.20
65T	Jerry Martin	.20
66T	Renie Martin	.20
67T	John Mayberry	.20
68T	Lee Mazzilli	.20
69T	Bake McBride	.20
70T	Dan Meyer	.20
71T	Larry Milbourne	.20

72T Eddie Milner .20
73T Sid Monge .20
74T John Montefusco .20
75T Jose Morales .20
76T Keith Moreland .20
77T Jim Morrison .20
78T Rance Mulliniks .20
79T Steve Mura .20
80T Gene Nelson .20
81T Joe Nolan .20
82T Dickie Noles .20
83T Al Oliver .20
84T Jorge Orta .20
85T Tom Paciorek .20
86T Larry Parrish .20
87T Jack Perconte .20
88T Gaylord Perry 2.50
89T Rob Picciolo .20
90T Joe Pittman .20
91T Hosken Powell .20
92T Mike Proly .20
93T Greg Pryor .20
94T Charlie Puleo .20
95T Shane Rawley .20
96T Johnny Ray .20
97T Dave Revering .20
98T Cal Ripken, Jr. 200.00
99T Allen Ripley .20
100T Bill Robinson .20
101T Aurelio Rodriguez .20
102T Joe Rudi .20
103T Steve Sax 1.00
104T Dan Schatzeder .20
105T Bob Shirley .20
106T Eric Show .20
107T Roy Smalley .20
108T Lonnie Smith .20
109T Ozzie Smith 25.00
110T Reggie Smith .20
111T Lary Sorensen .20
112T Elias Sosa .20
113T Mike Stanton .20
114T Steve Stroughter .20
115T Champ Summers .20
116T Rick Sutcliffe .20
117T Frank Tanana .20
118T Frank Taveras .20
119T Garry Templeton .20
120T Alex Trevino .20
121T Jerry Turner .20
122T Ed Vande Berg .20
123T Tom Veryzer .20
124T Ron Washington .20
125T Bob Watson .20
126T Dennis Werth .20
127T Eddie Whitson .20
128T Rob Wilfong .20
129T Bump Wills .20
130T Gary Woods .20
131T Butch Wynegar .20
132T Checklist 1-132 .20

1982 Topps Team Leaders Sheet

Available via a special mail-in offer, this 10-1/2" x 23" uncut sheet contained the 26 team batting and pitching leaders cards plus a card offering Topps collectors boxes. The team leader cards are identical to those issued in packs.

MT

Team Leaders sheet 12.00

1982 Topps Insert Stickers

This 48-player set is actually an abbreviated version of the regular 1982 Topps sticker set with different backs. Used to promote the 1982 sticker set, Topps inserted these stickers in its baseball card wax packs. They are identical to the regular 1982 stickers, except for the backs, which advertise that the Topps sticker album will be "Coming Soon." The 48 stickers retain the same numbers used in the regular sticker set, resulting in the smaller set being skip-numbered.

MT

Complete Set (48): 3.00
Common Player: .05
17 Chris Chambliss .05
21 Bruce Benedict .05
25 Leon Durham .05
29 Bill Buckner .05
33 Dave Collins .05
37 Dave Concepcion .05
41 Nolan Ryan 1.00
45 Bob Knepper .05
49 Ken Landreaux .05
53 Burt Hooton .05
57 Andre Dawson .15
61 Gary Carter .15
65 Joel Youngblood .05
69 Ellis Valentine .05
73 Garry Maddox .05
77 Bob Boone .05
81 Omar Moreno .05
85 Willie Stargell .20
89 Ken Oberkfell .05
93 Darrell Porter .05
97 Juan Eichelberger .05
101 Luis Salazar .05
105 Enos Cabell .05
109 Larry Herndon .05
143 Scott McGregor .05
148 Mike Flanagan .05
151 Mike Torrez .05
156 Carney Lansford .05
161 Fred Lynn .05
166 Rich Dotson .05
171 Tony Bernazard .05
176 Bo Diaz .05
181 Alan Trammell .10
186 Milt Wilcox .05
191 Dennis Leonard .05
196 Willie Aikens .05
201 Ted Simmons .05
206 Hosken Powell .05
211 Roger Erickson .05
215 Graig Nettles .05
216 Reggie Jackson .25
221 Rickey Henderson .25
226 Cliff Johnson .05
231 Jeff Burroughs .05
236 Tom Paciorek .05
241 Pat Putnam .05
246 Lloyd Moseby .05
251 Barry Bonnell .05

1982 Topps Stickers

The 1982 Topps sticker set is complete at 260 stickers and includes another series of "foil" All-Stars. The stickers measure 1-15/16" x 2-9/16" and feature full-color photos surrounded by a red border for American League players or a blue border for National League players. They are numbered on both the front and back and were designed to be mounted in a special album.

MT

Complete Set (260): 12.00
Common Player: .05
Sticker Album: 2.00
1 Bill Madlock .05
2 Carney Lansford .05
3 Mike Schmidt .25
4 Tony Armas, Dwight Evans, Bobby Grich, Eddie Murray .10
5 Mike Schmidt .25
6 Eddie Murray .20
7 Tim Raines .15
8 Rickey Henderson .25
9 Tom Seaver .20
10 Denny Martinez, Steve McCatty, Jack Morris, Pete Vuckovich .05
11 Fernando Valenzuela .05
12 Len Barker .05
13 Nolan Ryan .50
14 Steve McCatty .05
15 Bruce Sutter .05
16 Rollie Fingers .10
17 Chris Chambliss .05
18 Bob Horner .05
19 Dale Murphy .15
20 Phil Niekro .15
21 Bruce Benedict .05
22 Claudell Washington .05
23 Glenn Hubbard .05
24 Rick Camp .05
25 Leon Durham .05
26 Ken Reitz .05
27 Dick Tidrow .05
28 Tim Blackwell .05
29 Bill Buckner .05
30 Steve Henderson .05
31 Mike Krukow .05
32 Ivan DeJesus .05
33 Dave Collins .05
34 Ron Oester .05
35 Johnny Bench .25
36 Tom Seaver .20
37 Dave Concepcion .05
38 Ken Griffey .05
39 Ray Knight .05
40 George Foster .10
41 Nolan Ryan .50
42 Terry Puhl .05
43 Art Howe .05
44 Jose Cruz .05
45 Bob Knepper .05
46 Craig Reynolds .05
47 Cesar Cedeno .05
48 Alan Ashby .05
49 Ken Landreaux .05
50 Fernando Valenzuela .05
51 Ron Cey .05
52 Dusty Baker .05
53 Burt Hooton .05
54 Steve Garvey .15
55 Pedro Guerrero .05
56 Jerry Reuss .05
57 Andre Dawson .15
58 Chris Speier .05
59 Steve Rogers .05
60 Warren Cromartie .05
61 Gary Carter .15
62 Tim Raines .15
63 Scott Sanderson .05
64 Larry Parrish .05
65 Joel Youngblood .05
66 Neil Allen .05
67 Lee Mazzilli .05
68 Hubie Brooks .05
69 Ellis Valentine .05
70 Doug Flynn .05
71 Pat Zachry .05
72 Dave Kingman .05
73 Garry Maddox .05
74 Mike Schmidt .25
75 Steve Carlton .20
76 Manny Trillo .05
77 Bob Boone .05
78 Pete Rose .40
79 Gary Matthews .05
80 Larry Bowa .05
81 Omar Moreno .05
82 Rick Rhoden .05
83 Bill Madlock .05
84 Mike Easler .05
85 Willie Stargell .20
86 Jim Bibby .05
87 Dave Parker .05
88 Tim Foli .05
89 Ken Oberkfell .05
90 Bob Forsch .05
91 George Hendrick .05
92 Keith Hernandez .05
93 Darrell Porter .05
94 Bruce Sutter .05
95 Sixto Lezcano .05
96 Garry Templeton .05
97 Juan Eichelberger .05
98 Broderick Perkins .05
99 Ruppert Jones .05
100 Terry Kennedy .05
101 Luis Salazar .05
102 Gary Lucas .05
103 Gene Richards .05
104 Ozzie Smith .25
105 Enos Cabell .05
106 Jack Clark .05
107 Greg Minton .05
108 Johnnie LeMaster .05
109 Larry Herndon .05
110 Milt May .05
111 Vida Blue .05
112 Darrell Evans .05
113 Len Barker .05
114 Julio Cruz .05
115 Billy Martin .10
116 Tim Raines .15
117 Pete Rose .40
118 Bill Stein .05
119 Fernando Valenzuela .05
120 Carl Yastrzemski .25
121 Pete Rose .40
122 Manny Trillo .05
123 Mike Schmidt .25
124 Dave Concepcion .05
125 Andre Dawson .15
126 George Foster .05
127 Dave Parker .05
128 Gary Carter .15
129 Steve Carlton .20
130 Bruce Sutter .05
131 Rod Carew .25
132 Jerry Remy .05
133 George Brett .30
134 Rick Burleson .05
135 Dwight Evans .05
136 Ken Singleton .05
137 Dave Winfield .30
138 Carlton Fisk .20
139 Jack Morris .05
140 Rich Gossage .10
141 Al Bumbry .05
142 Doug DeCinces .05
143 Scott McGregor .05
144 Ken Singleton .05
145 Eddie Murray .20
146 Jim Palmer .15
147 Rich Dauer .05
148 Mike Flanagan .05
149 Jerry Remy .05
150 Jim Rice .10
151 Mike Torrez .05
152 Tony Perez .10
153 Dwight Evans .05
154 Mark Clear .05
155 Carl Yastrzemski .25
156 Carney Lansford .05
157 Rick Burleson .05
158 Don Baylor .10
159 Ken Forsch .05
160 Rod Carew .20
161 Fred Lynn .05
162 Bob Grich .05
163 Dan Ford .05
164 Butch Hobson .05
165 Greg Luzinski .05
166 Rich Dotson .05
167 Billy Almon .05
168 Chet Lemon .05
169 Steve Trout .05
170 Carlton Fisk .15
171 Tony Bernazard .05
172 Ron LeFlore .05
173 Bert Blyleven .05
174 Andre Thornton .05
175 Jorge Orta .05
176 Bo Diaz .05
177 Toby Harrah .05
178 Len Barker .05
179 Rick Manning .05
180 Mike Hargrove .05
181 Alan Trammell .10
182 Al Cowens .05
183 Jack Morris .05
184 Kirk Gibson .05
185 Steve Kemp .05
186 Milt Wilcox .05
187 Lou Whitaker .05
188 Lance Parrish .05
189 Willie Wilson .05
190 George Brett .30
191 Dennis Leonard .05
192 John Wathan .05
193 Frank White .05
194 Amos Otis .05
195 Larry Gura .05
196 Willie Aikens .05
197 Ben Oglivie .05
198 Rollie Fingers .10
199 Cecil Cooper .05
200 Paul Molitor .20
201 Ted Simmons .05
202 Pete Vuckovich .05
203 Robin Yount .30
204 Gorman Thomas .05
205 Rob Wilfong .05
206 Hosken Powell .05
207 Roy Smalley .05
208 Butch Wynegar .05
209 John Castino .05
210 Doug Corbett .05
211 Roger Erickson .05
212 Mickey Hatcher .05
213 Dave Winfield .30
214 Tommy John .10
215 Graig Nettles .05
216 Reggie Jackson .25
217 Rich Gossage .10
218 Rick Cerone .05
219 Willie Randolph .05
220 Jerry Mumphrey .05
221 Rickey Henderson .25
222 Mike Norris .05
223 Jim Spencer .05
224 Tony Armas .05
225 Matt Keough .05
226 Cliff Johnson .05
227 Dwayne Murphy .05
228 Steve McCatty .05
229 Richie Zisk .05
230 Lenny Randle .05
231 Jeff Burroughs .05
232 Bruce Bochte .05
233 Gary Gray .05
234 Floyd Bannister .05
235 Julio Cruz .05
236 Tom Paciorek .05
237 Danny Darwin .05
238 Buddy Bell .05
239 Al Oliver .05
240 Jim Sundberg .05
241 Pat Putnam .05
242 Steve Comer .05
243 Mickey Rivers .05
244 Bump Wills .05
245 Damaso Garcia .05
246 Lloyd Moseby .05
247 Ernie Whitt .05
248 John Mayberry .05
249 Otto Velez .05
250 Dave Stieb .05
251 Barry Bonnell .05
252 Alfredo Griffin .05
253 1981 N.L. Championship (Gary Carter) .10
254 1981 A.L. Championship (Mike Heath, Larry Milbourne) .05
255 1981 World Champions (Los Angeles Dodgers Team) .05
256 1981 World Champions (Los Angeles Dodgers Team) .05
257 1981 World Series - Game 3 (Fernando Valenzuela) .05
258 1981 World Series - Game 4 (Steve Garvey) .10
259 1981 World Series - Game 5 (Jerry Reuss, Steve Yeager) .05
260 1981 World Series - Game 6 (Pedro Guerrero) .05

1983 Topps

The 1983 Topps set totals 792 cards. Missing among the regular 2-1/2" x 3-1/2" cards are some form of future stars cards, as Topps was saving them for the now-established late season "Traded" set. The 1983 cards carry a large color photo as well as a smaller color photo on the front, quite similar in design to the 1963 set. Team colors frame the card, which, at the bottom, have the player's name, position and team. At the upper right-hand corner is a Topps logo. The backs are horizontal and include statistics, personal information and 1982 highlights. Specialty cards include record-breaking performances, league leaders, All-Stars, numbered checklists "Team Leaders" and "Super Veteran" cards which are horizontal with a current and first-season picture of the honored player.

MT

Complete Set (792): 125.00
Common Player: .08
Wax Box: 225.00
1 Tony Armas (Record Breaker) .08
2 Rickey Henderson (Record Breaker) .75
3 Greg Minton (Record Breaker) .08
4 Lance Parrish (Record Breaker) .08
5 Manny Trillo (Record Breaker) .08
6 John Wathan (Record Breaker) .08
7 Gene Richards .08
8 Steve Balboni .08
9 Joey McLaughlin .08
10 Gorman Thomas .08
11 Billy Gardner .08
12 Paul Mirabella .08
13 Larry Herndon .08
14 Frank LaCorte .08
15 Ron Cey .08
16 George Vukovich .08

17	Kent Tekulve	.08
18	Kent Tekulve (Super Veteran)	.08
19	Oscar Gamble	.08
20	Carlton Fisk	.75
21	Orioles Batting & Pitching Ldrs. (Eddie Murray, Jim Palmer)	.25
22	Randy Martz	.08
23	Mike Heath	.08
24	Steve Mura	.08
25	Hal McRae	.08
26	Jerry Royster	.08
27	Doug Corbett	.08
28	Bruce Bochte	.08
29	Randy Jones	.08
30	Jim Rice	.15
31	Bill Gullickson	.08
32	Dave Bergman	.08
33	Jack O'Connor	.08
34	Paul Householder	.08
35	Rollie Fingers	.65
36	Rollie Fingers (Super Veteran)	.15
37	Darrell Johnson	.08
38	Tim Flannery	.08
39	Terry Puhl	.08
40	Fernando Valenzuela	.15
41	Jerry Turner	.08
42	Dale Murray	.08
43	Bob Dernier	.08
44	Don Robinson	.08
45	John Mayberry	.08
46	Richard Dotson	.08
47	Dave McKay	.08
48	Lary Sorensen	.08
49	*Willie McGee*	1.50
50	Bob Horner	.08
51	Cubs Batting & Pitching Ldrs. (Leon Durham, Fergie Jenkins)	.08
52	*Onix Concepcion*	.08
53	Mike Witt	.08
54	Jim Maler	.08
55	Mookie Wilson	.08
56	Chuck Rainey	.08
57	Tim Blackwell	.08
58	Al Holland	.08
59	Benny Ayala	.08
60	Johnny Bench	1.50
61	Johnny Bench (Super Veteran)	.60
62	Bob McClure	.08
63	Rick Monday	.08
64	Bill Stein	.08
65	Jack Morris	.08
66	Bob Lillis	.08
67	Sal Butera	.08
68	*Eric Show*	.15
69	Lee Lacy	.08
70	Steve Carlton	1.00
71	Steve Carlton (Super Veteran)	.30
72	Tom Paciorek	.08
73	Allen Ripley	.08
74	Julio Gonzalez	.08
75	Amos Otis	.08
76	Rick Mahler	.08
77	Hosken Powell	.08
78	Bill Caudill	.08
79	Mick Kelleher	.08
80	George Foster	.08
81	Yankees Batting & Pitching Ldrs. (Jerry Mumphrey, Dave Righetti)	.08
82	Bruce Hurst	.08
83	*Ryne Sandberg*	27.50
84	Milt May	.08
85	Ken Singleton	.08
86	Tom Hume	.08
87	Joe Rudi	.08
88	Jim Gantner	.08
89	Leon Roberts	.08
90	Jerry Reuss	.08
91	Larry Milbourne	.08
92	Mike LaCoss	.08
93	John Castino	.08
94	Dave Edwards	.08
95	Alan Trammell	.50
96	Dick Howser	.08
97	Ross Baumgarten	.08
98	Vance Law	.08
99	Dickie Noles	.08
100	Pete Rose	3.00
101	Pete Rose (Super Veteran)	1.50
102	Dave Beard	.08
103	Darrell Porter	.08
104	Bob Walk	.08
105	Don Baylor	.15
106	Gene Nelson	.08
107	Mike Jorgensen	.08
108	Glenn Hoffman	.08
109	Luis Leal	.08
110	Ken Griffey	.08
111	Expos Batting & Pitching Ldrs. (Al Oliver, Steve Rogers)	.08
112	Bob Shirley	.08
113	Ron Roenicke	.08
114	Jim Slaton	.08
115	Chili Davis	.50
116	Dave Schmidt	.08
117	Alan Knicely	.08
118	Chris Welsh	.08
119	Tom Brookens	.08
120	Len Barker	.08
121	Mickey Hatcher	.08
122	Jimmy Smith	.08
123	George Frazier	.08
124	Marc Hill	.08
125	Leon Durham	.08
126	Joe Torre	.15
127	Preston Hanna	.08
128	Mike Ramsey	.08
129	Checklist 1-132	.08
130	Dave Stieb	.08
131	Ed Ott	.08
132	Todd Cruz	.08
133	Jim Barr	.08
134	Hubie Brooks	.08
135	Dwight Evans	.08
136	Willie Aikens	.08
137	Woodie Fryman	.08
138	Rick Dempsey	.08
139	Bruce Berenyi	.08
140	Willie Randolph	.08
141	Indians Batting & Pitching Ldrs. (Toby Harrah, Rick Sutcliffe)	.08
142	Mike Caldwell	.08
143	Joe Pettini	.08
144	Mark Wagner	.08
145	Don Sutton	.75
146	Don Sutton (Super Veteran)	.20
147	Rick Leach	.08
148	Dave Roberts	.08
149	Johnny Ray	.08
150	Bruce Sutter	.08
151	Bruce Sutter (Super Veteran)	.08
152	Jay Johnstone	.08
153	Jerry Koosman	.08
154	Johnnie LeMaster	.08
155	Dan Quisenberry	.08
156	Billy Martin	.15
157	Steve Bedrosian	.08
158	Rob Wilfong	.08
159	Mike Stanton	.08
160	Dave Kingman	.08
161	Dave Kingman (Super Veteran)	.08
162	Mark Clear	.08
163	Cal Ripken, Jr.	15.00
164	Dave Palmer	.08
165	Dan Driessen	.08
166	John Pacella	.08
167	Mark Brouhard	.08
168	Juan Eichelberger	.08
169	Doug Flynn	.08
170	Steve Howe	.08
171	Giants Batting & Pitching Ldrs. (Bill Laskey, Joe Morgan)	.08
172	Vern Ruhle	.08
173	Jim Morrison	.08
174	Jerry Ujdur	.08
175	Bo Diaz	.08
176	Dave Righetti	.08
177	Harold Baines	.60
178	Luis Tiant	.08
179	Luis Tiant (Super Veteran)	.08
180	Rickey Henderson	3.00
181	Terry Felton	.08
182	Mike Fischlin	.08
183	*Ed Vande Berg*	.08
184	Bob Clark	.08
185	Tim Lollar	.08
186	Whitey Herzog	.08
187	Terry Leach	.08
188	Rick Miller	.08
189	Dan Schatzeder	.08
190	Cecil Cooper	.08
191	Joe Price	.08
192	Floyd Rayford	.08
193	Harry Spilman	.08
194	Cesar Geronimo	.08
195	Bob Stoddard	.08
196	Bill Fahey	.08
197	*Jim Eisenreich*	.50
198	Kiko Garcia	.08
199	Marty Bystrom	.08
200	Rod Carew	1.00
201	Rod Carew (Super Veteran)	.35
202	Blue Jays Batting & Pitching Ldrs. (Damaso Garcia, Dave Stieb)	.08
203	Mike Morgan	.08
204	Junior Kennedy	.08
205	Dave Parker	.15
206	Ken Oberkfell	.08
207	Rick Camp	.08
208	Dan Meyer	.08
209	*Mike Moore*	.40
210	Jack Clark	.08
211	John Denny	.08
212	John Stearns	.08
213	Tom Burgmeier	.08
214	Jerry White	.08
215	Mario Soto	.08
216	Tony LaRussa	.08
217	Tim Stoddard	.08
218	Roy Howell	.08
219	Mike Armstrong	.08
220	Dusty Baker	.08
221	Joe Niekro	.08
222	Damaso Garcia	.08
223	John Montefusco	.08
224	Mickey Rivers	.08
225	Enos Cabell	.08
226	Enrique Romo	.08
227	Chris Bando	.08
228	Joaquin Andujar	.08
229	Phillies Batting/Pitching Leaders (Steve Carlton, Bo Diaz)	.15
230	Fergie Jenkins	.75
231	Fergie Jenkins (Super Veteran)	.20
232	Tom Brunansky	.08
233	Wayne Gross	.08
234	Larry Andersen	.08
235	Claudell Washington	.08
236	Steve Renko	.08
237	Dan Norman	.08
238	*Bud Black*	.55
239	Dave Stapleton	.08
240	Rich Gossage	.08
241	Rich Gossage (Super Veteran)	.08
242	Joe Nolan	.08
243	Duane Walker	.08
244	Dwight Bernard	.08
245	Steve Sax	.08
246	George Bamberger	.08
247	Dave Smith	.08
248	Bake McBride	.08
249	Checklist 133-264	.08
250	Bill Buckner	.08
251	*Alan Wiggins*	.08
252	Luis Aguayo	.08
253	Larry McWilliams	.08
254	Rick Cerone	.08
255	Gene Garber	.08
256	Gene Garber (Super Veteran)	.08
257	Jesse Barfield	.08
258	Manny Castillo	.08
259	Jeff Jones	.08
260	Steve Kemp	.08
261	Tigers Batting & Pitching Ldrs. (Larry Herndon, Dan Petry)	.08
262	Ron Jackson	.08
263	Renie Martin	.08
264	Jamie Quirk	.08
265	Joel Youngblood	.08
266	Paul Boris	.08
267	Terry Francona	.08
268	*Storm Davis*	.08
269	Ron Oester	.08
270	Dennis Eckersley	.75
271	Ed Romero	.08
272	Frank Tanana	.08
273	Mark Belanger	.08
274	Terry Kennedy	.08
275	Ray Knight	.08
276	Gene Mauch	.08
277	Rance Mulliniks	.08
278	Kevin Hickey	.08
279	Greg Gross	.08
280	Bert Blyleven	.15
281	Andre Robertson	.08
282	Reggie Smith	.08
283	Reggie Smith (Super Veteran)	.08
284	Jeff Lahti	.08
285	Lance Parrish	.08
286	Rick Langford	.08
287	Bobby Brown	.08
288	*Joe Cowley*	.08
289	Jerry Dybzinski	.08
290	Jeff Reardon	.20
291	Pirates Batting & Pitching Ldrs. (John Candelaria, Bill Madlock)	.08
292	Craig Swan	.08
293	Glenn Gulliver	.08
294	Dave Engle	.08
295	Jerry Remy	.08
296	Greg Harris	.08
297	Ned Yost	.08
298	Floyd Chiffer	.08
299	George Wright	.08
300	Mike Schmidt	3.50
301	Mike Schmidt (Super Veteran)	1.00
302	Ernie Whitt	.08
303	Miguel Dilone	.08
304	Dave Rucker	.08
305	Larry Bowa	.08
306	Tom Lasorda	.25
307	Lou Piniella	.08
308	Jesus Vega	.08
309	Jeff Leonard	.08
310	Greg Luzinski	.08
311	Glenn Brummer	.08
312	Brian Kingman	.08
313	Gary Gray	.08
314	Ken Dayley	.08
315	Rick Burleson	.08
316	Paul Splittorff	.08
317	Gary Rajsich	.08
318	John Tudor	.08
319	Lenn Sakata	.08
320	Steve Rogers	.08
321	Brewers Batting & Pitching Ldrs. (Pete Vuckovich, Robin Yount)	.20
322	Dave Van Gorder	.08
323	Luis DeLeon	.08
324	Mike Marshall	.08
325	Von Hayes	.08
326	Garth Iorg	.08
327	Bobby Castillo	.08
328	Craig Reynolds	.08
329	Randy Niemann	.08
330	Buddy Bell	.08
331	Mike Krukow	.08
332	*Glenn Wilson*	.08
333	Dave LaRoche	.08
334	Dave LaRoche (Super Veteran)	.08
335	Steve Henderson	.08
336	Rene Lachemann	.08
337	Tito Landrum	.08
338	Bob Owchinko	.08
339	Terry Harper	.08
340	Larry Gura	.08
341	Doug DeCinces	.08
342	Atlee Hammaker	.08
343	Bob Bailor	.08
344	Roger LaFrancois	.08
345	Jim Clancy	.08
346	Joe Pittman	.08
347	Sammy Stewart	.08
348	Alan Bannister	.08
349	Checklist 265-396	.08
350	Robin Yount	3.00
351	Reds Batting & Pitching Ldrs. (Cesar Cedeno, Mario Soto)	.08
352	Mike Scioscia	.08
353	Steve Comer	.08
354	Randy S. Johnson	.08
355	Jim Bibby	.08
356	Gary Woods	.08
357	*Len Matuszek*	.08
358	Jerry Garvin	.08
359	Dave Collins	.08
360	Nolan Ryan	12.00
361	Nolan Ryan (Super Veteran)	5.00
362	Bill Almon	.08
363	*John Stuper*	.08
364	Brett Butler	.50
365	Dave Lopes	.08
366	Dick Williams	.08
367	Bud Anderson	.08
368	Richie Zisk	.08
369	Jesse Orosco	.08
370	Gary Carter	.25
371	Mike Richardt	.08
372	Terry Crowley	.08
373	Kevin Saucier	.08
374	Wayne Krenchicki	.08
375	Pete Vuckovich	.08
376	Ken Landreaux	.08
377	Lee May	.08
378	Lee May (Super Veteran)	.08
379	Guy Sularz	.08
380	Ron Davis	.08
381	Red Sox Batting & Pitching Ldrs. (Jim Rice, Bob Stanley)	.08
382	Bob Knepper	.08
383	Ozzie Virgil	.08
384	*Dave Dravecky*	.50
385	Mike Easler	.08
386	Rod Carew (All-Star)	.40
387	Bob Grich (All-Star)	.08
388	George Brett (All-Star)	1.25
389	Robin Yount (All-Star)	.60
390	Reggie Jackson (All-Star)	.75
391	Rickey Henderson (All-Star)	.50
392	Fred Lynn (All-Star)	.08
393	Carlton Fisk (All-Star)	.15
394	Pete Vuckovich (All-Star)	.08
395	Larry Gura (All-Star)	.08
396	Dan Quisenberry (All-Star)	.08
397	Pete Rose (All-Star)	1.00
398	Manny Trillo (All-Star)	.08
399	Mike Schmidt (All-Star)	1.00
400	Dave Concepcion (All-Star)	.08
401	Dale Murphy (All-Star)	.20
402	Andre Dawson (All-Star)	.40
403	Tim Raines (All-Star)	.25
404	Gary Carter (All-Star)	.20
405	Steve Rogers (All-Star)	.08
406	Steve Carlton (All-Star)	.50
407	Bruce Sutter (All-Star)	.08
408	Rudy May	.08
409	Marvis Foley	.08
410	Phil Niekro	.75
411	Phil Niekro (Super Veteran)	.25
412	Rangers Batting & Pitching Ldrs. (Buddy Bell, Charlie Hough)	.08
413	Matt Keough	.08
414	Julio Cruz	.08
415	Bob Forsch	.08
416	Joe Ferguson	.08
417	Tom Hausman	.08
418	Greg Pryor	.08
419	Steve Crawford	.08
420	Al Oliver	.08
421	Al Oliver (Super Veteran)	.08
422	George Cappuzzello	.08
423	*Tom Lawless*	.08
424	Jerry Augustine	.08
425	Pedro Guerrero	.08
426	Earl Weaver	.20
427	Roy Lee Jackson	.08
428	Champ Summers	.08
429	Eddie Whitson	.08
430	Kirk Gibson	.25
431	*Gary Gaetti*	.75
432	Porfirio Altamirano	.08
433	Dale Berra	.08
434	Dennis Lamp	.08
435	Tony Armas	.08
436	Bill Campbell	.08
437	Rick Sweet	.08
438	*Dave LaPoint*	.08
439	Rafael Ramirez	.08
440	Ron Guidry	.20
441	Astros Batting & Pitching Ldrs. (Ray Knight, Joe Niekro)	.08
442	Brian Downing	.08
443	Don Hood	.08
444	Wally Backman	.08
445	Mike Flanagan	.08
446	Reid Nichols	.08
447	Bryn Smith	.08
448	Darrell Evans	.08
449	*Eddie Milner*	.08
450	Ted Simmons	.08
451	Ted Simmons (Super Veteran)	.08
452	Lloyd Moseby	.08
453	Lamar Johnson	.08
454	Bob Welch	.08
455	Sixto Lezcano	.08
456	Lee Elia	.08
457	Milt Wilcox	.08
458	Ron Washington	.08
459	Ed Farmer	.08
460	Roy Smalley	.08
461	Steve Trout	.08
462	Steve Nicosia	.08
463	Gaylord Perry	.65
464	Gaylord Perry (Super Veteran)	.20
465	Lonnie Smith	.08
466	Tom Underwood	.08
467	Rufino Linares	.08
468	Dave Goltz	.08
469	Ron Gardenhire	.08
470	Greg Minton	.08
471	Royals Batting & Pitching Ldrs. (Vida Blue, Willie Wilson)	.08
472	Gary Allenson	.08
473	John Lowenstein	.08
474	Ray Burris	.08
475	Cesar Cedeno	.08
476	Rob Picciolo	.08
477	Tom Niedenfuer	.08
478	Phil Garner	.08
479	Charlie Hough	.08
480	Toby Harrah	.08
481	Scot Thompson	.08
482	*Tony Gwynn*	60.00
483	Lynn Jones	.08
484	Dick Ruthven	.08
485	Omar Moreno	.08
486	Clyde King	.08
487	Jerry Hairston	.08
488	Alfredo Griffin	.08
489	Tom Herr	.08
490	Jim Palmer	.90
491	Jim Palmer (Super Veteran)	.20
492	Paul Serna	.08
493	Steve McCatty	.08
494	Bob Brenly	.08
495	Warren Cromartie	.08
496	Tom Veryzer	.08
497	Rick Sutcliffe	.08
498	*Wade Boggs*	30.00
499	Jeff Little	.08
500	Reggie Jackson	2.00
501	Reggie Jackson (Super Veteran)	.75
502	Braves Batting & Pitching Ldrs. (Dale Murphy, Phil Niekro)	.30
503	Moose Haas	.08
504	Don Werner	.08
505	Garry Templeton	.08
506	*Jim Gott*	.25
507	Tony Scott	.08
508	Tom Filer	.08
509	Lou Whitaker	.08
510	Tug McGraw	.08
511	Tug McGraw (Super Veteran)	.08
512	Doyle Alexander	.08
513	Fred Stanley	.08
514	Rudy Law	.08
515	Gene Tenace	.08
516	Bill Virdon	.08
517	Gary Ward	.08
518	Bill Laskey	.08
519	Terry Bulling	.08
520	Fred Lynn	.08
521	Bruce Benedict	.08
522	Pat Zachry	.08

523 Carney Lansford .08
524 Tom Brennan .08
525 Frank White .08
526 Checklist 397-528 .08
527 Larry Biittner .08
528 Jamie Easterly .08
529 Tim Laudner .08
530 Eddie Murray 3.00
531 Athletics Batting & Pitching Ldrs. (Rickey Henderson, Rick Langford) .15
532 Dave Stewart .50
533 Luis Salazar .08
534 John Butcher .08
535 Manny Trillo .08
536 Johnny Wockenfuss .08
537 Rod Scurry .08
538 Danny Heep .08
539 Roger Erickson .08
540 Ozzie Smith 3.00
541 Britt Burns .08
542 Jody Davis .08
543 Alan Fowlkes .08
544 Larry Whisenton .08
545 Floyd Bannister .08
546 Dave Garcia .08
547 Geoff Zahn .08
548 Brian Giles .08
549 *Charlie Puleo* .08
550 Carl Yastrzemski 1.00
551 Carl Yastrzemski (Super Veteran) .50
552 Tim Wallach .20
553 Denny Martinez .08
554 Mike Vail .08
555 Steve Yeager .08
556 Willie Upshaw .08
557 Rick Honeycutt .08
558 Dickie Thon .08
559 Pete Redfern .08
560 Ron LeFlore .08
561 Cardinals Batting & Pitching Ldrs. (Joaquin Andujar, Lonnie Smith) .08
562 Dave Rozema .08
563 Juan Bonilla .08
564 Sid Monge .08
565 Bucky Dent .08
566 Manny Sarmiento .08
567 Joe Simpson .08
568 Willie Hernandez .08
569 Jack Perconte .08
570 Vida Blue .08
571 Mickey Klutts .08
572 Bob Watson .08
573 Andy Hassler .08
574 Glenn Adams .08
575 Neil Allen .08
576 Frank Robinson .15
577 Luis Aponte .08
578 David Green .08
579 Rich Dauer .08
580 Tom Seaver 1.50
581 Tom Seaver (Super Veteran) .50
582 Marshall Edwards .08
583 Terry Forster .08
584 Dave Hostetler .08
585 Jose Cruz .08
586 *Frank Viola* 1.50
587 Ivan DeJesus .08
588 Pat Underwood .08
589 Alvis Woods .08
590 Tony Pena .08
591 White Sox Batting & Pitching Ldrs. (LaMarr Hoyt, Greg Luzinski) .08
592 Shane Rawley .08
593 Broderick Perkins .08
594 Eric Rasmussen .08
595 Tim Raines .60
596 Randy S. Johnson .08
597 Mike Proly .08
598 Dwayne Murphy .08
599 Don Aase .08
600 George Brett 4.00
601 Ed Lynch .08
602 Rich Gedman .08
603 Joe Morgan .75
604 Joe Morgan (Super Veteran) .15
605 Gary Roenicke .08
606 Bobby Cox .08
607 Charlie Leibrandt .08
608 Don Money .08
609 Danny Darwin .08
610 Steve Garvey .75
611 Bert Roberge .08
612 Steve Swisher .08
613 Mike Ivie .08
614 Ed Glynn .08
615 Garry Maddox .08
616 Bill Nahorodny .08
617 Butch Wynegar .08
618 LaMarr Hoyt .08
619 Keith Moreland .08
620 Mike Norris .08
621 Mets Batting & Pitching Ldrs. (Craig Swan, Mookie Wilson) .08
622 Dave Edler .08
623 Luis Sanchez .08
624 Glenn Hubbard .08
625 Ken Forsch .08
626 Jerry Martin .08
627 Doug Bair .08
628 Julio Valdez .08
629 Charlie Lea .08
630 Paul Molitor 3.00
631 Tippy Martinez .08
632 Alex Trevino .08
633 Vicente Romo .08
634 Max Venable .08
635 Graig Nettles .08
636 Graig Nettles (Super Veteran) .08
637 Pat Corrales .08
638 Dan Petry .08
639 Art Howe .08
640 Andre Thornton .08
641 Billy Sample .08
642 Checklist 529-660 .08
643 Bump Wills .08
644 Joe Lefebvre .08
645 Bill Madlock .08
646 Jim Essian .08
647 Bobby Mitchell .08
648 Jeff Burroughs .08
649 Tommy Boggs .08
650 George Hendrick .08
651 Angels Batting & Pitching Ldrs. (Rod Carew, Mike Witt) .08
652 Butch Hobson .08
653 Ellis Valentine .08
654 Bob Ojeda .08
655 Al Bumbry .08
656 Dave Frost .08
657 Mike Gates .08
658 Frank Pastore .08
659 Charlie Moore .08
660 Mike Hargrove .08
661 Bill Russell .08
662 Joe Sambito .08
663 Tom O'Malley .08
664 Bob Molinaro .08
665 Jim Sundberg .08
666 Sparky Anderson .15
667 Dick Davis .08
668 Larry Christenson .08
669 Mike Squires .08
670 Jerry Mumphrey .08
671 Lenny Faedo .08
672 Jim Kaat .20
673 Jim Kaat (Super Veteran) .08
674 Kurt Bevacqua .08
675 Jim Beattie .08
676 Biff Pocoroba .08
677 Dave Revering .08
678 Juan Beniquez .08
679 Mike Scott .08
680 Andre Dawson .75
681 Dodgers Batting & Pitching Ldrs. (Pedro Guerrero, Fernando Valenzuela) .08
682 Bob Stanley .08
683 Dan Ford .08
684 Rafael Landestoy .08
685 Lee Mazzilli .08
686 Randy Lerch .08
687 U.L. Washington .08
688 Jim Wohlford .08
689 Ron Hassey .08
690 Kent Hrbek .75
691 Dave Tobik .08
692 Denny Walling .08
693 Sparky Lyle .08
694 Sparky Lyle (Super Veteran) .08
695 Ruppert Jones .08
696 Chuck Tanner .08
697 Barry Foote .08
698 Tony Bernazard .08
699 Lee Smith 1.50
700 Keith Hernandez .08
701 Batting Leaders (Al Oliver, Willie Wilson) .08
702 Home Run Leaders (Reggie Jackson, Dave Kingman, Gorman Thomas) .15
703 Runs Batted In Leaders (Hal McRae, Dale Murphy, Al Oliver) .08
704 Stolen Base Leaders (Rickey Henderson, Tim Raines) .20
705 Victory Leaders (Steve Carlton, LaMarr Hoyt) .08
706 Strikeout Leaders (Floyd Bannister, Steve Carlton) .08
707 Earned Run Average Leaders (Steve Rogers, Rick Sutcliffe) .08
708 Leading Firemen (Dan Quisenberry, Bruce Sutter) .08
709 Jimmy Sexton .08
710 Willie Wilson .08
711 Mariners Batting & Pitching Ldrs. (Jim Beattie, Bruce Bochte) .08
712 Bruce Kison .08
713 Ron Hodges .08
714 Wayne Nordhagen .08
715 Tony Perez .15
716 Tony Perez (Super Veteran) .08
717 Scott Sanderson .08
718 Jim Dwyer .08
719 Rich Gale .08
720 Dave Concepcion .08
721 John Martin .08
722 Jorge Orta .08
723 Randy Moffitt .08
724 Johnny Grubb .08
725 Dan Spillner .08
726 Harvey Kuenn .08
727 Chet Lemon .08
728 Ron Reed .08
729 Jerry Morales .08
730 Jason Thompson .08
731 Al Williams .08
732 Dave Henderson .08
733 Buck Martinez .08
734 Steve Braun .08
735 Tommy John .25
736 Tommy John (Super Veteran) .08
737 Mitchell Page .08
738 Tim Foli .08
739 Rick Ownbey .08
740 Rusty Staub .08
741 Rusty Staub (Super Veteran) .08
742 Padres Batting & Pitching Ldrs. (Terry Kennedy, Tim Lollar) .08
743 Mike Torrez .08
744 Brad Mills .08
745 Scott McGregor .08
746 John Wathan .08
747 Fred Breining .08
748 Derrel Thomas .08
749 Jon Matlack .08
750 Ben Oglivie .08
751 Brad Havens .08
752 Luis Pujols .08
753 Elias Sosa .08
754 Bill Robinson .08
755 John Candelaria .08
756 Russ Nixon .08
757 Rick Manning .08
758 Aurelio Rodriguez .08
759 Doug Bird .08
760 Dale Murphy .75
761 Gary Lucas .08
762 Cliff Johnson .08
763 Al Cowens .08
764 Pete Falcone .08
765 Bob Boone .08
766 Barry Bonnell .08
767 Duane Kuiper .08
768 Chris Speier .08
769 Checklist 661-792 .08
770 Dave Winfield 2.50
771 Twins Batting & Pitching Ldrs. (Bobby Castillo, Kent Hrbek) .08
772 Jim Kern .08
773 Larry Hisle .08
774 Alan Ashby .08
775 Burt Hooton .08
776 Larry Parrish .08
777 John Curtis .08
778 Rich Hebner .08
779 Rick Waits .08
780 Gary Matthews .08
781 Rick Rhoden .08
782 Bobby Murcer .08
783 Bobby Murcer (Super Veteran) .08
784 Jeff Newman .08
785 Dennis Leonard .08
786 Ralph Houk .08
787 Dick Tidrow .08
788 Dane Iorg .08
789 Bryan Clark .08
790 Bob Grich .08
791 Gary Lavelle .08
792 Chris Chambliss .08

1983 Topps Traded

These 2-1/2" x 3-1/2" cards mark a continuation of the traded set introduced in 1981. The 132 cards retain the basic design of the year's regular issue, with their numbering being 1-132 with the "T" suffix. Cards in the set include traded players, new managers and promising rookies. Sold only through dealers, the set was in heavy demand as it contained the first cards of Darryl Strawberry, Ron Kittle, Julio Franco and Mel Hall. While some of those cards were very hot in 1983, it seems likely that some of the rookies may not live up to their initial promise.

MT
Complete Set (132): 25.00
Common Player: .10
1T Neil Allen .10
2T Bill Almon .10
3T Joe Altobelli .10
4T Tony Armas .10
5T Doug Bair .10
6T Steve Baker .10
7T Floyd Bannister .10
8T Don Baylor .50
9T Tony Bernazard .10
10T Larry Biittner .10
11T Dann Bilardello .10
12T Doug Bird .10
13T Steve Boros .10
14T Greg Brock .10
15T Mike Brown .10
16T Tom Burgmeier .10
17T Randy Bush .10
18T Bert Campaneris .10
19T Ron Cey .10
20T Chris Codiroli .10
21T Dave Collins .10
22T Terry Crowley .10
23T Julio Cruz .10
24T Mike Davis .10
25T Frank DiPino .10
26T Bill Doran .25
27T Jerry Dybzinski .10
28T Jamie Easterly .10
29T Juan Eichelberger .10
30T Jim Essian .10
31T Pete Falcone .10
32T Mike Ferraro .10
33T Terry Forster .10
34T *Julio Franco* 3.00
35T Rich Gale .10
36T Kiko Garcia .10
37T Steve Garvey 2.00
38T Johnny Grubb .10
39T Mel Hall .25
40T Von Hayes .25
41T Danny Heep .10
42T Steve Henderson .10
43T Keith Hernandez .15
44T Leo Hernandez .10
45T Willie Hernandez .10
46T Al Holland .10
47T Frank Howard .15
48T Bobby Johnson .10
49T Cliff Johnson .10
50T Odell Jones .10
51T Mike Jorgensen .10
52T Bob Kearney .10
53T Steve Kemp .10
54T Matt Keough .10
55T Ron Kittle .10
56T Mickey Klutts .10
57T Alan Knicely .10
58T Mike Krukow .10
59T Rafael Landestoy .10
60T Carney Lansford .10
61T Joe Lefebvre .10
62T Bryan Little .10
63T Aurelio Lopez .10
64T Mike Madden .10
65T Rick Manning .10
66T Billy Martin .40
67T Lee Mazzilli .10
68T Andy McGaffigan .10
69T Craig McMurtry .10
70T John McNamara .10
71T Orlando Mercado .10
72T Larry Milbourne .10
73T Randy Moffitt .10
74T Sid Monge .10
75T Jose Morales .10
76T Omar Moreno .10
77T Joe Morgan 4.00
78T Mike Morgan .10
79T Dale Murray .10
80T Jeff Newman .10
81T Pete O'Brien .25
82T Jorge Orta .10
83T Alejandro Pena .10
84T Pascual Perez .15
85T Tony Perez 1.50
86T Broderick Perkins .10
87T *Tony Phillips* 3.00
88T Charlie Puleo .10
89T Pat Putnam .10
90T Jamie Quirk .10
91T Doug Rader .10
92T Chuck Rainey .10
93T Bobby Ramos .10
94T Gary Redus .10
95T Steve Renko .10
96T Leon Roberts .10
97T Aurelio Rodriguez .10
98T Dick Ruthven .10
99T Daryl Sconiers .10
100T Mike Scott .10
101T Tom Seaver 7.50
102T John Shelby .10
103T Bob Shirley .10
104T Joe Simpson .10
105T Doug Sisk .10
106T Mike Smithson .10
107T Elias Sosa .10
108T *Darryl Strawberry* 10.00
109T Tom Tellmann .10
110T Gene Tenace .10
111T Gorman Thomas .10
112T Dick Tidrow .10
113T Dave Tobik .10
114T Wayne Tolleson .10
115T Mike Torrez .10
116T Manny Trillo .10
117T Steve Trout .10
118T Lee Tunnell .10
119T Mike Vail .10
120T Ellis Valentine .10
121T Tom Veryzer .10
122T George Vukovich .10
123T Rick Waits .10
124T Greg Walker .10
125T Chris Welsh .10
126T Len Whitehouse .10
127T Eddie Whitson .10
128T Jim Wohlford .10
129T Matt Young .10
130T Joel Youngblood .10
131T Pat Zachry .10
132T Checklist 1-132 .10

1983 Topps 1982 League Leaders Sheet

The leaders in various major statistical categories in 1982 are featured on this 7-1/2" x 10-1/2" blank-back sheet. Most of the cards on the sheet are identical to the players' regular 1983 Topps cards except for a white strip at upper-left identifying their statistical accomplishment. Reggie Jackson and Gorman Thomas who shared the A.L. home run record for 1982 share a card on this sheet. Available via a mail-in offer, huge quantities of these sheets are readily available.

MT
Uncut Sheet:
(1) Willie Wilson, Reggie Jackson, Gorman Thomas, Al Oliver, LaMarr Hoyt, Steve Carlton, Dan Quisenberry, Dave Kingman, Bruce Sutter 2.00

1983 Topps All-Star Glossy Set of 40

This set was a "consolation prize" in a scratch-off contest in regular packs of 1983 cards. The 2-1/2" x 3-1/2" cards have a large color photo surrounded by a yellow frame on the front. In very small type on a white border is printed the player's name. Backs carry the player's name, team, position and the card number along with a Topps identification. A major feature is that the surface of the front is glossy, which most collectors find very attractive. With many top stars, the set is a popular one, but the price has not moved too far above the issue price.

		MT
Complete Set (40):		13.00
Common Player:		.15
1	Carl Yastrzemski	.75
2	Mookie Wilson	.15
3	Andre Thornton	.15
4	Keith Hernandez	.15
5	Robin Yount	.60
6	Terry Kennedy	.15
7	Dave Winfield	.50
8	Mike Schmidt	.75
9	Buddy Bell	.15
10	Fernando Valenzuela	.15
11	Rich Gossage	.15
12	Bob Horner	.15
13	Toby Harrah	.15
14	Pete Rose	1.00
15	Cecil Cooper	.15
16	Dale Murphy	.35
17	Carlton Fisk	.30
18	Ray Knight	.15
19	Jim Palmer	.45
20	Gary Carter	.25
21	Richard Zisk	.15
22	Dusty Baker	.15
23	Willie Wilson	.15
24	Bill Buckner	.15
25	Dave Stieb	.15
26	Bill Madlock	.15
27	Lance Parrish	.15
28	Nolan Ryan	1.50
29	Rod Carew	.60
30	Al Oliver	.15
31	George Brett	.75
32	Jack Clark	.15
33	Rickey Henderson	.60
34	Dave Concepcion	.15
35	Kent Hrbek	.15
36	Steve Carlton	.50
37	Eddie Murray	.60
38	Ruppert Jones	.15
39	Reggie Jackson	.75
40	Bruce Sutter	.15

1983 Topps Foldouts

Another Topps test issue, these 3-1/2" x 5-5/16" cards were printed in booklets like souvenir postcards. Each of the booklets have a theme of currently playing statistical leaders in a specific category such as home runs. The cards feature a color player photo on each side. A black strip at the bottom gives the player's name, position and team along with statistics in the particular category. A facsimile autograph crosses the photograph. Booklets carry nine cards, with eight having players on both sides and one doubling as the back cover, for a total of 17 cards per booklet. There are 85 cards in the set, although some players appear in more than one category. Naturally, most of the players pictured are stars. Even so, the set is a problem as it seems to be most valuable when complete and unseparated, so the cards are difficult to display.

		MT
Complete Set (5):		24.00
Common Folder:		4.00
1	Pitching Leaders (Vida Blue, Bert Blyleven, Steve Carlton, Fergie Jenkins, Tommy John, Jim Kaat, Jerry Koosman, Joe Niekro, Phil Niekro, Jim Palmer, Gaylord Perry, Jerry Reuss, Nolan Ryan, Tom Seaver, Paul Splittorff, Don Sutton, Mike Torrez)	9.00
2	Home Run Leaders (Johnny Bench, Ron Cey, Darrell Evans, George Foster, Reggie Jackson, Dave Kingman, Greg Luzinski, John Mayberry, Rick Monday, Joe Morgan, Bobby Murcer, Graig Nettles, Tony Perez, Jim Rice, Mike Schmidt, Rusty Staub, Carl Yastrzemski)	6.00
3	Batting Leaders (George Brett, Rod Carew, Cecil Cooper, Steve Garvey, Ken Griffey, Pedro Guerrero, Keith Hernandez, Dane Iorg, Fred Lynn, Bill Madlock, Bake McBride, Al Oliver, Dave Parker, Jim Rice, Pete Rose, Lonnie Smith, Willie Wilson)	6.00
4	Relief Aces (Tom Burgmeier, Bill Campbell, Ed Farmer, Rollie Fingers, Terry Forster, Gene Garber, Rich Gossage, Jim Kern, Gary Lavelle, Tug McGraw, Greg Minton, Randy Moffitt, Dan Quisenberry, Ron Reed, Elias Sosa, Bruce Sutter, Kent Tekulve)	4.00
5	Stolen Base Leaders (Don Baylor, Larry Bowa, Al Bumbry, Rod Carew, Cesar Cedeno, Dave Concepcion, Jose Cruz, Julio Cruz, Rickey Henderson, Ron LeFlore, Davey Lopes, Garry Maddox, Omar Moreno, Joe Morgan, Amos Otis, Mickey Rivers, Willie Wilson)	4.00

1983 Topps Stickers

Topps increased the number of stickers in its set to 330 in 1983, but retained the same 1-15/16" x 2-9/16" size. The stickers are again numbered on both the front and back. Similar in style to previous sticker issues, the set includes 28 "foil" stickers, and various special stickers highlighting the 1982 season, playoffs and World Series. An album was also available.

		MT
Complete Set (330):		17.00
Common Player:		.05
Sticker Album:		2.00
1	Hank Aaron	.50
2	Babe Ruth	.75
3	Willie Mays	.50
4	Frank Robinson	.20
5	Reggie Jackson	.20
6	Carl Yastrzemski	.20
7	Johnny Bench	.20
8	Tony Perez	.10
9	Lee May	.05
10	Mike Schmidt	.35
11	Dave Kingman	.05
12	Reggie Smith	.05
13	Graig Nettles	.05
14	Rusty Staub	.05
15	Willie Wilson	.05
16	LaMarr Hoyt	.05
17	Reggie Jackson, Gorman Thomas	.15
18	Floyd Bannister	.05
19	Hal McRae	.05
20	Rick Sutcliffe	.05
21	Rickey Henderson	.25
22	Dan Quisenberry	.05
23	Jim Palmer	.20
24	John Lowenstein	.05
25	Mike Flanagan	.05
26	Cal Ripken, Jr.	1.00
27	Rich Dauer	.05
28	Ken Singleton	.05
29	Eddie Murray	.20
30	Rick Dempsey	.05
31	Carl Yastrzemski	.25
32	Carney Lansford	.05
33	Jerry Remy	.05
34	Dennis Eckersley	.05
35	Dave Stapleton	.05
36	Mark Clear	.05
37	Jim Rice	.10
38	Dwight Evans	.05
39	Rod Carew	.20
40	Don Baylor	.10
41	Reggie Jackson	.25
42	Geoff Zahn	.05
43	Bobby Grich	.05
44	Fred Lynn	.05
45	Bob Boone	.05
46	Doug DeCinces	.05
47	Tom Paciorek	.05
48	Britt Burns	.05
49	Tony Bernazard	.05
50	Steve Kemp	.05
51	Greg Luzinski	.05
52	Harold Baines	.05
53	LaMarr Hoyt	.05
54	Carlton Fisk	.15
55	Andre Thornton	.05
56	Mike Hargrove	.05
57	Len Barker	.05
58	Toby Harrah	.05
59	Dan Spillner	.05
60	Rick Manning	.05
61	Rick Sutcliffe	.05
62	Ron Hassey	.05
63	Lance Parrish	.05
64	John Wockenfuss	.05
65	Lou Whitaker	.05
66	Alan Trammell	.10
67	Kirk Gibson	.05
68	Larry Herndon	.05
69	Jack Morris	.05
70	Dan Petry	.05
71	Frank White	.05
72	Amos Otis	.05
73	Willie Wilson	.05
74	Dan Quisenberry	.05
75	Hal McRae	.05
76	George Brett	.35
77	Larry Gura	.05
78	John Wathan	.05
79	Rollie Fingers	.10
80	Cecil Cooper	.05
81	Robin Yount	.35
82	Ben Oglivie	.05
83	Paul Molitor	.25
84	Gorman Thomas	.05
85	Ted Simmons	.05
86	Pete Vuckovich	.05
87	Gary Gaetti	.05
88	Kent Hrbek	.05
89	John Castino	.05
90	Tom Brunansky	.05
91	Bobby Mitchell	.05
92	Gary Ward	.05
93	Tim Laudner	.05
94	Ron Davis	.05
95	Willie Randolph	.05
96	Roy Smalley	.05
97	Jerry Mumphrey	.05
98	Ken Griffey	.05
99	Dave Winfield	.20
100	Rich Gossage	.05
101	Butch Wynegar	.05
102	Ron Guidry	.05
103	Rickey Henderson	.20
104	Mike Heath	.05
105	Dave Lopes	.05
106	Rick Langford	.05
107	Dwayne Murphy	.05
108	Tony Armas	.05
109	Matt Keough	.05
110	Dan Meyer	.05
111	Bruce Bochte	.05
112	Julio Cruz	.05
113	Floyd Bannister	.05
114	Gaylord Perry	.15
115	Al Cowens	.05
116	Richie Zisk	.05
117	Jim Essian	.05
118	Bill Caudill	.05
119	Buddy Bell	.05
120	Larry Parrish	.05
121	Danny Darwin	.05
122	Bucky Dent	.05
123	Johnny Grubb	.05
124	George Wright	.05
125	Charlie Hough	.05
126	Jim Sundberg	.05
127	Dave Stieb	.05
128	Willie Upshaw	.05
129	Alfredo Griffin	.05
130	Lloyd Moseby	.05
131	Ernie Whitt	.05
132	Jim Clancy	.05
133	Barry Bonnell	.05
134	Damaso Garcia	.05
135	Jim Kaat	.05
136	Jim Kaat	.05
137	Greg Minton	.05
138	Greg Minton	.05
139	Paul Molitor	.20
140	Paul Molitor	.15
141	Manny Trillo	.05
142	Manny Trillo	.05
143	Joel Youngblood	.05
144	Joel Youngblood	.05
145	Robin Yount	.35
146	Robin Yount	.35
147	Willie McGee	.05
148	Darrell Porter	.05
149	Darrell Porter	.05
150	Robin Yount	.35
151	Bruce Benedict	.05
152	Bruce Benedict	.05
153	George Hendrick	.05
154	Bruce Benedict	.05
155	Doug DeCinces	.05
156	Paul Molitor	.25
157	Charlie Moore	.05
158	Fred Lynn	.05
159	Rickey Henderson	.25
160	Dale Murphy	.15
161	Willie Wilson	.05
162	Jack Clark	.05
163	Reggie Jackson	.20
164	Andre Dawson	.10
165	Dan Quisenberry	.05
166	Bruce Sutter	.05
167	Robin Yount	.35
168	Ozzie Smith	.15
169	Frank White	.05
170	Phil Garner	.05
171	Doug DeCinces	.05
172	Mike Schmidt	.25
173	Cecil Cooper	.05
174	Al Oliver	.05
175	Jim Palmer	.15
176	Steve Carlton	.15
177	Carlton Fisk	.15
178	Gary Carter	.15
179	Joaquin Andujar	.05
180	Ozzie Smith	.15
181	Cecil Cooper	.05
182	Darrell Porter	.05
183	Darrell Porter	.05
184	Mike Caldwell	.05
185	Mike Caldwell	.05
186	Ozzie Smith	.15
187	Bruce Sutter	.05
188	Keith Hernandez	.05
189	Dane Iorg	.05
190	Dane Iorg	.05
191	Tony Armas	.05
192	Tony Armas	.05
193	Lance Parrish	.05
194	Lance Parrish	.05
195	John Wathan	.05
196	John Wathan	.05
197	Rickey Henderson	.15
198	Rickey Henderson	.15
199	Rickey Henderson	.15
200	Rickey Henderson	.15
201	Rickey Henderson	.15
202	Rickey Henderson	.15
203	Steve Carlton	.15
204	Steve Carlton	.15
205	Al Oliver	.05
206	Dale Murphy, Al Oliver	.10
207	Dave Kingman	.05
208	Steve Rogers	.05
209	Bruce Sutter	.05
210	Tim Raines	.10
211	Dale Murphy	.15
212	Chris Chambliss	.05
213	Gene Garber	.05
214	Bob Horner	.05
215	Glenn Hubbard	.05
216	Claudell Washington	.05
217	Bruce Benedict	.05
218	Phil Niekro	.10
219	Leon Durham	.05
220	Jay Johnstone	.05
221	Larry Bowa	.05
222	Keith Moreland	.05
223	Bill Buckner	.05
224	Fergie Jenkins	.10
225	Dick Tidrow	.05
226	Jody Davis	.05
227	Dave Concepcion	.05
228	Dan Driessen	.05
229	Johnny Bench	.20
230	Ron Oester	.05
231	Cesar Cedeno	.05
232	Alex Trevino	.05
233	Tom Seaver	.20
234	Mario Soto	.05
235	Nolan Ryan	1.00
236	Art Howe	.05
237	Phil Garner	.05
238	Ray Knight	.05
239	Terry Puhl	.05
240	Joe Niekro	.05
241	Alan Ashby	.05
242	Jose Cruz	.05
243	Steve Garvey	.15
244	Ron Cey	.05
245	Dusty Baker	.05
246	Ken Landreaux	.05
247	Jerry Reuss	.05
248	Pedro Guerrero	.05
249	Bill Russell	.05
250	Fernando Valenzuela	.10
251	Al Oliver	.05
252	Andre Dawson	.10
253	Tim Raines	.10
254	Jeff Reardon	.05
255	Gary Carter	.15
256	Steve Rogers	.05
257	Tim Wallach	.05
258	Chris Speier	.05
259	Dave Kingman	.05
260	Bob Bailor	.05
261	Hubie Brooks	.05
262	Craig Swan	.05
263	George Foster	.05
264	John Stearns	.05
265	Neil Allen	.05
266	Mookie Wilson	.05
267	Steve Carlton	.20
268	Manny Trillo	.05
269	Gary Matthews	.05
270	Mike Schmidt	.25
271	Ivan DeJesus	.05
272	Pete Rose	.50
273	Bo Diaz	.05
274	Sid Monge	.05
275	Bill Madlock	.05
276	Jason Thompson	.05
277	Don Robinson	.05
278	Omar Moreno	.05
279	Dale Berra	.05
280	Dave Parker	.05
281	Tony Pena	.05
282	John Candelaria	.05
283	Lonnie Smith	.05
284	Bruce Sutter	.05
285	George Hendrick	.05
286	Tom Herr	.05
287	Ken Oberkfell	.05
288	Ozzie Smith	.15
289	Bob Forsch	.05
290	Keith Hernandez	.05
291	Garry Templeton	.05
292	Broderick Perkins	.05
293	Terry Kennedy	.05
294	Gene Richards	.05
295	Ruppert Jones	.05
296	Tim Lollar	.05
297	John Montefusco	.05
298	Sixto Lezcano	.05
299	Greg Minton	.05
300	Jack Clark	.05
301	Milt May	.05
302	Reggie Smith	.05
303	Joe Morgan	.10
304	John LeMaster	.05
305	Darrell Evans	.05
306	Al Holland	.05
307	Jesse Barfield	.05
308	Wade Boggs	.30
309	Tom Brunansky	.05
310	Storm Davis	.05
311	Von Hayes	.05
312	Dave Hostetler	.05
313	Kent Hrbek	.05
314	Tim Laudner	.05
315	Cal Ripken, Jr.	1.00
316	Andre Robertson	.05
317	Ed Vande Berg	.05
318	Glenn Wilson	.05
319	Chili Davis	.05
320	Bob Dernier	.05
321	Terry Francona	.05
322	Brian Giles	.05
323	David Green	.05
324	Atlee Hammaker	.05
325	Bill Laskey	.05
326	Willie McGee	.05
327	Johnny Ray	.05
328	Ryne Sandberg	.30
329	Steve Sax	.05
330	Eric Show	.05

Player names in *Italic* type indicate a rookie card.

1983 Topps Stickers Boxes

These eight cards were printed on the back panels of 1983 Topps sticker boxes, one card per box. The blank-backed cards measure the standard 2-1/2" x 3-1/2" and feature a full-color photo with the player's name at the top. The rest of the back panel advertises the sticker album, while the front of the box has an action photo of Reggie Jackson. The boxes are numbered on the front. Prices in the checklist that follows are for complete boxes.

		MT
Complete Set (8):		6.50
Common Player:		.75
1	Fernando Valenzuela	.75
2	Gary Carter	.75
3	Mike Schmidt	1.00
4	Reggie Jackson	1.00
5	Jim Palmer	.75
6	Rollie Fingers	.75
7	Pete Rose	1.50
8	Rickey Henderson	1.00

1983 Topps Traded Steve Carlton Bronze

The first in a series of 1/4-size metal replicas of Topps star cards was issued to dealers who purchased cases of 1983 Topps Traded sets. Each detail of the 1983 Steve Carlton card is reproduced on the 5/8" x 7/8" bronze metal mini-card, right down to the stats.

		MT
(1)	Steve Carlton	10.00

1983 Topps 1952 Reprint Set

The first of several reprint/retro sets in different sports issued by Topps, the 403-card reprinting of its classic 1952 baseball card set was controversial at the time of issue, but has since gained hobby acceptance and market value. To avoid possible confusion of the reprints for originals, the reprints were done in the now-standard 2-1/2" x 3-1/2" format instead of the original 2-5/8" x 3-3/4". Backs, printed in red, carry a line "Topps 1952 Reprint Series" at bottom, though there is no indication of the year of reprinting. Fronts have a semi-gloss finish, which also differs from the originals. Because of inability to come to terms with five of the players from the original 1952 Topps set, they were not included in the reprint series. Those cards which weren't issued are: #20 Billy Loes, #22 Dom DiMaggio, #159 Saul Rogovin, #196 Solly Hemus, and #289 Tommy Holmes. Two checklist cards were added to the reprint set. The '52 reprints were available only as a complete boxed set with a retail price of about $40 at issue.

		MT
Complete Sealed Boxed Set:		450.00
Complete Set (403):		300.00
Common Player:		.25
Minor Stars:		.50
Typical Hall of Famers:		2.00
Superstar Hall of Famers:		8.00
311	Mickey Mantle	75.00
407	Eddie Mathews (sample card)	12.00

(See 1952 Topps for checklist)

1984 Topps

Another 792-card regular set from Topps. For the second straight year, the 2-1/2" x 3-1/2" cards featured a color action photo on the front along with a small portrait photo in the lower left. The team name runs in big letters down the left side, while the player's name and position runs under the large action photo. In the upper right-hand corner is the Topps logo. Backs have a team logo in the upper right corner, along with statistics, personal information and a few highlights. The backs have an unusual and hard-to-read red and purple coloring. Specialty cards include past season highlights, team leaders, major league statistical leaders, All-Stars, active career leaders and numbered checklists. Again, promising rookies were saved for the traded set. Late in 1984, Topps introduced a specially boxed "Tiffany" edition of the 1984 set, with the cards printed on white cardboard with a glossy finish. A total of 10,000 sets were produced. Prices for Tiffany edition super-stars can run from six to eight times the value of the "regular" edition, while common cards sell in the 40¢ range.

		MT
Complete Set (792):		40.00
Common Player:		.08
Wax Box:		75.00
1	Steve Carlton (1983 Highlight)	.25
2	Rickey Henderson (1983 Highlight)	.40
3	Dan Quisenberry (1983 Highlight)	.08
4	Steve Carlton, Gaylord Perry, Nolan Ryan (1983 Highlight)	.75
5	Bob Forsch , Dave Righetti, Mike Warren (1983 Highlight)	.08
6	Johnny Bench, Gaylord Perry, Carl Yastrzemski (1983 Highlight)	.30
7	Gary Lucas	.08
8	*Don Mattingly*	10.00
9	Jim Gott	.08
10	Robin Yount	2.00
11	Twins Batting & Pitching Leaders (Kent Hrbek, Ken Schrom)	.08
12	Billy Sample	.08
13	Scott Holman	.08
14	Tom Brookens	.08
15	Burt Hooton	.08
16	Omar Moreno	.08
17	John Denny	.08
18	Dale Berra	.08
19	*Ray Fontenot*	.08
20	Greg Luzinski	.08
21	Joe Altobelli	.08
22	Bryan Clark	.08
23	Keith Moreland	.08
24	John Martin	.08
25	Glenn Hubbard	.08
26	Bud Black	.08
27	Daryl Sconiers	.08
28	Frank Viola	.08
29	Danny Heep	.08
30	Wade Boggs	4.00
31	Andy McGaffigan	.08
32	Bobby Ramos	.08
33	Tom Burgmeier	.08
34	Eddie Milner	.08
35	Don Sutton	.35
36	Denny Walling	.08
37	Rangers Batting & Pitching Leaders (Buddy Bell, Rick Honeycutt)	.08
38	Luis DeLeon	.08
39	Garth Iorg	.08
40	Dusty Baker	.08
41	Tony Bernazard	.08
42	Johnny Grubb	.08
43	Ron Reed	.08
44	Jim Morrison	.08
45	Jerry Mumphrey	.08
46	Ray Smith	.08
47	Rudy Law	.08
48	Julio Franco	.45
49	John Stuper	.08
50	Chris Chambliss	.08
51	Jim Frey	.08
52	Paul Splittorff	.08
53	Juan Beniquez	.08
54	Jesse Orosco	.08
55	Dave Concepcion	.08
56	Gary Allenson	.08
57	Dan Schatzeder	.08
58	Max Venable	.08
59	Sammy Stewart	.08
60	Paul Molitor	2.00
61	*Chris Codiroli*	.08
62	Dave Hostetler	.08
63	Ed Vande Berg	.08
64	Mike Scioscia	.08
65	Kirk Gibson	.08
66	Astros Batting & Pitching Leaders (Jose Cruz, Nolan Ryan)	.25
67	Gary Ward	.08
68	Luis Salazar	.08
69	Rod Scurry	.08
70	Gary Matthews	.08
71	Leo Hernandez	.08
72	Mike Squires	.08
73	Jody Davis	.08
74	Jerry Martin	.08
75	Bob Forsch	.08
76	Alfredo Griffin	.08
77	Brett Butler	.08
78	Mike Torrez	.08
79	Rob Wilfong	.08
80	Steve Rogers	.08
81	Billy Martin	.15
82	Doug Bird	.08
83	Richie Zisk	.08
84	Lenny Faedo	.08
85	Atlee Hammaker	.08
86	*John Shelby*	.08
87	Frank Pastore	.08
88	Rob Picciolo	.08
89	*Mike Smithson*	.08
90	Pedro Guerrero	.08
91	Dan Spillner	.08
92	Lloyd Moseby	.08
93	Bob Knepper	.08
94	Mario Ramirez	.08
95	Aurelio Lopez	.08
96	Royals Batting & Pitching Leaders (Larry Gura, Hal McRae)	.08
97	LaMarr Hoyt	.08
98	Steve Nicosia	.08
99	*Craig Lefferts*	.25
100	Reggie Jackson	1.50
101	Porfirio Altamirano	.08
102	Ken Oberkfell	.08
103	Dwayne Murphy	.08
104	Ken Dayley	.08
105	Tony Armas	.08
106	Tim Stoddard	.08
107	Ned Yost	.08
108	Randy Moffitt	.08
109	Brad Wellman	.08
110	Ron Guidry	.08
111	Bill Virdon	.08
112	Tom Niedenfuer	.08
113	Kelly Paris	.08
114	Checklist 1-132	.08
115	Andre Thornton	.08
116	George Bjorkman	.08
117	Tom Veryzer	.08
118	Charlie Hough	.08
119	Johnny Wockenfuss	.08
120	Keith Hernandez	.08
121	*Pat Sheridan*	.08
122	Cecilio Guante	.08
123	Butch Wynegar	.08
124	Damaso Garcia	.08
125	Britt Burns	.08
126	Braves Batting & Pitching Leaders (Craig McMurtry, Dale Murphy)	.08
127	Mike Madden	.08
128	Rick Manning	.08
129	Bill Laskey	.08
130	Ozzie Smith	2.00
131	Batting Leaders (Wade Boggs, Bill Madlock)	.25
132	Home Run Leaders (Jim Rice, Mike Schmidt)	.30
133	RBI Leaders (Cecil Cooper, Dale Murphy, Jim Rice)	.20
134	Stolen Base Leaders (Rickey Henderson, Tim Raines)	.25
135	Victory Leaders (John Denny, LaMarr Hoyt)	.08
136	Strikeout Leaders (Steve Carlton, Jack Morris)	.08
137	Earned Run Average Leaders (Atlee Hammaker, Rick Honeycutt)	.08
138	Leading Firemen (Al Holland, Dan Quisenberry)	.08
139	Bert Campaneris	.08
140	Storm Davis	.08
141	Pat Corrales	.08
142	Rich Gale	.08
143	Jose Morales	.08
144	*Brian Harper*	.35
145	Gary Lavelle	.08
146	Ed Romero	.08
147	Dan Petry	.08
148	Joe Lefebvre	.08
149	Jon Matlack	.08
150	Dale Murphy	.50
151	Steve Trout	.08
152	Glenn Brummer	.08
153	Dick Tidrow	.08
154	Dave Henderson	.08
155	Frank White	.08
156	Athletics Batting & Pitching Leaders (Tim Conroy, Rickey Henderson)	.15
157	Gary Gaetti	.08
158	John Curtis	.08
159	Darryl Cias	.08
160	Mario Soto	.08
161	*Junior Ortiz*	.08
162	Bob Ojeda	.08
163	Lorenzo Gray	.08
164	Scott Sanderson	.08
165	Ken Singleton	.08
166	Jamie Nelson	.08
167	Marshall Edwards	.08
168	Juan Bonilla	.08
169	Larry Parrish	.08
170	Jerry Reuss	.08
171	Frank Robinson	.15
172	Frank DiPino	.08
173	*Marvell Wynne*	.08
174	Juan Berenguer	.08
175	Graig Nettles	.08
176	Lee Smith	.08
177	Jerry Hairston	.08
178	Bill Krueger	.08
179	Buck Martinez	.08
180	Manny Trillo	.08
181	Roy Thomas	.08
182	Darryl Strawberry	1.50
183	Al Williams	.08
184	Mike O'Berry	.08
185	Sixto Lezcano	.08
186	Cardinals Batting & Pitching Leaders (Lonnie Smith, John Stuper)	.08
187	Luis Aponte	.08
188	Bryan Little	.08
189	*Tim Conroy*	.08
190	Ben Oglivie	.08
191	Mike Boddicker	.08
192	*Nick Esasky*	.08
193	Darrell Brown	.08
194	Domingo Ramos	.08
195	Jack Morris	.08
196	Don Slaught	.08
197	Garry Hancock	.08
198	*Bill Doran*	.15
199	Willie Hernandez	.08
200	Andre Dawson	.60
201	Bruce Kison	.08
202	Bobby Cox	.08
203	Matt Keough	.08
204	*Bobby Meacham*	.08
205	Greg Minton	.08
206	*Andy Van Slyke*	.75
207	Donnie Moore	.08
208	*Jose Oquendo*	.15
209	Manny Sarmiento	.08
210	Joe Morgan	.30
211	Rick Sweet	.08
212	Broderick Perkins	.08
213	Bruce Hurst	.08
214	Paul Householder	.08
215	Tippy Martinez	.08
216	White Sox Batting & Pitching Leaders (Richard Dotson, Carlton Fisk)	.08
217	Alan Ashby	.08
218	Rick Waits	.08
219	Joe Simpson	.08
220	Fernando Valenzuela	.08
221	Cliff Johnson	.08
222	Rick Honeycutt	.08
223	Wayne Krenchicki	.08
224	Sid Monge	.08
225	Lee Mazzilli	.08
226	Juan Eichelberger	.08
227	Steve Braun	.08
228	John Rabb	.08
229	Paul Owens	.08
230	Rickey Henderson	1.75
231	Gary Woods	.08
232	Tim Wallach	.08
233	Checklist 133-264	.08
234	Rafael Ramirez	.08
235	*Matt Young*	.08
236	Ellis Valentine	.08
237	John Castino	.08
238	Reid Nichols	.08
239	Jay Howell	.08
240	Eddie Murray	1.50
241	Billy Almon	.08
242	Alex Trevino	.08
243	Pete Ladd	.08
244	Candy Maldonado	.08
245	Rick Sutcliffe	.08
246	Mets Batting & Pitching Leaders (Tom Seaver, Mookie Wilson)	.25
247	Onix Concepcion	.08
248	*Bill Dawley*	.08
249	Jay Johnstone	.08
250	Bill Madlock	.08
251	Tony Gwynn	6.00
252	Larry Christenson	.08
253	Jim Wohlford	.08
254	Shane Rawley	.08
255	Bruce Benedict	.08
256	Dave Geisel	.08
257	Julio Cruz	.08
258	Luis Sanchez	.08
259	Sparky Anderson	.15

260	Scott McGregor	.08
261	Bobby Brown	.08
262	*Tom Candiotti*	.25
263	Jack Fimple	.08
264	Doug Frobel	.08
265	*Donnie Hill*	.08
266	Steve Lubratich	.08
267	*Carmelo Martinez*	.08
268	Jack O'Connor	.08
269	Aurelio Rodriguez	.08
270	*Jeff Russell*	.20
271	Moose Haas	.08
272	Rick Dempsey	.08
273	Charlie Puleo	.08
274	Rick Monday	.08
275	Len Matuszek	.08
276	Angels Batting & Pitching Leaders (Rod Carew, Geoff Zahn)	.20
277	Eddie Whitson	.08
278	Jorge Bell	.20
279	Ivan DeJesus	.08
280	Floyd Bannister	.08
281	Larry Milbourne	.08
282	Jim Barr	.08
283	Larry Biittner	.08
284	Howard Bailey	.08
285	Darrell Porter	.08
286	Lary Sorensen	.08
287	Warren Cromartie	.08
288	Jim Beattie	.08
289	Randy S. Johnson	.08
290	Dave Dravecky	.08
291	Chuck Tanner	.08
292	Tony Scott	.08
293	Ed Lynch	.08
294	U.L. Washington	.08
295	Mike Flanagan	.08
296	Jeff Newman	.08
297	Bruce Berenyi	.08
298	Jim Gantner	.08
299	John Butcher	.08
300	Pete Rose	2.00
301	Frank LaCorte	.08
302	Barry Bonnell	.08
303	Marty Castillo	.08
304	Warren Brusstar	.08
305	Roy Smalley	.08
306	Dodgers Batting & Pitching Leaders (Pedro Guerrero, Bob Welch)	.08
307	Bobby Mitchell	.08
308	Ron Hassey	.08
309	Tony Phillips	.25
310	Willie McGee	.08
311	Jerry Koosman	.08
312	Jorge Orta	.08
313	Mike Jorgensen	.08
314	Orlando Mercado	.08
315	Bob Grich	.08
316	Mark Bradley	.08
317	Greg Pryor	.08
318	Bill Gullickson	.08
319	Al Bumbry	.08
320	Bob Stanley	.08
321	Harvey Kuenn	.08
322	Ken Schrom	.08
323	Alan Knicely	.08
324	*Alejandro Pena*	.15
325	Darrell Evans	.15
326	Bob Kearney	.08
327	Ruppert Jones	.08
328	Vern Ruhle	.08
329	Pat Tabler	.08
330	John Candelaria	.08
331	Bucky Dent	.08
332	*Kevin Gross*	.15
333	Larry Herndon	.08
334	Chuck Rainey	.08
335	Don Baylor	.15
336	Mariners Batting & Pitching Leaders (Pat Putnam, Matt Young)	.08
337	Kevin Hagen	.08
338	Mike Warren	.08
339	Roy Lee Jackson	.08
340	Hal McRae	.08
341	Dave Tobik	.08
342	Tim Foli	.08
343	Mark Davis	.08
344	Rick Miller	.08
345	Kent Hrbek	.25
346	Kurt Bevacqua	.08
347	Allan Ramirez	.08
348	Toby Harrah	.08
349	Bob L. Gibson	.08
350	George Foster	.08
351	Russ Nixon	.08
352	Dave Stewart	.08
353	Jim Anderson	.08
354	Jeff Burroughs	.08
355	Jason Thompson	.08
356	Glenn Abbott	.08
357	Ron Cey	.08
358	Bob Dernier	.08
359	*Jim Acker*	.08
360	Willie Randolph	.08
361	Dave Smith	.08
362	David Green	.08
363	Tim Laudner	.08
364	Scott Fletcher	.15
365	Steve Bedrosian	.08
366	Padres Batting & Pitching Leaders (Dave Dravecky, Terry Kennedy)	.08
367	Jamie Easterly	.08
368	Hubie Brooks	.08
369	Steve McCatty	.08
370	Tim Raines	.50
371	Dave Gumpert	.08
372	Gary Roenicke	.08
373	Bill Scherrer	.08
374	Don Money	.08
375	Dennis Leonard	.08
376	*Dave Anderson*	.08
377	Danny Darwin	.08
378	Bob Brenly	.08
379	Checklist 265-396	.08
380	Steve Garvey	.45
381	Ralph Houk	.08
382	Chris Nyman	.08
383	Terry Puhl	.08
384	*Lee Tunnell*	.08
385	Tony Perez	.15
386	George Hendrick (All-Star)	.08
387	Johnny Ray (All-Star)	.08
388	Mike Schmidt (All-Star)	.50
389	Ozzie Smith (All-Star)	.40
390	Tim Raines (All-Star)	.25
391	Dale Murphy (All-Star)	.20
392	Andre Dawson (All-Star)	.25
393	Gary Carter (All-Star)	.15
394	Steve Rogers (All-Star)	.08
395	Steve Carlton (All-Star)	.25
396	Jesse Orosco (All-Star)	.08
397	Eddie Murray (All-Star)	.40
398	Lou Whitaker (All-Star)	.08
399	George Brett (All-Star)	.75
400	Cal Ripken, Jr. (All-Star)	2.00
401	Jim Rice (All-Star)	.08
402	Dave Winfield (All-Star)	.30
403	Lloyd Moseby (All-Star)	.08
404	Ted Simmons (All-Star)	.08
405	LaMarr Hoyt (All-Star)	.08
406	Ron Guidry (All-Star)	.08
407	Dan Quisenberry (All-Star)	.08
408	Lou Piniella	.08
409	*Juan Agosto*	.08
410	Claudell Washington	.08
411	Houston Jimenez	.08
412	Doug Rader	.08
413	*Spike Owen*	.20
414	Mitchell Page	.08
415	Tommy John	.15
416	Dane Iorg	.08
417	Mike Armstrong	.08
418	Ron Hodges	.08
419	John Henry Johnson	.08
420	Cecil Cooper	.08
421	Charlie Lea	.08
422	Jose Cruz	.08
423	Mike Morgan	.08
424	Dann Bilardello	.08
425	Steve Howe	.08
426	Orioles Batting & Pitching Leaders (Mike Boddicker, Cal Ripken, Jr.)	1.00
427	Rick Leach	.08
428	Fred Breining	.08
429	*Randy Bush*	.08
430	Rusty Staub	.08
431	Chris Bando	.08
432	*Charlie Hudson*	.08
433	Rich Hebner	.08
434	Harold Baines	.15
435	Neil Allen	.08
436	Rick Peters	.08
437	Mike Proly	.08
438	Biff Pocoroba	.08
439	Bob Stoddard	.08
440	Steve Kemp	.08
441	Bob Lillis	.08
442	Byron McLaughlin	.08
443	Benny Ayala	.08
444	Steve Renko	.08
445	Jerry Remy	.08
446	Luis Pujols	.08
447	Tom Brunansky	.08
448	Ben Hayes	.08
449	Joe Pettini	.08
450	Gary Carter	.30
451	Bob Jones	.08
452	Chuck Porter	.08
453	Willie Upshaw	.08
454	Joe Beckwith	.08
455	Terry Kennedy	.08
456	Cubs Batting & Pitching Leaders (Fergie Jenkins, Keith Moreland)	.08
457	Dave Rozema	.08
458	Kiko Garcia	.08
459	Kevin Hickey	.08
460	Dave Winfield	1.50
461	Jim Maler	.08
462	Lee Lacy	.08
463	Dave Engle	.08
464	Jeff Jones	.08
465	Mookie Wilson	.08
466	Gene Garber	.08
467	Mike Ramsey	.08
468	Geoff Zahn	.08
469	Tom O'Malley	.08
470	Nolan Ryan	7.00
471	Dick Howser	.08
472	Mike Brown	.08
473	Jim Dwyer	.08
474	Greg Bargar	.08
475	*Gary Redus*	.15
476	Tom Tellmann	.08
477	Rafael Landestoy	.08
478	Alan Bannister	.08
479	Frank Tanana	.08
480	Ron Kittle	.08
481	*Mark Thurmond*	.08
482	Enos Cabell	.08
483	Fergie Jenkins	.25
484	Ozzie Virgil	.08
485	Rick Rhoden	.08
486	Yankees Batting & Pitching Leaders (Don Baylor, Ron Guidry)	.08
487	Ricky Adams	.08
488	Jesse Barfield	.08
489	Dave Von Ohlen	.08
490	Cal Ripken, Jr.	7.00
491	Bobby Castillo	.08
492	Tucker Ashford	.08
493	Mike Norris	.08
494	Chili Davis	.08
495	Rollie Fingers	.25
496	Terry Francona	.08
497	Bud Anderson	.08
498	Rich Gedman	.08
499	Mike Witt	.08
500	George Brett	2.00
501	Steve Henderson	.08
502	Joe Torre	.08
503	Elias Sosa	.08
504	Mickey Rivers	.08
505	Pete Vuckovich	.08
506	Ernie Whitt	.08
507	Mike LaCoss	.08
508	Mel Hall	.08
509	Brad Havens	.08
510	Alan Trammell	.15
511	Marty Bystrom	.08
512	Oscar Gamble	.08
513	Dave Beard	.08
514	Floyd Rayford	.08
515	Gorman Thomas	.08
516	Expos Batting & Pitching Leaders (Charlie Lea, Al Oliver)	.08
517	John Moses	.08
518	*Greg Walker*	.08
519	Ron Davis	.08
520	Bob Boone	.08
521	Pete Falcone	.08
522	Dave Bergman	.08
523	Glenn Hoffman	.08
524	Carlos Diaz	.08
525	Willie Wilson	.08
526	Ron Oester	.08
527	Checklist 397-528	.08
528	Mark Brouhard	.08
529	*Keith Atherton*	.08
530	Dan Ford	.08
531	Steve Boros	.08
532	Eric Show	.08
533	Ken Landreaux	.08
534	Pete O'Brien	.08
535	Bo Diaz	.08
536	Doug Bair	.08
537	Johnny Ray	.08
538	Kevin Bass	.08
539	George Frazier	.08
540	George Hendrick	.08
541	Dennis Lamp	.08
542	Duane Kuiper	.08
543	*Craig McMurtry*	.08
544	Cesar Geronimo	.08
545	Bill Buckner	.08
546	Indians Batting & Pitching Leaders (Mike Hargrove, Lary Sorensen)	.08
547	Mike Moore	.08
548	Ron Jackson	.08
549	*Walt Terrell*	.20
550	Jim Rice	.15
551	Scott Ullger	.08
552	Ray Burris	.08
553	Joe Nolan	.08
554	Ted Power	.08
555	Greg Brock	.08
556	Joey McLaughlin	.08
557	Wayne Tolleson	.08
558	Mike Davis	.08
559	Mike Scott	.08
560	Carlton Fisk	.60
561	Whitey Herzog	.08
562	Manny Castillo	.08
563	Glenn Wilson	.08
564	Al Holland	.08
565	Leon Durham	.08
566	Jim Bibby	.08
567	Mike Heath	.08
568	Pete Filson	.08
569	Bake McBride	.08
570	Dan Quisenberry	.08
571	Bruce Bochy	.08
572	Jerry Royster	.08
573	Dave Kingman	.08
574	Brian Downing	.08
575	Jim Clancy	.08
576	Giants Batting & Pitching Leaders (Atlee Hammaker, Jeff Leonard)	.08
577	Mark Clear	.08
578	Lenn Sakata	.08
579	Bob James	.08
580	Lonnie Smith	.08
581	*Jose DeLeon*	.08
582	Bob McClure	.08
583	Derrel Thomas	.08
584	Dave Schmidt	.08
585	Dan Driessen	.08
586	Joe Niekro	.08
587	Von Hayes	.08
588	Milt Wilcox	.08
589	Mike Easler	.08
590	Dave Stieb	.08
591	Tony LaRussa	.08
592	Andre Robertson	.08
593	Jeff Lahti	.08
594	Gene Richards	.08
595	Jeff Reardon	.08
596	Ryne Sandberg	4.00
597	Rick Camp	.08
598	Rusty Kuntz	.08
599	*Doug Sisk*	.08
600	Rod Carew	.75
601	John Tudor	.08
602	John Wathan	.08
603	Renie Martin	.08
604	John Lowenstein	.08
605	Mike Caldwell	.08
606	Blue Jays Batting & Pitching Leaders (Lloyd Moseby, Dave Stieb)	.08
607	Tom Hume	.08
608	Bobby Johnson	.08
609	Dan Meyer	.08
610	Steve Sax	.08
611	Chet Lemon	.08
612	Harry Spilman	.08
613	Greg Gross	.08
614	Len Barker	.08
615	Garry Templeton	.08
616	Don Robinson	.08
617	Rick Cerone	.08
618	Dickie Noles	.08
619	Jerry Dybzinski	.08
620	Al Oliver	.08
621	Frank Howard	.08
622	Al Cowens	.08
623	Ron Washington	.08
624	Terry Harper	.08
625	Larry Gura	.08
626	Bob Clark	.08
627	Dave LaPoint	.08
628	Ed Jurak	.08
629	Rick Langford	.08
630	Ted Simmons	.08
631	Denny Martinez	.08
632	Tom Foley	.08
633	Mike Krukow	.08
634	Mike Marshall	.08
635	Dave Righetti	.08
636	Pat Putnam	.08
637	Phillies Batting & Pitching Leaders (John Denny, Gary Matthews)	.08
638	George Vukovich	.08
639	Rick Lysander	.08
640	Lance Parrish	.08
641	Mike Richardt	.08
642	Tom Underwood	.08
643	Mike Brown	.08
644	Tim Lollar	.08
645	Tony Pena	.08
646	Checklist 529-660	.08
647	Ron Roenicke	.08
648	Len Whitehouse	.08
649	Tom Herr	.08
650	Phil Niekro	.50
651	John McNamara	.08
652	Rudy May	.08
653	Dave Stapleton	.08
654	Bob Bailor	.08
655	Amos Otis	.08
656	Bryn Smith	.08
657	Thad Bosley	.08
658	Jerry Augustine	.08
659	Duane Walker	.08
660	Ray Knight	.08
661	Steve Yeager	.08
662	Tom Brennan	.08
663	Johnnie LeMaster	.08
664	Dave Stegman	.08
665	Buddy Bell	.08
666	Tigers Batting & Pitching Leaders (Jack Morris, Lou Whitaker)	.08
667	Vance Law	.08
668	Larry McWilliams	.08
669	Dave Lopes	.08
670	Rich Gossage	.08
671	Jamie Quirk	.08
672	Ricky Nelson	.08
673	Mike Walters	.08
674	Tim Flannery	.08
675	Pascual Perez	.08
676	Brian Giles	.08
677	Doyle Alexander	.08
678	Chris Speier	.08
679	Art Howe	.08
680	Fred Lynn	.08
681	Tom Lasorda	.25
682	Dan Morogiello	.08
683	*Marty Barrett*	.08
684	Bob Shirley	.08
685	Willie Aikens	.08
686	Joe Price	.08
687	Roy Howell	.08
688	George Wright	.08
689	Mike Fischlin	.08
690	Jack Clark	.08
691	*Steve Lake*	.08
692	Dickie Thon	.08
693	Alan Wiggins	.08
694	Mike Stanton	.08
695	Lou Whitaker	.08
696	Pirates Batting & Pitching Leaders (Bill Madlock, Rick Rhoden)	.08
697	Dale Murray	.08
698	Marc Hill	.08
699	Dave Rucker	.08
700	Mike Schmidt	2.00
701	NL Active Career Batting Leaders (Bill Madlock, Dave Parker, Pete Rose)	.25
702	NL Active Career Hit Leaders (Tony Perez, Pete Rose, Rusty Staub)	.25
703	NL Active Career Home Run Leaders (Dave Kingman, Tony Perez, Mike Schmidt)	.15
704	NL Active Career RBI Leaders (Al Oliver, Tony Perez, Rusty Staub)	.08
705	NL Active Career Stolen Bases Leaders (Larry Bowa, Cesar Cedeno, Joe Morgan)	.08
706	NL Active Career Victory Leaders (Steve Carlton, Fergie Jenkins, Tom Seaver)	.08
707	NL Active Career Strikeout Leaders (Steve Carlton, Nolan Ryan, Tom Seaver)	.35
708	NL Active Career ERA Leaders (Steve Carlton, Steve Rogers, Tom Seaver)	.08
709	NL Active Career Save Leaders (Gene Garber, Tug McGraw, Bruce Sutter)	.08
710	AL Active Career Batting Leaders (George Brett, Rod Carew, Cecil Cooper)	.30
711	AL Active Career Hit Leaders (Bert Campaneris, Rod Carew, Reggie Jackson)	.15
712	AL Active Career Home Run Leaders (Reggie Jackson, Greg Luzinski, Graig Nettles)	.20
713	AL Active Career RBI Leaders (Reggie Jackson, Graig Nettles, Ted Simmons)	.15
714	AL Active Career Stolen Bases Leaders (Bert Campaneris, Dave Lopes, Omar Moreno)	.08
715	AL Active Career Victory Leaders (Tommy John, Jim Palmer, Don Sutton)	.08
716	AL Active Strikeout Leaders (Bert Blyleven, Jerry Koosman, Don Sutton)	.08
717	AL Active Career ERA Leaders (Rollie Fingers, Ron Guidry, Jim Palmer)	.08
718	AL Active Career Save Leaders (Rollie Fingers, Rich Gossage, Dan Quisenberry)	.08
719	Andy Hassler	.08
720	Dwight Evans	.08
721	Del Crandall	.08
722	Bob Welch	.08
723	Rich Dauer	.08
724	Eric Rasmussen	.08

725	Cesar Cedeno	.08
726	Brewers Batting & Pitching Leaders (Moose Haas, Ted Simmons)	.08
727	Joel Youngblood	.08
728	Tug McGraw	.08
729	Gene Tenace	.08
730	Bruce Sutter	.08
731	Lynn Jones	.08
732	Terry Crowley	.08
733	Dave Collins	.08
734	Odell Jones	.08
735	Rick Burleson	.08
736	Dick Ruthven	.08
737	Jim Essian	.08
738	*Bill Schroeder*	.08
739	Bob Watson	.08
740	Tom Seaver	1.00
741	Wayne Gross	.08
742	Dick Williams	.08
743	Don Hood	.08
744	Jamie Allen	.08
745	Dennis Eckersley	.08
746	Mickey Hatcher	.08
747	Pat Zachry	.08
748	Jeff Leonard	.08
749	Doug Flynn	.08
750	Jim Palmer	1.00
751	Charlie Moore	.08
752	Phil Garner	.08
753	Doug Gwosdz	.08
754	Kent Tekulve	.08
755	Garry Maddox	.08
756	Reds Batting & Pitching Leaders (Ron Oester, Mario Soto)	.08
757	Larry Bowa	.08
758	Bill Stein	.08
759	Richard Dotson	.08
760	Bob Horner	.08
761	John Montefusco	.08
762	Rance Mulliniks	.08
763	Craig Swan	.08
764	Mike Hargrove	.08
765	Ken Forsch	.08
766	Mike Vail	.08
767	Carney Lansford	.08
768	Champ Summers	.08
769	Bill Caudill	.08
770	Ken Griffey	.08
771	Billy Gardner	.08
772	Jim Slaton	.08
773	Todd Cruz	.08
774	Tom Gorman	.08
775	Dave Parker	.08
776	Craig Reynolds	.08
777	Tom Paciorek	.08
778	*Andy Hawkins*	.15
779	Jim Sundberg	.08
780	Steve Carlton	1.00
781	Checklist 661-792	.08
782	Steve Balboni	.08
783	Luis Leal	.08
784	Leon Roberts	.08
785	Joaquin Andujar	.08
786	Red Sox Batting & Pitching Leaders (Wade Boggs, Bob Ojeda)	.30
787	Bill Campbell	.08
788	Milt May	.08
789	Bert Blyleven	.08
790	Doug DeCinces	.08
791	Terry Forster	.08
792	Bill Russell	.08

1984 Topps Tiffany

In 1984 Topps introduced a specially boxed, limited edition version of its baseball card set. Sold only through hobby dealers, the cards differed from regular-issue 1984 Topps cards in their use of white cardboard stock and the application of a high-gloss finish to the front of the card. Production was limited to a reported 10,000 sets. The nickname "Tiffany" was coined by collectors to identify the glossy collectors edition.

	MT
Complete Set (792):	200.00
Common Player:	.15
Stars: 6X	

(See 1984 Topps for checklist and base card values.)

1984 Topps Traded

The popular Topps Traded set returned for its fourth year in 1984 with another 132-card set. The 2-1/2" x 3-1/2" cards have an identical design to the regular Topps cards except that the back cardboard is white and the card numbers carry a "T" suffix. As before, the set was sold only through hobby dealers. Also as before, players who changed teams, new managers and promising rookies are included in the set. The presence of several promising young rookies in especially high demand from investors and speculators had made this one of the most expensive Topps issues of recent years. A glossy-finish "Tiffany" version of the set was also issued, valued at four to five times the price of the normal Traded cards.

		MT
Complete Set (132):		35.00
Common Player:		.25
1T	Willie Aikens	.25
2T	Luis Aponte	.25
3T	Mike Armstrong	.25
4T	Bob Bailor	.25
5T	Dusty Baker	.50
6T	Steve Balboni	.25
7T	Alan Bannister	.25
8T	Dave Beard	.25
9T	Joe Beckwith	.25
10T	Bruce Berenyi	.25
11T	Dave Bergman	.25
12T	Tony Bernazard	.25
13T	Yogi Berra	.60
14T	Barry Bonnell	.25
15T	Phil Bradley	.25
16T	Fred Breining	.25
17T	Bill Buckner	.25
18T	Ray Burris	.25
19T	John Butcher	.25
20T	Brett Butler	.25
21T	Enos Cabell	.25
22T	Bill Campbell	.25
23T	Bill Caudill	.25
24T	Bob Clark	.25
25T	Bryan Clark	.25
26T	Jaime Cocanower	.25
27T	*Ron Darling*	1.00
28T	Alvin Davis	.25
29T	Ken Dayley	.25
30T	Jeff Dedmon	.25
31T	Bob Dernier	.25
32T	Carlos Diaz	.25
33T	Mike Easler	.25
34T	Dennis Eckersley	4.00
35T	Jim Essian	.25
36T	Darrell Evans	.35
37T	Mike Fitzgerald	.25
38T	Tim Foli	.25
39T	George Frazier	.25
40T	Rich Gale	.25
41T	Barbaro Garbey	.25
42T	*Dwight Gooden*	4.00
43T	Rich Gossage	.40
44T	Wayne Gross	.25
45T	Mark Gubicza	.90
46T	Jackie Gutierrez	.25
47T	Mel Hall	.25
48T	Toby Harrah	.25
49T	Ron Hassey	.25
50T	Rich Hebner	.25
51T	Willie Hernandez	.25
52T	Ricky Horton	.25
53T	Art Howe	.25
54T	Dane Iorg	.25
55T	Brook Jacoby	.25
56T	Mike Jeffcoat	.25
57T	Dave Johnson	.25
58T	Lynn Jones	.25
59T	Ruppert Jones	.25
60T	Mike Jorgensen	.25
61T	Bob Kearney	.25
62T	*Jimmy Key*	3.00
63T	Dave Kingman	.25
64T	Jerry Koosman	.25
65T	Wayne Krenchicki	.25
66T	Rusty Kuntz	.25
67T	Rene Lachemann	.25
68T	Frank LaCorte	.25
69T	Dennis Lamp	.25
70T	*Mark Langston*	3.00
71T	Rick Leach	.25
72T	Craig Lefferts	.25
73T	Gary Lucas	.25
74T	Jerry Martin	.25
75T	Carmelo Martinez	.25
76T	Mike Mason	.25
77T	Gary Matthews	.25
78T	Andy McGaffigan	.25
79T	Larry Milbourne	.25
80T	Sid Monge	.25
81T	Jackie Moore	.25
82T	Joe Morgan	3.00
83T	Graig Nettles	.25
84T	Phil Niekro	3.00
85T	Ken Oberkfell	.25
86T	Mike O'Berry	.25
87T	Al Oliver	.25
88T	Jorge Orta	.25
89T	Amos Otis	.25
90T	Dave Parker	1.50
91T	Tony Perez	1.00
92T	Gerald Perry	.50
93T	Gary Pettis	.25
94T	Rob Picciolo	.25
95T	Vern Rapp	.25
96T	Floyd Rayford	.25
97T	Randy Ready	.25
98T	Ron Reed	.25
99T	Gene Richards	.25
100T	*Jose Rijo*	1.50
101T	Jeff Robinson	.25
102T	Ron Romanick	.25
103T	Pete Rose	8.00
104T	*Bret Saberhagen*	6.00
105T	Juan Samuel	.50
106T	Scott Sanderson	.25
107T	Dick Schofield	.25
108T	Tom Seaver	6.00
109T	Jim Slaton	.25
110T	Mike Smithson	.25
111T	Lary Sorensen	.25
112T	Tim Stoddard	.25
113T	Champ Summers	.25
114T	Jim Sundberg	.25
115T	Rick Sutcliffe	.25
116T	Craig Swan	.25
117T	Tim Teufel	.35
118T	Derrel Thomas	.25
119T	Gorman Thomas	.25
120T	Alex Trevino	.25
121T	Manny Trillo	.25
122T	John Tudor	.25
123T	Tom Underwood	.25
124T	Mike Vail	.25
125T	Tom Waddell	.25
126T	Gary Ward	.25
127T	Curt Wilkerson	.25
128T	Frank Williams	.25
129T	Glenn Wilson	.25
130T	Johnny Wockenfuss	.25
131T	Ned Yost	.25
132T	Checklist 1-132	.25

1984 Topps Traded Tiffany

Following up on its inaugural Tiffany collectors edition, Topps produced a special glossy version of its Traded set for 1984 as well. Cards in this special boxed set differ from regular Traded cards only in the use of white cardboard stock with a high-gloss finish coat on front.

	MT
Complete Set (132):	50.00
Common Player:	.15
Stars: 4X	

(See 1984 Topps Traded for checklist and base card values.)

1984 Topps All-Star Glossy Set of 22

These 2-1/2" x 3-1/2" cards were a result of the success of Topps' efforts the previous year with glossy cards on a mail-in basis. A 22-card set, the cards are divided evenly between the two leagues. Each All-Star Game starter for both leagues, the managers and the honorary team captains have an All-Star Glossy card. The cards feature a large color photo on the front with an All-Star banner across the top and the league emblem in the lower left. The player's name and position appear below the photo. Backs have a name, team, position and card number along with the phrase "1983 All-Star Game Commemorative Set". The '84 Glossy All-Stars were distributed one card per pack in Topps rack packs that year.

		MT
Complete Set (22):		4.00
Common Player:		.10
1	Harvey Kuenn	.10
2	Rod Carew	.50
3	Manny Trillo	.10
4	George Brett	.75
5	Robin Yount	.75
6	Jim Rice	.25
7	Fred Lynn	.10
8	Dave Winfield	.50
9	Ted Simmons	.10
10	Dave Stieb	.10
11	Carl Yastrzemski	.50
12	Whitey Herzog	.10
13	Al Oliver	.10
14	Steve Sax	.10
15	Mike Schmidt	.75
16	Ozzie Smith	.50
17	Tim Raines	.35
18	Andre Dawson	.35
19	Dale Murphy	.35
20	Gary Carter	.35
21	Mario Soto	.10
22	Johnny Bench	.60

1984 Topps All-Star Glossy Set of 40

For the second straight year in 1984, Topps produced a 40-card All-Star "Collector's Edition" set as a "consolation prize" for its sweepstakes game. By collecting game cards and sending them in with a bit of cash, the collector could receive one of eight different five-card series. As the previous year, the 2-1/2" x 3-1/2" cards feature a nearly full-frame color photo on its glossy finish front. Backs are printed in red and blue.

		MT
Complete Set (40):		16.00
Common Player:		.15
1	Pete Rose	2.00
2	Lance Parrish	.15
3	Steve Rogers	.15
4	Eddie Murray	.90
5	Johnny Ray	.15
6	Rickey Henderson	.75
7	Atlee Hammaker	.15
8	Wade Boggs	.90
9	Gary Carter	.30
10	Jack Morris	.15
11	Darrell Evans	.15
12	George Brett	1.50
13	Bob Horner	.15
14	Ron Guidry	.15
15	Nolan Ryan	4.00
16	Dave Winfield	.50
17	Ozzie Smith	.75
18	Ted Simmons	.15
19	Bill Madlock	.15
20	Tony Armas	.15
21	Al Oliver	.15
22	Jim Rice	.25
23	George Hendrick	.15
24	Dave Stieb	.15
25	Pedro Guerrero	.15
26	Rod Carew	.60
27	Steve Carlton	.50
28	Dave Righetti	.15
29	Darryl Strawberry	.30
30	Lou Whitaker	.15
31	Dale Murphy	.35
32	LaMarr Hoyt	.15
33	Jesse Orosco	.15
34	Cecil Cooper	.15
35	Andre Dawson	.25
36	Robin Yount	1.00
37	Tim Raines	.25
38	Dan Quisenberry	.15
39	Mike Schmidt	1.50
40	Carlton Fisk	.25

1984 Topps Cereal Series

The Topps-produced 1984 Cereal Series set is identical to the Ralston Purina set from the same year in nearly all aspects. On the card fronts the words "Ralston Purina Company" were replaced by "Cereal Series" and Topps logos were substituted for Ralston checkerboard logos. The set is comprised of 33 cards, each measuring 2-1/2" x 3-1/2." The cards were inserted in unmarked boxes of Chex brand cereals.

		MT
Complete Set (33):		10.00
Common Player:		.10
1	Eddie Murray	.50
2	Ozzie Smith	.60
3	Ted Simmons	.10
4	Pete Rose	1.00
5	Greg Luzinski	.10
6	Andre Dawson	.35
7	Dave Winfield	.45
8	Tom Seaver	.50
9	Jim Rice	.25
10	Fernando Valenzuela	.10
11	Wade Boggs	.60
12	Dale Murphy	.35
13	George Brett	1.00
14	Nolan Ryan	2.00
15	Rickey Henderson	.50
16	Steve Carlton	.45
17	Rod Carew	.50
18	Steve Garvey	.35
19	Reggie Jackson	.65
20	Dave Concepcion	.10
21	Robin Yount	.75
22	Mike Schmidt	1.00
23	Jim Palmer	.50
24	Bruce Sutter	.10
25	Dan Quisenberry	.10
26	Bill Madlock	.10
27	Cecil Cooper	.10
28	Gary Carter	.30
29	Fred Lynn	.10
30	Pedro Guerrero	.10
31	Ron Guidry	.10
32	Keith Hernandez	.10
33	Carlton Fisk	.30

1984 Topps Gallery of Immortals

The Gallery of Immortals set of bronze and silver replicas was the first miniature set of 12 from Topps and the start of an annual tradition (in 1985, the name was changed to Gallery of Champions). Each mini is an exact replica (one-quarter scale) of the featured player's 1994 Topps baseball card, both front and back, in minute detail. The three-dimensional raised metal cards were packaged in a velvet-lined case that bears the title of the set in gold-embossed letters. A certificate of authenticity is included with each set. A Tom Seaver pewter metal mini-card was given as a premium to dealers who purchased sets. A Darryl Strawberry bronze was given as a premium to dealers who purchased cases of the 1984 Topps Traded sets. Issue price was about $100 for the cased bronze set, $500 for the silver edition of 1,000. Earlier listings of aluminum versions of the Gallery of Immortals ingots were in error.

	MT
Complete Bronze Set (12):	200.00
Complete Silver Set (12):	600.00
(1b) George Brett (bronze)	25.00
(1s) George Brett (silver)	75.00
(2b) Rod Carew (bronze)	15.00
(2s) Rod Carew (silver)	45.00
(3b) Steve Carlton (bronze)	15.00
(3s) Steve Carlton (silver)	45.00
(4b) Rollie Fingers (bronze)	10.00
(4s) Rollie Fingers (silver)	30.00
(5b) Steve Garvey (bronze)	10.00
(5s) Steve Garvey (silver)	30.00
(6b) Reggie Jackson (bronze)	17.50
(6s) Reggie Jackson (silver)	50.00
(7b) Joe Morgan (bronze)	10.00
(7s) Joe Morgan (silver)	30.00
(8b) Jim Palmer (bronze)	10.00
(8s) Jim Palmer (silver)	30.00
(9b) Pete Rose (bronze)	25.00
(9s) Pete Rose (silver)	100.00
(10b) Nolan Ryan (bronze)	75.00
(10s) Nolan Ryan (silver)	225.00
(11b) Mike Schmidt (bronze)	25.00
(11s) Mike Schmidt (silver)	75.00
(12b) Tom Seaver (bronze)	15.00
(12s) Tom Seaver (silver)	45.00
(12p) Tom Seaver (pewter)	45.00
(13) Darryl Strawberry (bronze)	7.50

1984 Topps Rub Downs

This set consists of 32 "Rub Down" sheets featuring 112 different players. Each sheet measures 2-3/8" x 3-15/16" and includes small, color baseball player figures along with bats, balls and gloves. The pictures can be transferred to another surface by rubbing the paper backing. The sheets, which were sold as a separate issue, are somewhat reminiscent of earlier tattoo sets issued by Topps. The sheets are not numbered.

	MT
Complete Set (32):	8.00
Common Player:	.25
(1) Steve Bedrosian, Bruce Benedict, Tony Armas, Harold Baines, Lonnie Smith	.25
(2) Chris Chambliss, Bob Horner, Don Baylor, George Hendrick, Ron Kittle, Johnnie LeMaster	.25
(3) Glenn Hubbard, Rafael Ramirez, Buddy Bell, Ray Knight, Lloyd Moseby	.25
(4) Craig McMurtry, Bruce Benedict, Atlee Hammaker, Frank White	.25
(5) Wade Boggs, Rick Dempsey, Keith Hernandez	.40
(6) George Brett, Andre Dawson, Paul Molitor, Alan Wiggins	.75
(7) Tom Brunansky, Pedro Guerrero, Darryl Strawberry	.25
(8) Bill Buckner, Rich Gossage, Dave Stieb, Rick Sutcliffe	.25
(9) Rod Carew, Carlton Fisk, Johnny Ray, Matt Young	.25
(10) Steve Carlton, Bob Horner, Dan Quisenberry	.25
(11) Gary Carter, Phil Garner, Ron Guidry	.25
(12) Ron Cey, Steve Kemp, Greg Luzinski, Kent Tekulve	.25
(13) Chris Chambliss, Dwight Evans, Julio Franco	.25
(14) Jack Clark, Damaso Garcia, Hal McRae, Lance Parrish	.25
(15) Dave Concepcion, Cecil Cooper, Fred Lynn, Jesse Orosco	.25
(16) Jose Cruz, Gary Matthews, Jack Morris, Jim Rice	.25
(17) Ron Davis, Kent Hrbek, Tom Seaver	.30
(18) John Denny, Carney Lansford, Mario Soto, Lou Whitaker	.25
(19) Leon Durham, Dave Lopes, Steve Sax	.25
(20) George Foster, Gary Gaetti, Bobby Grich, Gary Redus	.25
(21) Steve Garvey, Bill Russell, Jerry Remy, George Wright	.25
(22) Moose Haas, Bruce Sutter, Dickie Thon, Andre Thornton	.25
(23) Toby Harrah, Pat Putnam, Tim Raines, Mike Schmidt	.35
(24) Rickey Henderson, Dave Righetti, Pete Rose	.75
(25) Steve Henderson, Bill Madlock, Alan Trammell	.25
(26) LaMarr Hoyt, Larry Parrish, Nolan Ryan	.75
(27) Reggie Jackson, Eric Show, Jason Thompson	.30
(28) Tommy John, Terry Kennedy, Eddie Murray, Ozzie Smith	.30
(29) Jeff Leonard, Dale Murphy, Ken Singleton, Dave Winfield	.30
(30) Craig McMurtry, Cal Ripken, Steve Rogers, Willie Upshaw	.90
(31) Ben Oglivie, Jim Palmer, Darrell Porter	.25
(32) Tony Pena, Fernando Valenzuela, Robin Yount	.35

1984 Topps Stickers

The largest sticker set issued by Topps, the 1984 set consists of 386 stickers, each measuring 1-15/16" x 2-9/16". The full color photos have stars in each of the corners and are numbered on both the front and the back. The back includes information about the sticker album and a promotion to order stickers through the mail. The back of the album is a tribute to Carl Yastrzemski, including a large photo and reproductions of his 1960-1983 cards in miniature.

		MT
Complete Set (386):		15.00
Common Player:		.05
Sticker Album:		2.00
1	Steve Carlton	.15
2	Steve Carlton	.15
3	Rickey Henderson	.25
4	Rickey Henderson	.20
5	Fred Lynn	.05
6	Fred Lynn	.05
7	Greg Luzinski	.05
8	Greg Luzinski	.05
9	Dan Quisenberry	.05
10	Dan Quisenberry	.05
11	1983 Championship (LaMarr Hoyt)	.05
12	1983 Championship (Mike Flanagan)	.05
13	1983 Championship (Mike Boddicker)	.05
14	1983 Championship (Tito Landrum)	.05
15	1983 Championship (Steve Carlton)	.10
16	1983 Championship (Fernando Valenzuela)	.05
17	1983 Championship (Charlie Hudson)	.05
18	1983 Championship (Gary Matthews)	.05
19	1983 World Series (John Denny)	.05
20	1983 World Series (John Lowenstein)	.05
21	1983 World Series (Jim Palmer)	.10
22	1983 World Series (Benny Ayala)	.05
23	1983 World Series (Rick Dempsey)	.05
24	1983 World Series (Cal Ripken)	.50
25	1983 World Series (Sammy Stewart)	.05
26	1983 World Series (Eddie Murray)	.20
27	Dale Murphy	.15
28	Chris Chambliss	.05
29	Glenn Hubbard	.05
30	Bob Horner	.05
31	Phil Niekro	.10
32	Claudell Washington	.05
33	Rafael Ramirez	.05
34	Bruce Benedict	.05
35	Gene Garber	.05
36	Pascual Perez	.05
37	Jerry Royster	.05
38	Steve Bedrosian	.05
39	Keith Moreland	.05
40	Leon Durham	.05
41	Ron Cey	.05
42	Bill Buckner	.05
43	Jody Davis	.05
44	Lee Smith	.05
45	Ryne Sandberg	.35
46	Larry Bowa	.05
47	Chuck Rainey	.05
48	Fergie Jenkins	.10
49	Dick Ruthven	.05
50	Jay Johnstone	.05
51	Mario Soto	.05
52	Gary Redus	.05
53	Ron Oester	.05
54	Cesar Cedeno	.05
55	Dan Driessen	.05
56	Dave Concepcion	.05
57	Dann Bilardello	.05
58	Joe Price	.05
59	Tom Hume	.05
60	Eddie Milner	.05
61	Paul Householder	.05
62	Bill Scherrer	.05
63	Phil Garner	.05
64	Dickie Thon	.05
65	Jose Cruz	.05
66	Nolan Ryan	.60
67	Terry Puhl	.05
68	Ray Knight	.05
69	Joe Niekro	.05
70	Jerry Mumphrey	.05
71	Bill Dawley	.05
72	Alan Ashby	.05
73	Denny Walling	.05
74	Frank DiPino	.05
75	Pedro Guerrero	.05
76	Ken Landreaux	.05
77	Bill Russell	.05
78	Steve Sax	.05
79	Fernando Valenzuela	.05
80	Dusty Baker	.05
81	Jerry Reuss	.05
82	Alejandro Pena	.05
83	Rick Monday	.05
84	Rick Honeycutt	.05
85	Mike Marshall	.05
86	Steve Yeager	.05
87	Al Oliver	.05
88	Steve Rogers	.05
89	Jeff Reardon	.05
90	Gary Carter	.15
91	Tim Raines	.15
92	Andre Dawson	.10
93	Manny Trillo	.05
94	Tim Wallach	.05
95	Chris Speier	.05
96	Bill Gullickson	.05
97	Doug Flynn	.05
98	Charlie Lea	.05
99	Bill Madlock	.05
100	Wade Boggs	.30
101	Mike Schmidt	.30
102a	Jim Rice	.10
102b	Reggie Jackson	.15
103	Hubie Brooks	.05
104	Jesse Orosco	.05
105	George Foster	.05
106	Tom Seaver	.20
107	Keith Hernandez	.05
108	Mookie Wilson	.05
109	Bob Bailor	.05
110	Walt Terrell	.05
111	Brian Giles	.05
112	Jose Oquendo	.05
113	Mike Torrez	.05
114	Junior Ortiz	.05
115	Pete Rose	.50
116	Joe Morgan	.15
117	Mike Schmidt	.30
118	Gary Matthews	.05
119	Steve Carlton	.15
120	Bo Diaz	.05
121	Ivan DeJesus	.05
122	John Denny	.05
123	Garry Maddox	.05
124	Von Hayes	.05
125	Al Holland	.05
126	Tony Perez	.10
127	John Candelaria	.05
128	Jason Thompson	.05
129	Tony Pena	.05
130	Dave Parker	.05
131	Bill Madlock	.05
132	Kent Tekulve	.05
133	Larry McWilliams	.05
134	Johnny Ray	.05
135	Marvell Wynne	.05
136	Dale Berra	.05
137	Mike Easler	.05
138	Lee Lacy	.05
139	George Hendrick	.05
140	Lonnie Smith	.05
141	Willie McGee	.05
142	Tom Herr	.05
143	Darrell Porter	.05
144	Ozzie Smith	.30
145	Bruce Sutter	.05
146	Dave LaPoint	.05
147	Neil Allen	.05
148	Ken Oberkfell	.05
149	David Green	.05
150	Andy Van Slyke	.05
151	Garry Templeton	.05
152	Juan Bonilla	.05
153	Alan Wiggins	.05
154	Terry Kennedy	.05
155	Dave Dravecky	.05
156	Steve Garvey	.15
157	Bobby Brown	.05
158	Ruppert Jones	.05
159	Luis Salazar	.05
160	Tony Gwynn	.40
161	Gary Lucas	.05
162	Eric Show	.05
163	Darrell Evans	.10
164	Gary Lavelle	.05
165	Atlee Hammaker	.05
166	Jeff Leonard	.05
167	Jack Clark	.05
168	Johnny LeMaster	.05
169	Duane Kuiper	.05
170	Tom O'Malley	.05
171	Chili Davis	.05
172	Bill Laskey	.05
173	Joel Youngblood	.05
174	Bob Brenly	.05
175	Atlee Hammaker	.05
176	Rick Honeycutt	.05
177	John Denny	.05
178	LaMarr Hoyt	.05
179	Tim Raines	.15
180	Dale Murphy	.15
181	Andre Dawson	.10
182	Steve Rogers	.05
183	Gary Carter	.10
184	Steve Carlton	.25
185	George Hendrick	.05
186	Johnny Ray	.05
187	Ozzie Smith	.25
188	Mike Schmidt	.30
189	Jim Rice	.10
190	Dave Winfield	.15
191	Lloyd Moseby	.05
192	LaMarr Hoyt	.05
193	Ted Simmons	.05
194	Ron Guidry	.05
195	Eddie Murray	.25
196	Lou Whitaker	.05
197	Cal Ripken, Jr.	.60
198	George Brett	.45
199	Dale Murphy	.15
200a	Cecil Cooper	.05
200b	Jim Rice	.10
201	Tim Raines	.10
202	Rickey Henderson	.20
203	Eddie Murray	.30
204	Cal Ripken	.60
205	Gary Roenicke	.05
206	Ken Singleton	.05
207	Scott McGregor	.05
208	Tippy Martinez	.05
209	John Lowenstein	.05
210	Mike Flanagan	.05
211	Jim Palmer	.10
212	Dan Ford	.05
213	Rick Dempsey	.05
214	Rich Dauer	.05
215	Jerry Remy	.05
216	Wade Boggs	.25
217	Jim Rice	.10
218	Tony Armas	.05
219	Dwight Evans	.05
220	Bob Stanley	.05
221	Dave Stapleton	.05
222	Rich Gedman	.05
223	Glenn Hoffman	.05
224	Dennis Eckersley	.05
225	John Tudor	.05
226	Bruce Hurst	.05
227	Rod Carew	.20
228	Bobby Grich	.05
229	Doug DeCinces	.05
230	Fred Lynn	.05
231	Reggie Jackson	.20
232	Tommy John	.05
233	Luis Sanchez	.05
234	Bob Boone	.05
235	Bruce Kison	.05
236	Brian Downing	.05
237	Ken Forsch	.05
238	Rick Burleson	.05
239	Dennis Lamp	.05
240	LaMarr Hoyt	.05
241	Richard Dotson	.05
242	Harold Baines	.05
243	Carlton Fisk	.15
244	Greg Luzinski	.05
245	Rudy Law	.05
246	Tom Paciorek	.05
247	Floyd Bannister	.05
248	Julio Cruz	.05
249	Vance Law	.05
250	Scott Fletcher	.05
251	Toby Harrah	.05
252	Pat Tabler	.05
253	Gorman Thomas	.05
254	Rick Sutcliffe	.05
255	Andre Thornton	.05
256	Bake McBride	.05
257	Alan Bannister	.05
258	Jamie Easterly	.05
259	Lary Sorenson	.05
260	Mike Hargrove	.05
261	Bert Blyleven	.05
262	Ron Hassey	.05
263	Jack Morris	.05
264	Larry Herndon	.05
265	Lance Parrish	.05
266	Alan Trammell	.05
267	Lou Whitaker	.05
268	Aurelio Lopez	.05
269	Dan Petry	.05
270	Glenn Wilson	.05
271	Chet Lemon	.05
272	Kirk Gibson	.05
273	Enos Cabell	.05
274	Johnny Wockenfuss	.05
275	George Brett	.35
276	Willie Aikens	.05

277	Frank White	.05
278	Hal McRae	.05
279	Dan Quisenberry	.05
280	Willie Wilson	.05
281	Paul Splitorff	.05
282	U.L. Washington	.05
283	Bud Black	.05
284	John Wathan	.05
285	Larry Gura	.05
286	Pat Sheridan	.05
287a	Rusty Staub	.05
287b	Dave Righetti	.05
288a	Bob Forsch	.05
288b	Mike Warren	.05
289	Al Holland	.05
290	Dan Quisenberry	.05
291	Cecil Cooper	.05
292	Moose Haas	.05
293	Ted Simmons	.05
294	Paul Molitor	.25
295	Robin Yount	.35
296	Ben Oglivie	.05
297	Tom Tellmann	.05
298	Jim Gantner	.05
299	Rick Manning	.05
300	Don Sutton	.15
301	Charlie Moore	.05
302	Jim Slaton	.05
303	Gary Ward	.05
304	Tom Brunansky	.05
305	Kent Hrbek	.05
306	Gary Gaetti	.05
307	John Castino	.05
308	Ken Schrom	.05
309	Ron Davis	.05
310	Lenny Faedo	.05
311	Darrell Brown	.05
312	Frank Viola	.05
313	Dave Engle	.05
314	Randy Bush	.05
315	Dave Righetti	.05
316	Rich Gossage	.05
317	Ken Griffey	.05
318	Ron Guidry	.05
319	Dave Winfield	.20
320	Don Baylor	.10
321	Butch Wynegar	.05
322	Omar Moreno	.05
323	Andre Robertson	.05
324	Willie Randolph	.05
325	Don Mattingly	.40
326	Graig Nettles	.05
327	Rickey Henderson	.20
328	Carney Lansford	.05
329	Jeff Burroughs	.05
330	Chris Codiroli	.05
331	Dave Lopes	.05
332	Dwayne Murphy	.05
333	Wayne Gross	.05
334	Bill Almon	.05
335	Tom Underwood	.05
336	Dave Beard	.05
337	Mike Heath	.05
338	Mike Davis	.05
339	Pat Putnam	.05
340	Tony Bernazard	.05
341	Steve Henderson	.05
342	Richie Zisk	.05
343	Dave Henderson	.05
344	Al Cowens	.05
345	Bill Caudill	.05
346	Jim Beattie	.05
347	Ricky Nelson	.05
348	Roy Thomas	.05
349	Spike Owen	.05
350	Jamie Allen	.05
351	Buddy Bell	.05
352	Billy Sample	.05
353	George Wright	.05
354	Larry Parrish	.05
355	Jim Sundberg	.05
356	Charlie Hough	.05
357	Pete O'Brien	.05
358	Wayne Tolleson	.05
359	Danny Darwin	.05
360	Dave Stewart	.05
361	Mickey Rivers	.05
362	Bucky Dent	.05
363	Willie Upshaw	.05
364	Damaso Garcia	.05
365	Lloyd Moseby	.05
366	Cliff Johnson	.05
367	Jim Clancy	.05
368	Dave Stieb	.05
369	Alfredo Griffin	.05
370	Barry Bonnell	.05
371	Luis Leal	.05
372	Jesse Barfield	.05
373	Ernie Whitt	.05
374	Rance Mulliniks	.05
375	Mike Boddicker	.05
376	Greg Brock	.05
377	Bill Doran	.05
378	Nick Esasky	.05
379	Julio Franco	.05
380	Mel Hall	.05
381	Bob Kearney	.05
382	Ron Kittle	.05
383	Carmelo Martinez	.05
384	Craig McMurtry	.05
385	Darryl Strawberry	.15
386	Matt Young	.05

1984 Topps Stickers Boxes

For the second straight year, Topps printed baseball cards on the back of its sticker boxes. The 1984 set, titled "The Super Bats" features 24 hitting leaders. The cards are blank-backed and measure 2-1/2" x 3-1/2". Two cards were printed on each of 12 different boxes. The player's name appears inside a bat above his photo. Prices listed are for complete boxes.

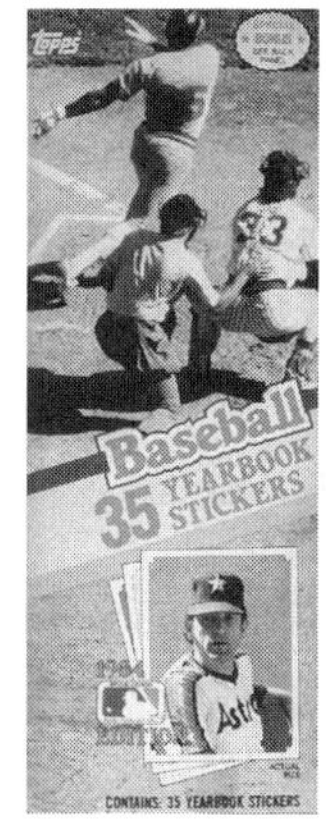

		MT
Complete Set (12):		8.50
Common Player:		.75
1	Al Oliver, Lou Whitaker	.75
2	Ken Oberkfell, Ted Simmons	.75
3	Hal McRae, Alan Wiggins	.75
4	Lloyd Moseby, Tim Raines	.75
5	Lonnie Smith, Willie Wilson	.75
6	Keith Hernandez, Robin Yount	1.50
7	Wade Boggs, Johnny Ray	1.00
8	Willie McGee, Ken Singleton	.75
9	Ray Knight, Alan Trammell	.75
10	Not issued	
11	Rod Carew, George Hendrick	1.00
12	Bill Madlock, Eddie Murray	1.00
13	Jose Cruz, Cal Ripken, Jr.	3.00

1984 Topps Super

The next installment in Topps' continuing production of large-format cards, these 4-7/8" x 6-7/8" cards were sold in cellophane packs with a complete set being 30 cards. Other than their size and the change in card number on the back, there is nothing to distinguish the Supers from the regular 1984 Topps cards of the same players. One plus is that the players are all big name stars, and are likely to remain in demand.

		MT
Complete Set (30):		12.00
Common Player:		.25
1	Cal Ripken, Jr.	4.00
2	Dale Murphy	.45
3	LaMarr Hoyt	.25
4	John Denny	.25
5	Jim Rice	.30
6	Mike Schmidt	1.00
7	Wade Boggs	.60
8	Bill Madlock	.25
9	Dan Quisenberry	.25
10	Al Holland	.25
11	Ron Kittle	.25
12	Darryl Strawberry	.40
13	George Brett	1.00
14	Bill Buckner	.25
15	Carlton Fisk	.30
16	Steve Carlton	.50
17	Ron Guidry	.25
18	Gary Carter	.35
19	Rickey Henderson	.50
20	Andre Dawson	.35
21	Reggie Jackson	.75
22	Steve Garvey	.30
23	Fred Lynn	.25
24	Pedro Guerrero	.25
25	Eddie Murray	.60
26	Keith Hernandez	.25
27	Dave Winfield	.45
28	Nolan Ryan	4.00
29	Robin Yount	.75
30	Fernando Valenzuela	.30

1984 "1977" Topps Dale Murphy Aluminum

Authorized by Topps to be issued in 1984 as a fund raiser for Huntington's Disease research, this aluminum card is a full size replica of 1977 Topps card #476, Dale Murphy's rookie card. Front features rather crude black etchings of the player portraits found on the cardboard version, while back reproduces the biographical data and includes a serial number. The cards were originally sold for $10.

		MT
476	Rookie Catchers (Gary Alexander, Rick Cerone, Dale Murphy, Kevin Pasley)	8.00

1985 Topps

Holding the line at 792 cards, Topps did initiate some major design changes in its 2-1/2" x 3-1/2" cards in 1985. The use of two photos on the front was discontinued in favor of one large color photo. The Topps logo appears in the upper left-hand corner. At the bottom runs a diagonal rectangular box with the team name. It joins a team logo, and below that point runs the player's position and name. The backs feature statistics, biographical information and a trivia question. Some interesting specialty sets were introduced in 1985, including the revival of the father/son theme from 1976, a subset of the 1984 U.S. Olympic Baseball Team members and a set featuring #1 draft choices since the inception of the baseball draft in 1965. Again in 1985, a glossy-finish "Tiffany" edition of the regular set was produced, though the number was cut back to 5,000 sets. Values range from four times regular value for common cards to five-six times for high-demand stars and rookie cards.

		MT
Complete Set (792):		240.00
Complete Set, Uncut Sheets (5):		450.00
Common Player:		.05
Wax Box:		375.00
1	Carlton Fisk (Record Breaker)	.25
2	Steve Garvey (Record Breaker)	.05
3	Dwight Gooden (Record Breaker)	.25
4	Cliff Johnson (Record Breaker)	.05
5	Joe Morgan (Record Breaker)	.05
6	Pete Rose (Record Breaker)	.50
7	Nolan Ryan (Record Breaker)	1.50
8	Juan Samuel (Record Breaker)	.05
9	Bruce Sutter (Record Breaker)	.05
10	Don Sutton (Record Breaker)	.05
11	Ralph Houk	.05
12	Dave Lopes	.05
13	Tim Lollar	.05
14	Chris Bando	.05
15	Jerry Koosman	.05
16	Bobby Meacham	.05
17	Mike Scott	.05
18	Mickey Hatcher	.05
19	George Frazier	.05
20	Chet Lemon	.05
21	Lee Tunnell	.05
22	Duane Kuiper	.05
23	Bret Saberhagen	1.25
24	Jesse Barfield	.05
25	Steve Bedrosian	.05
26	Roy Smalley	.05
27	Bruce Berenyi	.05
28	Dann Bilardello	.05
29	Odell Jones	.05
30	Cal Ripken, Jr.	4.00
31	Terry Whitfield	.05
32	Chuck Porter	.05
33	Tito Landrum	.05
34	Ed Nunez	.05
35	Graig Nettles	.05
36	Fred Breining	.05
37	Reid Nichols	.05
38	Jackie Moore	.05
39	Johnny Wockenfuss	.05
40	Phil Niekro	.40
41	Mike Fischlin	.05
42	Luis Sanchez	.05
43	Andre David	.05
44	Dickie Thon	.05
45	Greg Minton	.05
46	Gary Woods	.05
47	Dave Rozema	.05
48	Tony Fernandez	.15
49	Butch Davis	.05
50	John Candelaria	.05
51	Bob Watson	.05
52	Jerry Dybzinski	.05
53	Tom Gorman	.05
54	Cesar Cedeno	.05
55	Frank Tanana	.05
56	Jim Dwyer	.05
57	Pat Zachry	.05
58	Orlando Mercado	.05
59	Rick Waits	.05
60	George Hendrick	.05
61	Curt Kaufman	.05
62	Mike Ramsey	.05
63	Steve McCatty	.05
64	*Mark Bailey*	.05
65	Bill Buckner	.05
66	Dick Williams	.05
67	*Rafael Santana*	.05
68	Von Hayes	.05
69	*Jim Winn*	.05
70	Don Baylor	.10
71	Tim Laudner	.05
72	Rick Sutcliffe	.05
73	Rusty Kuntz	.05
74	Mike Krukow	.05
75	Willie Upshaw	.05
76	Alan Bannister	.05
77	Joe Beckwith	.05
78	Scott Fletcher	.05
79	Rick Mahler	.05
80	Keith Hernandez	.05
81	Lenn Sakata	.05
82	Joe Price	.05
83	Charlie Moore	.05
84	Spike Owen	.05
85	Mike Marshall	.05
86	Don Aase	.05
87	David Green	.05
88	Bryn Smith	.05
89	Jackie Gutierrez	.05
90	Rich Gossage	.05
91	Jeff Burroughs	.05
92	Paul Owens	.05
93	*Don Schulze*	.05
94	Toby Harrah	.05
95	Jose Cruz	.05
96	Johnny Ray	.05
97	Pete Filson	.05
98	Steve Lake	.05
99	Milt Wilcox	.05
100	George Brett	2.00
101	Jim Acker	.05
102	Tommy Dunbar	.05
103	Randy Lerch	.05
104	Mike Fitzgerald	.05
105	Ron Kittle	.05
106	Pascual Perez	.05
107	Tom Foley	.05
108	Darnell Coles	.05
109	Gary Roenicke	.05
110	Alejandro Pena	.05
111	Doug DeCinces	.05
112	Tom Tellmann	.05
113	Tom Herr	.05
114	Bob James	.05
115	Rickey Henderson	1.00
116	Dennis Boyd	.10
117	Greg Gross	.05
118	Eric Show	.05
119	Pat Corrales	.05
120	Steve Kemp	.05
121	Checklist 1-132	.05
122	Tom Brunansky	.05
123	Dave Smith	.05
124	Rich Hebner	.05
125	Kent Tekulve	.05
126	Ruppert Jones	.05
127	*Mark Gubicza*	.25
128	Ernie Whitt	.05
129	Gene Garber	.05
130	Al Oliver	.05
131	Father - Son (Buddy Bell, Gus Bell)	.10
132	Father - Son (Dale Berra, Yogi Berra)	.20
133	Father - Son (Bob Boone, Ray Boone)	.10
134	Father - Son (Terry Francona, Tito Francona)	.05
135	Father - Son (Bob Kennedy, Terry Kennedy)	.05
136	Father - Son (Bill Kunkel, Jeff Kunkel)	.05
137	Father - Son (Vance Law, Vern Law)	.10
138	Father - Son (Dick Schofield, Dick Schofield, Jr.)	.05
139	Father - Son (Bob Skinner, Joel Skinner)	.05
140	Father - Son (Roy Smalley, Jr., Roy Smalley III)	.05
141	Father - Son (Dave Stenhouse, Mike Stenhouse)	.05
142	Father - Son (Dizzy Trout, Steve Trout)	.05
143	Father - Son (Ozzie Virgil, Ozzie Virgil)	.05
144	Ron Gardenhire	.05
145	*Alvin Davis*	.05
146	Gary Redus	.05
147	Bill Swaggerty	.05
148	Steve Yeager	.05
149	Dickie Noles	.05
150	Jim Rice	.10
151	Moose Haas	.05
152	Steve Braun	.05
153	Frank LaCorte	.05
154	Argenis Salazar	.05
155	Yogi Berra	.10
156	Craig Reynolds	.05
157	Tug McGraw	.05
158	Pat Tabler	.05
159	Carlos Diaz	.05
160	Lance Parrish	.05
161	Ken Schrom	.05
162	*Benny Distefano*	.05
163	Dennis Eckersley	.10
164	Jorge Orta	.05
165	Dusty Baker	.05
166	Keith Atherton	.05
167	Rufino Linares	.05
168	Garth Iorg	.05
169	Dan Spillner	.05
170	George Foster	.05
171	Bill Stein	.05
172	Jack Perconte	.05

173	Mike Young	.05
174	Rick Honeycutt	.05
175	Dave Parker	.05
176	Bill Schroeder	.05
177	Dave Von Ohlen	.05
178	Miguel Dilone	.05
179	Tommy John	.10
180	Dave Winfield	1.00
181	Roger Clemens	25.00
182	Tim Flannery	.05
183	Larry McWilliams	.05
184	Carmen Castillo	.05
185	Al Holland	.05
186	Bob Lillis	.05
187	Mike Walters	.05
188	Greg Pryor	.05
189	Warren Brusstar	.05
190	Rusty Staub	.05
191	Steve Nicosia	.05
192	Howard Johnson	.10
193	Jimmy Key	1.00
194	Dave Stegman	.05
195	Glenn Hubbard	.05
196	Pete O'Brien	.05
197	Mike Warren	.05
198	Eddie Milner	.05
199	Denny Martinez	.05
200	Reggie Jackson	.75
201	Burt Hooton	.05
202	Gorman Thomas	.05
203	Bob McClure	.05
204	Art Howe	.05
205	Steve Rogers	.05
206	Phil Garner	.05
207	Mark Clear	.05
208	Champ Summers	.05
209	Bill Campbell	.05
210	Gary Matthews	.05
211	Clay Christiansen	.05
212	George Vukovich	.05
213	Billy Gardner	.05
214	John Tudor	.05
215	Bob Brenly	.05
216	Jerry Don Gleaton	.05
217	Leon Roberts	.05
218	Doyle Alexander	.05
219	Gerald Perry	.05
220	Fred Lynn	.05
221	Ron Reed	.05
222	Hubie Brooks	.05
223	Tom Hume	.05
224	Al Cowens	.05
225	Mike Boddicker	.05
226	Juan Beniquez	.05
227	Danny Darwin	.05
228	Dion James	.05
229	Dave LaPoint	.05
230	Gary Carter	.25
231	Dwayne Murphy	.05
232	Dave Beard	.05
233	Ed Jurak	.05
234	Jerry Narron	.05
235	Garry Maddox	.05
236	Mark Thurmond	.05
237	Julio Franco	.10
238	Jose Rijo	.10
239	Tim Teufel	.05
240	Dave Stieb	.05
241	Jim Frey	.05
242	Greg Harris	.05
243	Barbaro Garbey	.05
244	Mike Jones	.05
245	Chili Davis	.10
246	Mike Norris	.05
247	Wayne Tolleson	.05
248	Terry Forster	.05
249	Harold Baines	.05
250	Jesse Orosco	.05
251	Brad Gulden	.05
252	Dan Ford	.05
253	*Sid Bream*	.10
254	Pete Vuckovich	.05
255	Lonnie Smith	.05
256	Mike Stanton	.05
257	Brian Little (Bryan)	.05
258	Mike Brown	.05
259	Gary Allenson	.05
260	Dave Righetti	.05
261	Checklist 133-264	.05
262	*Greg Booker*	.05
263	Mel Hall	.05
264	Joe Sambito	.05
265	Juan Samuel	.10
266	Frank Viola	.10
267	*Henry Cotto*	.05
268	Chuck Tanner	.05
269	*Doug Baker*	.05
270	Dan Quisenberry	.05
271	Tim Foli (#1 Draft Pick)	.05
272	Jeff Burroughs (#1 Draft Pick)	.05
273	Bill Almon (#1 Draft Pick)	.05
274	Floyd Bannister (#1 Draft Pick)	.05
275	Harold Baines (#1 Draft Pick)	.10
276	Bob Horner (#1 Draft Pick)	.10
277	Al Chambers (#1 Draft Pick)	.05
278	Darryl Strawberry (#1 Draft Pick)	.30
279	Mike Moore (#1 Draft Pick)	.10
280	*Shawon Dunston* (#1 Draft Pick)	.40
281	*Tim Belcher* (#1 Draft Pick)	.30
282	*Shawn Abner* (#1 Draft Pick)	.05
283	Fran Mullins	.05
284	Marty Bystrom	.05
285	Dan Driessen	.05
286	Rudy Law	.05
287	Walt Terrell	.05
288	*Jeff Kunkel*	.05
289	Tom Underwood	.05
290	Cecil Cooper	.05
291	Bob Welch	.05
292	Brad Komminsk	.05
293	*Curt Young*	.05
294	*Tom Nieto*	.05
295	Joe Niekro	.05
296	Ricky Nelson	.05
297	Gary Lucas	.05
298	Marty Barrett	.05
299	Andy Hawkins	.05
300	Rod Carew	.40
301	John Montefusco	.05
302	Tim Corcoran	.05
303	*Mike Jeffcoat*	.05
304	Gary Gaetti	.05
305	Dale Berra	.05
306	Rick Reuschel	.05
307	Sparky Anderson	.10
308	John Wathan	.05
309	Mike Witt	.05
310	Manny Trillo	.05
311	Jim Gott	.05
312	Marc Hill	.05
313	Dave Schmidt	.05
314	Ron Oester	.05
315	Doug Sisk	.05
316	John Lowenstein	.05
317	*Jack Lazorko*	.05
318	Ted Simmons	.05
319	Jeff Jones	.05
320	Dale Murphy	.25
321	*Ricky Horton*	.05
322	Dave Stapleton	.05
323	Andy McGaffigan	.05
324	Bruce Bochy	.05
325	John Denny	.05
326	Kevin Bass	.05
327	Brook Jacoby	.05
328	Bob Shirley	.05
329	Ron Washington	.05
330	Leon Durham	.05
331	Bill Laskey	.05
332	Brian Harper	.05
333	Willie Hernandez	.05
334	Dick Howser	.05
335	Bruce Benedict	.05
336	Rance Mulliniks	.05
337	Billy Sample	.05
338	Britt Burns	.05
339	Danny Heep	.05
340	Robin Yount	.75
341	Floyd Rayford	.05
342	Ted Power	.05
343	Bill Russell	.05
344	Dave Henderson	.05
345	Charlie Lea	.05
346	*Terry Pendleton*	.75
347	Rick Langford	.05
348	Bob Boone	.05
349	Domingo Ramos	.05
350	Wade Boggs	1.50
351	Juan Agosto	.05
352	Joe Morgan	.40
353	Julio Solano	.05
354	Andre Robertson	.05
355	Bert Blyleven	.05
356	Dave Meier	.05
357	Rich Bordi	.05
358	Tony Pena	.05
359	Pat Sheridan	.05
360	Steve Carlton	.45
361	Alfredo Griffin	.05
362	Craig McMurtry	.05
363	Ron Hodges	.05
364	Richard Dotson	.05
365	Danny Ozark	.05
366	Todd Cruz	.05
367	Keefe Cato	.05
368	Dave Bergman	.05
369	*R.J. Reynolds*	.10
370	Bruce Sutter	.05
371	Mickey Rivers	.05
372	Roy Howell	.05
373	Mike Moore	.05
374	Brian Downing	.05
375	Jeff Reardon	.05
376	Jeff Newman	.05
377	Checklist 265-396	.05
378	Alan Wiggins	.05
379	Charles Hudson	.05
380	Ken Griffey	.05
381	Roy Smith	.05
382	Denny Walling	.05
383	Rick Lysander	.05
384	Jody Davis	.05
385	Jose DeLeon	.05
386	*Dan Gladden*	.30
387	*Buddy Biancalana*	.05
388	Bert Roberge	.05
389	Rod Dedeaux (Team USA)	.05
390	Sid Akins (Team USA)	.05
391	Flavio Alfaro (Team USA)	.05
392	Don August (Team USA)	.10
393	*Scott Bankhead* (Team USA)	.10
394	Bob Caffrey (Team USA)	.05
395	Mike Dunne (Team USA)	.10
396	Gary Green (Team USA)	.10
397	John Hoover (Team USA)	.05
398	*Shane Mack* (Team USA)	.25
399	John Marzano (Team USA)	.10
400	Oddibe McDowell (Team USA)	.10
401	*Mark McGwire* (Team USA)	175.00
402	Pat Pacillo (Team USA)	.05
403	*Cory Snyder* (Team USA)	.30
404	*Billy Swift* (Team USA)	.40
405	Tom Veryzer	.05
406	Len Whitehouse	.05
407	Bobby Ramos	.05
408	Sid Monge	.05
409	Brad Wellman	.05
410	Bob Horner	.05
411	Bobby Cox	.05
412	Bud Black	.05
413	Vance Law	.05
414	Gary Ward	.05
415	Ron Darling	.05
416	Wayne Gross	.05
417	*John Franco*	.45
418	Ken Landreaux	.05
419	Mike Caldwell	.05
420	Andre Dawson	.60
421	Dave Rucker	.05
422	Carney Lansford	.05
423	Barry Bonnell	.05
424	*Al Nipper*	.05
425	Mike Hargrove	.05
426	Verne Ruhle	.05
427	Mario Ramirez	.05
428	Larry Andersen	.05
429	Rick Cerone	.05
430	Ron Davis	.05
431	U.L. Washington	.05
432	Thad Bosley	.05
433	Jim Morrison	.05
434	Gene Richards	.05
435	Dan Petry	.05
436	Willie Aikens	.05
437	Al Jones	.05
438	Joe Torre	.10
439	Junior Ortiz	.05
440	Fernando Valenzuela	.10
441	Duane Walker	.05
442	Ken Forsch	.05
443	George Wright	.05
444	Tony Phillips	.05
445	Tippy Martinez	.05
446	Jim Sundberg	.05
447	Jeff Lahti	.05
448	Derrel Thomas	.05
449	*Phil Bradley*	.10
450	Steve Garvey	.25
451	Bruce Hurst	.05
452	John Castino	.05
453	Tom Waddell	.05
454	Glenn Wilson	.05
455	Bob Knepper	.05
456	Tim Foli	.05
457	Cecilio Guante	.05
458	Randy S. Johnson	.05
459	Charlie Leibrandt	.05
460	Ryne Sandberg	2.50
461	Marty Castillo	.05
462	Gary Lavelle	.05
463	Dave Collins	.05
464	*Mike Mason*	.05
465	Bob Grich	.05
466	Tony LaRussa	.10
467	Ed Lynch	.05
468	Wayne Krenchicki	.05
469	Sammy Stewart	.05
470	Steve Sax	.05
471	Pete Ladd	.05
472	Jim Essian	.05
473	Tim Wallach	.05
474	Kurt Kepshire	.05
475	Andre Thornton	.05
476	*Jeff Stone*	.05
477	Bob Ojeda	.05
478	Kurt Bevacqua	.05
479	Mike Madden	.05
480	Lou Whitaker	.10
481	Dale Murray	.05
482	Harry Spilman	.05
483	Mike Smithson	.05
484	Larry Bowa	.05
485	Matt Young	.05
486	Steve Balboni	.05
487	*Frank Williams*	.05
488	Joel Skinner	.05
489	Bryan Clark	.05
490	Jason Thompson	.05
491	Rick Camp	.05
492	Dave Johnson	.05
493	*Orel Hershiser*	1.50
494	Rich Dauer	.05
495	Mario Soto	.05
496	Donnie Scott	.05
497	Gary Pettis	.05
498	Ed Romero	.05
499	Danny Cox	.05
500	Mike Schmidt	1.50
501	Dan Schatzeder	.05
502	Rick Miller	.05
503	Tim Conroy	.05
504	Jerry Willard	.05
505	Jim Beattie	.05
506	*Franklin Stubbs*	.05
507	Ray Fontenot	.05
508	John Shelby	.05
509	Milt May	.05
510	Kent Hrbek	.05
511	Lee Smith	.10
512	Tom Brookens	.05
513	Lynn Jones	.05
514	Jeff Cornell	.05
515	Dave Concepcion	.05
516	Roy Lee Jackson	.05
517	Jerry Martin	.05
518	Chris Chambliss	.05
519	Doug Rader	.05
520	LaMarr Hoyt	.05
521	Rick Dempsey	.05
522	Paul Molitor	.75
523	Candy Maldonado	.05
524	Rob Wilfong	.05
525	Darrell Porter	.05
526	Dave Palmer	.05
527	Checklist 397-528	.05
528	Bill Krueger	.05
529	Rich Gedman	.05
530	Dave Dravecky	.05
531	Joe Lefebvre	.05
532	Frank DiPino	.05
533	Tony Bernazard	.05
534	Brian Dayett	.05
535	Pat Putnam	.05
536	Kirby Puckett	7.00
537	Don Robinson	.05
538	Keith Moreland	.05
539	Aurelio Lopez	.05
540	Claudell Washington	.05
541	Mark Davis	.05
542	Don Slaught	.05
543	Mike Squires	.05
544	Bruce Kison	.05
545	Lloyd Moseby	.05
546	Brent Gaff	.05
547	Pete Rose	1.00
548	Larry Parrish	.05
549	Mike Scioscia	.05
550	Scott McGregor	.05
551	Andy Van Slyke	.05
552	Chris Codiroli	.05
553	Bob Clark	.05
554	Doug Flynn	.05
555	Bob Stanley	.05
556	Sixto Lezcano	.05
557	Len Barker	.05
558	Carmelo Martinez	.05
559	Jay Howell	.05
560	Bill Madlock	.05
561	Darryl Motley	.05
562	Houston Jimenez	.05
563	Dick Ruthven	.05
564	Alan Ashby	.05
565	Kirk Gibson	.05
566	Ed Vande Berg	.05
567	Joel Youngblood	.05
568	Cliff Johnson	.05
569	Ken Oberkfell	.05
570	Darryl Strawberry	.30
571	Charlie Hough	.05
572	Tom Paciorek	.05
573	*Jay Tibbs*	.05
574	Joe Altobelli	.05
575	Pedro Guerrero	.05
576	Jaime Cocanower	.05
577	Chris Speier	.05
578	Terry Francona	.05
579	*Ron Romanick*	.05
580	Dwight Evans	.05
581	Mark Wagner	.05
582	Ken Phelps	.05
583	Bobby Brown	.05
584	Kevin Gross	.05
585	Butch Wynegar	.05
586	Bill Scherrer	.05
587	Doug Frobel	.05
588	Bobby Castillo	.05
589	Bob Dernier	.05
590	Ray Knight	.05
591	Larry Herndon	.05
592	*Jeff Robinson*	.05
593	Rick Leach	.05
594	Curt Wilkerson	.05
595	Larry Gura	.05
596	Jerry Hairston	.05
597	Brad Lesley	.05
598	Jose Oquendo	.05
599	Storm Davis	.05
600	Pete Rose	1.00
601	Tom Lasorda	.20
602	*Jeff Dedmon*	.05
603	Rick Manning	.05
604	Daryl Sconiers	.05
605	Ozzie Smith	.75
606	Rich Gale	.05
607	Bill Almon	.05
608	Craig Lefferts	.05
609	Broderick Perkins	.05
610	Jack Morris	.05
611	Ozzie Virgil	.05
612	Mike Armstrong	.05
613	Terry Puhl	.05
614	Al Williams	.05
615	Marvell Wynne	.05
616	Scott Sanderson	.05
617	Willie Wilson	.05
618	Pete Falcone	.05
619	Jeff Leonard	.05
620	Dwight Gooden	1.00
621	Marvis Foley	.05
622	Luis Leal	.05
623	Greg Walker	.05
624	Benny Ayala	.05
625	Mark Langston	1.00
626	German Rivera	.05
627	*Eric Davis*	.45
628	Rene Lachemann	.05
629	Dick Schofield	.05
630	Tim Raines	.15
631	Bob Forsch	.05
632	Bruce Bochte	.05
633	Glenn Hoffman	.05
634	Bill Dawley	.05
635	Terry Kennedy	.05
636	Shane Rawley	.05
637	Brett Butler	.05
638	*Mike Pagliarulo*	.10
639	Ed Hodge	.05
640	Steve Henderson	.05
641	Rod Scurry	.05
642	Dave Owen	.05
643	Johnny Grubb	.05
644	Mark Huismann	.05
645	Damaso Garcia	.05
646	Scot Thompson	.05
647	Rafael Ramirez	.05
648	Bob Jones	.05
649	Sid Fernandez	.05
650	Greg Luzinski	.05
651	Jeff Russell	.05
652	Joe Nolan	.05
653	Mark Brouhard	.05
654	Dave Anderson	.05
655	Joaquin Andujar	.05
656	Chuck Cottier	.05
657	Jim Slaton	.05
658	Mike Stenhouse	.05
659	Checklist 529-660	.05
660	Tony Gwynn	3.00
661	Steve Crawford	.05
662	Mike Heath	.05
663	Luis Aguayo	.05
664	*Steve Farr*	.20
665	Don Mattingly	3.00
666	Mike LaCoss	.05
667	Dave Engle	.05
668	Steve Trout	.05
669	Lee Lacy	.05
670	Tom Seaver	.40
671	Dane Iorg	.05
672	Juan Berenguer	.05
673	Buck Martinez	.05
674	Atlee Hammaker	.05
675	Tony Perez	.10
676	*Albert Hall*	.05
677	Wally Backman	.05
678	Joey McLaughlin	.05
679	Bob Kearney	.05
680	Jerry Reuss	.05
681	Ben Oglivie	.05
682	Doug Corbett	.05
683	Whitey Herzog	.05
684	Bill Doran	.05
685	Bill Caudill	.05
686	Mike Easler	.05
687	Bill Gullickson	.05
688	Len Matuszek	.05
689	Luis DeLeon	.05
690	Alan Trammell	.10
691	Dennis Rasmussen	.05
692	Randy Bush	.05
693	Tim Stoddard	.05
694	Joe Carter	3.00
695	Rick Rhoden	.05
696	John Rabb	.05
697	Onix Concepcion	.05
698	Jorge Bell	.10
699	Donnie Moore	.05
700	Eddie Murray	1.25
701	Eddie Murray (All-Star)	.40
702	Damaso Garcia (All-Star)	.05
703	George Brett (All-Star)	.50
704	Cal Ripken, Jr. (All-Star)	2.00
705	Dave Winfield (All-Star)	.50
706	Rickey Henderson (All-Star)	.25
707	Tony Armas (All-Star)	.05
708	Lance Parrish (All-Star)	.05
709	Mike Boddicker (All-Star)	.05
710	Frank Viola (All-Star)	.05
711	Dan Quisenberry (All-Star)	.05
712	Keith Hernandez (All-Star)	.05
713	Ryne Sandberg (All-Star)	.60
714	Mike Schmidt (All-Star)	.45
715	Ozzie Smith (All-Star)	.25
716	Dale Murphy (All-Star)	.15
717	Tony Gwynn (All-Star)	.75
718	Jeff Leonard (All-Star)	.05
719	Gary Carter (All-Star)	.10

720	Rick Sutcliffe (All-Star)	.05
721	Bob Knepper (All-Star)	.05
722	Bruce Sutter (All-Star)	.05
723	Dave Stewart	.05
724	Oscar Gamble	.05
725	Floyd Bannister	.05
726	Al Bumbry	.05
727	Frank Pastore	.05
728	Bob Bailor	.05
729	Don Sutton	.30
730	Dave Kingman	.05
731	Neil Allen	.05
732	John McNamara	.05
733	Tony Scott	.05
734	John Henry Johnson	.05
735	Garry Templeton	.05
736	Jerry Mumphrey	.05
737	Bo Diaz	.05
738	Omar Moreno	.05
739	Ernie Camacho	.05
740	Jack Clark	.05
741	John Butcher	.05
742	Ron Hassey	.05
743	Frank White	.05
744	Doug Bair	.05
745	Buddy Bell	.05
746	Jim Clancy	.05
747	Alex Trevino	.05
748	Lee Mazzilli	.05
749	Julio Cruz	.05
750	Rollie Fingers	.25
751	Kelvin Chapman	.05
752	Bob Owchinko	.05
753	Greg Brock	.05
754	Larry Milbourne	.05
755	Ken Singleton	.05
756	Rob Picciolo	.05
757	Willie McGee	.05
758	Ray Burris	.05
759	Jim Fanning	.06
760	Nolan Ryan	5.00
761	Jerry Remy	.05
762	Eddie Whitson	.05
763	Kiko Garcia	.05
764	Jamie Easterly	.05
765	Willie Randolph	.05
766	Paul Mirabella	.05
767	Darrell Brown	.05
768	Ron Cey	.05
769	Joe Cowley	.05
770	Carlton Fisk	.45
771	Geoff Zahn	.05
772	Johnnie LeMaster	.05
773	Hal McRae	.05
774	Dennis Lamp	.05
775	Mookie Wilson	.05
776	Jerry Royster	.05
777	Ned Yost	.05
778	Mike Davis	.05
779	Nick Esasky	.05
780	Mike Flanagan	.05
781	Jim Gantner	.05
782	Tom Niedenfuer	.05
783	Mike Jorgensen	.05
784	Checklist 661-792	.05
785	Tony Armas	.05
786	Enos Cabell	.05
787	Jim Wohlford	.05
788	Steve Comer	.05
789	Luis Salazar	.05
790	Ron Guidry	.10
791	Ivan DeJesus	.05
792	Darrell Evans	.10

1985 Topps Tiffany

In its second year of producing a high-gloss collectors edition of its regular baseball card set, Topps cut production to a reported 5,000 sets. Other than the use of white cardboard stock and the glossy front coating, the cards in this specially boxed set are identical to regular 1985 Topps cards.

	MT
Complete Unopened Set (792):	1250.
Complete Set, Opened (792):	700.00
Common Player:	.25
Stars: 4X	
(See 1985 Topps for checklist and base card values.)	

1985 Topps Traded

By 1985, the Topps Traded set had become a yearly feature, and Topps continued the tradition with another 132-card set. The 2-1/2" x 3-1/2" cards followed the pattern of being virtually identical in design to the regular cards issued by Topps. Sold only through established hobby dealers, the set features traded veterans and promising rookies. A glossy-finish "Tiffany" edition of the set is valued at four times normal Traded card value for commons, up to five or six times normal value for superstars and hot rookies. Cards are numbered with a "T" suffix.

		MT
Complete Set (132):		8.00
Common Player:		.10
1	Don Aase	.10
2	Bill Almon	.10
3	Benny Ayala	.10
4	Dusty Baker	.15
5	George Bamberger	.10
6	Dale Berra	.10
7	Rich Bordi	.10
8	Daryl Boston	.10
9	Hubie Brooks	.10
10	Chris Brown	.10
11	Tom Browning	.50
12	Al Bumbry	.10
13	Ray Burris	.10
14	Jeff Burroughs	.10
15	Bill Campbell	.10
16	Don Carman	.10
17	Gary Carter	.45
18	Bobby Castillo	.10
19	Bill Caudill	.10
20	Rick Cerone	.10
21	Bryan Clark	.10
22	Jack Clark	.10
23	Pat Clements	.10
24	*Vince Coleman*	.60
25	Dave Collins	.10
26	Danny Darwin	.10
27	Jim Davenport	.10
28	Jerry Davis	.10
29	Brian Dayett	.10
30	Ivan DeJesus	.10
31	Ken Dixon	.10
32	Mariano Duncan	.50
33	John Felske	.10
34	Mike Fitzgerald	.10
35	Ray Fontenot	.10
36	Greg Gagne	.35
37	Oscar Gamble	.10
38	Scott Garrelts	.15
39	Bob L. Gibson	.10
40	Jim Gott	.10
41	David Green	.10
42	Alfredo Griffin	.10
43	*Ozzie Guillen*	1.25
44	Eddie Haas	.10
45	Terry Harper	.10
46	Toby Harrah	.10
47	Greg Harris	.10
48	Ron Hassey	.10
49	Rickey Henderson	2.00
50	Steve Henderson	.10
51	George Hendrick	.10
52	Joe Hesketh	.10
53	Teddy Higuera	.10
54	Donnie Hill	.10
55	Al Holland	.10
56	Burt Hooton	.10
57	Jay Howell	.10
58	Ken Howell	.15
59	LaMarr Hoyt	.10
60	Tim Hulett	.10
61	Bob James	.10
62	Steve Jeltz	.10
63	Cliff Johnson	.10
64	Howard Johnson	.25
65	Ruppert Jones	.10
66	Steve Kemp	.10
67	Bruce Kison	.10
68	Alan Knicely	.10
69	Mike LaCoss	.10
70	Lee Lacy	.10
71	Dave LaPoint	.10
72	Gary Lavelle	.10
73	Vance Law	.10
74	Johnnie LeMaster	.10
75	Sixto Lezcano	.10
76	Tim Lollar	.10
77	Fred Lynn	.15
78	Billy Martin	.25
79	Ron Mathis	.10
80	Len Matuszek	.10
81	Gene Mauch	.10
82	Oddibe McDowell	.10
83	Roger McDowell	.50
84	John McNamara	.10
85	Donnie Moore	.10
86	Gene Nelson	.10
87	Steve Nicosia	.10
88	Al Oliver	.10
89	Joe Orsulak	.15
90	Rob Picciolo	.10
91	Chris Pittaro	.10
92	Jim Presley	.10
93	Rick Reuschel	.10
94	Bert Roberge	.10
95	Bob Rodgers	.10
96	Jerry Royster	.10
97	Dave Rozema	.10
98	Dave Rucker	.10
99	Vern Ruhle	.10
100	Paul Runge	.10
101	Mark Salas	.10
102	Luis Salazar	.10
103	Joe Sambito	.10
104	Rick Schu	.10
105	Donnie Scott	.10
106	Larry Sheets	.10
107	Don Slaught	.10
108	Roy Smalley	.10
109	Lonnie Smith	.10
110	Nate Snell	.10
111	Chris Speier	.10
112	Mike Stenhouse	.10
113	Tim Stoddard	.10
114	Jim Sundberg	.10
115	Bruce Sutter	.10
116	Don Sutton	1.00
117	Kent Tekulve	.10
118	Tom Tellmann	.10
119	Walt Terrell	.10
120	*Mickey Tettleton*	1.00
121	Derrel Thomas	.10
122	Rich Thompson	.10
123	Alex Trevino	.10
124	John Tudor	.10
125	Jose Uribe	.10
126	Bobby Valentine	.10
127	Dave Von Ohlen	.10
128	U.L. Washington	.10
129	Earl Weaver	.25
130	Eddie Whitson	.10
131	Herm Winningham	.10
132	Checklist 1-132	.10

1985 Topps Traded Tiffany

This specially boxed collectors version of the Topps Traded sets features cards that differ only in the use of a high-gloss finish coat on the fronts.

	MT
Complete Set (132):	40.00
Common Player:	.25
Stars: 4X	
(See 1985 Topps Traded for checklist and base card values.)	

1985 Topps All-Star Glossy Set of 22

This was the second straight year for this set of 22 cards featuring the starting players, honorary captains and managers in the All-Star Game. The set is virtually identical to that of the previous year in design with a color photo, All-Star banner, league emblem, and player ID on the front. Fronts have a high-gloss finish. The cards were available as inserts in Topps rack packs.

		MT
Complete Set (22):		3.00
Common Player:		.10
1	Paul Owens	.10
2	Steve Garvey	.30
3	Ryne Sandberg	.60
4	Mike Schmidt	.75
5	Ozzie Smith	.50
6	Tony Gwynn	.75
7	Dale Murphy	.30
8	Darryl Strawberry	.30
9	Gary Carter	.30
10	Charlie Lea	.10
11	Willie McCovey	.35
12	Joe Altobelli	.10
13	Rod Carew	.40
14	Lou Whitaker	.10
15	George Brett	.75
16	Cal Ripken, Jr.	1.00
17	Dave Winfield	.35
18	Chet Lemon	.10
19	Reggie Jackson	.45
20	Lance Parrish	.10
21	Dave Stieb	.10
22	Hank Greenberg	.25

1985 Topps All-Star Glossy Set of 40

Similar to previous years' glossy sets, the 1985 All-Star "Collector's Edition" set of 40 could be obtained through the mail in eight five-card subsets. To obtain the 2-1/2" x 3-1/2" cards, collectors had to accumulate sweepstakes insert cards from Topps packs, and pay 75¢ postage and handling. Under the circumstances, the complete set of 40 cards was not inexpensive.

		MT
Complete Set (40):		8.00
Common Player:		.10
1	Dale Murphy	.30
2	Jesse Orosco	.10
3	Bob Brenly	.10
4	Mike Boddicker	.10
5	Dave Kingman	.10
6	Jim Rice	.25
7	Frank Viola	.10
8	Alvin Davis	.10
9	Rick Sutcliffe	.10
10	Pete Rose	1.50
11	Leon Durham	.10
12	Joaquin Andujar	.10
13	Keith Hernandez	.10
14	Dave Winfield	.40
15	Reggie Jackson	.50
16	Alan Trammell	.25
17	Bert Blyleven	.10
18	Tony Armas	.10
19	Rich Gossage	.10
20	Jose Cruz	.10
21	Ryne Sandberg	.75
22	Bruce Sutter	.10
23	Mike Schmidt	1.00
24	Cal Ripken, Jr.	2.00
25	Dan Petry	.10
26	Jack Morris	.10
27	Don Mattingly	1.00
28	Eddie Murray	.60
29	Tony Gwynn	.75
30	Charlie Lea	.10
31	Juan Samuel	.10
32	Phil Niekro	.25
33	Alejandro Pena	.10
34	Harold Baines	.10
35	Dan Quisenberry	.10
36	Gary Carter	.20
37	Mario Soto	.10
38	Dwight Gooden	.25
39	Tom Brunansky	.10
40	Dave Stieb	.10

1985 Topps All-Time Record Holders

This 44-card boxed set was produced by Topps for the Woolworth's chain stores. Many hobbyists refer to this as the "Woolworth's" set, but that name does not appear anywhere on the cards. Featuring a combination of black-and-white and color photos of baseball record holders from all eras, the set is in the standard 2-1/2" x 3-1/2" format. Backs, printed in blue and orange, give career details and personal data. Because it combined old-timers with current players, the set did not achieve a great deal of collector popularity.

		MT
Complete Set (44):		6.00
Common Player:		.05
1	Hank Aaron	.25
2	Grover Alexander	.10
3	Ernie Banks	.15
4	Yogi Berra	.15
5	Lou Brock	.10
6	Steve Carlton	.10
7	Jack Chesbro	.05
8	Ty Cobb	.30
9	Sam Crawford	.05
10	Rollie Fingers	.05
11	Whitey Ford	.15
12	Johnny Frederick	.05
13	Frankie Frisch	.05
14	Lou Gehrig	.30
15	Jim Gentile	.05
16	Dwight Gooden	.10
17	Rickey Henderson	.25
18	Rogers Hornsby	.05
19	Frank Howard	.05
20	Cliff Johnson	.05
21	Walter Johnson	.10
22	Hub Leonard	.05
23	Mickey Mantle	1.00
24	Roger Maris	.50
25	Christy Mathewson	.10
26	Willie Mays	.20
27	Stan Musial	.20
28	Dan Quisenberry	.05
29	Frank Robinson	.10
30	Pete Rose	.50
31	Babe Ruth	.60
32	Nolan Ryan	.75
33	George Sisler	.05
34	Tris Speaker	.05
35	Ed Walsh	.05
36	Lloyd Waner	.05
37	Earl Webb	.05
38	Ted Williams	.30
39	Maury Wills	.05
40	Hack Wilson	.05
41	Owen Wilson	.05
42	Willie Wilson	.05
43	Rudy York	.05
44	Cy Young	.10

1985 Topps Gallery of Champions

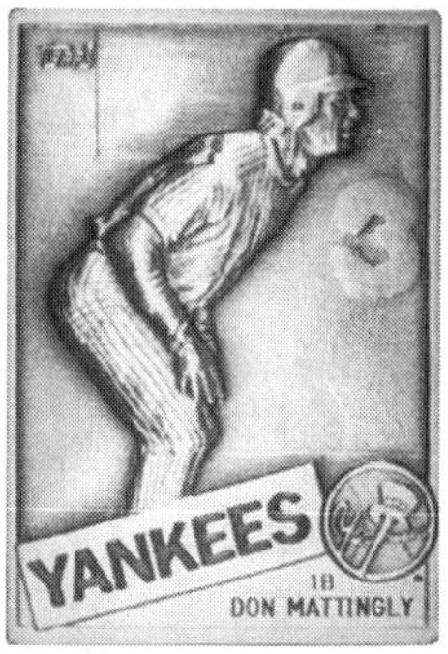

This second annual metallic miniatures issue honors 12 award winners from the previous season (MVP, Cy Young, Rookie of Year, Fireman, etc.). Each mini is an exact reproduction at one-quarter scale of the player's 1985 Topps card, both front and back. The sets (editions of 1,000) were issued in a specially-designed velvet-like case. A Dwight Gooden pewter replica was given as a premium to dealers who bought the sets. A Pete Rose bronze was issued as a premium to dealers purchasing cases of

1985 Topps Traded sets. Earlier listings of an aluminum version of the Gallery of Champions set were in error.

		MT
Complete Bronze Set (12):		200.00
Complete Silver Set (12):		485.00
(1b)	Tony Armas (bronze)	7.50
(1s)	Tony Armas (silver)	18.50
(2b)	Alvin Davis (bronze)	7.50
(2s)	Alvin Davis (silver)	18.50
(3b)	Dwight Gooden (bronze)	22.00
(3s)	Dwight Gooden (silver)	55.00
(3p)	Dwight Gooden (pewter)	35.00
(4b)	Tony Gwynn (bronze)	60.00
(4s)	Tony Gwynn (silver)	125.00
(5b)	Willie Hernandez (bronze)	7.50
(5s)	Willie Hernandez (silver)	18.50
(6b)	Don Mattingly (bronze)	45.00
(6s)	Don Mattingly (silver)	110.00
(7b)	Dale Murphy (bronze)	30.00
(7s)	Dale Murphy (silver)	75.00
(8b)	Dan Quisenberry (bronze)	7.50
(8s)	Dan Quisenberry (silver)	18.50
(9b)	Ryne Sandberg (bronze)	30.00
(9s)	Ryne Sandberg (silver)	75.00
(10b)	Mike Schmidt (bronze)	35.00
(10s)	Mike Schmidt (silver)	85.00
(11b)	Rick Sutcliffe (bronze)	7.50
(11s)	Rick Sutcliffe (silver)	18.50
(12b)	Bruce Sutter (bronze)	7.50
(12s)	Bruce Sutter (silver)	18.50
(13)	Pete Rose (bronze)	22.00

1985 Topps Minis

Never released for public sale, quantities of these enigmatic cards nevertheless reached the hobby market. Smaller than the standard 2-1/2" x 3-1/2" Topps cards, the "mini" version measures 2-3/8" x 3-9/32", 10% smaller than regular cards. Printed in Canada, the minis use a whiter cardboard stock than the regular '85 Topps, making the color printing more vibrant. The minis were the result of a test of new printing equipment by O-Pee-Chee, Topps' Canadian licensee. Only 132 of the 792 cards in the '85 Topps set are found in mini version. Only about 100 of each mini card are known, including about 15% blank-backs.

		MT
Complete Set (132):		4500.
Common Player:		7.50
12	Dave Lopes	7.50
15	Jerry Koosman	7.50
17	Mike Scott	7.50
25	Steve Bedrosian	7.50
44	Dickie Thon	7.50
65	Bill Buckner	7.50
68	Von Hayes	7.50
72	Rick Sutcliffe	7.50
75	Willie Upshaw	7.50
82	Joe Price	7.50
88	Bryn Smith	7.50
91	Jeff Burroughs	7.50
95	Jose Cruz	7.50
96	Johnny Ray	7.50
109	Gary Roenicke	7.50
113	Tom Herr	7.50
114	Bob James	7.50
117	Greg Gross	7.50
120	Steve Kemp	7.50
121	Checklist 1-132	3.00
128	(Ernie Whitt)	7.50
148	(Steve Yaeger)	7.50
150	Jim Rice	25.00
151	Moose Haas	7.50
154	Argenis Salazar	7.50
156	Craig Reynolds	7.50
160	Lance Parrish	10.00
165	Dusty Baker	9.00
170	George Foster	12.00
178	Miguel Dilone	7.50
185	Al Holland	7.50
190	Rusty Staub	15.00
198	Eddie Milner	7.50
201	Burt Hooton	7.50
205	Steve Rogers	7.50
209	Bill Campbell	7.50
210	Gary Matthews	7.50
218	Doyle Alexander	7.50
222	Hubie Brooks	7.50
223	Tom Hume	7.50
225	Mike Boddicker	7.50
229	Dave LaPoint	7.50
230	Gary Carter	30.00
235	Garry Maddox	7.50
236	Mark Thurmond	7.50
237	Julio Franco	10.00
239	Tim Teufel	7.50
248	Terry Forster	7.50
250	Jesse Orosco	7.50
251	Brad Gulden	7.50
255	Lonnie Smith	7.50
261	Checklist 133-264	3.00
263	(Mel Hall)	7.50
266	Frank Viola	7.50
287	Walt Terrell	7.50
306	Rick Reuschel	7.50
310	Manny Trillo	7.50
313	Dave Schmidt	7.50
325	John Denny	7.50
330	Leon Durham	7.50
333	Willie Hernandez	7.50
340	Robin Yount	125.00
343	Bill Russell	7.50
345	Charlie Lea	7.50
352	Joe Morgan	60.00
355	Bert Blyleven	7.50
358	Tony Pena	7.50
360	Steve Carlton	135.00
362	Craig McMurtry	7.50
375	Jeff Reardon	7.50
379	Charles Hudson	7.50
415	Ron Darling	9.00
445	Tippy Martinez	7.50
446	Jim Sundberg	7.50
450	Steve Garvey	45.00
452	John Castino	7.50
464	Mike Mason	7.50
470	Steve Sax	7.50
485	Matt Young	7.50
487	Frank Williams	7.50
489	Bryan Clark	7.50
491	Rick Camp	7.50
495	Mario Soto	7.50
500	Mike Schmidt	400.00
501	Dan Schatzeder	7.50
504	Jerry Willard	7.50
511	Lee Smith	12.00
515	Dave Concepcion	7.50
520	LaMarr Hoyt	7.50
526	Dave Palmer	7.50
530	Dave Dravecky	7.50
538	Keith Moreland	7.50
545	Lloyd Moseby	7.50
551	Andy Van Slyke	12.00
554	Doug Flynn	7.50
556	Sixto Lezcano	7.50
560	Bill Madlock	7.50
563	Dick Ruthven	7.50
566	Ed Vande Berg	7.50
568	Cliff Johnson	7.50
569	Ken Oberkfell	7.50
575	Pedro Guerrero	7.50
580	Dwight Evans	7.50
589	Bob Dernier	7.50
592	Jeff Robinson	7.50
603	Rick Manning	7.50
608	Craig Lefferts	7.50
610	Jack Morris	12.00
613	Terry Puhl	7.50
615	Marvell Wynne	7.50
619	Jeff Leonard	7.50
625	Mark Langston	12.00
630	Tim Raines	20.00
634	Bill Dawley	7.50
670	Tom Seaver	200.00
673	Buck Martinez	7.50
674	Atlee Hammaker	7.50
685	Bill Caudill	7.50
700	Eddie Murray	100.00
725	Floyd Bannister	7.50
729	Don Sutton	25.00
731	Neil Allen	7.50
736	Jerry Mumphrey	7.50
748	Lee Mazzilli	7.50
753	Greg Brock	7.50
755	Ken Singleton	7.50
757	Willie McGee	10.00
760	Nolan Ryan	850.00
762	Eddie Whitson	7.50
775	Mookie Wilson	7.50
780	Mike Flanagan	7.50
782	Tom Niedenfuer	7.50

1985 Topps Rub Downs

Similar in size and design to the Rub Downs of the previous year, the 1985 set again consisted of 32 unnumbered sheets featuring 112 different players. The set was sold by Topps as a separate issue.

		MT
Complete Set (32):		8.00
Common Player:		.25
(1)	Tony Armas, Harold Baines, Lonnie Smith	.25
(2)	Don Baylor, George Hendrick, Ron Kittle, Johnnie LeMaster	.25
(3)	Buddy Bell, Tony Gwynn, Lloyd Moseby	.30
(4)	Bruce Benedict, Atlee Hammaker, Frank White	.25
(5)	Mike Boddicker, Rod Carew, Carlton Fisk, Johnny Ray	.30
(6)	Wade Boggs, Rick Dempsey, Keith Hernandez	.40
(7)	George Brett, Andre Dawson, Paul Molitor, Alan Wiggins	.75
(8)	Tom Brunansky, Pedro Guerrero, Darryl Strawberry	.25
(9)	Bill Buckner, Tim Raines, Ryne Sandberg, Mike Schmidt	.50
(10)	Steve Carlton, Bob Horner, Dan Quisenberry	.25
(11)	Gary Carter, Phil Garner, Ron Guidry	.25
(12)	Jack Clark, Damaso Garcia, Hal McRae, Lance Parrish	.25
(13)	Dave Concepcion, Cecil Cooper, Fred Lynn, Jesse Orosco	.25
(14)	Jose Cruz, Jack Morris, Jim Rice, Rick Sutcliffe	.25
(15)	Alvin Davis, Steve Kemp, Greg Luzinski, Kent Tekulve	.25
(16)	Ron Davis, Kent Hrbek, Juan Samuel	.25
(17)	John Denny, Carney Lansford, Mario Soto, Lou Whitaker	.25
(18)	Leon Durham, Willie Hernandez, Steve Sax	.25
(19)	Dwight Evans, Julio Franco, Dwight Gooden	.25
(20)	George Foster, Gary Gaetti, Bobby Grich, Gary Redus	.25
(21)	Steve Garvey, Jerry Remy, Bill Russell, George Wright	.25
(22)	Kirk Gibson, Rich Gossage, Don Mattingly, Dave Stieb	.75
(23)	Moose Haas, Bruce Sutter, Dickie Thon, Andre Thornton	.25
(24)	Rickey Henderson, Dave Righetti, Pete Rose	.75
(25)	Steve Henderson, Bill Madlock, Alan Trammell	.25
(26)	LaMarr Hoyt, Larry Parrish, Nolan Ryan	.75
(27)	Reggie Jackson, Eric Show, Jason Thompson	.30
(28)	Terry Kennedy, Eddie Murray, Tom Seaver, Ozzie Smith	.40
(29)	Mark Langston, Ben Oglivie, Darrell Porter	.25
(30)	Jeff Leonard, Gary Matthews, Dale Murphy, Dave Winfield	.30
(31)	Craig McMurtry, Cal Ripken, Jr., Steve Rogers, Willie Upshaw	1.00
(32)	Tony Pena, Fernando Valenzuela, Robin Yount	.45

1985 Topps Stickers

Topps went to a larger size for its stickers in 1985. Each of the 376 stickers measures 2-1/8" x 3" and is numbered on both the front and the back. The backs contain either an offer to obtain an autographed team ball or a poster. An album was also available.

		MT
Complete Set (376):		16.00
Common Player:		.05
Sticker Album:		2.00
1	Steve Garvey	.10
2	Steve Garvey	.10
3	Dwight Gooden	.10
4	Dwight Gooden	.10
5	Joe Morgan	.10
6	Joe Morgan	.10
7	Don Sutton	.10
8	Don Sutton	.10
9	1984 A.L. Championships (Jack Morris)	.05
10	1984 A.L. Championships (Milt Wilcox)	.05
11	1984 A.L. Championships (Kirk Gibson)	.05
12	1984 N.L. Championships (Gary Matthews)	.05
13	1984 N.L. Championships (Steve Garvey)	.05
14	1984 N.L. Championships (Steve Garvey)	.05
15	1984 World Series (Jack Morris)	.05
16	1984 World Series (Kurt Bevacqua)	.05
17	1984 World Series (Milt Wilcox)	.05
18	1984 World Series (Alan Trammell)	.05
19	1984 World Series (Kirk Gibson)	.05
20	1984 World Series (Alan Trammell)	.05
21	1984 World Series (Chet Lemon)	.05
22	Dale Murphy	.15
23	Steve Bedrosian	.05
24	Bob Horner	.05
25	Claudell Washington	.05
26	Rick Mahler	.05
27	Rafael Ramirez	.05
28	Craig McMurtry	.05
29	Chris Chambliss	.05
30	Alex Trevino	.05
31	Bruce Benedict	.05
32	Ken Oberkfell	.05
33	Glenn Hubbard	.05
34	Ryne Sandberg	.40
35	Rick Sutcliffe	.05
36	Leon Durham	.05
37	Jody Davis	.05
38	Bob Dernier	.05
39	Keith Moreland	.05
40	Scott Sanderson	.05
41	Lee Smith	.05
42	Ron Cey	.05
43	Steve Trout	.05
44	Gary Matthews	.05
45	Larry Bowa	.05
46	Mario Soto	.05
47	Dave Parker	.05
48	Dave Concepcion	.05
49	Gary Redus	.05
50	Ted Power	.05
51	Nick Esasky	.05
52	Duane Walker	.05
53	Eddie Milner	.05
54	Ron Oester	.05
55	Cesar Cedeno	.05
56	Joe Price	.05
57	Pete Rose	.50
58	Nolan Ryan	.75
59	Jose Cruz	.05
60	Jerry Mumphrey	.05
61	Enos Cabell	.05
62	Bob Knepper	.05
63	Dickie Thon	.05
64	Phil Garner	.05
65	Craig Reynolds	.05
66	Frank DiPino	.05
67	Terry Puhl	.05
68	Bill Doran	.05
69	Joe Niekro	.05
70	Pedro Guerrero	.05
71	Fernando Valenzuela	.05
72	Mike Marshall	.05
73	Alejandro Pena	.05
74	Orel Hershiser	.10
75	Ken Landreaux	.05
76	Bill Russell	.05
77	Steve Sax	.05
78	Rick Honeycutt	.05
79	Mike Scioscia	.05
80	Tom Niedenfuer	.05
81	Candy Maldonado	.05
82	Tim Raines	.15
83	Gary Carter	.10
84	Charlie Lea	.05
85	Jeff Reardon	.05
86	Andre Dawson	.10
87	Tim Wallach	.05
88	Terry Francona	.05
89	Steve Rogers	.05
90	Bryn Smith	.05
91	Bill Gullickson	.05
92	Dan Driessen	.05
93	Doug Flynn	.05
94	Mike Schmidt	.25
95	Tony Armas	.05
96	Dale Murphy	.10
97	Rick Sutcliffe	.05
98	Keith Hernandez	.05
99	George Foster	.05
100	Darryl Strawberry	.10
101	Jesse Orosco	.05
102	Mookie Wilson	.05
103	Doug Sisk	.05
104	Hubie Brooks	.05
105	Ron Darling	.05
106	Wally Backman	.05
107	Dwight Gooden	.10
108	Mike Fitzgerald	.05
109	Walt Terrell	.05
110	Ozzie Virgil	.05
111	Mike Schmidt	.25
112	Steve Carlton	.20
113	Al Holland	.05
114	Juan Samuel	.05
115	Von Hayes	.05
116	Jeff Stone	.05
117	Jerry Koosman	.05
118	Al Oliver	.05
119	John Denny	.05
120	Charles Hudson	.05
121	Garry Maddox	.05
122	Bill Madlock	.05
123	John Candelaria	.05
124	Tony Pena	.05
125	Jason Thompson	.05
126	Lee Lacy	.05
127	Rick Rhoden	.05
128	Doug Frobel	.05
129	Kent Tekulve	.05
130	Johnny Ray	.05
131	Marvell Wynne	.05
132	Larry McWilliams	.05
133	Dale Berra	.05
134	George Hendrick	.05
135	Bruce Sutter	.05
136	Joaquin Andujar	.05
137	Ozzie Smith	.20
138	Andy Van Slyke	.05
139	Lonnie Smith	.05
140	Darrell Porter	.05
141	Willie McGee	.05
142	Tom Herr	.05
143	Dave LaPoint	.05
144	Neil Allen	.05
145	David Green	.05
146	Tony Gwynn	.50
147	Rich Gossage	.05
148	Terry Kennedy	.05
149	Steve Garvey	.15
150	Alan Wiggins	.05
151	Garry Templeton	.05
152	Ed Whitson	.05
153	Tim Lollar	.05
154	Dave Dravecky	.05
155	Graig Nettles	.05
156	Eric Show	.05
157	Carmelo Martinez	.05
158	Bob Brenly	.05

159	Gary Lavelle	.05
160	Jack Clark	.05
161	Jeff Leonard	.05
162	Chili Davis	.05
163	Mike Krukow	.05
164	Johnnie LeMaster	.05
165	Atlee Hammaker	.05
166	Dan Gladden	.05
167	Greg Minton	.05
168	Joel Youngblood	.05
169	Frank Williams	.05
170	Tony Gwynn	.50
171	Don Mattingly	.60
172	Bruce Sutter	.05
173	Dan Quisenberry	.05
174	Tony Gwynn	.50
175	Ryne Sandberg	.40
176	Steve Garvey	.15
177	Dale Murphy	.15
178	Mike Schmidt	.25
179	Darryl Strawberry	.10
180	Gary Carter	.10
181	Ozzie Smith	.20
182	Charlie Lea	.05
183	Lou Whitaker	.05
184	Rod Carew	.25
185	Cal Ripken, Jr.	.75
186	Dave Winfield	.30
187	Reggie Jackson	.25
188	George Brett	.45
189	Lance Parrish	.05
190	Chet Lemon	.05
191	Dave Stieb	.05
192	Gary Carter	.10
193	Mike Schmidt	.25
194	Tony Armas	.05
195	Mike Witt	.05
196	Eddie Murray	.20
197	Cal Ripken, Jr.	.75
198	Scott McGregor	.05
199	Rick Dempsey	.05
200	Tippy Martinez	.05
201	Ken Singleton	.05
202	Mike Boddicker	.05
203	Rich Dauer	.05
204	John Shelby	.05
205	Al Bumbry	.05
206	John Lowenstein	.05
207	Mike Flanagan	.05
208	Jim Rice	.10
209	Tony Armas	.05
210	Wade Boggs	.30
211	Bruce Hurst	.05
212	Dwight Evans	.05
213	Mike Easler	.05
214	Bill Buckner	.05
215	Bob Stanley	.05
216	Jackie Gutierrez	.05
217	Rich Gedman	.05
218	Jerry Remy	.05
219	Marty Barrett	.05
220	Reggie Jackson	.25
221	Geoff Zahn	.05
222	Doug DeCinces	.05
223	Rod Carew	.15
224	Brian Downing	.05
225	Fred Lynn	.05
226	Gary Pettis	.05
227	Mike Witt	.05
228	Bob Boone	.05
229	Tommy John	.05
230	Bobby Grich	.05
231	Ron Romanick	.05
232	Ron Kittle	.05
233	Richard Dotson	.05
234	Harold Baines	.05
235	Tom Seaver	.15
236	Greg Walker	.05
237	Roy Smalley	.05
238	Greg Luzinski	.05
239	Julio Cruz	.05
240	Scott Fletcher	.05
241	Rudy Law	.05
242	Vance Law	.05
243	Carlton Fisk	.15
244	Andre Thornton	.05
245	Julio Franco	.05
246	Brett Butler	.05
247	Bert Blyleven	.05
248	Mike Hargrove	.05
249	George Vukovich	.05
250	Pat Tabler	.05
251	Brook Jacoby	.05
252	Tony Bernazard	.05
253	Ernie Camacho	.05
254	Mel Hall	.05
255	Carmen Castillo	.05
256	Jack Morris	.05
257	Willie Hernandez	.05
258	Alan Trammell	.10
259	Lance Parrish	.05
260	Chet Lemon	.05
261	Lou Whitaker	.05
262	Howard Johnson	.05
263	Barbaro Garbey	.05
264	Dan Petry	.05
265	Aurelio Lopez	.05
266	Larry Herndon	.05
267	Kirk Gibson	.05
268	George Brett	.45
269	Dan Quisenberry	.05
270	Hal McRae	.05
271	Steve Balboni	.05
272	Pat Sheridan	.05
273	Jorge Orta	.05
274	Frank White	.05
275	Bud Black	.05
276	Darryl Motley	.05
277	Willie Wilson	.05
278	Larry Gura	.05
279	Don Slaught	.05
280	Dwight Gooden	.10
281	Mark Langston	.10
282	Tim Raines	.15
283	Rickey Henderson	.15
284	Robin Yount	.30
285	Rollie Fingers	.10
286	Jim Sundberg	.05
287	Cecil Cooper	.05
288	Jaime Cocanower	.05
289	Mike Caldwell	.05
290	Don Sutton	.10
291	Rick Manning	.05
292	Ben Oglivie	.05
293	Moose Haas	.05
294	Ted Simmons	.05
295	Jim Gantner	.05
296	Kent Hrbek	.10
297	Ron Davis	.05
298	Dave Engle	.05
299	Tom Brunansky	.05
300	Frank Viola	.05
301	Mike Smithson	.05
302	Gary Gaetti	.05
303	Tim Teufel	.05
304	Mickey Hatcher	.05
305	John Butcher	.05
306	Darrell Brown	.05
307	Kirby Puckett	.50
308	Dave Winfield	.20
309	Phil Niekro	.10
310	Don Mattingly	.60
311	Don Baylor	.10
312	Willie Randolph	.05
313	Ron Guidry	.05
314	Dave Righetti	.05
315	Bobby Meacham	.05
316	Butch Wynegar	.05
317	Mike Pagliarulo	.05
318	Joe Cowley	.05
319	John Montefusco	.05
320	Dave Kingman	.05
321	Rickey Henderson	.15
322	Bill Caudill	.05
323	Dwayne Murphy	.05
324	Steve McCatty	.05
325	Joe Morgan	.10
326	Mike Heath	.05
327	Chris Codiroli	.05
328	Ray Burris	.05
329	Tony Phillips	.10
330	Carney Lansford	.05
331	Bruce Bochte	.05
332	Alvin Davis	.05
333	Al Cowens	.05
334	Jim Beattie	.05
335	Bob Kearney	.05
336	Ed Vande Berg	.05
337	Mark Langston	.05
338	Dave Henderson	.05
339	Spike Owen	.05
340	Matt Young	.05
341	Jack Perconte	.05
342	Barry Bonnell	.05
343	Mike Stanton	.05
344	Pete O'Brien	.05
345	Charlie Hough	.05
346	Larry Parrish	.05
347	Buddy Bell	.05
348	Frank Tanana	.05
349	Curt Wilkerson	.05
350	Jeff Kunkel	.05
351	Billy Sample	.05
352	Danny Darwin	.05
353	Gary Ward	.05
354	Mike Mason	.05
355	Mickey Rivers	.05
356	Dave Stieb	.05
357	Damaso Garcia	.05
358	Willie Upshaw	.05
359	Lloyd Moseby	.05
360	George Bell	.05
361	Luis Leal	.05
362	Jesse Barfield	.05
363	Dave Collins	.05
364	Roy Lee Jackson	.05
365	Doyle Alexander	.05
366	Alfredo Griffin	.05
367	Cliff Johnson	.05
368	Alvin Davis	.05
369	Juan Samuel	.05
370	Brook Jacoby	.05
371	Dwight Gooden, Mark Langston	.05
372	Mike Fitzgerald	.05
373	Jackie Gutierrez	.05
374	Dan Gladden	.05
375	Carmelo Martinez	.05
376	Kirby Puckett	.50

1985 Topps Super

Still trying to sell collectors on the idea of jumbo-sized cards, Topps returned for a second year with its 4-7/8" x 6-7/8" "Super" set. In fact, the set size was doubled from the previous year, to 60 cards. The Supers are identical to the regular-issue 1985 cards of the same players, only the card numbers on back were changed. The cards were again sold three per pack for 50¢.

		MT
Complete Set (60):		15.00
Common Player:		.25
1	Ryne Sandberg	1.50
2	Willie Hernandez	.25
3	Rick Sutcliffe	.25
4	Don Mattingly	2.00
5	Tony Gwynn	2.00
6	Alvin Davis	.25
7	Dwight Gooden	.50
8	Dan Quisenberry	.25
9	Bruce Sutter	.25
10	Tony Armas	.25
11	Dale Murphy	.50
12	Mike Schmidt	2.00
13	Gary Carter	.40
14	Rickey Henderson	1.00
15	Tim Raines	.50
16	Mike Boddicker	.25
17	Alejandro Pena	.25
18	Eddie Murray	.75
19	Gary Matthews	.25
20	Mark Langston	.25
21	Mario Soto	.25
22	Dave Stieb	.25
23	Nolan Ryan	3.00
24	Steve Carlton	.75
25	Alan Trammell	.30
26	Steve Garvey	.40
27	Kirk Gibson	.25
28	Juan Samuel	.25
29	Reggie Jackson	.75
30	Darryl Strawberry	.60
31	Tom Seaver	.75
32	Pete Rose	2.50
33	Dwight Evans	.25
34	Jose Cruz	.25
35	Bert Blyleven	.25
36	Keith Hernandez	.25
37	Robin Yount	.75
38	Joaquin Andujar	.25
39	Lloyd Moseby	.25
40	Chili Davis	.25
41	Kent Hrbek	.25
42	Dave Parker	.25
43	Jack Morris	.25
44	Pedro Guerrero	.25
45	Mike Witt	.25
46	George Brett	2.00
47	Ozzie Smith	.75
48	Cal Ripken, Jr.	3.00
49	Rich Gossage	.25
50	Jim Rice	.35
51	Harold Baines	.35
52	Fernando Valenzuela	.25
53	Buddy Bell	.25
54	Jesse Orosco	.25
55	Lance Parrish	.25
56	Jason Thompson	.25
57	Tom Brunansky	.25
58	Dave Righetti	.25
59	Dave Kingman	.25
60	Dave Winfield	.65

1985 Topps 3-D

These 4-1/4" x 6" cards were something new. Printed on plastic, rather than paper, the player picture on the card is actually raised above the surface much like might be found on a relief map; a true 3-D baseball card. The plastic cards include the player's name, a Topps logo and card number across the top, and a team logo on the side. The backs are blank but have two peel-off adhesive strips so that the card may be attached to a flat surface. There are 30 cards in the set, mostly stars. Cards were sold one per pack for 50 cents.

		MT
Complete Set (30):		20.00
Common Player:		.25
1	Mike Schmidt	2.00
2	Eddie Murray	.75
3	Dale Murphy	.50
4	George Brett	2.00
5	Pete Rose	3.00
6	Jim Rice	.40
7	Ryne Sandberg	1.50
8	Don Mattingly	3.00
9	Darryl Strawberry	.40
10	Rickey Henderson	.50
11	Keith Hernandez	.25
12	Dave Kingman	.25
13	Tony Gwynn	2.00
14	Reggie Jackson	.60
15	Gary Carter	.35
16	Cal Ripken, Jr.	4.00
17	Tim Raines	.35
18	Dave Winfield	.50
19	Dwight Gooden	.35
20	Dave Stieb	.25
21	Fernando Valenzuela	.25
22	Mark Langston	.25
23	Bruce Sutter	.25
24	Dan Quisenberry	.25
25	Steve Carlton	.45
26	Mike Boddicker	.25
27	Goose Gossage	.25
28	Jack Morris	.25
29	Rick Sutcliffe	.25
30	Tom Seaver	.45

1986 Topps

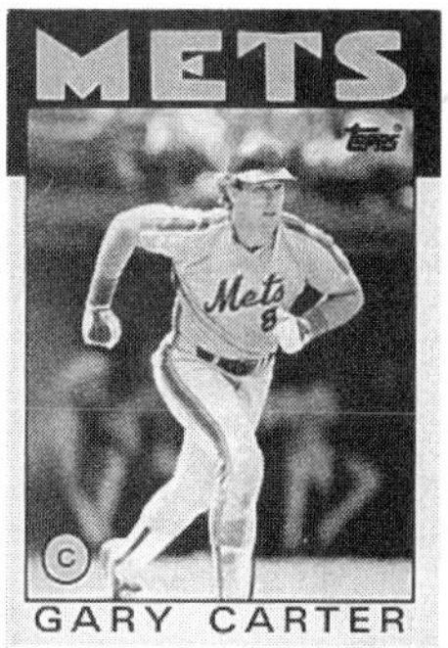

The 1986 Topps set consists of 792 cards. Fronts of the 2-1/2" x 3-1/2" cards feature color photos with the Topps logo in the upper right-hand corner while the player's position is in the lower left-hand corner. Above the picture is the team name, while below it is the player's name. The borders are a departure from previous practice, as the top 7/8" is black, while the remainder is white. There are no card numbers 51 and 171 in the set; the card that should have been #51, Bobby Wine, shares #57 with Bill Doran, while #171, Bob Rodgers, shares #141 with Chuck Cottier. Once again, a 5,000-set glossy-finish "Tiffany" edition was produced. Values are four to six times higher than the same card in the regular issue.

		MT
Complete Set (792):		25.00
Common Player:		.05
Wax Box:		30.00
1	Pete Rose	.50
2	Pete Rose (Special 1963-66)	.25
3	Pete Rose (Special 1967-70)	.25
4	Pete Rose (Special 1971-74)	.25
5	Pete Rose (Special 1975-78)	.25
6	Pete Rose (Special 1972-82)	.25
7	Pete Rose (Special 1983-85)	.25
8	Dwayne Murphy	.05
9	Roy Smith	.05
10	Tony Gwynn	1.00
11	Bob Ojeda	.05
12	*Jose Uribe*	.05
13	Bob Kearney	.05
14	Julio Cruz	.05
15	Eddie Whitson	.05
16	Rick Schu	.05
17	Mike Stenhouse	.05
18	Brent Gaff	.05
19	Rich Hebner	.05
20	Lou Whitaker	.05
21	George Bamberger	.05
22	Duane Walker	.05
23	*Manny Lee*	.05
24	Len Barker	.05
25	Willie Wilson	.05
26	Frank DiPino	.05
27	Ray Knight	.05
28	Eric Davis	.10
29	Tony Phillips	.05
30	Eddie Murray	.40
31	Jamie Easterly	.05
32	Steve Yeager	.05
33	Jeff Lahti	.05
34	Ken Phelps	.05
35	Jeff Reardon	.05
36	Tigers Leaders (Lance Parrish)	.05
37	Mark Thurmond	.05
38	Glenn Hoffman	.05
39	Dave Rucker	.05
40	Ken Griffey	.10
41	Brad Wellman	.05
42	Geoff Zahn	.05
43	Dave Engle	.05
44	*Lance McCullers*	.05
45	Damaso Garcia	.05
46	Billy Hatcher	.05
47	Juan Berenguer	.05
48	Bill Almon	.05
49	Rick Manning	.05
50	Dan Quisenberry	.05
51	Not issued, see #57	
52	Chris Welsh	.05
53	*Len Dykstra*	.50
54	John Franco	.05
55	Fred Lynn	.05
56	Tom Niedenfuer	.05
57a	Bill Doran	.05
57b	Bobby Wine (supposed to be #51)	.05
58	Bill Krueger	.05
59	Andre Thornton	.05
60	Dwight Evans	.05
61	Karl Best	.05
62	Bob Boone	.05
63	Ron Roenicke	.05
64	Floyd Bannister	.05
65	Dan Driessen	.05
66	Cardinals Leaders (Bob Forsch)	.05
67	Carmelo Martinez	.05
68	Ed Lynch	.05
69	Luis Aguayo	.05
70	Dave Winfield	.40
71	Ken Schrom	.05
72	Shawon Dunston	.05
73	Randy O'Neal	.05
74	Rance Mulliniks	.05
75	Jose DeLeon	.05
76	Dion James	.05
77	Charlie Leibrandt	.05
78	Bruce Benedict	.05
79	Dave Schmidt	.05
80	Darryl Strawberry	.20
81	Gene Mauch	.05
82	Tippy Martinez	.05
83	Phil Garner	.05
84	Curt Young	.05
85	Tony Perez	.25
86	Tom Waddell	.05
87	Candy Maldonado	.05
88	Tom Nieto	.05
89	Randy St. Claire	.05
90	Garry Templeton	.05
91	Steve Crawford	.05
92	Al Cowens	.05
93	Scot Thompson	.05
94	Rich Bordi	.05
95	Ozzie Virgil	.05
96	Blue Jay Leaders (Jim Clancy)	.05
97	Gary Gaetti	.10
98	Dick Ruthven	.05
99	Buddy Biancalana	.05
100	Nolan Ryan	2.00
101	Dave Bergman	.05
102	*Joe Orsulak*	.15
103	Luis Salazar	.05
104	Sid Fernandez	.05
105	Gary Ward	.05
106	Ray Burris	.05
107	Rafael Ramirez	.05
108	Ted Power	.05
109	Len Matuszek	.05
110	Scott McGregor	.05

111	Roger Craig	.05
112	Bill Campbell	.05
113	U.L. Washington	.05
114	Mike Brown	.05
115	Jay Howell	.05
116	Brook Jacoby	.05
117	Bruce Kison	.05
118	Jerry Royster	.05
119	Barry Bonnell	.05
120	Steve Carlton	.30
121	Nelson Simmons	.05
122	Pete Filson	.05
123	Greg Walker	.05
124	Luis Sanchez	.05
125	Dave Lopes	.05
126	Mets Leaders (Mookie Wilson)	.05
127	*Jack Howell*	.05
128	John Wathan	.05
129	Jeff Dedmon	.05
130	Alan Trammell	.15
131	Checklist 1-132	.05
132	Razor Shines	.05
133	Andy McGaffigan	.05
134	Carney Lansford	.05
135	Joe Niekro	.05
136	Mike Hargrove	.05
137	Charlie Moore	.05
138	Mark Davis	.05
139	Daryl Boston	.05
140	John Candelaria	.05
141a	Chuck Cottier	.05
141b	Bob Rodgers (supposed to be #171)	.05
142	Bob Jones	.05
143	Dave Van Gorder	.05
144	Doug Sisk	.05
145	Pedro Guerrero	.05
146	Jack Perconte	.05
147	Larry Sheets	.05
148	Mike Heath	.05
149	Brett Butler	.05
150	Joaquin Andujar	.05
151	Dave Stapleton	.05
152	Mike Morgan	.05
153	Ricky Adams	.05
154	Bert Roberge	.05
155	Bob Grich	.05
156	White Sox Leaders (Richard Dotson)	.05
157	Ron Hassey	.05
158	Derrel Thomas	.05
159	Orel Hershiser	.15
160	Chet Lemon	.05
161	Lee Tunnell	.05
162	Greg Gagne	.05
163	Pete Ladd	.05
164	Steve Balboni	.05
165	Mike Davis	.05
166	Dickie Thon	.05
167	Zane Smith	.05
168	Jeff Burroughs	.05
169	George Wright	.05
170	Gary Carter	.20
171	Not issued, see #141	
172	Jerry Reed	.05
173	Wayne Gross	.05
174	Brian Snyder	.05
175	Steve Sax	.05
176	Jay Tibbs	.05
177	Joel Youngblood	.05
178	Ivan DeJesus	.05
179	*Stu Cliburn*	.05
180	Don Mattingly	.75
181	Al Nipper	.05
182	Bobby Brown	.05
183	Larry Andersen	.05
184	Tim Laudner	.05
185	Rollie Fingers	.20
186	Astros Leader (Jose Cruz)	.05
187	Scott Fletcher	.05
188	Bob Dernier	.05
189	Mike Mason	.05
190	George Hendrick	.05
191	Wally Backman	.05
192	Milt Wilcox	.05
193	Daryl Sconiers	.05
194	Craig McMurtry	.05
195	Dave Concepcion	.05
196	Doyle Alexander	.05
197	Enos Cabell	.05
198	Ken Dixon	.05
199	Dick Howser	.05
200	Mike Schmidt	.75
201	Vince Coleman (Record Breaker)	.05
202	Dwight Gooden (Record Breaker)	.05
203	Keith Hernandez (Record Breaker)	.05
204	Phil Niekro (Record Breaker)	.15
205	Tony Perez (Record Breaker)	.10
206	Pete Rose (Record Breaker)	.25
207	Fernando Valenzuela (Record Breaker)	.05
208	Ramon Romero	.05
209	Randy Ready	.05
210	Calvin Schiraldi	.05
211	Ed Wojna	.05
212	Chris Speier	.05
213	Bob Shirley	.05
214	Randy Bush	.05
215	Frank White	.05
216	A's Leaders (Dwayne Murphy)	.05
217	Bill Scherrer	.05
218	Randy Hunt	.05
219	Dennis Lamp	.05
220	Bob Horner	.05
221	Dave Henderson	.05
222	Craig Gerber	.05
223	Atlee Hammaker	.05
224	Cesar Cedeno	.05
225	Ron Darling	.05
226	Lee Lacy	.05
227	Al Jones	.05
228	Tom Lawless	.05
229	Bill Gullickson	.05
230	Terry Kennedy	.05
231	Jim Frey	.05
232	Rick Rhoden	.05
233	Steve Lyons	.05
234	Doug Corbett	.05
235	Butch Wynegar	.05
236	Frank Eufemia	.05
237	Ted Simmons	.05
238	Larry Parrish	.05
239	Joel Skinner	.05
240	Tommy John	.10
241	Tony Fernandez	.05
242	Rich Thompson	.05
243	Johnny Grubb	.05
244	Craig Lefferts	.05
245	Jim Sundberg	.05
246	Phillies Leaders (Steve Carlton)	.10
247	Terry Harper	.05
248	Spike Owen	.05
249	Rob Deer	.05
250	Dwight Gooden	.25
251	Rich Dauer	.05
252	Bobby Castillo	.05
253	Dann Bilardello	.05
254	*Ozzie Guillen*	.30
255	Tony Armas	.05
256	Kurt Kepshire	.05
257	Doug DeCinces	.05
258	*Tim Burke*	.05
259	Dan Pasqua	.05
260	Tony Pena	.05
261	Bobby Valentine	.05
262	Mario Ramirez	.05
263	Checklist 133-264	.05
264	Darren Daulton	.15
265	Ron Davis	.05
266	Keith Moreland	.05
267	Paul Molitor	.75
268	Mike Scott	.05
269	Dane Iorg	.05
270	Jack Morris	.05
271	Dave Collins	.05
272	Tim Tolman	.05
273	Jerry Willard	.05
274	Ron Gardenhire	.05
275	Charlie Hough	.05
276	Yankees Leaders (Willie Randolph)	.05
277	Jaime Cocanower	.05
278	Sixto Lezcano	.05
279	Al Pardo	.05
280	Tim Raines	.12
281	Steve Mura	.05
282	Jerry Mumphrey	.05
283	Mike Fischlin	.05
284	Brian Dayett	.05
285	Buddy Bell	.05
286	Luis DeLeon	.05
287	*John Christensen*	.05
288	Don Aase	.05
289	Johnnie LeMaster	.05
290	Carlton Fisk	.30
291	Tom Lasorda	.20
292	Chuck Porter	.05
293	Chris Chambliss	.05
294	Danny Cox	.05
295	Kirk Gibson	.05
296	Geno Petralli	.05
297	Tim Lollar	.05
298	Craig Reynolds	.05
299	Bryn Smith	.05
300	George Brett	.75
301	Dennis Rasmussen	.05
302	Greg Gross	.05
303	Curt Wardle	.05
304	*Mike Gallego*	.12
305	Phil Bradley	.05
306	Padres Leaders (Terry Kennedy)	.05
307	Dave Sax	.05
308	Ray Fontenot	.05
309	John Shelby	.05
310	Greg Minton	.05
311	Dick Schofield	.05
312	Tom Filer	.05
313	Joe DeSa	.05
314	Frank Pastore	.05
315	Mookie Wilson	.05
316	Sammy Khalifa	.05
317	Ed Romero	.05
318	Terry Whitfield	.05
319	Rick Camp	.05
320	Jim Rice	.10
321	Earl Weaver	.20
322	Bob Forsch	.05
323	Jerry Davis	.05
324	Dan Schatzeder	.05
325	Juan Beniquez	.05
326	Kent Tekulve	.05
327	Mike Pagliarulo	.05
328	Pete O'Brien	.05
329	Kirby Puckett	2.00
330	Rick Sutcliffe	.05
331	Alan Ashby	.05
332	Darryl Motley	.05
333	Tom Henke	.05
334	Ken Oberkfell	.05
335	Don Sutton	.25
336	Indians Leaders (Andre Thornton)	.05
337	Darnell Coles	.05
338	Jorge Bell	.10
339	Bruce Berenyi	.05
340	Cal Ripken, Jr.	2.00
341	Frank Williams	.05
342	Gary Redus	.05
343	Carlos Diaz	.05
344	Jim Wohlford	.05
345	Donnie Moore	.05
346	Bryan Little	.05
347	*Teddy Higuera*	.10
348	Cliff Johnson	.05
349	Mark Clear	.05
350	Jack Clark	.05
351	Chuck Tanner	.05
352	Harry Spilman	.05
353	Keith Atherton	.05
354	Tony Bernazard	.05
355	Lee Smith	.10
356	Mickey Hatcher	.05
357	Ed Vande Berg	.05
358	Rick Dempsey	.05
359	Mike LaCoss	.05
360	Lloyd Moseby	.05
361	Shane Rawley	.05
362	Tom Paciorek	.05
363	Terry Forster	.05
364	Reid Nichols	.05
365	Mike Flanagan	.05
366	Reds Leaders (Dave Concepcion)	.05
367	Aurelio Lopez	.05
368	Greg Brock	.05
369	Al Holland	.05
370	*Vince Coleman*	.35
371	Bill Stein	.05
372	Ben Oglivie	.05
373	*Urbano Lugo*	.05
374	Terry Francona	.05
375	Rich Gedman	.05
376	Bill Dawley	.05
377	Joe Carter	.15
378	Bruce Bochte	.05
379	Bobby Meacham	.05
380	LaMarr Hoyt	.05
381	Ray Miller	.05
382	*Ivan Calderon*	.05
383	*Chris Brown*	.05
384	Steve Trout	.05
385	Cecil Cooper	.05
386	*Cecil Fielder*	.75
387	Steve Kemp	.05
388	Dickie Noles	.05
389	Glenn Davis	.05
390	Tom Seaver	.35
391	Julio Franco	.10
392	John Russell	.05
393	Chris Pittaro	.05
394	Checklist 265-396	.05
395	Scott Garrelts	.05
396	Red Sox Leaders (Dwight Evans)	.05
397	*Steve Buechele*	.20
398	*Earnie Riles*	.05
399	Bill Swift	.05
400	Rod Carew	.30
401	Fernando Valenzuela (Turn Back the Clock)	.05
402	Tom Seaver (Turn Back the Clock)	.15
403	Willie Mays (Turn Back the Clock)	.20
404	Frank Robinson (Turn Back the Clock)	.15
405	Roger Maris (Turn Back the Clock)	.25
406	Scott Sanderson	.05
407	Sal Butera	.05
408	Dave Smith	.05
409	*Paul Runge*	.05
410	Dave Kingman	.10
411	Sparky Anderson	.10
412	Jim Clancy	.05
413	Tim Flannery	.05
414	Tom Gorman	.05
415	Hal McRae	.05
416	Denny Martinez	.05
417	R.J. Reynolds	.05
418	Alan Knicely	.05
419	Frank Wills	.05
420	Von Hayes	.05
421	Dave Palmer	.05
422	Mike Jorgensen	.05
423	Dan Spillner	.05
424	Rick Miller	.05
425	Larry McWilliams	.05
426	Brewers Leaders (Charlie Moore)	.05
427	Joe Cowley	.05
428	Max Venable	.05
429	Greg Booker	.05
430	Kent Hrbek	.10
431	George Frazier	.05
432	Mark Bailey	.05
433	Chris Codiroli	.05
434	Curt Wilkerson	.05
435	Bill Caudill	.05
436	Doug Flynn	.05
437	Rick Mahler	.05
438	Clint Hurdle	.05
439	Rick Honeycutt	.05
440	Alvin Davis	.05
441	Whitey Herzog	.05
442	Ron Robinson	.05
443	Bill Buckner	.05
444	Alex Trevino	.05
445	Bert Blyleven	.05
446	Lenn Sakata	.05
447	Jerry Don Gleaton	.05
448	*Herm Winningham*	.05
449	Rod Scurry	.05
450	Graig Nettles	.05
451	Mark Brown	.05
452	Bob Clark	.05
453	Steve Jeltz	.05
454	Burt Hooton	.05
455	Willie Randolph	.05
456	Braves Leaders (Dale Murphy)	.10
457	Mickey Tettleton	.10
458	Kevin Bass	.05
459	Luis Leal	.05
460	Leon Durham	.05
461	Walt Terrell	.05
462	Domingo Ramos	.05
463	Jim Gott	.05
464	Ruppert Jones	.05
465	Jesse Orosco	.05
466	Tom Foley	.05
467	Bob James	.05
468	Mike Scioscia	.05
469	Storm Davis	.05
470	Bill Madlock	.05
471	Bobby Cox	.05
472	Joe Hesketh	.05
473	Mark Brouhard	.05
474	John Tudor	.05
475	Juan Samuel	.05
476	Ron Mathis	.05
477	Mike Easler	.05
478	Andy Hawkins	.05
479	*Bob Melvin*	.05
480	*Oddibe McDowell*	.05
481	Scott Bradley	.05
482	Rick Lysander	.05
483	George Vukovich	.05
484	Donnie Hill	.05
485	Gary Matthews	.05
486	Angels Leaders (Bob Grich)	.05
487	Bret Saberhagen	.25
488	Lou Thornton	.05
489	Jim Winn	.05
490	Jeff Leonard	.05
491	Pascual Perez	.05
492	Kelvin Chapman	.05
493	Gene Nelson	.05
494	Gary Roenicke	.05
495	Mark Langston	.10
496	Jay Johnstone	.05
497	John Stuper	.05
498	Tito Landrum	.05
499	Bob L. Gibson	.05
500	Rickey Henderson	.40
501	Dave Johnson	.05
502	Glen Cook	.05
503	Mike Fitzgerald	.05
504	Denny Walling	.05
505	Jerry Koosman	.05
506	Bill Russell	.05
507	*Steve Ontiveros*	.10
508	Alan Wiggins	.05
509	Ernie Camacho	.05
510	Wade Boggs	.50
511	Ed Nunez	.05
512	Thad Bosley	.05
513	Ron Washington	.05
514	Mike Jones	.05
515	Darrell Evans	.05
516	Giants Leaders (Greg Minton)	.05
517	*Milt Thompson*	.05
518	Buck Martinez	.05
519	Danny Darwin	.05
520	Keith Hernandez	.05
521	Nate Snell	.05
522	Bob Bailor	.05
523	Joe Price	.05
524	Darrell Miller	.05
525	Marvell Wynne	.05
526	Charlie Lea	.05
527	Checklist 397-528	.05
528	Terry Pendleton	.10
529	Marc Sullivan	.05
530	Rich Gossage	.10
531	Tony LaRussa	.05
532	*Don Carman*	.05
533	Billy Sample	.05
534	Jeff Calhoun	.05
535	Toby Harrah	.05
536	Jose Rijo	.05
537	Mark Salas	.05
538	Dennis Eckersley	.10
539	Glenn Hubbard	.05
540	Dan Petry	.05
541	Jorge Orta	.05
542	Don Schulze	.05
543	Jerry Narron	.05
544	Eddie Milner	.05
545	Jimmy Key	.10
546	Mariners Leaders (Dave Henderson)	.05
547	*Roger McDowell*	.12
548	Mike Young	.05
549	Bob Welch	.05
550	Tom Herr	.05
551	Dave LaPoint	.05
552	Marc Hill	.05
553	Jim Morrison	.05
554	Paul Householder	.05
555	Hubie Brooks	.05
556	John Denny	.05
557	Gerald Perry	.05
558	Tim Stoddard	.05
559	Tommy Dunbar	.05
560	Dave Righetti	.05
561	Bob Lillis	.05
562	Joe Beckwith	.05
563	Alejandro Sanchez	.05
564	Warren Brusstar	.05
565	Tom Brunansky	.05
566	Alfredo Griffin	.05
567	Jeff Barkley	.05
568	Donnie Scott	.05
569	Jim Acker	.05
570	Rusty Staub	.10
571	Mike Jeffcoat	.05
572	Paul Zuvella	.05
573	Tom Hume	.05
574	Ron Kittle	.05
575	Mike Boddicker	.05
576	Expos Leaders (Andre Dawson)	.10
577	Jerry Reuss	.05
578	Lee Mazzilli	.05
579	Jim Slaton	.05
580	Willie McGee	.05
581	Bruce Hurst	.05
582	Jim Gantner	.05
583	Al Bumbry	.05
584	*Brian Fisher*	.05
585	Garry Maddox	.05
586	Greg Harris	.05
587	Rafael Santana	.05
588	Steve Lake	.05
589	Sid Bream	.05
590	Bob Knepper	.05
591	Jackie Moore	.05
592	Frank Tanana	.05
593	Jesse Barfield	.05
594	Chris Bando	.05
595	Dave Parker	.15
596	Onix Concepcion	.05
597	Sammy Stewart	.05
598	Jim Presley	.05
599	*Rick Aguilera*	.25
600	Dale Murphy	.15
601	Gary Lucas	.05
602	*Mariano Duncan*	.25
603	Bill Laskey	.05
604	Gary Pettis	.05
605	Dennis Boyd	.05
606	Royals Leaders (Hal McRae)	.05
607	Ken Dayley	.05
608	Bruce Bochy	.05
609	Barbaro Garbey	.05
610	Ron Guidry	.05
611	Gary Woods	.05
612	Richard Dotson	.05
613	Roy Smalley	.05
614	Rick Waits	.05
615	Johnny Ray	.05
616	Glenn Brummer	.05
617	Lonnie Smith	.05
618	Jim Pankovits	.05
619	Danny Heep	.05
620	Bruce Sutter	.05
621	John Felske	.05
622	Gary Lavelle	.05
623	Floyd Rayford	.05
624	Steve McCatty	.05
625	Bob Brenly	.05
626	Roy Thomas	.05
627	Ron Oester	.05
628	*Kirk McCaskill*	.15
629	*Mitch Webster*	.05
630	Fernando Valenzuela	.05
631	Steve Braun	.05
632	Dave Von Ohlen	.05
633	Jackie Gutierrez	.05
634	Roy Lee Jackson	.05
635	Jason Thompson	.05
636	Cubs Leaders (Lee Smith)	.05
637	Rudy Law	.05
638	John Butcher	.05
639	Bo Diaz	.05
640	Jose Cruz	.05
641	Wayne Tolleson	.05
642	Ray Searage	.05
643	Tom Brookens	.05
644	Mark Gubicza	.12
645	Dusty Baker	.05
646	Mike Moore	.05
647	Mel Hall	.05
648	Steve Bedrosian	.05
649	Ronn Reynolds	.05
650	Dave Stieb	.05
651	Billy Martin	.10
652	Tom Browning	.05
653	Jim Dwyer	.05
654	Ken Howell	.05
655	Manny Trillo	.05
656	Brian Harper	.05
657	Juan Agosto	.05
658	Rob Wilfong	.05
659	Checklist 529-660	.05
660	Steve Garvey	.15
661	Roger Clemens	4.00
662	Bill Schroeder	.05
663	Neil Allen	.05
664	Tim Corcoran	.05
665	Alejandro Pena	.05
666	Rangers Leaders (Charlie Hough)	.05
667	Tim Teufel	.05
668	Cecilio Guante	.05
669	Ron Cey	.05

670	Willie Hernandez	.05
671	Lynn Jones	.05
672	Rob Picciolo	.05
673	Ernie Whitt	.05
674	Pat Tabler	.05
675	Claudell Washington	.05
676	Matt Young	.05
677	Nick Esasky	.05
678	Dan Gladden	.05
679	Britt Burns	.05
680	George Foster	.05
681	Dick Williams	.05
682	Junior Ortiz	.05
683	Andy Van Slyke	.05
684	Bob McClure	.05
685	Tim Wallach	.05
686	Jeff Stone	.05
687	Mike Trujillo	.05
688	Larry Herndon	.05
689	Dave Stewart	.12
690	Ryne Sandberg	.75
691	Mike Madden	.05
692	Dale Berra	.05
693	Tom Tellmann	.05
694	Garth Iorg	.05
695	Mike Smithson	.05
696	Dodgers Leaders (Bill Russell)	.05
697	Bud Black	.05
698	Brad Komminsk	.05
699	Pat Corrales	.05
700	Reggie Jackson	.25
701	Keith Hernandez (All-Star)	.05
702	Tom Herr (All-Star)	.05
703	Tim Wallach (All-Star)	.05
704	Ozzie Smith (All-Star)	.15
705	Dale Murphy (All-Star)	.10
706	Pedro Guerrero (All-Star)	.05
707	Willie McGee (All-Star)	.05
708	Gary Carter (All-Star)	.10
709	Dwight Gooden (All-Star)	.10
710	John Tudor (All-Star)	.05
711	Jeff Reardon (All-Star)	.05
712	Don Mattingly (All-Star)	.40
713	Damasco Garcia (All-Star)	.05
714	George Brett (All-Star)	.35
715	Cal Ripken, Jr. (All-Star)	.75
716	Rickey Henderson (All-Star)	.20
717	Dave Winfield (All-Star)	.20
718	George Bell (All-Star)	.05
719	Carlton Fisk (All-Star)	.15
720	Bret Saberhagen (All-Star)	.15
721	Ron Guidry (All-Star)	.10
722	Dan Quisenberry (All-Star)	.05
723	Marty Bystrom	.05
724	Tim Hulett	.05
725	Mario Soto	.05
726	Orioles Leaders (Rick Dempsey)	.05
727	David Green	.05
728	Mike Marshall	.05
729	Jim Beattie	.05
730	Ozzie Smith	.30
731	Don Robinson	.05
732	*Floyd Youmans*	.05
733	Ron Romanick	.05
734	Marty Barrett	.05
735	Dave Dravecky	.05
736	Glenn Wilson	.05
737	Pete Vuckovich	.05
738	Andre Robertson	.05
739	Dave Rozema	.05
740	Lance Parrish	.05
741	Pete Rose	.50
742	Frank Viola	.05
743	Pat Sheridan	.05
744	Lary Sorensen	.05
745	Willie Upshaw	.05
746	Denny Gonzalez	.05
747	Rick Cerone	.05
748	Steve Henderson	.05
749	Ed Jurak	.05
750	Gorman Thomas	.05
751	Howard Johnson	.05
752	Mike Krukow	.05
753	Dan Ford	.05
754	*Pat Clements*	.05
755	Harold Baines	.10
756	Pirates Leaders (Rick Rhoden)	.05
757	Darrell Porter	.05
758	Dave Anderson	.05
759	Moose Haas	.05
760	Andre Dawson	.30
761	Don Slaught	.05
762	Eric Show	.05
763	Terry Puhl	.05
764	Kevin Gross	.05
765	Don Baylor	.10
766	Rick Langford	.05
767	Jody Davis	.05
768	Vern Ruhle	.05
769	*Harold Reynolds*	.25
770	Vida Blue	.05
771	John McNamara	.05
772	Brian Downing	.05
773	Greg Pryor	.05
774	Terry Leach	.05
775	Al Oliver	.05
776	Gene Garber	.05
777	Wayne Krenchicki	.05
778	Jerry Hairston	.05
779	Rick Reuschel	.05
780	Robin Yount	.50
781	Joe Nolan	.05
782	Ken Landreaux	.05
783	Ricky Horton	.05
784	Alan Bannister	.05
785	Bob Stanley	.05
786	Twins Leaders (Mickey Hatcher)	.05
787	Vance Law	.05
788	Marty Castillo	.05
789	Kurt Bevacqua	.05
790	Phil Niekro	.30
791	Checklist 661-792	.05
792	Charles Hudson	.05

1986 Topps Tiffany

A total of only 5,000 of these specially boxed collectors edition sets was reported produced. Sold only through hobby dealers the cards differ from the regular-issue 1986 Topps cards only in the use of white cardboard stock and the application of a high-gloss finish on the cards' fronts.

	MT
Complete Set (792):	125.00
Common Player:	.25

(Star cards valued at 4X-6X corresponding cards in regular 1986 Topps issue)

1986 Topps Traded

This 132-card set of 2-1/2" x 3-1/2" cards was, at issue, one of the most popular sets of recent times. As always, the set features traded veterans, including such players as Phil Niekro and Tom Seaver. They were not, however, the reason for the excitement. The demand stemmed from a better than usual crop of rookies appearing in the set. Among those are Jose Canseco, Wally Joyner, Will Clark, Barry Bonds and the first card of Bo Jackson. As in the previous two years, a glossy-finish "Tiffany" edition of 5,000 Traded sets was produced. The "Tiffany" cards are worth three to five times the value of the regular Traded cards.

		MT
Complete Set (132):		15.00
Common Player:		.10
1T	Andy Allanson	.10
2T	Neil Allen	.10
3T	Joaquin Andujar	.10
4T	Paul Assenmacher	.10
5T	Scott Bailes	.10
6T	Don Baylor	.15
7T	Steve Bedrosian	.10
8T	Juan Beniquez	.10
9T	Juan Berenguer	.10
10T	Mike Bielecki	.10
11T	*Barry Bonds*	8.00
12T	*Bobby Bonilla*	.75
13T	Juan Bonilla	.10
14T	Rich Bordi	.10
15T	Steve Boros	.10
16T	Rick Burleson	.10
17T	Bill Campbell	.10
18T	Tom Candiotti	.10
19T	John Cangelosi	.10
20T	*Jose Canseco*	6.00
21T	Carmen Castillo	.10
22T	Rick Cerone	.10
23T	John Cerutti	.10
24T	*Will Clark*	1.50
25T	Mark Clear	.10
26T	Darnell Coles	.10
27T	Dave Collins	.10
28T	Tim Conroy	.10
29T	Joe Cowley	.10
30T	Joel Davis	.10
31T	Rob Deer	.10
32T	John Denny	.10
33T	Mike Easler	.10
34T	Mark Eichhorn	.15
35T	Steve Farr	.10
36T	Scott Fletcher	.10
37T	Terry Forster	.10
38T	Terry Francona	.10
39T	Jim Fregosi	.10
40T	Andres Galarraga	1.50
41T	Ken Griffey	.15
42T	Bill Gullickson	.10
43T	Jose Guzman	.10
44T	Moose Haas	.10
45T	Billy Hatcher	.10
46T	Mike Heath	.10
47T	Tom Hume	.10
48T	*Pete Incaviglia*	.20
49T	Dane Iorg	.10
50T	*Bo Jackson*	1.00
51T	*Wally Joyner*	.75
52T	Charlie Kerfeld	.10
53T	Eric King	.10
54T	Bob Kipper	.10
55T	Wayne Krenchicki	.10
56T	*John Kruk*	.35
57T	Mike LaCoss	.10
58T	Pete Ladd	.10
59T	Mike Laga	.10
60T	Hal Lanier	.10
61T	Dave LaPoint	.10
62T	Rudy Law	.10
63T	Rick Leach	.10
64T	Tim Leary	.10
65T	Dennis Leonard	.10
66T	Jim Leyland	.10
67T	Steve Lyons	.10
68T	Mickey Mahler	.10
69T	Candy Maldonado	.10
70T	Roger Mason	.10
71T	Bob McClure	.10
72T	Andy McGaffigan	.10
73T	Gene Michael	.10
74T	*Kevin Mitchell*	.25
75T	Omar Moreno	.10
76T	Jerry Mumphrey	.10
77T	Phil Niekro	.25
78T	Randy Niemann	.10
79T	Juan Nieves	.10
80T	Otis Nixon	.10
81T	Bob Ojeda	.10
82T	Jose Oquendo	.10
83T	Tom Paciorek	.10
84T	Dave Palmer	.10
85T	Frank Pastore	.10
86T	Lou Piniella	.10
87T	Dan Plesac	.10
88T	Darrell Porter	.10
89T	Rey Quinones	.10
90T	Gary Redus	.10
91T	Bip Roberts	.10
92T	Billy Jo Robidoux	.10
93T	Jeff Robinson	.10
94T	Gary Roenicke	.10
95T	Ed Romero	.10
96T	Argenis Salazar	.10
97T	Joe Sambito	.10
98T	Billy Sample	.10
99T	Dave Schmidt	.10
100T	Ken Schrom	.10
101T	Tom Seaver	.50
102T	Ted Simmons	.10
103T	Sammy Stewart	.10
104T	Kurt Stillwell	.10
105T	Franklin Stubbs	.10
106T	Dale Sveum	.10
107T	Chuck Tanner	.10
108T	Danny Tartabull	.10
109T	Tim Teufel	.10
110T	Bob Tewksbury	.15
111T	Andres Thomas	.10
112T	Milt Thompson	.10
113T	Robby Thompson	.10
114T	Jay Tibbs	.10
115T	Wayne Tolleson	.10
116T	Alex Trevino	.10
117T	Manny Trillo	.10
118T	Ed Vande Berg	.10
119T	Ozzie Virgil	.10
120T	Bob Walk	.10
121T	Gene Walter	.10
122T	Claudell Washington	.10
123T	Bill Wegman	.10
124T	Dick Williams	.10
125T	Mitch Williams	.15
126T	Bobby Witt	.15
127T	Todd Worrell	.15
128T	George Wright	.10
129T	Ricky Wright	.10
130T	Steve Yeager	.10
131T	Paul Zuvella	.10
132T	Checklist	.10

1986 Topps Traded Tiffany

This collectors edition differs from the regular 1986 Topps Traded set only in the use of a high-gloss front finish. The set was sold only through hobby channels in a specially design box.

	MT
Complete Set (132):	200.00
Common Player:	.25

(Star cards valued at 3X-4X corresponding cards in regular Topps Traded)

1986 Topps Box Panels

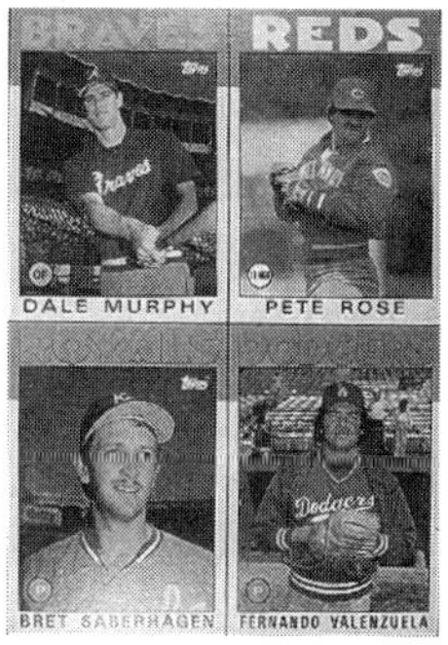

Following the lead of Donruss, which introduced the concept in 1985, Topps produced special cards on the bottom panels of wax boxes. Individual cards measure 2-1/2" x 3-1/2", the same as regular cards. Design of the cards is virtually identical with regular '86 Topps, though the top border is in red, rather than black. The cards are lettered "A" through "P", rather than numbered on the back.

		MT
Complete Panel Set:		10.00
Complete Singles Set:		5.00
Common Panel:		1.50
Common Single Player:		.10
Panel		3.25
A	Jorge Bell	.10
B	Wade Boggs	.50
C	George Brett	.75
D	Vince Coleman	.25
Panel		1.50
E	Carlton Fisk	.45
F	Dwight Gooden	.20
G	Pedro Guerrero	.10
H	Ron Guidry	.10
Panel		3.00
I	Reggie Jackson	.75
J	Don Mattingly	1.00
K	Oddibe McDowell	.10
L	Willie McGee	.10
Panel		2.50
M	Dale Murphy	.35
N	Pete Rose	1.00
O	Bret Saberhagen	.15
P	Fernando Valenzuela	.10

1986 Topps All-Star Glossy Set of 22

As in previous years, Topps continued to make the popular glossy-surfaced cards as an insert in rack packs. The All-Star Glossy set of 2-1/2" x 3-1/2" cards shows little design change from previous years. Cards feature a front color photo and All-Star banner at the top. The bottom has the player's name and position. The set includes the All-Star starting teams as well as the managers and honorary captains.

		MT
Complete Set (22):		4.00
Common Player:		.20
1	Sparky Anderson	.20
2	Eddie Murray	.50
3	Lou Whitaker	.20
4	George Brett	.80
5	Cal Ripken, Jr.	1.00
6	Jim Rice	.25
7	Rickey Henderson	.50
8	Dave Winfield	.50
9	Carlton Fisk	.50
10	Jack Morris	.20
11	A.L. All-Star Team	.20
12	Dick Williams	.20
13	Steve Garvey	.30
14	Tom Herr	.20
15	Graig Nettles	.20
16	Ozzie Smith	.50
17	Tony Gwynn	.75
18	Dale Murphy	.40
19	Darryl Strawberry	.25
20	Terry Kennedy	.20
21	LaMarr Hoyt	.20
22	N.L. All-Star Team	.20

1986 Topps All-Star Glossy Set of 60

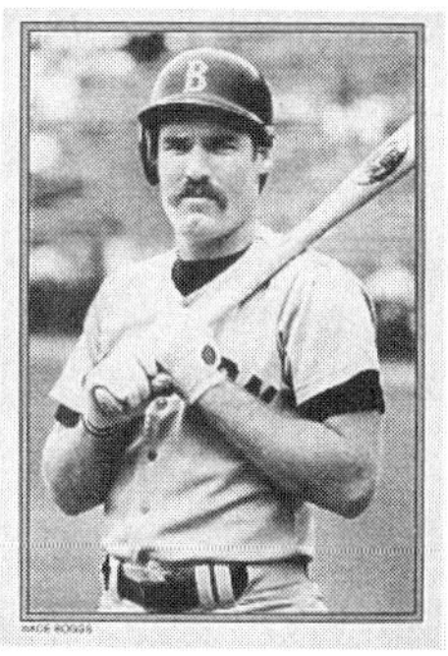

The Topps All-Star & Hot Prospects glossy set of 60 cards represents an expansion of a good idea. The 2-1/2" x 3-1/2" cards had a good following when they were limited to stars, but Topps realized that the addition of top young players would spice up the set even further, so in 1986 it was expanded from 40 to 60 cards. The cards themselves are basically all color glossy pictures with the player's name in very small print in the lower left-hand corner. To obtain the set, it was necessary to send $1 plus six special offer cards from wax packs to Topps for each series. At 60 cards, that meant the process had to be repeated six times as there were 10 cards in each series, making the set quite expensive from the outset.

		MT
Complete Set (60):		7.00
Common Player:		.15
1	Oddibe McDowell	.15
2	Reggie Jackson	.50
3	Fernando Valenzuela	.15
4	Jack Clark	.15
5	Rickey Henderson	.45
6	Steve Balboni	.15
7	Keith Hernandez	.15

8	Lance Parrish	.15
9	Willie McGee	.15
10	Chris Brown	.15
11	Darryl Strawberry	.25
12	Ron Guidry	.15
13	Dave Parker	.15
14	Cal Ripken	1.00
15	Tim Raines	.25
16	Rod Carew	.50
17	Mike Schmidt	.75
18	George Brett	.75
19	Joe Hesketh	.15
20	Dan Pasqua	.15
21	Vince Coleman	.20
22	Tom Seaver	.50
23	Gary Carter	.35
24	Orel Hershiser	.25
25	Pedro Guerrero	.15
26	Wade Boggs	.60
27	Bret Saberhagen	.20
28	Carlton Fisk	.50
29	Kirk Gibson	.15
30	Brian Fisher	.15
31	Don Mattingly	.90
32	Tom Herr	.15
33	Eddie Murray	.50
34	Ryne Sandberg	.60
35	Dan Quisenberry	.15
36	Jim Rice	.20
37	Dale Murphy	.35
38	Steve Garvey	.35
39	Roger McDowell	.15
40	Earnie Riles	.15
41	Dwight Gooden	.30
42	Dave Winfield	.45
43	Dave Stieb	.15
44	Bob Horner	.15
45	Nolan Ryan	1.00
46	Ozzie Smith	.45
47	Jorge Bell	.15
48	Gorman Thomas	.15
49	Tom Browning	.15
50	Larry Sheets	.15
51	Pete Rose	.90
52	Brett Butler	.25
53	John Tudor	.15
54	Phil Bradley	.15
55	Jeff Reardon	.15
56	Rich Gossage	.15
57	Tony Gwynn	.75
58	Ozzie Guillen	.15
59	Glenn Davis	.15
60	Darrell Evans	.15

1986 Topps Gallery of Champions

For the third consecutive year Topps issued 12 metal "mini cards," adding an aluminum version to the bronze and silver. The metal replicas were minted 1/4-size (approximately 1-1/4" x 1-3/4") of the regular cards. The bronze and silver sets were issued in leather-like velvet-lined display cases, the alumnium in individual cello packs. A bronze 1952 Topps Mickey Mantle was given as a premium for dealers purchasing 1986 Traded sets, while a pewter Don Mattingly was issued as a premium to those ordering the sets.

		MT
Complete Aluminum Set:		45.00
Complete Bronze Set:		135.00
Complete Silver Set:		300.00
(1a)	Wade Boggs (aluminum)	5.00
(1b)	Wade Boggs (bronze)	17.50
(1s)	Wade Boggs (silver)	37.00
(2a)	Vince Coleman (aluminum)	2.50
(2b)	Vince Coleman (bronze)	7.50
(2s)	Vince Coleman (silver)	15.00
(3a)	Darrell Evans (aluminum)	2.50
(3b)	Darrell Evans (bronze)	7.50
(3s)	Darrell Evans (silver)	15.00
(4a)	Dwight Gooden (aluminum)	5.00
(4b)	Dwight Gooden (bronze)	17.50
(4s)	Dwight Gooden (silver)	37.00
(5a)	Ozzie Guillen (aluminum)	2.50
(5b)	Ozzie Guillen (bronze)	7.50
(5s)	Ozzie Guillen (silver)	15.00
(6a)	Don Mattingly (aluminum)	10.00
(6b)	Don Mattingly (bronze)	32.00
(6s)	Don Mattingly (silver)	75.00
(6p)	Don Mattingly (pewter)	60.00
(7a)	Willie McGee (aluminum)	2.50
(7b)	Willie McGee (bronze)	7.50
(7s)	Willie McGee (silver)	15.00
(8a)	Dale Murphy (aluminum)	5.00
(8b)	Dale Murphy (bronze)	17.50
(8s)	Dale Murphy (silver)	37.00
(9a)	Dan Quisenberry	2.50
(9b)	Dan Quisenberry (bronze)	7.50
(9s)	Dan Quisenberry (silver)	15.00
(10a)	Jeff Reardon (aluminum)	2.50
(10b)	Jeff Reardon (bronze)	7.50
(10s)	Jeff Reardon (silver)	15.00
(11a)	Pete Rose (aluminum)	12.50
(11b)	Pete Rose (bronze)	37.00
(11s)	Pete Rose (silver)	100.00
(12a)	Bret Saberhagen (aluminum)	2.50
(12b)	Bret Saberhagen (bronze)	7.50
(12s)	Bret Saberhagen (silver)	15.00
(13)	Mickey Mantle (1952, bronze)	20.00

1986 Topps Mini League Leaders

Topps had long experimented with bigger cards, but in 1986, they also decided to try smaller ones. These 2-1/8" x 2-15/16" cards feature top players in a number of categories. Sold in plastic packs as a regular Topps issue, the 66-card set is attractive as well as innovative. The cards feature color photos and a minimum of added information on the fronts where only the player's name and Topps logo appear. Backs limited information as well, but do feature enough to justify the player's inclusion in a set of league leaders.

		MT
Complete Set (66):		6.00
Common Player:		.10
1	Eddie Murray	.35
2	Cal Ripken, Jr.	1.00
3	Wade Boggs	.50
4	Dennis Boyd	.10
5	Dwight Evans	.10
6	Bruce Hurst	.10
7	Gary Pettis	.10
8	Harold Baines	.15
9	Floyd Bannister	.10
10	Britt Burns	.10
11	Carlton Fisk	.35
12	Brett Butler	.10
13	Darrell Evans	.10
14	Jack Morris	.10
15	Lance Parrish	.10
16	Walt Terrell	.10
17	Steve Balboni	.10
18	George Brett	.75
19	Charlie Leibrandt	.10
20	Bret Saberhagen	.15
21	Lonnie Smith	.10
22	Willie Wilson	.10
23	Bert Blyleven	.10
24	Mike Smithson	.10
25	Frank Viola	.10
26	Ron Guidry	.10
27	Rickey Henderson	.35
28	Don Mattingly	.90
29	Dave Winfield	.30
30	Mike Moore	.10
31	Gorman Thomas	.10
32	Toby Harrah	.10
33	Charlie Hough	.10
34	Doyle Alexander	.10
35	Jimmy Key	.10
36	Dave Stieb	.10
37	Dale Murphy	.30
38	Keith Moreland	.10
39	Ryne Sandberg	.50
40	Tom Browning	.10
41	Dave Parker	.10
42	Mario Soto	.10
43	Nolan Ryan	1.00
44	Pedro Guerrero	.10
45	Orel Hershiser	.15
46	Mike Scioscia	.10
47	Fernando Valenzuela	.10
48	Bob Welch	.10
49	Tim Raines	.15
50	Gary Carter	.15
51	Sid Fernandez	.10
52	Dwight Gooden	.25
53	Keith Hernandez	.10
54	Juan Samuel	.10
55	Mike Schmidt	.75
56	Glenn Wilson	.10
57	Rick Reuschel	.10
58	Joaquin Andujar	.10
59	Jack Clark	.10
60	Vince Coleman	.10
61	Danny Cox	.10
62	Tom Herr	.10
63	Willie McGee	.10
64	John Tudor	.10
65	Tony Gwynn	.75
66	Checklist	.10

1986 Topps Stickers

The 1986 Topps stickers are 2-1/8" x 3". The 200- piece set features 316 different subjects, with some stickers including two or three players. Numbers run only to 315, however. The set includes some specialty stickers such as League Championships and World Series themes. Stickers are numbered both front and back and included a chance to win a trip to spring training as well as an offer to buy a complete 1986 Topps regular set. An album for the stickers was available in stores. It features Pete Rose in action on the front cover and reproductions of his Topps cards on back.

		MT
Complete Set (315):		9.00
Common Player:		.05
Sticker Album:		1.50
1	Pete Rose	.90
2	Pete Rose	.90
3	George Brett	.75
4	Rod Carew	.10
5	Vince Coleman	.10
6	Dwight Gooden	.15
7	Phil Niekro	.15
8	Tony Perez	.20
9	Nolan Ryan	1.00
10	Tom Seaver	.10
11	N.L. Championship Series (Ozzie Smith)	.10
12	N.L. Championship Series (Bill Madlock)	.05
13	N.L. Championship Series (Cardinals Celebrate)	.05
14	A.L. Championship Series (Al Oliver)	.05
15	A.L. Championship Series (Jim Sundberg)	.05
16	A.L. Championship Series (George Brett)	.10
17	World Series (Bret Saberhagen)	.05
18	World Series (Dane Iorg)	.05
19	World Series (Tito Landrum)	.05
20	World Series (John Tudor)	.05
21	World Series (Buddy Biancalana)	.05
22	World Series (Darryl Motley, Darrell Porter)	.05
23	World Series (George Brett, Frank White)	.10
24	Nolan Ryan	1.00
25	Bill Doran	.05
26	Jose Cruz	.05
27	Mike Scott	.05
28	Kevin Bass	.05
29	Glenn Davis	.05
30	Mark Bailey	.05
31	Dave Smith	.05
32	Phil Garner	.05
33	Dickie Thon	.05
34	Bob Horner	.05
35	Dale Murphy	.15
36	Glenn Hubbard	.05
37	Bruce Sutter	.05
38	Ken Oberkfell	.05
39	Claudell Washington	.05
40	Steve Bedrosian	.05
41	Terry Harper	.05
42	Rafael Ramirez	.05
43	Rick Mahler	.05
44	Joaquin Andujar	.05
45	Willie McGee	.05
46	Ozzie Smith	.35
47	Vince Coleman	.05
48	Danny Cox	.05
49	Tom Herr	.05
50	Jack Clark	.05
51	Andy Van Slyke	.05
52	John Tudor	.05
53	Terry Pendleton	.05
54	Keith Moreland	.05
55	Ryne Sandberg	.30
56	Lee Smith	.05
57	Steve Trout	.05
58	Jody Davis	.05
59	Gary Matthews	.05
60	Leon Durham	.05
61	Rick Sutcliffe	.05
62	Dennis Eckersley	.05
63	Bob Dernier	.05
64	Fernando Valenzuela	.10
65	Pedro Guerrero	.05
66	Jerry Reuss	.05
67	Greg Brock	.05
68	Mike Scioscia	.05
69	Ken Howell	.05
70	Bill Madlock	.05
71	Mike Marshall	.05
72	Steve Sax	.05
73	Orel Hershiser	.10
74	Andre Dawson	.10
75	Tim Raines	.10
76	Jeff Reardon	.05
77	Hubie Brooks	.05
78	Bill Gullickson	.05
79	Bryn Smith	.05
80	Terry Francona	.05
81	Vance Law	.05
82	Tim Wallach	.05
83	Herm Winningham	.05
84	Jeff Leonard	.05
85	Chris Brown	.05
86	Scott Garrelts	.05
87	Jose Uribe	.05
88	Manny Trillo	.05
89	Dan Driessen	.05
90	Dan Gladden	.05
91	Mark Davis	.05
92	Bob Brenly	.05
93	Mike Krukow	.05
94	Dwight Gooden	.15
95	Darryl Strawberry	.20
96	Gary Carter	.10
97	Wally Backman	.05
98	Ron Darling	.05
99	Keith Hernandez	.05
100	George Foster	.05
101	Howard Johnson	.05
102	Rafael Santana	.05
103	Roger McDowell	.05
104	Steve Garvey	.10
105	Tony Gwynn	.75
106	Graig Nettles	.05
107	Rich Gossage	.05
108	Andy Hawkins	.05
109	Carmelo Martinez	.05
110	Garry Templeton	.05
111	Terry Kennedy	.05
112	Tim Flannery	.05
113	LaMarr Hoyt	.05
114	Mike Schmidt	.45
115	Ozzie Virgil	.05
116	Steve Carlton	.10
117	Garry Maddox	.05
118	Glenn Wilson	.05
119	Kevin Gross	.05
120	Von Hayes	.05
121	Juan Samuel	.05
122	Rick Schu	.05
123	Shane Rawley	.05
124	Johnny Ray	.05
125	Tony Pena	.05
126	Rick Reuschel	.05
127	Sammy Khalifa	.05
128	Marvell Wynne	.05
129	Jason Thompson	.05
130	Rick Rhoden	.05
131	Bill Almon	.05
132	Joe Orsulak	.05
133	Jim Morrison	.05
134	Pete Rose	.90
135	Dave Parker	.10
136	Mario Soto	.05
137	Dave Concepcion	.05
138	Ron Oester	.05
139	Buddy Bell	.05
140	Ted Power	.05
141	Tom Browning	.05
142	John Franco	.05
143	Tony Perez	.20
144	Willie McGee	.05
145	Dale Murphy	.15
146	Tony Gwynn	.75
147	Tom Herr	.05
148	Steve Garvey	.15
149	Dale Murphy	.25
150	Darryl Strawberry	.20
151	Graig Nettles	.05
152	Terry Kennedy	.05
153	Ozzie Smith	.40
154	LaMarr Hoyt	.05
155	Rickey Henderson	.40
156	Lou Whitaker	.05
157	George Brett	.75
158	Eddie Murray	.40
159	Cal Ripken, Jr.	1.00
160	Dave Winfield	.30
161	Jim Rice	.10
162	Carlton Fisk	.20
163	Jack Morris	.05
164	Wade Boggs	.30
165	Darrell Evans	.05
166	Mike Davis	.05
167	Dave Kingman	.05
168	Alfredo Griffin	.05
169	Carney Lansford	.05
170	Bruce Bochte	.05
171	Dwayne Murphy	.05
172	Dave Collins	.05
173	Chris Codiroli	.05
174	Mike Heath	.05
175	Jay Howell	.05
176	Rod Carew	.20
177	Reggie Jackson	.35
178	Doug DeCinces	.05
179	Bob Boone	.05
180	Ron Romanick	.05
181	Bob Grich	.05
182	Donnie Moore	.05
183	Brian Downing	.05
184	Ruppert Jones	.05
185	Juan Beniquez	.05
186	Dave Stieb	.05
187	Jorge Bell	.05
188	Willie Upshaw	.05
189	Tom Henke	.05
190	Damaso Garcia	.05
191	Jimmy Key	.05
192	Jesse Barfield	.05
193	Dennis Lamp	.05
194	Tony Fernandez	.05
195	Lloyd Moseby	.05
196	Cecil Cooper	.05
197	Robin Yount	.45
198	Rollie Fingers	.10
199	Ted Simmons	.05
200	Ben Oglivie	.05
201	Moose Haas	.05
202	Jim Gantner	.05
203	Paul Molitor	.35
204	Charlie Moore	.05
205	Danny Darwin	.05
206	Brett Butler	.05
207	Brook Jacoby	.05
208	Andre Thornton	.05
209	Tom Waddell	.05
210	Tony Bernazard	.05
211	Julio Franco	.05
212	Pat Tabler	.05
213	Joe Carter	.10
214	George Vukovich	.05
215	Rich Thompson	.05
216	Gorman Thomas	.05
217	Phil Bradley	.05
218	Alvin Davis	.05
219	Jim Presley	.05
220	Matt Young	.05
221	Mike Moore	.05
222	Dave Henderson	.05
223	Ed Nunez	.05
224	Spike Owen	.05
225	Mark Langston	.05
226	Cal Ripken, Jr.	1.00
227	Eddie Murray	.20
228	Fred Lynn	.05
229	Lee Lacy	.05
230	Scott McGregor	.05
231	Storm Davis	.05
232	Rick Dempsey	.05
233	Mike Boddicker	.05
234	Mike Young	.05
235	Sammy Stewart	.05
236	Pete O'Brien	.05
237	Oddibe McDowell	.05
238	Toby Harrah	.05
239	Gary Ward	.05
240	Larry Parrish	.05
241	Charlie Hough	.05

242	Burt Hooton	.05
243	Don Slaught	.05
244	Curt Wilkerson	.05
245	Greg Harris	.05
246	Jim Rice	.10
247	Wade Boggs	.40
248	Rich Gedman	.05
249	Dennis Boyd	.05
250	Marty Barrett	.05
251	Dwight Evans	.05
252	Bill Buckner	.05
253	Bob Stanley	.05
254	Tony Armas	.05
255	Mike Easler	.05
256	George Brett	.75
257	Dan Quisenberry	.05
258	Willie Wilson	.05
259	Jim Sundberg	.05
260	Bret Saberhagen	.05
261	Bud Black	.05
262	Charlie Leibrandt	.05
263	Frank White	.05
264	Lonnie Smith	.05
265	Steve Balboni	.05
266	Kirk Gibson	.10
267	Alan Trammell	.10
268	Jack Morris	.05
269	Darrell Evans	.05
270	Dan Petry	.05
271	Larry Herndon	.05
272	Lou Whitaker	.05
273	Lance Parrish	.05
274	Chet Lemon	.05
275	Willie Hernandez	.05
276	Tom Brunansky	.05
277	Kent Hrbek	.10
278	Mark Salas	.05
279	Bert Blyleven	.05
280	Tim Teufel	.05
281	Ron Davis	.05
282	Mike Smithson	.05
283	Gary Gaetti	.05
284	Frank Viola	.05
285	Kirby Puckett	.60
286	Carlton Fisk	.25
287	Tom Seaver	.15
288	Harold Baines	.05
289	Ron Kittle	.05
290	Bob James	.05
291	Rudy Law	.05
292	Britt Burns	.05
293	Greg Walker	.05
294	Ozzie Guillen	.05
295	Tim Hulett	.05
296	Don Mattingly	.70
297	Rickey Henderson	.20
298	Dave Winfield	.30
299	Butch Wynegar	.05
300	Don Baylor	.05
301	Eddie Whitson	.05
302	Ron Guidry	.05
303	Dave Righetti	.05
304	Bobby Meacham	.05
305	Willie Randolph	.05
306	Vince Coleman	.05
307	Oddibe McDowell	.05
308	Larry Sheets	.05
309	Ozzie Guillen	.05
310	Earnie Riles	.05
311	Chris Brown	.05
312	Brian Fisher, Roger McDowell	.05
313	Tom Browning	.05
314	Glenn Davis	.05
315	Mark Salas	.05

1986 Topps Super

A third year of oversize (4-7/8" x 6-7/8") versions of Topps' regular issue cards saw the set once again hit the 60-card mark. Besides being four times the size of a normal card, the Supers differ only in the number on the back of the card.

		MT
Complete Set (60):		16.00
Common Player:		.25
1	Don Mattingly	1.00
2	Willie McGee	.25
3	Bret Saberhagen	.25
4	Dwight Gooden	.35
5	Dan Quisenberry	.25
6	Jeff Reardon	.25
7	Ozzie Guillen	.25
8	Vince Coleman	.25
9	Harold Baines	.25
10	Jorge Bell	.25
11	Bert Blyleven	.25
12	Wade Boggs	.75
13	Phil Bradley	.25
14	George Brett	1.00
15	Hubie Brooks	.25
16	Tom Browning	.25
17	Bill Buckner	.25
18	Brett Butler	.30
19	Gary Carter	.35
20	Cecil Cooper	.25
21	Darrell Evans	.25
22	Dwight Evans	.25
23	Carlton Fisk	.50
24	Steve Garvey	.40
25	Kirk Gibson	.25
26	Rich Gossage	.25
27	Pedro Guerrero	.25
28	Ron Guidry	.25
29	Tony Gwynn	.90
30	Rickey Henderson	.50
31	Keith Hernandez	.25
32	Tom Herr	.25
33	Orel Hershiser	.30
34	Jay Howell	.25
35	Reggie Jackson	.75
36	Bob James	.25
37	Charlie Leibrandt	.25
38	Jack Morris	.25
39	Dale Murphy	.45
40	Eddie Murray	.65
40p	Eddie Murray (sample card)	4.00
41	Dave Parker	.30
42	Tim Raines	.35
43	Jim Rice	.40
44	Dave Righetti	.25
45	Cal Ripken, Jr.	3.00
46	Pete Rose	1.50
47	Nolan Ryan	3.00
48	Ryne Sandberg	.75
49	Mike Schmidt	1.00
50	Tom Seaver	.75
51	Bryn Smith	.25
52	Lee Smith	.35
53	Ozzie Smith	.75
54	Dave Stieb	.25
55	Darryl Strawberry	.35
56	Gorman Thomas	.25
57	John Tudor	.25
58	Fernando Valenzuela	.30
59	Willie Wilson	.25
60	Dave Winfield	.60

1986 Topps Super Star

Labeled "Topps' Collector Series" in a red band at the top of the front, this set marked the second year of Topps' production of a special boxed set for the Woolworth chain of stores, though Woolworth's name does not appear anywhere on the card. The 2-1/2" x 3-1/2" cards feature a color photo with its lower-right corner rolled up to reveal the words "Super Star" on a bright yellow border. The player's name appears in the lower-left corner.

		MT
Complete Set (33):		5.00
Common Player:		.10
1	Tony Armas	.10
2	Don Baylor	.12
3	Wade Boggs	.60
4	George Brett	.80
5	Bill Buckner	.10
6	Rod Carew	.30
7	Gary Carter	.15
8	Cecil Cooper	.10
9	Darrell Evans	.10
10	Dwight Evans	.10
11	George Foster	.10
12	Bobby Grich	.10
13	Tony Gwynn	.75
14	Keith Hernandez	.10
15	Reggie Jackson	.40
16	Dave Kingman	.12
17	Carney Lansford	.10
18	Fred Lynn	.10
19	Bill Madlock	.10
20	Don Mattingly	1.00
21	Willie McGee	.10
22	Hal McRae	.10
23	Dale Murphy	.20
24	Eddie Murray	.40
25	Ben Oglivie	.10
26	Al Oliver	.10
27	Dave Parker	.12
28	Jim Rice	.12
29	Pete Rose	1.00
30	Mike Schmidt	.80
31	Gorman Thomas	.10
32	Willie Wilson	.10
33	Dave Winfield	.30

1986 Topps Tattoos

Topps returned to tattoos in 1986, marketing a set of 24 different tattoo sheets. Each sheet of tattoos measures 3-7/16" x 14" and includes both player and smaller action tattoos. As the action tattoos were uniform and not of any particular player, they add little value to the sheet. The player tattoos measure 1-3/16" x 2-3/8". With 24 sheets, eight players per sheet, there are 192 players represented in the set. The sheets are numbered.

		MT
Complete Set (24):		5.00
Common Player:		.25
1	Julio Franco, Rich Gossage, Keith Hernandez, Charlie Leibrandt, Jack Perconte, Lee Smith, Dickie Thon, Dave Winfield	.25
2	Jesse Barfield, Shawon Dunston, Dennis Eckersley, Brian Fisher, Moose Haas, Mike Moore, Dale Murphy, Bret Saberhagen	.30
3	George Bell, Bob Brenly, Steve Carlton, Jose DeLeon, Bob Horner, Bob James, Dan Quisenberry, Andre Thornton	.25
4	Mike Davis, Leon Durham, Darrell Evans, Glenn Hubbard, Johnny Ray, Cal Ripken, Ted Simmons	.45
5	John Candelaria, Rick Dempsey, Steve Garvey, Ozzie Guillen, Gary Matthews, Jesse Orosco, Tony Pena	.25
6	Bruce Bochte, George Brett, Cecil Cooper, Sammy Khalifa, Ron Kittle, Scott McGregor, Pete Rose, Mookie Wilson	.40
7	John Franco, Carney Lansford, Don Mattingly, Graig Nettles, Rick Reuschel, Mike Schmidt, Larry Sheets, Don Sutton	.45
8	Cecilio Guante, Willie Hernandez, Mike Krukow, Fred Lynn, Phil Niekro, Ed Nunez, Ryne Sandberg, Pat Tabler	.30
9	Brett Butler, Chris Codiroli, Jim Gantner, Charlie Hough, Dave Parker, Rick Rhoden, Glenn Wilson, Robin Yount	.25
10	Tom Browning, Ron Darling, Von Hayes, Chet Lemon, Tom Seaver, Mike Smithson, Bruce Sutter, Alan Trammell	.25
11	Tony Armas, Jose Cruz, Jay Howell, Rick Mahler, Jack Morris, Rafael Ramirez, Dave Righetti, Mike Young	.25
12	Alvin Davis, Doug DeCinces, Andy Hawkins, Dennis Lamp, Keith Moreland, Jim Presley, Mario Soto, John Tudor	.25
13	Hubie Brooks, Jody Davis, Dwight Evans, Ron Hassey, Charles Hudson, Kirby Puckett, Jose Uribe	.30
14	Tony Bernazard, Phil Bradley, Bill Buckner, Brian Downing, Dan Driessen, Ron Guidry, LaMarr Hoyt, Garry Maddox	.25
15	Buddy Bell, Joe Carter, Tony Fernandez, Tito Landrum, Jeff Leonard, Hal McRae, Willie Randolph, Juan Samuel	.25
16	Dennis Boyd, Vince Coleman, Scott Garrelts, Alfredo Griffin, Donnie Moore, Tony Perez, Ozzie Smith, Frank White	.25
17	Rich Gedman, Kent Hrbek, Reggie Jackson, Mike Marshall, Terry Pendleton, Tim Raines, Mark Salas, Claudell Washington	.30
18	Chris Brown, Tom Brunansky, Glenn Davis, Ron Davis, Burt Hooton, Darryl Strawberry, Frank Viola, Tim Wallach	.25
19	Jack Clark, Bill Doran, Toby Harrah, Bill Madlock, Pete O'Brien, Larry Parrish, Mike Scioscia, Garry Templeton	.25
20	Gary Carter, Andre Dawson, Dwight Gooden, Orel Hershiser, Oddibe McDowell, Roger McDowell, Dwayne Murphy, Jim Rice	.35
21	Steve Balboni, Mike Easler, Charlie Lea, Lloyd Moseby, Steve Sax, Rick Sutcliffe, Gary Ward, Willie Wilson	.25
22	Wade Boggs, Dave Concepcion, Kirk Gibson, Tom Herr, Lance Parrish, Jeff Reardon, Bryn Smith, Gorman Thomas	.30
23	Carlton Fisk, Bob Grich, Pedro Guerrero, Willie McGee, Paul Molitor, Mike Scott, Dave Stieb, Lou Whitaker	.30
24	Bert Blyleven, Damaso Garcia, Phil Garner, Tony Gwynn, Rickey Henderson, Ben Oglivie, Nolan Ryan, Fernando Valenzuela	.45

1986 Topps 3-D

This set is a second effort in the production of over-size (4-1/2" x 6") plastic cards on which the player figure is embossed. Cards were sold one per pack for 50¢. The 30 players in the set are among the game's top stars. The embossed color photo is bordered at bottom by a strip of contrasting color on which the player name appears. At the top, a row of white baseballs each contain a letter of the team nickname. Backs have no printing, and contain two self-adhesive strips with which the cards can be attached to a hard surface.

		MT
Complete Set (30):		15.00
Common Player:		.25
1	Bert Blyleven	.25
2	Gary Carter	.35
3	Wade Boggs	.65
4	Dwight Gooden	.30
5	George Brett	1.00
6	Rich Gossage	.25
7	Darrell Evans	.25
8	Pedro Guerrero	.25
9	Ron Guidry	.25
10	Keith Hernandez	.25
11	Rickey Henderson	.50
12	Orel Hershiser	.30
13	Reggie Jackson	.75
14	Willie McGee	.25
15	Don Mattingly	1.00
16	Dale Murphy	.40
17	Jack Morris	.25
18	Dave Parker	.25
19	Eddie Murray	.60
20	Jeff Reardon	.25
21	Dan Quisenberry	.25
22	Pete Rose	1.50
23	Jim Rice	.40
24	Mike Schmidt	1.00
25	Bret Saberhagen	.30
26	Darryl Strawberry	.30
27	Dave Stieb	.25
28	John Tudor	.25
29	Dave Winfield	.40
30	Fernando Valenzuela	.25

1987 Topps

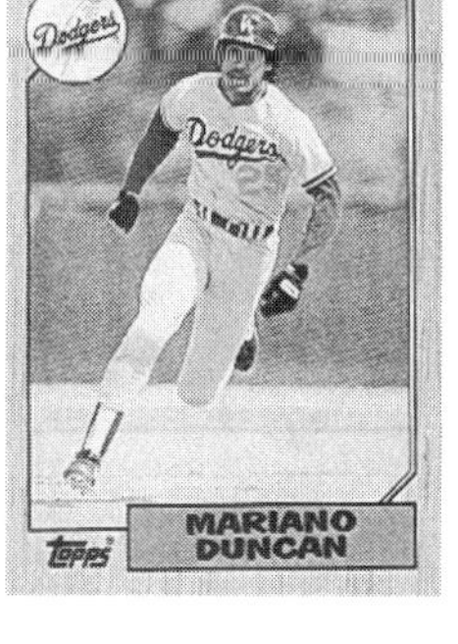

Many collectors feel that Topps' 1987 set of 792 cards is a future classic. The 2-1/2" x 3-1/2" design is closely akin to the 1962 set in that the player photo is set against a woodgrain border. Instead of a rolling corner, as in 1962, the player photos in '87 feature a couple of clipped corners at top left and bottom right, where the team logo and player name appear. The player's position is not given on the front of the card. For the first time in several years, the trophy which designates members of Topps All-Star Rookie Team returned to the card design. As in the previous three years, Topps issued a glossy-finish "Tiffany" edition of their 792-card set. However, it was speculated that as many as 50,000 sets were produced as opposed to the 5,000 sets printed in 1985 and 1986. Because of the large print run, the values for the Tiffany cards are only 3-4 times higher than the same card in the regular issue.

		MT
Complete Set (792):		12.00
Common Player:		.05
Wax Box:		15.00
1	Roger Clemens (Record Breaker)	.30
2	Jim Deshaies (Record Breaker)	.05
3	Dwight Evans (Record Breaker)	.05
4	Dave Lopes (Record Breaker)	.05
5	Dave Righetti (Record Breaker)	.05
6	Ruben Sierra (Record Breaker)	.05
7	Todd Worrell (Record Breaker)	.05
8	Terry Pendleton	.05
9	Jay Tibbs	.05
10	Cecil Cooper	.05
11	Indians Leaders (Jack Aker, Chris Bando, Phil Niekro)	.10
12	*Jeff Sellers*	.05
13	Nick Esasky	.05
14	Dave Stewart	.05
15	Claudell Washington	.05
16	Pat Clements	.05
17	Pete O'Brien	.05
18	Dick Howser	.05
19	Matt Young	.05
20	Gary Carter	.10
21	Mark Davis	.05
22	Doug DeCinces	.05
23	Lee Smith	.05
24	Tony Walker	.05
25	Bert Blyleven	.05
26	Greg Brock	.05
27	Joe Cowley	.05
28	Rick Dempsey	.05
29	Jimmy Key	.05
30	Tim Raines	.15
31	Braves Leaders (Glenn Hubbard, Rafael Ramirez)	.05
32	Tim Leary	.05
33	Andy Van Slyke	.05
34	Jose Rijo	.05
35	Sid Bream	.05
36	*Eric King*	.05
37	Marvell Wynne	.05
38	Dennis Leonard	.05
39	Marty Barrett	.05
40	Dave Righetti	.05
41	Bo Diaz	.05
42	Gary Redus	.05
43	Gene Michael	.05
44	Greg Harris	.05
45	Jim Presley	.05
46	Danny Gladden	.05
47	Dennis Powell	.05
48	Wally Backman	.05
49	Terry Harper	.05
50	Dave Smith	.05
51	Mel Hall	.05
52	Keith Atherton	.05
53	Ruppert Jones	.05
54	Bill Dawley	.05
55	Tim Wallach	.05
56	Brewers Leaders (Jamie Cocanower, Paul Molitor, Charlie Moore, Herm Starrette)	.10
57	*Scott Nielsen*	.05
58	Thad Bosley	.05
59	Ken Dayley	.05
60	Tony Pena	.05
61	*Bobby Thigpen*	.05
62	Bobby Meacham	.05
63	Fred Toliver	.05
64	Harry Spilman	.05
65	Tom Browning	.05
66	Marc Sullivan	.05
67	Bill Swift	.05
68	Tony LaRussa	.05
69	Lonnie Smith	.05
70	Charlie Hough	.05
71	*Mike Aldrete*	.05
72	Walt Terrell	.05
73	Dave Anderson	.05
74	Dan Pasqua	.05
75	Ron Darling	.05
76	Rafael Ramirez	.05
77	Bryan Oelkers	.05
78	Tom Foley	.05
79	Juan Nieves	.05
80	*Wally Joyner*	.35
81	Padres Leaders (Andy Hawkins, Terry Kennedy)	.05
82	*Rob Murphy*	.05
83	Mike Davis	.05
84	Steve Lake	.05
85	Kevin Bass	.05
86	Nate Snell	.05
87	Mark Salas	.05
88	Ed Wojna	.05
89	Ozzie Guillen	.05
90	Dave Stieb	.05
91	Harold Reynolds	.05
92a	Urbano Lugo (no trademark on front)	.10
92b	Urbano Lugo (trademark on front)	.05
93	Jim Leyland	.05
94	Calvin Schiraldi	.05
95	Oddibe McDowell	.05
96	Frank Williams	.05
97	Glenn Wilson	.05
98	Bill Scherrer	.05
99	Darryl Motley	.05
100	Steve Garvey	.15
101	*Carl Willis*	.05
102	Paul Zuvella	.05
103	Rick Aguilera	.05
104	Billy Sample	.05
105	Floyd Youmans	.05
106	Blue Jays Leaders (George Bell, Willie Upshaw)	.05
107	John Butcher	.05
108	Jim Gantner (photo reversed)	.05
109	R.J. Reynolds	.05
110	John Tudor	.05
111	Alfredo Griffin	.05
112	Alan Ashby	.05
113	Neil Allen	.05
114	Billy Beane	.05
115	Donnie Moore	.05
116	*Mike Stanley*	.05
117	Jim Beattie	.05
118	Bobby Valentine	.05
119	Ron Robinson	.05
120	Eddie Murray	.40
121	*Kevin Romine*	.05
122	Jim Clancy	.05
123	John Kruk	.10
124	Ray Fontenot	.05
125	Bob Brenly	.05
126	*Mike Loynd*	.05
127	Vance Law	.05
128	Checklist 1-132	.05
129	Rick Cerone	.05
130	Dwight Gooden	.10
131	Pirates Leaders (Sid Bream, Tony Pena)	.05
132	*Paul Assenmacher*	.05
133	Jose Oquendo	.05
134	*Rich Yett*	.05
135	Mike Easler	.05
136	Ron Romanick	.05
137	Jerry Willard	.05
138	Roy Lee Jackson	.05
139	*Devon White*	.40
140	Bret Saberhagen	.10
141	Herm Winningham	.05
142	Rick Sutcliffe	.05
143	Steve Boros	.05
144	Mike Scioscia	.05
145	Charlie Kerfeld	.05
146	*Tracy Jones*	.05
147	Randy Niemann	.05
148	Dave Collins	.05
149	Ray Searage	.05
150	Wade Boggs	.40
151	Mike LaCoss	.05
152	Toby Harrah	.05
153	*Duane Ward*	.25
154	Tom O'Malley	.05
155	Eddie Whitson	.05
156	Mariners Leaders (Bob Kearney, Phil Regan, Matt Young)	.05
157	Danny Darwin	.05
158	Tim Teufel	.05
159	Ed Olwine	.05
160	Julio Franco	.05
161	Steve Ontiveros	.05
162	*Mike LaValliere*	.10
163	Kevin Gross	.05
164	Sammy Khalifa	.05
165	Jeff Reardon	.05
166	Bob Boone	.05
167	*Jim Deshaies*	.10
168	Lou Piniella	.05
169	Ron Washington	.05
170	Bo Jackson (Future Stars)	.50
171	*Chuck Cary*	.05
172	Ron Oester	.05
173	Alex Trevino	.05
174	Henry Cotto	.05
175	Bob Stanley	.05
176	Steve Buechele	.05
177	Keith Moreland	.05
178	Cecil Fielder	.10
179	Bill Wegman	.05
180	Chris Brown	.05
181	Cardinals Leaders (Mike LaValliere, Ozzie Smith, Ray Soff)	.10
182	Lee Lacy	.05
183	Andy Hawkins	.05
184	Bobby Bonilla	.15
185	Roger McDowell	.05
186	Bruce Benedict	.05
187	Mark Huismann	.05
188	Tony Phillips	.05
189	Joe Hesketh	.05
190	Jim Sundberg	.05
191	Charles Hudson	.05
192	Cory Snyder	.05
193	Roger Craig	.05
194	Kirk McCaskill	.05
195	Mike Pagliarulo	.05
196	Randy O'Neal	.05
197	Mark Bailey	.05
198	Lee Mazzilli	.05
199	Mariano Duncan	.05
200	Pete Rose	.40
201	*John Cangelosi*	.05
202	Ricky Wright	.05
203	*Mike Kingery*	.05
204	Sammy Stewart	.05
205	Graig Nettles	.05
206	Twins Leaders (Tim Laudner, Frank Viola)	.05
207	George Frazier	.05
208	John Shelby	.05
209	Rick Schu	.05
210	Lloyd Moseby	.05
211	John Morris	.05
212	Mike Fitzgerald	.05
213	*Randy Myers*	.25
214	Omar Moreno	.05
215	Mark Langston	.05
216	*B.J. Surhoff* (Future Stars)	.15
217	Chris Codiroli	.05
218	Sparky Anderson	.15
219	Cecilio Guante	.05
220	Joe Carter	.10
221	Vern Ruhle	.05
222	Denny Walling	.05
223	Charlie Leibrandt	.05
224	Wayne Tolleson	.05
225	Mike Smithson	.05
226	Max Venable	.05
227	*Jamie Moyer*	.05
228	Curt Wilkerson	.05
229	*Mike Birkbeck*	.05
230	Don Baylor	.10
231	Giants Leaders (Bob Brenly, Mike Krukow)	.05
232	*Reggie Williams*	.05
233	*Russ Morman*	.05
234	Pat Sheridan	.05
235	Alvin Davis	.05
236	Tommy John	.10
237	Jim Morrison	.05
238	Bill Krueger	.05
239	Juan Espino	.05
240	Steve Balboni	.05
241	Danny Heep	.05
242	Rick Mahler	.05
243	Whitey Herzog	.05
244	Dickie Noles	.05
245	Willie Upshaw	.05
246	Jim Dwyer	.05
247	Jeff Reed	.05
248	Gene Walter	.05
249	Jim Pankovits	.05
250	Teddy Higuera	.05
251	Rob Wilfong	.05
252	Denny Martinez	.05
253	Eddie Milner	.05
254	*Bob Tewksbury*	.20
255	Juan Samuel	.05
256	Royals Leaders (George Brett, Frank White)	.15
257	Bob Forsch	.05
258	Steve Yeager	.05
259	*Mike Greenwell*	.25
260	Vida Blue	.05
261	Ruben Sierra	.10
262	Jim Winn	.05
263	Stan Javier	.05
264	Checklist 133-264	.05
265	Darrell Evans	.05
266	*Jeff Hamilton*	.05
267	Howard Johnson	.05
268	Pat Corrales	.05
269	Cliff Speck	.05
270	Jody Davis	.05
271	Mike Brown	.05
272	Andres Galarraga	.40
273	Gene Nelson	.05
274	*Jeff Hearron*	.05
275	LaMarr Hoyt	.05
276	Jackie Gutierrez	.05
277	Juan Agosto	.05
278	Gary Pettis	.05
279	*Dan Plesac*	.05
280	Jeffrey Leonard	.05
281	Reds Leaders (Bo Diaz, Bill Gullickson, Pete Rose)	.10
282	Jeff Calhoun	.05
283	*Doug Drabek*	.25
284	John Moses	.05
285	Dennis Boyd	.05
286	Mike Woodard	.05
287	Dave Von Ohlen	.05
288	Tito Landrum	.05
289	Bob Kipper	.05
290	Leon Durham	.05
291	*Mitch Williams*	.25
292	Franklin Stubbs	.05
293	Bob Rodgers	.05
294	Steve Jeltz	.05
295	Len Dykstra	.10
296	*Andres Thomas*	.05
297	Don Schulze	.05
298	Larry Herndon	.05
299	Joel Davis	.05
300	Reggie Jackson	.25
301	*Luis Aquino*	.05
302	Bill Schroeder	.05
303	Juan Berenguer	.05
304	Phil Garner	.05
305	John Franco	.05
306	Red Sox Leaders (Rich Gedman, John McNamara, Tom Seaver)	.10
307	*Lee Guetterman*	.05
308	Don Slaught	.05
309	Mike Young	.05
310	Frank Viola	.05
311	Rickey Henderson (Turn Back the Clock)	.15
312	Reggie Jackson (Turn Back the Clock)	.10
313	Roberto Clemente (Turn Back the Clock)	.45
314	Carl Yastrzemski (Turn Back the Clock)	.10
315	Maury Wills (Turn Back the Clock)	.05
316	Brian Fisher	.05
317	Clint Hurdle	.05
318	Jim Fregosi	.05
319	*Greg Swindell*	.10
320	Barry Bonds	1.50
321	Mike Laga	.05
322	Chris Bando	.05
323	*Al Newman*	.05
324	Dave Palmer	.05
325	Garry Templeton	.05
326	Mark Gubicza	.05
327	*Dale Sveum*	.05
328	Bob Welch	.05
329	Ron Roenicke	.05
330	Mike Scott	.05
331	Mets Leaders (Gary Carter, Keith Hernandez, Dave Johnson, Darryl Strawberry)	.10
332	Joe Price	.05
333	Ken Phelps	.05
334	*Ed Correa*	.05
335	Candy Maldonado	.05
336	*Allan Anderson*	.05
337	Darrell Miller	.05
338	Tim Conroy	.05
339	Donnie Hill	.05
340	Roger Clemens	.75
341	Mike Brown	.05
342	Bob James	.05
343	Hal Lanier	.05
344a	Joe Niekro (copyright outside yellow on back)	.25
344b	Joe Niekro (copyright inside yellow on back)	.05
345	Andre Dawson	.15
346	Shawon Dunston	.05
347	Mickey Brantley	.05
348	Carmelo Martinez	.05
349	Storm Davis	.05
350	Keith Hernandez	.05
351	Gene Garber	.05
352	Mike Felder	.05
353	Ernie Camacho	.05
354	Jamie Quirk	.05
355	Don Carman	.05
356	White Sox Leaders (Ed Brinkman, Julio Cruz)	.05
357	*Steve Fireovid*	.05
358	Sal Butera	.05
359	Doug Corbett	.05
360	Pedro Guerrero	.05
361	Mark Thurmond	.05
362	*Luis Quinones*	.05
363	Jose Guzman	.05
364	Randy Bush	.05
365	Rick Rhoden	.05
366	Mark McGwire	5.00
367	Jeff Lahti	.05
368	John McNamara	.05
369	Brian Dayett	.05
370	Fred Lynn	.05
371	*Mark Eichhorn*	.05
372	Jerry Mumphrey	.05
373	Jeff Dedmon	.05
374	Glenn Hoffman	.05
375	Ron Guidry	.10
376	Scott Bradley	.05
377	John Henry Johnson	.05
378	Rafael Santana	.05
379	John Russell	.05
380	Rich Gossage	.05
381	Expos Leaders (Mike Fitzgerald, Bob Rodgers)	.05
382	Rudy Law	.05
383	Ron Davis	.05
384	Johnny Grubb	.05
385	Orel Hershiser	.10
386	Dickie Thon	.05
387	*T.R. Bryden*	.05
388	Geno Petralli	.05
389	Jeff Robinson	.05
390	Gary Matthews	.05
391	Jay Howell	.05
392	Checklist 265-396	.05
393	Pete Rose	.35
394	Mike Bielecki	.05
395	Damaso Garcia	.05
396	Tim Lollar	.05
397	Greg Walker	.05
398	Brad Havens	.05
399	Curt Ford	.05
400	George Brett	.50
401	Billy Jo Robidoux	.05
402	Mike Trujillo	.05
403	Jerry Royster	.05
404	Doug Sisk	.05
405	Brook Jacoby	.05
406	Yankees Leaders (Rickey Henderson, Don Mattingly)	.25
407	Jim Acker	.05
408	John Mizerock	.05
409	Milt Thompson	.05
410	Fernando Valenzuela	.05
411	Darnell Coles	.05
412	Eric Davis	.05
413	Moose Haas	.05
414	Joe Orsulak	.05
415	*Bobby Witt*	.10
416	Tom Nieto	.05
417	Pat Perry	.05
418	Dick Williams	.05
419	*Mark Portugal*	.10
420	Will Clark	.75
421	Jose DeLeon	.05
422	Jack Howell	.05
423	Jaime Cocanower	.05
424	Chris Speier	.05
425	Tom Seaver	.30
426	Floyd Rayford	.05
427	Ed Nunez	.05
428	Bruce Bochy	.05
429	*Tim Pyznarski* (Future Stars)	.05
430	Mike Schmidt	.50
431	Dodgers Leaders (Tom Niedenfuer, Ron Perranoski, Alex Trevino)	.05
432	Jim Slaton	.05
433	*Ed Hearn*	.05
434	Mike Fischlin	.05
435	Bruce Sutter	.05
436	*Andy Allanson*	.05
437	Ted Power	.05
438	*Kelly Downs*	.05
439	Karl Best	.05
440	Willie McGee	.05
441	*Dave Leiper*	.05
442	Mitch Webster	.05
443	John Felske	.05
444	Jeff Russell	.05
445	Dave Lopes	.05
446	*Chuck Finley*	.25
447	Bill Almon	.05
448	*Chris Bosio*	.10
449	*Pat Dodson* (Future Stars)	.05
450	Kirby Puckett	.50
451	Joe Sambito	.05
452	Dave Henderson	.05
453	*Scott Terry*	.05
454	Luis Salazar	.05
455	Mike Boddicker	.05
456	A's Leaders (Carney Lansford, Tony LaRussa, Mickey Tettleton, Dave Von Ohlen)	.05
457	Len Matuszek	.05
458	Kelly Gruber	.05
459	Dennis Eckersley	.10
460	Darryl Strawberry	.10
461	Craig McMurtry	.05
462	Scott Fletcher	.05
463	Tom Candiotti	.05
464	Butch Wynegar	.05
465	Todd Worrell	.05
466	Kal Daniels	.05
467	Randy St. Claire	.05
468	George Bamberger	.05
469	*Mike Diaz*	.05
470	Dave Dravecky	.05
471	Ronn Reynolds	.05
472	Bill Doran	.05
473	Steve Farr	.05

474	Jerry Narron	.05
475	Scott Garrelts	.05
476	Danny Tartabull	.05
477	Ken Howell	.05
478	Tim Laudner	.05
479	*Bob Sebra*	.05
480	Jim Rice	.10
481	Phillies Leaders (Von Hayes, Juan Samuel, Glenn Wilson)	.05
482	Daryl Boston	.05
483	Dwight Lowry	.05
484	Jim Traber	.05
485	Tony Fernandez	.05
486	Otis Nixon	.05
487	Dave Gumpert	.05
488	Ray Knight	.05
489	Bill Gullickson	.05
490	Dale Murphy	.15
491	*Ron Karkovice*	.10
492	Mike Heath	.05
493	Tom Lasorda	.10
494	*Barry Jones*	.05
495	Gorman Thomas	.05
496	Bruce Bochte	.05
497	*Dale Mohorcic*	.05
498	Bob Kearney	.05
499	*Bruce Ruffin*	.05
500	Don Mattingly	.50
501	Craig Lefferts	.05
502	Dick Schofield	.05
503	Larry Andersen	.05
504	Mickey Hatcher	.05
505	Bryn Smith	.05
506	Orioles Leaders (Rich Bordi, Rick Dempsey, Earl Weaver)	.10
507	Dave Stapleton	.05
508	*Scott Bankhead*	.05
509	Enos Cabell	.05
510	Tom Henke	.05
511	Steve Lyons	.05
512	*Dave Magadan* (Future Stars)	.20
513	Carmen Castillo	.05
514	Orlando Mercado	.05
515	Willie Hernandez	.05
516	Ted Simmons	.05
517	Mario Soto	.05
518	Gene Mauch	.05
519	Curt Young	.05
520	Jack Clark	.05
521	Rick Reuschel	.05
522	Checklist 397-528	.05
523	Earnie Riles	.05
524	Bob Shirley	.05
525	Phil Bradley	.05
526	Roger Mason	.05
527	Jim Wohlford	.05
528	Ken Dixon	.05
529	*Alvaro Espinoza*	.05
530	Tony Gwynn	.50
531	Astros Leaders (Yogi Berra, Hal Lanier, Denis Menke, Gene Tenace)	.05
532	Jeff Stone	.05
533	Argenis Salazar	.05
534	Scott Sanderson	.05
535	Tony Armas	.05
536	*Terry Mulholland*	.25
537	Rance Mulliniks	.05
538	Tom Niedenfuer	.05
539	Reid Nichols	.05
540	Terry Kennedy	.05
541	*Rafael Belliard*	.05
542	Ricky Horton	.05
543	Dave Johnson	.05
544	Zane Smith	.05
545	Buddy Bell	.05
546	Mike Morgan	.05
547	Rob Deer	.05
548	*Bill Mooneyham*	.05
549	Bob Melvin	.05
550	Pete Incaviglia	.25
551	Frank Wills	.05
552	Larry Sheets	.05
553	*Mike Maddux*	.05
554	Buddy Biancalana	.05
555	Dennis Rasmussen	.05
556	Angels Leaders (Bob Boone, Marcel Lachemann, Mike Witt)	.05
557	*John Cerutti*	.05
558	Greg Gagne	.05
559	Lance McCullers	.05
560	Glenn Davis	.05
561	*Rey Quinones*	.05
562	*Bryan Clutterbuck*	.05
563	John Stefero	.05
564	Larry McWilliams	.05
565	Dusty Baker	.05
566	Tim Hulett	.05
567	*Greg Mathews*	.05
568	Earl Weaver	.10
569	Wade Rowdon	.05
570	Sid Fernandez	.05
571	Ozzie Virgil	.05
572	Pete Ladd	.05
573	Hal McRae	.05
574	Manny Lee	.05
575	Pat Tabler	.05
576	Frank Pastore	.05
577	Dann Bilardello	.05
578	Billy Hatcher	.05
579	Rick Burleson	.05
580	Mike Krukow	.05
581	Cubs Leaders (Ron Cey, Steve Trout)	.05
582	Bruce Berenyi	.05
583	Junior Ortiz	.05
584	Ron Kittle	.05
585	*Scott Bailes*	.05
586	Ben Oglivie	.05
587	Eric Plunk	.05
588	Wallace Johnson	.05
589	Steve Crawford	.05
590	Vince Coleman	.05
591	Spike Owen	.05
592	Chris Welsh	.05
593	Chuck Tanner	.05
594	Rick Anderson	.05
595	Keith Hernandez (All-Star)	.05
596	Steve Sax (All-Star)	.05
597	Mike Schmidt (All-Star)	.20
598	Ozzie Smith (All-Star)	.10
599	Tony Gwynn (All-Star)	.20
600	Dave Parker (All-Star)	.05
601	Darryl Strawberry (All-Star)	.05
602	Gary Carter (All-Star)	.05
603a	Dwight Gooden (All-Star, no trademark on front)	.25
603b	Dwight Gooden (All-Star, trademark on front)	.10
604	Fernando Valenzuela (All-Star)	.05
605	Todd Worrell (All-Star)	.05
606a	Don Mattingly (All-Star, no trademark on front)	.75
606b	Don Mattingly (All-Star, trademark on front)	.25
607	Tony Bernazard (All-Star)	.05
608	Wade Boggs (All-Star)	.20
609	Cal Ripken, Jr. (All-Star)	.60
610	Jim Rice (All-Star)	.05
611	Kirby Puckett (All-Star)	.40
612	George Bell (All-Star)	.05
613	Lance Parrish (All-Star)	.05
614	Roger Clemens (All-Star)	.20
615	Teddy Higuera (All-Star)	.05
616	Dave Righetti (All-Star)	.05
617	Al Nipper	.05
618	Tom Kelly	.05
619	Jerry Reed	.05
620	Jose Canseco	1.00
621	Danny Cox	.05
622	*Glenn Braggs*	.10
623	*Kurt Stillwell*	.05
624	Tim Burke	.05
625	Mookie Wilson	.05
626	Joel Skinner	.05
627	Ken Oberkfell	.05
628	Bob Walk	.05
629	Larry Parrish	.05
630	John Candelaria	.05
631	Tigers Leaders (Sparky Anderson, Mike Heath, Willie Hernandez)	.05
632	Rob Woodward	.05
633	Jose Uribe	.05
634	*Rafael Palmeiro*	1.50
635	Ken Schrom	.05
636	Darren Daulton	.10
637	*Bip Roberts*	.15
638	Rich Bordi	.05
639	Gerald Perry	.05
640	Mark Clear	.05
641	Domingo Ramos	.05
642	Al Pulido	.05
643	Ron Shepherd	.05
644	John Denny	.05
645	Dwight Evans	.05
646	Mike Mason	.05
647	Tom Lawless	.05
648	*Barry Larkin*	.75
649	Mickey Tettleton	.10
650	Hubie Brooks	.05
651	Benny Distefano	.05
652	Terry Forster	.05
653	Kevin Mitchell	.05
654	Checklist 529-660	.05
655	Jesse Barfield	.05
656	Rangers Leaders (Bobby Valentine, Rickey Wright)	.05
657	Tom Waddell	.05
658	*Robby Thompson*	.15
659	Aurelio Lopez	.05
660	Bob Horner	.05
661	Lou Whitaker	.05
662	Frank DiPino	.05
663	Cliff Johnson	.05
664	Mike Marshall	.05
665	Rod Scurry	.05
666	Von Hayes	.05
667	Ron Hassey	.05
668	Juan Bonilla	.05
669	Bud Black	.05
670	Jose Cruz	.05
671a	Ray Soff (no "D*" before copyright line)	.20
671b	Ray Soff ("D*" before copyright line)	.05
672	Chili Davis	.05
673	Don Sutton	.20
674	Bill Campbell	.05
675	Ed Romero	.05
676	Charlie Moore	.05
677	Bob Grich	.05
678	Carney Lansford	.05
679	Kent Hrbek	.05
680	Ryne Sandberg	.50
681	George Bell	.05
682	Jerry Reuss	.05
683	Gary Roenicke	.05
684	Kent Tekulve	.05
685	Jerry Hairston	.05
686	Doyle Alexander	.05
687	Alan Trammell	.10
688	Juan Beniquez	.05
689	Darrell Porter	.05
690	Dane Iorg	.05
691	Dave Parker	.10
692	Frank White	.05
693	Terry Puhl	.05
694	Phil Niekro	.25
695	Chico Walker	.05
696	Gary Lucas	.05
697	Ed Lynch	.05
698	Ernie Whitt	.05
699	Ken Landreaux	.05
700	Dave Bergman	.05
701	Willie Randolph	.05
702	Greg Gross	.05
703	Dave Schmidt	.05
704	Jesse Orosco	.05
705	Bruce Hurst	.05
706	Rick Manning	.05
707	Bob McClure	.05
708	Scott McGregor	.05
709	Dave Kingman	.05
710	Gary Gaetti	.05
711	Ken Griffey	.05
712	Don Robinson	.05
713	Tom Brookens	.05
714	Dan Quisenberry	.05
715	Bob Dernier	.05
716	Rick Leach	.05
717	Ed Vande Berg	.05
718	Steve Carlton	.20
719	Tom Hume	.05
720	Richard Dotson	.05
721	Tom Herr	.05
722	Bob Knepper	.05
723	Brett Butler	.05
724	Greg Minton	.05
725	George Hendrick	.05
726	Frank Tanana	.05
727	Mike Moore	.05
728	Tippy Martinez	.05
729	Tom Paciorek	.05
730	Eric Show	.05
731	Dave Concepcion	.05
732	Manny Trillo	.05
733	Bill Caudill	.05
734	Bill Madlock	.05
735	Rickey Henderson	.25
736	Steve Bedrosian	.05
737	Floyd Bannister	.05
738	Jorge Orta	.05
739	Chet Lemon	.05
740	Rich Gedman	.05
741	Paul Molitor	.25
742	Andy McGaffigan	.05
743	Dwayne Murphy	.05
744	Roy Smalley	.05
745	Glenn Hubbard	.05
746	Bob Ojeda	.05
747	Johnny Ray	.05
748	Mike Flanagan	.05
749	Ozzie Smith	.40
750	Steve Trout	.05
751	Garth Iorg	.05
752	Dan Petry	.05
753	Rick Honeycutt	.05
754	Dave LaPoint	.05
755	Luis Aguayo	.05
756	Carlton Fisk	.20
757	Nolan Ryan	.75
758	Tony Bernazard	.05
759	Joel Youngblood	.05
760	Mike Witt	.05
761	Greg Pryor	.05
762	Gary Ward	.05
763	Tim Flannery	.05
764	Bill Buckner	.05
765	Kirk Gibson	.05
766	Don Aase	.05
767	Ron Cey	.05
768	Dennis Lamp	.05
769	Steve Sax	.05
770	Dave Winfield	.20
771	Shane Rawley	.05
772	Harold Baines	.05
773	Robin Yount	.30
774	Wayne Krenchicki	.05
775	Joaquin Andujar	.05
776	Tom Brunansky	.05
777	Chris Chambliss	.05
778	Jack Morris	.05
779	Craig Reynolds	.05
780	Andre Thornton	.05
781	Atlee Hammaker	.05
782	Brian Downing	.05
783	Willie Wilson	.05
784	Cal Ripken, Jr.	.75
785	Terry Francona	.05
786	Jimy Williams	.05
787	Alejandro Pena	.05
788	Tim Stoddard	.05
789	Dan Schatzeder	.05
790	Julio Cruz	.05
791	Lance Parrish	.05
792	Checklist 661-792	.05

1987 Topps Tiffany

Produced in much greater quantity (reportedly 30,000 sets) than the previous years' sets, this specially boxed collectors edition differs from the regular 1987 Topps cards only in its use of white cardboard stock and a high-gloss finish on the cards' fronts.

	MT
Complete Set (792):	110.00
Common Player:	.15
(Star cards valued at 3X-5X corresponding cards in regular 1987 Topps)	

1987 Topps Traded

The Topps Traded set consists of 132 cards as have all Traded sets issued by Topps since 1981. The cards measure the standard 2-1/2" x 3-1/2" and are identical in design to the regular edition set. The purpose of the set is to update player trades and feature rookies not included in the regular issue. As they had done the previous three years, Topps produced a glossy-coated "Tiffany" edition of the Traded set. The Tiffany edition cards are valued at two to three times greater than the regular Traded cards. Cards are numbered with a "T" suffix.

		MT
Complete Set (132):		7.00
Common Player:		.08
1	Bill Almon	.08
2	Scott Bankhead	.08
3	Eric Bell	.08
4	Juan Beniquez	.08
5	Juan Berenguer	.08
6	Greg Booker	.08
7	Thad Bosley	.08
8	Larry Bowa	.08
9	Greg Brock	.08
10	Bob Brower	.08
11	Jerry Browne	.10
12	Ralph Bryant	.08
13	DeWayne Buice	.08
14	Ellis Burks	.50
15	Ivan Calderon	.08
16	Jeff Calhoun	.08
17	Casey Candaele	.08
18	John Cangelosi	.08
19	Steve Carlton	.30
20	Juan Castillo	.08
21	Rick Cerone	.08
22	Ron Cey	.08
23	John Christensen	.08
24	Dave Cone	1.00
25	Chuck Crim	.08
26	Storm Davis	.08
27	Andre Dawson	.25
28	Rick Dempsey	.08
29	Doug Drabek	.15
30	Mike Dunne	.08
31	Dennis Eckersley	.25
32	Lee Elia	.08
33	Brian Fisher	.08
34	Terry Francona	.08
35	Willie Fraser	.08
36	Billy Gardner	.08
37	Ken Gerhart	.08
38	Danny Gladden	.08
39	Jim Gott	.08
40	Cecilio Guante	.08
41	Albert Hall	.08
42	Terry Harper	.08
43	Mickey Hatcher	.08
44	Brad Havens	.08
45	Neal Heaton	.08
46	Mike Henneman	.20
47	Donnie Hill	.08
48	Guy Hoffman	.08
49	Brian Holton	.08
50	Charles Hudson	.08
51	Danny Jackson	.08
52	Reggie Jackson	.50
53	Chris James	.08
54	Dion James	.08
55	Stan Jefferson	.08
56	Joe Johnson	.08
57	Terry Kennedy	.08
58	Mike Kingery	.08
59	Ray Knight	.08
60	Gene Larkin	.10
61	Mike LaValliere	.08
62	Jack Lazorko	.08
63	Terry Leach	.08
64	Tim Leary	.08
65	Jim Lindeman	.08
66	Steve Lombardozzi	.08
67	Bill Long	.08
68	Barry Lyons	.08
69	Shane Mack	.10
70	*Greg Maddux*	4.00
71	Bill Madlock	.08
72	Joe Magrane	.08
73	Dave Martinez	.08
74	Fred McGriff	.50
75	Mark McLemore	.15
76	Kevin McReynolds	.10
77	Dave Meads	.08
78	Eddie Milner	.08
79	Greg Minton	.08
80	John Mitchell	.08
81	Kevin Mitchell	.10
82	Charlie Moore	.08
83	Jeff Musselman	.08
84	Gene Nelson	.08
85	Graig Nettles	.08
86	Al Newman	.08
87	Reid Nichols	.08
88	Tom Niedenfuer	.08
89	Joe Niekro	.08
90	Tom Nieto	.08
91	Matt Nokes	.10
92	Dickie Noles	.08
93	Pat Pacillo	.08
94	Lance Parrish	.10
95	Tony Pena	.08
96	Luis Polonia	.08
97	Randy Ready	.08
98	Jeff Reardon	.08
99	Gary Redus	.08
100	Jeff Reed	.08
101	Rick Rhoden	.08
102	Cal Ripken, Sr.	.08
103	Wally Ritchie	.08
104	Jeff Robinson	.08
105	Gary Roenicke	.08
106	Jerry Royster	.08
107	Mark Salas	.08
108	Luis Salazar	.08
109	Benny Santiago	.25
110	Dave Schmidt	.08
111	Kevin Seitzer	.10
112	John Shelby	.08
113	Steve Shields	.08
114	John Smiley	.20
115	Chris Speier	.08
116	Mike Stanley	.10
117	Terry Steinbach	.25
118	Les Straker	.08
119	Jim Sundberg	.08
120	Danny Tartabull	.10
121	Tom Trebelhorn	.08
122	Dave Valle	.08
123	Ed Vande Berg	.08
124	Andy Van Slyke	.08
125	Gary Ward	.08
126	Alan Wiggins	.08
127	Bill Wilkinson	.08
128	Frank Williams	.08
129	*Matt Williams*	1.50
130	Jim Winn	.08
131	Matt Young	.08
132	Checklist 1T-132T	.08

1987 Topps Traded Tiffany

The cards in this specially boxed limited edition version of the Traded set differ from the regular-issue cards only in the application of a high-gloss finish to the cards' fronts. Production was reported as 30,000 sets.

	MT
Complete Set (132):	50.00
Common Player:	.25
(Star cards valued at 2X-3X corresponding cards in regular Topps Traded)	

1987 Topps Box Panels

Offering baseball cards on retail boxes for a second straight year, Topps reduced the size of the cards to 2-1/8" x 3". Four different wax pack boxes were available, each featuring two cards that were placed on the sides of the boxes. The card fronts are identical in design to the regular issue cards. The backs are printed in blue and yellow and carry a commentary imitating a newspaper format. The cards are numbered A through H.

		MT
Complete Singles Set (8):		1.00
Complete Panel Set (4):		4.00
Common Panel:		.75
Common Single Player:		.15
Panel		1.00
A	Don Baylor	.15
B	Steve Carlton	.30
Panel		.75
C	Ron Cey	.15
D	Cecil Cooper	.15
Panel		1.00
E	Rickey Henderson	.30
F	Jim Rice	.20
Panel		1.25
G	Don Sutton	.25
H	Dave Winfield	.35

1987 Topps All-Star Glossy Set of 22

For the fourth consecutive year, Topps produced an All-Star Game commemorative set of 22 cards. The glossy cards, 2-1/2" x 3-1/2", were included in rack packs. Using the same basic design as in previous efforts with a few minor changes, the 1987 edition features American and National League logos on the card fronts. Cards #1-12 feature representatives from the American League, while #13-22 are National Leaguers.

		MT
Complete Set (22):		4.00
Common Player:		.15
1	Whitey Herzog	.15
2	Keith Hernandez	.15
3	Ryne Sandberg	.50
4	Mike Schmidt	.70
5	Ozzie Smith	.50
6	Tony Gwynn	.75
7	Dale Murphy	.25
8	Darryl Strawberry	.20
9	Gary Carter	.25
10	Dwight Gooden	.20
11	Fernando Valenzuela	.15
12	Dick Howser	.15
13	Wally Joyner	.25
14	Lou Whitaker	.15
15	Wade Boggs	.40
16	Cal Ripken, Jr.	1.00
17	Dave Winfield	.40
18	Rickey Henderson	.35
19	Kirby Puckett	.50
20	Lance Parrish	.15
21	Roger Clemens	.50
22	Teddy Higuera	.15

1987 Topps All-Star Glossy Set of 60

Using the same design as the previous year, the 1987 Topps All-Star glossy set includes 48 All-Star performers plus 12 potential superstars branded as "Hot Prospects". The card fronts are uncluttered, save the player's name found in very small print at the bottom. The set was available via a mail-in offer. Six subsets make up the 60-card set, with each subset being available for $1.00 plus six special offer cards that were found in wax packs.

		MT
Complete Set (60):		12.00
Common Player:		.15
1	Don Mattingly	.90
2	Tony Gwynn	.75
3	Gary Gaetti	.15
4	Glenn Davis	.15
5	Roger Clemens	.60
6	Dale Murphy	.25
7	Lou Whitaker	.15
8	Roger McDowell	.15
9	Cory Snyder	.15
10	Todd Worrell	.15
11	Gary Carter	.20
12	Eddie Murray	.45
13	Bob Knepper	.15
14	Harold Baines	.15
15	Jeff Reardon	.15
16	Joe Carter	.15
17	Dave Parker	.20
18	Wade Boggs	.60
19	Danny Tartabull	.15
20	Jim Deshaies	.15
21	Rickey Henderson	.50
22	Rob Deer	.15
23	Ozzie Smith	.60
24	Dave Righetti	.15
25	Kent Hrbek	.20
26	Keith Hernandez	.15
27	Don Baylor	.20
28	Mike Schmidt	.75
29	Pete Incaviglia	.20
30	Barry Bonds	1.00
31	George Brett	.75
32	Darryl Strawberry	.20
33	Mike Witt	.15
34	Kevin Bass	.15
35	Jesse Barfield	.15
36	Bob Ojeda	.15
37	Cal Ripken, Jr.	2.00
38	Vince Coleman	.15
39	Wally Joyner	.20
40	Robby Thompson	.15
41	Pete Rose	.90
42	Jim Rice	.20
43	Tony Bernazard	.15
44	Eric Davis	.20
45	George Bell	.15
46	Hubie Brooks	.15
47	Jack Morris	.15
48	Tim Raines	.20
49	Mark Eichhorn	.15
50	Kevin Mitchell	.15
51	Dwight Gooden	.20
52	Doug DeCinces	.15
53	Fernando Valenzuela	.15
54	Reggie Jackson	.50
55	Johnny Ray	.15
56	Mike Pagliarulo	.15
57	Kirby Puckett	.75
58	Lance Parrish	.15
59	Jose Canseco	.45
60	Greg Mathews	.15

1987 Topps Baseball Highlights

The "Baseball Highlights" boxed set of 33 cards was prepared by Topps for distribution at stores in the Woolworth's chain, although the retailer's name does not appear on the cards. Each card measures 2-1/2" x 3-1/2" in size and features a memorable baseball event that occurred during the 1986 season. The glossy set sold for $1.99.

		MT
Complete Set (33):		4.00
Common Player:		.10
1	Steve Carlton	.30
2	Cecil Cooper	.10
3	Rickey Henderson	.35
4	Reggie Jackson	.30
5	Jim Rice	.15
6	Don Sutton	.25
7	Roger Clemens	.75
8	Mike Schmidt	.75
9	Jesse Barfield	.10
10	Wade Boggs	.50
11	Tim Raines	.15
12	Jose Canseco	.35
13	Todd Worrell	.10
14	Dave Righetti	.10
15	Don Mattingly	.90
16	Tony Gwynn	.50
17	Marty Barrett	.10
18	Mike Scott	.10
19	World Series Game #1 (Bruce Hurst)	.10
20	World Series Game #1 (Calvin Schiraldi)	.10
21	World Series Game #2 (Dwight Evans)	.10
22	World Series Game #2 (Dave Henderson)	.10
23	World Series Game #3 (Len Dykstra)	.10
24	World Series Game #3 (Bob Ojeda)	.10
25	World Series Game #4 (Gary Carter)	.10
26	World Series Game #4 (Ron Darling)	.10
27	Jim Rice	.15
28	Bruce Hurst	.10
29	World Series Game #6 (Darryl Strawberry)	.20
30	World Series Game #6 (Ray Knight)	.10
31	World Series Game #6 (Keith Hernandez)	.10
32	World Series Games #7 (Mets Celebrate)	.10
33	Ray Knight	.10

1987 Topps Coins

For the first time since 1971, Topps issued a set of baseball "coins." Similar in design to the 1964 edition, the metal discs measure 1-1/2" in diameter. The aluminum coins were sold on a limited basis in retail outlets. Three coins and three sticks of gum were found in a pack. The coin fronts feature a full-color photo along with the player's name, team and position in a white band at the bottom. Gold-colored rims are found for American League players; National League players have silver-colored rims. Backs are silvered and carry the coin number, player's name and personal and statistical information.

		MT
Complete Set (48):		12.50
Common Player:		.15
1	Harold Baines	.15
2	Jesse Barfield	.15
3	George Bell	.15
4	Wade Boggs	.50
5	George Brett	.75
6	Jose Canseco	.50
7	Joe Carter	.15
8	Roger Clemens	.65
9	Alvin Davis	.15
10	Rob Deer	.15
11	Kirk Gibson	.15
12	Rickey Henderson	.40
13	Kent Hrbek	.15
14	Pete Incaviglia	.15
15	Reggie Jackson	.45
16	Wally Joyner	.20
17	Don Mattingly	.75
18	Jack Morris	.15
19	Eddie Murray	.45
20	Kirby Puckett	.50
21	Jim Rice	.20
22	Dave Righetti	.15
23	Cal Ripken, Jr.	2.00
24	Cory Snyder	.15
25	Danny Tartabull	.15
26	Dave Winfield	.45
27	Hubie Brooks	.15
28	Gary Carter	.25
29	Vince Coleman	.15
30	Eric Davis	.15
31	Glenn Davis	.15
32	Steve Garvey	.25
33	Dwight Gooden	.20
34	Tony Gwynn	.65
35	Von Hayes	.15
36	Keith Hernandez	.15
37	Dale Murphy	.25
38	Dave Parker	.15
39	Tony Pena	.15
40	Nolan Ryan	2.00
41	Ryne Sandberg	.90
42	Steve Sax	.15
43	Mike Schmidt	.75
44	Mike Scott	.15
45	Ozzie Smith	.45
46	Darryl Strawberry	.15
47	Fernando Valenzuela	.15
48	Todd Worrell	.15

1987 Topps Gallery of Champions

Designed as a tribute to 1986's winners of baseball's most prestigious awards, the Gallery of Champions are metal "cards" that are one-quarter size replicas of the regular issue Topps cards. The bronze and silver sets were issued in leather-like velvet-lined display cases; the aluminum sets came cello-wrapped. Hobby dealers who purchased one bronze set or a 16-set case of aluminum "cards" received one free Jose Canseco pewter metal mini-card. The purchase of a silver set included five Canseco pewters. A 1953 Willie Mays bronze was given to dealers who brought cases of 1987 Topps Traded sets.

		MT
Complete Aluminum Set (12):		40.00
Complete Bronze Set (12):		125.00
Complete Silver Set (12):		250.00
(1a)	Jesse Barfield (aluminum)	2.50
(1b)	Jesse Barfield (bronze)	7.50
(1s)	Jesse Barfield (silver)	15.00
(2a)	Wade Boggs (aluminum)	5.00
(2b)	Wade Boggs (bronze)	15.00
(2s)	Wade Boggs (silver)	30.00
(3a)	Jose Canseco (aluminum)	5.00
(3b)	Jose Canseco (bronze)	15.00
(3s)	Jose Canseco (silver)	30.00
(3p)	Jose Canseco (pewter)	15.00
(4a)	Joe Carter (aluminum)	3.00
(4b)	Joe Carter (bronze)	8.75
(4s)	Joe Carter (silver)	17.50
(5a)	Roger Clemens (aluminum)	6.00
(5b)	Roger Clemens (bronze)	17.50
(5s)	Roger Clemens (silver)	37.00
(6a)	Tony Gwynn (aluminum)	6.00
(6b)	Tony Gwynn (bronze)	17.50
(6s)	Tony Gwynn (silver)	37.00
(7a)	Don Mattingly (aluminum)	7.50
(7b)	Don Mattingly (bronze)	25.00
(7s)	Don Mattingly (silver)	75.00
(8a)	Tim Raines (aluminum)	2.50
(8b)	Tim Raines (bronze)	7.50
(8s)	Tim Raines (silver)	15.00
(9a)	Dave Righetti (aluminum)	2.50
(9b)	Dave Righetti (bronze)	7.50
(9s)	Dave Righetti (silver)	15.00
(10a)	Mike Schmidt (aluminum)	6.00
(10b)	Mike Schmidt (bronze)	20.00
(10s)	Mike Schmidt (silver)	50.00
(11a)	Mike Scott (aluminum)	2.50
(11b)	Mike Scott (bronze)	7.50
(11s)	Mike Scott (silver)	15.00
(12a)	Todd Worrell (aluminum)	2.50
(12b)	Todd Worrell (bronze)	7.50
(12s)	Todd Worrell (silver)	15.00
(13)	Willie Mays (1953, bronze)	12.50

1987 Topps Glossy Rookies

The 1987 Topps Glossy Rookies set of 22 cards was introduced with Topps' new 100-card "Jumbo Packs". Intended for sale in supermarkets, the jumbo packs contained one glossy card. Measuring the standard 2-1/2" x 3-1/2" size, the special insert cards feature the top rookies from the previous season.

		MT
Complete Set (22):		4.00
Common Player:		.10
1	Andy Allanson	.10
2	John Cangelosi	.10
3	Jose Canseco	2.00
4	Will Clark	1.50
5	Mark Eichhorn	.10
6	Pete Incaviglia	.15
7	Wally Joyner	.30
8	Eric King	.10
9	Dave Magadan	.10
10	John Morris	.10
11	Juan Nieves	.10
12	Rafael Palmeiro	1.50
13	Billy Jo Robidoux	.10
14	Bruce Ruffin	.10
15	Ruben Sierra	.10
16	Cory Snyder	.10
17	Kurt Stillwell	.10
18	Dale Sveum	.10
19	Danny Tartabull	.10
20	Andres Thomas	.10
21	Robby Thompson	.10
22	Todd Worrell	.10

1987 Topps Mini League Leaders

Returning for 1987, the Topps "Major League Leaders" set was increased in size from 66 to 76 cards. The 2-1/8" x 3" cards feature woodgrain borders that encompass a white-bordered color photo. Backs are printed in yellow, orange and brown and list the player's official ranking based on his 1986 American or National League statistics. The players featured are those who finished the top five in their leagues' various batting and pitching categories. The cards were sold in plastic-wrapped packs, seven cards plus a game card per pack.

		MT
Complete Set (77):		4.00
Common Player:		.05
1	Bob Horner	.05
2	Dale Murphy	.15
3	Lee Smith	.05
4	Eric Davis	.05
5	John Franco	.05
6	Dave Parker	.05
7	Kevin Bass	.05
8	Glenn Davis	.05
9	Bill Doran	.05
10	Bob Knepper	.05
11	Mike Scott	.05
12	Dave Smith	.05
13	Mariano Duncan	.05
14	Orel Hershiser	.05
15	Steve Sax	.05
16	Fernando Valenzuela	.05
17	Tim Raines	.10
18	Jeff Reardon	.05
19	Floyd Youmans	.05
20	Gary Carter	.10
21	Ron Darling	.05
22	Sid Fernandez	.05
23	Dwight Gooden	.05
24	Keith Hernandez	.05
25	Bob Ojeda	.05
26	Darryl Strawberry	.10
27	Steve Bedrosian	.05
28	Von Hayes	.05
29	Juan Samuel	.05
30	Mike Schmidt	.40
31	Rick Rhoden	.05
32	Vince Coleman	.05
33	Danny Cox	.05
34	Todd Worrell	.05
35	Tony Gwynn	.40
36	Mike Krukow	.05
37	Candy Maldonado	.05
38	Don Aase	.05
39	Eddie Murray	.20
40	Cal Ripken, Jr.	1.00
41	Wade Boggs	.30
42	Roger Clemens	.45
43	Bruce Hurst	.05
44	Jim Rice	.10
45	Wally Joyner	.10
46	Donnie Moore	.05
47	Gary Pettis	.05
48	Mike Witt	.05
49	John Cangelosi	.05
50	Tom Candiotti	.05
51	Joe Carter	.05
52	Pat Tabler	.05
53	Kirk Gibson	.05
54	Willie Hernandez	.05
55	Jack Morris	.05
56	Alan Trammell	.05
57	George Brett	.45
58	Willie Wilson	.05
59	Rob Deer	.05
60	Teddy Higuera	.05
61	Bert Blyleven	.05
62	Gary Gaetti	.05
63	Kirby Puckett	.40
64	Rickey Henderson	.20
65	Don Mattingly	.45
66	Dennis Rasmussen	.05
67	Dave Righetti	.05
68	Jose Canseco	.30
69	Dave Kingman	.05
70	Phil Bradley	.05
71	Mark Langston	.05
72	Pete O'Brien	.05
73	Jesse Barfield	.05
74	George Bell	.05
75	Tony Fernandez	.05
76	Tom Henke	.05
77	Checklist	.05

1987 Topps Stickers

For the seventh consecutive year, Topps issued stickers to be housed in a specially designed yearbook. The 2-1/8" x 3" stickers offer a full-color front with a peel-off back printed in blue. Fronts feature either one full-size player picture or two half-size individual stickers. The yearbook contains 36 glossy, magazine-style pages, all printed in full color. Mike Schmidt, 1986 National League MVP, is featured on the covers. The yearbook sold in retail outlets for 35¢, while stickers were sold five in a pack for 25¢. The number in parentheses in the following checklist is the sticker number the player shares the sticker with. Besides the common soft-back sticker made for Topps by Panini, there was a test issue of hard-back stickercards, valued at 2x to 3x the price of the regular stickers.

		MT
Complete Set (313):		18.00
Common Player:		.05
Sticker Album:		1.50
1	1986 Highlights (Jim Deshaies) (172)	.05
2	1986 Highlights (Roger Clemens) (175)	.25
3	1986 Highlights (Roger Clemens) (176)	.25
4	1986 Highlights (Dwight Evans) (177)	.05
5	1986 Highlights (Dwight Gooden) (178)	.05
6	1986 Highlights (Dwight Gooden) (180)	.05
7	1986 Highlights (Dave Lopes) (181)	.05
8	1986 Highlights (Dave Righetti) (182)	.05
9	1986 Highlights (Dave Righetti) (183)	.05
10	1986 Highlights (Ruben Sierra) (185)	.05
11	1986 Highlights (Todd Worrell) (186)	.05
12	1986 Highlights (Todd Worrell) (187)	.05
13	N.L. Championship Series (Lenny Dykstra)	.10
14	N.L. Championship Series (Gary Carter)	.05
15	N.L. Championship Series (Mike Scott)	.05
16	A.L. Championship Series (Gary Pettis)	.05
17	A.L. Championship Series (Jim Rice)	.05
18	A.L. Championship Series (Bruce Hurst)	.05
19	1986 World Series (Bruce Hurst)	.05
20	1986 World Series (Wade Boggs)	.10
21	1986 World Series (Lenny Dykstra)	.10
22	1986 World Series (Gary Carter)	.05
23	1986 World Series (Dave Henderson)	.05
24	1986 World Series (Howard Johnson)	.05
25	1986 World Series (Mets Celebrate)	.05
26	Glenn Davis	.05
27	Nolan Ryan (188)	.75
28	Charlie Kerfeld (189)	.05
29	Jose Cruz (190)	.05
30	Phil Garner (191)	.05
31	Bill Doran (192)	.05
32	Bob Knepper (195)	.05
33	Denny Walling (196)	.05
34	Kevin Bass (197)	.05
35	Mike Scott	.05
36	Dale Murphy	.12
37	Paul Assenmacher (198)	.05
38	Ken Oberkfell (200)	.05
39	Andres Thomas (201)	.05
40	Gene Garber (202)	.05
41	Bob Horner	.05
42	Rafael Ramirez (203)	.05
43	Rick Mahler (204)	.05
44	Omar Moreno (205)	.05
45	Dave Palmer (206)	.05
46	Ozzie Smith	.35
47	Bob Forsch (207)	.05
48	Willie McGee (209)	.05
49	Tom Herr (210)	.05
50	Vince Coleman (211)	.05
51	Andy Van Slyke (212)	.05
52	Jack Clark (215)	.05
53	John Tudor (216)	.05
54	Terry Pendleton (217)	.05
55	Todd Worrell	.05
56	Lee Smith	.05
57	Leon Durham (218)	.05
58	Jerry Mumphrey (219)	.05
59	Shawon Dunston (220)	.10
60	Scott Sanderson (221)	.05
61	Ryne Sandberg	.25
62	Gary Matthews (222)	.05
63	Dennis Eckersley (225)	.05
64	Jody Davis (226)	.05
65	Keith Moreland (227)	.05
66	Mike Marshall (228)	.05
67	Bill Madlock (229)	.05
68	Greg Brock (230)	.05
69	Pedro Guerrero (231)	.05
70	Steve Sax	.05
71	Rick Honeycutt (232)	.05
72	Franklin Stubbs (235)	.05
73	Mike Scioscia (236)	.05
74	Mariano Duncan (237)	.05
75	Fernando Valenzuela	.05
76	Hubie Brooks	.05
77	Andre Dawson (238)	.10
78	Tim Burke (240)	.05
79	Floyd Youmans (241)	.05
80	Tim Wallach (242)	.05
81	Jeff Reardon (243)	.05
82	Mitch Webster (244)	.05
83	Bryn Smith (245)	.05
84	Andres Galarraga (246)	.12
85	Tim Raines	.12
86	Chris Brown	.05
87	Bob Brenly (247)	.05
88	Will Clark (249)	.35
89	Scott Garrelts (250)	.05
90	Jeffrey Leonard (251)	.05
91	Robby Thompson (252)	.05
92	Mike Krukow (255)	.05
93	Danny Gladden (256)	.05
94	Candy Maldonado (257)	.05
95	Chili Davis	.05
96	Dwight Gooden	.12
97	Sid Fernandez (258)	.05
98	Len Dykstra (259)	.10
99	Bob Ojeda (260)	.05
100	Wally Backman (261)	.05
101	Gary Carter	.15
102	Keith Hernandez (262)	.05
103	Darryl Strawberry (265)	.10
104	Roger McDowell (266)	.05
105	Ron Darling (267)	.05
106	Tony Gwynn	.35
107	Dave Dravecky (268)	.05
108	Terry Kennedy (269)	.05
109	Rich Gossage (270)	.05
110	Garry Templeton (271)	.05
111	Lance McCullers (272)	.05
112	Eric Show (275)	.05
113	John Kruk (276)	.05
114	Tim Flannery (277)	.05
115	Steve Garvey	.15
116	Mike Schmidt	.35
117	Glenn Wilson (278)	.05
118	Kent Tekulve (280)	.05
119	Gary Redus (281)	.05
120	Shane Rawley (282)	.05
121	Von Hayes	.05
122	Don Carman (283)	.05
123	Bruce Ruffin (285)	.05
124	Steve Bedrosian (286)	.05
125	Juan Samuel (287)	.05
126	Sid Bream (288)	.05
127	Cecilio Guante (289)	.05
128	Rick Reuschel (290)	.05
129	Tony Pena (291)	.05
130	Rick Rhoden	.05
131	Barry Bonds (292)	.40
132	Joe Orsulak (295)	.05
133	Jim Morrison (296)	.05
134	R.J. Reynolds (297)	.05
135	Johnny Ray	.05
136	Eric Davis	.10
137	Tom Browning (298)	.05
138	John Franco (300)	.05
139	Pete Rose (301)	.35
140	Bill Gullickson (302)	.05
141	Ron Oester (303)	.05
142	Bo Diaz (304)	.05
143	Buddy Bell (305)	.05
144	Eddie Milner (306)	.05
145	Dave Parker	.05
146	Kirby Puckett	.35
147	Rickey Henderson	.20
148	Wade Boggs	.25
149	Lance Parrish	.05
150	Wally Joyner	.10
151	Cal Ripken, Jr.	.75
152	Dave Winfield	.30
153	Lou Whitaker	.05
154	Roger Clemens	.35
155	Tony Gwynn	.35
156	Ryne Sandberg	.35
157	Keith Hernandez	.05
158	Gary Carter	.10
159	Darryl Strawberry	.15
160	Mike Schmidt	.35
161	Dale Murphy	.15
162	Ozzie Smith	.35
163	Dwight Gooden	.10
164	Jose Canseco	.30
165	Curt Young (307)	.05
166	Alfredo Griffin (308)	.05
167	Dave Stewart (309)	.05
168	Mike Davis (310)	.05
169	Bruce Bochte (311)	.05
170	Dwayne Murphy (312)	.05
171	Carney Lansford (313)	.05
172	Joaquin Andujar (1)	.05
173	Dave Kingman	.05
174	Wally Joyner	.10
175	Gary Pettis (2)	.05
176	Dick Schofield (3)	.05
177	Donnie Moore (4)	.05
178	Brian Downing (5)	.05
179	Mike Witt	.05
180	Bob Boone (6)	.05
181	Kirk McCaskill (7)	.05
182	Doug DeCinces (8)	.05
183	Don Sutton (9)	.20
184	Jessie Barfield	.05
185	Tom Henke (10)	.05
186	Willie Upshaw (11)	.05
187	Mark Eichhorn (12)	.05
188	Damaso Garcia (27)	.05
189	Jim Clancy (28)	.05
190	Lloyd Moseby (29)	.05
191	Tony Fernandez (30)	.05
192	Jimmy Key (31)	.05
193	George Bell	.05
194	Rob Deer	.05
195	Mark Clear (32)	.05
196	Robin Yount (33)	.35
197	Jim Gantner (34)	.05
198	Cecil Cooper (37)	.05
199	Teddy Higuera	.05
200	Paul Molitor (38)	.30
201	Dan Plesac (39)	.05
202	Billy Jo Robidoux (40)	.05
203	Earnie Riles (42)	.05
204	Ken Schrom (43)	.05
205	Pat Tabler (44)	.05
206	Mel Hall (45)	.05
207	Tony Bernazard (47)	.05
208	Joe Carter	.10
209	Ernie Camacho (48)	.05
210	Julio Franco (49)	.05
211	Tom Candiotti (50)	.05
212	Brook Jacoby (51)	.05
213	Cory Snyder	.05
214	Jim Presley	.05
215	Mike Moore (52)	.05
216	Harold Reynolds (53)	.05
217	Scott Bradley (54)	.05
218	Matt Young (57)	.05
219	Mark Langston (58)	.05
220	Alvin Davis (59)	.05
221	Phil Bradley (60)	.05
222	Ken Phelps (62)	.05
223	Danny Tartabull	.05
224	Eddie Murray	.25
225	Rick Dempsey (63)	.05
226	Fred Lynn (64)	.05
227	Mike Boddicker (65)	.05
228	Don Aase (66)	.05
229	Larry Sheets (67)	.05
230	Storm Davis (68)	.05
231	Lee Lacy (69)	.05
232	Jim Traber (71)	.05
233	Cal Ripken, Jr.	.75
234	Larry Parrish	.05
235	Gary Ward (72)	.05
236	Pete Incaviglia (73)	.05
237	Scott Fletcher (74)	.05
238	Greg Harris (77)	.05
239	Pete O'Brien	.05
240	Charlie Hough (78)	.05
241	Don Slaught (79)	.05
242	Steve Buechele (80)	.05
243	Oddibe McDowell (81)	.05
244	Roger Clemens (82)	.35
245	Bob Stanley (83)	.05
246	Tom Seaver (84)	.20
247	Rich Gedman (87)	.05
248	Jim Rice	.10
249	Dennis Boyd (88)	.05
250	Bill Buckner (89)	.05
251	Dwight Evans (90)	.05
252	Don Baylor (91)	.05
253	Wade Boggs	.25
254	George Brett	.35
255	Steve Farr (92)	.05
256	Jim Sundberg (93)	.05
257	Dan Quisenberry (94)	.05
258	Charlie Leibrandt (97)	.05
259	Argenis Salazar (98)	.05
260	Frank White (99)	.05
261	Willie Wilson (100)	.05
262	Lonnie Smith (102)	.05
263	Steve Balboni	.05
264	Darrell Evans	.05
265	Johnny Grubb (103)	.05
266	Jack Morris (104)	.05
267	Lou Whitaker (105)	.05
268	Chet Lemon (107)	.05
269	Lance Parrish (108)	.05
270	Alan Trammell (109)	.10
271	Darnell Coles (110)	.05
272	Willie Hernandez (111)	.05
273	Kirk Gibson	.05
274	Kirby Puckett	.35
275	Mike Smithson (112)	.05
276	Mickey Hatcher (113)	.05
277	Frank Viola (114)	.05
278	Bert Blyleven (117)	.05
279	Gary Gaetti	.05
280	Tom Brunansky (118)	.05
281	Kent Hrbek (119)	.05
282	Roy Smalley (120)	.05
283	Greg Gagne (122)	.05
284	Harold Baines	.05
285	Ron Hassey (123)	.05
286	Floyd Bannister (124)	.05
287	Ozzie Guillen (125)	.05
288	Carlton Fisk (126)	.25
289	Tim Hulett (127)	.05
290	Joe Cowley (128)	.05
291	Greg Walker (129)	.05
292	Neil Allen (131)	.05
293	John Cangelosi	.05
294	Don Mattingly	.40
295	Mike Easler (132)	.05
296	Rickey Henderson (133)	.20
297	Dan Pasqua (134)	.05
298	Dave Winfield (137)	.15
299	Dave Righetti	.05
300	Mike Pagliarulo (138)	.05
301	Ron Guidry (139)	.05
302	Willie Randolph (140)	.05
303	Dennis Rasmussen (141)	.05
304	Jose Canseco (142)	.30
305	Andres Thomas (143)	.05
306	Danny Tartabull (144)	.05
307	Robby Thompson (165)	.05
308	Pete Incaviglia, Cory Snyder (166)	.05
309	Dale Sveum (167)	.05
310	Todd Worrell (168)	.05
311	Andy Allanson (169)	.05
312	Bruce Ruffin (170)	.05

313 Wally Joyner (171) .10

1988 Topps

The 1988 Topps set features a clean, attractive design. The full-color player photo is surrounded by a thin color frame which is encompassed by a white border. The player's name appears in the lower-right corner in a diagonal colored strip. The team nickname is in large letters at the top of the card. Backs feature black print on orange and gray stock and include the usual player personal and career statistics. Many of the cards contain a new feature titled "This Way To The Clubhouse", which explains how the player joined his current team. The 792-card set includes a number of special subsets including "Future Stars", "Turn Back The Clock", All-Star teams, All-Star rookie selections, and Record Breakers. All cards measure 2-1/2" x 3-1/2".

MT
Complete Set (792): 15.00
Common Player: .05
Wax Box: 8.00
1 Vince Coleman (Record Breakers) .05
2 Don Mattingly (Record Breakers) .15
3a Mark McGwire (Record Breakers, white triangle by left foot) 1.00
3b Mark McGwire (Record Breakers, no white triangle) .50
4a Eddie Murray (Record Breakers, no mention of record on front) .25
4b Eddie Murray (Record Breakers, record in box on front) .20
5 Joe Niekro, Phil Niekro (Record Breakers) .10
6 Nolan Ryan (Record Breakers) .40
7 Benito Santiago (Record Breakers) .05
8 Kevin Elster (Future Stars) .05
9 Andy Hawkins .05
10 Ryne Sandberg .40
11 Mike Young .05
12 Bill Schroeder .05
13 Andres Thomas .05
14 Sparky Anderson .10
15 Chili Davis .05
16 Kirk McCaskill .05
17 Ron Oester .05
18a *Al Leiter* (Future Stars, no "NY" on shirt, photo actually Steve George) .40
18b *Al Leiter* (Future Stars, "NY" on shirt, correct photo) .10
19 *Mark Davidson* .05
20 Kevin Gross .05
21 Red Sox Leaders (Wade Boggs, Spike Owen) .10
22 Greg Swindell .05
23 Ken Landreaux .05
24 Jim Deshaies .05
25 Andres Galarraga .25
26 Mitch Williams .05
27 R.J. Reynolds .05
28 *Jose Nunez* .05
29 Argenis Salazar .05
30 Sid Fernandez .05
31 Bruce Bochy .05
32 Mike Morgan .05
33 Rob Deer .05
34 Ricky Horton .05
35 Harold Baines .05
36 Jamie Moyer .05
37 Ed Romero .05
38 Jeff Calhoun .05
39 Gerald Perry .05
40 Orel Hershiser .05
41 Bob Melvin .05
42 *Bill Landrum* .05
43 Dick Schofield .05
44 Lou Piniella .05
45 Kent Hrbek .05
46 Darnell Coles .05
47 Joaquin Andujar .05
48 Alan Ashby .05
49 Dave Clark .05
50 Hubie Brooks .05
51 Orioles Leaders (Eddie Murray, Cal Ripken, Jr.) .25
52 Don Robinson .05
53 Curt Wilkerson .05
54 Jim Clancy .05
55 Phil Bradley .05
56 Ed Hearn .05
57 *Tim Crews* .05
58 Dave Magadan .05
59 Danny Cox .05
60 Rickey Henderson .15
61 *Mark Knudson* .05
62 Jeff Hamilton .05
63 Jimmy Jones .05
64 *Ken Caminiti* .50
65 Leon Durham .05
66 Shane Rawley .05
67 Ken Oberkfell .05
68 Dave Dravecky .05
69 *Mike Hart* .05
70 Roger Clemens .50
71 Gary Pettis .05
72 Dennis Eckersley .05
73 Randy Bush .05
74 Tom Lasorda .10
75 Joe Carter .10
76 Denny Martinez .05
77 Tom O'Malley .05
78 Dan Petry .05
79 Ernie Whitt .05
80 Mark Langston .05
81 Reds Leaders (John Franco, Ron Robinson) .05
82 *Darrel Akerfelds* .05
83 Jose Oquendo .05
84 Cecilio Guante .05
85 Howard Johnson .05
86 Ron Karkovice .05
87 Mike Mason .05
88 Earnie Riles .05
89 *Gary Thurman* .05
90 Dale Murphy .15
91 *Joey Cora* .20
92 Len Matuszek .05
93 Bob Sebra .05
94 *Chuck Jackson* .05
95 Lance Parrish .05
96 *Todd Benzinger* .10
97 Scott Garrelts .05
98 *Rene Gonzales* .05
99 Chuck Finley .05
100 Jack Clark .05
101 Allan Anderson .05
102 Barry Larkin .20
103 Curt Young .05
104 Dick Williams .05
105 Jesse Orosco .05
106 *Jim Walewander* .05
107 Scott Bailes .05
108 Steve Lyons .05
109 Joel Skinner .05
110 Teddy Higuera .05
111 Expos Leaders (Hubie Brooks, Vance Law) .05
112 *Les Lancaster* .05
113 Kelly Gruber .05
114 Jeff Russell .05
115 Johnny Ray .05
116 Jerry Don Gleaton .05
117 *James Steels* .05
118 Bob Welch .05
119 *Robbie Wine* .05
120 Kirby Puckett .40
121 Checklist 1-132 .05
122 Tony Bernazard .05
123 Tom Candiotti .05
124 Ray Knight .05
125 Bruce Hurst .05
126 Steve Jeltz .05
127 Jim Gott .05
128 Johnny Grubb .05
129 Greg Minton .05
130 Buddy Bell .05
131 Don Schulze .05
132 Donnie Hill .05
133 Greg Mathews .05
134 Chuck Tanner .05
135 Dennis Rasmussen .05
136 Brian Dayett .05
137 Chris Bosio .05
138 Mitch Webster .05
139 Jerry Browne .05
140 Jesse Barfield .05
141 Royals Leaders (George Brett, Bret Saberhagen) .20
142 Andy Van Slyke .05
143 Mickey Tettleton .05
144 *Don Gordon* .05
145 Bill Madlock .05
146 *Donell Nixon* .05
147 Bill Buckner .05
148 Carmelo Martinez .05
149 Ken Howell .05
150 Eric Davis .05
151 Bob Knepper .05
152 *Jody Reed* .15
153 John Habyan .05
154 Jeff Stone .05
155 Bruce Sutter .05
156 Gary Matthews .05
157 Atlee Hammaker .05
158 Tim Hulett .05
159 *Brad Arnsberg* .05
160 Willie McGee .05
161 Bryn Smith .05
162 Mark McLemore .05
163 Dale Mohorcic .05
164 Dave Johnson .05
165 Robin Yount .25
166 *Rick Rodriguez* .05
167 Rance Mulliniks .05
168 Barry Jones .05
169 *Ross Jones* .05
170 Rich Gossage .05
171 Cubs Leaders (Shawon Dunston, Manny Trillo) .05
172 *Lloyd McClendon* .05
173 Eric Plunk .05
174 Phil Garner .05
175 Kevin Bass .05
176 Jeff Reed .05
177 Frank Tanana .05
178 Dwayne Henry .05
179 Charlie Puleo .05
180 Terry Kennedy .05
181 Dave Cone .20
182 Ken Phelps .05
183 Tom Lawless .05
184 Ivan Calderon .05
185 Rick Rhoden .05
186 Rafael Palmeiro .30
187 Steve Kiefer .05
188 John Russell .05
189 *Wes Gardner* .05
190 Candy Maldonado .05
191 John Cerutti .05
192 Devon White .05
193 Brian Fisher .05
194 Tom Kelly .05
195 Dan Quisenberry .05
196 Dave Engle .05
197 Lance McCullers .05
198 Franklin Stubbs .05
199 *Dave Meads* .05
200 Wade Boggs .25
201 Rangers Leaders (Steve Buechele, Pete Incaviglia, Pete O'Brien, Bobby Valentine) .05
202 Glenn Hoffman .05
203 Fred Toliver .05
204 Paul O'Neill .20
205 *Nelson Liriano* .05
206 Domingo Ramos .05
207 *John Mitchell* .05
208 Steve Lake .05
209 Richard Dotson .05
210 Willie Randolph .05
211 Frank DiPino .05
212 Greg Brock .05
213 Albert Hall .05
214 Dave Schmidt .05
215 Von Hayes .05
216 Jerry Reuss .05
217 Harry Spilman .05
218 Dan Schatzeder .05
219 Mike Stanley .05
220 Tom Henke .05
221 Rafael Belliard .05
222 Steve Farr .05
223 Stan Jefferson .05
224 Tom Trebelhorn .05
225 Mike Scioscia .05
226 Dave Lopes .05
227 Ed Correa .05
228 Wallace Johnson .05
229 Jeff Musselman .05
230 Pat Tabler .05
231 Pirates Leaders (Barry Bonds, Bobby Bonilla) .20
232 Bob James .05
233 Rafael Santana .05
234 Ken Dayley .05
235 Gary Ward .05
236 Ted Power .05
237 Mike Heath .05
238 *Luis Polonia* .10
239 Roy Smalley .05
240 Lee Smith .05
241 Damaso Garcia .05
242 Tom Niedenfuer .05
243 Mark Ryal .05
244 Jeff Robinson .05
245 Rich Gedman .05
246 *Mike Campbell* (Future Stars) .05
247 Thad Bosley .05
248 Storm Davis .05
249 Mike Marshall .05
250 Nolan Ryan .75
251 Tom Foley .05
252 Bob Brower .05
253 Checklist 133-264 .05
254 Lee Elia .05
255 Mookie Wilson .05
256 Ken Schrom .05
257 Jerry Royster .05
258 Ed Nunez .05
259 Ron Kittle .05
260 Vince Coleman .05
261 Giants Leaders (Will Clark, Candy Maldonado, Kevin Mitchell, Robby Thompson, Jose Uribe) .10
262 Drew Hall .05
263 Glenn Braggs .05
264 *Les Straker* .05
265 Bo Diaz .05
266 Paul Assenmacher .05
267 *Billy Bean* .05
268 Bruce Ruffin .05
269 *Ellis Burks* .25
270 Mike Witt .05
271 Ken Gerhart .05
272 Steve Ontiveros .05
273 Garth Iorg .05
274 Junior Ortiz .05
275 Kevin Seitzer .05
276 Luis Salazar .05
277 Alejandro Pena .05
278 Jose Cruz .05
279 Randy St. Claire .05
280 Pete Incaviglia .05
281 Jerry Hairston .05
282 Pat Perry .05
283 Phil Lombardi .05
284 Larry Bowa .05
285 Jim Presley .05
286 *Chuck Crim* .05
287 Manny Trillo .05
288 *Pat Pacillo* .05
289 Dave Bergman .05
290 Tony Fernandez .05
291 Astros Leaders (Kevin Bass, Billy Hatcher) .05
292 Carney Lansford .05
293 *Doug Jones* .15
294 *Al Pedrique* .05
295 Bert Blyleven .05
296 Floyd Rayford .05
297 Zane Smith .05
298 Milt Thompson .05
299 Steve Crawford .05
300 Don Mattingly .50
301 Bud Black .05
302 Jose Uribe .05
303 Eric Show .05
304 George Hendrick .05
305 Steve Sax .05
306 Billy Hatcher .05
307 Mike Trujillo .05
308 Lee Mazzilli .05
309 *Bill Long* .05
310 Tom Herr .05
311 Scott Sanderson .05
312 Joey Meyer (Future Stars) .05
313 Bob McClure .05
314 Jimy Williams .05
315 Dave Parker .10
316 Jose Rijo .05
317 Tom Nieto .05
318 Mel Hall .05
319 Mike Loynd .05
320 Alan Trammell .05
321 White Sox Leaders (Harold Baines, Carlton Fisk) .10
322 *Vicente Palacios* .05
323 Rick Leach .05
324 Danny Jackson .05
325 Glenn Hubbard .05
326 Al Nipper .05
327 Larry Sheets .05
328 *Greg Cadaret* .05
329 Chris Speier .05
330 Eddie Whitson .05
331 Brian Downing .05
332 Jerry Reed .05
333 Wally Backman .05
334 Dave LaPoint .05
335 Claudell Washington .05
336 Ed Lynch .05
337 Jim Gantner .05
338 Brian Holton .05
339 Kurt Stillwell .05
340 Jack Morris .05
341 Carmen Castillo .05
342 Larry Andersen .05
343 Greg Gagne .05
344 Tony LaRussa .05
345 Scott Fletcher .05
346 Vance Law .05
347 Joe Johnson .05
348 Jim Eisenreich .05
349 Bob Walk .05
350 Will Clark .25
351 Cardinals Leaders (Tony Pena, Red Schoendienst) .05
352 *Billy Ripken* .05
353 Ed Olwine .05
354 Marc Sullivan .05
355 Roger McDowell .05
356 Luis Aguayo .05
357 Floyd Bannister .05
358 Rey Quinones .05
359 Tim Stoddard .05
360 Tony Gwynn .30
361 Greg Maddux 1.00
362 Juan Castillo .05
363 Willie Fraser .05
364 Nick Esasky .05
365 Floyd Youmans .05
366 Chet Lemon .05
367 Tim Leary .05
368 *Gerald Young* .05
369 Greg Harris .05
370 Jose Canseco .40
371 Joe Hesketh .05
372 Matt Williams .75
373 Checklist 265-396 .05
374 Doc Edwards .05
375 Tom Brunansky .05
376 *Bill Wilkinson* .05
377 *Sam Horn* .05
378 *Todd Frohwirth* .05
379 Rafael Ramirez .05
380 *Joe Magrane* .05
381 Angels Leaders (Jack Howell, Wally Joyner) .05
382 *Keith Miller* .05
383 Eric Bell .05
384 Neil Allen .05
385 Carlton Fisk .25
386 Don Mattingly (All-Star) .15
387 Willie Randolph (All-Star) .05
388 Wade Boggs (All-Star) .15
389 Alan Trammell (All-Star) .05
390 George Bell (All-Star) .05
391 Kirby Puckett (All-Star) .20
392 Dave Winfield (All-Star) .10
393 Matt Nokes (All-Star) .05
394 Roger Clemens (All-Star) .15
395 Jimmy Key (All-Star) .05
396 Tom Henke (All-Star) .05
397 Jack Clark (All-Star) .05
398 Juan Samuel (All-Star) .05
399 Tim Wallach (All-Star) .05
400 Ozzie Smith (All-Star) .15
401 Andre Dawson (All-Star) .10
402 Tony Gwynn (All-Star) .15
403 Tim Raines (All-Star) .05
404 Benny Santiago (All-Star) .05
405 Dwight Gooden (All-Star) .10
406 Shane Rawley (All-Star) .05
407 Steve Bedrosian (All-Star) .05
408 Dion James .05
409 Joel McKeon .05
410 Tony Pena .05
411 Wayne Tolleson .05
412 Randy Myers .10
413 John Christensen .05
414 John McNamara .05
415 Don Carman .05
416 Keith Moreland .05
417 *Mark Ciardi* .05
418 Joel Youngblood .05
419 Scott McGregor .05
420 Wally Joyner .10
421 Ed Vande Berg .05
422 Dave Concepcion .05
423 *John Smiley* .20
424 Dwayne Murphy .05
425 Jeff Reardon .05
426 Randy Ready .05
427 *Paul Kilgus* .05
428 John Shelby .05
429 Tigers Leaders (Kirk Gibson, Alan Trammell) .05
430 Glenn Davis .05
431 Casey Candaele .05
432 Mike Moore .05
433 *Bill Pecota* .05
434 Rick Aguilera .05
435 Mike Pagliarulo .05
436 Mike Bielecki .05
437 *Fred Manrique* .05
438 *Rob Ducey* .05
439 Dave Martinez .05
440 Steve Bedrosian .05
441 Rick Manning .05
442 *Tom Bolton* .05
443 Ken Griffey .05
444 Cal Ripken, Sr. .05
445 Mike Krukow .05
446 Doug DeCinces .05
447 *Jeff Montgomery* .20
448 Mike Davis .05
449 *Jeff Robinson* .05
450 Barry Bonds .50
451 Keith Atherton .05
452 Willie Wilson .05

453 Dennis Powell .05
454 Marvell Wynne .05
455 *Shawn Hillegas* .05
456 Dave Anderson .05
457 Terry Leach .05
458 Ron Hassey .05
459 Yankees Leaders (Willie Randolph, Dave Winfield) .05
460 Ozzie Smith .25
461 Danny Darwin .05
462 Don Slaught .05
463 Fred McGriff .25
464 Jay Tibbs .05
465 Paul Molitor .25
466 Jerry Mumphrey .05
467 Don Aase .05
468 Darren Daulton .05
469 Jeff Dedmon .05
470 Dwight Evans .05
471 Donnie Moore .05
472 Robby Thompson .05
473 Joe Niekro .05
474 Tom Brookens .05
475 Pete Rose .30
476 Dave Stewart .05
477 Jamie Quirk .05
478 Sid Bream .05
479 Brett Butler .05
480 Dwight Gooden .10
481 Mariano Duncan .05
482 Mark Davis .05
483 *Rod Booker* .05
484 Pat Clements .05
485 Harold Reynolds .05
486 *Pat Keedy* .05
487 Jim Pankovits .05
488 Andy McGaffigan .05
489 Dodgers Leaders (Pedro Guerrero, Fernando Valenzuela) .05
490 Larry Parrish .05
491 B.J. Surhoff .05
492 Doyle Alexander .05
493 Mike Greenwell .05
494 *Wally Ritchie* .05
495 Eddie Murray .20
496 Guy Hoffman .05
497 Kevin Mitchell .05
498 Bob Boone .05
499 Eric King .05
500 Andre Dawson .10
501 Tim Birtsas .05
502 Danny Gladden .05
503 *Junior Noboa* .05
504 Bob Rodgers .05
505 Willie Upshaw .05
506 John Cangelosi .05
507 Mark Gubicza .05
508 Tim Teufel .05
509 Bill Dawley .05
510 Dave Winfield .15
511 Joel Davis .05
512 Alex Trevino .05
513 Tim Flannery .05
514 Pat Sheridan .05
515 Juan Nieves .05
516 Jim Sundberg .05
517 Ron Robinson .05
518 Greg Gross .05
519 Mariners Leaders (Phil Bradley, Harold Reynolds) .05
520 Dave Smith .05
521 Jim Dwyer .05
522 *Bob Patterson* .05
523 Gary Roenicke .05
524 Gary Lucas .05
525 Marty Barrett .05
526 Juan Berenguer .05
527 Steve Henderson .05
528a Checklist 397-528 (#455 is Steve Carlton) .05
528b Checklist 397-528 (#455 is Shawn Hillegas) .05
529 Tim Burke .05
530 Gary Carter .10
531 Rich Yett .05
532 Mike Kingery .05
533 *John Farrell* .05
534 John Wathan .05
535 Ron Guidry .05
536 John Morris .05
537 Steve Buechele .05
538 Bill Wegman .05
539 Mike LaValliere .05
540 Bret Saberhagen .10
541 Juan Beniquez .05
542 *Paul Noce* .05
543 Kent Tekulve .05
544 Jim Traber .05
545 Don Baylor .10
546 John Candelaria .05
547 *Felix Fermin* .05
548 *Shane Mack* .10
549 Braves Leaders (Ken Griffey, Dion James, Dale Murphy, Gerald Perry) .05
550 Pedro Guerrero .05
551 Terry Steinbach .05
552 Mark Thurmond .05
553 Tracy Jones .05
554 Mike Smithson .05
555 Brook Jacoby .05
556 *Stan Clarke* .05
557 Craig Reynolds .05
558 Bob Ojeda .05
559 *Ken Williams* .05
560 Tim Wallach .05
561 Rick Cerone .05
562 Jim Lindeman .05
563 Jose Guzman .05
564 Frank Lucchesi .05
565 Lloyd Moseby .05
566 *Charlie O'Brien* .05
567 Mike Diaz .05
568 Chris Brown .05
569 Charlie Leibrandt .05
570 Jeffrey Leonard .05
571 *Mark Williamson* .05
572 Chris James .05
573 Bob Stanley .05
574 Graig Nettles .05
575 Don Sutton .10
576 *Tommy Hinzo* .05
577 Tom Browning .05
578 Gary Gaetti .05
579 Mets Leaders (Gary Carter, Kevin McReynolds) .05
580 Mark McGwire 1.50
581 Tito Landrum .05
582 *Mike Henneman* .15
583 Dave Valle .05
584 Steve Trout .05
585 Ozzie Guillen .05
586 Bob Forsch .05
587 Terry Puhl .05
588 *Jeff Parrett* .05
589 Geno Petralli .05
590 George Bell .05
591 Doug Drabek .05
592 Dale Sveum .05
593 Bob Tewksbury .05
594 Bobby Valentine .05
595 Frank White .05
596 John Kruk .05
597 Gene Garber .05
598 Lee Lacy .05
599 Calvin Schiraldi .05
600 Mike Schmidt .25
601 Jack Lazorko .05
602 Mike Aldrete .05
603 Rob Murphy .05
604 Chris Bando .05
605 Kirk Gibson .05
606 Moose Haas .05
607 Mickey Hatcher .05
608 Charlie Kerfeld .05
609 Twins Leaders (Gary Gaetti, Kent Hrbek) .05
610 Keith Hernandez .05
611 Tommy John .05
612 Curt Ford .05
613 Bobby Thigpen .05
614 Herm Winningham .05
615 Jody Davis .05
616 *Jay Aldrich* .05
617 Oddibe McDowell .05
618 Cecil Fielder .10
619 *Mike Dunne* .05
620 Cory Snyder .05
621 Gene Nelson .05
622 Kal Daniels .05
623 Mike Flanagan .05
624 Jim Leyland .05
625 Frank Viola .05
626 Glenn Wilson .05
627 *Joe Boever* .05
628 Dave Henderson .05
629 Kelly Downs .05
630 Darrell Evans .05
631 Jack Howell .05
632 *Steve Shields* .05
633 *Barry Lyons* .05
634 Jose DeLeon .05
635 Terry Pendleton .05
636 Charles Hudson .05
637 *Jay Bell* .25
638 Steve Balboni .05
639 Brewers Leaders (Glenn Braggs, Tony Muser) .05
640 Garry Templeton .05
641 Rick Honeycutt .05
642 Bob Dernier .05
643 *Rocky Childress* .05
644 Terry McGriff .05
645 *Matt Nokes* .10
646 Checklist 529-660 .05
647 Pascual Perez .05
648 Al Newman .05
649 *DeWayne Buice* .05
650 Cal Ripken, Jr. .60
651 *Mike Jackson* .10
652 Bruce Benedict .05
653 Jeff Sellers .05
654 Roger Craig .05
655 Len Dykstra .10
656 Lee Guetterman .05
657 Gary Redus .05
658 Tim Conroy .05
659 Bobby Meacham .05
660 Rick Reuschel .05
661 Nolan Ryan (Turn Back the Clock) .35
662 Jim Rice (Turn Back the Clock) .05
663 Ron Blomberg (Turn Back the Clock) .05
664 Bob Gibson (Turn Back the Clock) .10
665 Stan Musial (Turn Back the Clock) .15
666 Mario Soto .05
667 Luis Quinones .05
668 Walt Terrell .05
669 Phillies Leaders (Lance Parrish, Mike Ryan) .05
670 Dan Plesac .05
671 Tim Laudner .05
672 *John Davis* .05
673 Tony Phillips .05
674 Mike Fitzgerald .05
675 Jim Rice .10
676 Ken Dixon .05
677 Eddie Milner .05
678 Jim Acker .05
679 Darrell Miller .05
680 Charlie Hough .05
681 Bobby Bonilla .10
682 Jimmy Key .05
683 Julio Franco .05
684 Hal Lanier .05
685 Ron Darling .05
686 Terry Francona .05
687 Mickey Brantley .05
688 Jim Winn .05
689 *Tom Pagnozzi* .05
690 Jay Howell .05
691 Dan Pasqua .05
692 Mike Birkbeck .05
693 Benny Santiago .05
694 *Eric Nolte* .05
695 Shawon Dunston .15
696 Duane Ward .05
697 Steve Lombardozzi .05
698 Brad Havens .05
699 Padres Leaders (Tony Gwynn, Benny Santiago) .15
700 George Brett .40
701 Sammy Stewart .05
702 Mike Gallego .05
703 Bob Brenly .05
704 Dennis Boyd .05
705 Juan Samuel .05
706 Rick Mahler .05
707 Fred Lynn .05
708 Gus Polidor .05
709 George Frazier .05
710 Darryl Strawberry .10
711 Bill Gullickson .05
712 John Moses .05
713 Willie Hernandez .05
714 Jim Fregosi .05
715 Todd Worrell .05
716 Lenn Sakata .05
717 Jay Baller .05
718 Mike Felder .05
719 Denny Walling .05
720 Tim Raines .10
721 Pete O'Brien .05
722 Manny Lee .05
723 Bob Kipper .05
724 Danny Tartabull .05
725 Mike Boddicker .05
726 Alfredo Griffin .05
727 Greg Booker .05
728 Andy Allanson .05
729 Blue Jays Leaders (George Bell, Fred McGriff) .10
730 John Franco .05
731 Rick Schu .05
732 Dave Palmer .05
733 Spike Owen .05
734 Craig Lefferts .05
735 Kevin McReynolds .05
736 Matt Young .05
737 Butch Wynegar .05
738 Scott Bankhead .05
739 Daryl Boston .05
740 Rick Sutcliffe .05
741 Mike Easler .05
742 Mark Clear .05
743 Larry Herndon .05
744 Whitey Herzog .05
745 Bill Doran .05
746 *Gene Larkin* .10
747 Bobby Witt .05
748 Reid Nichols .05
749 Mark Eichhorn .05
750 Bo Jackson .20
751 Jim Morrison .05
752 Mark Grant .05
753 Danny Heep .05
754 Mike LaCoss .05
755 Ozzie Virgil .05
756 Mike Maddux .05
757 *John Marzano* .05
758 *Eddie Williams* .05
759 A's Leaders (Jose Canseco, Mark McGwire) .75
760 Mike Scott .05
761 Tony Armas .05
762 Scott Bradley .05
763 Doug Sisk .05
764 Greg Walker .05
765 Neal Heaton .05
766 Henry Cotto .05
767 *Jose Lind* (Future Stars) .15
768 Dickie Noles .05
769 Cecil Cooper .05
770 Lou Whitaker .05
771 Ruben Sierra .05
772 Sal Butera .05
773 Frank Williams .05
774 Gene Mauch .05
775 Dave Stieb .05
776 Checklist 661-792 .05
777 Lonnie Smith .05
778a *Keith Comstock* (white team letters) .40
778b *Keith Comstock* (blue team letters) .15
779 *Tom Glavine* .75
780 Fernando Valenzuela .05
781 *Keith Hughes* .05
782 *Jeff Ballard* .05
783 Ron Roenicke .05
784 Joe Sambito .05
785 Alvin Davis .05
786 Joe Price .05
787 Bill Almon .05
788 Ray Searage .05
789 Indians Leaders (Joe Carter, Cory Snyder) .10
790 Dave Righetti .05
791 Ted Simmons .05
792 John Tudor .05

1988 Topps Tiffany

Sharing a checklist with the regular issue 1988 Topps baseball set, this specially boxed, limited-edition (25,000 sets) features cards printed on white cardboard stock with high-gloss front finish. Topps offered the sets directly to the public in ads in USA Today and Sporting News at a price of $99.

	MT
Complete Set (792):	85.00
Common Player:	.15

(Star cards valued at 3X-5X corresponding cards in regular 1988 Topps issue)

1988 Topps Traded

In addition to new players and traded veterans, 21 members of the U.S.A. Olympic Baseball team are showcased in this 132-card set, numbered 1T-132T. The 2-1/2" x 3-1/2" cards follow the same design as the basic Topps issue - white borders, large full-color photos, team name (or U.S.A.) in large bold letters at the top of the card face, player name on a diagonal stripe across the lower-right corner. Topps had issued its traded series each year since 1981 in boxed complete sets available only through hobby dealers.

	MT
Complete Set (132):	12.00
Common Player:	.05

1 *Jim Abbott* (USA) .25
2 Juan Agosto .05
3 Luis Alicea .05
4 *Roberto Alomar* 3.00
5 *Brady Anderson* 1.00
6 Jack Armstrong .05
7 Don August .05
8 Floyd Bannister .05
9 Bret Barberie (USA) .20
10 Jose Bautista .05
11 Don Baylor .15
12 Tim Belcher .05
13 Buddy Bell .05
14 *Andy Benes* (USA) .50
15 Damon Berryhill .05
16 Bud Black .05
17 Pat Borders .05
18 Phil Bradley .05
19 Jeff Branson (USA) .05
20 Tom Brunansky .05
21 *Jay Buhner* 1.00
22 Brett Butler .10
23 Jim Campanis (USA) .10
24 Sil Campusano .05
25 John Candelaria .05
26 Jose Cecena .05
27 Rick Cerone .05
28 Jack Clark .05
29 Kevin Coffman .05
30 Pat Combs (USA) .10
31 Henry Cotto .05
32 Chili Davis .05
33 Mike Davis .05
34 Jose DeLeon .05
35 Richard Dotson .05
36 Cecil Espy .05
37 Tom Filer .05
38 Mike Fiore (USA) .05
39 *Ron Gant* .50
40 Kirk Gibson .05
41 Rich Gossage .05
42 *Mark Grace* 3.00
43 Alfredo Griffin .05
44 Ty Griffin (USA) .10
45 Bryan Harvey .10
46 Ron Hassey .05
47 Ray Hayward .05
48 Dave Henderson .05
49 Tom Herr .05
50 Bob Horner .05
51 Ricky Horton .05
52 Jay Howell .05
53 Glenn Hubbard .05
54 Jeff Innis .10
55 Danny Jackson .05
56 Darrin Jackson .10
57 Roberto Kelly .10
58 Ron Kittle .05
59 Ray Knight .05
60 Vance Law .05
61 Jeffrey Leonard .05
62 Mike Macfarlane .10
63 Scotti Madison .05
64 Kirt Manwaring .10
65 Mark Marquess (USA) .05
66 *Tino Martinez* (USA) 3.00
67 Billy Masse (USA) .05
68 *Jack McDowell* .25
69 Jack McKeon .05
70 Larry McWilliams .05
71 Mickey Morandini (USA) .15
72 Keith Moreland .05
73 Mike Morgan .05
74 Charles Nagy (USA) .50
75 Al Nipper .05
76 Russ Nixon .05
77 Jesse Orosco .05
78 Joe Orsulak .05
79 Dave Palmer .05
80 Mark Parent .10
81 Dave Parker .10
82 Dan Pasqua .10
83 Melido Perez .05
84 Steve Peters .05
85 Dan Petry .05
86 Gary Pettis .05
87 Jeff Pico .05
88 Jim Poole (USA) .10
89 Ted Power .05
90 Rafael Ramirez .05
91 Dennis Rasmussen .05
92 Jose Rijo .05
93 Earnie Riles .05
94 Luis Rivera .05
95 Doug Robbins (USA) .05
96 Frank Robinson .15
97 Cookie Rojas .05
98 Chris Sabo .10
99 Mark Salas .05
100 Luis Salazar .05
101 Rafael Santana .05
102 Nelson Santovenia .05
103 Mackey Sasser .05
104 Calvin Schiraldi .05
105 Mike Schooler .05
106 Scott Servais (USA) .10
107 Dave Silvestri (USA) .10
108 Don Slaught .05
109 Joe Slusarski (USA) .10
110 Lee Smith .10
111 Pete Smith .10
112 Jim Snyder .05
113 Ed Sprague (USA) .40
114 Pete Stanicek .05
115 Kurt Stillwell .05
116 Todd Stottlemyre .15
117 Bill Swift .05
118 Pat Tabler .05
119 Scott Terry .05
120 Mickey Tettleton .10
121 Dickie Thon .05
122 Jeff Treadway .05
123 Willie Upshaw .05
124 *Robin Ventura* 4.00
125 Ron Washington .05
126 Walt Weiss .25
127 Bob Welch .05
128 David Wells 1.00
129 Glenn Wilson .05
130 Ted Wood (USA) .05
131 Don Zimmer .05
132 Checklist 1T-132T .05

1988 Topps Traded Tiffany

The high-gloss front surface is all that distinguishes this limited-edition, hobby-only collectors version from the regular Topps Traded boxed set.

	MT
Complete Set (132):	55.00
Common Player:	.15
(Star cards valued at 3X-4X corresponding cards in regular Topps Traded issue)	

1988 Topps Box Panels

After a one-year hiatus during which they appeared on the sides of Topps wax pack display boxes, Topps retail box cards returned to box bottoms in 1988. The series includes 16 standard-size baseball cards, four cards per each of four different display boxes. Card fronts follow the same design as the 1988 Topps basic issue; full-color player photos, framed in yellow, surrounded by a white border; diagonal player name lower-right; team name in large letters at the top. Card backs are "numbered" A through P and are printed in black and orange.

		MT
Complete Panel Set (4):		3.00
Complete Singles Set (16):		1.50
Common Panel:		.50
Common Single Player:		.05
	Panel	.50
A	Don Baylor	.05
B	Steve Bedrosian	.05
C	Juan Beniquez	.05
D	Bob Boone	.05
	Panel	.70
E	Darrell Evans	.05
F	Tony Gwynn	.50
G	John Kruk	.05
H	Marvell Wynne	.05
	Panel	.60
I	Joe Carter	.10
J	Eric Davis	.05
K	Howard Johnson	.05
L	Darryl Strawberry	.10
	Panel	2.00
M	Rickey Henderson	.20
N	Nolan Ryan	1.00
O	Mike Schmidt	.35
P	Kent Tekulve	.05

1988 Topps All-Star Glossy Set of 22

The fifth edition of Topps' special All-Star inserts was included in the company's 1988 rack packs. The 1987 American and National League All-Star lineup, plus honorary captains Jim Hunter and Billy Williams, are featured on the 2-1/2" x 3-1/2" cards. The glossy full-color fronts contain player photos centered between a red and yellow "1987 All-Star" logo at top and the player name (also red and yellow) which is printed in the bottom margin. A league logo is in the lower-left corner. Card backs are printed in red and blue on a white background, with the title and All-Star logo emblem printed above the player name and card number.

		MT
Complete Set (22):		3.00
Common Player:		.15
1	John McNamara	.15
2	Don Mattingly	1.00
3	Willie Randolph	.15
4	Wade Boggs	.65
5	Cal Ripken, Jr.	1.50
6	George Bell	.15
7	Rickey Henderson	.50
8	Dave Winfield	.40
9	Terry Kennedy	.15
10	Bret Saberhagen	.15
11	Catfish Hunter	.15
12	Davey Johnson	.15
13	Jack Clark	.15
14	Ryne Sandberg	.65
15	Mike Schmidt	.75
16	Ozzie Smith	.50
17	Eric Davis	.15
18	Andre Dawson	.20
19	Darryl Strawberry	.15
20	Gary Carter	.20
21	Mike Scott	.15
22	Billy Williams	.15

1988 Topps All-Star Glossy Set of 60

This collectors set includes 60 full-color glossy cards featuring All-Stars and Prospects in six separate 10-card sets. Card fronts have a white border and a thin red line framing the player photo, with the player's name in the lower-left corner. Backs, in red and blue, include basic player identification along with the set logo and card number. Sets were marketed via a special offer printed on a card packaged in all Topps wax packs. For six special offer cards and $1.25, collectors received one of the six 10-card sets; 18 special offer cards and $7.50 earned the entire 60-card collection.

		MT
Complete Set (60):		12.00
Common Player:		.15
1	Andre Dawson	.20
2	Jesse Barfield	.15
3	Mike Schmidt	.75
4	Ruben Sierra	.15
5	Mike Scott	.15
6	Cal Ripken, Jr.	1.50
7	Gary Carter	.20
8	Kent Hrbek	.15
9	Kevin Seitzer	.15
10	Mike Henneman	.15
11	Don Mattingly	1.00
12	Tim Raines	.20
13	Roger Clemens	.75
14	Ryne Sandberg	.60
15	Tony Fernandez	.15
16	Eric Davis	.15
17	Jack Morris	.15
18	Tim Wallach	.15
19	Mike Dunne	.15
20	Mike Greenwell	.15
21	Dwight Evans	.15
22	Darryl Strawberry	.20
23	Cory Snyder	.15
24	Pedro Guerrero	.15
25	Rickey Henderson	.50
26	Dale Murphy	.30
27	Kirby Puckett	.75
28	Steve Bedrosian	.15
29	Devon White	.15
30	Benny Santiago	.15
31	George Bell	.15
32	Keith Hernandez	.15
33	Dave Stewart	.15
34	Dave Parker	.15
35	Tom Henke	.15
36	Willie McGee	.15
37	Alan Trammell	.15
38	Tony Gwynn	.75
39	Mark McGwire	2.00
40	Joe Magrane	.15
41	Jack Clark	.15
42	Willie Randolph	.15
43	Juan Samuel	.15
44	Joe Carter	.25
45	Shane Rawley	.15
46	Dave Winfield	.40
47	Ozzie Smith	.50
48	Wally Joyner	.20
49	B.J. Surhoff	.15
50	Ellis Burks	.25
51	Wade Boggs	.65
52	Howard Johnson	.15
53	George Brett	.75
54	Dwight Gooden	.20
55	Jose Canseco	.65
56	Lee Smith	.15
57	Paul Molitor	.45
58	Andres Galarraga	.25
59	Matt Nokes	.15
60	Casey Candaele	.15

1988 Topps American Baseball

This set, ostensibly issued for sale in the United Kingdom, was also made available for distribution by U.S. hobby dealers. Cards were packaged in checklist-backed boxes with an American flag on the top flap. The 2-1/4" x 3" cards feature full-color photos printed on white stock. The team name, printed in team colors, intersects the red frame at the top of the card. A yellow name banner appears below the photo. Backs have blue borders and cartoon-style horizontal layouts which include a team logo, stats, caricature of the player and a one-line caption. Below the cartoon, a short "Talkin' Baseball" paragraph provides elementary information, designed to acquaint soccer-playing European collectors with baseball rules and terminology.

		MT
Complete Set (88):		8.00
Common Player:		.10
1	Harold Baines	.10
2	Steve Bedrosian	.10
3	George Bell	.10
4	Wade Boggs	.65
5	Barry Bonds	.80
6	Bob Boone	.10
7	George Brett	.80
8	Hubie Brooks	.10
9	Ivan Calderon	.10
10	Jose Canseco	.50
11	Gary Carter	.20
12	Joe Carter	.10
13	Jack Clark	.10
14	Will Clark	.45
15	Roger Clemens	.75
16	Vince Coleman	.10
17	Alvin Davis	.10
18	Eric Davis	.10
19	Glenn Davis	.10
20	Andre Dawson	.15
21	Mike Dunne	.10
22	Dwight Evans	.10
23	Tony Fernandez	.10
24	John Franco	.10
25	Gary Gaetti	.10
26	Kirk Gibson	.10
27	Dwight Gooden	.15
28	Pedro Guerrero	.10
29	Tony Gwynn	.75
30	Billy Hatcher	.10
31	Rickey Henderson	.35
32	Tom Henke	.10
33	Keith Hernandez	.10
34	Orel Hershiser	.10
35	Teddy Higuera	.10
36	Charlie Hough	.10
37	Kent Hrbek	.10
38	Brook Jacoby	.10
39	Dion James	.10
40	Wally Joyner	.15
41	John Kruk	.10
42	Mark Langston	.10
43	Jeffrey Leonard	.10
44	Candy Maldonaldo	.10
45	Don Mattingly	1.00
46	Willie McGee	.10
47	Mark McGwire	2.00
48	Kevin Mitchell	.10
49	Paul Molitor	.50
50	Jack Morris	.10
51	Lloyd Moseby	.10
52	Dale Murphy	.20
53	Eddie Murray	.40
54	Matt Nokes	.10
55	Dave Parker	.10
56	Larry Parrish	.10
57	Kirby Puckett	.75
58	Tim Raines	.15
59	Willie Randolph	.10
60	Harold Reynolds	.10
61	Cal Ripken, Jr.	1.50
62	Nolan Ryan	1.50
63	Bret Saberhagen	.10
64	Juan Samuel	.10
65	Ryne Sandberg	.65
66	Benny Santiago	.10
67	Mike Schmidt	.75
68	Mike Scott	.10
69	Kevin Seitzer	.10
70	Larry Sheets	.10
71	Ruben Sierra	.10
72	Ozzie Smith	.45
73	Zane Smith	.10
74	Cory Snyder	.10
75	Dave Stewart	.10
76	Darryl Strawberry	.15
77	Rick Sutcliffe	.10
78	Danny Tartabull	.10
79	Alan Trammell	.10
80	Fernando Valenzuela	.10
81	Andy Van Slyke	.10
82	Frank Viola	.10
83	Greg Walker	.10
84	Tim Wallach	.10
85	Dave Winfield	.30
86	Mike Witt	.10
87	Robin Yount	.35
88	Checklist	.10

1988 Topps American Baseball Tiffany

This glossy "Tiffany" edition of the Topps American Baseball set is a complete parallel of the regular-issue.

	MT
Complete Set (88):	30.00
Common Player:	.40
(Stars and rookies valued at 4-5X regular edition cards.)	

1988 Topps Big Baseball

Topps Big Baseball cards (2-5/8" x 3-3/4") were issued in three series, 88 cards per series (a total set of 264 cards) sold in seven-card packs. The glossy cards are similar in format, both front and back, to the 1956 Topps set. Each card features a portrait and a game-action photo on the front, framed by a wide white border. A white outline highlights the portrait. The player's name appears at bottom on a splash of color that fades from yellow to orange to red to pink. On the card back, the player's name is printed in large red letters across the top, followed by his team name and position in black. Personal info is printed in a red rectangle beside a Topps baseball logo bearing the card number. A triple cartoon strip, in full-color, illustrates career highlights, performance, personal background, etc. A red, white and blue statistics box (pitching, batting, fielding) is printed across the bottom.

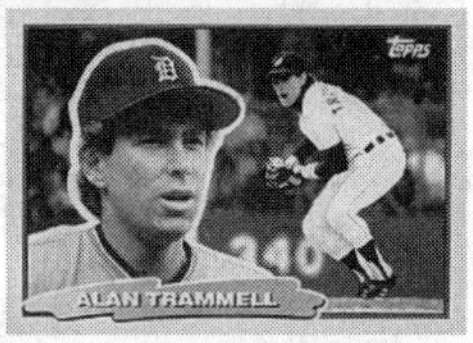

		MT
Complete Set (264):		21.00
Common Player:		.05
1	Paul Molitor	.50
2	Milt Thompson	.05
3	Billy Hatcher	.05
4	Mike Witt	.05
5	Vince Coleman	.05
6	Dwight Evans	.05
7	Tim Wallach	.05
8	Alan Trammell	.10
9	Will Clark	.50
10	Jeff Reardon	.05
11	Dwight Gooden	.15
12	Benny Santiago	.05
13	Jose Canseco	.50
14	Dale Murphy	.15
15	George Bell	.05
16	Ryne Sandberg	.60
17	Brook Jacoby	.05
18	Fernando Valenzuela	.05
19	Scott Fletcher	.05
20	Eric Davis	.10
21	Willie Wilson	.05
22	B.J. Surhoff	.05
23	Steve Bedrosian	.05
24	Dave Winfield	.45
25	Bobby Bonilla	.10
26	Larry Sheets	.05
27	Ozzie Guillen	.05
28	Checklist 1-88	.05
29	Nolan Ryan	2.00
30	Bob Boone	.05
31	Tom Herr	.05
32	Wade Boggs	.60
33	Neal Heaton	.05
34	Doyle Alexander	.05
35	Candy Maldonado	.05
36	Kirby Puckett	.85
37	Gary Carter	.10
38	Lance McCullers	.05
39a	Terry Steinbach (black Topps logo on front)	.15
39b	Terry Steinbach (white Topps logo on front)	.15
40	Gerald Perry	.05
41	Tom Henke	.05
42	Leon Durham	.05
43	Cory Snyder	.05
44	Dale Sveum	.05
45	Lance Parrish	.05
46	Steve Sax	.05
47	Charlie Hough	.05
48	Kal Daniels	.05
49	Bo Jackson	.25
50	Ron Guidry	.05
51	Bill Doran	.05
52	Wally Joyner	.10
53	Terry Pendleton	.05
54	Marty Barrett	.05
55	Andres Galarraga	.15
56	Larry Herndon	.05

57	Kevin Mitchell	.05
58	Greg Gagne	.05
59	Keith Hernandez	.05
60	John Kruk	.05
61	Mike LaValliere	.05
62	Cal Ripken, Jr.	2.00
63	Ivan Calderon	.05
64	Alvin Davis	.05
65	Luis Polonia	.05
66	Robin Yount	.45
67	Juan Samuel	.05
68	Andres Thomas	.05
69	Jeff Musselman	.05
70	Jerry Mumphrey	.05
71	Joe Carter	.10
72	Mike Scioscia	.05
73	Pete Incaviglia	.05
74	Barry Larkin	.15
75	Frank White	.05
76	Willie Randolph	.05
77	Kevin Bass	.05
78	Brian Downing	.05
79	Willie McGee	.05
80	Ellis Burks	.10
81	Hubie Brooks	.05
82	Darrell Evans	.05
83	Robby Thompson	.05
84	Kent Hrbek	.05
85	Ron Darling	.05
86	Stan Jefferson	.05
87	Teddy Higuera	.05
88	Mike Schmidt	.85
89	Barry Bonds	.75
90	Jim Presley	.05
91	Orel Hershiser	.05
92	Jesse Barfield	.05
93	Tom Candiotti	.05
94	Bret Saberhagen	.05
95	Jose Uribe	.05
96	Tom Browning	.05
97	Johnny Ray	.05
98	Mike Morgan	.05
100	Jim Sundberg	.05
101	Roger McDowell	.05
102	Randy Ready	.05
103	Mike Gallego	.05
104	Steve Buechele	.05
105	Greg Walker	.05
106	Jose Lind	.05
107	Steve Trout	.05
108	Rick Rhoden	.05
109	Jim Pankovits	.05
110	Ken Griffey	.05
111	Danny Cox	.05
112	Franklin Stubbs	.05
113	Lloyd Moseby	.05
114	Mel Hall	.05
115	Kevin Seitzer	.05
116	Tim Raines	.15
117	Juan Castillo	.05
118	Roger Clemens	.75
119	Mike Aldrete	.05
120	Mario Soto	.05
121	Jack Howell	.05
122	Rick Schu	.05
123	Jeff Robinson	.05
124	Doug Drabek	.05
125	Henry Cotto	.05
126	Checklist 89-176	.05
127	Gary Gaetti	.05
128	Rick Sutcliffe	.05
129	Howard Johnson	.05
130	Chris Brown	.05
131	Dave Henderson	.05
132	Curt Wilkerson	.05
133	Mike Marshall	.05
134	Kelly Gruber	.05
135	Julio Franco	.05
136	Kurt Stillwell	.05
137	Donnie Hill	.05
138	Mike Pagliarulo	.05
139	Von Hayes	.05
140	Mike Scott	.05
141	Bob Kipper	.05
142	Harold Reynolds	.05
143	Bob Brenly	.05
144	Dave Concepcion	.05
145	Devon White	.10
146	Jeff Stone	.05
147	Chet Lemon	.05
148	Ozzie Virgil	.05
149	Todd Worrell	.05
150	Mitch Webster	.05
151	Rob Deer	.05
152	Rich Gedman	.05
153	Andre Dawson	.10
154	Mike Davis	.05
155	Nelson Liriano	.05
156	Greg Swindell	.05
157	George Brett	.75
158	Kevin McReynolds	.05
159	Brian Fisher	.05
160	Mike Kingery	.05
161	Tony Gwynn	.75
162	Don Baylor	.05
163	Jerry Browne	.05
164	Dan Pasqua	.05
165	Rickey Henderson	.25
166	Brett Butler	.05
167	Nick Esasky	.05
168	Kirk McCaskill	.05
169	Fred Lynn	.05
170	Jack Morris	.05
171	Pedro Guerrero	.05
172	Dave Stieb	.05
173	Pat Tabler	.05
174	Floyd Bannister	.05
175	Rafael Belliard	.05
176	Mark Langston	.05
177	Greg Mathews	.05
178	Claudell Washington	.05
179	Mark McGwire	2.50
180	Bert Blyleven	.05
181	Jim Rice	.10
182	Mookie Wilson	.05
183	Willie Fraser	.05
184	Andy Van Slyke	.05
185	Matt Nokes	.05
186	Eddie Whitson	.05
187	Tony Fernandez	.05
188	Rick Reuschel	.05
189	Ken Phelps	.05
190	Juan Nieves	.05
191	Kirk Gibson	.05
192	Glenn Davis	.05
193	Zane Smith	.05
194	Jose DeLeon	.05
195	Gary Ward	.05
196	Pascual Perez	.05
197	Carlton Fisk	.25
198	Oddibe McDowell	.05
199	Mark Gubicza	.05
200	Glenn Hubbard	.05
201	Frank Viola	.05
202	Jody Reed	.05
203	Len Dykstra	.05
204	Dick Schofield	.05
205	Sid Bream	.05
206	Guillermo Hernandez	.05
207	Keith Moreland	.05
208	Mark Eichhorn	.05
209	Rene Gonzales	.05
210	Dave Valle	.05
211	Tom Brunansky	.05
212	Charles Hudson	.05
213	John Farrell	.05
214	Jeff Treadway	.05
215	Eddie Murray	.35
216	Checklist 177-264	.05
217	Greg Brock	.05
218	John Shelby	.05
219	Craig Reynolds	.05
220	Dion James	.05
221	Carney Lansford	.05
222	Juan Berenguer	.05
223	Luis Rivera	.05
224	Harold Baines	.10
225	Shawon Dunston	.05
226	Luis Aguayo	.05
227	Pete O'Brien	.05
228	Ozzie Smith	.50
229	Don Mattingly	.90
230	Danny Tartabull	.05
231	Andy Allanson	.05
232	John Franco	.05
233	Mike Greenwell	.05
234	Bob Ojeda	.05
235	Chili Davis	.05
236	Mike Dunne	.05
237	Jim Morrison	.05
238	Carmelo Martinez	.05
239	Ernie Whitt	.05
240	Scott Garrelts	.05
241	Mike Moore	.05
242	Dave Parker	.05
243	Tim Laudner	.05
244	Bill Wegman	.05
245	Bob Horner	.05
246	Rafael Santana	.05
247	Alfredo Griffin	.05
248	Mark Bailey	.05
249	Ron Gant	.15
250	Bryn Smith	.05
251	Lance Johnson	.05
252	Sam Horn	.05
253	Darryl Strawberry	.15
254	Chuck Finley	.05
255	Darnell Coles	.05
256	Mike Henneman	.05
257	Andy Hawkins	.05
258	Jim Clancy	.05
259	Atlee Hammaker	.05
260	Glenn Wilson	.05
261	Larry McWilliams	.05
262	Jack Clark	.05
263	Walt Weiss	.05
264	Gene Larkin	.05

1988 Topps Cloth Experimental

This is a true experimental issue from Topps: Baseball cards printed on heavy textured paper, much like high-quality paper towels. The cloth cards are the standard 2-1/2" x 3-1/2" in size and feature the fronts as used on Topps' regular '88 baseball card issue. Overprinted across the fronts of some cards are parts of the legend, "SAMPLE ONLY NOT FOR SALE". Backs are blank, and unlike earlier Topps cloth issues, are not gummed for use as stickers. The checklist presented here in alphabetical order may not be complete

		MT
Complete Set (121)		1250.
Common Player:		9.00
(1)	A's Team Leaders (Jose Canseco, Mark McGwire)	25.00
(2)	Rick Aguilera	9.00
(3)	Andy Allanson	9.00
(4)	Tony Armas	9.00
(5)	Keith Atherton	9.00
(6)	Steve Balboni	9.00
(7)	Billy Bean	9.00
(8)	Steve Bedrosian (AS)	9.00
(9)	George Bell (All-Star)	9.00
(10)	Bruce Benedict	9.00
(11)	Dave Bergman	9.00
(12)	Mike Bielecki	9.00
(13)	Tim Birtsas	9.00
(14)	Bruce Bochy	9.00
(15)	Wade Boggs (AS)	35.00
(16)	Rod Booker	9.00
(17)	Dennis Boyd	9.00
(18)	Braves Leaders (Ken Griffey, Dion James, Dale Murphy, Gerald Perry)	12.00
(19)	Tom Browning	9.00
(20)	Carmen Castillo	9.00
(21)	Rick Cerone	9.00
(22)	Jack Clark (AS)	9.00
(23)	Mark Clear	9.00
(24)	Roger Clemens (AS)	35.00
(25)	Pat Clements	9.00
(26)	Keith Comstock	9.00
(27)	Cecil Cooper	9.00
(28)	Joey Cora	9.00
(29)	Ed Correa	9.00
(30)	Mark Davidson	9.00
(31)	Mark Davis	9.00
(32)	Jeff Dedmon	9.00
(33)	Jim Dwyer	9.00
(34)	Doc Edwards	9.00
(35)	John Farrell	9.00
(36)	Mike Felder	9.00
(37)	Curt Ford	9.00
(38)	Bob Forsch	9.00
(39)	Damaso Garcia	9.00
(40)	Tom Glavine	24.00
(41)	Mark Grant	9.00
(42)	Tony Gwynn (AS)	35.00
(43)	Drew Hall	9.00
(44)	Jeff Hamilton	9.00
(45)	Mike Hart	9.00
(46)	Andy Hawkins	9.00
(47)	Ed Hearn	9.00
(48)	Tom Henke (AS)	9.00
(49)	Whitey Herzog	9.00
(50)	Shawn Hillegas	9.00
(51)	Charles Hudson	9.00
(52)	Dave Johnson	9.00
(53)	Ron Karkovice	9.00
(54)	Pat Keedy	9.00
(55)	Jimmy Key (AS)	9.00
(56)	Mark Kiefer	9.00
(57)	Bob Kipper	9.00
(58)	Les Lancaster	9.00
(59)	Ken Landreaux	9.00
(60)	Craig Lefferts	9.00
(61)	Jim Leyland	9.00
(62)	Jose Lind	9.00
(63)	Gary Lucas	9.00
(64)	Frank Lucchesi	9.00
(65)	Barry Lyons	9.00
(66)	John Marzano	9.00
(67)	Greg Mathews	9.00
(68)	Don Mattingly (AS)	45.00
(69)	Len Matuszek	9.00
(70)	Kirk McCaskill	9.00
(71)	Terry McGriff	9.00
(72)	Joey Meyer	9.00
(73)	John Mitchell	9.00
(74)	Jeff Montgomery	9.00
(75)	John Morris	9.00
(76)	John Moses	9.00
(77)	Tom Nieto	9.00
(78)	Matt Nokes (AS)	9.00
(79)	Charlie O'Brien	9.00
(80)	Ed Olwine	9.00
(81)	Paul O'Neill	15.00
(82)	Steve Ontiveros	9.00
(83)	Pat Pacillo	9.00
(84)	Tom Pagnozzi	9.00
(85)	Jim Pankovitz	9.00
(86)	Bill Pecota	9.00
(87)	Geno Petralli	9.00
(88)	Eric Plunk	9.00
(89)	Gus Polidor	9.00
(90)	Dennis Powell	9.00
(91)	Terry Puhl	9.00
(92)	Charlie Puleo	9.00
(93)	Shane Rawley (AS)	9.00
(94)	Rick Rodriguez	9.00
(95)	Ron Roenicke	9.00
(96)	Pete Rose	125.00
(97)	Lenn Sakata	9.00
(98)	Joe Sambito	9.00
(99)	Juan Samuel (AS)	9.00
(100)	Rafael Santana	9.00
(101)	Dan Schatzeder	9.00
(102)	Pat Sheridan	9.00
(103)	Steve Shields	9.00
(104)	Ted Simmons	9.00
(105)	Doug Sisk	9.00
(106)	Joel Skinner	9.00
(107)	Ozzie Smith (AS)	30.00
(108)	Chris Speier	9.00
(109)	Jim Sundberg	9.00
(110)	Don Sutton	12.00
(111)	Chuck Tanner	9.00
(112)	Mickey Tettleton	9.00
(113)	Tim Teufel	9.00
(114)	Gary Thurman	9.00
(115)	Alex Trevino	9.00
(116)	Mike Trujillo	9.00
(117)	Twins Leaders (Gary Gaetti, Kent Hrbek)	12.00
(118)	Tim Wallach (AS)	9.00
(119)	Frank Williams	9.00
(120)	Dave Winfield (AS)	25.00
(121)	Butch Wynegar	9.00

1988 Topps Coins

This edition of 60 lightweight metal coins is similar in design to Topps' 1964 set. The 1988 coins are 1-1/2" in diameter and feature full-color player portraits under crimped edges in silver, gold and pink. Curved under the photo is a red and white player name banner pinned by two gold stars. Coin backs list the coin number, player name, personal information and career summary in black letters on a silver background.

		MT
Complete Set (60):		12.00
Common Player:		.15
1	George Bell	.15
2	Roger Clemens	.75
3	Mark McGwire	3.00
4	Wade Boggs	.60
5	Harold Baines	.20
6	Ivan Calderon	.15
7	Jose Canseco	.50
8	Joe Carter	.15
9	Jack Clark	.15
10	Alvin Davis	.15
11	Dwight Evans	.15
12	Tony Fernandez	.15
13	Gary Gaetti	.15
14	Mike Greenwell	.15
15	Charlie Hough	.15
16	Wally Joyner	.25
17	Jimmy Key	.15
18	Mark Langston	.15
19	Don Mattingly	1.50
20	Paul Molitor	.50
21	Jack Morris	.15
22	Eddie Murray	.50
23	Kirby Puckett	1.00
24	Cal Ripken, Jr.	2.50
25	Bret Saberhagen	.15
26	Ruben Sierra	.15
27	Cory Snyder	.15
28	Terry Steinbach	.15
29	Danny Tartabull	.15
30	Alan Trammell	.15
31	Devon White	.20
32	Robin Yount	.75
33	Andre Dawson	.25
34	Steve Bedrosian	.15
35	Benny Santiago	.15
36	Tony Gwynn	.75
37	Bobby Bonilla	.20
38	Will Clark	.50
39	Eric Davis	.15
40	Mike Dunne	.15
41	John Franco	.15
42	Dwight Gooden	.25
43	Pedro Guerrero	.15
44	Dion James	.15
45	John Kruk	.15
46	Jeffrey Leonard	.15
47	Carmelo Martinez	.15
48	Dale Murphy	.25
49	Tim Raines	.20
50	Nolan Ryan	2.50
51	Juan Samuel	.15
52	Ryne Sandberg	.65
53	Mike Schmidt	1.00
54	Mike Scott	.15
55	Ozzie Smith	.75
56	Darryl Strawberry	.25
57	Rick Sutcliffe	.15
58	Fernando Valenzuela	.15
59	Tim Wallach	.15
60	Todd Worrell	.15

1988 Topps Gallery of Champions

These metal replicas are exact reproductions at one-quarter scale of Topps 1988 cards, both front and back. The set includes 12 three-dimensional raised metal cards packaged in a velvet-lined case that bears the title of the set in gold embossed letters. A deluxe limited edition of the set (1,000) was produced in in sterling silver and an economy version in aluminum. A Mark McGwire pewter replica was given as a premium to dealers ordering the aluminum, bronze and silver sets. The special pewter card is distinguished from the regular issue by a diagonal name banner in the lower-right corner; regular replicas have a rectangular name banner parallel to the lower edge of the card). A 1955 Topps Duke Snider bronze was available to dealers purchasing cases of the 1988 Topps Traded sets.

		MT
Complete Aluminum Set (12):		75.00
Complete Bronze Set (12):		225.00
Complete Silver Set (12):		550.00
(1a)	Steve Bedrosian (aluminum)	3.00
(1b)	Steve Bedrosian (bronze)	10.00
(1s)	Steve Bedrosian (silver)	25.00
(2a)	George Bell (aluminum)	3.00
(2b)	George Bell (bronze)	10.00
(2s)	George Bell (silver)	25.00
(3a)	Wade Boggs (aluminum)	10.00
(3b)	Wade Boggs (bronze)	30.00
(3s)	Wade Boggs (silver)	65.00
(4a)	Jack Clark (aluminum)	3.00
(4b)	Jack Clark (bronze)	10.00
(4s)	Jack Clark (silver)	25.00
(5a)	Roger Clemens (aluminum)	12.00
(5b)	Roger Clemens (bronze)	30.00
(5s)	Roger Clemens (silver)	75.00
(6a)	Andre Dawson (aluminum)	5.00
(6b)	Andre Dawson (bronze)	15.00
(6s)	Andre Dawson (silver)	40.00
(7a)	Tony Gwynn (aluminum)	15.00
(7b)	Tony Gwynn (bronze)	35.00
(7s)	Tony Gwynn (silver)	75.00
(8a)	Mark Langston (aluminum)	3.00
(8b)	Mark Langston (bronze)	10.00

(8s)	Mark Langston (silver)	25.00
(9a)	Mark McGwire (aluminum)	20.00
(9b)	Mark McGwire (bronze)	50.00
(9s)	Mark McGwire (silver)	100.00
(9p)	Mark McGwire (pewter)	125.00
(10a)	Dave Righetti (aluminum)	3.00
(10b)	Dave Righetti (bronze)	10.00
(10s)	Dave Righetti (silver)	25.00
(11a)	Nolan Ryan (aluminum)	25.00
(11b)	Nolan Ryan (bronze)	100.00
(11s)	Nolan Ryan (silver)	250.00
(12a)	Benny Santiago (aluminum)	4.00
(12b)	Benny Santiago (bronze)	10.00
(12s)	Benny Santiago (silver)	35.00
(13)	Duke Snider (bronze)	15.00

1988 Topps Glossy Rookies

The Topps 1988 Rookies special insert cards follow the same basic design as the All-Star inserts. The set consists of 22 standard-size cards found one per pack in 100-card jumbo cellos. Large, glossy color player photos are printed on a white background below a red, yellow and blue "1987 Rookies" banner. A red and yellow player name appears beneath the photo. Red, white and blue card backs bear the title of the special insert set, the Rookies logo emblem, player name and card number.

		MT
Complete Set (22):		5.00
Common Player:		.20
1	Billy Ripken	.20
2	Ellis Burks	.50
3	Mike Greenwell	.25
4	DeWayne Buice	.20
5	Devon White	.25
6	Fred Manrique	.20
7	Mike Henneman	.20
8	Matt Nokes	.20
9	Kevin Seitzer	.20
10	B.J. Surhoff	.25
11	Casey Candaele	.20
12	Randy Myers	.30
13	Mark McGwire	4.00
14	Luis Polonia	.20
15	Terry Steinbach	.25
16	Mike Dunne	.20
17	Al Pedrique	.20
18	Benny Santiago	.25
19	Kelly Downs	.20
20	Joe Magrane	.20
21	Jerry Browne	.20
22	Jeff Musselman	.20

1988 Topps Mini League Leaders

The third consecutive issue of Topps mini-cards (2-1/8" x 3") includes 77 cards spotlighting the top five ranked pitchers and batters. This set is unique in that it was the first time Topps included full-color player photos on both the front and back. Glossy action shots on the card fronts fade into a white border with a Topps logo in an upper corner. The player's name is printed in bold black letters beneath the photo. Horizontal reverses feature circular player photos on a blue and white background with the card number, player name, personal information, 1987 ranking and lifetime/1987 stats printed in red, black and yellow lettering.

		MT
Complete Set (77):		4.00
Common Player:		.10
1	Wade Boggs	.65
2	Roger Clemens	.75
3	Dwight Evans	.10
4	DeWayne Buice	.10
5	Brian Downing	.10
6	Wally Joyner	.15
7	Ivan Calderon	.10
8	Carlton Fisk	.40
9	Gary Redus	.10
10	Darrell Evans	.10
11	Jack Morris	.10
12	Alan Trammell	.15
13	Lou Whitaker	.10
14	Bret Saberhagen	.10
15	Kevin Seitzer	.10
16	Danny Tartabull	.10
17	Willie Wilson	.10
18	Teddy Higuera	.10
19	Paul Molitor	.50
20	Dan Plesac	.10
21	Robin Yount	.65
22	Kent Hrbek	.10
23	Kirby Puckett	.75
24	Jeff Reardon	.10
25	Frank Viola	.10
26	Rickey Henderson	.45
27	Don Mattingly	.90
28	Willie Randolph	.10
29	Dave Righetti	.10
30	Jose Canseco	.55
31	Mark McGwire	2.00
32	Dave Stewart	.10
33	Phil Bradley	.10
34	Mark Langston	.10
35	Harold Reynolds	.10
36	Charlie Hough	.10
37	George Bell	.10
38	Tom Henke	.10
39	Jimmy Key	.10
40	Dion James	.10
41	Dale Murphy	.15
42	Zane Smith	.10
43	Andre Dawson	.15
44	Lee Smith	.10
45	Rick Sutcliffe	.10
46	Eric Davis	.10
47	John Franco	.10
48	Dave Parker	.10
49	Billy Hatcher	.10
50	Nolan Ryan	1.50
51	Mike Scott	.10
52	Pedro Guerrero	.10
53	Orel Hershiser	.10
54	Fernando Valenzuela	.10
55	Bob Welch	.10
56	Andres Galarraga	.15
57	Tim Raines	.15
58	Tim Wallach	.10
59	Len Dykstra	.10
60	Dwight Gooden	.15
61	Howard Johnson	.10
62	Roger McDowell	.10
63	Darryl Strawberry	.15
64	Steve Bedrosian	.10
65	Shane Rawley	.10
66	Juan Samuel	.10
67	Mike Schmidt	.65
68	Mike Dunne	.10
69	Jack Clark	.10
70	Vince Coleman	.10
71	Willie McGee	.15
72	Ozzie Smith	.60
73	Todd Worrell	.10
74	Tony Gwynn	.70
75	John Kruk	.10
76	Rick Rueschel	.10
77	Checklist	.10

1988 Topps Stickercards

Actually a part of the 1988 Topps Stickers issue, this set consists of 67 cards. The cards are the backs of the peel-off stickers and measure 2-1/8" x 3". To determine total value, combine the prices of the stickers (found in the 1988 Topps Stickers checklist) on the stickercard front with the value assigned to the stickercard in the following checklist.

		MT
Complete Set (67):		2.50
Common Player:		.05
1	Jack Clark	.05
2	Andres Galarraga	.10
3	Keith Hernandez	.05
4	Tom Herr	.05
5	Juan Samuel	.05
6	Ryne Sandberg	.35
7	Terry Pendleton	.05
8	Mike Schmidt	.25
9	Tim Wallach	.05
10	Hubie Brooks	.05
11	Shawon Dunston	.05
12	Ozzie Smith	.30
13	Andre Dawson	.10
14	Eric Davis	.05
15	Pedro Guerrero	.05
16	Tony Gwynn	.50
17	Jeffrey Leonard	.05
18	Dale Murphy	.10
19	Dave Parker	.05
20	Tim Raines	.10
21	Darryl Strawberry	.10
22	Gary Carter	.10
23	Jody Davis	.05
24	Ozzie Virgil	.05
25	Dwight Gooden	.10
26	Mike Scott	.05
27	Rick Sutcliffe	.05
28	Sid Fernandez	.05
29	Neal Heaton	.05
30	Fernando Valenzuela	.05
31	Steve Bedrosian	.05
32	John Franco	.05
33	Lee Smith	.05
34	Wally Joyner	.10
35	Don Mattingly	.40
36	Mark McGwire	1.50
37	Willie Randolph	.05
38	Lou Whitaker	.05
39	Frank White	.05
40	Wade Boggs	.35
41	George Brett	.50
42	Paul Molitor	.35
43	Tony Fernandez	.05
44	Cal Ripken, Jr.	.90
45	Alan Trammell	.05
46	Jesse Barfield	.05
47	George Bell	.05
48	Jose Canseco	.30
49	Joe Carter	.10
50	Dwight Evans	.05
51	Rickey Henderson	.15
52	Kirby Puckett	.40
53	Cory Snyder	.05
54	Dave Winfield	.20
55	Terry Kennedy	.05
56	Matt Nokes	.05
57	B.J. Surhoff	.05
58	Roger Clemens	.50
59	Jack Morris	.05
60	Bret Saberhagen	.10
61	Ron Guidry	.05
62	Bruce Hurst	.05
63	Mark Langston	.05
64	Tom Henke	.05
65	Dan Plesac	.05
66	Dave Righetti	.05
67	Checklist	.05

1988 Topps Stickers

This set of 313 stickers (on 198 cards) offers an addition for 1988 - 66 different players are pictured on the backs of the sticker cards. The stickers come in two sizes (2-1/8" x 3" or 1-1/2" x 2-1/8"). Larger stickers fill and entire card, smaller ones are attached in pairs. A 36-page sticker yearbook has a designated space inside for each sticker, with one page per team and special pages of 1987 Highlights, World Series, All-Stars and Future Stars. No printing appears on the full-color action shot stickers except for a small black number in the lower left corner. Stickers were sold in packs of five (with gum) for 25 cents per pack. Unlike the 1987 Topps Stickers set, different pairings can be found, rather than the same two players/numbers always sharing the same sticker. To determine total value, combine the value of the stickercard (found in the 1988 Topps Stickercard checklist) with the values assigned the stickers in the following checklist.

		MT
Complete Set (313):		15.00
Common Player:		.05
Sticker Album:		1.50
1	1987 Highlights (Mark McGwire)	.25
2	1987 Highlights (Benny Santiago)	.05
3	1987 Highlights (Don Mattingly)	.25
4	1987 Highlights (Vince Coleman)	.05
5	1987 Highlights (Bob Boone)	.05
6	1987 Highlights (Steve Bedrosian)	.05
7	1987 Highlights (Nolan Ryan)	.40
8	1987 Highlights (Darrell Evans)	.05
9	1987 Highlights (Mike Schmidt)	.10
10	1987 Highlights (Don Baylor)	.05
11	1987 Highlights (Eddie Murray)	.10
12	1987 Highlights (Juan Beniquez)	.05
13	1987 Championship Series (John Tudor)	.05
14	1987 Championship Series (Jeff Reardon)	.05
15	1987 Championship Series (Tom Brunansky)	.05
16	1987 Championship Series (Jeffrey Leonard)	.05
17	1987 Championship Series (Gary Gaetti)	.05
18	1987 Championship Series (Cardinals Celebrate)	.05
19	1987 World Series (Danny Gladden)	.05
20	1987 World Series (Bert Blyleven)	.05
21	1987 World Series (John Tudor)	.05
22	1987 World Series (Tom Lawless)	.05
23	1987 World Series (Curt Ford)	.05
24	1987 World Series (Kent Hrbek)	.10
25	1987 World Series (Frank Viola)	.05
26	Dave Smith	.05
27	Jim Deshaies	.05
28	Billy Hatcher	.05
29	Kevin Bass	.05
30	Mike Scott	.05
31	Danny Walling	.05
32	Alan Ashby	.05
33	Ken Caminiti	.10
34	Bill Doran	.05
35	Glenn Davis	.05
36	Ozzie Virgil	.05
37	Ken Oberkfell	.05
38	Ken Griffey	.05
39	Albert Hall	.05
40	Zane Smith	.05
41	Andres Thomas	.05
42	Dion James	.05
43	Jim Acker	.05
44	Tom Glavine	.20
45	Dale Murphy	.15
46	Jack Clark	.05
47	Vince Coleman	.05
48	Ricky Horton	.05
49	Terry Pendleton	.05
50	Tom Herr	.05
51	Joe Magrane	.05
52	Tony Pena	.05
53	Ozzie Smith	.20
54	Todd Worrell	.05
55	Willie McGee	.05
56	Andre Dawson	.10
57	Ryne Sandberg	.25
58	Keith Moreland	.05
59	Greg Maddux	.60
60	Jody Davis	.05
61	Rick Sutcliffe	.05
62	Jamie Moyer	.05
63	Leon Durham	.05
64	Lee Smith	.05
65	Shawon Dunston	.10
66	Franklin Stubbs	.05
67	Mike Scioscia	.05
68	Orel Hershiser	.05
69	Mike Marshall	.05
70	Fernando Valenzuela	.05
71	Mickey Hatcher	.05
72	Matt Young	.05
73	Bob Welch	.05
74	Steve Sax	.05
75	Pedro Guerrero	.05
76	Tim Raines	.10
77	Casey Candaele	.05
78	Mike Fitzgerald	.05
79	Andres Galarraga	.10
80	Neal Heaton	.05
81	Hubie Brooks	.05
82	Floyd Youmans	.05
83	Herm Winningham	.05
84	Denny Martinez	.05
85	Tim Wallach	.05
86	Jeffrey Leonard	.05
87	Will Clark	.15
88	Kevin Mitchell	.05
89	Mike Aldrete	.05
90	Scott Garrelts	.05
91	Jose Uribe	.05
92	Bob Brenly	.05
93	Robby Thompson	.05
94	Don Robinson	.05
95	Candy Maldonado	.05
96	Darryl Strawberry	.10
97	Keith Hernandez	.05
98	Ron Darling	.05
99	Howard Johnson	.05
100	Roger McDowell	.05
101	Dwight Gooden	.10
102	Kevin McReynolds	.05
103	Sid Fernandez	.05
104	Dave Magadan	.05
105	Gary Carter	.10
106	Carmelo Martinez	.05
107	Eddie Whitson	.05
108	Tim Flannery	.05
109	Stan Jefferson	.05
110	John Kruk	.05
111	Chris Brown	.05
112	Benny Santiago	.05
113	Garry Templeton	.05
114	Lance McCullers	.05
115	Tony Gwynn	.45
116	Steve Bedrosian	.05
117	Von Hayes	.05
118	Kevin Gross	.05
119	Bruce Ruffin	.05
120	Juan Samuel	.05
121	Shane Rawley	.05
122	Chris James	.05
123	Lance Parrish	.05
124	Glenn Wilson	.05
125	Mike Schmidt	.25
126	Andy Van Slyke	.05
127	Jose Lind	.05
128	Al Pedrique	.05
129	Bobby Bonilla	.10
130	Sed Bream	.05
131	Mike LaValliere	.05
132	Mike Dunne	.05
133	Jeff Robinson	.05
134	Doug Drabek	.05
135	Barry Bonds	.60
136	Dave Parker	.05
137	Nick Esasky	.05
138	Buddy Bell	.05
139	Kal Daniels	.05
140	Barry Larkin	.20
141	Eric Davis	.05
142	John Franco	.05
143	Bo Diaz	.05
144	Ron Oester	.05
145	Dennis Rasmussen	.05
146	Eric Davis	.05
147	Ryne Sandberg	.30
148	Andre Dawson	.10
149	Mike Schmidt	.40
150	Jack Clark	.05
151	Darryl Strawberry	.15
152	Gary Carter	.10
153	Ozzie Smith	.20
154	Mike Scott	.05
155	Rickey Henderson	.20
156	Don Mattingly	.65
157	Wade Boggs	.40
158	George Bell	.05
159	Dave Winfield	.30
160	Cal Ripken, Jr.	.75
161	Terry Kennedy	.05
162	Willie Randolph	.05

163 Bret Saberhagen .05
164 Mark McGwire 1.00
165 Tony Phillips .05
166 Jay Howell .05
167 Carney Lansford .05
168 Dave Stewart .05
169 Alfredo Griffin .05
170 Dennis Eckersley .05
171 Mike Davis .05
172 Luis Polonia .05
173 Jose Canseco .35
174 Mike Witt .05
175 Jack Howell .05
176 Greg Minton .05
177 Dick Schofield .05
178 Gary Pettis .05
179 Wally Joyner .10
180 DeWayne Buice .05
181 Brian Downing .05
182 Bob Boone .05
183 Devon White .05
184 Jim Clancy .05
185 Willie Upshaw .05
186 Tom Henke .05
187 Ernie Whitt .05
188 George Bell .05
189 Lloyd Moseby .05
190 Jimmy Key .05
191 Dave Stieb .05
192 Jesse Barfield .05
193 Tony Fernandez .05
194 Paul Molitor .25
195 Jim Gantner .05
196 Teddy Higuera .05
197 Glenn Braggs .05
198 Rob Deer .05
199 Dale Sveum .05
200 Bill Wegman .05
201 Robin Yount .25
202 B.J. Surhoff .05
203 Dan Plesac .05
204 Pat Tabler .05
205 Mel Hall .05
206 Scott Bailes .05
207 Julio Franco .05
208 Cory Snyder .05
209 Chris Bando .05
210 Greg Swindell .05
211 Brook Jacoby .05
212 Brett Butler .05
213 Joe Carter .10
214 Mark Langston .05
215 Rey Quinones .05
216 Ed Nunez .05
217 Jim Presley .05
218 Phil Bradley .05
219 Alvin Davis .05
220 Dave Valle .05
221 Harold Reynolds .05
222 Scott Bradley .05
223 Gary Matthews .05
224 Eric Bell .05
225 Terry Kennedy .05
226 Dave Schmidt .05
227 Billy Ripken .05
228 Cal Ripken, Jr. .75
229 Ray Knight .05
230 Larry Sheets .05
231 Mike Boddicker .05
232 Tom Niedenfuer .05
233 Eddie Murray .25
234 Ruben Sierra .05
235 Steve Buechele .05
236 Charlie Hough .05
237 Oddibe McDowell .05
238 Mike Stanley .05
239 Pete Incaviglia .05
240 Pete O'Brien .05
241 Scott Fletcher .05
242 Dale Mohorcic .05
243 Larry Parrish .05
244 Wade Boggs .30
245 Dwight Evans .05
246 Sam Horn .05
247 Jim Rice .10
248 Marty Barrett .05
249 Mike Greenwell .05
250 Ellis Burks .10
251 Roger Clemens .25
252 Rich Gedman .05
253 Bruce Hurst .05
254 Bret Saberhagen .05
255 Frank White .05
256 Dan Quisenberry .05
257 Danny Tartabull .05
258 Bo Jackson .10
259 George Brett .25
260 Charlie Leibrandt .05
261 Kevin Seitzer .05
262 Mark Gubicza .05
263 Willie Wilson .05
264 Frank Tanana .05
265 Darrell Evans .05
266 Bill Madlock .05
267 Kirk Gibson .05
268 Jack Morris .05
269 Matt Nokes .05
270 Lou Whitaker .05
271 Eric King .05
272 Jim Morrison .05
273 Alan Trammell .10
274 Kent Hrbek .05
275 Tom Brunansky .05
276 Bert Blyleven .05
277 Gary Gaetti .05
278 Tim Laudner .05
279 Gene Larkin .05
280 Jeff Reardon .05
281 Danny Gladden .05
282 Frank Viola .05
283 Kirby Puckett .45
284 Ozzie Guillen .05
285 Ivan Calderon .05
286 Donnie Hill .05
287 Ken Williams .05
288 Jim Winn .05
289 Bob James .05
290 Carlton Fisk .25
291 Richard Dotson .05
292 Greg Walker .05
293 Harold Baines .10
294 Willie Randolph .05
295 Mike Pagliarulo .05
296 Ron Guidry .05
297 Rickey Henderson .15
298 Rick Rhoden .05
299 Don Mattingly .65
300 Dave Righetti .05
301 Claudell Washington .05
302 Dave Winfield .15
303 Gary Ward .05
304 Al Pedrique .05
305 Casey Candaele .05
306 Kevin Seitzer .05
307 Mike Dunne .05
308 Jeff Musselman .05
309 Mark McGwire 1.00
310 Ellis Burks .10
311 Matt Nokes .05
312 Mike Greenwell .05
313 Devon White .05

1988 Topps/Sports Shots Portfolios

One hundred and thirty of the biggest names from Topps' 1988 baseball card set were reproduced in the form of 9-1/2" x 11-3/4" cardboard folders. The folders reproduce both front and back of the '88 Topps cards and open to offer two pockets for storage. Various manufacturer and licensor logos are the only printing inside. The folders carried a suggested retail price of $1 apiece and were distributed in either team packs of or all-star assortments of 50 pieces each. By 1992, the folders were being wholesaled within the hobby at less than 30 cents apiece.

MT
Complete Set (130): 150.00
Common Player: 1.00
10 Ryne Sandberg 2.50
15 Chili Davis 1.00
25 Andres Galarraga 1.50
35 Harold Baines 1.00
39 Gerald Perry 1.00
40 Orel Hershiser 1.00
45 Kent Hrbek 1.00
50 Hubie Brooks 1.00
55 Phil Bradley 1.00
60 Rickey Henderson 2.00
70 Roger Clemens 3.00
75 Joe Carter 1.00
80 Mark Langston 1.00
90 Dale Murphy 1.50
95 Lance Parrish 1.00
100 Jack Clark 1.00
102 Barry Larkin 1.00
110 Teddy Higuera 1.00
118 Bob Welch 1.00
120 Kirby Puckett 3.00
130 Buddy Bell 1.00
138 Mitch Webster 1.00
140 Jesse Barfield 1.00
142 Andy Van Slyke 1.00
150 Eric Davis 1.00
165 Robin Yount 2.00
170 Goose Gossage 1.00
180 Terry Kennedy 1.00
184 Ivan Calderon 1.00
192 Devon White 1.00
193 Brian Fisher 1.00
195 Dan Quisenberry 1.00
197 Lance McCullers 1.00
200 Wade Boggs 2.50
210 Willie Randolph 1.00
215 Von Hayes 1.00
230 Pat Tabler 1.00
238 Luis Polonia 1.00
240 Lee Smith 1.00
250 Nolan Ryan 4.00
260 Vince Coleman 1.00
265 Bo Diaz 1.00
270 Mike Witt 1.00
280 Pete Incaviglia 1.00
285 Jim Presley 1.00
297 Zane Smith 1.00
300 Don Mattingly 3.00
305 Steve Sax 1.00
306 Billy Hatcher 1.00
320 Alan Trammell 1.00
327 Larry Sheets 1.00
331 Brian Downing 1.00
340 Jack Morris 1.00
343 Greg Gagne 1.00
350 Will Clark 1.50
360 Tony Gwynn 2.50
370 Jose Canseco 1.75
385 Carlton Fisk 2.50
408 Dion James 1.00
410 Tony Pena 1.00
420 Wally Joyner 1.25
424 Dwayne Murphy 1.00
430 Glenn Davis 1.00
440 Steve Bedrosian 1.00
450 Barry Bonds 3.00
452 Willie Wilson 1.00
460 Ozzie Smith 2.00
465 Paul Molitor 2.00
470 Dwight Evans 1.00
476 Dave Stewart 1.00
479 Brett Butler 1.00
480 Dwight Gooden 1.25
485 Harold Reynolds 1.00
490 Larry Parrish 1.00
491 B.J. Surhoff 1.00
495 Eddie Murray 2.00
497 Kevin Mitchell 1.00
500 Andre Dawson 1.00
510 Dave Winfield 1.50
525 Marty Barrett 1.00
530 Gary Carter 1.25
540 Bret Saberhagen 1.00
550 Pedro Guerrero 1.00
555 Brook Jacoby 1.00
560 Tim Wallach 1.00
565 Lloyd Moseby 1.00
570 Jeffrey Leonard 1.00
578 Gary Gaetti 1.00
580 Mark McGwire 5.00
590 George Bell 1.00
596 John Kruk 1.00
600 Mike Schmidt 2.50
605 Kirk Gibson 1.00
610 Keith Hernandez 1.00
613 Bobby Thigpen 1.00
615 Jody Davis 1.00
619 Mike Dunne 1.00
620 Cory Snyder 1.00
625 Frank Viola 1.00
645 Matt Nokes 1.00
649 De Wayne Buice 1.00
650 Cal Ripken Jr. 4.00
660 Rick Reuschel 1.00
670 Dan Plesac 1.00
675 Jim Rice 1.50
680 Charlie Hough 1.00
681 Bobby Bonilla 1.25
682 Jimmy Key 1.00
685 Ron Darling 1.00
693 Benito Santiago 1.00
700 George Brett 3.00
705 Juan Samuel 1.00
710 Darryl Strawberry 1.50
715 Todd Worrell 1.00
720 Tim Raines 1.25
721 Pete O'Brien 1.00
725 Mike Boddicker 1.00
730 John Franco 1.00
740 Rick Sutcliffe 1.00
745 Bill Doran 1.00
750 Bo Jackson 1.50
755 Ozzie Virgil 1.00
760 Mike Scott 1.00
764 Greg Walker 1.00
770 Lou Whitaker 1.00
771 Ruben Sierra 1.00
775 Dave Steib 1.00
780 Fernando Valenzuela 1.00
785 Alvin Davis 1.00
790 Dave Righetti 1.00

1989 Topps

Ten top young players from the June, 1988, draft are featured on "#1 Draft Pick" cards in this full-color basic set of 792 standard-size baseball cards. An additional five cards salute 1989 Future Stars, 22 cards highlight All-Stars, seven contain Record Breakers, five are designated Turn Back The Clock, and six contain checklists. This set features the familiar white borders, but upper-left and lower-right photo corners have been rounded off. A curved name banner in bright red or blue is beneath the team name in large script in the lower-right corner. The card backs are printed in black on a red background and include personal information and complete minor and major league stats. Another new addition in this set is the special Monthly Scoreboard chart that lists monthly stats (April through September) in two of several categories (hits, run, home runs, stolen bases, RBIs, wins, strikeouts, games or saves).

MT
Complete Set (792): 10.00
Common Player: .05
Wax Box: 9.00
1 George Bell (Record Breaker) .05
2 Wade Boggs (Record Breaker) .15
3 Gary Carter (Record Breaker) .05
4 Andre Dawson (Record Breaker) .05
5 Orel Hershiser (Record Breaker) .05
6 Doug Jones (Record Breaker) .05
7 Kevin McReynolds (Record Breaker) .05
8 *Dave Eiland* .05
9 Tim Teufel .05
10 Andre Dawson .10
11 Bruce Sutter .05
12 Dale Sveum .05
13 Doug Sisk .05
14 Tom Kelly .05
15 Robby Thompson .05
16 Ron Robinson .05
17 Brian Downing .05
18 Rick Rhoden .05
19 Greg Gagne .05
20 Steve Bedrosian .05
21 White Sox Leaders (Greg Walker) .05
22 Tim Crews .05
23 Mike Fitzgerald .05
24 Larry Andersen .05
25 Frank White .05
26 Dale Mohorcic .05
27 *Orestes Destrade* .05
28 Mike Moore .05
29 Kelly Gruber .05
30 Dwight Gooden .10
31 Terry Francona .05
32 Dennis Rasmussen .05
33 B.J. Surhoff .05
34 Ken Williams .05
35 John Tudor .05
36 Mitch Webster .05
37 Bob Stanley .05
38 Paul Runge .05
39 Mike Maddux .05
40 Steve Sax .05
41 Terry Mulholland .05
42 Jim Eppard .05
43 Guillermo Hernandez .05
44 Jim Snyder .05
45 Kal Daniels .05
46 Mark Portugal .05
47 Carney Lansford .05
48 Tim Burke .05
49 Craig Biggio .50
50 George Bell .05
51 Angels Leaders (Mark McLemore) .05
52 Bob Brenly .05
53 Ruben Sierra .05
54 Steve Trout .05
55 Julio Franco .05
56 Pat Tabler .05
57 Alejandro Pena .05
58 Lee Mazzilli .05
59 Mark Davis .05
60 Tom Brunansky .05
61 Neil Allen .05
62 Alfredo Griffin .05
63 Mark Clear .05
64 Alex Trevino .05
65 Rick Reuschel .05
66 Manny Trillo .05
67 Dave Palmer .05
68 Darrell Miller .05
69 Jeff Ballard .05
70 Mark McGwire 1.50
71 Mike Boddicker .05
72 John Moses .05
73 Pascual Perez .05
74 Nick Leyva .05
75 Tom Henke .05
76 *Terry Blocker* .05
77 Doyle Alexander .05
78 Jim Sundberg .05
79 Scott Bankhead .05
80 Cory Snyder .05
81 Expos Leaders (Tim Raines) .05
82 Dave Leiper .05
83 Jeff Blauser .05
84 *Bill Bene* (#1 Draft Pick) .05
85 Kevin McReynolds .05
86 Al Nipper .05
87 Larry Owen .05
88 *Darryl Hamilton* .10
89 Dave LaPoint .05
90 Vince Coleman .05
91 Floyd Youmans .05
92 Jeff Kunkel .05
93 Ken Howell .05
94 Chris Speier .05
95 Gerald Young .05
96 Rick Cerone .05
97 Greg Mathews .05
98 Larry Sheets .05
99 *Sherman Corbett* .05
100 Mike Schmidt .25
101 Les Straker .05
102 Mike Gallego .05
103 Tim Birtsas .05
104 Dallas Green .05
105 Ron Darling .05
106 Willie Upshaw .05
107 Jose DeLeon .05
108 Fred Manrique .05
109 *Hipolito Pena* .05
110 Paul Molitor .25
111 Reds Leaders (Eric Davis) .05
112 Jim Presley .05
113 Lloyd Moseby .05
114 Bob Kipper .05
115 Jody Davis .05
116 Jeff Montgomery .05
117 Dave Anderson .05
118 Checklist 1-132 .05
119 Terry Puhl .05
120 Frank Viola .05
121 Garry Templeton .05
122 Lance Johnson .05
123 Spike Owen .05
124 Jim Traber .05
125 Mike Krukow .05
126 Sid Bream .05
127 Walt Terrell .05
128 Milt Thompson .05
129 *Terry Clark* .05
130 Gerald Perry .05
131 Dave Otto .05
132 Curt Ford .05
133 Bill Long .05
134 Don Zimmer .05
135 Jose Rijo .05
136 Joey Meyer .05
137 Geno Petralli .05
138 Wallace Johnson .05
139 Mike Flanagan .05
140 Shawon Dunston .05
141 Indians Leaders (Brook Jacoby) .05
142 Mike Diaz .05
143 Mike Campbell .05
144 Jay Bell .05
145 Dave Stewart .05
146 Gary Pettis .05
147 DeWayne Buice .05
148 Bill Pecota .05
149 *Doug Dascenzo* .05
150 Fernando Valenzuela .05
151 Terry McGriff .05
152 Mark Thurmond .05
153 Jim Pankovits .05
154 Don Carman .05
155 Marty Barrett .05
156 *Dave Gallagher* .05
157 Tom Glavine .20
158 Mike Aldrete .05
159 Pat Clements .05
160 Jeffrey Leonard .05
161 *Gregg Olson* (#1 Draft Pick) .10
162 John Davis .05
163 Bob Forsch .05
164 Hal Lanier .05
165 Mike Dunne .05
166 *Doug Jennings* .05
167 *Steve Searcy* (Future Star) .05
168 Willie Wilson .05
169 Mike Jackson .05
170 Tony Fernandez .05
171 Braves Leaders (Andres Thomas) .05
172 Frank Williams .05

173	Mel Hall	.05
174	*Todd Burns*	.05
175	John Shelby	.05
176	Jeff Parrett	.05
177	*Monty Fariss* (#1 Draft Pick)	.10
178	Mark Grant	.05
179	Ozzie Virgil	.05
180	Mike Scott	.05
181	*Craig Worthington*	.05
182	Bob McClure	.05
183	Oddibe McDowell	.05
184	*John Costello*	.05
185	Claudell Washington	.05
186	Pat Perry	.05
187	Darren Daulton	.05
188	Dennis Lamp	.05
189	Kevin Mitchell	.05
190	Mike Witt	.05
191	*Sil Campusano*	.05
192	Paul Mirabella	.05
193	Sparky Anderson	.10
194	*Greg Harris*	.10
195	Ozzie Guillen	.05
196	Denny Walling	.05
197	Neal Heaton	.05
198	Danny Heep	.05
199	*Mike Schooler*	.05
200	George Brett	.30
201	Blue Jays Leaders (Kelly Gruber)	.05
202	*Brad Moore*	.05
203	Rob Ducey	.05
204	Brad Havens	.05
205	Dwight Evans	.05
206	Roberto Alomar	.50
207	Terry Leach	.05
208	Tom Pagnozzi	.05
209	*Jeff Bittiger*	.05
210	Dale Murphy	.10
211	Mike Pagliarulo	.05
212	Scott Sanderson	.05
213	Rene Gonzales	.05
214	Charlie O'Brien	.05
215	Kevin Gross	.05
216	Jack Howell	.05
217	Joe Price	.05
218	Mike LaValliere	.05
219	Jim Clancy	.05
220	Gary Gaetti	.05
221	Cecil Espy	.05
222	*Mark Lewis* (#1 Draft Pick)	.10
223	Jay Buhner	.15
224	Tony LaRussa	.05
225	*Ramon Martinez*	.25
226	Bill Doran	.05
227	John Farrell	.05
228	*Nelson Santovenia*	.05
229	Jimmy Key	.05
230	Ozzie Smith	.25
231	Padres Leaders (Roberto Alomar)	.15
232	Ricky Horton	.05
233	Gregg Jefferies (Future Star)	.25
234	Tom Browning	.05
235	John Kruk	.05
236	Charles Hudson	.05
237	Glenn Hubbard	.05
238	Eric King	.05
239	Tim Laudner	.05
240	Greg Maddux	.50
241	Brett Butler	.05
242	Ed Vande Berg	.05
243	Bob Boone	.05
244	Jim Acker	.05
245	Jim Rice	.10
246	Rey Quinones	.05
247	Shawn Hillegas	.05
248	Tony Phillips	.05
249	Tim Leary	.05
250	Cal Ripken, Jr.	.60
251	*John Dopson*	.05
252	Billy Hatcher	.05
253	*Jose Alvarez*	.05
254	Tom LaSorda	.15
255	Ron Guidry	.10
256	Benny Santiago	.05
257	Rick Aguilera	.05
258	Checklist 133-264	.05
259	Larry McWilliams	.05
260	Dave Winfield	.15
261	Cardinals Leaders (Tom Brunansky)	.05
262	*Jeff Pico*	.05
263	Mike Felder	.05
264	*Rob Dibble*	.10
265	Kent Hrbek	.05
266	Luis Aquino	.05
267	Jeff Robinson	.05
268	Keith Miller	.05
269	Tom Bolton	.05
270	Wally Joyner	.10
271	Jay Tibbs	.05
272	Ron Hassey	.05
273	Jose Lind	.05
274	Mark Eichhorn	.05
275	Danny Tartabull	.05
276	Paul Kilgus	.05
277	Mike Davis	.05
278	Andy McGaffigan	.05
279	Scott Bradley	.05
280	Bob Knepper	.05
281	Gary Redus	.05
282	*Cris Carpenter*	.10
283	Andy Allanson	.05
284	Jim Leyland	.05
285	John Candelaria	.05
286	Darrin Jackson	.05
287	Juan Nieves	.05
288	Pat Sheridan	.05
289	Ernie Whitt	.05
290	John Franco	.05
291	Mets Leaders (Darryl Strawberry)	.10
292	*Jim Corsi*	.05
293	Glenn Wilson	.05
294	Juan Berenguer	.05
295	Scott Fletcher	.05
296	Ron Gant	.10
297	*Oswald Peraza*	.05
298	Chris James	.05
299	*Steve Ellsworth*	.05
300	Darryl Strawberry	.10
301	Charlie Leibrandt	.05
302	Gary Ward	.05
303	Felix Fermin	.05
304	Joel Youngblood	.05
305	Dave Smith	.05
306	Tracy Woodson	.05
307	Lance McCullers	.05
308	Ron Karkovice	.05
309	Mario Diaz	.05
310	Rafael Palmeiro	.25
311	Chris Bosio	.05
312	Tom Lawless	.05
313	Denny Martinez	.05
314	Bobby Valentine	.05
315	Greg Swindell	.05
316	Walt Weiss	.05
317	*Jack Armstrong*	.05
318	Gene Larkin	.05
319	Greg Booker	.05
320	Lou Whitaker	.05
321	Red Sox Leaders (Jody Reed)	.05
322	John Smiley	.05
323	Gary Thurman	.05
324	*Bob Milacki*	.05
325	Jesse Barfield	.05
326	Dennis Boyd	.05
327	*Mark Lemke*	.05
328	Rick Honeycutt	.05
329	Bob Melvin	.05
330	Eric Davis	.10
331	Curt Wilkerson	.05
332	Tony Armas	.05
333	Bob Ojeda	.05
334	Steve Lyons	.05
335	Dave Righetti	.05
336	Steve Balboni	.05
337	Calvin Schiraldi	.05
338	Jim Adduci	.05
339	Scott Bailes	.05
340	Kirk Gibson	.05
341	Jim Deshaies	.05
342	Tom Brookens	.05
343	*Gary Sheffield* (Future Star)	.75
344	Tom Trebelhorn	.05
345	Charlie Hough	.05
346	Rex Hudler	.05
347	John Cerutti	.05
348	Ed Hearn	.05
349	*Ron Jones*	.05
350	Andy Van Slyke	.05
351	Giants Leaders (Bob Melvin)	.05
352	Rick Schu	.05
353	Marvell Wynne	.05
354	Larry Parrish	.05
355	Mark Langston	.05
356	Kevin Elster	.05
357	Jerry Reuss	.05
358	*Ricky Jordan*	.05
359	Tommy John	.10
360	Ryne Sandberg	.30
361	Kelly Downs	.05
362	Jack Lazorko	.05
363	Rich Yett	.05
364	Rob Deer	.05
365	Mike Henneman	.05
366	Herm Winningham	.05
367	*Johnny Paredes*	.05
368	Brian Holton	.05
369	Ken Caminiti	.10
370	Dennis Eckersley	.10
371	Manny Lee	.05
372	Craig Lefferts	.05
373	Tracy Jones	.05
374	John Wathan	.05
375	Terry Pendleton	.05
376	Steve Lombardozzi	.05
377	Mike Smithson	.05
378	Checklist 265-396	.05
379	Tim Flannery	.05
380	Rickey Henderson	.10
381	Orioles Leaders (Larry Sheets)	.05
382	John Smoltz	.50
383	Howard Johnson	.05
384	Mark Salas	.05
385	Von Hayes	.05
386	Andres Galarraga (All-Star)	.10
387	Ryne Sandberg (All-Star)	.15
388	Bobby Bonilla (All-Star)	.05
389	Ozzie Smith (All-Star)	.15
390	Darryl Strawberry (All-Star)	.10
391	Andre Dawson (All-Star)	.05
392	Andy Van Slyke (All-Star)	.05
393	Gary Carter (All-Star)	.05
394	Orel Hershiser (All-Star)	.05
395	Danny Jackson (All-Star)	.05
396	Kirk Gibson (All-Star)	.05
397	Don Mattingly (All-Star)	.20
398	Julio Franco (All-Star)	.05
399	Wade Boggs (All-Star)	.15
400	Alan Trammell (All-Star)	.05
401	Jose Canseco (All-Star)	.20
402	Mike Greenwell (All-Star)	.05
403	Kirby Puckett (All-Star)	.20
404	Bob Boone (All-Star)	.05
405	Roger Clemens (All-Star)	.25
406	Frank Viola (All-Star)	.05
407	Dave Winfield (All-Star)	.10
408	Greg Walker	.05
409	Ken Dayley	.05
410	Jack Clark	.05
411	Mitch Williams	.05
412	Barry Lyons	.05
413	Mike Kingery	.05
414	Jim Fregosi	.05
415	Rich Gossage	.10
416	Fred Lynn	.05
417	Mike LaCoss	.05
418	Bob Dernier	.05
419	Tom Filer	.05
420	Joe Carter	.10
421	Kirk McCaskill	.05
422	Bo Diaz	.05
423	Brian Fisher	.05
424	Luis Polonia	.05
425	Jay Howell	.05
426	Danny Gladden	.05
427	Eric Show	.05
428	Craig Reynolds	.05
429	Twins Leaders (Greg Gagne)	.05
430	Mark Gubicza	.05
431	Luis Rivera	.05
432	*Chad Kreuter*	.10
433	Albert Hall	.05
434	*Ken Patterson*	.10
435	Len Dykstra	.05
436	Bobby Meacham	.05
437	Andy Benes (#1 Draft Pick)	.25
438	Greg Gross	.05
439	Frank DiPino	.05
440	Bobby Bonilla	.10
441	Jerry Reed	.05
442	Jose Oquendo	.05
443	*Rod Nichols*	.05
444	Moose Stubing	.05
445	Matt Nokes	.05
446	Rob Murphy	.05
447	Donell Nixon	.05
448	Eric Plunk	.05
449	Carmelo Martinez	.05
450	Roger Clemens	.50
451	Mark Davidson	.05
452	*Israel Sanchez*	.05
453	Tom Prince	.05
454	Paul Assenmacher	.05
455	Johnny Ray	.05
456	Tim Belcher	.05
457	Mackey Sasser	.05
458	*Donn Pall*	.05
459	Mariners Leaders (Dave Valle)	.05
460	Dave Stieb	.05
461	Buddy Bell	.05
462	Jose Guzman	.05
463	Steve Lake	.05
464	Bryn Smith	.05
465	Mark Grace	.20
466	Chuck Crim	.05
467	Jim Walewander	.05
468	Henry Cotto	.05
469	*Jose Bautista*	.05
470	Lance Parrish	.05
471	*Steve Curry*	.05
472	Brian Harper	.05
473	Don Robinson	.05
474	Bob Rodgers	.05
475	Dave Parker	.05
476	Jon Perlman	.05
477	Dick Schofield	.05
478	Doug Drabek	.05
479	*Mike Macfarlane*	.10
480	Keith Hernandez	.05
481	Chris Brown	.05
482	*Steve Peters*	.05
483	Mickey Hatcher	.05
484	Steve Shields	.05
485	Hubie Brooks	.05
486	Jack McDowell	.05
487	Scott Lusader	.05
488	Kevin Coffman	.05
489	Phillies Leaders (Mike Schmidt)	.15
490	*Chris Sabo*	.15
491	Mike Birkbeck	.05
492	Alan Ashby	.05
493	Todd Benzinger	.05
494	Shane Rawley	.05
495	Candy Maldonado	.05
496	Dwayne Henry	.05
497	Pete Stanicek	.05
498	Dave Valle	.05
499	*Don Heinkel*	.05
500	Jose Canseco	.25
501	Vance Law	.05
502	Duane Ward	.05
503	Al Newman	.05
504	Bob Walk	.05
505	Pete Rose	.30
506	Kirt Manwaring	.05
507	Steve Farr	.05
508	Wally Backman	.05
509	Bud Black	.05
510	Bob Horner	.05
511	Richard Dotson	.05
512	Donnie Hill	.05
513	Jesse Orosco	.05
514	Chet Lemon	.05
515	Barry Larkin	.25
516	Eddie Whitson	.05
517	Greg Brock	.05
518	Bruce Ruffin	.05
519	Yankees Leaders (Willie Randolph)	.05
520	Rick Sutcliffe	.05
521	Mickey Tettleton	.05
522	*Randy Kramer*	.05
523	Andres Thomas	.05
524	Checklist 397-528	.05
525	Chili Davis	.05
526	Wes Gardner	.05
527	Dave Henderson	.05
528	*Luis Medina*	.05
529	Tom Foley	.05
530	Nolan Ryan	.75
531	Dave Hengel	.05
532	Jerry Browne	.05
533	Andy Hawkins	.05
534	Doc Edwards	.05
535	Todd Worrell	.05
536	Joel Skinner	.05
537	Pete Smith	.05
538	Juan Castillo	.05
539	Barry Jones	.05
540	Bo Jackson	.20
541	Cecil Fielder	.10
542	Todd Frohwirth	.05
543	Damon Berryhill	.05
544	Jeff Sellers	.05
545	Mookie Wilson	.05
546	Mark Williamson	.05
547	Mark McLemore	.05
548	Bobby Witt	.05
549	Cubs Leaders (Jamie Moyer)	.05
550	Orel Hershiser	.05
551	Randy Ready	.05
552	Greg Cadaret	.05
553	Luis Salazar	.05
554	Nick Esasky	.05
555	Bert Blyleven	.05
556	Bruce Fields	.05
557	*Keith Miller*	.05
558	Dan Pasqua	.05
559	Juan Agosto	.05
560	Tim Raines	.10
561	Luis Aguayo	.05
562	Danny Cox	.05
563	Bill Schroeder	.05
564	Russ Nixon	.05
565	Jeff Russell	.05
566	Al Pedrique	.05
567	David Wells	.10
568	Mickey Brantley	.05
569	*German Jimenez*	.05
570	Tony Gwynn	.50
571	Billy Ripken	.05
572	Atlee Hammaker	.05
573	Jim Abbott (#1 Draft Pick)	.15
574	Dave Clark	.05
575	Juan Samuel	.05
576	Greg Minton	.05
577	Randy Bush	.05
578	John Morris	.05
579	Astros Leaders (Glenn Davis)	.05
580	Harold Reynolds	.05
581	Gene Nelson	.05
582	Mike Marshall	.05
583	*Paul Gibson*	.05
584	Randy Velarde	.05
585	Harold Baines	.05
586	Joe Boever	.05
587	Mike Stanley	.05
588	*Luis Alicea*	.10
589	Dave Meads	.05
590	Andres Galarraga	.25
591	Jeff Musselman	.05
592	John Cangelosi	.05
593	Drew Hall	.05
594	Jimy Williams	.05
595	Teddy Higuera	.05
596	Kurt Stillwell	.05
597	*Terry Taylor*	.05
598	Ken Gerhart	.05
599	Tom Candiotti	.05
600	Wade Boggs	.25
601	Dave Dravecky	.05
602	Devon White	.05
603	Frank Tanana	.05
604	Paul O'Neill	.20
605a	Bob Welch (missing Complete Major League Pitching Record line)	1.00
605b	Bob Welch (contains Complete Major League Pitching Record line)	.05
606	Rick Dempsey	.05
607	*Willie Ansley* (#1 Draft Pick)	.05
608	Phil Bradley	.05
609	Tigers Leaders (Frank Tanana)	.05
610	Randy Myers	.05
611	Don Slaught	.05
612	Dan Quisenberry	.05
613	*Gary Varsho*	.05
614	Joe Hesketh	.05
615	Robin Yount	.25
616	*Steve Rosenberg*	.05
617	*Mark Parent*	.05
618	Rance Mulliniks	.05
619	Checklist 529-660	.05
620	Barry Bonds	.40
621	Rick Mahler	.05
622	Stan Javier	.05
623	Fred Toliver	.05
624	Jack McKeon	.05
625	Eddie Murray	.15
626	Jeff Reed	.05
627	Greg Harris	.05
628	Matt Williams	.25
629	Pete O'Brien	.05
630	Mike Greenwell	.05
631	Dave Bergman	.05
632	*Bryan Harvey*	.10
633	Daryl Boston	.05
634	Marvin Freeman	.05
635	Willie Randolph	.05
636	Bill Wilkinson	.05
637	Carmen Castillo	.05
638	Floyd Bannister	.05
639	Athletics Leaders (Walt Weiss)	.05
640	Willie McGee	.05
641	Curt Young	.05
642	Argenis Salazar	.05
643	*Louie Meadows*	.05
644	Lloyd McClendon	.05
645	Jack Morris	.05
646	Kevin Bass	.05
647	*Randy Johnson*	1.50
648	*Sandy Alomar* (Future Star)	.25
649	Stewart Cliburn	.05
650	Kirby Puckett	.35
651	Tom Niedenfuer	.05
652	Rich Gedman	.05
653	*Tommy Barrett*	.05
654	Whitey Herzog	.05
655	Dave Magadan	.05
656	Ivan Calderon	.05
657	Joe Magrane	.05
658	R.J. Reynolds	.05
659	Al Leiter	.05
660	Will Clark	.20
661	Dwight Gooden (Turn Back the Clock)	.10
662	Lou Brock (Turn Back the Clock)	.05
663	Hank Aaron (Turn Back the Clock)	.15
664	Gil Hodges (Turn Back the Clock)	.05
665	Tony Oliva (Turn Back the Clock)	.05
666	Randy St. Claire	.05
667	Dwayne Murphy	.05
668	Mike Bielecki	.05
669	Dodgers Leaders (Orel Hershiser)	.05
670	Kevin Seitzer	.05
671	Jim Gantner	.05
672	Allan Anderson	.05
673	Don Baylor	.10
674	Otis Nixon	.05
675	Bruce Hurst	.05
676	Ernie Riles	.05
677	Dave Schmidt	.05
678	Dion James	.05
679	Willie Fraser	.05
680	Gary Carter	.10
681	Jeff Robinson	.05
682	Rick Leach	.05
683	*Jose Cecena*	.05
684	Dave Johnson	.05
685	Jeff Treadway	.05
686	Scott Terry	.05
687	Alvin Davis	.05
688	Zane Smith	.05
689	Stan Jefferson	.05
690	Doug Jones	.05
691	Roberto Kelly	.05
692	Steve Ontiveros	.05
693	*Pat Borders*	.15
694	Les Lancaster	.05
695	Carlton Fisk	.25
696	Don August	.05
697	Franklin Stubbs	.05
698	Keith Atherton	.05
699	Pirates Leaders (Al Pedrique)	.05
700	Don Mattingly	.35
701	Storm Davis	.05
702	Jamie Quirk	.05
703	Scott Garrelts	.05
704	*Carlos Quintana*	.05
705	Terry Kennedy	.05
706	Pete Incaviglia	.05
707	Steve Jeltz	.05
708	Chuck Finley	.05
709	Tom Herr	.05
710	Dave Cone	.20
711	*Candy Sierra*	.05
712	Bill Swift	.05

713	*Ty Griffin* (#1 Draft Pick)	.05
714	Joe M. Morgan	.05
715	Tony Pena	.05
716	Wayne Tolleson	.05
717	Jamie Moyer	.05
718	Glenn Braggs	.05
719	Danny Darwin	.05
720	Tim Wallach	.05
721	*Ron Tingley*	.05
722	Todd Stottlemyre	.05
723	Rafael Belliard	.05
724	Jerry Don Gleaton	.05
725	Terry Steinbach	.05
726	Dickie Thon	.05
727	Joe Orsulak	.05
728	Charlie Puleo	.05
729	Rangers Leaders (Steve Buechele)	.05
730	Danny Jackson	.05
731	Mike Young	.05
732	Steve Buechele	.05
733	*Randy Bockus*	.05
734	Jody Reed	.05
735	Roger McDowell	.05
736	Jeff Hamilton	.05
737	*Norm Charlton*	.15
738	Darnell Coles	.05
739	Brook Jacoby	.05
740	Dan Plesac	.05
741	Ken Phelps	.05
742	*Mike Harkey* (Future Star)	.05
743	Mike Heath	.05
744	Roger Craig	.05
745	Fred McGriff	.15
746	*German Gonzalez*	.05
747	Wil Tejada	.05
748	Jimmy Jones	.05
749	Rafael Ramirez	.05
750	Bret Saberhagen	.05
751	Ken Oberkfell	.05
752	Jim Gott	.05
753	Jose Uribe	.05
754	Bob Brower	.05
755	Mike Scioscia	.05
756	*Scott Medvin*	.05
757	Brady Anderson	.25
758	Gene Walter	.05
759	Brewers Leaders (Rob Deer)	.05
760	Lee Smith	.05
761	*Dante Bichette*	.50
762	Bobby Thigpen	.05
763	Dave Martinez	.05
764	Robin Ventura (#1 Draft Pick)	.75
765	Glenn Davis	.05
766	Cecilio Guante	.05
767	*Mike Capel*	.05
768	Bill Wegman	.05
769	Junior Ortiz	.05
770	Alan Trammell	.10
771	Ron Kittle	.05
772	Ron Oester	.05
773	Keith Moreland	.05
774	Frank Robinson	.15
775	Jeff Reardon	.05
776	Nelson Liriano	.05
777	Ted Power	.05
778	Bruce Benedict	.05
779	Craig McMurtry	.05
780	Pedro Guerrero	.05
781	*Greg Briley*	.05
782	Checklist 661-792	.05
783	*Trevor Wilson*	.10
784	*Steve Avery* (#1 Draft Pick)	.20
785	Ellis Burks	.10
786	Melido Perez	.05
787	*Dave West*	.10
788	Mike Morgan	.05
789	Royals Leaders (Bo Jackson)	.10
790	Sid Fernandez	.05
791	Jim Lindeman	.05
792	Rafael Santana	.05

1989 Topps Tiffany

This special hobby-only edition shares the checklist with the regular 1989 Topps set. Cards are identical except for the use of white cardboard stock and the high-gloss front coating. Production has been reported as 25,000 sets.

	MT
Complete Set (792):	100.00
Common Player:	.10
(Star cards valued at 3x-4X corresponding cards in regular 1989 Topps issue)	

1989 Topps Traded

For the ninth straight year, Topps issued its annual 132-card "Traded" set at the end of the 1989 baseball season. The set, which was packaged in a special box and sold by hobby dealers, includes traded players and rookies who were not in the regular 1989 Topps set.

		MT
Complete Set (132):		30.00
Common Player:		.05
1T	Don Aase	.05
2T	Jim Abbott	.15
3T	Kent Anderson	.05
4T	Keith Atherton	.05
5T	Wally Backman	.05
6T	Steve Balboni	.05
7T	Jesse Barfield	.05
8T	Steve Bedrosian	.05
9T	Todd Benzinger	.05
10T	Geronimo Berroa	.10
11T	Bert Blyleven	.05
12T	Bob Boone	.05
13T	Phil Bradley	.05
14T	Jeff Brantley	.05
15T	Kevin Brown	.15
16T	Jerry Browne	.05
17T	Chuck Cary	.05
18T	Carmen Castillo	.05
19T	Jim Clancy	.05
20T	Jack Clark	.05
21T	Bryan Clutterbuck	.05
22T	Jody Davis	.05
23T	Mike Devereaux	.05
24T	Frank DiPino	.05
25T	Benny Distefano	.05
26T	John Dopson	.05
27T	Len Dykstra	.05
28T	Jim Eisenreich	.05
29T	Nick Esasky	.05
30T	Alvaro Espinoza	.05
31T	Darrell Evans	.05
32T	Junior Felix	.05
33T	Felix Fermin	.05
34T	Julio Franco	.05
35T	Terry Francona	.05
36T	Cito Gaston	.05
37T	Bob Geren (photo actually Mike Fennell)	.05
38T	*Tom Gordon*	.20
39T	Tommy Gregg	.05
40T	Ken Griffey	.10
41T	*Ken Griffey, Jr.*	25.00
42T	Kevin Gross	.05
43T	Lee Guetterman	.05
44T	Mel Hall	.05
45T	Erik Hanson	.15
46T	Gene Harris	.05
47T	Andy Hawkins	.05
48T	Rickey Henderson	.25
49T	Tom Herr	.05
50T	*Ken Hill*	.25
51T	Brian Holman	.05
52T	Brian Holton	.05
53T	Art Howe	.05
54T	Ken Howell	.05
55T	Bruce Hurst	.05
56T	Chris James	.05
57T	Randy Johnson	1.00
58T	Jimmy Jones	.05
59T	Terry Kennedy	.05
60T	Paul Kilgus	.05
61T	Eric King	.05
62T	Ron Kittle	.05
63T	John Kruk	.05
64T	Randy Kutcher	.05
65T	Steve Lake	.05
66T	Mark Langston	.10
67T	Dave LaPoint	.05
68T	Rick Leach	.05
69T	Terry Leach	.05
70T	Jim Levebvre	.05
71T	Al Leiter	.05
72T	Jeffrey Leonard	.05
73T	Derek Lilliquist	.05
74T	Rick Mahler	.05
75T	Tom McCarthy	.05
76T	Lloyd McClendon	.05
77T	Lance McCullers	.05
78T	Oddibe McDowell	.05
79T	Roger McDowell	.05
80T	Larry McWilliams	.05
81T	Randy Milligan	.05
82T	Mike Moore	.05
83T	Keith Moreland	.05
84T	Mike Morgan	.05
85T	Jamie Moyer	.05
86T	Rob Murphy	.05
87T	Eddie Murray	.40
88T	Pete O'Brien	.05
89T	Gregg Olson	.05
90T	Steve Ontiveros	.05
91T	Jesse Orosco	.05
92T	Spike Owen	.05
93T	Rafael Palmeiro	.30
94T	Clay Parker	.05
95T	Jeff Parrett	.05
96T	Lance Parrish	.05
97T	Dennis Powell	.05
98T	Rey Quinones	.05
99T	Doug Rader	.05
100T	Willie Randolph	.05
101T	Shane Rawley	.05
102T	Randy Ready	.05
103T	Bip Roberts	.05
104T	Kenny Rogers	.25
105T	Ed Romero	.05
106T	Nolan Ryan	1.50
107T	Luis Salazar	.05
108T	Juan Samuel	.05
109T	Alex Sanchez	.05
110T	*Deion Sanders*	.75
111T	Steve Sax	.05
112T	Rick Schu	.05
113T	Dwight Smith	.05
114T	Lonnie Smith	.05
115T	Billy Spiers	.10
116T	Kent Tekulve	.05
117T	Walt Terrell	.05
118T	Milt Thompson	.05
119T	Dickie Thon	.05
120T	Jeff Torborg	.05
121T	Jeff Treadway	.05
122T	*Omar Vizquel*	.50
123T	Jerome Walton	.05
124T	Gary Ward	.05
125T	Claudell Washington	.05
126T	Curt Wilkerson	.05
127T	Eddie Williams	.05
128T	Frank Williams	.05
129T	Ken Williams	.05
130T	Mitch Williams	.05
131T	Steve Wilson	.05
---	Topps Magazine subscription offer card	.05

1989 Topps Traded Tiffany

The Topps Traded set was issued in a specially boxed, hobby-only editions. Cards are identical to the regular-issue Topps Traded cards except for the application of a high-gloss to the fronts. Production has been reported as 15,000 sets.

	MT
Complete Set (132):	350.00
Common Player:	.15
(Star cards valued at 3X-4X corresponding cards in regular Topps Traded issue)	

1989 Topps Box Panels

Continuing its practice of printing baseball cards on the bottom panels of its wax pack boxes, Topps in 1989 issued a special 16-card set, printing four cards on each of four different box-bottom panels. The cards are identical in design to the regular 1989 Topps cards. They are designated by letter (from A through P) rather than by number.

		MT
Complete Panel Set (4):		10.00
Complete Singles Set: (16):		7.50
Common Panel:		1.50
Common Single Player:		.10
	PANEL	1.50
A	George Bell	.10
B	Bill Buckner	.15
C	Darrell Evans	.10
D	Goose Gossage	.10
	PANEL	1.50
E	Greg Gross	.10
F	Rickey Henderson	.40
G	Keith Hernandez	.20
H	Tommy Lasorda	.10
	PANEL	7.50
I	Jim Rice	.20
J	Cal Ripken Jr.	2.00
K	Nolan Ryan	2.00
L	Mike Schmidt	.75
	PANEL	1.50
M	Bruce Sutter	.10
N	Don Sutton	.20
O	Kent Tekulve	.10
P	Dave Winfield	.50

1989 Topps All-Star Glossy Set of 22

The glossy All-Stars were included in the Topps 1989 rack packs. Format was very similar to the sets produced since 1984. Besides the starting lineups of the 1988 All-Star Game, the set included the managers and honorary team captains, Bobby Doerr and Willie Stargell.

		MT
Complete Set (22):		2.50
Common Player:		.05
1	Tom Kelly	.05
2	Mark McGwire	1.50
3	Paul Molitor	.25
4	Wade Boggs	.30
5	Cal Ripken, Jr.	.90
6	Jose Canseco	.30
7	Rickey Henderson	.15
8	Dave Winfield	.15
9	Terry Steinbach	.05
10	Frank Viola	.05
11	Bobby Doerr	.05
12	Whitey Herzog	.05
13	Will Clark	.20
14	Ryne Sandberg	.40
15	Bobby Bonilla	.05
16	Ozzie Smith	.30
17	Vince Coleman	.05
18	Andre Dawson	.10
19	Darryl Strawberry	.10
20	Gary Carter	.10
21	Dwight Gooden	.10
22	Willie Stargell	.10

1989 Topps All-Star Glossy Set of 60

For the seventh straight year Topps issued this "send-away" glossy set. Divided into six 10-card sets, it was available only by sending in special offer cards from wax packs. The 2-1/2" x 3-1/2" cards feature full-color photos bordered in white with a thin yellow frame. The player's name appears in small print in the lower-right corner. Red-and-blue-printed flip sides provide basic information. Any of the six 10-card sets were available for $1.25 and six special offer cards. The set was also made available in its complete 60-card set form for $7.50 and 18 special offer cards.

		MT
Complete Set (60):		10.00
Common Player:		.15
1	Kirby Puckett	.75
2	Eric Davis	.15
3	Joe Carter	.15
4	Andy Van Slyke	.15
5	Wade Boggs	.70
6	Dave Cone	.15
7	Kent Hrbek	.15
8	Darryl Strawberry	.20
9	Jay Buhner	.15
10	Ron Gant	.15
11	Will Clark	.50
12	Jose Canseco	.50
13	Juan Samuel	.15
14	George Brett	.75
15	Benny Santiago	.15
16	Dennis Eckersley	.15
17	Gary Carter	.20
18	Frank Viola	.15
19	Roberto Alomar	.35
20	Paul Gibson	.15
21	Dave Winfield	.35
22	Howard Johnson	.15
23	Roger Clemens	.75
24	Bobby Bonilla	.15
25	Alan Trammell	.15
26	Kevin McReynolds	.15
27	George Bell	.15
28	Bruce Hurst	.15
29	Mark Grace	.35
30	Tim Belcher	.15
31	Mike Greenwell	.15
32	Glenn Davis	.15
33	Gary Gaetti	.15
34	Ryne Sandberg	.60
35	Rickey Henderson	.50
36	Dwight Evans	.15
37	Doc Gooden	.20
38	Robin Yount	.60
39	Damon Berryhill	.15
40	Chris Sabo	.15
41	Mark McGwire	1.50
42	Ozzie Smith	.50
43	Paul Molitor	.35
44	Andres Galarraga	.25
45	Dave Stewart	.15
46	Tom Browning	.15
47	Cal Ripken, Jr.	2.00
48	Orel Hershiser	.15
49	Dave Gallagher	.15
50	Walt Weiss	.15
51	Don Mattingly	1.00
52	Tony Fernandez	.15
53	Tim Raines	.20
54	Jeff Reardon	.15
55	Kirk Gibson	.15
56	Jack Clark	.15
57	Danny Jackson	.15
58	Tony Gwynn	.75
59	Cecil Espy	.15
60	Jody Reed	.15

1989 Topps American Baseball

For the second consecutive year Topps released an 88-

card set of baseball cards available in both the United States and the United Kingdom. The mini-sized cards (2-1/4" x 3") are printed on white stock with a low-gloss finish. The game-action color player photo is outlined in red, white, and blue and framed in white. Backs are horizontal and include a characterization cartoon along with biographical information and statistics. The cards were sold in packs of five with a stick of bubble gum.

		MT
Complete Set (88):		9.00
Common Player:		.10
1	Brady Anderson	.25
2	Harold Baines	.10
3	George Bell	.10
4	Wade Boggs	.60
5	Barry Bonds	.90
6	Bobby Bonilla	.10
7	George Brett	.80
8	Hubie Brooks	.10
9	Tom Brunansky	.10
10	Jay Buhner	.10
11	Brett Butler	.10
12	Jose Canseco	.50
13	Joe Carter	.10
14	Jack Clark	.10
15	Will Clark	.45
16	Roger Clemens	.65
17	Dave Cone	.10
18	Alvin Davis	.10
19	Eric Davis	.10
20	Glenn Davis	.10
21	Andre Dawson	.15
22	Bill Doran	.10
23	Dennis Eckersley	.10
24	Dwight Evans	.10
25	Tony Fernandez	.10
26	Carlton Fisk	.30
27	John Franco	.10
28	Andres Galarraga	.10
29	Ron Gant	.10
30	Kirk Gibson	.10
31	Dwight Gooden	.15
32	Mike Greenwell	.10
33	Mark Gubicza	.10
34	Pedro Gurrero	.10
35	Ozzie Guillen	.10
36	Tony Gwynn	.75
37	Rickey Henderson	.25
38	Orel Hershiser	.10
39	Teddy Higuera	.10
40	Charlie Hough	.10
41	Kent Hrbek	.10
42	Bruce Hurst	.10
43	Bo Jackson	.20
44	Gregg Jefferies	.10
45	Ricky Jordan	.10
46	Wally Joyner	.15
47	Mark Langston	.10
48	Mike Marshall	.10
49	Don Mattingly	1.00
50	Fred McGriff	.25
51	Mark McGwire	2.00
52	Kevin McReynolds	.10
53	Paul Molitor	.45
54	Jack Morris	.10
55	Dale Murphy	.15
56	Eddie Murray	.30
57	Pete O'Brien	.10
58	Rafael Palmeiro	.25
59	Gerald Perry	.10
60	Kirby Puckett	.75
61	Tim Raines	.15
62	Johnny Ray	.10
63	Rick Reuschel	.10
64	Cal Ripken	1.50
65	Chris Sabo	.10
66	Juan Samuel	.10
67	Ryne Sandberg	.60
68	Benny Santiago	.10
69	Steve Sax	.10
70	Mike Schmidt	.90
71	Ruben Sierra	.10
72	Ozzie Smith	.45
73	Cory Snyder	.10
74	Dave Stewart	.10
75	Darryl Strawberry	.15
76	Greg Swindell	.10
77	Alan Trammell	.10
78	Fernando Valenzuela	.10
79	Andy Van Slyke	.10
80	Frank Viola	.10
81	Claudell Washington	.10
82	Walt Weiss	.10
83	Lou Whitaker	.10
84	Dave Winfield	.35
85	Mike Witt	.10
86	Gerald Young	.10
87	Robin Yount	.45
88	Checklist	.10

1989 Topps Batting Leaders

The active career batting leaders are showcased in this 22-card set. The 2-1/2" x 3-1/2" cards are printed on super glossy stock with full-color photos and bright red borders. A "Top Active Career Batting Leaders" cup is displayed in a lower corner. The player's name appears above the photo. This set is specially numbered in accordance to career batting average. Wade Boggs is featured on card #1 as the top active career batting leader. The flip sides present batting statistics. One batting leader card was included in each K-Mart blister pack, which also includes 100 cards from the 1989 regular Topps set.

		MT
Complete Set (22):		19.00
Common Player:		.50
1	Wade Boggs	1.50
2	Tony Gwynn	2.50
3	Don Mattingly	2.50
4	Kirby Puckett	2.50
5	George Brett	2.00
6	Pedro Guerrero	.50
7	Tim Raines	.60
8	Keith Hernandez	.50
9	Jim Rice	.65
10	Paul Molitor	1.50
11	Eddie Murray	1.00
12	Willie McGee	.50
13	Dave Parker	.50
14	Julio Franco	.50
15	Rickey Henderson	.90
16	Kent Hrbek	.50
17	Willie Wilson	.50
18	Johnny Ray	.50
19	Pat Tabler	.50
20	Carney Lansford	.50
21	Robin Yount	1.50
22	Alan Trammell	.50

1989 Topps Big Baseball

Known by collectors as Topps "Big Baseball," the cards in this 330-card set measure 2-5/8" x 3-3/4" and are patterned after the 1956 Topps cards. The glossy card fronts are horizontally-designed and include two photos of each player, a portrait alongside an action photo. The backs include 1988 and career stats, but are dominated by a color cartoon featuring the player. Members of the 1988 Team U.S.A. Olympic baseball team are included in the set, which was issued in three series of 110 cards each.

		MT
Complete Set (330):		22.00
Common Player:		.05
1	Orel Hershiser	.10
2	Harold Reynolds	.05
3	Jody Davis	.05
4	Greg Walker	.05
5	Barry Bonds	.60
6	Bret Saberhagen	.10
7	Johnny Ray	.05
8	Mike Fiore	.05
9	Juan Castillo	.05
10	Todd Burns	.05
11	Carmelo Martinez	.05
12	Geno Petralli	.05
13	Mel Hall	.05
14	Tom Browning	.05
15	Fred McGriff	.15
16	Kevin Elster	.05
17	Tim Leary	.05
18	Jim Rice	.10
19	Bret Barberie	.10
20	Jay Buhner	.05
21	Atlee Hammaker	.05
22	Lou Whitaker	.05
23	Paul Runge	.05
24	Carlton Fisk	.20
25	Jose Lind	.05
26	Mark Gubicza	.05
27	Billy Ripken	.05
28	Mike Pagliarulo	.05
29	Jim Deshaies	.05
30	Mark McLemore	.05
31	Scott Terry	.05
32	Franklin Stubbs	.05
33	Don August	.05
34	Mark McGwire	1.50
35	Eric Show	.05
36	Cecil Espy	.05
37	Ron Tingley	.05
38	Mickey Brantley	.05
39	Paul O'Neill	.10
40	Ed Sprague	.10
41	Len Dykstra	.05
42	Roger Clemens	.60
43	Ron Gant	.10
44	Dan Pasqua	.05
45	Jeff Robinson	.05
46	George Brett	.70
47	Bryn Smith	.05
48	Mike Marshall	.05
49	Doug Robbins	.05
50	Don Mattingly	.90
51	Mike Scott	.05
52	Steve Jeltz	.05
53	Dick Schofield	.05
54	Tom Brunansky	.05
55	Gary Sheffield	.75
56	Dave Valle	.05
57	Carney Lansford	.05
58	Tony Gwynn	.75
59	Checklist	.05
60	Damon Berryhill	.05
61	Jack Morris	.05
62	Brett Butler	.05
63	Mickey Hatcher	.05
64	Bruce Sutter	.05
65	Robin Ventura	.50
66	Junior Oritiz	.05
67	Pat Tabler	.05
68	Greg Swindell	.05
69	Jeff Branson	.10
70	Manny Lee	.05
71	Dave Magadan	.05
72	Rich Gedman	.05
73	Tim Raines	.10
74	Mike Maddux	.05
75	Jim Presley	.05
76	Chuck Finley	.05
77	Jose Oquendo	.05
78	Rob Deer	.05
79	Jay Howell	.05
80	Terry Steinbach	.05
81	Eddie Whitson	.05
82	Ruben Sierra	.05
83	Bruce Benedict	.05
84	Fred Manrique	.05
85	John Smiley	.05
86	Mike Macfarlane	.05
87	Rene Gonzales	.05
88	Charles Hudson	.05
90	Les Straker	.05
91	Carmen Castillo	.05
92	Tracy Woodson	.05
93	Tino Martinez	.65
94	Herm Winningham	.05
95	Kelly Gruber	.05
96	Terry Leach	.05
97	Jody Reed	.05
98	Nelson Santovenia	.05
99	Tony Armas	.05
100	Greg Brock	.05
101	Dave Stewart	.05
102	Roberto Alomar	.25
103	Jim Sundberg	.05
104	Albert Hall	.05
105	Steve Lyons	.05
106	Sid Bream	.05
107	Danny Tartabull	.05
108	Rick Dempsey	.05
109	Rich Renteria	.05
110	Ozzie Smith	.25
111	Steve Sax	.05
112	Kelly Downs	.05
113	Larry Sheets	.05
114	Andy Benes	.50
115	Pete O'Brien	.05
116	Kevin McReynolds	.05
117	Juan Berenguer	.05
118	Billy Hatcher	.05
119	Rick Cerone	.05
120	Andre Dawson	.10
121	Storm Davis	.05
122	Devon White	.05
123	Alan Trammell	.05
124	Vince Coleman	.05
125	Al Leiter	.05
126	Dale Sveum	.05
127	Pete Incaviglia	.05
128	Dave Stieb	.05
129	Kevin Mitchell	.05
130	Dave Schmidt	.05
131	Gary Redus	.05
132	Ron Robinson	.05
133	Darnell Coles	.05
134	Benny Santiago	.05
135	John Farrell	.05
136	Willie Wilson	.05
137	Steve Bedrosian	.05
138	Don Slaught	.05
139	Darryl Strawberry	.15
140	Frank Viola	.05
141	Dave Silvestri	.10
142	Carlos Quintana	.05
143	Vance Law	.05
144	Dave Parker	.05
145	Tim Belcher	.05
146	Will Clark	.35
147	Mark Williamson	.05
148	Ozzie Guillen	.05
149	Kirk McCaskill	.05
150	Pat Sheridan	.05
151	Terry Pendleton	.05
152	Roberto Kelly	.05
153	Joey Meyer	.05
154	Mark Grant	.05
155	Joe Carter	.10
156	Steve Buechele	.05
157	Tony Fernandez	.05
158	Jeff Reed	.05
159	Bobby Bonilla	.10
160	Henry Cotto	.05
161	Kurt Stillwell	.05
162	Mickey Morandini	.15
163	Robby Thompson	.05
164	Rick Schu	.05
165	Stan Jefferson	.05
166	Ron Darling	.05
167	Kirby Puckett	.50
168	Bill Doran	.05
169	Dennis Lamp	.05
170	Ty Griffin	.10
171	Ron Hassey	.05
172	Dale Murphy	.10
173	Andres Galarraga	.10
174	Tim Flannery	.05
175	Cory Snyder	.05
176	Checklist	.05
177	Tommy Barrett	.05
178	Dan Petry	.05
179	Billy Masse	.05
180	Terry Kennedy	.05
181	Joe Orsulak	.05
182	Doyle Alexander	.05
183	Willie McGee	.05
184	Jim Gantner	.05
185	Keith Hernandez	.05
186	Greg Gagne	.05
187	Kevin Bass	.05
188	Mark Eichhorn	.05
189	Mark Grace	.30
190	Jose Canseco	.50
191	Bobby Witt	.05
192	Rafael Santana	.05
193	Dwight Evans	.05
194	Greg Booker	.05
195	Brook Jacoby	.05
196	Rafael Belliard	.05
197	Candy Maldonado	.05
198	Mickey Tettleton	.05
199	Barry Larkin	.10
200	Frank White	.05
201	Wally Joyner	.10
202	Chet Lemon	.05
203	Joe Magrane	.05
204	Glenn Braggs	.05
205	Scott Fletcher	.05
206	Gary Ward	.05
207	Nelson Liriano	.05
208	Howard Johnson	.05
209	Kent Hrbek	.05
210	Ken Caminiti	.10
211	Mike Greenwell	.05
212	Ryne Sandberg	.50
213	Joe Slusarski	.10
214	Donnell Nixon	.05
215	Tim Wallach	.05
216	John Kruk	.05
217	Charles Nagy	.25
218	Alvin Davis	.05
219	Oswald Peraza	.05
220	Mike Schmidt	.50
221	Spike Owen	.05
222	Mike Smithson	.05
223	Dion James	.05
224	Ernie Whitt	.05
225	Mike Davis	.05
226	Gene Larkin	.05
227	Pat Combs	.15
228	Jack Howell	.05
229	Ron Oester	.05
230	Paul Gibson	.05
231	Mookie Wilson	.05
232	Glenn Hubbard	.05
233	Shawon Dunston	.05
234	Otis Nixon	.05
235	Melido Perez	.05
236	Jerry Browne	.05
237	Rick Rhoden	.05
238	Bo Jackson	.20
239	Randy Velarde	.05
240	Jack Clark	.05
241	Wade Boggs	.60
242	Lonnie Smith	.05
243	Mike Flanagan	.05
244	Willie Randolph	.05
245	Oddibe McDowell	.05
246	Ricky Jordan	.05
247	Greg Briley	.05
248	Rex Hudler	.05
249	Robin Yount	.35
250	Lance Parrish	.05
251	Chris Sabo	.05
252	Mike Henneman	.05
253	Gregg Jefferies	.10
254	Curt Young	.05
255	Andy Van Slyke	.05
256	Rod Booker	.05
257	Rafael Palmeiro	.20
258	Jose Uribe	.05
259	Ellis Burks	.10
260	John Smoltz	.10
261	Tom Foley	.05
262	Lloyd Moseby	.05
263	Jim Poole	.10
264	Gary Gaetti	.05
265	Bob Dernier	.05
266	Harold Baines	.05
267	Tom Candiotti	.05
268	Rafael Ramirez	.05
269	Bob Boone	.05
270	Buddy Bell	.05
271	Rickey Henderson	.20
272	Willie Fraser	.05
273	Eric Davis	.05
274	Jeff Robinson	.05
275	Damaso Garcia	.05
276	Sid Fernandez	.05
277	Stan Javier	.05
278	Marty Barrett	.05
279	Gerald Perry	.05
280	Rob Ducey	.05
281	Mike Scioscia	.05
282	Randy Bush	.05
283	Tom Herr	.05
284	Glenn Wilson	.05
285	Pedro Guerrero	.05
286	Cal Ripken, Jr.	.95
287	Randy Johnson	.25
288	Julio Franco	.05
289	Ivan Calderon	.05
290	Rich Yett	.05
291	Scott Servais	.10
292	Bill Pecota	.05
293	Ken Phelps	.05
294	Chili Davis	.05
295	Manny Trillo	.05
296	Mike Boddicker	.05
297	Geronimo Berroa	.05
298	Todd Stottlemyre	.05
299	Kirk Gibson	.05
300	Wally Backman	.05
301	Hubie Brooks	.05
302	Von Hayes	.05
303	Matt Nokes	.05
304	Dwight Gooden	.10
305	Walt Weiss	.05
306	Mike LaValliere	.05
307	Cris Carpenter	.10
308	Ted Wood	.05
309	Jeff Russell	.05
310	Dave Gallagher	.05
311	Andy Allanson	.05
312	Craig Reynolds	.05
313	Kevin Seitzer	.05
314	Dave Winfield	.25
315	Andy McGaffigan	.05
316	Nick Esasky	.05
317	Jeff Blauser	.05
318	George Bell	.05
319	Eddie Murray	.25
320	Mark Davidson	.05
321	Juan Samuel	.05
322	Jim Abbott	.10
323	Kal Daniels	.05
324	Mike Brumley	.05
325	Gary Carter	.10
326	Dave Henderson	.05
327	Checklist	.05
328	Garry Templeton	.05
329	Pat Perry	.05
330	Paul Molitor	.25

1989 Topps Coins

Similar in format to previous Topps coins, this 60-piece set features 1-1/2" diameter coins with rolled colored edges. A shooting star device printed over the player photo gives his name, team and position. Backs have a few biographical details and a summary of the player's previous season performance printed in black on silver. The coins were sold three per pack, with each pack including an offer card for an album to house the pieces.

		MT
Complete Set (60):		9.00
Common Player:		.10
1	Kirk Gibson	.10
2	Orel Herhiser	.10
3	Chris Sabo	.10
4	Tony Gwynn	.50
5	Brett Butler	.10
6	Bobby Bonilla	.10
7	Jack Clark	.10
8	Will Clark	.30
9	Eric Davis	.10
10	Glenn Davis	.10
11	Andre Dawson	.15
12	John Franco	.10
13	Andres Galarraga	.15
14	Dwight Gooden	.15
15	Mark Grace	.15
16	Pedro Guerrero	.10
17	Ricky Jordan	.10
18	Mike Marshall	.10
19	Dale Murphy	.15
20	Eddie Murray	.35
21	Gerald Perry	.10
22	Tim Raines	.15
23	Juan Samuel	.10
24	Bonito Santiago	.10
25	Ozzie Smith	.35
26	Darryl Strawberry	.15
27	Andy Van Slyke	.10
28	Gerald Young	.10
29	Jose Canseco	.45
30	Frank Viola	.10
31	Walt Weiss	.10
32	Wade Boggs	.35
33	Harold Baines	.10
34	George Brett	.75
35	Jay Buhner	.10
36	Joe Carter	.10
37	Roger Clemens	.50
38	Alvin Davis	.10
39	Tony Fernandez	.10
40	Carlton Fisk	.20
41	Mike Greenwell	.10
42	Kent Hrbek	.10
43	Don Mattingly	.80
44	Fred McGriff	.25
45	Mark McGwire	2.00
46	Paul Molitor	.40
47	Rafael Palmeiro	.20
48	Kirby Puckett	.50
49	Johnny Ray	.10
50	Cal Ripken, Jr.	1.00
51	Ruben Sierra	.10
52	Pete Stanicek	.10
53	Dave Stewart	.10
54	Greg Swindell	.10
55	Danny Tartabull	.10
56	Alan Trammell	.10
57	Lou Whitaker	.10
58	Dave Winfield	.30
59	Mike Witt	.10
60	Robin Yount	.40

1989 Topps Double Headers All-Stars

This scarce test issue was produced in two versions, an All-Stars set and a set of exclusively Mets and Yankees players. The "cards" are two-sided miniature (1-5/8" x 2-1/4") reproductions of the player's 1989 Topps card and his Topps rookie card, encased in a clear plastic stand.

		MT
Complete Set (24):		45.00
Common Player:		1.00
(1)	Alan Ashby	1.00
(2)	Wade Boggs	3.00
(3)	Bobby Bonilla	1.00
(4)	Jose Canseco	3.00
(5)	Will Clark	3.00
(6)	Roger Clemens	4.00
(7)	Andre Dawson	1.00
(8)	Dennis Eckersley	1.00
(9)	Carlton Fisk	2.00
(10)	John Franco	1.00
(11)	Julio Franco	1.00
(12)	Kirk Gibson	1.00
(13)	Mike Greenwell	1.00
(14)	Orel Hershiser	1.00
(15)	Danny Jackson	1.00
(16)	Don Mattingly	5.00
(17)	Mark McGwire	6.00
(18)	Kirby Puckett	5.00
(19)	Ryne Sandberg	3.00
(20)	Ozzie Smith	3.00
(21)	Darryl Strawberry	1.50
(22)	Alan Trammell	1.00
(23)	Andy Van Slyke	1.00
(24)	Frank Viola	1.00

1989 Topps Double Headers Mets/Yankees

This was a regionally issued test for the concept of two "mini" baseball cards of a player encapsulated in clear plastic. Only New York players are represented in the set. Each double header plastic frame holds miniature (1-5/8" x 2-1/4") versions of the player's 1989 Topps card, and his first Topps card, printed on thin paper. The Double Headers of players who also appeared in the All-Star issue are indistinguishable in this version. The stand-ups were sold in boxes of 24 paper-wrapped pieces. It is reported that each box contains a full set. The unnumbered pieces are checklisted here in alphabetical order by team.

		MT
Complete Set (24):		400.00
Common Player:		15.00
	New York Mets team set:	225.00
(1)	Gary Carter	20.00
(2)	David Cone	25.00
(3)	Ron Darling	15.00
(4)	Len Dykstra	15.00
(5)	Doc Gooden	25.00
(6)	Keith Hernandez	15.00
(7)	Gregg Jefferies	20.00
(8)	Howard Johnson	15.00
(9)	Kevin McReynolds	15.00
(10)	Randy Myers	15.00
(11)	Darryl Strawberry	2.00
(12)	Tim Teufel	15.00
(13)	Mookie Wilson	15.00
	New York Yankees team set:	175.00
(14)	Richard Dotson	15.00
(15)	Rickey Henderson	25.00
(16)	Don Mattingly	6.00
(17)	Mike Pagliarulo	15.00
(18)	Ken Phelps	15.00
(19)	Rick Rhoden	15.00
(20)	Dave Righetti	15.00
(21)	Rafael Santana	15.00
(22)	Steve Sax	15.00
(23)	Claudell Washington	15.00
(24)	Dave Winfield	25.00

1989 Topps Double Headers Mets/Yankees Proofs

In advance of its special Mets/Yankees Double Headers novelty issue, Topps prepared a series of proof versions featuring four players from each of the New York teams. Like the later issues, these Double Headers feature miniature versions of the players' Topps rookie cards in a small plastic stand-up frame. However, the proof versions have the rookie cards back-to-back with the players' 1988 Topps cards, rather than 1989 as on the regularly issued pieces. Two different types of wrappers are found for the proofs, an opaque paper envelope picturing Gary Carter's piece and a cellophane wrapper with the proof issue's checklist.

		MT
Complete Set (8):		1000.
Common Player:		100.00
	N.Y. METS	
(1)	Gary Carter	150.00
(2)	Ron Darling	100.00
(3)	Dwight Gooden	150.00
(4)	Darryl Strawberry	200.00
	N.Y. YANKEES	
(1)	Rickey Henderson	200.00
(2)	Don Mattingly	400.00
(3)	Dave Righetti	100.00
(4)	Dave Winfield	250.00

1989 Topps Gallery of Champions

Topps continued its issue of 1/4-size metallic ingot reproductions of current-year baseball cards with aluminum, bronze and sterling silver sets in 1989. Again the players represented major award winners from the previous season. The metal mini-cards were sold only as complete sets. Dealers who ordered bronze and silver sets could receive as a bonus a pewter version of the Jose Canseco ingot. A bronze replica of Jackie Robinson's Topps debut card was offered to dealers who purchased Topps Traded sets for '89.

		MT
Complete Aluminum Set (12):		60.00
Complete Bronze Set (12):		175.00
Complete Silver Set (12):		450.00
(1a)	Wade Boggs (aluminum)	9.00
(1b)	Wade Boggs (bronze)	30.00
(1s)	Wade Boggs (silver)	65.00
(2a)	Jose Canseco (aluminum)	10.00
(2b)	Jose Canseco (bronze)	30.00
(2s)	Jose Canseco (silver)	75.00
(2p)	Jose Canseco (pewter)	30.00
(3a)	Will Clark (aluminum)	9.00
(3b)	Will Clark (bronze)	25.00
(3s)	Will Clark (silver)	65.00
(4a)	Dennis Eckersley (aluminum)	6.00
(4b)	Dennis Eckersley (bronze)	20.00
(4s)	Dennis Eckersley (silver)	50.00
(5a)	John Franco (aluminum)	3.00
(5b)	John Franco (bronze)	10.00
(5s)	John Franco (silver)	25.00
(6a)	Kirk Gibson (aluminum)	5.00
(6b)	Kirk Gibson (bronze)	15.00
(6s)	Kirk Gibson (silver)	40.00
(7a)	Tony Gwynn (aluminum)	10.00
(7b)	Tony Gwynn (bronze)	30.00
(7s)	Tony Gwynn (silver)	75.00
(8a)	Orel Hershiser (aluminum)	8.00
(8b)	Orel Hershiser (bronze)	25.00
(8s)	Orel Hershiser (silver)	50.00
(9a)	Chris Sabo (aluminum)	3.00
(9b)	Chris Sabo (bronze)	10.00
(9s)	Chris Sabo (silver)	25.00
(10a)	Darryl Strawberry (aluminum)	6.00
(10b)	Darryl Strawberry (bronze)	20.00
(10s)	Darryl Strawberry (silver)	50.00
(11a)	Frank Viola	3.00
(11b)	Frank Viola (bronze)	10.00
(11s)	Frank Viola (silver)	25.00
(12a)	Walt Weiss (aluminum)	3.00
(12b)	Walt Weiss (bronze)	10.00
(12s)	Walt Weiss (silver)	25.00
(13)	Jackie Robinson (1952, bronze)	20.00

1989 Topps Glossy Rookies Set of 22

Bearing the same design and style of the past two years, Topps featured the top first-year players from the 1988 season in this glossy set. The full-color player photo appears beneath the "1988 Rookies" banner. The player's name is displayed beneath the photo. The flip side features the "1988 Rookies Commemorative Set" logo followed by the player ID and card number. Glossy rookies were found only in 100-card jumbo cello packs.

		MT
Complete Set (22):		9.00
Common Player:		.30
1	Roberto Alomar	1.00
2	Brady Anderson	.50
3	Tim Belcher	.30
4	Damon Berryhill	.30
5	Jay Buhner	.50
6	Kevin Elster	.30
7	Cecil Espy	.30
8	Dave Gallagher	.30
9	Ron Gant	.50
10	Paul Gibson	.30
11	Mark Grace	1.50
12	Darrin Jackson	.30
13	Gregg Jefferies	.60
14	Ricky Jordan	.30
15	Al Leiter	.65
16	Melido Perez	.30
17	Chris Sabo	.30
18	Nelson Santovenia	.30
19	Mackey Sasser	.30
20	Gary Sheffield	1.00
21	Walt Weiss	.60
22	David Wells	.90

1989 Topps Heads Up! Test Issue

Much rarer than the 1990 issue, this 24-card test set debuted the bizarre "shrunken head" format of a die-cut player's head and cap printed on heavy cardboard, approximately 4-1/2" x 6-1/2" in size and sold one per pack. Backs feature both a small plastic suction cup and an adhesive strip for hanging the card. The player's name and team are printed in black on the back.

		MT
Complete Set (24):		3000.
Common Player:		75.00
1	Tony Gwynn	250.00
2	Will Clark	185.00
3	Dwight Gooden	95.00
4	Ken Griffey, Jr.	400.00
5	Darryl Strawberry	95.00
6	Ricky Jordan	75.00
7	Frank Viola	75.00
8	Bo Jackson	125.00
9	Ryne Sandberg	185.00
10	Gregg Jefferies	95.00
11	Wade Boggs	185.00
12	Ellis Burks	75.00
13	Gary Sheffield	155.00
14	Mark McGwire	375.00
15	Mark Grace	185.00
16	Jim Abbott	95.00
17	Ozzie Smith	185.00
18	Jose Canseco	155.00
19	Don Mattingly	250.00
20	Kirby Puckett	250.00
21	Eric Davis	75.00
22	Mike Greenwell	75.00
23	Dale Murphy	110.00
24	Mike Schmidt	185.00

1989 Topps Mini League Leaders

This 77-card set features baseball's statistical leaders from the 1988 season. It is referred to as a "mini" set because of the cards' small (2-1/8" x 3") size. The glossy cards feature action photos that have a soft focus on all edges. The player's team and name appear along the bottom of the card. The back features a head- shot of the player along with his 1988 season ranking and stats.

		MT
Complete Set (77):		4.00
Common Player:		.10
1	Dale Murphy	.15
2	Gerald Perry	.10
3	Andre Dawson	.15
4	Greg Maddux	.90
5	Rafael Palmeiro	.25
6	Tom Browning	.10
7	Kal Daniels	.10
8	Eric Davis	.10
9	John Franco	.10
10	Danny Jackson	.10
11	Barry Larkin	.20
12	Jose Rijo	.10
13	Chris Sabo	.10
14	Nolan Ryan	1.00
15	Mike Scott	.10
16	Gerald Young	.10
17	Kirk Gibson	.10
18	Orel Hershiser	.10
19	Steve Sax	.10
20	John Tudor	.10
21	Hubie Brooks	.10
22	Andres Galarraga	.15
23	Otis Nixon	.10
24	Dave Cone	.15
25	Sid Fernandez	.10
26	Dwight Gooden	.15
27	Kevin McReynolds	.10
28	Darryl Strawberry	.15
29	Juan Samuel	.10
30	Bobby Bonilla	.10
31	Sid Bream	.10
32	Jim Gott	.10
33	Andy Van Slyke	.10
34	Vince Coleman	.10
35	Jose DeLeon	.10
36	Joe Magrane	.10
37	Ozzie Smith	.45
38	Todd Worrell	.10
39	Tony Gwynn	.65
40	Brett Butler	.10

41	Will Clark	.50
42	Rick Reuschel	.10
43	Checklist	.10
44	Eddie Murray	.30
45	Wade Boggs	.60
46	Roger Clemens	.65
47	Dwight Evans	.10
48	Mike Greenwell	.10
49	Bruce Hurst	.10
50	Johnny Ray	.10
51	Doug Jones	.10
52	Greg Swindell	.10
53	Gary Pettis	.10
54	George Brett	.75
55	Mark Gubicza	.10
56	Willie Wilson	.10
57	Teddy Higuera	.10
58	Paul Molitor	.45
59	Robin Yount	.50
60	Allan Anderson	.10
61	Gary Gaetti	.10
62	Kirby Puckett	.65
63	Jeff Reardon	.10
64	Frank Viola	.10
65	Jack Clark	.10
66	Rickey Henderson	.25
67	Dave Winfield	.35
68	Jose Canseco	.50
69	Dennis Eckersley	.10
70	Mark McGwire	1.50
71	Dave Stewart	.10
72	Alvin Davis	.10
73	Mark Langston	.10
74	Harold Reynolds	.10
75	George Bell	.10
76	Tony Fernandez	.10
77	Fred McGriff	.20

1989 Topps Stickercards

Once again in 1989 Topps used a stickercard as cardboard backing for its paper sticker issue. Measuring 2-1/8" x 3", the cards are found with either one or two player stickers on back. The stickercards have a player photo on a background of graduated color. Minimal stats and biographic data are presented at the bottom of the card. Values shown are for complete stickercard/sticker(s), without regard to which stickers are on back.

		MT
Complete Set (66):		8.00
Common Player:		.10
1	George Brett	.65
2	Don Mattingly	.65
3	Mark McGwire	1.00
4	Julio Franco	.10
5	Harold Reynolds	.10
6	Lou Whitaker	.10
7	Wade Boggs	.50
8	Gary Gaetti	.10
9	Paul Molitor	.45
10	Tony Fernandez	.10
11	Cal Ripken Jr.	.90
12	Alan Trammell	.10
13	Jose Canseco	.30
14	Joe Carter	.10
15	Dwight Evans	.10
16	Mike Greenwell	.10
17	Dave Henderson	.10
18	Rickey Henderson	.20
19	Kirby Puckett	.50
20	Dave Winfield	.25
21	Robin Yount	.45
22	Bob Boone	.10
23	Carlton Fisk	.25
24	Geno Petralli	.10
25	Roger Clemens	.50
26	Mark Gubicza	.10
27	Dave Stewart	.10
28	Teddy Higuera	.10
29	Bruce Hurst	.10
30	Frank Viola	.10
31	Dennis Eckersley	.10
32	Doug Jones	.10
33	Jeff Reardon	.10
34	Will Clark	.25
35	Glenn Davis	.10
36	Andres Galarraga	.15
37	Juan Samuel	.10
38	Ryne Sandberg	.35
39	Steve Sax	.10
40	Bobby Bonilla	.10
41	Howard Johnson	.10
42	Vance Law	.10
43	Shawon Dunston	.10
44	Barry Larkin	.15
45	Ozzie Smith	.35
46	Barry Bonds	.50
47	Eric Davis	.10
48	Andre Dawson	.15
49	Kirk Gibson	.10
50	Tony Gwynn	.65
51	Kevin McReynolds	.10
52	Rafael Palmeiro	.25
53	Darryl Strawberry	.15
54	Andy Van Slyke	.10
55	Gary Carter	.15
56	Mike LaValliere	.10
57	Benito Santiago	.10
58	David Cone	.10
59	Dwight Gooden	.15
60	Orel Hershiser	.10
61	Tom Browning	.10
62	Danny Jackson	.10
63	Bob Knepper	.10
64	Mark Davis	.10
65	John Franco	.10
66	Randy Myers	.10

1989 Topps Stickers

Topps' 1989 baseball player stickers were produced in two formats. Some measure 2-1/8" x 3" while there are 128 pairs of half-size (1-1/2" x 2-1/8") stickers. All stickers are attached to Super Star stickers cards from which they can be peeled and affixed in a special Baseball Sticker Yearbook which was sold separately for 50 cents. Stickers have large center photos with white borders. Above and below are zipping fastball graphics trailing graduated color bars (blues for N.L., reds for A.L.)ing graduated color bars A tiny black sticker number is in the lower-right corner. There is no player name on the stickers; the albums have a box under each space with player data. The half-size stickers are printed in pairs and are checklisted in that fashion. Values given are for complete sticker(s)/stickercard combinations, but without regard for which stickercard is on back.

		MT
Complete Set (326):		16.00
Common Player/Pair:		.05
Album:		2.00
1-230	George Bell, Jeff Ballard	.05
2-272	Gary Carter, Steve Farr	.05
3-324	Doug Jones, Mark Grace	.10
4-320	John Franco, Cecil Espy	.05
5-322	Andre Dawson, Ron Gant	.20
6-326	Pat Tabler, Walt Weiss	.05
7-317	Tom Browning, Tim Belcher	.05
8-239	Jeff Reardon, Larry Sheets	.05
9-325	Wade Boggs, Chris Sabo	.25
10-319	Kevin McReynolds, Jay Buhner	.10
11-323	Jose Canseco, Paul Gibson	.20
12-318	Orel Hershiser, Damon Berryhill	.05
13-231	Dave Smith, Mickey Tettleton	.05
14-302	Kevin Bass, Jack McDowell	.05
15-232	Mike Scott, Pete Stanicek	.05
16-256	Bill Doran, Jim Rice	.05
17-207	Rafael Ramirez, Andy Allanson	.05
18-181	Buddy Bell, Jack Howell	.05
19-214	Billy Hatcher, John Farrell	.05
20-275	Nolan Ryan, Frank Tanana	1.00
21	Glenn Davis	.05
22	Bob Knepper	.05
23-211	Gerald Young, Tom Candiotti	.05
24-208	Dion James, Julio Franco	.05
25-243	Bruce Sutter, Jeff Russell	.05
26-310	Andres Thomas, Tommy John	.05
27-200	Zane Smith, B.J. Surhoff	.05
28-198	Ozzie Virgil, Teddy Higuera	.05
29-269	Rick Mahler, Floyd Bannister	.05
30-219	Albert Hall, Mickey Brantley	.05
31-203	Pete Smith, Jim Gantner	.05
32	Dale Murphy	.15
33	Gerald Perry	.05
34-177	Ron Gant, Chili Davis	.20
35-244	Bob Horner, Mike Stanley	.05
36-313	Willie McGee, Rafael Santana	.05
37-288	Luis Alicea, Greg Gagne	.05
38-279	Tony Pena, Gary Pettis	.05
39-184	Todd Worrell, Kirk McCaskill	.05
40-228	Pedro Guerrero, Bill Swift	.05
41-174	Tom Brunansky, Dick Schofield	.05
42-262	Terry Pendleton, Frank White	.05
43	Vince Coleman	.05
44	Ozzie Smith	.30
45-240	Jose Oquendo, Cecil Espy	.05
46-191	Vance Law, Pat Borders	.05
47-258	Rafael Palmeiro, Bob Stanley	.10
48-213	Greg Maddux, Greg Swindell	.45
49-229	Shawon Dunston, Jose Bautista	.10
50-210	Mark Grace, Cory Snyder	.10
51-187	Damon Berryhill, Kelly Gruber	.05
52-192	Rick Sutcliffe, Rance Mulliniks	.05
53-291	Jamie Moyer, Juan Berenguer	.05
54	Andre Dawson	.15
55	Ryne Sandberg	.45
56-284	Calvin Schiraldi, Jeff Reardon	.05
57-308	Steve Sax, Jack Clark	.05
58-263	Mike Scioscia, Bret Saberhagen	.05
59-298	Alfredo Griffin, Steve Lyons	.05
60-202	Fernando Valenzuela, Rob Deer	.05
61-286	Jay Howell, Dan Gladden	.05
62-305	Tim Leary, Bobby Thigpen	.05
63-212	John Shelby, Brook Jacoby	.05
64-306	John Tudor, John Candelaria	.05
65	Orel Hershiser	.10
66	Kirk Gibson	.05
67-223	Mike Marshall, Jim Presley	.05
68-206	Luis Rivera, Dale Sveum	.05
69-311	Tim Burke, Mike Pagliarulo	.05
70-253	Tim Wallach, Rich Gedman	.05
71-265	Pascual Perez, Bo Jackson	.10
72-185	Hubie Brooks, Fred McGriff	.10
73-250	Jeff Parrett, Steve Buechele	.05
74-316	Dennis Martinez, Rich Dotson	.05
75-285	Andy McGaffigan, Bert Blyleven	.05
76	Andres Galarraga	.10
77	Rock Raines	.10
78-287	Nelson Santovenia, Kent Hrbek	.05
79-261	Rick Reuschel, Mike Boddicker	.05
80-276	Mike Aldrete, Luis Salazar	.05
81-247	Kelly Downs, Mitch Williams	.05
82-283	Jose Uribe, Chet Lemon	.05
83-190	Mike Krukow, Mike Flanagan	.05
84-179	Kevin Mitchell, Devon White	.05
85-195	Brett Butler, Tom Henke	.05
86-252	Don Robinson, Dwight Evans	.05
87	Robby Thompson	.05
88	Will Clark	.25
89-188	Candy Maldonado, Lloyd Moseby	.05
90-180	Len Dykstra, Bryan Harvey	.05
91-234	Howard Johnson, Rene Gonzalez	.05
92-266	Roger McDowell, Kurt Stillwell	.05
93-222	Keith Hernandez, Steve Balboni	.05
94-178	Gary Carter, Brian Downing	.05
95-277	Kevin McReynolds, Jack Morris	.05
96-307	David Cone, Dave Righetti	.05
97-175	Randy Myers, Bob Boone	.05
98	Darryl Strawberry	.10
99	Doc Gooden	.10
100-257	Ron Darling, Marty Barrett	.05
101-201	Benny Santiago, Greg Brock	.05
102-273	John Kruk, Mike Henneman	.05
103-242	Chris Brown, Ruben Sierra	.05
104-255	Roberto Alomar, Mike Greenwell	.20
105-290	Keith Moreland, Tim Laudner	.05
106-217	Randy Ready, Scott Bailes	.05
107-267	Marvell Wynne, Danny Tartabull	.05
108-176	Lance McCullers, Mike Witt	.05
109	Tony Gwynn	.35
110	Mark Davis	.05
111-236	Andy Hawkins, Tom Niedenfeur	.05
112-233	Steve Bedrosian, Jim Traber	.05
113-196	Phil Bradley, Glenn Braggs	.05
114-189	Steve Jeltz, Tony Fernandez	.05
115-209	Von Hayes, Bud Black	.05
116-245	Kevin Gross, Charlie Hough	.05
117-218	Juan Samuel, Henry Cotto	.05
118-274	Shane Rawley, Doyle Alexander	.05
119-186	Chris James, Jimmy Key	.05
120	Mike Schmidt	.60
121	Don Carman	.05
122-280	Bruce Ruffin, Matt Nokes	.05
123-246	Bob Walk, Scott Fletcher	.05
124-278	John Smiley, Tom Brookens	.05
125-301	Sid Bream, Dan Pasqua	.05
126-251	Jose Lind, Lee Smith	.05
127-309	Barry Bonds, Willie Randolph	.25
128-294	Mike LaValliere, Gene Larkin	.05
129-225	Jeff D. Robinson, Scott Bradley	.05
130-295	Mike Dunne, Dave Gallagher	.05
131	Bobby Bonilla	.10
132	Andy Van Slyke	.05
133-241	Rafael Belliard, Jose Guzman	.05
134-197	Nick Esasky, Dan Plesac	.05
135-300	Bo Diaz, Fred Manrique	.05
136-221	John Franco, Mark Langston	.05
137-312	Barry Larkin, Rickey Henderson	.20
138-173	Eric Davis, Ron Hassey	.05
139-299	Jeff Treadway, Carlton Fisk	.05
140-254	Jose Rijo, Ellis Burks	.05
141-220	Tom Browning, Mike Moore	.05
142	Chris Sabo	.05
143	Danny Jackson	.05
144-199	Kal Daniels, Jeffrey Leonard	.05
145	Rickey Henderson (All-Star)	.10
146	Paul Molitor (All-Star)	.10
147	Wade Boggs (All-Star)	.20
148	Jose Canseco (All-Star)	.25
149	Dave Winfield (All-Star)	.15
150	Cal Ripken Jr. (All-Star)	.65
151	Mark McGwire (All-Star)	.75
152	Terry Steinbach (All-Star)	.05
153	Frank Viola (All-Star)	.05
154	Vince Coleman (All-Star)	.05
155	Ryne Sandberg (All-Star)	.25
156	Andre Dawson (All-Star)	.10
157	Darryl Strawberry (All-Star)	.10
158	Bobby Bonilla (All-Star)	.05
159	Will Clark (All-Star)	.20
160	Gary Carter (All-Star)	.05
161	Ozzie Smith (All-Star)	.25
162	Doc Gooden (All-Star)	.10
163-268	Dave Stewart, Willie Wilson	.05
164-297	Dave Henderson, Ivan Calderon	.05
165-321	Terry Steinbach, Dave Gallagher	.05
166-264	Bob Welch, Kevin Seitzer	.05
167-224	Dennis Eckersley, Rey Quinones	.05
168-235	Walt Weiss, Terry Kennedy	.05
169-296	Dave Parker, Melido Perez	.05
170-289	Carney Lansford, Gary Gaetti	.05
171	Jose Canseco	.25
172	Mark McGwire	1.00
182	Johnny Ray	.05
183	Wally Joyner	.10
193	George Bell	.05
194	Dave Steib	.05
204	Paul Molitor	.25
205	Robin Yount	.25
215	Doug Jones	.05
216	Joe Carter	.10
226	Harold Reynolds	.05
227	Alvin Davis	.05
237	Cal Ripken Jr.	1.00
238	Eddie Murray	.20
248	Pete O'Brien	.05
249	Pete Incaviglia	.05
259	Roger Clemens	.35
260	Wade Boggs	.25
270	George Brett	.50
271	Mark Gubicza	.05
281	Alan Trammell	.10
282	Lou Whitaker	.05
292	Frank Viola	.05
293	Kirby Puckett	.35
303	Ozzie Guillen	.05
304	Harold Baines	.05
314	Don Mattingly	.50
315	Dave Winfield	.15

1989 Topps/LJN Baseball Talk

Another generation of "talking baseball cards" was produced by Topps and the LJN Toy Co. in 1989. After purchasing a hand-held player, collectors could buy sets of four "Baseball Talk Collection" cards for about $4. The 3-1/4" x 5-1/4" cards had a plastic sheet laminated on their backs containing information about the player which could be heard by inserting the card into the player. Fronts of the cards of players active in 1989 reproduced their 1989 Topps cards. The cards of earlier stars reproduced various older Topps cards of those players. Narrators on the cards were Don Drysdale, Joe Torre and Mel Allen.

		MT
Complete Set (164):		150.00
Common Player:		.50
(1)	Hank Aaron (1954)	4.00
(2)	Hank Aaron (1976)	3.00
(3)	ALCS Game 5 1986	.50
(4)	Sparky Anderson	.60
(5)	Harold Baines	.60
(6)	Ernie Banks	1.50
(7)	Kevin Bass	.50
(8)	Steve Bedrosian	.50
(9)	George Bell	.50
(10)	Johnny Bench	1.50
(11)	Bert Blyleven	.50
(12)	Wade Boggs	1.50
(13)	Barry Bonds	2.00
(14)	Bobby Bonilla	.60
(15)	Bob Boone	.50
(16)	George Brett	2.50
(17)	Lou Brock	.75
(18)	Hubie Brooks	.50
(19)	Tom Brunansky	.50
(20)	Brett Butler	.60
(21)	Jose Canseco	1.50
(22)	Rod Carew	2.00
(23)	Steve Carlton	1.50
(24)	Gary Carter	.60
(25)	Joe Carter	.65
(26)	Jack Clark	.50
(27)	Will Clark	1.25
(28)	Roger Clemens	1.75
(29)	Roberto Clemente	5.00
(30)	Ty Cobb	2.50
(31)	Vince Coleman	.50
(32)	Roger Craig	.50
(33)	Kal Daniels	.50
(34)	Ron Darling	.50
(35)	Alvin Davis	.50
(36)	Chili Davis	.50
(37)	Eric Davis	.60
(38)	Glenn Davis	.50
(39)	Andre Dawson	.75
(40)	Don Drysdale	1.50
(41)	Dennis Eckersley	.60
(42)	Dwight Evans	.50
(43)	Carlton Fisk	.60
(44)	Tony Fernandez	.50
(45)	Mike Flanagan	.50
(46)	Whitey Ford	1.50
(47)	John Franco	.50
(48)	Gary Gaetti	.50
(49)	Andres Galarraga	.60
(50)	Lou Gehrig	4.00
(51)	Bob Gibson	1.50
(52)	Kirk Gibson	.50
(53)	Dwight Gooden	.60
(54)	Rich Gossage	.50
(55)	Mike Greenwell	.50
(56)	Pedro Guerrero	.50
(57)	Ron Guidry	.50
(58)	Ozzie Guillen	.50
(59)	Tony Gwynn	1.75
(60)	Rickey Henderson	.90
(61)	Tom Henke	.50
(62)	Keith Hernandez	.50
(63)	Orel Hershiser	.50
(64)	Charlie Hough	.50
(65)	Kent Hrbek	.50
(66)	Bruce Hurst	.50
(67)	Pete Incaviglia	.50
(68)	Danny Jackson	.50
(69)	Reggie Jackson	1.50
(70)	Gregg Jefferies	.50
(71)	Doug Jones	.50
(72)	Tommy John	.50
(73)	Wally Joyner	.50
(74)	Al Kaline	1.50
(75)	Jimmy Key	.50
(76)	Harmon Killebrew	1.50
(77)	Ralph Kiner	.90
(78)	John Kruk	.50
(79)	Mark Langston	.50
(80)	Carney Lansford	.50
(81)	Barry Larkin	.60
(82)	Tony LaRussa	.50
(83)	Tommy Lasorda	.65
(84)	Mike LaValliere	.50
(85)	Fred Lynn	.50
(86)	Joe Magrane	.50
(87)	Candy Maldonado	.50
(88)	Mike Marshall	.50
(89)	Eddie Mathews	1.50
(90)	Don Mattingly	2.50
(91)	Bill Mazeroski	1.25
(92)	Willie McCovey	1.50
(93)	Oddibe McDowell	.50
(94)	Roger McDowell	.50
(95)	Willie McGee	.50
(96)	Mark McGwire	6.00
(97)	Kevin Mitchell	.60
(98)	Paul Molitor	1.50
(99)	Joe Morgan	1.00
(100)	Jack Morris	.50
(101)	Dale Murphy	.90
(102)	Eddie Murray	.90
(103)	Stan Musial	2.50
(104)	Randy Myers	.50
(105)	NLCS Game 6 1986	.50
(106)	Dave Parker	.50
(107)	Gaylord Perry	.75
(108)	Gerald Perry	.50
(109)	Dan Plesac	.50
(110)	Kirby Puckett	1.50
(111)	Tim Raines	.50
(112)	Jeff Reardon	.50
(113)	Rick Reuschel	.50
(114)	Harold Reynolds	.50
(115)	Jim Rice	.50
(116)	Dave Righetti	.50
(117)	Cal Ripken, Jr.	5.00
(118)	Robin Roberts	1.25
(119)	Brooks Robinson	1.75
(120)	Pete Rose	2.50
(121)	Babe Ruth	5.00
(122)	Nolan Ryan	5.00
(123)	Bret Saberhagen	.50
(124)	Chris Sabo	.50
(125)	Juan Samuel	.50
(126)	Ryne Sandberg	2.00
(127)	Benito Santiago	.50
(128)	Steve Sax	.50
(129)	Mike Schmidt	2.00
(130)	Mike Scott	.50
(131)	Tom Seaver	1.50
(132)	Kevin Seitzer	.50
(133)	Lonnie Smith	.50
(134)	Ozzie Smith	1.50
(135)	Duke Snider	1.75
(136)	Cory Snyder	.50
(137)	Willie Stargell	1.25
(138)	Darryl Strawberry	.75
(139)	Rick Sutcliffe	.50
(140)	Bruce Sutter	.50
(141)	Frank Tanana	.50
(142)	Bobby Thomson	.50
(143)	Alan Trammell	.60
(144)	John Tudor	.50
(145)	Fernando Valenzuela	.60
(146)	Andy Van Slyke	.50
(147)	Frank Viola	.50
(148)	Tim Wallach	.50
(149)	Bob Welch	.50
(150)	Lou Whitaker	.50
(151)	Frank White	.50
(152)	Billy Williams	1.00
(153)	Dave Winfield	1.00
(154)	Mike Witt	.50
(155)	Todd Worrell	.50
(156)	World Series Game 5 1956	.50
(157)	World Series Game 5 1969	.50
(158)	World Series Game 6 1975	.50
(159)	World Series Game 5 1984	.50
(160)	World Series Game 6 1986	.50
(161)	World Series Game 1 1988	.50
(162)	Carl Yastrzemski	1.75
(163)	Robin Yount	1.00
(164)	Checklist	.25

1989 Topps/Sport Shots Portfolios

In its second year, the number of baseball card folders produced by Shaeffer Eaton reproducing current Topps baseball cards was drastically reduced, from 130 to 39. The format remains the same, a 9-1/2" x 11-3/4" cardboard two-pocket folder. The 1989 portfolios are considerably scarcer than the 1988s.

		MT
Complete Set (39):		45.00
Common Player:		1.00
10	Andre Dawson	1.00
30	Doc Gooden	1.25
70	Mark McGwire	4.00
85	Kevin McReynolds	1.00
110	Paul Molitor	1.50
120	Frank Viola	1.00
145	Dave Stewart	1.00
180	Mike Scott	1.00
200	George Brett	2.00
205	Dwight Evans	1.00
230	Ozzie Smith	2.00
233	Gregg Jefferies	1.00
260	Dave Winfield	1.50
300	Darryl Strawberry	1.00
330	Eric Davis	1.00
335	Dave Righetti	1.00
340	Kirk Gibson	1.00
370	Dennis Eckersley	1.00
380	Rickey Henderson	1.50
425	Jay Howell	1.00
450	Roger Clemens	2.00
480	Keith Hernandez	1.00
500	Jose Canseco	1.50
527	Dave Henderson	1.00
550	Orel Hershiser	1.00
570	Tony Gwynn	2.50
582	Mike A. Marshall	1.00
590	Andres Galarraga	1.00
600	Wade Boggs	1.50
630	Mike Greenwell	1.00
650	Kirby Puckett	2.00
660	Will Clark	1.50
700	Don Mattingly	2.50
710	David Cone	1.00
725	Terry Steinbach	1.00
730	Danny Jackson	1.00
755	Mike Scioscia	1.00
770	Alan Trammell	1.00
785	Ellis Burks	1.00

1990 Topps

The 1990 Topps set again included 792 cards, and sported a newly-designed front that featured six different color schemes. The set led off with a special four-card salute to Nolan Ryan, and features other specials including All-Stars, Number 1 Draft Picks, Record Breakers, managers, rookies, and "Turn Back the Clock" cards. The set also includes a special card commemorating A. Bartlett Giamatti, the late baseball commissioner. Backs are printed in black on a chartreuse background. The set features 725 different individual player cards, the most ever, including 138 players' first appearance in a regular Topps set.

		MT
Complete Set (792):		18.00
Common Player:		.05
Wax Box:		10.00
1	Nolan Ryan	.50
2	Nolan Ryan (Mets)	.20
3	Nolan Ryan (Angels)	.20
4	Nolan Ryan (Astros)	.20
5	Nolan Ryan (Rangers)	.20
6	Vince Coleman (Record Breaker)	.05
7	Rickey Henderson (Record Breaker)	.10
8	Cal Ripken, Jr. (Record Breaker)	.25
9	Eric Plunk	.05
10	Barry Larkin	.10
11	Paul Gibson	.05
12	Joe Girardi	.05
13	Mark Williamson	.05
14	*Mike Fetters*	.10
15	Teddy Higuera	.05
16	*Kent Anderson*	.05
17	Kelly Downs	.05
18	Carlos Quintana	.05
19	Al Newman	.05
20	Mark Gubicza	.05
21	Jeff Torborg	.05
22	Bruce Ruffin	.05
23	Randy Velarde	.05
24	Joe Hesketh	.05
25	Willie Randolph	.05
26	Don Slaught	.05
27	Rick Leach	.05
28	Duane Ward	.05
29	John Cangelosi	.05
30	David Cone	.20
31	Henry Cotto	.05
32	John Farrell	.05
33	Greg Walker	.05
34	*Tony Fossas*	.05
35	Benito Santiago	.05
36	John Costello	.05
37	Domingo Ramos	.05
38	Wes Gardner	.05
39	Curt Ford	.05
40	Jay Howell	.05
41	Matt Williams	.20
42	Jeff Robinson	.05
43	Dante Bichette	.10
44	*Roger Salkeld* (#1 Draft Pick)	.15
45	Dave Parker	.05
46	Rob Dibble	.05
47	Brian Harper	.05
48	Zane Smith	.05
49	Tom Lawless	.05
50	Glenn Davis	.05
51	Doug Rader	.05
52	*Jack Daugherty*	.10
53	Mike LaCoss	.05
54	Joel Skinner	.05
55	Darrell Evans	.05
56	Franklin Stubbs	.05
57	Greg Vaughn	.10
58	Keith Miller	.05
59	Ted Power	.05
60	George Brett	.25
61	Deion Sanders	.25
62	Ramon Martinez	.10
63	Mike Pagliarulo	.05
64	Danny Darwin	.05
65	Devon White	.05
66	*Greg Litton*	.05
67	Scott Sanderson	.05
68	Dave Henderson	.05
69	Todd Frohwirth	.05
70	Mike Greenwell	.05
71	Allan Anderson	.05
72	*Jeff Huson*	.10
73	Bob Milacki	.05
74	*Jeff Jackson* (#1 Draft Pick)	.05
75	Doug Jones	.05
76	Dave Valle	.05
77	Dave Bergman	.05
78	Mike Flanagan	.05
79	Ron Kittle	.05
80	Jeff Russell	.05
81	Bob Rodgers	.05
82	Scott Terry	.05
83	Hensley Meulens	.05
84	Ray Searage	.05
85	Juan Samuel	.05
86	Paul Kilgus	.05
87	*Rick Luecken*	.05
88	Glenn Braggs	.05
89	*Clint Zavaras*	.05
90	Jack Clark	.05
91	*Steve Frey*	.10
92	Mike Stanley	.05
93	Shawn Hillegas	.05
94	Herm Winningham	.05
95	Todd Worrell	.05
96	Jody Reed	.05
97	Curt Schilling	.10
98	Jose Gonzalez	.05
99	*Rich Monteleone*	.05
100	Will Clark	.30
101	Shane Rawley	.05
102	Stan Javier	.05
103	Marvin Freeman	.05
104	Bob Knepper	.05
105	Randy Myers	.05
106	Charlie O'Brien	.05
107	Fred Lynn	.05
108	Rod Nichols	.05
109	Roberto Kelly	.05
110	Tommy Helms	.05
111	Ed Whited	.05
112	Glenn Wilson	.05
113	Manny Lee	.05
114	Mike Bielecki	.05
115	Tony Pena	.05
116	Floyd Bannister	.05
117	Mike Sharperson	.05
118	Erik Hanson	.05
119	Billy Hatcher	.05
120	John Franco	.05
121	Robin Ventura	.15
122	Shawn Abner	.05
123	Rich Gedman	.05
124	Dave Dravecky	.05
125	Kent Hrbek	.05
126	Randy Kramer	.05
127	Mike Devereaux	.05
128	Checklist 1-132	.05
129	Ron Jones	.05
130	Bert Blyleven	.05
131	Matt Nokes	.05
132	Lance Blankenship	.05
133	Ricky Horton	.05
134	*Earl Cunningham* (#1 Draft Pick)	.05
135	Dave Magadan	.05
136	Kevin Brown	.20
137	*Marty Pevey*	.05
138	Al Leiter	.10
139	Greg Brock	.05
140	Andre Dawson	.10
141	John Hart	.05
142	*Jeff Wetherby*	.05
143	Rafael Belliard	.05
144	Bud Black	.05
145	Terry Steinbach	.05
146	*Rob Richie*	.05
147	Chuck Finley	.05
148	Edgar Martinez	.10
149	Steve Farr	.05
150	Kirk Gibson	.05
151	Rick Mahler	.05
152	Lonnie Smith	.05
153	Randy Milligan	.05
154	Mike Maddux	.05
155	Ellis Burks	.10
156	Ken Patterson	.05
157	Craig Biggio	.25
158	Craig Lefferts	.05
159	Mike Felder	.05
160	Dave Righetti	.05
161	Harold Reynolds	.05
162	*Todd Zeile*	.20
163	Phil Bradley	.05
164	*Jeff Juden* (#1 Draft Pick)	.15
165	Walt Weiss	.05
166	Bobby Witt	.05
167	Kevin Appier	.10
168	Jose Lind	.05
169	Richard Dotson	.05
170	George Bell	.05
171	Russ Nixon	.05
172	Tom Lampkin	.05
173	Tim Belcher	.05
174	Jeff Kunkel	.05
175	Mike Moore	.05
176	Luis Quinones	.05
177	Mike Henneman	.05
178	Chris James	.05
179	Brian Holton	.05
180	Rock Raines	.10
181	Juan Agosto	.05
182	Mookie Wilson	.05
183	Steve Lake	.05
184	Danny Cox	.05
185	Ruben Sierra	.05
186	Dave LaPoint	.05
187	*Rick Wrona*	.05
188	Mike Smithson	.05
189	Dick Schofield	.05
190	Rick Reuschel	.05
191	Pat Borders	.05
192	Don August	.05
193	Andy Benes	.15
194	Glenallen Hill	.10
195	Tim Burke	.05
196	Gerald Young	.05
197	Doug Drabek	.05
198	Mike Marshall	.05
199	*Sergio Valdez*	.05
200	Don Mattingly	.35
201	Cito Gaston	.05
202	Mike Macfarlane	.05
203	*Mike Roesler*	.05
204	Bob Dernier	.05
205	Mark Davis	.05
206	Nick Esasky	.05
207	Bob Ojeda	.05
208	Brook Jacoby	.05
209	Greg Mathews	.05
210	Ryne Sandberg	.30
211	John Cerutti	.05
212	Joe Orsulak	.05
213	Scott Bankhead	.05
214	Terry Francona	.05
215	Kirk McCaskill	.05
216	Ricky Jordan	.05
217	Don Robinson	.05
218	Wally Backman	.05
219	Donn Pall	.05
220	Barry Bonds	.40
221	*Gary Mielke*	.05
222	Kurt Stillwell	.05
223	Tommy Gregg	.05
224	*Delino DeShields*	.25
225	Jim Deshaies	.05
226	Mickey Hatcher	.05
227	*Kevin Tapani*	.25
228	Dave Martinez	.05
229	David Wells	.10
230	Keith Hernandez	.05
231	Jack McKeon	.05
232	Darnell Coles	.05
233	Ken Hill	.10
234	Mariano Duncan	.05
235	Jeff Reardon	.05
236	Hal Morris	.05
237	*Kevin Ritz*	.10
238	Felix Jose	.05
239	Eric Show	.05
240	Mark Grace	.15
241	Mike Krukow	.05
242	Fred Manrique	.05
243	Barry Jones	.05
244	Bill Schroeder	.05
245	Roger Clemens	.40
246	Jim Eisenreich	.05
247	Jerry Reed	.05
248	Dave Anderson	.05
249	*Mike Smith*	.05
250	Jose Canseco	.40
251	Jeff Blauser	.05
252	Otis Nixon	.05
253	Mark Portugal	.05
254	Francisco Cabrera	.05
255	Bobby Thigpen	.05
256	Marvell Wynne	.05
257	Jose DeLeon	.05
258	Barry Lyons	.05
259	Lance McCullers	.05
260	Eric Davis	.10
261	Whitey Herzog	.05
262	Checklist 133-264	.05
263	*Mel Stottlemyre, Jr.*	.10
264	Bryan Clutterbuck	.05
265	Pete O'Brien	.05
266	German Gonzalez	.05
267	Mark Davidson	.05
268	Rob Murphy	.05
269	Dickie Thon	.05
270	Dave Stewart	.05
271	Chet Lemon	.05
272	Bryan Harvey	.05
273	Bobby Bonilla	.10
274	*Goose Gozzo*	.05
275	Mickey Tettleton	.05
276	Gary Thurman	.05
277	Lenny Harris	.05
278	Pascual Perez	.05
279	Steve Buechele	.05
280	Lou Whitaker	.05
281	Kevin Bass	.05
282	Derek Lilliquist	.05

283 Albert Belle 1.00
284 *Mark Gardner* .10
285 Willie McGee .05
286 Lee Guetterman .05
287 Vance Law .05
288 Greg Briley .05
289 Norm Charlton .05
290 Robin Yount .30
291 Dave Johnson .05
292 Jim Gott .05
293 Mike Gallego .05
294 Craig McMurtry .05
295 Fred McGriff .25
296 Jeff Ballard .05
297 Tom Herr .05
298 Danny Gladden .05
299 Adam Peterson .05
300 Bo Jackson .20
301 Don Aase .05
302 *Marcus Lawton* .05
303 Rick Cerone .05
304 Marty Clary .05
305 Eddie Murray .25
306 Tom Niedenfuer .05
307 Bip Roberts .05
308 Jose Guzman .05
309 *Eric Yelding* .20
310 Steve Bedrosian .05
311 Dwight Smith .05
312 Dan Quisenberry .05
313 Gus Polidor .05
314 *Donald Harris* (#1 Draft Pick) .10
315 Bruce Hurst .05
316 Carney Lansford .05
317 *Mark Guthrie* .05
318 Wallace Johnson .05
319 Dion James .05
320 Dave Steib .05
321 Joe M. Morgan .05
322 Junior Ortiz .05
323 Willie Wilson .05
324 Pete Harnisch .05
325 Robby Thompson .05
326 *Tom McCarthy* .05
327 Ken Williams .05
328 Curt Young .05
329 Oddibe McDowell .05
330 Ron Darling .05
331 *Juan Gonzalez* 3.00
332 Paul O'Neill .15
333 Bill Wegman .05
334 Johnny Ray .05
335 Andy Hawkins .05
336 Ken Griffey, Jr. 2.50
337 Lloyd McClendon .05
338 Dennis Lamp .05
339 Dave Clark .05
340 Fernando Valenzuela .05
341 Tom Foley .05
342 Alex Trevino .05
343 Frank Tanana .05
344 *George Canale* .05
345 Harold Baines .05
346 Jim Presley .05
347 *Junior Felix* .05
348 *Gary Wayne* .05
349 *Steve Finley* .15
350 Bret Saberhagen .05
351 Roger Craig .05
352 Bryn Smith .05
353 Sandy Alomar .10
354 *Stan Belinda* .10
355 Marty Barrett .05
356 Randy Ready .05
357 Dave West .05
358 Andres Thomas .05
359 Jimmy Jones .05
360 Paul Molitor .25
361 *Randy McCament* .05
362 Damon Berryhill .05
363 Dan Petry .05
364 Rolando Roomes .05
365 Ozzie Guillen .05
366 Mike Heath .05
367 Mike Morgan .05
368 Bill Doran .05
369 Todd Burns .05
370 Tim Wallach .05
371 Jimmy Key .05
372 Terry Kennedy .05
373 Alvin Davis .05
374 *Steve Cummings* .05
375 Dwight Evans .05
376 Checklist 265-396 .05
377 *Mickey Weston* .05
378 Luis Salazar .05
379 Steve Rosenberg .05
380 Dave Winfield .20
381 Frank Robinson .10
382 Jeff Musselman .05
383 John Morris .05
384 *Pat Combs* .05
385 Fred McGriff (All-Star) .10
386 Julio Franco (All-Star) .05
387 Wade Boggs (All-Star) .15
388 Cal Ripken, Jr. (All-Star) .40
389 Robin Yount (All-Star) .15
390 Ruben Sierra (All-Star) .05
391 Kirby Puckett (All-Star) .20
392 Carlton Fisk (All-Star) .15
393 Bret Saberhagen (All-Star) .05
394 Jeff Ballard (All-Star) .05
395 Jeff Russell (All-Star) .05
396 A. Bartlett Giamatti .20
397 Will Clark (All-Star) .15
398 Ryne Sandberg (All-Star) .20
399 Howard Johnson (All-Star) .05
400 Ozzie Smith (All-Star) .15
401 Kevin Mitchell (All-Star) .05
402 Eric Davis (All-Star) .05
403 Tony Gwynn (All-Star) .20
404 Craig Biggio (All-Star) .10
405 Mike Scott (All-Star) .05
406 Joe Magrane (All-Star) .05
407 Mark Davis (All-Star) .05
408 Trevor Wilson .10
409 Tom Brunansky .05
410 Joe Boever .05
411 Ken Phelps .05
412 Jamie Moyer .05
413 *Brian DuBois* .10
414a *Frank Thomas* No *Name* (#1 Draft Pick, no name on front) 1200.
414b *Frank Thomas* (#1 Draft Pick, name on front) 3.00
415 Shawon Dunston .05
416 *Dave Johnson* .05
417 Jim Gantner .05
418 Tom Browning .05
419 *Beau Allred* .05
420 Carlton Fisk .20
421 Greg Minton .05
422 Pat Sheridan .05
423 Fred Toliver .05
424 Jerry Reuss .05
425 Bill Landrum .05
426 Jeff Hamilton .05
427 Carmem Castillo .05
428 *Steve Davis* .05
429 Tom Kelly .05
430 Pete Incaviglia .05
431 Randy Johnson .30
432 Damaso Garcia .05
433 *Steve Olin* .05
434 Mark Carreon .10
435 Kevin Seitzer .05
436 Mel Hall .05
437 Les Lancaster .05
438 Greg Myers .05
439 Jeff Parrett .05
440 Alan Trammell .05
441 Bob Kipper .05
442 Jerry Browne .05
443 Cris Carpenter .05
444 *Kyle Abbott* (FDP) .10
445 Danny Jackson .05
446 Dan Pasqua .05
447 Atlee Hammaker .05
448 Greg Gagne .05
449 Dennis Rasmussen .05
450 Rickey Henderson .20
451 Mark Lemke .05
452 Luis de los Santos .05
453 Jody Davis .05
454 Jeff King .10
455 Jeffrey Leonard .05
456 Chris Gwynn .05
457 Gregg Jefferies .15
458 Bob McClure .05
459 Jim Lefebvre .05
460 Mike Scott .05
461 *Carlos Martinez* .05
462 Denny Walling .05
463 Drew Hall .05
464 *Jerome Walton* .10
465 Kevin Gross .05
466 Rance Mulliniks .05
467 Juan Nieves .05
468 Billy Ripken .05
469 John Kruk .05
470 Frank Viola .05
471 Mike Brumley .05
472 Jose Uribe .05
473 Joe Price .05
474 Rich Thompson .05
475 Bob Welch .05
476 Brad Komminsk .05
477 Willie Fraser .05
478 Mike LaValliere .05
479 Frank White .05
480 Sid Fernandez .05
481 Garry Templeton .05
482 *Steve Carter* .05
483 Alejandro Pena .05
484 Mike Fitzgerald .05
485 John Candelaria .05
486 Jeff Treadway .05
487 Steve Searcy .05
488 Ken Oberkfell .05
489 Nick Leyva .05
490 Dan Plesac .05
491 *Dave Cochrane* .05
492 Ron Oester .05
493 *Jason Grimsley* .10
494 Terry Puhl .05
495 Lee Smith .05
496 Cecil Espy .05
497 Dave Schmidt .05
498 Rick Schu .05
499 Bill Long .05
500 Kevin Mitchell .05
501 Matt Young .05
502 Mitch Webster .05
503 Randy St. Claire .05
504 Tom O'Malley .05
505 Kelly Gruber .05
506 Tom Glavine .15
507 Gary Redus .05
508 Terry Leach .05
509 Tom Pagnozzi .05
510 Dwight Gooden .10
511 Clay Parker .05
512 Gary Pettis .05
513 Mark Eichhorn .05
514 Andy Allanson .05
515 Len Dykstra .05
516 Tim Leary .05
517 Roberto Alomar .30
518 Bill Krueger .05
519 Bucky Dent .05
520 Mitch Williams .05
521 Craig Worthington .05
522 Mike Dunne .05
523 Jay Bell .05
524 Daryl Boston .05
525 Wally Joyner .10
526 Checklist 397-528 .05
527 Ron Hassey .05
528 *Kevin Wickander* .10
529 Greg Harris .05
530 Mark Langston .05
531 Ken Caminiti .15
532 Cecilio Guante .05
533 Tim Jones .05
534 Louie Meadows .05
535 John Smoltz .15
536 *Bob Geren* .05
537 Mark Grant .05
538 *Billy Spiers* .05
539 Neal Heaton .05
540 Danny Tartabull .05
541 Pat Perry .05
542 Darren Daulton .05
543 Nelson Liriano .05
544 Dennis Boyd .05
545 Kevin McReynolds .05
546 Kevin Hickey .05
547 Jack Howell .05
548 Pat Clements .05
549 Don Zimmer .05
550 Julio Franco .05
551 Tim Crews .05
552 *Mike Smith* .05
553 *Scott Scudder* .05
554 Jay Buhner .10
555 Jack Morris .05
556 Gene Larkin .05
557 *Jeff Innis* .05
558 Rafael Ramirez .05
559 Andy McGaffigan .05
560 Steve Sax .05
561 Ken Dayley .05
562 Chad Kreuter .05
563 Alex Sanchez .05
564 *Tyler Houston* (#1 Draft Pick) .10
565 Scott Fletcher .05
566 Mark Knudson .05
567 Ron Gant .10
568 John Smiley .05
569 Ivan Calderon .05
570 Cal Ripken, Jr. .50
571 Brett Butler .05
572 Greg Harris .05
573 Danny Heep .05
574 Bill Swift .05
575 Lance Parrish .05
576 *Mike Dyer* .05
577 Charlie Hayes .05
578 Joe Magrane .05
579 Art Howe .05
580 Joe Carter .10
581 Ken Griffey .05
582 Rick Honeycutt .05
583 Bruce Benedict .05
584 *Phil Stephenson* .05
585 Kal Daniels .05
586 Ed Nunez .05
587 Lance Johnson .05
588 Rick Rhoden .05
589 Mike Aldrete .05
590 Ozzie Smith .30
591 Todd Stottlemyre .05
592 R.J. Reynolds .05
593 Scott Bradley .05
594 *Luis Sojo* .05
595 Greg Swindell .05
596 Jose DeJesus .05
597 Chris Bosio .05
598 Brady Anderson .20
599 Frank Williams .05
600 Darryl Strawberry .10
601 Luis Rivera .05
602 Scott Garrelts .05
603 Tony Armas .05
604 Ron Robinson .05
605 Mike Scioscia .05
606 Storm Davis .05
607 Steve Jeltz .05
608 *Eric Anthony* .25
609 Sparky Anderson .10
610 Pedro Guerrero .05
611 Walt Terrell .05
612 Dave Gallagher .05
613 Jeff Pico .05
614 Nelson Santovenia .05
615 Rob Deer .05
616 Brian Holman .05
617 Geronimo Berroa .05
618 Eddie Whitson .05
619 Rob Ducey .05
620 *Tony Castillo* .05
621 Melido Perez .05
622 Sid Bream .05
623 Jim Corsi .05
624 Darrin Jackson .05
625 Roger McDowell .05
626 Bob Melvin .05
627 Jose Rijo .05
628 Candy Maldonado .05
629 Eric Hetzel .05
630 Gary Gaetti .05
631 *John Wetteland* .25
632 Scott Lusader .05
633 Dennis Cook .05
634 Luis Polonia .05
635 Brian Downing .05
636 Jesse Orosco .05
637 Craig Reynolds .05
638 Jeff Montgomery .05
639 Tony LaRussa .05
640 Rick Sutcliffe .05
641 *Doug Strange* .05
642 Jack Armstrong .05
643 Alfredo Griffin .05
644 Paul Assenmacher .05
645 Jose Oquendo .05
646 Checklist 529-660 .05
647 Rex Hudler .05
648 Jim Clancy .05
649 *Dan Murphy* .05
650 Mike Witt .05
651 Rafael Santana .05
652 Mike Boddicker .05
653 John Moses .05
654 *Paul Coleman* (#1 Draft Pick) .05
655 Gregg Olson .05
656 Mackey Sasser .05
657 Terry Mulholland .05
658 Donell Nixon .05
659 Greg Cadaret .05
660 Vince Coleman .05
661 Dick Howser (Turn Back the Clock) .05
662 Mike Schmidt (Turn Back the Clock) .10
663 Fred Lynn (Turn Back the Clock) .05
664 Johnny Bench (Turn Back the Clock) .05
665 Sandy Koufax (Turn Back the Clock) .15
666 Brian Fisher .05
667 Curt Wilkerson .05
668 *Joe Oliver* .10
669 Tom Lasorda .15
670 Dennis Eckersley .05
671 Bob Boone .05
672 Roy Smith .05
673 Joey Meyer .05
674 Spike Owen .05
675 Jim Abbott .10
676 Randy Kutcher .05
677 Jay Tibbs .05
678 Kirt Manwaring .05
679 Gary Ward .05
680 Howard Johnson .05
681 Mike Schooler .05
682 Dann Bilardello .05
683 *Kenny Rogers* .10
684 *Julio Machado* .05
685 Tony Fernandez .05
686 Carmelo Martinez .05
687 Tim Birtsas .05
688 Milt Thompson .05
689 Rich Yett .05
690 Mark McGwire 1.50
691 Chuck Cary .05
692 *Sammy Sosa* 5.00
693 Calvin Schiraldi .05
694 *Mike Stanton* .05
695 Tom Henke .05
696 B.J. Surhoff .05
697 Mike Davis .05
698 *Omar Vizquel* .25
699 Jim Leyland .05
700 Kirby Puckett .25
701 *Bernie Williams* 1.50
702 Tony Phillips .05
703 *Jeff Brantley* .10
704 *Chip Hale* .10
705 Claudell Washington .05
706 Geno Petralli .05
707 Luis Aquino .05
708 Larry Sheets .05
709 Juan Berneguer .05
710 Von Hayes .05
711 Rick Aguilera .05
712 Todd Benzinger .05
713 *Tim Drummond* .10
714 *Marquis Grissom* .25
715 Greg Maddux .50
716 Steve Balboni .05
717 Ron Kakovice .05
718 Gary Sheffield .20
719 *Wally Whitehurst* .05
720 Andres Galarraga .20
721 Lee Mazzilli .05
722 Felix Fermin .05
723 Jeff Robinson .05
724 Juan Bell .10
725 Terry Pendleton .05
726 Gene Nelson .05
727 Pat Tabler .05
728 Jim Acker .05
729 Bobby Valentine .05
730 Tony Gwynn .40
731 Don Carman .05
732 Ernie Riles .05
733 John Dopson .05
734 Kevin Elster .05
735 Charlie Hough .05
736 Rick Dempsey .05
737 Chris Sabo .05
738 *Gene Harris* .05
739 Dale Sveum .05
740 Jesse Barfield .05
741 Steve Wilson .05
742 Ernie Whitt .05
743 Tom Candiotti .05
744 *Kelly Mann* .05
745 Hubie Brooks .05
746 Dave Smith .05
747 Randy Bush .05
748 Doyle Alexander .05
749 Mark Parent .05
750 Dale Murphy .15
751 Steve Lyons .05
752 Tom Gordon .05
753 Chris Speier .05
754 Bob Walk .05
755 Rafael Palmeiro .20
756 Ken Howell .05
757 *Larry Walker* 1.50
758 Mark Thurmond .05
759 Tom Trebelhorn .05
760 Wade Boggs .25
761 Mike Jackson .05
762 Doug Dascenzo .05
763 Denny Martinez .05
764 Tim Teufel .05
765 Chili Davis .05
766 Brian Meyer .05
767 Tracy Jones .05
768 Chuck Crim .05
769 *Greg Hibbard* .10
770 Cory Snyder .05
771 Pete Smith .05
772 Jeff Reed .05
773 Dave Leiper .05
774 *Ben McDonald* .20
775 Andy Van Slyke .05
776 Charlie Leibrandt .05
777 Tim Laudner .05
778 Mike Jeffcoat .05
779 Lloyd Moseby .05
780 Orel Hershiser .05
781 Mario Diaz .05
782 Jose Alvarez .05
783 Checklist 661-792 .05
784 Scott Bailes .05
785 Jim Rice .10
786 Eric King .05
787 Rene Gonzales .05
788 Frank DiPino .05
789 John Wathan .05
790 Gary Carter .15
791 Alvaro Espinoza .05
792 Gerald Perry .05

1990 Topps Tiffany

This specially boxed version of Topps' 1990 baseball card set was sold through hobby channels only. The checklist is identical to the regular-issue Topps set and the cards are nearly so. The Tiffany version features white cardboard stock and a high-gloss finish on the fronts.

	MT
Complete Set (792):	95.00
Common Player:	.10
(Star cards valued at 3X-4X corresponding cards in regular Topps issue)	

1990 Topps Traded

For the first time, Topps "Traded" series cards were made available nationwide in retail wax packs. The 132-card set was also sold in complete boxed form as it has been in recent years. The wax pack traded cards feature gray backs, while the boxed set cards feature white backs. The cards are numbered 1T-132T and showcase rookies, players who changed teams and new managers.

		MT
Complete Set (132):		4.00
Common Player:		.05
1	Darrel Akerfelds	.05
2	Sandy Alomar, Jr.	.20
3	Brad Arnsberg	.05
4	Steve Avery	.10
5	Wally Backman	.05
6	*Carlos Baerga*	.10
7	Kevin Bass	.05
8	Willie Blair	.05
9	Mike Blowers	.05
10	Shawn Boskie	.10
11	Daryl Boston	.05
12	Dennis Boyd	.05
13	Glenn Braggs	.05
14	Hubie Brooks	.05
15	Tom Brunansky	.05
16	John Burkett	.15
17	Casey Candaele	.05
18	John Candelaria	.05
19	Gary Carter	.15
20	Joe Carter	.15
21	Rick Cerone	.05
22	Scott Coolbaugh	.05
23	Bobby Cox	.05
24	Mark Davis	.05
25	Storm Davis	.05
26	Edgar Diaz	.05
27	Wayne Edwards	.05
28	Mark Eichhorn	.05
29	Scott Erickson	.25
30	Nick Esasky	.05
31	Cecil Fielder	.15
32	John Franco	.05
33	*Travis Fryman*	.40
34	Bill Gullickson	.05
35	Darryl Hamilton	.05
36	Mike Harkey	.05
37	Bud Harrelson	.05
38	Billy Hatcher	.05
39	Keith Hernandez	.05
40	Joe Hesketh	.05
41	Dave Hollins	.15
42	Sam Horn	.05
43	Steve Howard	.05
44	*Todd Hundley*	.50
45	Jeff Huson	.05
46	Chris James	.05
47	Stan Javier	.05
48	*Dave Justice*	1.00
49	Jeff Kaiser	.05
50	Dana Kiecker	.05
51	Joe Klink	.05
52	Brent Knackert	.05
53	Brad Komminsk	.05
54	Mark Langston	.05
55	Tim Layana	.10
56	Rick Leach	.05
57	Terry Leach	.05
58	Tim Leary	.05
59	Craig Lefferts	.05
60	Charlie Leibrandt	.05
61	Jim Leyritz	.25
62	Fred Lynn	.05
63	Kevin Maas	.05
64	Shane Mack	.05
65	Candy Maldonado	.05
66	Fred Manrique	.05
67	Mike Marshall	.05
68	Carmelo Martinez	.05
69	John Marzano	.05
70	Ben McDonald	.05
71	Jack McDowell	.05
72	John McNamara	.05
73	Orlando Mercado	.05
74	Stump Merrill	.05
75	Alan Mills	.05
76	Hal Morris	.10
77	Lloyd Moseby	.05
78	Randy Myers	.10
79	Tim Naehring	.10
80	Junior Noboa	.05
81	Matt Nokes	.05
82	Pete O'Brien	.05
83	*John Olerud*	1.00
84	Greg Olson	.05
85	Junior Ortiz	.05
86	Dave Parker	.10
87	Rick Parker	.10
88	Bob Patterson	.05
89	Alejandro Pena	.05
90	Tony Pena	.05
91	Pascual Perez	.05
92	Gerald Perry	.05
93	Dan Petry	.05
94	Gary Pettis	.05
95	Tony Phillips	.05
96	Lou Pinella	.05
97	Luis Polonia	.05
98	Jim Presley	.05
99	Scott Radinsky	.15
100	Willie Randolph	.05
101	Jeff Reardon	.05
102	Greg Riddoch	.05
103	Jeff Robinson	.05
104	Ron Robinson	.05
105	Kevin Romine	.05
106	Scott Ruskin	.05
107	John Russell	.05
108	Bill Sampen	.05
109	Juan Samuel	.05
110	Scott Sanderson	.05
111	Jack Savage	.05
112	Dave Schmidt	.05
113	Red Schoendienst	.10
114	Terry Shumpert	.05
115	Matt Sinatro	.05
116	Don Slaught	.05
117	Bryn Smith	.05
118	Lee Smith	.05
119	Paul Sorrento	.10
120	Franklin Stubbs	.05
121	Russ Swan	.05
122	Bob Tewksbury	.10
123	Wayne Tolleson	.05
124	John Tudor	.05
125	Randy Veres	.10
126	Hector Villanueva	.05
127	Mitch Webster	.05
128	Ernie Whitt	.05
129	Frank Wills	.05
130	Dave Winfield	.25
131	Matt Young	.05
132	Checklist	.05

1990 Topps Traded Tiffany

Identical to the regular Topps Traded issue except for the glossy front surface, this special hobby-only boxed set shares the same checklist.

	MT
Complete Set (132):	25.00
Common Player:	.15
(Star cards valued at 4X-6X corresponding cards in regular Topps Traded issue)	

1990 Topps Box Panels

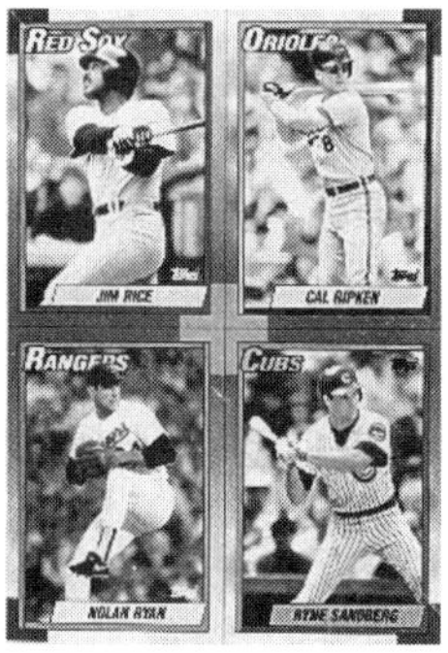

This special 16-card set features four cards on four different box-bottom panels. The cards are identical in design to the regular 1990 Topps cards. The cards are designated by letter.

		MT
Complete Panel Set (4):		7.00
Complete Singles Set (16):		5.00
Common Panel:		1.25
Common Single Player:		.10
Panel		2.00
A	Wade Boggs	.30
B	George Brett	.50
C	Andre Dawson	.15
D	Darrell Evans	.10
Panel		1.25
E	Dwight Gooden	.15
F	Rickey Henderson	.25
G	Tom Lasorda	.15
H	Fred Lynn	.10
Panel		1.25
I	Mark McGwire	2.00
J	Dave Parker	.10
K	Jeff Reardon	.10
L	Rick Reuschel	.10
Panel		6.00
M	Jim Rice	.15
N	Cal Ripken, Jr.	1.50
O	Nolan Ryan	1.50
P	Ryne Sandberg	.60

1990 Topps All-Star Glossy Set of 22

One glossy All-Star card was included in each 1990 Topps rack pack. The cards measure 2-1/2" x 3-1/2" and feature a similar style to past glossy All-Star cards. Special cards of All-Star team captains Carl Yastrzemski and Don Drysdale are included in the set.

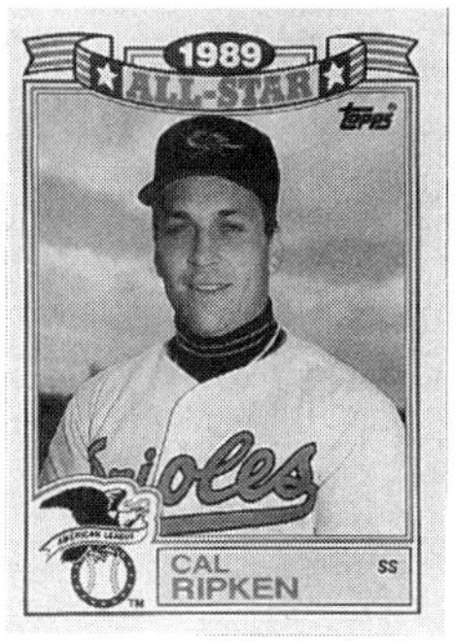

		MT
Complete Set (22):		4.00
Common Player:		.10
1	Tom Lasorda	.15
2	Will Clark	.25
3	Ryne Sandberg	.40
4	Howard Johnson	.10
5	Ozzie Smith	.40
6	Kevin Mitchell	.10
7	Eric Davis	.10
8	Tony Gwynn	.50
9	Benny Santiago	.10
10	Rick Rueschel	.10
11	Don Drysdale	.20
12	Tony LaRussa	.10
13	Mark McGwire	1.50
14	Julio Franco	.10
15	Wade Boggs	.30
16	Cal Ripken, Jr.	.90
17	Bo Jackson	.25
18	Kirby Puckett	.50
19	Ruben Sierra	.10
20	Terry Steinbach	.10
21	Dave Stewart	.10
22	Carl Yastrzemski	.20

1990 Topps All-Star Glossy Set of 60

Sharp color photographs and a clutter-free design are features of the cards in this 60-card send away set. Topps initiated the redemption series in 1983. Six special offer cards, included in Topps baseball wax packs, were necessary to obtain each of the six 10-card sets in the series.

		MT
Complete Set (60):		9.00
Common Player:		.10
1	Ryne Sandberg	.65
2	Nolan Ryan	1.25
3	Glenn Davis	.10
4	Dave Stewart	.10
5	Barry Larkin	.15
6	Carney Lansford	.10
7	Darryl Strawberry	.15
8	Steve Sax	.10
9	Carlos Martinez	.10
10	Gary Sheffield	.35
11	Don Mattingly	1.00
12	Mark Grace	.30
13	Bret Saberhagen	.10
14	Mike Scott	.10
15	Robin Yount	.50
16	Ozzie Smith	.60
17	Jeff Ballard	.10
18	Rick Reuschel	.10
19	Greg Briley	.10
20	Ken Griffey, Jr.	1.75
21	Kevin Mitchell	.10
22	Wade Boggs	.60
23	Dwight Gooden	.15
24	George Bell	.10
25	Eric Davis	.10
26	Ruben Sierra	.10
27	Roberto Alomar	.35
28	Gary Gaetti	.10
29	Gregg Olson	.10
30	Tom Gordon	.10
31	Jose Canseco	.60
32	Pedro Guerrero	.10
33	Joe Carter	.10
34	Mike Scioscia	.10
35	Julio Franco	.10
36	Joe Magrane	.10
37	Rickey Henderson	.25
38	Tim Raines	.15
39	Jerome Walton	.10
40	Bob Geren	.10
41	Andre Dawson	.10
42	Mark McGwire	1.50
43	Howard Johnson	.10
44	Bo Jackson	.25
45	Shawon Dunston	.10
46	Carlton Fisk	.25
47	Mitch Williams	.10
48	Kirby Puckett	.75
49	Craig Worthington	.10
50	Jim Abbott	.10
51	Cal Ripken, Jr.	1.25
52	Will Clark	.45
53	Dennis Eckersley	.10
54	Craig Biggio	.15
55	Fred McGriff	.30
56	Tony Gwynn	.75
57	Mickey Tettleton	.10
58	Mark Davis	.10
59	Omar Vizquel	.10
60	Gregg Jefferies	.10

1990 Topps Glossy Rookies

While the size of the annual glossy rookies set increased to 33 cards from previous years' issues of 22, the format remained identical in 1990. Above the player photo is a colored banner with "1989 Rookies." The player's name appears in red in a yellow bar beneath the photo. Backs are printed in red and blue and contain a shield design with the notation, "1989 Rookies Commemorative Set". The player's name, position and team are listed below, along with a card number. Cards are numbered alphabetically in the set. The glossy rookies were found one per pack in jumbo (100-card) cello packs.

		MT
Complete Set (33):		25.00
Common Player:		.50
1	Jim Abbott	.50
2	Joey Belle	6.00
3	Andy Benes	.75
4	Greg Briley	.50
5	Kevin Brown	4.50
6	Mark Carreon	.50
7	Mike Devereaux	.50
8	Junior Felix	.50
9	Bob Geren	.50
10	Tom Gordon	.75
11	Ken Griffey, Jr.	15.00
12	Pete Harnisch	.50
13	Greg W. Harris	.50
14	Greg Hibbard	.50
15	Ken Hill	.50
16	Gregg Jefferies	.60
17	Jeff King	.50
18	Derek Lilliquist	.50
19	Carlos Martinez	.50
20	Ramon Martinez	.75
21	Bob Milacki	.50
22	Gregg Olson	.50
23	Donn Pall	.50
24	Kenny Rogers	.50
25	Gary Sheffield	1.50
26	Dwight Smith	.50
27	Billy Spiers	.50
28	Omar Vizquel	.60
29	Jerome Walton	.50
30	Dave West	.50
31	John Wetteland	.60
32	Steve Wilson	.50
33	Craig Worthington	.50

1990 Topps Glossy Rookies Foil-test Cards

To test the use of metallic-foil highlights which it would debut on its 1991 Stadium Club and Desert Shield cards, Topps made a test run using as base cards the 33-piece "1989 Rookies Commemorative Set". The test consists of a 2-1/4" x 1/4" metallic strip with a "Topps" logotype punched out of the center. Cards can be found with the strip in many different locations horizontally on the cards' fronts, and in many colors including silver, gold, red, green, blue and purple. Color of foil does not affect values, though a complete set in matching color might command a premium.

		MT
Complete Set (33):		75.00
Common Player:		1.50
1	Jim Abbott	1.50
2	Joey Belle	9.00
3	Andy Benes	2.00
4	Greg Briley	1.50
5	Kevin Brown	12.50
6	Mark Carreon	1.50
7	Mike Devereaux	1.50
8	Junior Felix	1.50
9	Bob Geren	1.50
10	Tom Gordon	2.00
11	Ken Griffey, Jr.	35.00
12	Pete Harnisch	1.50
13	Greg W. Harris	1.50
14	Greg Hibbard	1.50
15	Ken Hill	1.75
16	Gregg Jefferies	2.00
17	Jeff King	1.50
18	Derek Lilliquist	1.50
19	Carlos Martinez	1.50
20	Ramon Martinez	3.00
21	Bob Milacki	1.50
22	Gregg Olson	1.50
23	Donn Pall	1.50
24	Kenny Rogers	1.50
25	Gary Sheffield	5.00
26	Dwight Smith	1.50
27	Billy Spiers	1.50
28	Omar Vizquel	2.00
29	Jerome Walton	1.50
30	Dave West	1.50
31	John Wetteland	2.00
32	Steve Wilson	1.50
33	Craig Worthington	1.50

1990 Topps Award Winners Commemorative Sheet

Six of 1989's top award winners are pictured in the style of 1990 Topps baseball cards on this sheet issued with blister packed sets of Topps baseball stickers. The cards are blank-backed and use photos which are different from those found on the same players' regular 1990 cards. Each player's award is noted in the panel beneath his name. The sheet measures 8-

3/4" x 8-1/8" with individual cards measuring the standard 2-1/2" x 3-1/2".

		MT
Complete Set, Sheet:		5.00
Complete Set, Singles (6):		3.00
Common Player:		.10
(1)	Mark Davis (N.L. Cy Young)	.10
(2)	Kevin Mitchell (N.L. MVP)	.15
(3)	Gregg Olson (A.L. R.O.Y.)	.10
(4)	Bret Saberhagen (A.L. Cy Young)	.25
(5)	Jerome Walton (N.L. R.O.Y.)	.10
(6)	Robin Yount (A.L. MVP)	1.50

1990 Topps Batting Leaders

Once again produced as an exclusive insert in jumbo blister packs for K-Mart stores, the 1990 career batting leaders cards are similar in concept and design to the previous year's issue; in fact, some of the same player photos were used. The 22 cards in the set are arranged roughly in order of the players' standings in lifetime batting average. Card fronts are bordered in bright green; backs are printed in red, white and dark green.

		MT
Complete Set (22):		36.00
Common Player:		1.00
1	Wade Boggs	5.00
2	Tony Gwynn	7.50
3	Kirby Puckett	5.00
4	Don Mattingly	5.00
5	George Brett	6.00
6	Pedro Guerrero	1.00
7	Tim Raines	1.25
8	Paul Molitor	5.00
9	Jim Rice	1.25
10	Keith Hernandez	1.00
11	Julio Franco	1.00
12	Carney Lansford	1.00
13	Dave Parker	1.00
14	Willie McGee	1.00
15	Robin Yount	5.00
16	Tony Fernandez	1.00
17	Eddie Murray	4.00
18	Johnny Ray	1.00
19	Lonnie Smith	1.00
20	Phil Bradley	1.00
21	Rickey Henderson	3.00
22	Kent Hrbek	1.00

1990 Topps Big Baseball

For the third consecutive year, Topps issued a 330-card set of oversized cards (2-5/8" x 3-3/4") in three 110-card series. The cards are reminiscent of Topps cards from the mid-1950s in that they feature players in portrait and action shots. The 1990 set has action photos in freeze frames. As in previous years, the cards are printed on white card stock with a glossy finish on the front. The card backs include 1989 and career hitting, fielding and pitching stats and a player cartoon.

		MT
Complete Set (330):		18.00
Common Player:		.05
1	Dwight Evans	.05
2	Kirby Puckett	.65
3	Kevin Gross	.05
4	Ron Hassey	.05
5	Lloyd McClendon	.05
6	Bo Jackson	.25
7	Lonnie Smith	.05
8	Alvaro Espinoza	.05
9	Roberto Alomar	.25
10	Glenn Braggs	.05
11	David Cone	.10
12	Claudell Washington	.05
13	Pedro Guerrero	.05
14	Todd Benzinger	.05
15	Jeff Russell	.05
16	Terry Kennedy	.05
17	Kelly Gruber	.05
18	Alfredo Griffin	.05
19	Mark Grace	.25
20	Dave Winfield	.20
21	Bret Saberhagen	.10
22	Roger Clemens	.45
23	Bob Walk	.05
24	Dave Magadan	.05
25	Spike Owen	.05
26	Jody Davis	.05
27	Kent Hrbek	.05
28	Mark McGwire	2.00
29	Eddie Murray	.25
30	Paul O'Neill	.10
31	Jose DeLeon	.05
32	Steve Lyons	.05
33	Dan Plesac	.05
34	Jack Howell	.05
35	Greg Briley	.05
36	Andy Hawkins	.05
37	Cecil Espy	.05
38	Rick Sutcliffe	.05
39	Jack Clark	.05
40	Dale Murphy	.15
41	Mike Henneman	.05
42	Rick Honeycutt	.05
43	Willie Randolph	.05
44	Marty Barrett	.05
45	Willie Wilson	.05
46	Wallace Johnson	.05
47	Greg Brock	.05
48	Tom Browning	.05
49	Gerald Young	.05
50	Dennis Eckersley	.05
51	Scott Garrelts	.05
52	Gary Redus	.05
53	Al Newman	.05
54	Darryl Boston	.05
55	Ron Oester	.05
56	Danny Tartabull	.05
57	Gregg Jefferies	.10
58	Tom Foley	.05
59	Robin Yount	.40
60	Pat Borders	.05
61	Mike Greenwell	.05
62	Shawon Dunston	.05
63	Steve Buechele	.05
64	Dave Stewart	.05
65	Jose Oquendo	.05
66	Ron Gant	.15
67	Mike Scioscia	.05
68	Randy Velarde	.05
69	Charlie Hayes	.05
70	Tim Wallach	.05
71	Eric Show	.05
72	Eric Davis	.05
73	Mike Gallego	.05
74	Rob Deer	.05
75	Ryne Sandberg	.50
76	Kevin Seitzer	.05
77	Wade Boggs	.45
78	Greg Gagne	.05
79	John Smiley	.05
80	Ivan Calderon	.05
81	Pete Incaviglia	.05
82	Orel Hershiser	.05
83	Carney Lansford	.05
84	Mike Fitzgerald	.05
85	Don Mattingly	.75
86	Chet Lemon	.05
87	Rolando Roomes	.05
88	Bill Spiers	.05
89	Pat Tabler	.05
90	Danny Heep	.05
91	Andre Dawson	.15
92	Randy Bush	.05
93	Tony Gwynn	.40
94	Tom Brunansky	.05
95	Johnny Ray	.05
96	Matt Williams	.30
97	Barry Lyons	.05
98	Jeff Hamilton	.05
99	Tom Glavine	.10
100	Ken Griffey, Sr.	.05
101	Tom Henke	.05
102	Dave Righetti	.05
103	Paul Molitor	.35
104	Mike LaValliere	.05
105	Frank White	.05
106	Bob Welch	.05
107	Ellis Burks	.05
108	Andres Galarraga	.15
109	Mitch Williams	.05
110	Checklist	.05
111	Craig Biggio	.10
112	Dave Steib	.05
113	Ron Darling	.05
114	Bert Blyleven	.05
115	Dickie Thon	.05
116	Carlos Martinez	.05
117	Jeff King	.05
118	Terry Steinbach	.05
119	Frank Tanana	.05
120	Mark Lemke	.05
121	Chris Sabo	.05
122	Glenn Davis	.05
123	Mel Hall	.05
124	Jim Gantner	.05
125	Benito Santiago	.05
126	Milt Thompson	.05
127	Rafael Palmeiro	.20
128	Barry Bonds	.75
129	Mike Bielecki	.05
130	Lou Whitaker	.05
131	Bob Ojeda	.05
132	Dion James	.05
133	Denny Martinez	.05
134	Fred McGriff	.25
135	Terry Pendleton	.05
136	Pat Combs	.05
137	Kevin Mitchell	.05
138	Marquis Grissom	.15
139	Chris Bosio	.05
140	Omar Vizquel	.05
141	Steve Sax	.05
142	Nelson Liriano	.05
143	Kevin Elster	.05
144	Dan Pasqua	.05
145	Dave Smith	.05
146	Craig Worthington	.05
147	Dan Gladden	.05
148	Oddibe McDowell	.05
149	Bip Roberts	.05
150	Randy Ready	.05
151	Dwight Smith	.05
152	Ed Whitson	.05
153	George Bell	.05
154	Tim Raines	.10
155	Sid Fernandez	.05
156	Henry Cotto	.05
157	Harold Baines	.05
158	Willie McGee	.05
159	Bill Doran	.05
160	Steve Balboni	.05
161	Pete Smith	.05
162	Frank Viola	.05
163	Gary Sheffield	.25
164	Bill Landrum	.05
165	Tony Fernandez	.05
166	Mike Heath	.05
167	Jody Reed	.05
168	Wally Joyner	.10
169	Robby Thompson	.05
170	Ken Caminiti	.10
171	Nolan Ryan	1.75
172	Ricky Jordan	.05
173	Lance Blankenship	.05
174	Dwight Gooden	.10
175	Ruben Sierra	.05
176	Carlton Fisk	.25
177	Garry Templeton	.05
178	Mike Devereaux	.05
179	Mookie Wilson	.05
180	Jeff Blauser	.05
181	Scott Bradley	.05
182	Luis Salazar	.05
183	Rafael Ramirez	.05
184	Vince Coleman	.05
185	Doug Drabek	.05
186	Darryl Strawberry	.10
187	Tim Burke	.05
188	Jesse Barfield	.05
189	Barry Larkin	.20
190	Alan Trammell	.05
191	Steve Lake	.05
192	Derek Lilliquist	.05
193	Don Robinson	.05
194	Kevin McReynolds	.05
195	Melido Perez	.05
196	Jose Lind	.05
197	Eric Anthony	.05
198	B.J. Surhoff	.05
199	John Olerud	.25
200	Mike Moore	.05
201	Mark Gubicza	.05
202	Phil Bradley	.05
203	Ozzie Smith	.35
204	Greg Maddux	.90
205	Julio Franco	.05
206	Tom Herr	.05
207	Scott Fletcher	.05
208	Bobby Bonilla	.10
209	Bob Geren	.05
210	Junior Felix	.05
211	Dick Schofield	.05
212	Jim Deshaies	.05
213	Jose Uribe	.05
214	John Kruk	.05
215	Ozzie Guillen	.05
216	Howard Johnson	.05
217	Andy Van Slyke	.05
218	Tim Laudner	.05
219	Manny Lee	.05
220	Checklist	.05
221	Cory Snyder	.05
222	Billy Hatcher	.05
223	Bud Black	.05
224	Will Clark	.30
225	Kevin Tapani	.05
226	Mike Pagliarulo	.05
227	Dave Parker	.05
228	Ben McDonald	.05
229	Carlos Baerga	.05
230	Roger McDowell	.05
231	Delino DeShields	.05
232	Mark Langston	.05
233	Wally Backman	.05
234	Jim Eisenreich	.05
235	Mike Schooler	.05
236	Kevin Bass	.05
237	John Farrell	.05
238	Kal Daniels	.05
239	Tony Phillips	.05
240	Todd Stottlemyre	.05
241	Greg Olson	.05
242	Charlie Hough	.05
243	Mariano Duncan	.05
244	Billy Ripken	.05
245	Joe Carter	.05
246	Tim Belcher	.05
247	Roberto Kelly	.05
248	Candy Maldonado	.05
249	Mike Scott	.05
250	Ken Griffey, Jr.	2.00
251	Nick Esasky	.05
252	Tom Gordon	.05
253	John Tudor	.05
254	Gary Gaetti	.05
255	Neal Heaton	.05
256	Jerry Browne	.05
257	Jose Rijo	.05
258	Mike Boddicker	.05
259	Brett Butler	.05
260	Andy Benes	.10
261	Kevin Brown	.15
262	Hubie Brooks	.05
263	Randy Milligan	.05
264	John Franco	.05
265	Sandy Alomar	.10
266	Dave Valle	.05
267	Jerome Walton	.05
268	Bob Boone	.05
269	Ken Howell	.05
270	Jose Canseco	.35
271	Joe Magrane	.05
272	Brian DuBois	.05
273	Carlos Quintana	.05
274	Lance Johnson	.05
275	Steve Bedrosian	.05
276	Brook Jacoby	.05
277	Fred Lynn	.05
278	Jeff Ballard	.05
279	Otis Nixon	.05
280	Chili Davis	.05
281	Joe Oliver	.05
282	Brian Holman	.05
283	Juan Samuel	.05
284	Rick Aguilera	.05
285	Jeff Reardon	.05
286	Sammy Sosa	1.50
287	Carmelo Martinez	.05
288	Greg Swindell	.05
289	Erik Hanson	.05
290	Tony Pena	.05
291	Pascual Perez	.05
292	Rickey Henderson	.20
293	Kurt Stillwell	.05
294	Todd Zeile	.15
295	Bobby Thigpen	.05
296	Larry Walker	.25
297	Rob Murphy	.05
298	Mitch Webster	.05
299	Devon White	.05
300	Len Dykstra	.05
301	Keith Hernandez	.05
302	Gene Larkin	.05
303	Jeffrey Leonard	.05
304	Jim Presley	.05
305	Lloyd Moseby	.05
306	John Smoltz	.10
307	Sam Horn	.05
308	Greg Litton	.05
309	Dave Henderson	.05
310	Mark McLemore	.05
311	Gary Pettis	.05
312	Mark Davis	.05
313	Cecil Fielder	.10
314	Jack Armstrong	.05
315	Alvin Davis	.05
316	Doug Jones	.05
317	Eric Yelding	.10
318	Joe Orsulak	.05
319	Chuck Finley	.05
320	Glenn Wilson	.05
321	Harold Reynolds	.05
322	Teddy Higuera	.05
323	Lance Parrish	.05
324	Bruce Hurst	.05
325	Dave West	.05
326	Kirk Gibson	.05
327	Cal Ripken, Jr.	1.75
328	Rick Reuschel	.05
329	Jim Abbott	.10
330	Checklist	.05

1990 Topps George Bush

As a favor to President George Bush, Topps produced a special run of cards in its 1990 design featuring a photo of the president in his Yale University baseball uniform. Some of the cards were inadvertently included in regular Topps packages and made their way into the hobby.

George Bush

1990 Topps Coins

Sixty of the game's top stars and promising rookies are featured in this fourth annual coin set. Fronts of the 1-1/2" diameter coins feature a player photo with a symbolic infield in front of and behind the photo. The player's name and team appear below. Most coins feature natural aluminum coloring on the rolled edges and on the back. Special coins of major award winners have different colors in the background and edges. Backs feature a coin number, minimal biographical data and a previous season career summary. Coins were sold three per pack which included an offer card for a coin holder and Topps magazine subscription offer.

		MT
Complete Set (60):		11.00
Common Player:		.15
1	Robin Yount	.50
2	Bret Saberhagen	.20
3	Gregg Olson	.15
4	Kirby Puckett	.75
5	George Bell	.15
6	Wade Boggs	.50
7	Jerry Browne	.15
8	Ellis Burks	.15
9	Ivan Calderon	.15
10	Tom Candiotti	.15
11	Alvin Davis	.15
12	Chili Davis	.15
13	Chuck Finley	.15
14	Gary Gaetti	.15
15	Tom Gordon	.20
16	Ken Griffey, Jr.	1.00
17	Rickey Henderson	.30
18	Kent Hrbek	.15
19	Bo Jackson	.25
20	Carlos Martinez	.15
21	Don Mattingly	.75
22	Fred McGriff	.30
23	Paul Molitor	.50
24	Cal Ripken, Jr.	.90
25	Nolan Ryan	.90
26	Steve Sax	.15
27	Gary Sheffield	.25

28	Ruben Sierra	.15
29	Dave Stewart	.15
30	Mickey Tettleton	.15
31	Alan Trammell	.15
32	Lou Whitaker	.15
33	Kevin Mitchell	.15
34	Mark Davis	.15
35	Jerome Walton	.15
36	Tony Gwynn	.50
37	Roberto Alomar	.30
38	Tim Belcher	.15
39	Craig Biggio	.20
40	Barry Bonds	.60
41	Bobby Bonilla	.15
42	Joe Carter	.15
43	Will Clark	.30
44	Eric Davis	.15
45	Glenn Davis	.15
46	Sid Fernandez	.15
47	Pedro Guerrero	.15
48	Von Hayes	.15
49	Tom Herr	.15
50	Howard Johnson	.15
51	Barry Larkin	.20
52	Joe Magrane	.15
53	Dale Murphy	.20
54	Tim Raines	.20
55	Willie Randolph	.15
56	Ryne Sandberg	.60
57	Dwight Smith	.15
58	Lonnie Smith	.15
59	Robby Thompson	.15
60	Tim Wallach	.15

1990 Topps Double Headers

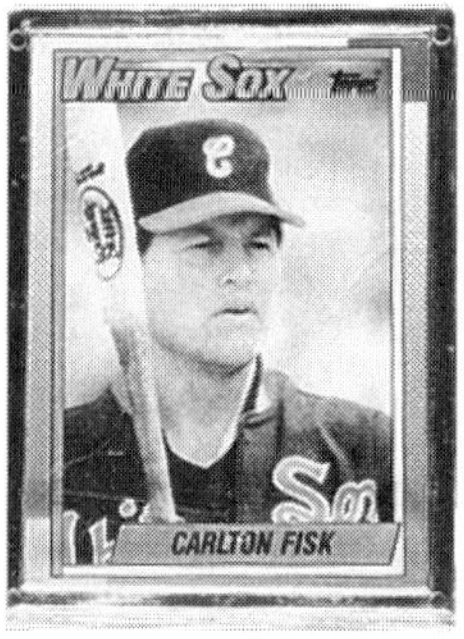

For a second (and final) year, Topps produced an issue of mini cards encased in plastic stands and marketed as Double Headers. Each piece features a 1-5/8" x 2-1/4" reproduction of the player's Topps rookie card, backed by a reproduction of his card from the regular 1990 Topps set. The size of the DH set was increased from 24 in 1989 to 72 for 1990. The novelties were sold for 50 cents apiece. The unnumbered cards are checklisted here alphabetically.

		MT
Complete Set (72):		40.00
Common Player:		.25
(1)	Jim Abbott	.25
(2)	Jeff Ballard	.25
(3)	George Bell	.25
(4)	Wade Boggs	1.00
(5)	Barry Bonds	2.00
(6)	Bobby Bonilla	.25
(7)	Ellis Burks	.25
(8)	Jose Canseco	1.50
(9)	Joe Carter	.25
(10)	Will Clark	.75
(11)	Roger Clemens	1.50
(12)	Vince Coleman	.25
(13)	Alvin Davis	.25
(14)	Eric Davis	.25
(15)	Glenn Davis	.25
(16)	Mark Davis	.25
(17)	Andre Dawson	.35
(18)	Shawon Dunston	.25
(19)	Dennis Eckersley	.25
(20)	Sid Fernandez	.25
(21)	Tony Fernandez	.25
(22)	Chuck Finley	.25
(23)	Carlton Fisk	.60
(24)	Julio Franco	.25
(25)	Gary Gaetti	.25
(26)	Dwight Gooden	.30
(27)	Mark Grace	.45
(28)	Mike Greenwell	.25
(29)	Ken Griffey, Jr.	4.00
(30)	Pedro Guerrero	.25
(31)	Tony Gwynn	1.50
(32)	Von Hayes	.25
(33)	Rickey Henderson	.50
(34)	Orel Hershiser	.25
(35)	Bo Jackson	.35
(36)	Gregg Jefferies	.25
(37)	Howard Johnson	.25
(38)	Ricky Jordan	.25
(39)	Carney Lansford	.25
(40)	Barry Larkin	.30
(41)	Greg Maddux	2.00
(42)	Joe Magrane	.25
(43)	Don Mattingly	2.00
(44)	Fred McGriff	.60
(45)	Mark McGwire	4.00
(46)	Kevin McReynolds	.25
(47)	Kevin Mitchell	.25
(48)	Gregg Olson	.25
(49)	Kirby Puckett	1.50
(50)	Tim Raines	.30
(51)	Harold Reynolds	.25
(52)	Cal Ripken, Jr.	3.00
(53)	Nolan Ryan	3.00
(54)	Bret Saberhagen	.30
(55)	Ryne Sandberg	1.50
(56)	Benito Santiago	.25
(57)	Steve Sax	.25
(58)	Mike Scioscia	.25
(59)	Mike Scott	.25
(60)	Ruben Sierra	.25
(61)	Lonnie Smith	.25
(62)	Ozzie Smith	1.00
(63)	Dave Stewart	.25
(64)	Darryl Strawberry	.30
(65)	Greg Swindell	.25
(66)	Alan Trammell	.25
(67)	Frank Viola	.25
(68)	Tim Wallach	.25
(69)	Jerome Walton	.25
(70)	Lou Whitaker	.25
(71)	Mitch Williams	.25
(72)	Robin Yount	1.50

1990 Topps Gallery of Champions

The 1990 Topps 1/4-size metal baseball mini-cards were issued only as complete sets in a special display case. As with earlier editions, the 1-1/4" x 1-3/4" ingots do a creditable job of reproducing the players' 1990 Topps cards, right down to the tiny stats on the back. Players in the set represent the winners of major awards and statistical leaders from the previous season. A pewter Nolan Ryan 1/4-size card and 1954 Hank Aaron bronze mini-replica were issued as sales incentives for dealers purchasing the Gallery of Champions sets or 1990 Topps Traded sets.

		MT
Complete Aluminum Set (12):		75.00
Complete Bronze Set (12):		150.00
Complete Silver Set (12):		375.00
(1a)	Mark Davis (aluminum)	3.00
(1b)	Mark Davis (bronze)	6.00
(1s)	Mark Davis (silver)	15.00
(2a)	Jose DeLeon (aluminum)	3.00
(2b)	Jose DeLeon (bronze)	6.00
(2s)	Jose DeLeon (silver)	15.00
(3a)	Tony Gwynn (aluminum)	12.00
(3b)	Tony Gwynn (bronze)	24.00
(3s)	Tony Gwynn (silver)	60.00
(4a)	Fred McGriff (aluminum)	7.50
(4b)	Fred McGriff (bronze)	15.00
(4s)	Fred McGriff (silver)	40.00
(5a)	Kevin Mitchell (aluminum)	3.00
(5b)	Kevin Mitchell (bronze)	6.00
(5s)	Kevin Mitchell (silver)	15.00
(6a)	Gregg Olson (aluminum)	3.00
(6b)	Gregg Olson (bronze)	6.00
(6s)	Gregg Olson (silver)	15.00
(7a)	Kirby Puckett (aluminum)	12.00
(7b)	Kirby Puckett (bronze)	24.00
(7s)	Kirby Puckett (silver)	60.00
(8a)	Jeff Russell (aluminum)	3.00
(8b)	Jeff Russell (bronze)	6.00
(8s)	Jeff Russell (silver)	15.00
(9a)	Nolan Ryan (aluminum)	35.00
(9b)	Nolan Ryan (bronze)	65.00
(9s)	Nolan Ryan (silver)	150.00
(9p)	Nolan Ryan (pewter)	125.00
(10a)	Bret Saberhagen (aluminum)	5.00
(10b)	Bret Saberhagen (bronze)	10.00
(10s)	Bret Saberhagen (silver)	25.00
(11a)	Jerome Walton (aluminum)	3.00
(11b)	Jerome Walton (bronze)	6.00
(11s)	Jerome Walton (silver)	15.00
(12a)	Robin Yount (aluminum)	12.00
(12b)	Robin Yount (bronze)	25.00
(12s)	Robin Yount (silver)	50.00
(13)	Hank Aaron (1954, bronze)	25.00

1990 Topps Golden Spikes Award

This one-card "set" was given out at the United States Baseball Federation awards luncheon in New York City on Nov. 14, 1990, honoring Alex Fernandez as the outstanding amateur baseball player of the year and winner of the Golden Spikes Award. The rough borders found on many of these cards indicates they were cut from the press sheet by hand. Production was reported as 600 cards.

	MT
Alex Fernandez	300.00

1990 Topps Heads Up!

Following up a much rarer test issue of the previous year, the Heads Up! Baseball Stars of 1990 was a 24-piece set which received much wider distribution, but proved unpopular with collectors. On heavy cardboard, die-cut to approximately 5" x 6", these novelties featured only a head-and-cap photo of the player. Backs have the player's name and team, along with an adhesive strip and plastic suction cup which could be used to "hang" the player.

		MT
Complete Set (24):		7.50
Common Player:		.25
1	Tony Gwynn	1.00
2	Will Clark	.40
3	Dwight Gooden	.25
4	Dennis Eckersley	.25
5	Ken Griffey, Jr.	2.00
6	Craig Biggio	.25
7	Bret Saberhagen	.25
8	Bo Jackson	.35
9	Ryne Sandberg	1.00
10	Gregg Olson	.25
11	John Franco	.25
12	Rafael Palmeiro	.35
13	Gary Sheffield	.45
14	Mark McGwire	2.00
15	Kevin Mitchell	.25
16	Jim Abbott	.30
17	Harold Reynolds	.25
18	Jose Canseco	.35
19	Don Mattingly	1.00
20	Kirby Puckett	1.00
21	Tom Gordon	.25
22	Craig Worthington	.25
23	Dwight Smith	.25
24	Jerome Walton	.25

1990 Topps 1989 Major League Debut

This 150-card set chronicles the debut date of all 1989 Major League rookies. Two checklist cards are also included in this boxed set, listing the players in order of debut date, though the cards are numbered alphabetically. The card fronts resemble the 1990 Topps cards in style. A debut banner appears in an upper corner. The flip sides are horizontal and are printed in black on yellow stock, providing an overview of the player's first game. The set is packaged in a special collectors box and was only available through hobby dealers.

		MT
Complete Set (150):		45.00
Common Player:		.10
1	Jim Abbott	.15
2	Beau Allred	.10
3	Wilson Alvarez	.15
4	Kent Anderson	.10
5	Eric Anthony	.20
6	Kevin Appier	.20
7	Larry Arndt	.10
8	John Barfield	.10
9	Billy Bates	.10
10	Kevin Batiste	.10
11	Blaine Beatty	.10
12	Stan Belinda	.10
13	Juan Bell	.10
14	Joey Belle	2.00
15	Andy Benes	.20
16	Mike Benjamin	.10
17	Geronimo Berroa	.10
18	Mike Blowers	.10
19	Brian Brady	.10
20	Francisco Cabrera	.10
21	George Canale	.10
22	Jose Cano	.10
23	Steve Carter	.10
24	Pat Combs	.10
25	Scott Coolbaugh	.10
26	Steve Cummings	.10
27	Pete Dalena	.10
28	Jeff Datz	.10
29	Bobby Davidson	.10
30	Drew Denson	.10
31	Gary DiSarcina	.10
32	Brian DuBois	.10
33	Mike Dyer	.10
34	Wayne Edwards	.10
35	Junior Felix	.10
36	Mike Fetters	.10
37	Steve Finley	.20
38	Darren Fletcher	.15
39	LaVel Freeman	.10
40	Steve Frey	.10
41	Mark Gardner	.10
42	Joe Girardi	.20
43	Juan Gonzalez	3.00
44	Goose Gozzo	.10
45	Tommy Greene	.15
46	Ken Griffey, Jr.	9.00
47	Jason Grimsley	.10
48	Marquis Grissom	.75
49	Mark Guthrie	.10
50	Chip Hale	.10
51	John Hardy	.10
52	Gene Harris	.10
53	Mike Hartley	.10
54	Scott Hemond	.10
55	Xavier Hernandez	.10
56	Eric Hetzel	.10
57	Greg Hibbard	.10
58	Mark Higgins	.10
59	Glenallen Hill	.15
60	Chris Hoiles	.15
61	Shawn Holman	.10
62	Dann Howitt	.10
63	Mike Huff	.10
64	Terry Jorgenson	.10
65	Dave Justice	2.00
66	Jeff King	.15
67	Matt Kinzer	.10
68	Joe Kraemer	.10
69	Marcus Lawton	.10
70	Derek Lilliquist	.10
71	Scott Little	.10
72	Greg Litton	.10
73	Rick Lueken	.10
74	Julio Machado	.10
75	Tom Magrann	.10
76	Kelly Mann	.10
77	Randy McCament	.10
78	Ben McDonald	.10
79	Chuck McElroy	.10
80	Jeff McKnight	.10
81	Kent Mercker	.10
82	Matt Merullo	.10
83	Hensley Meulens	.10
84	Kevin Mmahat	.10
85	Mike Munoz	.10
86	Dan Murphy	.10
87	Jaime Navarro	.10
88	Randy Nosek	.10
89	John Olerud	.50
90	Steve Olin	.10
91	Joe Oliver	.10
92	Francisco Oliveras	.10
93	Greg Olson	.10
94	John Orton	.10
95	Dean Palmer	.10
96	Ramon Pena	.10
97	Jeff Peterek	.10
98	Marty Pevey	.10
99	Rusty Richards	.10
100	Jeff Richardson	.10
101	Rob Richie	.10
102	Kevin Ritz	.10
103	Rosario Rodriguez	.10
104	Mike Roesler	.10
105	Kenny Rogers	.15
106	Bobby Rose	.10
107	Alex Sanchez	.10
108	Deion Sanders	.60
109	Jeff Schaefer	.10
110	Jeff Schulz	.10
111	Mike Schwabe	.10
112	Dick Scott	.10
113	Scott Scudder	.10
114	Rudy Seanez	.10
115	Joe Skalski	.10
116	Dwight Smith	.10
117	Greg Smith	.10
118	Mike Smith	.10
119	Paul Sorrento	.10
120	Sammy Sosa	20.00
121	Billy Spiers	.10
122	Mike Stanton	.10
123	Phil Stephenson	.10
124	Doug Strange	.10
125	Russ Swan	.10
126	Kevin Tapani	.15
127	Stu Tate	.10
128	Greg Vaughn	.30
129	Robin Ventura	.40
130	Randy Veres	.10
131	Jose Vizcaino	.10
132	Omar Vizquel	.15
133	Larry Walker	1.00
134	Jerome Walton	.10
135	Gary Wayne	.10
136	Lenny Webster	.10
137	Mickey Weston	.10
138	Jeff Wetherby	.10
139	John Wetteland	.15
140	Ed Whited	.10
141	Wally Whitehurst	.10
142	Kevin Wickander	.10
143	Dean Wilkins	.10
144	Dana Williams	.10
145	Paul Wilmet	.10
146	Craig Wilson	.10
147	Matt Winters	.10
148	Eric Yelding	.10
149	Clint Zavaras	.10
150	Todd Zeile	.15
----	Checklist (1 of 2)	.05
----	Checklist (2 of 2)	.05

b1107-1990-93 Topps Magazine

Beginning with its debut issue dated Winter, 1990, Topps Magazine included sportscards in each of its quarterly issues. Generally printed on perforated panels which could be easily separated from the magazine and the other cards, six to eight cards were included in most issues. Most of the cards were original designs, but some depicted then-current players on Topps designs from previous years. For the duration of their issue, the cards were numbered consecutively with a "TM" prefix.

		MT
Complete Set (112):		60.00
Common Player:		.25
1	Dave Staton	.25
2	Dan Peltier	.25
3	Ken Griffey Jr.	3.00
4	Ruben Sierra	.25
5	Bret Saberhagen	.25
6	Jerome Walton	.25
7	Kevin Mitchell	.25
8	Mike Scott	.25
9	Bo Jackson	.35
10	Nolan Ryan	3.00
11	Will Clark	.50
12	Robin Yount	.50
13	Joe Morgan	.50
14	Jim Palmer	.50
15	Ben McDonald	.25
16	John Olerud	.35
17	Don Mattingly	2.00
18	Eric Davis, Barry Larkin, Chris Sabo	.25
19	Jim Abbott	.25
20	Sandy Alomar Jr.	.35
21	Jose Canseco	1.00
22	Delino DeShields	.25
23	Wade Boggs	1.00
24	Kirby Puckett	1.00
25	Ryne Sandberg	1.00
26	Roger Clemens	1.00
27	Ken Griffey Jr., Ken Griffey Sr.	1.50
28	Cecil Fielder	.25
29	Steve Avery	.25
30	Rickey Henderson	.35
31	Kevin Maas	.25
32	Len Dykstra	.25
33	Darryl Strawberry	.35
34	Mark McGwire	3.00
35	Matt Williams	.35
36	David Justice	.25
37	Cincinnati Reds	.25
38	Todd Van Poppel	.25
39	Jose Offerman	.25
40	Alex Fernandez	.25
41	Carlton Fisk	.35
42	Barry Bonds	1.00
43	Bobby Bonilla	.25
44	Bob Welch	.25
45	Mo Vaughn	.35
46	Tino Martinez	.35
47	D.J. Dozier	.25
48	Frank Thomas	1.50
49	Cal Ripken Jr. ('75 Topps style)	2.00
50	Dave Winfield ('75 Topps style)	.50
51	Dwight Gooden ('75 Topps style)	.40
52	Bo Jackson ('75 Topps style)	.40
53	Kirk Dressendorfer	.25
54	Gary Scott	.25
55	Steve Decker	.25
56	Ray Lankford	.25
57	Ozzie Smith ('86 Topps style)	1.00
58	Joe Carter ('86 Topps style)	.35
59	Dave Henderson ('86 Topps style)	.25
60	Tony Gwynn ('86 Topps style)	1.00
61	Jeff Bagwell	.65
62	Scott Erickson	.25
63	Pat Kelly	.25
64	Orlando Merced	.25
65	Andre Dawson	.35
66	Reggie Sanders	.25
67	Phil Plantier	.25
68	Paul Molitor	.50
69	Terry Pendleton	.25
70	Julio Franco	.25
71	Lee Smith	.25
72	'91 Minnesota Twins	.25
73	Royce Clayton	.25
74	Tom Glavine	.25
75	Roger Salkeld	.25
76	Robin Ventura	.35
77	John Goodman (as Babe Ruth)	.25
78	Jack Morris	.25
79	Brien Taylor	.25
80	Howard Johnson	.25
81	Barry Larkin	.25
82	Deion Sanders	.35
83	Mike Mussina	.65
84	Juan Gonzalez	1.00
85	Roberto Alomar	.35
86	Fred McGriff	.25
87	Doug Drabek	.25
88	George Brett	.60
89	Otis Nixon	.25
90	Brady Anderson	.25
91	Gary Sheffield	.35
92	Dave Fleming	.25
93	Jeff Reardon	.25
94	Mark McGwire	3.00
95	Larry Walker	.50
96	John Kruk	.25
97	Carlos Baerga	.25
98	Pat Listach	.25
99	'92 Toronto Blue Jays	.25
100	Eric Karros	.25
101	Bret Boone	.25
102	Al Martin	.25
103	Wil Cordero	.25
104	Tim Salmon	.35
105	Danny Tartabull	.25
106	J.T. Snow	.35
107	Mike Piazza	1.50
108	Frank Viola	.25
109	Nolan Ryan (Mets)	2.00
110	Nolan Ryan (Angels)	2.00
111	Nolan Ryan (Astros)	2.00
112	Nolan Ryan (Rangers)	2.00

1990 Topps Mini League Leaders

The last in a five-year string of mini cards, the 1990 league leaders' set offers players who were in the top five in major batting and pitching stats during the 1989 season. Fronts of the 2-1/8" x 3" cards mimic the regular Topps' design for 1990; featuring an action photo with multi-colored borders. Backs offer a round player portrait photo and information about the statistical achievement, all printed in full color. Cards are numbered alphabetically within teams. The 1990 minis are considerably scarcer than the previous years' offerings.

		MT
Complete Set (88):		15.00
Common Player:		.10
1	Jeff Ballard	.10
2	Phil Bradley	.10
3	Wade Boggs	.50
4	Roger Clemens	.75
5	Nick Esasky	.10
6	Jody Reed	.10
7	Bert Blyleven	.10
8	Chuck Finley	.10
9	Kirk McCaskill	.10
10	Devon White	.10
11	Ivan Calderon	.10
12	Bobby Thigpen	.10
13	Joe Carter	.10
14	Gary Pettis	.10
15	Tom Gordon	.10
16	Bo Jackson	.25
17	Bret Saberhagen	.15
18	Kevin Seitzer	.10
19	Chris Bosio	.10
20	Paul Molitor	.50
21	Dan Plesac	.10
22	Robin Yount	.50
23	Kirby Puckett	1.00
24	Don Mattingly	1.00
25	Steve Sax	.10
26	Storm Davis	.10
27	Dennis Eckersley	.10
28	Rickey Henderson	.25
29	Carney Lansford	.10
30	Mark McGwire	3.00
31	Mike Moore	.10
32	Dave Stewart	.10
33	Alvin Davis	.10
34	Harold Reynolds	.10
35	Mike Schooler	.10
36	Cecil Espy	.10
37	Julio Franco	.10
38	Jeff Russell	.10
39	Nolan Ryan	2.00
40	Ruben Sierra	.10
41	George Bell	.10
42	Tony Fernandez	.10
43	Fred McGriff	.25
44	Dave Steib	.10
45	Checklist	.05
46	Lonnie Smith	.10
47	John Smoltz	.15
48	Mike Bielecki	.10
49	Mark Grace	.25
50	Greg Maddux	1.50
51	Ryne Sandberg	.75
52	Mitch Williams	.10
53	Eric Davis	.10
54	John Franco	.10
55	Glenn Davis	.10
56	Mike Scott	.10
57	Tim Belcher	.10
58	Orel Hershiser	.10
59	Jay Howell	.10
60	Eddie Murray	.30
61	Tim Burke	.10
62	Mark Langston	.10
63	Tim Raines	.15
64	Tim Wallach	.10
65	David Cone	.15
66	Sid Fernandez	.10
67	Howard Johnson	.10
68	Juan Samuel	.10
69	Von Hayes	.10
70	Barry Bonds	1.00
71	Bobby Bonilla	.10
72	Andy Van Slyke	.10
73	Vince Coleman	.10
74	Jose DeLeon	.10
75	Pedro Guerrero	.10
76	Joe Magrane	.10
77	Roberto Alomar	.25
78	Jack Clark	.10
79	Mark Davis	.10
80	Tony Gwynn	.65
81	Bruce Hurst	.10
82	Eddie Whitson	.10
83	Brett Butler	.10
84	Will Clark	.25
85	Scott Garrelts	.10
86	Kevin Mitchell	.10
87	Rick Reuschel	.10
88	Robby Thompson	.10

1990 Topps Nolan Ryan Bronze

This full-size bronze reproduction of Ryan's 1990 Topps card was given to dealers who made early orders for Topps' 1991 "Tiffany" sets. A 2,500 piece limit was announced.

	MT
Nolan Ryan	125.00

1990 Topps Senior League

Topps was among several companies to produce a Senior League set in 1990. The set includes 132 cards and was sold as a boxed set. The card fronts have the Senior Baseball and Topps logo on top and the player's name and team logo on the bottom, with a woodgrain-like border surrounding the front photo. The backs of the card include traditional biographical information, plus career major league statistics, career ML bests and stats from any Senior League experience.

		MT
Complete Set (132):		4.00
Common Player:		.10
1	George Foster	.15
2	Dwight Lowry	.10
3	Bob Jones	.10
4	Clete Boyer	.10
5	Rafael Landestoy	.10
6	Bob Shirley	.10
7	Ivan Murrell	.10
8	Jerry White	.10
9	Steve Henderson	.10
10	Marty Castillo	.10
11	Bruce Kison	.10
12	George Hendrick	.10
13	Bernie Carbo	.10
14	Jerry Martin	.10
15	Al Hrabosky	.10
16	Luis Gomez	.10
17	Dick Drago	.10
18	Bobby Ramos	.10
19	Joe Pittman	.10
20	Ike Blessitt	.10
21	Bill Travers	.10
22	Dick Williams	.10
23	Randy Lerch	.10
24	Tom Spencer	.10
25	Graig Nettles	.10
26	Jim Gideon	.10
27	Al Bumbry	.10
28	Tom Murphy	.10
29	Rodney Scott	.10
30	Alan Bannister	.10
31	John D'Acquisto	.10
32	Bert Campaneris	.10
33	Bill Lee	.10
34	Jerry Grote	.10
35	Ken Reitz	.10
36	Al Oliver	.15
37	Tim Stoddard	.10
38	Lenny Randle	.10
39	Rick Manning	.10
40	Bobby Bonds	.15
41	Rick Wise	.10
42	Sal Butera	.10
43	Ed Figueroa	.10
44	Ron Washington	.10
45	Elias Sosa	.10
46	Dan Driessen	.10
47	Wayne Nordhagen	.10
48	Vida Blue	.15
49	Butch Hobson	.10
50	Randy Bass	.10
51	Paul Mirabella	.10
52	Steve Kemp	.10
53	Kim Allen	.10
54	Stan Cliburn	.10
55	Derrel Thomas	.10
56	Pete Falcone	.10
57	Willie Aikens	.10
58	Toby Harrah	.10
59	Bob Tolan	.10
60	Rick Waits	.10
61	Jim Morrison	.10
62	Stan Bahnsen	.10
63	Gene Richards	.10
64	Dave Cash	.10
65	Rollie Fingers	.50
66	Butch Benton	.10
67	Tim Ireland	.10
68	Rick Lysander	.10
69	Cesar Cedeno	.10
70	Jim Willoughby	.10
71	Bill Madlock	.15
72	Lee Lacy	.10
73	Milt Wilcox	.10
74	Ron Pruitt	.10
75	Wayne Krenchicki	.10
76	Earl Weaver	.25
77	Pedro Borbon	.10
78	Jose Cruz	.10
79	Steve Ontiveros	.10
80	Mike Easler	.10
81	Amos Otis	.10
82	Mickey Mahler	.10
83	Orlando Gonzalez	.10
84	Doug Simunic	.10
85	Felix Millan	.10
86	Garth Iorg	.10
87	Pete Broberg	.10
88	Roy Howell	.10
89	Dave LaRoche	.10
90	Jerry Manuel	.10
91	Tony Scott	.10
92	Larvell Blanks	.10
93	Joaquin Andujar	.10
94	Tito Landrum	.10
95	Joe Sambito	.10
96	Pat Dobson	.10
97	Dan Meyer	.10
98	Clint Hurdle	.10
99	Pete LaCock	.10
100	Bob Galasso	.10
101	Dave Kingman	.15
102	Jon Matlack	.10
103	Larry Harlow	.10
104	Rick Peterson	.10
105	Joe Hicks	.10
106	Bill Campbell	.10
107	Tom Paciorek	.10
108	Ray Burris	.10
109	Ken Landreaux	.10
110	Steve McCatty	.10
111	Ron LeFlore	.10
112	Joe Decker	.10
113	Leon Roberts	.10
114	Doug Corbett	.10
115	Mickey Rivers	.10
116	Dock Ellis	.10
117	Ron Jackson	.10
118	Bob Molinaro	.10
119	Fergie Jenkins	.50
120	U.L. Washington	.10
121	Roy Thomas	.10
122	Hal McRae	.20
123	Juan Eichelberger	.10
124	Gary Rajsich	.10
125	Dennis Leonard	.10
126	Walt Williams	.10
127	Rennie Stennett	.10
128	Jim Bibby	.10
129	Dyar Miller	.10
130	Luis Pujols	.10
131	Juan Beniquez	.10
132	Checklist	.10

1990 Topps Stickercards

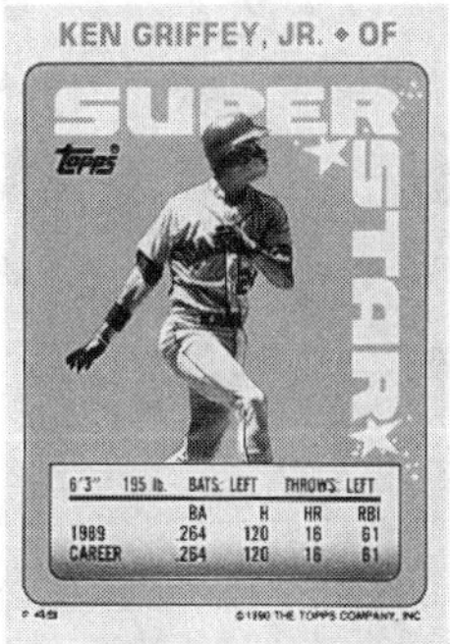

Providing a cardboard backing for its annual series of player stickers, the stickercards are a collectible in themselves. Each 2-1/8" x 3" card is backed by one or two player stickers which could be removed and placed into a special album. The card portion features a player photo set against a solid-color background. A few vital plus 1989 and career stats are presented in a graduated-color box toward the bottom. The stickercards are sequenced by position within league.

		MT
Complete Set (67):		9.00
Common Player:		.10
1	Will Clark	.25
2	Glenn Davis	.10
3	Pedro Guerrero	.10
4	Roberto Alomar	.35
5	Gregg Jefferies	.10
6	Ryne Sandberg	.25
7	Bobby Bonilla	.10
8	Howard Johnson	.10
9	Tim Wallach	.10
10	Shawon Dunston	.10
11	Barry Larkin	.15
12	Ozzie Smith	.45
13	Eric Davis	.10
14	Andre Dawson	.15
15	Tony Gwynn	.75
16	Von Hayes	.10
17	Kevin Mitchell	.10
18	Rock Raines	.15
19	Lonnie Smith	.10
20	Darryl Strawberry	.15
21	Jerome Walton	.10
22	Craig Biggio	.10
23	Benito Santiago	.10
24	Mike Scioscia	.10
25	Doc Gooden	.15
26	Rick Reuschel	.10
27	Mike Scott	.10
28	Sid Fernandez	.10
29	Mark Langston	.10

30	Joe Magrane	.10
31	Mark Davis	.10
32	Jay Howell	.10
33	Mitch Williams	.10
34	Don Mattingly	.90
35	Fred McGriff	.15
36	Mark McGwire	1.50
37	Julio Franco	.10
38	Steve Sax	.10
39	Lou Whitaker	.10
40	Wade Boggs	.35
41	Gary Gaetti	.10
42	Carney Lansford	.10
43	Tony Fernandez	.10
44	Cal Ripken Jr.	1.00
45	Alan Trammell	.10
46	George Bell	.10
47	Jose Canseco	.35
48	Joe Carter	.10
49	Ken Griffey Jr.	1.50
50	Rickey Henderson	.25
51	Bo Jackson	.15
52	Kirby Puckett	.80
53	Ruben Sierra	.10
54	Robin Yount	.45
55	Carlton Fisk	.30
56	Terry Steinbach	.10
57	Mickey Tettleton	.10
58	Nolan Ryan	1.25
59	Bret Saberhagen	.10
60	Dave Stewart	.10
61	Jeff Ballard	.10
62	Chuck Finley	.10
63	Greg Swindell	.10
64	Dennis Eckersley	.10
65	Gregg Olson	.10
66	Jeff Russell	.10
67	Checklist	.10

1990 Topps/OPC Stickers

Topps' 1990 baseball player stickers were produced in two formats. Some measure 2-1/8" x 3" while there are many pairs of half-size (1-1/2" x 2-1/8") stickers. All stickers are attached to Super Star stickerscards from which they can be peeled and affixed in a special Baseball Sticker Yearbook which was sold separately for 50 cents. Stickers have large center photos with a shadow box effect in the borders. (blues for N.L., reds for A.L.). A tiny black sticker number is in the lower-right corner. There is no player name on the stickers; the albums have a box under each space with player data. The half-size stickers are printed in pairs and are checklisted in that fashion. Values given are for complete sticker (s)/stickercard combinations, but without regard for which stickercard is on back. The checklist and values for the O-Pee-Chee version of this set are identical to those for the Topps brand. Packs of five stickers sold for a quarter; the album with Mattingly on the cover retailed for 50 cents.

		MT
Complete Set (328):		15.00
Common Sticker:		.05
Album:		2.00
1	Rick Cerone (Highlight) (321)	.05
2	Kevin Elster (Highlight) (322)	.05
3	Nolan Ryan (Highlight) (323)	.60
4	Vince Coleman (Highlight) (319)	.05
5	Cal Ripken Jr. (Highlight) (240)	.60
6	Jeff Reardon (Highlight) (328)	.05
7	Rickey Henderson (Highlight) (320)	.05
8	Wade Boggs (Highlight) (324)	.10
9	Barry Bonds (Highlight) (325)	.10
10	Gregg Olson (Highlight) (236)	.05
11	Tony Fernandez (Highlight) (327)	.05
12	Ryne Sandberg (Highlight) (326)	.10
13	Glenn Davis	.05
14	Danny Darwin (316)	.05
15	Bill Doran (298)	.05
16	Dave Smith (225)	.05
17	Kevin Bass (278)	.05
18	Rafael Ramirez (177)	.05
19	Mike Scott	.05
20	Ken Caminiti (235)	.10
21	Jim Deshaies (272)	.05
22	Gerald Young (314)	.05
23	Craig Biggio (186)	.10
24	Lonnie Smith	.05
25	Dale Murphy (210)	.15
26	Tom Glavine	.10
27	Gerald Perry (313)	.05
28	Jeff Blauser (269)	.05
29	Jeff Treadway (252)	.05
30	John Smoltz (299)	.10
31	Darrell Evans (295)	.05
32	Oddibe McDowell (265)	.05
33	Andres Thomas (304)	.05
34	Joe Boever (191)	.05
35	Pedro Guerrero	.05
36	Ken Dayley (226)	.05
37	Milt Thompson (188)	.05
38	Jose DeLeon (180)	.05
39	Vince Coleman (293)	.05
40	Terry Pendleton (225)	.05
41	Joe Magrane	.05
42	Ozzie Smith (179)	.15
43	Todd Worrell (195)	.05
44	Jose Oquendo (238)	.05
45	Tom Brunansky (287)	.05
46	Ryne Sandberg	.15
47	Andre Dawson (268)	.10
48	Mitch Williams	.05
49	Damon Berryhill (204)	.05
50	Jerome Walton (274)	.05
51	Greg Maddux (315)	.50
52	Dwight Smith (248)	.05
53	Shawon Dunston (194)	.05
54	Mike Bielecki (239)	.05
55	Rick Sutcliffe (305)	.05
56	Mark Grace (228)	.10
57	Eddie Murray	.15
58	Alfredo Griffin (197)	.05
59	Fernando Valenzuela (277)	.05
60	Kirk Gibson (201)	.05
61	Ramon Martinez (190)	.10
62	Mike Marshall (309)	.05
63	Orel Hershiser	.05
64	Mike Scioscia (271)	.05
65	Jay Howell (279)	.05
66	Willie Randolph (283)	.05
67	Jeff Hamilton (280)	.05
68	Denny Martinez	.05
69	Tim Raines (184)	.10
70	Mark Langston	.05
71	Dave Martinez (301)	.05
72	Tim Burke (258)	.05
73	Spike Owen (232)	.05
74	Tim Wallach (254)	.05
75	Andres Galarraga (208)	.10
76	Kevin Gross (234)	.05
77	Hubie Brooks (263)	.05
78	Bryn Smith (207)	.05
79	Kevin Mitchell	.05
80	Craig Lefferts (256)	.05
81	Ernest Riles (247)	.05
82	Scott Garrelts (185)	.05
83	Robby Thompson (251)	.05
84	Don Robinson (282)	.05
85	Will Clark	.10
86	Steve Bedrosian (183)	.05
87	Brett Butler (284)	.05
88	Matt Williams (227)	.10
89	Rick Reuschel (291)	.05
90	Howard Johnson	.05
91	Darryl Strawberry (246)	.10
92	Sid Fernandez	.05
93	David Cone (189)	.10
94	Kevin McReynolds (311)	.05
95	Frank Viola (229)	.05
96	Dwight Gooden (206)	.10
97	Kevin Elster (267)	.05
98	Ron Darling (289)	.05
99	Dave Magadan (257)	.05
100	Randy Myers (192)	.05
101	Tony Gwynn	.15
102	Mark Davis (312)	.05
103	Bip Roberts (212)	.05
104	Jack Clark (205)	.05
105	Chris James (211)	.05
106	Mike Pagliarulo (199)	.05
107	Ed Whitson	.05
108	Bruce Hurst (245)	.05
109	Roberto Alomar (202)	.10
110	Benito Santiago (224)	.05
111	Eric Show (307)	.05
112	Ricky Jordan	.05
113	Steve Jeltz (203)	.05
114	Von Hayes	.05
115	Dickie Thon (182)	.05
116	Ken Howell (213)	.05
117	John Kruk (306)	.05
118	Lenny Dykstra (302)	.05
119	Jeff Parrett (300)	.05
120	Randy Ready (230)	.05
121	Roger McDowell (262)	.05
122	Tom Herr (250)	.05
123	Barry Bonds	.25
124	Andy Van Slyke (219)	.05
125	Bob Walk (216)	.05
126	R.J. Reynolds (243)	.05
127	Gary Redus (249)	.05
128	Bill Landrum (276)	.05
129	Bobby Bonilla	.05
130	Doug Drabek (218)	.05
131	Jose Lind (221)	.05
132	John Smiley (241)	.05
133	Mike LaValliere (214)	.05
134	Eric Davis	.05
135	Tom Browning (270)	.05
136	Barry Larkin	.10
137	Jose Rijo (318)	.05
138	Todd Benzinger (292)	.05
139	Rick Mahler (217)	.05
140	Chris Sabo (196)	.05
141	Paul O'Neill (175)	.10
142	Danny Jackson (273)	.05
143	Rolando Roomes (261)	.05
144	John Franco (233)	.05
145	Ozzie Smith (All-Star)	.10
146	Tony Gwynn (All-Star)	.10
147	Will Clark (All-Star)	.05
148	Kevin Mitchell (All-Star)	.05
149	Eric Davis (All-Star)	.05
150	Howard Johnson (All-Star)	.05
151	Pedro Guerrero (All-Star)	.05
152	Ryne Sandberg (All-Star)	.10
153	Benito Santiago (All-Star)	.05
154	Rick Reuschel (All-Star)	.05
155	Bo Jackson (All-Star)	.10
156	Wade Boggs (All-Star)	.10
157	Kirby Puckett (All-Star)	.10
158	Harold Baines (All-Star)	.05
159	Julio Franco (All-Star)	.05
160	Cal Ripken Jr. (All-Star)	.60
161	Ruben Sierra (All-Star)	.05
162	Mark McGwire (All-Star)	.75
163	Terry Steinbach (All-Star)	.05
164	Dave Stewart (All-Star)	.05
165	Bert Blyleven	.05
166	Wally Joyner (285)	.10
167	Kirk McCaskill (290)	.05
168	Devon White (223)	.05
169	Brian Downing (294)	.05
170	Lance Parrish (296)	.05
171	Chuck Finley	.05
172	Jim Abbott (317)	.05
173	Chili Davis (181)	.05
174	Johnny Ray (260)	.05
175	Bryan Harvey (141)	.05
176	Mark McGwire	1.00
177	Jose Canseco (18)	.15
178	Mike Moore	.05
179	Dave Parker (42)	.05
180	Bob Welch (38)	.05
181	Rickey Henderson (173)	.10
182	Dennis Eckersley (115)	.05
183	Carney Lansford (86)	.05
184	Dave Henderson (69)	.05
185	Dave Stewart (82)	.05
186	Terry Steinbach (23)	.05
187	Fred McGriff	.10
188	Junior Felix (37)	.05
189	Ernie Whitt (93)	.05
190	Dave Smith (61)	.05
191	Jimmy Key (34)	.05
192	George Bell (100)	.05
193	Kelly Gruber	.05
194	Tony Fernandez (53)	.05
195	John Cerutti (43)	.05
196	Tom Henke (140)	.05
197	Nelson Liriano (58)	.05
198	Robin Yount	.15
199	Paul Molitor (106)	.15
200	Dan Plesac	.05
201	Teddy Higuera (60)	.05
202	Gary Sheffield (109)	.10
203	B.J. Surhoff (113)	.05
204	Rob Deer (49)	.05
205	Chris Bosio (104)	.05
206	Glenn Braggs (96)	.05
207	Jim Gantner (78)	.05
208	Greg Brock (75)	.05
209	Joe Carter	.05
210	Jerry Browne (25)	.05
211	Cory Snyder (105)	.05
212	Joey Belle (103)	.15
213	Bud Black (116)	.05
214	Greg Swindell (133)	.05
215	Doug Jones	.05
216	Tom Candiotti (125)	.05
217	John Farrell (139)	.05
218	Pete O'Brien (130)	.05
219	Brook Jacoby (124)	.05
220	Alvin Davis	.05
221	Harold Reynolds (131)	.05
222	Scott Bankhead	.05
223	Jeffrey Leonard (168)	.05
224	Jim Presley (110)	.05
225	Ken Griffey Jr. (40)	1.00
226	Greg Briley (36)	.05
227	Darnell Coles (88)	.05
228	Mike Schooler (56)	.05
229	Scott Bradley (95)	.05
230	Randy Johnson (120)	.20
231	Cal Ripken Jr.	.90
232	Jeff Ballard (73)	.05
233	Randy Milligan (144)	.05
234	Joe Orsulak (76)	.05
235	Billy Ripken (20)	.05
236	Mark Williamson (10)	.05
237	Mickey Tettleton	.05
238	Gregg Olson (44)	.05
239	Craig Worthington (54)	.05
240	Bob Milacki (5)	.05
241	Phil Bradley (132)	.05
242	Nolan Ryan	.90
243	Julio Franco (126)	.05
244	Ruben Sierra	.05
245	Harold Baines (128)	.05
246	Jeff Kunkel (91)	.05
247	Pete Incaviglia (81)	.05
248	Kevin Brown (52)	.05
249	Cecil Espy (127)	.05
250	Rafael Palmeiro (122)	.10
251	Steve Buechele (83)	.05
252	Jeff Russell (29)	.05
253	Wade Boggs	.15
254	Mike Greenwell (74)	.05
255	Roger Clemens (16)	.15
256	Marty Barrett (80)	.05
257	Dwight Evans (99)	.05
258	Mike Boddicker (72)	.05
259	Ellis Burks	.05
260	John Dopson (174)	.05
261	Rob Murphy (143)	.05
262	Lee Smith (121)	.05
263	Nick Esasky (77)	.05
264	Bo Jackson	.15
265	George Brett (32)	.60
266	Bret Saberhagen	.05
267	Kevin Seitzer (97)	.05
268	Tom Gordon (47)	.05
269	Kurt Stillwell (28)	.05
270	Steve Farr (135)	.05
271	Jim Eisenreich (64)	.05
272	Mark Gubicza (21)	.05
273	Jeff Montgomery (142)	.05
274	Danny Tartabull (50)	.05
275	Lou Whitaker	.05
276	Jack Morris (128)	.05
277	Frank Tanana (59)	.05
278	Chet Lemon (17)	.05
279	Fred Lynn (65)	.05
280	Mike Heath (67)	.05
281	Alan Trammell	.10
282	Mike Henneman (84)	.05
283	Gary Pettis (56)	.05
284	Jeff Robinson (87)	.05
285	Dave Bergman (166)	.05
286	Kirby Puckett	.50
287	Kent Hrbek (45)	.05
288	Gary Gaetti	.05
289	Jeff Reardon (98)	.05
290	Brian Harper (167)	.05
291	Gene Larkin (89)	.05
292	Dan Gladden (138)	.05
293	Al Newman (39)	.05
294	Randy Bush (169)	.05
295	Greg Gagne (31)	.05
296	Allan Anderson (170)	.05
297	Bobby Thigpen	.05
298	Ozzie Guillen (15)	.05
299	Ivan Calderon (30)	.05
300	Carlos Martinez (119)	.05
301	Steve Lyons (71)	.05
302	Ron Kittle (118)	.05
303	Carlton Fisk	.20
304	Melido Perez (33)	.05
305	Dave Gallagher (55)	.05
306	Dan Pasqua (117)	.05
307	Scott Fletcher (111)	.05
308	Don Mattingly	.50
309	Dave Righetti (62)	.05
310	Steve Sax	.05
311	Alvaro Espinoza (94)	.05
312	Roberto Kelly (102)	.05
313	Mel Hall (27)	.05
314	Jesse Barfield (22)	.05
315	Chuck Cary (51)	.05
316	Bob Geren (14)	.05
317	Andy Hawkins (172)	.05
318	Don Slaught (137)	.05
319	Jim Abbott (Future Star) (4)	.05
320	Greg Briley (Future Star) (7)	.05
321	Bob Geren (Future Star) (1)	.05
322	Tom Gordon (Future Star) (2)	.05
323	Ken Griffey Jr. (Future Star) (3)	.75
324	Gregg Jefferies (Future Star) (8)	.25
325	Carlos Martinez (Future Star) (9)	.05
326	Gary Sheffield (Future Star) (12)	.10
327	Jerome Walton (Future Star) (11)	.05
328	Craig Worthington (Future Star) (6)	.05

1990 Topps TV All-Stars

This 66-card boxed set was sold only through a television offer in limited markets. Consequently, production numbers are relatively low and single cards are seldom offered in the hobby market. Most of the game's top stars are included in the issue. Fronts feature a high-gloss surface. On the red-bordered backs there are several lines of biographical data plus each player's "Career Bests" in various statistical categories, set against a pastel background shield. Issue price was $22.90.

		MT
Complete Set (66):		75.00
Common Player:		.50
1	Mark McGwire	25.00
2	Julio Franco	.50
3	Ozzie Guillen	.50
4	Carney Lansford	.50
5	Bo Jackson	1.00
6	Kirby Puckett	10.00
7	Ruben Sierra	.50
8	Carlton Fisk	3.00
9	Nolan Ryan	24.00
10	Rickey Henderson	2.00
11	Jose Canseco	4.00
12	Mark Davis	.50
13	Dennis Eckersley	.50
14	Chuck Finley	.50
15	Bret Saberhagen	.75
16	Dave Stewart	.50
17	Don Mattingly	12.00
18	Steve Sax	.50
19	Cal Ripken, Jr.	24.00
20	Wade Boggs	7.00
21	George Bell	.50
22	Mike Greenwell	.50
23	Robin Yount	5.00
24	Mickey Tettleton	.50
25	Roger Clemens	10.00
26	Fred McGriff	3.00
27	Jeff Ballard	.50
28	Dwight Evans	.50
29	Paul Molitor	5.00
30	Gregg Olson	.50
31	Dan Plesac	.50
32	Greg Swindell	.50
33	Cito Gaston, Tony LaRussa	.50
34	Will Clark	3.00
35	Roberto Alomar	4.00
36	Barry Larkin	1.00
37	Ken Caminiti	.75
38	Eric Davis	.50
39	Tony Gwynn	12.00
40	Kevin Mitchell	.50
41	Craig Biggio	.75
42	Mike Scott	.50
43	Joe Carter	.50
44	Jack Clark	.50
45	Glenn Davis	.50
46	Orel Hershiser	.50
47	Jay Howell	.50
48	Bruce Hurst	.50
49	Dave Smith	.50
50	Pedro Guerrero	.50
51	Ryne Sandberg	5.00
52	Ozzie Smith	9.00
53	Howard Johnson	.50
54	Von Hayes	.50
55	Tim Raines	1.00
56	Darryl Strawberry	1.50
57	Mike LaValliere	.50
58	Dwight Gooden	1.50
59	Bobby Bonilla	.50
60	Tim Burke	.50
61	Sid Fernandez	.50
62	Andres Galarraga	1.00
63	Mark Grace	3.00
64	Joe Magrane	.50
65	Mitch Williams	.50
66	Roger Craig, Don Zimmer	.50

1990 Topps TV Cardinals Team Set

Available only as a boxed set via a limited television offer, this team set includes cards of all players on the opening day roster plus the manager, selected coaches and many of the organization's top prospects. In many cases this is the first card of a player in major league uniform, and in some cases represents the only card which will ever be issued of the player as a major leaguer. Cards feature a high-gloss front surface. Backs have a red border and feature a "ghost image" of the photo on the front as a background to the statistical and biographical data. Because of the relatively limited production and the fact it was sold as a boxed set only, single cards are seldom available.

		MT
Complete Set (66):		55.00
Common Player:		.50
1	Whitey Herzog	.75
2	Steve Braun	.50
3	Rich Hacker	.50
4	Dave Ricketts	.50
5	Jim Riggleman	1.50
6	Mike Roarke	.50
7	Cris Carpenter	.50
8	John Costello	.50
9	Danny Cox	.50
10	Ken Dayley	.50
11	Jose DeLeon	.50
12	Frank DiPino	.50
13	Ken Hill	1.50
14	Howard Hilton	.50
15	Ricky Horton	.50
16	Joe Magrane	.50
17	Greg Mathews	.50
18	Bryn Smith	.50
19	Scott Terry	.50
20	Bob Tewksbury	2.00
21	John Tudor	.50
22	Todd Worrell	1.00
23	Tom Pagnozzi	.50
24	Todd Zeile	3.00
25	Pedro Guerrero	.50
26	Tim Jones	.50
27	Jose Oquendo	.50
28	Terry Pendleton	1.50
29	Ozzie Smith	15.00
30	Denny Walling	.50
31	Tom Brunansky	.50
32	Vince Coleman	1.50
33	Dave Collins	.50
34	Willie McGee	1.50
35	John Morris	.50
36	Milt Thompson	.50
37	Gibson Alba	.50
38	Scott Arnold	.50
39	Rod Brewer	.50
40	Greg Carmona	.50
41	Mark Clark	1.50
42	Stan Clarke	.50
43	Paul Coleman	.50
44	Todd Crosby	.50
45	Brad DuVall	.50
46	John Ericks	.50
47	Bien Figueroa	.50
48	Terry Francona	.50
49	Ed Fulton	.50
50	Bernard Gilkey	5.00
51	Ernie Camacho	.50
52	Mike Hinkle	.50
53	Ray Lankford	5.00
54	Julian Martinez	.50
55	Jesus Mendez	.50
56	Mike Milchin	.50
57	Mauricio Nunez	.50
58	Omar Olivares	.75
59	Geronimo Pena	.50
60	Mike Perez	.75
61	Gaylen Pitts	.50
62	Mark Riggins	.50
63	Tim Sherrill	.50
64	Roy Silver	.50
65	Ray Stephens	.50
66	Craig Wilson	.50

1990 Topps TV Cubs Team Set

Sold only in boxed set form via a limited television offer, this 66-card issue includes all players on the team's 1990 opening day roster as well as the manager, selected coaches and some of the organization's top minor league prospects. For the latter group, this set offers the first - and in many cases the only - card of the player in a major league uniform. The cards have a high-gloss front surface. Card backs feature a "ghost image" of the color photo used on the front as a background to the stats and biographical information. A red border completes the back design. Because the set was sold only in boxed form, and production was relatively low, single cards are seldom seen in the market.

		MT
Complete Set (66):		65.00
Common Player:		.50
1	Don Zimmer	.75
2	Joe Altobelli	.50
3	Chuck Cottier	.50
4	Jose Martinez	.50
5	Dick Pole	.50
6	Phil Roof	.50
7	Paul Assenmacher	.50
8	Mike Bielecki	.50
9	Mike Harkey	.50
10	Joe Kraemer	.50
11	Les Lancaster	.50
12	Greg Maddux	35.00
13	Jose Nunez	.50
14	Jeff Pico	.50
15	Rick Sutcliffe	1.50
16	Dean Wilkins	.50
17	Mitch Williams	.50
18	Steve Wilson	.50
19	Damon Berryhill	.50
20	Joe Girardi	1.50
21	Rick Wrona	.50
22	Shawon Dunston	1.00
23	Mark Grace	10.00
24	Domingo Ramos	.50
25	Luis Salazar	.50
26	Ryne Sandberg	15.00
27	Greg Smith	.50
28	Curtis Wilkerson	.50
29	Dave Clark	.50
30	Doug Dascenzo	.50
31	Andre Dawson	6.00
32	Lloyd McClendon	.50
33	Dwight Smith	.50
34	Jerome Walton	.50
35	Marvell Wynne	.50
36	Alex Arias	.50
37	Bob Bafia	.50
38	Brad Bierley	.50
39	Shawn Boskie	1.00
40	Danny Clay	.50
41	Rusty Crockett	.50
42	Earl Cunningham	.50
43	Len Damian	.50
44	Darrin Duffy	.50
45	Ty Griffin	.50
46	Brian Guinn	.50
47	Phil Hannon	.50
48	Phil Harrison	.50
49	Jeff Hearron	.50
50	Greg Kallevig	.50
51	Cedric Landrum	.50
52	Bill Long	.50
53	Derrick May	.50
54	Ray Mullino	.50
55	Erik Pappas	.75
56	Steve Parker	.50
57	Dave Pavlas	.50
58	Laddie Renfroe	.50
59	Jeff Small	.50
60	Doug Strange	.50
61	Gary Varsho	.50
62	Hector Villanueva	.50
63	Rick Wilkins	1.00
64	Dana Williams	.50
65	Bill Wrona	.50
66	Fernando Zarranz	.50

1990 Topps TV Mets Team Set

This late-season issue, sold only as a boxed set via a television offer in limited areas, features all of the players on the 1990 opening day roster, plus the manager, selected coaches and many of the organization's top minor league prospects. For many of the prospects, this is the first, if not the only, card on which they appear in major league uniform. A highlight of the back design is a "ghost image" full-color reproduction of the front photo, used as a background to the statistical and biographical information. A red border dominates the remainder of the back design. Because it was sold only as a boxed set, and production was relatively limited, single cards are seldom available.

		MT
Complete Set (66):		40.00
Common Player:		.50
1	Dave Johnson	.75
2	Mike Cubbage	.50
3	Doc Edwards	.50
4	Bud Harrelson	.75
5	Greg Pavlick	.50
6	Mel Stottlemyre, Sr.	.75
7	Blaine Beatty	.50
8	David Cone	3.00
9	Ron Darling	.50
10	Sid Fernandez	.50
11	John Franco	1.50
12	Dwight Gooden	3.00
13	Jeff Innis	.50
14	Julio Machado	.50
15	Jeff Musselman	.50
16	Bob Ojeda	.50
17	Alejandro Pena	.50
18	Frank Viola	.50
19	Wally Whitehurst	.50
20	Barry Lyons	.50
21	Orlando Mercado	.50
22	Mackey Sasser	.50
23	Kevin Elster	.75
24	Gregg Jefferies	3.00
25	Howard Johnson	.50
26	Dave Magadan	.50
27	Mike Marshall	.50
28	Tom O'Malley	.50
29	Tim Teufel	.50
30	Mark Carreon	1.50
31	Kevin McReynolds	.50
32	Keith Miller	.50
33	Darryl Strawberry	3.00
34	Lou Thornton	.50
35	Shawn Barton	.50
36	Tim Bogar	.50
37	Terry Bross	.50
38	Kevin Brown	.50
39	Mike DeButch	.50
40	Alex Diaz	.50
41	Chris Donnels	.50
42	Jeff Gardner	.50
43	Denny Gonzalez	.50
44	Kenny Graves	.50
45	Manny Hernandez	.50
46	Keith Hughes	.50
47	Todd Hundley	5.00
48	Chris Jelic	.50
49	Dave Liddell	.50
50	Terry McDaniel	.50
51	Cesar Mejia	.50
52	Scott Nielsen	.50
53	Dale Plummer	.50
54	Darren Reed	1.00
55	Gil Roca	.50
56	Jaime Roseboro	.50
57	Roger Samuels	.50
58	Zoilo Sanchez	.50
59	Pete Schourek	1.00
60	Craig Shipley	.50
61	Ray Soff	.50
62	Steve Swisher	.50
63	Kelvin Torve	.50
64	Dave Trautwein	.50
65	Julio Valera	.50
66	Alan Zinter	.50

1990 Topps TV Red Sox Team Set

This 66-card set was available only via a television offer in certain limited areas. Production was relatively low and single cards are hard to find. Player selection includes all those on the team's opening day roster in 1990, plus the manager, selected coaches and the team's top minor league prospects. In many cases this represents the first, or even the only, appearance of these prospects on major league baseball cards. Fronts have a high-gloss surface. Card backs, bordered in red, feature a "ghost image" reproduction of the front photo as a background to the statistics and biographical data.

		MT
Complete Set (66):		65.00
Common Player:		.50
1	Joe Morgan	.50
2	Dick Berardino	.50
3	Al Bumbry	.50
4	Bill Fischer	.50
5	Richie Hebner	.50
6	Rac Slider	.50
7	Mike Boddicker	.50
8	Roger Clemens	30.00
9	John Dopson	.50
10	Wes Gardner	.50
11	Greg Harris	.50
12	Dana Kiecker	.50
13	Dennis Lamp	.50
14	Rob Murphy	.50
15	Jeff Reardon	.50
16	Mike Rochford	.50
17	Lee Smith	2.00
18	Rich Gedman	.50
19	John Marzano	.50
20	Tony Pena	.50
21	Marty Barrett	.50
22	Wade Boggs	25.00
23	Bill Buckner	.65
24	Danny Heep	.50
25	Jody Reed	1.50
26	Luis Rivera	.50
27	Billy Jo Robidoux	.50
28	Ellis Burks	2.00
29	Dwight Evans	.75
30	Mike Greenwell	.75
31	Randy Kutcher	.50
32	Carlos Quintana	.50
33	Kevin Romine	.50
34	Ed Nottle	.50
35	Mark Meleski	.50
36	Steve Bast	.50
37	Greg Blosser	.50
38	Tom Bolton	.50
39	Scott Cooper	.75
40	Zach Crouch	.50
41	Steve Curry	.50
42	Mike Dalton	.50
43	John Flaherty	.50
44	Angel Gonzalez	.50
45	Eric Hetzel	.50
46	Daryl Irvine	.50
47	Joe Johnson	.50
48	Rick Lancellotti	.50
49	John Leister	.50
50	Derek Livernois	.50
51	Josias Manzanillo	.50
52	Kevin Morton	.50
53	Julius McDougal	.50
54	Tim Naehring	.75
55	Jim Pankovits	.50
56	Mickey Pina	.50
57	Phil Plantier	.75
58	Jerry Reed	.50
59	Larry Shikles	.50
60	Tito Stewart	.50
61	Jeff Stone	.50
62	John Trautwein	.50
63	Gary Tremblay	.50
64	Mo Vaughn	15.00
65	Scott Wade	.50
66	Eric Wedge	.50

1990 Topps TV Yankees Team Set

The first - and in many cases the only - baseball card appearance of top minor league prospects occurs in this special 66-card boxed set which was sold only via a special television offer in limited markets. The set also includes all players on the team's opening day roster, plus the manager and selected coaches. Card fronts have a high-gloss surface. On back, framed by a red border, the design features a "ghost image" of the color front photo, used as a background to the statistical and biographical information. Because the cards were sold only as a complete set, single cards are seldom available.

		MT
Complete Set (66):		75.00
Common Player:		.50
1	Bucky Dent	.50
2	Mark Connor	.50
3	Billy Connors	.50
4	Mike Ferraro	.50
5	Joe Sparks	.50
6	Champ Summers	.50
7	Greg Cadaret	.50
8	Chuck Cary	.50
9	Lee Guetterman	.50
10	Andy Hawkins	.50
11	Dave LaPoint	.50
12	Tim Leary	.50
13	Lance McCullers	.50
14	Alan Mills	.50
15	Clay Parker	.50
16	Pascual Perez	.50
17	Eric Plunk	.50
18	Dave Righetti	.50
19	Jeff Robinson	.50
20	Rick Cerone	.50
21	Bob Geren	.50
22	Steve Balboni	.50
23	Mike Blowers	.50
24	Alvaro Espinoza	.50
25	Don Mattingly	25.00
26	Steve Sax	.50
27	Wayne Tolleson	.50
28	Randy Velarde	.50
29	Jesse Barfield	.50
30	Mel Hall	.50
31	Roberto Kelly	.75
32	Luis Polonia	.50
33	Deion Sanders	5.00
34	Dave Winfield	9.00
35	Steve Adkins	.50
36	Oscar Azocar	.50

37 Bob Brower .50
38 Britt Burns .50
39 Bob Davidson .50
40 Brian Dorsett .50
41 Dave Eiland .50
42 John Fishel .50
43 Andy Fox .50
44 John Habyan .50
45 Cullen Hartzog .50
46 Sterling Hitchcock 2.00
47 Brian Johnson .50
48 Jimmy Jones .50
49 Scott Kamieniecki .50
50 Mark Leiter .50
51 Jim Leyritz 2.00
52 Jason Maas .50
53 Kevin Maas .50
54 Hensley Meulens .50
55 Kevin Mmahat .50
56 Rich Monteleone .50
57 Vince Phillips .50
58 Carlos Rodriguez .50
59 Dave Sax .50
60 Willie Smith .50
61 Van Snider .50
62 Andy Stankiewicz .50
63 Wade Taylor .50
64 Ricky Torres .50
65 Jim Walewander .50
66 Bernie Williams 20.00

1991 Topps

Topps celebrated its 40th anniversary in 1991 with the biggest promotional campaign in baseball card history. More than 300,000 vintage Topps cards (or certificates redeemable for valuable older cards) produced from 1952 to 1990 were randomly inserted in packs. Also a grand prize winner received a complete set from each year, and others received a single set from 1952-1990. The 1991 Topps card fronts feature the "Topps 40 Years of Baseball" logo in the upper-left corner. Colored borders frame the player photos. All players of the same team have cards with the same frame/border colors. Both action and posed shots appear in full-color on the card fronts. The flip sides are printed horizontally and feature complete statistics. Record Breakers and other special cards were once again included in the set. The cards measure 2-1/2" x 3-1/2".

MT
Complete Set (792): 15.00
Common Player: .05
Wax Box: 9.00

1 Nolan Ryan .75
2 George Brett (Record Breaker) .15
3 Carlton Fisk (Record Breaker) .10
4 Kevin Maas (Record Breaker) .05
5 Cal Ripken, Jr. (Record Breaker) .25
6 Nolan Ryan (Record Breaker) .25
7 Ryne Sandberg (Record Breaker) .15
8 Bobby Thigpen (Record Breaker) .05
9 Darrin Fletcher .10
10 Gregg Olson .05
11 Roberto Kelly .05
12 Paul Assenmacher .05
13 Mariano Duncan .05
14 Dennis Lamp .05
15 Von Hayes .05
16 Mike Heath .05
17 Jeff Brantley .05
18 Nelson Liriano .05
19 Jeff Robinson .05
20 Pedro Guerrero .05
21 Joe M. Morgan .05
22 Storm Davis .05
23 Jim Gantner .05
24 Dave Martinez .05
25 Tim Belcher .05
26 Luis Sojo .05
27 Bobby Witt .05
28 Alvaro Espinoza .05
29 Bob Walk .05
30 Gregg Jefferies .15
31 *Colby Ward* .05
32 *Mike Simms* .05
33 Barry Jones .05
34 Atlee Hammaker .05
35 Greg Maddux .50
36 Donnie Hill .05
37 Tom Bolton .05
38 Scott Bradley .05
39 *Jim Neidlinger* .05
40 Kevin Mitchell .05
41 Ken Dayley .05
42a *Chris Hoiles* (white inner photo frame) .20
42b *Chris Hoiles* (gray inner photo frame) .20
43 Roger McDowell .05
44 Mike Felder .05
45 Chris Sabo .05
46 Tim Drummond .05
47 Brook Jacoby .05
48 Dennis Boyd .05
49a Pat Borders (40 stolen bases in Kinston 1986) .20
49b Pat Borders (0 stolen bases in Kinston 1986) .10
50 Bob Welch .05
51 Art Howe .05
52 *Francisco Oliveras* .05
53 Mike Sharperson .05
54 Gary Mielke .05
55 Jeffrey Leonard .05
56 Jeff Parrett .05
57 Jack Howell .05
58 Mel Stottlemyre .05
59 Eric Yelding .05
60 Frank Viola .05
61 Stan Javier .05
62 Lee Guetterman .05
63 Milt Thompson .05
64 Tom Herr .05
65 Bruce Hurst .05
66 Terry Kennedy .05
67 Rick Honeycutt .05
68 Gary Sheffield .20
69 Steve Wilson .05
70 Ellis Burks .10
71 Jim Acker .05
72 Junior Ortiz .05
73 Craig Worthington .05
74 *Shane Andrews* (#1 Draft Pick) .20
75 Jack Morris .05
76 Jerry Browne .05
77 Drew Hall .05
78 Geno Petralli .05
79 Frank Thomas .75
80a Fernando Valenzuela (no diamond after 104 ER in 1990) .25
80b Fernando Valenzuela (diamond after 104 ER in 1990) .10
81 Cito Gaston .05
82 Tom Glavine .20
83 Daryl Boston .05
84 Bob McClure .05
85 Jesse Barfield .05
86 Les Lancaster .05
87 Tracy Jones .05
88 Bob Tewksbury .05
89 Darren Daulton .05
90 Danny Tartabull .05
91 *Greg Colbrunn* (Future Star) .10
92 Danny Jackson .05
93 Ivan Calderon .05
94 John Dopson .05
95 Paul Molitor .20
96 Trevor Wilson .05
97a Brady Anderson (3H, 2RBI in Sept. scoreboard) .25
97b Brady Anderson (14H, 3 RBI in Sept. scoreboard) .15
98 Sergio Valdez .05
99 Chris Gwynn .05
100a Don Mattingly (10 hits 1990) .50
100b Don Mattingly (101 hits in 1990) .45
101 Rob Ducey .05
102 Gene Larkin .05
103 *Tim Costo* (#1 Draft Pick) .10
104 Don Robinson .05
105 Kevin McReynolds .05
106 Ed Nunez .05
107 Luis Polonia .05
108 Matt Young .05
109 Greg Riddoch .05
110 Tom Henke .05
111 Andres Thomas .05
112 Frank DiPino .05
113 *Carl Everett* (#1 Draft Pick) .50
114 *Lance Dickson* (Future Star) .10
115 Hubie Brooks .05
116 Mark Davis .05
117 Dion James .05
118 *Tom Edens* .05
119 Carl Nichols .05
120 Joe Carter .10
121 Eric King .05
122 Paul O'Neill .15
123 Greg Harris .05
124 Randy Bush .05
125 Steve Bedrosian .05
126 *Bernard Gilkey* .20
127 Joe Price .05
128 Travis Fryman .10
129 Mark Eichhorn .05
130 Ozzie Smith .25
131a Checklist 1 (Phil Bradley #727) .05
131b Checklist 1 (Phil Bradley #717) .05
132 Jamie Quirk .05
133 Greg Briley .05
134 Kevin Elster .05
135 Jerome Walton .05
136 Dave Schmidt .05
137 Randy Ready .05
138 Jamie Moyer .05
139 Jeff Treadway .05
140 Fred McGriff .15
141 Nick Leyva .05
142 Curtis Wilkerson .05
143 John Smiley .05
144 Dave Henderson .05
145 Lou Whitaker .05
146 Dan Plesac .05
147 Carlos Baerga .05
148 Rey Palacios .05
149 *Al Osuna* .05
150 Cal Ripken, Jr. .75
151 Tom Browning .05
152 Mickey Hatcher .05
153 Bryan Harvey .05
154 Jay Buhner .10
155a Dwight Evans (diamond after 162 G 1982) .10
155b Dwight Evans (no diamond after 162 G 1982) .05
156 Carlos Martinez .05
157 John Smoltz .10
158 Jose Uribe .05
159 Joe Boever .05
160 Vince Coleman .05
161 Tim Leary .05
162 *Ozzie Canseco* .10
163 Dave Johnson .05
164 Edgar Diaz .05
165 Sandy Alomar .10
166 Harold Baines .05
167a *Randy Tomlin* ("Harriburg" 1989-90) .10
167b *Randy Tomlin* ("Harrisburg" 1989-90) .05
168 John Olerud .25
169 Luis Aquino .05
170 Carlton Fisk .20
171 Tony LaRussa .05
172 Pete Incaviglia .05
173 Jason Grimsley .05
174 Ken Caminiti .10
175 Jack Armstrong .05
176 John Orton .05
177 *Reggie Harris* .10
178 Dave Valle .05
179 Pete Harnisch .05
180 Tony Gwynn .40
181 Duane Ward .05
182 Junior Noboa .05
183 Clay Parker .05
184 Gary Green .05
185 Joe Magrane .05
186 Rod Booker .05
187 Greg Cadaret .05
188 Damon Berryhill .05
189 *Daryl Irvine* .05
190 Matt Williams .15
191 *Willie Blair* .05
192 Rob Deer .05
193 Felix Fermin .05
194 Xavier Hernandez .10
195 Wally Joyner .10
196 *Jim Vatcher* .05
197 *Chris Nabholz* .10
198 R.J. Reynolds .05
199 Mike Hartley .05
200 Darryl Strawberry .10
201 Tom Kelly .05
202 *Jim Leyritz* .20
203 Gene Harris .05
204 Herm Winningham .05
205 *Mike Perez* .10
206 Carlos Quintana .05
207 Gary Wayne .05
208 Willie Wilson .05
209 Ken Howell .05
210 Lance Parrish .05
211 *Brian Barnes* (Future Star) .10
212 Steve Finley .05
213 Frank Wills .05
214 Joe Girardi .05
215 Dave Smith .05
216 Greg Gagne .05
217 Chris Bosio .05
218 *Rick Parker* .05
219 Jack McDowell .05
220 Tim Wallach .05
221 Don Slaught .05
222 *Brian McRae* .20
223 Allan Anderson .05
224 Juan Gonzalez .60
225 Randy Johnson .25
226 Alfredo Griffin .05
227 Steve Avery .05
228 Rex Hudler .05
229 Rance Mulliniks .05
230 Sid Fernandez .05
231 Doug Rader .05
232 Jose DeJesus .05
233 Al Leiter .05
234 *Scott Erickson* .20
235 Dave Parker .10
236a Frank Tanana (no diamond after 269 SO 1975) .10
236b Frank Tanana (diamond after 269 SO 1975) .05
237 Rick Cerone .05
238 Mike Dunne .05
239 *Darren Lewis* .20
240 Mike Scott .05
241 Dave Clark .05
242 Mike LaCoss .05
243 Lance Johnson .05
244 Mike Jeffcoat .05
245 Kal Daniels .05
246 Kevin Wickander .05
247 Jody Reed .05
248 Tom Gordon .05
249 Bob Melvin .05
250 Dennis Eckersley .05
251 Mark Lemke .05
252 *Mel Rojas* .10
253 Garry Templeton .05
254 *Shawn Boskie* .10
255 Brian Downing .05
256 Greg Hibbard .05
257 Tom O'Malley .05
258 Chris Hammond .10
259 Hensley Meulens .05
260 Harold Reynolds .05
261 Bud Harrelson .05
262 Tim Jones .05
263 Checklist 2 .05
264 *Dave Hollins* .20
265 Mark Gubicza .05
266 Carmen Castillo .05
267 Mark Knudson .05
268 Tom Brookens .05
269 Joe Hesketh .05
270a Mark McGwire (1987 SLG .618) 1.50
270b Mark McGwire (1987 SLG 618) 1.50
271 *Omar Olivares* .15
272 Jeff King .05
273 Johnny Ray .05
274 Ken Williams .05
275 Alan Trammell .05
276 Bill Swift .05
277 Scott Coolbaugh .05
278 *Alex Fernandez* (#1 Draft Pick) .35
279a Jose Gonzalez (photo of Billy Bean, left-handed batter) .15
279b Jose Gonzalez (correct photo, right-handed batter) .10
280 Bret Saberhagen .05
281 Larry Sheets .05
282 Don Carman .05
283 Marquis Grissom .10
284 Bill Spiers .05
285 Jim Abbott .05
286 Ken Oberkfell .05
287 Mark Grant .05
288 Derrick May .10
289 Tim Birtsas .05
290 Steve Sax .05
291 John Wathan .05
292 Bud Black .05
293 Jay Bell .05
294 Mike Moore .05
295 Rafael Palmeiro .20
296 Mark Williamson .05
297 Manny Lee .05
298 Omar Vizquel .05
299 *Scott Radinsky* .15
300 Kirby Puckett .25
301 Steve Farr .05
302 Tim Teufel .05
303 Mike Boddicker .05
304 Kevin Reimer .05
305 Mike Scioscia .05
306a Lonnie Smith (136 G 1990) .10
306b Lonnie Smith (135 G 1990) .05
307 Andy Benes .10
308 Tom Pagnozzi .05
309 Norm Charlton .05
310 Gary Carter .10
311 Jeff Pico .05
312 Charlie Hayes .05
313 Ron Robinson .05
314 Gary Pettis .05
315 Roberto Alomar .25
316 Gene Nelson .05
317 Mike Fitzgerald .05
318 Rick Aguilera .05
319 Jeff McKnight .05
320 Tony Fernandez .05
321 Bob Rodgers .05
322 *Terry Shumpert* .05
323 Cory Snyder .05
324a Ron Kittle ("6 Home Runs" in career summary) .10
324b Ron Kittle ("7 Home Runs" in career summary) .05
325 Brett Butler .05
326 Ken Patterson .05
327 Ron Hassey .05
328 Walt Terrell .05
329 Dave Justice .25
330 Dwight Gooden .10
331 Eric Anthony .05
332 Kenny Rogers .05
333 *Chipper Jones* (#1 Draft Pick) 6.00
334 Todd Benzinger .05
335 Mitch Williams .05
336 Matt Nokes .05
337a Keith Comstock (Mariners logo) .05
337b Keith Comstock (Cubs logo) .10
338 Luis Rivera .05
339 Larry Walker .25
340 Ramon Martinez .10
341 John Moses .05
342 *Mickey Morandini* .10
343 Jose Oquendo .05
344 Jeff Russell .05
345 Len Dykstra .05
346 Jesse Orosco .05
347 Greg Vaughn .05
348 Todd Stottlemyre .05
349 Dave Gallagher .05
350 Glenn Davis .05
351 Joe Torre .05
352 Frank White .05
353 Tony Castillo .05
354 Sid Bream .05
355 Chili Davis .05
356 Mike Marshall .05
357 Jack Savage .05
358 Mark Parent .05
359 Chuck Cary .05
360 Tim Raines .10
361 Scott Garrelts .05
362 *Hector Villanueva* .05
363 Rick Mahler .05
364 Dan Pasqua .05
365 Mike Schooler .05
366a Checklist 3 (Carl Nichols #19) .05
366b Checklist 3 (Carl Nichols #119) .05
367 *Dave Walsh* .05
368 Felix Jose .05
369 Steve Searcy .05
370 Kelly Gruber .05
371 Jeff Montgomery .05
372 Spike Owen .05
373 Darrin Jackson .05
374 *Larry Casian* .10
375 Tony Pena .05
376 Mike Harkey .05
377 Rene Gonzales .05
378a *Wilson Alvarez* (no 1989 Port Charlotte stats) .30
378b *Wilson Alvarez* (1989 Port Charlotte stats) .20
379 Randy Velarde .05
380 Willie McGee .05
381 Jim Leyland .05
382 Mackey Sasser .05
383 Pete Smith .05
384 Gerald Perry .05
385 Mickey Tettleton .05
386 Cecil Fielder (All-Star) .05
387 Julio Franco (All-Star) .05
388 Kelly Gruber (All-Star) .05
389 Alan Trammell (All-Star) .05
390 Jose Canseco (All-Star) .15
391 Rickey Henderson (All-Star) .10
392 Ken Griffey, Jr. (All-Star) .50
393 Carlton Fisk (All-Star) .10
394 Bob Welch (All-Star) .05
395 Chuck Finley (All-Star) .05
396 Bobby Thigpen (All-Star) .05
397 Eddie Murray (All-Star) .10
398 Ryne Sandberg (All-Star) .10
399 Matt Williams (All-Star) .05
400 Barry Larkin (All-Star) .05
401 Barry Bonds (All-Star) .15
402 Darryl Strawberry (All-Star) .05
403 Bobby Bonilla (All-Star) .05

404 Mike Scoscia (All-Star) .05
405 Doug Drabek (All-Star) .05
406 Frank Viola (All-Star) .05
407 John Franco (All-Star) .05
408 Ernie Riles .05
409 Mike Stanley .05
410 Dave Righetti .05
411 Lance Blankenship .05
412 Dave Bergman .05
413 Terry Mulholland .05
414 Sammy Sosa 1.50
415 Rick Sutcliffe .05
416 Randy Milligan .05
417 Bill Krueger .05
418 Nick Esasky .05
419 Jeff Reed .05
420 Bobby Thigpen .05
421 Alex Cole .05
422 Rick Rueschel .05
423 Rafael Ramirez .05
424 Calvin Schiraldi .05
425 Andy Van Slyke .05
426 *Joe Grahe* .10
427 Rick Dempsey .05
428 *John Barfield* .05
429 Stump Merrill .05
430 Gary Gaetti .05
431 Paul Gibson .05
432 Delino DeShields .05
433 Pat Tabler .05
434 Julio Machado .05
435 Kevin Maas .05
436 Scott Bankhead .05
437 Doug Dascenzo .05
438 Vicente Palacios .05
439 Dickie Thon .05
440 George Bell .05
441 Zane Smith .05
442 Charlie O'Brien .05
443 Jeff Innis .05
444 Glenn Braggs .05
445 Greg Swindell .05
446 *Craig Grebeck* .05
447 John Burkett .05
448 Craig Lefferts .05
449 Juan Berenguer .05
450 Wade Boggs .25
451 Neal Heaton .05
452 Bill Schroeder .05
453 Lenny Harris .05
454a Kevin Appier (no 1990 Omaha stats) .15
454b Kevin Appier (1990 Omaha stats) .10
455 Walt Weiss .05
456 Charlie Leibrandt .05
457 Todd Hundley .15
458 Brian Holman .05
459 Tom Trebelhorn .05
460 Dave Steib .05
461a Robin Ventura (gray inner photo frame at left) .15
461b Robin Ventura (red inner photo frame at left) .15
462 Steve Frey .05
463 Dwight Smith .05
464 Steve Buechele .05
465 Ken Griffey .05
466 Charles Nagy .10
467 Dennis Cook .05
468 Tim Hulett .05
469 Chet Lemon .05
470 Howard Johnson .05
471 *Mike Lieberthal* (#1 Draft Pick) .50
472 Kirt Manwaring .05
473 Curt Young .05
474 *Phil Plantier* .15
475 Teddy Higuera .05
476 Glenn Wilson .05
477 Mike Fetters .05
478 Kurt Stillwell .05
479 Bob Patterson .05
480 Dave Magadan .05
481 Eddie Whitson .05
482 Tino Martinez .15
483 Mike Aldrete .05
484 Dave LaPoint .05
485 Terry Pendleton .05
486 Tommy Greene .10
487 Rafael Belliard .05
488 Jeff Manto .10
489 Bobby Valentine .05
490 Kirk Gibson .05
491 *Kurt Miller* (#1 Draft Pick) .15
492 Ernie Whitt .05
493 Jose Rijo .05
494 Chris James .05
495 Charlie Hough .05
496 Marty Barrett .05
497 Ben McDonald .05
498 Mark Salas .05
499 Melido Perez .05
500 Will Clark .20
501 Mike Bielecki .05
502 Carney Lansford .05
503 Roy Smith .05
504 *Julio Valera* .05
505 Chuck Finley .05
506 Darnell Coles .05
507 Steve Jeltz .05
508 *Mike York* .05
509 Glenallen Hill .05
510 John Franco .05
511 Steve Balboni .05
512 Jose Mesa .05
513 Jerald Clark .05
514 Mike Stanton .05
515 Alvin Davis .05
516 *Karl Rhodes* .10
517 Joe Oliver .05
518 Cris Carpenter .05
519 Sparky Anderson .10
520 Mark Grace .20
521 Joe Orsulak .05
522 Stan Belinda .05
523 *Rodney McCray* .05
524 Darrel Akerfelds .05
525 Willie Randolph .05
526a Moises Alou (37 R 1990 Pirates) .20
526b Moises Alou (0 R 1990 Pirates) .10
527a Checklist 4 (Kevin McReynolds #719) .05
527b Checklist 4 (Kevin McReynolds #105) .05
528 Denny Martinez .05
529 *Mark Newfield* (#1 Draft Pick) .15
530 Roger Clemens .40
531 *Dave Rhode* .10
532 Kirk McCaskill .05
533 Oddibe McDowell .05
534 Mike Jackson .05
535 Ruben Sierra .05
536 Mike Witt .05
537 Jose Lind .05
538 Bip Roberts .05
539 Scott Terry .05
540 George Brett .30
541 Domingo Ramos .05
542 Rob Murphy .05
543 Junior Felix .05
544 Alejandro Pena .05
545 Dale Murphy .10
546 Jeff Ballard .05
547 Mike Pagliarulo .05
548 Jaime Navarro .05
549 John McNamara .05
550 Eric Davis .05
551 Bob Kipper .05
552 Jeff Hamilton .05
553 *Joe Klink* .05
554 Brian Harper .05
555 *Turner Ward* .10
556 Gary Ward .05
557 Wally Whitehurst .05
558 Otis Nixon .05
559 Adam Peterson .05
560 Greg Smith .05
561 Tim McIntosh (Future Star) .10
562 Jeff Kunkel .05
563 *Brent Knackert* .10
564 Dante Bichette .15
565 Craig Biggio .25
566 *Craig Wilson* .10
567 Dwayne Henry .05
568 Ron Karkovice .05
569 Curt Schilling .05
570 Barry Bonds .30
571 Pat Combs .05
572 Dave Anderson .05
573 *Rich Rodriguez* .10
574 John Marzano .05
575 Robin Yount .20
576 Jeff Kaiser .05
577 Bill Doran .05
578 Dave West .05
579 Roger Craig .05
580 Dave Stewart .05
581 Luis Quinones .05
582 Marty Clary .05
583 Tony Phillips .05
584 Kevin Brown .05
585 Pete O'Brien .05
586 Fred Lynn .05
587 Jose Offerman (Future Star) .10
588a Mark Whiten (hand inside left border) .15
588b Mark Whiten (hand over left border) .20
589 *Scott Ruskin* .10
590 Eddie Murray .15
591 Ken Hill .05
592 B.J. Surhoff .05
593a *Mike Walker* (No 1990 Canton-Akron stats) .15
593b *Mike Walker* (1990 Canton-Akron stats) .15
594 *Rich Garces* (Future Star) .10
595 Bill Landrum .05
596 *Ronnie Walden* (#1 Draft Pick) .10
597 Jerry Don Gleaton .05
598 Sam Horn .05
599a Greg Myers (no 1990 Syracuse stats) .10
599b Greg Myers (1990 Syracuse stats) .10
600 Bo Jackson .15
601 Bob Ojeda .05
602 Casey Candaele .05
603a *Wes Chamberlain* (photo of Louie Meadows, no bat) .20
603b *Wes Chamberlain* (correct photo, holding bat) .10
604 Billy Hatcher .05
605 Jeff Reardon .05
606 Jim Gott .05
607 Edgar Martinez .05
608 Todd Burns .05
609 Jeff Torborg .05
610 Andres Galarraga .20
611 Dave Eiland .05
612 Steve Lyons .05
613 Eric Show .05
614 Luis Salazar .05
615 Bert Blyleven .05
616 Todd Zeile .05
617 Bill Wegman .05
618 Sil Campusano .05
619 David Wells .05
620 Ozzie Guillen .05
621 Ted Power .05
622 Jack Daugherty .05
623 Jeff Blauser .05
624 Tom Candiotti .05
625 Terry Steinbach .05
626 Gerald Young .05
627 *Tim Layana* .10
628 Greg Litton .05
629 Wes Gardner .05
630 Dave Winfield .15
631 Mike Morgan .05
632 Lloyd Moseby .05
633 Kevin Tapani .05
634 Henry Cotto .05
635 Andy Hawkins .05
636 Geronimo Pena .05
637 Bruce Ruffin .05
638 Mike Macfarlane .05
639 Frank Robinson .05
640 Andre Dawson .10
641 Mike Henneman .05
642 Hal Morris .05
643 Jim Presley .05
644 Chuck Crim .05
645 Juan Samuel .05
646 *Andujar Cedeno* .10
647 Mark Portugal .05
648 Lee Stevens .05
649 *Bill Sampen* .05
650 Jack Clark .05
651 *Alan Mills* .10
652 Kevin Romine .05
653 *Anthony Telford* .15
654 Paul Sorrento .10
655 Erik Hanson .05
656a Checklist 5 (Vincente Palacios #348) .05
656b Checklist 5 (Palacios #433) .05
656c Checklist 5 (Palacios #438) .05
657 Mike Kingery .05
658 *Scott Aldred* .05
659 *Oscar Azocar* .05
660 Lee Smith .05
661 Steve Lake .05
662 Rob Dibble .05
663 Greg Brock .05
664 John Farrell .05
665 Mike LaValliere .05
666 Danny Darwin .05
667 Kent Anderson .05
668 Bill Long .05
669 Lou Pinella .05
670 Rickey Henderson .20
671 Andy McGaffigan .05
672 Shane Mack .05
673 *Greg Olson* .05
674a Kevin Gross (no diamond after 89 BB 1988) .10
674b Kevin Gross (diamond after 89 BB 1988) .10
675 Tom Brunansky .05
676 *Scott Chiamparino* .10
677 Billy Ripken .05
678 Mark Davidson .05
679 Bill Bathe .05
680 David Cone .15
681 *Jeff Schaefer* .05
682 *Ray Lankford* .20
683 Derek Lilliquist .05
684 Milt Cuyler .05
685 Doug Drabek .05
686 Mike Gallego .05
687a John Cerutti (4.46 ERA 1990) .05
687b John Cerutti (4.76 ERA 1990) .05
688 *Rosario Rodriguez* .05
689 John Kruk .05
690 Orel Hershiser .05
691 Mike Blowers .05
692a *Efrain Valdez* (no text below stats) .15
692b *Efrain Valdez* (two lines of text below stats) .15
693 Francisco Cabrera .05
694 Randy Veres .05
695 Kevin Seitzer .05
696 Steve Olin .05
697 Shawn Abner .05
698 Mark Guthrie .05
699 Jim Lefebvre .05
700 Jose Canseco .25
701 Pascual Perez .05
702 *Tim Naehring* .15
703 Juan Agosto .05
704 Devon White .05
705 Robby Thompson .05
706a Brad Arnsberg (68.2 IP Rangers 1990) .05
706b Brad Arnsberg (62.2 IP Rangers 1990) .05
707 Jim Eisenreich .05
708 John Mitchell .05
709 Matt Sinatro .05
710 Kent Hrbek .05
711 Jose DeLeon .05
712 Ricky Jordan .05
713 Scott Scudder .05
714 Marvell Wynne .05
715 Tim Burke .05
716 Bob Geren .05
717 Phil Bradley .05
718 Steve Crawford .05
719 Keith Miller .05
720 Cecil Fielder .10
721 *Mark Lee* .05
722 Wally Backman .05
723 Candy Maldonado .05
724 *David Segui* .10
725 Ron Gant .15
726 Phil Stephenson .05
727 Mookie Wilson .05
728 Scott Sanderson .05
729 Don Zimmer .05
730 Barry Larkin .20
731 *Jeff Gray* .05
732 Franklin Stubbs .05
733 Kelly Downs .05
734 John Russell .05
735 Ron Darling .05
736 Dick Schofield .05
737 Tim Crews .05
738 Mel Hall .05
739 *Russ Swan* .05
740 Ryne Sandberg .25
741 Jimmy Key .05
742 Tommy Gregg .05
743 Bryn Smith .05
744 Nelson Santovenia .05
745 Doug Jones .05
746 John Shelby .05
747 Tony Fossas .05
748 Al Newman .05
749 Greg Harris .05
750 Bobby Bonilla .10
751 *Wayne Edwards* .05
752 Kevin Bass .05
753 *Paul Marak* .05
754 Bill Pecota .05
755 Mark Langston .05
756 Jeff Huson .05
757 Mark Gardner .05
758 Mike Devereaux .05
759 Bobby Cox .05
760 Benny Santiago .05
761 Larry Andersen .05
762 Mitch Webster .05
763 *Dana Kiecker* .05
764 Mark Carreon .05
765 Shawon Dunston .05
766 Jeff Robinson .05
767 *Dan Wilson* (#1 Draft Pick) .15
768 Donn Pall .05
769 *Tim Sherrill* .05
770 Jay Howell .05
771 Gary Redus .05
772 Kent Mercker .05
773 Tom Foley .05
774 Dennis Rasmussen .05
775 Julio Franco .05
776 Brent Mayne .10
777 John Candelaria .05
778 Danny Gladden .05
779 Carmelo Martinez .05
780a Randy Myers (Career losses 15) .10
780b Randy Myers (Career losses 19) .10
781 Darryl Hamilton .05
782 Jim Deshaies .05
783 Joel Skinner .05
784 Willie Fraser .05
785 Scott Fletcher .05
786 Eric Plunk .05
787 Checklist 6 .05
788 Bob Milacki .05
789 Tom Lasorda .10
790 Ken Griffey, Jr. 1.50
791 Mike Benjamin .05
792 Mike Greenwell .05

1991 Topps Tiffany

Topps ended its annual run of special collectors edition boxed sets in 1991, producing the glossy sets in considerably more limited quantity than in previous years. Cards are identical to the regular 1991 Topps set except for the use of white cardboard stock and a high-gloss front finish.

MT
Complete Set (792): 150.00
Common Player: .10
(Star cards valued at 3X-4X corresponding regular issue Topps cards)

1991 Topps Traded

"Team USA" players are featured in the 1991 Topps Traded set. The cards feature the same style as the regular 1991 issue, including the 40th anniversary logo. The set includes 132 cards and showcases rookies and traded players along with "Team USA." The cards are numbered with a "T" designation in alphabetical order.

MT
Complete Set (132): 7.00
Common Player: .05
1 Juan Agosto .05
2 Roberto Alomar .25
3 Wally Backman .05
4 *Jeff Bagwell* 5.00
5 Skeeter Barnes .05
6 Steve Bedrosian .05
7 Derek Bell .25
8 George Bell .05
9 Rafael Belliard .05
10 Dante Bichette .20
11 Bud Black .05
12 Mike Boddicker .05
13 Sid Bream .05
14 Hubie Brooks .05
15 Brett Butler .10
16 Ivan Calderon .05
17 John Candelaria .05
18 Tom Candiotti .05
19 Gary Carter .10
20 Joe Carter .10
21 Rick Cerone .05
22 Jack Clark .05
23 Vince Coleman .05
24 Scott Coolbaugh .05
25 Danny Cox .05
26 Danny Darwin .05
27 Chili Davis .05
28 Glenn Davis .05
29 Steve Decker .10
30 Rob Deer .05
31 Rich DeLucia .05
32 *John Dettmer* (USA) .05
33 Brian Downing .05
34 *Darren Dreifort* (USA) .75
35 Kirk Dressendorfer .10
36 Jim Essian .05
37 Dwight Evans .05
38 Steve Farr .05
39 Jeff Fassero .10
40 Junior Felix .05
41 Tony Fernandez .05
42 Steve Finley .05
43 Jim Fregosi .05
44 Gary Gaetti .05
45 *Jason Giambi* (USA) 4.00
46 Kirk Gibson .05
47 Leo Gomez .10
48 Luis Gonzalez .15
49 *Jeff Granger* (USA) .15
50 *Todd Greene* (USA) .25
51 *Jeffrey Hammonds* (USA) .40
52 Mike Hargrove .05
53 Pete Harnisch .05
54 *Rick Helling* (USA) .15
55 Glenallen Hill .05
56 Charlie Hough .05
57 Pete Incaviglia .05
58 Bo Jackson .20
59 Danny Jackson .05
60 Reggie Jefferson .15
61 *Charles Johnson* (USA) 1.50
62 Jeff Johnson .10
63 *Todd Johnson* (USA) .10
64 Barry Jones .05
65 Chris Jones .05

66	Scott Kamieniecki	.05
67	*Pat Kelly*	.15
68	Darryl Kile	.10
69	Chuck Knoblauch	.40
70	Bill Krueger	.05
71	Scott Leius	.10
72	*Donnie Leshnock* (USA)	.10
73	Mark Lewis	.15
74	Candy Maldonado	.05
75	*Jason McDonald* (USA)	.10
76	Willie McGee	.05
77	Fred McGriff	.25
78	*Billy McMillon* (USA)	.10
79	Hal McRae	.05
80	*Dan Melendez* (USA)	.15
81	Orlando Merced	.15
82	Jack Morris	.05
83	*Phil Nevin* (USA)	.15
84	Otis Nixon	.05
85	Johnny Oates	.05
86	Bob Ojeda	.05
87	Mike Pagliarulo	.05
88	Dean Palmer	.25
89	Dave Parker	.05
90	Terry Pendleton	.05
91	*Tony Phillips* (USA)	.10
92	Doug Piatt	.10
93	Ron Polk (U.S.A.)	.05
94	Tim Raines	.10
95	Willie Randolph	.05
96	Dave Righetti	.05
97	Ernie Riles	.05
98	*Chris Roberts* (USA)	.15
99	Jeff Robinson (Angels)	.05
100	Jeff Robinson (Orioles)	.05
101	*Ivan Rodriguez*	4.00
102	*Steve Rodriguez* (USA)	.10
103	Tom Runnells	.05
104	Scott Sanderson	.05
105	Bob Scanlan	.05
106	Pete Schourek	.15
107	Gary Scott	.05
108	*Paul Shuey* (USA)	.15
109	*Doug Simons*	.10
110	Dave Smith	.05
111	Cory Snyder	.05
112	Luis Sojo	.05
113	*Kennie Steenstra* (USA)	.10
114	Darryl Strawberry	.20
115	Franklin Stubbs	.05
116	*Todd Taylor* (USA)	.10
117	Wade Taylor	.10
118	Garry Templeton	.05
119	Mickey Tettleton	.05
120	Tim Teufel	.05
121	Mike Timlin	.10
122	*David Tuttle* (USA)	.10
123	Mo Vaughn	.50
124	*Jeff Ware* (USA)	.10
125	Devon White	.05
126	Mark Whiten	.05
127	Mitch Williams	.05
128	*Craig Wilson* (USA)	.10
129	Willie Wilson	.05
130	*Chris Wimmer* (USA)	.10
131	*Ivan Zweig* (USA)	.10
132	Checklist	.05

1991 Topps Box Panel Cards

Styled like the standard 1991 Topps cards, this 16-card set honors milestones of the featured players. The cards were found on the bottom of wax pack boxes. The cards are designated in alphabetical order by (A-P) and are not numbered.

		MT
Complete Set (16):		2.50
Common Player:		.10
A	Bert Blyleven	.10
B	George Brett	.75
C	Brett Butler	.10
D	Andre Dawson	.15
E	Dwight Evans	.10
F	Carlton Fisk	.25
G	Alfredo Griffin	.10
H	Rickey Henderson	.25
I	Willie McGee	.10
J	Dale Murphy	.25
K	Eddie Murray	.25
L	Dave Parker	.10
M	Jeff Reardon	.10
N	Nolan Ryan	1.50
O	Juan Samuel	.10
P	Robin Yount	.50

1991 Topps All-Star Glossy Set of 22

Continuing the same basic format used since 1984, these glossy-front rack-pak inserts honor the players, manager and honorary captains of the previous year's All-Star Game. Fronts have a league logo in the lower-left corner, a 1990 All-Star banner above the photo and a Topps 40th anniversary logo superimposed over the photo. Backs have a shield and star design and the legend "1990 All-Star Commemorative Set" above the player's name, position and card number. Backs are printed in red and blue.

		MT
Complete Set (22):		5.00
Common Player:		.10
1	Tony LaRussa	.10
2	Mark McGwire	1.50
3	Steve Sax	.10
4	Wade Boggs	.40
5	Cal Ripken, Jr.	.90
6	Rickey Henderson	.30
7	Ken Griffey, Jr.	1.50
8	Jose Canseco	.40
9	Sandy Alomar, Jr.	.15
10	Bob Welch	.10
11	Al Lopez	.10
12	Roger Craig	.10
13	Will Clark	.25
14	Ryne Sandberg	.45
15	Chris Sabo	.10
16	Ozzie Smith	.40
17	Kevin Mitchell	.10
18	Len Dykstra	.10
19	Andre Dawson	.15
20	Mike Scoscia	.10
21	Jack Armstrong	.10
22	Juan Marichal	.10

1991 Topps Glossy Rookies

Similar in format to previous years' glossy rookies sets, this 33-card issue was available one per pack in 100-card jumbo cello packs. Card fronts have a colored "1990 Rookies" banner above the player photo, with the player's name in red in a yellow bar beneath. The Topps 40th anniversary logo appears in one of the upper corners of the photo. Backs are printed in red and blue and feature a "1990 Rookies Commemorative Set" shield logo. The player's name, position, team and card number are printed beneath. Cards are numbered alphabetically.

		MT
Complete Set (33):		11.00
Common Player:		.25
1	Sandy Alomar, Jr.	.35
2	Kevin Appier	.35
3	Steve Avery	.25
4	Carlos Baerga	.25
5	John Burkett	.25
6	Alex Cole	.25
7	Pat Combs	.25
8	Delino DeShields	.25
9	Travis Fryman	.25
10	Marquis Grissom	.50
11	Mike Harkey	.25
12	Glenallen Hill	.25
13	Jeff Huson	.25
14	Felix Jose	.25
15	Dave Justice	[illegible]
16	Jim Leyritz	.30
17	Kevin Maas	.25
18	Ben McDonald	.25
19	Kent Mercker	.25
20	Hal Morris	.25
21	Chris Nabholz	.25
22	Tim Naehring	.25
23	Jose Offerman	.25
24	John Olerud	.50
25	Scott Radinsky	.25
26	Scott Ruskin	.25
27	Kevin Tapani	.25
28	Frank Thomas	3.00
29	Randy Tomlin	.25
30	Greg Vaughn	.45
31	Robin Ventura	.45
32	Larry Walker	.50
33	Todd Zeile	.25

1991 Topps Desert Shield

As a special treat for U.S. armed services personnel serving in the Persian Gulf prior to and during the war with Iraq, Topps produced a special edition of its 1991 baseball card set featuring a gold-foil overprint honoring the military effort. Enough cards were produced to equal approximately 6,800 sets. While some cards actually reached the troops in the Middle East, many were shortstopped by military supply personnel stateside and sold into the hobby. Many of the cards sent to Saudi Arabia never returned to the U.S., however, making the supply of available cards somewhat scarce. At the peak of their popularity Desert Shield cards sold for price two to three times their current levels. The checklist cards in the set were not overprinted. At least two types of counterfeit overprint have been seen on genuine Topps cards in an attempt to cash in on the scarcity of these war "veterans."

	MT
Complete Set (792):	2000.
Common Player:	1.00
(Star cards valued at 100X corresponding cards in regular 1991 Topps issue)	

1991 Topps East Coast National Reprints

Produced in Topps' 40th anniversary year, this four-card set was issued at the 1991 East Coast National card show, the first card show in which Topps had ever participated. A total of 40,000 sets were reportedly issued in the now-standard 2-1/2" x 3-1/2" format. Fronts reproduce first Topps cards of four baseball greats while backs, printed in blue, carry a reprint notice, ad for the card show and Topps copyright.

		MT
Complete Set (4):		30.00
Common Card:		6.00
(1)	Mickey Mantle (1952)	20.00
(2)	Hank Aaron (1954)	12.00
(3)	Frank Robinson (1957)	7.50
(4)	Stan Musial (1958)	5.00

1991 Topps Gallery of Champions

Topps final issue of metallic mini-cards continued the theme of honoring the previous year's winners of major awards. The 1/4-size (1-1/4" x 1-3/4") ingots were issued in complete boxed sets of aluminum, bronze and silver in special display cases. To promote quantity sales, Topps offered a special pewter version of the Rickey Henderson ingot. A miniature replica of Brooks Robinson's 1957 Topps debut card was offered to dealers who bought Topps Traded sets.

		MT
Complete Aluminum Set (12).		125.00
Complete Bronze Set (12):		250.00
Complete Silver Set (12):		625.00
(1a)	Sandy Alomar Jr. (aluminum)	5.00
(1b)	Sandy Alomar Jr. (bronze)	10.00
(1s)	Sandy Alomar Jr. (silver)	25.00
(2a)	Barry Bonds (aluminum)	25.00
(2b)	Barry Bonds (bronze)	50.00
(2s)	Barry Bonds (silver)	125.00
(3a)	George Brett (aluminum)	25.00
(3b)	George Brett (bronze)	50.00
(3s)	George Brett (silver)	125.00
(4a)	Doug Drabek (aluminum)	5.00
(4b)	Doug Drabek (bronze)	10.00
(4s)	Doug Drabek (silver)	25.00
(5a)	Cecil Fielder (aluminum)	7.50
(5b)	Cecil Fielder (bronze)	15.00
(5s)	Cecil Fielder (silver)	35.00
(6a)	John Franco (aluminum)	5.00
(6b)	John Franco (bronze)	10.00
(6s)	John Franco (silver)	25.00
(7a)	Rickey Henderson (aluminum)	15.00
(7b)	Rickey Henderson (bronze)	30.00
(7s)	Rickey Henderson (silver)	75.00
(7p)	Rickey Henderson (pewter)	45.00
(8a)	Dave Justice (aluminum)	10.00
(8b)	Dave Justice (bronze)	20.00
(8s)	Dave Justice (silver)	50.00
(9a)	Willie McGee (aluminum)	5.00
(9b)	Willie McGee (bronze)	10.00
(9s)	Willie McGee (silver)	25.00
(10a)	Ryne Sandberg (aluminum)	15.00
(10b)	Ryne Sandberg (bronze)	30.00
(10s)	Ryne Sandberg (silver)	75.00
(11a)	Bobby Thigpen (aluminum)	5.00
(11b)	Bobby Thigpen (bronze)	10.00
(11s)	Bobby Thigpen (silver)	25.00
(12a)	Bob Welch (aluminum)	5.00
(12b)	Bob Welch (bronze)	10.00
(12s)	Bob Welch (silver)	25.00
(13)	Brooks Robinson (1957, bronze)	20.00

1991 Topps Golden Spikes Award

Each year the United States Baseball Federation honors the outstanding amateur player with the Golden Spikes Award. This card was handed out at the Nov. 20, 1991, awards banquet honoring Arizona State star Mike Kelly. Production was reported at 600 cards.

	MT
Mike Kelly	150.00

1991 Topps 1990 Major League Debut

This 171-card set features the players who made their Major League debut in 1990. The cards are styled like the 1991 Topps cards and are numbered in alphabetical order. The card backs are printed horizontally and feature information about the player's debut and statistics. The issue was sold only as a boxed set through hobby channels.

		MT
Complete Set (171):		25.00
Common Player:		.10
1	Paul Abbott	.10
2	Steve Adkins	.10
3	Scott Aldred	.10
4	Gerald Alexander	.10
5	Moises Alou	1.00
6	Steve Avery	.25
7	Oscar Azocar	.10
8	Carlos Baerga	.15
9	Kevin Baez	.10
10	Jeff Baldwin	.10
11	Brian Barnes	.15
12	Kevin Bearse	.10
13	Kevin Belcher	.20
14	Mike Bell	.10
15	Sean Berry	.20
16	Joe Bitker	.10
17	Willie Blair	.10
18	Brian Bohanon	.10
19	Mike Bordick	.25
20	Shawn Boskie	.25
21	Rod Brewer	.10
22	Kevin Brown	.25
23	Dave Burba	.10
24	Jim Campbell	.10
25	Ozzie Canseco	.20
26	Chuck Carr	.10
27	Larry Casian	.10
28	Andujar Cedeno	.25
29	Wes Chamberlain	.20
30	Scott Chiamparino	.10
31	Steve Chitren	.10
32	Pete Coachman	.10
33	Alex Cole	.10
34	Jeff Conine	.25
35	Scott Cooper	.25
36	Milt Cuyler	.10
37	Steve Decker	.10
38	Rich DeLucia	.10
39	Delino DeShields	.25
40	Mark Dewey	.10
41	Carlos Diaz	.10
42	Lance Dickson	.20
43	Narciso Elvira	.10
44	Luis Encarnacion	.10
45	Scott Erickson	.50
46	Paul Faries	.10
47	Howard Farmer	.10
48	Alex Fernandez	.25
49	Travis Fryman	.75
50	Rich Garces	.10
51	Carlos Garcia	.10
52	Mike Gardiner	.10
53	Bernard Gilkey	.25
54	Tom Gilles	.10
55	Jerry Goff	.10
56	Leo Gomez	.25
57	Luis Gonzalez	.75
58	Joe Grahe	.20
59	Craig Grebeck	.10
60	Kip Gross	.10
61	Eric Gunderson	.10
62	Chris Hammond	.20
63	Dave Hansen	.20
64	Reggie Harris	.10
65	Bill Haselman	.10
66	Randy Hennis	.10
67	Carlos Hernandez	.20
68	Howard Hilton	.10
69	Dave Hollins	.25
70	Darren Holmes	.20
71	John Hoover	.10
72	Steve Howard	.10
73	Thomas Howard	.10
74	Todd Hundley	.40
75	Daryl Irvine	.10
76	Chris Jelic	.10
77	Dana Kiecker	.10
78	Brent Knackert	.10
79	Jimmy Kremers	.10
80	Jerry Kutzler	.10
81	Ray Lankford	1.00
82	Tim Layana	.10
83	Terry Lee	.10
84	Mark Leiter	.10
85	Scott Leius	.25
86	Mark Leonard	.10
87	Darren Lewis	.25
88	Scott Lewis	.10
89	Jim Leyritz	.20
90	Dave Liddell	.10
91	Luis Lopez	.10
92	Kevin Maas	.10
93	Bob MacDonald	.10
94	Carlos Maldonado	.10
95	Chuck Malone	.10
96	Ramon Manon	.10
97	Jeff Manto	.10
98	Paul Marak	.10
99	Tino Martinez	1.00
100	Derrick May	.10
101	Brent Mayne	.20
102	Paul McClellan	.10
103	Rodney McCray	.10
104	Tim McIntosh	.10
105	Brian McRae	.25
106	Jose Melendez	.10
107	Orlando Merced	.25
108	Alan Mills	.10
109	Gino Minutelli	.10
110	Mickey Morandini	.15
111	Pedro Munoz	.15
112	Chris Nabholz	.10
113	Tim Naehring	.20
114	Charles Nagy	.25
115	Jim Neidlinger	.10
116	Rafael Novoa	.10
117	Jose Offerman	.25
118	Omar Olivares	.25
119	Javier Ortiz	.10
120	Al Osuna	.10
121	Rick Parker	.10
122	Dave Pavlas	.10
123	Geronimo Pena	.10
124	Mike Perez	.10
125	Phil Plantier	.15
126	Jim Poole	.10
127	Tom Quinlan	.10
128	Scott Radinsky	.10
129	Darren Reed	.20
130	Karl Rhodes	.10
131	Jeff Richardson	.10
132	Rich Rodriguez	.15
133	Dave Rohde	.10
134	Mel Rojas	.25
135	Vic Rosario	.10
136	Rich Rowland	.10
137	Scott Ruskin	.10
138	Bill Sampen	.10
139	Andres Santana	.10
140	David Segui	.25
141	Jeff Shaw	.10
142	Tim Sherrill	.10
143	Terry Shumpert	.10
144	Mike Simms	.10
145	Daryl Smith	.10
146	Luis Sojo	.10
147	Steve Springer	.10
148	Ray Stephens	.10
149	Lee Stevens	.10
150	Mel Stottlemyre, Jr.	.10
151	Glenn Sutko	.10
152	Anthony Telford	.15
153	Frank Thomas	6.00
154	Randy Tomlin	.25
155	Brian Traxler	.10
156	Efrain Valdez	.10
157	Rafael Valdez	.10
158	Julio Valera	.10
159	Jim Vatcher	.10
160	Hector Villanueva	.10
161	Hector Wagner	.10
162	Dave Walsh	.10
163	Steve Wapnick	.10
164	Colby Ward	.10
165	Turner Ward	.10
166	Terry Wells	.10
167	Mark Whiten	.10
168	Mike York	.10
169	Cliff Young	.10
170	Checklist	.10
171	Checklist	.10

1991 Topps Babe Ruth

This 11-card set by Topps was released in honor of the NBC movie about Babe Ruth. The cards were released on a limited basis. The card fronts feature full-color photos from the movie, while the flip sides are printed horizontally and describe the front photo. The cards are numbered on the back.

		MT
Complete Set (11):		15.00
Common Player:		2.00
1	Sunday Oct. 6, NBC	1.00
2	Stephen Lang as Babe Ruth	1.00
3	Bruce Weitz as Miller Huggins	1.00
4	Lisa Zane as Claire Ruth	1.00
5	Donald Moffat as Jacob Ruppert	1.00
6	Neil McDonough as Lou Gehrig	1.00
7	Pete Rose as Ty Cobb	7.50
8	Baseball Consultant (Rod Carew)	2.50
9	Miller Huggins, Babe Ruth	1.00
10	Ruth In Action	1.00
11	Babe Calls His Shot	1.00

1991 Topps Superstar Stand-Ups

Another of Topps' efforts over the years to market candy containers with a baseball player theme, the 1991 Superstar Stand-Ups were a test issue. Sold in a color-printed paper envelope, Stand-Ups are a hard plastic container filled with candy tablets. In bright see-through colors, the containers measure 2-1/16" x 2-9/16" and are vaguely shaped like a head and shoulders. A paper label attached to the front of the plastic has a player portrait with his team in a banner above and his name in a strip at bottom. Backs have a baseball design on the label with the Topps 40th anniversary logo at top. The player's name, team and position are in color bars at the bottom, with the item number at left. At center are the player's height, weight, birth date, batting and throwing preference and the year and number of his Topps rookie card. Clear (non-colored) plastic containers are also known for each player, though their relative scarcity to the colored pieces is currently undetermined.

		MT
Complete Set (36):		100.00
Common Player:		2.00
1	Jim Abbott	2.00
2	Sandy Alomar	2.00
3	Wade Boggs	6.00
4	Barry Bonds	9.00
5	Bobby Bonilla	2.00
6	George Brett	9.00
7	Jose Canseco	7.00
8	Will Clark	5.00
9	Roger Clemens	7.50
10	Eric Davis	2.00
11	Andre Dawson	2.00
12	Len Dykstra	2.00
13	Cecil Fielder	2.00
14	Carlton Fisk	3.00
15	Dwight Gooden	2.00
16	Mark Grace	3.00
17	Ken Griffey, Jr.	15.00
18	Tony Gwynn	9.00
19	Rickey Henderson	3.00
20	Bo Jackson	3.00
21	Dave Justice	4.00
22	Kevin Maas	2.00
23	Ramon Martinez	2.00
24	Don Mattingly	10.00
25	Ben McDonald	2.00
26	Mark McGwire	15.00
27	Kevin Mitchell	2.00
28	Cal Ripken, Jr.	12.50
29	Nolan Ryan	12.50
30	Ryne Sandberg	7.00
31	Ozzie Smith	7.50
32	Dave Stewart	2.00
33	Darryl Strawberry	2.00
34	Frank Viola	2.00
35	Matt Williams	2.00
36	Robin Yount	3.00

1991 "1953" Topps Archives Promos

This nine-card set was issued to promote Topps' 1953 Archives set. Besides seven of the cards being reprinted from the '53 set, the promo set included two of the "new" 1953-style cards which were included in the Archives issue - cards of Hank Aaron and Eleanor Engle, the first woman to sign a minor league contract in modern times. Card fronts are identical to the issued Archives cards, while the backs are white with red Archives logo and "Pre-production Sample" notation.

		MT
Complete Set (9):		150.00
Common Player:		15.00
(1)	Hank Aaron	24.00
(2)	Roy Campanella	20.00
(3)	Eleanor Engle	15.00
(4)	Bob Feller	15.00
(5)	Whitey Ford	15.00
(6)	Mickey Mantle	45.00
(7)	Willie Mays	24.00
(8)	Jackie Robinson	24.00
(9)	Satchell Paige	24.00

1991 "1953" Topps Archives

Billed as "The Ultimate 1953 Set," this issue reproduced 273 of the original 274-card 1953 Topps set. (Card #174, Billy Loes, was not reproduced due to lack of permission from the former Dodgers pitcher.) The Archives issue downsized the cards from their original 2-5/8" x 3-3/4" size to the now-standard 2-1/2" x 3-1/2" format. More than 50 cards of players who were not included in the 1953 Topps set were created as part of the Archives issue. Because Topps chose to use black-and-white photos and colorized backgrounds for most of the "extended" cards, rather than paintings as on the originals, collector interest in the Archives issue was diminished. Only 18,000 cases were reportedly produced.

		MT
Complete Set (337):		70.00
Common Player:		.20
Wax Box:		45.00
1	Jackie Robinson	8.00
2	Luke Easter	.20
3	George Crowe	.20
4	Ben Wade	.20
5	Joe Dobson	.20
6	Sam Jones	.20
7	Bob Borkowski	.20
8	Clem Koshorek	.20
9	Joe Collins	.20
10	Smoky Burgess	.20
11	Sal Yvars	.20
12	Howie Judson	.20
13	Conrado Marrero	.20
14	Clem Labine	.20
15	Bobo Newsom	.20
16	Peanuts Lowrey	.20
17	Billy Hitchcock	.20
18	Ted Lepcio	.20
19	Mel Parnell	.20
20	Hank Thompson	.20
21	Billy Johnson	.20
22	Howie Fox	.20
23	Toby Atwell	.20
24	Ferris Fain	.20
25	Ray Boone	.20
26	Dale Mitchell	.25
27	Roy Campanella	2.50
28	Eddie Pellagrini	.20
29	Hal Jeffcoat	.20
30	Willard Nixon	.20
31	Ewell Blackwell	.20
32	Clyde Vollmer	.20
33	Bob Kennedy	.20
34	George Shuba	.20
35	Irv Noren	.20
36	Johnny Groth	.20
37	Eddie Mathews	1.00
38	Jim Hearn	.20
39	Eddie Miksis	.20
40	John Lipon	.20
41	Enos Slaughter	.50
42	Gus Zernial	.20
43	Gil McDougald	.25
44	Ellis Kinder	.20
45	Grady Hatton	.20
46	Johnny Klippstein	.20
47	Bubba Church	.20
48	Bob Del Greco	.20
49	Faye Throneberry	.20
50	Chuck Dressen	.20
51	Frank Campos	.20
52	Ted Gray	.20
53	Sherman Lollar	.20
54	Bob Feller	1.00
55	Maurice McDermott	.20
56	Gerald Staley	.20
57	Carl Scheib	.20
58	George Metkovich	.20
59	Karl Drews	.20
60	Cloyd Boyer	.20
61	Early Wynn	.50
62	Monte Irvin	.50
63	Gus Niarhos	.20
64	Dave Philley	.20
65	Earl Harrist	.20
66	Orestes Minoso	.35
67	Roy Sievers	.20
68	Del Rice	.20
69	Dick Brodowski	.20
70	Ed Yuhas	.20
71	Tony Bartirome	.20
72	Fred Hutchinson	.20
73	Eddie Robinson	.20
74	Joe Rossi	.20
75	Mike Garcia	.20
76	Pee Wee Reese	2.00
77	John Mize	.75
78	Al Schoendienst	.50
79	Johnny Wyrostek	.20
80	Jim Hegan	.20
81	Joe Black	.20
82	Mickey Mantle	16.00
83	Howie Pollet	.20
84	Bob Hooper	.20
85	Bobby Morgan	.20
86	Billy Martin	.35
87	Ed Lopat	.25
88	Willie Jones	.20
89	Chuck Stobbs	.20
90	Hank Edwards	.20
91	Ebba St. Claire	.20
92	Paul Minner	.20
93	Hal Rice	.20
94	William Kennedy	.20
95	Willard Marshall	.20
96	Virgil Trucks	.20
97	Don Kolloway	.20
98	Cal Abrams	.20
99	Dave Madison	.20
100	Bill Miller	.20
101	Ted Wilks	.20
102	Connie Ryan	.20
103	Joe Astroth	.20
104	Yogi Berra	2.50
105	Joe Nuxhall	.20
106	John Antonelli	.20
107	Danny O'Connell	.20
108	Bob Porterfield	.20
109	Alvin Dark	.20
110	Herman Wehmeier	.20

111	Hank Sauer	.20
112	Ned Garver	.20
113	Jerry Priddy	.20
114	Phil Rizzuto	2.00
115	George Spencer	.20
116	Frank Smith	.20
117	Sid Gordon	.20
118	Gus Bell	.20
119	John Sain	.35
120	Davey Williams	.20
121	Walt Dropo	.20
122	Elmer Valo	.20
123	Tommy Byrne	.20
124	Sibby Sisti	.20
125	Dick Williams	.25
126	Bill Connelly	.20
127	Clint Courtney	.20
128	Wilmer Mizell	.20
129	Keith Thomas	.20
130	Turk Lown	.20
131	Harry Byrd	.20
132	Tom Morgan	.20
133	Gil Coan	.20
134	Rube Walker	.20
135	Al Rosen	.25
136	Ken Heintzelman	.20
137	John Rutherford	.20
138	George Kell	.50
139	Sammy White	.20
140	Tommy Glaviano	.20
141	Allie Reynolds	.35
142	Vic Wertz	.20
143	Billy Pierce	.25
144	Bob Schultz	.20
145	Harry Dorish	.20
146	Granville Hamner	.20
147	Warren Spahn	1.00
148	Mickey Grasso	.20
149	Dom DiMaggio	.25
150	Harry Simpson	.20
151	Hoyt Wilhelm	.75
152	Bob Adams	.20
153	Andy Seminick	.20
154	Dick Groat	.25
155	Dutch Leonard	.20
156	Jim Rivera	.20
157	Bob Addis	.20
158	John Logan	.20
159	Wayne Terwilliger	.20
160	Bob Young	.20
161	Vern Bickford	.20
162	Ted Kluszewski	.35
163	Fred Hatfield	.20
164	Frank Shea	.20
165	Billy Hoeft	.20
166	Bill Hunter	.20
167	Art Schult	.20
168	Willard Schmidt	.20
169	Dizzy Trout	.20
170	Bill Werle	.20
171	Bill Glynn	.20
172	Rip Repulski	.20
173	Preston Ward	.20
174	Not issued	
175	Ron Kline	.20
176	Don Hoak	.20
177	Jim Dyck	.20
178	Jim Waugh	.20
179	Gene Hermanski	.20
180	Virgil Stallcup	.20
181	Al Zarilla	.20
182	Bob Hofman	.20
183	Stu Miller	.20
184	Hal Brown	.20
185	Jim Pendleton	.20
186	Charlie Bishop	.20
187	Jim Fridley	.20
188	Andy Carey	.20
189	Ray Jablonski	.20
190	Dixie Walker	.20
191	Ralph Kiner	.50
192	Wally Westlake	.20
193	Mike Clark	.20
194	Eddie Kazak	.20
195	Ed McGhee	.20
196	Bob Keegan	.20
197	Del Crandall	.20
198	Forrest Main	.20
199	Marion Fricano	.20
200	Gordon Goldsberry	.20
201	Paul La Palme	.20
202	Carl Sawatski	.20
203	Cliff Fannin	.20
204	Dick Bokelmann	.20
205	Vern Benson	.20
206	Ed Bailey	.20
207	Whitey Ford	2.00
208	Jim Wilson	.20
209	Jim Greengrass	.20
210	Bob Cerv	.20
211	J.W. Porter	.20
212	Jack Dittmer	.20
213	Ray Scarborough	.20
214	Bill Bruton	.20
215	Gene Conley	.20
216	Jim Hughes	.20
217	Murray Wall	.20
218	Les Fusselman	.20
219	Pete Runnels	.20
220	Satchell Paige	4.00
221	Bob Milliken	.20
222	Vic Janowicz	.20
223	John O'Brien	.20
224	Lou Sleater	.20
225	Bobby Shantz	.25
226	Ed Erautt	.20
227	Morris Martin	.20
228	Hal Newhouser	.20
229	Rocky Krsnich	.20
230	Johnny Lindell	.20
231	Solly Hemus	.20
232	Dick Kokos	.20
233	Al Aber	.20
234	Ray Murray	.20
235	John Hetki	.20
236	Harry Perkowski	.20
237	Clarence Podbielan	.20
238	Cal Hogue	.20
239	Jim Delsing	.20
240	Freddie Marsh	.20
241	Al Sima	.20
242	Charlie Silvera	.20
243	Carlos Bernier	.20
244	Willie Mays	7.50
245	Bill Norman	.20
246	Roy Face	.20
247	Mike Sandlock	.20
248	Gene Stephens	.20
249	Ed O'Brien	.20
250	Bob Wilson	.20
251	Sid Hudson	.20
252	Henry Foiles	.20
253	Not issued	
254	Preacher Roe	.20
255	Dixie Howell	.20
256	Les Peden	.20
257	Bob Boyd	.20
258	Jim Gilliam	.35
259	Roy McMillan	.20
260	Sam Calderone	.20
261	Not issued	
262	Bob Oldis	.20
263	John Podres	.35
264	Gene Woodling	.35
265	Jackie Jensen	.35
266	Bob Cain	.20
267	Not issued	
268	Not issued	
269	Duane Pillette	.20
270	Vern Stephens	.20
271	Not issued	
272	Bill Antonello	.20
273	Harvey Haddix	.20
274	John Riddle	.20
275	Not issued	
276	Ken Raffensberger	.20
277	Don Lund	.20
278	Willie Miranda	.20
279	Joe Coleman	.20
280	Milt Bolling	.20
281	Jimmie Dykes	.20
282	Ralph Houk	.35
283	Frank Thomas	.20
284	Bob Lemon	.50
285	Joe Adcock	.20
286	Jimmy Piersall	.25
287	Mickey Vernon	.20
288	Robin Roberts	.50
289	Rogers Hornsby	.75
290	Hank Bauer	.20
291	Hoot Evers	.20
292	Whitey Lockman	.20
293	Ralph Branca	.25
294	Wally Post	.20
295	Phil Cavarretta	.20
296	Gil Hodges	.35
297	Roy Smalley	.20
298	Bob Friend	.20
299	Dusty Rhodes	.25
300	Eddie Stanky	.20
301	Harvey Kuenn	.25
302	Marty Marion	.20
303	Sal Maglie	.20
304	Lou Boudreau	.50
305	Carl Furillo	.35
306	Bobo Holloman	.20
307	Steve O'Neill	.20
308	Carl Erskine	.25
309	Leo Durocher	.25
310	Lew Burdette	.20
311	Richie Ashburn	.60
312	Hoyt Wilhelm	.60
313	Bucky Harris	.50
314	Joe Garagiola	.75
315	Johnny Pesky	.20
316	Fred Haney	.20
317	Hank Aaron	6.50
318	Curt Simmons	.20
319	Ted Williams	6.50
320	Don Newcombe	.35
321	Charlie Grimm	.20
322	Paul Richards	.20
323	Wes Westrum	.20
324	Vern Law	.20
325	Casey Stengel	1.00
326	Hall of Fame Inductees (Dizzy Dean, Al Simmons)	1.00
327	Duke Snider	2.00
328	Bill Rigney	.20
329	Al Lopez	.50
330	Bobby Thomson	.35
331	Nellie Fox	.40
332	Eleanor Engle	.20
333	Larry Doby	.50
334	Billy Goodman	.20
335	Checklist 1-140	.20
336	Checklist 141-280	.20
337	Checklist 281-337	.20

1992 Topps Promo Sheet

To preview its 1992 card set for dealers, Topps distributed a nine-card sheet in the basic format of its 1992 issue. The 8" x 10" sheets are often found cut into standard 2-1/2" x 3-1/2" singles. Card numbers on the backs of these promo cards do not correspond to the same cards in the regular set, and the stats for 1991 are not included. The preview cards have an orange oval on back, with the words, "1992 Pre-Production Sample".

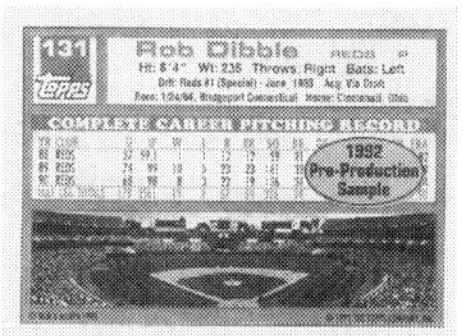

		MT
Complete Set (Sheet):		20.00
Complete Set (9):		12.00
Common Player:		2.00
3	Shawon Dunston	2.50
16	Mike Heath	2.00
18	Todd Frohwirth	2.00
20	Bip Roberts	2.50
131	Rob Dibble	2.50
174	Otis Nixon	2.50
273	Dennis Martinez	2.50
325	Brett Butler	2.50
798	Tom Lasorda	2.50

1992 Topps

This 792-card set features white stock much like the 1991 issue. The card fronts feature full-color action and posed photos with a gray inner frame and the player name and position at bottom. Backs feature biographical information, statistics and stadium photos on player cards where space is available. All-Star cards and #1 Draft Pick cards are once again included. Topps brought back four-player rookie cards in 1992. Nine Top Prospect cards of this nature can be found within the set. "Match the Stats" game cards were inserted into packs of 1992 Topps cards. Special bonus cards were given away to winners of this insert game. This was the first Topps regular-issue baseball card set since 1951 which was sold without bubble gum.

		MT
Complete Set (792):		25.00
Common Player:		.05
Golds: 6x to 12x		
Wax Box:		14.00
1	Nolan Ryan	.75
2	Rickey Henderson (Record Breaker)	.05
3	Jeff Reardon (Record Breaker)	.05
4	Nolan Ryan (Record Breaker)	.40
5	Dave Winfield (Record Breaker)	.05
6	*Brien Taylor* (Draft Pick)	.10
7	*Jim Olander*	.05
8	*Bryan Hickerson*	.05
9	John Farrell (Draft Pick)	.05
10	Wade Boggs	.20
11	Jack McDowell	.05
12	Luis Gonzalez	.10
13	Mike Scioscia	.05
14	Wes Chamberlain	.05
15	Denny Martinez	.05
16	Jeff Montgomery	.05
17	Randy Milligan	.05
18	Greg Cadaret	.05
19	Jamie Quirk	.05
20	Bip Roberts	.05
21	Buck Rodgers	.05
22	Bill Wegman	.05
23	Chuck Knoblauch	.15
24	Randy Myers	.05
25	Ron Gant	.10
26	Mike Bielecki	.05
27	Juan Gonzalez	.50
28	Mike Schooler	.05
29	Mickey Tettleton	.05
30	John Kruk	.05
31	Bryn Smith	.05
32	Chris Nabholz	.05
33	Carlos Baerga	.05
34	Jeff Juden	.05
35	Dave Righetti	.05
36	*Scott Ruffcorn* (Draft Pick)	.15
37	Luis Polonia	.05
38	Tom Candiotti	.05
39	Greg Olson	.05
40	Cal Ripken, Jr.	1.50
41	Craig Lefferts	.05
42	Mike Macfarlane	.05
43	Jose Lind	.05
44	Rick Aguilera	.05
45	Gary Carter	.10
46	Steve Farr	.05
47	Rex Hudler	.05
48	Scott Scudder	.05
49	Damon Berryhill	.05
50	Ken Griffey, Jr.	1.50
51	Tom Runnells	.05
52	Juan Bell	.05
53	Tommy Gregg	.05
54	David Wells	.05
55	Rafael Palmeiro	.20
56	Charlie O'Brien	.05
57	Donn Pall	.05
58	Top Prospects-Catchers *(Brad Ausmus), (Jim Campanis), (Dave Nilsson), (Doug Robbins)*	.15
59	Mo Vaughn	.30
60	Tony Fernandez	.05
61	Paul O'Neill	.15
62	Gene Nelson	.05
63	Randy Ready	.05
64	Bob Kipper	.05
65	Willie McGee	.05
66	*Scott Stahoviak* (Draft Pick)	.15
67	Luis Salazar	.05
68	Marvin Freeman	.05
69	Kenny Lofton	.40
70	Gary Gaetti	.05
71	Erik Hanson	.05
72	Eddie Zosky	.10
73	Brian Barnes	.05
74	Scott Leius	.05
75	Bret Saberhagen	.05
76	Mike Gallego	.05
77	Jack Armstrong	.05
78	Ivan Rodriguez	.40
79	Jesse Orosco	.05
80	Dave Justice	.20
81	*Ced Landrum*	.05
82	*Doug Simons*	.10
83	Tommy Greene	.05
84	Leo Gomez	.05
85	Jose DeLeon	.05
86	Steve Finley	.05
87	*Bob MacDonald*	.10
88	Darrin Jackson	.05
89	Neal Heaton	.05
90	Robin Yount	.20
91	Jeff Reed	.05
92	Lenny Harris	.05
93	Reggie Jefferson	.05
94	Sammy Sosa	1.00
95	Scott Bailes	.05
96	*Tom McKinnon* (Draft Pick)	.10
97	Luis Rivera	.05
98	Mike Harkey	.05
99	Jeff Treadway	.05
100	Jose Canseco	.25
101	Omar Vizquel	.05
102	*Scott Kamieniecki*	.10
103	Ricky Jordan	.05
104	Jeff Ballard	.05
105	Felix Jose	.05
106	Mike Boddicker	.05
107	Dan Pasqua	.05
108	*Mike Timlin*	.15
109	Roger Craig	.05
110	Ryne Sandberg	.25
111	Mark Carreon	.05
112	Oscar Azocar	.05
113	Mike Greenwell	.05
114	Mark Portugal	.05
115	Terry Pendleton	.05
116	Willie Randolph	.05
117	Scott Terry	.05
118	Chili Davis	.05
119	Mark Gardner	.05
120	Alan Trammell	.10
121	Derek Bell	.10
122	Gary Varsho	.05
123	Bob Ojeda	.05
124	*Shawn Livsey* (Draft Pick)	.10
125	Chris Hoiles	.05
126	Top Prospects-1st Baseman (Rico Brogna, John Jaha, Ryan Klesko, Dave Staton)	.25
127	Carlos Quintana	.05
128	Kurt Stillwell	.05
129	Melido Perez	.05
130	Alvin Davis	.05
131	Checklist 1	.05
132	Eric Show	.05
133	Rance Mulliniks	.05
134	Darryl Kile	.05
135	Von Hayes	.05
136	Bill Doran	.05
137	Jeff Robinson	.05
138	Monty Fariss	.05
139	Jeff Innis	.05
140	Mark Grace	.15
141	Jim Leyland	.05
142	Todd Van Poppel	.05
143	Paul Gibson	.05
144	Bill Swift	.05
145	Danny Tartabull	.05
146	Al Newman	.05
147	Cris Carpenter	.05
148	*Anthony Young*	.15
149	*Brian Bohanon*	.10
150	Roger Clemens	.50
151	Jeff Hamilton	.05
152	Charlie Leibrandt	.05
153	Ron Karkovice	.05
154	Hensley Meulens	.05
155	Scott Bankhead	.05
156	*Manny Ramirez* (Draft Pick)	3.00
157	Keith Miller	.05
158	Todd Frohwirth	.05
159	Darrin Fletcher	.05
160	Bobby Bonilla	.05
161	Casey Candaele	.05
162	Paul Faries	.05
163	Dana Kiecker	.05
164	Shane Mack	.05
165	Mark Langston	.05
166	Geronimo Pena	.05
167	Andy Allanson	.05
168	Dwight Smith	.05
169	Chuck Crim	.05
170	Alex Cole	.05
171	Bill Plummer	.05
172	Juan Berenguer	.05
173	Brian Downing	.05
174	Steve Frey	.05
175	Orel Hershiser	.05
176	*Ramon Garcia*	.10
177	Danny Gladden	.05
178	Jim Acker	.05
179	Top Prospects-2nd Baseman *(Cesar Bernhardt), (Bobby DeJardin), (Armando Moreno), (Andy Stankiewicz)*	.15
180	Kevin Mitchell	.05
181	Hector Villanueva	.05
182	Jeff Reardon	.05
183	Brent Mayne	.05
184	Jimmy Jones	.05
185	Benny Santiago	.05
186	*Cliff Floyd* (Draft Pick)	.40
187	Ernie Riles	.05
188	Jose Guzman	.05
189	Junior Felix	.05
190	Glenn Davis	.05
191	Charlie Hough	.05
192	*Dave Fleming*	.10
193	Omar Oliveras	.05
194	Eric Karros	.10
195	David Cone	.15
196	*Frank Castillo*	.05
197	Glenn Braggs	.05
198	Scott Aldred	.05
199	Jeff Blauser	.05
200	Len Dykstra	.05
201	Buck Showalter	.05
202	Rick Honeycutt	.05
203	Greg Myers	.05
204	Trevor Wilson	.05
205	Jay Howell	.05
206	Luis Sojo	.05
207	Jack Clark	.05
208	Julio Machado	.05
209	Lloyd McClendon	.05
210	Ozzie Guillen	.05
211	*Jeremy Hernandez*	.10
212	Randy Velarde	.05
213	Les Lancaster	.05
214	*Andy Mota*	.10
215	Rich Gossage	.05
216	*Brent Gates* (Draft Pick)	.20
217	Brian Harper	.05
218	Mike Flanagan	.05
219	Jerry Browne	.05
220	Jose Rijo	.05
221	Skeeter Barnes	.05
222	Jaime Navarro	.05
223	Mel Hall	.05
224	*Brett Barberie*	.10
225	Roberto Alomar	.25

226	Pete Smith	.05
227	Daryl Boston	.05
228	Eddie Whitson	.05
229	Shawn Boskie	.05
230	Dick Schofield	.05
231	*Brian Drahman*	.10
232	John Smiley	.05
233	Mitch Webster	.05
234	Terry Steinbach	.05
235	Jack Morris	.05
236	Bill Pecota	.05
237	*Jose Hernandez*	.10
238	Greg Litton	.05
239	Brian Holman	.05
240	Andres Galarraga	.15
241	Gerald Young	.05
242	Mike Mussina	.25
243	Alvaro Espinoza	.05
244	Darren Daulton	.05
245	John Smoltz	.15
246	*Jason Pruitt* (Draft Pick)	.10
247	Chuck Finley	.05
248	Jim Gantner	.05
249	Tony Fossas	.05
250	Ken Griffey	.05
251	Kevin Elster	.05
252	Dennis Rasmussen	.05
253	Terry Kennedy	.05
254	*Ryan Bowen*	.15
255	Robin Ventura	.20
256	Mike Aldrete	.05
257	Jeff Russell	.05
258	Jim Lindeman	.05
259	Ron Darling	.05
260	Devon White	.05
261	Tom Lasorda	.10
262	Terry Lee	.10
263	Bob Patterson	.05
264	Checklist 2	.05
265	Teddy Higuera	.05
266	Roberto Kelly	.05
267	Steve Bedrosian	.05
268	Brady Anderson	.10
269	*Ruben Amaro*	.10
270	Tony Gwynn	.50
271	Tracy Jones	.05
272	Jerry Don Gleaton	.05
273	Craig Grebeck	.05
274	*Bob Scanlan*	.10
275	Todd Zeile	.05
276	*Shawn Green* (Draft Pick)	3.00
277	Scott Chiamparino	.05
278	Darryl Hamilton	.05
279	Jim Clancy	.05
280	Carlos Martinez	.05
281	Kevin Appier	.05
282	*John Wehner*	.10
283	Reggie Sanders	.15
284	Gene Larkin	.05
285	Bob Welch	.05
286	Gilberto Reyes	.05
287	*Pete Schourek*	.15
288	Andujar Cedeno	.05
289	Mike Morgan	.05
290	Bo Jackson	.15
291	Phil Garner	.05
292	Ray Lankford	.10
293	Mike Henneman	.05
294	Dave Valle	.05
295	Alonzo Powell	.05
296	Tom Brunansky	.05
297	Kevin Brown	.05
298	Kelly Gruber	.05
299	Charles Nagy	.05
300	Don Mattingly	.40
301	Kirk McCaskill	.05
302	Joey Cora	.05
303	Dan Plesac	.05
304	Joe Oliver	.05
305	Tom Glavine	.15
306	*Al Shirley* (Draft Pick)	.10
307	Bruce Ruffin	.05
308	*Craig Shipley*	.05
309	Dave Martinez	.05
310	Jose Mesa	.05
311	Henry Cotto	.05
312	Mike LaValliere	.05
313	Kevin Tapani	.05
314	Jeff Huson	.05
315	Juan Samuel	.05
316	Curt Schilling	.10
317	Mike Bordick	.05
318	Steve Howe	.05
319	Tony Phillips	.05
320	George Bell	.05
321	Lou Pinella	.05
322	Tim Burke	.05
323	Milt Thompson	.05
324	Danny Darwin	.05
325	Joe Orsulak	.05
326	Eric King	.05
327	Jay Buhner	.10
328	*Joel Johnston*	.10
329	Franklin Stubbs	.05
330	Will Clark	.20
331	Steve Lake	.05
332	*Chris Jones*	.10
333	Pat Tabler	.05
334	Kevin Gross	.05
335	Dave Henderson	.05
336	*Greg Anthony* (Draft Pick)	.10
337	Alejandro Pena	.05
338	Shawn Abner	.05
339	Tom Browning	.05
340	Otis Nixon	.05
341	Bob Geren	.05
342	*Tim Spehr*	.10
343	*Jon Vander Wal*	.20
344	Jack Daugherty	.05
345	Zane Smith	.05
346	*Rheal Cormier*	.15
347	Kent Hrbek	.05
348	*Rick Wilkins*	.10
349	Steve Lyons	.05
350	Gregg Olson	.05
351	Greg Riddoch	.05
352	Ed Nunez	.05
353	*Braulio Castillo*	.05
354	Dave Bergman	.05
355	*Warren Newson*	.10
356	Luis Quinones	.05
357	Mike Witt	.05
358	*Ted Wood*	.10
359	Mike Moore	.05
360	Lance Parrish	.05
361	Barry Jones	.05
362	*Javier Ortiz*	.10
363	John Candelaria	.05
364	Glenallen Hill	.05
365	Duane Ward	.05
366	Checklist 3	.05
367	Rafael Belliard	.05
368	Bill Krueger	.05
369	*Steve Whitaker* (Draft Pick)	.10
370	Shawon Dunston	.05
371	Dante Bichette	.15
372	*Kip Gross*	.05
373	Don Robinson	.05
374	Bernie Williams	.30
375	Bert Blyleven	.05
376	*Chris Donnels*	.10
377	*Bob Zupcic*	.05
378	Joel Skinner	.05
379	Steve Chitren	.05
380	Barry Bonds	.35
381	Sparky Anderson	.10
382	Sid Fernandez	.05
383	Dave Hollins	.05
384	Mark Lee	.05
385	Tim Wallach	.05
386	Will Clark (All-Star)	.10
387	Ryne Sandberg (All-Star)	.10
388	Howard Johnson (All-Star)	.05
389	Barry Larkin (All-Star)	.05
390	Barry Bonds (All-Star)	.10
391	Ron Gant (All-Star)	.05
392	Bobby Bonilla (All-Star)	.05
393	Craig Biggio (All-Star)	.10
394	Denny Martinez (All-Star)	.05
395	Tom Glavine (All-Star)	.05
396	Lee Smith (All-Star)	.05
397	Cecil Fielder (All-Star)	.05
398	Julio Franco (All-Star)	.05
399	Wade Boggs (All-Star)	.10
400	Cal Ripken, Jr. (All-Star)	.25
401	Jose Canseco (All-Star)	.10
402	Joe Carter (All-Star)	.05
403	Ruben Sierra (All-Star)	.05
404	Matt Nokes (All-Star)	.05
405	Roger Clemens (All-Star)	.20
406	Jim Abbott (All-Star)	.05
407	Bryan Harvey (All-Star)	.05
408	Bob Milacki	.05
409	Geno Petralli	.05
410	Dave Stewart	.05
411	Mike Jackson	.05
412	Luis Aquino	.05
413	Tim Teufel	.05
414	Jeff Ware (Draft Pick)	.10
415	Jim Deshaies	.05
416	Ellis Burks	.10
417	Allan Anderson	.05
418	Alfredo Griffin	.05
419	Wally Whitehurst	.05
420	Sandy Alomar	.10
421	Juan Agosto	.05
422	Sam Horn	.05
423	*Jeff Fassero*	.10
424	*Paul McClellan*	.10
425	Cecil Fielder	.10
426	Tim Raines	.10
427	*Eddie Taubensee*	.20
428	Dennis Boyd	.05
429	Tony LaRussa	.05
430	Steve Sax	.05
431	Tom Gordon	.05
432	Billy Hatcher	.05
433	Cal Eldred	.10
434	Wally Backman	.05
435	Mark Eichhorn	.05
436	Mookie Wilson	.05
437	*Scott Servais*	.10
438	Mike Maddux	.05
439	*Chico Walker*	.05
440	Doug Drabek	.05
441	Rob Deer	.05
442	Dave West	.05
443	Spike Owen	.05
444	*Tyrone Hill* (Draft Pick)	.10
445	Matt Williams	.15
446	Mark Lewis	.05
447	David Segui	.05
448	Tom Pagnozzi	.05
449	*Jeff Johnson*	.10
450	Mark McGwire	1.50
451	Tom Henke	.05
452	Wilson Alvarez	.05
453	Gary Redus	.05
454	Darren Holmes	.05
455	Pete O'Brien	.05
456	Pat Combs	.05
457	Hubie Brooks	.05
458	Frank Tanana	.05
459	Tom Kelly	.05
460	Andre Dawson	.10
461	Doug Jones	.05
462	Rich Rodriguez	.05
463	*Mike Simms*	.10
464	Mike Jeffcoat	.05
465	Barry Larkin	.10
466	Stan Belinda	.05
467	Lonnie Smith	.05
468	Greg Harris	.05
469	Jim Eisenreich	.05
470	Pedro Guerrero	.05
471	Jose DeJesus	.05
472	*Rich Rowland*	.10
473	Top Prospects-3rd Baseman *(Frank Bolick)*, *(Craig Paquette)*, *(Tom Redington)*, *(Paul Russo)*	.15
474	*Mike Rossiter* (Draft Pick)	.15
475	Robby Thompson	.05
476	Randy Bush	.05
477	Greg Hibbard	.05
478	Dale Sveum	.05
479	*Chito Martinez*	.10
480	Scott Sanderson	.05
481	Tino Martinez	.10
482	Jimmy Key	.05
483	Terry Shumpert	.05
484	Mike Hartley	.05
485	Chris Sabo	.05
486	Bob Walk	.05
487	John Cerutti	.05
488	Scott Cooper	.10
489	Bobby Cox	.05
490	Julio Franco	.05
491	Jeff Brantley	.05
492	Mike Devereaux	.05
493	Jose.Offerman	.05
494	Gary Thurman	.05
495	Carney Lansford	.05
496	Joe Grahe	.05
497	*Andy Ashby*	.15
498	Gerald Perry	.05
499	Dave Otto	.05
500	Vince Coleman	.05
501	*Rob Mallicoat*	.05
502	Greg Briley	.05
503	Pascual Perez	.05
504	*Aaron Sele* (Draft Pick)	.40
505	Bobby Thigpen	.05
506	Todd Benzinger	.05
507	Candy Maldonado	.05
508	Bill Gullickson	.05
509	Doug Dascenzo	.05
510	Frank Viola	.05
511	Kenny Rogers	.05
512	Mike Heath	.05
513	Kevin Bass	.05
514	*Kim Batiste*	.10
515	Delino DeShields	.05
516	*Ed Sprague*	.10
517	Jim Gott	.05
518	*Jose Melendez*	.10
519	Hal McRae	.05
520	Jeff Bagwell	.50
521	Joe Hesketh	.05
522	Milt Cuyler	.05
523	Shawn Hillegas	.05
524	Don Slaught	.05
525	Randy Johnson	.20
526	*Doug Piatt*	.10
527	Checklist 4	.05
528	*Steve Foster*	.15
529	Joe Girardi	.05
530	Jim Abbott	.05
531	Larry Walker	.25
532	Mike Huff	.05
533	Mackey Sasser	.05
534	*Benji Gil* (Draft Pick)	.20
535	Dave Stieb	.05
536	Willie Wilson	.05
537	*Mark Leiter*	.05
538	Jose Uribe	.05
539	Thomas Howard	.05
540	Ben McDonald	.05
541	*Jose Tolentino*	.10
542	*Keith Mitchell*	.05
543	Jerome Walton	.05
544	*Cliff Brantley*	.10
545	Andy Van Slyke	.05
546	Paul Sorrento	.05
547	Herm Winningham	.05
548	Mark Guthrie	.05
549	Joe Torre	.05
550	Darryl Strawberry	.15
551	Top Prospects-Shortstops (Manny Alexander, Alex Arias, Wil Cordero, Chipper Jones)	1.50
552	Dave Gallagher	.05
553	Edgar Martinez	.05
554	Donald Harris	.05
555	Frank Thomas	.75
556	Storm Davis	.05
557	Dickie Thon	.05
558	Scott Garrelts	.05
559	Steve Olin	.05
560	Rickey Henderson	.15
561	Jose Vizcaino	.05
562	*Wade Taylor*	.10
563	Pat Borders	.05
564	*Jimmy Gonzalez* (Draft Pick)	.10
565	Lee Smith	.05
566	Bill Sampen	.05
567	Dean Palmer	.05
568	Bryan Harvey	.05
569	Tony Pena	.05
570	Lou Whitaker	.05
571	Randy Tomlin	.05
572	Greg Vaughn	.10
573	Kelly Downs	.05
574	Steve Avery	.05
575	Kirby Puckett	.35
576	*Heathcliff Slocumb*	.05
577	Kevin Seitzer	.05
578	Lee Guetterman	.05
579	Johnny Oates	.05
580	Greg Maddux	.75
581	Stan Javier	.05
582	Vicente Palacios	.05
583	Mel Rojas	.05
584	*Wayne Rosenthal*	.10
585	Lenny Webster	.05
586	Rod Nichols	.05
587	Mickey Morandini	.05
588	Russ Swan	.05
589	Mariano Duncan	.05
590	Howard Johnson	.05
591	Top Prospects-Outfielders *(Jacob Brumfield)*, *(Jeremy Burnitz)*, (*Alan Cockrell*, D.J. Dozier)	.25
592	*Denny Neagle*	.10
593	Steve Decker	.05
594	*Brian Barber* (Draft Pick)	.10
595	Bruce Hurst	.05
596	Kent Mercker	.05
597	*Mike Magnante*	.05
598	Jody Reed	.05
599	Steve Searcy	.05
600	Paul Molitor	.20
601	Dave Smith	.05
602	Mike Fetters	.05
603	*Luis Mercedes*	.10
604	Chris Gwynn	.05
605	Scott Erickson	.05
606	Brook Jacoby	.05
607	Todd Stottlemyre	.05
608	Scott Bradley	.05
609	Mike Hargrove	.05
610	Eric Davis	.05
611	*Brian Hunter*	.05
612	Pat Kelly	.05
613	Pedro Munoz	.10
614	Al Osuna	.05
615	Matt Merullo	.05
616	Larry Andersen	.05
617	Junior Ortiz	.05
618	Top Prospects-Outfielders (*Cesar Hernandez*, Steve Hosey, Dan Peltier), *(Jeff McNeely)*	.20
619	Danny Jackson	.05
620	George Brett	.40
621	*Dan Gakeler*	.10
622	Steve Buechele	.05
623	Bob Tewksbury	.05
624	*Shawn Estes* (Draft Pick)	.25
625	Kevin McReynolds	.05
626	*Chris Haney*	.05
627	Mike Sharperson	.05
628	Mark Williamson	.05
629	Wally Joyner	.10
630	Carlton Fisk	.20
631	*Armando Reynoso*	.10
632	Felix Fermin	.05
633	Mitch Williams	.05
634	Manuel Lee	.05
635	Harold Baines	.05
636	Greg Harris	.05
637	Orlando Merced	.05
638	Chris Bosio	.05
639	*Wayne Housie*	.10
640	Xavier Hernandez	.05
641	*David Howard*	.10
642	Tim Crews	.05
643	Rick Cerone	.05
644	Terry Leach	.05
645	Deion Sanders	.15
646	Craig Wilson	.10
647	Marquis Grissom	.10
648	Scott Fletcher	.05
649	Norm Charlton	.05
650	Jesse Barfield	.05
651	*Joe Slusarski*	.10
652	Bobby Rose	.05
653	Dennis Lamp	.05
654	*Allen Watson* (Draft Pick)	.20
655	Brett Butler	.05
656	Top Prospects-Outfielders *(Rudy Pemberton,* Henry Rodriguez), *(Lee Tinsley)*, *(Gerald Williams)*	.25
657	Dave Johnson	.05
658	Checklist 5	.05
659	Brian McRae	.05
660	Fred McGriff	.15
661	Bill Landrum	.05
662	Juan Guzman	.05
663	Greg Gagne	.05
664	Ken Hill	.05
665	*Dave Haas*	.05
666	Tom Foley	.05
667	*Roberto Hernandez*	.10
668	Dwayne Henry	.05
669	Jim Fregosi	.05
670	Harold Reynolds	.05
671	Mark Whiten	.05
672	Eric Plunk	.05
673	Todd Hundley	.10
674	*Mo Sanford*	.10
675	Bobby Witt	.05
676	Top Prospects-Pitchers *(Pat Mahomes)*, *(Sam Militello,* Roger Salkeld), *(Turk Wendell)*	.15
677	John Marzano	.05
678	Joe Klink	.05
679	Pete Incaviglia	.05
680	Dale Murphy	.10
681	Rene Gonzales	.05
682	Andy Benes	.05
683	Jim Poole	.05
684	*Trever Miller* (Draft Pick)	.15
685	*Scott Livingstone*	.15
686	Rich DeLucia	.05
687	*Harvey Pulliam*	.10
688	Tim Belcher	.05
689	Mark Lemke	.05
690	John Franco	.05
691	Walt Weiss	.05
692	Scott Ruskin	.05
693	Jeff King	.05
694	Mike Gardiner	.05
695	Gary Sheffield	.15
696	Joe Boever	.05
697	Mike Felder	.05
698	John Habyan	.05
699	Cito Gaston	.05
700	Ruben Sierra	.05
701	Scott Radinsky	.05
702	Lee Stevens	.05
703	*Mark Wohlers*	.10
704	Curt Young	.05
705	Dwight Evans	.05
706	Rob Murphy	.05
707	Gregg Jefferies	.05
708	Tom Bolton	.05
709	Chris James	.05
710	Kevin Maas	.05
711	*Ricky Bones*	.10
712	Curt Wilkerson	.05
713	Roger McDowell	.05
714	*Calvin Reese* (Draft Pick)	.20
715	Craig Biggio	.25
716	*Kirk Dressendorfer*	.10
717	Ken Dayley	.05
718	B.J. Surhoff	.10
719	Terry Mulholland	.05
720	Kirk Gibson	.05
721	Mike Pagliarulo	.05
722	Walt Terrell	.05
723	Jose Oquendo	.05
724	Kevin Morton	.05
725	Dwight Gooden	.10
726	Kirt Manwaring	.05
727	Chuck McElroy	.05
728	Dave Burba	.05
729	Art Howe	.05
730	Ramon Martinez	.10
731	Donnie Hill	.05
732	Nelson Santovenia	.05
733	Bob Melvin	.05
734	*Scott Hatteberg* (Draft Pick)	.10
735	Greg Swindell	.05
736	Lance Johnson	.05
737	Kevin Reimer	.05
738	Dennis Eckersley	.05
739	Rob Ducey	.05
740	Ken Caminiti	.10
741	Mark Gubicza	.05
742	Billy Spiers	.05
743	Darren Lewis	.05
744	Chris Hammond	.05
745	Dave Magadan	.05
746	Bernard Gilkey	.10
747	Willie Banks	.05
748	Matt Nokes	.05
749	Jerald Clark	.05
750	Travis Fryman	.05
751	Steve Wilson	.05
752	Billy Ripken	.05
753	Paul Assenmacher	.05
754	Charlie Hayes	.05
755	Alex Fernandez	.10
756	Gary Pettis	.05
757	Rob Dibble	.05
758	Tim Naehring	.05
759	Jeff Torborg	.05
760	Ozzie Smith	.25

761 Mike Fitzgerald .05
762 John Burkett .05
763 Kyle Abbott .05
764 *Tyler Green* (Draft Pick) .20
765 Pete Harnisch .05
766 Mark Davis .05
767 Kal Daniels .05
768 Jim Thome .50
769 Jack Howell .05
770 Sid Bream .05
771 *Arthur Rhodes* .10
772 Garry Templeton .05
773 Hal Morris .05
774 Bud Black .05
775 Ivan Calderon .05
776 *Doug Henry* .05
777 John Olerud .20
778 Tim Leary .05
779 Jay Bell .05
780 Eddie Murray .15
781 Paul Abbott .05
782 Phil Plantier .05
783 Joe Magrane .05
784 Ken Patterson .05
785 Albert Belle .30
786 Royce Clayton .10
787 Checklist 6 .05
788 Mike Stanton .05
789 Bobby Valentine .05
790 Joe Carter .10
791 Danny Cox .05
792 Dave Winfield .15

1992 Topps Gold Promo Sheet

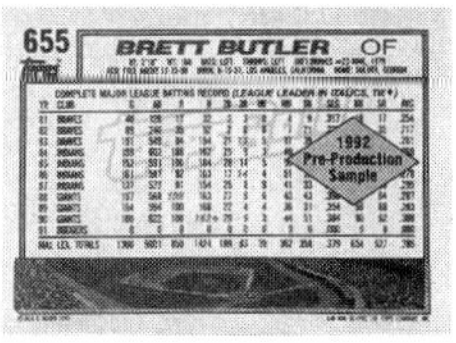

Similar in form and function to the nine-card promo sheet issued for the regular 1992 Topps set, this 8" x 11" sheet previewed the Topps Gold cards for dealers. Fronts are identical to the regular-issue '92 Topps cards. Backs differ in that actual 1991 stats are not printed, and there is a diamond over the stat box which reads, "1992 Pre-Production Sample". Card numbers on the gold preview cards correspond to the regular Topps cards. Single cards in the standard 2-1/2" x 3-1/2" size are frequently offered cut from these sheets.

	MT
Complete Set (Sheet):	30.00
Complete Set (9):	24.00
Common Player:	2.00
1 Nolan Ryan	10.00
15 Dennis Martinez	2.00
20 Bip Roberts	2.00
40 Cal Ripken, Jr.	10.00
261 Tom Lasorda	2.00
370 Shawon Dunston	2.00
512 Mike Heath	2.00
655 Brett Butler	2.00
757 Rob Dibble	2.00

1992 Topps Gold

Topps Gold cards share a checklist and format with the regular-issue 1992 Topps baseball issue except the color bars with the player's name and team printed beneath the photo have been replaced with gold foil. On back the light blue Topps logo printed beneath the stats has been replaced with a gold "Topps Gold" logo. Topps Gold cards were random inserts in all forms of packs. Additionally, factory sets of Gold cards were sold which included an autographed card of Yankees #1 draft pick Brien Taylor, and which had the checklist cards replaced with player cards. Several errors connected with the gold name/team strips are noted; no corrected versions were issued.

	MT
Complete Set (792):	120.00
Complete Factory Set (793):	130.00
Common Player:	.20
(Star cards valued at 10X-15X corresponding cards in regular-issue 1992 Topps)	.20
86 Steve Finley (incorrect name, Mark Davidson, on gold strip)	.20
131 Terry Mathews	.20
264 Rod Beck	1.50
288 Andujar Cedeno (incorrect team, Yankees, listed on gold strip)	.60
366 Tony Perezchica	.20
465 Barry Larkin (incorrect team, Astros, listed on gold strip)	2.00
527 Terry McDaniel	.20
532 Mike Huff (incorrect team, Red Sox, listed on gold strip)	.20
658 John Ramos	.20
787 Brian Williams	.20
793 Brien Taylor (autographed edition of 12,000; factory sets only)	20.00

1992 Topps Gold Winners

A second gold-foil enhanced parallel version of the regular 1992 Topps issue was the Gold Winner cards awarded as prizes in a scratch-off contest found in each pack. Winner cards are identical to the Topps Gold cards except for the addition of a gold-foil "Winner" and star added above the team name. Due to a flaw in the design of the scratch-off game cards, it was easy to win every time and the Winner cards had to be produced in quantities far greater than originally planned, making them rather common. Six checklist cards from the regular issue were replaced with player cards in the Winners edition.

	MT
Complete Set (792):	40.00
Common Player:	.15
(Star cards valued at 5X-7X corresponding cards in regular 1992 Topps issue)	
131 Terry Mathews	.15
264 Rod Beck	.90
366 Tony Perezchica	.15
465a Barry Larkin (team name incorrect, Astros)	.90
465b Barry Larkin (team name correct, Reds)	.35
527 Terry McDaniel	.15
658 John Ramos	.15
787 Brian Williams	.15

1992 Topps Traded

Members of the United States baseball team are featured in this 132-card boxed set released by Topps. The cards are styled after the regular 1992 Topps cards and are numbered alphabetically. Several United States baseball players featured in this set were also featured in the 1991 Topps Traded set.

	MT
Complete Set (132):	120.00
Common Player:	.05
1 *Willie Adams* (USA)	.20
2 Jeff Alkire (USA)	.20
3 Felipe Alou	.05
4 Moises Alou	.50
5 Ruben Amaro	.05
6 Jack Armstrong	.05
7 Scott Bankhead	.05
8 Tim Belcher	.05
9 George Bell	.05
10 Freddie Benavides	.10
11 Todd Benzinger	.05
12 Joe Boever	.05
13 Ricky Bones	.05
14 Bobby Bonilla	.10
15 Hubie Brooks	.05
16 Jerry Browne	.05
17 Jim Bullinger	.05
18 Dave Burba	.05
19 Kevin Campbell	.10
20 Tom Candiotti	.05
21 Mark Carreon	.05
22 Gary Carter	.10
23 Archi Cianfrocco	.05
24 Phil Clark	.05
25 *Chad Curtis*	.50
26 Eric Davis	.10
27 Tim Davis (USA)	.10
28 Gary DiSarcina	.05
29 Darren Dreifort (USA)	.40
30 Mariano Duncan	.05
31 Mike Fitzgerald	.05
32 John Flaherty	.10
33 Darrin Fletcher	.10
34 Scott Fletcher	.05
35 Ron Fraser (USA)	.05
36 Andres Galarraga	.25
37 Dave Gallagher	.05
38 Mike Gallego	.05
39 *Nomar Garciaparra* (USA)	100.00
40 Jason Giambi (USA)	1.50
41 Danny Gladden	.05
42 Rene Gonzales	.05
43 Jeff Granger (USA)	.40
44 Rick Greene (USA)	.10
45 Jeffrey Hammonds (USA)	.40
46 Charlie Hayes	.05
47 Von Hayes	.05
48 Rick Helling (USA)	.10
49 Butch Henry	.10
50 Carlos Hernandez	.10
51 Ken Hill	.05
52 Butch Hobson	.05
53 Vince Horsman	.10
54 Pete Incaviglia	.05
55 Gregg Jefferies	.10
56 Charles Johnson (USA)	1.00
57 Doug Jones	.05
58 *Brian Jordan*	5.00
59 Wally Joyner	.10
60 *Daron Kirkreit* (USA)	.20
61 Bill Krueger	.05
62 Gene Lamont	.05
63 Jim Lefebvre	.05
64 *Danny Leon*	.05
65 Pat Listach	.05
66 Kenny Lofton	1.00
67 Dave Martinez	.05
68 Derrick May	.05
69 Kirk McCaskill	.05
70 *Chad McConnell* (USA)	.25
71 Kevin McReynolds	.05
72 Rusty Meacham	.05
73 Keith Miller	.05
74 Kevin Mitchell	.05
75 *Jason Moler* (USA)	.25
76 Mike Morgan	.05
77 Jack Morris	.05
78 *Calvin Murray* (USA)	.50
79 Eddie Murray	.20
80 Randy Myers	.05
81 Denny Neagle	.10
82 Phil Nevin (USA)	.20
83 Dave Nilsson	.10
84 Junior Ortiz	.05
85 Donovan Osborne	.05
86 Bill Pecota	.05
87 Melido Perez	.05
88 Mike Perez	.05
89 Hipolito Pena	.05
90 Willie Randolph	.05
91 Darren Reed	.10
92 Bip Roberts	.05
93 Chris Roberts (USA)	.25
94 Steve Rodriguez (USA)	.10
95 Bruce Ruffin	.05
96 Scott Ruskin	.05
97 Bret Saberhagen	.10
98 Rey Sanchez	.10
99 Steve Sax	.05
100 Curt Schilling	.10
101 Dick Schofield	.05
102 Gary Scott	.05
103 Kevin Seitzer	.05
104 Frank Seminara	.10
105 Gary Sheffield	.20
106 John Smiley	.05
107 Cory Snyder	.05
108 Paul Sorrento	.05
109 Sammy Sosa	4.00
110 *Matt Stairs*	2.50
111 Andy Stankiewicz	.10
112 Kurt Stillwell	.05
113 Rick Sutcliffe	.05
114 Bill Swift	.05
115 Jeff Tackett	.10
116 Danny Tartabull	.05
117 Eddie Taubensee	.15
118 Dickie Thon	.05
119 *Michael Tucker* (USA)	.75
120 Scooter Tucker	.10
121 *Marc Valdes* (USA)	.10
122 Julio Valera	.10
123 *Jason Varitek* (USA)	3.00
124 *Ron Villone* (USA)	.20
125 Frank Viola	.05
126 *B.J. Wallace* (USA)	.30
127 Dan Walters	.10
128 Craig Wilson (USA)	.10
129 Chris Wimmer (USA)	.10
130 Dave Winfield	.15
131 Herm Winningham	.05
132 Checklist	.05

1992 Topps Traded Gold

A reported 6,000 sets of 1992 Topps Traded were produced in a gold edition, with gold-foil strips on front bearing the player and team names. The cards are in all other respects identical to the regular boxed Traded issue.

	MT
Complete Set (132):	300.00
Common Player:	.25
Stars/Rookies: 2X	
(See 1992 Topps Traded for checklist and base card values.)	

1992 Topps Golden Spikes Award

At a Nov. 17, 1992, awards ceremony, Phil Nevin was presented with the U.S. Baseball Federation's Golden Spikes Award, emblematic of his selection as the outstanding amatuer player in the nation. Topps created and handed out at the affair this one-card "set." Production was reported at 600 cards.

	MT
Phil Nevin	150.00

1992 Topps Kids

In a market which had increasingly become the province of adult collectors, Topps in 1992 offered an issue unashamedly aimed at the youngster. Called "Topps Kids," the 132-card set features bright colors, garish graphics and the game's top stars. Sold at 35 cents per pack (with bubble gum), the issue was even priced for the young collector. Unfortunately, the concept was a flop and was not repeated in subsequent years. Card fronts feature player photos, sometimes only the player's head on a cartoon body, against a background of wild designs or cartoon ballpark action. Player names at bottom were rendered in superhero comic-book style. Backs feature a few 1991 and career stats, and/or a cartoon or two about the player or baseball trivia.

	MT
Complete Set (132):	8.00
Common Player:	.05
1 Ryne Sandberg	.35
2 Andre Dawson	.10
3 George Bell	.05
4 Mark Grace	.10
5 Shawon Dunston	.05
6 Tim Wallach	.05
7 Ivan Calderon	.05
8 Marquis Grissom	.10
9 Delino DeShields	.05
10 Denny Martinez	.05
11 Dwight Gooden	.10
12 Howard Johnson	.05
13 John Franco	.05
14 Gregg Jefferies	.05
15 Kevin McReynolds	.05
16 David Cone	.05
17 Len Dykstra	.05
18 John Kruk	.05
19 Von Hayes	.05
20 Mitch Williams	.05
21 Barry Bonds	.40
22 Bobby Bonilla	.05
23 Andy Van Slyke	.05
24 Doug Drabek	.05
25 Ozzie Smith	.30
26 Pedro Guerrero	.05
27 Todd Zelle	.05
28 Lee Smith	.05
29 Felix Jose	.05

30	Jose DeLeon	.05
31	David Justice	.15
32	Ron Gant	.10
33	Terry Pendleton	.05
34	Tom Glavine	.10
35	Otis Nixon	.05
36	Steve Avery	.05
37	Barry Larkin	.10
38	Eric Davis	.05
39	Chris Sabo	.05
40	Rob Dibble	.05
41	Paul O'Neill	.10
42	Jose Rijo	.05
43	Craig Biggio	.10
44	Jeff Bagwell	.25
45	Ken Caminiti	.10
46	Steve Finley	.05
47	Darryl Strawberry	.10
48	Ramon Martinez	.10
49	Brett Butler	.05
50	Eddie Murray	.15
51	Kal Daniels	.05
52	Orel Hershiser	.05
53	Tony Gwynn	.30
54	Benny Santiago	.05
55	Fred McGriff	.15
56	Bip Roberts	.05
57	Tony Fernandez	.05
58	Will Clark	.15
59	Kevin Mitchell	.05
60	Matt Williams	.15
61	Willie McGee	.05
62	Dave Righetti	.05
63	Cal Ripken, Jr.	.75
64	Ben McDonald	.05
65	Glenn Davis	.05
66	Gregg Olson	.05
67	Roger Clemens	.30
68	Wade Boggs	.25
69	Mike Greenwell	.05
70	Ellis Burks	.05
71	Sandy Alomar	.10
72	Greg Swindell	.05
73	Albert Belle	.30
74	Mark Whiten	.05
75	Alan Trammell	.05
76	Cecil Fielder	.10
77	Lou Whitaker	.05
78	Travis Fryman	.05
79	Tony Phillips	.05
80	Robin Yount	.30
81	Paul Molitor	.30
82	B.J. Surhoff	.05
83	Greg Vaughn	.05
84	Don Mattingly	.40
85	Steve Sax	.05
86	Kevin Maas	.05
87	Mel Hall	.05
88	Roberto Kelly	.05
89	Joe Carter	.05
90	Roberto Alomar	.20
91	Dave Stieb	.05
92	Kelly Gruber	.05
93	Tom Henke	.05
94	Chuck Finley	.05
95	Wally Joyner	.10
96	Dave Winfield	.25
97	Jim Abbott	.05
98	Mark Langston	.05
99	Frank Thomas	.50
100	Ozzie Guillen	.05
101	Bobby Thigpen	.05
102	Robin Ventura	.10
103	Bo Jackson	.15
104	Tim Raines	.10
105	George Brett	.40
106	Danny Tartabull	.05
107	Bret Saberhagen	.05
108	Brian McRae	.05
109	Kirby Puckett	.40
110	Scott Erickson	.05
111	Kent Hrbek	.05
112	Chuck Knoblauch	.10
113	Chili Davis	.05
114	Rick Aguilera	.05
115	Jose Canseco	.25
116	Dave Henderson	.05
117	Dave Stewart	.05
118	Rickey Henderson	.15
119	Dennis Eckersley	.05
120	Harold Baines	.05
121	Mark McGwire	1.00
122	Ken Griffey, Jr.	1.00
123	Harold Reynolds	.05
124	Erik Hanson	.05
125	Edgar Martinez	.05
126	Randy Johnson	.15
127	Nolan Ryan	.75
128	Ruben Sierra	.05
129	Julio Franco	.05
130	Rafael Palmeiro	.10
131	Juan Gonzalez	.30
132	Checklist	.05

1992 Topps Triple Header Photo Balls

Picture a slightly oversize ping pong ball painted like a baseball with the heads and facsimile autographs of three different players on it and you've got the idea behind the Triple Headers test issue. Very limited in distribution, the team balls were sold in a small box with a package of candy.

		MT
Complete Set (26):		125.00
Common Ball:		3.00
(1)	California Angels (Chuck Finley, Dave Winfield, Wally Joyner)	3.50
(2)	Houston Astros (Jeff Bagwell, Craig Biggio, Ken Caminiti)	10.00
(3)	Oakland Athletics (Dave Henderson, Jose Canseco, Rickey Henderson)	4.00
(4)	Toronto Blue Jays (Roberto Alomar, Kelly Gruber, Joe Carter)	3.50
(5)	Atlanta Braves (Ron Gant, Tom Glavine, Dave Justice)	3.50
(6)	Milwaukee Brewers (Greg Vaughn, Paul Molitor, Robin Yount)	5.00
(7)	St. Louis Cardinals (Todd Zeile, Pedro Guerrero, Ozzie Smith)	3.50
(8)	Chicago Cubs (Ryne Sandberg, George Bell, Mark Grace)	10.00
(9)	Los Angeles Dodgers (Ramon Martinez, Eddie Murray, Darryl Strawberry)	4.00
(10)	Montreal Expos (Delino DeShields, Dennis Martinez, Ivan Calderon)	3.00
(11)	San Francisco Giants (Will Clark, Kevin Mitchell, Matt Williams)	3.50
(12)	Cleveland Indians (Sandy Alomar Jr., Alex Cole, Mark Lewis)	3.00
(13)	Seattle Mariners (Ken Griffey Jr., Harold Reynolds, Ken Griffey Sr.)	15.00
(14)	New York Mets (Vince Coleman, Dwight Gooden, Howard Johnson)	3.00
(15)	Baltimore Orioles (Ben McDonald, Cal Ripken Jr., Gregg Olson)	12.00
(16)	San Diego Padres (Benito Santiago, Fred McGriff, Tony Gwynn)	8.00
(17)	Philadelphia Phillies (Len Dykstra, John Kruk, Dale Murphy)	3.00
(18)	Pittsburgh Pirates (Andy Van Slyke, Barry Bonds, Bobby Bonilla)	4.00
(19)	Cincinnati Reds (Chris Sabo, Eric Davis, Barry Larkin)	3.00
(20)	Boston Red Sox (Wade Boggs, Mike Greenwell, Roger Clemens)	5.00
(21)	Kansas City Royals (George Brett, Danny Tartabull, Bret Saberhagen)	3.50
(22)	Texas Rangers (Julio Franco, Nolan Ryan, Juan Gonzalez)	12.00
(23)	Minnesota Twins (Scott Erickson, Kirby Puckett, Kent Hrbek)	3.50
(24)	Detroit Tigers (Cecil Fielder, Tony Phillips, Alan Trammell)	3.00
(25)	Chicago White Sox (Carlton Fisk, Robin Ventura, Frank Thomas)	12.00
(26)	New York Yankees (Don Mattingly, Steve Sax, Willie Randolph)	5.00

1992 Topps 1991 Major League Debut

This 194-card set highlights the debut date of 1991 Major League rookies. Two checklist cards are also included in this boxed set. The card fronts resemble the 1992 Topps cards. A debut banner appears in the lower-right corner of the card front. The set is packaged in an attractive collector box and the cards are numbered alphabetically. This set was available only through hobby dealers.

		MT
Complete Set (194):		30.00
Common Player:		.15
1	Kyle Abbott	.15
2	Dana Allison	.15
3	Rich Amaral	.15
4	Ruben Amaro	.15
5	Andy Ashby	.30
6	Jim Austin	.15
7	Jeff Bagwell	5.00
8	Jeff Banister	.15
9	Willie Banks	.15
10	Bret Barberie	.15
11	Kim Batiste	.15
12	Chris Beasley	.15
13	Rod Beck	.20
14	Derek Bell	.40
15	Esteban Beltre	.15
16	Freddie Benavides	.15
17	Rickey Bones	.15
18	Denis Boucher	.15
19	Ryan Bowen	.20
20	Cliff Brantley	.20
21	John Briscoe	.15
22	Scott Brosius	.25
23	Terry Bross	.15
24	Jarvis Brown	.15
25	Scott Bullett	.15
26	Kevin Campbell	.15
27	Amalio Carreno	.15
28	Matias Carrillo	.15
29	Jeff Carter	.15
30	Vinny Castilla	1.00
31	Braulio Castillo	.15
32	Frank Castillo	.15
33	Darrin Chapin	.15
34	Mike Christopher	.15
35	Mark Clark	.20
36	Royce Clayton	.30
37	Stu Cole	.15
38	Gary Cooper	.15
39	Archie Corbin	.15
40	Rheal Cormier	.20
41	Chris Cron	.15
42	Mike Dalton	.15
43	Mark Davis	.15
44	Francisco de la Rosa	.15
45	Chris Donnels	.20
46	Brian Drahman	.20
47	Tom Drees	.15
48	Kirk Dressendorfer	.15
49	Bruce Egloff	.15
50	Cal Eldred	.25
51	Jose Escobar	.15
52	Tony Eusebio	.20
53	Hector Fajardo	.20
54	Monty Farriss	.20
55	Jeff Fassero	.30
56	Dave Fleming	.20
57	Kevin Flora	.15
58	Steve Foster	.15
59	Dan Gakeler	.15
60	Ramon Garcia	.15
61	Chris Gardner	.15
62	Jeff Gardner	.20
63	Chris George	.20
64	Ray Giannelli	.15
65	Tom Goodwin	.25
66	Mark Grater	.15
67	Johnny Guzman	.15
68	Juan Guzman	.25
69	Dave Haas	.15
70	Chris Haney	.15
71	Shawn Hare	.20
72	Donald Harris	.20
73	Doug Henry	.20
74	Pat Hentgen	.40
75	Gil Heredia	.20
76	Jeremy Hernandez	.15
77	Jose Hernandez	.15
78	Roberto Hernandez	.20
79	Bryan Hickerson	.20
80	Milt Hill	.15
81	Vince Horsman	.15
82	Wayne Housie	.15
83	Chris Howard	.15
84	David Howard	.20
85	Mike Humphreys	.15
86	Brian Hunter	.15
87	Jim Hunter	.15
88	Mike Ignasiak	.15
89	Reggie Jefferson	.25
90	Jeff Johnson	.20
91	Joel Johnson	.15
92	Calvin Jones	.15
93	Chris Jones	.20
94	Stacy Jones	.15
95	Jeff Juden	.15
96	Scott Kamieniecki	.20
97	Eric Karros	1.00
98	Pat Kelly	.20
99	John Kiely	.15
100	Darryl Kile	.40
101	Wayne Kirby	.20
102	Garland Kiser	.15
103	Chuck Knoblauch	1.00
104	Randy Knorr	.15
105	Tom Kramer	.15
106	Ced Landrum	.15
107	Patrick Lennon	.15
108	Jim Lewis	.15
109	Mark Lewis	.15
110	Doug Lindsey	.15
111	Scott Livingstone	.20
112	Kenny Lofton	1.50
113	Ever Magallanes	.15
114	Mike Magnante	.20
115	Barry Manuel	.15
116	Josias Manzanillo	.20
117	Chito Martinez	.20
118	Terry Mathews	.15
119	Rob Mauer	.15
120	Tim Mauser	.15
121	Terry McDaniel	.15
122	Rusty Meacham	.15
123	Luis Mercedes	.20
124	Paul Miller	.20
125	Keith Mitchell	.15
126	Bobby Moore	.15
127	Kevin Morton	.20
128	Andy Mota	.15
129	Jose Mota	.15
130	Mike Mussina	3.00
131	Jeff Mutis	.15
132	Denny Neagle	.15
133	Warren Newson	.20
134	Jim Olander	.15
135	Erik Pappas	.20
136	Jorge Pedre	.15
137	Yorkis Perez	.20
138	Mark Petkovsek	.20
139	Doug Piatt	.15
140	Jeff Plympton	.15
141	Harvey Pulliam	.15
142	John Ramos	.15
143	Mike Remlinger	.15
144	Laddie Renfroe	.15
145	Armando Reynoso	.20
146	Arthur Rhodes	.15
147	Pat Rice	.20
148	Nikco Riesgo	.15
149	Carlos Rodriguez	.15
150	Ivan Rodriguez	5.00
151	Wayne Rosenthal	.15
152	Rico Rossy	.15
153	Stan Royer	.20
154	Rey Sanchez	.20
155	Reggie Sanders	.40
156	Mo Sanford	.15
157	Bob Scanlan	.20
158	Pete Schourek	.20
159	Gary Scott	.20
160	Tim Scott	.15
161	Tony Scruggs	.15
162	Scott Servais	.20
163	Doug Simons	.15
164	Heathcliff Slocumb	.15
165	Joe Slusarski	.20
166	Tim Spehr	.20
167	Ed Sprague	.25
168	Jeff Tackett	.20
169	Eddie Taubensee	.25
170	Wade Taylor	.20
171	Jim Thome	2.50
172	Mike Timlin	.25
173	Jose Tolentino	.15
174	John Vander Wal	.20
175	Todd Van Poppel	.20
176	Mo Vaughn	1.50
177	Dave Wainhouse	.15
178	Don Wakamatsu	.15
179	Bruce Walton	.15
180	Kevin Ward	.15
181	Dave Weathers	.15
182	Eric Wedge	.15
183	John Wehner	.15
184	Rick Wilkins	.20
185	Bernie Williams	1.50
186	Brian Williams	.15
187	Ron Witmeyer	.15
188	Mark Wohlers	.15
189	Ted Wood	.15
190	Anthony Young	.15
191	Eddie Zosky	.20
192	Bob Zupcic	.15
193	Checklist	.15
194	Checklist	.15

1993 Topps Promos

Specially marked 1992 Topps factory sets included this nine-card preview of the coming year's issue. The preview cards are identical to the regular-issue versions except the backs have a gray oval over the stats box with the notation, "1993 Pre-Production Sample".

		MT
Complete Set (9):		4.00
Common Player:		.25
1	Robin Yount	.50
2	Barry Bonds	.50
11	Eric Karros	.25
32	Don Mattingly	.75
100	Mark McGwire	3.00
150	Frank Thomas	1.50
179	Ken Griffey, Jr.	3.00
230	Carlton Fisk	.40
250	Chuck Knoblauch	.35

1993 Topps Promo Sheet

Originally produced as an 8" x 11" nine-card sheet, these pre-production sample cards are rarely found as singles. Cards are in the same basic format as the regular-issue 1993 Topps cards. Backs differ in that all cards are numbered "000" with all zeroes for 1992 stats and bogus career highlights. A large gray circle over the stats box reads "1993 Pre-Production Sample For General Look Only".

		MT
Complete Set (Sheet):		20.00
Complete Set (9):		16.00
Common Player:		1.00
(1)	Roberto Alomar	3.00
(2)	Bobby Bonilla	1.50
(3)	Gary Carter	1.50
(4)	Andre Dawson	1.50
(5)	Dave Fleming	1.00
(6)	Ken Griffey, Jr.	6.00
(7)	Pete Incaviglia	1.00
(8)	Spike Owen	1.00
(9)	Larry Walker	3.00

1993 Topps

Topps issued in a two-series format in 1993. Series I includes cards #1-396; Series II comprises #397-825. The card fronts feature full-color photos enclosed by a white border. The player's name and team appear at the bottom. The backs feature an additional player photo and biographical information at the top. The bottom box includes statistics and player information. The cards are numbered in red in a yellow flag on the back.

		MT
Complete Set (825):		30.00
Common Player:		.05
Golds: 2x to 4x		
Series 1 or 2 Wax Box:		20.00
1	Robin Yount	.35
2	Barry Bonds	.50
3	Ryne Sandberg	.40
4	Roger Clemens	.75
5	Tony Gwynn	.75
6	*Jeff Tackett*	.10
7	Pete Incaviglia	.05
8	Mark Wohlers	.05
9	Kent Hrbek	.05
10	Will Clark	.20
11	Eric Karros	.10
12	Lee Smith	.05
13	Esteban Beltre	.05
14	Greg Briley	.05
15	Marquis Grissom	.10
16	Dan Plesac	.05
17	Dave Hollins	.05
18	Terry Steinbach	.05
19	Ed Nunez	.05
20	Tim Salmon	.35
21	Luis Salazar	.05
22	Jim Eisenreich	.05
23	Todd Stottlemyre	.05
24	Tim Naehring	.05
25	John Franco	.05
26	Skeeter Barnes	.05
27	*Carlos Garcia*	.15
28	Joe Orsulak	.05
29	Dwayne Henry	.05
30	Fred McGriff	.20
31	Derek Lilliquist	.05
32	Don Mattingly	.40
33	B.J. Wallace (1992 Draft Pick)	.15
34	Juan Gonzalez	.50
35	John Smoltz	.15
36	Scott Servais	.05
37	Lenny Webster	.05
38	Chris James	.05
39	Roger McDowell	.05
40	Ozzie Smith	.40
41	Alex Fernandez	.10
42	Spike Owen	.05
43	Ruben Amaro	.05
44	Kevin Seitzer	.05
45	Dave Fleming	.05
46	*Eric Fox*	.05
47	Bob Scanlan	.05
48	Bert Blyleven	.05
49	Brian McRae	.05
50	Roberto Alomar	.30
51	Mo Vaughn	.30
52	Bobby Bonilla	.10
53	Frank Tanana	.05
54	Mike LaValliere	.05
55	Mark McLemore	.05
56	*Chad Mottola* (1992 Draft Pick)	.15
57	Norm Charlton	.05
58	Jose Melendez	.05
59	Carlos Martinez	.05
60	Roberto Kelly	.05
61	Gene Larkin	.05
62	Rafael Belliard	.05
63	Al Osuna	.05
64	Scott Chiamparino	.05
65	Brett Butler	.05
66	John Burkett	.05
67	Felix Jose	.05
68	Omar Vizquel	.05
69	*John Vander Wal*	.10
70	Roberto Hernandez	.05
71	Ricky Bones	.05
72	*Jeff Grotewold*	.10
73	Mike Moore	.05
74	Steve Buechele	.05
75	Juan Guzman	.05
76	Kevin Appier	.05
77	Junior Felix	.05
78	Greg Harris	.05
79	Dick Schofield	.05
80	Cecil Fielder	.10
81	Lloyd McClendon	.05
82	David Segui	.05
83	Reggie Sanders	.10
84	Kurt Stillwell	.05
85	Sandy Alomar	.10
86	John Habyan	.05
87	Kevin Reimer	.05
88	Mike Stanton	.05
89	Eric Anthony	.05
90	Scott Erickson	.05
91	Craig Colbert	.05
92	Tom Pagnozzi	.05
93	*Pedro Astacio*	.20
94	Lance Johnson	.05
95	Larry Walker	.30
96	Russ Swan	.05
97	Scott Fletcher	.05
98	*Derek Jeter* (1992 Draft Pick)	8.00
99	*Mike Williams*	.05
100	Mark McGwire	2.00
101	*Jim Bullinger*	.15
102	Brian Hunter	.05
103	Jody Reed	.05
104	*Mike Butcher*	.10
105	Gregg Jefferies	.05
106	Howard Johnson	.05
107	*John Kiely*	.10
108	Jose Lind	.05
109	Sam Horn	.05
110	Barry Larkin	.20
111	Bruce Hurst	.05
112	Brian Barnes	.05
113	Thomas Howard	.05
114	Mel Hall	.05
115	Robby Thompson	.05
116	Mark Lemke	.05
117	Eddie Taubensee	.05
118	David Hulse	.05
119	Pedro Munoz	.05
120	Ramon Martinez	.10
121	Todd Worrell	.05
122	Joey Cora	.05
123	Moises Alou	.20
124	Franklin Stubbs	.05
125	Pete O'Brien	.05
126	*Bob Ayrault*	.10
127	Carney Lansford	.05
128	Kal Daniels	.05
129	Joe Grahe	.05
130	Jeff Montgomery	.05
131	Dave Winfield	.15
132	*Preston Wilson* (1992 Draft Pick)	1.00
133	Steve Wilson	.05
134	Lee Guetterman	.05
135	Mickey Tettleton	.05
136	Jeff King	.05
137	Alan Mills	.05
138	Joe Oliver	.05
139	Gary Gaetti	.05
140	Gary Sheffield	.15
141	Dennis Cook	.05
142	Charlie Hayes	.05
143	Jeff Huson	.05
144	Kent Mercker	.05
145	*Eric Young*	.25
146	Scott Leius	.05
147	Bryan Hickerson	.05
148	Steve Finley	.05
149	Rheal Cormier	.05
150	Frank Thomas	.75
151	*Archi Cianfrocco*	.05
152	Rich DeLucia	.05
153	Greg Vaughn	.20
154	Wes Chamberlain	.05
155	Dennis Eckersley	.05
156	Sammy Sosa	1.25
157	Gary DiSarcina	.05
158	*Kevin Koslofski*	.10
159	*Doug Linton*	.10
160	Lou Whitaker	.05
161	Chad McDonnell (1992 Draft Pick)	.15
162	Joe Hesketh	.05
163	*Tim Wakefield*	.10
164	Leo Gomez	.05
165	Jose Rijo	.05
166	*Tim Scott*	.10
167	Steve Olin	.05
168	Kevin Maas	.05
169	Kenny Rogers	.05
170	Dave Justice	.25
171	Doug Jones	.05
172	*Jeff Reboulet*	.10
173	Andres Galarraga	.20
174	Randy Velarde	.05
175	Kirk McCaskill	.05
176	Darren Lewis	.05
177	Lenny Harris	.05
178	Jeff Fassero	.05
179	Ken Griffey, Jr.	2.00
180	Darren Daulton	.05
181	John Jaha	.05
182	Ron Darling	.05
183	Greg Maddux	1.00
184	*Damion Easley*	.10
185	Jack Morris	.05
186	Mike Magnante	.05
187	John Dopson	.05
188	Sid Fernandez	.05
189	Tony Phillips	.05
190	Doug Drabek	.05
191	*Sean Lowe* (1992 Draft Pick)	.10
192	Bob Milacki	.05
193	*Steve Foster*	.05
194	Jerald Clark	.05
195	Pete Harnisch	.05
196	Pat Kelly	.05
197	Jeff Frye	.10
198	Alejandro Pena	.05
199	Junior Ortiz	.05
200	Kirby Puckett	.50
201	Jose Uribe	.05
202	Mike Scioscia	.05
203	Bernard Gilkey	.05
204	Dan Pasqua	.05
205	Gary Carter	.10
206	Henry Cotto	.05
207	Paul Molitor	.40
208	Mike Hartley	.05
209	Jeff Parrett	.05
210	Mark Langston	.05
211	Doug Dascenzo	.05
212	Rick Reed	.05
213	Candy Maldonado	.05
214	Danny Darwin	.05
215	*Pat Howell*	.10
216	Mark Leiter	.05
217	Kevin Mitchell	.05
218	Ben McDonald	.05
219	Bip Roberts	.05
220	Benny Santiago	.05
221	Carlos Baerga	.05
222	Bernie Williams	.30
223	*Roger Pavlik*	.10
224	Sid Bream	.05
225	Matt Williams	.25
226	Willie Banks	.05
227	Jeff Bagwell	.50
228	Tom Goodwin	.05
229	Mike Perez	.05
230	Carlton Fisk	.20
231	John Wetteland	.05
232	Tino Martinez	.15
233	*Rick Greene* (1992 Draft Pick)	.10
234	Tim McIntosh	.05
235	Mitch Williams	.05
236	*Kevin Campbell*	.10
237	Jose Vizcaino	.05
238	Chris Donnels	.05
239	Mike Boddicker	.05
240	John Olerud	.20
241	Mike Gardiner	.05
242	Charlie O'Brien	.05
243	Rob Deer	.05
244	Denny Neagle	.05
245	Chris Sabo	.05
246	Gregg Olson	.05
247	Frank Seminara	.05
248	Scott Scudder	.05
249	Tim Burke	.05
250	Chuck Knoblauch	.25
251	Mike Bielecki	.05
252	Xavier Hernandez	.05
253	Jose Guzman	.05
254	Cory Snyder	.05
255	Orel Hershiser	.05
256	Wil Cordero	.10
257	Luis Alicea	.05
258	Mike Schooler	.05
259	Craig Grebeck	.05
260	Duane Ward	.05
261	Bill Wegman	.05
262	Mickey Morandini	.05
263	*Vince Horsman*	.10
264	Paul Sorrento	.05
265	Andre Dawson	.15
266	Rene Gonzales	.05
267	Keith Miller	.05
268	Derek Bell	.10
269	*Todd Steverson* (1992 Draft Pick)	.15
270	Frank Viola	.05
271	Wally Whitehurst	.05
272	*Kurt Knudsen*	.05
273	*Dan Walters*	.15
274	Rick Sutcliffe	.05
275	Andy Van Slyke	.05
276	Paul O'Neill	.15
277	Mark Whiten	.05
278	Chris Nabholz	.05
279	Todd Burns	.05
280	Tom Glavine	.15
281	*Butch Henry*	.10
282	Shane Mack	.05
283	Mike Jackson	.05
284	Henry Rodriguez	.10
285	Bob Tewksbury	.05
286	Ron Karkovice	.05
287	Mike Gallego	.05
288	Dave Cochrane	.05
289	Jesse Orosco	.05
290	Dave Stewart	.05
291	Tommy Greene	.05
292	Rey Sanchez	.05
293	Rob Ducey	.05
294	Brent Mayne	.05
295	Dave Stieb	.05
296	Luis Rivera	.05
297	Jeff Innis	.05
298	Scott Livingstone	.05
299	Bob Patterson	.05
300	Cal Ripken, Jr.	1.50
301	Cesar Hernandez	.05
302	Randy Myers	.05
303	Brook Jacoby	.05
304	Melido Perez	.05
305	Rafael Palmeiro	.20
306	Damon Berryhill	.05
307	*Dan Serafini* (1992 Draft Pick)	.10
308	Darryl Kile	.05
309	*J.T. Bruett*	.05
310	Dave Righetti	.05
311	Jay Howell	.05
312	Geronimo Pena	.05
313	Greg Hibbard	.05
314	Mark Gardner	.05
315	Edgar Martinez	.05
316	Dave Nilsson	.05
317	Kyle Abbott	.05
318	Willie Wilson	.05
319	Paul Assenmacher	.05
320	*Tim Fortugno*	.10
321	Rusty Meacham	.05
322	Pat Borders	.05
323	Mike Greenwell	.05
324	Willie Randolph	.05
325	Bill Gullickson	.05
326	Gary Varsho	.05
327	Tim Hulett	.05
328	Scott Ruskin	.05
329	Mike Maddux	.05
330	Danny Tartabull	.05
331	Kenny Lofton	.30
332	Geno Petralli	.05
333	Otis Nixon	.05
334	*Jason Kendall* (1992 Draft Pick)	1.50
335	Mark Portugal	.05
336	Mike Pagliarulo	.05
337	Kirt Manwaring	.05
338	Bob Ojeda	.05
339	*Mark Clark*	.10
340	John Kruk	.05
341	Mel Rojas	.05
342	Erik Hanson	.05
343	Doug Henry	.05
344	Jack McDowell	.05
345	Harold Baines	.05
346	Chuck McElroy	.05
347	Luis Sojo	.05
348	Andy Stankiewicz	.05
349	*Hipolito Pichardo*	.10
350	Joe Carter	.05
351	Ellis Burks	.05
352	Pete Schourek	.05
353	*Buddy Groom*	.10
354	Jay Bell	.05
355	Brady Anderson	.15
356	Freddie Benavides	.05
357	Phil Stephenson	.05
358	Kevin Wickander	.05
359	Mike Stanley	.05
360	Ivan Rodriguez	.50
361	Scott Bankhead	.05
362	Luis Gonzalez	.10
363	John Smiley	.05
364	Trevor Wilson	.05
365	Tom Candiotti	.05
366	Craig Wilson	.05
367	Steve Sax	.05
368	Delino Deshields	.10
369	Jaime Navarro	.05
370	Dave Valle	.05
371	Mariano Duncan	.05
372	Rod Nichols	.05
373	Mike Morgan	.05
374	Julio Valera	.05
375	Wally Joyner	.10
376	Tom Henke	.05
377	Herm Winningham	.05
378	Orlando Merced	.05
379	Mike Munoz	.05
380	Todd Hundley	.05
381	Mike Flanagan	.05
382	Tim Belcher	.05
383	Jerry Browne	.05
384	Mike Benjamin	.05
385	Jim Leyritz	.05
386	Ray Lankford	.10
387	Devon White	.05
388	Jeremy Hernandez	.05
389	Brian Harper	.05
390	Wade Boggs	.25
391	Derrick May	.05
392	Travis Fryman	.05
393	Ron Gant	.10
394	Checklist 1-132	.05
395	Checklist 133-264	.05
396	Checklist 265-396	.05
397	George Brett	.50
398	Bobby Witt	.05
399	Daryl Boston	.05
400	Bo Jackson	.15
401	Fred McGriff, Frank Thomas (All-Star)	.30
402	Ryne Sandberg, Carlos Baerga (All-Star)	.15
403	Gary Sheffield, Edgar Martinez (All-Star)	.05
404	Barry Larkin, Travis Fryman (All-Star)	.10
405	Andy Van Slyke, Ken Griffey, Jr. (All-Star)	.50
406	Larry Walker, Kirby Puckett (All-Star)	.25
407	Barry Bonds, Joe Carter (All-Star)	.15
408	Darren Daulton, Brian Harper (All-Star)	.05
409	Greg Maddux, Roger Clemens (All-Star)	.40
410	Tom Glavine, Dave Fleming (All-Star)	.10
411	Lee Smith, Dennis Eckersley (All-Star)	.05
412	Jamie McAndrew	.05
413	Pete Smith	.05
414	Juan Guerrero	.05
415	Todd Frohwirth	.05
416	Randy Tomlin	.05
417	B.J. Surhoff	.10
418	Jim Gott	.05
419	Mark Thompson (1992 Draft Pick)	.10
420	Kevin Tapani	.05
421	Curt Schilling	.05
422	*J.T. Snow*	.50
423	Top Prospects 1B (Ryan Klesko, Ivan Cruz, Bubba Smith, Larry Sutton)	.25
424	John Valentin	.05
425	Joe Girardi	.05
426	*Nigel Wilson*	.15
427	Bob MacDonald	.05
428	Todd Zeile	.05
429	Milt Cuyler	.05
430	Eddie Murray	.20
431	Rich Amaral	.05
432	Pete Young	.05
433	Rockies Future Stars (Roger Bailey, Tom Schmidt)	.15
434	Jack Armstrong	.05
435	Willie McGee	.05
436	Greg Harris	.05
437	Chris Hammond	.05
438	*Ritchie Moody* (1992 Draft Pick)	.15
439	Bryan Harvey	.05
440	Ruben Sierra	.05
441	Marlins Future Stars (Don Lemon, Todd Pridy)	.10
442	Kevin McReynolds	.05
443	Terry Leach	.05
444	David Nied	.10
445	Dale Murphy	.15
446	Luis Mercedes	.05
447	*Keith Shepherd*	.10
448	Ken Caminiti	.15
449	James Austin	.05
450	Darryl Strawberry	.10
451	Top Prospects 2B (Ramon Caraballo, Jon Shave, Brent Gates, *Quinton McCracken*)	.15
452	Bob Wickman	.05
453	Victor Cole	.05
454	*John Johnstone*	.10
455	Chili Davis	.05
456	Scott Taylor	.05
457	Tracy Woodson	.05
458	David Wells	.05
459	*Derek Wallace* (1992 Draft Pick)	.20
460	Randy Johnson	.35
461	*Steve Reed*	.05
462	Felix Fermin	.05
463	Scott Aldred	.05
464	Greg Colbrunn	.05
465	Tony Fernandez	.05
466	Mike Felder	.05
467	Lee Stevens	.05
468	Matt Whiteside	.05
469	Dave Hansen	.05
470	Rob Dibble	.05
471	Dave Gallagher	.05
472	Chris Gwynn	.05
473	Dave Henderson	.05
474	Ozzie Guillen	.05
475	Jeff Reardon	.05
476	Rockies Future Stars (Mark Voisard, Will Scalzitti)	.15
477	Jimmy Jones	.05
478	Greg Cadaret	.05
479	Todd Pratt	.05
480	Pat Listach	.05
481	*Ryan Luzinski* (1992 Draft Pick)	.10
482	Darren Reed	.05
483	*Brian Griffiths*	.10
484	John Wehner	.05
485	Glenn Davis	.05
486	*Eric Wedge*	.05
487	Jesse Hollins	.05
488	Manuel Lee	.05
489	*Scott Fredrickson*	.10
490	Omar Olivares	.05
491	Shawn Hare	.05
492	Tom Lampkin	.05
493	Jeff Nelson	.05
494	Top Prospects 3B (Kevin Young, Adell Davenport, Eduardo Perez, Lou Lucca)	.15
495	Ken Hill	.05
496	Reggie Jefferson	.05
497	Marlins Future Stars (Matt Petersen, Willie Brown)	.10
498	Bud Black	.05
499	Chuck Crim	.05
500	Jose Canseco	.50
501	Major League Managers (Johnny Oates, Bobby Cox)	.05
502	Major League Managers (Butch Hobson, Jim Lefebvre)	.05
503	Major League Managers (Buck Rodgers, Tony Perez)	.05
504	Major League Managers (Gene Lamont, Don Baylor)	.05

505 Major League Managers (Mike Hargrove, Rene Lachemann) .05
506 Major League Managers (Sparky Anderson, Art Howe) .10
507 Major League Managers (Hal McRae, Tommy Lasorda) .15
508 Major League Manager (Phil Garner, Felipe Alou) .05
509 Major League Managers (Tom Kelly, Jeff Torborg) .05
510 Major League Managers (Buck Showalter, Jim Fregosi) .05
511 Major League Managers (Tony LaRussa, Jim Leyland) .05
512 Major League Managers (Lou Piniella, Joe Torre) .05
513 Major League Managers (Toby Harrah, Jim Riggleman) .05
514 Major League Managers (Cito Gaston, Dusty Baker) .05
515 Greg Swindell .05
516 Alex Arias .05
517 Bill Pecota .05
518 *Benji Grigsby* (1992 Draft Pick) .15
519 David Howard .05
520 Charlie Hough .05
521 Kevin Flora .05
522 Shane Reynolds .10
523 *Doug Bochtler* .10
524 Chris Hoiles .05
525 Scott Sanderson .05
526 Mike Sharperson .05
527 Mike Fetters .05
528 Paul Quantrill .05
529 Top Prospects SS (Dave Silvestri, Chipper Jones, Benji Gil, Jeff Patzke) 2.00
530 Sterling Hitchcock .05
531 Joe Millette .05
532 Tom Brunansky .05
533 Frank Castillo .05
534 Randy Knorr .05
535 Jose Oquendo .05
536 Dave Haas .05
537 Rockies Future Stars (Jason Hutchins, Ryan Turner) .15
538 Jimmy Baron (1992 Draft Pick) .10
539 Kerry Woodson .05
540 Ivan Calderon .05
541 Denis Boucher .05
542 Royce Clayton .10
543 Reggie Williams .05
544 Steve Decker .05
545 Dean Palmer .05
546 Hal Morris .05
547 *Ryan Thompson* .10
548 Lance Blankenship .05
549 Hensley Meulens .05
550 Scott Radinsky .05
551 *Eric Young* .25
552 Jeff Blauser .05
553 Andujar Cedeno .05
554 Arthur Rhodes .05
555 Terry Mulholland .05
556 Darryl Hamilton .05
557 Pedro Martinez .75
558 Marlins Future Stars (Ryan Whitman, Mark Skeels) .15
559 *Jamie Arnold* (1992 Draft Pick) .15
560 Zane Smith .05
561 Matt Nokes .05
562 Bob Zupcic .05
563 Shawn Boskie .05
564 Mike Timlin .05
565 Jerald Clark .05
566 Rod Brewer .05
567 Mark Carreon .05
568 Andy Benes .05
569 Shawn Barton .05
570 Tim Wallach .05
571 Dave Mlicki .05
572 Trevor Hoffman .10
573 John Patterson .05
574 DeShawn Warren (1992 Draft Pick) .15
575 Monty Fariss .05
576 Top Prospects OF (Darrell Sherman, Damon Buford, Cliff Floyd, Michael Moore) .15
577 Tim Costo .05
578 Dave Magadan .05
579 Rockies Future Stars (Neil Garret, Jason Bates) .15
580 Walt Weiss .05
581 Chris Haney .05
582 Shawn Abner .05
583 Marvin Freeman .05
584 Casey Candaele .05
585 Ricky Jordan .05
586 Jeff Tabaka .05
587 Manny Alexander .05
588 Mike Trombley .05
589 Carlos Hernandez .05
590 Cal Eldred .05
591 Alex Cole .05
592 Phil Plantier .05
593 Brett Merriman .05
594 Jerry Nielsen .05
595 Shawon Dunston .05
596 Jimmy Key .05
597 Gerald Perry .05
598 Rico Brogna .05
599 Marlins Future Stars (Clemente Nunez, Dan Robinson) .15
600 Bret Saberhagen .10
601 Craig Shipley .05
602 Henry Mercedes .05
603 Jim Thome .30
604 Rod Beck .05
605 Chuck Finley .05
606 J. Owens .05
607 Dan Smith .05
608 Bill Doran .05
609 Lance Parrish .05
610 Denny Martinez .05
611 Tom Gordon .05
612 Byron Mathews (1992 Draft Pick) .10
613 Joel Adamson .05
614 Brian Williams .05
615 Steve Avery .05
616 Top Prospects OF (Matt Mieske, Tracy Sanders, Midre Cummings, Ryan Freeburg) .15
617 Craig Lefferts .05
618 Tony Pena .05
619 Billy Spiers .05
620 Todd Benzinger .05
621 Rockies Future Stars (Mike Kotarski, Greg Boyd) .15
622 Ben Rivera .05
623 Al Martin .10
624 Sam Militello .05
625 Rick Aguilera .05
626 Danny Gladden .05
627 Andres Berumen .05
628 Kelly Gruber .05
629 Cris Carpenter .05
630 Mark Grace .15
631 Jeff Brantley .05
632 Chris Widger (1992 Draft Pick) .10
633 Russian Angels (Rodolf Razjigaev, Evgenyi Puchkov, Ilya Bogatyrev) .10
634 Mo Sanford .05
635 Albert Belle .40
636 Tim Teufel .05
637 Greg Myers .05
638 Brian Bohanon .05
639 Mike Bordick .05
640 Dwight Gooden .10
641 Marlins Future Stars (Pat Leahy, Gavin Baugh) .10
642 Milt Hill .05
643 Luis Aquino .05
644 Dante Bichette .15
645 Bobby Thigpen .05
646 Rich Scheid .05
647 Brian Sackinsky (1992 Draft Pick) .10
648 Ryan Hawblitzel .05
649 Tom Marsh .05
650 Terry Pendleton .05
651 *Rafael Bournigal* .10
652 Dave West .05
653 Steve Hosey .05
654 Gerald Williams .05
655 Scott Cooper .05
656 Gary Scott .05
657 Mike Harkey .05
658 Top Prospects OF (Jeromy Burnitz, Melvin Nieves, Rich Becker, Shon Walker) .25
659 Ed Sprague .05
660 Alan Trammell .05
661 Rockies Future Stars (Garvin Alston, Mike Case) .15
662 Donovan Osborne .05
663 Jeff Gardner .05
664 Calvin Jones .05
665 Darrin Fletcher .05
666 Glenallen Hill .05
667 Jim Rosenbohm (1992 Draft Pick) .10
668 Scott Lewis .05
669 Kip Yaughn .05
670 Julio Franco .05
671 Dave Martinez .05
672 Kevin Bass .05
673 Todd Van Poppel .10
674 Mark Gubicza .05
675 Tim Raines .10
676 Rudy Seanez .05
677 Charlie Leibrandt .05
678 Randy Milligan .05
679 Kim Batiste .05
680 Craig Biggio .25
681 Darren Holmes .05
682 John Candelaria .05
683 Marlins Future Stars (Jerry Stafford, Eddie Christian) .15
684 Pat Mahomes .05
685 Bob Walk .05
686 Russ Springer .05
687 Tony Sheffield (1992 Draft Picks) .10
688 Dwight Smith .05
689 Eddie Zosky .05
690 Bien Figueroa .05
691 Jim Tatum .05
692 Chad Kreuter .05
693 Rich Rodriguez .05
694 Shane Turner .05
695 Kent Bottenfield .05
696 Jose Mesa .05
697 *Darrell Whitmore* .10
698 Ted Wood .05
699 Chad Curtis .05
700 Nolan Ryan 1.50
701 Top Prospects C (Mike Piazza, Carlos Delgado, Brook Fordyce, Donnie Leshnock) 2.00
702 *Tim Pugh* .15
703 Jeff Kent .10
704 Rockies Future Stars (Jon Goodrich, Danny Figueroa) .15
705 Bob Welch .05
706 Sherard Clinkscales (1992 Draft Pick) .05
707 Donn Pall .05
708 Greg Olson .05
709 Jeff Juden .05
710 Mike Mussina .30
711 Scott Chiamparino .05
712 Stan Javier .05
713 John Doherty .05
714 Kevin Gross .05
715 Greg Gagne .05
716 Steve Cooke .05
717 Steve Farr .05
718 Jay Buhner .10
719 Butch Henry .05
720 David Cone .15
721 Rick Wilkins .05
722 Chuck Carr .05
723 *Kenny Felder* (1992 Draft Pick) .10
724 Guillermo Velasquez .05
725 Billy Hatcher .05
726 Marlins Future Stars (Mike Veneziale, Ken Kendrena) .15
727 Jonathan Hurst .05
728 Steve Frey .05
729 Mark Leonard .05
730 Charles Nagy .05
731 Donald Harris .05
732 Travis Buckley .05
733 Tom Browning .05
734 Anthony Young .05
735 Steve Shifflett .05
736 Jeff Russell .05
737 Wilson Alvarez .05
738 Lance Painter .05
739 Dave Weathers .05
740 Len Dykstra .05
741 Mike Devereaux .05
742 Top Prospects SP (Rene Arocha, Alan Embree), *(Tim Crabtree,* Brien Taylor) .20
743 Dave Landaker (1992 Draft Pick) .05
744 Chris George .05
745 Eric Davis .05
746 Rockies Future Stars *(Mark Strittmatter,* LaMarr Rogers) .15
747 Carl Willis .05
748 Stan Belinda .05
749 Scott Kamieniecki .05
750 Rickey Henderson .25
751 Eric Hillman .05
752 Pat Hentgen .05
753 Jim Corsi .05
754 Brian Jordan .10
755 Bill Swift .05
756 Mike Henneman .05
757 Harold Reynolds .05
758 Sean Berry .05
759 Charlie Hayes .05
760 Luis Polonia .05
761 Darrin Jackson .05
762 Mark Lewis .05
763 Rob Maurer .05
764 Willie Greene .05
765 Vince Coleman .05
766 Todd Revenig .05
767 Rich Ireland (1992 Draft Pick) .10
768 Mike MacFarlane .05
769 Francisco Cabrera .05
770 Robin Ventura .25
771 Kevin Ritz .05
772 Chito Martinez .05
773 Cliff Brantley .05
774 Curtis Leskanic .05
775 Chris Bosio .05
776 Jose Offerman .05
777 Mark Guthrie .05
778 Don Slaught .05
779 Rich Monteleone .05
780 Jim Abbott .10
781 Jack Clark .05
782 Marlins Future Stars (Rafael Mendoza, Dan Roman) .15
783 Heathcliff Slocumb .05
784 Jeff Branson .05
785 Kevin Brown .15
786 Top Prospects RP (Mike Christopher, Ken Ryan, Aaron Taylor, Gus Gandarillas) .15
787 Mike Matthews (1992 Draft Pick) .05
788 Mackey Sasser .05
789 Jeff Conine .10
790 George Bell .05
791 Pat Rapp .05
792 Joe Boever .05
793 Jim Poole .05
794 Andy Ashby .10
795 Deion Sanders .20
796 Scott Brosius .10
797 Brad Pennington (Coming Attraction) .10
798 Greg Blosser (Coming Attraction) .10
799 *Jim Edmonds* (Coming Attraction) 1.00
800 Shawn Jeter (Coming Attraction) .15
801 Jesse Levis (Coming Attraction) .05
802 Phil Clark (Coming Attraction) .10
803 Ed Pierce (Coming Attraction) .05
804 *Jose Valentin* (Coming Attraction) .20
805 Terry Jorgensen (Coming Attraction) .05
806 Mark Hutton (Coming Attraction) .05
807 Troy Neel (Coming Attraction) .10
808 Bret Boone (Coming Attraction) .20
809 Chris Colon (Coming Attraction) .05
810 *Domingo Martinez* (Coming Attraction) .10
811 Javier Lopez (Coming Attraction) .30
812 Matt Walbeck (Coming Attraction) .10
813 Dan Wilson (Coming Attraction) .10
814 Scooter Tucker (Coming Attraction) .10
815 *Billy Ashley* (Coming Attraction) .05
816 *Tim Laker* (Coming Attraction) .10
817 Bobby Jones (Coming Attraction) .10
818 Brad Brink (Coming Attraction) .05
819 William Pennyfeather (Coming Attraction) .05
820 Stan Royer (Coming Attraction) .10
821 Doug Brocail (Coming Attraction) .10
822 Kevin Rogers (Coming Attraction) .05
823 Checklist 397-528 .05
824 Checklist 541-691 .05
825 Checklist 692-825 .05

1993 Topps Gold

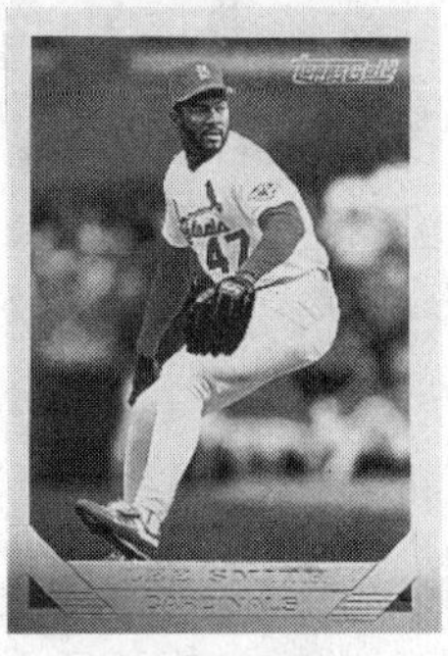

Expanding on the concept begun in 1992, Topps issued a "gold" version of each of its regular 1993 cards as a pack-age insert. One Gold card was found in each wax pack; three per rack-pack and five per jumbo cello pack. Ten Gold cards were included in each factory set. Identical in format to the regular-issue 1993 Topps cards, the Gold version replaces the black or white Topps logo on front with a "ToppsGold" logo in gold-foil. The color bars and angled strips beneath the player pho-to which carry the player and team ID on regular cards are replaced with a gold-foil ver-sion on the insert cards. Backs are identical to the regular cards. The six checklist cards in the regular issue were re-placed in the Gold version with cards of players who do not appear in the 1993 Topps set.

		MT
Complete Set (825):		70.00
Common Player:		.25
(Star cards valued at 3X-4X corresponding cards in regular 1993 Topps issue)		
394	Bernardo Brito	.25
395	Jim McNamara	.25
396	Rich Sauveur	.25
823	Keith Brown	.25
824	Russ McGinnis	.25
825	Mike Walker	.25

1993 Topps Black Gold

Randomly inserted in regu-lar 1993 Topps packs, as well as 10 per factory set, Black Gold cards are found in both single-player versions and "Winner" cards. The single-player cards feature an action photo set against a black back-ground and highlighted at top and bottom with gold foil. Backs have another player photo at left, again on a black back-ground. A career summary is printed in a blue box at right. A "Topps Black Gold" logo ap-pears at top-left, and the play-er's name is printed in gold foil in an art deco device at top-right. The Winner cards picture tiny versions of the Black Gold player cards for which they could be redeemed by mail.

		MT
Complete Set (44):		10.00
Common Player:		.25
Winner A (1-11):		.50
Winner B (12-22):		.50
Winner C (23-33):		.50
Winner D (34-44):		.50
Winner AB (1-22):		2.00
Winner CD (23-44):		2.00
Winner ABCD (1-44):		8.00
1	Barry Bonds	.75
2	Will Clark	.30
3	Darren Daulton	.25
4	Andre Dawson	.25
5	Delino DeShields	.25
6	Tom Glavine	.30
7	Marquis Grissom	.25
8	Tony Gwynn	.75
9	Eric Karros	.25
10	Ray Lankford	.25
11	Barry Larkin	.30

12	Greg Maddux	1.50
13	Fred McGriff	.30
14	Joe Oliver	.25
15	Terry Pendleton	.25
16	Bip Roberts	.25
17	Ryne Sandberg	.50
18	Gary Sheffield	.30
19	Lee Smith	.25
20	Ozzie Smith	.50
21	Andy Van Slyke	.25
22	Larry Walker	.40
23	Roberto Alomar	.40
24	Brady Anderson	.30
25	Carlos Baerga	.25
26	Joe Carter	.25
27	Roger Clemens	.75
28	Mike Devereaux	.25
29	Dennis Eckersley	.25
30	Cecil Fielder	.25
31	Travis Fryman	.25
32	Juan Gonzalez	.75
33	Ken Griffey Jr.	3.00
34	Brian Harper	.25
35	Pat Listach	.25
36	Kenny Lofton	.40
37	Edgar Martinez	.25
38	Jack McDowell	.25
39	Mark McGwire	2.50
40	Kirby Puckett	.65
41	Mickey Tettleton	.25
42	Frank Thomas	1.50
43	Robin Ventura	.35
44	Dave Winfield	.30

1993 Topps Traded

The 1993 Topps Traded baseball set features many players in their new uniforms as a result of trades, free agent signings and rookie call-ups. The set also features 35 expansion players from the Colorado Rockies and Florida Marlins, as well as 22 Team USA members exclusive to Topps. The 132-card set is packed in a color deluxe printed box.

		MT
Complete Set (132):		35.00
Common Player:		.05
1	Barry Bonds	.50
2	Rich Renteria	.05
3	Aaron Sele	.30
4	*Carlton Loewer* (USA)	.15
5	Erik Pappas	.05
6	*Greg McMichael*	.15
7	Freddie Benavides	.05
8	Kirk Gibson	.10
9	Tony Fernandez	.05
10	*Jay Gainer* (USA)	.20
11	Orestes Destrade	.05
12	*A.J. Hinch* (USA)	1.50
13	Bobby Munoz	.05
14	Tom Henke	.05
15	Rob Butler	.05
16	Gary Wayne	.05
17	David McCarty	.15
18	Walt Weiss	.05
19	*Todd Helton* (USA)	18.00
20	Mark Whiten	.05
21	Ricky Gutierrez	.15
22	*Dustin Hermanson* (USA)	1.00
23	*Sherman Obando*	.10
24	Mike Piazza	3.00
25	Jeff Russell	.05
26	Jason Bere	.15
27	*Jack Voight*	.10
28	Chris Bosio	.05
29	Phil Hiatt	.15
30	*Matt Beaumont* (USA)	.10
31	Andres Galarraga	.40
32	Greg Swindell	.05
33	Vinny Castilla	.15
34	*Pat Clougherty* (USA)	.10
35	Greg Briley	.05
36	Dallas Green, Davey Johnson	.05
37	Tyler Green	.10
38	Craig Paquette	.05
39	Danny Sheaffer	.05
40	Jim Converse	.05
41	Terry Harvey	.05
42	Phil Plantier	.10
43	*Doug Saunders*	.10
44	Benny Santiago	.05
45	*Dante Powell* (USA)	1.00
46	Jeff Parrett	.05
47	Wade Boggs	.50
48	Paul Molitor	.50
49	Turk Wendell	.05
50	David Wells	.10
51	Gary Sheffield	.25
52	Kevin Young	.15
53	Nelson Liriano	.05
54	Greg Maddux	1.50
55	Derek Bell	.10
56	*Matt Turner*	.20
57	*Charlie Nelson* (USA)	.10
58	Mike Hampton	.05
59	*Troy O'Leary*	1.50
60	Benji Gil	.15
61	*Mitch Lyden*	.15
62	J.T. Snow	.25
63	Damon Buford	.10
64	Gene Harris	.05
65	Randy Myers	.05
66	Felix Jose	.05
67	*Todd Dunn* (USA)	.10
68	Jimmy Key	.05
69	Pedro Castellano	.05
70	*Mark Merila* (USA)	.10
71	Rich Rodriguez	.05
72	Matt Mieske	.05
73	Pete Incaviglia	.05
74	Carl Everett	.25
75	Jim Abbott	.15
76	Luis Aquino	.05
77	*Rene Arocha*	.15
78	*Jon Shave*	.10
79	*Todd Walker* (USA)	4.00
80	Jack Armstrong	.05
81	Jeff Richardson	.05
82	Blas Minor	.05
83	Dave Winfield	.25
84	Paul O'Neill	.25
85	*Steve Reich* (USA)	.10
86	Chris Hammond	.05
87	*Hilly Hathaway*	.10
88	Fred McGriff	.25
89	*Dave Telgheder*	.10
90	*Richie Lewis*	.15
91	Brent Gates	.10
92	Andre Dawson	.15
93	*Andy Barkett* (USA)	.10
94	Doug Drabek	.05
95	Joe Klink	.05
96	Willie Blair	.05
97	*Danny Graves* (USA)	.10
98	Pat Meares	.05
99	Mike Lansing	.10
100	*Marcos Armas*	.10
101	*Darren Grass* (USA)	.10
102	Chris Jones	.05
103	*Ken Ryan*	.15
104	Ellis Burks	.10
105	Bobby Kelly	.05
106	Dave Magadan	.05
107	*Paul Wilson* (USA)	.40
108	Rob Natal	.05
109	Paul Wagner	.05
110	Jeromy Burnitz	.25
111	Monty Fariss	.05
112	Kevin Mitchell	.05
113	*Scott Pose*	.15
114	Dave Stewart	.05
115	*Russ Johnson* (USA)	.25
116	Armando Reynoso	.05
117	Geronimo Berroa	.05
118	*Woody Williams*	.25
119	*Tim Bogar*	.15
120	*Bob Scafa* (USA)	.15
121	Henry Cotto	.05
122	Gregg Jefferies	.10
123	Norm Charlton	.05
124	*Bret Wagner* (USA)	.05
125	David Cone	.25
126	Daryl Boston	.05
127	Tim Wallach	.05
128	*Mike Martin* (USA)	.10
129	*John Cummings*	.15
130	Ryan Bowen	.05
131	*John Powell* (USA)	.20
132	Checklist 1	.05

1993 Topps Colorado Rockies Inaugural Year

To mark the team's inaugural year in the Major Leagues, Topps produced a special run of 10,000 of its 1993 factory sets in which each card was embossed with a special gold seal incorporating the Rockies logo. Sets sold for $100 at the team's normal souvenir outlets. The factory sets were sealed with a sticker featuring the inaugural year logo.

	MT
Complete Set (825):	100.00
Common Player:	.50
(Star cards valued at 10X-15X the same card in regular 1993 Topps)	

1993 Topps Florida Marlins Inaugural Year

To commemorate the team's inaugural year in the Major Leagues, Topps produced a special edition of 6,000 of its 1993 factory sets in which every card was embossed with a special gold seal incorporating the Marlins logo. The sets were sold for $100 at the team's normal souvenir outlets. Factory sets are sealed with a sticker incorporating the inaugural year logo.

	MT
Complete Set (825):	100.00
Common Player:	.50
(Star players 10X to 20X same card in regular 1993 Topps)	

1993 Topps Full Shot Super

Just as rivals Upper Deck and Donruss did, Topps issued a set of 21 oversized cards (3-1/2" x 5") that was available in retail outlets in packages that contained one of the large cards and two packs of regular issue Topps cards from the same year. The Topps Full Shot cards feature many of the top players in the game, and unlike the Upper Deck oversized cards, the Topps cards were not enlarged versions of existing cards but rather photos and a design that appeared only in this format.

		MT
Complete Set (21):		100.00
Common Player:		3.00
1	Frank Thomas	7.50
2	Ken Griffey, Jr.	12.00
3	Barry Bonds	7.50
4	Juan Gonzalez	7.50
5	Roberto Alomar	5.00
6	Mike Piazza	8.00
7	Tony Gwynn	9.00
8	Jeff Bagwell	7.50
9	Tim Salmon	4.00
10	John Olerud	4.00
11	Cal Ripken, Jr.	10.00
12	David McCarty	3.00
13	Darren Daulton	3.00
14	Carlos Baerga	3.00
15	Roger Clemens	6.00
16	John Kruk	3.00
17	Barry Larkin	4.00
18	Gary Sheffield	5.00
19	Tom Glavine	4.00
20	Andres Galarraga	4.00
21	Fred McGriff	5.00

1993 Topps Magazine Jumbo Rookies

The final four issues of Topps' Magazine in 1993 substituted a 5" x 7" enlargement of a player's Topps rookie card in place of four of the standard-size inserts found previously. The jumbo rookie cards are identical, front and back, to the original rookie cards but carry a reprint notice on front. In an attempt to increase sales to subscribers and at the newsstands, the stars pictured autographed 100 of their cards to be randomly bound into the magazine.

		MT
Complete Set (4):		15.00
Common Player:		2.00
(1)	Dennis Eckersley (1976 Topps)	2.00
(2)	Dave Winfield (1974 Topps)	3.00
(3)	George Brett (1975 Topps)	4.00
(4)	Jerry Koosman, Nolan Ryan (1968 Topps)	6.00

1993 Topps/R&N China Nolan Ryan

Thin porcelain versions of a dozen of Nolan Ryan's Topps cards from 1968-92 were produced for sale as "The Nolan Ryan Collector's Edition." The cards are faithfully reproduced, front and back, in slightly larger than 2-1/2" x 3-1/2" format on thin china plates. Issue price was about $20 each.

	MT
Complete Set (12):	250.00
Common Card:	20.00
1968 Nolan Ryan, Jerry Koosman (Rookie Stars)	30.00
1969 Nolan Ryan	20.00
1972 Nolan Ryan	20.00
1974 Nolan Ryan	20.00
1975 Nolan Ryan	20.00
1978 Nolan Ryan	20.00
1980 Nolan Ryan	20.00
1982 Nolan Ryan (Highlight)	20.00
1985 Nolan Ryan (Record Breaker)	20.00
1986 Nolan Ryan	20.00
1990 Nolan Ryan	20.00
1992 Nolan Ryan	20.00

1993 Topps/R&N China Nolan Ryan Commemorative Series

Thin porcelain versions of eight of Nolan Ryan's Topps cards from 1968-93 were produced for sale as "The Nolan Ryan Commemorative Edition," honoring his all-time strikeout record. The cards are faithfully reproduced, front and back, in slightly larger than 2-1/2" x 3-1/2" format on thin china plates. Issue price was about $15-20 each. Cards were produced in a serially numbered edition of 10,000 apiece.

		MT
Complete Set (8):		100.00
Common Card:		15.00
(1)	Nolan Ryan, Jerry Koosman (1968 #177)	20.00
(2)	Nolan Ryan (1989 #530)	15.00
(3)	Nolan Ryan (1990 #1)	15.00
(4)	Nolan Ryan (1990 #2)	15.00
(5)	Nolan Ryan (1990 #3)	15.00
(6)	Nolan Ryan (1990 #4)	15.00
(7)	Nolan Ryan (1990 #5)	15.00
(8)	Nolan Ryan (1993 #700)	15.00

Player names in *Italic* type indicate a rookie card.

1994 Topps Preview

Two different versions of this nine-card set exist. A cello-wrapped version, designated (a) in the checklist, was given away to dealers and the hobby press. A second version, designated (b), was included in 1993 Topps factory sets. It is currently unknown which version, if either, will become more valuable due to demand and perceived scarcity. Both versions are similar to the regular-issue '94 Topps cards, except for the sample notation on back.

	MT
Complete Set (a) (9):	7.50
Complete Set (b) (9):	7.50
Common Player (a):	.25
Common Player (b):	.25
2a Barry Bonds (vertical format)	1.50
2b Barry Bonds (horizontal)	1.50
6a Jeff Tackett (full bat label visible)	.25
6b Jeff Tackett (partial bat label)	.25
34a Juan Gonzalez (green triangle behind "Juan")	1.50
34b Juan Gonzalez (brown triangle)	1.50
225a Matt Williams (green triangle behind "Matt")	.50
225b Matt Williams (blue triangle)	.50
294a Carlos Quintana (team/position yellow)	.25
294b Carlos Quintana (team/position black)	.25
331a Ken Lofton (team/position white)	.75
331b Ken Lofton (team/position black)	.75
390a Wade Boggs (team/position yellow)	.75
390b Wade Boggs (team/position black)	.75
397a George Brett (vertical format)	1.50
397b George Brett (horizontal)	1.50
700a Nolan Ryan (vertical format)	2.50
700b Nolan Ryan (horizontal)	2.50

1994 Topps

Once again released in two series of 396 cards each, Topps' basic baseball issue for 1994 offers a standard mix of regular player cards, Future Stars, multi-player rookie cards and double-header All-Star cards. On most cards the player photo on front is framed in a home-plate shaped design. The player's name appears in script beneath the photo and a team color-coded strip at bottom carries the team name and position designation. On back is a player photo, a red box at top with biographical details and a marbled panel which carries the stats and a career highlight. Cards are UV coated on each side. Inserts include a gold-foil enhanced parallel card in every pack, plus random Black Gold cards.

	MT
Complete Set (792):	30.00
Complete Factory Set (808):	60.00
Common Player:	.05
Complete Gold Set (792):	75.00
Golds: 1.5x to 3x	
Series 1 or 2 Wax Box:	18.00
1 Mike Piazza (All-Star Rookie)	1.00
2 Bernie Williams	.40
3 Kevin Rogers	.05
4 Paul Carey (Future Star)	.10
5 Ozzie Guillen	.05
6 Derrick May	.05
7 Jose Mesa	.05
8 Todd Hundley	.05
9 Chris Haney	.05
10 John Olerud	.20
11 Andujar Cedeno	.05
12 John Smiley	.05
13 Phil Plantier	.05
14 Willie Banks	.05
15 Jay Bell	.05
16 Doug Henry	.05
17 Lance Blankenship	.05
18 Greg Harris	.05
19 Scott Livingstone	.05
20 Bryan Harvey	.05
21 Wil Cordero (All-Star Rookie)	.10
22 Roger Pavlik	.05
23 Mark Lemke	.05
24 Jeff Nelson	.05
25 Todd Zeile	.05
26 Billy Hatcher	.05
27 Joe Magrane	.05
28 Tony Longmire (Future Star)	.10
29 Omar Daal	.05
30 Kirt Manwaring	.05
31 Melido Perez	.05
32 Tim Hulett	.05
33 Jeff Schwarz	.05
34 Nolan Ryan	1.00
35 Jose Guzman	.05
36 Felix Fermin	.05
37 Jeff Innis	.05
38 Brent Mayne	.05
39 *Huck Flener*	.05
40 Jeff Bagwell	.50
41 Kevin Wickander	.05
42 Ricky Gutierrez	.05
43 Pat Mahomes	.05
44 Jeff King	.05
45 Cal Eldred	.05
46 Craig Paquette	.05
47 Richie Lewis	.05
48 Tony Phillips	.05
49 Armando Reynoso	.05
50 Moises Alou	.20
51 Manuel Lee	.05
52 Otis Nixon	.05
53 Billy Ashley (Future Star)	.10
54 Mark Whiten	.05
55 Jeff Russell	.05
56 Chad Curtis	.05
57 Kevin Stocker	.05
58 Mike Jackson	.05
59 Matt Nokes	.05
60 Chris Bosio	.05
61 Damon Buford	.05
62 Tim Belcher	.05
63 Glenallen Hill	.05
64 Bill Wertz	.05
65 Eddie Murray	.25
66 Tom Gordon	.05
67 Alex Gonzalez (Future Star)	.15
68 Eddie Taubensee	.05
69 Jacob Brumfield	.05
70 Andy Benes	.05
71 Rich Becker (Future Star)	.10
72 Steve Cooke (All-Star Rookie)	.05
73 Billy Spiers	.05
74 Scott Brosius	.10
75 Alan Trammell	.05
76 Luis Aquino	.05
77 Jerald Clark	.05
78 Mel Rojas	.05
79 OF Prospects (Billy Masse, Stanton Cameron, Tim Clark, Craig McClure)	.15
80 Jose Canseco	.50
81 Greg McMichael (All-Star Rookie)	.05
82 Brian Turang	.05
83 Tom Urban	.05
84 Garret Anderson (Future Star)	.15
85 Tony Pena	.05
86 Ricky Jordan	.05
87 Jim Gott	.05
88 Pat Kelly	.05
89 Bud Black	.05
90 Robin Ventura	.20
91 Rick Sutcliffe	.05
92 Jose Bautista	.05
93 Bob Ojeda	.05
94 Phil Hiatt	.05
95 Tim Pugh	.05
96 Randy Knorr	.05
97 Todd Jones (Future Star)	.05
98 Ryan Thompson	.05
99 Tim Mauser	.05
100 Kirby Puckett	.75
101 Mark Dewey	.05
102 B.J. Surhoff	.05
103 Sterling Hitchcock	.05
104 Alex Arias	.05
105 David Wells	.10
106 Daryl Boston	.05
107 Mike Stanton	.05
108 Gary Redus	.05
109a Delino DeShields (red "Expos, 2B")	.15
109b Delino DeShields (yellow "Expos, 2B")	.05
110 Lee Smith	.05
111 Greg Litton	.05
112 Frank Rodriguez (Future Star)	.10
113 Russ Springer	.05
114 Mitch Williams	.05
115 Eric Karros	.15
116 Jeff Brantley	.05
117 Jack Voight	.05
118 Jason Bere	.10
119 Kevin Roberson	.10
120 Jimmy Key	.05
121 Reggie Jefferson	.05
122 Jeremy Burnitz	.15
123 Billy Brewer (Future Star)	.05
124 Willie Canate	.05
125 Greg Swindell	.05
126 Hal Morris	.05
127 Brad Ausmus	.05
128 George Tsamis	.05
129 Denny Neagle	.05
130 Pat Listach	.05
131 Steve Karsay	.05
132 Bret Barberie	.05
133 Mark Leiter	.05
134 Greg Colbrunn	.05
135 David Nied	.05
136 Dean Palmer	.05
137 Steve Avery	.05
138 Bill Haselman	.05
139 Tripp Cromer (Future Star)	.10
140 Frank Viola	.05
141 Rene Gonzales	.05
142 Curt Schilling	.15
143 Tim Wallach	.05
144 Bobby Munoz	.05
145 Brady Anderson	.10
146 Rod Beck	.05
147 Mike LaValliere	.05
148 Greg Hibbard	.05
149 Kenny Lofton	.40
150 Dwight Gooden	.10
151 Greg Gagne	.05
152 Ray McDavid (Future Star)	.10
153 Chris Donnels	.05
154 Dan Wilson	.05
155 Todd Stottlemyre	.10
156 David McCarty	.05
157 Paul Wagner	.05
158 SS Prospects (Orlando Miller, Brandon Wilson, Derek Jeter, Mike Neal)	1.50
159 Mike Fetters	.05
160 Scott Lydy	.05
161 Darrell Whitmore	.05
162 Bob MacDonald	.05
163 Vinny Castilla	.10
164 Denis Boucher	.05
165 Ivan Rodriguez	.50
166 Ron Gant	.10
167 Tim Davis	.05
168 Steve Dixon	.05
169 Scott Fletcher	.05
170 Terry Mulholland	.05
171 Greg Myers	.05
172 Brett Butler	.05
173 Bob Wickman	.05
174 Dave Martinez	.05
175 Fernando Valenzuela	.05
176 Craig Grebeck	.05
177 Shawn Boskie	.05
178 Albie Lopez	.05
179 Butch Huskey (Future Star)	.15
180 George Brett	.50
181 Juan Guzman	.05
182 Eric Anthony	.05
183 Bob Dibble	.05
184 Craig Shipley	.05
185 Kevin Tapani	.05
186 Marcus Moore	.05
187 Graeme Lloyd	.05
188 Mike Bordick	.05
189 Chris Hammond	.05
190 Cecil Fielder	.05
191 Curtis Leskanic	.05
192 Lou Frazier	.05
193 Steve Dreyer	.05
194 Javier Lopez (Future Star)	.25
195 Edgar Martinez	.05
196 Allen Watson	.10
197 John Flaherty	.05
198 Kurt Stillwell	.05
199 Danny Jackson	.05
200 Cal Ripken, Jr.	1.50
201 Mike Bell (Draft Pick)	.05
202 *Alan Benes* (Draft Pick)	.25
203 Matt Farner (Draft Pick)	.05
204 *Jeff Granger* (Draft Pick)	.15
205 *Brooks Kieschnick* (Draft Pick)	.20
206 Jeremy Lee (Draft Pick)	.05
207 *Charles Peterson* (Draft Pick)	.05
208 Andy Rice (Draft Pick)	.05
209 *Billy Wagner* (Draft Pick)	.50
210 Kelly Wunsch (Draft Pick)	.15
211 Tom Candiotti	.05
212 Domingo Jean (Draft Pick)	.05
213 John Burkett	.05
214 George Bell	.05
215 Dan Plesac	.05
216 Manny Ramirez (Future Star)	1.00
217 Mike Maddux	.05
218 Kevin McReynolds	.05
219 Pat Borders	.05
220 Doug Drabek	.05
221 Larry Luebbers	.05
222 Trevor Hoffman	.10
223 Pat Meares	.05
224 Danny Miceli (Future Star)	.10
225 Greg Vaughn	.15
226 Scott Hemond	.05
227 Pat Rapp	.05
228 Kirk Gibson	.05
229 Lance Painter	.05
230 Larry Walker	.40
231 Benji Gil (Future Star)	.10
232 Mark Wohlers	.05
233 Rich Amaral	.05
234 Erik Pappas	.05
235 Scott Cooper	.05
236 Mike Butcher	.05
237 OF Prospects (*Curtis Pride*, Shawn Green, Mark Sweeney, Eddie Davis)	.50
238 Kim Batiste	.05
239 Paul Assenmacher	.05
240 Will Clark	.25
241 Jose Offerman	.05
242 Todd Frohwirth	.05
243 Tim Raines	.10
244 Rick Wilkins	.05
245 Bret Saberhagen	.05
246 Thomas Howard	.05
247 Stan Belinda	.05
248 Rickey Henderson	.30
249 Brian Williams	.05
250 Barry Larkin	.20
251 Jose Valentin (Future Star)	.05
252 Lenny Webster	.05
253 Blas Minor	.05
254 Tim Teufel	.05
255 Bobby Witt	.05
256 Walt Weiss	.05
257 Chad Kreuter	.05
258 Roberto Mejia	.05
259 Cliff Floyd (Future Star)	.15
260 Julio Franco	.05
261 Rafael Belliard	.05
262 Marc Newfield	.05
263 Gerald Perry	.05
264 Ken Ryan	.05
265 Chili Davis	.05
266 Dave West	.05
267 Royce Clayton	.05
268 Pedro Martinez	.50
269 Mark Hutton	.05
270 Frank Thomas	.75
271 Brad Pennington	.05
272 Mike Harkey	.05
273 Sandy Alomar	.15
274 Dave Gallagher	.05
275 Wally Joyner	.10
276 Ricky Trlicek	.05
277 Al Osuna	.05
278 Calvin Reese (Future Star)	.15
279 Kevin Higgins	.05
280 Rick Aguilera	.05
281 Orlando Merced	.05
282 Mike Mohler	.05
283 John Jaha	.10
284 Robb Nen	.05
285 Travis Fryman	.10
286 Mark Thompson (Future Star)	.05
287 Mike Lansing (All-Star Rookie)	.10
288 Craig Lefferts	.05
289 Damon Berryhill	.05
290 Randy Johnson	.30
291 Jeff Reed	.05
292 Danny Darwin	.05
293 J.T. Snow (All-Star Rookie)	.10
294 Tyler Green	.05
295 Chris Hoiles	.05
296 Roger McDowell	.05
297 Spike Owen	.05
298 Salomon Torres (Future Star)	.05
299 Wilson Alvarez	.05
300 Ryne Sandberg	.40
301 Derek Lilliquist	.05
302 Howard Johnson	.05
303 Greg Cadaret	.05
304 Pat Hentgen	.05
305 Craig Biggio	.20
306 Scott Service	.05
307 Melvin Nieves	.05
308 Mike Trombley	.05
309 Carlos Garcia (All-Star Rookie)	.05
310 Robin Yount	.35
311 Marcos Armas	.05
312 Rich Rodriguez	.05
313 Justin Thompson (Future Star)	.05
314 Danny Sheaffer	.05
315 Ken Hill	.05
316 P Propsects (*Chad Ogea*), (*Duff Brumley*, *Terrell Wade*), (*Chris Michalak*)	.25
317 Cris Carpenter	.05
318 Jeff Blauser	.05
319 Ted Power	.05
320 Ozzie Smith	.40
321 John Dopson	.05
322 Chris Turner	.05
323 Pete Incaviglia	.05
324 Alan Mills	.05
325 Jody Reed	.05
326 Rich Monteleone	.05
327 Mark Carreon	.05
328 Donn Pall	.05
329 Matt Walbeck (Future Star)	.05
330 Charles Nagy	.05
331 Jeff McKnight	.05
332 Jose Lind	.05
333 Mike Timlin	.05
334 Doug Jones	.05
335 Kevin Mitchell	.05
336 Luis Lopez	.05
337 Shane Mack	.05
338 Randy Tomlin	.05
339 Matt Mieske	.05
340 Mark McGwire	2.00
341 Nigel Wilson (Future Star)	.05
342 Danny Gladden	.05
343 Mo Sanford	.05
344 Sean Berry	.05
345 Kevin Brown	.15
346 Greg Olson	.05
347 Dave Magadan	.05
348 Rene Arocha	.05
349 Carlos Quintana	.05
350 Jim Abbott	.05
351 Gary DiSarcina	.05
352 Ben Rivera	.05
353 Carlos Hernandez	.05
354 Darren Lewis	.05
355 Harold Reynolds	.05
356 Scott Ruffcorn (Future Star)	.10
357 Mark Gubicza	.05
358 Paul Sorrento	.05
359 Anthony Young	.05
360 Mark Grace	.20
361 Rob Butler	.05
362 Kevin Bass	.05
363 Eric Helfand (Future Star)	.05
364 Derek Bell	.05
365 Scott Erickson	.10
366 Al Martin	.05
367 Ricky Bones	.05
368 Jeff Branson	.05
369 3B Prospects (Luis Ortiz, David Bell, Jason Giambi, *George Arias*)	.40
370a Benny Santiago	.05
370b Mark McLemore (originally checklisted as #379)	.05

371 John Doherty .05
372 Joe Girardi .05
373 Tim Scott .05
374 Marvin Freeman .05
375 Deion Sanders .25
376 Roger Salkeld .05
377 Bernard Gilkey .05
378 Tony Fossas .05
379 (Not issued, see #370)
380 Darren Daulton .05
381 Chuck Finley .05
382 Mitch Webster .05
383 Gerald Williams .05
384 Frank Thomas, Fred McGriff (All Star) .30
385 Roberto Alomar, Robby Thompson (All Star) .20
386 Wade Boggs, Matt Williams (All Star) .15
387 Cal Ripken, Jr., Jeff Blauser (All Star) .40
388 Ken Griffey, Jr., Len Dykstra (All Star) .50
389 Juan Gonzalez, Dave Justice (All Star) .30
390 Albert Belle, Barry Bonds (All Star) .30
391 Mike Stanley, Mike Piazza (All Star) .40
392 Jack McDowell, Greg Maddux (All Star) .25
393 Jimmy Key, Tom Glavine (All Star) .10
394 Jeff Montgomery, Randy Myers (All Star) .05
395 Checklist 1 .05
396 Checklist 2 .05
397 Tim Salmon (All-Star Rookie) .25
398 Todd Benzinger .05
399 Frank Castillo .05
400 Ken Griffey, Jr. 2.00
401 John Kruk .05
402 Dave Telgheder .05
403 Gary Gaetti .05
404 Jim Edmonds .15
405 Don Slaught .05
406 Jose Oquendo .05
407 Bruce Ruffin .05
408 Phil Clark .05
409 Joe Klink .05
410 Lou Whitaker .05
411 Kevin Seitzer .05
412 Darrin Fletcher .05
413 Kenny Rogers .05
414 Bill Pecota .05
415 Dave Fleming .05
416 Luis Alicea .05
417 Paul Quantrill .05
418 Damion Easley .05
419 Wes Chamberlain .05
420 Harold Baines .10
421 Scott Radinsky .05
422 Rey Sanchez .05
423 Junior Ortiz .05
424 Jeff Kent .05
425 Brian McRae .05
426 Ed Sprague .05
427 Tom Edens .05
428 Willie Greene .05
429 Bryan Hickerson .05
430 Dave Winfield .25
431 Pedro Astacio .05
432 Mike Gallego .05
433 Dave Burba .05
434 Bob Walk .05
435 Darryl Hamilton .05
436 Vince Horsman .05
437 Bob Natal .05
438 Mike Henneman .05
439 Willie Blair .05
440 Denny Martinez .05
441 Dan Peltier .05
442 Tony Tarasco .05
443 John Cummings .05
444 Geronimo Pena .05
445 Aaron Sele .10
446 Stan Javier .05
447 Mike Williams .05
448 1B Prospects (Greg Pirkl, Roberto Petagine, D.J. Boston, Shawn Wooten) .10
449 Jim Poole .05
450 Carlos Baerga .05
451 Bob Scanlan .05
452 Lance Johnson .05
453 Eric Hillman .05
454 Keith Miller .05
455 Dave Stewart .05
456 Pete Harnisch .05
457 Roberto Kelly .05
458 Tim Worrell .05
459 Pedro Munoz .05
460 Orel Hershiser .05
461 Randy Velarde .05
462 Trevor Wilson .05
463 Jerry Goff .05
464 Bill Wegman .05
465 Dennis Eckersley .10
466 Jeff Conine (All-Star Rookie) .10
467 Joe Boever .05
468 Dante Bichette .15
469 Jeff Shaw .05
470 Rafael Palmeiro .25
471 *Phil Leftwich* .10
472 Jay Buhner .10
473 Bob Tewksbury .05
474 Tim Naehring .05
475 Tom Glavine .15
476 Dave Hollins .05
477 Arthur Rhodes .05
478 Joey Cora .05
479 Mike Morgan .05
480 Albert Belle .40
481 John Franco .05
482 Hipolito Pichardo .05
483 Duane Ward .05
484 Luis Gonzalez .10
485 Joe Oliver .05
486 Wally Whitehurst .05
487 Mike Benjamin .05
488 Eric Davis .05
489 Scott Kamieniecki .05
490 Kent Hrbek .05
491 *John Hope* .15
492 Jesse Orosco .05
493 Troy Neel .05
494 Ryan Bowen .05
495 Mickey Tettleton .05
496 Chris Jones .05
497 John Wetteland .05
498 David Hulse .05
499 Greg Maddux 1.00
500 Bo Jackson .10
501 Donovan Osborne .05
502 Mike Greenwell .05
503 Steve Frey .05
504 Jim Eisenreich .05
505 Robby Thompson .05
506 Leo Gomez .05
507 Dave Staton .05
508 Wayne Kirby (All-Star Rookie) .05
509 Tim Bogar .05
510 David Cone .15
511 Devon White .05
512 Xavier Hernandez .05
513 Tim Costo .05
514 Gene Harris .05
515 Jack McDowell .05
516 Kevin Gross .05
517 Scott Leius .05
518 Lloyd McClendon .05
519 *Alex Diaz* .10
520 Wade Boggs .25
521 Bob Welch .05
522 Henry Cotto .05
523 Mike Moore .05
524 Tim Laker .05
525 Andres Galarraga .20
526 Jamie Moyer .05
527 2B Prospects (Norberto Martin, Ruben Santana, Jason Hardtke, Chris Sexton) .10
528 Sid Bream .05
529 Erik Hanson .05
530 Ray Lankford .05
531 Rob Deer .05
532 Rod Correia .05
533 Roger Mason .05
534 Mike Devereaux .05
535 Jeff Montgomery .05
536 Dwight Smith .05
537 Jeremy Hernandez .05
538 Ellis Burks .05
539 Bobby Jones .15
540 Paul Molitor .40
541 Jeff Juden .05
542 Chris Sabo .05
543 Larry Casian .05
544 Jeff Gardner .05
545 Ramon Martinez .10
546 Paul O'Neill .15
547 Steve Hosey .05
548 Dave Nilsson .05
549 Ron Darling .05
550 Matt Williams .20
551 Jack Armstrong .05
552 Bill Krueger .05
553 Freddie Benavides .05
554 Jeff Fassero .05
555 Chuck Knoblauch .15
556 Guillermo Velasquez .05
557 Joel Johnston .05
558 Tom Lampkin .05
559 Todd Van Poppel .05
560 Gary Sheffield .15
561 Skeeter Barnes .05
562 Darren Holmes .05
563 John Vander Wal .05
564 Mike Ignasiak .05
565 Fred McGriff .20
566 Luis Polonia .05
567 Mike Perez .05
568 John Valentin .05
569 Mike Felder .05
570 Tommy Greene .05
571 David Segui .05
572 Roberto Hernandez .05
573 Steve Wilson .05
574 Willie McGee .05
575 Randy Myers .05
576 Darrin Jackson .05
577 Eric Plunk .05
578 Mike MacFarlane .05
579 Doug Brocail .05
580 Steve Finley .05
581 John Roper .05
582 Danny Cox .05
583 Chip Hale .05
584 Scott Bullett .05
585 Kevin Reimer .05
586 Brent Gates .05
587 Matt Turner .05
588 Rich Rowland .05
589 Kent Bottenfield .05
590 Marquis Grissom .10
591 Doug Strange .05
592 Jay Howell .05
593 Omar Vizquel .10
594 Rheal Cormier .05
595 Andre Dawson .15
596 Hilly Hathaway .05
597 Todd Pratt .05
598 Mike Mussina .20
599 Alex Fernandez .10
600 Don Mattingly .75
601 Frank Thomas (Measures of Greatness) .30
602 Ryne Sandberg (Measures of Greatness) .20
603 Wade Boggs (Measures of Greatness) .15
604 Cal Ripken, Jr. (Measures of Greatness) .75
605 Barry Bonds (Measures of Greatness) .25
606 Ken Griffey, Jr. (Measures of Greatness) 1.00
607 Kirby Puckett (Measures of Greatness) .25
608 Darren Daulton (Measures of Greatness) .05
609 Paul Molitor (Measures of Greatness) .15
610 Terry Steinbach .05
611 Todd Worrell .05
612 Jim Thome .40
613 Chuck McElroy .05
614 John Habyan .05
615 Sid Fernandez .05
616 OF Prospects (Eddie Zambrano, Glenn Murray, Chad Mottola, *Jermaine Allensworth*) .25
617 Steve Bedrosian .05
618 Rob Ducey .05
619 Tom Browning .05
620 Tony Gwynn .75
621 Carl Willis .05
622 Kevin Young .05
623 Rafael Novoa .05
624 Jerry Browne .05
625 Charlie Hough .05
626 Chris Gomez .05
627 Steve Reed .05
628 Kirk Rueter .05
629 Matt Whiteside .05
630 Dave Justice .25
631 Brad Holman .05
632 Brian Jordan .05
633 Scott Bankhead .05
634 Torey Lovullo .05
635 Len Dykstra .05
636 Ben McDonald .05
637 Steve Howe .05
638 Jose Vizcaino .05
639 Bill Swift .05
640 Darryl Strawberry .15
641 Steve Farr .05
642 Tom Kramer .05
643 Joe Orsulak .05
644 Tom Henke .05
645 Joe Carter .05
646 Ken Caminiti .15
647 Reggie Sanders .10
648 Andy Ashby .10
649 Derek Parks .05
650 Andy Van Slyke .05
651 Juan Bell .05
652 Roger Smithberg .05
653 Chuck Carr .05
654 Bill Gullickson .05
655 Charlie Hayes .05
656 Chris Nabholz .05
657 Karl Rhodes .05
658 Pete Smith .05
659 Bret Boone .05
660 Gregg Jefferies .10
661 Bob Zupcic .05
662 Steve Sax .05
663 Mariano Duncan .05
664 Jeff Tackett .05
665 Mark Langston .05
666 Steve Buechele .05
667 Candy Maldonado .05
668 Woody Williams .05
669 Tim Wakefield .05
670 Danny Tartabull .05
671 Charlie O'Brien .05
672 Felix Jose .05
673 Bobby Ayala .05
674 Scott Servais .05
675 Roberto Alomar .40
676 Pedro Martinez .05
677 Eddie Guardado .05
678 Mark Lewis .05
679 Jaime Navarro .05
680 Ruben Sierra .05
681 Rick Renteria .05
682 Storm Davis .05
683 Cory Snyder .05
684 Ron Karkovice .05
685 Juan Gonzalez .50
686 C Prospects (Chris Howard, Carlos Delgado, Jason Kendall, Paul Bako) .40
687 John Smoltz .15
688 Brian Dorsett .05
689 Omar Olivares .05
690 Mo Vaughn .30
691 Joe Grahe .05
692 Mickey Morandini .05
693 Tino Martinez .10
694 Brian Barnes .05
695 Mike Stanley .05
696 Mark Clark .05
697 Dave Hansen .05
698 Willie Wilson .05
699 Pete Schourek .05
700 Barry Bonds .45
701 Kevin Appier .05
702 Tony Fernandez .05
703 Darryl Kile .05
704 Archi Cianfrocco .05
705 Jose Rijo .05
706 Brian Harper .05
707 Zane Smith .05
708 Dave Henderson .05
709 Angel Miranda .05
710 Orestes Destrade .05
711 Greg Gohr .05
712 Eric Young .05
713 P Prospects (Todd Williams, Ron Watson, Kirk Bullinger, Mike Welch) .15
714 Tim Spehr .05
715 Hank Aaron (20th Anniversary #715) .50
716 Nate Minchey .05
717 Mike Blowers .05
718 Kent Mercker .05
719 Tom Pagnozzi .05
720 Roger Clemens .75
721 Eduardo Perez .05
722 Milt Thompson .05
723 Gregg Olson .05
724 Kirk McCaskill .05
725 Sammy Sosa 1.00
726 Alvaro Espinoza .05
727 Henry Rodriguez .05
728 Jim Leyritz .05
729 Steve Scarsone .05
730 Bobby Bonilla .10
731 Chris Gwynn .05
732 Al Leiter .10
733 Bip Roberts .05
734 Mark Portugal .05
735 Terry Pendleton .05
736 Dave Valle .05
737 Paul Kilgus .05
738 Greg Harris .05
739 *Jon Ratliff* (Draft Pick) .15
740 *Kirk Presley* (Draft Pick) .10
741 *Josue Estrada* (Draft Pick) .10
742 *Wayne Gomes* (Draft Pick) .20
743 *Pat Watkins* (Draft Pick) .15
744 *Jamey Wright* (Draft Pick) .20
745 *Jay Powell* (Draft Pick) .15
746 *Ryan McGuire* (Draft Pick) .15
747 *Marc Barcelo* (Draft Pick) .10
748 *Sloan Smith* (Draft Pick) .15
749 *John Wasdin* (Draft Pick) .15
750 Marc Valdes (Draft Pick) .10
751 *Dan Ehler* (Draft Pick) .10
752 *Andre King* (Draft Pick) .15
753 *Greg Keagle* (Draft Pick) .20
754 *Jason Myers* (Draft Pick) .10
755 *Dax Winslett* (Draft Pick) .10
756 *Casey Whitten* (Draft Pick) .15
757 *Tony Fuduric* (Draft Pick) .10
758 *Greg Norton* (Draft Pick) .10
759 *Jeff D'Amico* (Draft Pick) .10
760 *Ryan Hancock* (Draft Pick) .15
761 *David Cooper* (Draft Pick) .10
762 *Kevin Orie* (Draft Pick) .15
763 John O'Donoghue, Mike Oquist (Coming Attractions) .10
764 Cory Bailey, Scott Hatteberg (Coming Attractions) .10
765 Mark Holzemer, Paul Swingle (Coming Attractions) .10
766 James Baldwin, Rod Bolton (Coming Attractions) .15
767 *Jerry DiPoto,Julian Tavarez* (Coming Attractions) .20
768 Danny Bautista, Sean Bergman (Coming Attractions) .10
769 Bob Hamelin, Joe Vitiello (Coming Attractions) .20
770 Mark Kiefer, Troy O'Leary (Coming Attractions) .15
771 Denny Hocking, Oscar Munoz (Coming Attractions) .15
772 Russ Davis, Brien Taylor (Coming Attractions) .20
773 Kurt Abbott, Miguel Jimenez (Coming Attractions) .20
774 Kevin King, Eric Plantenberg (Coming Attractions) .15
775 Jon Shave, Desi Wilson (Coming Attractions) .15
776 Domingo Cedeno, Paul Spoljaric (Coming Attractions) .10
777 Chipper Jones, Ryan Klesko (Coming Attractions) .75
778 Steve Trachsel, Turk Wendell (Coming Attractions) .20
779 Johnny Ruffin, Jerry Spradlin (Coming Attractions) .10
780 Jason Bates, John Burke (Coming Attractions) .15
781 Carl Everett, Dave Weathers (Coming Attractions) .35
782 Gary Mota, James Mouton (Coming Attractions) .15
783 Raul Mondesi, Ben Van Ryn (Coming Attractions) .25
784 Gabe White, Rondell White (Coming Attractions) .25
785 Brook Fordyce, Bill Pulsipher (Coming Attractions) .20
786 Kevin Foster, Gene Schall (Coming Attractions) .10
787 Rich Aude, Midre Cummings (Coming Attractions) .15
788 Brian Barber, Richard Batchelor (Coming Attractions) .10
789 *Brian Johnson*, Scott Sanders (Coming Attractions) .10
790 Rikkert Faneyte, J.R. Phillips (Coming Attractions) .10
791 Checklist 3 .05
792 Checklist 4 .05

1994 Topps Gold

This premium parallel set was issued as inserts in virtually all forms of Topps packaging. Identical in all other ways to the regular Topps cards, the Gold version replaces the white or black Topps logo on front with a gold-foil "Topps Gold" logo, and prints either the player name or card title in gold foil. The four checklist cards from the regular issue are replaced with cards of players not found in the regular Topps set.

		MT
Complete Set (792):		75.00
Common Player:		.15
(Star cards valued at 4X-5X corresponding cards in regular Topps issue)		

1994 Topps Traded

Topps Traded consists of 132 cards featuring many top prospects and rookies, as well as traded veterans. Also included with this boxed set was an eight-card Topps Finest subset, including six MVPs and two Rookie of the Year cards. Regular cards have the same design as the previously released 1994 Topps set. Players are featured on a white bordered card, with their name across the bottom in white. "Anatomy of a Trade" is a two-card subset that includes Roberto Kelly/Deion Sanders and Pedro Martinez/Delino DeShields on a split, puzzle-like front. There is also a Prospect card, showcasing a top prospect from AAA, AA and A, as well as a top-rated draft pick. In addition, there are 12 Draft Pick cards included in the Topps Traded set. Finally, there are two cards that pay tribute to Ryne Sandberg, one in a Phillies uniform, one with the Cubs.

		MT
Complete Set (132):		60.00
Common Player:		.05
1	Paul Wilson (Draft Pick)	.25
2	Bill Taylor	.05
3	Dan Wilson	.10
4	Mark Smith	.05
5	Toby Borland	.10
6	Dave Clark	.05
7	Denny Martinez	.05
8	Dave Gallagher	.05
9	Josias Manzanillo	.05
10	Brian Anderson	.10
11	Damon Berryhill	.05
12	Alex Cole	.05
13	Jacob Shumate (Draft Pick)	.15
14	Oddibe McDowell	.05
15	Willie Banks	.05
16	Jerry Browne	.05
17	Donnie Elliott	.05
18	Ellis Burks	.05
19	Chuck McElroy	.05
20	Luis Polonia	.05
21	Brian Harper	.05
22	Mark Portugal	.05
23	Dave Henderson	.05
24	Mark Acre	.15
25	Julio Franco	.05
26	Darren Hall	.05
27	Eric Anthony	.05
28	Sid Fernandez	.05
29	Rusty Greer	5.00
30	Riccardo Ingram	.15
31	Gabe White	.10
32	Tim Belcher	.05
33	*Terrence Long* (Draft Pick)	.25
34	Mark Dalesandro	.10
35	Mike Kelly	.05
36	Jack Morris	.05
37	Jeff Brantley	.05
38	Larry Barnes (Draft Pick)	.15
39	Brian Hunter	.10
40	Otis Nixon	.05
41	Bret Wagner (Draft pick)	.05
42	Anatomy of a Trade (Pedro Martinez, Delino DeShields)	.25
43	Heathcliff Slocumb	.05
44	*Ben Grieve* (Draft Pick)	30.00
45	John Hudek	.15
46	Shawon Dunston	.05
47	Greg Colbrunn	.05
48	Joey Hamilton	.25
49	Marvin Freeman	.05
50	Terry Mulholland	.05
51	Keith Mitchell	.05
52	Dwight Smith	.05
53	Shawn Boskie	.05
54	*Kevin Witt* (Draft Pick)	1.50
55	Ron Gant	.15
56	1994 Prospects (Trenidad Hubbard, Jason Schmidt, Larry Sutton, Stephen Larkin)	1.00
57	Jody Reed	.05
58	Rick Helling	.05
59	John Powell (Draft Pick)	.10
60	Eddie Murray	.35
61	Joe Hall	.10
62	Jorge Fabregas	.10
63	Mike Mordecai	.10
64	Ed Vosberg	.05
65	Rickey Henderson	.25
66	Tim Grieve (Draft pick)	.15
67	Jon Lieber	.05
68	Chris Howard	.05
69	Matt Walbeck	.05
70	Chan Ho Park	4.00
71	Bryan Eversgerd	.10
72	John Dettmer	.05
73	Erik Hanson	.05
74	Mike Thurman (Draft pick)	.15
75	Bobby Ayala	.05
76	Rafael Palmeiro	.40
77	Bret Boone	.15
78	Paul Shuey (Future Star)	.10
79	Kevin Foster	.10
80	Dave Magadan	.05
81	Bip Roberts	.05
82	Howard Johnson	.05
83	Xavier Hernandez	.05
84	Ross Powell	.05
85	*Doug Million* (Draft Pick)	.05
86	Geronimo Berroa	.05
87	Mark Farris (Draft Pick)	.15
88	Butch Henry	.05
89	Junior Felix	.05
90	Bo Jackson	.10
91	Hector Carrasco	.10
92	Charlie O'Brien	.05
93	Omar Vizquel	.10
94	David Segui	.10
95	Dustin Hermanson (Draft Pick)	.50
96	Gar Finnvold	.05
97	Dave Stevens	.05
98	Corey Pointer (Draft Pick)	.15
99	Felix Fermin	.05
100	Lee Smith	.05
101	Reid Ryan (Draft Pick)	.15
102	Bobby Munoz	.05
103	Anatomy of a Trade (Deion Sanders, Roberto Kelly)	.10
104	Turner Ward	.05
105	William Van Landingham	.05
106	Vince Coleman	.05
107	Stan Javier	.05
108	Darrin Jackson	.05
109	C.J. Nitkowski (Draft Pick)	.10
110	Anthony Young	.05
111	Kurt Miller	.05
112	*Paul Konerko* (Draft Pick)	10.00
113	Walt Weiss	.05
114	Daryl Boston	.05
115	Will Clark	.40
116	Matt Smith (Draft Pick)	.05
117	Mark Leiter	.05
118	Gregg Olson	.05
119	Tony Pena	.05
120	Jose Vizcaino	.05
121	Rick White	.10
122	Rich Rowland	.05
123	Jeff Reboulet	.10
124	Greg Hibbard	.05
125	Chris Sabo	.05
126	Doug Jones	.05
127	Tony Fernandez	.05
128	Carlos Reyes	.10
129	Kevin Brown (Draft Pick)	.15
130	Commemorative (Ryne Sandberg)	1.00
131	Commemorative (Ryne Sandberg)	1.00
132	Checklist 1-132	.05

1994 Topps Traded Finest Inserts

Eight Topps Finest cards were included in the 1994 Topps Traded set. Cards picture the player on a blue and gold Finest card. Either Rookie of the Year or MVP is printed across the bottom on the opposite side of the player's name, indicating the player's candidacy for such an award in 1994. Backs offer a portrait photo, stats through the All-Star break and comments on the player's season to that point.

		MT
Complete Set (8):		9.00
Common Player:		1.50
1	Greg Maddux	1.50
2	Mike Piazza	2.00
3	Matt Williams	.25
4	Raul Mondesi	.50
5	Ken Griffey Jr.	3.00
6	Kenny Lofton	.50
7	Frank Thomas	1.50
8	Manny Ramirez	1.00

1994 Topps Black Gold

The Black Gold insert set returned for 1994 randomly included in all types of Topps packaging. Single Black Gold cards, as well as cards redeemable by mail for 11, 22 or 44 Black Gold cards, were produced. The basic single-player card features an action photo, the background of which has been almost completely blacked out. At top is the team name in black letters against a gold prismatic foil background. The player name at bottom is in the same gold foil. On back, bordered in white, is a background which fades from black at top to gray at the bottom and is gridded with white lines. To the left is another color player action photo. The Topps Black Gold logo and player name appear in gold foil; the latter printed on a simulated wooden board "hanging" from the top of the card. A second hanging plank has player stats and rankings from the 1993 season. The multi-card redemption cards comes in two versions. The type found in packs has all 11, 22 or 44 of the cards pictured on front in miniature and redemption details printed on back. A second version, returned with the single cards won, has on back a checklist and non-redemption notice. Stated odds of winning Black Gold cards were one in 72 packs for single cards; one in 180 packs for 11-card winners and one in 720 packs (one per foil-pack case) for a 22-card winner.

		MT
Complete Set (44):		25.00
Complete Series 1 (22):		15.00
Complete Series 2 (22):		10.00
Common Player:		.25
1	Roberto Alomar	.50
2	Carlos Baerga	.25
3	Albert Belle	.65
4	Joe Carter	.25
5	Cecil Fielder	.25
6	Travis Fryman	.25
7	Juan Gonzalez	.75
8	Ken Griffey, Jr.	4.00
9	Chris Hoiles	.25
10	Randy Johnson	.40
11	Kenny Lofton	.40
12	Jack McDowell	.25
13	Paul Molitor	.50
14	Jeff Montgomery	.25
15	John Olerud	.30
16	Rafael Palmeiro	.40
17	Kirby Puckett	1.00
18	Cal Ripken, Jr.	3.00
19	Tim Salmon	.40
20	Mike Stanley	.25
21	Frank Thomas	.75
22	Robin Ventura	.30
23	Jeff Bagwell	1.00
24	Jay Bell	.25
25	Craig Biggio	.35
26	Jeff Blauser	.25
27	Barry Bonds	.75
28	Darren Daulton	.25
29	Len Dykstra	.25
30	Andres Galarraga	.25
31	Ron Gant	.25
32	Tom Glavine	.30
33	Mark Grace	.40
34	Marquis Grissom	.25
35	Gregg Jefferies	.25
36	Dave Justice	.35
37	John Kruk	.25
38	Greg Maddux	1.50
39	Fred McGriff	.40
40	Randy Myers	.25
41	Mike Piazza	2.00
42	Sammy Sosa	2.00
43	Robby Thompson	.25
44	Matt Williams	.30
---	Winner A	.75
---	Winner B	.75
---	Winner C	.75
---	Winner D	.75
---	Winner A/B	1.00
---	Winner C/D	1.00
---	Winner A/B/C/D	1.00

1994 Topps Bilingual

Produced in a limited edition said to be 5,000 sets, this issue is a close parallel to the regular 1994 Topps baseball card issue. Each card is virtually identical to the regular Topps card except that backs are printed in English and Spanish. The set was test marketed in areas with a high percentage of Hispanic population and was also sold through Topps' Stadium Club. The bilingual edition was sold only in factory set form. A special feature of the set was the inclusion of 10 "Topps Leyendas/Legends" cards of former Latin stars.

		MT
Factory Set (792+10):		125.00
Common Player:		.50
(Star cards valued at 10X-20X corresponding cards in regular issue)		
Topps Leyendas/ Legends		
1	Felipe Alou	1.50
2	Ruben Amaro	.50
3	Luis Aparicio	4.00
4	Rod Carew	3.00
5	Chico Carrasquel	.75
6	Orlando Cepeda	3.00
7	Juan Marichal	3.00
8	Minnie Minoso	2.50
9	Cookie Rojas	.50
10	Luis Tiant	1.00

1994 Topps "1954" Archives

Marketed as "The Ultimate 1954 Series," the Archives set was a virtual reproduction of the popular 1954 Topps issue. Of the 250 cards in the original set 248 were included in the Archives release. Ted Williams, who was on cards #1 and 250 in the '54 set, was contractually prohibited by Upper Deck from appearing in the Archives issue. Eight "1954 Prospect" cards featuring future Hall of Famers and star players were appended to the reproduction cards to create a 256-card Archives issue. Cards were sold in 12-card packs, with one Gold card in each pack. There were 1,954 personally autographed cards of Henry Aaron inserted at random, along with cards that could be redeemed for genuine 1954 Topps cards and complete sets of Gold Archives cards. The Archives cards were produced in the now-standard 2-1/2" x 3-1/2" size, instead of the original 1954 dimensions of 2-5/8" x 3-3/4". That format allowed the Archives cards to have a white border at top which the originals lack. While the card backs identify the Archives issue, they do not specify a 1994 production date anywhere.

		MT
Complete Set (256):		60.00
Common Player:		.20
2	Gus Zernial	.20
3	Monte Irvin	.30
4	Hank Sauer	.20
5	Ed Lopat	.25
6	Pete Runnels	.20
7	Ted Kluszewski	.25
8	Bobby Young	.20

9	Harvey Haddix	.20
10	Jackie Robinson	1.00
11	Paul Smith	.20
12	Del Crandall	.20
13	Billy Martin	.35
14	Preacher Roe	.25
15	Al Rosen	.20
16	Vic Janowicz	.20
17	Phil Rizzuto	.40
18	Walt Dropo	.20
19	Johnny Lipon	.20
20	Warren Spahn	.30
21	Bobby Shantz	.20
22	Jim Greengrass	.20
23	Luke Easter	.20
24	Granny Hamner	.20
25	Harvey Kuenn	.20
26	Ray Jablonski	.20
27	Ferris Fain	.20
28	Paul Minner	.20
29	Jim Hegan	.20
30	Eddie Mathews	.30
31	Johnny Klippstein	.20
32	Duke Snider	.60
33	Johnny Schmitz	.20
34	Jim Rivera	.20
35	Junior Gilliam	.25
36	Hoyt Wilhelm	.30
37	Whitey Ford	.45
38	Eddie Stanky	.20
39	Sherman Lollar	.20
40	Mel Parnell	.20
41	Willie Jones	.20
42	Don Mueller	.20
43	Dick Groat	.20
44	Ned Garver	.20
45	Richie Ashburn	.35
46	Ken Raffensberger	.20
47	Ellis Kinder	.20
48	Billy Hunter	.20
49	Ray Murray	.20
50	Yogi Berra	.60
51	Johnny Lindell	.20
52	Vic Power	.20
53	Jack Dittmer	.20
54	Vern Stephens	.20
55	Phil Cavarretta	.20
56	Willie Miranda	.25
57	Luis Aloma	.20
58	Bob Wilson	.20
59	Gene Conley	.20
60	Frank Baumholtz	.20
61	Bob Cain	.20
62	Eddie Robinson	.25
63	Johnny Pesky	.20
64	Hank Thompson	.20
65	Bob Swift	.20
66	Ted Lepcio	.20
67	Jim Willis	.20
68	Sam Calderone	.20
69	Bud Podbielan	.20
70	Larry Doby	.40
71	Frank Smith	.20
72	Preston Ward	.20
73	Wayne Terwilliger	.20
74	Bill Taylor	.20
75	Fred Haney	.20
76	Bob Scheffing	.20
77	Ray Boone	.20
78	Ted Kazanski	.20
79	Andy Pafko	.20
80	Jackie Jensen	.25
81	Dave Hoskins	.20
82	Milt Bolling	.20
83	Joe Collins	.25
84	Dick Cole	.20
85	Bob Turley	.30
86	Billy Herman	.25
87	Roy Face	.20
88	Matt Batts	.20
89	Howie Pollet	.20
90	Willie Mays	2.00
91	Bob Oldis	.20
92	Wally Westlake	.20
93	Sid Hudson	.20
94	Ernie Banks	2.50
95	Hal Rice	.20
96	Charlie Silvera	.25
97	Jerry Lane	.20
98	Joe Black	.20
99	Bob Hofman	.20
100	Bob Keegan	.20
101	Gene Woodling	.25
102	Gil Hodges	.30
103	*Jim Lemon*	.20
104	Mike Sandlock	.20
105	Andy Carey	.25
106	Dick Kokos	.20
107	Duane Pillette	.20
108	Thornton Kipper	.20
109	Bill Bruton	.20
110	Harry Dorish	.20
111	Jim Delsing	.20
112	Bill Renna	.20
113	Bob Boyd	.20
114	Dean Stone	.20
115	"Rip" Repulski	.20
116	Steve Bilko	.20
117	Solly Hemus	.20
118	Carl Scheib	.20
119	Johnny Antonelli	.20
120	Roy McMillan	.20
121	Clem Labine	.25
122	Johnny Logan	.20
123	Bobby Adams	.20
124	Marion Fricano	.20
125	Harry Perkowski	.20
126	Ben Wade	.20
127	Steve O'Neill	.20
128	Hank Aaron	3.00
129	Forrest Jacobs	.20
130	Hank Bauer	.30
131	Reno Bertoia	.20
132	Tom Lasorda	1.25
133	Del Baker	.20
134	Cal Hogue	.20
135	Joe Presko	.20
136	Connie Ryan	.20
137	Wally Moon	.20
138	Bob Borkowski	.20
139	Ed & Johnny O'Brien	.25
140	Tom Wright	.20
141	Joe Jay	.20
142	Tom Poholsky	.20
143	Rollie Hemsley	.20
144	Bill Werle	.20
145	Elmer Valo	.20
146	Don Johnson	.20
147	John Riddle	.20
148	Bob Trice	.20
149	Jim Robertson	.20
150	Dick Kryhoski	.20
151	Alex Grammas	.20
152	Mike Blyzka	.20
153	Rube Walker	.20
154	Mike Fornieles	.20
155	Bob Kennedy	.20
156	Joe Coleman	.20
157	Don Lenhardt	.20
158	Peanuts Lowrey	.20
159	Dave Philley	.20
160	Red Kress	.20
161	John Hetki	.20
162	Herman Wehmeier	.20
163	Frank House	.20
164	Stu Miller	.20
165	Jim Pendleton	.20
166	Johnny Podres	.30
167	Don Lund	.20
168	Morrie Martin	.20
169	Jim Hughes	.20
170	Dusty Rhodes	.20
171	Leo Kiely	.20
172	Hal Brown	.20
173	Jack Harshman	.20
174	Tom Qualters	.20
175	Frank Leja	.25
176	Bob Keely	.20
177	Bob Milliken	.20
178	Bill Glynn	.20
179	Gair Allie	.20
180	Wes Westrum	.20
181	Mel Roach	.20
182	Chuck Harmon	.20
183	Earle Combs	.20
184	Ed Bailey	.20
185	Chuck Stobbs	.20
186	Karl Olson	.20
187	Heinie Manush	.20
188	Dave Jolly	.20
189	Bob Ross	.20
190	Ray Herbert	.20
191	*Dick Schofield*	.20
192	Cot Deal	.20
193	Johnny Hopp	.20
194	Bill Sarni	.20
195	Bill Consolo	.20
196	Stan Jok	.20
197	Schoolboy Rowe	.20
198	Carl Sawatski	.20
199	Rocky Nelson	.20
200	Larry Jansen	.20
201	Al Kaline	2.00
202	Bob Purkey	.20
203	Harry Brecheen	.20
204	Angel Scull	.20
205	Johnny Sain	.30
206	Ray Crone	.20
207	Tom Oliver	.20
208	Grady Hatton	.20
209	Charlie Thompson	.20
210	Bob Buhl	.20
211	Don Hoak	.25
212	Mickey Micelotta	.20
213	John Fitzpatrick	.20
214	Arnold Portocarrero	.20
215	Ed McGhee	.20
216	Al Sima	.20
217	Paul Schreiber	.20
218	Fred Marsh	.20
219	Charlie Kress	.20
220	Ruben Gomez	.20
221	Dick Brodowski	.20
222	Bill Wilson	.20
223	Joe Haynes	.20
224	Dick Weik	.20
225	Don Liddle	.20
226	Jehosie Heard	.20
227	Buster Mills	.20
228	Gene Hermanski	.20
229	Bob Talbot	.20
230	Bob Kuzava	.25
231	Roy Smalley	.20
232	Lou Limmer	.20
233	Augie Galan	.20
234	Jerry Lynch	.20
235	Vern Law	.20
236	Paul Penson	.20
237	Mike Ryba	.20
238	Al Aber	.20
239	Bill Skowron	.30
240	Sam Mele	.20
241	Bob Miller	.20
242	Curt Roberts	.20
243	Ray Blades	.20
244	Leroy Wheat	.20
245	Roy Sievers	.20
246	Howie Fox	.20
247	Eddie Mayo	.20
248	*Al Smith*	.20
249	Wilmer Mizell	.20
251	Roberto Clemente	3.00
252	Bob Grim	.25
253	Elston Howard	.30
254	Harmon Killebrew	1.00
255	Camilo Pascual	.20
256	Herb Score	.20
257	Bill Virdon	.20
258	Don Zimmer	.30

1994 Topps "1954" Archives Gold

Issued as a premium Insert at the rate of one per foil pack, gold versions of each of the cards in the 1954 Archives set differ from the regular cards only in that the team logo at top and player facsimile autograph on bottom are printed in gold foil. Redemption cards for complete Archives gold sets were also randomly inserted into Archives packs.

		MT
Complete Set (256):		150.00
Common Player:		.50
(Star cards valued at 5X-10X same cards in regular Archives series)		
128	Hank Aaron (autographed)	150.00

1994 Topps/R&N China Nolan Ryan Porcelain

The 27-year career of Nolan Ryan and his final regular-issue Topps card are remembered on this thin porcelain version of Ryan's card #34 (his uniform number) in the 1994 Topps baseball set. The 2-1/2" x 3-1/2" round-cornered card exactly replicates both the front and back of the original Topps card in full color. The edition was advertised as limited to 5,000; issue price was about $20 per piece.

		MT
34	Nolan Ryan	20.00

1995 Topps Pre-production

The "Baker's Dozen" version of Topps' 1994 factory baseball card set includes a 10-card pre-production sample of the company's 1995 issue. The sample features nine regular-issue cards and one of them in its Spectralite foil-printed version, as used on the Cyberstats insert cards. Cards are virtually identical to the regular '95 Topps except the backs have a "PP" prefix to the card number and "PRE-PRODUCTION SAMPLE" instead of 1994 season stats.

		MT
Complete Set (9):		19.00
Complete Set, Cyberstats (9):		72.00
1	Larry Walker	1.00
1	Larry Walker (Spectralite)	4.00
2	Mike Piazza	5.00
2	Mike Piazza (Spectralite)	20.00
3	Greg Vaughn	2.50
3	Greg Vaughn (Spectralite)	4.00
4	Sandy Alomar Jr.	2.50
4	Sandy Alomar Jr. (Spectralite)	4.00
5	Travis Fryman	1.00
5	Travis Fryman (Spectralite)	3.00
6	Ken Griffey Jr.	9.00
6	Ken Griffey Jr. (Spectralite)	35.00
7	Mike Devereaux	1.00
7	Mike Devereaux (Spectralite)	3.00
8	Roberto Hernandez	1.00
8	Roberto Hernandez (Spectralite)	3.00
9	Alex Fernandez	1.50
9	Alex Fernandez (Spectralite)	3.00

1995 Topps

Topps 1995 baseball arrived offering Cyberstats, which projected full-season statistics for the strike shortened year, as well as League Leaders and Stadium Club First Day Issue preproduction inserts. The entire Series I set was composed of 396 cards, including subsets like 1994 Draft Picks, Star Tracks, a Babe Ruth commemorative card and the Topps All-Stars, featuring two players per card at each position, as selected by Topps. Regular cards have a jagged white border around the color picture of the player, with his name in gold foil under the picture. Series II concluded the Cyberstats inserts and added 264 cards to the regular set. Subsets in Series II included a continuation of the Draft Picks from Series I, as well as two-player On Deck cards and four-player Prospects cards, arranged by position.

		MT
Complete Set (660):		40.00
Complete Series 1 (396):		20.00
Complete Series 2 (264):		20.00
Common Player:		.05
Series 1 or 2 Wax Box:		35.00
1	Frank Thomas	1.00
2	Mickey Morandini	.05
3a	Babe Ruth (100th Birthday, no gold "Topps" logo)	2.00
3b	Babe Ruth (100th Birthday, gold "Topps" logo)	2.00
4	Scott Cooper	.05
5	David Cone	.15
6	Jacob Shumate (Draft Pick)	.10
7	Trevor Hoffman	.10
8	Shane Mack	.05
9	Delino DeShields	.05
10	Matt Williams	.25
11	Sammy Sosa	1.50
12	Gary DiSarcina	.05
13	Kenny Rogers	.05
14	Jose Vizcaino	.05
15	Lou Whitaker	.05
16	Ron Darling	.05
17	Dave Nilsson	.05
18	Chris Hammond	.05
19	Sid Bream	.05
20	Denny Martinez	.05
21	Orlando Merced	.05
22	John Wetteland	.05
23	Mike Devereaux	.05
24	Rene Arocha	.05
25	Jay Buhner	.10
26	Darren Holmes	.05
27	Hal Morris	.05
28	*Brian Buchanan* (Draft Pick)	.15
29	Keith Miller	.05
30	Paul Molitor	.40
31	Dave West	.05
32	Tony Tarasco	.05
33	Scott Sanders	.05
34	Eddie Zambrano	.05
35	Ricky Bones	.05
36	John Valentin	.05
37	Kevin Tapani	.05
38	Tim Wallach	.05
39	Darren Lewis	.05
40	Travis Fryman	.10
41	Mark Leiter	.05
42	Jose Bautista	.05
43	Pete Smith	.05
44	Bret Barberie	.05
45	Dennis Eckersley	.10
46	Ken Hill	.05
47	Chad Ogea (Star Track)	.12
48	Pete Harnisch	.05
49	James Baldwin (Future Star)	.15
50	Mike Mussina	.30
51	Al Martin	.05
52	Mark Thompson (Star Track)	.05
53	Matt Smith (Draft Pick)	.10
54	Joey Hamilton (All Star Rookie)	.10
55	Edgar Martinez	.05
56	John Smiley	.05
57	Rey Sanchez	.05
58	Mike Timlin	.05
59	Ricky Bottalico (Star Track)	.10
60	Jim Abbott	.05
61	Mike Kelly	.05
62	Brian Jordan	.15
63	Ken Ryan	.10
64	Matt Mieske	.05
65	Rick Aguilera	.05
66	Ismael Valdes	.05
67	Royce Clayton	.05
68	Junior Felix	.05
69	Harold Reynolds	.05
70	Juan Gonzalez	1.00
71	Kelly Stinnett	.05
72	Carlos Reyes	.05
73	Dave Weathers	.05
74	Mel Rojas	.05
75	Doug Drabek	.05
76	Charles Nagy	.05
77	Tim Raines	.10
78	Midre Cummings	.05
79	1B Prospects (Gene Schall), *(Scott Talanoa, Harold Williams, Ray Brown)*	.15
80	Rafael Palmeiro	.25
81	Charlie Hayes	.05
82	Ray Lankford	.15
83	Tim Davis	.05

84 *C.J. Nitkowski* (Draft Pick) .15
85 Andy Ashby .05
86 Gerald Williams .05
87 Terry Shumpert .05
88 Heathcliff Slocumb .05
89 Domingo Cedeno .05
90 Mark Grace .20
91 *Brad Woodall* (Star Track) .10
92 Gar Finnvold .05
93 Jaime Navarro .05
94 Carlos Hernandez .05
95 Mark Langston .05
96 Chuck Carr .05
97 Mike Gardiner .05
98 David McCarty .05
99 Cris Carpenter .05
100 Barry Bonds .60
101 David Segui .05
102 Scott Brosius .05
103 Mariano Duncan .05
104 Kenny Lofton .30
105 Ken Caminiti .20
106 Darrin Jackson .05
107 Jim Poole .05
108 Wil Cordero .05
109 Danny Miceli .05
110 Walt Weiss .05
111 Tom Pagnozzi .05
112 Terrence Long (Draft Pick) .05
113 Bret Boone .05
114 Daryl Boston .05
115 Wally Joyner .10
116 Rob Butler .05
117 Rafael Belliard .05
118 Luis Lopez .05
119 Tony Fossas .05
120 Len Dykstra .05
121 Mike Morgan .05
122 Denny Hocking .05
123 Kevin Gross .05
124 Todd Benzinger .05
125 John Doherty .05
126 Eduardo Perez .05
127 Dan Smith .05
128 Joe Orsulak .05
129 Brent Gates .05
130 Jeff Conine .10
131 Doug Henry .05
132 Paul Sorrento .05
133 Mike Hampton .05
134 Tim Spehr .05
135 Julio Franco .05
136 Mike Dyer .05
137 Chris Sabo .05
138 Rheal Cormier .05
139 Paul Konerko (Draft Pick) .75
140 Dante Bichette .15
141 Chuck McElroy .05
142 Mike Stanley .05
143 Bob Hamelin (All Star Rookie) .05
144 Tommy Greene .05
145 John Smoltz .15
146 Ed Sprague .05
147 Ray McDavid (Star Track) .10
148 Otis Nixon .05
149 Turk Wendell .05
150 Chris James .05
151 Derek Parks .05
152 Jose Offerman .05
153 Tony Clark (Future Star) .50
154 Chad Curtis .05
155 Mark Portugal .05
156 Bill Pulsipher (Future Star) .15
157 Troy Neel .05
158 Dave Winfield .15
159 Bill Wegman .05
160 Benny Santiago .05
161 Jose Mesa .05
162 Luis Gonzalez .10
163 Alex Fernandez .10
164 Freddie Benavides .05
165 Ben McDonald .05
166 Blas Minor .05
167 Bret Wagner (Draft Pick) .05
168 Mac Suzuki (Future Star) .10
169 Roberto Mejia .05
170 Wade Boggs .30
171 Calvin Reese (Future Star) .15
172 Hipolito Pichardo .05
173 Kim Batiste .05
174 Darren Hall .05
175 Tom Glavine .15
176 Phil Plantier .05
177 Chris Howard .05
178 Karl Rhodes .05
179 LaTroy Hawkins (Future Star) .15
180 Raul Mondesi (All Star Rookie) .40
181 Jeff Reed .05
182 Milt Cuyler .05
183 Jim Edmonds .15
184 Hector Fajardo .05
185 Jeff Kent .05
186 Wilson Alvarez .05
187 Geronimo Berroa .05
188 Billy Spiers .05
189 Derek Lilliquist .05
190 Craig Biggio .20
191 Roberto Hernandez .05
192 Bob Natal .05
193 Bobby Ayala .05
194 *Travis Miller* (Draft Pick) .20
195 Bob Tewksbury .05
196 Rondell White .15
197 Steve Cooke .05
198 Jeff Branson .05
199 Derek Jeter (Future Star) 2.00
200 Tim Salmon .25
201 Steve Frey .05
202 Kent Mercker .05
203 Randy Johnson .40
204 Todd Worrell .05
205 Mo Vaughn .30
206 Howard Johnson .05
207 John Wasdin (Future Star) .10
208 Eddie Williams .05
209 Tim Belcher .05
210 Jeff Montgomery .05
211 Kirt Manwaring .05
212 Ben Grieve (Draft Pick) 1.50
213 Pat Hentgen .05
214 Shawon Dunston .05
215 Mike Greenwell .05
216 Alex Diaz .05
217 Pat Mahomes .05
218 Dave Hanson .05
219 Kevin Rogers .05
220 Cecil Fielder .10
221 Andrew Lorraine (Star Track) .10
222 Jack Armstrong .05
223 Todd Hundley .15
224 Mark Acre .05
225 Darrell Whitmore .05
226 Randy Milligan .05
227 Wayne Kirby .05
228 Darryl Kile .05
229 Bob Zupcic .05
230 Jay Bell .05
231 Dustin Hermanson (Draft Pick) .15
232 Harold Baines .05
233 Alan Benes (Future Star) .15
234 Felix Fermin .05
235 Ellis Burks .05
236 Jeff Brantley .05
237 OF Prospects (Brian Hunter, Jose Malave, Shane Pullen, *Karim Garcia*) .40
238 Matt Nokes .05
239 Ben Rivera .05
240 Joe Carter .10
241 Jeff Granger (Star Track) .05
242 Terry Pendleton .05
243 Melvin Nieves .05
244 Frank Rodriguez (Future Star) .10
245 Darryl Hamilton .05
246 Brooks Kieschnick (Future Star) .25
247 Todd Hollandsworth (Future Star) .15
248 Joe Rosselli (Future Star) .10
249 Bill Gullickson .05
250 Chuck Knoblauch .15
251 Kurt Miller (Star Track) .05
252 Bobby Jones .10
253 Lance Blankenship .05
254 Matt Whiteside .05
255 Darrin Fletcher .05
256 Eric Plunk .05
257 Shane Reynolds .10
258 Norberto Martin .05
259 Mike Thurman (Draft Pick) .05
260 Andy Van Slyke .05
261 Dwight Smith .05
262 Allen Watson .10
263 Dan Wilson .05
264 Brent Mayne .05
265 Bip Roberts .05
266 Sterling Hitchcock .05
267 Alex Gonzalez (Star Track) .15
268 Greg Harris .05
269 Ricky Jordan .05
270 Johnny Ruffin .05
271 Mike Stanton .05
272 Rich Rowland .05
273 Steve Trachsel .10
274 Pedro Munoz .05
275 Ramon Martinez .10
276 Dave Henderson .05
277 Chris Gomez (All Star Rookie) .10
278 Joe Grahe .05
279 Rusty Greer .05
280 John Franco .05
281 Mike Bordick .05
282 Jeff D'Amico (Future Star) .10
283 Dave Magadan .05
284 Tony Pena .05
285 Greg Swindell .05
286 Doug Million (Draft Pick) .05
287 Gabe White (Star Track) .15
288 Trey Beamon (Future Star) .15
289 Arthur Rhodes .05
290 Juan Guzman .05
291 Jose Oquendo .05
292 Willie Blair .05
293 Eddie Taubensee .05
294 Steve Howe .05
295 Greg Maddux 1.50
296 Mike MacFarlane .05
297 Curt Schilling .10
298 Phil Clark .05
299 Woody Williams .05
300 Jose Canseco .50
301 Aaron Sele .10
302 Carl Willis .05
303 Steve Buechele .05
304 Dave Burba .05
305 Orel Hershiser .05
306 Damion Easley .05
307 Mike Henneman .05
308 Josias Manzanillo .05
309 Kevin Seitzer .05
310 Ruben Sierra .05
311 Bryan Harvey .05
312 Jim Thome .25
313 *Ramon Castro* (Draft Pick) .15
314 Lance Johnson .05
315 Marquis Grissom .10
316 SP Prospects (Terrell Wade, Juan Acevedo, Matt Arrandale, *Eddie Priest*) .10
317 Paul Wagner .05
318 Jamie Moyer .05
319 Todd Zeile .10
320 Chris Bosio .05
321 Steve Reed .05
322 Erik Hanson .05
323 Luis Polonia .05
324 Ryan Klesko .20
325 Kevin Appier .05
326 Jim Eisenreich .05
327 Randy Knorr .05
328 Craig Shipley .05
329 Tim Naehring .05
330 Randy Myers .05
331 Alex Cole .05
332 Jim Gott .05
333 Mike Jackson .05
334 John Flaherty .05
335 Chili Davis .05
336 Benji Gil (Star Track) .10
337a Jason Jacome (No Diamond Vision logo on back photo) .15
337b Jason Jacome (Diamond Vision logo on back photo) .15
338 Stan Javier .05
339 Mike Fetters .05
340 Rick Renteria .05
341 Kevin Witt (Draft Pick) .05
342 Scott Servais .05
343 Craig Grebeck .05
344 Kirk Rueter .05
345 Don Slaught .05
346 *Armando Benitez* (Star Track) .15
347 Ozzie Smith .40
348 Mike Blowers .05
349 Armando Reynoso .05
350 Barry Larkin .15
351 Mike Williams .05
352 Scott Kamieniecki .05
353 Gary Gaetti .05
354 Todd Stottlemyre .05
355 Fred McGriff .20
356 Tim Mauser .05
357 Chris Gwynn .05
358 Frank Castillo .05
359 Jeff Reboulet .10
360 Roger Clemens .75
361 Mark Carreon .05
362 Chad Kreuter .05
363 Mark Farris (Draft Pick) .05
364 Bob Welch .05
365 Dean Palmer .05
366 Jeromy Burnitz .05
367 B.J. Surhoff .05
368 Mike Butcher .05
369 RP Prospects (Brad Clontz, Steve Phoenix, Scott Gentile, Bucky Buckles) .10
370 Eddie Murray .20
371 Orlando Miller (Star Track) .05
372 Ron Karkovice .05
373 Richie Lewis .05
374 Lenny Webster .05
375 Jeff Tackett .05
376 Tom Urbani .05
377 Tino Martinez .15
378 Mark Dewey .05
379 Charlie O'Brien .05
380 Terry Mulholland .05
381 Thomas Howard .05
382 Chris Haney .05
383 Billy Hatcher .05
384 Jeff Bagwell, Frank Thomas (All Stars) .50
385 Bret Boone, Carlos Baerga (All Stars) .10
386 Matt Williams, Wade Boggs (All Stars) .15
387 Wil Cordero, Cal Ripken Jr. (All Stars) .50
388 Barry Bonds, Ken Griffey Jr. (All Stars) .75
389 Tony Gwynn, Albert Belle (All Stars) .40
390 Dante Bichette, Kirby Puckett (All Stars) .25
391 Mike Piazza, Mike Stanley (All Stars) .40
392 Greg Maddux, David Cone (All Stars) .40
393 Danny Jackson, Jimmy Key (All Stars) .05
394 John Franco, Lee Smith (All Stars) .05
395 Checklist 1-198 .05
396 Checklist 199-396 .05
397 Ken Griffey Jr. 3.00
398 *Rick Heiserman* (Draft Pick) .10
399 Don Mattingly .75
400 Henry Rodriguez .05
401 Lenny Harris .05
402 Ryan Thompson .05
403 Darren Oliver .05
404 Omar Vizquel .10
405 Jeff Bagwell .60
406 *Doug Webb* (Draft Pick) .10
407 Todd Van Poppel .05
408 Leo Gomez .05
409 Mark Whiten .05
410 Pedro Martinez .05
411 Reggie Sanders .10
412 Kevin Foster .05
413 Danny Tartabull .05
414 Jeff Blauser .05
415 Mike Magnante .05
416 Tom Candiotti .05
417 Rod Beck .05
418 Jody Reed .05
419 Vince Coleman .05
420 Danny Jackson .05
421 *Ryan Nye* (Draft Pick) .15
422 Larry Walker .30
423 Russ Johnson (Draft Pick) .15
424 Pat Borders .05
425 Lee Smith .05
426 Paul O'Neill .15
427 Devon White .05
428 Jim Bullinger .05
429 SP Prospects (Greg Hansell, Brian Sackinsky, Carey Paige, Rob Welch) .10
430 Steve Avery .05
431 Tony Gwynn 1.00
432 Pat Meares .05
433 Bill Swift .05
434 David Wells .05
435 John Briscoe .05
436 Roger Pavlik .05
437 *Jayson Peterson* (Draft Pick) .15
438 Roberto Alomar .40
439 Billy Brewer .05
440 Gary Sheffield .20
441 Lou Frazier .05
442 Terry Steinbach .05
443 *Jay Payton* (Draft Pick) .25
444 Jason Bere .05
445 Denny Neagle .05
446 Andres Galarraga .15
447 Hector Carrasco .05
448 Bill Risley .05
449 Andy Benes .05
450 Jim Leyritz .05
451 Jose Oliva .05
452 Greg Vaughn .05
453 Rich Monteleone .05
454 Tony Eusebio .05
455 Chuck Finley .05
456 Kevin Brown .15
457 Joe Boever .05
458 Bobby Munoz .05
459 Bret Saberhagen .05
460 Kurt Abbott .05
461 Bobby Witt .05
462 Cliff Floyd .10
463 Mark Clark .05
464 Andujar Cedeno .05
465 Marvin Freeman .05
466 Mike Piazza 1.50
467 Willie Greene .05
468 Pat Kelly .05
469 Carlos Delgado .40
470 Willie Banks .05
471 Matt Walbeck .05
472 Mark McGwire 3.00
473 McKay Christensen (Draft Pick) .15
474 Alan Trammell .10
475 Tom Gordon .05
476 Greg Colbrunn .05
477 Darren Daulton .05
478 Albie Lopez .05
479 Robin Ventura .25
480 C Prospects (*Eddie Perez*, Jason Kendall, *Einar Diaz*, Bret Hemphill) .20
481 Bryan Eversgerd .05
482 Dave Fleming .05
483 Scott Livingstone .05
484 Pete Schourek .05
485 Bernie Williams .30
486 Mark Lemke .05
487 Eric Karros .10
488 Scott Ruffcorn .05
489 Billy Ashley .05
490 Rico Brogna .05
491 John Burkett .05
492 *Cade Gaspar* (Draft Pick) .15
493 Jorge Fabregas .05
494 Greg Gagne .05
495 Doug Jones .05
496 Troy O'Leary .05
497 Pat Rapp .05
498 Butch Henry .05
499 John Olerud .20
500 John Hudek .05
501 Jeff King .05
502 Bobby Bonilla .10
503 Albert Belle .30
504 Rick Wilkins .05
505 John Jaha .05
506 Nigel Wilson .05
507 Sid Fernandez .05
508 Deion Sanders .20
509 Gil Heredia .05
510 *Scott Elarton* (Draft Pick) .75
511 Melido Perez .05
512 Greg McMichael .05
513 Rusty Meacham .05
514 Shawn Green .40
515 Carlos Garcia .05
516 Dave Stevens .05
517 Eric Young .05
518 Omar Daal .05
519 Kirk Gibson .05
520 Spike Owen .05
521 *Jacob Cruz* (Draft Pick) .40
522 Sandy Alomar .10
523 Steve Bedrosian .05
524 Ricky Gutierrez .05
525 Dave Veres .05
526 Gregg Jefferies .10
527 Jose Valentin .05
528 Robb Nen .05
529 Jose Rijo .05
530 Sean Berry .05
531 Mike Gallego .05
532 Roberto Kelly .05
533 Kevin Stocker .05
534 Kirby Puckett .75
535 Chipper Jones 1.00
536 Russ Davis .05
537 Jon Lieber .05
538 *Trey Moore* (Draft Pick) .10
539 Joe Girardi .05
540 2B Prospects (Quilvio Veras, Arquimedez Pozo, Miguel Cairo, Jason Camilli) .20
541 Tony Phillips .05
542 Brian Anderson .15
543 Ivan Rodriguez .75
544 Jeff Cirillo .05
545 Joey Cora .05
546 Chris Hoiles .05
547 Bernard Gilkey .10
548 Mike Lansing .05
549 Jimmy Key .05
550 Mark Wohlers .05
551 *Chris Clemons* (Draft Pick) .15
552 Vinny Castilla .15
553 Mark Guthrie .05
554 Mike Lieberthal .10
555 *Tommy Davis* (Draft Pick) .15
556 Robby Thompson .05
557 Danny Bautista .05
558 Will Clark .30
559 Rickey Henderson .25
560 Todd Jones .05
561 Jack McDowell .05
562 Carlos Rodriguez .05
563 Mark Eichhorn .05
564 Jeff Nelson .05
565 Eric Anthony .05
566 Randy Velarde .05
567 Javy Lopez .15
568 Kevin Mitchell .05
569 Steve Karsay .05
570 *Brian Meadows* (Draft Pick) .20
571 SS Prospects (*Rey Ordonez*, Mike Metcalfe, Ray Holbert, Kevin Orie) 1.00
572 John Kruk .05
573 Scott Leius .05
574 John Patterson .05
575 Kevin Brown .15
576 Mike Moore .05
577 Manny Ramirez .75
578 Jose Lind .05
579 Derrick May .05
580 Cal Eldred .05
581 3B Prospects (David Bell, Joel Chelmis, Lino Diaz, *Aaron Boone*) .15
582 J.T. Snow .10
583 Luis Sojo .05
584 Moises Alou .20

585	Dave Clark	.05
586	Dave Hollins	.05
587	Nomar Garciaparra (Draft Pick)	4.00
588	Cal Ripken Jr.	2.50
589	Pedro Astacio	.05
590	J.R. Phillips	.05
591	Jeff Frye	.05
592	Bo Jackson	.15
593	Steve Ontiveros	.05
594	David Nied	.05
595	Brad Ausmus	.05
596	Carlos Baerga	.05
597	James Mouton	.05
598	Ozzie Guillen	.05
599	OF Prospects (Ozzie Timmons, Curtis Goodwin, Johnny Damon, *Jeff Abbott*)	.20
600	Yorkis Perez	.05
601	Rich Rodriguez	.05
602	Mark McLemore	.05
603	Jeff Fassero	.05
604	John Roper	.05
605	*Mark Johnson* (Draft Pick)	.20
606	Wes Chamberlain	.05
607	Felix Jose	.05
608	Tony Longmire	.05
609	Duane Ward	.05
610	Brett Butler	.05
611	William Van Landingham	.05
612	Mickey Tettleton	.05
613	Brady Anderson	.15
614	Reggie Jefferson	.05
615	Mike Kingery	.05
616	Derek Bell	.10
617	Scott Erickson	.05
618	Bob Wickman	.05
619	Phil Leftwich	.05
620	Dave Justice	.20
621	Paul Wilson (Draft Pick)	.15
622	Pedro Martinez	.75
623	Terry Mathews	.05
624	Brian McRae	.05
625	Bruce Ruffin	.05
626	Steve Finley	.05
627	Ron Gant	.15
628	Rafael Bournigal	.05
629	Darryl Strawberry	.15
630	Luis Alicea	.05
631	Mark Smith, Scott Klingenbeck (On Deck)	.10
632	Cory Bailey, Scott Hatteberg (On Deck)	.15
633	Todd Greene, Troy Percival (On Deck)	.10
634	Rod Bolton, Olmedo Saenz (On Deck)	.10
635	Herb Perry, Steve Kline (On Deck)	.10
636	Sean Bergman, Shannon Penn (On Deck)	.10
637	Joe Vitiello, Joe Randa (On Deck)	.10
638	Jose Mercedes, Duane Singleton (On Deck)	.05
639	Marty Cordova, Marc Barcelo (On Deck)	.10
640	Ruben Rivera, Andy Pettitte (On Deck)	1.00
641	Willie Adams, Scott Spiezio (On Deck)	.10
642	Eddie Diaz, Desi Relaford (On Deck)	.10
643	Jon Shave, Terrell Lowery (On Deck)	.10
644	Paul Spoljaric, Angel Martinez (On Deck)	.05
645	Damon Hollins, Tony Graffanino (On Deck)	.10
646	Darron Cox, Doug Glanville (On Deck)	.10
647	Tim Belk, Pat Watkins (On Deck)	.10
648	Rod Pedraza, Phil Schneider (On Deck)	.10
649	Marc Valdes, Vic Darensbourg (On Deck)	.10
650	Rick Huisman, Roberto Petagine (On Deck)	.05
651	Ron Coomer, Roger Cedeno (On Deck)	.20
652	*Carlos Perez*, Shane Andrews (On Deck)	.30
653	Jason Isringhausen, Chris Roberts (On Deck)	.10
654	Kevin Jordan, Wayne Gomes (On Deck)	.10
655	Esteban Loaiza, Steve Pegues (On Deck)	.10
656	John Frascatore, Terry Bradshaw (On Deck)	.10
657	Bryce Florie, Andres Berumen (On Deck)	.10
658	Keith Williams, Dan Carlson (On Deck)	.10
659	Checklist	.05
660	Checklist	.05

1995 Topps Cyberstats

		MT
Complete Set (396):		60.00
Series 1 (198):		30.00
Series 2 (198):		30.00
Common Player:		.15
(Valued at 2x their regular Topps card.)		

1995 Topps Cyberstat Season in Review

This special edition of Cyberstat cards was available only in Topps factory sets. Carrying forward the idea of computerized projections to complete the strike-shortened 1994 season, the Season in Review cards speculate on career milestones and the playoffs that never happened. The Season in Review cards have player action photos printed on a foil background resembling the U.S. flag. Names are in gold foil. Backs have a black background and a recap of the computer simulation.

		MT
Complete Set (7):		8.00
Common Player:		1.50
1	Barry Bonds (61 Home Runs)	3.00
2	Jose Canseco (AL West One-Game Playoff)	2.00
3	Juan Gonzalez (AL Divisional Playoffs)	3.00
4	Fred McGriff (NL Divisional Playoffs)	1.50
5	Carlos Baerga (ALCS MVP)	1.00
6	Ryan Klesko (NLCS MVP)	1.00
7	Kenny Lofton (World Series MVP)	1.50

1995 Topps League Leaders

League Leaders is a 50-card insert set found in one of every six retail packs only of both Series I and II. The set includes the top five players in each league across 10 statistical categories. Cards featured the statistical category running up the right side, with the player's name across the bottom. Photo backgrounds have been darkened and posterized to make the player action stand out. Backs have the player's stat rankings within his division and league, and a bar graph at bottom gives his performance in that statistical category for the previous five seasons.

		MT
Complete Set (50):		30.00
Complete Series 1 (25):		15.00
Complete Series 2 (25):		15.00
Common Player:		.25
1	Albert Belle	.75
2	Kevin Mitchell	.25
3	Wade Boggs	.50
4	Tony Gwynn	1.50
5	Moises Alou	.40
6	Andres Galarraga	.40
7	Matt Williams	.40
8	Barry Bonds	1.00
9	Frank Thomas	1.00
10	Jose Canseco	.75
11	Jeff Bagwell	1.00
12	Kirby Puckett	1.00
13	Julio Franco	.25
14	Albert Belle	.75
15	Fred McGriff	.40
16	Kenny Lofton	.50
17	Otis Nixon	.25
18	Brady Anderson	.25
19	Deion Sanders	.40
20	Chuck Carr	.25
21	Pat Hentgen	.25
22	Andy Benes	.25
23	Roger Clemens	1.50
24	Greg Maddux	2.00
25	Pedro Martinez	1.00
26	Paul O'Neill	.40
27	Jeff Bagwell	1.00
28	Frank Thomas	1.00
29	Hal Morris	.25
30	Kenny Lofton	.50
31	Ken Griffey Jr.	4.00
32	Jeff Bagwell	1.00
33	Albert Belle	75.00
34	Fred McGriff	.50
35	Cecil Fielder	.25
36	Matt Williams	.40
37	Joe Carter	.25
38	Dante Bichette	.45
39	Frank Thomas	1.00
40	Mike Piazza	2.00
41	Craig Biggio	.50
42	Vince Coleman	.25
43	Marquis Grissom	.25
44	Chuck Knoblauch	.45
45	Darren Lewis	.25
46	Randy Johnson	.50
47	Jose Rijo	.25
48	Chuck Finley	.25
49	Bret Saberhagen	.25
50	Kevin Appier	.25

1995 Topps Total Bases Finest

Printed in Topps Finest technology, including a peel-off plastic protector coating on the front, these cards honor the 1994 statistical leaders in total bases. The cards have a silver waffle-texture background on front as a background to the color action photo. At bottom is a team logo and team-color bar with the player's name. Backs feature a portrait photo and the player's total base stats. These inserts are found in Series II Topps packs at an average rate of one per 36 packs (one box).

		MT
Complete Set (15):		60.00
Common Player:		1.00
1	Jeff Bagwell	4.00
2	Albert Belle	3.00
3	Ken Griffey Jr.	10.00
4	Frank Thomas	4.00
5	Matt Williams	1.50
6	Dante Bichette	1.50
7	Barry Bonds	4.00
8	Moises Alou	1.00
9	Andres Galarraga	1.00
10	Kenny Lofton	1.50
11	Rafael Palmeiro	2.00
12	Tony Gwynn	4.00
13	Kirby Puckett	4.00
14	Jose Canseco	2.00
15	Jeff Conine	1.00

1995 Topps Traded and Rookies

Traded players, free agents who signed with new teams and all the up-and-coming rookies are the meat of the 1995 Topps Traded and Rookies set, sold for the first time exclusively in foil pack form. Maintaining the same format used in Series 1 and 2 Topps, the updates also re-used the Future Star, Draft Pick and Star Track subsets, along with four-player Prospects cards. New subsets included Rookie of the Year Candidates, All-Stars, On Deck and "At the Break," 10 cards chronicling star players' performances through the first half of the 1995 season. A double-thick, foil-printed version of the "At the Break" cards called "Power Boosters" were the only inserts in the Traded/Rookies set.

		MT
Complete Set (165):		50.00
Common Player:		.10
Wax Box:		100.00
1	Frank Thomas (At The Break)	.40
2	Ken Griffey Jr. (At The Break)	1.50
3	Barry Bonds (At The Break)	.40
4	Albert Belle (At The Break)	.25
5	Cal Ripken Jr. (At The Break)	1.00
6	Mike Piazza (At The Break)	.75
7	Tony Gwynn (At The Break)	.40
8	Jeff Bagwell (At The Break)	.25
9	Mo Vaughn (At The Break)	.25
10	Matt Williams (At The Break)	.15
11	Ray Durham	.10
12	*Juan LeBron* (Draft Pick)	4.00
13	Shawn Green (Rookie of the Year Candidate)	.50
14	Kevin Gross	.10
15	Jon Nunnally	.10
16	*Brian Maxcy*	.10
17	Mark Kiefer	.10
18	*Carlos Beltran* (Draft Pick) (photo actually Juan Beltran)	20.00
19	*Mike Mimbs*	.10
20	Larry Walker	.40
21	Chad Curtis	.10
22	Jeff Barry	.10
23	Joe Oliver	.10
24	*Tomas Perez*	.10
25	*Michael Barrett* (Draft Pick)	6.00
26	Brian McRae	.10
27	Derek Bell	.10
28	Ray Durham (Rookie of the Year Candidate)	.10
29	Todd Williams	.10
30	*Ryan Jaroncyk* (Draft Pick)	.20
31	Todd Steverson	.10
32	Mike Devereaux	.10
33	Rheal Cormier	.10
34	Benny Santiago	.10
35	*Bobby Higginson*	1.50
36	Jack McDowell	.10
37	Mike Macfarlane	.10
38	*Tony McKnight* (Draft Pick)	.20
39	Brian Hunter (Rookie of the Year Candidate)	.15
40	*Hideo Nomo* (Star Track)	2.00
41	Brett Butler	.10
42	Donovan Osborne	.10
43	Scott Karl	.10
44	Tony Phillips	.10
45	Marty Cordova (Rookie of the Year Candidate)	.20
46	Dave Mlicki	.10
47	*Bronson Arroyo* (Draft Pick)	1.50
48	John Burkett	.10
49	*J.D. Smart* (Draft Pick)	.25
50	Mickey Tettleton	.10
51	Todd Stottlemyre	.15
52	Mike Perez	.10
53	Terry Mulholland	.10
54	Edgardo Alfonzo	.25
55	Zane Smith	.10
56	Jacob Brumfield	.10
57	Andujar Cedeno	.10
58	Jose Parra	.10
59	Manny Alexander	.10
60	Tony Tarasco	.10
61	Orel Hershiser	.10
62	Tim Scott	.10
63	*Felix Rodriguez*	.10
64	Ken Hill	.10
65	Marquis Grissom	.15
66	Lee Smith	.10
67	Jason Bates (Rookie of the Year Candidate)	.10
68	Felipe Lira	.10
69	*Alex Hernandez* (Draft Pick)	1.50
70	Tony Fernandez	.10
71	Scott Radinsky	.10
72	Jose Canseco	.50
73	*Mark Grudzielanek*	.50
74	*Ben Davis* (Draft Pick)	8.00
75	Jim Abbott	.10
76	Roger Bailey	.10
77	Gregg Jefferies	.10
78	Erik Hanson	.10
79	*Brad Radke*	1.00
80	Jaime Navarro	.10
81	John Wetteland	.10
82	*Chad Fonville*	.15
83	John Mabry	.10
84	Glenallen Hill	.10
85	Ken Caminiti	.20
86	Tom Goodwin	.10
87	Darren Bragg	.10
88	1995 Prospects (Pitchers) (*Pat Ahearne*), (*Gary Rath*), (*Larry Wimberly*, *Robbie Bell*)	2.00
89	Jeff Russell	.10
90	Dave Gallagher	.10
91	Steve Finley	.10
92	Vaughn Eshelman	.10
93	Kevin Jarvis	.10
94	Mark Gubicza	.10
95	Tim Wakefield	.10

96	Bob Tewksbury	.10
97	*Sid Roberson*	.10
98	Tom Henke	.10
99	Michael Tucker (Future Star)	.15
100	Jason Bates	.10
101	Otis Nixon	.10
102	Mark Whiten	.10
103	Dilson Torres	.10
104	*Melvin Bunch*	.10
105	Terry Pendleton	.10
106	*Corey Jenkins* (Draft Pick)	.20
107	On Deck (*Glenn Dishman, Rob Grable*)	.15
108	*Reggie Taylor* (Draft Pick)	2.00
109	Curtis Goodwin (Rookie of the Year Candidate)	.10
110	David Cone	.20
111	Antonio Osuna	.10
112	Paul Shuey	.10
113	Doug Jones	.10
114	Mark McLemore	.10
115	Kevin Ritz	.10
116	John Kruk	.10
117	Trevor Wilson	.10
118	Jerald Clark	.10
119	Julian Tavarez	.10
120	Tim Pugh	.10
121	Todd Zeile	.10
122	1995 Prospects (Fielders) (*Mark Sweeney*, George Arias, *Richie Sexson, Brian Schneider*)	8.00
123	Bobby Witt	.10
124	Hideo Nomo (Rookie of the Year Candidate)	.40
125	Joey Cora	.10
126	*Jim Scharrer* (Draft Pick)	.10
127	Paul Quantrill	.10
128	Chipper Jones (Rookie of the Year Candidate)	1.00
129	*Kenny James* (Draft Pick)	.10
130	On Deck (Lyle Mouton, Mariano Rivera)	.10
131	Tyler Green (Rookie of the Year Candidate)	.10
132	Brad Clontz	.10
133	Jon Nunnally (Rookie of the Year Candidate)	.10
134	Dave Magadan	.10
135	Al Leiter	.20
136	Bret Barberie	.10
137	Bill Swift	.10
138	Scott Cooper	.10
139	Roberto Kelly	.10
140	Charlie Hayes	.10
141	Pete Harnisch	.10
142	Rich Amaral	.10
143	Rudy Seanez	.10
144	Pat Listach	.10
145	Quilvio Veras (Rookie of the Year Candidate)	.15
146	*Jose Olmeda* (Draft Pick)	.10
147	Roberto Petagine	.10
148	Kevin Brown	.20
149	Phil Plantier	.10
150	*Carlos Perez* (Rookie of the Year Candidate)	.40
151	Pat Borders	.10
152	Tyler Green	.10
153	Stan Belinda	.10
154	Dave Stewart	.10
155	Andre Dawson	.15
156	Frank Thomas, Fred McGriff (All-Star)	.25
157	Carlos Baerga, Craig Biggio (All-Star)	.15
158	Wade Boggs, Matt Williams (All-Star)	.10
159	Cal Ripken Jr., Ozzie Smith (All-Star)	.50
160	Ken Griffey Jr., Tony Gwynn (All-Star)	.75
161	Albert Belle, Barry Bonds (All-Star)	.25
162	Kirby Puckett, Len Dykstra (All-Star)	.25
163	Ivan Rodriguez, Mike Piazza (All-Star)	.25
164	Randy Johnson, Hideo Nomo (All-Star)	.25
165	Checklist	.10

1995 Topps Traded and Rookies Power Boosters

Virtually identical to the first 10 cards of the 1995 Topps Traded and Rookies issue, the "At the Break" subset is the only insert found in Traded packs. Cards are printed on double-thick cardboard stock on metallized foil. The chase cards are found at an average rate of one per 36 packs.

		MT
Complete Set (10):		37.00
Common Player:		1.50
1	Frank Thomas	6.00
2	Ken Griffey Jr.	12.50
3	Barry Bonds	4.00
4	Albert Belle	3.00
5	Cal Ripken Jr.	10.00
6	Mike Piazza	7.50
7	Tony Gwynn	6.00
8	Jeff Bagwell	3.00
9	Mo Vaughn	1.50
10	Matt Williams	1.50

1995 Topps Opening Day

This 10-card set featuring top performers on the belated opening day of the 1995 season was available exclusively in retail factory sets. Card fronts feature color action photos printed on textured foil in a U.S. flag-like design. A large colorful Opening Day logo appears in an upper corner while the player's key stats from that game appear in a foil box at lower-right. Backs have a portrait photo along with complete details and a stats line of the opening day performance.

		MT
Complete Set (10):		16.00
Common Player:		2.00
1	Kevin Appier	2.00
2	Dante Bichette	3.00
3	Ken Griffey Jr.	8.00
4	Todd Hundley	3.00
5	John Jaha	2.00
6	Fred McGriff	3.00
7	Raul Mondesi	3.00
8	Manny Ramirez	4.00
9	Danny Tartabull	2.00
10	Devon White	2.50

1995 Topps/Archives Brooklyn Dodgers

In a departure from its program of complete set reissues, Topps' Archives baseball series for 1995 was a tribute to the 40th anniversary of the Brooklyn Dodgers' 1955 World's Series victory over the archrival Yankees. Besides reprinting all of the Dodgers' cards from the 1952-56 Topps sets and the 1955 Bowman issue, the Archives release included some 30 "cards that never were," done in the styles of the 1952-55 Topps issues. Those cards are designated with an "N" suffix in parentheses. The old larger format of the vintage cards has been reduced to the standard 2-1/2" x 3-1/2" format for the Archives versions. Cards are UV coated on each side. Each card carries its original or an "extended" card number in the normal location, plus a tiny Archives series card number at the bottom in the fine print. The numbers on cards #97-109 do not coincide with those listed on the checklist card. The only chase cards in the issue were autographed versions of Sandy Koufax's 1956 Archives card. Cards #111-165 are short-printed in relation to cards #1-110.

		MT
Complete Set (165):		50.00
Common Player:		.10
1	Andy Pafko (52T)	.25
2	Wayne Terwilliger (52T)	.10
3	Billy Loes (52T)	.25
4	Gil Hodges (52T)	.50
5	Duke Snider (52T)	.75
6	Jim Russell (52T)	.10
7	Chris Van Cuyk (52T)	.10
8	Preacher Roe (52T)	.10
9	Johnny Schmitz (52T)	.10
10	Bud Podbielan (52T)	.10
11	Phil Haugstad (52T)	.10
12	Clyde King (52T)	.10
13	Billy Cox (52T)	.10
14	Rocky Bridges (52T)	.10
15	Carl Erskine (52T)	.10
16	Erv Palica (52T)	.10
17	Ralph Branca (52T)	.10
18	Jackie Robinson (52T)	2.00
19	Roy Campanella (52T)	.75
20	Rube Walker (52T)	.10
21	Johnny Rutherford (52T)	.10
22	Joe Black (52T)	.25
23	George Shuba (52T)	.10
24	Pee Wee Reese (52T)	.75
25	Clem Labine (52T)	.10
26	Bobby Morgan (52T)	.10
27	Cookie Lavagetto (52T)	.10
28	Chuck Dressen (52T)	.10
29	Ben Wade (52T)	.10
30	Rocky Nelson (52T)	.10
31	Billy Herman (52T)	.10
32	Jake Pitler (52T)	.10
33	Dick Williams (52T)	.10
34	Cal Abrams (52N)	.25
35	Carl Furillo (52N)	.25
36	Don Newcombe (52N)	.25
37	Jackie Robinson (53T)	2.00
38	Ben Wade (53T)	.10
39	Clem Labine (53T)	.10
40	Roy Campanella (53T)	.75
41	George Shuba (53T)	.10
42	Chuck Dressen (53T)	.10
43	Pee Wee Reese (53T)	.75
44	Joe Black (53T)	.25
45	Bobby Morgan (53T)	.10
46	Dick Williams (53T)	.10
47	Rube Walker (53T)	.10
48	Johnny Rutherford (53T)	.10
49	Billy Loes (53T)	.15
50	Don Hoak (53T)	.10
51	Jim Hughes (53T)	.10
52	Bob Milliken (53T)	.10
53	Preacher Roe (53T)	.10
54	Dixie Howell (53T)	.10
55	Junior Gilliam (53T)	.25
56	Johnny Podres (53T)	.25
57	Bill Antonello (53T)	.10
58	Ralph Branca (53N)	.25
59	Gil Hodges (53N)	.60
60	Carl Furillo (53N)	.45
61	Carl Erskine (53N)	.25
62	Don Newcombe (53N)	.35
63	Duke Snider (53N)	.75
64	Billy Cox (53N)	.25
65	Russ Meyer (53N)	.25
66	Jackie Robinson (54T)	2.00
67	Preacher Roe (54T)	.10
68	Duke Snider (54T)	.75
69	Junior Gilliam (54T)	.10
70	Billy Herman (54T)	.10
71	Joe Black (54T)	.15
72	Gil Hodges (54T)	.50
73	Clem Labine (54T)	.10
74	Ben Wade (54T)	.10
75	Tommy Lasorda (54T)	1.00
76	Rube Walker (54T)	.10
77	Johnny Podres (54T)	.10
78	Jim Hughes (54T)	.10
79	Bob Milliken (54T)	.10
80	Charlie Thompson (54T)	.10
81	Don Hoak (54T)	.10
82	Roberto Clemente (54N)	1.00
83	Don Zimmer (54N)	.25
84	Roy Campanella (54N)	1.00
85	Billy Cox (54N)	.45
86	Carl Erskine (54N)	.45
87	Carl Furillo (54N)	.45
88	Don Newcombe (54N)	.45
89	Pee Wee Reese (54N)	1.00
90	George Shuba (54N)	.25
91	Junior Gilliam (55T)	.10
92	Billy Herman (55T)	.10
93	Johnny Podres (55T)	.10
94	Don Hoak (55T)	.10
95	Jackie Robinson (55T)	2.00
96	Jim Hughes (55T)	.10
97	Bob Borkowski (55N)	.10
98	Sandy Amoros (55T)	.10
99	Karl Spooner (55T)	.10
100	Don Zimmer (55T)	.10
101	Rube Walker (55T)	.10
102	Bob Milliken (55T)	.10
103	Sandy Koufax (55T)	2.00
104	Joe Black (55T)	.20
105	Clem Labine (55T)	.10
106	Gil Hodges (55T)	.50
107	Ed Roebuck (55T)	.10
108	Bert Hamric (55T)	.10
109	Duke Snider (55T)	.75
110	Walter Alston (55N)	.25
111	Roger Craig (55N)	.45
112	Don Drysdale (55N)	1.50
113	Dixie Howell (55N)	.35
114	Frank Kellert (55N)	.35
115	Tommy Lasorda (55N)	.50
116	Chuck Templeton (55N)	.35
117	World Series Game 3, Dodgers Stay Alive (Jackie Robinson) (55N)	.45
118	World Series Game 4, Series Knotted (Gil Hodges) (55N)	.15
119	World Series Game 5, Dodgers Lead (Duke Snider) (55N)	.15
120	World Series Game 7, Dodgers Reign (Johnny Podres) (55N)	.15
121	Don Hoak (55B)	.15
122	Roy Campanella (55B)	.90
123	Pee Wee Reese (55B)	.90
124	Bob Darnell (55B)	.15
125	Don Zimmer (55B)	.15
126	George Shuba (55B)	.15
127	Johnny Podres (55B)	.15
128	Junior Gilliam (55B)	.15
129	Don Newcombe (55B)	.15
130	Jim Hughes (55B)	.15
131	Gil Hodges (55B)	.60
132	Carl Furillo (55B)	.35
133	Carl Erskine (55B)	.15
134	Erv Palica (55B)	.15
135	Russ Meyer (55B)	.15
136	Billy Loes (55B)	.15
137	Walt Moryn (55B)	.15
138	Chico Fernandez (55B)	.15
139	Charley Neal (55B)	.15
140	Ken Lehman (55B)	.15
141	Walter Alston (56T)	.25
142	Jackie Robinson (56T)	3.00
143	Sandy Amoros (56T)	.15
144	Ed Roebuck (56T)	.15
145	Roger Craig (56T)	.15
146	Sandy Koufax (56T)	1.00
146a	Sandy Koufax (56T, autographed)	200.00
147	Karl Spooner (56T)	.15
148	Don Zimmer (56T)	.15
149	Roy Campanella (56T)	.90
150	Gil Hodges (56T)	.60
151	Duke Snider (56T)	.90
152	Team photo (56T)	2.50
153	Johnny Podres (56T)	.15
154	Don Bessent (56T)	.15
155	Carl Furillo (56T)	.20
156	Randy Jackson (56T)	.15
157	Carl Erskine (56T)	.15
158	Don Newcombe (56T)	.15
159	Pee Wee Reese (56T)	.90
160	Billy Loes (56T)	.15
161	Junior Gilliam (56T)	.15
162	Clem Labine (56T)	.15
163	Charley Neal (56T)	.15
164	Rube Walker (56T)	.15
165	Checklist	.05

1995 Topps/DIII

Describing its cards as featuring "infinite depth perspectives" with game-action photos, Topps entered the 3-D card market with its Dimension III product. Utilizing "super thick laminated construction" to provide the illusion of depth, the cards feature borderless action photos on front. Backs are conventionally printed with a color portrait photo and several sets of stats that go beyond the usual to the provide a more in-depth look at the player's performance.

		MT
Complete Set (59):		27.50
Common Player:		.25
Retail Wax Box:		35.00
Hobby Wax Box:		50.00
1	Dave Justice	.40
2	Cal Ripken Jr.	5.00
3	Ruben Sierra	.25
4	Roberto Alomar	1.00
5	Dennis Martinez	.25
6	Todd Zeile	.25
7	Albert Belle	1.00
8	Chuck Knoblauch	.50
9	Roger Clemens	1.00
10	Cal Eldred	.25
11	Dennis Eckersley	.25
12	Andy Benes	.25
13	Moises Alou	.35
14	Andres Galarraga	.35
15	Jim Thome	.40
16	Tim Salmon	.40
17	Carlos Garcia	.25
18	Scott Leius	.25
19	Jeff Montgomery	.25
20	Brian Anderson	.25
21	Will Clark	.50
22	Bobby Bonilla	.25
23	Mike Stanley	.25
24	Barry Bonds	1.50
25	Jeff Conine	.25
26	Paul O'Neill	.25
27	Mike Piazza	2.50
28	Tom Glavine	.35
29	Jim Edmonds	.35
30	Lou Whitaker	.25
31	Jeff Frye	.25

32 Ivan Rodriguez .50
33 Bret Boone .25
34 Mike Greenwell .25
35 Mark Grace .45
36 Darren Lewis .25
37 Don Mattingly 2.50
38 Jose Rijo .25
39 Robin Ventura .35
40 Bob Hamelin .25
41 Tim Wallach .25
42 Tony Gwynn 1.50
43 Ken Griffey Jr. 6.00
44 Doug Drabek .25
45 Rafael Palmeiro .35
46 Dean Palmer .25
47 Bip Roberts .25
48 Barry Larkin .25
49 Dave Nilsson .25
50 Wil Cordero .25
51 Travis Fryman .25
52 Chuck Carr .25
53 Rey Sanchez .25
54 Walt Weiss .25
55 Joe Carter .25
56 Len Dykstra .25
57 Orlando Merced .25
58 Ozzie Smith .75
59 Chris Gomez .25

1995 Topps/DIII Zone

A barrage of baseballs in the background, behind a player action photo, are featured on the front of this DIII chase set. Backs have a blazing baseball across the top and a description and stats of the pictured player's hot streaks of the previous season -- those times when athletes are said to be "in the zone." The inserts are found on average of one per six packs.

MT
Complete Set (6): 22.00
Common Player: 2.00
1 Frank Thomas 5.00
2 Kirby Puckett 3.50
3 Jeff Bagwell 3.00
4 Fred McGriff 2.50
5 Raul Mondesi 2.00
6 Kenny Lofton 2.00

1995 Topps/Embossed

Taking the embossed sportscard idea which Action Packed developed years earlier to a new level, Topps Embossed baseball features the tactile image on both sides of the card. Fronts have a lightly textured border while the central player photo is deeply embossed. The player name is embossed in gold-foil letters at bottom. Backs have another embossed player photo and various levels of embossing around the borders and boxes which contain stats and trivia.

MT
Complete Set (140): 20.00
Common Player: .10
Comp. Embossed Gold Set (140): 70.00
Embossed Golds: 2X to 4X
Wax Box: 40.00
1 Kenny Lofton .50
2 Gary Sheffield .20
3 Hal Morris .10
4 Cliff Floyd .15
5 Pat Hentgen .10
6 Tony Gwynn 1.50
7 Jose Valentin .10
8 Jason Bere .10
9 Jeff Kent .10
10 John Valentin .10
11 Brian Anderson .10
12 Deion Sanders .40
13 Ryan Thompson .10
14 Ruben Sierra .10
15 Jay Bell .10
16 Chuck Carr .10
17 Brent Gates .10
18 Bret Boone .10
19 Paul Molitor .25
20 Chili Davis .10
21 Ryan Klesko .20
22 Will Clark .35
23 Greg Vaughn .10
24 Moises Alou .10
25 Ray Lankford .10
26 Jose Rijo .10
27 Bobby Jones .10
28 Rick Wilkins .10
29 Cal Eldred .10
30 Juan Gonzalez 1.50
31 Royce Clayton .10
32 Bryan Harvey .10
33 Dave Nilsson .10
34 Chris Hoiles .10
35 David Nied .10
36 Javy Lopez .15
37 Tim Wallach .10
38 Bobby Bonilla .10
39 Danny Tartabull .10
40 Andy Benes .10
41 Dean Palmer .10
42 Chris Gomez .10
43 Kevin Appier .10
44 Brady Anderson .15
45 Alex Fernandez .10
46 Roberto Kelly .10
47 Dave Hollins .10
48 Chuck Finley .10
49 Wade Boggs .30
50 Travis Fryman .10
51 Ken Griffey Jr. 3.00
52 John Olerud .15
53 Delino DeShields .10
54 Ivan Rodriguez .25
55 Tommy Greene .10
56 Tom Pagnozzi .10
57 Bip Roberts .10
58 Luis Gonzalez .10
59 Rey Sanchez .10
60 Ken Ryan .10
61 Darren Daulton .10
62 Rick Aguilera .10
63 Wally Joyner .10
64 Mike Greenwell .10
65 Jay Buhner .10
66 Craig Biggio .10
67 Charles Nagy .10
68 Devon White .10
69 Randy Johnson .25
70 Shawon Dunston .10
71 Kirby Puckett 1.00
72 Paul O'Neill .10
73 Tino Martinez .15
74 Carlos Garcia .10
75 Ozzie Smith .60
76 Cecil Fielder .10
77 Mike Stanley .10
78 Lance Johnson .10
79 Tony Phillips .10
80 Bobby Munoz .10
81 Kevin Tapani .10
82 William Van Landingham .10
83 Dante Bichette .25
84 Tom Candiotti .10
85 Wil Cordero .10
86 Jeff Conine .10
87 Joey Hamilton .10
88 Mark Whiten .10
89 Jeff Montgomery .10
90 Andres Galarraga .10
91 Roberto Alomar .50
92 Orlando Merced .10
93 Mike Mussina .30
94 Pedro Martinez .10
95 Carlos Baerga .10
96 Steve Trachsel .10
97 Lou Whitaker .10
98 David Cone .10
99 Chuck Knoblauch .15
100 Frank Thomas 2.00
101 Dave Justice .20
102 Raul Mondesi .30
103 Rickey Henderson .25
104 Doug Drabek .10
105 Sandy Alomar .10
106 Roger Clemens .60
107 Mark McGwire 3.00
108 Tim Salmon .25
109 Greg Maddux 1.50
110 Mike Piazza 2.00
111 Tom Glavine .10
112 Walt Weiss .10
113 Cal Ripken Jr. 2.50
114 Eddie Murray .40
115 Don Mattingly 1.50
116 Ozzie Guillen .10
117 Bob Hamelin .10
118 Jeff Bagwell 1.50
119 Eric Karros .10
120 Barry Bonds .75
121 Mickey Tettleton .10
122 Mark Langston .10
123 Robin Ventura .10
124 Bret Saberhagen .10
125 Albert Belle .75
126 Rafael Palmeiro .10
127 Fred McGriff .25
128 Jimmy Key .10
129 Barry Larkin .10
130 Tim Raines .10
131 Len Dykstra .10
132 Todd Zeile .10
133 Joe Carter .10
134 Matt Williams .25
135 Terry Steinbach .10
136 Manny Ramirez .75
137 John Wetteland .10
138 Rod Beck .10
139 Mo Vaughn .50
140 Darren Lewis .10

1995 Topps/Embossed Golden Idols

The only insert in the Topps Embossed baseball set was a parallel set of the 140 cards rendered in gold tones on front and inserted at the rate of one per pack. Backs are identical to the regular version.

MT
Complete Set (140): 70.00
Common Player: .25
(Star cards valued at 2X-4X corresponding regular Embossed cards)

1995 Topps Legends of the '60s

Twelve of the true superstars of the 1960s are featured on one of their best Topps card designs in this collection of 6-oz. bronze metal cards. In 2-1/2" x 3-1/2" size, the ingots' fronts reproduce one of the player's 1960s Topps cards. Backs have been modified to present entire career stats. The set was sold in a mail-order subscription plan and included a custom wood box to house the collection.

MT
Complete Set (12): 550.00
Common Player: 40.00
(1) Hank Aaron (1965) 40.00
(2) Roberto Clemente (1965) 40.00
(3) Don Drysdale (1965) 40.00
(4) Bob Gibson (1964) 40.00
(5) Harmon Killebrew (1968) 40.00
(6) Juan Marichal (1966) 40.00
(7) Willie Mays (1964) 40.00
(8) Willie McCovey (1961) 40.00
(9) Brooks Robinson (1969) 40.00
(10) Frank Robinson (1962) 40.00
(11) Billy Williams (1967) 40.00
(12) Carl Yastrzemski (1966) 40.00

1995 Topps Ted Williams Tunnel Opening Commemorative

This card was produced as the header for a 13-card set distributed at a luncheon in conjunction with Dec. 15, 1995, opening day ceremonies for the Ted Williams Tunnel, connecting South Boston with the city's airport, running beneath Boston Harbor. Just 3,000 sets were reported produced. This card is in the style of Topps' regular 1996 baseball card set and features gold-foil highlights on front. A career summary is on back. The card was later offered free with a $75 purchase from Topps Stadium Club. (See also 1995 Choice Marketing Ted Williams Tunnel Opening Day Set.)

MT
9 Ted Williams 50.00

1995 Topps "1952" Gold Mickey Mantle

This down-sized (2-1/2" x 3-1/2") version of Topps' first Mickey Mantle card was produced with embossed 22k. gold-foil design on front and back and individually serial numbered.

MT
311 Mickey Mantle 15.00

1996 Topps

At 440 cards, the basic Topps set for 1996 was the smallest regular-issue from the company since it adopted the 2-1/2" x 3-1/2" format in 1957. Honoring the late Mickey Mantle on card No. 7, Topps announced it would hereafter retire that card number. Subsets in the 220-card Series 1 are Star Power, Commemoratives, Draft Picks, Tribute, AAA Stars and Future Stars. Series 2 subsets repeat Star Power and Draft Picks and add Prospects, Now Appearing and Rookie All-Stars.

MT
Complete Set (440): 40.00
Complete Series 1 (220): 25.00
Complete Series 2 (220): 15.00
Common Player: .05
Series 1 Wax Box: 60.00
Series 2 Wax Box: 70.00
1 Tony Gwynn (Star Power) .25
2 Mike Piazza (Star Power) .40
3 Greg Maddux (Star Power) .50
4 Jeff Bagwell (Star Power) .30
5 Larry Walker (Star Power) .20
6 Barry Larkin (Star Power) .10
7 Mickey Mantle (Commemorative) 5.00
8 Tom Glavine (Star Power) .10
9 Craig Biggio (Star Power) .05
10 Barry Bonds (Star Power) .20
11 Heathcliff Slocumb (Star Power) .05
12 Matt Williams (Star Power) .15
13 Todd Helton (Draft Pick) 1.00
14 Mark Redman (Draft Pick) .15
15 Michael Barrett (Draft Pick) .50
16 Ben Davis (Draft Pick) .25
17 Juan LeBron (Draft Pick) .20
18 Tony McKnight (Draft Pick) .10
19 Ryan Jaroncyk (Draft Pick) .05
20 Corey Jenkins (Draft Pick) .15
21 Jim Scharrer (Draft Pick) .05
22 *Mark Bellhorn* (Draft Pick) .25
23 *Jarrod Washburn* (Draft Pick) .40
24 *Geoff Jenkins* (Draft Pick) .75
25 *Sean Casey* (Draft Pick) 12.00
26 *Brett Tomko* (Draft Pick) .20
27 Tony Fernandez .05
28 Rich Becker .05
29 Andujar Cedeno .05
30 Paul Molitor .25
31 Brent Gates .05
32 Glenallen Hill .05
33 Mike MacFarlane .05
34 Manny Alexander .05
35 Todd Zeile .05
36 Joe Girardi .05
37 Tony Tarasco .05
38 Tim Belcher .05
39 Tom Goodwin .05
40 Orel Hershiser .05
41 Tripp Cromer .05
42 Sean Bergman .05
43 Troy Percival .05
44 Kevin Stocker .05
45 Albert Belle .60
46 Tony Eusebio .05
47 Sid Roberson .05
48 Todd Hollandsworth .05
49 Mark Wohlers .05
50 Kirby Puckett .65
51 Darren Holmes .05
52 Ron Karkovice .05
53 Al Martin .05
54 Pat Rapp .05
55 Mark Grace .15
56 Greg Gagne .05
57 Stan Javier .05
58 Scott Sanders .05
59 J.T. Snow .05
60 David Justice .15
61 Royce Clayton .05
62 Kevin Foster .05
63 Tim Naehring .05
64 Orlando Miller .05
65 Mike Mussina .30

66	Jim Eisenreich	.05
67	Felix Fermin	.05
68	Bernie Williams	.30
69	Robb Nen	.05
70	Ron Gant	.10
71	Felipe Lira	.05
72	Jacob Brumfield	.05
73	John Mabry	.05
74	Mark Carreon	.05
75	Carlos Baerga	.05
76	Jim Dougherty	.05
77	Ryan Thompson	.05
78	Scott Leius	.05
79	Roger Pavlik	.05
80	Gary Sheffield	.35
81	Julian Tavarez	.05
82	Andy Ashby	.05
83	Mark Lemke	.05
84	Omar Vizquel	.05
85	Darren Daulton	.05
86	Mike Lansing	.05
87	Rusty Greer	.05
88	Dave Stevens	.05
89	Jose Offerman	.05
90	Tom Henke	.05
91	Troy O'Leary	.05
92	Michael Tucker	.05
93	Marvin Freeman	.05
94	Alex Diaz	.05
95	John Wetteland	.05
96	Cal Ripken Jr. (Tribute Card)	2.00
97	Mike Mimbs	.05
98	Bobby Higginson	.10
99	Edgardo Alfonzo	.10
100	Frank Thomas	.75
101	Steve Gibralter, Bob Abreu (AAA Stars)	.15
102	Brian Givens, T.J. Mathews (AAA Stars)	.05
103	Chris Pritchett, Trenidad Hubbard (AAA Stars)	.10
104	Eric Owens, Butch Huskey (AAA Stars)	.15
105	Doug Drabek	.05
106	Tomas Perez	.05
107	Mark Leiter	.05
108	Joe Oliver	.05
109	Tony Castillo	.05
110	Checklist	.05
111	Kevin Seitzer	.05
112	Pete Schourek	.05
113	Sean Berry	.05
114	Todd Stottlemyre	.05
115	Joe Carter	.05
116	Jeff King	.05
117	Dan Wilson	.05
118	Kurt Abbott	.05
119	Lyle Mouton	.05
120	Jose Rijo	.05
121	Curtis Goodwin	.05
122	*Jose Valentin*	.05
123	Ellis Burks	.05
124	David Cone	.10
125	Eddie Murray	.25
126	Brian Jordan	.10
127	Darrin Fletcher	.05
128	Curt Schilling	.05
129	Ozzie Guillen	.05
130	Kenny Rogers	.05
131	Tom Pagnozzi	.05
132	Garret Anderson	.05
133	Bobby Jones	.05
134	Chris Gomez	.05
135	Mike Stanley	.05
136	Hideo Nomo	.50
137	Jon Nunnally	.05
138	Tim Wakefield	.05
139	Steve Finley	.05
140	Ivan Rodriguez	.50
141	Quilvio Veras	.05
142	Mike Fetters	.05
143	Mike Greenwell	.05
144	Bill Pulsipher	.10
145	Mark McGwire	2.50
146	Frank Castillo	.05
147	Greg Vaughn	.05
148	Pat Hentgen	.05
149	Walt Weiss	.05
150	Randy Johnson	.30
151	David Segui	.05
152	Benji Gil	.05
153	Tom Candiotti	.05
154	Geronimo Berroa	.05
155	John Franco	.05
156	Jay Bell	.05
157	Mark Gubicza	.05
158	Hal Morris	.05
159	Wilson Alvarez	.05
160	Derek Bell	.10
161	Ricky Bottalico	.05
162	Bret Boone	.05
163	Brad Radke	.05
164	John Valentin	.05
165	Steve Avery	.05
166	Mark McLemore	.05
167	Danny Jackson	.05
168	Tino Martinez	.10
169	Shane Reynolds	.05
170	Terry Pendleton	.05
171	Jim Edmonds	.10
172	Esteban Loaiza	.05
173	Ray Durham	.05
174	Carlos Perez	.05
175	Raul Mondesi	.25
176	Steve Ontiveros	.05
177	Chipper Jones	1.00
178	Otis Nixon	.05
179	John Burkett	.05
180	Gregg Jefferies	.05
181	Denny Martinez	.05
182	Ken Caminiti	.15
183	Doug Jones	.05
184	Brian McRae	.05
185	Don Mattingly	.75
186	Mel Rojas	.05
187	Marty Cordova	.05
188	Vinny Castilla	.15
189	John Smoltz	.15
190	Travis Fryman	.10
191	Chris Hoiles	.05
192	Chuck Finley	.05
193	Ryan Klesko	.15
194	Alex Fernandez	.05
195	Dante Bichette	.25
196	Eric Karros	.10
197	Roger Clemens	1.00
198	Randy Myers	.05
199	Tony Phillips	.05
200	Cal Ripken Jr.	2.00
201	Rod Beck	.05
202	Chad Curtis	.05
203	Jack McDowell	.05
204	Gary Gaetti	.05
205	Ken Griffey Jr.	2.50
206	Ramon Martinez	.10
207	Jeff Kent	.05
208	Brad Ausmus	.05
209	Devon White	.05
210	Jason Giambi (Future Star)	.15
211	Nomar Garciaparra (Future Star)	1.50
212	Billy Wagner (Future Star)	.10
213	Todd Greene (Future Star)	.15
214	Paul Wilson (Future Star)	.15
215	Johnny Damon (Future Star)	.10
216	Alan Benes (Future Star)	.15
217	Karim Garcia (Future Star)	.30
218	Dustin Hermanson (Future Star)	.10
219	Derek Jeter (Future Star)	1.50
220	Checklist	.05
221	Kirby Puckett (Star Power)	.25
222	Cal Ripken Jr. (Star Power)	.75
223	Albert Belle (Star Power)	.25
224	Randy Johnson (Star Power)	.15
225	Wade Boggs (Star Power)	.10
226	Carlos Baerga (Star Power)	.05
227	Ivan Rodriguez (Star Power)	.25
228	Mike Mussina (Star Power)	.15
229	Frank Thomas (Star Power)	.30
230	Ken Griffey Jr. (Star Power)	1.00
231	Jose Mesa (Star Power)	.05
232	*Matt Morris* (Draft Pick)	.25
233	Craig Wilson (Draft Pick)	.05
234	*Alvie Shepherd* (Draft Pick)	.10
235	*Randy Winn* (Draft Pick)	.05
236	*David Yocum* (Draft Pick)	.15
237	*Jason Brester* (Draft Pick)	.20
238	*Shane Monahan* (Draft Pick)	.25
239	*Brian McNichol* (Draft Pick)	.20
240	Reggie Taylor (Draft Pick)	.05
241	Garrett Long (Draft Pick)	.05
242	*Jonathan Johnson* (Draft Pick)	.20
243	*Jeff Liefer* (Draft Pick)	.25
244	*Brian Powell* (Draft Pick)	.05
245	Brian Buchanan (Draft Pick)	.10
246	Mike Piazza	1.25
247	Edgar Martinez	.05
248	Chuck Knoblauch	.15
249	Andres Galarraga	.20
250	Tony Gwynn	1.00
251	Lee Smith	.05
252	Sammy Sosa	1.50
253	Jim Thome	.30
254	Frank Rodriguez	.05
255	Charlie Hayes	.05
256	Bernard Gilkey	.10
257	John Smiley	.05
258	Brady Anderson	.15
259	Rico Brogna	.05
260	Kirt Manwaring	.05
261	Len Dykstra	.05
262	Tom Glavine	.15
263	Vince Coleman	.05
264	John Olerud	.15
265	Orlando Merced	.05
266	Kent Mercker	.05
267	Terry Steinbach	.05
268	Brian Hunter	.05
269	Jeff Fassero	.05
270	Jay Buhner	.10
271	Jeff Brantley	.05
272	Tim Raines	.05
273	Jimmy Key	.05
274	Mo Vaughn	.30
275	Andre Dawson	.10
276	Jose Mesa	.05
277	Brett Butler	.05
278	Luis Gonzalez	.10
279	Steve Sparks	.05
280	Chili Davis	.05
281	Carl Everett	.10
282	Jeff Cirillo	.10
283	Thomas Howard	.05
284	Paul O'Neill	.20
285	Pat Meares	.05
286	Mickey Tettleton	.05
287	Rey Sanchez	.05
288	Bip Roberts	.05
289	Roberto Alomar	.40
290	Ruben Sierra	.05
291	John Flaherty	.05
292	Bret Saberhagen	.10
293	Barry Larkin	.15
294	Sandy Alomar	.10
295	Ed Sprague	.05
296	Gary DiSarcina	.05
297	Marquis Grissom	.10
298	John Frascatore	.05
299	Will Clark	.25
300	Barry Bonds	.50
301	Ozzie Smith	.40
302	Dave Nilsson	.05
303	Pedro Martinez	.50
304	Joey Cora	.05
305	Rick Aguilera	.05
306	Craig Biggio	.25
307	Jose Vizcaino	.05
308	Jeff Montgomery	.05
309	Moises Alou	.15
310	Robin Ventura	.15
311	David Wells	.05
312	Delino DeShields	.05
313	Trevor Hoffman	.05
314	Andy Benes	.05
315	Deion Sanders	.20
316	Jim Bullinger	.05
317	John Jaha	.05
318	Greg Maddux	1.00
319	Tim Salmon	.20
320	Ben McDonald	.05
321	*Sandy Martinez*	.10
322	Dan Miceli	.05
323	Wade Boggs	.25
324	Ismael Valdes	.05
325	Juan Gonzalez	.75
326	Charles Nagy	.05
327	Ray Lankford	.10
328	Mark Portugal	.05
329	Bobby Bonilla	.10
330	Reggie Sanders	.10
331	Jamie Brewington	.05
332	Aaron Sele	.05
333	Pete Harnisch	.05
334	Cliff Floyd	.05
335	Cal Eldred	.05
336	Jason Bates (Now Appearing)	.05
337	Tony Clark (Now Appearing)	.25
338	Jose Herrera (Now Appearing)	.05
339	Alex Ochoa (Now Appearing)	.10
340	Mark Loretta (Now Appearing)	.05
341	*Donne Wall* (Now Appearing)	.05
342	Jason Kendall (Now Appearing)	.10
343	Shannon Stewart (Now Appearing)	.10
344	Brooks Kieschnick (Now Appearing)	.10
345	Chris Snopek (Now Appearing)	.10
346	Ruben Rivera (Now Appearing)	.10
347	Jeff Suppan (Now Appearing)	.05
348	Phil Nevin (Now Appearing)	.05
349	John Wasdin (Now Appearing)	.05
350	Jay Payton (Now Appearing)	.05
351	Tim Crabtree (Now Appearing)	.05
352	Rick Krivda (Now Appearing)	.05
353	Bob Wolcott (Now Appearing)	.05
354	Jimmy Haynes (Now Appearing)	.05
355	Herb Perry	.05
356	Ryne Sandberg	.40
357	Harold Baines	.05
358	Chad Ogea	.05
359	Lee Tinsley	.05
360	Matt Williams	.25
361	Randy Velarde	.05
362	Jose Canseco	.50
363	Larry Walker	.35
364	Kevin Appier	.05
365	Darryl Hamilton	.05
366	Jose Lima	.05
367	Javy Lopez	.15
368	Dennis Eckersley	.10
369	Jason Isringhausen	.10
370	Mickey Morandini	.05
371	Scott Cooper	.05
372	Jim Abbott	.05
373	Paul Sorrento	.05
374	Chris Hammond	.05
375	Lance Johnson	.05
376	Kevin Brown	.10
377	Luis Alicea	.05
378	Andy Pettitte	.25
379	Dean Palmer	.05
380	Jeff Bagwell	.50
381	Jaime Navarro	.05
382	Rondell White	.10
383	Erik Hanson	.05
384	Pedro Munoz	.05
385	Heathcliff Slocumb	.05
386	Wally Joyner	.10
387	Bob Tewksbury	.05
388	David Bell	.05
389	Fred McGriff	.25
390	Mike Henneman	.05
391	Robby Thompson	.05
392	Norm Charlton	.05
393	Cecil Fielder	.10
394	Benito Santiago	.05
395	Rafael Palmeiro	.20
396	Ricky Bones	.05
397	Rickey Henderson	.25
398	C.J. Nitkowski	.05
399	Shawon Dunston	.05
400	Manny Ramirez	.75
401	Bill Swift	.05
402	Chad Fonville	.05
403	Joey Hamilton	.05
404	Alex Gonzalez	.05
405	Roberto Hernandez	.05
406	Jeff Blauser	.05
407	LaTroy Hawkins	.05
408	Greg Colbrunn	.05
409	Todd Hundley	.10
410	Glenn Dishman	.05
411	Joe Vitiello	.05
412	Todd Worrell	.05
413	Wil Cordero	.05
414	Ken Hill	.05
415	Carlos Garcia	.05
416	Bryan Rekar	.05
417	Shawn Green (Topps Rookie All-Star)	.40
418	Tyler Green	.05
419	Mike Blowers	.05
420	Kenny Lofton	.30
421	Denny Neagle	.05
422	Jeff Conine	.05
423	Mark Langston	.05
424	Steve Cox, *Jesse Ibarra*, Derrek Lee, *Ron Wright* (Prospects)	.25
425	*Jim Bonnici*, Billy Owens, Richie Sexson, *Daryle Ward* (Prospects)	3.00
426	Kevin Jordan, *Bobby Morris*, Desi Relaford, *Adam Riggs* (Prospects)	.05
427	Tim Harkrider, Rey Ordonez, Neifi Perez, Enrique Wilson (Prospects)	.25
428	Bartolo Colon, Doug Million, Rafael Orellano, *Ray Ricken* (Prospects)	.10
429	Jeff D'Amico, *Marty Janzen*, Gary Rath, Clint Sodowsky (Prospects)	.10
430	Matt Drews, *Rich Hunter*, *Matt Ruebel*, Bret Wagner (Prospects)	.10
431	Jaime Bluma, *Dave Coggin*, Steve Montgomery, Brandon Reed (Prospects)	.10
432	Mike Figga, *Raul Ibanez*, Paul Konerko, Julio Mosquera (Prospects)	.20
433	Brian Barber, Marc Kroon, Marc Valdes, Don Wengert (Prospects)	.05
434	George Arias, *Chris Haas*, Scott Rolen, Scott Spiezio (Prospects)	1.00
435	*Brian Banks*, Vladimir Guerrero, Andruw Jones, Billy McMillon (Prospects)	2.00
436	Roger Cedeno, Derrick Gibson, Ben Grieve, *Shane Spencer* (Prospects)	1.50
437	Anton French, Demond Smith, *Darond Stovall*, Keith Williams (Prospects)	.20
438	*Michael Coleman*, Jacob Cruz, Richard Hidalgo, Charles Peterson (Prospects)	.40
439	Trey Beamon, Yamil Benitez, Jermaine Dye, Angel Echevarria (Prospects)	.15
440	Checklist	.05

1996 Topps Classic Confrontations

Head-to-head stats among baseball's top pitchers and hitters are featured in this insert set. The cards were seeded one per pack in the special 50-cent packs sold exclusively at Wal-Mart during the T206 Honus Wagner card giveaway promotion. Fronts have player action poses against a granite background and are highlighted in gold foil. Backs have a portrait photo and stats.

		MT
	Complete Set (15):	6.00
	Common Player:	.25
1	Ken Griffey Jr.	1.50
2	Cal Ripken Jr.	1.00
3	Edgar Martinez	.25
4	Kirby Puckett	.75
5	Frank Thomas	.60
6	Barry Bonds	.50
7	Reggie Sanders	.25
8	Andres Galarraga	.25
9	Tony Gwynn	.75
10	Mike Piazza	1.00
11	Randy Johnson	.35
12	Mike Mussina	.25
13	Roger Clemens	.75
14	Tom Glavine	.25
15	Greg Maddux	.90

1996 Topps Mickey Mantle Reprint Cards

One of Mickey Mantle's regular-issue Bowman or Topps cards from each year

1951-1969 was reproduced in 2-1/2" x 3-1/2" format as a Series 1 insert. Each card carries a gold-foil commemorative seal in one corner of the front. The reprints are found one per six retail packs and, in hobby, once per nine packs. The 1965-69 reprints were somewhat shortprinted (four 1965-69 cards for each five 1951-1964) and are 20% scarcer.

		MT
Complete Set (19):		100.00
Common Mantle:		5.00
Common SP Mantle (15-19):		8.00
1	1951 Bowman #253	10.00
2	1952 Topps #311	15.00
3	1953 Topps #82	6.00
4	1954 Bowman #65	5.00
5	1955 Bowman #202	5.00
6	1956 Topps #135	5.00
7	1957 Topps #95	5.00
8	1958 Topps #150	5.00
9	1959 Topps #10	5.00
10	1960 Topps #350	5.00
11	1961 Topps #300	5.00
12	1962 Topps #200	5.00
13	1963 Topps #200	5.00
14	1964 Topps #50	5.00
15	1965 Topps #350	8.00
16	1966 Topps #50	8.00
17	1967 Topps #150	8.00
18	1968 Topps #280	8.00
19	1969 Topps #500	8.00

1996 Topps/Finest Mickey Mantle

Nineteen of Mickey Mantle's regular-issue Bowman and Topps cards from 1951-1969 were printed in Finest technology for this Series 2 insert set. Each card's chrome front is protected with a peel-off plastic layer. Average insertion rate for the Mantle Finest reprints is one per 18 packs. The 1965-69 reprints were printed in a ratio of four for every five 1951-64 reprints, making them 20% scarcer.

		MT
Complete Set (19):		140.00
Common Mantle:		6.00
Common Shortprint Mantle (15-19):		10.00
1	1951 Bowman #253	12.00
2	1952 Topps #311	20.00
3	1953 Topps #82	10.00
4	1954 Bowman #65	6.00
5	1955 Bowman #202	6.00
6	1956 Topps #135	6.00
7	1957 Topps #95	6.00
8	1958 Topps #150	6.00
9	1959 Topps #10	6.00
10	1960 Topps #350	6.00
11	1961 Topps #300	6.00
12	1962 Topps #200	6.00
13	1963 Topps #200	6.00
14	1964 Topps #50	6.00
15	1965 Topps #350	10.00
16	1966 Topps #50	10.00
17	1967 Topps #150	10.00
18	1968 Topps #280	10.00
19	1969 Topps #500	10.00

1996 Topps/Finest Mickey Mantle Refractors

Each of the 19 Mickey Mantle Finest reprints in Series 2 can also be found in an unmarked Refractor version. Average insertion rate of these super scarce inserts is one per 144 packs.

		MT
Complete Set (19):		725.00
Common Mantle:		40.00
Common SP Mantle (15-19):		48.00
1	1951 Bowman #253	80.00
2	1952 Topps #311	120.00
3	1953 Topps #82	48.00
4	1954 Bowman #65	40.00
5	1955 Bowman #202	40.00
6	1956 Topps #135	40.00
7	1957 Topps #95	40.00
8	1958 Topps #150	40.00
9	1959 Topps #10	40.00
10	1960 Topps #350	40.00
11	1961 Topps #300	40.00
12	1962 Topps #200	40.00
13	1963 Topps #200	40.00
14	1964 Topps #50	40.00
15	1965 Topps #350	48.00
16	1966 Topps #50	48.00
17	1967 Topps #150	48.00
18	1968 Topps #280	48.00
19	1969 Topps #500	48.00

1996 Topps Mickey Mantle Redemption

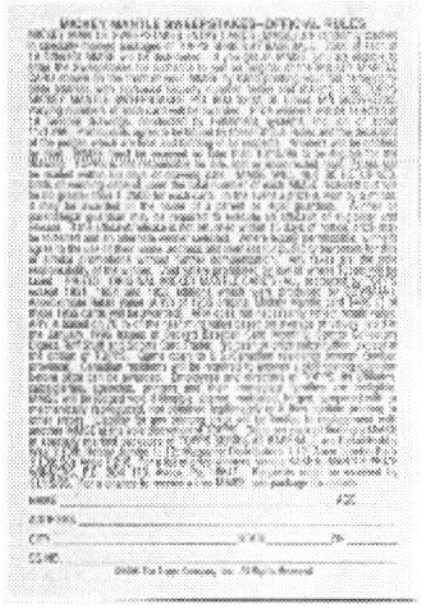

Each of the 19 Mantle reprint cards, minus the commemorative gold-foil stamp on front, was also issued in a sweepstakes set. Seeded one per 108 packs, these cards could be sent in for a chance to win the authentic Mantle card pictured on front. Between one and 10 genuine Mantles were awarded for each of the 19 years. Cards entered in the sweepstakes were not returned when the contest ended Oct. 15, 1996. The sweepstakes cards are a Series 2 exclusive insert.

		MT
Complete Set (19):		200.00
Common Mantle:		10.00
1	1951 Bowman #253	25.00
2	1952 Topps #311	35.00
3	1953 Topps #82	15.00
4	1954 Bowman #65	10.00
5	1955 Bowman #202	10.00
6	1956 Topps #135	10.00
7	1957 Topps #95	10.00
8	1958 Topps #150	10.00
9	1959 Topps #10	10.00
10	1960 Topps #350	10.00
11	1961 Topps #300	10.00
12	1962 Topps #200	10.00
13	1963 Topps #200	10.00
14	1964 Topps #50	10.00
15	1965 Topps #350	10.00
16	1966 Topps #50	10.00
17	1967 Topps #150	10.00
18	1968 Topps #280	10.00
19	1969 Topps #500	10.00

1996 Topps Mickey Mantle Case Inserts

Inserted one per case of Series 2 Topps, these special versions of the 19 Mickey Mantle reprint cards come pre-packaged in a hard plastic holder. The cards are identical to the other reprints except for the inclusion of a foil stamp at bottom-back indicating that it is a case card. Like the other Mantle reprints, the 1965-69 cards are somewhat scarcer due to short-printing.

		MT
Complete Set (19):		700.00
Common Mantle:		40.00
Common SP Mantle (15-19):		50.00
1	1951 Bowman #253	60.00
2	1952 Topps #311	75.00
3	1953 Topps #82	50.00
4	1954 Bowman #65	40.00
5	1955 Bowman #202	40.00
6	1956 Topps #135	40.00
7	1957 Topps #95	40.00
8	1958 Topps #150	40.00
9	1959 Topps #10	40.00
10	1960 Topps #350	40.00
11	1961 Topps #300	40.00
12	1962 Topps #200	40.00
13	1963 Topps #200	40.00
14	1964 Topps #50	40.00
15	1965 Topps #350	50.00
16	1966 Topps #50	50.00
17	1967 Topps #150	50.00
18	1968 Topps #280	50.00
19	1969 Topps #500	50.00

1996 Topps Mickey Mantle Foundation Card

This black-and-white card was an insert exclusive to specially marked 1996 Topps factory sets. In standard 2-1/2" x 3-1/2" format, the card offers on its back information about the foundation and it work in health care and organ donation causes.

	MT
Mickey Mantle	6.00

1996 Topps Masters of the Game

Appearing at a one per 18 pack rate, these inserts are exclusive to Series 1 hobby packs.

		MT
Complete Set (20):		25.00
Common Player:		.50
1	Dennis Eckersley	.50
2	Denny Martinez	.50
3	Eddie Murray	1.00
4	Paul Molitor	1.50
5	Ozzie Smith	1.50
6	Rickey Henderson	1.00
7	Tim Raines	.50
8	Lee Smith	.50
9	Cal Ripken Jr.	8.00
10	Chili Davis	.50
11	Wade Boggs	1.00
12	Tony Gwynn	4.00
13	Don Mattingly	2.00
14	Bret Saberhagen	.50
15	Kirby Puckett	1.50
16	Joe Carter	.50
17	Roger Clemens	3.00
18	Barry Bonds	3.00
19	Greg Maddux	5.00
20	Frank Thomas	2.00

1996 Topps Mystery Finest

Each Mystery Finest insert has an opaque black film over the card front, concealing the identity of the player until removed. The inserts are seeded at the rate of one per 36 packs.

		MT
Complete Set (21)		60.00
Common Player:		1.00
Refractors: 3X to 6X		
M1	Hideo Nomo	1.50
M2	Greg Maddux	5.00
M3	Randy Johnson	1.50
M4	Chipper Jones	6.00
M5	Marty Cordova	1.00
M6	Garret Anderson	1.00
M7	Cal Ripken Jr.	7.50
M8	Kirby Puckett	2.50
M9	Tony Gwynn	4.00
M10	Manny Ramirez	3.00
M11	Jim Edmonds	1.00
M12	Mike Piazza	6.00
M13	Barry Bonds	3.00
M14	Raul Mondesi	1.00
M15	Sammy Sosa	6.00
M16	Ken Griffey Jr.	10.00
M17	Albert Belle	2.00
M18	Dante Bichette	1.00
M10	Mo Vaughn	1.50
M20	Jeff Bagwell	2.50
M21	Frank Thomas	4.00

1996 Topps 5-Star Mystery Finest

The 5-Star Mystery Finest inserts have an opaque black film over the card front, like the regular Mystery Finest, but has the words "5-Star" in large letters across the background. They are inserted at the average rate of one per 36 packs.

		MT
Complete Set (5):		40.00
Common Player:		2.00
Refractors: 3X to 5X		
M22	Hideo Nomo	3.00
M23	Cal Ripken Jr.	12.00
M24	Mike Piazza	12.00
M25	Ken Griffey Jr.	20.00
M26	Frank Thomas	5.00

1996 Topps Power Boosters

This insert set is printed in Topps' "Power Matrix" technology, replacing two regular cards when found on the average of once per 36 packs. The Power Boosters reproduce the Star Power and Draft Picks subsets on a double-thick card.

		MT
Complete Set (26):		60.00
Common Player:		1.25
1	Tony Gwynn (Star Power)	4.00
2	Mike Piazza (Star Power)	6.00
3	Greg Maddux (Star Power)	5.00
4	Jeff Bagwell (Star Power)	2.50
5	Larry Walker (Star Power)	2.00
6	Barry Larkin (Star Power)	1.25
8	Tom Glavine (Star Power)	1.25
9	Craig Biggio (Star Power)	2.00
10	Barry Bonds (Star Power)	2.50
11	Heathcliff Slocumb (Star Power)	1.25
12	Matt Williams (Star Power)	1.25
13	Todd Helton (Draft Pick)	5.00
14	Mark Redman (Draft Pick)	1.25
15	Michael Barrett (Draft Pick)	3.00
16	Ben Davis (Draft Pick)	4.00
17	Juan LeBron (Draft Pick)	1.25
18	Tony McKnight (Draft Pick)	1.25
19	Ryan Jaroncyk (Draft Pick)	1.25
20	Corey Jenkins (Draft Pick)	1.25
21	Jim Scharrer (Draft Pick)	1.25
22	Mark Bellhorn (Draft Pick)	1.25
23	Jarrod Washburn (Draft Pick)	1.25

24	Geoff Jenkins (Draft Pick)	5.00
25	Sean Casey (Draft Pick)	40.00
26	Brett Tomko (Draft Pick)	1.25

1996 Topps Profiles-AL

Ten cards from this insert issue can be found in each of Topps Series 1 and 2. Analyzing an up-and-coming star, the cards are found every 12th pack, on average.

		MT
Complete Set (20):		20.00
Complete Series 1 (10):		10.00
Complete Series 2 (10):		10.00
Common Player:		.50
1	Roberto Alomar	1.00
2	Carlos Baerga	.50
3	Albert Belle	.75
4	Cecil Fielder	.50
5	Ken Griffey Jr.	5.00
6	Randy Johnson	.60
7	Paul O'Neill	.50
8	Cal Ripken Jr.	3.00
9	Frank Thomas	1.50
10	Mo Vaughn	.50
11	Jay Buhner	.50
12	Marty Cordova	.50
13	Jim Edmonds	.50
14	Juan Gonzalez	1.50
15	Kenny Lofton	.50
16	Edgar Martinez	.50
17	Don Mattingly	1.50
18	Mark McGwire	5.00
19	Rafael Palmeiro	1.00
20	Tim Salmon	.75

1996 Topps Profiles-NL

Projected future stars of the National League are featured in this insert set. Ten players each are found in Series 1 and 2 packs at the rate of one per 12, on average.

		MT
Complete Set (20):		15.00
Complete Series 1 (10):		10.00
Complete Series 2 (10):		5.00
Common Player:		.50
1	Jeff Bagwell	1.50
2	Derek Bell	.50
3	Barry Bonds	1.50
4	Greg Maddux	3.00
5	Fred McGriff	.75
6	Raul Mondesi	.50
7	Mike Piazza	3.00
8	Reggie Sanders	.50
9	Sammy Sosa	3.00
10	Larry Walker	1.00
11	Dante Bichette	.75
12	Andres Galarraga	.75
13	Ron Gant	.50
14	Tom Glavine	.50
15	Chipper Jones	3.00
16	David Justice	.50
17	Barry Larkin	.50
18	Hideo Nomo	.75
19	Gary Sheffield	.75
20	Matt Williams	.75

1996 Topps Road Warriors

These inserts feature top hitters and were only found in Series 2 packs sold at Wal-Mart stores. Cards have an RW prefix to their number. Fronts have action photos and gold foil highlights. Backs feature a portrait photo and hitting stats from the player's favorite out-of-town ballparks.

		MT
Complete Set (20):		12.00
Common Player:		.25
1	Derek Bell	.25
2	Albert Belle	1.00
3	Craig Biggio	.50
4	Barry Bonds	2.00
5	Jay Buhner	.25
6	Jim Edmonds	.25
7	Gary Gaetti	.25
8	Ron Gant	.25
9	Edgar Martinez	.25
10	Tino Martinez	.40
11	Mark McGwire	3.00
12	Mike Piazza	2.50
13	Manny Ramirez	1.00
14	Tim Salmon	.50
15	Reggie Sanders	.25
16	Frank Thomas	1.50
17	John Valentin	.25
18	Mo Vaughn	1.00
19	Robin Ventura	.50
20	Matt Williams	.40

1996 Topps Wrecking Crew

Printed on foilboard stock, cards of 15 players known for their hitting prowess are featured in this insert set. Found only in Series 2 hobby packs, the inserts are a one per 72 packs find, on average. Cards are numbered with a "WC" prefix.

		MT
Complete Set (15):		40.00
Common Player:		1.00
1	Jeff Bagwell	2.50
2	Albert Belle	2.00
3	Barry Bonds	2.50
4	Jose Canseco	2.00
5	Joe Carter	1.00
6	Cecil Fielder	1.00
7	Ron Gant	1.00
8	Juan Gonzalez	2.50
9	Ken Griffey Jr.	10.00
10	Fred McGriff	1.50
11	Mark McGwire	10.00
12	Mike Piazza	5.00
13	Frank Thomas	2.50
14	Mo Vaughn	1.50
15	Matt Williams	1.50

1996 Topps Team Topps

Some of baseball's most popular players and their teammates are featured on specially marked cards sold in blister packed team sets along with a jumbo "Big Topps" version of the team superstar's card. The team sets were a Wal-Mart exclusive, selling for around $5. Most of the Team Topps cards are identical to the regular-issue versions except for the addition of a gold-foil Team Topps logo on the card front. Several cards in this special issue have had their regular and Star Power backs transposed. Individual team set values shown do not include the Big Topps card packaged with it.

		MT
Complete Set (79):		20.00
Common Player:		.10
	Orioles team set (18):	5.00
	Cal Ripken, Jr. Big Topps:	3.50
34	Manny Alexander	.10
65	Mike Mussina (Star Power front, regular back)	.25
96	Cal Ripken Jr. (2,131)	2.00
121	Curtis Goodwin	.10
183	Doug Jones	.10
191	Chris Hoiles	.10
200	Cal Ripken Jr.	2.50
222	Cal Ripken Jr. (Star Power)	1.00
228	Mike Mussina (Regular-card front, Star Power back)	.25
234	Alvie Shepherd (Draft Pick)	.15
258	Brady Anderson	.20
320	Ben McDonald	.10
329	Bobby Bonilla	.10
352	Rick Krivda (Now Appearing)	.10
354	Jimmy Haynes (Now Appearing)	.15
357	Harold Baines	.10
376	Kevin Brown	.10
395	Rafael Palmeiro	.15
	Cubs team set (15):	3.00
	Ryne Sandberg Big Topps:	2.50
35	Todd Zeile	.10
55	Mark Grace	.25
62	Kevin Foster	.10
146	Frank Castillo	.10
184	Brian McRae	.10
198	Randy Myers	.10
239	Brian McNichol (Draft Pick)	.15
252	Sammy Sosa	1.50
278	Luis Gonzalez	.10
287	Rey Sanchez	.10
316	Jim Bullinger	.10
344	Brooks Kieshnick (Now Appearing)	.30
356	Ryne Sandberg	.75
381	Jaime Navarro	.10
399	Shawon Dunston	.10
	White Sox team set (14):	3.00
	Frank Thomas Big Topps:	4.00
52	Ron Karkovice	.10
100	Frank Thomas	1.50
119	Lyle Mouton	.10
129	Ozzie Guillen	.10
159	Wilson Alvarez	.10
173	Ray Durham (All-Star Rookie)	.20
194	Alex Fernandez	.10
229	Frank Thomas (Star Power)	.50
243	Jeff Liefer (Draft Pick)	.15
272	Tim Raines	.15
310	Robin Ventura	.15
345	Chris Snopek (Now Appearing)	.15
375	Lance Johnson	.10
405	Roberto Hernandez	.10
	Yankees team set (18):	7.50
	Derek Jeter Big Topps:	2.50
7	Mickey Mantle	6.00
27	Tony Fernandez	.10
68	Bernie Williams	.40
95	John Wetteland	.10
124	David Cone	.10
135	Mike Stanley	.10
185	Don Mattingly	1.00
203	Jack McDowell	.10
219	Derek Jeter (Future Star)	1.00
225	Wade Boggs (Star Power)	.25
245	Brian Buchanan (Draft Pick)	.15
273	Jimmy Key	.10
284	Paul O'Neill	.10
290	Ruben Sierra	.10
323	Wade Boggs	.45
346	Ruben Rivera (Now Appearing)	.30
361	Randy Velarde	.10
378	Andy Pettitte	.15
	Rangers team set (14):	2.00
	Juan Gonzalez Big Topps:	2.50
79	Roger Pavlik	.10
87	Rusty Greer	.10
130	Kenny Rogers	.10
140	Ivan Rodriguez	.45
152	Benji Gil	.10
166	Mark McLemore	.10
178	Otis Nixon	.10
227	Ivan Rodriguez (Star Power)	.20
242	Jonathan Johnson (Draft Pick)	.15
286	Mickey Tettleton	.10
299	Will Clark	.25
325	Juan Gonzalez	1.00
387	Bob Tewksbury	.10
379	Dean Palmer	.10

1996 Topps American League Champion Cleveland Indians

Sold in a blister pack at Wal-Mart stores, this team set features specially overprinted versions of the Indians' regular '96 Topps cards, along with a super-size "Big Topps" card of Albert Belle. Each card carries a color logo recognizing the Tribe's A.L. Championship season of 1995. Sets sold for around $5.

		MT
Complete Set (21):		3.00
Common Player:		.10
Albert Belle Big Topps:		3.00
25	Sean Casey	.75
40	Orel Hershiser	.15
45	Albert Belle	.50
75	Carlos Baerga	.15
81	Julian Tavarez	.10
84	Omar Vizquel	.10
125	Eddie Murray	.25
181	Denny Martinez	.15
223	Albert Belle (Star Power)	.40
226	Carlos Baerga (Star Power)	.15
231	Jose Mesa (Star Power)	.10
253	Jim Thome	.25
276	Jose Mesa	.10
294	Sandy Alomar	.15
326	Charles Nagy	.10
355	Herb Perry	.10
358	Chad Ogea	.10
373	Paul Sorrento	.10
400	Manny Ramirez	.75
414	Ken Hill	.10
420	Kenny Lofton	.35

1996 Topps A.L. West Champion Seattle Mariners

These specially marked versions of Topps' regular '96 cards were sold for around $5 in a blister pack with a Ken Griffey, Jr. "Big Topps" card. The team sets were a Wal-Mart exclusive. Each of the Mariners' cards is overprinted with a color A.L. West Champions logo. Cards are otherwise identical to the regular issue.

		MT
Complete Set (18):		3.00
Common Player:		.10
Ken Griffey, Jr. Big Topps:		4.00
38	Tim Belcher	.10
67	Felix Fermin	.10
94	Alex Diaz	.10
117	Dan Wilson	.15
150	Randy Johnson	.30
168	Tino Martinez	.15
205	Ken Griffey Jr.	2.50
224	Randy Johnson (Star Power)	.20
230	Ken Griffey Jr. (Star Power)	1.00
238	Shane Monahan (Draft Pick)	.15
247	Edgar Martinez	.15
263	Vince Coleman	.10
270	Jay Buhner	.20
304	Joey Cora	.10
314	Andy Benes	.15
353	Bob Wolcott (Now Appearing)	.10
392	Norm Charlton	.10
419	Mike Blowers	.10

1996 Topps Dodger Stadium 35th Anniversary L.A. Dodgers

Celebrating 35 seasons of play in Chavez Ravine, this team set of specially marked cards was issued in a blister pack with a jumbo Hideo Nomo "Big Topps" card. Selling for about $5, the team set was a Wal-Mart exclusive. Otherwise identical to the regular '96 Topps cards, these are overprinted with a colorful 35 Seasons logo. The backs of the two Mike Piazza cards in the set were switched. His regular card has the Star Power back (#2) while his Star Power card (#246) has the regular-issue back.

		MT
Complete Set (16):		3.00
Common Player:		.10
Hideo Nomo Big Topps:		2.00
2	Mike Piazza (Star Power back)	.75
48	Todd Hollandsworth	.15
89	Jose Offerman	.10
136	Hideo Nomo (All-Star Rookie)	1.00
153	Tom Candiotti	.10
175	Raul Mondesi	.40
196	Eric Karros	.10
206	Ramon Martinez	.15
217	Karim Garcia (Future Star)	.40
236	David Yocum (Draft Pick)	.15
246	Mike Piazza (Star Power front)	.75
277	Brett Butler	.10
312	Delino DeShields	.10
324	Ismael Valdes	.10
402	Chad Fonville	.10
412	Todd Worrell	.10

1996 Topps World Champions Atlanta Braves

These specially marked versions of Topps regular 1996 cards feature a color World Champions logo overprinted on the front of each card. They were sold as a team set along with a 3-1/2" x 5" "Big Topps" card at Wal-Mart stores for around $5.

		MT
Complete Set (17):		3.00
Common Player:		.10
Greg Maddux Big Topps:		2.50
3	Greg Maddux (Star Power)	.50
8	Tom Glavine (Star Power)	.15
12	Jim Scharrer (Draft Pick)	.15
49	Mark Wohlers	.10
60	David Justice	.25
83	Mark Lemke	.10
165	Steve Avery	.10
177	Chipper Jones (All-Star Rookie)	1.50
189	John Smoltz	.15
193	Ryan Klesko	.25
262	Tom Glavine	.15
266	Kent Mercker	.10
297	Marquis Grissom	.10
318	Greg Maddux	1.50
367	Javy Lopez	.15
389	Fred McGriff	.35
406	Jeff Blauser	.10

1996 Topps Big Topps

These double-size (3-1/2" x 5") cards are found exclusively in team-set blister packs prepared by Treat Entertainments for sale at Wal-Mart stores. Suggested retail price was just under $5. The Big Topps cards feature the fronts of the players' regular 1996 Topps card set against a marbled green background. Backs are in black-and-white with copyright data and licensors' logos. The unnumbered cards are checklisted here alphabetically.

		MT
Complete Set (9):		24.00
Common Player:		2.50
(1)	Albert Belle	1.50
(2)	Juan Gonzalez	2.50
(3)	Ken Griffey Jr.	4.00
(4)	Derek Jeter	3.00
(5)	Greg Maddux	2.00
(6)	Hideo Nomo	1.00
(7)	Cal Ripken Jr.	3.50
(8)	Ryne Sandberg	2.00
(9)	Frank Thomas	2.00

1996 Topps/Chrome Promo Sheet

This promotional sheet was issued to promote the first annual issue of Topps Chrome baseball cards. The 8" x 5" sheet reproduces three of the card fronts from the forthcoming set in Topps' "Brilliant Chromium" technology. Back of the sheet is conventionally printed and advertises the set and its chase cards.

	MT
Sheet:	8.00
Tom Glavine (Star Power)	
Mike Piazza	
Cal Ripken Jr. (2131 Tribute)	

1996 Topps/Chrome

In conjunction with baseball's Post-season, Topps introduced the premiere edition of Chrome Baseball. The set has 165 of the elite players from 1996 Topps Baseball Series I and II. Card #7 is a Mickey Mantle tribute card, similar to Topps' Series I card. There are four insert sets: Masters of the Game and Wrecking Crew, and scarcer Refractor versions for both types.

		MT
Complete Set (165):		75.00
Common Player:		.25
Complete Refractor Set (165):		2500.
Common Refractor:		5.00
Refractors: 4x to 8x		
Wax Box:		100.00
1	Tony Gwynn (Star Power)	2.00
2	Mike Piazza (Star Power)	2.50
3	Greg Maddux (Star Power)	2.50
4	Jeff Bagwell (Star Power)	1.50
5	Larry Walker (Star Power)	.75
6	Barry Larkin (Star Power)	.50
7	Mickey Mantle (Commemorative)	10.00
8	Tom Glavine (Star Power)	.40
9	Craig Biggio (Star Power)	.50
10	Barry Bonds (Star Power)	1.00
11	Heathcliff Slocumb (Star Power)	.25
12	Matt Williams (Star Power)	.50
13	Todd Helton (Draft Pick)	8.00
14	Paul Molitor	1.50
15	Glenallen Hill	.25
16	Troy Percival	.25
17	Albert Belle	1.50
18	Mark Wohlers	.25
19	Kirby Puckett	2.00
20	Mark Grace	.50
21	J.T. Snow	.25
22	David Justice	.50
23	Mike Mussina	1.50
24	Bernie Williams	1.50
25	Ron Gant	.25
26	Carlos Baerga	.25
27	Gary Sheffield	.75
28	Cal Ripken Jr. (Tribute Card)	6.00
29	Frank Thomas	2.50
30	Kevin Seitzer	.25
31	Joe Carter	.30
32	Jeff King	.25
33	David Cone	.40
34	Eddie Murray	.75
35	Brian Jordan	.25
36	Garret Anderson	.25
37	Hideo Nomo	.50
38	Steve Finley	.25
39	Ivan Rodriguez	2.00
40	Quilvio Veras	.25
41	Mark McGwire	8.00
42	Greg Vaughn	.25
43	Randy Johnson	1.50
44	David Segui	.25
45	Derek Bell	.25
46	John Valentin	.25
47	Steve Avery	.25
48	Tino Martinez	.25
49	Shane Reynolds	.50
50	Jim Edmonds	.40
51	Raul Mondesi	.60
52	Chipper Jones	5.00
53	Gregg Jefferies	.25
54	Ken Caminiti	.75
55	Brian McRae	.25
56	Don Mattingly	2.00
57	Marty Cordova	.25
58	Vinny Castilla	.40
59	John Smoltz	.60
60	Travis Fryman	.30
61	Ryan Klesko	.35
62	Alex Fernandez	.25
63	Dante Bichette	.50
64	Eric Karros	.30
65	Roger Clemens	3.00
66	Randy Myers	.25
67	Cal Ripken Jr.	6.00
68	Rod Beck	.25
69	Jack McDowell	.25
70	Ken Griffey Jr.	8.00
71	Ramon Martinez	.30
72	Jason Giambi (Future Star)	.50
73	Nomar Garciaparra (Future Star)	5.00
74	Billy Wagner (Future Star)	.50
75	Todd Greene (Future Star)	.25
76	Paul Wilson (Future Star)	.40
77	Johnny Damon (Future Star)	.25
78	Alan Benes (Future Star)	.50
79	Karim Garcia (Future Star)	.75
80	Derek Jeter (Future Star)	5.00
81	Kirby Puckett (Star Power)	1.00
82	Cal Ripken Jr. (Star Power)	3.00
83	Albert Belle (Star Power)	1.00
84	Randy Johnson (Star Power)	.50
85	Wade Boggs (Star Power)	.40
86	Carlos Baerga (Star Power)	.25
87	Ivan Rodriguez (Star Power)	1.00
88	Mike Mussina (Star Power)	.75
89	Frank Thomas (Star Power)	1.00
90	Ken Griffey Jr. (Star Power)	4.00
91	Jose Mesa (Star Power)	.25
92	*Matt Morris* (Draft Pick)	3.00
93	Mike Piazza	5.00
94	Edgar Martinez	.25
95	Chuck Knoblauch	.50
96	Andres Galarraga	.75
97	Tony Gwynn	4.00
98	Lee Smith	.25
99	Sammy Sosa	5.00
100	Jim Thome	.75
101	Bernard Gilkey	.25
102	Brady Anderson	.35
103	Rico Brogna	.25
104	Lenny Dykstra	.25
105	Tom Glavine	.50
106	John Olerud	.75
107	Terry Steinbach	.25
108	Brian Hunter	.25
109	Jay Buhner	.30
110	Mo Vaughn	1.50
111	Jose Mesa	.25
112	Brett Butler	.25
113	Chili Davis	.25
114	Paul O'Neill	.75
115	Roberto Alomar	1.50
116	Barry Larkin	.50
117	Marquis Grissom	.25
118	Will Clark	.50
119	Barry Bonds	2.00
120	Ozzie Smith	1.50
121	Pedro Martinez	2.50
122	Craig Biggio	1.00
123	Moises Alou	.50
124	Robin Ventura	.50
125	Greg Maddux	5.00
126	Tim Salmon	.50
127	Wade Boggs	.50
128	Ismael Valdes	.25
129	Juan Gonzalez	2.00
130	Ray Lankford	.25
131	Bobby Bonilla	.30
132	Reggie Sanders	.25
133	Alex Ochoa (Now Appearing)	.25
134	Mark Loretta (Now Appearing)	.25
135	Jason Kendall (Now Appearing)	.25
136	Brooks Kieschnick (Now Appearing)	.25
137	Chris Snopek (Now Appearing)	.25
138	Ruben Rivera (Now Appearing)	.50
139	Jeff Suppan (Now Appearing)	.25
140	John Wasdin (Now Appearing)	.25
141	Jay Payton (Now Appearing)	.40
142	Rick Krivda (Now Appearing)	.25
143	Jimmy Haynes (Now Appearing)	.25
144	Ryne Sandberg	1.50
145	Matt Williams	.50
146	Jose Canseco	1.50
147	Larry Walker	1.50
148	Kevin Appier	.25
149	Javy Lopez	.40
150	Dennis Eckersley	.25
151	Jason Isringhausen	.25
152	Dean Palmer	.25
153	Jeff Bagwell	2.00
154	Rondell White	.40
155	Wally Joyner	.25
156	Fred McGriff	.50
157	Cecil Fielder	.30
158	Rafael Palmeiro	1.00
159	Rickey Henderson	.50
160	Shawon Dunston	.25
161	Manny Ramirez	2.00
162	Alex Gonzalez	.25
163	Shawn Green	1.00
164	Kenny Lofton	1.50
165	Jeff Conine	.25

1996 Topps/Chrome Masters of the Game

These 1996 Topps Chrome inserts were seeded one per every 12 packs. Each of the cards is also reprinted in a Refractor version; these cards are seeded one per every 36 packs.

		MT
Complete Set (20):		55.00
Common Player:		1.50
Refractors: 1.5x to 2x		
1	Dennis Eckersley	1.50
2	Denny Martinez	1.50
3	Eddie Murray	3.00
4	Paul Molitor	3.50
5	Ozzie Smith	3.50
6	Rickey Henderson	2.00
7	Tim Raines	1.50
8	Lee Smith	1.50
9	Cal Ripken Jr.	11.00
10	Chili Davis	1.50
11	Wade Boggs	2.25
12	Tony Gwynn	7.50
13	Don Mattingly	6.00
14	Bret Saberhagen	1.50
15	Kirby Puckett	6.00
16	Joe Carter	2.25
17	Roger Clemens	6.00
18	Barry Bonds	4.50
19	Greg Maddux	9.00
20	Frank Thomas	4.50

1996 Topps/Chrome Wrecking Crew

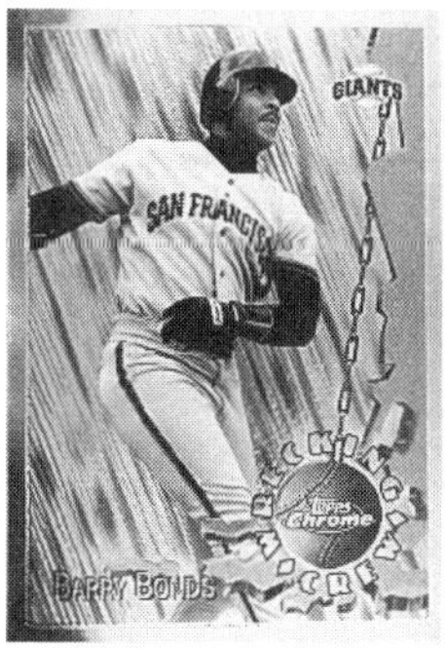

Wrecking Crew insert cards were inserted one per every 24 packs of 1996 Topps Chrome Baseball. Refractor versions were also made for these cards; they are seeded one per every 72 packs. Cards are numbered with a "WC" prefix.

		MT
Complete Set (15):		45.00
Common Player:		1.50
Refractors: 1.5x to 2x		
1	Jeff Bagwell	5.00
2	Albert Belle	2.00
3	Barry Bonds	3.00
4	Jose Canseco	2.00
5	Joe Carter	1.50
6	Cecil Fielder	1.50
7	Ron Gant	1.50
8	Juan Gonzalez	6.00
9	Ken Griffey Jr.	12.50
10	Fred McGriff	2.00
11	Mark McGwire	12.50
12	Mike Piazza	7.50
13	Frank Thomas	4.00
14	Mo Vaughn	2.00
15	Matt Williams	2.00

1996 Topps Landmark Medallions

Milestones of the 1995 season are recalled in this set

of limited edition (2,000) medallions. Each of the 2-1/2" x 3-1/2" pieces features a Topps Finest technology card bonded to a 1/8" thick, 4-oz. burnished bronze ingot, then clear-coated. Backs have career stats and a description of the milestone minted into the bronze. The issue was sold only as complete sets through Topps Stadium Club; issue price was $100.

		MT
Complete Set (4):		100.00
Common Player:		15.00
1	Greg Maddux (4th straight Cy Young)	25.00
2	Albert Belle (First 50 HR/50 2B season)	20.00
3	Cal Ripken, Jr. (2,131 consecutive games)	50.00
4	Eddie Murray (3,000 hits)	15.00

1996 Topps League Leaders Finest Bronze

Specially designed Topps Finest cards are bedded to a slab of bronze and clear-coated in this set honoring major award winners from the 1995 season. A "League Leaders" logo at top has the player's award inscribed. Backs of the 2-3/4" x 3-3/4" ingots are silk-screened with season and career stats. The issue was sold only in complete sets (2,000 limit) through Topps Stadium Club for $80.

		MT
Complete Set (6):		80.00
Common Player:		10.00
(1)	Mo Vaughn (A.L. MVP)	15.00
(2)	Barry Larkin (N.L. MVP)	10.00
(3)	Randy Johnson (A.L. CY)	10.00
(4)	Greg Maddux (N.L. CY)	35.00
(5)	Marty Cordova (A.L. ROY)	10.00
(6)	Hideo Nomo (N.L. ROY)	20.00

1996 Topps Legends of the '50s

A dozen of the greatest players of the 1950s ever to grace a Topps card are featured in this set of bronze replicas. Each player's card is reproduced in a 4-oz. bronze version in 2-1/2" x 3-1/2" format. The card fronts are faithfully reproduced on each ingot, while the backs have been modified to present the player's lifetime stats. The ingots were sold through Topps' Stadium Club for about $45 apiece through a monthly subscription plan. The complete set was housed in a special wooden display case. The ingots are checklisted here alphabetically, with the year of Topps card reproduced noted parenthetically.

		MT
Complete Set (12):		550.00
Common Player:		45.00
(1)	Ernie Banks (1954)	45.00
(2)	Yogi Berra (1952)	45.00
(3)	Roy Campanella (1952)	45.00
(4)	Whitey Ford (1953)	45.00
(5)	Mickey Mantle (1952)	75.00
(6)	Eddie Mathews (1952)	45.00
(7)	Willie Mays (1953)	50.00
(8)	Stan Musial (1959)	45.00
(9)	Jackie Robinson (1952)	60.00
(10)	Duke Snider (1955)	45.00
(11)	Warren Spahn (1952)	45.00
(12)	Ted Williams (1954, #250)	50.00

1996 Topps/Gallery

This 180-card set is printed on 24-point stock utilizing metallic inks and a high-definition printing process. Then a high-gloss film is applied to each card, followed by foil stamping. The regular set is broken down into five subsets - The Classics, The Modernists, The Futurists, The Masters and New Editions. Each theme has a different design. Gallery also has four insert sets. Player's Private Issue cards are a parallel set to the main issue; these cards are seeded one per every 12 packs. The backs are sequentially numbered from 0-999, with the first 100 cards sent to the players; the rest are inserted into packs. The backs are UV coated on the photo only, to allow for autographing. The other insert sets are Expressionists, Photo Gallery and a Mickey Mantle Masterpiece card.

		MT
Complete Set (180):		35.00
Common Player:		.25
Complete Players Private Issue (180):		800.00
Private Issue: 6X to 15X		
1	Tom Glavine	.50
2	Carlos Baerga	.25
3	Dante Bichette	.40
4	Mark Langston	.25
5	Ray Lankford	.25
6	Moises Alou	.40
7	Marquis Grissom	.25
8	Ramon Martinez	.25
8p	Ramon Martinez (unmarked promo, "Pitcher" spelled out under photo on back)	5.00
9	Steve Finley	.25
10	Todd Hundley	.25
11	Brady Anderson	.25
12	John Valentin	.25
13	Heathcliff Slocumb	.25
14	Ruben Sierra	.25
15	Jeff Conine	.25
16	Jay Buhner	.35
16p	Jay Buhner (unmarked promo; height, weight and "Bats" on same line)	5.00
17	Sammy Sosa	3.00
18	Doug Drabek	.25
19	Jose Mesa	.25
20	Jeff King	.25
21	Mickey Tettleton	.25
22	Jeff Montgomery	.25
23	Alex Fernandez	.25
24	Greg Vaughn	.25
25	Chuck Finley	.25
26	Terry Steinbach	.25
27	Rod Beck	.25
28	Jack McDowell	.25
29	Mark Wohlers	.25
30	Lenny Dykstra	.25
31	Bernie Williams	.75
32	Travis Fryman	.25
33	Jose Canseco	1.25
34	Ken Caminiti	.40
35	Devon White	.25
36	Bobby Bonilla	.25
37	Paul Sorrento	.25
38	Ryne Sandberg	1.00
39	Derek Bell	.25
40	Bobby Jones	.25
41	J.T. Snow	.25
42	Denny Neagle	.25
43	Tim Wakefield	.25
44	Andres Galarraga	.75
45	David Segui	.25
46	Lee Smith	.25
47	Mel Rojas	.25
48	John Franco	.25
49	Pete Schourek	.25
50	John Wetteland	.25
51	Paul Molitor	.75
52	Ivan Rodriguez	1.50
53	Chris Hoiles	.25
54	Mike Greenwell	.25
55	Orel Hershiser	.25
56	Brian McRae	.25
57	Geronimo Berroa	.25
58	Craig Biggio	.75
59	David Justice	.40
59p	David Justice (unmarked promo; height,weight and "Bats" on same line)	5.00
60	Lance Johnson	.25
61	Andy Ashby	.25
62	Randy Myers	.25
63	Gregg Jefferies	.25
64	Kevin Appier	.25
65	Rick Aguilera	.25
66	Shane Reynolds	.40
67	John Smoltz	.40
68	Ron Gant	.25
69	Eric Karros	.25
70	Jim Thome	.40
71	Terry Pendleton	.25
72	Kenny Rogers	.25
73	Robin Ventura	.50
74	Dave Nilsson	.25
75	Brian Jordan	.25
76	Glenallen Hill	.25
77	Greg Colbrunn	.25
78	Roberto Alomar	1.00
79	Rickey Henderson	.50
80	Carlos Garcia	.25
81	Dean Palmer	.25
82	Mike Stanley	.25
83	Hal Morris	.25
84	Wade Boggs	.75
85	Chad Curtis	.25
86	Roberto Hernandez	.25
87	John Olerud	.75
88	Frank Castillo	.25
89	Rafael Palmeiro	1.00
90	Trevor Hoffman	.25
91	Marty Cordova	.25
92	Hideo Nomo	.50
93	Johnny Damon	.25
94	Bill Pulsipher	.25
95	Garret Anderson	.25
96	Ray Durham	.25
97	Ricky Bottalico	.25
98	Carlos Perez	.25
99	Troy Percival	.25
100	Chipper Jones	3.00
101	Esteban Loaiza	.25
102	John Mabry	.25
103	Jon Nunnally	.25
104	Andy Pettitte	.75
105	Lyle Mouton	.25
106	Jason Isringhausen	.25
107	Brian Hunter	.25
108	Quilvio Veras	.25
109	Jim Edmonds	.25
110	Ryan Klesko	.40
111	Pedro Martinez	1.50
112	Joey Hamilton	.25
113	Vinny Castilla	.40
114	Alex Gonzalez	.25
115	Raul Mondesi	.40
116	Rondell White	.40
117	Dan Miceli	.25
118	Tom Goodwin	.25
119	Bret Boone	.25
120	Shawn Green	1.00
121	Jeff Cirillo	.25
122	Rico Brogna	.25
123	Chris Gomez	.25
124	Ismael Valdes	.25
125	Javy Lopez	.40
126	Manny Ramirez	1.50
127	Paul Wilson	.25
128	Billy Wagner	.25
129	Eric Owens	.25
130	Todd Greene	.25
131	Karim Garcia	.25
132	Jimmy Haynes	.25
133	Michael Tucker	.25
134	John Wasdin	.25
135	Brooks Kieschnick	.25
136	Alex Ochoa	.25
137	Ariel Prieto	.25
138	Tony Clark	.40
139	Mark Loretta	.25
140	Rey Ordonez	.50
141	Chris Snopek	.25
142	Roger Cedeno	.25
143	Derek Jeter	3.00
144	Jeff Suppan	.25
145	Greg Maddux	2.50
146	Ken Griffey Jr.	5.00
147	Tony Gwynn	2.50
148	Darren Daulton	.25
149	Will Clark	.50
150	Mo Vaughn	.75
151	Reggie Sanders	.25
152	Kirby Puckett	1.50
153	Paul O'Neill	.50
154	Tim Salmon	.50
155	Mark McGwire	5.00
156	Barry Bonds	1.50
157	Albert Belle	1.00
158	Edgar Martinez	.25
159	Mike Mussina	.75
160	Cecil Fielder	.25
161	Kenny Lofton	.75
162	Randy Johnson	1.00
163	Juan Gonzalez	1.50
164	Jeff Bagwell	1.50
165	Joe Carter	.25
166	Mike Piazza	3.00
167	Eddie Murray	.50
168	Cal Ripken Jr.	3.00
169	Barry Larkin	.50
170	Chuck Knoblauch	.40
171	Chili Davis	.25
172	Fred McGriff	.50
173	Matt Williams	.40
174	Roger Clemens	2.00
175	Frank Thomas	1.50
176	Dennis Eckersley	.25
177	Gary Sheffield	.40
178	David Cone	.40
179	Larry Walker	1.00
180	Mark Grace	.50

1996 Topps/Gallery Players Private Issue

The first 999 examples of each of the base cards in the Gallery issue are designated on the front with a gold-foil stamp as "Players Private Issue." The first 100 of those cards were given to the depicted player, the others are randomly packed. Besides the logo on front, the PPI cards are identified on back with an individual serial number.

	MT
Complete Set (180):	475.00
Common Player:	1.50
(Star cards valued at 8X to 15X regular Gallery versions)	

1996 Topps/Gallery Expressionists

These 1996 Topps Gallery inserts feature 20 team leaders printed on triple foil-stamped and texture-embossed cards. Cards are seeded one per every 24 packs.

		MT
Complete Set (20):		45.00
Common Player:		.75
1	Mike Piazza	6.00
2	J.T. Snow	.75
3	Ken Griffey Jr.	10.00
4	Kirby Puckett	2.50
5	Carlos Baerga	.75
6	Chipper Jones	6.00
7	Hideo Nomo	.75
8	Mark McGwire	10.00
9	Gary Sheffield	1.00
10	Randy Johnson	2.00
11	Ray Lankford	.75
12	Sammy Sosa	6.00
13	Denny Martinez	.75
14	Jose Canseco	2.00
15	Tony Gwynn	5.00
16	Edgar Martinez	.75
17	Reggie Sanders	.75
18	Andres Galarraga	1.50
19	Albert Belle	2.50
20	Barry Larkin	1.00

1996 Topps/Gallery Masterpiece

Topps continues its tribute to Mickey Mantle with this 1996 Topps Gallery insert card. The card, seeded one per every 48 packs, has three photos of Mantle on the front, with his comprehensive career statistics on the back.

		MT
MP1	Mickey Mantle	10.00

1996 Topps/Gallery Photo Gallery

Photo Gallery is a collection of 15 cards featuring photography of baseball's biggest stars and greatest moments from the last season. The text on the card includes details of the card's front and back photos. The cards are seeded one per every 30 packs. Cards are numbered with a "PG" prefix.

		MT
Complete Set (15):		30.00
Common Player:		1.00
1	Eddie Murray	1.00
2	Randy Johnson	2.00
3	Cal Ripken Jr.	7.50
4	Bret Boone	1.00
5	Frank Thomas	2.50
6	Jeff Conine	1.00
7	Johnny Damon	1.00
8	Roger Clemens	4.00
9	Albert Belle	2.00
10	Ken Griffey Jr.	10.00
11	Kirby Puckett	2.50
12	David Justice	1.50
13	Bobby Bonilla	1.00
14	Larry Walker, Andres Galarraga, Vinny Castilla, Dante Bichette	1.50
15	Mark Wohlers, Javier Lopez	1.00

1996 Topps/Laser

Topps' 1996 Laser Baseball was the first set to use laser-cut technology on every card, creating surgically-precise lattice-work across the entire card. Every card in the 128-card regular issue set features one of four designs laser-cut into 20-point stock. One card from each of the four different designs is found in each four-card pack. Three different laser-cut insert sets were also produced: Bright Spots, Power Cuts and Stadium Stars. Cards 1-8 from each insert set were in Series 1 packs; cards 9-16 were seeded in Series 2 packs. A slightly oversize (1-5/8" x 3-5/8") checklist card in each pack helped protect the delicate die-cut details from damage.

		MT
Complete Set (128):		100.00
Complete Series 1 Set (64):		50.00
Complete Series 2 Set (64):		50.00
Common Player:		.25
Wax Box:		65.00
1	Moises Alou	.75
2	Derek Bell	.25
3	Joe Carter	.25
4	Jeff Conine	.25
5	Darren Daulton	.25
6	Jim Edmonds	.25
7	Ron Gant	.35
8	Juan Gonzalez	2.00
9	Brian Jordan	.25
10	Ryan Klesko	.35
11	Paul Molitor	1.50
12	Tony Phillips	.25
13	Manny Ramirez	2.00
14	Sammy Sosa	5.00
15	Devon White	.25
16	Bernie Williams	1.00
17	Garret Anderson	.25
18	Jay Bell	.25
19	Craig Biggio	1.00
20	Bobby Bonilla	.25
21	Ken Caminiti	.40
22	Shawon Dunston	.25
23	Mark Grace	.75
23p	Mark Grace (unmarked promo, plain, rather than brushed, gold foil)	4.00
24	Gregg Jefferies	.25
25	Jeff King	.25
26	Javy Lopez	.25
27	Edgar Martinez	.25
28	Dean Palmer	.25
29	J.T. Snow	.25
30	Mike Stanley	.25
30p	Mike Stanley (unmarked promo; plain, rather than brushed, gold foil)	3.00
31	Terry Steinbach	.25
32	Robin Ventura	.75
33	Roberto Alomar	1.50
34	Jeff Bagwell	2.00
35	Dante Bichette	.75
36	Wade Boggs	.75
37	Barry Bonds	2.00
38	Jose Canseco	1.50
39	Vinny Castilla	.25
40	Will Clark	1.00
41	Marty Cordova	.25
42	Ken Griffey Jr.	8.00
43	Tony Gwynn	4.00
44	Rickey Henderson	.75
45	Chipper Jones	5.00
46	Mark McGwire	8.00
47	Brian McRae	.25
48	Ryne Sandberg	2.00
49	Andy Ashby	.25
50	Alan Benes	.25
51	Andy Benes	.25
52	Roger Clemens	3.00
53	Doug Drabek	.25
54	Dennis Eckersley	.25
55	Tom Glavine	.50
56	Randy Johnson	1.50
57	Mark Langston	.25
58	Denny Martinez	.25
59	Jack McDowell	.25
60	Hideo Nomo	.50
61	Shane Reynolds	.40
62	John Smoltz	.40
63	Paul Wilson	.25
64	Mark Wohlers	.25
65	Shawn Green	1.00
66	Marquis Grissom	.25
67	Dave Hollins	.25
68	Todd Hundley	.25
69	David Justice	.50
70	Eric Karros	.25
71	Ray Lankford	.25
72	Fred McGriff	.50
73	Hal Morris	.25
74	Eddie Murray	.50
75	Paul O'Neill	.50
76	Rey Ordonez	.50
77	Reggie Sanders	.25
78	Gary Sheffield	.50
79	Jim Thome	1.00
80	Rondell White	.50
81	Travis Fryman	.30
82	Derek Jeter	5.00
83	Chuck Knoblauch	.60
84	Barry Larkin	.50
85	Tino Martinez	.50
86	Raul Mondesi	1.00
87	John Olerud	.75
88	Rafael Palmeiro	1.00
89	Mike Piazza	5.00
90	Cal Ripken Jr.	6.00
91	Ivan Rodriguez	2.00
92	Frank Thomas	2.00
93	John Valentin	.25
94	Mo Vaughn	1.50
95	Quilvio Veras	.25
96	Matt Williams	.75
97	Brady Anderson	.40
98	Carlos Baerga	.25
99	Albert Belle	1.50
100	Jay Buhner	.35
101	Johnny Damon	.25
102	Chili Davis	.25
103	Ray Durham	.25
104	Lenny Dykstra	.25
105	Cecil Fielder	.25
106	Andres Galarraga	.75
107	Brian Hunter	.25
108	Kenny Lofton	1.50
109	Kirby Puckett	2.00
110	Tim Salmon	.50
111	Greg Vaughn	.30
112	Larry Walker	1.50
113	Rick Aguilera	.25
114	Kevin Appier	.25
115	Kevin Brown	.40
116	David Cone	.50
117	Alex Fernandez	.25
118	Chuck Finley	.25
119	Joey Hamilton	.25
120	Jason Isringhausen	.25
121	Greg Maddux	4.00
122	Pedro Martinez	2.00
123	Jose Mesa	.25
124	Jeff Montgomery	.25
125	Mike Mussina	1.50
126	Randy Myers	.25
127	Kenny Rogers	.25
128	Ismael Valdes	.25
	Series 1 checklist	.05
	Series 2 Checklist	.05

1996 Topps/Laser Bright Spots

Top young stars are featured on these 1996 Topps Laser cards, which use etched silver and gold diffraction foil. The cards are seeded one per every 20 packs. Numbers 1-8 are in Series I packs; cards 9-16 are in Series II packs.

		MT
Complete Set (16):		35.00
Complete Series 1 Set (8):		15.00
Complete Series 2 Set (8):		20.00
Common Player:		1.50
1	Brian Hunter	1.50
2	Derek Jeter	7.50
3	Jason Kendall	2.50
4	Brooks Kieschnick	1.50
5	Rey Ordonez	2.00
6	Jason Schmidt	1.50
7	Chris Snopek	1.50
8	Bob Wolcott	1.50
9	Alan Benes	2.00
10	Marty Cordova	1.50
11	Jimmy Haynes	1.50
12	Todd Hollandsworth	1.50
13	Derek Jeter	7.50
14	Chipper Jones	6.00
15	Hideo Nomo	2.00
16	Paul Wilson	1.50

1996 Topps/Laser Power Cuts

This 1996 Topps Laser insert set spotlights 16 of the game's top power hitters on etched foil and gold diffraction foil cards. These cards were seeded one per every 40 packs; numbers 1-8 were in Series I packs; cards 9-16 were in Series II packs.

		MT
Complete Set (8):		80.00
Complete Series 1 Set (8):		37.00
Complete Series 2 Set (8):		45.00
Common Player:		2.00
1	Albert Belle	5.00
2	Jay Buhner	2.00
3	Fred McGriff	2.00
4	Mike Piazza	12.50
5	Tim Salmon	2.50
6	Frank Thomas	7.50
7	Mo Vaughn	5.00
8	Matt Williams	2.50
9	Jeff Bagwell	6.00
10	Barry Bonds	6.00
11	Jose Canseco	3.00
12	Cecil Fielder	2.00
13	Juan Gonzalez	10.00
14	Ken Griffey Jr.	20.00
15	Sammy Sosa	12.50
16	Larry Walker	3.00

1996 Topps/Laser Stadium Stars

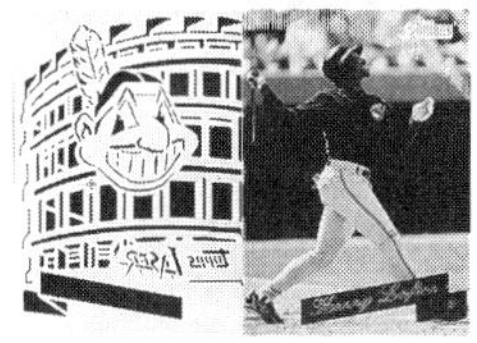

These 1996 Topps Laser cards are the most difficult to find; they are seeded one per every 60 packs. The 16 cards feature a laser-sculpted cover that folds back to reveal striated silver and gold etched diffraction foil on each card front. Cards 1-8 were in Series I packs; numbers 9-16 were Series II inserts.

		MT
Complete Set (8):		75.00
Complete Series 1 Set (8):		45.00
Complete Series 2 Set (8):		35.00
Common Player:		2.50
1	Carlos Baerga	2.50
2	Barry Bonds	5.00
3	Andres Galarraga	4.00
4	Ken Griffey Jr.	20.00
5	Barry Larkin	3.00
6	Raul Mondesi	2.50
7	Kirby Puckett	5.00
8	Cal Ripken Jr.	15.00
9	Will Clark	4.00
10	Roger Clemens	7.50
11	Tony Gwynn	10.00
12	Randy Johnson	3.00
13	Kenny Lofton	3.00
14	Edgar Martinez	2.50
15	Ryne Sandberg	5.00
16	Frank Thomas	7.50

1996 Topps/R&N China Mickey Mantle Porcelains

Eight of Mantle's most popular Bowman and Topps cards were reproduced by L&N China for this special collection. Each of the 2-3/4" x 3-3/4" ceramics is printed on thin, round-cornered porcelain, hand-numbered on the back from within an edition of 1,000 sets and sold through Topps Stadium Club with a certificate of authenticity and a display case. Issue price was $100 per set.

		MT
Complete Set:		50.00
Common Card:		5.00
(1)	Mickey Mantle (1951 Bowman)	10.00
(2)	Mickey Mantle (1952 Topps)	15.00
(3)	Mickey Mantle (1953 Topps)	10.00
(4)	Mickey Mantle (1954 Bowman)	5.00
(5)	Mickey Mantle (1956 Topps)	5.00
(6)	Mickey Mantle (1957 Topps)	5.00
(7)	Mickey Mantle (1967 Topps)	5.00
(8)	Mickey Mantle (1969 Topps)	5.00

1996 Topps/R&N China Cal Ripken Porcelains

In a salute to Ripken's record-setting career L&N China produced this pair of Topps card reproductions. The 2-3/4" x 3-3/4" round-cornered ceramics are dipped in 22-karat gold before the printing is applied. The issue was sold only as a complete set in a plexiglass holder for $70. The issue was limited to 1,000 sets.

		MT
Complete Set:		70.00
(1)	Cal Ripken Jr. (1982 Topps Traded)	55.00
(2)	Cal Ripken Jr. (1996 Topps 2,131)	25.00

1996 Topps/R&N China Stadium Club Porcelains

One card from each of the first six years of Topps Stadium Club Baseball issues was reproduced by R&N China for this special collection. On thin porcelain, 2-3/4" x 3-3/4" with rounded corners, the cards were sold only as a complete set through Topps Stadium Club. Issue price was $79 for the set. The back of each card carries a serial number from within an edition of 750 sets.

		MT
Complete Set:		80.00
Common Player:		10.00
(1)	Ken Griffey Jr. (1991)	30.00
(2)	Frank Thomas (1992)	25.00
(3)	Kenny Lofton (1993)	10.00
(4)	Dante Bichette (1994)	10.00
(5)	Paul Molitor (1995)	10.00
(6)	Randy Johnson (1996)	10.00

1996 Topps "1952" Gold Willie Mays

This reproduction of Topps' 1952 card #261 is embossed and covered in 22 karat gold foil. Each full-size replica card is serially numbered within an edition of 50,000.

		MT
261	Willie Mays	20.00

1996 Topps "1954" Ted Williams Gold

This reproduction of Topps' 1954 card #1, Ted Williams, is embossed and covered in 22 karat gold foil. Each full-size replica card is serially numbered within an edition of 50,000.

		MT
1	Ted Williams	20.00

1996 Topps "1959" Stan Musial Gold

Topps' first regular-issue card of Stan Musial was reproduced in a full-size (2-12/" x 3-1/2") 22-karat gold foil edition sold through Topps' Stadium Club. Each of the gold replicas bears a unique serial number. Issue price of the card was about $30.

		MT
150	Stan Musial	20.00

1997 Topps

Topps' 1997 set includes the first-ever player cards of the expansion Diamondbacks and Devil Rays; 16 Mickey Mantle reprints; a special Jackie Robinson tribute card; 27 Willie Mays Topps and Bowman reprints; randomly-inserted Willie Mays autographed reprint cards; and Inter-League Finest and Finest Refractors cards. The base set has 275 cards in each series. Each card front has a gloss coating on the photo and a spot matte finish on the outside border. Gold foil stamping is also used. Card backs have informative text, complete player stats and biographies, and a second photo. The Jackie Robinson card pays tribute to the 50th anniversary of his breaking the color line. This card is #42 in the regular issue. Mantle reprints, seeded one per every 12 packs, feature the 16 remaining Mantle cards which were not reprinted in 1996 Topps baseball. The cards, each stamped with a gold foil logo, are numbered from #21 to #36. Willie Mays has 27 of his cards reprinted and seeded one per every eight packs. Each card also has a gold foil stamp. As a special hobby-exclusive bonus, 1,000 randomly-selected Mays reprints will be autographed and randomly inserted in packs. Five other insert sets were made: All-Stars, Inter-League Finest and Inter-League Finest Refractors, Sweet Strokes and Hobby Masters.

		MT
Complete Set (496):		40.00
Complete Series 1 Set (276):		20.00
Complete Series 2 Set (220):		20.00
Common Player:		.05
Series I & II Wax Box:		40.00
1	Barry Bonds	.50
2	Tom Pagnozzi	.05
3	Terrell Wade	.05
4	Jose Valentin	.05
5	Mark Clark	.05
6	Brady Anderson	.15
7	Not issued	
8	Wade Boggs	.25
9	Scott Stahoviak	.05
10	Andres Galarraga	.25
11	Steve Avery	.05
12	Rusty Greer	.05
13	Derek Jeter	1.50
14	Ricky Bottalico	.05
15	Andy Ashby	.05
16	Paul Shuey	.05
17	F.P. Santangelo	.05
18	Royce Clayton	.05
19	Mike Mohler	.05
20	Mike Piazza	1.50
21	Jaime Navarro	.05
22	Billy Wagner	.10
23	Mike Timlin	.05
24	Garret Anderson	.05
25	Ben McDonald	.05
26	Mel Rojas	.05
27	John Burkett	.05
28	Jeff King	.05
29	Reggie Jefferson	.05
30	Kevin Appier	.05
31	Felipe Lira	.05
32	Kevin Tapani	.05
33	Mark Portugal	.05
34	Carlos Garcia	.05
35	Joey Cora	.05
36	David Segui	.05
37	Mark Grace	.25
38	Erik Hanson	.05
39	Jeff D'Amico	.05
40	Jay Buhner	.05
41	B.J. Surhoff	.05
42	Jackie Robinson	3.00
43	Roger Pavlik	.05
44	Hal Morris	.05
45	Mariano Duncan	.05
46	Harold Baines	.10
47	Jorge Fabregas	.05
48	Jose Herrera	.05
49	Jeff Cirillo	.05
50	Tom Glavine	.15
51	Pedro Astacio	.05
52	Mark Gardner	.05
53	Arthur Rhodes	.05
54	Troy O'Leary	.05
55	Bip Roberts	.05
56	Mike Lieberthal	.05
57	Shane Andrews	.05
58	Scott Karl	.05
59	Gary DiSarcina	.05
60	Andy Pettitte	.25
61a	Kevin Elster	.05
61b	Mike Fetters (should be #84)	.05
62	Mark McGwire	2.50
63	Dan Wilson	.05
64	Mickey Morandini	.05
65	Chuck Knoblauch	.20
66	Tim Wakefield	.05
67	Raul Mondesi	.25
68	Todd Jones	.05
69	Albert Belle	.50
70	Trevor Hoffman	.05
71	Eric Young	.10
72	Robert Perez	.05
73	Butch Huskey	.05
74	Brian McRae	.05
75	Jim Edmonds	.10
76	Mike Henneman	.05
77	Frank Rodriguez	.05
78	Danny Tartabull	.05
79	Robby Nen	.05
80	Reggie Sanders	.10
81	Ron Karkovice	.05
82	Benny Santiago	.05
83	Mike Lansing	.05
84	Not issued - see #61b	
85	Craig Biggio	.25
86	Mike Bordick	.05
87	Ray Lankford	.10
88	Charles Nagy	.05
89	Paul Wilson	.05
90	John Wetteland	.05
91	Tom Candiotti	.05
92	Carlos Delgado	.40
93	Derek Bell	.10
94	Mark Lemke	.05
95	Edgar Martinez	.05
96	Rickey Henderson	.25
97	Greg Myers	.05
98	Jim Leyritz	.05
99	Mark Johnson	.05
100	Dwight Gooden (Season Highlights)	.05
101	Al Leiter (Season Highlights)	.05
102a	John Mabry (Season Highlights) (last line on back ends "... Mabry"))	.05
102b	John Mabry (Season Highlights) (last line on back ends "...walked.")	.05
103	Alex Ochoa (Season Highlights)	.05
104	Mike Piazza (Season Highlights)	.60
105	Jim Thome	.30
106	Ricky Otero	.05
107	Jamey Wright	.05
108	Frank Thomas	.50
109	Jody Reed	.05
110	Orel Hershiser	.10
111	Terry Steinbach	.05
112	Mark Loretta	.05
113	Turk Wendell	.05
114	Marvin Benard	.05
115	Kevin Brown	.05
116	Robert Person	.05
117	Joey Hamilton	.05
118	Francisco Cordova	.10
119	John Smiley	.05
120	Travis Fryman	.15
121	Jimmy Key	.05
122	Tom Goodwin	.05
123	Mike Greenwell	.05
124	Juan Gonzalez	.75
125	Pete Harnisch	.05
126	Roger Cedeno	.05
127	Ron Gant	.15
128	Mark Langston	.05
129	Tim Crabtree	.05
130	Greg Maddux	1.50
131	William VanLandingham	.05
132	Wally Joyner	.10
133	Randy Myers	.05
134	John Valentin	.10
135	Bret Boone	.05
136	Bruce Ruffin	.05
137	Chris Snopek	.05
138	Paul Molitor	.40
139	Mark McLemore	.05
140	Rafael Palmeiro	.25
141	Herb Perry	.05
142	Luis Gonzalez	.10
143	Doug Drabek	.05
144	Ken Ryan	.05
145	Todd Hundley	.10
146	Ellis Burks	.05
147	Ozzie Guillen	.05
148	Rich Becker	.05
149	Sterling Hitchcock	.05
150	Bernie Williams	.40
151	Mike Stanley	.05
152	Roberto Alomar	.40
153	Jose Mesa	.05
154	Steve Trachsel	.05
155	Alex Gonzalez	.05
156	Troy Percival	.05
157	John Smoltz	.20
158	Pedro Martinez	.50
159	Jeff Conine	.10
160	Bernard Gilkey	.05
161	Jim Eisenreich	.05
162	Mickey Tettleton	.05
163	Justin Thompson	.05
164	Jose Offerman	.05
165	Tony Phillips	.05
166	Ismael Valdes	.05
167	Ryne Sandberg	.50
168	Matt Mieske	.05
169	Geronimo Berroa	.05
170	Otis Nixon	.05
171	John Mabry	.05
172	Shawon Dunston	.05
173	Omar Vizquel	.10
174	Chris Holles	.05
175	Doc Gooden	.10
176	Wilson Alvarez	.05
177	Todd Hollandsworth	.10
178	Roger Salkeld	.05
179	Rey Sanchez	.05
180	Rey Ordonez	.15
181	Denny Martinez	.05
182	Ramon Martinez	.10
183	Dave Nilsson	.05
184	Marquis Grissom	.10
185	Randy Velarde	.05
186	Ron Coomer	.05
187	Tino Martinez	.15
188	Jeff Brantley	.05
189	Steve Finley	.05
190	Andy Benes	.10
191	Terry Adams	.05
192	Mike Blowers	.05
193	Russ Davis	.05
194	Darryl Hamilton	.05
195	Jason Kendall	.15
196	Johnny Damon	.10
197	Dave Martinez	.05
198	Mike Macfarlane	.05
199	Norm Charlton	.05
200	Doug Million, Damian Moss, Bobby Rodgers (Prospect)	.20
201	Geoff Jenkins, Raul Ibanez, Mike Cameron (Prospect)	.25
202	Sean Casey, Jim Bonnici, Dmitri Young (Prospect)	1.00
203	Jed Hansen, Homer Bush, Felipe Crespo (Prospect)	.10
204	Kevin Orie, Gabe Alvarez, Aaron Boone (Prospect)	.25
205	Ben Davis, Kevin Brown, Bobby Estalella (Prospect)	.10
206	Billy McMillon, *Bubba Trammell*, Dante Powell (Prospect)	.25
207	Jarrod Washburn, *Marc Wilkins*, Glendon Rusch (Prospect)	.15
208	Brian Hunter	.05
209	Jason Giambi	.10
210	Henry Rodriguez	.05
211	Edgar Renteria	.20
212	Edgardo Alfonzo	.15
213	Fernando Vina	.05
214	Shawn Green	.40
215	Ray Durham	.05
216	Joe Randa	.05
217	Armando Reynoso	.05
218	Eric Davis	.05
219	Bob Tewksbury	.05
220	Jacob Cruz	.05
221	Glenallen Hill	.05
222	Gary Gaetti	.05
223	Donne Wall	.05
224	Brad Clontz	.05
225	Marty Janzen	.05
226	Todd Worrell	.05
227	John Franco	.05
228	David Wells	.05
229	Gregg Jefferies	.10
230	Tim Naehring	.05
231	Thomas Howard	.05
232	Roberto Hernandez	.05
233	Kevin Ritz	.05
234	Julian Tavarez	.05
235	Ken Hill	.05
236	Greg Gagne	.05
237	Bobby Chouinard	.05
238	Joe Carter	.05
239	Jermaine Dye	.05
240	Antonio Osuna	.05
241	Julio Franco	.05
242	Mike Grace	.05
243	Aaron Sele	.05
244	David Justice	.20
245	Sandy Alomar	.10
246	Jose Canseco	.50
247	Paul O'Neill	.20
248	Sean Berry	.05
249	*Nick Bierbrodt, Kevin Sweeney* (Diamond Backs)	.35
250	*Larry Rodriguez, Vladimir Nunez* (Diamond Backs)	.25
251	Ron Hartman, David Hayman (Diamond Backs)	.20
252	Alex Sanchez, Matt Quatraro (Devil Rays)	.20
253	Ronni Seberino, *Pablo Ortega* (Devil Rays)	.25
254	Rex Hudler	.05
255	Orlando Miller	.05
256	Mariano Rivera	.25
257	Brad Radke	.05
258	Bobby Higginson	.05
259	Jay Bell	.05
260	Mark Grudzielanek	.05
261	Lance Johnson	.05
262	Ken Caminiti	.15
263	J.T. Snow	.05
264	Gary Sheffield	.20
265	Darrin Fletcher	.05
266	Eric Owens	.05
267	Luis Castillo	.10
268	Scott Rolen	.75
269	*Todd Noel*, John Oliver (Draft Pick)	.25
270	*Robert Stratton, Corey Lee* (Draft Pick)	.25
271	*Gil Meche, Matt Halloran* (Draft Pick)	1.00
272	*Eric Milton*, Dermal Brown (Draft Pick)	.50
273	*Josh Garrett, Chris Reitsma* (Draft Pick)	.25
274	*A.J. Zapp, Jason Marquis* (Draft Pick)	.50
275	Checklist	.05
276a	Checklist	.05
276b	Chipper Jones (should be #277)	1.50
277	Not issued	
278	Orlando Merced	.05
279	Ariel Prieto	.05
280	Al Leiter	.15
281	Pat Meares	.05
282	Darryl Strawberry	.15
283	Jamie Moyer	.05
284	Scott Servais	.05
285	Delino DeShields	.05
286	Danny Graves	.05
287	Gerald Williams	.05
288	Todd Greene	.05
289	Rico Brogna	.05
290	Derrick Gibson	.05
291	Joe Girardi	.05
292	Darren Lewis	.05
293	Nomar Garciaparra	1.50
294	Greg Colbrunn	.05
295	Jeff Bagwell	.50
296	Brent Gates	.05
297	Jose Vizcaino	.05
298	Alex Ochoa	.05
299	Sid Fernandez	.05
300	Ken Griffey Jr.	2.50
301	Chris Gomez	.05
302	Wendell Magee	.05
303	Darren Oliver	.05
304	Mel Nieves	.05
305	Sammy Sosa	1.50
306	George Arias	.05
307	Jack McDowell	.05
308	Stan Javier	.05
309	Kimera Bartee	.05
310	James Baldwin	.05
311	Rocky Coppinger	.05
312	Keith Lockhart	.05
313	C.J. Nitkowski	.05
314	Allen Watson	.05
315	Darryl Kile	.05
316	Amaury Telemaco	.05
317	Jason Isringhausen	.05
318	Manny Ramirez	.50
319	Terry Pendleton	.05
320	Tim Salmon	.15
321	Eric Karros	.10
322	Mark Whiten	.05
323	Rick Krivda	.05
324	Brett Butler	.05
325	Randy Johnson	.30
326	Eddie Taubensee	.05
327	Mark Leiter	.05
328	Kevin Gross	.05
329	Ernie Young	.05
330	Pat Hentgen	.05
331	Rondell White	.15
332	Bobby Witt	.05
333	Eddie Murray	.30
334	Tim Raines	.10
335	Jeff Fassero	.05
336	Chuck Finley	.05
337	Willie Adams	.05
338	Chan Ho Park	.15
339	Jay Powell	.05
340	Ivan Rodriguez	.50
341	Jermaine Allensworth	.05
342	Jay Payton	.15
343	T.J. Mathews	.05
344	Tony Batista	.05
345	Ed Sprague	.05
346	Jeff Kent	.05
347	Scott Erickson	.05
348	Jeff Suppan	.05
349	Pete Schourek	.05
350	Kenny Lofton	.40
351	Alan Benes	.05
352	Fred McGriff	.25
353	Charlie O'Brien	.05
354	Darren Bragg	.05
355	Alex Fernandez	.05
356	Al Martin	.05
357	Bob Wells	.05
358	Chad Mottola	.05
359	Devon White	.05
360	David Cone	.15
361	Bobby Jones	.05
362	Scott Sanders	.05
363	Karim Garcia	.10
364	Kirt Manwaring	.05
365	Chili Davis	.05
366	Mike Hampton	.05
367	Chad Ogea	.05
368	Curt Schilling	.15
369	Phil Nevin	.05
370	Roger Clemens	1.00
371	Willie Greene	.05
372	Kenny Rogers	.05
373	Jose Rijo	.05
374	Bobby Bonilla	.05
375	Mike Mussina	.40
376	Curtis Pride	.05
377	Todd Walker	.15
378	Jason Bere	.05
379	Heathcliff Slocumb	.05
380	Dante Bichette	.20
381	Carlos Baerga	.05
382	Livan Hernandez	.05
383	Jason Schmidt	.05
384	Kevin Stocker	.05
385	Matt Williams	.20
386	Bartolo Colon	.15
387	Will Clark	.25
388	Dennis Eckersley	.10
389	Brooks Kieschnick	.10
390	Ryan Klesko	.15
391	Mark Carreon	.05
392	Tim Worrell	.05
393	Dean Palmer	.05
394	Wil Cordero	.05
395	Javy Lopez	.15
396	Rich Aurilla	.05
397	Greg Vaughn	.15
398	Vinny Castilla	.15
399	Jeff Montgomery	.05
400	Cal Ripken Jr.	1.50
401	Walt Weiss	.05
402	Brad Ausmus	.05
403	Ruben Rivera	.15
404	Mark Wohlers	.05
405	Rick Aguilera	.05
406	Tony Clark	.20
407	Lyle Mouton	.05
408	Bill Pulsipher	.05
409	Jose Rosado	.05
410	Tony Gwynn	1.00
411	Cecil Fielder	.10
412	John Flaherty	.05
413	Lenny Dykstra	.05
414	Ugueth Urbina	.05
415	Brian Jordan	.15
416	Bob Abreu	.10
417	Craig Paquette	.05
418	Sandy Martinez	.05
419	Jeff Blauser	.05
420	Barry Larkin	.10
421	Kevin Seitzer	.05
422	Tim Belcher	.05
423	Paul Sorrento	.05
424	Cal Eldred	.05
425	Robin Ventura	.15
426	John Olerud	.20
427	Bob Wolcott	.05
428	Matt Lawton	.05
429	Rod Beck	.05
430	Shane Reynolds	.15
431	Mike James	.05
432	Steve Wojciechowski	.05
433	Vladimir Guerrero	.75
434	Dustin Hermanson	.10
435	Marty Cordova	.05
436	Marc Newfield	.05
437	Todd Stottlemyre	.05
438	Jeffrey Hammonds	.05
439	Dave Stevens	.05
440	Hideo Nomo	.20
441	Mark Thompson	.05
442	Mark Lewis	.05
443	Quinton McCracken	.05
444	Cliff Floyd	.05
445	Denny Neagle	.05
446	John Jaha	.05
447	Mike Sweeney	.05
448	John Wasdin	.05
449	Chad Curtis	.05
450	Mo Vaughn	.40
451	Donovan Osborne	.05
452	Ruben Sierra	.05
453	Michael Tucker	.05
454	Kurt Abbott	.05
455	Andruw Jones	.50
456	Shannon Stewart	.05
457	Scott Brosius	.05
458	Juan Guzman	.05
459	Ron Villone	.05
460	Moises Alou	.15
461	Larry Walker	.40
462	Eddie Murray (Season Highlights)	.20
463	Paul Molitor (Season Highlights)	.20
464	Hideo Nomo (Season Highlights)	.25
465	Barry Bonds (Season Highlights)	.40
466	Todd Hundley (Season Highlights)	.05
467	Rheal Cormier	.05
468	*Jason Conti*	.50
469	Rod Barajas	.05
470	Jared Sandberg, *Cedric Bowers*	.50
471	Paul Wilders, *Chie Gunner*	.20
472	Mike Decelle, *Marcus McCain*	.20
473	Todd Zeile	.05
474	Neifi Perez	.05
475	Jeromy Burnitz	.05
476	Trey Beamon	.05
477	John Patterson, *Braden Looper* (Draft Picks)	.50
478	*Danny Peoples, Jake Westbrook* (Draft Picks)	.25
479	*Eric Chavez*, Adam Eaton (Draft Picks)	1.50
480	*Joe Lawrence*, Pete Tucci (Draft Picks)	.50
481	Kris Benson, *Billy Koch* (Draft Picks)	.50
482	John Nicholson, Andy Prater (Draft Picks)	.25
483	*Mark Kotsay*, Mark Johnson (Draft Picks)	.50
484	Armando Benitez	.05
485	Mike Matheny	.05
486	Jeff Reed	.05

487	Mark Bellhorn, Russ Johnson, Enrique Wilson (Prospects)	.05
488	Ben Grieve, Richard Hidalgo, *Scott Morgan* (Prospects)	.75
489	Paul Konerko, Derrek Lee, Ron Wright (Prospects)	.25
490	Wes Helms, *Bill Mueller*, Brad Seitzer (Prospects)	.50
491	Jeff Abbott, Shane Monahan, Edgard Velazquez (Prospects)	.20
492	*Jimmy Anderson*, Ron Blazier, Gerald Witasick, Jr. (Prospects)	.25
493	Darin Blood, Heath Murray, Carl Pavano (Prospects)	.05
494	Mark Redman, *Mike Villano*, Nelson Figueroa (Prospects)	.20
495	Checklist	.05
496	Checklist	.05
NNO	Derek Jeter (Auto)	100.00

1997 Topps All-Stars

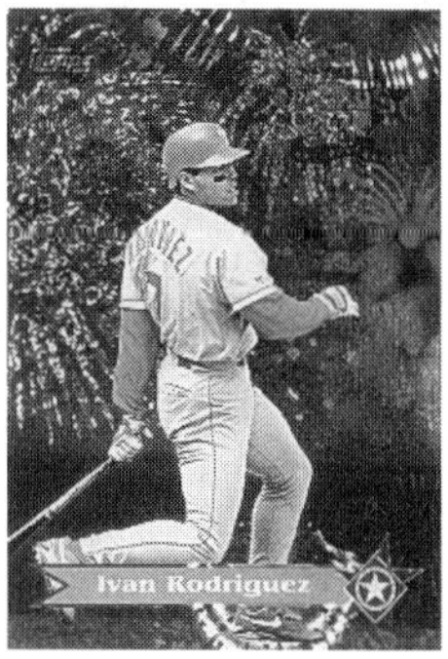

Topps' 1997 All-Stars insert cards, printed on a dazzling rainbow foilboard, feature the top players from each position. There are 22 cards, 11 from each league, which showcase the top three players from each position as voted by Topps' sports department. On the front of each card is a photo of a "first team" all-star player; the back has a different photo of that player, who appears alongside the "second team" and "third team" selections. These cards are seeded one per every 18 1997 Topps Series I packs. Cards are numbered with an "AS" prefix.

		MT
Complete Set (22):		40.00
Common Player:		1.00
1	Ivan Rodriguez	3.00
2	Todd Hundley	1.00
3	Frank Thomas	5.00
4	Andres Galarraga	1.25
5	Chuck Knoblauch	1.25
6	Eric Young	1.25
7	Jim Thome	1.25
8	Chipper Jones	7.00
9	Cal Ripken Jr.	8.00
10	Barry Larkin	1.25
11	Albert Belle	3.00
12	Barry Bonds	3.00
13	Ken Griffey Jr.	10.00
14	Ellis Burks	1.00
15	Juan Gonzalez	3.00
16	Gary Sheffield	1.25
17	Andy Pettitte	1.25
18	Tom Glavine	1.25
19	Pat Hentgen	1.00
20	John Smoltz	1.25
21	Roberto Hernandez	1.00
22	Mark Wohlers	1.00

1997 Topps Awesome Impact

This flashy insert exclusive to Series 2 retail packaging features young players who have quickly made their mark in the big leagues. Fronts have player action photos against a background of silver primatic geometric shapes. Backs are horizontal with a player portrait photo, recent stats and a few words about the player's current and projected impact. Stated odds of finding this insert are one per 18 packs. Cards are numbered with an "AI" prefix.

		MT
Complete Set (20):		50.00
Common Player:		1.00
1	Jaime Bluma	1.00
2	Tony Clark	2.00
3	Jermaine Dye	1.00
4	Nomar Garciaparra	12.00
5	Vladimir Guerrero	8.00
6	Todd Hollandsworth	1.00
7	Derek Jeter	15.00
8	Andruw Jones	4.00
9	Chipper Jones	12.00
10	Jason Kendall	2.00
11	Brooks Kieschnick	1.00
12	Alex Ochoa	1.00
13	Rey Ordonez	1.50
14	Neifi Perez	1.00
15	Edgar Renteria	1.50
16	Mariano Rivera	1.50
17	Ruben Rivera	1.00
18	Scott Rolen	5.00
19	Billy Wagner	1.00
20	Todd Walker	1.00

1997 Topps Hobby Masters

These 10 cards lead the way as dealers' top selections. The cards, printed on 28-point diffraction foilboard, replace two regular cards in every 36th pack of 1997 Topps Series I product. Cards are numbered with a "HM" prefix.

		MT
Complete Set (20):		60.00
Complete Series 1 (10):		33.00
Complete Series 2 (10):		29.00
Common Player:		1.00
1	Ken Griffey Jr.	9.50
2	Cal Ripken Jr.	6.50
3	Greg Maddux	5.00
4	Albert Belle	2.00
5	Tony Gwynn	5.00
6	Jeff Bagwell	2.50
7	Randy Johnson	1.50
8	Raul Mondesi	1.00
9	Juan Gonzalez	2.50
10	Kenny Lofton	1.50
11	Frank Thomas	2.50
12	Mike Piazza	6.00
13	Chipper Jones	6.00
14	Brady Anderson	1.00
15	Ken Caminiti	1.25
16	Barry Bonds	2.50
17	Mo Vaughn	1.00
18	Derek Jeter	6.00
19	Sammy Sosa	6.00
20	Andres Galarraga	1.00

1997 Topps Inter-League Match Ups

The double-sided Inter-League Finest and Inter-League Finest Refractors (seeded one in 36 and one in 216 Topps Series I packs respectively) feature top individual matchups from inter-league rivalries. One player from each major league team is represented, for a total of 28 players on 14 different cards. Each card is covered with a Finest clear protector. Cards are numbered with an "ILM" prefix.

		MT
Complete Set (14):		35.00
Common Player:		1.00
Refractors: 2X		
1	Mark McGwire, Barry Bonds	7.50
2	Tim Salmon, Mike Piazza	5.00
3	Ken Griffey Jr., Dante Bichette	7.50
4	Juan Gonzalez, Tony Gwynn	4.00
5	Frank Thomas, Sammy Sosa	5.00
6	Albert Belle, Barry Larkin	2.00
7	Johnny Damon, Brian Jordan	1.00
8	Paul Molitor, Jeff King	1.50
9	John Jaha, Jeff Bagwell	2.50
10	Bernie Williams, Todd Hundley	1.00
11	Joe Carter, Henry Rodriguez	1.00
12	Cal Ripken Jr., Gregg Jefferies	6.00
13	Mo Vaughn, Chipper Jones	5.00
14	Travis Fryman, Gary Sheffield	1.00

1997 Topps Mickey Mantle Reprints

All 16 remaining Mickey Mantle cards that were not reprinted in 1996 Topps Baseball are found in this insert, seeded every 12 packs of Series I Topps. The set starts off with No. 21 and runs through No. 36 since the '96 reprints were numbered 1-20.

		MT
Complete Set (16):		60.00
Common Card:		5.00
21	1953 Bowman #44	5.00
22	1953 Bowman #59	6.00
23	1957 Topps #407	5.00
24	1958 Topps #418	5.00
25	1958 Topps #487	5.00
26	1959 Topps #461	5.00
27	1959 Topps #564	5.00
28	1960 Topps #160	5.00
29	1960 Topps #563	5.00
30	1961 Topps #406	5.00
31	1961 Topps #475	5.00
32	1961 Topps #578	5.00
33	1962 Topps #18	5.00
34	1962 Topps #318	5.00
35	1962 Topps #471	5.00
36	1964 Topps #331	5.00

1997 Topps Mickey Mantle Finest

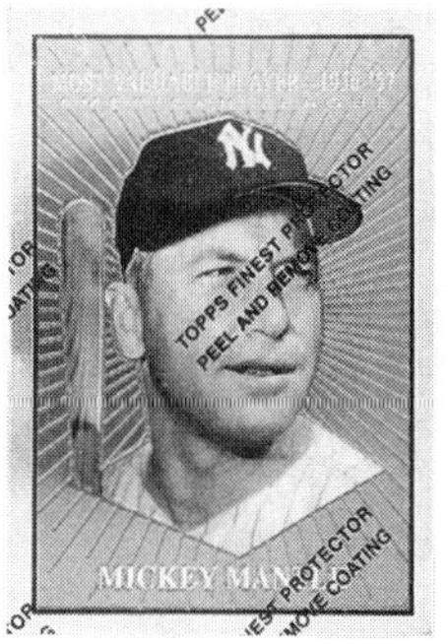

The 16-card Mickey Mantle reprints insert that was found in Series I was re-issued in Series II in the Topps Finest technology. The Finest versions are found on average of every 24 packs.

		MT
Complete Set (16):		90.00
Common Mantle:		6.00
21	1953 Bowman #44	6.00
22	1953 Bowman #59	9.00
23	1957 Topps #407	6.00
24	1958 Topps #418	6.00
25	1958 Topps #487	6.00
26	1959 Topps #461	6.00
27	1959 Topps #564	6.00
28	1960 Topps #160	6.00
29	1960 Topps #563	6.00
30	1961 Topps #406	6.00
31	1961 Topps #475	6.00
32	1961 Topps #578	6.00
33	1962 Topps #18	6.00
34	1962 Topps #318	6.00
35	1962 Topps #471	6.00
36	1964 Topps #331	6.00

1997 Topps Mickey Mantle Finest Refractors

Each of the 16 Mantle Finest reprints from Series II can also be found in a Refractor version. Refractors are found every 216 packs, on average.

		MT
Complete Set (16):		400.00
Common Mantle:		25.00
21	1953 Bowman #44	25.00
22	1953 Bowman #59	40.00
23	1957 Topps #407	25.00
24	1958 Topps #418	25.00
25	1958 Topps #487	25.00
26	1959 Topps #461	25.00
27	1959 Topps #564	25.00
28	1960 Topps #160	25.00
29	1960 Topps #563	25.00
30	1961 Topps #406	25.00
31	1961 Topps #475	25.00
32	1961 Topps #578	25.00
33	1962 Topps #18	25.00
34	1962 Topps #318	25.00
35	1962 Topps #471	25.00
36	1964 Topps #331	25.00

Player names in *Italic* type indicate a rookie card.

1997 Topps Willie Mays Reprints

There are 27 different Willie Mays cards reprinted in Topps Series I and seeded every eight packs. The inserts form a collection of Topps and Bowman cards from throughout Mays' career and each is highlighted by a special commemorative gold foil stamp. Each of the Mays reprints can also be found in an autographed edition, bearing a special "Certified Autograph Issue" gold-foil logo.

		MT
Complete Set (27):		60.00
Common Card:		2.25
Autographed Card:		100.00
1	1951 Bowman #305	4.50
2	1952 Topps #261	3.00
3	1953 Topps #244	3.00
4	1954 Bowman #89	2.25
5	1954 Topps #90	2.25
6	1955 Bowman #184	2.25
7	1955 Topps #194	2.25
8	1956 Topps #130	2.25
9	1957 Topps #10	2.25
10	1958 Topps #5	2.25
11	1959 Topps #50	2.25
12	1960 Topps #200	2.25
13	1961 Topps #150	2.25
14	1961 Topps #579	2.25
15	1962 Topps #300	2.25
16	1963 Topps #300	2.25
17	1964 Topps #150	2.25
18	1965 Topps #250	2.25
19	1966 Topps #1	2.25
20	1967 Topps #200	2.25
21	1968 Topps #50	2.25
22	1969 Topps #190	2.25
23	1970 Topps #600	2.25
24	1971 Topps #600	2.25
25	1971 Topps #600	2.25
26	1972 Topps #49	2.25
27	1973 Topps #305	2.25

1997 Topps Willie Mays Finest

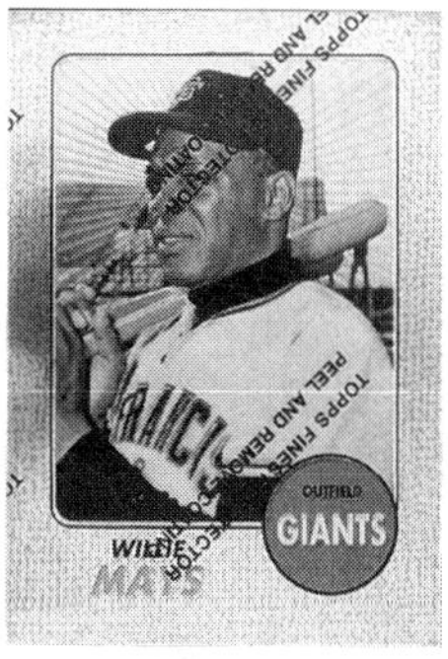

The introduction of Series II Topps offered collectors a chance to find Finest technology versions of each of the 27 commemorative reprint Topps and Bowman cards from throughout Mays' career. The Finest Mays reprints are found one in every 30 packs, on average.

		MT
Complete Set (27):		75.00
Common Card:		4.00
1	1951 Bowman #305	8.00
2	1952 Topps #261	6.00

3	1953 Topps #244	6.00
4	1954 Bowman #89	4.00
5	1954 Topps #90	4.00
6	1955 Bowman #184	4.00
7	1955 Topps #194	4.00
8	1956 Topps #130	4.00
9	1957 Topps #10	4.00
10	1958 Topps #5	4.00
11	1959 Topps #50	4.00
12	1960 Topps #200	4.00
13	1961 Topps #150	4.00
14	1961 Topps #579	4.00
15	1962 Topps #300	4.00
16	1963 Topps #300	4.00
17	1964 Topps #150	4.00
18	1965 Topps #250	4.00
19	1966 Topps #1	4.00
20	1967 Topps #200	4.00
21	1968 Topps #50	4.00
22	1969 Topps #190	4.00
23	1970 Topps #600	4.00
24	1971 Topps #600	4.00
25	1971 Topps #600	4.00
26	1972 Topps #49	4.00
27	1973 Topps #305	4.00

1997 Topps Willie Mays Finest Refractors

A high-end parallel set to the Willie Mays 27-card commemorative reprint issue is the Finest Refractor version issued in Series II. Refractors are found on average of once per 180 packs.

		MT
Complete Set (27):		250.00
Common Card:		10.00
1	1951 Bowman #305	25.00
2	1952 Topps #261	20.00
3	1953 Topps #244	20.00
4	1954 Bowman #89	15.00
5	1954 Topps #90	15.00
6	1955 Bowman #184	15.00
7	1955 Topps #194	15.00
8	1956 Topps #130	15.00
9	1957 Topps #10	15.00
10	1958 Topps #5	15.00
11	1959 Topps #50	15.00
12	1960 Topps #200	15.00
13	1961 Topps #150	15.00
14	1961 Topps #579	15.00
15	1962 Topps #300	15.00
16	1963 Topps #300	15.00
17	1964 Topps #150	15.00
18	1965 Topps #250	15.00
19	1966 Topps #1	15.00
20	1967 Topps #200	15.00
21	1968 Topps #50	15.00
22	1969 Topps #190	15.00
23	1970 Topps #600	15.00
24	1971 Topps #600	15.00
25	1971 Topps #600	15.00
26	1972 Topps #49	15.00
27	1973 Topps #305	15.00

1997 Topps Willie Mays Commemorative Super

This oversize (4-1/4" x 5-3/4") version of card #2 (1952 Topps) in the Willie Mays Commemorative Reprint series was available exclusively in a special retail packaging of 10 1997 Topps Series I foil packs. Like the regular-size reprints, it has a gold-foil commemorative stamp on front.

		MT
2	Willie Mays (1952 Topps)	5.00

1997 Topps Season's Best

Season's Best features 25 players on prismatic illusion foilboard, and can be found every six packs. The set has the top five players from five statistical categories: home runs, RBIs, batting average, steals, and wins. Season's Best were found in packs of Topps Series II, and later reprinted on chromium stock as part of Topps Chrome.

		MT
Complete Set (25):		15.00
Common Player:		.25
1	Tony Gwynn	2.00
2	Frank Thomas	2.00
3	Ellis Burks	.25
4	Paul Molitor	.75
5	Chuck Knoblauch	.40
6	Mark McGwire	4.00
7	Brady Anderson	.25
8	Ken Griffey Jr.	4.00
9	Albert Belle	.75
10	Andres Galarraga	.50
11	Andres Galarraga	.50
12	Albert Belle	.75
13	Juan Gonzalez	1.00
14	Mo Vaughn	.60
15	Rafael Palmeiro	.50
16	John Smoltz	.25
17	Andy Pettitte	.25
18	Pat Hentgen	.25
19	Mike Mussina	.60
20	Andy Benes	.25
21	Kenny Lofton	.60
22	Tom Goodwin	.25
23	Otis Nixon	.25
24	Eric Young	.25
25	Lance Johnson	.25

1997 Topps Sweet Strokes

These retail-exclusive Sweet Strokes insert cards consist of 15 Power Matrix foil cards of the top hitters in the game. These players have the swings to produce game winning-hits. The cards were seeded one per every 12 1997 Topps Series I retail packs. Cards are numbered with a "SS" prefix.

		MT
Complete Set (15):		40.00
Common Player:		1.00
1	Roberto Alomar	2.00
2	Jeff Bagwell	4.00
3	Albert Belle	2.50
4	Barry Bonds	2.50
5	Mark Grace	1.50
6	Ken Griffey Jr.	12.00
7	Tony Gwynn	4.00
8	Chipper Jones	6.00
9	Edgar Martinez	1.00
10	Mark McGwire	12.00
11	Rafael Palmeiro	1.50
12	Mike Piazza	6.00
13	Gary Sheffield	1.50
14	Frank Thomas	4.00
15	Mo Vaughn	1.50

1997 Topps Team Timber

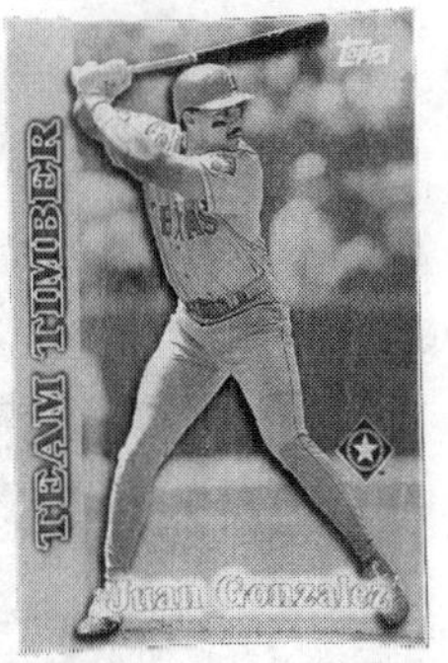

Team Timber was a 16-card insert that was exclusive to retail packs and inserted one per 36. The set displays the game's top sluggers on laminated litho wood cards. Cards are numbered with a "TT" prefix.

		MT
Complete Set (16):		50.00
Common Player:		1.00
1	Ken Griffey Jr.	10.00
2	Ken Caminiti	1.50
3	Bernie Williams	2.00
4	Jeff Bagwell	4.00
5	Frank Thomas	4.00
6	Andres Galarraga	1.00
7	Barry Bonds	3.00
8	Rafael Palmeiro	1.50
9	Brady Anderson	1.00
10	Juan Gonzalez	5.00
11	Mo Vaughn	2.00
12	Mark McGwire	10.00
13	Gary Sheffield	1.50
14	Albert Belle	2.50
15	Chipper Jones	6.50
16	Mike Piazza	6.50

1997 Topps Series 2 Supers

At 3-3/4" x 5-1/4", these premium cards are nearly identical to the regular-issue versions except for size. Also, whereas the regular cards have a front format which combines a high-gloss central area with a matte finish near the borders, the supers have just one finish on the front which is a semi-gloss. The supers also have different card numbers on back. One of the supers was included in each boxed lot of 15 Series II foil packs sold at large retail outlets with a price tag of about $15.

		MT
Complete Set (3):		25.00
1	Chipper Jones	9.00
2	Ken Griffey Jr.	12.00
3	Cal Ripken Jr.	10.00

1997 Topps/Chrome

Chrome Baseball reprinted the top 165 cards from Topps Series I and II baseball on a chromium, metallized stock. Chrome sold in four-card packs and included three insert sets: Diamond Duos, which was created exclusively for this product, Season's Best and Topps All-Stars, which were both reprinted from Topps products. Refractor versions of each card were found every 12 packs.

		MT
Complete Set (165):		70.00
Common Player:		.25
Common Refractors:		5.00
Star Refractors: 6X		
Young Stars and RCs: 4X		
Wax Box:		90.00
1	Barry Bonds	2.00
2	Jose Valentin	.25
3	Brady Anderson	.35
4	Wade Boggs	.50
5	Andres Galarraga	.75
6	Rusty Greer	.25
7	Derek Jeter	5.00
8	Ricky Bottalico	.25
9	Mike Piazza	5.00
10	Garret Anderson	.25
11	Jeff King	.25
12	Kevin Appier	.25
13	Mark Grace	.40
14	Jeff D'Amico	.25
15	Jay Buhner	.30
16	Hal Morris	.25
17	Harold Baines	.25
18	Jeff Cirillo	.25
19	Tom Glavine	.40
20	Andy Pettitte	.60
21	Mark McGwire	8.00
22	Chuck Knoblauch	.50
23	Raul Mondesi	.50
24	Albert Belle	1.50
25	Trevor Hoffman	.25
26	Eric Young	.25
27	Brian McRae	.25
28	Jim Edmonds	.25
29	Robb Nen	.25
30	Reggie Sanders	.25
31	Mike Lansing	.25
32	Craig Biggio	1.00
33	Ray Lankford	.25
34	Charles Nagy	.25
35	Paul Wilson	.25
36	John Wetteland	.25
37	Derek Bell	.25
38	Edgar Martinez	.25
39	Rickey Henderson	.75
40	Jim Thome	.75
41	Frank Thomas	2.00
42	Jackie Robinson (Tribute)	6.00
43	Terry Steinbach	.25
44	Kevin Brown	.40
45	Joey Hamilton	.25
46	Travis Fryman	.30
47	Juan Gonzalez	2.00
48	Ron Gant	.30
49	Greg Maddux	4.00
50	Wally Joyner	.30
51	John Valentin	.25
42	Bret Boone	.25
53	Paul Molitor	1.00
54	Rafael Palmeiro	1.00
55	Todd Hundley	.25
56	Ellis Burks	.25
57	Bernie Williams	1.50
58	Roberto Alomar	1.50
59	Jose Mesa	.25
60	Troy Percival	.25
61	John Smoltz	.50
62	Jeff Conine	.25
63	Bernard Gilkey	.25
64	Mickey Tettleton	.25
65	Justin Thompson	.25
66	Tony Phillips	.25
67	Ryne Sandberg	1.50
68	Geronimo Berroa	.25
69	Todd Hollandsworth	.25
70	Rey Ordonez	.25
71	Marquis Grissom	.25
72	Tino Martinez	.30
73	Steve Finley	.25
74	Andy Benes	.25
75	Jason Kendall	.40
76	Johnny Damon	.25
77	Jason Giambi	.25
78	Henry Rodriguez	.25
79	Edgar Renteria	.25
80	Ray Durham	.25
81	Gregg Jefferies	.25
82	Roberto Hernandez	.25
83	Joe Carter	.30
84	Jermaine Dye	.25
85	Julio Franco	.25
86	David Justice	.50
87	Jose Canseco	1.50
88	Paul O'Neill	.50
89	Mariano Rivera	.40
90	Bobby Higginson	.25
91	Mark Grudzielanek	.25
92	Lance Johnson	.25
93	Ken Caminiti	.40
94	Gary Sheffield	.40
95	Luis Castillo	.25
96	Scott Rolen	2.50
97	Chipper Jones	5.00
98	Darryl Strawberry	.50
99	Nomar Garciaparra	5.00
100	Jeff Bagwell	2.00
101	Ken Griffey Jr.	8.00
102	Sammy Sosa	5.00
103	Jack McDowell	.25
104	James Baldwin	.25
105	Rocky Coppinger	.25
106	Manny Ramirez	2.00
107	Tim Salmon	.40
108	Eric Karros	.25
109	Brett Butler	.25
110	Randy Johnson	1.50
111	Pat Hentgen	.25
112	Rondell White	.40
113	Eddie Murray	.50
114	Ivan Rodriguez	2.00
115	Jermaine Allensworth	.25
116	Ed Sprague	.25
117	Kenny Lofton	1.00
118	Alan Benes	.25
119	Fred McGriff	.50
120	Alex Fernandez	.25
121	Al Martin	.25
122	Devon White	.25
123	David Cone	.40
124	Karim Garcia	.25
125	Chili Davis	.25
126	Roger Clemens	3.00
127	Bobby Bonilla	.25
128	Mike Mussina	1.00
129	Todd Walker	.40
130	Dante Bichette	.40
131	Carlos Baerga	.25
132	Matt Williams	.50
133	Will Clark	.50
134	Dennis Eckersley	.25
135	Ryan Klesko	.40
136	Dean Palmer	.25
137	Javy Lopez	.40
138	Greg Vaughn	.40
139	Vinny Castilla	.40
140	Cal Ripken Jr.	6.00
141	Ruben Rivera	.25
142	Mark Wohlers	.25
143	Tony Clark	1.00
144	Jose Rosado	.25
145	Tony Gwynn	4.00
146	Cecil Fielder	.25
147	Brian Jordan	.25
148	Bob Abreu	.25
149	Barry Larkin	.50
150	Robin Ventura	.40
151	John Olerud	.75
152	Rod Beck	.25
153	Vladimir Guerrero	3.00
154	Marty Cordova	.25
155	Todd Stottlemyre	.25
156	Hideo Nomo	.40
157	Denny Neagle	.25
158	John Jaha	.25
159	Mo Vaughn	1.00
160	Andruw Jones	1.50
161	Moises Alou	.40
162	Larry Walker	1.00
163	Eddie Murray (Season Highlights)	.50
164	Paul Molitor (Season Highlights)	.75
165	Checklist	.25

1997 Topps/Chrome All-Stars

Topps Chrome All-Stars display the same 22 cards found in Topps Series I, however these are reprinted on a Chrome stock. Regular versions are seeded every 24 packs, while Refractor versions arrive every 72 packs. Cards are numbered with an "AS" prefix.

		MT
Complete Set (22):		90.00
Common Player:		2.00
Refractors: 3X		
1	Ivan Rodriguez	5.00
2	Todd Hundley	3.00
3	Frank Thomas	6.00
4	Andres Galarraga	4.00
5	Chuck Knoblauch	2.00
6	Eric Young	2.00
7	Jim Thome	3.00
8	Chipper Jones	12.00
9	Cal Ripken Jr.	15.00
10	Barry Larkin	3.00
11	Albert Belle	4.00
12	Barry Bonds	5.00
13	Ken Griffey Jr.	20.00
14	Ellis Burks	2.00
15	Juan Gonzalez	10.00
16	Gary Sheffield	3.00
17	Andy Pettitte	3.00
18	Tom Glavine	3.00
19	Pat Hentgen	2.00
20	John Smoltz	2.00
21	Roberto Hernandez	2.00
22	Mark Wohlers	2.00

1997 Topps/Chrome Diamond Duos

Diamond Duos is the only one of the three insert sets in Chrome Baseball that was developed exclusively for this product. The set has 10 cards featuring two superstar teammates on double-sided chromium cards. Diamond Duos are found every 36 packs, while Refractor versions are found every 108 packs. Cards are numbered with a "DD" prefix.

		MT
Complete Set (10):		70.00
Common Player:		3.00
Refractors: 2X		
1	Chipper Jones, Andruw Jones	10.00
2	Derek Jeter, Bernie Williams	10.00
3	Ken Griffey Jr., Jay Buhner	20.00
4	Kenny Lofton, Manny Ramirez	5.00
5	Jeff Bagwell, Craig Biggio	5.00
6	Juan Gonzalez, Ivan Rodriguez	6.00
7	Cal Ripken Jr., Brady Anderson	15.00
8	Mike Piazza, Hideo Nomo	10.00
9	Andres Galarraga, Dante Bichette	3.00
10	Frank Thomas, Albert Belle	5.00

1997 Topps/Chrome Season's Best

Season's Best includes the 25 players found in Topps Series II, but in a chromium version. The top five players from five statistical categories, including Leading Looters, Bleacher Reachers and Kings of Swing. Regular versions are seeded every 18 packs, with Refractors every 54 packs.

		MT
Complete Set (25):		100.00
Common Player:		2.00
Refractors: 3X		
1	Tony Gwynn	10.00
2	Frank Thomas	5.00
3	Ellis Burks	2.00
4	Paul Molitor	4.00
5	Chuck Knoblauch	3.00
6	Mark McGwire	20.00
7	Brady Anderson	2.50
8	Ken Griffey Jr.	20.00
9	Albert Belle	4.00
10	Andres Galarraga	4.00
11	Andres Galarraga	4.00
12	Albert Belle	4.00
13	Juan Gonzalez	5.00
14	Mo Vaughn	4.00
15	Rafael Palmeiro	4.00
16	John Smoltz	2.00
17	Andy Pettitte	3.00
18	Pat Hentgen	2.00
19	Mike Mussina	4.00
20	Andy Benes	2.00
21	Kenny Lofton	4.00
22	Tom Goodwin	2.00
23	Otis Nixon	2.00
24	Eric Young	2.00
25	Lance Johnson	2.00

1997 Topps/Chrome Jumbos

These large-format (3-3/4" x 5-1/4") Topps Chrome cards were produced for sale in special retail packaging offering one jumbo card and five packs of Topps Chrome for about $15. The jumbos are identical in design to the regular-issue Chrome cards of the same players. Because they were offered in a windowed retail package, it was easy for collectors to pick the card they wanted.

		MT
Complete Set (6):		22.00
Common Player:		2.00
9	Mike Piazza	4.50
94	Gary Sheffield	2.00
97	Chipper Jones	4.50
101	Ken Griffey Jr.	7.50
102	Sammy Sosa	5.00
140	Cal Ripken Jr.	6.00

1997 Topps/Gallery Pre-production

In its second year Topps Gallery was produced in a greatly improved combination of card stock, graphic highlights and inserts. To reintroduce the hobby to the issue, Topps distributed these promotional samples to dealers and the press. Except for the "PP" prefix to the card number on front, the samples are virtually identical to the issued versions.

		MT
Complete Set (4):		25.00
Common Player:		3.00
1	Andruw Jones	5.00
2	Derek Jeter	9.00
3	Mike Piazza	10.00
4	Craig Biggio	3.00

1997 Topps/Gallery

The second year of Gallery features 180 cards printed on extra-thick 24-point stock. Card fronts feature a player photo surrounded by an embossed foil "frame" to give each card the look of a piece of artwork. Backs contain career stats and biographical information on each player. Inserts include Peter Max Serigraphs, Signature Series Serigraphs, Player's Private Issue (parallel set), Photo Gallery and Gallery of Heroes. Cards were sold exclusively in hobby shops in eight-card packs for $4 each.

		MT
Complete Set (180):		50.00
Common Player:		.15
Unlisted Semistars: .30 to .50		
Wax Box:		60.00
1	Paul Molitor	1.00
2	Devon White	.15
3	Andres Galarraga	.50
4	Cal Ripken Jr.	3.00
5	Tony Gwynn	2.00
6	Mike Stanley	.15
7	Orel Hershiser	.15
8	Jose Canseco	1.00
9	Chili Davis	.15
10	Harold Baines	.15
11	Rickey Henderson	.25
12	Darryl Strawberry	.15
13	Todd Worrell	.15
14	Cecil Fielder	.15
15	Gary Gaetti	.15
16	Bobby Bonilla	.15
17	Will Clark	.50
18	Kevin Brown	.15
19	Tom Glavine	.40
20	Wade Boggs	.40
21	Edgar Martinez	.15
22	Lance Johnson	.15
23	Gregg Jefferies	.15
24	Bip Roberts	.15
25	Tony Phillips	.15
26	Greg Maddux	2.50
27	Mickey Tettleton	.15
28	Terry Steinbach	.15
29	Ryne Sandberg	1.00
30	Wally Joyner	.15
31	Joe Carter	.15
32	Ellis Burks	.15
33	Fred McGriff	.40
34	Barry Larkin	.25
35	John Franco	.15
36	Rafael Palmeiro	.50
37	Mark McGwire	5.00
38	Ken Caminiti	.25
39	David Cone	.25
40	Julio Franco	.15
41	Roger Clemens	2.00
42	Barry Bonds	1.25
43	Dennis Eckersley	.15
44	Eddie Murray	.50
45	Paul O'Neill	.20
46	Craig Biggio	.20
47	Roberto Alomar	1.00
48	Mark Grace	.40
49	Matt Williams	.40
50	Jay Buhner	.15
51	John Smoltz	.25
52	Randy Johnson	.75
53	Ramon Martinez	.15
54	Curt Schilling	.15
55	Gary Sheffield	.50
56	Jack McDowell	.15
57	Brady Anderson	.15
58	Dante Bichette	.30
59	Ron Gant	.20
60	Alex Fernandez	.25
61	Moises Alou	.15
62	Travis Fryman	.15
63	Dean Palmer	.15
64	Todd Hundley	.20
65	Jeff Brantley	.15
66	Bernard Gilkey	.15
67	Geronimo Berroa	.15
68	John Wetteland	.15
69	Robin Ventura	.20
70	Ray Lankford	.15
71	Kevin Appier	.15
72	Larry Walker	.75
73	Juan Gonzalez	1.25
74	Jeff King	.15
75	Greg Vaughn	.15
76	Steve Finley	.15
77	Brian McRae	.15
78	Paul Sorrento	.15
79	Ken Griffey Jr.	5.00
80	Omar Vizquel	.15
81	Jose Mesa	.15
82	Albert Belle	1.00
83	Glenallen Hill	.15
84	Sammy Sosa	3.00
85	Andy Benes	.15
86	David Justice	.40
87	Marquis Grissom	.15
88	John Olerud	.20
89	Tino Martinez	.20
90	Frank Thomas	1.50
91	Raul Mondesi	.40
92	Steve Trachsel	.15
93	Jim Edmonds	.15
94	Rusty Greer	.15
95	Joey Hamilton	.15
96	Ismael Valdes	.15
97	Dave Nilsson	.15
98	John Jaha	.15
99	Alex Gonzalez	.15
100	Javy Lopez	.25
101	Ryan Klesko	.25
102	Tim Salmon	.25
103	Bernie Williams	.75
104	Roberto Hernandez	.15
105	Chuck Knoblauch	.35
106	Mike Lansing	.15
107	Vinny Castilla	.15
108	Reggie Sanders	.15
109	Mo Vaughn	.75
110	Rondell White	.15
111	Ivan Rodriguez	1.25
112	Mike Mussina	.75
113	Carlos Baerga	.15
114	Jeff Conine	.15
115	Jim Thome	.50
116	Manny Ramirez	1.25
117	Kenny Lofton	.75
118	Wilson Alvarez	.15
119	Eric Karros	.15
120	Robb Nen	.15
121	Mark Wohlers	.15
122	Ed Sprague	.15
123	Pat Hentgen	.15
124	Juan Guzman	.15
125	Derek Bell	.15
126	Jeff Bagwell	1.25
127	Eric Young	.15
128	John Valentin	.15
129	Al Martin (photo actually Javy Lopez)	.25
130	Trevor Hoffman	.15
131	Henry Rodriguez	.15
132	Pedro Martinez	1.25
133	Mike Piazza	3.00
134	Brian Jordan	.15
135	Jose Valentin	.15
136	Jeff Cirillo	.15
137	Chipper Jones	3.00
138	Ricky Bottalico	.15
139	Hideo Nomo	.40
140	Troy Percival	.15
141	Rey Ordonez	.15
142	Edgar Renteria	.15
143	Luis Castillo	.15
144	Vladimir Guerrero	1.50
145	Jeff D'Amico	.15
146	Andruw Jones	.50
147	Darin Erstad	.50
148	Bob Abreu	.15
149	Carlos Delgado	.75
150	Jamey Wright	.15
151	Nomar Garciaparra	3.00
152	Jason Kendall	.25
153	Jermaine Allensworth	.15
154	Scott Rolen	1.25
155	Rocky Coppinger	.15
156	Paul Wilson	.15
157	Garret Anderson	.15
158	Mariano Rivera	.30
159	Ruben Rivera	.25
160	Andy Pettitte	.35
161	Derek Jeter	3.00
162	Neifi Perez	.15
163	Ray Durham	.15
164	James Baldwin	.15
165	Marty Cordova	.15
166	Tony Clark	.40
167	Michael Tucker	.15
168	Mike Sweeney	.15
169	Johnny Damon	.15
170	Jermaine Dye	.15
171	Alex Ochoa	.15
172	Jason Isringhausen	.15
173	Mark Grudzielanek	.15
174	Jose Rosado	.15
175	Todd Hollandsworth	.15
176	Alan Benes	.30
177	Jason Giambi	.15
178	Billy Wagner	.15
179	Justin Thompson	.15
180	Todd Walker	.25

1997 Topps/Gallery Players Private Issue

A parallel version of the Gallery issue called Players Private Issue was produced as a 1:12 pack insert. The PPI cards differ from the regular version in the use of a "PPI-" prefix to the card number on front and the application of a small silver PPI seal in a lower corner. On back, the line "One of 250 Issued" has been added.

	MT
Common Player:	4.00
Stars: 10X	
(See 1997 Topps/ Gallery for checklist and base card values.)	

1997 Topps/Gallery Peter Max

Noted artist Peter Max has painted renditions of 10 superstar players and offered his commentary about those players on the backs. Cards were inserted 1:24 packs. In addition, Max-autographed cards signed and numbered from an edition of 40 are inserted 1:1,200 packs.

		MT
Complete Set (10):		50.00
Common Player:		2.00
Complete Autographed Set (10):		2000.
Common Autographed Player:		75.00
1	Ken Griffey Jr.	10.00
1	Ken Griffey Jr. (autographed)	275.00
2	Frank Thomas	4.00
2	Frank Thomas (autographed)	150.00
3	Albert Belle	3.00
3	Albert Belle (autographed)	75.00
4	Barry Bonds	3.00
4	Barry Bonds (autographed)	75.00
5	Derek Jeter	6.00
5	Derek Jeter (autographed)	175.00
6	Ken Caminiti	2.00
6	Ken Caminiti (autographed)	75.00
7	Mike Piazza	6.00
7	Mike Piazza (autographed)	200.00
8	Cal Ripken Jr.	7.50
8	Cal Ripken Jr. (autographed)	225.00

9	Mark McGwire	10.00
9	Mark McGwire (autographed)	275.00
10	Chipper Jones	6.00
10	Chipper Jones (autographed)	200.00

1997 Topps/Gallery of Heroes

This 10-card die-cut insert features a design resembling stained glass. Cards were inserted 1:36 packs. Cards are numbered with a "GH" prefix.

		MT
Complete Set (10):		135.00
Common Player:		6.00
1	Derek Jeter	20.00
2	Chipper Jones	20.00
3	Frank Thomas	7.50
4	Ken Griffey Jr.	30.00
5	Cal Ripken Jr.	22.50
6	Mark McGwire	30.00
7	Mike Piazza	20.00
8	Jeff Bagwell	7.50
9	Tony Gwynn	12.00
10	Mo Vaughn	6.00

1997 Topps/Gallery Photo Gallery

This 21-card set features full-bleed, high-gloss action photos of some of the game's top stars. Cards were inserted 1:24 packs. They are numbered with a "PG" prefix.

		MT
Complete Set (16):		130.00
Common Player:		3.50
1	World Series	8.00
2	Paul Molitor	7.00
3	Eddie Murray	6.00
4	Ken Griffey Jr.	30.00
5	Chipper Jones	17.00
6	Derek Jeter	17.00
7	Frank Thomas	12.00
8	Mark McGwire	30.00
9	Kenny Lofton	6.00
10	Gary Sheffield	5.00
11	Mike Piazza	17.00
12	Vinny Castilla	3.50
13	Andres Galarraga	3.50
14	Andy Pettitte	6.00
15	Robin Ventura	3.50
16	Barry Larkin	3.50

1997 Topps Porcelain

Six of 1997's most popular players are featured in this set of porcelain reproductions of their regular '97 Topps cards. Topps contracted with R&M China Co. to manufacture the ultra-thin ceramic "cards." Each porcelain card is trimmed in 22k gold and is limited to an edition of 500; a serial number appears on the back of each piece. Original issue price was $25 and the cards were available exclusively through Topps Stadium Club program.

		MT
Complete Set (6):		150.00
Common Player:		25.00
13	Derek Jeter	25.00
108	Frank Thomas	25.00
130	Greg Maddux	25.00
277	Chipper Jones	25.00
300	Ken Griffey Jr.	25.00
400	Cal Ripken	25.00

1997 Topps Screenplays

Twenty of the game's top stars were featured in this multi-part collectible. The packaging is a 5-1/8" diameter lithographed steel can. The can was shrink-wrapped at the factory with a round checklist disc covering the color player photo on top of the can. The top has a woodgrain border around the photo and a gold facsimile autograph. The back of the topper disc has a career summary of the player. Inside the tin is a 2-1/2" x 3-1/2" plastic motion card with several seconds of game action shown as the angle of view changes. The card is covered by a peel-off protective layer on front and back. Foam pieces in the package allow both the can and card to be displayed upright. Issue price was about $10 per can. The unnumbered cans are checklisted here alphabetically. Values shown are for can/card combinations.

		MT
Complete Set (20):		50.00
Common Player:		1.00
Box:		45.00
(1)	Jeff Bagwell	2.50
(2)	Albert Belle	2.50
(3)	Barry Bonds	2.50
(4)	Andres Galarraga	2.00
(5)	Nomar Garciaparra	5.00
(6)	Juan Gonzalez	2.50
(7)	Ken Griffey Jr.	7.50
(8)	Tony Gwynn	4.00
(9)	Derek Jeter	5.00
(10)	Randy Johnson	2.00
(11)	Andruw Jones	2.00
(12)	Chipper Jones	5.00
(13)	Kenny Lofton	2.00
(14)	Mark McGwire	7.50
(15)	Paul Molitor	2.00
(16)	Hideo Nomo	1.00
(17)	Cal Ripken Jr.	6.00
(18)	Sammy Sosa	5.00
(19)	Frank Thomas	2.50
(20)	Jim Thome	1.00

1997 Topps Screenplays Inserts

		MT
Complete Set (6):		75.00
Common Player:		9.25
1	Larry Walker	5.00
2	Cal Ripken Jr.	17.50
3	Chipper Jones	15.00
4	Frank Thomas	7.50
5	Mike Piazza	15.00
6	Ken Griffey Jr.	25.00

1997 Topps Stars Promos

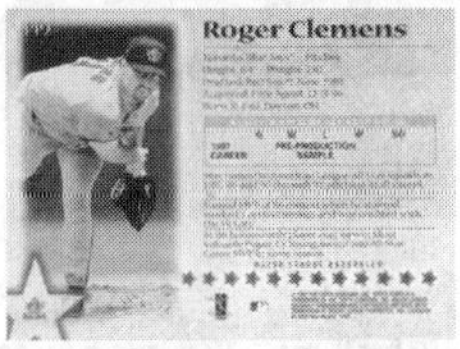

These promo cards introduced Topps' new line of premium cards. They are in the same basic format as the regular issue, but are marked "PRE-PRODUCTION / SAMPLE" in the stats box on back.

		MT
Complete Set (3):		8.00
Common Player:		2.00
PP1	Larry Walker	2.00
PP2	Roger Clemens	3.00
PP3	Frank Thomas	5.00

1997 Topps Stars

The premiere version of this product was sold only to hobby shops that were members of the Topps Home Team Advantage program. Each of the 125 regular cards in the set is printed on 20-point stock. Card fronts feature spot UV coating with a textured star pattern running down one side of the card. Inserts include the parallel Always Mint set, as well as '97 All-Stars, Future All-Stars, All-Star memories, and Autographed Rookie Reprints. Cards were sold in seven-card packs for $3 each.

		MT
Complete Set (125):		50.00
Common Player:		.15
Always Mint Stars, RCs: 10X		
Wax Box:		50.00
1	Larry Walker	.75
2	Tino Martinez	.25
3	Cal Ripken Jr.	3.00
4	Ken Griffey Jr.	4.00
5	Chipper Jones	2.50
6	David Justice	.25
7	Mike Piazza	2.50
8	Jeff Bagwell	1.00
9	Ron Gant	.25
10	Sammy Sosa	2.50
11	Tony Gwynn	2.00
12	Carlos Baerga	.15
13	Frank Thomas	1.00
14	Moises Alou	.25
15	Barry Larkin	.25
16	Ivan Rodriguez	1.00
17	Greg Maddux	2.00
18	Jim Edmonds	.20
19	Jose Canseco	.75
20	Rafael Palmeiro	.40
21	Paul Molitor	.75
22	Kevin Appier	.15
23	Raul Mondesi	.25
24	Lance Johnson	.15
25	Edgar Martinez	.15
26	Andres Galarraga	.40
27	Mo Vaughn	.60
28	Ken Caminiti	.25
29	Cecil Fielder	.15
30	Harold Baines	.15
31	Roberto Alomar	.60
32	Shawn Estes	.15
33	Tom Glavine	.25
34	Dennis Eckersley	.15
35	Manny Ramirez	1.00
36	John Olerud	.40
37	Juan Gonzalez	1.00
38	Chuck Knoblauch	.30
39	Albert Belle	.75
40	Vinny Castilla	.20
41	John Smoltz	.20
42	Barry Bonds	1.00
43	Randy Johnson	.60
44	Brady Anderson	.20
45	Jeff Blauser	.15
46	Craig Biggio	.40
47	Jeff Conine	.15
48	Marquis Grissom	.20
49	Mark Grace	.30
50	Roger Clemens	1.50
51	Mark McGwire	4.00
52	Fred McGriff	.25
53	Gary Sheffield	.30
54	Bobby Jones	.15
55	Eric Young	.15
56	Robin Ventura	.25
57	Wade Boggs	.25
58	Joe Carter	.15
59	Ryne Sandberg	.75
60	Matt Williams	.30
61	Todd Hundley	.20
62	Dante Bichette	.25
63	Chili Davis	.15
64	Kenny Lofton	.60
65	Jay Buhner	.15
66	Will Clark	.25
67	Travis Fryman	.20
68	Pat Hentgen	.15
69	Ellis Burks	.15
70	Mike Mussina	.60
71	Hideo Nomo	.25
72	Sandy Alomar	.20
73	Bobby Bonilla	.15
74	Rickey Henderson	.25
75	David Cone	.25
76	Terry Steinbach	.15
77	Pedro Martinez	1.25
78	Jim Thome	.50
79	Rod Beck	.15
80	Randy Myers	.15
81	Charles Nagy	.15
82	Mark Wohlers	.15
83	Paul O'Neill	.25
84	Curt Shilling	.25
85	Joey Cora	.15
86	John Franco	.15
87	Kevin Brown	.25
88	Benito Santiago	.15
89	Ray Lankford	.20
90	Bernie Williams	.60
91	Jason Dickson	.15
92	Jeff Cirillo	.15
93	Nomar Garciaparra	2.50
94	Mariano Rivera	.25
95	Javy Lopez	.20
96	*Tony Womack*	.75
97	Jose Rosado	.15
98	Denny Neagle	.15
99	Darryl Kile	.15
100	Justin Thompson	.15
101	Juan Encarnacion	.25
102	Brad Fullmer	.15
103	*Kris Benson*	4.00
104	Todd Helton	1.00
105	Paul Konerko	.25
106	*Travis Lee*	6.00
107	Todd Greene	.15
108	*Mark Kotsay*	2.00
109	Carl Pavano	.20
110	*Kerry Wood*	6.00
111	*Jason Romano*	1.50
112	*Geoff Goetz*	.75
113	*Scott Hodges*	.75
114	*Aaron Akin*	.50
115	*Vernon Wells*	6.00
116	*Chris Stowe*	.50
117	*Brett Caradonna*	.50
118	*Adam Kennedy*	3.00
119	*Jayson Werth*	4.00
120	*Glenn Davis*	.75
121	*Troy Cameron*	2.00
122	*J.J. Davis*	2.00
123	*Jason Dellaero*	.75
124	*Jason Standridge*	2.00
125	*Lance Berkman*	6.00

1997 Topps Stars Always Mint

This set parallels the regular Topps Stars issue and was inserted at the announced rate of one card per 12 packs. Identical in design to the regular version, the Always Mint cards have metallic foil background on the player portion of the front photos. Backs of the Always Mint parallels have a shiny metallic silver background.

	MT
Complete Set (125):	600.00
Common Player:	1.00
(Star cards and rookies valued about 10X regular version.)	

1997 Topps Stars All-Star Memories

This 10-card insert features stars who have had memorable performances in previous All-Star Games. Cards feature a laser-cut cascade of stars on a foilboard stock. Backs have another photo and a description of the All-Star memory. The cards were inserted 1:24 packs. Cards are numbered with an "ASM" prefix.

		MT
Complete Set (10):		50.00
Common Player:		2.00
1	Cal Ripken Jr.	15.00
2	Jeff Conine	2.00
3	Mike Piazza	12.00
4	Randy Johnson	4.00
5	Ken Griffey Jr.	20.00
6	Fred McGriff	3.00
7	Moises Alou	2.50
8	Hideo Nomo	2.50
9	Larry Walker	4.00
10	Sandy Alomar	2.00

1997 Topps Stars Future All-Stars

This 15-card set showcases the top candidates to make their All-Star Game debut in 1998. Cards feature a prismatic rainbow foil background and were inserted 1:12 packs. Cards are numbered with a "FAS" prefix.

		MT
Complete Set (15):		40.00
Common Player:		2.00
1	Derek Jeter	12.00
2	Andruw Jones	4.00
3	Vladimir Guerrero	6.00
4	Scott Rolen	5.00
5	Jose Guillen	2.00
6	Jose Cruz, Jr.	2.00
7	Darin Erstad	3.00
8	Tony Clark	3.00
9	Scott Spiezio	2.00
10	Kevin Orie	2.00
11	Calvin Reese	2.00
12	Billy Wagner	2.00
13	Matt Morris	2.00
14	Jeremi Gonzalez	2.00
15	Hideki Irabu	2.00

1997 Topps Stars Rookie Reprints

Fifteen Topps rookie cards of Hall of Famers were reprinted as a one-per-six-packs insert. Regardless of original size, all reprints are 2-1/2" x 3-1/2" with a reprint notice on back.

		MT
Complete Set (15):		25.00
Common Player:		2.50
(1)	Luis Aparicio	3.00
(2)	Richie Ashburn	2.50
(3)	Jim Bunning	2.50
(4)	Bob Feller	3.00
(5)	Rollie Fingers	2.50
(6)	Monte Irvin	2.50
(7)	Al Kaline	5.00
(8)	Ralph Kiner	2.50
(9)	Eddie Mathews	4.00
(10)	Hal Newhouser	2.50
(11)	Gaylord Perry	2.50
(12)	Robin Roberts	2.50
(13)	Brooks Robinson	5.00
(14)	Enos Slaughter	2.50
(15)	Earl Weaver	2.50

1997 Topps Stars Autographed Rookie Reprints

Fourteen different Hall of Famers autographed reprinted versions of their Topps rookie cards as a one-per-30-pack insert. Each card features a special certified stamp. Richie Ashburn was to have been card #2, but he died before he could autograph them.

		MT
Complete Set (14):		300.00
Common Player:		20.00
(1)	Luis Aparicio	35.00
(3)	Jim Bunning	25.00
(4)	Bob Feller	35.00
(5)	Rollie Fingers	20.00
(6)	Monte Irvin	20.00
(7)	Al Kaline	40.00
(8)	Ralph Kiner	25.00
(9)	Eddie Mathews	40.00
(10)	Hal Newhouser	20.00
(11)	Gaylord Perry	20.00
(12)	Robin Roberts	20.00
(13)	Brooks Robinson	40.00
(14)	Enos Slaughter	20.00
(15)	Earl Weaver	35.00

1997 Topps Stars 1997 All-Stars

This 20-card insert honors participants of the 1997 All-Star Game in Cleveland. Cards were inserted 1:24 packs. Fronts are printed on prismatic foil with hundreds of stars in the background. On back is another player photo and his All-Star Game 1997 and career stats. Cards are numbered with an "AS" prefix.

		MT
Complete Set (20):		200.00
Common Player:		6.00
1	Greg Maddux	30.00
2	Randy Johnson	8.00
3	Tino Martinez	6.00
4	Jeff Bagwell	15.00
5	Ivan Rodriguez	12.00
6	Mike Piazza	30.00
7	Cal Ripken Jr.	40.00
8	Ken Caminiti	6.00
9	Tony Gwynn	25.00
10	Edgar Martinez	6.00
11	Craig Biggio	6.00
12	Roberto Alomar	10.00
13	Larry Walker	8.00
14	Brady Anderson	6.00
15	Barry Bonds	12.00
16	Ken Griffey Jr.	50.00
17	Ray Lankford	6.00
18	Paul O'Neill	6.00
19	Jeff Blauser	6.00
20	Sandy Alomar	6.00

1997 Topps Dodger Rookie of the Year Collection

Available only through Topps Stadium Club and at Dodger Stadium, this set of special cards honors the five consecutive (1992-96) N.L. Rookies of the Year - all L.A. Dodgers - as well as the first-ever Rookie of the Year, Jackie Robinson. The cards feature reproductions of the players' rookie cards printed on front in metallic foil and with an N.L. Rookie of the Year logo and year banner. Backs are virtually identical to the regular-issue cards, but include a reprint line in the fine print. Raul Mondesi's card is a different version of the '94 Topps Coming Attractions subset card which he shared with Ben Van Ryn. Production was reported at 4,000 sets.

		MT
Complete Set (6):		30.00
Common Player:		3.00
1	Jackie Robinson (1952 Topps)	15.00
2	Mike Piazza (1992 Bowman)	15.00
3	Eric Karros (1993 Topps)	3.00
4	Raul Mondesi (1994 Topps)	3.50
5	Hideo Nomo (1995 Topps Traded)	4.00
6	Todd Hollandsworth (1996 Topps)	3.00

1997 Topps 22k Gold

These 22-karat gold-foil cards were created for direct sale by Topps. They reproduce, front and back, Griffey's and Ripken's regular-issue 1997 Topps cards, and feature a 1997-style card of Irabu, who did not appear on a regular Topps card that year. The 2-1/2" x 3-1/2" cards are individually serial numbered and were sold in a protective display holder. Initially priced at $30 apiece, they were discounted in a later offer to $19.95.

		MT
Complete Set (3):		60.00
Common Player:		20.00
300	Ken Griffey Jr.	20.00
400	Cal Ripken Jr.	20.00
----	Hideki Irabu	15.00

1998 Topps Pre-Production

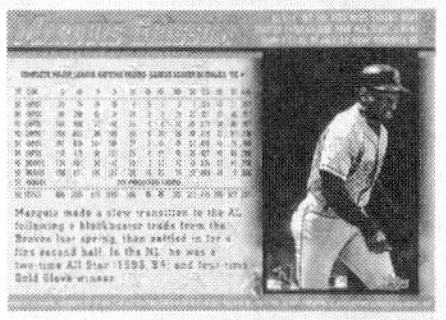

To give potential customers a feel for its 1998 baseball cards, Topps issued this series of pre-production samples. Cards are identical in format to the issued versions except they are numbered with a "PP" prefix and the 1997 stats line reads "PRE-PRODUCTION SAMPLE".

		MT
Complete Set (6):		15.00
Common Player:		1.00
PP1	Carlos Baerga	1.00
PP2	Jeff Bagwell	4.00
PP3	Marquis Grissom	1.50
PP4	Derek Jeter	6.00
PP5	Randy Johnson	2.00
PP6	Mike Piazza	5.00

1998 Topps

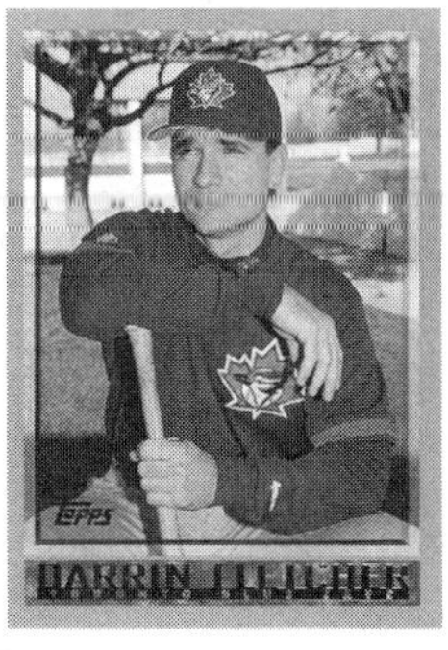

Topps was issued in two series in 1998 that totalled 503 cards, with 282 in Series I and 220 in Series II. Cards featured a gold border instead of the traditional white used in past years and the product featured Roberto Clemente inserts and a tribute card No. 21 in the base set. Series Highlights, Expansion Team Prospects, Interleague Highlights, Season Highlights, Prospects and Draft Picks. Subsets in Series II included: Expansion Teams, InterLeague Preview, Season Highlights, Prospects and Draft Picks. Every card in the set is paralleled in a Minted in Cooperstown insert that was stamped on-site at the Baseball Hall of Fame in Cooperstown. Inserts in Series I include: Roberto Clemente Reprints, Clemente Finest, Clemente Tribute, Memorabilia Madness, Etch a Sketch, Mystery Finest, Flashback and Baby Boomers. Inserts in Series II included: Clemente Reprints, Clemente Finest, 1998 Rookie Class, Mystery Finest, Milestones, Focal Points, and Clout 9.

		MT
Complete Set (503):		40.00
Complete Series 1 (282):		20.00
Complete Series 2 (220):		20.00
Common Player:		.05
Minted: 10X		
Inserted 1:8		
Wax Box:		45.00
1	Tony Gwynn	1.25
2	Larry Walker	.25
3	Billy Wagner	.05
4	Denny Neagle	.05
5	Vladimir Guerrero	.75
6	Kevin Brown	.15
7	NOT ISSUED	
8	Mariano Rivera	.15
9	Tony Clark	.25
10	Deion Sanders	.15
11	Francisco Cordova	.05
12	Matt Williams	.20
13	Carlos Baerga	.05
14	Mo Vaughn	.40
15	Bobby Witt	.05
16	Matt Stairs	.05
17	Chan Ho Park	.10
18	Mike Bordick	.05
19	Michael Tucker	.05
20	Frank Thomas	.75
21	Roberto Clemente	1.50
22	Dmitri Young	.05
23	Steve Trachsel	.05
24	Jeff Kent	.05
25	Scott Rolen	.75
26	John Thomson	.05
27	Joe Vitiello	.05
28	Eddie Guardado	.05
29	Charlie Hayes	.05
30	Juan Gonzalez	.75
31	Garret Anderson	.05
32	John Jaha	.05
33	Omar Vizquel	.05
34	Brian Hunter	.05
35	Jeff Bagwell	.75
36	Mark Lemke	.05
37	Doug Glanville	.05
38	Dan Wilson	.05
39	Steve Cooke	.05
40	Chili Davis	.05
41	Mike Cameron	.05
42	F.P. Santangelo	.05
43	Brad Ausmus	.05
44	Gary DiSarcina	.05
45	Pat Hentgen	.05
46	Wilton Guerrero	.05
47	Devon White	.05
48	Danny Patterson	.05
49	Pat Meares	.05
50	Rafael Palmeiro	.25
51	Mark Gardner	.05
52	Jeff Blauser	.05
53	Dave Hollins	.05
54	Carlos Garcia	.05
55	Ben McDonald	.05
56	John Mabry	.05
57	Trevor Hoffman	.05
58	Tony Fernandez	.05
59	Rich Loiselle	.05
60	Mark Leiter	.05
61	Pat Kelly	.05
62	John Flaherty	.05
63	Roger Bailey	.05
64	Tom Gordon	.05
65	Ryan Klesko	.15
66	Darryl Hamilton	.05
67	Jim Eisenreich	.05
68	Butch Huskey	.05
69	Mark Grudzielanek	.05
70	Marquis Grissom	.10
71	Mark McLemore	.05
72	Gary Gaetti	.05
73	Greg Gagne	.05
74	Lyle Mouton	.05
75	Jim Edmonds	.10
76	Shawn Green	.50
77	Greg Vaughn	.10
78	Terry Adams	.05
79	*Kevin Polcovich*	.20
80	Troy O'Leary	.05
81	Jeff Shaw	.05
82	Rich Becker	.05
83	David Wells	.05
84	Steve Karsay	.05
85	Charles Nagy	.05
86	B.J. Surhoff	.05
87	Jamey Wright	.05
88	James Baldwin	.05
89	Edgardo Alfonzo	.15
90	Jay Buhner	.10
91	Brady Anderson	.15
92	Scott Servais	.05
93	Edgar Renteria	.05
94	Mike Lieberthal	.10
95	Rick Aguilera	.05
96	Walt Weiss	.05
97	Deivi Cruz	.05
98	Kurt Abbott	.05
99	Henry Rodriguez	.05
100	Mike Piazza	1.50
101	Bill Taylor	.05
102	Todd Zeile	.05
103	Rey Ordonez	.05
104	Willie Greene	.05
105	Tony Womack	.05
106	Mike Sweeney	.05
107	Jeffrey Hammonds	.05
108	Kevin Orie	.05
109	Alex Gonzalez	.05
110	Jose Canseco	.50
111	Paul Sorrento	.05
112	Joey Hamilton	.05
113	Brad Radke	.05
114	Steve Avery	.05
115	Esteban Loaiza	.05
116	Stan Javier	.05
117	Chris Gomez	.05
118	Royce Clayton	.05
119	Orlando Merced	.05
120	Kevin Appier	.05
121	Mel Nieves	.05
122	Joe Girardi	.05
123	Rico Brogna	.05
124	Kent Mercker	.05
125	Manny Ramirez	.75
126	Jeromy Burnitz	.05
127	Kevin Foster	.05
128	Matt Morris	.05
129	Jason Dickson	.05
130	Tom Glavine	.15
131	Wally Joyner	.05
132	Rick Reed	.05
133	Todd Jones	.05
134	Dave Martinez	.05
135	Sandy Alomar	.05
136	Mike Lansing	.05
137	Sean Berry	.05
138	Doug Jones	.05
139	Todd Stottlemyre	.05
140	Jay Bell	.05
141	Jaime Navarro	.05
142	Chris Hoiles	.05
143	Joey Cora	.05
144	Scott Spiezio	.05
145	Joe Carter	.05
146	Jose Guillen	.15
147	Damion Easley	.05
148	Lee Stevens	.05
149	Alex Fernandez	.05
150	Randy Johnson	.40
151	J.T. Snow	.10
152	Chuck Finley	.05
153	Bernard Gilkey	.05
154	David Segui	.05
155	Dante Bichette	.15
156	Kevin Stocker	.05
157	Carl Everett	.15
158	Jose Valentin	.05
159	Pokey Reese	.05
160	Derek Jeter	1.50
161	Roger Pavlik	.05
162	Mark Wohlers	.05
163	Ricky Bottalico	.05
164	Ozzie Guillen	.05
165	Mike Mussina	.40
166	Gary Sheffield	.15
167	Hideo Nomo	.25
168	Mark Grace	.20
169	Aaron Sele	.05
170	Darryl Kile	.10
171	Shawn Estes	.05
172	Vinny Castilla	.10
173	Ron Coomer	.05
174	Jose Rosado	.05
175	Kenny Lofton	.40
176	Jason Giambi	.10
177	Hal Morris	.05
178	Darren Bragg	.05
179	Orel Hershiser	.05
180	Ray Lankford	.05
181	Hideki Irabu	.15
182	Kevin Young	.05
183	Javy Lopez	.15
184	Jeff Montgomery	.05
185	Mike Holtz	.05
186	George Williams	.05
187	Cal Eldred	.05
188	Tom Candiotti	.05
189	Glenallen Hill	.05

190 Brian Giles .05
191 Dave Mlicki .05
192 Garrett Stephenson .05
193 Jeff Frye .05
194 Joe Oliver .05
195 Bob Hamelin .05
196 Luis Sojo .05
197 LaTroy Hawkins .05
198 Kevin Elster .05
199 Jeff Reed .05
200 Dennis Eckersley .05
201 Bill Mueller .05
202 Russ Davis .05
203 Armando Benitez .05
204 Quilvio Veras .05
205 Tim Naehring .05
206 Quinton McCracken .05
207 Raul Casanova .05
208 Matt Lawton .05
209 Luis Alicea .05
210 Luis Gonzalez .10
211 Allen Watson .05
212 Gerald Williams .05
213 David Bell .05
214 Todd Hollandsworth .05
215 Wade Boggs .15
216 Jose Mesa .05
217 Jamie Moyer .05
218 Darren Daulton .05
219 Mickey Morandini .05
220 Rusty Greer .10
221 Jim Bullinger .05
222 Jose Offerman .05
223 Matt Karchner .05
224 Woody Williams .05
225 Mark Loretta .05
226 Mike Hampton .05
227 Willie Adams .05
228 Scott Hatteberg .05
229 Rich Amaral .05
230 Terry Steinbach .05
231 Glendon Rusch .05
232 Bret Boone .05
233 Robert Person .05
234 Jose Hernandez .05
235 Doug Drabek .05
236 Jason McDonald .05
237 Chris Widger .05
238 *Tom Martin* .05
239 Dave Burba .05
240 Pete Rose II .05
241 Bobby Ayala .05
242 Tim Wakefield .05
243 Dennis Springer .05
244 Tim Belcher .05
245 Jon Garland, Geoff Goetz (Draft Pick) .15
246 Glenn Davis, Lance Berkman (Draft Pick) .25
247 Vernon Wells, Aaron Akin (Draft Pick) .25
248 Adam Kennedy, Jason Romano (Draft Pick) .10
249 Jason Dellaero, Troy Cameron (Draft Pick) .20
250 Alex Sanchez, *Jared Sandberg* (Expansion Team Prospects) .20
251 Pablo Ortega, Jim Manias (Expansion Team Prospects) .15
252 Jason Conti, *Mike Stoner* (Expansion Team Prospects) .40
253 John Patterson, Larry Rodriguez (Expansion Team Prospects) .20
254 Adrian Beltre, *Ryan Minor*, Aaron Boone (Prospect) .75
255 Ben Grieve, Brian Buchanan, Dermal Brown (Prospect) .50
256 Carl Pavano, Kerry Wood, Gil Meche (Prospect) .50
257 David Ortiz, Daryle Ward, Richie Sexson (Prospect) .15
258 Randy Winn, Juan Encarnacion, Andrew Vessel (Prospect) .15
259 Kris Benson, Travis Smith, Courtney Duncan (Prospect) .15
260 Chad Hermansen, Brent Butler, *Warren Morris* (Prospect) .50
261 Ben Davis, Elieser Marrero, Ramon Hernandez (Prospect) .10
262 Eric Chavez, Russell Branyan, Russ Johnson (Prospect) .15
263 Todd Dunwoody, John Barnes, *Ryan Jackson* (Prospect) .25
264 Matt Clement, Roy Halladay, *Brian Fuentes* (Prospect) .25
265 Randy Johnson (Season Highlight) .10
266 Kevin Brown (Season Highlight) .05
267 Ricardo Rincon, Francisco Cordova (Season Highlight) .05
268 Nomar Garciaparra (Season Highlight) .65
269 Tino Martinez (Season Highlight) .05
270 Chuck Knoblauch (Interleague) .05
271 Pedro Martinez (Interleague) .40
272 Denny Neagle (Interleague) .05
273 Juan Gonzalez (Interleague) .40
274 Andres Galarraga (Interleague) .05
275 Checklist .05
276 Checklist .05
277 Moises Alou (World Series) .05
278 Sandy Alomar (World Series) .05
279 Gary Sheffield (World Series) .05
280 Matt Williams (World Series) .05
281 Livan Hernandez (World Series) .05
282 Chad Ogea (World Series) .05
283 Marlins Win (World Series) .05
284 Tino Martinez .10
285 Roberto Alomar .50
286 Jeff King .05
287 Brian Jordan .05
288 Darin Erstad .15
289 Ken Caminiti .20
290 Jim Thome .30
291 Paul Molitor .50
292 Ivan Rodriguez .75
293 Bernie Williams .40
294 Todd Hundley .10
295 Andres Galarraga .40
296 Greg Maddux 1.25
297 Edgar Martinez .05
298 Ron Gant .10
299 Derek Bell .05
300 Roger Clemens 1.00
301 Rondell White .15
302 Barry Larkin .15
303 Robin Ventura .20
304 Jason Kendall .15
305 Chipper Jones 1.50
306 John Franco .05
307 Sammy Sosa 1.50
308 Troy Percival .05
309 Chuck Knoblauch .15
310 Ellis Burks .05
311 Al Martin .05
312 Tim Salmon .20
313 Moises Alou .15
314 Lance Johnson .05
315 Justin Thompson .10
316 Will Clark .25
317 Barry Bonds .60
318 Craig Biggio .25
319 John Smoltz .15
320 Cal Ripken Jr. 2.00
321 Ken Griffey Jr. 2.50
322 Paul O'Neill .15
323 Todd Helton .50
324 John Olerud .25
325 Mark McGwire 2.50
326 Jose Cruz Jr. .10
327 Jeff Cirillo .05
328 Dean Palmer .05
329 John Wetteland .05
330 Steve Finley .05
331 Albert Belle .50
332 Curt Schilling .10
333 Raul Mondesi .20
334 Andruw Jones .40
335 Nomar Garciaparra 1.50
336 David Justice .20
337 Andy Pettitte .20
338 Pedro Martinez .75
339 Travis Miller .05
340 Chris Stynes .05
341 Gregg Jefferies .05
342 Jeff Fassero .05
343 Craig Counsell .05
344 Wilson Alvarez .05
345 Bip Roberts .05
346 Kelvim Escobar .05
347 Mark Bellhorn .05
348 *Cory Lidle* .05
349 Fred McGriff .15
350 Chuck Carr .05
351 Bob Abreu .05
352 Juan Guzman .05
353 Fernando Vina .05
354 Andy Benes .05
355 Dave Nilsson .05
356 Bobby Bonilla .05
357 Ismael Valdes .05
358 Carlos Perez .05
359 Kirk Rueter .05
360 Bartolo Colon .15
361 Mel Rojas .05
362 Johnny Damon .05
363 Geronimo Berroa .05
364 Reggie Sanders .05
365 Jermaine Allensworth .05
366 Orlando Cabrera .05
367 Jorge Fabregas .05
368 Scott Stahoviak .05
369 Ken Cloude .05
370 Donovan Osborne .05
371 Roger Cedeno .05
372 Neifi Perez .05
373 Chris Holt .05
374 Cecil Fielder .05
375 Marty Cordova .05
376 Tom Goodwin .05
377 Jeff Suppan .05
378 Jeff Brantley .05
379 Mark Langston .05
380 Shane Reynolds .10
381 Mike Fetters .05
382 Todd Greene .05
383 Ray Durham .05
384 Carlos Delgado .50
385 Jeff D'Amico .05
386 Brian McRae .05
387 Alan Benes .10
388 Heathcliff Slocumb .05
389 Eric Young .05
390 Travis Fryman .05
391 David Cone .10
392 Otis Nixon .05
393 Jereml Gonzalez .05
394 Jeff Juden .05
395 Jose Vizcaino .05
396 Ugueth Urbina .05
397 Ramon Martinez .10
398 Robb Nen .05
399 Harold Baines .05
400 Delino DeShields .05
401 John Burkett .05
402 Sterling Hitchcock .05
403 Mark Clark .05
404 Terrell Wade .05
405 Scott Brosius .05
406 Chad Curtis .05
407 Brian Johnson .05
408 Roberto Kelly .05
409 *Dave Dellucci* .05
410 Michael Tucker .05
411 Mark Kotsay .10
412 Mark Lewis .05
413 Ryan McGuire .05
414 Shawon Dunston .05
415 Brad Rigby .05
416 Scott Erickson .05
417 Bobby Jones .05
418 Darren Oliver .05
419 John Smiley .05
420 T.J. Mathews .05
421 Dustin Hermanson .05
422 Mike Timlin .05
423 Willie Blair .05
424 Manny Alexander .05
425 Bob Tewksbury .05
426 Pete Schourek .05
427 Reggie Jefferson .05
428 Ed Sprague .05
429 Jeff Conine .05
430 Roberto Hernandez .05
431 Tom Pagnozzi .05
432 Jaret Wright .20
433 Livan Hernandez .10
434 Andy Ashby .05
435 Todd Dunn .05
436 Bobby Higginson .05
437 Rod Beck .05
438 Jim Leyritz .05
439 Matt Williams .20
440 Brett Tomko .05
441 Joe Randa .05
442 Chris Carpenter .05
443 Dennis Reyes .05
444 Al Leiter .10
445 Jason Schmidt .05
446 Ken Hill .05
447 Shannon Stewart .05
448 Enrique Wilson .05
449 Fernando Tatis .15
450 Jimmy Key .05
451 Darrin Fletcher .05
452 John Valentin .05
453 Kevin Tapani .05
454 Eric Karros .10
455 Jay Bell .05
456 Walt Weiss .05
457 Devon White .05
458 Carl Pavano .05
459 Mike Lansing .05
460 John Flaherty .05
461 Richard Hidalgo .05
462 Quinton McCracken .05
463 Karim Garcia .10
464 Miguel Cairo .05
465 Edwin Diaz .05
466 Bobby Smith .05
467 Yamil Benitez .05
468 *Rich Butler* .25
469 *Ben Ford* .05
470 Bubba Trammell .05
471 Brent Brede .05
472 Brooks Kieschnick .05
473 Carlos Castillo .05
474 Brad Radke (Season Highlight) .05
475 Roger Clemens (Season Highlight) .50
476 Curt Schilling (Season Highlight) .05
477 John Olerud (Season Highlight) .05
478 Mark McGwire (Season Highlight) 1.25
479 Mike Piazza, Ken Griffey Jr. (Interleague) 1.00
480 Jeff Bagwell, Frank Thomas (Interleague) .50
481 Chipper Jones, Nomar Garciaparra (Interleague) .75
482 Larry Walker, Juan Gonzalez (Interleague) .40
483 Gary Sheffield, Tino Martinez (Interleague) .05
484 Derrick Gibson, Michael Coleman, Norm Hutchins (Prospect) .10
485 Braden Looper, Cliff Politte, Brian Rose (Prospect) .15
486 Eric Milton, Jason Marquis, Corey Lee (Prospect) .15
487 A.J. Hinch, Mark Osborne, *Robert Fick* (Prospect) .50
488 Aramis Ramirez, Alex Gonzalez, Sean Casey (Prospect) .60
489 *Donnie Bridges*, *Tim Drew* (Draft Pick) .40
490 *Ntema Ndungidi*, *Darnell McDonald* (Draft Pick) .50
491 *Ryan Anderson*, Mark Mangum (Draft Pick) .75
492 J.J. Davis, *Troy Glaus* (Draft Pick) 1.50
493 Jayson Werth, *Dan Reichert* (Draft Pick) .25
494 *John Curtice*, *Mike Cuddyer* (Draft Pick) .50
495 *Jack Cust*, Jason Standridge (Draft Pick) .50
496 Brian Anderson (Expansion Team Prospect) .05
497 Tony Saunders (Expansion Team Prospect) .05
498 Vladimir Nunez, *Jhensy Sandoval* (Expansion Team Prospect) .10
499 Brad Penny, Nick Bierbrodt (Expansion Team Prospect) .15
500 *Dustin Carr*, *Luis Cruz* (Expansion Team Prospect) .20
501 *Marcus McCain*, *Cedrick Bowers* (Expansion Team Prospect) .20
502 Checklist .05
503 Checklist .05
504 Alex Rodriguez 2.00

1998 Topps Minted in Cooperstown

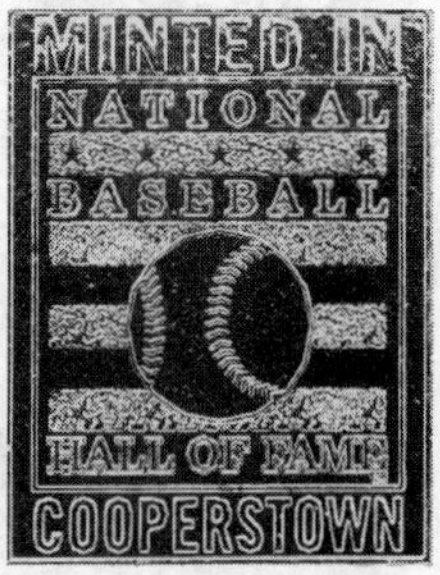

As part of an effort to promote interest in the various major sports' halls of fame, Topps produced this parallel version of its Series 1 baseball set. A special embossing machine was set up at the National Baseball Hall of Fame in Cooperstown to apply a bronze-foil "MINTED IN COOPERSTOWN" logo to cards. Twenty-card sheets of the logoed cards were sold on the premises and single cards were inserted into foil packs.

	MT
Common Card:	.25

(Star and rookie cards valued at 10X corresponding card in regular issue.)

1998 Topps Arizona Diamondbacks Inaugural Season

To mark the team's inaugural year in the Major Leagues, Topps produced a special run of 5,000 factory sets in which each card was embossed with a special gold seal incorporating the D-Backs logo. Sets were sold only at the team's normal souvenir outlets.

	MT
Complete Set (503):	100.00
Common Player:	.50

(Star players' cards valued at 10X-15X same card in regular Topps version.)

1998 Topps Tampa Bay Devil Rays Inaugural Season

To mark the team's inaugural year in the Major Leagues, Topps produced a special run of 5,000 factory sets in which each card was embossed with a special gold seal incorporating the D-Rays logo. Sets were sold only at the team's normal souvenir outlets.

	MT
Complete Set (503):	100.00
Common Player:	.50

(Star players' cards valued at 10X-15X same card in regular Topps version.)

1998 Topps Baby Boomers

This 15-card retail exclusive insert was seeded one

per 36 packs of Series I. It featured some of the top young players in the game and was numbered with a "BB" prefix.

		MT
Complete Set (15):		30.00
Common Player:		.75
Inserted 1:36 retail		
1	Derek Jeter	5.00
2	Scott Rolen	2.00
3	Nomar Garciaparra	5.00
4	Jose Cruz Jr.	.75
5	Darin Erstad	1.50
6	Todd Helton	2.00
7	Tony Clark	1.00
8	Jose Guillen	.75
9	Andruw Jones	1.50
10	Vladimir Guerrero	2.50
11	Mark Kotsay	.75
12	Todd Greene	.75
13	Andy Pettitte	.75
14	Justin Thompson	.75
15	Alan Benes	.75

1998 Topps Roberto Clemente Reprints

Nineteen different Topps Clemente cards were reprinted with a gold foil stamp and included 1998 Topps. Odd numbers were included in Series I, while even numbers were inserted into Series II, both at a rate of one per 18 packs. The insert was created to honor the memory of the 25th anniversary of Clemente's death.

		MT
Complete Set (19):		70.00
Common Clemente:		4.00
Inserted 1:18		
1	1955	10.00
2	1956	4.00
3	1957	4.00
4	1958	4.00
5	1959	4.00
6	1960	4.00
7	1961	4.00
8	1962	4.00
9	1963	4.00
10	1964	4.00
11	1965	4.00
12	1966	4.00
13	1967	4.00
14	1968	4.00
15	1969	4.00
16	1970	4.00
17	1971	4.00
18	1972	4.00
19	1973	4.00

1998 Topps Roberto Clemente Finest

Clemente Finest inserts were included in both Series I and II at a rate of one per 72 packs. There were a total of 19 different, with odd numbers in Series I and even numbers in Series II. The insert helped honor the memory of the 25th anniversary of his death.

		MT
Complete Set (19):		150.00
Common Card:		10.00
Inserted 1:72		
Refractors: 2.5X		
Inserted 1:288		
1	1955	15.00
2	1956	10.00
3	1957	10.00
4	1958	10.00
5	1959	10.00
6	1960	10.00
7	1961	10.00
8	1962	10.00
9	1963	10.00
10	1964	10.00
11	1965	10.00
12	1966	10.00
13	1967	10.00
14	1968	10.00
15	1969	10.00
16	1970	10.00
17	1971	10.00
18	1972	10.00
19	1973	10.00

1998 Topps Roberto Clemente "Tin" Reprints

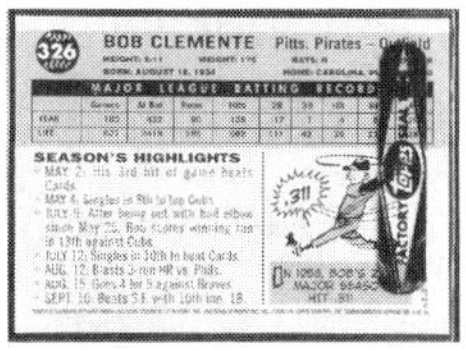

		MT
Complete Set (19):		70.00
Common Card:		4.00
1	1955	10.00
2	1956	4.00
3	1957	4.00
4	1958	4.00
5	1959	4.00
6	1960	4.00
7	1961	4.00
8	1962	4.00
9	1963	4.00
10	1964	4.00
11	1965	4.00
12	1966	4.00
13	1967	4.00
14	1968	4.00
15	1969	4.00
16	1970	4.00
17	1971	4.00
18	1972	4.00
19	1973	4.00

1998 Topps Roberto Clemente Commemorative Tins

This series of commemorative tin card "packs" reproduces in an enlarged (about 3" x 4-5/8" x 3/4") format the front and back of four of Roberto Clemente's Topps cards. Each tin, originally retailing for about $5, contains a plastic-sealed Clemente reprint card.

	MT
Complete Set (4):	20.00
Roberto Clemente (1955)	7.50
Roberto Clemente (1956)	5.00
Roberto Clemente (1965)	5.00
Roberto Clemente (1971)	5.00

1998 Topps Roberto Clemente Tribute

Five Clemente Tribute cards were produced for Series I and inserted in one per 12 packs. The set features some classic photos of Clemente and honor his memory in the 25th anniversary of his death. Clemente Tribute cards are numbered with an "RC" prefix.

		MT
Complete Set (5):		6.00
Common Clemente:		1.50
Inserted 1:12		
1	Roberto Clemente	1.50
2	Roberto Clemente	1.50
3	Roberto Clemente	1.50
4	Roberto Clemente	1.50
5	Roberto Clemente	1.50

1998 Topps Clout 9

Clout 9 captured nine players known for their statistical supremacy. Cards were numbered with a "C" prefix and inserted one per 72 packs of Series II.

		MT
Complete Set (9):		50.00
Common Player:		3.00
Inserted 1:72		
1	Edgar Martinez	3.00
2	Mike Piazza	12.00
3	Frank Thomas	7.50
4	Craig Biggio	4.00
5	Vinny Castilla	3.00
6	Jeff Blauser	3.00
7	Barry Bonds	7.50
8	Ken Griffey Jr.	20.00
9	Larry Walker	4.00

1998 Topps Etch-A-Sketch

Etch a Sketch featured nine different players depicted by nationally acclaimed artist George Vlosich III. Known as "The Etch a Sketch Kid," Vlosich created each one of these Series I inserts, which were inserted at a rate of one per 36 packs. Cards are numbered with an "ES" prefix.

		MT
Complete Set (9):		30.00
Common Player:		1.50
Inserted 1:36		
1	Albert Belle	2.00
2	Barry Bonds	3.00
3	Ken Griffey Jr.	10.00
4	Greg Maddux	5.00
5	Hideo Nomo	1.50
6	Mike Piazza	6.00
7	Cal Ripken Jr.	8.00
8	Frank Thomas	3.00
9	Mo Vaughn	2.00

1998 Topps Flashback

This double-sided insert showed "then and now" photos of 10 top major leaguers. One side contained a shot of the player in 1998, while the other side showed him at the beginning of his major league career. Flashback inserts were seeded one per 72 packs and numbered with an "FB" prefix.

		MT
Complete Set (10):		70.00
Common Player:		3.00
Inserted 1:72		
1	Barry Bonds	8.00
2	Ken Griffey Jr.	25.00
3	Paul Molitor	4.00
4	Randy Johnson	4.00
5	Cal Ripken Jr.	15.00
6	Tony Gwynn	12.00
7	Kenny Lofton	4.00
8	Gary Sheffield	4.00
9	Deion Sanders	3.00
10	Brady Anderson	3.00

1998 Topps Focal Point

This hobby exclusive insert contained 15 top players and focused on the skills that have made that player great. Focal Point inserts were available in Series II packs and seeded one per 36 packs, and were numbered with an "FP" prefix.

		MT
Complete Set (15):		80.00
Common Player:		2.00
Inserted 1:36		
1	Juan Gonzalez	6.00
2	Nomar Garciaparra	12.00
3	Jose Cruz Jr.	2.00
4	Cal Ripken Jr.	15.00
5	Ken Griffey Jr.	20.00
6	Ivan Rodriguez	5.00
7	Larry Walker	4.00
8	Barry Bonds	5.00
9	Roger Clemens	6.00
10	Frank Thomas	5.00
11	Chuck Knoblauch	2.00
12	Mike Piazza	12.00
13	Greg Maddux	10.00
14	Vladimir Guerrero	6.00
15	Andruw Jones	4.00

1998 Topps Hallbound

Hallbound featured 15 top players who are considered locks to be inducted into the Hall of Fame when there career is over. This insert was exclusive to Series I hobby packs and seeded one per 36 packs. Cards are numbered with an "HB" prefix.

		MT
Complete Set (15):		75.00
Common Player:		1.50
1	Paul Molitor	3.00
2	Tony Gwynn	8.00
3	Wade Boggs	2.00
4	Roger Clemens	6.00
5	Dennis Eckersley	1.50
6	Cal Ripken Jr.	12.00
7	Greg Maddux	8.00
8	Rickey Henderson	2.00
9	Ken Griffey Jr.	15.00
10	Frank Thomas	6.00
11	Mark McGwire	15.00
12	Barry Bonds	5.00
13	Mike Piazza	10.00
14	Juan Gonzalez	5.00
15	Randy Johnson	3.00

1998 Topps Inter-League Mystery Finest

Five of the 1997 season's most intriguing inter-league matchups are showcased with four cards each in Inter-League Mystery Finest. Regular versions of this Series 1 insert are seeded one per 36 packs, while Refractor versions are seeded one per 144 packs. Cards are numbered with an "ILM" prefix.

		MT
Complete Set (20):		100.00
Common Player:		1.50
Inserted 1:36		
Refractors: 5X		
Inserted 1:144		
1	Chipper Jones	12.00
2	Cal Ripken Jr.	15.00
3	Greg Maddux	10.00
4	Rafael Palmeiro	3.00
5	Todd Hundley	1.50
6	Derek Jeter	12.00
7	John Olerud	2.50
8	Tino Martinez	2.00
9	Larry Walker	4.00
10	Ken Griffey Jr.	20.00
11	Andres Galarraga	2.00
12	Randy Johnson	4.00
13	Mike Piazza	12.00
14	Jim Edmonds	1.50
15	Eric Karros	2.00
16	Tim Salmon	3.00
17	Sammy Sosa	12.00
18	Frank Thomas	9.00
19	Mark Grace	3.00
20	Albert Belle	4.00

Checklists with card numbers in parentheses ( ) indicates the numbers do not appear on the card.

1998 Topps Milestones

Milestones features 10 records that could be broken during the 1998 season and the player's who have the best shot at breaking them. This retail exclusive insert is seeded one per 36 packs and is numbered with an "MS" prefix.

	MT
Complete Set (10):	60.00
Common Player:	1.50
MS1 Barry Bonds	5.00
MS2 Roger Clemens	5.00
MS3 Dennis Eckersley	1.50
MS4 Juan Gonzalez	5.00
MS5 Ken Griffey Jr.	15.00
MS6 Tony Gwynn	7.50
MS7 Greg Maddux	10.00
MS8 Mark McGwire	15.00
MS9 Cal Ripken Jr.	12.00
MS10Frank Thomas	4.00

1998 Topps Mystery Finest

This 20-card insert set features top players on bordered and borderless designs, with Refractor versions of each. Exclusive to Series 2 packs, bordered cards are seeded 1:36 packs, borderless are seeded 1:72 packs, bordered Refractors are 1:108 and borderless Refractors are seeded 1:288 packs. Mystery Finest inserts are numbered with an "M" prefix.

		MT
Complete Set (20):		125.00
Common Player:		2.50
Inserted 1:36		
Borderless 1:72: 1.5X		
Bordered Refractors 1:108: 3X		
Borderless Refractors 1:288: 5X		
1	Nomar Garciaparra	12.00
2	Chipper Jones	12.00
3	Scott Rolen	5.00
4	Albert Belle	4.00
5	Mo Vaughn	3.00
6	Jose Cruz Jr.	2.50
7	Mark McGwire	20.00
8	Derek Jeter	12.00
9	Tony Gwynn	10.00
10	Frank Thomas	7.50
11	Tino Martinez	3.00
12	Greg Maddux	10.00
13	Juan Gonzalez	6.00
14	Larry Walker	4.00
15	Mike Piazza	12.00
16	Cal Ripken Jr.	15.00
17	Jeff Bagwell	6.00
18	Andruw Jones	4.00
19	Barry Bonds	6.00
20	Ken Griffey Jr.	20.00

Player names in *Italic* type indicate a rookie card.

1998 Topps Rookie Class

Rookie Class features 10 young stars from 1998 and was exclusive to Series II packs. The cards were inserted one per 12 packs and numbered with an "R" prefix.

		MT
Complete Set (10):		9.00
Common Player:		.50
Inserted 1:12		
1	Travis Lee	2.50
2	Richard Hidalgo	.50
3	Todd Helton	1.50
4	Paul Konerko	1.50
5	Mark Kotsay	1.00
6	Derrek Lee	.75
7	Eli Marrero	.50
8	Fernando Tatis	.60
9	Juan Encarnacion	.60
10	Ben Grieve	2.00

1998 Topps Chrome

All 502 cards from Topps Series 1 and 2 were reprinted in chromium versions for Topps Chrome. Chrome was released in two series, with Series 1 containing 282 cards and Series 2 including 220 cards. Four-card packs were sold for a suggested retail price of $3. Chrome also included a sampling of the inserts from Topps, along with Refractor versions of every card and insert. Series 1 inserts included Flashbacks, Baby Boomers and Hall Bound. Series 2 inserts included Milestones, '98 Rookie Class and Clout 9.

	MT
Complete Set (502):	300.00
Complete Series 1 (282):	150.00
Complete Series 2 (220):	150.00
Common Player:	.25
Star Refractors: 8X	
Rookie Refractors: 5X	
Wax Box:	100.00
(See 1998 Topps for checklist and base card values.)	

1998 Topps Chrome Refractors

Each card in the regular Topps Series 1 and Series 2 Chrome issue could also be found in a refractor version seeded approximately one per 12 packs. Refractor versions are so designated above the card number of back.

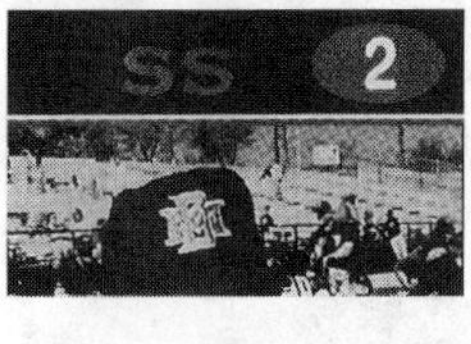

	MT
Common Player:	4.00
(Stars and rookies valued at 5-8X regular Chrome version.)	

1998 Topps Chrome Baby Boomers

This 15-card insert featured players with less than three years of experience. Cards were inserted one per 24 packs, with Refractor versions found every 72 packs of Series I. Cards were numbered with a "BB" prefix.

		MT
Complete Set (15):		60.00
Common Player:		2.00
Inserted 1:24		
Refractors: 4X		
Inserted 1:72		
1	Derek Jeter	15.00
2	Scott Rolen	6.00
3	Nomar Garciaparra	12.00
4	Jose Cruz Jr.	2.00
5	Darin Erstad	3.00
6	Todd Helton	5.00
7	Tony Clark	3.00
8	Jose Guillen	3.00
9	Andruw Jones	4.00
10	Vladimir Guerrero	8.00
11	Mark Kotsay	3.00
12	Todd Greene	2.00
13	Andy Pettitte	3.00
14	Justin Thompson	2.00
15	Alan Benes	2.00

1998 Topps Chrome Clout 9

This nine-card insert included players for their statistical supremacy. Clout 9 cards were found in Series II packs at a rate of one per 24 packs, with Refractor versions every 72 packs. Cards are numbered with a "C" prefix.

		MT
Complete Set (9):		70.00
Common Player:		3.00
Inserted 1:24		
Refractors: 4X		
Inserted 1:72		
1	Edgar Martinez	3.00
2	Mike Piazza	20.00
3	Frank Thomas	10.00
4	Craig Biggio	5.00
5	Vinny Castilla	4.00
6	Jeff Blauser	3.00
7	Barry Bonds	10.00
8	Ken Griffey Jr.	30.00
9	Larry Walker	5.00

1998 Topps Chrome Flashback

This 10-card double-sided insert features top players as they looked in 1998 on one side, and how they looked when they first appeared in the majors on the other side. Flashback inserts were seeded one per 24 packs of Series I, with Refractors every 72 packs. This insert was numbered with an "FB" prefix.

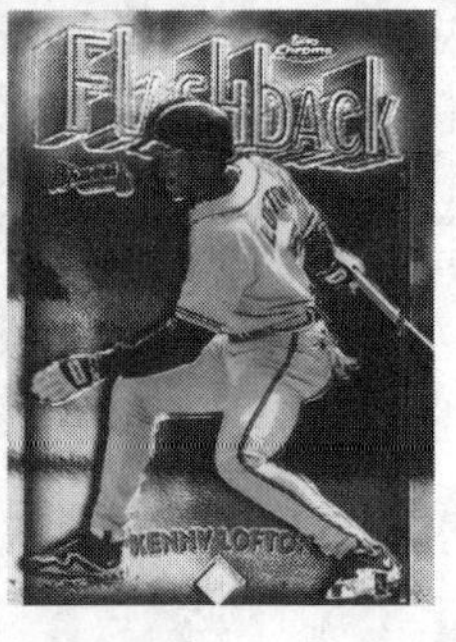

		MT
Complete Set (10):		50.00
Common Player:		3.00
Inserted 1:24		
Refractors: 4X		
Inserted 1:72		
1	Barry Bonds	8.00
2	Ken Griffey Jr.	20.00
3	Paul Molitor	4.00
4	Randy Johnson	4.00
5	Cal Ripken Jr.	12.00
6	Tony Gwynn	10.00
7	Kenny Lofton	3.00
8	Gary Sheffield	3.00
9	Deion Sanders	3.00
10	Brady Anderson	3.00

1998 Topps Chrome Hallbound

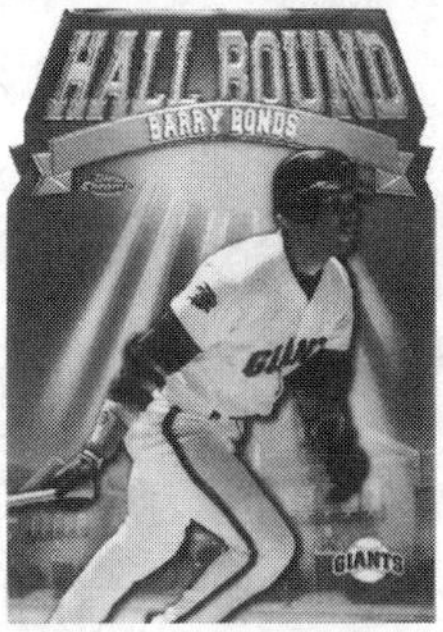

Hall Bound highlighted 15 players destined for the Hall of Fame on die-cut cards. Inserted at a rate of one per 24 packs of Series I, with Refractors every 72 packs, these were numbered with an "HB" prefix.

		MT
Complete Set (15):		125.00
Common Player:		3.00
Inserted 1:24		
Refractors: 4X		
Inserted 1:72		
1	Paul Molitor	5.00
2	Tony Gwynn	12.00
3	Wade Boggs	4.00
4	Roger Clemens	10.00
5	Dennis Eckersley	3.00
6	Cal Ripken Jr.	20.00
7	Greg Maddux	12.00
8	Rickey Henderson	3.00
9	Ken Griffey Jr.	30.00
10	Frank Thomas	10.00
11	Mark McGwire	30.00
12	Barry Bonds	8.00
13	Mike Piazza	15.00
14	Juan Gonzalez	10.00
15	Randy Johnson	5.00

1998 Topps Chrome Milestones

Ten superstars who were within reach of major records for the 1998 season are featured in Milestones. This Series II insert was seeded one per 24 packs, with Refractor versions seeded one per 72 packs. Milestones were numbered with an "MS" prefix.

		MT
Complete Set (10):		120.00
Common Player:		3.00
Inserted 1:24		
Refractors: 4X		
Inserted 1:72		
1	Barry Bonds	8.00
2	Roger Clemens	10.00
3	Dennis Eckersley	3.00
4	Juan Gonzalez	8.00
5	Ken Griffey Jr.	30.00
6	Tony Gwynn	15.00
7	Greg Maddux	12.00
8	Mark McGwire	30.00
9	Cal Ripken Jr.	25.00
10	Frank Thomas	8.00

1998 Topps Chrome Rookie Class

This insert featured 10 players with less than one year of major league experience. Inserted in Series II packs at a rate of one per 12 packs, with Refractors every 24 packs, '98 Rookie Class inserts were numbered with an "R" prefix.

		MT
Complete Set (10):		20.00
Common Player:		1.50
Inserted 1:12		
Refractors: 2.5X		
Inserted 1:24		
1	Travis Lee	3.00
2	Richard Hidalgo	1.50
3	Todd Helton	5.00
4	Paul Konerko	3.00
5	Mark Kotsay	2.00
6	Derrek Lee	2.00
7	Eli Marrero	1.50
8	Fernando Tatis	3.00
9	Juan Encarnacion	1.50
10	Ben Grieve	4.00

1998 Topps Super Chrome

This 36-card oversized set featured some of the top players from Chrome on 4-1/8" x 5-3/4" cards. The product sold in three-card packs and featured the same photography as Topps and Topps Chrome before it, but added a Super Chrome logo. Refractor versions of each card were also available, inserted one per 12 packs.

		MT
Complete Set (36):		30.00
Common Player:		.25
Refractors: 8X		
Inserted 1:12		
Wax Box:		15.00
1	Tony Gwynn	2.00
2	Larry Walker	.50
3	Vladimir Guerrero	1.00
4	Mo Vaughn	.75
5	Frank Thomas	1.50
6	Barry Larkin	.40
7	Scott Rolen	1.00
8	Juan Gonzalez	2.00
9	Jeff Bagwell	1.00
10	Ryan Klesko	.25
11	Mike Piazza	2.50
12	Randy Johnson	.50
13	Derek Jeter	2.50
14	Gary Sheffield	.40
15	Hideo Nomo	.40

16	Tino Martinez	.25
17	Ivan Rodriguez	.75
18	Bernie Williams	.50
19	Greg Maddux	2.00
20	Roger Clemens	1.50
21	Roberto Clemente	1.50
22	Chipper Jones	2.50
23	Sammy Sosa	2.50
24	Tony Clark	.50
25	Barry Bonds	1.00
26	Craig Biggio	.25
27	Cal Ripken Jr.	3.00
28	Ken Griffey Jr.	4.00
29	Todd Helton	1.00
30	Mark McGwire	4.00
31	Jose Cruz	.75
32	Albert Belle	.75
33	Andruw Jones	1.00
34	Nomar Garciaparra	2.00
35	Andy Pettitte	.50
36	Alex Rodriguez	3.00

1998 Topps/Fruit Roll-Ups All-Stars

(See "Fruit Roll-Ups")

1998 Topps Gallery Pre-Production Samples

To introduce its premium Gallery line for 1998, Topps issued this set of pre-production samples showcasing several of the different technologies to be found in the issue. The samples are virtually identical to the issued versions except for the use of a "PP" prefix to the card number.

		MT
Complete Set (5):		25.00
Common Player:		5.00
PP1	Andruw Jones (Portraits)	5.00
PP2	Juan Gonzalez (Permanent Collection)	7.50
PP3	Barry Bonds (Expressionists)	5.00
PP4	Derek Jeter (Exhibitions)	10.00
PP5	Nomar Garciaparra (Impressions)	7.50

1998 Topps Gallery

Gallery returned in 1998 with a 150-card set broken up into five different subsets - Exhibitions, Impressions, Expressionists, Portraits and Permanent Collection. The set was paralleled twice - first in a Player's Private Issue set and, second in Gallery Proofs. Gallery cards were made to look like works of art instead of simply a photo of the player on cardboard, and were sold in six-card packs. Inserts in this single-series product include: Photo Gallery, Gallery of Heroes and Awards Gallery.

		MT
Complete Set (150):		50.00
Common Player:		.20
Wax Box:		65.00
1	Andruw Jones	1.00
2	Fred McGriff	.40
3	Wade Boggs	.40
4	Pedro Martinez	1.50
5	Matt Williams	.50
6	Wilson Alvarez	.20
7	Henry Rodriguez	.20
8	Jay Bell	.20
9	Marquis Grissom	.20
10	Darryl Kile	.20
11	Chuck Knoblauch	.30
12	Kenny Lofton	.75
13	Quinton McCracken	.20
14	Andres Galarraga	.75
15	Brian Jordan	.20
16	Mike Lansing	.20
17	Travis Fryman	.30
18	Tony Saunders	.20
19	Moises Alou	.40
20	Travis Lee	.50
21	Garret Anderson	.20
22	Ken Caminiti	.35
23	Pedro Astacio	.20
24	Ellis Burks	.20
25	Albert Belle	.75
26	Alan Benes	.25
27	Jay Buhner	.20
28	Derek Bell	.20
29	Jeromy Burnitz	.20
30	Kevin Appier	.20
31	Jeff Cirillo	.20
32	Bernard Gilkey	.20
33	David Cone	.40
34	Jason Dickson	.20
35	Jose Cruz Jr.	.30
36	Marty Cordova	.20
37	Ray Durham	.20
38	Jaret Wright	.35
39	Billy Wagner	.20
40	Roger Clemens	2.00
41	Juan Gonzalez	1.50
42	Jeremi Gonzalez	.20
43	Mark Grudzielanek	.20
44	Tom Glavine	.40
45	Barry Larkin	.30
46	Lance Johnson	.20
47	Bobby Higginson	.20
48	Mike Mussina	.75
49	Al Martin	.20
50	Mark McGwire	5.00
51	Todd Hundley	.20
52	Ray Lankford	.20
53	Jason Kendall	.30
54	Javy Lopez	.30
55	Ben Grieve	.50
56	Randy Johnson	.75
57	Jeff King	.20
58	Mark Grace	.40
59	Rusty Greer	.20
60	Greg Maddux	2.50
61	Jeff Kent	.20
62	Rey Ordonez	.25
63	Hideo Nomo	.40
64	Charles Nagy	.20
65	Rondell White	.40
66	Todd Helton	1.25
67	Jim Thome	.75
68	Denny Neagle	.20
69	Ivan Rodriguez	1.25
70	Vladimir Guerrero	1.50
71	Jorge Posada	.20
72	J.T. Snow Jr.	.20
73	Reggie Sanders	.20
74	Scott Rolen	1.25
75	Robin Ventura	.40
76	Mariano Rivera	.40
77	Cal Ripken Jr.	4.00
78	Justin Thompson	.20
79	Mike Piazza	3.00
80	Kevin Brown	.40
81	Sandy Alomar	.40
82	Craig Biggio	.75
83	Vinny Castilla	.40
84	Eric Young	.20
85	Bernie Williams	.65
86	Brady Anderson	.20
87	Bobby Bonilla	.20
88	Tony Clark	.40
89	Dan Wilson	.20
90	John Wetteland	.20
91	Barry Bonds	1.50
92	Chan Ho Park	.40
93	Carlos Delgado	.75
94	David Justice	.40
95	Chipper Jones	3.00
96	Shawn Estes	.20
97	Jason Giambi	.20
98	Ron Gant	.20
99	John Olerud	.50
100	Frank Thomas	1.50
101	Jose Guillen	.20
102	Brad Radke	.20
103	Troy Percival	.20
104	John Smoltz	.40
105	Edgardo Alfonzo	.40
106	Dante Bichette	.40
107	Larry Walker	.75
108	John Valentin	.20
109	Roberto Alomar	.75
110	Mike Cameron	.20
111	Eric Davis	.20
112	Johnny Damon	.20
113	Darin Erstad	.40
114	Omar Vizquel	.20
115	Derek Jeter	3.00
116	Tony Womack	.20
117	Edgar Renteria	.20
118	Raul Mondesi	.40
119	Tony Gwynn	2.50
120	Ken Griffey Jr.	5.00
121	Jim Edmonds	.20
122	Brian Hunter	.20
123	Neifi Perez	.20
124	Dean Palmer	.20
125	Alex Rodriguez	4.00
126	Tim Salmon	.40
127	Curt Schilling	.20
128	Kevin Orie	.20
129	Andy Pettitte	.30
130	Gary Sheffield	.40
131	Jose Rosado	.20
132	Manny Ramirez	1.50
133	Rafael Palmeiro	.75
134	Sammy Sosa	3.00
135	Jeff Bagwell	1.25
136	Delino DeShields	.20
137	Ryan Klesko	.40
138	Mo Vaughn	.75
139	Steve Finley	.20
140	Nomar Garciaparra	3.00
141	Paul Molitor	.75
142	Pat Hentgen	.20
143	Eric Karros	.25
144	Bobby Jones	.20
145	Tino Martinez	.25
146	Matt Morris	.20
147	Livan Hernandez	.25
148	Edgar Martinez	.20
149	Paul O'Neill	.40
150	Checklist	.20

1998 Topps Gallery Player's Private Issue

Players Private Issue inserts parallel the 150-card base set with a distinct design and embossing. The average insertion rate is one per 12 packs.

	MT
Common Player:	5.00
Stars: 25X	
Young Stars/RCs 15X	
Production 250 sets	

(See 1998 Topps Gallery for checklist and base card values.)

1998 Topps Gallery Awards Gallery

Awards Gallery featured 10 players who earned the highest honors in the game on a horizontal design. Fronts featured a shot of the player and the award he won on silver foilboard. These were inserted every 24 packs and numbered with an "AG" prefix.

		MT
Complete Set (10):		80.00
Common Player:		3.00
Inserted 1:24		
1	Ken Griffey Jr.	25.00
2	Larry Walker	5.00
3	Roger Clemens	8.00
4	Pedro Martinez	6.00
5	Nomar Garciaparra	15.00
6	Scott Rolen	6.00
7	Frank Thomas	8.00
8	Tony Gwynn	12.00
9	Mark McGwire	25.00
10	Livan Hernandez	3.00

1998 Topps Gallery Gallery Proofs

This hobby-only parallel set included all 150 cards in the base set. Gallery Proofs were sequentially numbered to 125 sets.

	MT
Common Player:	5.00
Gallery Proof Stars: 30X	
Young Stars/RCs: 15X	
Production 125 sets	

(See 1998 Topps Gallery for checklist and base card values.)

1998 Topps Gallery of Heroes

Gallery of Heroes is a 15-card insert printed on colored, die-cut plastic that resembles a stained glass window. Cards were inserted one per 24 packs and numbered with a "GH" prefix. More is less in the case in the jumbo (3-1/4" x 4-1/2") version of the cards which were inserted one per hobby box. Cards are numbered with a "GH" prefix.

		MT
Complete Set (15):		150.00
Common Player:		2.50
Inserted 1:24		
Jumbo Version (1:24): 75%		
1	Ken Griffey Jr.	25.00
2	Derek Jeter	15.00
3	Barry Bonds	7.00
4	Alex Rodriguez	17.50
5	Frank Thomas	7.00
6	Nomar Garciaparra	15.00
7	Mark McGwire	25.00
8	Mike Piazza	15.00
9	Cal Ripken Jr.	17.50
10	Jose Cruz Jr.	2.50
11	Jeff Bagwell	7.00
12	Chipper Jones	15.00
13	Juan Gonzalez	7.00
14	Hideo Nomo	3.50
15	Greg Maddux	12.50

1998 Topps Gallery Photo Gallery

This 10-card insert captured unique shots of players on a silver foilboard design. Photo Gallery inserts were seeded one per 24 packs and numbered with a "PG" prefix.

		MT
Complete Set (10):		90.00
Common Player:		3.00
Inserted 1:24		
1	Alex Rodriguez	20.00
2	Frank Thomas	10.00
3	Derek Jeter	15.00
4	Cal Ripken Jr.	20.00
5	Ken Griffey Jr.	25.00
6	Mike Piazza	15.00
7	Nomar Garciaparra	15.00
8	Tim Salmon	3.00
9	Jeff Bagwell	10.00
10	Barry Bonds	10.00

1998 Topps Gold Label Class 1 (Fielding, Follow-thru)

Topps debuted its Gold Label brand with 100 cards printed on 30-point "spectral-reflective stock" with gold foil stamping and two shots of the player on each card front. Cards arrived in Gold Label, Black Label and Red Label versions, each with varying levels of scarcity. The rarity of the cards was determined by the photo and foil stamping on the cards. In the foreground of each card front, the photograph is the same, but in the background one of three shots is featured. Class 1, fielding, are considered base cards; Class 2: running (inserted 1:4 packs) and Class 3, hitting (inserted 1:8 packs) are seeded levels. For pitching the levels are: Class 1, set position (base); Class 2, throwing (inserted 1:4 packs) and Class 3, follow-through (inserted 1:8 packs). Black Label cards are scarcer, while Red Label cards are scarcer yet. In addition, 1 of 1 cards exist for each Class and version. Class 1 cards have matte gold-foil graphic highlights on front. Black Label Class 1 cards were inserted one per eight packs. Red Label Class 1 cards are a 1:99 insert and are serially numbered to 100.

		MT
Complete Gold Label Set (100):		50.00
Gold Label Common Player:		.25
Black Label Common Player:		1.00
Black Label Stars/RCs: 6X		
Red Label Common Player:		5.00
Red Label Stars/RCs: 15X		
1	Kevin Brown	.30
2	Greg Maddux	2.00
3	Albert Belle	.75
4	Andres Galarraga	.50
5	Craig Biggio	.50
6	Matt Williams	.40
7	Derek Jeter	2.50
8	Randy Johnson	.60
9	Jay Bell	.25
10	Jim Thome	.40
11	Roberto Alomar	.75
12	Tom Glavine	.30
13	Reggie Sanders	.25
14	Tony Gwynn	2.00
15	Mark McGwire	5.00
16	Jeromy Burnitz	.25
17	Andruw Jones	.50

18 Jay Buhner .30
19 Robin Ventura .30
20 Jeff Bagwell 1.00
21 Roger Clemens 1.50
22 *Masato Yoshii* .40
23 Travis Fryman .25
24 Rafael Palmeiro .40
25 Alex Rodriguez 3.00
26 Sandy Alomar .25
27 Chipper Jones 2.50
28 Rusty Greer .25
29 Cal Ripken Jr. 3.00
30 Tony Clark .40
31 Derek Bell .25
32 Fred McGriff .40
33 Paul O'Neill .40
34 Moises Alou .30
35 Henry Rodriguez .25
36 Steve Finley .25
37 Marquis Grissom .25
38 Jason Giambi .25
39 Javy Lopez .25
40 Damion Easley .25
41 Mariano Rivera .30
42 Mo Vaughn .60
43 Mike Mussina .60
44 Jason Kendall .25
45 Pedro Martinez 1.25
46 Frank Thomas 1.00
47 Jim Edmonds .25
48 Hideki Irabu .30
49 Eric Karros .25
50 Juan Gonzalez 1.00
51 Ellis Burks .25
52 Dean Palmer .25
53 Scott Rolen .75
54 Raul Mondesi .30
55 Quinton McCracken .25
56 John Olerud .40
57 Ken Caminiti .30
58 Brian Jordan .25
59 Wade Boggs .40
60 Mike Piazza 2.50
61 Darin Erstad .40
62 Curt Schilling .25
63 David Justice .40
64 Kenny Lofton .60
65 Barry Bonds 1.00
66 Ray Lankford .25
67 Brian Hunter .25
68 Chuck Knoblauch .30
69 Vinny Castilla .25
70 Vladimir Guerrero 1.25
71 Tim Salmon .30
72 Larry Walker .60
73 Paul Molitor .50
74 Barry Larkin .30
75 Edgar Martinez .25
76 Bernie Williams .60
77 Dante Bichette .30
78 Nomar Garciaparra 2.50
79 Ben Grieve .40
80 Ivan Rodriguez 1.00
81 Todd Helton .50
82 Ryan Klesko .25
83 Sammy Sosa 2.50
84 Travis Lee .30
85 Jose Cruz .25
86 Mark Kotsay .25
87 Richard Hidalgo .25
88 Rondell White .25
89 Greg Vaughn .25
90 Gary Sheffield .30
91 Paul Konerko .25
92 Mark Grace .35
93 *Kevin Millwood* 3.00
94 Manny Ramirez 1.00
95 Tino Martinez .25
96 Brad Fullmer .25
97 Todd Walker .35
98 Carlos Delgado .40
99 Kerry Wood .40
100 Ken Griffey Jr. 5.00

1998 Topps Gold Label Class 2 (Running, Set Position)

Class 2 Gold Label and parallels feature background photos on front of position players running and pitchers in the set position. Class 2 cards have sparkling silver-foil graphic highlights on front and were inserted one per two packs. Black Label Class 2 cards were inserted one per 16 packs. Red Label Class 2 cards are a 1:198 insert and are serially numbered to 50.

	MT
Complete Gold Label Set (100):	100.00
Gold Label Common Player:	.50
Gold Label Stars/RCs: 2.5X	
Black Label Common Player:	2.00
Black Label Stars/RCs: 6X	
Red Label Common Player:	10.00
Red Label Stars/RCs: 25X	

(See 1998 Topps Gold Label Class 1 for checklist and base card values.)

1998 Topps Gold Label Class 3 (Hitting, Throwing)

Class 3 Gold Label and parallels feature background photos on front of position players hitting and pitchers throwing. Class 3 cards have sparkling gold-foil graphic highlights on front and were inserted one per four packs. Black Label Class 3 cards were inserted one per 32 packs. Red Label Class 2 cards are a 1:396 insert and are serially numbered to 25.

	MT
Complete Gold Label Set (100):	200.00
Common Player:	1.00
Gold Label Stars/RCs: 4X	
Black Label Common Player:	3.00
Black Label Stars/RCs 8X	
Red Label Common Player:	10.00
Red Label Stars/RCs: 40X	

(See 1998 Topps Gold Label Class 1 for checklist and base card values.)

1998 Topps Gold Label Home Run Race

Home Run Race of '98 was a four-card insert set. Each of the current players' cards features a background photo of Roger Maris, while the fourth card features two shots of Maris. Gold, Black and Red Label versions are identified by the different foil-stamp logos. Gold cards were inserted 1:12 packs, Black Label cards were inserted 1:48 packs and Red Label cards were sequentially numbered to 61 and inserted 1:4,055 packs. The Home Run Race inserts are exclusive to Topps Home Team Advantage boxes.

		MT
Complete Set (4):		40.00
Common Player:		10.00
Black Label: 2X		
Red Label: 15X		
HR1	Roger Maris	8.00
HR2	Mark McGwire	15.00
HR3	Ken Griffey Jr.	15.00
HR4	Sammy Sosa	8.00

1998 Topps Gold Label 1 of 1

Each of the Classes and color versions of Topps Gold Label cards was paralleled in a 1 of 1 insert which was to be found on average of one per 1,085 packs. Each player, thus, can be found on nine different 1 of 1 cards in the issue.

(Due to scarcity and variance in demand, values cannot be quoted.)

1998 Topps Opening Day

Topps Opening Day was a retail exclusive product included 165 cards, with 110 from Series I and 55 from Series II. The 55 cards from Series II were available in this product prior to the cards being released. Opening Day cards featured a silver border vs. the gold border in the base set, and included a silver Opening Day stamp.

	MT
Complete Set (165):	15.00
Common Player:	.05

1 Tony Gwynn 1.00
2 Larry Walker .40
3 Billy Wagner .10
4 Denny Neagle .05
5 Vladimir Guerrero .60
6 Kevin Brown .15
7 Mariano Rivera .15
8 Tony Clark .25
9 Deion Sanders .10
10 Matt Williams .15
11 Carlos Baerga .05
12 Mo Vaughn .40
13 Chan Ho Park .10
14 Frank Thomas .75
15 John Jaha .05
16 Steve Trachsel .05
17 Jeff Kent .05
18 Scott Rolen .60
19 Juan Gonzalez .75
20 Garret Anderson .05
21 Roberto Clemente 1.50
22 Omar Vizquel .05
23 Brian Hunter .05
24 Jeff Bagwell .50
25 Chili Davis .05
26 Mike Cameron .10
27 Pat Hentgen .05
28 Wilton Guerrero .05
29 Devon White .05
30 Rafael Palmeiro .25
31 Jeff Blauser .05
32 Dave Hollins .05
33 Trevor Hoffman .10
34 Ryan Klesko .10
35 Butch Huskey .05
36 Mark Grudzielanek .05
37 Marquis Grissom .05
38 Jim Edmonds .15
39 Greg Vaughn .10
40 David Wells .05
41 Charles Nagy .05
42 B.J. Surhoff .05
43 Edgardo Alfonzo .15
44 Jay Buhner .05
45 Brady Anderson .15
46 Edgar Renteria .05
47 Rick Aguilera .05
48 Henry Rodriguez .05
49 Mike Piazza 1.25
50 Todd Zeile .05
51 Rey Ordonez .10
52 Tony Womack .05
53 Mike Sweeney .05
54 Jeffrey Hammonds .05
55 Kevin Orie .05
56 Alex Gonzalez .05
57 Jose Canseco .40
58 Joey Hamilton .05
59 Brad Radke .05
60 Kevin Appier .05
61 Manny Ramirez .50
62 Jeromy Burnitz .05
63 Matt Morris .05
64 Jason Dickson .05
65 Tom Glavine .15
66 Wally Joyner .05
67 Todd Jones .05
68 Sandy Alomar .10
69 Mike Lansing .05
70 Todd Stottlemyre .05
71 Jay Bell .05
72 Joey Cora .05
73 Scott Spiezio .05
74 Joe Carter .05
75 Jose Guillen .10
76 Damion Easley .05
77 Alex Fernandez .05
78 Randy Johnson .40
79 J.T. Snow .15
80 Bernard Gilkey .05
81 David Segui .05
82 Dante Bichette .15
83 Derek Jeter 1.25
84 Mark Wohlers .05
85 Ricky Bottalico .05
86 Mike Mussina .40
87 Gary Sheffield .15
88 Hideo Nomo .20
89 Mark Grace .20
90 Darryl Kile .05
91 Shawn Estes .15
92 Vinny Castilla .10
93 Jose Rosado .05
94 Kenny Lofton .40
95 Jason Giambi .05
96 Ray Lankford .05
97 Hideki Irabu .15
98 Javy Lopez .05
99 Jeff Montgomery .05
100 Dennis Eckersley .05
101 Armando Benitez .05
102 Tim Naehring .05
103 Luis Gonzalez .05
104 Todd Hollandsworth .05
105 Wade Boggs .20
106 Mickey Morandini .05
107 Rusty Greer .10
108 Terry Steinbach .05
109 Pete Rose II .25
110 Checklist .05
111 Tino Martinez .20
112 Roberto Alomar .40
113 Jeff King .05
114 Brian Jordan .05
115 Darin Erstad .25
116 Ken Caminiti .15
117 Jim Thome .30
118 Paul Molitor .40
119 Ivan Rodriguez .50
120 Bernie Williams .40
121 Todd Hundley .15
122 Andres Galarraga .25
123 Greg Maddux 1.00
124 Edgar Martinez .05
125 Ron Gant .10
126 Derek Bell .05
127 Roger Clemens .75
128 Rondell White .15
129 Barry Larkin .20
130 Robin Ventura .15
131 Jason Kendall .10
132 Chipper Jones 1.25
133 John Franco .05
134 Sammy Sosa 1.25
135 Chuck Knoblauch .20
136 Ellis Burks .05
137 Al Martin .05
138 Tim Salmon .20
139 Moises Alou .15
140 Lance Johnson .05
141 Justin Thompson .05
142 Will Clark .15
143 Barry Bonds .50
144 Craig Biggio .25
145 John Smoltz .15
146 Cal Ripken Jr. 1.50
147 Ken Griffey Jr. 2.50
148 Paul O'Neill .15
149 Todd Helton .50
150 John Olerud .15
151 Mark McGwire 2.50
152 Jose Cruz Jr. .10
153 Jeff Cirillo .05
154 Dean Palmer .05
155 John Wetteland .05
156 Eric Karros .10
157 Steve Finley .05
158 Albert Belle .50
159 Curt Schilling .10
160 Raul Mondesi .15
161 Andruw Jones .40
162 Nomar Garciaparra 1.25
163 David Justice .15
164 Andy Pettitte .10
165 Pedro Martinez .60

1998 Topps "Own the Game" mobile

Large (8" x 11-1/2") reproductions on heavy cardboard of eight different Topps 1998 baseball cards are featured on this point-of-purchase promotional mobile. Several regular-issue cards are featured along with inserts or subset cards. The piece features a Topps slogan header and necessary string and a hook for hanging.

	MT
Complete Mobile:	30.00

(1) Barry Bonds (Flashback front)
(2) Barry Bonds (Flashback back)
(3) Kevin Brown (Highlight)
(4) Roberto Clemente (Tribute)
(5) Juan Gonzalez (regular)
(6) Cal Ripken Jr. (Hall Bound)
(7) Larry Walker (Mystery Finest)
(8) John Patterson, Michael Stoner (Diamond Backs rookies)

1998 Topps/R&N China

This series of ceramic card reproductions presents rookie and other cards of some of the game's top names. Printed front and back on a thin 2-3/4" x 3-3/4" porcelain plate (slightly larger than the actual cards), these cards can be found in three versions: A standard format featuring white or normal colored borders; a gold version with gold borders and hand-numbered within an edition of 10,000, and, a platinum version with platinum borders and numbered to 7,500. Each card was sold with a custom protective holder and certificate of authenticity. Original issue price was about $20 for standard cards, $27 for gold, and $35 for platinum.

	MT
Complete Set, Standard (11):	225.00
Common Player:	20.00
Gold: 1.5X	
Platinum: 1.75X	
98T Cal Ripken Jr. (1982 Topps Traded)	20.00
401 Mark McGwire (1985 Topps)	20.00
70T Greg Maddux (1987 Topps Traded)	20.00
41T Ken Griffey Jr. (1989 Topps Traded)	20.00
692 Sammy Sosa (1990 Topps)	20.00
701 Bernie Williams (1990 Topps)	20.00
219 Derek Jeter (1996 Topps)	20.00
96 Cal Ripken Jr. (1996 Topps Tribute)	20.00
307 Sammy Sosa (1998 Topps)	20.00
325 Mark McGwire (1998 Topps)	20.00
504 Alex Rodriguez (1998 Topps)	20.00

1998 Topps/R&N China Rookie Collection

Capitalizing on the home-run record chase, Topps and R&N China issued this series of porcelain versions of top stars' rookie cards. Measuring slightly larger than the actual cards (about 2-3/4" x 3-3/4"), the commemoratives exactly reproduce both fronts and backs on a round-cornered, thin ceramic format. Cards were originally offered with a protective holder and certificate of authenticity for about $20. The porcelain cards are checklisted here by year of issue.

	MT
Complete Set (6):	120.00
Common Player:	20.00
98T Cal Ripken Jr. (1982 Traded)	20.00
401 Mark McGwire (1985)	20.00
41T Ken Griffey Jr. (1989 Traded)	20.00
414 Frank Thomas (1990)	20.00
692 Sammy Sosa (1990)	20.00
219 Derek Jeter (1996)	20.00

1998 Topps Stars

Topps Stars adopted an all-sequential numbering format in 1998 with a 150-card set. Every card was available in a bronze (numbered to 9,799), red (9,799), silver (4,399), gold (2,299) and gold rainbow format (99) with different color foil to distinguish the groups. Players were each judged in five categories: arm strength, hit for average, power, defense and speed. Inserts in the product include: Galaxy, Luminaries, Supernovas, Rookie Reprints and Rookie Reprint Autographs. All regular-issue cards and inserts were individually numbered except the Rookie Reprints.

		MT
Complete Set, Red or Bronze (150):		75.00
Common Player, Red or Bronze:		.25
Production 9,799 sets each		
1	Greg Maddux	5.00
2	Darryl Kile	.25
3	Rod Beck	.25
4	Ellis Burks	.25
5	Gary Sheffield	.50
6	David Ortiz	.25
7	Marquis Grissom	.30
8	Tony Womack	.25
9	Mike Mussina	1.50
10	Bernie Williams	1.50
11	Andy Benes	.25
12	Rusty Greer	.30
13	Carlos Delgado	1.50
14	Jim Edmonds	.30
15	Raul Mondesi	.50
16	Andres Galarraga	1.00
17	Wade Boggs	.60
18	Paul O'Neill	.75
19	Edgar Renteria	.25
20	Tony Clark	.75
21	Vladimir Guerrero	3.00
22	Moises Alou	.50
23	Bernard Gilkey	.25
24	Lance Johnson	.25
25	Ben Grieve	.75
26	Sandy Alomar	.25
27	Ray Durham	.25
28	Shawn Estes	.25
29	David Segui	.25
30	Javy Lopez	.35
31	Steve Finley	.25
32	Rey Ordonez	.25
33	Derek Jeter	6.00
34	Henry Rodriguez	.25
35	Mo Vaughn	1.50
36	Richard Hidalgo	.25
37	Omar Vizquel	.25
38	Johnny Damon	.25
39	Brian Hunter	.25
40	Matt Williams	.60
41	Chuck Finley	.25
42	Jeromy Burnitz	.25
43	Livan Hernandez	.25
44	Delino DeShields	.25
45	Charles Nagy	.25
46	Scott Rolen	2.50
47	Neifi Perez	.25
48	John Wetteland	.25
49	Eric Milton	.25
50	Mike Piazza	6.00
51	Cal Ripken Jr.	7.50
52	Mariano Rivera	.50
53	Butch Huskey	.25
54	Quinton McCracken	.25
55	Jose Cruz Jr.	.25
56	Brian Jordan	.25
57	Hideo Nomo	.50
58	Masato Yoshii	.25
59	Cliff Floyd	.25
60	Jose Guillen	.50
61	Jeff Shaw	.25
62	Edgar Martinez	.25
63	Rondell White	.50
64	Hal Morris	.25
65	Barry Larkin	.60
66	Eric Young	.25
67	Ray Lankford	.25
68	Derek Bell	.25
69	Charles Johnson	.25
70	Robin Ventura	.50
71	Chuck Knoblauch	.60
72	Kevin Brown	.50
73	Jose Valentin	.25
74	Jay Buhner	.25
75	Tony Gwynn	5.00
76	Andy Pettitte	.30
77	Edgardo Alfonzo	.50
78	Kerry Wood	.75
79	Darin Erstad	.40
80	Paul Konerko	.50
81	Jason Kendall	.30
82	Tino Martinez	.30
83	Brad Radke	.25
84	Jeff King	.25
85	Travis Lee	.50
86	Jeff Kent	.25
87	Trevor Hoffman	.25
88	David Cone	.35
89	Jose Canseco	2.00
90	Juan Gonzalez	2.50
91	Todd Hundley	.25
92	John Valentin	.25
93	Sammy Sosa	6.00
94	Jason Giambi	.25
95	Chipper Jones	6.00
96	Jeff Blauser	.25
97	Brad Fullmer	.30
98	Derrek Lee	.25
99	Denny Neagle	.25
100	Ken Griffey Jr.	9.00
101	David Justice	.50
102	Tim Salmon	.40
103	J.T. Snow	.25
104	Fred McGriff	.50
105	Brady Anderson	.30
106	Larry Walker	1.50
107	Jeff Cirillo	.25
108	Andruw Jones	1.00
109	Manny Ramirez	2.50
110	Justin Thompson	.25
111	Vinny Castilla	.50
112	Chan Ho Park	.50
113	Mark Grudzielanek	.25
114	Mark Grace	.50
115	Ken Caminiti	.50
116	Ryan Klesko	.30
117	Rafael Palmeiro	.75
118	Pat Hentgen	.25
119	Eric Karros	.30
120	Randy Johnson	1.50
121	Roberto Alomar	1.50
122	John Olerud	.75
123	Paul Molitor	1.50
124	Dean Palmer	.25
125	Nomar Garciaparra	6.00
126	Curt Schilling	.40
127	Jay Bell	.25
128	Craig Biggio	1.50
129	Marty Cordova	.25
130	Ivan Rodriguez	2.50
131	Todd Helton	1.50
132	Jim Thome	.75
133	Albert Belle	1.50
134	Mike Lansing	.25
135	Mark McGwire	9.00
136	Roger Clemens	4.00
137	Tom Glavine	.50
138	Ron Gant	.25
139	Alex Rodriguez	7.50
140	Jeff Bagwell	2.50
141	John Smoltz	.50
142	Kenny Lofton	1.50
143	Dante Bichette	.50
144	Pedro Martinez	2.50
145	Barry Bonds	2.50
146	Travis Fryman	.35
147	Bobby Jones	.25
148	Bobby Higginson	.25
149	Reggie Sanders	.25
150	Frank Thomas	2.50

1998 Topps Stars Silver

	MT
Common Silver:	.75
Silver Stars: 1.5X	
Production 4,399 sets	
(See 1998 Topps Stars for checklist and base card values.)	

1998 Topps Stars Gold

	MT
Common Gold:	1.00
Gold Stars: 2.5X	
Production 2,299 sets	
(See 1998 Topps Stars for checklist and base card values.)	

1998 Topps Stars Gold Rainbow

	MT
Common Gold Rainbow:	8.00
Gold Rainbow Stars: 15X	
Production 99 sets	
(See 1998 Topps Stars for checklist and base card values.)	

1998 Topps Stars Galaxy

Galaxy featured 10 players who possess all five skills featured in Topps Stars Baseball. Four versions were available and sequentially numbered, including: Bronze (numbered to 100, inserted 1:682 packs), Silver (numbered to 75, inserted 1:910), Gold (numbered to 50, inserted 1:1,364) and Gold Rainbow (numbered to 5, inserted 1:13,643).

		MT
Complete Set (10):		500.00
Common Player:		10.00
Production 100 sets		
Silvers: 1.5X		
Production 75 sets		
Golds: 2X		
Production 50 sets		
G1	Barry Bonds	40.00
G2	Jeff Bagwell	40.00
G3	Nomar Garciaparra	100.00
G4	Chipper Jones	100.00
G5	Ken Griffey Jr.	175.00
G6	Sammy Sosa	100.00
G7	Larry Walker	30.00
G8	Alex Rodriguez	135.00
G9	Craig Biggio	25.00
G10	Raul Mondesi	10.00

1998 Topps Stars Luminaries

Luminaries featured three top players in each tool group in Topps Stars. The 15-card insert arrived in four different versions and were sequentially numbered. They were inserted as follows: bronze (numbered to 100, inserted 1:455), silver (numbered to 75, inserted 1:606), gold (numbered to 50, inserted 1:910) and gold rainbow (numbered to 5, inserted 1:9,095).

		MT
Complete Set (15):		900.00
Common Player:		12.50
Production 100 sets		
Silver: 1.5X		
Production 75 sets		
Gold: 1.5X		
Production 50 sets		
Gold Rainbow: ?		
Production 5 sets		
L1	Ken Griffey Jr.	150.00
L2	Mark McGwire	150.00
L3	Juan Gonzalez	60.00
L4	Tony Gwynn	80.00
L5	Frank Thomas	75.00
L6	Mike Piazza	100.00
L7	Chuck Knoblauch	12.50
L8	Kenny Lofton	20.00
L9	Barry Bonds	60.00
L10	Matt Williams	12.50
L11	Raul Mondesi	15.00
L12	Ivan Rodriguez	50.00
L13	Alex Rodriguez	125.00
L14	Nomar Garciaparra	90.00
L15	Ken Caminiti	15.00

1998 Topps Stars Rookie Reprints

Topps reprinted the rookie cards of five Hall of Famers in Rookie Reprints. The cards are inserted one per 24 packs and have UV coating.

	MT
Complete Set (5):	20.00
Common Player:	3.00
Johnny Bench	6.00
Whitey Ford	3.00
Joe Morgan	3.00
Mike Schmidt	8.00
Carl Yastrzemski	6.00

1998 Topps Stars Rookie Reprints Autographs

Autographed versions of all five Rookie Reprint inserts were available and seeded one per 273 packs. Each card arrive with a Topps "Certified Autograph Issue" stamp to ensure its authenticity.

	MT
Complete Set (5):	300.00
Common Player:	40.00
Johnny Bench	75.00
Whitey Ford	40.00
Joe Morgan	40.00
Mike Schmidt	100.00
Carl Yastrzemski	75.00

1998 Topps Stars Supernovas

Supernovas was a 10-card insert in Topps Stars and included rookies and prospects who either have all five tools focused on in the product, or excel dramatically in one of the five. Four sequentially numbered levels were available, with insert rates as follows: bronze (numbered to 100, inserted 1:682), silver (numbered to 75, inserted 1:910), gold (numbered to 50, inserted 1:1,364) and gold rainbow (numbered to 5, inserted 1:13,643).

		MT
Complete Set (10):		175.00
Common Player:		10.00
Production 100 sets		
Silver: 1.5X		
Production 75 sets		
Gold: 2X		
Production 50 sets		
S1	Ben Grieve	40.00
S2	Travis Lee	20.00
S3	Todd Helton	40.00
S4	Adrian Beltre	20.00
S5	Derrek Lee	10.00
S6	David Ortiz	10.00
S7	Brad Fullmer	15.00
S8	Mark Kotsay	15.00
S9	Paul Konerko	15.00
S10	Kerry Wood	40.00

1998 Topps Stars N' Steel

Stars 'N Steel was a 44-card set printed on four-colored textured film laminate bonded to a sheet of 25-gauge metal. Regular cards featured a silver colored border while gold versions were also available and seeded one per 12 packs. Stars 'N Steel was available only to Home Team Advantage members and was packaged in three-card packs that arrived in sturdy, tri-fold stand-up display unit. A second parallel version was also available featuring gold holographic technology and was seeded one per 40 packs.

		MT
Complete Set (44):		150.00
Common Player:		2.00
Golds: 3X		
Holographics: 10X		
Wax Box:		100.00
1	Roberto Alomar	5.00
2	Jeff Bagwell	8.00
3	Albert Belle	5.00
4	Dante Bichette	2.00
5	Barry Bonds	8.00
6	Jay Buhner	2.00
7	Ken Caminiti	2.00
8	Vinny Castilla	2.00
9	Roger Clemens	10.00
10	Jose Cruz Jr.	2.00
11	Andres Galarraga	3.00
12	Nomar Garciaparra	15.00
13	Juan Gonzalez	8.00
14	Mark Grace	4.00
15	Ken Griffey Jr.	25.00
16	Tony Gwynn	12.00
17	Todd Hundley	2.00
18	Derek Jeter	15.00
19	Randy Johnson	4.00
20	Andruw Jones	4.00
21	Chipper Jones	15.00
22	David Justice	2.00
23	Ray Lankford	2.00
24	Barry Larkin	2.00
25	Kenny Lofton	4.00
26	Greg Maddux	12.00
27	Edgar Martinez	2.00
28	Tino Martinez	2.00
29	Mark McGwire	25.00
30	Paul Molitor	5.00
31	Rafael Palmeiro	4.00
32	Mike Piazza	15.00
33	Manny Ramirez	6.00
34	Cal Ripken Jr.	20.00
35	Ivan Rodriguez	5.00
36	Scott Rolen	5.00
37	Tim Salmon	2.00
38	Gary Sheffield	2.00
39	Sammy Sosa	15.00
40	Frank Thomas	7.50
41	Jim Thome	4.00
42	Mo Vaughn	4.00
43	Larry Walker	5.00
44	Bernie Williams	4.00

1998 Topps TEK

A myriad of collecting methods was created with this innovative product which features 90 different players each printed on an acetate stock with 90 different background patterns. A parallel series utilizing Diffraction technology was inserted at the rate of one per six packs. Each of the 8,100 different cards was created in the same quantity, so there is no differentiation in value among patterns.

		MT
Complete Set (90):		125.00
Common Player:		.25
1	Ben Grieve	1.00
2	Kerry Wood	1.00
3	Barry Bonds	2.50
4	John Olerud	.75
5	Ivan Rodriguez	2.50
6	Frank Thomas	2.50
7	Bernie Williams	1.50
8	Dante Bichette	.75
9	Alex Rodriguez	7.50
10	Tom Glavine	.50
11	Eric Karros	.40
12	Craig Biggio	.75
13	Mark McGwire	10.00
14	Derek Jeter	6.00
15	Nomar Garciaparra	5.00
16	Brady Anderson	.25
17	Vladimir Guerrero	3.00
18	David Justice	.75
19	Chipper Jones	6.00
20	Jim Edmonds	.25
21	Roger Clemens	4.00
22	Mark Kotsay	.25
23	Tony Gwynn	5.00
24	Todd Walker	.40
25	Tino Martinez	.50
26	Andruw Jones	1.50
27	Sandy Alomar	.25
28	Sammy Sosa	6.00
29	Gary Sheffield	.50
30	Ken Griffey Jr.	10.00
31	Aramis Ramirez	.35
32	Curt Schilling	.50
33	Robin Ventura	.50
34	Larry Walker	1.50
35	Darin Erstad	.75
36	Todd Dunwoody	.25
37	Paul O'Neill	.60
38	Vinny Castilla	.50
39	Randy Johnson	2.00
40	Rafael Palmeiro	1.00
41	Pedro Martinez	3.00
42	Derek Bell	.25
43	Carlos Delgado	.75
44	Matt Williams	.60
45	Kenny Lofton	1.50
46	Edgar Renteria	.25
47	Albert Belle	2.00
48	Jeromy Burnitz	.25
49	Adrian Beltre	.75
50	Greg Maddux	5.00
51	Cal Ripken Jr.	7.50
52	Jason Kendall	.40
53	Ellis Burks	.25
54	Paul Molitor	1.50
55	Moises Alou	.50
56	Raul Mondesi	.50
57	Barry Larkin	.50
58	Tony Clark	.75
59	Travis Lee	.75
60	Juan Gonzalez	2.50
61	*Troy Glaus*	4.00
62	Jose Cruz Jr.	.35
63	Paul Konerko	.50
64	Edgar Martinez	.25
65	Javy Lopez	.50
66	Manny Ramirez	2.50
67	Roberto Alomar	1.50
68	Ken Caminiti	.50
69	Todd Helton	1.00
70	Chuck Knoblauch	.50
71	Kevin Brown	.50
72	Tim Salmon	.50
73	*Orlando Hernandez*	4.00
74	Jeff Bagwell	2.50
75	Brian Jordan	.25
76	Derrek Lee	.25
77	Brad Fullmer	.35
78	Mark Grace	.75
79	Jeff King	.25
80	Mike Mussina	1.50
81	Jay Buhner	.25
82	Quinton McCracken	.25
83	A.J. Hinch	.25
84	Richard Hidalgo	.25
85	Andres Galarraga	.75
86	Mike Piazza	6.00
87	Mo Vaughn	1.50
88	Scott Rolen	2.50
89	Jim Thome	.75
90	Ray Lankford	.25

1998 Topps TEK Diffraction

Not only can each of the 90 cards in Topps TEK be found in 90 different background patterns, but each can be found in a parallel edition printed with diffraction foil. The parallels are inserted on an average of one per six packs. Like the regular issue TEKs, all patterns were produced equally and there is no value differentiation among them.

	MT
Complete Set (90):	600.00
Common Player:	3.00
Stars/RCs: 4X	
(See 1998 Topps TEK for checklist and base card values.)	

1999 Topps Pre-Production

To give potential customers a feel for its 1999 baseball cards, Topps issued this series of pre-production samples. Cards are identical in format to the issued versions except they are numbered with a "PP" prefix and the 1998 stats line reads "PRE-PRODUCTION SAMPLE".

		MT
Complete Set (6):		12.00
Common Player:		1.00
PP1	Roger Clemens	3.00
PP2	Sammy Sosa	3.00
PP3	Derek Jeter	5.00
PP4	Walt Weiss	1.00
PP5	Darin Erstad	2.50
PP6	Jason Kendall	1.00

1999 Topps

Released in two series, the 462-card set includes two home run record subsets, featuring McGwire and Sosa. McGwire's subset card #220 has 70 different versions, commemorating each of his home runs, including where it was hit, the pitcher, date and estimated distance. Sosa's subset card #461 has 66 different versions. Other subsets include World Series Highlights, Prospects, Draft Picks and Season Highlights. Each pack contains 11 cards with an SRP of $1.29. MVPs are the only parallel. They feature a special Topps MVP logo; 100 cards of each player exist. If the player on the card was named a weekly Topps MVP, collectors won a special set of redemption cards.

		MT
Complete Set (462):		55.00
Complete Series 1 (241):		30.00
Complete Series 2 (221):		25.00
Common Player:		.10
Complete Hobby Set (462):		60.00
Complete X-Mas Set (463):		60.00
MVP Stars: 60X		
Young Stars/RCs: 40X		
Series 1 H Wax Box:		75.00
Series 2 H Wax Box:		50.00
1	Roger Clemens	1.00
2	Andres Galarraga	.30
3	Scott Brosius	.10
4	John Flaherty	.10
5	Jim Leyritz	.10
6	Ray Durham	.10
7	not issued	
8	Joe Vizcaino	.10
9	Will Clark	.25
10	David Wells	.10
11	Jose Guillen	.15
12	Scott Hatteberg	.10
13	Edgardo Alfonzo	.25
14	Mike Bordick	.10
15	Manny Ramirez	.75
16	Greg Maddux	1.25
17	David Segui	.10
18	Darryl Strawberry	.20
19	Brad Radke	.10
20	Kerry Wood	.40
21	Matt Anderson	.10
22	Derrek Lee	.10
23	Mickey Morandini	.10
24	Paul Konerko	.20
25	Travis Lee	.25
26	Ken Hill	.10
27	Kenny Rogers	.10
28	Paul Sorrento	.10
29	Quilvio Veras	.10
30	Todd Walker	.15
31	Ryan Jackson	.10
32	John Olerud	.25
33	Doug Glanville	.10
34	Nolan Ryan	2.50
35	Ray Lankford	.10
36	Mark Loretta	.10
37	Jason Dickson	.10
38	Sean Bergman	.10
39	Quinton McCracken	.10
40	Bartolo Colon	.15
41	Brady Anderson	.15
42	Chris Stynes	.10
43	Jorge Posada	.10
44	Justin Thompson	.10
45	Johnny Damon	.10
46	Armando Benitez	.10
47	Brant Brown	.10
48	Charlie Hayes	.10
49	Darren Dreifort	.10
50	Juan Gonzalez	.75
51	Chuck Knoblauch	.25
52	Todd Helton (Rookie All-Star)	.40
53	Rick Reed	.10
54	Chris Gomez	.10
55	Gary Sheffield	.25
56	Rod Beck	.10
57	Rey Sanchez	.10
58	Garret Anderson	.10
59	Jimmy Haynes	.10
60	Steve Woodard	.10
61	Rondell White	.20
62	Vladimir Guerrero	.75
63	Eric Karros	.20
64	Russ Davis	.10
65	Mo Vaughn	.50
66	Sammy Sosa	1.50
67	Troy Percival	.10
68	Kenny Lofton	.40
69	Bill Taylor	.10
70	Mark McGwire	3.00
71	Roger Cedeno	.10
72	Javy Lopez	.20
73	Damion Easley	.10
74	Andy Pettitte	.25
75	Tony Gwynn	1.25
76	Ricardo Rincon	.10
77	F.P. Santangelo	.10
78	Jay Bell	.10
79	Scott Servais	.10
80	Jose Canseco	.40
81	Roberto Hernandez	.10
82	Todd Dunwoody	.10
83	John Wetteland	.10
84	Mike Caruso (Rookie All-Star)	.10
85	Derek Jeter	1.50
86	Aaron Sele	.10
87	Jose Lima	.10
88	Ryan Christenson	.10
89	Jeff Cirillo	.10
90	Jose Hernandez	.10
91	Mark Kotsay (Rookie All-Star)	.20
92	Darren Bragg	.10
93	Albert Belle	.50
94	Matt Lawton	.10
95	Pedro Martinez	.50
96	Greg Vaughn	.20
97	Neifi Perez	.10
98	Gerald Williams	.10
99	Derek Bell	.10
100	Ken Griffey Jr.	3.00
101	David Cone	.20
102	Brian Johnson	.10
103	Dean Palmer	.10
104	Javier Valentin	.10
105	Trevor Hoffman	.10
106	Butch Huskey	.10
107	Dave Martinez	.10
108	Billy Wagner	.10
109	Shawn Green	.40
110	Ben Grieve (Rookie All-Star)	.25
111	Tom Goodwin	.10
112	Jaret Wright	.20
113	Aramis Ramirez	.15
114	Dmitri Young	.10
115	Hideki Irabu	.20
116	Roberto Kelly	.10
117	Jeff Fassero	.10
118	Mark Clark	.10
119	Jason McDonald	.10
120	Matt Williams	.25
121	Dave Burba	.10
122	Bret Saberhagen	.10
123	Deivi Cruz	.10
124	Chad Curtis	.10
125	Scott Rolen	.50
126	Lee Stevens	.10
127	J.T. Snow Jr.	.10
128	Rusty Greer	.10
129	Brian Meadows	.10
130	Jim Edmonds	.20
131	Ron Gant	.20
132	A.J. Hinch (Rookie All-Star)	.10
133	Shannon Stewart	.10
134	Brad Fullmer	.15
135	Cal Eldred	.10
136	Matt Walbeck	.10
137	Carl Everett	.15
138	Walt Weiss	.10
139	Fred McGriff	.20
140	Darin Erstad	.25
141	Dave Nilsson	.10
142	Eric Young	.10
143	Dan Wilson	.10
144	Jeff Reed	.10
145	Brett Tomko	.10
146	Terry Steinbach	.10
147	Seth Greisinger	.10
148	Pat Meares	.10
149	Livan Hernandez	.10
150	Jeff Bagwell	.75
151	Bob Wickman	.10
152	Omar Vizquel	.10
153	Eric Davis	.15
154	Larry Sutton	.10
155	Magglio Ordonez (Rookie All-Star)	.15
156	Eric Milton	.10
157	Darren Lewis	.10
158	Rick Aguilera	.10
159	Mike Lieberthal	.10
160	Robb Nen	.10
161	Brian Giles	.20
162	Jeff Brantley	.10
163	Gary DiSarcina	.10
164	John Valentin	.10
165	David Dellucci	.10
166	Chan Ho Park	.15
167	Masato Yoshii	.10
168	Jason Schmidt	.10
169	LaTroy Hawkins	.10
170	Bret Boone	.10
171	Jerry DiPoto	.10
172	Mariano Rivera	.20
173	Mike Cameron	.10
174	Scott Erickson	.10
175	Charles Johnson	.10
176	Bobby Jones	.10
177	Francisco Cordova	.10
178	Todd Jones	.10
179	Jeff Montgomery	.10
180	Mike Mussina	.50
181	Bob Abreu	.20
182	Ismael Valdes	.10
183	Andy Fox	.10
184	Woody Williams	.10
185	Denny Neagle	.10
186	Jose Valentin	.10
187	Darrin Fletcher	.10
188	Gabe Alvarez	.10
189	Eddie Taubensee	.10
190	Edgar Martinez	.10
191	Jason Kendall	.20
192	Darryl Kile	.10
193	Jeff King	.10
194	Rey Ordonez	.10
195	Andruw Jones	.25
196	Tony Fernandez	.10
197	Jamey Wright	.10
198	B.J. Surhoff	.10
199	Vinny Castilla	.20
200	David Wells (Season Highlight)	.10
201	Mark McGwire (Season Highlight)	1.00
202	Sammy Sosa (Season Highlight)	.75
203	Roger Clemens (Season Highlight)	.50
204	Kerry Wood (Season Highlight)	.25
205	Lance Berkman, Mike Frank, Gabe Kapler (Prospects)	.25
206	*Alex Escobar*, Ricky Ledee, Mike Stoner (Prospects)	.75
207	*Peter Bergeron*, Jeremy Giambi, George Lombard (Prospects)	.40
208	Michael Barrett, Ben Davis, Robert Fick (Prospects)	.15
209	Pat Cline, Ramon Hernandez, Jayson Werth (Prospects)	.25
210	Bruce Chen, Chris Enochs, Ryan Anderson (Prospects)	.25
211	Mike Lincoln, Octavio Dotel, Brad Penny (Prospects)	.20
212	Chuck Abbott, Brent Butler, Danny Klassen (Prospects)	.25
213	Chris Jones,*Jeff Urban* (Draft Pick)	.25
214	*Arturo McDowell,Tony Torcato* (Draft Pick)	.25
215	*Josh McKinley,Jason Tyner* (Draft Pick)	.40
216	*Matt Burch,Seth Etherton* (Draft Pick)	.40
217	*Mamon Tucker,Rick Elder* (Draft Pick)	.50
218	*J.M. Gold,Ryan Mills* (Draft Pick)	.50
219	*Adam Brown,Choo Freeman* (Draft Pick)	.40
220	Home Run Record #1 (M. McGwire)	25.00
220	HR Record #2-60 (M. McGwire)	15.00
220	HR Record #61-62 (M. McGwire)	40.00
220	HR Record #63-69 (M. McGwire)	15.00
220	HR Record #70 (Mark McGwire)	90.00
221	Larry Walker (League Leader)	.25
222	Bernie Williams (League Leader)	.30
223	Mark McGwire (League Leader)	1.00
224	Ken Griffey Jr. (League Leader)	1.00
225	Sammy Sosa (League Leader)	.75
226	Juan Gonzalez (League Leader)	.40
227	Dante Bichette (League Leader)	.25
228	Alex Rodriguez (League Leader)	.75
229	Sammy Sosa (League Leader)	1.00
230	Derek Jeter (League Leader)	.75
231	Greg Maddux (League Leader)	.50
232	Roger Clemens (League Leader)	.50
233	Ricky Ledee (World Series)	.10
234	Chuck Knoblauch (World Series)	.20
235	Bernie Williams (World Series)	.25
236	Tino Martinez (World Series)	.20
237	Orlando Hernandez (World Series)	.25
238	Scott Brosius (World Series)	.10
239	Andy Pettitte (World Series)	.25
240	Mariano Rivera (World Series)	.20
241	Checklist	.10
242	Checklist	.10
243	Tom Glavine	.25
244	Andy Benes	.10
245	Sandy Alomar	.20
246	Wilton Guerrero	.10
247	Alex Gonzalez	.10
248	Roberto Alomar	.40
249	Ruben Rivera	.10
250	Eric Chavez	.20
251	Ellis Burks	.10
252	Richie Sexson	.15
253	Steve Finley	.10
254	Dwight Gooden	.10
255	Dustin Hermanson	.10
256	Kirk Rueter	.10
257	Steve Trachsel	.10
258	Gregg Jefferies	.10
259	Matt Stairs	.10
260	Shane Reynolds	.15
261	Gregg Olson	.10
262	Kevin Tapani	.10
263	Matt Morris	.10
264	Carl Pavano	.10
265	Nomar Garciaparra	1.50
266	Kevin Young	.10
267	Rick Helling	.10
268	Mark Leiter	.10
269	Brian McRae	.10
270	Cal Ripken Jr.	2.00
271	Jeff Abbott	.10

272	Tony Batista	.10
273	Bill Simas	.10
274	Brian Hunter	.10
275	John Franco	.10
276	Devon White	.10
277	Rickey Henderson	.25
278	Chuck Finley	.10
279	Mike Blowers	.10
280	Mark Grace	.25
281	Randy Winn	.10
282	Bobby Bonilla	.20
283	David Justice	.25
284	Shane Monahan	.10
285	Kevin Brown	.25
286	Todd Zeile	.10
287	Al Martin	.10
288	Troy O'Leary	.10
289	Darryl Hamilton	.10
290	Tino Martinez	.25
291	David Ortiz	.10
292	Tony Clark	.25
293	Ryan Minor	.25
294	Reggie Sanders	.10
295	Wally Joyner	.10
296	Cliff Floyd	.10
297	Shawn Estes	.10
298	Pat Hentgen	.10
299	Scott Elarton	.10
300	Alex Rodriguez	2.00
301	Ozzie Guillen	.10
302	Manny Martinez	.10
303	Ryan McGuire	.10
304	Brad Ausmus	.10
305	Alex Gonzalez	.10
306	Brian Jordan	.10
307	John Jaha	.10
308	Mark Grudzielanek	.10
309	Juan Guzman	.10
310	Tony Womack	.10
311	Dennis Reyes	.10
312	Marty Cordova	.10
313	Ramiro Mendoza	.10
314	Robin Ventura	.20
315	Rafael Palmeiro	.30
316	Ramon Martinez	.10
317	John Mabry	.10
318	Dave Hollins	.10
319	Tom Candiotti	.10
320	Al Leiter	.20
321	Rico Brogna	.10
322	Jimmy Key	.10
323	Bernard Gilkey	.10
324	Jason Giambi	.10
325	Craig Biggio	.30
326	Troy Glaus	.25
327	Delino DeShields	.10
328	Fernando Vina	.10
329	John Smoltz	.20
330	Jeff Kent	.10
331	Roy Halladay	.15
332	Andy Ashby	.10
333	Tim Wakefield	.10
334	Tim Belcher	.10
335	Bernie Williams	.40
336	Desi Relaford	.10
337	John Burkett	.10
338	Mike Hampton	.10
339	Royce Clayton	.10
340	Mike Piazza	1.50
341	Jeremi Gonzalez	.10
342	Mike Lansing	.10
343	Jamie Moyer	.10
344	Ron Coomer	.10
345	Barry Larkin	.30
346	Fernando Tatis	.20
347	Chili Davis	.10
348	Bobby Higginson	.10
349	Hal Morris	.10
350	Larry Walker	.40
351	Carlos Guillen	.10
352	Miguel Tejada	.10
353	Travis Fryman	.20
354	Jarrod Washburn	.10
355	Chipper Jones	1.25
356	Todd Stottlemyre	.15
357	Henry Rodriguez	.10
358	Eli Marrero	.10
359	Alan Benes	.10
360	Tim Salmon	.25
361	Luis Gonzalez	.10
362	Scott Spiezio	.10
363	Chris Carpenter	.10
364	Bobby Howry	.10
365	Raul Mondesi	.20
366	Ugueth Urbina	.10
367	Tom Evans	.10
368	*Kerry Ligtenberg*	.25
369	Adrian Beltre	.25
370	Ryan Klesko	.25
371	Wilson Alvarez	.10
372	John Thomson	.10
373	Tony Saunders	.10
374	Mike Stanley	.10
375	Ken Caminiti	.20
376	Jay Buhner	.20
377	Bill Mueller	.10
378	Jeff Blauser	.10
379	Edgar Renteria	.10
380	Jim Thome	.25
381	Joey Hamilton	.10
382	Calvin Pickering	.15
383	Marquis Grissom	.10
384	Omar Daal	.10
385	Curt Schilling	.20
386	Jose Cruz Jr.	.15
387	Chris Widger	.10
388	Pete Harnisch	.10
389	Charles Nagy	.10
390	Tom Gordon	.10
391	Bobby Smith	.10
392	Derrick Gibson	.10
393	Jeff Conine	.10
394	Carlos Perez	.10
395	Barry Bonds	.50
396	Mark McLemore	.10
397	Juan Encarnacion	.20
398	Wade Boggs	.25
399	Ivan Rodriguez	.50
400	Moises Alou	.25
401	Jeromy Burnitz	.10
402	Sean Casey	.25
403	Jose Offerman	.10
404	Joe Fontenot	.10
405	Kevin Millwood	.20
406	Lance Johnson	.10
407	Richard Hidalgo	.10
408	Mike Jackson	.10
409	Brian Anderson	.10
410	Jeff Shaw	.10
411	Preston Wilson	.10
412	Todd Hundley	.10
413	Jim Parque	.10
414	Justin Baughman	.10
415	Dante Bichette	.20
416	Paul O'Neill	.30
417	Miguel Cairo	.10
418	Randy Johnson	.40
419	Jesus Sanchez	.10
420	Carlos Delgado	.40
421	Ricky Ledee	.25
422	Orlando Hernandez	.15
423	Frank Thomas	.75
424	Pokey Reese	.10
425	Carlos Lee, Mike Lowell,*Kit Pellow* (Prospect)	.25
426	Michael Cuddyer, Mark DeRosa, Jerry Hairston (Prospect)	.10
427	Marlon Anderson, Ron Belliard, Orlando Cabrera (Prospect)	.10
428	*Micah Bowie,Phil Norton*, Randy Wolf (Prospect)	.25
429	Jack Cressend, Jason Rakers, John Rocker (Prospect)	.20
430	Ruben Mateo, Scott Morgan,*Mike Zywica* (Prospect)	.40
431	Jason LaRue, Matt LeCroy, Mitch Meluskey (Prospect)	.15
432	Gabe Kapler, Armando Rios, Fernando Seguignol (Prospect)	.20
433	Adam Kennedy,*Mickey Lopez*, Jackie Rexrode (Prospect)	.25
434	*Jose Fernandez*, Jeff Liefer, Chris Truby (Prospect)	.25
435	Corey Koskie, Doug Mientkiewicz, Damon Minor (Prospect)	.25
436	*Roosevelt Brown*, Dernell Stenson, Vernon Wells (Prospect)	.25
437	*A.J. Burnett*, John Nicholson, Billy Koch (Prospect)	.50
438	*Matt Belisle,Matt Roney* (Draft Pick)	.50
439	*Austin Kearns*, Chris George (Draft Pick)	.50
440	*Nate Bump,Nate Cornejo* (Draft Pick)	.40
441	*Brad Lidge,Mike Nannini* (Draft Pick)	.50
442	*Matt Holiday,Jeff Winchester* (Draft Pick)	.50
443	*Adam Everett,Chip Ambres* (Draft Pick)	.50
444	*Pat Burrell,Eric Valent* (Draft Pick)	2.00
445	Roger Clemens (Strikeout Kings)	.50
446	Kerry Wood (Strikeout Kings)	.20
447	Curt Schilling (Strikeout Kings)	.10
448	Randy Johnson (Strikeout Kings)	.20
449	Pedro Martinez (Strikeout Kings)	.25
450	Jeff Bagwell, Andres Galarraga, Mark McGwire (All-Topps)	1.00
451	John Olerud, Jim Thome, Tino Martinez (All-Topps)	.20
452	Alex Rodriguez, Nomar Garciaparra, Derek Jeter (All-Topps)	.40
453	Vinny Castilla, Chipper Jones, Scott Rolen (All-Topps)	.25
454	Sammy Sosa, Ken Griffey Jr., Juan Gonzalez (All-Topps)	.75
455	Barry Bonds, Manny Ramirez, Larry Walker (All-Topps)	.40
456	Frank Thomas, Tim Salmon, David Justice (All-Topps)	.40
457	Travis Lee, Todd Helton, Ben Grieve (All-Topps)	.20
458	Vladimir Guerrero, Greg Vaughn, Bernie Williams (All-Topps)	.25
459	Mike Piazza, Ivan Rodriguez, Jason Kendall (All-Topps)	.40
460	Roger Clemens, Kerry Wood, Greg Maddux (All-Topps)	.25
461	Home Run Parade #1 (Sammy Sosa)	8.00
461	HR Parade #2-60 (Sammy Sosa)	4.00
461	HR Parade #61-62 (Sammy Sosa)	15.00
461	HR Parade #63-65 (Sammy Sosa)	6.00
461	HR Parade #66 (Sammy Sosa)	20.00
462	Checklist	.10
463	Checklist	.10

1999 Topps All-Matrix

This 30-card set features holo-foil card fronts and features the top stars in the game. Each card is numbered with an "AM" prefix on card backs and are seeded 1:18 packs.

		MT
Complete Set (30):		90.00
Common Player:		1.50
Inserted 1:18		
AM1	Mark McGwire	15.00
AM2	Sammy Sosa	10.00
AM3	Ken Griffey Jr.	15.00
AM4	Greg Vaughn	1.50
AM5	Albert Belle	3.50
AM6	Vinny Castilla	1.50
AM7	Jose Canseco	4.00
AM8	Juan Gonzalez	4.00
AM9	Manny Ramirez	4.00
AM10	Andres Galarraga	3.00
AM11	Rafael Palmeiro	3.00
AM12	Alex Rodriguez	10.00
AM13	Mo Vaughn	2.00
AM14	Eric Chavez	2.00
AM15	Gabe Kapler	3.00
AM16	Calvin Pickering	1.50
AM17	Ruben Mateo	3.00
AM18	Roy Halladay	1.50
AM19	Jeremy Giambi	1.50
AM20	Alex Gonzalez	1.50
AM21	Ron Belliard	1.50
AM22	Marlon Anderson	1.50
AM23	Carlos Lee	1.50
AM24	Kerry Wood	2.50
AM25	Roger Clemens	6.00
AM26	Curt Schilling	1.50
AM27	Kevin Brown	2.00
AM28	Randy Johnson	2.00
AM29	Pedro Martinez	5.00
AM30	Orlando Hernandez	2.50

1999 Topps All-Topps Mystery Finest

This 33-card set features a black opaque covering that collectors peel off to reveal the player. Each card is numbered with an "M" prefix and inserted 1:36 packs. A parallel Refractor version is also randomly seeded and inserted 1:144 packs.

		MT
Complete Set (33):		250.00
Common Player:		3.00
Inserted 1:36		
Refractors: 2X		
Inserted 1:144		
M1	Jeff Bagwell	8.00
M2	Andres Galarraga	5.00
M3	Mark McGwire	30.00
M4	John Olerud	4.00
M5	Jim Thome	5.00
M6	Tino Martinez	5.00
M7	Alex Rodriguez	20.00
M8	Nomar Garciaparra	15.00
M9	Derek Jeter	15.00
M10	Vinny Castilla	3.00
M11	Chipper Jones	15.00
M12	Scott Rolen	8.00
M13	Sammy Sosa	15.00
M14	Ken Griffey Jr.	30.00
M15	Juan Gonzalez	8.00
M16	Barry Bonds	8.00
M17	Manny Ramirez	8.00
M18	Larry Walker	6.00
M19	Frank Thomas	8.00
M20	Tim Salmon	4.00
M21	David Justice	4.00
M22	Travis Lee	4.00
M23	Todd Helton	6.00
M24	Ben Grieve	5.00
M25	Bernie Williams	5.00
M26	Greg Vaughn	3.00
M27	Vladimir Guerrero	10.00
M28	Mike Piazza	15.00
M29	Ivan Rodriguez	8.00
M30	Jason Kendall	3.00
M31	Roger Clemens	12.00
M32	Kerry Wood	6.00
M33	Greg Maddux	12.00

1999 Topps Autographs

Autographs were inserted exclusively in hobby packs in both Topps series I and II. Each series had eight cards with each one carrying the Topps Certified Autograph Issue stamp. Series I Autographs were seeded 1:532 packs while Series II were found 1:501 packs.

		MT
Complete Set (16):		700.00
Complete Series 1 (8):		450.00
Complete Series 2 (8):		250.00
Common Player:		25.00
Series 1 Inserted 1:532 H		
Series 2 Inserted 1:501 H		
A1	Roger Clemens	75.00
A2	Chipper Jones	80.00
A3	Scott Rolen	50.00
A4	Alex Rodriguez	150.00
A5	Andres Galarraga	30.00
A6	Rondell White	20.00
A7	Ben Grieve	30.00
A8	Troy Glaus	30.00
A9	Moises Alou	20.00
A10	Barry Bonds	75.00
A11	Vladimir Guerrero	50.00
A12	Andruw Jones	40.00
A13	Darin Erstad	25.00
A14	Shawn Green	35.00
A15	Eric Chavez	20.00
A16	Pat Burrell	60.00

1999 Topps Hall of Fame

Found exclusively in hobby packs, Hall of Fame Collection is a ten-card set featured on cards that silhouette their images against their respective Hall of Fame plaques. Featured players include Yogi Berra, Reggie Jackson and Ernie Banks among others. These were seeded 1:12 packs.

		MT
Complete Set (10):		20.00
Common Player:		1.00
Inserted 1:12 H		
HOF1	Mike Schmidt	4.00
HOF2	Brooks Robinson	2.00
HOF3	Stan Musial	3.00
HOF4	Willie McCovey	1.00
HOF5	Eddie Mathews	1.50
HOF6	Reggie Jackson	4.00
HOF7	Ernie Banks	2.50
HOF8	Whitey Ford	1.50
HOF9	Bob Feller	1.00
HOF10	Yogi Berra	2.50

1999 Topps Lords of the Diamond

Inserted in every 18 packs this 15-card set features the top players in the game including Barry Bonds and Ken Griffey Jr. Card fronts include a holographic look with die-cutting across the top of the card on a silver background.

		MT
Complete Set (15):		50.00
Common Player:		1.00
Inserted 1:18		
LD1	Ken Griffey Jr.	10.00
LD2	Chipper Jones	6.00
LD3	Sammy Sosa	6.00
LD4	Frank Thomas	3.50
LD5	Mark McGwire	10.00
LD6	Jeff Bagwell	2.50
LD7	Alex Rodriguez	8.00
LD8	Juan Gonzalez	2.50
LD9	Barry Bonds	2.50
LD10	Nomar Garciaparra	6.00
LD11	Darin Erstad	1.50
LD12	Tony Gwynn	5.00
LD13	Andres Galarraga	1.00
LD14	Mike Piazza	6.00
LD15	Greg Maddux	5.00

1999 Topps MVP Promotion

Each of the 198 players cards in Series 1 and Series 2 was issued in a parallel version of 100 each for use in an MVP of the Week sweepstakes. Overprinted with a large gold-foil seal on front, the MVP cards have contest rules on back. The MVP cards were inserted at ratios of between 1:142 (HTA) and 1:515 (Hobby) packs. Cards of players who won MVP of the Week during the 1999 season could be redeemed for a special set of MVP cards prior to the Dec. 31, 1999 deadline.

	MT
Common Player:	4.00
Stars: 60X	
Rookies: 40X	
(See 1999 Topps for checklist and base card values.)	

1999 Topps MVP Redemption

Person redeeming winning MVP contest cards prior to the Dec. 31, 1999, deadline received this set of 25 star and rookie cards. Card numbers have an MVP prefix.

		MT
Complete Set (25):		45.00
Common Player:		.75
1	Raul Mondesi	1.00
2	Tim Salmon	.75
3	Fernando Tatis	.75
4	Larry Walker	1.00
5	Fred McGriff	1.00
6	Nomar Garciaparra	5.00
7	Rafael Palmeiro	1.50
8	Randy Johnson	1.00
9	Mike Lieberthal	.75
10	B.J. Surhoff	.75
11	Todd Helton	1.00
12	Tino Martinez	.75
13	Scott Rolen	2.00
14	Mike Piazza	5.00
15	David Cone	.75
16	Tony Clark	.75
17	Roberto Alomar	.75
18	Miguel Tejada	.75
19	Alex Rodriguez	7.50
20	J.T. Snow	.75
21	Ray Lankford	.75
22	Mo Vaughn	.75
23	Paul O'Neill	.75
24	Chipper Jones	4.00
25	Mark McGwire	10.00

1999 Topps New Breed

The next generation of stars are featured in this 15-card set that showcases the young talent on a silver foil card. These are seeded 1:18 packs.

		MT
Complete Set (15):		20.00
Common Player:		.50
Inserted 1:18		
NB1	Darin Erstad	1.00
NB2	Brad Fullmer	.75
NB3	Kerry Wood	1.50
NB4	Nomar Garciaparra	5.00
NB5	Travis Lee	1.00
NB6	Scott Rolen	2.00
NB7	Todd Helton	1.50
NB8	Vladimir Guerrero	3.00
NB9	Derek Jeter	5.00
NB10	Alex Rodriguez	7.50
NB11	Ben Grieve	1.50
NB12	Andruw Jones	1.50
NB13	Paul Konerko	.50
NB14	Aramis Ramirez	.50
NB15	Adrian Beltre	.75

1999 Topps Picture Perfect

This 10-card set features a full bleed photo of baseball's biggest stars, including Derek Jeter and Ken Griffey Jr. These are found one per eight packs.

		MT
Complete Set (10):		12.00
Common Player:		.50
Inserted 1:8		
P1	Ken Griffey Jr.	5.00
P2	Kerry Wood	.75
P3	Pedro Martinez	1.00
P4	Mark McGwire	5.00
P5	Greg Maddux	2.00
P6	Sammy Sosa	2.50
P7	Greg Vaughn	.50
P8	Juan Gonzalez	1.00
P9	Jeff Bagwell	1.00
P10	Derek Jeter	2.50

1999 Topps Power Brokers

This 20-card set features baseball's biggest superstars including McGwire, Sosa and Chipper Jones. The cards are die-cut at the top and printed on Finest technology. Power Brokers are inserted in every 36 packs. A Refractor parallel version also exists, which are seeded 1:144 packs.

		MT
Complete Set (20):		100.00
Common Player:		1.25
Inserted 1:36		
Refractors: 2X		
Inserted 1:144		
PB1	Mark McGwire	15.00
PB2	Andres Galarraga	2.00
PB3	Ken Griffey Jr.	15.00
PB4	Sammy Sosa	10.00
PB5	Juan Gonzalez	4.00
PB6	Alex Rodriguez	12.00
PB7	Frank Thomas	4.00
PB8	Jeff Bagwell	4.00
PB9	Vinny Castilla	1.25
PB10	Mike Piazza	10.00
PB11	Greg Vaughn	1.25
PB12	Barry Bonds	4.00
PB13	Mo Vaughn	2.50
PB14	Jim Thome	2.00
PB15	Larry Walker	2.00
PB16	Chipper Jones	10.00
PB17	Nomar Garciaparra	10.00
PB18	Manny Ramirez	4.00
PB19	Roger Clemens	6.00
PB20	Kerry Wood	3.00

1999 Topps Record Numbers

This 10-card set highlights achievements from the game's current stars, including Nomar Garciaparra's 30 game hitting streak, the longest by a rookie in major league history. These inserts are randomly seeded 1:8 packs, each card is numbered on the back with an "RN" prefix.

		MT
Complete Set (10):		20.00
Common Player:		.75
Inserted 1:8		
RN1	Mark McGwire	5.00
RN2	Mike Piazza	3.00
RN3	Curt Schilling	.50
RN4	Ken Griffey Jr.	5.00
RN5	Sammy Sosa	3.00
RN6	Alex Rodriguez	4.00
RN7	Kerry Wood	1.00
RN8	Roger Clemens	1.50
RN9	Cal Ripken Jr.	4.00
RN10	Mark McGwire	5.00

1999 Topps Record Numbers Gold

This is a parallel of the Record Numbers insert set, each card features the appropriate sequential numbering based on the featured players' highlighted record. Each card is numbered with an "RN" prefix on the back.

		MT
Complete Set (10):		1200.
Common Player:		8.00
RN1	Mark McGwire (70)	250.00
RN2	Mike Piazza (362)	40.00
RN3	Curt Schilling (319)	8.00
RN4	Ken Griffey Jr. (350)	60.00
RN5	Sammy Sosa (20)	350.00
RN6	Nomar Garciaparra (30)	300.00
RN7	Kerry Wood (20)	100.00
RN8	Roger Clemens (20)	250.00
RN9	Cal Ripken Jr. (2,632)	25.00
RN10	Mark McGwire (162)	125.00

1999 Topps Nolan Ryan Reprints

Topps reprinted all 27 of Nolan Ryan's basic Topps cards, with 14 odd numbers appearing in Series I and the remaining 13 even cards inserted into Series II packs. Each card is stamped with a gold Topps commemorative stamp on the front for identification. Reprints were seeded in every 18 packs. Nolan Ryan also autographed a number of the reprints for both series. Series I Ryan autographs are seeded 1:4,260 with Series II autographs found 1:5,007 packs. Ryan autographs were inserted exclusively in hobby packs.

		MT
Complete Set (27):		100.00
Common Ryan:		5.00
Inserted 1:18		
Nolan Ryan Autograph:		200.00
1	Nolan Ryan (1968)	15.00
2	Nolan Ryan (1969)	10.00
3	Nolan Ryan (1970)	5.00
4	Nolan Ryan (1971)	5.00
5	Nolan Ryan (1972)	5.00
6	Nolan Ryan (1973)	5.00
7	Nolan Ryan (1974)	5.00
8	Nolan Ryan (1975)	5.00
9	Nolan Ryan (1976)	5.00
10	Nolan Ryan (1977)	5.00
11	Nolan Ryan (1978)	5.00
12	Nolan Ryan (1979)	5.00
13	Nolan Ryan (1980)	5.00
14	Nolan Ryan (1981)	5.00
15	Nolan Ryan (1982)	5.00
16	Nolan Ryan (1983)	5.00
17	Nolan Ryan (1984)	5.00
18	Nolan Ryan (1985)	5.00
19	Nolan Ryan (1986)	5.00
20	Nolan Ryan (1987)	5.00
21	Nolan Ryan (1988)	5.00
22	Nolan Ryan (1989)	5.00
23	Nolan Ryan (1990)	5.00
24	Nolan Ryan (1991)	5.00
25	Nolan Ryan (1992)	5.00
26	Nolan Ryan (1993)	5.00
27	Nolan Ryan (1994)	5.00

1999 Topps Nolan Ryan Finest Reprints

This 27-card set reprinted all 27 of Ryan's basic Topps cards. Odd numbers were distributed in Series I packs, with even numbers distributed in Series II packs. These are seeded 1:72 packs in both series I and II packs. A Refractor parallel version is inserted 1:288 packs.

		MT
Complete Set (27):		250.00
Common Card:		12.00
Inserted 1:72		
Refractors: 2X		
Inserted 1:288		
1	1968	20.00
2	1969	12.00
3	1970	12.00
4	1971	12.00
5	1972	12.00
6	1973	12.00
7	1974	12.00
8	1975	12.00
9	1976	12.00
10	1977	12.00
11	1978	12.00
12	1979	12.00
13	1980	12.00
14	1981	12.00
15	1982	12.00
16	1983	12.00
17	1984	12.00
18	1985	12.00
19	1986	12.00
20	1987	12.00
21	1988	12.00
22	1989	12.00
23	1990	12.00
24	1991	12.00
25	1992	12.00
26	1992	12.00
27	1992	12.00

1999 Topps Traded and Rookies

Identical in design to the base 1999 Topps cards the 121- card set includes players involved in pre and mid-season transactions as well as top prospects and 1999 Draft Picks. Released in a boxed set, each set also includes one autographed card from the 75 rookie/draft pick cards in the set.

		MT
Complete Set (121):		40.00
Common Player:		.15
1	*Seth Etherton*	1.00
2	*Mark Harriger*	.50
3	*Matt Wise*	.50
4	*Carlos Hernandez*	.50
5	*Julio Lugo*	.75
6	*Mike Nannini*	1.00
7	*Justin Bowles*	.40
8	*Mark Mulder*	2.00
9	*Roberto Vaz*	.40
10	*Felipe Lopez*	.75
11	*Matt Belisle*	.75
12	Micah Bowie	.15
13	*Ruben Quevedo*	.50
14	*Jose Garcia*	.50
15	*David Kelton*	.75
16	*Phillip Norton*	.25
17	*Corey Patterson*	5.00
18	*Ron Walker*	.50
19	*Paul Hoover*	1.00
20	*Ryan Rupe*	.75
21	*J.D. Closser*	.75
22	*Rob Ryan*	.40
23	*Steve Colyer*	.50
24	*Bubba Crosby*	.50
25	*Luke Prokopec*	.75
26	*Matt Blank*	.50
27	*Josh McKinley*	1.00
28	*Nate Bump*	.75
29	*Giuseppe Chiaramonte*	.75
30	*Arturo McDowell*	.50
31	*Tony Torcato*	.50
32	Dave Roberts	.75
33	*C.C. Sabathia*	1.50
34	*Sean Spencer*	.50
35	*Chip Ambres*	1.00
36	*A.J. Burnett*	1.50
37	*Mo Bruce*	.50
38	*Jason Tyner*	.40
39	*Mamon Tucker*	.75
40	*Sean Burroughs*	5.00
41	*Kevin Eberwein*	.25
42	*Junior Herndon*	.25
43	*Bryan Wolff*	.25
44	*Pat Burrell*	4.00
45	*Eric Valent*	1.00
46	*Carlos Pena*	1.00
47	*Mike Zywica*	.50
48	*Adam Everett*	1.00
49	*Juan Pena*	.40
50	*Adam Dunn*	1.50
51	*Austin Kearns*	1.00
52	*Jacobo Sequea*	.25
53	*Choo Freeman*	.50
54	*Jeff Winchester*	.40
55	*Matt Burch*	.50
56	*Chris George*	.50
57	*Scott Mullen*	.25
58	*Kit Pellow*	.50
59	*Mark Quinn*	2.00
60	*Nate Cornejo*	.50

61	*Ryan Mills*	1.00
62	*Kevin Beirne*	.25
63	*Kip Wells*	2.00
64	*Juan Rivera*	.75
65	*Alfonso Soriano*	5.00
66	*Josh Hamilton*	6.00
67	*Josh Girdley*	.75
68	*Kyle Snyder*	1.50
69	*Mike Paradis*	.75
70	*Jason Jennings*	.75
71	*David Walling*	1.50
72	*Omar Ortiz*	.25
73	*Jay Gehrke*	.50
74	*Casey Burns*	.25
75	*Carl Crawford*	1.00
76	Reggie Sanders	.15
77	Will Clark	.25
78	David Wells	.15
79	Paul Konerko	.15
80	Armando Benitez	.15
81	Brant Brown	.15
82	Mo Vaughn	.50
83	Jose Canseco	.75
84	Albert Belle	.50
85	Dean Palmer	.15
86	Greg Vaughn	.25
87	Mark Clark	.15
88	Pat Meares	.15
89	Eric Davis	.15
90	Brian Giles	.15
91	Jeff Brantley	.15
92	Bret Boone	.15
93	Ron Gant	.15
94	Mike Cameron	.15
95	Charles Johnson	.15
96	Denny Neagle	.15
97	Brian Hunter	.15
98	Jose Hernandez	.15
99	Rick Aguilera	.15
100	Tony Batista	.15
101	Roger Cedeno	.15
102	Creighton Gubanich	.15
103	Tim Belcher	.15
104	Bruce Aven	.15
105	*Brian Daubach*	2.50
106	Ed Sprague	.15
107	Michael Tucker	.15
108	Homer Bush	.15
109	Armando Reynoso	.15
110	Brook Fordyce	.15
111	Matt Mantei	.15
112	Jose Guillen	.15
113	Kenny Rogers	.15
114	Livan Hernandez	.15
115	Butch Huskey	.15
116	David Segui	.15
117	Darryl Hamilton	.15
118	Jim Leyritz	.15
119	Randy Velarde	.15
120	Bill Taylor	.15
121	Kevin Appier	.15

1999 Topps Traded and Rookies Autographs

These autographs have identical photos and design from the Traded and Rookies set. Seeded one per boxed set, each card has a "Topps Certified Autograph Issue" stamp ensuring its authenticity. 75 of the rookie/draft picks included in the 121-card boxed set signed.

		MT
Common Player:		8.00
Inserted 1:set		
1	Seth Etherton	20.00
2	Mark Harriger	8.00
3	Matt Wise	8.00
4	Carlos Hernandez	8.00
5	Julio Lugo	8.00
6	Mike Nannini	8.00
7	Justin Bowles	8.00
8	Mark Mulder	25.00
9	Roberto Vaz	8.00
10	Felipe Lopez	15.00
11	Matt Belisle	8.00
12	Micah Bowie	8.00
13	Ruben Quevedo	8.00
14	Jose Garcia	8.00
15	David Kelton	15.00
16	Phillip Norton	8.00
17	Corey Patterson	70.00
18	Ron Walker	8.00
19	Paul Hoover	15.00
20	Ryan Rupe	15.00
21	J.D. Closser	15.00
22	Rob Ryan	8.00
23	Steve Colyer	8.00
24	Bubba Crosby	8.00
25	Luke Prokopec	8.00
26	Matt Blank	8.00
27	Josh McKinley	15.00
28	Nate Bump	8.00
29	Giuseppe Chiaramonte	15.00
30	Arturo McDowell	8.00
31	Tony Torcato	8.00
32	Dave Roberts	8.00
33	C.C. Sabathia	20.00
34	Sean Spencer	8.00
35	Chip Ambres	15.00
36	A.J. Burnett	20.00
37	Mo Bruce	8.00
38	Jason Tyner	8.00
39	Mamon Tucker	8.00
40	Sean Burroughs	60.00
41	Kevin Eberwein	8.00
42	Junior Herndon	8.00
43	Bryan Wolff	8.00
44	Pat Burrell	50.00
45	Eric Valent	20.00
46	Carlos Pena	20.00
47	Mike Zywica	8.00
48	Adam Everett	15.00
49	Juan Pena	8.00
50	Adam Dunn	25.00
51	Austin Kearns	20.00
52	Jacobo Sequea	8.00
53	Choo Freeman	8.00
54	Jeff Winchester	8.00
55	Matt Burch	8.00
56	Chris George	8.00
57	Scott Mullen	8.00
58	Kit Pellow	8.00
59	Mark Quinn	20.00
60	Nate Cornejo	8.00
61	Ryan Mills	15.00
62	Kevin Beirne	8.00
63	Kip Wells	20.00
64	Juan Rivera	8.00
65	Alfonso Soriano	50.00
66	Josh Hamilton	60.00
67	Josh Girdley	15.00
68	Kyle Snyder	20.00
69	Mike Paradis	8.00
70	Jason Jennings	8.00
71	David Walling	20.00
72	Omar Ortiz	8.00
73	Jay Gehrke	8.00
74	Casey Burns	8.00
75	Carl Crawford	15.00

1999 Topps Action Flats

"Dynamic action poses . . . painstakingly capturing one of their signature plays" are featured in this issue of plastic player figures. The figures are about 3" tall by 2-1/2" wide and stand on a plastic base. In the manner of early 20th Century tin soldiers, there is little depth to the figures. Each handpainted figure is sold in a plastic-windowed box which includes a special foil-stamped version of the player's 1999 Topps card inside. Each figure was also produced in a short-printed "away" jersey version, with 10 of the players seeded at the rate of one per 12 figures, Sosa at a 1:24 rate and McGwire at a 1:36 rate. Suggested retail price at issue was $2.99. Values shown are for unopened packages.

		MT
Complete Set, "Home" (12):		35.00
Compkete Set, "Away" (12):		75.00
Common Player, "Home":		3.00
Common Player, "Away":		4.50
	HOME JERSEY	
1	Chipper Jones	3.50
2	Greg Maddux	3.00
3	Mark McGwire	4.00
4	Sammy Sosa	3.50
5	Kerry Wood	3.00
6	Bobby Bonds	3.00
7	Alex Rodriguez	3.50
8	Ken Griffey Jr.	5.00
9	Cal Ripken Jr.	4.00
10	Juan Gonzalez	3.50
11	Nomar Garciaparra	3.50
12	Derek Jeter	3.50
	AWAY JERSEY	
1	Chipper Jones	5.00
2	Greg Maddux	4.50
3	Mark McGwire	12.50
4	Sammy Sosa	7.50
5	Kerry Wood	4.50
6	Bobby Bonds	4.50
7	Alex Rodriguez	5.00
8	Ken Griffey Jr.	7.50
9	Cal Ripken Jr.	6.00
10	Juan Gonzalez	5.00
11	Nomar Garciaparra	5.00
12	Derek Jeter	5.00

1999 Topps Opening Day

This retail exclusive product is comprised of 165 cards. Base cards have a silver border, and the Opening Day logo stamped with silver foil. Packs are pre-priced at $.99, each pack has seven cards. Hank Aaron autographs are randomly seeded and are stamped with the Topps "Certified Autograph Issue" stamp. The insertion rate for the autograph is 1:29,642 packs.

		MT
Complete Set (165):		30.00
Common Player:		.15
Hank Aaron Autograph:		200.00
Wax Box:		25.00
1	Hank Aaron	2.00
2a	Roger Clemens	1.00
2b	Andres Galarraga (should be #3)	.50
4	Scott Brosius	.15
5	Ray Durham	.15
6	Will Clark	.40
7	David Wells	.15
8	Jose Guillen	.15
9	Edgardo Alfonzo	.15
10	Manny Ramirez	1.00
11	Greg Maddux	2.00
12	David Segui	.15
13	Darryl Strawberry	.25
14	Brad Radke	.15
15	Kerry Wood	.75
16	Paul Konerko	.25
17	Travis Lee	.50
18	Kenny Rogers	.15
19	Todd Walker	.25
20	John Olerud	.25
21	Nolan Ryan	3.00
22	Ray Lankford	.15
23	Bartolo Colon	.15
24	Brady Anderson	.15
25	Jorge Posada	.15
26	Justin Thompson	.15
27	Juan Gonzalez	1.50
28	Chuck Knoblauch	.40
29	Todd Helton	.60
30	Gary Sheffield	.30
31	Rod Beck	.15
32	Garret Anderson	.15
33	Rondell White	.25
34	Vladimir Guerrero	1.00
35	Eric Karros	.15
36	Mo Vaughn	.60
37	Sammy Sosa	2.50
38	Kenny Lofton	.60
39	Mark McGwire	4.00
40	Javy Lopez	.25
41	Damion Easley	.15
42	Andy Pettitte	.40
43	Tony Gwynn	1.50
44	Jay Bell	.15
45	Jose Canseco	.40
46	John Wetteland	.15
47	Mike Caruso	.15
48	Derek Jeter	2.00
49	Aaron Sele	.15
50	Jeff Cirillo	.15
51	Mark Kotsay	.15
52	Albert Belle	.75
53	Matt Lawton	.15
54	Pedro Martinez	.50
55	Greg Vaughn	.25
56	Neifi Perez	.15
57	Derek Bell	.15
58	Ken Griffey Jr.	4.00
59	David Cone	.25
60	Dean Palmer	.15
61	Trevor Hoffman	.15
62	Billy Wagner	.15
63	Shawn Green	.15
64	Ben Grieve	.75
65	Tom Goodwin	.15
66	Jaret Wright	.40
67	Dmitri Young	.15
68	Hideki Irabu	.25
69	Jeff Fassero	.15
70	Matt Williams	.30
71	Bret Saberhagen	.15
72	Chad Curtis	.15
73	Scott Rolen	.75
74	J.T. Snow Jr.	.15
75	Rusty Greer	.15
76	Jim Edmonds	.15
77	Ron Gant	.15
78	A.J. Hinch	.15
79	Shannon Stewart	.15
80	Brad Fullmer	.25
81	Walt Weiss	.15
82	Fred McGriff	.25
83	Darin Erstad	.75
84	Eric Young	.15
85	Livan Hernandez	.15
86	Jeff Bagwell	1.00
87	Omar Vizquel	.15
88	Eric Davis	.15
89	Magglio Ordonez	.15
90	John Valentin	.15
91	Dave Dellucci	.15
92	Chan Ho Park	.25
93	Masato Yoshii	.15
94	Bret Boone	.15
95	Mariano Rivera	.25
96	Bobby Jones	.15
97	Francisco Cordova	.15
98	Mike Mussina	.50
99	Denny Neagle	.15
100	Edgar Martinez	.15
101	Jason Kendall	.25
102	Jeff King	.15
103	Rey Ordonez	.15
104	Andruw Jones	.75
105	Vinny Castilla	.15
106	Troy Glaus	1.00
107	Tom Glavine	.25
108	Moises Alou	.25
109	Carlos Delgado	.25
110	Raul Mondesi	.25
111	Shane Reynolds	.15
112	Jason Giambi	.15
113	Jose Cruz Jr.	.15
114	Craig Biggio	.40
115	Tim Salmon	.40
116	Chipper Jones	2.00
117	Andy Benes	.15
118	John Smoltz	.25
119	Jeromy Burnitz	.15
120	Randy Johnson	.50
121	Mark Grace	.25
122	Henry Rodriguez	.15
123	Ryan Klesko	.15
124	Kevin Millwood	.50
125	Sean Casey	.15
126	Brian Jordan	.15
127	Kevin Brown	.25
128	Orlando Hernandez	1.50
129	Barry Bonds	.75
130	David Justice	.25
131	Carlos Perez	.15
132	Andy Ashby	.15
133	Paul O'Neill	.30
134	Curt Schilling	.25
135	Alex Rodriguez	3.00
136	Cliff Floyd	.15
137	Rafael Palmeiro	.30
138	Nomar Garciaparra	2.00
139	Mike Piazza	2.00
140	Roberto Alomar	.50
141	Todd Hundley	.15
142	Jeff Kent	.15
143	Barry Larkin	.25
144	Cal Ripken Jr.	3.00
145	Jay Buhner	.25
146	Kevin Young	.15
147	Ivan Rodriguez	.75
148	Al Leiter	.15
149	Sandy Alomar	.15
150	Bernie Williams	.50
151	Ellis Burks	.15
152	Wally Joyner	.15
153	Bobby Higginson	.15
154	Tony Clark	.50
155	Larry Walker	.40
156	Frank Thomas	1.50
157	Tino Martinez	.40
158	Jim Thome	.40
159	Dante Bichette	.25
160	David Wells (Season Highlights)	.15
161	Roger Clemens (Season Highlights)	.60
162	Kerry Wood (Season Highlights)	.50
163	Mark McGwire (HR Record #70)	5.00
164	Sammy Sosa (HR Record #66)	3.00
165	Checklist	.15

1999 Topps Chrome

The 462-card base set is a chromium parallel version of Topps baseball. Included are the Mark McGwire #220 and Sammy Sosa #461 home run subset cards, which commemorate each of his home runs. Each pack contains four cards with a S.R.P. of $3.00 per pack.

		MT
Complete Set (461):		280.00
Series 1 Set (242):		160.00
Series 2 Set (221):		125.00
Common Player:		.40
Star Refractors: 10X		
Young Stars/RCs: 6X		
McGwire Refractors #220: 4X		
Sosa Refractors #461: 4X		
Inserted 1:12		
Series 1 Wax Box:		120.00
Series 2 Wax Box:		70.00
1	Roger Clemens	3.00
2	Andres Galarraga	1.60
3	Scott Brosius	.40
4	John Flaherty	.40
5	Jim Leyritz	.40
6	Ray Durham	.40
7	not issued	
8	Joe Vizcaino	.40
9	Will Clark	1.00
10	David Wells	.40
11	Jose Guillen	.60
12	Scott Hatteberg	.40
13	Edgardo Alfonzo	.75
14	Mike Bordick	.40
15	Manny Ramirez	2.00
16	Greg Maddux	4.00
17	David Segui	.40
18	Darryl Strawberry	.75
19	Brad Radke	.40
20	Kerry Wood	1.00
21	Matt Anderson	.40
22	Derrek Lee	.40
23	Mickey Morandini	.40
24	Paul Konerko	.60
25	Travis Lee	.75
26	Ken Hill	.40
27	Kenny Rogers	.40
28	Paul Sorrento	.40
29	Quilvio Veras	.40
30	Todd Walker	.50
31	Ryan Jackson	.40
32	John Olerud	.75
33	Doug Glanville	.40
34	Nolan Ryan	8.00
35	Ray Lankford	.40
36	Mark Loretta	.40
37	Jason Dickson	.40
38	Sean Bergman	.40
39	Quinton McCracken	.40
40	Bartolo Colon	.75
41	Brady Anderson	.40
42	Chris Stynes	.40
43	Jorge Posada	.60
44	Justin Thompson	.40
45	Johnny Damon	.40
46	Armando Benitez	.40
47	Brant Brown	.40
48	Charlie Hayes	.40
49	Darren Dreifort	.40
50	Juan Gonzalez	2.00
51	Chuck Knoblauch	.75
52	Todd Helton (Rookie All-Star)	1.50
53	Rick Reed	.40
54	Chris Gomez	.40
55	Gary Sheffield	.75
56	Rod Beck	.40
57	Rey Sanchez	.40
58	Garret Anderson	.40
59	Jimmy Haynes	.40
60	Steve Woodard	.40
61	Rondell White	.60
62	Vladimir Guerrero	3.00
63	Eric Karros	.60
64	Russ Davis	.40
65	Mo Vaughn	1.50
66	Sammy Sosa	6.00
67	Troy Percival	.40
68	Kenny Lofton	1.50
69	Bill Taylor	.40
70	Mark McGwire	10.00
71	Roger Cedeno	.40
72	Javy Lopez	.60
73	Damion Easley	.40
74	Andy Pettitte	.75
75	Tony Gwynn	4.00
76	Ricardo Rincon	.40
77	F.P. Santangelo	.40

78 Jay Bell .40
79 Scott Servais .40
80 Jose Canseco 1.50
81 Roberto Hernandez .40
82 Todd Dunwoody .40
83 John Wetteland .40
84 Mike Caruso (Rookie All-Star) .40
85 Derek Jeter 5.00
86 Aaron Sele .40
87 Jose Lima .40
88 Ryan Christenson .40
89 Jeff Cirillo .40
90 Jose Hernandez .40
91 Mark Kotsay (Rookie All-Star) .60
92 Darren Bragg .40
93 Albert Belle 2.00
94 Matt Lawton .40
95 Pedro Martinez 2.00
96 Greg Vaughn .60
97 Neifi Perez .40
98 Gerald Williams .40
99 Derek Bell .40
100 Ken Griffey Jr. 8.00
101 David Cone .60
102 Brian Johnson .40
103 Dean Palmer .40
104 Javier Valentin .40
105 Trevor Hoffman .40
106 Butch Huskey .40
107 Dave Martinez .40
108 Billy Wagner .40
109 Shawn Green 1.00
110 Ben Grieve (Rookie All-Star) 1.00
111 Tom Goodwin .40
112 Jaret Wright .50
113 Aramis Ramirez .75
114 Dmitri Young .40
115 Hideki Irabu .50
116 Roberto Kelly .40
117 Jeff Fassero .40
118 Mark Clark .40
119 Jason McDonald .40
120 Matt Williams .75
121 Dave Burba .40
122 Bret Saberhagen .40
123 Deivi Cruz .40
124 Chad Curtis .40
125 Scott Rolen 2.00
126 Lee Stevens .40
127 J.T. Snow Jr. .40
128 Rusty Greer .40
129 Brian Meadows .40
130 Jim Edmonds .60
131 Ron Gant .60
132 A.J. Hinch (Rookie All-Star) .40
133 Shannon Stewart .40
134 Brad Fullmer .60
135 Cal Eldred .40
136 Matt Walbeck .40
137 Carl Everett .40
138 Walt Weiss .40
139 Fred McGriff .60
140 Darin Erstad .75
141 Dave Nilsson .40
142 Eric Young .40
143 Dan Wilson .40
144 Jeff Reed .40
145 Brett Tomko .40
146 Terry Steinbach .40
147 Seth Greisinger .40
148 Pat Meares .40
149 Livan Hernandez .40
150 Jeff Bagwell 2.00
151 Bob Wickman .40
152 Omar Vizquel .40
153 Eric Davis .40
154 Larry Sutton .40
155 Magglio Ordonez (Rookie All-Star) .75
156 Eric Milton .40
157 Darren Lewis .40
158 Rick Aguilera .40
159 Mike Lieberthal .40
160 Robb Nen .40
161 Brian Giles .40
162 Jeff Brantley .40
163 Gary DiSarcina .40
164 John Valentin .40
165 David Dellucci .40
166 Chan Ho Park .60
167 Masato Yoshii .40
168 Jason Schmidt .40
169 LaTroy Hawkins .40
170 Bret Boone .40
171 Jerry DiPoto .40
172 Mariano Rivera .60
173 Mike Cameron .40
174 Scott Erickson .40
175 Charles Johnson .40
176 Bobby Jones .40
177 Francisco Cordova .40
178 Todd Jones .40
179 Jeff Montgomery .40
180 Mike Mussina 1.50
181 Bob Abreu .40
182 Ismael Valdes .40
183 Andy Fox .40
184 Woody Williams .40
185 Denny Neagle .40
186 Jose Valentin .40
187 Darrin Fletcher .40
188 Gabe Alvarez .40
189 Eddie Taubensee .40
190 Edgar Martinez .40
191 Jason Kendall .60
192 Darryl Kile .40
193 Jeff King .40
194 Rey Ordonez .40
195 Andruw Jones 1.00
196 Tony Fernandez .40
197 Jamey Wright .40
198 B.J. Surhoff .40
199 Vinny Castilla .40
200 David Wells (Season Highlight) .40
201 Mark McGwire (Season Highlight) 5.00
202 Sammy Sosa (Season Highlight) 3.00
203 Roger Clemens (Season Highlight) 1.50
204 Kerry Wood (Season Highlight) .50
205 Lance Berkman, Mike Frank, Gabe Kapler (Prospects) 4.00
206 *Alex Escobar*, Ricky Ledee, Mike Stoner (Prospects) 4.00
207 *Peter Bergeron*, Jeremy Giambi, George Lombard (Prospects) 3.00
208 Michael Barrett, Ben Davis, Robert Fick (Prospects) 1.00
209 Pat Cline, Ramon Hernandez, Jayson Werth (Prospects) 1.00
210 Bruce Chen, Chris Enochs, Ryan Anderson (Prospects) 2.00
211 Mike Lincoln, Octavio Dotel, Brad Penny (Prospects) 1.00
212 Chuck Abbott, Brent Butler, Danny Klassen (Prospects) 1.50
213 Chris Jones,*Jeff Urban* (Draft Pick) 2.00
214 *Arturo McDowell,Tony Torcato* (Draft Pick) 2.00
215 *Josh McKinley,Jason Tyner* (Draft Pick) 2.00
216 *Matt Burch,Seth Etherton* (Draft Pick) 2.00
217 *Mamon Tucker,Rick Elder* (Draft Pick) 5.00
218 *J.M. Gold,Ryan Mills* (Draft Pick) 4.00
219 *Adam Brown,Choo Freeman* (Draft Pick) 2.50
220 Mark McGwire HR #1 (Record Breaker) 60.00
220 Mark McGwire HR #2-60 30.00
220 McGwire HR #61-62 75.00
220 McGwire HR #63-69 50.00
220 McGwire HR #70 250.00
221 Larry Walker (League Leader) .75
222 Bernie Williams (League Leader) 1.00
223 Mark McGwire (League Leader) 6.00
224 Ken Griffey Jr. (League Leader) 5.00
225 Sammy Sosa (League Leader) 3.00
226 Juan Gonzalez (League Leader) 1.00
227 Dante Bichette (League Leader) .50
228 Alex Rodriguez (League Leader) 3.00
229 Sammy Sosa (League Leader) 3.00
230 Derek Jeter (League Leader) 3.00
231 Greg Maddux (League Leader) 2.00
232 Roger Clemens (League Leader) 1.50
233 Ricky Ledee (World Series) .50
234 Chuck Knoblauch (World Series) .75
235 Bernie Williams (World Series) 1.00
236 Tino Martinez (World Series) .75
237 Orlando Hernandez (World Series) .50
238 Scott Brosius (World Series) .40
239 Andy Pettitte (World Series) .75
240 Mariano Rivera (World Series) .60
241 Checklist .40
242 Checklist .40
243 Tom Glavine .60
244 Andy Benes .40
245 Sandy Alomar .60
246 Wilton Guerrero .40
247 Alex Gonzalez .40
248 Roberto Alomar 1.50
249 Ruben Rivera .40
250 Eric Chavez .40
251 Ellis Burks .40
252 Richie Sexson .50
253 Steve Finley .40
254 Dwight Gooden .60
255 Dustin Hermanson .40
256 Kirk Rueter .40
257 Steve Trachsel .40
258 Gregg Jefferies .40
259 Matt Stairs .40
260 Shane Reynolds .40
261 Gregg Olson .40
262 Kevin Tapani .40
263 Matt Morris .40
264 Carl Pavano .40
265 Nomar Garciaparra 5.00
266 Kevin Young .40
267 Rick Helling .40
268 Matt Franco .40
269 Brian McRae .40
270 Cal Ripken Jr. 6.00
271 Jeff Abbott .40
272 Tony Batista .40
273 Bill Simas .40
274 Brian Hunter .40
275 John Franco .40
276 Devon White .40
277 Rickey Henderson .75
278 Chuck Finley .40
279 Mike Blowers .40
280 Mark Grace .75
281 Randy Winn .40
282 Bobby Bonilla .60
283 David Justice .75
284 Shane Monahan .40
285 Kevin Brown .75
286 Todd Zeile .40
287 Al Martin .40
288 Troy O'Leary .40
289 Darryl Hamilton .40
290 Tino Martinez 1.00
291 David Ortiz .40
292 Tony Clark 1.00
293 Ryan Minor .60
294 Reggie Sanders .40
295 Wally Joyner .40
296 Cliff Floyd .40
297 Shawn Estes .40
298 Pat Hentgen .40
299 Scott Elarton .40
300 Alex Rodriguez 5.00
301 Ozzie Guillen .40
302 Hideo Martinez .40
303 Ryan McGuire .40
304 Brad Ausmus .40
305 Alex Gonzalez .40
306 Brian Jordan .40
307 John Jaha .40
308 Mark Grudzielanek .40
309 Juan Guzman .40
310 Tony Womack .40
311 Dennis Reyes .40
312 Marty Cordova .40
313 Ramiro Mendoza .40
314 Robin Ventura .75
315 Rafael Palmeiro 1.50
316 Ramon Martinez .40
317 Pedro Astacio .40
318 Dave Hollins .40
319 Tom Candiotti .40
320 Al Leiter .60
321 Rico Brogna .40
322 Reggie Jefferson .40
323 Bernard Gilkey .40
324 Jason Giambi .40
325 Craig Biggio 1.50
326 Troy Glaus 1.50
327 Delino DeShields .40
328 Fernando Vina .40
329 John Smoltz .75
330 Jeff Kent .40
331 Roy Halladay .75
332 Andy Ashby .40
333 Tim Wakefield .40
334 Roger Clemens 4.00
335 Bernie Williams 1.50
336 Desi Relaford .40
337 John Burkett .40
338 Mike Hampton .40
339 Royce Clayton .40
340 Mike Piazza 5.00
341 Jeremi Gonzalez .40
342 Mike Lansing .40
343 Jamie Moyer .40
344 Ron Coomer .40
345 Barry Larkin 1.00
346 Fernando Tatis 1.00
347 Chili Davis .40
348 Bobby Higginson .40
349 Hal Morris .40
350 Larry Walker 1.50
351 Carlos Guillen .40
352 Miguel Tejada .60
353 Travis Fryman .60
354 Jarrod Washburn .40
355 Chipper Jones 4.00
356 Todd Stottlemyre .60
357 Henry Rodriguez .40
358 Eli Marrero .40
359 Alan Benes .40
360 Tim Salmon .75
361 Luis Gonzalez .40
362 Scott Spiezio .40
363 Chris Carpenter .40
364 Bobby Howry .40
365 Raul Mondesi .75
366 Ugueth Urbina .40
367 Tom Evans .40
368 *Kerry Ligtenberg* 2.00
369 Adrian Beltre 1.00
370 Ryan Klesko .50
371 Wilson Alvarez .40
372 John Thomson .40
373 Tony Saunders .40
374 Mike Stanley .40
375 Ken Caminiti .75
376 Jay Buhner .75
377 Bill Mueller .40
378 Jeff Blauser .40
379 Edgar Renteria .40
380 Jim Thome 1.00
381 Joey Hamilton .40
382 Calvin Pickering .40
383 Marquis Grissom .40
384 Omar Daal .40
385 Curt Schilling .75
386 Jose Cruz Jr. .50
387 Chris Widger .40
388 Pete Harnisch .40
389 Charles Nagy .40
390 Tom Gordon .40
391 Bobby Smith .40
392 Derrick Gibson .40
393 Jeff Conine .40
394 Carlos Perez .40
395 Barry Bonds 2.00
396 Mark McLemore .40
397 Juan Encarnacion .75
398 Wade Boggs 1.00
399 Ivan Rodriguez 2.00
400 Moises Alou .75
401 Jeromy Burnitz .40
402 Sean Casey 1.00
403 Jose Offerman .40
404 Joe Fontenot .40
405 Kevin Millwood .75
406 Lance Johnson .40
407 Richard Hidalgo .40
408 Mike Jackson .40
409 Brian Anderson .40
410 Jeff Shaw .40
411 Preston Wilson .40
412 Todd Hundley .40
413 Jim Parque .40
414 Justin Baughman .40
415 Dante Bichette .75
416 Paul O'Neill .75
417 Miguel Cairo .40
418 Randy Johnson 1.50
419 Jesus Sanchez .40
420 Carlos Delgado 1.50
421 Ricky Ledee .75
422 Orlando Hernandez 1.00
423 Frank Thomas 2.00
424 Pokey Reese .40
425 Carlos Lee, Mike Lowell,*Kit Pellow* (Prospect) 4.00
426 Michael Cuddyer, Mark DeRosa,*Jerry Hairston Jr.* (Prospect) 1.50
427 Marlon Anderson, Ron Belliard, Orlando Cabrera (Prospect) 1.50
428 *Micah Bowie,Phil Norton*, Randy Wolf (Prospect) 2.50
429 Jack Cressend, Jason Rakers, John Rocker (Prospect) 2.00
430 Ruben Mateo, Scott Morgan,*Mike Zywica* (Prospect) 6.00
431 Jason LaRue, Matt LeCroy,*Mitch Meluskey* (Prospect) 2.00
432 Gabe Kapler,*Armando Rios*, Fernando Seguignol (Prospect) 3.00
433 Adam Kennedy,*Mickey Lopez*, Jackie Rexrode (Prospect) 2.00
434 *Jose Fernandez*, Jeff Liefer, Chris Truby (Prospect) 2.00
435 Corey Koskie,*Doug Mientkiewicz*, Damon Minor (Prospect) 2.50
436 *Roosevelt Brown*, Dernell Stenson, Vernon Wells (Prospect) 3.00
437 *A.J. Burnett*, John Nicholson, Billy Koch (Prospect) 4.00
438 *Matt Belisle,Matt Roney* (Draft Pick) 4.00
439 *Austin Kearns,Chris George* (Draft Pick) 4.00
440 *Nate Bump,Nate Cornejo* (Draft Pick) 4.00
441 *Brad Lidge,Mike Nannini* (Draft Pick) 4.00
442 *Matt Holliday,Jeff Winchester* (Draft Pick) 5.00
443 *Adam Everett,Chip Ambres* (Draft Pick) 3.00
444 *Pat Burrell,Eric Valent* (Draft Pick) 15.00
445 Roger Clemens (Strikeout Kings) 1.50
446 Kerry Wood (Strikeout Kings) .75
447 Curt Schilling (Strikeout Kings) .40
448 Randy Johnson (Strikeout Kings) .75
449 Pedro Martinez (Strikeout Kings) 1.00
450 Jeff Bagwell, Andres Galarraga, Mark McGwire (All-Topps) 4.00
451 John Olerud, Jim Thome, Tino Martinez (All-Topps) .40
452 Alex Rodriguez, Nomar Garciaparra, Derek Jeter (All-Topps) 2.50
453 Vinny Castilla, Chipper Jones, Scott Rolen (All-Topps) 2.00
454 Sammy Sosa, Ken Griffey Jr., Juan Gonzalez (All-Topps) 4.00
455 Barry Bonds, Manny Ramirez, Larry Walker (All-Topps) 1.50
456 Frank Thomas, Tim Salmon, David Justice (All-Topps) 1.50
457 Travis Lee, Todd Helton, Ben Grieve (All-Topps) .75
458 Vladimir Guerrero, Greg Vaughn, Bernie Williams (All-Topps) 1.00
459 Mike Piazza, Ivan Rodriguez, Jason Kendall (All-Topps) 2.00
460 Roger Clemens, Kerry Wood, Greg Maddux (All-Topps) 1.00
461 Sammy Sosa #1 (Home Run Parade) 25.00
461 Sammy Sosa HR #2-60 12.00
461 S. Sosa HR #61-62 30.00
461 S. Sosa HR #63-65 15.00
461 S. Sosa HR #66 60.00
--- Checklist 1-100 .40
--- Checklist - inserts .40

1999 Topps Chrome All-Etch

Inserted in Series II packs, All-Etch has three different levels of inserts, all printed on All-Etch technology. The three levels include '99 Rookie Rush which features rookies who have the best shot of winning '99 Rookie of the Year. Club 40 features 13 players who hit 40 homers or more from the '98 season and Club K features seven pitchers who are known for their strikeout abilities including Roger Clemens and Pedro Martinez. Each of these three levels are inserted 1:6 packs while the Refractor versions are all seeded 1:24 packs.

		MT
Complete Set (30):		60.00
Common Player:		1.00
Inserted 1:6		
Refractors: 2X		
Inserted 1:24		
1	Mark McGwire	12.00
2	Sammy Sosa	6.00
3	Ken Griffey Jr.	12.00
4	Greg Vaughn	1.00
5	Albert Belle	2.00
6	Vinny Castilla	1.00
7	Jose Canseco	2.00
8	Juan Gonzalez	5.00
9	Manny Ramirez	3.00

10	Andres Galarraga	1.50
11	Rafael Palmeiro	1.50
12	Alex Rodriguez	8.00
13	Mo Vaughn	1.50
14	Eric Chavez	2.50
15	Gabe Kapler	3.00
16	Calvin Pickering	1.00
17	Ruben Mateo	2.50
18	Roy Halladay	1.50
19	Jeremy Giambi	1.50
20	Alex Gonzalez	1.00
21	Ron Belliard	1.00
22	Marlon Anderson	1.00
23	Carlos Lee	1.00
24	Kerry Wood	2.50
25	Roger Clemens	4.00
26	Curt Schilling	1.00
27	Kevin Brown	1.50
28	Randy Johnson	1.50
29	Pedro Martinez	2.00
30	Orlando Hernandez	2.50

1999 Topps Chrome Early Road to the Hall

This insert set spotlights 10 players with less than 10 years in the Majors but are gunning towards their respective spots in Cooperstown. Utilizing Chromium technology featured players include Alex Rodriguez and Derek Jeter, with an insert rate of 1:12 packs. A Refractor parallel edition, numbered to 100 each, was a 1:944 hobby-pack insert.

		MT
Complete Set (10):		75.00
Common Player:		3.00
Inserted 1:12		
Refractors (#d to 100): 8X		
ER1	Nomar Garciaparra	12.00
ER2	Derek Jeter	12.00
ER3	Alex Rodriguez	15.00
ER4	Juan Gonzalez	10.00
ER5	Ken Griffey Jr.	20.00
ER6	Chipper Jones	12.00
ER7	Vladimir Guerrero	6.00
ER8	Jeff Bagwell	6.00
ER9	Ivan Rodriguez	5.00
ER10	Frank Thomas	8.00

1999 Topps Chrome Fortune 15

Fortune 15 showcases the baseball's best players and hot rookies. They are inserted in Series 2 packs at a rate of 1:12. A Refractor version also exists found exclusively in hobby packs at a rate of 1:627 packs. Refractors are sequentially numbered to 100.

		MT
Complete Set (15):		100.00
Common Player:		2.50
Inserted 1:12		
Refractors: 8X		
Production 100 sets H		
1	Alex Rodriguez	15.00
2	Nomar Garciaparra	10.00
3	Derek Jeter	10.00
4	Troy Glaus	5.00
5	Ken Griffey Jr.	20.00
6	Vladimir Guerrero	5.00
7	Kerry Wood	4.00
8	Eric Chavez	4.00
9	Greg Maddux	10.00
10	Mike Piazza	10.00
11	Sammy Sosa	10.00
12	Mark McGwire	20.00
13	Ben Grieve	4.00
14	Chipper Jones	10.00
15	Manny Ramirez	5.00

1999 Topps Chrome Home Run Heroes

These cards were part of an unannounced multi-manufacturer (Fleer, Upper Deck, Topps, Pacific) insert program which was exclusive to Wal-Mart. Each company produced cards of Mark McGwire and Sammy Sosa, along with two other premier sluggers. Each company's cards share a "Power Elite" logo at top and "Home Run Heroes" logo vertically at right.

		MT
Complete Set (4):		8.00
Common Player:		1.00
9	Mark McGwire	4.00
10	Sammy Sosa	2.50
11	Alex Rodriguez	2.50
12	Vladimir Guerrero	1.00

1999 Topps Chrome Lords of the Diamond

Parallel to the Topps version, the 15-card set features die-cutting across the card top and are seeded 1:8 in Series 1 packs. Refractor versions can be found 1:24 packs.

		MT
Complete Set (15):		60.00
Common Player:		1.00
Inserted 1:8		
Refractors: 2X		
Inserted 1:24		
LD1	Ken Griffey Jr.	12.00
LD2	Chipper Jones	6.00
LD3	Sammy Sosa	8.00
LD4	Frank Thomas	4.00
LD5	Mark McGwire	12.00
LD6	Jeff Bagwell	3.00
LD7	Alex Rodriguez	8.00
LD8	Juan Gonzalez	5.00
LD9	Barry Bonds	3.00
LD10	Nomar Garciaparra	6.00
LD11	Darin Erstad	2.50
LD12	Tony Gwynn	5.00
LD13	Andres Galarraga	1.00
LD14	Mike Piazza	6.00
LD15	Greg Maddux	6.00

1999 Topps Chrome New Breed

A parallel version of Topps New Breed utilizing Chromium technology. The 15-card set features the top young stars in the game and are seeded 1:24 packs. A Refractor version also exists which are found 1:72 packs.

		MT
Complete Set (15):		35.00
Common Player:		.50
Inserted 1:24		
Refractors: 1.5X		
Inserted 1:72		
NB1	Darin Erstad	2.50
NB2	Brad Fullmer	1.00
NB3	Kerry Wood	2.50
NB4	Nomar Garciaparra	6.00
NB5	Travis Lee	2.00
NB6	Scott Rolen	2.50
NB7	Todd Helton	1.00
NB8	Vladimir Guerrero	3.00
NB9	Derek Jeter	6.00
NB10	Alex Rodriguez	8.00
NB11	Ben Grieve	2.50
NB12	Andruw Jones	2.50
NB13	Paul Konerko	.50
NB14	Aramis Ramirez	.50
NB15	Adrian Beltre	.75

1999 Topps Chrome Record Numbers

This 10-card insert set salutes 10 record-setters who have earned a mark of distinction, including Cal Ripken Jr. for his record setting consecutive game streak. Inserted randomly in series II packs at a rate of 1:36 packs. Refractor parallel versions are seeded 1:144 packs.

		MT
Complete Set (10):		120.00
Common Player:		3.00
Inserted 1:36		
Refractors: 2X		
Inserted 1:144		
1	Mark McGwire	25.00
2	Craig Biggio	3.00
3	Barry Bonds	6.00
4	Ken Griffey Jr.	25.00
5	Sammy Sosa	15.00
6	Alex Rodriguez	20.00
7	Kerry Wood	6.00
8	Roger Clemens	9.00
9	Cal Ripken Jr.	20.50
10	Mark McGwire	25.00

1999 Topps Chrome Traded and Rookies

Actually issued in 2000, this parallel of the Topps Traded set utilizing Chromium technology was issued only in complete set form.

		MT
Complete Set (121):		125.00
Common Player:		.40
1	*Seth Etherton*	3.00
2	*Mark Harriger*	2.00
3	*Matt Wise*	2.00
4	*Carlos Hernandez*	2.00
5	*Julio Lugo*	2.50
6	*Mike Nannini*	3.00
7	*Justin Bowles*	1.50
8	*Mark Mulder*	6.00
9	*Roberto Vaz*	1.50
10	*Felipe Lopez*	6.00
11	*Matt Belisle*	3.00
12	Micah Bowie	.40
13	*Ruben Quevedo*	2.00
14	*Jose Garcia*	2.00
15	*David Kelton*	3.00
16	*Phillip Norton*	1.00
17	*Corey Patterson*	30.00
18	*Ron Walker*	2.00
19	*Paul Hoover*	4.00
20	*Ryan Rupe*	3.00
21	*J.D. Closser*	3.00
22	*Rob Ryan*	1.50
23	*Steve Colyer*	2.00
24	*Bubba Crosby*	2.00
25	*Luke Prokopec*	3.00
26	*Matt Blank*	2.00
27	*Josh McKinley*	3.00
28	*Nate Bump*	2.50
29	*Giuseppe Chiaramonte*	2.50
30	*Arturo McDowell*	2.00
31	*Tony Torcato*	2.00
32	Dave Roberts	.75
33	*C.C. Sabathia*	5.00
34	*Sean Spencer*	2.00
35	*Chip Ambres*	3.00
36	*A.J. Burnett*	6.00
37	*Mo Bruce*	2.00
38	*Jason Tyner*	1.50
39	*Mamon Tucker*	2.50
40	*Sean Burroughs*	15.00
41	*Kevin Eberwein*	1.00
42	*Junior Herndon*	1.00
43	*Bryan Wolff*	1.00
44	*Pat Burrell*	15.00
45	*Eric Valent*	6.00
46	*Carlos Pena*	3.00
47	*Mike Zywica*	2.00
48	*Adam Everett*	3.00
49	*Juan Pena*	1.50
50	*Adam Dunn*	8.00
51	*Austin Kearns*	4.00
52	*Jacobo Sequea*	1.00
53	*Choo Freeman*	2.00
54	*Jeff Winchester*	1.50
55	*Matt Burch*	2.00
56	*Chris George*	2.00
57	*Scott Mullen*	1.00
58	*Kit Pellow*	2.00
59	*Mark Quinn*	4.00
60	*Nate Cornejo*	2.00
61	*Ryan Mills*	4.00
62	*Kevin Beirne*	1.00
63	*Kip Wells*	6.00
64	*Juan Rivera*	1.50
65	*Alfonso Soriano*	20.00
66	*Josh Hamilton*	20.00
67	*Josh Girdley*	2.50
68	*Kyle Snyder*	4.00
69	*Mike Paradis*	2.50
70	*Jason Jennings*	2.50
71	*David Walling*	5.00
72	*Omar Ortiz*	1.00
73	*Jay Gehrke*	2.00
74	*Casey Burns*	1.00
75	*Carl Crawford*	3.00
76	Reggie Sanders	.40
77	Will Clark	.75
78	David Wells	.40
79	Paul Konerko	.40
80	Armando Benitez	.40
81	Brant Brown	.40
82	Mo Vaughn	.75
83	Jose Canseco	1.50
84	Albert Belle	.75
85	Dean Palmer	.40
86	Greg Vaughn	.50
87	Mark Clark	.40
88	Pat Meares	.40
89	Eric Davis	.40
90	Brian Giles	.40
91	Jeff Brantley	.40
92	Bret Boone	.40
93	Ron Gant	.40
94	Mike Cameron	.40
95	Charles Johnson	.40
96	Denny Neagle	.40
97	Brian Hunter	.40
98	Jose Hernandez	.40
99	Rick Aguilera	.40
100	Tony Batista	.40
101	Roger Cedeno	.40
102	Creighton Gubanich	.40
103	Tim Belcher	.40
104	Bruce Aven	.40
105	*Brian Daubach*	8.00
106	Ed Sprague	.40
107	Michael Tucker	.40
108	Homer Bush	.40
109	Armando Reynoso	.40
110	Brook Fordyce	.40
111	Matt Mantei	.40
112	Jose Guillen	.40
113	Kenny Rogers	.40
114	Livan Hernandez	.40
115	Butch Huskey	.40
116	David Segui	.40
117	Darryl Hamilton	.40
118	Jim Leyritz	.40
119	Randy Velarde	.40
120	Bill Taylor	.40
121	Kevin Appier	.40

1999 Topps Super Chrome

Using identical photos from Topps Chrome Baseball, Topps supersized 36 players to 4-1/8" x 5-3/4" card size. The cards are done on standard chromium technology. Each pack contains three oversized cards and sells for S.R.P. of $4.99. There also is a Refractor parallel set, which are seeded 1:12 packs.

		MT
Complete Set (36):		50.00
Common Player:		.50
Refractors: 4X		
Inserted 1:12		
1	Roger Clemens	2.00
2	Andres Galarraga	.75
3	Manny Ramirez	1.50
4	Greg Maddux	3.00
5	Kerry Wood	1.50
6	Travis Lee	1.00
7	Nolan Ryan	5.00
8	Juan Gonzalez	2.50
9	Vladimir Guerrero	1.50
10	Sammy Sosa	3.00
11	Mark McGwire	6.00
12	Javy Lopez	.50
13	Tony Gwynn	2.50
14	Derek Jeter	3.00
15	Albert Belle	1.00
16	Pedro Martinez	1.00
17	Greg Vaughn	.50
18	Ken Griffey Jr.	6.00
19	Ben Grieve	1.25
20	Vinny Castilla	.50
21	Moises Alou	.50
22	Barry Bonds	1.25
23	Nomar Garciaparra	3.00
24	Chipper Jones	3.00
25	Mike Piazza	3.00
26	Alex Rodriguez	5.00
27	Ivan Rodriguez	1.25
28	Frank Thomas	3.00
29	Larry Walker	1.00
30	Troy Glaus	1.25
31	David Wells (Season Highlight)	.50
32	Roger Clemens (Season Highlight)	1.50
33	Kerry Wood (Season Highlight)	.75
34	Mark McGwire (Home Run Record)	8.00
35	Sammy Sosa (Home Run Parade)	4.00
36	World Series	.50

1999 Topps Gallery Pre-Production

Topps debuted its 1999 Gallery set with this trio of sample cards. Format is virtually identical to issued cards except for the use of a "PP" prefix to the card numbers on back.

		MT
Complete Set (3):		7.50
Common Player:		3.00
PP1	Scott Rolen	3.00
PP2	Andres Galarraga (Masters)	3.00
PP3	Brad Fullmer (Artisans)	3.00

1999 Topps Gallery

This 150-card base set features a white textured border surrounding the player image with the player's name, team name and Topps Gallery logo stamped with gold foil. The first 100 cards in the set portray veteran players while the next 50 cards are broken down into three subsets: Masters, Artisans and Apprentices. Card backs have a monthly batting or pitching record from the '98 season, one player photo and vital information.

		MT
Complete Set (150):		120.00
Common Player (1-100):		.20
Common Player (101-150):		.50
Wax Box:		140.00
1	Mark McGwire	4.00
2	Jim Thome	.75
3	Bernie Williams	.75
4	Larry Walker	.75
5	Juan Gonzalez	1.00
6	Ken Griffey Jr.	4.00
7	Raul Mondesi	.40
8	Sammy Sosa	2.50
9	Greg Maddux	2.00
10	Jeff Bagwell	1.00
11	Vladimir Guerrero	1.50
12	Scott Rolen	1.00
13	Nomar Garciaparra	2.50
14	Mike Piazza	2.50
15	Travis Lee	.40
16	Carlos Delgado	.75
17	Darin Erstad	.40
18	David Justice	.40
19	Cal Ripken Jr.	2.50
20	Derek Jeter	2.50
21	Tony Clark	.40
22	Barry Larkin	.50
23	Greg Vaughn	.40
24	Jeff Kent	.20
25	Wade Boggs	.50
26	Andres Galarraga	.50
27	Ken Caminiti	.30
28	Jason Kendall	.40
29	Todd Helton	.50
30	Chuck Knoblauch	.50
31	Roger Clemens	1.50
32	Jeromy Burnitz	.20
33	Javy Lopez	.20
34	Roberto Alomar	.75
35	Eric Karros	.30
36	Ben Grieve	.50
37	Eric Davis	.30
38	Rondell White	.40
39	Dmitri Young	.20
40	Ivan Rodriguez	1.25
41	Paul O'Neill	.50
42	Jeff Cirillo	.20
43	Kerry Wood	.50
44	Albert Belle	1.00
45	Frank Thomas	1.00
46	Manny Ramirez	1.00
47	Tom Glavine	.40
48	Mo Vaughn	.75
49	Jose Cruz Jr.	.25
50	Sandy Alomar	.20
51	Edgar Martinez	.20
52	John Olerud	.40
53	Todd Walker	.20
54	Tim Salmon	.40
55	Derek Bell	.20
56	Matt Williams	.50
57	Alex Rodriguez	2.50
58	Rusty Greer	.20
59	Vinny Castilla	.40
60	Jason Giambi	.20
61	Mark Grace	.40
62	Jose Canseco	1.00
63	Gary Sheffield	.40
64	Brad Fullmer	.20
65	Trevor Hoffman	.20
66	Mark Kotsay	.20
67	Mike Mussina	.75
68	Johnny Damon	.20
69	Tino Martinez	.75
70	Curt Schilling	.40
71	Jay Buhner	.40
72	Kenny Lofton	.75
73	Randy Johnson	.75
74	Kevin Brown	.50
75	Brian Jordan	.20
76	Craig Biggio	.75
77	Barry Bonds	1.00
78	Tony Gwynn	2.00
79	Jim Edmonds	.20
80	Shawn Green	.75
81	Todd Hundley	.20
82	Cliff Floyd	.20
83	Jose Guillen	.20
84	Dante Bichette	.40
85	Moises Alou	.40
86	Chipper Jones	2.50
87	Ray Lankford	.20
88	Fred McGriff	.40
89	Rod Beck	.20
90	Dean Palmer	.30
91	Pedro Martinez	1.00
92	Andruw Jones	.75
93	Robin Ventura	.40
94	Ugueth Urbina	.20
95	Orlando Hernandez	.50
96	Sean Casey	.75
97	Denny Neagle	.20
98	Troy Glaus	.75
99	John Smoltz	.30
100	Al Leiter	.30
101	Ken Griffey Jr.	6.00
102	Frank Thomas	1.50
103	Mark McGwire	6.00
104	Sammy Sosa	4.00
105	Chipper Jones	4.00
106	Alex Rodriguez	4.00
107	Nomar Garciaparra	4.00
108	Juan Gonzalez	1.50
109	Derek Jeter	4.00
110	Mike Piazza	4.00
111	Barry Bonds	1.50
112	Tony Gwynn	3.00
113	Cal Ripken Jr.	4.00
114	Greg Maddux	3.00
115	Roger Clemens	2.00
116	Brad Fullmer	.50
117	Kerry Wood	1.00
118	Ben Grieve	1.00
119	Todd Helton	.75
120	Kevin Millwood	.50
121	Sean Casey	1.00
122	Vladimir Guerrero	2.00
123	Travis Lee	.50
124	Troy Glaus	.75
125	Bartolo Colon	.50
126	Andruw Jones	1.00
127	Scott Rolen	1.50
128	*Alfonso Soriano*	10.00
129	*Nick Johnson*	8.00
130	*Matt Belisle*	1.00
131	*Jorge Toca*	3.00
132	*Masao Kida*	.50
133	*Carlos Pena*	2.50
134	Adrian Beltre	.50
135	Eric Chavez	.50
136	Carlos Beltran	1.50
137	Alex Gonzalez	.50
138	Ryan Anderson	.50
139	Ruben Mateo	1.50
140	Bruce Chen	.50
141	*Pat Burrell*	10.00
142	Michael Barrett	.50
143	Carlos Lee	.50
144	*Mark Mulder*	2.50
145	*Choo Freeman*	2.00
146	Gabe Kapler	.50
147	Juan Encarnacion	.50
148	Jeremy Giambi	.50
149	*Jason Tyner*	1.50
150	George Lombard	.50
	Checklist folder 1 (1:3 packs)	.10
	Checklist folder 2 (1:3)	.10
	Checklist folder 3 (1:3)	.10
	Checklist folder 4 (1:12)	.25
	Checklist folder 5 (1:240)	3.00
	Checklist folder 6 (1:640)	6.00

1999 Topps Gallery Player's Private Issue

This parallel to the 150 regular cards in 1999 Gallery is limited to 250 serially numbered cards of each. Stated odds of insertion were one per 17 packs.

	MT
Common Player:	3.00
Stars: 10X	
SPs (101-127): 6X	
SP rookies (128-150): 3X	
Production 250 sets	

(See 1999 Topps Gallery for checklist and base card values.)

1999 Topps Gallery Autograph Cards

Three of baseball's top young third baseman are featured in this autographed set, Eric Chavez, Troy Glaus and Adrian Beltre. The insertion odds are 1:209.

		MT
Complete Set (3):		55.00
Common Player:		40.00
Inserted 1:209		
GA1	Troy Glaus	25.00
GA2	Adrian Beltre	20.00
GA3	Eric Chavez	15.00

1999 Topps Gallery Awards Gallery

This 10-card set features players who have earned the highest honors in baseball. Each insert commemorates the player's award by stamping his achievement on the bottom of the card front. Card fronts have silver borders surrounding the player's image. These are seeded 1:12 and card numbers have an "AG" prefix.

		MT
Complete Set (10):		50.00
Common Player:		2.00
Inserted 1:12		
AG1	Kerry Wood	3.00
AG2	Ben Grieve	3.00
AG3	Roger Clemens	5.00
AG4	Tom Glavine	2.00
AG5	Juan Gonzalez	4.00
AG6	Sammy Sosa	10.00
AG7	Ken Griffey Jr.	15.00
AG8	Mark McGwire	15.00
AG9	Bernie Williams	2.00
AG10	Larry Walker	3.00

1999 Topps Gallery Exhibitions

This 20-card set is done on textured 24-point stock and features baseball's top stars. Exhibitions are seeded 1:48 packs.

		MT
Complete Set (20):		200.00
Common Player:		3.50
Inserted 1:48		
E1	Sammy Sosa	18.00
E2	Mark McGwire	25.00
E3	Greg Maddux	12.50
E4	Roger Clemens	10.00
E5	Ben Grieve	5.00
E6	Kerry Wood	5.00
E7	Ken Griffey Jr.	25.00
E8	Tony Gwynn	12.50
E9	Cal Ripken Jr.	18.00
E10	Frank Thomas	8.00
E11	Jeff Bagwell	7.50
E12	Derek Jeter	15.00
E13	Alex Rodriguez	18.00
E14	Nomar Garciaparra	15.00
E15	Manny Ramirez	6.00
E16	Vladimir Guerrero	10.00
E17	Darin Erstad	3.50
E18	Scott Rolen	6.00
E19	Mike Piazza	15.00
E20	Andres Galarraga	3.50

1999 Topps Gallery Gallery of Heroes

This 10-card set is done on card stock that simulates medieval stained glass. Gallery of Heroes are found 1:24 packs.

		MT
Complete Set (10):		90.00
Common Player:		3.00
Inserted 1:24		
GH1	Mark McGwire	20.00
GH2	Sammy Sosa	12.00
GH3	Ken Griffey Jr.	20.00
GH4	Mike Piazza	12.00
GH5	Derek Jeter	12.00
GH6	Nomar Garciaparra	12.00
GH7	Kerry Wood	3.00
GH8	Ben Grieve	3.00
GH9	Chipper Jones	12.00
GH10	Alex Rodriguez	15.00

1999 Topps Gallery Heritage

Nineteen contemporary legends and Hall of Famer Hank Aaron are artistically depicted using the 1953 Topps design as a template. For a chance to bid on the original art used in the development of this insert set, collectors were able to enter the Topps Gallery Auction. Collectors could accumulate auction points found in Topps Gallery packs. Heritages are seeded 1:12 packs. A parallel called Heritage Proofs are also randomly inserted 1:48 packs and have a chrome styrene finish.

		MT
Complete Set (20):		400.00
Common Player:		8.00
Inserted 1:12		
Heritage Proofs: 2X		
Inserted 1:48		
TH1	Hank Aaron	40.00
TH2	Ben Grieve	10.00
TH3	Nomar Garciaparra	30.00
TH4	Roger Clemens	15.00
TH5	Travis Lee	8.00
TH6	Tony Gwynn	25.00
TH7	Alex Rodriguez	35.00
TH8	Ken Griffey Jr.	50.00
TH9	Derek Jeter	30.00
TH10	Sammy Sosa	30.00
TH11	Scott Rolen	10.00
TH12	Chipper Jones	25.00
TH13	Cal Ripken Jr.	40.00
TH14	Kerry Wood	10.00
TH15	Barry Bonds	12.00
TH16	Juan Gonzalez	15.00
TH17	Mike Piazza	30.00
TH18	Greg Maddux	25.00
TH19	Frank Thomas	15.00
TH20	Mark McGwire	50.00

1999 Topps Gallery Heritage Proofs

Heritage Proofs are a parallel to the 1953-style inserts. Printed on chrome styrene, the proofs have a silver metallic background on front and the notation on bottom-back, "1953 TOPPS HERITAGE PROOF". The proof versions are found on average of one per 48 packs.

		MT
Complete Set (20):		750.00
Common Player:		12.00
TH1	Hank Aaron	50.00
TH2	Ben Grieve	20.00
TH3	Nomar Garciaparra	40.00
TH4	Roger Clemens	30.00
TH5	Travis Lee	12.00
TH6	Tony Gwynn	40.00
TH7	Alex Rodriguez	60.00
TH8	Ken Griffey Jr.	100.00
TH9	Derek Jeter	40.00
TH10	Sammy Sosa	40.00
TH11	Scott Rolen	20.00
TH12	Chipper Jones	60.00
TH13	Cal Ripken Jr.	60.00
TH14	Kerry Wood	20.00
TH15	Barry Bonds	30.00
TH16	Juan Gonzalez	30.00
TH17	Mike Piazza	40.00
TH18	Greg Maddux	40.00
TH19	Frank Thomas	30.00
TH20	Mark McGwire	100.00

Checklists with card numbers in parentheses ( ) indicates the numbers do not appear on the card.

1999 Topps Gallery Heritage Lithographs

Eight of the paintings used to create the Heritage inserts for 1999 Topps Gallery were reproduced as enlarged limited-edition offset lithographs. The paintings of Bill Purdom and James Fiorentino were reproduced in an 18" x 25" serially-numbered, artist-signed edition of 600 pieces each. The lithos were offered through Bill Goff Inc / Good Sports at $60 each unframed.

		MT
Complete Set (8):		480.00
Single Player:		60.00
(1)	Roger Clemens	60.00
(2)	Nomar Garciaparra	60.00
(3)	Ken Griffey Jr.	60.00
(4)	Derek Jeter	60.00
(5)	Mark McGwire	60.00
(6)	Mike Piazza	60.00
(7)	Cal Ripken Jr.	60.00
(8)	Sammy Sosa	60.00

1999 Topps Gallery Press Plates

The aluminum press plates used to print the Gallery cards were inserted at a rate of one per 985 packs. Each card's front and back can be found in four different color variations. Because of the unique nature of each plate, assignment of catalog values in not feasible.

(See 1999 Topps Gallery for checklist.)

1999 Topps Gold Label Pre-Production

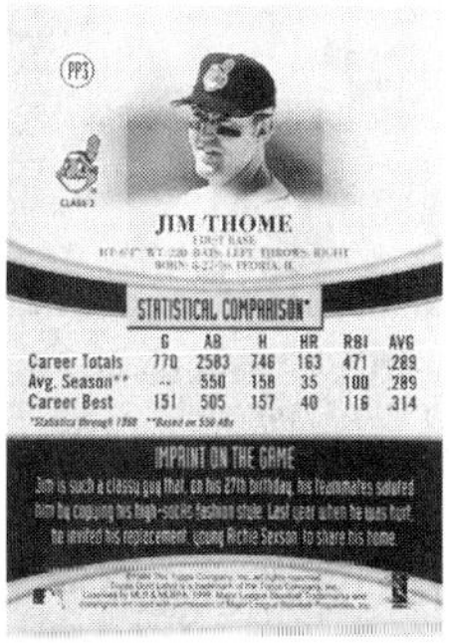

This trio of pre-production samples previews Topps' 1999 version of its high-end Gold Label brand. Cards are nearly identical in format to the issued version except for the "PP" prefix to card numbers on back.

		MT
Complete Set (3):		9.00
Common Player:		3.00
PP1	Tom Glavine	5.00
PP2	Tino Martinez	3.00
PP3	Jim Thome	3.00

1999 Topps Gold Label Class 1

This set consists of 100 cards on 35-point spectral-reflective rainbow stock with gold foil stamping. All cards are available in three versions each with the same foreground photo, but with different background photos that vary by category: Class 1 (fielding), Class 2 (running, 1:2), Class 3 (hitting, 1:4). In addition each variation has a different version of the player's team logo in the background. Variations for pitchers are Class 1, set position; Class 2, wind-up, and Class 3, throwing. Black Label parallels were inserted at the rate of between 1:8 and 1:12, depending on packaging. Red Label parallels, serially numbered to 100 each were inserted at rates from 1:118 to 1:148. A One to One parallel version also exists and is limited to one numbered card for each variation and color (Gold, Black and Red), for a total of 900 cards inserted about one per 1,500 packs.

		MT
Complete Gold Label Set (100):		60.00
Common Gold Label:		.25
Common Black Label:		.50
Black Label Stars: 2X		
Common Red Label:		4.00
Red Label Stars: 15X		
Wax Box:		125.00
1	Mike Piazza	3.00
2	Andres Galarraga	.75
3	Mark Grace	.40
4	Tony Clark	.40
5	Jim Thome	.75
6	Tony Gwynn	2.50
7	*Kelly Dransfeldt*	.50
8	Eric Chavez	.40
9	Brian Jordan	.25
10	Todd Hundley	.25
11	Rondell White	.40
12	Dmitri Young	.25
13	Jeff Kent	.25
14	Derek Bell	.25
15	Todd Helton	.75
16	Chipper Jones	2.50
17	Albert Belle	1.00
18	Barry Larkin	.50
19	Dante Bichette	.40
20	Gary Sheffield	.40
21	Cliff Floyd	.25
22	Derek Jeter	3.00
23	Jason Giambi	.25
24	Ray Lankford	.25
25	Alex Rodriguez	3.00
26	Ruben Mateo	.50
27	Wade Boggs	.50
28	Carlos Delgado	1.00
29	Tim Salmon	.40
30	*Alfonso Soriano*	4.00
31	Javy Lopez	.25
32	Jason Kendall	.40
33	*Nick Johnson*	4.00
34	*A.J. Burnett*	.75
35	Troy Glaus	1.00
36	*Pat Burrell*	5.00
37	Jeff Cirillo	.25
38	David Justice	.40
39	Ivan Rodriguez	1.25
40	Bernie Williams	1.00
41	Jay Buhner	.40
42	Mo Vaughn	1.00
43	Randy Johnson	1.00
44	Pedro Martinez	1.25
45	Larry Walker	.75
46	Todd Walker	.25
47	Roberto Alomar	1.00
48	Kevin Brown	.40
49	Mike Mussina	1.00
50	Tom Glavine	.40
51	Curt Schilling	.40
52	Ken Caminiti	.40
53	Brad Fullmer	.25
54	*Bobby Seay*	.50
55	Orlando Hernandez	.75
56	Sean Casey	.50
57	Al Leiter	.25
58	Sandy Alomar	.25
59	Mark Kotsay	.25
60	Matt Williams	.50
61	Raul Mondesi	.40
62	*Joe Crede*	.50
63	Jim Edmonds	.25
64	Jose Cruz Jr.	.25
65	Juan Gonzalez	1.50
66	Sammy Sosa	3.00
67	Cal Ripken Jr.	4.00
68	Vinny Castilla	.40
69	Craig Biggio	.75
70	Mark McGwire	5.00
71	Greg Vaughn	.40
72	Greg Maddux	2.50
73	Paul O'Neill	.40
74	Scott Rolen	1.25
75	Ben Grieve	.50
76	Vladimir Guerrero	1.50
77	John Olerud	.40
78	Eric Karros	.25
79	Jeromy Burnitz	.25
80	Jeff Bagwell	1.25
81	Kenny Lofton	1.00
82	Manny Ramirez	1.50
83	Andruw Jones	.75
84	Travis Lee	.40
85	Darin Erstad	.40
86	Nomar Garciaparra	3.00
87	Frank Thomas	1.25
88	Moises Alou	.40
89	Tino Martinez	.50
90	*Carlos Pena*	1.00
91	Shawn Green	1.00
92	Rusty Greer	.25
93	*Matt Belisle*	.50
94	Adrian Beltre	.40
95	Roger Clemens	1.50
96	John Smoltz	.40
97	*Mark Mulder*	1.00
98	Kerry Wood	.75
99	Barry Bonds	1.25
100	Ken Griffey Jr.	5.00
	Checklist folder	.05

1999 Topps Gold Label Class 2

Background photos for Class 2 Gold Label and color parallels show position players running and pitchers in their windup. Class 2 Gold Label cards are inserted at the rate of one in two Home Team Advantage packs, and one in four retail packs. Black Label versions are inserted 1:16 HTA and 1:24 R. Red Labels, numbered to 50 each, are found in HTA at a 1:237 rate, and in retail at 1:296.

	MT
Complete Gold Label Set (100):	150.00
Common Gold Label:	.50
Gold Label Stars: 2X	
Common Black Label:	2.00
Black Label Stars: 4X	
Common Red Label:	6.00
Red Label Stars: 24X	

(See 1999 Topps Gold Label Class 1 for checklist and base card values.)

1999 Topps Gold Label Class 3

Background photos for Class 3 Gold Label and color parallels show position players hitting and pitchers pitching. Class 3 Gold Label cards are inserted at the rate of one in four Home Team Advantage packs, and one in eight retail packs. Black Label versions are inserted 1:32 HTA and 1:48 R. Red Labels, numbered to 25 each, are found in HTA at a 1:473 rate, and in retail at 1:591.

	MT
Complete Gold Label Set (100):	250.00
Common Gold Label:	.75
Gold Label Stars: 3X	
Common Black Label:	3.00
Black Label Stars: 8X	
Common Red Label:	12.00
Red Label Stars: 35X	

(See 1999 Topps Gold Label Class 1 for checklist and base card values.)

1999 Topps Gold Label Race to Aaron

This 10-card set features the best current players who are chasing Hank Aaron's career home run and career RBI records. Each player is pictured in the foreground with Aaron silhouetted in the background on the card front. These are seeded 1:12 packs. Two parallel versions also exist: Black and Red. Blacks have black foil stamping and are seeded 1:48 packs. Reds have red foil stamping and are limited to 44 sequentially numbered sets.

		MT
Complete Set (10):		90.00
Common Player:		3.00
Blacks: 2X		
Reds: 12X		
1	Mark McGwire	20.00
2	Ken Griffey Jr.	20.00
3	Alex Rodriguez	15.00
4	Vladimir Guerrero	8.00
5	Albert Belle	3.00
6	Nomar Garciaparra	12.00
7	Ken Griffey Jr.	20.00
8	Alex Rodriguez	15.00
9	Juan Gonzalez	4.00
10	Barry Bonds	4.00

1999 Topps Gold Label One to One

Depending on type of packaging, these rare parallels are found at the rate of only one per approximately 1,200-1,600 packs. Each of the three Classes in Gold, Red and Black versions can be found as a One to One insert, for a total of nine "unique" cards for each player in the base set and three in the Race to Aaron insert series. Backs of the One to One cards are printed in silver foil with a "1/1" foil serial number.

	MT
Common Player, Base Set:	50.00
Common Player, Race to Aaron:	150.00

(Star/rookie card values cannot be determined due to scarcity.)

1999 Topps Stars Pre-Production

Five-card cello packs of pre-production samples were distributed to introduce Topps' new concept for its Stars brand. The samples follow the format of the issued versions except for the use of a "PP" prefix to the card number on back.

		MT
Complete Set (5):		12.00
Common Player:		2.50
PP1	Paul O'Neill (base card)	2.00
PP2	Vinny Castilla (one-star)	2.00
PP3	Darin Erstad (two-star)	3.00
PP4	Kerry Wood (three-star)	2.50
PP5	Chipper Jones (four-star)	4.00

1999 Topps Stars

Topps Stars consists of 180 cards, on 20-point stock with foil stamping and metallic inks. Within the base set there are 150 base cards and 30 subset cards, Luminaries and Supernovas. Packs contain six cards; three base cards, two One-Star cards and one Two-Star card on the average.

		MT
Complete Set (180):		90.00
Common Player:		.25
Wax Box:		43.00
1	Ken Griffey Jr.	5.00
2	Chipper Jones	2.50
3	Mike Piazza	2.50
4	Nomar Garciaparra	2.50
5	Derek Jeter	2.50
6	Frank Thomas	1.00
7	Ben Grieve	.75
8	Mark McGwire	5.00
9	Sammy Sosa	2.50
10	Alex Rodriguez	3.75
11	Troy Glaus	.75
12	Eric Chavez	.50
13	Kerry Wood	.50

14 Barry Bonds 1.00
15 Vladimir Guerrero 1.50
16 Albert Belle .75
17 Juan Gonzalez 1.00
18 Roger Clemens 1.50
19 Ruben Mateo .75
20 Cal Ripken Jr. 3.75
21 Darin Erstad .40
22 Jeff Bagwell 1.00
23 Roy Halladay .25
24 Todd Helton .75
25 Michael Barrett .25
26 Manny Ramirez 1.00
27 Fernando Seguignol .25
28 *Pat Burrell* 4.00
29 Andruw Jones .75
30 Randy Johnson .60
31 Jose Canseco .60
32 Brad Fullmer .25
33 *Alex Escobar* 1.25
34 *Alfonso Soriano* 4.00
35 Larry Walker .60
36 Matt Clement .25
37 Mo Vaughn .50
38 Bruce Chen .25
39 Travis Lee .40
40 Adrian Beltre .40
41 Alex Gonzalez .25
42 *Jason Tyner* .50
43 George Lombard .25
44 Scott Rolen 1.00
45 *Mark Mulder* 1.25
46 Gabe Kapler 1.00
47 *Choo Freeman* .60
48 Tony Gwynn 2.00
49 *A.J. Burnett* 1.00
50 *Matt Belisle* .40
51 Greg Maddux 2.00
52 John Smoltz .25
53 Mark Grace .40
54 Wade Boggs .40
55 Bernie Williams .50
56 Pedro Martinez 1.00
57 Barry Larkin .50
58 Orlando Hernandez .40
59 Jason Kendall .25
60 Mark Kotsay .25
61 Jim Thome .50
62 Gary Sheffield .25
63 Preston Wilson .25
64 Rafael Palmeiro .60
65 David Wells .25
66 Shawn Green .75
67 Tom Glavine .25
68 Jeromy Burnitz .25
69 Kevin Brown .40
70 Rondell White .40
71 Roberto Alomar .60
72 Cliff Floyd .25
73 Craig Biggio .60
74 Greg Vaughn .25
75 Ivan Rodriguez 1.00
76 Vinny Castilla .25
77 Todd Walker .25
78 Paul Konerko .25
79 *Andy Brown* .40
80 Todd Hundley .25
81 Dmitri Young .25
82 Tony Clark .50
83 *Nick Johnson* 2.50
84 Mike Caruso .25
85 David Ortiz .25
86 Matt Williams .50
87 Raul Mondesi .25
88 Kenny Lofton .50
89 Miguel Tejada .25
90 Dante Bichette .40
91 Jorge Posada .25
92 Carlos Beltran 1.50
93 Carlos Delgado .50
94 Javy Lopez .25
95 Aramis Ramirez .25
96 Neifi Perez .25
97 Marlon Anderson .25
98 David Cone .25
99 Moises Alou .25
100 John Olerud .40
101 Tim Salmon .25
102 Jason Giambi .25
103 Sandy Alomar .25
104 Curt Schilling .25
105 Andres Galarraga .50
106 Rusty Greer .25
107 *Bobby Seay* .40
108 Eric Young .25
109 Brian Jordan .25
110 Eric Davis .25
111 Will Clark .40
112 Andy Ashby .25
113 Edgardo Alfonzo .50
114 Paul O'Neill .25
115 Denny Neagle .25
116 Eric Karros .25
117 Ken Caminiti .25
118 Garret Anderson .25
119 Todd Stottlemyre .25
120 David Justice .25
121 Francisco Cordova .25
122 Robin Ventura .25
123 Mike Mussina .50
124 Hideki Irabu .25
125 Justin Thompson .25
126 Mariano Rivera .25
127 Delino DeShields .25
128 Steve Finley .25
129 Jose Cruz Jr. .25
130 Ray Lankford .25
131 Jim Edmonds .25
132 Charles Johnson .25
133 Al Leiter .25
134 Jose Offerman .25
135 Eric Milton .25
136 Dean Palmer .25
137 Johnny Damon .25
138 Andy Pettitte .25
139 Ray Durham .25
140 Ugueth Urbina .25
141 Marquis Grissom .25
142 Ryan Klesko .25
143 Brady Anderson .25
144 Bobby Higginson .25
145 Chuck Knoblauch .40
146 Rickey Henderson .40
147 Kevin Millwood .40
148 Fred McGriff .25
149 Damion Easley .25
150 Tino Martinez .25
151 Greg Maddux (Luminaries) 1.00
152 Scott Rolen (Luminaries) .50
153 Pat Burrell (Luminaries) 2.00
154 Roger Clemens (Luminaries) .60
155 Albert Belle (Luminaries) .40
156 Troy Glaus (Luminaries) .50
157 Cal Ripken Jr. (Luminaries) 2.00
158 Alfonso Soriano (Luminaries) 2.00
159 Manny Ramirez (Luminaries) .50
160 Eric Chavez (Luminaries) .25
161 Kerry Wood (Luminaries) .25
162 Tony Gwynn (Luminaries) 1.00
163 Barry Bonds (Luminaries) .50
164 Ruben Mateo (Luminaries) .40
165 Todd Helton (Luminaries) .25
166 Darin Erstad (Luminaries) .25
167 Jeff Bagwell (Luminaries) .50
168 Juan Gonzalez (Luminaries) .50
169 Mo Vaughn (Luminaries) .25
170 Vladimir Guerrero (Luminaries) .60
171 Nomar Garciaparra (Supernovas) 1.25
172 Derek Jeter (Supernovas) 1.25
173 Alex Rodriguez (Supernovas) 1.50
174 Ben Grieve (Supernovas) .25
175 Mike Piazza (Supernovas) 1.25
176 Chipper Jones (Supernovas) 1.25
177 Frank Thomas (Supernovas) .50
178 Ken Griffey Jr. (Supernovas) 2.00
179 Sammy Sosa (Supernovas) 1.50
180 Mark McGwire (Supernovas) 2.50

Checklist 1 (1-45) .05
Checklist 2 (46-136) .05
Checklist 3 (137-150, inserts) .05

1999 Topps Stars Foil

Metallic foil in the background and a serial number on back from within a specific edition identifies this parallel. Stated odds of insertion were one in 15 packs for parallels of the 180 base cards, numbered to 299 each. One-Star foil parallels are numbered to 249 and inserted 1:33. The Two-Star Foils are numbered to 199 each and found on average of one per 82 packs. With insertion odds of 1:410, the Three-Star Foil parallels are numbered within an edition of 99. At the top of the scarcity scale, the Foil Four-Star parallels are sequentially numbered to 49 and are a one per 650-pack find.

MT
Complete Base Set (180): 125.00
Common Foil Player: .25
Foil Stars: 4X
One-Star Foils: 10X
Two-Star Foils: 12X
Three-Star Foils: 15X
Four-Star Foils: 25X
(Stars/rookies valued about 3-8X base card values.)

1999 Topps Stars One-Star

One-Star inserts include card numbers 1-100 from the base set and have silver foil stamping with one star on the bottom left portion of the card front. These are seeded two per pack. A foil One-Star parallel also is randomly seeded and sequentially numbered to 249 sets. These are a 1:33 pack insert.

MT
Complete Set (100): 40.00
Common Player: .25
Foils (249 each): 10X
1 Ken Griffey Jr. 4.00
2 Chipper Jones 2.00
3 Mike Piazza 2.50
4 Nomar Garciaparra 2.50
5 Derek Jeter 2.50
6 Frank Thomas 1.50
7 Ben Grieve .75
8 Mark McGwire 5.00
9 Sammy Sosa 2.50
10 Alex Rodriguez 2.50
11 Troy Glaus 1.00
12 Eric Chavez .50
13 Kerry Wood .50
14 Barry Bonds 1.00
15 Vladimir Guerrero 1.50
16 Albert Belle .75
17 Juan Gonzalez 2.00
18 Roger Clemens 1.50
19 Ruben Mateo .75
20 Cal Ripken Jr. 3.00
21 Darin Erstad .75
22 Jeff Bagwell 1.00
23 Roy Halladay .25
24 Todd Helton .75
25 Michael Barrett .25
26 Manny Ramirez 1.00
27 Fernando Seguignol .25
28 Pat Burrell 4.00
29 Andruw Jones .75
30 Randy Johnson .75
31 Jose Canseco .75
32 Brad Fullmer .25
33 Alex Escobar 2.00
34 Alfonso Soriano 4.00
35 Larry Walker .75
36 Matt Clement .25
37 Mo Vaughn .75
38 Bruce Chen .25
39 Travis Lee .60
40 Adrian Beltre .50
41 Alex Gonzalez .25
42 Jason Tyner .60
43 George Lombard .25
44 Scott Rolen 1.00
45 Mark Mulder 2.00
46 Gabe Kapler 1.00
47 Choo Freeman .50
48 Tony Gwynn 2.00
49 A.J. Burnett 1.00
50 Matt Belisle .75
51 Greg Maddux 2.50
52 John Smoltz .25
53 Mark Grace .40
54 Wade Boggs .40
55 Bernie Williams .75
56 Pedro Martinez 1.00
57 Barry Larkin .40
58 Orlando Hernandez .40
59 Jason Kendall .25
60 Mark Kotsay .25
61 Jim Thome .60
62 Gary Sheffield .40
63 Preston Wilson .25
64 Rafael Palmeiro .75
65 David Wells .25
66 Shawn Green .60
67 Tom Glavine .25
68 Jeromy Burnitz .25
69 Kevin Brown .40
70 Rondell White .40
71 Roberto Alomar .75
72 Cliff Floyd .25
73 Craig Biggio .60
74 Greg Vaughn .40
75 Ivan Rodriguez 1.00
76 Vinny Castilla .25
77 Todd Walker .25
78 Paul Konerko .25
79 *Andy Brown* .50
80 Todd Hundley .25
81 Dmitri Young .25
82 Tony Clark .50
83 *Nick Johnson* 2.00
84 Mike Caruso .25
85 David Ortiz .25
86 Matt Williams .50
87 Raul Mondesi .40
88 Kenny Lofton .75
89 Miguel Tejada .25
90 Dante Bichette .40
91 Jorge Posada .40
92 Carlos Beltran 1.00
93 Carlos Delgado .75
94 Javy Lopez .25
95 Aramis Ramirez .25
96 Neifi Perez .25
97 Marlon Anderson .25
98 David Cone .25
99 Moises Alou .25
100 John Olerud .40

1999 Topps Stars Two-Star

Two-Stars are inserted one per pack and feature light gold metallic inks and foil stamping. Two-Stars include card numbers 1-50 from the base set. A Two-Star parallel is also randomly seeded and limited to 199 sequentially numbered sets.

MT
Complete Set (50): 30.00
Common Player: .25
Foils: 12X
1 Ken Griffey Jr. 4.00
2 Chipper Jones 2.00
3 Mike Piazza 2.50
4 Nomar Garciaparra 2.50
5 Derek Jeter 2.50
6 Frank Thomas 1.50
7 Ben Grieve .75
8 Mark McGwire 5.00
9 Sammy Sosa 2.50
10 Alex Rodriguez 2.50
11 Troy Glaus 1.00
12 Eric Chavez .60
13 Kerry Wood .50
14 Barry Bonds 1.00
15 Vladimir Guerrero 1.50
16 Albert Belle .75
17 Juan Gonzalez 2.00
18 Roger Clemens 1.50
19 Ruben Mateo .75
20 Cal Ripken Jr. 3.00
21 Darin Erstad .75
22 Jeff Bagwell 1.00
23 Roy Halladay .25
24 Todd Helton .75
25 Michael Barrett .25
26 Manny Ramirez 1.00
27 Fernando Seguignol .25
28 Pat Burrell 3.00
29 Andruw Jones .75
30 Randy Johnson .75
31 Jose Canseco .75
32 Brad Fullmer .25
33 Alex Escobar 2.00
34 Alfonso Soriano 4.00
35 Larry Walker .75
36 Matt Clement .25
37 Mo Vaughn .75
38 Bruce Chen .25
39 Travis Lee .50
40 Adrian Beltre .40
41 Alex Gonzalez .25
42 Jason Tyner .50
43 George Lombard .25
44 Scott Rolen 1.00
45 Mark Mulder 2.00
46 Gabe Kapler 1.00
47 Choo Freeman .50
48 Tony Gwynn 2.00
49 A.J. Burnett 1.00
50 Matt Belisle .75

1999 Topps Stars Three-Star

Three-Star inserts are a partial parallel from the base set including cards 1-20. Inserted 1:5 packs, these cards feature refractive silver foil stamping along with gold metallic inks. A Three-Star parallel also is randomly inserted featuring gold stamping and limited to 99 serial numbered sets, inserted one per 410 packs.

MT
Complete Set (20): 60.00
Common Player: 1.00
Foils (99 each): 15X
1 Ken Griffey Jr. 8.00
2 Chipper Jones 4.00
3 Mike Piazza 5.00
4 Nomar Garciaparra 5.00
5 Derek Jeter 5.00
6 Frank Thomas 3.00
7 Ben Grieve 1.50
8 Mark McGwire 10.00
9 Sammy Sosa 5.00
10 Alex Rodriguez 5.00
11 Troy Glaus 2.00
12 Eric Chavez 1.00
13 Kerry Wood 1.00
14 Barry Bonds 2.00
15 Vladimir Guerrero 3.00
16 Albert Belle 1.50
17 Juan Gonzalez 4.00
18 Roger Clemens 3.00
19 Ruben Mateo 1.50
20 Cal Ripken Jr. 6.00

1999 Topps Stars Four-Star

Four-Star inserts include cards numbered 1-10 from the base set and are seeded 1:10 packs. The cards feature dark metallic inks and refractive foil stamping on front. A Four-Star parallel is also randomly seeded and has gold metallic inks. Sequentially numbered to 49, it is inserted at the rate of one per 650 packs.

MT
Complete Set (10): 40.00
Common Player: 1.50
Foils (49 each): 25X
1 Ken Griffey Jr. 8.00
2 Chipper Jones 4.00
3 Mike Piazza 5.00
4 Nomar Garciaparra 5.00
5 Derek Jeter 5.00
6 Frank Thomas 3.00
7 Ben Grieve 1.50
8 Mark McGwire 10.00
9 Sammy Sosa 5.00
10 Alex Rodriguez 5.00

1999 Topps Stars Bright Futures

This 10-card set features top prospects with a brilliant future ahead of them. Each card features foil stamping and is sequentially numbered to 1,999. Cards have a "BF" prefix to the number. A metalized foil parallel version is also randomly seeded (1:2702) and limited to 30 numbered sets.

MT
Complete Set (10): 50.00
Common Player: 2.00
Production 1,999 sets
Foil (30 each): 8X
1 Troy Glaus 8.00
2 Eric Chavez 4.00
3 Adrian Beltre 4.00
4 Michael Barrett 4.00
5 Fernando Seguignol 2.00
6 Alex Gonzalez 3.00
7 Matt Clement 2.00

8	Pat Burrell	15.00
9	Ruben Mateo	8.00
10	Alfonso Soriano	15.00

1999 Topps Stars Galaxy

This 10-card set highlights the top players in baseball with foil stamping and limited to 1,999 numbered sets, inserted at the rate of one per 41 packs. Each card is numbered on the back with a "G" prefix. A Galaxy parallel version is randomly seeded (1:2,702) and sequentially numbered to 30 sets.

		MT
Complete Set (10):		150.00
Common Player:		5.00
Production 1,999 sets		
Foil (30 each): 8X		
1	Mark McGwire	30.00
2	Roger Clemens	10.00
3	Nomar Garciaparra	20.00
4	Alex Rodriguez	25.00
5	Kerry Wood	5.00
6	Ben Grieve	5.00
7	Derek Jeter	20.00
8	Vladimir Guerrero	10.00
9	Ken Griffey Jr.	30.00
10	Sammy Sosa	20.00

1999 Topps Stars Rookie Reprints

Topps reprinted five Hall of Famers' rookie cards. The rookie reprints are inserted 1:65 packs and limited to 2,500 numbered sets.

		MT
Complete Set (5):		50.00
Common Player:		10.00
Production 2,500 sets		
1	Frank Robinson	10.00
2	Ernie Banks	12.50
3	Yogi Berra	12.50
4	Bob Gibson	10.00
5	Tom Seaver	17.50

1999 Topps Stars Rookie Reprints Autographs

These foil stamped inserts feature the "Topps Certified Autograph Issue" stamp and are inserted 1:406 packs. The Ernie Banks autograph is inserted 1:812 packs.

		MT
Complete Set (5):		400.00
Common Player:		60.00
Inserted 1:406		
Banks inserted 1:812		
1	Frank Robinson	80.00
2	Ernie Banks	90.00
3	Yogi Berra	80.00
4	Bob Gibson	60.00
5	Tom Seaver	125.00

1999 Topps Stars 'N Steel

Using Serilusion technology, each borderless card features a four-colored textured film laminate bonded to a sheet of strong 25-gauge metal. Each pack contains three cards, packaged in a stand-up tri-fold display unit, at a S.R.P. of $9.99. There are two parallels to the 44-card set, Gold and Holographics. Golds are seeded 1:12 packs, Holographics are found every 24 packs.

		MT
Complete Set (44):		125.00
Common Player:		2.00
Gold: 2X		
Inserted 1:12		
Holographic Dome: 4X		
Inserted 1:24		
1	Kerry Wood	4.00
2	Ben Grieve	4.00
3	Chipper Jones	12.00
4	Alex Rodriguez	20.00
5	Mo Vaughn	4.00
6	Bernie Williams	4.00
7	Juan Gonzalez	6.00
8	Vinny Castilla	2.00
9	Tony Gwynn	12.00
10	Manny Ramirez	6.00
11	Raul Mondesi	2.00
12	Roger Clemens	10.00
13	Darin Erstad	2.50
14	Barry Bonds	6.00
15	Cal Ripken Jr.	20.00
16	Barry Larkin	3.00
17	Scott Rolen	6.00
18	Albert Belle	4.00
19	Craig Biggio	4.00
20	Tony Clark	2.50
21	Mark McGwire	25.00
22	Andres Galarraga	3.00
23	Kenny Lofton	4.00
24	Pedro Martinez	6.00
25	Paul O'Neill	2.00
26	Ken Griffey Jr.	25.00
27	Travis Lee	2.50
28	Tim Salmon	3.00
29	Frank Thomas	6.00
30	Larry Walker	4.00
31	Moises Alou	2.00
32	Vladimir Guerrero	8.00
33	Ivan Rodriguez	6.00
34	Derek Jeter	15.00
35	Greg Vaughn	3.00
36	Gary Sheffield	3.00
37	Carlos Delgado	3.00
38	Greg Maddux	12.00
39	Sammy Sosa	15.00
40	Mike Piazza	15.00
41	Nomar Garciaparra	15.00
42	Dante Bichette	3.00
43	Jeff Bagwell	6.00
44	Jim Thome	3.00

1999 Topps Stars 'N Steel Gold Domed Holographics

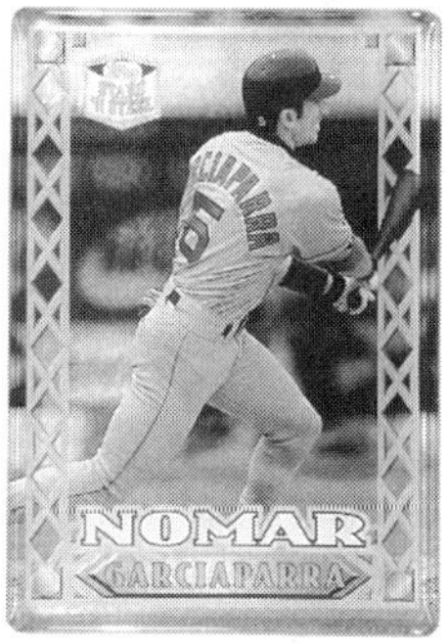

This parallel edition was inserted at a rate of one per box. Cards are basically the same as the regular-issue, except for the use of holographic foil highlights on front and the presence of a thick plastic dome which covers the front.

	MT
Complete Set (44):	1500.
Common Player:	6.00
Stars: 4X	
(See 1999 Topps Stars 'N Steel for checklist and base card values.)	

1999 Topps TEK Pre-Production

The second edition of Topps TEK was introduced with this trio of star cards. The preview cards are virtually identical in format to the issued version, except for the use of "PP" prefixes to card numbers on back.

	MT
Complete Set (3):	9.00
Common Player:	3.00
PP1ADerek Jeter	6.00
PP2AMoises Alou	3.00
PP3ATony Clark	3.00

1999 Topps TEK

Topps TEK baseball contains 45 players, with all cards printed on a transparent, 27-point stock. Each player is featured in two different versions (A & B), which are noted on the card back. The versions are differentiated by type of player uniform (home is version A and away uniforms are version B). Each version also has 30 different baseball focused background patterns; as a result every player in the 45-card set has 60 total cards. There also is a Gold parallel set that has a gold design and all versions are paralleled. Each gold card is numbered to 10, with an insertion rate of 1:15 packs.

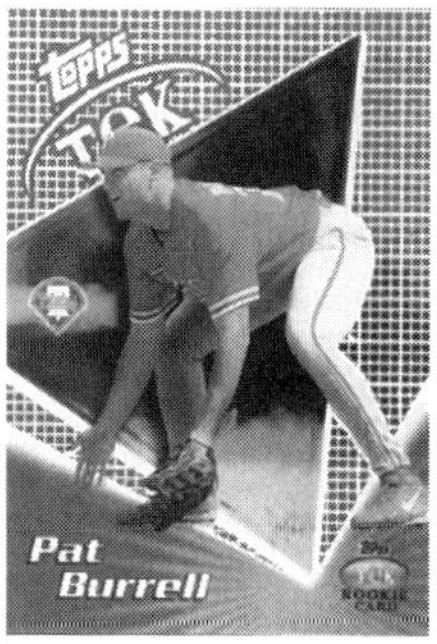

		MT
Complete Set (45):		80.00
Common Player:		.50
Gold (10 each variation): 8X		
Wax Box:		80.00
1	Ben Grieve	1.50
2	Andres Galarraga	1.50
3	Travis Lee	1.00
4	Larry Walker	2.00
5	Ken Griffey Jr.	10.00
6	Sammy Sosa	6.00
7	Mark McGwire	10.00
8	Roberto Alomar	2.00
9	Wade Boggs	1.00
10	Troy Glaus	1.50
11	Craig Biggio	1.50
12	Kerry Wood	1.50
13	Vladimir Guerrero	3.00
14	Albert Belle	2.50
15	Mike Piazza	6.00
16	Chipper Jones	5.00
17	Randy Johnson	2.00
18	Adrian Beltre	1.00
19	Barry Bonds	2.50
20	Jim Thome	1.50
21	Greg Vaughn	.75
22	Scott Rolen	2.50
23	Ivan Rodriguez	2.50
24	Derek Jeter	6.00
25	Cal Ripken Jr.	7.50
26	Mark Grace	.75
27	Bernie Williams	2.00
28	Darin Erstad	1.00
29	Eric Chavez	1.00
30	Tom Glavine	.75
31	Jeff Bagwell	2.50
32	Manny Ramirez	2.50
33	Tino Martinez	1.50
34	Todd Helton	1.50
35	Jason Kendall	.75
36	*Pat Burrell*	6.00
37	Tony Gwynn	5.00
38	Nomar Garciaparra	6.00
39	Frank Thomas	3.00
40	Orlando Hernandez	1.00
41	Juan Gonzalez	2.50
42	Alex Rodriguez	6.00
43	Greg Maddux	5.00
44	Mo Vaughn	2.00
45	Roger Clemens	3.00
	Version A checklist folder (orange)	.05
	Version B checklist folder (green)	.05

1999 Topps TEK Gold

Each of the two player versions on each of the 30 background patterns was paralleled in a gold insert version. Cards share the same front and back designs and photos but feature gold graphics. Each card is serially numbered within an edition of just 10. Insertion rate is one per 15 packs.

Gold Parallels 5X-8X
(See 1999 Topps TEK for checklist, base card values.)

1999 Topps TEK Fantastek Phenoms

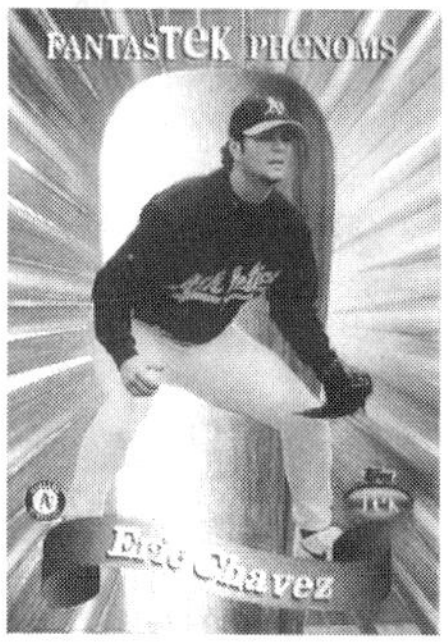

This 10-card set highlights top young prospects on a transparent plastic stock with silver and blue highlighting. These are inserted 1:18 packs.

		MT
Complete Set (10):		35.00
Common Player:		2.00
Inserted 1:18		
F1	Eric Chavez	3.00
F2	Troy Glaus	4.00
F3	Pat Burrell	15.00
F4	Alex Gonzalez	2.00
F5	Carlos Lee	2.00
F6	Ruben Mateo	3.00
F7	Carlos Beltran	6.00
F8	Adrian Beltre	4.00
F9	Bruce Chen	2.00
F10	Ryan Anderson	4.00

1999 Topps TEK Teknicians

This 10-card set focuses on baseball's top stars on a clear, plastic stock utilizing metallic blue, silver and red inks. These are inserted 1:18 packs.

		MT
Complete Set (10):		90.00
Common Player:		2.00
Inserted 1:18		
T1	Ken Griffey Jr.	20.00
T2	Mark McGwire	20.00
T3	Kerry Wood	4.00
T4	Ben Grieve	4.00
T5	Sammy Sosa	12.00
T6	Derek Jeter	12.00
T7	Alex Rodriguez	15.00
T8	Roger Clemens	6.00
T9	Nomar Garciaparra	12.00
T10	Vladimir Guerrero	6.00

2000 Topps

Released in two series the card fronts have a silver border with the Topps logo, player name and position stamped with gold foil. Card backs have complete year-by-year statistics along with a small photo in the upper right portion and the player's vital information. Subsets within the first series 239-card set include Draft Picks, Prospects, Magic Moments, Season Highlights and 20th Century's Best. The Topps MVP promotion is a parallel of 200 of the base cards, excluding subsets, with a special Topps MVP logo. 100 cards of each player was produced and if the featured player is named MVP for a week, collectors win a prize.

		MT
Complete Set (478):		50.00
Complete Series I set (239):		25.00
Complete Series II set (239):		25.00
Common Player:		.10
MVP Stars: 30x to 60x		
Yng Stars & RCs: 20x to 40x		
Production 100 sets		
5 Versions for 236-240, 475-479		
Wax Box:		38.00
1	Mark McGwire	2.50
2	Tony Gwynn	1.25
3	Wade Boggs	.25
4	Cal Ripken Jr.	2.00
5	Matt Williams	.25
6	Jay Buhner	.20
7	Not Issued	.10
8	Jeff Conine	.10
9	Todd Greene	.10
10	Mike Lieberthal	.10
11	Steve Avery	.10
12	Bret Saberhagen	.10
13	Magglio Ordonez	.20
14	Brad Radke	.10
15	Derek Jeter	1.25
16	Javy Lopez	.25
17	Russ David	.10
18	Armando Benitez	.10
19	B.J. Surhoff	.10
20	Darryl Kile	.10
21	Mark Lewis	.10
22	Mike Williams	.10
23	Mark McLemore	.10
24	Sterling Hitchcock	.10
25	Darin Erstad	.25
26	Ricky Gutierrez	.10
27	John Jaha	.10
28	Homer Bush	.10
29	Darrin Fletcher	.10
30	Mark Grace	.25
31	Fred McGriff	.25
32	Omar Daal	.10
33	Eric Karros	.20
34	Orlando Cabrera	.10
35	J.T. Snow Jr.	.10
36	Luis Castillo	.10
37	Rey Ordonez	.10
38	Bob Abreu	.10
39	Warren Morris	.10
40	Juan Gonzalez	.60
41	Mike Lansing	.10
42	Chili Davis	.10
43	Dean Palmer	.10
44	Hank Aaron	2.00
45	Jeff Bagwell	.50
46	Jose Valentin	.10
47	Shannon Stewart	.10
48	Kent Bottenfield	.10
49	Jeff Shaw	.10
50	Sammy Sosa	1.25
51	Randy Johnson	.40
52	Benny Agbayani	.10
53	Dante Bichette	.25
54	Pete Harnisch	.10
55	Frank Thomas	.60
56	Jorge Posada	.10
57	Todd Walker	.10
58	Juan Encarnacion	.10
59	Mike Sweeney	.10
60	Pedro Martinez	.60
61	Lee Stevens	.10
62	Brian Giles	.10
63	Chad Ogea	.10
64	Ivan Rodriguez	.50
65	Roger Cedeno	.10
66	David Justice	.20
67	Steve Trachsel	.10
68	Eli Marrero	.10
69	Dave Nilsson	.10
70	Ken Caminiti	.20
71	Tim Raines	.10
72	Brian Jordan	.10
73	Jeff Blauser	.10
74	Bernard Gilkey	.10
75	John Flaherty	.10
76	Brent Mayne	.10
77	Jose Vidro	.10
78	Jeff Fassero	.10
79	Bruce Aven	.10
80	John Olerud	.25
81	Juan Guzman	.10
82	Woody Williams	.10
83	Ed Sprague	.10
84	Joe Girardi	.10
85	Barry Larkin	.40
86	Mike Caruso	.10
87	Bobby Higginson	.10
88	Roberto Kelly	.10
89	Edgar Martinez	.20
90	Mark Kotsay	.10
91	Paul Sorrento	.10
92	Eric Young	.10
93	Carlos Delgado	.40
94	Troy Glaus	.40
95	Ben Grieve	.25
96	Jose Lima	.10
97	Garret Anderson	.10
98	Luis Gonzalez	.10
99	Carl Pavano	.10
100	Alex Rodriguez	1.25
101	Preston Wilson	.10
102	Ron Gant	.10
103	Harold Baines	.10
104	Rickey Henderson	.25
105	Gary Sheffield	.25
106	Mickey Morandini	.10
107	Jim Edmonds	.10
108	Kris Benson	.10
109	Adrian Beltre	.25
110	Alex Fernandez	.10
111	Dan Wilson	.10
112	Mark Clark	.10
113	Greg Vaughn	.25
114	Neifi Perez	.10
115	Paul O'Neill	.25
116	Jermaine Dye	.10
117	Todd Jones	.10
118	Terry Steinbach	.10
119	Greg Norton	.10
120	Curt Schilling	.20
121	Todd Zeile	.10
122	Edgardo Alfonzo	.25
123	Ryan McGuire	.10
124	Stan Javier	.10
125	John Smoltz	.20
126	Bob Wickman	.10
127	Richard Hidalgo	.10
128	Chuck Finley	.10
129	Billy Wagner	.10
130	Todd Hundley	.10
131	Dwight Gooden	.10
132	Russ Ortiz	.10
133	Mike Lowell	.10
134	Reggie Sanders	.10
135	John Valentin	.10
136	Brad Ausmus	.10
137	Chad Kreuter	.10
138	David Cone	.25
139	Brook Fordyce	.10
140	Roberto Alomar	.40
141	Charles Nagy	.10
142	Brian Hunter	.10
143	Mike Mussina	.40
144	Robin Ventura	.25
145	Kevin Brown	.25
146	Pat Hentgen	.10
147	Ryan Klesko	.20
148	Derek Bell	.10
149	Andy Sheets	.10
150	Larry Walker	.40
151	Scott Williamson	.10
152	Jose Offerman	.10
153	Doug Mientkiewicz	.10
154	John Snyder	.10
155	Sandy Alomar	.25
156	Joe Nathan	.10
157	Lance Johnson	.10
158	Odalis Perez	.10
159	Hideo Nomo	.25
160	Steve Finley	.10
161	Dave Martinez	.10
162	Matt Walbeck	.10
163	Bill Spiers	.10
164	Fernando Tatis	.25
165	Kenny Lofton	.50
166	Paul Byrd	.10
167	Aaron Sele	.10
168	Eddie Taubensee	.10
169	Reggie Jefferson	.10
170	Roger Clemens	1.00
171	Francisco Cordova	.10
172	Mike Bordick	.10
173	Wally Joyner	.10
174	Marvin Benard	.10
175	Jason Kendall	.10
176	Mike Stanley	.10
177	Chad Allen	.10
178	Carlos Beltran	.25
179	Deivi Cruz	.10
180	Chipper Jones	1.25
181	Vladimir Guerrero	.60
182	Dave Burba	.10
183	Tom Goodwin	.10
184	Brian Daubach	.10
185	Jay Bell	.10
186	Roy Halladay	.10
187	Miguel Tejada	.10
188	Armando Rios	.10
189	Fernando Vina	.10
190	Eric Davis	.10
191	Henry Rodriguez	.10
192	Joe McEwing	.10
193	Jeff Kent	.10
194	Mike Jackson	.10
195	Mike Morgan	.10
196	Jeff Montgomery	.10
197	Jeff Zimmerman	.10
198	Tony Fernandez	.10
199	Jason Giambi	.10
200	Jose Canseco	.50
201	Alex Gonzalez	.10
202	Jack Cust, Mike Colangelo, Dee Brown	.20
203	Felipe Lopez, Alfonso Soriano, Pablo Ozuna	.75
204	Erubiel Durazo, Pat Burrell, Nick Johnson	.50
205	*John Sneed*, Kip Wells, Matt Blank	.40
206	Josh Kalinowski,*Michael Tejera*, Chris Mears	.25
207	Roosevelt Brown, Corey Patterson, Lance Berkman	.75
208	Kit Pellow, Kevin Barker, Russ Branyan	.25
209	*B.J. Garbe,Larry Bigbie*	1.00
210	Eric Munson, *Bobby Bradley*	1.00
211	Josh Girdley, Kyle Snyder	.40
212	*Chance Caple*, Jason Jennings	.40
213	*Ryan Christiansen Brett Myers*	.40
214	*Jason Stumm Rob Purvis*	.50
215	David Walling, Mike Paradis	.40
216	Omar Ortiz, Jay Gehrke	.20
217	David Cone (Season Highlights)	.10
218	Jose Jimenez (Season Highlights)	.10
219	Chris Singleton (Season Highlights)	.10
220	Fernando Tatis (Season Highlights)	.10
221	Todd Helton (Season Highlights)	.20
222	Kevin Millwood (Post-Season Highlights)	.20
223	Todd Pratt (Post-Season Highlights)	.10
224	Orlando Hernandez (Post-Season Highlights)	.20
225	(Post-Season Highlights)	.10
226	(Post-Season Highlights)	.10
227	Bernie Williams (Post-Season Highlights)	.40
228	Mariano Rivera (Post-Season Highlights)	.20
229	Tony Gwynn (20th Century's Best)	.50
230	Wade Boggs (20th Century's Best)	.25
231	Tim Raines (20th Century's Best)	.10
232	Mark McGwire (20th Century's Best)	2.00
233	Rickey Henderson (20th Century's Best)	.25
234	Rickey Henderson (20th Century's Best)	.25
235	Roger Clemens (20th Century's Best)	.50
236	Mark McGwire (Magic Moments)	3.00
237	Hank Aaron (Magic Moments)	2.00
238	Cal Ripken Jr. (Magic Moments)	2.00
239	Wade Boggs (Magic Moments)	.50
240	Tony Gwynn (Magic Moments)	1.00
	Series 1 checklist (1-201)	.05
	Series 1 checklist (202-240, inserts)	.05
241	Tom Glavine	.25
242	David Wells	.10
243	Kevin Appier	.10
244	Troy Percival	.10
245	Ray Lankford	.10
246	Marquis Grissom	.10
247	Randy Winn	.10
248	Miguel Batista	.10
249	Darren Dreifort	.10
250	Barry Bonds	.60
251	Harold Baines	.10
252	Cliff Floyd	.10
253	Freddy Garcia	.20
254	Kenny Rogers	.10
255	Ben Davis	.10
256	Charles Johnson	.10
257	John Burkett	.10
258	Desi Relaford	.10
259	Al Martin	.10
260	Andy Pettitte	.20
261	Carlos Lee	.10
262	Matt Lawton	.10
263	Andy Fox	.10
264	Chan Ho Park	.10
265	Billy Koch	.10
266	Dave Roberts	.10
267	Carl Everett	.20
268	Orel Hershiser	.10
269	Trot Nixon	.10
270	Rusty Greer	.10
271	Will Clark	.25
272	Quilvio Veras	.10
273	Rico Brogna	.10
274	Devon White	.10
275	Tim Hudson	.25
276	Mike Hampton	.10
277	Miguel Cairo	.10
278	Darren Oliver	.10
279	Jeff Cirillo	.10
280	Al Leiter	.20
281	Brant Brown	.10
282	Carlos Febles	.10
283	Pedro Astacio	.10
284	Juan Guzman	.10
285	Orlando Hernandez	.25
286	Paul Konerko	.20
287	Tony Clark	.20
288	Aaron Boone	.10
289	Ismael Valdes	.10
290	Moises Alou	.20
291	Kevin Tapani	.10
292	John Franco	.10
293	Todd Zeile	.20
294	Jason Schmidt	.10
295	Johnny Damon	.10
296	Scott Brosius	.10
297	Travis Fryman	.20
298	Jose Vizcaino	.10
299	Eric Chavez	.20
300	Mike Piazza	1.50
301	Matt Clement	.10
302	Cristian Guzman	.10
303	Darryl Strawberry	.20
304	Jeff Abbott	.10
305	Brett Tomko	.10
306	Mike Lansing	.10
307	Eric Owens	.10
308	Livan Hernandez	.10
309	Rondell White	.20
310	Todd Stottlemyre	.20
311	Chris Carpenter	.10
312	Ken Hill	.10
313	Mark Loretta	.10
314	John Rocker	.10
315	Richie Sexson	.10
316	Ruben Mateo	.25
317	Ramon Martinez	.10
318	Mike Sirotka	.10
319	Jose Rosado	.10
320	Matt Mantei	.10
321	Kevin Millwood	.20
322	Gary DiSarcina	.10
323	Dustin Hermanson	.10
324	Mike Stanton	.10
325	Kirk Rueter	.10
326	Damian Miller	.10
327	Doug Glanville	.10
328	Scott Rolen	.60
329	Ray Durham	.10
330	Butch Huskey	.10
331	Mariano Rivera	.20
332	Darren Lewis	.10
333	Ramiro Mendoza	.10
334	Mark Grudzielanek	.10
335	Mike Cameron	.10
336	Kelvim Escobar	.10
337	Bret Boone	.10
338	Mo Vaughn	.40
339	Craig Biggio	.40
340	Michael Barrett	.10
341	Marlon Anderson	.10
342	Bobby Jones	.10
343	John Halama	.10
344	Todd Ritchie	.10
345	Chuck Knoblauch	.20
346	Rick Reed	.10
347	Kelly Stinnett	.10
348	Tim Salmon	.20
349	A.J. Hinch	.10
350	Jose Cruz Jr.	.10
351	Roberto Hernandez	.10
352	Edgar Renteria	.10
353	Jose Hernandez	.10
354	Brad Fullmer	.20
355	Trevor Hoffman	.10
356	Troy O'Leary	.10
357	Justin Thompson	.10
358	Kevin Young	.10
359	Hideki Irabu	.10
360	Jim Thome	.25
361	Todd Dunwoody	.10
362	Octavio Dotel	.10
363	Omar Vizquel	.20
364	Raul Mondesi	.20
365	Shane Reynolds	.20
366	Bartolo Colon	.20
367	Chris Widger	.10
368	Gabe Kapler	.20
369	Bill Simas	.10
370	Tino Martinez	.25
371	John Thomson	.10
372	Delino DeShields	.10
373	Carlos Perez	.10
374	Eddie Perez	.10
375	Jeromy Burnitz	.20
376	Jimmy Haynes	.10
377	Travis Lee	.20
378	Darryl Hamilton	.10
379	Jamie Moyer	.10
380	Alex Gonzalez	.10
381	John Wetteland	.10
382	Vinny Castilla	.20
383	Jeff Suppan	.10
384	Chad Curtis	.10
385	Robb Nen	.10
386	Wilson Alvarez	.10
387	Andres Galarraga	.25
388	Mike Remlinger	.10
389	Geoff Jenkins	.20
390	Matt Stairs	.10
391	Bill Mueller	.10
392	Mike Lowell	.10
393	Andy Ashby	.10
394	Ruben Rivera	.10
395	Todd Helton	.25
396	Bernie Williams	.50
397	Royce Clayton	.10
398	Manny Ramirez	.60
399	Kerry Wood	.25
400	Ken Griffey Jr.	2.50
401	Enrique Wilson	.10
402	Joey Hamilton	.10
403	Shawn Estes	.10
404	Ugueth Urbina	.10
405	Albert Belle	.40
406	Rick Helling	.10
407	Steve Parris	.10
408	Eric Milton	.10
409	Dave Mlicki	.10
410	Shawn Green	.50
411	Jaret Wright	.10
412	Tony Womack	.10
413	Vernon Wells	.10
414	Ron Belliard	.10
415	Ellis Burks	.10
416	Scott Erickson	.10
417	Rafael Palmeiro	.30
418	Damion Easley	.10
419	Jamey Wright	.10
420	Corey Koskie	.10
421	Bobby Howry	.10
422	Ricky Ledee	.10
423	Dmitri Young	.10
424	Sidney Ponson	.10
425	Greg Maddux	1.25
426	Jose Guillen	.10
427	Jon Lieber	.10
428	Andy Benes	.20
429	Randy Velarde	.10
430	Sean Casey	.25
431	Torii Hunter	.10
432	Ryan Rupe	.10
433	David Segui	.10
434	Rich Aurilia	.10
435	Nomar Garciaparra	1.50
436	Denny Neagle	.10
437	Ron Coomer	.10
438	Chris Singleton	.10
439	Tony Batista	.10
440	Andruw Jones	.40
441	Adam Piatt, Aubrey Huff, Sean Burroughs (Prospects)	.40
442	Rafael Furcal, Jason Dallero, Travis Dawkins (Prospects)	.25
443	Wilton Veras, Joe Crede, Mike Lamb (Prospects)	.10
444	Julio Zuleta, Dernell Stenson, Jorge Toca (Prospects)	.10
445	Tim Raines, Jr., Gary Mathews Jr.,*Garry Maddox Jr.* (Prospects)	.10
446	Matt Riley, Mark Mulder, C.C. Sabathia (Prospects)	.10
447	*Scott Downs*, Chris George, Matt Belisle (Prospects)	.10
448	Doug Mirabelli, Ben Petrick, Jayson Werth (Prospects)	.10
449	Josh Hamilton,*Corey Myers* (Draft Picks)	.40
450	*Ben Christensen,Brett Myers* (Draft Picks)	.40
451	*Barry Zito,Ben Sheets* (Draft Picks)	.25
452	*Ty Howington,Kurt Ainsworth* (Draft Picks)	.25
453	*Rick Asadoorian,Vince Faison* (Draft Picks)	1.00
454	*Keith Reed,Jeff Heaverlo* (Draft Picks)	.25
455	*Mike MacDougal*, Jay Gehrke (Draft Picks)	.25
456	Mark McGwire (Season Highlights)	1.50
457	Cal Ripken Jr. (Season Highlights)	1.00
458	Wade Boggs (Season Highlights)	.25
459	Tony Gwynn (Season Highlights)	.75

460	Jesse Orosco (Season Highlights)	.10
461	Nomar Garciaparra, Larry Walker (League Leaders)	.50
462	Mark McGwire, Ken Griffey Jr. (League Leaders)	1.00
463	Mark McGwire, Manny Ramirez (League Leaders)	.75
464	Randy Johnson, Pedro Martinez (League Leaders)	.25
465	Randy Johnson, Pedro Martinez (League Leaders)	.25
466	Luis Gonzalez, Derek Jeter (League Leaders)	.50
467	Manny Ramirez, Larry Walker (League Leaders)	.25
468	Tony Gwynn (20th Century's Best)	1.00
469	Mark McGwire (20th Century's Best)	2.00
470	Frank Thomas (20th Century's Best)	.75
471	Harold Baines (20th Century's Best)	.10
472	Roger Clemens (20th Century's Best)	.75
473	John Franco (20th Century's Best)	.10
474	John Franco (20th Century's Best)	.10
475	Ken Griffey Jr. (Magic Moments)	3.00
476	Barry Bonds (Magic Moments)	.75
477	Sammy Sosa (Magic Moments)	2.00
478	Derek Jeter (Magic Moments)	2.00
479	Alex Rodriguez (Magic Moments)	2.00

2000 Topps Hank Aaron Reprints

This 23-card set reprints all of Aaron's 23-regular issued Topps cards and are seeded 1:18 packs.

		MT
Complete Set (23):		120.00
Common Aaron:		6.00
Inserted 1:18		
1	Hank Aaron - 1954	10.00
2	Hank Aaron - 1955	6.00
3	Hank Aaron - 1956	6.00
4	Hank Aaron - 1957	6.00
5	Hank Aaron - 1958	6.00
6	Hank Aaron - 1959	6.00
7	Hank Aaron - 1960	6.00
8	Hank Aaron - 1961	6.00
9	Hank Aaron - 1962	6.00
10	Hank Aaron - 1963	6.00
11	Hank Aaron - 1964	6.00
12	Hank Aaron - 1965	6.00
13	Hank Aaron - 1966	6.00
14	Hank Aaron - 1967	6.00
15	Hank Aaron - 1968	6.00
16	Hank Aaron - 1969	6.00
17	Hank Aaron - 1970	6.00
18	Hank Aaron - 1971	6.00
19	Hank Aaron - 1972	6.00
20	Hank Aaron - 1973	6.00
21	Hank Aaron - 1974	6.00
22	Hank Aaron - 1975	6.00
23	Hank Aaron - 1976	6.00

2000 Topps Hank Aaron Chrome Reprints

This 23-card set reprints Aaron's regular issued Topps cards utilizing Chromium technology. Each card has a commemorative logo and are seeded 1:72 packs. A Refractor parallel version is also randomly inserted 1:288 packs and have Refractor printed underneath the number on the card back.

		MT
Complete Set (23):		200.00
Common Aaron:		10.00
Inserted 1:72		
Refractors: 2x to 3x		
Inserted 1:288		
1	Hank Aaron - 1954	20.00
2	Hank Aaron - 1955	10.00
3	Hank Aaron - 1956	10.00
4	Hank Aaron - 1957	10.00
5	Hank Aaron - 1958	10.00
6	Hank Aaron - 1959	10.00
7	Hank Aaron - 1960	10.00
8	Hank Aaron - 1961	10.00
9	Hank Aaron - 1962	10.00
10	Hank Aaron - 1963	10.00
11	Hank Aaron - 1964	10.00
12	Hank Aaron - 1965	10.00
13	Hank Aaron - 1966	10.00
14	Hank Aaron - 1967	10.00
15	Hank Aaron - 1968	10.00
16	Hank Aaron - 1969	10.00
17	Hank Aaron - 1970	10.00
18	Hank Aaron - 1971	10.00
19	Hank Aaron - 1972	10.00
20	Hank Aaron - 1973	10.00
21	Hank Aaron - 1974	10.00
22	Hank Aaron - 1975	10.00
23	Hank Aaron - 1976	10.00

2000 Topps All-Star Rookie Team

		MT
Complete Set (10):		35.00
Common Player:		.50
Inserted 1:36		
1	Mark McGwire	8.00
2	Chuck Knoblauch	1.00
3	Chipper Jones	4.00
4	Cal Ripken Jr.	6.00
5	Manny Ramirez	2.00
6	Jose Canseco	2.00
7	Ken Griffey Jr.	8.00
8	Mike Piazza	5.00
9	Dwight Gooden	.50
10	Billy Wagner	.50

2000 Topps All-Topps Team

This 10-card set spotlights 10 National League players who are deemed the best at their respective position. Card fronts have gold foil stamping, while card backs make comparisons to Hall of Fame greats at their respective position. These were seeded 1:12 packs. Cards are numbered with an "AT" prefix.

		MT
Complete Set (20):		25.00
Common Player:		.50
Inserted 1:12		
1	Greg Maddux	2.00
2	Mike Piazza	2.50
3	Mark McGwire	4.00
4	Craig Biggio	.50
5	Chipper Jones	2.00
6	Barry Larkin	.50
7	Barry Bonds	1.00
8	Andruw Jones	.75
9	Sammy Sosa	2.50
10	Larry Walker	.75
11	Pedro Martinez	1.00
12	Ivan Rodriguez	1.00
13	Rafael Palmeiro	.75
14	Roberto Alomar	.75
15	Cal Ripken Jr.	3.00
16	Derek Jeter	2.50
17	Albert Belle	.75
18	Ken Griffey Jr.	4.00
19	Manny Ramirez	1.00
20	Jose Canseco	1.00

2000 Topps Century Best

		MT
Common Player:		15.00
Ser. 1 1:869 H		
Ser. 2 1:362		
CB1	Tony Gwynn (339)	80.00
CB2	Wade Boggs (578)	35.00
CB3	Lance Johnson (117)	20.00
CB4	Mark McGwire (522)	90.00
CB5	Rickey Henderson (1,334)	20.00
CB6	Rickey Henderson (2,103)	15.00
CB7	Roger Clemens (247)	80.00
CB8	Tony Gwynn (3,067)	25.00
CB9	Mark McGwire (587)	90.00
CB10	Frank Thomas (440)	40.00
CB11	Harold Baines (1,583)	15.00
CB12	Roger Clemens (3,316)	25.00
CB13	John Franco (264)	25.00
CB14	John Franco (416)	20.00

2000 Topps Combos

		MT
Complete Set (10):		40.00
Common Player:		1.00
Inserted 1:18		
1	Roberto Alomar, Manny Ramirez, Kenny Lofton, Jim Thome	2.00
2	Tom Glavine, Greg Maddux, John Smoltz	4.00
3	Derek Jeter, Bernie Williams, Tino Martinez	5.00
4	Ivan Rodriguez, Mike Piazza	5.00
5	Nomar Garciaparra, Alex Rodriguez, Derek Jeter	6.00
6	Sammy Sosa, Mark McGwire	8.00
7	Pedro Martinez, Randy Johnson	2.00
8	Barry Bonds, Ken Griffey Jr.	8.00
9	Chipper Jones, Ivan Rodriguez	4.00
10	Cal Ripken Jr., Tony Gwynn, Wade Boggs	6.00

2000 Topps Hands of Gold

This seven-card insert set highlights players who have won at least five gold gloves. Each card is foil stamped and die-cut and is seeded 1:18 packs.

		MT
Complete Set (7):		10.00
Common Player:		.50
Inserted 1:18		
1	Barry Bonds	1.00
2	Ivan Rodriguez	1.00
3	Ken Griffey Jr.	4.00
4	Roberto Alomar	.75
5	Tony Gwynn	2.00
6	Omar Vizquel	.50
7	Greg Maddux	2.00

2000 Topps Mark McGwire 1985 Rookie Reprint

This insert pays tribute to baseball reigning single season home run record holder by reprinting his '85 Topps Rookie card. Card fronts have a commemorative gold stamp and is seeded 1:36 packs.

	MT
Complete Set (1):	8.00
Mark McGwire	8.00

2000 Topps Oversize Cards

		MT
Complete Set (8):		15.00
Common Player:		1.00
Inserted 1:box		
1	Barry Bonds	1.25
2	Orlando Hernandez	1.00
3	Mike Piazza	3.00
4	Manny Ramirez	1.25
5	Ken Griffey Jr.	5.00
6	Rafael Palmeiro	1.00
7	Greg Maddux	2.50
8	Nomar Garciaparra	3.00

2000 Topps Own the Game

		MT
Complete Set (30):		75.00
Common Player:		.75
Inserted 1:12		
1	Derek Jeter	5.00
2	B.J. Surhoff	.75
3	Luis Gonzalez	.75
4	Manny Ramirez	2.00
5	Rafael Palmeiro	1.25
6	Mark McGwire	8.00
7	Mark McGwire	8.00
8	Sammy Sosa	5.00
9	Ken Griffey Jr.	8.00
10	Larry Walker	1.50
11	Nomar Garciaparra	5.00
12	Derek Jeter	5.00
13	Larry Walker	1.50
14	Mark McGwire	8.00
15	Manny Ramirez	2.00
16	Pedro Martinez	2.00
17	Randy Johnson	1.50
18	Kevin Millwood	1.00
19	Pedro Martinez	2.00
20	Randy Johnson	1.50
21	Kevin Brown	1.00
22	Chipper Jones	4.00
23	Ivan Rodriguez	2.00
24	Mariano Rivera	1.00
25	Scott Williamson	.75
26	Carlos Beltran	1.00
27	Randy Johnson	1.50
28	Pedro Martinez	2.00
29	Sammy Sosa	5.00
30	Manny Ramirez	2.00

2000 Topps Power Players

This 20-card set highlights the top power hitters in the game and are printed on a holographic silver foil front. They are numbered with a "P" prefix and are seeded 1:8 packs.

		MT
Complete Set (20):		25.00
Common Player:		.50
Inserted 1:8		
1	Juan Gonzalez	1.00
2	Ken Griffey Jr.	4.00
3	Mark McGwire	4.00
4	Nomar Garciaparra	2.50
5	Barry Bonds	1.00
6	Mo Vaughn	.75
7	Larry Walker	.75
8	Alex Rodriguez	2.50
9	Jose Canseco	1.00
10	Jeff Bagwell	1.00
11	Manny Ramirez	1.00
12	Albert Belle	.75

13	Frank Thomas	1.50
14	Mike Piazza	2.50
15	Chipper Jones	2.00
16	Sammy Sosa	2.50
17	Vladimir Guerrero	1.50
18	Scott Rolen	1.00
19	Raul Mondesi	.50
20	Derek Jeter	2.50

2000 Topps Perennial All-Stars

This 10-card set highlights 10 superstars who have consistently achieved All-Star recognition. Card fronts feature a silver holographic foil throughout, while card backs have the featured player's career All-Star statistics. These were seeded 1:18 packs. Cards are numbered with a "PA" prefix.

		MT
Complete Set (10):		20.00
Common Player:		.50
Inserted 1:18		
1	Ken Griffey Jr.	4.00
2	Derek Jeter	2.50
3	Sammy Sosa	2.50
4	Cal Ripken Jr.	3.00
5	Mike Piazza	2.50
6	Nomar Garciaparra	2.50
7	Jeff Bagwell	1.00
8	Barry Bonds	1.00
9	Alex Rodriguez	2.50
10	Mark McGwire	4.00

2000 Topps Stadium Relics

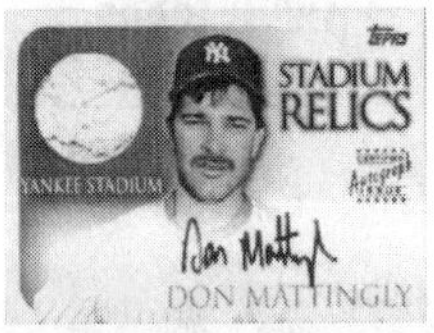

Inserted exclusively in Home-Team Advantage packs, this five-card set features historical baseball stadiums and the autograph of the players who made them sacred. Besides the player autograph, the cards also have a piece of base from the featured stadium embedded into each card. These were seeded 1:165 HTA packs and are numbered with an "SR" prefix.

		MT
Common Player:		125.00
Inserted 1:165 HTA		
1	Don Mattingly	200.00
2	Carl Yastrzemski	125.00
3	Ernie Banks	125.00
4	Johnny Bench	150.00
5	Willie Mays	250.00
6	Mike Schmidt	
7	Lou Brock	
8	Al Kaline	
9	Paul Molitor	
10	Eddie Matthews	

2000 Topps Supers

Each box of Topps foil packs includes one upwrapped box-topper card in an oversize (3-1/2" x 5") format. Except for its size, the super version differs from the same players' issued cards only in the numbering on back which designates each card "x of 8".

		MT
Complete Set (8):		25.00
Common Player:		2.00
Inserted 1:box		
1	Mark McGwire	5.00
2	Hank Aaron	5.00
3	Derek Jeter	3.00
4	Sammy Sosa	3.00
5	Alex Rodriguez	3.00
6	Chipper Jones	4.00
7	Cal Ripken Jr.	4.00
8	Pedro Martinez	2.00

2000 Topps 21st Century Topps

Printed on a silver holographic foil front, this 10-card set highlights young players who are poised to thrive into the next millennium. These are seeded 1:18 packs and are numbered on the card backs with a "C" prefix.

		MT
Complete Set (10):		10.00
Common Player:		.50
Inserted 1:18		
1	Ben Grieve	.75
2	Alex Gonzalez	.50
3	Derek Jeter	3.00
4	Sean Casey	.75
5	Nomar Garciaparra	3.00
6	Alex Rodriguez	3.00
7	Scott Rolen	1.25
8	Andruw Jones	1.00
9	Vladimir Guerrero	1.50
10	Todd Helton	1.00

2000 Topps Chrome

The base set consists of 478 cards utilizing Topps Chromium technology and features the same photos and basic design as the 2000 Topps base set. Subsets include Prospects, Draft Picks, 20th Century's Best, Magic Moments and Post Season Highlights. A parallel Refractor version is also available 1:12 packs.

		MT
Complete Series I Set (239):		150.00
Common Player:		.40
5 versions for cards #236-240		
Wax Box:		65.00
1	Mark McGwire	8.00
2	Tony Gwynn	4.00
3	Wade Boggs	1.00
4	Cal Ripken Jr.	6.00
5	Matt Williams	1.00
6	Jay Buhner	.50
7	Not Issued	
8	Jeff Conine	.40
9	Todd Greene	.40
10	Mike Lieberthal	.40
11	Steve Avery	.40
12	Bret Saberhagen	.40
13	Magglio Ordonez	.40
14	Brad Radke	.40
15	Derek Jeter	5.00
16	Javy Lopez	.50
17	Russ David	.40
18	Armando Benitez	.40
19	B.J. Surhoff	.40
20	Darryl Kile	.40
21	Mark Lewis	.40
22	Mike Williams	.40
23	Mark McLemore	.40
24	Sterling Hitchcock	.40
25	Darin Erstad	.60
26	Ricky Gutierrez	.40
27	John Jaha	.40
28	Homer Bush	.40
29	Darrin Fletcher	.40
30	Mark Grace	.75
31	Fred McGriff	.75
32	Omar Daal	.40
33	Eric Karros	.60
34	Orlando Cabrera	.40
35	J.T. Snow Jr.	.40
36	Luis Castillo	.40
37	Rey Ordonez	.40
38	Bob Abreu	.40
39	Warren Morris	.40
40	Juan Gonzalez	2.00
41	Mike Lansing	.40
42	Chili Davis	.40
43	Dean Palmer	.40
44	Hank Aaron	8.00
45	Jeff Bagwell	2.00
46	Jose Valentin	.40
47	Shannon Stewart	.40
48	Kent Bottenfield	.40
49	Jeff Shaw	.40
50	Sammy Sosa	5.00
51	Randy Johnson	1.50
52	Benny Agbayani	.40
53	Dante Bichette	.75
54	Pete Harnisch	.40
55	Frank Thomas	2.00
56	Jorge Posada	.75
57	Todd Walker	.40
58	Juan Encarnacion	.40
59	Mike Sweeney	.40
60	Pedro Martinez	2.00
61	Lee Stevens	.40
62	Brian Giles	.40
63	Chad Ogea	.40
64	Ivan Rodriguez	2.00
65	Roger Cedeno	.40
66	David Justice	.75
67	Steve Trachsel	.40
68	Eli Marrero	.40
69	Dave Nilsson	.40
70	Ken Caminiti	.60
71	Tim Raines	.40
72	Brian Jordan	.40
73	Jeff Blauser	.40
74	Bernard Gilkey	.40
75	John Flaherty	.40
76	Brent Mayne	.40
77	Jose Vidro	.40
78	Jeff Fassero	.40
79	Bruce Aven	.40
80	John Olerud	.75
81	Juan Guzman	.40
82	Woody Williams	.40
83	Ed Sprague	.40
84	Joe Girardi	.40
85	Barry Larkin	1.00
86	Mike Caruso	.40
87	Bobby Higginson	.40
88	Roberto Kelly	.40
89	Edgar Martinez	.20
90	Mark Kotsay	.40
91	Paul Sorrento	.40
92	Eric Young	.40
93	Carlos Delgado	1.50
94	Troy Glaus	1.00
95	Ben Grieve	.75
96	Jose Lima	.40
97	Garret Anderson	.40
98	Luis Gonzalez	.40
99	Carl Pavano	.40
100	Alex Rodriguez	5.00
101	Preston Wilson	.40
102	Ron Gant	.60
103	Harold Baines	.40
104	Rickey Henderson	1.00
105	Gary Sheffield	.75
106	Mickey Morandini	.40
107	Jim Edmonds	.40
108	Kris Benson	.40
109	Adrian Beltre	.60
110	Alex Fernandez	.40
111	Dan Wilson	.40
112	Mark Clark	.40
113	Greg Vaughn	.75
114	Neifi Perez	.40
115	Paul O'Neill	.75
116	Jermaine Dye	.40
117	Todd Jones	.40
118	Terry Steinbach	.40
119	Greg Norton	.40
120	Curt Schilling	.60
121	Todd Zeile	.40
122	Edgardo Alfonzo	.75
123	Ryan McGuire	.40
124	Stan Javier	.40
125	John Smoltz	.60
126	Bob Wickman	.40
127	Richard Hidalgo	.40
128	Chuck Finley	.40
129	Billy Wagner	.40
130	Todd Hundley	.40
131	Dwight Gooden	.60
132	Russ Ortiz	.40
133	Mike Lowell	.40
134	Reggie Sanders	.40
135	John Valentin	.40
136	Brad Ausmus	.40
137	Chad Kreuter	.40
138	David Cone	.75
139	Brook Fordyce	.40
140	Roberto Alomar	1.50
141	Charles Nagy	.40
142	Brian Hunter	.40
143	Mike Mussina	1.50
144	Robin Ventura	.75
145	Kevin Brown	.60
146	Pat Hentgen	.40
147	Ryan Klesko	.60
148	Derek Bell	.40
149	Andy Sheets	.40
150	Larry Walker	1.50
151	Scott Williamson	.40
152	Jose Offerman	.40
153	Doug Mientkiewicz	.40
154	John Snyder	.40
155	Sandy Alomar	.25
156	Joe Nathan	.40
157	Lance Johnson	.40
158	Odalis Perez	.40
159	Hideo Nomo	.75
160	Steve Finley	.40
161	Dave Martinez	.40
162	Matt Walbeck	.40
163	Bill Spiers	.40
164	Fernando Tatis	.75
165	Kenny Lofton	1.25
166	Paul Byrd	.40
167	Aaron Sele	.40
168	Eddie Taubensee	.40
169	Reggie Jefferson	.40
170	Roger Clemens	3.00
171	Francisco Cordova	.40
172	Mike Bordick	.40
173	Wally Joyner	.40
174	Marvin Benard	.40
175	Jason Kendall	.60
176	Mike Stanley	.40
177	Chad Allen	.40
178	Carlos Beltran	.75
179	Deivi Cruz	.40
180	Chipper Jones	4.00
181	Vladimir Guerrero	2.50
182	Dave Burba	.40
183	Tom Goodwin	.40
184	Brian Daubach	.40
185	Jay Bell	.40
186	Roy Halladay	.40
187	Miguel Tejada	.40
188	Armando Rios	.40
189	Fernando Vina	.40
190	Eric Davis	.60
191	Henry Rodriguez	.40
192	Joe McEwing	.40
193	Jeff Kent	.40
194	Mike Jackson	.40
195	Mike Morgan	.40
196	Jeff Montgomery	.40
197	Jeff Zimmerman	.40
198	Tony Fernandez	.40
199	Jason Giambi	.40
200	Jose Canseco	2.00
201	Alex Gonzalez	.40
202	Jack Cust, Mike Colangelo, Dee Brown	1.50
203	Felipe Lopez, Alfonso Soriano, Pablo Ozuna	4.00
204	Erubiel Durazo, Pat Burrell, Nick Johnson	4.00
205	*John Sneed*, Kip Wells, Matt Blank	1.50
206	Josh Kalinowski,*Michael Tejera*, Chris Mears	1.00
207	Roosevelt Brown, Corey Patterson, Lance Berkman	8.00
208	Kit Pellow, Kevin Barker, Russ Branyan	1.00
209	*B.J. Garbe,Larry Bigbie*	3.00
210	Eric Munson, *Bobby Bradley*	4.00
211	Josh Girdley, Kyle Snyder	1.50
212	*Chance Caple*, Jason Jennings	2.00
213	*Ryan Christiansen, Brett Myers*	4.00
214	*Jason Stumm, Rob Purvis*	8.00
215	David Walling, Mike Paradis	1.50
216	Omar Ortiz, Jay Gehrke	.75
217	David Cone (Season Highlights)	.75
218	Jose Jimenez (Season Highlights)	.40
219	Chris Singleton (Season Highlights)	.40
220	Fernando Tatis (Season Highlights)	.75
221	Todd Helton (Season Highlights)	.75
222	Kevin Millwood (Post-Season Highlights)	.60
223	Todd Pratt (Post-Season Highlights)	.40
224	Orlando Hernandez (Post-Season Highlights)	.75
225	Post-Season Highlights	.40
226	Post-Season Highlights	.40
227	Bernie Williams (Post-Season Highlights)	1.00
228	Mariano Rivera (Post-Season Highlights)	.75
229	Tony Gwynn (20th Century's Best)	2.00
230	Wade Boggs (20th Century's Best)	1.00
231	Tim Raines (20th Century's Best)	.40
232	Mark McGwire (20th Century's Best)	8.00
233	Rickey Henderson (20th Century's Best)	.75
234	Rickey Henderson (20th Century's Best)	.75
235	Roger Clemens (20th Century's Best)	3.00
236	Mark McGwire (Magic Moments)	15.00
237	Hank Aaron (Magic Moments)	8.00
238	Cal Ripken Jr. (Magic Moments)	10.00
239	Wade Boggs (Magic Moments)	4.00
240	Tony Gwynn (Magic Moments)	8.00
	Series 1 checklist (1-201)	.05
	Series 1 checklist (202-240, inserts)	.05
241	Tom Glavine	.40
242	David Wells	.40
243	Kevin Appier	.40
244	Troy Percival	.40
245	Ray Lankford	.40
246	Marquis Grissom	.40
247	Randy Winn	.40
248	Miguel Batista	.40
249	Darren Dreifort	.40
250	Barry Bonds	.40
251	Harold Baines	.40
252	Cliff Floyd	.40
253	Freddy Garcia	.40
254	Kenny Rogers	.40
255	Ben Davis	.40
256	Charles Johnson	.40
257	John Burkett	.40
258	Desi Relaford	.40
259	Al Martin	.40
260	Andy Pettitte	.40
261	Carlos Lee	.40
262	Matt Lawton	.40
263	Andy Fox	.40
264	Chan Ho Park	.40
265	Billy Koch	.40
266	Dave Roberts	.40
267	Carl Everett	.40
268	Orel Hershiser	.40
269	Trot Nixon	.40
270	Rusty Greer	.40
271	Will Clark	.40
272	Quilvio Veras	.40
273	Rico Brogna	.40
274	Devon White	.40
275	Tim Hudson	.40
276	Mike Hampton	.40
277	Miguel Cairo	.40
278	Darren Oliver	.40
279	Jeff Cirillo	.40
280	Al Leiter	.40
281	Brant Brown	.40
282	Carlos Febles	.40
283	Pedro Astacio	.40
284	Juan Guzman	.40
285	Orlando Hernandez	.40
286	Paul Konerko	.40
287	Tony Clark	.40
288	Aaron Boone	.40
289	Ismael Valdes	.40
290	Moises Alou	.40
291	Kevin Tapani	.40
292	John Franco	.40
293	Todd Zeile	.40
294	Jason Schmidt	.40
295	Johnny Damon	.40
296	Scott Brosius	.40
297	Travis Fryman	.40
298	Jose Vizcaino	.40
299	Eric Chavez	.40
300	Mike Piazza	.40
301	Matt Clement	.40
302	Cristian Guzman	.40
303	Darryl Strawberry	.40
304	Jeff Abbott	.40
305	Brett Tomko	.40
306	Mike Lansing	.40
307	Eric Owens	.40

308 Livan Hernandez .40
309 Rondell White .40
310 Todd Stottlemyre .40
311 Chris Carpenter .40
312 Ken Hill .40
313 Mark Loretta .40
314 John Rocker .40
315 Richie Sexson .40
316 Ruben Mateo .40
317 Ramon Martinez .40
318 Mike Sirotka .40
319 Jose Rosado .40
320 Matt Mantei .40
321 Kevin Millwood .40
322 Gary DiSarcina .40
323 Dustin Hermanson .40
324 Mike Stanton .40
325 Kirk Rueter .40
326 Damian Miller .40
327 Doug Glanville .40
328 Scott Rolen .40
329 Ray Durham .40
330 Butch Huskey .40
331 Mariano Rivera .40
332 Darren Lewis .40
333 Ramiro Mendoza .40
334 Mark Grudzielanek .40
335 Mike Cameron .40
336 Kelvim Escobar .40
337 Bret Boone .40
338 Mo Vaughn .40
339 Craig Biggio .40
340 Michael Barrett .40
341 Marlon Anderson .40
342 Bobby Jones .40
343 John Halama .40
344 Todd Ritchie .40
345 Chuck Knoblauch .40
346 Rick Reed .40
347 Kelly Stinnett .40
348 Tim Salmon .40
349 A.J. Hinch .40
350 Jose Cruz Jr. .40
351 Roberto Hernandez .40
352 Edgar Renteria .40
353 Jose Hernandez .40
354 Brad Fullmer .40
355 Trevor Hoffman .40
356 Troy O'Leary .40
357 Justin Thompson .40
358 Kevin Young .40
359 Hideki Irabu .40
360 Jim Thome .40
361 Todd Dunwoody .40
362 Octavio Dotel .40
363 Omar Vizquel .40
364 Raul Mondesi .40
365 Shane Reynolds .40
366 Bartolo Colon .40
367 Chris Widger .40
368 Gabe Kapler .40
369 Bill Simas .40
370 Tino Martinez .40
371 John Thomson .40
372 Delino DeShields .40
373 Carlos Perez .40
374 Eddie Perez .40
375 Jeromy Burnitz .40
376 Jimmy Haynes .40
377 Travis Lee .40
378 Darryl Hamilton .40
379 Jamie Moyer .40
380 Alex Gonzalez .40
381 John Wetteland .40
382 Vinny Castilla .40
383 Jeff Suppan .40
384 Chad Curtis .40
385 Robb Nen .40
386 Wilson Alvarez .40
387 Andres Galarraga .40
388 Mike Remlinger .40
389 Geoff Jenkins .40
390 Matt Stairs .40
391 Bill Mueller .40
392 Mike Lowell .40
393 Andy Ashby .40
394 Ruben Rivera .40
395 Todd Helton .40
396 Bernie Williams .40
397 Royce Clayton .40
398 Manny Ramirez .40
399 Kerry Wood .40
400 Ken Griffey Jr. .40
401 Enrique Wilson .40
402 Joey Hamilton .40
403 Shawn Estes .40
404 Ugueth Urbina .40
405 Albert Belle .40
406 Rick Helling .40
407 Steve Parris .40
408 Eric Milton .40
409 Dave Mlicki .40
410 Shawn Green .40
411 Jaret Wright .40
412 Tony Womack .40
413 Vernon Wells .40
414 Ron Belliard .40
415 Ellis Burks .40
416 Scott Erickson .40
417 Rafael Palmeiro .40
418 Damion Easley .40
419 Jamey Wright .40
420 Corey Koskie .40
421 Bobby Howry .40
422 Ricky Ledee .40
423 Dmitri Young .40
424 Sidney Ponson .40
425 Greg Maddux .40
426 Jose Guillen .40
427 Jon Lieber .40
428 Andy Benes .40
429 Randy Velarde .40
430 Sean Casey .40
431 Torii Hunter .40
432 Ryan Rupe .40
433 David Segui .40
434 Rich Aurilia .40
435 Nomar Garciaparra .40
436 Denny Neagle .40
437 Ron Coomer .40
438 Chris Singleton .40
439 Tony Batista .40
440 Andruw Jones .40
441 Adam Piatt, Aubrey Huff, Sean Burroughs (Prospects) .40
442 Rafael Furcal, Jason Dallero, Travis Dawkins (Prospects) .40
443 Wilton Veras, Joe Crede, Mike Lamb (Prospects) .40
444 Julio Zuleta, Dernell Stenson, Jorge Toca (Prospects) .40
445 Tim Raines, Jr., Gary Mathews Jr., *Garry Maddox Jr.* (Prospects) .40
446 Matt Riley, Mark Mulder, C.C. Sabathia (Prospects) .40
447 *Scott Downs*, Chris George, Matt Belisle (Prospects) .40
448 Doug Mirabelli, Ben Petrick, Jayson Werth (Prospects) .40
449 Josh Hamilton, *Corey Myers* (Draft Picks) .40
450 *Ben Christensen, Brett Myers* (Draft Picks) .40
451 *Barry Zito, Ben Sheets* (Draft Picks) .40
452 *Ty Howington, Kurt Ainsworth* (Draft Picks) .40
453 *Rick Asadoorian, Vince Faison* (Draft Picks) .40
454 *Keith Reed, Jeff Heaverlo* (Draft Picks) .40
455 *Mike MacDougal*, Jay Gehrke (Draft Picks) .40
456 Mark McGwire (Season Highlights) .40
457 Cal Ripken Jr. (Season Highlights) .40
458 Wade Boggs (Season Highlights) .40
459 Tony Gwynn (Season Highlights) .40
460 Jesse Orosco (Season Highlights) .40
461 Nomar Garciaparra, Larry Walker (League Leaders) .40
462 Mark McGwire, Ken Griffey Jr. (League Leaders) .40
463 Mark McGwire, Manny Ramirez (League Leaders) .40
464 Randy Johnson, Pedro Martinez (League Leaders) .40
465 Randy Johnson, Pedro Martinez (League Leaders) .40
466 Luis Gonzalez, Derek Jeter (League Leaders) .40
467 Manny Ramirez, Larry Walker (League Leaders) .40
468 Tony Gwynn (20th Century's Best) .40
469 Mark McGwire (20th Century's Best) .40
470 Frank Thomas (20th Century's Best) .40
471 Harold Baines (20th Century's Best) .40
472 Roger Clemens (20th Century's Best) .40
473 John Franco (20th Century's Best) .40
474 John Franco (20th Century's Best) .40
475 Ken Griffey Jr. (Magic Moments) .40
476 Barry Bonds (Magic Moments) .40
477 Sammy Sosa (Magic Moments) .40
478 Derek Jeter (Magic Moments) .40
479 Alex Rodriguez (Magic Moments) .40

2000 Topps Chrome Refractors

A parallel to the base set, Refractors have a reflective sheen to them when held up to light. They are seeded 1:12 packs and have "Refractor" written underneath the card number on the back.

Stars: 5x-10x
Young Stars/RCs: 3x-5x
Inserted 1:12
(See 2000 Topps Chrome for checklist and base card values.)

2000 Topps Chrome Allegiance

Allegiance features 20 stars who have spent their entire career with one team. They are seeded 1:16 and are numbered with a "TA" prefix. There is also a hobby-exclusive Refractor parallel version, sequentially numbered to 100 and inserted 1:424 packs.

		MT
Complete Set (20):		100.00
Common Player:		2.00
Inserted 1:16		
1	Derek Jeter	12.00
2	Ivan Rodriguez	5.00
3	Alex Rodriguez	12.00
4	Cal Ripken Jr.	15.00
5	Mark Grace	2.00
6	Tony Gwynn	10.00
7	Juan Gonzalez	5.00
8	Frank Thomas	5.00
9	Manny Ramirez	5.00
10	Barry Larkin	4.00
11	Bernie Williams	4.00
12	Raul Mondesi	2.00
13	Vladimir Guerrero	6.00
14	Craig Biggio	3.00
15	Nomar Garciaparra	12.00
16	Andruw Jones	4.00
17	Jim Thome	3.00
18	Scott Rolen	5.00
19	Chipper Jones	10.00
20	Ken Griffey Jr.	20.00

2000 Topps Chrome Allegiance Refractors

A parallel to the Allegiance inserts, these were limited to 100 sequentially numbered sets and inserted 1:424 packs.

		MT
Common Player:		2.00
Production 100 sets		
1	Derek Jeter	100.00
2	Ivan Rodriguez	40.00
3	Alex Rodriguez	100.00
4	Cal Ripken Jr.	120.00
5	Mark Grace	15.00
6	Tony Gwynn	75.00
7	Juan Gonzalez	40.00
8	Frank Thomas	40.00
9	Manny Ramirez	40.00
10	Barry Larkin	30.00
11	Bernie Williams	30.00
12	Raul Mondesi	15.00
13	Vladimir Guerrero	50.00
14	Craig Biggio	30.00
15	Nomar Garciaparra	100.00
16	Andruw Jones	30.00
17	Jim Thome	25.00
18	Scott Rolen	40.00
19	Chipper Jones	75.00
20	Ken Griffey Jr.	150.00

2000 Topps Chrome All-Topps N.L. Team

These feature top National League players and picks a top player for each position. They have a brown border utilizing Topps Chromium technology. Card backs have a small photo along with statistical comparisons made to current and former greats for their respective position. Backs are numbered with an "AT" prefix and are seeded 1:32 packs. A Refractor parallel is inserted 1:160 packs.

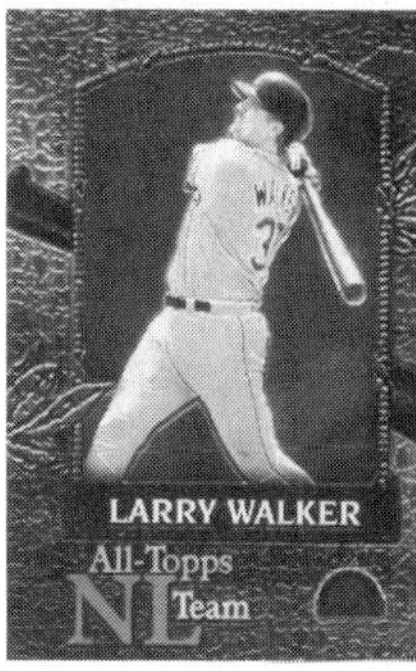

		MT
Complete Set (10):		70.00
Common Player:		3.00
Inserted 1:32		
Refractors: 2x-3x		
Inserted 1:160		
1	Greg Maddux	10.00
2	Mike Piazza	12.00
3	Mark McGwire	20.00
4	Craig Biggio	3.00
5	Chipper Jones	10.00
6	Barry Larkin	4.00
7	Barry Bonds	5.00
8	Andruw Jones	4.00
9	Sammy Sosa	12.00
10	Larry Walker	4.00

2000 Topps Chrome Mark McGwire 1985 Rookie Reprint

This insert is a chromium reprinted version of McGwire's 1985 Topps rookie card. Each card features a commemorative gold-foil stamp. The insertion rate is 1:32 packs. A hobby-exclusive Refractor version is also inserted, limited to 70 sequentially numbered sets and seeded 1:12,116 packs.

	MT
Inserted 1:32	
Refractor:	250.00
Production 70 cards	
Mark McGwire	10.00

2000 Topps Chrome Power Players

Twenty of the leading power hitters are featured on a colorful design. They are seeded 1:8 packs and are numbered with a "P" prefix. A Refractor parallel is also randomly seeded 1:40 packs.

		MT
Complete Set (20):		75.00
Common Player:		1.00
Inserted 1:8		
Refractors: 2x-3x		
Inserted 1:40		
1	Juan Gonzalez	3.00
2	Ken Griffey Jr.	12.00
3	Mark McGwire	12.00
4	Nomar Garciaparra	8.00
5	Barry Bonds	3.00
6	Mo Vaughn	2.00
7	Larry Walker	2.00
8	Alex Rodriguez	8.00
9	Jose Canseco	3.00
10	Jeff Bagwell	3.00
11	Manny Ramirez	3.00
12	Albert Belle	2.00
13	Frank Thomas	4.00
14	Mike Piazza	8.00
15	Chipper Jones	6.00
16	Sammy Sosa	8.00
17	Vladimir Guerrero	4.00
18	Scott Rolen	3.00
19	Raul Mondesi	1.00
20	Derek Jeter	8.00

2000 Topps Chrome 21st Century Topps

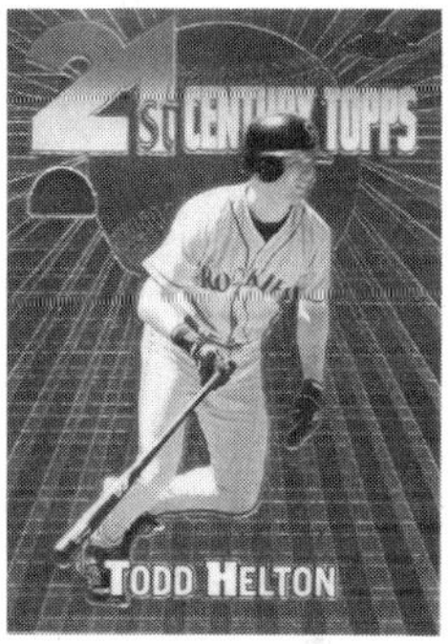

This 10-card set focuses on the top young stars in baseball heading into the next century. These were seeded 1:16 packs and are numbered with a "C" prefix on the card back. A Refractor parallel version is also seeded 1:80 packs.

		MT
Complete Set (10):		40.00
Common Player:		1.50
Inserted 1:16		
Refractors: 2x-3x		
Inserted 1:80		
1	Ben Grieve	2.00
2	Alex Gonzalez	1.50
3	Derek Jeter	10.00
4	Sean Casey	2.50
5	Nomar Garciaparra	10.00
6	Alex Rodriguez	10.00
7	Scott Rolen	4.00
8	Andruw Jones	3.00
9	Vladimir Guerrero	4.00
10	Todd Helton	2.00

2000 Topps HD

This super-premium product consists of 100 regular base cards comprised of 88 veterans and 12 rookies. The base cards feature hyper-color technology and printed on a very thick 50-pt. card stock. Card backs have a small photo, career highlight and complete year-by-year statistics. A

Platinum parallel to the base set is also randomly seeded and are sequentially numbered to 99 sets.

		MT
Complete Set (100):		100.00
Common Player:		.50
Platinums: 10x to 20x		
Production 99 sets		
Wax Box:		70.00
1	Derek Jeter	6.00
2	Andruw Jones	1.50
3	Ben Grieve	1.00
4	Carlos Beltran	1.00
5	Randy Johnson	2.00
6	Javy Lopez	.50
7	Gary Sheffield	.75
8	John Olerud	.75
9	Vinny Castilla	.50
10	Barry Larkin	1.00
11	Tony Clark	.75
12	Roberto Alomar	2.00
13	Brian Jordan	.50
14	Wade Boggs	1.00
15	Carlos Febles	.50
16	Alfonso Soriano	1.50
17	A.J. Burnett	.50
18	Matt Williams	1.00
19	Alex Gonzalez	.50
20	Larry Walker	2.00
21	Jeff Bagwell	2.50
22	Al Leiter	.50
23	Ken Griffey Jr.	10.00
24	Ruben Mateo	.75
25	Mark Grace	.75
26	Carlos Delgado	2.00
27	Vladimir Guerrero	3.00
28	Kenny Lofton	2.00
29	Rusty Greer	.50
30	Pedro Martinez	2.50
31	Todd Helton	1.00
32	Ray Lankford	.50
33	Jose Canseco	2.00
34	Raul Mondesi	.75
35	Mo Vaughn	2.00
36	Eric Chavez	.75
37	Manny Ramirez	2.50
38	Jason Kendall	.50
39	Mike Mussina	2.00
40	Dante Bichette	.75
41	Troy Glaus	.75
42	Rickey Henderson	1.00
43	Pablo Ozuna	.50
44	Michael Barrett	.50
45	Tony Gwynn	5.00
46	John Smoltz	.50
47	Rafael Palmeiro	1.50
48	Curt Schilling	.50
49	Todd Walker	.50
50	Greg Vaughn	.75
51	Orlando Hernandez	1.00
52	Jim Thome	1.00
53	Pat Burrell	1.50
54	Tim Salmon	.75
55	Tom Glavine	.75
56	Travis Lee	.50
57	Gabe Kapler	.50
58	Greg Maddux	5.00
59	Scott Rolen	2.50
60	Cal Ripken Jr.	6.00
61	Preston Wilson	.50
62	Ivan Rodriguez	2.50
63	Johnny Damon	.50
64	Bernie Williams	2.00
65	Barry Bonds	2.50
66	Sammy Sosa	6.00
67	Robin Ventura	.75
68	Tony Fernandez	.50
69	Jay Bell	.50
70	Mark McGwire	10.00
71	Jeromy Burnitz	.50
72	Chipper Jones	6.00
73	Josh Hamilton	1.00
74	Darin Erstad	.50
75	Alex Rodriguez	6.00
76	Sean Casey	1.00
77	Tino Martinez	1.00
78	Juan Gonzalez	2.50
79	Cliff Floyd	.50
80	Craig Biggio	1.00
81	Shawn Green	1.00
82	Adrian Beltre	.50
83	Mike Piazza	6.00
84	Nomar Garciaparra	6.00
85	Kevin Brown	.75
86	Roger Clemens	4.00
87	Frank Thomas	2.50
88	Albert Belle	2.50
89	Erubiel Durazo	.50
90	David Walling	.50
91	*John Sneed*	3.00
92	*Larry Bigbie*	4.00
93	*B.J. Garbe*	5.00
94	*Bobby Bradley*	4.00
95	*Ryan Christiansen*	1.50
96	*Jay Gerhke*	1.00
97	*Jason Stumm*	2.00
98	*Brett Myers*	1.50
99	*Chance Caple*	2.00
100	*Corey Myers*	4.00

2000 Topps HD Autographs

This two-card set features Cal Ripken Jr. and Derek Jeter. Card fronts include the Topps "Certified Autograph Issue" logo stamp as well as the Topps 3M authentication sticker to verify its authenticity. The insert rate for Jeter is 1:859 and Ripken Jr. 1:4,386.

		MT
Complete Set (2):		600.00
Jeter 1:859		
Ripken 1:4,386		
1	Derek Jeter	250.00
2	Cal Ripken Jr.	400.00

2000 Topps HD Ballpark Figures

This 10-card set features a baseball field designed die-cut. These are seeded 1:11 packs and are numbered with a "BF" prefix on the card back.

		MT
Complete Set (10):		50.00
Common Player:		1.50
Inserted 1:11		
1	Mark McGwire	12.00
2	Ken Griffey Jr.	12.00
3	Nomar Garciaparra	8.00
4	Derek Jeter	8.00
5	Sammy Sosa	8.00
6	Mike Piazza	8.00
7	Juan Gonzalez	3.00
8	Larry Walker	2.50
9	Ben Grieve	1.50
10	Barry Bonds	3.00

2000 Topps HD Clearly Refined

This 10-card set focuses on baseball's top young stars heading into the 2000 season. They are printed on high definition card stock and are seeded 1:20 packs. These are numbered with a "CR" prefix on the card back.

		MT
Complete Set (10):		40.00
Common Player:		2.00
Inserted 1:20		
1	Alfonso Soriano	10.00
2	Ruben Mateo	3.00
3	Josh Hamilton	6.00
4	Chad Hermansen	2.00
5	Ryan Anderson	3.00
6	Nick Johnson	8.00
7	Octavio Dotel	2.00
8	Peter Bergeron	2.00
9	Adam Piatt	5.00
10	Pat Burrell	10.00

2000 Topps HD Image

This 10-card insert set highlights those batters with the best eyes at the plate. These were seeded 1:44 packs and are numbered with an "HD" prefix on the card back.

		MT
Complete Set (10):		180.00
Common Player:		8.00
Inserted 1:44		
1	Sammy Sosa	25.00
2	Mark McGwire	40.00
3	Derek Jeter	25.00
4	Albert Belle	10.00
5	Vladimir Guerrero	12.00
6	Ken Griffey Jr.	40.00
7	Mike Piazza	25.00
8	Alex Rodriguez	25.00
9	Barry Bonds	10.00
10	Nomar Garciaparra	25.00

2000 Topps HD On The Cutting Edge

This 10-card insert set is die-cut down the right hand side of the card highlighting the five-tool stars top five baseball attributes. These are inserted 1:22 packs and are numbered with a "CE" prefix on the card back.

		MT
Complete Set (10):		75.00
Common Player:		3.00
Inserted 1:22		
1	Andruw Jones	3.00
2	Nomar Garciaparra	12.00
3	Barry Bonds	5.00
4	Larry Walker	4.00
5	Vladimir Guerrero	6.00
6	Jeff Bagwell	5.00
7	Derek Jeter	12.00
8	Sammy Sosa	12.00
9	Alex Rodriguez	12.00
10	Ken Griffey Jr.	20.00

2000 Topps Opening Day

Essentially identical in design to 2000 Topps regular cards, Opening Day has a silver border with "2000 Opening Day" stamped in silver foil on the card front. The checklist is made up of cards from series I and II from Topps base set with identical photos.

		MT
Complete Set (165):		40.00
Common Player:		.15
1	Mark McGwire	3.00
2	Tony Gwynn	1.50
3	Wade Boggs	.40
4	Cal Ripken Jr.	2.50
5	Matt Williams	.50
6	Jay Buhner	.15
7	Mike Lieberthal	.15
8	Magglio Ordonez	.25
9	Derek Jeter	2.00
10	Javy Lopez	.15
11	Armando Benitez	.15
12	Darin Erstad	.25
13	Mark Grace	.25
14	Eric Karros	.15
15	J.T. Snow Jr.	.15
16	Luis Castillo	.15
17	Rey Ordonez	.15
18	Bob Abreu	.15
19	Warren Morris	.15
20	Juan Gonzalez	1.00
21	Dean Palmer	.15
22	Hank Aaron	3.00
23	Jeff Bagwell	.75
24	Sammy Sosa	2.00
25	Randy Johnson	.50
26	Dante Bichette	.15
27	Frank Thomas	1.00
28	Pedro Martinez	.75
29	Brian Giles	.15
30	Ivan Rodriguez	.75
31	Roger Cedeno	.15
32	David Justice	.40
33	Ken Caminiti	.15
34	Brian Jordan	.15
35	John Olerud	.25
36	Pokey Reese	.15
37	Barry Larkin	.40
38	Edgar Martinez	.15
39	Carlos Delgado	.50
40	Troy Glaus	.25
41	Ben Grieve	.25
42	Jose Lima	.15
43	Luis Gonzalez	.15
44	Alex Rodriguez	2.00
45	Preston Wilson	.15
46	Rickey Henderson	.40
47	Gary Sheffield	.25
48	Jim Edmonds	.15
49	Greg Vaughn	.25
50	Neifi Perez	.15
51	Paul O'Neill	.25
52	Jermaine Dye	.15
53	Curt Schilling	.25
54	Edgardo Alfonzo	.15
55	John Smoltz	.15
56	Chuck Finley	.15
57	Billy Wagner	.15
58	David Cone	.25
59	Roberto Alomar	.50
60	Charles Nagy	.15
61	Mike Mussina	.50
62	Robin Ventura	.25
63	Kevin Brown	.15
64	Pat Hentgen	.15
65	Ryan Klesko	.15
66	Derek Bell	.15
67	Larry Walker	.50
68	Scott Williamson	.15
69	Jose Offerman	.15
70	Doug Mientkiewicz	.15
71	John Snyder	.15
72	Sandy Alomar	.15
73	Joe Nathan	.15
74	Steve Finley	.15
75	Dave Martinez	.15
76	Fernando Tatis	.15
77	Kenny Lofton	.40
78	Paul Byrd	.15
79	Aaron Sele	.15
80	Roger Clemens	1.00
81	Francisco Cordova	.15
82	Wally Joyner	.15
83	Jason Kendall	.25
84	Carlos Beltran	.25
85	Chipper Jones	1.50
86	Vladimir Guerrero	1.00
87	Tom Goodwin	.15
88	Brian Daubach	.15
89	Jay Bell	.15
90	Roy Halladay	.15
91	Miguel Tejada	.15
92	Eric Davis	.15
93	Henry Rodriguez	.15
94	Joe McEwing	.15
95	Jeff Kent	.15
96	Jeff Zimmerman	.15
97	Tony Fernandez	.15
98	Jason Giambi	.15
99	Jose Canseco	.75
100	Alex Gonzalez	.15
101	Erubiel Durazo, Pat Burrell, Nick Johnson (Prospects)	1.00
102	Corey Patterson, Roosevelt Brown, Lance Berkman (Prospects)	2.50
103	Eric Munson, *Bobby Bradley* (Draft Picks)	1.00
104	Josh Hamilton, *Corey Myers* (Draft Picks)	1.00
105	Mark McGwire (Magic Moments)	3.00
106	Hank Aaron (Magic Moments)	3.00
107	Cal Ripken Jr. (Magic Moments)	2.50
108	Wade Boggs (Magic Moments)	.40
109	Tony Gwynn (Magic Moments)	1.50
110	Hank Aaron (Rookie Reprint)	3.00
111	Tom Glavine	.40
112	Mo Vaughn	.50
113	Tino Martinez	.25
114	Craig Biggio	.40
115	Tim Hudson	.25
116	John Wetteland	.15
117	Ellis Burks	.15
118	David Wells	.15
119	Rico Brogna	.15
120	Greg Maddux	1.50
121	Jeromy Burnitz	.15
122	Raul Mondesi	.25
123	Rondell White	.25
124	Barry Bonds	.75
125	Orlando Hernandez	.40
126	Bartolo Colon	.15
127	Tim Salmon	.25
128	Kevin Young	.15
129	Troy O'Leary	.15
130	Jim Thome	.40
131	Ray Durham	.15
132	Tony Clark	.40
133	Mariano Rivera	.25
134	Omar Vizquel	.15
135	Ken Griffey Jr.	3.00
136	Shawn Green	.50
137	Cliff Floyd	.15
138	Al Leiter	.15
139	Mike Hampton	.15
140	Mike Piazza	2.00
141	Andy Pettitte	.25
142	Albert Belle	.50
143	Scott Rolen	.75
144	Rusty Greer	.15
145	Kevin Millwood	.25
146	Ivan Rodriguez	.75
147	Nomar Garciaparra	2.00
148	Denny Neagle	.15
149	Manny Ramirez	.75
150	Vinny Castilla	.15
151	Andruw Jones	.50
152	Johnny Damon	.15
153	Eric Milton	.15
154	Todd Helton	.40
155	Rafael Palmeiro	.40
156	Damion Easley	.15
157	Carlos Febles	.15
158	Paul Konerko	.25
159	Bernie Williams	.50
160	Ken Griffey Jr. (Magic Moments)	3.00
161	Barry Bonds (Magic Moments)	.75
162	Sammy Sosa (Magic Moments)	2.00
163	Derek Jeter (Magic Moments)	2.00
164	Alex Rodriguez (Magic Moments)	2.00
165	Checklist (Magic Moments)	.15

2000 Topps Opening Day 2K

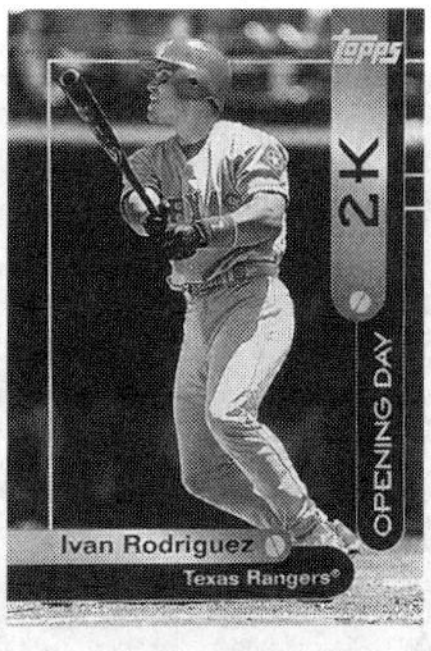

As part of a multi-manufacturer promotion, Topps issued eight cards of an "Opening Day 2K" set. Packages containing some of the 32 cards in the issue were distributed by MLB teams early in the season. The cards were also available exclusively as inserts in Topps Opening Day packs sold at Kmart stores early in the season. The Topps OD2K cards have gold-foil graphic highlights on front. Backs have portrait photos, stats and are numbered with an "OD" prefix.

		MT
Complete Set (8):		6.00
Common Player:		.50
1	Mark McGwire	2.00
2	Barry Bonds	.75
3	Ivan Rodriguez	.75
4	Sean Casey	.65
5	Derek Jeter	1.00
6	Vladimir Guerrero	1.00
7	Preston Wilson	.65
8	Ben Grieve	.50

1984 Toronto Blue Jays Fire Safety

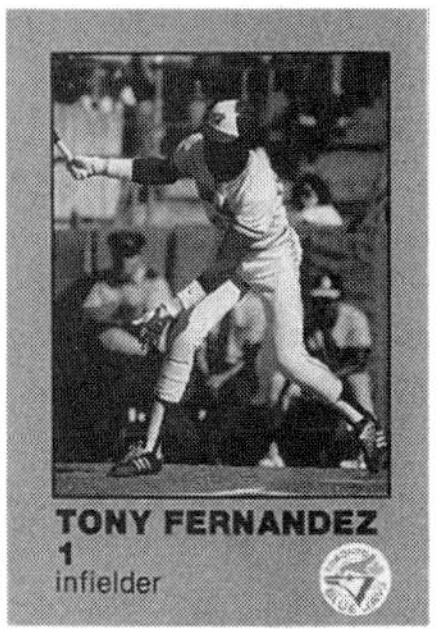

This 35-card set was issued in conjuction with the Toronto Sun newspaper and various Ontario area fire departments. The cards feature full-color action photos on the fronts, along with the player name, number and position. Rather than the customary wide white border on front, the Blue Jays fire safety set features bright blue borders. The card backs include brief player biographies and a fire safety tip. The 2-1/2" x 3-1/2" cards were distributed five at a time at two-week intervals during the summer of 1984.

		MT
Complete Set (35):		7.00
Common Player:		.25
1	Tony Fernandez	.30
3	Jimy Williams	.25
4	Alfredo Griffin	.25
5	Rance Mulliniks	.25
6	Bobby Cox	.50
7	Damaso Garcia	.25
8	John Sullivan	.25
9	Rick Leach	.25
10	Dave Collins	.25
11	George Bell	.40
12	Ernie Whitt	.25
13	Buck Martinez	.25
15	Lloyd Moseby	.25
16	Garth Iorg	.25
17	Kelly Gruber	.25
18	Jim Clancy	.25
23	Mitch Webster	.25
24	Willie Aikens	.25
25	Roy Lee Jackson	.25
26	Willie Upshaw	.25
27	Jimmy Key	1.00
29	Jesse Barfield	.30
31	Jim Acker	.25
33	Doyle Alexander	.25
34	Stan Clarke	.25
35	Bryan Clark	.25
37	Dave Stieb	.40
38	Jim Gott	.25
41	Al Widmar	.25
42	Billy Smith	.25
43	Cito Gaston	.40
44	Cliff Johnson	.25
48	Luis Leal	.25
53	Dennis Lamp	.25
---	Team Logo/Checklist	.25

1985 Toronto Blue Jays Fire Safety

The Toronto Blue Jays issued a 35-card fire safety set for the second year in a row in 1985. Cards feature players, coaches, managers, checklist and team picture. The full-color photos are on the card fronts with a blue border. The backs feature player stats and a safety tip. The cards measure 2-1/2" x 3-1/2" and were distributed throughout the Province of Ontario, Canada.

		MT
Complete Set (36):		5.00
Common Player:		.25
1	Tony Fernandez	.35
3	Jimy Williams	.25
4	Manny Lee	.25
5	Rance Mulliniks	.25
6	Bobby Cox	.45
7	Damaso Garcia	.25
8	John Sullivan	.25
11	George Bell	.30
12	Ernie Whitt	.25
13	Buck Martinez	.25
15	Lloyd Moseby	.25
16	Garth Iorg	.25
17	Kelly Gruber	.25
18	Jim Clancy	.25
22	Jimmy Key	.50
23	Mitch Webster	.25
24	Willie Aikens	.25
25	Len Matuszek	.25
26	Willie Upshaw	.25
28	Lou Thornton	.25
29	Jesse Barfield	.30
30	Ron Musselman	.25
31	Jim Acker	.25
33	Doyle Alexander	.25
36	Bill Caudill	.25
37	Dave Stieb	.30
41	Al Widmar	.25
42	Billy Smith	.25
43	Cito Gaston	.25
44	Jeff Burroughs	.25
46	Gary Lavelle	.25
48	Luis Leal	.25
50	Tom Henke	.35
53	Dennis Lamp	.25
---	Team logo/checklist	.25
---	Team photo/schedule	.25

1986 Toronto Blue Jays Fire Safety

This was the third consecutive year the Toronto Blue Jays issued a fire safety set of 36 baseball cards. The cards were given out at many fire stations in Ontario, Canada. The cards are printed in full color and include players and other personnel. The set was co-sponsored by the local fire departments, Bubble Yum and the Toronto Star. The cards measure 2-1/2" x 3-1/2".

		MT
Complete Set (36):		9.00
Common Player:		.25
1	Tony Fernandez	.30
3	Jimy Williams	.25
5	Rance Mulliniks	.25
7	Damaso Garcia	.25
8	John Sullivan	.25
9	Rick Leach	.25
11	George Bell	.30
12	Ernie Whitt	.25
13	Buck Martinez	.25
15	Lloyd Moseby	.25
16	Garth Iorg	.25
17	Kelly Gruber	.25
18	Jim Clancy	.25
22	Jimmy Key	.50
23	Cecil Fielder	3.50
24	John McLaren	.25
25	Steve Davis	.25
26	Willie Upshaw	.25
29	Jesse Barfield	.30
31	Jim Acker	.25
33	Doyle Alexander	.25
36	Bill Caudill	.25
37	Dave Stieb	.30
38	Mark Eichhorn	.25
39	Don Gordon	.25
41	Al Widmar	.25
42	Billy Smith	.25
43	Cito Gaston	.25
44	Cliff Johnson	.25
46	Gary Lavelle	.25
49	Tom Filer	.25
50	Tom Henke	.25
53	Dennis Lamp	.25
54	Jeff Hearron	.25
---	Team Photo	.25
---	10th Anniversary Logo Card	.25

1987 Toronto Blue Jays Fire Safety

For the fourth consecutive year, the Toronto Blue Jays issued a fire safety set of 36 cards. As in 1986, the set was sponsored by the local fire departments and governing agencies, Bubble Yum and the Toronto Star. The card fronts feature a full-color photo surrounded by a white border. The backs carry a fire safety tip and logos of all sponsors, plus player personal data and statistics. Produced on thin stock, cards in the set are the standard 2-1/2" x 3-1/2" size.

		MT
Complete Set (36):		7.00
Common Player:		.15
1	Tony Fernandez	.25
3	Jimy Williams	.15
5	Rance Mulliniks	.15
8	John Sullivan	.15
9	Rick Leach	.15
10	Mike Sharperson	.15
11	George Bell	.20
12	Ernie Whitt	.15
15	Lloyd Moseby	.15
16	Garth Iorg	.15
17	Kelly Gruber	.15
18	Jim Clancy	.15
19	Fred McGriff	4.00
22	Jimmy Key	.25
23	Cecil Fielder	1.00
24	John McLaren	.15
26	Willie Upshaw	.15
29	Jesse Barfield	.25
31	Duane Ward	.15
33	Joe Johnson	.15
35	Jeff Musselman	.15
37	Dave Stieb	.20
38	Mark Eichhorn	.15
40	Rob Ducey	.15
41	Al Widmar	.15
42	Billy Smith	.15
43	Cito Gaston	.15
45	Jose Nunez	.15
46	Gary Lavelle	.15
47	Matt Stark	.15
48	Craig McMurtry	.15
50	Tom Henke	.15
54	Jeff Hearron	.15
55	John Cerutti	.15
---	Logo/Won-Loss Record	.15
---	Team Photo/ Checklist	.15

1988 Toronto Blue Jays Fire Safety

This 36-card set features full-color action photos on 3-1/2" x 5" cards with white borders and a thin black line framing the photos. Card numbers (player's uniform #) appear lower left, team logo lower right; player's name and position are printed bottom center. Card backs are blue on white and include personal and career info, 1987 and career stats, sponsor logos and a fire safety tip. The set includes 31 player cards, a team photo checklist card and a team logo card with a year-by-year won/loss record. The set was sponsored by the Ontario Fire Chiefs Association, Ontario's Solicitor General, The Toronto Star and Bubble Yum and was distributed free as part of a community service project.

		MT
Complete Set (36):		7.00
Common Player:		.15
1	Tony Fernandez	.30
2	Nelson Liriano	.15
3	Jimy Williams	.15
4	Manny Lee	.15
5	Rance Mulliniks	.15
6	Silvestre Campusano	.15
7	John McLaren	.15
8	John Sullivan	.15
9	Rick Leach	.15
10	Pat Borders	.25
11	George Bell	.25
12	Ernie Whitt	.15
13	Jeff Musselman	.15
15	Lloyd Moseby	.15
16	Todd Stottlemyre	.75
17	Kelly Gruber	.15
18	Jim Clancy	.15
19	Fred McGriff	2.50
21	Juan Beniquez	.15
22	Jimmy Key	.25
23	Cecil Fielder	.75
29	Jesse Barfield	.30
31	Duane Ward	.15
36	David Wells	.75
37	Dave Stieb	.20
38	Mark Eichhorn	.15
40	Rob Ducey	.15
41	Al Widmar	.15
42	Billy Smith	.15
43	Cito Gaston	.15
46	Mike Flanagan	.15
50	Tom Henke	.15
55	John Cerutti	.15
57	Winston Llenas	.15
---	Team photo	.15
---	Team logo	.15

1989 Toronto Blue Jays Fire Safety

The 1989 Blue Jays safety set consists of 36 standard-size cards co-sponsored by the Ontario Association of Fire Chiefs, Oh Henry! candy bars and A&P supermarkets. Card fronts feature color photos with the player's uniform number in large type in the upper left corner. His name and position are to the right above the photo. The Blue Jays "On the Move" logo is centered at the bottom. The backs of the cards include fire safety messages.

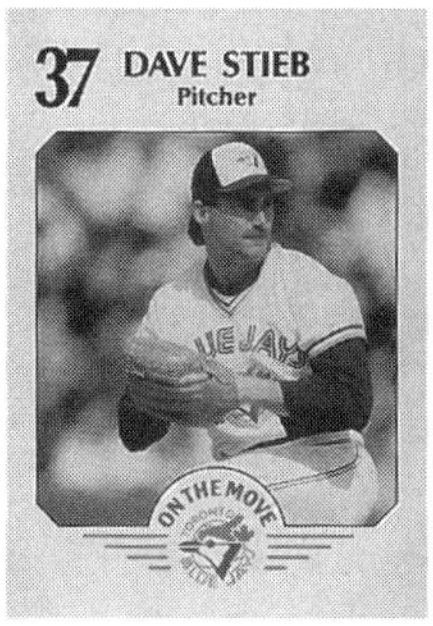

		MT
Complete Set (36):		6.00
Common Player:		.15
1	Tony Fernandez	.25
2	Nelson Liriano	.15
3	Jimy Williams	.15
4	Manny Lee	.15
5	Rance Mulliniks	.15
6	Silvestre Campusano	.15
7	John McLaren	.15
8	John Sullivan	.15
9	Bob Brenly	.15
10	Pat Borders	.15
11	George Bell	.25
12	Ernie Whitt	.15
13	Jeff Musselman	.15
15	Lloyd Moseby	.15
16	Greg Myers	.15
17	Kelly Gruber	.15
18	Tom Lawless	.15
19	Fred McGriff	2.50
22	Jimmy Key	.20
25	Mike Squires	.15
26	Sal Butera	.15
29	Jesse Barfield	.20
30	Todd Stottlemyre	.35
31	Duane Ward	.15
36	David Wells	.45
37	Dave Steib	.20
40	Rob Ducey	.15
41	Al Widman	.15
43	Cito Gaston	.15
44	Frank Wills	.15
45	Jose Nunez	.15
46	Mike Flanagan	.15
50	Tom Henke	.15
55	John Cerutti	.15
---	Team photo	.15
---	Team logo	.15

1990 Toronto Blue Jays Fire Safety

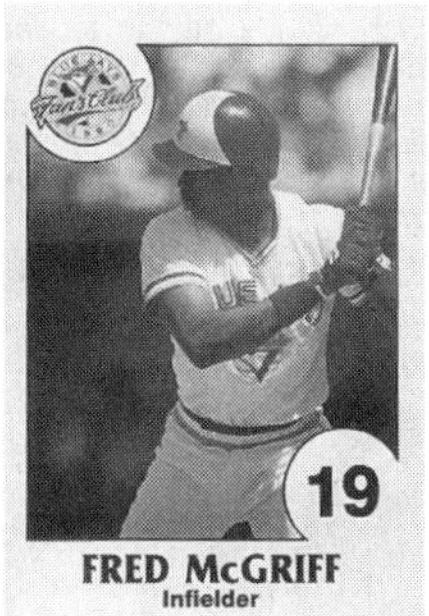

This 35-card set was cosponsored by the Ontario Association of Fire Chiefs, The Ministry of the Solicitor General, A & P/Dominion, Oh Henry and the Toronto Blue Jays. The card fronts feature full-color photos on white stock and display a special Blue Jays fan club logo in the upper left corner. The flip sides feature biographical information, statistics, and a fire fact. The cards are numbered according to the respective player or coaches' uniform number.

		MT
Complete Set (35):		7.00
Common Player:		.15
1	Tony Fernandez	.20
2	Nelson Liriano	.15
3	Mookie Wilson	.20

4	Manny Lee	.15
5	Rance Mulliniks	.15
7	John McLaren	.15
8	John Sullivan	.15
9	John Olerud	2.00
10	Pat Borders	.15
11	George Bell	.20
15	Gene Tenace	.15
18	Tom Lawless	.15
19	Fred McGriff	2.00
21	Greg Myers	.15
22	Jimmy Key	.20
23	Alex Sanchez	.15
24	Glenallen Hill	.35
25	Mike Squires	.15
26	Ozzie Virgil	.15
27	Willie Blair	.15
28	Al Leiter	.20
30	Todd Stottlemyre	.25
31	Duane Ward	.15
34	Jim Acker	.15
36	David Wells	.40
37	Dave Steib	.20
39	Paul Kilgus	.15
42	Galen Cisco	.15
43	Cito Gaston	.15
44	Frank Wills	.15
47	Junior Felix	.15
50	Tom Henke	.15
55	John Cerutti	.15
---	Skydome/checklist	.15
---	Logo/schedule	.15

1991 Toronto Blue Jays Fire Safety

The Blue Jays played host to the 1991 All-Star Game and the team's annual fire safety set prominently featured that honor. A headercard with the Jays All-Star logo was included in the set and each card carried the logo in full color on the front. The 2-1/2" x 3-1/2" cards have a color action photo at top which bleeds off the top and sides. Beneath the photo is a white border with the player's name, position and uniform number. Backs are printed in black-and-white and have a few biographical notes, 1990 and career stats, a Fire Fact safety message and logos of the cards' sponsors.

		MT
Complete Set (36):		6.00
Common Player:		.15
3	Mookie Wilson	.15
4	Manuel Lee	.15
5	Rance Mulliniks	.15
6	MIke Squires	.15
7	Rich Hacker	.15
8	John Sullivan	.15
9	John Olerud	.50
10	Pat Borders	.15
12	Roberto Alomar	3.00
13	Kenny Williams	.15
15	Pat Tabler	.15
17	Kelly Gruber	.15
18	Gene Tenace	.15
20	Rob Ducey	.15
21	Greg Myers	.15
22	Jimmy Key	.20
23	Mark Whiten	.25
24	Glenallen Hill	.15
25	Devon White	.25
28	Al Leiter	.20
29	Joe Carter	.50
30	Todd Stottlemyre	.20
31	Duane Ward	.15
34	Jim Acker	.15
35	Denis Boucher	.15
36	David Wells	.30
37	Dave Steib	.20
42	Galen Cisco	.15
43	Cito Gaston	.15
44	Frank Wills	.15
46	Ken Dayley	.15
50	Tom Henke	.15
56	Hector Torres	.15
88	Rene Gonzales	.15
---	BJ Birdy (Mascot)	.15
---	All-Star Season header/checklist card	.15

1992 Toronto Blue Jays Fire Safety

Hidden amid the myriad sponsors' logos on the backs of these cards is a fire safety message. The 2-1/2" x 3-1/2" cards are printed on thin cardboard and feature color player photos on front, along with a red, white and blue "Toronto Blue Jays Fanatic" logo. Fronts also carry uniform numbers, by which the set is checklisted here. Backs are printed in black-and-white with a few biographical details, 1991 and career stats.

		MT
Complete Set (36):		10.00
Common Player:		.25
1	Eddie Zosky	.25
2	Manuel Lee	.25
3	Bob Bailor	.25
4	Alfredo Griffin	.25
5	Rance Mulliniks	.25
7	Rich Hacker	.25
8	John Sullivan	.25
9	John Olerud	.50
10	Pat Borders	.25
12	Roberto Alomar	2.00
14	Derek Bell	.50
15	Pat Tabler	.25
17	Kelly Gruber	.25
18	Gene Tenace	.25
20	Rob Ducey	.25
21	Greg Myers	.25
22	Jimmy Key	.35
23	Candy Maldonado	.25
24	Turner Ward	.25
25	Devon White	.40
29	Joe Carter	.35
30	Todd Stottlemyre	.30
31	Duane Ward	.25
32	Dave Winfield	2.00
36	David Wells	.45
37	Dave Steib	.30
39	Larry Hisle	.25
40	Mike Timlin	.25
42	Galen Cisco	.25
43	Cito Gaston	.25
45	Bob MacDonald	.25
46	Ken Dayley	.25
47	Jack Morris	.25
50	Tom Henke	.25
66	Juan Guzman	.25
---	Checklist	.25

1993 Toronto Blue Jays Fire Safety

The Blue Jays produced a fire safety set for the 10th year in a row in 1993. In the first year of offering the item as a boxed set, the cards feature a full-bleed color photo on the front, with the player's name printed in white over a blue stripe across the top of the card. The Blue Jay's 1992 World Champions logo appears in the upper left corner in the 35-card set.

		MT
Complete Set (35):		4.00
Common Player:		.25
(1)	Eddie Zosky	.25
(2)	Luis Sojo	.25
(3)	Bob Bailor	.25
(4)	Alfredo Griffin	.25
(5)	Domingo Martinez	.25
(6)	Rich Hacker	.25
(7)	John Sullivan	.25
(8)	John Olerud	.40
(9)	Pat Borders	.25
(10)	Darnell Coles	.25
(11)	Roberto Alomar	.75
(12)	Darrin Jackson	.25
(13)	Tom Quinlin	.25
(14)	Gene Tenace	.25
(15)	Paul Molitor	1.00
(16)	Dick Schofield	.25
(17)	Turner Ward	.25
(18)	Devon White	.35
(19)	Randy Knorr	.25
(20)	Al Leiter	.35
(21)	Joe Carter	.30
(22)	Todd Stottlemyre	.30
(23)	Duane Ward	.25
(24)	Ed Sprague	.30
(25)	Dave Stewart	.25
(26)	Larry Hisle	.25
(27)	Mike Timlin	.25
(28)	Pat Hentgen	.50
(29)	Galen Cisco	.25
(30)	Cito Gaston	.25
(31)	Ken Davley	.25
(32)	Jack Morris	.25
(33)	Mark Eichhorn	.25
(34)	Danny Cox	.25
(35)	Juan Guzman	.25

1997 Toronto Blue Jays Jackie Robinson

The 50th anniversary of Jackie Robinson's entry to the major leagues was commemorated by this card given to fans attending the April 15 game at SkyDome. The 3-1/2" x 5" card has a sepia portrait of Robinson framed in black and bordered in blue. The 50th anniversary commemorative logo is at lower-right. Back has quotes by and about Robinson, along with his career stats, a repeat of the anniversary logo and the team logo.

		MT
(1)	Jackie Robinson	8.00

Player names in *Italic* type indicate a rookie card.

1987 Toys "R" Us

Marked as a collectors' edition set and titled "Baseball Rookies," the 1987 Toys "R" Us issue was produced by Topps for the toy store chain. The set is comprised of 33 glossy-coated cards, each measuring 2-1/2" x 3-1/2". The card fronts are very colorful, employing nine different colors including deep black borders. The backs, printed in blue and orange, contain career highlights and composite minor and major league statistics. The set was distributed in a specially designed box and sold for $1.99 in retail outlets.

		MT
Complete Set (33):		3.00
Common Player:		.10
1	Andy Allanson	.10
2	Paul Assenmacher	.10
3	Scott Bailes	.10
4	Barry Bonds	1.50
5	Jose Canseco	.75
6	John Cerutti	.10
7	Will Clark	.50
8	Kal Daniels	.10
9	Jim Deshaies	.10
10	Mark Eichhorn	.10
11	Ed Hearn	.10
12	Pete Incaviglia	.10
13	Bo Jackson	.30
14	Wally Joyner	.15
15	Charlie Kerfeld	.10
16	Eric King	.10
17	John Kruk	.10
18	Barry Larkin	.15
19	Mike LaValliere	.10
20	Greg Mathews	.10
21	Kevin Mitchell	.10
22	Dan Plesac	.10
23	Bruce Ruffin	.10
24	Ruben Sierra	.10
25	Cory Snyder	.10
26	Kurt Stillwell	.10
27	Dale Sveum	.10
28	Danny Tartabull	.10
29	Andres Thomas	.10
30	Robby Thompson	.10
31	Jim Traber	.10
32	Mitch Williams	.10
33	Todd Worrell	.10

1988 Toys "R" Us Rookies

This 33-card boxed edition was produced by Topps for exclusive distribution at Toys "R" Us stores. The glossy standard-size cards spotlight rookies in both close-ups and action photos on a bright blue background inlaid with yellow. The Toys "R" Us logo frames the top left corner, above a curving white banner that reads "Topps 1988 Collectors' Edition Rookies". A black Topps logo hugs the upper right-hand edge of the photo. The player name, red-lettered on a tube of yellow, frames the bottom. Card backs are horizontal, blue and pink on a bright pink background and include the player's name, personal information and career highlights and stats.

		MT
Complete Set (33):		3.50
Common Player:		.10
1	Todd Benzinger	.10
2	Bob Brower	.10
3	Jerry Browne	.10
4	DeWayne Buice	.10
5	Ellis Burks	.25
6	Ken Caminiti	.20
7	Casey Candaele	.10
8	Dave Cone	.30
9	Kelly Downs	.10
10	Mike Dunne	.10
11	Ken Gerhart	.10
12	Mike Greenwell	.10
13	Mike Henneman	.10
14	Sam Horn	.10
15	Joe Magrane	.10
16	Fred Manrique	.10
17	John Marzano	.10
18	Fred McGriff	.40
19	Mark McGwire	3.00
20	Jeff Musselman	.10
21	Randy Myers	.20
22	Matt Nokes	.10
23	Al Pedrique	.10
24	Luis Polonia	.10
25	Billy Ripken	.10
26	Benny Santiago	.10
27	Kevin Seitzer	.10
28	John Smiley	.10
29	Mike Stanley	.10
30	Terry Steinbach	.10
31	B.J. Surhoff	.10
32	Bobby Thigpen	.10
33	Devon White	.20

1989 Toys "R" Us Rookies

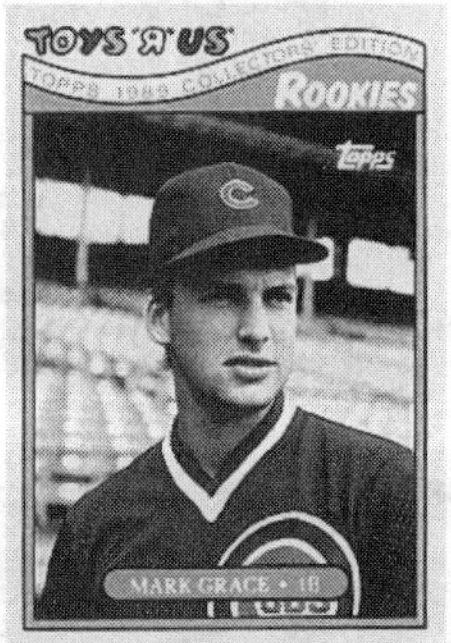

This glossy set of 33 top rookies was produced by Topps for the Toys "R" Us chain and was sold in a special box. Each player's name and position appear below the full-color photo, while the Toys "R" Us logo and "Topps 1989 Collector's Edition" appear along the top. Major and minor league stats are on the back. The set is numbered alphabetically.

		MT
Complete Set (33):		3.00
Common Player:		.10
1	Roberto Alomar	.50
2	Brady Anderson	.20
3	Tim Belcher	.10
4	Damon Berryhill	.10
5	Jay Buhner	.20
6	Sherman Corbett	.10
7	Kevin Elster	.10
8	Cecil Espy	.10
9	Dave Gallagher	.10
10	Ron Gant	.30
11	Paul Gibson	.10
12	Mark Grace	.50
13	Bryan Harvey	.10
14	Darrin Jackson	.10

15	Gregg Jefferies	.40
16	Ron Jones	.10
17	Ricky Jordan	.10
18	Roberto Kelly	.10
19	Al Leiter	.20
20	Jack McDowell	.20
21	Melido Perez	.10
22	Jeff Pico	.10
23	Jody Reed	.10
24	Chris Sabo	.10
25	Nelson Santovenia	.10
26	Mackey Sasser	.10
27	Mike Schooler	.10
28	Gary Sheffield	.50
29	Pete Smith	.10
30	Pete Stanicek	.10
31	Jeff Treadway	.10
32	Walt Weiss	.10
33	Dave West	.10

1990 Toys "R" Us Rookies

This 33-card set marks the fourth straight year that Topps has produced a set to be sold exclusively at Toys "R" Us stores. The card fronts contain full-color photos of 1989 rookies. The flip sides are horizontal and provide both minor and major league totals. The complete set is packaged in a special box which features a checklist on the back.

		MT
Complete Set (33):		4.00
Common Player:		.10
1	Jim Abbott	.30
2	Eric Anthony	.10
3	Joey Belle	.75
4	Andy Benes	.25
5	Greg Briley	.10
6	Kevin Brown	.10
7	Mark Carreon	.10
8	Mike Devereaux	.10
9	Junior Felix	.10
10	Mark Gardner	.10
11	Bob Geren	.10
12	Tom Gordon	.15
13	Ken Griffey, Jr.	3.00
14	Pete Harnisch	.10
15	Ken Hill	.15
16	Gregg Jefferies	.30
17	Derek Lilliquist	.10
18	Carlos Martinez	.10
19	Ramon Martinez	.20
20	Bob Milacki	.10
21	Gregg Olson	.10
22	Kenny Rogers	.10
23	Alex Sanchez	.10
24	Gary Sheffield	.25
25	Dwight Smith	.10
26	Billy Spiers	.10
27	Greg Vaughn	.25
28	Robin Ventura	.40
29	Jerome Walton	.10
30	Dave West	.10
31	John Wetteland	.10
32	Craig Worthington	.10
33	Todd Zeile	.20

1991 Toys "R" Us Rookies

Produced by Topps, this 33-card set features baseball's top young players. The cards are styled much like past Toys "R" Us issues feature glossy photos. The backs are printed horizontally and include player information and statistics. This set is the fifth of its kind produced by Topps for Toys "R" Us.

		MT
Complete Set (33):		4.00
Common Player:		.10
1	Sandy Alomar, Jr.	.25
2	Kevin Appier	.15
3	Steve Avery	.10
4	Carlos Baerga	.10
5	Alex Cole	.10
6	Pat Combs	.10
7	Delino DeShields	.10
8	Travis Fryman	.20
9	Marquis Grissom	.30
10	Mike Harkey	.10
11	Glenallen Hill	.10
12	Jeff Huson	.10
13	Felix Jose	.10
14	Dave Justice	.60
15	Dana Kiecker	.10
16	Kevin Maas	.10
17	Ben McDonald	.10
18	Brian McRae	.10
19	Kent Mercker	.10
20	Hal Morris	.10
21	Chris Nabholz	.10
22	Tim Naehring	.10
23	Jose Offerman	.10
24	John Olerud	.35
25	Scott Radinsky	.10
26	Bill Sampen	.10
27	Frank Thomas	2.00
28	Randy Tomlin	.10
29	Greg Vaughn	.10
30	Robin Ventura	.30
31	Larry Walker	.30
32	Wally Whitehurst	.10
33	Todd Zeile	.15

1993 Toys "R" Us Ty Cobb

This special gold-foil bordered card was available exclusively at TRU stores as part of a package of 65 plastic sheets sold by Megacards. The card is in the design of the contemporary Conlon Collection issue from Megacards and features on its front the classic photo of Cobb sliding into base. On the back, Conlon describes how he came to take the photo.

	MT
Ty Cobb	7.00

1993 Toys "R" Us Master Photos

Each boxed set of Toys "R" Us Stadium Club cards comes with a set of 12 Master Photos. Similar to the regular 1993 S.C. Master Photos, they feature at center a larger 2-3/4" x 3-3/4"), uncropped version of the photo used on the Toys "R" Us card. A gold holographic box on the photo delineates the dimensions of the regular card, while another separates the photo from the 5" by 7" white background. Topps, Toys "R" Us, and Master Photo logos appear at the top of the card. Blank white backs have a few logos and copyrights printed in black.

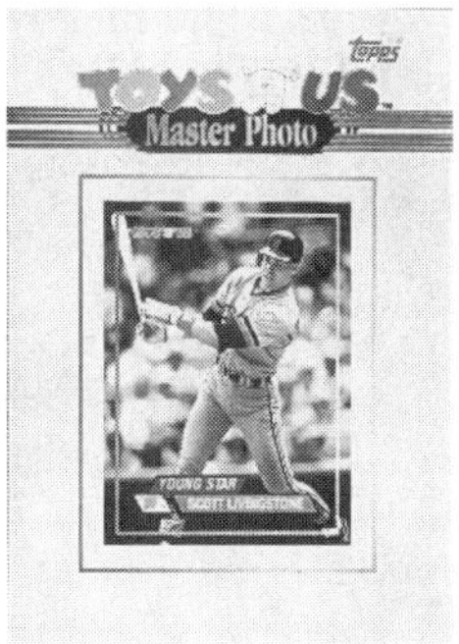

		MT
Complete Set (12):		6.00
Common Player:		.50
(1)	Willie Greene	.50
(2)	Frank Thomas	1.50
(3)	Chuck Knoblauch	.75
(4)	Marquis Grissom	.60
(5)	Scott Livingstone	.50
(6)	Ken Griffey, Jr.	2.00
(7)	Carlos Baerga	.50
(8)	Ivan Rodriguez	1.00
(9)	Moises Alou	.60
(10)	Sam Militello	.50
(11)	Eric Anthony	.50
(12)	Gary Sheffield	.75

1993 Toys "R" Us Topps Stadium Club

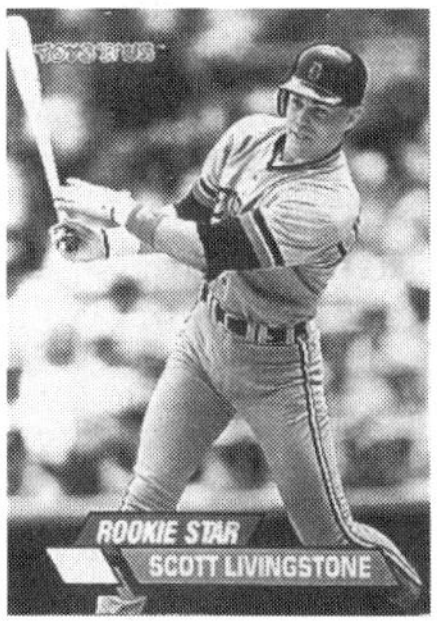

Featuring subsets labeled "Young Stars," "Future Stars" and "Rookie Stars," this 100-card set was sold in a plastic replica of a Toys "R" Us store, packaged with a dozen "Master Photos." Similar to regular 1993 Topps Stadium Club cards, the Toys "R" Us version features full-bleed photos on front, highlighted with gold-foil and a color Toys "R" Us logo in one of the upper corners. Backs have a background of a cloud-filled blue sky and green grass. A small player photo is at upper-right. Back information offers a few personal details, 1992 and career stats and a few career highlights. At bottom are the logos of all involved parties. The cards are UV-coated front and back. Each card is designated on the front as "Rookie Star," "Young Star" or "Future Star" in gold foil.

		MT
Complete Set (100):		15.00
Common Player:		.10
1	Ken Griffey, Jr.	2.00
2	Chad Curtis	.15
3	Mike Bordick	.10
4	Ryan Klesko	.45
5	Pat Listach	.10
6	Jim Bullinger	.10
7	Tim Laker	.10
8	Mike Devereaux	.10
9	Kevin Young	.10
10	John Valentin	.15
11	Pat Mahomes	.10
12	Todd Hundley	.15
13	Roberto Alomar	.35
14	David Justice	.30
15	Mike Perez	.10
16	Royce Clayton	.10
17	Ryan Thompson	.10
18	Dave Hollins	.15
19	Brien Taylor	.15
20	Melvin Nieves	.10
21	Rheal Cormier	.10
22	Mike Piazza	1.00
23	Larry Walker	.30
24	Tim Wakefield	.10
25	Tim Costo	.10
26	Pedro Munoz	.10
27	Reggie Sanders	.15
28	Arthur Rhodes	.10
29	Scott Cooper	.10
30	Marquis Grissom	.15
31	Dave Nilsson	.10
32	John Patterson	.10
33	Ivan Rodriguez	.30
34	Andy Stankiewicz	.10
35	Bret Boone	.15
36	Gerald Williams	.10
37	Mike Mussina	.25
38	Henry Rodriguez	.15
39	Chuck Knoblauch	.25
40	Bob Wickman	.10
41	Donovan Osborne	.10
42	Mike Timlin	.10
43	Damion Easley	.10
44	Pedro Astacio	.10
45	David Segui	.15
46	Willie Greene	.10
47	Mike Trombley	.10
48	Bernie Williams	.75
49	Eric Anthony	.10
50	Tim Naehring	.10
51	Carlos Baerga	.10
52	Brady Anderson	.15
53	Mo Vaughn	.30
54	Willie Banks	.10
55	Mark Wohlers	.10
56	Jeff Bagwell	.90
57	Frank Seminara	.10
58	Robin Ventura	.20
59	Alan Embree	.10
60	Rey Sanchez	.10
61	Delino DeShields	.10
62	Todd Van Poppel	.10
63	Eric Karros	.15
64	Gary Sheffield	.30
65	Dan Wilson	.10
66	Frank Thomas	1.50
67	Tim Salmon	.75
68	Dan Smith	.10
69	Kenny Lofton	.30
70	Carlos Garcia	.10
71	Scott Livingstone	.10
72	Sam Militello	.10
73	Juan Guzman	.10
74	Greg Colbrunn	.10
75	David Hulse	.10
76	Rusty Meacham	.10
77	Dave Fleming	.10
78	Rene Arocha	.10
79	Derrick May	.10
80	Cal Eldred	.10
81	Bernard Gilkey	.10
82	Deion Sanders	.20
83	Reggie Jefferson	.10
84	Jeff Kent	.10
85	Juan Gonzalez	1.00
86	Bill Ashley	.10
87	Travis Fryman	.15
88	Roberto Hernandez	.10
89	Hipolito Pichardo	.10
90	Wil Cordero	.10
91	John Jaha	.10
92	Javy Lopez	.25
93	Derek Bell	.15
94	Jeff Juden	.10
95	Steve Avery	.10
96	Moises Alou	.20
97	Brian Jordan	.15
98	Brian Williams	.10
99	Bob Zupcic	.10
100	Ray Lankford	.10

1992 Triple Play Previews

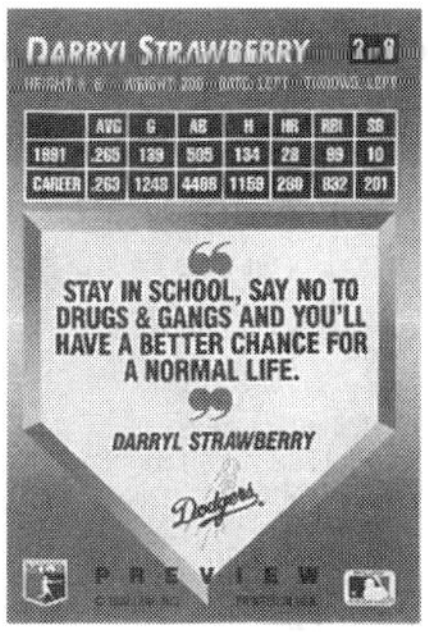

To introduce its base-brand Triple Play set in 1992, Donruss issued these preview cards. The format and photos on the previews are exactly like the issued versions; backs, however, differ in the numbering "X of 8" and the appearance of the word "PREVIEW" between the MLBPA and MLB logos at bottom.

		MT
Complete Set (8):		87.00
Common Player:		3.50
1	Ken Griffey Jr.	30.00
2	Darryl Strawberry	5.50
3	Andy Van Slyke (Little Hotshots)	3.50
4	Don Mattingly	15.00
5	Awesome Action (Gary Carter, Steve Finley)	3.50
6	Frank Thomas	20.00
7	Kirby Puckett	12.50
8	Fun at the Ballpark	3.50

1992 Triple Play

This set was released only in wax pack form. Cards feature red borders. Boyhood photos, mascots and ballparks are among the featured cards. This set was designed to give collectors an alternative product to the high-end card sets. The cards are standard size.

		MT
Complete Set (264):		10.00
Common Player:		.05
Wax Box:		10.00
1	SkyDome	.05
2	Tom Foley	.05
3	Scott Erickson	.05
4	Matt Williams	.15
5	Dave Valle	.05
6	Andy Van Slyke (Little Hotshot)	.05
7	Tom Glavine	.10
8	Kevin Appier	.05
9	Pedro Guerrero	.05
10	Terry Steinbach	.05
11	Terry Mulholland	.05
12	Mike Boddicker	.05
13	Gregg Olson	.05
14	Tim Burke	.05
15	Candy Maldonado	.05
16	Orlando Merced	.05
17	Robin Ventura	.10
18	Eric Anthony	.05
19	Greg Maddux	.75
20	Erik Hanson	.05
21	Bob Ojeda	.05
22	Nolan Ryan	.50
23	Dave Righetti	.05
24	Reggie Jefferson	.05
25	Jody Reed	.05
26	Awesome Action (Steve Finley, Gary Carter)	.05
27	Chili Davis	.05
28	Hector Villanueva	.05
29	Cecil Fielder	.05
30	Hal Morris	.05
31	Barry Larkin	.10
32	Bobby Thigpen	.05
33	Andy Benes	.10
34	Harold Baines	.05
35	David Cone	.10
36	Mark Langston	.05
37	Bryan Harvey	.05
38	John Kruk	.05
39	Scott Sanderson	.05
40	Lonnie Smith	.05
41	Awesome Action (Rex Hudler)	.05
42	George Bell	.05
43	Steve Finley	.05
44	Mickey Tettleton	.05

45 Robby Thompson .05
46 Pat Kelly .05
47 Marquis Grissom .10
48 Tony Pena .05
49 Alex Cole .05
50 Steve Buechele .05
51 Ivan Rodriguez .25
52 John Smiley .05
53 Gary Sheffield .15
54 Greg Olson .05
55 Ramon Martinez .10
56 B.J. Surhoff .05
57 Bruce Hurst .05
58 Todd Stottlemyre .05
59 Brett Butler .05
60 Glenn Davis .05
61 Awesome Action (Glenn Braggs, Kirt Manwaring) .05
62 Lee Smith .05
63 Rickey Henderson .15
64 Fun at the Ballpark (David Cone, Jeff Innis, John Franco) .05
65 Rick Aguilera .05
66 Kevin Elster .05
67 Dwight Evans .05
68 Andujar Cedeno .05
69 Brian McRae .05
70 Benito Santiago .05
71 Randy Johnson .20
72 Roberto Kelly .05
73 Awesome Action (Juan Samuel) .05
74 Alex Fernandez .05
75 Felix Jose .05
76 Brian Harper .05
77 Scott Sanderson (Little Hotshot) .05
78 Ken Caminiti .10
79 Mo Vaughn .15
80 Roger McDowell .05
81 Robin Yount .20
82 Dave Magadan .05
83 Julio Franco .05
84 Roberto Alomar .25
85 Steve Avery .05
86 Travis Fryman .10
87 Fred McGriff .15
88 Dave Stewart .05
89 Larry Walker .15
90 Chris Sabo .05
91 Chuck Finley .05
92 Dennis Martinez .05
93 Jeff Johnson .05
94 Len Dykstra .05
95 Mark Whiten .05
96 Wade Taylor .05
97 Lance Dickson .05
98 Kevin Tapani .05
99 Awesome Action (Luis Polonia, Tony Phillips) .05
100 Milt Cuyler .05
101 Willie McGee .05
102 Awesome Action (Tony Fernandez, Ryne Sandberg) .05
103 Albert Belle .25
104 Todd Hundley .05
105 Ben McDonald .05
106 Doug Drabek .05
107 Tim Raines .10
108 Joe Carter .05
109 Reggie Sanders .05
110 John Olerud .10
111 Darren Lewis .05
112 Juan Gonzalez .30
113 Awesome Action (Andre Dawson) .05
114 Mark Grace .15
115 George Brett .25
116 Barry Bonds .30
117 Lou Whitaker .05
118 Jose Oquendo .05
119 Lee Stevens .05
120 Phil Plantier .05
121 Awesome Action (Devon White, Matt Merullo) .05
122 Greg Vaughn .10
123 Royce Clayton .05
124 Bob Welch .05
125 Juan Samuel .05
126 Ron Gant .10
127 Edgar Martinez .05
128 Andy Ashby .05
129 Jack McDowell .05
130 Awesome Action (Dave Henderson, Jerry Browne) .05
131 Leo Gomez .05
132 Checklist 1-88 .05
133 Phillie Phanatic .05
134 Bret Barbarie .05
135 Kent Hrbek .05
136 Hall of Fame .05
137 Omar Vizquel .05
138 The Famous Chicken .05
139 Terry Pendleton .05
140 Jim Eisenreich .05
141 Todd Zeile .05
142 Todd Van Poppel .05
143 Darren Daulton .05
144 Mike Macfarlane .05
145 Luis Mercedes .05
146 Trevor Wilson .05
147 Dave Steib .05
148 Andy Van Slyke .05
149 Carlton Fisk .20
150 Craig Biggio .15
151 Joe Girardi .05
152 Ken Griffey, Jr. 1.25
153 Jose Offerman .05
154 Bobby Witt .05
155 Will Clark .20
156 Steve Olin .05
157 Greg Harris .05
158 Dale Murphy (Little Hotshot) .05
159 Don Mattingly .30
160 Shawon Dunston .05
161 Bill Gullickson .05
162 Paul O'Neill .10
163 Norm Charlton .05
164 Bo Jackson .15
165 Tony Fernandez .05
166 Dave Henderson .05
167 Dwight Gooden .10
168 Junior Felix .05
169 Lance Parrish .05
170 Pat Combs .05
171 Chuck Knoblauch .15
172 John Smoltz .10
173 Wrigley Field .05
174 Andre Dawson .10
175 Pete Harnisch .05
176 Alan Trammell .10
177 Kirk Dressendorfer .05
178 Matt Nokes .05
179 Wil Cordero .05
180 Scott Cooper .05
181 Glenallen Hill .05
182 John Franco .05
183 Rafael Palmeiro .15
184 Jay Bell .05
185 Bill Wegman .05
186 Deion Sanders .15
187 Darryl Strawberry .10
188 Jaime Navarro .05
189 Darren Jackson .05
190 Eddie Zosky .05
191 Mike Scioscia .05
192 Chito Martinez .05
193 Awesome Action (Pat Kelly, Ron Tingley) .05
194 Ray Lankford .05
195 Dennis Eckersley .05
196 Awesome Action (Ivan Calderon, Mike Maddux) .05
197 Shane Mack .05
198 Checklist 89-176 .05
199 Cal Ripken, Jr. 1.00
200 Jeff Bagwell .40
201 David Howard .05
202 Kirby Puckett .30
203 Harold Reynolds .05
204 Jim Abbott .05
205 Mark Lewis .05
206 Frank Thomas .50
207 Rex Hudler .05
208 Vince Coleman .05
209 Delino DeShields .05
210 Luis Gonzalez .05
211 Wade Boggs .15
212 Orel Hershiser .05
213 Cal Eldred .05
214 Jose Canseco .30
215 Jose Guzman .05
216 Roger Clemens .35
217 Dave Justice .15
218 Tony Phillips .05
219 Tony Gwynn .40
220 Mitch Williams .05
221 Bill Sampen .05
222 Billy Hatcher .05
223 Gary Gaetti .05
224 Tim Wallach .05
225 Kevin Maas .05
226 Kevin Brown .10
227 Sandy Alomar .10
228 John Habyan .05
229 Ryne Sandberg .25
230 Greg Gagne .05
231 Autographs (Mark McGwire) 1.00
232 Mike LaValliere .05
233 Mark Gubicza .05
234 Lance Parrish (Little Hotshot) .05
235 Carlos Baerga .05
236 Howard Johnson .05
237 Mike Mussina .10
238 Ruben Sierra .05
239 Lance Johnson .05
240 Devon White .05
241 Dan Wilson .05
242 Kelly Gruber .05
243 Brett Butler (Little Hotshot) .05
244 Ozzie Smith .25
245 Chuck McElroy .05
246 Shawn Boskie .05
247 Mark Davis .05
248 Bill Landrum .05
249 Frank Tanana .05
250 Darryl Hamilton .05
251 Gary DiSarcina .05
252 Mike Greenwell .05
253 Cal Ripken, Jr. (Little Hotshot) .25
254 Paul Molitor .15
255 Tim Teufel .05
256 Chris Hoiles .05
257 Rob Dibble .05
258 Sid Bream .05
259 Chito Martinez .05
260 Dale Murphy .15
261 Greg Hibbard .05
262 Mark McGwire 1.00
263 Oriole Park .05
264 Checklist 177-264 .05

1992 Triple Play Gallery of Stars

Two levels of scarcity are represented in this insert issue. Cards #1-6 (all cards have a GS prefix to the card number) feature in their new uniforms players who changed teams for 1993. Those inserts were found in the standard Triple Play foil packs and are somewhat more common than cards #7-12, which were found only in jumbo packs and which feature a better selection of established stars and rookies. All of the inserts feature the artwork of Dick Perez, with player portraits set against a colorful background. Silver-foil accents highlight the front design. Backs are red with a white "tombstone" containing a career summary.

MT
Complete Set (12): 9.00
Common Player: .40
1 Bobby Bonilla .40
2 Wally Joyner .40
3 Jack Morris .40
4 Steve Sax .40
5 Danny Tartabull .40
6 Frank Viola .40
7 Jeff Bagwell 1.00
8 Ken Griffey, Jr. 3.50
9 David Justice .50
10 Ryan Klesko .50
11 Cal Ripken, Jr. 2.50
12 Frank Thomas 1.25

1993 Triple Play Promos

Other than the fact they bear different card numbers than the same players in the regular-issue, nothing distinguishes these preview cards.

MT
Complete Set (12): 70.00
Common Player: 3.50
1 Ken Griffey Jr. 20.00
2 Roberto Alomar 7.50
3 Cal Ripken Jr. 17.50
4 Eric Karros 5.00
5 Cecil Fielder 3.50
6 Gary Sheffield 5.00
7 Darren Daulton 3.50
8 Andy Van Slyke 3.50
9 Dennis Eckersley 3.50
10 Ryne Sandberg 7.50
11 Mark Grace 6.00
12 Awesome Action (David Segui, Luis Polonia) 3.50

1993 Triple Play

For the second year, Leaf-Donruss used the "Triple Play" brand name for its base-level card set aimed at the younger collector. The 264-card set was available in several types of retail packaging and included a number of special subsets, such as childhood photos (labeled LH - Little Hotshots - in the checklist) and insert sets. Checklist card #264 incorrectly shows card #129, Joe Robbie Stadium, as #259. There is a second card, "Equipment," which also bears #129. An "Action Baseball" scratch-off game card was included in each foil pack.

MT
Complete Set (264): 10.00
Common Player: .05
Wax Box: 14.00
1 Ken Griffey, Jr. 1.50
2 Roberto Alomar .25
3 Cal Ripken, Jr. 1.00
4 Eric Karros .10
5 Cecil Fielder .05
6 Gary Sheffield .15
7 Darren Daulton .05
8 Andy Van Slyke .05
9 Dennis Eckersley .05
10 Ryne Sandberg .30
11 Mark Grace (Little Hotshots) .10
12 Awesome Action #1 (Luis Polonia, David Segui) .05
13 Mike Mussina .15
14 Vince Coleman .05
15 Rafael Belliard .05
16 Ivan Rodriguez .25
17 Eddie Taubensee .05
18 Cal Eldred .05
19 Rick Wilkins .05
20 Edgar Martinez .05
21 Brian McRae .05
22 Darren Holmes .05
23 Mark Whiten .05
24 Todd Zeile .05
25 Scott Cooper .05
26 Frank Thomas .50
27 Wil Cordero .05
28 Juan Guzman .05
29 Pedro Astacio .05
30 Steve Avery .05
31 Barry Larkin .15
32 President Clinton .25
33 Scott Erickson .05
34 Mike Devereaux .05
35 Tino Martinez .10
36 Brent Mayne .05
37 Tim Salmon .15
38 Dave Hollins .05
39 Royce Clayton .05
40 Shawon Dunston .05
41 Eddie Murray .15
42 Larry Walker .15
43 Jeff Bagwell .25
44 Milt Cuyler .05
45 Mike Bordick .05
46 Mike Greenwell .05
47 Steve Sax .05
48 Chuck Knoblauch .10
49 Charles Nagy .05
50 Tim Wakefield .05
51 Tony Gwynn .40
52 Rob Dibble .05
53 Mickey Morandini .05
54 Steve Hosey .05
55 Mike Piazza .75
56 Bill Wegman .05
57 Kevin Maas .05
58 Gary DiSarcina .05
59 Travis Fryman .10
60 Ruben Sierra .05
61 Awesome Action #2 (Ken Caminiti) .05
62 Brian Jordan .05
63 Scott Chiamparino .05
64 Awesome Action #3 (Mike Bordick, George Brett) .05
65 Carlos Garcia .05
66 Checklist 1-66 .05
67 John Smoltz .10
68 Awesome Action #4 (Mark McGwire, Brian Harper) .75
69 Kurt Stillwell .05
70 Chad Curtis .05
71 Rafael Palmeiro .15
72 Kevin Young .05
73 Glenn Davis .05
74 Dennis Martinez .05
75 Sam Militello .05
76 Mike Morgan .05
77 Frank Thomas (Little Hotshots) .25
78 Staying Fit (Bip Roberts, Mike Devereaux) .05
79 Steve Buechele .05
80 Carlos Baerga .05
81 Robby Thompson .05
82 Kirk McCaskill .05
83 Lee Smith .05
84 Gary Scott .05
85 Tony Pena .05
86 Howard Johnson .05
87 Mark McGwire 1.50
88 Bip Roberts .05
89 Devon White .05
90 John Franco .05
91 Tom Browning .05
92 Mickey Tettleton .05
93 Jeff Conine .05
94 Albert Belle .20
95 Fred McGriff .15
96 Nolan Ryan 1.00
97 Paul Molitor (Little Hotshots) .15
98 Juan Bell .05
99 Dave Fleming .05
100 Craig Biggio .15
101a Andy Stankiewicz (white name on front) .05
101b Andy Stankiewicz (red name on front) .25
102 Delino DeShields .05
103 Damion Easley .05
104 Kevin McReynolds .05
105 David Nied .05
106 Rick Sutcliffe .05
107 Will Clark .15
108 Tim Raines .10
109 Eric Anthony .05
110 Mike LaValliere .05
111 Dean Palmer .05
112 Eric Davis .05
113 Damon Berryhill .05
114 Felix Jose .05
115 Ozzie Guillen .05
116 Pat Listach .05
117 Tom Glavine .15
118 Roger Clemens .40
119 Dave Henderson .05
120 Don Mattingly .50
121 Orel Hershiser .05
122 Ozzie Smith .20
123 Joe Carter .05
124 Bret Saberhagen .10
125 Mitch Williams .05
126 Jerald Clark .05
127 Mile High Stadium .05
128 Kent Hrbek .05
129a Equipment (Curt Schilling, Mark Whiten) .05
129b Joe Robbie Stadium .05
130 Gregg Jefferies .05
131 John Orton .05
132 Checklist 67-132 .05
133 Bret Boone .05
134 Pat Borders .05
135 Gregg Olson .05
136 Brett Butler .05
137 Rob Deer .05
138 Darrin Jackson .05
139 John Kruk .05
140 Jay Bell .05
141 Bobby Witt .05
142 New Cubs (Dan Plesac, Randy Myers, Jose Guzman) .05
143 Wade Boggs (Little Hotshots) .15
144 Awesome Action #5 (Kenny Lofton) .05
145 Ben McDonald .05
146 Dwight Gooden .10
147 Terry Pendleton .05
148 Julio Franco .05
149 Ken Caminiti .10
150 Greg Vaughn .10
151 Sammy Sosa .75
152 David Valle .05
153 Wally Joyner .05
154 Dante Bichette .10
155 Mark Lewis .05
156 Bob Tewksbury .05
157 Billy Hatcher .05
158 Jack McDowell .05
159 Marquis Grissom .05
160 Jack Morris .05
161 Ramon Martinez .10
162 Deion Sanders .10
163 Tim Belcher .05
164 Mascots .10
165 Scott Leius .05
166 Brady Anderson .10
167 Randy Johnson .15
168 Mark Gubicza .05
169 Chuck Finley .05
170 Terry Mulholland .05
171 Matt Williams .10

172	Dwight Smith	.05
173	Bobby Bonilla	.05
174	Ken Hill	.05
175	Doug Jones	.05
176	Tony Phillips	.05
177	Terry Steinbach	.05
178	Frank Viola	.05
179	Robin Ventura	.10
180	Shane Mack	.05
181	Kenny Lofton	.20
182	Jeff King	.05
183	Tim Teufel	.05
184	Chris Sabo	.05
185	Lenny Dykstra	.05
186	Trevor Wilson	.05
187	Darryl Strawberry	.10
188	Robin Yount	.25
189	Bob Wickman	.05
190	Luis Polonia	.05
191	Alan Trammell	.10
192	Bob Welch	.05
193	Awesome Action #6	.05
194	Tom Pagnozzi	.05
195	Bret Barberie	.05
196	Awesome Action #7 (Mike Scioscia)	.05
197	Randy Tomlin	.05
198	Checklist 133-198	.05
199	Ron Gant	.10
200	Awesome Action #8 (Roberto Alomar)	.05
201	Andy Benes	.10
202	Pepper	.05
203	Steve Finley	.05
204	Steve Olin	.05
205	Chris Hoiles	.05
206	John Wetteland	.05
207	Danny Tartabull	.05
208	Bernard Gilkey	.05
209	Tom Glavine (Little Hotshots)	.05
210	Benito Santiago	.05
211	Mark Grace	.15
212	Glenallen Hill	.05
213	Jeff Brantley	.05
214	George Brett	.40
215	Mark Lemke	.05
216	Ron Karkovice	.05
217	Tom Brunansky	.05
218	Todd Hundley	.05
219	Rickey Henderson	.20
220	Joe Oliver	.05
221	Juan Gonzalez	.50
222	John Olerud	.15
223	Hal Morris	.05
224	Lou Whitaker	.05
225	Bryan Harvey	.05
226	Mike Gallego	.05
227	Willie McGee	.05
228	Jose Oquendo	.05
229	Darren Daulton (Little Hotshots)	.05
230	Curt Schilling	.05
231	Jay Buhner	.05
232	New Astros (Doug Drabek, Greg Swindell)	.05
233	Jaime Navarro	.05
234	Kevin Appier	.05
235	Mark Langston	.05
236	Jeff Montgomery	.05
237	Joe Girardi	.05
238	Ed Sprague	.05
239	Dan Walters	.05
240	Kevin Tapani	.05
241	Pete Harnisch	.05
242	Al Martin	.05
243	Jose Canseco	.25
244	Moises Alou	.10
245	Mark McGwire (Little Hotshots)	.75
246	Luis Rivera	.05
247	George Bell	.05
248	B.J. Surhoff	.05
249	Dave Justice	.15
250	Brian Harper	.05
251	Sandy Alomar, Jr.	.10
252	Kevin Brown	.10
253	New Dodgers (Tim Wallach, Jody Reed, Todd Worrell)	.05
254	Ray Lankford	.05
255	Derek Bell	.05
256	Joe Grahe	.05
257	Charlie Hayes	.05
258	New Yankees (Wade Boggs, Jim Abbott)	.15
259	Joe Robbie Stadium	.05
260	Kirby Puckett	.40
261	Fun at the Ballpark (Jay Bell, Vince Coleman)	.05
262	Bill Swift	.05
263	Fun at the Ballpark (Roger McDowell)	.05
264	Checklist 199-264	.05

1993 Triple Play Action Baseball

These game folders were inserted in each 1993 Triple Play foil pack. Because collation of the folders was very bad, few collectors bothered to save them. Measuring 2-1/2" x 5", fronts have an action photo of an unnamed player. Printed over the bottom of the photo are two full-color team logos, with a white "Versus" between. Inside the folder is a baseball diamond diagram, a three-inning scoreboard, rules for playing the game and 32 scratch-off squares for playing. Backs have a number designating the folder as "of 30."

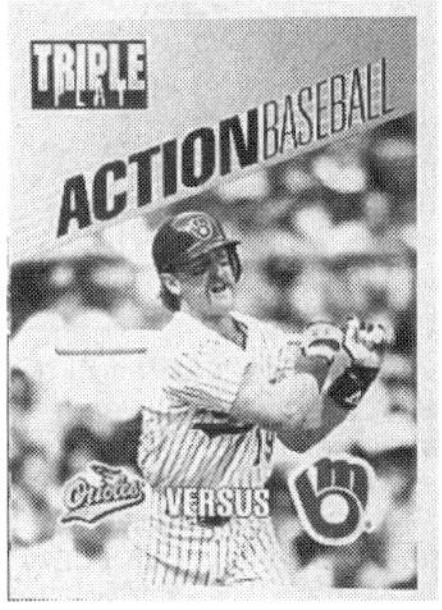

		MT
Complete Set (30):		5.00
Common Player:		.10
1	Andy Van Slyke	.10
2	Bobby Bonilla	.10
3	Ozzie Smith	.20
4	Ryne Sandberg	.25
5	Darren Daulton	.10
6	Larry Walker	.15
7	Eric Karros	.10
8	Barry Larkin	.10
9	Deion Sanders	.15
10	Gary Sheffield	.20
11	Will Clark	.20
12	Jeff Bagwell	.25
13	Roberto Alomar	.15
14	Roger Clemens	.25
15	Cecil Fielder	.10
16	Robin Yount	.25
17	Cal Ripken, Jr.	.45
18	Carlos Baerga	.10
19	Don Mattingly	.30
20	Kirby Puckett	.30
21	Frank Thomas	.25
22	Juan Gonzalez	.25
23	Mark McGwire	.50
24	Ken Griffey, Jr.	.50
25	Wally Joyner	.10
26	Chad Curtis	.10
27	Batting glove	.10
28	Juan Guzman	.10
29	Dave Justice	.15
30	Joe Carter	.10

1993 Triple Play Gallery

The Gallery of Stars cards were found as random inserts in Triple Play jumbo packs. The cards feature Dick Perez painted representations of the players.

		MT
Complete Set (10):		7.50
Common Player:		.40
1	Barry Bonds	1.50
2	Andre Dawson	.40
3	Wade Boggs	1.00
4	Greg Maddux	2.50
5	Dave Winfield	.75
6	Paul Molitor	1.50
7	Jim Abbott	.40
8	J.T. Snow	.40
9	Benito Santiago	.40
10	David Nied	.40

1993 Triple Play League Leaders

These "double-headed" cards feature one player on each side. The six cards were random inserts in Triple Play retail packs.

		MT
Complete Set (6):		7.00
Common Player:		.50
1	Barry Bonds, Dennis Eckersley	1.50
2	Greg Maddux, Dennis Eckersley	2.50
3	Eric Karros, Pat Listach	.50
4	Fred McGriff, Juan Gonzalez	2.00
5	Darren Daulton, Cecil Fielder	.50
6	Gary Sheffield, Edgar Martinez	.50

1993 Triple Play Nicknames

Popular nicknames of 10 of the game's top stars are featured in silver foil on this insert set found in Triple Play foil packs.

		MT
Complete Set (10):		18.00
Common Player:		1.00
1	Frank Thomas (Big Hurt)	2.00
2	Roger Clemens (Rocket)	2.00
3	Ryne Sandberg (Ryno)	1.50
4	Will Clark (Thrill)	1.50
5	Ken Griffey, Jr. (Junior)	6.00
6	Dwight Gooden (Doc)	1.00
7	Nolan Ryan (Express)	4.50
8	Deion Sanders (Prime Time)	1.00
9	Ozzie Smith (Wizard)	1.50
10	Fred McGriff (Crime Dog)	1.00

1994 Triple Play Promos

This set was given to dealers to preview the 1994 Donruss Triple Play issue. Cards are virtually identical to the regular-issue cards except for a large black "Promotional Sample" printed diagonally in black on both front and back. Cards are numbered as "X of 10" on the promos.

		MT
Complete Set (10):		20.00
Common Player:		1.50
1	Juan Gonzalez	2.00
2	Frank Thomas	2.00
3	Barry Bonds	2.50
4	Ken Griffey, Jr.	4.00
5	Paul Molitor	2.00
6	Mike Piazza	3.00
7	Tim Salmon	1.50
8	Lenny Dykstra	1.50
9	Don Mattingly	3.00
10	Greg Maddux	2.50

1994 Triple Play

Triple Play cards returned for a third year in 1994, this time with a borderless design. According to company officials, production was less than 1994 Donruss Series I baseball, which was roughly 17,500 20-box cases. In the regular-issue 300-card set, 10 players from each team were featured, along with a 17-card Rookie Review subset and several insert sets.

		MT
Complete Set (300):		14.00
Common Player:		.05
Wax Box:		22.00
1	Mike Bordick	.05
2	Dennis Eckersley	.05
3	Brent Gates	.05
4	Rickey Henderson	.20
5	Mark McGwire	1.50
6	Troy Neel	.05
7	Craig Paquette	.05
8	Ruben Sierra	.05
9	Terry Steinbach	.05
10	Bobby Witt	.05
11	Chad Curtis	.05
12	Chili Davis	.05
13	Gary DiSarcina	.05
14	Damion Easley	.05
15	Chuck Finley	.05
16	Joe Grahe	.05
17	Mark Langston	.05
18	Eduardo Perez	.05
19	Tim Salmon	.15
20	J.T. Snow	.10
21	Jeff Bagwell	.50
22	Craig Biggio	.20
23	Ken Caminiti	.10
24	Andujar Cedeno	.05
25	Doug Drabek	.05
26	Steve Finley	.05
27	Luis Gonzalez	.05
28	Pete Harnisch	.05
29	Darryl Kile	.05
30	Mitch Williams	.05
31	Roberto Alomar	.25
32	Joe Carter	.05
33	Juan Guzman	.05
34	Pat Hentgen	.05
35	Paul Molitor	.25
36	John Olerud	.15
37	Ed Sprague	.05
38	Dave Stewart	.05
39	Duane Ward	.05
40	Devon White	.05
41	Steve Avery	.05
42	Jeff Blauser	.05
43	Ron Gant	.10
44	Tom Glavine	.15
45	Dave Justice	.15
46	Greg Maddux	.75
47	Fred McGriff	.15
48	Terry Pendleton	.05
49	Deion Sanders	.15
50	John Smoltz	.10
51	Ricky Bones	.05
52	Cal Eldred	.05
53	Darryl Hamilton	.05
54	John Jaha	.05
55	Pat Listach	.05
56	Jaime Navarro	.05
57	Dave Nilsson	.05
58	B.J. Surhoff	.05
59	Greg Vaughn	.10
60	Robin Yount	.25
61	Bernard Gilkey	.05
62	Gregg Jefferies	.10
63	Brian Jordan	.05
64	Ray Lankford	.05
65	Tom Pagnozzi	.05
66	Ozzie Smith	.30
67	Bob Tewksbury	.05
68	Allen Watson	.05
69	Mark Whiten	.05
70	Todd Zeile	.05
71	Steve Buechele	.05
72	Mark Grace	.15
73	Jose Guzman	.05
74	Derrick May	.05
75	Mike Morgan	.05
76	Randy Myers	.05
77	Ryne Sandberg	.30
78	Sammy Sosa	1.00
79	Jose Vizcaino	.05
80	Rick Wilkins	.05
81	Pedro Astacio	.05
82	Brett Butler	.05
83	Delino DeShields	.05
84	Orel Hershiser	.05
85	Eric Karros	.05
86	Ramon Martinez	.10
87	Jose Offerman	.05
88	Mike Piazza	.60
89	Darryl Strawberry	.10
90	Tim Wallach	.05
91	Moises Alou	.10
92	Wil Cordero	.05
93	Jeff Fassero	.05
94	Darrin Fletcher	.05
95	Marquis Grissom	.10
96	Ken Hill	.05
97	Mike Lansing	.05
98	Kirk Rueter	.05
99	Larry Walker	.20
100	John Wetteland	.05
101	Rod Beck	.05
102	Barry Bonds	.40
103	John Burkett	.05
104	Royce Clayton	.05
105	Darren Lewis	.05
106	Kirt Manwaring	.05
107	Willie McGee	.05
108	Bill Swift	.05
109	Robby Thompson	.05
110	Matt Williams	.15
111	Sandy Alomar Jr.	.10
112	Carlos Baerga	.05
113	Albert Belle	.35
114	Wayne Kirby	.05
115	Kenny Lofton	.20
116	Jose Mesa	.05
117	Eddie Murray	.15
118	Charles Nagy	.05
119	Paul Sorrento	.05
120	Jim Thome	.15
121	Rich Amaral	.05
122	Eric Anthony	.05
123	Mike Blowers	.05
124	Chris Bosio	.05
125	Jay Buhner	.05
126	Dave Fleming	.05
127	Ken Griffey, Jr.	1.50
128	Randy Johnson	.25
129	Edgar Martinez	.05
130	Tino Martinez	.10
131	Bret Barberie	.05
132	Ryan Bowen	.05
133	Chuck Carr	.05
134	Jeff Conine	.10
135	Orestes Destrade	.05
136	Chris Hammond	.05
137	Bryan Harvey	.05
138	Dave Magadan	.05
139	Benito Santiago	.05
140	Gary Sheffield	.15
141	Bobby Bonilla	.05
142	Jeromy Burnitz	.05
143	Dwight Gooden	.10
144	Todd Hundley	.10
145	Bobby Jones	.05
146	Jeff Kent	.05
147	Joe Orsulak	.05
148	Bret Saberhagen	.05
149	Pete Schourek	.05
150	Ryan Thompson	.05
151	Brady Anderson	.10
152	Harold Baines	.05
153	Mike Devereaux	.05
154	Chris Hoiles	.05
155	Ben McDonald	.05
156	Mark McLemore	.05
157	Mike Mussina	.15
158	Rafael Palmeiro	.20
159	Cal Ripken, Jr.	1.00
160	Chris Sabo	.05
161	Brad Ausmus	.05
162	Derek Bell	.05
163	Andy Benes	.05
164	Doug Brocail	.05

165	Archi Cianfrocco	.05
166	Ricky Gutierrez	.05
167	Tony Gwynn	.50
168	Gene Harris	.05
169	Pedro Martinez	.50
170	Phil Plantier	.05
171	Darren Daulton	.05
172	Mariano Duncan	.05
173	Len Dykstra	.05
174	Tommy Greene	.05
175	Dave Hollins	.05
176	Danny Jackson	.05
177	John Kruk	.05
178	Terry Mulholland	.05
179	Curt Schilling	.10
180	Kevin Stocker	.05
181	Jay Bell	.05
182	Steve Cooke	.05
183	Carlos Garcia	.05
184	Joel Johnston	.05
185	Jeff King	.05
186	Al Martin	.05
187	Orlando Merced	.05
188	Don Slaught	.05
189	Andy Van Slyke	.05
190	Kevin Young	.05
191	Kevin Brown	.10
192	Jose Canseco	.30
193	Will Clark	.20
194	Juan Gonzalez	.40
195	Tom Henke	.05
196	David Hulse	.05
197	Dean Palmer	.05
198	Roger Pavlik	.05
199	Ivan Rodriguez	.40
200	Kenny Rogers	.05
201	Roger Clemens	.40
202	Scott Cooper	.05
203	Andre Dawson	.10
204	Mike Greenwell	.05
205	Billy Hatcher	.05
206	Jeff Russell	.05
207	Aaron Sele	.05
208	John Valentin	.05
209	Mo Vaughn	.25
210	Frank Viola	.05
211	Rob Dibble	.05
212	Willie Greene	.05
213	Roberto Kelly	.05
214	Barry Larkin	.15
215	Kevin Mitchell	.05
216	Hal Morris	.05
217	Joe Oliver	.05
218	Jose Rijo	.05
219	Reggie Sanders	.05
220	John Smiley	.05
221	Dante Bichette	.10
222	Ellis Burks	.05
223	Andres Galarraga	.15
224	Joe Girardi	.05
225	Charlie Hayes	.05
226	Darren Holmes	.05
227	Howard Johnson	.05
228	Roberto Mejia	.05
229	David Nied	.05
230	Armando Reynoso	.05
231	Kevin Appier	.05
232	David Cone	.10
233	Greg Gagne	.05
234	Tom Gordon	.05
235	Felix Jose	.05
236	Wally Joyner	.05
237	Jose Lind	.05
238	Brian McRae	.05
239	Mike MacFarlane	.05
240	Jeff Montgomery	.05
241	Eric Davis	.05
242	John Doherty	.05
243	Cecil Fielder	.05
244	Travis Fryman	.10
245	Bill Gullickson	.05
246	Mike Henneman	.05
247	Tony Phillips	.05
248	Mickey Tettleton	.05
249	Alan Trammell	.10
250	Lou Whitaker	.05
251	Rick Aguilera	.05
252	Scott Erickson	.05
253	Kent Hrbek	.05
254	Chuck Knoblauch	.10
255	Shane Mack	.05
256	Dave McCarty	.05
257	Pat Meares	.05
258	Kirby Puckett	.40
259	Kevin Tapani	.05
260	Dave Winfield	.20
261	Wilson Alvarez	.05
262	Jason Bere	.05
263	Alex Fernandez	.05
264	Ozzie Guillen	.05
265	Roberto Hernandez	.05
266	Lance Johnson	.05
267	Jack McDowell	.05
268	Tim Raines	.10
269	Frank Thomas	.50
270	Robin Ventura	.10
271	Jim Abbott	.05
272	Wade Boggs	.25
273	Mike Gallego	.05
274	Pat Kelly	.05
275	Jimmy Key	.05
276	Don Mattingly	.50
277	Paul O'Neill	.15
278	Mike Stanley	.05
279	Danny Tartabull	.05
280	Bernie Williams	.25
281	Chipper Jones	.60
282	Ryan Klesko	.15
283	Javier Lopez	.10
284	Jeffrey Hammonds	.10
285	Jeff McNeely	.05
286	Manny Ramirez	.50
287	Billy Ashley	.05
288	Raul Mondesi	.15
289	Cliff Floyd	.10
290	Rondell White	.10
291	Steve Karsay	.05
292	Midre Cummings	.10
293	Salomon Torres	.05
294	J.R. Phillips	.05
295	Marc Newfield	.05
296	Carlos Delgado	.25
297	Butch Huskey	.10
298	Checklist (Frank Thomas)	.05
299	Checklist (Barry Bonds)	.05
300	Checklist (Juan Gonzalez)	.05

1994 Triple Play Bomb Squad

Ten of the top major league home run hitters are included in this insert set. Fronts feature sepia-toned player photos within a wide brown frame. Gold foil enhances the typography. Backs have a white background with representations of vintage airplanes. A bar chart at left gives the player's home run totals by year. A small color portrait photo is at upper-right. Below are a few words about his homer history.

		MT
Complete Set (10):		15.00
Common Player:		.50
1	Frank Thomas	2.00
2	Cecil Fielder	.50
3	Juan Gonzalez	3.00
4	Barry Bonds	2.00
5	Dave Justice	.75
6	Fred McGriff	.75
7	Ron Gant	.50
8	Ken Griffey, Jr.	6.00
9	Albert Belle	1.50
10	Matt Williams	.50

1994 Triple Play Medalists

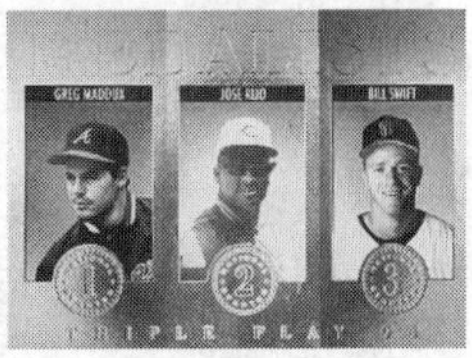

Statistical performance over the 1992-93 seasons was used to rank the players appearing in the Medalists insert set. Horizontal format cards have photos of the first, second and third place winners in appropriate boxes of gold, silver and bronze foil. "Medalists," the "medals" and "Triple Play 94" are embossed on the front. Backs have color action photos of each player along with team logos and a few stats.

		MT
Complete Set (15):		10.00
Common Player:		.50
1	A.L. Catchers (Chris Hoiles, Mickey Tettleton, Brian Harper)	.50
2	N.L. Catchers (Darren Daulton, Rick Wilkins, Kirt Manwaring)	.50
3	A.L. First Basemen (Frank Thomas, Rafael Palmeiro, John Olerud)	.75
4	N.L. First Basemen (Mark Grace, Fred McGriff, Jeff Bagwell)	1.50
5	A.L. Second Basemen (Roberto Alomar, Carlos Baerga, Lou Whitaker)	.50
6	N.L. Second Basemen (Ryne Sandberg, Craig Biggio, Robby Thompson)	1.00
7	A.L. Shortstops (Tony Fernandez, Cal Ripken, Jr., Alan Trammell)	2.00
8	N.L. Shortstops (Barry Larkin, Jay Bell, Jeff Blauser)	.50
9	A.L. Third Basemen (Robin Ventura, Travis Fryman, Wade Boggs)	.60
10	N.L. Third Basemen (Terry Pendleton, Dave Hollins, Gary Sheffield)	.50
11	A.L. Outfielders (Ken Griffey, Jr., Kirby Puckett, Albert Belle)	2.50
12	N.L. Outfielders (Barry Bonds, Andy Van Slyke, Len Dykstra)	.75
13	A.L. Starters (Jack McDowell, Kevin Brown, Randy Johnson)	.65
14	N.L. Starters (Greg Maddux, Jose Rijo, Billy Swift)	1.00
15	Designated Hitters (Paul Molitor, Dave Winfield, Harold Baines)	.60

1994 Triple Play Nicknames

Eight of baseball's most colorful team nicknames are featured in this insert set. Fronts feature a background photo representative of the nickname, with a player photo superimposed over that. Backs have another player photo and a history of the team's nickname.

		MT
Complete Set (8):		15.00
Common Player:		1.50
1	Cecil Fielder	1.00
2	Ryne Sandberg	2.00
3	Gary Sheffield	1.00
4	Joe Carter	1.00
5	John Olerud	1.50
6	Cal Ripken, Jr.	4.00
7	Mark McGwire	6.00
8	Gregg Jefferies	1.00

Player names in *Italic* type indicate a rookie card.

1990 Tropicana Team Mets

In 1990, Tropicana orange juice took over as sponsor of the junior Mets fan club. One of the membership perks was a nine-card sheet. Action photos were surrounded by team-color stripes of blue and orange and a white outer border. Backs have Team Mets and Tropicana logos, 1989 highlights and stats, career numbers and personal data. Individual cards measure 2-1/2" x 3-1/2", though they are not often sold other than as an original 7-1/2" x 10-1/2" sheet. Cards are checklisted here on the basis of uniform numbers found on the cards' fronts.

		MT
Complete Set (9):		4.00
Common Player:		.50
9	Gregg Jefferies	.75
16	Dwight Gooden	.60
18	Darryl Strawberry	.60
20	Howard Johnson	.50
21	Kevin Elster	.50
25	Keith Miller	.50
29	Frank Viola	.50
44	David Cone	.75
50	Sid Fernandez	.50

1991 Tropicana Team Mets

This nine-card sheet was a perk for members of the junior Mets fan club - Team Mets. Sponsored by Tropicana fruit juices for the second straight year, the 2-1/2" x 3-1/2" individual cards on the 7-1/2" x 10-1/2" sheet feature color action photos of the players, surrounded by team-color blue and orange stripes and an outer white border. Backs have 1990 highlights and stats, career stats and biographical details, along with the Team Mets and Tropicana logos. Cards are checklisted here according to the uniform numbers found on the front.

		MT
Complete Set (9):		4.00
Common Player:		.50
2	Mackey Sasser	.50
9	Gregg Jefferies	.75
10	Dave Magadan	.50
16	Dwight Gooden	.60
20	Howard Johnson	.50
22	Kevin McReynolds	.50
29	Frank Viola	.50
31	John Franco	.50
44	David Cone	.60

1983 True Value White Sox

Issued by the White Sox and True Value hardware stores, these 2-5/8" x 4-1/8" cards are among the scarcer early 1980s regional sets. The issue was originally scheduled as part of a promotion in which cards were given out at special Tuesday night games. The idea was sound, but rainouts forced the cancellation of some games so those scheduled cards were never given out. They were, however, smuggled out to hobby channels making it possible, although not easy, to assemble complete sets. The cards feature a large color photo with a wide white border. A team logo is at lower-left while the player's name, position and uniform number are in the lower right. Backs feature a True Value ad along with statistics. The three cards which were never given out through the normal channels are considered scarcer than the others. They are Marc Hill, Harold Baines and Salome Barojas.

		MT
Complete Set (23):		24.00
Common Player:		.50
1	Scott Fletcher	.50
2	Harold Baines	7.00
5	Vance Law	.50
7	Marc Hill	3.25
10	Tony LaRussa	1.00
11	Rudy Law	.50
14	Tony Bernazard	.50
17	Jerry Hairston	.50
19	Greg Luzinski	.75
24	Floyd Bannister	.50
25	Mike Squires	.50
30	Salome Barojas	3.50
31	LaMarr Hoyt	.50
34	Richard Dotson	.50
36	Jerry Koosman	.50
40	Britt Burns	.50
41	Dick Tidrow	.50
42	Ron Kittle	.50
44	Tom Paciorek	.50
45	Kevin Hickey	.50
53	Dennis Lamp	.50
67	Jim Kern	.50
72	Carlton Fisk	3.00

1984 True Value White Sox

True Value hardware stores and the White Sox gave the Tuesday night baseball card promotion at Comiskey Park another try in 1984. The cards measure 2-5/8" x 4-1/8". In addition to the players, there are cards for manager Tony LaRussa, the coaching staff, and former Sox greats Luis Aparicio and Minnie Minoso. Card design is very similar to the 1983 cards. As the cards were given out two at a time, it was very difficult to acquire a complete set. Additionally, as numbers available vary because of attendance, some cards are scarcer than others.

		MT
Complete Set (30):		25.00
Common Player:		.50
1	Scott Fletcher	.50
3	Harold Baines	2.00
5	Vance Law	.50
7	Marc Hill	.50
8	Dave Stegman	.50
10	Tony LaRussa	1.00
11	Rudy Law	.50
16	Julio Cruz	.50
17	Jerry Hairston	.50
19	Greg Luzinski	.75
20	Jerry Dybzinski	.50
24	Floyd Bannister	.50
25	Mike Squires	.50
27	Ron Reed	.50
29	Greg Walker	.50
30	Salome Barojas	.50
31	LaMarr Hoyt	.50
32	Tim Hulett	.50
34	Richard Dotson	.50
40	Britt Burns	.50
41	Tom Seaver	5.00
42	Ron Kittle	.50
44	Tom Paciorek	.50
50	Juan Agosto	.50
59	Tom Brennan	.50
72	Carlton Fisk	2.00
---	Minnie Minoso	3.00
---	Luis Aparicio	3.00
---	Nancy Faust (organist)	1.00
---	The Coaching Staff (Ed Brinkman, Dave Duncan, Art Kusnyer, Tony LaRussa, Jim Leyland, Dave Nelson, Joe Nossek)	.50

1986 True Value

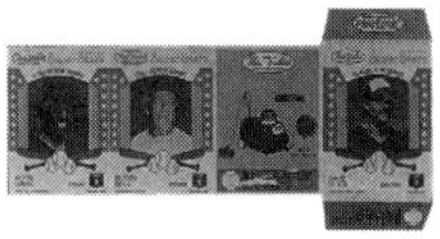

A 30-card set of 2-1/2" x 3-1/2" cards was available in three-card folders at True Value hardware stores with a purchase of $5 or more. Cards feature a photo enclosed by stars and a ball and bat at the bottom. The player's ID and a Major League Players Association logo are at bottom. Team insignia have been removed from the uniforms. Backs feature some personal information and brief 1985 statistics. Along with the player cards, the folders contained a sweepstakes card offering trips to post-season games and other prizes.

		MT
Complete Panel Set:		10.00
Complete Singles Set:		5.00
Common Panel:		.40
Common Single Player:		.05
Panel 1		1.00
1	Pedro Guerrero	.05
2	Steve Garvey	.15
3	Eddie Murray	.30
Panel 2		3.00
4	Pete Rose	.90
5	Don Mattingly	.90
6	Fernando Valenzuela	.10
Panel 3		.75
7	Jim Rice	.10
8	Kirk Gibson	.08
9	Ozzie Smith	.50
Panel 4		1.25
10	Dale Murphy	.20
11	Robin Yount	.45
12	Tom Seaver	.25
Panel 5		1.25
13	Reggie Jackson	.20
14	Ryne Sandberg	.35
15	Bruce Sutter	.05
Panel 6		1.50
16	Gary Carter	.10
17	George Brett	.75
18	Rick Sutcliffe	.05
Panel 7		.40
19	Dave Stieb	.05
20	Buddy Bell	.05
21	Alvin Davis	.05
Panel 8		2.50
22	Cal Ripken, Jr.	1.00
23	Bill Madlock	.05
24	Kent Hrbek	.10
Panel 9		2.00
25	Lou Whitaker	.05
26	Nolan Ryan	1.00
27	Dwayne Murphy	.05
Panel 10		2.00
28	Mike Schmidt	.60
29	Andre Dawson	.10
30	Wade Boggs	.45

U

1991 Ultra

This 400-card set was originally going to be called the Elite set, but Fleer chose to use the Ultra label. The card fronts feature gray borders surrounding full-color action photos. The backs feature three player photos and statistics. Hot Prospects and Great Performers are among the special cards featured within the set.

		MT
Complete Set (400):		20.00
Common Player:		.05
Wax Box:		17.00
1	Steve Avery	.05
2	Jeff Blauser	.05
3	Francisco Cabrera	.05
4	Ron Gant	.20
5	Tom Glavine	.15
6	Tommy Gregg	.05
7	Dave Justice	.25
8	Oddibe McDowell	.05
9	Greg Olson	.05
10	Terry Pendleton	.05
11	Lonnie Smith	.05
12	John Smoltz	.15
13	Jeff Treadway	.05
14	Glenn Davis	.05
15	Mike Devereaux	.05
16	Leo Gomez	.05
17	Chris Hoiles	.05
18	Dave Johnson	.05
19	Ben McDonald	.05
20	Randy Milligan	.05
21	Gregg Olson	.05
22	Joe Orsulak	.05
23	Bill Ripken	.05
24	Cal Ripken, Jr.	2.00
25	David Segui	.05
26	Craig Worthington	.05
27	Wade Boggs	.25
28	Tom Bolton	.05
29	Tom Brunansky	.05
30	Ellis Burks	.05
31	Roger Clemens	1.00
32	Mike Greenwell	.05
33	Greg Harris	.05
34	Daryl Irvine	.05
35	Mike Marshall	.05
36	Tim Naehring	.05
37	Tony Pena	.05
38	*Phil Plantier*	.05
39	Carlos Quintana	.05
40	Jeff Reardon	.05
41	Jody Reed	.05
42	Luis Rivera	.05
43	Jim Abbott	.05
44	Chuck Finley	.05
45	Bryan Harvey	.05
46	Donnie Hill	.05
47	Jack Howell	.05
48	Wally Joyner	.05
49	Mark Langston	.05
50	Kirk McCaskill	.05
51	Lance Parrish	.05
52	Dick Schofield	.05
53	Lee Stevens	.05
54	Dave Winfield	.20
55	George Bell	.05
56	Damon Berryhill	.05
57	Mike Bielecki	.05
58	Andre Dawson	.15
59	Shawon Dunston	.05
60	Joe Girardi	.05
61	Mark Grace	.20
62	Mike Harkey	.05
63	Les Lancaster	.05
64	Greg Maddux	1.50
65	Derrick May	.05
66	Ryne Sandberg	.60
67	Luis Salazar	.05
68	Dwight Smith	.05
69	Hector Villanueva	.05
70	Jerome Walton	.05
71	Mitch Williams	.05
72	Carlton Fisk	.20
73	Scott Fletcher	.05
74	Ozzie Guillen	.05
75	Greg Hibbard	.05
76	Lance Johnson	.05
77	Steve Lyons	.05
78	Jack McDowell	.05
79	Dan Pasqua	.05
80	Melido Perez	.05
81	Tim Raines	.10
82	Sammy Sosa	2.00
83	Cory Snyder	.05
84	Bobby Thigpen	.05
85	Frank Thomas	1.50
86	Robin Ventura	.20
87	Todd Benzinger	.05
88	Glenn Braggs	.05
89	Tom Browning	.05
90	Norm Charlton	.05
91	Eric Davis	.05
92	Rob Dibble	.05
93	Bill Doran	.05
94	Mariano Duncan	.05
95	Billy Hatcher	.05
96	Barry Larkin	.15
97	Randy Myers	.05
98	Hal Morris	.05
99	Joe Oliver	.05
100	Paul O'Neill	.20
101a	Jeff Reed	.05
101b	Beau Allred (Should be #104)	.05
102	Jose Rijo	.05
103a	Chris Sabo	.05
103b	Carlos Baerga (Should be #106)	.05
104	Not Issued (Not issued, see #101b)	
105	Sandy Alomar,Jr.	.15
106	Not Issued (Not issued, see #103b)	
107	Albert Belle	.75
108	Jerry Browne	.05
109	Tom Candiotti	.05
110	Alex Cole	.05
111a	John Farrell	.05
111b	Chris James (Should be #114)	.05
112	Felix Fermin	.05
113	Brook Jacoby	.05
114	Not Issued (Not issued, see #111b)	
115	Doug Jones	.05
116a	Steve Olin	.05
116b	Mitch Webster (Should be #119)	.05
117	Greg Swindell	.05
118	Turner Ward	.05
119	Not Issued (Not issued, see #116b)	
120	Dave Bergman	.05
121	Cecil Fielder	.05
122	Travis Fryman	.15
123	Mike Henneman	.05
124	Lloyd Moseby	.05
125	Dan Petry	.05
126	Tony Phillips	.05
127	Mark Salas	.05
128	Frank Tanana	.05
129	Alan Trammell	.10
130	Lou Whitaker	.05
131	Eric Anthony	.05
132	Craig Biggio	.40
133	Ken Caminiti	.20
134	Casey Candaele	.05
135	Andujar Cedeno	.05
136	Mark Davidson	.05
137	Jim Deshaies	.05
138	Mark Portugal	.05
139	Rafael Ramirez	.05
140	Mike Scott	.05
141	Eric Yelding	.05
142	Gerald Young	.05
143	Kevin Appier	.05
144	George Brett	.50
145	*Jeff Conine*	.40
146	Jim Eisenreich	.05
147	Tom Gordon	.05
148	Mark Gubicza	.05
149	Bo Jackson	.20
150	Brent Mayne	.05
151	Mike Macfarlane	.05
152	*Brian McRae*	.35
153	Jeff Montgomery	.05
154	Bret Saberhagen	.05
155	Kevin Seitzer	.05
156	Terry Shumpert	.05
157	Kurt Stillwell	.05
158	Danny Tartabull	.05
159	Tim Belcher	.05
160	Kal Daniels	.05
161	Alfredo Griffin	.05
162	Lenny Harris	.05
163	Jay Howell	.05
164	Ramon Martinez	.10
165	Mike Morgan	.05
166	Eddie Murray	.30
167	Jose Offerman	.05
168	Juan Samuel	.05
169	Mike Scioscia	.05
170	Mike Sharperson	.05
171	Darryl Strawberry	.15
172	Greg Brock	.05
173	Chuck Crim	.05
174	Jim Gantner	.05
175	Ted Higuera	.05
176	Mark Knudson	.05
177	Tim McIntosh	.05
178	Paul Molitor	.30
179	Dan Plesac	.05
180	Gary Sheffield	.25
181	Bill Spiers	.05
182	B.J. Surhoff	.05
183	Greg Vaughn	.10
184	Robin Yount	.25
185	Rick Aguilera	.05
186	Greg Gagne	.05
187	Dan Gladden	.05
188	Brian Harper	.05
189	Kent Hrbek	.05
190	Gene Larkin	.05
191	Shane Mack	.05
192	Pedro Munoz	.05
193	Al Newman	.05
194	Junior Ortiz	.05
195	Kirby Puckett	.60
196	Kevin Tapani	.05
197	Dennis Boyd	.05
198	Tim Burke	.05
199	Ivan Calderon	.05
200	Delino DeShields	.05
201	Mike Fitzgerald	.05
202	Steve Frey	.05
203	Andres Galarraga	.25
204	Marquis Grissom	.10
205	Dave Martinez	.05
206	Dennis Martinez	.05
207	Junior Noboa	.05
208	Spike Owen	.05
209	Scott Ruskin	.05
210	Tim Wallach	.05
211	Daryl Boston	.05
212	Vince Coleman	.05
213	David Cone	.20
214	Ron Darling	.05
215	Kevin Elster	.05
216	Sid Fernandez	.05
217	John Franco	.05
218	Dwight Gooden	.10
219	Tom Herr	.05
220	Todd Hundley	.20
221	Gregg Jefferies	.10
222	Howard Johnson	.05
223	Dave Magadan	.05
224	Kevin McReynolds	.05
225	Keith Miller	.05
226	Mackey Sasser	.05
227	Frank Viola	.05
228	Jesse Barfield	.05
229	Greg Cadaret	.05
230	Alvaro Espinoza	.05
231	Bob Geren	.05
232	Lee Guetterman	.05
233	Mel Hall	.05
234	Andy Hawkins	.05
235	Roberto Kelly	.05
236	Tim Leary	.05
237	Jim Leyritz	.05
238	Kevin Maas	.05
239	Don Mattingly	.75
240	Hensley Meulens	.05
241	Eric Plunk	.05
242	Steve Sax	.05
243	Todd Burns	.05
244	Jose Canseco	.50
245	Dennis Eckersley	.05
246	Mike Gallego	.05
247	Dave Henderson	.05
248	Rickey Henderson	.30
249	Rick Honeycutt	.05
250	Carney Lansford	.05
251	Mark McGwire	3.00
252	Mike Moore	.05
253	Terry Steinbach	.05
254	Dave Stewart	.05
255	Walt Weiss	.05
256	Bob Welch	.05
257	Curt Young	.05
258	Wes Chamberlain	.05
259	Pat Combs	.05
260	Darren Daulton	.05
261	Jose DeJesus	.05
262	Len Dykstra	.05
263	Charlie Hayes	.05
264	Von Hayes	.05
265	Ken Howell	.05
266	John Kruk	.05
267	Roger McDowell	.05
268	Mickey Morandini	.05
269	Terry Mulholland	.05
270	Dale Murphy	.10
271	Randy Ready	.05
272	Dickie Thon	.05
273	Stan Belinda	.05
274	Jay Bell	.05
275	Barry Bonds	.60
276	Bobby Bonilla	.05
277	Doug Drabek	.05
278	*Carlos Garcia*	.15
279	Neal Heaton	.05
280	Jeff King	.05
281	Bill Landrum	.05
282	Mike LaValliere	.05
283	Jose Lind	.05
284	*Orlando Merced*	.20
285	Gary Redus	.05
286	Don Slaught	.05
287	Andy Van Slyke	.05
288	Jose DeLeon	.05
289	Pedro Guerrero	.05
290	Ray Lankford	.05
291	Joe Magrane	.05
292	Jose Oquendo	.05
293	Tom Pagnozzi	.05
294	Bryn Smith	.05
295	Lee Smith	.05
296	Ozzie Smith	.40
297	Milt Thompson	.05
298	*Craig Wilson*	.05
299	Todd Zeile	.10
300	Shawn Abner	.05
301	Andy Benes	.10
302	Paul Faries	.05
303	Tony Gwynn	1.00
304	Greg Harris	.05
305	Thomas Howard	.05
306	Bruce Hurst	.05
307	Craig Lefferts	.05
308	Fred McGriff	.35
309	Dennis Rasmussen	.05
310	Bip Roberts	.05
311	Benito Santiago	.05
312	Garry Templeton	.05
313	Ed Whitson	.05
314	Dave Anderson	.05
315	Kevin Bass	.05
316	Jeff Brantley	.05
317	John Burkett	.05
318	Will Clark	.25
319	Steve Decker	.05
320	Scott Garrelts	.05
321	Terry Kennedy	.05
322	Mark Leonard	.05
323	Darren Lewis	.05
324	Greg Litton	.05
325	Willie McGee	.05
326	Kevin Mitchell	.05
327	Don Robinson	.05
328	Andres Santana	.05
329	Robby Thompson	.05
330	Jose Uribe	.05
331	Matt Williams	.15
332	Scott Bradley	.05
333	Henry Cotto	.05
334	Alvin Davis	.05
335	Ken Griffey, Sr.	.05
336	Ken Griffey, Jr.	3.00
337	Erik Hanson	.05
338	Brian Holman	.05
339	Randy Johnson	.40
340	Edgar Martinez	.05
341	Tino Martinez	.20
342	Pete O'Brien	.05
343	Harold Reynolds	.05
344	David Valle	.05
345	Omar Vizquel	.05
346	Brad Arnsberg	.05
347	Kevin Brown	.15
348	Julio Franco	.05
349	Jeff Huson	.05
350	Rafael Palmeiro	.30
351	Geno Petralli	.05
352	Gary Pettis	.05
353	Kenny Rogers	.05
354	Jeff Russell	.05
355	Nolan Ryan	2.00
356	Ruben Sierra	.05
357	Bobby Witt	.05
358	Roberto Alomar	.35
359	Pat Borders	.05
360	Joe Carter	.05
361	Kelly Gruber	.05
362	Tom Henke	.05
363	Glenallen Hill	.05
364	Jimmy Key	.05
365	Manny Lee	.05
366	Rance Mulliniks	.05
367	John Olerud	.25
368	Dave Stieb	.05
369	Duane Ward	.05
370	David Wells	.10
371	Mark Whiten	.05
372	Mookie Wilson	.05
373	Willie Banks	.05
374	Steve Carter	.05
375	Scott Chiamparino	.05
376	Steve Chitren	.05
377	Darrin Fletcher	.05
378	Rich Garces	.05
379	Reggie Jefferson	.05
380	*Eric Karros*	.75
381	Pat Kelly	.05
382	Chuck Knoblauch	.50
383	Denny Neagle	.05
384	Dan Opperman	.05
385	John Ramos	.05
386	*Henry Rodriguez*	.50
387	Mo Vaughn	1.00
388	Gerald Williams	.05
389	Mike York	.05
390	Eddie Zosky	.05
391	Barry Bonds (Great Performer)	.30
392	Cecil Fielder (Great Performer)	.05
393	Rickey Henderson (Great Performer)	.10
394	Dave Justice (Great Performer)	.20
395	Nolan Ryan (Great Performer)	1.00

396	Bobby Thigpen (Great Performer)	.05
397	Checklist	.05
398	Checklist	.05
399	Checklist	.05
400	Checklist	.05

1991 Ultra Gold

A pair of action photos flanking and below a portrait in a home plate frame at top-center are featured on these cards. Background is a graduated gold coloring. The Fleer Ultra Team logo is in the upper-left corner. Backs have narrative career information. The Puckett and Sandberg cards feature incorrect historical information on the backs.

		MT
Complete Set (10):		7.50
Common Player:		.25
1	Barry Bonds	1.50
2	Will Clark	.50
3	Doug Drabek	.25
4	Ken Griffey, Jr.	4.00
5	Rickey Henderson	.50
6	Bo Jackson	.40
7	Ramon Martinez	.30
8	Kirby Puckett	1.25
9	Chris Sabo	.25
10	Ryne Sandberg	1.00

1991 Ultra Update

This 120-card set was produced as a supplement to the premier Fleer Ultra set. Cards feature the same style as the regular Fleer Ultra cards. The cards were sold only as complete sets in full color, shrink-wrapped boxes.

		MT
Complete Set (120):		40.00
Common Player:		.15
1	Dwight Evans	.15
2	Chito Martinez	.15
3	Bob Melvin	.15
4	*Mike Mussina*	6.00
5	Jack Clark	.15
6	Dana Kiecker	.15
7	Steve Lyons	.15
8	Gary Gaetti	.15
9	Dave Gallagher	.15
10	Dave Parker	.20
11	Luis Polonia	.15
12	Luis Sojo	.15
13	Wilson Alvarez	.40
14	Alex Fernandez	.25
15	Craig Grebeck	.15
16	Ron Karkovice	.15
17	Warren Newson	.15
18	Scott Radinsky	.15
19	Glenallen Hill	.15
20	Charles Nagy	.40
21	Mark Whiten	.15
22	Milt Cuyler	.15
23	Paul Gibson	.15
24	Mickey Tettleton	.15
25	Todd Benzinger	.15
26	Storm Davis	.15
27	Kirk Gibson	.15
28	Bill Pecota	.15
29	Gary Thurman	.15
30	Darryl Hamilton	.15
31	Jaime Navarro	.15
32	Willie Randolph	.15
33	Bill Wegman	.15
34	Randy Bush	.15
35	Chili Davis	.15
36	Scott Erickson	.25
37	Chuck Knoblauch	1.00
38	Scott Leius	.15
39	Jack Morris	.15
40	John Habyan	.15
41	Pat Kelly	.15
42	Matt Nokes	.15
43	Scott Sanderson	.15
44	Bernie Williams	3.00
45	Harold Baines	.20
46	Brook Jacoby	.15
47	Ernest Riles	.15
48	Willie Wilson	.15
49	Jay Buhner	.15
50	Rich DeLucia	.15
51	Mike Jackson	.15
52	Bill Krueger	.15
53	Bill Swift	.15
54	Brian Downing	.15
55	Juan Gonzalez	15.00
56	Dean Palmer	.50
57	Kevin Reimer	.15
58	*Ivan Rodriguez*	15.00
59	Tom Candiotti	.15
60	Juan Guzman	.15
61	Bob MacDonald	.15
62	Greg Myers	.15
63	Ed Sprague	.15
64	Devon White	.20
65	Rafael Belliard	.15
66	Juan Berenguer	.15
67	Brian Hunter	.15
68	Kent Mercker	.15
69	Otis Nixon	.15
70	Danny Jackson	.15
71	Chuck McElroy	.15
72	Gary Scott	.15
73	Heathcliff Slocumb	.15
74	Chico Walker	.15
75	Rick Wilkins	.15
76	Chris Hammond	.15
77	Luis Quinones	.15
78	Herm Winningham	.15
79	*Jeff Bagwell*	15.00
80	Jim Corsi	.15
81	Steve Finley	.15
82	*Luis Gonzalez*	2.00
83	Pete Harnisch	.15
84	Darryl Kile	.15
85	Brett Butler	.15
86	Gary Carter	.25
87	Tim Crews	.15
88	Orel Hershiser	.15
89	Bob Ojeda	.15
90	Bret Barberie	.15
91	Barry Jones	.15
92	Gilberto Reyes	.15
93	Larry Walker	3.00
94	Hubie Brooks	.15
95	Tim Burke	.15
96	Rick Cerone	.15
97	Jeff Innis	.15
98	Wally Backman	.15
99	Tommy Greene	.15
100	Ricky Jordan	.15
101	Mitch Williams	.15
102	John Smiley	.15
103	Randy Tomlin	.15
104	Gary Varsho	.15
105	Cris Carpenter	.15
106	Ken Hill	.15
107	Felix Jose	.15
108	*Omar Oliveras*	.75
109	Gerald Perry	.15
110	Jerald Clark	.15
111	Tony Fernandez	.15
112	Darrin Jackson	.15
113	Mike Maddux	.15
114	Tim Teufel	.15
115	Bud Black	.15
116	Kelly Downs	.15
117	Mike Felder	.15
118	Willie McGee	.15
119	Trevor Wilson	.15
120	Checklist	.15

1992 Ultra Pre-Production Samples

These cards were produced and distributed to hobby dealers to give them a preview of Ultra's second-year offering, including the Award Winners and Tony Gwynn inserts. Cards are virtually identical to the issued versions except for a white oval on back which has a "1992 / PRE-PRODUCTION / SAMPLE" notice printed in black. Each card (except the Gwynn) can also be found in a version with no card number on back; they are worth a small premium over the numbered promos.

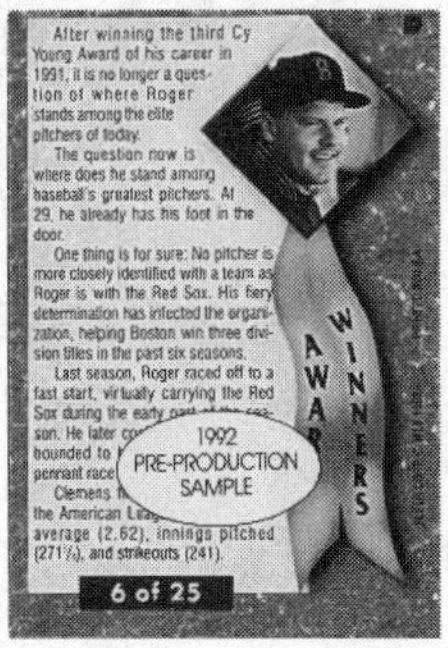

		MT
Complete Set (6):		125.00
Common Player:		7.50
118	Todd Van Poppel	7.50
180	Rey Sanchez	7.50
271	Ozzie Smith	45.00
288	Royce Clayton	7.50
6/25	Roger Clemens (Award Winners)	45.00
2/10	Tony Gwynn (Commermorative Series)	35.00

1992 Ultra

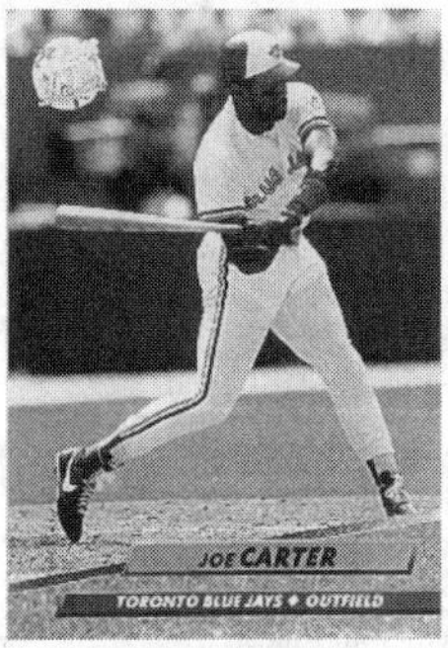

Fleer released its second annual Ultra set in 1992. Card fronts feature full-color action photos with a marble accent at the card bottom. The flip sides are horizontal with two additional player photos. Many insert sets were randomly included in foil packs as premiums. These included rookie, All-Star and award winners, among others. A two-card Tony Gwynn send-away set was also available through an offer from Fleer. For $1 and 10 Ultra wrappers, collectors could receive the Gwynn cards. The set is numbered by team; cards #1-300 comprise Series I, cards #301-600 are Series II.

		MT
Complete Set (600):		30.00
Series 1 (300):		20.00
Series 2 (300):		10.00
Common Player:		.10
Series 1 Wax Box:		40.00
Series 2 Wax Box:		30.00
1	Glenn Davis	.10
2	Mike Devereaux	.10
3	Dwight Evans	.10
4	Leo Gomez	.10
5	Chris Hoiles	.10
6	Sam Horn	.10
7	Chito Martinez	.10
8	Randy Milligan	.10
9	Mike Mussina	.60
10	Billy Ripken	.10
11	Cal Ripken, Jr.	2.00
12	Tom Brunansky	.10
13	Ellis Burks	.10
14	Jack Clark	.10
15	Roger Clemens	1.00
16	Mike Greenwell	.10
17	Joe Hesketh	.10
18	Tony Pena	.10
19	Carlos Quintana	.10
20	Jeff Reardon	.10
21	Jody Reed	.10
22	Luis Rivera	.10
23	Mo Vaughn	.40
24	Gary DiSarcina	.10
25	Chuck Finley	.10
26	Gary Gaetti	.10
27	Bryan Harvey	.10
28	Lance Parrish	.10
29	Luis Polonia	.10
30	Dick Schofield	.10
31	Luis Sojo	.10
32	Wilson Alvarez	.10
33	Carlton Fisk	.40
34	Craig Grebeck	.10
35	Ozzie Guillen	.10
36	Greg Hibbard	.10
37	Charlie Hough	.10
38	Lance Johnson	.10
39	Ron Karkovice	.10
40	Jack McDowell	.10
41	Donn Pall	.10
42	Melido Perez	.10
43	Tim Raines	.15
44	Frank Thomas	1.00
45	Sandy Alomar, Jr.	.20
46	Carlos Baerga	.10
47	Albert Belle	.40
48	Jerry Browne	.10
49	Felix Fermin	.10
50	Reggie Jefferson	.10
51	Mark Lewis	.10
52	Carlos Martinez	.10
53	Steve Olin	.10
54	Jim Thome	.75
55	Mark Whiten	.10
56	Dave Bergman	.10
57	Milt Cuyler	.10
58	Rob Deer	.10
59	Cecil Fielder	.10
60	Travis Fryman	.25
61	Scott Livingstone	.10
62	Tony Phillips	.10
63	Mickey Tettleton	.10
64	Alan Trammell	.15
65	Lou Whitaker	.10
66	Kevin Appier	.10
67	Mike Boddicker	.10
68	George Brett	.75
69	Jim Eisenreich	.10
70	Mark Gubicza	.10
71	David Howard	.10
72	Joel Johnston	.10
73	Mike Macfarlane	.10
74	Brent Mayne	.10
75	Brian McRae	.10
76	Jeff Montgomery	.10
77	Terry Shumpert	.10
78	Don August	.10
79	Dante Bichette	.25
80	Ted Higuera	.10
81	Paul Molitor	.40
82	Jamie Navarro	.10
83	Gary Sheffield	.25
84	Bill Spiers	.10
85	B.J. Surhoff	.10
86	Greg Vaughn	.10
87	Robin Yount	.40
88	Rick Aguilera	.10
89	Chili Davis	.10
90	Scott Erickson	.10
91	Brian Harper	.10
92	Kent Hrbek	.10
93	Chuck Knoblauch	.15
94	Scott Leius	.10
95	Shane Mack	.10
96	Mike Pagliarulo	.10
97	Kirby Puckett	.75
98	Kevin Tapani	.10
99	Jesse Barfield	.10
100	Alvaro Espinoza	.10
101	Mel Hall	.10
102	Pat Kelly	.10
103	Roberto Kelly	.10
104	Kevin Maas	.10
105	Don Mattingly	1.00
106	Hensley Meulens	.10
107	Matt Nokes	.10
108	Steve Sax	.10
109	Harold Baines	.10
110	Jose Canseco	.50
111	Ron Darling	.10
112	Mike Gallego	.10
113	Dave Henderson	.10
114	Rickey Henderson	.40
115	Mark McGwire	3.00
116	Terry Steinbach	.10
117	Dave Stewart	.10
118	Todd Van Poppel	.10
119	Bob Welch	.10
120	Greg Briley	.10
121	Jay Buhner	.10
122	Rich DeLucia	.10
123	Ken Griffey, Jr.	3.00
124	Erik Hanson	.10
125	Randy Johnson	.40
126	Edgar Martinez	.10
127	Tino Martinez	.15
128	Pete O'Brien	.10
129	Harold Reynolds	.10
130	Dave Valle	.10
131	Julio Franco	.10
132	Juan Gonzalez	1.00
133	Jeff Huson	.10
134	Mike Jeffcoat	.10
135	Terry Mathews	.10
136	Rafael Palmeiro	.40
137	Dean Palmer	.10
138	Geno Petralli	.10
139	Ivan Rodriguez	.75
140	Jeff Russell	.10
141	Nolan Ryan	2.00
142	Ruben Sierra	.10
143	Roberto Alomar	.50
144	Pat Borders	.10
145	Joe Carter	.10
146	Kelly Gruber	.10
147	Jimmy Key	.10
148	Manny Lee	.10
149	Rance Mulliniks	.10
150	Greg Myers	.10
151	John Olerud	.25
152	Dave Stieb	.10
153	Todd Stottlemyre	.10
154	Duane Ward	.10
155	Devon White	.10
156	Eddie Zosky	.10
157	Steve Avery	.10
158	Rafael Belliard	.10
159	Jeff Blauser	.10
160	Sid Bream	.10
161	Ron Gant	.10
162	Tom Glavine	.25
163	Brian Hunter	.10
164	Dave Justice	.25
165	Mark Lemke	.10
166	Greg Olson	.10
167	Terry Pendleton	.10
168	Lonnie Smith	.10
169	John Smoltz	.15
170	Mike Stanton	.10
171	Jeff Treadway	.10
172	Paul Assenmacher	.10
173	George Bell	.10
174	Shawon Dunston	.10
175	Mark Grace	.20
176	Danny Jackson	.10
177	Les Lancaster	.10
178	Greg Maddux	1.50
179	Luis Salazar	.10
180	Rey Sanchez	.10
181	Ryne Sandberg	.50
182	Jose Vizcaino	.10
183	Chico Walker	.10
184	Jerome Walton	.10
185	Glenn Braggs	.10
186	Tom Browning	.10
187	Rob Dibble	.10
188	Bill Doran	.10
189	Chris Hammond	.10
190	Billy Hatcher	.10
191	Barry Larkin	.15
192	Hal Morris	.10
193	Joe Oliver	.10
194	Paul O'Neill	.25
195	Jeff Reed	.10
196	Jose Rijo	.10
197	Chris Sabo	.10
198	Jeff Bagwell	1.00
199	Craig Biggio	.20
200	Ken Caminiti	.25
201	Andujar Cedeno	.10
202	Steve Finley	.10
203	Luis Gonzalez	.10
204	Pete Harnisch	.10
205	Xavier Hernandez	.10
206	Darryl Kile	.10
207	Al Osuna	.10
208	Curt Schilling	.10
209	Brett Butler	.10
210	Kal Daniels	.10
211	Lenny Harris	.10
212	Stan Javier	.10
213	Ramon Martinez	.15
214	Roger McDowell	.10
215	Jose Offerman	.10
216	Juan Samuel	.10
217	Mike Scioscia	.10
218	Mike Sharperson	.10
219	Darryl Strawberry	.20
220	Delino DeShields	.10
221	Tom Foley	.10
222	Steve Frey	.10
223	Dennis Martinez	.10
224	Spike Owen	.10
225	Gilberto Reyes	.10
226	Tim Wallach	.10
227	Daryl Boston	.10
228	Tim Burke	.10
229	Vince Coleman	.10
230	David Cone	.25
231	Kevin Elster	.10
232	Dwight Gooden	.15
233	Todd Hundley	.10
234	Jeff Innis	.10
235	Howard Johnson	.10
236	Dave Magadan	.10
237	Mackey Sasser	.10
238	Anthony Young	.10
239	Wes Chamberlain	.10
240	Darren Daulton	.10
241	Len Dykstra	.10
242	Tommy Greene	.10
243	Charlie Hayes	.10
244	Dave Hollins	.10
245	Ricky Jordan	.10
246	John Kruk	.10
247	Mickey Morandini	.10
248	Terry Mulholland	.10
249	Dale Murphy	.20
250	Jay Bell	.10
251	Barry Bonds	.75
252	Steve Buechele	.10
253	Doug Drabek	.10
254	Mike LaValliere	.10
255	Jose Lind	.10
256	Lloyd McClendon	.10
257	Orlando Merced	.10
258	Don Slaught	.10

259	John Smiley	.10
260	Zane Smith	.10
261	Randy Tomlin	.10
262	Andy Van Slyke	.10
263	Pedro Guerrero	.10
264	Felix Jose	.10
265	Ray Lankford	.10
266	Omar Olivares	.10
267	Jose Oquendo	.10
268	Tom Pagnozzi	.10
269	Bryn Smith	.10
270	Lee Smith	.10
271	Ozzie Smith	.50
272	Milt Thompson	.10
273	Todd Zeile	.10
274	Andy Benes	.15
275	Jerald Clark	.10
276	Tony Fernandez	.10
277	Tony Gwynn	.75
278	Greg Harris	.10
279	Thomas Howard	.10
280	Bruce Hurst	.10
281	Mike Maddux	.10
282	Fred McGriff	.40
283	Benito Santiago	.10
284	Kevin Bass	.10
285	Jeff Brantley	.10
286	John Burkett	.10
287	Will Clark	.40
288	Royce Clayton	.10
289	Steve Decker	.10
290	Kelly Downs	.10
291	Mike Felder	.10
292	Darren Lewis	.10
293	Kirt Manwaring	.10
294	Willie McGee	.10
295	Robby Thompson	.10
296	Matt Williams	.30
297	Trevor Wilson	.10
298	Checklist 1-108 (Sandy Alomar, Jr.)	.10
299	Checklist 109-208 (Rey Sanchez)	.10
300	Checklist 209-300 (Nolan Ryan)	.15
301	Brady Anderson	.15
302	Todd Frohwirth	.10
303	Ben McDonald	.10
304	Mark McLemore	.10
305	Jose Mesa	.10
306	Bob Milacki	.10
307	Gregg Olson	.10
308	David Segui	.10
309	Rick Sutcliffe	.10
310	Jeff Tackett	.10
311	Wade Boggs	.40
312	Scott Cooper	.10
313	John Flaherty	.10
314	Wayne Housie	.10
315	Peter Hoy	.10
316	John Marzano	.10
317	Tim Naehring	.10
318	Phil Plantier	.10
319	Frank Viola	.10
320	Matt Young	.10
321	Jim Abbott	.10
322	Hubie Brooks	.10
323	*Chad Curtis*	.40
324	Alvin Davis	.10
325	Junior Felix	.10
326	Von Hayes	.10
327	Mark Langston	.10
328	Scott Lewis	.10
329	Don Robinson	.10
330	Bobby Rose	.10
331	Lee Stevens	.10
332	George Bell	.10
333	Esteban Beltre	.10
334	Joey Cora	.10
335	Alex Fernandez	.20
336	Roberto Hernandez	.10
337	Mike Huff	.10
338	Kirk McCaskill	.10
339	Dan Pasqua	.10
340	Scott Radinsky	.10
341	Steve Sax	.10
342	Bobby Thigpen	.10
343	Robin Ventura	.25
344	Jack Armstrong	.10
345	Alex Cole	.10
346	Dennis Cook	.10
347	Glenallen Hill	.10
348	Thomas Howard	.10
349	Brook Jacoby	.10
350	Kenny Lofton	.40
351	Charles Nagy	.10
352	Rod Nichols	.10
353	Junior Ortiz	.10
354	Dave Otto	.10
355	Tony Perezchica	.10
356	Scott Scudder	.10
357	Paul Sorrento	.10
358	Skeeter Barnes	.10
359	Mark Carreon	.10
360	John Doherty	.10
361	Dan Gladden	.10
362	Bill Gullickson	.10
363	Shawn Hare	.10
364	Mike Henneman	.10
365	Chad Kreuter	.10
366	Mark Leiter	.10
367	Mike Munoz	.10
368	Kevin Ritz	.10
369	Mark Davis	.10
370	Tom Gordon	.10
371	Chris Gwynn	.10
372	Gregg Jefferies	.15
373	Wally Joyner	.10
374	Kevin McReynolds	.10
375	Keith Miller	.10
376	Rico Rossy	.10
377	Curtis Wilkerson	.10
378	Ricky Bones	.10
379	Chris Bosio	.10
380	Cal Eldred	.10
381	Scott Fletcher	.10
382	Jim Gantner	.10
383	Darryl Hamilton	.10
384	Doug Henry	.10
385	*Pat Listach*	.10
386	Tim McIntosh	.10
387	Edwin Nunez	.10
388	Dan Plesac	.10
389	Kevin Seitzer	.10
390	Franklin Stubbs	.10
391	William Suero	.10
392	Bill Wegman	.10
393	Willie Banks	.10
394	Jarvis Brown	.10
395	Greg Gagne	.10
396	Mark Guthrie	.10
397	Bill Krueger	.10
398	*Pat Mahomes*	.25
399	Pedro Munoz	.10
400	John Smiley	.10
401	Gary Wayne	.10
402	Lenny Webster	.10
403	Carl Willis	.10
404	Greg Cadaret	.10
405	Steve Farr	.10
406	Mike Gallego	.10
407	Charlie Hayes	.10
408	Steve Howe	.10
409	Dion James	.10
410	Jeff Johnson	.10
411	Tim Leary	.10
412	Jim Leyritz	.10
413	Melido Perez	.10
414	Scott Sanderson	.10
415	Andy Stankiewicz	.10
416	Mike Stanley	.10
417	Danny Tartabull	.10
418	Lance Blankenship	.10
419	Mike Bordick	.10
420	*Scott Brosius*	.40
421	Dennis Eckersley	.10
422	Scott Hemond	.10
423	Carney Lansford	.10
424	Henry Mercedes	.10
425	Mike Moore	.10
426	Gene Nelson	.10
427	Randy Ready	.10
428	Bruce Walton	.10
429	Willie Wilson	.10
430	Rich Amaral	.10
431	Dave Cochrane	.10
432	Henry Cotto	.10
433	Calvin Jones	.10
434	Kevin Mitchell	.10
435	Clay Parker	.10
436	Omar Vizquel	.10
437	Floyd Bannister	.10
438	Kevin Brown	.20
439	John Cangelosi	.10
440	Brian Downing	.10
441	Monty Fariss	.10
442	Jose Guzman	.10
443	Donald Harris	.10
444	Kevin Reimer	.10
445	Kenny Rogers	.10
446	Wayne Rosenthal	.10
447	Dickie Thon	.10
448	Derek Bell	.10
449	Juan Guzman	.10
450	Tom Henke	.10
451	Candy Maldonado	.10
452	Jack Morris	.10
453	David Wells	.10
454	Dave Winfield	.35
455	Juan Berenguer	.10
456	Damon Berryhill	.10
457	Mike Bielecki	.10
458	Marvin Freeman	.10
459	Charlie Leibrandt	.10
460	Kent Mercker	.10
461	Otis Nixon	.10
462	Alejandro Pena	.10
463	Ben Rivera	.10
464	Deion Sanders	.20
465	Mark Wohlers	.10
466	Shawn Boskie	.10
467	Frank Castillo	.10
468	Andre Dawson	.15
469	Joe Girardi	.10
470	Chuck McElroy	.10
471	Mike Morgan	.10
472	Ken Patterson	.10
473	Bob Scanlan	.10
474	Gary Scott	.10
475	Dave Smith	.10
476	Sammy Sosa	1.50
477	Hector Villanueva	.10
478	Scott Bankhead	.10
479	Tim Belcher	.10
480	Freddie Benavides	.10
481	Jacob Brumfield	.10
482	Norm Charlton	.10
483	Dwayne Henry	.10
484	Dave Martinez	.10
485	Bip Roberts	.10
486	Reggie Sanders	.10
487	Greg Swindell	.10
488	Ryan Bowen	.10
489	Casey Candaele	.10
490	Juan Guerrero	.10
491	Pete Incaviglia	.10
492	Jeff Juden	.10
493	Rob Murphy	.10
494	Mark Portugal	.10
495	Rafael Ramirez	.10
496	Scott Servais	.10
497	Ed Taubensee	.10
498	Brian Williams	.10
499	Todd Benzinger	.10
500	John Candelaria	.10
501	Tom Candiotti	.10
502	Tim Crews	.10
503	Eric Davis	.10
504	Jim Gott	.10
505	Dave Hansen	.10
506	Carlos Hernandez	.10
507	Orel Hershiser	.10
508	Eric Karros	.15
509	Bob Ojeda	.10
510	Steve Wilson	.10
511	Moises Alou	.20
512	Bret Barberie	.10
513	Ivan Calderon	.10
514	Gary Carter	.15
515	Archi Cianfrocco	.10
516	Jeff Fassero	.10
517	Darrin Fletcher	.10
518	Marquis Grissom	.10
519	Chris Haney	.10
520	Ken Hill	.10
521	Chris Nabholz	.10
522	Bill Sampen	.10
523	John VanderWal	.10
524	David Wainhouse	.10
525	Larry Walker	.40
526	John Wetteland	.10
527	Bobby Bonilla	.10
528	Sid Fernandez	.10
529	John Franco	.10
530	Dave Gallagher	.10
531	Paul Gibson	.10
532	Eddie Murray	.35
533	Junior Noboa	.10
534	Charlie O'Brien	.10
535	Bill Pecota	.10
536	Willie Randolph	.10
537	Bret Saberhagen	.10
538	Dick Schofield	.10
539	Pete Schourek	.10
540	Ruben Amaro	.10
541	Andy Ashby	.15
542	Kim Batiste	.10
543	Cliff Brantley	.10
544	Mariano Duncan	.10
545	Jeff Grotewold	.10
546	Barry Jones	.10
547	Julio Peguero	.10
548	Curt Schilling	.10
549	Mitch Williams	.10
550	Stan Belinda	.10
551	Scott Bullett	.10
552	Cecil Espy	.10
553	Jeff King	.10
554	Roger Mason	.10
555	Paul Miller	.10
556	Denny Neagle	.10
557	Vocente Palacios	.10
558	Bob Patterson	.10
559	Tom Prince	.10
560	Gary Redus	.10
561	Gary Varsho	.10
562	Juan Agosto	.10
563	Cris Carpenter	.10
564	*Mark Clark*	.20
565	Jose DeLeon	.10
566	Rich Gedman	.10
567	Bernard Gilkey	.10
568	Rex Hudler	.10
569	Tim Jones	.10
570	Donovan Osborne	.10
571	Mike Perez	.10
572	Gerald Perry	.10
573	Bob Tewksbury	.10
574	Todd Worrell	.10
575	Dave Eiland	.10
576	Jeremy Hernandez	.10
577	Craig Lefferts	.10
578	Jose Melendez	.10
579	Randy Myers	.10
580	Gary Pettis	.10
581	Rich Rodriguez	.10
582	Gary Sheffield	.30
583	Craig Shipley	.10
584	Kurt Stillwell	.10
585	Tim Teufel	.10
586	*Rod Beck*	.25
587	Dave Burba	.10
588	Craig Colbert	.10
589	Bryan Hickerson	.10
590	Mike Jackson	.10
591	Mark Leonard	.10
592	Jim McNamara	.10
593	John Patterson	.10
594	Dave Righetti	.10
595	Cory Snyder	.10
596	Bill Swift	.10
597	Ted Wood	.10
598	Checklist 301-403 (Scott Sanderson)	.10
599	Checklist 404-498 (Junior Ortiz)	.10
600	Checklist 499-600 (Mike Morgan)	.10

1992 Ultra All-Rookies

The 10 promising rookies in this set could be found on special cards inserted in Ultra Series 2 foil packs.

		MT
Complete Set (10):		8.00
Common Player:		.50
1	Eric Karros	2.00
2	Andy Stankiewicz	.50
3	Gary DiSarcina	.50
4	Archi Cianfrocco	.50
5	Jim McNamara	.50
6	Chad Curtis	1.50
7	Kenny Lofton	2.50
8	Reggie Sanders	1.00
9	Pat Mahomes	.50
10	Donovan Osborne	.50

1992 Ultra All-Stars

An All-Star team from each league, with two pitchers, could be assembled by collecting these inserts from Ultra Series 2 foil packs.

		MT
Complete Set (20):		25.00
Common Player:		.50
1	Mark McGwire	6.00
2	Roberto Alomar	1.00
3	Cal Ripken, Jr.	4.00
4	Wade Boggs	1.00
5	Mickey Tettleton	.50
6	Ken Griffey, Jr.	6.00
7	Roberto Kelly	.50
8	Kirby Puckett	1.50
9	Frank Thomas	2.00
10	Jack McDowell	.50
11	Will Clark	1.00
12	Ryne Sandberg	1.50
13	Barry Larkin	.60
14	Gary Sheffield	.75
15	Tom Pagnozzi	.50
16	Barry Bonds	2.00
17	Deion Sanders	.75
18	Darryl Strawberry	.60
19	David Cone	.75
20	Tom Glavine	.75

1992 Ultra Award Winners

The 25 cards in this insert issue were randomly packaged with Series 1 Ultra. One of the Cal Ripken cards (#21) can be found with a photo made from a reversed negative, as well as with the proper orientation. Neither version carries a premium.

		MT
Complete Set (26):		40.00
Common Player:		.60
1	Jack Morris	.60
2	Chuck Knoblauch	1.00
3	Jeff Bagwell	2.50
4	Terry Pendleton	.60
5	Cal Ripken, Jr.	5.00
6	Roger Clemens	2.50
7	Tom Glavine	.75
8	Tom Pagnozzi	.60
9	Ozzie Smith	1.50
10	Andy Van Slyke	.60
11	Barry Bonds	2.50
12	Tony Gwynn	3.50
13	Matt Williams	.60
14	Will Clark	.75
15	Robin Ventura	.75
16	Mark Langston	.60
18	Devon White	.60
19	Don Mattingly	2.50
20	Roberto Alomar	1.50
21a	Cal Ripken, Jr. (reversed negative)	5.00
21b	Cal Ripken, Jr. (correct)	5.00
22	Ken Griffey, Jr.	8.00
23	Kirby Puckett	2.00
24	Greg Maddux	4.00
25	Ryne Sandberg	1.50

1992 Ultra Tony Gwynn

This 12-card subset of Ultra's spokesman features 10 cards which were available as inserts in Series I foil packs, plus two cards labeled "Special No. 1" and "Special No. 2" which could only be obtained in a send-away offer. Some 2,000 of these cards carry a "certified" Gwynn autograph. Not part of the issue, but similar in format were a pair of extra Tony Gwynn cards. One pictures him with Fleer CEO Paul Mullan, the other shows him with the poster child for Casa de Amparo, a children's shelter in San Diego County.

		MT
Complete Set (12):		10.00
Common Card:		1.00
Certified Autograph Card:		90.00
	INSERT CARDS	1.00
1	Tony Gwynn (fielding)	1.00
2	Tony Gwynn (batting)	1.00
3	Tony Gwynn (fielding)	1.00
4	Tony Gwynn (batting)	1.00
5	Tony Gwynn (base-running)	1.00
6	Tony Gwynn (awards)	1.00
7	Tony Gwynn (bunting)	1.00
8	Tony Gwynn (batting)	1.00
9	Tony Gwynn (running)	1.00

10	Tony Gwynn (batting)	1.00
	SEND-AWAY CARDS	1.00
1	Tony Gwynn (batting)	4.00
2	Tony Gwynn (fielding)	4.00
	SPECIAL CARDS	1.00
---	Tony Gwynn, Paul Mullan	6.00
---	Tony Gwynn (Casa de Amparo)	15.00

1993 Ultra

The first series of 300 cards retains Fleer's successful features from 1992, including additional gold foil stamping, UV coating, and team color-coded marbled bars on the fronts. The backs feature a stylized ballpark background, which creates a 3-D effect, stats and portrait and an action photo. Dennis Eckersley is featured in a limited-edition "Career Highlights" set and personally autographed more than 2,000 of his cards, to be randomly inserted into both series' packs. A 10-card Home Run Kings subset and 25-card Ultra Awards Winners subset were also randomly inserted in packs. Ultra Rookies cards are included in both series. Ultra's second series has three limited-edition subsets: Ultra All-Stars, Ultra All-Rookie Team, and Strikeout Kings, plus cards featuring Colorado Rockies and Florida Marlins players.

		MT
Complete Set (650):		30.00
Series 1 (300):		15.00
Series 2 (350):		15.00
Common Player:		.10
Series 1 or 2 Wax Box:		45.00
1	Steve Avery	.10
2	Rafael Belliard	.10
3	Damon Berryhill	.10
4	Sid Bream	.10
5	Ron Gant	.15
6	Tom Glavine	.20
7	Ryan Klesko	.25
8	Mark Lemke	.10
9	Javier Lopez	.25
10	Greg Olson	.10
11	Terry Pendleton	.10
12	Deion Sanders	.25
13	Mike Stanton	.10
14	Paul Assenmacher	.10
15	Steve Buechele	.10
16	Frank Castillo	.10
17	Shawon Dunston	.10
18	Mark Grace	.35
19	Derrick May	.10
20	Chuck McElroy	.10
21	Mike Morgan	.10
22	Bob Scanlan	.10
23	Dwight Smith	.10
24	Sammy Sosa	1.50
25	Rick Wilkins	.10
26	Tim Belcher	.10
27	Jeff Branson	.10
28	Bill Doran	.10
29	Chris Hammond	.10
30	Barry Larkin	.20
31	Hal Morris	.10
32	Joe Oliver	.10
33	Jose Rijo	.10
34	Bip Roberts	.10
35	Chris Sabo	.10
36	Reggie Sanders	.15
37	Craig Biggio	.40
38	Ken Caminiti	.20
39	Steve Finley	.10
40	Luis Gonzalez	.10
41	Juan Guerrero	.10
42	Pete Harnisch	.10
43	Xavier Hernandez	.10
44	Doug Jones	.10
45	Al Osuna	.10
46	Eddie Taubensee	.10
47	Scooter Tucker	.10
48	Brian Williams	.10
49	Pedro Astacio	.10
50	Rafael Bournigal	.10
51	Brett Butler	.10
52	Tom Candiotti	.10
53	Eric Davis	.10
54	Lenny Harris	.10
55	Orel Hershiser	.10
56	Eric Karros	.20
57	Pedro Martinez	1.00
58	Roger McDowell	.10
59	Jose Offerman	.10
60	Mike Piazza	3.00
61	Moises Alou	.20
62	Kent Bottenfield	.10
63	Archi Cianfrocco	.10
64	Greg Colbrunn	.10
65	Wil Cordero	.10
66	Delino DeShields	.10
67	Darrin Fletcher	.10
68	Ken Hill	.10
69	Chris Nabholz	.10
70	Mel Rojas	.10
71	Larry Walker	.40
72	Sid Fernandez	.10
73	John Franco	.10
74	Dave Gallagher	.10
75	Todd Hundley	.15
76	Howard Johnson	.10
77	Jeff Kent	.15
78	Eddie Murray	.25
79	Bret Saberhagen	.15
80	Chico Walker	.10
81	Anthony Young	.10
82	Kyle Abbott	.10
83	Ruben Amaro Jr.	.10
84	Juan Bell	.10
85	Wes Chamberlain	.10
86	Darren Daulton	.10
87	Mariano Duncan	.10
88	Dave Hollins	.10
89	Ricky Jordan	.10
90	John Kruk	.10
91	Mickey Morandini	.10
92	Terry Mulholland	.10
93	Ben Rivera	.10
94	Mike Williams	.10
95	Stan Belinda	.10
96	Jay Bell	.10
97	Jeff King	.10
98	Mike LaValliere	.10
99	Lloyd McClendon	.10
100	Orlando Merced	.10
101	Zane Smith	.10
102	Randy Tomlin	.10
103	Andy Van Slyke	.10
104	Tim Wakefield	.10
105	John Wehner	.10
106	Bernard Gilkey	.10
107	Brian Jordan	.15
108	Ray Lankford	.10
109	Donovan Osborne	.10
110	Tom Pagnozzi	.10
111	Mike Perez	.10
112	Lee Smith	.10
113	Ozzie Smith	.50
114	Bob Tewksbury	.10
115	Todd Zeile	.10
116	Andy Benes	.15
117	Greg Harris	.10
118	Darrin Jackson	.10
119	Fred McGriff	.25
120	Rich Rodriguez	.10
121	Frank Seminara	.10
122	Gary Sheffield	.25
123	Craig Shipley	.10
124	Kurt Stillwell	.10
125	Dan Walters	.10
126	Rod Beck	.10
127	Mike Benjamin	.10
128	Jeff Brantley	.10
129	John Burkett	.10
130	Will Clark	.25
131	Royce Clayton	.10
132	Steve Hosey	.10
133	Mike Jackson	.10
134	Darren Lewis	.10
135	Kirt Manwaring	.10
136	Bill Swift	.10
137	Robby Thompson	.10
138	Brady Anderson	.20
139	Glenn Davis	.10
140	Leo Gomez	.10
141	Chito Martinez	.10
142	Ben McDonald	.10
143	Alan Mills	.10
144	Mike Mussina	.50
145	Gregg Olson	.10
146	David Segui	.10
147	Jeff Tackett	.10
148	Jack Clark	.10
149	Scott Cooper	.10
150	Danny Darwin	.10
151	John Dopson	.10
152	Mike Greenwell	.10
153	Tim Naehring	.10
154	Tony Pena	.10
155	Paul Quantrill	.10
156	Mo Vaughn	.40
157	Frank Viola	.10
158	Bob Zupcic	.10
159	Chad Curtis	.10
160	Gary DiSarcina	.10
161	Damion Easley	.10
162	Chuck Finley	.10
163	Tim Fortugno	.10
164	Rene Gonzales	.10
165	Joe Grahe	.10
166	Mark Langston	.10
167	John Orton	.10
168	Luis Polonia	.10
169	Julio Valera	.10
170	Wilson Alvarez	.10
171	George Bell	.10
172	Joey Cora	.10
173	Alex Fernandez	.15
174	Lance Johnson	.10
175	Ron Karkovice	.10
176	Jack McDowell	.10
177	Scott Radinsky	.10
178	Tim Raines	.15
179	Steve Sax	.10
180	Bobby Thigpen	.10
181	Frank Thomas	1.50
182	Sandy Alomar Jr.	.20
183	Carlos Baerga	.10
184	Felix Fermin	.10
185	Thomas Howard	.10
186	Mark Lewis	.10
187	Derek Lilliquist	.10
188	Carlos Martinez	.10
189	Charles Nagy	.15
190	Scott Scudder	.10
191	Paul Sorrento	.10
192	Jim Thome	.40
193	Mark Whiten	.10
194	Milt Cuyler	.10
195	Rob Deer	.10
196	John Doherty	.10
197	Travis Fryman	.20
198	Dan Gladden	.10
199	Mike Henneman	.10
200	John Kiely	.10
201	Chad Kreuter	.10
202	Scott Livingstone	.10
203	Tony Phillips	.10
204	Alan Trammell	.15
205	Mike Boddicker	.10
206	George Brett	.75
207	Tom Gordon	.10
208	Mark Gubicza	.10
209	Gregg Jefferies	.15
210	Wally Joyner	.10
211	Kevin Koslofski	.10
212	Brent Mayne	.10
213	Brian McRae	.10
214	Kevin McReynolds	.10
215	Rusty Meacham	.10
216	Steve Shifflett	.10
217	James Austin	.10
218	Cal Eldred	.10
219	Darryl Hamilton	.10
220	Doug Henry	.10
221	John Jaha	.10
222	Dave Nilsson	.10
223	Jesse Orosco	.10
224	B.J. Surhoff	.10
225	Greg Vaughn	.15
226	Bill Wegman	.10
227	Robin Yount	.25
228	Rick Aguilera	.10
229	J.T. Bruett	.10
230	Scott Erickson	.10
231	Kent Hrbek	.10
232	Terry Jorgensen	.10
233	Scott Leius	.10
234	Pat Mahomes	.10
235	Pedro Munoz	.10
236	Kirby Puckett	1.00
237	Kevin Tapani	.10
238	Lenny Webster	.10
239	Carl Willis	.10
240	Mike Gallego	.10
241	John Habyan	.10
242	Pat Kelly	.10
243	Kevin Maas	.10
244	Don Mattingly	1.00
245	Hensley Meulens	.10
246	Sam Militello	.10
247	Matt Nokes	.10
248	Melido Perez	.10
249	Andy Stankiewicz	.10
250	Randy Velarde	.10
251	Bob Wickman	.10
252	Bernie Williams	.40
253	Lance Blankenship	.10
254	Mike Bordick	.10
255	Jerry Browne	.10
256	Ron Darling	.10
257a	Dennis Eckersley	.10
257b	Dennis Eckersley (Wt. 195; no "MLBPA" on back - unmarked sample card)	3.00
257c	Dennis Eckersley (Wt, 195; no "Printed in USA" on back - unmarked sample card)	3.00
258	Rickey Henderson	.40
259	Vince Horsman	.10
260	Troy Neel	.10
261	Jeff Parrett	.10
262	Terry Steinbach	.10
263	Bob Welch	.10
264	Bobby Witt	.10
265	Rich Amaral	.10
266	Bret Boone	.20
267	Jay Buhner	.10
268	Dave Fleming	.10
269	Randy Johnson	.40
270	Edgar Martinez	.10
271	Mike Schooler	.10
272	Russ Swan	.10
273	Dave Valle	.10
274	Omar Vizquel	.10
275	Kerry Woodson	.10
276	Kevin Brown	.20
277	Julio Franco	.10
278	Jeff Frye	.10
279	Juan Gonzalez	1.25
280	Jeff Huson	.10
281	Rafael Palmeiro	.40
282	Dean Palmer	.10
283	Roger Pavlik	.10
284	Ivan Rodriguez	.75
285	Kenny Rogers	.10
286	Derek Bell	.10
287	Pat Borders	.10
288	Joe Carter	.10
289	Bob MacDonald	.10
290	Jack Morris	.10
291	John Olerud	.25
292	Ed Sprague	.10
293	Todd Stottlemyre	.10
294	Mike Timlin	.10
295	Duane Ward	.10
296	David Wells	.10
297	Devon White	.10
298	Checklist	.10
299	Checklist	.10
300	Checklist	.10
301	Steve Bedrosian	.10
302	Jeff Blauser	.10
303	Francisco Cabrera	.10
304	Marvin Freeman	.10
305	Brian Hunter	.10
306	Dave Justice	.25
307	Greg Maddux	1.50
308	*Greg McMichael*	.10
309	Kent Mercker	.10
310	Otis Nixon	.10
311	Pete Smith	.10
312	John Smoltz	.20
313	Jose Guzman	.10
314	Mike Harkey	.10
315	Greg Hibbard	.10
316	Candy Maldonado	.10
317	Randy Myers	.10
318	Dan Plesac	.10
319	Rey Sanchez	.10
320	Ryne Sandberg	.60
321	*Tommy Shields*	.10
322	Jose Vizcaino	.10
323	*Matt Walbeck*	.15
324	Willie Wilson	.10
325	Tom Browning	.10
326	Tim Costo	.10
327	Rob Dibble	.10
328	Steve Foster	.10
329	Roberto Kelly	.10
330	Randy Milligan	.10
331	Kevin Mitchell	.10
332	*Tim Pugh*	.15
333	Jeff Reardon	.10
334	*John Roper*	.10
335	Juan Samuel	.10
336	John Smiley	.10
337	San Wilson	.10
338	Scott Aldred	.10
339	Andy Ashby	.10
340	Freddie Benavides	.10
341	Dante Bichette	.20
342	Willie Blair	.10
343	Daryl Boston	.10
344	Vinny Castilla	.20
345	Jerald Clark	.10
346	Alex Cole	.10
347	Andres Galarraga	.25
348	Joe Girardi	.10
349	*Ryan Hawblitzel*	.10
350	Charlie Hayes	.10
351	Butch Henry	.10
352	Darren Holmes	.10
353	Dale Murphy	.20
354	David Nied	.10
355	Jeff Parrett	.10
356	*Steve Reed*	.15
357	Bruce Ruffin	.10
358	*Danny Sheaffer*	.15
359	Bryn Smith	.10
360	*Jim Tatum*	.10
361	Eric Young	.10
362	Gerald Young	.10
363	Luis Aquino	.10
364	*Alex Arias*	.10
365	Jack Armstrong	.10
366	Bret Barberie	.10
367	Ryan Bowen	.10
368	Greg Briley	.10
369	Cris Carpenter	.10
370	Chuck Carr	.10
371	*Jeff Conine*	.25
372	Steve Decker	.10
373	Orestes Destrade	.10
374	Monty Fariss	.10
375	Junior Felix	.10
376	Chris Hammond	.10
377	Bryan Harvey	.10
378	*Trevor Hoffman*	.25
379	Charlie Hough	.10
380	Joe Klink	.10
381	*Richie Lewis*	.10
382	Dave Magadan	.10
383	Bob McCLure	.10
384	*Scott Pose*	.15
385	*Rich Renteria*	.15
386	Benito Santiago	.10
387	Walt Weiss	.10
388	Nigel Wilson	.10
389	Eric Anthony	.10
390	Jeff Bagwell	1.25
391	Andujar Cedeno	.10
392	Doug Drabek	.10
393	Darryl Kile	.10
394	Mark Portugal	.10
395	Karl Rhodes	.10
396	Scott Servais	.10
397	Greg Swindell	.10
398	Tom Goodwin	.10
399	Kevin Gross	.10
400	Carlos Hernandez	.10
401	Ramon Martinez	.15
402	Raul Mondesi	.40
403	Jody Reed	.10
404	Mike Sharperson	.10
405	Cory Snyder	.10
406	Darryl Strawberry	.20
407	*Rick Trlicek*	.10
408	Tim Wallach	.10
409	Todd Worrell	.10
410	Tavo Alvarez	.10
411	*Sean Berry*	.15
412	*Frank Bolick*	.10
413	Cliff Floyd	.15
414	Mike Gardiner	.10
415	Marquis Grissom	.15
416	*Tim Laker*	.10
417	*Mike Lansing*	.25
418	Dennis Martinez	.10
419	John Vander Wal	.10
420	John Wetteland	.10
421	Rondell White	.15
422	Bobby Bonilla	.10
423	Jeromy Burnitz	.15
424	*Vince Burnitz*	.10
425	*Mike Draper*	.10
426	Tony Fernandez	.10
427	Dwight Gooden	.15
428	Jeff Innis	.10
429	Bobby Jones	.15
430	Mike Maddux	.10
431	Charlie O'Brien	.10
432	Joe Orsulak	.10
433	Pete Schourek	.10
434	Frank Tanana	.10
435	*Ryan Thompson*	.15
436	Kim Batiste	.10
437	Mark Davis	.10
438	Jose DeLeon	.10
439	Len Dykstra	.10
440	Jim Eisenreich	.10
441	Tommy Greene	.10
442	Pete Incaviglia	.10
443	Danny Jackson	.10
444	*Todd Pratt*	.20
445	Curt Schilling	.15
446	Milt Thompson	.10
447	David West	.10
448	Mitch Williams	.10
449	Steve Cooke	.10
450	Carlos Garcia	.10
451	Al Martin	.15
452	*Blas Minor*	.15
453	Dennis Moeller	.10
454	Denny Neagle	.10
455	Don Slaught	.10
456	Lonnie Smith	.10
457	Paul Wagner	.10
458	Bob Walk	.10
459	Kevin Young	.10
460	*Rene Arocha*	.15
461	Brian Barber	.10
462	Rheal Cormier	.10
463	Gregg Jefferies	.15
464	Joe Magrane	.10
465	Omar Olivares	.10
466	Geronimo Pena	.10
467	Allen Watson	.10
468	Mark Whiten	.10
469	Derek Bell	.10
470	Phil Clark	.10
471	*Pat Gomez*	.20
472	Tony Gwynn	1.25
473	Jeremy Hernandez	.10
474	Bruce Hurst	.10
475	Phil Plantier	.10
476	*Scott Sanders*	.20
477	*Tim Scott*	.10
478	*Darrell Sherman*	.10
479	Guillermo Velasquez	.10
480	*Tim Worrell*	.10
481	Todd Benzinger	.10
482	Bud Black	.10
483	Barry Bonds	.75
484	Dave Burba	.10
485	Bryan Hickerson	.10
486	Dave Martinez	.10
487	Willie McGee	.10
488	Jeff Reed	.10
489	Kevin Rogers	.10
490	Matt Williams	.20
491	Trevor Wilson	.10
492	Harold Baines	.10
493	Mike Devereaux	.10
494	Todd Frohwirth	.10
495	Chris Hoiles	.10
496	Luis Mercedes	.10
497	*Sherman Obando*	.15
498	*Brad Pennington*	.15
499	Harold Reynolds	.10
500	Arthur Rhodes	.10
501	Cal Ripken, Jr.	2.50
502	Rick Sutcliffe	.10
503	Fernando Valenzuela	.10
504	Mark Williamson	.10

505	Scott Bankhead	.10
506	Greg Blosser	.10
507	Ivan Calderon	.10
508	Roger Clemens	1.25
509	Andre Clemens	.10
510	Scott Fletcher	.10
511	Greg Harris	.10
512	Billy Hatcher	.10
513	Bob Melvin	.10
514	Carlos Quintana	.10
515	Luis Rivera	.10
516	Jeff Russell	.10
517	*Ken Ryan*	.20
518	Chili Davis	.10
519	*Jim Edmonds*	1.50
520	Gary Gaetti	.10
521	Torey Lovullo	.10
522	*Tony Percival*	.10
523	Tim Salmon	.40
524	Scott Sanderson	.10
525	*J.T. Snow*	.75
526	Jerome Walton	.10
527	Jason Bere	.10
528	*Rod Bolton*	.10
529	Ellis Burks	.10
530	Carlton Fisk	.25
531	Craig Grebeck	.10
532	Ozzie Guillen	.10
533	Roberto Hernandez	.10
534	Bo Jackson	.25
535	Kirk McCaskill	.10
536	Dave Stieb	.10
537	Robin Ventura	.25
538	Albert Belle	.50
539	Mike Bielecki	.10
540	Glenallen Hill	.10
541	Reggie Jefferson	.10
542	Kenny Lofton	.40
543	*Jeff Mutis*	.15
544	Junior Ortiz	.10
545	Manny Ramirez	1.50
546	Jeff Treadway	.10
547	Kevin Wickander	.10
548	Cecil Fielder	.10
549	Kirk Gibson	.10
550	*Greg Gohr*	.10
551	David Haas	.10
552	Bill Krueger	.10
553	Mike Moore	.10
554	Mickey Tettleton	.10
555	Lou Whitaker	.10
556	Kevin Appier	.10
557	*Billy Brewer*	.10
558	David Cone	.25
559	Greg Gagne	.10
560	Mark Gardner	.10
561	Phil Hiatt	.10
562	Felix Jose	.10
563	Jose Lind	.10
564	Mike Macfarlane	.10
565	Keith Miller	.10
566	Jeff Montgomery	.10
567	Hipolito Pechardo	.10
568	Ricky Bones	.10
569	Tom Brunansky	.10
570	*Joe Kmak*	.10
571	Pat Listach	.10
572	*Graeme Lloyd*	.20
573	*Carlos Maldonado*	.10
574	Josias Manzanillo	.10
575	Matt Mieske	.10
576	Kevin Reimer	.10
577	Bill Spiers	.10
578	Dickie Thon	.10
579	Willie Banks	.10
580	Jim Deshaies	.10
581	Mark Guthrie	.10
582	Brian Harper	.10
583	Chuck Knoblauch	.25
584	Gene Larkin	.10
585	Shane Mack	.10
586	David McCarty	.10
587	Mike Pagliarulo	.10
588	Mike Trombley	.10
589	Dave Winfield	.25
590	Jim Abbott	.10
591	Wade Boggs	.30
592	*Russ Davis*	.20
593	Steve Farr	.10
594	Steve Howe	.10
595	*Mike Humphreys*	.10
596	Jimmy Key	.10
597	Jim Leyritz	.10
598	*Bobby Munoz*	.15
599	Paul O'Neill	.25
600	Spike Owen	.10
601	Mike Stanley	.10
602	Danny Tartabull	.10
603	Scott Brosius	.10
604	Storm Davis	.10
605	Eric Fox	.10
606	Goose Gossage	.10
607	Scott Hammond	.10
608	Dave Henderson	.10
609	Mark McGwire	3.00
610	*Mike Mohler*	.10
611	Edwin Nunez	.10
612	Kevin Seitzer	.10
613	Ruben Sierra	.10
614	Chris Bosio	.10
615	Norm Charlton	.10
616	*Jim Converse*	.10
617	*John Cummings*	.10
618	Mike Felder	.10
619	Ken Griffey, Jr.	3.00
620	*Mike Hampton*	.10
621	Erik Hanson	.10
622	Bill Haselman	.10
623	Tino Martinez	.20
624	Lee Tinsley	.10
625	*Fernando Vina*	.25
626	*David Wainhouse*	.15
627	Jose Canseco	.75
628	Benji Gil	.10
629	Tom Henke	.10
630	*David Hulse*	.20
631	Manuel Lee	.10
632	Craig Lefferts	.10
633	*Robb Nen*	.15
634	Gary Redus	.10
635	Bill Ripken	.10
636	Nolan Ryan	2.50
637	Dan Smith	.10
638	*Matt Whiteside*	.10
639	Roberto Alomar	.50
640	Juan Guzman	.10
641	Pat Hentgen	.15
642	Darrin Jackson	.10
643	Randy Knorr	.10
644	*Domingo Martinez*	.20
645	Paul Molitor	.40
646	Dick Schofield	.10
647	Dave Stewart	.10
648	Checklist	.10
649	Checklist	.10
650	Checklist	.10

1993 Ultra All-Rookies

These insert cards are foil stamped on both sides and were randomly inserted into Series II packs. The cards have black fronts, with six different colors of type. The player's uniform number and position are located in the upper righthand corner. The player's name and Ultra logo are gold-foil stamped. Backs have a black background on which is a player photo and a career summary.

		MT
Complete Set (10):		15.00
Common Player:		1.00
1	Rene Arocha	.50
2	Jeff Conine	1.00
3	Phil Hiatt	.50
4	Mike Lansing	.75
5	Al Martin	.75
6	David Nied	.50
7	Mike Piazza	10.00
8	Tim Salmon	3.00
9	J.T. Snow	2.50
10	Kevin Young	.75

1993 Ultra All-Stars

This 20-card set features 10 of the top players from each league. Cards were randomly inserted into Series II packs and are foil stamped on both sides.

		MT
Complete Set (20):		45.00
Common Player:		.75
1	Darren Daulton	.75
2	Will Clark	1.50
3	Ryne Sandberg	3.00
4	Barry Larkin	1.00
5	Gary Sheffield	1.00
6	Barry Bonds	3.00
7	Ray Lankford	.75
8	Larry Walker	1.50
9	Greg Maddux	6.00
10	Lee Smith	.75
11	Ivan Rodriguez	3.00
12	Mark McGwire	10.00
13	Carlos Baerga	.75
14	Cal Ripken, Jr.	8.00
15	Edgar Martinez	.75
16	Juan Gonzalez	4.00
17	Ken Griffey, Jr.	10.00
18	Kirby Puckett	3.00
19	Frank Thomas	3.00
20	Mike Mussina	1.50

1993 Ultra Award Winners

This insert set features 18 Top Glove players (nine from each league), two rookies of the year, three MVPs (both leagues and World Series), both Cy Young Award winners and one Player of the Year. All cards are UV coated and foil stamped on both sides and were found in Series I packs. Fronts have a black background with "Fleer Ultra Award Winners" splashed around in trendy colors. The Ultra logo, player's name and his award are spelled out in gold foil. The horizontally arranged backs have much the same elements, plus a summary of the season's performance which led to the award. There is a close-up player photo, as well.

		MT
Complete Set (25):		40.00
Common Player:		.75
1	Greg Maddux	6.00
2	Tom Pagnozzi	.75
3	Mark Grace	1.00
4	Jose Lind	.75
5	Terry Pendleton	.75
6	Ozzie Smith	2.00
7	Barry Bonds	3.00
8	Andy Van Slyke	.75
9	Larry Walker	1.50
10	Mark Langston	.75
11	Ivan Rodriguez	3.00
12	Don Mattingly	3.00
13	Roberto Alomar	2.00
14	Robin Ventura	1.00
15	Cal Ripken, Jr.	8.00
16	Ken Griffey, Jr.	10.00
17	Kirby Puckett	3.00
18	Devon White	.75
19	Pat Listach	.75
20	Eric Karros	.75
21	Pat Borders	.75
22	Greg Maddux	6.00
23	Dennis Eckersley	.75
24	Barry Bonds	3.00
25	Gary Sheffield	1.00

1993 Ultra Career Highlights Promo Sheet

To introduce its "Career Highlights" insert cards in Fleer and Fleer Ultra, the company distributed this promo sheet picturing one card each from the Tom Glavine and Dennis Eckersley sets, overprinted with a gray "PROMOTIONAL SAMPLE" across front and back. A third panel on the sheet provides details of the mail-in offer through which additional cards from the sets could be ordered. The sheet measures 7-1/2" x 3-1/2".

	MT
Three-panel Strip: Dennis Eckersley, Tom Glavine	4.00

1993 Ultra Commemorative

Photos of Fleer's CEO and the company's spokesman, 1992 Cy Young/MVP winner Dennis Eckersley are superimposed on a background of Oakland-Alameda Country Stadium on this promo card. The back gives details of the forthcoming 1993 Fleer Ultra issue.

	MT
Dennis Eckersley, Paul Mullan	10.00

1993 Ultra Dennis Eckersley Career Highlights

This limited-edition subset chronicles Dennis Eckersley's illustrious career. Cards, which are UV coated and silver foil-stamped on both sides, were randomly inserted into both series' packs. Eckersley autographed more than 2,000 of the cards, which were also randomly inserted into packs. By sending in 10 Fleer Ultra wrappers plus $1, collectors could receive two additional Eckersley cards which were not available in regular packs. Card fronts have a color action photo, the background of which has been colorized into shades of purple. A black marble strip at bottom has the city name and years he was with the team in silver foil. A large black marble box in one corner has the "Dennis Eckersley Career Highlights" logo in silver foil. On back, a purple box is dropped out of a color photo, and silver-foil typography describes some phrase of Eck's career.

		MT
Complete Set (12):		5.00
Common Card:		.50
Autographed Card:		40.00
1	"Perfection" (A's 1987-92)	.50
2	"The Kid" (Indians 1975-77)	.50
3	"The Warrior" (Indians 1975-77)	.50
4	"Beantown Blazer" (Red Sox 1978-84)	.50
5	"Eckspeak" (Red Sox 1978-84)	.50
6	"Down to Earth" (Red Sox 1978-84)	.50
7	"Wrigley Bound" (Cubs 1984-86)	.50
8	"No Relief" (A's 1987-92)	.50
9	"In Control" (A's 1987-92)	.50
10	"Simply the Best" (A's 1987-92)	.50
11	"Reign of Perfection" (A's 1987-92)	.50
12	"Leaving His Mark" (A's 1987-92)	.50

1993 Ultra Home Run Kings

This insert set features top home run kings. Cards, which are UV coated and have gold foil stamping on both sides, were inserts in Series I packs.

		MT
Complete Set (10):		15.00
Common Player:		1.00
1	Juan Gonzalez	4.00
2	Mark McGwire	10.00
3	Cecil Fielder	1.00
4	Fred McGriff	1.50
5	Albert Belle	2.00
6	Barry Bonds	3.00
7	Joe Carter	1.00
8	Gary Sheffield	1.00
9	Darren Daulton	1.00
10	Dave Hollins	1.00

1993 Ultra Performers

An Ultra Performers set of Fleer Ultra baseball cards was offered directly to collectors in 1993. The set, available only by mail, was limited to 150,000 sets. The cards featured gold-foil stamping and UV coating on each side and a six-photo design, including five on the front of the card. Each card was identified on the back by set serial number jet-printed in black in a strip at bottom.

		MT
Complete Set (10):		12.00
Common Player:		1.00
1	Barry Bonds	2.00
2	Juan Gonzalez	2.00
3	Ken Griffey, Jr.	6.00
4	Eric Karros	.75
5	Pat Listach	.75
6	Greg Maddux	3.00
7	David Nied	.75
8	Gary Sheffield	.75
9	J.T. Snow	.75
10	Frank Thomas	2.00

1993 Ultra Strikeout Kings

Five of baseball's top strikeout pitchers are featured in this second-series Ultra insert set. Cards are UV coated and foil stamped on both sides. Each card front has a picture of a pitcher winding up to throw. A baseball is in the background, with the pitcher in the forefront.

		MT
Complete Set (5):		15.00
Common Player:		1.00
1	Roger Clemens	4.00
2	Juan Guzman	1.00
3	Randy Johnson	2.50
4	Nolan Ryan	10.00
5	John Smoltz	1.50

1994 Ultra

Issued in two series of 300 cards each, Ultra for 1994 represented a new highwater mark in production values for a mid-priced brand. Each side of the basic cards is UV coated and gold-foil embossed. Fronts feature full-bleed action photos. At bottom the player name, team, position and Fleer Ultra logo appear in gold-foil above a gold-foil strip. Some rookie cards are specially designated with a large gold "ROOKIE" above the Ultra logo. Backs feature a basic background that is team color coordinated. Three more player action photos are featured on the back, along with a team logo and a modicum of stats and personal data. There is a gold stripe along the left edge and the player's name and card number appear in gold in the lower-left corner. The set features seven types of insert cards, packaged one per pack.

		MT
Complete Set (600):		30.00
Common Player:		.10
Series 1 or 2 Wax Box:		45.00
1	Jeffrey Hammonds	.15
2	Chris Hoiles	.10
3	Ben McDonald	.10
4	Mark McLemore	.10
5	Alan Mills	.10
6	Jamie Moyer	.10
7	Brad Pennington	.10
8	Jim Poole	.10
9	Cal Ripken, Jr.	2.50
10	Jack Voigt	.10
11	Roger Clemens	1.00
12	Danny Darwin	.10
13	Andre Dawson	.20
14	Scott Fletcher	.10
15	Greg Harris	.10
16	Billy Hatcher	.10
17	Jeff Russell	.10
18	Aaron Sele	.15
19	Mo Vaughn	.50
20	Mike Butcher	.10
21	Rod Correia	.10
22	Steve Frey	.10
23	*Phil Leftwich*	.10
24	Torey Lovullo	.10
25	Ken Patterson	.10
26	Eduardo Perez	.10
27	Tim Salmon	.25
28	J.T. Snow	.20
29	Chris Turner	.10
30	Wilson Alvarez	.10
31	Jason Bere	.10
32	Joey Cora	.10
33	Alex Fernandez	.15
34	Roberto Hernandez	.10
35	Lance Johnson	.10
36	Ron Karkovice	.10
37	Kirk McCaskill	.10
38	Jeff Schwarz	.10
39	Frank Thomas	1.00
40	Sandy Alomar Jr.	.15
41	Albert Belle	.75
42	Felix Fermin	.10
43	Wayne Kirby	.10
44	Tom Kramer	.10
45	Kenny Lofton	.50
46	Jose Mesa	.10
47	Eric Plunk	.10
48	Paul Sorrento	.10
49	Jim Thome	.40
50	Bill Wertz	.10
51	John Doherty	.10
52	Cecil Fielder	.10
53	Travis Fryman	.15
54	Chris Gomez	.10
55	Mike Henneman	.10
56	Chad Kreuter	.10
57	Bob MacDonald	.10
58	Mike Moore	.10
59	Tony Phillips	.10
60	Lou Whitaker	.10
61	Kevin Appier	.10
62	Greg Gagne	.10
63	Chris Gwynn	.10
64	Bob Hamelin	.10
65	Chris Haney	.10
66	Phil Hiatt	.10
67	Felix Jose	.10
68	Jose Lind	.10
69	Mike Macfarlane	.10
70	Jeff Montgomery	.10
71	Hipolito Pichardo	.10
72	Juan Bell	.10
73	Cal Eldred	.10
74	Darryl Hamilton	.10
75	Doug Henry	.10
76	Mike Ignasiak	.10
77	John Jaha	.15
78	Graeme Lloyd	.10
79	Angel Miranda	.10
80	Dave Nilsson	.10
81	Troy O'Leary	.10
82	Kevin Reimer	.10
83	Willie Banks	.10
84	Larry Casian	.10
85	Scott Erickson	.15
86	Eddie Guardado	.10
87	Kent Hrbek	.10
88	Terry Jorgensen	.10
89	Chuck Knoblauch	.25
90	Pat Meares	.10
91	Mike Trombley	.10
92	Dave Winfield	.20
93	Wade Boggs	.20
94	Scott Kamieniecki	.10
95	Pat Kelly	.10
96	Jimmy Key	.10
97	Jim Leyritz	.10
98	Bobby Munoz	.10
99	Paul O'Neill	.25
100	Melido Perez	.10
101	Mike Stanley	.10
102	Danny Tartabull	.10
103	Bernie Williams	.40
104	*Kurt Abbott*	.25
105	Mike Bordick	.10
106	Ron Darling	.10
107	Brent Gates	.10
108	Miguel Jimenez	.10
109	Steve Karsay	.10
110	Scott Lydy	.10
111	Mark McGwire	3.00
112	Troy Neel	.10
113	Craig Paquette	.10
114	Bob Welch	.10
115	Bobby Witt	.10
116	Rich Amaral	.10
117	Mike Blowers	.10
118	Jay Buhner	.10
119	Dave Fleming	.10
120	Ken Griffey, Jr.	3.00
121	Tino Martinez	.15
122	Marc Newfield	.10
123	Ted Power	.10
124	Mackey Sasser	.10
125	Omar Vizquel	.15
126	Kevin Brown	.20
127	Juan Gonzalez	1.00
128	Tom Henke	.10
129	David Hulse	.10
130	Dean Palmer	.10
131	Roger Pavlik	.10
132	Ivan Rodriguez	.75
133	Kenny Rogers	.10
134	Doug Strange	.10
135	Pat Borders	.10
136	Joe Carter	.10
137	Darnell Coles	.10
138	Pat Hentgen	.10
139	Al Leiter	.15
140	Paul Molitor	.40
141	John Olerud	.25
142	Ed Sprague	.10
143	Dave Stewart	.10
144	Mike Timlin	.10
145	Duane Ward	.10
146	Devon White	.10
147	Steve Avery	.10
148	Steve Bedrosian	.10
149	Damon Berryhill	.10
150	Jeff Blauser	.10
151	Tom Glavine	.25
152	Chipper Jones	2.00
153	Mark Lemke	.10
154	Fred McGriff	.25
155	Greg McMichael	.10
156	Deion Sanders	.25
157	John Smoltz	.20
158	Mark Wohlers	.10
159	Jose Bautista	.10
160	Steve Buechele	.10
161	Mike Harkey	.10
162	Greg Hibbard	.10
163	Chuck McElroy	.10
164	Mike Morgan	.10
165	Kevin Roberson	.10
166	Ryne Sandberg	.75
167	Jose Vizcaino	.10
168	Rick Wilkins	.10
169	Willie Wilson	.10
170	Willie Greene	.10
171	Roberto Kelly	.10
172	Larry Luebbers	.10
173	Kevin Mitchell	.10
174	Joe Oliver	.10
175	John Roper	.10
176	Johnny Ruffin	.10
177	Reggie Sanders	.15
178	John Smiley	.10
179	Jerry Spradlin	.10
180	Freddie Benavides	.10
181	Dante Bichette	.25
182	Willie Blair	.10
183	Kent Bottenfield	.10
184	Jerald Clark	.10
185	Joe Girardi	.10
186	Roberto Mejia	.10
187	Steve Reed	.10
188	Armando Reynoso	.10
189	Bruce Ruffin	.10
190	Eric Young	.15
191	Luis Aquino	.10
192	Bret Barberie	.10
193	Ryan Bowen	.10
194	Chuck Carr	.10
195	Orestes Destrade	.10
196	Richie Lewis	.10
197	Dave Magadan	.10
198	Bob Natal	.10
199	Gary Sheffield	.20
200	Matt Turner	.10
201	Darrell Whitmore	.10
202	Jesus Tavarez	.10
203	Jeff Bagwell	1.00
204	Andujar Cedeno	.10
205	Luis Gonzalez	.15
206	Xavier Hernandez	.10
207	Doug Jones	.10
208	Darryl Kile	.10
209	Scott Servais	.10
210	Greg Swindell	.10
211	Brian Williams	.10
212	Pedro Astacio	.10
213	Brett Butler	.10
214	Omar Daal	.10
215	Jim Gott	.10
216	Raul Mondesi	.25
217	Jose Offerman	.10
218	Mike Piazza	2.00
219	Cory Snyder	.10
220	Tim Wallach	.10
221	Todd Worrell	.10
222	Moises Alou	.15
223	Sean Berry	.10
224	Wil Cordero	.10
225	Jeff Fassero	.10
226	Darrin Fletcher	.10
227	Cliff Floyd	.15
228	Marquis Grissom	.15
229	Ken Hill	.10
230	Mike Lansing	.10
231	Kirk Rueter	.10
232	John Wetteland	.10
233	Rondell White	.25
234	Tim Bogar	.10
235	Jeromy Burnitz	.10
236	Dwight Gooden	.20
237	Todd Hundley	.15
238	Jeff Kent	.10
239	Josias Manzanillo	.10
240	Joe Orsulak	.10
241	Ryan Thompson	.10
242	Kim Batiste	.10
243	Darren Daulton	.10
243a	Darren Daulton (promotional sample)	.50
244	Tommy Greene	.10
245	Dave Hollins	.10
246	Pete Incaviglia	.10
247	Danny Jackson	.10
248	Ricky Jordan	.10
249	John Kruk	.10
249a	John Kruk (promotional sample)	.50
250	Mickey Morandini	.10
251	Terry Mulholland	.10
252	Ben Rivera	.10
253	Kevin Stocker	.10
254	Jay Bell	.10
255	Steve Cooke	.10
256	Jeff King	.10
257	Al Martin	.10
258	Danny Micelli	.10
259	Blas Minor	.10
260	Don Slaught	.10
261	Paul Wagner	.10
262	Tim Wakefield	.10
263	Kevin Young	.10
264	Rene Arocha	.10
265	*Richard Batchelor*	.10
266	Gregg Jefferies	.15
267	Brian Jordan	.15
268	Jose Oquendo	.10
269	Donovan Osborne	.10
270	Erik Pappas	.10
271	Mike Perez	.10
272	Bob Tewksbury	.10
273	Mark Whiten	.10
274	Todd Zeile	.15
275	Andy Ashby	.10
276	Brad Ausmus	.10
277	Phil Clark	.10
278	Jeff Gardner	.10
279	Ricky Gutierrez	.10
280	Tony Gwynn	1.00
281	Tim Mauser	.10
282	Scott Sanders	.10
283	Frank Seminara	.10
284	Wally Whitehurst	.10
285	Rod Beck	.10
286	Barry Bonds	1.00
287	Dave Burba	.10
288	Mark Carreon	.10
289	Royce Clayton	.10
290	Mike Jackson	.10
291	Darren Lewis	.10
292	Kirt Manwaring	.10
293	Dave Martinez	.10
294	Billy Swift	.10
295	Salomon Torres	.10
296	Matt Williams	.20
297	Checklist 1-103 (Joe Orsulak)	.10
298	Checklist 104-201 (Pete Incaviglia)	.10
299	Checklist 202-300 (Todd Hundley)	.10
300	Checklist - Inserts (John Doherty)	.10
301	Brady Anderson	.25
302	Harold Baines	.10
303	Damon Buford	.10
304	Mike Devereaux	.10
305	Sid Fernandez	.10
306	Rick Krivda	.10
307	Mike Mussina	.50
308	Rafael Palmeiro	.30
309	Arthur Rhodes	.10
310	Chris Sabo	.10
311	Lee Smith	.10
312	*Gregg Zaun*	.15
313	Scott Cooper	.10
314	Mike Greenwell	.10
315	Tim Naehring	.10
316	Otis Nixon	.10
317	Paul Quantrill	.10
318	John Valentin	.15
319	Dave Valle	.10
320	Frank Viola	.10
321	*Brian Anderson*	.15
322	Garret Anderson	.10
323	Chad Curtis	.10
324	Chili Davis	.10
325	Gary DiSarcina	.10
326	Damion Easley	.10
327	Jim Edmonds	.20
328	Chuck Finley	.10
329	Joe Grahe	.10
330	Bo Jackson	.20
331	Mark Langston	.10
332	Harold Reynolds	.10
333	James Baldwin	.10
334	*Ray Durham*	.75
335	Julio Franco	.10
336	Craig Grebeck	.10
337	Ozzie Guillen	.10
338	Joe Hall	.10
339	Darrin Jackson	.10
340	Jack McDowell	.10
341	Tim Raines	.10
342	Robin Ventura	.20
343	Carlos Baerga	.10
344	Derek Lilliquist	.10
345	Dennis Martinez	.10
346	Jack Morris	.10
347	Eddie Murray	.20
348	Chris Nabholz	.10
349	Charles Nagy	.10
350	Chad Ogea	.10
351	Manny Ramirez	1.00
352	Omar Vizquel	.10
353	Tim Belcher	.10
354	Eric Davis	.10
355	Kirk Gibson	.10
356	Rick Greene	.10
357	Mickey Tettleton	.10
358	Alan Trammell	.15
359	David Wells	.10
360	Stan Belinda	.10
361	Vince Coleman	.10
362	David Cone	.15
363	Gary Gaetti	.10
364	Tom Gordon	.10
365	Dave Henderson	.10
366	Wally Joyner	.10
367	Brent Mayne	.10
368	Brian McRae	.10
369	Michael Tucker	.10
370	Ricky Bones	.10
371	Brian Harper	.10
372	Tyrone Hill	.10
373	Mark Kiefer	.10
374	Pat Listach	.10
375	*Mike Matheny*	.15
376	*Jose Mercedes*	.10
377	Jody Reed	.10
378	Kevin Seitzer	.10
379	B.J. Surhoff	.10
380	Greg Vaughn	.20
381	Turner Ward	.10
382	*Wes Weger*	.10
383	Bill Wegman	.10
384	Rick Aguilera	.10
385	Rich Becker	.10
386	Alex Cole	.10
387	Steve Dunn	.10
388	*Keith Garagozzo*	.10
389	*LaTroy Hawkins*	.20
390	Shane Mack	.10
391	David McCarty	.10
392	Pedro Munoz	.10
393	*Derek Parks*	.20
394	Kirby Puckett	1.00
395	Kevin Tapani	.10
396	Matt Walbeck	.10
397	Jim Abbott	.10
398	Mike Gallego	.10
399	Xavier Hernandez	.10
400	Don Mattingly	1.00
401	Terry Mulholland	.10
402	Matt Nokes	.10
403	Luis Polonia	.10
404	Bob Wickman	.10
405	Mark Acre	.10
406	*Fausto Cruz*	.20
407	Dennis Eckersley	.10
408	Rickey Henderson	.40
409	Stan Javier	.10
410	*Carlos Reyes*	.10
411	Ruben Sierra	.10
412	Terry Steinbach	.10
413	Bill Taylor	.10
414	Todd Van Poppel	.10
415	Eric Anthony	.10
416	Bobby Ayala	.10
417	Chris Bosio	.10
418	Tim Davis	.10
419	Randy Johnson	.40
420	Kevin King	.10
421	*Anthony Manahan*	.15
422	Edgar Martinez	.10
423	Keith Mitchell	.10
424	Roger Salkeld	.10
425	*Mac Suzuki*	.15
426	Dan Wilson	.10
427	*Duff Brumley*	.10
428	Jose Canseco	.50
429	Will Clark	.40

430	Steve Dreyer	.10
431	Rick Helling	.10
432	Chris James	.10
433	Matt Whiteside	.10
434	Roberto Alomar	.50
435	Scott Brow	.10
436	*Domingo Cedeno*	.15
437	Carlos Delgado	.50
438	Juan Guzman	.10
439	Paul Spoljaric	.10
440	Todd Stottlemyre	.10
441	Woody Williams	.10
442	Dave Justice	.20
443	Mike Kelly	.10
444	Ryan Klesko	.15
445	Javier Lopez	.15
446	Greg Maddux	1.50
447	Kent Mercker	.10
448	Charlie O'Brien	.10
449	Terry Pendleton	.10
450	Mike Stanton	.10
451	Tony Tarasco	.10
452	*Terrell Wade*	.10
453	Willie Banks	.10
454	Shawon Dunston	.10
455	Mark Grace	.20
456	Jose Guzman	.10
457	Jose Hernandez	.10
458	Glenallen Hill	.10
459	Blaise Ilsley	.10
460	*Brooks Kieschnick*	.40
461	Derrick May	.10
462	Randy Myers	.10
463	Karl Rhodes	.10
464	Sammy Sosa	2.00
465	*Steve Trachsel*	.25
466	Anthony Young	.10
467	*Eddie Zambrano*	.15
468	Bret Boone	.10
469	Tom Browning	.10
470	*Hector Carrasco*	.15
471	Rob Dibble	.10
472	Erik Hanson	.10
473	Thomas Howard	.10
474	Barry Larkin	.20
475	Hal Morris	.10
476	Jose Rijo	.10
477	John Burke	.10
478	Ellis Burks	.10
479	Marvin Freeman	.10
480	Andres Galarraga	.25
481	Greg Harris	.10
482	Charlie Hayes	.10
483	Darren Holmes	.10
484	Howard Johnson	.10
485	*Marcus Moore*	.15
486	David Nied	.10
487	Mark Thompson	.10
488	Walt Weiss	.10
489	Kurt Abbott	.10
490	Matias Carrillo	.10
491	Jeff Conine	.15
492	Chris Hammond	.10
493	Bryan Harvey	.10
494	Charlie Hough	.10
495	*Yorkis Perez*	.15
496	Pat Rapp	.15
497	Benito Santiago	.10
498	David Weathers	.10
499	Craig Biggio	.40
500	Ken Caminiti	.25
501	Doug Drabek	.10
502	*Tony Eusebio*	.20
503	Steve Finley	.10
504	Pete Harnisch	.10
505	Brian Hunter	.10
506	Domingo Jean	.10
507	Todd Jones	.10
508	Orlando Miller	.10
509	James Mouton	.10
510	Roberto Petagine	.10
511	Shane Reynolds	.10
512	Mitch Williams	.10
513	Billy Ashley	.10
514	Tom Candiotti	.10
515	Delino DeShields	.10
516	Kevin Gross	.10
517	Orel Hershiser	.10
518	Eric Karros	.15
519	Ramon Martinez	.15
520	*Chan Ho Park*	.50
521	Henry Rodriguez	.10
522	Joey Eischen	.10
523	Rod Henderson	.10
524	Pedro Martinez	1.00
525	Mel Rojas	.10
526	Larry Walker	.50
527	*Gabe White*	.20
528	Bobby Bonilla	.10
529	Jonathan Hurst	.10
530	Bobby Jones	.10
531	Kevin McReynolds	.10
532	Bill Pulsipher	.10
533	Bret Saberhagen	.10
534	David Segui	.10
535	Pete Smith	.10
536	*Kelly Stinnett*	.15
537	Dave Telgheder	.10
538	*Quilvio Veras*	.25
539	Jose Vizcaino	.10
540	Pete Walker	.10
541	Ricky Bottalico	.10
542	Wes Chamberlain	.10
543	Mariano Duncan	.10
544	Len Dykstra	.10
545	Jim Eisenreich	.10
546	*Phil Geisler*	.10
547	*Wayne Gomes*	.15
548	Doug Jones	.10
549	Jeff Juden	.10
550	Mike Lieberthal	.20
551	*Tony Longmire*	.15
552	Tom Marsh	.10
553	Bobby Munoz	.10
554	Curt Schilling	.10
555	Carlos Garcia	.10
556	*Ravelo Manzanillo*	.10
557	Orlando Merced	.10
558	*Will Pennyfeather*	.10
559	Zane Smith	.10
560	Andy Van Slyke	.10
561	Rick White	.10
562	Luis Alicea	.10
563	*Brian Barber*	.15
564	*Clint Davis*	.10
565	Bernard Gilkey	.10
566	Ray Lankford	.10
567	Tom Pagnozzi	.10
568	Ozzie Smith	.50
569	Rick Sutcliffe	.10
570	Allen Watson	.10
571	Dmitri Young	.10
572	Derek Bell	.10
573	Andy Benes	.15
574	Archi Cianfrocco	.10
575	Joey Hamilton	.10
576	Gene Harris	.10
577	Trevor Hoffman	.15
578	*Tim Hyers*	.15
579	*Brian Johnson*	.15
580	*Keith Lockhart*	.20
581	Pedro Martinez	.25
582	Ray McDavid	.10
583	Phil Plantier	.10
584	Bip Roberts	.10
585	Dave Staton	.10
586	Todd Benzinger	.10
587	John Burkett	.10
588	Bryan Hickerson	.10
589	Willie McGee	.10
590	John Patterson	.10
591	Mark Portugal	.10
592	Kevin Rogers	.10
593	*Joe Rosselli*	.10
594	*Steve Soderstrom*	.10
595	Robby Thompson	.10
596	125th Anniversary card	.10
597	Checklist	.10
598	Checklist	.10
599	Checklist	.10
600	Checklist	.10

1994 Ultra All-Rookie Team

A stylized sunrise landscape is the background for this insert set featuring top rookies and inserted into Ultra Series II packs at the rate of about one per 10. Backs repeat the motif with an action photo. Both sides are gold-foil enhanced and UV-coated.

		MT
Complete Set (10):		6.00
Common Player:		.50
1	Kurt Abbott	.50
2	Carlos Delgado	2.50
3	Cliff Floyd	.50
4	Jeffrey Hammonds	.50
5	Ryan Klesko	.75
6	Javier Lopez	1.00
7	Raul Mondesi	1.00
8	James Mouton	.50
9	Chan Ho Park	1.00
10	Dave Staton	.50

1994 Ultra All-Rookie Team Supers

This super-size (3-1/2" x 5-1/2") version of the Fleer Ultra II insert set featuring top rookies was included one per case of hobby packaging. Cards are identical to the smaller version. Both sides are gold-foil enhanced and UV-coated.

		MT
Complete Set (10):		12.50
Common Player:		.75
1	Kurt Abbott	.90
2	Carlos Delgado	3.00
3	Cliff Floyd	.90
4	Jeffrey Hammonds	.90
5	Ryan Klesko	2.00
6	Javier Lopez	2.00
7	Raul Mondesi	2.00
8	James Mouton	.75
9	Chan Ho Park	2.00
10	Dave Staton	.75

1994 Ultra All-Stars

Fleer's opinion of the top 20 players in 1994 are featured in this most common of the Series II Ultra insert sets. Silver-foil highlights enhance the chase cards, found, according to stated odds, once per three packs, on average. National Leaguers have purple backgrounds front and back, American Leaguers have red.

		MT
Complete Set (20):		15.00
Common Player:		.50
1	Chris Hoiles	.50
2	Frank Thomas	1.50
3	Roberto Alomar	.75
4	Cal Ripken, Jr.	3.00
5	Robin Ventura	.75
6	Albert Belle	1.00
7	Juan Gonzalez	1.50
8	Ken Griffey, Jr.	4.00
9	John Olerud	.75
10	Jack McDowell	.50
11	Mike Piazza	2.50
12	Fred McGriff	.75
13	Ryne Sandberg	1.00
14	Jay Bell	.50
15	Matt Williams	.60
16	Barry Bonds	1.00
17	Len Dykstra	.50
18	Dave Justice	.75
19	Tom Glavine	.60
20	Greg Maddux	2.00

1994 Ultra Award Winners

The most common of the Fleer Ultra insert sets for 1994 is the 25-card "Award Winners." Horizontal format cards feature front and back background with a gold-embossed look. A player action photo appears on the front. A gold-foil seal on the front has a symbolic player representation flanked by the pictured player's name and award. A gold Fleer Ultra logo is at top. Backs have a player portrait photo and a write-up about the award. The name of the award and the player's name appear in gold foil at the top. Stated odds of finding an Award Winners card were one in three packs.

		MT
Complete Set (25):		18.00
Common Player:		.40
1	Ivan Rodriguez	1.00
2	Don Mattingly	1.00
3	Roberto Alomar	.75
4	Robin Ventura	.60
5	Omar Vizquel	.40
6	Ken Griffey, Jr.	4.00
7	Kenny Lofton	.60
8	Devon White	.50
9	Mark Langston	.40
10	Kirt Manwaring	.40
11	Mark Grace	.60
12	Robby Thompson	.40
13	Matt Williams	.50
14	Jay Bell	.40
15	Barry Bonds	1.00
16	Marquis Grissom	.40
17	Larry Walker	.75
18	Greg Maddux	2.00
19	Frank Thomas	1.50
20	Barry Bonds	1.00
21	Paul Molitor	.75
22	Jack McDowell	.40
23	Greg Maddux	2.00
24	Tim Salmon	.50
25	Mike Piazza	3.00

1994 Ultra Career Achievement Awards

The outstanding careers of five of baseball's top veteran stars are recognized in this chase set, inserted on average once every 21 packs of Ultra Series II. The gold-highlighted horizontal fronts combine a current color photo with a background single-tint photo from the player's earlier days. Backs flip-flop the photo use, with the current photo in the background and the earlier photo in full color in the foreground. The gold Ultra Career Achievement Award seal is repeated on back, as well.

		MT
Complete Set (5):		8.00
Common Player:		1.00
1	Joe Carter	1.00
2	Paul Molitor	1.50
3	Cal Ripken, Jr.	5.00
4	Ryne Sandberg	1.50
5	Dave Winfield	1.50

1994 Ultra Firemen

Ten of the major leagues' leading relief pitchers are featured in this Ultra insert set. Cards have an action photo of the player superimposed over a background photo of a fire truck. A shield at top, in gold foil, has a smoke-eater's helmet, stylized flames and proclaims the player an "Ultra Fireman." Backs are horizontal in format and feature the pumper's control panel in the background photo. A color player portrait photo appears on one side, with a description of his relief role and successes in a whitened box. Fireman cards are found, on average, once per 11 packs, according to stated odds.

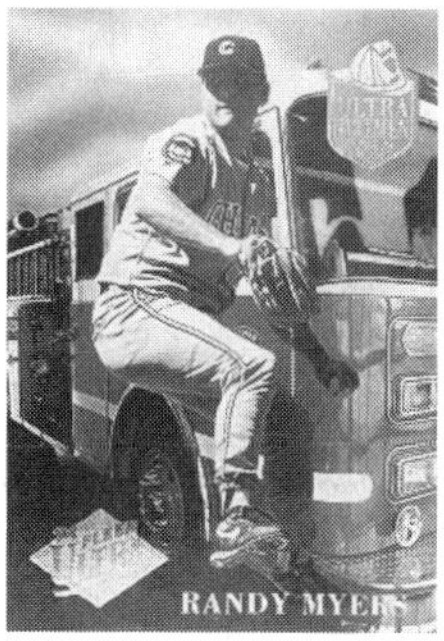

		MT
Complete Set (10):		5.00
Common Player:		.50
1	Jeff Montgomery	.50
2	Duane Ward	.50
3	Tom Henke	.50
4	Roberto Hernandez	.50
5	Dennis Eckersley	1.00
6	Randy Myers	.50
7	Rod Beck	.50
8	Bryan Harvey	.50
9	John Wetteland	.50
10	Mitch Williams	.50

1994 Ultra Hitting Machines

A heavy metal background of gears and iron-letter logo is featured in this insert set honoring the game's top hitters. The cards turn up about once in every five packs of Ultra Series II. Both front and back are highlighted in silver foil.

		MT
Complete Set (10):		10.00
Common Player:		.50
1	Roberto Alomar	1.00
2	Carlos Baerga	.50
3	Barry Bonds	1.25
4	Andres Galarraga	.75
5	Juan Gonzalez	1.50
6	Tony Gwynn	1.50
7	Paul Molitor	.75
8	John Olerud	.75
9	Mike Piazza	2.50
10	Frank Thomas	1.50

1994 Ultra Home Run Kings

One of two high-end insert sets in '94 Ultra is the 12-card "Home Run Kings" found exclusively in 14-card foil packs, on an average of once per 36-pack box. Featuring the technology Fleer calls "etched metallization," the cards have a black background with a red and blue foil representation of a batter. An action photo of a player taking a mighty cut or starting his home-run trot is featured. A large gold-foil "Home Run King" crown-and-shield device are in an upper corner, while the Ultra logo and player name are in gold foil at bottom. Backs have a white background with the red and blue batter symbol. The player's name appears in gold foil at the top, along with a portrait photo and a summary of his home run prowess.

		MT
Complete Set (12):		60.00
Common Player:		3.00
1	Juan Gonzalez	7.50
2	Ken Griffey, Jr.	20.00
3	Frank Thomas	7.50
4	Albert Belle	5.00
5	Rafael Palmeiro	3.00
6	Joe Carter	2.00
7	Barry Bonds	6.00
8	Dave Justice	2.50
9	Matt Williams	2.50
10	Fred McGriff	2.50
11	Ron Gant	2.00
12	Mike Piazza	12.00

1994 Ultra League Leaders

Arguably the least attractive of the '94 Fleer Ultra inserts are the 10 "League Leaders." Fronts feature a full-bleed action photo on which the bottom has been re-colored to a team hue giving the effect of teal, purple and magenta miasmas rising from the turf. An Ultra logo appear in gold foil in an upper corner, with the player's name in gold foil at about the dividing line between the natural color and colorized portions of the photo. A large "League Leader" appears in the bottom half of the photo, with the category led printed in the lower-left. Backs repeat the team color at top, fading to white at the bottom. In gold foil are "League Leader" and the category. A portrait-type player photo appears at bottom. Several paragraphs detail the league leading performance of the previous season.

		MT
Complete Set (10):		5.00
Common Player:		.50
1	John Olerud	.75
2	Rafael Palmeiro	.75
3	Kenny Lofton	.75
4	Jack McDowell	.50
5	Randy Johnson	1.00
6	Andres Galarraga	.75
7	Len Dykstra	.50
8	Chuck Carr	.50
9	Tom Glavine	.75
10	Jose Rijo	.50

1994 Ultra On-Base Leaders

One of the lesser-known, but most valuable, stats - on-base percentage - is featured in this subset found exclusively in 17-card packs, at the rate of about one per 37 packs. The fronts feature color photos against a stat-filled printed-foil background.

		MT
Complete Set (12):		100.00
Common Player:		5.00
1	Roberto Alomar	10.00
2	Barry Bonds	15.00
3	Len Dykstra	5.00
4	Andres Galarraga	8.00
5	Mark Grace	8.00
6	Ken Griffey, Jr.	40.00
7	Gregg Jefferies	5.00
8	Orlando Merced	5.00
9	Paul Molitor	10.00
10	John Olerud	8.00
11	Tony Phillips	5.00
12	Frank Thomas	15.00

1994 Ultra Phillies Finest

As a tribute to two of Fleer's home-team heroes, the Philadelphia-based card company created an Ultra insert set featuring 12 cards each of "Phillies Finest," John Kruk and Darren Daulton. Twenty of the cards were issued as Series 1 and 2 inserts, about one in every eight packs, while four were available only by a mail-in offer. Fronts feature action photos with large block letters popping out of the background. The Ultra logo and player name appear in gold foil. Backs have portrait photos and career summaries, with the player's name and card number in gold foil. Daulton and Kruk each autographed 1,000 of the inserts. Stated odds of finding the autographed cards were one in 11,000 packs. Values listed are per card.

		MT
Complete Set (24):		10.00
Common player:		.50
Autographed Daulton or Kruk:		25.00
1-5	Darren Daulton	.50
6-10	John Kruk	.50
11-15	Darren Daulton	.50
16-20	John Kruk	.50
9a	John Kruk (PROMOTIONAL SAMPLE) MAIL-IN CARDS	3.00
1M, 3M	Darren Daulton	1.50
2M, 4M	John Kruk	1.50
1	Darren Daulton (holding mask and glove)	.50
2	Darren Daulton (power swing, home uniform)	.50
3	Darren Daulton (blocking home plate)	.50
4	Darren Daulton (home run trot, home uniform)	.50
1M	Darren Daulton (standing, throwing)	1.50
2M	John Kruk (ready to field)	1.50
3M	Darren Daulton (awaiting pitch)	1.50
4M	John Kruk (running)	1.50

1994 Ultra RBI Kings

Exclusive to the 19-card jumbo packs of Fleer Ultra are a series of 12 "RBI Kings" insert cards, found, according to stated odds, one per 36 packs. The horizontal-format card front uses Fleer's "etched metallized" technology to produce a sepia-toned background action photo, in front of which is a color player photo. An Ultra logo appears in gold foil in an upper corner while a fancy shield-and-scroll "RBI King" logo and the player's name are in gold at the bottom. Backs repeat the basic front motif and include a color player portrait photo, his name in gold foil and a paragraph justifying his selection as an RBI King.

		MT
Complete Set (12):		80.00
Common Player:		6.00
1	Albert Belle	10.00
2	Frank Thomas	12.00
3	Joe Carter	5.00
4	Juan Gonzalez	12.00
5	Cecil Fielder	5.00
6	Carlos Baerga	5.00
7	Barry Bonds	12.00
8	David Justice	6.00
9	Ron Gant	5.00
10	Mike Piazza	20.00
11	Matt Williams	8.00
12	Darren Daulton	5.00

1994 Ultra Rising Stars

An outer space background printed on metallic foil sets this chase set apart from most of the rest of the Ultra Series II inserts. The silver-foil enhanced cards of projected superstars of tomorrow are found on average once every 37 packs.

		MT
Complete Set (12):		65.00
Common Player:		4.00
1	Carlos Baerga	3.00
2	Jeff Bagwell	12.00
3	Albert Belle	10.00
4	Cliff Floyd	4.00
5	Travis Fryman	4.00
6	Marquis Grissom	3.00
7	Kenny Lofton	10.00
8	John Olerud	4.00
9	Mike Piazza	20.00
10	Kirk Rueter	3.00
11	Tim Salmon	8.00
12	Aaron Sele	3.00

1994 Ultra Second Year Standouts

Approximately once every 11 packs, the Ultra insert find is a "Second Year Standout" card. Ten of the game's sophomore stars are featured. Fronts feature a pair of action photos against a team-color background. Gold-foil highlights are the Ultra logo, the player's name and a "Second Year Standout" shield. The shield and player name are repeated in gold foil on the back, as is the team color background. There is a player portrait photo at bottom and a summary of the player's 1993 season.

		MT
Complete Set (10):		10.00
Common Player:		.50
1	Jason Bere	.75
2	Brent Gates	.50
3	Jeffrey Hammonds	.75
4	Tim Salmon	2.00
5	Aaron Sele	.75
6	Chuck Carr	.50
7	Jeff Conine	.75
8	Greg McMichael	.50
9	Mike Piazza	8.00
10	Kevin Stocker	.50

1994 Ultra Strikeout Kings

A gold-foil "Strikeout Kings" crown-and-shield logo is featured on the front of this chase set. Cards are found on average once per seven packs. Each of the cards features the K-king in sequential action photos. Backs have a larger action photo with a large version of the Strikeout King shield in the background.

		MT
Complete Set (5):		4.00
Common Player:		.75
1	Randy Johnson	1.25
2	Mark Langston	.75
3	Greg Maddux	2.50
4	Jose Rijo	.75
5	John Smoltz	1.00

1995 Ultra

A clean design enhanced with three different colors of metallic foil graphics is featured on the basic cards of 1995 Fleer Ultra. Two series of 250 cards each were issued with cards arranged alphabetically within team, also sequenced alphabetically. Fronts have a gold-foil Ultra logo in an upper corner, with the player's name and team logo in a team-color coded foil at bottom. There are no other graphic elements on the borderless photos. Backs have a large photo rendered in a single color, again team-coded. A postage-stamp sized color photo in one corner is flanked by a few vital stats in silver foil. Career and '94 stats are printed at bottom, enhanced by the foil color from the front. Cards were issued in 12-card retail and hobby packs at $1.99 and jumbo pre-priced ($2.69) magazine packs. Each pack contains one of the several insert series from the appropriate series.

		MT
Complete Set (450):		30.00
Series 1 (250):		20.00
Series 2 (200):		15.00
Common Player:		.10
Series 1 or 2 Wax Box:		50.00
1	Brady Anderson	.15
2	Sid Fernandez	.10
3	Jeffrey Hammonds	.10
4	Chris Hoiles	.10
5	Ben McDonald	.10
6	Mike Mussina	.50
7	Rafael Palmeiro	.40
8	Jack Voigt	.10
9	Wes Chamberlain	.10
10	Roger Clemens	1.25
11	Chris Howard	.10
12	Tim Naehring	.10
13	Otis Nixon	.10

14	Rich Rowland	.10
15	Ken Ryan	.10
16	John Valentin	.10
17	Mo Vaughn	.50
18	Brian Anderson	.10
19	Chili Davis	.10
20	Damion Easley	.10
21	Jim Edmonds	.10
22	Mark Langston	.10
23	Tim Salmon	.25
24	J.T. Snow	.15
25	Chris Turner	.10
26	Wilson Alvarez	.10
27	Joey Cora	.10
28	Alex Fernandez	.10
29	Roberto Hernandez	.10
30	Lance Johnson	.10
31	Ron Karkovice	.10
32	Kirk McCaskill	.10
33	Tim Raines	.15
34	Frank Thomas	1.25
35	Sandy Alomar	.15
36	Albert Belle	.75
37	Mark Clark	.10
38	Kenny Lofton	.50
39	Eddie Murray	.40
40	Eric Plunk	.10
41	Manny Ramirez	1.00
42	Jim Thome	.30
43	Omar Vizquel	.10
44	Danny Bautista	.10
45	Junior Felix	.10
46	Cecil Fielder	.10
47	Chris Gomez	.10
48	Chad Kreuter	.10
49	Mike Moore	.10
50	Tony Phillips	.10
51	Alan Trammell	.15
52	David Wells	.10
53	Kevin Appier	.10
54	Billy Brewer	.10
55	David Cone	.15
56	Greg Gagne	.10
57	Bob Hamelin	.10
58	Jose Lind	.10
59	Brent Mayne	.10
60	Brian McRae	.10
61	Terry Shumpert	.10
62	Ricky Bones	.10
63	Mike Fetters	.10
64	Darryl Hamilton	.10
65	John Jaha	.10
66	Graeme Lloyd	.10
67	Matt Mieske	.10
68	Kevin Seitzer	.10
69	Jose Valentin	.10
70	Turner Ward	.10
71	Rick Aguilera	.10
72	Rich Becker	.10
73	Alex Cole	.10
74	Scott Leius	.10
75	Pat Meares	.10
76	Kirby Puckett	.75
77	Dave Stevens	.10
78	Kevin Tapani	.10
79	Matt Walbeck	.10
80	Wade Boggs	.35
81	Scott Kamieniecki	.10
82	Pat Kelly	.10
83	Jimmy Key	.10
84	Paul O'Neill	.25
85	Luis Polonia	.10
86	Mike Stanley	.10
87	Danny Tartabull	.10
88	Bob Wickman	.10
89	Mark Acre	.10
90	Geronimo Berroa	.10
91	Mike Bordick	.10
92	Ron Darling	.10
93	Stan Javier	.10
94	Mark McGwire	3.00
95	Troy Neel	.10
96	Ruben Sierra	.10
97	Terry Steinbach	.10
98	Eric Anthony	.10
99	Chris Bosio	.10
100	Dave Fleming	.10
101	Ken Griffey Jr.	3.00
102	Reggie Jefferson	.10
103	Randy Johnson	.40
104	Edgar Martinez	.10
105	Bill Risley	.10
106	Dan Wilson	.10
107	Cris Carpenter	.10
108	Will Clark	.35
109	Juan Gonzalez	1.00
110	Rusty Greer	.10
111	David Hulse	.10
112	Roger Pavlik	.10
113	Ivan Rodriguez	.75
114	Doug Strange	.10
115	Matt Whiteside	.10
116	Roberto Alomar	.50
117	Brad Cornett	.10
118	Carlos Delgado	.50
119	Alex Gonzalez	.10
120	Darren Hall	.10
121	Pat Hentgen	.10
122	Paul Molitor	.40
123	Ed Sprague	.10
124	Devon White	.10
125	Tom Glavine	.25
126	Dave Justice	.20
127	Roberto Kelly	.10
128	Mark Lemke	.10
129	Greg Maddux	1.50
130	Charles Johnson	.10
131	Kent Mercker	.10
132	Charlie O'Brien	.10
133	John Smoltz	.25
134	Willie Banks	.10
135	Steve Buechele	.10
136	Kevin Foster	.10
137	Glenallen Hill	.10
138	Ray Sanchez	.10
139	Sammy Sosa	2.00
140	Steve Trachsel	.10
141	Rick Wilkins	.10
142	Jeff Brantley	.10
143	Hector Carrasco	.10
144	Kevin Jarvis	.10
145	Barry Larkin	.15
146	Chuck McElroy	.10
147	Jose Rijo	.10
148	Johnny Ruffin	.10
149	Deion Sanders	.20
150	Eddie Taubensee	.10
151	Dante Bichette	.20
152	Ellis Burks	.10
153	Joe Girardi	.10
154	Charlie Hayes	.10
155	Mike Kingery	.10
156	Steve Reed	.10
157	Kevin Ritz	.10
158	Bruce Ruffin	.10
159	Eric Young	.15
160	Kurt Abbott	.10
161	Chuck Carr	.10
162	Chris Hammond	.10
163	Bryan Harvey	.10
164	Terry Mathews	.10
165	Yorkis Perez	.10
166	Pat Rapp	.10
167	Gary Sheffield	.20
168	Dave Weathers	.10
169	Jeff Bagwell	.75
170	Ken Caminiti	.20
171	Doug Drabek	.10
172	Steve Finley	.10
173	John Hudek	.10
174	Todd Jones	.10
175	James Mouton	.10
176	Shane Reynolds	.15
177	Scott Servais	.10
178	Tom Candiotti	.10
179	Omar Daal	.10
180	Darren Dreifort	.10
181	Eric Karros	.10
182	Ramon Martinez	.15
183	Raul Mondesi	.25
184	Henry Rodriguez	.10
185	Todd Worrell	.10
186	Moises Alou	.20
187	Sean Berry	.10
188	Wil Cordero	.10
189	Jeff Fassero	.10
190	Darrin Fletcher	.10
191	Butch Henry	.10
192	Ken Hill	.10
193	Mel Rojas	.10
194	John Wetteland	.10
195	Bobby Bonilla	.10
196	Rico Brogna	.10
197	Bobby Jones	.10
198	Jeff Kent	.10
199	Josias Manzanillo	.10
200	Kelly Stinnett	.10
201	Ryan Thompson	.10
202	Jose Vizcaino	.10
203	Lenny Dykstra	.10
204	Jim Eisenreich	.10
205	Dave Hollins	.10
206	Mike Lieberthal	.20
207	Mickey Morandini	.10
208	Bobby Munoz	.10
209	Curt Schilling	.10
210	Heathcliff Slocumb	.10
211	David West	.10
212	Dave Clark	.10
213	Steve Cooke	.10
214	Midre Cummings	.10
215	Carlos Garcia	.10
216	Jeff King	.10
217	Jon Lieber	.10
218	Orlando Merced	.10
219	Don Slaught	.10
220	Rick White	.10
221	Rene Arocha	.10
222	Bernard Gilkey	.10
223	Brian Jordan	.15
224	Tom Pagnozzi	.10
225	Vicente Palacios	.10
226	Geronimo Pena	.10
227	Ozzie Smith	.50
228	Allen Watson	.10
229	Mark Whiten	.10
230	Brad Ausmus	.10
231	Derek Bell	.10
232	Andy Benes	.10
233	Tony Gwynn	1.50
234	Joey Hamilton	.10
235	Luis Lopez	.10
236	Pedro A. Martinez	.10
237	Scott Sanders	.10
238	Eddie Williams	.10
239	Rod Beck	.10
240	Dave Burba	.10
241	Darren Lewis	.10
242	Kirt Manwaring	.10
243	Mark Portugal	.10
244	Darryl Strawberry	.20
245	Robby Thompson	.10
246	William VanLandingham	.10
247	Matt Williams	.20
248	Checklist	.10
249	Checklist	.10
250	Checklist	.10
251	Harold Baines	.10
252	Bret Barberie	.10
253	Armando Benitez	.10
254	Mike Devereaux	.10
255	Leo Gomez	.10
256	Jamie Moyer	.10
257	Arthur Rhodes	.10
258	Cal Ripken Jr.	2.00
259	Luis Alicea	.10
260	Jose Canseco	.75
261	Scott Cooper	.10
262	Andre Dawson	.20
263	Mike Greenwell	.10
264	Aaron Sele	.10
265	Garret Anderson	.10
266	Chad Curtis	.10
267	Gary DiSarcina	.10
268	Chuck Finley	.10
269	Rex Hudler	.10
270	Andrew Lorraine	.10
271	Spike Owen	.10
272	Lee Smith	.10
273	Jason Bere	.10
274	Ozzie Guillen	.10
275	Norberto Martin	.10
276	Scott Ruffcorn	.10
277	Robin Ventura	.25
278	Carlos Baerga	.10
279	Jason Grimsley	.10
280	Dennis Martinez	.10
281	Charles Nagy	.10
282	Paul Sorrento	.10
283	Dave Winfield	.25
284	John Doherty	.10
285	Travis Fryman	.15
286	Kirk Gibson	.10
287	Lou Whitaker	.10
288	Gary Gaetti	.10
289	Tom Gordon	.10
290	Mark Gubicza	.10
291	Wally Joyner	.10
292	Mike Macfarlane	.10
293	Jeff Montgomery	.10
294	Jeff Cirillo	.10
295	Cal Eldred	.10
296	Pat Listach	.10
297	Jose Mercedes	.10
298	Dave Nilsson	.10
299	Duane Singleton	.10
300	Greg Vaughn	.15
301	Scott Erickson	.15
302	Denny Hocking	.10
303	Chuck Knoblauch	.15
304	Pat Mahomes	.10
305	Pedro Munoz	.10
306	Erik Schullstrom	.10
307	Jim Abbott	.10
308	Tony Fernandez	.10
309	Sterling Hitchcock	.10
310	Jim Leyritz	.10
311	Don Mattingly	.75
312	Jack McDowell	.10
313	Melido Perez	.10
314	Bernie Williams	.40
315	Scott Brosius	.10
316	Dennis Eckersley	.10
317	Brent Gates	.10
318	Rickey Henderson	.50
319	Steve Karsay	.10
320	Steve Ontiveros	.10
321	Bill Taylor	.10
322	Todd Van Poppel	.10
323	Bob Welch	.10
324	Bobby Ayala	.10
325	Mike Blowers	.10
326	Jay Buhner	.10
327	Felix Fermin	.10
328	Tino Martinez	.15
329	Marc Newfield	.10
330	Greg Pirkl	.10
331	Alex Rodriguez	2.00
332	Kevin Brown	.20
333	John Burkett	.10
334	Jeff Frye	.10
335	Kevin Gross	.10
336	Dean Palmer	.10
337	Joe Carter	.10
338	Shawn Green	.50
339	Juan Guzman	.10
340	Mike Huff	.10
341	Al Leiter	.15
342	John Olerud	.25
343	Dave Stewart	.10
344	Todd Stottlemyre	.10
345	Steve Avery	.10
346	Jeff Blauser	.10
347	Chipper Jones	1.50
348	Mike Kelly	.10
349	Ryan Klesko	.15
350	Javier Lopez	.15
351	Fred McGriff	.20
352	Jose Oliva	.10
353	Terry Pendleton	.10
354	Mike Stanton	.10
355	Tony Tarasco	.10
356	Mark Wohlers	.10
357	Jim Bullinger	.10
358	Shawon Dunston	.10
359	Mark Grace	.25
360	Derrick May	.10
361	Randy Myers	.10
362	Karl Rhodes	.10
363	Bret Boone	.10
364	Brian Dorsett	.10
365	Ron Gant	.10
366	Brian R. Hunter	.10
367	Hal Morris	.10
368	Jack Morris	.10
369	John Roper	.10
370	Reggie Sanders	.10
371	Pete Schourek	.10
372	John Smiley	.10
373	Marvin Freeman	.10
374	Andres Galarraga	.25
375	Mike Munoz	.10
376	David Nied	.10
377	Walt Weiss	.10
378	Greg Colbrunn	.10
379	Jeff Conine	.10
380	Charles Johnson	.15
381	Kurt Miller	.10
382	Robb Nen	.10
383	Benito Santiago	.10
384	Craig Biggio	.40
385	Tony Eusebio	.10
386	Luis Gonzalez	.15
387	Brian L. Hunter	.10
388	Darryl Kile	.10
389	Orlando Miller	.10
390	Phil Plantier	.10
391	Greg Swindell	.10
392	Billy Ashley	.10
393	Pedro Astacio	.10
394	Brett Butler	.10
395	Delino DeShields	.10
396	Orel Hershiser	.10
397	Garey Ingram	.10
398	Chan Ho Park	.15
399	Mike Piazza	1.50
400	Ismael Valdes	.10
401	Tim Wallach	.10
402	Cliff Floyd	.10
403	Marquis Grissom	.15
404	Mike Lansing	.10
405	Pedro Martinez	1.00
406	Kirk Rueter	.10
407	Tim Scott	.10
408	Jeff Shaw	.10
409	Larry Walker	.50
410	Rondell White	.15
411	John Franco	.10
412	Todd Hundley	.10
413	Jason Jacome	.10
414	Joe Orsulak	.10
415	Bret Saberhagen	.15
416	David Segui	.10
417	Darren Daulton	.10
418	Mariano Duncan	.10
419	Tommy Greene	.10
420	Gregg Jefferies	.10
421	John Kruk	.10
422	Kevin Stocker	.10
423	Jay Bell	.10
424	Al Martin	.10
425	Denny Neagle	.10
426	Zane Smith	.10
427	Andy Van Slyke	.10
428	Paul Wagner	.10
429	Tom Henke	.10
430	Danny Jackson	.10
431	Ray Lankford	.10
432	John Mabry	.10
433	Bob Tewksbury	.10
434	Todd Zeile	.10
435	Andy Ashby	.10
436	Andujar Cedeno	.10
437	Donnie Elliott	.10
438	Bryce Florie	.10
439	Trevor Hoffman	.10
440	Melvin Nieves	.10
441	Bip Roberts	.10
442	Barry Bonds	.75
443	Royce Clayton	.10
444	Mike Jackson	.10
445	John Patterson	.10
446	J.R. Phillips	.10
447	Bill Swift	.10
448	Checklist	.10
449	Checklist	.10
450	Checklist	.10

1995 Ultra Gold Medallion

Less than 10% of the production run of Fleer Ultra (regular and insert sets) was produced in a special parallel Gold Medallion edition. On these special cards an embossed round gold seal replaces the Fleer Ultra logo in the upper corner. One Gold Medallion card was inserted into each Ultra foil pack.

	MT
Complete Set (450):	100.00
Series 1 (1-250):	60.00
Series 2 (251-450)	40.00
Common Player:	.25

(Star cards valued at 2X regular Fleer Ultra version.)

1995 Ultra All-Rookies

Enlarged pieces of the central color action photo, set on a white background, make up the front design on these inserts. The player's name, card title and Ultra logo are printed in silver foil. Horizontal backs have another color photo, which is also repeated in single-color fashion. A career summary is printed over the larger photo. The All-Rookie inserts are found only in 12-card packs, at the rate of about one per four packs.

		MT
Complete Set (10):		6.00
Common Player:		.40
Gold Medallion: 2X		
1	Cliff Floyd	.50
2	Chris Gomez	.40
3	Rusty Greer	.50
4	Bob Hamelin	.50
5	Joey Hamilton	.50
6	John Hudek	.40
7	Ryan Klesko	.75
8	Raul Mondesi	1.00
9	Manny Ramirez	4.00
10	Steve Trachsel	.50

1995 Ultra All-Stars

Twenty of the top players in the majors were chosen as Ultra All-Stars in this Series II chase set. Fronts have a color player photo at left. At right is a second photo, printed in only one color. A large "ALL-STAR" is at bottom, with the player's name above and team below in silver foil. An Ultra logo is at left. Backs have another color photo, with a '94 season summary printed in a black panel at right.

These cards were found one per five packs, on average.

		MT
Complete Set (20):		15.00
Common Player:		.25
Gold Medallion: 2X		
1	Moises Alou	.25
2	Albert Belle	.75
3	Craig Biggio	.50
4	Wade Boggs	.50
5	Barry Bonds	1.00
6	David Cone	.25
7	Ken Griffey Jr.	5.00
8	Tony Gwynn	2.00
9	Chuck Knoblauch	.35
10	Barry Larkin	.35
11	Kenny Lofton	.60
12	Greg Maddux	2.50
13	Fred McGriff	.50
14	Paul O'Neill	.25
15	Mike Piazza	2.50
16	Kirby Puckett	1.50
17	Cal Ripken Jr.	3.00
18	Ivan Rodriguez	1.00
19	Frank Thomas	1.50
20	Matt Williams	.35

1995 Ultra Award Winners

Various official and unofficial award winners from the 1994 season are featured in this Series I insert set. Horizontal cards have a color player photo on the right side, with a single-color, vertically compressed action photo at left. The player's award is printed in a white strip at top, while his name and team logo, along with the Ultra logo, are at bottom. All front typography is in gold foil. Backs repeat the compressed photo at left, combined with another color photo at right. A season summary is printed over the photo at left. The Award Winners inserts were common to all types of packaging, found at the rate of about one per four packs.

		MT
Complete Set (25):		18.00
Common Player:		.25
Gold Medallion: 2x		
1	Ivan Rodriguez	1.25
2	Don Mattingly	1.50
3	Roberto Alomar	1.00
4	Wade Boggs	.40
5	Omar Vizquel	.25
6	Ken Griffey Jr.	5.00
7	Kenny Lofton	1.00
8	Devon White	.25
9	Mark Langston	.25
10	Tom Pagnozzi	.25
11	Jeff Bagwell	1.50
12	Craig Biggio	.50
13	Matt Williams	.40
14	Barry Larkin	.40
15	Barry Bonds	1.25
16	Marquis Grissom	.25
17	Darren Lewis	.25
18	Greg Maddux	2.50
19	Frank Thomas	1.50
20	Jeff Bagwell	1.50
21	David Cone	.35
22	Greg Maddux	2.50
23	Bob Hamelin	.25
24	Raul Mondesi	.40
25	Moises Alou	.25

1995 Ultra Golden Prospects

A hobby-pack exclusive, found at the rate of one per eight packs on average in Series I. Fronts feature a player photo at right, with three horizontally and vertically compressed versions of the same photo at right. The photo's background has been rendered in a single color. All typography - Ultra logo, card title, name and team - is in gold foil. Backs are also horizontal and have a color player photo and career summary.

		MT
Complete Set (10):		10.00
Common Player:		.35
Gold Medallion: 2X		
1	James Baldwin	.50
2	Alan Benes	.35
3	Armando Benitez	.35
4	Ray Durham	.75
5	LaTroy Hawkins	.35
6	Brian Hunter	.35
7	Derek Jeter	4.00
8	Charles Johnson	.50
9	Alex Rodriguez	5.00
10	Michael Tucker	.35

1995 Ultra Gold Medallion Rookies Mail-in

This set of 20 was available only by mailing in 10 Fleer Ultra wrappers plus $5.95. A reported 100,000 sets were produced. The cards are in the same format as the regular-issue Fleer Ultra. Each card has a team logo, player name and "ROOKIE" notation in gold foil at bottom, and the round Gold Medallion seal in an upper-corner of the borderless game-action photo front. Backs have two more action photos, a large one-in-one-color and a small one in full-color. Much of the typography on back is rendered in gold foil. Card numbers have an M prefix.

		MT
Complete Set (20):		9.00
Common Player:		.25
M-1	Manny Alexander	.25
M-2	Edgardo Alfonzo	1.50
M-3	Jason Bates	.25
M-4	Andres Berumen	.25
M-5	Darren Bragg	.25
M-6	Jamie Brewington	.25
M-7	Jason Christiansen	.25
M-8	Brad Clontz	.25
M-9	Marty Cordova	1.00
M-10	Johnny Damon	1.00
M-11	Vaughn Eshelman	.25
M-12	Chad Fonville	.25
M-13	Curtis Goodwin	.35
M-14	Tyler Green	.35
M-15	Bob Higginson	.50
M-16	Jason Isringhausen	.75
M-17	Hideo Nomo	4.00
M-18	Jon Nunnally	.50
M-19	Carlos Perez	.25
M-20	Julian Tavarez	.25

1995 Ultra Hitting Machines

Various mechanical devices and dynamics make up the letters of "HITTING MACHINE" behind the color player action photo in this insert set. Both of those elements, along with the gold-foil player name, team and Ultra logo are in UV-coated contrast to the matte-finish gray background. Backs are also horizontal in format and feature a portrait photo at right, against a gray-streaked background. A career summary is printed at right. The Hitting Machines series is found only in Series II Ultra retail packs, at the rate of one card per eight packs, on average.

		MT
Complete Set (10):		15.00
Common Player:		.50
Gold Medallion: 2X		
1	Jeff Bagwell	1.50
2	Albert Belle	1.00
3	Dante Bichette	.75
4	Barry Bonds	1.50
5	Jose Canseco	1.00
6	Ken Griffey Jr.	5.00
7	Tony Gwynn	2.50
8	Fred McGriff	.75
9	Mike Piazza	3.00
10	Frank Thomas	1.50

1995 Ultra Home Run Kings

Retail packaging of Fleer Ultra Series I was the hiding place for this sluggers' chase set. An average of one out of eight packs yielded a Home Run King insert. Fronts have a photo of the player's home run cut, while large letters "H," "R" and "K" are stacked vertically down one side. All front typography is in gold foil. Backs have another batting photo and a couple of sentences of recent career slugging prowess.

		MT
Complete Set (10):		25.00
Common Player:		.75
Gold Medallion: 2X		
1	Ken Griffey Jr.	10.00
2	Frank Thomas	4.00
3	Albert Belle	2.00
4	Jose Canseco	2.50
5	Cecil Fielder	.75
6	Matt Williams	1.00
7	Jeff Bagwell	4.00
8	Barry Bonds	4.00
9	Fred McGriff	1.00
10	Andres Galarraga	1.00

1995 Ultra League Leaders

Top performers in major statistical categories are featured in this Series I insert. Cards were seeded in all types of Ultra packaging at the rate of about one card per three packs. Cards have a horizontal orientation with a color player action photo printed over a black logo of the appropriate league. American Leaguers' cards have a light brown overall background color, National Leaguers have dark green. The player's name, team and Ultra logos, and box with his league-leading category are printed in silver foil. The background from the front is carried over to the back, where a color portrait photo is at left, and a '94 season summary printed at right.

		MT
Complete Set (10):		4.00
Common Player:		.25
Gold Medallion: 2X		
1	Paul O'Neill	.50
2	Kenny Lofton	.75
3	Jimmy Key	.25
4	Randy Johnson	.75
5	Lee Smith	.25
6	Tony Gwynn	1.50
7	Craig Biggio	.75
8	Greg Maddux	1.50
9	Andy Benes	.25
10	John Franco	.25

1995 Ultra On-Base Leaders

Numerous smaller versions in several sizes of the central action photo against a graduated color background from the front design of this Series II insert set. The player name, card title and Ultra logo are printed in gold foil down one side. Backs have a horizontal player photo with a large team logo at top, a smaller version at bottom and a 1994 season summary. One out of eight (on average) prepriced packs yielded an On-Base Leaders insert.

		MT
Complete Set (10):		40.00
Common Player:		2.50
Gold Medallion: 2X		
1	Jeff Bagwell	6.00
2	Albert Belle	4.00
3	Craig Biggio	4.00
4	Wade Boggs	4.00
5	Barry Bonds	5.00
6	Will Clark	3.00
7	Tony Gwynn	8.00
8	Dave Justice	3.00
9	Paul O'Neill	3.00
10	Frank Thomas	6.00

Player names in *Italic* type indicate a rookie card.

1995 Ultra Power Plus

The scarcest of the Series I Ultra inserts are the Power Plus cards, printed on 100% etched foil and inserted at the rate of less than one per box. Fronts have a player action photo overprinted on a background of "POWER PLUS" logos in various metallic colors. A team logo and player name are at bottom in gold foil, as is the Ultra logo at top. Backs are conventionally printed and have a player photo on one side and season summary on the other.

		MT
Complete Set (6):		35.00
Common Player:		3.00
Gold Medallion: 2X		
1	Albert Belle	4.00
2	Ken Griffey Jr.	15.00
3	Frank Thomas	5.00
4	Jeff Bagwell	5.00
5	Barry Bonds	4.00
6	Matt Williams	3.00

1995 Ultra RBI Kings

A bright aura surrounds the central player action photo on these cards, separating the player image from an indistinct colored background. At center is a large gold-foil "RBI KING" with the player's name above and team below. Backs have a similar design with a white box at bottom covering the player's RBI abilities. This set is found only in Series I jumbo packs, at an average rate of one per eight packs.

		MT
Complete Set (10):		40.00
Common Player:		2.00
Gold Medallion: 2X		
1	Kirby Puckett	3.00
2	Joe Carter	2.00
3	Albert Belle	3.00
4	Frank Thomas	6.00
5	Julio Franco	2.00
6	Jeff Bagwell	5.00
7	Matt Williams	2.50
8	Dante Bichette	2.50
9	Fred McGriff	3.00
10	Mike Piazza	10.00

1995 Ultra Rising Stars

The top of the line among Series II chase cards is this set

printed on 100% etched foil and seeded at the rate of less than one per box, on average. Horizontal-format cards have two player photos on a background of multi-colored rays. The Ultra logo, card title, player name and team are printed in gold foil. Backs repeat the colored rays, have another player photo and a career summary.

		MT
Complete Set (9):		45.00
Common Player:		2.50
Gold Medallion: 2X		
1	Moises Alou	2.50
2	Jeff Bagwell	7.50
3	Albert Belle	5.00
4	Juan Gonzalez	10.00
5	Chuck Knoblauch	2.50
6	Kenny Lofton	5.00
7	Raul Mondesi	3.00
8	Mike Piazza	15.00
9	Frank Thomas	10.00

1995 Ultra Second Year Standouts

Fifteen of the game's sophomore stars are featured in this Series I insert set. Horizontal-format cards have player action photos front and back set against a background of orange and yellow rays. Besides the player name, card title and Ultra logo in gold-foil, the front features a pair of leafed branches flanking a team logo, all in embossed gold-foil. Backs have a career summary. The series was seeded at the average rate of one per six packs.

		MT
Complete Set (15):		8.00
Common Player:		.25
Gold Medallion: 2X		
1	Cliff Floyd	.40
2	Chris Gomez	.25
3	Rusty Greer	.35
4	Darren Hall	.25
5	Bob Hamelin	.25
6	Joey Hamilton	.40
7	Jeffrey Hammonds	.35
8	John Hudek	.25
9	Ryan Klesko	.50
10	Raul Mondesi	1.00
11	Manny Ramirez	5.00
12	Bill Risley	.25
13	Steve Trachsel	.35
14	William Van Landingham	.25
15	Rondell White	1.00

1995 Ultra Strikeout Kings

A purple background with several types of concentric and overlapping circular designs in white are the background of this Series II chase set. An action color photo of the K-King is at center, while down one side are stacked photos of the grips used for various pitches. The player name, card title and Ultra logo are in silver foil. Backs have a portrait photo and career summary with purple circles behind and a black background. Stated odds of finding a Strikeout King card are one in five packs, on average.

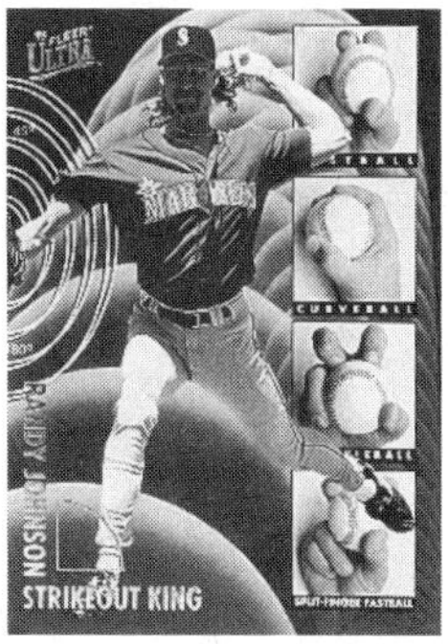

		MT
Complete Set (6):		6.00
Common Player:		.50
Gold Medallion: 2X		
1	Andy Benes	.50
2	Roger Clemens	1.50
3	Randy Johnson	1.00
4	Greg Maddux	3.00
5	Pedro Martinez	1.50
6	Jose Rijo	.50

1996 Ultra Promotional Samples

A six-page glossy folder which was die-cut to hold three sample cards introduced Fleer's Ultra line for 1996. The fronts of all three cards are similar in format to the issued versions, but only the back of the basic-card sample replicates the issued version. Backs of the chase card samples contained product information.

		MT
Complete Set (8):		50.00
Common Player:		4.00
(1)	Ken Griffey Jr. (basic card)	7.50
(2)	Matt Williams (basic card)	4.00
(3)	Barry Bonds (HR King)	7.50
(4)	Frank Thomas (HR King)	5.00
(5)	Roberto Alomar (Prime Leather)	4.00
(6)	Cal Ripken Jr. (Prime Leather)	12.50
2	Tony Gwynn (Season Crown)	6.00
4	Kenny Lofton (Season Crown)	6.00

1996 Ultra

A 40% thicker cardboard stock and silver-foil highlights are featured in this year's edition. Fronts are very basic with a borderless action photo and silver-foil graphics. Backs feature a three-photo montage along with 1995 and career stats. The set was released in two 300-card series; each card is also reprinted as part of a limited-edition Gold Medallion parallel set. One Gold Medallion card is found in every pack. Each series has eight insert sets. Series I inserts are RBI Kings, Home Run Kings, Fresh Foundations, Diamond Producers, Power Plus, Season Crowns, Golden Prospects and Prime Leather. Series II inserts are Call to the Hall, Golden Prospects, Hitting Machines, On-Base Leaders, RESPECT, Rawhide, Rising Stars and Thunderclap. Checklist cards were also randomly inserted into packs from both series.

		MT
Complete Set (600):		55.00
Series 1 (300):		30.00
Series 2 (300):		25.00
Common Player:		.10
2X		
Wax Box:		45.00
1	Manny Alexander	.10
2	Brady Anderson	.15
3	Bobby Bonilla	.10
4	Scott Erickson	.10
5	Curtis Goodwin	.10
6	Chris Hoiles	.10
7	Doug Jones	.10
8	Jeff Manto	.10
9	Mike Mussina	.50
10	Rafael Palmeiro	.40
11	Cal Ripken Jr.	3.00
12	Rick Aguilera	.10
13	Luis Alicea	.10
14	Stan Belinda	.10
15	Jose Canseco	.75
16	Roger Clemens	1.50
17	Mike Greenwell	.10
18	Mike Macfarlane	.10
19	Tim Naehring	.10
20	Troy O'Leary	.10
21	John Valentin	.10
22	Mo Vaughn	.50
23	Tim Wakefield	.10
24	Brian Anderson	.10
25	Garret Anderson	.10
26	Chili Davis	.10
27	Gary DiSarcina	.10
28	Jim Edmonds	.10
29	Jorge Fabregas	.10
30	Chuck Finley	.10
31	Mark Langston	.10
32	Troy Percival	.10
33	Tim Salmon	.25
34	Lee Smith	.10
35	Wilson Alvarez	.10
36	Ray Durham	.15
37	Alex Fernandez	.10
38	Ozzie Guillen	.10
39	Roberto Hernandez	.10
40	Lance Johnson	.10
41	Ron Karkovice	.10
42	Lyle Mouton	.10
43	Tim Raines	.10
44	Frank Thomas	1.00
45	Carlos Baerga	.10
46	Albert Belle	.60
47	Orel Hershiser	.10
48	Kenny Lofton	.50
49	Dennis Martinez	.10
50	Jose Mesa	.10
51	Eddie Murray	.40
52	Chad Ogea	.10
53	Manny Ramirez	1.00
54	Jim Thome	.35
55	Omar Vizquel	.10
56	Dave Winfield	.25
57	Chad Curtis	.10
58	Cecil Fielder	.10
59	John Flaherty	.10
60	Travis Fryman	.15
61	Chris Gomez	.10
62	Bob Higginson	.10
63	Felipe Lira	.10
64	Brian Maxcy	.10
65	Alan Trammell	.15
66	Lou Whitaker	.10
67	Kevin Appier	.10
68	Gary Gaetti	.10
69	Tom Goodwin	.10
70	Tom Gordon	.10
71	Jason Jacome	.10
72	Wally Joyner	.10
73	Brent Mayne	.10
74	Jeff Montgomery	.10
75	Jon Nunnally	.10
76	Joe Vitiello	.10
77	Ricky Bones	.10
78	Jeff Cirillo	.10
79	Mike Fetters	.10
80	Darryl Hamilton	.10
81	David Hulse	.10
82	Dave Nilsson	.10
83	Kevin Seitzer	.10
84	Steve Sparks	.10
85	B.J. Surhoff	.10
86	Jose Valentin	.10
87	Greg Vaughn	.10
88	Marty Cordova	.15
89	Chuck Knoblauch	.25
90	Pat Meares	.10
91	Pedro Munoz	.10
92	Kirby Puckett	.75
93	Brad Radke	.10
94	Scott Stahoviak	.10
95	Dave Stevens	.10
96	Mike Trombley	.10
97	Matt Walbeck	.10
98	Wade Boggs	.25
99	Russ Davis	.10
100	Jim Leyritz	.10
101	Don Mattingly	1.00
102	Jack McDowell	.10
103	Paul O'Neill	.25
104	Andy Pettitte	.50
105	Mariano Rivera	.20
106	Ruben Sierra	.10
107	Darryl Strawberry	.15
108	John Wetteland	.10
109	Bernie Williams	.50
110	Geronimo Berroa	.10
111	Scott Brosius	.10
112	Dennis Eckersley	.10
113	Brent Gates	.10
114	Rickey Henderson	.40
115	Mark McGwire	4.00
116	Ariel Prieto	.10
117	Terry Steinbach	.10
118	Todd Stottlemyre	.10
119	Todd Van Poppel	.10
120	Steve Wojciechowski	.10
121	Rich Amaral	.10
122	Bobby Ayala	.10
123	Mike Blowers	.10
124	Chris Bosio	.10
125	Joey Cora	.10
126	Ken Griffey Jr.	4.00
127	Randy Johnson	.40
128	Edgar Martinez	.10
129	Tino Martinez	.15
130	Alex Rodriguez	3.00
131	Dan Wilson	.10
132	Will Clark	.30
133	Jeff Frye	.10
134	Benji Gil	.10
135	Juan Gonzalez	1.50
136	Rusty Greer	.10
137	Mark McLemore	.10
138	Roger Pavlik	.10
139	Ivan Rodriguez	.75
140	Kenny Rogers	.10
141	Mickey Tettleton	.10
142	Roberto Alomar	.50
143	Joe Carter	.10
144	Tony Castillo	.10
145	Alex Gonzalez	.10
146	Shawn Green	.50
147	Pat Hentgen	.15
148	*Sandy Martinez*	.10
149	Paul Molitor	.40
150	John Olerud	.25
151	Ed Sprague	.10
152	Jeff Blauser	.10
153	Brad Clontz	.10
154	Tom Glavine	.20
155	Marquis Grissom	.15
156	Chipper Jones	2.00
157	David Justice	.20
158	Ryan Klesko	.15
159	Javier Lopez	.15
160	Greg Maddux	1.50
161	John Smoltz	.20
162	Mark Wohlers	.10
163	Jim Bullinger	.10
164	Frank Castillo	.10
165	Shawon Dunston	.10
166	Kevin Foster	.10
167	Luis Gonzalez	.15
168	Mark Grace	.20
169	Rey Sanchez	.10
170	Scott Servais	.10
171	Sammy Sosa	2.00
172	Ozzie Timmons	.10
173	Steve Trachsel	.10
174	Bret Boone	.10
175	Jeff Branson	.10
176	Jeff Brantley	.10
177	Dave Burba	.10
178	Ron Gant	.10
179	Barry Larkin	.25
180	Darren Lewis	.10
181	Mark Portugal	.10
182	Reggie Sanders	.10
183	Pete Schourek	.10
184	John Smiley	.10
185	Jason Bates	.10
186	Dante Bichette	.25
187	Ellis Burks	.10
188	Vinny Castilla	.15
189	Andres Galarraga	.30
190	Darren Holmes	.10
191	Armando Reynoso	.10
192	Kevin Ritz	.10
193	Bill Swift	.10
194	Larry Walker	.50
195	Kurt Abbott	.10
196	John Burkett	.10
197	Greg Colbrunn	.10
198	Jeff Conine	.15
199	Andre Dawson	.20
200	Chris Hammond	.10
201	Charles Johnson	.15
202	Robb Nen	.10
203	Terry Pendleton	.10
204	Quilvio Veras	.10
205	Jeff Bagwell	1.00
206	Derek Bell	.10
207	Doug Drabek	.10
208	Tony Eusebio	.10
209	Mike Hampton	.10
210	Brian Hunter	.10
211	Todd Jones	.10
212	Orlando Miller	.10
213	James Mouton	.10
214	Shane Reynolds	.15
215	Dave Veres	.10
216	Billy Ashley	.10
217	Brett Butler	.10
218	Chad Fonville	.10
219	Todd Hollandsworth	.10
220	Eric Karros	.15
221	Ramon Martinez	.15
222	Raul Mondesi	.20
223	Hideo Nomo	.25
224	Mike Piazza	2.00
225	Kevin Tapani	.10
226	Ismael Valdes	.10
227	Todd Worrell	.10
228	Moises Alou	.20
229	Wil Cordero	.10
230	Jeff Fassero	.10
231	Darrin Fletcher	.10
232	Mike Lansing	.10
233	Pedro Martinez	1.00
234	Carlos Perez	.10
235	Mel Rojas	.10
236	David Segui	.10
237	Tony Tarasco	.10
238	Rondell White	.20
239	Edgardo Alfonzo	.25
240	Rico Brogna	.10
241	Carl Everett	.10
242	Todd Hundley	.15
243	Butch Huskey	.10
244	Jason Isringhausen	.20
245	Bobby Jones	.10
246	Jeff Kent	.10
247	Bill Pulsipher	.10
248	Jose Vizcaino	.10
249	Ricky Bottalico	.10
250	Darren Daulton	.10
251	Jim Eisenreich	.10
252	Tyler Green	.10
253	Charlie Hayes	.10
254	Gregg Jefferies	.15
255	Tony Longmire	.10
256	Michael Mimbs	.10
257	Mickey Morandini	.10
258	Paul Quantrill	.10
259	Heathcliff Slocumb	.10
260	Jay Bell	.10
261	Jacob Brumfield	.10
262	*Angelo Encarnacion*	.15
263	John Ericks	.10
264	Mark Johnson	.10
265	Esteban Loaiza	.10
266	Al Martin	.10
267	Orlando Merced	.10
268	Dan Miceli	.10
269	Denny Neagle	.10
270	Brian Barber	.10
271	Scott Cooper	.10
272	Tripp Cromer	.10
273	Bernard Gilkey	.10
274	Tom Henke	.10
275	Brian Jordan	.10
276	John Mabry	.10
277	Tom Pagnozzi	.10
278	*Mark Petkovsek*	.10
279	Ozzie Smith	.50
280	Andy Ashby	.10
281	Brad Ausmus	.10
282	Ken Caminiti	.20
283	Glenn Dishman	.10
284	Tony Gwynn	1.50
285	Joey Hamilton	.10
286	Trevor Hoffman	.10
287	Phil Plantier	.10
288	Jody Reed	.10
289	Eddie Williams	.10
290	Barry Bonds	.75
291	Jamie Brewington	.10
292	Mark Carreon	.10
293	Royce Clayton	.10
294	Glenallen Hill	.10
295	Mark Leiter	.10
296	Kirt Manwaring	.10
297	J.R. Phillips	.10
298	Deion Sanders	.25
299	William VanLandingham	.10
300	Matt Williams	.20
301	Roberto Alomar	.60
302	Armando Benitez	.10

303	Mike Devereaux	.10
304	Jeffrey Hammonds	.10
305	Jimmy Haynes	.10
306	*Scott McClain*	.10
307	Kent Mercker	.10
308	Randy Myers	.10
309	B.J. Surhoff	.10
310	Tony Tarasco	.10
311	David Wells	.10
312	Wil Cordero	.10
313	Alex Delgado	.10
314	Tom Gordon	.10
315	Dwayne Hosey	.10
316	Jose Malave	.10
317	Kevin Mitchell	.10
318	Jamie Moyer	.10
319	Aaron Sele	.10
320	Heathcliff Slocumb	.10
321	Mike Stanley	.10
322	Jeff Suppan	.10
323	Jim Abbott	.10
324	George Arias	.10
325	Todd Greene	.10
326	Bryan Harvey	.10
327	J.T. Snow	.15
328	Randy Velarde	.10
329	Tim Wallach	.10
330	Harold Baines	.10
331	Jason Bere	.10
332	Darren Lewis	.10
333	Norberto Martin	.10
334	Tony Phillips	.10
335	Bill Simas	.10
336	Chris Snopek	.10
337	Kevin Tapani	.10
338	Danny Tartabull	.10
339	Robin Ventura	.25
340	Sandy Alomar	.15
341	Julio Franco	.10
342	Jack McDowell	.10
343	Charles Nagy	.10
344	Julian Tavarez	.10
345	Kimera Bartee	.10
346	Greg Keagle	.10
347	Mark Lewis	.10
348	Jose Lima	.10
349	Melvin Nieves	.10
350	Mark Parent	.10
351	Eddie Williams	.10
352	Johnny Damon	.15
353	Sal Fasano	.10
354	Mark Gubicza	.10
355	Bob Hamelin	.10
356	Chris Haney	.10
357	Keith Lockhart	.10
358	Mike Macfarlane	.10
359	Jose Offerman	.10
360	Bip Roberts	.10
361	Michael Tucker	.10
362	Chuck Carr	.10
363	Bobby Hughes	.10
364	John Jaha	.10
365	Mark Loretta	.10
366	Mike Matheny	.10
367	Ben McDonald	.10
368	Matt Mieske	.10
369	Angel Miranda	.10
370	Fernando Vina	.10
371	Rick Aguilera	.10
372	Rich Becker	.10
373	LaTroy Hawkins	.10
374	Dave Hollins	.10
375	Roberto Kelly	.10
376	*Matt Lawton*	.20
377	Paul Molitor	.40
378	*Dan Naulty*	.10
379	Rich Robertson	.10
380	Frank Rodriguez	.10
381	David Cone	.20
382	Mariano Duncan	.10
383	*Andy Fox*	.10
384	Joe Girardi	.10
385	Dwight Gooden	.15
386	Derek Jeter	2.00
387	Pat Kelly	.10
388	Jimmy Key	.10
389	*Matt Luke*	.10
390	Tino Martinez	.15
391	Jeff Nelson	.10
392	Melido Perez	.10
393	Tim Raines	.15
394	Ruben Rivera	.15
395	Kenny Rogers	.10
396	*Tony Batista*	2.00
397	Allen Battle	.10
398	Mike Bordick	.10
399	Steve Cox	.10
400	Jason Giambi	.10
401	Doug Johns	.10
402	Pedro Munoz	.10
403	Phil Plantier	.10
404	Scott Spiezio	.10
405	George Williams	.10
406	Ernie Young	.10
407	Darren Bragg	.10
408	Jay Buhner	.10
409	Norm Charlton	.10
410	Russ Davis	.10
411	Sterling Hitchcock	.10
412	Edwin Hurtado	.10
413	*Raul Ibanez*	.10
414	Mike Jackson	.10
415	Luis Sojo	.10
416	Paul Sorrento	.10
417	Bob Wolcott	.10
418	Damon Buford	.10
419	Kevin Gross	.10
420	Darryl Hamilton	.10
421	Mike Henneman	.10
422	Ken Hill	.10
423	Dean Palmer	.10
424	Bobby Witt	.10
425	Tilson Brito	.10
426	Giovanni Carrara	.10
427	Domingo Cedeno	.10
428	Felipe Crespo	.10
429	Carlos Delgado	.50
430	Juan Guzman	.10
431	Erik Hanson	.10
432	*Marty Janzen*	.10
433	Otis Nixon	.10
434	Robert Perez	.10
435	Paul Quantrill	.10
436	Bill Risley	.10
437	Steve Avery	.10
438	Jermaine Dye	.10
439	Mark Lemke	.10
440	*Marty Malloy*	.10
441	Fred McGriff	.20
442	Greg McMichael	.10
443	Wonderful Monds	.10
444	Eddie Perez	.10
445	Jason Schmidt	.10
446	Terrell Wade	.10
447	Terry Adams	.10
448	Scott Bullett	.10
449	*Robin Jennings*	.10
450	Doug Jones	.10
451	Brooks Kieschnick	.10
452	Dave Magadan	.10
453	*Jason Maxwell*	.10
454	Brian McRae	.10
455	Rodney Myers	.10
456	Jaime Navarro	.10
457	Ryne Sandberg	.75
458	Vince Coleman	.10
459	Eric Davis	.10
460	Steve Gibralter	.10
461	Thomas Howard	.10
462	Mike Kelly	.10
463	Hal Morris	.10
464	Eric Owens	.10
465	Jose Rijo	.10
466	Chris Sabo	.10
467	Eddie Taubensee	.10
468	Trenidad Hubbard	.10
469	Curt Leskanic	.10
470	Quinton McCracken	.10
471	Jayhawk Owens	.10
472	Steve Reed	.10
473	Bryan Rekar	.10
474	Bruce Ruffin	.10
475	Bret Saberhagen	.10
476	Walt Weiss	.10
477	Eric Young	.10
478	Kevin Brown	.20
479	Al Leiter	.15
480	Pat Rapp	.10
481	Gary Sheffield	.20
482	Devon White	.10
483	Bob Abreu	.10
484	Sean Berry	.10
485	Craig Biggio	.40
486	Jim Dougherty	.10
487	Richard Hidalgo	.10
488	Darryl Kile	.10
489	Derrick May	.10
490	Greg Swindell	.10
491	Rick Wilkins	.10
492	Mike Blowers	.10
493	Tom Candiotti	.10
494	Roger Cedeno	.10
495	Delino DeShields	.10
496	Greg Gagne	.10
497	Karim Garcia	.15
498	*Wilton Guerrero*	.30
499	Chan Ho Park	.15
500	Israel Alcantara	.10
501	Shane Andrews	.10
502	Yamil Benitez	.10
503	Cliff Floyd	.10
504	Mark Grudzielanek	.10
505	Ryan McGuire	.10
506	Sherman Obando	.10
507	Jose Paniagua	.10
508	Henry Rodriguez	.10
509	Kirk Rueter	.10
510	Juan Acevedo	.10
511	John Franco	.10
512	Bernard Gilkey	.10
513	Lance Johnson	.10
514	Rey Ordonez	.25
515	Robert Person	.10
516	Paul Wilson	.15
517	Toby Borland	.10
518	*David Doster*	.10
519	Lenny Dykstra	.10
520	Sid Fernandez	.10
521	*Mike Grace*	.10
522	*Rich Hunter*	.10
523	Benito Santiago	.10
524	Gene Schall	.10
525	Curt Schilling	.15
526	*Kevin Sefcik*	.10
527	Lee Tinsley	.10
528	David West	.10
529	Mark Whiten	.10
530	Todd Zeile	.10
531	Carlos Garcia	.10
532	Charlie Hayes	.10
533	Jason Kendall	.15
534	Jeff King	.10
535	Mike Kingery	.10
536	Nelson Liriano	.10
537	Dan Plesac	.10
538	Paul Wagner	.10
539	Luis Alicea	.10
540	David Bell	.10
541	Alan Benes	.10
542	Andy Benes	.15
543	*Mike Busby*	.10
544	Royce Clayton	.10
545	Dennis Eckersley	.10
546	Gary Gaetti	.10
547	Ron Gant	.10
548	Aaron Holbert	.10
549	Ray Lankford	.10
550	T.J. Mathews	.10
551	Willie McGee	.10
552	*Miguel Mejia*	.10
553	Todd Stottlemyre	.10
554	Sean Bergman	.10
555	Willie Blair	.10
556	Andujar Cedeno	.10
557	Steve Finley	.10
558	Rickey Henderson	.40
559	Wally Joyner	.10
560	Scott Livingstone	.10
561	Marc Newfield	.10
562	Bob Tewksbury	.10
563	Fernando Valenzuela	.10
564	Rod Beck	.10
565	Doug Creek	.10
566	Shawon Dunston	.10
567	*Osvaldo Fernandez*	.20
568	Stan Javier	.10
569	Marcus Jensen	.10
570	Steve Scarsone	.10
571	Robby Thompson	.10
572	Allen Watson	.10
573	Roberto Alomar (Ultra Stars)	.25
574	Jeff Bagwell (Ultra Stars)	.50
575	Albert Belle (Ultra Stars)	.30
576	Wade Boggs (Ultra Stars)	.20
577	Barry Bonds (Ultra Stars)	.40
578	Juan Gonzalez (Ultra Stars)	.50
579	Ken Griffey Jr. (Ultra Stars)	1.50
580	Tony Gwynn (Ultra Stars)	.75
581	Randy Johnson (Ultra Stars)	.25
582	Chipper Jones (Ultra Stars)	1.00
583	Barry Larkin (Ultra Stars)	.10
584	Kenny Lofton (Ultra Stars)	.25
585	Greg Maddux (Ultra Stars)	1.00
586	Raul Mondesi (Ultra Stars)	.10
587	Mike Piazza (Ultra Stars)	1.00
588	Cal Ripken Jr. (Ultra Stars)	1.25
589	Tim Salmon (Ultra Stars)	.20
590	Frank Thomas (Ultra Stars)	.50
591	Mo Vaughn (Ultra Stars)	.25
592	Matt Williams (Ultra Stars)	.10
593	Marty Cordova (Raw Power)	.10
594	Jim Edmonds (Raw Power)	.10
595	Cliff Floyd (Raw Power)	.10
596	Chipper Jones (Raw Power)	1.00
597	Ryan Klesko (Raw Power)	.25
598	Raul Mondesi (Raw Power)	.20
599	Manny Ramirez (Raw Power)	.50
600	Ruben Rivera (Raw Power)	.15

1996 Ultra Gold Medallion

Limited to less than 10% of the regular edition's production, the Gold Medallion parallel set replaces the front photo's background with gold foil featuring a large embossed Fleer Ultra Gold Medallion seal at center. One Gold Medallion card is found in each foil pack.

	MT
Complete Set (600):	100.00
Common Player:	.25
(Star cards valued at 2X regular edition Fleer Ultra.)	

1996 Ultra Call to the Hall

Ten probable future Hall of Famers are featured on these cards, which use classic style original illustrations of the players. The cards were seeded one per every 24 Series 2 packs.

		MT
Complete Set (10):		60.00
Common Player:		2.50
Gold Medallion Edition: 2X		
1	Barry Bonds	5.00
2	Ken Griffey Jr.	20.00
3	Tony Gwynn	10.00
4	Rickey Henderson	4.00
5	Greg Maddux	10.00
6	Eddie Murray	3.00
7	Cal Ripken Jr.	12.00
8	Ryne Sandberg	5.00
9	Ozzie Smith	4.00
10	Frank Thomas	7.50

1996 Ultra Checklists

Fleer Ultra featured 10 checklist cards that were inserted every four packs. These cards featured a superstar player on the front and, throughout the set, a full checklist of all cards in the 1996 Ultra set on the back.

		MT
Complete Set (20):		20.00
Common Player:		.25
	SERIES 1	
1	Jeff Bagwell	.75
2	Barry Bonds	.75
3	Juan Gonzalez	.75
4	Ken Griffey Jr.	3.00
5	Chipper Jones	2.00
6	Mike Piazza	2.00
7	Manny Ramirez	1.00
8	Cal Ripken Jr.	2.50
9	Frank Thomas	1.50
10	Matt Williams	.25
	SERIES 2	
1	Albert Belle	1.00
2	Cecil Fielder	.25
3	Ken Griffey Jr.	3.00
4	Tony Gwynn	1.50
5	Derek Jeter	2.00
6	Jason Kendall	.25
7	Ryan Klesko	.50
8	Greg Maddux	1.50
9	Cal Ripken Jr.	2.50
10	Frank Thomas	1.50

1996 Ultra Diamond Dust

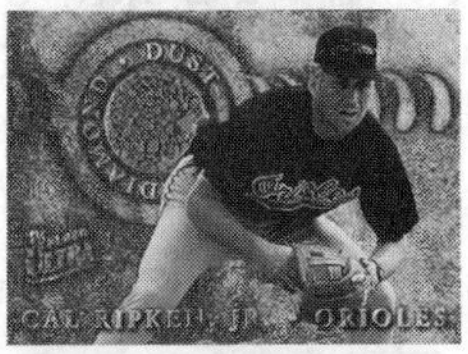

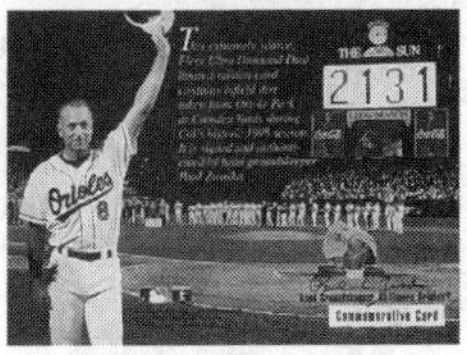

This card commemorates Cal Ripken's history-making 1995 record of playing in 2,131 consecutive regular-season games. Horizontal in format, the front has a color action photo of Ripken on a simulated leather background. Back has a photo of Ripken on the night he set the new record. Sandwiched between front and back is a dime-sized plastic capsule of dirt certified, according to the facsimile autograph on back of the team's head groundskeeper, to have been used on the infield at Oriole Park in Camden Yards during the 1995 season. Two versions of the card were made. A hand-numbered version limited to 2,131 was offered direct to dealers for $39.99. An unnumbered version was available to collectors as a wrapper redemption for $24.99.

	MT
Cal Ripken Jr. (numbered)	250.00
Cal Ripken Jr. (unnumbered)	150.00

1996 Ultra Diamond Producers

A horizontal layout and two versions of the same photo printed on holographic foil are featured in this insert set. Stated odds of finding a Diamond Producers card are one per every 20 Series I packs.

		MT
Complete Set (12):		60.00
Common Player:		2.00
Gold Medallions: 2X		
1	Albert Belle	4.00
2	Barry Bonds	5.00
3	Ken Griffey Jr.	15.00
4	Tony Gwynn	7.00
5	Greg Maddux	8.00
6	Hideo Nomo	2.00
7	Mike Piazza	10.00

8	Kirby Puckett	4.00
9	Cal Ripken Jr.	12.00
10	Frank Thomas	5.00
11	Mo Vaughn	3.00
12	Matt Williams	3.00

1996 Ultra Fresh Foundations

Rising stars who can carry their teams' fortunes into the next century are featured in this foil-printed insert set, found on average of one card per every three Series I foil packs.

		MT
Complete Set (10):		5.00
Common Player:		.50
Gold Medallions: 2X		
1	Garret Anderson	.50
2	Marty Cordova	.50
3	Jim Edmonds	.50
4	Brian Hunter	.50
5	Chipper Jones	3.00
6	Ryan Klesko	.75
7	Raul Mondesi	.75
8	Hideo Nomo	.75
9	Manny Ramirez	1.50
10	Rondell White	.50

1996 Ultra Golden Prospects, Series 1

A hobby-pack-only insert, these horizontal format cards have rainbow foil ballpark backgrounds and feature 1996's rookie crop. They are found on average of one per every five Series I packs.

		MT
Complete Set (10):		5.00
Common Player:		.25
Gold Medallions: 2X		
1	Yamil Benitez	.30
2	Alberto Castillo	.25
3	Roger Cedeno	.50
4	Johnny Damon	.50
5	Micah Franklin	.25
6	Jason Giambi	.75
7	Jose Herrera	.25
8	Derek Jeter	4.00
9	Kevin Jordan	.25
10	Ruben Rivera	.75

1996 Ultra Golden Prospects, Series 2

The Golden Prospects insert series continued with 15 more young stars found exclusively in Series 2 hobby packs, though in much lower numbers than the Series 1 inserts.

		MT
Complete Set (15):		45.00
Common Player:		2.00
Gold Medallions: 2X		
1	Bob Abreu	12.00
2	Israel Alcantara	2.00
3	Tony Batista	5.00
4	Mike Cameron	4.00
5	Steve Cox	2.00
6	Jermaine Dye	4.00
7	Wilton Guerrero	3.00
8	Richard Hidalgo	5.00
9	Raul Ibanez	3.00
10	Marty Janzen	2.00
11	Robin Jennings	2.00
12	Jason Maxwell	2.00
13	Scott McClain	2.00
14	Wonderful Monds	2.00
15	Chris Singleton	6.00

1996 Ultra Hitting Machines

These die-cut 1996 Fleer Ultra Series II insert cards showcase the heaviest hitters on cards featuring a machine-gear design. The cards were seeded one per every 288 Series II packs.

		MT
Complete Set (10):		200.00
Common Player:		10.00
Gold Medallion: 2X		
1	Albert Belle	15.00
2	Barry Bonds	20.00
3	Juan Gonzalez	30.00
4	Ken Griffey Jr.	75.00
5	Edgar Martinez	10.00
6	Rafael Palmeiro	10.00
7	Mike Piazza	50.00
8	Tim Salmon	10.00
9	Frank Thomas	25.00
10	Matt Williams	12.00

1996 Ultra Home Run Kings Exchange Cards

Printed on a thin wood veneer, these super-scarce inserts are found at the rate of only one per 75 packs. Because of quality control problems, the cards were initially released as exchange cards, with instructions on back for a mail-in redemption offer for the actual wooden card. The redemption period expired Dec. 1, 1996.

		MT
Complete Set (12):		16.00
Common Player:		.75
Gold Medallions: 2X		
1	Jeff Bagwell	2.00
2	Albert Belle	1.00
3	Dante Bichette	1.00
4	Barry Bonds	2.00
5	Ron Gant	.75
6	Ken Griffey Jr.	4.00
7	Manny Ramirez	1.00
8	Tim Salmon	.75
9	Frank Thomas	2.00
10	Mo Vaughn	.75
11	Larry Walker	.75
12	Matt Williams	.75

1996 Ultra Home Run Kings

Printed on a thin wood veneer, these super-scarce inserts are seeded one per every 75 Series I packs. Because of quality control problems, the cards were initially released as exchange cards, with instructions on back for a mail-in redemption offer for the actual wooden card.

		MT
Complete Set (12):		50.00
Common Player:		4.00
Gold Medallions: 2X		
1	Jeff Bagwell	8.00
2	Albert Belle	5.00
3	Dante Bichette	3.00
4	Barry Bonds	6.00
5	Ron Gant	3.00
6	Ken Griffey Jr.	20.00
7	Manny Ramirez	8.00
8	Tim Salmon	3.00
9	Frank Thomas	8.00
10	Mo Vaughn	4.00
11	Larry Walker	4.00
12	Matt Williams	3.00

1996 Ultra On-Base Leaders

These 1996 Fleer Ultra Series II inserts feature 10 of the game's top on-base leaders. The cards were seeded one per every four packs.

		MT
Complete Set (10):		6.00
Common Player:		.50
Gold Medallion: 2X		
1	Wade Boggs	.75
2	Barry Bonds	1.50
3	Tony Gwynn	1.50
4	Rickey Henderson	.75
5	Chuck Knoblauch	.50
6	Edgar Martinez	.50
7	Mike Piazza	2.50
8	Tim Salmon	.50
9	Frank Thomas	1.50
10	Jim Thome	.50

1996 Ultra Power Plus

Etched-foil backgrounds, multiple player photos and a horizontal format are featured in this chase set. Stated odds of finding one of the dozen Power Plus cards are one per every 10 Series I packs.

		MT
Complete Set (12):		20.00
Common Player:		.50
Gold Medallions: 2X		
1	Jeff Bagwell	4.00
2	Barry Bonds	2.50
3	Ken Griffey Jr.	9.00
4	Raul Mondesi	.75
5	Rafael Palmeiro	1.00
6	Mike Piazza	6.00
7	Manny Ramirez	2.50
8	Tim Salmon	.75
9	Reggie Sanders	.50
10	Frank Thomas	4.00
11	Larry Walker	1.00
12	Matt Williams	.75

1996 Ultra Prime Leather

An embossed leather-feel background is featured on these cards of top fielders, seeded one per every eight Series I packs, on average.

		MT
Complete Set (18):		35.00
Common Player:		.75
Gold Medallions: 2X		
1	Ivan Rodriguez	3.00
2	Will Clark	1.50
3	Roberto Alomar	2.00
4	Cal Ripken Jr.	7.50
5	Wade Boggs	1.00
6	Ken Griffey Jr.	9.00
7	Kenny Lofton	1.50
8	Kirby Puckett	3.00
9	Tim Salmon	.75
10	Mike Piazza	6.00
11	Mark Grace	.75
12	Craig Biggio	1.00
13	Barry Larkin	.75
14	Matt Williams	.75
15	Barry Bonds	3.00
16	Tony Gwynn	5.00
17	Brian McRae	.75
18	Raul Mondesi	.75

1996 Ultra Rawhide

Ten top fielders are featured on these 1996 Fleer Ultra Series II inserts. The cards were seeded one per every eight packs.

		MT
Complete Set (10):		15.00
Common Player:		1.00
Gold Medallion: 2X		
1	Roberto Alomar	.75
2	Barry Bonds	1.50
3	Mark Grace	.75
4	Ken Griffey Jr.	6.00
5	Kenny Lofton	.75
6	Greg Maddux	2.50
7	Raul Mondesi	.75
8	Mike Piazza	3.00
9	Cal Ripken Jr.	4.00
10	Matt Williams	.75

1996 Ultra RBI Kings

Retail packs are the exclusive provenance of this 10-card set of top RBI men. Stated odds of finding an RBI King card are one per every five Series I packs.

		MT
Complete Set (10):		18.00
Common Player:		.40
Gold Medallions: 2X		
1	Derek Bell	.50
2	Albert Belle	2.00
3	Dante Bichette	.75
4	Barry Bonds	3.00
5	Jim Edmonds	.50
6	Manny Ramirez	3.00
7	Reggie Sanders	.50
8	Sammy Sosa	10.00
9	Frank Thomas	4.00
10	Mo Vaughn	2.00

1996 Ultra R-E-S-P-E-C-T

These cards feature 10 players held in high esteem by

their major league peers. The cards were seeded one per every 18 1996 Ultra Series II packs.

		MT
Complete Set (10):		50.00
Common Player:		1.50
Gold Medallion: 2X		
1	Joe Carter	1.50
2	Ken Griffey Jr.	15.00
3	Tony Gwynn	7.00
4	Greg Maddux	8.00
5	Eddie Murray	3.00
6	Kirby Puckett	4.00
7	Cal Ripken Jr.	10.00
8	Ryne Sandberg	4.00
9	Frank Thomas	6.00
10	Mo Vaughn	3.00

1996 Ultra Rising Stars

Ten of baseball's best young players are spotlighted on these 1996 Fleer Ultra Series II inserts. Cards were seeded one per every four packs.

		MT
Complete Set (10):		5.00
Common Player:		.25
Gold Medallion: 2X		
1	Garret Anderson	.35
2	Marty Cordova	.50
3	Jim Edmonds	.40
4	Cliff Floyd	.25
5	Brian Hunter	.35
6	Chipper Jones	2.50
7	Ryan Klesko	.40
8	Hideo Nomo	.75
9	Manny Ramirez	2.00
10	Rondell White	.50

1996 Ultra Season Crowns

Large coats-of-arms printed on "Ultra Crystal" clear plastic are the background for player action photos in this insert set. Odds of one per every 10 Series II packs were stated.

		MT
Complete Set (10):		25.00
Common Player:		1.00
Gold Medallions: 2X		
1	Barry Bonds	2.50
2	Tony Gwynn	5.00
3	Randy Johnson	2.00
4	Kenny Lofton	1.50
5	Greg Maddux	5.00
6	Edgar Martinez	1.00
7	Hideo Nomo	1.50
8	Cal Ripken Jr.	7.50
9	Frank Thomas	4.00
10	Tim Wakefield	1.00

1996 Ultra Thunderclap

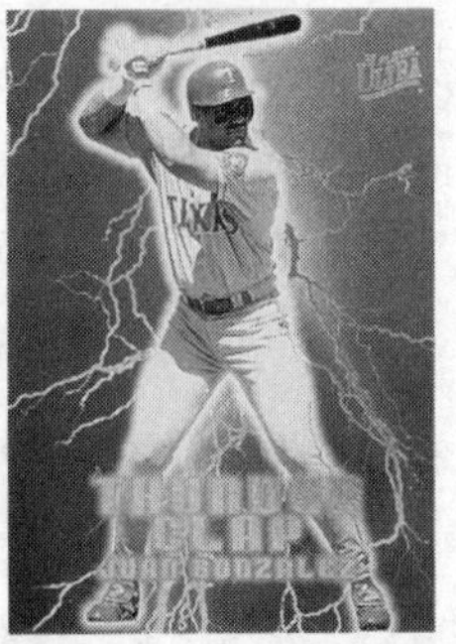

The active career home run leaders are featured in this retail-exclusive Ultra insert set. Seeded only one per 72 packs, the Thunderclap cards have action photos on front with simulated lightning in the background and other graphic highlights rendered in holographic foil. Backs have a large portrait photo and career summary. Each of these scarce retail inserts can also be found in an even more elusive Gold Medallion version.

		MT
Complete Set (20):		275.00
Common Player:		4.50
Gold Medallion: 2X		
1	Albert Belle	12.00
2	Barry Bonds	20.00
3	Bobby Bonilla	4.50
4	Jose Canseco	12.00
5	Joe Carter	4.50
6	Will Clark	7.50
7	Andre Dawson	4.50
8	Cecil Fielder	4.50
9	Andres Galarraga	6.00
10	Juan Gonzalez	30.00
11	Ken Griffey Jr.	55.00
12	Fred McGriff	6.00
13	Mark McGwire	55.00
14	Eddie Murray	9.00
15	Rafael Palmeiro	9.00
16	Kirby Puckett	15.00
17	Cal Ripken Jr.	45.00
18	Ryne Sandberg	15.00
19	Frank Thomas	[illegible]
20	Matt Williams	5.00

1997 Ultra Promo Strip

To introduce the concept of its new non-parallel parallel set, Fleer issued this three-card promo strip picturing regular (left), Gold Medallion (center) and Platinum Medallion (right) Cal Ripken, Jr., cards. Fronts have a "PROMOTIONAL SAMPLE," overprint in foil to match the cards' graphic highlights (silver, gold and prismatic). Backs, which have stats only through the 1995 season, have the same overprint in red.

		MT
Three-card Strip:		25.00
11	Cal Ripken Jr.	
G11	Cal Ripken Jr. (Gold Medallion)	
P11	Cal Ripken Jr. (Platinum Medallion)	

1997 Ultra

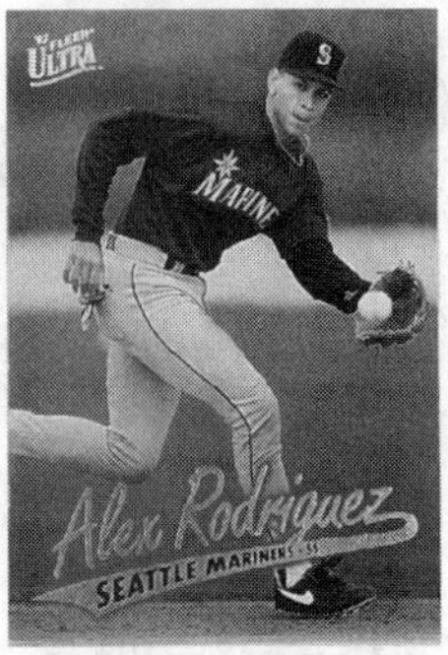

Ultra arrived in a 300-card Series I issue with two parallel sets, Gold and Platinum, which featured "G" and "P" prefixes on the card number, respectively. Cards were issued in 10-card packs. Player names and the Ultra logo are in silver holographic foil. Backs contains complete year-by-year statistics, plus two photos of the player. This also marked the first time that the Gold and Platinum parallel sets displayed a different photo than the base cards. Inserts in Ultra included: Rookie Reflections, Double Trouble, Checklists, Season Crowns, RBI Kings, Power Plus, Fielder's Choice, Diamond Producers, HR Kings and Baseball Rules.

		MT
Complete Set (553):		55.00
Series 1 (300):		30.00
Series 2 (253):		25.00
Common Player:		.10
Series 1 or 2 Wax Box:		60.00
1	Roberto Alomar	.50
2	Brady Anderson	.10
3	Rocky Coppinger	.10
4	Jeffrey Hammonds	.10
5	Chris Hoiles	.10
6	Eddie Murray	.40
7	Mike Mussina	.60
8	Jimmy Myers	.10
9	Randy Myers	.10
10	Arthur Rhodes	.10
11	Cal Ripken Jr.	2.50
12	Jose Canseco	.75
13	Roger Clemens	1.25
14	Tom Gordon	.10
15	Jose Malave	.10
16	Tim Naehring	.10
17	Troy O'Leary	.10
18	Bill Selby	.10
19	Heathcliff Slocumb	.10
20	Mike Stanley	.10
21	Mo Vaughn	.50
22	Garret Anderson	.10
23	George Arias	.10
24	Chili Davis	.10
25	Jim Edmonds	.20
26	Darin Erstad	.25
27	Chuck Finley	.10
28	Todd Greene	.10
29	Troy Percival	.10
30	Tim Salmon	.20
31	Jeff Schmidt	.10
32	Randy Velarde	.10
33	Shad Williams	.10
34	Wilson Alvarez	.10
35	Harold Baines	.10
36	James Baldwin	.10
37	Mike Cameron	.10
38	Ray Durham	.10
39	Ozzie Guillen	.10
40	Roberto Hernandez	.10
41	Darren Lewis	.10
42	Jose Munoz	.10
43	Tony Phillips	.10
44	Frank Thomas	1.50
45	Sandy Alomar Jr.	.15
46	Albert Belle	.75
47	Mark Carreon	.10
48	Julio Franco	.10
49	Orel Hershiser	.10
50	Kenny Lofton	.50
51	Jack McDowell	.15
52	Jose Mesa	.10
53	Charles Nagy	.10
54	Manny Ramirez	1.00
55	Julian Tavarez	.10
56	Omar Vizquel	.15
57	Raul Casanova	.10
58	Tony Clark	.30
59	Travis Fryman	.20
60	Bob Higginson	.10
61	Melvin Nieves	.10
62	Curtis Pride	.10
63	Justin Thompson	.10
64	Alan Trammell	.15
65	Kevin Appier	.10
66	Johnny Damon	.20
67	Keith Lockhart	.10
68	Jeff Montgomery	.10
69	Jose Offerman	.10
70	Bip Roberts	.10
71	Jose Rosado	.10
72	Chris Stynes	.10
73	Mike Sweeney	.10
74	Jeff Cirillo	.10
75	Jeff D'Amico	.10
76	John Jaha	.10
77	Scott Karl	.10
78	Mike Matheny	.10
79	Ben McDonald	.10
80	Matt Mieske	.10
81	Marc Newfield	.10
82	Dave Nilsson	.10
83	Jose Valentin	.10
84	Fernando Vina	.10
85	Rick Aguilera	.10
86	Marty Cordova	.10
87	Chuck Knoblauch	.20
88	Matt Lawton	.10
89	Pat Meares	.10
90	Paul Molitor	.40
91	Greg Myers	.10
92	Dan Naulty	.10
93	Kirby Puckett	1.00
94	Frank Rodriguez	.10
95	Wade Boggs	.20
96	Cecil Fielder	.15
97	Joe Girardi	.10
98	Dwight Gooden	.15
99	Derek Jeter	2.00
100	Tino Martinez	.30
101	*Ramiro Mendoza*	.50
102	Andy Pettitte	.40
103	Mariano Rivera	.20
104	Ruben Rivera	.15
105	Kenny Rogers	.10
106	Darryl Strawberry	.15
107	Bernie Williams	.50
108	Tony Batista	.20
109	Geronimo Berroa	.10
110	Bobby Chouinard	.10
111	Brent Gates	.10
112	Jason Giambi	.10
113	*Damon Mashore*	.10
114	Mark McGwire	3.00
115	Scott Spiezio	.10
116	John Wasdin	.10
117	Steve Wojciechowski	.10
118	Ernie Young	.10
119	Norm Charlton	.10
120	Joey Cora	.10
121	Ken Griffey Jr.	3.00
122	Sterling Hitchcock	.10
123	Raul Ibanez	.10
124	Randy Johnson	.50
125	Edgar Martinez	.15
126	Alex Rodriguez	2.50
127	Matt Wagner	.10
128	Bob Wells	.10
129	Dan Wilson	.10
130	Will Clark	.25
131	Kevin Elster	.10
132	Juan Gonzalez	1.25
133	Rusty Greer	.10
134	Darryl Hamilton	.10
135	Mike Henneman	.10
136	Ken Hill	.10
137	Mark McLemore	.10
138	Dean Palmer	.20
139	Roger Pavlik	.10
140	Ivan Rodriguez	.75
141	Joe Carter	.20
142	Carlos Delgado	.50
143	Alex Gonzalez	.10
144	Juan Guzman	.10
145	Pat Hentgen	.10
146	Marty Janzen	.10
147	Otis Nixon	.10
148	Charlie O'Brien	.10
149	John Olerud	.25
150	Robert Perez	.10
151	Jermaine Dye	.15
152	Tom Glavine	.20
153	Andruw Jones	.75
154	Chipper Jones	2.00
155	Ryan Klesko	.20
156	Javier Lopez	.20
157	Greg Maddux	1.50
158	Fred McGriff	.25
159	Wonderful Monds	.10
160	John Smoltz	.20
161	Terrell Wade	.10
162	Mark Wohlers	.10
163	Brant Brown	.10
164	Mark Grace	.20
165	Tyler Houston	.10
166	Robin Jennings	.10
167	Jason Maxwell	.10
168	Ryne Sandberg	.75
169	Sammy Sosa	2.00
170	Amaury Telemaco	.10
171	Steve Trachsel	.10
172	*Pedro Valdes*	.10
173	Tim Belk	.10
174	Bret Boone	.10
175	Jeff Brantley	.10
176	Eric Davis	.15
177	Barry Larkin	.25
178	Chad Mottola	.10
179	Mark Portugal	.10
180	Reggie Sanders	.10
181	John Smiley	.10
182	Eddie Taubensee	.10
183	Dante Bichette	.20
184	Ellis Burks	.15
185	Andres Galarraga	.25
186	Curt Leskanic	.10
187	Quinton McCracken	.10
188	Jeff Reed	.10
189	Kevin Ritz	.10
190	Walt Weiss	.10
191	Jamey Wright	.10
192	Eric Young	.10
193	Kevin Brown	.20
194	Luis Castillo	.25
195	Jeff Conine	.10
196	Andre Dawson	.15
197	Charles Johnson	.10
198	Al Leiter	.15
199	Ralph Milliard	.10
200	Robb Nen	.10
201	Edgar Renteria	.15
202	Gary Sheffield	.25
203	Bob Abreu	.10
204	Jeff Bagwell	1.00
205	Derek Bell	.10
206	Sean Berry	.10
207	Richard Hidalgo	.10
208	Todd Jones	.10
209	Darryl Kile	.10
210	Orlando Miller	.10
211	Shane Reynolds	.15
212	Billy Wagner	.10
213	Donne Wall	.10
214	Roger Cedeno	.10
215	Greg Gagne	.10
216	Karim Garcia	.15
217	Wilton Guerrero	.15
218	Todd Hollandsworth	.10
219	Ramon Martinez	.15
220	Raul Mondesi	.20
221	Hideo Nomo	.25
222	Chan Ho Park	.15
223	Mike Piazza	2.00
224	Ismael Valdes	.10
225	Moises Alou	.20
226	Derek Aucoin	.10
227	Yamil Benitez	.10
228	Jeff Fassero	.10
229	Darrin Fletcher	.10
230	Mark Grudzielanek	.10
231	Barry Manuel	.10
232	Pedro Martinez	1.00
233	Henry Rodriguez	.10
234	Ugueth Urbina	.10
235	Rondell White	.15
236	Carlos Baerga	.10
237	John Franco	.10
238	Bernard Gilkey	.10
239	Todd Hundley	.10
240	Butch Huskey	.10
241	Jason Isringhausen	.10
242	Lance Johnson	.10
243	Bobby Jones	.10
244	Alex Ochoa	.10
245	Rey Ordonez	.20
246	Paul Wilson	.15
247	Ron Blazier	.10
248	David Doster	.10
249	Jim Eisenreich	.10
250	Mike Grace	.15
251	Mike Lieberthal	.10
252	Wendell Magee	.10
253	Mickey Morandini	.10
254	Ricky Otero	.10
255	Scott Rolen	1.00
256	Curt Schilling	.15
257	Todd Zeile	.10
258	Jermaine Allensworth	.10
259	Trey Beamon	.10
260	Carlos Garcia	.10
261	Mark Johnson	.10
262	Jason Kendall	.20
263	Jeff King	.10
264	Al Martin	.10
265	Denny Neagle	.10
266	Matt Ruebel	.10
267	*Marc Wilkins*	.10
268	Alan Benes	.10
269	Dennis Eckersley	.15
270	Ron Gant	.15
271	Aaron Holbert	.10
272	Brian Jordan	.10
273	Ray Lankford	.15
274	John Mabry	.10
275	T.J. Mathews	.10
276	Ozzie Smith	.50
277	Todd Stottlemyre	.15
278	Mark Sweeney	.10
279	Andy Ashby	.10
280	Steve Finley	.10
281	John Flaherty	.10
282	Chris Gomez	.10
283	Tony Gwynn	1.50
284	Joey Hamilton	.10
285	Rickey Henderson	.25
286	Trevor Hoffman	.10
287	Jason Thompson	.10

288 Fernando Valenzuela .10
289 Greg Vaughn .20
290 Barry Bonds .75
291 Jay Canizaro .10
292 Jacob Cruz .10
293 Shawon Dunston .10
294 Shawn Estes .10
295 Mark Gardner .10
296 Marcus Jensen .10
297 *Bill Mueller* .40
298 Chris Singleton .10
299 Allen Watson .10
300 Matt Williams .25
301 Rod Beck .10
302 Jay Bell .10
303 Shawon Dunston .10
304 Reggie Jefferson .10
305 Darren Oliver .10
306 Benito Santiago .10
307 Gerald Williams .10
308 Damon Buford .10
309 Jeromy Burnitz .10
310 Sterling Hitchcock .10
311 Dave Hollins .10
312 Mel Rojas .10
313 Robin Ventura .25
314 David Wells .10
315 Cal Eldred .10
316 Gary Gaetti .10
317 John Hudek .10
318 Brian Johnson .10
319 Denny Neagle .10
320 Larry Walker .50
321 Russ Davis .10
322 Delino DeShields .10
323 Charlie Hayes .10
324 Jermaine Dye .10
325 John Ericks .10
326 Jeff Fassero .10
327 Nomar Garciaparra 2.00
328 Willie Greene .10
329 Greg McMichael .10
330 Damion Easley .10
331 Ricky Bones .10
332 John Burkett .10
333 Royce Clayton .10
334 Greg Colbrunn .10
335 Tony Eusebio .10
336 Gregg Jefferies .10
337 Wally Joyner .10
338 Jim Leyritz .10
339 Paul O'Neill .25
340 Bruce Ruffin .10
341 Michael Tucker .10
342 Andy Benes .10
343 Craig Biggio .40
344 Rex Hudler .10
345 Brad Radke .10
346 Deion Sanders .25
347 Moises Alou .20
348 Brad Ausmus .10
349 Armando Benitez .10
350 Mark Gubicza .10
351 Terry Steinbach .10
352 Mark Whiten .10
353 Ricky Bottalico .10
354 *Brian Giles* 1.50
355 Eric Karros .20
356 Jimmy Key .10
357 Carlos Perez .10
358 Alex Fernandez .10
359 J.T. Snow .10
360 Bobby Bonilla .15
361 Scott Brosius .10
362 Greg Swindell .10
363 Jose Vizcaino .10
364 Matt Williams .30
365 Darren Daulton .10
366 Shane Andrews .10
367 Jim Eisenreich .10
368 Ariel Prieto .10
369 Bob Tewksbury .10
370 Mike Bordick .10
371 Rheal Cormier .10
372 Cliff Floyd .10
373 David Justice .20
374 John Wetteland .10
375 Mike Blowers .10
376 Jose Canseco .75
377 Roger Clemens 1.25
378 Kevin Mitchell .10
379 Todd Zeile .10
380 Jim Thome .50
381 Turk Wendell .10
382 Rico Brogna .10
383 Eric Davis .15
384 Mike Lansing .10
385 Devon White .10
386 Marquis Grissom .10
387 Todd Worrell .10
388 Jeff Kent .10
389 Mickey Tettleton .10
390 Steve Avery .10
391 David Cone .20
392 Scott Cooper .10
393 Lee Stevens .10
394 Kevin Elster .10
395 Tom Goodwin .10
396 Shawn Green .40
397 Pete Harnisch .10
398 Eddie Murray .40
399 Joe Randa .10
400 Scott Sanders .10
401 John Valentin .10
402 Todd Jones .10
403 Terry Adams .10
404 Brian Hunter .10
405 Pat Listach .10
406 Kenny Lofton .50
407 Hal Morris .10
408 Ed Sprague .10
409 Rich Becker .10
410 Edgardo Alfonzo .25
411 Albert Belle .75
412 Jeff King .10
413 Kirt Manwaring .10
414 Jason Schmidt .10
415 Allen Watson .10
416 Lee Tinsley .10
417 Brett Butler .10
418 Carlos Garcia .10
419 Mark Lemke .10
420 Jaime Navarro .10
421 David Segui .10
422 Ruben Sierra .10
423 B.J. Surhoff .10
424 Julian Tavarez .10
425 Billy Taylor .10
426 Ken Caminiti .25
427 Chuck Carr .10
428 Benji Gil .10
429 Terry Mulholland .10
430 Mike Stanton .10
431 Wil Cordero .10
432 Chili Davis .10
433 Mariano Duncan .10
434 Orlando Merced .10
435 Kent Mercker .10
436 John Olerud .25
437 Quilvio Veras .10
438 Mike Fetters .10
439 Glenallen Hill .10
440 Bill Swift .10
441 Tim Wakefield .10
442 Pedro Astacio .10
443 Vinny Castilla .15
444 Doug Drabek .10
445 Alan Embree .10
446 Lee Smith .10
447 Darryl Hamilton .10
448 Brian McRae .10
449 Mike Timlin .10
450 Bob Wickman .10
451 Jason Dickson .15
452 Chad Curtis .10
453 Mark Leiter .10
454 Damon Berryhill .10
455 Kevin Orie .10
456 Dave Burba .10
457 Chris Holt .10
458 *Ricky Ledee* 2.50
459 Mike Devereaux .10
460 Pokey Reese .10
461 Tim Raines .15
462 Ryan Jones .10
463 Shane Mack .10
464 Darren Dreifort .10
465 Mark Parent .10
466 Mark Portugal .10
467 Dante Powell .15
468 Craig Grebeck .10
469 Ron Villone .10
470 Dmitri Young .10
471 Shannon Stewart .10
472 Rick Helling .10
473 Bill Haselman .10
474 Albie Lopez .10
475 Glendon Rusch .10
476 Derrick May .10
477 Chad Ogea .10
478 Kirk Reuter .10
479 Chris Hammond .10
480 Russ Johnson .10
481 James Mouton .10
482 Mike Macfarlane .10
483 Scott Ruffcorn .10
484 Jeff Frye .10
485 Richie Sexson .10
486 *Emil Brown* .40
487 Desi Wilson .10
488 Brent Gates .10
489 Tony Graffanino .10
490 Dan Miceli .10
491 *Orlando Cabrera* .25
492 *Tony Womack* .75
493 Jerome Walton .10
494 Mark Thompson .10
495 Jose Guillen .15
496 Willie Blair .10
497 *T.J. Staton* .25
498 Scott Kamieniecki .10
499 Vince Coleman .10
500 Jeff Abbott .10
501 Chris Widger .10
502 Kevin Tapani .10
503 *Carlos Castillo* .40
504 Luis Gonzalez .10
505 Tim Belcher .10
506 Armando Reynoso .10
507 Jamie Moyer .10
508 *Randall Simon* .60
509 Vladimir Guerrero 1.00
510 Wady Almonte .10
511 Dustin Hermanson .10
512 *Deivi Cruz* .25
513 Luis Alicea .10
514 *Felix Heredia* .25
515 Don Slaught .10
516 Shigetosi Hasegawa .10
517 Matt Walbeck .10
518 *David Arias* (last name actually Ortiz) 1.00
519 *Brady Raggio* .10
520 Rudy Pemberton .10
521 Wayne Kirby .10
522 Calvin Maduro .10
523 Mark Lewis .10
524 Mike Jackson .10
525 Sid Fernandez .10
526 Mike Bielecki .10
527 *Bubba Trammell* .25
528 *Brent Brede* .10
529 Matt Morris .15
530 Joe Borowski .10
531 Orlando Miller .10
532 Jim Bullinger .10
533 Robert Person .10
534 Doug Glanville .10
535 Terry Pendleton .10
536 Jorge Posada .20
537 *Marc Sagmoen* .10
538 *Fernando Tatis* 3.00
539 Aaron Sele .10
540 Brian Banks .10
541 Derrek Lee .10
542 John Wasdin .10
543 *Justin Towle* .40
544 Pat Cline .10
545 Dave Magadan .10
546 Jeff Blauser .10
547 Phil Nevin .10
548 Todd Walker .15
549 Elieser Marrero .10
550 Bartolo Colon .20
551 *Jose Cruz Jr.* .75
552 Todd Dunwoody .15
553 *Hideki Irabu* 1.00

1997 Ultra Gold Medallion Edition

A new concept in parallel editions was debuted by Ultra in Series I. While sharing the card numbers with regular-issue Ultra cards, the Gold Medallion Edition features a "G" prefix to the card number and gold-foil highlights on front. Unlike past parallels, however, the '97 Ultra Gold Medallion and Platinum Medallion inserts share a photograph which is entirely different from the regular Ultra base cards. Gold Medallion Edition cards are identified as such in the lower-right corner and were inserted at a rate of one per pack.

	MT
Complete Set (553):	200.00
Common Player:	.25
(Gold Medallion Edition stars valued at 2X regular Fleer Ultra.)	

1997 Ultra Platinum Medallion Edition

A new concept in parallel editions was debuted by Ultra in Series I. While sharing the card numbers with regular-issue Ultra cards, the Platinum Medallion Edition features a "P" prefix to the card number and holographic-foil highlights on front. Unlike past parallels, however, the '97 Ultra Gold Medallion and Platinum Medallion inserts share a photograph which is entirely different from the regular Ultra. Base cards are identified as such in the lower-right corner and were inserted at a rate of one per 100 packs.

	MT
Complete Set (553):	1200.
Common Player:	3.00
(Platinum Medallion Edition stars valued at 15X regular Fleer Ultra.)	

1997 Ultra Baseball "Rules"!

Baseball Rules was a 10-card insert that was found only in retail packs at a rate of one per 36 packs. The cards are die-cut with a player in front of a mound of baseballs with embossed seams on the front, while each card back explains a baseball term or rule.

		MT
Complete Set (10):		100.00
Common Player:		3.00
1	Barry Bonds	6.00
2	Ken Griffey Jr.	25.00
3	Derek Jeter	15.00
4	Chipper Jones	15.00
5	Greg Maddux	12.00
6	Mark McGwire	25.00
7	Troy Percival	3.00
8	Mike Piazza	15.00
9	Cal Ripken Jr.	20.00
10	Frank Thomas	8.00

1997 Ultra Checklists

There are 10 Checklist cards in each series of Ultra baseball covering all regular-issue cards and inserts. The front of the card features a superstar, while the back contains a portion of the set checklist. The cards have the player's name and "CHECKLIST" in bold, all caps across the bottom in silver foil.

		MT
Complete Set (20):		15.00
Common Player:		.25
	SERIES 1	
1	Dante Bichette	.25
2	Barry Bonds	.60
3	Ken Griffey Jr.	2.00
4	Greg Maddux	1.00
5	Mark McGwire	2.00
6	Mike Piazza	1.50
7	Cal Ripken Jr.	1.50
8	John Smoltz	.25
9	Sammy Sosa	1.50
10	Frank Thomas	1.00
	SERIES 2	
1	Andruw Jones	.75
2	Ken Griffey Jr.	2.00
3	Frank Thomas	1.00
4	Alex Rodriguez	1.50
5	Cal Ripken Jr.	1.50
6	Mike Piazza	1.50
7	Greg Maddux	1.00
8	Chipper Jones	1.50
9	Derek Jeter	1.50
10	Juan Gonzalez	.75

1997 Ultra Diamond Producers

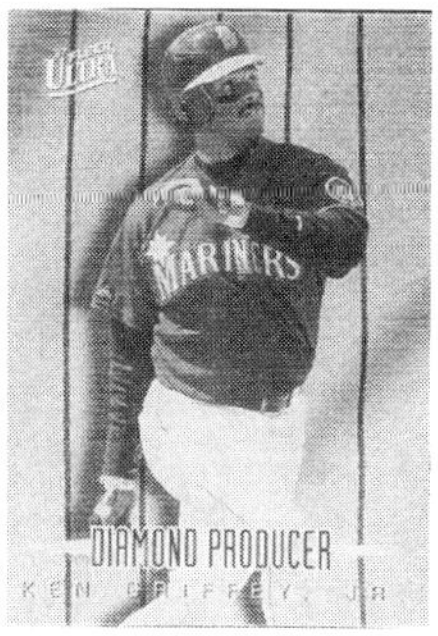

Printed on textured, uniform-like matterial, this 12-card insert contains some of the most consistent producers in baseball. Horizontal backs are conventionally printed with another color player photo on a pin-striped background and a few words about him. This was the most difficult insert Ultra foil-pack insert, with a ratio of one per 288.

		MT
Complete Set (12):		400.00
Common Player:		10.00
1	Jeff Bagwell	20.00
2	Barry Bonds	20.00
3	Ken Griffey Jr.	75.00
4	Chipper Jones	50.00
5	Kenny Lofton	15.00
6	Greg Maddux	40.00
7	Mark McGwire	75.00
8	Mike Piazza	50.00
9	Cal Ripken Jr.	60.00
10	Alex Rodriguez	60.00
11	Frank Thomas	35.00
12	Matt Williams	10.00

1997 Ultra Double Trouble

Double Trouble is a 20-card, team color coded set pairing two stars from the same team on a horizontal front. These inserts were found every four packs.

	MT
Complete Set (20):	9.00
Common Player:	.15

1	Roberto Alomar, Cal Ripken Jr.	1.25
2	Mo Vaughn, Jose Canseco	.45
3	Jim Edmonds, Tim Salmon	.15
4	Harold Baines, Frank Thomas	.60
5	Albert Belle, Kenny Lofton	.30
6	Chuck Knoblauch, Marty Cordova	.15
7	Andy Pettitte, Derek Jeter	1.25
8	Jason Giambi, Mark McGwire	1.75
9	Ken Griffey Jr., Alex Rodriguez	2.50
10	Juan Gonzalez, Will Clark	.60
11	Greg Maddux, Chipper Jones	.90
12	Mark Grace, Sammy Sosa	1.00
13	Dante Bichette, Andres Galarraga	.15
14	Jeff Bagwell, Derek Bell	.45
15	Hideo Nomo, Mike Piazza	.90
16	Henry Rodriguez, Moises Alou	.15
17	Rey Ordonez, Alex Ochoa	.15
18	Ray Lankford, Ron Gant	.15
19	Tony Gwynn, Rickey Henderson	.90
20	Barry Bonds, Matt Williams	.45

1997 Ultra Fame Game

This eight-card hobby-exclusive insert showcases players who have displayed Hall of Fame potential. The player photo on front and Fame Game logo are embossed and highlighted in gold and silver foil. Backs have a color portrait photo and a few words about the player. Cards were inserted 1:8 packs.

		MT
	Complete Set (18):	55.00
	Common Player:	.75
1	Ken Griffey Jr.	10.00
2	Frank Thomas	4.00
3	Alex Rodriguez	8.00
4	Cal Ripken Jr.	8.00
5	Mike Piazza	6.00
6	Greg Maddux	5.00
7	Derek Jeter	6.00
8	Jeff Bagwell	3.00
9	Juan Gonzalez	4.00
10	Albert Belle	2.50
11	Tony Gwynn	4.00
12	Mark McGwire	10.00
13	Andy Pettitte	1.50
14	Kenny Lofton	1.50
15	Roberto Alomar	2.00
16	Ryne Sandberg	2.50
17	Barry Bonds	2.50
18	Eddie Murray	1.00

1997 Ultra Fielder's Choice

Fielder's Choice highlights 18 of the top defensive players in baseball. Fronts of the horizontal cards have a leather look and feel and are highlighted in gold foil. Backs are conventionally printed with another player photo and some words about his fielding ability. Fielder's Choice inserts were found every 144 packs.

		MT
	Complete Set (18):	240.00
	Common Player:	3.00
1	Roberto Alomar	10.00
2	Jeff Bagwell	15.00
3	Wade Boggs	7.50
4	Barry Bonds	15.00
5	Mark Grace	5.00
6	Ken Griffey Jr.	60.00
7	Marquis Grissom	3.00
8	Charles Johnson	3.00
9	Chuck Knoblauch	3.00
10	Barry Larkin	6.00
11	Kenny Lofton	10.00
12	Greg Maddux	30.00
13	Raul Mondesi	3.00
14	Rey Ordonez	3.00
15	Cal Ripken Jr.	50.00
16	Alex Rodriguez	50.00
17	Ivan Rodriguez	15.00
18	Matt Williams	6.00

1997 Ultra Golden Prospects

This 10-card set was exclusive to hobby shop packs and highlighted the top young players in baseball. Action photos on front and portraits on back are set on a sepia background. Cards were inserted 1:4 packs.

		MT
	Complete Set (10):	4.00
	Common Player:	.25
1	Andruw Jones	1.00
2	Vladimir Guerrero	1.50
3	Todd Walker	.50
4	Karim Garcia	.25
5	Kevin Orie	.25
6	Brian Giles	.25
7	Jason Dickson	.25
8	Jose Guillen	.25
9	Ruben Rivera	.40
10	Derrek Lee	.25

1997 Ultra Hitting Machines

This 36-card insert was only found in hobby packs and showcases the game's top hitters. Cards were inserted at a ratio of 1:36 packs.

		MT
	Complete Set (18):	200.00
	Common Player:	3.00
1	Andruw Jones	6.00
2	Ken Griffey Jr.	30.00
3	Frank Thomas	12.00
4	Alex Rodriguez	25.00
5	Cal Ripken Jr.	25.00
6	Mike Piazza	20.00
7	Derek Jeter	20.00
8	Albert Belle	4.00
9	Tony Gwynn	15.00
10	Jeff Bagwell	9.00
11	Mark McGwire	30.00
12	Kenny Lofton	4.00
13	Manny Ramirez	9.00
14	Roberto Alomar	4.00
15	Ryne Sandberg	8.00
16	Eddie Murray	4.00
17	Sammy Sosa	20.00
18	Ken Caminiti	3.00

1997 Ultra HR Kings

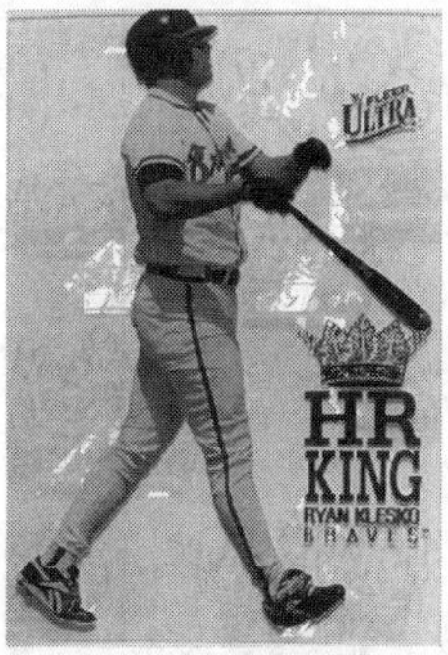

HR Kings are printed on clear plastic with transparent refractive holofoil crowns and other objects in the plastic. Backs contain a white silhouette of the player with career summary and logos within the figure. Stated odds of finding an HR King card were one per 36 packs.

		MT
	Complete Set (12):	100.00
	Common Player:	3.00
1	Albert Belle	5.00
2	Barry Bonds	7.50
3	Juan Gonzalez	8.00
4	Ken Griffey Jr.	25.00
5	Todd Hundley	3.00
6	Ryan Klesko	3.00
7	Mark McGwire	25.00
8	Mike Piazza	15.00
9	Sammy Sosa	15.00
10	Frank Thomas	8.00
11	Mo Vaughn	5.00
12	Matt Williams	4.00

1997 Ultra Leather Shop

Baseball's best fielders are honored in this 12-card hobby-exclusive insert. Cards were inserted at a ratio of 1:6 packs and feature an embossed grain-like finish on the fronts.

		MT
	Complete Set (12):	15.00
	Common Player:	.50
1	Ken Griffey Jr.	4.00
2	Alex Rodriguez	3.00
3	Cal Ripken Jr.	3.00
4	Derek Jeter	2.50
5	Juan Gonzalez	1.25
6	Tony Gwynn	2.00
7	Jeff Bagwell	1.25
8	Roberto Alomar	.75
9	Ryne Sandberg	1.00
10	Ken Caminiti	.50
11	Kenny Lofton	.75
12	John Smoltz	.50

1997 Ultra Power Plus Series 1

Series 1 Power Plus is a 12-card insert utilizing silver rainbow holofoil in the background, with the featured player in the foreground. Backs contain another action photo and the player's credentials. The insert captures power hitters that also excel in other areas of the game. Power Plus inserts can be found every 24 packs.

		MT
	Complete Set (12):	80.00
	Common Player:	2.50
1	Jeff Bagwell	4.00
2	Barry Bonds	4.00
3	Juan Gonzalez	6.00
4	Ken Griffey Jr.	15.00
5	Chipper Jones	10.00
6	Mark McGwire	15.00
7	Mike Piazza	10.00
8	Cal Ripken Jr.	12.00
9	Alex Rodriguez	12.00
10	Sammy Sosa	10.00
11	Frank Thomas	6.00
12	Matt Williams	3.00

1997 Ultra Power Plus Series 2

Similar in design to the Power Plus insert in Series I, this 12-card insert salutes the game's top sluggers and was found only in hobby packs. Cards were inserted at a ratio of 1:8 packs. Front design features gold holographic foil graphics. Backs have another photo and a description of the player's skills.

		MT
	Complete Set (12):	30.00
	Common Player:	1.00
1	Ken Griffey Jr.	6.00
2	Frank Thomas	2.50
3	Alex Rodriguez	5.00
4	Cal Ripken Jr.	5.00
5	Mike Piazza	4.00
6	Chipper Jones	4.00
7	Albert Belle	1.00
8	Juan Gonzalez	2.50
9	Jeff Bagwell	1.50
10	Mark McGwire	6.00
11	Mo Vaughn	1.00
12	Barry Bonds	1.50

1997 Ultra RBI Kings

Ten different players are featured in RBI Kings, which contain a metallic paisley background, with an English shield of armor and Latin words in the background. RBI Kings were inserted every 18 packs of Series I.

		MT
	Complete Set (10):	40.00
	Common Player:	2.00
1	Jeff Bagwell	4.00
2	Albert Belle	3.00
3	Dante Bichette	2.00
4	Barry Bonds	4.00
5	Jay Buhner	2.00
6	Juan Gonzalez	5.00
7	Ken Griffey Jr.	15.00
8	Sammy Sosa	10.00
9	Frank Thomas	5.00
10	Mo Vaughn	3.00

1997 Ultra Rookie Reflections

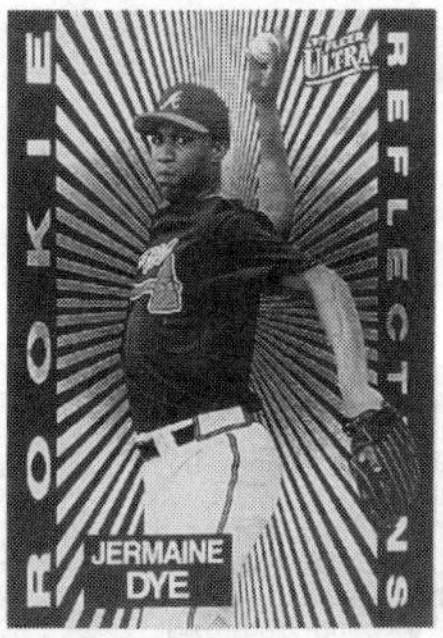

Rookie Reflections features 10 of the 1996 season's top first-year stars. Cards are inserted every four packs. Front features an action photo on a black-and-silver starburst pattern. Horizontal backs have another photo and a career summary of the prospect.

		MT
	Complete Set (10):	5.00
	Common Player:	.25
1	James Baldwin	.25
2	Jermaine Dye	.25
3	Darin Erstad	.50
4	Todd Hollandsworth	.25
5	Derek Jeter	3.00
6	Jason Kendall	.40
7	Alex Ochoa	.25
8	Rey Ordonez	.50
9	Edgar Renteria	.25
10	Scott Rolen	1.00

Player names in *Italic* type indicate a rookie card.

1997 Ultra Season Crowns

Season Crowns were found at a rate of one per eight packs of Ultra I Baseball. This etched, silver-foil insert contained 12 statistical leaders and award winners from the 1996 season.

		MT
Complete Set (12):		10.00
Common Player:		.50
1	Albert Belle	.75
2	Dante Bichette	.50
3	Barry Bonds	1.00
4	Kenny Lofton	.75
5	Edgar Martinez	.50
6	Mark McGwire	3.50
7	Andy Pettitte	.50
8	Mike Piazza	2.00
9	Alex Rodriguez	2.50
10	John Smoltz	.50
11	Sammy Sosa	2.00
12	Frank Thomas	1.00

1997 Ultra Starring Role

Another hobby-exclusive insert, these 12 cards salute baseball's clutch performers and were found 1:288 packs.

		MT
Complete Set (12):		260.00
Common Player:		10.00
1	Andruw Jones	10.00
2	Ken Griffey Jr.	50.00
3	Frank Thomas	15.00
4	Alex Rodriguez	40.00
5	Cal Ripken Jr.	40.00
6	Mike Piazza	30.00
7	Greg Maddux	25.00
8	Chipper Jones	30.00
9	Derek Jeter	30.00
10	Juan Gonzalez	15.00
11	Albert Belle	10.00
12	Tony Gwynn	25.00

1997 Ultra Thunderclap

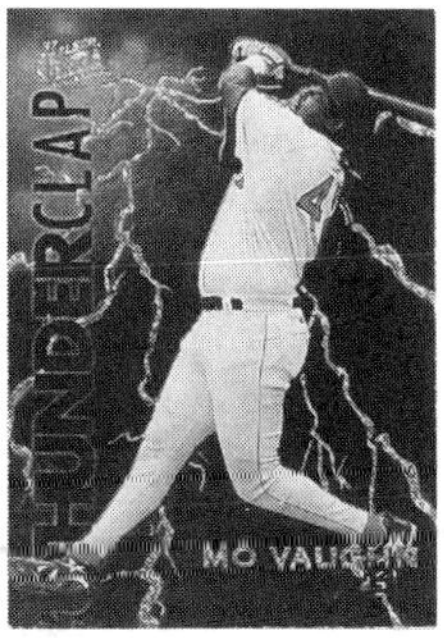

This 10-card hobby-exclusive insert showcases hitters who strike fear in opposing pitchers. Cards were inserted 1:18 packs. Fronts are highlighted by streaks of gold prismatic foil lightning in a stormy sky. Backs have another player photo and a few words about him.

		MT
Complete Set (10):		60.00
Common Player:		3.00
1	Barry Bonds	4.00
2	Mo Vaughn	3.00
3	Mark McGwire	15.00
4	Jeff Bagwell	4.00
5	Juan Gonzalez	5.00
6	Alex Rodriguez	12.00
7	Chipper Jones	9.00
8	Ken Griffey Jr.	15.00
9	Mike Piazza	9.00
10	Frank Thomas	5.00

1997 Ultra Top 30

This 30-card insert was found only in retail store packs and salutes the 30 most collectible players in the game. Cards were inserted one per pack. A Top 30 Gold Medallion parallel set was also produced and inserted 1:18 packs.

		MT
Complete Set (30):		35.00
Common Player:		.50
Gold Medallions: 5X		
1	Andruw Jones	1.50
2	Ken Griffey Jr.	6.00
3	Frank Thomas	2.00
4	Alex Rodriguez	4.00
5	Cal Ripken Jr.	4.00
6	Mike Piazza	3.00
7	Greg Maddux	2.50
8	Chipper Jones	3.00
9	Derek Jeter	3.00
10	Juan Gonzalez	2.00
11	Albert Belle	1.00
12	Tony Gwynn	2.50
13	Jeff Bagwell	1.50
14	Mark McGwire	6.00
15	Andy Pettitte	1.00
16	Mo Vaughn	1.00
17	Kenny Lofton	1.00
18	Manny Ramirez	1.50
19	Roberto Alomar	1.00
20	Ryne Sandberg	1.00
21	Hideo Nomo	.60
22	Barry Bonds	1.50
23	Eddie Murray	.75
24	Ken Caminiti	.50
25	John Smoltz	.50
26	Pat Hentgen	.50
27	Todd Hollandsworth	.50
28	Matt Williams	.60
29	Bernie Williams	1.00
30	Brady Anderson	.50

1997 Ultra FanFest Larry Doby

In the same basic style as its regular-issue Ultra baseball series of 1997, Fleer issued a special Larry Doby card in conjunction with the All-Star FanFest in Cleveland, recognizing Doby's 50th anniversary of breaking the American League color barrier. The card has a black-and-white batting pose of Doby on front with his name, team and Fleer Ultra logo in red-shaded silver holographic foil. A color All-Star Game logo also appears on front. Backs have a red duotone photo of Doby fielding, his career stats and a few words about his career.

	MT
Larry Doby	8.00

1998 Ultra

Ultra was released in two series and contained a total of 501 cards, with 250 in Series I and 251 in Series II. The product sold in 10-card packs for an SRP of $2.59 and three parallel sets - Gold Medallion, Platinum Medallion and Masterpieces. Series I has 210 regular cards, 25 Prospects (seeded 1:4 packs), 10 Season's Crowns (seeded 1:12) and five Checklists (1:8). Series II had 202 regular cards, 25 Pizzazz (seeded 1:4), 20 New Horizons and three checklists. Series II also added a Mike Piazza N.Y. Mets card that was added to the set as card No. 501 and inserted every 20 packs. Inserts in Series I include: Big Shots, Double Trouble, Kid Gloves, Back to the Future, Artistic Talents, Fall Classics, Power Plus, Prime Leather, Diamond Producers, Diamond Ink and Million Dollar Moments. Series II included: Notables, Rocket to Stardom, Millennium Men, Win Now, Ticket Studs, Diamond Immortals, Diamond Ink, Top 30 and 750 sequentially numbered Alex Rodriguez autographed cards.

		MT
Complete Set (501):		175.00
Series 1 Set (250):		100.00
Series 2 Set (251):		75.00
Common Player:		.10
Alex Rodriguez Autograph (750):		125.00
Wax Box:		55.00
1	Ken Griffey Jr.	3.00
2	Matt Morris	.10
3	Roger Clemens	1.00
4	Matt Williams	.25
5	Roberto Hernandez	.10
6	Rondell White	.10
7	Tim Salmon	.20
8	Brad Radke	.10
9	Brett Butler	.10
10	Carl Everett	.10
11	Chili Davis	.10
12	Chuck Finley	.10
13	Darryl Kile	.10
14	Deivi Cruz	.10
15	Gary Gaetti	.10
16	Matt Stairs	.10
17	Pat Meares	.10
18	Will Cunnane	.10
19	*Steve Woodard*	.30
20	Andy Ashby	.10
21	Bobby Higginson	.20
22	Brian Jordan	.10
23	Craig Biggio	.20
24	Jim Edmonds	.20
25	Ryan McGuire	.10
26	Scott Hatteberg	.10
27	Willie Greene	.10
28	Albert Belle	.75
29	Ellis Burks	.10
30	Hideo Nomo	.50
31	Jeff Bagwell	1.25
32	Kevin Brown	.10
33	Nomar Garciaparra	2.00
34	Pedro Martinez	.75
35	Raul Mondesi	.25
36	Ricky Bottalico	.10
37	Shawn Estes	.10
38	Shawon Dunston	.10
39	Terry Steinbach	.10
40	Tom Glavine	.20
41	Todd Dunwoody	.10
42	Deion Sanders	.25
43	Gary Sheffield	.35
44	Mike Lansing	.10
45	Mike Lieberthal	.10
46	Paul Sorrento	.10
47	Paul O'Neill	.20
48	Tom Goodwin	.10
49	Andruw Jones	1.50
50	Barry Bonds	.75
51	Bernie Williams	.50
52	Jeremi Gonzalez	.20
53	Mike Piazza	2.00
54	Russ Davis	.10
55	Vinny Castilla	.10
56	Rod Beck	.10
57	Andres Galarraga	.20
58	Ben McDonald	.10
59	Billy Wagner	.10
60	Charles Johnson	.10
61	Fred McGriff	.25
62	Dean Palmer	.10
63	Frank Thomas	1.50
64	Ismael Valdes	.10
65	Mark Bellhorn	.10
66	Jeff King	.10
67	John Wetteland	.10
68	Mark Grace	.25
69	Mark Kotsay	.50
70	Scott Rolen	1.50
71	Todd Hundley	.20
72	Todd Worrell	.10
73	Wilson Alvarez	.10
74	Bobby Jones	.10
75	Jose Canseco	.25
76	Kevin Appier	.10
77	Neifi Perez	.10
78	Paul Molitor	.50
79	Quilvio Veras	.10
80	Randy Johnson	.50
81	Glendon Rusch	.10
82	Curt Schilling	.10
83	Alex Rodriguez	2.50
84	Rey Ordonez	.10
85	Jeff Juden	.10
86	Mike Cameron	.10
87	Ryan Klesko	.25
88	Trevor Hoffman	.10
89	Chuck Knoblauch	.25
90	Larry Walker	.30
91	Mark McLemore	.10
92	B.J. Surhoff	.10
93	Darren Daulton	.10
94	Ray Durham	.10
95	Sammy Sosa	2.00
96	Eric Young	.10
97	Gerald Williams	.10
98	Javy Lopez	.15
99	John Smiley	.10
100	Juan Gonzalez	1.50
101	Shawn Green	.10
102	Charles Nagy	.10
103	David Justice	.25
104	Joey Hamilton	.10
105	Pat Hentgen	.10
106	Raul Casanova	.10
107	Tony Phillips	.10
108	Tony Gwynn	1.50
109	Will Clark	.25
110	Jason Giambi	.10
111	Jay Bell	.10
112	Johnny Damon	.10
113	Alan Benes	.10
114	Jeff Suppan	.10
115	*Kevin Polcovich*	.25
116	Shigetosi Hasegawa	.10
117	Steve Finley	.10
118	Tony Clark	.40
119	David Cone	.20
120	Jose Guillen	.40
121	*Kevin Millwood*	4.00
122	Greg Maddux	2.00
123	Dave Nilsson	.10
124	Hideki Irabu	.50
125	Jason Kendall	.10
126	Jim Thome	.40
127	Delino DeShields	.10
128	Edgar Renteria	.20
129	Edgardo Alfonzo	.10
130	J.T. Snow	.10
131	Jeff Abbott	.10
132	Jeffrey Hammonds	.10
133	Rich Loiselle	.10
134	Vladimir Guerrero	1.50
135	Jay Buhner	.20
136	Jeff Cirillo	.10
137	Jeromy Burnitz	.10
138	Mickey Morandini	.10
139	Tino Martinez	.25
140	Jeff Shaw	.10
141	Rafael Palmeiro	.20
142	Bobby Bonilla	.20
143	Cal Ripken Jr.	2.50
144	*Chad Fox*	.25
145	Dante Bichette	.20
146	Dennis Eckersley	.20
147	Mariano Rivera	.20
148	Mo Vaughn	.75
149	Reggie Sanders	.10
150	Derek Jeter	2.00
151	Rusty Greer	.20
152	Brady Anderson	.20
153	Brett Tomko	.10
154	Jaime Navarro	.10
155	Kevin Orie	.10
156	Roberto Alomar	.60
157	Edgar Martinez	.10
158	John Olerud	.10
159	John Smoltz	.20
160	Ryne Sandberg	.75
161	Billy Taylor	.10
162	Chris Holt	.10
163	Damion Easley	.10
164	Darin Erstad	.75
165	Joe Carter	.20
166	Kelvim Escobar	.10
167	Ken Caminiti	.25
168	Pokey Reese	.10
169	Ray Lankford	.10
170	Livan Hernandez	.20
171	Steve Kline	.10
172	Tom Gordon	.10
173	Travis Fryman	.10
174	Al Martin	.10
175	Andy Pettitte	.50
176	Jeff Kent	.10
177	Jimmy Key	.10
178	Mark Grudzielanek	.10
179	Tony Saunders	.20
180	Barry Larkin	.25
181	Bubba Trammell	.20
182	Carlos Delgado	.50
183	Carlos Baerga	.10
184	Derek Bell	.10
185	Henry Rodriguez	.10
186	Jason Dickson	.10
187	Ron Gant	.10
188	Tony Womack	.10
189	Justin Thompson	.10
190	Fernando Tatis	.30
191	Mark Wohlers	.10
192	Takashi Kashiwada	.50
193	Garret Anderson	.10
194	Jose Cruz, Jr.	.25
195	Ricardo Rincon	.10
196	Tim Naehring	.10
197	Moises Alou	.20
198	Eric Karros	.10
199	John Jaha	.10
200	Marty Cordova	.10
201	Travis Lee	.75
202	Mark Davis	.10
203	Vladimir Nunez	.10
204	Stanton Cameron	.10
205	*Mike Stoner*	1.00
206	*Rolando Arrojo*	.40
207	Rick White	.10
208	Luis Polonia	.10
209	Greg Blosser	.10
210	Cesar Devarez	.10
211	Jeff Bagwell (Season Crown)	3.00
212	Barry Bonds (Season Crown)	2.50
213	Roger Clemens (Season Crown)	4.00
214	Nomar Garciaparra (Season Crown)	6.00
215	Ken Griffey Jr. (Season Crown)	10.00
216	Tony Gwynn (Season Crown)	5.00
217	Randy Johnson (Season Crown)	1.50
218	Mark McGwire (Season Crown)	12.00
219	Scott Rolen (Season Crown)	3.00
220	Frank Thomas (Season Crown)	3.00
221	Matt Perisho (Prospect)	.10
222	Wes Helms (Prospect)	1.00
223	*David Dellucci* (Prospect)	2.00
224	Todd Helton (Prospect)	3.00
225	Brian Rose (Prospect)	.75
226	Aaron Boone (Prospect)	.25
227	Keith Foulke (Prospect)	.50
228	Homer Bush (Prospect)	.40
229	Shannon Stewart (Prospect)	.25
230	Richard Hidalgo (Prospect)	.75
231	Russ Johnson (Prospect)	.50
232	*Henry Blanco* (Prospect)	.40
233	Paul Konerko (Prospect)	.75

234	Antone Williamson (Prospect)	.50
235	*Shane Bowers* (Prospect)	.50
236	Jose Vidro (Prospect)	.25
237	Derek Wallace (Prospect)	.25
238	Ricky Ledee (Prospect)	1.00
239	Ben Grieve (Prospect)	3.00
240	Lou Collier (Prospect)	.50
241	Derrek Lee (Prospect)	.75
242	Ruben Rivera (Prospect)	.50
243	Jorge Velandia (Prospect)	.25
244	Andrew Vessel (Prospect)	.40
245	Chris Carpenter (Prospect)	.50
246	Checklist (Ken Griffey Jr.)	1.50
247	Checklist (Andruw Jones)	.75
248	Checklist (Alex Rodriguez)	1.00
249	Checklist (Frank Thomas)	.75
250	Checklist (Cal Ripken Jr.)	1.00
251	Carlos Perez	.10
252	Larry Sutton	.10
253	Brad Rigby	.10
254	Wally Joyner	.10
255	Todd Stottlemyre	.10
256	Nerio Rodriguez	.10
257	Jeff Frye	.10
258	Pedro Astacio	.10
259	Cal Eldred	.10
260	Chili Davis	.10
261	Freddy Garcia	.10
262	Bobby Witt	.10
263	Michael Coleman	.10
264	Mike Caruso	.20
265	Mike Lansing	.10
266	Dennis Reyes	.10
267	F.P. Santangelo	.10
268	Darryl Hamilton	.10
269	Mike Fetters	.10
270	Charlie Hayes	.10
271	Royce Clayton	.10
272	Doug Drabek	.10
273	James Baldwin	.10
274	Brian Hunter	.10
275	Chan Ho Park	.20
276	John Franco	.10
277	David Wells	.10
278	Eli Marrero	.10
279	Kerry Wood	.75
280	Donnie Sadler	.10
281	*Scott Winchester*	.25
282	Hal Morris	.10
283	Brad Fullmer	.25
284	Bernard Gilkey	.10
285	Ramiro Mendoza	.10
286	Kevin Brown	.20
287	David Segui	.10
288	Willie McGee	.10
289	Darren Oliver	.10
290	Antonio Alfonseca	.10
291	Eric Davis	.10
292	Mickey Morandini	.10
293	*Frank Catalanotto*	.20
294	Derrek Lee	.10
295	Todd Zeile	.10
296	Chuck Knoblauch	.25
297	Wilson Delgado	.10
298	Raul Ibanez	.10
299	Orel Hershiser	.10
300	Ozzie Guillen	.10
301	Aaron Sele	.10
302	Joe Carter	.20
303	Darryl Kile	.10
304	Shane Reynolds	.10
305	Todd Dunn	.10
306	Bob Abreu	.10
307	Doug Strange	.10
308	Jose Canseco	.30
309	Lance Johnson	.10
310	Harold Baines	.10
311	Todd Pratt	.10
312	Greg Colbrunn	.10
313	*Masato Yoshii*	.40
314	Felix Heredia	.10
315	Dennis Martinez	.10
316	Geronimo Berroa	.10
317	Darren Lewis	.10
318	Billy Ripken	.10
319	Enrique Wilson	.10
320	Alex Ochoa	.10
321	Doug Glanville	.10
322	Mike Stanley	.10
323	Gerald Williams	.10
324	Pedro Martinez	.75
325	Jaret Wright	.20
326	Terry Pendleton	.10
327	LaTroy Hawkins	.10
328	Emil Brown	.10
329	Walt Weiss	.10
330	Omar Vizquel	.10
331	Carl Everett	.10
332	Fernando Vina	.10
333	Mike Blowers	.10
334	Dwight Gooden	.20
335	Mark Lewis	.10
336	Jim Leyritz	.10
337	Kenny Lofton	.75
338	*John Halama*	.30
339	Jose Valentin	.10
340	Desi Relaford	.10
341	Dante Powell	.10
342	Ed Sprague	.10
343	Reggie Jefferson	.10
344	Mike Hampton	.10
345	Marquis Grissom	.10
346	Heathcliff Slocumb	.10
347	Francisco Cordova	.10
348	Ken Cloude	.25
349	Benito Santiago	.10
350	Denny Neagle	.10
351	Sean Casey	.50
352	Robb Nen	.10
353	Orlando Merced	.10
354	Adrian Brown	.10
355	Gregg Jefferies	.10
356	Otis Nixon	.10
357	Michael Tucker	.10
358	Eric Milton	.25
359	Travis Fryman	.10
360	Gary DiSarcina	.10
361	Mario Valdez	.10
362	Craig Counsell	.10
363	Jose Offerman	.10
364	Tony Fernandez	.10
365	Jason McDonald	.10
366	Sterling Hitchcock	.10
367	Donovan Osborne	.10
368	Troy Percival	.10
369	Henry Rodriguez	.10
370	Dmitri Young	.10
371	Jay Powell	.10
372	Jeff Conine	.10
373	Orlando Cabrera	.10
374	Butch Huskey	.10
375	*Mike Lowell*	.40
376	Kevin Young	.10
377	Jamie Moyer	.10
378	Jeff D'Amico	.10
379	Scott Erickson	.10
380	*Magglio Ordonez*	2.00
381	Melvin Nieves	.10
382	Ramon Martinez	.20
383	A.J. Hinch	.50
384	Jeff Brantley	.10
385	Kevin Elster	.10
386	Allen Watson	.10
387	Moises Alou	.20
388	Jeff Blauser	.10
389	Pete Harnisch	.10
390	Shane Andrews	.10
391	Rico Brogna	.10
392	Stan Javier	.10
393	David Howard	.10
394	Darryl Strawberry	.20
395	Kent Mercker	.10
396	Juan Encarnacion	.25
397	Sandy Alomar	.20
398	Al Leiter	.20
399	Tony Graffanino	.10
400	Terry Adams	.10
401	Bruce Aven	.10
402	Derrick Gibson	.10
403	Jose Cabrera	.10
404	Rich Becker	.10
405	David Ortiz	.40
406	Brian McRae	.10
407	Bobby Estalella	.10
408	Bill Mueller	.10
409	Dennis Eckersley	.20
410	Sandy Martinez	.10
411	Jose Vizcaino	.10
412	Jermaine Allensworth	.10
413	Miguel Tejada	.40
414	Turner Ward	.10
415	Glenallen Hill	.10
416	Lee Stevens	.10
417	Cecil Fielder	.25
418	Ruben Sierra	.10
419	Jon Nunnally	.10
420	Rod Myers	.10
421	Dustin Hermanson	.10
422	James Mouton	.10
423	Dan Wilson	.10
424	Roberto Kelly	.10
425	Antonio Osuna	.10
426	Jacob Cruz	.10
427	Brent Mayne	.10
428	Matt Karchner	.10
429	Damian Jackson	.10
430	Roger Cedeno	.10
431	Rickey Henderson	.40
432	Joe Randa	.10
433	Greg Vaughn	.10
434	Andres Galarraga	.40
435	Rod Beck	.10
436	Curtis Goodwin	.10
437	Brad Ausmus	.10
438	Bob Hamelin	.10
439	Todd Walker	.30
440	Scott Brosius	.10
441	Lenny Dykstra	.10
442	Abraham Nunez	.10
443	Brian Johnson	.10
444	Randy Myers	.10
445	Bret Boone	.10
446	Oscar Henriquez	.10
447	Mike Sweeney	.10
448	Kenny Rogers	.10
449	Mark Langston	.10
450	Luis Gonzalez	.10
451	John Burkett	.10
452	Bip Roberts	.10
453	Travis Lee (New Horizons)	.40
454	Felix Rodriguez (New Horizons)	.10
455	Andy Benes (New Horizons)	.10
456	Willie Blair (New Horizons)	.10
457	Brian Anderson (New Horizons)	.10
458	Jay Bell (New Horizons)	.10
459	Matt Williams (New Horizons)	.25
460	Devon White (New Horizons)	.10
461	Karim Garcia (New Horizons)	.10
462	Jorge Fabregas (New Horizons)	.10
463	Wilson Alvarez (New Horizons)	.10
464	Roberto Hernandez (New Horizons)	.10
465	Tony Saunders (New Horizons)	.10
466	*Rolando Arrojo* (New Horizons)	.40
467	Wade Boggs (New Horizons)	.25
468	Fred McGriff (New Horizons)	.25
469	Paul Sorrento (New Horizons)	.10
470	Kevin Stocker (New Horizons)	.10
471	Bubba Trammell (New Horizons)	.25
472	Quinton McCracken (New Horizons)	.10
473	Checklist (Ken Griffey Jr.)	1.00
474	Checklist (Cal Ripken Jr.)	.75
475	Checklist (Frank Thomas)	.40
476	Ken Griffey Jr. (Pizzazz)	6.00
477	Cal Ripken Jr. (Pizzazz)	5.00
478	Frank Thomas (Pizzazz)	2.00
479	Alex Rodriguez (Pizzazz)	4.00
480	Nomar Garciaparra (Pizzazz)	4.00
481	Derek Jeter (Pizzazz)	4.00
482	Andruw Jones (Pizzazz)	1.50
483	Chipper Jones (Pizzazz)	4.00
484	Greg Maddux (Pizzazz)	3.00
485	Mike Piazza (Pizzazz)	4.00
486	Juan Gonzalez (Pizzazz)	2.00
487	Jose Cruz (Pizzazz)	.75
488	Jaret Wright (Pizzazz)	.75
489	Hideo Nomo (Pizzazz)	.75
490	Scott Rolen (Pizzazz)	1.50
491	Tony Gwynn (Pizzazz)	3.00
492	Roger Clemens (Pizzazz)	2.00
493	Darin Erstad (Pizzazz)	.75
494	Mark McGwire (Pizzazz)	8.00
495	Jeff Bagwell (Pizzazz)	1.50
496	Mo Vaughn (Pizzazz)	1.25
497	Albert Belle (Pizzazz)	1.50
498	Kenny Lofton (Pizzazz)	1.25
499	Ben Grieve (Pizzazz)	1.00
500	Barry Bonds (Pizzazz)	1.50
501	Mike Piazza (mets)	3.00

1998 Ultra Gold Medallion

This parallel to the Ultra set is found seeded on a one per pack ratio. Cards are similar to the regular-issue Ultra except for a gold presentation of the embossed player name on front and a shower of gold specks in the photo background. Backs have a "G" suffix to the card number and a "GOLD MEDALLION EDITION" notation at bottom. The short-printed subset cards from the regular Ultra edition are not short-printed in Gold Medallion.

	MT
Complete Set (501):	300.00
Common Player:	.25
Stars/RCs: 2X	
Checklists: 3X	
Season Crowns: 50%	
Prospects: 50%	
Pizzazz: 1X	

(See 1998 Ultra for checklist and base card values.)

1998 Ultra Platinum Medallion

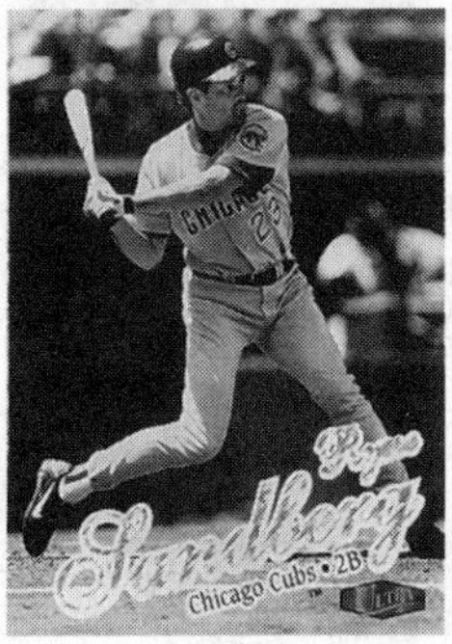

Insertion odds on this super-scarce insert set are not given but each card is produced and serially numbered in an edition of only 100. Fronts are similar to regular Ultra cards except the photo is black-and-white and the name is rendered in silver prismatic foil. Backs are in color with the serial number printed in silver foil at bottom. Series 2 checklist cards #473-475 were never printed in the Platinum Medallion edition.

	MT
Common Player:	6.00
Stars/RCs: 30X	
Checklists: 3X	
Season Crowns: 6X	
Prospects: 8X	
Pizzazz: 8X	

(See 1998 Ultra for checklist and base card values.)

1998 Ultra Masterpiece

This top of the line parallel to '98 Ultra consists of a 1 of 1 version of each regular card.

	MT
Common Player:	100.00

(Individual players cannot be priced due to scarcity and fluctuating demand.)

1998 Ultra Artistic Talents

This 18-card insert featured top players in the game on a canvas-like surface with the insert name in silver holographic letters across the top. The backs are done in black and white and numbered with an "AT" suffix. Artistic Talents are inserted one per eight packs.

		MT
Complete Set (18):		60.00
Common Player:		1.50
Inserted 1:8		
1	Ken Griffey Jr.	8.00
2	Andruw Jones	2.00
3	Alex Rodriguez	6.00
4	Frank Thomas	4.00
5	Cal Ripken Jr.	6.00
6	Derek Jeter	5.00
7	Chipper Jones	5.00
8	Greg Maddux	4.00
9	Mike Piazza	5.00
10	Albert Belle	1.50
11	Darin Erstad	1.50
12	Juan Gonzalez	3.00
13	Jeff Bagwell	3.00
14	Tony Gwynn	4.00
15	Mark McGwire	8.00
16	Scott Rolen	2.00
17	Barry Bonds	2.00
18	Kenny Lofton	1.50

1998 Ultra Back to the Future

This 15-card insert was printed in a horizontal format with a baseball field background. Cards were numbered with a "BF" suffix and seeded one per six packs.

		MT
Complete Set (15):		15.00
Common Player:		.40
Inserted 1:6		
1	Andruw Jones	.75
2	Alex Rodriguez	4.00
3	Derek Jeter	3.00
4	Darin Erstad	.60
5	Mike Cameron	.40
6	Scott Rolen	1.50
7	Nomar Garciaparra	3.00
8	Hideki Irabu	.60
9	Jose Cruz, Jr.	.40
10	Vladimir Guerrero	1.50
11	Mark Kotsay	.60
12	Tony Womack	.40
13	Jason Dickson	.40
14	Jose Guillen	.60
15	Tony Clark	.75

1998 Ultra Big Shots

Big Shots was a 15-card insert displaying some of the top home run hitters in baseball. A generic stadium is pictured across the bottom with the insert name running up the left side. Cards were numbered with a "BS" suffix and inserted one per four Series I packs.

		MT
Complete Set (15):		10.00
Common Player:		.25
Inserted 1:4		
1	Ken Griffey Jr.	3.00
2	Frank Thomas	1.00
3	Chipper Jones	2.00
4	Albert Belle	.60
5	Juan Gonzalez	1.00
6	Jeff Bagwell	.75
7	Mark McGwire	3.00
8	Barry Bonds	.75
9	Manny Ramirez	.75
10	Mo Vaughn	.50
11	Matt Williams	.35
12	Jim Thome	.25
13	Tino Martinez	.25
14	Mike Piazza	2.00
15	Tony Clark	.25

1998 Ultra Diamond Immortals

This Series II insert showcased 15 top player on an intricate silver holographic foil design that frames each player. Cards were numbered with a "DI" suffix and inserted one per 288 packs.

		MT
Complete Set (15):		425.00
Common Player:		7.50
Inserted 1:288		
1	Ken Griffey Jr.	80.00
2	Frank Thomas	20.00
3	Alex Rodriguez	60.00
4	Cal Ripken Jr.	60.00
5	Mike Piazza	50.00
6	Mark McGwire	80.00
7	Greg Maddux	40.00
8	Andruw Jones	15.00
9	Chipper Jones	50.00
10	Derek Jeter	50.00
11	Tony Gwynn	40.00
12	Juan Gonzalez	25.00
13	Jose Cruz	7.50
14	Roger Clemens	25.00
15	Barry Bonds	20.00

1998 Ultra Diamond Producers

This 15-card insert captured players on a prismatic silver design, with a wood backdrop and a black felt frame around the border. Cards were seeded one per 288 Series I packs and numbered with a "DP" suffix.

		MT
Complete Set (15):		575.00
Common Player:		7.50
Inserted 1:288		
1	Ken Griffey Jr.	90.00
2	Andruw Jones	15.00
3	Alex Rodriguez	70.00
4	Frank Thomas	25.00
5	Cal Ripken Jr.	70.00
6	Derek Jeter	55.00
7	Chipper Jones	55.00
8	Greg Maddux	45.00
9	Mike Piazza	55.00
10	Juan Gonzalez	25.00
11	Jeff Bagwell	22.50
12	Tony Gwynn	45.00
13	Mark McGwire	90.00
14	Barry Bonds	22.50
15	Jose Cruz, Jr.	7.50

1998 Ultra Double Trouble

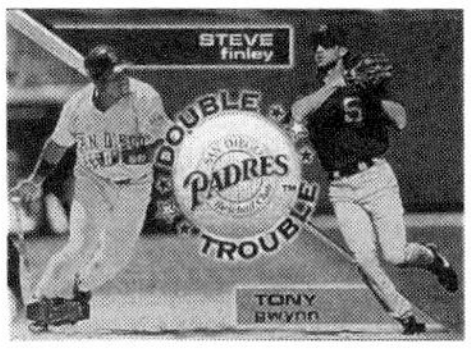

Double Trouble includes 20 cards and pairs two teammates on a horizontal format with the team's logo and the insert name featured in a silver holographic circle in the middle. These were numbered with a "DT" suffix and exclusive to Series I packs at a rate of one per four.

		MT
Complete Set (20):		10.00
Common Player:		.15
Inserted 1:4		
1	Ken Griffey Jr., Alex Rodriguez	2.00
2	Vladimir Guerrero, Pedro Martinez	.75
3	Andruw Jones, Kenny Lofton	.50
4	Chipper Jones, Greg Maddux	1.00
5	Derek Jeter, Tino Martinez	1.00
6	Frank Thomas, Albert Belle	.75
7	Cal Ripken Jr., Roberto Alomar	1.25
8	Mike Piazza, Hideo Nomo	.75
9	Darin Erstad, Jason Dickson	.15
10	Juan Gonzalez, Ivan Rodriguez	.75
11	Jeff Bagwell, Darryl Kile	.75
12	Tony Gwynn, Steve Finley	.75
13	Mark McGwire, Ray Lankford	2.00
14	Barry Bonds, Jeff Kent	.50
15	Andy Pettitte, Bernie Williams	.25
16	Mo Vaughn, Nomar Garciaparra	1.00
17	Matt Williams, Jim Thome	.15
18	Hideki Irabu, Mariano Rivera	.25
19	Roger Clemens, Jose Cruz, Jr.	.75
20	Manny Ramirez, David Justice	.60

1998 Ultra Fall Classics

This Series I insert pictures 15 stars over a green holographic background that contains the insert name in script. Fall Classics were inserted one per 18 packs and numbered with an "FC" suffix.

		MT
Complete Set (15):		100.00
Common Player:		3.00
Inserted 1:18		
1	Ken Griffey Jr.	15.00
2	Andruw Jones	4.00
3	Alex Rodriguez	12.00
4	Frank Thomas	7.50
5	Cal Ripken Jr.	12.00
6	Derek Jeter	10.00
7	Chipper Jones	10.00
8	Greg Maddux	8.00
9	Mike Piazza	10.00
10	Albert Belle	3.00
11	Juan Gonzalez	5.00
12	Jeff Bagwell	4.00
13	Tony Gwynn	8.00
14	Mark McGwire	15.00
15	Barry Bonds	4.00

1998 Ultra Kid Gloves

Kid Gloves featured top fielders in the game over an embossed glove background. Exclusive to Series I packs, they were inserted in one per eight packs and numbered with a "KG" suffix.

		MT
Complete Set (12):		15.00
Common Player:		.50
Inserted 1:8		
1	Andruw Jones	1.25
2	Alex Rodriguez	3.50
3	Derek Jeter	3.00
4	Chipper Jones	3.00
5	Darin Erstad	.75
6	Todd Walker	.50
7	Scott Rolen	1.50
8	Nomar Garciaparra	3.00
9	Jose Cruz, Jr.	.50
10	Charles Johnson	.50
11	Rey Ordonez	.50
12	Vladimir Guerrero	1.50

1998 Ultra Millennium Men

Millennium Men was a 15-card hobby-only insert exclusive to Series II packs. These tri-fold cards featured an embossed wax seal design and could be unfolded to reveal another shot of the player, team logo and statistics. They were numbered with an "MM" suffix and inserted every 35 packs.

		MT
Complete Set (15):		125.00
Common Player:		3.00
Inserted 1:35		
1	Jose Cruz	3.00
2	Ken Griffey Jr.	25.00
3	Cal Ripken Jr.	20.00
4	Derek Jeter	15.00
5	Andruw Jones	5.00
6	Alex Rodriguez	20.00
7	Chipper Jones	15.00
8	Scott Rolen	6.00
9	Nomar Garciaparra	15.00
10	Frank Thomas	8.00
11	Mike Piazza	15.00
12	Greg Maddux	12.00
13	Juan Gonzalez	8.00
14	Ben Grieve	4.00
15	Jaret Wright	3.00

1998 Ultra Notables

This 20-card insert pictured a player over a holographic background with either an American League or National League logo in the background. Notables were seeded one per four Series II packs and numbered with an "N" suffix.

		MT
Complete Set (20):		25.00
Common Player:		.50
Inserted 1:4		
1	Frank Thomas	1.50
2	Ken Griffey Jr.	5.00
3	Edgar Renteria	.50
4	Albert Belle	1.00
5	Juan Gonzalez	1.50
6	Jeff Bagwell	1.25
7	Mark McGwire	5.00
8	Barry Bonds	1.00
9	Scott Rolen	1.00
10	Mo Vaughn	.75
11	Andruw Jones	1.00
12	Chipper Jones	2.50
13	Tino Martinez	.50
14	Mike Piazza	2.50
15	Tony Clark	.50
16	Jose Cruz	.50
17	Nomar Garciaparra	2.50
18	Cal Ripken Jr.	3.50
19	Alex Rodriguez	3.50
20	Derek Jeter	2.50

1998 Ultra Power Plus

This 10-card insert was exclusive to Series I packs and seeded one per 36 packs. Cards pictured the player over an embossed blue background featuring plus signs. These were numbered with a "PP" suffix.

		MT
Complete Set (10):		75.00
Common Player:		3.00
Inserted 1:36		
1	Ken Griffey Jr.	25.00
2	Andruw Jones	6.00
3	Alex Rodriguez	15.00
4	Frank Thomas	8.00
5	Mike Piazza	10.00
6	Albert Belle	4.00
7	Juan Gonzalez	8.00
8	Jeff Bagwell	6.00
9	Barry Bonds	6.00
10	Jose Cruz, Jr.	3.00

1998 Ultra Prime Leather

This 18-card insert features top fielders on a leather-like card stock, with a large baseball in the background. Cards are seeded one per 144 Series I packs and numbered with a "PL" suffix.

		MT
Complete Set (18):		400.00
Common Player:		8.00
Inserted 1:144		
1	Ken Griffey Jr.	75.00
2	Andruw Jones	10.00
3	Alex Rodriguez	50.00
4	Frank Thomas	25.00
5	Cal Ripken Jr.	50.00
6	Derek Jeter	40.00
7	Chipper Jones	40.00
8	Greg Maddux	35.00
9	Mike Piazza	40.00
10	Albert Belle	15.00
11	Darin Erstad	10.00
12	Juan Gonzalez	25.00
13	Jeff Bagwell	20.00
14	Tony Gwynn	35.00
15	Roberto Alomar	15.00
16	Barry Bonds	20.00
17	Kenny Lofton	15.00
18	Jose Cruz, Jr.	8.00

1998 Ultra Rocket to Stardom

This 15-card insert set was exclusive to Series II packs and inserted one per 20 packs. Cards were in black-and-white and were die-cut and embossed. The insert contained a collection of top young stars and was numbered with an "RS" suffix.

		MT
Complete Set (15):		25.00
Common Player:		1.00
Inserted 1:20		
1	Ben Grieve	3.00
2	Magglio Ordonez	8.00
3	Travis Lee	1.50
4	Carl Pavano	1.00
5	Brian Rose	1.00
6	Brad Fullmer	1.50
7	Michael Coleman	1.00
8	Juan Encarnacion	1.00
9	Karim Garcia	1.00
10	Todd Helton	4.00
11	Richard Hildalgo	1.00
12	Paul Konerko	1.50
13	Rod Myers	1.00
14	Jaret Wright	1.50
15	Miguel Tejada	2.00

1998 Ultra Ticket Studs

Fifteen players are featured on fold-out game ticket-like cards in Ticket Studs. The cards arrived folded across the middle and open to reveal a full-length shot of the player with prismatic team color stripes in over a white background that has section, seat and row numbers. Cards were inserted one per 144 Series II packs and are numbered with a "TS" suffix.

		MT
Complete Set (15):		500.00
Common Player:		8.00
Inserted 1:144		
1	Travis Lee	8.00
2	Tony Gwynn	35.00
3	Scott Rolen	20.00
4	Nomar Garciaparra	50.00
5	Mike Piazza	50.00
6	Mark McGwire	75.00
7	Ken Griffey Jr.	75.00
8	Juan Gonzalez	25.00
9	Jose Cruz	8.00
10	Frank Thomas	25.00
11	Derek Jeter	50.00
12	Chipper Jones	50.00
13	Cal Ripken Jr.	60.00
14	Andruw Jones	15.00
15	Alex Rodriguez	60.00

Checklists with card numbers in parentheses ( ) indicates the numbers do not appear on the card.

1998 Ultra Top 30

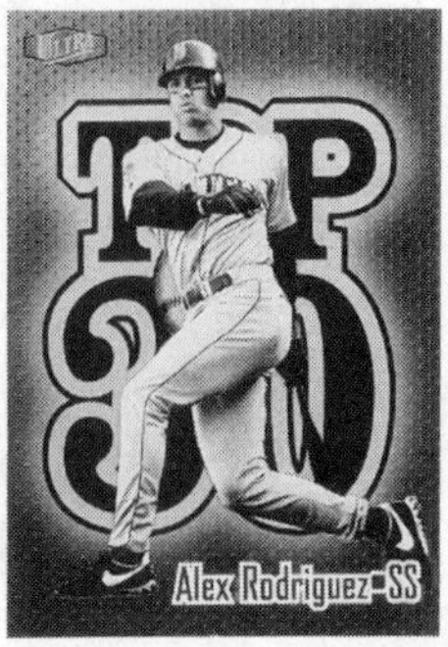

		MT
Complete Set (30):		30.00
Common Player:		.25
Inserted 1:1 R		
1	Barry Bonds	1.00
2	Ivan Rodriguez	1.00
3	Kenny Lofton	.75
4	Albert Belle	1.00
5	Mo Vaughn	.75
6	Jeff Bagwell	1.25
7	Mark McGwire	4.00
8	Darin Erstad	.50
9	Roger Clemens	1.50
10	Tony Gwynn	2.00
11	Scott Rolen	1.00
12	Hideo Nomo	.40
13	Juan Gonzalez	1.50
14	Mike Piazza	2.50
15	Greg Maddux	2.00
16	Chipper Jones	2.50
17	Andruw Jones	.75
18	Derek Jeter	2.50
19	Nomar Garciaparra	2.50
20	Alex Rodriguez	3.00
21	Frank Thomas	1.50
22	Cal Ripken Jr.	3.00
23	Ken Griffey Jr.	4.00
24	Jose Cruz Jr.	.25
25	Jaret Wright	.50
26	Travis Lee	.50
27	Wade Boggs	.40
28	Chuck Knoblauch	.25
29	Joe Carter	.25
30	Ben Grieve	.75

1998 Ultra Win Now

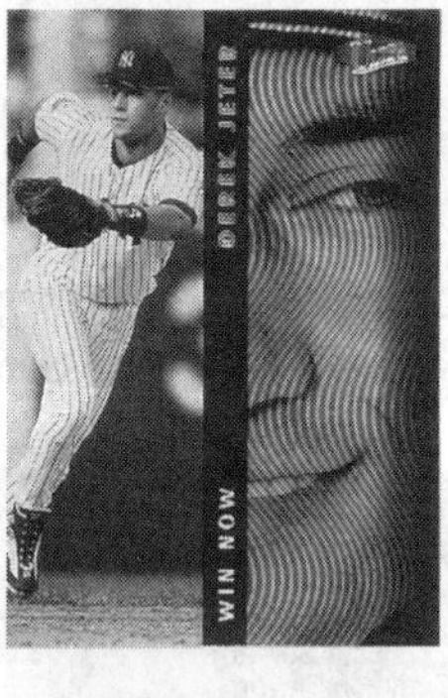

This Series II insert has 20 top players printed on plastic card stock, with a color shot of the player on the left side and a close-up shot on the right with black lines through it. Win Now cards were seeded one per 72 packs and numbered with a "WN" suffix.

		MT
Complete Set (20):		375.00
Common Player:		5.00
Inserted 1:72		
1	Alex Rodriguez	40.00
2	Andruw Jones	10.00
3	Cal Ripken Jr.	40.00
4	Chipper Jones	30.00
5	Darin Erstad	6.00
6	Derek Jeter	30.00
7	Frank Thomas	15.00
8	Greg Maddux	25.00
9	Hideo Nomo	5.00
10	Jeff Bagwell	12.00
11	Jose Cruz	5.00
12	Juan Gonzalez	15.00
13	Ken Griffey Jr.	50.00
14	Mark McGwire	50.00
15	Mike Piazza	30.00
16	Mo Vaughn	8.00
17	Nomar Garciaparra	30.00
18	Roger Clemens	15.00
19	Scott Rolen	10.00
20	Tony Gwynn	25.00

1999 Ultra Sample Sheet

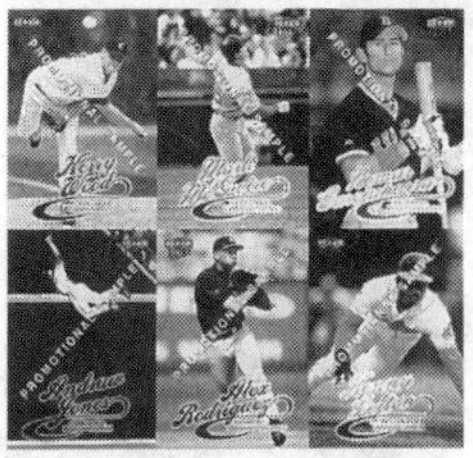

This six-card sheet was issued to introduce potential customers to '99 Ultra's base cards. The sheet measures 7-1/2" x 7". Cards are virtually identical to the issued version, except for the diagonal black-and-white "PROMOTIONAL SAMPLE" overprint on front and back.

		MT
Complete Sheet:		12.00
25	Andruw Jones	
69	Nomar Garciaparra	
70	Mark McGwire	
100	Kerry Wood	
113	Kenny Lofton	
173	Alex Rodriguez	

1999 Ultra

Base cards feature the full career stats by year in 15 categories and career highlights. There are short-printed subsets including Season Crowns (216-225) found 1:8 packs and Prospects (226-250) found 1:4 packs. Card fronts feature full bleed photography, and metallic foil stamping. There are three parallel versions: Gold Medallion seeded 1 per pack with Prospects 1:40 and Season Crowns 1:80. Platinum Medallions are numbered to 99 with Prospects numbered to 65 and Season Crowns numbered to 50 sets. One of One Masterpiece parallels also exist. Packs consist of 10 cards with an SRP of $2.69.

		MT
Complete Set (250):		80.00
Common Player:		.10
Common Season Crown:		.50
Inserted 1:8		
Common Prospect:		.25
Inserted 1:4		
Wax Box:		55.00
1	Greg Maddux	1.50
2	Greg Vaughn	.20
3	John Wetteland	.10
4	Tino Martinez	.25
5	Todd Walker	.15
6	Troy O'Leary	.10
7	Barry Larkin	.30
8	Mike Lansing	.10
9	Delino DeShields	.10
10	Brett Tomko	.10
11	Carlos Perez	.10
12	Mark Langston	.10
13	Jamie Moyer	.10
14	Jose Guillen	.15
15	Bartolo Colon	.10
16	Brady Anderson	.15
17	Walt Weiss	.10
18	Shane Reynolds	.15
19	David Segui	.10
20	Vladimir Guerrero	1.00
21	Freddy Garcia	.10
22	Carl Everett	.15
23	Jose Cruz Jr.	.20
24	David Ortiz	.10
25	Andruw Jones	.50
26	Darren Lewis	.10
27	Ray Lankford	.10
28	Wally Joyner	.10
29	Charles Johnson	.10
30	Derek Jeter	2.00
31	Sean Casey	.40
32	Bobby Bonilla	.15
33	Todd Zelle	.10
34	Todd Helton	.50
35	David Wells	.10
36	Darin Erstad	.25
37	Ivan Rodriguez	.75
38	Antonio Osuna	.10
39	Mickey Morandini	.10
40	Rusty Greer	.10
41	Rod Beck	.10
42	Larry Sutton	.10
43	Edgar Renteria	.10
44	Otis Nixon	.10
45	Eli Marrero	.10
46	Reggie Jefferson	.10
47	Trevor Hoffman	.10
48	Andres Galarraga	.40
49	Scott Brosius	.10
50	Vinny Castilla	.15
51	Bret Boone	.10
52	Masato Yoshii	.10
53	Matt Williams	.25
54	Robin Ventura	.20
55	Jay Powell	.10
56	Dean Palmer	.15
57	Eric Milton	.10
58	Willie McGee	.10
59	Tony Gwynn	1.50
60	Tom Gordon	.10
61	Dante Bichette	.25
62	Jaret Wright	.20
63	Devon White	.10
64	Frank Thomas	1.00
65	Mike Piazza	2.00
66	Jose Offerman	.10
67	Pat Meares	.10
68	Brian Meadows	.10
69	Nomar Garciaparra	2.00
70	Mark McGwire	4.00
71	Tony Graffanino	.10
72	Ken Griffey Jr.	3.00
73	Ken Caminiti	.20
74	Todd Jones	.10
75	A.J. Hinch	.10
76	Marquis Grissom	.10
77	Jay Buhner	.20
78	Albert Belle	.65
79	Brian Anderson	.10
80	Quinton McCracken	.10
81	Omar Vizquel	.15
82	Todd Stottlemyre	.15
83	Cal Ripken Jr.	2.50
84	Magglio Ordonez	.25
85	John Olerud	.25
86	Hal Morris	.10
87	Derrek Lee	.10
88	Doug Glanville	.10
89	Marty Cordova	.10
90	Kevin Brown	.20
91	Kevin Young	.10
92	Rico Brogna	.10
93	Wilson Alvarez	.10
94	Bob Wickman	.10
95	Jim Thome	.50
96	Mike Mussina	.50
97	Al Leiter	.15
98	Travis Lee	.25
99	Jeff King	.10
100	Kerry Wood	.50
101	Cliff Floyd	.10
102	Jose Valentin	.10
103	Manny Ramirez	1.00
104	Butch Huskey	.10
105	Scott Erickson	.15
106	Ray Durham	.10
107	Johnny Damon	.10
108	Craig Counsell	.10
109	Rolando Arrojo	.10
110	Bob Abreu	.10
111	Tony Womack	.10
112	Mike Stanley	.10
113	Kenny Lofton	.50
114	Eric Davis	.15
115	Jeff Conine	.10
116	Carlos Baerga	.10
117	Rondell White	.20
118	Billy Wagner	.10
119	Ed Sprague	.10
120	Jason Schmidt	.10
121	Edgar Martinez	.15
122	Travis Fryman	.15
123	Armando Benitez	.10
124	Matt Stairs	.10
125	Roberto Hernandez	.10
126	Jay Bell	.10
127	Justin Thompson	.10
128	John Jaha	.10
129	Mike Caruso	.10
130	Miguel Tejada	.20
131	Geoff Jenkins	.10
132	Wade Boggs	.25
133	Andy Benes	.10
134	Aaron Sele	.10
135	Bret Saberhagen	.10
136	Mariano Rivera	.20
137	Neifi Perez	.10
138	Paul Konerko	.20
139	Barry Bonds	.75
140	Garret Anderson	.10
141	Bernie Williams	.50
142	Gary Sheffield	.25
143	Rafael Palmeiro	.40
144	Orel Hershiser	.10
145	Craig Biggio	.30
146	Dmitri Young	.10
147	Damion Easley	.10
148	Henry Rodriguez	.10
149	Brad Radke	.10
150	Pedro Martinez	.75
151	Mike Lieberthal	.10
152	Jim Leyritz	.10
153	Chuck Knoblauch	.25
154	Darryl Kile	.10
155	Brian Jordan	.10
156	Chipper Jones	2.00
157	Pete Harnisch	.10
158	Moises Alou	.20
159	Ismael Valdes	.10
160	Stan Javier	.10
161	Mark Grace	.20
162	Jason Giambi	.10
163	Chuck Finley	.10
164	Juan Encarnacion	.10
165	Chan Ho Park	.15
166	Randy Johnson	.50
167	J.T. Snow	.10
168	Tim Salmon	.25
169	Brian Hunter	.10
170	Rickey Henderson	.25
171	Cal Eldred	.10
172	Curt Schilling	.20
173	Alex Rodriguez	2.50
174	Dustin Hermanson	.10
175	Mike Hampton	.10
176	Shawn Green	.40
177	Roberto Alomar	.50
178	Sandy Alomar Jr.	.20
179	Larry Walker	.40
180	Mo Vaughn	.50
181	Raul Mondesi	.25
182	Hideki Irabu	.20
183	Jim Edmonds	.20
184	Shawn Estes	.10
185	Tony Clark	.25
186	Dan Wilson	.10
187	Michael Tucker	.10
188	Jeff Shaw	.10
189	Mark Grudzielanek	.10
190	Roger Clemens	1.50
191	Juan Gonzalez	1.00
192	Sammy Sosa	2.00
193	Troy Percival	.10
194	Robb Nen	.10
195	Bill Mueller	.10
196	Ben Grieve	.40
197	Luis Gonzalez	.10
198	Will Clark	.25
199	Jeff Cirillo	.10
200	Scott Rolen	.75
201	Reggie Sanders	.10
202	Fred McGriff	.25
203	Denny Neagle	.10
204	Brad Fullmer	.15
205	Royce Clayton	.10
206	Jose Canseco	.60
207	Jeff Bagwell	1.00
208	Hideo Nomo	.25
209	Karim Garcia	.10
210	Kenny Rogers	.10
211	Checklist (Kerry Wood)	.40
212	Checklist (Alex Rodriguez)	1.00
213	Checklist (Cal Ripken Jr.)	1.00
214	Checklist (Frank Thomas)	.50
215	Checklist (Ken Griffey Jr.)	1.50
216	Alex Rodriguez (Season Crowns)	5.00
217	Greg Maddux (Season Crowns)	3.00
218	Juan Gonzalez (Season Crowns)	2.00
219	Ken Griffey Jr. (Season Crowns)	6.00
220	Kerry Wood (Season Crowns)	1.00
221	Mark McGwire (Season Crowns)	6.00
222	Mike Piazza (Season Crowns)	4.00
223	Rickey Henderson (Season Crowns)	.50
224	Sammy Sosa (Season Crowns)	4.00
225	Travis Lee (Season Crowns)	.50
226	Gabe Alvarez (Prospects)	.25
227	Matt Anderson (Prospects)	1.00
228	Adrian Beltre (Prospects)	.75
229	Orlando Cabrera (Prospects)	.25
230	Orlando Hernandez (Prospects)	2.50

231 Aramis Ramirez (Prospects) .50
232 Troy Glaus (Prospects) 4.00
233 Gabe Kapler (Prospects) 3.00
234 Jeremy Giambi (Prospects) 1.50
235 Derrick Gibson (Prospects) .25
236 Carlton Loewer (Prospects) .25
237 Mike Frank (Prospects) .25
238 Carlos Guillen (Prospects) .25
239 Alex Gonzalez (Prospects) .25
240 Enrique Wilson (Prospects) .25
241 J.D. Drew (Prospects) 6.00
242 Bruce Chen (Prospects) .25
243 Ryan Minor (Prospects) 1.50
244 Preston Wilson (Prospects) .25
245 Josh Booty (Prospects) .25
246 Luis Ordaz (Prospects) .25
247 George Lombard (Prospects) .75
248 Matt Clement (Prospects) .25
249 Eric Chavez (Prospects) .75
250 Corey Koskie (Prospects) .75

1999 Ultra Gold Medallion

The basic cards (#1-215) in this parallel set are found one per pack, while the short-printed versions are seen one per 40 packs (Prospects) or one per 80 packs (Season Crowns). Sharing the photos and format of the regular-issue cards, these inserts have a gold-foil background on front. On back, "GOLD MEDALLION EDITION" is printed in gold foil.

MT
Common Player (1-215): .50
Stars/RCs 2X
Season Crowns (216-225): 4X
Prospects (226-250): 3X
(See 1999 Ultra for checklist and base card values.)

1999 Ultra Platinum Medallion

The basic cards (#1-215) in this parallel set are found in an individually serial numbered edition of 99. The short-printed cards were released in editions of 65 (Prospects) and 50 (Season Crowns). Sharing the photos and format of the regular-issue cards, these inserts have a silver-foil background on front. On back, "PLATINUM MEDALLION" is printed in silver foil along with the serial number.

MT
Common Player (1-215): 6.00
Stars/RCs: 30X
Season Crowns (216-225): 30X
Prospects (226-250): 6X
(See 1999 Ultra for checklist and base card values.)

1999 Ultra Masterpiece

This top-of-the-line parallel to '99 Ultra consists of a 1 of 1 version of each regular card.

MT
Common Player: 100.00
(Individual player cards cannot be valued due to scarcity and fluctuating demand.)

1999 Ultra Book On

This 20-card set features insider scouting reports on the game's best players, utilizing embossing and gold foil stamping. These are found 1:6 packs.

MT
Complete Set (20): 50.00
Common Player: 1.00
Inserted 1:6
1 Kerry Wood 1.50
2 Ken Griffey Jr. 8.00
3 Frank Thomas 2.50
4 Albert Belle 1.50
5 Juan Gonzalez 3.00
6 Jeff Bagwell 2.50
7 Mark McGwire 8.00
8 Barry Bonds 2.00
9 Andruw Jones 1.50
10 Mo Vaughn 1.00
11 Scott Rolen 1.50
12 Travis Lee 1.00
13 Tony Gwynn 4.00
14 Greg Maddux 4.00
15 Mike Piazza 5.00
16 Chipper Jones 5.00
17 Nomar Garciaparra 5.00
18 Cal Ripken Jr. 6.50
19 Derek Jeter 5.00
20 Alex Rodriguez 6.50

1999 Ultra Damage Inc.

This 15-card insert set has a business card design, for players who mean business. These are seeded 1:72 packs.

MT
Complete Set (15): 275.00
Common Player: 8.00
Inserted 1:72
1 Alex Rodriguez 30.00
2 Greg Maddux 20.00
3 Cal Ripken Jr. 30.00
4 Chipper Jones 25.00
5 Derek Jeter 25.00
6 Frank Thomas 12.00
7 Juan Gonzalez 15.00
8 Ken Griffey Jr. 40.00
9 Kerry Wood 8.00
10 Mark McGwire 40.00
11 Mike Piazza 25.00
12 Nomar Garciaparra 25.00
13 Scott Rolen 10.00
14 Tony Gwynn 20.00
15 Travis Lee 8.00

1999 Ultra Diamond Producers

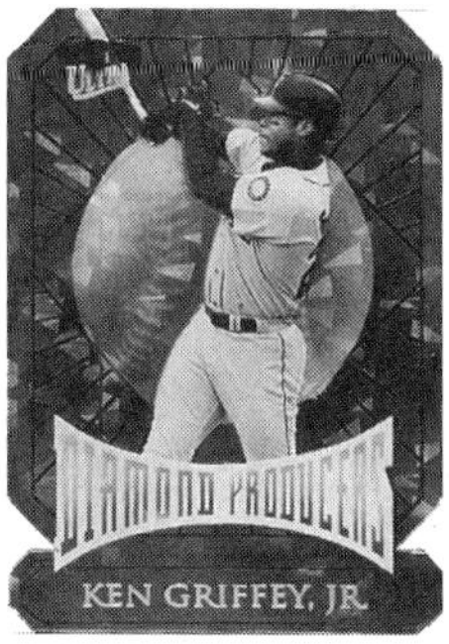

This die-cut set uses full-foil plastic with custom embossing. Baseball's biggest stars comprise this 10-card set, which are seeded 1:288 packs.

MT
Complete Set (10): 400.00
Common Player: 20.00
Inserted 1:288
1 Ken Griffey Jr. 80.00
2 Frank Thomas 25.00
3 Alex Rodriguez 50.00
4 Cal Ripken Jr. 50.00
5 Mike Piazza 40.00
6 Mark McGwire 80.00
7 Greg Maddux 40.00
8 Kerry Wood 20.00
9 Chipper Jones 40.00
10 Derek Jeter 40.00

1999 Ultra RBI Kings

Found exclusively in retail packs, this 30-card set showcases baseball's top run producers. These are seeded one per retail pack.

MT
Complete Set (30): 25.00
Common Player: .25
Inserted 1:1 R
1 Rafael Palmeiro .50
2 Mo Vaughn .75
3 Ivan Rodriguez 1.00
4 Barry Bonds 1.00
5 Albert Belle .75
6 Jeff Bagwell 1.50
7 Mark McGwire 4.00
8 Darin Erstad .50
9 Manny Ramirez 1.50
10 Chipper Jones 2.50
11 Jim Thome .40
12 Scott Rolen 1.00
13 Tony Gwynn 2.00
14 Juan Gonzalez 1.50
15 Mike Piazza 2.50
16 Sammy Sosa 3.00
17 Andruw Jones .50
18 Derek Jeter 2.50
19 Nomar Garciaparra 2.50
20 Alex Rodriguez 3.00
21 Frank Thomas 1.50
22 Cal Ripken Jr. 3.00
23 Ken Griffey Jr. 4.00
24 Travis Lee .40
25 Paul O'Neill .25
26 Greg Vaughn .25
27 Andres Galarraga .50
28 Tino Martinez .40
29 Jose Canseco .75
30 Ben Grieve .75

1999 Ultra Thunderclap

This set highlights the top hitters in the game, such as Nomar Garciaparra. Card fronts feature a lightning bolt in the background and are seeded 1:36 packs.

MT
Complete Set (15): 120.00
Common Player: 3.00
Inserted 1:36
1 Alex Rodriguez 15.00
2 Andruw Jones 4.00
3 Cal Ripken Jr. 15.00
4 Chipper Jones 12.00
5 Darin Erstad 3.00
6 Derek Jeter 12.00
7 Frank Thomas 8.00
8 Jeff Bagwell 8.00
9 Juan Gonzalez 9.00
10 Ken Griffey Jr. 25.00
11 Mark McGwire 25.00
12 Mike Piazza 12.00
13 Travis Lee 3.00
14 Nomar Garciaparra 12.00
15 Scott Rolen 5.00

1999 Ultra World Premiere

This 15-card set highlights rookies who made debuts in 1998, including J.D. Drew and Ben Grieve. These are seeded 1:18 packs.

MT
Complete Set (15): 20.00
Common Player: 1.00
Inserted 1:18
1 Gabe Alvarez 1.00
2 Kerry Wood 1.50
3 Orlando Hernandez 2.50
4 Mike Caruso 1.00
5 Matt Anderson 1.00
6 Randall Simon 1.00
7 Adrian Beltre 1.50
8 Scott Elarton 1.00
9 Karim Garcia 1.00
10 Mike Frank 1.00
11 Richard Hidalgo 1.00
12 Paul Konerko 1.00
13 Travis Lee 1.50
14 J.D. Drew 5.00
15 Miguel Tejada 1.00

2000 Ultra Sample

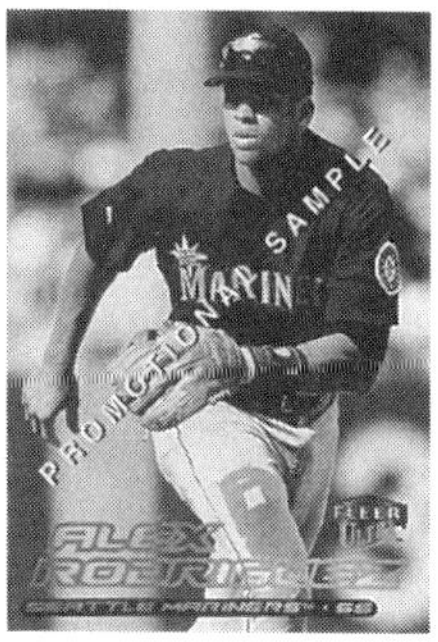

MT
1 Alex Rodriguez 3.00

2000 Ultra

The 300-card base set features a borderless design with silver holographic foil stamping on the card front. Card backs have an action image along with complete year-by-year statistics. The base set includes a 50-card short-printed Prospects (1:4) subset. A Masterpiece one-of-one parallel was produced.

MT
Complete Set (300): 120.00
Common Player: .10
Common Player (251-300): .75
Inserted 1:4
Wax Box: 70.00
1 Alex Rodriguez 2.00
2 Shawn Green .40
3 Magglio Ordonez .40
4 Tony Gwynn 1.50
5 Joe McEwing .10
6 Jose Rosado .10
7 Sammy Sosa 2.00
8 Gary Sheffield .25
9 Mickey Morandini .10
10 Mo Vaughn .60
11 Todd Hollandsworth .10
12 Tom Gordon .10
13 Charles Johnson .10
14 Derek Bell .10
15 Kevin Young .10
16 Jay Buhner .20
17 J.T. Snow .10

18	Jay Bell	.10
19	John Rocker	.10
20	Ivan Rodriguez	.75
21	Pokey Reese	.10
22	Paul O'Neill	.25
23	Ronnie Belliard	.10
24	Ryan Rupe	.10
25	Travis Fryman	.20
26	Trot Nixon	.10
27	Wally Joyner	.10
28	Andy Pettitte	.25
29	Dan Wilson	.10
30	Orlando Hernandez	.25
31	Dmitri Young	.10
32	Edgar Renteria	.10
33	Eric Karros	.20
34	Fernando Seguignol	.10
35	Jason Kendall	.20
36	Jeff Shaw	.10
37	Matt Lawton	.10
38	Robin Ventura	.25
39	Scott Williamson	.10
40	Ben Grieve	.40
41	Billy Wagner	.10
42	Javy Lopez	.20
43	Joe Randa	.10
44	Neifi Perez	.10
45	David Justice	.25
46	Ray Durham	.10
47	Dustin Hermanson	.10
48	Andres Galarraga	.50
49	Brad Fullmer	.10
50	Nomar Garciaparra	2.00
51	David Cone	.20
52	David Nilsson	.10
53	David Wells	.10
54	Miguel Tejada	.10
55	Ismael Valdes	.10
56	Jose Lima	.10
57	Juan Encarnacion	.10
58	Fred McGriff	.25
59	Kenny Rogers	.10
60	Vladimir Guerrero	1.00
61	Benito Santiago	.10
62	Chris Singleton	.10
63	Carlos Lee	.10
64	Sean Casey	.40
65	Tom Goodwin	.10
66	Todd Hundley	.10
67	Ellis Burks	.10
68	Tim Hudson	.50
69	Matt Stairs	.10
70	Chipper Jones	2.00
71	Craig Biggio	.50
72	Brian Rose	.10
73	Carlos Delgado	.50
74	Eddie Taubensee	.10
75	John Smoltz	.20
76	Ken Caminiti	.20
77	Rafael Palmeiro	.50
78	Sidney Ponson	.10
79	Todd Helton	.40
80	Juan Gonzalez	.75
81	Bruce Aven	.10
82	Desi Relaford	.10
83	Johnny Damon	.10
84	Albert Belle	.60
85	Mark McGwire	4.00
86	Rico Brogna	.10
87	Tom Glavine	.20
88	Harold Baines	.10
89	Chad Allen	.10
90	Barry Bonds	.75
91	Mark Grace	.25
92	Paul Byrd	.10
93	Roberto Alomar	.50
94	Roberto Hernandez	.10
95	Steve Finley	.10
96	Bret Boone	.10
97	Charles Nagy	.10
98	Eric Chavez	.10
99	Jamie Moyer	.10
100	Ken Griffey Jr.	3.00
101	J.D. Drew	.75
102	Todd Stottlemyre	.10
103	Tony Fernandez	.10
104	Jeromy Burnitz	.10
105	Jeremy Giambi	.10
106	Livan Hernandez	.10
107	Marlon Anderson	.10
108	Troy Glaus	.40
109	Troy O'Leary	.10
110	Scott Rolen	.75
111	Bernard Gilkey	.10
112	Brady Anderson	.20
113	Chuck Knoblauch	.30
114	Jeff Weaver	.25
115	B.J. Surhoff	.10
116	Alex Gonzalez	.10
117	Vinny Castilla	.10
118	Tim Salmon	.25
119	Brian Jordan	.10
120	Corey Koskie	.10
121	Dean Palmer	.10
122	Gabe Kapler	.25
123	Jim Edmonds	.10
124	John Jaha	.10
125	Mark Grudzielanek	.10
126	Mike Bordick	.10
127	Mike Lieberthal	.10
128	Pete Harnisch	.10
129	Russ Ortiz	.10
130	Kevin Brown	.20
131	Troy Percival	.10
132	Alex Gonzalez	.10
133	Bartolo Colon	.10
134	John Valentin	.10
135	Jose Hernandez	.10
136	Marquis Grissom	.10
137	Wade Boggs	.40
138	Dante Bichette	.25
139	Bobby Higginson	.10
140	Frank Thomas	1.00
141	Geoff Jenkins	.10
142	Jason Giambi	.10
143	Jeff Cirillo	.10
144	Sandy Alomar Jr.	.20
145	Luis Gonzalez	.10
146	Preston Wilson	.10
147	Carlos Beltran	.40
148	Greg Vaughn	.25
149	Carlos Febles	.10
150	Jose Canseco	.75
151	Kris Benson	.10
152	Chuck Finley	.10
153	Michael Barrett	.10
154	Rey Ordonez	.10
155	Adrian Beltre	.25
156	Andruw Jones	.50
157	Barry Larkin	.40
158	Brian Giles	.10
159	Carl Everett	.10
160	Manny Ramirez	.75
161	Darryl Kile	.10
162	Edgar Martinez	.10
163	Jeff Kent	.10
164	Matt Williams	.25
165	Mike Piazza	2.00
166	Pedro J. Martinez	.75
167	Ray Lankford	.10
168	Roger Cedeno	.10
169	Ron Coomer	.10
170	Cal Ripken Jr.	2.50
171	Jose Offerman	.10
172	Kenny Lofton	.60
173	Kent Bottenfield	.10
174	Kevin Millwood	.25
175	Omar Daal	.10
176	Orlando Cabrera	.10
177	Pat Hentgen	.10
178	Tino Martinez	.40
179	Tony Clark	.25
180	Roger Clemens	1.00
181	Brad Radke	.10
182	Darin Erstad	.30
183	Jose Jimenez	.10
184	Jim Thome	.40
185	John Wetteland	.10
186	Justin Thompson	.10
187	John Hamala	.10
188	Lee Stevens	.10
189	Miguel Cairo	.10
190	Mike Mussina	.60
191	Raul Mondesi	.20
192	Armando Rios	.10
193	Trevor Hoffman	.10
194	Tony Batista	.10
195	Will Clark	.40
196	Brad Ausmus	.10
197	Chili Davis	.10
198	Cliff Floyd	.10
199	Curt Schilling	.20
200	Derek Jeter	2.00
201	Henry Rodriguez	.10
202	Jose Cruz Jr.	.10
203	Omar Vizquel	.10
204	Randy Johnson	.50
205	Reggie Sanders	.10
206	Al Leiter	.20
207	Damion Easley	.10
208	David Bell	.10
209	Fernando Tatis	.25
210	Kerry Wood	.25
211	Kevin Appier	.10
212	Mariano Rivera	.25
213	Mike Caruso	.10
214	Moises Alou	.25
215	Randy Winn	.10
216	Roy Halladay	.10
217	Shannon Stewart	.10
218	Todd Walker	.10
219	Jim Parque	.10
220	Travis Lee	.25
221	Andy Ashby	.10
222	Ed Sprague	.10
223	Larry Walker	.50
224	Rick Helling	.10
225	Rusty Greer	.10
226	Todd Zeile	.10
227	Freddy Garcia	.50
228	Hideo Nomo	.25
229	Marty Cordova	.10
230	Greg Maddux	1.50
231	Rondell White	.25
232	Paul Konerko	.20
233	Warren Morris	.10
234	Bernie Williams	.50
235	Bobby Abreu	.10
236	John Olerud	.25
237	Doug Glanville	.10
238	Eric Young	.10
239	Robb Nen	.10
240	Jeff Bagwell	.75
241	Sterling Hitchcock	.10
242	Todd Greene	.10
243	Bill Mueller	.10
244	Rickey Henderson	.25
245	Chan Ho Park	.20
246	Jason Schmidt	.10
247	Jeff Zimmerman	.10
248	Jermaine Dye	.10
249	Randall Simon	.10
250	Richie Sexson	.10
251	Micah Bowie	.75
252	Joe Nathan	.75
253	Chris Woodward	.75
254	Lance Berkman	.75
255	Ruben Mateo	2.00
256	Russell Branyan	.75
257	Randy Wolf	1.00
258	A.J. Burnett	3.00
259	Mark Quinn	3.00
260	Buddy Carlyle	.75
261	Ben Davis	.75
262	Yamid Haad	.75
263	Mike Colangelo	.75
264	Rick Ankiel	25.00
265	Jacque Jones	.75
266	Kelly Dransfeldt	.75
267	Matt Riley	4.00
268	Adam Kennedy	.75
269	Octavio Dotel	.75
270	Francisco Cordero	.75
271	Wilton Veras	2.00
272	Calvin Pickering	1.50
273	Alex Sanchez	.75
274	Tony Armas, Jr.	1.50
275	Pat Burrell	8.00
276	Chad Meyers	1.00
277	Ben Petrick	.10
278	Ramon Hernandez	.75
279	Ed Yarnall	1.50
280	Erubiel Durazo	2.00
281	Vernon Wells	1.50
282	Gary Matthews	.75
283	Kip Wells	1.50
284	Peter Bergeron	1.00
285	Travis Dawkins	3.00
286	Jorge Toca	3.00
287	Cole Liniak	1.00
288	Chad Hermansen	3.00
289	Eric Gagne	2.00
290	Chad Hutchinson	2.00
291	Eric Munson	8.00
292	(Wiki Gonzalez)	1.50
293	(Alfonso Soriano)	8.00
294	Trent Durrington	.75
295	(Ben Molina)	1.00
296	Aaron Myette	.75
297	(Willi Mo Pena)	6.00
298	Kevin Barker	.75
299	(Geoff Blum)	.75
300	Josh Beckett	10.00

2000 Ultra Gold Medallion

A parallel to the 300-card base set these have gold foil stamping over a metallic gold background. Cards 1-250 are seeded one per pack, Prospects 251-300 are seeded 1:24 packs. Card backs are numbered with a "G" suffix.

Stars: 2x
Young Stars: 1.5x
Inserted 1:1
Prospects (251-300): 2x to 4x
Inserted 1:24
(See 2000 Ultra for checklist and base card values.)

2000 Ultra Platinum Medallion

Platinum Medallion are a parallel to the 300-card base set and are die-cut like the Gold Medallion parallel inserts. Card fronts are stamped with silver foil over a metallic silver background. Card backs are serially numbered with cards 1-250 limited to 50 sets and Prospects limited to 25 numbered sets. Card backs are numbered with a "P" suffix.

Stars: 50x to 75x
Young Stars: 30x to 50x
Production 50 sets
Prospects (251-300): 6x to 12x
Production 25 sets
(See 2000 Ultra for checklist and base card values.)

2000 Ultra Club 3000

This three-card set is die-cut around the number 3,000 and commemorates 3,000 hit club members Wade Boggs, Tony Gwynn and Carl Yastrzemski. These were seeded 1:24 packs.

	MT
Complete Set (3):	10.00
Common Player:	3.00
Inserted 1:24	
Wade Boggs	4.00
Tony Gwynn	6.00
Carl Yastrzemski	3.00

2000 Ultra Club 3000 Memorabilia

Each featured player has a total of four different memorabilia based inserts: hat, jersey, bat/jersey and bat/hat/jersey.

	MT
Common Card:	75.00
Wade Boggs bat (250)	90.00
Wade Boggs hat (100)	120.00
Wade Boggs jersey (440)	75.00
Wade Boggs bat/jersey (100)	150.00
W Boggs bat/hat/jersey (25)	400.00
Tony Gwynn bat (260)	150.00
Tony Gwynn hat (115)	200.00
Tony Gwynn jersey (450)	100.00
T Gwynn bat/jersey (100)	250.00
T Gwynn bat/jersey/hat (25)	700.00
C. Yaz (bat (250)	125.00
C. Yaz hat (100)	200.00
C. Yaz jersey (440)	100.00
C. Yaz bat/jersey (100)	200.00
C. Yaz bat/hat/jersey (25)	600.00

2000 Ultra Crunch Time

This 15-card insert set is printed on suede stock with gold foil stamping. These were seeded 1:72 packs and numbered with a "CT" suffix on the card back.

		MT
Complete Set (15):		250.00
Common Player:		6.00
Inserted 1:72		
1	Nomar Garciaparra	25.00
2	Ken Griffey Jr.	40.00
3	Mark McGwire	50.00
4	Alex Rodriguez	25.00
5	Derek Jeter	25.00
6	Sammy Sosa	25.00
7	Mike Piazza	25.00
8	Cal Ripken Jr.	30.00
9	Frank Thomas	12.00
10	Juan Gonzalez	10.00
11	J.D. Drew	10.00
12	Greg Maddux	20.00
13	Tony Gwynn	20.00
14	Vladimir Guerrero	12.00
15	Ben Grieve	6.00

Checklists with card numbers in parentheses ( ) indicates the numbers do not appear on the card.

2000 Ultra Diamond Mine

These were printed on a silver foil card front with Diamond Mine stamped in the background of the player image. These were inserted 1:6 packs and numbered with a "DM" suffix on the card back.

		MT
Complete Set (15):		45.00
Common Player:		1.00
Inserted 1:6		
1	Greg Maddux	3.00
2	Mark McGwire	8.00
3	Ken Griffey Jr.	6.00
4	Cal Ripken Jr.	5.00
5	Nomar Garciaparra	4.00
6	Mike Piazza	4.00
7	Alex Rodriguez	4.00
8	Frank Thomas	2.00
9	Juan Gonzalez	1.50
10	Derek Jeter	4.00
11	Tony Gwynn	3.00
12	Chipper Jones	4.00
13	Sammy Sosa	4.00
14	Roger Clemens	2.00
15	Vladimir Guerrero	2.00

2000 Ultra Feel the Game

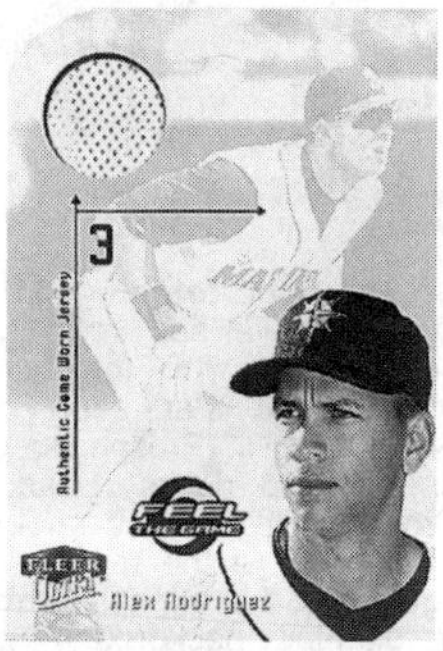

These memorabilia based inserts have a piece of game worn jersey or batting glove embedded into the card front.

	MT
Complete Set (15):	1400.
Common Player:	40.00
Roberto Alomar	75.00
J.D. Drew	75.00
Tony Gwynn	150.00
Randy Johnson	75.00
Greg Maddux	175.00
Edgar Martinez	40.00
Pedro Martinez	100.00
Kevin Millwood	60.00
Cal Ripken Jr.	200.00
Alex Rodriguez	200.00
Scott Rolen	75.00
Curt Schilling	40.00
Chipper Jones	175.00
Frank Thomas	125.00
Robin Ventura	50.00

2000 Ultra Fresh Ink

These autographed cards have the words "Fresh Ink" printed continually in the background image of the player. The signature is in a designated blank box intended for the autograph. Production numbers vary from player to player and are listed in parentheses after the player name.

		MT
Common Player:		10.00
1	Bobby Abreu (400)	10.00
2	Chad Allen (1,000)	10.00
3	Marlon Anderson (1,000)	10.00
4	Glen Barker (1,000)	10.00
5	Michael Barrett (1,000)	15.00
6	Carlos Beltran (1,000)	30.00
7	Adrian Beltre (1,000)	20.00
8	Wade Boggs (250)	50.00
9	Barry Bonds (250)	75.00
10	Peter Bergeron (1,000)	10.00
11	Pat Burrell (500)	75.00
12	Roger Cedeno (500)	10.00
13	Eric Chavez (750)	20.00
14	Bruce Chen (600)	15.00
15	Johnny Damon (750)	15.00
16	Ben Davis (1,000)	10.00
17	Carlos Delgado (300)	40.00
18	Einar Diaz (1,000)	10.00
19	Octavio Dotel (1,000)	10.00
20	J.D. Drew (600)	50.00
21	Scott Elarton (1,000)	10.00
22	Freddy Garcia (500)	25.00
23	Jeremy Giambi (1,000)	10.00
24	Troy Glaus (500)	30.00
25	Shawn Green (350)	30.00
26	Tony Gwynn (250)	120.00
27	Richard Hidalgo (500)	10.00
28	Bobby Higginson (1,000)	15.00
29	Tim Hudson (1,000)	20.00
30	Norm Hutchins (1,000)	10.00
31	Derek Jeter (95)	300.00
32	Randy Johnson (150)	50.00
33	Gabe Kapler (750)	25.00
34	Jason Kendall (400)	20.00
35	Paul Konerko (500)	15.00
36	Matt Lawton (1,000)	10.00
37	Carlos Lee (1,000)	15.00
38	Jose Macias (1,000)	10.00
39	Greg Maddux (250)	160.00
40	Ruben Mateo (250)	25.00
41	Kevin Millwood (500)	20.00
42	Warren Morris (1,000)	10.00
43	Eric Munson (1,000)	30.00
44	Heath Murray (1,000)	10.00
45	Joe Nathan (1,000)	10.00
46	Magglio Ordonez (350)	20.00
47	Angel Pena (1,000)	10.00
48	Cal Ripken Jr. (350)	200.00
49	Alex Rodriguez (350)	150.00
50	Scott Rolen (250)	50.00
51	Ryan Rupe (1,000)	10.00
52	Curt Schilling (375)	20.00
53	Randall Simon (1,000)	10.00
54	Alfonso Soriano (1,000)	40.00
55	Shannon Stewart (300)	10.00
56	Miguel Tejada (1,000)	10.00
57	Frank Thomas (150)	140.00
58	Jeff Weaver (1,000)	15.00
59	Randy Wolf (1,000)	10.00
60	Ed Yarnall (1,000)	20.00
61	Kevin Young (1,000)	10.00
62	Tony Gwynn, Wade Boggs, Nolan Ryan (100)	600.00
63	Rick Ankiel (500)	75.00

2000 Ultra Swing King

Printed on a clear, plastic stock this 10-card set features the top hitters in the game. Card fronts also utilize silver foil stamping. These were seeded 1:24 packs and are numbered on the card back with an "SK" suffix.

		MT
Complete Set (10):		90.00
Common Player:		3.00
Inserted 1:24		
1	Cal Ripken Jr.	12.00
2	Nomar Garciaparra	10.00
3	Frank Thomas	5.00
4	Tony Gwynn	8.00
5	Ken Griffey Jr.	15.00
6	Chipper Jones	10.00
7	Mark McGwire	20.00
8	Sammy Sosa	10.00
9	Derek Jeter	10.00
10	Alex Rodriguez	10.00

2000 Ultra Ultra Talented

Available exclusively in hobby packs these were printed on a holofoil background with gold foil stamping. Each card is serially numbered to 100 and are numbered on the card back with a "UT" suffix.

		MT
Complete Set (10):		850.00
Common Player:		15.00
Production 100 sets		
1	Sammy Sosa	100.00
2	Derek Jeter	100.00
3	Alex Rodriguez	100.00
4	Mike Piazza	100.00
5	Ken Griffey Jr.	160.00
6	Nomar Garciaparra	100.00
7	Mark McGwire	180.00
8	Cal Ripken Jr.	120.00
9	Frank Thomas	50.00
10	J.D. Drew	40.00

2000 Ultra World Premiere

This insert set highlights ten young potential stars on a die-cut, silver foil etched design. These were inserted 1:12 packs and are numbered with a "WP" suffix on the card back.

		MT
Complete Set (10):		30.00
Common Player:		.75
Inserted 1:12		
1	Ruben Mateo	2.00
2	Lance Berkman	.75
3	Octavio Dotel	.75
4	Joe McEwing	1.50
5	Ben Davis	.75
6	Warren Morris	.75
7	Carlos Lee	1.00
8	Rick Ankiel	15.00
9	Adam Kennedy	.75
10	Tim Hudson	4.00

1992 Ultra-Pro

This 18-card set was issued one per box of Rembrandt's Ultra-Pro sportscard plastic sheets. Because no license was obtained from Major League Baseball, the players are pictured either in street clothes or in photos from which uniform logos have been removed. Cards measure the standard 2-1/2" x 3-1/2" and have black borders on front and back. Backs have a second color photo, along with a paragraph about the player and a large Ultra-Pro hologram. Backs of some cards mention a "limited edition" of 250,000. Complete sets were available by mail from Rembrandt for about $40 plus proofs of purchase.

		MT
Complete Set (20):		10.00
Common Player:		.50
P1	Bobby Bonilla (holding bat behind neck)	.50
P2	Bobby Bonilla (waist-up portrait)	.50
P3	Bobby Bonilla (swinging golf club)	.50
P4	Jose Canseco (in car)	1.50
P5	Jose Canseco (batting)	1.50
P6	Jose Canseco (bat on shoulder)	1.50
P7	Hal Morris (bat on shoulder)	.50
P8	Hal Morris (holding tennis racket)	.50
P9	Hal Morris (waist-up pose)	.50
P10	Scott Erickson (skis on shoulder)	.50
P11	Scott Erickson (waist-up pose)	.50
P12	Scott Erickson (batting)	.50
P13	Danny Tartabull (batting)	.50
P14	Danny Tartabull (bat on shoulder)	.50
P15	Danny Tartabull (holding dumbbell)	.50
P16	Bobby Bonilla, Danny Tartabull (posed in tuxedos)	.50
P17	Bobby Bonilla (in tuxedo)	.50
P18	Bobby Bonilla, Danny Tartabull (hologram)	1.50
P20	Bobby Bonilla, Danny Tartabull	.50

1993 Ultra-Pro Eric Karros

The 1992 National League Rookie of the Year, Los Angeles Dodgers first baseman Eric Karros, is featured in this set from Rembrandt, makers of Ultra-Pro sportscard plastic pages. Because the cards are not licensed by MLB, the team logo has been removed from the uniforms, or photos are taken in street clothes. Card backs feature a portrait photo along with a paragraph about the player, and a few stats. A large Ultra-Pro hologram is at bottom, along with a notation that each card is from a "limited edition" of 100,000.

		MT
Complete Set (5):		2.00
Common Card:		.50
1	Eric Karros (batting)	.50
2	Eric Karros (fielding)	.50
3	Eric Karros (lifting dumbbells)	.50
4	Eric Karros (posed in tuxedo)	.50
5	Eric Karros, Dave Hansen (in tuxedos, bats on shoulders)	.50

1994 Ultra-Pro Mike Piazza

This set, featuring 1993 N.L. Rookie of the Year Mike Piazza, was issued at the rate of one card per 200-count box of Ultra-Pro card holders and one per box of the company's plastic sheets. Additionally, complete sets were available via a mail-in offer in hobby publications. Seven of the cards feature traditional printing while a sixth card, scarcer than the others, was produced with chromium technology. Because the cards are licensed only by the player, and not Major League Baseball, Piazza appears in street clothes or in uniforms on which Dodgers logos are not shown. Each of the five regular cards states on back that it is from a limited edition of 100,000, the chromium card has an announced production of 20,000. All cards carry an Ultra-Pro hologram on back.

		MT
Complete Set (8):		35.00
Common Card:		3.00
1	Mike Piazza (tuxedo)	3.00
2	Mike Piazza (blocking ball)	3.00
3	Mike Piazza (with golf club)	3.00
4	Mike Piazza (throwing)	3.00
5	Mike Piazza (with free weight)	3.00
6	Mike Piazza (chromium)	10.00
--	Mike Piazza (holding chrome card)	5.00
--	Mike Piazza (holding cards in sheet)	5.00

1996 Ultra-Pro Mike Piazza

This puzzle set of cards was distributed one per box of 100-count plastic sheets. When arranged numerically in a nine-pocket sheet, the fronts form a painting of spokesman Mike Piazza in action. Backs also form a composite picture with action photos of the Dodgers catcher on each card. Because the set is not licensed by Major League Baseball, Dodgers uniform logos are not shown. Special versions of the cards were also issued with silver or gold seals embossed. A set of gold-seal cards could be redeemed for $250; silvers for $100. Complete regular sets of nine cards could be exchanged for an uncut sheet of the puzzle set.

		MT
Complete Set (9):		9.00
Single Card:		1.00
1-9	Mike Piazza	

1982 Union Oil Dodgers Premium Pictures

A whole new generation of Los Angeles Dodgers was portrayed in the pastel renderings by sports artist Nicholas Volpe found on these large-format (8-1/2" x 11") premiums sponsored by Union Oil Co. Fronts featured large portraits and smaller action pictures. Backs, in black-and-white, have player data, complete minor and major league stats, a profile of the artist and a Union Oil/Union 76 ad. The Unnumbered pictures are checklisted here alphabetically.

		MT
Complete Set (26):		12.00
Common Player:		.25
(1)	Dusty Baker	.50
(2)	Mark Belanger	.25
(3)	Ron Cey	.50
(4)	Terry Forster	.25
(5)	Steve Garvey	3.00
(6)	Pedro Guerrero	.40
(7)	Burt Hooton	.25

(8)	Steve Howe	.50
(9)	Ken Landreaux	.25
(10)	Tom Lasorda	.75
(11)	Mike Marshall	.25
(12)	Rick Monday	.50
(13)	Jose Morales	.25
(14)	Tom Niedenfeur	.25
(15)	Jorge Orta	.25
(16)	Jerry Reuss	.35
(17)	Ron Roenicke	.25
(18)	Bill Russell	.35
(19)	Steve Sax	.35
(20)	Mike Scioscia	.35
(21)	Vin Scully (announcer)	.25
(22)	Dave Stewart	1.00
(23)	Derrell Thomas	.25
(24)	Fernando Valenzuela	1.00
(25)	Bob Welch	.50
(26)	Steve Yaeger	.25

1984 Union Oil Dodgers Most Memorable Moments

Sixteen highlights of the Dodgers' first 25 years in Los Angeles are featured in this series of color prints given away one per week at Union Oil gas stations at the beginning of the season. Local sports media were polled to choose the "Most Memorable Moments" and four prominent Southern California artists were chosen to do the paintings. The 8-1/2" x 11" premiums have detailed descriptions of the highlights on back, along with a biography of the artist who did the color front. The unnumbered prints are listed here chronologically.

		MT
Complete Set (16):		40.00
Common Print:		2.00
(1)	Coliseum Tribute (Roy Campanella)	6.00
(2)	1959 World Championship	4.00
(3)	104th Stolen Base (Maury Wills)	4.00
(4)	1963 World Championship	4.00
(5)	1965 World Championship	4.00
(6)	58-2/3 Scoreless Innings (Don Drysdale)	5.00
(7)	31-Game Hitting Streak (Willie Davis)	3.00
(8)	30-Home Run Foursome (Dusty Baker, Ron Cey, Steve Garvey, Reggie Smith)	4.00
(9)	1977 N.L. Championship Series	4.00
(10)	Welch Strikes Out Reggie Jackson (Bob Welch)	2.00
(11)	145th Pinch Hit (Manny Mota)	2.00
(12)	Three-Game Sweep of Houston	2.00
(13)	No-Hitters (Jerry Reuss, Bill Singer)	2.00
(14)	Record-Setting Infield (Ron Cey, Steve Garvey, Davey Lopes, Bill Russell)	3.00
(15)	Cy Young Season (Fernando Valenzuela)	4.00
(16)	1981 World Championship	4.00

1991 United Way Ruben Sierra

Six different sponsors' versions of this one-card set can be found. Presumably given away for a donation to United Way the 2-1/2" x 3-1/2" card has a color photo on front with UW and team logos. Backs have a portrait photo, career data and stats, along with sponsors' names.

	MT
Common Card:	1.00
Ruben Sierra (County Seat/Dallas Times)	1.00
Ruben Sierra (John Deere/NCNB)	1.00
Ruben Sierra (Etheridge Printing)	1.00
Ruben Sierra (ElectroCom/Gen'l Dynamics)	1.00
Ruben Sierra (Nat'l Semi-Conductor/ Pier 1)	1.00
Ruben Sierra (Stripling Cox/ Tandy)	1.00

1986 Unocal 76 Dodgers Playmakers Posters

Large game-action color photos on a Dodger-blue background are featured in this set of gas station giveaways. Once a week through much of the season collectors in Southern California could receive one of these 11" x 8-1/2" posters. Back feature lengthy career summaries and full professional stats, plus an in-depth look at the player's 1985 season stats. The posters are checklisted here by uniform number.

		MT
Complete Set (24):		30.00
Common Player:		2.00
2	Tom Lasorda	2.00
3	Steve Sax	2.00
5	Mike Marshall	2.00
9	Greg Brock	2.00
10	Dave Anderson	2.00
12	Bill Madlock	2.00
14	Mike Scioscia	2.00
18	Bill Russell	2.00
21	Reggie Williams	2.00
22	Franklin Stubbs	2.00
23	Enos Cabell	2.00
25	Mariano Duncan	2.00
27	Carlos Diaz	2.00
28	Pedro Guerrero	2.00
29	Alex Trevino	2.00
31	Ed Vande Berg	2.00
34	Fernando Valenzuela	3.00
35	Bob Welch	2.00
40	Rick Honeycutt	2.00
41	Jerry Reuss	2.00
43	Ken Howell	2.00
44	Ken Landreaux	2.00
49	Tom Niedenfuer	2.00
55	Orel Hershiser	3.00

1989 Upper Deck Promos

In 1988 Upper Deck produced a two-card test set to be distributed as samples for the 1989 set; 18,000 of each card were produced. The cards were distributed to dealers at the 1988 National Sports Collectors Convention. Two other variations of the promo cards exist. Both variations involve differences in where the hologram was placed. Fewer than 5,000 of one of the hologram variations exist, while less than 1,000 of the third variation exist. Joyner and Buice were selected for the promo cards because of a reported investment interest in Upper Deck; they were later required to sell their interest in the card company due to their active-player status.

		MT
Complete Set A (2):		150.00
Complete Set B (2):		300.00
Complete Set C (2):		500.00
1a	DeWayne Buice (1/2" x 3/16" hologram at bottom)	50.00
1b	DeWayne Buice (hologram extends to bottom edge)	100.00
1c	DeWayne Buice (hologram at top)	150.00
700a	Wally Joyner (1/2" x 3/16" hologram at bottom)	75.00
700b	Wally Joyner (hologram extends to bottom edge)	200.00
700c	Wally Joyner (hologram at top)	350.00

1989 Upper Deck

This premiere "Collector's Choice" issue from Upper Deck contains 700 cards (2-1/2" by 3-1/2") with full-color photos on both sides. The first 26 cards feature Star Rookies. The set also includes 26 special portrait cards with team checklist backs and seven numberical checklist cards. Major 1988 award winners (Cy Young, Rookie of Year, MVP) are honored on 10 cards in the set, in addition to their individual player cards. There are also special cards for the Most Valuable Players in both League Championship series and the World Series. The card fronts feature player photos framed by a white border. A vertical brown and green artist's rendition of the runner's lane that leads from home plate to first base is found along the right margin. Backs carry full-color action poses that fill the card back, except for a compact (yet complete) stats chart. A high-number series, cards 701-800, featuring rookies and traded players, was released in mid-season in foil packs mixed within the complete set, in boxed complete sets and in high number set boxes.

		MT
Complete Set (800):		175.00
Unopened Factory Set (800):		250.00
Complete Low Set (700):		160.00
Complete High Set (100):		15.00
Common Player:		.10
Low Wax Box:		360.00
High Wax Box:		250.00
1	*Ken Griffey, Jr.*	160.00
2	*Luis Medina*	.10
3	*Tony Chance*	.10
4	*Dave Otto*	.10
5	*Sandy Alomar, Jr.*	1.50
6	*Rolando Roomes*	.10
7	*David West*	.10
8	*Cris Carpenter*	.15
9	Gregg Jefferies	.40
10	*Doug Dascenzo*	.10
11	*Ron Jones*	.10
12	*Luis de los Santos*	.10
13a	*Gary Sheffield* ("SS" upside-down)	3.00
13b	*Gary Sheffield* ("SS" correct)	3.00
14	*Mike Harkey*	.10
15	*Lance Blankenship*	.15
16	*William Brennan*	.10
17	John Smoltz	3.00
18	*Ramon Martinez*	1.00
19	*Mark Lemke*	.20
20	*Juan Bell*	.10
21	*Rey Palacios*	.10
22	*Felix Jose*	.15
23	*Van Snider*	.10
24	*Dante Bichette*	2.00
25	*Randy Johnson*	8.00
26	*Carlos Quintana*	.15
27	Star Rookie Checklist 1-26	.10
28	*Mike Schooler*	.10
29	Randy St. Claire	.10
30	*Jerald Clark*	.15
31	Kevin Gross	.10
32	*Dan Firova*	.10
33	Jeff Calhoun	.10
34	Tommy Hinzo	.10
35	*Ricky Jordan*	.20
36	Larry Parrish	.10
37	Bret Saberhagen	.15
38	Mike Smithson	.10
39	Dave Dravecky	.10
40	Ed Romero	.10
41	Jeff Musselman	.10
42	Ed Hearn	.10
43	Rance Mulliniks	.10
44	Jim Eisenreich	.10
45	*Sil Campusano*	.10
46	Mike Krukow	.10
47	*Paul Gibson*	.10
48	Mike LaCoss	.10
49	Larry Herndon	.10
50	Scott Garrelts	.10
51	Dwayne Henry	.10
52	Jim Acker	.10
53	Steve Sax	.10
54	Pete O'Brien	.10
55	Paul Runge	.10
56	Rick Rhoden	.10
57	*John Dopson*	.10
58	Casey Candaele	.10
59	Dave Righetti	.10
60	Joe Hesketh	.10
61	Frank DiPino	.10
62	Tim Laudner	.10
63	Jamie Moyer	.10
64	Fred Toliver	.10
65	Mitch Webster	.10
66	John Tudor	.10
67	John Cangelosi	.10
68	Mike Devereaux	.10
69	Brian Fisher	.10
70	Mike Marshall	.10
71	Zane Smith	.10
72a	Brian Holton (ball not visible on card front, photo actually Shawn Hillegas)	1.50
72b	Brian Holton (ball visible, correct photo)	.10
73	Jose Guzman	.10
74	Rick Mahler	.10
75	John Shelby	.10
76	Jim Deshaies	.10
77	Bobby Meacham	.10
78	Bryn Smith	.10
79	Joaquin Andujar	.10
80	Richard Dotson	.10
81	Charlie Lea	.10
82	Calvin Schiraldi	.10
83	Les Straker	.10
84	Les Lancaster	.10
85	Allan Anderson	.10
86	Junior Ortiz	.10
87	Jesse Orosco	.10
88	Felix Fermin	.10
89	Dave Anderson	.10
90	Rafael Belliard	.10
91	Franklin Stubbs	.10
92	Cecil Espy	.10
93	Albert Hall	.10
94	Tim Leary	.10
95	Mitch Williams	.10
96	Tracy Jones	.10
97	Danny Darwin	.10
98	Gary Ward	.10
99	Neal Heaton	.10
100	Jim Pankovits	.10
101	Bill Doran	.10
102	Tim Wallach	.10
103	Joe Magrane	.10
104	Ozzie Virgil	.10
105	Alvin Davis	.10
106	Tom Brookens	.10
107	Shawon Dunston	.10
108	Tracy Woodson	.10
109	Nelson Liriano	.10
110	Devon White	.15
111	Steve Balboni	.10
112	Buddy Bell	.10
113	*German Jimenez*	.10
114	Ken Dayley	.10
115	Andres Galarraga	.60
116	Mike Scioscia	.10
117	Gary Pettis	.10
118	Ernie Whitt	.10
119	Bob Boone	.10
120	Ryne Sandberg	1.00
121	Bruce Benedict	.10
122	Hubie Brooks	.10
123	Mike Moore	.10
124	Wallace Johnson	.10
125	Bob Horner	.10
126	Chili Davis	.10
127	Manny Trillo	.10
128	Chet Lemon	.10
129	John Cerutti	.10
130	Orel Hershiser	.10
131	Terry Pendleton	.10
132	Jeff Blauser	.10
133	Mike Fitzgerald	.10
134	Henry Cotto	.10
135	Gerald Young	.10
136	Luis Salazar	.10
137	Alejandro Pena	.10
138	Jack Howell	.10
139	Tony Fernandez	.10
140	Mark Grace	.60
141	Ken Caminiti	1.00
142	Mike Jackson	.10
143	Larry McWilliams	.10
144	Andres Thomas	.10
145	Nolan Ryan	3.00
146	Mike Davis	.10
147	DeWayne Buice	.10
148	Jody Davis	.10
149	Jesse Barfield	.10
150	Matt Nokes	.10
151	Jerry Reuss	.10
152	Rick Cerone	.10
153	Storm Davis	.10
154	Marvell Wynne	.10
155	Will Clark	.75
156	Luis Aguayo	.10
157	Willie Upshaw	.10
158	Randy Bush	.10
159	Ron Darling	.10
160	Kal Daniels	.10
161	Spike Owen	.10
162	Luis Polonia	.10
163	Kevin Mitchell	.10
164	*Dave Gallagher*	.10
165	Benito Santiago	.10
166	Greg Gagne	.10
167	Ken Phelps	.10
168	Sid Fernandez	.10
169	Bo Diaz	.10
170	Cory Snyder	.10
171	Eric Show	.10
172	Robby Thompson	.10
173	Marty Barrett	.10
174	Dave Henderson	.10
175	Ozzie Guillen	.10
176	Barry Lyons	.10
177	*Kelvin Torve*	.10
178	Don Slaught	.10
179	Steve Lombardozzi	.10
180	*Chris Sabo*	.20
181	Jose Uribe	.10
182	Shane Mack	.10

183 Ron Karkovice .10
184 Todd Benzinger .10
185 Dave Stewart .10
186 Julio Franco .10
187 Ron Robinson .10
188 Wally Backman .10
189 Randy Velarde .10
190 Joe Carter .20
191 Bob Welch .10
192 Kelly Paris .10
193 Chris Brown .10
194 Rick Reuschel .10
195 Roger Clemens 2.00
196 Dave Concepcion .10
197 Al Newman .10
198 Brook Jacoby .10
199 Mookie Wilson .10
200 Don Mattingly 1.50
201 Dick Schofield .10
202 Mark Gubicza .10
203 Gary Gaetti .10
204 Dan Pasqua .10
205 Andre Dawson .25
206 Chris Speier .10
207 Kent Tekulve .10
208 Rod Scurry .10
209 Scott Bailes .10
210 Rickey Henderson .50
211 Harold Baines .10
212 Tony Armas .10
213 Kent Hrbek .10
214 Darrin Jackson .10
215 George Brett 1.50
216 Rafael Santana .10
217 Andy Allanson .10
218 Brett Butler .10
219 Steve Jeltz .10
220 Jay Buhner .30
221 Bo Jackson .25
222 Angel Salazar .10
223 Kirk McCaskill .10
224 Steve Lyons .10
225 Bert Blyleven .10
226 Scott Bradley .10
227 Bob Melvin .10
228 Ron Kittle .10
229 Phil Bradley .10
230 Tommy John .10
231 Greg Walker .10
232 Juan Berenguer .10
233 Pat Tabler .10
234 *Terry Clark* .10
235 Rafael Palmeiro 1.00
236 Paul Zuvella .10
237 Willie Randolph .10
238 Bruce Fields .10
239 Mike Aldrete .10
240 Lance Parrish .10
241 Greg Maddux 3.00
242 John Moses .10
243 Melido Perez .10
244 Willie Wilson .10
245 Mark McLemore .10
246 Von Hayes .10
247 Matt Williams .60
248 John Candelaria .10
249 Harold Reynolds .10
250 Greg Swindell .10
251 Juan Agosto .10
252 Mike Felder .10
253 Vince Coleman .10
254 Larry Sheets .10
255 George Bell .10
256 Terry Steinbach .10
257 *Jack Armstrong* .10
258 Dickie Thon .10
259 Ray Knight .10
260 Darryl Strawberry .25
261 Doug Sisk .10
262 Alex Trevino .10
263 Jeff Leonard .10
264 Tom Henke .10
265 Ozzie Smith 1.00
266 Dave Bergman .10
267 Tony Phillips .10
268 Mark Davis .10
269 Kevin Elster .10
270 Barry Larkin .30
271 Manny Lee .10
272 Tom Brunansky .10
273 Craig Biggio 4.00
274 Jim Gantner .10
275 Eddie Murray .40
276 Jeff Reed .10
277 Tim Teufel .10
278 Rick Honeycutt .10
279 Guillermo Hernandez .10
280 John Kruk .10
281 *Luis Alicea* .20
282 Jim Clancy .10
283 Billy Ripken .10
284 Craig Reynolds .10
285 Robin Yount .50
286 Jimmy Jones .10
287 Ron Oester .10
288 Terry Leach .10
289 Dennis Eckersley .20
290 Alan Trammell .10
291 Jimmy Key .15
292 Chris Bosio .10
293 Jose DeLeon .10
294 Jim Traber .10
295 Mike Scott .10
296 Roger McDowell .10
297 Garry Templeton .10
298 Doyle Alexander .10
299 Nick Esasky .10
300 Mark McGwire 6.00

301 *Darryl Hamilton* .20
302 Dave Smith .10
303 Rick Sutcliffe .10
304 Dave Stapleton .10
305 Alan Ashby .10
306 Pedro Guerrero .10
307 Ron Guidry .10
308 Steve Farr .10
309 Curt Ford .10
310 Claudell Washington .10
311 Tom Prince .10
312 *Chad Kreuter* .15
313 Ken Oberkfell .10
314 Jerry Browne .10
315 R.J. Reynolds .10
316 Scott Bankhead .10
317 Milt Thompson .10
318 Mario Diaz .10
319 Bruce Ruffin .10
320 Dave Valle .10
321a *Gary Varsho* (batting righty on card back, photo actually Mike Bielecki) 2.00
321b *Gary Varsho* (batting lefty on card back, correct photo) .10
322 Paul Mirabella .10
323 Chuck Jackson .10
324 Drew Hall .10
325 Don August .10
326 *Israel Sanchez* .10
327 Denny Walling .10
328 Joel Skinner .10
329 Danny Tartabull .10
330 Tony Pena .10
331 Jim Sundberg .10
332 Jeff Robinson .10
333 Odibbe McDowell .10
334 Jose Lind .10
335 Paul Kilgus .10
336 Juan Samuel .10
337 Mike Campbell .10
338 Mike Maddux .10
339 Darnell Coles .10
340 Bob Dernier .10
341 Rafael Ramirez .10
342 Scott Sanderson .10
343 B.J. Surhoff .10
344 Billy Hatcher .10
345 Pat Perry .10
346 Jack Clark .10
347 Gary Thurman .10
348 *Timmy Jones* .10
349 Dave Winfield .25
350 Frank White .10
351 Dave Collins .10
352 Jack Morris .10
353 Eric Plunk .10
354 Leon Durham .10
355 Ivan DeJesus .10
356 *Brian Holman* .15
357a Dale Murphy (reversed negative) 25.00
357b Dale Murphy (corrected) .25
358 Mark Portugal .10
359 Andy McGaffigan .10
360 Tom Glavine 1.00
361 Keith Moreland .10
362 Todd Stottlemyre .20
363 Dave Leiper .10
364 Cecil Fielder .15
365 Carmelo Martinez .10
366 Dwight Evans .10
367 Kevin McReynolds .10
368 Rich Gedman .10
369 Len Dykstra .10
370 Jody Reed .10
371 Jose Canseco 1.00
372 Rob Murphy .10
373 Mike Henneman .10
374 Walt Weiss .10
375 *Rob Dibble* .15
376 Kirby Puckett 1.00
377 Denny Martinez .10
378 Ron Gant .30
379 Brian Harper .10
380 *Nelson Santovenia* .10
381 Lloyd Moseby .10
382 Lance McCullers .10
383 Dave Stieb .10
384 Tony Gwynn 1.50
385 Mike Flanagan .10
386 Bob Ojeda .10
387 Bruce Hurst .10
388 Dave Magadan .10
389 Wade Boggs .25
390 Gary Carter .15
391 Frank Tanana .10
392 Curt Young .10
393 Jeff Treadway .10
394 Darrell Evans .10
395 Glenn Hubbard .10
396 Chuck Cary .10
397 Frank Viola .10
398 Jeff Parrett .10
399 *Terry Blocker* .10
400 Dan Gladden .10
401 *Louie Meadows* .10
402 Tim Raines .15
403 Joey Meyer .10
404 Larry Andersen .10
405 Rex Hudler .10
406 Mike Schmidt 1.50
407 John Franco .10
408 Brady Anderson .50
409 Don Carman .10

410 Eric Davis .10
411 Bob Stanley .10
412 Pete Smith .10
413 Jim Rice .15
414 Bruce Sutter .10
415 Oil Can Boyd .10
416 Ruben Sierra .10
417 Mike LaValliere .10
418 Steve Buechele .10
419 Gary Redus .10
420 Scott Fletcher .10
421 Dale Sveum .10
422 Bob Knepper .10
423 Luis Rivera .10
424 Ted Higuera .10
425 Kevin Bass .10
426 Ken Gerhart .10
427 Shane Rawley .10
428 Paul O'Neill .25
429 Joe Orsulak .10
430 Jackie Gutierrez .10
431 Gerald Perry .10
432 Mike Greenwell .10
433 Jerry Royster .10
434 Ellis Burks .30
435 Ed Olwine .10
436 Dave Rucker .10
437 Charlie Hough .10
438 Bob Walk .10
439 Bob Brower .10
440 Barry Bonds 1.25
441 Tom Foley .10
442 Rob Deer .10
443 Glenn Davis .10
444 Dave Martinez .10
445 Bill Wegman .10
446 Lloyd McClendon .10
447 Dave Schmidt .10
448 Darren Daulton .10
449 Frank Williams .10
450 Don Aase .10
451 Lou Whitaker .10
452 Goose Gossage .10
453 Ed Whitson .10
454 Jim Walewander .10
455 Damon Berryhill .10
456 Tim Burke .10
457 Barry Jones .10
458 Joel Youngblood .10
459 Floyd Youmans .10
460 Mark Salas .10
461 Jeff Russell .10
462 Darrell Miller .10
463 Jeff Kunkel .10
464 *Sherman Corbett* .10
465 Curtis Wilkerson .10
466 Bud Black .10
467 Cal Ripken, Jr. 3.00
468 John Farrell .10
469 Terry Kennedy .10
470 Tom Candiotti .10
471 Roberto Alomar 1.00
472 Jeff Robinson .10
473 Vance Law .10
474 Randy Ready .10
475 Walt Terrell .10
476 Kelly Downs .10
477 *Johnny Paredes* .10
478 Shawn Hillegas .10
479 Bob Brenly .10
480 Otis Nixon .10
481 Johnny Ray .10
482 Geno Petralli .10
483 Stu Cliburn .10
484 Pete Incaviglia .10
485 Brian Downing .10
486 Jeff Stone .10
487 Carmen Castillo .10
488 Tom Niedenfuer .10
489 Jay Bell .10
490 Rick Schu .10
491 *Jeff Pico* .10
492 *Mark Parent* .15
493 Eric King .10
494 Al Nipper .10
495 Andy Hawkins .10
496 Daryl Boston .10
497 Ernie Riles .10
498 Pascual Perez .10
499 Bill Long .10
500 Kirt Manwaring .10
501 Chuck Crim .10
502 Candy Maldonado .10
503 Dennis Lamp .10
504 Glenn Braggs .10
505 Joe Price .10
506 Ken Williams .10
507 Bill Pecota .10
508 Rey Quinones .10
509 *Jeff Bittiger* .10
510 Kevin Seitzer .10
511 Steve Bedrosian .10
512 Todd Worrell .10
513 Chris James .10
514 Jose Oquendo .10
515 David Palmer .10
516 John Smiley .10
517 Dave Clark .10
518 Mike Dunne .10
519 Ron Washington .10
520 Bob Kipper .10
521 Lee Smith .15
522 Juan Castillo .10
523 Don Robinson .10
524 Kevin Romine .10
525 Paul Molitor .50
526 Mark Langston .15
527 Donnie Hill .10

528 Larry Owen .10
529 Jerry Reed .10
530 Jack McDowell .10
531 Greg Mathews .10
532 John Russell .10
533 Dan Quisenberry .10
534 Greg Gross .10
535 Danny Cox .10
536 Terry Francona .10
537 Andy Van Slyke .10
538 Mel Hall .10
539 Jim Gott .10
540 Doug Jones .10
541 Criag Lefferts .10
542 Mike Boddicker .10
543 Greg Brock .10
544 Atlee Hammaker .10
545 Tom Bolton .10
546 *Mike Macfarlane* .25
547 *Rich Renteria* .10
548 John Davis .10
549 Floyd Bannister .10
550 Mickey Brantley .10
551 Duane Ward .10
552 Dan Petry .10
553 Mickey Tettleton .10
554 Rick Leach .10
555 Mike Witt .10
556 Sid Bream .10
557 Bobby Witt .10
558 Tommy Herr .10
559 Randy Milligan .10
560 *Jose Cecena* .10
561 Mackey Sasser .10
562 Carney Lansford .10
563 Rick Aguilera .10
564 Ron Hassey .10
565 Dwight Gooden .20
566 Paul Assenmacher .10
567 Neil Allen .10
568 Jim Morrison .10
569 Mike Pagliarulo .10
570 Ted Simmons .10
571 Mark Thurmond .10
572 Fred McGriff .40
573 Wally Joyner .10
574 *Jose Bautista* .10
575 Kelly Gruber .10
576 Cecilio Guante .10
577 Mark Davidson .10
578 Bobby Bonilla .15
579 Mike Stanley .10
580 Gene Larkin .10
581 Stan Javier .10
582 Howard Johnson .10
583a Mike Gallego (photo on card back reversed) 1.00
583b Mike Gallego (correct photo) .10
584 David Cone .50
585 *Doug Jennings* .10
586 Charlie Hudson .10
587 Dion James .10
588 Al Leiter .20
589 Charlie Puleo .10
590 Roberto Kelly .10
591 Thad Bosley .10
592 Pete Stanicek .10
593 *Pat Borders* .25
594 *Bryan Harvey* .15
595 Jeff Ballard .10
596 Jeff Reardon .10
597 Doug Drabek .10
598 Edwin Correa .10
599 Keith Atherton .10
600 Dave LaPoint .10
601 Don Baylor .15
602 Tom Pagnozzi .10
603 Tim Flannery .10
604 Gene Walter .10
605 Dave Parker .15
606 Mike Diaz .10
607 Chris Gwynn .10
608 Odell Jones .10
609 Carlton Fisk .40
610 Jay Howell .10
611 Tim Crews .10
612 Keith Hernandez .10
613 Willie Fraser .10
614 Jim Eppard .10
615 Jeff Hamilton .10
616 Kurt Stillwell .10
617 Tom Browning .10
618 Jeff Montgomery .10
619 Jose Rijo .10
620 Jamie Quirk .10
621 Willie McGee .10
622 Mark Grant .10
623 Bill Swift .10
624 Orlando Mercado .10
625 *John Costello* .10
626 Jose Gonzalez .10
627a Bill Schroeder (putting on shin guards on card back, photo actually Ronn Reynolds) 1.25
627b Bill Schroeder (arms crossed on card back, correct photo) .10
628a Fred Manrique (throwing on card back, photo actually Ozzie Guillen) 1.00
628b Fred Manrique (batting on card back, correct photo) .10

629 Ricky Horton .10
630 Dan Plesac .10
631 Alfredo Griffin .10
632 Chuck Finley .15
633 Kirk Gibson .10
634 Randy Myers .10
635 Greg Minton .10
636 Herm Winningham .10
637 Charlie Leibrandt .10
638 Tim Birtsas .10
639 Bill Buckner .10
640 Danny Jackson .10
641 Greg Booker .10
642 Jim Presley .10
643 Gene Nelson .10
644 Rod Booker .10
645 Dennis Rasmussen .10
646 Juan Nieves .10
647 Bobby Thigpen .10
648 Tim Belcher .10
649 Mike Young .10
650 Ivan Calderon .10
651 *Oswaldo Peraza* .10
652a Pat Sheridan (no position on front) 15.00
652b Pat Sheridan (position on front) .10
653 Mike Morgan .10
654 Mike Heath .10
655 Jay Tibbs .10
656 Fernando Valenzuela .10
657 Lee Mazzilli .10
658 Frank Viola .10
659 Jose Canseco .50
660 Walt Weiss .10
661 Orel Hershiser .10
662 Kirk Gibson .10
663 Chris Sabo .10
664 Dennis Eckersley .10
665 Orel Hershiser .10
666 Kirk Gibson .10
667 Orel Hershiser .10
668 Wally Joyner (TC) .10
669 Nolan Ryan (TC) .60
670 Jose Canseco (TC) .20
671 Fred McGriff (TC) .15
672 Dale Murphy (TC) .10
673 Paul Molitor (TC) .20
674 Ozzie Smith (TC) .20
675 Ryne Sandberg (TC) .30
676 Kirk Gibson (TC) .10
677 Andres Galarraga (TC) .15
678 Will Clark (TC) .20
679 Cory Snyder (TC) .10
680 Alvin Davis (TC) .10
681 Darryl Strawberry (TC) .10
682 Cal Ripken, Jr. (TC) .40
683 Tony Gwynn (TC) .40
684 Mike Schmidt (TC) .25
685 Andy Van Slyke (TC) .10
686 Ruben Sierra (TC) .10
687 Wade Boggs (TC) .20
688 Eric Davis (TC) .10
689 George Brett (TC) .30
690 Alan Trammell (TC) .10
691 Frank Viola (TC) .10
692 Harold Baines (TC) .10
693 Don Mattingly (TC) .30
694 Checklist 1-100 .10
695 Checklist 101-200 .10
696 Checklist 201-300 .10
697 Checklist 301-400 .10
698 Checklist 401-500 .10
699 Checklist 501-600 .10
700 Checklist 601-700 .10
701 Checklist 701-800 .10
702 Jessie Barfield .10
703 Walt Terrell .10
704 Dickie Thon .10
705 Al Leiter .10
706 Dave LaPoint .10
707 *Charlie Hayes* .40
708 Andy Hawkins .10
709 Mickey Hatcher .10
710 Lance McCullers .10
711 Ron Kittle .10
712 Bert Blyleven .10
713 Rick Dempsey .10
714 Ken Williams .10
715 Steve Rosenberg .10
716 Joe Skalski .10
717 Spike Owen .10
718 Todd Burns .10
719 Kevin Gross .10
720 Tommy Herr .10
721 Rob Ducey .10
722 Gary Green .10
723 *Gregg Olson* .25
724 Greg Harris .10
725 Craig Worthington .10
726 Tom Howard .10
727 Dale Mohorcic .10
728 Rich Yett .10
729 Mel Hall .10
730 Floyd Youmans .10
731 Lonnie Smith .10
732 Wally Backman .10
733 Trevor Wilson .10
734 Jose Alvarez .10
735 Bob Milacki .10
736 *Tom Gordon* .50
737 Wally Whitehurst .10
738 Mike Aldrete .10
739 Keith Miller .10
740 Randy Milligan .10
741 Jeff Parrett .10

742	*Steve Finley*	1.50
743	*Junior Felix*	.15
744	*Pete Harnisch*	.25
745	Bill Spiers	.10
746	Hensley Meulens	.10
747	Juan Bell	.10
748	Steve Sax	.10
749	Phil Bradley	.10
750	Rey Quinones	.10
751	Tommy Gregg	.10
752	Kevin Brown	2.00
753	Derek Lilliquist	.10
754	*Todd Zeile*	.75
755	Jim Abbott	.15
756	*Ozzie Canseco*	.10
757	Nick Esasky	.10
758	Mike Moore	.10
759	Rob Murphy	.10
760	Rick Mahler	.10
761	Fred Lynn	.10
762	*Kevin Blankenship*	.10
763	Eddie Murray	.40
764	*Steve Searcy*	.10
765	*Jerome Walton*	.10
766	*Erik Hanson*	.25
767	Bob Boone	.15
768	Edgar Martinez	.60
769	*Jose DeJesus*	.10
770	*Greg Briley*	.10
771	*Steve Peters*	.10
772	Rafael Palmeiro	1.00
773	Jack Clark	.10
774	Nolan Ryan	3.00
775	Lance Parrish	.10
776	*Joe Girardi*	.40
777	Willie Randolph	.10
778	Mitch Williams	.10
779	*Dennis Cook*	.10
780	*Dwight Smith*	.15
781	*Lenny Harris*	.15
782	*Torey Lovullo*	.15
783	*Norm Charlton*	.25
784	Chris Brown	.10
785	Todd Benzinger	.10
786	Shane Rawley	.10
787	*Omar Vizquel*	3.00
788	*LaVel Freeman*	.10
789	Jeffrey Leonard	.10
790	*Eddie Williams*	.15
791	Jamie Moyer	.10
792	Bruce Hurst	.10
793	Julio Franco	.10
794	Claudell Washington	.10
795	Jody Davis	.10
796	Oddibe McDowell	.10
797	Paul Kilgus	.10
798	Tracy Jones	.10
799	Steve Wilson	.20
800	Pete O'Brien	.10

1989 Upper Deck Souvenir Sheets

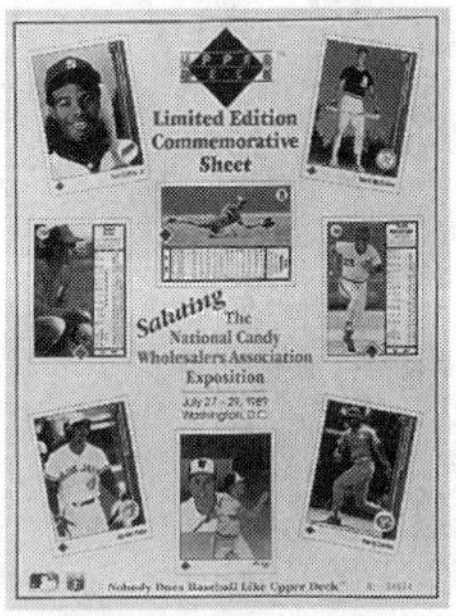

In conjunction with the card company's participation at three conventions in 1989, Upper Deck produced this series of 11" x 8-1/2" souvenir cards. Each depicts reproductions of eight of UD's premiere edition cards in full size and color. Backs are blank. Each sheet carries a serial number, but information on the size of the edition is not available.

		MT
Complete Set (3):		35.00
(1)	1989 Nat'l Sports Collector Convention (Jim Abbott, Harold Baines, Wade Boggs, Will Clark, Dwight Gooden, Mark Grace, Kevin Mitchell, (Mickey Tettleton) (Chicago)	10.00
(2)	Nat'l Candy Wholesalers Expo (Todd Benzinger, Junior Felix, Ken Griffey Jr., Barry Larkin, Mark McGwire), (Tim Raines, Cal Ripken, Jr., (Todd Zeile) (Washington, D.C.)	25.00
(3)	Sun-Times Baseball Show (Tom Browning, Andre Dawson, Gary Gaetti, Andres Galarraga, Ken Griffey Jr., Don Mattingly, Kevin Mitchell, (Kevin Seitzer) (Chicago) (Pictures 1990 cards)	15.00

1990 Upper Deck

Tom Gordon

Following the success of its first issue, Upper Deck released another 800-card set in 1990. The cards feature full-color photos on both sides in the standard 2-1/2" x 3-1/2" format. The artwork of Vernon Wells Sr. is featured on the front of all team checklist cards. The 1990 set also introduces two new Wells illustrations — a tribute to Mike Schmidt upon his retirement and one commemorating Nolan Ryan's 5,000 career strikeouts. The cards are similar in design to the 1989 issue. The high-number series (701-800) was released as a boxed set, in factory sets and in foil packs at mid-season. Cards #101-199 can be found either with or without the copyright line on back; no premium attaches to either.

		MT
Complete Set (800):		25.00
Complete Low Set (700):		20.00
Complete High Set (100):		5.00
Common Player:		.05
Low or High Wax Box:		20.00
1	Star Rookie Checklist	.05
2	*Randy Nosek*	.05
3	*Tom Drees*	.05
4	Curt Young	.05
5	Angels checklist (Devon White)	.05
6	Luis Salazar	.05
7	Phillies checklist (Von Hayes)	.05
8	Jose Bautista	.05
9	*Marquis Grissom*	.50
10	Dodgers checklist (Orel Hershiser)	.05
11	Rick Aguilera	.05
12	Padres checklist (Benito Santiago)	.05
13	Deion Sanders	.50
14	Marvell Wynne	.05
15	David West	.05
16	Pirates checklist (Bobby Bonilla)	.05
17	*Sammy Sosa*	10.00
18	Yankees checklist (Steve Sax)	.05
19	Jack Howell	.05
20	Mike Schmidt Retires (Mike Schmidt)	.50
21	Robin Ventura	.40
22	Brian Meyer	.05
23	*Blaine Beatty*	.05
24	Mariners checklist (Ken Griffey, Jr.)	.75
25	Greg Vaughn	.15
26	*Xavier Hernandez*	.10
27	*Jason Grimsley*	.10
28	*Eric Anthony*	.10
29	Expos checklist (Tim Raines)	.05
30	David Wells	.10
31	Hal Morris	.10
32	Royals checklist (Bo Jackson)	.15
33	*Kelly Mann*	.05
34	Nolan Ryan 5000 Strikeouts (Nolan Ryan)	1.00
35	*Scott Service*	.05
36	Athletics checklist (Mark McGwire)	1.00
37	Tino Martinez	.20
38	Chili Davis	.05
39	Scott Sanderson	.05
40	Giants checklist (Kevin Mitchell)	.05
41	Tigers checklist (Lou Whitaker)	.05
42	*Scott Coolbaugh*	.05
43	*Jose Cano*	.05
44	*Jose Vizcaino*	.25
45	*Bob Hamelin*	.15
46	*Jose Offerman*	.50
47	Kevin Blankenship	.05
48	Twins checklist (Kirby Puckett)	.20
49	*Tommy Greene*	.15
50	N.L. Top Vote Getter (Will Clark)	.10
51	Rob Nelson	.05
52	*Chris Hammond*	.15
53	Indians checklist (Joe Carter)	.05
54a	*Ben McDonald* (Orioles Logo)	1.50
54b	*Ben McDonald* (Star Rookie logo)	.25
55	Andy Benes	.50
56	*John Olerud*	1.00
57	Red Sox checklist (Roger Clemens)	.25
58	Tony Armas	.05
59	*George Canale*	.05
60a	Orioles checklist (Mickey Tettleton) (#683 Jamie Weston)	4.00
60b	Orioles checklist (Mickey Tettleton) (#683 Mickey Weston)	.05
61	*Mike Stanton*	.15
62	Mets checklist (Dwight Gooden)	.05
63	*Kent Mercker*	.10
64	*Francisco Cabrera*	.05
65	Steve Avery	.05
66	Jose Canseco	.40
67	*Matt Merullo*	.05
68	Cardinals checklist (Vince Coleman)	.05
69	Ron Karkovice	.05
70	*Kevin Maas*	.05
71	Dennis Cook	.05
72	*Juan Gonzalez*	5.00
73	Cubs checklist (Andre Dawson)	.05
74	*Dean Palmer*	.75
75	A.L. Top Vote Getter (Bo Jackson)	.15
76	*Rob Richie*	.05
77	*Bobby Rose*	.05
78	*Brian DuBois*	.05
79	White Sox checklist (Ozzie Guillen)	.05
80	Gene Nelson	.05
81	Bob McClure	.05
82	Rangers checklist (Julio Franco)	.05
83	Greg Minton	.05
84	Braves checklist (John Smoltz)	.10
85	Willie Fraser	.05
86	Neal Heaton	.05
87	*Kevin Tapani*	.30
88	Astros checklist (Mike Scott)	.05
89a	Jim Gott (incorrect photo)	4.00
89b	Jim Gott (correct photo)	.05
90	Lance Johnson	.05
91	Brewers checklist (Robin Yount)	.10
92	Jeff Parrett	.05
93	*Julio Machado*	.05
94	Ron Jones	.05
95	Blue Jays checklist (George Bell)	.05
96	Jerry Reuss	.05
97	Brian Fisher	.05
98	*Kevin Ritz*	.10
99	Reds checklist (Barry Larkin)	.10
100	Checklist 1-100	.05
101	Gerald Perry	.05
102	Kevin Appier	.10
103	Julio Franco	.05
104	Craig Biggio	.20
105	Bo Jackson	.20
106	*Junior Felix*	.05
107	Mike Harkey	.05
108	Fred McGriff	.35
109	Rick Sutcliffe	.05
110	Pete O'Brien	.05
111	Kelly Gruber	.05
112	Pat Borders	.05
113	Dwight Evans	.05
114	Dwight Gooden	.10
115	*Kevin Batiste*	.05
116	Eric Davis	.05
117	Kevin Mitchell	.05
118	Ron Oester	.05
119	Brett Butler	.05
120	Danny Jackson	.05
121	Tommy Gregg	.05
122	Ken Caminiti	.25
123	Kevin Brown	.10
124	George Brett	.50
125	Mike Scott	.05
126	Cory Snyder	.05
127	George Bell	.05
128	Mark Grace	.30
129	Devon White	.05
130	Tony Fernandez	.05
131	Don Aase	.05
132	Rance Mulliniks	.05
133	Marty Barrett	.05
134	Nelson Liriano	.05
135	Mark Carreon	.10
136	Candy Maldonado	.05
137	Tim Birtsas	.05
138	Tom Brookens	.05
139	John Franco	.05
140	Mike LaCoss	.05
141	Jeff Treadway	.05
142	Pat Tabler	.05
143	Darrell Evans	.05
144	Rafael Ramirez	.05
145	Oddibe McDowell	.05
146	Brian Downing	.05
147	Curtis Wilkerson	.05
148	Ernie Whitt	.05
149	Bill Schroeder	.05
150	Domingo Ramos	.05
151	Rick Honeycutt	.05
152	Don Slaught	.05
153	Mitch Webster	.05
154	Tony Phillips	.05
155	Paul Kilgus	.05
156	Ken Griffey, Jr.	6.00
157	Gary Sheffield	.35
158	Wally Backman	.05
159	B.J. Surhoff	.05
160	Louie Meadows	.05
161	Paul O'Neill	.10
162	*Jeff McKnight*	.05
163	Alvaro Espinoza	.05
164	*Scott Scudder*	.05
165	Jeff Reed	.05
166	Gregg Jefferies	.20
167	Barry Larkin	.15
168	Gary Carter	.10
169	Robby Thompson	.05
170	Rolando Roomes	.05
171	Mark McGwire	2.50
172	Steve Sax	.05
173	Mark Williamson	.05
174	Mitch Williams	.05
175	Brian Holton	.05
176	Rob Deer	.05
177	Tim Raines	.10
178	Mike Felder	.05
179	Harold Reynolds	.05
180	Terry Francona	.05
181	Chris Sabo	.05
182	Darryl Strawberry	.10
183	Willie Randolph	.05
184	Billy Ripken	.05
185	Mackey Sasser	.05
186	Todd Benzinger	.05
187	Kevin Elster	.05
188	Jose Uribe	.05
189	Tom Browning	.05
190	Keith Miller	.05
191	Don Mattingly	.40
192	Dave Parker	.10
193	Roberto Kelly	.05
194	Phil Bradley	.05
195	Ron Hassey	.05
196	Gerald Young	.05
197	Hubie Brooks	.05
198	Bill Doran	.05
199	Al Newman	.05
200	Checklist 101-200	.05
201	Terry Puhl	.05
202	Frank DiPino	.05
203	Jim Clancy	.05
204	Bob Ojeda	.05
205	Alex Trevino	.05
206	Dave Henderson	.05
207	Henry Cotto	.05
208	Rafael Belliard	.05
209	Stan Javier	.05
210	Jerry Reed	.05
211	Doug Dascenzo	.05
212	Andres Thomas	.05
213	Greg Maddux	1.00
214	Mike Schooler	.05
215	Lonnie Smith	.05
216	Jose Rijo	.05
217	Greg Gagne	.05
218	Jim Gantner	.05
219	Allan Anderson	.05
220	Rick Mahler	.05
221	Jim Deshaies	.05
222	Keith Hernandez	.05
223	Vince Coleman	.05
224	David Cone	.25
225	Ozzie Smith	.35
226	Matt Nokes	.05
227	Barry Bonds	.75
228	Felix Jose	.05
229	Dennis Powell	.05
230	Mike Gallego	.05
231	Shawon Dunston	.05
232	Ron Gant	.15
233	Omar Vizquel	.10
234	Derek Lilliquist	.05
235	Erik Hanson	.05
236	Kirby Puckett	.75
237	Bill Spiers	.05
238	Dan Gladden	.05
239	Bryan Clutterbuck	.05
240	John Moses	.05
241	Ron Darling	.05
242	Joe Magrane	.05
243	Dave Magadan	.05
244	Pedro Guerrero	.05
245	Glenn Davis	.05
246	Terry Steinbach	.05
247	Fred Lynn	.05
248	Gary Redus	.05
249	Kenny Williams	.05
250	Sid Bream	.05
251	Bob Welch	.05
252	Bill Buckner	.05
253	Carney Lansford	.05
254	Paul Molitor	.35
255	Jose DeJesus	.05
256	Orel Hershiser	.05
257	Tom Brunansky	.05
258	Mike Davis	.05
259	Jeff Ballard	.05
260	Scott Terry	.05
261	Sid Fernandez	.05
262	Mike Marshall	.05
263	Howard Johnson	.05
264	Kirk Gibson	.05
265	Kevin McReynolds	.05
266	Cal Ripken, Jr.	1.50
267	Ozzie Guillen	.05
268	Jim Traber	.05
269	Bobby Thigpen	.05
270	Joe Orsulak	.05
271	Bob Boone	.10
272	Dave Stewart	.05
273	Tim Wallach	.05
274	Luis Aquino	.05
275	Mike Moore	.05
276	Tony Pena	.05
277	Eddie Murray	.30
278	Milt Thompson	.05
279	Alejandro Pena	.05
280	Ken Dayley	.05
281	Carmen Castillo	.05
282	Tom Henke	.05
283	Mickey Hatcher	.05
284	Roy Smith	.05
285	Manny Lee	.05
286	Dan Pasqua	.05
287	Larry Sheets	.05
288	Garry Templeton	.05
289	Eddie Williams	.05
290	Brady Anderson	.15
291	Spike Owen	.05
292	Storm Davis	.05
293	Chris Bosio	.05
294	Jim Eisenreich	.05
295	Don August	.05
296	Jeff Hamilton	.05
297	Mickey Tettleton	.05
298	Mike Scioscia	.05
299	Kevin Hickey	.05
300	Checklist 201-300	.05
301	Shawn Abner	.05
302	Kevin Bass	.05
303	Bip Roberts	.05
304	Joe Girardi	.05
305	Danny Darwin	.05
306	Mike Heath	.05
307	Mike Macfarlane	.05
308	Ed Whitson	.05
309	Tracy Jones	.05
310	Scott Fletcher	.05
311	Darnell Coles	.05
312	Mike Brumley	.05
313	Bill Swift	.05
314	Charlie Hough	.05
315	Jim Presley	.05
316	Luis Polonia	.05
317	Mike Morgan	.05
318	Lee Guetterman	.05
319	Jose Oquendo	.05
320	Wayne Tollenson	.05
321	Jody Reed	.05
322	Damon Berryhill	.05
323	Roger Clemens	.75
324	Ryne Sandberg	.40
325	Benito Santiago	.05
326	Bret Saberhagen	.10
327	Lou Whitaker	.05
328	Dave Gallagher	.05
329	Mike Pagliarulo	.05
330	Doyle Alexander	.05
331	Jeffrey Leonard	.05
332	Torey Lovullo	.05
333	Pete Incaviglia	.05
334	Rickey Henderson	.25
335	Rafael Palmeiro	.25
336	Ken Hill	.05
337	Dave Winfield	.30
338	Alfredo Griffin	.05
339	Andy Hawkins	.05
340	Ted Power	.05
341	Steve Wilson	.05
342	Jack Clark	.05
343	Ellis Burks	.10
344	Tony Gwynn	.75
345	Jerome Walton	.05
346	Roberto Alomar	.60
347	*Carlos Martinez*	.05
348	Chet Lemon	.05
349	Willie Wilson	.05

350	Greg Walker	.05
351	Tom Bolton	.05
352	German Gonzalez	.05
353	Harold Baines	.05
354	Mike Greenwell	.05
355	Ruben Sierra	.05
356	Andres Galarraga	.25
357	Andre Dawson	.15
358	*Jeff Brantley*	.15
359	Mike Bielecki	.05
360	Ken Oberkfell	.05
361	Kurt Stillwell	.05
362	Brian Holman	.05
363	Kevin Seitzer	.05
364	Alvin Davis	.05
365	Tom Gordon	.05
366	Bobby Bonilla	.10
367	Carlton Fisk	.35
368	*Steve Carter*	.05
369	Joel Skinner	.05
370	John Cangelosi	.05
371	Cecil Espy	.05
372	*Gary Wayne*	.05
373	Jim Rice	.10
374	*Mike Dyer*	.05
375	Joe Carter	.10
376	Dwight Smith	.05
377	*John Wetteland*	.35
378	Ernie Riles	.05
379	Otis Nixon	.05
380	Vance Law	.05
381	Dave Bergman	.05
382	Frank White	.05
383	Scott Bradley	.05
384	Israel Sanchez	.05
385	Gary Pettis	.05
386	Donn Pall	.05
387	John Smiley	.05
388	Tom Candiotti	.05
389	Junior Ortiz	.05
390	Steve Lyons	.05
391	Brian Harper	.05
392	Fred Manrique	.05
393	Lee Smith	.05
394	Jeff Kunkel	.05
395	Claudell Washington	.05
396	John Tudor	.05
397	Terry Kennedy	.05
398	Lloyd McClendon	.05
399	Craig Lefferts	.05
400	Checklist 301-400	.05
401	Keith Moreland	.05
402	Rich Gedman	.05
403	Jeff Robinson	.05
404	Randy Ready	.05
405	Rick Cerone	.05
406	Jeff Blauser	.05
407	Larry Andersen	.05
408	Joe Boever	.05
409	Felix Fermin	.05
410	Glenn Wilson	.05
411	Rex Hudler	.05
412	Mark Grant	.05
413	Dennis Martinez	.05
414	Darrin Jackson	.05
415	Mike Aldrete	.05
416	Roger McDowell	.05
417	Jeff Reardon	.05
418	Darren Daulton	.05
419	Tim Laudner	.05
420	Don Carman	.05
421	Lloyd Moseby	.05
422	Doug Drabek	.05
423	Lenny Harris	.05
424	Jose Lind	.05
425	*Dave Johnson*	.05
426	Jerry Browne	.05
427	*Eric Yelding*	.05
428	Brad Komminsk	.05
429	Jody Davis	.05
430	Mariano Duncan	.05
431	Mark Davis	.05
432	Nelson Santovenia	.05
433	Bruce Hurst	.05
434	*Jeff Huson*	.05
435	Chris James	.05
436	*Mark Guthrie*	.05
437	Charlie Hayes	.05
438	Shane Rawley	.05
439	Dickie Thon	.05
440	Juan Berenguer	.05
441	Kevin Romine	.05
442	Bill Landrum	.05
443	Todd Frohwirth	.05
444	Craig Worthington	.05
445	Fernando Valenzuela	.05
446	Albert Belle	1.00
447	*Ed Whited*	.05
448	Dave Smith	.05
449	Dave Clark	.05
450	Juan Agosto	.05
451	Dave Valle	.05
452	Kent Hrbek	.05
453	Von Hayes	.05
454	Gary Gaetti	.05
455	Greg Briley	.05
456	Glenn Braggs	.05
457	Kirt Manwaring	.05
458	Mel Hall	.05
459	Brook Jacoby	.05
460	Pat Sheridan	.05
461	Rob Murphy	.05
462	Jimmy Key	.10
463	Nick Esasky	.05
464	Rob Ducey	.05
465	Carlos Quintana	.05
466	*Larry Walker*	1.50
467	Todd Worrell	.05
468	Kevin Gross	.05
469	Terry Pendleton	.05
470	Dave Martinez	.05
471	Gene Larkin	.05
472	Len Dykstra	.05
473	Barry Lyons	.05
474	Terry Mulholland	.05
475	*Chip Hale*	.05
476	Jesse Barfield	.05
477	Dan Plesac	.05
478a	Scott Garrelts (Photo actually Bill Bathe)	2.00
478b	Scott Garrelts (Correct photo)	.05
479	Dave Righetti	.05
480	Gus Polidor	.05
481	Mookie Wilson	.05
482	Luis Rivera	.05
483	Mike Flanagan	.05
484	Dennis "Oil Can" Boyd	.05
485	John Cerutti	.05
486	John Costello	.05
487	Pascual Perez	.05
488	Tommy Herr	.05
489	Tom Foley	.05
490	Curt Ford	.05
491	Steve Lake	.05
492	Tim Teufel	.05
493	Randy Bush	.05
494	Mike Jackson	.05
495	Steve Jeltz	.05
496	Paul Gibson	.05
497	Steve Balboni	.05
498	Bud Black	.05
499	Dale Sveum	.05
500	Checklist 401-500	.05
501	Timmy Jones	.05
502	Mark Portugal	.05
503	Ivan Calderon	.05
504	Rick Rhoden	.05
505	Willie McGee	.05
506	Kirk McCaskill	.05
507	Dave LaPoint	.05
508	Jay Howell	.05
509	Johnny Ray	.05
510	Dave Anderson	.05
511	Chuck Crim	.05
512	Joe Hesketh	.05
513	Dennis Eckersley	.05
514	Greg Brock	.05
515	Tim Burke	.05
516	Frank Tanana	.05
517	Jay Bell	.10
518	Guillermo Hernandez	.05
519	Randy Kramer	.05
520	Charles Hudson	.05
521	Jim Corsi	.05
522	Steve Rosenberg	.05
523	Cris Carpenter	.05
524	*Matt Winters*	.05
525	Melido Perez	.05
526	Chris Gwynn	.05
527	Bert Blyleven	.05
528	Chuck Cary	.05
529	Daryl Boston	.05
530	Dale Mohorcic	.05
531	Geronimo Berroa	.05
532	Edgar Martinez	.10
533	Dale Murphy	.15
534	Jay Buhner	.10
535	John Smoltz	.50
536	Andy Van Slyke	.05
537	Mike Henneman	.05
538	Miguel Garcia	.05
539	Frank Williams	.05
540	R.J. Reynolds	.05
541	Shawn Hillegas	.05
542	Walt Weiss	.05
543	*Greg Hibbard*	.10
544	Nolan Ryan	1.50
545	Todd Zeile	.10
546	Hensley Meulens	.05
547	Tim Belcher	.05
548	Mike Witt	.05
549	Greg Cadaret	.05
550	Franklin Stubbs	.05
551	*Tony Castillo*	.05
552	Jeff Robinson	.05
553	*Steve Olin*	.05
554	Alan Trammell	.10
555	Wade Boggs	.30
556	Will Clark	.40
557	Jeff King	.05
558	Mike Fitzgerald	.05
559	Ken Howell	.05
560	Bob Kipper	.05
561	Scott Bankhead	.05
562a	*Jeff Innis* (Photo actually David West)	1.00
562b	*Jeff Innis* (Correct photo)	.05
563	Randy Johnson	.50
564	*Wally Whithurst*	.05
565	*Gene Harris*	.05
566	Norm Charlton	.05
567	Robin Yount	.50
568	*Joe Oliver*	.05
569	Mark Parent	.05
570	John Farrell	.05
571	Tom Glavine	.40
572	Rod Nichols	.05
573	Jack Morris	.05
574	Greg Swindell	.05
575	Steve Searcy	.05
576	Ricky Jordan	.05
577	Matt Williams	.30
578	Mike LaValliere	.05
579	Bryn Smith	.05
580	Bruce Ruffin	.05
581	Randy Myers	.10
582	*Rick Wrona*	.05
583	Juan Samuel	.05
584	Les Lancaster	.05
585	Jeff Musselman	.05
586	Rob Dibble	.05
587	Eric Show	.05
588	Jesse Orosco	.05
589	Herm Winningham	.05
590	Andy Allanson	.05
591	Dion James	.05
592	Carmelo Martinez	.05
593	Luis Quinones	.05
594	Dennis Rasmussen	.05
595	Rich Yett	.05
596	Bob Walk	.05
597a	Andy McGaffigan (player #48, photo actually Rich Thompson)	.75
597b	Andy McGaffigan (player #27, correct photo)	.05
598	Billy Hatcher	.05
599	Bob Knepper	.05
600	Checklist 501-600	.05
601	Joey Cora	.05
602	*Steve Finley*	.20
603	Kal Daniels	.05
604	Gregg Olson	.05
605	Dave Steib	.05
606	*Kenny Rogers*	.10
607	Zane Smith	.05
608	*Bob Geren*	.05
609	Chad Kreuter	.05
610	Mike Smithson	.05
611	*Jeff Wetherby*	.05
612	*Gary Mielke*	.05
613	Pete Smith	.05
614	*Jack Daugherty*	.05
615	Lance McCullers	.05
616	Don Robinson	.05
617	Jose Guzman	.05
618	Steve Bedrosian	.05
619	Jamie Moyer	.05
620	Atlee Hammaker	.05
621	*Rick Luecken*	.05
622	Greg W. Harris	.05
623	Pete Harnisch	.05
624	Jerald Clark	.05
625	Jack McDowell	.05
626	Frank Viola	.05
627	Ted Higuera	.05
628	*Marty Pevey*	.05
629	Bill Wegman	.05
630	Eric Plunk	.05
631	Drew Hall	.05
632	Doug Jones	.05
633	Geno Petralli	.05
634	Jose Alvarez	.05
635	Bob Milacki	.05
636	Bobby Witt	.05
637	Trevor Wilson	.05
638	Jeff Russell	.05
639	Mike Krukow	.05
640	Rick Leach	.05
641	Dave Schmidt	.05
642	Terry Leach	.05
643	Calvin Schiraldi	.05
644	Bob Melvin	.05
645	Jim Abbott	.10
646	*Jaime Navarro*	.10
647	Mark Langston	.05
648	Juan Nieves	.05
649	Damaso Garcia	.05
650	Charlie O'Brien	.05
651	Eric King	.05
652	Mike Boddicker	.05
653	Duane Ward	.05
654	Bob Stanley	.05
655	Sandy Alomar, Jr.	.10
656	Danny Tartabull	.05
657	Randy McCament	.05
658	Charlie Leibrandt	.05
659	Dan Quisenberry	.05
660	Paul Assenmacher	.05
661	Walt Terrell	.05
662	Tim Leary	.05
663	Randy Milligan	.05
664	Bo Diaz	.05
665	Mark Lemke	.05
666	Jose Gonzalez	.05
667	Chuck Finley	.10
668	John Kruk	.05
669	Dick Schofield	.05
670	Tim Crews	.05
671	John Dopson	.05
672	*John Orton*	.05
673	Eric Hetzel	.05
674	Lance Parrish	.05
675	Ramon Martinez	.20
676	Mark Gubicza	.05
677	Greg Litton	.05
678	Greg Mathews	.05
679	Dave Dravecky	.05
680	Steve Farr	.05
681	Mike Devereaux	.05
682	Ken Griffey, Sr.	.05
683a	*Jamie Weston* (first name incorrect)	3.00
683b	*Mickey Weston* (corrected)	.05
684	Jack Armstrong	.05
685	Steve Buechele	.05
686	Bryan Harvey	.05
687	Lance Blankenship	.05
688	Dante Bichette	.50
689	Todd Burns	.05
690	Dan Petry	.05
691	*Kent Anderson*	.05
692	Todd Stottlemyre	.10
693	Wally Joyner	.05
694	Mike Rochford	.05
695	Floyd Bannister	.05
696	Rick Reuschel	.05
697	Jose DeLeon	.05
698	Jeff Montgomery	.05
699	Kelly Downs	.05
700a	Checklist 601-700 (#683 Jamie Weston)	.05
700b	Checklist 601-700 (# 683 Mickey Weston)	.05
701	Jim Gott	.05
702	"Rookie Threats" (Delino DeShields, Larry Walker, Marquis Grissom)	.40
703	Alejandro Pena	.05
704	Willie Randolph	.05
705	Tim Leary	.05
706	Chuck McElroy	.05
707	Gerald Perry	.05
708	Tom Brunansky	.05
709	John Franco	.05
710	Mark Davis	.05
711	*Dave Justice*	1.00
712	Storm Davis	.05
713	Scott Ruskin	.05
714	Glenn Braggs	.05
715	Kevin Bearse	.05
716	Jose Nunez	.05
717	Tim Layana	.05
718	Greg Myers	.05
719	Pete O'Brien	.05
720	John Candelaria	.05
721	Craig Grebeck	.05
722	Shawn Boskie	.05
723	Jim Leyritz	.10
724	Bill Sampen	.05
725	Scott Radinsky	.05
726	*Todd Hundley*	.40
727	Scott Hemond	.05
728	Lenny Webster	.05
729	Jeff Reardon	.05
730	Mitch Webster	.05
731	Brian Bohanon	.05
732	Rick Parker	.05
733	Terry Shumpert	.05
734a	Nolan Ryan (300-win stripe on front)	2.00
734b	Nolan Ryan (no stripe)	8.00
735	John Burkett	.05
736	*Derrick May*	.10
737	*Carlos Baerga*	.10
738	Greg Smith	.05
739	Joe Kraemer	.05
740	Scott Sanderson	.05
741	Hector Villanueva	.05
742	Mike Fetters	.05
743	Mark Gardner	.10
744	Matt Nokes	.05
745	Dave Winfield	.25
746	*Delino DeShields*	.15
747	Dann Howitt	.05
748	Tony Pena	.05
749	Oil Can Boyd	.05
750	Mike Benjamin	.05
751	Alex Cole	.05
752	Eric Gunderson	.05
753	Howard Farmer	.05
754	Joe Carter	.10
755	*Ray Lankford*	.75
756	Sandy Alomar,Jr.	.10
757	Alex Sanchez	.05
758	Nick Esasky	.05
759	Stan Belinda	.05
760	Jim Presley	.05
761	Gary DiSarcina	.10
762	Wayne Edwards	.05
763	Pat Combs	.10
764	Mickey Pina	.05
765	*Wilson Alvarez*	.40
766	Dave Parker	.15
767	Mike Blowers	.10
768	Tony Phillips	.05
769	Pascual Perez	.05
770	Gary Pettis	.05
771	Fred Lynn	.05
772	*Mel Rojas*	.10
773	David Segui	.40
774	Gary Carter	.10
775	Rafael Valdez	.05
776	Glenallen Hill	.10
777	Keith Hernandez	.05
778	Billy Hatcher	.05
779	Marty Clary	.05
780	Candy Maldonado	.05
781	Mike Marshall	.05
782	Billy Jo Robidoux	.05
783	Mark Langston	.10
784	*Paul Sorrento*	.25
785	*Dave Hollins*	.20
786	Cecil Fielder	.10
787	Matt Young	.05
788	Jeff Huson	.05
789	Lloyd Moseby	.05
790	Ron Kittle	.05
791	Hubie Brooks	.05
792	Craig Lefferts	.05
793	Kevin Bass	.05
794	Bryn Smith	.05
795	Juan Samuel	.05
796	Sam Horn	.05
797	Randy Myers	.10
798	Chris James	.05
799	Bill Gullickson	.05
800	Checklist 701-800	.05

1990 Upper Deck Reggie Jackson Heroes

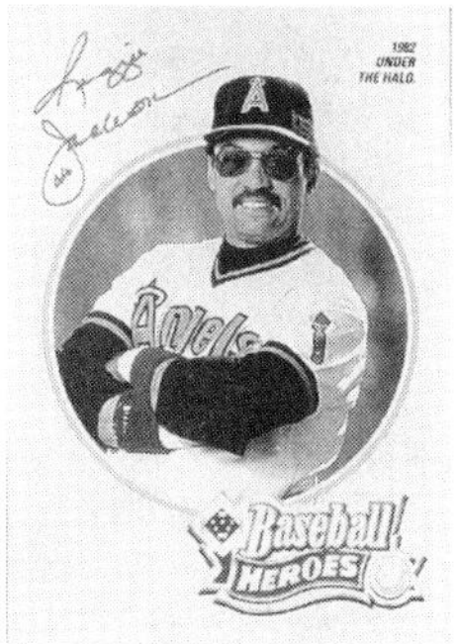

This Baseball Heroes set is devoted to Reggie Jackson. The cards, numbered 1-9, are the first in a continuing series of cards issued in subsequent years. An unnumbered cover card that says "Baseball Heroes" was also issued. The Jackson cards were randomly inserted in high number foil packs only. Jackson also autographed 2,500 numbered cards, which were randomly included in high number packs.

		MT
Complete Set (10):		8.00
Common Player:		1.00
Autographed Card:		125.00
1	1969 Emerging Superstar (Reggie Jackson)	1.00
2	1973 An MVP Year (Reggie Jackson)	1.00
3	1977 "Mr. October" (Reggie Jackson)	1.00
4	1978 Jackson vs. Welch (Reggie Jackson)	1.00
5	1982 Under the Halo (Reggie Jackson)	1.00
6	1984 500! (Reggie Jackson)	1.00
7	1986 Moving Up the List (Reggie Jackson)	1.00
8	1987 A Great Career Ends (Reggie Jackson)	1.00
9	Heroes Checklist 1-9 (Reggie Jackson)	1.00
----	Header card	1.00

1990 Upper Deck Souvenir Sheets

UD continued its program of souvenir sheet production for two major card shows in 1990. Sheets were also bound into copies of Street and Smith's baseball annual magazine on a regional basis. Sheets again feature full-size, full-color photos of UD cards on an 11" x 8-1/2" format. Backs are blank. Sheets are serially numbered from within an unknown number issued.

		MT
Complete Set (5):		45.00
(1)	Street and Smith - East (Wade Boggs, Jose Canseco, Will Clark, Carlton Fisk, Gregg Jefferies, Gregg Olson, Tim Raines)	10.00
(2)	Street and Smith - Midwest (Jose Canseco, Will Clark, Carlton Fisk, Tom Gordon, Pedro Guerrero, Tim Raines, Ryne Sandberg)	10.00
(3)	Street and Smith - West (Roberto Alomar, Bert Blyleven, Jose Canseco, Will Clark, Carlton Fisk, Ken Griffey Jr., Tim Raines)	15.00
(4)	1990 Nat'l Sports Collectors Convention (Bugs Bunny (Comic Ball), Pat Combs, Bill Doran, Daffy Duck (Comic Ball) Howard Johnson, Mark McGwire, Nolan Ryan, Ruben Sierra) (Arlington) (26,000)	10.00
(5)	San Francisco Card Show (Delino DeShields, Cecil Fielder, Marquis Grissom, Reggie Jackson, Kevin Maas), Nolan Ryan, Larry Walker, Bob Welch, Matt Williams)	10.00

1991 Upper Deck

More than 110 rookies are included among the first 700 cards in the 1991 Upper Deck set. A 100-card high-number series was released in late summer. Cards feature top quality white stock and color photos on front and back. A nine-card "Baseball Heroes" bonus set honoring Nolan Ryan, is among the many insert specials in the '91 UD set. Others include a card of Chicago Bulls superstar Michael Jordan. Along with the Ryan bonus cards, 2,500 cards personally autographed and numbered by Ryan were randomly inserted. Upper Deck cards are packaged in tamper-proof foil packs. Each pack contains 15 cards and a 3-1/2" x 2-1/2" 3-D team logo hologram sticker.

		MT
Complete Set (800):		20.00
Complete Low Series (1-700):		15.00
Complete High Series (701-800):		5.00
Common Player:		.05
Low or High Wax Box:		15.00
1	Star Rookie Checklist	.05
2	*Phil Plantier*	.10
3	*D.J. Dozier*	.05
4	Dave Hansen	.05
5	Mo Vaughn	.50
6	*Leo Gomez*	.10
7	*Scott Aldred*	.05
8	*Scott Chiamparino*	.05
9	*Lance Dickson*	.05
10	*Sean Berry*	.15
11	Bernie Williams	.50
12	*Brian Barnes*	.05
13	*Narciso Elvira*	.05
14	*Mike Gardiner*	.10
15	*Greg Colbrunn*	.15
16	*Bernard Gilkey*	.25
17	Mark Lewis	.10
18	*Mickey Morandini*	.10
19	Charles Nagy	.15
20	*Geronimo Pena*	.10
21	*Henry Rodriguez*	.40
22	Scott Cooper	.05
23	*Andujar Cedeno*	.10
24	*Eric Karros*	.75
25	*Steve Decker*	.05
26	*Kevin Belcher*	.10
27	*Jeff Conine*	.25
28	Oakland Athletics checklist (Dave Stewart)	.05
29	Chicago White Sox checklist (Carlton Fisk)	.10
30	Texas Rangers checklist (Rafael Palmeiro)	.10
31	California Angels checklist (Chuck Finley)	.05
32	Seattle Mariners checklist (Harold Reynolds)	.05
33	Kansas City Royals checklist (Bret Saberhagen)	.05
34	Minnesota Twins checklist (Gary Gaetti)	.05
35	Scott Leius	.05
36	Neal Heaton	.05
37	*Terry Lee*	.05
38	Gary Redus	.05
39	Barry Jones	.05
40	Chuck Knoblauch	.40
41	Larry Andersen	.05
42	Darryl Hamilton	.05
43	Boston Red Sox checklist (Mike Greenwell)	.05
44	Toronto Blue Jays checklist (Kelly Gruber)	.05
45	Detroit Tigers checklist (Jack Morris)	.05
46	Cleveland Indians checklist (Sandy Alomar Jr.)	.05
47	Baltimore Orioles checklist (Gregg Olson)	.05
48	Milwaukee Brewers checklist (Dave Parker)	.05
49	New York Yankees checklist (Roberto Kelly)	.05
50	Top Prospect '91 checklist	.05
51	*Kyle Abbott* (Top Prospect)	.10
52	Jeff Juden (Top Prospect)	.15
53	*Todd Van Poppel* (Top Prospect)	.15
54	*Steve Karsay* (Top Prospect)	.15
55	*Chipper Jones* (Top Prospect)	4.00
56	*Chris Johnson* (Top Prospect)	.05
57	*John Ericks* (Top Prospect)	.05
58	*Gary Scott* (Top Prospect)	.05
59	Kiki Jones (Top Prospect)	.05
60	*Wil Cordero* (Top Prospect)	.25
61	*Royce Clayton* (Top Prospect)	.20
62	*Tim Costo* (Top Prospect)	.10
63	Roger Salkeld (Top Prospect)	.10
64	*Brook Fordyce* (Top Prospect)	.05
65	*Mike Mussina* (Top Prospect)	1.50
66	*Dave Staton* (Top Prospect)	.15
67	*Mike Lieberthal* (Top Prospect)	.60
68	*Kurt Miller* (Top Prospect)	.15
69	*Dan Peltier* (Top Prospect)	.05
70	Greg Blosser (Top Prospect)	.05
71	*Reggie Sanders* (Top Prospect)	.25
72	Brent Mayne (Top Prospect)	.10
73	*Rico Brogna* (Top Prospect)	.25
74	*Willie Banks* (Top Prospect)	.10
75	*Len Brutcher* (Top Prospect)	.05
76	*Pat Kelly* (Top Prospect)	.10
77	Cincinnati Reds checklist (Chris Sabo)	.05
78	Los Angeles Dodgers checklist (Ramon Martinez)	.10
79	San Francisco Giants checklist (Matt Williams)	.10
80	San Diego Padres checklist (Roberto Alomar)	.10
81	Houston Astros checklist (Glenn Davis)	.05
82	Atlanta Braves checklist (Ron Gant)	.10
83	"Fielder's Feat" (Cecil Fielder)	.10
84	*Orlando Merced*	.20
85	Domingo Ramos	.05
86	Tom Bolton	.05
87	*Andres Santana*	.05
88	John Dopson	.05
89	Kenny Williams	.05
90	Marty Barrett	.05
91	Tom Pagnozzi	.05
92	Carmelo Martinez	.05
93	"Save Master" (Bobby Thigpen)	.05
94	Pittsburgh Pirates checklist (Barry Bonds)	.30
95	New York Mets checklist (Gregg Jefferies)	.05
96	Montreal Expos checklist (Tim Wallach)	.05
97	Philadelphia Phillies checklist (Lenny Dykstra)	.05
98	St. Louis Cardinals checklist (Pedro Guerrero)	.05
99	Chicago Cubs checklist (Mark Grace)	.10
100	Checklist 1-100	.05
101	Kevin Elster	.05
102	Tom Brookens	.05
103	Mackey Sasser	.05
104	Felix Fermin	.05
105	Kevin McReynolds	.05
106	Dave Steib	.05
107	Jeffrey Leonard	.05
108	Dave Henderson	.05
109	Sid Bream	.05
110	Henry Cotto	.05
111	Shawon Dunston	.05
112	Mariano Duncan	.05
113	Joe Girardi	.05
114	Billy Hatcher	.05
115	Greg Maddux	.75
116	Jerry Browne	.05
117	Juan Samuel	.05
118	Steve Olin	.05
119	Alfredo Griffin	.05
120	Mitch Webster	.05
121	Joel Skinner	.05
122	Frank Viola	.05
123	Cory Snyder	.05
124	Howard Johnson	.05
125	Carlos Baerga	.05
126	Tony Fernandez	.05
127	Dave Stewart	.05
128	Jay Buhner	.05
129	Mike LaValliere	.05
130	Scott Bradley	.05
131	Tony Phillips	.05
132	Ryne Sandberg	.30
133	Paul O'Neill	.20
134	Mark Grace	.20
135	Chris Sabo	.05
136	Ramon Martinez	.15
137	Brook Jacoby	.05
138	Candy Maldonado	.05
139	Mike Scioscia	.05
140	Chris James	.05
141	Craig Worthington	.05
142	Manny Lee	.05
143	Tim Raines	.10
144	Sandy Alomar, Jr.	.10
145	John Olerud	.20
146	*Ozzie Canseco*	.10
147	Pat Borders	.05
148	Harold Reynolds	.05
149	Tom Henke	.05
150	R.J. Reynolds	.05
151	Mike Gallego	.05
152	Bobby Bonilla	.05
153	Terry Steinbach	.05
154	Barry Bonds	.60
155	Jose Canseco	.40
156	Gregg Jefferies	.10
157	Matt Williams	.20
158	Craig Biggio	.25
159	Daryl Boston	.05
160	Ricky Jordan	.05
161	Stan Belinda	.05
162	Ozzie Smith	.50
163	Tom Brunansky	.05
164	Todd Zeile	.10
165	Mike Greenwell	.05
166	Kal Daniels	.05
167	Kent Hrbek	.05
168	Franklin Stubbs	.05
169	Dick Schofield	.05
170	Junior Ortiz	.05
171	*Hector Villanueva*	.05
172	Dennis Eckersley	.05
173	Mitch Williams	.05
174	Mark McGwire	2.00
175	Fernando Valenzuela	.05
176	Gary Carter	.10
177	Dave Magadan	.05
178	Robby Thompson	.05
179	Bob Ojeda	.05
180	Ken Caminiti	.15
181	Don Slaught	.05
182	Luis Rivera	.05
183	Jay Bell	.05
184	Jody Reed	.05
185	Wally Backman	.05
186	Dave Martinez	.05
187	Luis Polonia	.05
188	Shane Mack	.05
189	Spike Owen	.05
190	Scott Bailes	.05
191	John Russell	.05
192	Walt Weiss	.05
193	Jose Oquendo	.05
194	Carney Lansford	.05
195	Jeff Huson	.05
196	Keith Miller	.05
197	Eric Yelding	.05
198	Ron Darling	.05
199	John Kruk	.05
200	Checklist 101-200	.05
201	John Shelby	.05
202	Bob Geren	.05
203	Lance McCullers	.05
204	Alvaro Espinoza	.05
205	Mark Salas	.05
206	Mike Pagliarulo	.05
207	Jose Uribe	.05
208	Jim Deshaies	.05
209	Ron Karkovice	.05
210	Rafael Ramirez	.05
211	Donnie Hill	.05
212	Brian Harper	.05
213	Jack Howell	.05
214	Wes Gardner	.05
215	Tim Burke	.05
216	Doug Jones	.05
217	Hubie Brooks	.05
218	Tom Candiotti	.05
219	Gerald Perry	.05
220	Jose DeLeon	.05
221	Wally Whitehurst	.05
222	*Alan Mills*	.10
223	Alan Trammell	.10
224	Dwight Gooden	.10
225	Travis Fryman	.10
226	Joe Carter	.05
227	Julio Franco	.05
228	Craig Lefferts	.05
229	Gary Pettis	.05
230	Dennis Rasmussen	.05
231a	Brian Downing (no position on front)	.50
231b	Brian Downing (DH on front)	.05
232	Carlos Quintana	.05
233	Gary Gaetti	.05
234	Mark Langston	.05
235	Tim Wallach	.05
236	Greg Swindell	.05
237	Eddie Murray	.25
238	Jeff Manto	.05
239	Lenny Harris	.05
240	Jesse Orosco	.05
241	Scott Lusader	.05
242	Sid Fernandez	.05
243	*Jim Leyritz*	.20
244	Cecil Fielder	.10
245	Darryl Strawberry	.10
246	Frank Thomas	1.00
247	Kevin Mitchell	.05
248	Lance Johnson	.05
249	Rick Rueschel	.05
250	Mark Portugal	.05
251	Derek Lilliquist	.05
252	Brian Holman	.05
253	Rafael Valdez	.05
254	B.J. Surhoff	.05
255	Tony Gwynn	.60
256	Andy Van Slyke	.05
257	Todd Stottlemyre	.10
258	Jose Lind	.05
259	Greg Myers	.05
260	Jeff Ballard	.05
261	Bobby Thigpen	.05
262	*Jimmy Kremers*	.05
263	Robin Ventura	.20
264	John Smoltz	.15
265	Sammy Sosa	1.00
266	Gary Sheffield	.20
267	Len Dykstra	.05
268	Bill Spiers	.05
269	Charlie Hayes	.05
270	Brett Butler	.05
271	Bip Roberts	.05
272	Rob Deer	.05
273	Fred Lynn	.05
274	Dave Parker	.10
275	Andy Benes	.10
276	Glenallen Hill	.10
277	*Steve Howard*	.10
278	Doug Drabek	.05
279	Joe Oliver	.05
280	Todd Benzinger	.05
281	Eric King	.05
282	Jim Presley	.05
283	Ken Patterson	.05
284	Jack Daugherty	.05
285	Ivan Calderon	.05
286	*Edgar Diaz*	.05
287	Kevin Bass	.05
288	Don Carman	.05
289	Greg Brock	.05
290	John Franco	.05
291	Joey Cora	.05
292	Bill Wegman	.05
293	Eric Show	.05
294	Scott Bankhead	.05
295	Garry Templeton	.05
296	Mickey Tettleton	.05
297	Luis Sojo	.05
298	Jose Rijo	.05
299	Dave Johnson	.05
300	Checklist 201-300	.05
301	Mark Grant	.05
302	Pete Harnisch	.10
303	Greg Olson	.05
304	*Anthony Telford*	.10
305	Lonnie Smith	.05
306	Chris Hoiles	.05
307	Bryn Smith	.05
308	Mike Devereaux	.05
309a	Milt Thompson ("86" in stats obscured by "bull's eye")	.50
309b	Milt Thompson ("86" visible)	.05
310	Bob Melvin	.05
311	Luis Salazar	.05
312	Ed Whitson	.05
313	Charlie Hough	.05
314	Dave Clark	.05
315	*Eric Gunderson*	.05
316	Dan Petry	.05
317	Dante Bichette	.20
318	Mike Heath	.05
319	Damon Berryhill	.05
320	Walt Terrell	.05
321	Scott Fletcher	.05
322	Dan Plesac	.05
323	Jack McDowell	.05
324	Paul Molitor	.35
325	Ozzie Guillen	.05
326	Gregg Olson	.05
327	Pedro Guerrero	.05
328	Bob Milacki	.05
329	John Tudor	.05
330	Steve Finley	.05
331	Jack Clark	.05
332	Jerome Walton	.05
333	Andy Hawkins	.05
334	Derrick May	.05
335	Roberto Alomar	.35
336	Jack Morris	.05
337	Dave Winfield	.20
338	Steve Searcy	.05
339	Chili Davis	.05
340	Larry Sheets	.05
341	Ted Higuera	.05
342	*David Segui*	.15
343	Greg Cadaret	.05
344	Robin Yount	.35
345	Nolan Ryan	1.00
346	Ray Lankford	.10
347	Cal Ripken, Jr.	1.00
348	Lee Smith	.05
349	Brady Anderson	.15
350	Frank DiPino	.05
351	Hal Morris	.05
352	Deion Sanders	.20
353	Barry Larkin	.15
354	Don Mattingly	.50
355	Eric Davis	.05
356	Jose Offerman	.05
357	Mel Rojas	.05
358	Rudy Seanez	.05
359	Oil Can Boyd	.05
360	Nelson Liriano	.05
361	Ron Gant	.10
362	*Howard Farmer*	.05
363	Dave Justice	.20
364	Delino DeShields	.05
365	Steve Avery	.05
366	David Cone	.10
367	Lou Whitaker	.05
368	Von Hayes	.05
369	Frank Tanana	.05
370	Tim Teufel	.05
371	Randy Myers	.05
372	Roberto Kelly	.05
373	Jack Armstrong	.05
374	Kelly Gruber	.05
375	Kevin Maas	.05
376	Randy Johnson	.25
377	David West	.05
378	*Brent Knackert*	.05
379	Rick Honeycutt	.05
380	Kevin Gross	.05
381	Tom Foley	.05
382	Jeff Blauser	.05
383	*Scott Ruskin*	.05
384	Andres Thomas	.05
385	Dennis Martinez	.05
386	Mike Henneman	.05
387	Felix Jose	.05
388	Alejandro Pena	.05
389	Chet Lemon	.05
390	*Craig Wilson*	.10
391	Chuck Crim	.05
392	Mel Hall	.05

393	Mark Knudson	.05
394	Norm Charlton	.05
395	Mike Felder	.05
396	*Tim Layana*	.05
397	Steve Frey	.05
398	Bill Doran	.05
399	Dion James	.05
400	Checklist 301-400	.05
401	Ron Hassey	.05
402	Don Robinson	.05
403	Gene Nelson	.05
404	Terry Kennedy	.05
405	Todd Burns	.05
406	Roger McDowell	.05
407	Bob Kipper	.05
408	Darren Daulton	.05
409	Chuck Cary	.05
410	Bruce Ruffin	.05
411	Juan Berenguer	.05
412	Gary Ward	.05
413	Al Newman	.05
414	Danny Jackson	.05
415	Greg Gagne	.05
416	Tom Herr	.05
417	Jeff Parrett	.05
418	Jeff Reardon	.05
419	Mark Lemke	.05
420	Charlie O'Brien	.05
421	Willie Randolph	.05
422	Steve Bedrosian	.05
423	Mike Moore	.05
424	Jeff Brantley	.05
425	Bob Welch	.05
426	Terry Mulholland	.05
427	*Willie Blair*	.10
428	Darrin Fletcher	.10
429	Mike Witt	.05
430	Joe Boever	.05
431	Tom Gordon	.05
432	*Pedro Munoz*	.10
433	Kevin Seitzer	.05
434	Kevin Tapani	.05
435	Bret Saberhagen	.10
436	Ellis Burks	.10
437	Chuck Finley	.05
438	Mike Boddicker	.05
439	Francisco Cabrera	.05
440	Todd Hundley	.15
441	Kelly Downs	.05
442	*Dann Howitt*	.05
443	Scott Garrelts	.05
444	Rickey Henderson	.25
445	Will Clark	.30
446	Ben McDonald	.05
447	Dale Murphy	.10
448	Dave Righetti	.05
449	Dickie Thon	.05
450	Ted Power	.05
451	Scott Coolbaugh	.05
452	Dwight Smith	.05
453	Pete Incaviglia	.05
454	Andre Dawson	.10
455	Ruben Sierra	.05
456	Andres Galarraga	.20
457	Alvin Davis	.05
458	Tony Castillo	.05
459	Pete O'Brien	.05
460	Charlie Leibrandt	.05
461	Vince Coleman	.05
462	Steve Sax	.05
463	*Omar Oliveras*	.05
464	*Oscar Azocar*	.05
465	Joe Magrane	.05
466	*Karl Rhodes*	.10
467	Benito Santiago	.05
468	*Joe Klink*	.05
469	Sil Campusano	.05
470	Mark Parent	.05
471	*Shawn Boskie*	.10
472	Kevin Brown	.10
473	Rick Sutcliffe	.05
474	Rafael Palmeiro	.25
475	Mike Harkey	.05
476	Jaime Navarro	.05
477	Marquis Grissom	.10
478	Marty Clary	.05
479	Greg Briley	.05
480	Tom Glavine	.15
481	Lee Guetterman	.05
482	Rex Hudler	.05
483	Dave LaPoint	.05
484	Terry Pendleton	.05
485	Jesse Barfield	.05
486	Jose DeJesus	.05
487	*Paul Abbott*	.05
488	Ken Howell	.05
489	Greg W. Harris	.05
490	Roy Smith	.05
491	Paul Assenmacher	.05
492	Geno Petralli	.05
493	Steve Wilson	.05
494	Kevin Reimer	.05
495	Bill Long	.05
496	Mike Jackson	.05
497	Oddibe McDowell	.05
498	Bill Swift	.05
499	Jeff Treadway	.05
500	Checklist 401-500	.05
501	Gene Larkin	.05
502	Bob Boone	.05
503	Allan Anderson	.05
504	Luis Aquino	.05
505	Mark Guthrie	.05
506	Joe Orsulak	.05
507	*Dana Kiecker*	.05
508	Dave Gallagher	.05
509	Greg A. Harris	.05
510	Mark Williamson	.05
511	Casey Candaele	.05
512	Mookie Wilson	.05
513	Dave Smith	.05
514	*Chuck Carr*	.05
515	Glenn Wilson	.05
516	Mike Fitzgerald	.05
517	Devon White	.05
518	Dave Hollins	.05
519	Mark Eichhorn	.05
520	Otis Nixon	.05
521	*Terry Shumpert*	.05
522	*Scott Erickson*	.25
523	Danny Tartabull	.05
524	Orel Hershiser	.05
525	George Brett	.40
526	Greg Vaughn	.05
527	Tim Naehring	.05
528	Curt Schilling	.10
529	Chris Bosio	.05
530	Sam Horn	.05
531	Mike Scott	.05
532	George Bell	.05
533	Eric Anthony	.05
534	*Julio Valera*	.05
535	Glenn Davis	.05
536	Larry Walker	.25
537	Pat Combs	.05
538	*Chris Nabholz*	.05
539	Kirk McCaskill	.05
540	Randy Ready	.05
541	Mark Gubicza	.05
542	Rick Aguilera	.05
543	*Brian McRae*	.25
544	Kirby Puckett	.50
545	Bo Jackson	.20
546	Wade Boggs	.20
547	Tim McIntosh	.05
548	Randy Milligan	.05
549	Dwight Evans	.05
550	Billy Ripken	.05
551	Erik Hanson	.05
552	Lance Parrish	.05
553	Tino Martinez	.10
554	Jim Abbott	.05
555	Ken Griffey, Jr.	2.00
556	Milt Cuyler	.05
557	*Mark Leonard*	.05
558	Jay Howell	.05
559	Lloyd Moseby	.05
560	Chris Gwynn	.05
561	*Mark Whiten*	.15
562	Harold Baines	.05
563	Junior Felix	.05
564	Darren Lewis	.05
565	Fred McGriff	.20
566	Kevin Appier	.05
567	*Luis Gonzalez*	.50
568	Frank White	.05
569	Juan Agosto	.05
570	Mike Macfarlane	.05
571	Bert Blyleven	.05
572	Ken Griffey, Sr.	.05
573	Lee Stevens	.05
574	Edgar Martinez	.05
575	Wally Joyner	.05
576	Tim Belcher	.05
577	John Burkett	.05
578	Mike Morgan	.05
579	Paul Gibson	.05
580	Jose Vizcaino	.05
581	Duane Ward	.05
582	Scott Sanderson	.05
583	David Wells	.10
584	Willie McGee	.05
585	John Cerutti	.05
586	Danny Darwin	.05
587	Kurt Stillwell	.05
588	Rich Gedman	.05
589	Mark Davis	.05
590	Bill Gullickson	.05
591	Matt Young	.05
592	Bryan Harvey	.05
593	Omar Vizquel	.05
594	*Scott Lewis*	.05
595	Dave Valle	.05
596	Tim Crews	.05
597	Mike Bielecki	.05
598	Mike Sharperson	.05
599	Dave Bergman	.05
600	Checklist 501-600	.05
601	Steve Lyons	.05
602	Bruce Hurst	.05
603	Donn Pall	.05
604	*Jim Vatcher*	.05
605	Dan Pasqua	.05
606	Kenny Rogers	.05
607	*Jeff Schulz*	.05
608	Brad Arnsberg	.05
609	Willie Wilson	.05
610	Jamie Moyer	.05
611	Ron Oester	.05
612	Dennis Cook	.05
613	Rick Mahler	.05
614	Bill Landrum	.05
615	Scott Scudder	.05
616	*Tom Edens*	.05
617	"1917 Revisited" (Chicago White Sox team photo)	.10
618	Jim Gantner	.05
619	Darrel Akerfelds	.05
620	Ron Robinson	.05
621	Scott Radinsky	.05
622	Pete Smith	.05
623	Melido Perez	.05
624	Jerald Clark	.05
625	Carlos Martinez	.05
626	*Wes Chamberlain*	.10
627	Bobby Witt	.05
628	Ken Dayley	.05
629	*John Barfield*	.05
630	Bob Tewksbury	.05
631	Glenn Braggs	.05
632	*Jim Neidlinger*	.05
633	Tom Browning	.05
634	Kirk Gibson	.05
635	Rob Dibble	.05
636	"Stolen Base Leaders" (Lou Brock, Rickey Henderson)	.15
637	Jeff Montgomery	.05
638	Mike Schooler	.05
639	Storm Davis	.05
640	*Rich Rodriguez*	.05
641	Phil Bradley	.05
642	Kent Mercker	.05
643	Carlton Fisk	.25
644	Mike Bell	.05
645	*Alex Fernandez*	.15
646	Juan Gonzalez	.75
647	Ken Hill	.05
648	Jeff Russell	.05
649	*Chuck Malone*	.05
650	Steve Buechele	.05
651	Mike Benjamin	.05
652	Tony Pena	.05
653	Trevor Wilson	.05
654	Alex Cole	.05
655	Roger Clemens	.50
656	"The Bashing Years" (Mark McGwire)	.75
657	*Joe Grahe*	.05
658	Jim Eisenreich	.05
659	Dan Gladden	.05
660	Steve Farr	.05
661	*Bill Sampen*	.05
662	*Dave Rohde*	.05
663	Mark Gardner	.05
664	*Mike Simms*	.05
665	Moises Alou	.15
666	Mickey Hatcher	.05
667	Jimmy Key	.10
668	John Wetteland	.05
669	John Smiley	.05
670	Jim Acker	.05
671	Pascual Perez	.05
672	*Reggie Harris*	.10
673	Matt Nokes	.05
674	*Rafael Novoa*	.05
675	Hensley Meulens	.05
676	Jeff M. Robinson	.05
677	"Ground Breaking" (New Comiskey Park)	.15
678	Johnny Ray	.05
679	Greg Hibbard	.05
680	Paul Sorrento	.05
681	Mike Marshall	.05
682	Jim Clancy	.05
683	Rob Murphy	.05
684	Dave Schmidt	.05
685	*Jeff Gray*	.05
686	Mike Hartley	.05
687	Jeff King	.05
688	Stan Javier	.05
689	Bob Walk	.05
690	Jim Gott	.05
691	Mike LaCoss	.05
692	John Farrell	.05
693	Tim Leary	.05
694	*Mike Walker*	.05
695	Eric Plunk	.05
696	Mike Fetters	.05
697	Wayne Edwards	.05
698	Tim Drummond	.05
699	Willie Fraser	.05
700	Checklist 601-700	.05
701	Mike Heath	.05
702	"Rookie Threats" (Luis Gonzalez, Karl Rhodes, Jeff Bagwell)	.60
703	Jose Mesa	.05
704	Dave Smith	.05
705	Danny Darwin	.05
706	Rafael Belliard	.05
707	Rob Murphy	.05
708	Terry Pendleton	.05
709	Mike Pagliarulo	.05
710	Sid Bream	.05
711	Junior Felix	.05
712	Dante Bichette	.20
713	Kevin Gross	.05
714	Luis Sojo	.05
715	Bob Ojeda	.05
716	Julio Machado	.05
717	Steve Farr	.05
718	Franklin Stubbs	.05
719	Mike Boddicker	.05
720	Willie Randolph	.05
721	Willie McGee	.05
722	Chili Davis	.05
723	Danny Jackson	.05
724	Cory Snyder	.05
725	"MVP Lineup" (Andre Dawson, George Bell, Ryne Sandberg)	.15
726	Rob Deer	.05
727	Rich DeLucia	.05
728	Mike Perez	.05
729	Mickey Tettleton	.05
730	Mike Blowers	.05
731	Gary Gaetti	.05
732	Brett Butler	.05
733	Dave Parker	.10
734	Eddie Zosky	.05
735	Jack Clark	.05
736	Jack Morris	.05
737	Kirk Gibson	.05
738	Steve Bedrosian	.05
739	Candy Maldonado	.05
740	Matt Young	.05
741	Rich Garces	.05
742	George Bell	.05
743	Deion Sanders	.20
744	Bo Jackson	.20
745	Luis Mercedes	.05
746	Reggie Jefferson	.05
747	Pete Incaviglia	.05
748	Chris Hammond	.05
749	Mike Stanton	.05
750	Scott Sanderson	.05
751	Paul Faries	.05
752	Al Osuna	.05
753	Steve Chitren	.05
754	Tony Fernandez	.05
755	*Jeff Bagwell*	3.00
756	Kirk Dressendorfer	.05
757	Glenn Davis	.05
758	Gary Carter	.05
759	Zane Smith	.05
760	Vance Law	.05
761	Denis Boucher	.05
762	Turner Ward	.05
763	Roberto Alomar	.30
764	Albert Belle	.40
765	Joe Carter	.10
766	Pete Schourek	.05
767	Heathcliff Slocumb	.05
768	Vince Coleman	.05
769	Mitch Williams	.05
770	Brian Downing	.05
771	Dana Allison	.05
772	Pete Harnisch	.05
773	Tim Raines	.10
774	Darryl Kile	.10
775	Fred McGriff	.20
776	Dwight Evans	.05
777	Joe Slusarski	.05
778	Dave Righetti	.05
779	Jeff Hamilton	.05
780	Ernest Riles	.05
781	Ken Dayley	.05
782	Eric King	.05
783	Devon White	.05
784	Beau Allred	.05
785	Mike Timlin	.10
786	Ivan Calderon	.05
787	Hubie Brooks	.05
788	Juan Agosto	.05
789	Barry Jones	.05
790	Wally Backman	.05
791	Jim Presley	.05
792	Charlie Hough	.05
793	Larry Andersen	.05
794	Steve Finley	.05
795	Shawn Abner	.05
796	Jeff M. Robinson	.05
797	Joe Bitker	.05
798	Eric Show	.05
799	Bud Black	.05
800	Checklist 701-800	.05
SP1	Michael Jordan	15.00
SP2	"A Day to Remember" (Rickey Henderson, Nolan Ryan)	1.50
HH1	Hank Aaron (hologram)	1.50

1991 Upper Deck Hank Aaron Heroes

This set devoted to Hank Aaron is numbered 19-27 and includes an unnumbered "Baseball Heroes" cover card. The cards are found in foil and jumbo packs of Upper Deck high-number cards.

		MT
Complete Set (10):		6.00
Common Aaron:		.50
Autographed Card:		150.00
Aaron Header:		2.50
19	1954 Rookie Year	.50
20	1957 MVP	.50
21	1966 Move to Atlanta	.50
22	1970 3,000	.50
23	1974 715	.50
24	1975 Return to Milwaukee	.50
25	1976 755	.50
26	1982 Hall of Fame	.50
27	Checklist - Heroes 19-27	.50

1991 Upper Deck Heroes of Baseball

This four-card set features three members of Baseball's Hall of Fame: Harmon Killebrew, Gaylord Perry and Ferguson Jenkins. Each has a card for himself, plus there's a card which features all three players. The cards were found in specially-marked low number foil packs. The cards are numbered H1-H4. Upper Deck also produced 3,000 autographed and numbered cards for each player.

		MT
Complete Set (4):		12.50
Autographed Card:		37.00
1	Harmon Killebrew	4.00
2	Gaylord Perry	4.00
3	Ferguson Jenkins	4.00
4	Gaylord Perry, Ferguson Jenkins, Harmon Killebrew	4.00

1991 Upper Deck Nolan Ryan Heroes

This set devoted to Nolan Ryan is numbered 10-18 and includes an unnumbered "Baseball Heroes" cover card. The cards are found in low-number foil and jumbo boxes.

		MT
Complete Set (10):		6.00
Common Player:		.50
Ryan header Card:		2.50
Autographed Card:		300.00
10	1968 Victory #1	.50
11	1973 A Career Year	.50
12	1975 Double Milestone	.50
13	1979 Back Home	.50
14	1981 All-Time Leader	.50
15	1989 5,000	.50
16	1990 The Sixth	.50
17	1990 ... and Still Counting	.50
18	Checklist - Heroes 10-18	.50

1991 Upper Deck Silver Sluggers

Each year the "Silver Slugger" award is presented

to the player at each position with the highest batting average in each league. Upper Deck produced special cards in honor of the 1990 season award winners. The cards were randomly inserted in jumbo packs of Upper Deck cards. The cards feature an "SS" designation along with the card number. The cards are designed like the regular issue Upper Deck cards from 1991, but feature a Silver Slugger bat along the left border of the card.

		MT
Complete Set (18):		15.00
Common Player:		.50
1	Julio Franco	.50
2	Alan Trammell	.50
3	Rickey Henderson	1.00
4	Jose Canseco	2.50
5	Barry Bonds	3.50
6	Eddie Murray	1.00
7	Kelly Gruber	.50
8	Ryne Sandberg	1.50
9	Darryl Strawberry	.50
10	Ellis Burks	.50
11	Lance Parrish	.50
12	Cecil Fielder	.50
13	Matt Williams	.75
14	Dave Parker	.50
15	Bobby Bonilla	.50
16	Don Robinson	.50
17	Benito Santiago	.50
18	Barry Larkin	.75

1991 Upper Deck Final Edition

Upper Deck surprised the hobby with the late-season release of this 100-card boxed set. The cards are numbered with an "F" designation. A special "Minor League Diamond Skills" subset (cards #1-21) features several top prospects. An All-Star subset (cards #79-99) is also included in this set. The cards are styled like the regular 1991 Upper Deck issue Special team hologram cards are included with the set.

		MT
Complete Set (100):		15.00
Common Player:		.05
1	Ryan Klesko, Reggie Sanders (Minor League Diamond Skills Checklist)	.50
2	*Pedro Martinez*	8.00
3	Lance Dickson	.05
4	Royce Clayton	.10
5	Scott Bryant	.05
6	Dan Wilson	.25
7	*Dmitri Young*	.25
8	*Ryan Klesko*	.40
9	Tom Goodwin	.10
10	*Rondell White*	.50
11	Reggie Sanders	.20
12	Todd Van Poppel	.05
13	Arthur Rhodes	.05
14	Eddie Zosky	.05
15	Gerald Williams	.10
16	Robert Eenhoorn	.05
17	*Jim Thome*	1.50
18	*Marc Newfield*	.10
19	Kerwin Moore	.05
20	Jeff McNeely	.05
21	Frankie Rodriguez	.10
22	Andy Mota	.05
23	Chris Haney	.05
24	*Kenny Lofton*	.50
25	Dave Nilsson	.25
26	Derek Bell	.15
27	Frank Castillo	.10
28	Candy Maldonado	.05
29	Chuck McElroy	.05
30	Chito Martinez	.05
31	Steve Howe	.05
32	Freddie Benavides	.05
33	Scott Kamieniecki	.10
34	Denny Neagle	.20
35	Mike Humphreys	.05
36	Mike Remlinger	.05
37	Scott Coolbaugh	.05
38	Darren Lewis	.10
39	Thomas Howard	.10
40	John Candelaria	.05
41	Todd Benzinger	.05
42	Wilson Alvarez	.15
43	Patrick Lennon	.05
44	Rusty Meacham	.05
45	*Ryan Bowen*	.05
46	*Rick Wilkins*	.10
47	*Ed Sprague*	.15
48	*Bob Scanlan*	.05
49	Tom Candiotti	.05
50	Dennis Martinez (Perfecto)	.10
51	Oil Can Boyd	.05
52	Glenallen Hill	.05
53	*Scott Livingstone*	.05
54	*Brian Hunter*	.20
55	*Ivan Rodriguez*	2.00
56	*Keith Mitchell*	.05
57	Roger McDowell	.05
58	Otis Nixon	.05
59	*Juan Bell*	.05
60	Bill Krueger	.05
61	*Chris Donnels*	.05
62	Tommy Greene	.05
63	Doug Simons	.05
64	*Andy Ashby*	.15
65	*Anthony Young*	.05
66	*Kevin Morton*	.05
67	*Bret Barberie*	.10
68	*Scott Servais*	.15
69	Ron Darling	.05
70	Vicente Palacios	.05
71	*Tim Burke*	.05
72	*Gerald Alexander*	.05
73	Reggie Jefferson	.05
74	Dean Palmer	.05
75	Mark Whiten	.05
76	Randy Tomlin	.05
77	*Mark Wohlers*	.25
78	Brook Jacoby	.05
79	Ken Griffey Jr., Ryne Sandberg (All-Star Checklist)	.40
80	Jack Morris (AS)	.05
81	Sandy Alomar, Jr. (AS)	.05
82	Cecil Fielder (AS)	.05
83	Roberto Alomar (AS)	.20
84	Wade Boggs (AS)	.15
85	Cal Ripken, Jr. (AS)	.50
86	Rickey Henderson (AS)	.10
87	Ken Griffey, Jr. (AS)	.75
88	Dave Henderson (AS)	.05
89	Danny Tartabull (AS)	.05
90	Tom Glavine (AS)	.10
91	Benito Santiago (AS)	.05
92	Will Clark (AS)	.15
93	Ryne Sandberg (AS)	.20
94	Chris Sabo (AS)	.05
95	Ozzie Smith (AS)	.20
96	Ivan Calderon (AS)	.05
97	Tony Gwynn (AS)	.25
98	Andre Dawson (AS)	.05
99	Bobby Bonilla (AS)	.05
100	Checklist	.05

1991 Upper Deck Souvenir Sheets

In conjunction with its sponsorship of a series of old-timers' benefit game around the leagues, Upper Deck produced a series of 11" x 8-1/2" souvenir sheets given to fans attending the events. Fronts feature color artwork of players involved in the contests. Backs are blank. Each sheet is serially numbered from within a stated edition. Sheets are listed here alphabetically by title. Editions are indicated in parentheses. The Jackson header sheet can be found indicating either 10,000 or 20,000 pieces and is common to each set.

		MT
Complete Set (23):		100.00
Common Sheet:		5.00
(1)	All-Star Joes vs. All-Star Bobs (Bobby Bonds, Bobby Doerr, Bob Gibson, Joe Pepitone, Joe Rudi) (San Diego) (27,000)	5.00
(2)	American League vs. National League (Don Kessinger, Dave Kingman, Ferguson Jenkins, Ron Santo, Billy Williams) (Wrigley Field) (22,000)	5.00
(3)	Atlanta Braves vs. National League (Lou Brock, Jeff Burroughs, Rico Carty, Chris Chambliss, Darrell Evans) (22,000)	5.00
(4)	Battle of Missouri (Lou Brock, Bob Gibson, Al Hrabosky, Red Schoendienst, Mike Shannon) (St. Louis) (17,000)	5.00
(5)	Cincinnati Reds vs. World Series Heroes (Ed Bailey, Leo Cardenas, John Edwards, Joe Nuxhall, Tony Perez) (Cincinnati) (22,000)	5.00
(6)	David vs. Goliath (Lou Brock, Cesar Cedeno, Eddie Mathews, Gaylord Perry, Billy Williams) (Houston) (17,000)	7.50
(7)	Giants Reunion (Gaylord Perry) (SF) (42,000)	5.00
(8a)	Header Sheet (Reggie Jackson) (10,000)	3.00
(8b)	Header Sheet (Reggie Jackson) (20,000)	3.00
(9)	Heroes of the '70s (Mark Fidrych, Ray Fosse, Reggie Jackson, Gaylord Perry, Boog Powell) (Cleveland) (22,000)	5.00
(10)	Philadelphia Scholars Fund Sports Show (Charles Barkley, Mike Schmidt, Rick Tocchet, Reggie White) (21,500)	25.00
(11)	Tribute to All-Star Heroes (Lou Brock, Bob Gibson, Reggie Jackson, Ferguson Jenkins, Brooks Robinson) (Toronto) (95,000)	5.00
(12)	Tribute to Baltimore Orioles Heroes (Boog Powell, Robin Roberts, Brooks Robinson, Frank Robinson, Earl Weaver) (17,000)	7.50
(13)	Tribute to Hall of Famers (Ferguson Jenkins, Gaylord Perry) (Arlington) (17,000)	5.00
(14)	Tribute to Home Run Hitters (Bobby Bonds, George Foster, Bobby Grich, Reggie Jackson, Billy Williams) (Anaheim) (44,000)	5.00
(15)	Tribute to DiMaggio/ Williams 1941 (Dom DiMaggio, Bobby Doerr, Ken Keltner, Mickey Owen, Johnny Pesky) (Boston) (17,000)	5.00
(16)	Tribute to Jim "Catfish" Hunter (Jim "Catfish" Hunter) (Oakland) (22,000)	5.00
(17)	Tribute to 1971 Heroes (Bill Freehan, Willie Horton, Al Kaline, Mickey Lolich) (Detroit) (32,000)	7.50
(18)	World Series Heroes (Yogi Berra, Donn Clendenon, Ray Knight, Tug McGraw, Ron Swoboda) (Shea) (47,000)	7.50
(19)	10th Anniversary, Expos Division Champs (Charlie Lea, Larry Parrish, Steve Rogers, Chris Speier, Jerry White) (22,000)	5.00
(20)	45th Annual Old-Timers Day Classic (Ron Guidry, Catfish Hunter, Bobby Murcer, Joe Pepitone, Bobby Richardson) (Yankees) (47,000)	7.50
(21)	1971 Phillies vs. Upper Deck Heroes (Larry Bowa, Jim Bunning, Don Money, Willie Montanez) (Phila.) (42,000)	5.00
(22)	1971 Pirates vs. the Baltimore Orioles (Steve Blass, Richie Hebner, Bruce Kison, Al Oliver, Willie Stargell) (18,000)	6.50
(23)	1981 A.L. Division Playoff Heroes (Cecil Cooper, Rollie Fingers, Ben Oglivie, Charlie Moore, Gorman Thomas) (Milwaukee) (27,000)	5.00

1991 Upper Deck Comic Ball 2 Promos

Among the most sought-after promo cards in the promo-card mania that marked the 1991 National Sports Collectors Convention in Anaheim, Calif., was this set of Upper Deck preview cards for its Comic Ball 2 set. One card was given out each day of the National, from July 4-7, with the giveaway date noted in a banner at top. Fronts picture Reggie Jackson and Nolan Ryan with various Looney Tunes cartoon characters. Backs have information on the upcoming Comic Ball 2 issue against a cartoon puzzle background.

		MT
Complete Set (4):		25.00
Common Player:		4.00
7/4/91	Nolan Ryan (w/ Bugs Bunny, Daffy Duck)	10.00
7/5/91	Reggie Jackson (w/ Taz)	4.00
7/6/91	Nolan Ryan (w/ Speedy Gonzalez)	10.00
7/7/91	Reggie Jackson (w/ Sylvester, Elmer Fudd)	4.00

1991 Upper Deck Comic Ball 2

Despite featuring two popular superstars on dozens of the cards, this 198-piece issue has found little favor with collectors. Most cards are arranged in 18-card sequences which tell a baseball-related cartoon tale starring Bugs Bunny, Daffy Duck, Wile E. Coyote and the rest of the Looney Tune characters. Actual-photo "guest appearances" by Nolan Ryan and Reggie Jackson highlight these presentations. There are also "Seventh Inning Stretch" cards featuring the ballplayers in scenes with the cartoon figures. When arranged in nine-pocket plastic sheets, card backs form a cartoon picture puzzle. Cards are typical Upper Deck quality with semi-gloss front and back surfaces and a circular hologram on the backs in the standard 2-1/2" x 3-1/2" format. Nine hologram stickers featuring Ryan and Jackson along with the cartoon characters were produced as random pack inserts. Because the cards are licensed by Major League Baseball, the players and cartoon critters are depicted in Major League uniforms.

	MT
Complete Set (198):	9.00
Common Card, Cartoon:	.05
Common Card, Ryan/Jackson:	.10
Hologram Sticker:	2.00

1992 Upper Deck

Upper Deck introduced a new look in 1992. The baseline style was no longer used. The cards feature full-color action photos on white stock, with the player's name and the Upper Deck logo along the top border. The team name is in the photo's bottom-right corner. Once again a 100-card high number series was released in late summer. Ted Williams autographed 2,500 Baseball Heroes cards which were randomly inserted into packs. Subsets featured in the 1992 issue include Star Rookies and Top Prospects. Cards originating from factory sets have gold-foil holograms on back, rather than silver.

	MT
Complete Set (800):	15.00
Complete Low Series (1-700):	15.00
Complete High Series (701-800):	5.00
Common Player:	.05
Low or High Wax Box:	20.00

1 Star Rookie Checklist (Ryan Klesko, Jim Thome) .40
2 Royce Clayton (Star Rookie) .15
3 *Brian Jordan* (Star Rookie) .40
4 *Dave Fleming* (Star Rookie) .10
5 Jim Thome (Star Rookie) .50
6 Jeff Juden (Star Rookie) .10
7 *Roberto Hernandez* (Star Rookie) .12
8 Kyle Abbott (Star Rookie) .10
9 *Chris George* (Star Rookie) .05
10 *Rob Maurer* (Star Rookie) .05
11 *Donald Harris* (Star Rookie) .05
12 *Ted Wood* (Star Rookie) .05
13 *Patrick Lennon* (Star Rookie) .05
14 Willie Banks (Star Rookie) .05
15 Roger Salkeld (Star Rookie) .10
16 Wil Cordero (Star Rookie) .20
17 *Arthur Rhodes* (Star Rookie) .10
18 Pedro Martinez (Star Rookie) 1.50
19 *Andy Ashby* (Star Rookie) .10
20 Tom Goodwin (Star Rookie) .10
21 *Braulio Castillo* (Star Rookie) .05
22 Todd Van Poppel (Star Rookie) .05
23 *Brian Williams* (Star Rookie) .05
24 Ryan Klesko (Star Rookie) .25
25 Kenny Lofton (Star Rookie) .25
26 Derek Bell (Star Rookie) .15
27 Reggie Sanders (Star Rookie) .15
28 Dave Winfield (Winfield's 400th) .10
29 Atlanta Braves Checklist (Dave Justice) .10
30 Cincinnati Reds Checklist (Rob Dibble) .05
31 Houston Astros Checklist (Craig Biggio) .10
32 Los Angeles Dodgers Checklist (Eddie Murray) .10
33 San Diego Padres Checklist (Fred McGriff) .10
34 San Francisco Giants Checklist (Willie McGee) .05
35 Chicago Cubs Checklist (Shawon Dunston) .05
36 Montreal Expos Checklist (Delino DeShields) .05
37 New York Mets Checklist (Howard Johnson) .05
38 Philadelphia Phillies Checklist (John Kruk) .05
39 Pittsburgh Pirates Checklist (Doug Drabek) .05
40 St. Louis Cardinals Checklist (Todd Zeile) .05
41 Steve Avery (Playoff Perfection) .05
42 *Jeremy Hernandez* .05
43 *Doug Henry* .10
44 *Chris Donnels* .05
45 *Mo Sanford* .05
46 *Scott Kamieniecki* .15
47 Mark Lemke .05
48 Steve Farr .05
49 Francisco Oliveras .05
50 *Ced Landrum* .05
51 Top Prospect Checklist (Rondell White, Marc Newfield) .20
52 *Eduardo Perez* (Top Prospect) .10
53 *Tom Nevers* (Top Prospect) .05
54 *David Zancanaro* (Top Prospect) .05
55 *Shawn Green* (Top Prospect) 3.00
56 *Mark Wohlers* (Top Prospect) .05
57 Dave Nilsson (Top Prospect) .15
58 Dmitri Young (Top Prospect) .15
59 *Ryan Hawblitzel* (Top Prospect) .10
60 Raul Mondesi (Top Prospect) .40
61 Rondell White (Top Prospect) .15
62 Steve Hosey (Top Prospect) .05
63 *Manny Ramirez* (Top Prospect) 3.00
64 Marc Newfield (Top Prospect) .05
65 Jeromy Burnitz (Top Prospect) .25
66 *Mark Smith* (Top Prospect) .05
67 *Joey Hamilton* (Top Prospect) .40
68 *Tyler Green* (Top Prospect) .10
69 *John Farrell* (Top Prospect) .05
70 *Kurt Miller* (Top Prospect) .10
71 *Jeff Plympton* (Top Prospect) .05
72 Dan Wilson (Top Prospect) .15
73 *Joe Vitiello* (Top Prospect) .10
74 Rico Brogna (Top Prospect) .15
75 *David McCarty* (Top Prospect) .10
76 *Bob Wickman* (Top Prospect) .10
77 *Carlos Rodriguez* (Top Prospect) .10
78 Jim Abbott (Stay in School) .10
79 Bloodlines (Pedro Martinez, Ramon Martinez) .40
80 Bloodlines (Kevin Mitchell, Keith Mitchell) .05
81 Bloodlines (Sandy Jr. & Roberto Alomar, Sandy Jr. & Roberto Alomar) .15
82 Bloodlines (Cal Jr. & Billy Ripken, Cal Jr. & Billy Ripken) .40
83 Bloodlines (Tony & Chris Gwynn, Tony & Chris Gwynn) .20
84 Bloodlines (Dwight Gooden, Gary Sheffield) .15
85 Bloodlines (Ken, Sr.; Ken, Jr.; & Craig Griffey, Ken, Sr.; Ken, Jr.; & Craig Griffey, Ken, Sr.; Ken, Jr.; & Craig Griffey) .50
86 California Angels Checklist (Jim Abbott) .05
87 Chicago White Sox Checklist (Frank Thomas) .20
88 Kansas City Royals Checklist (Danny Tartabull) .05
89 Minnesota Twins Checklist (Scott Erickson) .05
90 Oakland Athletics Checklist (Rickey Henderson) .10
91 Seattle Mariners Checklist (Edgar Martinez) .05
92 Texas Rangers Checklist (Nolan Ryan) .50
93 Baltimore Orioles Checklist (Ben McDonald) .05
94 Boston Red Sox Checklist (Ellis Burks) .05
95 Cleveland Indians Checklist (Greg Swindell) .05
96 Detroit Tigers Checklist (Cecil Fielder) .05
97 Milwaukee Brewers Checklist (Greg Vaughn) .05
98 New York Yankees Checklist (Kevin Maas) .05
99 Toronto Blue Jays Checklist (Dave Steib) .05
100 Checklist 1-100 .05
101 Joe Oliver .05
102 Hector Villanueva .05
103 Ed Whitson .05
104 Danny Jackson .05
105 Chris Hammond .05
106 Ricky Jordan .05
107 Kevin Bass .05
108 Darrin Fletcher .05
109 Junior Ortiz .05
110 Tom Bolton .05
111 Jeff King .05
112 Dave Magadan .05
113 Mike LaValliere .05
114 Hubie Brooks .05
115 Jay Bell .05
116 David Wells .05
117 Jim Leyritz .05
118 Manuel Lee .05
119 Alvaro Espinoza .05
120 B.J. Surhoff .05
121 Hal Morris .05
122 Shawon Dunston .05
123 Chris Sabo .05
124 Andre Dawson .10
125 Eric Davis .05
126 Chili Davis .05
127 Dale Murphy .10
128 Kirk McCaskill .05
129 Terry Mulholland .05
130 Rick Aguilera .05
131 Vince Coleman .05
132 Andy Van Slyke .05
133 Gregg Jefferies .05
134 Barry Bonds .40
135 Dwight Gooden .10
136 Dave Stieb .05
137 Albert Belle .30
138 Teddy Higuera .05
139 Jesse Barfield .05
140 Pat Borders .05
141 Bip Roberts .05
142 Rob Dibble .05
143 Mark Grace .20
144 Barry Larkin .10
145 Ryne Sandberg .30
146 Scott Erickson .05
147 Luis Polonia .05
148 John Burkett .05
149 Luis Sojo .05
150 Dickie Thon .05
151 Walt Weiss .05
152 Mike Scioscia .05
153 Mark McGwire 1.50
154 Matt Williams .10
155 Rickey Henderson .20
156 Sandy Alomar, Jr. .10
157 Brian McRae .05
158 Harold Baines .05
159 Kevin Appier .05
160 Felix Fermin .05
161 Leo Gomez .05
162 Craig Biggio .25
163 Ben McDonald .05
164 Randy Johnson .30
165 Cal Ripken, Jr. 1.00
166 Frank Thomas .50
167 Delino DeShields .05
168 Greg Gagne .05
169 Ron Karkovice .05
170 Charlie Leibrandt .05
171 Dave Righetti .05
172 Dave Henderson .05
173 Steve Decker .05
174 Darryl Strawberry .10
175 Will Clark .25
176 Ruben Sierra .05
177 Ozzie Smith .25
178 Charles Nagy .05
179 Gary Pettis .05
180 Kirk Gibson .05
181 Randy Milligan .05
182 Dave Valle .05
183 Chris Hoiles .05
184 Tony Phillips .05
185 Brady Anderson .10
186 Scott Fletcher .05
187 Gene Larkin .05
188 Lance Johnson .05
189 Greg Olson .05
190 Melido Perez .05
191 Lenny Harris .05
192 Terry Kennedy .05
193 Mike Gallego .05
194 Willie McGee .05
195 Juan Samuel .05
196 Jeff Huson .05
197 Alex Cole .05
198 Ron Robinson .05
199 Joel Skinner .05
200 Checklist 101-200 .05
201 Kevin Reimer .05
202 Stan Belinda .05
203 Pat Tabler .05
204 Jose Guzman .05
205 Jose Lind .05
206 Spike Owen .05
207 Joe Orsulak .05
208 Charlie Hayes .05
209 Mike Devereaux .05
210 Mike Fitzgerald .05
211 Willie Randolph .05
212 Rod Nichols .05
213 Mike Boddicker .05
214 Bill Spiers .05
215 Steve Olin .05
216 *David Howard* .05
217 Gary Varsho .05
218 Mike Harkey .05
219 Luis Aquino .05
220 Chuck McElroy .05
221 Doug Drabek .05
222 Dave Winfield .15
223 Rafael Palmeiro .25
224 Joe Carter .05
225 Bobby Bonilla .05
226 Ivan Calderon .05
227 Gregg Olson .05
228 Tim Wallach .05
229 Terry Pendleton .05
230 Gilberto Reyes .05
231 Carlos Baerga .05
232 Greg Vaughn .05
233 Bret Saberhagen .05
234 Gary Sheffield .15
235 Mark Lewis .05
236 George Bell .05
237 Danny Tartabull .05
238 Willie Wilson .05
239 Doug Dascenzo .05
240 Bill Pecota .05
241 Julio Franco .05
242 Ed Sprague .05
243 Juan Gonzalez .50
244 Chuck Finley .05
245 Ivan Rodriguez .50
246 Len Dykstra .05
247 Deion Sanders .15
248 Dwight Evans .05
249 Larry Walker .25
250 Billy Ripken .05
251 Mickey Tettleton .05
252 Tony Pena .05
253 Benito Santiago .05
254 Kirby Puckett .40
255 Cecil Fielder .05
256 Howard Johnson .05
257 Andujar Cedeno .05
258 Jose Rijo .05
259 Al Osuna .05
260 Todd Hundley .10
261 Orel Hershiser .05
262 Ray Lankford .05
263 Robin Ventura .15
264 Felix Jose .05
265 Eddie Murray .25
266 Kevin Mitchell .05
267 Gary Carter .05
268 Mike Benjamin .05
269 Dick Schofield .05
270 Jose Uribe .05
271 Pete Incaviglia .05
272 Tony Fernandez .05
273 Alan Trammell .10
274 Tony Gwynn .40
275 Mike Greenwell .05
276 Jeff Bagwell .50
277 Frank Viola .05
278 Randy Myers .05
279 Ken Caminiti .15
280 Bill Doran .05
281 Dan Pasqua .05
282 Alfredo Griffin .05
283 Jose Oquendo .05
284 Kal Daniels .05
285 Bobby Thigpen .05
286 Robby Thompson .05
287 Mark Eichhorn .05
288 Mike Felder .05
289 Dave Gallagher .05
290 Dave Anderson .05
291 Mel Hall .05
292 Jerald Clark .05
293 Al Newman .05
294 Rob Deer .05
295 Matt Nokes .05
296 Jack Armstrong .05
297 Jim Deshaies .05
298 Jeff Innis .05
299 Jeff Reed .05
300 Checklist 201-300 .05
301 Lonnie Smith .05
302 Jimmy Key .05
303 Junior Felix .05
304 Mike Heath .05
305 Mark Langston .05
306 Greg W. Harris .05
307 Brett Butler .05
308 Luis Rivera .05
309 Bruce Ruffin .05
310 Paul Faries .05
311 Terry Leach .05
312 *Scott Brosius* .25
313 Scott Leius .05
314 Harold Reynolds .05
315 Jack Morris .05
316 David Segui .05
317 Bill Gullickson .05
318 Todd Frohwirth .05
319 *Mark Leiter* .05
320 Jeff M. Robinson .05
321 Gary Gaetti .05
322 John Smoltz .15
323 Andy Benes .10
324 Kelly Gruber .05
325 Jim Abbott .05
326 John Kruk .05
327 Kevin Seitzer .05
328 Darrin Jackson .05
329 Kurt Stillwell .05
330 Mike Maddux .05
331 Dennis Eckersley .05
332 Dan Gladden .05
333 Jose Canseco .25
334 Kent Hrbek .05
335 Ken Griffey, Sr. .05
336 Greg Swindell .05
337 Trevor Wilson .05
338 Sam Horn .05
339 Mike Henneman .05
340 Jerry Browne .05
341 Glenn Braggs .05
342 Tom Glavine .15
343 Wally Joyner .05
344 Fred McGriff .15
345 Ron Gant .10
346 Ramon Martinez .10
347 Wes Chamberlain .05
348 Terry Shumpert .05
349 Tim Teufel .05
350 Wally Backman .05
351 Joe Girardi .05
352 Devon White .05
353 Greg Maddux .75
354 *Ryan Bowen* .10
355 Roberto Alomar .30
356 Don Mattingly .50
357 Pedro Guerrero .05
358 Steve Sax .05
359 Joey Cora .05
360 Jim Gantner .05
361 Brian Barnes .05
362 Kevin McReynolds .05
363 *Bret Barberie* .10
364 David Cone .10
365 Dennis Martinez .05
366 *Brian Hunter* .10
367 Edgar Martinez .05
368 Steve Finley .05
369 Greg Briley .05
370 Jeff Blauser .05
371 Todd Stottlemyre .10
372 Luis Gonzalez .05
373 Rick Wilkins .05
374 *Darryl Kile* .10
375 John Olerud .20
376 Lee Smith .05
377 Kevin Maas .05
378 Dante Bichette .15
379 Tom Pagnozzi .05
380 Mike Flanagan .05
381 Charlie O'Brien .05
382 Dave Martinez .05
383 Keith Miller .05
384 Scott Ruskin .05
385 Kevin Elster .05
386 Alvin Davis .05
387 Casey Candaele .05
388 Pete O'Brien .05
389 Jeff Treadway .05
390 Scott Bradley .05
391 Mookie Wilson .05
392 Jimmy Jones .05
393 Candy Maldonado .05
394 Eric Yelding .05
395 Tom Henke .05
396 Franklin Stubbs .05
397 Milt Thompson .05
398 Mark Carreon .05
399 Randy Velarde .05
400 Checklist 301-400 .05
401 Omar Vizquel .05
402 Joe Boever .05
403 Bill Krueger .05
404 Jody Reed .05
405 Mike Schooler .05
406 Jason Grimsley .05
407 Greg Myers .05
408 Randy Ready .05
409 *Mike Timlin* .15
410 Mitch Williams .05
411 Garry Templeton .05
412 Greg Cadaret .05
413 Donnie Hill .05
414 Wally Whitehurst .05
415 Scott Sanderson .05
416 Thomas Howard .05
417 Neal Heaton .05
418 Charlie Hough .05
419 Jack Howell .05
420 Greg Hibbard .05
421 Carlos Quintana .05
422 *Kim Batiste* .05
423 Paul Molitor .30
424 Ken Griffey, Jr. 1.50
425 Phil Plantier .05
426 Denny Neagle .05

427 Von Hayes .05
428 Shane Mack .05
429 Darren Daulton .05
430 Dwayne Henry .05
431 Lance Parrish .05
432 *Mike Humphreys* .05
433 Tim Burke .05
434 Bryan Harvey .05
435 Pat Kelly .05
436 Ozzie Guillen .05
437 Bruce Hurst .05
438 Sammy Sosa .75
439 Dennis Rasmussen .05
440 Ken Patterson .05
441 Jay Buhner .05
442 Pat Combs .05
443 Wade Boggs .20
444 George Brett .30
445 Mo Vaughn .15
446 Chuck Knoblauch .15
447 Tom Candiotti .05
448 Mark Portugal .05
449 Mickey Morandini .05
450 Duane Ward .05
451 Otis Nixon .05
452 Bob Welch .05
453 Rusty Meacham .05
454 Keith Mitchell .05
455 Marquis Grissom .10
456 Robin Yount .25
457 *Harvey Pulliam* .05
458 Jose DeLeon .05
459 Mark Gubicza .05
460 Darryl Hamilton .05
461 Tom Browning .05
462 Monty Fariss .05
463 Jerome Walton .05
464 Paul O'Neill .15
465 Dean Palmer .05
466 Travis Fryman .10
467 John Smiley .05
468 Lloyd Moseby .05
469 *John Wehner* .05
470 Skeeter Barnes .05
471 Steve Chitren .05
472 Kent Mercker .05
473 Terry Steinbach .05
474 Andres Galarraga .20
475 Steve Avery .05
476 Tom Gordon .05
477 Cal Eldred .05
478 Omar Olivares .05
479 Julio Machado .05
480 Bob Milacki .05
481 Les Lancaster .05
482 John Candelaria .05
483 Brian Downing .05
484 Roger McDowell .05
485 Scott Scudder .05
486 Zane Smith .05
487 John Cerutti .05
488 Steve Buechele .05
489 Paul Gibson .05
490 Curtis Wilkerson .05
491 Marvin Freeman .05
492 Tom Foley .05
493 Juan Berenguer .05
494 Ernest Riles .05
495 Sid Bream .05
496 Chuck Crim .05
497 Mike Macfarlane .05
498 Dale Sveum .05
499 Storm Davis .05
500 Checklist 401-500 .05
501 Jeff Reardon .05
502 Shawn Abner .05
503 Tony Fossas .05
504 Cory Snyder .05
505 Matt Young .05
506 Allan Anderson .05
507 Mark Lee .05
508 Gene Nelson .05
509 Mike Pagliarulo .05
510 Rafael Belliard .05
511 Jay Howell .05
512 Bob Tewksbury .05
513 Mike Morgan .05
514 John Franco .05
515 Kevin Gross .05
516 Lou Whitaker .05
517 Orlando Merced .05
518 Todd Benzinger .05
519 Gary Redus .05
520 Walt Terrell .05
521 Jack Clark .05
522 Dave Parker .10
523 Tim Naehring .05
524 Mark Whiten .05
525 Ellis Burks .05
526 *Frank Castillo* .10
527 Brian Harper .05
528 Brook Jacoby .05
529 Rick Sutcliffe .05
530 Joe Klink .05
531 Terry Bross .05
532 Jose Offerman .05
533 Todd Zeile .05
534 Eric Karros .10
535 *Anthony Young* .05
536 Milt Cuyler .05
537 Randy Tomlin .05
538 *Scott Livingstone* .05
539 Jim Eisenreich .05
540 Don Slaught .05
541 Scott Cooper .05
542 Joe Grahe .05
543 Tom Brunansky .05
544 Eddie Zosky .05
545 Roger Clemens .50
546 Dave Justice .20
547 Dave Stewart .05
548 David West .05
549 Dave Smith .05
550 Dan Plesac .05
551 Alex Fernandez .10
552 Bernard Gilkey .05
553 Jack McDowell .05
554 Tino Martinez .10
555 Bo Jackson .15
556 Bernie Williams .20
557 Mark Gardner .05
558 Glenallen Hill .05
559 Oil Can Boyd .05
560 Chris James .05
561 *Scott Servais* .10
562 *Rey Sanchez* .15
563 *Paul McClellan* .05
564 *Andy Mota* .05
565 Darren Lewis .05
566 *Jose Melendez* .05
567 Tommy Greene .05
568 Rich Rodriguez .05
569 *Heathcliff Slocumb* .05
570 Joe Hesketh .05
571 Carlton Fisk .20
572 Erik Hanson .05
573 Wilson Alvarez .05
574 *Rheal Cormier* .05
575 Tim Raines .05
576 Bobby Witt .05
577 Roberto Kelly .05
578 Kevin Brown .10
579 Chris Nabholz .05
580 Jesse Orosco .05
581 Jeff Brantley .05
582 Rafael Ramirez .05
583 Kelly Downs .05
584 Mike Simms .05
585 *Mike Remlinger* .05
586 Dave Hollins .05
587 Larry Andersen .05
588 Mike Gardiner .05
589 Craig Lefferts .05
590 Paul Assenmacher .05
591 Bryn Smith .05
592 Donn Pall .05
593 Mike Jackson .05
594 Scott Radinsky .05
595 Brian Holman .05
596 Geronimo Pena .05
597 Mike Jeffcoat .05
598 Carlos Martinez .05
599 Geno Petralli .05
600 Checklist 501-600 .05
601 Jerry Don Gleaton .05
602 Adam Peterson .05
603 Craig Grebeck .05
604 Mark Guthrie .05
605 Frank Tanana .05
606 Hensley Meulens .05
607 Mark Davis .05
608 Eric Plunk .05
609 Mark Williamson .05
610 Lee Guetterman .05
611 Bobby Rose .05
612 Bill Wegman .05
613 Mike Hartley .05
614 *Chris Beasley* .05
615 Chris Bosio .05
616 Henry Cotto .05
617 *Chico Walker* .05
618 Russ Swan .05
619 Bob Walk .05
620 Billy Swift .05
621 *Warren Newson* .05
622 Steve Bedrosian .05
623 *Ricky Bones* .05
624 Kevin Tapani .05
625 *Juan Guzman* .10
626 *Jeff Johnson* .05
627 Jeff Montgomery .05
628 Ken Hill .05
629 Gary Thurman .05
630 Steve Howe .05
631 Jose DeJesus .05
632 Bert Blyleven .05
633 Jaime Navarro .05
634 Lee Stevens .05
635 Pete Harnisch .05
636 Bill Landrum .05
637 Rich DeLucia .05
638 Luis Salazar .05
639 Rob Murphy .05
640 A.L. Diamond Skills Checklist (Rickey Henderson, Jose Canseco) .05
641 Roger Clemens (Diamond Skills) .25
642 Jim Abbott (Diamond Skills) .05
643 Travis Fryman (Diamond Skills) .05
644 Jesse Barfield (Diamond Skills) .05
645 Cal Ripken, Jr. (Diamond Skills) .50
646 Wade Boggs (Diamond Skills) .10
647 Cecil Fielder (Diamond Skills) .05
648 Rickey Henderson (Diamond Skills) .10
649 Jose Canseco (Diamond Skills) .20
650 Ken Griffey, Jr. (Diamond Skills) .50
651 Kenny Rogers .05
652 *Luis Mercedes* .05
653 Mike Stanton .05
654 Glenn Davis .05
655 Nolan Ryan 1.00
656 Reggie Jefferson .05
657 *Javier Ortiz* .05
658 Greg A. Harris .05
659 Mariano Duncan .05
660 Jeff Shaw .05
661 Mike Moore .05
662 *Chris Haney* .05
663 *Joe Slusarski* .05
664 *Wayne Housie* .05
665 Carlos Garcia .05
666 Bob Ojeda .05
667 *Bryan Hickerson* .05
668 Tim Belcher .05
669 Ron Darling .05
670 Rex Hudler .05
671 Sid Fernandez .05
672 *Chito Martinez* .05
673 *Pete Schourek* .15
674 *Armando Renoso* .05
675 Mike Mussina .35
676 Kevin Morton .05
677 Norm Charlton .05
678 Danny Darwin .05
679 Eric King .05
680 Ted Power .05
681 Barry Jones .05
682 Carney Lansford .05
683 Mel Rojas .05
684 Rick Honeycutt .05
685 *Jeff Fassero* .15
686 Cris Carpenter .05
687 Tim Crews .05
688 Scott Terry .05
689 Chris Gwynn .05
690 Gerald Perry .05
691 John Barfield .05
692 Bob Melvin .05
693 Juan Agosto .05
694 Alejandro Pena .05
695 Jeff Russell .05
696 Carmelo Martinez .05
697 Bud Black .05
698 Dave Otto .05
699 Billy Hatcher .05
700 Checklist 601-700 .05
701 Clemente Nunez .15
702 "Rookie Threats" (Donovan Osborne, Brian Jordan, Mark Clark) .10
703 Mike Morgan .05
704 Keith Miller .05
705 Kurt Stillwell .05
706 Damon Berryhill .05
707 Von Hayes .05
708 Rick Sutcliffe .05
709 Hubie Brooks .05
710 Ryan Turner .05
711 N.L. Diamond Skills Checklist (Barry Bonds, Andy Van Slyke) .15
712 Jose Rijo (Diamond Skills) .05
713 Tom Glavine (Diamond Skills) .05
714 Shawon Dunston (Diamond Skills) .05
715 Andy Van Slyke (Diamond Skills) .05
716 Ozzie Smith (Diamond Skills) .10
717 Tony Gwynn (Diamond Skills) .20
718 Will Clark (Diamond Skills) .05
719 Marquis Grissom (Diamond Skills) .05
720 Howard Johnson (Diamond Skills) .05
721 Barry Bonds (Diamond Skills) .20
722 Kirk McCaskill .05
723 Sammy Sosa .75
724 George Bell .05
725 Gregg Jefferies .05
726 Gary DiSarcina .05
727 Mike Bordick .05
728 Eddie Murray (400 Home Run Club) .15
729 Rene Gonzales .05
730 Mike Bielecki .05
731 Calvin Jones .05
732 Jack Morris .05
733 Frank Viola .05
734 Dave Winfield .15
735 Kevin Mitchell .05
736 Billy Swift .05
737 Dan Gladden .05
738 Mike Jackson .05
739 Mark Carreon .05
740 Kirt Manwaring .05
741 Randy Myers .05
742 Kevin McReynolds .05
743 Steve Sax .05
744 Wally Joyner .05
745 Gary Sheffield .15
746 Danny Tartabull .05
747 Julio Valera .05
748 Denny Neagle .10
749 Lance Blankenship .05
750 Mike Gallego .05
751 Bret Saberhagen .05
752 Ruben Amaro .05
753 Eddie Murray .15
754 Kyle Abbott .10
755 Bobby Bonilla .05
756 Eric Davis .05
757 Eddie Taubensee .10
758 Andres Galarraga .15
759 Pete Incaviglia .05
760 Tom Candiotti .05
761 Tim Belcher .05
762 Ricky Bones .05
763 Bip Roberts .05
764 Pedro Munoz .05
765 Greg Swindell .05
766 Kenny Lofton .25
767 Gary Carter .05
768 Charlie Hayes .05
769 Dickie Thon .05
770 Diamond Debuts Checklist (Donovan Osborne) .05
771 Bret Boone (Diamond Debuts) .15
772 *Archi Cianfrocco* (Diamond Debuts) .05
773 *Mark Clark* (Diamond Debuts) .05
774 *Chad Curtis* (Diamond Debuts) .20
775 *Pat Listach* (Diamond Debuts) .05
776 *Pat Mahomes* (Diamond Debuts) .05
777 *Donovan Osborne* (Diamond Debuts) .05
778 *John Patterson* (Diamond Debuts) .05
779 *Andy Stankiewicz* (Diamond Debuts) .05
780 *Turk Wendell* (Diamond Debuts) .05
781 Bill Krueger .05
782 Rickey Henderson (Grand Theft) .10
783 Kevin Seitzer .05
784 Dave Martinez .05
785 John Smiley .05
786 Matt Stairs .20
787 Scott Scudder .05
788 John Wetteland .05
789 Jack Armstrong .05
790 Ken Hill .05
791 Dick Schofield .05
792 Mariano Duncan .05
793 Bill Pecota .05
794 *Mike Kelly* .05
795 Willie Randolph .05
796 *Butch Henry* .05
797 *Carlos Hernandez* .05
798 Doug Jones .05
799 Melido Perez .05
800 Checklist .05
SP3 "Prime Time's Two" (Deion Sanders) 1.00
SP4 "Mr. Baseball" (Tom Selleck, Frank Thomas) 2.00
HH2 (Ted Williams) (hologram) 2.00

1992 Upper Deck Bench/Morgan Heroes

This set is devoted to two of the vital cogs in Cincinnati's Big Red Machine: Hall of Famers Johnny Bench and Joe Morgan. Cards, numbered 37-45, were included in high number packs. An unnumbered cover card was also produced. Both players autographed 2,500 of card #45, the painting of the Reds duo by sports artist Vernon Wells.

	MT
Complete Set (10):	8.00
Common Card:	.40
Header Card:	1.50
Autographed Card:	100.00
37 1968 Rookie of the Year (Johnny Bench)	.75
38 1968-77 Ten Straight Gold Gloves (Johnny Bench)	.75
39 1970 & 1972 MVP (Johnny Bench)	.75
40 1965 Rookie Year (Joe Morgan)	.40
41 1975-76 Back-to-Back MVP (Joe Morgan)	.40
42 1980-83 The Golden Years (Joe Morgan)	.40
43 1972-79 Big Red Machine (Johnny Bench, Joe Morgan)	.60
44 1989 & 1990 Hall of Fame (Johnny Bench, Joe Morgan)	.60
45 Checklist - Heroes 37-45 (Johnny Bench, Joe Morgan)	.60

1992 Upper Deck College POY Holograms

This three-card hologram set features the College Player of the Year winners from 1989-91. Cards were randomly inserted in high number foil packs and have a CP prefix for numbering.

	MT
Complete Set (3):	.75
Common Player:	.25
1 David McCarty	.25
2 Mike Kelly	.25
3 Ben McDonald	.25

1992 Upper Deck Hall of Fame Heroes

This set features three top players from the 1970s: Vida Blue, Lou Brock and Rollie Fingers. The cards continue from last year's set by using numbers H5-H8. The three players are each on one card; the fourth card features all three. They were found in low-number foil packs and specially-marked jumbo packs. Both types of packs could also contain autographed cards; each player signed 3,000 cards.

	MT
Complete Set (4):	3.00
Common Player:	4.00
Vida Blue Autograph:	15.00
Lou Brock Autograph:	30.00
Rollie Fingers Autograph:	15.00
5 Vida Blue	.40
6 Lou Brock	2.00
7 Rollie Fingers	.50
8 Vida Blue, Lou Brock, Rollie Fingers	1.00

1992 Upper Deck Heroes Highlights

Special packaging of 1992 Upper Deck high numbers produced for sales to dealers at its Heroes of Baseball show series included these cards of former players as inserts. Cards have a Heroes Highlights banner including the player's name and the date of his career highlight beneath the photo. In a tombstone frame on back, the highlight is chronicled. Cards are numbered alphabetically by player name, with the card number carrying an "HI" prefix.

		MT
Complete Set (10):		15.00
Common Player:		1.00
1	Bobby Bonds	1.00
2	Lou Brock	1.00
3	Rollie Fingers	1.00
4	Bob Gibson	1.25
5	Reggie Jackson	2.00
6	Gaylord Perry	1.00
7	Robin Roberts	1.00
8	Brooks Robinson	1.50
9	Billy Williams	1.00
10	Ted Williams	3.50

1992 Upper Deck Home Run Heroes

This 26-card set features a top home-run hitter from each major league team. The cards, numbered HR1-HR26, were found in low-number jumbo packs, one per pack.

		MT
Complete Set (26):		15.00
Common Player:		.40
1	Jose Canseco	1.00
2	Cecil Fielder	.40
3	Howard Johnson	.40
4	Cal Ripken, Jr.	3.00
5	Matt Williams	.75
6	Joe Carter	.40
7	Ron Gant	.40
8	Frank Thomas	1.00
9	Andre Dawson	.40
10	Fred McGriff	.75
11	Danny Tartabull	.40
12	Chili Davis	.40
13	Albert Belle	.75
14	Jack Clark	.40
15	Paul O'Neill	.60
16	Darryl Strawberry	.50
17	Dave Winfield	.65
18	Jay Buhner	.40
19	Juan Gonzalez	1.00
20	Greg Vaughn	.40
21	Barry Bonds	1.00
22	Matt Nokes	.40
23	John Kruk	.40
24	Ivan Calderon	.40
25	Jeff Bagwell	1.00
26	Todd Zeile	.40

1992 Upper Deck Scouting Report

These cards were randomly inserted in Upper Deck high-number jumbo packs. The set is numbered SR1-SR25 and features 25 top prospects, including 1992 Rookies of the Year Pat Listach and Eric Karros. "Scouting Report" is written down the side on the front in silver lettering. The back features a clipboard which shows a photo, a player profile and a major league scouting report.

		MT
Complete Set (25):		12.00
Common Player:		.25
1	Andy Ashby	.35
2	Willie Banks	.25
3	Kim Batiste	.25
4	Derek Bell	.50
5	Archi Cianfrocco	.25
6	Royce Clayton	.25
7	Gary DiSarcina	.25
8	Dave Fleming	.25
9	Butch Henry	.25
10	Todd Hundley	.50
11	Brian Jordan	.50
12	Eric Karros	.50
13	Pat Listach	.25
14	Scott Livingstone	.25
15	Kenny Lofton	3.00
16	Pat Mahomes	.25
17	Denny Neagle	.25
18	Dave Nilsson	.35
19	Donovan Osborne	.25
20	Reggie Sanders	.35
21	Andy Stankiewicz	.25
22	Jim Thome	5.00
23	Julio Valera	.25
24	Mark Wohlers	.25
25	Anthony Young	.25

1992 Upper Deck Ted Williams' Best

Twenty of the best hitters in baseball according to legend Ted Williams are featured in this special insert set from Upper Deck. The cards are styled much like the 1992 FanFest cards and showcase each chosen player. Each card is numbered with a "T" designation.

		MT
Complete Set (20):		20.00
Common Player:		.50
1	Wade Boggs	1.00
2	Barry Bonds	1.50
3	Jose Canseco	1.50
4	Will Clark	.75
5	Cecil Fielder	.50
6	Tony Gwynn	3.00
7	Rickey Henderson	.75
8	Fred McGriff	.75
9	Kirby Puckett	2.00
10	Ruben Sierra	.50
11	Roberto Alomar	1.00
12	Jeff Bagwell	2.00
13	Albert Belle	1.00
14	Juan Gonzalez	2.00
15	Ken Griffey, Jr.	6.00
16	Chris Hoiles	.50
17	Dave Justice	.75
18	Phil Plantier	.50
19	Frank Thomas	2.00
20	Robin Ventura	.65

1992 Upper Deck Ted Williams Heroes

This Baseball Heroes set devoted to Ted Williams continues where previous efforts left off by numbering it from 28-36. An unnumbered "Baseball Heroes" cover card is also included. Cards were found in low-number foil and jumbo packs. Williams also autographed 2,500 cards, which were numbered and randomly inserted in low-number packs.

		MT
Complete Set (10):		6.00
Common Player:		.50
Autographed Card:		400.00
Williams Header:		2.50
28	1939 Rookie Year	.50
29	1941 .406!	.50
30	1942 Triple Crown Year	.50
31	1946 & 1949 MVP	.50
32	1947 Second Triple Crown	.50
33	1950s Player of the Decade	.50
34	1960 500 Home Run Club	.50
35	1966 Hall of Fame	.50
36	Checklist - Heroes 28-36	.50

1992 Upper Deck Ted Williams Box Bottoms

Foil-pack boxes of low-number 1992 Upper Deck baseball featured on their bottom an oversize reproduction of the front of one of the Ted Williams "Baseball Heroes" insert cards. Eight different box-bottom cards were produced, measuring 5" x 7" and printed on a mottled orange background. The box-bottom cards are blank-backed and unnumbered. They are checklisted here by the chronology of the featured highlight.

		MT
Complete Set (8):		6.00
Common Player:		1.00
(1)	1936 - Rookie Year (Ted Williams)	1.00
(2)	1941 - .406 (Ted Williams)	1.00
(3)	1942 - Triple Crown Year (Ted Williams)	1.00
(4)	1946, 1949 - MVP (Ted Williams)	1.00
(5)	1947 - Second Triple Crown (Ted Williams)	1.00
(6)	1950s - Player of the Decade (Ted Williams)	1.00
(7)	1960 - 500 Hokme Run Club (Ted Williams)	1.00
(8)	1966 - Hall of Fame (Ted Williams)	1.00

1992 Upper Deck High Number Promo Sheet

This 11" x 8-1/2" glossy photo print was created to showcase UD's high-number series for 1992. Eight of the high-number cards, including several from the specialty subsets are featured on the sheet. The players appearing on the blank-back sheet are checklisted here alphabetically.

		MT
Sheet:		12.00
(1)	Barry Bonds (Diamond Skills)	
(2)	Eric Davis	
(3)	Wally Joyner	
(4)	Kenny Lofton (Scouting Report)	
(5)	Pat Mahomes (Diamond Debuts)	
(6)	Eddie Murray (400 HR Club)	
(7)	Gary Sheffield	
(8)	Frank Thomas (Ted Williams Best Hitters)	

> Checklists with card numbers in parentheses ( ) indicates the numbers do not appear on the card.

1992 Upper Deck Poster

This 14-3/4" x 21" color poster was issued as an in-store promotion for Upper Deck's 1992 baseball card series. It is blank-backed.

	MT
Ken Griffey Jr.	15.00

1992 Upper Deck Souvenir Sheets

All 26 major league teams participated in UD's Heroes of Baseball tour and series of old-timers' games to raise funds for the Baseball Assistance Team. Individually serial numbered sheets were given away to fans attending the special games. Announced editions sizes are listed here in parentheses. The 8-1/2" x 11" color sheets feature artwork of several players on front. Backs are blank. The sheets are listed here alphabetically according to title.

		MT
Complete Set (34):		175.00
Common Sheet:		5.00
(1)	All-Star FanFest (Larry Doby, Rollie Fingers, Steve Garvey) (San Diego) (12,000)	9.00
(2)	All-Star Game Heroes (Roy Face, Chuck Tanner, Kent Tekulve, Frank Thomas, Bob Veale) (Pittsburg) (27,000)	5.00
(3)	A.L Heroes vs N.L. Heroes (Jose Cruz, Mark Fidrych, Joe Niekro, Tony Oliva, Jim Wynn) (Houston) (17,000)	5.00
(4)	A.L. Heroes vs. N.L. Heroes (Ernie Banks, Randy Hundley, Don Kessinger, Ron Santo, Billy Williams) (Wrigley) (22,000)	7.50
(5)	Blue Jays Heroes vs. UD Heroes (Bob Bailor, Rick Bosetti, Garth Iorg, John Mayberry, Balor Moore) (Toronto) (52,000)	5.00
(6)	Cardinals' 100th Anniversary (Lou Brock, Bob Gibson, Red Schoendienst, Enos Slaughter) (St. Louis) (22,000)	7.50

(7)	Cubs Heroes vs. Reds Heroes (Pedro Borbon, Bernie Carbo, Cesar Cedeno, George Foster, Gary Nolan) (Cincinnati) (27,000)	5.00
(8)	Harvey's Wallbangers (Cecil Cooper, Harvey Kuenn, Ben Oglivie, Gorman Thomas) (Milwaukee) (32,000)	5.00
(9)	Heroes of Baseball - All-Star Game (Bob Feller, Rollie Fingers, Steve Garvey, Reggie Jackson, Brooks Robinson) (San Diego) (67,000)	5.00
(10)	Minnesota Twins "World Series Heroes" (Bob Gibson, Jim (Mudcat) Grant, Tony Oliva, Zoilo Versalles, Maury Wills) (22,000)	5.00
(11)	More Than 100 Years of Montreal Baseball (Claude Raymond, Steve Rogers, Jean-Pierre Roy, Duke Snider), (Rusty Staub) (22,000)	5.00
(12)	Nickname Heroes of the 'Stick (Orlando Cepeda, Jim Davenport, Dave Kingman, Juan Marichal, John Montefusco) (S.F.) (37,000)	7.50
(13)	N.L. Heroes vs. A.L. Heroes (Toby Harrah, Jim Kern, Al Oliver, Jim Spencer, Jim Sundberg) (Arlington) (47,000)	5.00
(14)	Opening Day Oriole Park at Camden Yards (Four views of ballpark) (Baltimore) (17,000)	10.00
(15)	Rangers Heroes vs. White Sox Heroes (Dick Allen, Carlos May, Bill Melton, Chuck Tanner, Wilbur Wood) (Comiskey) (22,000)	7.50
(16)	Record Setters (Jim Abbott, Jimmie Reese, Nolan Ryan) (Anaheim) (52,000)	15.00
(17)	Record-Setting Infield (Ron Cey, Steve Garvey, Davey Lopes, Bill Russell) (L.A.) (62,000)	12.00
(18)	Rollie Fingers Hall of Fame Day (Rollie Fingers) (Milwaukee) (32,000)	5.00
(19)	Royals Hall of Fame Inductees (Joe Burke, Larry Gura, Fred Patek) (K.C.) (42,000)	5.00
(20)	Silver Anniversary of Impossible Dream (Tony Conigliaro, Jim Lonborg, George Scott, Dick Williams, Carl Yastrzemski) (Boston) (38,000)	9.00
(21)	Ted Williams Triple Crown Winner (Ted Williams) (Heroes schedule card)	6.50
(22)	Tribute to Rocky Colavito (Rocky Colavito) (Cleveland) (22,000)	7.50
(23)	Upper Deck Heroes of Baseball Shows (Bobby Bonds, Lou Brock, Bob Gibson, Robin Roberts, Billy Williams) (76,400)	5.00
(24)	Upper Deck Heroes of Baseball Shows (Rollie Fingers, Reggie Jackson, Gaylord Perry, Brooks Robinson, Ted Williams) (76,400)	5.00
(25)	Upper Deck Honors (Vida Blue, Lou Brock, Rollie Fingers) (50,000)	5.00
(26)	Yankee Fan Festival (Alvaro Espinoza, Mel Hall, Pat Kelly, Don Mattingly, Matt Nokes, Bernie Williams) (12,500) (player cards reproduced)	10.00
(27)	25th Anniversary of Oakland Athletics (Vida Blue, Bert Campaneris, Rollie Fingers, Jim (Catfish) Hunter), Reggie Jackson) (22,000)	5.00
(28)	30 Years of Mets Baseball (Bud Harrelson, Cleon Jones, Jerry Koosman, Ed Kranepool, Rusty Staub) (47,000)	7.50
(29)	46th Anniversary Old-Timers Day Classic (Hank Bauer, Bobby Brown, Tom Henrich, Allie Reynolds, Phil Rizzuto) (Yankees) (50,000)	7.50
(30)	50 Year Anniversary of Triple Crown (Ted Williams) (unknown edition)	9.00
(31)	'70 A's vs. '76 Phillies (Dick Allen, Larry Bowa, Steve Carlton, Greg Luzinski, Tug McGraw) (Phila.) (44,000)	7.50
(32)	'72 UD Heroes vs. Atlanta Braves Heroes (Bruce Benedict, Darrell Evans, Glenn Hubbard, Reggie Jackson, Dave Johnson) (Atlanta) (22,000)	5.00
(33)	200 Club (Luis Aparicio, Bill Buckner, Milt Pappas, J.R. Richard, Brooks Robinson) (Baltimore) (50,000)	5.00
(34)	1972 Division Winners - Detroit Tigers (Sparky Anderson, Bert Campaneris, Al Oliver, Aurelio Rodriguez) (32,000)	6.50

1992 Upper Deck FanFest

This 54-card boxed set was made available through special offers at the 1992 National Sports Collectors Convention and at the 1992 All-Star FanFest in San Diego. Card fronts feature a glossy UV finish, silver-foil stamping and the All-Star FanFest logo. The card backs include a player profile. Both "Future Heroes" and past and present "All-Star Heroes" are featured. The complete set was packaged in an attractive blue box with white pinstripes.

		MT
Complete Set (54):		10.00
Common Player:		.10
1	Steve Avery	.10
2	Ivan Rodriguez	.60
3	Jeff Bagwell	.75
4	Delino DeShields	.10
5	Royce Clayton	.10
6	Robin Ventura	.20
7	Phil Plantier	.10
8	Ray Lankford	.10
9	Juan Gonzalez	1.00
10	Frank Thomas	1.00
11	Roberto Alomar	.65
12	Sandy Alomar, Jr.	.15
13	Wade Boggs	.40
14	Barry Bonds	1.00
15	Bobby Bonilla	.10
16	George Brett	.75
17	Jose Canseco	.40
18	Will Clark	.50
19	Roger Clemens	.75
20	Eric Davis	.10
21	Rob Dibble	.10
22	Cecil Fielder	.10
23	Dwight Gooden	.10
24	Ken Griffey, Jr.	1.50
25	Tony Gwynn	.75
26	Bryan Harvey	.10
27	Rickey Henderson	.20
28	Howard Johnson	.10
29	Wally Joyner	.10
30	Barry Larkin	.25
31	Don Mattingly	1.00
32	Mark McGwire	1.50
33	Dale Murphy	.15
34	Rafael Palmeiro	.20
35	Kirby Puckett	.65
36	Cal Ripken, Jr.	1.25
37	Nolan Ryan	1.00
38	Chris Sabo	.10
39	Ryne Sandberg	.50
40	Benito Santiago	.10
41	Ruben Sierra	.10
42	Ozzie Smith	.40
43	Darryl Strawberry	.10
44	Robin Yount	.40
45	Rollie Fingers	.10
46	Reggie Jackson	.40
47	Billy Williams	.15
48	Lou Brock	.10
49	Gaylord Perry	.10
50	Ted Williams	1.00
51	Brooks Robinson	.50
52	Bob Gibson	.20
53	Bobby Bonds	.10
54	Robin Roberts	.15

1992 Upper Deck FanFest Gold

One out of every 60 sets of Upper Deck FanFest All-Stars was produced with gold-foil printing highlights rather than silver. The sets were randomly inserted into cases.

	MT
Complete Set (54):	190.00
Common Player:	1.50
(Gold cards valued at 12X-15X the same cards in the regular FanFest set.)	

1992 Upper Deck FanFest Ted Williams Super

This large-format (8-1/2" x 11") card is essentially an enlargement of Ted Williams' card issued with the FanFest All-Star Heroes boxed set by UD. The Williams super cards were distributed at the FanFest event and are serially numbered on back within an edition of 2,500.

	MT
Ted Williams	25.00

1992 Upper Deck MVP Holograms

State of the art holography is presented in this 54-card plastic-cased set featuring a top pitcher and a top position player from each major league team, plus 1991 MVPs Terry Pendleton and Cal Ripken, Jr. The hologram on the front of each card features a close-up and a field-action photo of the player; his name and position are in a strip at bottom. Full-color backs have a player photo on the right and career summary on the left. A custom album for the set was available via a mail offer for $10. Each set includes a numbered certificate of authenticity, verifying its position within a total issue of 216,000 sets.

		MT
Complete Set (54):		20.00
Common Player:		.25
1	A.L. Checklist (Cal Ripken, Jr.)	1.00
2	N.L. Checkklist (Terry Pendleton)	.25
3	Jim Abbott	.25
4	Roberto Alomar	.75
5	Kevin Appier	.25
6	Steve Avery	.25
7	Jeff Bagwell	1.50
8	Albert Belle	.60
9	Andy Benes	.25
10	Wade Boggs	.50
11	Barry Bonds	1.00
12	George Brett	1.00
13	Ivan Calderon	.25
14	Jose Canseco	.75
15	Will Clark	.50
16	Roger Clemens	1.00
17	David Cone	.30
18	Doug Drabek	.25
19	Dennis Eckersley	.25
20	Scott Erickson	.25
21	Cecil Fielder	.25
22	Ken Griffey, Jr.	3.50
23	Bill Gullickson	.25
24	Juan Guzman	.25
25	Pete Harnisch	.25
26	Howard Johnson	.25
27	Randy Johnson	.50
28	John Kruk	.25
29	Barry Larkin	.30
30	Greg Maddux	2.00
31	Dennis Martinez	.25
32	Ramon Martinez	.30
33	Don Mattingly	1.00
34	Jack McDowell	.25
35	Fred McGriff	.50
36	Paul Molitor	.50
37	Charles Nagy	.30
38	Gregg Olson	.25
39	Terry Pendleton	.25
40	Luis Polonia	.25
41	Kirby Puckett	1.00
42	Dave Righetti	.25
43	Jose Rijo	.25
44	Cal Ripken, Jr.	3.00
45	Nolan Ryan	3.00
46	Ryne Sandberg	.90
47	Scott Sanderson	.25
48	Ruben Sierra	.25
49	Lee Smith	.25
50	Ozzie Smith	.75
51	Darryl Strawberry	.30
52	Frank Thomas	1.50
53	Bill Wegman	.25
54	Mitch Williams	.25

1992 Upper Deck Comic Ball 3

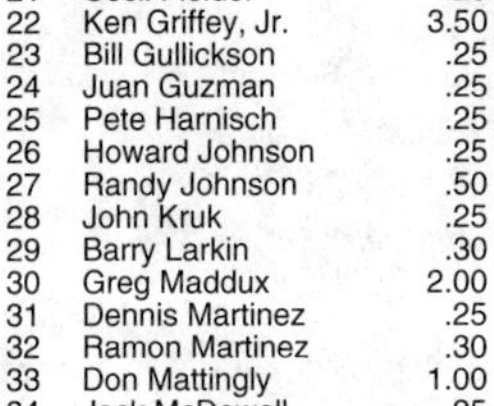

The third series of Comic Ball cards was issued in 1992 and was the second to combine photos of real ballplayers with Looney Tune cartoon characters in several cartoon strip-style series. Players featured in the set with Bugs, Taz and the gang were Jim Abbott and the Ken Griffeys, Sr. and Jr. Each of the 198 regular cards features a puzzle-piece back. A special album to house the set was sold separately. A series of holograms which also combined the players and cartoon figures was issued as pack inserts.

	MT
Complete Set (198):	6.00
Common Player:	.05
Hologram:	2.00

1992 Upper Deck Comic Ball 3 Holograms

These blank-back holograms which combine player pictures with those of cartoon characters were issued as inserts in Comic Ball 3 foil packs.

		MT
Common Hologram:		.50
(1)	Jim Abbott (w/Tweety)	1.00
(2)	Ken Griffey Jr. (w/Bugs)	2.50
(3)	Ken Griffey Jr. (w/Wile E. Coyote)	2.50
(4)	Chuck Jones (artist) (w/Bugs)	.50

1993 Upper Deck

Upper Deck introduced its 1993 set in a two-series format to adjust to expansion. Cards 1-420 make up the first series. Special subsets in Series 1 include rookies, teammates and community heroes. Fronts feature color player photos surrounded by a white border. "Upper Deck" appears at the top of the photo and the player ID at the bottom. Backs feature vertical photos, which is a change from the past, and more complete statistics than what Upper Deck has had in the past. The hologram appears in the lower-left corner on the card back.

		MT
Complete Set (840):		35.00
Complete Series 1 (420):		20.00
Complete Series 2 (420):		20.00
Common Player:		.05
Gold Hologram: 4X		
Distributed 1:20 in Factory Set form		
Series 1 or 2 Wax Box:		25.00
1	Tim Salmon (Checklist)	.25
2	Mike Piazza (Star Rookie)	2.00
3	*Rene Arocha* (Star Rookie)	.15
4	*Willie Greene* (Star Rookie)	.15
5	*Manny Alexander* (Star Rookie)	.10
6	Dan Wilson (Star Rookie)	.10
7	*Dan Smith* (Star Rookie)	.05
8	*Kevin Rogers* (Star Rookie)	.05

9	*Nigel Wilson* (Star Rookie)	.05
10	*Joe Vitko* (Star Rookie)	.10
11	Tim Costo (Star Rookie)	.15
12	Alan Embree (Star Rookie)	.15
13	*Jim Tatum* (Star Rookie)	.05
14	*Cris Colon* (Star Rookie)	.10
15	Steve Hosey (Star Rookie)	.10
16	*Sterling Hitchcock* (Star Rookie)	.15
17	*Dave Mlicki* (Star Rookie)	.15
18	*Jessie Hollins* (Star Rookie)	.10
19	*Bobby Jones* (Star Rookie)	.15
20	*Kurt Miller* (Star Rookie)	.15
21	*Melvin Nieves* (Star Rookie)	.15
22	*Billy Ashley* (Star Rookie)	.15
23	*J.T. Snow* (Star Rookie)	.50
24	Chipper Jones (Star Rookie)	1.25
25	Tim Salmon (Star Rookie)	.25
26	*Tim Pugh* (Star Rookie)	.10
27	David Nied (Star Rookie)	.05
28	*Mike Trombley* (Star Rookie)	.10
29	Javier Lopez (Star Rookie)	.25
30	Community Heroes Checklist (Jim Abbott)	.05
31	Jim Abbott (Community Heroes)	.10
32	Dale Murphy (Community Heroes)	.10
33	Tony Pena (Community Heroes)	.05
34	Kirby Puckett (Community Heroes)	.40
35	Harold Reynolds (Community Heroes)	.10
36	Cal Ripken, Jr. (Community Heroes)	.50
37	Nolan Ryan (Community Heroes)	.50
38	Ryne Sandberg (Community Heroes)	.25
39	Dave Stewart (Community Heroes)	.05
40	Dave Winfield (Community Heroes)	.10
41	Teammates Checklist (Joe Carter, Mark McGwire)	1.00
42	Blockbuster Trade (Joe Carter, Roberto Alomar)	.15
43	Brew Crew (Pat Listach, Robin Yount, Paul Molitor)	.15
44	Iron and Steal (Brady Anderson, Cal Ripken, Jr.)	.25
45	Youthful Tribe (Albert Belle, Sandy Alomar Jr., Jim Thome, Carlos Baerga, Kenny Lofton)	.15
46	Motown Mashers (Cecil Fielder, Mickey Tettleton)	.10
47	Yankee Pride (Roberto Kelly, Don Mattingly)	.20
48	Boston Cy Sox (Frank Viola, Roger Clemens)	.25
49	Bash Brothers (Ruben Sierra, Mark McGwire)	1.00
50	Twin Titles (Kent Hrbek, Kirby Puckett)	.20
51	Southside Sluggers (Robin Ventura, Frank Thomas)	.25
52	Latin Stars (Jose Canseco, Ivan Rodriguez, Rafael Palmeiro, Juan Gonzalez)	.25
53	Lethal Lefties (Mark Langston, Jim Abbott, Chuck Finley)	.10
54	Royal Family (Gregg Jefferies, George Brett, Wally Joyner)	.20
55	Pacific Sox Exchange (Kevin Mitchell, Jay Buhner, Ken Griffey, Jr.)	.50
56	George Brett	.50
57	Scott Cooper	.05
58	Mike Maddux	.05
59	*Rusty Meacham*	.05
60	Wil Cordero	.10
61	Tim Teufel	.05
62	Jeff Montgomery	.05
63	Scott Livingstone	.05
64	Doug Dascenzo	.05
65	Bret Boone	.10
66	*Tim Wakefield*	.10
67	Curt Schilling	.10
68	Frank Tanana	.05
69	Len Dykstra	.05
70	Derek Lilliquist	.05
71	Anthony Young	.05
72	*Hipolito Pichardo*	.05
73	Rod Beck	.05
74	Kent Hrbek	.05
75	Tom Glavine	.15
76	Kevin Brown	.10
77	Chuck Finley	.05
78	Bob Walk	.05
79	Rheal Cormier	.05
80	Rick Sutcliffe	.05
81	Harold Baines	.05
82	Lee Smith	.05
83	Geno Petralli	.05
84	Jose Oquendo	.05
85	Mark Gubicza	.05
86	Mickey Tettleton	.05
87	Bobby Witt	.05
88	Mark Lewis	.05
89	Kevin Appier	.10
90	Mike Stanton	.05
91	Rafael Belliard	.05
92	Kenny Rogers	.05
93	Randy Velarde	.05
94	Luis Sojo	.05
95	Mark Leiter	.05
96	Jody Reed	.05
97	Pete Harnisch	.05
98	Tom Candiotti	.05
99	Mark Portugal	.05
100	Dave Valle	.05
101	Shawon Dunston	.05
102	B.J. Surhoff	.05
103	Jay Bell	.05
104	Sid Bream	.05
105	Checklist 1-105 (Frank Thomas)	.20
106	Mike Morgan	.05
107	Bill Doran	.05
108	Lance Blankenship	.05
109	Mark Lemke	.05
110	Brian Harper	.05
111	Brady Anderson	.15
112	Bip Roberts	.05
113	Mitch Williams	.05
114	Craig Biggio	.20
115	Eddie Murray	.20
116	Matt Nokes	.05
117	Lance Parrish	.05
118	Bill Swift	.05
119	Jeff Innis	.05
120	Mike LaValliere	.05
121	Hal Morris	.05
122	Walt Weiss	.05
123	Ivan Rodriguez	.50
124	Andy Van Slyke	.05
125	Roberto Alomar	.30
126	Robby Thompson	.05
127	Sammy Sosa	1.00
128	Mark Langston	.05
129	Jerry Browne	.05
130	Chuck McElroy	.05
131	Frank Viola	.05
132	Leo Gomez	.05
133	Ramon Martinez	.10
134	Don Mattingly	.60
135	Roger Clemens	1.00
136	Rickey Henderson	.35
137	Darren Daulton	.05
138	Ken Hill	.05
139	Ozzie Guillen	.05
140	Jerald Clark	.05
141	Dave Fleming	.05
142	Delino DeShields	.05
143	Matt Williams	.20
144	Larry Walker	.25
145	Ruben Sierra	.05
146	Ozzie Smith	.40
147	Chris Sabo	.05
148	*Carlos Hernandez*	.10
149	Pat Borders	.05
150	Orlando Merced	.05
151	Royce Clayton	.05
152	Kurt Stillwell	.05
153	Dave Hollins	.05
154	Mike Greenwell	.05
155	Nolan Ryan	1.00
156	Felix Jose	.05
157	Junior Felix	.05
158	Derek Bell	.10
159	Steve Buechele	.05
160	John Burkett	.05
161	*Pat Howell*	.05
162	Milt Cuyler	.05
163	Terry Pendleton	.05
164	Jack Morris	.05
165	Tony Gwynn	.75
166	Deion Sanders	.15
167	Mike Devereaux	.05
168	Ron Darling	.05
169	Orel Hershiser	.05
170	Mike Jackson	.05
171	Doug Jones	.05
172	*Dan Walters*	.05
173	Darren Lewis	.05
174	Carlos Baerga	.05
175	Ryne Sandberg	.35
176	Gregg Jefferies	.10
177	John Jaha	.05
178	Luis Polonia	.05
179	Kirt Manwaring	.05
180	Mike Magnante	.05
181	Billy Ripken	.05
182	Mike Moore	.05
183	Eric Anthony	.05
184	Lenny Harris	.05
185	Tony Pena	.05
186	Mike Felder	.05
187	Greg Olson	.05
188	Rene Gonzales	.05
189	Mike Bordick	.05
190	Mel Rojas	.05
191	Todd Frohwirth	.05
192	Darryl Hamilton	.05
193	Mike Fetters	.05
194	Omar Olivares	.05
195	Tony Phillips	.05
196	Paul Sorrento	.05
197	Trevor Wilson	.05
198	Kevin Gross	.05
199	Ron Karkovice	.05
200	Brook Jacoby	.05
201	Mariano Duncan	.05
202	Dennis Cook	.05
203	Daryl Boston	.05
204	Mike Perez	.05
205	Manuel Lee	.05
206	Steve Olin	.05
207	Charlie Hough	.05
208	Scott Scudder	.05
209	Charlie O'Brien	.05
210	Checklist 106-210 (Barry Bonds)	.10
211	Jose Vizcaino	.05
212	Scott Leius	.05
213	Kevin Mitchell	.05
214	Brian Barnes	.05
215	Pat Kelly	.05
216	Chris Hammond	.05
217	Rob Deer	.05
218	Cory Snyder	.05
219	Gary Carter	.10
220	Danny Darwin	.05
221	Tom Gordon	.05
222	Gary Sheffield	.20
223	Joe Carter	.05
224	Jay Buhner	.05
225	Jose Offerman	.05
226	Jose Rijo	.05
227	Mark Whiten	.05
228	Randy Milligan	.05
229	Bud Black	.05
230	Gary DiSarcina	.05
231	Steve Finley	.05
232	Dennis Martinez	.05
233	Mike Mussina	.20
234	Joe Oliver	.05
235	Chad Curtis	.05
236	Shane Mack	.05
237	Jaime Navarro	.05
238	Brian McRae	.05
239	Chili Davis	.05
240	Jeff King	.05
241	Dean Palmer	.05
242	Danny Tartabull	.05
243	Charles Nagy	.05
244	Ray Lankford	.05
245	Barry Larkin	.15
246	Steve Avery	.05
247	John Kruk	.05
248	Derrick May	.05
249	Stan Javier	.05
250	Roger McDowell	.05
251	Dan Gladden	.05
252	Wally Joyner	.10
253	Pat Listach	.05
254	Chuck Knoblauch	.20
255	Sandy Alomar Jr.	.10
256	Jeff Bagwell	.60
257	Andy Stankiewicz	.05
258	Darrin Jackson	.05
259	Brett Butler	.05
260	Joe Orsulak	.05
261	Andy Benes	.10
262	Kenny Lofton	.25
263	Robin Ventura	.15
264	Ron Gant	.10
265	Ellis Burks	.05
266	Juan Guzman	.05
267	Wes Chamberlain	.05
268	John Smiley	.05
269	Franklin Stubbs	.05
270	Tom Browning	.05
271	Dennis Eckersley	.05
272	Carlton Fisk	.20
273	Lou Whitaker	.05
274	Phil Plantier	.05
275	Bobby Bonilla	.05
276	Ben McDonald	.05
277	Bob Zupcic	.05
278	Terry Steinbach	.05
279	Terry Mulholland	.05
280	Lance Johnson	.05
281	Willie McGee	.05
282	Bret Saberhagen	.10
283	Randy Myers	.05
284	Randy Tomlin	.05
285	Mickey Morandini	.05
286	Brian Williams	.05
287	Tino Martinez	.10
288	Jose Melendez	.05
289	Jeff Huson	.05
290	Joe Grahe	.05
291	Mel Hall	.05
292	Otis Nixon	.05
293	Todd Hundley	.10
294	Casey Candaele	.05
295	Kevin Seitzer	.05
296	Eddie Taubensee	.05
297	Moises Alou	.15
298	Scott Radinsky	.05
299	Thomas Howard	.05
300	Kyle Abbott	.05
301	Omar Vizquel	.10
302	Keith Miller	.05
303	Rick Aguilera	.05
304	Bruce Hurst	.05
305	Ken Caminiti	.15
306	Mike Pagiarulo	.05
307	Frank Seminara	.05
308	Andre Dawson	.10
309	Jose Lind	.05
310	Joe Boever	.05
311	Jeff Parrett	.05
312	Alan Mills	.05
313	Kevin Tapani	.05
314	Darryl Kile	.05
315	Checklist 211-315 (Will Clark)	.05
316	Mike Sharperson	.05
317	John Orton	.05
318	Bob Tewksbury	.05
319	Xavier Hernandez	.05
320	Paul Assenmacher	.05
321	John Franco	.05
322	Mike Timlin	.05
323	Jose Guzman	.05
324	Pedro Martinez	.75
325	Bill Spiers	.05
326	Melido Perez	.05
327	Mike Macfarlane	.05
328	Ricky Bones	.05
329	Scott Bankhead	.05
330	Rich Rodriguez	.05
331	Geronimo Pena	.05
332	Bernie Williams	.30
333	Paul Molitor	.25
334	Roger Mason	.05
335	David Cone	.15
336	Randy Johnson	.30
337	Pat Mahomes	.05
338	Erik Hanson	.05
339	Duane Ward	.05
340	Al Martin	.05
341	Pedro Munoz	.05
342	Greg Colbrunn	.05
343	Julio Valera	.05
344	John Olerud	.15
345	George Bell	.05
346	Devon White	.05
347	Donovan Osborne	.05
348	Mark Gardner	.05
349	Zane Smith	.05
350	Wilson Alvarez	.05
351	*Kevin Koslofski*	.05
352	Roberto Hernandez	.05
353	Glenn Davis	.05
354	Reggie Sanders	.10
355	Ken Griffey, Jr.	2.00
355a	Ken Griffey Jr. (promo, 1992-dated hologram on back)	6.00
355b	Ken Griffey, Jr. (8-1/2" x 11" limited edition of 1,000)	25.00
356	Marquis Grissom	.10
357	Jack McDowell	.05
358	Jimmy Key	.05
359	Stan Belinda	.05
360	Gerald Williams	.05
361	Sid Fernandez	.05
362	Alex Fernandez	.10
363	John Smoltz	.15
364	Travis Fryman	.10
365	Jose Canseco	.50
366	Dave Justice	.20
367	*Pedro Astacio*	.15
368	Tim Belcher	.05
369	Steve Sax	.05
370	Gary Gaetti	.05
371	Jeff Frye	.10
372	Bob Wickman	.05
373	*Ryan Thompson*	.10
374	*David Hulse*	.10
375	Cal Eldred	.05
376	Ryan Klesko	.20
377	*Damion Easley*	.10
378	*John Kiely*	.10
379	*Jim Bullinger*	.10
380	Brian Bohanon	.05
381	Rod Brewer	.05
382	*Fernando Ramsey*	.05
383	Sam Militello	.05
384	Arthur Rhodes	.05
385	Eric Karros	.10
386	Rico Brogna	.05
387	*John Valentin*	.25
388	*Kerry Woodson*	.05
389	*Ben Rivera*	.05
390	*Matt Whiteside*	.10
391	Henry Rodriguez	.05
392	John Wetteland	.05
393	Kent Mercker	.05
394	Bernard Gilkey	.05
395	Doug Henry	.05
396	Mo Vaughn	.30
397	Scott Erickson	.05
398	Bill Gullickson	.05
399	Mark Guthrie	.05
400	Dave Martinez	.05
401	*Jeff Kent*	.15
402	Chris Hoiles	.05
403	Mike Henneman	.05
404	Chris Nabholz	.05
405	Tom Pagnozzi	.05
406	Kelly Gruber	.05
407	Bob Welch	.05
408	Frank Castillo	.05
409	John Dopson	.05
410	Steve Farr	.05
411	Henry Cotto	.05
412	Bob Patterson	.05
413	Todd Stottlemyre	.10
414	Greg A. Harris	.05
415	Denny Neagle	.05
416	Bill Wegman	.05
417	Willie Wilson	.05
418	Terry Leach	.05
419	Willie Randolph	.05
420	Checklist 316-420 (Mark McGwire)	1.00
421	Calvin Murray (Top Prospects Checklist)	.10
422	*Pete Janicki* (Top Prospect)	.05
423	Todd Jones (Top Prospect)	.05
424	Mike Neill (Top Prospect)	.05
425	Carlos Delgado (Top Prospect)	.50
426	Jose Oliva (Top Prospect)	.05
427	Tyrone Hill (Top Prospect)	.05
428	Dmitri Young (Top Prospect)	.15
429	*Derek Wallace* (Top Prospect)	.10
430	*Michael Moore* (Top Prospect)	.05
431	Cliff Floyd (Top Prospect)	.10
432	Calvin Murray (Top Prospect)	.10
433	Manny Ramirez (Top Prospect)	1.00
434	Marc Newfield (Top Prospect)	.05
435	Charles Johnson (Top Prospect)	.15
436	Butch Huskey (Top Prospect)	.10
437	Brad Pennington (Top Prospect)	.10
438	*Ray McDavid* (Top Prospect)	.10
439	Chad McConnell (Top Prospect)	.10
440	*Midre Cummings* (Top Prospect)	.15
441	Benji Gil (Top Prospect)	.10
442	Frank Rodriguez (Top Prospect)	.05
443	*Chad Mottola* (Top Prospect)	.10
444	*John Burke* (Top Prospect)	.15
445	Michael Tucker (Top Prospect)	.10
446	Rick Greene (Top Prospect)	.10
447	Rich Becker (Top Prospect)	.10
448	Mike Robertson (Top Prospect)	.05
449	*Derek Jeter* (Top Prospect)	8.00
450	Checklist 451-470 Inside the Numbers (David McCarty, Ivan Rodriguez)	.15
451	Jim Abbott (Inside the Numbers)	.05
452	Jeff Bagwell (Inside the Numbers)	.25
453	Jason Bere (Inside the Numbers)	.05
454	Delino DeShields (Inside the Numbers)	.05
455	Travis Fryman (Inside the Numbers)	.05
456	Alex Gonzalez (Inside the Numbers)	.05
457	Phil Hiatt (Inside the Numbers)	.05
458	Dave Hollins (Inside the Numbers)	.05
459	Chipper Jones (Inside the Numbers)	.40
460	Dave Justice (Inside the Numbers)	.15
461	Ray Lankford (Inside the Numbers)	.05

462	David McCarty (Inside the Numbers)	.05
463	Mike Mussina (Inside the Numbers)	.20
464	Jose Offerman (Inside the Numbers)	.05
465	Dean Palmer (Inside the Numbers)	.05
466	Geronimo Pena (Inside the Numbers)	.05
467	Eduardo Perez (Inside the Numbers)	.05
468	Ivan Rodriguez (Inside the Numbers)	.20
469	Reggie Sanders (Inside the Numbers)	.05
470	Bernie Williams (Inside the Numbers)	.20
471	Checklist 472-485 Team Stars (Barry Bonds, Matt Williams, Will Clark)	.20
472	Strike Force (John Smoltz, Steve Avery, Greg Maddux, Tom Glavine)	.15
473	Red October (Jose Rijo, Rob Dibble, Roberto Kelly, Reggie Sanders, Barry Larkin)	.10
474	Four Corners (Gary Sheffield, Phil Plantier, Tony Gwynn, Fred McGriff)	.20
475	Shooting Stars (Doug Drabek, Craig Biggio, Jeff Bagwell)	.15
476	Giant Sticks (Will Clark, Barry Bonds, Matt Williams)	.20
477	Boyhood Friends (Darryl Strawberry, Eric Davis)	.05
478	Rock Solid (Dante Bichette, David Nied, Andres Galarraga)	.10
479	Inaugural Catch (Dave Magadan, Orestes Destrade, Bret Barbarie, Jeff Conine)	.05
480	Steel City Champions (Tim Wakefield, Andy Van Slyke, Jay Bell)	.05
481	"Les Grandes Etoiles" (Marquis Grissom, Delino DeShields, Dennis Martinez, Larry Walker)	.10
482	Runnin' Redbirds (Geronimo Pena, Ray Lankford, Ozzie Smith, Bernard Gilkey)	.10
483	Ivy Leaguers (Ryne Sandberg, Mark Grace, Randy Myers)	.15
484	Big Apple Power Switch (Eddie Murray, Bobby Bonilla, Howard Johnson)	.10
485	Hammers & Nails (John Kruk, Dave Hollins, Darren Daulton, Len Dykstra)	.05
486	Barry Bonds (Award Winners)	.15
487	Dennis Eckersley (Award Winners)	.05
488	Greg Maddux (Award Winners)	.35
489	Dennis Eckersley (Award Winners)	.05
490	Eric Karros (Award Winners)	.05
491	Pat Listach (Award Winners)	.05
492	Gary Sheffield (Award Winners)	.10
493	Mark McGwire (Award Winners)	1.00
494	Gary Sheffield (Award Winners)	.10
495	Edgar Martinez (Award Winners)	.05
496	Fred McGriff (Award Winners)	.15
497	Juan Gonzalez (Award Winners)	.25
498	Darren Daulton (Award Winners)	.05
499	Cecil Fielder (Award Winners)	.05
500	Checklist 501-510 Diamond Debuts (Brent Gates)	.10
501	Tavo Alvarez (Diamond Debuts)	.05
502	Rod Bolton (Diamond Debuts)	.05
503	*John Cummings* (Diamond Debuts)	.10
504	Brent Gates (Diamond Debuts)	.05
505	Tyler Green (Diamond Debuts)	.10
506	*Jose Martinez* (Diamond Debuts)	.10
507	Troy Percival (Diamond Debuts)	.05
508	Kevin Stocker (Diamond Debuts)	.05
509	*Matt Walbeck* (Diamond Debuts)	.15
510	Rondell White (Diamond Debuts)	.20
511	Billy Ripken	.05
512	Mike Moore	.05
513	Jose Lind	.05
514	Chito Martinez	.05
515	Jose Guzman	.05
516	Kim Batiste	.05
517	Jeff Tackett	.05
518	Charlie Hough	.05
519	Marvin Freeman	.05
520	Carlos Martinez	.05
521	Eric Young	.10
522	Pete Incaviglia	.05
523	Scott Fletcher	.05
524	Orestes Destrade	.05
525	Checklist 421-525 (Ken Griffey, Jr.)	.20
526	Ellis Burks	.05
527	Juan Samuel	.05
528	Dave Magadan	.05
529	Jeff Parrett	.05
530	Bill Krueger	.05
531	Frank Bolick	.05
532	Alan Trammell	.10
533	Walt Weiss	.05
534	David Cone	.15
535	Greg Maddux	.75
536	Kevin Young	.05
537	Dave Hansen	.05
538	Alex Cole	.05
539	Greg Hibbard	.05
540	Gene Larkin	.05
541	Jeff Reardon	.05
542	Felix Jose	.05
543	Jimmy Key	.05
544	Reggie Jefferson	.05
545	Gregg Jefferies	.05
546	Dave Stewart	.05
547	Tim Wallach	.05
548	Spike Owen	.05
549	Tommy Greene	.05
550	Fernando Valenzuela	.05
551	Rich Amaral	.05
552	Bret Barberie	.05
553	Edgar Martinez	.05
554	Jim Abbott	.05
555	Frank Thomas	.75
556	Wade Boggs	.20
557	Tom Henke	.05
558	Milt Thompson	.05
559	Lloyd McClendon	.05
560	Vinny Castilla	.25
561	Ricky Jordan	.05
562	Andujar Cedeno	.05
563	Greg Vaughn	.10
564	Cecil Fielder	.05
565	Kirby Puckett	.50
566	Mark McGwire	2.00
567	Barry Bonds	.40
568	Jody Reed	.05
569	Todd Zeile	.05
570	Mark Carreon	.05
571	Joe Girardi	.05
572	Luis Gonzalez	.10
573	Mark Grace	.20
574	Rafael Palmeiro	.20
575	Darryl Strawberry	.10
576	Will Clark	.25
577	Fred McGriff	.20
578	Kevin Reimer	.05
579	Dave Righetti	.05
580	Juan Bell	.05
581	Jeff Brantley	.05
582	Brian Hunter	.05
583	Tim Naehring	.05
584	Glenallen Hill	.05
585	Cal Ripken, Jr.	1.50
586	Albert Belle	.40
587	Robin Yount	.20
588	Chris Bosio	.05
589	Pete Smith	.05
590	Chuck Carr	.05
591	Jeff Blauser	.05
592	Kevin McReynolds	.05
593	Andres Galarraga	.15
594	Kevin Maas	.05
595	Eric Davis	.05
596	Brian Jordan	.10
597	Tim Raines	.05
598	Rick Wilkins	.05
599	Steve Cooke	.05
600	Mike Gallego	.05
601	Mike Munoz	.05
602	Luis Rivera	.05
603	Junior Ortiz	.05
604	Brent Mayne	.05
605	Luis Alicea	.05
606	Damon Berryhill	.05
607	Dave Henderson	.05
608	Kirk McCaskill	.05
609	Jeff Fassero	.05
610	Mike Harkey	.05
611	Francisco Cabrera	.05
612	Rey Sanchez	.05
613	Scott Servais	.05
614	Darrin Fletcher	.05
615	Felix Fermin	.05
616	Kevin Seitzer	.05
617	Bob Scanlan	.05
618	Billy Hatcher	.05
619	John Vander Wal	.05
620	Joe Hesketh	.05
621	Hector Villanueva	.05
622	Randy Milligan	.05
623	*Tony Tarasco*	.10
624	Russ Swan	.05
625	Willie Wilson	.05
626	Frank Tanana	.05
627	Pete O'Brien	.05
628	Lenny Webster	.05
629	Mark Clark	.05
630	Checklist 526-630 (Roger Clemens)	.25
631	Alex Arias	.05
632	Chris Gwynn	.05
633	Tom Bolton	.05
634	Greg Briley	.05
635	Kent Bottenfield	.05
636	Kelly Downs	.05
637	Manuel Lee	.05
638	Al Leiter	.10
639	Jeff Gardner	.05
640	Mike Gardiner	.05
641	Mark Gardner	.05
642	Jeff Branson	.05
643	Paul Wagner	.05
644	Sean Berry	.05
645	Phil Hiatt	.05
646	Kevin Mitchell	.05
647	Charlie Hayes	.05
648	Jim Deshaies	.05
649	Dan Pasqua	.05
650	Mike Maddux	.05
651	*Domingo Martinez*	.10
652	*Greg McMichael*	.10
653	*Eric Wedge*	.05
654	Mark Whiten	.05
655	Bobby Kelly	.05
656	Julio Franco	.05
657	Gene Harris	.05
658	Pete Schourek	.05
659	Mike Bielecki	.05
660	Ricky Gutierrez	.05
661	Chris Hammond	.05
662	Tim Scott	.05
663	Norm Charlton	.05
664	Doug Drabek	.05
665	Dwight Gooden	.10
666	Jim Gott	.05
667	Randy Myers	.05
668	Darren Holmes	.05
669	Tim Spehr	.05
670	Bruce Ruffin	.05
671	Bobby Thigpen	.05
672	Tony Fernandez	.05
673	Darrin Jackson	.05
674	Gregg Olson	.05
675	Rob Dibble	.05
676	Howard Johnson	.05
677	*Mike Lansing*	.15
678	Charlie Leibrandt	.05
679	Kevin Bass	.05
680	Hubie Brooks	.05
681	Scott Brosius	.05
682	Randy Knorr	.05
683	Dante Bichette	.15
684	Bryan Harvey	.05
685	Greg Gohr	.05
686	Willie Banks	.05
687	Robb Nen	.05
688	Mike Scioscia	.05
689	John Farrell	.05
690	John Candelaria	.05
691	Damon Buford	.05
692	Todd Worrell	.05
693	Pat Hentgen	.05
694	John Smiley	.05
695	Greg Swindell	.05
696	Derek Bell	.10
697	Terry Jorgensen	.05
698	Jimmy Jones	.05
699	David Wells	.10
700	Dave Martinez	.05
701	Steve Bedrosian	.05
702	Jeff Russell	.05
703	Joe Magrane	.05
704	Matt Mieske	.05
705	Paul Molitor	.25
706	Dale Murphy	.15
707	Steve Howe	.05
708	Greg Gagne	.05
709	Dave Eiland	.05
710	David West	.05
711	Luis Aquino	.05
712	Joe Orsulak	.05
713	Eric Plunk	.05
714	Mike Felder	.05
715	Joe Klink	.05
716	Lonnie Smith	.05
717	Monty Fariss	.05
718	Craig Lefferts	.05
719	John Habyan	.05
720	Willie Blair	.05
721	Darnell Coles	.05
722	Mark Williamson	.05
723	Bryn Smith	.05
724	Greg W. Harris	.05
725	*Graeme Lloyd*	.10
726	Cris Carpenter	.05
727	Chico Walker	.05
728	Tracy Woodson	.05
729	Jose Uribe	.05
730	Stan Javier	.05
731	Jay Howell	.05
732	Freddie Benavides	.05
733	Jeff Reboulet	.05
734	Scott Sanderson	.05
735	Checklist 631-735 (Ryne Sandberg)	.10
736	Archi Cianfrocco	.05
737	Daryl Boston	.05
738	Craig Grebeck	.05
739	Doug Dascenzo	.05
740	Gerald Young	.05
741	Candy Maldonado	.05
742	Joey Cora	.05
743	Don Slaught	.05
744	Steve Decker	.05
745	Blas Minor	.05
746	Storm Davis	.05
747	Carlos Quintana	.05
748	Vince Coleman	.05
749	Todd Burns	.05
750	Steve Frey	.05
751	Ivan Calderon	.05
752	*Steve Reed*	.10
753	Danny Jackson	.05
754	Jeff Conine	.05
755	Juan Gonzalez	.50
756	Mike Kelly	.05
757	John Doherty	.05
758	Jack Armstrong	.05
759	John Wehner	.05
760	Scott Bankhead	.05
761	Jim Tatum	.05
762	*Scott Pose*	.10
763	Andy Ashby	.05
764	Ed Sprague	.05
765	Harold Baines	.05
766	Kirk Gibson	.05
767	Troy Neel	.05
768	Dick Schofield	.05
769	Dickie Thon	.05
770	Butch Henry	.05
771	Junior Felix	.05
772	*Ken Ryan*	.10
773	Trevor Hoffman	.10
774	Phil Plantier	.05
775	Bo Jackson	.15
776	Benito Santiago	.05
777	Andre Dawson	.10
778	Bryan Hickerson	.05
779	Dennis Moeller	.05
780	Ryan Bowen	.05
781	Eric Fox	.05
782	Joe Kmak	.05
783	Mike Hampton	.05
784	*Darrell Sherman*	.10
785	J.T. Snow	.10
786	Dave Winfield	.20
787	Jim Austin	.05
788	Craig Shipley	.05
789	Greg Myers	.05
790	Todd Benzinger	.05
791	Cory Snyder	.05
792	David Segui	.05
793	Armando Reynoso	.05
794	Chili Davis	.05
795	Dave Nilsson	.05
796	Paul O'Neill	.15
797	Jerald Clark	.05
798	Jose Mesa	.05
799	Brian Holman	.05
800	Jim Eisenreich	.05
801	Mark McLemore	.05
802	Luis Sojo	.05
803	Harold Reynolds	.05
804	Dan Plesac	.05
805	Dave Stieb	.05
806	Tom Brunansky	.05
807	Kelly Gruber	.05
808	Bob Ojeda	.05
809	Dave Burba	.05
810	Joe Boever	.05
811	Jeremy Hernandez	.05
812	Angels Checklist (Tim Salmon)	.10
813	Astros Checklist (Jeff Bagwell)	.25
814	Athletics Checklist (Mark McGwire)	.75
815	Blue Jays Checklist (Roberto Alomar)	.15
816	Braves Checklist (Steve Avery)	.05
817	Brewers Checklist (Pat Listach)	.05
818	Cardinals Checklist (Gregg Jefferies)	.05
819	Cubs Checklist (Sammy Sosa)	.50
820	Dodgers Checklist (Darryl Strawberry)	.05
821	Expos Checklist (Dennis Martinez)	.05
822	Giants Checklist (Robby Thompson)	.05
823	Indians Checklist (Albert Belle)	.20
824	Mariners Checklist (Randy Johnson)	.15
825	Marlins Checklist (Nigel Wilson)	.05
826	Mets Checklist (Bobby Bonilla)	.05
827	Orioles Checklist (Glenn Davis)	.05
828	Padres Checklist (Gary Sheffield)	.10
829	Phillies Checklist (Darren Daulton)	.05
830	Pirates Checklist (Jay Bell)	.05
831	Rangers Checklist (Juan Gonzalez)	.25
832	Red Sox Checklist (Andre Dawson)	.05
833	Reds Checklist (Hal Morris)	.05
834	Rockies Checklist (David Nied)	.05
835	Royals Checklist (Felix Jose)	.05
836	Tigers Checklist (Travis Fryman)	.05
837	Twins Checklist (Shane Mack)	.05
838	White Sox Checklist (Robin Ventura)	.05
839	Yankees Checklist (Danny Tartabull)	.05
840	Checklist 736-840 (Roberto Alomar)	.15
SP5	3,000 Hits (Robin Yount, George Brett)	2.00
SP6	Nolan Ryan	3.00

1993 Upper Deck Gold Holograms

Unlike 1992, when gold holograms were found on the back of every card originating in a factory set, in 1993 the use of gold holograms was limited to just one factory set per 20-set case, creating a scarce parallel version.

	MT
Complete Factory Set (840):	200.00
Common Player:	.50

(Star cards valued at 5X regular version; see 1993 UD for base values.)

1993 Upper Deck Clutch Performers

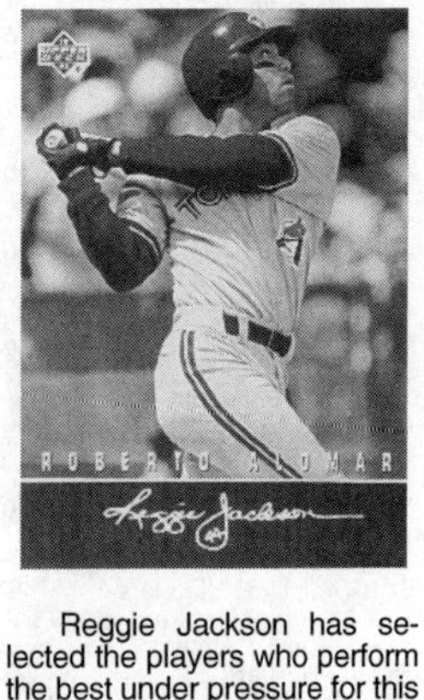

Reggie Jackson has selected the players who perform the best under pressure for this 20-card insert set. Cards were available only in Series II retail packs and use the prefix "R" for numbering. Fronts have a black bottom panel with "Clutch Performers" printed in dark gray. Jackson's facsimile autograph is overprinted in gold foil. On back, under a second player photo, is Jackson's picture and his assessment of the player. There are a few lines of stats to support the player's selection to this exclusive company.

		MT
Complete Set (20):		15.00
Common Player:		.25
1	Roberto Alomar	1.00
2	Wade Boggs	.40
3	Barry Bonds	1.25
4	Jose Canseco	1.50
5	Joe Carter	.25
6	Will Clark	.75
7	Roger Clemens	2.00
8	Dennis Eckersley	.25
9	Cecil Fielder	.25
10	Juan Gonzalez	2.00
11	Ken Griffey, Jr.	5.00
12	Rickey Henderson	.50
13	Barry Larkin	.40
14	Don Mattingly	1.50
15	Fred McGriff	.50
16	Terry Pendleton	.25
17	Kirby Puckett	1.50
18	Ryne Sandberg	1.00
19	John Smoltz	.25
20	Frank Thomas	1.50

1993 Upper Deck 5th Anniversary

This 15-card insert set replicates 15 of Upper Deck's most popular cards from its first five years. Foil stamping and a fifth-anniversary logo appear on the cards, which are otherwise reproductions of the originals. The prefix "A" appears before each card number. The cards were available in Series II hobby packs only.

		MT
Complete Set (15):		20.00
Common Player:		.50
1	Ken Griffey, Jr.	6.00
2	Gary Sheffield	.75
3	Roberto Alomar	1.00
4	Jim Abbott	.50
5	Nolan Ryan	4.00
6	Juan Gonzalez	2.00
7	Dave Justice	.75
8	Carlos Baerga	.50
9	Reggie Jackson	.75
10	Eric Karros	.50
11	Chipper Jones	2.50
12	Ivan Rodriguez	1.50
13	Pat Listach	.50
14	Frank Thomas	2.00
15	Tim Salmon	.75

1993 Upper Deck 5th Anniversary Supers

This set of oversized (3-1/2" x 5") cards is simply an enlarged version of the Upper Deck 5th Anniversary subset that was inserted with the company's 1993 cards. There are 15 cards in the set, which are reprinted versions of some of the most popular cards in the last five years from Upper Deck. Each of the cards carries a number on the back out of an edition of 10,000. The cards were sold individually in blister packs at retail outlets along with two packs of 1993 Upper Deck.

		MT
Complete Set (15):		50.00
Common Player:		2.50
1	Ken Griffey, Jr.	9.00
2	Gary Sheffield	3.00
3	Roberto Alomar	3.00
4	Jim Abbott	2.50
5	Nolan Ryan	7.50
6	Juan Gonzalez	5.00
7	David Justice	2.50
8	Carlos Baerga	2.50
9	Reggie Jackson	3.00
10	Eric Karros	2.50
11	Chipper Jones	6.00
12	Ivan Rodriguez	4.00
13	Pat Listach	2.50
14	Frank Thomas	5.00
15	Tim Salmon	3.00

1993 Upper Deck Future Heroes

This insert set includes eight player cards, a checklist and an unnumbered header card. The cards are numbered 55-63 as a continuation of previous Heroes sets, but this one features more than one player; previous sets featured only one player. Card fronts have a Future Heroes logo and a facsimile autograph. The player's name is revealed using a peeled-back paper effect. Cards were randomly inserted in Series II foil packs.

		MT
Complete Set (10):		15.00
Common Player:		1.25
Header Card:		.25
55	Roberto Alomar	1.00
56	Barry Bonds	1.50
57	Roger Clemens	2.00
58	Juan Gonzalez	2.00
59	Ken Griffey, Jr.	5.00
60	Mark McGwire	5.00
61	Kirby Puckett	2.00
62	Frank Thomas	2.00
63	Checklist	.10

1993 Upper Deck Heroes of Baseball Players' Plaque

This special presentation piece was distributed to players participating in UD's "Heroes of Baseball '93" tour of Major League ballparks to raise funds for the Baseball Assistance Team. The 8" x 4-1/2" plastic holder has sealed inside a lable indicating at which game it was distributed, a 1-1/2" bronze medal of Mickey Mantle, Ted Williams or Willie Mays, and a serially-numbered 5-1/4" x 3-3/4" card picturing Mantle, Williams and Reggie Jackson in action. Back of the card has the schedule for upcoming events overprinted on a color photo of Camden Yards, along with the B.A.T. logo.

	MT
Reggie Jackson, Mickey Mantle, Ted Williams	200.00

1993 Upper Deck Highlights

These 20 insert cards commemorate highlights from the 1992 season. Cards, which were randomly inserted in Series II packs, have a '92 Season Highlights logo on the bottom, with the player's name inside a banner trailing from the logo. The date of the significant event is under the player's name. Card backs have the logo at the top and are numbered with an "HI" prefix. A headline describes what highlight occurred, while the text describes the event.

		MT
Complete Set (20):		100.00
Common Player:		2.00
1	Roberto Alomar	6.00
2	Steve Avery	2.00
3	Harold Baines	2.00
4	Damon Berryhill	2.00
5	Barry Bonds	8.00
6	Bret Boone	2.00
7	George Brett	8.00
8	Francisco Cabrera	2.00
9	Ken Griffey, Jr.	30.00
10	Rickey Henderson	5.00
11	Kenny Lofton	6.00
12	Mickey Morandini	2.00
13	Eddie Murray	4.00
14	David Nied	2.00
15	Jeff Reardon	2.00
16	Bip Roberts	2.00
17	Nolan Ryan	25.00
18	Ed Sprague	2.00
19	Dave Winfield	4.00
20	Robin Yount	5.00

Player names in *Italic* type indicate a rookie card.

1993 Upper Deck Home Run Heroes

This 28-card insert set features the top home run hitters from each team for 1992. Cards, inserted in Series I jumbo packs, are numbered with an "HR" prefix. The card fronts have "Home Run Heroes" printed vertically at the left edge and an embossed bat with the player's name and Upper Deck trademark at bottom. Backs have a purple or pink posterized photo and a few words about the player.

		MT
Complete Set (28):		15.00
Common Player:		.25
1	Juan Gonzalez	2.00
2	Mark McGwire	5.00
3	Cecil Fielder	.25
4	Fred McGriff	.50
5	Albert Belle	1.00
6	Barry Bonds	1.50
7	Joe Carter	.25
8	Darren Daulton	.25
9	Ken Griffey, Jr.	5.00
10	Dave Hollins	.25
11	Ryne Sandberg	1.00
12	George Bell	.25
13	Danny Tartabull	.25
14	Mike Devereaux	.25
15	Greg Vaughn	.25
16	Larry Walker	.75
17	Dave Justice	.50
18	Terry Pendleton	.25
19	Eric Karros	.35
20	Ray Lankford	.25
21	Matt Williams	.60
22	Eric Anthony	.25
23	Bobby Bonilla	.25
24	Kirby Puckett	2.00
25	Mike Macfarlane	.25
26	Tom Brunansky	.25
27	Paul O'Neill	.40
28	Gary Gaetti	.25

1993 Upper Deck Iooss Collection

Sports photographer Walter Iooss Jr. has captured 26 current players in this insert set featuring their candid portraits. Cards have full-bleed photos and gold foil stamping. Backs have biographical sketches and are numbered using a WI prefix. They are available in Series I retail packs.

		MT
Complete Set (27):		18.00
Common Player:		.50
Header Card:		1.00
1	Tim Salmon	.75
2	Jeff Bagwell	2.00
3	Mark McGwire	5.00
4	Roberto Alomar	1.00
5	Steve Avery	.50
6	Paul Molitor	1.00
7	Ozzie Smith	1.00
8	Mark Grace	.75
9	Eric Karros	.60
10	Delino DeShields	.50
11	Will Clark	.75
12	Albert Belle	1.00
13	Ken Griffey, Jr.	5.00
14	Howard Johnson	.50
15	Cal Ripken, Jr.	4.00
16	Fred McGriff	.75
17	Darren Daulton	.50
18	Andy Van Slyke	.50
19	Nolan Ryan	4.00
20	Wade Boggs	.75
21	Barry Larkin	.60
22	George Brett	1.50
23	Cecil Fielder	.50
24	Kirby Puckett	1.50
25	Frank Thomas	2.00
26	Don Mattingly	1.50

1993 Upper Deck Iooss Collection Supers

Upper Deck issued a series of 27 individually numbered oversized cards identical to the Iooss Collection inserts from the regular 1993 Upper Deck set. The cards are 3-1/2" x 5" and each is numbered on back to a limit of 10,000. The cards were available in retail outlets such as Wal-Mart, packaged in blister packs with two foil packs of 1993 Upper Deck cards for around $5. Authentically autographed and numbered (on card fronts) of some players' cards were sold by Upper Deck Authenticated.

		MT
Complete Set (27):		85.00
Common Player:		3.00
Header Card:		3.00
1	Tim Salmon	4.00
2	Jeff Bagwell	6.00
3	Mark McGwire	10.00
4	Roberto Alomar	3.50
5	Steve Avery	3.00
6	Paul Molitor	4.00
7	Ozzie Smith	4.00
8	Mark Grace	4.00
9	Eric Karros	3.00
10	Delino DeShields	3.00
11	Will Clark	4.00
12	Albert Belle	5.00
13	Ken Griffey, Jr.	10.00
14	Howard Johnson	3.00
15	Cal Ripken, Jr.	8.00
16	Fred McGriff	3.50
17	Darren Daulton	3.00
18	Andy Van Slyke	3.00
19	Nolan Ryan	8.00
20	Wade Boggs	3.50
21	Barry Larkin	3.00
22	George Brett	5.00
23	Cecil Fielder	3.00
24	Kirby Puckett	5.00
25	Frank Thomas	5.00
26	Don Mattingly	6.00

1993 Upper Deck Reggie Jackson Heroes Supers

Upper Deck issued a large version of its 1990 Heroes Reggie Jackson cards that was available in retail outlets. Just as in the case of the regular issue Jackson insert cards, there are 10 cards (nine numbered and one unnumbered header card). The cards are 3-1/2" x 5" and identical to the smaller Heroes cards in every other respect. Each of the individual cards carries a sequential number out of a limit of 10,000. The cards were sold one to a package that also included two packs of

1993 Upper Deck cards for about $5.

		MT
Complete Set (10):		30.00
Common Card:		4.00
1	1969 Emerging Superstar (Reggie Jackson)	4.00
2	1973 An MVP Year (Reggie Jackson)	4.00
3	1977 "Mr. October" (Reggie Jackson)	4.00
4	1978 Jackson vs. Welch (Reggie Jackson)	4.00
5	1982 Under the Halo (Reggie Jackson)	4.00
6	1984 500! (Reggie Jackson)	4.00
7	1986 Moving Up the List (Reggie Jackson)	4.00
8	1987 A Great Career Ends (Reggie Jackson)	4.00
9	Heroes Checklist (Reggie Jackson)	4.00
---	Header card	4.00

1993 Upper Deck Reggie Jackson Souvenir Sheet

Upper Deck marked the induction of its spokesman Reggie Jackson into the Hall of Fame in 1983 with the issue of an autographed souvenir sheet. The 10" x 8" sheet is titled, "Reggie Jackson, Mr. October," and pictures him in N.Y. Yankees livery in a home run swing. At left are personal data and career stats. Each sheet is serially numbered from within an edition of 5,000.

	MT
Reggie Jackson	30.00

1993 Upper Deck Willie Mays Heroes

This 10-card insert set includes eight individually-titled cards, an illustrated checklist and one header card. The set is a continuation of Upper Deck's previous Heroes efforts, honoring greats such as Hank Aaron, Nolan Ryan and Reggie Jackson, and is numbered 46-54. Cards were randomly inserted into Series 1 foil packs.

		MT
Complete Set (10):		5.00
Common Mays:		.50
Header Card:		3.00
46	1951 Rookie-of-the-Year	.50
47	1954 The Catch	.50
48	1956-57 30-30 Club	.50
49	1961 Four-Homer Game	.50
50	1965 Most Valuable Player	.50
51	1969 600-Home Run Club	.50
52	1972 New York Homecoming	.50
53	1979 Hall of Fame	.50
54	Checklist - Heroes 46-54	.50

1993 Upper Deck On Deck

These UV-coated cards feature 25 of the game's top players. Each card has a full-bleed photo on the front and questions and answers on the back. Available only in Series II jumbo packs, the cards have a "D" prefix for numbering.

		MT
Complete Set (25):		24.00
Common Player:		.25
1	Jim Abbott	.25
2	Roberto Alomar	1.00
3	Carlos Baerga	.25
4	Albert Belle	1.00
5	Wade Boggs	.75
6	George Brett	1.50
7	Jose Canseco	1.25
8	Will Clark	.75
9	Roger Clemens	2.00
10	Dennis Eckersley	.25
11	Cecil Fielder	.25
12	Juan Gonzalez	2.00
13	Ken Griffey, Jr.	5.00
14	Tony Gwynn	2.50
15	Bo Jackson	.50
16	Chipper Jones	3.00
17	Eric Karros	.40
18	Mark McGwire	5.00
19	Kirby Puckett	1.50
20	Nolan Ryan	4.00
21	Tim Salmon	.50
22	Ryne Sandberg	1.00
23	Darryl Strawberry	.25
24	Frank Thomas	2.00
25	Andy Van Slyke	.25

1993 Upper Deck Supers

A series of six 1993 Upper Deck cards and one from 1991 was re-issued in an 8-1/2" x 11" format, though the manner of distribution is unclear. The cards are virtually identical in design to the regularly issued versions, except for the size, the lack of a hologram on back, and a 1993 dated seal with an individual serial number. The Ryan card was issued in an edition of 5,000, the Karros and Finley cards were issued in an edition of 2,500; the others were limited to 1,000 each.

		MT
Complete Set (7):		80.00
6	Kirby Puckett (Triple Crown Contender)	15.00
10	Barry Bonds (SP)	12.00
24	Eric Karros (1991)	10.00
75	Tom Glavine (1993)	10.00
77	Chuck Finley	10.00
155	Nolan Ryan	25.00
199	Roger Clemens (SP)	15.00

1993 Upper Deck Then And Now

This 18-card lithogram set features both Hall of Famers and current players. The cards feature a combination of four-color player photos and a holographic background. They were random inserts in both Series I and Series II packs. Numbering includes the prefix TN. A limited edition of 2,500 super size 5" by 7" Mickey Mantle Then And Now cards was created for sale through Upper Deck Authenticated.

		MT
Complete Set (18):		50.00
Complete Series 1 (9):		20.00
Complete Series 2 (9):		30.00
Common Player:		.75
1	Wade Boggs	1.50
2	George Brett	2.50
3	Rickey Henderson	1.00
4	Cal Ripken, Jr.	9.00
5	Nolan Ryan	9.00
6	Ryne Sandberg	2.00
7	Ozzie Smith	2.00
8	Darryl Strawberry	.75
9	Dave Winfield	1.00
10	Dennis Eckersley	.75
11	Tony Gwynn	4.00
12	Howard Johnson	.75
13	Don Mattingly	2.50
14	Eddie Murray	1.00
15	Robin Yount	1.50
16	Reggie Jackson	1.50
17	Mickey Mantle	12.00
17a	Mickey Mantle (5" x 7")	40.00
18	Willie Mays	6.00

1993 Upper Deck Triple Crown

These insert cards were available in 1993 Upper Deck Series I foil packs sold by hobby dealers. The set features 10 players who are candidates to win baseball's Triple Crown. Card fronts have a crown and the player's name at the bottom. Backs put that material at the top and explain why the player might lead the league in home runs, batting average and runs batted in.

		MT
Complete Set (10):		15.00
Common Player:		.75
1	Barry Bonds	2.00
2	Jose Canseco	1.50
3	Will Clark	1.00
4	Ken Griffey, Jr.	5.00
5	Fred McGriff	.75
6	Kirby Puckett	2.00
7	Cal Ripken, Jr.	4.00
8	Gary Sheffield	.75
9	Frank Thomas	2.00
10	Larry Walker	1.00

1993 Upper Deck Souvenir Sheets

Once again in 1993, old-timers' benefit games sponsored by the card company were the principal venue for distribution of these 11" x 8-1/2" souvenir sheets. The blank-back sheets feature color artwork on front, usually depicting a handful of players. Each sheet is serially numbered from within a defined edition. Sheets are listed here alphabetically by title. Editions are listed in parentheses.

		MT
Complete Set (27):		125.00
Common Sheet:		5.00
(1)	All-Time Home Run Hitters (Dick Allen, George Foster, Willie Horton, Harmon Killebrew, Tony Oliva) (Minneapolis) (21,600)	5.00
(2)	Blue Jays Heroes vs. UD Heroes (Andy Ashby, Bob Bailor, Reggie Jackson, Ferguson Jenkins) (53.600)	5.00
(3)	Braves Heroes vs. UD Award Winners (Jeff Burroughs, Ralph Garr, George Kell, Gary Matthews, Earl Williams) (44,000)	5.00
(4)	Celebration of Early Black Baseball (Roy Campanella, Ray Dandridge, Piper Davis, Leon Day, Henry Kimbro), Buck Leonard, Verdell Mathis, Buck O'Neil, Andy Porter, Ted Radcliffe, Luis Villodas, Bill Wright) (Baltimore) (50,000) (two-sided)	12.00
(5)	Colorado Rockies Inaugural Season (Johnny Blanchard, Roger Freed, Graig Nettles, J.R. Richard) (21,600)	5.00
(6)	Ewing Kauffman Induction to Royals HoF (Ewing Kauffman) (K.C.) (42,600)	5.00
(7)	Expos' 25th Anniversary (Gary Carter, Warren Cromartie, Gene Mauch, Steve Rogers, Rusty Staub) (41,600)	6.00
(8)	Florida Marlins Inaugural Season (Orlando Cepeda, Minnie Minoso, Tony Perez, Cookie Rojas, Luis Tiant) (47,600)	7.50
(9)	Heroes of Arlington Stadium (46,600)	5.00
(10)	Heroes of the '60s (Orlando Cepeda, Jim Davenport, Tom Haller, Jim Ray Hart, Juan Marichal) (S.F.) (31,600)	6.00
(11)	Nickname Heroes (Jerry Augustine, Cecil Cooper, Mark Fidrych, Bill Madlock, John Montefusco) (Milwaukee) (31,600)	5.00
(12)	Reggie Jackson Hall of Fame Induction (Reggie Jackson) (Anaheim) (51,600)	6.00
(13)	Tribute to Billy Ball (Billy Martin) (Oakland) (46,600)	5.00
(14)	Tribute to Cleveland Stadium (Lou Boudreau, Bob Feller, Mel Harder, Andre Thornton) (76,600)	6.00
(15)	UD Heroes of Baseball All-Star Game (Reggie Jackson, Al Kaline, Jim Palmer, Brooks Robinson, Frank Robinson) (Baltimore) (unnumbered)	5.00
(16)	UD Heroes vs. Red Sox Heroes (Ernie Banks, Minnie Minoso, Billy Williams, Carl Yastrzemski) (36,600)	5.00
(17)	UD Heroes vs. St. Louis Cardinals (Bob Feller, Ken Holtzman, Reggie Jackson, Art Shamsky, Earl Weaver, Dick Williams) (51,600)	5.00
(18)	White Sox Winning Ugly vs. Orioles 1983 (Floyd Bannister, Julio Cruz, Rich Dotson, Tom Paciorek, Dick Tidrow) (Chicago) (21,600)	6.00
(19)	World Children's Baseball Fair (Orlando Cepeda, George Foster, Randy Jones, Sachio Kinugasa, Bill Madlock, Minnie Minoso, Sadaharu Oh) (San Diego) (61,000)	9.00
(20)	20th Anniversary of 1973 World Series (Vida Blue, Wayne Garrett, Jerry Grote, Felix Millan, Dick Williams) (Shea) (46,000)	5.00
(21)	25 Years of Padres (Nate Colbert, Steve Garvey, Randy Jones, Graig Nettles, Dick Williams) (41,600)	5.00
(22)	25th Anniversary of 1968 World Series (Lou Brock, Curt Flood, Willie Horton, Mickey Lolich, Jim Northrup) (Detroit) (31,600)	7.50
(23)	'69 Royals vs. '69 Twins (Moe Drabowsky, Dick Drago, Joe Keough, Bob Oliver, Ellie Rodriguez) (K.C.) (42,600)	5.00
(24)	'83 Phillies vs. '83 Heroes (John Denny, Al Holland, Gary Matthews, Joe Morgan, Mike Schmidt) (56,000)	5.00
(25)	125 Years of Cincinnati Baseball (Gordy Coleman, Tommy Helms, Brooks Lawrence, Bobby Tolan) (51,600)	5.00

(26)	1978 Yankees 22nd World Championship (Steve Garvey, Reggie Jackson, Dennis Leonard, Thurman Munson, Mike Torrez) (51,000)	7.50
(27)	1993 UD All-Star FanFest Autograph Sheet (Camden Yards) (Baltimore) (unnumbered)	5.00
(28)	1993 National Convention (Ken Griffey Jr., Juan Gonzalez, Dave Justice, Ivan Rodriguez, Nolan Ryan, Tim Salmon, Gary Sheffield, Frank Thomas) (Chicago) (unnumbered)	4.00

1993 Upper Deck World Series Contenders

A key player from each team contending for the 1993 World Series was featured on this pair of retail-exclusive 5" x 3-1/2" cards. Fronts have postage-stamp size color photos and the logo of UD Authenticated, along with a serial number from within an edition of 5,000. Backs have a brief summary of each team in the pennant race.

	MT
Complete Set (2):	10.00
AMERICAN LEAGUE Jim Abbott, Juan Gonzalez, John Olerud, Cal Ripken Jr., Frank Thomas	6.00
NATIONAL LEAGUE Barry Bonds, Lenny Dykstra, Marquis Grissom, Fred McGriff	4.00

1993 Upper Deck Heroes of Baseball Previews

This four-card preview set was produced in conjunction with the All-Star FanFest in Baltimore to re-introduce the concept of T202-style "triple-folder" baseball cards. The preview set came in a specially decorated box. The 5-1/4" x 2-1/4" cards feature Ted Williams, Mickey Mantle and Reggie Jackson in various combinations of photos and artwork on each card. Backs are printed in red and gold and include an infield-shaped hologram. Written summaries of the players and their careers are featured. Cards have an "HOB" prefix to their number.

		MT
Complete Set (4):		12.00
Common Player:		2.00
1	Triple Threat (Mickey Mantle, Ted Williams)	5.00
2	Changing of the Guard (Mickey Mantle, Reggie Jackson)	4.00
3	Night and Day (Reggie Jackson, Ted Williams)	3.00
4	Hall-of-Fame Trio (Reggie Jackson, Mickey Mantle, Ted Williams)	4.00

1993 Upper Deck All-Time Heroes

This 1993 set pays homage to one of the classiest, turn-of-the-century card sets, the T202 Hassan Triplefolders. The All-Time Heroes cards are 2-1/4" x 5-1/4" and feature two side panels and a larger middle panel, which features an action shot of the player. A portrait of the player and the Baseball Assistance Team (BAT) logo flank the action photo. Card backs have a biography and career summary. A Classic Combinations subset of 35 cards features artwork or photographs of two or more great players together, plus individual photos on the side panels. Production was limited to 5,140 numbered cases of 12-card foil packs. Ten T202 reprints were also produced and were randomly inserted in the foil packs.

		MT
Complete Set (165):		45.00
Common Player:		.10
1	Hank Aaron	2.00
2	Tommie Agee	.10
3	Bob Allison	.10
4	Matty Alou	.10
5	Sal Bando	.10
6	Hank Bauer	.15
7	Don Baylor	.10
8	Glenn Beckert	.10
9	Yogi Berra	.50
10	Buddy Biancalana	.10
11	Jack Billingham	.10
12	Joe Black	.10
13	Paul Blair	.10
14	Steve Blass	.10
15	Ray Boone	.10
16	Lou Boudreau	.10
17	Ken Brett	.10
18	Nellie Briles	.10
19	Bobby Brown	.10
20	Bill Buckner	.10
21	Don Buford	.10
22	Al Bumbry	.10
23	Lew Burdette	.10
24	Jeff Burroughs	.10
25	Johnny Callison	.10
26	Bert Campaneris	.10
27	Rico Carty	.10
28	Dave Cash	.10
29	Cesar Cedeno	.10
30	Frank Chance	.25
31	Joe Charboneau	.15
32	Ty Cobb	2.00
33	Jerry Coleman	.10
34	Cecil Cooper	.10
35	Frankie Crossetti	.10
36	Alvin Dark	.10
37	Tommy Davis	.10
38	Dizzy Dean	.25
39	Doug DeCinces	.10
40	Bucky Dent	.10
41	Larry Dierker	.10
42	Larry Doby	.20
43	Moe Drabowsky	.10
44	Dave Dravecky	.10
45	Del Ennis	.10
46	Carl Erskine	.10
47	Johnny Evers	.25
48	Elroy Face	.10
49	Rick Ferrell	.10
50	Mark Fidrych	.15
51	Curt Flood	.10
52	Whitey Ford	.50
53	George Foster	.10
54	Jimmie Foxx	.25
55	Jim Fregosi	.10
56	Phil Garner	.10
57	Ralph Garr	.10
58	Lou Gehrig	2.00
59	Bobby Grich	.10
60	Jerry Grote	.10
61	Harvey Haddix	.10
62	Toby Harrah	.10
63	Bud Harrelson	.10
64	Jim Hegan	.10
65	Gil Hodges	.25
66	Ken Holtzman	.10
67	Bob Horner	.10
68	Rogers Hornsby	.25
69	Carl Hubbell	.25
70	Ron Hunt	.10
71	Monte Irvin	.10
72a	Reggie Jackson (regular issue, black printing on back)	.50
72b	Reggie Jackson (dealer promo, red printing on back)	8.00
73	Larry Jansen	.10
74	Ferguson Jenkins	.10
75	Tommy John	.10
76	Cliff Johnson	.10
77	Davey Johnson	.10
78	Walter Johnson	.45
79	George Kell	.10
80	Don Kessinger	.10
81	Vern Law	.10
82	Dennis Leonard	.10
83	Johnny Logan	.10
84	Mickey Lolich	.10
85	Jim Lonborg	.10
86	Bill Madlock	.10
87	Mickey Mantle	4.00
88	Billy Martin	.25
89	Christy Mathewson	.45
90	Lee May	.10
91	Willie Mays	2.00
92	Bill Mazeroski	.15
93	Gil McDougald	.15
94	Sam McDowell	.10
95	Minnie Minoso	.15
96	Johnny Mize	.25
97	Rick Monday	.10
98	Wally Moon	.10
99	Manny Mota	.10
100	Bobby Murcer	.10
101	Ron Necciai	.10
102	Al Oliver	.10
103	Mel Ott	.15
104	Mel Parnell	.10
105	Jimmy Piersall	.10
106	Johnny Podres	.15
107	Bobby Richardson	.15
108	Robin Roberts	.15
109	Al Rosen	.10
110	Babe Ruth	3.00
111	Joe Sambito	.10
112	Manny Sanguillen	.10
113	Ron Santo	.10
114	Bill Skowron	.15
115	Enos Slaughter	.15
116	Warren Spahn	.20
117	Tris Speaker	.20
118	Frank Thomas	.10
119	Bobby Thomson	.10
120	Andre Thornton	.10
121	Marv Throneberry	.10
122	Luis Tiant	.10
123	Joe Tinker	.25
124	Honus Wagner	.50
125	Bill White	.10
126	Ted Williams	1.00
127	Earl Wilson	.10
128	Joe Wood	.10
129	Cy Young	.40
130	Richie Zisk	.10
131	Babe Ruth, Lou Gehrig	2.00
132	Ted Williams, Rogers Hornsby	1.00
133	Lou Gehrig, Babe Ruth	2.00
134	Babe Ruth, Mickey Mantle	3.00
135	Mickey Mantle, Reggie Jackson	1.00
136	Mel Ott, Carl Hubbell	.25
137	Mickey Mantle, Willie Mays	2.00
138	Cy Young, Walter Johnson	.25
139	Honus Wagner, Rogers Hornsby	.25
140	Mickey Mantle, Whitey Ford	2.00
141	Mickey Mantle, Billy Martin	2.00
142	Cy Young, Walter Johnson	.25
143	Christy Mathewson, Walter Johnson	.25
144	Warren Spahn, Christy Mathewson	.15
145	Honus Wagner, Ty Cobb	.50
146	Babe Ruth, Ty Cobb	1.00
147	Joe Tinker, Johnny Evers	.15
148	Johnny Evers, Frank Chance	.15
149	Hank Aaron, Babe Ruth	1.00
150	Willie Mays, Hank Aaron	1.00
151	Babe Ruth, Willie Mays	1.00
152	Babe Ruth, Whitey Ford	1.00
153	Larry Doby, Minnie Minoso	.25
154	Joe Black, Monte Irvin	.10
155	Joe Wood, Christy Mathewson	.15
156	Christy Mathewson, Cy Young	.25
157	Cy Young, Joe Wood	.15
158	Cy Young, Whitey Ford	.20
159	Cy Young, Ferguson Jenkins	.15
160	Ty Cobb, Rogers Hornsby	.45
161	Tris Speaker, Ted Williams	1.00
162	Rogers Hornsby, Ted Williams	1.00
163	Willie Mays, Monte Irvin	.50
164	Willie Mays, Bobby Thomson	.50
165	Reggie Jackson, Mickey Mantle	2.00

1993 Upper Deck All-Time Heroes T202 Reprints

A series of 10 reprints of the classic 1912 Hassan "Triplefolders" baseball cards on which the All-Time Heroes set was patterned was included as random inserts in the Upper Deck old-timers set. The reprints measure 5-1/4" x 2-1/4" (same as the originals). The Hassan cigarette ads on the backs of the originals have been replaced on the reprints by an Upper Deck hologram and the logos of the card company, B.A.T., Major League Baseball and the Cooperstown Collection. The Hassan cards are known as T202, their designation in the "American Card Catalog." The reprints are unnumbered and are checklisted here alphabetically in order of the player appearing on the left end of each card.

		MT
Complete Set (10):		10.00
Common Player:		.50
(1)	Art Devlin, Christy Mathewson	1.00
(2)	Hugh Jennings, Ty Cobb	2.00
(3)	John Kling, Cy Young	1.00
(4)	Jack Knight, Walter Johnson	.75
(5)	John McGraw, Hugh Jennings	.50
(6)	George Moriarty, Ty Cobb	2.00
(7)	Charley O'Leary, Ty Cobb	2.00
(8)	Charley O'Leary, Ty Cobb	2.00
(9)	Joe Tinker, Frank Chance	1.00
(10)	Joe Wood, Tris Speaker	.50

1993 Upper Deck Diamond Gallery

Utilizing something the company calls lithogram technology, Upper Deck produced a 36-card set that combines four-color photography and a holographic image. The set features one star from each of the 28 teams, along with a subset spotlighting top rookies from 1993 and cards saluting Nolan Ryan, Rickey Henderson and Ozzie Smith. The set comes in a specially-designed box, with a numbered checklist card. The set was limited to a total of 123,600.

		MT
Complete Set (36):		25.00
Common Player:		.50
1	Tim Salmon	1.50
2	Jeff Bagwell	2.00
3	Mark McGwire	6.00
4	Roberto Alomar	1.50
5	Terry Pendleton	.50
6	Robin Yount	1.50
7	Ray Lankford	.60
8	Ryne Sandberg	2.50
9	Darryl Strawberry	.60
10	Marquis Grissom	.50
11	Barry Bonds	2.50
12	Carlos Baerga	.50
13	Ken Griffey, Jr.	6.00
14	Benito Santiago	.50
15	Dwight Gooden	.50
16	Cal Ripken, Jr.	5.00
17	Tony Gwynn	2.00
18	Dave Hollins	.50
19	Andy Van Slyke	.50
20	Juan Gonzalez	2.50
21	Roger Clemens	2.00
22	Barry Larkin	.60
23	Dave Nied	.50
24	George Brett	3.00
25	Travis Fryman	.60
26	Kirby Puckett	3.00
27	Frank Thomas	2.50
28	Don Mattingly	3.00
29	Rickey Henderson	1.25
30	Nolan Ryan	5.00
31	Ozzie Smith	2.00
32	Wil Cordero	.50
33	Phil Hiatt	.50
34	Mike Piazza	4.00
35	J.T. Snow	.75
36	Kevin Young	.50

1993 Upper Deck Fun Packs

Aimed at the younger audience, this Upper Deck product features 150 "regular" player cards and 75 specialty cards in a variety of subsets, plus two different types of insert cards. The basic player cards feature a photo (generally an action shot) set onto a background of purple, green and red, highlighted by yellow and orange stripes. On back is a white panel set against a red, yellow and orange blended stripes. In the panel are a cartoon, a trivia question and answer about the player, and some brief biographical details, stats and career summary. The basic player cards are arranged within the set in alphabetical order by team. The teams are also arranged alphabetically, according to their popular nickname. Leading off each team's roster in the set is a "Glow Stars" sticker, featuring a color player photo against a parti-colored background. The area around the photo is die-cut to allow the player's picture to be separated from the background and stuck to a wall, where the white and green outlines glow in the dark. Cards #1-9 are designated as "Stars of Tomorrow". Both front and back have a background of a star-studded purple sky. On front, the player's name appears in white in a stadium setting at bottom. The player is pictured in an action pose above the stadium, outlined as a constellation. On back is a portrait photo, a prediction of future greatness and a few stats and biographical details. Cards 10-21 are "Hot Shots" - heat-sensitive cards. When touched, the black textured ink which surrounds the player photo turns clear, revealing a colored pattern beneath. Backs, which are not heat-sensitive, have a short career write-up. Cards 22-27 are "Kid Stars" and feature a childhood photo and a clue to the player's identity; backs have a color photo of the player. Cards 28-37 are checklisted as "Upper Deck Heroes", though that designation does not appear on the cards. The subset is done in comic-book art style, and features a blackboard motif on front and back, on which player photos are superimposed and annotated with baseball playing tips. Cards 216-220 are designated "Fold-outs" and are double-size (2-1/2"x7"). Fronts have a purple background photo of the player, with a full-color action photo superimposed. Backs have previous year and career stats and a player profile. Inside the Foldout is a full-color version of the front background photo, showing the player leaping or diving to make a play. The five checklist cards which conclude the set have player photos on front.

		MT
	Complete Set (225):	24.00
	Common Player:	.05
1	Wil Cordero (Stars of Tomorrow)	.20
2	Brent Gates (Stars of Tomorrow)	.15
3	Benji Gil (Stars of Tomorrow)	.10
4	Phil Hiatt (Stars of Tomorrow)	.10
5	David McCarty (Stars of Tomorrow)	.10
6	Mike Piazza (Stars of Tomorrow)	2.00
7	Tim Salmon (Stars of Tomorrow)	1.00
8	*J.T. Snow* (Stars of Tomorrow)	.75
9	Kevin Young (Stars of Tomorrow)	.15
10	Roberto Alomar (Hot Shots)	.40
11	Barry Bonds (Hot Shots)	.50
12	Jose Canseco (Hot Shots)	.40
13	Will Clark (Hot Shots)	.25
14	Roger Clemens (Hot Shots)	.50
15	Juan Gonzalez (Hot Shots)	.75
16	Ken Griffey, Jr. (Hot Shots)	1.50
17	Mark McGwire (Hot Shots)	1.50
18	Nolan Ryan (Hot Shots)	1.00
19	Ryne Sandberg (Hot Shots)	.75
20	Gary Sheffield (Hot Shots)	.25
21	Frank Thomas (Hot Shots)	1.00
22	Roberto Alomar (Kid Stars)	.20
23	Roger Clemens (Kid Stars)	.25
24	Ken Griffey, Jr. (Kid Stars)	1.00
25	Gary Sheffield (Kid Stars)	.10
26	Nolan Ryan (Kid Stars)	.75
27	Frank Thomas (Kid Stars)	.50
28	Reggie Jackson (Heroes)	.15
29	Roger Clemens (Heroes)	.25
30	Ken Griffey, Jr. (Heroes)	1.00
31	Bo Jackson (Heroes)	.15
32	Cal Ripken, Jr. (Heroes)	.75
33	Nolan Ryan (Heroes)	.75
34	Deion Sanders (Heroes)	.25
35	Ozzie Smith (Heroes)	.25
36	Frank Thomas (Heroes)	.50
37	Tim Salmon (Glow Stars)	.25
38	Chili Davis	.05
39	Chuck Finley	.05
40	Mark Langston	.05
41	Luis Polonia	.05
42	Jeff Bagwell (Glow Stars)	.40
43	Jeff Bagwell	.75
44	Craig Biggio	.15
45	Ken Caminiti	.15
46	Doug Drabek	.05
47	Steve Finley	.05
48	Mark McGwire (Glow Stars)	1.00
49	Dennis Eckersley	.05
50	Rickey Henderson	.15
51	Mark McGwire	2.50
52	Ruben Sierra	.05
53	Terry Steinbach	.05
54	Roberto Alomar (Glow Stars)	.30
55	Roberto Alomar	.25
56	Joe Carter	.05
57	Juan Guzman	.05
58	Paul Molitor	.25
59	Jack Morris	.05
60	John Olerud	.15
61	Tom Glavine (Glow Stars)	.20
62	Steve Avery	.05
63	Tom Glavine	.10
64	Dave Justice	.20
65	Greg Maddux	.50
66	Terry Pendleton	.05
67	Deion Sanders	.20
68	John Smoltz	.10
69	Robin Yount (Glow Stars)	.25
70	Cal Eldred	.05
71	Pat Listach	.05
72	Greg Vaughn	.05
73	Robin Yount	.15
74	Ozzie Smith (Glow Stars)	.25
75	Gregg Jefferies	.15
76	Ray Lankford	.10
77	Lee Smith	.05
78	Ozzie Smith	.30
79	Bob Tewksbury	.05
80	Ryne Sandberg (Glow Stars)	.25
81	Mark Grace	.15
82	Mike Morgan	.05
83	Randy Myers	.05
84	Ryne Sandberg	.50
85	Sammy Sosa	.75
86	Eric Karros (Glow Stars)	.20
87	Brett Butler	.10
88	Orel Hershiser	.10
89	Eric Karros	.15
90	Ramon Martinez	.10
91	Jose Offerman	.05
92	Darryl Strawberry	.10
93	Marquis Grissom (Glow Stars)	.15
94	Delino DeShields	.05
95	Marquis Grissom	.10
96	Ken Hill	.05
97	Dennis Martinez	.05
98	Larry Walker	.25
99	Barry Bonds (Glow Stars)	.40
100	Barry Bonds	.40
101	Will Clark	.25
102	Bill Swift	.05
103	Robby Thompson	.05
104	Matt Williams	.10
105	Carlos Baerga (Glow Stars)	.05
106	Sandy Alomar, Jr.	.10
107	Carlos Baerga	.05
108	Albert Belle	.30
109	Kenny Lofton	.30
110	Charles Nagy	.05
111	Ken Griffey, Jr. (Glow Stars)	1.50
112	Jay Buhner	.05
113	Dave Fleming	.05
114	Ken Griffey, Jr.	2.50
115	Randy Johnson	.30
116	Edgar Martinez	.05
117	Benito Santiago (Glow Stars)	.15
118	Bret Barberie	.05
119	Jeff Conine	.15
120	Brian Harvey	.05
121	Benito Santiago	.05
122	Walt Weiss	.05
123	Dwight Gooden (Glow Stars)	.15
124	Bobby Bonilla	.05
125	Tony Fernandez	.05
126	Dwight Gooden	.10
127	Howard Johnson	.05
128	Eddie Murray	.20
129	Bret Saberhagen	.05
130	Cal Ripken, Jr. (Glow Stars)	1.00
131	Brady Anderson	.15
132	Mike Devereaux	.05
133	Ben McDonald	.05
134	Mike Mussina	.25
135	Cal Ripken, Jr.	1.50
136	Fred McGriff (Glow Stars)	.20
137	Andy Benes	.10
138	Tony Gwynn	.40
139	Fred McGriff	.15
140	Phil Plantier	.05
141	Gary Sheffield	.20
142	Darren Daulton (Glow Stars)	.10
143	Darren Daulton	.05
144	Len Dykstra	.05
145	Dave Hollins	.05
146	John Kruk	.05
147	Mitch Williams	.05
148	Andy Van Slyke (Glow Stars)	.05
149	Jay Bell	.05
150	Zane Smith	.05
151	Andy Van Slyke	.05
152	Tim Wakefield	.05
153	Juan Gonzalez (Glow Stars)	.60
154	Kevin Brown	.10
155	Jose Canseco	.25
156	Juan Gonzalez	.50
157	Rafael Palmeiro	.15
158	Dean Palmer	.05
159	Ivan Rodriguez	.25
160	Nolan Ryan	1.50
161	Roger Clemens (Glow Stars)	.40
162	Roger Clemens	.40
163	Andre Dawson	.10
164	Mike Greenwell	.05
165	Tony Pena	.05
166	Frank Viola	.05
167	Barry Larkin (Glow Stars)	.15
168	Rob Dibble	.05
169	Roberto Kelly	.05
170	Barry Larkin	.15
171	Kevin Mitchell	.05
172	Bip Roberts	.05
173	Andres Galarraga (Glow Stars)	.15
174	Dante Bichette	.15
175	Jerald Clark	.05
176	Andres Galarraga	.15
177	Charlie Hayes	.05
178	David Nied	.05
179	David Cone (Glow Stars)	.10
180	Kevin Appler	.05
181	George Brett	.40
182	David Cone	.05
183	Felix Jose	.05
184	Wally Joyner	.05
185	Cecil Fielder (Glow Stars)	.15
186	Cecil Fielder	.15
187	Travis Fryman	.05
188	Tony Phillips	.05
189	Mickey Tettleton	.05
190	Lou Whitaker	.05
191	Kirby Puckett (Glow Stars)	.40
192	Scott Erickson	.05
193	Chuck Knoblauch	.15
194	Shane Mack	.05
195	Kirby Puckett	.50
196	Dave Winfield	.15
197	Frank Thomas (Glow Stars)	.50
198	George Bell	.05
199	Bo Jackson	.15
200	Jack McDowell	.05
201	Tim Raines	.10
202	Frank Thomas	1.00
203	Robin Ventura	.15
204	Jim Abbott (Glow Stars)	.15
205	Jim Abbott	.15
206	Wade Boggs	.25
207	Jimmy Key	.05
208	Don Mattingly	.75
209	Danny Tartabull	.05
210	Brett Butler (All-Star Advice)	.05
211	Tony Gwynn (All-Star Advice)	.15
212	Rickey Henderson (All-Star Advice)	.05
213	Ramon Martinez (All-Star Advice)	.05
214	Nolan Ryan (All-Star Advice)	.60
215	Ozzie Smith (All-Star Advice)	.15
216	Marquis Grissom (Fold-Out)	.15
217	Dean Palmer (Fold-Out)	.15
218	Cal Ripken, Jr. (Fold-Out)	1.00
219	Deion Sanders (Fold-Out)	.20
220	Darryl Strawberry (Fold-Out)	.15
221	David McCarty (Checklist)	.10
222	Barry Bonds (Checklist)	.25
223	Juan Gonzalez (Checklist)	.20
224	Ken Griffey, Jr. (Checklist)	.50
225	Frank Thomas (Checklist)	.25

1993 Upper Deck Fun Packs All-Star Scratch-Off

Randomly inserted into Fun Packs was a series of nine "All-Star Scratch-Off" game cards. Fronts and backs have a star-studded blue background. Inside the folded, double-size (2-1/2" x 7") cards are American and National League line-ups which can be used to play a baseball game, the rules of which are explained on the card backs. On front are photos of two of the players in the line-up, matched by position from each league. The inserts are numbered with an "AS" prefix.

		MT
	Complete Set (9):	12.00
	Common Player:	.60
1	Fred McGriff, Frank Thomas	2.00
2	Darren Daulton, Ivan Rodriguez	.75
3	Mark McGwire, Will Clark	3.00
4	Ryne Sandberg, Roberto Alomar	1.50
5	Robin Ventura, Terry Pendleton	.60
6	Cal Ripken Jr., Ozzie Smith	2.00
7	Barry Bonds, Juan Gonzalez	1.75
8	Marquis Grissom, Ken Griffey, Jr.	3.00
9	Tony Gwynn, Kirby Puckett	1.75

1993 Upper Deck Fun Packs Mascot Madness

Upper Deck's high-tech lithogram process of combining color photos and holograms was used to create the five-card "Mascot Madness" inserts which were randomly found in Fun Packs. Backs have a description of the mascot and explain his role with the team.

		MT
	Complete Set (5):	5.00
	Common Player:	1.00
1	Phillie Phanatic	1.00
2	Pirate Parrot	1.00
3	Fredbird	1.00
4	BJ Birdy	1.00
5	Youppi (mascot)	1.00

1993 Upper Deck/ Mead memo books

The well-known school/office supply company, Mead, teamed with UD in 1993 to produce a series of pocket notebooks. The 3" x 5" books have 120 lined pages, spiral-bound at top. The front and back of the cover reproduce the front and back of a player's card from the '93 UD baseball set. The back cover features lists of recent leaders in various statistical categories (11 different lists can be found for each notebook). Individual notebooks are numbered in a series of 12.

		MT
	Complete Set (12):	18.00
	Common Player:	2.00
1	Kirby Puckett (Triple Crown Contenders)	2.00
2	Gary Sheffield (Triple Crown Contenders)	2.00
3	Nolan Ryan (Looss Collection)	3.00
4	David Justice	2.00
5	Deion Sanders	2.00
6	Eric Karros	2.00
7	Ryne Sandberg	2.50
8	Will Clark (Triple Crown Contenders)	2.00
9	Bobby Bonilla	2.00
10	Barry Larkin	2.00
11	Cal Ripken Jr. (Triple Crown Contenders)	3.00
12	Ken Griffey Jr. (Triple Crown Contenders)	4.00

Player names in *Italic* type indicate a rookie card.

1994 Upper Deck

Upper Deck's 1994 offering was a typical presentation for the company, combining high-quality regular-issue cards with innovative subsets and high-tech chase cards. Series I, besides the standard player cards, features subsets including 30 Star Rookies, with metallic borders, 10 "Fantasy Team" stars who excelled in Rotisserie League stats, 14 Home Field Advantage cards showcasing National League stadiums and hometeam stars, and, 15 stars under the age of 25 in a subset titled, "The Future is Now." Regular issue cards feature a color photo on front and a second, black-and-white version of the same photo at left in a vertically stretched format. The player's name, team and Upper Deck logo appear on front in copper foil. Backs have a color photo, recent and career major league stats and an infield-shaped hologram. Series II offered, in addition to regular cards, subsets of 14 American League Home Field Advantage cards, a group of "Classic Alumni" minor league players, a selection of "Diamond Debuts" cards and a group of "Top Prospects." Retail packaging contained a special Mickey Mantle/Ken Griffey, Jr. card which could be found bearing either one or both of the players' autographs in an edition of 1,000 each. Series II retail packs offered a chance to find an autographed version of Alex Rodriguez' Classic Alumni card.

		MT
Complete Set (550):		45.00
Complete Series 1 (280):		30.00
Complete Series 2 (270):		18.00
Common Player:		.10
Series 1 E/W Wax Box:		50.00
Series 1 Cen. Wax Box:		70.00
Series 2 E/W Wax Box:		35.00
Series 2 Cen. Wax Box:		45.00
1	*Brian Anderson* (Star Rookie)	.15
2	Shane Andrews (Star Rookie)	.25
3	James Baldwin (Star Rookie)	.15
4	Rich Becker (Star Rookie)	.10
5	Greg Blosser (Star Rookie)	.10
6	*Ricky Bottalico* (Star Rookie)	.15
7	Midre Cummings (Star Rookie)	.10
8	Carlos Delgado (Star Rookie)	.75
9	*Steve Dreyer* (Star Rookie)	.10
10	*Joey Eischen* (Star Rookie)	.15
11	Carl Everett (Star Rookie)	.20
12	Cliff Floyd (Star Rookie)	.15
13	Alex Gonzalez (Star Rookie)	.20
14	Jeff Granger (Star Rookie)	.10
15	Shawn Green (Star Rookie)	1.00
16	Brian Hunter (Star Rookie)	.15
17	Butch Huskey (Star Rookie)	.15
18	Mark Hutton (Star Rookie)	.10
19	*Michael Jordan* (Star Rookie)	12.00
20	Steve Karsay (Star Rookie)	.15
21	Jeff McNeely (Star Rookie)	.10
22	Marc Newfield (Star Rookie)	.10
23	Manny Ramirez (Star Rookie)	1.50
24	*Alex Rodriguez* (Star Rookie)	15.00
25	Scott Ruffcorn (Star Rookie)	.10
26	Paul Spoljaric (Star Rookie)	.10
27	*Salomon Torres* (Star Rookie)	.10
28	Steve Trachsel (Star Rookie)	.15
29	*Chris Turner* (Star Rookie)	.10
30	Gabe White (Star Rookie)	.10
31	Randy Johnson (Fantasy Team)	.30
32	John Wetteland (Fantasy Team)	.10
33	Mike Piazza (Fantasy Team)	1.00
34	Rafael Palmeiro (Fantasy Team)	.20
35	Roberto Alomar (Fantasy Team)	.30
36	Matt Williams (Fantasy Team)	.20
37	Travis Fryman (Fantasy Team)	.10
38	Barry Bonds (Fantasy Team)	.40
39	Marquis Grissom (Fantasy Team)	.10
40	Albert Belle (Fantasy Team)	.30
41	Steve Avery (Future/Now)	.10
42	Jason Bere (Future/Now)	.10
43	Alex Fernandez (Future/Now)	.15
44	Mike Mussina (Future/Now)	.30
45	Aaron Sele (Future/Now)	.10
46	Rod Beck (Future/Now)	.10
47	Mike Piazza (Future/Now)	1.00
48	John Olerud (Future/Now)	.15
49	Carlos Baerga (Future/Now)	.10
50	Gary Sheffield (Future/Now)	.10
51	Travis Fryman (Future/Now)	.10
52	Juan Gonzalez (Future/Now)	.60
53	Ken Griffey, Jr. (Future/Now)	2.00
54	Tim Salmon (Future/Now)	.25
55	Frank Thomas (Future/Now)	.50
56	Tony Phillips	.10
57	Julio Franco	.10
58	Kevin Mitchell	.10
59	Raul Mondesi	.40
60	Rickey Henderson	.40
61	Jay Buhner	.10
62	Bill Swift	.10
63	Brady Anderson	.10
64	Ryan Klesko	.20
65	Darren Daulton	.10
66	Damion Easley	.10
67	Mark McGwire	3.00
68	John Roper	.10
69	Dave Telgheder	.10
70	Dave Nied	.10
71	Mo Vaughn	.50
72	Tyler Green	.10
73	Dave Magadan	.10
74	Chili Davis	.10
75	Archi Cianfrocco	.10
76	Joe Girardi	.10
77	Chris Hoiles	.10
78	Ryan Bowen	.10
79	Greg Gagne	.10
80	Aaron Sele	.10
81	Dave Winfield	.20
82	Chad Curtis	.10
83	Andy Van Slyke	.10
84	Kevin Stocker	.10
85	Deion Sanders	.15
86	Bernie Williams	.40
87	John Smoltz	.20
88	*Ruben Santana*	.10
89	Dave Stewart	.10
90	Don Mattingly	.75
91	Joe Carter	.10
92	Ryne Sandberg	.40
93	Chris Gomez	.10
94	Tino Martinez	.25
95	Terry Pendleton	.10
96	Andre Dawson	.15
97	Wil Cordero	.10
98	Kent Hrbek	.10
99	John Olerud	.25
100	Kirt Manwaring	.10
101	Tim Bogar	.10
102	Mike Mussina	.40
103	Nigel Wilson	.10
104	Ricky Gutierrez	.10
105	Roberto Mejia	.10
106	Tom Pagnozzi	.10
107	Mike Macfarlane	.10
108	Jose Bautista	.10
109	Luis Ortiz	.10
110	Brent Gates	.10
111	Tim Salmon	.25
112	Wade Boggs	.25
113	*Tripp Cromer*	.10
114	Denny Hocking	.10
115	Carlos Baerga	.10
116	*J.R. Phillips*	.10
117	Bo Jackson	.15
118	Lance Johnson	.10
119	Bobby Jones	.15
120	Bobby Witt	.10
121	Ron Karkovice	.10
122	Jose Vizcaino	.10
123	Danny Darwin	.10
124	Eduardo Perez	.10
125	Brian Looney	.10
126	Pat Hentgen	.10
127	Frank Viola	.10
128	Darren Holmes	.10
129	Wally Whitehurst	.10
130	Matt Walbeck	.10
131	Albert Belle	.75
132	Steve Cooke	.10
133	Kevin Appier	.10
134	Joe Oliver	.10
135	Benji Gil	.10
136	Steve Buechele	.10
137	Devon White	.10
138	Sterling Hitchcock	.10
139	*Phil Leftwich*	.10
140	Jose Canseco	.60
141	Rick Aguilera	.10
142	Rod Beck	.10
143	Jose Rijo	.10
144	Tom Glavine	.20
145	Phil Plantier	.10
146	Jason Bere	.10
147	Jamie Moyer	.10
148	Wes Chamberlain	.10
149	Glenallen Hill	.10
150	Mark Whiten	.10
151	Bret Barberie	.10
152	Chuck Knoblauch	.20
153	Trevor Hoffman	.15
154	Rick Wilkins	.10
155	Juan Gonzalez	1.00
156	Ozzie Guillen	.10
157	Jim Eisenreich	.10
158	Pedro Astacio	.10
159	Joe Magrane	.10
160	Ryan Thompson	.10
161	Jose Lind	.10
162	Jeff Conine	.10
163	Todd Benzinger	.10
164	Roger Salkeld	.10
165	Gary DiSarcina	.10
166	Kevin Gross	.10
167	Charlie Hayes	.10
168	Tim Costo	.10
169	Wally Joyner	.10
170	Johnny Ruffin	.10
171	*Kirk Rueter*	.10
172	Len Dykstra	.10
173	Ken Hill	.10
174	Mike Bordick	.10
175	Billy Hall	.10
176	Rob Butler	.10
177	Jay Bell	.10
178	Jeff Kent	.10
179	David Wells	.10
180	Dean Palmer	.10
181	Mariano Duncan	.10
182	Orlando Merced	.10
183	Brett Butler	.10
184	Milt Thompson	.10
185	Chipper Jones	2.00
186	Paul O'Neill	.25
187	Mike Greenwell	.10
188	Harold Baines	.10
189	Todd Stottlemyre	.15
190	Jeromy Burnitz	.15
191	Rene Arocha	.10
192	Jeff Fassero	.10
193	Robby Thompson	.10
194	Greg W. Harris	.10
195	Todd Van Poppel	.10
196	Jose Guzman	.10
197	Shane Mack	.10
198	Carlos Garcia	.10
199	Kevin Roberson	.10
200	David McCarty	.10
201	Alan Trammell	.15
202	Chuck Carr	.10
203	Tommy Greene	.10
204	Wilson Alvarez	.15
205	Dwight Gooden	.15
206	*Tony Tarasco*	.10
207	Darren Lewis	.10
208	Eric Karros	.15
209	Chris Hammond	.10
210	Jeffrey Hammonds	.15
211	Rich Amaral	.10
212	Danny Tartabull	.10
213	Jeff Russell	.10
214	Dave Staton	.10
215	Kenny Lofton	.50
216	Manuel Lee	.10
217	Brian Koelling	.10
218	Scott Lydy	.10
219	Tony Gwynn	1.50
220	Cecil Fielder	.10
221	Royce Clayton	.10
222	Reggie Sanders	.15
223	Brian Jordan	.10
224	Ken Griffey, Jr.	3.00
224a	Ken Griffey, Jr. (promo card)	4.00
225	Fred McGriff	.20
226	Felix Jose	.10
227	Brad Pennington	.10
228a	Chris Bosio ("ARINERS")	.10
228b	Chris Bosio ("MARINERS")	.10
229	Mike Stanley	.10
230	Willie Greene	.10
231	Alex Fernandez	.15
232	Brad Ausmus	.10
233	Darrell Whitmore	.10
234	Marcus Moore	.10
235	Allen Watson	.10
236	Jose Offerman	.10
237	Rondell White	.20
238	Jeff King	.10
239	Luis Alicea	.10
240	Dan Wilson	.10
241	Ed Sprague	.10
242	Todd Hundley	.15
243	Al Martin	.10
244	Mike Lansing	.10
245	Ivan Rodriguez	.75
246	Dave Fleming	.10
247	John Doherty	.10
248	Mark McLemore	.10
249	Bob Hamelin	.10
250	*Curtis Pride*	.20
251	Zane Smith	.10
252	Eric Young	.20
253	Brian McRae	.10
254	Tim Raines	.10
255	Javier Lopez	.25
256	Melvin Nieves	.10
257	Randy Myers	.10
258	Willie McGee	.10
259	Jimmy Key	.10
260	Tom Candiotti	.10
261	Eric Davis	.10
262	Craig Paquette	.10
263	Robin Ventura	.20
264	Pat Kelly	.10
265	Gregg Jefferies	.10
266	Cory Snyder	.10
267	Dave Justice (Home Field Advantage)	.20
268	Sammy Sosa (Home Field Advantage)	1.50
269	Barry Larkin (Home Field Advantage)	.10
270	Andres Galarraga (Home Field Advantage)	.10
271	Gary Sheffield (Home Field Advantage)	.10
272	Jeff Bagwell (Home Field Advantage)	.40
273	Mike Piazza (Home Field Advantage)	.75
274	Larry Walker (Home Field Advantage)	.25
275	Bobby Bonilla (Home Field Advantage)	.10
276	John Kruk (Home Field Advantage)	.10
277	Jay Bell (Home Field Advantage)	.10
278	Ozzie Smith (Home Field Advantage)	.30
279	Tony Gwynn (Home Field Advantage)	.75
280	Barry Bonds (Home Field Advantage)	.40
281	Cal Ripken, Jr. (Home Field Advantage)	1.00
282	Mo Vaughn (Home Field Advantage)	.30
283	Tim Salmon (Home Field Advantage)	.25
284	Frank Thomas (Home Field Advantage)	.50
285	Albert Belle (Home Field Advantage)	.30
286	Cecil Fielder (Home Field Advantage)	.10
287	Wally Joyner (Home Field Advantage)	.10
288	Greg Vaughn (Home Field Advantage)	.10
289	Kirby Puckett (Home Field Advantage)	.75
290	Don Mattingly (Home Field Advantage)	.75
291	Terry Steinbach (Home Field Advantage)	.10
292	Ken Griffey, Jr. (Home Field Advantage)	1.50
293	Juan Gonzalez (Home Field Advantage)	.75
294	Paul Molitor (Home Field Advantage)	.25
295	Tavo Alvarez (Classic Alumni)	.10
296	Matt Brunson (Classic Alumni)	.10
297	Shawn Green (Classic Alumni)	.40
298	Alex Rodriguez (Classic Alumni)	3.00
299	Shannon Stewart (Classic Alumni)	.15
300	Frank Thomas	1.00
301	Mickey Tettleton	.10
302	Pedro Munoz	.10
303	Jose Valentin	.10
304	Orestes Destrade	.10
305	Pat Listach	.10
306	Scott Brosius	.10
307	*Kurt Miller*	.10
308	Rob Dibble	.10
309	Mike Blowers	.10
310	Jim Abbott	.10
311	Mike Jackson	.10
312	Craig Biggio	.40
313	*Kurt Abbott*	.20
314	Chuck Finley	.10
315	Andres Galarraga	.25
316	Mike Moore	.10
317	Doug Strange	.10
318	Pedro J. Martinez	1.00
319	Kevin McReynolds	.10
320	Greg Maddux	1.50
321	Mike Henneman	.10
322	Scott Leius	.10
323	John Franco	.10
324	Jeff Blauser	.10
325	Kirby Puckett	.75
326	Darryl Hamilton	.10
327	John Smiley	.10
328	Derrick May	.10
329	Jose Vizcaino	.10
330	Randy Johnson	.50
331	Jack Morris	.10
332	Graeme Lloyd	.10
333	Dave Valle	.10
334	Greg Myers	.10
335	John Wetteland	.10
336	Jim Gott	.10
337	Tim Naehring	.10
338	Mike Kelly	.10
339	Jeff Montgomery	.10
340	Rafael Palmeiro	.40
341	Eddie Murray	.25
342	Xavier Hernandez	.10
343	Bobby Munoz	.10
344	Bobby Bonilla	.10
345	Travis Fryman	.15
346	Steve Finley	.10
347	Chris Sabo	.10
348	Armando Reynoso	.10
349	Ramon Martinez	.15
350	Will Clark	.35
351	Moises Alou	.15
352	Jim Thome	.40
353	Bob Tewksbury	.10
354	Andujar Cedeno	.10
355	Orel Hershiser	.10
356	Mike Devereaux	.10
357	Mike Perez	.10
358	Dennis Martinez	.10
359	Dave Nilsson	.10
360	Ozzie Smith	.50
361	Eric Anthony	.10
362	Scott Sanders	.10
363	Paul Sorrento	.10
364	Tim Belcher	.10
365	Dennis Eckersley	.10
366	Mel Rojas	.10
367	Tom Henke	.10
368	Randy Tomlin	.10
369	B.J. Surhoff	.10
370	Larry Walker	.50
371	Joey Cora	.10
372	Mike Harkey	.10
373	John Valentin	.10
374	Doug Jones	.10
375	Dave Justice	.20
376	Vince Coleman	.10
377	David Hulse	.10
378	Kevin Seitzer	.10
379	Pete Harnisch	.10
380	Ruben Sierra	.10
381	Mark Lewis	.10
382	Bip Roberts	.10
383	Paul Wagner	.10
384	Stan Javier	.10
385	Barry Larkin	.15
386	Mark Portugal	.10
387	Roberto Kelly	.10
388	Andy Benes	.15
389	Felix Fermin	.10
390	Marquis Grissom	.10
391	Troy Neel	.10
392	Chad Kreuter	.10
393	Gregg Olson	.10
394	Charles Nagy	.10
395	Jack McDowell	.10
396	Luis Gonzalez	.10
397	Benito Santiago	.10
398	Chris James	.10
399	Terry Mulholland	.10
400	Barry Bonds	.75
401	Joe Grahe	.10
402	Duane Ward	.10

403	John Burkett	.10
404	Scott Servais	.10
405	Bryan Harvey	.10
406	Bernard Gilkey	.10
407	Greg McMichael	.10
408	Tim Wallach	.10
409	Ken Caminiti	.20
410	John Kruk	.10
411	Darrin Jackson	.10
412	Mike Gallego	.10
413	David Cone	.20
414	Lou Whitaker	.10
415	Sandy Alomar Jr.	.15
416	Bill Wegman	.10
417	Pat Borders	.10
418	Roger Pavlik	.10
419	Pete Smith	.10
420	Steve Avery	.10
421	David Segui	.10
422	Rheal Cormier	.10
423	Harold Reynolds	.10
424	Edgar Martinez	.10
425	Cal Ripken, Jr.	2.00
426	Jaime Navarro	.10
427	Sean Berry	.10
428	Bret Saberhagen	.10
429	Bob Welch	.10
430	Juan Guzman	.10
431	Cal Eldred	.10
432	Dave Hollins	.10
433	Sid Fernandez	.10
434	Willie Banks	.10
435	Darryl Kile	.10
436	Henry Rodriguez	.10
437	Tony Fernandez	.10
438	Walt Weiss	.10
439	Kevin Tapani	.10
440	Mark Grace	.20
441	Brian Harper	.10
442	Kent Mercker	.10
443	Anthony Young	.10
444	Todd Zeile	.10
445	Greg Vaughn	.10
446	Ray Lankford	.10
447	David Weathers	.10
448	Bret Boone	.10
449	Charlie Hough	.10
450	Roger Clemens	1.50
451	Mike Morgan	.10
452	Doug Drabek	.10
453	Danny Jackson	.10
454	Dante Bichette	.25
455	Roberto Alomar	.60
456	Ben McDonald	.10
457	Kenny Rogers	.10
458	Bill Gullickson	.10
459	Darrin Fletcher	.10
460	Curt Schilling	.15
461	Billy Hatcher	.10
462	Howard Johnson	.10
463	Mickey Morandini	.10
464	Frank Castillo	.10
465	Delino DeShields	.10
466	Gary Gaetti	.10
467	Steve Farr	.10
468	Roberto Hernandez	.10
469	Jack Armstrong	.10
470	Paul Molitor	.30
471	Melido Perez	.10
472	Greg Hibbard	.10
473	Jody Reed	.10
474	Tom Gordon	.10
475	Gary Sheffield	.20
476	John Jaha	.10
477	Shawon Dunston	.10
478	Reggie Jefferson	.10
479	Don Slaught	.10
480	Jeff Bagwell	.75
481	Tim Pugh	.10
482	Kevin Young	.10
483	Ellis Burks	.10
484	Greg Swindell	.10
485	Mark Langston	.10
486	Omar Vizquel	.10
487	Kevin Brown	.15
488	Terry Steinbach	.10
489	Mark Lemke	.10
490	Matt Williams	.30
491	Pete Incaviglia	.10
492	Karl Rhodes	.10
493	Shawn Green	.50
494	Hal Morris	.10
495	Derek Bell	.10
496	Luis Polonia	.10
497	Otis Nixon	.10
498	Ron Darling	.10
499	Mitch Williams	.10
500	Mike Piazza	2.00
501	Pat Meares	.10
502	Scott Cooper	.10
503	Scott Erickson	.15
504	Jeff Juden	.10
505	Lee Smith	.10
506	Bobby Ayala	.10
507	Dave Henderson	.10
508	Erik Hanson	.10
509	Bob Wickman	.10
510	Sammy Sosa	2.00
511	Hector Carrasco (Diamond Debuts)	.10
512	Tim Davis (Diamond Debuts)	.10
513	Joey Hamilton (Diamond Debuts)	.25
514	Robert Eenhoorn (Diamond Debuts)	.10
515	Jorge Fabregas (Diamond Debuts)	.10
516	Tim Hyers (Diamond Debuts)	.10
517	John Hudek (Diamond Debuts)	.10
518	*James Mouton* (Diamond Debuts)	.10
519	Herbert Perry (Diamond Debuts)	.10
520	*Chan Ho Park* (Diamond Debuts)	1.00
521	Bill VanLandingham (Diamond Debuts)	.10
522	Paul Shuey (Diamond Debuts)	.15
523	*Ryan Hancock* (Top Prospects)	.20
524	*Billy Wagner* (Top Prospects)	1.00
525	Jason Giambi (Top Prospects)	.25
526	*Jose Silva* (Top Prospects)	.10
527	*Terrell Wade* (Top Prospects)	.10
528	Todd Dunn (Top Prospects)	.15
529	*Alan Benes* (Top Prospects)	.40
530	*Brooks Kieschnick* (Top Prospects)	.30
531	Todd Hollandsworth (Top Prospects)	.15
532	*Brad Fullmer* (Top Prospects)	.75
533	*Steve Soderstrom* (Top Prospects)	.10
534	Daron Kirkreit (Top Prospects)	.10
535	*Arquimedez Pozo* (Top Prospects)	.15
536	Charles Johnson (Top Prospects)	.20
537	Preston Wilson (Top Prospects)	.25
538	Alex Ochoa (Top Prospects)	.15
539	*Derrek Lee* (Top Prospects)	.75
540	*Wayne Gomes* (Top Prospects)	.20
541	*Jermaine Allensworth* (Top Prospects)	.50
542	*Mike Bell* (Top Prospects)	.30
543	*Trot Nixon* (Top Prospects)	1.50
544	Pokey Reese (Top Prospects)	.25
545	*Neifi Perez* (Top Prospects)	.75
546	Johnny Damon (Top Prosepcts)	.15
547	Matt Brunson (Top Prospects)	.15
548	*LaTroy Hawkins* (Top Prospects)	.25
549	*Eddie Pearson* (Top Prosepcts)	.10
550	Derek Jeter	2.00
A298	Alex Rodriguez (autographed)	175.00
MM1	(Mickey Mantle, Ken Griffey Jr.) (Mantle autograph)	450.00
KG1	(Mickey Mantle, Ken Griffey Jr.) (Griffey autograph)	250.00
GM1	(Mickey Mantle, Ken Griffey Jr.) (both autographs)	1000.

1994 Upper Deck Diamond Collection

The premium chase cards in 1994 Upper Deck are a series of Diamond Collection cards issued in regional subsets. Ten cards are found unique to each of three geographic areas of distribution. Western region cards carry a "W" prefix to the card number, Central cards have a "C" prefix and Eastern cards have an "E" prefix. The region is also indicated in silver foil printing on the front of the card, with a large "W", "C" or "E" in a compass design. The player's name and team are presented in a foil strip at bottom. A "Diamond Collection" logo is shown in embossed-look typography in the background. Diamond Collection cards are inserted only in hobby packs.

		MT
Complete Set (30):		180.00
Common Player:		1.50
Complete Central (10):		65.00
	CENTRAL REGION	
1	Michael Jordan	25.00
2	Jeff Bagwell	10.00
3	Barry Larkin	2.50
4	Kirby Puckett	7.50
5	Manny Ramirez	12.00
6	Ryne Sandberg	7.50
7	Ozzie Smith	7.00
8	Frank Thomas	10.00
9	Andy Van Slyke	1.50
10	Robin Yount	6.00
Complete East (10):		40.00
	EASTERN REGION	
1	Roberto Alomar	4.00
2	Roger Clemens	10.00
3	Len Dykstra	1.50
4	Cecil Fielder	1.50
5	Cliff Floyd	1.50
6	Dwight Gooden	2.00
7	Dave Justice	2.50
8	Don Mattingly	8.00
9	Cal Ripken, Jr.	20.00
10	Gary Sheffield	3.00
Complete West (10):		80.00
	WESTERN REGION	
1	Barry Bonds	8.00
2	Andres Galarraga	3.00
3	Juan Gonzalez	12.00
4	Ken Griffey, Jr.	25.00
5	Tony Gwynn	12.00
6	Rickey Henderson	3.00
7	Bo Jackson	3.00
8	Mark McGwire	25.00
9	Mike Piazza	15.00
10	Tim Salmon	2.50

1994 Upper Deck Electric Diamond

Each of the regular-issue and subset cards from 1994 Upper Deck was also produced in a limited edition premium pack insert "Electric Diamond" version. Where the regular cards have the Upper Deck logo, player and team name in copper foil, the Electric Diamond version has those elements in a silver prismatic foil, along with an "Electric Diamond" identification line next to the UD logo. Backs are identical to the regular cards. (Many of the first series cards can be found with player names on back in either silver or copper.) Electric Diamond cards are found, on average, about every other pack.

	MT
Complete Set (550):	100.00
Complete Series 1 (1-280):	60.00
Complete Series 2 (281-550):	40.00
Stars: 2X	
Common Player:	.25
(See 1994 Upper Deck for checklist and base card values.)	

1994 Upper Deck Jumbo Checklists

Each hobby foil box of 1994 Upper Deck cards contains one jumbo checklist card. Each of the 5" x 7" cards features Ken Griffey, Jr. There is a large color action photo along with a hologram of the player on front, highlighted by copper-foil printing. Backs have one of four checklists and are numbered with a "CL" prefix.

		MT
Complete Set (4):		12.00
Common Card:		3.00
1	Numerical Checklist (Ken Griffey, Jr.)	3.00
2	Alphabetical Checklist (Ken Griffey, Jr.)	3.00
3	Team Checklist (Ken Griffey, Jr.)	3.00
4	Insert Checklist (Ken Griffey, Jr.)	3.00

1994 Upper Deck Mantle Heroes

Mickey Mantle Baseball Hero is a 10-card set that chronicles his career. The cards, which include an unnumbered header card, were randomly inserted into both hobby and retail packs of Series II Upper Deck Baseball. This set starts with his rookie season in 1951 and concludes with his induction into The Hall of Fame. It is numbered 64-72 and was the eighth in the continuing "Baseball Heroes" series, which began in 1990.

		MT
Complete Set (10):		75.00
Common Card:		8.00
64	1951 - The Early Years (Mickey Mantle)	8.00
65	1953 - Tape Measure Home Runs (Mickey Mantle)	8.00
66	1956 - Triple Crown Season (Mickey Mantle)	8.00
67	1957 - 2nd Consecutive MVP (Mickey Mantle)	8.00
68	1961 - Chases The Babe (Mickey Mantle)	8.00
69	1964 - Series Home Run Record (Mickey Mantle)	8.00
70	1967 - 500th Home Run (Mickey Mantle)	8.00
----	Header card (Mickey Mantle)	8.00

1994 Upper Deck Mickey Mantle's Long Shots

Retail packaging was the exclusive venue for this insert set of contemporary long-ball sluggers. Horizontal fronts feature game-action photos with holographic foil rendering of the background. In one of the lower corners appears the logo "1994 Mickey Mantle's Long Shots". Backs have a color player photo at top, with a photo of Mantle beneath and a statement by him about the featured player. Previous season and career stats are included. Cards are numbered with an "MM" prefix. Besides the 20 current player cards there is a Mickey Mantle card and two trade cards which could be redeemed for complete insert card sets.

		MT
Complete Set (21):		45.00
Common Player:		.75
(1)	Mickey Mantle Trade Card (silver): (Redeemable for 21-card Mantle Long Shots set)	4.00
(2)	Mickey Mantle Trade Card (blue): (Redeemable for Electric Diamond version Mantle Long Shots set)	4.00
1	Jeff Bagwell	3.00
2	Albert Belle	2.50
3	Barry Bonds	2.50
4	Jose Canseco	2.00
5	Joe Carter	1.00
6	Carlos Delgado	2.00
7	Cecil Fielder	.75
8	Cliff Floyd	.75
9	Juan Gonzalez	3.00
10	Ken Griffey, Jr.	10.00
11	Dave Justice	1.50
12	Fred McGriff	1.50
13	Mark McGwire	10.00
14	Dean Palmer	.75
15	Mike Piazza	6.00
16	Manny Ramirez	3.00
17	Tim Salmon	1.00
18	Frank Thomas	2.50
19	Mo Vaughn	2.00
20	Matt Williams	1.50
21	Mickey Mantle (Header)	12.00

1994 Upper Deck Next Generation

Next Generation linked 20 of the top current stars with all-time greats, using the HoloView card printing technology.

Next Generation trade cards could be redeemed for a complete set matching the cards found in retail packs. This insert set was inserted at a rate of one per 20 packs, while the Trade Card was inserted one per case.

		MT
Complete Set (18):		80.00
Common Player:		1.25
1	Roberto Alomar	3.00
2	Carlos Delgado	2.50
3	Cliff Floyd	1.25
4	Alex Gonzalez	1.25
5	Juan Gonzalez	6.50
6	Ken Griffey, Jr.	16.00
7	Jeffrey Hammonds	1.25
8	Michael Jordan	20.00
9	Dave Justice	2.50
10	Ryan Klesko	1.25
11	Javier Lopez	1.25
12	Raul Mondesi	1.50
13	Mike Piazza	12.00
14	Kirby Puckett	4.00
15	Manny Ramirez	6.50
16	Alex Rodriguez	24.00
17	Tim Salmon	1.50
18	Gary Sheffield	2.00

1994 Upper Deck SP Insert

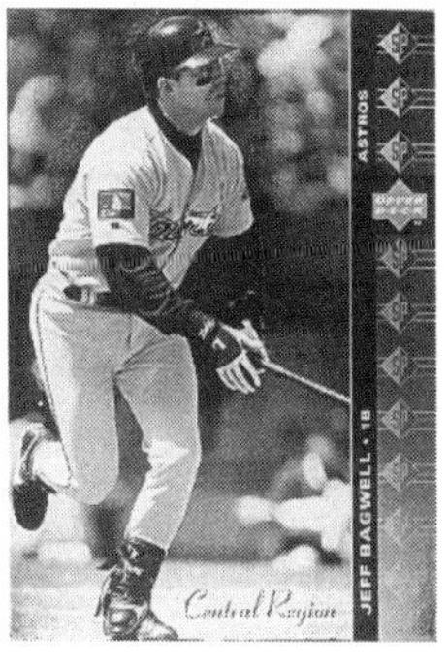

Fifteen SP Preview cards were inserted into Series II packs of Upper Deck baseball. The cards were inserted with regional distribution and gave collectors a chance to see what the SP super-premium cards would look like. There were five cards available in the East, Central and West and were inserted at a rate of about one per 36 packs. Most of the preview inserts have different front and back photos than the regularly issued SPs, along with other differences in typography and graphics elements.

		MT
Complete Set (15):		130.00
Common Player:		.75
EASTERN REGION		
1	Roberto Alomar	4.00
2	Cliff Floyd	.75
3	Javier Lopez	2.00
4	Don Mattingly	10.00
5	Cal Ripken, Jr.	20.00
CENTRAL REGION		
1	Jeff Bagwell	5.00
2	Michael Jordan	25.00
3	Kirby Puckett	7.50
4	Manny Ramirez	5.00
5	Frank Thomas	9.00
WESTERN REGION		
1	Barry Bonds	9.00
2	Juan Gonzalez	10.00
3	Ken Griffey, Jr.	25.00
4	Mike Piazza	15.00
5	Tim Salmon	2.50

1994 Upper Deck Ken Griffey Jr. 5th Anniversary Jumbo

The origin of this card is unknown. Besides producing 15-card sets of top players in a black-bordered 5th Anniversary insert set in regular and 3-1/2" x 5-1/2" formats, UD issued an 8-1/2" x 11" 5th Anniversary card of Griffey. In virtually all respects except size, the jumbo card is identical to the others. It is, however, numbered on back from within an edition of 5,000.

	MT
Ken Griffey Jr.	25.00

1994 Upper Deck Souvenir Sheets

Again benefiting the Baseball Assistance Team by sponsoring old-timers' games, UD issued a series of color artwork souvenir cards, generally picturing participants in the contests. The 11" x 8-1/2" cards are blank-backed. Card fronts are serially numbered within specific edition limits (shown here in parentheses).

		MT
Complete Set (5):		21.00
(1)	Heroes of Baseball All-Star Game (Steve Garvey, Reggie Jackson, Bill Mazeroski, Willie Stargell, Chuck Tanner) (Pittsburgh) (60,000)	6.00
(2)	Tribute to the 1964 Season (Lou Brock, Bob Gibson, Dick Groat, Bobby Richardson) (St. Louis) (50,000)	6.00
(3)	UD Heroes and Hollywood Softball Game (Bo Belinsky, Ken Brett, Reggie Jackson, Harmon Killebrew) (Annaheim) (40,000)	6.50
(4)	Upper Deck Heroes All-Time HR Kings (Orlando Cepeda, Reggie Jackson, Harmon Killebrew, Dave Kingman), Mickey Mantle) (Denver) (70,000)	10.00
(5)	25th Anniversary of the Miracle Mets (Tommie Agee, Ernie Banks, Rico Carty, Donn Clendenon, Earl Weaver) (Shea) (50,000)	7.50

1994 Upper Deck World Cup Soccer

Honorary captains of the 1994 USA World Cup soccer team (who coincidentally happened to also be UD spokesmen) were featured as the first cards in the company's soccer set. Reggie is the only baseball player.

		MT
HC1	Reggie Jackson	2.00

1994 Upper Deck/ All-Stars

Produced in commemoration of the 1994 All-Star Game, this boxed set features photography by Walter Looss, Jr. on most cards, shown to its best advantage on a large 3-1/2" x 5" format. The front of each card has a foil seal of the Pittsburgh All-Star Game logo. On most sets, the seal is in green foil; every 40th set has the seals in gold. The left side of the card backs feature a smaller version of the front photo and a few sentences about the player. Some cards feature a second, larger photo of the player on back, but most have a photo and write-up of a teammate. The last six cards in the set honor the 125th anniversary of professional baseball. An album to house the set was made available for $10 via a mail-in offer card in the set.

		MT
Complete Set (48):		15.00
Common Player:		.25
1	Ken Griffey, Jr.	4.00
2	Ruben Sierra, Todd Van Poppel	.25
3	Bryan Harvey, Gary Sheffield	.25
4	Gregg Jefferies, Brian Jordan	.25
5	Ryne Sandberg	1.00
6	Matt Williams, John Burkett	.40
7	Darren Daulton, John Kruk	.25
8	Don Mattingly, Wade Boggs	1.00
9	Pat Listach, Greg Vaughn	.25
10	Tim Salmon, Eduardo Perez	.40
11	Fred McGriff, Tom Glavine	.50
12	Mo Vaughn, Andre Dawson	.50
13	Brian McRae, Kevin Appier	.25
14	Kirby Puckett, Kent Hrbek	.75
15	Cal Ripken, Jr.	3.00
16	Roberto Alomar, Paul Molitor	.50
17	Tony Gwynn, Phil Plantier	.75
18	Greg Maddux, Steve Avery	1.00
19	Mike Mussina, Chris Hoiles	.40
20	Randy Johnson	.50
21	Roger Clemens, Aaron Sele	.50
22	Will Clark, Dean Palmer	.40
23	Cecil Fielder, Travis Fryman	.35
24	John Olerud, Joe Carter	.30
25	Juan Gonzalez	1.25
26	Jose Rijo, Barry Larkin	.30
27	Andy Van Slyke, Jeff King	.25
28	Larry Walker, Marquis Grissom	.40
29	Kenny Lofton, Albert Belle	1.00
30	Mark Grace, Sammy Sosa	1.50
31	Mike Piazza	1.50
32	Ramon Martinez, Orel Hershiser	.25
33	Dave Justice, Terry Pendleton	.35
34	Ivan Rodriguez, Jose Canseco	.50
35	Barry Bonds	1.00
36	Jeff Bagwell, Craig Biggio	1.25
37	Jay Bell, Orlando Merced	.25
38	Jeff Kent, Dwight Gooden	.25
39	Andres Galarraga, Charlie Hayes	.25
40	Frank Thomas	1.50
41	Bobby Bonilla	.25
42	Jack McDowell, Tim Raines	.25
43	1869 Red Stockings	.25
44	Ty Cobb	.50
45	Babe Ruth	2.00
46	Mickey Mantle	4.00
47	Reggie Jackson	.40
48	Ken Griffey, Jr.	4.00
48a	Ken Griffey, Jr. (promo card)	3.00

1994 Upper Deck/ All-Stars Gold

Identical to Upper Deck's regular (green foil) All-Star commemorative set in all respects except for the use of gold foil for the logo on front, the gold set is found on an average of one per 40 sets.

		MT
Complete Set (48):		100.00
Common Player:		1.00
1	Ken Griffey, Jr.	15.00
2	Ruben Sierra, Todd Van Poppel	1.00
3	Bryan Harvey, Gary Sheffield	1.50
4	Gregg Jefferies, Brian Jordan	1.50
5	Ryne Sandberg	3.00
6	Matt Williams, John Burkett	1.50
7	Darren Daulton, John Kruk	1.00
8	Don Mattingly, Wade Boggs	4.00
9	Pat Listach, Greg Vaughn	1.00
10	Tim Salmon, Eduardo Perez	2.00
11	Fred McGriff, Tom Glavine	2.50
12	Mo Vaughn, Andre Dawson	2.50
13	Brian McRae, Kevin Appier	1.50
14	Kirby Puckett, Kent Hrbek	4.00
15	Cal Ripken, Jr.	12.50
16	Roberto Alomar, Paul Molitor	2.50
17	Tony Gwynn, Phil Plantier	2.50
18	Greg Maddux, Steve Avery	3.00
19	Mike Mussina, Chris Hoiles	2.00
20	Randy Johnson	2.00
21	Roger Clemens, Aaron Sele	2.50
22	Will Clark, Dean Palmer	2.00
23	Cecil Fielder, Travis Fryman	1.50
24	John Olerud, Joe Carter	1.50
25	Juan Gonzalez	4.00
26	Jose Rijo, Barry Larkin	2.00
27	Andy Van Slyke, Jeff King	1.00
28	Larry Walker, Marquis Grissom	2.50
29	Kenny Lofton, Albert Belle	3.00
30	Mark Grace, Sammy Sosa	7.50
31	Mike Piazza	4.00
32	Ramon Martinez, Orel Hershiser	1.50
33	Dave Justice, Terry Pendleton	2.50
34	Ivan Rodriguez, Jose Canseco	3.00
35	Barry Bonds	4.00
36	Jeff Bagwell, Craig Biggio	4.00
37	Jay Bell, Orlando Merced	1.00
38	Jeff Kent, Dwight Gooden	1.00
39	Andres Galarraga, Charlie Hayes	1.50
40	Frank Thomas	8.00
41	Bobby Bonilla	1.00
42	Jack McDowell, Tim Raines	1.00
43	1869 Red Stockings	1.00
44	Ty Cobb	3.00
45	Babe Ruth	9.00
46	Mickey Mantle	15.00
47	Reggie Jackson	2.00
48	Ken Griffey, Jr.	15.00

1994 Upper Deck/ All-Time Heroes

The All-Time Heroes set provided collectors with both Ted Williams cards from Topps 1954 reprint set, from which they were absent due to a contractual obligation between Ted Williams and the Upper Deck Co. An agreement between Topps and Upper Deck allowed both Williams' cards to be offered in the All-Time Heroes set. There is also a 1954 Mickey Mantle inserted that has no number, but bears the same design as original 1954 Topps cards. The basic All-Time Heroes of Baseball set contains 225 cards. The cards were patterned after cards from the early 60s', with black borders across the top and bottom. Black-and-white photographs give the 2-1/2" x 3-1/2" cards a nostalgic appearance. All-Time Heroes also has autographed cards of Mantle, Brett, Jackson, Seaver and Ryan, along with a Next in Line insert set and a parallel, bronze-foil 125th anniversary set.

		MT
Complete Set (225):		15.00
Common Player:		.05
1	Ted Williams	.50
2	Johnny Vander Meer	.05
3	Lou Brock	.10
4	Lou Gehrig	.75
5	Hank Aaron	.50
6	Tommie Agee	.05
7	Mickey Mantle	1.50
8	Bill Mazeroski	.10
9	Reggie Jackson, Bud Harrelson	.15
10	Mays & Mantle (Willie Mays, Mickey Mantle)	.75
11	Roy Campanella	.15
12	Harvey Haddix	.05
13	Jimmy Piersall	.10
14	Enos Slaughter	.10
15	Nolan Ryan	.75
16	Bobby Thomson	.05
17	Willie Mays	.50
18	Bucky Dent	.05
19	Joe Garagiola	.10
20	George Brett	.35
21	Cecil Cooper	.05
22	Ray Boone	.05
23	King Kelly	.05
24	Willie Mays	.50
25	Napoleon Lajoie	.05
26	Gil McDougald	.05
27	Nelson Briles	.05
28	Bucky Dent	.05
29	Manny Sanguillen	.05
30	Ty Cobb	.50
31	Jim Grant	.05
32	Del Ennis	.05
33	Ron Hunt	.05
34	Nolan Ryan	1.00
35	Christy Mathewson	.15
36	Robin Roberts	.10

37	Frank Crosetti	.05
38	Johnny Vander Meer	.05
39	Virgil Trucks	.05
40	Lou Gehrig	.75
41	Luke Appling	.05
42	Rico Petrocelli	.05
43	Harry Walker	.05
44	Reggie Jackson	.35
44a	Reggie Jackson (promo card)	2.00
45	Mel Ott	.05
46	Phil Cavaretta	.05
47	Larry Doby	.15
48	Johnny Mize	.10
49	Ralph Kiner	.10
50	Ted Williams	.75
51	Bobby Thomson	.05
52	Joe Black	.05
53	Monte Irvin	.10
54	Bill Virdon	.05
55	Honus Wagner	.30
56	Herb Score	.10
57	Jerry Coleman	.05
58	Jimmie Foxx	.15
59	Elroy Face	.05
60	Babe Ruth	1.50
61	Jimmy Piersall	.10
62	Ed Charles	.05
63	Johnny Podres	.05
64	Charlie Neal	.05
65	Bill White	.05
66	Bill Skowron	.05
67	Al Rosen	.05
68	Eddie Lopat	.05
69	Bud Harrelson	.05
70	Steve Carlton	.15
71	Vida Blue	.05
72	Don Newcombe	.05
73	Al Bumbry	.05
74	Bill Madlock	.05
75	Checklist 1-75	.05
76	Bill Mazeroski	.10
77	Ron Cey	.05
78	Tommy John	.05
79	Lou Brock	.10
80	Walter Johnson	.40
81	Harvey Haddix	.05
82	Al Oliver	.05
83	Johnny Logan	.05
84	Dave Dravecky	.05
85	Tony Oliva	.05
86	Dave Kingman	.05
87	Luis Tiant	.05
88	Sal Bando	.05
89	Cesar Cedeno	.05
90	Warren Spahn	.10
91	Mickey Lolich	.05
92	Lew Burdette	.05
93	Hank Bauer	.05
94	Marv Throneberry	.05
95	Willie Stargell	.10
96	George Kell	.05
97	Fergie Jenkins	.10
98	Al Kaline	.15
99	Billy Martin	.05
100	Mickey Mantle	1.50
101	1869 - Red Stockings	.10
102	1892 (King Kelly)	.05
103	1901 (Nap Lajoie)	.05
104	1905 (Christy Mathewson)	.10
105	1910 (Cy Young)	.10
106	1915 (Ty Cobb)	.40
(107)	Checklist (Reggie Jackson)	.05
108	1924 (Rogers Hornsby)	.15
109	1926 (Walter Johnson)	.15
110	1927 (Babe Ruth)	1.00
111	1930 (Hack Wilson)	.05
112	1939 (Lou Gehrig)	.50
113	1941 (Ted Williams)	.40
114	1949 (Yogi Berra)	.15
115	1951 (Bobby Thomson)	.05
116	1953 (Mickey Mantle)	1.00
117	1954 (Willie Mays)	.50
118	1960 (Bill Mazeroski)	.10
119	1967 (Bob Gibson)	.10
120	1969 Miracle Mets	.10
121	1974 (Hank Aaron)	.50
122	1977 (Reggie Jackson)	.15
123	1980 (George Brett)	.10
124	1982 (Steve Carlton)	.10
125	1991 (Nolan Ryan)	.75
126	Frank Thomas	.05
127	Sam McDowell	.05
128	Jim Lonberg	.05
129	Bert Campaneris	.05
130	Bob Gibson	.10
131	Bobby Richardson	.05
132	Bobby Grich	.05
133	Billy Pierce	.05
134	Enos Slaughter	.05
(135)	Honus Wagner	.05
136	Orlando Cepeda	.10
137	Rennie Stennett	.05
138	Gene Alley	.05
139	Manny Mota	.05
140	Rogers Hornsby	.15
141	Joe Charboneau	.05
142	Rick Farrell	.05
143	Toby Harrah	.05
144	Hank Aaron	.50
145	Yogi Berra	.15
146	Whitey Ford	.15
147	Roy Campanella	.15
148	Graig Nettles	.05
149	Bobby Brown	.05
150	Checklist 76-150	.05
151	Cy Young	.30
152	Walter Johnson	.20
153	Christy Mathewson	.15
154	Warren Spahn	.10
155	Steve Carlton	.10
156	Bob Gibson	.10
157	Whitey Ford	.10
158	Yogi Berra	.10
159	Roy Campanella	.10
160	Lou Gehrig	.75
161	Johnny Mize	.05
162	Rogers Hornsby	.10
163	Honus Wagner	.15
164	Hank Aaron	.50
165	Babe Ruth	1.00
166	Willie Mays	.50
167	Reggie Jackson	.15
168	Mickey Mantle	1.00
169	Jimmie Foxx	.10
170	Ted Williams	.50
171	Mel Ott	.05
172	Willie Stargell	.05
173	Al Kaline	.10
174	Ty Cobb	.50
175	Napoleon Lajoie	.10
176	Lou Brock	.10
177	Tom Seaver	.10
178	Mark Fidrych	.05
179	Don Baylor	.05
180	Tom Seaver	.10
181	Jerry Grote	.05
182	George Foster	.05
183	Buddy Bell	.05
184	Ralph Garr	.05
185	Steve Garvey	.10
186	Joe Torre	.05
187	Carl Erskine	.05
188	Tommy Davis	.05
189	Bill Buckner	.05
190	Hack Wilson	.05
191	Steve Bass	.05
192	Ken Brett	.05
193	Lee May	.05
194	Bob Horner	.05
195	Boog Powell	.05
196	Darrell Evans	.05
197	Paul Blair	.05
198	Johnny Callison	.05
199	Jimmie Reese	.05
200	Cy Young	.30
201	Ron Santo	.05
202	Rico Carty	.05
203	Ron Necciai	.05
204	Lou Boudreau	.05
205	Minnie Minoso	.05
206	Eddie Yost	.05
207	Tommie Agee	.05
208	Dave Kingman	.05
209	Tony Oliva	.05
210	Reggie Jackson	.15
211	Paul Blair	.05
212	Fergie Jenkins	.10
213	Steve Garvey	.10
214	Bert Campaneris	.05
215	Orlando Cepeda	.05
216	Bill Madlock	.05
217	Rennie Stennett	.05
218	Frank Thomas	.05
219	Bob Gibson	.10
220	Lou Brock	.10
221	Rico Carty	.05
222	Mickey Mantle	1.00
223	Robin Roberts	.10
224	Manny Sanguillen	.05
225	Checklist 151-225	.05

1994 Upper Deck/ All-Time Heroes 125th Anniversary

This parallel set was issued at the rate of one card per pack of Upper Deck All-Time Heroes cards. They are identical to the regular-issue version except for the presence on front of bronze-foil stamping which reads, "Major League Baseball / 125th Anniversary".

		MT
Complete Set (225):		50.00
Common Player:		.25

(Star cards valued at 3X-5X corresponding card in regular ATH issue)

1994 Upper Deck/ All-Time Heroes Autographed Inserts

Five players' autographed cards were randomly inserted into select packs of All-Time Heroes. Mickey Mantle, Tom Seaver, Nolan Ryan, Reggie Jackson, and George Brett are the superstars who have autographed cards.

		MT
Complete Set (5):		425.00
Common Player:		60.00
(1)	Mickey Mantle	150.00
(2)	Reggie Jackson	60.00
(3)	George Brett	80.00
(4)	Tom Seaver	75.00
(5)	Nolan Ryan	125.00

1994 Upper Deck/ All-Time Heroes Next In Line

The Next in Line insert set includes 20 top minor leaguers. These cards were randomly inserted into every 39 packs with only 2,500 of each card produced.

		MT
Complete Set (20):		60.00
Common Player:		2.00
1	Mike Bell	2.00
2	Alan Benes	5.00
3	D.J. Boston	2.00
4	Johnny Damon	2.50
5	Brad Fullmer	5.00
6	LaTroy Hawkins	2.50
7	Derek Jeter	15.00
8	Daron Kirkreit	2.00
9	Trot Nixon	2.00
10	Alex Ochoa	2.00
11	Kirk Presley	2.00
12	Jose Silva	2.00
13	Terrell Wade	2.00
14	Billy Wagner	2.50
15	Glenn Williams	3.00
16	Preston Wilson	2.50
17	Wayne Gomes	2.00
18	Ben Grieve	7.50
19	Dustin Hermanson	2.50
20	Paul Wilson	3.00

1994 Upper Deck/ All-Time Heroes 1954 Topps Archives

Two cards that were not included in the Topps 1954 Archives Set and one that wasn't even in the original 1954 set were randomly inserted into All-Time Heroes foil packs. Both Ted Williams cards, numbers 1 and 250, were left out of the Archives set because of contractual obligations of Williams with Upper Deck. In addition, an unnumbered Mickey Mantle card with the original 1954 design was randomly inserted. Mantle was signed exclusively with Bowman in 1954 and 1955, and therefore, was not in either Topps set.

		MT
Complete Set (3):		90.00
1	Ted Williams	25.00
250	Ted Williams	25.00
259	Mickey Mantle	50.00

1994 Upper Deck/ American Epic

Baseball, The American Epic traces the history of the game, highlighting players, personalities, events and stadiums that have contributed to the national pastime. The set was patterned after a 1994 18-hour TV documentary which divided baseball history into nine distinct "innings." This boxed set contains 80 cards, beginning with the "First Inning," which covers the 19th century. It explains the roots of the game and showcases some of baseball's first great players like Cap Anson and King Kelly. Baseball is chronicled from the infamous "Black Sox" scandal and Ebbets Field, on through the great Yankee teams, Mazeroski's historic homerun and, then concludes with Mr. October and Nolan Ryan. Each set contains a randomly inserted card of either Michael Jordan, Babe Ruth or Mickey Mantle. Cards from the regular set are in black-and-white, with the player name and the featured year running down the left side in white print. Card backs contain half color, depending on what "inning" the card is from, and half white. The color side tells a story of how that player, field or personality contributed to the making of baseball. The white side gives statistics and brief career highlights.

		MT
Complete Set (81):		18.00
Common Player:		.15
1	1880s - Our Game	.15
2	1845 - Alexander Cartwright	.15
3	1857 - Henry Chadwick	.15
4	1866 - The Fair Sex	.15
5	1869 - Harry Wright	.15
6	1876 - Albert Goodwill Spalding	.15
7	1883 - Cap Anson	.15
8	1884 - Moses Fleetwood Walker	.25
9	1886 - King Kelly	.15
10	1890 - John Montgomery Ward	.15
11	1909 - Ty Cobb	.65
12	1904 - John McGraw	.15
13	1904 - Rube Waddell	.15
14	1905 - Christy Mathewson	.15
15	1907 - Walter Johnson	.20
16	1908 - Alta Weiss	.15
17	1908 - Fred Merkle	.15
18	1908 - Take Me Out To The Ball Game	.15
19	1909 - John Henry Lloyd	.15
20	1909 - Honus Wagner	.40
21	1915 - Woodrow Wilson	.15
22	1910 - Napoleon Lajoie	.15
23	1911 - Addie Joss	.15
24	1912 - Joe Wood	.15
25	1912 - Royal Rooters	.15
26	1913 - Ebbets Field	.15
27	1914 - Johnny Evers	.15
28	1918 - World War II	.15
29	1919 - Joe Jackson	.65
30	1927 - Babe Ruth	2.00
31	1920 - Rube Foster	.30
32	1920 - Ray Chapman	.15
33	1921 - Kenesaw M. Landis	.15
34	1923 - Yankee Stadium	.15
35	1924 - Rogers Hornsby	.30
36	1923 - Warren G. Harding	.15
37	1925 - Lou Gehrig	1.00
38	1926 - Grover C. Alexander	.15
39	1929 - House of David	.15
40	1933 - Satchel Paige	.50
41	1931 - Lefty Grove	.15
42	1932 - Jimmie Foxx	.15
43	1932 - Connie Mack	.15
44	1937 - Josh Gibson	.25
45	1934 - Dizzy Dean	.15
46	1934 - Carl Hubbell	.15
47	1937 - Franklin D. Roosevelt	.15
48	1938 - Bob Feller	.25
49	1939 - Cool Papa Bell	.30
50	1947 - Jackie Robinson	1.00
51	1941 - Ted Williams	.75
52	1941 - Sym-Phony Band	.15
53	1944 - Annabel Lee	.15
54	1945 - Hank Greenberg	.15
55	1947 - Branch Rickey	.15
56	1948 - Harry S. Truman	.15
57	1953 - Casey Stengel	.25
58	1951 - Bobby Thomson	.15
59	1952 - Dwight D. Eisenhower	.15
60	1952 - Mario Cuomo	.15
61	1952 - Buck O'Neil	.25
62	1955 - Yogi Berra	.25
63	1956 - Mickey Mantle	1.50
64	1956 - Don Larsen	.15
65	1961 - John F. Kennedy	.15
66	1960 - Bill Mazeroski	.15
67	1961 - Roger Maris	.35
68	1966 - Frank Robinson	.25

69	1969 - Bob Gibson	.25
70	1970 - Tom Seaver	.25
71	1969 - Curt Flood	.15
72	1972 - Roberto Clemente	.50
73	1975 - Luis Tiant	.15
74	1975 - Marvin Miller	.15
75	1977 - Reggie Jackson	.25
76	1979 - Willie Stargell	.15
77	1985 - Pete Rose	.45
78	1994 - Bill Clinton	.15
79	1991 - Nolan Ryan	.75
80	1993 - George Brett	.25
----	Checklist	.15

1994 Upper Deck/ American Epic Inserts

In addition to the regular 80-card set, each boxed set contains one special insert card, depending on where it was purchased. At retail locations, an additional Babe Ruth card was included. Michael Jordan was included in sets purchased through direct mail outlets. Mickey Mantle was featured in sets purchased from QVC (sets purchased from Upper Deck Authenticated included an autographed card of Mantle). The inserts are numbered BC1- BC3.

		MT
Complete Set (3):		12.00
Common Player:		4.00
1	Mickey Mantle	4.00
2	Michael Jordan	4.00
3	Babe Ruth	4.00

1994 Upper Deck/ American Epic Little Debbie Mail-in

Fifteen of the cards from Upper Deck's "An American Epic" card set were chosen for use in a mail-in promotion with Little Debbie snack cakes. These cards are identical to the Epic versions except for the card numbers, which include an "LD" prefix. The back of card LD1 is a checklist for the set and includes a Little Debbie logo. Sets sold for about $4, with proofs of purchase.

		MT
Complete Set (15):		9.00
Common Player:		.50
1	Our Game/Checklist	.25
2	Alexander Cartwright	.50
3	King Kelly	.50
4	John McGraw	.50
5	Christy Mathewson	.75
6	Walter Johnson	.75
7	Ted Williams	1.50
8	Annabel Lee	.50
9	Jackie Robinson	1.00
10	Bobby Thomson	.50
11	Buck O'Neil	.50
12	Mickey Mantle	3.00
13	Bob Gibson	.50
14	Curt Flood	.50
15	Reggie Jackson	.75

1994 Upper Deck/ Fun Packs

In its second year, this product aimed at the young collector, again offered a basic set of some 160 players, surrounded by several special subsets. The first nine cards feature Stars of Tomorrow. There is a group of 18 Stand Out cards on which the background can be folded to create a player figure. Profiles cards feature playing tips from six young stars. A group of nine Headline Stars cards features two players on each which fold back to reveal a holographic photo. What's the Call cards offer game problems and cartoon caricatures of nine players. There are nine Fold Outs cards which open to reveal action photos. The subsets concluded with seven heat-activated Fun Cards on which the background temporarily appears when body heat is applied. Each five-card foil pack also includes a scratch-off game card; one for each major league team and one All-Star team for each league.

		MT
Complete Set (240):		50.00
Common Player:		.05
1	Manny Ramirez (Stars of Tomorrow)	.75
2	Cliff Floyd (Stars of Tomorrow)	.10
3	Rondell White (Stars of Tomorrow)	.25
4	Carlos Delgado (Stars of Tomorrow)	.25
5	Chipper Jones (Stars of Tomorrow)	1.00
6	Javier Lopez (Stars of Tomorrow)	.35
7	Ryan Klesko (Stars of Tomorrow)	.30
8	Steve Karsay (Stars of Tomorrow)	.05
9	Rich Becker (Stars of Tomorrow)	.05
10	Gary Sheffield	.15
11	Jeffrey Hammonds	.05
12	Roberto Alomar	.40
13	Brent Gates	.05
14	Andres Galarraga	.10
15	Tim Salmon	.25
16	Dwight Gooden	.05
17	Mark Grace	.15
18	Andy Van Slyke	.05
19	Juan Gonzalez	.50
20	Mickey Tettleton	.05
21	Roger Clemens	.50
22	Will Clark	.25
23	Dave Justice	.15
24	Ken Griffey, Jr.	2.50
24a	Ken Griffey, Jr. (promo card)	3.00
25	Barry Bonds	.60
26	Bill Swift	.05
27	Fred McGriff	.25
28	Randy Myers	.05
29	Joe Carter	.05
30	Nigel Wilson	.05
31	Mike Piazza	1.50
32	Dave Winfield	.20
33	Steve Avery	.05
34	Kirby Puckett	.60
35	Frank Thomas	1.00
36	Aaron Sele	.10
37	Ricky Gutierrez	.05
38	Curt Schilling	.10
39	Mike Greenwell	.05
40	Andy Benes	.05
41	Kevin Brown	.10
42	Mo Vaughn	.25
43	Dennis Eckersley	.05
44	Ken Hill	.05
45	Cecil Fielder	.05
46	Bobby Jones	.10
47	Tom Glavine	.10
48	Wally Joyner	.05
49	Ellis Burks	.05
50	Jason Bere	.05
51	Randy Johnson	.25
52	Darryl Kile	.05
53	Jeff Montgomery	.05
54	Alex Fernandez	.10
55	Kevin Appier	.05
56	Brian McRae	.05
57	John Wetteland	.05
58	Bob Tewksbury	.05
59	Todd Van Poppel	.05
60	Ryne Sandberg	.35
61	Bret Barberie	.05
62	Phil Plantier	.05
63	Chris Hoiles	.05
64	Tony Phillips	.05
65	Salomon Torres	.05
66	Juan Guzman	.05
67	Paul O'Neill	.10
68	Dante Bichette	.20
69	Len Dykstra	.05
70	Ivan Rodriguez	.25
71	Dean Palmer	.05
72a	Brett Butler	.05
72b	Phil Hiatt (checklisted as #172)	.05
73	Rick Aguilera	.05
74	Robby Thompson	.05
75	Jim Abbott	.05
76	Al Martin	.05
77	Roberto Hernandez	.05
78	Jay Buhner	.05
79	Devon White	.05
80	Travis Fryman	.05
81	Jeromy Burnitz	.05
82	John Burkett	.05
83	Orlando Merced	.05
84	Jose Rijo	.05
85	Eddie Murray	.25
86	Howard Johnson	.05
87	Chuck Carr	.05
88	Pedro J. Martinez	.10
89	Charlie Hayes	.05
90	Matt Williams	.15
91	Steve Finley	.05
92	Pat Listach	.05
93	Sandy Alomar, Jr.	.10
94	Delino DeShields	.05
95	Rod Beck	.05
96	Not issued	
97	Todd Zeile (Checklisted as #96)	.05
98a	Darryl Hamilton	.05
98b	Duane Ward (Checklisted as #97)	.05
99	John Olerud	.10
100	Andre Dawson	.10
101	Ozzie Smith	.25
102	Rick Wilkins	.05
103	Alan Trammell	.05
104	Jeff Blauser	.05
105	Bret Boone	.05
106	J.T. Snow	.10
107	Kenny Lofton	.30
108	Cal Ripken, Jr.	2.50
109	Carlos Baerga	.05
110	Bip Roberts	.05
111	Barry Larkin	.10
112	Mark Langston	.05
113	Ozzie Guillen	.05
114	Chad Curtis	.05
115	Dave Hollins	.05
116	Reggie Sanders	.05
117	Jeff Conine	.05
118	Mark Whiten	.05
119	Tony Gwynn	.45
120	John Kruk	.05
121	Eduardo Perez	.05
122	Walt Weiss	.05
123	Don Mattingly	.60
124	Rickey Henderson	.15
125	Mark McGwire	1.50
126	Wade Boggs	.15
127	Bobby Bonilla	.05
128	Jeff King	.05
129	Jack McDowell	.05
130	Albert Belle	.40
131	Greg Maddux	1.00
132	Dennis Martinez	.05
133	Jose Canseco	.35
134	Bryan Harvey	.05
135	Dave Fleming	.05
136	Larry Walker	.20
137	Ken Caminiti	.10
138	Doug Drabek	.05
139	Ron Gant	.10
140	Darren Daulton	.05
141	Ruben Sierra	.05
142	Kirk Rueter	.05
143	Raul Mondesi	.50
144	Greg Vaughn	.05
145	Danny Tartabull	.05
146	Eric Karros	.10
147	Chuck Knoblauch	.10
148	Mike Mussina	.25
149	Brady Anderson	.10
150	Paul Molitor	.20
151	Bo Jackson	.10
152	Jeff Bagwell	.50
153	Gregg Jefferies	.05
154	Rafael Palmeiro	.10
155	Orel Hershiser	.05
156	Derek Bell	.05
157	Jeff Kent	.05
158	Craig Biggio	.10
159	Marquis Grissom	.05
160	Matt Mieske	.05
161	Jay Bell	.05
162	Sammy Sosa	.75
163	Robin Ventura	.10
164	Deion Sanders	.25
165	Jimmy Key	.05
166	Cal Eldred	.05
167	David McCarty	.05
168	Carlos Garcia	.05
169	Willie Greene	.05
170	*Michael Jordan*	9.00
171	Roberto Mejia	.05
172	Not issued	
173	Marc Newfield	.05
174	Kevin Stocker	.05
175	Randy Johnson (Standouts)	.10
176	Ivan Rodriguez (Standouts)	.25
177	Frank Thomas (Standouts)	.50
178	Roberto Alomar (Standouts)	.20
179	Travis Fryman (Standouts)	.05
180	Cal Ripken, Jr. (Standouts)	1.00
181	Juan Gonzalez (Standouts)	.25
182	Ken Griffey, Jr. (Standouts)	1.00
183	Albert Belle (Standouts)	.20
184	Greg Maddux (Standouts)	.50
185	Mike Piazza (Standouts)	.50
186	Fred McGriff (Standouts)	.15
187	Robby Thompson (Standouts)	.05
188	Matt Williams (Standouts)	.10
189	Jeff Blauser (Standouts)	.05
190	Barry Bonds (Standouts)	.30
191	Len Dykstra (Standouts)	.05
192	Dave Justice (Standouts)	.15
193	Ken Griffey, Jr. (Profiles)	1.00
194	Barry Bonds (Profiles)	.30
195	Frank Thomas (Profiles)	.50
196	Juan Gonzalez (Profiles)	.45
197	Randy Johnson (Profiles)	.10
198	Chuck Carr (Profiles)	.05
199	Barry Bonds, Juan Gonzalez (Headline Stars)	.60
200	Ken Griffey, Jr., Don Mattingly (Headline Stars)	2.50
201	Roberto Alomar, Carlos Baerga (Headline Stars)	.40
202	Dave Winfield, Robin Yount (Headline Stars)	.50
203	Mike Piazza, Tim Salmon (Headline Stars)	1.00
204	Albert Belle, Frank Thomas (Headline Stars)	1.00
205	Cliff Floyd, Rondell White (Headline Stars)	.25
206	Kirby Puckett, Tony Gwynn (Headline Stars)	.00
207	Roger Clemens, Greg Maddux (Headline Stars)	2.00
208	Mike Piazza (What's The Call)	.40
209	Jose Canseco (What's The Call)	.15
210	Frank Thomas (What's The Call)	.50
211	Roberto Alomar (What's The Call)	.15
212	Barry Bonds (What's The Call)	.30
213	Rickey Henderson (What's The Call)	.10
214	John Kruk (What's The Call)	.05
215	Juan Gonzalez (What's The Call)	.40
216	Ken Griffey, Jr. (What's The Call)	1.00
217	Roberto Alomar (Foldouts)	.30
218	Craig Biggio (Foldouts)	.25
219	Cal Ripken, Jr. (Foldouts)	1.00
220	Mike Piazza (Foldouts)	.60
221	Brent Gates (Foldouts)	.10
222	Walt Weiss (Foldouts)	.10
223	Bobby Bonilla (Foldouts)	.10
224	Ken Griffey, Jr. (Foldouts)	2.50
225	Barry Bonds (Foldouts)	.30
226	Barry Bonds (Fun Cards)	.30
227	Joe Carter (Fun Cards)	.10
228	Mike Greenwell (Fun Cards)	.10
229	Ken Griffey, Jr. (Fun Cards)	1.00
230	John Kruk (Fun Cards)	.10
231	Mike Piazza (Fun Cards)	.60
232	Kirby Puckett (Fun Cards)	.40
233	John Smoltz (Fun Cards)	.10
234	Rick Wilkins (Fun Cards)	.10
235	Checklist 1-40 (Ken Griffey, Jr.)	1.00
236	Checklist 41-80 (Frank Thomas)	.50
237	Checklist 81-120 (Barry Bonds)	.25
238	Checklist 121-160 (Mike Piazza)	.35
239	Checklist 161-200 (Tim Salmon)	.15
240	Checklist 201-240 (Juan Gonzalez)	.25
Scratch-off Game Cards:		
(1)	National League	.05
(2)	Atlanta Braves	.05
(3)	Chicago Cubs	.05
(4)	Cincinnati Reds	.05
(5)	Colorado Rockies	.05
(6)	Florida Marlins	.05
(7)	Houston Astros	.05
(8)	Los Angeles Dodgers	.05
(9)	Montreal Expos	.05
(10)	New York Mets	.05
(11)	Philadelphia Phillies	.05
(12)	Pittsburgh Pirates	.05
(13)	St. Louis Cardinals	.05
(14)	San Diego Padres	.05
(15)	San Francisco Giants	.05
(1)	American League	.05
(2)	Baltimore Orioles	.05
(3)	Boston Red Sox	.05
(4)	California Angels	.05
(5)	Chicago White Sox	.05
(6)	Cleveland Indians	.05
(7)	Detroit Tigers	.05
(8)	Kansas City Royals	.05
(9)	Milwaukee Brewers	.05
(10)	Minnesota Twins	.05
(11)	New York Yankees	.05
(12)	Seattle Mariners	.05
(13)	Texas Rangers	.05
(14)	Toronto Blue Jays	.05

1994 Upper Deck/GM "Baseball" Previews

This nine-card set is closely related to the 80-card issue subsequently released in conjunction with the public television series "Baseball" by Ken Burns. This preview issue, carrying the logo of General Motors (principal sponsor of the TV series), was issued in cello and foil packs and was available, generally with a test drive, at GM automobile dealerships. Card backs have some biographical and statistical highlights and a career summary.

		MT
Complete Set (9):		10.00
Common Player:		.90
1	Hank Aaron	1.25
2	Roberto Clemente	2.00
3	Ty Cobb	.90
4	Hank Greenberg	.90
5	Mickey Mantle	4.00
6	Satchel Paige	.90
7	Jackie Robinson	1.25
8	Babe Ruth	2.50
9	Ted Williams	1.25

1994 Upper Deck/GTS Mickey Mantle Phone Cards

Upper Deck and Global Telecommunication Solutions combined to produce this set of phone cards paralleling the Mantle Heroes insert cards found in the regular UD issue. The phone cards were sold in two series of five cards each for $59.95 per series. Fronts of the 2-1/8" x 3-3/8" plastic cards feature black-and-white or color photos of Mantle, along with mention of a career highlight. Backs are printed in black and have instructions for use of the card. A card picturing the 1869 Cincinnati Red Stockings was included as a random insert in the first series of Mantle phone card sets.

		MT
Complete Set (10):		90.00
Common Player (Series 1):		60.00
Common Player (Series 2):		30.00
(1)	Mickey Mantle (portrait)	12.00
(2)	Mickey Mantle (1951: The Early Years)	12.00
(3)	Mickey Mantle (1953: Tape Measure Home Runs)	12.00
(4)	Mickey Mantle (1956: Triple Crown Season)	12.00
(5)	Mickey Mantle (1957: Second Consecutive MVP)	12.00
(6)	Mickey Mantle (1961: Chasing the Babe)	7.50
(7)	Mickey Mantle (1964: Series Home Run Record)	7.50
(8)	Mickey Mantle (1967: 500th Home Run)	7.50
(9)	Mickey Mantle (1974: Hall of Fame)	7.50
(10)	Mickey Mantle (portrait)	7.50
(11)	1869 Cincinnati Red Stockings	25.00

1995 Upper Deck

Issued in two series of 225 base cards each, with loads of subsets and inserts, the 1995 Upper Deck set was a strong collector favorite from the outset. Basic cards feature a borderless front photo with the player's name and UD logo in bronze foil. Backs have another large color photo, recent stats and career totals and appropriate logos, along with the infield-shaped hologram. Subsets in each series include Star Rookies and Top Prospects, each with special designs highlighting the game's young stars. Series I has a "'90s Midpoint Analysis" subset studying the decade's superstars, and Series II has another hot rookies' subset, Diamond Debuts. The set closes with a five-card "Final Tribute" subset summarizing the careers of five recently retired superstars. Retail and hobby versions were sold with each featuring some unique insert cards. Basic packaging of each type was the 12-card foil pack at $1.99, though several other configurations were also released.

		MT
Complete Set (450):		60.00
Complete Series 1 (225):		30.00
Complete Series 2 (225):		30.00
Common Player:		.10
Series 1 or 2 Wax Box:		55.00
1	Ruben Rivera (Top Prospect)	.15
2	Bill Pulsipher (Top Prospect)	.15
3	Ben Grieve (Top Prospect)	1.50
4	Curtis Goodwin (Top Prospect)	.15
5	Damon Hollins (Top Prospect)	.10
6	Todd Greene (Top Prospect)	.15
7	Glenn Williams (Top Prospect)	.10
8	Bret Wagner (Top Prospect)	.10
9	*Karim Garcia* (Top Prospect)	.50
10	Nomar Garciaparra (Top Prospect)	3.00
11	*Raul Casanova* (Top Prospect)	.20
12	Matt Smith (Top Prospect)	.15
13	Paul Wilson (Top Prospect)	.15
14	Jason Isringhausen (Top Prospect)	.15
15	Reid Ryan (Top Prospect)	.10
16	Lee Smith	.10
17	Chili Davis	.10
18	Brian Anderson	.10
19	Gary DiSarcina	.10
20	Bo Jackson	.15
21	Chuck Finley	.10
22	Darryl Kile	.10
23	Shane Reynolds	.15
24	Tony Eusebio	.10
25	Craig Biggio	.40
26	Doug Drabek	.10
27	Brian L. Hunter	.10
28	James Mouton	.10
29	Geronimo Berroa	.10
30	Rickey Henderson	.40
31	Steve Karsay	.10
32	Steve Ontiveros	.10
33	Ernie Young	.10
34	Dennis Eckersley	.10
35	Mark McGwire	3.00
36	Dave Stewart	.10
37	Pat Hentgen	.10
38	Carlos Delgado	.50
39	Joe Carter	.10
40	Roberto Alomar	.60
41	John Olerud	.25
42	Devon White	.10
43	Roberto Kelly	.10
44	Jeff Blauser	.10
45	Fred McGriff	.25
46	Tom Glavine	.25
47	Mike Kelly	.10
48	Javy Lopez	.20
49	Greg Maddux	1.50
50	Matt Mieske	.10
51	Troy O'Leary	.10
52	Jeff Cirillo	.15
53	Cal Eldred	.10
54	Pat Listach	.10
55	Jose Valentin	.10
56	John Mabry	.10
57	Bob Tewksbury	.10
58	Brian Jordan	.15
59	Gregg Jefferies	.10
60	Ozzie Smith	.50
61	Geronimo Pena	.10
62	Mark Whiten	.10
63	Rey Sanchez	.10
64	Willie Banks	.10
65	Mark Grace	.20
66	Randy Myers	.10
67	Steve Trachsel	.15
68	Derrick May	.10
69	Brett Butler	.10
70	Eric Karros	.10
71	Tim Wallach	.10
72	Delino DeShields	.10
73	Darren Dreifort	.10
74	Orel Hershiser	.10
75	Billy Ashley	.10
76	Sean Berry	.10
77	Ken Hill	.10
78	John Wetteland	.10
79	Moises Alou	.20
80	Cliff Floyd	.10
81	Marquis Grissom	.15
82	Larry Walker	.50
83	Rondell White	.20
84	William VanLandingham	.10
85	Matt Williams	.30
86	Rod Beck	.10
87	Darren Lewis	.10
88	Robby Thompson	.10
89	Darryl Strawberry	.20
90	Kenny Lofton	.50
91	Charles Nagy	.10
92	Sandy Alomar Jr.	.15
93	Mark Clark	.10
94	Dennis Martinez	.10
95	Dave Winfield	.25
96	Jim Thome	.30
97	Manny Ramirez	1.00
98	Goose Gossage	.10
99	Tino Martinez	.15
100	Ken Griffey Jr.	3.00
100a	Ken Griffey Jr. (overprinted "For Promotional Use Only")	3.00
101	Greg Maddux (Analysis: '90s Midpoint)	1.00
102	Randy Johnson (Analysis: '90s Midpoint)	.15
103	Barry Bonds (Analysis: '90s Midpoint)	.30
104	Juan Gonzalez (Analysis: '90s Midpoint)	.50
105	Frank Thomas (Analysis: '90s Midpoint)	.50
106	Matt Williams (Analysis: '90s Midpoint)	.15
107	Paul Molitor (Analysis: '90s Midpoint)	.25
108	Fred McGriff (Analysis: '90s Midpoint)	.15
109	Carlos Baerga (Analysis: '90s Midpoint)	.10
110	Ken Griffey Jr. (Analysis: '90s Midpoint)	1.50
111	Reggie Jefferson	.10
112	Randy Johnson	.40
113	Marc Newfield	.10
114	Robb Nen	.10
115	Jeff Conine	.10
116	Kurt Abbott	.10
117	Charlie Hough	.10
118	Dave Weathers	.10
119	Juan Castillo	.10
120	Bret Saberhagen	.10
121	Rico Brogna	.10
122	John Franco	.10
123	Todd Hundley	.10
124	Jason Jacome	.10
125	Bobby Jones	.10
126	Bret Barberie	.10
127	Ben McDonald	.10
128	Harold Baines	.10
129	Jeffrey Hammonds	.10
130	Mike Mussina	.40
131	Chris Hoiles	.10
132	Brady Anderson	.15
133	Eddie Williams	.10
134	Andy Benes	.15
135	Tony Gwynn	1.50
136	Bip Roberts	.10
137	Joey Hamilton	.15
138	Luis Lopez	.10
139	Ray McDavid	.10
140	Lenny Dykstra	.10
141	Mariano Duncan	.10
142	Fernando Valenzuela	.10
143	Bobby Munoz	.10
144	Kevin Stocker	.10
145	John Kruk	.10
146	Jon Lieber	.10
147	Zane Smith	.10
148	Steve Cooke	.10
149	Andy Van Slyke	.10
150	Jay Bell	.10
151	Carlos Garcia	.10
152	John Dettmer	.10
153	Darren Oliver	.10
154	Dean Palmer	.10
155	Otis Nixon	.10
156	Rusty Greer	.10
157	Rick Helling	.10
158	Jose Canseco	.75
159	Roger Clemens	1.50
160	Andre Dawson	.20
161	Mo Vaughn	.60
162	Aaron Sele	.10
163	John Valentin	.10
164	Brian Hunter	.10
165	Bret Boone	.10
166	Hector Carrasco	.10
167	Pete Schourek	.10
168	Willie Greene	.10
169	Kevin Mitchell	.10
170	Deion Sanders	.20
171	John Roper	.10
172	Charlie Hayes	.10
173	David Nied	.10
174	Ellis Burks	.10
175	Dante Bichette	.25
176	Marvin Freeman	.10
177	Eric Young	.15
178	David Cone	.20
179	Greg Gagne	.10
180	Bob Hamelin	.10
181	Wally Joyner	.10
182	Jeff Montgomery	.10
183	Jose Lind	.10
184	Chris Gomez	.10
185	Travis Fryman	.15
186	Kirk Gibson	.10
187	Mike Moore	.10
188	Lou Whitaker	.10
189	Sean Bergman	.10
190	Shane Mack	.10
191	Rick Aguilera	.10
192	Denny Hocking	.10
193	Chuck Knoblauch	.20
194	Kevin Tapani	.10
195	Kent Hrbek	.10
196	Ozzie Guillen	.10
197	Wilson Alvarez	.10
198	Tim Raines	.10
199	Scott Ruffcorn	.10
200	Michael Jordan	3.00
201	Robin Ventura	.25
202	Jason Bere	.10
203	Darrin Jackson	.10
204	Russ Davis	.10
205	Jimmy Key	.10
206	Jack McDowell	.10
207	Jim Abbott	.10
208	Paul O'Neill	.25
209	Bernie Williams	.40
210	Don Mattingly	1.00
211	Orlando Miller (Star Rookie)	.10
212	Alex Gonzalez (Star Rookie)	.15
213	Terrell Wade (Star Rookie)	.10
214	Jose Oliva (Star Rookie)	.10
215	Alex Rodriguez (Star Rookie)	3.00
216	Garret Anderson (Star Rookie)	.15
217	Alan Benes (Star Rookie)	.10
218	Armando Benitez (Star Rookie)	.10
219	Dustin Hermanson (Star Rookie)	.10
220	Charles Johnson (Star Rookie)	.15
221	Julian Tavarez (Star Rookie)	.10
222	Jason Giambi (Star Rookie)	.25
223	LaTroy Hawkins (Star Rookie)	.10
224	Todd Hollandsworth (Star Rookie)	.10
225	Derek Jeter (Star Rookie)	2.00
226	*Hideo Nomo* (Star Rookie)	1.00
227	Tony Clark (Star Rookie)	.40
228	Roger Cedeno (Star Rookie)	.10
229	Scott Stahoviak (Star Rookie)	.10
230	Michael Tucker (Star Rookie)	.15
231	Joe Rosselli (Star Rookie)	.10
232	Antonio Osuna (Star Rookie)	.10
233	*Bobby Higginson* (Star Rookie)	1.00
234	*Mark Grudzielanek* (Star Rookie)	.25
235	Ray Durham (Star Rookie)	.25
236	Frank Rodriguez (Star Rookie)	.10
237	Quilvio Veras (Star Rookie)	.10
238	Darren Bragg (Star Rookie)	.10
239	Ugueth Urbina (Star Rookie)	.10
240	Jason Bates (Star Rookie)	.10
241	David Bell (Diamond Debuts)	.10
242	Ron Villone (Diamond Debuts)	.10
243	Joe Randa (Diamond Debuts)	.10
244	*Carlos Perez* (Diamond Debuts)	.25
245	Brad Clontz (Diamond Debuts)	.10
246	Steve Rodriguez (Diamond Debuts)	.10
247	Joe Vitiello (Diamond Debuts)	.10
248	Ozzie Timmons (Diamond Debuts)	.10
249	Rudy Pemberton (Diamond Debuts)	.10
250	Marty Cordova (Diamond Debuts)	.15
251	Tony Graffanino (Top Prospect)	.10
252	*Mark Johnson* (Top Prospect)	.20
253	*Tomas Perez* (Top Prospect)	.20
254	Jimmy Hurst (Top Prospect)	.10
255	Edgardo Alfonzo (Top Prospect)	.40
256	Jose Malave (Top Prospect)	.10
257	*Brad Radke* (Top Prospect)	.20
258	Jon Nunnally (Top Prospect)	.10
259	Dilson Torres (Top Prospect)	.15
260	Esteban Loaiza (Top Prospect)	.15
261	*Freddy Garcia* (Top Prospect)	.20
262	Don Wengert (Top Prospect)	.10
263	*Robert Person* (Top Prospect)	.10
264	*Tim Unroe* (Top Prospect)	.15
265	Juan Acevedo (Top Prospect)	.10
266	Eduardo Perez	.10
267	Tony Phillips	.10
268	Jim Edmonds	.15
269	Jorge Fabregas	.10
270	Tim Salmon	.20
271	Mark Langston	.10
272	J.T. Snow	.15
273	Phil Plantier	.10
274	Derek Bell	.10
275	Jeff Bagwell	1.00
276	Luis Gonzalez	.15
277	John Hudek	.10
278	Todd Stottlemyre	.15
279	Mark Acre	.10
280	Ruben Sierra	.10
281	Mike Bordick	.10
282	Ron Darling	.10
283	Brent Gates	.10
284	Todd Van Poppel	.10
285	Paul Molitor	.40
286	Ed Sprague	.10
287	Juan Guzman	.10
288	David Cone	.20
289	Shawn Green	.50
290	Marquis Grissom	.15
291	Kent Mercker	.10
292	Steve Avery	.10
293	Chipper Jones	2.00
294	John Smoltz	.20
295	Dave Justice	.20
296	Ryan Klesko	.20
297	Joe Oliver	.10
298	Ricky Bones	.10
299	John Jaha	.10
300	Greg Vaughn	.15
301	Dave Nilsson	.10
302	Kevin Seitzer	.10
303	Bernard Gilkey	.10
304	Allen Battle	.10
305	Ray Lankford	.10
306	Tom Pagnozzi	.10
307	Allen Watson	.10
308	Danny Jackson	.10
309	Ken Hill	.10

310 Todd Zeile .10
311 Kevin Roberson .10
312 Steve Buechele .10
313 Rick Wilkins .10
314 Kevin Foster .10
315 Sammy Sosa 2.00
316 Howard Johnson .10
317 Greg Hansell .10
318 Pedro Astacio .10
319 Rafael Bournigal .10
320 Mike Piazza 2.00
321 Ramon Martinez .15
322 Raul Mondesi .25
323 Ismael Valdes .15
324 Wil Cordero .10
325 Tony Tarasco .10
326 Roberto Kelly .10
327 Jeff Fassero .10
328 Mike Lansing .10
329 Pedro J. Martinez 1.00
330 Kirk Rueter .10
331 Glenallen Hill .10
332 Kirt Manwaring .10
333 Royce Clayton .10
334 J.R. Phillips .10
335 Barry Bonds .75
336 Mark Portugal .10
337 Terry Mulholland .10
338 Omar Vizquel .15
339 Carlos Baerga .10
340 Albert Belle .60
341 Eddie Murray .30
342 Wayne Kirby .10
343 Chad Ogea .10
344 Tim Davis .10
345 Jay Buhner .10
346 Bobby Ayala .10
347 Mike Blowers .10
348 Dave Fleming .10
349 Edgar Martinez .10
350 Andre Dawson .15
351 Darrell Whitmore .10
352 Chuck Carr .10
353 John Burkett .10
354 Chris Hammond .10
355 Gary Sheffield .40
356 Pat Rapp .10
357 Greg Colbrunn .10
358 David Segui .10
359 Jeff Kent .10
360 Bobby Bonilla .10
361 Pete Harnisch .10
362 Ryan Thompson .10
363 Jose Vizcaino .10
364 Brett Butler .10
365 Cal Ripken Jr. 2.50
366 Rafael Palmeiro .40
367 Leo Gomez .10
368 Andy Van Slyke .10
369 Arthur Rhodes .10
370 Ken Caminiti .25
371 Steve Finley .10
372 Melvin Nieves .10
373 Andujar Cedeno .10
374 Trevor Hoffman .15
375 Fernando Valenzuela .10
376 Ricky Bottalico .10
377 Dave Hollins .10
378 Charlie Hayes .10
379 Tommy Greene .10
380 Darren Daulton .10
381 Curt Schilling .15
382 Midre Cummings .10
383 Al Martin .10
384 Jeff King .10
385 Orlando Merced .10
386 Denny Neagle .10
387 Don Slaught .10
388 Dave Clark .10
389 Kevin Gross .10
390 Will Clark .30
391 Ivan Rodriguez .75
392 Benji Gil .10
393 Jeff Frye .10
394 Kenny Rogers .10
395 Juan Gonzalez 1.00
396 Mike Macfarlane .10
397 Lee Tinsley .10
398 Tim Naehring .10
399 Tim Vanegmond .10
400 Mike Greenwell .10
401 Ken Ryan .10
402 John Smiley .10
403 Tim Pugh .10
404 Reggie Sanders .15
405 Barry Larkin .15
406 Hal Morris .10
407 Jose Rijo .10
408 Lance Painter .10
409 Joe Girardi .10
410 Andres Galarraga .25
411 Mike Kingery .10
412 Roberto Mejia .10
413 Walt Weiss .10
414 Bill Swift .10
415 Larry Walker .50
416 Billy Brewer .10
417 Pat Borders .10
418 Tom Gordon .10
419 Kevin Appier .10
420 Gary Gaetti .10
421 Greg Gohr .10
422 Felipe Lira .10
423 John Doherty .10
424 Chad Curtis .10
425 Cecil Fielder .10
426 Alan Trammell .15
427 David McCarty .10
428 Scott Erickson .15
429 Pat Mahomes .10
430 Kirby Puckett 1.00
431 Dave Stevens .10
432 Pedro Munoz .10
433 Chris Sabo .10
434 Alex Fernandez .15
435 Frank Thomas 1.00
436 Roberto Hernandez .10
437 Lance Johnson .10
438 Jim Abbott .10
439 John Wetteland .10
440 Melido Perez .10
441 Tony Fernandez .10
442 Pat Kelly .10
443 Mike Stanley .10
444 Danny Tartabull .10
445 Wade Boggs .20
446 Robin Yount (Final Tribute) .40
447 Ryne Sandberg (Final Tribute) .50
448 Nolan Ryan (Final Tribute) 2.00
449 George Brett (Final Tribute) .75
450 Mike Schmidt (Final Tribute) .50

1995 Upper Deck Electric Diamond

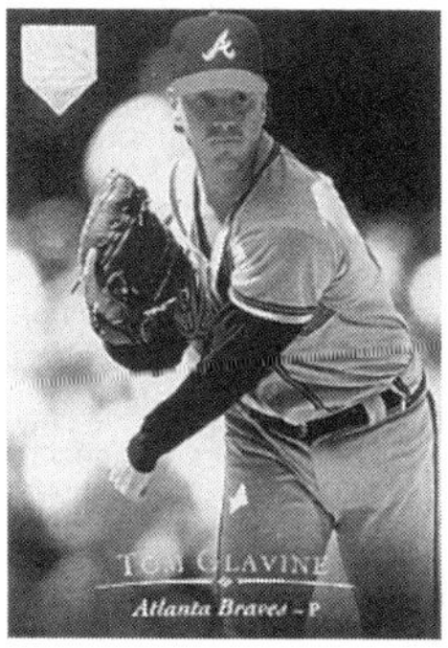

Included as an insert at the rate of one per retail foil pack and two per jumbo pack, this set parallels the regular issue. The only differences are that the Electric Diamond cards utilize silver-foil highlights on front, compared to the copper foil on the regular cards. The Electric Diamond cards also include a home-plate shaped logo printed in silver foil in one of the upper corners.

	MT
Complete Set (1-450):	100.00
Common Player:	.25
Stars/Rookies: 2X	

(See 1995 Upper Deck for checklist and base card values.)

1995 Upper Deck Electric Diamond Gold

A parallel set of a parallel set, the Electric Diamond Gold cards were found at an average rate of one per 36 retail packs. They differ from the standard ED inserts in that the home plate-shaped Electric Diamond logo in the upper corner and the player's name at bottom are printed in gold foil, rather than the silver of the ED cards or the copper of the regular-issue UD cards.

	MT
Complete Set (450):	1500.
Common Player:	3.00
Stars/Rookies: 10X	

(See 1995 Upper Deck for checklist and base card values.)

Player names in *Italic* type indicate a rookie card.

1995 Upper Deck Update Trade Cards

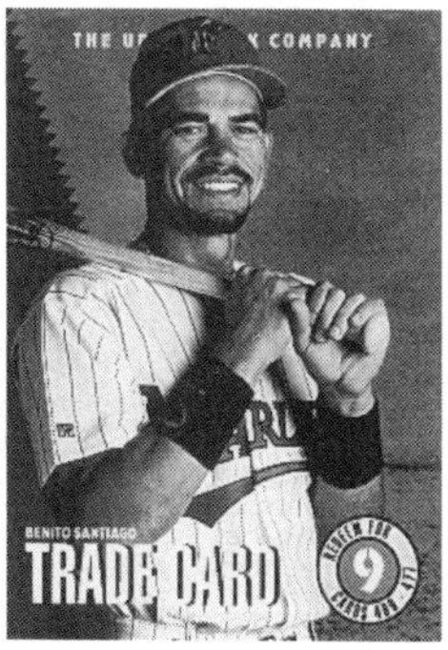

Inserted into Series II at the rate of about one per 11 packs was this five-card series of trade cards. Each card could be mailed in with $2 to receive nine cards from a special UD Update set picturing traded or free agent players in the uniforms of their new teams. The front of each trade card pictures one of the traded players in his old uniform against a red and blue background. Backs have instructions for redeeming the trade cards. The mail-in offer expired Feb. 1, 1996. Cards are numbered with a "TC" prefix.

		MT
Complete Set (5):		6.00
Common Player:		1.00
1	Orel Hershiser	1.00
2	Terry Pendleton	1.00
3	Benito Santiago	1.00
4	Kevin Brown	1.00
5	Gregg Jefferies	1.00

1995 Upper Deck Update

These 45 cards depicting traded and free agent players in the uniforms of their new 1995 teams were available only by redeeming trade-in cards found in Series II packs. Each trade-in card was good for one nine-card segment of the Update series when sent with $2 prior to the Feb. 1, 1996, deadline. Update cards share the same format as the regular 1995 Upper Deck set. The Updates are sequenced according to team nickname.

	MT
Complete Set (45):	9.00
Common Player:	.15

451 Jim Abbott .15
452 Danny Tartabull .15
453 Ariel Prieto .15
454 Scott Cooper .15
455 Tom Henke .15
456 Todd Zeile .30
457 Brian McRae .25
458 Luis Gonzalez .15
459 Jaime Navarro .15
460 Todd Worrell .15
461 Roberto Kelly .15
462 Chad Fonville .20
463 Shane Andrews .50
464 David Segui .15
465 Deion Sanders .50
466 Orel Hershiser .25
467 Ken Hill .15
468 Andy Benes .25
469 Terry Pendleton .15
470 Bobby Bonilla .20
471 Scott Erickson .25
472 Kevin Brown .25
473 Glenn Dishman .15
474 Phil Plantier .15
475 Gregg Jefferies .30
476 Tyler Green .15
477 Heathcliff Slocumb .15
478 Mark Whiten .15
479 Mickey Tettleton .15
480 Tim Wakefield .15
481 Vaughn Eshelman .15
482 Rick Aguilera .15
483 Erik Hanson .15
484 Willie McGee .20
485 Troy O'Leary .15
486 Benito Santiago .15
487 Darren Lewis .15
488 Dave Burba .15
489 Ron Gant .25
490 Bret Saberhagen .25
491 Vinny Castilla .50
492 Frank Rodriguez .15
493 Andy Pettitte 3.00
494 Ruben Sierra .15
495 David Cone .50

1995 Upper Deck Autograph Trade Cards

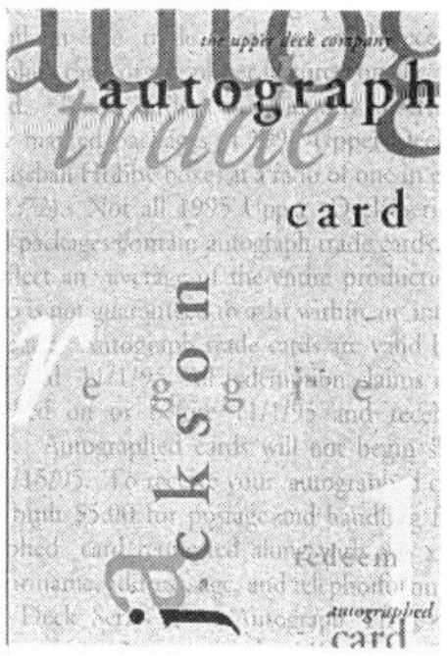

On the average of once every 72 packs (two boxes) of Series II hobby, a trade card good for an autographed player card could be found as an insert. The cards feature the player name, but no picture, on front, while the reverse has instructions for redeeming the card for a $5 fee. The autograph trade cards expired on Nov. 1, 1995.

		MT
Complete Set (5):		10.00
Common Player:		2.00
(1)	Roger Clemens	2.00
(2)	Reggie Jackson	1.00
(3)	Willie Mays	3.00
(4)	Raul Mondesi	2.00
(5)	Frank Robinson	2.00

1995 Upper Deck Autograph Redemption Cards

These cards were sent to collectors who redeemed Autograph Trade cards found in Series II Upper Deck baseball. A certificate of authenticity with a holographic serial number matching that on the card back was issued with each card.

		MT
Complete Set (5):		180.00
Common Player:		25.00
(1)	Roger Clemens	60.00
(2)	Reggie Jackson	30.00
(3)	Willie Mays	75.00
(4)	Raul Mondesi	25.00
(5)	Frank Robinson	35.00

1995 Upper Deck Autographed Jumbos

By sending in quantities of foil wrappers from Upper Deck baseball cards, collectors could receive a jumbo 5" x 7" blow-up of a player's card. The offer was limited to 8,000 Roger Clemens cards (Series I) and 6,000 Alex Rodriguez cards (Series II). Each card bears a serial number hologram on back and comes with a matching Upper Deck Authenticated auhtenticity guarantee card.

		MT
Complete Set (2):		150.00
Common Player:		30.00
(1)	Roger Clemens	60.00
(2)	Alex Rodriguez	100.00

1995 Upper Deck Award Winners Predictors

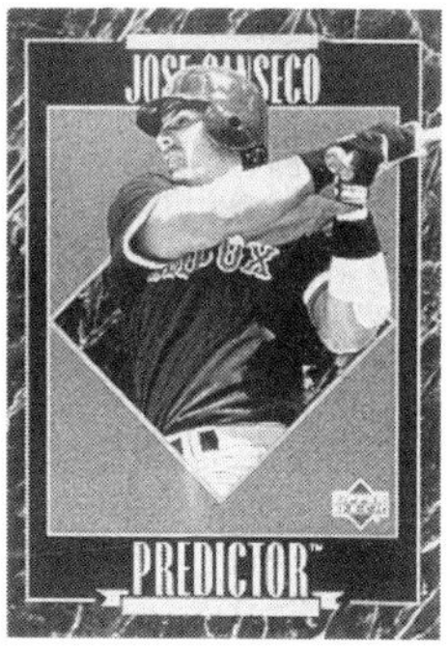

Candidates for 1995 MVP and Rookie of the Year in each league are featured in the interactive insert series called Predictors. Twenty potential award winners were released in each of Series I and II at the rate of one per 30 packs on average. Cards feature on front a player photo inside a diamond cutout on a rich looking black and marbled background. In gold foil are his name and team at top, and "PREDICTOR" and the category at bottom. Backs feature game rules and details for redeeming the card if the pictured player wins the specified award. Winners could trade in the card for a foil-enhanced set of Predictor cards. The trade-in offer expired at the end of 1995. Cards are numbered with a "H" prefix.

		MT
Complete Set (40):		45.00
Common Player:		.50
1	Albert Belle	1.00
2	Juan Gonzalez	2.00
3	Ken Griffey Jr.	6.00
4	Kirby Puckett	2.00
5	Frank Thomas	2.00
6	Jeff Bagwell	1.50
7	Barry Bonds	1.50
8	Mike Piazza	4.00
9	Matt Williams	.75
10	1995 MVP Long Shot	.50
11	Armando Benitez	.50
12	Alex Gonzalez	.50
13	Shawn Green	1.50
14	Derek Jeter	4.00
15	Alex Rodriguez	5.00
16	Alan Benes	.50
17	Brian L. Hunter	.50
18	Charles Johnson	.50
19	Jose Oliva	.50
20	1995 ROY Long Shot	.50
21	Cal Ripken Jr.	5.00
22	Don Mattingly	1.50
23	Roberto Alomar	1.00
24	Kenny Lofton	.75
25	Will Clark	1.00
26	Mark McGwire	6.00
27	Greg Maddux	3.00
28	Fred McGriff	.75
29	Andres Galarraga	1.00
30	Jose Canseco	1.50
31	Ray Durham	.50
32	Mark Grudzielanek	.50
33	Scott Ruffcorn	.50
34	Michael Tucker	.50
35	Garret Anderson	.50
36	Darren Bragg	.50
37	Quilvio Veras	.50
38	Hideo Nomo	.75
39	Chipper Jones	4.00
40	Marty Cordova	.50

1995 Upper Deck Checklists

Upscale checklists for the 1995 UD set were part of the insert card program, seeded about one per 17 packs, on average. Horizontally formatted fronts are printed on metallic foil and include a career highlight of the pictured player. Backs have the checklist data. Five checklists were issued in each of Series I and Series II.

		MT
Complete Set (10):		15.00
Common Player:		
	Series I	
1	Checklist 1-75 (Montreal Expos)	1.00
2	Checklist 76-150 (Fred McGriff)	1.50
3	Checklist 151-225 (John Valentin) (unassisted triple play)	1.00
4	Special Edition Checklist (Greg Maddux)	3.00
5	Special Edition Checklist 69-135 (Kenny Rogers) (perfect game)	1.00
	Series II	
1	Checklist 226-300 (Cecil Fielder)	1.00
2	Checklist 301-375 (Tony Gwynn)	2.50
3	Checklist 376-450 (Greg Maddux)	3.00
4	Special Edition Checklist 136-203 (Randy Johnson)	1.50
5	Special Edition Checklist 204-270 (Mike Schmidt)	3.00

Checklists with card numbers in parentheses ( ) indicates the numbers do not appear on the card.

1995 Upper Deck Babe Ruth Baseball Heroes

In the 100th anniversary year of his birth, Babe Ruth was the featured star in Upper Deck continuing "Heroes" insert set. Ten cards, including an unnumbered header, were issued in Series II packs. The cards featured colorized photos printed on metallic foil on the front. Backs have stats and/or biographical data. On average, one Babe Ruth Heroes card is found per 34 packs.

		MT
Complete Set (10):		100.00
Common Player:		10.00
73	1914-18 Pitching Career (Babe Ruth)	10.00
74	1919 - Move to Outfield (Babe Ruth)	10.00
75	1920 - Renaissance Man (Babe Ruth)	10.00
76	1923 - House That Ruth Built (Babe Ruth)	10.00
77	1927 - 60-Homer Season (Babe Ruth)	10.00
78	1928 - Three-homer Game (Babe Ruth)	10.00
79	1932 - The Called Shot (Babe Ruth)	10.00
80	1930-35 - Milestones (Babe Ruth)	10.00
81	1935 - The Last Hurrah (Babe Ruth)	10.00
---	Header card	3.00

1995 Upper Deck League Leaders Predictors

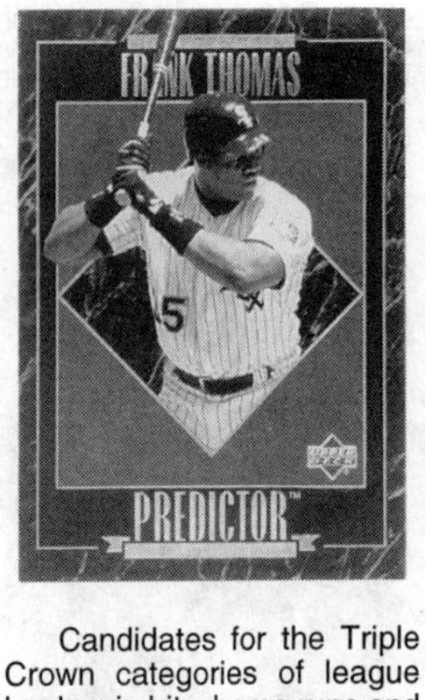

Candidates for the Triple Crown categories of league leaders in hits, home runs and RBIs are featured in this retail-only insert set, found at the average rate of one per 30 packs in both Series I and II. If the player pictured on the card front won the category specified on his card, it could be redeemed for a special foil-enhanced version of the subset prior to the Dec. 31, 1995, deadline. Cards are numbered with a "R" prefix.

		MT
Complete Set (60):		70.00
Common Player:		.50
1	Albert Belle	1.00
2	Jose Canseco	1.50
3	Juan Gonzalez	2.00
4	Ken Griffey Jr.	6.00
5	Frank Thomas	2.00
6	Jeff Bagwell	1.50
7	Barry Bonds	1.50
8	Fred McGriff	1.00
9	Matt Williams	.75
10	1995 Home Run Long Shot	.50
11	Albert Belle	1.00
12	Joe Carter	.50
13	Cecil Fielder	.50
14	Kirby Puckett	1.50
15	Frank Thomas	2.00
16	Jeff Bagwell	1.50
17	Barry Bonds	1.50
18	Mike Piazza	4.00
19	Matt Williams	.75
20	1995 RBI Long Shot	.50
21	Wade Boggs	1.00
22	Kenny Lofton	.75
23	Paul Molitor	1.50
24	Paul O'Neill	.75
25	Frank Thomas	2.00
26	Jeff Bagwell	1.50
27	Tony Gwynn	3.00
28	Gregg Jefferies	.50
29	Hal Morris	.50
30	1995 Batting Long Shot	.50
31	Joe Carter	.50
32	Cecil Fielder	.50
33	Rafael Palmeiro	1.00
34	Larry Walker	1.00
35	Manny Ramirez	2.00
36	Tim Salmon	.75
37	Mike Piazza	4.00
38	Andres Galarraga	1.00
39	Dave Justice	.75
40	Gary Sheffield	.75
41	Juan Gonzalez	2.00
42	Jose Canseco	1.50
43	Will Clark	1.00
44	Rafael Palmeiro	1.00
45	Ken Griffey Jr.	6.00
46	Ruben Sierra	.50
47	Larry Walker	1.00
48	Fred McGriff	1.00
49	Dante Bichette	.65
50	Darren Daulton	.50
51	Will Clark	1.00
52	Ken Griffey Jr.	6.00
53	Don Mattingly	1.50
54	John Olerud	1.00
55	Kirby Puckett	1.50
56	Raul Mondesi	.75
57	Moises Alou	.75
58	Bret Boone	.50
59	Albert Belle	1.00
60	Mike Piazza	4.00

1995 Upper Deck Steal of a Deal

A horizontal format with an action photo printed over a green foil background and a large bronze seal indicating how the player was acquired are featured in this 15-card insert set. The front has a terra-cotta border, which is carried over to the back. A large green box on back details the transaction and describes why it can be categorized as a "steal" for the player's new team. These top-of-the-line chase cards were seeded in both hobby and retail packs of Series I at the average rate of one per 34 packs. Cards are numbered with a "SD" prefix.

		MT
Complete Set (15):		80.00
Common Player:		2.00
1	Mike Piazza	15.00
2	Fred McGriff	4.00
3	Kenny Lofton	6.00
4	Jose Oliva	2.00
5	Jeff Bagwell	10.00
6	Roberto Alomar, Joe Carter	4.00
7	Steve Karsay	2.00
8	Ozzie Smith	6.00
9	Dennis Eckersley	2.00
10	Jose Canseco	6.00
11	Carlos Baerga	2.00
12	Cecil Fielder	2.00
13	Don Mattingly	10.00
14	Bret Boone	2.00
15	Michael Jordan	30.00

1995 Upper Deck Special Edition

Printed on metallic foil on front, and inserted into hobby packs only at the rate of one per pack, this insert series is found in both Series I (#1-135) and Series II (#136-270). A silver stripe at top has the name of the issue and the issuers, while stacked black and silver bars at bottom have the player name, team and position. Backs are conventionally printed and have another color photo, career data and 1994 and lifetime stats.

		MT
Complete Set (270):		150.00
Common Player:		.25
1	Cliff Floyd	.25
2	Wil Cordero	.25
3	Pedro Martinez	2.50
4	Larry Walker	1.50
5	Derek Jeter	6.00
6	Mike Stanley	.25
7	Melido Perez	.25
8	Jim Leyritz	.25
9	Danny Tartabull	.25
10	Wade Boggs	1.00
11	Ryan Klesko	.50
12	Steve Avery	.25
13	Damon Hollins	.25
14	Chipper Jones	6.00
15	Dave Justice	.50
16	Glenn Williams	.25
17	Jose Oliva	.25
18	Terrell Wade	.25
19	Alex Fernandez	.25
20	Frank Thomas	3.00
21	Ozzie Guillen	.25
22	Roberto Hernandez	.25
23	Albie Lopez	.25
24	Eddie Murray	.75
25	Albert Belle	2.00
26	Omar Vizquel	.30
27	Carlos Baerga	.25
28	Jose Rijo	.25
29	Hal Morris	.25
30	Reggie Sanders	.25
31	Jack Morris	.25
32	Raul Mondesi	.50
33	Karim Garcia	.25
34	Todd Hollandsworth	.25
35	Mike Piazza	6.00
36	Chan Ho Park	.50
37	Ramon Martinez	.25
38	Kenny Rogers	.25
39	Will Clark	.75
40	Juan Gonzalez	3.00
41	Ivan Rodriguez	2.50
42	Orlando Miller	.25
43	John Hudek	.25
44	Luis Gonzalez	.25
45	Jeff Bagwell	3.00
46	Cal Ripken Jr.	8.00
47	Mike Oquist	.25
48	Armando Benitez	.25
49	Ben McDonald	.25
50	Rafael Palmeiro	1.00
51	Curtis Goodwin	.25
52	Vince Coleman	.25
53	Tom Gordon	.25
54	Mike Macfarlane	.25
55	Brian McRae	.25
56	Matt Smith	.25
57	David Segui	.25
58	Paul Wilson	.25
59	Bill Pulsipher	.25
60	Bobby Bonilla	.25
61	Jeff Kent	.25
62	Ryan Thompson	.25
63	Jason Isringhausen	.25
64	Ed Sprague	.25
65	Paul Molitor	1.50
66	Juan Guzman	.25
67	Alex Gonzalez	.25
68	Shawn Green	1.50
69	Mark Portugal	.25
70	Barry Bonds	2.50
71	Robby Thompson	.25
72	Royce Clayton	.25
73	Ricky Bottalico	.25
74	Doug Jones	.25
75	Darren Daulton	.25
76	Gregg Jefferies	.25
77	Scott Cooper	.25
78	Nomar Garciaparra	6.00
79	Ken Ryan	.25
80	Mike Greenwell	.25
81	LaTroy Hawkins	.25
82	Rich Becker	.25
83	Scott Erickson	.25
84	Pedro Munoz	.25
85	Kirby Puckett	3.00
86	Orlando Merced	.25
87	Jeff King	.25
88	Midre Cummings	.25
89	Bernard Gilkey	.25
90	Ray Lankford	.25
91	Todd Zeile	.25
92	Alan Benes	.25
93	Bret Wagner	.25
94	Rene Arocha	.25
95	Cecil Fielder	.25
96	Alan Trammell	.25
97	Tony Phillips	.25
98	Junior Felix	.25
99	Brian Harper	.25
100	Greg Vaughn	.30
101	Ricky Bones	.25
102	Walt Weiss	.25
103	Lance Painter	.25
104	Roberto Mejia	.25
105	Andres Galarraga	1.00
106	Todd Van Poppel	.25
107	Ben Grieve	1.50
108	Brent Gates	.25
109	Jason Giambi	.50
110	Ruben Sierra	.25
111	Terry Steinbach	.25
112	Chris Hammond	.25
113	Charles Johnson	.25
114	Jesus Tavarez	.25
115	Gary Sheffield	.40
116	Chuck Carr	.25
117	Bobby Ayala	.25
118	Randy Johnson	2.00
119	Edgar Martinez	.25
120	Alex Rodriguez	8.00
121	Kevin Foster	.25
122	Kevin Roberson	.25
123	Sammy Sosa	6.00
124	Steve Trachsel	.25
125	Eduardo Perez	.25
126	Tim Salmon	.40
127	Todd Greene	.25
128	Jorge Fabregas	.25
129	Mark Langston	.25
130	Mitch Williams	.25
131	Raul Casanova	.25
132	Mel Nieves	.25
133	Andy Benes	.25
134	Dustin Hermanson	.25
135	Trevor Hoffman	.25
136	Mark Grudzielanek	.25
137	Ugueth Urbina	.25
138	Moises Alou	.40
139	Roberto Kelly	.25
140	Rondell White	.40
141	Paul O'Neill	.50
142	Jimmy Key	.25
143	Jack McDowell	.25
144	Ruben Rivera	.25
145	Don Mattingly	3.00
146	John Wetteland	.25
147	Tom Glavine	.75
148	Marquis Grissom	.25
149	Javy Lopez	.40
150	Fred McGriff	1.00
151	Greg Maddux	5.00
152	Chris Sabo	.25
153	Ray Durham	.25
154	Robin Ventura	.50
155	Jim Abbott	.25
156	Jimmy Hurst	.25
157	Tim Raines	.25
158	Dennis Martinez	.25
159	Kenny Lofton	2.00
160	Dave Winfield	.40
161	Manny Ramirez	3.00
162	Jim Thome	.60
163	Barry Larkin	.40
164	Bret Boone	.25
165	Deion Sanders	.40
166	Ron Gant	.30
167	Benito Santiago	.25
168	Hideo Nomo	.50
169	Billy Ashley	.25
170	Roger Cedeno	.25
171	Ismael Valdes	.25
172	Eric Karros	.30
173	Rusty Greer	.25
174	Rick Helling	.25
175	Nolan Ryan	8.00
176	Dean Palmer	.25
177	Phil Plantier	.25

178	Darryl Kile	.25
179	Derek Bell	.25
180	Doug Drabek	.25
181	Craig Biggio	1.00
182	Kevin Brown	.40
183	Harold Baines	.25
184	Jeffrey Hammonds	.25
185	Chris Hoiles	.25
186	Mike Mussina	1.50
187	Bob Hamelin	.25
188	Jeff Montgomery	.25
189	Michael Tucker	.25
190	George Brett	2.50
191	Edgardo Alfonzo	.50
192	Brett Butler	.25
193	Bobby Jones	.25
194	Todd Hundley	.25
195	Bret Saberhagen	.25
196	Pat Hentgen	.25
197	Roberto Alomar	2.00
198	David Cone	.40
199	Carlos Delgado	1.50
200	Joe Carter	.25
201	William Van Landingham	.25
202	Rod Beck	.25
203	J.R. Phillips	.25
204	Darren Lewis	.25
205	Matt Williams	.60
206	Lenny Dykstra	.25
207	Dave Hollins	.25
208	Mike Schmidt	1.50
209	Charlie Hayes	.25
210	Mo Vaughn	2.00
211	Jose Malave	.25
212	Roger Clemens	3.00
213	Jose Canseco	2.00
214	Mark Whiten	.25
215	Marty Cordova	.25
216	Rick Aguilera	.25
217	Kevin Tapani	.25
218	Chuck Knoblauch	.50
219	Al Martin	.25
220	Jay Bell	.25
221	Carlos Garcia	.25
222	Freddy Garcia	.25
223	Jon Lieber	.25
224	Danny Jackson	.25
225	Ozzie Smith	1.50
226	Brian Jordan	.25
227	Ken Hill	.25
228	Scott Cooper	.25
229	Chad Curtis	.25
230	Lou Whitaker	.25
231	Kirk Gibson	.25
232	Travis Fryman	.35
233	Jose Valentin	.25
234	Dave Nilsson	.25
235	Cal Eldred	.25
236	Matt Mieske	.25
237	Bill Swift	.25
238	Marvin Freeman	.25
239	Jason Bates	.25
240	Larry Walker	1.50
241	David Nied	.25
242	Dante Bichette	.50
243	Dennis Eckersley	.25
244	Todd Stottlemyre	.25
245	Rickey Henderson	.75
246	Geronimo Berroa	.25
247	Mark McGwire	10.00
248	Quilvio Veras	.25
249	Terry Pendleton	.25
250	Andre Dawson	.40
251	Jeff Conine	.25
252	Kurt Abbott	.25
253	Jay Buhner	.30
254	Darren Bragg	.25
255	Ken Griffey Jr.	10.00
256	Tino Martinez	.50
257	Mark Grace	.50
258	Ryne Sandberg	1.50
259	Randy Myers	.25
260	Howard Johnson	.25
261	Lee Smith	.25
262	J.T. Snow	.35
263	Chili Davis	.25
264	Chuck Finley	.25
265	Eddie Williams	.25
266	Joey Hamilton	.25
267	Ken Caminiti	.75
268	Andujar Cedeno	.25
269	Steve Finley	.25
270	Tony Gwynn	5.00

1995 Upper Deck Special Edition Gold

An insert set within an insert set, gold-foil enhanced versions of the Special Edition cards were seeded into hobby packs at the rate of about one per box. The substitution of gold ink for silver is also carried over onto the background of the card back.

	MT
Complete Set (270):	700.00
Common Player:	2.00

Stars/Rookies: 4X
(See 1995 Upper Deck Special Edition for checklist and base card values.)

1995 Upper Deck Cal Ripken Commemorative Jumbo

To commemorate Cal Ripken's 2,131st consecutive game, UD issued this 5" x 3" die-cut card. Five thousand of the cards were issued with silver foil highlights; 2,131 with gold trim. Each card is serially numbered in the lower-right corner on back.

	MT
Cal Ripken Jr. (silver edition of 5,000)	20.00
Cal Ripken Jr. (gold edition of 2,131)	30.00

1995 Upper Deck Auto Racing

Several of Upper Deck's spokesmen from other sports were included in a "Pit Crew" subset in the company's premiere auto racing product. The two baseball players among them are listed here.

		MT
134	Reggie Jackson	1.00
136	Ken Griffey Jr.	3.00

1995 Upper Deck/ Eagle Snacks Ballpark Legends

Nine Hall of Famers comprise this set which was produced by UD for the Eagle snack food company. Sets were available via mail-in redemption for proofs of purchase and $1. Fronts have sepia photos on which uniform logos have been removed. The Eagle Ballpark Legends is at upper-left, the UD logo is at lower-left, followed by the player name. Backs of the 2-1/2" x 3-1/2" cards have career summary and personal data. Autographed cards of Harmon Killebrew were random inserts.

		MT
Complete Set (9):		3.00
Common Player:		.25
1	Nolan Ryan	1.00
2	Reggie Jackson	.50
3	Tom Seaver	.50
4	Harmon Killebrew	.25
4a	Harmon Killebrew (autographed)	20.00
5	Ted Williams	.75
6	Whitey Ford	.50
7	Al Kaline	.50
8	Willie Stargell	.25
9	Bob Gibson	.25

1995 Upper Deck/GTS Phone Cards

In conjunction with Global Telecommunications Service, Upper Deck issued a series of 15 phone cards described as being the first licensed by Major League Baseball and the Players Association. Measuring about 2-1/8" x 3-3/8" with round corners, the cards were printed on heavy plastic and utilized the basic format and photos from the players' 1994 Upper Deck baseball cards. Issue price, with phone time, was $12 each. Cards are numbered with a "MLB" prefix.

		MT
Complete Set (15):		45.00
Common Player:		3.00
01	Tony Gwynn	4.50
02	Fred McGriff	3.00
03	Frank Thomas	4.00
04	Ken Griffey Jr.	6.00
05	Cecil Fielder	3.00
06	Barry Bonds	4.50
07	Don Mattingly	5.00
08	Dave Justice	3.00
09	Roger Clemens	4.50
10	Cal Ripken Jr.	5.00
11	Roberto Alomar	3.00
12	Gary Sheffield	3.00
13	Jeff Bagwell	3.50
14	Kirby Puckett	4.50
15	Ozzie Smith	3.50

1995 Upper Deck/ Metallic Impressions Michael Jordan

Michael Jordan's brief, highly publicized baseball career is chronicled in this metallic card set produced for UD by Metallic Impressions and sold in a special lithographed tin box. Each of the 2-5/8" x 3-9/16" cards has a gold-tone rolled edge. Fronts feature photos of Jordan in action. Backs have another photo and a career summary in a horizontal format. Cards are numbered with a "JT" prefix.

		MT
Complete Boxed Set (5):		12.00
Common Player:		4.00
1	Starting Out (Michael Jordan)	4.00
2	West to Arizona (Michael Jordan)	4.00
3	Hitting (Michael Jordan)	4.00
4	Baserunning (Michael Jordan)	4.00
5	Fielding (Michael Jordan)	4.00

1995 Upper Deck/ Metallic Impressions Mickey Mantle

Sharing the card-front images with the UD phone cards of 1994, these metal cards trace the career of Mickey Mantle. Sold in an embossed metal box, the cards measure 2-5/8" x 3-9/16" and have rolled gold-tone metal borders. Fronts have black-and-white or color photos of Mantle. Backs have a career summary in a red box against a background of pin-striped flannel, along with a small color photo of Mantle. The issue was reportedly limited to 19,950 sets.

		MT
Complete Boxed Set (10):		25.00
Common Player:		4.00
1	The Commerce Comet (Mickey Mantle)	4.00
2	1951 - The Early Years (Mickey Mantle)	4.00
3	1953 - Tape-Measure Home Runs (Mickey Mantle)	4.00
4	1956 - Triple Crown Season (Mickey Mantle)	4.00
5	1957 - Second Consecutive MVP (Mickey Mantle)	4.00
6	1961 - Chasing the Babe (Mickey Mantle)	4.00
7	1964 - Series Home Run Record (Mickey Mantle)	4.00
8	1967 - 500th Home Run (Mickey Mantle)	4.00
9	1974 - Hall of Famer (Mickey Mantle)	4.00
10	Checklist (Mickey Mantle)	4.00

1996 Upper Deck

Upper Deck Series I consists of 240 regular-issue cards. There are 187 regular player cards plus subsets of Star Rookies, Young at Heart, Beat the Odds, Milestones, Post-season, checklists and expansion logos. The issue was marketed in 10-card foil packs in hobby and retail versions. Hobby packs feature a Special Edition insert while retail packs offer Electric Diamond parallel cards. Series I insert sets are Blue Chip Prospects, Future Shock and Power Driven. Cal Ripken Jr. Collection cards are inserted in both series, as are Retail Predictor (home runs, batting average and RBIs) and Hobby Predictor (Player of the Month, Pitcher of the Month and rookie hits leaders) cards. Series II has 240 cards, including subsets for Star Rookies, Diamond Debuts, Strange But True, Managerial Salutes and Best of a Generation. Additional insert sets include Hot Commodities, Hideo Nomo Highlights, Run Producers and the Lovero Collection.

		MT
Complete Set (480):		60.00
Complete Series 1 (240):		30.00
Complete Series 2 (240):		30.00
Common Player:		.10
Wax Box:		45.00
1	Cal Ripken Jr. (Milestones)	2.50
2	Eddie Murray (Milestones)	.40
3	Mark Wohlers	.10
4	Dave Justice	.20
5	Chipper Jones	2.00
6	Javier Lopez	.20
7	Mark Lemke	.10
8	Marquis Grissom	.10
9	Tom Glavine	.25
10	Greg Maddux	1.50
11	Manny Alexander	.10
12	Curtis Goodwin	.10
13	Scott Erickson	.10
14	Chris Hoiles	.10
15	Rafael Palmeiro	.40
16	Rick Krivda	.10
17	Jeff Manto	.10
18	Mo Vaughn	.60
19	Tim Wakefield	.10
20	Roger Clemens	1.50
21	Tim Naehring	.10
22	Troy O'Leary	.10
23	Mike Greenwell	.10
24	Stan Belinda	.10
25	John Valentin	.10
26	J.T. Snow	.15
27	Gary DiSarcina	.10
28	Mark Langston	.10
29	Brian Anderson	.10
30	Jim Edmonds	.15
31	Garret Anderson	.10
32	Orlando Palmeiro	.10
33	Brian McRae	.10
34	Kevin Foster	.10
35	Sammy Sosa	2.00
36	Todd Zeile	.10
37	Jim Bullinger	.10

38	Luis Gonzalez	.15
39	Lyle Mouton	.10
40	Ray Durham	.10
41	Ozzie Guillen	.10
42	Alex Fernandez	.10
43	Brian Keyser	.10
44	Robin Ventura	.20
45	Reggie Sanders	.10
46	Pete Schourek	.10
47	John Smiley	.10
48	Jeff Brantley	.10
49	Thomas Howard	.10
50	Bret Boone	.10
51	Kevin Jarvis	.10
52	Jeff Branson	.10
53	Carlos Baerga	.10
54	Jim Thome	.40
55	Manny Ramirez	1.00
56	Omar Vizquel	.15
57	Jose Mesa	.10
58	Julian Tavarez	.10
59	Orel Hershiser	.10
60	Larry Walker	.50
61	Bret Saberhagen	.15
62	Vinny Castilla	.15
63	Eric Young	.15
64	Bryan Rekar	.10
65	Andres Galarraga	.25
66	Steve Reed	.10
67	Chad Curtis	.10
68	Bobby Higginson	.10
69	Phil Nevin	.10
70	Cecil Fielder	.10
71	Felipe Lira	.10
72	Chris Gomez	.10
73	Charles Johnson	.20
74	Quilvio Veras	.10
75	Jeff Conine	.10
76	John Burkett	.10
77	Greg Colbrunn	.10
78	Terry Pendleton	.10
79	Shane Reynolds	.15
80	Jeff Bagwell	1.00
81	Orlando Miller	.10
82	Mike Hampton	.10
83	James Mouton	.10
84	Brian L. Hunter	.10
85	Derek Bell	.10
86	Kevin Appier	.10
87	Joe Vitiello	.10
88	Wally Joyner	.10
89	Michael Tucker	.10
90	Johnny Damon	.15
91	Jon Nunnally	.10
92	Jason Jacome	.10
93	Chad Fonville	.10
94	Chan Ho Park	.20
95	Hideo Nomo	.25
96	Ismael Valdes	.10
97	Greg Gagne	.10
98	Diamondbacks-Devil Rays (Expansion Card)	.25
99	Raul Mondesi	.25
100	Dave Winfield (Young at Heart)	.15
101	Dennis Eckersley (Young at Heart)	.10
102	Andre Dawson (Young at Heart)	.10
103	Dennis Martinez (Young at Heart)	.10
104	Lance Parrish (Young at Heart)	.10
105	Eddie Murray (Young at Heart)	.25
106	Alan Trammell (Young at Heart)	.10
107	Lou Whitaker (Young at Heart)	.10
108	Ozzie Smith (Young at Heart)	.25
109	Paul Molitor (Young at Heart)	.20
110	Rickey Henderson (Young at Heart)	.20
111	Tim Raines (Young at Heart)	.10
112	Harold Baines (Young at Heart)	.10
113	Lee Smith (Young at Heart)	.10
114	Fernando Valenzuela (Young at Heart)	.10
115	Cal Ripken Jr. (Young at Heart)	1.50
116	Tony Gwynn (Young at Heart)	.75
117	Wade Boggs (Young at Heart)	.15
118	Todd Hollandsworth	.15
119	Dave Nilsson	.10
120	*Jose Valentin*	.20
121	Steve Sparks	.10
122	Chuck Carr	.10
123	John Jaha	.10
124	Scott Karl	.10
125	Chuck Knoblauch	.25
126	Brad Radke	.10
127	Pat Meares	.10
128	Ron Coomer	.10
129	Pedro Munoz	.10
130	Kirby Puckett	1.00
131	David Segui	.10
132	Mark Grudzielanek	.10
133	Mike Lansing	.10
134	Sean Berry	.10
135	Rondell White	.15
136	Pedro Martinez	.75
137	Carl Everett	.15
138	Dave Mlicki	.10
139	Bill Pulsipher	.10
140	Jason Isringhausen	.10
141	Rico Brogna	.10
142	Edgardo Alfonzo	.25
143	Jeff Kent	.10
144	Andy Pettitte	.25
145	Mike Piazza (Beat the Odds)	1.00
146	Cliff Floyd (Beat the Odds)	.10
147	Jason Isringhausen (Beat the Odds)	.10
148	Tim Wakefield (Beat the Odds)	.10
149	Chipper Jones (Beat the Odds)	1.00
150	Hideo Nomo (Beat the Odds)	.15
151	Mark McGwire (Beat the Odds)	2.00
152	Ron Gant (Beat the Odds)	.10
153	Gary Gaetti (Beat the Odds)	.10
154	Don Mattingly	1.00
155	Paul O'Neill	.25
156	Derek Jeter	2.50
157	Joe Girardi	.10
158	Ruben Sierra	.10
159	Jorge Posada	.20
160	Geronimo Berroa	.10
161	Steve Ontiveros	.10
162	George Williams	.10
163	Doug Johns	.10
164	Ariel Prieto	.10
165	Scott Brosius	.10
166	Mike Bordick	.10
167	Tyler Green	.10
168	Mickey Morandini	.10
169	Darren Daulton	.10
170	Gregg Jefferies	.10
171	Jim Eisenreich	.10
172	Heathcliff Slocumb	.10
173	Kevin Stocker	.10
174	Esteban Loaiza	.10
175	Jeff King	.10
176	Mark Johnson	.10
177	Denny Neagle	.10
178	Orlando Merced	.10
179	Carlos Garcia	.10
180	Brian Jordan	.10
181	Mike Morgan	.10
182	Mark Petkovsek	.10
183	Bernard Gilkey	.10
184	John Mabry	.10
185	Tom Henke	.10
186	Glenn Dishman	.10
187	Andy Ashby	.10
188	Bip Roberts	.10
189	Melvin Nieves	.10
190	Ken Caminiti	.20
191	Brad Ausmus	.10
192	Deion Sanders	.20
193	Jamie Brewington	.10
194	Glenallen Hill	.10
195	Barry Bonds	.75
196	William VanLandingham	.10
197	Mark Carreon	.10
198	Royce Clayton	.10
199	Joey Cora	.10
200	Ken Griffey Jr.	3.00
201	Jay Buhner	.10
202	Alex Rodriguez	2.50
203	Norm Charlton	.10
204	Andy Benes	.10
205	Edgar Martinez	.10
206	Juan Gonzalez	1.00
207	Will Clark	.25
208	Kevin Gross	.10
209	Roger Pavlik	.10
210	Ivan Rodriguez	.75
211	Rusty Greer	.10
212	Angel Martinez	.10
213	Tomas Perez	.10
214	Alex Gonzalez	.10
215	Joe Carter	.10
216	Shawn Green	.50
217	Edwin Hurtado	.10
218	(Edgar Martinez, Tony Pena) (Post Season Checklist)	.10
219	Chipper Jones, Barry Larkin (Post Season Checklist)	.25
220	Orel Hershiser (Post Season Checklist)	.10
221	Mike Devereaux (Post Season Checklist)	.10
222	Tom Glavine (Post Season Checklist)	.10
223	Karim Garcia (Star Rookies)	.15
224	Arquimedez Pozo (Star Rookies)	.10
225	Billy Wagner (Star Rookies)	.15
226	John Wasdin (Star Rookies)	.10
227	Jeff Suppan (Star Rookies)	.10
228	Steve Gibralter (Star Rookies)	.10
229	Jimmy Haynes (Star Rookies)	.10
230	Ruben Rivera (Star Rookies)	.15
231	Chris Snopek (Star Rookies)	.15
232	Alex Ochoa (Star Rookies)	.10
233	Shannon Stewart (Star Rookies)	.10
234	Quinton McCracken (Star Rookies)	.15
235	Trey Beamon (Star Rookies)	.10
236	Billy McMillon (Star Rookies)	.10
237	Steve Cox (Star Rookies)	.10
238	George Arias (Star Rookies)	.10
239	Yamil Benitez (Star Rookies)	.10
240	Todd Greene (Star Rookies)	.20
241	Jason Kendall (Star Rookie)	.20
242	Brooks Kieschnick (Star Rookie)	.15
243	*Osvaldo Fernandez* (Star Rookie)	.15
244	*Livan Hernandez* (Star Rookie)	.75
245	Rey Ordonez (Star Rookie)	.20
246	*Mike Grace* (Star Rookie)	.10
247	Jay Canizaro (Star Rookie)	.10
248	Bob Wolcott (Star Rookie)	.10
249	Jermaine Dye (Star Rookie)	.15
250	Jason Schmidt (Star Rookie)	.10
251	*Mike Sweeney* (Star Rookie)	1.00
252	Marcus Jensen (Star Rookie)	.10
253	Mendy Lopez (Star Rookie)	.10
254	*Wilton Guerrero* (Star Rookie)	.50
255	Paul Wilson (Star Rookie)	.10
256	Edgar Renteria (Star Rookie)	.20
257	Richard Hidalgo (Star Rookie)	.10
258	Bob Abreu (Star Rookie)	.15
259	*Robert Smith* (Diamond Debuts)	.30
260	Sal Fasano (Diamond Debuts)	.10
261	Enrique Wilson (Diamond Debuts)	.10
262	*Rich Hunter* (Diamond Debuts)	.10
263	Sergio Nunez (Diamond Debuts)	.10
264	Dan Serafini (Diamond Debuts)	.10
265	*David Doster* (Diamond Debuts)	.10
266	Ryan McGuire (Diamond Debuts)	.10
267	Scott Spiezio (Diamond Debuts)	.10
268	Rafael Orellano (Diamond Debuts)	.10
269	Steve Avery	.10
270	Fred McGriff	.30
271	John Smoltz	.20
272	Ryan Klesko	.15
273	Jeff Blauser	.10
274	Brad Clontz	.10
275	Roberto Alomar	.60
276	B.J. Surhoff	.10
277	Jeffrey Hammonds	.10
278	Brady Anderson	.15
279	Bobby Bonilla	.10
280	Cal Ripken Jr.	2.50
281	Mike Mussina	.60
282	Wil Cordero	.10
283	Mike Stanley	.10
284	Aaron Sele	.10
285	Jose Canseco	.60
286	Tom Gordon	.10
287	Heathcliff Slocumb	.10
288	Lee Smith	.10
289	Troy Percival	.10
290	Tim Salmon	.25
291	Chuck Finley	.10
292	Jim Abbott	.10
293	Chili Davis	.10
294	Steve Trachsel	.10
295	Mark Grace	.25
296	Rey Sanchez	.10
297	Scott Servais	.10
298	Jaime Navarro	.10
299	Frank Castillo	.10
300	Frank Thomas	1.50
301	Jason Bere	.10
302	Danny Tartabull	.10
303	Darren Lewis	.10
304	Roberto Hernandez	.10
305	Tony Phillips	.10
306	Wilson Alvarez	.10
307	Jose Rijo (NEW)	.10
308	Hal Morris	.10
309	Mark Portugal	.10
310	Barry Larkin	.15
311	Dave Burba	.10
312	Eddie Taubensee	.10
313	Sandy Alomar Jr.	.15
314	Dennis Martinez	.10
315	Albert Belle	.75
316	Eddie Murray	.40
317	Charles Nagy	.10
318	Chad Ogea	.10
319	Kenny Lofton	.50
320	Dante Bichette	.25
321	Armando Reynoso	.10
322	Walt Weiss	.10
323	Ellis Burks	.10
324	Kevin Ritz	.10
325	Bill Swift	.10
326	Jason Bates	.10
327	Tony Clark	.40
328	Travis Fryman	.15
329	Mark Parent	.10
330	Alan Trammell	.10
331	C.J. Nitkowski	.10
332	Jose Lima	.10
333	Phil Plantier	.10
334	Kurt Abbott	.10
335	Andre Dawson (NEW)	.15
336	Chris Hammond	.10
337	Robb Nen	.10
338	Pat Rapp	.10
339	Al Leiter	.15
340	Gary Sheffield	.20
341	Todd Jones	.10
342	Doug Drabek	.10
343	Greg Swindell (NEW)	.10
344	Tony Eusebio	.10
345	Craig Biggio	.40
346	Darryl Kile	.10
347	Mike Macfarlane	.10
348	Jeff Montgomery	.10
349	Chris Haney	.10
350	Bip Roberts	.10
351	Tom Goodwin	.10
352	Mark Gubicza	.10
353	Joe Randa (NEW)	.10
354	Ramon Martinez	.10
355	Eric Karros	.15
356	Delino DeShields	.10
357	Brett Butler	.10
358	Todd Worrell	.10
359	Mike Blowers	.10
360	Mike Piazza	2.00
361	Ben McDonald	.10
362	Ricky Bones	.10
363	Greg Vaughn	.15
364	Matt Mieske	.10
365	Kevin Seitzer	.10
366	Jeff Cirillo	.10
367	LaTroy Hawkins	.10
368	Frank Rodriguez	.10
369	Rick Aguilera	.10
370	Roberto Alomar (Best of a Generation)	.40
371	Albert Belle (Best of a Generation)	.40
372	Wade Boggs (Best of a Generation)	.15
373	Barry Bonds (Best of a Generation)	.40
374	Roger Clemens (Best of a Generation)	.75
375	Dennis Eckersley (Best of a Generation)	.10
376	Ken Griffey Jr. (Best of a Generation)	2.00
377	Tony Gwynn (Best of a Generation)	.75
378	Rickey Henderson (Best of a Generation)	.20
379	Greg Maddux (Best of a Generation)	.75
380	Fred McGriff (Best of a Generation)	.20
381	Paul Molitor (Best of a Generation)	.20
382	Eddie Murray (Best of a Generation)	.25
383	Mike Piazza (Best of a Generation)	1.00
384	Kirby Puckett (Best of a Generation)	.50
385	Cal Ripken Jr. (Best of a Generation)	1.50
386	Ozzie Smith (Best of a Generation)	.30
387	Frank Thomas (Best of a Generation)	.50
388	Matt Walbeck	.10
389	Dave Stevens	.10
390	Marty Cordova	.10
391	Darrin Fletcher	.10
392	Cliff Floyd	.10
393	Mel Rojas	.10
394	Shane Andrews	.15
395	Moises Alou	.20
396	Carlos Perez	.10
397	Jeff Fassero	.10
398	Bobby Jones	.10
399	Todd Hundley	.15
400	John Franco	.10
401	Jose Vizcaino	.10
402	Bernard Gilkey	.10
403	Pete Harnisch	.10
404	Pat Kelly	.10
405	David Cone	.20
406	Bernie Williams	.40
407	John Wetteland	.10
408	Scott Kamieniecki	.10
409	Tim Raines	.10
410	Wade Boggs	.30
411	Terry Steinbach	.10
412	Jason Giambi	.10
413	Todd Van Poppel	.10
414	Pedro Munoz	.10
415	Eddie Murray-1990 (Strange But True)	.25
416	Dennis Eckersley-1990 (Strange But True)	.10
417	Bip Roberts-1992 (Strange But True)	.10
418	Glenallen Hill-1992 (Strange But True)	.10
419	John Hudek-1994 (Strange But True)	.10
420	Derek Bell-1995 (Strange But True)	.10
421	Larry Walker-1995 (Strange But True)	.25
422	Greg Maddux-1995 (Strange But True)	.75
423	Ken Caminiti-1995 (Strange But True)	.20
424	Brent Gates	.10
425	Mark McGwire	3.00
426	Mark Whiten	.10
427	Sid Fernandez	.10
428	Ricky Bottalico	.10
429	Mike Mimbs	.10
430	Lenny Dykstra	.10
431	Todd Zeile	.10
432	Benito Santiago	.10
433	Danny Miceli	.10
434	Al Martin	.10
435	Jay Bell	.10
436	Charlie Hayes	.10
437	Mike Kingery	.10
438	Paul Wagner	.10
439	Tom Pagnozzi	.10
440	Ozzie Smith	.60
441	Ray Lankford	.10
442	Dennis Eckersley	.10
443	Ron Gant	.10
444	Alan Benes	.10
445	Rickey Henderson	.40
446	Jody Reed	.10
447	Trevor Hoffman	.10
448	Andujar Cedeno	.10
449	Steve Finley	.10
450	Tony Gwynn	1.50
451	Joey Hamilton	.10
452	Mark Leiter	.10
453	Rod Beck	.10
454	Kirt Manwaring	.10
455	Matt Williams	.25
456	Robby Thompson	.10
457	Shawon Dunston	.10
458	Russ Davis	.10
459	Paul Sorrento	.10
460	Randy Johnson	.40
461	Chris Bosio	.10
462	Luis Sojo	.10
463	Sterling Hitchcock	.10
464	Benji Gil	.10
465	Mickey Tettleton	.10
466	Mark McLemore	.10
467	Darryl Hamilton	.10
468	Ken Hill	.10
469	Dean Palmer	.10
470	Carlos Delgado	.50
471	Ed Sprague	.10
472	Otis Nixon	.10
473	Pat Hentgen	.10
474	Juan Guzman	.10
475	John Olerud	.25
476	Checklist (Buck Showalter)	.10
477	Checklist (Bobby Cox)	.10
478	Checklist (Tommy Lasorda)	.25
479	Checklist (Jim Leyland)	.10
480	Checklist (Sparky Anderson)	.15

1996 Upper Deck A Cut Above

(See 1996 Collector's Choice A Cut Above.)

1996 Upper Deck Blue Chip Prospects

Twenty top young stars who could make a major impact in the major leagues in upcoming seasons are featured in this insert set. Each card is highlighted with blue-foil printing and double die-cut technology, which includes a zig-zag pattern around the top and a die-cut around both bottom corners. The cards are found one per 20 packs in Series 1 foil packs. Cards are numbered with a "BC" prefix.

		MT
Complete Set (20):		150.00
Common Player:		3.00
1	Hideo Nomo	5.00
2	Johnny Damon	4.00
3	Jason Isringhausen	3.00
4	Bill Pulsipher	3.00
5	Marty Cordova	4.00
6	Michael Tucker	4.00
7	John Wasdin	3.00
8	Karim Garcia	4.00
9	Ruben Rivera	4.00
10	Chipper Jones	20.00
11	Billy Wagner	5.00
12	Brooks Kieschnick	3.00
13	Alex Ochoa	4.00
14	Roger Cedeno	4.00
15	Alex Rodriguez	35.00
16	Jason Schmidt	4.00
17	Derek Jeter	35.00
18	Brian L. Hunter	3.00
19	Garret Anderson	4.00
20	Manny Ramirez	10.00

1996 Upper Deck Diamond Destiny

This late-season release is found exclusively in retail foil packs labeled "Upper Deck Tech." They are inserted at a rate of one per pack, sold with eight regular 1996 Upper Deck cards at a suggested retail of around $3. The cards have three versions of the same action photo; in color and black-and-white on front, and in black-and-white on back. A large team logo also appears on front and back. In the upper half of the card is a 1-3/16" diameter round color transparency portrait of the player. The basic version of this chase set had bronze foil highlights. Parallel silver and gold versions are found on average of one per 35 and one per 140 packs, respectively. Cards are numbered with a "DD" prefix.

		MT
Complete Set (Bronze):		75.00
Common Player (Bronze):		.60
Silver: 8X		
Gold: 25X		
1	Chipper Jones	5.00
2	Fred McGriff	1.25
3	Ryan Klesko	.60
4	John Smoltz	.60
5	Greg Maddux	4.00
6	Cal Ripken Jr.	6.00
7	Roberto Alomar	1.75
8	Eddie Murray	1.25
9	Brady Anderson	.60
10	Mo Vaughn	1.50
11	Roger Clemens	3.00
12	Darin Erstad	3.00
13	Sammy Sosa	5.00
14	Frank Thomas	2.50
15	Barry Larkin	1.00
16	Albert Belle	2.00
17	Manny Ramirez	2.50
18	Kenny Lofton	1.50
19	Dante Bichette	.75
20	Gary Sheffield	.75
21	Jeff Bagwell	2.50
22	Hideo Nomo	.60
23	Mike Piazza	5.00
24	Kirby Puckett	2.00
25	Paul Molitor	2.00
26	Chuck Knoblauch	.75
27	Wade Boggs	1.50
28	Derek Jeter	5.00
29	Rey Ordonez	.60
30	Mark McGwire	8.00
31	Ozzie Smith	2.00
32	Tony Gwynn	4.00
33	Barry Bonds	2.00
34	Matt Williams	1.00
35	Ken Griffey Jr.	8.00
36	Jay Buhner	.60
37	Randy Johnson	1.75
38	Alex Rodriguez	6.00
39	Juan Gonzalez	2.50
40	Joe Carter	.60

1996 Upper Deck Future Stock

Future Stock inserts are found on average of one per six packs of Series 1, highlighting 20 top young stars on a die-cut design. Each card has a blue border, vertical photo and silver-foil stamping on the front. Cards are numbered with a "FS" prefix.

		MT
Complete Set (20):		9.00
Common Player:		.60
1	George Arias	.60
2	Brian Barnes	.60
3	Trey Beamon	.60
4	Yamil Benitez	.60
5	Jamie Brewington	.60
6	Tony Clark	1.00
7	Steve Cox	.60
8	Carlos Delgado	2.00
9	Chad Fonville	.60
10	Steve Gibralter	.60
11	Curtis Goodwin	.60
12	Todd Greene	.60
13	Jimmy Haynes	.60
14	Quinton McCracken	.60
15	Billy McMillon	.60
16	Chan Ho Park	1.00
17	Arquimedez Pozo	.60
18	Chris Snopek	.60
19	Shannon Stewart	.75
20	Jeff Suppan	.60

The election of former players to the Hall of Fame does not always have an immediate upward effect on card prices. The hobby market generally has done a good job of predicting those inductions and adjusting values over the course of several years.

1996 Upper Deck Gameface

		MT
Complete Set (10):		8.00
Common Player:		.25
1	Ken Griffey Jr.	2.00
2	Frank Thomas	1.00
3	Barry Bonds	.65
4	Albert Belle	.50
5	Cal Ripken Jr.	1.75
6	Mike Piazza	1.50
7	Chipper Jones	1.50
8	Matt Williams	.25
9	Hideo Nomo	.25
10	Greg Maddux	1.00

1996 Upper Deck Hobby Predictor

These inserts depict 60 top players as possible winners in the categories of Player of the Month, Pitcher of the Month and Rookie Hits Leader. If the pictured player won that category any month of the season the card was redeemable for a 10-card set with a different look, action photos and printed on silver-foil stock. Hobby Predictor inserts are found on average once per dozen packs in both series. Winning cards are indicated by (W). Cards are numbered with a "H" prefix.

		MT
Complete Set (60):		55.00
Common Player:		.50
1	Albert Belle	1.00
2	Kenny Lofton	1.00
3	Rafael Palmeiro	1.00
4	Ken Griffey Jr.	5.00
5	Tim Salmon	.75
6	Cal Ripken Jr.	4.00
7	Mark McGwire (W)	5.00
8	Frank Thomas (W)	1.50
9	Mo Vaughn (W)	1.00
10	Player of the Month Long Shot (W)	.50
11	Roger Clemens	2.00
12	David Cone	.75
13	Jose Mesa	.50
14	Randy Johnson	1.00
15	Steve Finley	.50
16	Mike Mussina	1.00
17	Kevin Appier	.50
18	Kenny Rogers	.50
19	Lee Smith	.50
20	Pitcher of the Month Long Shot (W)	.50
21	George Arias	.50
22	Jose Herrera	.50
23	Tony Clark	.75
24	Todd Greene	.50
25	Derek Jeter (W)	4.00
26	Arquimedez Pozo	.50
27	Matt Lawton	.50
28	Shannon Stewart	.75
29	Chris Snopek	.50
30	Rookie Hits Long Shot	.50
31	Jeff Bagwell (W)	1.50
32	Dante Bichette	.75
33	Barry Bonds (W)	1.50
34	Tony Gwynn	2.50
35	Chipper Jones	3.00
36	Eric Karros	.60
37	Barry Larkin	.60
38	Mike Piazza	3.00
39	Matt Williams	.75
40	Player of the Month Long Shot (W)	.50
41	Osvaldo Fernandez	.50
42	Tom Glavine	.75
43	Jason Isringhausen	.50
44	Greg Maddux	2.50
45	Pedro Martinez	1.50
46	Hideo Nomo	1.00
47	Pete Schourek	.50
48	Paul Wilson	.50
49	Mark Wohlers	.50
50	Pitcher of the Month Long Shot	.50
51	Bob Abreu	.75
52	Trey Beamon	.50
53	Yamil Benitez	.50
54	Roger Cedeno (W)	.50
55	Todd Hollandsworth	.50
56	Marvin Benard	.50
57	Jason Kendall	.75
58	Brooks Kieschnick	.50
59	Rey Ordonez (W)	.90
60	Rookie Hits Long Shot (W)	.50

1996 Upper Deck Hobby Predictor Redemption

Persons who redeemed winning cards from UD's interactive Predictor insert series received a 10-card set of the top players in various statistical categories. The redemption cards are similar in format to the Predictor cards, but have fronts printed on silver-foil. In palce of the contest rules found on the backs of Predictor cards, the redemption cards have a career summary.

		MT
Complete Set (30):		12.00
Common Player:		.25
H31	Jeff Bagwell	1.00
H32	Dante Bichette	.40
H33	Barry Bonds	.75
H34	Tony Gwynn	1.00
H35	Chipper Jones	1.50
H36	Eric Karros	.25
H37	Barry Larkin	.25
H38	Mike Piazza	1.50
H39	Matt Williams	.25
H40	Player of the Month Long Shot	.25
H41	Osvaldo Fernandez	.25
H42	Tom Glavine	.40
H43	Jason Isringhausen	.25
H44	Greg Maddux	1.00
H45	Pedro Martinez	.50
H46	Hideo Nomo	.50
H47	Pete Schourek	.25
H48	Paul Wilson	.35
H49	Mark Wohlers	.25
H50	Pitcher of the Month Long Shot	.25
H51	Bob Abreu	.35
H52	Trey Beamon	.25
H53	Yamil Benitez	.25
H54	Roger Cedeno	.25
H55	Todd Hollandsworth	.25
H56	Marvin Benard	.25
H57	Jason Kendall	.35
H58	Brooks Kieschnick	.25
H59	Rey Ordonez	.60
H60	Rookie Hits Long Shot	.25

1996 Upper Deck Hot Commodities

These 20 die-cut cards were seeded one per every 37 1996 Upper Deck Series II packs. Cards are numbered with a "HC" prefix.

		MT
Complete Set (20):		150.00
Common Player:		3.50
1	Ken Griffey Jr.	25.00
2	Hideo Nomo	3.50
3	Roberto Alomar	5.00
4	Paul Wilson	3.50
5	Albert Belle	5.00
6	Manny Ramirez	9.00
7	Kirby Puckett	7.50
8	Johnny Damon	3.50
9	Randy Johnson	5.00
10	Greg Maddux	12.50
11	Chipper Jones	15.00
12	Barry Bonds	7.50
13	Mo Vaughn	5.00
14	Mike Piazza	15.00
15	Cal Ripken Jr.	20.00
16	Tim Salmon	4.00
17	Sammy Sosa	15.00
18	Kenny Lofton	5.00
19	Tony Gwynn	12.50
20	Frank Thomas	9.00

1996 Upper Deck Lovero Collection

Every sixth pack of 1996 Upper Deck Series II has a V.J. Lovero insert card. This 20-card set features unique shots from Lovero, one of the most well-known photographers in the country. Some of the cards feature Randy Johnson wearing a conehead, Frank Thomas blowing a bubble while throwing the ball, and Jay Buhner and his child both chewing on a bat. Cards are numbered with a "VJ" prefix.

		MT
Complete Set (20):		25.00
Common Player:		.35
1	Rod Carew	.50
2	Hideo Nomo	.75
3	Derek Jeter	3.50
4	Barry Bonds	1.50
5	Greg Maddux	2.75
6	Mark McGwire	5.00
7	Jose Canseco	1.50
8	Ken Caminiti	.35
9	Raul Mondesi	.50
10	Ken Griffey Jr.	5.00
11	Jay Buhner	.35
12	Randy Johnson	.75
13	Roger Clemens	2.25
14	Brady Anderson	.35
15	Frank Thomas	2.50
16	Angels Outfielders	.35

17	Mike Piazza	3.50
18	Dante Bichette	.50
19	Tony Gwynn	2.25
20	Jim Abbott	.35

1996 Upper Deck Nomo Highlights

The 1995 rookie season of Los Angeles Dodgers' pitcher Hideo Nomo is recapped in this five-card 1996 Upper Deck insert set. The cards were seeded one per every 23 Series 2 packs. A 5" x 7" version of each card was also issued as a retail box insert. Values are the same as for small cards.

		MT
Complete Set (5):		10.00
Common Nomo:		2.50
1	Hideo Nomo	2.00
2	Hideo Nomo	2.00
3	Hideo Nomo	2.00
4	Hideo Nomo	2.00
5	Hideo Nomo	2.00

1996 Upper Deck Power Driven

Twenty of the game's top power hitters are analyzed in depth by baseball writer Peter Gammons on these Series 1 insert cards. Found once per 36 packs, on average, the cards are printed on an embossed light F/X design. Cards are numbered with a "PD" prefix.

		MT
Complete Set (20):		125.00
Common Player:		2.50
1	Albert Belle	6.00
2	Barry Bonds	7.50
3	Jay Buhner	2.50
4	Jose Canseco	5.00
5	Cecil Fielder	2.50
6	Juan Gonzalez	9.00
7	Ken Griffey Jr.	25.00
8	Eric Karros	2.50
9	Fred McGriff	4.00
10	Mark McGwire	25.00
11	Rafael Palmeiro	4.00
12	Mike Piazza	17.50
13	Manny Ramirez	9.00
14	Tim Salmon	3.00
15	Reggie Sanders	2.50
16	Sammy Sosa	16.00
17	Frank Thomas	9.00
18	Mo Vaughn	3.00
19	Larry Walker	5.00
20	Matt Williams	3.00

1996 Upper Deck Retail Predictor

Retail Predictor inserts feature 60 possible winners in the categories of monthly leader in home runs, batting average and RBIs. If the pictured player led a category in any month, his card was redeemable for a 10-card set featuring action photos on silver foil. Retail Predictors are found on average once per 12 packs in each series. Winning cards are indicated by (W). Cards are numbered with a "R" prefix.

		MT
Complete Set (60):		90.00
Common Player:		.75
1	Albert Belle (W)	1.50
2	Jay Buhner (W)	.75
3	Juan Gonzalez	3.00
4	Ken Griffey Jr.	7.50
5	Mark McGwire (W)	7.50
6	Rafael Palmeiro	1.00
7	Tim Salmon	.75
8	Frank Thomas	3.00
9	Mo Vaughn (W)	1.50
10	Home Run Long Shot (W)	.75
11	Albert Belle (W)	1.50
12	Jay Buhner	.75
13	Jim Edmonds	.75
14	Cecil Fielder	.75
15	Ken Griffey Jr.	7.50
16	Edgar Martinez	.75
17	Manny Ramirez	2.00
18	Frank Thomas	3.00
19	Mo Vaughn ((W))	1.50
20	RBI Long Shot (W)	.75
21	Roberto Alomar (W)	1.50
22	Carlos Baerga	.75
23	Wade Boggs	1.00
24	Ken Griffey Jr.	7.50
25	Chuck Knoblauch	.90
26	Kenny Lofton	1.50
27	Edgar Martinez	.75
28	Tim Salmon	.75
29	Frank Thomas	3.00
30	Batting Average Long Shot (W)	.75
31	Dante Bichette	.75
32	Barry Bonds (W)	2.00
33	Ron Gant	.75
34	Chipper Jones	5.00
35	Fred McGriff	1.00
36	Mike Piazza	5.00
37	Sammy Sosa	3.00
38	Larry Walker	1.00
39	Matt Williams	.90
40	Home Run Long Shot	.75
41	Jeff Bagwell (W)	3.00
42	Dante Bichette	.75
43	Barry Bonds (W)	2.00
44	Jeff Conine	.75
45	Andres Galarraga	.75
46	Mike Piazza	5.00
47	Reggie Sanders	.75
48	Sammy Sosa	3.00
49	Matt Williams	.90
50	RBI Long Shot	.75
51	Jeff Bagwell	3.00
52	Derek Bell	.75
53	Dante Bichette	.75
54	Craig Biggio	.90
55	Barry Bonds	2.00
56	Bret Boone	.75
57	Tony Gwynn	3.00
58	Barry Larkin	.90
59	Mike Piazza (W)	5.00
60	AVG Long Shot	.75

1996 Upper Deck Retail Predictor Redemption

Persons who redeemed winning cards from UD's interactive Predictor insert series received a 10-card set of the top players in various statistical categories. The redemption cards are similar in format to the Predictor cards, but have fronts printed on silver-foil. In palce of the contest rules found on the backs of Predictor cards, the redemption cards have a career summary.

		MT
Complete Set (30):		12.00
Common Player:		.25
R31	Dante Bichette	.25
R32	Barry Bonds	.75
R33	Ron Gant	.25
R34	Chipper Jones	1.50
R35	Fred McGriff	.40
R36	Mike Piazza	1.50
R37	Sammy Sosa	1.50
R38	Larry Walker	.35
R39	Matt Williams	.25
R40	Home Run Long Shot	.25
R41	Jeff Bagwell	1.00
R42	Dante Bichette	.25
R43	Barry Bonds	.75
R44	Jeff Conine	.25
R45	Andres Galarraga	.25
R46	Mike Piazza	1.50
R47	Reggie Sanders	.25
R48	Sammy Sosa	1.50
R49	Matt Williams	.25
R50	RBI Long Shot	.25
R51	Jeff Bagwell	1.00
R52	Derek Bell	.25
R53	Dante Bichette	.25
R54	Craig Biggio	.25
R55	Barry Bonds	.75
R56	Bret Boone	.25
R57	Tony Gwynn	1.00
R58	Barry Larkin	.25
R59	Mike Piazza	1.50
R60	AVG Long Shot	.25

1996 Upper Deck Cal Ripken Collection

Part of a cross-brand insert set, four cards are included as Series I inserts at the rate of one per 24 packs. Five cards are also included in Series II, one per every 23 packs. They chronicle Cal Ripken's career and highlights.

		MT
Complete Set (5-8, 13-17):		45.00
Common Card:		6.00
Header:		6.00
5	Cal Ripken Jr.	6.00
6	Cal Ripken Jr.	6.00
7	Cal Ripken Jr.	6.00
8	Cal Ripken Jr.	6.00
13	Cal Ripken Jr.	6.00
14	Cal Ripken Jr.	6.00
15	Cal Ripken Jr.	6.00
16	Cal Ripken Jr.	6.00
17	Cal Ripken Jr.	6.00

1996 Upper Deck Cal Ripken Jr. Collection Jumbos

The career of Cal Ripken Jr. to the point of his 2,131st consecutive major league game is chronicled in this boxed set of 3-1/2" x 5" cards. The tale is told in reverse order, with card #1 marking the record and #22 detailing Ripken's first major league experience. Fronts have photos of Ripken in various stages of his career and feature a gold-foil facsimile autograph. Backs have a green and black background with a portrait of Ripken at top. At center are a few sentences about his career and a season's stats.

		MT
Complete Set (22):		15.00
Common Player:		1.00
1	Cal Ripken Jr.	1.00
2	Cal Ripken Jr. (w/Barry Bonds)	1.25
3	Cal Ripken Jr.	1.00
4	Cal Ripken Jr.	1.00
5	Cal Ripken Jr.	1.00
6	Cal Ripken Jr.	1.00
7	Cal Ripken Jr.	1.00
8	Cal Ripken Jr.	1.00
9	Cal Ripken Jr.	1.00
10	Cal Ripken Jr.	1.00
11	Cal Ripken Jr.	1.00
12	Cal Ripken Jr.	1.00
13	Cal Ripken Jr.	1.00
14	Cal Ripken Jr.	1.00
15	Cal Ripken Jr.	1.00
16	Cal Ripken Jr.	1.00
17	Cal Ripken Jr.	1.00
18	Cal Ripken Jr.	1.00
19	Cal Ripken Jr.	1.00
20	Cal Ripken Jr.	1.00
21	Cal Ripken Jr.	1.00
22	Cal Ripken Jr. (w/ Eddie Murray)	1.25

1996 Upper Deck Run Producers

These double die-cut, embossed and color foil-stamped cards feature 20 of the game's top RBI men. The cards were seeded one per every 71 packs of 1996 Upper Deck Series II. Cards are numbered with a "RP" prefix.

		MT
Complete Set (20):		200.00
Common Player:		4.00
1	Albert Belle	8.00
2	Dante Bichette	5.00
3	Barry Bonds	10.00
4	Jay Buhner	4.00
5	Jose Canseco	8.00
6	Juan Gonzalez	15.00
7	Ken Griffey Jr.	40.00
8	Tony Gwynn	20.00
9	Kenny Lofton	6.00
10	Edgar Martinez	4.00
11	Fred McGriff	5.00
12	Mark McGwire	40.00
13	Rafael Palmeiro	6.00
14	Mike Piazza	25.00
15	Manny Ramirez	10.00
16	Tim Salmon	4.00
17	Sammy Sosa	25.00
18	Frank Thomas	15.00
19	Mo Vaughn	6.00
20	Matt Williams	4.00

1996 Upper Deck All-Star Supers

The starting line-ups of the 1996 All-Star Game are featured in super-size (3-1/2" x 5")_versions of their 1996 Upper Deck cards in this special boxed set sold at Wal-Mart late in the year for around $18. Other than a large silver-foil All-Star Game logo in the lower-left corner of each photo, these cards are identical to the regular-issue versions, right down to the silver- and bronze-foil highlights on front and the card numbers on back.

		MT
Complete Set (18):		18.00
Common Player:		.50
80	Jeff Bagwell	1.00
195	Barry Bonds	1.00
200	Ken Griffey Jr.	4.00
271	John Smoltz	.50
275	Roberto Alomar	.75
280	Cal Ripken Jr.	3.00
300	Frank Thomas	2.00
310	Barry Larkin	.50
313	Sandy Alomar Jr.	.50
315	Albert Belle	.75
317	Charles Nagy	.50
319	Kenny Lofton	.50
320	Dante Bichette	.60
345	Craig Biggio	.60
360	Mike Piazza	2.00
410	Wade Boggs	.75
450	Tony Gwynn	1.00
455	Matt Williams	.50

1996 Upper Deck Authenticated Life-size Stand-ups

Marketed through Upper Deck Authenticated, the large (about 6' x 2') stand-ups feature die-cut figures with an easel on back allowing it to stand. Front has a facsimile autograph, MLB and UD logos.

	MT
Ken Griffey Jr.	30.00
Cal Ripken Jr.	30.00

Player names in *Italic* type indicate a rookie card.

1996 Upper Deck Ken Griffey Jr. All-Star

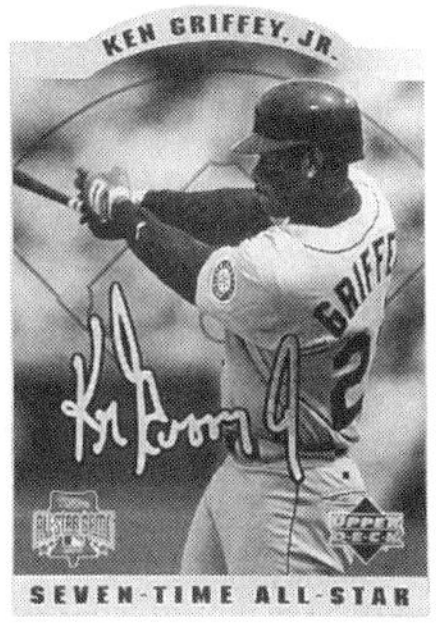

Junior's seventh All-Star team selection was marked with the issue of this special jumbo (3-1/2" x 5") card. The front has an action photo with the 1996 All-Star Game logo and is highlighted in silver foil, including a reproduction of his autograph. The top is die-cut. On back is a portrait photo with Griffey's All-Star history overprinted, and a serial number from within an edition of 2,500. The card was an exclusive to a TV shopping network.

	MT
Ken Griffey Jr.	18.00

1996 Upper Deck Hideo Nomo R.O.Y.

The Japanese pitcher's 1995 Rookie of the Year season was commemorated with this large-format (3-1/2" x 5"), die-cut card sold only via TV shopping programs. The card has an action photo of Nomo on front and is highlighted in gold foil, including a replica of his autograph. On back is an action photo, major league career summary and stats and a serial number from within an edition of 5,000 pieces.

	MT
Hideo Nomo	20.00

1996 Upper Deck Meet the Stars

These 7" x 5" cards were issued in conjunction with UD's "Meet the

		MT
Complete Set (2):		12.00
(1)	Dynamic Debut - 1989 (Ken Griffey Jr.)	6.00
(2)	Magic Memories - 1995 (Ken Griffey Jr.)	6.00

1996 Upper Deck National Heroes

Two baseball stars are included in this series of collector issues believed to have been a TV shop-at-home exclusive. Measuring 3-1/2" x 5", the cards are die-cut into a torn ticket shape. Fronts have color action photos on a gold-foil background. Two versions of each card were issued, an edition of 5,000 unsigned cards and an autographed edition serially numbered on front to a limit of 250.

		MT
Complete Set (2):		25.00
Complete Set, Autographed (2):		245.00
(1)	Ken Griffey Jr.	15.00
(1a)	Ken Griffey Jr. (autographed)	125.00
(2)	Cal Ripken Jr.	10.00
(2a)	Cal Ripken Jr. (autographed)	120.00

1996 Upper Deck Statistics Leaders

National League and American League winners of important statistical categories, along with major award winners for the 1996 season are featured in this boxed set of large-format (3-1/2" x 5") cards. Besides the size, these cards differ from the regular-issue 1996 UD cards of the same players only in the additional of a silver-foil award shield on front and the card number on back. Players with multiple awards have identical cards. The set was sold only at retail outlets with a suggested price of about $20.

		MT
Complete Set (23):		20.00
Common Player:		.50
1	Alex Rodriguez (AL batting)	5.00
2	Tony Gwynn (NL batting)	3.00
3	Mark McGwire (AL HR)	5.00
4	Andres Galarraga (NL HR)	.50
5	Albert Belle (AL RBI)	1.00
6	Andres Galarraga (NL RBI)	.50
7	Kenny Lofton (AL steals)	.50
8	Eric Young (NL steals)	.50
9	Andy Pettitte (AL wins)	.50
10	John Smoltz (NL wins)	.50
11	Roger Clemens (AL Ks)	2.00
12	John Smoltz (NL Ks)	.50
13	Juan Guzman (AL ERA)	.50
14	Kevin Brown (NL ERA)	.50
15	John Wetteland (AL saves)	.50
16	Jeff Brantley (NL saves)	.50
17	Todd Worrell (NL saves)	.50
18	Derek Jeter (AL ROY)	4.00
19	Todd Hollandsworth (NL ROY)	.50
20	Juan Gonzalez (AL MVP)	2.50
21	Ken Caminiti (NL MVP)	.50
22	Pat Hentgen (AL CY)	.50
23	John Smoltz (NL CY)	.50

1997 Upper Deck

The 520-card, regular-sized set was available in 12-card packs. The base card fronts feature a full action shot with the player's name near the bottom edge above a bronze-foil, wood-grain stripe. The player's team logo is in the lower left corner in silver foil. Each card front has the date of the game pictured with a brief description. The card backs contain more detailed game highlight descriptions and statistics, along with a small action shot in the upper left quadrant. Subsets are: Jackie Robinson Tribute (1-9), Strike Force (65-72), Defensive Gems (136-153), Global Impact (181-207), Season Highlights Checklist (214-222) and Star Rookies (223-240). Inserts are: Game Jerseys, Ticket To Stardom, Power Package, Amazing Greats and Rock Solid Foundation. A 30-card update to Series I was released early in the season featuring 1996 post-season highlights and star rookies. The card faces had red or purple borders and were numbered 241 to 270. A second update set of 30 was released near the end of the 1997 season, numbered 521-550 and featuring traded players and rookies in a format identical to Series I and II UD. Both of the update sets were available only via a mail-in redemption offer.

		MT
Complete Set (550):		140.00
Complete Series 1 Set (240):		30.00
Complete Update Set (241-270):		35.00
Common Update (241-270):		.50
Complete Series 2 Set (250):		60.00
Complete Update Set (521-550):		15.00
Common Player:		.10
Hobby Box:		60.00
1	Jackie Robinson	1.00
2	Jackie Robinson	1.00
3	Jackie Robinson	1.00
4	Jackie Robinson	1.00
5	Jackie Robinson	1.00
6	Jackie Robinson	1.00
7	Jackie Robinson	1.00
8	Jackie Robinson	1.00
9	Jackie Robinson	1.00
10	Chipper Jones	2.00
11	Marquis Grissom	.10
12	Jermaine Dye	.10
13	Mark Lemke	.10
14	Terrell Wade	.10
15	Fred McGriff	.30
16	Tom Glavine	.25
17	Mark Wohlers	.10
18	Randy Myers	.10
19	Roberto Alomar	.60
20	Cal Ripken Jr.	3.00
21	Rafael Palmeiro	.30
22	Mike Mussina	.40
23	Brady Anderson	.15
24	Jose Canseco	.50
25	Mo Vaughn	.60
26	Roger Clemens	1.00
27	Tim Naehring	.10
28	Jeff Suppan	.10
29	Troy Percival	.10
30	Sammy Sosa	2.00
31	Amaury Telemaco	.10
32	Rey Sanchez	.10
33	Scott Servais	.10
34	Steve Trachsel	.10
35	Mark Grace	.20
36	Wilson Alvarez	.10
37	Harold Baines	.10
38	Tony Phillips	.10
39	James Baldwin	.10
40	Frank Thomas (wrong (Ken Griffey Jr.'s) vital data)	1.00
41	Lyle Mouton	.10
42	Chris Snopek	.10
43	Hal Morris	.10
44	Eric Davis	.10
45	Barry Larkin	.20
46	Reggie Sanders	.10
47	Pete Schourek	.10
48	Lee Smith	.10
49	Charles Nagy	.10
50	Albert Belle	.75
51	Julio Franco	.10
52	Kenny Lofton	.60
53	Orel Hershiser	.10
54	Omar Vizquel	.10
55	Eric Young	.15
56	Curtis Leskanic	.10
57	Quinton McCracken	.10
58	Kevin Ritz	.10
59	Walt Weiss	.10
60	Dante Bichette	.25
61	Marc Lewis	.10
62	Tony Clark	.40
63	Travis Fryman	.15
64	John Smoltz (Strike Force)	.15
65	Greg Maddux (Strike Force)	.75
66	Tom Glavine (Strike Force)	.15
67	Mike Mussina (Strike Force)	.20
68	Andy Pettitte (Strike Force)	.40
69	Mariano Rivera (Strike Force)	.15
70	Hideo Nomo (Strike Force)	.25
71	Kevin Brown (Strike Force)	.10
72	Randy Johnson (Strike Force)	.15
73	Felipe Lira	.10
74	Kimera Bartee	.10
75	Alan Trammell	.10
76	Kevin Brown	.15
77	Edgar Renteria	.15
78	Al Leiter	.15
79	Charles Johnson	.15
80	Andre Dawson	.15
81	Billy Wagner	.15
82	Donne Wall	.10
83	Jeff Bagwell	1.00
84	Keith Lockhart	.10
85	Jeff Montgomery	.10
86	Tom Goodwin	.10
87	Tim Belcher	.10
88	Mike Macfarlane	.10
89	Joe Randa	.10
90	Brett Butler	.10
91	Todd Worrell	.10
92	Todd Hollandsworth	.10
93	Ismael Valdes	.10
94	Hideo Nomo	.25
95	Mike Piazza	2.00
96	Jeff Cirillo	.10
97	Ricky Bones	.10
98	Fernando Vina	.10
99	Ben McDonald	.10
100	John Jaha	.10
101	Mark Loretta	.10
102	Paul Molitor	.50
103	Rick Aguilera	.10
104	Marty Cordova	.10
105	Kirby Puckett	.50
106	Dan Naulty	.10
107	Frank Rodriguez	.10
108	Shane Andrews	.15
109	Henry Rodriguez	.10
110	Mark Grudzielanek	.10
111	Pedro Martinez	.75
112	Ugueth Urbina	.10
113	David Segui	.10
114	Rey Ordonez	.15
115	Bernard Gilkey	.10
116	Butch Huskey	.10
117	Paul Wilson	.10
118	Alex Ochoa	.10
119	John Franco	.10
120	Dwight Gooden	.10
121	Ruben Rivera	.15
122	Andy Pettitte	.75
123	Tino Martinez	.20
124	Bernie Williams	.40
125	Wade Boggs	.25
126	Paul O'Neill	.20
127	Scott Brosius	.10
128	Ernie Young	.10
129	Doug Johns	.10
130	Geronimo Berroa	.10
131	Jason Giambi	.10
132	John Wasdin	.10
133	Jim Eisenreich	.10
134	Ricky Otero	.10
135	Ricky Bottalico	.10
136	Mark Langston (Defensive Gems)	.10
137	Greg Maddux (Defensive Gems)	.75
138	Ivan Rodriguez (Defensive Gems)	.30
139	Charles Johnson (Defensive Gems)	.10
140	J.T. Snow (Defensive Gems)	.10
141	Mark Grace (Defensive Gems)	.15
142	Roberto Alomar (Defensive Gems)	.40
143	Craig Biggio (Defensive Gems)	.15
144	Ken Caminiti (Defensive Gems)	.10
145	Matt Williams (Defensive Gems)	.10
146	Omar Vizquel (Defensive Gems)	.10
147	Cal Ripken Jr. (Defensive Gems)	1.50
148	Ozzie Smith (Defensive Gems)	.25
149	Rey Ordonez (Defensive Gems)	.15
150	Ken Griffey Jr. (Defensive Gems)	1.50
151	Devon White (Defensive Gems)	.10
152	Barry Bonds (Defensive Gems)	.50
153	Kenny Lofton (Defensive Gems)	.40
154	Mickey Morandini	.10
155	Gregg Jefferies	.10
156	Curt Schilling	.15
157	Jason Kendall	.10
158	Francisco Cordova	.10
159	Dennis Eckersley	.10
160	Ron Gant	.15
161	Ozzie Smith	.50
162	Brian Jordan	.10
163	John Mabry	.10
164	Andy Ashby	.10
165	Steve Finley	.10
166	Fernando Valenzuela	.10
167	Archi Cianfrocco	.10
168	Wally Joyner	.10
169	Greg Vaughn	.15
170	Barry Bonds	.75
171	William VanLandingham	.10
172	Marvin Benard	.10
173	Rich Aurilia	.10
174	Jay Canizaro	.10
175	Ken Griffey Jr.	4.00
176	Bob Wells	.10
177	Jay Buhner	.10
178	Sterling Hitchcock	.10
179	Edgar Martinez	.10
180	Rusty Greer	.10
181	Dave Nilsson (Global Impact)	.10
182	Larry Walker (Global Impact)	.35
183	Edgar Renteria (Global Impact)	.15
184	Rey Ordonez (Global Impact)	.15

185 Rafael Palmeiro (Global Impact) .20
186 Osvaldo Fernandez (Global Impact) .10
187 Raul Mondesi (Global Impact) .15
188 Manny Ramirez (Global Impact) .50
189 Sammy Sosa (Global Impact) 1.00
190 Robert Eenhoorn (Global Impact) .10
191 Devon White (Global Impact) .10
192 Hideo Nomo (Global Impact) .25
193 Mac Suzuki (Global Impact) .10
194 Chan Ho Park (Global Impact) .10
195 Fernando Valenzuela (Global Impact) .10
196 Andruw Jones (Global Impact) .50
197 Vinny Castilla (Global Impact) .10
198 Dennis Martinez (Global Impact) .10
199 Ruben Rivera (Global Impact) .15
200 Juan Gonzalez (Global Impact) .50
201 Roberto Alomar (Global Impact) .40
202 Edgar Martinez (Global Impact) .10
203 Ivan Rodriguez (Global Impact) .30
204 Carlos Delgado (Global Impact) .50
205 Andres Galarraga (Global Impact) .15
206 Ozzie Guillen (Global Impact) .10
207 Midre Cummings (Global Impact) .10
208 Roger Pavlik .10
209 Darren Oliver .10
210 Dean Palmer .10
211 Ivan Rodriguez .75
212 Otis Nixon .10
213 Pat Hentgen .10
214 Ozzie Smith, Andre Dawson, Kirby Puckett CL (Season Highlights) .25
215 Barry Bonds, Gary Sheffield, Brady Anderson CL (Season Highlights) .25
216 Ken Caminiti CL (Season Highlights) .10
217 John Smoltz CL (Season Highlights) .10
218 Eric Young CL (Season Highlights) .10
219 Juan Gonzalez CL (Season Highlights) .50
220 Eddie Murray CL (Season Highlights) .20
221 Tommy Lasorda CL (Season Highlights) .15
222 Paul Molitor CL (Season Highlights) .15
223 Luis Castillo .10
224 Justin Thompson .10
225 Rocky Coppinger .10
226 Jermaine Allensworth .10
227 Jeff D'Amico .10
228 Jamey Wright .10
229 Scott Rolen 1.00
230 Darin Erstad .50
231 Marty Janzen .10
232 Jacob Cruz .10
233 Raul Ibanez .10
234 Nomar Garciaparra 2.00
235 Todd Walker .10
236 *Brian Giles* 1.50
237 Matt Beech .10
238 Mike Cameron .10
239 Jose Paniagua .10
240 Andruw Jones 1.00
241 Brant Brown (Star Rookies) .50
242 Robin Jennings (Star Rookies) .50
243 Willie Adams (Star Rookies) .50
244 Ken Caminiti (Division Series) .50
245 Brian Jordan (Division Series) .50
246 Chipper Jones (Division Series) 6.00
247 Juan Gonzalez (Division Series) 3.00
248 Bernie Williams (Division Series) 1.50
249 Roberto Alomar (Division Series) 1.50
250 Bernie Williams (Post-Season) 1.50
251 David Wells (Post-Season) .50
252 Cecil Fielder (Post-Season) .50
253 Darryl Strawberry (Post-Season) .75
254 Andy Pettitte (Post-Season) 1.00
255 Javier Lopez (Post-Season) .75
256 Gary Gaetti (Post-Season) .50
257 Ron Gant (Post-Season) .75
258 Brian Jordan (Post-Season) .50
259 John Smoltz (Post-Season) .50
260 Greg Maddux (Post-Season) 5.00
261 Tom Glavine (Post-Season) .75
262 Chipper Jones (World Series) 6.00
263 Greg Maddux (World Series) 5.00
264 David Cone (World Series) .75
265 Jim Leyritz (World Series) .50
266 Andy Pettitte (World Series) 1.00
267 John Wetteland (World Series) .50
268 *Dario Veras* (Star Rookie) .50
269 Neifi Perez (Star Rookie) .50
270 Bill Mueller (Star Rookie) .50
271 Vladimir Guerrero (Star Rookie) 1.00
272 Dmitri Young (Star Rookie) .10
273 *Nerio Rodriguez* (Star Rookie) .20
274 Kevin Orie (Star Rookie) .15
275 Felipe Crespo (Star Rookie) .10
276 Danny Graves (Star Rookie) .10
277 Roderick Myers (Star Rookie) .10
278 *Felix Heredia* (Star Rookie) .25
279 Ralph Milliard (Star Rookie) .10
280 Greg Norton (Star Rookie) .10
281 Derek Wallace (Star Rookie) .10
282 Trot Nixon (Star Rookie) .15
283 Bobby Chouinard (Star Rookie) .10
284 Jay Witasick (Star Rookie) .10
285 Travis Miller (Star Rookie) .10
286 Brian Bevil (Star Rookie) .10
287 Bobby Estalella (Star Rookie) .10
288 Steve Soderstrom (Star Rookie) .10
289 Mark Langston .10
290 Tim Salmon .20
291 Jim Edmonds .10
292 Garret Anderson .10
293 George Arias .10
294 Gary DiSarcina .10
295 Chuck Finley .10
296 Todd Greene .10
297 Randy Velarde .10
298 David Justice .25
299 Ryan Klesko .20
300 John Smoltz .20
301 Javier Lopez .15
302 Greg Maddux 1.50
303 Denny Neagle .10
304 B.J. Surhoff .10
305 Chris Hoiles .10
306 Eric Davis .10
307 Scott Erickson .10
308 Mike Bordick .10
309 John Valentin .10
310 Heathcliff Slocumb .10
311 Tom Gordon .10
312 Mike Stanley .10
313 Reggie Jefferson .10
314 Darren Bragg .10
315 Troy O'Leary .10
316 John Mabry (Season Highlight) .10
317 Mark Whiten (Season Highlight) .10
318 Edgar Martinez (Season Highlight) .10
319 Alex Rodriguez (Season Highlight) 2.00
320 Mark McGwire (Season Highlight) 2.00
321 Hideo Nomo (Season Highlight) .25
322 Todd Hundley (Season Highlight) .15
323 Barry Bonds (Season Highlight) .40
324 Andruw Jones (Season Highlight) 1.00
325 Ryne Sandberg .75
326 Brian McRae .10
327 Frank Castillo .10
328 Shawon Dunston .10
329 Ray Durham .10
330 Robin Ventura .20
331 Ozzie Guillen .10
332 Roberto Hernandez .10
333 Albert Belle .75
334 Dave Martinez .10
335 Willie Greene .10
336 Jeff Brantley .10
337 Kevin Jarvis .10
338 John Smiley .10
339 Eddie Taubensee .10
340 Bret Boone .10
341 Kevin Seitzer .10
342 Jack McDowell .10
343 Sandy Alomar Jr. .15
344 Chad Curtis .10
345 Manny Ramirez 1.00
346 Chad Ogea .10
347 Jim Thome .40
348 Mark Thompson .10
349 Ellis Burks .10
350 Andres Galarraga .25
351 Vinny Castilla .15
352 Kirt Manwaring .10
353 Larry Walker .50
354 Omar Olivares .10
355 Bobby Higginson .10
356 Melvin Nieves .10
357 Brian Johnson .10
358 Devon White .10
359 Jeff Conine .10
360 Gary Sheffield .20
361 Robb Nen .10
362 Mike Hampton .10
363 Bob Abreu .10
364 Luis Gonzalez .15
365 Derek Bell .10
366 Sean Berry .10
367 Craig Biggio .40
368 Darryl Kile .10
369 Shane Reynolds .10
370 Jeff Bagwell (Capture the Flag) .50
371 Ron Gant (Capture the Flag) .10
372 Andy Benes (Capture the Flag) .10
373 Gary Gaetti (Capture the Flag) .10
374a Ramon Martinez (Capture the Flag) (gold back) .10
374b Ramon Martinez (Capture the Flag) (white back) .10
375 Raul Mondesi (Capture the Flag) .10
376a Steve Finley (Capture the Flag) (gold back) .10
376b Steve Finley (Capture the Flag) (white back) .10
377 Ken Caminiti (Capture the Flag) .15
378 Tony Gwynn (Capture the Flag) .75
379 Dario Veras (Capture the Flag) .10
380 Andy Pettitte (Capture the Flag) .40
381 Ruben Rivera (Capture the Flag) .10
382 David Cone (Capture the Flag) .10
383 Roberto Alomar (Capture the Flag) .30
384 Edgar Martinez (Capture the Flag) .10
385 Ken Griffey Jr. (Capture the Flag) 2.00
386 Mark McGwire (Capture the Flag) 2.00
387 Rusty Greer (Capture the Flag) .10
388 Jose Rosado .10
389 Kevin Appier .10
390 Johnny Damon .10
391 Jose Offerman .10
392 Michael Tucker .10
393 Craig Paquette .10
394 Bip Roberts .10
395 Ramon Martinez .10
396 Greg Gagne .10
397 Chan Ho Park .20
398 Karim Garcia .10
399 Wilton Guerrero .10
400 Eric Karros .15
401 Raul Mondesi .20
402 Matt Mieske .10
403 Mike Fetters .10
404 Dave Nilsson .10
405 Jose Valentin .10
406 Scott Karl .10
407 Marc Newfield .10
408 Cal Eldred .10
409 Rich Becker .10
410 Terry Steinbach .10
411 Chuck Knoblauch .20
412 Pat Meares .10
413 Brad Radke .10
414 not issued
415a Kirby Puckett (should be #414) 1.00
415b Andruw Jones (Griffey Hot List) 3.00
416 Chipper Jones (Griffey Hot List) 6.00
417 Mo Vaughn (Griffey Hot List) 1.50
418 Frank Thomas (Griffey Hot List) 3.00
419 Albert Belle (Griffey Hot List) 1.50
420 Mark McGwire (Griffey Hot List) 12.00
421 Derek Jeter (Griffey Hot List) 8.00
422 Alex Rodriguez (Griffey Hot List) 10.00
423 Juan Gonzalez (Griffey Hot List) 4.00
424 Ken Griffey Jr. (Griffey Hot List) 12.00
425 Rondell White .15
426 Darrin Fletcher .10
427 Cliff Floyd .10
428 Mike Lansing .10
429 F.P. Santangelo .10
430 Todd Hundley .10
431 Mark Clark .10
432 Pete Harnisch .10
433 Jason Isringhausen .10
434 Bobby Jones .10
435 Lance Johnson .10
436 Carlos Baerga .10
437 Mariano Duncan .10
438 David Cone .20
439 Mariano Rivera .20
440 Derek Jeter 2.00
441 Joe Girardi .10
442 Charlie Hayes .15
443 Tim Raines .15
444 Darryl Strawberry .15
445 Cecil Fielder .10
446 Ariel Prieto .10
447 Tony Batista .15
448 Brent Gates .10
449 Scott Spiezio .10
450 Mark McGwire 4.00
451 Don Wengert .10
452 Mike Lieberthal .10
453 Lenny Dykstra .10
454 Rex Hudler .10
455 Darren Daulton .10
456 Kevin Stocker .10
457 Trey Beamon .10
458 Midre Cummings .10
459 Mark Johnson .10
460 Al Martin .10
461 Kevin Elster .10
462 Jon Lieber .10
463 Jason Schmidt .10
464 Paul Wagner .10
465 Andy Benes .10
466 Alan Benes .10
467 Royce Clayton .10
468 Gary Gaetti .10
469 Curt Lyons (Diamond Debuts) .10
470 Eugene Kingsale (Diamond Debuts) .10
471 Damian Jackson (Diamond Debuts) .10
472 Wendell Magee (Diamond Dubuts) .10
473 Kevin L. Brown (Diamond Debuts) .10
474 Raul Casanova (Diamond Debuts) .10
475 Ramiro Mendoza (Diamond Debuts) .10
476 Todd Dunn (Diamond Debuts) .10
477 Chad Mottola (Diamond Debuts) .10
478 Andy Larkin (Diamond Debuts) .10
479 Jaime Bluma (Diamond Debuts) .10
480 Mac Suzuki (Diamond Debuts) .10
481 Brian Banks (Diamond Debuts) .10
482 Desi Wilson (Diamond Debuts) .10
483 Einar Diaz (Diamond Debuts) .10
484 Tom Pagnozzi .10
485 Ray Lankford .10
486 Todd Stottlemyre .10
487 Donovan Osborne .10
488 Trevor Hoffman .10
489 Chris Gomez .10
490 Ken Caminiti .20
491 John Flaherty .10
492 Tony Gwynn 1.50
493 Joey Hamilton .10
494 Rickey Henderson .40
495 Glenallen Hill .10
496 Rod Beck .10
497 Osvaldo Fernandez .10
498 Rick Wilkins .10
499 Joey Cora .10
500 Alex Rodriguez 3.00
501 Randy Johnson .60
502 Paul Sorrento .10
503 Dan Wilson .10
504 Jamie Moyer .10
505 Will Clark .25
506 Mickey Tettleton .10
507 John Burkett .10
508 Ken Hill .10
509 Mark McLemore .10
510 Juan Gonzalez 1.00
511 Bobby Witt .10
512 Carlos Delgado .50
513 Alex Gonzalez .10
514 Shawn Green .50
515 Joe Carter .10
516 Juan Guzman .10
517 Charlie O'Brien .10
518 Ed Sprague .10
519 Mike Timlin .10
520 Roger Clemens 1.00
521 Eddie Murray .25
522 Jason Dickson .10
523 Jim Leyritz .10
524 Michael Tucker .10
525 Kenny Lofton .60
526 Jimmy Key .10
527 Mel Rojas .10
528 Deion Sanders .25
529 Bartolo Colon .10
530 Matt Williams .30
531 Marquis Grissom .10
532 David Justice .25
533 *Bubba Trammell* .25
534 Moises Alou .15
535 Bobby Bonilla .10
536 Alex Fernandez .10
537 Jay Bell .10
538 Chili Davis .10
539 Jeff King .10
540 Todd Zeile .10
541 John Olerud .25
542 Jose Guillen .10
543 Derrek Lee .10
544 Dante Powell .10
545 J.T. Snow .15
546 Jeff Kent .10
547 *Jose Cruz Jr.* 2.00
548 John Wetteland .10
549 Orlando Merced .10
550 *Hideki Irabu* 1.00

1997 Upper Deck Amazing Greats

The 20-card, regular-sized insert set was included every 138 packs of 1997 Upper Deck baseball. The cards include real wood with two player shots imaged on the card front. The team logo appears in the upper right corner of the horizontal card. The cards are numbered with the "AG" prefix.

		MT
Complete Set (20):		350.00
Common Player:		8.00
1	Ken Griffey Jr.	50.00
2	Roberto Alomar	10.00
3	Alex Rodriguez	40.00
4	Paul Molitor	10.00
5	Chipper Jones	30.00
6	Tony Gwynn	25.00
7	Kenny Lofton	8.00
8	Albert Belle	8.00
9	Matt Williams	8.00
10	Frank Thomas	20.00
11	Greg Maddux	25.00
12	Sammy Sosa	30.00
13	Kirby Puckett	15.00
14	Jeff Bagwell	15.00
15	Cal Ripken Jr.	40.00
16	Manny Ramirez	15.00
17	Barry Bonds	15.00
18	Mo Vaughn	8.00
19	Eddie Murray	8.00
20	Mike Piazza	30.00

1997 Upper Deck Blue Chip Prospects

This 20-card insert was found in packs of Series II and features a die-cut design. Cards appear to have a photo slide attached to them featuring a portrait shot of the promising youngster depicted on the card. A total of 500 of each card were produced. Cards are numbered with a "BC" prefix.

		MT
Complete Set (20):		300.00
Common Player:		7.50
1	Andruw Jones	20.00
2	Derek Jeter	50.00
3	Scott Rolen	20.00
4	Manny Ramirez	20.00
5	Todd Walker	7.50
6	Rocky Coppinger	5.00
7	Nomar Garciaparra	50.00
8	Darin Erstad	10.00
9	Jermaine Dye	5.00
10	Vladimir Guerrero	30.00
11	Edgar Renteria	7.50
12	Bob Abreu	7.50
13	Karim Garcia	5.00
14	Jeff D'Amico	5.00
15	Chipper Jones	35.00
16	Todd Hollandsworth	5.00
17	Andy Pettitte	9.00
18	Ruben Rivera	5.00
19	Jason Kendall	7.50
20	Alex Rodriguez	60.00

1997 Upper Deck Game Jersey

The three-card, regular-sized set was inserted every 800 packs of Upper Deck Series I. The cards contained a square of the player's game-used jersey, and carried a "GJ" card number prefix.

		MT
Complete Set (3):		600.00
Common Player:		100.00
GJ1	Ken Griffey Jr.	400.00
GJ2	Tony Gwynn	150.00
GJ3	Rey Ordonez	100.00

1997 Upper Deck Hot Commodities

This 20-card insert from Series II features a flame pattern behind the image of the player depicted on the front of the card. Odds of finding a card were 1:13 packs. Cards are numbered with a "HC" prefix.

		MT
Complete Set (20):		70.00
Common Player:		2.50
1	Alex Rodriguez	8.00
2	Andruw Jones	2.00
3	Derek Jeter	6.00
4	Frank Thomas	5.00
5	Ken Griffey Jr.	10.00
6	Chipper Jones	6.00
7	Juan Gonzalez	4.00
8	Cal Ripken Jr.	8.00
9	John Smoltz	1.00
10	Mark McGwire	10.00
11	Barry Bonds	2.50
12	Albert Belle	1.75
13	Mike Piazza	6.00
14	Manny Ramirez	4.00
15	Mo Vaughn	1.50
16	Tony Gwynn	5.00
17	Vladimir Guerrero	3.00
18	Hideo Nomo	1.50
19	Greg Maddux	5.00
20	Kirby Puckett	2.50

1997 Upper Deck Long Distance Connection

This 20-card insert from Series II features the top home run hitters in the game. Odds of finding a card were 1:35 packs. Cards are numbered with a "LD" prefix.

		MT
Complete Set (20):		150.00
Common Player:		4.00
1	Mark McGwire	25.00
2	Brady Anderson	2.00
3	Ken Griffey Jr.	25.00
4	Albert Belle	5.00
5	Juan Gonzalez	8.00
6	Andres Galarraga	4.00
7	Jay Buhner	2.00
8	Mo Vaughn	5.00
9	Barry Bonds	6.00
10	Gary Sheffield	2.50
11	Todd Hundley	2.00
12	Frank Thomas	8.00
13	Sammy Sosa	15.00
14	Rafael Palmeiro	4.00
15	Alex Rodriguez	20.00
16	Mike Piazza	15.00
17	Ken Caminiti	3.00
18	Chipper Jones	15.00
19	Manny Ramirez	8.00
20	Andruw Jones	5.00

1997 Upper Deck Memorable Moments

This issue was a one per pack insert in special Series 1 and 2 Collector's Choice six-card retail packs. In standard 2-1/2" x 3-1/2", the cards are die-cut at top and bottom in a wave pattern. Fronts, highlighted in matte bronze foil, have action photos and a career highlight. Backs have another photo and a more complete explanation of the Memorable Moment.

		MT
Complete Set (20):		18.00
Common Player:		.50
		.50
	SERIES 1	
1	Andruw Jones	.75
2	Chipper Jones	2.00
3	Cal Ripken Jr.	2.50
4	Frank Thomas	1.00
5	Manny Ramirez	.75
6	Mike Piazza	2.00
7	Mark McGwire	3.00
8	Ken Griffey Jr.	3.00
9	Barry Bonds	.75
10	Alex Rodriguez	2.50
	SERIES 2	
1	Ken Griffey Jr.	3.00
2	Albert Belle	.60
3	Derek Jeter	2.00
4	Greg Maddux	1.50
5	Tony Gwynn	1.50
6	Ryne Sandberg	.75
7	Juan Gonzalez	1.00
8	Roger Clemens	1.50
9	Jose Cruz Jr.	.50
10	Mo Vaughn	.50

1997 Upper Deck Power Package

The 20-card, regular-sized, die-cut set was inserted every 23 packs of 1997 Upper Deck baseball. The player's name is printed in gold foil along the top border of the card face, which also features Light F/X. The die-cut cards have a silver-foil border and team-color frame with a "Power Package" logo in gold foil centered on the bottom border. The card backs have a short highlight in a brown box bordered by team colors and are numbered with the "PP" prefix.

		MT
Complete Set (20):		100.00
Common Player:		3.00
1	Ken Griffey Jr.	20.00
2	Joe Carter	2.00
3	Rafael Palmeiro	3.00
4	Jay Buhner	2.00
5	Sammy Sosa	12.00
6	Fred McGriff	2.50
7	Jeff Bagwell	5.00
8	Albert Belle	4.00
9	Matt Williams	3.00
10	Mark McGwire	20.00
11	Gary Sheffield	2.00
12	Tim Salmon	3.00
13	Ryan Klesko	2.00
14	Manny Ramirez	5.00
15	Mike Piazza	12.00
16	Barry Bonds	5.00
17	Mo Vaughn	4.00
18	Jose Canseco	5.00
19	Juan Gonzalez	6.00
20	Frank Thomas	6.00

1997 Upper Deck Power Package Jumbos

Unlike the regular Power Package inserts found in Series I packs, these jumbo versions are not die-cut. The 5" x 7" jumbos are found one per retail foil box of Series I. Cards are numbered with a "PP" prefix.

		MT
Complete Set (20):		75.00
Common Player:		1.75
1	Ken Griffey Jr.	9.00
2	Joe Carter	1.75
3	Rafael Palmeiro	1.75
4	Jay Buhner	1.75
5	Sammy Sosa	6.00
6	Fred McGriff	2.50
7	Jeff Bagwell	5.00
8	Albert Belle	3.50
9	Matt Williams	1.75
10	Mark McGwire	9.00
11	Gary Sheffield	1.75
12	Tim Salmon	1.75
13	Ryan Klesko	3.00
14	Manny Ramirez	5.00
15	Mike Piazza	7.00
16	Barry Bonds	6.00
17	Mo Vaughn	4.00
18	Jose Canseco	3.00
19	Juan Gonzalez	6.00
20	Frank Thomas	5.00

1997 Upper Deck Predictor

A new concept in interactive cards was UD's Series II Predictor inserts. Each player's card has four scratch-off baseball bats at the top-right. Under each bat is printed a specific accomplishment - hit for cycle, CG shutout, etc. - If the player attained that goal during the '97 season, and if the collector had scratched off the correct bat among the four, the Predictor card could be redeemed (with $2) for a premium TV cel card of the player. Thus if the player made one of his goals, the collector had a 25% chance of choosing the right bat. Two goals gave a 50% chance, etc. The Predictor cards have color action photos of the players at the left end of the horizontal format. The background at left and bottom is a red scorecard motif. Behind the bats is a black-and-white stadium scene. Backs repeat the red scorecard design with contest rules printed in white. A (W) in the checklist here indicates the player won one or more of his goals making his cards eligible for redemption. The redemption period ended Nov. 22, 1997. Values shown are for unscratched cards.

		MT
Complete Set (30):		25.00
Common Player:		.50
Values for Unscratched Cards		
1	Andruw Jones	.50
2	Chipper Jones	1.50
3	Greg Maddux (W)	1.50
4	Fred McGriff (W)	.50
5	John Smoltz (W)	.50
6	Brady Anderson (W)	.50
7	Cal Ripken Jr. (W)	2.50
8	Mo Vaughn (W)	.50
9	Sammy Sosa	2.00
10	Albert Belle (W)	.75
11	Frank Thomas	1.00
12	Kenny Lofton (W)	.50
13	Jim Thome	.50
14	Dante Bichette (W)	.50
15	Andres Galarraga	.50
16	Gary Sheffield	.50
17	Hideo Nomo (W)	.50
18	Mike Piazza (W)	2.00
19	Derek Jeter (W)	2.00
20	Bernie Williams	.50
21	Mark McGwire (W)	3.00
22	Ken Caminiti (W)	.50
23	Tony Gwynn (W)	1.50
24	Barry Bonds (W)	.75
25	Jay Buhner (W)	.50
26	Ken Griffey Jr. (W)	3.00
27	Alex Rodriguez (W)	2.50
28	Juan Gonzalez (W)	1.00
29	Dean Palmer (W)	.50
30	Roger Clemens (W)	1.00

1997 Upper Deck Predictor Prize Cards

Persons who redeemed winning Predictor scratch-off cards prior to the Nov. 22, 1997, deadline received a premium version of that player's card. A $2 per card handling fee was charged. The Predictor prize cards are in a format similar to the scratch-off cards, with a red background on front and back depicting the motif of a baseball score card. The prize cards are printed on plastic in 3-1/2" x 2-1/2" format. Fronts have a player portrait photo at left. At right is a large semi-circular mirrored window with an action photo visible when held to the light. Backs have a few stats, copyright data, logos, etc., with a reverse image in the window. Card fronts were covered with a sheet of peel-off protection plastic. The prize cards are numbered on back with a "P" prefix.

		MT
Complete Set (22):		250.00
Common Player:		3.00
3	Greg Maddux	16.00
4	Fred McGriff	4.50
5	John Smoltz	4.50
6	Brady Anderson	3.00
7	Cal Ripken Jr.	24.00
8	Mo Vaughn	6.00
11	Frank Thomas	15.00
12	Kenny Lofton	6.00
14	Dante Bichette	3.50
17	Hideo Nomo	6.00
18	Mike Piazza	18.00
19	Derek Jeter	16.00
21	Mark McGwire	30.00
22	Ken Caminiti	4.50
23	Tony Gwynn	15.00
24	Barry Bonds	7.50
25	Jay Buhner	3.00
26	Ken Griffey Jr.	30.00
27	Alex Rodriguez	24.00
28	Juan Gonzalez	15.00
29	Dean Palmer	3.00
30	Roger Clemens	12.00

1997 Upper Deck Rock Solid Foundation

The 20-card, regular-sized set was inserted every seven packs of 1997 Upper Deck baseball. The card fronts feature rainbow foil with the player's name in silver foil along the top border. The team logo appears in gold foil in the lower right corner with "Rock Solid Foundation" also printed in gold foil over a marbled background. The card backs have the same marbled background with a close-up shot on the upper half. A short text is also included and the cards are numbered with the "RS" prefix.

		MT
Complete Set (20):		40.00
Common Player:		1.25
1	Alex Rodriguez	12.00
2	Rey Ordonez	1.50
3	Derek Jeter	9.50
4	Darin Erstad	2.50
5	Chipper Jones	8.00
6	Johnny Damon	1.25
7	Ryan Klesko	1.25
8	Charles Johnson	1.25
9	Andy Pettitte	2.00
10	Manny Ramirez	4.00
11	Ivan Rodriguez	3.25
12	Jason Kendall	1.50
13	Rondell White	1.50
14	Alex Ochoa	1.25
15	Javy Lopez	1.50
16	Pedro Martinez	3.25
17	Carlos Delgado	2.50
18	Paul Wilson	1.25
19	Alan Benes	1.25
20	Raul Mondesi	1.25

1997 Upper Deck Run Producers

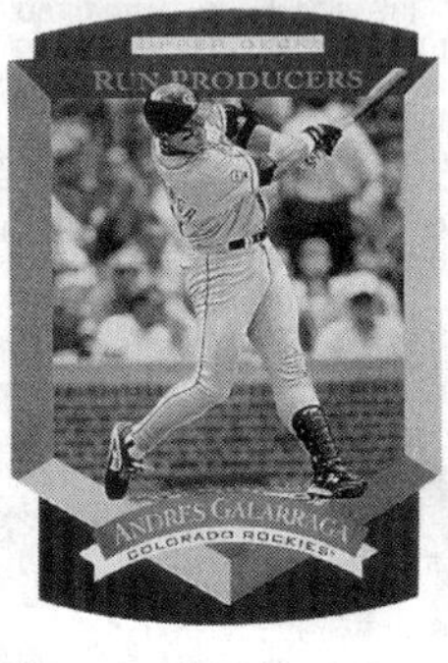

A 24-card insert found in Series II, Run Producers salutes the top offensive players in the game. Cards were inserted 1:69 packs. Die-cut into a shield shape, the cards have an action photo in a home-plate shaped center section and several colors of foil highlights. Backs have recent stats and career highlights. Cards are numbered with a "RP" prefix.

		MT
Complete Set (24):		250.00
Common Player:		4.50
1	Ken Griffey Jr.	36.00
2	Barry Bonds	9.00
3	Albert Belle	8.00
4	Mark McGwire	36.00
5	Frank Thomas	15.00
6	Juan Gonzalez	12.00
7	Brady Anderson	4.50
8	Andres Galarraga	7.00
9	Rafael Palmeiro	7.00
10	Alex Rodriguez	32.00
11	Jay Buhner	4.50
12	Gary Sheffield	4.50
13	Sammy Sosa	24.00
14	Dante Bichette	4.50
15	Mike Piazza	24.00
16	Manny Ramirez	12.00
17	Kenny Lofton	7.50
18	Mo Vaughn	7.50
19	Tim Salmon	4.50
20	Chipper Jones	24.00
21	Jim Thome	6.00
22	Ken Caminiti	4.50
23	Jeff Bagwell	15.00
24	Paul Molitor	7.50

1997 Upper Deck Star Attractions

These die-cut cards were inserted one per pack of retail "Memorabila Madness" Collector's Choice (#11-20) and Upper Deck (#1-10) cards. Fronts have action photos, backs have portrait photos.

		MT
Complete Set (20):		25.00
Common Player:		.50
1	Ken Griffey Jr.	4.00
2	Barry Bonds	1.00
3	Jeff Bagwell	1.00
4	Nomar Garciaparra	2.00
5	Tony Gwynn	2.00
6	Roger Clemens	1.50
7	Chipper Jones	2.50
8	Tino Martinez	.50
9	Albert Belle	.75
10	Kenny Lofton	.75
11	Alex Rodriguez	3.00
12	Mark McGwire	4.00
13	Cal Ripken Jr.	3.00
14	Larry Walker	.75
15	Mike Piazza	2.50
16	Frank Thomas	2.00
17	Juan Gonzalez	1.00
18	Greg Maddux	1.50
19	Jose Cruz Jr.	.50
20	Mo Vaughn	.75

1997 Upper Deck Ticket to Stardom

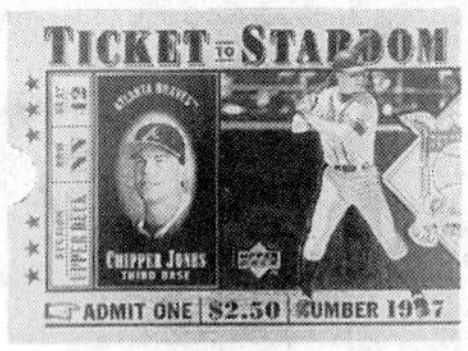

The 20-card, regular-sized, die-cut set was inserted every 34 packs of 1997 Upper Deck baseball. Card fronts have a gold-foil border on three sides with a portrait and action photo. Half of the player's league emblem appears on either the left or right border of the horizontal cards, as two cards can be placed together to form a "ticket." The card backs feature an in-depth text with the same headshot as the card front and are numbered with the "TS" prefix.

		MT
Complete Set (20):		90.00
Common Player:		2.50
1	Chipper Jones	15.00
2	Jermaine Dye	2.00
3	Rey Ordonez	2.50
4	Alex Ochoa	2.00
5	Derek Jeter	20.00
6	Ruben Rivera	2.00
7	Billy Wagner	2.50
8	Jason Kendall	2.50
9	Darin Erstad	4.00
10	Alex Rodriguez	25.00
11	Bob Abreu	2.50
12	Richard Hidalgo	2.00
13	Karim Garcia	2.00
14	Andruw Jones	4.00
15	Carlos Delgado	3.00
16	Rocky Coppinger	2.00
17	Jeff D'Amico	2.00
18	Johnny Damon	2.00
19	John Wasdin	2.00
20	Manny Ramirez	8.00

1997 Upper Deck Ticket to Stardom Retail

Double-size "full ticket" versions of Upper Deck's Series 1 Ticket to Stardom inserts were produced as an incentive for collectors to buy a boxed three-pack of Collector's Choice cards in a special retail-only packaging. Unlike the insert Ticket cards which feature only one player and measure 3-1/2" x 2-1/2", the retail version measures 5" x 2-1/2" and features two players. The basic format of the retail cards follows the inserts, with gold-foil background, a vignetted player portrait at one end with an action photo toward center and a league logo at center. Arrangement of graphics on the retail ticket prevent unscrupulous persons from cutting them in half and passing them off as the more valuable insert cards. Backs repeat the player portrait photo and present a career summary. Cards are numbered in the upper-left corner. Seven players were dropped from the original Ticket checklist and replaced in the retail issue with new faces. Cards are numbered with a "TS" prefix.

		MT
Complete Set (10):		55.00
Common Player:		4.00
1	Chipper Jones, Andruw Jones	12.00
2	Rey Ordonez, Kevin Orie	4.00
3	Derek Jeter, Nomar Garciaparra	12.00
4	Billy Wagner, Jason Kendall	4.00
5	Darin Erstad, Alex Rodriguez	15.00
6	Bob Abreu, Jose Guillen	4.00
7	Wilton Guerrero, Vladimir Guerrero	9.00
8	Carlos Delgado, Rocky Coppinger	4.00
9	Jason Dickson, Johnny Damon	4.00
10	Bartolo Colon, Manny Ramirez	8.00

1997 Upper Deck Florida Marlins World Champions

This special large-format (5" x 3-1/2") card commemorates the 1997 World Series win by the Florida Marlins. In keeping with the U.S. flag background on both front and back, the card is cut in a wave pattern. Front is printed on prismatic foil and features three player action photos and the World Series logo. Back is conventionally printed with three more player photos, details of the Series victory and a serial number from within an editon of 5,000. The card was a retail exclusive.

	MT
	12.00
Moises Alou, Bobby Bonilla, Kevin Brown, Alex Fernandez, Charles Johnson, Gary Sheffield	

1997 Upper Deck Ken Griffey Jr. Highlight Reel

Using its trademarked Diamond Vision technology to provide action scenes on these 5" x 3-1/2" plastic cards. Each card has two scenes which go into action as the angle of vision is changed. Cards were sold in retail outlets in plastic blister packs at a suggested $9.99 price.

		MT
Complete Set (5):		50.00
Common Card:		10.00
1	Record Setter (Ken Griffey Jr.)	10.00
2	Long Distance Connection (Ken Griffey Jr.)	10.00
3	Home Run Derby (Ken Griffey Jr.)	10.00
4	Swing for the Ages (Ken Griffey Jr.)	10.00
5	Postseason Power (Ken Griffey Jr.)	10.00

1997 Upper Deck Ken Griffey Jr. Standup

This 6" x 11" cardboard standup figure commemorates Junior's new major league record for home runs through the month of May: 23. The figure was found in retail-only collectors' kits along with eight packs of Collector's Choice cards and a jumbo version of one of Griffey's Clearly Dominant cards, with a sticker price of about $15.

	MT
Ken Griffey Jr.	6.00

1997 Upper Deck Tony Gwynn Commemorative

Tony Gwynn's record-tying eighth batting title in 1997 is commemorated on this 3-1/2" x 4-7/8" card marketed by UD Authenticated. The card has a batting pose on front with a die-cut background of bats citing the year and average of each of his batting titles. The back has three color photos and is numbered within an edition of 2,500.

	MT
Tony Gwynn	10.00

1997 Upper Deck Home Team Heroes

These large-format cards were issued both as a 12-card boxed set (original price about $20) and as a blister-pack insert to enhance the sales of special Collector's Choice team sets at Wal-Mart. Each $4.99 pack contains a 14-card team set and a Home Team Heroes card of one of 12 teams, plus a random assortment of Collector's Choice cards. The Heroes cards are 5" x 3-1/2" with a die-cut pattern at top. Fronts are rendered in team colors with two player action photos superimposed on a background of the players' home ballpark. The ballpark scene is executed in etched silver foil and there are silver-foil graphics around the card front. Backs are conventionally printed with small photos and a few sentences about each player.

		MT
Complete Set (12):		15.00
Common Player:		1.50
1	Alex Rodriguez, Ken Griffey Jr.	3.50
2	Bernie Williams, Derek Jeter	2.50
3	Bernard Gilkey, Randy Hundley	1.50
4	Hideo Nomo, Mike Piazza	2.00
5	Andruw Jones, Chipper Jones	2.50
6	John Smoltz, Greg Maddux	2.25
7	Mike Mussina, Cal Ripken Jr.	2.50
8	Andres Galarraga, Dante Bichette	1.50
9	Juan Gonzalez, Ivan Rodriguez	2.25
10	Albert Belle, Frank Thomas	1.50
11	Jim Thome, Manny Ramirez	2.00
12	Ken Caminiti, Tony Gwynn	2.25

1997 Upper Deck Jackie Robinson Jumbos

The nine Jackie Robinson commemorative cards which lead off the '97 Upper Deck set were also issued in a large-format (3-1/2" x 5") version as a complete boxed set. The jumbos are printed in sepia tones on gold-foil backgrounds and, like the standard-size cards, are highlighted with silver-foil graphics on front. Backs are also identical to the regular cards. Complete sets only were sold in a gold-foil stamped box with the 50th anniversary logo.

		MT
Complete Set (10):		20.00
Common Player:		3.00
1	The Beginnings (Jackie Robinson)	3.00
2	Breaking the Barrier (Jackie Robinson)	3.00
3	The MVP Season (Jackie Robinson)	3.00
4	The '51 Season (Jackie Robinson)	3.00
5	The '52 and '53 Seasons (Jackie Robinson)	3.00
6	The '54 Season (Jackie Robinson)	3.00
7	The '55 Season (Jackie Robinson)	3.00
8	The '56 Season (Jackie Robinson)	3.00
9	The Hall of Fame (Jackie Robinson)	3.00
--	Checklist	.10

1997 Upper Deck Jackie Robinson Tribute

This retail exclusive card commemorates the 50th anniversary of Robinson's major league debut. The 5" x 3-1/2" card has a tombstone contour top edge and a sepia photo on front of Robinson at bat. Also on front are 50th anniversary and UD logos and a large gold-foil facsimile autograph. Back has a photo of Robinson sliding into home plate, his career stats and a serial number from within an edition of 5,000.

	MT
Jackie Robinson	10.00

1997 Upper Deck UD3

Released in April, this 60-card set is broken down into three different 20-card subsets, each utilizing a different print technology. There are 20 PROmotion cards (Light F/X cards featuring a special foil stock), 20 Future Impact cards (Cel-Chrome cards that feature a 3-D image on transparent chromium), and 20 Homerun Heroes (Electric Wood cards printed on an embossed wood/paper stock). Cards were sold in three-card packs (with one subset card per pack) for $3.99 each. Inserts include Superb Signatures, Generation Next and Marquee Attraction.

		MT
Complete Set (60):		50.00
Common Player:		.40
Wax Box:		80.00
1	Mark McGwire	6.00
2	Brady Anderson	.50
3	Ken Griffey Jr.	6.00
4	Albert Belle	1.00
5	Andres Galarraga	.75
6	Juan Gonzalez	1.50
7	Jay Buhner	.50
8	Mo Vaughn	1.00
9	Barry Bonds	1.25
10	Gary Sheffield	.75
11	Todd Hundley	.40
12	Ellis Burks	.40
13	Ken Caminiti	.75
14	Vinny Castilla	.40
15	Sammy Sosa	3.00
16	Frank Thomas	2.00
17	Rafael Palmeiro	.75
18	Mike Piazza	3.00
19	Matt Williams	.60
20	Eddie Murray	.75
21	Roger Clemens	2.00
22	Tim Salmon	.50
23	Robin Ventura	.50
24	Ron Gant	.40
25	Cal Ripken Jr.	5.00
26	Bernie Williams	1.00
27	Hideo Nomo	.75
28	Ivan Rodriguez	1.50
29	John Smoltz	.50
30	Paul Molitor	1.00
31	Greg Maddux	2.50
32	Raul Mondesi	.50
33	Roberto Alomar	1.00
34	Barry Larkin	.60
35	Tony Gwynn	2.50
36	Jim Thome	.60
37	Kenny Lofton	1.00
38	Jeff Bagwell	1.50
39	Ozzie Smith	.75
40	Kirby Puckett	1.50
41	Andruw Jones	1.00
42	Vladimir Guerrero	1.50
43	Edgar Renteria	.40
44	Luis Castillo	.40
45	Darin Erstad	.75
46	Nomar Garciaparra	3.00
47	Todd Greene	.40
48	Jason Kendall	.40
49	Rey Ordonez	.40
50	Alex Rodriguez	5.00
51	Manny Ramirez	1.50
52	Todd Walker	.40
53	Ruben Rivera	.40
54	Andy Pettitte	.60
55	Derek Jeter	3.00
56	Todd Hollandsworth	.40
57	Rocky Coppinger	.40
58	Scott Rolen	1.50
59	Jermaine Dye	.40
60	Chipper Jones	3.00

1997 Upper Deck UD3 Generation Next

A 20-card insert saluting the game's up-and-coming stars with two different photos of the player on each card front. Odds of finding these cards were 1:11 packs. Cards are numbered with a "GN" prefix.

		MT
Complete Set (20):		125.00
Common Player:		4.00
1	Alex Rodriguez	25.00
2	Vladimir Guerrero	10.00
3	Luis Castillo	4.00
4	Rey Ordonez	4.00
5	Andruw Jones	5.00
6	Darin Erstad	5.00
7	Edgar Renteria	4.00
8	Jason Kendall	4.00
9	Jermaine Dye	4.00
10	Chipper Jones	20.00
11	Rocky Coppinger	4.00
12	Andy Pettitte	5.00
13	Todd Greene	4.00
14	Todd Hollandsworth	4.00
15	Derek Jeter	20.00
16	Ruben Rivera	4.00
17	Todd Walker	4.00
18	Nomar Garciaparra	15.00
19	Scott Rolen	10.00
20	Manny Ramirez	10.00

1997 Upper Deck UD3 Marquee Attraction

The game's top names are featured in this insert set, inserted 1:144 packs. Cards featured a peel-off protector that would expose a holographic image on the card fronts. Cards are numbered with a "MA" prefix.

		MT
Complete Set (10):		275.00
Common Player:		15.00
1	Ken Griffey Jr.	60.00
2	Mark McGwire	60.00
3	Juan Gonzalez	15.00
4	Barry Bonds	15.00
5	Frank Thomas	25.00
6	Albert Belle	12.00
7	Mike Piazza	40.00
8	Cal Ripken Jr.	50.00
9	Mo Vaughn	10.00
10	Alex Rodriguez	50.00

1997 Upper Deck UD3 Superb Signatures

Autographed cards of Ken Griffey Jr., Ken Caminiti, Vladimir Guerrero and Derek Jeter were inserted 1:1,500 packs.

		MT
Complete Set (4):		800.00
Common Autograph:		50.00
1	Ken Caminiti	50.00
2	Ken Griffey Jr.	500.00
3	Vladimir Guerrero	150.00
4	Derek Jeter	300.00

1997 Upper Deck/ Pepsi Mariners

This team set, sponsored by Pepsi, was given away to the first 20,000 fans attending the July 12 game at the Kingdome. Format of the cards is similar to UD's regular 1997 issue, with borderless color photos on front and back. At bottom-front is a Mariners-blue foil area with the player identification. Backs differ from the regular '97 UD cards in the use of a "P" prefix to the card number and the inclusion of a Pepsi logo at lower-left.

		MT
Complete Set (21):		20.00
Common Player:		.50
1	Joey Cora	.50
2	Ken Griffey Jr.	10.00
3	Jay Buhner	1.00
4	Alex Rodriguez	9.00
5	Norm Charlton	.50
6	Edgar Martinez	.75
7	Paul Sorrento	.50
8	Randy Johnson	2.00
9	Rich Amaral	.50
10	Russ Davis	.50
11	Greg McCarthy	.50
12	Jamie Moyer	.50
13	Jeff Fassero	.50
14	Scott Sanders	.50
15	Dan Wilson	.50
16	Mike Blowers	.50
17	Bobby Ayala	.50
18	Brent Gates	.50
19	John Marzano	.50
20	Lou Piniella	.50
---	Pepsi header card/ coupon	.05

1997 Upper Deck/ Shimano

Two ballplayers are included with four professional fishermen in this set produced by Upper Deck as a premium with the purchase of Shimano fishing reels. Fronts have pictures of the fishermen displaying their trophy. Backs have a portrait photo, baseball and fishing stats and data.

		MT
Complete Set (6):		12.00
Common Player:		1.00
1	Bob Izumi	1.00
2	Jimmy Houston	1.00
3	Jose Wejebe	1.00
4	Larry Dahlberg	1.00
5	Jay Buhner	3.00
6	Tony Gwynn	8.00

1998 Upper Deck

Upper Deck Baseball was released in three series. Series One consisted of 270 base cards, with five subsets. Inserts included A Piece of the Action, Amazing Greats, National Pride, Ken Griffey Jr.'s Home Run Chronicles and 10th Anniversary Preview. The 270-card second series also had five subsets. Inserts include Prime Nine, Ken Griffey Jr.'s Home Run Chronicles, Tape Measure Titans, Blue Chip Prospects, Clearly Dominant and A Piece of the Action. The third series, Upper Deck Rookie Edition, had a 210-card base set. Insert sets were Ken Griffey Jr. Game Jersey, Game Jersey Rookie Cards, Unparalleled, Destination Stardom, All-Star Credentials and Retrospectives.

		MT
Complete Set (750):		150.00
Complete Series 1 Set (270):		30.00
Complete Series 2 Set (270):		30.00
Complete Series 3 Set (210):		90.00
Common Emminent Prestige (601-630):		1.00
Common Player:		.10
Series 1,2 & 3 Box:		55.00
1	Tino Martinez (History in the Making)	.10
2	Jimmy Key (History in the Making)	.10
3	Jay Buhner (History in the Making)	.10
4	Mark Gardner (History in the Making)	.10
5	Greg Maddux (History in the Making)	.75
6	Pedro Martinez (History in the Making)	.40
7	Hideo Nomo, Shigetosi Hasegawa (History in the Making)	.20
8	Sammy Sosa (History in the Making)	1.50
9	Mark McGwire (Griffey Hot List)	4.00
10	Ken Griffey Jr. (Griffey Hot List)	4.00
11	Larry Walker (Griffey Hot List)	.40
12	Tino Martinez (Griffey Hot List)	.20
13	Mike Piazza (Griffey Hot List)	2.00
14	Jose Cruz, Jr. (Griffey Hot List)	.50
15	Tony Gwynn (Griffey Hot List)	1.00
16	Greg Maddux (Griffey Hot List)	1.00
17	Roger Clemens (Griffey Hot List)	1.50
18	Alex Rodriguez (Griffey Hot List)	1.50
19	Shigetosi Hasegawa	.10
20	Eddie Murray	.25
21	Jason Dickson	.10
22	Darin Erstad	.40
23	Chuck Finley	.10
24	Dave Hollins	.10
25	Garret Anderson	.10
26	Michael Tucker	.10
27	Kenny Lofton	.75
28	Javier Lopez	.20
29	Fred McGriff	.25
30	Greg Maddux	1.50
31	Jeff Blauser	.10
32	John Smoltz	.20
33	Mark Wohlers	.10
34	Scott Erickson	.10
35	Jimmy Key	.10
36	Harold Baines	.10
37	Randy Myers	.10
38	B.J. Surhoff	.10
39	Eric Davis	.10
40	Rafael Palmeiro	.40
41	Jeffrey Hammonds	.10
42	Mo Vaughn	.75
43	Tom Gordon	.10
44	Tim Naehring	.10
45	Darren Bragg	.10
46	Aaron Sele	.10
47	Troy O'Leary	.10
48	John Valentin	.10

49	Doug Glanville	.10
50	Ryne Sandberg	.75
51	Steve Trachsel	.10
52	Mark Grace	.25
53	Kevin Foster	.10
54	Kevin Tapani	.10
55	Kevin Orie	.10
56	Lyle Mouton	.10
57	Ray Durham	.10
58	Jaime Navarro	.10
59	Mike Cameron	.10
60	Albert Belle	.75
61	Doug Drabek	.10
62	Chris Snopek	.10
63	Eddie Taubensee	.10
64	Terry Pendleton	.10
65	Barry Larkin	.30
66	Willie Greene	.10
67	Deion Sanders	.20
68	Pokey Reese	.10
69	Jeff Shaw	.10
70	Jim Thome	.40
71	Orel Hershiser	.10
72	Omar Vizquel	.10
73	Brian Giles	.20
74	David Justice	.25
75	Bartolo Colon	.20
76	Sandy Alomar Jr.	.20
77	Neifi Perez	.10
78	Eric Young	.15
79	Vinny Castilla	.15
80	Dante Bichette	.20
81	Quinton McCracken	.10
82	Jamey Wright	.10
83	John Thomson	.10
84	Damion Easley	.10
85	Justin Thompson	.10
86	Willie Blair	.10
87	Raul Casanova	.10
88	Bobby Higginson	.10
89	Bubba Trammell	.15
90	Tony Clark	.40
91	Livan Hernandez	.20
92	Charles Johnson	.10
93	Edgar Renteria	.10
94	Alex Fernandez	.10
95	Gary Sheffield	.25
96	Moises Alou	.20
97	Tony Saunders	.20
98	Robb Nen	.10
99	Darryl Kile	.10
100	Craig Biggio	.40
101	Chris Holt	.10
102	Bob Abreu	.10
103	Luis Gonzalez	.10
104	Billy Wagner	.10
105	Brad Ausmus	.10
106	Chili Davis	.10
107	Tim Belcher	.10
108	Dean Palmer	.10
109	Jeff King	.10
110	Jose Rosado	.10
111	Mike Macfarlane	.10
112	Jay Bell	.10
113	Todd Worrell	.10
114	Chan Ho Park	.10
115	Raul Mondesi	.25
116	Brett Butler	.10
117	Greg Gagne	.10
118	Hideo Nomo	.25
119	Todd Zeile	.10
120	Eric Karros	.20
121	Cal Eldred	.10
122	Jeff D'Amico	.10
123	Antone Williamson	.10
124	Doug Jones	.10
125	Dave Nilsson	.10
126	Gerald Williams	.10
127	Fernando Vina	.10
128	Ron Coomer	.10
129	Matt Lawton	.10
130	Paul Molitor	.40
131	Todd Walker	.10
132	Rick Aguilera	.10
133	Brad Radke	.10
134	Bob Tewksbury	.10
135	Vladimir Guerrero	1.00
136	Tony Gwynn (Define The Game)	.75
137	Roger Clemens (Define The Game)	.75
138	Dennis Eckersley (Define The Game)	.10
139	Brady Anderson (Define The Game)	.10
140	Ken Griffey Jr. (Define The Game)	1.50
141	Derek Jeter (Define The Game)	1.50
142	Ken Caminiti (Define The Game)	.15
143	Frank Thomas (Define The Game)	.75
144	Barry Bonds (Define The Game)	.40
145	Cal Ripken Jr. (Define The Game)	1.25
146	Alex Rodriguez (Define The Game)	1.25
147	Greg Maddux (Define The Game)	1.00
148	Kenny Lofton (Define The Game)	.40
149	Mike Piazza (Define The Game)	1.50
150	Mark McGwire (Define The Game)	2.00
151	Andruw Jones (Define The Game)	.75
152	Rusty Greer (Define The Game)	.10
153	F.P. Santangelo (Define The Game)	.10
154	Mike Lansing	.10
155	Lee Smith	.10
156	Carlos Perez	.10
157	Pedro Martinez	.75
158	Ryan McGuire	.10
159	F.P. Santangelo	.10
160	Rondell White	.20
161	*Takashi Kashiwada*	.40
162	Butch Huskey	.10
163	Edgardo Alfonzo	.25
164	John Franco	.10
165	Todd Hundley	.20
166	Rey Ordonez	.10
167	Armando Reynoso	.10
168	John Olerud	.25
169	Bernie Williams	.50
170	Andy Pettitte	.40
171	Wade Boggs	.25
172	Paul O'Neill	.25
173	Cecil Fielder	.10
174	Charlie Hayes	.10
175	David Cone	.20
176	Hideki Irabu	.75
177	Mark Bellhorn	.10
178	Steve Karsay	.10
179	Damon Mashore	.10
180	Jason McDonald	.10
181	Scott Spiezio	.10
182	Ariel Prieto	.10
183	Jason Giambi	.10
184	Wendell Magee	.10
185	Rico Brogna	.10
186	Garrett Stephenson	.10
187	Wayne Gomes	.10
188	Ricky Bottalico	.10
189	Mickey Morandini	.10
190	Mike Lieberthal	.10
191	*Kevin Polcovich*	.25
192	Francisco Cordova	.10
193	Kevin Young	.10
194	Jon Lieber	.10
195	Kevin Elster	.10
196	Tony Womack	.10
197	Lou Collier	.10
198	*Mike Defelice*	.20
199	Gary Gaetti	.10
200	Dennis Eckersley	.10
201	Alan Benes	.10
202	Willie McGee	.10
203	Ron Gant	.15
204	Fernando Valenzuela	.10
205	Mark McGwire	4.00
206	Archi Cianfrocco	.10
207	Andy Ashby	.10
208	Steve Finley	.10
209	Quilvio Veras	.10
210	Ken Caminiti	.25
211	Rickey Henderson	.50
212	Joey Hamilton	.10
213	Derrek Lee	.10
214	Bill Mueller	.10
215	Shawn Estes	.10
216	J.T. Snow	.10
217	Mark Gardner	.10
218	Terry Mulholland	.10
219	Dante Powell	.10
220	Jeff Kent	.10
221	Jamie Moyer	.10
222	Joey Cora	.10
223	Jeff Fassero	.10
224	Dennis Martinez	.10
225	Ken Griffey Jr.	4.00
226	Edgar Martinez	.10
227	Russ Davis	.10
228	Dan Wilson	.10
229	Will Clark	.25
230	Ivan Rodriguez	.75
231	Benji Gil	.10
232	Lee Stevens	.10
233	Mickey Tettleton	.10
234	Julio Santana	.10
235	Rusty Greer	.10
236	Bobby Witt	.10
237	Ed Sprague	.10
238	Pat Hentgen	.10
239	Kevin Escobar	.10
240	Joe Carter	.10
241	Carlos Delgado	.50
242	Shannon Stewart	.10
243	Benito Santiago	.10
244	Tino Martinez (Season Highlights)	.10
245	Ken Griffey Jr. (Season Highlights)	1.50
246	Kevin Brown (Season Highlights)	.15
247	Ryne Sandberg (Season Highlights)	.40
248	Mo Vaughn (Season Highlights)	.40
249	Darryl Hamilton (Season Highlights)	.10
250	Randy Johnson (Season Highlights)	.30
251	Steve Finley (Season Highlights)	.10
252	Bobby Higginson (Season Highlights)	.10
253	Brett Tomko (Star Rookie)	.10
254	Mark Kotsay (Star Rookie)	.25
255	Jose Guillen (Star Rookie)	.25
256	Elieser Marrero (Star Rookie)	.10
257	Dennis Reyes (Star Rookie)	.25
258	Richie Sexson (Star Rookie)	.15
259	Pat Cline (Star Rookie)	.15
260	Todd Helton (Star Rookie)	.75
261	Juan Melo (Star Rookie)	.10
262	Matt Morris (Star Rookie)	.10
263	Jeremi Gonzalez (Star Rookie)	.20
264	Jeff Abbott (Star Rookie)	.10
265	Aaron Boone (Star Rookie)	.10
266	Todd Dunwoody (Star Rookie)	.10
267	Jaret Wright (Star Rookie)	.25
268	Derrick Gibson (Star Rookie)	.10
269	Mario Valdez (Star Rookie)	.10
270	Fernando Tatis (Star Rookie)	.25
271	Craig Counsell (Star Rookie)	.10
272	Brad Rigby (Star Rookie)	.10
273	Danny Clyburn (Star Rookie)	.10
274	Brian Rose (Star Rookie)	.25
275	Miguel Tejada (Star Rookie)	.25
276	Jason Varitek (Star Rookie)	.20
277	*David Dellucci* (Star Rookie)	.50
278	Michael Coleman (Star Rookie)	.10
279	Adam Riggs (Star Rookie)	.10
280	Ben Grieve (Star Rookie)	.25
281	Brad Fullmer (Star Rookie)	.10
282	Ken Cloude (Star Rookie)	.25
283	Tom Evans (Star Rookie)	.10
284	*Kevin Millwood* (Star Rookie)	4.00
285	Paul Konerko (Star Rookie)	.75
286	Juan Encarnacion (Star Rookie)	.10
287	Chris Carpenter (Star Rookie)	.10
288	Tom Fordham (Star Rookie)	.10
289	Gary DiSarcina	.10
290	Tim Salmon	.30
291	Troy Percival	.10
292	Todd Greene	.10
293	Ken Hill	.10
294	Dennis Springer	.10
295	Jim Edmonds	.20
296	Allen Watson	.10
297	Brian Anderson	.10
298	Keith Lockhart	.10
299	Tom Glavine	.25
300	Chipper Jones	2.00
301	Randall Simon	.10
302	Mark Lemke	.10
303	Ryan Klesko	.25
304	Denny Neagle	.10
305	Andruw Jones	.50
306	Mike Mussina	.60
307	Brady Anderson	.15
308	Chris Hoiles	.10
309	Mike Bordick	.10
310	Cal Ripken Jr.	2.50
311	Geronimo Berroa	.10
312	Armando Benitez	.10
313	Roberto Alomar	.60
314	Tim Wakefield	.10
315	Reggie Jefferson	.10
316	Jeff Frye	.10
317	Scott Hatteberg	.10
318	Steve Avery	.10
319	Robinson Checo	.10
320	Nomar Garciaparra	2.00
321	Lance Johnson	.10
322	Tyler Houston	.10
323	Mark Clark	.10
324	Terry Adams	.10
325	Sammy Sosa	2.00
326	Scott Servais	.10
327	Manny Alexander	.10
328	Norberto Martin	.10
329	*Scott Eyre*	.25
330	Frank Thomas	1.00
331	Robin Ventura	.20
332	Matt Karchner	.10
333	Keith Foulke	.10
334	James Baldwin	.10
335	Chris Stynes	.10
336	Bret Boone	.10
337	Jon Nunnally	.10
338	Dave Burba	.10
339	Eduardo Perez	.10
340	Reggie Sanders	.10
341	Mike Remlinger	.10
342	Pat Watkins	.10
343	Chad Ogea	.10
344	John Smiley	.10
345	Kenny Lofton	.75
346	Jose Mesa	.10
347	Charles Nagy	.10
348	Bruce Aven	.10
349	Enrique Wilson	.10
350	Manny Ramirez	1.00
351	Jerry DiPoto	.10
352	Ellis Burks	.10
353	Kirt Manwaring	.10
354	Vinny Castilla	.20
355	Larry Walker	.50
356	Kevin Ritz	.10
357	Pedro Astacio	.10
358	Scott Sanders	.10
359	Deivi Cruz	.10
360	Brian L. Hunter	.10
361	Pedro Martinez (History in the Making)	.40
362	Tom Glavine (History in the Making)	.10
363	Willie McGee (History in the Making)	.10
364	J.T. Snow (History in the Making)	.10
365	Rusty Greer (History in the Making)	.10
366	Mike Grace (History in the Making)	.10
367	Tony Clark (History in the Making)	.20
368	Ben Grieve (History in the Making)	.75
369	Gary Sheffield (History in the Making)	.20
370	Joe Oliver	.10
371	Todd Jones	.10
372	*Frank Catalanotto*	.20
373	Brian Moehler	.10
374	Cliff Floyd	.10
375	Bobby Bonilla	.10
376	Al Leiter	.15
377	Josh Booty	.10
378	Darren Daulton	.10
379	Jay Powell	.10
380	Felix Heredia	.10
381	Jim Eisenreich	.10
382	Richard Hidalgo	.10
383	Mike Hampton	.10
384	Shane Reynolds	.10
385	Jeff Bagwell	1.00
386	Derek Bell	.10
387	Ricky Gutierrez	.10
388	Bill Spiers	.10
389	Jose Offerman	.10
390	Johnny Damon	.10
391	Jermaine Dye	.10
392	Jeff Montgomery	.10
393	Glendon Rusch	.10
394	Mike Sweeney	.10
395	Kevin Appier	.10
396	Joe Vitiello	.10
397	Ramon Martinez	.20
398	Darren Dreifort	.10
399	Wilton Guerrero	.10
400	Mike Piazza	2.00
401	Eddie Murray	.25
402	Ismael Valdes	.10
403	Todd Hollandsworth	.10
404	Mark Loretta	.10
405	Jeromy Burnitz	.10
406	Jeff Cirillo	.10
407	Scott Karl	.10
408	Mike Matheny	.10
409	Jose Valentin	.10
410	John Jaha	.10
411	Terry Steinbach	.10
412	Torii Hunter	.10
413	Pat Meares	.10
414	Marty Cordova	.10
415	Jaret Wright (Postseason Headliners)	.15
416	Mike Mussina (Postseason Headliners)	.25
417	John Smoltz (Postseason Headliners)	.10
418	Devon White (Postseason Headliners)	.10
419	Denny Neagle (Postseason Headliners)	.10
420	Livan Hernandez (Postseason Headliners)	.20
421	Kevin Brown (Postseason Headliners)	.10
422	Marquis Grissom (Postseason Headliners)	.10
423	Mike Mussina (Postseason Headliners)	.25
424	Eric Davis (Postseason Headliners)	.10
425	Tony Fernandez (Postseason Headliners)	.10
426	Moises Alou (Postseason Headliners)	.10
427	Sandy Alomar Jr. (Postseason Headliners)	.10
428	Gary Sheffield (Postseason Headliners)	.20
429	Jaret Wright (Postseason Headliners)	.20
430	Livan Hernandez (Postseason Headliners)	.20
431	Chad Ogea (Postseason Headliners)	.10
432	Edgar Renteria (Postseason Headliners)	.10
433	LaTroy Hawkins	.10
434	Rich Robertson	.10
435	Chuck Knoblauch	.25
436	Jose Vidro	.10
437	Dustin Hermanson	.10
438	Jim Bullinger	.10
439	Orlando Cabrera (Star Rookie)	.10
440	Vladimir Guerrero	1.00
441	Ugueth Urbina	.10
442	Brian McRae	.10
443	Matt Franco	.10
444	Bobby Jones	.10
445	Bernard Gilkey	.10
446	Dave Mlicki	.10
447	Brian Bohanon	.10
448	Mel Rojas	.10
449	Tim Raines	.10
450	Derek Jeter	2.00
451	Roger Clemens (Upper Echelon)	.75
452	Nomar Garciaparra (Upper Echelon)	1.50
453	Mike Piazza (Upper Echelon)	1.50
454	Mark McGwire (Upper Echelon)	2.00
455	Ken Griffey Jr. (Upper Echelon)	1.50
456	Larry Walker (Upper Echelon)	.25
457	Alex Rodriguez (Upper Echelon)	1.50
458	Tony Gwynn (Upper Echelon)	1.00
459	Frank Thomas (Upper Echelon)	.75
460	Tino Martinez	.25
461	Chad Curtis	.10
462	Ramiro Mendoza	.10
463	Joe Girardi	.10
464	David Wells	.10
465	Mariano Rivera	.20
466	Willie Adams	.10
467	George Williams	.10
468	Dave Telgheder	.10
469	Dave Magadan	.10
470	Matt Stairs	.10
471	Billy Taylor	.10
472	Jimmy Haynes	.10
473	Gregg Jefferies	.10
474	Midre Cummings	.10
475	Curt Schilling	.20
476	Mike Grace	.10
477	Mark Leiter	.10
478	Matt Beech	.10
479	Scott Rolen	.75
480	Jason Kendall	.20
481	Esteban Loaiza	.10
482	Jermaine Allensworth	.10
483	Mark Smith	.10
484	Jason Schmidt	.10
485	Jose Guillen	.20
486	Al Martin	.10
487	Delino DeShields	.10
488	Todd Stottlemyre	.10
489	Brian Jordan	.10
490	Ray Lankford	.10
491	Matt Morris	.10
492	Royce Clayton	.10
493	John Mabry	.10
494	Wally Joyner	.10
495	Trevor Hoffman	.10
496	Chris Gomez	.10
497	Sterling Hitchcock	.10
498	Pete Smith	.10
499	Greg Vaughn	.15
500	Tony Gwynn	1.50
501	Will Cunnane	.10
502	Darryl Hamilton	.10
503	Brian Johnson	.10
504	Kirk Rueter	.10
505	Barry Bonds	.75
506	Osvaldo Fernandez	.10
507	Stan Javier	.10
508	Julian Tavarez	.10
509	Rich Aurilia	.10
510	Alex Rodriguez	2.50
511	David Segui	.10
512	Rich Amaral	.10
513	Raul Ibanez	.10
514	Jay Buhner	.10
515	Randy Johnson	.50
516	Heathcliff Slocumb	.10

517	Tony Saunders	.10
518	Kevin Elster	.10
519	John Burkett	.10
520	Juan Gonzalez	1.00
521	John Wetteland	.10
522	Domingo Cedeno	.10
523	Darren Oliver	.10
524	Roger Pavlik	.10
525	Jose Cruz Jr.	.75
526	Woody Williams	.10
527	Alex Gonzalez	.10
528	Robert Person	.10
529	Juan Guzman	.10
530	Roger Clemens	1.00
531	Shawn Green	.75
532	Cordova, Ricon, Smith (Season Highlights)	.10
533	Nomar Garciaparra (Season Highlights)	1.50
534	Roger Clemens (Season Highlights)	.75
535	Mark McGwire (Season Highlights)	2.00
536	Larry Walker (Season Highlights)	.25
537	Mike Piazza (Season Highlights)	1.50
538	Curt Schilling (Season Highlights)	.10
539	Tony Gwynn (Season Highlights)	.75
540	Ken Griffey Jr. (Season Highlights)	1.50
541	Carl Pavano (Star Rookies)	.10
542	Shane Monahan (Star Rookies)	.10
543	*Gabe Kapler* (Star Rookies)	3.00
544	Eric Milton (Star Rookies)	.25
545	*Gary Matthews Jr.* (Star Rookies)	.50
546	*Mike Kinkade* (Star Rookies)	.50
547	*Ryan Christenson* (Star Rookies)	.25
548	*Corey Koskie* (Star Rookies)	.50
549	Norm Hutchins (Star Rookies)	.10
550	Russell Branyan (Star Rookies)	.10
551	*Masato Yoshii* (Star Rookies)	.50
552	*Jesus Sanchez* (Star Rookies)	.30
553	Anthony Sanders (Star Rookies)	.20
554	Edwin Diaz (Star Rookies)	.10
555	Gabe Alvarez (Star Rookies)	.10
556	*Carlos Lee* (Star Rookies)	1.50
557	Mike Darr (Star Rookies)	.10
558	Kerry Wood (Star Rookies)	.75
559	Carlos Guillen (Star Rookies)	.10
560	Sean Casey (Star Rookies)	1.00
561	*Manny Aybar* (Star Rookies)	.40
562	Octavio Dotel (Star Rookies)	.15
563	Jarrod Washburn (Star Rookies)	.10
564	Mark L. Johnson (Star Rookies)	.10
565	Ramon Hernandez (Star Rookies)	.10
566	*Rich Butler* (Star Rookies)	.50
567	Mike Caruso (Star Rookies)	.25
568	Cliff Politte (Star Rookies)	.10
569	Scott Elarton (Star Rookies)	.10
570	*Magglio Ordonez* (Star Rookies)	4.00
571	*Adam Butler* (Star Rookies)	.40
572	Marlon Anderson (Star Rookies)	.15
573	*Julio Ramirez* (Star Rookies)	1.00
574	*Darron Ingram* (Star Rookies)	.20
575	Bruce Chen (Star Rookies)	.10
576	*Steve Woodard* (Star Rookies)	.25
577	Hiram Bocachica (Star Rookies)	.10
578	Kevin Witt (Star Rookies)	.10
579	Javier Vazquez (Star Rookies)	.10
580	Alex Gonzalez (Star Rookies)	.15
581	Brian Powell (Star Rookies)	.10
582	Wes Helms (Star Rookies)	.10
583	Ron Wright (Star Rookies)	.10
584	Rafael Medina (Star Rookies)	.10
585	Daryle Ward (Star Rookies)	.15
586	Geoff Jenkins (Star Rookies)	.10
587	Preston Wilson (Star Rookies)	.15
588	*Jim Chamblee* (Star Rookies)	.25
589	*Mike Lowell* (Star Rookies)	.50
590	A.J. Hinch (Star Rookies)	.25
591	*Francisco Cordero* (Star Rookies)	.25
592	*Rolando Arrojo* (Star Rookies)	.50
593	Braden Looper (Star Rookies)	.10
594	Sidney Ponson (Star Rookies)	.10
595	Matt Clement (Star Rookies)	.25
596	Carlton Loewer (Star Rookies)	.10
597	Brian Meadows (Star Rookies)	.10
598	Danny Klassen (Star Rookies)	.20
599	Larry Sutton (Star Rookies)	.10
600	Travis Lee (Star Rookies)	.25
601	Randy Johnson (Eminent Prestige)	1.50
602	Greg Maddux (Eminent Prestige)	5.00
603	Roger Clemens (Eminent Prestige)	4.00
604	Jaret Wright (Eminent Prestige)	1.00
605	Mike Piazza (Eminent Prestige)	6.00
606	Tino Martinez (Eminent Prestige)	1.50
607	Frank Thomas (Eminent Prestige)	3.00
608	Mo Vaughn (Eminent Prestige)	1.50
609	Todd Helton (Eminent Prestige)	2.50
610	Mark McGwire (Eminent Prestige)	10.00
611	Jeff Bagwell (Eminent Prestige)	3.00
612	Travis Lee (Eminent Prestige)	2.00
613	Scott Rolen (Eminent Prestige)	3.00
614	Cal Ripken Jr. (Eminent Prestige)	8.00
615	Chipper Jones (Eminent Prestige)	6.00
616	Nomar Garciaparra (Eminent Prestige)	6.00
617	Alex Rodriguez (Eminent Prestige)	8.00
618	Derek Jeter (Eminent Prestige)	6.00
619	Tony Gwynn (Eminent Prestige)	5.00
620	Ken Griffey Jr. (Eminent Prestige)	10.00
621	Kenny Lofton (Eminent Prestige)	1.50
622	Juan Gonzalez (Eminent Prestige)	4.00
623	Jose Cruz Jr. (Eminent Prestige)	1.00
624	Larry Walker (Eminent Prestige)	1.50
625	Barry Bonds (Eminent Prestige)	2.50
626	Ben Grieve (Eminent Prestige)	2.00
627	Andruw Jones (Eminent Prestige)	1.50
628	Vladimir Guerrero (Eminent Prestige)	2.50
629	Paul Konerko (Eminent Prestige)	1.00
630	Paul Molitor (Eminent Prestige)	2.00
631	Cecil Fielder	.10
632	Jack McDowell	.10
633	Mike James	.10
634	Brian Anderson	.10
635	Jay Bell	.10
636	Devon White	.10
637	Andy Stankiewicz	.10
638	Tony Batista	.10
639	Omar Daal	.10
640	Matt Williams	.25
641	Brent Brede	.10
642	Jorge Fabregas	.10
643	Karim Garcia	.10
644	Felix Rodriguez	.10
645	Andy Benes	.10
646	Willie Blair	.10
647	Jeff Suppan	.10
648	Yamil Benitez	.10
649	Walt Weiss	.10
650	Andres Galarraga	.40
651	Doug Drabek	.10
652	Ozzie Guillen	.10
653	Joe Carter	.10
654	Dennis Eckersley	.10
655	Pedro Martinez	.75
656	Jim Leyritz	.10
657	Henry Rodriguez	.10
658	Rod Beck	.10
659	Mickey Morandini	.10
660	Jeff Blauser	.10
661	Ruben Sierra	.10
662	Mike Sirotka	.10
663	Pete Harnisch	.10
664	Damian Jackson	.10
665	Dmitri Young	.10
666	Steve Cooke	.10
667	Geronimo Berroa	.10
668	Shawon Dunston	.10
669	Mike Jackson	.10
670	Travis Fryman	.20
671	Dwight Gooden	.10
672	Paul Assenmacher	.10
673	Eric Plunk	.10
674	Mike Lansing	.10
675	Darryl Kile	.10
676	Luis Gonzalez	.20
677	Frank Castillo	.10
678	Joe Randa	.10
679	Bip Roberts	.10
680	Derrek Lee	.10
681	Mike Piazza	4.00
682	Sean Berry	.10
683	Ramon Garcia	.10
684	Carl Everett	.10
685	Moises Alou	.20
686	Hal Morris	.10
687	Jeff Conine	.10
688	Gary Sheffield LA	.25
689	Jose Vizcaino	.10
690	Charles Johnson	.10
691	Bobby Bonilla LA	.15
692	Marquis Grissom	.10
693	Alex Ochoa	.10
694	Mike Morgan	.10
695	Orlando Merced	.10
696	David Ortiz	.15
697	Brent Gates	.10
698	Otis Nixon	.10
699	Trey Moore	.10
700	Derrick May	.10
701	Rich Becker	.10
702	Al Leiter	.20
703	Chili Davis	.10
704	Scott Brosius	.10
705	Chuck Knoblauch	.30
706	Kenny Rogers	.10
707	Mike Blowers	.10
708	Mike Fetters	.10
709	Tom Candiotti	.10
710	Rickey Henderson	.50
711	Bob Abreu	.10
712	Mark Lewis	.10
713	Doug Glanville	.10
714	Desi Relaford	.10
715	Kent Mercker	.10
716	J. Kevin Brown	.20
717	James Mouton	.10
718	Mark Langston	.10
719	Greg Myers	.10
720	Orel Hershiser	.10
721	Charlie Hayes	.10
722	Robb Nen	.10
723	Glenallen Hill	.10
724	Tony Saunders	.10
725	Wade Boggs	.40
726	Kevin Stocker	.10
727	Wilson Alvarez	.10
728	Albie Lopez	.10
729	Dave Martinez	.10
730	Fred McGriff	.25
731	Quinton McCracken	.10
732	Bryan Rekar	.10
733	Paul Sorrento	.10
734	Roberto Hernandez	.10
735	Bubba Trammell	.10
736	Miguel Cairo	.10
737	John Flaherty	.10
738	Terrell Wade	.10
739	Roberto Kelly	.10
740	Mark Mclemore (McLemore)	.10
741	Danny Patterson	.10
742	Aaron Sele	.10
743	Tony Fernandez	.10
744	Randy Myers	.10
745	Jose Canseco	.60
746	Darrin Fletcher	.10
747	Mike Stanley	.10
748	Marquis Grissom (Season Highlights)	.10
749	Fred McGriff (Season Highlights)	.20
750	Travis Lee (Season Highlights)	.25

1998 Upper Deck Amazing Greats

The 30-card Amazing Greats insert is printed on acetate. The cards are numbered to 2,000. A die-cut parallel was sequentially numbered to 250. Amazing Greats was an insert in Upper Deck Series One packs. Cards carry an "AG" prefix.

		MT
Complete Set (30):		550.00
Common Player:		5.00
Die-Cuts (250): 1.5X		
1	Ken Griffey Jr.	60.00
2	Derek Jeter	40.00
3	Alex Rodriguez	50.00
4	Paul Molitor	12.00
5	Jeff Bagwell	15.00
6	Larry Walker	10.00
7	Kenny Lofton	10.00
8	Cal Ripken Jr.	50.00
9	Juan Gonzalez	15.00
10	Chipper Jones	40.00
11	Greg Maddux	30.00
12	Roberto Alomar	12.00
13	Mike Piazza	40.00
14	Andres Galarraga	10.00
15	Barry Bonds	15.00
16	Andy Pettitte	8.00
17	Nomar Garciaparra	35.00
18	Hideki Irabu	5.00
19	Tony Gwynn	30.00
20	Frank Thomas	15.00
21	Roger Clemens	20.00
22	Sammy Sosa	40.00
23	Jose Cruz, Jr.	5.00
24	Manny Ramirez	15.00
25	Mark McGwire	60.00
26	Randy Johnson	10.00
27	Mo Vaughn	10.00
28	Gary Sheffield	6.00
29	Andruw Jones	12.00
30	Albert Belle	10.00

1998 Upper Deck A Piece of the Action

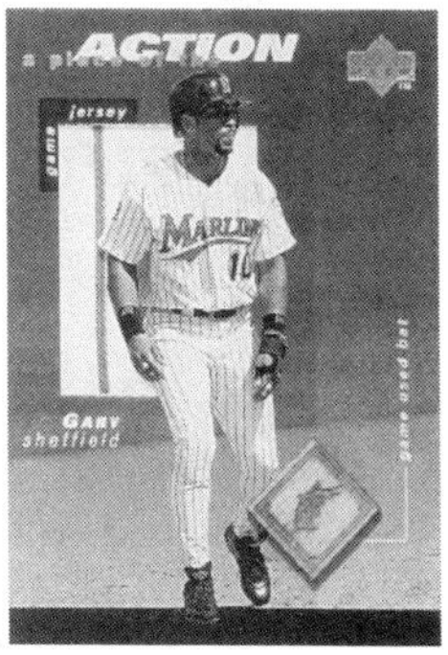

A Piece of the Action was inserted in Series One, Two and Three packs. Series One featured 10 cards: five with a piece of game-used jersey and five with a piece of game-used bat. Series Two offered a piece of game-used bat and jersey on four cards. Series Three inserts featured a piece of jersey only. The cards were inserted one per 2,500 packs in Series 1 and 2; the insertion rate in Series 3 was not revealed.

		MT
Complete Set (18):		1600.
Complete Series 1 Set (10):		1250.
Complete Series 2 Set (4):		350.00
Common Player:		40.00
Inserted 1:2,500		
(1)	Tony Gwynn (Jersey)	200.00
(2)	Tony Gwynn (Bat)	150.00
(3)	Alex Rodriguez (Jersey)	300.00
(4)	Alex Rodriguez (Bat)	250.00
(5)	Gary Sheffield (Jersey)	60.00
(6)	Gary Sheffield (Bat)	50.00
(7)	Todd Hollandsworth (Jersey)	50.00
(8)	Todd Hollandsworth (Bat)	40.00
(9)	Greg Maddux (Jersey)	250.00
(10)	Jay Buhner (Bat)	50.00
RA	Roberto Alomar	150.00
JB	Jay Buhner	75.00
AJ	Andruw Jones	200.00
GS	Gary Sheffield	75.00

1998 Upper Deck Blue Chip Prospects

Inserted in Series Two packs, Blue Chip Prospects is printed on die-cut acetate. The cards are sequentially numbered to 2,000. They carry a "BC" prefix.

		MT
Complete Set (30):		250.00
Common Player:		3.00
1	Nomar Garciaparra	40.00
2	Scott Rolen	15.00
3	Jason Dickson	3.00
4	Darin Erstad	8.00
5	Brad Fullmer	3.00
6	Jaret Wright	4.00
7	Justin Thompson	3.00
8	Matt Morris	3.00
9	Fernando Tatis	3.00
10	Alex Rodriguez	50.00
11	Todd Helton	8.00
12	Andy Pettitte	6.00
13	Jose Cruz Jr.	3.00
14	Mark Kotsay	3.00
15	Derek Jeter	40.00
16	Paul Konerko	5.00
17	Todd Dunwoody	3.00
18	Vladimir Guerrero	20.00
19	Miguel Tejada	6.00
20	Chipper Jones	35.00
21	Kevin Orie	3.00
22	Juan Encarnacion	3.00
23	Brian Rose	3.00
24	Andruw Jones	10.00
25	Livan Hernandez	3.00
26	Brian Giles	4.00
27	Brett Tomko	3.00
28	Jose Guillen	3.00
29	Aaron Boone	3.00
30	Ben Grieve	8.00

1998 Upper Deck Clearly Dominant

Clearly Dominant was an insert in Series Two. Printed on Light F/X plastic stock, the 30-card set is sequentially numbered to 250. They carry a "CD" prefix.

		MT
Complete Set (30):		1500.
Common Player:		10.00
Production 250 sets		
1	Mark McGwire	150.00
2	Derek Jeter	100.00
3	Alex Rodriguez	120.00
4	Paul Molitor	30.00
5	Jeff Bagwell	40.00
6	Ivan Rodriguez	40.00
7	Kenny Lofton	30.00
8	Cal Ripken Jr.	120.00
9	Albert Belle	30.00
10	Chipper Jones	100.00
11	Gary Sheffield	15.00
12	Roberto Alomar	30.00
13	Mo Vaughn	30.00
14	Andres Galarraga	30.00
15	Nomar Garciaparra	100.00
16	Randy Johnson	30.00
17	Mike Mussina	30.00
18	Greg Maddux	75.00
19	Tony Gwynn	80.00
20	Frank Thomas	40.00
21	Roger Clemens	75.00
22	Dennis Eckersley	10.00
23	Juan Gonzalez	40.00
24	Tino Martinez	15.00
25	Andruw Jones	20.00
26	Larry Walker	30.00
27	Ken Caminiti	10.00
28	Mike Piazza	100.00
29	Barry Bonds	40.00
30	Ken Griffey Jr.	150.00

1998 Upper Deck Ken Griffey Jr.'s HR Chronicles

Griffey's Home Run Chronicles was inserted in both Series 1 and 2 packs. Series 1 had cards spotlighting one of Junior's first 30 home runs of the 1997 season. Series 2 had 26 cards highlighting the rest of his 1997 home run output. In both series, the cards were inserted one per nine packs. Cards are numbered "XX of 56" and printed on silver-metallic foil on front.

		MT
Complete Set (56):		190.00
Common Card:		4.00
Inserted 1:9		
1	Ken Griffey Jr.	5.00
2	Ken Griffey Jr.	5.00
3	Ken Griffey Jr.	5.00
4	Ken Griffey Jr.	5.00
5	Ken Griffey Jr.	5.00
6	Ken Griffey Jr.	5.00
7	Ken Griffey Jr.	5.00
8	Ken Griffey Jr.	5.00
9	Ken Griffey Jr.	5.00
10	Ken Griffey Jr.	5.00
11	Ken Griffey Jr.	5.00
12	Ken Griffey Jr.	5.00
13	Ken Griffey Jr.	5.00
14	Ken Griffey Jr.	5.00
15	Ken Griffey Jr.	5.00
16	Ken Griffey Jr.	5.00
17	Ken Griffey Jr.	5.00
18	Ken Griffey Jr.	5.00
19	Ken Griffey Jr.	5.00
20	Ken Griffey Jr.	5.00
21	Ken Griffey Jr.	5.00
22	Ken Griffey Jr.	5.00
23	Ken Griffey Jr.	5.00
24	Ken Griffey Jr.	5.00
25	Ken Griffey Jr.	5.00
26	Ken Griffey Jr.	5.00
27	Ken Griffey Jr.	5.00
28	Ken Griffey Jr.	5.00
29	Ken Griffey Jr.	5.00
30	Ken Griffey Jr.	5.00

1998 Upper Deck National Pride

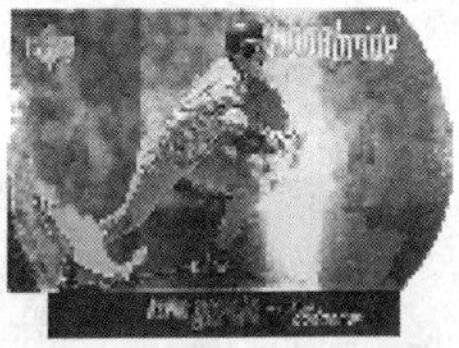

National Pride is a 42-card insert printed on die-cut rainbow foil. The set honors the nationality of the player with their country's flag in the background. The cards were inserted one per 24 packs. Cards are numbered with a "NP" prefix.

		MT
Complete Set (42):		250.00
Common Player:		2.25
1	Dave Nilsson	2.25
2	Larry Walker	6.00
3	Edgar Renteria	2.25
4	Jose Canseco	7.50
5	Rey Ordonez	2.25
6	Rafael Palmeiro	5.00
7	Livan Hernandez	2.25
8	Andruw Jones	5.00
9	Manny Ramirez	15.00
10	Sammy Sosa	25.00
11	Raul Mondesi	3.00
12	Moises Alou	3.00
13	Pedro Martinez	12.00
14	Vladimir Guerrero	12.00
15	Chili Davis	2.25
16	Hideo Nomo	3.00
17	Hideki Irabu	2.25
18	Shigetosi Hasegawa	2.25
19	Takashi Kashiwada	2.25
20	Chan Ho Park	2.50
21	Fernando Valenzuela	2.25
22	Vinny Castilla	2.50
23	Armando Reynoso	2.25
24	Karim Garcia	2.25
25	Marvin Benard	2.25
26	Mariano Rivera	2.25
27	Juan Gonzalez	12.00
28	Roberto Alomar	6.00
29	Ivan Rodriguez	9.00
30	Carlos Delgado	4.00
31	Bernie Williams	6.00
32	Edgar Martinez	2.25
33	Frank Thomas	12.00
34	Barry Bonds	9.00
35	Mike Piazza	25.00
36	Chipper Jones	25.00
37	Cal Ripken Jr.	30.00
38	Alex Rodriguez	30.00
39	Ken Griffey Jr.	35.00
40	Andres Galarraga	4.00
41	Omar Vizquel	2.25
42	Ozzie Guillen	2.25

1998 Upper Deck Prime Nine

Nine of the most popular players are featured in this insert set. The cards are printed on silver foil stock and inserted 1:5.

	MT
Complete Set (60):	150.00
Common Griffey (PN1-PN7):	5.00
Common Piazza (PN8-PN14):	3.00
Common Thomas (PN15-PN21):	2.00
Common McGwire (PN22-PN28):	5.00
Common Ripken (PN29-PN35):	4.00
Common Gonzalez (PN36-PN42):	2.00
Common Gwynn (PN43-PN49):	3.00
Common Bonds (PN50-PN55):	2.00
Common Maddux (PN56-PN60):	3.00
Inserted 1:5	
(Values indicated are per card)	

1998 Upper Deck Tape Measure Titans

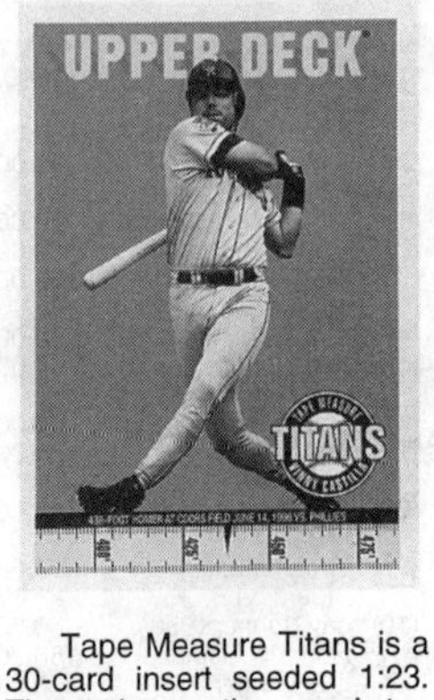

Tape Measure Titans is a 30-card insert seeded 1:23. The set honors the game's top home run hitters.

		MT
Complete Set (30):		240.00
Common Player:		2.50
Inserted 1:23		
1	Mark McGwire	30.00
2	Andres Galarraga	4.00
3	Jeff Bagwell	10.00
4	Larry Walker	5.00
5	Frank Thomas	10.00
6	Rafael Palmeiro	5.00
7	Nomar Garciaparra	20.00
8	Mo Vaughn	5.00
9	Albert Belle	6.00
10	Ken Griffey Jr.	30.00
11	Manny Ramirez	10.00
12	Jim Thome	5.00
13	Tony Clark	4.00
14	Juan Gonzalez	10.00
15	Mike Piazza	20.00
16	Jose Canseco	7.50
17	Jay Buhner	2.50
18	Alex Rodriguez	25.00
19	Jose Cruz Jr.	3.00
20	Tino Martinez	2.50
21	Carlos Delgado	3.00
22	Andruw Jones	6.00
23	Chipper Jones	20.00
24	Fred McGriff	4.00
25	Matt Williams	3.00
26	Sammy Sosa	20.00
27	Vinny Castilla	2.50
28	Tim Salmon	3.00
29	Ken Caminiti	3.00
30	Barry Bonds	8.00

1998 Upper Deck 10th Anniversary Preview

10th Anniversary Preview is a 60-card set. The foil cards have the same design as the 1989 Upper Deck base cards. The set was inserted one per five packs.

		MT
Complete Set (60):		120.00
Common Player:		.75
1	Greg Maddux	8.00
2	Mike Mussina	2.00
3	Roger Clemens	4.00
4	Hideo Nomo	1.50
4	David Cone	.75
6	Tom Glavine	.75
7	Andy Pettitte	2.00
8	Jimmy Key	.75
9	Randy Johnson	2.00
10	Dennis Eckersley	.75
11	Lee Smith	.75
12	John Franco	.75
13	Randy Myers	.75
14	Mike Piazza	8.00
15	Ivan Rodriguez	3.00
16	Todd Hundley	1.00
17	Sandy Alomar Jr.	.75
18	Frank Thomas	5.00
19	Rafael Palmeiro	1.00
20	Mark McGwire	12.00
21	Mo Vaughn	2.00
22	Fred McGriff	1.25
23	Andres Galarraga	1.25
24	Mark Grace	1.25
25	Jeff Bagwell	5.00
26	Roberto Alomar	2.50
27	Chuck Knoblauch	1.50
28	Ryne Sandberg	3.00
29	Eric Young	.75
30	Craig Biggio	1.00
31	Carlos Baerga	.75
32	Robin Ventura	.75
33	Matt Williams	.75
34	Wade Boggs	1.00
35	Dean Palmer	.75
36	Chipper Jones	8.00
37	Vinny Castilla	.75
38	Ken Caminiti	1.25
39	Omar Vizquel	.75
40	Cal Ripken Jr.	10.00
41	Derek Jeter	8.00
42	Alex Rodriguez	10.00
43	Barry Larkin	.75
44	Mark Grudzielanek	.75
45	Albert Belle	2.00
46	Manny Ramirez	4.00
47	Jose Canseco	1.50
48	Ken Griffey Jr.	12.00
49	Juan Gonzalez	6.00
50	Kenny Lofton	2.00
51	Sammy Sosa	5.00
52	Larry Walker	1.50
53	Gary Sheffield	1.50
54	Rickey Henderson	1.00
55	Tony Gwynn	5.00
56	Barry Bonds	3.00
57	Paul Molitor	2.50
58	Edgar Martinez	.75
59	Chili Davis	.75
60	Eddie Murray	1.00

1998 Upper Deck Jumbos

For $3 and 10 foil-pack wrappers, collectors could receive this set of large-format (3-1/2" x 5") cards in a mail-in redemption. The cards are identical to the standard-size versions.

		MT
Complete Set (15):		8.00
Common Player:		.25
27	Kenny Lofton	.25
30	Greg Maddux	.75
40	Rafael Palmeiro	.35
50	Ryne Sandberg	.40
60	Albert Belle	.40
65	Barry Larkin	.25
67	Deion Sanders	.25
95	Gary Sheffield	.25
130	Paul Molitor	.35
135	Vladimir Guerrero	.50
176	Hideki Irabu	.25
205	Mark McGwire	3.00
211	Rickey Henderson	.35
225	Ken Griffey Jr.	3.00
230	Ivan Rodriguez	.45

1998 Upper Deck 5x7 Inserts

Each box of specially marked Series 2 retail packs contains one of these oversize (5" x 7") versions of UD cards. Besides being four times the size of the regular cards, the jumbo versions do not have the metallic-foil highlights on front nor the hologram on back.

		MT
Complete Set (10):		18.00
Common Player:		1.00
310	Cal Ripken Jr.	4.00
320	Nomar Garciaparra	3.00
330	Frank Thomas	2.00
355	Larry Walker	1.00
385	Jeff Bagwell	2.00
400	Mike Piazza	3.00
450	Derek Jeter	3.00
500	Tony Gwynn	2.50
510	Alex Rodriguez	4.00
530	Roger Clemens	2.00

1998 Upper Deck 5x7 Mail-In Offer

Via a wrapper redemption offer, collectors could obtain this 15-card set of oversize (5" x 7") versions of Series 1 UD cards. Besides being four times the size of the regular cards, the jumbo versions do not have the metallic-foil highlights on front nor the hologram on back.

		MT
Complete Set (15):		12.00
Common Player:		.50
27	Kenny Lofton	.50
30	Greg Maddux	2.50
40	Rafael Palmeiro	.60
50	Ryne Sandberg	1.50
60	Albert Belle	.75
65	Barry Larkin	.50
68	Deion Sanders	.50
95	Gary Sheffield	.50
130	Paul Molitor	1.00
135	Vladimir Guerrero	1.00
176	Hideki Irabu	.50
205	Mark McGwire	5.00
211	Rickey Henderson	.75
225	Ken Griffey Jr.	5.00
230	Ivan Rodriguez	.75

1998 Upper Deck Richie Ashburn Tribute

As part of the company's participation at SportsFest in May, 1998, the company issued a tribute card for Phillies Hall of Famer and broadcasting great Richie Ashburn. The card front features a color action photo, part of which is repeated on the back along with Ashburn's career stats and highlights.

		MT
1	Richie Ashburn	4.00

1998 Upper Deck Mark McGwire's Chase for 62

This boxed set chronicles the Cardinal slugger's quest for the single-season home run record. Sold only as a boxed set of 30 cards in standard 2-1/2" x 3-1/2" format, plus a 3-1/2" x 5" card picturing home runs No. 61 and 62, these sets were offered only on a television home shopping show (individually serial numbered red box) and in selected retail stores (unnumbered yellow box). The cards in each version are identical. Issue price was about $20. Card fronts have color poses or action photos at right; at left is a monochrome portrait photo in red. Backs repeat the large front photo, also in red monochrome, and have a few words about a McGwire homer or other highlight. Each card has a silver-foil UD logo on front and a diamond-shaped hologram on back.

	MT
Complete Boxed Set:	20.00
Common Card:	1.00
1-30 Mark McGwire	1.50
--- Mark McGwire (3-1/2" x 5" HR #61/62)	6.00

1998 Upper Deck PowerDeck Audio Card

A late-1990s reinvention of the "talking" baseball card, this was the first application of UD's "PowerDeck" technology to the trading card field. Specially marked hobby boxes of '98 UD baseball could contain one of three Ken Griffey, Jr., audio cards. The cards are standard 2-1/2" x 3-1/2" and were made to be inserted into a "dummy" plastic disc which could then be played in any audio CD, offering comments from Griffey, trivia, and career highlights. Insertion rate of each of the Griffey cards varies and is detailed in the listings.

Complete Set (3):
Common Card:
(1) Ken Griffey Jr. (gray jersey, 1:46 packs)
(2) Ken Griffey Jr. (blue jersey, 1:500 packs)
(3) Ken Griffey Jr. (white jersey, 1:2,400 packs)

1998 UD Retro

The 129-card set is comprised of 99 regular player cards and 30 Futurama subset cards. Card fronts have a white border encasing the player photo. Retro is packaged in a lunchbox featuring one of six players. Each lunchbox contains 24 six-card packs.

	MT
Complete Set (129):	50.00
Common Player:	.15
1 Jim Edmonds	.25
2 Darin Erstad	.40
3 Tim Salmon	.50
4 Jay Bell	.15
5 Matt Williams	.45
6 Andres Galarraga	.75
7 Andruw Jones	.75
8 Chipper Jones	2.50
9 Greg Maddux	2.00
10 Rafael Palmeiro	.50
11 Cal Ripken Jr.	3.00
12 Brooks Robinson	.50
13 Nomar Garciaparra	3.00
14 Pedro Martinez	1.00
15 Mo Vaughn	.60
16 Ernie Banks	.60
17 Mark Grace	.40
18 Gary Matthews	.15
19 Sammy Sosa	3.00
20 Albert Belle	.75
21 Carlton Fisk	.30
22 Frank Thomas	1.00
23 Ken Griffey Sr.	.15
24 Paul Konerko	.30
25 Barry Larkin	.35
26 Sean Casey	.75
27 Tony Perez	.25
28 Bob Feller	.25
29 Kenny Lofton	.60
30 Manny Ramirez	1.00
31 Jim Thome	.60
32 Omar Vizquel	.15
33 Dante Bichette	.40
34 Larry Walker	.75
35 Tony Clark	.50
36 Damion Easley	.15
37 Cliff Floyd	.15
38 Livan Hernandez	.15
39 Jeff Bagwell	1.00
40 Craig Biggio	.40
41 Al Kaline	.30
42 Johnny Damon	.15
43 Dean Palmer	.15
44 Charles Johnson	.15
45 Eric Karros	.15
46 Gaylord Perry	.15
47 Raul Mondesi	.30
48 Gary Sheffield	.30
49 Eddie Mathews	.50
50 Warren Spahn	.50
51 Jeromy Burnitz	.15
52 Jeff Cirillo	.15
53 Marquis Grissom	.15
54 Paul Molitor	.75
55 Kirby Puckett	1.00
56 Brad Radke	.15
57 Todd Walker	.25
58 Vladimir Guerrero	1.50
59 Brad Fullmer	.40
60 Rondell White	.25
61 Bobby Jones	.15
62 Hideo Nomo	.50
63 Mike Piazza	2.50
64 Tom Seaver	.50
65 Frank J. Thomas	.30
66 Yogi Berra	.60
67 Derek Jeter	2.50
68 Tino Martinez	.30
69 Paul O'Neill	.30
70 Andy Pettitte	.45
71 Rollie Fingers	.15
72 Rickey Henderson	.40
73 Matt Stairs	.15
74 Scott Rolen	1.00
75 Curt Schilling	.25
76 Jose Guillen	.15
77 Jason Kendall	.15
78 Lou Brock	.35
79 Bob Gibson	.50
80 Ray Lankford	.15
81 Mark McGwire	4.00
83 Kevin Brown	.25
84 Ken Caminiti	.25
85 Tony Gwynn	2.00
86 Greg Vaughn	.25
87 Barry Bonds	1.00
88 Willie Stargell	.50
89 Willie McCovey	.40
90 Ken Griffey Jr.	4.00
91 Randy Johnson	.60
92 Alex Rodriguez	3.00
93 Quinton McCracken	.15
94 Fred McGriff	.30
95 Juan Gonzalez	1.00
96 Ivan Rodriguez	1.00
97 Nolan Ryan	3.00
98 Jose Canseco	1.00
99 Roger Clemens	1.50
100 Jose Cruz Jr.	.50
101 *Justin Baughman*	.50
102 *David Dellucci* (Futurama)	.75
103 Travis Lee (Futurama)	.50
104 *Troy Glaus* (Futurama)	3.00
105 Kerry Wood (Futurama)	1.00
106 Mike Caruso (Futurama)	.15
107 *Jim Parque* (Futurama)	.50
108 Brett Tomko (Futurama)	.15
109 Russell Branyan (Futurama)	.15
110 Jaret Wright (Futurama)	.25
111 Todd Helton (Futurama)	1.00
112 Gabe Alvarez (Futurama)	.15
113 *Matt Anderson* (Futurama)	.50
114 Alex Gonzalez (Futurama)	.15
115 Mark Kotsay (Futurama)	.30
116 Derrek Lee (Futurama)	.15
117 Richard Hidalgo (Futurama)	.15
118 Adrian Beltre (Futurama)	1.00
119 Geoff Jenkins (Futurama)	.15
120 Eric Milton (Futurama)	.15
121 Brad Fullmer (Futurama)	.25
122 Vladimir Guerrero (Futurama)	1.50
123 Carl Pavano (Futurama)	.15
124 *Orlando Hernandez* (Futurama)	2.00
125 Ben Grieve (Futurama)	.50
126 A.J. Hinch (Futurama)	.15
127 Matt Clement (Futurama)	.15
128 *Gary Matthews Jr.* (Futurama)	.50
129 Aramis Ramirez (Futurama)	.40
130 Rolando Arrojo (Futurama)	.75

1998 UD Retro Big Boppers

The game's heavy hitters are the focus of this insert set. Cards have a color action photo on a sepia background. Each card is individually serial numbered in red foil in the upper-right, within an edition of 500. Backs repeat part of the front photo, in sepia only, and have recent stats and hitting highlights. Cards are numbered with a "B" prefix.

	MT
Complete Set (30):	500.00
Common Player:	5.00
Production 500 sets	
B1 Darin Erstad	5.00
B2 Rafael Palmeiro	8.00
B3 Cal Ripken Jr.	50.00
B4 Nomar Garciaparra	40.00
B5 Mo Vaughn	10.00
B6 Frank Thomas	15.00
B7 Albert Belle	10.00
B8 Jim Thome	10.00
B9 Manny Ramirez	15.00
B10 Tony Clark	8.00
B11 Tino Martinez	5.00
B12 Ben Grieve	8.00
B13 Ken Griffey Jr.	60.00
B14 Alex Rodriguez	50.00
B15 Jay Buhner	5.00
B16 Juan Gonzalez	15.00
B17 Jose Cruz Jr.	5.00
B18 Jose Canseco	12.00
B19 Travis Lee	5.00
B20 Chipper Jones	40.00
B21 Andres Galarraga	10.00
B22 Andruw Jones	12.00
B23 Sammy Sosa	40.00
B24 Vinny Castilla	5.00
B25 Larry Walker	10.00
B26 Jeff Bagwell	15.00
B27 Gary Sheffield	6.00
B28 Mike Piazza	40.00
B29 Mark McGwire	60.00
B30 Barry Bonds	12.00

Player names in *Italic* type indicate a rookie card.

1998 UD Retro Groovy Kind of Glove

This 30-card set showcases baseball's top defensive players on a psychadelic, wavy and colorful background. They were inserted 1:7 packs.

	MT
Complete Set (30):	125.00
Common Player:	1.50
Inserted 1:7	
G1 Roberto Alomar	3.00
G2 Cal Ripken Jr.	12.00
G3 Nomar Garciaparra	10.00
G4 Frank Thomas	6.00
G5 Robin Ventura	1.50
G6 Omar Vizquel	1.50
G7 Kenny Lofton	2.00
G8 Ben Grieve	2.50
G9 Alex Rodriguez	12.00
G10 Ken Griffey Jr.	15.00
G11 Ivan Rodriguez	5.00
G12 Travis Lee	2.50
G13 Matt Williams	2.00
G14 Greg Maddux	8.00
G15 Andres Galarraga	3.00
G16 Andruw Jones	4.00
G17 Kerry Wood	4.00
G18 Mark Grace	2.00
G19 Craig Biggio	2.00
G20 Charles Johnson	1.50
G21 Raul Mondesi	2.00
G22 Mike Piazza	10.00
G23 Rey Ordonez	1.50
G24 Derek Jeter	10.00
G25 Scott Rolen	4.00
G26 Mark McGwire	15.00
G27 Ken Caminiti	2.00
G28 Tony Gwynn	8.00
G29 J.T. Snow	1.50
G30 Barry Bonds	4.00

1998 UD Retro Legendary Cut

This insert features an actual Babe Ruth cut signature and is limited to a total of three cards.

Complete Set (1):
Value Undetermined
LC Babe Ruth (3 total)

1998 UD Retro New Frontier

This 30-card set spotlights 30 of baseball's top young prospects and is limited to 1,000 sequentially numbered sets.

	MT
Complete Set (30):	120.00
Common Player:	2.50
Production 1,000 sets	
NF1 Justin Baughman	2.50
NF2 David Dellucci	4.00
NF3 Travis Lee	5.00
NF4 Troy Glaus	15.00
NF5 Mike Caruso	2.50
NF6 Jim Parque	2.50
NF7 Kerry Wood	8.00
NF8 Brett Tomko	2.50
NF9 Russell Branyan	2.50
NF10 Jaret Wright	4.00
NF11 Todd Helton	8.00
NF12 Gabe Alvarez	2.50
NF13 Matt Anderson	4.00
NF14 Alex Gonzalez	2.50
NF15 Mark Kotsay	3.00
NF16 Derrek Lee	2.50
NF17 Richard Hidalgo	2.50
NF18 Adrian Beltre	8.00
NF19 Geoff Jenkins	2.50
NF20 Eric Milton	2.50
NF21 Brad Fullmer	4.00
NF22 Vladimir Guerrero	20.00
NF23 Carl Pavano	2.50
NF24 Orlando Hernandez	15.00
NF25 Ben Grieve	6.00
NF26 A.J. Hinch	2.50
NF27 Matt Clement	2.50
NF28 Gary Matthews	4.00
NF29 Aramis Ramirez	4.00
NF30 Rolando Arrojo	5.00

1998 UD Retro Quantum Leap

This 30-card insert set highlights the technology advancements of current Upper Deck products on a horizontal format. A total of 500 serially numbered sets were produced.

	MT
Complete Set (30):	4500.
Common Player:	60.00
Production 50 sets	
Q1 Darin Erstad	75.00
Q2 Cal Ripken Jr.	400.00
Q3 Nomar Garciaparra	250.00
Q4 Frank Thomas	150.00
Q5 Kenny Lofton	75.00
Q6 Ben Grieve	75.00
Q7 Ken Griffey Jr.	500.00
Q8 Alex Rodriguez	400.00
Q9 Juan Gonzalez	125.00
Q10 Jose Cruz Jr.	60.00
Q11 Roger Clemens	150.00
Q12 Travis Lee	75.00
Q13 Chipper Jones	250.00
Q14 Greg Maddux	200.00
Q15 Kerry Wood	75.00
Q16 Jeff Bagwell	125.00
Q17 Mike Piazza	250.00
Q18 Scott Rolen	100.00
Q19 Mark McGwire	500.00
Q20 Tony Gwynn	200.00
Q21 Larry Walker	75.00
Q22 Derek Jeter	250.00
Q23 Sammy Sosa	300.00
Q24 Barry Bonds	100.00
Q25 Mo Vaughn	75.00
Q26 Roberto Alomar	75.00
Q27 Todd Helton	75.00
Q28 Ivan Rodriguez	100.00
Q29 Vladimir Guerrero	150.00
Q30 Albert Belle	75.00

1998 UD Retro Sign of the Times

This retro-style autographed set featured both retired legends and current players. They were inserted 1:36 packs.

		MT
Common Autograph:		20.00
Inserted 1:36		
EB	Ernie Banks (300)	65.00
YB	Yogi Berra (150)	100.00
RB	Russell Branyan (750)	20.00
LB	Lou Brock (300)	60.00
JC	Jose Cruz Jr. (300)	30.00
RF	Rollie Fingers (600)	30.00
BF	Bob Feller (600)	40.00
CF	Carlton Fisk (600)	50.00
BGi	Bob Gibson (300)	60.00
BGr	Ben Grieve (300)	40.00
KGj	Ken Griffey Jr. (100)	600.00
KGs	Ken Griffey Sr. (600)	30.00
JG	Jose Guillen	20.00
TG	Tony Gwynn (200)	150.00
AK	Al Kaline (600)	50.00
PK	Paul Konerko (750)	20.00
TLe	Travis Lee (300)	25.00
EM	Eddie Mathews (600)	50.00
GMj	Gary Matthews Jr. (750)	20.00
GMs	Gary Matthews (600)	20.00
WM	Willie McCovey (600)	50.00
TP	Tony Perez (600)	40.00
GP	Gaylord Perry (1,000)	35.00
KP	Kirby Puckett (450)	100.00
BR	Brooks Robinson (300)	60.00
SR	Scott Rolen (300)	60.00
NR	Nolan Ryan (500)	250.00
TS	Tom Seaver (300)	80.00
WS	Warren Spahn (600)	50.00
WiS	Willie Stargell (600)	40.00
FT	Frank Thomas (600)	50.00
KW	Kerry Wood (200)	60.00

1998 UD Retro 1990s Time Capsule

Another retro-styled card that featured current stars who were destined to earn a place in baseball history. They were inserted 1:2 packs.

		MT
Complete Set (50):		100.00
Common Player:		.75
Inserted 1:2		
TC1	Mike Mussina	1.50
TC2	Rafael Palmeiro	1.50
TC3	Cal Ripken Jr.	8.00
TC4	Nomar Garciaparra	6.00
TC5	Pedro Martinez	2.50
TC6	Mo Vaughn	1.50
TC7	Albert Belle	1.50
TC8	Frank Thomas	3.00
TC9	David Justice	1.00
TC10	Kenny Lofton	1.50
TC11	Manny Ramirez	3.00
TC12	Jim Thome	1.50
TC13	Derek Jeter	6.00
TC14	Tino Martinez	1.00
TC15	Ben Grieve	1.50
TC16	Rickey Henderson	1.00
TC17	Ken Griffey Jr.	10.00
TC18	Randy Johnson	1.50
TC19	Alex Rodriguez	8.00
TC20	Wade Boggs	1.50
TC21	Fred McGriff	.90
TC22	Juan Gonzalez	3.00
TC23	Ivan Rodriguez	2.50
TC24	Nolan Ryan	8.00
TC25	Jose Canseco	2.00
TC26	Roger Clemens	4.00
TC27	Jose Cruz Jr.	.75
TC28	Travis Lee	1.00
TC29	Matt Williams	1.00
TC30	Andres Galarraga	1.50
TC31	Andruw Jones	2.00
TC32	Chipper Jones	6.00
TC33	Greg Maddux	5.00
TC34	Kerry Wood	2.00
TC35	Barry Larkin	1.00
TC36	Dante Bichette	1.00
TC37	Larry Walker	1.50
TC38	Livan Hernandez	.75
TC39	Jeff Bagwell	2.50
TC40	Craig Biggio	.75
TC41	Charles Johnson	.75
TC42	Gary Sheffield	1.00
TC43	Marquis Grissom	.75
TC44	Mike Piazza	6.00
TC45	Scott Rolen	2.00
TC46	Curt Schilling	.75
TC47	Mark McGwire	10.00
TC48	Ken Caminiti	.75
TC49	Tony Gwynn	5.00
TC50	Barry Bonds	2.50

1998 UD Retro Lunchbox

Lunchboxes were the form of packaging for UD Retro. Six different players are featured with each lunchbox containing 24 six-card packs, with a SRP of $4.99.

	MT
Complete Set (6):	75.00
Common Lunchbox:	8.00
Nomar Garciaparra	12.00
Ken Griffey Jr.	20.00
Chipper Jones	12.00
Travis Lee	8.00
Mark McGwire	20.00
Cal Ripken Jr.	15.00

1998 Upper Deck Rookie Edition Preview

		MT
Complete Set (10):		6.00
Common Player:		.40
1	Nomar Garciaparra	2.00
2	Scott Rolen	1.00
3	Mark Kotsay	.50
4	Todd Helton	.75
5	Paul Konerko	.50
6	Juan Encarnacion	.40
7	Brad Fullmer	.50
8	Miguel Tejada	.75
9	Richard Hidalgo	.40
10	Ben Grieve	.75

1998 Upper Deck Rookie Edition All-Star Credentials

All-Star Credentials is a 30-card insert seeded 1:9. It features the game's top players.

		MT
Complete Set (30):		100.00
Common Player:		.75
Inserted 1:9		
AS1	Ken Griffey Jr.	12.00
AS2	Travis Lee	2.00
AS3	Ben Grieve	2.00
AS4	Jose Cruz Jr.	.75
AS5	Andruw Jones	2.00
AS6	Craig Biggio	1.50
AS7	Hideo Nomo	1.50
AS8	Cal Ripken Jr.	10.00
AS9	Jaret Wright	1.50
AS10	Mark McGwire	12.00
AS11	Derek Jeter	8.00
AS12	Scott Rolen	3.00
AS13	Jeff Bagwell	3.00
AS14	Manny Ramirez	3.00
AS15	Alex Rodriguez	12.00
AS16	Chipper Jones	8.00
AS17	Larry Walker	2.50
AS18	Barry Bonds	3.00
AS19	Tony Gwynn	6.00
AS20	Mike Piazza	8.00
AS21	Roger Clemens	4.00
AS22	Greg Maddux	6.00
AS23	Jim Thome	2.00
AS24	Tino Martinez	1.00
AS25	Nomar Garciaparra	8.00
AS26	Juan Gonzalez	4.00
AS27	Kenny Lofton	2.50
AS28	Randy Johnson	2.50
AS29	Todd Helton	2.50
AS30	Frank Thomas	4.00

1998 Upper Deck Rookie Edition A Piece of the Action

A Piece of the Action consists of five Game Jersey cards. Three rookie Game Jersey cards were sequentially numbered to 200, while a Ken Griffey Jr. Game Jersey card was numbered to 300. Griffey also signed and hand-numbered 24 Game Jersey cards.

		MT
Common Card:		75.00
KG	Ken Griffey Jr. (300)	450.00
KGS	Ken Griffey Jr. (24) (Signed)	3000.
BG	Ben Grieve (200)	125.00
JC	Jose Cruz Jr. (200)	60.00
TL	Travis Lee (200)	80.00

1998 Upper Deck Rookie Edition Destination Stardom

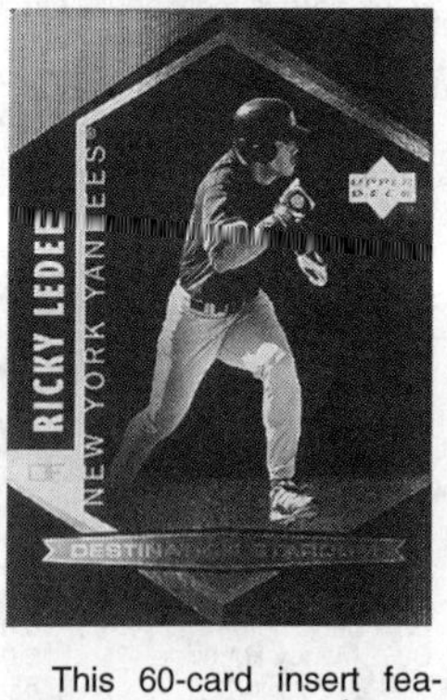

This 60-card insert features top young players. Fronts are printed on a foil background. The insertion rate was one card per five packs.

		MT
Complete Set (60):		75.00
Common Player:		.50
Inserted 1:5		
DS1	Travis Lee	1.50
DS2	Nomar Garciaparra	8.00
DS3	Alex Gonzalez	.75
DS4	Richard Hidalgo	.50
DS5	Jaret Wright	.50
DS6	Mike Kinkade	.50
DS7	Matt Morris	.50
DS8	Gary Mathews Jr.	.50
DS9	Brett Tomko	.50
DS10	Todd Helton	2.50
DS11	Scott Elarton	.50
DS12	Scott Rolen	3.00
DS13	Jose Cruz Jr.	1.00
DS14	Jarrod Washburn	.50
DS15	Sean Casey	4.00
DS16	Magglio Ordonez	6.00
DS17	Gabe Alvarez	.50
DS18	Todd Dunwoody	.50
DS19	Kevin Witt	.50
DS20	Ben Grieve	1.50
DS21	Daryle Ward	.50
DS22	Matt Clement	.50
DS23	Carlton Loewer	.50
DS24	Javier Vazquez	.50
DS25	Paul Konerko	1.00
DS26	Preston Wilson	1.00
DS27	Wes Helms	.50
DS28	Derek Jeter	8.00
DS29	Corey Koskie	.75
DS30	Russell Branyan	.50
DS31	Vladimir Guerrero	5.00
DS32	Ryan Christenson	.50
DS33	Carlos Lee	2.00
DS34	David Dellucci	.50
DS35	Bruce Chen	.50
DS36	Ricky Ledee	1.00
DS37	Ron Wright	.50
DS38	Derrek Lee	.50
DS39	Miguel Tejada	2.50
DS40	Brad Fullmer	1.00
DS41	Rich Butler	.50
DS42	Chris Carpenter	.50
DS43	Alex Rodriguez	10.00
DS44	Darron Ingram	.50
DS45	Kerry Wood	3.00
DS46	Jason Varitek	.50
DS47	Ramon Hernandez	.50
DS48	Aaron Boone	.50
DS49	Juan Encarnacion	.50
DS50	A.J. Hinch	.50
DS51	Mike Lowell	.50
DS52	Fernando Tatis	1.00
DS53	Jose Guillen	.50
DS54	Mike Caruso	.50
DS55	Carl Pavano	.50
DS56	Chris Clemons	.50
DS57	Mark L. Johnson	.50
DS58	Ken Cloude	.50
DS59	Rolando Arrojo	1.00
DS60	Mark Kotsay	1.00

1998 Upper Deck Rookie Edition Eminent Prestige 5x7

Complete Set (10):	
Common Player:	
605	Mike Piazza
607	Frank Thomas
610	Mark McGwire
611	Jeff Bagwell
612	Travis Lee
614	Cal Ripken Jr.
616	Nomar Garciaparra
617	Alex Rodriguez
619	Tony Gwynn
620	Ken Griffey Jr.

1998 Upper Deck Rookie Edition Retrospectives

Retrospectives is a 30-card insert seeded 1:24. The cards offer a look back at the careers of baseball's top stars.

		MT
Complete Set (30):		200.00
Common Player:		2.50
Inserted 1:24		
1	Dennis Eckersley	2.50
2	Rickey Henderson	5.00
3	Harold Baines	2.50
4	Cal Ripken Jr.	25.00
5	Tony Gwynn	15.00
6	Wade Boggs	4.00
7	Orel Hershiser	2.50
8	Joe Carter	2.50
9	Roger Clemens	10.00
10	Barry Bonds	8.00
11	Mark McGwire	30.00
12	Greg Maddux	15.00
13	Fred McGriff	3.00
14	Rafael Palmeiro	5.00
15	Craig Biggio	3.00
16	Brady Anderson	2.50
17	Randy Johnson	5.00
18	Gary Sheffield	3.00
19	Albert Belle	6.00
20	Ken Griffey Jr.	30.00
21	Juan Gonzalez	8.00
22	Larry Walker	5.00
23	Tino Martinez	3.00
24	Frank Thomas	8.00
25	Jeff Bagwell	8.00
26	Kenny Lofton	6.00
27	Mo Vaughn	6.00
28	Mike Piazza	20.00
29	Alex Rodriguez	25.00
30	Chipper Jones	20.00

1998 Upper Deck Rookie Edition Unparalleled

Unparalleled is a 20-card, hobby-only insert. The set consists of holo-pattern foil-stamped cards. They were inserted one per 72 packs.

		MT
Complete Set (20):		375.00
Common Player:		5.00
Inserted 1:72		
1	Ken Griffey Jr.	50.00
2	Travis Lee	8.00
3	Ben Grieve	8.00
4	Jose Cruz Jr.	6.00
5	Nomar Garciaparra	30.00
6	Hideo Nomo	6.00
7	Kenny Lofton	10.00
8	Cal Ripken Jr.	40.00
9	Roger Clemens	20.00
10	Mike Piazza	30.00
11	Jeff Bagwell	15.00
12	Chipper Jones	30.00
13	Greg Maddux	25.00
14	Randy Johnson	10.00
15	Alex Rodriguez	40.00
16	Barry Bonds	12.00
17	Frank Thomas	15.00
18	Juan Gonzalez	15.00
19	Tony Gwynn	25.00
20	Mark McGwire	50.00

1998 Upper Deck Special F/X

Special F/X is a retail-only product. The 150-card set consists of 125 regular cards, the 15-card Star Rookies subset and a 10-card subset called Ken Griffey Jr.'s Hot List. The base cards are printed on 20-point stock. The only insert is Power Zone which has four levels: Level One, Level Two - Octoberbest, Level Three - Power Driven and Level Four - Superstar Xcitement.

	MT
Complete Set (150):	50.00
Common Player:	.25
Unlisted Stars: .75 to 1.00	
1 Ken Griffey Jr. (Griffey Hot List)	4.00
2 Mark McGwire (Griffey Hot List)	4.00
3 Alex Rodriguez (Griffey Hot List)	4.00
4 Larry Walker (Griffey Hot List)	.75
5 Tino Martinez (Griffey Hot List)	.60
6 Mike Piazza (Griffey Hot List)	3.00
7 Jose Cruz Jr. (Griffey Hot List)	.50
8 Greg Maddux (Griffey Hot List)	3.00
9 Tony Gwynn (Griffey Hot List)	2.50
10 Roger Clemens (Griffey Hot List)	2.50
11 Jason Dickson	.25
12 Darin Erstad	1.50
13 Chuck Finley	.25
14 Dave Hollins	.25
15 Garret Anderson	.25
16 Michael Tucker	.25
17 Javier Lopez	.40
18 John Smoltz	.40
19 Mark Wohlers	.25
20 Greg Maddux	3.00
21 Scott Erickson	.25
22 Jimmy Key	.25
23 B.J. Surhoff	.25
24 Eric Davis	.25
25 Rafael Palmeiro	.50
26 Tim Naehring	.25
27 Darren Bragg	.25
28 Troy O'Leary	.25
29 John Valentin	.25
30 Mo Vaughn	1.00
31 Mark Grace	.75
32 Kevin Foster	.25
33 Kevin Tapani	.25
34 Kevin Orie	.25
35 Albert Belle	1.50
36 Ray Durham	.25
37 Jaime Navarro	.25
38 Mike Cameron	.25
39 Eddie Taubensee	.25
40 Barry Larkin	.50
41 Willie Greene	.25
42 Jeff Shaw	.25
43 Omar Vizquel	.25
44 Brian Giles	.25
45 Jim Thome	1.00
46 David Justice	.75
47 Sandy Alomar Jr.	.50
48 Neifi Perez	.25
49 Dante Bichette	.50
50 Vinny Castilla	.50
51 John Thomson	.25
52 Damion Easley	.25
53 Justin Thompson	.25
54 Bobby Higginson	.25
55 Tony Clark	1.00
56 Charles Johnson	.25
57 Edgar Renteria	.25
58 Alex Fernandez	.25
59 Gary Sheffield	.60
60 Livan Hernandez	.25
61 Craig Biggio	.75
62 Chris Holt	.25
63 Billy Wagner	.25
64 Brad Ausmus	.25
65 Dean Palmer	.25
66 Tim Belcher	.25
67 Jeff King	.25
68 Jose Rosado	.25
69 Chan Ho Park	.75
70 Raul Mondesi	.50
71 Hideo Nomo	.75
72 Todd Zeile	.25
73 Eric Karros	.35
74 Cal Eldred	.25
75 Jeff D'Amico	.25
76 Doug Jones	.25
77 Dave Nilsson	.25
78 Todd Walker	.25
79 Rick Aguilera	.25
80 Paul Molitor	1.00
81 Brad Radke	.25
82 Vladimir Guerrero	1.50
83 Carlos Perez	.25
84 F.P. Santangelo	.25
85 Rondell White	.40
86 Butch Huskey	.25
87 Edgardo Alfonzo	.30
88 John Franco	.25
89 John Olerud	.40
90 Todd Hundley	.25
91 Bernie Williams	.75
92 Andy Pettitte	.75
93 Paul O'Neill	.50
94 David Cone	.40
95 Jason Giambi	.25
96 Damon Mashore	.25
97 Scott Spiezio	.25
98 Ariel Prieto	.25
99 Rico Brogna	.25
100 Mike Lieberthal	.25
101 Garrett Stephenson	.25
102 Ricky Bottalico	.25
103 Kevin Polcovich	.25
104 Jon Lieber	.25
105 Kevin Young	.25
106 Tony Womack	.25
107 Gary Gaetti	.25
108 Alan Benes	.40
109 Willie McGee	.25
110 Mark McGwire	5.00
111 Ron Gant	.35
112 Andy Ashby	.25
113 Steve Finley	.25
114 Quilvio Veras	.25
115 Ken Caminiti	.50
116 Joey Hamilton	.25
117 Bill Mueller	.25
118 Mark Gardner	.25
119 Shawn Estes	.25
120 J.T. Snow	.25
121 Dante Powell	.25
122 Jeff Kent	.25
123 Jamie Moyer	.25
124 Joey Cora	.25
125 Ken Griffey Jr.	5.00
126 Jeff Fassero	.25
127 Edgar Martinez	.25
128 Will Clark	.50
129 Lee Stevens	.25
130 Ivan Rodriguez	1.50
131 Rusty Greer	.35
132 Ed Sprague	.25
133 Pat Hentgen	.25
134 Shannon Stewart	.25
135 Carlos Delgado	.75
136 Brett Tomko (Star Rookie)	.25
137 Jose Guillen (Star Rookie)	.50
138 Elieser Marrero (Star Rookie)	.25
139 Dennis Reyes (Star Rookie)	.25
140 Mark Kotsay (Star Rookie)	.75
141 Richie Sexson (Star Rookie)	.35
142 Todd Helton (Star Rookie)	1.50
143 Jeremi Gonzalez (Star Rookie)	.25
144 Jeff Abbott (Star Rookie)	.25
145 Matt Morris (Star Rookie)	.25
146 Aaron Boone (Star Rookie)	.25
147 Todd Dunwoody (Star Rookie)	.25
148 Mario Valdez (Star Rookie)	.25
149 Fernando Tatis (Star Rookie)	.35
150 Jaret Wright (Star Rookie)	2.00

1998 Upper Deck Special F/X OctoberBest

OctoberBest is Level Two of the Power Zone insert. This 20-card insert is die-cut and printed on silver foil. Inserted one per 34 packs, the set features the postseason exploits of 20 players from Power Zone Level One.

	MT
Complete Set (15):	160.00
Common Player:	3.00
Inserted 1:34	
PZ1 Frank Thomas	12.00
PZ2 Juan Gonzalez	15.00
PZ3 Mike Piazza	20.00
PZ4 Mark McGwire	30.00
PZ5 Jeff Bagwell	12.00
PZ6 Barry Bonds	8.00
PZ7 Ken Griffey Jr.	30.00
PZ8 John Smoltz	3.00
PZ9 Andruw Jones	8.00
PZ10 Greg Maddux	17.50
PZ11 Sandy Alomar Jr.	3.00
PZ12 Roberto Alomar	6.00
PZ13 Chipper Jones	20.00
PZ14 Kenny Lofton	6.00
PZ15 Tom Glavine	3.00

1998 Upper Deck Special F/X Power Driven

Power Driven is Level Three of the Power Zone insert. Inserted 1:69, the set features the top 10 power hitters from Power Zone Level Two. The cards feature gold Light F/X Technology.

	MT
Complete Set (10):	150.00
Common Player:	4.00
Inserted 1:69	
PZ1 Frank Thomas	15.00
PZ2 Juan Gonzalez	20.00
PZ3 Mike Piazza	25.00
PZ4 Larry Walker	5.00
PZ5 Mark McGwire	40.00
PZ6 Jeff Bagwell	15.00
PZ7 Mo Vaughn	8.00
PZ8 Barry Bonds	10.00
PZ9 Tino Martinez	4.00
PZ10 Ken Griffey Jr.	40.00

1998 Upper Deck Special F/X Power Zone

Power Zone Level One is a 30-card insert seeded one per seven packs. The cards are printed using silver Light F/X technology.

	MT
Complete Set (20):	50.00
Common Player:	.75
Inserted 1:7	
PZ1 Jose Cruz Jr.	1.00
PZ2 Frank Thomas	4.00
PZ3 Juan Gonzalez	5.00
PZ4 Mike Piazza	6.00
PZ5 Mark McGwire	10.00
PZ6 Barry Bonds	3.00
PZ7 Greg Maddux	6.00
PZ8 Alex Rodriguez	8.00
PZ9 Nomar Garciaparra	6.00
PZ10 Ken Griffey Jr.	10.00
PZ11 John Smoltz	.75
PZ12 Andruw Jones	2.50
PZ13 Sandy Alomar Jr.	.75
PZ14 Roberto Alomar	2.00
PZ15 Chipper Jones	6.00
PZ16 Kenny Lofton	2.00
PZ17 Larry Walker	1.50
PZ18 Jeff Bagwell	4.00
PZ19 Mo Vaughn	2.00
PZ20 Tom Glavine	.75

1998 Upper Deck Special F/X Superstar Xcitement

Printed on Light F/X gold foil, this 10-card set features the same players as the Power Driven insert. This set is Power Zone Level Four and is sequentially numbered to 250.

	MT
Complete Set (10):	600.00
Common Player:	12.00
Production 250 sets	
PZ1 Jose Cruz Jr.	12.00
PZ2 Frank Thomas	40.00
PZ3 Juan Gonzalez	40.00
PZ4 Mike Piazza	75.00
PZ5 Mark McGwire	125.00
PZ6 Barry Bonds	30.00
PZ7 Greg Maddux	75.00
PZ8 Alex Rodriguez	90.00
PZ9 Nomar Garciaparra	75.00
PZ10 Ken Griffey Jr.	125.00

Player names in *Italic* type indicate a rookie card.

1998 Upper Deck UD 3

	MT
Complete Set (270):	700.00
Common Future Impact (1-30):	.50
Inserted 1:12	
Die-Cuts (2,000 sets): 1X	
Common Power Corps (31-60):	.25
Inserted 1:1.5	
Die-Cuts (2,000 sets): 3X	
Common Establishment (61-90):	.50
Inserted 1:6	
Die-Cuts (2,000 sets): 2X	
Common Future Impact Embossed (91-120):	.40
Inserted 1:6	
Die-Cuts (1,000 sets): 3X	
Common Power Corps Embossed (121-150):	.25
Inserted 1:4	
Die-Cuts (1,000 sets): 6X	
Common Establishment Embossed (151-180):	.25
Inserted 1:1	
Die-Cuts (1,000 sets): 12X	
Common Future Impact Rainbow (181-210):	.25
Inserted 1:1	
Die-Cuts (100 sets): 15X	
Common Power Corps Rainbow (211-240):	1.50
Inserted 1:12	
Die-Cuts (100 sets): 8X	
Common Establishment Rainbow (241-270):	2.00
Inserted 1:24	
Die-Cuts (100 sets): 5X	
1 Travis Lee	6.00
2 A.J. Hinch	.50
3 Mike Caruso	.50
4 Miguel Tejada	1.50
5 Brad Fullmer	1.50
6 Eric Milton	.50
7 Mark Kotsay	2.00
8 Darin Erstad	6.00
9 Magglio Ordonez	2.00
10 Ben Grieve	8.00
11 Brett Tomko	.50
12 *Mike Kinkade*	1.00
13 Rolando Arrojo	5.00
14 Todd Helton	1.50
15 Scott Rolen	4.00
16 Bruce Chen	.50
17 Daryle Ward	.50
18 Jaret Wright	4.00
19 Cliff Politte	.50
20 Paul Konerko	.75
21 Kerry Wood	4.00
22 Russell Branyan	.50
23 Gabe Alvarez	.50
24 Juan Encarnacion	.50
25 Andruw Jones	4.00
26 Vladimir Guerrero	5.00
27 Eli Marrero	.25
28 Matt Clement	.25
29 Gary Matthews Jr.	1.00
30 Derrek Lee	.50
31 Ken Caminiti	.75
32 Gary Sheffield	1.00
33 Jay Buhner	.75
34 Ryan Klesko	.75
35 Nomar Garciaparra	5.00
36 Vinny Castilla	.25
37 Tony Clark	.75
38 Sammy Sosa	5.00
39 Tino Martinez	.75
40 Mike Piazza	5.00
41 Manny Ramirez	3.00
42 Larry Walker	.75
43 Jose Cruz Jr.	1.50
44 Matt Williams	.75
45 Frank Thomas	3.00
46 Jim Edmonds	.25
47 Raul Mondesi	.60
48 Alex Rodriguez	5.00
49 Albert Belle	2.00
50 Mark McGwire	10.00
51 Tim Salmon	.75
52 Andres Galarraga	.75
53 Jeff Bagwell	3.00
54 Jim Thome	1.00
55 Barry Bonds	2.00
56 Carlos Delgado	.50
57 Mo Vaughn	2.00
58 Chipper Jones	4.00
59 Juan Gonzalez	4.00
60 Ken Griffey Jr.	8.00
61 David Cone	.40
62 Hideo Nomo	2.00
63 Edgar Martinez	.25
64 Fred McGriff	1.00
65 Cal Ripken Jr.	10.00
66 Todd Hundley	.25
67 Barry Larkin	.75
68 Dennis Eckersley	.25
69 Randy Johnson	3.00
70 Paul Molitor	3.00
71 Eric Karros	.25
72 Rafael Palmeiro	.75
73 Chuck Knoblauch	2.00
74 Ivan Rodriguez	4.00
75 Greg Maddux	8.00
76 Dante Bichette	1.50
77 Brady Anderson	.25
78 Craig Biggio	.75
79 Derek Jeter	7.00
80 Roger Clemens	6.00
81 Roberto Alomar	2.50
82 Wade Boggs	.75
83 Charles Johnson	.25
84 Mark Grace	.75
85 Kenny Lofton	4.00
86 Mike Mussina	3.00
87 Pedro Martinez	3.00
88 Curt Schilling	.50
89 Bernie Williams	2.50
90 Tony Gwynn	6.00
91 Travis Lee	3.00
92 A.J. Hinch	.50
93 Mike Caruso	.40
94 Miguel Tejada	1.00
95 Brad Fullmer	1.50
96 Eric Milton	.25
97 Mark Kotsay	1.50
98 Darin Erstad	3.00
99 Magglio Ordonez	1.50
100 Ben Grieve	5.00
101 Brett Tomko	.40
102 Mike Kinkade	.40
103 Rolando Arrojo	4.00
104 Todd Helton	2.50
105 Scott Rolen	4.00
106 Bruce Chen	.40
107 Daryle Ward	.40
108 Jaret Wright	3.00
109 Sean Casey	.50
110 Paul Konerko	.75
111 Kerry Wood	4.00
112 Russell Branyan	.40
113 Gabe Alvarez	.40
114 Juan Encarnacion	.40
115 Andruw Jones	3.00
116 Vladimir Guerrero	4.00
117 Eli Marrero	.40
118 Matt Clement	.40
119 Gary Matthews Jr.	1.00
120 Derrek Lee	.25
121 Ken Caminiti	.50
122 Gary Sheffield	.75
123 Jay Buhner	.50
124 Ryan Klesko	.50
125 Nomar Garciaparra	5.00
126 Vinny Castilla	.25
127 Tony Clark	1.00
128 Sammy Sosa	5.00
129 Tino Martinez	1.00
130 Mike Piazza	5.00
131 Manny Ramirez	3.00
132 Larry Walker	1.00
133 Jose Cruz Jr.	1.50
134 Matt Williams	.75
135 Frank Thomas	3.00
136 Jim Edmonds	.25
137 Raul Mondesi	.40
138 Alex Rodriguez	5.00
139 Albert Belle	2.00
140 Mark McGwire	10.00
141 Tim Salmon	.50
142 Andres Galarraga	.75
143 Jeff Bagwell	2.50
144 Jim Thome	.75
145 Barry Bonds	2.00
146 Carlos Delgado	.50
147 Mo Vaughn	2.00
148 Chipper Jones	4.00
149 Juan Gonzalez	4.00
150 Ken Griffey Jr.	8.00
151 David Cone	.40
152 Hideo Nomo	.75
153 Edgar Martinez	.25
154 Fred McGriff	.25
155 Cal Ripken Jr.	3.00
156 Todd Hundley	.25
157 Barry Larkin	.40
158 Dennis Eckersley	.25
159 Randy Johnson	1.00
160 Paul Molitor	1.00
161 Eric Karros	.40
162 Rafael Palmeiro	.40
163 Chuck Knoblauch	.75
164 Ivan Rodriguez	1.25
165 Greg Maddux	2.50
166 Dante Bichette	.50
167 Brady Anderson	.25
168 Craig Biggio	.25
169 Derek Jeter	2.50
170 Roger Clemens	2.00
171 Roberto Alomar	1.00
172 Wade Boggs	.50
173 Charles Johnson	.25
174 Mark Grace	.50
175 Kenny Lofton	1.25
176 Mike Mussina	1.00
177 Pedro Martinez	1.00
178 Curt Schilling	.40
179 Bernie Williams	.75
180 Tony Gwynn	2.00
181 Travis Lee	1.50
182 A.J. Hinch	.25

183	Mike Caruso	.40
184	Miguel Tejada	.75
185	Brad Fullmer	.75
186	Eric Milton	.25
187	Mark Kotsay	.75
188	Darin Erstad	1.50
189	Magglio Ordonez	1.00
190	Ben Grieve	2.00
191	Brett Tomko	.25
192	Mike Kinkade	.25
193	Rolando Arrojo	2.00
194	Todd Helton	1.00
195	Scott Rolen	1.50
196	Bruce Chen	.25
197	Daryle Ward	.25
198	Jaret Wright	1.25
199	Cliff Politte	.25
200	Paul Konerko	.50
201	Kerry Wood	2.00
202	Russell Branyan	.25
203	Gabe Alvarez	.25
204	Juan Encarnacion	.25
205	Andruw Jones	1.00
206	Vladimir Guerrero	1.50
207	Eli Marrero	.25
208	Matt Clement	.25
209	Gary Matthews Jr.	.25
210	Derrek Lee	.25
211	Ken Caminiti	1.50
212	Gary Sheffield	2.50
213	Jay Buhner	2.50
214	Ryan Klesko	2.50
215	Nomar Garciaparra	15.00
216	Vinny Castilla	1.50
217	Tony Clark	4.00
218	Sammy Sosa	15.00
219	Tino Martinez	3.00
220	Mike Piazza	15.00
221	Manny Ramirez	8.00
222	Larry Walker	3.00
223	Jose Cruz Jr.	2.00
224	Matt Williams	2.50
225	Frank Thomas	6.00
226	Jim Edmonds	1.50
227	Raul Mondesi	2.00
228	Alex Rodriguez	15.00
229	Albert Belle	6.00
230	Mark McGwire	30.00
231	Tim Salmon	2.50
232	Andres Galarraga	3.00
233	Jeff Bagwell	8.00
234	Jim Thome	4.00
235	Barry Bonds	6.00
236	Carlos Delgado	3.00
267	Mo Vaughn	6.00
238	Chipper Jones	12.00
239	Juan Gonzalez	12.00
240	Ken Griffey Jr.	25.00
241	David Cone	2.50
242	Hideo Nomo	4.00
243	Edgar Martinez	2.00
244	Fred McGriff	2.50
245	Cal Ripken Jr.	30.00
246	Todd Hundley	2.00
247	Barry Larkin	2.50
248	Dennis Eckersley	2.00
249	Randy Johnson	8.00
250	Paul Molitor	8.00
251	Eric Karros	2.00
252	Rafael Palmeiro	3.00
253	Chuck Knoblauch	4.00
254	Ivan Rodriguez	10.00
255	Greg Maddux	25.00
256	Dante Bichette	3.00
257	Brady Anderson	2.00
258	Craig Biggio	2.00
259	Derek Jeter	25.00
260	Roger Clemens	20.00
261	Roberto Alomar	8.00
262	Wade Boggs	4.00
263	Charles Johnson	2.00
264	Mark Grace	3.00
265	Kenny Lofton	10.00
266	Mike Mussina	8.00
267	Pedro Martinez	8.00
268	Curt Schilling	2.00
269	Bernie Williams	6.00
270	Tony Gwynn	20.00

1998 Upper Deck UD 3 Die-Cut

Die-cut versions of all 270 cards in UD 3 were available and sequentially numbered. FX subset cards (1-90) were numbered to 2,000 sets, Embossed cards (91-180) were numbered to 1,000 and Rainbow foil cards (181-270) were numbered to 100.

Future Impact (1-30): 1X
Power Corps (31-60): 3X
Establishment (61-90): 2X
Regular Production
2,000 sets each
Future Impact Embossed (91-120): 3X
Power Corps Embossed (121-150): 6X
Establishment Embossed (151-180): 12X
Embossed Production
1,000 sets each
Future Impact Rainbow (181-210): 15X
Power Corps Rainbow (211-240): 8X
Establishment Rainbow (241-270): 5X
Rainbow Production 100 sets each
(See 1998 UD3 for checklist and base card values.)

1998 Upper Deck UD 3 Power Corps Blowup

Complete Set (10):
Common Player:

60	Ken Griffey Jr.
50	Mark McGwire
38	Sammy Sosa
58	Chipper Jones
45	Frank Thomas
40	Mike Piazza
59	Juan Gonzalez
55	Barry Bonds
48	Alex Rodriguez
35	Nomar Garciaparra

1999 Upper Deck

Released in two series, card fronts feature a textured silver border along the left and right sides of the base card. The player name and Upper Deck logo also are stamped with silver foil. Card backs have a small photo, with year by year stats and a brief highlight caption of the player's career. Randomly seeded in packs are 100 Ken Griffey Jr. rookie cards that were bought back by Upper Deck from the hobby and autographed by Griffey Jr. Upper Deck also reinserted one pack of '89 Upper Deck inside every hobby box. 10-card hobby packs carry a S.R.P. of $2.99.

	MT
Complete Set (525):	90.00
Complete Series 1 (255):	50.00
Complete Series 2 (270):	40.00
Common Player:	.10
Common SR (1-18):	.50
Exclusive Stars/RCs: 20X	
Production 100 each	
Ser 1 H Wax Box:	90.00
Ser 2 H Wax Box:	75.00

1	Troy Glaus (Star Rookies)	2.50
2	Adrian Beltre (Star Rookies)	1.00
3	Matt Anderson (Star Rookies)	.50
4	Eric Chavez (Star Rookies)	3.00
5	Jin Cho (Star Rookies)	.50
6	*Robert Smith* (Star Rookies)	.50
7	George Lombard (Star Rookies)	1.00
8	Mike Kinkade (Star Rookies)	.75
9	Seth Greisinger (Star Rookies)	.50
10	J.D. Drew (Star Rookies)	3.00
11	Aramis Ramirez (Star Rookies)	.75
12	Carlos Guillen (Star Rookies)	.50
13	Justin Baughman (Star Rookies)	.50
14	Jim Parque (Star Rookies)	.50
15	Ryan Jackson (Star Rookies)	.50
16	Ramon Martinez (Star Rookies)	.50
17	Orlando Hernandez (Star Rookies)	3.00
18	Jeremy Giambi (Star Rookies)	1.00
19	Gary DiSarcina	.10
20	Darin Erstad	.75
21	Troy Glaus	1.00
22	Chuck Finley	.10
23	Dave Hollins	.10
24	Troy Percival	.10
25	Tim Salmon	.25
26	Brian Anderson	.10
27	Jay Bell	.10
28	Andy Benes	.10
29	Brent Brede	.10
30	David Dellucci	.10
31	Karim Garcia	.10
32	Travis Lee	.75
33	Andres Galarraga	.30
34	Ryan Klesko	.25
35	Keith Lockhart	.10
36	Kevin Millwood	.40
37	Denny Neagle	.10
38	John Smoltz	.25
39	Michael Tucker	.10
40	Walt Weiss	.10
41	Dennis Martinez	.10
42	Javy Lopez	.10
43	Brady Anderson	.10
44	Harold Baines	.10
45	Mike Bordick	.10
46	Roberto Alomar	.50
47	Scott Erickson	.10
48	Mike Mussina	.50
49	Cal Ripken Jr.	2.50
50	Darren Bragg	.10
51	Dennis Eckersley	.10
52	Nomar Garciaparra	2.00
53	Scott Hatteberg	.10
54	Troy O'Leary	.10
55	Bret Saberhagen	.10
56	John Valentin	.10
57	Rod Beck	.10
58	Jeff Blauser	.10
59	Brant Brown	.10
60	Mark Clark	.10
61	Mark Grace	.25
62	Kevin Tapani	.10
63	Henry Rodriguez	.10
64	Mike Cameron	.10
65	Mike Caruso	.10
66	Ray Durham	.10
67	Jaime Navarro	.10
68	Magglio Ordonez	.25
69	Mike Sirotka	.10
70	Sean Casey	.20
71	Barry Larkin	.25
72	Jon Nunnally	.10
73	Paul Konerko	.25
74	Chris Stynes	.10
75	Brett Tomko	.10
76	Dmitri Young	.10
77	Sandy Alomar	.10
78	Bartolo Colon	.10
79	Travis Fryman	.10
80	Brian Giles	.10
81	David Justice	.25
82	Omar Vizquel	.10
83	Jaret Wright	.50
84	Jim Thome	.40
85	Charles Nagy	.10
86	Pedro Astacio	.10
87	Todd Helton	.60
88	Darryl Kile	.10
89	Mike Lansing	.10
90	Neifi Perez	.10
91	John Thomson	.10
92	Larry Walker	.40
93	Tony Clark	.40
94	Deivi Cruz	.10
95	Damion Easley	.10
96	Brian L. Hunter	.10
97	Todd Jones	.10
98	Brian Moehler	.10
99	Gabe Alvarez	.10
100	Craig Counsell	.10
101	Cliff Floyd	.10
102	Livan Hernandez	.10
103	Andy Larkin	.10
104	Derrek Lee	.10
105	Brian Meadows	.10
106	Moises Alou	.25
107	Sean Berry	.10
108	Craig Biggio	.25
109	Ricky Gutierrez	.10
110	Mike Hampton	.10
111	Jose Lima	.10
112	Billy Wagner	.10
113	Hal Morris	.10
114	Johnny Damon	.10
115	Jeff King	.10
116	Jeff Montgomery	.10
117	Glendon Rusch	.10
118	Larry Sutton	.10
119	Bobby Bonilla	.20
120	Jim Eisenreich	.10
121	Eric Karros	.20
122	Matt Luke	.10
123	Ramon Martinez	.20
124	Gary Sheffield	.25
125	Eric Young	.10
126	Charles Johnson	.10
127	Jeff Cirillo	.10
128	Marquis Grissom	.10
129	Jeremy Burnitz	.10
130	Bob Wickman	.10
131	Scott Karl	.10
132	Mark Loretta	.10
133	Fernando Vina	.10
134	Matt Lawton	.10
135	Pat Meares	.10
136	Eric Milton	.10
137	Paul Molitor	.50
138	David Ortiz	.10
139	Todd Walker	.25
140	Shane Andrews	.10
141	Brad Fullmer	.25
142	Vladimir Guerrero	1.00
143	Dustin Hermanson	.10
144	Ryan McGuire	.10
145	Ugueth Urbina	.10
146	John Franco	.10
147	Butch Huskey	.10
148	Bobby Jones	.10
149	John Olerud	.25
150	Rey Ordonez	.10
151	Mike Piazza	2.00
152	Hideo Nomo	.40
153	Masato Yoshii	.10
154	Derek Jeter	2.00
155	Chuck Knoblauch	.25
156	Paul O'Neill	.25
157	Andy Pettitte	.50
158	Mariano Rivera	.20
159	Darryl Strawberry	.25
160	David Wells	.20
161	Jorge Posada	.20
162	Ramiro Mendoza	.20
163	Miguel Tejada	.25
164	Ryan Christenson	.10
165	Rickey Henderson	.40
166	A.J. Hinch	.10
167	Ben Grieve	.75
168	Kenny Rogers	.10
169	Matt Stairs	.10
170	Bob Abreu	.10
171	Rico Brogna	.10
172	Doug Glanville	.10
173	Mike Grace	.10
174	Desi Relaford	.10
175	Scott Rolen	.75
176	Jose Guillen	.20
177	Francisco Cordova	.10
178	Al Martin	.10
179	Jason Schmidt	.10
180	Turner Ward	.10
181	Kevin Young	.10
182	Mark McGwire	3.00
183	Delino DeShields	.10
184	Eli Marrero	.10
185	Tom Lampkin	.10
186	Ray Lankford	.10
187	Willie McGee	.10
188	Matt Morris	.10
189	Andy Ashby	.10
190	Kevin Brown	.20
191	Ken Caminiti	.20
192	Trevor Hoffman	.10
193	Wally Joyner	.10
194	Greg Vaughn	.20
195	Danny Darwin	.10
196	Shawn Estes	.10
197	Orel Hershiser	.10
198	Jeff Kent	.10
199	Bill Mueller	.10
200	Robb Nen	.10
201	J.T. Snow	.10
202	Ken Cloude	.10
203	Russ Davis	.10
204	Jeff Fassero	.10
205	Ken Griffey Jr.	3.00
206	Shane Monahan	.10
207	David Segui	.10
208	Dan Wilson	.10
209	Wilson Alvarez	.10
210	Wade Boggs	.25
211	Miguel Cairo	.10
212	Bubba Trammell	.10
213	Quinton McCracken	.10
214	Paul Sorrento	.10
215	Kevin Stocker	.10
216	Will Clark	.25
217	Rusty Greer	.10
218	Rick Helling	.10
219	Mike McLemore	.10
220	Ivan Rodriguez	.75
221	John Wetteland	.10
222	Jose Canseco	.60
223	Roger Clemens	1.50
224	Carlos Delgado	.50
225	Darrin Fletcher	.10
226	Alex Gonzalez	.10
227	Jose Cruz Jr.	.50
228	Shannon Stewart	.10
229	Rolando Arrojo (Foreign Focus)	.20
230	Livan Hernandez (Foreign Focus)	.10
231	Orlando Hernandez (Foreign Focus)	1.00
232	Raul Mondesi (Foreign Focus)	.20
233	Moises Alou (Foreign Focus)	.20
234	Pedro Martinez (Foreign Focus)	.75
235	Sammy Sosa (Foreign Focus)	1.25
236	Vladimir Guerrero (Foreign Focus)	.50
237	Bartolo Colon (Foreign Focus)	.10
238	Miguel Tejada (Foreign Focus)	.10
239	Ismael Valdes (Foreign Focus)	.10
240	Mariano Rivera (Foreign Focus)	.10
241	Jose Cruz Jr. (Foreign Focus)	.25
242	Juan Gonzalez (Foreign Focus)	.75
243	Ivan Rodriguez (Foreign Focus)	.40
244	Sandy Alomar (Foreign Focus)	.10
245	Roberto Alomar (Foreign Focus)	.25
246	Magglio Ordonez (Foreign Focus)	.20
247	Kerry Wood (Highlights Checklist)	.75
248	Mark McGwire (Highlights Checklist)	2.00
249	David Wells (Highlights Checklist)	.10
250	Rolando Arrojo (Highlights Checklist)	.20
251	Ken Griffey Jr. (Highlights Checklist)	1.50
252	Trevor Hoffman (Highlights Checklist)	.10
253	Travis Lee (Highlights Checklist)	.40
254	Roberto Alomar (Highlights Checklist)	.25
255	Sammy Sosa (Highlights Checklist)	1.25
256	Not Issued	
257	Not Issued	
258	Not Issued	
259	Not Issued	
260	Not Issued	
261	Not Issued	
262	Not Issued	
263	Not Issued	
264	Not Issued	
265	Not Issued	
266	*Pat Burrell* (Star Rookie)	5.00
267	*Shea Hillenbrand* (Star Rookie)	.50
268	Robert Fick (Star Rookie)	.10
269	Roy Halladay (Star Rookie)	.25
270	Ruben Mateo (Star Rookie)	.50
271	Bruce Chen (Star Rookie)	.25
272	Angel Pena (Star Angel)	.75
273	Michael Barrett (Star Rookie)	.50
274	Kevin Witt (Star Rookie)	.10
275	Damon Minor (Star Rookie)	.10
276	Ryan Minor (Star Rookie)	.40
277	A.J. Pierzynski (Star Rookie)	.10
278	*A.J. Burnett* (Star Rookie)	2.00
279	Dermal Brown (Star Rookie)	.10
280	Joe Lawrence (Star Rookie)	.10
281	Derrick Gibson (Star Rookie)	.10
282	Carlos Febles (Star Rookie)	.75
283	Chris Haas (Star Rookie)	.10
284	Cesar King (Star Rookie)	.10
285	Calvin Pickering (Star Rookie)	.10
286	Mitch Meluskey (Star Rookie)	.15
287	Carlos Beltran (Star Rookie)	2.00
288	Ron Belliard (Star Rookie)	.25

289 Jerry Hairston Jr. (Star Rookie) .10
290 Fernando Seguignol (Star Rookie) .50
291 Kris Benson (Star Rookie) .10
292 *Chad Hutchinson* (Star Rookie) 2.50
293 Jarrod Washburn .10
294 Jason Dickson .10
295 Mo Vaughn .75
296 Garrett Anderson .10
297 Jim Edmonds .10
298 Ken Hill .10
299 Shigetosi Hasegawa .10
300 Todd Stottlemyre .10
301 Randy Johnson .50
302 Omar Daal .10
303 Steve Finley .10
304 Matt Williams .25
305 Danny Klassen .10
306 Tony Batista .10
307 Brian Jordan .10
308 Greg Maddux 2.00
309 Chipper Jones 1.50
310 Bret Boone .10
311 Ozzie Guillen .10
312 John Rocker .10
313 Tom Glavine .20
314 Andruw Jones .75
315 Albert Belle .75
316 Charles Johnson .10
317 Will Clark .40
318 B.J. Surhoff .10
319 Delino DeShields .10
320 Heathcliff Slocumb .10
321 Sidney Ponson .10
322 Juan Guzman .10
323 Reggie Jefferson .10
324 Mark Portugal .10
325 Tim Wakefield .10
326 Jason Varitek .10
327 Jose Offerman .10
328 Pedro Martinez .75
329 Trot Nixon .10
330 Kerry Wood .40
331 Sammy Sosa 2.00
332 Glenallen Hill .10
333 Gary Gaetti .10
334 Mickey Morandini .10
335 Benito Santiago .10
336 Jeff Blauser .10
337 Frank Thomas 1.00
338 Paul Konerko .10
339 Jaime Navarro .10
340 Carlos Lee .10
341 Brian Simmons .10
342 Mark Johnson .10
343 Jeff Abbot .10
344 Steve Avery .10
345 Mike Cameron .10
346 Michael Tucker .10
347 Greg Vaughn .10
348 Hal Morris .10
349 Pete Harnisch .10
350 Denny Neagle .10
351 Manny Ramirez 1.00
352 Roberto Alomar .50
353 Dwight Gooden .10
354 Kenny Lofton .75
355 Mike Jackson .10
356 Charles Nagy .10
357 Enrique Wilson .10
358 Russ Branyan .10
359 Richie Sexson .10
360 Vinny Castilla .20
361 Dante Bichette .30
362 Kirt Manwaring .10
363 Darryl Hamilton .10
364 Jamey Wright .10
365 Curt Leskanic .10
366 Jeff Reed .10
367 Bobby Higginson .10
368 Justin Thompson .10
369 Brad Ausmus .10
370 Dean Palmer .10
371 Gabe Kapler 1.50
372 Juan Encarnacion .10
373 Karim Garcia .10
374 Alex Gonzalez .10
375 Braden Looper .10
376 Preston Wilson .10
377 Todd Dunwoody .10
378 Alex Fernandez .10
379 Mark Kotsay .10
380 Mark Mantei .10
381 Ken Caminiti .10
382 Scott Elarton .10
383 Jeff Bagwell .75
384 Derek Bell .10
385 Ricky Gutierrez .10
386 Richard Hildalgo .10
387 Shane Reynolds .10
388 Carl Everett .10
389 Scott Service .10
390 Jeff Suppan .10
391 Joe Randa .10
392 Kevin Appier .10
393 Shane Halter .10
394 Chad Kreuter .10
395 Mike Sweeney .10
396 Kevin Brown .25
397 Devon White .10
398 Todd Hollandsworth .10
399 Todd Hundley .10
400 Chan Ho Park .20
401 Mark Grudzielanek .10
402 Raul Mondesi .25
403 Ismael Valdes .10
404 Rafael Roque .10
405 Sean Berry .10
406 Kevin Barker .10
407 Dave Nilsson .10
408 Geoff Jenkins .10
409 Jim Abbott .10
410 Bobby Hughes .10
411 Corey Koskie .10
412 Rick Aguilera .10
413 LaTroy Hawkins .10
414 Ron Coomer .10
415 Denny Hocking .10
416 Marty Cordova .10
417 Terry Steinbach .10
418 Rondell White .20
419 Wilton Guerrero .10
420 Shane Andrews .10
421 Orlando Cabrerra .10
422 Carl Pavano .10
423 Jeff Vasquez .10
424 Chris Widger .10
425 Robin Ventura .20
426 Rickey Henderson .20
427 Al Leiter .20
428 Bobby Jones .10
429 Brian McRae .10
430 Roger Cedeno .10
431 Bobby Bonilla .10
432 Edgardo Alfonzo .10
433 Bernie Williams .50
434 Ricky Ledee .10
435 Chili Davis .10
436 Tino Martinez .40
437 Scott Brosius .10
438 David Cone .20
439 Joe Girardi .10
440 Roger Clemens 1.00
441 Chad Curtis .10
442 Hideki Irabu .10
443 Jason Giambi .10
444 Scott Spezio .10
445 Tony Phillips .10
446 Ramon Hernandez .10
447 Mike Macfarlane .10
448 Tom Candiotti .10
449 Billy Taylor .10
450 Bobby Estella .10
451 Curt Schilling .20
452 Carlton Loewer .10
453 Marlon Anderson .10
454 Kevin Jordan .10
455 Ron Gant .10
456 Chad Ogea .10
457 Abraham Nunez .10
458 Jason Kendall .20
459 Pat Meares .10
460 Brant Brown .10
461 Brian Giles .10
462 Chad Hermansen .10
463 Freddy Garcia 3.00
464 Edgar Renteria .10
465 Fernando Tatis .10
466 Eric Davis .10
467 Darren Bragg .10
468 Donovan Osborne .10
469 Manny Aybar .10
470 Jose Jimenez .10
471 Kent Mercker .10
472 Reggie Sanders .10
473 Ruben Rivera .10
474 Tony Gwynn 1.50
475 Jim Leyritz .10
476 Chris Gomez .10
477 Matt Clement .10
478 Carlos Hernandez .10
479 Sterling Hitchcock .10
480 Ellis Burks .10
481 Barry Bonds .75
482 Marvin Bernard .10
483 Kirk Rueter .10
484 F.P. Santangelo .10
485 Stan Javier .10
486 Jeff Kent .10
487 Alex Rodriguez 2.50
488 Tom Lampkin .10
489 Jose Mesa .10
490 Jay Buhner .20
491 Edgar Martinez .10
492 Butch Huskey .10
493 John Mabry .10
494 Jamie Moyer .10
495 Roberto Hernandez .10
496 Tony Saunders .10
497 Fred McGriff .25
498 Dave Martinez .10
499 Jose Canseco .60
500 Rolando Arrojo .10
501 Esteban Yan .10
502 Juan Gonzalez 1.50
503 Rafael Palmeiro .40
504 Aaron Sele .10
505 Royce Clayton .10
506 Todd Zeile .10
507 Tom Goodwin .10
508 Lee Stevens .10
509 Esteban Loaiza .10
510 Joey Hamilton .10
511 Homer Bush .10
512 Willie Greene .10
513 Shawn Green .50
514 David Wells .10
515 Kelvim Escobar .10
516 Tony Fernandez .10
517 Pat Hentgen .10
518 Mark McGwire 3.00
519 Ken Griffey Jr. 1.50
520 Sammy Sosa 1.00
521 Juan Gonzalez .75
522 J.D. Drew .50
523 Chipper Jones .75
524 Alex Rodriguez 1.00
525 Mike Piazza 1.00
526 Nomar Garciaparra 1.00
527 Season Highlights Checklist (Mark McGwire) 2.00
528 Season Highlights Checklist (Sammy Sosa) 1.00
529 Season Highlights Checklist (Scott Brosius) .10
530 Season Highlights Checklist (Cal Ripken Jr.) 1.00
531 Season Highlights Checklist (Barry Bonds) .40
532 Season Highlights Checklist (Roger Clemens) .50
533 Season Highlights Checklist (Ken Griffey Jr.) 1.50
534 Season Highlights Checklist (Alex Rodriguez) 1.00
535 Season Highlights Checklist (Curt Schilling) .10

1999 Upper Deck Crowning Glory

These double-sided cards feature players who reached milestones during the '98 season. There are three cards in the set, with four different versions of each card. The regular version is seeded 1:23 packs. Doubles are numbered to 1,000, Triples numbered to 25 and Home Runs are limited to one each.

	MT
Complete Set (3):	60.00
Common Player:	10.00
Inserted 1:23	
Doubles (1,000 sets): 2X	
Triples (25 sets): 8X	
Home Runs (1 set): Values Undetermined	
CG1 Roger Clemens, Kerry Wood	15.00
CG2 Mark McGwire, Barry Bonds	25.00
CG3 Ken Griffey Jr., Mark McGwire	30.00

1999 Upper Deck Exclusives

Randomly inserted into hobby packs, this parallel issue is individually serial numbered on back from within an edition of 100 of each card. Besides the serial number, the inserts are readily apparent by the use of copper metallic foil graphic highlights on front. A parallel of this parallel with only one card of each player, was also issued but is not priced here because of rarity. Series 1 Exclusive cards have the serial number on back in gold foil; Series 2 Exclusives have the number ink-jetted in black.

	MT
Common Player:	5.00
Stars: 15X	
Rookies: 8X	
(See 1999 Upper Deck for checklist, base card values.)	

1999 Upper Deck Forte

This 30-card set features the top players in the game, highlighted by blue holofoil treatment. Numbers on card backs have a "F" prefix and are seeded 1:23 packs. There are also die-cut parallels to Forte: Double, Triple and Home Run. Doubles are sequentially numbered to 2,000 sets, Triples are limited to 100 numbered sets and Home Runs are limited to 10 numbered sets.

		MT
Complete Set (30):		250.00
Common Player:		3.00
Inserted 1:23		
Doubles (2,000 sets): 2X		
Triples (100 sets): 5X		
Quadruples (10 sets): Value Undetermined		
1	Darin Erstad	4.00
2	Troy Glaus	5.00
3	Mo Vaughn	4.00
4	Greg Maddux	12.00
5	Andres Galarraga	5.00
6	Chipper Jones	15.00
7	Cal Ripken Jr.	20.00
8	Albert Belle	5.00
9	Nomar Garciaparra	15.00
10	Sammy Sosa	15.00
11	Kerry Wood	5.00
12	Frank Thomas	8.00
13	Jim Thome	4.00
14	Jeff Bagwell	6.00
15	Vladimir Guerrero	8.00
16	Mike Piazza	15.00
17	Derek Jeter	15.00
18	Ben Grieve	4.00
19	Eric Chavez	3.00
20	Scott Rolen	6.00
21	Mark McGwire	25.00
22	J.D. Drew	6.00
23	Tony Gwynn	12.00
24	Barry Bonds	6.00
25	Alex Rodriguez	15.00
26	Ken Griffey Jr.	25.00
27	Ivan Rodriguez	6.00
28	Juan Gonzalez	8.00
29	Roger Clemens	8.00
30	Andruw Jones	5.00

1999 Upper Deck Game Jersey

Inserted in both hobby and retail packs, this five-card set features a swatch of game-used jersey on each card. These are seeded 1:2,500 packs.

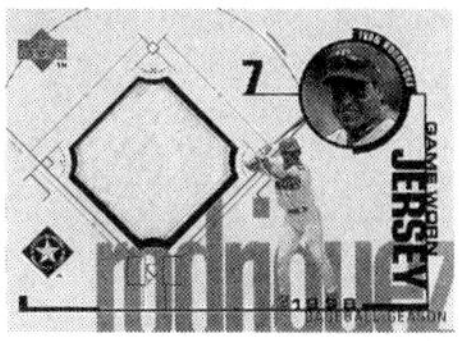

		MT
Complete Set (9):		1900.
Complete Series 1 (5):		850.00
Complete Series 2 (4):		1100.
Common Player:		50.00
Inserted 1:2,500		
GJKW	Kerry Wood	100.00
GJCJ	Charles Johnson	50.00
GJMP	Mike Piazza	300.00
GJAR	Alex Rodriguez	300.00
GJJG	Juan Gonzalez	200.00
GJKWs	Kerry Wood (autographed)	1000.
GJKGs	Ken Griffey Jr. (autographed)	4000.
GM	Greg Maddux	250.00
JR	Ken Griffey Jr.	400.00
NRb	Nolan Ryan	450.00
FT	Frank Thomas	180.00
JRS	Ken Griffey Jr. (autographed)	4000.

1999 Upper Deck Game Jersey-Hobby

This six-card set features a swatch of game-used jersey on each card and are available exclusively in hobby packs. The insert ratio is 1:288 packs.

		MT
Complete Set (14):		1800.
Common Player:		50.00
Inserted 1:288		
GJKG	Ken Griffey Jr.	400.00
GJAB	Adrian Beltre	50.00
GJBG	Ben Grieve	75.00
GJTL	Travis Lee	50.00
GJIV	Ivan Rodriguez	125.00
GJDE	Darin Erstad	60.00
GJKGs	Ken Griffey Jr. (autographed)	4000.
BF	Brad Fullmer	50.00
BT	Bubba Trammell	50.00
EC	Eric Chavez	50.00
JD	J.D. Drew	100.00
MR	Manny Ramirez	150.00
NRa	Nolan Ryan	400.00
TGw	Tony Gwynn	150.00
CJ	Chipper Jones	150.00
JDs	J.D. Drew (auto, 8)	
NRaS	Nolan Ryan (autographed edition of 34)	4000.
TH	Todd Helton	60.00

1999 Upper Deck Immaculate Perception

Done in a horizontal format, this 27-card set features baseball's most celebrated players. Card fronts are enhanced with copper and silver foil stamping, encasing the player's image. The cards are numbered with an I prefix and are seeded 1:23 packs. There are also three parallel versions: Doubles numbered to

1,000, Triples numbered to 25 and Home Runs which are limited to one.

		MT
	Complete Set (27):	220.00
	Common Player:	2.50
	Inserted 1:23	
	Doubles (1,000 sets): 1.5X	
	Triples (25 sets): 8X	
	Home Runs (1 sets): Values Undetermined	
101	Jeff Bagwell	6.00
102	Craig Biggio	4.00
103	Barry Bonds	6.00
104	Roger Clemens	12.00
105	Jose Cruz Jr.	2.50
106	Nomar Garciaparra	20.00
107	Tony Clark	4.00
108	Ben Grieve	6.00
109	Ken Griffey Jr.	30.00
110	Tony Gwynn	15.00
111	Randy Johnson	5.00
112	Chipper Jones	20.00
113	Travis Lee	4.00
114	Kenny Lofton	4.00
115	Greg Maddux	15.00
116	Mark McGwire	30.00
117	Hideo Nomo	3.00
118	Mike Piazza	20.00
119	Manny Ramirez	8.00
120	Cal Ripken Jr.	25.00
121	Alex Rodriguez	25.00
122	Scott Rolen	6.00
123	Frank Thomas	8.00
124	Kerry Wood	6.00
125	Larry Walker	5.00
126	Vinny Castilla	2.50
127	Derek Jeter	20.00

1999 Upper Deck Babe Ruth Piece of History Bat

Limited to approximately 400, this unique card has a chip of a bat in it, from an actual game-used Louisville Slugger swung by the Bambino himself. A signed version of this card also exists, which incorporates both a "cut" signature of Ruth along with a piece of his game-used bat; only three exist.

	MT
Babe Ruth Piece of History:	1800.
Babe Ruth Legendary Cut: (Production of bat-piece card reported as 400; Legendary Cut - only three.)	

1999 Upper Deck Textbook Excellence

This 30-card set features the game's most fundamentally sound performers. Card fronts have a photo of the featured player with a silver foil stamped grid surrounding the player. The left portion of the insert has the player name, team and his postion on a brown background. These are seeded 1:23 packs. There are three parallels as well: Double, Triple and Home Run. Doubles are hobby exclusive and numbered to 2,000 sets, Triples are hobby-only and limited to 100 numbered sets and Home Runs are hobby-only and limited to 10 numbered sets.

		MT
	Complete Set (30):	60.00
	Common Player:	.75
	Inserted 1:4	
	Doubles (2,000 sets): 3X	
	Triples (100 sets): 15X	
	Quadruples (10 sets): Value Undetermined	
1	Mo Vaughn	1.00
2	Greg Maddux	4.00
3	Chipper Jones	5.00
4	Andruw Jones	1.50
5	Cal Ripken Jr.	8.00
6	Albert Belle	1.50
7	Roberto Alomar	1.50
8	Nomar Garciaparra	5.00
9	Kerry Wood	1.50
10	Sammy Sosa	5.00
11	Greg Vaughn	.75
12	Jeff Bagwell	2.00
13	Kevin Brown	.75
14	Vladimir Guerrero	2.50
15	Mike Piazza	5.00
16	Bernie Williams	1.50
17	Derek Jeter	5.00
18	Ben Grieve	1.50
19	Eric Chavez	1.00
20	Scott Rolen	2.00
21	Mark McGwire	10.00
22	David Wells	.75
23	J.D. Drew	2.00
24	Tony Gwynn	4.00
25	Barry Bonds	2.00
26	Alex Rodriguez	8.00
27	Ken Griffey Jr.	10.00
28	Juan Gonzalez	2.50
29	Ivan Rodriguez	2.00
30	Roger Clemens	3.00

1999 Upper Deck View to a Thrill

This 30-card set focuses on baseball's best overall athletes. There are two photos of the featured player on the card front, highlighted by silver foil and some embossing. These are inserted 1:7 packs.

		MT
	Complete Set (30):	100.00
	Common Player:	1.00
	Inserted 1:7	
	Doubles (2,000 sets): 2X	
	Triples (100 sets): 10X	
	Quadruples (10 sets): Value Undetermined	
1	Mo Vaughn	2.00
2	Darin Erstad	1.50
3	Travis Lee	1.50
4	Chipper Jones	8.00
5	Greg Maddux	6.00
6	Gabe Kapler	2.50
7	Cal Ripken Jr.	10.00
8	Nomar Garciaparra	8.00
9	Kerry Wood	2.50
10	Frank Thomas	6.00
11	Manny Ramirez	3.00
12	Larry Walker	2.50
13	Tony Clark	1.00
14	Jeff Bagwell	3.00
15	Craig Biggio	1.50
16	Vladimir Guerrero	5.00
17	Mike Piazza	8.00
18	Bernie Williams	2.00
19	Derek Jeter	8.00
20	Ben Grieve	2.00
21	Eric Chavez	1.00
22	Scott Rolen	3.00
23	Mark McGwire	15.00
24	Tony Gwynn	6.00
25	Barry Bonds	3.00
26	Ken Griffey Jr.	15.00
27	Alex Rodriguez	10.00
28	J.D. Drew	3.00
29	Juan Gonzalez	4.00
30	Roger Clemens	4.00

1999 Upper Deck Wonder Years

These inserts look like a throwback to the groovin' '70s, with its bright, striped, green and pink border. Wonder Years is across the top of the card front in yellow lettering. Card backs have the player's three best seasons statistics along with a mention of a milestone. The cards are numbered with a WY prefix and are seeded 1:7 packs. There are three parallel versions: Doubles which are numbered to 1,000, Triples numbered to 25 and Home Run's which are limited to one.

		MT
	Complete Set (30):	80.00
	Common Player:	1.00
	Inserted 1:7	
	Doubles (2,000 sets): 2X	
	Triples (50 sets): 15X	
	Home Runs (1 set): Values Undetermined	
W01	Kerry Wood	2.00
W02	Travis Lee	1.25
W03	Jeff Bagwell	2.50
W04	Barry Bonds	2.50
W05	Roger Clemens	5.00
W06	Jose Cruz Jr.	1.00
W07	Andres Galarraga	1.25
W08	Nomar Garciaparra	7.50
W09	Juan Gonzalez	3.50
W10	Ken Griffey Jr.	10.00
W11	Tony Gwynn	5.00
W12	Derek Jeter	7.50
W13	Randy Johnson	1.50
W14	Andruw Jones	2.00
W15	Chipper Jones	7.50
W16	Kenny Lofton	1.50
W17	Greg Maddux	5.00
W18	Tino Martinez	1.00
W19	Mark McGwire	10.00
W20	Paul Molitor	1.50
W21	Mike Piazza	7.50
W22	Manny Ramirez	3.50
W23	Cal Ripken Jr.	8.00
W24	Alex Rodriguez	8.00
W25	Sammy Sosa	7.50
W26	Frank Thomas	3.50
W27	Mo Vaughn	1.50
W28	Larry Walker	1.25
W29	Scott Rolen	2.50
W30	Ben Grieve	1.25

1999 Upper Deck 10th Anniversary Team

This 30-card set commemorates Upper Deck's 10th Anniversary, as collectors selected their favorite players for this set. Regular versions are seeded 1:4 packs, Doubles numbered to 4,000, Triples numbered to 100 and Home Runs which are limited to one set.

		MT
	Complete Set (30):	50.00
	Common Player:	.35
	Inserted 1:4	
	Doubles (4,000 sets): 2X	
	Triples (100 sets): 20X	
	Home Runs (1 set): Values Undetermined	
X1	Mike Piazza	3.50
X2	Mark McGwire	7.00
X3	Roberto Alomar	.75
X4	Chipper Jones	3.50
X5	Cal Ripken Jr.	5.00
X6	Ken Griffey Jr.	7.00
X7	Barry Bonds	1.50
X8	Tony Gwynn	2.75
X9	Nolan Ryan	6.00
X10	Randy Johnson	.75
X11	Dennis Eckersley	.35
X12	Ivan Rodriguez	1.50
X13	Frank Thomas	2.25
X14	Craig Biggio	.50
X15	Wade Boggs	.50
X16	Alex Rodriguez	5.00
X17	Albert Belle	1.00
X18	Juan Gonzalez	2.75
X19	Rickey Henderson	.50
X20	Greg Maddux	3.00
X21	Tom Glavine	.50
X22	Randy Myers	.35
X23	Sandy Alomar	.50
X24	Jeff Bagwell	1.50
X25	Derek Jeter	3.50
X26	Matt Williams	.35
X27	Kenny Lofton	.75
X28	Sammy Sosa	4.50
X29	Larry Walker	.50
X30	Roger Clemens	2.75

1999 Upper Deck Ken Griffey Jr. Supers

These large-format (5" x 7") reproductions of each of Junior's regular-issue UD cards from 1989-98 were issued as Wal-Mart exclusive in Series 1 UD baseball. Autographed versions of the super-sized Griffey cards were also found in the boxes. The supers were also distributed at the July, 1999, National Sports Collectors Convention as a wrapper-redemption premium at the card company's booth. Other than the lack of a hologram on back, the cards are identical 4X blow-ups of the issued cards.

		MT
	Complete Set (10):	15.00
	Common Card:	2.00
	Autographed Card:	200.00
1	Ken Griffey Jr. (1989)	5.00
156	Ken Griffey Jr. (1990)	2.00
555	Ken Griffey Jr. (1991)	2.00
424	Ken Griffey Jr. (1992)	2.00
355	Ken Griffey Jr. (1993)	2.00
224	Ken Griffey Jr. (1994)	2.00
100	Ken Griffey Jr. (1995)	2.00
200	Ken Griffey Jr. (1996)	2.00
175	Ken Griffey Jr. (1997)	2.00
225	Ken Griffey Jr. (1998)	2.00

1999 Upper Deck Ken Griffey Jr. 1989 UD Autograph

	MT
Complete Set (1):	1200.
Ken Griffey Jr. (100)	1200.

1999 Upper Deck Black Diamond

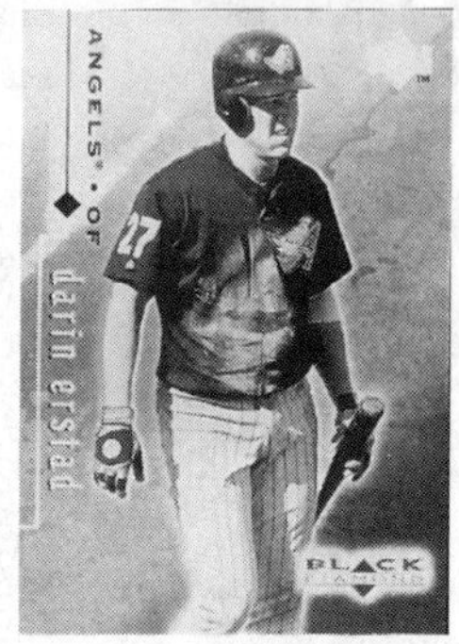

This 120-card base set features metallic foil fronts, while card backs have the featured player's vital information along with a close-up photo. The Diamond Debut subset (91-120) are short-printed and seeded 1:4 packs.

		MT
	Complete Set (120):	120.00
	Common Player:	.25
	Common Diamond Debut (91-120):	1.00
	Inserted 1:4	
	Wax Box:	120.00
1	Darin Erstad	.75
2	Tim Salmon	.50
3	Jim Edmonds	.25
4	Matt Williams	.40
5	David Dellucci	.25
6	Jay Bell	.25
7	Andres Galarraga	.75
8	Chipper Jones	2.50
9	Greg Maddux	2.50
10	Andruw Jones	.75
11	Cal Ripken Jr.	4.00
12	Rafael Palmeiro	.75
13	Brady Anderson	.25
14	Mike Mussina	1.00
15	Nomar Garciaparra	3.00
16	Mo Vaughn	1.00
17	Pedro Martinez	1.00
18	Sammy Sosa	3.00
19	Henry Rodriguez	.25
20	Frank Thomas	1.50
21	Magglio Ordonez	.75
22	Albert Belle	1.00
23	Paul Konerko	.25
24	Sean Casey	.75
25	Jim Thome	.75
26	Kenny Lofton	1.00
27	Sandy Alomar Jr.	.25
28	Jaret Wright	.25
29	Larry Walker	.75
30	Todd Helton	1.00
31	Vinny Castilla	.25
32	Tony Clark	.50
33	Damion Easley	.25
34	Mark Kotsay	.25
35	Derrek Lee	.25
36	Moises Alou	.40
37	Jeff Bagwell	1.50
38	Craig Biggio	.75
39	Randy Johnson	1.00
40	Dean Palmer	.25
41	Johnny Damon	.25
42	Chan Ho Park	.40
43	Raul Mondesi	.40
44	Gary Sheffield	.40
45	Jeromy Burnitz	.25
46	Marquis Grissom	.25
47	Jeff Cirillo	.25
48	Paul Molitor	1.00
49	Todd Walker	.25
50	Vladimir Guerrero	1.50
51	Brad Fullmer	.25
52	Mike Piazza	3.00
53	Hideo Nomo	.25
54	Carlos Baerga	.25
55	John Olerud	.50
56	Derek Jeter	3.00
57	Hideki Irabu	.40
58	Tino Martinez	.50
59	Bernie Williams	.75
60	Miguel Tejada	.40
61	Ben Grieve	.75
62	Jason Giambi	.25
63	Scott Rolen	1.25
64	Doug Glanville	.25
65	Desi Relaford	.25
66	Tony Womack	.25
67	Jason Kendall	.40
68	Jose Guillen	.25
69	Tony Gwynn	2.50
70	Ken Caminiti	.40
71	Greg Vaughn	.40
72	Kevin Brown	.40
73	Barry Bonds	1.25
74	J.T. Snow	.25
75	Jeff Kent	.25

76	Ken Griffey Jr.	5.00
77	Alex Rodriguez	3.00
78	Edgar Martinez	.25
79	Jay Buhner	.40
80	Mark McGwire	5.00
81	Delino DeShields	.25
82	Brian Jordan	.25
83	Quinton McCracken	.25
84	Fred McGriff	.50
85	Juan Gonzalez	1.50
86	Ivan Rodriguez	1.25
87	Will Clark	.50
88	Roger Clemens	2.00
89	Jose Cruz Jr.	.40
90	Babe Ruth	5.00
91	Troy Glaus (Diamond Debut)	6.00
92	Jarrod Washburn (Diamond Debut)	1.00
93	Travis Lee (Diamond Debut)	2.00
94	Bruce Chen (Diamond Debut)	1.00
95	Mike Caruso (Diamond Debut)	1.00
96	Jim Parque (Diamond Debut)	1.00
97	Kerry Wood (Diamond Debut)	4.00
98	Jeremy Giambi (Diamond Debut)	2.50
99	Matt Anderson (Diamond Debut)	1.00
100	Seth Greisinger (Diamond Debut)	1.00
101	Gabe Alvarez (Diamond Debut)	1.00
102	Rafael Medina (Diamond Debut)	1.00
103	Daryle Ward (Diamond Debut)	1.00
104	Alex Cora (Diamond Debut)	1.00
105	Adrian Beltre (Diamond Debut)	2.00
106	Geoff Jenkins (Diamond Debut)	1.50
107	Eric Milton (Diamond Debut)	1.00
108	Carl Pavano (Diamond Debut)	1.00
109	Eric Chavez (Diamond Debut)	1.50
110	Orlando Hernandez (Diamond Debut)	3.00
111	A.J. Hinch (Diamond Debut)	1.00
112	Carlton Loewer (Diamond Debut)	1.00
113	Aramis Ramirez (Diamond Debut)	1.00
114	Cliff Politte (Diamond Debut)	1.00
115	Matt Clement (Diamond Debut)	1.00
116	Alex Gonzalez (Diamond Debut)	1.00
117	J.D. Drew (Diamond Debut)	10.00
118	Shane Monahan (Diamond Debut)	1.00
119	Rolando Arrojo (Diamond Debut)	1.50
120	George Lombard (Diamond Debut)	1.00

1999 Upper Deck Black Diamond Double Diamond

Double Diamonds are the most common of the parallels to the Black Diamond base cards. The regular player cards (#1-90) feature a red metallic foil background and are serially numbered on back from within an edition of 3,000 each. Diamond Debut cards (#91-120) also feature red foil highlights on front and are individually numbered within an edition of 2,500 each.

	MT
Complete Set (120):	450.00
Common Player (1-90):	1.00
Common Diamond Debut (91-120):	3.00

(See 1999 Upper Deck Black Diamond for checklist, base card values. Stars and rookies #1-90 valued at 3X; #91-120 at 1x)

1999 Upper Deck Black Diamond Triple Diamond

Triple Diamonds are the second most common of the parallel inserts to the Black Diamond base cards. The regular player cards (#1-90) feature a yellow metallic foil background and are serially numbered on back from within an edition of 1,500 each. Diamond Debut cards (#91-120) also feature yellow foil highlights on front and are individually numbered within an edition of 1,000 each.

	MT
Common Player (1-90):	2.00
Common Diamond Debut (91-120):	3.00

(See 1999 Upper Deck Black Diamond for checklist, base card values. Stars and rookies #1-90 valued at 6X; #91-120 at 3x)

1999 Upper Deck Black Diamond Quadruple Diamond

Quadruple Diamonds are the scarcest of the parallel inserts to the Black Diamond base cards. The regular player cards (#1-90) feature a green metallic foil background and are serially numbered on back from within an edition of 150 each. Diamond Debut cards (#91-120) also feature green foil highlights on front and are individually numbered within an edition of 100 each.

		MT
Common Player (#1-90):		5.00
Production 150 each		
Common Diamond Debut (#91-120):		6.00
Production 100 each		
Griffey, Sosa & McGwire SP's		
18	Sammy Sosa/66	100.00
76	Ken Griffey Jr. /56	200.00
80	Mark McGwire/70	200.00

Checklists with card numbers in parentheses ( ) indicates the numbers do not appear on the card.

1999 Upper Deck Black Diamond Piece of History 500 Club

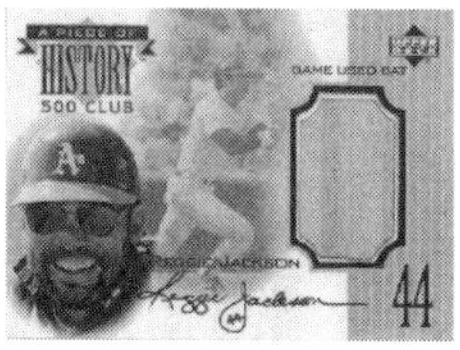

A veneer of lumber from one of Mr. October's war clubs is included in this special insert card. A facsimile autograph is also featured on front. A premium version with an authentic autographed serially numbered from within an edition of 44 (his uniform number) was also issued. Backs have a congratulatory authentication message from US CEO Richard McWilliam.

	MT
Reggie Jackson	450.00
Reggie Jackson (autographed)	750.00

1999 Upper Deck Black Diamond Diamond Dominance

This 30-card set features full-bleed metallic foil fronts and includes the top stars of the game along with Babe Ruth. Each card is numbered with a "D" prefix and is limited to 1,500 sequentially numbered sets.

		MT
Complete Set (30):		400.00
Common Player:		2.00
Production 1,500 sets		
D01	Kerry Wood	10.00
D02	Derek Jeter	25.00
D03	Alex Rodriguez	25.00
D04	Frank Thomas	15.00
D05	Jeff Bagwell	10.00
D06	Mo Vaughn	6.00
D07	Ivan Rodriguez	10.00
D08	Cal Ripken Jr.	30.00
D09	Rolando Arrojo	2.00
D10	Chipper Jones	20.00
D11	Kenny Lofton	6.00
D12	Paul Konerko	2.00
D13	Mike Piazza	25.00
D14	Ben Grieve	6.00
D15	Nomar Garciaparra	25.00
D16	Travis Lee	5.00
D17	Scott Rolen	10.00
D18	Juan Gonzalez	12.00
D19	Tony Gwynn	20.00
D20	Tony Clark	3.00
D21	Roger Clemens	15.00
D22	Sammy Sosa	25.00
D23	Larry Walker	6.00
D24	Ken Griffey Jr.	40.00
D25	Mark McGwire	40.00
D26	Barry Bonds	10.00
D27	Vladimir Guerrero	15.00
D28	Tino Martinez	2.00
D29	Greg Maddux	20.00
D30	Babe Ruth	40.00

1999 Upper Deck Black Diamond Mystery Numbers

The player's card number determines scarcity in this hobby-only insert set. The basic set has an action photo set against a silver-foil background of repeated numerals. Backs have a portrait photo and significant stat numbers from the 1998 season. Each base Mystery Numbers card is individually numbered within an edition of 100 cards times the card number within the 30-card set (i.e., card #24 has an edition of 2,400) for a total of 46,500 cards. An emerald version of the Mystery Numbers cards has a total issue of 465 cards, with cards issued to a limit of the player's card number multiplied by 1.

		MT
Complete Set (30):		750.00
Common Player:		3.00
M01	Babe Ruth (100)	175.00
M02	Ken Griffey Jr. (200)	150.00
M03	Kerry Wood (300)	30.00
M04	Mark McGwire (400)	75.00
M05	Alex Rodriguez (500)	50.00
M06	Chipper Jones (600)	30.00
M07	Nomar Garciaparra (700)	35.00
M08	Derek Jeter (800)	35.00
M09	Mike Piazza (900)	30.00
M10	Roger Clemens (1,000)	20.00
M11	Greg Maddux (1,100)	25.00
M12	Scott Rolen (1,200)	12.00
M13	Cal Ripken Jr. (1,300)	30.00
M14	Ben Grieve (1,400)	8.00
M15	Troy Glaus (1,500)	12.00
M16	Sammy Sosa (1,600)	20.00
M17	Darin Erstad (1,700)	6.00
M18	Juan Gonzalez (1,800)	12.00
M19	Pedro Martinez (1,900)	8.00
M20	Larry Walker (2,000)	6.00
M21	Vladimir Guerrero (2,100)	10.00
M22	Jeff Bagwell (2,200)	8.00
M23	Jaret Wright (2,300)	4.00
M24	Travis Lee (2,400)	5.00
M25	Barry Bonds (2,500)	6.00
M26	Orlando Hernandez (2,600)	10.00
M27	Frank Thomas (2,700)	8.00
M28	Tony Gwynn (2,800)	10.00
M29	Andres Galarraga (2,900)	5.00
M30	Craig Biggio (3,000)	4.00

1999 Upper Deck Black Diamond A Piece of History

This six-card set features green metallic foil fronts with a diamond-shaped piece of game-used bat from the featured player embedded on the card front. No insertion ratio was released.

		MT
Complete Set (6):		1200.
Common Player:		75.00
JG	Juan Gonzalez	125.00
TG	Tony Gwynn	175.00
BW	Bernie Williams	75.00
MM	Mark McGwire	800.00
MV	Mo Vaughn	75.00
SS	Sammy Sosa	300.00

1999 Upper Deck Century Legends

The first 47 cards in the 131-card set are taken from the Sporting News' list of Baseball's 100 Greatest Players. Each card bears a Sporting News photo of the featured player and his ranking in silver and copper foil. The next 50 cards tout Upper Deck's rankings of the Top 50 contemporary players. Rounding out the base set are two subsets: "21st Century Phenoms" and "Century Memories".

		MT
Complete Set (131):		50.00
Common Player:		.20
Century Collection: 25X		
Production 100 sets		
Wax Box:		150.00
1	Babe Ruth (Sporting News Top 50)	4.00
1	Babe Ruth (SAMPLE overprint on back)	4.00
2	Willie Mays (Sporting News Top 50)	2.00
3	Ty Cobb (Sporting News Top 50)	2.00
4	Walter Johnson (Sporting News Top 50)	.75
5	Hank Aaron (Sporting News Top 50)	1.50
6	Lou Gehrig (Sporting News Top 50)	3.00
7	Christy Mathewson (Sporting News Top 50)	.75
8	Ted Williams (Sporting News Top 50)	2.00
9	Rogers Hornsby (Sporting News Top 50)	.50
10	Stan Musial (Sporting News Top 50)	1.00
12	Grover Alexander (Sporting News Top 50)	.50
13	Honus Wagner (Sporting News Top 50)	.75
14	Cy Young (Sporting News Top 50)	.75
15	Jimmie Foxx (Sporting News Top 50)	.75
16	Johnny Bench (Sporting News Top 50)	.75
17	Mickey Mantle (Sporting News Top 50)	4.00
18	Josh Gibson (Sporting News Top 50)	.75
19	Satchel Paige (Sporting News Top 50)	1.00
20	Roberto Clemente (Sporting News Top 50)	3.00
21	Warren Spahn (Sporting News Top 50)	.50
22	Frank Robinson (Sporting News Top 50)	.50

23	Lefty Grove (Sporting News Top 50)	.50
24	Eddie Collins (Sporting News Top 50)	.50
27	Tris Speaker (Sporting News Top 50)	.50
28	Mike Schmidt (Sporting News Top 50)	.75
29	Napoleon LaJoie (Sporting News Top 50)	.50
30	Steve Carlton (Sporting News Top 50)	.50
31	Bob Gibson (Sporting News Top 50)	.50
32	Tom Seaver (Sporting News Top 50)	.50
33	George Sisler (Sporting News Top 50)	.50
34	Barry Bonds (Sporting News Top 50)	.75
35	Joe Jackson (Sporting News Top 50)	2.00
36	Bob Feller (Sporting News Top 50)	.50
37	Hank Greenberg (Sporting News Top 50)	.50
38	Ernie Banks (Sporting News Top 50)	.75
39	Greg Maddux (Sporting News Top 50)	1.50
40	Yogi Berra (Sporting News Top 50)	.75
41	Nolan Ryan (Sporting News Top 50)	3.00
42	Mel Ott (Sporting News Top 50)	.50
43	Al Simmons (Sporting News Top 50)	.50
44	Jackie Robinson (Sporting News Top 50)	2.50
45	Carl Hubbell (Sporting News Top 50)	.50
46	Charley Gehringer (Sporting News Top 50)	.50
47	Buck Leonard (Sporting News Top 50)	.50
48	Reggie Jackson (Sporting News Top 50)	.75
49	Tony Gwynn (Sporting News Top 50)	1.00
50	Roy Campanella (Sporting News Top 50)	.75
51	Ken Griffey Jr. (Contemporaries)	4.00
52	Barry Bonds (Contemporaries)	.75
53	Roger Clemens (Contemporaries)	1.00
54	Tony Gwynn (Contemporaries)	1.50
55	Cal Ripken Jr. (Contemporaries)	2.50
56	Greg Maddux (Contemporaries)	1.50
57	Frank Thomas (Contemporaries)	1.50
58	Mark McGwire (Contemporaries)	4.00
59	Mike Piazza (Contemporaries)	2.00
60	Wade Boggs (Contemporaries)	.40
61	Alex Rodriguez (Contemporaries)	3.00
62	Juan Gonzalez (Contemporaries)	1.50
63	Mo Vaughn (Contemporaries)	.60
64	Albert Belle (Contemporaries)	.75
65	Sammy Sosa (Contemporaries)	2.00
66	Nomar Garciaparra (Contemporaries)	2.00
67	Derek Jeter (Contemporaries)	2.00
68	Kevin Brown (Contemporaries)	.30
69	Jose Canseco (Contemporaries)	.50
70	Randy Johnson (Contemporaries)	.40
71	Tom Glavine (Contemporaries)	.20
72	Barry Larkin (Contemporaries)	.30
73	Curt Schilling (Contemporaries)	.20
74	Moises Alou (Contemporaries)	.20
75	Fred McGriff (Contemporaries)	.20
76	Pedro Martinez (Contemporaries)	.50
77	Andres Galarraga (Contemporaries)	.30
78	Will Clark (Contemporaries)	.30
79	Larry Walker (Contemporaries)	.50
80	Ivan Rodriguez (Contemporaries)	.75
81	Chipper Jones (Contemporaries)	2.00
82	Jeff Bagwell (Contemporaries)	.75
83	Craig Biggio (Contemporaries)	.40
84	Kerry Wood (Contemporaries)	.75
85	Roberto Alomar (Contemporaries)	.50
86	Vinny Castilla (Contemporaries)	.20
87	Kenny Lofton (Contemporaries)	.60
88	Rafael Palmeiro (Contemporaries)	.30
89	Manny Ramirez (Contemporaries)	1.00
90	David Wells (Contemporaries)	.20
91	Mark Grace (Contemporaries)	.30
92	Bernie Williams (Contemporaries)	.25
93	David Cone (Contemporaries)	.20
94	John Olerud (Contemporaries)	.20
95	John Smoltz (Contemporaries)	.20
96	Tino Martinez (Contemporaries)	.25
97	Raul Mondesi (Contemporaries)	.30
98	Gary Sheffield (Contemporaries)	.25
99	Orel Hershiser (Contemporaries)	.20
100	Rickey Henderson (Contemporaries)	.30
101	J.D. Drew (21st Century Phenoms)	1.00
102	Troy Glaus (21st Century Phenoms)	1.00
103	Nomar Garciaparra (21st Century Phenoms)	2.00
104	Scott Rolen (21st Century Phenoms)	.75
105	Ryan Minor (21st Century Phenoms)	.20
106	Travis Lee (21st Century Phenoms)	.75
107	Roy Halladay (21st Century Phenoms)	.20
108	Carlos Beltran (21st Century Phenoms)	.75
109	Alex Rodriguez (21st Century Phenoms)	3.00
110	Eric Chavez (21st Century Phenoms)	.75
111	Vladimir Guerrero (21st Century Phenoms)	1.00
112	Ben Grieve (21st Century Phenoms)	.75
113	Kerry Wood (21st Century Phenoms)	.75
114	Alex Gonzalez (21st Century Phenoms)	.20
115	Darin Erstad (21st Century Phenoms)	.75
116	Derek Jeter (21st Century Phenoms)	2.00
117	Jaret Wright (21st Century Phenoms)	.40
118	Jose Cruz Jr. (21st Century Phenoms)	.40
119	Chipper Jones (21st Century Phenoms)	2.00
120	Gabe Kapler (21st Century Phenoms)	1.50
121	Satchel Paige (Century Memories)	1.00
122	Willie Mays (Century Memories)	1.50
123	Roberto Clemente (Century Memories)	3.00
124	Lou Gehrig (Century Memories)	2.50
125	Mark McGwire (Century Memories)	4.00
127	Bob Gibson (Century Memories)	.50
128	Johnny Vander Meer (Century Memories)	.20
129	Walter Johnson (Century Memories)	.50
130	Ty Cobb (Century Memories)	1.50
131	Don Larsen (Century Memories)	.40
132	Jackie Robinson (Century Memories)	2.00
133	Tom Seaver (Century Memories)	.50
134	Johnny Bench (Century Memories)	.50
135	Frank Robinson (Century Memories)	.50

1999 Upper Deck Century Legends All-Century Team

This 10-card set highlights Upper Deck's all-time all-star team. These were seeded 1:23 packs.

		MT
Complete Set (10):		50.00
Common Player:		4.00
Inserted 1:23		
1	Babe Ruth	15.00
2	Ty Cobb	6.00
3	Willie Mays	6.00
4	Lou Gehrig	10.00
5	Jackie Robinson	8.00
6	Mike Schmidt	4.00
7	Ernie Banks	4.00
8	Johnny Bench	4.00
9	Cy Young	4.00
10	Lineup Sheet	1.00

1999 Upper Deck Century Legends Century Artifacts

A total of nine cards were inserted, which were redeemable for memorabilia from some of the top players of the century. Due to the limited nature of these one-of-one inserts no pricing is available.

1900s	Framed Cut of Cobb w/Cent. Card
1910s	Framed Cut of Ruth w/Cent. Card
1920s	Framed Cut of Hornsby w/Cent. Card
1930s	Framed Cut of Paige w/Cent. Card
1950s	Auto. Ball Coll. Aaron, Mays, Mantle
1960s	Auto. Ball Coll. Banks, Gibson, Bench
1970s	Auto. Ball Col. Seaver, Schmidt, Carlton
1980s	Auto. Ball Coll. Nolan Ryan/Ken Griffey
1990s	Ken Griffey Autographed Jersey

1999 Upper Deck Century Legends Century MVPs

This 100-card collection takes 100 cards from Upper Deck's '99 MVP brand and adds a rainbow-foil shift to each card. These are limited to only one numbered set.

One Set Produced, Values Undetermined

1	Mo Vaughn
2	Troy Glaus
3	Darin Erstad
4	Randy Johnson
5	Travis Lee
6	Chipper Jones
7	Greg Maddux
8	Tom Glavine
9	John Smoltz
10	Cal Ripken Jr.
11	Charles Johnson
12	Albert Belle
13	Nomar Garciaparra
14	Pedro Martinez
15	Kerry Wood
16	Sammy Sosa
17	Mark Grace
18	Frank Thomas
19	Paul Konerko
20	Ray Durham
21	Denny Neagle
22	Sean Casey
23	Barry Larkin
24	Roberto Alomar
25	Kenny Lofton
26	Travis Fryman
27	Jim Thome
28	Manny Ramirez
29	Vinny Castilla
30	Todd Helton
31	Dante Bichette
32	Larry Walker
33	Gabe Kapler
34	Dean Palmer
35	Tony Clark
36	Juan Encarnacion
37	Alex Gonzalez
38	Preston Wilson
39	Derrek Lee
40	Ken Caminiti
41	Jeff Bagwell
42	Moises Alou
43	Craig Biggio
44	Carlos Beltran
45	Jeremy Giambi
46	Johnny Damon
47	Kevin Brown
48	Chan Ho Park
49	Raul Mondesi
50	Gary Sheffield
51	Sean Berry
52	Jeromy Burnitz
53	Brad Radke
54	Eric Milton
55	Todd Walker
56	Vladimir Guerrero
57	Rondell White
58	Mike Piazza
59	Rickey Henderson
60	Rey Ordonez
61	Derek Jeter
62	Bernie Williams
63	Paul O'Neill
64	Scott Brosius
65	Tino Martinez
66	Roger Clemens
67	Orlando Hernandez
68	Ben Grieve
69	Eric Chavez
70	Jason Giambi
71	Curt Schilling
72	Scott Rolen
73	Pat Burrell
74	Jason Kendall
75	Aramis Ramirez
76	Mark McGwire
77	J.D. Drew
78	Edgar Renteria
79	Tony Gwynn
80	Sterling Hitchcock
81	Ruben Rivera
82	Trevor Hoffman
83	Barry Bonds
84	Ellis Burks
85	Robb Nen
86	Ken Griffey Jr.
87	Alex Rodriguez
88	Carlos Guillen
89	Edgar Martinez
90	Jose Canseco
91	Rolando Arrojo
92	Wade Boggs
93	Fred McGriff
94	Juan Gonzalez
95	Ivan Rodriguez
96	Rafael Palmeiro
97	David Wells
98	Roy Halladay
99	Carlos Delgado
100	Jose Cruz Jr.

1999 Upper Deck Century Legends Epic Milestones

This nine-card set showcases nine of the most impressive milestones established in major league history. Each card is numbered with a "EM" prefix and are seeded 1:12 packs.

		MT
Complete Set (9):		45.00
Common Player:		2.00
Inserted 1:12		
2	Jackie Robinson	6.00
3	Nolan Ryan	10.00
4	Mark McGwire	12.00
5	Roger Clemens	4.00
6	Sammy Sosa	6.00
7	Cal Ripken Jr.	10.00
8	Rickey Henderson	2.00
9	Hank Aaron	4.00
10	Barry Bonds	3.00

1999 Upper Deck Century Legends Epic Signatures

This 30-card set features autographs from retired and current stars on a horizonal format. These autographed cards are seeded 1:24 packs.

		MT
Complete Set (30):		2000.
Common Player:		15.00
Inserted 1:24		
EB	Ernie Banks	50.00
JB	Johnny Bench	75.00
YB	Yogi Berra	60.00
BB	Barry Bonds	75.00
SC	Steve Carlton	40.00
BD	Bucky Dent	15.00
BF	Bob Feller	25.00
CF	Carlton Fisk	35.00
BG	Bob Gibson	30.00
JG	Juan Gonzalez	75.00
Jr.	Ken Griffey Jr.	250.00
Sr.	Ken Griffey Sr.	15.00
VG	Vladimir Guerrero	50.00
TG	Tony Gwynn	125.00
RJ	Reggie Jackson	125.00
HK	Harmon Killebrew	40.00
DL	Don Larsen	15.00
GM	Greg Maddux	150.00
EMa	Eddie Mathews	50.00
BM	Bill Mazeroski	15.00
WMc	Willie McCovey	30.00
SM	Stan Musial	80.00
FR	Frank Robinson	50.00
AR	Alex Rodriguez	175.00
NR	Nolan Ryan	350.00
MS	Mike Schmidt	60.00
TS	Tom Seaver	80.00
WS	Warren Spahn	50.00
FT	Frank Thomas	100.00
BT	Bobby Thomson	15.00

1999 Upper Deck Century Legends Century Epic Signatures

This 32-card autographed set features signatures from retired and current stars. The cards have a horizontal format and have gold foil stamping. Each card is hand numbered to 100.

		MT
Common Player:		25.00
Production 100 sets		
EB	Ernie Banks	80.00
JB	Johnny Bench	125.00
YB	Yogi Berra	125.00
BB	Barry Bonds	125.00
SC	Steve Carlton	80.00
BD	Bucky Dent	40.00
BF	Bob Feller	50.00
CF	Carlton Fisk	75.00
BG	Bob Gibson	75.00
JG	Juan Gonzalez	150.00
Jr.	Ken Griffey Jr.	400.00
Sr.	Ken Griffey Sr.	35.00
VG	Vladimir Guerrero	80.00
TG	Tony Gwynn	150.00
RJ	Reggie Jackson	175.00
HK	Harmon Killebrew	60.00
DL	Don Larsen	35.00
GM	Greg Maddux	250.00
EMa	Eddie Mathews	60.00
WM	Willie Mays	250.00
BM	Bill Mazeroski	35.00
WMc	Willie McCovey	50.00
SM	Stan Musial	150.00
FR	Frank Robinson	60.00
AR	Alex Rodriguez	300.00
NR	Nolan Ryan	400.00
MS	Mike Schmidt	125.00
TS	Tom Seaver	100.00
WS	Warren Spahn	60.00
FT	Frank Thomas	150.00
BT	Bobby Thomson	35.00
TW	Ted Williams	600.00

1999 Upper Deck Century Legends Jerseys of the Century

This eight-card set features a swatch of game-worn jersey from the featured player, which includes current and retired players. These are seeded 1:418 packs.

		MT
Common Player:		100.00
Inserted 1:418		
GB	George Brett	200.00
RC	Roger Clemens	200.00
TG	Tony Gwynn	200.00
GM	Greg Maddux	250.00
EM	Eddie Murray	100.00
NR	Nolan Ryan	600.00
MS	Mike Schmidt	200.00
OZ	Ozzie Smith	150.00
DW	Dave Winfield	100.00

1999 Upper Deck Century Legends Legendary Cuts

A total of nine of these inserts exist. These special inserts an actual "cut" signature from some of baseball's all-time greats, including Ty Cobb and Satchel Paige.

Complete Set (9):	
Common Player:	
Values Undetermined Due to Scarcity	
RC	Roy Campanella
TY	Ty Cobb
XX	Jimmie Foxx
LG	Lefty Grove
WJ	Walter Johnson
MO	Mel Ott
SP	Satchel Paige
BR	Babe Ruth
CY	Cy Young

1999 Upper Deck Century Legends Memorable Shots

This 10-card insert set focuses on the most memorable home runs launched during this century. The player's image is framed in an embossed foil, frame-like design. These are seeded 1:12 packs, each card back is numbered with a "HR" prefix.

		MT
Complete Set (10):		40.00
Common Player:		2.00
Inserted 1:12		
1	Babe Ruth	10.00
2	Bobby Thomson	2.00
3	Kirk Gibson	2.00
4	Carlton Fisk	2.00
5	Bill Mazeroski	2.00
6	Bucky Dent	1.00
7	Mark McGwire	10.00
8	Mickey Mantle	12.00
9	Joe Carter	1.00
10	Mark McGwire	10.00

1999 Upper Deck Century Legends 500 Club Piece History

This Jimmie Foxx insert has a piece of of a game-used Louisville Slugger once swung by Foxx, embedded into the card front. An estimated 350 cards of this one exist.

	MT
534 HRJimmie Foxx	300.00

1999 Upper Deck Challengers for 70

Celebrating Mark McGwire's record-setting season of 1998, and featuring those who would chase his single-season home run crown in 1999, Upper Deck issued this specialty product. The base set of 90 cards is fractured into subsets of Power Elite (#1-10), Power Corps (#11-40), Rookie Power (#41-45), and Home Run Highlights (#46-90). Several styles of inserts and numbered parallels were included in the 5-card foil packs.

		MT
Complete Set (90):		40.00
Common Player:		.15
McGwire (#61-71):		1.50
1	Mark McGwire (Power Elite)	3.00
2	Sammy Sosa (Power Elite)	2.00
3	Ken Griffey Jr. (Power Elite)	3.00
4	Alex Rodriguez (Power Elite)	2.50
5	Albert Belle (Power Elite)	.60
6	Mo Vaughn (Power Elite)	.50
7	Mike Piazza (Power Elite)	2.00
8	Frank Thomas (Power Elite)	1.00
9	Juan Gonzalez (Power Elite)	1.00
10	Barry Bonds (Power Elite)	.75
11	Rafael Palmeiro (Power Corps)	.40
12	Jose Canseco (Power Corps)	.75
13	Nomar Garciaparra (Power Corps)	2.00
14	Carlos Delgado (Power Corps)	.50
15	Brian Jordan (Power Corps)	.15
16	Vladimir Guerrero (Power Corps)	1.00
17	Vinny Castilla (Power Corps)	.25
18	Chipper Jones (Power Corps)	2.00
19	Jeff Bagwell (Power Corps)	.75
20	Moises Alou (Power Corps)	.25
21	Tony Clark (Power Corps)	.40
22	Jim Thome (Power Corps)	.40
23	Tino Martinez (Power Corps)	.25
24	Greg Vaughn (Power Corps)	.25
25	Javy Lopez (Power Corps)	.15
26	Jeromy Burnitz (Power Corps)	.15
27	Cal Ripken Jr. (Power Corps)	2.50
28	Manny Ramirez (Power Corps)	.75
29	Darin Erstad (Power Corps)	.25
30	Ken Caminiti (Power Corps)	.15
31	Edgar Martinez (Power Corps)	.15
32	Ivan Rodriguez (Power Corps)	.75
33	Larry Walker (Power Corps)	.50
34	Todd Helton (Power Corps)	.50
35	Andruw Jones (Power Corps)	.50
36	Ray Lankford (Power Corps)	.15
37	Travis Lee (Power Corps)	.25
38	Raul Mondesi (Power Corps)	.25
39	Scott Rolen (Power Corps)	.75
40	Ben Grieve (Power Corps)	.25
41	J.D. Drew (Rookie Power)	.25
42	Troy Glaus (Rookie Power)	.25
43	Eric Chavez (Rookie Power)	.15
44	Gabe Kapler (Rookie Power)	.15
45	Michael Barrett (Rookie Power)	.15
46	Mark McGwire (Home Run Highlights)	1.50
47	Jose Canseco (Home Run Highlights)	.40
48	Greg Vaughn (Home Run Highlights)	.15
49	Albert Belle (Home Run Highlights)	.30
50	Mark McGwire (Home Run Highlights)	1.50
51	Vinny Castilla (Home Run Highlights)	.15
52	Vladimir Guerrero (Home Run Highlights)	.50
53	Andres Galarraga (Home Run Highlights)	.25
54	Rafael Palmeiro (Home Run Highlights)	.25
55	Juan Gonzalez (Home Run Highlights)	.50
56	Ken Griffey Jr. (Home Run Highlights)	1.50
57	Barry Bonds (Home Run Highlights)	.40
58	Mo Vaughn (Home Run Highlights)	.20
59	Nomar Garciaparra (Home Run Highlights)	1.00
60	Tino Martinez (Home Run Highlights)	.15
61	Mark McGwire (Home Run Highlights)	1.50
62	Mark McGwire (Home Run Highlights)	1.50
63	Mark McGwire (Home Run Highlights)	1.50
64	Mark McGwire (Home Run Highlights)	1.50
65	Mark McGwire (Home Run Highlights)	1.50
66	Sammy Sosa (Home Run Highlights)	1.00
67	Mark McGwire (Home Run Highlights)	1.50
68	Mark McGwire (Home Run Highlights)	1.50
69	Mark McGwire (Home Run Highlights)	1.50
70	Mark McGwire (Home Run Highlights)	1.50
71	Mark McGwire (Home Run Highlights)	1.50
72	Scott Brosius (Home Run Highlights)	.15
73	Tony Gwynn (Home Run Highlights)	.75
74	Chipper Jones (Home Run Highlights)	1.00
75	Jeff Bagwell (Home Run Highlights)	.40
76	Moises Alou (Home Run Highlights)	.15
77	Manny Ramirez (Home Run Highlights)	.40
78	Carlos Delgado (Home Run Highlights)	.25
79	Kerry Wood (Home Run Highlights)	.15
80	Ken Griffey Jr. (Home Run Highlights)	1.50
81	Cal Ripken Jr. (Home Run Highlights)	1.25
82	Alex Rodriguez (Home Run Highlights)	1.25
83	Barry Bonds (Home Run Highlights)	.40
84	Ken Griffey Jr. (Home Run Highlights)	1.50
85	Travis Lee (Home Run Highlights)	.15
86	George Lombard (Home Run Highlights)	.15
87	Michael Barrett (Home Run Highlights)	.15
88	Jeremy Giambi (Home Run Highlights)	.15
89	Troy Glaus (Home Run Highlights)	.25
90	J.D. Drew (Home Run Highlights)	.35

1999 Upper Deck Challengers for 70 Challengers for 70

Found one per pack, this insert series identifies 30 of the top contenders for the 1999 home run crown. Action photos on front are highlighted by red graphics and silver-foil. Backs repeat a detail of the front photo and present a capsule of the player's 1998 season. Cards have a "C" prefix to the number. A parallel edition, utilizing refractive foil details on front, is serially numbered within an edition of 70 each.

		MT
Complete Set (30):		40.00
Common Player:		.40
1	Mark McGwire	3.00
2	Sammy Sosa	2.00
3	Ken Griffey Jr.	3.00
4	Alex Rodriguez	2.50
5	Albert Belle	.60
6	Mo Vaughn	.50
7	Mike Piazza	2.00
8	Frank Thomas	1.50
9	Juan Gonzalez	1.00
10	Barry Bonds	.75
11	Rafael Palmeiro	.40
12	Nomar Garciaparra	2.00
13	Vladimir Guerrero	1.00
14	Vinny Castilla	.40
15	Chipper Jones	2.00
16	Jeff Bagwell	.75
17	Moises Alou	.40
18	Tony Clark	.40
19	Jim Thome	.40
20	Tino Martinez	.40
21	Greg Vaughn	.40
22	Manny Ramirez	.75
23	Darin Erstad	.40
24	Ken Caminiti	.40
25	Ivan Rodriguez	.75
26	Andruw Jones	.60
27	Travis Lee	.40
28	Scott Rolen	.75
29	Ben Grieve	.40
30	J.D. Drew	.75

1999 Upper Deck Challengers for 70 Challengers Edition

In this parallel of the 90-card base set, each card is serially numbered within an edition of 600 each.

	MT
Complete Set (90):	375.00
Commons:	4.00
Stars: 6X	
(See 1999 Challengers for 70 for checklist and base card values.)	

1999 Upper Deck Challengers for 70 Longball Legends

Top home-run threats are featured in this insert series. The action photos on front are repeated in a diffused version on back, where they are joined by a second photo and a bar-graph of the player's home run production in recent seasons. Cards have an "L" prefix to the number. Stated odds of picking a Longball Legends card are one per 39 packs.

		MT
Complete Set (30):		225.00
Common Player:		4.00
1	Ken Griffey Jr.	25.00
2	Mark McGwire	25.00
3	Sammy Sosa	15.00
4	Cal Ripken Jr.	20.00
5	Barry Bonds	6.00
6	Larry Walker	5.00
7	Fred McGriff	4.00
8	Alex Rodriguez	20.00
9	Frank Thomas	12.00
10	Juan Gonzalez	8.00
11	Jeff Bagwell	6.00
12	Mo Vaughn	4.00
13	Albert Belle	5.00
14	Mike Piazza	15.00
15	Vladimir Guerrero	8.00
16	Chipper Jones	15.00
17	Ken Caminiti	4.00
18	Rafael Palmeiro	5.00
19	Nomar Garciaparra	15.00
20	Jim Thome	4.00
21	Edgar Martinez	4.00
22	Ivan Rodriguez	6.00
23	Andres Galarraga	4.00
24	Scott Rolen	6.00
25	Darin Erstad	4.00
26	Moises Alou	4.00
27	J.D. Drew	6.00
28	Andruw Jones	5.00
29	Manny Ramirez	6.00
30	Tino Martinez	4.00

Player names in *Italic* type indicate a rookie card.

1999 Upper Deck Challengers for 70 Mark on History

The details of Mark McGwire successful assault on the single-season home run record are captured in this 25-card insert set, found on average of one per five packs. Cards have action photos set against split red and black backgrounds and are highlighted in red metallic foil. Backs have details of the home run featured on front, a quote from McGwire and another photo. Cards have an "M" prefix to the number. A parallel edition number to 70 was also issued.

		MT
Complete Set (25):		75.00
Common McGwire:		4.00
Parallel: 8X		
01	Mark McGwire	4.00
02	Mark McGwire	4.00
03	Mark McGwire	4.00
04	Mark McGwire	4.00
05	Mark McGwire	4.00
06	Mark McGwire	4.00
07	Mark McGwire	4.00
08	Mark McGwire	4.00
09	Mark McGwire	4.00
10	Mark McGwire	4.00
11	Mark McGwire	4.00
12	Mark McGwire	4.00
13	Mark McGwire	4.00
14	Mark McGwire	4.00
15	Mark McGwire	4.00
16	Mark McGwire	4.00
17	Mark McGwire	4.00
18	Mark McGwire	4.00
19	Mark McGwire	4.00
20	Mark McGwire	4.00
21	Mark McGwire	4.00
22	Mark McGwire	4.00
23	Mark McGwire	4.00
24	Mark McGwire	4.00
25	Mark McGwire	4.00

1999 Upper Deck Challengers for 70 Swinging/Fences

Fifteen top sluggers are included in this insert set. The players' power swing is captured on a muted textured-look background. Back has a color portrait photo and an "S" prefix to the card number. Stated insertion rate is one per 19 packs.

		MT
Complete Set (15):		90.00
Common Player:		3.00
1	Ken Griffey Jr.	15.00
2	Mark McGwire	15.00
3	Sammy Sosa	10.00
4	Alex Rodriguez	12.00
5	Nomar Garciaparra	10.00
6	J.D. Drew	4.00
7	Vladimir Guerrero	6.00
8	Ben Grieve	3.00
9	Chipper Jones	10.00
10	Gabe Kapler	3.00
11	Travis Lee	3.00
12	Todd Helton	3.00
13	Juan Gonzalez	5.00
14	Mike Piazza	10.00
15	Mo Vaughn	3.00

1999 Upper Deck Challengers for 70 Autographed Swinging

A total of 2,700 autographed versions of Swinging for the Fences inserts were featured in the Challengers for 70 issue. Only six of the 15 players' cards were included in this premium version.

		MT
Common Player:		20.00
JR	Ken Griffey Jr.	350.00
VG	Vladimir Guerrero	60.00
TH	Todd Helton	30.00
GK	Gabe Kapler	20.00
TL	Travis Lee	20.00
AR	Alex Rodriguez	200.00

1999 Upper Deck Challengers for 70 Piece/History 500

A piece of game-used bat from 500-HR club member Harmon Killebrew is featured on these inserts. Only 350 cards were issued, along with three (his uniform number) authentically autographed versions. Backs have an action photo and a congratulatory authentication message from UD CEO Richard McWilliam.

	MT
Harmon Killebrew	300.00
Harmon Killebrew (autographed - value not determined)	

1999 Upper Deck UD Choice Previews

A month prior to the release of its new UD Choice brand baseball series, Upper Deck issued this 55-card Preview version. Sold in five-card cello packs for about 75 cents only at retail outlets, the cards are identical to the issued versions of the same players except for the appearance at top front of a gold foil-stamped "PREVIEW".

		MT
Complete Set (55):		12.50
Common Player:		.10
46	Tim Salmon	.25
48	Chuck Finley	.10
50	Matt Williams	.25
52	Travis Lee	.50
54	Andres Galarraga	.25
56	Greg Maddux	.90
58	Cal Ripken Jr.	1.50
60	Rafael Palmeiro	.25
62	Nomar Garciaparra	1.00
64	Pedro Martinez	.35
66	Kerry Wood	.50
67	Sammy Sosa	1.00
70	Albert Belle	.50
72	Frank Thomas	1.00
74	Pete Harnisch	.10
76	Manny Ramirez	.60
78	Travis Fryman	.10
80	Kenny Lofton	.25
82	Larry Walker	.35
84	Gabe Alvarez	.10
86	Damion Easley	.10
88	Mark Kotsay	.10
90	Jeff Bagwell	.60
93	Craig Biggio	.25
94	Larry Sutton	.10
96	Johnny Damon	.10
98	Gary Sheffield	.20
100	Mark Grudzielanek	.10
102	Jeff Cirillo	.10
104	Mark Loretta	.10
106	David Ortiz	.10
108	Brad Fullmer	.30
110	Vladimir Guerrero	.60
112	Brian McRae	.10
114	Rey Ordonez	.10
115	Derek Jeter	1.00
118	Paul O'Neill	.10
120	A.J. Hinch	.10
122	Miguel Tejada	.10
124	Scott Rolen	.35
126	Bobby Abreu	.10
128	Jason Kendall	.10
130	Mark McGwire	2.00
132	Eli Marrero	.10
136	Kevin Brown	.20
137	Tony Gwynn	.75
138	Bill Mueller	.10
140	Barry Bonds	.65
142	Ken Griffey Jr.	2.00
143	Alex Rodriguez	1.50
146	Rolando Arrojo	.25
148	Quinton McCracken	.10
150	Will Clark	.35
152	Juan Gonzalez	.65
154	Carlos Delgado	.10

1999 Upper Deck UD Choice

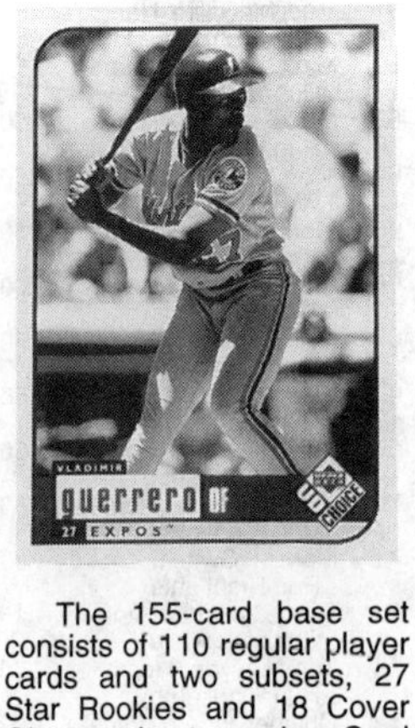

The 155-card base set consists of 110 regular player cards and two subsets, 27 Star Rookies and 18 Cover Glory subset cards. Card fronts have a white border, with the Upper Deck UD Choice logo on the bottom right of the front. Card backs have complete year-by-year stats along with some vital information. Each pack contains 12 cards. A parallel version also exists, called Prime Choice Reserve and are numbered to 100.

		MT
Complete Set (155):		15.00
Common Player:		.10
Wax Box:		40.00
1	Gabe Kapler (Rookie Class)	.75
2	Jin Ho Cho (Rookie Class)	.15
3	Matt Anderson (Rookie Class)	.20
4	Ricky Ledee (Rookie Class)	.20
5	Bruce Chen (Rookie Class)	.10
6	Alex Gonzalez (Rookie Class)	.10
7	Ryan Minor (Rookie Class)	.25
8	Michael Barrett (Rookie Class)	.10
9	Carlos Beltran (Rookie Class)	.20
10	Ramon Martinez (Rookie Class)	.10
11	Dermal Brown (Rookie Class)	.10
12	Robert Fick (Rookie Class)	.10
13	Preston Wilson (Rookie Class)	.15
14	Orlando Hernandez (Rookie Class)	1.50
15	Troy Glaus (Rookie Class)	1.00
16	Calvin Pickering (Rookie Class)	.10
17	Corey Koskie (Rookie Class)	.10
18	Fernando Seguignol (Rookie Class)	.20
19	Carlos Guillen (Rookie Class)	.10
20	Kevin Witt (Rookie Class)	.10
21	Mike Kinkade (Rookie Class)	.10
22	Eric Chavez (Rookie Class)	.30
23	Mike Lowell (Rookie Class)	.10
24	Adrian Beltre (Rookie Class)	.25
25	George Lombard (Rookie Class)	.10
26	Jeremy Giambi (Rookie Class)	.10
27	J.D. Drew (Rookie Class)	.75
28	Mark McGwire (Cover Glory)	1.25
29	Kerry Wood (Cover Glory)	.40
30	David Wells (Cover Glory)	.10
31	Juan Gonzalez (Cover Glory)	.50
32	Randy Johnson (Cover Glory)	.20
33	Derek Jeter (Cover Glory)	.50
34	Tony Gwynn (Cover Glory)	.50
35	Greg Maddux (Cover Glory)	.60
36	Cal Ripken Jr. (Cover Glory)	.75
37	Ken Griffey Jr. (Cover Glory)	1.25
38	Bartolo Colon (Cover Glory)	.10
39	Troy Glaus (Cover Glory)	.25
40	Ben Grieve (Cover Glory)	.25
41	Roger Clemens (Cover Glory)	.30
42	Chipper Jones (Cover Glory)	.50
43	Scott Rolen (Cover Glory)	.25
44	Nomar Garciaparra (Cover Glory)	.60
45	Sammy Sosa (Cover Glory)	.75
46	Tim Salmon	.20
47	Darin Erstad	.50
48	Chuck Finley	.10
49	Garrett Anderson	.10
50	Matt Williams	.20
51	Jay Bell	.10
52	Travis Lee	.50
53	Andruw Jones	.50
54	Andres Galarraga	.25
55	Chipper Jones	1.25
56	Greg Maddux	1.00
57	Javy Lopez	.15
58	Cal Ripken Jr.	2.00
59	Brady Anderson	.10
60	Rafael Palmeiro	.20
61	B.J. Surhoff	.10
62	Nomar Garciaparra	1.25
63	Troy O'Leary	.10
64	Pedro Martinez	.40
65	Jason Varitek	.10
66	Kerry Wood	.75
67	Sammy Sosa	1.50
68	Mark Grace	.20
69	Mickey Morandini	.10
70	Albert Belle	.50
71	Mike Caruso	.10
72	Frank Thomas	.75
73	Sean Casey	.25
74	Pete Harnisch	.10
75	Dmitri Young	.10
76	Manny Ramirez	.75
77	Omar Vizquel	.10
78	Travis Fryman	.10
79	Jim Thome	.35
80	Kenny Lofton	.35
81	Todd Helton	.40
82	Larry Walker	.35
83	Vinny Castilla	.10
84	Gabe Alvarez	.10
85	Tony Clark	.40
86	Damion Easley	.10
87	Livan Hernandez	.10
88	Mark Kotsay	.20
89	Cliff Floyd	.10
90	Jeff Bagwell	.60
91	Moises Alou	.20
92	Randy Johnson	.35
93	Craig Biggio	.20
94	Larry Sutton	.10
95	Dean Palmer	.10
96	Johnny Damon	.10
97	Charles Johnson	.10
98	Gary Sheffield	.20
99	Raul Mondesi	.20
100	Mark Grudzielanek	.10
101	Jeromy Burnitz	.10
102	Jeff Cirillo	.10
103	Jose Valentin	.10
104	Mark Loretta	.10
105	Todd Walker	.20
106	David Ortiz	.10
107	Brad Radke	.10
108	Brad Fullmer	.20
109	Rondell White	.20
110	Vladimir Guerrero	.75
111	Mike Piazza	1.25
112	Brian McRae	.10
113	John Olerud	.20
114	Rey Ordonez	.10
115	Derek Jeter	1.50
116	Bernie Williams	.30
117	David Wells	.10
118	Paul O'Neill	.20
119	Tino Martinez	.20
120	A.J. Hinch	.10
121	Jason Giambi	.10
122	Miguel Tejada	.10
123	Ben Grieve	.50
124	Scott Rolen	.50
125	Desi Relaford	.10
126	Bobby Abreu	.10
127	Jose Guillen	.10
128	Jason Kendall	.15
129	Aramis Ramirez	.20
130	Mark McGwire	2.50
131	Ray Lankford	.10
132	Eli Marrero	.10
133	Wally Joyner	.10
134	Greg Vaughn	.10
135	Trevor Hoffman	.10
136	Kevin Brown	.15
137	Tony Gwynn	1.00
138	Bill Mueller	.10
139	Ellis Burks	.10
140	Barry Bonds	.50
141	Robb Nen	.10
142	Ken Griffey Jr.	2.50
143	Alex Rodriguez	2.00
144	Jay Buhner	.10
145	Edgar Martinez	.10
146	Rolando Arrojo	.15
147	Robert Smith	.10
148	Quinton McCracken	.10
149	Ivan Rodriguez	.50
150	Will Clark	.25
151	Mark McLemore	.10
152	Juan Gonzalez	1.00
153	Jose Cruz Jr.	.35
154	Carlos Delgado	.25
155	Roger Clemens	.75

1999 Upper Deck UD Choice Prime Choice Reserve

Each card in the UD Choice set is also found in a parallel version with the words "Prime Choice Reserve" repeated in the background of the photo on front in refractive foil. On back, the parallels are individually serial numbered from within an edition of 100 each.

	MT
Common Player:	3.00
(PCR stars valued at 60X regular version; young stars and rookies about 25X. See 1999 UD Choice for base	

1999 Upper Deck UD Choice Mini Bobbing Head

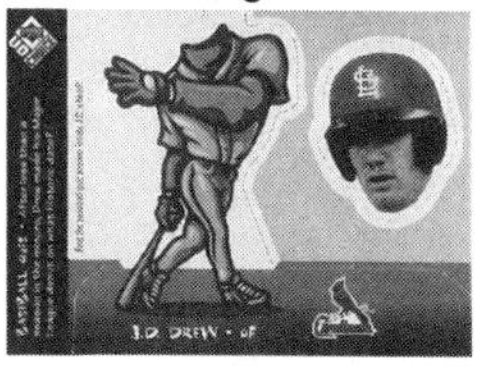

Inserted 1:5 packs, some of the game's best players can be assembled into a miniature bobbing head figure by following the instructions on the card backs.

		MT
Complete Set (30):		25.00
Common Player:		.40
Inserted 1:5		
B01	Randy Johnson	.60
B02	Troy Glaus	.75
B03	Chipper Jones	2.00
B04	Cal Ripken Jr.	3.00
B05	Nomar Garciaparra	2.00
B06	Pedro Martinez	.60
B07	Kerry Wood	.75
B08	Sammy Sosa	2.50
B09	Frank Thomas	1.00
B10	Paul Konerko	.40
B11	Omar Vizquel	.40
B12	Kenny Lofton	.60
B13	Gabe Kapler	1.50
B14	Adrian Beltre	.40
B15	Orlando Hernandez	1.50
B16	Derek Jeter	2.00
B17	Mike Piazza	2.00
B18	Tino Martinez	.40
B19	Ben Grieve	.75
B20	Rickey Henderson	.50
B21	Scott Rolen	.75
B22	Aramis Ramirez	.40
B23	Greg Vaughn	.40
B24	Tony Gwynn	1.50
B25	Barry Bonds	.75
B26	Alex Rodriguez	3.00
B27	Ken Griffey Jr.	4.00
B28	Mark McGwire	4.00
B29	J.D. Drew	1.50
B30	Juan Gonzalez	1.50

1999 Upper Deck UD Choice Piece of History 500 Club

A piece from a Eddie Murray game-used bat was incorporated into each of these cards, which are limited to 350.

		MT
		200.00
EM	Eddie Murray (350)	200.00

1999 Upper Deck UD Choice StarQuest

This four-tiered 30-card set features four different colors for each of the levels. Singles are seeded one per pack and have blue foil etching, Doubles (1:8) have green foil etching, Triples (1:23) have red foil etching and Home Runs are limited to 100 numbered sets with gold foil etching.

		MT
Complete Set (30):		18.00
Common Player:		.25
Inserted 1:1		
Green: 2X		
Inserted 1:8		
Red: 4X		
Inserted 1:23		
Gold: 50X		
Production 100 sets		
SQ1	Ken Griffey Jr.	2.50
SQ2	Sammy Sosa	1.50
SQ3	Alex Rodriguez	2.00
SQ4	Derek Jeter	1.25
SQ5	Troy Glaus	.75
SQ6	Mike Piazza	1.25
SQ7	Barry Bonds	.50
SQ8	Tony Gwynn	1.00
SQ9	Juan Gonzalez	1.00
SQ10	Chipper Jones	1.25
SQ11	Greg Maddux	1.00
SQ12	Randy Johnson	.40
SQ13	Roger Clemens	.75
SQ14	Ben Grieve	.50
SQ15	Nomar Garciaparra	1.25
SQ16	Travis Lee	.50
SQ17	Frank Thomas	.75
SQ18	Vladimir Guerrero	.75
SQ19	Scott Rolen	.50
SQ20	Ivan Rodriguez	.50
SQ21	Cal Ripken Jr.	2.00
SQ22	Mark McGwire	2.50
SQ23	Jeff Bagwell	.60
SQ24	Tony Clark	.40
SQ25	Kerry Wood	.50
SQ26	Kenny Lofton	.40
SQ27	Adrian Beltre	.40
SQ28	Larry Walker	.40
SQ29	Curt Schilling	.25
SQ30	Jim Thome	.40

1999 Upper Deck UD Choice Yard Work

This 30-card set showcases the top power hitters in the game. The right side of the card is covered in bronze foil and stamped with Yard Work. They are numbered with a Y-prefix and seeded 1:13 packs.

		MT
Complete Set (30):		75.00
Common Player:		1.00
Inserted 1:13		
Y01	Andres Galarraga	2.00
Y02	Chipper Jones	6.00
Y03	Rafael Palmeiro	1.50
Y04	Nomar Garciaparra	6.00
Y05	Sammy Sosa	7.50
Y06	Frank Thomas	4.50
Y07	J.D. Drew	2.50
Y08	Albert Belle	2.00
Y09	Jim Thome	1.50
Y10	Manny Ramirez	3.50
Y11	Larry Walker	1.50
Y12	Vinny Castilla	1.25
Y13	Tony Clark	1.50
Y14	Jeff Bagwell	3.50
Y15	Moises Alou	1.25
Y16	Dean Palmer	1.25
Y17	Gary Sheffield	1.25
Y18	Vladimir Guerrero	3.00
Y19	Mike Piazza	6.00
Y20	Tino Martinez	1.50
Y21	Ben Grieve	2.25
Y22	Greg Vaughn	1.25
Y23	Ken Caminiti	1.25
Y24	Barry Bonds	2.25
Y25	Ken Griffey Jr.	10.00
Y26	Alex Rodriguez	7.50
Y27	Mark McGwire	10.00
Y28	Juan Gonzalez	4.50
Y29	Jose Canseco	1.75
Y30	Jose Cruz Jr.	1.50

1999 Upper Deck Encore

Encore is essentially a 180-card partial parallel of Upper Deck Series I, that utilizes a special holo-foil treatment on each card. The 180-card base set consists of 90 base cards and three short-printed subsets: 45 Star Rookie (1:4), 30 Homer Odyssey (1:6) and 15 Stroke of Genius (1:8).

		MT
Complete Set (180):		250.00
Common Player (1-90):		.20
Common Player (91-135):		1.00
Inserted 1:4		
Common Player (136-165):		.75
Inserted 1:6		
Common Player (166-180):		1.00
Inserted 1:8		
Wax Box:		65.00
1	Darin Erstad	.40
2	Mo Vaughn	.75
3	Travis Lee	.50
4	Randy Johnson	.75
5	Matt Williams	.40
6	John Smoltz	.20
7	Greg Maddux	2.00
8	Chipper Jones	2.00
9	Tom Glavine	.40
10	Andruw Jones	.75
11	Cal Ripken Jr.	3.00
12	Mike Mussina	.75
13	Albert Belle	.75
14	Nomar Garciaparra	2.50
15	Jose Offerman	.20
16	Pedro J. Martinez	1.00
17	Trot Nixon	.20
18	Kerry Wood	.50
19	Sammy Sosa	2.50
20	Frank Thomas	1.00
21	Paul Konerko	.20
22	Sean Casey	.75
23	Barry Larkin	.50
24	Greg Vaughn	.40
25	Travis Fryman	.40
26	Jaret Wright	.20
27	Jim Thome	.50
28	Manny Ramirez	1.00
29	Roberto Alomar	.75
30	Kenny Lofton	.60
31	Todd Helton	.75
32	Larry Walker	.75
33	Vinny Castilla	.20
34	Dante Bichette	.40
35	Tony Clark	.50
36	Dean Palmer	.20
37	Gabe Kapler	.50
38	Juan Encarnacion	.20
39	Alex Gonzalez	.20
40	Preston Wilson	.20
41	Mark Kotsay	.20
42	Moises Alou	.40
43	Craig Biggio	.50
44	Ken Caminiti	.30
45	Jeff Bagwell	1.00
46	Johnny Damon	.20
47	Gary Sheffield	.40
48	Kevin Brown	.40
49	Raul Mondesi	.30
50	Jeff Cirillo	.20
51	Jeromy Burnitz	.20
52	Todd Walker	.20
53	Corey Koskie	.20
54	Brad Fullmer	.20
55	Vladimir Guerrero	1.50
56	Mike Piazza	2.50
57	Robin Ventura	.40
58	Rickey Henderson	.60
59	Derek Jeter	2.50
60	Paul O'Neill	.40
61	Bernie Williams	.75
62	Tino Martinez	.40
63	Roger Clemens	1.50
64	Ben Grieve	.50
65	Jason Giambi	.20
66	Bob Abreu	.20
67	Scott Rolen	1.00
68	Curt Schilling	.40
69	Marlon Anderson	.20
70	Kevin Young	.20
71	Jason Kendall	.40
72	Brian Giles	.20
73	Mark McGwire	4.00
74	Fernando Tatis	.40
75	Eric Davis	.20
76	Trevor Hoffman	.20
77	Tony Gwynn	2.00
78	Matt Clement	.20
79	Robb Nen	.20
80	Barry Bonds	1.00
81	Ken Griffey Jr.	4.00
82	Alex Rodriguez	3.00
83	Wade Boggs	.50
84	Fred McGriff	.40
85	Jose Canseco	1.00
86	Ivan Rodriguez	1.00
87	Juan Gonzalez	1.50
88	Rafael Palmeiro	.75
89	Carlos Delgado	.75
90	David Wells	.20
91	Troy Glaus (Star Rookies)	3.00
92	Adrian Beltre (Star Rookies)	1.50
93	Matt Anderson (Star Rookies)	1.00
94	Eric Chavez (Star Rookies)	1.50
95	*Jeff Weaver* (Star Rookies)	5.00
96	Warren Morris (Star Rookies)	1.50
97	George Lombard (Star Rookies)	1.00
98	Mike Kinkade (Star Rookies)	1.00
99	*Kyle Farnsworth* (Star Rookies)	2.00
100	J.D. Drew (Star Rookies)	4.00
101	*Joe McEwing* (Star Rookies)	3.00
102	Carlos Guillen (Star Rookies)	1.00
103	*Kelly Dransfeldt* (Star Rookies)	2.50
104	*Eric Munson* (Star Rookies)	20.00
105	Armando Rios (Star Rookies)	1.00
106	Ramon Martinez (Star Rookies)	1.00
107	Orlando Hernandez (Star Rookies)	2.50
108	Jeremy Giambi (Star Rookies)	2.00
109	*Pat Burrell* (Star Rookies)	20.00
110	Shea Hillenbrand (Star Rookies)	2.50
111	Billy Koch (Star Rookies)	1.00
112	Roy Halladay (Star Rookies)	1.00
113	Ruben Mateo (Star Rookies)	4.00
114	Bruce Chen (Star Rookies)	1.00
115	Angel Pena (Star Rookies)	1.50
116	Michael Barrett (Star Rookies)	1.50
117	Kevin Witt (Star Rookies)	1.00
118	Damon Minor (Star Rookies)	1.00
119	Ryan Minor (Star Rookies)	2.00
120	A.J. Pierzynski (Star Rookies)	1.00
121	*A.J. Burnett* (Star Rookies)	4.00
122	Christian Guzman (Star Rookies)	1.00
123	Joe Lawrence (Star Rookies)	1.00
124	Derrick Gibson (Star Rookies)	1.00
125	Carlos Febles (Star Rookies)	3.00
126	Chris Haas (Star Rookies)	1.00
127	Cesar King (Star Rookies)	1.00
128	Calvin Pickering (Star Rookies)	1.00
129	Mitch Meluskey (Star Rookies)	1.00
130	Carlos Beltran (Star Rookies)	6.00
131	Ron Belliard (Star Rookies)	1.50
132	Jerry Hairston Jr. (Star Rookies)	1.00
133	Fernando Seguignol (Star Rookies)	1.50
134	Kris Benson (Star Rookies)	1.00
135	*Chad Hutchinson* (Star Rookies)	5.00
136	Ken Griffey Jr. (Homer Odyssey)	8.00
137	Mark McGwire (Homer Odyssey)	8.00
138	Sammy Sosa (Homer Odyssey)	5.00
139	Albert Belle (Homer Odyssey)	1.50
140	Mo Vaughn (Homer Odyssey)	1.50
141	Alex Rodriguez (Homer Odyssey)	6.00
142	Manny Ramirez (Homer Odyssey)	2.00
143	J.D. Drew (Homer Odyssey)	2.00
144	Juan Gonzalez (Homer Odyssey)	2.50
145	Vladimir Guerrero (Homer Odyssey)	3.00
146	Fernando Tatis (Homer Odyssey)	.75
147	Mike Piazza (Homer Odyssey)	5.00
148	Barry Bonds (Homer Odyssey)	2.00
149	Ivan Rodriguez (Homer Odyssey)	2.00
150	Jeff Bagwell (Homer Odyssey)	2.00
151	Raul Mondesi (Homer Odyssey)	.75
152	Nomar Garciaparra (Homer Odyssey)	5.00
153	Jose Canseco (Homer Odyssey)	2.00
154	Greg Vaughn (Homer Odyssey)	.75
155	Scott Rolen (Homer Odyssey)	2.00
156	Vinny Castilla (Homer Odyssey)	.75
157	Troy Glaus (Homer Odyssey)	2.00
158	Craig Biggio (Homer Odyssey)	1.50
159	Tino Martinez (Homer Odyssey)	1.00
160	Jim Thome (Homer Odyssey)	1.50
161	Frank Thomas (Homer Odyssey)	2.50
162	Tony Clark (Homer Odyssey)	1.00
163	Ben Grieve (Homer Odyssey)	1.50
164	Matt Williams (Homer Odyssey)	1.00
165	Derek Jeter (Homer Odyssey)	5.00
166	Ken Griffey Jr. (Strokes of Genius)	8.00
167	Tony Gwynn (Strokes of Genius)	4.00
168	Mike Piazza (Strokes of Genius)	5.00
169	Mark McGwire (Strokes of Genius)	8.00
170	Sammy Sosa (Strokes of Genius)	5.00
171	Juan Gonzalez (Strokes of Genius)	2.50
172	Mo Vaughn (Strokes of Genius)	1.50
173	Derek Jeter (Strokes of Genius)	5.00
174	Bernie Williams (Strokes of Genius)	1.50
175	Ivan Rodriguez (Strokes of Genius)	2.00
176	Barry Bonds (Strokes of Genius)	2.00
177	Scott Rolen (Strokes of Genius)	2.00
178	Larry Walker (Strokes of Genius)	1.50
179	Chipper Jones (Strokes of Genius)	4.00
180	Alex Rodriguez (Strokes of Genius)	5.00

1999 Upper Deck Encore Gold

This is a 180-card parallel to the base set featuring gold holo-foil treatment and limited to 125 sequentially numbered sets.

Gold (1-90): 15X
Gold (91-135): 2X
Gold (136-165): 4X
Gold (166-180): 5X
(See 1999 Upper Deck Encore for checklist and base card values.)

1999 Upper Deck Encore Batting Practice Caps

This 15-card set features actual swatch pieces of the highlighted players' batting practice cap embedded into each card. These are seeded 1:750 packs.

		MT
Common Player:		40.00
Inserted 1:750		
CB	Carlos Beltran	75.00
BB	Barry Bonds	120.00
VC	Vinny Castilla	50.00
EC	Eric Chavez	40.00
TC	Tony Clark	50.00
JD	J.D. Drew	100.00
VG	Vladimir Guerrero	125.00
TG	Tony Gwynn	150.00
TH	Todd Helton	60.00
GK	Gabe Kapler	50.00
JK	Jason Kendall	40.00
DP	Dean Palmer	40.00
BH	Frank Thomas	150.00
GV	Greg Vaughn	40.00
TW	Todd Walker	40.00

1999 Upper Deck Encore Driving Forces

This 15-card set is highlighted by holo-foil treatment on the card fronts on a thick card stock. Baseball's top performers are featured in this set and are seeded 1:23 packs. A Gold parallel exists and is limited to 10 sets.

		MT
Complete Set (15):		100.00
Common Player:		1.50
Inserted 1:23		
1	Ken Griffey Jr.	15.00
2	Mark McGwire	15.00
3	Sammy Sosa	10.00
4	Albert Belle	3.00
5	Alex Rodriguez	12.00
6	Mo Vaughn	3.00
7	Juan Gonzalez	5.00
8	Jeff Bagwell	4.00
9	Mike Piazza	10.00
10	Frank Thomas	4.00
11	Barry Bonds	4.00
12	Vladimir Guerrero	5.00
13	Chipper Jones	10.00
14	Tony Gwynn	8.00
15	J.D. Drew	4.00

Player names in *Italic* type indicate a rookie card.

1999 Upper Deck Encore McGwired!

This 10-card set salutes baseball's reigning single season home run king. These are seeded 1:23 packs. A gold parallel also is randomly seeded and is limited to 500 sequentially numbered sets. A small photo of the pitcher McGwire hit the historic home run off of is pictured as well.

		MT
Complete Set (10):		70.00
Common Card:		8.00
Inserted 1:23		
Parallel: 2X		
Production 500 sets		
1	Mark McGwire, Carl Pavano	8.00
2	Mark McGwire, Michael Morgan	8.00
3	Mark McGwire, Steve Trachsel	8.00
4	Mark McGwire	8.00
5	Mark McGwire	8.00
6	Mark McGwire, Scott Elarton	8.00
7	Mark McGwire, Jim Parque	8.00
8	Mark McGwire	8.00
9	Mark McGwire, Rafael Roque	8.00
10	Mark McGwire, Jaret Wright	8.00

1999 Upper Deck Encore Pure Excitement

This 30-card set features Light F/X technology and includes the top players in baseball. These are seeded 1:7 packs.

		MT
Complete Set (30):		100.00
Common Player:		1.00
Inserted 1:7		
1	Mo Vaughn	1.50
2	Darin Erstad	1.50
3	Travis Lee	1.50
4	Chipper Jones	6.00
5	Greg Maddux	5.00
6	Gabe Kapler	1.50
7	Cal Ripken Jr.	8.00
8	Nomar Garciaparra	6.00
9	Kerry Wood	1.50
10	Frank Thomas	3.00
11	Manny Ramirez	2.50
12	Larry Walker	2.00
13	Tony Clark	1.00
14	Jeff Bagwell	2.50
15	Craig Biggio	1.50
16	Vladimir Guerrero	3.50
17	Mike Piazza	6.00
18	Bernie Williams	1.50
19	Derek Jeter	6.00
20	Ben Grieve	2.00
21	Eric Chavez	1.00
22	Scott Rolen	2.50
23	Mark McGwire	10.00
24	Tony Gwynn	5.00
25	Barry Bonds	2.50
26	Ken Griffey Jr.	10.00
27	Alex Rodriguez	8.00
28	J.D. Drew	2.50
29	Juan Gonzalez	3.00
30	Roger Clemens	3.00

1999 Upper Deck Encore Rookie Encore

This 10-card set highlights the top rookie prospects in 1999, including J.D. Drew and Gabe Kapler. These are seeded 1:23 packs. A parallel version is also randomly seeded and limited to 500 sequentially numbered sets.

		MT
Complete Set (10):		25.00
Common Player:		1.50
Inserted 1:23		
Parallel: 2X		
Production 500 sets		
1	J.D. Drew	5.00
2	Eric Chavez	1.50
3	Gabe Kapler	2.00
4	Bruce Chen	1.50
5	Carlos Beltran	4.00
6	Troy Glaus	3.00
7	Roy Halladay	1.50
8	Adrian Beltre	2.00
9	Michael Barrett	1.50
10	Pat Burrell	10.00

1999 Upper Deck Encore UD Authentics

This six-card autographed set features signatures of Griffey Jr. and Nomar Garciaparra. These are seeded 1:288 packs.

		MT
Complete Set (6):		525.00
Common Player:		20.00
Inserted 1:288		
MB	Michael Barrett	20.00
PB	Pat Burrell	50.00
JD	J.D. Drew	40.00
NG	Nomar Garciaparra	125.00
TG	Troy Glaus	25.00
JR	Ken Griffey Jr.	350.00

1999 Upper Deck Encore Upper Realm

This 15-card set focuses on the top stars of the game. Card fronts utilize holo-foil treatment, with the initials UR lightly foiled. Card backs are numbered with an "U" prefix and are seeded 1:11 packs.

		MT
Complete Set (15):		60.00
Common Player:		1.00
Inserted 1:11		
1	Ken Griffey Jr.	8.00
2	Mark McGwire	8.00
3	Sammy Sosa	5.00
4	Tony Gwynn	4.00
5	Alex Rodriguez	6.00
6	Juan Gonzalez	2.50
7	J.D. Drew	2.00
8	Roger Clemens	3.00
9	Greg Maddux	4.00
10	Randy Johnson	1.50
11	Mo Vaughn	1.50
12	Derek Jeter	5.00
13	Vladimir Guerrero	2.50
14	Cal Ripken Jr.	6.00
15	Nomar Garciaparra	5.00

1999 Upper Deck Encore 2K Countdown

This set recognizes the countdown to the next century with a salute to baseball's next century of superstars including Derek Jeter and Alex Rodriguez. These are done on a horizontal format and inserted 1:11 packs.

		MT
Complete Set (10):		35.00
Common Player:		1.50
Inserted 1:11		
1	Ken Griffey Jr.	6.00
2	Derek Jeter	4.00
3	Mike Piazza	4.00
4	J.D. Drew	1.50
5	Vladimir Guerrero	2.00
6	Chipper Jones	4.00
7	Alex Rodriguez	5.00
8	Nomar Garciaparra	4.00
9	Mark McGwire	6.00
10	Sammy Sosa	4.00

1999 Upper Deck HoloGrFX Sample

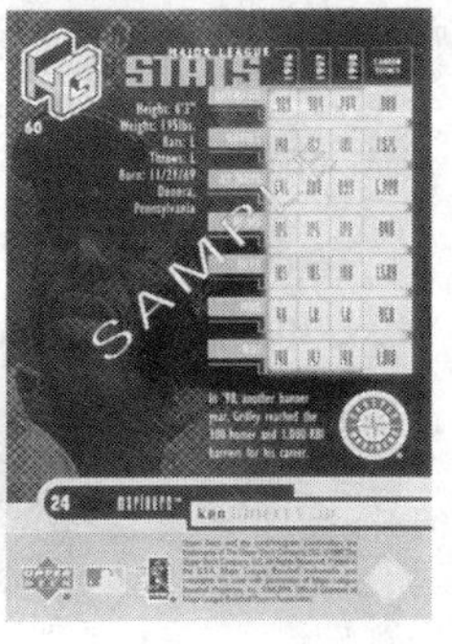

Numbered 60, rather than 56 as in the regular-issue version, this card, which also bears a white "SAMPLE" notation on back, was issued to preview the new UD brand.

		MT
60	Ken Griffey Jr.	6.00

1999 Upper Deck HoloGrFX

HoloGrFX was distributed exclusively to retail and the base set is comprised of 60 base cards, each utilizing holographic technology.

		MT
Complete Set (60):		30.00
Common Player:		.25
AUsome: 3X		
Inserted 1:8		
Wax Box:		65.00
1	Mo Vaughn	.60
2	Troy Glaus	1.00
3	Tim Salmon	.50
4	Randy Johnson	.75
5	Travis Lee	.60
6	Chipper Jones	2.50
7	Greg Maddux	2.00
8	Andruw Jones	.75
9	Tom Glavine	.25
10	Cal Ripken Jr.	3.00
11	Albert Belle	.75
12	Nomar Garciaparra	2.50
13	Pedro J. Martinez	1.00
14	Sammy Sosa	2.50
15	Frank Thomas	1.50
16	Greg Vaughn	.25
17	Kenny Lofton	.60
18	Jim Thome	.50
19	Manny Ramirez	1.00
20	Todd Helton	.50
21	Larry Walker	.75
22	Tony Clark	.50
23	Juan Encarnacion	.25
24	Mark Kotsay	.25
25	Jeff Bagwell	1.00
26	Craig Biggio	.60
27	Ken Caminiti	.40
28	Carlos Beltran	1.00
29	Jeremy Giambi	.25
30	Raul Mondesi	.40
31	Kevin Brown	.25
32	Jeromy Burnitz	.25
33	Corey Koskie	.25
34	Todd Walker	.25
35	Vladimir Guerrero	1.00
36	Mike Piazza	2.50
37	Robin Ventura	.25
38	Derek Jeter	2.50
39	Roger Clemens	1.50
40	Bernie Williams	.60
41	Orlando Hernandez	.50
42	Ben Grieve	.50
43	Eric Chavez	.50
44	Scott Rolen	1.00
45	*Pat Burrell*	4.00
46	Warren Morris	.25
47	Jason Kendall	.25
48	Mark McGwire	4.00
49	J.D. Drew	1.00
50	Tony Gwynn	2.00
51	Trevor Hoffman	.25
52	Barry Bonds	1.00
53	Ken Griffey Jr.	4.00
54	Alex Rodriguez	3.00
55	Jose Canseco	.75
56	Juan Gonzalez	1.50
57	Ivan Rodriguez	1.00
58	Rafael Palmeiro	.60
59	David Wells	.25
60	Carlos Delgado	.75

1999 Upper Deck HoloGrFX Future Fame

This six-card set focuses on players who are destined for Hall of Fame greatness. Card fronts feature a horizontal format on a die-cut design. These are seeded 1:34 packs. A parallel Gold (AU) version is also randomly seeded in every 1:432 packs.

		MT
Complete Set (6):		50.00
Common Player:		8.00
Inserted 1:34		
Gold: 3X		
Inserted 1:210		
1	Tony Gwynn	8.00
2	Cal Ripken Jr.	12.00
3	Mark McGwire	15.00
4	Ken Griffey Jr.	15.00
5	Greg Maddux	8.00
6	Roger Clemens	6.00

1999 Upper Deck HoloGrFX Launchers

This 15-card set highlights the top home run hitters on holographic patterned foil fronts, including McGwire and Sosa. These are seeded 1:3 packs. A Gold (AU) parallel version is also seeded 1:105 packs.

		MT
Complete Set (15):		40.00
Common Player:		1.00
Inserted 1:3		
Gold: 4X		
Inserted 1:105		
1	Mark McGwire	7.50
2	Ken Griffey Jr.	7.50
3	Sammy Sosa	4.00
4	J.D. Drew	1.50
5	Mo Vaughn	1.00
6	Juan Gonzalez	2.00
7	Mike Piazza	4.00
8	Alex Rodriguez	5.00
9	Chipper Jones	4.00
10	Nomar Garciaparra	4.00
11	Vladimir Guerrero	2.00
12	Albert Belle	1.00
13	Barry Bonds	1.50
14	Frank Thomas	2.00
15	Jeff Bagwell	1.50

1999 Upper Deck HoloGrFX StarView

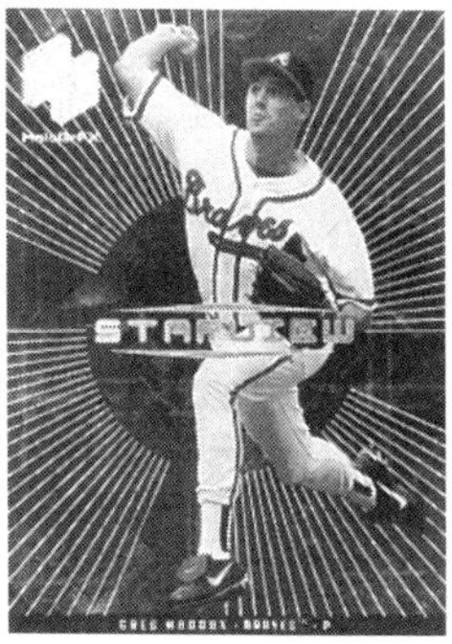

This nine-card set highlights the top players in the game on a rainbow foil, full bleed design. These are seeded 1:17 packs. A Gold parallel version is also randomly seeded 1:210 packs.

		MT
Complete Set (9):		50.00
Common Player:		4.00
Inserted 1:17		
Gold: 3X		
Inserted 1:210		
1	Mark McGwire	10.00
2	Ken Griffey Jr.	10.00
3	Sammy Sosa	6.00
4	Nomar Garciaparra	6.00
5	Roger Clemens	4.00
6	Greg Maddux	5.00
7	Mike Piazza	6.00
8	Alex Rodriguez	6.00
9	Chipper Jones	6.00

1999 Upper Deck HoloGrFX UD Authentics

This 12-card autographed set is done on a horizontal format, with the player signature across the front of a shadow image, of the featured player in the background. These are inserted 1:431 packs.

		MT
Common Player:		10.00
Inserted 1:431		
CB	Carlos Beltran	50.00
BC	Bruce Chen	20.00
JD	J.D. Drew	40.00
AG	Alex Gonzalez	15.00
JR	Ken Griffey Jr.	300.00
CJ	Chipper Jones	125.00
GK	Gabe Kapler	30.00
MK	Mike Kinkade	10.00
CK	Corey Koskie	15.00
GL	George Lombard	15.00
RM	Ryan Minor	20.00
SM	Shane Monahan	10.00

1999 Upper Deck HoloGrFX 500 Club Piece of History

This two card collection features game-used bat chips from bats swung by Willie McCovey and Eddie Mathews embedded into each card. 350 cards of each player exist. Each player also autographed these inserts to their respective jersey numbers: McCovey (44) and Mathews (41).

	MT
Willie McCovey:	250.00
Production 350 cards	
McCovey Autograph (44 issued):	400.00
Eddie Mathews:	300.00
Production 350 cards	
Mathews Autograph (41 issued):	425.00

1999 Upper Deck Home Run Heroes

These cards were part of an unannounced multi-manufacturer (Fleer, Upper Deck, Topps, Pacific) insert program which was exclusive to Wal-Mart. Each company produced cards of Mark McGwire and Sammy Sosa, along with two other premier sluggers. Each company's cards share a "Power Elite" logo at top and "Home Run Heroes" logo vertically at right.

		MT
Complete Set (4):		10.00
Common Player:		2.00
5	Mark McGwire	4.00
6	Sammy Sosa	2.50
7	Ken Griffey Jr.	4.00
8	Frank Thomas	2.00

1999 UD Ionix

Ionix is a 90-card set that includes a 30-card "Techno" subset that was short-printed (1:4 packs). Packs were sold for $4.99, and contain four cards. The first 60 cards of the set are included in a parallel set in which the photo from the back of the regular card was put on the front of a rainbow-foil Reciprocal card. These cards are sequentially numbered to 750. The remaining 30 cards in the set were also paralleled on a Reciprocal card sequentially numbered to 100. The set also includes 350 Frank Robinson "500 Club Piece of History" bat cards, with a piece of a Robinson game-used bat. Another version of the bat cards includes Robinson's autograph, and are hand-numbered to 20. Insert sets included Hyper, Nitro, Cyber, Warp Zone, and HoloGrFX.

		MT
Complete Set (90):		150.00
Common Player (1-60):		.50
Common Techno (61-90):		1.50
Inserted 1:4		
Reciprocals (1-60): 6x to 8x		
Production 750 sets		
Techno Reciprocals (61-90): 6x to 10x		
Production 100 sets		
Wax Box:		85.00
1	Troy Glaus	1.00
2	Darin Erstad	.50
3	Travis Lee	.50
4	Matt Williams	.60
5	Chipper Jones	3.00
6	Greg Maddux	2.50
7	Andruw Jones	1.00
8	Andres Galarraga	1.00
9	Tom Glavine	.75
10	Cal Ripken Jr.	4.00
11	Ryan Minor	.50
12	Nomar Garciaparra	3.00
13	Mo Vaughn	1.00
14	Pedro Martinez	1.50
15	Sammy Sosa	3.00
16	Kerry Wood	1.00
17	Albert Belle	1.00
18	Frank Thomas	1.50
19	Sean Casey	.75
20	Kenny Lofton	1.00
21	Manny Ramirez	1.50
22	Jim Thome	.75
23	Bartolo Colon	.50
24	Jaret Wright	.50
25	Larry Walker	1.00
26	Tony Clark	.75
27	Gabe Kapler	1.00
28	Edgar Renteria	.50
29	Randy Johnson	1.00
30	Craig Biggio	.75
31	Jeff Bagwell	1.50
32	Moises Alou	.50
33	Johnny Damon	.50
34	Adrian Beltre	.75
35	Jeromy Burnitz	.50
36	Todd Walker	.50
37	Corey Koskie	.50
38	Vladimir Guerrero	2.00
39	Mike Piazza	3.00
40	Hideo Nomo	.50
41	Derek Jeter	3.00
42	Tino Martinez	.75
43	Orlando Hernandez	1.00
44	Ben Grieve	.75
45	Rickey Henderson	.75
46	Scott Rolen	1.25
47	Curt Schilling	.75
48	Aramis Ramirez	.50
49	Tony Gwynn	2.50
50	Kevin Brown	.75
51	Barry Bonds	1.50
52	Ken Griffey Jr.	5.00
53	Alex Rodriguez	3.00
54	Mark McGwire	5.00
55	J.D. Drew	1.00
56	Rolando Arrojo	.50
57	Ivan Rodriguez	1.50
58	Juan Gonzalez	1.50
59	Roger Clemens	2.00
60	Jose Cruz Jr.	.50
61	Travis Lee (Techno)	1.50
62	Andres Galarraga (Techno)	2.00
63	Andruw Jones (Techno)	2.50
64	Chipper Jones (Techno)	10.00
65	Greg Maddux (Techno)	8.00
66	Cal Ripken Jr. (Techno)	12.00
67	Nomar Garciaparra (Techno)	10.00
68	Mo Vaughn (Techno)	3.00
69	Sammy Sosa (Techno)	10.00
70	Frank Thomas (Techno)	5.00
71	Kerry Wood (Techno)	2.50
72	Kenny Lofton (Techno)	2.50
73	Manny Ramirez (Techno)	4.00
74	Larry Walker (Techno)	3.00
75	Jeff Bagwell (Techno)	4.00
76	Randy Johnson (Techno)	3.00
77	Paul Molitor (Techno)	3.00
78	Derek Jeter (Techno)	10.00
79	Tino Martinez (Techno)	1.50
80	Mike Piazza (Techno)	10.00
81	Ben Grieve (Techno)	2.50
82	Scott Rolen (Techno)	4.00
83	Mark McGwire (Techno)	15.00
84	Tony Gwynn (Techno)	8.00
85	Barry Bonds (Techno)	4.00
86	Ken Griffey Jr. (Techno)	15.00
87	Alex Rodriguez (Techno)	12.00
88	Juan Gonzalez (Techno)	5.00
89	Roger Clemens (Techno)	5.00
90	J.D. Drew (Techno)	4.00
		.75
100	Ken Griffey Jr. (SAMPLE)	6.00

1999 UD Ionix Cyber

This insert set consisted of 25-cards of baseball's superstars and red-hot rookies. One card was inserted every 53 packs.

		MT
Complete Set (25):		600.00
Common Player:		10.00
C01	Ken Griffey Jr.	65.00
C02	Cal Ripken Jr.	50.00
C03	Frank Thomas	20.00
C04	Greg Maddux	35.00
C05	Mike Piazza	40.00
C06	Alex Rodriguez	45.00
C07	Chipper Jones	35.00
C08	Derek Jeter	45.00
C09	Mark McGwire	65.00
C10	Juan Gonzalez	25.00
C11	Kerry Wood	10.00
C12	Tony Gwynn	35.00
C13	Scott Rolen	15.00
C14	Nomar Garciaparra	40.00
C15	Roger Clemens	25.00
C16	Sammy Sosa	40.00
C17	Travis Lee	10.00
C18	Ben Grieve	10.00
C19	Jeff Bagwell	15.00
C20	Ivan Rodriguez	15.00
C21	Barry Bonds	15.00
C22	J.D. Drew	20.00
C23	Kenny Lofton	10.00
C24	Andruw Jones	10.00
C25	Vladimir Guerrero	25.00

1999 UD Ionix HoloGrFX

This insert set consisted of 10-cards, and featured only the best players in the game. The cards in this set were holographically enhanced. Those cards were rare with one card inserted every 1,500 packs.

		MT
Complete Set (10):		1250.
Common Player:		75.00
Inserted 1:1,500		
HG01	Ken Griffey Jr.	250.00
HG02	Cal Ripken Jr.	200.00
HG03	Frank Thomas	75.00
HG04	Greg Maddux	125.00
HG05	Mike Piazza	150.00
HG06	Alex Rodriguez	150.00
HG07	Chipper Jones	125.00
HG08	Derek Jeter	150.00
HG09	Mark McGwire	250.00
HG10	Juan Gonzalez	75.00

1999 UD Ionix Hyper

This insert set featured the top players in baseball, and consisted of 20-cards. Hyper cards were inserted one per nine packs.

		MT
Complete Set (20):		120.00
Common Player:		3.00
Inserted 1:9		
H01	Ken Griffey Jr.	15.00
H02	Cal Ripken Jr.	12.00
H03	Frank Thomas	5.00
H04	Greg Maddux	8.00
H05	Mike Piazza	10.00
H06	Alex Rodriguez	10.00
H07	Chipper Jones	8.00
H08	Derek Jeter	10.00
H09	Mark McGwire	15.00
H10	Juan Gonzalez	5.00
H11	Kerry Wood	3.00
H12	Tony Gwynn	8.00
H13	Scott Rolen	4.00
H14	Nomar Garciaparra	10.00
H15	Roger Clemens	5.00
H16	Sammy Sosa	10.00
H17	Travis Lee	3.00
H18	Ben Grieve	3.00
H19	Jeff Bagwell	4.00
H20	J.D. Drew	4.00

1999 UD Ionix Nitro

Baseball's ten most collectible players are featured in this 10-card insert set. Each card features Ionix technology with rainbow foil and a unique color pattern. Nitro cards were inserted one per 18 packs.

		MT
Complete Set (10):		100.00
Common Player:		6.00
Inserted 1:18		
N01	Ken Griffey Jr.	18.00
N02	Cal Ripken Jr.	12.00
N03	Frank Thomas	6.00
N04	Greg Maddux	10.00
N05	Mike Piazza	10.00
N06	Alex Rodriguez	12.00
N07	Chipper Jones	10.00
N08	Derek Jeter	12.00
N09	Mark McGwire	18.00
N10	J.D. Drew	5.00

1999 UD Ionix Warp Zone

This 15-card insert set contained a special holographic foil enhancement. Warp Zone cards were inserted one per 216 packs.

		MT
Complete Set (15):		900.00
Common Player:		30.00
Inserted 1:216		
WZ01	Ken Griffey Jr.	125.00
WZ02	Cal Ripken Jr.	100.00
WZ03	Frank Thomas	40.00
WZ04	Greg Maddux	60.00
WZ05	Mike Piazza	80.00
WZ06	Alex Rodriguez	100.00
WZ07	Chipper Jones	60.00
WZ08	Derek Jeter	80.00
WZ09	Mark McGwire	125.00
WZ10	Juan Gonzalez	40.00
WZ11	Kerry Wood	30.00
WZ12	Tony Gwynn	60.00
WZ13	Scott Rolen	30.00
WZ14	Nomar Garciaparra	80.00
WZ15	J.D. Drew	30.00

1999 UD Ionix 500 Club Piece of History

These cards feature an actual piece of game-used bat from one of Hall-of-Famer Frank Robinson's Louisville Sluggers. Approximately 350 were made. Robinson also autographed 20 of his Piece of History inserts.

		MT
FR	Frank Robinson/350	200.00
FRA	Frank Robinson Auto./20	750.00

1999 Upper Deck MVP Samples

		MT
S3	Ken Griffey Jr.	2.00
S3	Ken Griffey Jr. (silver signature)	2.00

1999 Upper Deck MVP

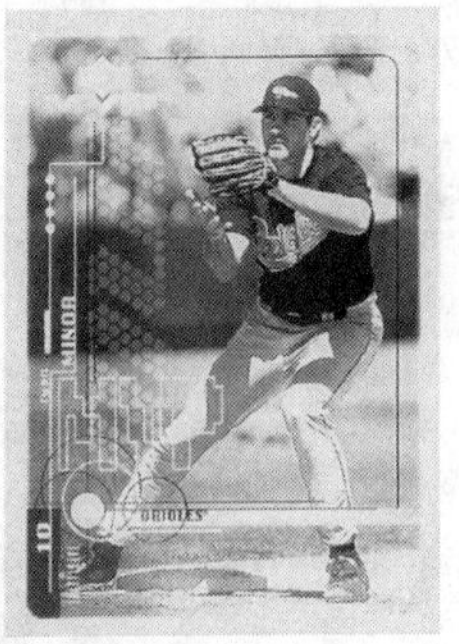

Card fronts of the 220-card set feature silver foil stamping and a white border. Card backs feature year-by-year statistics, a small photo of the featured player and a brief career note. MVP was distributed in 24-pack boxes, with a SRP of $1.59 for 10-card packs.

		MT
Complete Set (220):		30.00
Common Player:		.15
Wax Box:		45.00
1	Mo Vaughn	.60
2	Tim Belcher	.15
3	Jack McDowell	.15
4	Troy Glaus	.75
5	Darin Erstad	.75
6	Tim Salmon	.30
7	Jim Edmonds	.15
8	Randy Johnson	.50
9	Steve Finley	.15
10	Travis Lee	.75
11	Matt Williams	.25
12	Todd Stottlemyre	.15
13	Jay Bell	.15
14	David Dellucci	.15
15	Chipper Jones	2.00
16	Andruw Jones	.50
17	Greg Maddux	1.50
18	Tom Glavine	.25
19	Javy Lopez	.15
20	Brian Jordan	.15
21	George Lombard	.25
22	John Smoltz	.25
23	Cal Ripken Jr.	2.50
24	Charles Johnson	.15
25	Albert Belle	.75
26	Brady Anderson	.15
27	Mike Mussina	.60
28	Calvin Pickering	.15
29	Ryan Minor	.25
30	Jerry Hairston Jr.	.15
31	Nomar Garciaparra	2.00
32	Pedro Martinez	.60
33	Jason Varitek	.15
34	Troy O'Leary	.15
35	Donnie Sadler	.15
36	Mark Portugal	.15
37	John Valentin	.15
38	Kerry Wood	.75
39	Sammy Sosa	2.00
40	Mark Grace	.25
41	Henry Rodriguez	.15
42	Rod Beck	.15
43	Benito Santiago	.15
44	Kevin Tapani	.15
45	Frank Thomas	1.50
46	Mike Caruso	.15
47	Magglio Ordonez	.25
48	Paul Konerko	.25
49	Ray Durham	.15
50	Jim Parque	.15
51	Carlos Lee	.25
52	Denny Neagle	.15
53	Pete Harnisch	.15
54	Michael Tucker	.15
55	Sean Casey	.30
56	Eddie Taubenese	.15
57	Barry Larkin	.20
58	Pokey Reese	.15
59	Sandy Alomar	.25
60	Roberto Alomar	.60
61	Bartolo Colon	.15
62	Kenny Lofton	.60
63	Omar Vizquel	.15
64	Travis Fryman	.15
65	Jim Thome	.40
66	Manny Ramirez	1.00
67	Jaret Wright	.25
68	Darryl Kile	.15
69	Kirt Manwaring	.15
70	Vinny Castilla	.25
71	Todd Helton	.40
72	Dante Bichette	.25
73	Larry Walker	.50
74	Derrick Gibson	.15
75	Gabe Kapler	.75
76	Dean Palmer	.15
77	Matt Anderson	.15
78	Bobby Higginson	.15
79	Damion Easley	.15
80	Tony Clark	.40
81	Juan Encarnacion	.15
82	Livan Hernandez	.15
83	Alex Gonzalez	.15
84	Preston Wilson	.15
85	Derrek Lee	.15
86	Mark Kotsay	.15
87	Todd Dunwoody	.15
88	Cliff Floyd	.15
89	Ken Caminiti	.15
90	Jeff Bagwell	.75
91	Moises Alou	.25
92	Craig Biggio	.40
93	Billy Wagner	.15
94	Richard Hidalgo	.15
95	Derek Bell	.15
96	Hipolito Pichardo	.15
97	Jeff King	.15
98	Carlos Beltran	.20
99	Jeremy Giambi	.25
100	Larry Sutton	.15
101	Johnny Damon	.15
102	Dee Brown	.15
103	Kevin Brown	.25
104	Chan Ho Park	.25
105	Raul Mondesi	.30
106	Eric Karros	.15
107	Adrian Beltre	.30
108	Devon White	.15
109	Gary Sheffield	.20
110	Sean Berry	.15
111	Alex Ochoa	.15
112	Marquis Grissom	.15
113	Fernando Vina	.15
114	Jeff Cirillo	.15
115	Geoff Jenkins	.15
116	Jeromy Burnitz	.15
117	Brad Radke	.15
118	Eric Milton	.15
119	A.J. Pierzynski	.15
120	Todd Walker	.25
121	David Ortiz	.15
122	Corey Koskie	.15
123	Vladimir Guerrero	1.00
124	Rondell White	.20
125	Brad Fullmer	.20
126	Ugueth Urbina	.15
127	Dustin Hermanson	.15
128	Michael Barrett	.25
129	Fernando Seguignol	.20
130	Mike Piazza	2.00
131	Rickey Henderson	.30
132	Rey Ordonez	.15
133	John Olerud	.25
134	Robin Ventura	.15
135	Hideo Nomo	.25
136	Mike Kinkade	.15
137	Al Leiter	.25
138	Brian McRae	.15
139	Derek Jeter	2.00
140	Bernie Williams	.40
141	Paul O'Neill	.30
142	Scott Brosius	.15
143	Tino Martinez	.30
144	Roger Clemens	1.00
145	Orlando Hernandez	1.00
146	Mariano Rivera	.25
147	Ricky Ledee	.15
148	A.J. Hinch	.15
149	Ben Grieve	.75
150	Eric Chavez	.75
151	Miguel Tejada	.25
152	Matt Stairs	.15
153	Ryan Christenson	.15
154	Jason Giambi	.15
155	Curt Schilling	.25
156	Scott Rolen	.75
157	*Pat Burrell*	5.00
158	Doug Glanville	.15
159	Bobby Abreu	.15
160	Rico Brogna	.15
161	Ron Gant	.15
162	Jason Kendall	.25
163	Aramis Ramirez	.15
164	Jose Guillen	.15
165	Emil Brown	.15
166	Pat Meares	.15
167	Kevin Young	.15
168	Brian Giles	.15
169	Mark McGwire	3.00
170	J.D. Drew	.75
171	Edgar Renteria	.15
172	Fernando Tatis	.20
173	Matt Morris	.15
174	Eli Marrero	.15
175	Ray Lankford	.15
176	Tony Gwynn	1.50
177	Sterling Hitchcock	.15
178	Ruben Rivera	.15
179	Wally Joyner	.15
180	Trevor Hoffman	.15
181	Jim Leyritz	.15
182	Carlos Hernandez	.15
183	Barry Bonds	.75
184	Ellis Burks	.15
185	F.P. Santangelo	.15
186	J.T. Snow	.15
187	Ramon Martinez	.15
188	Jeff Kent	.15
189	Robb Nen	.15
190	Ken Griffey Jr.	3.00
191	Alex Rodriguez	2.50
192	Shane Monahan	.15
193	Carlos Guillen	.15
194	Edgar Martinez	.15
195	David Segui	.15
196	Jose Mesa	.15
197	Jose Canseco	.75
198	Rolando Arrojo	.15
199	Wade Boggs	.25
200	Fred McGriff	.25
201	Quinton McCracken	.15
202	Bobby Smith	.15
203	Bubba Trammell	.15
204	Juan Gonzalez	1.50
205	Ivan Rodriguez	.75
206	Rafael Palmeiro	.30
207	Royce Clayton	.15
208	Rick Helling	.15
209	Todd Zeile	.15
210	Rusty Greer	.15
211	David Wells	.15
212	Roy Halladay	.25
213	Carlos Delgado	.40
214	Darrin Fletcher	.15
215	Shawn Green	.50
216	Kevin Witt	.15
217	Jose Cruz Jr.	.20
218	Ken Griffey Jr.	1.50
219	Sammy Sosa	.65
220	Mark McGwire	1.50

1999 Upper Deck MVP Scripts/Super Scripts

Three different parallels of the 220 base cards in MVP are inserted bearing a metallic-foil facsimile autograph on front. Silver Script cards are found about every other pack. Gold Script cards are hobby-only and serially numbered to 100 apiece. Also hobby-only are Super Script versions on which the autograph is in holographic foil and the cards are numbered on the back to 25 apiece.

Silver Script: 2X
Gold Script: 25X
Super Script: 75X
(See 1999 UD MVP for checklist and base card values.)

1999 Upper Deck MVP Dynamics

This 15-card set features holofoil treatment on the card fronts with silver foil stamping. Card backs are numbered with a "D" prefix and are inserted 1:28 packs.

		MT
Complete Set (15):		125.00
Common Player:		3.00
Inserted 1:28		
1	Ken Griffey Jr.	20.00
2	Alex Rodriguez	15.00
3	Nomar Garciaparra	12.00
4	Mike Piazza	12.00
5	Mark McGwire	20.00
6	Sammy Sosa	12.00
7	Chipper Jones	12.00
8	Mo Vaughn	4.00
9	Tony Gwynn	10.00
10	Vladimir Guerrero	7.50
11	Derek Jeter	12.00
12	Jeff Bagwell	5.00
13	Cal Ripken Jr.	15.00
14	Juan Gonzalez	10.00
15	J.D. Drew	5.00

1999 Upper Deck MVP Game Used Souvenirs

This 10-card set have a piece of game-used bat from the featured player embedded into each card. These are found exclusively in hobby packs at a rate of 1:144 packs.

		MT
Complete Set (9):		750.00
Common Player:		50.00
Inserted 1:144		
JB	Jeff Bagwell	60.00
BB	Barry Bonds	50.00
JD	J.D. Drew	60.00
KGj	Ken Griffey Jr.	200.00
CJ	Chipper Jones	125.00
MP	Mike Piazza	125.00
CR	Cal Ripken Jr.	160.00
SR	Scott Rolen	50.00
MV	Mo Vaughn	50.00

1999 Upper Deck MVP Signed Game Used Souvenirs

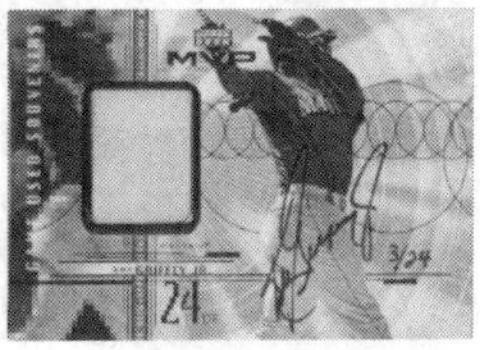

Ken Griffey Jr. and Chipper Jones both signed their Game Used Souvenir inserts to their jersey number, Griffey (24) and Jones (10). These were seeded exclusively in hobby packs.

		MT
Complete Set (2):		1600.
KGj	Ken Griffey Jr.	1200.
CJ	Chipper Jones	500.00

1999 Upper Deck MVP Power Surge

This 15-card set features baseball's top home run hitters, utilizing rainbow foil technology. Card backs are numbered with a "P" prefix and are seeded 1:9 packs.

		MT
Complete Set (15):		30.00
Common Player:		.70
Inserted 1:9		
1	Mark McGwire	5.00
2	Sammy Sosa	3.00
3	Ken Griffey Jr.	5.00
4	Alex Rodriguez	4.00
5	Juan Gonzalez	2.50
6	Nomar Garciaparra	3.00
7	Vladimir Guerrero	1.50
8	Chipper Jones	3.00
9	Albert Belle	1.00
10	Frank Thomas	1.50
11	Mike Piazza	3.00
12	Jeff Bagwell	1.25
13	Manny Ramirez	1.25
14	Mo Vaughn	1.25
15	Barry Bonds	1.50

1999 Upper Deck MVP ProSign

This 30-card autographed set is randomly seeded exclusively in retail packs at a rate of 1:216 packs. Card backs are numbered with the featured player's initials.

		MT
Common Player:		10.00
Inserted 1:216 R		
MA	Matt Anderson	15.00
CB	Carlos Beltran	50.00
RB	Russ Branyan	20.00
EC	Eric Chavez	25.00
BC	Bruce Chen	20.00
BF	Brad Fuller	15.00
NG	Nomar Garciaparra	140.00
JG	Jeremy Giambi	20.00
DG	Derrick Gibson	15.00
CG	Chris Gomez	10.00
AG	Alex Gonzalez	15.00
BG	Ben Grieve	40.00
JR.	Ken Griffey Jr.	400.00
RH	Richard Hidalgo	15.00
SH	Shea Hillenbrand	10.00
CJ	Chipper Jones	125.00
GK	Gabe Kapler	40.00
SK	Scott Karl	10.00
CK	Corey Koskie	15.00
RL	Ricky Ledee	15.00
ML	Mike Lincoln	10.00
GL	George Lombard	20.00
MLo	Mike Lowell	20.00
RM	Ryan Minor	20.00
SM	Shane Monahan	10.00
AN	Abraham Nunez	10.00
JP	Jim Parque	10.00
CP	Calvin Pickering	20.00
JRa	Jason Rakers	10.00
RR	Ruben Rivera	10.00
IR	Ivan Rodriguez	80.00
KW	Kevin Witt	10.00

1999 Upper Deck MVP Scout's Choice

Utilizing Light F/X technology, this 15-card set highlights the top young prospects in the game. Card backs are numbered with a "SC" prefix and are seeded 1:9 packs.

		MT
Complete Set (15):		20.00
Common Player:		.50
Inserted 1:9		
1	J.D. Drew	1.25
2	Ben Grieve	1.25
3	Troy Glaus	2.00
4	Gabe Kapler	1.50
5	Carlos Beltran	1.00
6	Aramis Ramirez	.50
7	Pat Burrell	5.00
8	Kerry Wood	1.25
9	Ryan Minor	.50
10	Todd Helton	1.00
11	Eric Chavez	1.25
12	Russ Branyon	.50
13	Travis Lee	1.25
14	Ruben Mateo	1.50
15	Roy Halladay	.50

1999 Upper Deck MVP Super Tools

This 15-card insert set focuses on baseball's top stars and utilizes holo foil technology on the card fronts. Card backs are numbered with a "T" prefix and are seeded 1:14 packs.

		MT
Complete Set (15):		60.00
Common Player:		2.00
Inserted 1:14		
1	Ken Griffey Jr.	12.00
2	Alex Rodriguez	10.00
3	Sammy Sosa	8.00
4	Derek Jeter	8.00
5	Vladimir Guerrero	4.00
6	Ben Grieve	2.50
7	Mike Piazza	8.00
8	Kenny Lofton	2.00
9	Barry Bonds	2.50
10	Darin Erstad	2.00
11	Nomar Garciaparra	8.00
12	Cal Ripken Jr.	10.00
13	J.D. Drew	2.50
14	Larry Walker	2.00
15	Chipper Jones	8.00

1999 Upper Deck MVP Swing Time

This 12-card set focuses on top hitters in the game and points out three aspects why the featured player is such a successful hitter. Printed on a full foiled front these are seeded 1:6 packs. Card backs are numbered with a "S" prefix.

		MT
Complete Set (12):		20.00
Common Player:		.90
Inserted 1:6		
1	Ken Griffey Jr.	3.50
2	Mark McGwire	3.50
3	Sammy Sosa	2.25
4	Tony Gwynn	1.75
5	Alex Rodriguez	2.75
6	Nomar Garciaparra	2.25
7	Barry Bonds	.90
8	Frank Thomas	1.50
9	Chipper Jones	2.25
10	Ivan Rodriguez	.90
11	Mike Piazza	2.25
12	Derek Jeter	2.25

1999 Upper Deck MVP 500 Club Piece of History

This insert has a piece of game-used bat once swung by Mike Schmidt embedded into each card. A total of 350 of this insert was produced. Schmidt also signed 20 of the inserts.

	MT
548HRMike Schmidt	350.00
548HRMike Schmidt (autographed edition of 20)	900.00

1999 Upper Deck Ovation

Cards 1-60 in the base set have the look and feel of an actual baseball. A player photo is in the foreground with a partial image of a baseball in the background on the card front. Cards 61-90 make up two subsets: World Premiere (61-80) is a 20-card collection consisting of 20 rookie prospects and Superstar Spotlight (81-90) is a 10-card lineup of baseball's biggest stars. Both subsets are short-printed, World Premiere are seeded 1:3.5 packs and Superstar Spotlight 1:6 packs. Five card packs carry a S.R.P. of $3.99 per pack.

		MT
Complete Set (90):		150.00
Common Player:		.40
Common World Premiere:		1.00
Inserted 1:3.5		
Common Superstar Spotlight:		4.00
Inserted 1:6		
Wax Box:		110.00
1	Ken Griffey Jr.	6.00
2	Rondell White	.40
3	Tony Clark	.75
4	Barry Bonds	1.25
5	Larry Walker	.75
6	Greg Vaughn	.40
7	Mark Grace	.50
8	John Olerud	.50
9	Matt Williams	.60
10	Craig Biggio	.65
11	Quinton McCracken	.40
12	Kerry Wood	1.00
13	Derek Jeter	3.00
14	Frank Thomas	1.50
15	Tino Martinez	.75
16	Albert Belle	.75
17	Ben Grieve	1.25
18	Cal Ripken Jr.	4.00
19	Johnny Damon	.40
20	Jose Cruz Jr.	.75
21	Barry Larkin	.60
22	Jason Giambi	.40
23	Sean Casey	.75
24	Scott Rolen	1.25
25	Jim Thome	.75
26	Curt Schilling	.50
27	Moises Alou	.75
28	Alex Rodriguez	4.00
29	Mark Kotsay	.45
30	Darin Erstad	.75
31	Mike Mussina	.65
32	Todd Walker	.50
33	Nomar Garciaparra	3.00
34	Vladimir Guerrero	1.50
35	Jeff Bagwell	1.25
36	Mark McGwire	6.00
37	Travis Lee	.75
38	Dean Palmer	.40
39	Fred McGriff	.50
40	Sammy Sosa	3.00
41	Mike Piazza	3.00
42	Andres Galarraga	.75
43	Pedro Martinez	1.50
44	Juan Gonzalez	1.50
45	Greg Maddux	2.50
46	Jeromy Burnitz	.40
47	Roger Clemens	2.00
48	Vinny Castilla	.40
49	Kevin Brown	.50
50	Mo Vaughn	.65
51	Raul Mondesi	.50
52	Randy Johnson	.75
53	Ray Lankford	.40
54	Jaret Wright	.40
55	Tony Gwynn	2.50
56	Chipper Jones	3.00
57	Gary Sheffield	.60
58	Ivan Rodriguez	1.25
59	Kenny Lofton	.65
60	Jason Kendall	.40
61	J.D. Drew (World Premiere)	5.00
62	Gabe Kapler (World Premiere)	3.00
63	Adrian Beltre (World Premiere)	2.00
64	Carlos Beltran (World Premiere)	4.00
65	Eric Chavez (World Premiere)	1.50
66	Mike Lowell (World Premiere)	1.00
67	Troy Glaus (World Premiere)	4.00
68	George Lombard (World Premiere)	1.00
69	Alex Gonzalez (World Premiere)	1.00
70	Mike Kinkade (World Premiere)	1.50
71	Jeremy Giambi (World Premiere)	1.50
72	Bruce Chen (World Premiere)	1.50
73	Preston Wilson (World Premiere)	1.25
74	Kevin Witt (World Premiere)	1.00
75	Carlos Guillen (World Premiere)	1.00
76	Ryan Minor (World Premiere)	2.50
77	Corey Koskie (World Premiere)	1.00
78	Robert Fick (World Premiere)	1.00
79	Michael Barrett (World Premiere)	2.00
80	Calvin Pickering (World Premiere)	1.00
81	Ken Griffey Jr. (Superstar Spotlight)	12.00
82	Mark McGwire (Superstar Spotlight)	15.00
83	Cal Ripken Jr. (Superstar Spotlight)	10.00
84	Derek Jeter (Superstar Spotlight)	8.00
85	Chipper Jones (Superstar Spotlight)	6.00
86	Nomar Garciaparra (Superstar Spotlight)	8.00
87	Sammy Sosa (Superstar Spotlight)	8.00
88	Juan Gonzalez (Superstar Spotlight)	4.00
89	Mike Piazza (Superstar Spotlight)	8.00
90	Alex Rodriguez (Superstar Spotlight)	10.00

Modern cards in Near Mint condition are valued at about 75% of the Mint value shown here. Excellent-condition cards are worth 50%. Cards in lower grades are not generally collectible.

1999 Upper Deck Ovation Standing Ovation

	MT
Common Player:	3.00
Stars (1-60): 5X	
World Premiere (61-80): 1.5X	
Superstar Spotlight (81-90): 2X	
Production 500 sets	
(See 1999 Upper Deck Ovation for checklist and base card values.)	

1999 Upper Deck Ovation Curtain Calls

This 20-card set focuses on the most memorable accomplishments posted during the '98 season. Card fronts have two images of the player, one on the right half and a smaller image on the bottom left. Copper foil stamping is used to enhance the card front. These are numbered with a R-prefix and are seeded 1:8 packs.

		MT
Complete Set (20):		80.00
Common Player:		1.25
Inserted 1:8		
R01	Mark McGwire	12.50
R02	Sammy Sosa	6.00
R03	Ken Griffey Jr.	12.50
R04	Alex Rodriguez	8.00
R05	Roger Clemens	4.00
R06	Cal Ripken Jr.	8.00
R07	Barry Bonds	3.00
R08	Kerry Wood	2.00
R09	Nomar Garciaparra	6.00
R10	Derek Jeter	6.00
R11	Juan Gonzalez	5.00
R12	Greg Maddux	5.00
R13	Pedro Martinez	2.00
R14	David Wells	1.25
R15	Moises Alou	1.25
R16	Tony Gwynn	5.00
R17	Albert Belle	2.50
R18	Mike Piazza	6.00
R19	Ivan Rodriguez	2.75
R20	Randy Johnson	1.75

1999 Upper Deck Ovation Major Production

This 20-card set utilizes thermography technology to simulate the look and feel of home plate and highlights some of the game's most productive players. These are inserted 1:45 packs and are numbered with a S prefix.

		MT
Complete Set (20):		400.00
Common Player:		6.00
Inserted 1:45		
S01	Mike Piazza	35.00
S02	Mark McGwire	50.00
S03	Chipper Jones	35.00
S04	Cal Ripken Jr.	40.00
S05	Ken Griffey Jr.	50.00
S06	Barry Bonds	12.00
S07	Tony Gwynn	25.00
S08	Randy Johnson	8.00
S09	Ivan Rodriguez	12.00
S10	Frank Thomas	20.00
S11	Alex Rodriguez	40.00
S12	Albert Belle	10.00
S13	Juan Gonzalez	25.00
S14	Greg Maddux	30.00
S15	Jeff Bagwell	12.00
S16	Derek Jeter	35.00
S17	Matt Williams	6.00
S18	Kenny Lofton	8.00
S19	Sammy Sosa	35.00
S20	Roger Clemens	16.00

1999 Upper Deck Ovation Piece of History

This 14-card set has actual pieces of game-used bat, from the featured player, imbedded into the card. These are inserted 1:247 packs. Ben Grieve autographed 25 versions of his Piece of History insert cards. Although there is no regular Piece of History Kerry Wood card, Upper Deck inserted 25 autographed Piece of History game-used baseball cards. These have a piece of one of Wood's game-hurled baseballs from the 1998 season.

		MT
Complete Set (14):		2500.
Common Player:		75.00
Inserted 1:247		
BB	Barry Bonds	150.00
CJ	Chipper Jones	250.00
BW	Bernie Williams	90.00
KGj	Ken Griffey Jr.	450.00
NG	Nomar Garciaparra	250.00
JG	Juan Gonzalez	150.00
DJ	Derek Jeter	300.00
SS	Sammy Sosa	300.00
TG	Tony Gwynn	160.00
AR	Alex Rodriguez	300.00
CR	Cal Ripken Jr.	350.00
BG	Ben Grieve	75.00
VG	Vladimir Guerrero	120.00
MP	Mike Piazza	250.00
BGAU	Ben Grieve (auto, 25)	850.00
KWAU	Kerry Wood (auto, 25)	600.00

1999 Upper Deck Ovation ReMarkable

This three-tiered 15-card insert showcases Mark McGwire's historic '98 season. Cards #1-5 are Bronze and inserted 1:9 packs; cards #6-10 are Silver and inserted 1:25 packs; and cards #11-15 are Gold and inserted 1:99 packs.

		MT
Complete Set (15):		150.00
Common #1-5:		6.00
Inserted 1:9		
Common #6-10:		12.00
Inserted 1:25		
Common # 11-15		25.00
Inserted 1:99		
MM01	Mark McGwire	6.00
MM02	Mark McGwire	6.00
MM03	Mark McGwire	6.00
MM04	Mark McGwire	6.00
MM05	Mark McGwire	6.00
MM06	Mark McGwire	12.00
MM07	Mark McGwire	12.00
MM08	Mark McGwire	12.00
MM09	Mark McGwire	12.00
MM10	Mark McGwire	12.00
MM11	Mark McGwire	25.00
MM12	Mark McGwire	25.00
MM13	Mark McGwire	25.00
MM14	Mark McGwire	25.00
MM15	Mark McGwire	25.00

1999 Upper Deck Ovation 500 Club Piece of History

Each of these cards actually have a piece of game-used Louisville Slugger, once swung by Mickey Mantle, imbedded in them. Approximately 350 cards exist. There also is one card with a cut signature of Mantle and a piece of his game-used bat on it.

		MT
Production 350 cards		
MIC-P	Mickey Mantle	1200.

1999 Upper Deck PowerDeck

This 25-card set is comprised of 25 digital PowerDeck interactive trading cards, complete with video and audio content. There is also a parallel "paper" version of the base set called Auxiliary Power. Each digital card includes 32 megabytes of information and is compatible with almost any internet ready computer. One PowerDeck digital card comes in every three-card pack.

		MT
Complete Set (25):		80.00
Common Player:		2.00
1	Ken Griffey Jr.	10.00
2	Mark McGwire	10.00
3	Cal Ripken Jr.	8.00
4	Sammy Sosa	6.00
5	Derek Jeter	6.00
6	Mike Piazza	6.00
7	Nomar Garciaparra	6.00
8	Greg Maddux	5.00
9	Tony Gwynn	5.00
10	Roger Clemens	4.00
11	Scott Rolen	2.50
12	Alex Rodriguez	8.00
13	Manny Ramirez	2.50
14	Chipper Jones	6.00
15	Juan Gonzalez	3.00
16	Ivan Rodriguez	2.50
17	Frank Thomas	3.00
18	Mo Vaughn	2.00
19	Barry Bonds	2.50
20	Vladimir Guerrero	3.00
21	Jose Canseco	2.00
22	Jeff Bagwell	2.50
23	Pedro Martinez	2.50
24	Gabe Kapler	2.00
25	J.D. Drew	2.50
	Checklist card	.10

1999 Upper Deck PowerDeck Auxiliary Power

A "paper" parallel version of the 25-card digital set. These have a horizontal format with silver foil stamping. Backs have a close-up photo along with the featured player's past five years of statistics and a brief career highlight.

		MT
Complete Set (25):		25.00
Common Player:		.50
1	Ken Griffey Jr.	4.00
2	Mark McGwire	4.00
3	Cal Ripken Jr.	2.50
4	Sammy Sosa	2.00
5	Derek Jeter	2.00
6	Mike Piazza	2.00
7	Nomar Garciaparra	2.00
8	Greg Maddux	1.50
9	Tony Gwynn	1.50
10	Roger Clemens	1.00
11	Scott Rolen	.75
12	Alex Rodriguez	2.50
13	Manny Ramirez	.75
14	Chipper Jones	2.00
15	Juan Gonzalez	.75
16	Ivan Rodriguez	.75
17	Frank Thomas	1.00
18	Mo Vaughn	.50
19	Barry Bonds	.75
20	Vladimir Guerrero	1.00
21	Jose Canseco	.75
22	Jeff Bagwell	.75
23	Pedro Martinez	.75
24	Gabe Kapler	.50
25	J.D. Drew	.75

1999 Upper Deck PowerDeck Most Valuable Performances

This seven-card digital insert set consists of capturing true MVP performances from some of baseball's greatest players, including Ken Griffey Jr. These were seeded 1:287 packs.

		MT
Complete Set (7):		300.00
Common Player:		25.00
Inserted 1:287		
1	Sammy Sosa	50.00
2	Barry Bonds	25.00
3	Cal Ripken Jr.	60.00
4	Juan Gonzalez	25.00
5	Ken Griffey Jr.	80.00
6	Roger Clemens	35.00
7	Mark McGwire, Sammy Sosa	100.00

1999 Upper Deck PowerDeck Most Valuable Performanes-Aux

A "paper" parallel version of the digital set, these also were inserted 1:287 packs. They have a horizontal format using silver holofoil and also have different photos from the digital version.

		MT
Complete Set (7):		180.00
Common Player:		10.00
Inserted 1:287		
1	Sammy Sosa	30.00
2	Barry Bonds	15.00
3	Cal Ripken Jr.	35.00
4	Juan Gonzalez	15.00
5	Ken Griffey Jr.	50.00
6	Roger Clemens	20.00
7	Mark McGwire, Sammy Sosa	60.00

1999 Upper Deck PowerDeck Powerful Moments

This six-card digital interactive set has game-action footage pinpointing specific milestones in each of the featured players' careers. These were inserted 1:7 packs.

		MT
Complete Set (6):		60.00
Common Player:		4.00
Inserted 1:7		
1	Mark McGwire	20.00
2	Sammy Sosa	10.00
3	Cal Ripken Jr.	12.00
4	Ken Griffey Jr.	15.00
5	Derek Jeter	10.00
6	Alex Rodriguez	10.00

1999 Upper Deck PowerDeck Powerful Moments-Aux. Power

This "paper" parallel version of the digital set is also inserted 1:7 packs on a horizontal format. Different photos were used from the digital set.

		MT
Complete Set (6):		30.00
Common Player:		4.00
Inserted 1:7		
Gold (one each): Value Undetermined		
1	Mark McGwire	8.00
2	Sammy Sosa	5.00
3	Cal Ripken Jr.	6.00
4	Ken Griffey Jr.	8.00
5	Derek Jeter	5.00
6	Alex Rodriguez	6.00

1999 Upper Deck PowerDeck Time Capsule

Five previous MLB Rookies of the Year are honored in this digital set with the digital content going back to the rookie seasons of the featured players. These were seeded 1:23 packs.

		MT
Complete Set (6):		70.00
Common Player:		6.00
Inserted 1:23		
1	Ken Griffey Jr.	20.00
2	Mike Piazza	12.00
3	Mark McGwire	20.00
4	Derek Jeter	12.00
5	Jose Canseco	6.00
6	Nomar Garciaparra	12.00

1999 Upper Deck PowerDeck Time Capsule-Auxiliary Power

This "paper' parallel set of the digital version utilizes a similar design as the digital insert and uses different photos as well. These were also inserted 1:23 packs.

		MT
Complete Set (6):		45.00
Common Player:		5.00
Inserted 1:23		
Gold (one of each): Values Undetermined		
1	Ken Griffey Jr.	15.00
2	Mike Piazza	8.00
3	Mark McGwire	15.00
4	Derek Jeter	8.00
5	Jose Canseco	5.00
6	Nomar Garciaparra	8.00

1999 Upper Deck World Series Power Deck

This CD-Rom card titled "Season to Remember" was distributed at Yankee Stadium during Game 4 of the 1999 World Series and features highlights of the Yankees championship season.

	MT
Season to Remember (1999 Yankees)	20.00

1999 UD Retro

The 110-card base set is comprised of 88 current stars and 22 retired greats. Card fronts have a tan, speckled border while card backs have a year-by-year compilation of the player's stats along with a career note. Retro is packaged in lunchboxes, 24 packs to a box with a SRP of $4.99 per six-card pack.

		MT
Complete Set (110):		30.00
Common Player:		.20
Wax Box:		90.00
1	Mo Vaughn	.75
2	Troy Glaus	.75
3	Tim Salmon	.40
4	Randy Johnson	.75
5	Travis Lee	.40
6	Matt Williams	.50
7	Greg Maddux	2.00
8	Chipper Jones	2.50
9	Andruw Jones	.75
10	Tom Glavine	.40
11	Javy Lopez	.40
12	Albert Belle	.75
13	Cal Ripken Jr.	3.00
14	Brady Anderson	.20
15	Nomar Garciaparra	2.50
16	Pedro J. Martinez	1.50
17	Sammy Sosa	2.50
18	Mark Grace	.60
19	Frank Thomas	1.50
20	Ray Durham	.20
21	Sean Casey	.50
22	Greg Vaughn	.30
23	Barry Larkin	.30
24	Manny Ramirez	1.00
25	Jim Thome	.50
26	Jaret Wright	.20
27	Kenny Lofton	.75
28	Larry Walker	.75
29	Todd Helton	.75
30	Vinny Castilla	.40
31	Tony Clark	.40
32	Juan Encarnacion	.20
33	Dean Palmer	.20
34	Mark Kotsay	.20
35	Alex Gonzalez	.20
36	Shane Reynolds	.20
37	Ken Caminiti	.40
38	Jeff Bagwell	1.00
39	Craig Biggio	.50
40	Carlos Febles	.40
41	Carlos Beltran	2.00
42	Jeremy Giambi	.20
43	Raul Mondesi	.40
44	Adrian Beltre	.40
45	Kevin Brown	.40
46	Jeromy Burnitz	.30
47	Jeff Cirillo	.20
48	Corey Koskie	.20
49	Todd Walker	.20
50	Vladimir Guerrero	1.50
51	Michael Barrett	.50
52	Mike Piazza	2.50
53	Robin Ventura	.50
54	Edgardo Alfonzo	.50
55	Derek Jeter	2.50
56	Roger Clemens	1.50
57	Tino Martinez	.60
58	Orlando Hernandez	.50
59	Chuck Knoblauch	.50
60	Bernie Williams	.60
61	Eric Chavez	.50
62	Ben Grieve	.50
63	Jason Giambi	.20
64	Scott Rolen	1.00
65	Curt Schilling	.40
66	Bobby Abreu	.20
67	Jason Kendall	.40
68	Kevin Young	.30
69	Mark McGwire	5.00
70	J.D. Drew	1.00
71	Eric Davis	.20
72	Tony Gwynn	2.00
73	Trevor Hoffman	.20
74	Barry Bonds	1.00
75	Robb Nen	.20
76	Ken Griffey Jr.	5.00
77	Alex Rodriguez	3.00
78	Jay Buhner	.20
79	Carlos Guillen	.20
80	Jose Canseco	1.00
81	Bobby Smith	.20
82	Juan Gonzalez	2.00
83	Ivan Rodriguez	1.00
84	Rafael Palmeiro	.75
85	Rick Helling	.20

86	Jose Cruz Jr.	.40
87	David Wells	.20
88	Carlos Delgado	.75
89	Nolan Ryan	4.00
90	George Brett	1.50
91	Robin Yount	1.00
92	Paul Molitor	1.00
93	Dave Winfield	.50
94	Steve Garvey	.20
95	Ozzie Smith	1.00
96	Ted Williams	4.00
97	Don Mattingly	1.00
98	Mickey Mantle	4.00
99	Harmon Killebrew	.50
100	Rollie Fingers	.20
101	Kirk Gibson	.20
102	Bucky Dent	.20
103	Willie Mays	2.00
104	Babe Ruth	4.00
105	Gary Carter	.20
106	Reggie Jackson	1.50
107	Frank Robinson	1.00
108	Ernie Banks	1.50
109	Eddie Murray	.50
110	Mike Schmidt	1.50

1999 UD Retro Gold/Platinum

This is a 110-card parallel to the base set. Cards have a gold foil front and are sequentially numbered to 250 sets. A one-of-one Platinum parallel to the base set also is randomly seeded.

	MT
Common Gold:	2.00
Gold Stars: 12X	
Platinum 1/1:	
Values Undetermined	
(See 1999 UD Retro for checklist and base card values.)	

1999 UD Retro Distant Replay

This 15-card set recounts the 15 most memorable plays from the 1998 season. Card fronts have a black and white photo of the player and along the bottom of the photo a date of the memorable play and brief description are given. These are seeded 1:8 packs. A parallel version, Level II is also randomly seeded, limited to 100 sequentially numbered sets.

		MT
Complete Set (15):		60.00
Common Player:		2.00
Inserted 1:8		
Level 2: 10x to 20x		
Production 100 sets		
1	Ken Griffey Jr.	8.00
2	Mark McGwire	8.00
3	Cal Ripken Jr.	6.00
4	Greg Maddux	4.00
5	Nomar Garciaparra	5.00
6	Roger Clemens	3.00
7	Alex Rodriguez	6.00
8	Frank Thomas	3.00
9	Mike Piazza	5.00
10	Chipper Jones	5.00
11	Juan Gonzalez	4.00
12	Tony Gwynn	4.00
13	Barry Bonds	2.00
14	Ivan Rodriguez	2.00
15	Derek Jeter	5.00

Player names in *Italic* type indicate a rookie card.

1999 UD Retro INKredible

INKredible is an autographed insert set that consists of both current players and retired stars. Card fronts have a small photo in the upper left portion of the featured player and a large signing area. These are seeded 1:23 packs.

		MT
Common Player:		12.00
Inserted 1:23		
CBe	Carlos Beltran	50.00
GB	George Brett	125.00
PB	Pat Burrell	50.00
SC	Sean Casey	40.00
TC	Tony Clark	25.00
BD	Bucky Dent	15.00
DE	Darin Erstad	30.00
RF	Rollie Fingers	15.00
SG	Steve Garvey	25.00
KG	Kirk Gibson	25.00
RG	Rusty Greer	15.00
JR	Ken Griffey Jr.	350.00
TG	Tony Gwynn	150.00
CJ	Chipper Jones	125.00
GK	Gabe Kapler	30.00
HK	Harmon Killebrew	35.00
FL	Fred Lynn	20.00
DM	Don Mattingly	100.00
PM	Paul Molitor	50.00
EM	Eddie Murray	50.00
PO	Paul O'Neill	25.00
AP	Angel Pena	12.00
MR	Manny Ramirez	75.00
IR	Ivan Rodriguez	50.00
NR	Nolan Ryan	250.00
OZ	Ozzie Smith	75.00
DWe	David Wells	15.00
BW	Bernie Williams	50.00
DW	Dave Winfield	40.00
RY	Robin Yount	75.00

1999 UD Retro INKredible Level 2

A parallel to INKredible autographed inserts, these are hand-numbered to the featured player's jersey number.

		MT
Common Player:		12.00
Limited to player's jersey #		
CBe	Carlos Beltran (36)	150.00
GB	George Brett (5)	
PB	Pat Burrell (76)	150.00
SC	Sean Casey (21)	175.00
TC	Tony Clark (17)	75.00
BD	Bucky Dent (20)	75.00
DE	Darin Erstad (17)	100.00
RF	Rollie Fingers (34)	60.00
SG	Steve Garvey (6)	
KG	Kirk Gibson (23)	90.00
RG	Rusty Greer (29)	75.00
JR	Ken Griffey Jr. (24)	
TG	Tony Gwynn (19)	500.00
CJ	Chipper Jones (10)	
GK	Gabe Kapler (23)	125.00
HK	Harmon Killebrew (3)	
FL	Fred Lynn (19)	90.00
DM	Don Mattingly (23)	450.00
PM	Paul Molitor (4)	
EM	Eddie Murray (33)	150.00
PO	Paul O'Neill (21)	100.00
AP	Angel Pena (36)	40.00
MR	Manny Ramirez (24)	250.00
IR	Ivan Rodriguez (7)	
NR	Nolan Ryan (34)	
OZ	Ozzie Smith (1)	
DWe	David Wells (33)	75.00
BW	Bernie Williams (51)	100.00
DW	Dave Winfield (31)	125.00
RY	Robin Yount (19)	220.00

1999 UD Retro Old/New School

This 30-card insert set captures 15 Old School players and 15 New School players. Each card is sequentially numbered to 1,000. A parallel version is also randomly seeded and is limited to 50 sequentially numbered sets.

		MT
Complete Set (30):		300.00
Common Player:		3.00
Production 1,000 sets		
Level 2: 5x to 10x		
Production 50 sets		
1	Ken Griffey Jr.	30.00
2	Alex Rodriguez	25.00
3	Frank Thomas	8.00
4	Cal Ripken Jr.	25.00
5	Chipper Jones	20.00
6	Craig Biggio	6.00
7	Greg Maddux	15.00
8	Jeff Bagwell	8.00
9	Juan Gonzalez	15.00
10	Mark McGwire	30.00
11	Mike Piazza	20.00
12	Mo Vaughn	4.00
13	Roger Clemens	10.00
14	Sammy Sosa	20.00
15	Tony Gwynn	15.00
16	Gabe Kapler	5.00
17	J.D. Drew	8.00
18	Pat Burrell	15.00
19	Roy Halladay	3.00
20	Jeff Weaver	3.00
21	Troy Glaus	5.00
22	Vladimir Guerrero	10.00
23	Michael Barrett	3.00
24	Carlos Beltran	10.00
25	Scott Rolen	8.00
26	Nomar Garciaparra	20.00
27	Warren Morris	3.00
28	Alex Gonzalez	3.00
29	Kyle Farnsworth	3.00
30	Derek Jeter	20.00

1999 UD Retro Throwback Attack

This 15-card set has a "Retro" look, like trading cards from yesteryear. The set highlights the top players and feature card fronts with a player photo encircled, "throwback attack" across the top and a white border. Card backs are numbered with a "T" prefix and are seeded 1:5 packs. A parallel version is also randomly seeded and limited to 500 numbered sets.

		MT
Complete Set (15):		40.00
Common Player:		1.00
Inserted 1:5		
Level 2: 5x to 10x		
Production 500 sets		
1	Ken Griffey Jr.	7.50
2	Mark McGwire	7.50
3	Sammy Sosa	4.00
4	Roger Clemens	2.00
5	J.D. Drew	2.00
6	Alex Rodriguez	5.00
7	Greg Maddux	3.00
8	Mike Piazza	4.00
9	Juan Gonzalez	2.00
10	Mo Vaughn	1.00
11	Cal Ripken Jr.	5.00
12	Frank Thomas	2.00
13	Nomar Garciaparra	4.00
14	Vladimir Guerrero	2.00
15	Tony Gwynn	3.00

1999 UD Retro Piece of History 500 Club

Each one of these inserts features a piece of game-used bat swung by Ted Williams embedded into each card. A total of 350 of these were issued. Williams also autographed nine of the 500 Club Piece of History cards.

		MT
TW	Ted Williams (edition of 350)	700.00
TWA	Ted Williams (autographed edition of nine)	

1999 UD Retro Lunchbox

Lunchboxes was the packaging for UD Retro. Each lunchbox contains 24 six-card packs and features 17 different current or retired baseball legends including Babe Ruth.

	MT
Complete Set (17):	300.00
Common lunchbox:	10.00
1 dual player per case	
Roger Clemens	12.00
Ken Griffey Jr.	20.00
Mickey Mantle	20.00
Mark McGwire	20.00
Mike Piazza	15.00
Alex Rodriguez	17.50
Babe Ruth	20.00
Sammy Sosa	15.00
Ted Williams	20.00
Ken Griffey Jr., Mark McGwire	30.00
Ken Griffey Jr., Babe Ruth	30.00
Ken Griffey Jr., Ted Williams	30.00
Mickey Mantle, Babe Ruth	30.00
Mark McGwire, Mickey Mantle	30.00
Mark McGwire, Babe Ruth	30.00
Mark McGwire, Ted Williams	30.00

1999 Upper Deck Ultimate Victory

The 180-card base set includes two 30-card shortprinted (1:4) subsets: McGwire Magic (151-180) and 1999 Rookie (121-150). The base cards have a silver foil border with the featured players' last five seasons of statistics along with a brief career highlight. There are two parallels randomly inserted: Victory Collection and Ultimate Collection. Victory Collection are seeded 1:12 packs with a holographic, prismatic look. Ultimate Collection have a gold holographic, prismatic look and are serially numbered "xxx/100" on the card front.

		MT
Complete Set (180):		300.00
Common Player:		.20
Common SP (121-150):		2.00
Common McGwire Magic (151-180):		2.00
Victory (1-120): 4X		
Victory SP (121-150): 1.5X		
Inserted 1:12		
Ultimate (1-120): 12X		
Ultimate SP (121-150): 2X		
Production 100 sets		
1	Troy Glaus	.50
2	Tim Salmon	.40
3	Mo Vaughn	.75
4	Garret Anderson	.20
5	Darin Erstad	.50
6	Randy Johnson	.75
7	Matt Williams	.40
8	Travis Lee	.40
9	Jay Bell	.20
10	Steve Finley	.20
11	Luis Gonzalez	.20
12	Greg Maddux	2.00
13	Chipper Jones	2.50
14	Javy Lopez	.40
15	Tom Glavine	.40
16	John Smoltz	.20
17	Cal Ripken Jr.	3.00
18	Charles Johnson	.20
19	Albert Belle	.75
20	Mike Mussina	.75
21	Pedro Martinez	1.00
22	Nomar Garciaparra	2.50
23	Jose Offerman	.20
24	Sammy Sosa	2.50
25	Mark Grace	.40
26	Kerry Wood	.50
27	Frank Thomas	1.00
28	Ray Durham	.20
29	Paul Konerko	.20
30	Pete Harnisch	.20
31	Greg Vaughn	.25
32	Sean Casey	.50
33	Manny Ramirez	1.00
34	Jim Thome	.40
35	Sandy Alomar	.40
36	Roberto Alomar	.75
37	Travis Fryman	.20
38	Kenny Lofton	.75
39	Omar Vizquel	.20
40	Larry Walker	.75
41	Todd Helton	.75
42	Vinny Castilla	.40
43	Tony Clark	.40
44	Juan Encarnacion	.20
45	Dean Palmer	.20
46	Damion Easley	.20
47	Mark Kotsay	.20
48	Cliff Floyd	.20
49	Jeff Bagwell	1.00
50	Ken Caminiti	.40
51	Craig Biggio	.75
52	Moises Alou	.40
53	Johnny Damon	.20
54	Larry Sutton	.20
55	Kevin Brown	.40
56	Adrian Beltre	.40
57	Raul Mondesi	.40
58	Gary Sheffield	.40
59	Jeromy Burnitz	.20
60	Sean Berry	.20
61	Jeff Cirillo	.20
62	Brad Radke	.20
63	Todd Walker	.20
64	Matt Lawton	.20
65	Vladimir Guerrero	1.50
66	Rondell White	.40
67	Dustin Hermanson	.20
68	Mike Piazza	2.50
69	Rickey Henderson	.50
70	Robin Ventura	.50
71	John Olerud	.50
72	Derek Jeter	2.50
73	Roger Clemens	1.50
74	Orlando Hernandez	.50
75	Paul O'Neill	.50
76	Bernie Williams	.60
77	Chuck Knoblauch	.40
78	Tino Martinez	.25
79	Jason Giambi	.20
80	Ben Grieve	.50
81	Matt Stairs	.20
82	Scott Rolen	1.00
83	Ron Gant	.20
84	Bobby Abreu	.20
85	Curt Schilling	.40
86	Brian Giles	.20
87	Jason Kendall	.40
88	Kevin Young	.20
89	Mark McGwire	5.00
90	Fernando Tatis	.50
91	Ray Lankford	.20
92	Eric Davis	.20
93	Tony Gwynn	2.00
94	Reggie Sanders	.20
95	Wally Joyner	.20
96	Trevor Hoffman	.20
97	Robb Nen	.20
98	Barry Bonds	1.00
99	Jeff Kent	.20
100	J.T. Snow	.20
101	Ellis Burks	.20
102	Ken Griffey Jr	5.00
103	Alex Rodriguez	3.00
104	Jay Buhner	.40
105	Edgar Martinez	.20
106	David Bell	.20
107	Bobby Smith	.20
108	Wade Boggs	.50
109	Fred McGriff	.50
110	Rolando Arrojo	.20
111	Jose Canseco	.75
112	Ivan Rodriguez	1.00
113	Juan Gonzalez	1.00
114	Rafael Palmeiro	.75
115	Rusty Greer	.20
116	Todd Zeile	.20
117	Jose Cruz Jr.	.25
118	Carlos Delgado	.75
119	Shawn Green	.50
120	David Wells	.20

121	*Eric Munson* (99 Rookie)	30.00
122	Lance Berkman (99 Rookie)	2.00
123	Ed Yarnall (99 Rookie)	2.00
124	Jacque Jones (99 Rookie)	2.00
125	Kyle Farnsworth (99 Rookie)	3.00
126	Ryan Rupe (99 Rookie)	2.00
127	*Jeff Weaver* (99 Rookie)	5.00
128	Gabe Kapler (99 Rookie)	3.00
129	Alex Gonzalez (99 Rookie)	2.00
130	Randy Wolf (99 Rookie)	2.00
131	Ben Davis (99 Rookie)	2.00
132	Carlos Beltran (99 Rookie)	5.00
133	Jim Morris (99 Rookie)	2.00
134	Jeff Zimmerman (99 Rookie)	4.00
135	Bruce Aven (99 Rookie)	2.00
136	*Alfonso Soriano* (99 Rookie)	25.00
137	*Tim Hudson* (99 Rookie)	10.00
138	*Josh Beckett* (99 Rookie)	25.00
139	Michael Barrett (99 Rookie)	2.00
140	Eric Chavez (99 Rookie)	2.00
141	*Pat Burrell* (99 Rookie)	30.00
142	Kris Benson (99 Rookie)	2.00
143	J.D. Drew (99 Rookie)	5.00
144	Matt Clement (99 Rookie)	2.00
145	*Rick Ankiel* (99 Rookie)	75.00
146	Vernon Wells (99 Rookie)	2.50
147	Ruben Mateo (99 Rookie)	2.00
148	Roy Halladay (99 Rookie)	2.00
149	Joe McEwing (99 Rookie)	4.00
150	Freddy Garcia (99 Rookie)	15.00
151	Mark McGwire (McGwire Magic)	2.00
152	Mark McGwire (McGwire Magic)	2.00
153	Mark McGwire (McGwire Magic)	2.00
154	Mark McGwire (McGwire Magic)	2.00
155	Mark McGwire (McGwire Magic)	2.00
156	Mark McGwire (McGwire Magic)	2.00
157	Mark McGwire (McGwire Magic)	2.00
158	Mark McGwire (McGwire Magic)	2.00
159	Mark McGwire (McGwire Magic)	2.00
160	Mark McGwire (McGwire Magic)	2.00
161	Mark McGwire (McGwire Magic)	2.00
162	Mark McGwire (McGwire Magic)	2.00
163	Mark McGwire (McGwire Magic)	2.00
164	Mark McGwire (McGwire Magic)	2.00
165	Mark McGwire (McGwire Magic)	2.00
166	Mark McGwire (McGwire Magic)	2.00
167	Mark McGwire (McGwire Magic)	2.00
168	Mark McGwire (McGwire Magic)	2.00
169	Mark McGwire (McGwire Magic)	2.00
170	Mark McGwire (McGwire Magic)	2.00
171	Mark McGwire (McGwire Magic)	2.00
172	Mark McGwire (McGwire Magic)	2.00
173	Mark McGwire (McGwire Magic)	2.00
174	Mark McGwire (McGwire Magic)	2.00
175	Mark McGwire (McGwire Magic)	2.00
176	Mark McGwire (McGwire Magic)	2.00
177	Mark McGwire (McGwire Magic)	2.00
178	Mark McGwire (McGwire Magic)	2.00
179	Mark McGwire (McGwire Magic)	2.00
180	Mark McGwire (McGwire Magic)	2.00

1999 Upper Deck Ultimate Victory Bleacher Reachers

This 11-card set focuses on the hitters who were vying for the 1999 home run title. They have a horizontal format with a holographic foil card front. Card backs have a small photo along with his 3-year statistical totals. They are numbered with a "BR" prefix and were inserted 1:23 packs.

		MT
Complete Set (11):		60.00
Common Player:		3.00
Inserted 1:23		
1	Ken Griffey Jr.	12.00
2	Mark McGwire	12.00
3	Sammy Sosa	8.00
4	Barry Bonds	3.00
5	Nomar Garciaparra	8.00
6	Juan Gonzalez	4.00
7	Jose Canseco	3.00
8	Manny Ramirez	4.00
9	Mike Piazza	8.00
10	Jeff Bagwell	4.00
11	Alex Rodriguez	10.00

1999 Upper Deck Ultimate Victory Fame-Used Memorabilia

This four-card set has a piece of game-used bat embedded into each card, from either George Brett, Robin Yount, Nolan Ryan and Orlando Cepeda. A total of approximately 350 bat cards of each player was produced.

		MT
Complete Set (4):		500.00
Common Player:		50.00
Production 350 cards		
GB	George Brett	125.00
OC	Orlando Cepeda	50.00
NR	Nolan Ryan	250.00
RY	Robin Yount	100.00

1999 Upper Deck Ultimate Victory Fame-Used Combo

This insert has a piece of game-used bat from each of the 1999 Hall of Fame inductees and is limited to 99 sequentially numbered singles.

	MT
Edition of 99:	
HOF Nolan Ryan, George Brett, Robin Yount, Orlando Cepeda	650.00

1999 Upper Deck Ultimate Victory Frozen Ropes

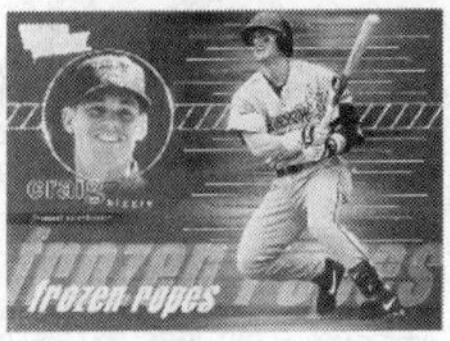

This 10-card set spotlights baseball's top hitters and are seeded 1:23 packs.

		MT
Complete Set (10):		60.00
Common Player:		2.00
Inserted 1:23		
1	Ken Griffey Jr.	12.00
2	Mark McGwire	12.00
3	Sammy Sosa	8.00
4	Derek Jeter	8.00
5	Tony Gwynn	6.00
6	Nomar Garciaparra	8.00
7	Alex Rodriguez	10.00
8	Mike Piazza	8.00
9	Mo Vaughn	2.50
10	Craig Biggio	2.00

1999 Upper Deck Ultimate Victory STATure

This 15-card set highlights 15 players with outstanding statistical achievements. The featured stat for the player runs down the right side of the card. The card backs are numbered with an "S" prefix. These were seeded 1:6 packs.

		MT
Complete Set (15):		25.00
Common Player:		1.00
Inserted 1:6		
1	Ken Griffey Jr.	5.00
2	Mark McGwire	5.00
3	Sammy Sosa	2.50
4	Nomar Garciaparra	2.50
5	Roger Clemens	1.50
6	Greg Maddux	2.00
7	Alex Rodriguez	3.50
8	Derek Jeter	2.50
9	Juan Gonzalez	1.25
10	Manny Ramirez	1.25
11	Mike Piazza	2.50
12	Tony Gwynn	2.00
13	Chipper Jones	2.50
14	Pedro Martinez	1.00
15	Frank Thomas	1.50

1999 Upper Deck Ultimate Victory Tribute 1999

This four-card set is devoted to 1999's Hall of Fame inductees. Card fronts have a horizontal format over a holographic foil design. Card backs have the featured players' year-by-year statistics and are numbered with a "T" prefix.

		MT
Complete Set (4):		15.00
Common Player:		1.50
Inserted 1:11		
1	Nolan Ryan	10.00
2	Robin Yount	3.00
3	George Brett	4.00
4	Orlando Cepeda	1.50

1999 Upper Deck Ultimate Victory Ultimate Competitors

This 12-card set has a close-up photo, along with two miniature action photos in the foreground inside a white border. These were seeded 1:23 packs and are numbered with a "U" prefix on the card back.

		MT
Complete Set (12):		60.00
Common Player:		2.00
Inserted 1:23		
1	Ken Griffey Jr.	15.00
2	Roger Clemens	5.00
3	Scott Rolen	3.00
4	Greg Maddux	6.00
5	Mark McGwire	15.00
6	Derek Jeter	8.00
7	Randy Johnson	2.00
8	Cal Ripken Jr.	10.00
9	Craig Biggio	2.00
10	Kevin Brown	2.00
11	Chipper Jones	8.00
12	Vladimir Guerrero	4.00

1999 Upper Deck Ultimate Victory Ultimate Hit Men

This insert set spotlights the eight candidates who competed for the 1999 batting titles. Inserted on the average of 1:23 packs they were numbered with an "H" prefix on the card back.

		MT
Complete Set (8):		30.00
Common Player:		2.00
Inserted 1:23		
1	Tony Gwynn	5.00
2	Cal Ripken Jr.	8.00
3	Wade Boggs	2.00
4	Larry Walker	2.00
5	Alex Rodriguez	8.00
6	Derek Jeter	6.00
7	Ivan Rodriguez	2.50
8	Ken Griffey Jr.	10.00

1999 Upper Deck Victory

This 470-card base set is printed on 20-point stock and has a white border with UV coating. The set consists of a number of subsets including, 30-card Mark McGwire Magic, 30 team checklist cards, 50 '99 rookies, 15 Power Trip, 20 Rookie Flashback, 15 Big Play Makers and 10 History in the Making. Packs have a SRP of $.99.

		MT
Complete Set (470):		40.00
Common Player:		.05
Wax Box:		32.00
1	Anaheim Angels (Team Checklist)	.05
2	*Mark Harriger* (99 Rookie)	.25
3	Mo Vaughn (Power Trip)	.20
4	Darin Erstad (Big Play Makers)	.15
5	Troy Glaus	.25
6	Tim Salmon	.20
7	Mo Vaughn	.30
8	Darin Erstad	.25
9	Garret Anderson	.05
10	Todd Greene	.05
11	Troy Percival	.05
12	Chuck Finley	.05
13	Jason Dickson	.05
14	Jim Edmonds	.05
15	Arizona Diamondbacks (Team Checklist)	.05
16	Randy Johnson	.30
17	Matt Williams	.25
18	Travis Lee	.25
19	Jay Bell	.05
20	Tony Womack	.05
21	Steve Finley	.05
22	Bernard Gilkey	.05
23	Tony Batista	.05
24	Todd Stottlemyre	.05
25	Omar Daal	.05
26	Atlanta Braves (Team Checklist)	.05
27	Bruce Chen (99 Rookie)	.15
28	George Lombard (99 Rookie)	.05
29	Chipper Jones (Power Trip)	.50
30	Chipper Jones (Big Play Makers)	.50
31	Greg Maddux	1.00
32	Chipper Jones	1.00
33	Javy Lopez	.15
34	Tom Glavine	.20
35	John Smoltz	.15
36	Andruw Jones	.30
37	Brian Jordan	.05
38	Walt Weiss	.05
39	Bret Boone	.05
40	Andres Galarraga	.25
41	Baltimore Orioles (Team Checklist)	.05
42	Ryan Minor (99 Rookie)	.20
43	Jerry Hairston Jr. (99 Rookie)	.05
44	Calvin Pickering (99 Rookie)	.05
45	Cal Ripken Jr. (History in the Making)	.50
46	Cal Ripken Jr.	1.25
47	Charles Johnson	.05
48	Albert Belle	.40
49	Delino DeShields	.05
50	Mike Mussina	.30
51	Scott Erickson	.05
52	Brady Anderson	.10
53	B.J. Surhoff	.05
54	Harold Baines	.10
55	Will Clark	.25
56	Boston Red Sox (Team Checklist)	.05
57	Shea Hillenbrand (99 Rookie)	.05
58	Trot Nixon (99 Rookie)	.05
59	Jin Ho Cho (99 Rookie)	.05
60	Nomar Garciaparra (Power Trip)	.50
61	Nomar Garciaparra (Big Play Makers)	.50
62	Pedro Martinez	.40
63	Nomar Garciaparra	1.00
64	Jose Offerman	.05
65	Jason Varitek	.05
66	Darren Lewis	.05
67	Troy O'Leary	.05
68	Donnie Sadler	.05
69	John Valentin	.05
70	Tim Wakefield	.05
71	Bret Saberhagen	.05
72	Chicago Cubs (Team Checklist)	.05
73	*Kyle Farnsworth* (99 Rookie)	.20
74	Sammy Sosa (Power Trip)	.50
75	Sammy Sosa (Big Play Makers)	.50
76	Sammy Sosa (History in the Making)	.50
77	Kerry Wood (History in the Making)	.15
78	Sammy Sosa	1.00
79	Mark Grace	.20
80	Kerry Wood	.25
81	Kevin Tapani	.05
82	Benito Santiago	.05
83	Gary Gaetti	.05
84	Mickey Morandini	.05
85	Glenallen Hill	.05
86	Henry Rodriguez	.05
87	Rod Beck	.05
88	Chicago White Sox (Team Checklist)	.05

89	Carlos Lee (99 Rookie)	.15
90	Mark Johnson (99 Rookie)	.05
91	Frank Thomas (Power Trip)	.25
92	Frank Thomas	.50
93	Jim Parque	.05
94	Mike Sirotka	.05
95	Mike Caruso	.05
96	Ray Durham	.10
97	Magglio Ordonez	.20
98	Paul Konerko	.10
99	Bob Howry	.05
100	Brian Simmons	.05
101	Jaime Navarro	.05
102	Cincinnati Reds (Team Checklist)	.05
103	Denny Neagle	.05
104	Pete Harnisch	.05
105	Greg Vaughn	.15
106	Brett Tomko	.05
107	Mike Cameron	.05
108	Sean Casey	.25
109	Aaron Boone	.05
110	Michael Tucker	.05
111	Dmitri Young	.05
112	Barry Larkin	.25
113	Cleveland Indians (Team Checklist)	.05
114	Russ Branyan (99 Rookie)	.05
115	Jim Thome (Power Trip)	.15
116	Manny Ramirez (Power Trip)	.20
117	Manny Ramirez	.40
118	Jim Thome	.25
119	David Justice	.20
120	Sandy Alomar	.10
121	Roberto Alomar	.30
122	Jaret Wright	.10
123	Bartolo Colon	.10
124	Travis Fryman	.10
125	Kenny Lofton	.30
126	Omar Vizquel	.10
127	Colorado Rockies (Team Checklist)	.05
128	Derrick Gibson (99 Rookie)	.05
129	Larry Walker (Big Play Makers)	.15
130	Larry Walker	.30
131	Dante Bichette	.20
132	Todd Helton	.25
133	Neifi Perez	.05
134	Vinny Castilla	.10
135	Darryl Kile	.05
136	Pedro Astacio	.10
137	Darryl Hamilton	.05
138	Mike Lansing	.05
139	Kirt Manwaring	.05
140	Detroit Tigers (Team Checklist)	.05
141	*Jeff Weaver* (99 Rookie)	.50
142	Gabe Kapler (99 Rookie)	.30
143	Tony Clark (Power Trip)	.10
144	Tony Clark	.20
145	Juan Encarnacion	.05
146	Dean Palmer	.10
147	Damion Easley	.05
148	Bobby Higginson	.05
149	Karim Garcia	.05
150	Justin Thompson	.05
151	Matt Anderson	.05
152	Willie Blair	.05
153	Brian Hunter	.05
154	Florida Marlins (Team Checklist)	.05
155	Alex Gonzalez (99 Rookie)	.05
156	Mark Kotsay	.05
157	Livan Hernandez	.05
158	Cliff Floyd	.05
159	Todd Dunwoody	.05
160	Alex Fernandez	.05
161	Mark Mantei	.05
162	Derrek Lee	.05
163	Kevin Orie	.05
164	Craig Counsell	.05
165	Rafael Medina	.05
166	Houston Astros (Team Checklist)	.05
167	Daryle Ward (99 Rookie)	.05
168	Mitch Meluskey (99 Rookie)	.10
169	Jeff Bagwell (Power Trip)	.25
170	Jeff Bagwell	.50
171	Ken Caminiti	.15
172	Craig Biggio	.25
173	Derek Bell	.05
174	Moises Alou	.15
175	Billy Wagner	.10
176	Shane Reynolds	.10
177	Carl Everett	.05
178	Scott Elarton	.05
179	Richard Hidalgo	.05
180	Kansas City Royals (Team Checklist)	.05
181	Carlos Beltran (99 Rookie)	.40
182	Carlos Febles (99 Rookie)	.20
183	Jeremy Giambi (99 Rookie)	.15
184	Johnny Damon	.05
185	Joe Randa	.05
186	Jeff King	.05
187	Hipolito Pichardo	.05
188	Kevin Appier	.05
189	Chad Kreuter	.05
190	Rey Sanchez	.05
191	Larry Sutton	.05
192	Jeff Montgomery	.05
193	Jermaine Dye	.05
194	Los Angeles Dodgers (Team Checklist)	.05
195	Adam Riggs (99 Rookie)	.05
196	Angel Pena (99 Rookie)	.05
197	Todd Hundley	.05
198	Kevin Brown	.15
199	Ismael Valdes	.10
200	Chan Ho Park	.10
201	Adrian Beltre	.20
202	Mark Grudzielanek	.05
203	Raul Mondesi	.15
204	Gary Sheffield	.15
205	Eric Karros	.15
206	Devon White	.05
207	Milwaukee Brewers (Team Checklist)	.05
208	Ron Belliard (99 Rookie)	.10
209	Rafael Roque (99 Rookie)	.05
210	Jeromy Burnitz	.10
211	Fernando Vina	.05
212	Scott Karl	.05
213	Jim Abbott	.05
214	Sean Berry	.05
215	Marquis Grissom	.10
216	Geoff Jenkins	.05
217	Jeff Cirillo	.05
218	Dave Nilsson	.05
219	Jose Valentin	.05
220	Minnesota Twins (Team Checklist)	.05
221	Corey Koskie (99 Rookie)	.05
222	Christian Guzman (99 Rookie)	.05
223	A.J. Pierzynski (99 Rookie)	.05
224	David Ortiz	.05
225	Brad Radke	.05
226	Todd Walker	.05
227	Matt Lawton	.05
228	Rick Aguilera	.05
229	Eric Milton	.05
230	Marty Cordova	.05
231	Torii Hunter	.05
232	Ron Coomer	.05
233	LaTroy Hawkins	.05
234	Montreal Expos (Team Checklist)	.05
235	Fernando Seguignol (99 Rookie)	.15
236	Michael Barrett (99 Rookie)	.25
237	Vladimir Guerrero (Big Play Makers)	.25
238	Vladimir Guerrero	.50
239	Brad Fullmer	.05
240	Rondell White	.10
241	Ugueth Urbina	.05
242	Dustin Hermanson	.10
243	Orlando Cabrera	.05
244	Wilton Guerrero	.05
245	Carl Pavano	.05
246	Javier Vasquez	.05
247	Chris Widger	.05
248	New York Mets (Team Checklist)	.05
249	Mike Kinkade (99 Rookie)	.05
250	Octavio Dotel (99 Rookie)	.05
251	Mike Piazza (Power Trip)	.50
252	Mike Piazza	1.00
253	Rickey Henderson	.10
254	Edgardo Alfonzo	.10
255	Robin Ventura	.15
256	Al Leiter	.15
257	Brian McRae	.05
258	Rey Ordonez	.10
259	Bobby Bonilla	.10
260	Orel Hershiser	.10
261	John Olerud	.15
262	New York Yankees (Team Checklist)	.15
263	Ricky Ledee (99 Rookie)	.10
264	Bernie Williams (Big Play Makers)	.15
265	Derek Jeter (Big Play Makers)	.50
266	Scott Brosius (History in the Making)	.05
267	Derek Jeter	1.00
268	Roger Clemens	.50
269	Orlando Hernandez	.25
270	Scott Brosius	.05
271	Paul O'Neill	.15
272	Bernie Williams	.30
273	Chuck Knoblauch	.15
274	Tino Martinez	.25
275	Mariano Rivera	.15
276	Jorge Posada	.10
277	Oakland Athletics (Team Checklist)	.05
278	Eric Chavez (99 Rookie)	.15
279	Ben Grieve (History in the Making)	.20
280	Jason Giambi	.05
281	John Jaha	.05
282	Miguel Tejada	.15
283	Ben Grieve	.30
284	Matt Stairs	.05
285	Ryan Christenson	.05
286	A.J. Hinch	.05
287	Kenny Rogers	.05
288	Tom Candiotti	.05
289	Scott Spezio	.05
290	Philadelphia Phillies (Team Checklist)	.05
291	*Pat Burrell* (99 Rookie)	2.00
292	Marlon Anderson (99 Rookie)	.05
293	Scott Rolen (Big Play Makers)	.20
294	Scott Rolen	.40
295	Doug Glanville	.05
296	Rico Brogna	.05
297	Ron Gant	.15
298	Bobby Abreu	.05
299	Desi Relaford	.05
300	Curt Schilling	.15
301	Chad Ogea	.05
302	Kevin Jordan	.05
303	Carlton Loewer	.05
304	Pittsburgh Pirates (Team Checklist)	.05
305	Kris Benson (99 Rookie)	.15
306	Brian Giles	.05
307	Jason Kendall	.15
308	Jose Guillen	.05
309	Pat Meares	.05
310	Brant Brown	.05
311	Kevin Young	.05
312	Ed Sprague	.05
313	Francisco Cordova	.05
314	Aramis Ramirez	.05
315	Freddy Garcia	1.00
316	Saint Louis Cardinals (Team Checklist)	.05
317	J.D. Drew (99 Rookie)	.50
318	*Chad Hutchinson* (99 Rookie)	.40
319	Mark McGwire (Power Trip)	1.00
320	J.D. Drew (Power Trip)	.25
321	Mark McGwire (Big Play Makers)	1.00
322	Mark McGwire (History in the Making)	1.00
323	Mark McGwire	1.50
324	Fernando Tatis	.15
325	Edgar Renteria	.05
326	Ray Lankford	.05
327	Willie McGee	.05
328	Ricky Bottalico	.05
329	Eli Marrero	.05
330	Matt Morris	.05
331	Eric Davis	.15
332	Darren Bragg	.05
333	Padres (Team Checklist)	.05
334	Matt Clement (99 Rookie)	.05
335	Ben Davis (99 Rookie)	.15
336	Gary Matthews Jr. (99 Rookie)	.05
337	Tony Gwynn (Big Play Makers)	.40
338	Tony Gwynn (History in the Making)	.40
339	Tony Gwynn	.75
340	Reggie Sanders	.05
341	Ruben Rivera	.05
342	Wally Joyner	.05
343	Sterling Hitchcock	.05
344	Carlos Hernandez	.05
345	Andy Ashby	.05
346	Trevor Hoffman	.05
347	Chris Gomez	.05
348	Jim Leyritz	.05
349	San Francisco Giants (Team Checklist)	.05
350	Armando Rios (99 Rookie)	.15
351	Barry Bonds (Power Trip)	.20
352	Barry Bonds (Big Play Makers)	.20
353	Barry Bonds (History in the Making)	.20
354	Robb Nen	.05
355	Bill Mueller	.05
356	Barry Bonds	.40
357	Jeff Kent	.15
358	J.T. Snow	.05
359	Ellis Burks	.10
360	F.P. Santangelo	.05
361	Marvin Benard	.05
362	Stan Javier	.05
363	Shawn Estes	.05
364	Seattle Mariners (Team Checklist)	.05
365	Carlos Guillen (99 Rookie)	.15
366	Ken Griffey Jr. (Power Trip)	.75
367	Alex Rodriguez (Power Trip)	.50
368	Ken Griffey Jr. (Big Play Makers)	.75
369	Alex Rodriguez (Big Play Makers)	.50
370	Ken Griffey Jr. (History in the Making)	.75
371	Alex Rodriguez (History in the Making)	.75
372	Ken Griffey Jr.	1.50
373	Alex Rodriguez	1.25
374	Jay Buhner	.15
375	Edgar Martinez	.15
376	Jeff Fassero	.05
377	David Bell	.05
378	David Segui	.05
379	Russ Davis	.05
380	Dan Wilson	.05
381	Jamie Moyer	.05
382	Tampa Bay Devil Rays (Team Checklist)	.05
383	Roberto Hernandez	.05
384	Bobby Smith	.05
385	Wade Boggs	.20
386	Fred McGriff	.20
387	Rolando Arrojo	.05
388	Jose Canseco	.40
389	Wilson Alvarez	.05
390	Kevin Stocker	.05
391	Miguel Cairo	.05
392	Quinton McCracken	.05
393	Texas Rangers (Team Checklist)	.05
394	Ruben Mateo (99 Rookie)	.40
395	Cesar King (99 Rookie)	.05
396	Juan Gonzalez (Power Trip)	.25
397	Juan Gonzalez (Big Play Makers)	.25
398	Ivan Rodriguez	.40
399	Juan Gonzalez	.50
400	Rafael Palmeiro	.25
401	Rick Helling	.05
402	Aaron Sele	.05
403	John Wetteland	.10
404	Rusty Greer	.10
405	Todd Zeile	.10
406	Royce Clayton	.05
407	Tom Goodwin	.05
408	Toronto Blue Jays (Team Checklist)	.05
409	Kevin Witt (99 Rookie)	.05
410	Roy Halladay (99 Rookie)	.15
411	Jose Cruz Jr.	.15
412	Carlos Delgado	.25
413	Willie Greene	.05
414	Shawn Green	.20
415	Homer Bush	.05
416	Shannon Stewart	.10
417	David Wells	.05
418	Kelvim Escobar	.05
419	Joey Hamilton	.05
420	Alex Gonzalez	.05
421	Mark McGwire (McGwire Magic)	.40
422	Mark McGwire (McGwire Magic)	.40
423	Mark McGwire (McGwire Magic)	.40
424	Mark McGwire (McGwire Magic)	.40
425	Mark McGwire (McGwire Magic)	.40
426	Mark McGwire (McGwire Magic)	.40
427	Mark McGwire (McGwire Magic)	.40
428	Mark McGwire (McGwire Magic)	.40
429	Mark McGwire (McGwire Magic)	.40
430	Mark McGwire (McGwire Magic)	.40
431	Mark McGwire (McGwire Magic)	.40
432	Mark McGwire (McGwire Magic)	.40
433	Mark McGwire (McGwire Magic)	.40
434	Mark McGwire (McGwire Magic)	.40
435	Mark McGwire (McGwire Magic)	.40
436	Mark McGwire (McGwire Magic)	.40
437	Mark McGwire (McGwire Magic)	.40
438	Mark McGwire (McGwire Magic)	.40
439	Mark McGwire (McGwire Magic)	.40
440	Mark McGwire (McGwire Magic)	.40
441	Mark McGwire (McGwire Magic)	.40
442	Mark McGwire (McGwire Magic)	.40
443	Mark McGwire (McGwire Magic)	.40
444	Mark McGwire (McGwire Magic)	.40
445	Mark McGwire (McGwire Magic)	.40
446	Mark McGwire (McGwire Magic)	.40
447	Mark McGwire (McGwire Magic)	.40
448	Mark McGwire (McGwire Magic)	.40
449	Mark McGwire (McGwire Magic)	.40
450	Mark McGwire (McGwire Magic)	.40
451	Chipper Jones '93 (Rookie Flashback)	.40
452	Cal Ripken Jr. '81 (Rookie Flashback)	.50
453	Roger Clemens '84 (Rookie Flashback)	.25
454	Wade Boggs '82 (Rookie Flashback)	.15
455	Greg Maddux '86 (Rookie Flashback)	.50
456	Frank Thomas '90 (Rookie Flashback)	.25
457	Jeff Bagwell '91 (Rookie Flashback)	.20
458	Mike Piazza '92 (Rookie Flashback)	.50
459	Randy Johnson '88 (Rookie Flashback)	.15
460	Mo Vaughn '91 (Rookie Flashback)	.15
461	Mark McGwire '86 (Rookie Flashback)	1.00
462	Rickey Henderson '79 (Rookie Flashback)	.10
463	Barry Bonds '86 (Rookie Flashback)	.20
464	Tony Gwynn '82 (Rookie Flashback)	.40
465	Ken Griffey Jr. '89 (Rookie Flashback)	.75
466	Alex Rodriguez '94 (Rookie Flashback)	.50
467	Sammy Sosa '89 (Rookie Flashback)	.50
468	Juan Gonzalez '89 (Rookie Flashback)	.25
469	Kevin Brown '86 (Rookie Flashback)	.05
470	Fred McGriff '86 (Rookie Flashback)	.10

2000 Upper Deck

		MT
Complete Set (270):		40.00
Common Player:		.15
Comm. Silver Exclusive:		4.00
Silver Stars: 10x to 20x		
Rookies: 5x to 10x		
Hobby Box:		85.00
1	Rick Ankiel (Star Rookie)	8.00
2	Vernon Wells (Star Rookie)	.75
3	Ryan Anderson (Star Rookie)	.75
4	Ed Yarnall (Star Rookie)	.50
5	Brian McNichol (Star Rookie)	.25
6	Ben Petrick (Star Rookie)	.50
7	Kip Wells (Star Rookie)	.40
8	Eric Munson (Star Rookie)	2.50
9	Matt Riley (Star Rookie)	1.00
10	Peter Bergeron (Star Rookie)	.40
11	Eric Gagne (Star Rookie)	.25
12	Ramon Ortiz (Star Rookie)	.50

13	Josh Beckett (Star Rookie)	3.00
14	Alfonso Soriano (Star Rookie)	2.00
15	Jorge Toca (Star Rookie)	.50
16	Buddy Carlyle (Star Rookie)	.40
17	Chad Hermansen (Star Rookie)	.50
18	Matt Perisho (Star Rookie)	.40
19	*Tomokazu Ohka* (Star Rookie)	.75
20	Jacque Jones (Star Rookie)	.50
21	Josh Paul (Star Rookie)	.40
22	Dermal Brown (Star Rookie)	.50
23	Adam Kennedy (Star Rookie)	.50
24	Chad Harville (Star Rookie)	.40
25	Calvin Murray (Star Rookie)	.40
26	Chad Meyers (Star Rookie)	.40
27	Brian Cooper (Star Rookie)	.40
28	Troy Glaus	.40
29	Ben Molina	.25
30	Troy Percival	.15
31	Ken Hill	.15
32	Chuck Finley	.15
33	Todd Greene	.15
34	Tim Salmon	.25
35	Gary DiSarcina	.15
36	Luis Gonzalez	.15
37	Tony Womack	.15
38	Omar Daal	.15
39	Randy Johnson	.50
40	Erubiel Durazo	.40
41	Jay Bell	.15
42	Steve Finley	.15
43	Travis Lee	.25
44	Greg Maddux	1.50
45	Bret Boone	.15
46	Brian Jordan	.15
47	Kevin Millwood	.25
48	Odalis Perez	.15
49	Javy Lopez	.25
50	John Smoltz	.25
51	Bruce Chen	.25
52	Albert Belle	.60
53	Jerry Hairston Jr.	.15
54	Will Clark	.40
55	Sidney Ponson	.15
56	Charles Johnson	.15
57	Cal Ripken Jr.	2.50
58	Ryan Minor	.25
59	Mike Mussina	.50
60	Tom Gordon	.15
61	Jose Offerman	.15
62	Trot Nixon	.15
63	Pedro Martinez	1.00
64	John Valentin	.15
65	Jason Varitek	.15
66	Juan Pena	.15
67	Troy O'Leary	.15
68	Sammy Sosa	2.00
69	Henry Rodriguez	.15
70	Kyle Farnsworth	.15
71	Glenallen Hill	.15
72	Lance Johnson	.15
73	Mickey Morandini	.15
74	Jon Lieber	.15
75	Kevin Tapani	.15
76	Carlos Lee	.15
77	Ray Durham	.15
78	Jim Parque	.15
79	Bob Howry	.15
80	Magglio Ordonez	.40
81	Paul Konerko	.25
82	Mike Caruso	.15
83	Chris Singleton	.15
84	Sean Casey	.40
85	Barry Larkin	.40
86	Pokey Reese	.15
87	Eddie Taubensee	.15
88	Scott Williamson	.15
89	Jason LaRue	.15
90	Aaron Boone	.15
91	Jeffrey Hammonds	.15
92	Omar Vizquel	.15
93	Manny Ramirez	.75
94	Kenny Lofton	.60
95	Jaret Wright	.20
96	Einar Diaz	.15
97	Charles Nagy	.15
98	David Justice	.25
99	Richie Sexson	.15
100	Steve Karsay	.15
101	Todd Helton	.40
102	Dante Bichette	.25
103	Larry Walker	.50
104	Pedro Astacio	.15
105	Neifi Perez	.15
106	Brian Bohanon	.15
107	Edgard Clemente	.15
108	Dave Veres	.15
109	Gabe Kapler	.25
110	Juan Encarnacion	.15
111	Jeff Weaver	.25
112	Damion Easley	.15
113	Justin Thompson	.15
114	Brad Ausmus	.15
115	Frank Catalanotto	.15
116	Todd Jones	.15
117	Preston Wilson	.15
118	Cliff Floyd	.15
119	Mike Lowell	.15
120	Jorge Fabregas	.15
121	Alex Gonzalez	.15
122	Braden Looper	.15
123	Bruce Aven	.15
124	Richard Hidalgo	.15
125	Mitch Meluskey	.15
126	Jeff Bagwell	.75
127	Jose Lima	.15
128	Derek Bell	.15
129	Billy Wagner	.15
130	Shane Reynolds	.15
131	Moises Alou	.25
132	Carlos Beltran	.40
133	Carlos Febles	.15
134	Jermaine Dye	.15
135	Jeremy Giambi	.15
136	Joe Randa	.15
137	Jose Rosado	.15
138	Chad Kreuter	.15
139	Jose Vizcaino	.15
140	Adrian Beltre	.25
141	Kevin Brown	.25
142	Ismael Valdes	.15
143	Angel Pena	.15
144	Chan Ho Park	.25
145	Mark Grudzielanek	.15
146	Jeff Shaw	.15
147	Geoff Jenkins	.15
148	Jeromy Burnitz	.15
149	Hideo Nomo	.25
150	Ron Belliard	.15
151	Sean Berry	.15
152	Mark Loretta	.15
153	Steve Woodard	.15
154	Joe Mays	.15
155	Eric Milton	.15
156	Corey Koskie	.15
157	Ron Coomer	.15
158	Brad Radke	.15
159	Terry Steinbach	.15
160	Christian Guzman	.15
161	Vladimir Guerrero	1.00
162	Wilton Guerrero	.15
163	Michael Barrett	.25
164	Chris Widger	.15
165	Fernando Seguignol	.25
166	Ugueth Urbina	.15
167	Dustin Hermanson	.15
168	Kenny Rogers	.15
169	Edgardo Alfonzo	.25
170	Orel Hershiser	.15
171	Robin Ventura	.40
172	Octavio Dotel	.15
173	Rickey Henderson	.25
174	Roger Cedeno	.15
175	John Olerud	.30
176	Derek Jeter	2.00
177	Tino Martinez	.40
178	Orlando Hernandez	.25
179	Chuck Knoblauch	.30
180	Bernie Williams	.50
181	Chili Davis	.15
182	David Cone	.25
183	Ricky Ledee	.15
184	Paul O'Neill	.25
185	Jason Giambi	.15
186	Eric Chavez	.15
187	Matt Stairs	.15
188	Miguel Tejada	.15
189	Olmedo Saenz	.15
190	Tim Hudson	.40
191	John Jaha	.15
192	Randy Velarde	.15
193	Rico Brogna	.15
194	Mike Lieberthal	.15
195	Marlon Anderson	.15
196	Bobby Abreu	.15
197	Ron Gant	.15
198	Randy Wolf	.15
199	Desi Relaford	.15
200	Doug Glanville	.15
201	Warren Morris	.15
202	Kris Benson	.15
203	Kevin Young	.15
204	Brian Giles	.15
205	Jason Schmidt	.15
206	Ed Sprague	.15
207	Francisco Cordova	.15
208	Mark McGwire	4.00
209	Jose Jimenez	.15
210	Fernando Tatis	.40
211	Kent Bottenfield	.15
212	Eli Marrero	.15
213	Edgar Renteria	.15
214	Joe McEwing	.15
215	J.D. Drew	.75
216	Tony Gwynn	1.50
217	Gary Matthews Jr.	.15
218	Eric Owens	.15
219	Damian Jackson	.15
220	Reggie Sanders	.15
221	Trevor Hoffman	.15
222	Ben Davis	.15
223	Shawn Estes	.15
224	F.P. Santangelo	.15
225	Livan Hernandez	.15
226	Ellis Burks	.15
227	J.T. Snow	.15
228	Jeff Kent	.15
229	Robb Nen	.15
230	Marvin Benard	.15
231	Ken Griffey Jr.	3.00
232	John Halama	.15
233	Gil Meche	.15
234	David Bell	.15
235	Brian L. Hunter	.15
236	Jay Buhner	.25
237	Edgar Martinez	.25
238	Jose Mesa	.15
239	Wilson Alvarez	.15
240	Wade Boggs	.40
241	Fred McGriff	.25
242	Jose Canseco	.75
243	Kevin Stocker	.15
244	Roberto Hernandez	.15
245	Bubba Trammell	.15
246	John Flaherty	.15
247	Ivan Rodriguez	.75
248	Rusty Greer	.15
249	Rafael Palmeiro	.40
250	Jeff Zimmerman	.15
251	Royce Clayton	.15
252	Todd Zeile	.15
253	John Wetteland	.15
254	Ruben Mateo	.40
255	Kelvim Escobar	.15
256	David Wells	.15
257	Shawn Green	.50
258	Homer Bush	.15
259	Shannon Stewart	.15
260	Carlos Delgado	.50
261	Roy Halladay	.15
262	Fernando Tatis CL	.25
263	Jose Jimenez CL	.15
264	Tony Gwynn CL	.75
265	Wade Boggs CL	.25
266	Cal Ripken Jr. CL	1.00
267	David Cone CL	.15
268	Mark McGwire CL	2.00
269	Pedro Martinez CL	.50
270	Nomar Garciaparra CL	1.00

2000 Upper Deck Faces of the Game

		MT
Complete Set (20):		90.00
Common Player:		1.50
Inserted 1:11		
Silver: 6x to 12x		
Production 100 sets		
1	Ken Griffey Jr.	12.00
2	Mark McGwire	12.00
3	Sammy Sosa	8.00
4	Alex Rodriguez	8.00
5	Manny Ramirez	3.00
6	Derek Jeter	8.00
7	Jeff Bagwell	3.00
8	Roger Clemens	4.00
9	Scott Rolen	3.00
10	Tony Gwynn	6.00
11	Nomar Garciaparra	8.00
12	Randy Johnson	2.50
13	Greg Maddux	6.00
14	Mike Piazza	8.00
15	Frank Thomas	3.00
16	Cal Ripken Jr.	8.00
17	Ivan Rodriguez	3.00
18	Mo Vaughn	2.50
19	Chipper Jones	8.00
20	Sean Casey	2.00

2000 Upper Deck Game Jersey

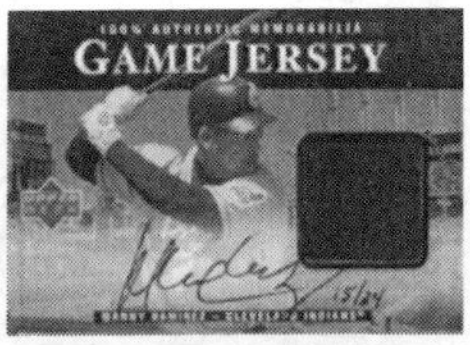

		MT
Common Player:		50.00
Inserted 1:2,500		
JC	Jose Canseco	100.00
JG	Juan Gonzalez	100.00
VG	Vladimir Guerrero	150.00
TH	Todd Helton	75.00
CJ	Chipper Jones	200.00
GK	Gabe Kapler	50.00
GM	Greg Maddux	175.00
MR	Manny Ramirez	125.00
CR	Cal Ripken Jr.	250.00
GV	Greg Vaughn	50.00

The election of former players to the Hall of Fame does not always have an immediate upward effect on card prices. The hobby market generally has done a good job of predicting those inductions and adjusting values over the course of several years.

2000 Upper Deck Game Jersey Hobby

		MT
Common Player:		50.00
Inserted 1:288		50.00
JB	Jeff Bagwell	150.00
TG	Troy Glaus	50.00
CY	Tom Glavine	80.00
Jr.	Ken Griffey Jr.	350.00
DJ	Derek Jeter	275.00
PM	Pedro J. Martinez	150.00
MP	Mike Piazza	250.00
AR	Alex Rodriguez	250.00
FT	Frank Thomas	125.00
LW	Larry Walker	80.00

2000 Upper Deck Game Jersey Patch

		MT
Common Player:		100.00
Inserted 1:10,000		
JB	Jeff Bagwell	500.00
JC	Jose Canseco	500.00
TG	Troy Glaus	150.00
CY	Tom Glavine	300.00
Jr.	Ken Griffey Jr.	1000.
VG	Vladimir Guerrero	400.00
TH	Todd Helton	150.00
DJ	Derek Jeter	700.00
CJ	Chipper Jones	500.00
GK	Gabe Kapler	100.00
GM	Greg Maddux	500.00
PM	Pedro J. Martinez	500.00
MP	Mike Piazza	500.00
MR	Manny Ramirez	400.00
CR	Cal Ripken Jr.	800.00
AR	Alex Rodriguez	600.00
FT	Frank Thomas	400.00
GV	Greg Vaughn	150.00
LW	Larry Walker	150.00

2000 Upper Deck Hit Brigade

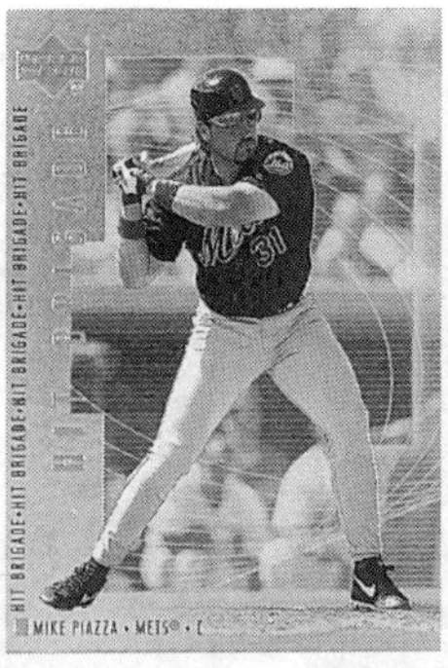

		MT
Complete Set (15):		35.00
Common Player:		.75
Inserted 1:8		
Silver: 10x to 20x		
Production 100 sets		
1	Ken Griffey Jr.	6.00
2	Tony Gwynn	3.00
3	Alex Rodriguez	4.00
4	Derek Jeter	4.00
5	Mike Piazza	4.00
6	Sammy Sosa	4.00
7	Juan Gonzalez	1.50
8	Scott Rolen	1.50
9	Nomar Garciaparra	4.00
10	Barry Bonds	1.50
11	Craig Biggio	.75
12	Chipper Jones	4.00
13	Frank Thomas	1.50
14	Larry Walker	1.25
15	Mark McGwire	6.00

2000 Upper Deck Power MARK

		MT
Complete Set (10):		80.00
Common McGwire:		10.00
Inserted 1:23		
Silver: 8x to 15x		
Production 100 sets		
1	Mark McGwire	10.00
2	Mark McGwire	10.00
3	Mark McGwire	10.00
4	Mark McGwire	10.00
5	Mark McGwire	10.00
6	Mark McGwire	10.00
7	Mark McGwire	10.00
8	Mark McGwire	10.00
9	Mark McGwire	10.00
10	Mark McGwire	10.00

2000 Upper Deck Power Rally

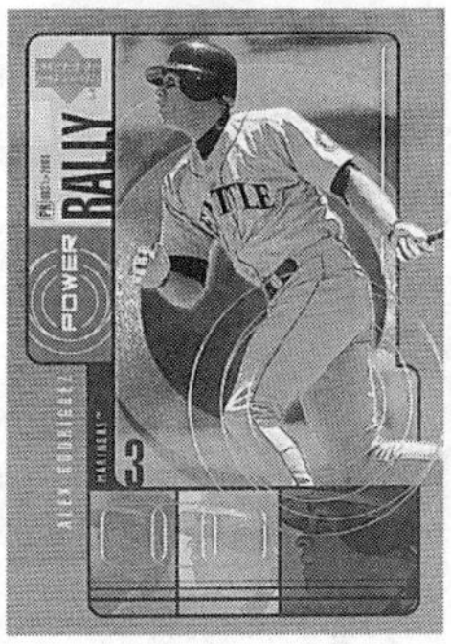

		MT
Complete Set (15):		60.00
Common Player:		1.50
Inserted 1:11		
Silver: 8x to 15x		
Production 100 sets		
1	Ken Griffey Jr.	10.00
2	Mark McGwire	10.00
3	Sammy Sosa	6.00
4	Jose Canseco	2.50
5	Juan Gonzalez	2.50
6	Bernie Williams	2.00
7	Jeff Bagwell	2.50
8	Chipper Jones	6.00
9	Vladimir Guerrero	3.00
10	Mo Vaughn	2.00
11	Derek Jeter	6.00
12	Mike Piazza	6.00
13	Barry Bonds	2.50
14	Alex Rodriguez	6.00
15	Nomar Garciaparra	6.00

2000 Upper Deck STATitude

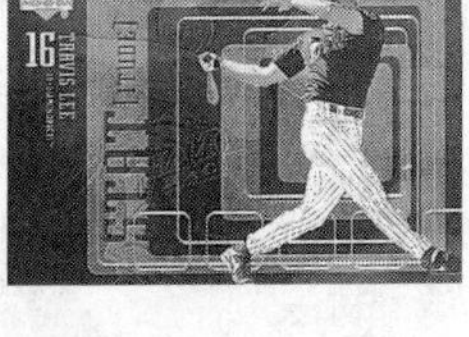

2000 UD Ionix

		MT
Complete Set (90):		125.00
Common Player:		.20
Common Futuristic:		2.00
Inserted 1:4		
Wax Box:		85.00
Reciprocal (1-60): 1.5x-4x		
Reciprocal (61-90): 1x-1.5x		
Inserted 1:4		
Future Recip. 1:11		
1	Mo Vaughn	.75
2	Troy Glaus	.50
3	Jeff Bagwell	1.00
4	Craig Biggio	.50
5	Jose Lima	.20
6	Jason Giambi	.20
7	Tim Hudson	.40
8	Shawn Green	.75
9	Carlos Delgado	.75
10	Chipper Jones	2.00
11	Andruw Jones	.75
12	Greg Maddux	2.00
13	Jeromy Burnitz	.20
14	Mark McGwire	4.00
15	J.D. Drew	1.00
16	Sammy Sosa	2.50
17	Jose Canseco	1.00
18	Fred McGriff	.50
19	Randy Johnson	.75
20	Matt Williams	.50
21	Kevin Brown	.40
22	Gary Sheffield	.40
23	Vladimir Guerrero	1.50
24	Barry Bonds	1.00
25	Jim Thome	.50
26	Manny Ramirez	1.00
27	Roberto Alomar	.75
28	Kenny Lofton	.75
29	Ken Griffey Jr.	4.00
30	Alex Rodriguez	2.50
31	Alex Gonzalez	.20
32	Preston Wilson	.20
33	Mike Piazza	2.50
34	Robin Ventura	.40
35	Cal Ripken Jr.	2.50
36	Albert Belle	.75
37	Tony Gwynn	2.00
38	Scott Rolen	1.00
39	Curt Schilling	.40
40	Brian Giles	.20
41	Juan Gonzalez	1.00
42	Ivan Rodriguez	1.00
43	Rafael Palmeiro	.60
44	Pedro J. Martinez	1.00
45	Nomar Garciaparra	2.50
46	Sean Casey	.50
47	Aaron Boone	.20
48	Barry Larkin	.50
49	Larry Walker	.75
50	Vinny Castilla	.30
51	Carlos Beltran	.50
52	Gabe Kapler	.40
53	Dean Palmer	.30
54	Eric Milton	.20
55	Corey Koskie	.20
56	Frank Thomas	1.00
57	Magglio Ordonez	.50
58	Roger Clemens	1.50
59	Bernie Williams	.75
60	Derek Jeter	2.50
61	Josh Beckett (Futuristics)	8.00
62	Eric Munson (Futuristics)	8.00
63	Rick Ankiel (Futuristics)	15.00
64	Matt Riley (Futuristics)	5.00
65	Robert Ramsay (Futuristics)	2.00
66	Vernon Wells (Futuristics)	3.00
67	Eric Gagne (Futuristics)	2.00
68	Robert Fick (Futuristics)	2.00
69	Mark Quinn (Futuristics)	4.00
70	Kip Wells (Futuristics)	2.00
71	Peter Bergeron (Futuristics)	2.00
72	Ed Yarnall (Futuristics)	2.00
73	Jorge Luis Toca (Futuristics)	3.00
74	Alfonso Soriano (Futuristics)	6.00
75	Calvin Murray (Futuristics)	2.00
76	Ramon Ortiz (Futuristics)	3.00
77	Chad Meyers (Futuristics)	3.00
78	Jason LaRue (Futuristics)	2.00
79	Pat Burrell (Futuristics)	6.00
80	Chad Hermansen (Futuristics)	2.00
81	Lance Berkman (Futuristics)	2.00
82	Erubiel Durazo (Futuristics)	3.00
83	Juan Pena (Futuristics)	2.00
84	Adam Kennedy (Futuristics)	2.00
85	Ben Petrick (Futuristics)	2.00
86	Kevin Barker (Futuristics)	2.00
87	Bruce Chen (Futuristics)	2.00
88	Jerry Hairston Jr. (Futuristics)	2.00
89	A.J. Burnett (Futuristics)	3.00
90	Gary Matthews Jr. (Futuristics)	2.00

2000 UD Ionix Atomic

		MT
Complete Set (15):		60.00
Common Player:		2.00
Inserted 1:8		
1	Pedro J. Martinez	2.50
2	Mark McGwire	10.00
3	Ken Griffey Jr.	10.00
4	Jeff Bagwell	2.50
5	Greg Maddux	5.00
6	Derek Jeter	6.00
7	Cal Ripken Jr.	6.00
8	Manny Ramirez	2.50
9	Randy Johnson	2.00
10	Nomar Garciaparra	6.00
11	Tony Gwynn	5.00
12	Bernie Williams	2.00
13	Mike Piazza	6.00
14	Roger Clemens	4.00
15	Alex Rodriguez	6.00

2000 UD Ionix Awesome Powers

		MT
Complete Set (15):		150.00
Common Player:		4.00
Inserted 1:23		
1	Ken Griffey Jr.	25.00
2	Mike Piazza	15.00
3	Carlos Delgado	4.00
4	Mark McGwire	25.00
5	Chipper Jones	12.00
6	Scott Rolen	6.00
7	Cal Ripken Jr.	15.00
8	Alex Rodriguez	15.00
9	Larry Walker	5.00
10	Sammy Sosa	15.00
11	Barry Bonds	6.00
12	Nomar Garciaparra	15.00
13	Jose Canseco	6.00
14	Manny Ramirez	6.00
15	Jeff Bagwell	6.00

2000 UD Ionix BIOrhythm

		MT
Complete Set (15):		75.00
Common Player:		2.00
Inserted 1:11		
1	Randy Johnson	2.50
2	Derek Jeter	8.00
3	Sammy Sosa	8.00
4	Jose Lima	2.00
5	Chipper Jones	6.00
6	Barry Bonds	3.00
7	Ken Griffey Jr.	12.00
8	Nomar Garciaparra	8.00
9	Frank Thomas	3.00
10	Pedro Martinez	3.00
11	Larry Walker	2.50
12	Greg Maddux	6.00
13	Alex Rodriguez	8.00
14	Mark McGwire	12.00
15	Cal Ripken Jr.	8.00

2000 UD Ionix Pyrotechnics

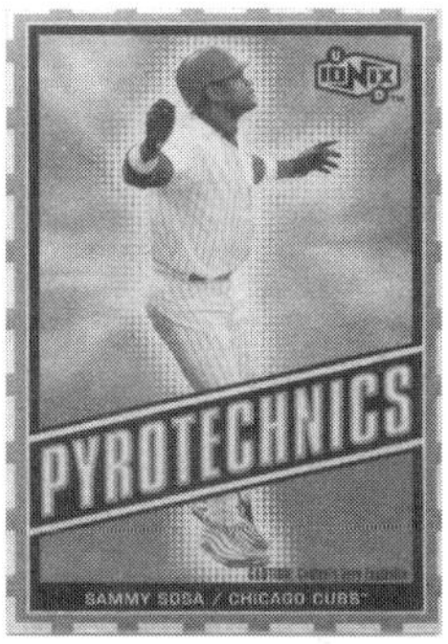

		MT
Complete Set (15):		320.00
Common Player:		12.00
Inserted 1:72		
1	Roger Clemens	20.00
2	Chipper Jones	25.00
3	Alex Rodriguez	30.00
4	Jeff Bagwell	12.00
5	Mark McGwire	50.00
6	Pedro Martinez	12.00
7	Manny Ramirez	12.00
8	Cal Ripken Jr.	30.00
9	Mike Piazza	30.00
10	Derek Jeter	30.00
11	Ken Griffey Jr.	50.00
12	Frank Thomas	12.00
13	Sammy Sosa	30.00
14	Nomar Garciaparra	30.00
15	Greg Maddux	25.00

2000 UD Ionix Shockwave

		MT
Complete Set (15):		25.00
Common Player:		.75
Inserted 1:4		
1	Mark McGwire	5.00
2	Sammy Sosa	3.00
3	Manny Ramirez	1.50
4	Ken Griffey Jr.	5.00
5	Vladimir Guerrero	2.00
6	Barry Bonds	1.50
7	Albert Belle	1.00
8	Ivan Rodriguez	1.50
9	Chipper Jones	2.50
10	Mo Vaughn	1.00
11	Jose Canseco	1.50
12	Jeff Bagwell	1.50
13	Matt Williams	.75
14	Alex Rodriguez	3.00
15	Carlos Delgado	.75

2000 UD Ionix UD Authentics

		MT
Common Player:		20.00
Inserted 1:144		
CBE	Carlos Beltran	40.00
AB	Adrian Beltre	25.00
CB	Craig Biggio	50.00
PB	Pat Burrell	60.00
JC	Jose Canseco	100.00
SC	Sean Casey	40.00
BD	Ben Davis	20.00
NG	Nomar Garciaparra	
SG	Shawn Green	75.00
JR	Ken Griffey Jr.	
VG	Vladimir Guerrero	60.00
DJ	Derek Jeter	200.00
CJ	Chipper Jones	125.00
GK	Gabe Kapler	40.00
PM	Pedro Martinez	
RM	Ruben Mateo	25.00
RB	Joe McEwing	30.00
MR	Manny Ramirez	75.00
SR	Scott Rolen	50.00
MW	Matt Williams	50.00

2000 UD Ionix Warp Zone

		MT
Complete Set (15):		875.00
Common Player:		25.00
Inserted 1:288		
1	Cal Ripken Jr.	75.00
2	Barry Bonds	30.00
3	Ken Griffey Jr.	120.00
4	Nomar Garciaparra	75.00
5	Chipper Jones	60.00
6	Ivan Rodriguez	30.00
7	Greg Maddux	60.00
8	Derek Jeter	75.00
9	Mike Piazza	75.00
10	Sammy Sosa	75.00
11	Roger Clemens	40.00
12	Alex Rodriguez	75.00
13	Vladimir Guerrero	40.00
14	Pedro Martinez	30.00
15	Mark McGwire	120.00

2000 UD Ionix 3,000-Hit Club Piece of History

		MT
RC1	Roberto Clemente	500.00
RC2	Roberto Clemente Bat/Cut/5	
RC3	Roberto Clemente Cut/4	

2000 Upper Deck Opening Day 2K

As part of a multi-manufacturer promotion, UD issued eight cards of an "Opening Day 2K" set. Packages containing some of the 32 cards in the issue were distributed by MLB teams early in the season. The cards were also available exclusively as inserts in Upper Deck Victory and Hitters Club packs sold at KMart stores early in the season. The Upper Deck OD2K cards have gold-foil graphic highlights on front. Backs have portrait photos, stats and are numbered with an "OD" prefix.

		MT
Complete Set (8):		6.00
Common Player:		.50
17	Ken Griffey Jr.	2.00
18	Sammy Sosa	1.00
19	Pedro Martinez	.75
20	Manny Ramirez	.65
21	Shawn Green	.65
22	Carlos Beltran	.65
23	Juan Gonzalez	.65
24	Jeromy Burnitz	.50

2000 Upper Deck Ovation

		MT
Complete Set (89):		125.00
Common Player:		.25
Common World Prem. (61-80):		2.00
Inserted 1:3		
Common Super. Spot (81-90):		3.00
Inserted 1:6		
Wax Box:		70.00
1	Mo Vaughn	.75
2	Troy Glaus	.50
3	Jeff Bagwell	1.00
4	Craig Biggio	.50
5	Mike Hampton	.25
6	Jason Giambi	.25
7	Tim Hudson	.50
8	Chipper Jones	2.00
9	Greg Maddux	2.00
10	Kevin Millwood	.50
11	Brian Jordan	.25
12	Jeromy Burnitz	.25
13	David Wells	.25
14	Carlos Delgado	.75
15	Sammy Sosa	2.50
16	Mark McGwire	4.00
17	Matt Williams	.50
18	Randy Johnson	.75
19	Erubiel Durazo	.50
20	Kevin Brown	.25
21	Shawn Green	.75
22	Gary Sheffield	.40
23	Jose Canseco	1.00
24	Vladimir Guerrero	1.50
25	Barry Bonds	1.00
26	Manny Ramirez	1.00
27	Roberto Alomar	.75
28	Richie Sexson	.25
29	Jim Thome	.50
30	Alex Rodriguez	2.50
31	Ken Griffey Jr.	4.00
32	Preston Wilson	.25
33	Mike Piazza	2.50
34	Al Leiter	.25
35	Robin Ventura	.40
36	Cal Ripken Jr.	3.00
37	Albert Belle	.75
38	Tony Gwynn	2.00
39	Brian Giles	.25
40	Jason Kendall	.40
41	Scott Rolen	1.00
42	Bob Abreu	.25
43	Ken Griffey Jr.	8.00
44	Sean Casey	.40
45	Carlos Beltran	.50
46	Gabe Kapler	.40
47	Ivan Rodriguez	1.00
48	Rafael Palmeiro	.50
49	Larry Walker	.75
50	Nomar Garciaparra	2.50
51	Pedro J. Martinez	1.00

52	Eric Milton	.25
53	Juan Gonzalez	1.25
54	Tony Clark	.50
55	Frank Thomas	1.25
56	Magglio Ordonez	.40
57	Roger Clemens	1.50
58	Derek Jeter	2.50
59	Bernie Williams	.75
60	Orlando Hernandez	.50
61	Rick Ankiel (World Premiere)	15.00
62	Josh Beckett (World Premiere)	10.00
63	Vernon Wells (World Premiere)	3.00
64	Alfonso Soriano (World Premiere)	8.00
65	Pat Burrell (World Premiere)	8.00
66	Eric Munson (World Premiere)	8.00
67	Chad Hutchinson (World Premiere)	3.00
68	Eric Gagne (World Premiere)	2.00
69	Peter Bergeron (World Premiere)	2.00
71	A.J. Burnett (World Premiere)	2.00
72	Jorge Luis Toca (World Premiere)	3.00
73	Matt Riley (World Premiere)	5.00
74	Chad Hermansen (World Premiere)	2.00
75	Doug Davis (World Premiere)	2.00
76	Jim Morris (World Premiere)	2.00
77	Ben Petrick (World Premiere)	3.00
78	Mark Quinn (World Premiere)	3.00
79	Ed Yarnall (World Premiere)	3.00
80	Ramon Ortiz (World Premiere)	3.00
81	Ken Griffey Jr. (Superstar Spotlight)	12.00
82	Mark McGwire (Superstar Spotlight)	12.00
83	Derek Jeter (Superstar Spotlight)	8.00
84	Jeff Bagwell (Superstar Spotlight)	3.00
85	Nomar Garciaparra (Superstar Spotlight)	8.00
86	Sammy Sosa (Superstar Spotlight)	8.00
87	Mike Piazza (Superstar Spotlight)	8.00
88	Alex Rodriguez (Superstar Spotlight)	8.00
89	Cal Ripken Jr. (Superstar Spotlight)	10.00
90	Pedro Martinez (Superstar Spotlight)	3.00

2000 Upper Deck Ovation Standing Ovation

Stars (1-60): 25x-50x
World Prem. (61-80): 3x-6x
Super. Spot. (81-90): 8x-15x
Production 50 sets
(See 2000 UD Ovation for checklist and base card values.)

2000 Upper Deck Ovation A Piece of History

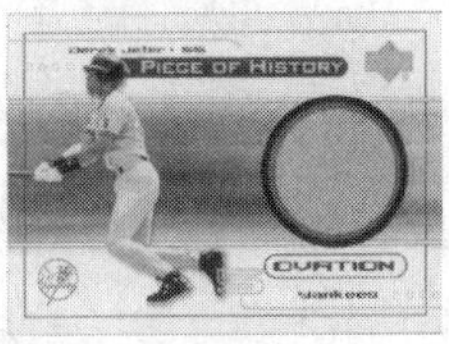

		MT
Common Player:		40.00
Production 400 sets		
JB	Jeff Bagwell	60.00
CB	Carlos Beltran	50.00
SC	Sean Casey	40.00
KG	Ken Griffey Jr.	250.00
DJ	Derek Jeter	175.00
AJ	Andruw Jones	50.00
CJ	Chipper Jones	120.00
RP	Rafael Palmeiro	50.00
MP	Mike Piazza	150.00
MR	Manny Ramirez	75.00
CR	Cal Ripken Jr.	200.00
AR	Alex Rodriguez	150.00
SR	Scott Rolen	60.00
SS	Sammy Sosa	150.00
FT	Frank Thomas	75.00

2000 Upper Deck Ovation A Piece of History - Signed

Values Undetermined
Complete Set (7):
Common Player:

KG	Ken Griffey Jr.
TG	Tony Gwynn
DJ	Derek Jeter
CJ	Chipper Jones
CR	Cal Ripken Jr.
AR	Alex Rodriguez
IR	Ivan Rodriguez

2000 Upper Deck Ovation Center Stage

		MT
Complete Set (10):		75.00
Common Player:		2.00
Inserted 1:9		
Gold: 2x		
Inserted 1:39		
Rainbow: 3x-4x		
Inserted 1:99		
1	Jeff Bagwell	3.00
2	Ken Griffey Jr.	12.00
3	Nomar Garciaparra	8.00
4	Mike Piazza	8.00
5	Mark McGwire	12.00
6	Alex Rodriguez	8.00
7	Cal Ripken Jr.	10.00
8	Derek Jeter	8.00
9	Chipper Jones	6.00
10	Sammy Sosa	8.00

The election of former players to the Hall of Fame does not always have an immediate upward effect on card prices. The hobby market generally has done a good job of predicting those inductions and adjusting values over the course of several years.

2000 Upper Deck Ovation Curtain Calls

		MT
Complete Set (20):		50.00
Common Player:		1.00
Inserted 1:3		
1	David Cone	1.00
2	Mark McGwire	8.00
3	Sammy Sosa	5.00
4	Eric Milton	1.00
5	Bernie Williams	1.50
6	Tony Gwynn	4.00
7	Nomar Garciaparra	5.00
8	Manny Ramirez	2.00
9	Wade Boggs	1.50
10	Randy Johnson	1.50
11	Cal Ripken Jr.	6.00
12	Pedro J. Martinez	2.00
13	Alex Rodriguez	5.00
14	Fernando Tatis	1.00
15	Vladimir Guerrero	3.00
16	Robin Ventura	1.00
17	Larry Walker	1.50
18	Carlos Beltran	1.50
19	Jose Canseco	2.00
20	Ken Griffey Jr.	8.00

2000 Upper Deck Ovation Diamond Futures

		MT
Complete Set (10):		40.00
Common Player:		2.00
Inserted 1:6		
1	J.D. Drew	5.00
2	Alfonso Soriano	5.00
3	Preston Wilson	2.00
4	Erubiel Durazo	3.00
5	Rick Ankiel	20.00
6	Octavio Dotel	2.00
7	A.J. Burnett	2.00
8	Carlos Beltran	3.00
9	Vernon Wells	2.00
10	Troy Glaus	2.00

2000 Upper Deck Ovation Lead Performers

		MT
Complete Set (10):		75.00
Common Player:		3.00
Inserted 1:19		
1	Mark McGwire	15.00
2	Derek Jeter	10.00
3	Vladimir Guerrero	5.00
4	Mike Piazza	10.00
5	Cal Ripken Jr.	12.00
6	Sammy Sosa	10.00
7	Jeff Bagwell	4.00
8	Nomar Garciaparra	10.00
9	Chipper Jones	8.00
10	Ken Griffey Jr.	15.00

2000 Upper Deck Ovation Super Signatures

Values Undetermined

Jr	Ken Griffey Jr.
MP	Mike Piazza

2000 Upper Deck Ovation Superstar Theatre

		MT
Complete Set (20):		90.00
Common Player:		3.00
Inserted 1:19		
1	Ivan Rodriguez	6.00
2	Brian Giles	3.00
3	Bernie Williams	5.00
4	Greg Maddux	12.00
5	Frank Thomas	8.00
6	Sean Casey	4.00
7	Mo Vaughn	5.00
8	Carlos Delgado	5.00
9	Tony Gwynn	12.00
10	Pedro Martinez	6.00
11	Scott Rolen	6.00
12	Mark McGwire	25.00
13	Manny Ramirez	6.00
14	Rafael Palmeiro	5.00
15	Jose Canseco	6.00
16	Randy Johnson	5.00
17	Gary Sheffield	3.00
18	Larry Walker	5.00
19	Barry Bonds	6.00
20	Roger Clemens	8.00

2000 Upper Deck Ovation 3,000 Hit Club

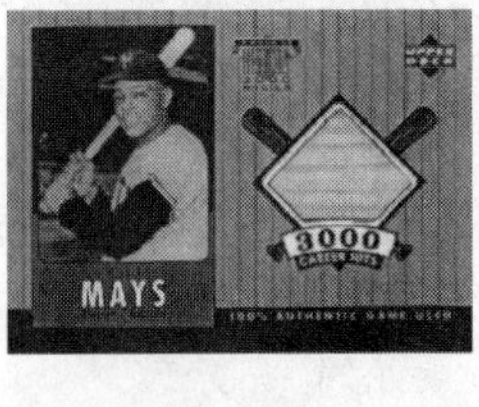

		MT
1	Willie Mays (Jersey Card/350)	315.00
2	Willie Mays (Bat Card/300)	340.00
3	Willie Mays (Jersey+Bat Card/ 50)	1100.
4	Willie Mays (Signed Jersey+Bat Card/ 24)	1600.

2000 Upper Deck Power Deck

		MT
Complete Set (11):		50.00
Common Player:		2.00
Inserted 1:23		
1	Ken Griffey Jr.	10.00
2	Cal Ripken Jr.	6.00
3	Mark McGwire	10.00
4	Tony Gwynn	5.00
5	Roger Clemens	4.00
6	Alex Rodriguez	6.00
7	Sammy Sosa	6.00
8	Derek Jeter	6.00
9	Ken Griffey Jr.	40.00
10	Mark McGwire	40.00
11	Reggie Jackson	10.00

2000 Upper Deck Victory

		MT
Complete Set (440):		50.00
Common Player:		.10
Common Griffey (391-440):		.50
1	Mo Vaughn	.30
2	Garret Anderson	.10
3	Tim Salmon	.20
4	Troy Percival	.10
5	Orlando Palmeiro	.10
6	Darin Erstad	.20
7	Ramon Ortiz	.10
8	Ben Molina	.10
9	Troy Glaus	.20
10	Jim Edmonds	.10
11	Mo Vaughn, Troy Percival	.15
12	Craig Biggio	.25
13	Roger Cedeno	.10
14	Shane Reynolds	.10
15	Jeff Bagwell	.50
16	Octavio Dotel	.10
17	Moises Alou	.15
18	Jose Lima	.10
19	Ken Caminiti	.15
20	Richard Hidalgo	.10
21	Billy Wagner	.10
22	Lance Berkman	.10
23	Jeff Bagwell, Jose Lima	.25
24	Jason Giambi	.10
25	Randy Velarde	.10
26	Miguel Tejada	.10
27	Matt Stairs	.10
28	A.J. Hinch	.10
29	Olmedo Saenz	.10
30	Ben Grieve	.20
31	Ryan Christenson	.10
32	Eric Chavez	.10
33	Tim Hudson	.20
34	John Jaha	.10
35	Jason Giambi, Matt Stairs	.10
36	Raul Mondesi	.20
37	Tony Batista	.10
38	David Wells	.10
39	Homer Bush	.10
40	Carlos Delgado	.40
41	Billy Koch	.10
42	Darrin Fletcher	.10
43	Tony Fernandez	.10
44	Shannon Stewart	.20
45	Roy Halladay	.10
46	Chris Carpenter	.10
47	Carlos Delgado, David Wells	.20
48	Chipper Jones	1.00
49	Greg Maddux	1.00
50	Andruw Jones	.40
51	Andres Galarraga	.30
52	Tom Glavine	.20
53	Brian Jordan	.10
54	John Smoltz	.10
55	John Rocker	.10
56	Javy Lopez	.15
57	Eddie Perez	.10
58	Kevin Millwood	.10
59	Chipper Jones, Greg Maddux	.50
60	Jeromy Burnitz	.20
61	Steve Woodard	.10
62	Ron Belliard	.10
63	Geoff Jenkins	.20
64	Bob Wickman	.10
65	Marquis Grissom	.10
66	Henry Blanco	.10
67	Mark Loretta	.10
68	Alex Ochoa	.10
69	Marquis Grissom, Jeromy Burnitz	.10
70	Mark McGwire	2.00
71	Edgar Renteria	.10
72	Dave Veres	.10
73	Eli Marrero	.10
74	Fernando Tatis	.20
75	J.D. Drew	.20
76	Ray Lankford	.10
77	Daryle Kile	.10
78	Kent Bottenfield	.10
79	Joe McEwing	.10
80	Mark McGwire, Ray Lankford	1.00
81	Sammy Sosa	1.25
82	Jose Nieves	.10
83	Jon Lieber	.10
84	Henry Rodriguez	.10
85	Mark Grace	.20
86	Eric Young	.10
87	Kerry Wood	.25
88	Ismael Valdes	.10
89	Glenallen Hill	.10

90	Sammy Sosa, Mark Grace	.60
91	Greg Vaughn	.20
92	Fred McGriff	.20
93	Ryan Rupe	.10
94	Bubba Trammell	.10
95	Miguel Cairo	.10
96	Roberto Hernandez	.10
97	Jose Canseco	.50
98	Wilson Alvarez	.10
99	John Flaherty	.10
100	Vinny Castilla	.15
101	Jose Canseco, Roberto Hernandez	.25
102	Randy Johnson	.40
103	Matt Williams	.20
104	Matt Mantei	.10
105	Steve Finley	.10
106	Luis Gonzalez	.10
107	Travis Lee	.10
108	Omar Daal	.10
109	Jay Bell	.10
110	Erubiel Durazo	.10
111	Tony Womack	.10
112	Todd Stottlemyre	.10
113	Randy Johnson, Matt Williams	.10
114	Gary Sheffield	.25
115	Adrian Beltre	.10
116	Kevin Brown	.20
117	Todd Hundley	.10
118	Eric Karros	.20
119	Shawn Green	.40
120	Chan Ho Park	.10
121	Mark Grudzielanek	.10
122	Todd Hollandsworth	.10
123	Jeff Shaw	.10
124	Darren Dreifort	.10
125	Gary Sheffield, Kevin Brown	.15
126	Vladimir Guerrero	.75
127	Michael Barrett	.10
128	Dustin Hermanson	.10
129	Jose Vidro	.10
130	Chris Widger	.10
131	Mike Thurman	.10
132	Wilton Guerrero	.10
133	Brad Fullmer	.10
134	Rondell White	.20
135	Ugueth Urbina	.10
136	Vladimir Guerrero, Rondell White	.40
137	Barry Bonds	.50
138	Russ Ortiz	.10
139	J.T. Snow	.10
140	Joe Nathan	.10
141	Rich Aurilia	.10
142	Jeff Kent	.10
143	Armando Rios	.10
144	Ellis Burks	.10
145	Robb Nen	.10
146	Marvin Benard	.10
147	Barry Bonds, Russ Ortiz	.25
148	Manny Ramirez	.50
149	Bartolo Colon	.10
150	Kenny Lofton	.35
151	Sandy Alomar Jr.	.15
152	Travis Fryman	.15
153	Omar Vizquel	.10
154	Roberto Alomar	.40
155	Richie Sexson	.10
156	David Justice	.20
157	Jim Thome	.30
158	Manny Ramirez, Roberto Alomar	.25
159	Ken Griffey Jr.	2.00
160	Edgar Martinez	.15
161	Fred Garcia	.10
162	Alex Rodriguez	1.50
163	John Halama	.10
164	Russ Davis	.10
165	David Bell	.10
166	Gil Meche	.10
167	Jamie Moyer	.10
168	John Olerud	.20
169	Ken Griffey Jr., Fred Garcia	1.00
170	Preston Wilson	.10
171	Antonio Alfonseca	.10
172	A.J. Burnett	.10
173	Luis Castillo	.10
174	Mike Lowell	.10
175	Alex Fernandez	.10
176	Mike Redmond	.10
177	Alex Gonzalez	.10
178	Vladimir Nunez	.10
179	Mark Kotsay	.10
180	Preston Wilson, Luis Castillo	.10
181	Mike Piazza	1.25
182	Darryl Hamilton	.10
183	Al Leiter	.20
184	Robin Ventura	.20
185	Rickey Henderson	.20
186	Rey Ordonez	.10
187	Edgardo Alfonzo	.15
188	Derek Bell	.10
189	Mike Hampton	.10
190	Armando Benitez	.10
191	Mike Piazza, Rickey Henderson	.50
192	Cal Ripken Jr.	1.50
193	B.J. Surhoff	.10
194	Mike Mussina	.40
195	Albert Belle	.40
196	Jerry Hairston	.10
197	Will Clark	.20
198	Sidney Ponson	.10
199	Brady Anderson	.15
200	Scott Erickson	.10
201	Ryan Minor	.10
202	Cal Ripken Jr., Albert Belle	.75
203	Tony Gwynn	1.00
204	Bret Boone	.10
205	Ryan Klesko	.10
206	Ben Davis	.10
207	Matt Clement	.10
208	Eric Owens	.10
209	Trevor Hoffman	.10
210	Sterling Hitchcock	.10
211	Phil Nevin	.10
212	Tony Gwynn, Trevor Hoffman	.50
213	Scott Rolen	.50
214	Bob Abreu	.20
215	Curt Schilling	.20
216	Rico Brogna	.10
217	Robert Person	.10
218	Doug Glanville	.10
219	Mike Lieberthal	.10
220	Andy Ashby	.10
221	Randy Wolf	.10
222	Bob Abreu, Curt Schilling	.15
223	Brian Giles	.20
224	Jason Kendall	.20
225	Kris Benson	.10
226	Warren Morris	.10
227	Kevin Young	.10
228	Al Martin	.10
229	Wil Cordero	.10
230	Bruce Aven	.10
231	Todd Ritchie	.10
232	Jason Kendall, Brian Giles	.10
233	Ivan Rodriguez	.50
234	Rusty Greer	.10
235	Ruben Mateo	.10
236	Justin Thompson	.10
237	Rafael Palmeiro	.25
238	Chad Curtis	.10
239	Royce Clayton	.10
240	Gabe Kapler	.20
241	Jeff Zimmerman	.10
242	John Wetteland	.10
243	Ivan Rodriguez, Rafael Palmeiro	.25
244	Nomar Garciaparra	1.25
245	Pedro Martinez	.50
246	Jose Offerman	.10
247	Jason Varitek	.10
248	Troy O'Leary	.10
249	John Valentin	.10
250	Trot Nixon	.10
251	Carl Everett	.10
252	Wilton Veras	.10
253	Bret Saberhagen	.10
254	Nomar Garciaparra, Pedro J. Martinez	.60
255	Sean Casey	.10
256	Barry Larkin	.25
257	Pokey Reese	.10
258	Pete Harnisch	.10
259	Aaron Boone	.10
260	Dante Bichette	.20
261	Scott Williamson	.10
262	Steve Parris	.10
263	Dmitri Young	.10
264	Mike Cameron	.10
265	Sean Casey, Scott Williamson	.10
266	Larry Walker	.40
267	Rolando Arrojo	.10
268	Pedro Astacio	.10
269	Todd Helton	.25
270	Jeff Cirillo	.10
271	Neifi Perez	.10
272	Brian Bohanon	.10
273	Jeffrey Hammonds	.10
274	Tom Goodwin	.10
275	Larry Walker, Todd Helton	.20
276	Carlos Beltran	.20
277	Jermaine Dye	.10
278	Mike Sweeney	.10
279	Joe Randa	.10
280	Jose Rosado	.10
281	Carlos Febles	.10
282	Jeff Suppan	.10
283	Johnny Damon	.10
284	Jeremy Giambi	.10
285	Mike Sweeney, Carlos Beltran	.10
286	Tony Clark	.20
287	Damion Easley	.10
288	Jeff Weaver	.10
289	Dean Palmer	.10
290	Juan Gonzalez	.50
291	Juan Encarnacion	.10
292	Todd Jones	.10
293	Karim Garcia	.10
294	Deivi Cruz	.10
295	Dean Palmer, Juan Encarnacion	.10
296	Corey Koskie	.10
297	Brad Radke	.10
298	Doug Mientkiewicz	.10
299	Ron Coomer	.10
300	Joe Mays	.10
301	Eric Milton	.10
302	Jacque Jones	.10
303	Chad Allen	.10
304	Cristian Guzman	.10
305	Jason Ryan	.10
306	Todd Walker	.10
307	Corey Koskie, Eric Milton	.10
308	Frank Thomas	.75
309	Paul Konerko	.10
310	Mike Sirotka	.10
311	Jim Parque	.10
312	Magglio Ordonez	.10
313	Bob Howry	.10
314	Carlos Lee	.10
315	Ray Durham	.10
316	Chris Singleton	.10
317	Brook Fordyce	.10
318	Frank Thomas, Magglio Ordonez	.25
319	Derek Jeter	1.25
320	Roger Clemens	.75
321	Paul O'Neill	.20
322	Bernie Williams	.40
323	Mariano Rivera	.20
324	Tino Martinez	.20
325	David Cone	.20
326	Chuck Knoblauch	.20
327	Darryl Strawberry	.20
328	Orlando Hernandez	.10
329	Ricky Ledee	.10
330	Derek Jeter, Bernie Williams	.50
331	Pat Burrell (Rookie 2000)	.60
332	Alfonso Soriano (Rookie 2000)	.60
333	Josh Beckett (Rookie 2000)	.75
334	Matt Riley (Rookie 2000)	.50
335	Brian Cooper (Rookie 2000)	.10
336	Eric Munson (Rookie 2000)	.75
337	Vernon Wells (Rookie 2000)	.10
338	Juan Pena (Rookie 2000)	.10
339	Mark DeRosa (Rookie 2000)	.10
340	Kip Wells (Rookie 2000)	.10
341	Roosevelt Brown (Rookie 2000)	.10
342	Jason LaRue (Rookie 2000)	.10
343	Ben Petrick (Rookie 2000)	.10
344	Mark Quinn (Rookie 2000)	.10
345	Julio Ramirez (Rookie 2000)	.10
346	Rod Barajas (Rookie 2000)	.10
347	Robert Fick (Rookie 2000)	.10
348	David Newhan (Rookie 2000)	.10
349	Eric Gagne (Rookie 2000)	.10
350	Jorge Toca (Rookie 2000)	.10
351	Mitch Meluskey (Rookie 2000)	.10
352	Ed Yarnall (Rookie 2000)	.10
353	Chad Hermansen (Rookie 2000)	.10
354	Peter Bergeron (Rookie 2000)	.10
355	Dermal Brown (Rookie 2000)	.10
356	Adam Kennedy (Rookie 2000)	.10
357	Kevin Barker (Rookie 2000)	.10
358	Francisco Cordero (Rookie 2000)	.10
359	Travis Dawkins (Rookie 2000)	.10
360	Jeff Williams (Rookie 2000)	.10
361	Chad Hutchinson (Rookie 2000)	.10
362	D'Angelo Jimenez (Rookie 2000)	.10
363	Derrick Gibson (Rookie 2000)	.10
364	Calvin Murray (Rookie 2000)	.10
365	Doug Davis (Rookie 2000)	.10
366	Rob Ramsay (Rookie 2000)	.10
367	Mark Redman (Rookie 2000)	.10
368	Rick Ankiel (Rookie 2000)	2.00
369	Domingo Guzman (Rookie 2000)	.10
370	Eugene Kingsale (Rookie 2000)	.10
371	Nomar Garciaparra (Big Play Makers)	.60
372	Ken Griffey Jr. (Big Play Makers)	1.00
373	Randy Johnson (Big Play Makers)	.20
374	Jeff Bagwell (Big Play Makers)	.25
375	Ivan Rodriguez (Big Play Makers)	.25
376	Derek Jeter (Big Play Makers)	.60
377	Carlos Beltran (Big Play Makers)	.10
378	Vladimir Guerrero (Big Play Makers)	.40
379	Sammy Sosa (Big Play Makers)	.60
380	Barry Bonds (Big Play Makers)	.25
381	Pedro Martinez (Big Play Makers)	.25
382	Chipper Jones (Big Play Makers)	.50
383	Mo Vaughn (Big Play Makers)	.15
384	Mike Piazza (Big Play Makers)	.60
385	Alex Rodriguez (Big Play Makers)	.60
386	Manny Ramirez (Big Play Makers)	.25
387	Mark McGwire (Big Play Makers)	1.00
388	Tony Gwynn (Big Play Makers)	.50
389	Sean Casey (Big Play Makers)	.10
390	Cal Ripken Jr. (Big Play Makers)	.75
391	Ken Griffey Jr.	.50
392	Ken Griffey Jr.	.50
393	Ken Griffey Jr.	.50
394	Ken Griffey Jr.	.50
395	Ken Griffey Jr.	.50
396	Ken Griffey Jr.	.50
397	Ken Griffey Jr.	.50
398	Ken Griffey Jr.	.50
399	Ken Griffey Jr.	.50
400	Ken Griffey Jr.	.50
401	Ken Griffey Jr.	.50
402	Ken Griffey Jr.	.50
403	Ken Griffey Jr.	.50
404	Ken Griffey Jr.	.50
405	Ken Griffey Jr.	.50
406	Ken Griffey Jr.	.50
407	Ken Griffey Jr.	.50
408	Ken Griffey Jr.	.50
409	Ken Griffey Jr.	.50
410	Ken Griffey Jr.	.50
411	Ken Griffey Jr.	.50
412	Ken Griffey Jr.	.50
413	Ken Griffey Jr.	.50
414	Ken Griffey Jr.	.50
415	Ken Griffey Jr.	.50
416	Ken Griffey Jr.	.50
417	Ken Griffey Jr.	.50
418	Ken Griffey Jr.	.50
419	Ken Griffey Jr.	.50
420	Ken Griffey Jr.	.50
421	Ken Griffey Jr.	.50
422	Ken Griffey Jr.	.50
423	Ken Griffey Jr.	.50
424	Ken Griffey Jr.	.50
425	Ken Griffey Jr.	.50
426	Ken Griffey Jr.	.50
427	Ken Griffey Jr.	.50
428	Ken Griffey Jr.	.50
429	Ken Griffey Jr.	.50
430	Ken Griffey Jr.	.50
431	Ken Griffey Jr.	.50
432	Ken Griffey Jr.	.50
433	Ken Griffey Jr.	.50
434	Ken Griffey Jr.	.50
435	Ken Griffey Jr.	.50
436	Ken Griffey Jr.	.50
437	Ken Griffey Jr.	.50
438	Ken Griffey Jr.	.50
439	Ken Griffey Jr.	.50
440	Ken Griffey Jr.	.50

1993 USA Rice

To promote rice consumption and raise money for the pictured athletes' favorite charities, the USA Rice Council issued this multi-sport card set and made it available by mail for a $2 donation. All players are pictured in civilian clothes with either a blue or red border around. Backs of most cards have rice recipes and indicate the charity to which the athlete is donating their portion of the proceeds. Cards are standard 2-1/2" x 3-1/2".

		MT
Complete Set (10):		8.00
Common Card:		.50
1	Steve Sax (cooking)	1.00
2	Troy Aikman (football)	3.00
3	Roger Clemens	4.00
4	Zina Garrison (tennis)	.50
5	Warren Moon (football)	2.00
6	Summer Sanders (swimming)	.50
7	Steve Sax (lifting weights)	1.00
8	Brian Shimer (bobsledder)	.50
9	Food Guide Pyramid	.25
10	Healthy Eating Tips	.25

1999 U.S. Cellular Milwaukee Brewers

The four Milwaukee Brewers who have had their uniform numbers retired by the team, plus Jackie Robinson, whose #42 was retired by MLB edict, are honored on this foldout promotion given to fans Oct. 2 at County Stadium. Five 4" x 6" cards make up the panel, which is perforated between the cards for ease of separation. Cards have player action photos on front (color except for Robinson) on a muted blue-green stadium photo background. At lower-right is a gold-foil seal with the player's name and number. At top is a sponsor logo and part of the legend "COMMEMORATING GREATNESS" which runs contiguously across the panel. Backs have a black-and-white photo, career data and highlights.

		MT
Complete Set, Panel:		12.00
Complete Set, Singles:		8.00
Common Player:		1.00
4	Paul Molitor	4.00
19	Robin Yount	4.00
34	Rollie Fingers	1.00
42	Jackie Robinson	3.00
44	Hank Aaron	5.00

1993 U.S. Department of Transportation Safety Set

This six-card set (issued in three-card panels) was sponsored by the U.S. Department of Transportation and distributed at the Little League World Series. Standard size cards have red and blue borders on front, along with the Little League logo. Backs are printed in red and blue and include a highway safety message and sponsors/licensors logos.

		MT
Complete Set (6):		22.00
Common Player:		3.00
	Panel 1	10.00
(1)	(Orel Hershiser)	3.00
(2)	(Don Mattingly)	6.00
(3)	(Mike Mussina)	3.00
	Panel 2	12.00
(4)	Mike Piazza	5.00
(5)	Cal Ripken Jr.	8.00
(6)	Mo Vaughn	4.50

1987 U.S. Forestry Service Smokey Bear's Team

The U.S. Forestry Service and Major League Baseball united in an effort to promote National Smokey the Bear Day. Two perforated sheets of baseball cards, one each for the American and National Leagues, were produced. The sheet of American Leaguers measures 18" x 24" and contains 16 full-color cards. The National League sheet measures 20" x 18" and contains 15 cards. Each individual card is 4" x 6" and contains a fire prevention tip on the back. An average number of 25,000 sets was sent to all teams.

		MT
Complete Set (31):		12.00
Complete A.L. Sheet:		7.00
Complete N.L. Sheet:		7.00
Common Player:		.25
1A	Jose Canseco	.75
1N	Steve Sax	.25
2A	Dennis "Oil Can" Boyd	.25
2Na	Dale Murphy (shirttail out)	5.00
2Nb	Dale Murphy (shirttail in)	.90
3A	John Candelaria	.25
3Na	Jody Davis (standing)	3.00
3Nb	Jody Davis (kneeling)	.25
4A	Harold Baines	.25
4N	Bill Gullickson	.25
5A	Joe Carter	.25
5N	Mike Scott	.25
6A	Jack Morris	.25
6N	Roger McDowell	.25
7A	Buddy Biancalana	.25
7N	Steve Bedrosian	.25
8A	Kirby Puckett	3.00
8N	Johnny Ray	.25
9A	Mike Pagliarulo	.25
9N .	Ozzie Smith	3.00
10A	Larry Sheets	.25
10N	Steve Garvey	.50
11A	Mike Moore	.25
11N	Smokey Bear Logo Card	.05
12A	Charlie Hough	.25
12N	Mike Krukow	.25
13A	Smokey Bear Logo Card	.05
13N	Smokey Bear	.05
14A	Tom Henke	.25
14N	Mike Fitzgerald	.25
15A	Jim Gantner	.25
15N	National League Logo Card	.05
16A	American League Logo Card	.05

1997 U.S. Mint Jackie Robinson Legacy

This high-end cherrywood cased collectors set was offered to collectors in conjunction with the release of a pair of commemorative coins honoring Jackie Robinson on the 50th anniversary of his major league debut. The set contains a commemorative $5 gold piece, the 50th anniversary uniform patch worn during the season, a lapel pin of the patch and a Topps Finest reproduction of the 1952 Jackie Robinson card featuring the seal of the U.S. Mint at upper-left. Production of the set was reported at 50,000, with issue price of about $325.

	MT
Complete Set: Jackie Robinson	325.00

1997 U.S. Mint Jackie Robinson Coins

To commemorate the 50th anniversary of Jackie Robinson's debut in the major leagues, the U.S. Mint issued a pair of commemorative collectors issues. The $1 silver coin features Robinson sliding on front and has a version of the anniversary logo on back. The $5 gold piece has a portrait of an older Robinson on front and a baseball on back with his birth and death years and "Legacy of Courage". Each coin was produced in proof and uncirculated finishes and sold singly and in sets of two and four. Maximum mintage was 200,000 total for the silver dollars and 100,000 for the $5 gold pieces. Issue prices for the uncirculated pieces were $32 for silver, $205 for gold. Proofs originally sold for $37 and $225, respectively.

	MT
Silver Dollar, Uncirculated:	32.00
Silver Dollar, Proof:	200.00
$5 Gold Piece, Uncirculated:	200.00
$5 Gold Piece, Proof Jackie Robinson	225.00

1991 U.S. Oil Co. Milwaukee Brewers Pin/Card

Team highlights of the 1980s are featured in this set of pins/cards distributed by Wisconsin gas stations. Cards are 2-3/4" x 5-5/8", with a perforation at the depth of 4". The top portion of the cards has a color photo with the team logo superimposed, bordered in team colors of blue and yellow. The players' cards have uniform numbers in a star at top-right. On a white panel below the perforation, an enameled pin, about 1" x 1" is pinned, and a description of the highlight is printed. Backs are in black-and-white with player portrait photo, biographical data and career highlights, along with sponsor's logo. Prices shown are for complete pin/card combinations.

		MT
Complete Set (4):		15.00
Common Pin/Card:		2.00
1	Paul Molitor (39-Game Hitting Streak)	6.00
2	Robin Yount (A.L. MVP 1982, 1989)	7.50
3	Juan Nieves (1st Brewers No-Hitter)	2.00
4	Milwaukee County Stadium - 1982 (American League Championship)	2.00

1990 U.S. Playing Card All-Stars

Sold as a boxed set, these cards are the standard 2-1/2" x 3-1/2" format but feature rounded corners. Each card features a color player photo with the upper-left and lower-right corners inset to provide for playing card designations. A team logo appears in the lower-left corner. On American League players' cards (Clubs and Spades) the player's name and position appear in white in a blue box beneath the photo. On National Leaguers' cards (Hearts and Diamonds) the box is red and the printing black. Card backs are identical, with blue borders and a multi-colored "1990 Baseball Major League All-Stars" logo on a pinstriped white center panel. A premium version with the cards' edges silvered was also issued. These cards have a small diagonal "nip" at each rounded corner.

		MT
Complete Set (56):		5.00
Common Player:		.05
HEARTS		
J	Bobby Bonilla	.05
Q	Kevin Mitchell	.05
K	Darryl Strawberry	.10
A	Ramon Martinez	.10
2	Mike Scioscia	.05
3	Jeff Brantley	.05
4	Ryne Sandberg	.35
5	Chris Sabo	.05
6	Ozzie Smith	.45
7	John Franco	.05
8	Matt Williams	.10
9	Andre Dawson	.10
10	Benito Santiago	.05
CLUBS		
J	Wade Boggs	.35
Q	George Bell	.05
K	Rickey Henderson	.25
A	Bob Welch	.05
2	Lance Parrish	.05
3	Bret Saberhagen	.15
4	Gregg Olson	.05
5	Brook Jacoby	.05
6	Ozzie Guillen	.05
7	Ellis Burks	.05
8	Dennis Eckersley	.05
9	Bobby Thigpen	.05
10	Dave Stieb	.05
DIAMONDS		
J	Tony Gwynn	.50
Q	Will Clark	.30
K	Barry Bonds	.50
A	Frank Viola	.05
2	Greg Olson	.05
3	Dennis Martinez	.05
4	Roberto Alomar	.30
5	Tim Wallach	.05
6	Barry Larkin	.10
7	Neal Heaton	.05
8	Dave Smith	.05
9	Lenny Dykstra	.05
10	Shawon Dunston	.05
SPADES		
J	Ken Griffey, Jr.	1.00
Q	Dave Parker	.05
K	Cecil Fielder	.05
A	Roger Clemens	.45
2	Sandy Alomar	.10
3	Randy Johnson	.10
4	Steve Sax	.05
5	Kelly Gruber	.05
6	Chuck Finley	.05
7	Doug Jones	.05
8	Kirby Puckett	.50
9	Cal Ripken, Jr.	.75
10	Alan Trammell	.05
WILD CARDS/JOKERS		
---	Jack Armstrong (Joker)	.05
---	Julio Franco (Joker)	.05
---	Rob Dibble, Randy Myers (Wild Card)	.05
---	Mark McGwire, Jose Canseco (Wild Card)	1.00

1991 U.S. Playing Card All-Stars

In standard 2-1/2" x 3-1/2" format, though with rounded corners, this 56-card set was produced by the country's leading maker of playing cards and sold as a boxed set. Fronts have a color player photo with the top-left and bottom-right corners inset to include playing card designations. A team logo appears in the upper-right corner. On American Leaguers' cards (Hearts and Diamonds), the player's name and position appear in white in a green stripe beneath the photo. National League players (Clubs and Spades) have a yellow stripe with black printing. Backs are red-bordered with a colorful "1991 Baseball Major League All-Stars" logo on a pinstriped white center panel. A silver-edged premium version was also issued. These cards have a diagonal "nip" at each rounded corner.

		MT
Complete Set (56):		5.00
Common Player:		.05
HEARTS		
J	Rickey Henderson	.25
Q	Roberto Alomar	.25
K	Dave Henderson	.05
A	Jack Morris	.05
2	Ozzie Guillen	.05
3	Jack McDowell	.05
4	Joe Carter	.05
5	Mark Langston	.05
6	Julio Franco	.05
7	Rick Aguilera	.05
8	Paul Molitor	.35
9	Ruben Sierra	.05
10	Roger Clemens	.45
CLUBS		
J	Andre Dawson	.10
Q	Chris Sabo	.05
K	Ivan Calderon	.05
A	Tony Gwynn	.45
2	Paul O'Neill	.05
3	John Smiley	.05
4	Howard Johnson	.05
5	Mike Morgan	.05
6	Barry Larkin	.10
7	Frank Viola	.05
8	Juan Samuel	.05
9	Craig Biggio	.10
10	Lee Smith	.05
DIAMONDS		
J	Sandy Alomar	.10
Q	Cecil Fielder	.05
K	Cal Ripken, Jr.	.75
A	Ken Griffey, Jr.	1.00
2	Carlton Fisk	.10
3	Scott Sanderson	.05
4	Kirby Puckett	.50
5	Jeff Reardon	.05
6	Rafael Palmeiro	.20
7	Bryan Harvey	.05
8	Jimmy Key	.05
9	Harold Baines	.05
10	Dennis Eckersley	.05
SPADES		
J	Benito Santiago	.05
Q	Ryne Sandberg	.35
K	Ozzie Smith	.35
A	Tom Glavine	.15
2	Eddie Murray	.30
3	Pete Harnisch	.05
4	John Kruk	.05
5	Tom Browning	.05
6	George Bell	.05
7	Dennis Martinez	.05
8	Brett Butler	.05
9	Terry Pendleton	.05
10	Rob Dibble	.05
WILD CARDS/JOKERS		
---	Bobby Bonilla (Joker)	.05
---	Danny Tartabull	.05
---	Wade Boggs (Wild Card)	.25
---	Will Clark (Wild Card)	.20

1992 U.S. Playing Card Aces

This 56-card boxed set features 13 top players in each of four major statistical categories, ranked by performance. Hearts feature RBI leaders, Clubs depict home run hitters, batting average leaders are featured on Diamonds and Spades have pitchers with lowest ERAs. Card fronts feature full-bleed color photos, with the playing card suit and rank overprinted in opposing corners. A team logo is in the lower-left, along with a black box containing the player's name and position in gold. Backs have a red, white and gold "Major League Baseball 1992 Aces" against a black background. The 2-1/2" x 3-1/2" cards have rounded corners.

		MT
Complete Set (56):		5.00
Common Player:		.05
HEARTS		
J	Will Clark	.25
Q	Howard Johnson	.05
K	Jose Canseco	.35
A	Cecil Fielder	.05
2	Juan Gonzalez	.50
3	Andre Dawson	.10
4	Ron Gant	.05
5	Fred McGriff	.10
6	Joe Carter	.05
7	Frank Thomas	.60
8	Cal Ripkin (Ripken)	.75
9	Ruben Sierra	.05
10	Barry Bonds	.50
CLUBS		
J	Cal Ripkin (Ripken)	.75
Q	Howard Johnson	.05
K	Cecil Fielder	.05
A	Jose Canseco	.25
2	Chili Davis	.05
3	Mickey Tettleton	.05
4	Danny Tartabull	.05
5	Fred McGriff	.10
6	Andre Dawson	.10
7	Frank Thomas	.60
8	Ron Gant	.05
9	Cal Ripkin (Ripken)	.75
10	Matt Williams	.10
DIAMONDS		
J	Ken Griffey, Jr.	1.00
Q	Willie Randolph	.05
K	Wade Boggs	.25
A	Julio Franco	.05
2	Danny Tartabull	.05
3	Tony Gwynn	.50
4	Frank Thomas	.60
5	Hal Morris	.05
6	Kirby Puckett	.45
7	Terry Pendleton	.05
8	Rafael Palmeiro	.20
9	Cal Ripkin (Ripken)	.75
10	Paul Molitor	.35
SPADES		
J	Tim Belcher	.05
Q	Tom Glavine	.10
K	Jose Rijo	.05
A	Dennis Martinez	.05
2	Mike Moore	.05
3	Nolan Ryan	.75
4	Jim Abbott	.05
5	Bill Wegman	.05
6	Mike Morgan	.05
7	Jose DeLeon	.05
8	Pete Harnisch	.05
9	Tom Candiotti	.05
10	Roger Clemens	.50
JOKERS		
---	Roger Clemens (Joker)	.35
---	Tom Glavine (Joker)	.10
---	Home Run Rummy Game Instructions	.05
---	Header Card	.05

1992 U.S. Playing Card All-Stars

Players from the 1992 All-Star Game are featured in this set of 56 playing cards. In playing card format of 2-1/2" x 3-1/2" with rounded corners, the cards have a photo on front with a team logo in the upper-right corner. Traditional playing card suits and values are in the upper-left and lower-right corners. Player names are in a yellow (American League) or red (National League) box beneath the photo. Backs have a large product logo on a white background with a dark blue-green border. Appropriate licensor and manufacturer logos appear at bottom. The set was sold in a box featuring miniature representations of some of the cards.

		MT
Complete Set (56):		5.00
Common Player:		.05
AC	Roberto Alomar	.25
2C	Joe Carter	.05
3C	Juan Guzman	.05
4C	Charles Nagy	.05
5C	Robin Ventura	.10
6C	Chuck Knoblauch	.20
7C	Ruben Sierra	.05
8C	Paul Molitor	.35
9C	Carlos Baerga	.05
10C	Edgar Martinez	.05
JC	Sandy Alomar Jr.	.10
QC	Mark McGwire	1.00
KC	Wade Boggs	.35
AS	Ken Griffey Jr.	1.00
2S	Ivan Rodriguez	.20
3S	Roberto Kelly	.05
4S	Brady Anderson	.05
5S	Travis Fryman	.05
6S	Jeff Montgomery	.05
7S	Jack McDowell	.05
8S	Rick Aguilera	.05
9S	Kevin Brown	.10
10S	Roger Clemens	.40
JS	Jose Canseco	.35
QS	Cal Ripken Jr.	.75
KS	Kirby Puckett	.45
AH	Andy Van Slyke	.05
2H	Greg Maddux	.50
3H	Larry Walker	.15
4H	Tom Pagnozzi	.05
5H	David Cone	.05
6H	Tony Fernandez	.05
7H	Will Clark	.15
8H	Gary Sheffield	.20
9H	Mike Sharperson	.05
10H	John Kruk	.05
JH	Ryne Sandberg	.40
QH	Ozzie Smith	.35
KH	Fred McGriff	.10
AD	Tony Gwynn	.45
2D	Bob Tewksbury	.05
3D	Ron Gant	.05
4D	Doug Jones	.05
5D	Craig Biggio	.10
6D	Bip Roberts	.05
7D	Norm Charlton	.05
8D	John Smoltz	.10
9D	Lee Smith	.05
10D	Tom Glavine	.10
JD	Benito Santiago	.05
QD	Terry Pendleton	.05
KD	Barry Bonds	.45
WILD	Dennis Eckersley	.05
JOKER	Mike Mussina, Mark Langston	.05
JOKER	Darren Daulton, Dennis Martinez	.05
---	Advertising card	.05

1992 U.S. Playing Card Team Sets

Besides two All-Star sets, the U.S. Playing Card Co. in 1992 issued playing card team sets for five teams. All were issued as 56-card boxed sets in a similar format. Cards are 2-1/2" x 3-1/2" with rounded corners. Fronts feature player photos with insets at the upper-left and lower-right corners to allow playing card suit designations and ratings. The player's name and position appear in a colored strip beneath the photo. Backs feature a large color team logo set again a gray background with either dark blue or red pinstriping and heavy vertical side bars. A silver-edged World Series premium version of the Braves and Twins sets were also issued; on these cards each rounded corner has a diagonal "nip".

(Team sets listed individually)

Misspellings of names are not uncommon on modern minor league cards. Unless a corrected version was issued, such errors have no effect on value.

1992 U.S. Playing Card Atlanta Braves

		MT
Complete Set (56):		4.00
Common Player:		.05
HEARTS		
J	Dave Justice	.25
Q	Juan Berenguer	.05
K	Ron Gant	.10
A	Otis Nixon	.05
2	Deion Sanders	.25
3	Mike Stanton	.05
4	Sid Bream	.05
5	Armando Reynoso	.05
6	Brian Hunter	.05
7	Kent Mercker	.05
8	Lonnie Smith	.05
9	Jeff Treadway	.05
10	Tom Glavine	.10
CLUBS		
J	Pete Smith	.05
Q	Jeff Blauser	.05
K	Charlie Leibrandt	.05
A	Terry Pendleton	.05
2	Mark Lemke	.05
3	Armadno Reynoso	.05
4	Kent Mercker	.05
5	Marvin Freeman	.05
6	Rico Rossy	.05
7	Dave Justice	.25
8	Juan Berenguer	.05
9	Ron Gant	.10
10	Otis Nixon	.05
DIAMONDS		
J	Brian Hunter	.05
Q	Rafael Belliard	.05
K	Greg Olson	.05
A	Steve Avery	.05
2	Marvin Freeman	.05
3	Pete Smith	.05
4	Mike Heath	.05
5	Jeff Blauser	.05
6	Jim Clancy	.05
7	Rico Rossy	.05
8	John Smoltz	.15
9	Charlie Leibrandt	.05
10	Terry Pendleton	.05
SPADES		
J	John Smoltz	.15
Q	Lonnie Smith	.05
K	Jeff Treadway	.05
A	Tom Glavine	.10
2	Jim Clancy	.05
3	Deion Sanders	.25
4	Mark Lemke	.05
5	Mike Heath	.05
6	Mike Stanton	.05
7	Sid Bream	.05
8	Rafael Belliard	.05
9	Greg Olson	.05
10	Steve Avery	.05
JOKERS		
---	N.L. logo (Joker)	.05
---	N.L. logo (Joker)	.05
---	'92 Braves Home Schedule	.05
---	Atlanta Braves History	.05

1992 U.S. Playing Card World Series - Braves

		MT
Complete Set (56):		8.00
Common Player:		.10
AC	Charlie Leibrandt	.10
2C	Vinny Castilla	.15
3C	Alejandro Pena	.10
4C	Mark Lemke	.10
5C	Marvin Freeman	.10
6C	Dave Justice	.50
7C	Mike Stanton	.10
8C	Terry Pendleton	.10
9C	Jeff Treadway	.10
10C	Brian Hunter	.10
JC	Steve Avery	.10
QC	Jeff Blauser	.10
KC	Ron Gant	.15
AS	Terry Pendleton	.10
2S	Ryan Klesko	.50
3S	Jeff Treadway	.10
4S	Pete Smith	.10
5S	Ron Gant	.15
6S	Sid Bream	.10
7S	Deion Sanders	.50
8S	Tom Glavine	.20
9S	Kent Mercker	.10
10S	Lonnie Smith	.10
JS	Damon Berryhill	.10
QS	Marvin Freeman	.10
KS	John Smoltz	.15
AH	Dave Justice	.50
2H	Kent Mercker	.10
3H	Lonnie Smith	.10
4H	Greg Olson	.10
5H	Jeff Reardon	.10
6H	Steve Avery	.10
7H	Otis Nixon	.10
8H	Juan Berenguer	.10
9H	Greg Olson	.10
10H	Mike Bielecki	.10
JH	Mike Stanton	.10
QH	Deion Sanders	.50
KH	Pete Smith	.10
AD	Otis Nixon	.10
2D	Juan Berenguer	.10
3D	Francisco Cabrera	.10
4D	Damon Berryhill	.10
5D	Brian Hunter	.10
6D	Charlie Leibrandt	.10
7D	Jeff Blauser	.10
8D	John Smoltz	.15
9D	Alejandro Pena	.10
10D	Mark Lemke	.10
JD	Jeff Reardon	.10
QD	Sid Bream	.10
KD	Tom Glavine	.20
WILD	Mike Bielecki	.10
WILD	David Nied	.10
WILD	Mark Wohlers	.10
JOKER	Checklist	.10

Player names in *Italic* type indicate a rookie card.

1992 U.S. Playing Card Chicago Cubs

		MT
Complete Set (56):		4.50
Common Player:		.05
HEARTS		
J	Jerome Walton	.05
Q	Chico Walker	.05
K	Chuck McElroy	.05
A	Andre Dawson	.10
2	Dwight Smith	.05
3	Rick Wilkins	.05
4	Doug Dascenzo	.05
5	Bob Scanlan	.05
6	Chico Walker	.05
7	Paul Assenmacher	.05
8	Mark Grace	.35
9	Ryne Sandberg	.50
10	Danny Jackson	.05
CLUBS		
J	Hector Villanueva	.05
Q	Doug Dascenzo	.05
K	Shawon Dunston	.05
A	George Bell	.05
2	Greg Scott	.05
3	Jose Vizcaino	.05
4	Heathcliff Slocumb	.05
5	Danny Jackson	.05
6	Shawn Boskie	.05
7	Luis Salazar	.05
8	Chuck McElroy	.05
9	Andre Dawson	.10
10	Dave Smith	.05
DIAMONDS		
J	Frank Castillo	.05
Q	Les Lancaster	.05
K	Paul Assenmacher	.05
A	Greg Maddux	.75
2	Shawn Boskie	.05
3	Ced Landrum	.05
4	Gary Scott	.05
5	Ced Landrum	.05
6	Jose Vizcaino	.05
7	Mike Harkey	.05
8	Jerome Walton	.05
9	George Bell	.05
10	Frank Castillo	.05
SPADES		
J	Bob Scanlan	.05
Q	Luis Salazar	.05
K	Mark Grace	.35
A	Ryne Sandberg	.50
2	Frank Castillo	.05
3	Mike Harkey	.05
4	Dave Smith	.05
5	Les Lancaster	.05
6	Hector Villanueva	.05
7	Shawon Dunston	.05
8	Heathcliff Slocumb	.05
9	Greg Maddux	.75
10	Dwight Smith	.05
JOKERS		
---	N.L. logo (Joker)	.05
---	N.L. logo (Joker)	.05
---	'92 Cubs Home Schedule	.05
---	Chicago Cubs Team History	.05

1992 U.S. Playing Card Boston Red Sox

		MT
Complete Set (56):		4.50
Common Player:		.05
HEARTS		
J	Jack Clark	.05
Q	Jeff Gray	.05
K	Greg Harris	.05
A	Roger Clemens	.50
2	Matt Young	.05
3	John Marzano	.05
4	Dennis Lamp	.05
5	Danny Darwin	.05
6	Jeff Reardon	.05
7	Phil Plantier	.05
8	Tony Fossas	.05
9	Carlos Quintana	.05
10	Wade Boggs	.35
CLUBS		
J	Luis Rivera	.05
Q	John Marzano	.05
K	Jody Reed	.10
A	Mike Greenwell	.05
2	Danny Darwin	.05
3	Dan Petry	.05
4	Dana Kiecker	.05
5	Greg Harris	.05
6	Tony Pena	.05
7	Dan Petry	.05
8	Jeff Gray	.05
9	Jack Clark	.05
10	Roger Clemens	.50
DIAMONDS		
J	Tom Brunansky	.05
Q	Mo Vaughn	.40
K	Ellis Burks	.15
A	Joe Hesketh	.05
2	Steve Lyons	.05
3	Dana Kiecker	.05
4	Tony Fossas	.05
5	Matt Young	.05
6	Luis Rivera	.05
7	Tom Bolton	.05
8	Kevin Morton	.05
9	Jody Reed	.05
10	Mike Greenwell	.05
SPADES		
J	Tony Pena	.05
Q	Phil Plantier	.05
K	Carlos Quintana	.05
A	Wade Boggs	.35
2	Tom Bolton	.05
3	Mo Vaughn	.40
4	Kevin Morton	.05
5	Steve Lyons	.05
6	Tom Brunansky	.05
7	Dennis Lamp	.05
8	Joe Hesketh	.05
9	Ellis Burks	.15
10	Jeff Reardon	.05
JOKERS		
---	A.L. Logo (Joker)	.05
---	A.L. Logo (Joker)	.05
---	'92 Red Sox Home Schedule	.05
---	Boston Red Sox Team History	.05

1992 U.S. Playing Card Detroit Tigers

		MT
Complete Set (56):		4.50
Common Player:		.05
HEARTS		
J	Lloyd Moseby	.05
Q	Walt Terrell	.05
K	Mickey Tettleton	.05
A	Cecil Fielder	.10
2	Andy Allanson	.05
3	Dave Bergman	.05
4	Steve Searcy	.05
5	Dan Galeker	.05
6	Jerry Don Gleaton	.05
7	Paul Gibson	.05
8	Alan Trammell	.20
9	Frank Tanana	.05
10	John Cerutti	.05
CLUBS		
J	Rob Deer	.05
Q	Skeeter Barnes	.05
K	Pete Incaviglia	.05
A	Tony Phillips	.05
2	Dan Galeker	.05
3	Walt Terrell	.05
4	David Haas	.05
5	Pete Incaviglia	.05
6	Travis Fryman	.15
7	Scott Aldred	.05
8	Skeeter Barnes	.05
9	Mickey Tettleton	.05
10	Cecil Fielder	.10
DIAMONDS		
J	Milt Cuyler	.05
Q	Travis Fryman	.15
K	Lou Whitaker	.10
A	Bill Gullickson	.05
2	John Cerutti	.05
3	Steve Searcy	.05
4	David Haas	.05
5	Lloyd Moseby	.05

6	Scott Livingstone	.05
7	John Shelby	.05
8	Mike Henneman	.05
9	Dave Bergman	.05
10	Tony Phillips	.05
SPADES		
J	Alan Trammell	.20
Q	Jerry Don Gleaton	.05
K	Mike Henneman	.05
A	Frank Tanana	.05
2	Scott Aldred	.05
3	Scott Livingstone	.05
4	John Shelby	.05
5	Rob Deer	.05
6	Milt Cuyler	.05
7	Andy Allanson	.05
8	Paul Gibson	.05
9	Lou Whitaker	.10
10	Bill Gullickson	.05
JOKERS		
---	A.L. Logo (Joker)	.05
---	A.L. Logo (Joker)	.05
---	'92 Tigers Home Schedule	.05
---	Detroit Tigers team history	.05

1992 U.S. Playing Card Minnesota Twins

		MT
Complete Set (56):		4.00
Common Player:		.05
HEARTS		
J	Scott Leius	.05
Q	Rick Aguilera	.05
K	Jack Morris	.05
A	Kirby Puckett	.65
2	Junior Ortiz	.05
3	Paul Abbott	.05
4	Steve Bedrosian	.05
5	Pedro Munoz	.05
6	Mike Pagliarulo	.05
7	Greg Gagne	.05
8	Chuck Knoblauch	.25
9	Kevin Tapani	.05
10	Scott Erickson	.10
CLUBS		
J	Carl Willis	.05
Q	Dan Gladden	.05
K	Kent Hrbek	.15
A	Shane Mack	.05
2	Allan Anderson	.05
3	Al Newman	.05
4	Junior Ortiz	.05
5	Mike Pagliarulo	.05
6	Terry Leach	.05
7	Scott Leius	.05
8	Rick Aguilera	.05
9	Jack Morris	.05
10	Kirby Puckett	.65
DIAMONDS		
J	Gene Larkin	.05
Q	Randy Bush	.05
K	Chili Davis	.10
A	Brian Harper	.05
2	Al Newman	.05
3	Allan Anderson	.05
4	David West	.05
5	Terry Leach	.05
6	Mark Guthrie	.05
7	Carl Willis	.05
8	Dan Gladden	.05
9	Kent Hrbek	.15
10	Shane Mack	.05
SPADES		
J	Greg Gagne	.05
Q	Chuck Knoblauch	.25
K	Kevin Tapani	.05
A	Scott Erickson	.10
2	Paul Abbott	.05
3	David West	.05
4	Steve Bedrosian	.05
5	Mark Guthrie	.05
6	Pedro Munoz	.05
7	Gene Larkin	.05
8	Randy Bush	.05
9	Chili Davis	.10
10	Brian Harper	.05
JOKERS		
---	A.L. Logo (Joker)	.05
---	A.L. Logo (Joker)	.05
---	'92 Twins Home Schedule	.05
----	Minnesota Twins team history	.05

1993 U.S. Playing Card Aces

Major league superstars with the top 1992 statistical performance in four major categories are featured in this set of playing cards. Spades feature the 13 lowest ERAs; Hearts depict the baker's dozen stolen base leaders; the 13 players with highest home run totals and batting average are featured on clubs and diamonds, respectively. The 2-1/2" x 3-1/2" cards have rounded corners and traditional trading card suits and values in the upper-left and lower-right corners. Borderless color player photos are featured on front, with color team logos at lower-left. Player names and positions are printed in a black box at bottom. Backs have a red background with a large product logo and smaller licensor and manufacturer logos at bottom. The box in which the cards were sold is enhanced with gold foil and features miniature representations of some of the cards.

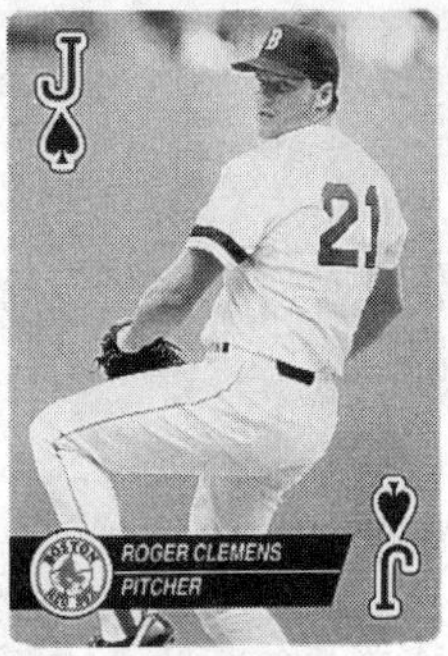

		MT
Complete Set (56):		5.00
Common Player:		.05
AC	Juan Gonzalez	.50
2C	Dave Hollins	.05
3C	Darren Daulton	.05
4C	Ken Griffey Jr.	1.00
5C	Rob Deer	.05
6C	Mickey Tettleton	.05
7C	Gary Sheffield	.25
8C	Joe Carter	.05
9C	Albert Belle	.25
10C	Barry Bonds	.45
JC	Fred McGriff	.10
QC	Cecil Fielder	.05
KC	Mark McGwire	1.00
AS	Bill Swift	.05
2S	Tom Glavine	.10
3S	Sid Fernandez	.05
4S	Greg Swindell	.05
5S	Juan Guzman	.05
6S	Jose Rijo	.05
7S	Mike Morgan	.05
8S	Mike Mussina	.10
9S	Dennis Martinez	.05
10S	Kevin Appier	.05
JS	Roger Clemens	.35
QS	Curt Schilling	.10
KS	Greg Maddux	.50
AH	Marquis Grissom	.05
2H	Chad Curtis	.05
3H	Ozzie Smith	.25
4H	Bip Roberts	.05
5H	Steve Finley	.05
6H	Tim Raines	.05
7H	Delino DeShields	.05
8H	Rickey Henderson	.25
9H	Roberto Alomar	.20
10H	Luis Polonia	.05
JH	Brady Anderson	.10
QH	Pat Listach	.05
KH	Kenny Lofton	.15
AD	Edgar Martinez	.05
2D	Roberto Alomar	.20
3D	Terry Pendleton	.05
4D	Carlos Baerga	.05
5D	Shane Mack	.05
6D	Tony Gwynn	.45
7D	Paul Molitor	.25
8D	Frank Thomas	.65
9D	Bip Roberts	.05
10D	John Kruk	.05
JD	Andy Van Slyke	.05
QD	Kirby Puckett	.45
KD	Gary Sheffield	.25
WILD	Cal Ripken Jr.	.75
JOKER	National League logo	.05
JOKER	American League logo	.05
---	Advertising card	.05

1993 U.S. Playing Card Team Sets

For a second year the leading U.S. manufacturer of playing cards produced several team sets depicting ballplayers. Each was sold as a 56-card set in standard 2-1/2" x 3-1/2" round-corner playing card format in a colorful flip-top box. Backs of each team set carry a team logo. Fronts have portrait or action photo and playing card suits and values. Most players are represented twice in each team set in different photos.

(Team sets listed individually)

1993 U.S. Playing Card Florida Marlins

		MT
Complete Set (56):		4.00
Common Player:		.05
AC	Walt Weiss	.05
2C	Dave Magadan	.05
3C	Chris Carpenter	.05
4C	Dave Magadan	.05
5C	Bob McClure	.05
6C	Junior Felix	.05
7C	Walt Weiss	.05
8C	Steve Decker	.05
9C	Jeff Conine	.20
10C	Bryan Harvey	.05
JC	Orestes Destrade	.05
QC	Chris Hammond	.05
KC	Monty Fariss	.05
AS	Alex Arias	.05
2S	Benito Santiago	.05
3S	Ryan Bowen	.05
4S	Steve Decker	.05
5S	Jeff Conine	.20
6S	Bret Barberie	.05
7S	Orestes Destrade	.05
8S	Greg Briley	.05
9S	Charlie Hough	.05
10S	Bob Natal	.05
JS	Jack Armstrong	.05
QS	Junior Felix	.05
KS	Richie Lewis	.05
AH	Benito Santiago	.05
2H	Walt Weiss	.05
3H	Monty Fariss	.05
4H	Chris Hammond	.05
5H	Joe Klink	.05
6H	Chuck Carr	.05
7H	Alex Arias	.05
8H	Charlie Hough	.05
9H	Junior Felix	.05
10H	Jim Corsi	.05
JH	Jeff Conine	.20
QH	Trevor Hoffman	.25
KH	Rich Renteria	.05
AD	Dave Magadan	.05
2D	Jack Armstrong	.05
3D	Bryan Harvey	.05
4D	Richie Lewis	.05
5D	Scott Pose	.05
6D	Rich Renteria	.05
7D	Trevor Hoffman	.25
8D	Jim Corsi	.05
9D	Ryan Bowen	.05
10D	Orestes Destrade	.05
JD	Bret Barberie	.05
QD	Chuck Carr	.05
KD	Chris Carpenter	.05
JOKER	N.L. logo	.05
JOKER	N.L. logo	.05
---	Opening Day roster	.05
---	Marlins schedule	.05

1993 U.S. Playing Card Cincinnati Reds

		MT
Complete Set (56):		3.00
Common Player:		.05
AC	Tim Belcher	.05
2C	Jacob Brumfield	.05
3C	Rob Dibble	.05
4C	Jose Rijo	.05
5C	Dan Wilson	.05
6C	Cecil Espy	.05
7C	Tom Browning	.05
8C	Steve Foster	.05
9C	Jacob Brumfield	.05
10C	Jeff Branson	.05
JC	Greg Cadaret	.05
QC	Hal Morris	.05
KC	Joe Oliver	.05
AS	Bip Roberts	.05
2S	Cesar Hernandez	.05
3S	Chris Hammond	.05
4S	Scott Ruskin	.05
5S	John Smiley	.05
6S	Roberto Kelly	.05
7S	Barry Larkin	.25
8S	Gary Varsho	.05
9S	Hal Morris	.05
10S	Dwayne Henry	.05
JS	Tommy Gregg	.05
QS	Kevin Mitchell	.05
KS	Rob Dibble	.05
AH	Barry Larkin	.25
2H	Willie Greene	.10
3H	Steve Foster	.05
4H	Greg Cadaret	.05
5H	Chris Sabo	.05
6H	Joe Oliver	.05
7H	Milton Hill	.05
8H	Tim Belcher	.05
9H	Scott Ruskin	.05
10H	Cecil Espy	.05
JH	Roberto Kelly	.05
QH	Tom Browning	.05
KH	Reggie Sanders	.15
AD	Jose Rijo	.05
2D	Dwayne Henry	.05
3D	Jeff Branson	.05
4D	Milton Hill	.05
5D	Tim Costo	.05
6D	Bip Roberts	.05
7D	Kevin Mitchell	.05
8D	Tim Pugh	.05
9D	Reggie Sanders	.15
10D	Chris Hammond	.05
JD	Gary Varsho	.05
QD	John Smiley	.05
KD	Chris Sabo	.05
WILD	Tony Perez	.40
JOKER	Riverfront Stadium	.05
JOKER	Reds schedule	.05
JOKER	Checklist	.05

1993 U.S. Playing Card Colorado Rockies

		MT
Complete Set (56):		4.00
Common Player:		.05
AC	Jim Tatum	.05
2C	Charlie Hayes	.05
3C	Dale Murphy	.50
4C	Scott Aldred	.05
5C	Braulio Castillo	.05
6C	Danny Sheaffer	.05
7C	Jerald Clark	.05
8C	Willie Blair	.05
9C	Daryl Boston	.05
10C	Andy Ashby	.05
JC	Butch Henry	.05
QC	Alex Cole	.05
KC	Vinny Castilla	.15
AS	David Nied	.05
2S	Andres Galarraga	.25
3S	Gary Wayne	.05
4S	Freddie Benavides	.05
5S	Butch Henry	.05
6S	Gerald Young	.05
7S	Jeff Parrett	.05
8S	Braulio Castillo	.05
9S	Darren Holmes	.05
10S	Dale Murphy	.50
JS	Eric Young	.10
QS	Bruce Ruffin	.05
KS	Joe Girardi	.05
AH	Charlie Hayes	.05
2H	Jim Tatum	.05
3H	Andy Ashby	.05
4H	Vinny Castilla	.15
5H	Steve Reed	.05
6H	Daryl Boston	.05
7H	Alex Cole	.05
8H	Bryn Smith	.05
9H	Danny Sheaffer	.05
10H	Willie Blair	.05
JH	Dante Bichette	.25
QH	Jerald Clark	.05
DH	Scott Aldred	.05
AD	Andres Galarraga	.25
2D	David Nied	.05
3D	Dante Bichette	.25
4D	Joe Girardi	.05
5D	Bryn Smith	.05
6D	Darren Holmes	.05
7D	Bruce Ruffin	.05
8D	Eric Young	.10
9D	Gerald Young	.05
10D	Gary Wayne	.05
JD	Steve Reed	.05
QD	Jeff Parrett	.05
KD	Freddie Benavides	.05

1993 U.S. Playing Card 1992 Rookies

Top rookies of the 1992 season are featured in full-color on the fronts of these playing cards. Player name and position are printed in white in a green stripe beneath the photo. A team logo is in the upper-right corner. Backs are printed in dark green with gold pinstripes and a large gold, red and purple logo.

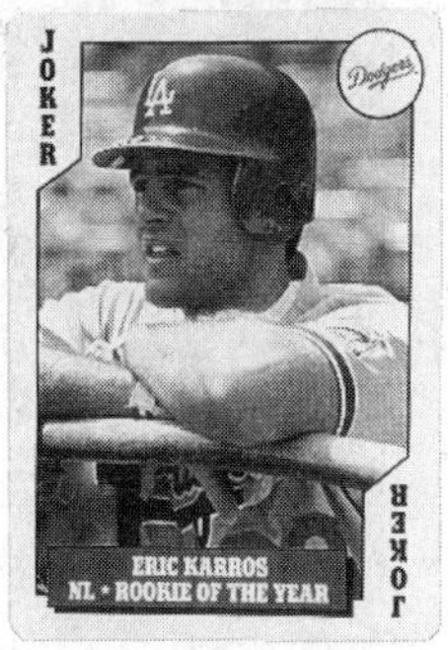

		MT
Complete Boxed Set (56):		4.00
Common Player:		.05
AC	Kenny Lofton	.45
2C	Eric Fox	.05
3C	Mark Wohlers	.05
4C	John Patterson	.05
5C	Eric Young	.15
6C	Arthur Rhodes	.05
7C	Jeff Frye	.05
8C	Scott Servais	.05
9C	Ruben Amaro, Jr.	.05
10C	Reggie Sanders	.15
JC	Alan Mills	.05
QC	Bob Zupcic	.05
KC	Cal Eldred	.05
AS	Eric Karros	.25
2S	Butch Henry	.05
3S	Wil Cordero	.05
4S	Pedro Astacio	.05
5S	Derek Bell	.10
6S	David Nied	.05
7S	Jeff Kent	.10
8S	David Haas	.05
9S	Ed Taubensee	.05
10S	Royce Clayton	.05
JS	Moises Alou	.20
QS	Rusty Meacham	.05
KS	Chad Curtis	.05
AH	Pat Listach	.05
2H	Pat Mahomes	.05
3H	Greg Colbrunn	.05
4H	Dan Walters	.05
5H	John Vander Wal	.05
6H	Jeff Branson	.05
7H	Monty Fariss	.05
8H	Rey Sanchez	.05
9H	Robert Wickman	.05
10H	Derrick May	.05
JH	Donovan Osborne	.05
QH	Scott Livingstone	.05
KH	Gary DiSarcina	.05
AD	Dave Fleming	.05
2D	Reggie Jefferson	.05
3D	Anthony Young	.05
4D	Kevin Koslofski	.05
5D	Brian Williams	.05
6D	Brian Jordan	.20
7D	John Doherty	.05
8D	Lenny Webster	.05
9D	Roberto Hernandez	.05
10D	Frank Seminara	.05
JD	Scott Cooper	.05
QD	Andy Stankiewicz	.05
KD	Tim Wakefield	.05
JOKER	Eric Karros (N.L. ROY)	.20
JOKER	Pat Listach (A.L. ROY)	.05
---	Rookie qualification rules	.05
---	Checklist	.05

1994 U.S. Playing Card 1993 Rookies

The top rookies from the 1993 season are featured on this deck of playing cards; several players appear on more than one card in the deck. Fronts have color player photos at center, with traditional playing card suits and values in the upper-left and lower-right borders. A team logo is at upper-right. The player's name and position appear in white in a purple strip at lower-left. Backs are purple with a large product logo at top-center and licensor/licensee logos at bottom. Cards measure 2-1/2" x 3-1/2" with rounded corners and were sold in a specially decorated cardboard box.

		MT
Complete Set (56):		5.00
Common Player:		.05
AC	Mike Piazza	.65
2C	Vinny Castilla	.15
3C	Wil Cordero	.05
4C	Ryan Thompson	.05
5C	Craig Paquette	.05
6C	Carlos Garcia	.05
7C	Jeff Conine	.15
8C	Bret Boone	.10
9C	Jeromy Burnitz	.05
10C	J.T. Snow	.15
JC	Al Martin	.05
QC	Troy Neel	.05
KC	Tim Salmon	.25
AS	Greg McMichael	.05
2S	Paul Quantrill	.05
3S	Steve Reed	.05
4S	Trevor Hoffman	.10
5S	Tim Pugh	.05
6S	Angel Miranda	.05
7S	Steve Cooke	.05
8S	Aaron Sele	.10
9S	Kirk Rueter	.05
10S	Rene Arocha	.05
JS	Pedro J. Martinez	.20
QS	Armadno Reynoso	.05
KS	Jason Bere	.05
AH	Kevin Stocker	.05
2H	Alex Arias	.05
3H	Carlos Garcia	.05
4H	Erik Pappas	.05
5H	Al Martin	.05
6H	Tim Salmon	.25
7H	Mike Lansing	.10
8H	Rich Amaral	.05
9H	Brent Gates	.05
10H	David Hulse	.05
JH	Troy Neel	.05
QH	Jeff Conine	.15
KH	Mike Piazza	.65
AD	Chuck Carr	.05
2D	Jeff McNeeley	.05
3D	Joe Kmak	.05
4D	Phil Hiatt	.05
5D	Brent Gates	.05
6D	Wil Cordero	.05
7D	Al Martin	.05
8D	Wayne Kirby	.05
9D	Lou Frazier	.05
10D	Carlos Garcia	.05
JD	Rich Amaral	.05
QD	Mike Lansing	.10
KD	David Hulse	.05
Joker	Tim Salmon (Rookie of the Year)	.20
Joker	Mike Piazza (Rookie of the Year)	.50
--	Checklist	.05
--	Rookie qualification rules	.05

1994 U.S. Playing Card Aces

Statistical leaders from the 1993 season were featured in this deck of playing cards. Pitchers with the lowest ERAs are shown on the spades; stolen base leaders are featured on the hearts; home run hitters are depicted on the clubs, and diamonds host the batting average leaders. Cards are 2-1/2" x 3-1/2" with rounded corners. Fronts have full-bleed photos with the suit and value of the playing card the upper-left and lower-right corners. The player's name, position and team logo are at lower-left. Backs are printed in dark blue with vertical silver stripes at each side and a red, white and blue "Baseball Aces" logo at top. Licensing logos appear at the bottom. Besides the 52 player cards in the boxed set, there is a checklist card, A.L. and N.L. logo cards and a U.S. Playing Card Co. advertising card.

		MT
Complete Set (56):		5.00
Common Player:		.05
AC	Barry Bonds	.50
2C	Phil Plantier	.05
3C	Bobby Bonilla	.05
4C	Mike Piazza	.60
5C	Ron Gant	.05
6C	Rafael Palmeiro	.20
7C	Fred McGriff	.10
8C	Matt Williams	.10
9C	Albert Belle	.25
10C	Dave Justice	.10
JC	Frank Thomas	.50
QC	Ken Griffey Jr.	.75
KC	Juan Gonzalez	.50
AS	Greg Maddux	.60
2S	Tom Candiotti	.05
3S	Jimmy Key	.05
4S	Jack McDowell	.05
5S	John Burkett	.05
6S	Tom Glavine	.10
7S	Pete Harnisch	.05
8S	Wilson Alvarez	.05
9S	Steve Avery	.05
10S	Bill Swift	.05
JS	Mark Portugal	.05
QS	Kevin Appier	.05
KS	Jose Rijo	.05
AH	Kenny Lofton	.10
2H	Brett Butler	.05
3H	Eric Young	.10
4H	Delino DeShields	.05
5H	Darren Lewis	.05
6H	Gregg Jefferies	.05
7H	Otis Nixon	.05
8H	Chad Curtis	.05
9H	Rickey Henderson	.10
10H	Marquis Grissom	.05
JH	Luis Polonia	.05
QH	Roberto Alomar	.15
KH	Chuck Carr	.05
AD	Andres Galarraga	.10
2D	John Kruk	.05
3D	Frank Thomas	.50
4D	Mike Piazza	.60
5D	Jeff Bagwell	.45
6D	Carlos Baerga	.05
7D	Mark Grace	.20
8D	Kenny Lofton	.10
9D	Roberto Alomar	.15
10D	Paul Molitor	.25
JD	Barry Bonds	.50
QD	Gregg Jefferies	.05
KD	John Olerud	.10
Joker	National League logo	.05
Joker	American League logo	.05
---	Checklist	.05
---	Advertising card	.05

1994 U.S. Playing Card Atlanta Braves

The most popular Braves are pictured on up to three of the cards in this deck. In 2-1/2" x 3-1/2" round-cornered format, the large color photos on the card fronts have their upper-left and lower-right corners clipped to display traditional playing card suits and values. The player name and position are printed in black in a gold strip below the photo. Backs have the Braves logo on a dark blue background with red stripes on the left and right edges. Brand and licensor logos are at bottom. The cards were sold in a colorful box.

		MT
Complete Set (56):		5.00
Common Player:		.05
AC	Ron Gant	.05
2C	Chipper Jones	.75
3C	Terry Pendleton	.05
4C	Mark Wohlers	.05
5C	Pedro Borbon	.05
6C	Steve Avery	.05
7C	Deion Sanders	.25
8C	Dave Justice	.25
9C	Dave Gallagher	.05
10C	Rafael Belliard	.05
JC	Greg McMichael	.05
QC	John Smoltz	.10
KC	Fred McGriff	.20
AS	Jeff Blauser	.05
2S	Mike Stanton	.05
3S	Ryan Klesko	.30
4S	Mike Potts	.05
5S	Charlie O'Brien	.05
6S	Steve Bedrosian	.05
7S	Javier Lopez	.20
8S	Greg Maddux	.60
9S	Deion Sanders	.25
10S	Ramon Caraballo	.05
JS	Kent Mercker	.05
QS	Mark Wohlers	.05
KS	Tom Glavine	.10
AH	Dave Justice	.25
2H	Mark Lemke	.05
3H	Javier Lopez	.20
4H	Rafael Belliard	.05
5H	Bill Pecota	.05
6H	Tom Glavine	.10
7H	Milt Hill	.05
8H	Jeff Blauser	.05
9H	Ryan Klesko	.30
10H	Terry Pendleton	.05
JH	Mike Stanton	.05
QH	Steve Avery	.05
KH	Deion Sanders	.25
AD	Greg Maddux	.60
2D	Ron Gant	.05
3D	Kent Mercker	.05
4D	Greg McMichael	.05
5D	Tony Tarasco	.05
6D	John Smoltz	.10
7D	Fred McGriff	.20
8D	Ron Gant	.05
9D	Mike Kelly	.05
10D	Steve Bedrosian	.05
JD	Bill Pecota	.05
QD	Mark Lemke	.05
KD	Terry Pendleton	.05
Joker	Atlanta Braves logo	.05
Joker	National League logo	.05
---	Checklist	.05
---	'94 Braves Home Schedule	.05

1994 U.S. Playing Card S.F. Giants

Veterans and rookies on the roster of the '94 Giants are featured in this deck of playing cards; the most popular players appear on up to three cards each. In standard 2-1/2" x 3-1/2" round-cornered format, the large color photos have their top-left and bottom-right corners clipped to display traditional playing card suits and values. The player's name and position are printed in white on an orange strip beneath the photo. Backs have a large Giants logo on a gray pinstriped background. Company and licensor logos are at bottom. The cards were sold in a decorative box.

		MT
Complete Set (56):		4.00
Common Player:		.05
AC	Matt Williams	.25
2C	John Patterson	.05
3C	Steve Hosey	.05
4C	Jeff Reed	.05
5C	Mike Jackson	.05
6C	Kirt Manwaring	.05
7C	Royce Clayton	.05
8C	Robby Thompson	.05
9C	Luis Mercedes	.05
10C	Mike Benjamin	.05
JC	Mark Carreon	.05
QC	Dave Burba	.05
KC	John Burkett	.10
AS	Barry Bonds	.75
2S	Salomon Torres	.05
3S	Kevin Rogers	.05
4S	Todd Benzinger	.05
5S	Dave Martinez	.05
6S	Darren Lewis	.05
7S	Willie McGee	.10
8S	Bill Swift	.05
9S	Paul Faries	.05
10S	Trevor Wilson	.05
JS	Steve Scarsone	.05
QS	Bryan Hickerson	.05
KS	Rod Beck	.10
AH	Robby Thompson	.05
2H	Paul Faries	.05
3H	Trevor Wilson	.05
4H	Steve Scarsone	.05
5H	Bryan Hickerson	.05
6H	Rod Beck	.10
7H	Barry Bonds	.75
8H	John Patterson	.05
9H	J.R. Phillips	.05
10H	Jeff Reed	.05
JH	Mike Jackson	.05
QH	Kirt Manwaring	.05
KH	Royce Clayton	.05
AD	Bill Swift	.05
2D	Luis Mercedes	.05
3D	Mike Benjamin	.05
4D	Mark Carreon	.05
5D	Dave Burba	.05
6D	John Burkett	.05
7D	Matt Williams	.25
8D	Salomon Torres	.05
9D	Kevin Rogers	.05
10D	Todd Benzinger	.05
JD	Dave Martinez	.05
QD	Darren Lewis	.05
KD	Willie McGee	.05
JOKER	Giants home schedule	.05
JOKER	Checklist	.05
---	N.L. logo	.05
---	Giants logo	.05

1994 U.S. Playing Card Baltimore Orioles

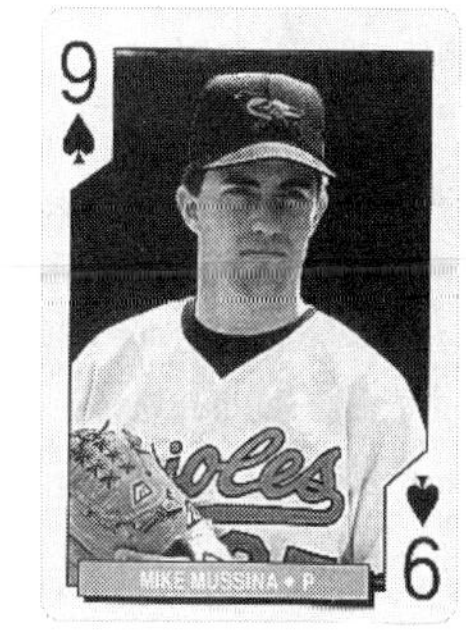

The 1994 Baltimore Orioles are featured in this deck of playing cards. Color photos of the players have clipped corners to display traditional playing card suits and values in the upper-left and lower-right corners. Beneath the photo is an orange strip with the player's name and position in white. Backs have a large Orioles logo on a pinstriped background. Company and licensor logos are at the bottom. Cards measure 2-1/2" x 3-1/2" with rounded corners. The set was sold in a colorful cardboard box.

		MT
Complete Set (56):		5.00
Common Player:		.05
AC	Chris Hoiles	.05
2C	Mike Cook	.05
3C	Paul Carey	.05
4C	Jeff Tackett	.05
5C	Arthur Rhodes	.05
6C	Damon Buford	.05
7C	David Segui	.05
8C	Ben McDonald	.05
9C	Cal Ripken Jr.	1.00
10C	Brad Pennington	.05
JC	Jack Voigt	.05
QC	Jeffrey Hammonds	.25
KC	Rafael Palmeiro	.40
AS	Mark McLemore	.05
2S	Manny Alexander	.05
3S	Kevin McGehee	.05
4S	Jim Poole	.05
5S	Leo Gomez	.05
6S	Tim Hulett	.05
7S	Mike Devereaux	.05
8S	Brady Anderson	.25
9S	Mike Mussina	.25
10S	Sherman Obando	.05
JS	Alan Mills	.05
QS	Jamie Moyer	.05
KS	Harold Baines	.10
AH	Cal Ripken Jr.	1.00
2H	Harold Baines	.10
3H	John O'Donoghue	.05
4H	Sid Fernandez	.05
5H	Alan Mills	.05
6H	Jamie Moyer	.05
7H	Harold Baines	.10
8H	Mark McLemore	.05
9H	Jeff Tackett	.05
10H	Arthur Rhodes	.05
JH	Damon Buford	.05
QH	David Segui	.05
KH	Ben McDonald	.05
AD	Mike Mussina	.25
2D	Mike Oquist	.05
3D	Brad Pennington	.05
4D	Jeffrey Hammonds	.25
5D	Jack Voigt	.05
6D	Chris Sabo	.05
7D	Rafael Palmeiro	.25
8D	Chris Hoiles	.05
9D	Jim Poole	.05
10D	Leo Gomez	.05
JD	Tim Hulett	.05
QD	Mike Devereaux	.05
KD	Brady Anderson	.25
Joker	Baltimore Orioles logo	.05
Joker	American League logo	.05
---	Checklist	.05
---	'94 Orioles Home Schedule	.05

1994 U.S. Playing Card Philadelphia Phillies

Veterans and rookies on the roster of the '94 Phils are featured in this deck of playing cards; the most popular players appear on up to three cards each. In standard 2-1/2" x 3-1/2" round-cornered format, the large color photos have their top-left and bottom-right corners clipped to display traditional playing card suits and values. The player's name and position are printed in black on a red strip beneath the photo. Backs have a large Phillies logo on a gray pin-striped background. Company and licensor logos are at bottom. The cards were sold in a decorative box.

		MT
Complete Set (56):		3.00
Common Player:		.05
AC	Pete Incaviglia	.05
2C	Lenny Dykstra	.10
3C	Milt Thompson	.05
4C	Mickey Morandini	.05
5C	Kevin Stocker	.05
6C	Terry Mulholland	.05
7C	Curt Schilling	.15
8C	Darren Daulton	.10
9C	Terry Mulholland	.05
10C	Roger Mason	.05
JC	Mariano Duncan	.05
QC	Ben Rivera	.05
KC	John Kruk	.10
AS	Dave Hollins	.15
2S	Danny Jackson	.05
3S	Todd Pratt	.05
4S	David West	.05
5S	Lenny Dykstra	.10
6S	Wes Chamberlain	.05
7S	Tommy Greene	.05
8S	Tony Longmire	.10
9S	Brad Brink	.05
10S	Ricky Jordan	.05
JS	Kim Batiste	.05
QS	Tyler Green	.05
KS	Jim Eisenreich	.05
AH	Lenny Dykstra	.10
2H	Tony Longmire	.10
3H	Kim Batiste	.05
4H	Pete Incaviglia	.05
5H	Ben Rivera	.05
6H	Ricky Jordan	.05
7H	Dave Hollins	.10
8H	Kevin Foster	.05
9H	Kevin Stocker	.05
10H	Mike Williams	.05
JH	Milt Thompson	.05
QH	Curt Schilling	.10
KH	Darren Daulton	.10
AD	Terry Mulholland	.10
2D	Brad Brink	.05
3D	Roger Mason	.05
4D	Mariano Duncan	.05
5D	Danny Jackson	.05
6D	Jim Eisenreich	.05
7D	John Kruk	.10
8D	David West	.05
9D	Todd Pratt	.05
10D	Wes Chamberlain	.05
JD	Jim Eisenreich	.05
QD	Mickey Morandini	.05
KD	Tommy Greene	.05
Joker	Phillies logo	.05
Joker	National League logo	.05
---	Checklist	.05
---	'94 Phillies Home Schedule	.05

1995 U.S. Playing Card Aces

Baseball's 1994 statistical leaders in home runs (clubs), ERA (spades), stolen bases (hearts) and batting average (diamonds) are featured in this deck of playing cards. Measuring a standard 2-1/2" x 3-1/2" with rounded corners, cards have borderless action photos on front with traditional playing card suits and denominations in the upper-left and lower-right corners. The player's color team logo, name and position appear in the lower-left corner. Backs are silver with black side stripes and a red-and-black Aces logo at center. Sets were sold in a colorful cardboard box.

		MT
Complete Set (56):		5.00
Common Player:		.05
AC	Matt Williams	.10
2C	Joe Carter	.05
3C	Dante Bichette	.05
4C	Cecil Fielder	.05
5C	Kevin Mitchell	.05
6C	Andres Galarraga	.10
7C	Jose Canseco	.35
8C	Fred McGriff	.10
9C	Albert Belle	.25
10C	Barry Bonds	.50
JC	Frank Thomas	.60
QC	Jeff Bagwell	.45
KC	Ken Griffey Jr.	1.00
AS	Greg Maddux	.65
2S	Steve Trachsel	.05
3S	Randy Johnson	.10
4S	Bobby Jones	.05
5S	Jose Rijo	.05
6S	Mike Mussina	.10
7S	Shane Reynolds	.05
8S	Jeff Fassero	.05
9S	David Cone	.05
10S	Roger Clemens	.45
JS	Doug Drabek	.05
QS	Bret Saberhagen	.05
KS	Steve Ontiveros	.05
AH	Kenny Lofton	.10
2H	Brian McRae	.05
3H	Alex Cole	.05
4H	Barry Bonds	.50
5H	Darren Lewis	.05
6H	Brady Anderson	.05
7H	Chuck Carr	.05
8H	Chuck Knoblauch	.05
9H	Marquis Grissom	.05
10H	Deion Sanders	.10
JH	Craig Biggio	.05
QH	Otis Nixon	.05
KH	Vince Coleman	.05
AD	Tony Gwynn	.50
2D	Gregg Jefferies	.05
3D	Kevin Mitchell	.05
4D	Will Clark	.20
5D	Hal Morris	.05
6D	Moises Alou	.05
7D	Paul Molitor	.25
8D	Wade Boggs	.25
9D	Kenny Lofton	.10
10D	Frank Thomas	.60
JD	Albert Belle	.25
QD	Paul O'Neill	.05
KD	Jeff Bagwell	.45
Joker	American League logo	.05
Joker	National League logo	.05
---	Checklist	.05
---	MicroMini Team card order form	.05

1989 U.S. Postal Service Legends

In 1989 the U.S. Postal Service offered to collectors a Legends set for $7.95. The set consists of a heavily illustrated 24-page "Baseball Scrapbook and Stamp Album," a set of the four U.S. postage stamps which had been issued to that time honoring individual players, and a set of cards matching the stamps. The 2-1/2" x 3-1/2" cards have color reproductions of the stamps on front, bordered in white with red and blue striping. Backs are in red, black and orange and feature player data and major league stats.

		MT
Complete Set, album, stamps, cards:		24.00
Card Set (4):		15.00
3	Babe Ruth	4.00
4	Lou Gehrig	3.00
21	Roberto Clemente	5.00
42	Jackie Robinson	3.00

1986 Utah Sports Card Wally Joyner

Officially titled "The Wonderful World of Wally Joyner at BYU," this collectors issue spotlighted the promising young slugger in his first major league season. The 14 cards in the set depict Joyner in color portrait and action photos with a red frame around. Card #1 has a "WALLY WORLD" sign at top. Backs are in black-and-white with personal data, highlights of his college career at BYU, or stats. The photo on card #3 was also produced as an 11" x 17" poster in a 1983 issue of BYU Sports Magazine.

		MT
Complete Set (14):		4.00
Common Card:		.50
Poster:		7.00
1-14	Wally Joyner	

V

1989 Very Fine Pirates

This 30-card Pirates set was sponsored by Veryfine fruit juices and issued in the form of two uncut, perforated panels, each containing 15 standard-size cards. A third panel featured color action photographs. The panels were distributed in a promotion to fans attending the April 23 game at Three Rivers Stadium. The cards display the Pirates' traditional black and gold color scheme. The backs include player data and complete stats.

		MT
Complete 3-Panel Set:		20.00
Complete Singles Set (30):		12.00
Common Player:		.25
0	Junior Ortiz	.25
2	Gary Redus	.25
3	Jay Bell	.50
5	Sid Bream	.25
6	Rafael Belliard	.25
10	Jim Leyland	.35
11	Glenn Wilson	.25
12	Mike La Valliere	.25
13	Jose Lind	.25
14	Ken Oberkfell	.25
15	Doug Drabek	.45
16	Bob Kipper	.25
17	Bob Walk	.25
18	Andy Van Slyke	.35
23	R.J. Reynolds	.25
24	Barry Bonds	6.00
25	Bobby Bonilla	1.00
26	Neal Heaton	.25
30	Benny Distefano	.25
35	Jim Gott	.25
41	Mike Dunne	.25
43	Bill Landrum	.25
44	John Cangelosi	.25
49	Jeff Robinson	.25
52	Dorn Taylor	.25
54	Brian Fisher	.25
57	John Smiley	.35
31/37	Ray Miller, Tommy Sandt	.25
32/36	Bruce Kimm, Gene Lamont	.25
39/45	Milt May, Rich Donnelly	.25
---	Rich Donnelly (39-45)	.25

1991 Vine Line Chicago Cubs

This set was produced in conjunction with the official fan magazine of the Chicago Cubs, "Vine Line." Issued in nine-card panels for insertion into issues of the magazine, the panels were apparently also offered as a complete set via a mail-in offer. Cards measure the standard 2-1/2" x 3-1/2" and will be perforated on two, three or four sides, depending on their placement on the panel. Fronts are bordered in black with white typography that has the player name, position and uniform number. The player photo is in color with the background in stippled black-and-white. Backs have a black-and-white player portrait, biographical data, career highlights, 1990 and career stats and a brown and green background. The cards are listed here by uniform number.

		MT
Complete Singles Set (36):		9.00
Complete Panel Set (4):		12.00
Common Card:		.25
3	Jose Martinez	.25
4	Don Zimmer	.25
5	Chuck Cottier	.25
6	Joe Altobelli	.25
7	Joe Girardi	.25
8	Andre Dawson	.45
9	Damon Berryhill	.25
10	Luis Salazar	.25
11	George Bell	.25
12	Shawon Dunston	.25
16	Jose Vizcaino	.25
17	Mark Grace	1.00
18	Dwight Smith	.25
19	Hector Villanueva	.25
20	Jerome Walton	.25
22	Mike Harkey	.25
23	Ryne Sandberg	1.50
24	Chico Walker	.25
25	Gary Scott	.25
29	Doug Dascenzo	.25
31	Greg Maddux	2.00
32	Danny Jackson	.25
34	Dick Pole	.25
35	Chuck McElroy	.25
36	Mike Bielecki	.25
37	Erik Pappas	.25
40	Rick Sutcliffe	.25
42	Dave Smith	.25
44	Steve Wilson	.25
45	Paul Assenmacher	.25
47	Shawn Boskie	.25
48	Phil Roof	.25
50	Les Lancaster	.25
51	Heathcliff Slocumb	.25
31	Fergie Jenkins (Hall of Fame)	.40
---	Most Valuable Players (Ryne Sandberg, Andre Dawson, George Bell)	.40

1998 Virginia Lottery Baseball Legends Cards

This set of cards was one of several consolation prizes available in the commonwealth's scratch-off lottery game featuring Hall of Famers who had played in Virginia. The 2-1/2" x 3-1/2" cards have larger versions of the player photos found on the tickets. Borders are in red, white, blue and black. Black-and-white backs have career highlights and stats. Cards can be found in either signed or autographed versions.

		MT
Complete Set (4):		4.00
Complete Set, Autographed (4):		25.00
Common Player:		1.00
Common Player, Autographed:		8.00
(1)	Yogi Berra	2.00
(1)	Yogi Berra (autographed)	15.00
(2)	Willie McCovey	1.00
(2)	Willie McCovey (autographed)	8.00
(3)	Phil Niekro	1.00
(3)	Phil Niekro (autographed)	8.00
(4)	Duke Snider	1.50
(4)	Duke Snider (autographed)	12.00

1998 Virginia Lottery Baseball Legends Tickets

Joining the parade of states using former stars to sell its lottery, Virginia issued this quartet of scratch-off tickets picturing Hall of Famers who played minor league ball in Virginia. Color photos, without uniform/cap logos, are featured on the fronts of the approximately 2-3/8" x 4-3/4" tickets. Besides cash prizes, winning tickets could be redeemed for baseball cards and memorabilia of the four players. Values shown are for unscratched tickets.

		MT
Complete Set (4):		6.00
Common Player:		1.50
(1)	Yogi Berra	2.00
(2)	Willie McCovey	1.50
(3)	Phil Niekro	1.50
(4)	Duke Snider	2.00

W

1992 Wal-Mart

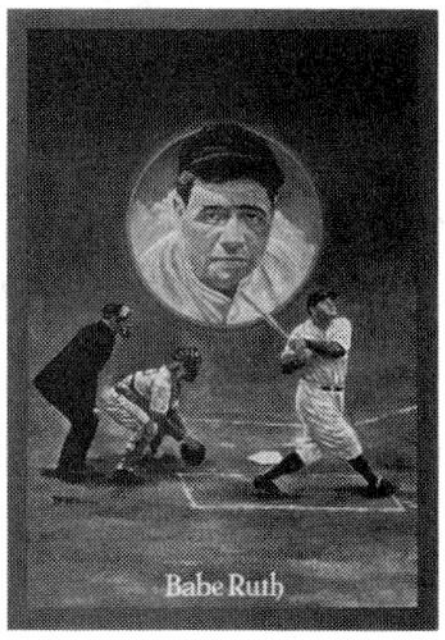

In conjunction with an exhibit of baseball cards which traveled to various Wal-Mart stores in 1992, souvenir cards were given to the first 500 visitors at each store. The 4-7/8" x 6-3/4" card features color portrait and action paintings on the front by Hall of Fame artist Dick Perez. The front is bordered in gold. Backs are printed in white on green with details of Ruth's career and the Wal-Mart exhibit and card.

	MT
Babe Ruth	10.00

1986 Waldenbooks "The Mick"

To introduce a mass-market paperback book ostensibly written by Mickey Mantle and Herb Gluck, the Waldenbooks chain issued this promotional card. In standard 2-1/2" x 3-1/2" format, the card has a color action photo of Mantle on front and complete major league statistics on back.

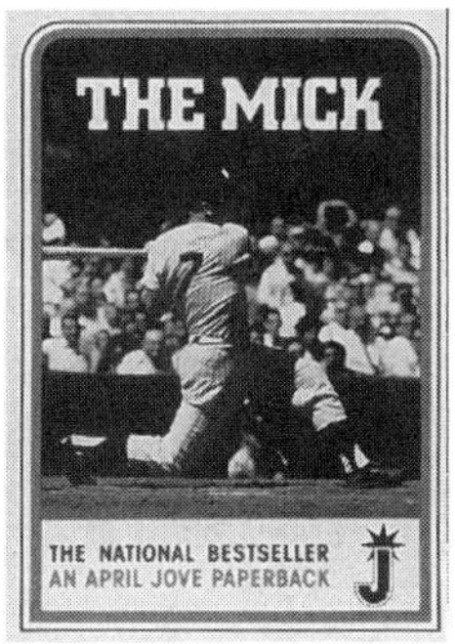

	MT
The Mick (Mickey Mantle)	6.00

1991 Waldo Candies

This is an unauthorized collectors' issue purporting to have been issued by "Hooking & Geek Bros, & Glickstein" and advertising Waldo Candies. The cards are standard 2-1/2" x 3-1/2" in a format reminiscent of the 1914-15 Cracker Jack baseball cards. Color player photos are shown on a red background. The player's last name, team and league are printed in the bottom border. Backs have career highlights, an ad for the fictitious candy company.

		MT
Complete Set (4):		2.00
Common Player:		.25
1	Ken Griffey Jr.	1.50
2	Ryne Sandberg	.75
3	David Justice	.50
4	Kevin Maas	.25

1997 Ted Walker Philadelphia A's

Philadelphia Athletics from the turn of the century until the team departed for Kansas City in 1955 are featured on this series of art cards by Ted Walker. The 4-1/4" x 5-1/4" cards have black-and-white line art portraits on front. On back, in blue on white, is a rampant elephant logo and details of the player's time with the A's. It was reported only 100 sets were produced, with most being sold to benefit the A's historical society.

		MT
Complete Set (44):		33.00
Common Player:		.50
(1)	Joe Astroth	.50
(2)	Frank Baker	.75
(3)	Chief Bender	1.00
(4)	Max Bishop	.50
(5)	Ty Cobb	3.00
(6)	Mickey Cochrane	.75
(7)	Eddie Collins	.75
(8)	Doc Cramer	.50
(9)	Joe DeMaestri	.50
(10)	Bill Dietrich	.50
(11)	Jimmy Dykes	.50
(12)	George Earnshaw	.50
(13)	Elmer Flick	.75
(14)	Nellie Fox	2.50
(15)	Jimmie Foxx	1.00
(16)	Walter French	.50
(17)	Lefty Grove	1.00
(18)	Mule Haas	.50
(19)	Sammy Hale	.50
(20)	Shoeless Joe Jackson	5.00
(21)	Bob Johnson	.50
(22)	Alex Kellner	.50
(23)	Nap Lajoie	.75
(24)	Connie Mack	1.00
(25)	Hank Majeski	.50
(26)	Stuffy McInnis	.50
(27)	Bing Miller	.50
(28)	Wally Moses	.50
(29)	Dave Philley	.50
(30)	Eddie Plank	.75
(31)	Jack Quinn	.50
(32)	Eddie Rommel	.50
(33)	Buddy Rosar	.50
(34)	Carl Scheib	.50
(35)	Wally Schang	.75
(36)	Bobby Shantz	1.00
(37)	Al Simmons	.75
(38)	Tris Speaker	1.00
(39)	Pete Suder	.50
(40)	Homer Summa	.50
(41)	Rube Waddell	.75
(42)	Rube Walberg	.50
(43)	Tom Walker	.50
(44)	Gus Zernial	.50

1990 Warner Bros. Bugs Bunny team logo stickers

It is believed these team logo stickers were produced for sale in vending machines. The 3" x 2-1/2" stickers have a cartoon of Bugs Bunny in a baseball uniform, along with a team logo. When the backing is peeled away, the sticker has a clear background. It is unknown whether any teams other than those listed were issued.

		MT
Common Sticker:		1.00
(1)	Atlanta Braves	1.00
(2)	Baltimore Orioles	1.00
(3)	Cincinnati Reds	1.00
(4)	Cleveland Indians	1.00
(5)	Milwaukee Brewers	1.00
(6)	Minnesota Twins	1.00
(7)	Philadelphia Phillies	1.00
(8)	Pittsburgh Pirates	1.00
(9)	St. Louis Cardinals	1.00

1998 Washington Mint Mark McGwire

In commemoration of McGwire's 62nd home run to set a new single-season record, this collector card was issued. The 3" x 5" card pictures the player on front, hitting the historic homer. Also on front are the date, red-foil graphic highlights and a gold-foil facsimile signature. On back is a list of McGwire's first 62 home runs of the 1998 season, with date, opponent and distance noted. Issue price was $29.95 plus $4.95 postage. An issue of 62,000 cards was announced.

	MT
Mark McGwire	30.00

1988 Weis Winners Super Stars Discs

(See 1988 Baseball Superstars Discs for checklist and price guide.)

1985 Wendy's Tigers

This set contains 22 cards measuring 2-1/2" x 3-1/2", which carry both Wendy's Hamburgers and Coca-Cola logos and were produced by Topps. The cards feature a color photo with the player's identification underneath the picture. Backs are identical to 1985 Topps cards except they have different card numbers and are done in a red and black color scheme. Cards were distributed three to a pack along with a "Header" checklist in a cellophane package at selected Wendy's outlets in Michigan only.

		MT
Complete Set (22):		7.00
Common Player:		.25
1	Sparky Anderson	.75
2	Doug Bair	.25
3	Juan Berenguer	.25
4	Dave Bergman	.25
5	Tom Brookens	.25
6	Marty Castillo	.25
7	Darrell Evans	.40
8	Barbaro Garbey	.25
9	Kirk Gibson	.65
10	Johnny Grubb	.25
11	Willie Hernandez	.25
12	Larry Herndon	.25
13	Rusty Kuntz	.25
14	Chet Lemon	.25
15	Aurelio Lopez	.25
16	Jack Morris	.40
17	Lance Parrish	.65
18	Dan Petry	.25
19	Bill Scherrer	.25
20	Alan Trammell	1.00
21	Lou Whitaker	.50
22	Milt Wilcox	.25

1994 Wendy's Roberto Clemente Hologram

This single-card set was issued by the restaurant chain in a stated edition of 90,000. The front has a black-bordered hologram picturing Clemente at bat, with the number 3,000 in a box at upper-right. The back has a couple of color photos of the Pirates' star along with biographical data and a career summary.

		MT
(1)	Roberto Clemente	8.00

1993 Whataburger Nolan Ryan

Issued in two-card cello packs at Whataburger restaurants, this set honors the career of Nolan Ryan. Cards have action photos set against colorized backgrounds and overlayed with ribbed plastic to create a 3-D effect. A card title is printed in white in the lower-left corner, with the logo of Triad (the card's maker) in the lower-right. In the upper-left corner is a red "Nolan Ryan's Recollections" logo. Backs have color logos of the hamburger chain, Triad, Coca-Cola and Major League Baseball, along with a quote from Ryan about the career highlight and a facsimile autograph. The cards are unnumbered.

		MT
Complete Set (10):		9.00
Common Card:		1.50
(1)	(Nolan Ryan) (1st No-hitter)	1.50
(2)	(Nolan Ryan) (2nd No-Hitter)	1.50
(3)	(Nolan Ryan) (3rd No-hitter)	1.50
(4)	(Nolan Ryan) (4th No-hitter)	1.50
(5)	(Nolan Ryan) (5th No-hitter)	1.50
(6)	(Nolan Ryan) (6th No-hitter)	1.50
(7)	(Nolan Ryan) (7th No-hitter)	1.50
(8)	(Nolan Ryan) (5,000th Strikeout)	1.50

(9)	(Nolan Ryan) (300th Win)	1.50
(10)	(Nolan Ryan) (on horse)	1.50

1982 Wheaties Indians

These 2-13/16" x 4-1/8" cards were given out ten at a time during three special promotional games; later the complete set was placed on sale at the Indians' gift shop. The cards represented the first time in 30 years that Wheaties had been associated with a baseball card set. Fronts feature color photos surrounded by a wide white border with the player's name and position below the picture. The Indians logo is in the lower-left corner while the Wheaties logo is in the lower-right. Card backs have a Wheaties ad.

		MT
Complete Set (30):		7.00
Common Player:		.25
(1)	Chris Bando	.25
(2)	Alan Bannister	.25
(3)	Len Barker	.25
(4)	Bert Blyleven	.50
(5)	Tom Brennan	.25
(6)	Joe Charboneau	.40
(7)	Rodney Craig	.25
(8)	John Denny	.25
(9)	Miguel Dilone	.25
(10)	Jerry Dybzinski	.25
(11)	Mike Fischlin	.25
(12)	Dave Garcia	.25
(13)	Johnny Goryl	.25
(14)	Mike Hargrove	.40
(15)	Toby Harrah	.40
(16)	Ron Hassey	.25
(17)	Von Hayes	.25
(18)	Dennis Lewallyn	.25
(19)	Rick Manning	.25
(20)	Bake McBride	.25
(21)	Tommy McCraw	.25
(22)	Jack Perconte	.25
(23)	Mel Queen	.25
(24)	Dennis Sommers	.25
(25)	Lary Sorensen	.25
(26)	Dan Spillner	.25
(27)	Rick Sutcliffe	.40
(28)	Andre Thornton	.40
(29)	Rick Waits	.25
(30)	Eddie Whitson	.25

1983 Wheaties Indians

A 32-card set marked the second year of Wheaties involvement with the Indians. Distribution of the 2-13/16" x 4-1/8" cards changed slightly in that the entire set was given away on the day of the special promotional game. As happened in 1982, the set was then placed on sale at the team's gift shop. The set includes 27 players, four coaches and the manager. The format of the cards remained basically the same on the front although the backs of player cards were changed to include complete major and minor league statistics.

		MT
Complete Set (32):		6.00
Common Player:		.25
(1)	Bud Anderson	.25
(2)	Jay Baller	.25
(3)	Chris Bando	.25
(4)	Alan Bannister	.25
(5)	Len Barker	.25
(6)	Bert Blyleven	.45
(7)	Wil Culmer	.25
(8)	Miguel Dilone	.25
(9)	Juan Eichelberger	.25
(10)	Jim Essian	.25
(11)	Mike Ferraro	.25
(12)	Mike Fischlin	.25
(13)	Julio Franco	.75
(14)	Ed Glynn	.25
(15)	Johnny Goryl	.25
(16)	Mike Hargrove	.35
(17)	Toby Harrah	.35
(18)	Ron Hassey	.25
(19)	Neal Heaton	.25
(20)	Rick Manning	.25
(21)	Bake McBride	.25
(22)	Don McMahon	.25
(23)	Ed Napoleon	.25
(24)	Broderick Perkins	.25
(25)	Dennis Sommers	.25
(26)	Lary Sorensen	.25
(27)	Dan Spillner	.25
(28)	Rick Sutcliffe	.35
(29)	Andre Thornton	.35
(30)	Manny Trillo	.25
(31)	George Vukovich	.25
(32)	Rick Waits	.25

1984 Wheaties Indians

The 2-13/16" x 4-1/8" cards again were given out at Municipal Stadium as part of a promotion involving Wheaties and the Indians on July 22. The set was down from 32 cards in 1983 to 29. There are 26 players as well as cards for the manager, coaches and team mascot. Design of the cards is virtually identical to prior years. The 1984 set is numbered by uniform number. A total of 15,000 sets were printed and any left over from the promotion were placed on sale in the team's gift shop.

		MT
Complete Set (29):		6.00
Common Player:		.25
2	Brett Butler	.50
4	Tony Bernazard	.25
8	Carmelo Castillo	.25
10	Pat Tabler	.25
13	Ernie Camacho	.25
14	Julio Franco	.50
15	Broderick Perkins	.25
16	Jerry Willard	.25
18	Pat Corrales	.25
21	Mike Hargrove	.35
22	Mike Fischlin	.25
23	Chris Bando	.25
24	George Vukovich	.25
26	Brook Jacoby	.25
27	Steve Farr	.25
28	Bert Blyleven	.40
29	Andre Thornton	.35
30	Joe Carter	2.00
31	Steve Comer	.25
33	Roy Smith	.25
34	Mel Hall	.25
36	Jamie Easterly	.25
37	Don Schulze	.25
38	Luis Aponte	.25
44	Neal Heaton	.25
46	Mike Jeffcoat	.25
54	Tom Waddell	.25
---	Coaching Staff (Bobby Bonds, John Goryl, Don McMahon, Ed Napoleon, Dennis Sommers)	.25
---	Tom-E-Hawk (mascot)	.25

1997 Wheaties All Stars

Forty-five years after it last printed baseball cards on its cereal boxes, Wheaties issued a cross-brand set of 30 cards in 1997. Top players are generally grouped by positions in groups of six on the box backs. Boxes also feature three player photos on front and an ad for obtaining a player photoball. The three series of cards found on 18 oz. boxes of Wheaties carry a Topps logo in upper-right corner. The top of the cards' fronts have action photos. A blue box below the photo has the player name and career highlights in white. A green, blue or orange border surrounds the card, which is separated from the rest of the box back by a black dotted line. Backs, printed inside the box, have limited personal data and full major league stats. Perfectly cut cards from these boxes measure about 2-1/2" x 3-13/16". Somewhat smaller at 2-1/16" x 3-3/8", though identical in format, are the cards found on the backs of Honey Frosted Wheaties and Crispy Wheaties 'n Raisins. Cards on the former carry a Pinnacle logo; the latter are marked Upper Deck. Both have orange borders surrounding the cards.

		MT
Complete Set, Boxes (5):		30.00
Complete Set, Singles (30):		24.00
	CRISPY WHEATIES 'N RAISINS (Upper Deck)	
	All Star Players Complete Box:	8.00
(1)	Ken Griffey Jr.	3.00
(2)	Greg Maddux	2.00
(3)	Paul Molitor	1.50
(4)	Cal Ripken Jr.	2.50
(5)	Frank Thomas	2.00
(6)	Mo Vaughn	.60
	HONEY FROSTED WHEATIES (Pinnacle)	
	All Star Players Complete Box:	7.50
(7)	Barry Bonds	1.50
(8)	Ken Caminiti	.50
(9)	Ken Griffey Jr.	3.00
(10)	Chipper Jones	2.00
(11)	Chuck Knoblauch	.50
(12)	Alex Rodriguez	2.50
	WHEATIES (Topps)	
	All Star Infielders Complete Box:	6.00
(13)	Jeff Bagwell	.75
(14)	Mark McGwire	3.00
(15)	Mike Piazza	2.00
(16)	Cal Ripken Jr.	2.50
(17)	Ryne Sandberg	1.00
(18)	Frank Thomas	2.00
	All Star Outfielders Complete Box:	6.00
(19)	Barry Bonds	1.50
(20)	Ellis Burks	.50
(21)	Juan Gonzalez	1.50
(22)	Ken Griffey Jr.	3.00
(23)	Tony Gwynn	1.50
(24)	Bernie Williams	.50
	All Star Pitchers Complete Box:	5.00
(25)	Andy Benes	.50
(26)	David Cone	.50
(27)	Greg Maddux	2.00
(28)	Mike Mussina	1.00
(29)	Hideo Nomo	.60
(30)	John Smoltz	.50

1997 Wheaties All Stars Fotoballs

In conjunction with its box-back baseball card issue, Wheaties offered a mail-in redemption program for player portrait Fotoballs. With $3 and a proof of purchase, collectors could obtain any one of 28 different balls. The standard size baseballs have a color portrait on one panel, with a Wheaties All Stars logo on the opposite panel. The balls were delivered in a cello bag with a small white plastic display stand. The unnumbered balls are listed here in alphabetical order.

		MT
Complete Set (28):		120.00
Common Player:		3.00
(1)	Jeff Bagwell	6.00
(2)	Andy Benes	3.00
(3)	Barry Bonds	5.00
(4)	Ellis Burks	3.00
(5)	Ken Caminiti	3.00
(6)	David Cone	3.00
(7)	Alex Fernandez	3.00
(8)	Andres Galarraga	3.00
(9)	Juan Gonzalez	7.50
(10)	Ken Griffey Jr.	12.00
(11)	Tony Gwynn	7.50
(12)	Chipper Jones	8.00
(13)	Chuck Knoblauch	4.00
(14)	Greg Maddux	8.00
(15)	Mark McGwire	8.00
(16)	Paul Molitor	4.00
(17)	Mike Mussina	3.00
(18)	Hideo Nomo	5.00
(19)	Mike Piazza	8.00
(20)	Cal Ripken Jr.	10.00
(21)	Mariano Rivera	3.00
(22)	Alex Rodriguez	9.00
(23)	Ivan Rodriguez	5.00
(24)	Ryne Sandberg	6.00
(25)	John Smoltz	3.00
(26)	Frank Thomas	10.00
(27)	Mo Vaughn	5.00
(28)	Bernie Williams	3.00

1992 Whitehall Collection Prototypes

These cards were issued to introduce the hobby to a series of baseball card holograms utilizing technologically enhanced photos of the game's greats. Fronts of the 2-1/2" x 3-1/2" prototype cards have color portrait photos with the player's name at bottom. Backs have a black-and-white version of the photo, an explanation of the company "Photonix" technique and a gray diagonal "PROTOTYPE". The unnumbered cards are checklisted here in alphabetical order.

		MT
Complete Set (5):		8.00
Common Player:		2.00
(1)	Ty Cobb	2.50
(2)	Lou Gehrig	2.50
(3)	Babe Ruth	3.00
(4)	Honus Wagner	2.00
(5)	Cy Young	2.00

1992 Whitehall Collection Holograms

This series of holographic baseball cards feature five of the game's greatest in high-quality color holograms. Fronts of the 2-1/2" x 3-1/2" cards have action photos and ornate borders. Conventionally printed backs have a color portrait photo, career summary, issuer and licensor data and a statement that each card is limited to an edition of 150,000. The unnumbered cards are checklisted here in alphabetical order.

		MT
Complete Set (5):		10.00
Common Player:		3.00
(1)	Ty Cobb	4.00
(2)	Lou Gehrig	4.00
(3)	Babe Ruth	5.00
(4)	Honus Wagner	3.00
(5)	Cy Young	3.00

1995 Wienerschnitzel L.A. Dodgers POGs

The Dodger Stadium hot dog concessionaire sponsored this promotion which was given away to youngsters attending a May 13 Dodgers game. The issue consists of 14 POGs die cut from an 8-1/2" x 10-3/4" cardboard sheet. The POGs picture the team's winners of the Rookie of the Year Award from Jackie Robinson in 1947 through Raul Mondesi in 1994. The individual POGs measure 1-5/8" in diameter. Fronts have a sepia or color player portrait at center, with a blue border of lighter blue stars. Backs are printed in red and blue on white and have a bit of player information plus the logos of the team, sponsor and World POG Federation.

		MT
Complete Set, Unpunched Panel:		9.00
Complete Set, Singles (14):		7.00
Common Player:		.25
1	Jackie Robinson	2.50
2	Don Newcombe	.50
3	Joe Black	.50
4	Jim Gilliam	.35
5	Frank Howard	.45
6	Jim Lefebvre	.25
7	Ted Sizemore	.25
8	Rick Sutcliffe	.25
9	Steve Howe	.25
10	Fernando Valenzuela	.35
11	Steve Sax	.25
12	Eric Karros	.50
13	Mike Piazza	1.50
14	Raul Mondesi	.75

1993 Ted Williams Card Co. Premier Edition

Without a license from the players' union, the premiere issue of the Ted Williams Card Company relied on innovative subsets to create interest in its "old-timers" set. The first 96 cards in the set comprise the base issue. Those cards feature a black-and-white or color action photo set against a background of a second ghost-image photo. The player's name is at bottom with the card company logo conspicuous at top. Backs have some biographical detail, a career summary, the player's five best seasons' and career stats. Subsets numbered contiguously with the base set include a 19-card Negro Leagues series highlighted with green-foil; five cards featuring the All-American Girls Professional Baseball League; a 10-card "Ted's Greatest Hitters" series; 10 "Barrier Breakers" cards featuring Negro Leagues veterans who later played in the majors; a 10-card "Goin' North" subset featuring major league stars of the 1940s-1970s in minor league photos, and, a pair of five-card "Dawning of a Legacy" series featuring Juan Gonzalez and Jeff Bagwell. There were also several insert card series which are listed separately. The cards were packaged with a pair of die-cut player or team logo pogs.

		MT
Complete Set (160):		20.00
Common Player:		.10
Wax Box:		25.00
1	Ted Williams	3.00
2	Rick Ferrell	.10
3	Jim Lonborg	.10
4	Mel Parnell	.10
5	Jim Piersall	.20
6	Luis Tiant	.10
7	Carl Yastrzemski	.50
8	Ralph Branca	.10
9	Roy Campanella	.50
10	Ron Cey	.10
11	Tommy Davis	.10
12	Don Drysdale	.50
13	Carl Erskine	.10
14	Steve Garvey	.20
15	Don Newcombe	.10
16	Duke Snider	.50
17	Maury Wills	.20
18	Jim Fregosi	.10
19	Bobby Grich	.10
20	Bill Buckner	.10
21	Billy Herman	.10
22	Ferguson Jenkins	.20
23	Ron Santo	.20
24	Billy Williams	.25
25	Luis Aparicio	.25
26	Luke Appling	.15
27	Minnie Minoso	.15
28	Johnny Bench	.50
29	George Foster	.10
30	Joe Morgan	.40
31	Buddy Bell	.10
32	Lou Boudreau	.25
33	Rocky Colavito	.25
34	Jim "Mudcat" Grant	.10
35	Tris Speaker	.30
36	Ray Boone	.10
37	Darrell Evans	.10
38	Al Kaline	.50
39	George Kell	.15
40	Mickey Lolich	.10
41	Cesar Cedeno	.10
42	Sal Bando	.10
43	Vida Blue	.10
44	Bert Campaneris	.10
45	Ken Holtzman	.10
46	Lew Burdette	.10
47	Bob Horner	.10
48	Warren Spahn	.50
49	Cecil Cooper	.10
50	Tony Oliva	.20
51	Bobby Bonds	.20
52	Alvin Dark	.10
53	Dave Dravecky	.10
54	Monte Irvin	.15
55	Willie Mays	1.00
56	Bud Harrelson	.10
57	Dave Kingman	.10
58	Yogi Berra	.50
59	Don Baylor	.10
60	Jim Bouton	.10
61	Bobby Brown	.10
62	Whitey Ford	.50
63	Lou Gehrig	1.50
64	Charlie Keller	.10
65	Eddie Lopat	.10
66	Johnny Mize	.40
67	Bobby Murcer	.10
68	Graig Nettles	.10
69	Bobby Shantz	.10
70	Richie Ashburn	.25
71	Larry Bowa	.10
72	Steve Carlton	.40
73	Robin Roberts	.30
74	Matty Alou	.10
75	Harvey Haddix	.10
76	Ralph Kiner	.25
77	Bill Madlock	.10
78	Bill Mazeroski	.25
79	Al Oliver	.10
80	Manny Sanguillen	.10
81	Willie Stargell	.20
82	Al Brumbry	.10
83	Davey Johnson	.10
84	Boog Powell	.15
85	Earl Weaver	.15
86	Lou Brock	.40
87	Orlando Cepeda	.25
88	Curt Flood	.10
89	Joe Garagiola	.25
90	Bob Gibson	.40
91	Rogers Hornsby	.25
92	Enos Slaughter	.25
93	Joe Torre	.20
94	Gaylord Perry	.10
95	Checklist 1-49	.10
96	Checklist 50-96	.10
97	Cool Papa Bell	.25
98	Garnett Blair	.10
99	Gene Benson	.10
100	Lyman Bostock, Sr.	.15
101	Marlin Carter	.10
102	Oscar Charleston	.15
103	Ray Dandridge	.15
104	Mahlon Duckett	.10
105	Josh Gibson	.50
106	Cowan Hyde	.10
107	"Judy" Johnson	.25
108	Buck Leonard	.25
109	Pop Lloyd	.25
110	Lester Lockett	.10
111	Max Manning	.10
112	Satchel Paige	.75
113	Armando Vazquez	.10
114	Smokey Joe Williams	.25
115	Negro Leagues Checklist	.10
116	Alice Hohlmeyer	.10
117	Dotty Kamenshek	.10
118	Pepper Davis	.10
119	Marge Wenzell	.10
120	AAGPBA Checklist	.10
121	The Babe (Babe Ruth)	1.50
122	The Iron Horse (Lou Gehrig)	.75
123	Double X (Jimmie Foxx)	.50
124	Rajah (Rogers Hornsby)	.50
125	The Georgia Peach (Ty Cobb)	.75
126	The Say Hey Kid (Willie Mays)	.75
127	Ralph (Ralph Kiner)	.30
128	The Grey Eagle (Tris Speaker)	.30
129	The Big Cat (Johnny Mize)	.30
130	Ted's Greatest Hitters Checklist	.10
131	Satchel Paige	.75
132	Joe Black	.10
133	Roy Campanella	.50
134	Larry Doby	.25
135	Jim Gilliam	.10
136	Monte Irvin	.15
137	Sam Jethroe	.10
138	Willie Mays	.75
139	Don Newcombe	.10
140	Barrier Breakers Checklist	.10
141	Roy Campanella	.50
142	Bob Gibson	.40
143	Boog Powell	.15
144	Willie Mays	.75
145	Johnny Mize	.15
146	Monte Irvin	.15
147	Earl Weaver	.15
148	Ted Williams	1.50
149	Jim Gilliam	.10
150	Goin' North Checklist	.10
151	Juan Gonzalez (Footsteps to Greatness)	1.50
151a	Juan Gonzalez (autographed, edition of 43)	200.00
152	Juan Gonzalez (Sign 'em Up)	1.50
152a	Juan Gonzalez (autographed, edition of 43)	200.00
153	Juan Gonzalez (The Road to Success)	1.50
153a	Juan Gonzalez (autographed, edition of 43)	200.00
154	Juan Gonzalez (Looking Ahead)	1.50
154a	Juan Gonzalez (autographed, edition of 43)	200.00
155	"Dawning of a Legacy" Checklist	.10
156	Jeff Bagwell (Born with Red Sox Blood)	.75
157	Jeff Bagwell (Movin' Up, Then Out)	.75
158	Jeff Bagwell (Year 1)	.75
159	Jeff Bagwell (Year 2)	.75
160	"Dawning of a Legacy" Checklist	.10

1993 Ted Williams Co. Etched in Stone

This 10-card insert set documents the career of Roberto Clemente, using sepia-toned and color photographs on the card front, highlighted by a gold-foil embossed "Tribute '93" logo in the lower-left corner and an "Etched in Stone" logo at upper-right. Backs have a detailed biography. Cards are numbered ES1 through ES10.

		MT
Complete Set (10):		20.00
Common Player:		3.00
1	Youth (Roberto Clemente)	3.00
2	Sign Up (Roberto Clemente)	3.00
3	Try-Out (Roberto Clemente)	3.00
4	Playing Mad (Roberto Clemente)	3.00
5	Minor Leagues (Roberto Clemente)	3.00
6	1955-1959 (Roberto Clemente)	3.00
7	1960 (Roberto Clemente)	3.00
8	1963 (Roberto Clemente)	3.00
9	1970 (Roberto Clemente)	3.00
10	Etched in Stone Checklist	3.00

1993 Ted Williams Co. Locklear Collection

The paintings of former major leaguer Gene Locklear are featured in this 10-card insert set. The central image of the player is set against a background of multiple player images in orange, red and purple tones. The player's name is in dark blue on the left edge and a "Gene Locklear Collection" logo is in lower-right. On back is a commentary on the player, a card number with an "LC" suffix and, at bottom center, a serial number. The cards of Ted Williams can be found in an autographed insert version numbered on back from within an edition of 406.

		MT
Complete Set (10):		12.50
Common Player:		.75
9LC Ted Williams Autographed:		300.00
1	Yogi Berra	1.00
2	Lou Brock	.75
3	Willie Mays	2.00
4	Johnny Mize	.75
5	Satchel Paige	2.00
6	Babe Ruth	3.00
7	Enos Slaughter	.75
8	Carl Yastrzemski	1.00
9	Ted Williams	3.50
10	Locklear Collection Checklist	.10

1993 Ted Williams Co. Memories

Four historical World Series of the 1950s-1970s are featured in five-card runs within the "Memories" insert set. Fronts have black-and-white or color player photos. In the lower-left corner is a vintage press camera with "Memories" and the year emanating from the flashbulb. The Ted Williams Card Co. logo is at upper-right. The player's name is in white at bottom-center. Cards are numbered with an "M" prefix on back and feature a headline announcing the team's World Series victory and a summary of the featured player's performance in that Fall Classic.

		MT
Complete Set (20):		10.00
Common Player:		1.00
1955 BROOKLYN DODGERS		
1	Roy Campanella	1.25
2	Jim Gilliam	.50
3	Gil Hodges	1.25
4	Duke Snider	1.25
5	1955 Dodgers Checklist	.25
1963 L.A. DODGERS		
6	Don Drysdale	1.50
7	Tommy Davis	.50
8	Johnny Podres	.50
9	Maury Wills	1.00
10	1963 Dodgers Checklist	.25
1971 PITTSBURGH PIRATES		
11	Roberto Clemente	2.00
12	Al Oliver	.40
13	Manny Sanguillen	.40
14	Willie Stargell	.50
15	1971 Pirates Checklist	.25
1975 CINCINNATI REDS		
16	Johnny Bench	1.00
17	George Foster	.40
18	Joe Morgan	.50
19	Tony Perez	.50
20	1975 Red Checklist	.25

1993 Ted Williams Co. POGs

These 26 cards featuring two die-cut POGs on each were issued as inserts in 1993 Ted Williams packs. Fronts of the extra-thick cardboard cards have a black background with the logos of the card company and the Cooperstown Collection. Two 1-5/8" diameter POGs appear on each card, picturing either players or team logos. Backs are blank. The unnumbered

POG cards are listed here alphabetically, with player POGs listed first.

		MT
	Complete Set (26):	4.00
	Common Player:	.25
(1)	Yogi Berra, Roy Campanella	1.00
(2)	Brooklyn Dodgers (Roy Campanella)	.50
(3)	Tommy Davis, George Foster	.25
(4)	Lou Gehrig, Ted Williams	2.00
(5)	New York Yankees (Lou Gehrig)	1.50
(6)	Ted Williams, #9 patch	.75
(7)	1993 All-Star patch 1993 World Series patch	.25
(8)	Atlanta Black Crackers, Baltimore Elite Giants	.25
(9)	Atlanta Braves, New York Mets	.25
(10)	Birmingham Black Barons, New York Cuban Stars	.25
(11)	Boston Red Sox, Minnesota Twins	.25
(12)	Brooklyn Dodgers, St. Louis Browns	.25
(13)	Chicago Cubs, Detroit Tigers	.25
(14)	Cincinnati Reds, Kansas City Royals	.25
(15)	Cleveland Buckeyes, Detroit Stars	.25
(16)	Cleveland Indians, Kansas City Athletics	.25
(17)	Colorado Rockies, Florida Marlins	.25
(18)	Homestead Grays, New York Black Yankees	.25
(19)	Houston Colt .45s New York Yankees	.25
(20)	Indianapolis ABCs, New York Harlem Stars	.25
(21)	Louisville Black Caps, Philadelphia Stars	.25
(22)	Milwaukee Braves, New York Giants	.25
(23)	Montreal Expos, San Diego Padres	.25
(24)	Negro League Baseball Players Assn., Negro Leagues Classic Teams	.25
(25)	Oakland A's, #21 (Clemente) patch	.25
(26)	Pittsburgh Pirates, St. Louis Cardinals	.25

1993 Ted Williams Co. Brooks Robinson

This 10-card insert set, numbered BR1 through BR10, traces the baseball career of Hall of Fame Orioles third baseman Brooks Robinson. Card fronts feature sepia-toned or color photos highlighted by the player's name in gold foil down the left side and a "Brooks Robinson Collection" diamond logo at lower-right. Backs include a career summary or batting or fielding stats.

		MT
	Complete Set (10):	3.00
	Common Player:	.50
1BR	Salad Days (Brooks Robinson)	.50
2BR	Career Batting Stats (Brooks Robinson)	.50
3BR	'66 World Series (Brooks Robinson)	.50
4BR	Career Fielding Stats (Brooks Robinson)	.50
5BR	'70 Series #2 (Brooks Robinson)	.50
6BR	'70 Series #1 (Brooks Robinson)	.50
7BR	Comin' Up (Brooks Robinson)	.50
8BR	All Star Games (Brooks Robinson)	.50
9BR	1964 (Brooks Robinson)	.50
10BR	Brooks Robinson Collection Checklist	.50

1994 Ted Williams Card Company

Lack of a players' association license again limited the company to using two major leaguers in its second annual card set, but it spiced up its 1994 edition with hot prospects in the minor leagues, more high-tech production values and innovative subsets and chase cards. The base set for 1994 includes 162 cards. The first 92 feature retured or deceased players. Those cards feature a color or colorized photo set against a background of a second ghost-image photo or the actual photo background. Vertically at right is a stone image on which the player's name is printed in extremely difficult to read gold letters. The edge of the stone and the card company logo are embossed. Backs have biographical and career details, and stats for the player's five top seasons. Subsets numbered consecutively with the base cards include a seven-card "Women of Baseball" series; 18 Negro Leaguers, 18 current minor leaguers in a series titled "The Campaign;" 10 "Goin' North" cards of former superstars as minor leaguers; nine "Swingin' for the Fences" cards of home run hitters, and, a nine-card "Dawning of a Legacy" series featuring Cliff Floyd and Tim Salmon. The several insert card series are listed separately.

		MT
	Complete Set (162):	12.00
	Common Player:	.10
	Wax Box:	20.00
1	Ted Williams	2.50
P1	Ted Williams (promo card)	3.00
2	Bernie Carbo	.10
3	Bobby Doerr	.10
4	Fred Lynn	.10
5	Johnny Pesky	.10
6	Rico Petrocelli	.10
7	Cy Young	.25
8	Paul Blair	.10
9	Andy Etchebarren	.10
10	Brooks Robinson	.50
11	Gil Hodges	.20
12	Tommy John	.10
13	Rick Monday	.10
14	Dean Chance	.10
15	Doug DeCinces	.10
16	Gabby Hartnett	.10
17	Don Kessinger	.10
18	Bruce Sutter	.10
19	Eddie Collins	.10
20	Nellie Fox	.20
21	Carlos May	.10
22	Ted Kluszewski	.15
23	Vada Pinson	.10
24	Johnny Vander Meer	.10
25	Bob Feller	.40
26	Mike Garcia	.10
27	Sam McDowell	.10
28	Al Rosen	.10
29	Norm Cash	.10
30	Ty Cobb	.60
31	Mark Fidrych	.15
32	Hank Greenberg	.20
33	Denny McLain	.10
34	Virgil Trucks	.10
35	Enos Cabell	.10
36	Mike Scott	.10
37	Bob Watson	.10
38	Amos Otis	.10
39	Frank White	.10
40	Joe Adcock	.10
41	Rico Carty	.10
42	Ralph Garr	.10
43	Eddie Mathews	.25
44	Ben Oglivie	.10
45	Gorman Thomas	.10
46	Earl Battey	.10
47	Rod Carew	.25
48	Jim Kaat	.10
49	Harmon Killebrew	.25
50	Gary Carter	.15
51	Steve Rogers	.10
52	Rusty Staub	.10
53	Sal Maglie	.10
54	Juan Marichal	.25
55	Mel Ott	.10
56	Bobby Thomson	.10
57	Tommie Agee	.10
58	Tug McGraw	.10
59	Elston Howard	.10
60	Sparky Lyle	.10
61	Billy Martin	.10
62	Thurman Munson	.20
63	Bobby Richardson	.10
64	Bill Skowron	.10
65	Mickey Cochrane	.10
66	Rollie Fingers	.10
67	Lefty Grove	.10
68	Catfish Hunter	.10
69	Connie Mack	.10
70	Al Simmons	.10
71	Dick Allen	.10
72	Bob Boone	.10
73	Del Ennis	.10
74	Chuck Klein	.10
75	Mike Schmidt	.50
76	Dock Ellis	.10
77	Elroy Face	.10
78	Phil Garner	.10
79	Bill Mazeroski	.15
80	Pie Traynor	.10
81	Honus Wagner	.50
82	Dizzy Dean	.25
83	Red Schoendienst	.10
84	Randy Jones	.10
85	Nate Colbert	.10
86	Jeff Burroughs	.10
87	Jim Sundberg	.10
88	Frank Howard	.10
89	Walter Johnson	.25
90	Eddie Yost	.10
91	Checklist 1-46	.10
92	Checklist 47-92	.10
93	Faye Dancer	.10
94	Snookie Doyle	.10
95	Maddy English	.10
96	Nickie Fox	.10
97	Sophie Kurys	.10
98	Alma Ziegler	.10
99	Women of Baseball Checklist	.10
100	Newton Allen	.10
101	Willard Brown	.10
102	Larry Brown	.10
103	Leon Day	.20
104	John Donaldson	.10
105	Rube Foster	.10
106	Bud Fowler	.10
107	Vic Harris	.10
108	Webster McDonald	.10
109	John "Buck" O'Neil	.15
110	Ted "Double Duty" Radcliffe	.10
111	Wilber "Bullet" Rogan	.15
112	Toni Stone	.10
113	Jim Taylor	.10
114	Moses "Fleetwood" Walker	.15
115	George Wilson	.10
116	Judson Wilson	.10
117	Negro Leagues Checklist	.10
118	Howard Battle	.10
119	John Burke	.10
120	Brian Dubose	.10
121	Alex Gonzalez	.25
122	Jose Herrera	.10
123	Jason Giambi	.25
124	Derek Jeter	2.50
125	Charles Johnson	.50
126	Daron Kirkreit	.10
127	Jason Moler	.10
128	Vince Moore	.10
129	Chad Mottola	.25
130	Jose Silva	.10
131	Makato Suzuki (Makoto)	.10
132	Brien Taylor	.10
133	Michael Tucker	.25
134	Billy Wagner	.15
135	The Campaign Checklist	.10
136	Gary Carter	.10
137	Tony Conigliaro	.10
138	Sparky Lyle	.10
139	Roger Maris	.50
140	Vada Pinson	.10
141	Mike Schmidt	.50
142	Frank White	.10
143	Ted Williams	2.50
144	Goin' North Checklist	.10
145	Joe Adcock	.10
146	Rocky Colavito	.25
147	Lou Gehrig	1.00
148	Gil Hodges	.20
149	Bob Horner	.10
150	Willie Mays	1.00
151	Mike Schmidt	.50
152	Pat Seery	.10
153	Swingin' for the Fences Checklist	.10
154	Cliff Floyd (The Honors Begin)	.15
155	Cliff Floyd (The Top Polecat)	.15
156	Cliff Floyd (Minor League Team of the Year)	.15
157	Cliff Floyd (Major League Debut)	.15
158	Tim Salmon (Award Winner)	.25
159	Tim Salmon (Early Professional Career)	.25
160	Tim Salmon (An MVP Season)	.25
161	Tim Salmon (Rookie of the Year)	.25
162	Dawning of a Legacy Checklist	.10

1994 Ted Williams Co. Etched in Stone

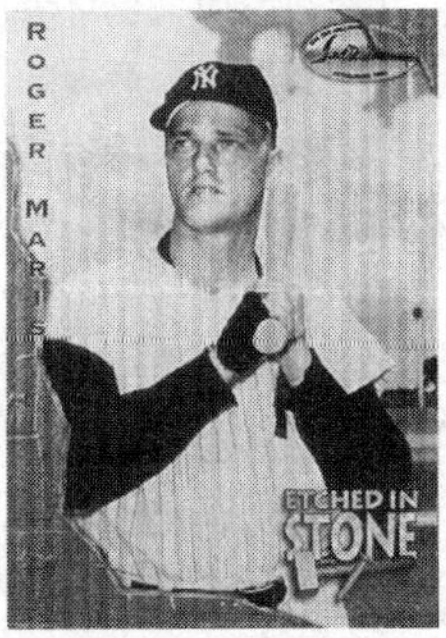

A metallized effect highlights the front design of this insert series commemorating the career of Roger Maris. Color (or colorized) photos appear to have been revealed by chiseling away a rock face which forms much of the front border. Backs have career write-ups overprinted on a design which forms a large "Etched in Stone" design when the cards are laid together in order. Cards have an "ES" prefix to the card number. Cards can be found with either brown or red "rock" borders. The red version is valued at double the brown.

		MT
	Complete Set (9):	8.00
	Common Player:	2.00
1	Roger Maris (Scouting Report)	2.00
2	Roger Maris (Traded)	2.00
3	Roger Maris (Career Year)	2.00
4	Roger Maris (1961)	2.00
5	Roger Maris (Silent Accomplishments)	2.00
6	Roger Maris (Team Player)	2.00
7	Roger Maris (Reborn)	2.00
8	Roger Maris (Hero's Welcome)	2.00
9	Checklist (Roger Maris)	.35

Player names in *Italic* type indicate a rookie card.

1994 Ted Williams Co. Dan Gardiner

Sports artist Dan Gardiner was commissioned to produce a series of nine insert cards depicting hot minor league prospects for this insert set. Players are depicted in posed portraits on front and in action paintings on the back. Cards carry a "DG" prefix to the card number and each card is serially numbered in the upper-left corner.

		MT
	Complete Set (9):	10.00
	Common Player:	1.00
1	Michael Jordan	4.00
2	Michael Tucker	1.00
3	Derek Jeter	3.00
4	Charles Johnson	1.50
5	Howard Battle	1.00
6	Quilvio Vergas (Veras)	1.00
7	Brian Hunter	1.00
8	Brien Taylor	1.00
9	Checklist	.25

1994 Ted Williams Co. Locklear Collection

Paintings of eight Hall of Famers plus a checklist are featured in this insert set. The art is the work of former major leaguer Gene Locklear. The cards are numbered with an "LC" suffix.

		MT
	Complete Set (9):	20.00
	Common Player:	2.00
11	Ty Cobb	3.00
12	Bob Feller	2.00
13	Lou Gehrig	5.00
14	Josh Gibson	2.00
15	Walter Johnson	2.00
16	Casey Stengel	2.00
17	Honus Wagner	4.00
18	Cy Young	2.50
19	Checklist	.50

1994 Ted Williams Co. LP Cards

Two premium insert cards in the 1994 Ted Williams Co. set carry an "LP" card number prefix. One depicts basketball superstar Larry Bird playing baseball during his college days at Indiana State University. The other card depicts Ted Williams speaking at the opening of the Ted Williams Museum. Fronts use a metalized technology. Backs describe the action.

		MT
Complete Set (2):		12.00
1	Larry Bird	4.00
2	Ted Williams	8.00

1994 Ted Williams Co. Mike Schmidt Collection

This nine-card insert set honors the career of Hall of Fame Phillies third baseman Mike Schmidt. Fronts feature full-bleed metallized color photos. Backs have a Phillies flag design with a career biography. Cards are numbered with an "MS" prefix.

		MT
Complete Set (9):		5.00
Common Player:		1.00
1	Mike Schmidt (Mike)	1.00
2	Mike Schmidt (The White House)	1.00
3	Mike Schmidt (Soaping Up)	1.00
4	Mike Schmidt (The Promised Land)	1.00
5	Mike Schmidt (Who's Who)	1.00
6	Mike Schmidt (The Call)	1.00
7	Mike Schmidt (Leading the Way)	1.00
8	Mike Schmidt (Award Winner)	1.00
9	Checklist	.35

1994 Ted Williams Co. The 500 Club

Major leaguers with 500 or more career home runs are featured in this nine-card insert set. Fronts have full-bleed metallized photos, some in color and some which have been colorized. A logo picturing a hanging "The 500 Club" sign appears at lower-left, with the player's name in gold. Backs have a basic design that looks for all the world like a toilet seat, in which the player's home run prowess is recalled. Cards are numbered with a "5C" prefix. Two versions of each card exist, one has brown graphic highlights on front, one has red. The red highlighted cards are worth about 25% more than the brown.

		MT
Complete Set (9):		12.00
Common Player:		1.00
1	Hank Aaron	1.75
2	Reggie Jackson	1.25
3	Harmon Killebrew	1.00
4	Mickey Mantle	3.00
5	Jimmie Foxx	1.00
6	Babe Ruth	2.50
7	Mike Schmidt	1.25
8	Ted Williams	2.50
9	Checklist	.25

1994 Ted Williams Co. Trade for Babe

This nine-card set was available to persons who found a randomly packaged "Trade for Babe" redemption card in packs of Ted Williams Co. cards. A $4.50 postage/handling fee was necessary for redemption and a reported 9,999 trade sets were available. Card fronts feature colorized photos of Ruth while backs have text concerning the front theme. Cards are numbered with a "TB" prefix.

		MT
Complete Set (9):		30.00
Common Player:		4.00
----	Babe Ruth (redemption card, expired Nov. 30, 1994)	5.00
1	Babe Ruth (George Herman Ruth)	5.00
2	Babe Ruth (King of the Hill)	5.00
3	Babe Ruth (On to New York)	5.00
4	Babe Ruth (Called Shot?)	5.00
5	Babe Ruth (The Bambino and the Iron Horse)	5.00
6	Babe Ruth (Larger Than Life)	5.00
7	Babe Ruth (Always a Yankee)	5.00
8	Babe Ruth (The Babe)	5.00
9	Babe Ruth (Checklist)	5.00

Player names in *Italic* type indicate a rookie card.

1994 Ted Williams Co. Memories

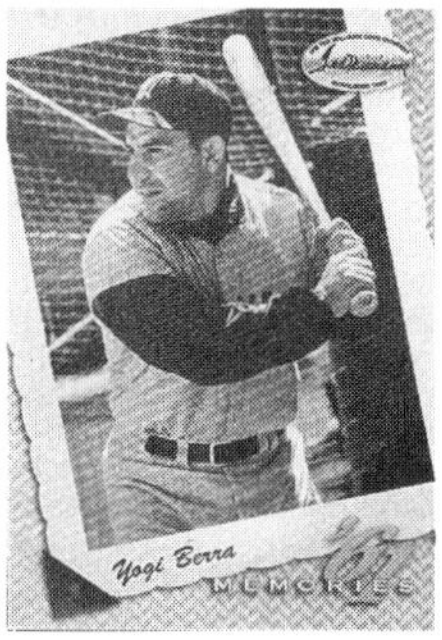

Continuing the card numbers from the 1993 Memories insert set, the 1994 version features highlights of the 1954, 1961, 1968 and 1975 World Series. Card fronts feature metallized images in a snapshot format. The year is noted in large pink numbers at lower-left. Backs describe each player's participation in that particular World Series and are numbered with an "M" prefix.

		MT
Complete Set (20):		22.00
Common Player:		1.00
	1954 N.Y. GIANTS	
21	Monte Irvin	1.00
22	Sal Maglie	1.00
23	Dusty Rhodes	1.00
24	Hank Thompson	1.00
	1961 N.Y. YANKEES	
25	Yogi Berra	2.50
26	Elston Howard	1.50
27	Roger Maris	3.50
28	Bobby Richardson	1.50
	1968 DETROIT TIGERS	
29	Norm Cash	1.50
30	Al Kaline	2.00
31	Mickey Lolich	1.00
32	Denny McLain	1.00
	1975 BOSTON RED SOX	
33	Bernie Carbo	1.00
34	Fred Lynn	1.00
35	Rico Petrocelli	1.00
36	Luis Tiant	1.00
37	Checklist	.25

1992 Willis Oil Jeff Treadway

This single-card issue was sponsored by Willis Oil, Tire & Auto and distributed to "boys that are members of the Boy Scouts of America and in good standing." The front carries the logo of Griffin, Georgia's Flint River Council of the B.S.A. Black borders surround the game-action photo of Treadway on front. Back is printed in red and blue and carries player information and sponsor's logos.

	MT
Jeff Treadway	2.00

1982-84 Wilson Glove Hang Tags

This series of hang-tag cards was found attached to baseball gloves by a plastic strip threaded through a hole punched in the card's corner. The variety of front designations and back variations is challenging to both collectors and catalogers. Generally, the hang tags measure about 3" x 5". Fronts have color action photos at center. The 1982 cards have full uniform logos; those issued 1983-84 have logos airbrushed away. In the wide white border at top is a red Wilson logo. A facsimile autograph appears either on the picture or in the border. Some cards were printed with regular finish, some with glossy. Each tag is designated at top as: "BASEBALL GLOVE", "FIELDER'S GLOVE" or YOUTH LEAGUE FIELDER'S GLOVE". Backs are found in three styles: 1) No picture; 2) Glove pictured, no closeup, and 3) Glove pictured w/ Power Snap closeup.

		MT
Complete Set (28):		150.00
Common Player:		4.00
	1982	
(1)	Buddy Bell (BASEBALL)	6.00
(2)	Buddy Bell (FIELDER'S)	6.00
(3)	George Brett (BASEBALL)	12.00
(4)	George Brett (FIELDER'S)	12.00
(5)	George Brett (YOUTH BASEBALL)	12.00
(6)	George Brett (YOUTH FIELDER'S, no UPC)	12.00
(7)	George Brett (YOUTH FIELDER'S, w/UPC)	10.00
(8)	Ron Guidry (BASEBALL)	6.00
(9)	Ron Guidry (FIELDER'S)	6.00
(10)	Tommy John (BASEBALL)	6.00
(11)	Tommy John (FIELDER'S)	6.00
(12)	Fred Lynn (BASEBALL)	7.50
(13)	Fred Lynn (FIELDER'S)	7.50
(14)	Jim Rice (BASEBALL)	7.50
(15)	Jim Rice (FIELDER'S)	7.50
	1983	
(1)	Buddy Bell (FIELDER'S, glossy)	4.00
(2)	Buddy Bell (YOUTH FIELDER'S)	4.00
(3)	Mike Flanagan (FIELDER'S)	4.00
(4)	Ron Guidry (FIELDER'S, glossy)	4.00
(5)	Tommy John (FIELDER'S, glossy)	4.00
(6)	Fred Lynn (FIELDER'S, glossy)	5.00
(7)	Jim Rice (YOUTH FIELDER'S)	5.00
(8)	Bruce Sutter (FIELDER'S)	4.00
(9)	Manny Trillo (FIELDER'S, glossy)	4.00
	1984	
(1)	George Brett (FIELDER'S, glossy)	9.00
(2)	George Brett (YOUTH FIELDER'S)	9.00
(3)	Mike Flanagan (FIELDER'S, glossy)	4.00
(4)	Bruce Sutter (FIELDER'S, glossy)	4.00

1984 Wilson Canada Hang Tag

This card of star Blue Jays pitcher Dave Steib was found attached to Wilson baseball gloves sold in Canada. The folded tag measures about 2-3/4" x 5-1/2" and is virtually identical on front and back. Each side features a color action photo at right center. At top is a "Win with Wilson" panel, at left is an announcement of a World Series prize trip. One side is printed in English, the other in French.

	MT
Dave Steib	8.00

1985 Wilson Glove Hang Tags

This series of hang tag cards was issued as an attachment to baseball gloves in retail sales outlets. Approximately 3" x 5" (folded), the front of each tag has a color action photo of a member of the Wilson Advisory Staff. Under the Wilson logo in the wide white border at top is "Performance Glove Series" in script. A facsimile autograph appears across the picture. The common back is a color photo of George Brett seated in the dugout with his glove outstretched and a few words of endorsement. Inside the hang tag folder is information about Wilson gloves. The 1985 tags have no pinstripes on front, and no UPC on back.

		MT
Complete Set (5):		20.00
Common Player:		4.00
(1)	George Brett	12.00
(2)	Ron Guidry	5.00
(3)	Tommy John	5.00
(4)	Bruce Sutter	4.00
(5)	Manny Trillo	4.00

1986 Wilson Glove Hang Tags

This series of hang tag cards was issued as an attachment to baseball gloves in retail sales outlets. Approximately 3" x 5" (folded), the front of each tag has a color action photo of a member of the Wilson Advisory Staff. Under the Wilson logo in the wide white border at top is "Performance Glove Series". A facsimile autograph appears across the front. The common back is a color photo of George Brett seated in the dugout with his glove outstretched and a few words of endorsement. Inside the hang tag folder is information about Wilson gloves. The 1986 tags have pinstripes on front, and a UPC on back.

		MT
Complete Set (4):		24.00
Common Player:		4.00
(1)	George Brett	12.00
(2)	Kirk Gibson	6.00
(3)	Eddie Murray	8.00
(4)	Bruce Sutter	4.00

1987-88 Wilson Glove Hang Tags

This series of hang tag cards was distributed as an attachment to baseball gloves sold in retail outlets. The folders measure about 2-7/8" x 4-1/8" (folded). Fronts have color action photos at center, from which uniform and cap logos have been eliminated. A facsimile autograph appears in white across the picture. Wilson logos are at top and bottom of the diagonally striped background. Backs are similar in design to the front, but have no picture. Inside, the folder has information about the glove and its care. Nine lines of gloves are advertised in this series. Those listed with (?) were advertised in Wilson's catalog, but the cards have not been verified.

		MT
Complete Set (19):		120.00
Common Player:		4.00
(1)	George Brett (Signature)	12.00
(2)	George Brett (Youth)	12.00
(3)	George Brett (MVP)	12.00
(4)	Roger Clemens (Fieldmaster) (?)	
(5)	Roger Clemens (MVP)	10.00
(6)	Roger Clemens (Cy Young)	10.00
(7)	Roger Clemens (20K)	10.00
(8)	Kal Daniels (Pro Special)	4.00
(9)	Shawon Dunston (Fieldmaster)	4.00
(10)	Kirk Gibson (Fieldmaster)	5.00
(11)	Kirk Gibson (Youth) (?)	
(12)	Kirk Gibson (MVP) (?)	
(13)	Kirk Gibson (Pro Special)	5.00
(14)	Pedro Guerrero (Classic)	4.00
(15)	Pedro Guerrero (Youth)	4.00
(16)	Ron Guidry (Fieldmaster)	5.00
(17)	Kevin McReynolds (Signature)	4.00
(18)	Kevin McReynolds (Autograph)	4.00
(19)	Eddie Murray (Signature)	8.00
(20)	Eddie Murray (Autograph) (?)	
(21)	Tony Pena (Autograph)	4.00
(22)	Kirby Puckett (Fieldmaster)	12.00
(23)	Dave Righetti (Fieldmaster)	4.00

1987 Wilson Vanguard Hang Tag

This card measures 3" x 5" (folded) and was issued as an attachment to Wilson gloves sold in retail outlets. Front of the folder is printed in red, blue and black and advertises the Vanguard line of baseball gloves. On back is a color photo of George Brett seated in the dugout with his glove outstretched. Inside the folder is information about the glove's features and care.

	MT
George Brett	8.00

1990 Windwalker discs

The origins of this disc set, even its name, are not recorded. The set is comprised on nine dual-headed 3-7/8" discs. Each disc features two players from the 1990 American League All-Star team. No similar issue is known for the National League. Each side has a color action photo and a facsimile autograph. The unnumbered discs are checklisted here alphabetically.

		MT
Complete Set (9):		12.00
Common Disc:		1.00
(1)	Sandy Alomar Jr., Dave Parker	1.00
(2)	George Bell, Julio Franco	1.00
(3)	Wade Boggs, Kirby Puckett	3.00
(4)	Jose Canseco, Rickey Henderson	2.00
(5)	Roger Clemens, Bob Welch	2.00
(6)	Cecil Fielder, Bret Saberhagen	1.00
(7)	Chuck Finley, Kelly Gruber	1.00
(8)	Ken Griffey Jr., Steve Sax	4.00
(9)	Ozzie Guillen, Cal Ripken Jr.	3.00

1999 Wisconsin Desert Classic Robin Yount Postcard

One doesn't often associate Wisconsin and desert, but the two words are joined as the name of a charitable golf tournament sponsored by Miller Lite and held near Phoenix on April 9, 1999. To promote the event, which benefits a Milwaukee cancer center, the sponsor issued a glossy color postcard. The 3-1/2" x 5-1/2" card pictures Robin Yount posed on a golf course. A green facsimile autograph is printed on front and the tournament logo is at upper-left. The black-and-white back has tournament and sponsor details.

	MT
Robin Yount	10.00

1991 Wiz Mets

This 450-card issue was one of several sponsored by the East Coast WIZ home entertainment stores in the early 1990s. Virtually every player in Mets history is included in the set. Each of three series of 15-card perforated sheets was co-sponsored by a large electronics manufacturer: AT&T, Fisher or Maxell. Sheets measure 10" x 9", with individual cards measuring 2" x 3". Card fronts have a black-and-white photo at center with the player's name at left and position at right. A color Mets logo is above and a WIZ logo below. Blue corner decorations complete the front design. Backs are printed in black-and-white, have Mets and sponsors' logos, years the player appeared with the Mets and his Mets career stats. Single cards from this set are seldom available.

		MT
Complete Set (450):		50.00
Common Player:		.10
1	Don Aase	.10
2	Tommie Agee	.15
3	Rick Aguilera	.15
4	Jack Aker	.10
5	Neil Allen	.10
6	Bill Almon	.10
7	Sandy Alomar	.10
8	Jesus Alou	.15
9	George Altman	.10
10	Luis Alvarado	.10
11	Craig Anderson	.10
12	Rick Anderson	.10
13	Bob Apodaca	.10
14	Gerry Arrigo	.10
15	Richie Ashburn	3.00
16	Tucker Ashford	.10
17	Bob Aspromonte	.10
18	Benny Ayala	.10
19	Wally Backman	.10
20	Kevin Baez	.10
21	Bob Bailor	.10
22	Rick Baldwin	.10
23	Billy Baldwin	.10
24	Lute Barnes	.10
25	Ed Bauta	.10
26	Billy Beane	.10
27	Larry Bearnarth	.10
28	Blaine Beatty	.10
29	Jim Beauchamp	.10
30	Gus Bell	.15
31	Dennis Bennett	.10
32	Butch Benton	.10
33	Juan Berenguer	.10
34	Bruce Berenyi	.10
35	Dwight Bernard	.10
36	Yogi Berra	3.00
37	Jim Bethke	.10
38	Mike Bishop	.10
39	Terry Blocker	.10
40	Bruce Bochy	.10
41	Bruce Boisclair	.10
42	Dan Boitano	.10
43	Mark Bomback	.10
44	Don Bosch	.10
45	Daryl Boston	.15
46	Ken Boswell	.10
47	Ed Bouchee	.10
48	Larry Bowa	.10
49	Ken Boyer	.35
50	Mark Bradley	.10
51	Eddie Bressoud	.10
52	Hubie Brooks	.15
53	Kevin Brown	.10
54	Leon Brown	.10
55	Mike Bruhert	.10
56	Jerry Buchek	.10
57	Larry Burright	.10
58	Ray Burris	.10
59	John Candelaria	.10
60	Chris Cannizzarro	.10
61	Buzz Capra	.10
62	Jose Cardenal	.10
63	Don Cardwell	.10
64	Duke Carmel	.10
65	Chuck Carr	.15
66	Mark Carreon	.15
67	Gary Carter	.75
68	Elio Chacon	.10
69	Dean Chance	.10
70	Kelvin Chapman	.10
71	Ed Charles	.20
72	Rich Chiles	.10
73	Harry Chiti	.10
74	John Christensen	.10
75	Joe Christopher	.10
76	Galen Cisco	.10
77	Donn Clendenon	.20
78	Gene Clines	.10
79	Choo Choo Coleman	.20
80	Kevin Collins	.10
81	David Cone	.35
82	Bill Connors	.10
83	Cliff Cook	.10
84	Tim Corcoran	.10
85	Mardie Cornejo	.10
86	Billy Cowan	.10
87	Roger Craig	.10
88	Jerry Cram	.10
89	Mike Cubbage	.10
90	Ron Darling	.15
91	Ray Daviault	.10
92	Tommie Davis	.15
93	John DeMerit	.10
94	Bill Denehy	.10
95	Jack DiLauro	.10
96	Carlos Diaz	.10
97	Mario Diaz	.10
98	Steve Dillon	.10
99	Sammy Drake	.10
100	Jim Dwyer	.10
101	Duffy Dyer	.10
102	Len Dykstra	.45
103	Tom Edens	.10
104	Dave Eilers	.10
105	Larry Elliot	.10
106	Dock Ellis	.10
107	Kevin Elster	.10
108	Nino Espinosa	.10
109	Chuck Estrada	.10
110	Francisco Estrada	.10
111	Pete Falcone	.10
112	Sid Fernandez	.15
113	Chico Fernandez	.10
114	Sergio Ferrer	.10
115	Jack Fisher	.10
116	Mike Fitzgerald	.10
117	Shaun Fitzmaurice	.10
118	Gil Flores	.10
119	Doug Flynn	.10
120	Tim Foli	.10
121	Rich Folkers	.10
122	Larry Foss	.10
123	George Foster	.15
124	Leo Foster	.10
125	Joe Foy	.10
126	John Franco	.15
127	Jim Fregosi	.15
128	Bob Friend	.10
129	Danny Frisella	.10
130	Brent Gaff	.10
131	Bob Gallagher	.10
132	Ron Gardenhire	.10
133	Rob Gardner	.10
134	Wes Gardner	.10
135	Wayne Garrett	.10
136	Rod Gaspar	.10
137	Gary Gentry	.10
138	Jim Gibbons	.10
139	Bob Gibson	.10
140	Brian Giles	.10
141	Joe Ginsberg	.10
142	Ed Glynn	.10
143	Jess Gonder	.15
144	Dwight Gooden	.75
145	Greg Goossen	.10
146	Tom Gorman	.10
147	Jim Gosger	.10
148	Bill Graham	.10
149	Wayne Graham	.10
150	Dallas Green	.15
151	Pumpsie Green	.10
152	Tom Grieve	.15
153	Jerry Grote	.15
154	Joe Grzenda	.10
155	Don Hahn	.10
156	Tom Hall	.10
157	Jack Hamilton	.10
158	Ike Hampton	.10
159	Tim Harkness	.10
160	Bud Harrelson	.20
161	Greg Harris	.10
162	Greg Harts	.10
163	Andy Hassler	.10
164	Tom Hausman	.10
165	Ed Hearn	.10
166	Richie Hebner	.15
167	Danny Heep	.10
168	Jack Heidemann	.10
169	Bob Heise	.10
170	Ken Henderson	.10
171	Steve Henderson	.10
172	Bob Hendley	.10
173	Phil Hennigan	.10
174	Bill Hepler	.10
175	Ron Herbel	.10
176	Manny Hernandez	.10
177	Keith Hernandez	.20
178	Tommy Herr	.10
179	Rick Herrscher	.10
180	Jim Hickman	.10
181	Joe Hicks	.10
182	Chuck Hiller	.10
183	Dave Hillman	.10
184	Jerry Hinsley	.10
185	Gil Hodges	.75
186	Ron Hodges	.10
187	Scott Holman	.10
188	Jay Hook	.10
189	Mike Howard	.10
190	Jesse Hudson	.10
191	Keith Hughes	.10
192	Todd Hundley	.35
193	Ron Hunt	.10
194	Willard Hunter	.10
195	Clint Hurdle	.10
196	Jeff Innis	.10
197	Al Jackson	.10
198	Roy Lee Jackson	.10
199	Gregg Jefferies	.50
200	Stan Jefferson	.10
201	Chris Jelic	.10
202	Bob Johnson	.10
203	Howard Johnson	.30
204	Bob W. Johnson	.10
205	Randy Jones	.10
206	Sherman Jones	.10
207	Cleon Jones	.15
208	Ross Jones	.10
209	Mike Jorgensen	.10
210	Rod Kanehl	.10
211	Dave Kingman	.20
212	Bobby Klaus	.10
213	Jay Kleven	.10
214	Lou Klimchock	.10
215	Ray Knight	.15
216	Kevin Kobel	.10
217	Gary Kolb	.10
218	Cal Koonce	.10
219	Jerry Koosman	.15
220	Ed Kranepool	.15
221	Gary Kroll	.10
222	Clem Labine	.15
223	Jack Lamabe	.10
224	Hobie Landrith	.10
225	Frank Lary	.10
226	Bill Latham	.10
227	Terry Leach	.10
228	Tim Leary	.10
229	John Lewis	.10
230	David Liddell	.10
231	Phil Linz	.10
232	Ron Locke	.10
233	Skip Lockwood	.10
234	Mickey Lolich	.30
235	Phil Lombardi	.10
236	Al Luplow	.10
237	Ed Lynch	.10
238	Barry Lyons	.10
239	Ken MacKenzie	.10
240	Julio Machado	.10
241	Elliot Maddox	.10
243	Dave Magadan	.20
244	Phil Mankowski	.10
245	Felix Mantilla	.10
246	Mike Marshall	.10
247	Dave Marshall	.10
248	Jim Marshall	.10
249	Mike A. Marshall	.10
250	J.C. Martin	.10
251	Jerry Martin	.10
252	Teddy Martinez	.10
253	Jon Matlack	.10
254	Jerry May	.10
255	Willie Mays	8.50
256	Lee Mazzilli	.15
257	Jim McAndrew	.10
258	Bob McClure	.10
259	Roger McDowell	.15
260	Tug McGraw	.20
261	Jeff McKnight	.10
262	Roy McMillan	.15
263	Kevin McReynolds	.15
264	George Medich	.10
265	Orlando Mercado	.10
266	Butch Metzger	.10
267	Felix Millan	.10

268 Bob G. Miller .10
269 Bob L. Miller .10
270 Dyar Miller .10
271 Larry Miller .10
272 Keith Miller .10
273 Randy Milligan .10
274 John Milner .10
275 John Mitchell .10
276 Kevin Mitchell .20
277 Wilmer Mizell .10
278 Herb Moford .10
279 Willie Montanez .10
280 Joe Moock .10
281 Tommy Moore .10
282 Bob Moorhead .10
283 Jerry Morales .10
284 Al Moran .10
285 Jose Moreno .10
286 Bill Murphy .10
287 Dale Murray .10
288 Dennis Musgraves .10
289 Jeff Musselman .10
290 Randy Myers .15
291 Bob Myrick .10
292 Danny Napoleon .10
293 Charlie Neal .10
294 Randy Niemann .10
295 Joe Nolan .10
296 Dan Norman .10
297 Ed Nunez .10
298 Charlie O'Brien .10
299 Tom O'Malley .10
300 Bob Ojeda .15
301 Jose Oquendo .10
302 Jesse Orosco .10
303 Junior Ortiz .10
304 Brian Ostrosser .10
305 Amos Otis .15
306 Rick Ownbey .10
307 John Pacella .10
308 Tom Paciorek .10
309 Harry Parker .10
310 Tom Parsons .10
311 Al Pedrique .10
312 Brock Pemberton .10
313 Alejandro Pena .10
314 Bobby Pfeil .10
315 Mike Phillips .10
316 Jim Piersall .35
317 Joe Pignatano .10
318 Grover Powell .10
319 Rich Puig .10
320 Charlie Puleo .10
321 Gary Rajsich .10
322 Mario Ramirez .10
323 Lenny Randle .10
324 Bob Rauch .10
325 Jeff Reardon .15
326 Darren Reed .10
327 Hal Reniff .10
328 Ronn Reynolds .10
329 Tom Reynolds .10
330 Dennis Ribant .10
331 Gordie Richardson .10
332 Dave Roberts .10
333 Les Rohr .10
334 Luis Rosado .10
335 Don Rose .10
336 Don Rowe .10
337 Dick Rusteck .10
338 Nolan Ryan 8.50
339 Ray Sadecki .10
340 Joe Sambito .10
341 Amado Samuel .10
342 Juan Samuel .15
343 Ken Sanders .10
344 Rafael Santana .10
345 Mackey Sasser .10
346 Mac Scarce .10
347 Jim Schaffer .10
348 Dan Schatzeder .10
349 Calvin Schiraldi .10
350 Al Schmelz .10
351 Dave Schneck .10
352 Ted Schreiber .10
353 Don Schulze .10
354 Mike Scott .15
355 Ray Searage .10
356 Tom Seaver 4.50
357 Dick Selma .10
358 Art Shamsky .15
359 Bob Shaw .10
360 Don Shaw .10
361 Norm Sherry .10
362 Craig Shipley .10
363 Bart Shirley .10
364 Bill Short .10
365 Paul Siebert .10
366 Ken Singleton .15
367 Doug Sisk .10
368 Bobby Gene Smith .10
369 Charley Smith .10
370 Dick Smith .10
371 Duke Snider 4.50
372 Warren Spahn 3.00
373 Larry Stahl .10
374 Roy Staiger .10
375 Tracy Stallard .10
376 Leroy Stanton .10
377 Rusty Staub .45
378 John Stearns .10
379 John Stephenson .10
380 Randy Sterling .10
381 George Stone .10
382 Darryl Strawberry .35
383 John Strohmayer .10
384 Brent Strom .10
385 Dick Stuart .20
386 Tom Sturdivant .10
387 Bill Sudakis .10
388 John Sullivan .10
389 Darrell Sutherland .10
390 Ron Swoboda .15
391 Craig Swan .10
392 Rick Sweet .10
393 Pat Tabler .10
394 Kevin Tapani .10
395 Randy Tate .10
396 Frank Taveras .10
397 Chuck Taylor .10
398 Ron Taylor .10
399 Bob Taylor .10
400 Sammy Taylor .10
401 Walt Terrell .10
402 Ralph Terry .10
403 Tim Teufel .15
404 George Theodore .10
405 Frank Thomas .10
406 Lou Thornton .10
407 Marv Throneberry .15
408 Dick Tidrow .10
409 Rusty Tillman .10
410 Jackson Todd .10
411 Joe Torre .40
412 Mike Torrez .10
413 Kelvin Torve .10
414 Alex Trevino .10
415 Wayne Twitchell .10
416 Del Unser .10
417 Mike Vail .10
418 Bobby Valentine .10
419 Ellis Valentine .10
420 Julio Valera .10
421 Tom Veryzer .10
422 Frank Viola .15
423 Bill Wakefield .10
424 Gene Walter .10
425 Claudell Washington .10
426 Hank Webb .10
427 Al Weis .10
428 Dave West .15
429 Wally Whitehurst .10
430 Carl Willey .10
431 Nick Willhite .10
432 Charlie Williams .10
433 Mookie Wilson .30
434 Herm Winningham .10
435 Gene Woodling .15
436 Billy Wynne .10
437 Joel Youngblood .10
438 Pat Zachry .10
439 Don Zimmer .15
(440) Checklist 1-40 .10
(441) Checklist 41-80 .10
(442) Checklist 81-120 .10
(443) Checklist 121-160 .10
(444) Checklist 161-200 .10
(445) Checklist 201-240 .10
(446) Checklist 241-280 .10
(447) Checklist 281-320 .10
(448) Checklist 321-360 .10
(449) Checklist 361-400 .10
(450) Checklist 401-439 .10

1992 Wiz Yankees Classics

More than 600 different Yankees players from the turn of the century through the 1980s are featured in this set. Produced and distributed in five series at various promotional games, the cards share a common design and theme. Originally in a 10" x 9" perforated sheet format, the 2" x 3" individual cards can be separated with ease. Fronts feature blue-and-white duo-tone photos with the familiar Yankee Stadium facade in blue at top and the player name in black below. Backs are printed in blue on white. The series name is printed beneath the top name bar, along with a line indicating the player's years with the Yankees and a few career stats. At bottom of all cards are the Yankees Classics and Wiz Home Entertainment Centers logos, along with the logo of the co-sponsor. The Yankees of the '60s and All-Star series were co-sponsored by American Express; the '70s series by Fisher; the '80s by Minolta and the Hall of Famers by Aiwa. The unnumbered cards are checklisted here alphabetically within series.

MT
Complete Set (638): 95.00
Common Player: .20
Complete series, Yankees of the '60s: 36.00
(1) Jack Aker .20
(2) Ruben Amaro .20
(3) Luis Arroyo .20
(4) Stan Bahnsen .20
(5) Steve Barber .20
(6) Ray Barker .20
(7) Rich Beck .20
(8) Yogi Berra 2.00
(9) Johnny Blanchard .50
(10) Gil Blanco .20
(11) Ron Blomberg .20
(12) Len Boehmer .20
(13) Jim Bouton .50
(14) Clete Boyer .50
(15) Jim Brenneman .20
(16) Marshall Bridges .20
(17) Harry Bright .20
(18) Hal Brown .20
(19) Billy Bryan .20
(20) Bill Burbach .20
(21) Andy Carey .20
(22) Duke Carmel .20
(23) Bob Cerv .20
(24) Horace Clarke .20
(25) Tex Clevenger .20
(26) Lu Clinton .20
(27) Jim Coates .20
(28) Rocky Colavito 1.50
(29) Billy Cowan .20
(30) Bobby Cox .50
(31) Jack Cullen .20
(32) John Cumberland .20
(33) Bud Daley .20
(34) Joe DeMaestri .20
(35) Art Ditmar .20
(36) Al Downing .30
(37) Ryne Duren .30
(38) Doc Edwards .20
(39) John Ellis .20
(40) Frank Fernandez .20
(41) Mike Ferraro .20
(42) Whitey Ford 2.00
(43) Bob Friend .20
(44) John Gabler .20
(45) Billy Gardner .20
(46) Jake Gibbs .20
(47) Jesse Gonder .20
(48) Pedro Gonzalez .20
(49) Eli Grba .20
(50) Kent Hadley .20
(51) Bob Hale .20
(52) Jimmie Hall .20
(53) Steve Hamilton .20
(54) Mike Hegan .30
(55) Bill Henry .20
(56) Elston Howard 1.00
(57) Dick Howser .50
(58) Ken Hunt .20
(59) Johnny James .20
(60) Elvio Jiminez .20
(61) Deron Johnson .30
(62) Ken Johnson .20
(63) Mike Jurewicz .50
(64) Mike Kekich .20
(65) John Kennedy .20
(66) Jerry Kenney .20
(67) Fred Kipp .20
(68) Ron Klimkowski .20
(69) Andy Kosco .20
(70) Tony Kubek .70
(71) Bill Kunkel .20
(72) Phil Linz .20
(73) Dale Long .30
(74) Art Lopez .20
(75) Hector Lopez .20
(76) Jim Lyttle .20
(77) Duke Maas .20
(78) Mickey Mantle 12.00
(79) Roger Maris 6.00
(80) Lindy McDaniel .20
(81) Danny McDevitt .20
(82) Dave McDonald .20
(83) Gil McDougald .50
(84) Tom Metcalf .20
(85) Bob Meyer .20
(86) Gene Michael .30
(87) Pete Mikkelsen .20
(88) John Miller .20
(89) Bill Monbouquette .20
(90) Archie Moore .20
(91) Ross Moschitto .20
(92) Thurman Munson 4.00
(93) Bobby Murcer .70
(94) Don Nottebart .20
(95) Nate Oliver .20
(96) Joe Pepitone .50
(97) Cecil Perkins .20
(98) Fritz Peterson .20
(99) Jim Pisoni .20
(100) Pedro Ramos .20
(101) Jack Reed .20
(102) Hal Reniff .20
(103) Roger Repoz .20
(104) Bobby Richardson .90
(105) Dale Roberts .50
(106) Bill Robinson .20
(107) Ellie Rodriguez .20
(108) Charlie Sands .20
(109) Bob Schmidt .20
(110) Dick Schofield .30
(111) Billy Shantz .20
(112) Bobby Shantz .30
(113) Rollie Sheldon .20
(114) Tom Shopay .20
(115) Bill Short .20
(116) Dick Simpson .20
(117) Bill Skowron .50
(118) Charley Smith .20
(119) Tony Solaita .20
(120) Bill Stafford .20
(121) Mel Stottlemyre .30
(122) Hal Stowe .20
(123) Fred Talbot .20
(124) Frank Tepedino .20
(125) Ralph Terry .20
(126) Lee Thomas .20
(127) Bobby Tiefenauer .20
(128) Bob Tillman .20
(129) Thad Tillotson .20
(130) Earl Torgeson .20
(131) Tom Tresh .50
(132) Bob Turley .30
(133) Elmer Valo .20
(134) Joe Verbanic .20
(135) Steve Whitaker .20
(136) Roy White .40
(137) Stan Williams .20
(138) Dooley Womack .20
(139) Ron Woods .20
(140) John Wyatt .20
Complete series, Yankees of the '70s 24.00
(1) Jack Aker .20
(2) Doyle Alexander .20
(3) Bernie Allen .20
(4) Sandy Alomar .20
(5) Felipe Alou .25
(6) Matty Alou .20
(7) Dell Alston .20
(8) Rick Anderson .20
(9) Stan Bahnsen .20
(10) Frank Baker .20
(11) Jim Beattie .20
(12) Fred Beene .20
(13) Juan Berenguer .20
(14) Dave Bergman .20
(15) Juan Bernhardt .20
(16) Rick Bladt .20
(17) Paul Blair .20
(18) Wade Blasingame .20
(19) Steve Blateric .20
(20) Curt Blefary .20
(21) Ron Blomberg .20
(22) Len Boehmer .20
(23) Bobby Bonds .30
(24) Ken Brett .20
(25) Ed Brinkman .20
(26) Bobby Brown .20
(27) Bill Burbach .20
(28) Ray Burris .20
(29) Tom Buskey .20
(30) Johnny Callison .20
(31) Danny Cater .20
(32) Chris Chambliss .30
(33) Horace Clarke .20
(34) Ken Clay .20
(35) Al Closter .20
(36) Rich Coggins .20
(37) Loyd Colson .20
(38) Casey Cox .20
(39) John Cumberland .20
(40) Ron Davis .20
(41) Jim Deidel .20
(42) Rick Dempsey .30
(43) Bucky Dent .40
(44) Kerry Dineen .20
(45) Pat Dobson .20
(46) Brian Doyle .20
(47) Rawly Eastwick .20
(48) Dock Ellis .20
(49) John Ellis .20
(50) Ed Figueroa .20
(51) Oscar Gamble .20
(52) Damaso Garcia .20
(53) Rob Gardner .20
(54) Jake Gibbs .20
(55) Fernando Gonzalez .20
(56) Rich Gossage .40
(57) Larry Gowell .20
(58) Wayne Granger .20
(59) Mike Griffin .20
(60) Ron Guidry .70
(61) Brad Gulden .20
(62) Don Gullett .20
(63) Larry Gura .20
(64) Roger Hambright .20
(65) Steve Hamilton .20
(66) Ron Hansen .20
(67) Jim Hardin .20
(68) Jim Ray Hart .20
(69) Fran Healy .20
(70) Mike Heath .20
(71) Mike Hegan .30
(72) Elrod Hendricks .20
(73) Ed Herrmann .20
(74) Rich Hinton .20
(75) Ken Holtzman .20
(76) Don Hood .20
(77) Catfish Hunter 1.00
(78) Grant Jackson .20
(79) Reggie Jackson 3.00
(80) Tommy John .90
(81) Alex Johnson .20
(82) Cliff Johnson .20
(83) Jay Johnstone .30
(84) Darryl Jones .20
(85) Gary Jones .20
(86) Jim Kaat .40
(87) Bob Kammeyer .20
(88) Mike Kekich .20
(89) Jerry Kenney .20
(90) Dave Kingman .50
(91) Ron Klimkowski .20
(92) Steve Kline .20
(93) Mickey Klutts .20
(94) Hal Lanier .20
(95) Eddie Leon .20
(96) Terry Ley .20
(97) Paul Lindblad .20
(98) Gene Locklear .20
(99) Sparky Lyle .40
(100) Jim Lyttle .20
(101) Elliott Maddox .20
(102) Jim Magnuson .20
(103) Tippy Martinez .20
(104) Jim Mason .20
(105) Carlos May .20
(106) Rudy May .20
(107) Larry McCall .20
(108) Mike McCormick .20
(109) Lindy McDaniel .20
(110) Sam McDowell .30
(111) Rich McKinney .20
(112) George Medich .20
(113) Andy Messersmith .30
(114) Gene Michael .20
(115) Paul Mirabolla .20
(116) Bobby Mitchell .20
(117) Gerry Moses .20
(118) Thurman Munson 4.00
(119) Bobby Murcer .70
(120) Larry Murray .20
(121) Jerry Narron .20
(122) Graig Nettles .40
(123) Bob Oliver .20
(124) Dave Pagan .20
(125) Gil Patterson .20
(126) Marty Perez .20
(127) Fritz Peterson .20
(128) Lou Piniella .50
(129) Dave Rajsich .20
(130) Domingo Ramos .20
(131) Lenny Randle .20
(132) Willie Randolph .50
(133) Dave Righetti .30
(134) Mickey Rivers .30
(135) Bruce Robinson .20
(136) Jim Roland .20
(137) Celerino Sanchez .20
(138) Rick Sawyer .20
(139) George Scott .30
(140) Duke Sims .20
(141) Roger Slagle .20
(142) Jim Spencer .20
(143) Charlie Spikes .20
(144) Roy Staiger .20
(145) Fred Stanley .30
(146) Bill Sudakis .20
(147) Ron Swoboda .20
(148) Frank Tepedino .20
(149) Stan Thomas .20
(150) Gary Thomasson .20
(151) Luis Tiant .40
(152) Dick Tidrow .20
(153) Rusty Torres .20
(154) Mike Torrez .30
(155) Cesar Tovar .20
(156) Cecil Upshaw .20
(157) Otto Velez .20
(158) Joe Verbanic .20
(159) Mike Wallace .20
(160) Danny Walton .20
(161) Pete Ward .20
(162) Gary Waslewski .20
(163) Dennis Werth .20
(164) Roy White .30
(165) Terry Whitfield .20
(166) Walt Williams .20
(167) Ron Woods .20
(168) Dick Woodson .20
(169) Ken Wright .20
(170) Jimmy Wynn .30
(171) Jim York .20
(172) George Zeber .20
Complete series, Yankees of the '80s: 24.00
(1) Luis Aguayo .20
(2) Doyle Alexander .20
(3) Neil Allen .20
(4) Mike Armstrong .20
(5) Brad Arnsberg .20
(6) Tucker Ashford .20
(7) Steve Balboni .20
(8) Jesse Barfield .30
(9) Don Baylor .40
(10) Dale Berra .20
(11) Doug Bird .20
(12) Paul Blair .30
(13) Mike Blowers .30
(14) Juan Bonilla .20

(15) Rich Bordi .20
(16) Scott Bradley .20
(17) Marshall Brant .20
(18) Tom Brookens .20
(19) Bob Brower .20
(20) Bobby Brown .20
(21) Curt Brown .20
(22) Jay Buhner .90
(23) Marty Bystrom .20
(24) Greg Cadaret .20
(25) Bert Campaneris .30
(26) John Candelaria .30
(27) Chuck Cary .20
(28) Bill Castro .20
(29) Rick Cerone .30
(30) Chris Chambliss .30
(31) Clay Christiansen .20
(32) Jack Clark .30
(33) Pat Clements .20
(34) Dave Collins .25
(35) Don Cooper .20
(36) Henry Cotto .20
(37) Joe Cowley .20
(38) Jose Cruz .30
(39) Bobby Davidson .20
(40) Ron Davis .20
(41) Brian Dayett .20
(42) Ivan DeJesus .30
(43) Bucky Dent .50
(44) Jim Deshaies .30
(45) Orestes Destrade .20
(46) Brian Dorsett .20
(47) Rich Dotson .20
(48) Brian Doyle .20
(49) Doug Drabek .30
(50) Mike Easler .20
(51) Dave Eiland .20
(52) Roger Erickson .20
(53) Juan Espino .20
(54) Alvaro Espinoza .20
(55) Barry Evans .20
(56) Ed Figueroa .20
(57) Pete Filson .20
(58) Mike Fischlin .20
(59) Brian Fisher .20
(60) Tim Foli .20
(61) Ray Fontenot .20
(62) Barry Foote .20
(63) George Frazier .20
(64) Bill Fulton .20
(65) Oscar Gamble .20
(66) Bob Geren .20
(67) Rich Gossage .40
(68) Mike Griffin .20
(69) Ken Griffey .30
(70) Cecilio Guante .20
(71) Lee Guetterman .20
(72) Ron Guidry .50
(73) Brad Gulden .20
(74) Don Gullett .20
(75) Bill Gullickson .20
(76) Mel Hall .30
(77) Toby Harrah .25
(78) Ron Hassey .20
(79) Andy Hawkins .20
(80) Rickey Henderson 1.50
(81) Leo Hernandez .20
(82) Butch Hobson .20
(83) Al Holland .20
(84) Roger Holt .20
(85) Jay Howell .25
(86) Rex Hudler .20
(87) Charles Hudson .20
(88) Keith Hughes .20
(89) Reggie Jackson 3.00
(90) Stan Javier .30
(91) Stan Jefferson .20
(92) Tommy John .50
(93) Jimmy Jones .20
(94) Ruppert Jones .20
(95) Jim Kaat .30
(96) Curt Kaufman .20
(97) Roberto Kelly .30
(98) Steve Kemp .25
(99) Matt Keough .20
(100) Steve Kiefer .20
(101) Ron Kittle .20
(102) Dave LaPoint .20
(103) Marcus Lawton .20
(104) Joe Lefebvre .20
(105) Al Leiter .20
(106) Jim Lewis .20
(107) Bryan Little .20
(108) Tim Lollar .20
(109) Phil Lombardi .20
(110) Vic Mata .20
(111) Don Mattingly 4.00
(112) Rudy May .20
(113) John Mayberry .20
(114) Lee Mazzilli .30
(115) Lance McCullers .20
(116) Andy McGaffigan .20
(117) Lynn McGlothen .20
(118) Bobby Meacham .20
(119) Hensley Muelens .30
(120) Larry Milbourne .20
(121) Kevin Mmahat .20
(122) Dale Mohorcic .20
(123) John Montefusco .20
(124) Omar Moreno .20
(125) Mike Morgan .20
(126) Jeff Moronko .20
(127) Hal Morris .30
(128) Jerry Mumphrey .20
(129) Bobby Murcer .30
(130) Dale Murray .20
(131) Gene Nelson .20
(132) Joe Niekro .30
(133) Phil Niekro .90
(134) Scott Nielsen .20
(135) Otis Nixon .20
(136) Johnny Oates .20
(137) Mike O'Berry .20
(138) Rowland Office .20
(139) John Pacella .20
(140) Mike Pagliarulo .30
(141) Clay Parker .20
(142) Dan Pasqua .20
(143) Mike Patterson .20
(144) Hipolito Pena .20
(145) Gaylord Perry .50
(146) Ken Phelps .20
(147) Lou Piniella .40
(148) Eric Plunk .20
(149) Luis Polonia .30
(150) Alfonso Pulido .20
(151) Jamie Quirk .20
(152) Bobby Ramos .20
(153) Willie Randolph .40
(154) Dennis Rasmussen .20
(155) Shane Rawley .20
(156) Rick Reuschel .20
(157) Dave Revering .20
(158) Rick Rhoden .20
(159) Dave Righetti .30
(160) Jose Rijo .40
(161) Andre Robertson .20
(162) Bruce Robinson .20
(163) Aurelio Rodriguez .20
(164) Edwin Rodriguez .20
(165) Gary Roenicke .20
(166) Jerry Royster .20
(167) Lenn Sakata .20
(168) Mark Salas .20
(169) Billy Sample .20
(170) Deion Sanders 3.00
(171) Rafael Santana .20
(172) Steve Sax .30
(173) Don Schulze .20
(174) Rodney Scott .20
(175) Rod Scurry .20
(176) Dennis Sherrill .20
(177) Steve Shields .20
(178) Bob Shirley .20
(179) Joel Skinner .20
(180) Don Slaught .30
(181) Roy Smalley .20
(182) Keith Smith .20
(183) Eric Soderholm .20
(184) Jim Spencer .20
(185) Fred Stanley .20
(186) Dave Stegman .20
(187) Tim Stoddard .20
(188) Walt Terrell .20
(189) Bob Tewksbury .40
(190) Luis Tiant .40
(191) Wayne Tolleson .20
(192) Steve Trout .20
(193) Tom Underwood .20
(194) Randy Velarde .30
(195) Gary Ward .20
(196) Claudell Washington .30
(197) Bob Watson .20
(198) Dave Wehrmeister .20
(199) Dennis Werth .20
(200) Stefan Wever .20
(201) Ed Whitson .20
(202) Ted Wilborn .20
(203) Dave Winfield 1.00
(204) Butch Wynegar .20
(205) Paul Zuvella .20
Complete series, Yankees All-Stars 24.00
(1) Luis Arroyo .20
(2) Hank Bauer .30
(3) Yogi Berra 2.00
(4) Bobby Bonds .30
(5) Ernie Bonham .20
(6) Hank Borowy .20
(7) Jim Bouton .30
(8) Tommy Byrne .20
(9) Chris Chambliss .20
(10) Spud Chandler .20
(11) Ben Chapman .20
(12) Jim Coates .20
(13) Jerry Coleman .20
(14) Frank Crosetti .20
(15) Ron Davis .20
(16) Bucky Dent .30
(17) Bill Dickey .50
(18) Joe DiMaggio 6.00
(19) Al Downing .20
(20) Ryne Duren .30
(21) Whitey Ford 2.00
(22) Lou Gehrig 6.00
(23) Lefty Gomez .40
(24) Joe Gordon .20
(25) Rich Gossage .30
(26) Bob Grim .20
(27) Ron Guidry .30
(28) Rollie Hemsley .20
(29) Rickey Henderson 1.50
(30) Tommy Henrich .20
(31) Elston Howard .30
(32) Catfish Hunter .30
(33) Reggie Jackson 3.00
(34) Tommy John .30
(35) Billy Johnson .20
(36) Charlie Keller .20
(37) Tony Kubek .30
(38) Johnny Kucks .20
(39) Tony Lazzeri .30
(40) Johnny Lindell .20
(41) Ed Lopat .30
(42) Sparky Lyle .30
(43) Mickey Mantle 12.00
(44) Roger Maris 6.00
(45) Billy Martin .70
(46) Don Mattingly 4.00
(47) Gil McDougald .30
(48) George McQuinn .20
(49) Johnny Mize .40
(50) Thurman Munson 4.00
(51) Bobby Murcer .30
(52) Johnny Murphy .20
(53) Graig Nettles .20
(54) Phil Niekro .80
(55) Irv Noren .20
(56) Joe Page .20
(57) Monte Pearson .20
(58) Joe Pepitone .30
(59) Fritz Peterson .20
(60) Willie Randolph .30
(61) Vic Raschi .20
(62) Allie Reynolds .30
(63) Bobby Richardson .30
(64) Dave Righetti .20
(65) Mickey Rivers .20
(66) Phil Rizzuto 2.00
(67) Aaron Robinson .20
(68) Red Rolfe .20
(69) Buddy Rosar .20
(70) Red Ruffing .20
(71) Marius Russo .20
(72) Babe Ruth 8.00
(73) Johnny Sain .40
(74) Scott Sanderson .20
(75) Steve Sax .20
(76) George Selkirk .20
(77) Bobby Shantz .20
(78) Spec Shea .20
(79) Bill Skowron .30
(80) Snuffy Stirnweiss .20
(81) Mel Stottlemyre .20
(82) Ralph Terry .20
(83) Tom Tresh .20
(84) Bob Turley .20
(85) Roy White .30
(86) Dave Winfield 1.00
Complete series, Yankees Hall of Famers 20.00
(1) Home Run Baker .50
(2) Ed Barrow .20
(3) Yogi Berra 2.00
(4) Frank Chance .50
(5) Jack Chesbro .20
(6) Earle Combs .20
(7) Stan Coveleski .20
(8) Bill Dickey .50
(9) Joe DiMaggio 6.00
(10) Whitey Ford 2.00
(11) Lou Gehrig 6.00
(12) Lefty Gomez .50
(13) Clark C. Griffith .20
(14) Burleigh Grimes .20
(15) Bucky Harris .20
(16) Waite Hoyt .20
(17) Miller Huggins .20
(18) Catfish Hunter .30
(19) Willie Keeler .20
(20) Tony Lazzeri .20
(21) Larry MacPhail .20
(22) Mickey Mantle 12.00
(23) Joe McCarthy .20
(24) Johnny Mize .30
(25) Herb Pennock .20
(26) Gaylord Perry .20
(27) Branch Rickey .20
(28) Red Ruffing .20
(29) Babe Ruth 8.00
(30) Joe Sewell .20
(31) Enos Slaughter .30
(32) Casey Stengel .30
(33) Dazzy Vance .20
(34) Paul Waner .20
(35) George M. Weiss .20

1990 Wonder Stars

The cards were found in specially marked loaves of Wonder Bread, in a special plastic pocket to protect them from product stains (and vice versa). Uncut sheets could also be obtained for $3 and proofs of purchase. Produced by Mike Schechter Associates, the photos at the center of the cards have had team logos airbrushed away for lack of a license from MLB. The cards are licensed by the players' union. A red border surrounds the photo on front. Backs are printed in red and blue on white and have up to five years' worth of stats, a few lines of career highlights and a facsimile autograph.

		MT
Complete Set (20):		12.00
Common Player:		.25
1	Bo Jackson	.35
2	Roger Clemens	.75
3	Jim Abbott	.25
4	Orel Hershiser	.25
5	Ozzie Smith	.50
6	Don Mattingly	1.00
7	Kevin Mitchell	.25
8	Jerome Walton	.25
9	Kirby Puckett	1.00
10	Darryl Strawberry	.30
11	Robin Yount	.50
12	Tony Gwynn	.75
13	Alan Trammell	.25
14	Jose Canseco	.60
15	Greg Swindell	.25
16	Nolan Ryan	2.00
17	Howard Johnson	.25
18	Ken Griffey Jr.	2.50
19	Will Clark	.40
20	Ryne Sandberg	.60

1988 Woolworth

This 33-card boxed set was produced by Topps for exclusive distribution at Woolworth stores. The set includes 18 individual player cards and 15 World Series game-action photo cards. World Series cards include two for each game of the Series, plus a card of 1987 Series MVP Frank Viola. A white-lettered caption beneath the photo consists of either the player's name or a World Series game notation. Card backs are red, white and blue and contain a brief description of the photo on the front.

		MT
Complete Set (33):		3.00
Common Player:		.10
1	Don Baylor	.15
2	Vince Coleman	.10
3	Darrell Evans	.10
4	Don Mattingly	.85
5	Eddie Murray	.35
6	Nolan Ryan	2.00
7	Mike Schmidt	.45
8	Andre Dawson	.20
9	George Bell	.10
10	Steve Bedrosian	.10
11	Roger Clemens	.50
12	Tony Gwynn	.50
13	Wade Boggs	.35
14	Benny Santiago	.10
15	Mark McGwire	2.00
16	Dave Righetti	.10
17	Jeffrey Leonard	.10
18	Gary Gaetti	.10
19	World Series Game #1 (Frank Viola)	.10
20	World Series Game #1 (Dan Gladden)	.10
21	World Series Game #2 (Bert Blyleven)	.10
22	World Series Game #2 (Gary Gaetti)	.10
23	World Series Game #3 (John Tudor)	.10
24	World Series Game #3 (Todd Worrell)	.10
25	World Series Game #4 (Tom Lawless)	.10
26	World Series Game #4 (Willie McGee)	.10
27	World Series Game #5 (Danny Cox)	.10
28	World Series Game #5 (Curt Ford)	.10
29	World Series Game #6 (Don Baylor)	.10
30	World Series Game #6 (Kent Hrbek)	.10
31	World Series Game #7 (Kirby Puckett)	.35
32	World Series Game #7 (Greg Gagne)	.10
33	World Series MVP (Frank Viola)	.10

1989 Woolworth

This 33-card set was produced by Topps for the Woolworth store chain and was sold in a special box with a checklist on the back. The glossy-coated cards commemorate the most memorable moments in baseball from the the 1988 season. The backs include a description of the various highlights.

		MT
Complete Set (33):		3.00
Common Player:		.10
1	Jose Canseco	.45
2	Kirk Gibson	.10
3	Frank Viola	.10
4	Orel Hershiser	.10
5	Walt Weiss	.10
6	Chris Sabo	.10
7	George Bell	.10
8	Wade Boggs	.45
9	Tom Browning	.10
10	Gary Carter	.15
11	Andre Dawson	.15
12	John Franco	.10
13	Randy Johnson	.30
14	Doug Jones	.10
15	Kevin McReynolds	.10
16	Gene Nelson	.10
17	Jeff Reardon	.10
18	Pat Tabler	.10
19	Tim Belcher	.10
20	Dennis Eckersley	.10
21	Orel Hershiser	.10
22	Gregg Jefferies	.10
23	Jose Canseco	.45
24	Kirk Gibson	.10
25	Orel Hershiser	.10
26	Mike Marshall	.10
27	Mark McGwire	2.00
28	Rick Honeycutt	.10
29	Tim Belcher	.10
30	Jay Howell	.10
31	Mickey Hatcher	.10
32	Mike Davis	.10
33	Orel Hershiser	.10

1990 Woolworth

This 33-card set highlights the great baseball moments of 1989. The cards are styled like past Woolworth sets. The set features award winners and regular and post-season highlights.

		MT
Complete Set (33):		3.00
Common Player:		.10
1	Robin Yount	.45
2	Kevin Mitchell	.10
3	Bret Saberhagen	.10
4	Mark Davis	.10
5	Gregg Olson	.10

6	Jerome Walton	.10
7	Bert Blyleven	.10
8	Wade Boggs	.35
9	George Brett	.65
10	Vince Coleman	.10
11	Andre Dawson	.15
12	Dwight Evans	.10
13	Carlton Fisk	.20
14	Rickey Henderson	.25
15	Dale Murphy	.20
16	Eddie Murray	.25
17	Jeff Reardon	.10
18	Rick Reuschel	.10
19	Cal Ripken, Jr.	1.00
20	Nolan Ryan	1.00
21	Ryne Sandberg	.40
22	Robin Yount	.45
23	Rickey Henderson	.25
24	Will Clark	.20
25	Dave Stewart	.10
26	Walt Weiss	.10
27	Mike Moore	.10
28	Terry Steinbach	.10
29	Dave Henderson	.10
30	Matt Williams	.15
31	Rickey Henderson	.25
32	Kevin Mitchell	.10
33	Dave Stewart	.10

1991 Woolworth

This 33-card boxed set was produced by Topps for distribution at Woolworth stores. Yellow borders are featured on the fronts of the glossy cards. The backs feature baseball highlights from the previous season. Award winners, regular season and World Series highlights are showcased.

		MT
Complete Set (33):		3.00
Common Player:		.10
1	Barry Bonds	.75
2	Rickey Henderson	.20
3	Doug Drabek	.10
4	Bob Welch	.10
5	Dave Justice	.25
6	Sandy Alomar, Jr.	.15
7	Bert Blyleven	.10
8	George Brett	.65
9	Andre Dawson	.15
10	Dwight Evans	.10
11	Alex Fernandez	.10
12	Carlton Fisk	.15
13	Kevin Maas	.10
14	Dale Murphy	.20
15	Eddie Murray	.30
16	Dave Parker	.10
17	Jeff Reardon	.10
18	Cal Ripken, Jr.	1.00
19	Nolan Ryan	1.00
20	Ryne Sandberg	.45
21	Bobby Thigpen	.10
22	Robin Yount	.45
23	Nasty Boys (Rob Dibble, Randy Myers)	.10
24	Dave Stewart	.10
25	Eric Davis	.10
26	Rickey Henderson	.20
27	Billy Hatcher	.10
28	Joe Oliver	.10
29	Chris Sabo	.10
30	Barry Larkin	.15
31	Jose Rijo	.10
32	Reds Celebrate	.10
33	Jose Rijo (World Series MVP)	.10

1986-88 World Wide Sports Conlon Collection

Marketed as complete series through World Wide Sports, five sets of black-and-white cards featuring the game's great players of the 1905-1935 era were made utilizing the photos of Charles Martin Conlon. The 2-1/2" x 3-1/2" cards carry the copyright of "The Sporting News," owner of the Conlon photos. The 60 cards of Series one each feature a Babe Ruth logo in the lower-left corner, the only graphic on the borderless card front. Series two has no front logo. Series 3-5 have a sliding Ty Cobb logo. Backs feature a line of career stats, a few bits of biographical data and a paragraph of highlights written by TSN historian Paul MacFarlane. The first two series were produced in an edition of 12,000 sets each; production of the other series was not announced. Cards in Series 3-5 are not numbered and are checklisted here alphabetically. Series designations are in small print at back-bottom.

		MT
Complete Set (211):		45.00
Common Player:		.25
Series 1 - 1986:		15.00
1	Lou Gehrig	1.00
2	Ty Cobb	1.00
3	Grover C. Alexander	.25
4	Walter Johnson	.50
5	Bill Klem	.25
6	Ty Cobb	1.00
7	Gordon S. Cochrane	.25
8	Paul Waner	.25
9	Joe Cronin	.25
10	Jay Hannah Dean	.25
11	Leo Durocher	.25
12	Jimmie Foxx	.25
13	Babe Ruth	1.50
14	Mike Gonzalez, Frank Frisch, Clyde Wares	.25
15	Carl Hubbell	.25
16	Miller Huggins	.25
17	Lou Gehrig	1.00
18	Connie Mack	.25
19	Heinie Manush	.25
20	Babe Ruth	1.50
21	Al Simmons	.25
22	Pepper Martin	.25
23	Christy Mathewson	.50
24	Ty Cobb	1.00
25	Stanley Harris	.25
26	Waite Hoyt	.25
27	Rube Marquard	.25
28	Joe McCarthy	.25
29	John McGraw	.25
30	Tris Speaker	.25
31	Bill Terry	.25
32	Christy Mathewson	.50
33	Casey Stengel	.25
34	Robert W. Meusel	.25
35	George Edward Waddell	.25
36	Mel Ott	.25
37	Roger Peckinpaugh	.25
38	Pie Traynor	.25
39	Chief Bender	.25
40	John W. Coombs	.25
41	Ty Cobb	1.00
42	Harry Heilmann	.25
43	Charlie Gehringer	.25
44	Rogers Hornsby	.25
45	Vernon Gomez	.25
46	Christy Mathewson	.50
47	Robert M. Grove	.25
48	Babe Ruth	1.50
49	Fred Merkle	.25
50	Babe Ruth	1.50
51	Herb Pennock	.25
52	Lou Gehrig	1.00
53	Fred Clarke	.25
54	Babe Ruth	1.50
55	John P. Wagner	.50
56	Hack Wilson	.25
57	Lou Gehrig	1.00
58	Lloyd Waner	.25
59	Charles Martin Conlon	.25
60	Charles & Margie Conlon	.25
---	Header card	.25
Series 2 - 1987:		10.00
1	Lou Gehrig	1.00
2	Vernon Gomez	.25
3	Christy Mathewson	.50
4	Grover Alexander	.25
5	Ty Cobb	1.00
6	Walter Johnson	.50
7	Charles (Babe) Adams	.25
8	Nick Altrock	.25
9	Al Schacht	.25
10	Hugh Critz	.25
11	Henry Cullop	.25
12	Jake Daubert	.25
13	Bill Donovan	.25
14	Chick Hafey	.25
15	Bill Hallahan	.25
16	Fred Haney	.25
17	Charles Hartnett	.25
18	Walter Henline	.25
19	Ed Rommel	.25
20	Ralph "Babe" Pinelli	.25
21	Bob Meusel	.25
22	Emil Meusel	.25
23	Smead Jolley	.25
24	Ike Boone	.25
25	Earl Webb	.25
26	Charles Comiskey	.25
27	Edward Collins	.25
28	Geroge (Buck) Weaver	.50
29	Eddie Cicotte	.50
30	Sam Crawford	.25
31	Chuck Dressen	.25
32	Arthur Fletcher	.25
33	Hugh Duffy	.25
34	Ira Flagstead	.25
35	Harry Hooper	.25
36	George E. Lewis	.25
37	James Dykes	.25
38	Leon Goslin	.25
39	Henry Gowdy	.25
40	Charles Grimm	.25
41	Mark Koenig	.25
42	James Hogan	.25
43	William Jacobson	.25
44	Fielder Jones	.25
45	George Kelly	.25
46	Adolfo Luque	.40
47	Walter Maranville	.25
48	Carl Mays	.25
49	Eddie Plank	.25
50	Hubert Pruett	.25
51	John (Picus) Quinn	.25
52	Charles (Flint) Rhem	.25
53	Amos Rusie	.25
54	Edd Roush	.25
55	Ray Schalk	.25
56	Ernie Shore	.25
57	Joe Wood	.25
58	George Sisler	.25
59	James Thorpe	1.00
60	Earl Whitehill	.25
Series 3 - 1988:		5.00
(1)	Ace Adams	.25
(2)	Grover C. Alexander	.25
(3)	Eldon Auker	.25
(4)	Jack Barry	.25
(5)	Wally Berger	.25
(6)	Ben Chapman	.25
(7)	Mickey Cochrane	.25
(8)	Frank Crosetti	.25
(9)	Paul Dean	.25
(10)	Leo Durocher	.25
(11)	Wes Ferrell	.25
(12)	Hank Gowdy	.25
(13)	Andy High	.25
(14)	Rogers Hornsby	.25
(15)	Carl Hubbell	.25
(16)	Joe Judge	.25
(17)	Tony Lazzeri	.25
(18)	Pepper Martin	.25
(19)	Lee Meadows	.25
(20)	Jimmy Murphy	.25
(21)	Steve O'Neill	.25
(22)	Ed Plank	.25
(23)	John P. Quinn	.25
(24)	Charlie Root	.25
(25)	Babe Ruth	1.50
(26)	Fred Snodgrass	.25
(27)	Tris Speaker	.25
(28)	Bill Terry	.25
(29)	Jeff Tesreau	.25
(30)	George Torporcer	.25
Series 4 - 1988:		5.00
(1)	Dale Alexander	.25
(2)	Morris Badgro	.25
(3)	Dick Bartell	.25
(4)	Max Bishop	.25
(5)	Hal Chase	.40
(6)	Ty Cobb	1.00
(7)	Nick Cullop	.25
(8)	Dizzy Dean	.40
(9)	Chuck Dressen	.25
(10)	Jimmy Dykes	.25
(11)	Art Fletcher	.25
(12)	Charlie Grimm	.25
(13)	Lefty Grove	.25
(14)	Baby Doll Jacobson	.25
(15)	Bill Klem	.25
(16)	Mark Koenig	.25
(17)	Duffy Lewis	.25
(18)	Carl Mays	.25
(19)	Fred Merkle	.25
(20)	Greasy Neale	.40
(21)	Mel Ott	.25
(22)	"Babe" Pinelli	.25
(23)	Flint Rhem	.25
(24)	Slim Sallee	.25
(25)	Al Simmons	.25
(26)	George Sisler	.25
(27)	Riggs Stephenson	.25
(28)	Jim Thorpe	1.00
(29)	Bill Wambsganss	.25
(30)	Cy Young	.40
Series 5 - 1988:		5.00
(1)	Nick Altrock	.25
(2)	Del Baker	.25
(3)	Moe Berg	1.00
(4)	Zeke Bonura	.25
(5)	Eddie Collins	.25
(6)	Hugh Critz	.25
(7)	George Dauss	.25
(8)	Joe Dugan	.25
(9)	Howard Ehmke	.25
(10)	Jimmie Foxx	.25
(11)	Frank Frisch	.25
(12)	Lou Gehrig	1.00
(13)	Charlie Gehringer	.25
(14)	Kid Gleason	.25
(15)	Lefty Gomez	.25
(16)	Babe Herman	.25
(17)	Bill James	.25
(18)	Joe Kuhel	.25
(19)	Dolf Luque	.40
(20)	John McGraw	.25
(21)	Stuffy McInnis	.25
(22)	Bob Meusel	.25
(23)	Lefty O'Doul	.25
(24)	Hub Pruett	.25
(25)	Paul Richards	.25
(26)	Bob Shawkey	.25
(27)	Gabby Street	.25
(28)	Johnny Tobin	.25
(29)	Rube Waddell	.25
(30)	Billy Werber	.25

1988 World Wide Sports 1933 All-Stars

The photos of Charles M. Conlon in The Sporting News' archive are the basis for this collectors issue depicting the players of the original All-Star Game of 1933. Fronts have sepia photo of the players on a 2-1/2" x 3-1/2" format. The only graphics added to the front are in the upper-right corner designating the league which the player represented. Backs have 1933 and career stats, along with a career summary. The unnumbered cards are checklisted here in alphabetical order within league.

		MT
Complete Set (48):		12.00
Common Player:		.25
	American League	6.00
(1)	Luke Appling	.25
(2)	Earl Averill	.25
(3)	Tommy Bridges	.25
(4)	Ben Chapman	.25
(5)	Mickey Cochrane	.25
(6)	Joe Cronin	.25
(7)	Alvin Crowder	.25
(8)	Bill Dickey	.35
(9)	Jimmie Foxx	.45
(10)	Lou Gehrig	1.00
(11)	Charlie Gehringer	.35
(12)	Lefty Gomez	.25
(13)	Lefty Grove	.25
(14)	Mel Harder	.25
(15)	Pinky Higgins	.25
(16)	Urban Hodapp	.25
(17)	Roy Johnson	.25
(18)	Joe Kuhel	.25
(19)	Tony Lazzeri	.25
(20)	Heinie Manush	.25
(21)	Babe Ruth	1.50
(22)	Al Simmons	.25
(23)	Evar Swanson	.25
(24)	Earl Whitehill	.25
	National League	6.00
(1)	Wally Berger	.25
(2)	Guy Bush	.25
(3)	Ripper Collins	.25
(4)	Spud Davis	.25
(5)	Dizzy Dean	.45
(6)	Johnny Frederick	.25
(7)	Larry French	.25
(8)	Frank Frisch	.25
(9)	Chick Fullis	.25
(10)	Chick Hafey	.25
(11)	Carl Hubbell	.25
(12)	Chuck Klein	.25
(13)	Freddie Lindstrom	.25
(14)	Pepper Martin	.25
(15)	Ducky Medwick	.25
(16)	Tony Piet	.25
(17)	Wes Schulmerich	.25
(18)	Hal Schumacher	.25
(19)	Riggs Stephenson	.25
(20)	Bill Terry	.25
(21)	Paul Traynor	.25
(22)	Arky Vaughan	.25
(23)	Paul Waner	.25
(24)	Lon Warneke	.25

1988 World Wide Sports 1933 Negro All Stars

The photos of Charles M. Conlon in The Sporting News' archive are the basis for this collectors issue depicting "1933 Negro All Stars. Fronts have borderless sepia photos of the players on a 2-1/2" x 3-1/2" format. The only graphics added to the front are in the upper-right corner designating the All-Star status. Backs have a few personal data along with a career summary. The unnumbered cards are checklisted here in alphabetical order.

		MT
Complete Set (12):		6.00
Common Player:		.50
(1)	Cool Papa Bell	.50
(2)	Oscar Charleston	.50
(3)	Martin Dihigo	.50
(4)	Andrew (Rube) Foster	.50
(5)	Josh Gibson	.75
(6)	Judy Johnson	.50
(7)	Buck Leonard	.50
(8)	Pop Lloyd	.50
(9)	Dave Malarcher	.50
(10)	Satchel Paige	1.00
(11)	Willie Wells	.50
(12)	Joe Williams	.50

1988 Worth Jose Canseco

This one-card "set" was issued in conjunction with Jose Canseco's endorsement of Worth bats in 1988. Printed in black-and-white on thin cardboard, the front features a photo of Canseco in civilian clothes with a white facsimile autograph at the bottom. His name appears in black block letters at the bottom. The back has a few biographical details and career highlights, along with the Worth logo. The card measures the standard 2-1/2" x 3-1/2". Thousands of the card made their way into the hobby via one New York dealer at the time of issue and it remains common today.

		MT
1	Jose Canseco	.50

1989 W/R Associates Mark Grace

This collectors' issue traces the career of Mark Grace

on a nine-card panel which includes eight standard 2-1/2" x 3-1/2" cards and a 5" x 7" card on a sheet with overall dimensions of 10-5/8" x 14". Because the issue was licensed only by the player, and not Major League Baseball, all Cubs uniform logos have been removed from the photos. Cards are numbered on front and back with a year identifying the photo. Backs are printed in red, white and blue and include biographical data and career summary. The large-format card offers complete major and minor league stats on back. The cards on the sheet are not perforated and individual cards are rarely encountered. Sheets were offered in either autographed or unautographed form with production limited to 15,000 sheets.

		MT
Complete Sheet:		9.00
Complete Sheet, Autographed:		35.00
Complete Set, Cut (9):		6.00
Common Card:		.50
73	Mark Grace (boyhood photo)	.50
83	Mark Grace (San Diego State)	.50
86	Mark Grace (minor league)	.50
87	Mark Grace (throwing)	.50
88a	Mark Grace (fielding)	.50
88b	Mark Grace (wedding)	.50
89a	Mark Grace, Mark Grace (batting batting)	.50
89b	Mark Grace (batting)	.50
----	Mark Grace (5" x 7" portrait, autographed)	25.00
----	Mark Grace (5" x 7" portrait, unsigned)	4.00

1985 WTBS Atlanta Braves

This set of large-format (8-1/4" x 10-3/4") cards was issued by the Braves' TV broadcaster, WTBS. The sets were given to potential sponsors as part of a "kit" inviting them to Florida to attend a spring training game. It was reported that only 600 sets were printed and 150 of them were destroyed. Fronts feature player portraits on brightly colored backgrounds. There is a facsimile autograph and a large star-boxed "AMERICA'S TEAM". Backs are in red and black and have some vital data and stats for the 1982-84 seasons. Cards are numbered according to uniform number.

		MT
Complete Set (4):		45.00
Common Player:		9.00
3	Dale Murphy	20.00
7	Brad Komminsk	9.00
15	Claudell Washington	9.00
42	Bruce Sutter	12.00

Y

1993 Yoo-Hoo

The Yoo Hoo beverage company, which had a promotional affiliation with Yogi Berra as far back as the 1950's, made Berra the #1 card in a 1993 set of 20 baseball legends that was released in two series. All of the players included in the set are retired, and all but five are Hall of Famers (at this printing). The unnumbered cards feature a yellow border with a color photo on the front; the backs have the player's statistics and biographical information.

		MT
Complete Set (20):		10.00
Common Player:		.25
Series 1		
(1)	Yogi Berra	.75
(2)	Joe Morgan	.35
(3)	Duke Snider	.75
(4)	Steve Garvey	.30
(5)	Jim Rice	.25
(6)	Bob Feller	.40
(7)	Pete Rose	.90
(8)	Rod Carew	.40
(9)	Gaylord Perry	.30
(10)	Graig Nettles	.25
Series 2		
(1)	Johnny Bench	.40
(2)	Lou Brock	.40
(3)	Stan Musial	1.00
(4)	Willie McCovey	.45
(5)	Whitey Ford	.50
(6)	Phil Rizzuto	.50
(7)	Tom Seaver	.50
(8)	Willie Stargell	.40
(9)	Brooks Robinson	.45
(10)	Al Kaline	.45

The election of former players to the Hall of Fame does not always have an immediate upward effect on card prices. The hobby market generally has done a good job of predicting those inductions and adjusting values over the course of several years.

1994 Yoo-Hoo

		MT
Complete Set (20):		16.00
Common Player:		.50
1	Luis Aparicio	.65
2	Bobby Bonds	.50
3	Bob Boone	.50
4	Steve Carlton	.75
5	Roberto Clemente	2.00
6	Bob Gibson	.75
7	Keith Hernandez	.50
8	Jim Kaat	.50
9	Roger Maris	1.50
10	Don Mattingly	1.25
11	Thurman Munson	.90
12	Phil Rizzuto	.75
13	Brooks Robinson	.75
14	Ryne Sandberg	1.00
15	Mike Schmidt	1.00
16	Carl Yastrzemski	.90
17	Fact Card	.25
18	Fact Card	.25
19	Fact Card	.25
20	Fact Card	.25

1999 Robin Yount Celebrity Golf Classic

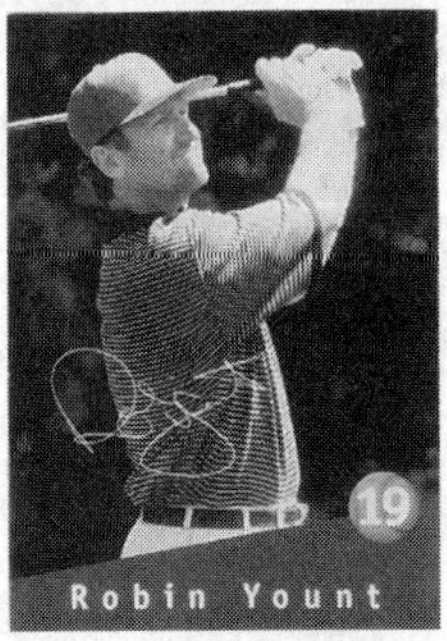

This card was distributed in an edition of 3,000 in conjunction with the Hall of Famer's golf benefit in Milwaukee, June 24-25. On front there is a facsimile autograph printed over a photo of Yount swinging a golf club. His uniform number appears in a circle at right. On back are printed his career achievements and information about charitable aspects of the tournament.

	MT
Robin Yount	15.00

Z

1982 Zellers Expos

Produced and distributed by the Zellers department stores in Canada, this 60-card set was produced in the form of 20 three-card panels. The cards feature a photo of the player surrounded by rings and a yellow background. A red "Zellers" is above the photo and on either side of it are the words "Baseball Pro Tips" in English on the left and in French on the right. The player's name and the title of the playing tip are under the photo. Backs have the playing tip in both languages. Single cards measure 2-1/2" x 3-1/2" while the whole panel is 7-1/2" x 3-1/2". Although a number of stars are depicted, this set is not terribly popular as collectors do not generally like the playing tips idea. Total panels are worth more than separated cards.

		MT
Complete Set (20):		8.00
Common Player:		.25
1	Gary Carter (Catching Position)	.75
2	Steve Rogers (Pitching Stance)	.25
3	Tim Raines (Sliding)	.60
4	Andre Dawson (Batting Stance)	1.00
5	Terry Francona (Contact Hitting)	.25
6	Gary Carter (Fielding Pop Fouls)	.75
7	Warren Cromartie (Fielding at First Base)	.25
8	Chris Speier (Fielding at Shortstop)	.25
9	Billy DeMars (Signals)	.25
10	Andre Dawson (Batting Stroke)	1.00
11	Terry Francona (Outfield Throws)	.25
12	Woodie Fryman (Holding the Runner-Left Handed)	.25
13	Gary Carter (Fielding Low Balls)	.75
14	Andre Dawson (Playing Centerfield)	1.00
15	Bill Gullickson (The Slurve)	.25
16	Gary Carter (Catching Stance)	.75
17	Scott Sanderson (Fielding as a Pitcher)	.25
18	Warren Cromartie (Handling Bad Throws)	.25
19	Gary Carter (Hitting Stride)	.75
20	Ray Burris (Holding the Runner-Right Handed)	.25

1995 Zenith Samples

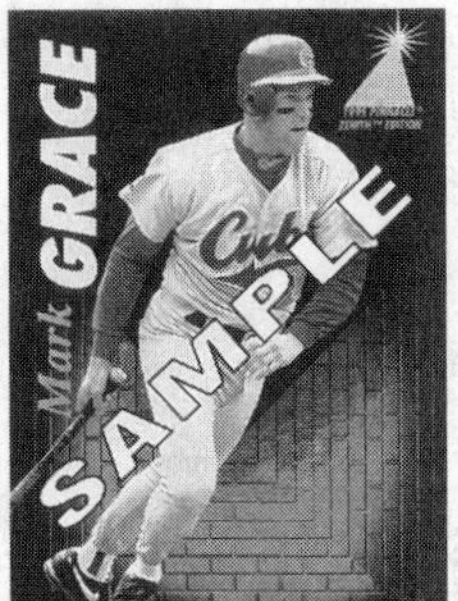

As Pinnacle extended its top-of-the-line brand name into baseball, this nine-card cello-wrapped samples set was sent to dealers to familiarize them with the product. Using the same state of the art all-foil metalized printing on extra heavy 24-point cardboard stock, the samples are virtually identical to the issued version, except for a white "SAMPLE" printed diagonally across front and back.

		MT
Complete Set (9):		30.00
Common Player:		3.00
12	Cal Ripken Jr.	7.00
20	Dante Bichette	3.00
51	Jim Thome	3.00
70	Mark Grace	4.00
97	Ryan Klesko	3.00
111	Chipper Jones (Rookie)	6.00
113	Curtis Goodwin (Rookie)	3.00
7	Hideo Nomo (Rookie Roll Call)	6.00
---	Header card	.15

1995 Zenith

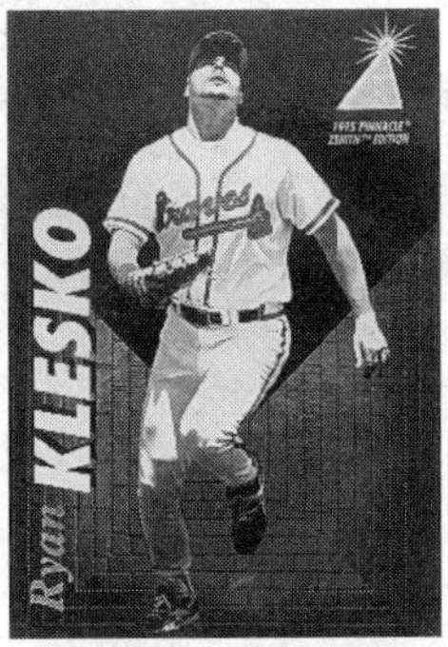

At the top of the pyramid of Pinnacle's baseball card lines for 1995 was Zenith, a super-premium brand utilizing all-foil metallized printing technology on double-thick 24-point cardboard stock to emphasize the quality look and feel. Six-card packs carried a retail price of $3.99. Two styles comprise the 150-card base set. The 110 veteran player cards are curiously arranged in alphabetical order according to the player's first names (with the exception of card #48, a special Japanese-language card of Hideo Nomo). These cards have a color player action photo on a black and gold background that is a view of a pyramid from its pinnacle. On the horizontal back, a portrait photo of the player in a partly-cloudy blue sky overlooks a playing field which offers his hit location preferences versus righty and lefty pitching. A scoreboard has his 1994 and career stats. The Pinnacle anti-counterfeiting optical-variable bar is in the lower-right corner. The rookie cards which comprise the final 40 cards in the set have a color photo at center with a gold-tone version of the same picture in the background. A large gold "ROOKIE" is vertically at right. Backs are similar to those on the verterans' cards except they have a scouting report in place of the hit-location chart.

		MT
Complete Set (150):		50.00
Common Player:		.25
Wax Box:		60.00
1	Albert Belle	1.00
2	Alex Fernandez	.25
3	Andy Benes	.25
4	Barry Larkin	.50
5	Barry Bonds	1.00
6	Ben McDonald	.25
7	Bernard Gilkey	.25
8	Billy Ashley	.25
9	Bobby Bonilla	.40
10	Bret Saberhagen	.25
11	Brian Jordan	.25

12	Cal Ripken Jr.	3.50
13	Carlos Baerga	.25
14	Carlos Delgado	.75
15	Cecil Fielder	.40
16	Chili Davis	.25
17	Chuck Knoblauch	.50
18	Craig Biggio	.60
19	Danny Tartabull	.25
20	Dante Bichette	.40
21	Darren Daulton	.25
22	Dave Justice	.40
23	Dave Winfield	.40
24	David Cone	.40
25	Dean Palmer	.25
26	Deion Sanders	.50
27	Dennis Eckersley	.25
28	Derek Bell	.25
29	Don Mattingly	1.50
30	Edgar Martinez	.40
31	Eric Karros	.35
32	Erik Hanson	.25
33	Frank Thomas	1.50
34	Fred McGriff	.50
35	Gary Sheffield	.50
36	Gary Gaetti	.25
37	Greg Maddux	2.50
38	Gregg Jefferies	.25
39	Ivan Rodriguez	1.00
40	Kenny Rogers	.25
41	J.T. Snow	.40
42	Hal Morris	.25
43	Eddie Murray (3,000 hit)	.75
44	Javier Lopez	.40
45	Jay Bell	.25
46	Jeff Conine	.25
47	Jeff Bagwell	1.50
48	*Hideo Nomo*	1.50
49	Jeff Kent	.25
50	Jeff King	.25
51	Jim Thome	.75
52	Jimmy Key	.25
53	Joe Carter	.40
54	John Valentin	.25
55	John Olerud	.50
56	Jose Canseco	1.00
57	Jose Rijo	.25
58	Jose Offerman	.25
59	Juan Gonzalez	1.50
60	Ken Caminiti	.40
61	Ken Griffey Jr.	5.00
62	Kenny Lofton	.75
63	Kevin Appier	.25
64	Kevin Seitzer	.25
65	Kirby Puckett	1.50
66	Kirk Gibson	.25
67	Larry Walker	.75
68	Lenny Dykstra	.25
69	Manny Ramirez	1.00
70	Mark Grace	.40
71	Mark McGwire	5.00
72	Marquis Grissom	.25
73	Jim Edmonds	.25
74	Matt Williams	.50
75	Mike Mussina	.75
76	Mike Piazza	3.00
77	Mo Vaughn	.75
78	Moises Alou	.40
79	Ozzie Smith	.75
80	Paul O'Neill	.50
81	Paul Molitor	.75
82	Rafael Palmeiro	.75
83	Randy Johnson	.75
84	Raul Mondesi	.40
85	Ray Lankford	.25
86	Reggie Sanders	.25
87	Rickey Henderson	.75
88	Rico Brogna	.25
89	Roberto Alomar	.75
90	Robin Ventura	.40
91	Roger Clemens	2.00
92	Ron Gant	.40
93	Rondell White	.40
94	Royce Clayton	.25
95	Ruben Sierra	.25
96	Rusty Greer	.40
97	Ryan Klesko	.40
98	Sammy Sosa	2.50
99	Shawon Dunston	.25
100	Steve Ontiveros	.25
101	Tim Naehring	.25
102	Tim Salmon	.50
103	Tino Martinez	.50
104	Tony Gwynn	2.00
105	Travis Fryman	.40
106	Vinny Castilla	.35
107	Wade Boggs	.75
108	Wally Joyner	.25
109	Wil Cordero	.25
110	Will Clark	.50
111	Chipper Jones	2.50
112	C.J. Nitkowski	.25
113	Curtis Goodwin	.25
114	Tim Unroe	.25
115	Vaughn Eshelman	.25
116	Marty Cordova	.25
117	Dustin Hermanson	.25
118	Rich Becker	.25
119	Ray Durham	.25
120	Shane Andrews	.25
121	Scott Ruffcorn	.25
122	*Mark Grudzielanek*	.75
123	James Baldwin	.25
124	*Carlos Perez*	.50
125	Julian Tavarez	.25
126	Joe Vitiello	.25
127	Jason Bates	.25
128	Edgardo Alfonzo	.50
129	Juan Acevedo	.25
130	Bill Pulsipher	.25
131	*Bob Higginson*	1.50
132	Russ Davis	.25
133	Charles Johnson	.25
134	Derek Jeter	3.00
135	Phil Nevin	.25
136	LaTroy Hawkins	.25
137	Brian Hunter	.25
138	Roberto Petagine	.25
139	Jim Pittsley	.25
140	Garret Anderon	.25
141	Ugueth Urbina	.25
142	Antonio Osuna	.25
143	Michael Tucker	.25
144	Benji Gil	.25
145	Jon Nunnally	.25
146	Alex Rodriguez	4.00
147	Todd Hollandworth	.25
148	Alex Gonzalez	.25
149	*Hideo Nomo*	2.00
150	Shawn Green	1.00
---	Numeric checklist	.25
---	Chase program checklist	.25

1995 Zenith All-Star Salute

The most common of the Zenith inserts is a series of 18 All-Star Salute cards. Fronts have action photos printed on foil. Backs have the 1995 All-Star Game logo and a large photo of the player taken at the game, with a few words about his All-Star history. The Salute cards are seeded at the rate of one per six packs, on average.

		MT
Complete Set (19):		40.00
Common Player:		1.00
1	Cal Ripken Jr.	6.00
2	Frank Thomas	2.50
3	Mike Piazza	5.00
4	Kirby Puckett	2.50
5	Manny Ramirez	2.00
6	Tony Gwynn	4.00
7	Hideo Nomo	1.50
8	Matt Williams	1.50
9	Randy Johnson	1.50
10	Raul Mondesi	1.00
11	Albert Belle	2.00
12	Ivan Rodriguez	2.00
13	Barry Bonds	2.00
14	Carlos Baerga	1.00
15	Ken Griffey Jr.	8.00
16	Jeff Conine	1.00
17	Frank Thomas	2.50
18	Cal Ripken Jr.	6.00
19	Barry Bonds	2.00

1995 Zenith Rookie Roll Call

Dufex foil printing technology on both front and back is featured on this insert set. Fronts have a large and a small player photo on a green background dominated by a large star. Backs have another photo on a green and gold background. A prestigious black and gold box at left in the horizontally formatted design has a few good words about the prospect. Stated odds of finding a Rookie Roll Call card are one per 24 packs, on average.

		MT
Complete Set (18):		110.00
Common Player:		2.50
1	Alex Rodriguez	35.00
2	Derek Jeter	30.00
3	Chipper Jones	20.00
4	Shawn Green	9.00
5	Todd Hollandsworth	2.50
6	Bill Pulsipher	2.50
7	Hideo Nomo	3.00
8	Ray Durham	3.00
9	Curtis Goodwin	2.50
10	Brian Hunter	2.50
11	Julian Tavarez	2.50
12	Marty Cordova	2.50
13	Michael Tucker	2.50
14	Edgardo Alfonzo	4.00
15	LaTroy Hawkins	2.50
16	Carlos Perez	2.50
17	Charles Johnson	4.00
18	Benji Gil	2.50

1996 Zenith Z-Team

The scarcest of the Zenith insert cards are those of 18 "living legends" profiled in the Z-Team series. Found at an average rate of only one per 72 packs, the cards are printed in technology Pinnacle calls 3-D Dufex.

		MT
Complete Set (18):		135.00
Common Player:		2.50
1	Cal Ripken Jr.	20.00
2	Ken Griffey Jr.	25.00
3	Frank Thomas	7.50
4	Matt Williams	5.00
5	Mike Piazza	15.00
6	Barry Bonds	7.50
7	Raul Mondesi	2.50
8	Greg Maddux	12.50
9	Jeff Bagwell	7.50
10	Manny Ramirez	7.50
11	Larry Walker	5.00
12	Tony Gwynn	12.50
13	Will Clark	5.00
14	Albert Belle	6.00
15	Kenny Lofton	6.00
16	Rafael Palmeiro	5.00
17	Don Mattingly	7.50
18	Carlos Baerga	2.50

1996 Zenith

Pinnacle's 1996 Zenith set has 150 cards in the regular set, including 30 Rookies, 20 Honor roll and two checklist cards. Each card in the set has a parallel Artist's Proof version (seeded one per every 35 packs). Insert sets include Z Team, Mozaics and two versions of Diamond Club. Normal Dufex versions of Diamond Club appear one every 24 packs; parallel versions, which have an actual diamond chip incorporated into the card design, were seeded one per every 350 packs.

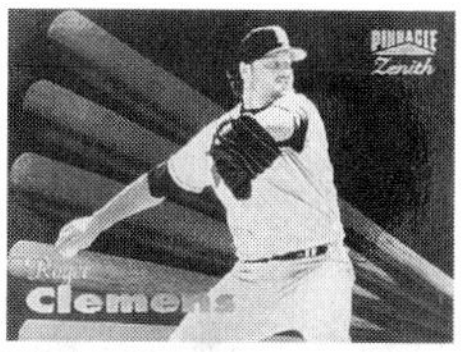

		MT
Complete Set (150):		40.00
Common Player:		.25
Artist's Proofs Comp. Set (150):		2000.
Common Artist's Proofs:		4.00
Veteran Star Artist's Proofs: 15x to 25x		
Rookies and Young Stars: 8x to 15x		
Wax Box:		50.00
1	Ken Griffey Jr.	4.00
2	Ozzie Smith	.75
3	Greg Maddux	2.00
4	Rondell White	.40
5	Mark McGwire	4.00
6	Jim Thome	.75
7	Ivan Rodriguez	1.00
8	Marc Newfield	.25
9	Travis Fryman	.40
10	Fred McGriff	.40
11	Shawn Green	1.00
12	Mike Piazza	2.50
13	Dante Bichette	.40
14	Tino Martinez	.50
15	Sterling Hitchcock	.25
16	Ryne Sandberg	1.00
17	Rico Brogna	.25
18	Roberto Alomar	.75
19	Barry Larkin	.50
20	Bernie Williams	.75
21	Gary Sheffield	.50
22	Frank Thomas	1.25
23	Gregg Jefferies	.25
24	Jeff Bagwell	1.25
25	Marty Cordova	.25
26	Jim Edmonds	.25
27	Jay Bell	.25
28	Ben McDonald	.25
29	Barry Bonds	1.00
30	Mo Vaughn	.75
31	Johnny Damon	.25
32	Dean Palmer	.25
33	Ismael Valdes	.25
34	Manny Ramirez	1.00
35	Edgar Martinez	.25
36	Cecil Fielder	.35
37	Ryan Klesko	.40
38	Ray Lankford	.25
39	Tim Salmon	.40
40	Joe Carter	.35
41	Jason Isringhausen	.25
42	Rickey Henderson	.75
43	Lenny Dykstra	.25
44	Andre Dawson	.40
45	Paul O'Neill	.50
46	Ray Durham	.25
47	Raul Mondesi	.40
48	Jay Buhner	.40
49	Eddie Murray	.75
50	Henry Rodriguez	.25
51	Hal Morris	.25
52	Mike Mussina	.75
53	Wally Joyner	.25
54	Will Clark	.50
55	Chipper Jones	2.50
56	Brian Jordan	.25
57	Larry Walker	.75
58	Wade Boggs	.75
59	Melvin Nieves	.25
60	Charles Johnson	.25
61	Juan Gonzalez	1.25
62	Carlos Delgado	.75
63	Reggie Sanders	.25
64	Brian Hunter	.25
65	Edgardo Alfonzo	.50
66	Kenny Lofton	.75
67	Paul Molitor	.75
68	Mike Bordick	.25
69	Garret Anderson	.25
70	Orlando Merced	.25
71	Craig Biggio	.60
72	Chuck Knoblauch	.50
73	Mark Grace	.40
74	Jack McDowell	.25
75	Randy Johnson	.75
76	Cal Ripken Jr.	3.00
77	Matt Williams	.50
78	Benji Gil	.25
79	Moises Alou	.40
80	Robin Ventura	.40
81	Greg Vaughn	.40
82	Carlos Baerga	.25
83	Roger Clemens	1.50
84	Hideo Nomo	.50
85	Pedro Martinez	1.00
86	John Valentin	.25
87	Andres Galarraga	.50
88	Andy Pettitte	.75
89	Derek Bell	.25
90	Kirby Puckett	1.25
91	Tony Gwynn	2.00
92	Brady Anderson	.35
93	Derek Jeter	3.00
94	Michael Tucker	.25
95	Albert Belle	.75
96	David Cone	.35
97	J.T. Snow	.25
98	Tom Glavine	.40
99	Alex Rodriguez	3.00
100	Sammy Sosa	2.50
101	Karim Garcia	.25
102	Alan Benes	.25
103	Chad Mottola	.25
104	*Robin Jennings*	.25
105	Bob Abreu	.25
106	Tony Clark	.50
107	George Arias	.25
108	Jermaine Dye	.25
109	Jeff Suppan	.25
110	*Ralph Milliard*	.25
111	Ruben Rivera	.25
112	Billy Wagner	.25
113	Jason Kendall	.25
114	*Mike Grace*	.50
115	Edgar Renteria	.25
116	Jason Schmidt	.25
117	Paul Wilson	.25
118	Rey Ordonez	.40
119	*Rocky Coppinger*	.40
120	*Wilton Guerrero*	.75
121	Brooks Kieschnick	.25
122	Raul Casanova	.25
123	Alex Ochoa	.25
124	Chan Ho Park	.35
125	John Wasdin	.25
126	Eric Owens	.25
127	Justin Thompson	.25
128	Chris Snopek	.25
129	Terrell Wade	.25
130	*Darin Erstad*	4.00
131	Albert Belle (Honor Roll)	.50
132	Cal Ripken Jr. (Honor Roll)	1.50
133	Frank Thomas (Honor Roll)	.60
134	Greg Maddux (Honor Roll)	1.00
135	Ken Griffey Jr. (Honor Roll)	2.00
136	Mo Vaughn (Honor Roll)	.40
137	Chipper Jones (Honor Roll)	1.00
138	Mike Piazza (Honor Roll)	1.25
139	Ryan Klesko (Honor Roll)	.25
140	Hideo Nomo (Honor Roll)	.25
141	Roberto Alomar (Honor Roll)	.40
142	Manny Ramirez (Honor Roll)	.50
143	Gary Sheffield (Honor Roll)	.25
144	Barry Bonds (Honor Roll)	.50
145	Matt Williams (Honor Roll)	.25
146	Jim Edmonds (Honor Roll)	.25
147	Derek Jeter (Honor Roll)	1.50
148	Sammy Sosa (Honor Roll)	1.00
149	Kirby Puckett (Honor Roll)	.75
150	Tony Gwynn (Honor Roll)	1.00

1996 Zenith Artist's Proofs

Each card in the '96 Zenith base set can also be found in a specially marked Artist's Proof version. The AP cards were found an average of one per 35 packs.

	MT
Complete Set (150):	2000.
Common Player:	4.00

(Veteran stars' Artist's Proofs 20X-30X regular Zenith; young stars and rookies 8X-15X.)

Player names in *Italic* type indicate a rookie card.

1996 Zenith Diamond Club

Twenty different players are featured on these two 1996 Pinnacle Zenith insert cards. Normal Dufex versions are inserted one per every 24 packs. Parallel versions of these cards, containing an actual diamond chip incorporated into the design, were seeded one per every 350 packs.

		MT
Complete Set (20):		125.00
Common Player:		4.00
Diamond Versions: 2x to 4x		
1	Albert Belle	5.00
2	Mo Vaughn	4.00
3	Ken Griffey Jr.	20.00
4	Mike Piazza	12.00
5	Cal Ripken Jr.	15.00
6	Jermaine Dye	2.50
7	Jeff Bagwell	5.00
8	Frank Thomas	6.00
9	Alex Rodriguez	15.00
10	Ryan Klesko	3.00
11	Roberto Alomar	4.00
12	Sammy Sosa	12.00
13	Matt Williams	4.00
14	Gary Sheffield	3.00
15	Ruben Rivera	2.50
16	Darin Erstad	5.00
17	Randy Johnson	4.00
18	Greg Maddux	10.00
19	Karim Garcia	2.50
20	Chipper Jones	10.00

1996 Zenith Mozaics

Each of these 1996 Pinnacle Zenith cards contains multiple player images for the team represented on the card. The cards were inserted one per every 10 packs.

		MT
Complete Set (25):		90.00
Common Player:		1.00
1	Greg Maddux, Chipper Jones, Ryan Klesko	8.00
2	Juan Gonzalez, Will Clark, Ivan Rodriguez	4.00
3	Frank Thomas, Robin Ventura, Ray Durham	4.00
4	Matt Williams, Barry Bonds, Osvaldo Fernandez	4.00
5	Ken Griffey Jr., Randy Johnson, Alex Rodriguez	15.00
6	Sammy Sosa, Ryne Sandberg, Mark Grace	10.00
7	Jim Edmonds, Tim Salmon, Garret Anderson	2.00
8	Cal Ripken Jr., Roberto Alomar, Mike Mussina	10.00
9	Mo Vaughn, Roger Clemens, John Valentin	6.00
10	Barry Larkin, Reggie Sanders, Hal Morris	2.00
11	Ray Lankford, Brian Jordan, Ozzie Smith	2.50
12	Dante Bichette, Larry Walker, Andres Galarraga	3.00
13	Mike Piazza, Hideo Nomo, Raul Mondesi	10.00
14	Ben McDonald, Greg Vaughn, Kevin Seitzer	1.50
15	Joe Carter, Carlos Delgado, Alex Gonzalez	1.00
16	Gary Sheffield, Charles Johnson, Jeff Conine	1.50
17	Rondell White, Moises Alou, Henry Rodriguez	1.00
18	Albert Belle, Manny Ramirez, Carlos Baerga	4.00
19	Kirby Puckett, Paul Molitor, Chuck Knoblauch	4.00
20	Tony Gwynn, Rickey Henderson, Wally Joyner	8.00
21	Mark McGwire, Mike Bordick, Scott Brosius	15.00
22	Paul O'Neill, Bernie Williams, Wade Boggs	3.00
23	Jay Bell, Orlando Merced, Jason Kendall	1.00
24	Rico Brogna, Paul Wilson, Jason Isringhausen	1.00
25	Jeff Bagwell, Craig Biggio, Derek Bell	4.00

1996 Zenith Z-Team Samples

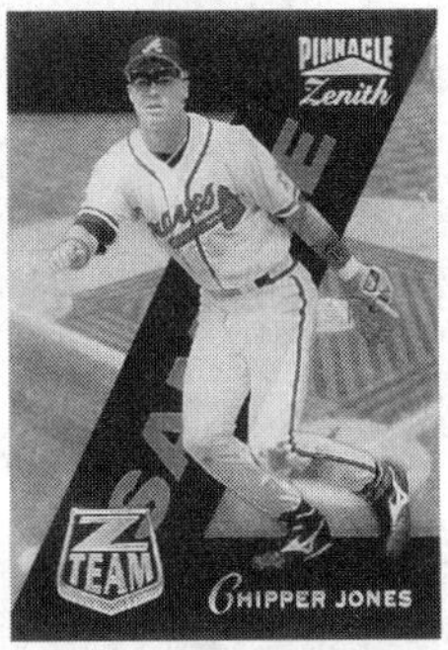

Each of the first nine micro-etched plastic-printed Z Team insert cards can also be found in an edition which is overprinted "SAMPLE" on the front. These cards were distributed to hobby dealers.

		MT
Complete Set (9):		65.00
Common Player:		3.00
1	Ken Griffey Jr.	12.50
2	Albert Belle	4.00
3	Cal Ripken Jr.	10.00
4	Frank Thomas	5.00
5	Greg Maddux	7.50
6	Mo Vaughn	4.00
7	Chipper Jones	7.50
8	Mike Piazza	7.50
9	Ryan Klesko	3.50

1996 Zenith Z-Team

Pinnacle's 1996 Zenith baseball continues the Z Team insert concept with a new clear plastic treatment that is micro-etched for a see-through design that allows light to shine through etched highlights and a green ball field background. The 18 cards were seeded one per every 72 packs.

		MT
Complete Set (18):		135.00
Common Player:		5.00
1	Ken Griffey Jr.	25.00
2	Albert Belle	7.50
3	Cal Ripken Jr.	20.00
4	Frank Thomas	7.50
5	Greg Maddux	12.50
6	Mo Vaughn	4.00
7	Chipper Jones	15.00
8	Mike Piazza	15.00
9	Ryan Klesko	2.50
10	Hideo Nomo	4.00
11	Roberto Alomar	5.00
12	Manny Ramirez	7.50
13	Gary Sheffield	4.00
14	Barry Bonds	7.50
15	Matt Williams	4.00
16	Jim Edmonds	2.50
17	Kirby Puckett	7.50
18	Sammy Sosa	15.00

1997 Zenith

This set combines standard size trading cards with cards in an 8" x 10" format. The standard size set consists of 60 cards. Card fronts feature full-bleed photos and the word "Zenith", but no reference to the player's name or team is found on the fronts. Backs have another player photo, a hit location chart and 1996/career stats. There are four inserts in the set, all of which are printed on the larger size format - 8" x 10", 8" x 10" Dufex, 8" x 10" V-2, and Z-Team. Each sale unit contained one pack of five standard-size cards and two larger size cards for a suggested retail price of $9.99.

		MT
Complete Set (50):		40.00
Common Player:		.25
Wax box:		50.00
1	Frank Thomas	1.25
2	Tony Gwynn	2.00
3	Jeff Bagwell	1.00
4	Paul Molitor	.75
5	Roberto Alomar	.75
6	Mike Piazza	2.50
7	Albert Belle	.75
8	Greg Maddux	2.00
9	Barry Larkin	.50
10	Tony Clark	.50
11	Larry Walker	.75
12	Chipper Jones	2.50
13	Juan Gonzalez	1.25
14	Barry Bonds	1.00
15	Ivan Rodriguez	1.00
16	Sammy Sosa	2.50
17	Derek Jeter	2.50
18	Hideo Nomo	.50
19	Roger Clemens	1.50
20	Ken Griffey Jr.	4.00
21	Andy Pettitte	.60
22	Alex Rodriguez	3.00
23	Tino Martinez	.60
24	Bernie Williams	.75
25	Ken Caminiti	.40
26	John Smoltz	.40
27	Javier Lopez	.40
28	Mark McGwire	4.00
29	Gary Sheffield	.50
30	David Justice	.50
30p	David Justice (marked SAMPLE)	2.00
31	Randy Johnson	.75
32	Chuck Knoblauch	.50
33	Mike Mussina	.75
34	Deion Sanders	.50
35	Cal Ripken Jr.	3.00
36	Darin Erstad	.75
37	Kenny Lofton	.60
38	Jay Buhner	.25
39	Brady Anderson	.40
40	Edgar Martinez	.25
41	Mo Vaughn	.60
42	Ryne Sandberg	1.00
43	Andruw Jones	.75
44	Nomar Garciaparra	2.50
45	*Hideki Irabu*	1.00
46	Wilton Guerrero	.25
47	*Jose Cruz Jr.*	.75
48	Vladimir Guerrero	1.50
49	Scott Rolen	1.25
50	Jose Guillen	.25

1997 Zenith V-2

This eight-card die-cut insert utilizes motion technology as well as foil printing to create a very high-tech 8" x 10" card. Cards were inserted 1:47 packs.

		MT
Complete Set (8):		100.00
Common Player:		5.00
1	Ken Griffey Jr.	25.00
2	Andruw Jones	5.00
3	Frank Thomas	7.50
4	Mike Piazza	15.00
5	Alex Rodriguez	20.00
6	Cal Ripken Jr.	20.00
7	Derek Jeter	15.00
8	Vladimir Guerrero	10.00

1997 Zenith Z-Team

This nine-card 8" x 10" insert is printed on a mirror gold mylar foil stock with each card sequentially numbered to 1,000.

		MT
Complete Set (9):		150.00
Common Player:		5.00
1	Ken Griffey Jr.	35.00
2	Larry Walker	7.50
3	Frank Thomas	10.00
4	Alex Rodriguez	30.00
5	Mike Piazza	25.00
6	Cal Ripken Jr.	30.00
7	Derek Jeter	25.00
8	Andruw Jones	5.00
9	Roger Clemens	15.00

1997 Zenith 8x10

This 24-card insert takes select cards from the standard set and blows them up to an 8" x 10" format. Cards were inserted one per pack. A Dufex version of each 8" x 10" insert card was also available at a rate of one per pack (except in packs which contained either a Z-Team or V-2 card).

		MT
Complete Set (24):		50.00
Common Player:		1.00
Dufex versions: 1x to 1.5x		
1	Frank Thomas	2.00
2	Tony Gwynn	3.00
3	Jeff Bagwell	1.50
4	Ken Griffey Jr.	6.00
5	Mike Piazza	4.00
6	Greg Maddux	2.50
7	Ken Caminiti	1.00
8	Albert Belle	1.00
9	Ivan Rodriguez	1.50
10	Sammy Sosa	4.00
11	Mark McGwire	6.00
12	Roger Clemens	2.00
13	Alex Rodriguez	5.00
14	Chipper Jones	3.00
15	Juan Gonzalez	2.00
16	Barry Bonds	1.50
17	Derek Jeter	4.00
18	Hideo Nomo	1.00
19	Cal Ripken Jr.	5.00
20	Hideki Irabu	1.00
21	Andruw Jones	1.00
22	Nomar Garciaparra	4.00
23	Vladimir Guerrero	2.00
24	Scott Rolen	1.50

1998 Zenith

Zenith Baseball was part of Pinnacle's "Dare to Tear" program. Sold in three-card packs, the set consisted of 5"-x-7" cards, each with a standard-size card inside. Collectors had to decide whether to keep the large cards or tear them open to get the smaller card inside. Eighty 5"-x-7" cards and 100 regular cards made up the set. The regular, or Z2, cards were paralleled twice - Z-Silver (1:7) and Z-Gold (numbered to 100). The large cards also had two parallels - Impulse (1:7) and Gold Impulse (numbered to 100). Inserts include Raising the Bar, Rookie Thrills, Epix, 5x7 Z Team, Z Team, Gold Z Team, Rookie Z Team and Gold Rookie Z Team.

		MT
Complete Set (100):		60.00
Common Player:		.25
Silvers: 2X		
Inserted 1:7		
Wax Box:		80.00
1	Larry Walker	1.00
2	Ken Griffey Jr.	5.00
2s	Ken Griffey Jr. (SAMPLE)	3.00
3	Cal Ripken Jr.	4.00
4	Sammy Sosa	3.00
5	Andruw Jones	1.00
6	Frank Thomas	1.50
7	Tony Gwynn	2.50
8	Rafael Palmeiro	.75
9	Tim Salmon	.50
10	Randy Johnson	1.00
11	Juan Gonzalez	1.50
12	Greg Maddux	2.50
13	Vladimir Guerrero	2.00
14	Mike Piazza	3.00
15	Andres Galarraga	.50
16	Alex Rodriguez	4.00
17	Derek Jeter	4.00
18	Nomar Garciaparra	3.00
19	Ivan Rodriguez	1.50
20	Chipper Jones	3.00
21	Barry Larkin	.75
22	Mo Vaughn	.75

23 Albert Belle 1.00
24 Scott Rolen 1.50
25 Sandy Alomar Jr. .40
26 Roberto Alomar .75
27 Andy Pettitte .50
28 Chuck Knoblauch .50
29 Jeff Bagwell 1.50
30 Mike Mussina .75
31 Fred McGriff .40
32 Roger Clemens 2.00
33 Rusty Greer .25
34 Edgar Martinez .25
35 Paul Molitor 1.00
36 Mark Grace .50
37 Darin Erstad .50
38 Kenny Lofton .75
39 Tom Glavine .40
40 Javier Lopez .25
41 Will Clark .75
42 Tino Martinez .50
43 Raul Mondesi .40
44 Brady Anderson .25
45 Chan Ho Park .40
46 Jason Giambi .25
47 Manny Ramirez 1.50
48 Jay Buhner .30
49 Dante Bichette .35
50 Jose Cruz Jr. .25
51 Charles Johnson .25
52 Bernard Gilkey .25
53 Johnny Damon .25
54 David Justice .40
55 Justin Thompson .25
56 Bobby Higginson .25
57 Todd Hundley .25
58 Gary Sheffield .50
59 Barry Bonds 1.50
60 Mark McGwire 5.00
61 John Smoltz .40
62 Tony Clark .50
63 Brian Jordan .25
64 Jason Kendall .25
65 Mariano Rivera .40
66 Pedro Martinez 1.50
67 Jim Thome .75
68 Neifi Perez .25
69 Kevin Brown .40
70 Hideo Nomo .50
71 Craig Biggio .75
72 Bernie Williams .75
73 Jose Guillen .25
74 Ken Caminiti .40
75 Livan Hernandez .25
76 Ray Lankford .25
77 Jim Edmonds .25
78 Matt Williams .75
79 Mark Kotsay .25
80 Moises Alou .40
81 Antone Williamson .25
82 Jaret Wright .40
83 Jacob Cruz .25
84 Abraham Nunez .25
85 Raul Ibanez .25
86 Miguel Tejada .25
87 Derek Lee .25
88 Juan Encarnacion .25
89 Todd Helton .75
90 Travis Lee .50
91 Ben Grieve .75
92 Ryan McGuire .25
93 Richard Hidalgo .25
94 Paul Konerko .50
95 Shannon Stewart .25
96 Homer Bush .25
97 Lou Collier .25
98 Jeff Abbott .25
99 Brett Tomko .25
100 Fernando Tatis .50

1998 Zenith 5x7

The 80 Zenith 5x7 cards all contained a regular-size card. Collectors could tear open the 5x7 to get at the smaller card inside. The set has two parallels: 5x7 Impulse (1:7) and 5x7 Gold Impulse (1:43).

MT
Complete Set (80): 75.00
Common Player: .50
Silvers: 2X
Inserted 1:7
1 Nomar Garciaparra 5.00
2 Andres Galarraga 1.00
3 Greg Maddux 4.00
4 Frank Thomas 2.50
5 Mark McGwire 8.00
6 Rafael Palmeiro 1.00
7 John Smoltz .50
8 Jeff Bagwell 2.00
9 Andruw Jones 1.50
10 Rusty Greer .50
11 Paul Molitor 1.50
12 Bernie Williams 1.50
13 Kenny Lofton 1.50
14 Alex Rodriguez 5.00
15 Derek Jeter 5.00
15s Derek Jeter ("SAMPLE" overprint on back) 4.00
16 Scott Rolen 2.00
17 Albert Belle 2.00
18 Mo Vaughn 1.50
19 Chipper Jones 5.00
20 Chuck Knoblauch .75
21 Mike Piazza 5.00
22 Tony Gwynn 4.00
22s Tony Gwynn ("SAMPLE" overprint on back) 3.00
23 Juan Gonzalez 2.50
24 Andy Pettitte .75
25 Tim Salmon .75
26 Brady Anderson .50
27 Mike Mussina 1.50
28 Edgar Martinez .50
29 Jose Guillen .50
30 Hideo Nomo .50
31 Jim Thome .75
32 Mark Grace .50
33 Darin Erstad .50
34 Bobby Higginson .50
35 Ivan Rodriguez 2.00
36 Todd Hundley .50
37 Sandy Alomar Jr. .50
38 Gary Sheffield .75
39 David Justice .75
40 Ken Griffey Jr. 8.00
40s Ken Griffey Jr. ("SAMPLE" overprint on back) 4.00
41 Vladimir Guerrero 2.50
42 Larry Walker 1.00
43 Barry Bonds 2.00
44 Randy Johnson 1.50
45 Roger Clemens 3.00
46 Raul Mondesi .50
47 Tino Martinez .75
48 Jason Giambi .50
49 Matt Williams .75
50 Cal Ripken Jr. 6.00
51 Barry Larkin 1.00
52 Jim Edmonds .50
53 Ken Caminiti .50
54 Sammy Sosa 5.00
55 Tony Clark .75
56 Manny Ramirez 2.00
57 Bernard Gilkey .50
58 Jose Cruz Jr. .50
59 Brian Jordan .50
60 Kevin Brown .50
61 Craig Biggio 1.00
62 Javier Lopez .50
63 Jay Buhner .75
64 Roberto Alomar 1.50
65 Justin Thompson .50
66 Todd Helton 1.50
67 Travis Lee .75
68 Paul Konerko .50
69 Jaret Wright .50
70 Ben Grieve 1.50
71 Juan Encarnacion .50
72 Ryan McGuire .50
73 Derrek Lee .50
74 Abraham Nunez .50
75 Richard Hidalgo .50
76 Miguel Tejada .50
77 Jacob Cruz .50
78 Homer Bush .50
79 Jeff Abbott .50
80 Lou Collier .50
Checklist .50

1998 Zenith Silver

This parallel set reprinted all 100 standard sized cards in Zenith on silver foilboard, with a "Z-Silver" logo across the bottom center. Z-Silvers were inserted one per seven packs.

Veteran Stars: 3X
Young Stars/RCs: 2X
Inserted 1:7
(See 1998 Zenith for checklist and base card values.)

1998 Zenith 5x7 Silver

These silver parallels reprinted each of the 80 cards in the 5" x 7" set. Cards were called Impulse and carried that logo on the front and were inserted one per seven packs. Since these cards contained other cards inside them, they are condition sensitive and only worth full price if left in mint condition and not cut open.

Veteran Stars: 3X
Young Stars/RCs: 2.5X
Inserted 1:7
(See 1998 Zenith 5x7 for checklist and base card values.)

1998 Zenith Z-Gold

MT
Common Player: 5.00
Stars/Rookies 20X
Production 100 sets
(See 1998 Zenith for checklist and base card values.)

1998 Zenith 5x7 Gold

The 5x7 Gold Impulse set parallels the 80-card 5x7 base set. The cards were inserted one per 43 packs.

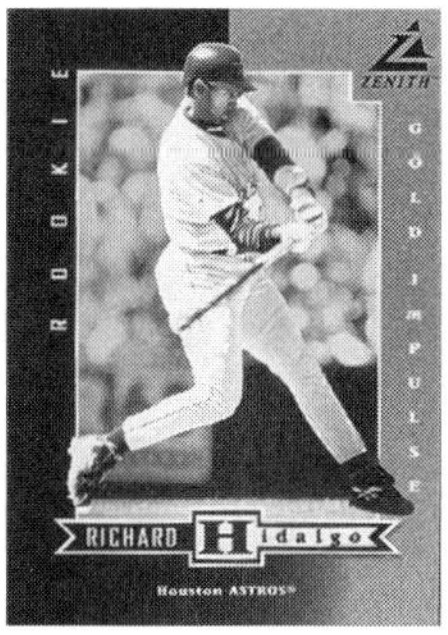

MT
Common Player: 10.00
Semistars: 25.00
Production 100 sets
1 Nomar Garciaparra 100.00
2 Andres Galarraga 30.00
3 Greg Maddux 100.00
4 Frank Thomas 60.00
5 Mark McGwire 200.00
6 Rafael Palmeiro 30.00
7 John Smoltz 15.00
8 Jeff Bagwell 50.00
9 Andruw Jones 30.00
10 Rusty Greer 20.00
11 Paul Molitor 30.00
12 Bernie Williams 30.00
13 Kenny Lofton 30.00
14 Alex Rodriguez 100.00
15 Derek Jeter 100.00
16 Scott Rolen 50.00
17 Albert Belle 30.00
18 Mo Vaughn 30.00
19 Chipper Jones 100.00
20 Chuck Knoblauch 25.00
21 Mike Piazza 100.00
22 Tony Gwynn 80.00
23 Juan Gonzalez 60.00
24 Andy Pettitte 20.00
25 Tim Salmon 20.00
26 Brady Anderson 15.00
27 Mike Mussina 30.00
28 Edgar Martinez 15.00
29 Jose Guillen 10.00
30 Hideo Nomo 20.00
31 Jim Thome 25.00
32 Mark Grace 20.00
33 Darin Erstad 30.00
34 Bobby Higginson 15.00
35 Ivan Rodriguez 40.00
36 Todd Hundley 10.00
37 Sandy Alomar Jr. 20.00
38 Gary Sheffield 20.00
39 David Justice 20.00
40 Ken Griffey Jr. 160.00
41 Vladimir Guerrero 60.00
42 Larry Walker 30.00
43 Barry Bonds 40.00
44 Randy Johnson 30.00
45 Roger Clemens 75.00
46 Raul Mondesi 15.00
47 Tino Martinez 20.00
48 Jason Giambi 10.00
49 Matt Williams 25.00
50 Cal Ripken Jr. 125.00
51 Barry Larkin 25.00
52 Jim Edmonds 15.00
53 Ken Caminiti 20.00
54 Sammy Sosa 100.00
55 Tony Clark 20.00
56 Manny Ramirez 40.00
57 Bernard Gilkey 10.00
58 Jose Cruz Jr. 20.00
59 Brian Jordan 10.00
60 Kevin Brown 20.00
61 Craig Biggio 30.00
62 Javier Lopez 20.00
63 Jay Buhner 20.00
64 Roberto Alomar 30.00
65 Justin Thompson 15.00
66 Todd Helton 30.00
67 Travis Lee 25.00
68 Paul Konerko 20.00
69 Jaret Wright 20.00
70 Ben Grieve 25.00
71 Juan Encarnacion 20.00
72 Ryan McGuire 15.00
73 Derrek Lee 10.00
74 Abraham Nunez 10.00
75 Richard Hidalgo 10.00
76 Miguel Tejada 20.00
77 Jacob Cruz 10.00
78 Homer Bush 10.00
79 Jeff Abbott 10.00
80 Lou Collier 10.00
Checklist 10.00

1998 Zenith Epix

Epix is a cross-brand insert. The set honors the top Plays, Games, Seasons and Moments in the careers of top baseball players. Epix consisted of 24 cards in Zenith, inserted 1:11. The cards have orange, purple and emerald versions.

MT
Common Card: 1.50
Purples: 1.5X
Emeralds: 2X
1 Ken Griffey Jr. S 30.00
2 Juan Gonzalez S 8.00
3 Jeff Bagwell S 6.00
4 Ivan Rodriguez S 6.00
5 Nomar Garciaparra S 15.00
6 Ryne Sandberg S 6.00
7 Frank Thomas M 15.00
8 Derek Jeter M 25.00
9 Tony Gwynn M 20.00
10 Albert Belle M 6.00
11 Scott Rolen M 8.00
12 Barry Larkin M 5.00
13 Alex Rodriguez P 6.00
14 Cal Ripken Jr. P 6.00
15 Chipper Jones P 5.00
16 Roger Clemens P 4.00
17 Mo Vaughn P 1.50
18 Mark McGwire P 8.00
19 Mike Piazza G 8.00
20 Andruw Jones G 2.50
21 Greg Maddux G 6.00
22 Barry Bonds G 3.00
23 Paul Molitor G 2.50
24 Eddie Murray G 2.50

1998 Zenith Raising the Bar

Raising the Bar is a 15-card insert seeded 1:25. The set features players who have set high standards for other players to follow.

MT
Complete Set (15): 150.00
Common Player: 6.00
Inserted 1:25
1 Ken Griffey Jr. 25.00
2 Frank Thomas 8.00
3 Alex Rodriguez 15.00
4 Tony Gwynn 12.00
5 Mike Piazza 15.00
6 Ivan Rodriguez 6.00
7 Cal Ripken Jr. 20.00
8 Greg Maddux 12.00
9 Hideo Nomo 5.00
10 Mark McGwire 25.00
11 Juan Gonzalez 8.00
12 Andruw Jones 5.00
13 Jeff Bagwell 6.00
14 Chipper Jones 15.00
15 Nomar Garciaparra 15.00

1998 Zenith Rookie Thrills

Rookie Thrills is a 15-card insert seeded 1:25. The set features many of the top rookies of 1998.

MT
Complete Set (15): 40.00
Common Player: 3.00
Inserted 1:25
1 Travis Lee 5.00
2 Juan Encarnacion 3.00
3 Derrek Lee 3.00
4 Raul Ibanez 3.00
5 Ryan McGuire 3.00
6 Todd Helton 6.00
7 Jacob Cruz 3.00
8 Abraham Nunez 3.00
9 Paul Konerko 4.00
10 Ben Grieve 6.00
11 Jeff Abbott 3.00
12 Richard Hidalgo 3.00
13 Jaret Wright 3.00
14 Lou Collier 3.00
15 Miguel Tejada 4.00

1998 Zenith Z-Team

The Z Team insert was created in 5x7 and standard-size versions, each inserted at a 1:35 pack rate. The nine Rookie Z Team cards were seeded 1:58 and gold versions of both were found 1:175.

MT
Complete Set (18): 200.00
Common Player: 6.00
Golds: 2X
Inserted 1:175
1 Frank Thomas 10.00
2 Ken Griffey Jr. 30.00
3 Mike Piazza 20.00
4 Cal Ripken Jr. 25.00
5 Alex Rodriguez 25.00
6 Greg Maddux 15.00
7 Derek Jeter 20.00
8 Chipper Jones 20.00
9 Roger Clemens 10.00
10 Ben Grieve 8.00
11 Derrek Lee 6.00
12 Jose Cruz Jr. 6.00
13 Nomar Garciaparra 20.00
14 Travis Lee 8.00
15 Todd Helton 8.00
16 Paul Konerko 6.00
17 Miguel Tejada 8.00
18 Scott Rolen 10.00

1998 Zenith 5x7 Z-Team

The 5x7 Z Team insert is a nine-card set seeded one per 35 packs.

MT
Complete Set (9): 250.00
Common Player: 15.00
Inserted 1:35
1 Frank Thomas 15.00
2 Ken Griffey Jr. 50.00
3 Mike Piazza 30.00

4	Cal Ripken Jr.	40.00
5	Alex Rodriguez	40.00
6	Greg Maddux	25.00
7	Derek Jeter	30.00
8	Chipper Jones	30.00
9	Roger Clemens	20.00

1992 Ziploc

Dow Brands produced an 11-card set of All-Stars in 1992 that featured mostly Hall of Famers, with the exception only of Nellie Fox. The cards were included in specially-marked Ziploc packages, and also could be purchased by mail.

		MT
Complete Set (11):		7.00
Common Player:		.50
1	Warren Spahn	.50
2	Bob Gibson	.50
3	Rollie Fingers	.50
4	Carl Yastrzemski	.75
5	Brooks Robinson	.75
6	Pee Wee Reese	.60
7	Willie McCovey	.60
8	Willie Mays	1.00
9	Nellie Fox	.60
10	Yogi Berra	.75
11	Hank Aaron	1.00

Player names in *Italic* type indicate a rookie card.

1994 Z Silk Cachets

Produced in limited quantities by Z Silk Cachets, known for its line of commemorative cacheted envelopes, this set includes both baseball and football players (only the baseball players are listed here). The cards are standard 2-1/2" x 3-1/2" and featured a colored silk piece attached to the front. The player's name is flanked by a pair of logos. Backs feature the same logos and a list of the company's products.

		MT
Complete Set (9):		60.00
Common Player:		5.00
(1)	Wade Boggs	9.00
(2)	Barry Bonds	10.00
(3)	Jose Canseco	9.00
(4)	Ken Griffey, Jr.	15.00
(5)	David Justice	8.00
(6)	Terry Pendleton	5.00
(7)	Kirby Puckett	10.00
(8)	Cal Ripken, Jr.	12.00
(9)	Dave Winfield	8.00

Checklists with card numbers in parentheses ( ) indicates the numbers do not appear on the card.

Minor League (1888-1969)

Prior to 1970 virtually all minor league baseball cards were issued as single cards rather than as complete sets. Like contemporary major league cards they were usually intended as premiums given away with the purchase of goods and services.

The listings which follow offer individual card prices in three grades of preservation to allow accurate valuations of superstar and other special interest cards, along with cards which were short-printed or otherwise are scarce.

A

1960 Armour Meats Denver Bears

Ten cards from this Class AA farm team of the Detroit Tigers have been checklisted, with others possibly to be discovered. The black-and-white blank-backed cards measure 2-1/2" x 3-1/4" and were issued with a coupon attached to the right side. The unnumbered cards are checklisted here alphabetically.

	NM	EX	VG
Complete Set (10):	650.00	325.00	195.00
Common Player:	75.00	37.00	22.00
(1) George Alusik	75.00	37.00	22.00
(2) Tony Bartirome	75.00	37.00	22.00
(3) Edward J. Donnelly	75.00	37.00	22.00
(4) James R. McDaniel	75.00	37.00	22.00
(5) Charlie Metro	75.00	37.00	22.00
(6) Harry Perkowski	75.00	37.00	22.00
(7) Vernon E. Rapp	75.00	37.00	22.00
(8) James Stump	75.00	37.00	22.00
(9) Ozzie Virgil	75.00	37.00	22.00
(10) Robert Walz	75.00	37.00	22.00

1940 Associated Stations San Francisco Seals

This album and sticker set was created as a premium by a Northern California gas company. Individual stickers were given away each week at participating service stations. The blank-backed, 1-3/4" x 2-5/8" stickers have the player's name in a black strip at the bottom. Pages in the accompanying 3-1/2" x 6" album have space for an autograph and a few career highlights for each player. The checklist is presented in page order of the album.

	NM	EX	VG
Complete Set With Album:	375.00	185.00	110.00
Common Player:	15.00	7.50	4.50
Album:	75.00	37.00	22.00
(1) "Lefty" O'Doul	37.00	18.50	11.00
(2) Sam Gibson	15.00	7.50	4.50
(3) Brooks Holder	15.00	7.50	4.50
(4) Ted Norbert	15.00	7.50	4.50
(5) Win Ballou	15.00	7.50	4.50
(6) Al Wright	15.00	7.50	4.50
(7) Al Epperly	15.00	7.50	4.50
(8) Orville Jorgens	15.00	7.50	4.50
(9) Larry Powell	15.00	7.50	4.50
(10) Joe Sprinz	15.00	7.50	4.50
(11) Harvey Storey	15.00	7.50	4.50
(12) Jack Burns	15.00	7.50	4.50
(13) Bob Price	15.00	7.50	4.50
(14) Larry Guay	15.00	7.50	4.50
(15) Frank Dasso	15.00	7.50	4.50
(16) Eddie Stutz	15.00	7.50	4.50
(17) John Barrett	15.00	7.50	4.50
(18) Eddie Botelho	15.00	7.50	4.50
(19) Ferris Fain	30.00	15.00	9.00
(20) Larry Woodall	15.00	7.50	4.50
(21) Ted Jennings	15.00	7.50	4.50
(22) Jack Warner	15.00	7.50	4.50
(23) Wil Leonard	15.00	7.50	4.50
(24) Gene Kiley	15.00	7.50	4.50
(25) Bob Jensen	15.00	7.50	4.50
(26) Wilfrid Le Febvre	15.00	7.50	4.50

1910 A.W.H. Caramels Virginia League

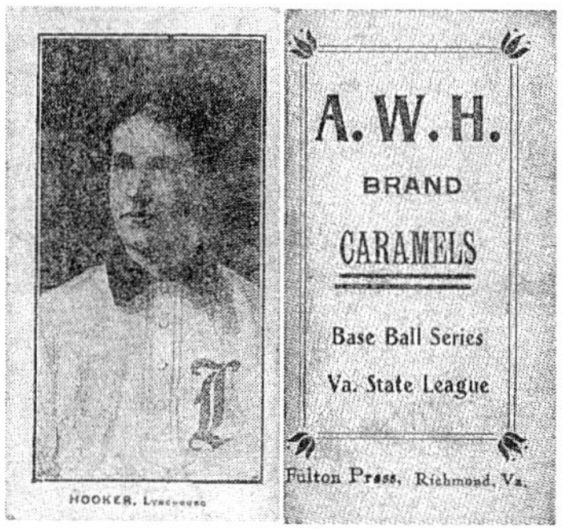

This rare set of cards picturing players from the Virginia League was issued by the A.W.H. Caramel Company in 1910. The cards measure 1-1/2"x 2-3/4" and feature player portraits in either red, black, brown, or blue and white. To date examples of 10 different cards have been found. The front of the card displays the player's last name and team below his photo. The back states "A.W.H. Brand Caramels" in large letters with "Base Ball Series/Va. State League" below.

	NM	EX	VG
Complete Set (12):	15500.	6500.	3750.
Common Player:	1500.	600.00	375.00
(1) Tom Guiheen	1500.	600.00	375.00
(2) Hooker	1500.	600.00	375.00
(3) Ison	1500.	600.00	375.00
(4) Lipe	1500.	600.00	375.00
(5) McCauley	1500.	600.00	375.00
(6) Otey	1500.	600.00	375.00
(7) Revelle	1500.	600.00	375.00
(8) Ryan	1500.	600.00	375.00
(9) Shaugnessy	1500.	600.00	375.00
(10) Sieber	1500.	600.00	375.00
(11) Smith	1500.	600.00	375.00
(12) Titman	1500.	600.00	375.00

The ratio of Excellent and Very Good prices to Near Mint can vary depending on relative collectibility for each grade in a specific set. Current listings reflect such adjustments.

1910 Baltimore News Orioles

The Eastern League Baltimore Orioles are featured in this set of schedule cards issued by a local newspaper. Cards measure 2-3/4" x 3-1/2" and feature player photographs on front, with a wide border. Player name, position, team and league are printed at the bottom of the photo. Backs have both the "Home" and "Abroad" schedule for the team, along with ads at top and bottom for the newspaper. All printing on front is in red-and-white; backs are in black-and-white. The checklist here is likely incomplete.

	NM	EX	VG
Common Player:	600.00	300.00	180.00
(1) Byers	600.00	300.00	180.00
(2) Maisel	600.00	300.00	180.00
(3) Malloy	600.00	300.00	180.00
(4) Jimmy Murray	600.00	300.00	180.00
(5) Russell	600.00	300.00	180.00

B

1914 Baltimore News Orioles

The International League Baltimore Orioles are one of two teams featured (along with the city's Federal League team) in this set of newspaper promotional cards. The 2-5/8" x 3-5/8" cards are monochrome printed in either blue or red with wide borders on front framing full-length action poses on which the background has been erased in favor of artificial shawdows. Player name, position and league are printed on front. Backs have a "HOME" and "ABROAD" schedule with an ad for the paper at top and a line at bottom which reads, "This Card is Given to," with space for a signature. At least one card, a Babe Ruth, has been seen with "Compliments Baltimore International League" replacing the newspaper ad at top. Only the minor league Orioles players are listed here, the Terrapins cards are listed in the major league section of this catalog. It is unlikely this checklist is complete.

		NM	EX	VG
Common Player:		1100.	550.00	325.00
(1)	Ensign Cottrell	1100.	550.00	325.00
(2)	Birdie Cree	1100.	550.00	325.00
(3)	Bert Daniels	1100.	550.00	325.00
(4)	Davidson	1100.	550.00	325.00
(5)	Jack Dunn	3000.	1500.	900.00
(6)	Jim Egan	1100.	550.00	325.00
(7)	Happy Finneran	1100.	550.00	325.00
(8)	Gleichmann	1100.	550.00	325.00
(9)	Allen Russell (Allan)	1100.	550.00	325.00
(10)	Babe Ruth		60000.	20000.
(11)	Ernie Shore	1100.	550.00	325.00
(12)	George Twombley (Twombly)	1100.	550.00	325.00

1923 Baltimore Shirt Co. Kansas City Blues

This unusual souvenir of the American Association Champion K.C. Blues is in the form of a 48" x 3-5/8" accordian-fold packet. Individual 1-7/8" x 3-1/4" black-and-white photos of the players are glued onto the black backing paper. Because the photos are rather easily removed, they may be encountered as singles. The players are checklisted here as they originally appeared, from left to right, on the foldout. There is no advertising on the individual pictures, just on the outer covers.

		NM	EX	VG
Complete Foldout:		600.00	300.00	180.00
Complete Set, Singles:		450.00	225.00	135.00
Common Player:		30.00	15.00	9.00
(1)	Wilbur Good	30.00	15.00	9.00
(2)	Bill Skiff	30.00	15.00	9.00
(3)	Lew McCarty	30.00	15.00	9.00
(4)	Dudley Branom	30.00	15.00	9.00
(5)	Lena Blackburne	32.50	16.00	9.75
(6)	Walter Hammond	30.00	15.00	9.00
(7)	Glen Wright (Glenn)	35.00	17.50	10.50
(8)	Geo. Armstrong	30.00	15.00	9.00
(9)	Beals Becker	30.00	15.00	9.00
(10)	"Dutch" Zwilling	30.00	15.00	9.00
(11)	Pete Scott	30.00	15.00	9.00
(12)	"Bunny" Brief	30.00	15.00	9.00
(13)	Jimmie Zinn	30.00	15.00	9.00
(14)	Ferd Schupp	30.00	15.00	9.00
(15)	Roy Wilkinson	30.00	15.00	9.00
(16)	Ray Caldwell	30.00	15.00	9.00
(17)	Joe Dawson	30.00	15.00	9.00
(18)	John Saladna	30.00	15.00	9.00
(19)	Herb Thormahlen	30.00	15.00	9.00
(20)	"Nick" Carter	30.00	15.00	9.00
(21)	George Muehlebach (president)	30.00	15.00	9.00

1961 Bee Hive Starch Toronto Maple Leafs

This 24-card set features players of the Toronto Maple Leafs, an independent team in the International League which featured future Hall of Fame Manager Sparky Anderson as its second baseman. The black-and-white cards are printed on thin, blank-backed stock and measure approximately 2-1/2" x 3-1/4" As the cards are not numbered, the checklist below is presented alphabetically.

		NM	EX	VG
Complete Set (24):		600.00	300.00	175.00
Common Player:		20.00	10.00	6.00
(1)	George Anderson	150.00	75.00	45.00
(2)	Fritzie Brickell	20.00	10.00	6.00
(3)	Ellis Burton	20.00	10.00	6.00
(4)	Bob Chakales	20.00	10.00	6.00
(5)	Rip Coleman	20.00	10.00	6.00
(6)	Steve Demeter	20.00	10.00	6.00
(7)	Joe Hannah	20.00	10.00	6.00
(8)	Earl Hersh	20.00	10.00	6.00
(9)	Lou Jackson	20.00	10.00	6.00
(10)	Ken Johnson	20.00	10.00	6.00
(11)	Lou Johnson	20.00	10.00	6.00
(12)	John Lipon	20.00	10.00	6.00
(13)	Carl Mathias	20.00	10.00	6.00
(14)	Bill Moran	20.00	10.00	6.00
(15)	Ron Negray	20.00	10.00	6.00
(16)	Herb Plews	20.00	10.00	6.00
(17)	Dave Pope	20.00	10.00	6.00
(18)	Steve Ridzik	20.00	10.00	6.00
(19)	Raul Sanchez	20.00	10.00	6.00
(20)	Pat Scantlebury	20.00	10.00	6.00
(21)	Bill Smith	20.00	10.00	6.00
(22)	Bob Smith	20.00	10.00	6.00
(23)	Chuck Tanner	40.00	20.00	12.00
(24)	Tim Thompson	20.00	10.00	6.00

1911 Big Eater Sacramento Solons

This very rare set was issued circa 1911 and includes only members of the Pacific Coast League Sacramento Solons. The black-and-white cards measure 2-1/8" x 4" and feature action photos. The lower part of the card contains a three-line caption that includes the player's last name, team designation (abbreviated to "Sac'to"), and the promotional line: "He Eats Big Eater"'. Although the exact origin is undetermined, it is believed that "Big Eaters" were a candy novelty.

		NM	EX	VG
Complete Set (20):		24000.	9500.	6000.
Common Player:		1500.	600.00	375.00
(1)	Frank Arellanes	1500.	600.00	375.00
(2)	Spider Baum	1500.	600.00	375.00
(3)	Herb Byram	1500.	600.00	375.00
(4)	Babe Danzig	1500.	600.00	375.00
(5)	Jack Fitzgerald	1500.	600.00	375.00
(6)	George Gaddy	1500.	600.00	375.00
(7)	Al Heister	1500.	600.00	375.00
(8)	Ben Hunt	1500.	600.00	375.00
(9)	Butch Kerns	1500.	600.00	375.00
(10)	Mickey LaLonge	1500.	600.00	375.00
(11)	Dutch Lerchen	1500.	600.00	375.00
(12)	Jimmy Lewis	1500.	600.00	375.00
(13)	Chris Mahoney	1500.	600.00	375.00
(14)	Dick Nebinger	1500.	600.00	375.00
(15)	Patsy O'Rourke	1500.	600.00	375.00
(16)	Jimmy Shinn	1500.	600.00	375.00
(17)	Chester Thomas	1500.	600.00	375.00
(18)	Fuller Thompson	1500.	600.00	375.00
(19)	Frank Thornton	1500.	600.00	375.00
(20)	Deacon Van Buren	1500.	600.00	375.00

1950 Big League Stars (V362)

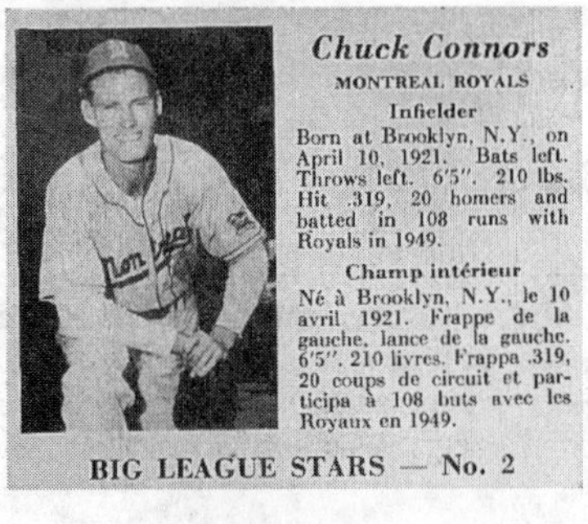
Chuck Connors
MONTREAL ROYALS
Infielder
Born at Brooklyn, N.Y., on April 10, 1921. Bats left. Throws left. 6'5". 210 lbs. Hit .319, 20 homers and batted in 108 runs with Royals in 1949.
Champ intérieur
Né à Brooklyn, N.Y., le 10 avril 1921. Frappe de la gauche, lance de la gauche. 6'5". 210 livres. Frappa .319, 20 coups de circuit et participa à 108 buts avec les Royaux en 1949.
BIG LEAGUE STARS — No. 2

International League players are featured in this 48-card set. Measuring 3-1/4" x 2-5/8", the blank-backed cards are printed in blue-on-white with English and French stats and biographical data.

		NM	EX	VG
Complete Set (48):		2800.	1400.	825.00
Common Player:		50.00	25.00	15.00
1	Rocky Bridges	85.00	42.00	25.00
2	Chuck Connors	500.00	250.00	150.00
3	Jake Wade	50.00	25.00	15.00
4	Al Cihocki	50.00	25.00	15.00
5	John Simmons	50.00	25.00	15.00
6	Frank Trechock	50.00	25.00	15.00
7	Steve Lembo	50.00	25.00	15.00
8	Johnny Welaj	50.00	25.00	15.00
9	Seymour Block	50.00	25.00	15.00
10	Pat McGlothlin	50.00	25.00	15.00
11	Bryan Stephens	50.00	25.00	15.00
12	Clarence Podbielan	50.00	25.00	15.00
13	Clem Hausmann	50.00	25.00	15.00
14	Turk Lown	50.00	25.00	15.00
15	Joe Payne	50.00	25.00	15.00
16	Coacker Triplett (Coaker)	50.00	25.00	15.00
17	Nick Strincevich	50.00	25.00	15.00
18	Charlie Thompson	50.00	25.00	15.00
19	Erick Silverman	50.00	25.00	15.00
20	George Schmees	50.00	25.00	15.00
21	George Binks	50.00	25.00	15.00
22	Gino Cimoli	75.00	37.00	22.00
23	Marty Tabacheck	50.00	25.00	15.00
24	Al Gionfriddo	65.00	32.00	19.50
25	Ronnie Lee	50.00	25.00	15.00
26	Clyde King	50.00	25.00	15.00
27	Harry Heslet	50.00	25.00	15.00
28	Jerry Scala	50.00	25.00	15.00
29	Boris Woyt	50.00	25.00	15.00
30	Jack Collum	50.00	25.00	15.00
31	Chet Laabs	50.00	25.00	15.00
32	Carden Gillwater	50.00	25.00	15.00
33	Irving Medlinger	50.00	25.00	15.00
34	Toby Atwell	50.00	25.00	15.00
35	Charlie Marshall	50.00	25.00	15.00
36	Johnny Mayo	50.00	25.00	15.00
37	Gene Markland	50.00	25.00	15.00
38	Russ Kerns	50.00	25.00	15.00
39	Jim Prendergast	50.00	25.00	15.00
40	Lou Welaj	50.00	25.00	15.00
41	Clyde Kluttz	50.00	25.00	15.00
42	Bill Glynn	50.00	25.00	15.00
43	Don Richmond	50.00	25.00	15.00
44	Hank Biasatti	50.00	25.00	15.00
45	Tom Lasorda	425.00	212.00	127.00
46	Al Roberge	50.00	25.00	15.00
47	George Byam	50.00	25.00	15.00
48	Dutch Mele	50.00	25.00	15.00

1910 Bishop & Co. P.C.L. (E99)

Hap. Hogan, c. Vernon

The first of two obscure sets produced by the Los Angeles candy maker Bishop & Co., this 30-card set was issued in 1910 and depicts players from the Pacific Coast League, showing five players from each of the six teams. The cards measure approximately 1-1/2" x 2-3/4" and feature black-and-white player photos with colored backgrounds (green, blue, purple, yellow, or rarely, black). The player's last name, position and team appear along the bottom. The backs of the cards contain the complete checklist in groups of five, according to team, with each name indented slightly more than the name above. Cards in the 1910 set do not contain the name "Bishop & Company, California" along the bottom on the back.

		NM	EX	VG
Complete Set (30):		10500.	4200.	2625.
Common Player:		425.00	175.00	100.00
(1)	Bodie	450.00	180.00	110.00
(2)	N. Brashear	425.00	175.00	100.00
(3)	Briggs	425.00	175.00	100.00
(4)	Byones (Byrnes)	425.00	175.00	100.00
(5)	Cameron	425.00	175.00	100.00
(6)	Casey	425.00	175.00	100.00
(7)	Cutshaw	425.00	175.00	100.00
(8)	Delmas	425.00	175.00	100.00
(9)	Dillon	425.00	175.00	100.00
(10)	Hasty	425.00	175.00	100.00
(11)	Hitt	425.00	175.00	100.00

(12)	Hap. Hogan	425.00	175.00	100.00
(13)	Hunt	425.00	175.00	100.00
(14)	Krapp	425.00	175.00	100.00
(15)	Lindsay	425.00	175.00	100.00
(16)	Maggert	425.00	175.00	100.00
(17)	McArdle	425.00	175.00	100.00
(18)	McCredie (McCreedie)	425.00	175.00	100.00
(19)	Melchoir	425.00	175.00	100.00
(20)	Mohler	425.00	175.00	100.00
(21)	Nagle	425.00	175.00	100.00
(22)	Nelson	425.00	175.00	100.00
(23)	Nourse	425.00	175.00	100.00
(24)	Olsen	425.00	175.00	100.00
(25)	Raymer	425.00	175.00	100.00
(26)	Smith	425.00	175.00	100.00
(27)	Tennent (Tennant)	425.00	175.00	100.00
(28)	Thorsen	425.00	175.00	100.00
(29)	Van Buren	425.00	175.00	100.00
(30)	Wolverton	425.00	175.00	100.00

1910 Bishop & Co. P.C.L. Teams (E221)

A very rare issue, this series of team pictures of clubs in the Pacific Coast League was distributed by Bishop & Company of Los Angeles in 1910. The team photos were printed on a thin, newsprint-type paper that measures an elongated 10" x 2-3/4". Although there were six teams in the PCL at the time, only five clubs have been found - the sixth team, Sacramento, was apparently never issued. The cards indicate that they were issued with five-cent packages of Bishop's Milk Chocolate and that the photos were taken by the Los Angeles Examiner. The black-and-white team photos are found with red, blue, yellow, purple or green background.

		NM	EX	VG
Complete Set (5):		12000.	4800.	2850.
Common Team:		2400.	1200.	720.00
(1)	Los Angeles	2500.	1000.	625.00
(2)	Oakland	2500.	1000.	625.00
(3)	Portland	2500.	1000.	625.00
(4)	San Francisco	2500.	1000.	625.00
(5)	Vernon	2500.	1000.	625.00

1911 Bishop & Co. P.C.L. Type I (E100)

This set was issued by the confectioner Bishop & Company of Los Angeles, which had produced a similar set a year earlier. Both sets showcased star players from the Pacific Coast League. The cards measure approximately 1-1/2" x 2-3/4" and feature black-and-white photos with a background of green, blue, yellow, purple or red. The backs contain the complete checklist of the set, listing the players in groups of five by team, with one line indented slightly more than the previous one. In addition to the checklist, the 1911 set can be differentiated from the previous year because the line "Bishop & Company, California" appears along the bottom. Variations have been discovered in recent years for many of the cards in this set. The variations, known as "Type II" have either orange or green backgrounds with more tightly cropped photos and blank backs.

		NM	EX	VG
Complete Set (30):		10000.	4000.	2500.
Common Player:		425.00	175.00	100.00
(1)	Spider Baum	425.00	175.00	100.00
(2)	Burrell	425.00	175.00	100.00
(3)	Carlisle	425.00	175.00	100.00
(4)	Cutshaw	425.00	175.00	100.00
(5)	Pete Daley	425.00	175.00	100.00
(6)	Danzig	425.00	175.00	100.00
(7)	Delhi	425.00	175.00	100.00
(8)	Delmas	425.00	175.00	100.00
(9)	Hitt	425.00	175.00	100.00
(10)	Hap Hogan (actually Walter Bray)	425.00	175.00	100.00
(11)	Lerchen	425.00	175.00	100.00
(12)	McCreddie (McCreedie)	425.00	175.00	100.00
(13)	Mohler	425.00	175.00	100.00
(14)	Moore	425.00	175.00	100.00
(15)	Slim Nelson	425.00	175.00	100.00
(16)	P. O'Rourke	425.00	175.00	100.00
(17)	Patterson	425.00	175.00	100.00
(18)	Bunny Pearce	425.00	175.00	100.00
(19)	Peckinpaugh	425.00	175.00	100.00
(20)	Monte Pfyle (Pfyl)	425.00	175.00	100.00
(21)	Powell	425.00	175.00	100.00
(22)	Rapps	425.00	175.00	100.00
(23)	Seaton	425.00	175.00	100.00
(24)	Steen	425.00	175.00	100.00
(25)	Suter	425.00	175.00	100.00
(26)	Tennant	425.00	175.00	100.00
(27)	Thomas	425.00	175.00	100.00
(28)	Tozer	425.00	175.00	100.00
(29)	Clyde Wares	425.00	175.00	100.00
(30)	Weaver	950.00	375.00	225.00

1911 Bishop & Co. P.C.L. Type II (E100)

		NM	EX	VG
Complete Set (17):		7000.	2800.	1750.
Common Player:		425.00	175.00	100.00
(1)	Burrell	425.00	175.00	100.00
(2)	Danzig	425.00	175.00	100.00
(3)	Delhi	425.00	175.00	100.00
(4)	Hitt	425.00	175.00	100.00
(5)	Lerchen	425.00	175.00	100.00
(6)	McCreddie (McCreedie)	425.00	175.00	100.00
(7)	Slim Nelson	425.00	175.00	100.00
(8)	P. O'Rourke	425.00	175.00	100.00
(9)	Patterson	425.00	175.00	100.00
(10)	Bunny Pearce	425.00	175.00	100.00
(11)	Monte Pfyle	425.00	175.00	100.00
(12)	Rapps	425.00	175.00	100.00
(13)	Seaton	425.00	175.00	100.00
(14)	Steen	425.00	175.00	100.00
(15)	Suter	425.00	175.00	100.00
(16)	Tennant	425.00	175.00	100.00
(17)	Weaver	950.00	375.00	225.00

1954 Blossom Dairy Charleston Senators

The Class AAA farm team of the Chicago White Sox is featured in this team set sponsored by a Charleston, W. Va., dairy. The 2-1/4" x 3-3/16" black-and-white cards are either a late issue by Globe Printing (which issued many minor league sets from 1951-52) or were patterned after the Globe issues, right down to the issue of an album to house the cards. A white box is superimposed over the posed action photos and contains the player and sponsor identification. Cards are blank-backed.

		NM	EX	VG
Complete Set (22):		1500.	750.00	450.00
Common Player:		75.00	37.00	22.00
Album:		150.00	75.00	45.00
(1)	Al Baro	75.00	37.00	22.00
(2)	Joe Becker	75.00	37.00	22.00
(3)	Joe Carroll	75.00	37.00	22.00
(4)	Gerald "Red" Fahr	75.00	37.00	22.00
(5)	Dick Fowler	75.00	37.00	22.00
(6)	Alex Garbowski	75.00	37.00	22.00
(7)	Gordon Goldsberry	75.00	37.00	22.00
(8)	Ross Grimsley	75.00	37.00	22.00
(9)	Sam Hairston	90.00	45.00	27.00
(10)	Phil Haugstad	75.00	37.00	22.00
(11)	Tom Hurd	80.00	40.00	24.00
(12)	Bill Killinger	75.00	37.00	22.00
(13)	John Kropf	75.00	37.00	22.00
(14)	Bob Masser	75.00	37.00	22.00
(15)	Danny Menendez	75.00	37.00	22.00
(16)	Bill Paolisso	75.00	37.00	22.00
(17)	Bill Pope	75.00	37.00	22.00
(18)	Lou Sleater	75.00	37.00	22.00
(19)	Dick Strahs	75.00	37.00	22.00
(20)	Joe Torpey	75.00	37.00	22.00
(21)	Bill Voiselle	75.00	37.00	22.00
(22)	Al Ware	75.00	37.00	22.00

1958 Bond Bread Buffalo Bisons

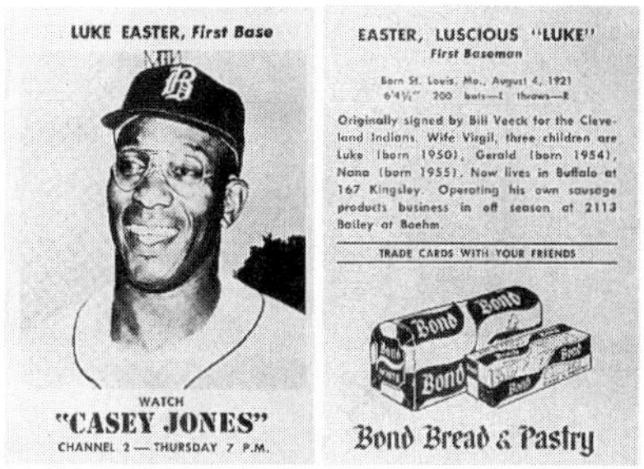

Nine members of the International League affiliate of the Kansas City Athletics are featured in this set. The 2-1/2" x 3-1/2" cards are printed on very thin cardboard. Fronts have a black-and-white player photo, the player's name and position, and an ad for a TV Western. Card backs are printed in red and blue and include a few biographical details and a career summary, along with an illustrated ad.

		NM	EX	VG
Complete Set (9):		225.00	110.00	65.00
Common Player:		25.00	12.50	7.50
(1)	Al Aber	25.00	12.50	7.50
(2)	Joe Caffie	25.00	12.50	7.50
(3)	Phil Cavaretta	25.00	12.50	7.50
(4)	Rip Coleman	25.00	12.50	7.50
(5)	Luke Easter	40.00	20.00	12.00
(6)	Ken Johnson	25.00	12.50	7.50
(7)	Lou Ortiz	25.00	12.50	7.50
(8)	Jack Phillips	25.00	12.50	7.50
(9)	Jim Small	25.00	12.50	7.50

1949 Bowman Pacific Coast League

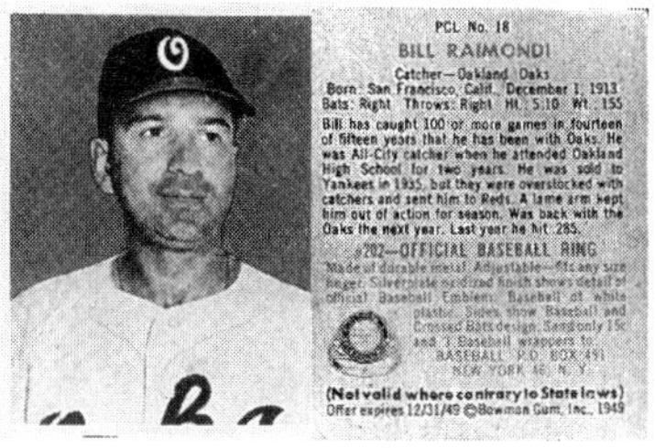

One of the scarcest issues of the post-war period, the 1949 Bowman PCL set was issued only on the West Coast. Like the 1949 Bowman regular issue, the cards contain black-and-white photos overprinted with various pastel colors. Thirty-six cards, which measure 2-1/16" x 2-1/2", make up the set. It is believed that the cards may have been issued only in sheets and not sold in gum packs. Consequently, many cards are found which display evidence of having been cut with a scissors.

		NM	EX	VG
Complete Set (36):		11000.	4500.	2900.
Common Player:		350.00	140.00	90.00
1	Lee Anthony	400.00	160.00	100.00
2	George Metkovich	400.00	160.00	100.00
3	Ralph Hodgin	400.00	160.00	100.00
4	George Woods	400.00	160.00	100.00
5	Xavier Rescigno	400.00	160.00	100.00
6	Mickey Grasso	400.00	160.00	100.00
7	Johnny Rucker	400.00	160.00	100.00
8	Jack Brewer	400.00	160.00	100.00
9	Dom D'Allessandro	400.00	160.00	100.00
10	Charlie Gassaway	400.00	160.00	100.00
11	Tony Freitas	400.00	160.00	100.00
12	Gordon Maltzberger	400.00	160.00	100.00
13	John Jensen	400.00	160.00	100.00
14	Joyner White	400.00	160.00	100.00
15	Harvey Storey	400.00	160.00	100.00
16	Dick Lajeski	400.00	160.00	100.00
17	Albie Glossop	400.00	160.00	100.00
18	Bill Raimondi	400.00	160.00	100.00
19	Ken Holcombe	400.00	160.00	100.00
20	Don Ross	400.00	160.00	100.00
21	Pete Coscarart	400.00	160.00	100.00
22	Tony York	400.00	160.00	100.00
23	Jake Mooty	400.00	160.00	100.00
24	Charles Adams	400.00	160.00	100.00
25	Les Scarsella	400.00	160.00	100.00
26	Joe Marty	400.00	160.00	100.00
27	Frank Kelleher	400.00	160.00	100.00
28	Lee Handley	400.00	160.00	100.00
29	Herman Besse	400.00	160.00	100.00
30	John Lazor	400.00	160.00	100.00
31	Eddie Malone	400.00	160.00	100.00
32	Maurice Van Robays	400.00	160.00	100.00
33	Jim Tabor	400.00	160.00	100.00
34	Gene Handley	400.00	160.00	100.00
35	Tom Seats	400.00	160.00	100.00
36	Ora Burnett	400.00	160.00	100.00

1933 Buffalo Bisons Jigsaw Puzzles

Produced as a stadium promotional giveaway, this set consists of 19 player puzzles and one for Hall of Fame Manager Ray Schalk. Each of the 11" x 14", 200-piece, black-and-white puzzles was produced in an edition of 10,000. Puzzles carried a red serial number, and certain numbers could be redeemed for tickets and other prizes. The known puzzles are checklisted below in alphabetical order.

		NM	EX	VG
Complete Set (13):		2900.	1450.	870.00
Common Player:		225.00	115.00	70.00
(1)	Joe Bartulis	225.00	115.00	70.00
(2)	Ollie Carnegie	225.00	115.00	70.00
(3)	Clyde "Buck" Crouse	225.00	115.00	70.00
(4)	Harry Danning	225.00	115.00	70.00
(5)	Gilbert English	225.00	115.00	70.00
(6)	Fred Fussell	225.00	115.00	70.00
(7)	Bob Gould	225.00	115.00	70.00
(8)	Len Koenecke	225.00	115.00	70.00
(9)	Clarence Mueller	225.00	115.00	70.00
(10)	Ray Schalk	350.00	175.00	105.00
(11)	Jack Smith	225.00	115.00	70.00
(12)	Roy Tarr	225.00	115.00	70.00
(13)	Johnny Wilson	225.00	115.00	70.00

1940 Buffalo Bisons team issue

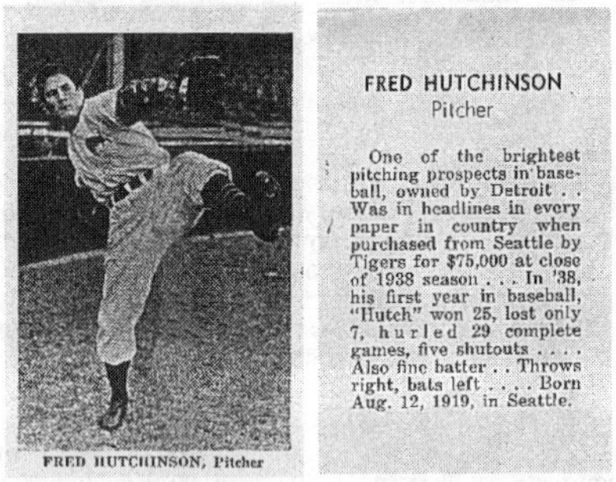

Many former and future big leaguers are included in this set of black-and-white, 2" x 3" cards. Fronts picture the players in poses at old Offerman Stadium. The player's name and position are printed in the white border at bottom. Backs have a career summary and highlights. The unnumbered cards are checklisted here alphabetically.

		NM	EX	VG
Complete Set (24):		950.00	475.00	285.00
Common Player:		60.00	30.00	18.50
(1)	Ollie Carnegie	60.00	30.00	18.50
(2)	Dan Carnevale	60.00	30.00	18.50
(3)	Earl Cook	60.00	30.00	18.50
(4)	Les Fleming	60.00	30.00	18.50
(5)	Floyd Giebel	60.00	30.00	18.50
(6)	Jimmy Hutch	60.00	30.00	18.50
(7)	Fred Hutchinson	75.00	37.00	22.00
(8)	Art Jacobs	60.00	30.00	18.50
(9)	John Kroner	60.00	30.00	18.50
(10)	Sal Maglie	80.00	40.00	24.00
(11)	Joe Martin	60.00	30.00	18.50
(12)	Clyde McCullough	60.00	30.00	18.50
(13)	Greg Mulleavy	60.00	30.00	18.50
(14)	Pat Mullin	60.00	30.00	18.50
(15)	Hank Nowak	60.00	30.00	18.50
(16)	Steve O'Neil	60.00	30.00	18.50
(17)	Jimmy Outlaw	60.00	30.00	18.50
(18)	Joe Rogalski	60.00	30.00	18.50
(19)	Les Scarsella	60.00	30.00	18.50
(20)	Mayo Smith	60.00	30.00	18.50
(21)	Floyd Stromme	60.00	30.00	18.50
(22)	Jim Trexler	60.00	30.00	18.50
(23)	Hal White	60.00	30.00	18.50
(24)	Frank Zubik			

C

1943 Centennial Flour Seattle Rainiers

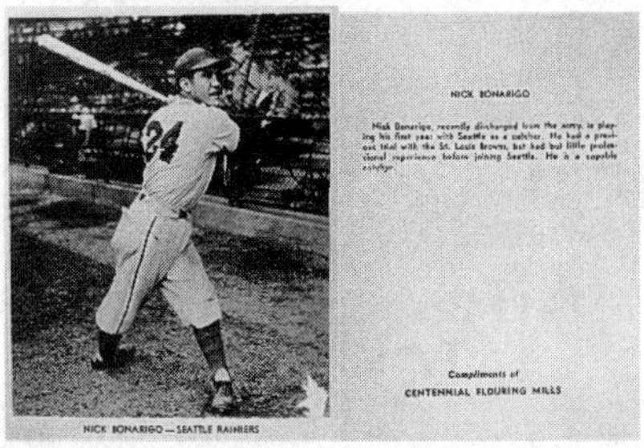

The 25 cards in this 4" x 5" black-and-white set feature players of the Pacific Coast League Seattle Rainiers. Identical in format to the set issued in 1944, the '43s can be identified by the lines of type at the bottom of the card back reading, "Compliments of/CENTENNIAL FLOURING MILLS."

		NM	EX	VG
Complete Set (25):		1000.	500.00	300.00
Common Player:		45.00	22.00	13.50
(1)	John Babich	45.00	22.00	13.50
(2)	Nick Bonarigo (Buonarigo)	45.00	22.00	13.50
(3)	Eddie Carnett	45.00	22.00	13.50
(4)	Lloyd Christopher	45.00	22.00	13.50
(5)	Joe Demoran	45.00	22.00	13.50
(6)	Joe Dobbins	45.00	22.00	13.50
(7)	Glenn Elliott	45.00	22.00	13.50
(8)	Carl Fischer	45.00	22.00	13.50
(9)	Leonard Gabrielson	45.00	22.00	13.50
(10)	Stanley Gray	45.00	22.00	13.50
(11)	Dick Gyselman	45.00	22.00	13.50
(12)	Jim Jewell	45.00	22.00	13.50
(13)	Syl Johnson	45.00	22.00	13.50
(14)	Pete Jonas	45.00	22.00	13.50
(15)	Bill Kats	45.00	22.00	13.50
(16)	Lynn King	45.00	22.00	13.50
(17)	Bill Lawrence	45.00	22.00	13.50
(18)	Clarence Marshall	45.00	22.00	13.50
(19)	Bill Matheson	45.00	22.00	13.50
(20)	Ford Mullen	45.00	22.00	13.50
(21)	Bill Skiff	45.00	22.00	13.50
(22)	Byron Speece	45.00	22.00	13.50
(23)	Hal Sueme	45.00	22.00	13.50
(24)	Hal Turpin	45.00	22.00	13.50
(25)	John Yelovic	45.00	22.00	13.50

1944 Centennial Flour Seattle Rainers

Identical in format to the previous year's issue, the 25 black-and-white 4" x 5" cards issued in 1944 can be differentiated from the 1943 set by the two lines of type at the bottom of each card's back. In the 1944 set, it reads, "Compliments of/CENTENNIAL HOTCAKE AND WAFFLE FLOUR."

		NM	EX	VG
Complete Set (25):		1000.	500.00	300.00
Common Player:		45.00	22.00	13.50
(1)	John Babich	45.00	22.00	13.50
(2)	Paul Carpenter	45.00	22.00	13.50
(3)	Lloyd Christopher	45.00	22.00	13.50
(4)	Joe Demoran	45.00	22.00	13.50
(5)	Joe Dobbins	45.00	22.00	13.50
(6)	Glenn Elliott	45.00	22.00	13.50
(7)	Carl Fischer	45.00	22.00	13.50
(8)	Bob Garbould (Gorbould)	45.00	22.00	13.50
(9)	Stanley Gray	45.00	22.00	13.50
(10)	Dick Gyselman	45.00	22.00	13.50
(11)	Gene Holt	45.00	22.00	13.50
(12)	Roy Johnson	45.00	22.00	13.50
(13)	Syl Johnson	45.00	22.00	13.50
(14)	Al Libke	45.00	22.00	13.50
(15)	Bill Lyman	45.00	22.00	13.50
(16)	Bill Matheson	45.00	22.00	13.50
(17)	Jack McClure	45.00	22.00	13.50
(18)	Jimmy Ripple	45.00	22.00	13.50
(19)	Bill Skiff	45.00	22.00	13.50
(20)	Byron Speece	45.00	22.00	13.50
(21)	Hal Sueme	45.00	22.00	13.50
(22)	Frank Tincup	45.00	22.00	13.50
(23)	Jack Treece	45.00	22.00	13.50
(24)	Hal Turpin	45.00	22.00	13.50
(25)	Sicks Stadium	45.00	22.00	13.50

Suffix letters following a card number indicate a variation card.

1945 Centennial Flour Seattle Rainiers

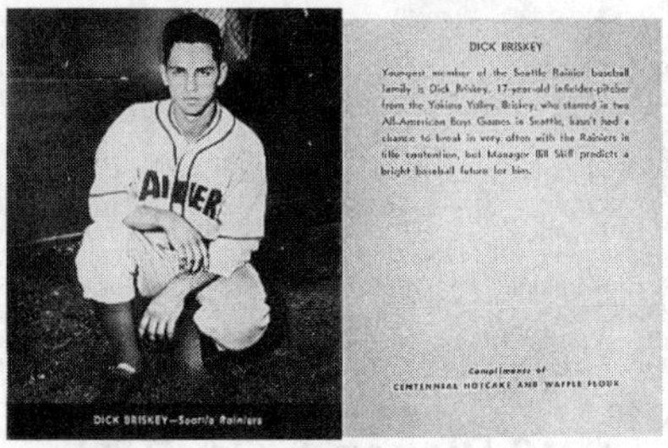

The 27 blue-and-white cards in the third consecutive issue for this Pacific Coast League team are distinguished from the two previous issues by the borderless photo on the front and the fact that the name and team are printed in a black bar at the bottom. The set can be distinguished from the 1947 issue by virtue of the fact that the player biography on back is not surrounded by a frame. The cards measure slightly narrower but longer than the 1943-44 issues, at 3-7/8" x 5-1/8".

		NM	EX	VG
Complete Set (27):		800.00	400.00	250.00
Common Player:		40.00	20.00	12.00
(1)	Charley Aleno	40.00	20.00	12.00
(2)	Dick Briskey	40.00	20.00	12.00
(3)	John Carpenter	40.00	20.00	12.00
(4)	Joe Demoran	40.00	20.00	12.00
(5)	Joe Dobbins	40.00	20.00	12.00
(6)	Glenn Elliott	40.00	20.00	12.00
(7)	Bob Finley	40.00	20.00	12.00
(8)	Carl Fischer	40.00	20.00	12.00
(9)	Keith Frazier	40.00	20.00	12.00
(10)	Johnny Gill	40.00	20.00	12.00
(11)	Bob Gorbould	40.00	20.00	12.00
(12)	Chet Johnson	40.00	20.00	12.00
(13)	Syl Johnson	40.00	20.00	12.00
(14)	Bill Kats	40.00	20.00	12.00
(15)	Billy Lyman	40.00	20.00	12.00
(16)	Bill Matheson	40.00	20.00	12.00
(17)	George McDonald	40.00	20.00	12.00
(18)	Ted Norbert	40.00	20.00	12.00
(19)	Alex Palica	40.00	20.00	12.00
(20)	Joe Passero	40.00	20.00	12.00
(21)	Hal Patchett	40.00	20.00	12.00
(22)	Bill Skiff	40.00	20.00	12.00
(23)	Byron Speece	40.00	20.00	12.00
(24)	Hal Sueme	40.00	20.00	12.00
(25)	Eddie Taylor	40.00	20.00	12.00
(26)	Hal Turpin	40.00	20.00	12.00
(27)	Jack Whipple	40.00	20.00	12.00

1947 Centennial Flour Seattle Rainiers

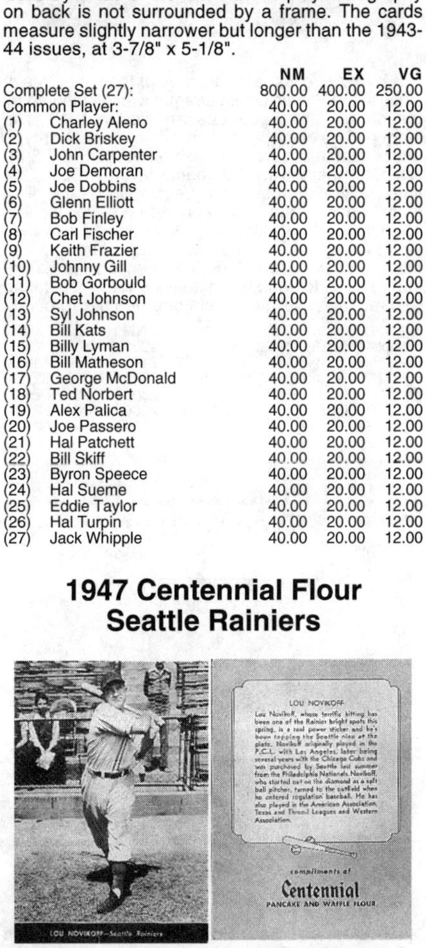

After a lapse of one year, Centennial Flour returned to issue a final black-and-white 32-card set for 1947. Identical in size (3-7/8" x 5-1/8") and front format to the 1945 issue, the '47s can be identified by the white framed box on back containing the player's biography.

		NM	EX	VG
Complete Set (32):		1200.	600.00	350.00
Common Player:		40.00	20.00	12.00
(1)	Dick Barrett	40.00	20.00	12.00
(2)	Joe Buzas	40.00	20.00	12.00
(3)	Paul Carpenter	40.00	20.00	12.00
(4)	Rex Cecil	40.00	20.00	12.00
(5)	Tony Criscola	40.00	20.00	12.00
(6)	Walter Dubiel	40.00	20.00	12.00
(7)	Doug Ford	40.00	20.00	12.00
(8)	Rollie Hemsley	45.00	22.00	13.50
(9)	Jim Hill	40.00	20.00	12.00
(10)	Jim Hopper	40.00	20.00	12.00
(11)	Sigmund Jakucki	40.00	20.00	12.00
(12)	Bob Johnson	60.00	30.00	18.00
(13)	Pete Jonas	40.00	20.00	12.00
(14)	Joe Kaney	40.00	20.00	12.00
(15)	Hillis Layne	40.00	20.00	12.00
(16)	Lou Novikoff	50.00	25.00	15.00

		NM	EX	VG
(17)	Johnny O'Neil	40.00	20.00	12.00
(18)	John Orphal	40.00	20.00	12.00
(19)	Ike Pearson	40.00	20.00	12.00
(20)	Bill Posedel	40.00	20.00	12.00
(21)	Don Pulford	40.00	20.00	12.00
(22)	Tom Reis	40.00	20.00	12.00
(23)	Charley Ripple	40.00	20.00	12.00
(24)	Mickey Rocco	40.00	20.00	12.00
(25)	Johnny Rucker	40.00	20.00	12.00
(26)	Earl Sheely	40.00	20.00	12.00
(27)	Bob Stagg	40.00	20.00	12.00
(28)	Hal Sueme	40.00	20.00	12.00
(29)	Eddie Taylor	40.00	20.00	12.00
(30)	Ed Vanni	40.00	20.00	12.00
(31)	JoJo White	40.00	20.00	12.00
(32)	Tony York	40.00	20.00	12.00

1910 Clement Bros. Bread (D380)

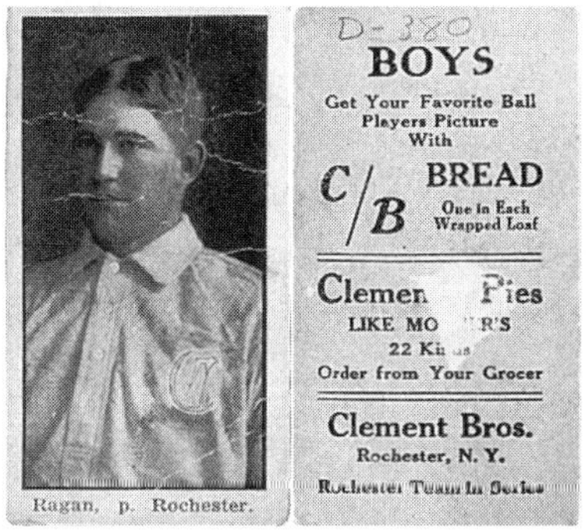

For the second of two annual issues, the bakery added seven major league players' cards to those of six of the hometeam Rochester club of the Eastern League. While the backs remained identical to the previous issue, featuring advertising for the bakery's bread and pies, the fronts adopted the standard format of the era, player photos surrounded by a white border, with the player's last name, position and city printed at bottom. Size remained 1-1/2" x 2-3/4".

		NM	EX	VG
Complete Set (13):		14000.	5600.	3500.
Common Player:		800.00	400.00	200.00
(1)	Whitey Alperman	800.00	400.00	200.00
(2)	Bailey	800.00	400.00	200.00
(3)	Blair	800.00	400.00	200.00
(4)	Ty Cobb	7500.	3000.	1875.
(5)	Eddie Collins	1400.	550.00	350.00
(6)	Addie Joss	2400.	960.00	600.00
(7)	McConnell	800.00	400.00	200.00
(8)	Osborn	800.00	400.00	200.00
(9)	Pattee	800.00	400.00	200.00
(10)	Don Carlos Ragan	800.00	400.00	200.00
(11)	Oscar Stanage	800.00	400.00	200.00
(12)	Ed Summers	800.00	400.00	200.00
(13)	Joe Tinker	1000.	400.00	250.00
(14)	Bert Tooley	800.00	400.00	200.00
(15)	Heinie Zimmerman	800.00	400.00	200.00

1909 Clement Bros. Bread (D380-1)

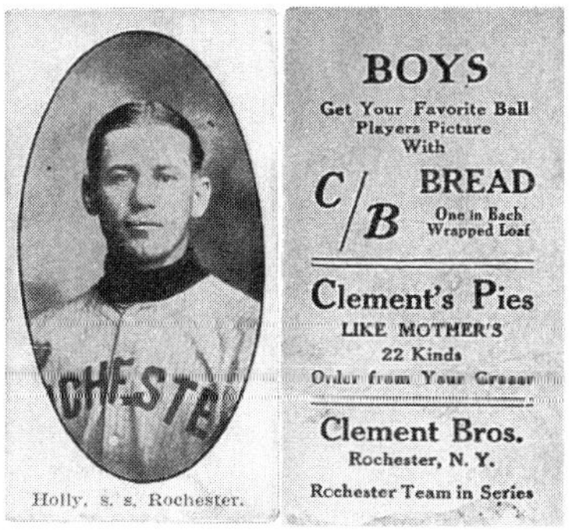

This set features only players of the Rochester team in the Eastern League. According to the bakery ad on back, the cards were distributed one per loaf of bread. The 1-1/2" x 2-3/4" cards feature a player photo on front in an oval frame against a white background. The player's last name, position and "Rochester" are printed beneath.

		NM	EX	VG
Complete Set (8):		6000.	3000.	1800.
Common Player:		800.00	400.00	225.00
(1)	Anderson	800.00	400.00	225.00
(2)	Heinie Batch	800.00	400.00	225.00
(3)	Butler	800.00	400.00	225.00
(4)	Ed Holly	800.00	400.00	225.00
(5)	Holmes	800.00	400.00	225.00
(6)	McConnell	800.00	400.00	225.00
(7)	Osborn	800.00	400.00	225.00
(8)	Partee	800.00	400.00	225.00

1955 Columbus Jets Photos

A top farm club of the Kansas City A's in 1955 the Columbus (Ohio) Jets issued these black-and-white glossy photocards. In 3-5/8" x 5-5/8" format, the cards have a facsimile autograph on front. It is possible that the checklist presented here in alphabetical order of the unnumbered cards may be incomplete.

		NM	EX	VG
Complete Set (21):		300.00	150.00	90.00
Common Player:		15.00	7.50	4.50
(1)	Hal Bevan	15.00	7.50	4.50
(2)	Paul Burris	15.00	7.50	4.50
(3)	Ted Del Guercio	15.00	7.50	4.50
(4)	Carl Duser	15.00	7.50	4.50
(5)	Charlie Haag	15.00	7.50	4.50
(6)	Forrest "Spook" Jacobs	20.00	10.00	6.00
(7)	Dick Kryhoski	15.00	7.50	4.50
(8)	Mike Kume	15.00	7.50	4.50
(9)	Al Lakeman	15.00	7.50	4.50
(10)	Jackie Mayo	15.00	7.50	4.50
(11)	Jim Miller	15.00	7.50	4.50
(12)	Al Pinkston	17.50	8.75	5.25
(13)	Al Romberger	15.00	7.50	4.50
(14)	Bill Stewart	15.00	7.50	4.50
(15)	Russ Sullivan	15.00	7.50	4.50
(16)	"Jake" Thies	15.00	7.50	4.50
(17)	Bob Trice	15.00	7.50	4.50
(18)	Ozzie VanBrabant	15.00	7.50	4.50
(19)	Frank Verdi	15.00	7.50	4.50
(20)	Leroy Wheat	15.00	7.50	4.50
(21)	Spider Wilhelm	15.00	7.50	4.50

1957 Columbus Jets Postcards

In 1957, the Columbus (Ohio) Jets began a long association as a top farm team of the Pittsburgh Pirates. That year, the team issued this set of postcards. The black-and-white glossy cards measure 3-9/16" x 5-1/2" and have the player name and position overprinted in black block letters near the bottom of the photo. Backs have postcard indicia and a notice of printing by the Howard Photo Service of New York City. The unnumbered cards are presented here alphabetically but it is unknown whether this checklist is complete at 20.

		NM	EX	VG
Complete Set (20):		300.00	150.00	90.00
Common Player:		15.00	7.50	4.50
(1)	Dick Barone	15.00	7.50	4.50
(2)	Ron Blackburn	17.50	8.75	5.25
(3)	Jackie Brown	15.00	7.50	4.50
(4)	Ed Burtschy	15.00	7.50	4.50
(5)	Whammy Douglas	17.50	8.75	5.25
(6)	Howie Goss	15.00	7.50	4.50
(7)	Al Grunwald	15.00	7.50	4.50
(8)	Gail Henley	15.00	7.50	4.50
(9)	Don Kildoo	15.00	7.50	4.50
(10)	Danny Kravitz	17.50	8.75	5.25
(11)	Bob Kuzava	17.50	8.75	5.25
(12)	Johnny Lipon	17.50	8.75	5.25
(13)	Cholly Naranjo	15.00	7.50	4.50
(14)	Eddie O'Brien	17.50	8.75	5.25
(15)	Frank Oceak	15.00	7.50	4.50
(16)	Harding Peterson	17.50	8.75	5.25
(17)	John Powers	15.00	7.50	4.50
(18)	James Rice	15.00	7.50	4.50
(19)	Russ Sullivan	15.00	7.50	4.50
(20)	Ken Toothman	15.00	7.50	4.50

1958 Columbus Jets Photos

In format similar to the postcard issue of the previous year, and sharing some of the same pictures, this set of photocards is smaller, at 4" x 5", and is blank-backed. It is unknown whether the alphabetical checklist of the unnumbered cards presented here is complete.

		NM	EX	VG
Complete Set (17):		200.00	100.00	60.00
Common Player:		12.00	6.00	3.50
(1)	Gair Allie	12.00	6.00	3.50
(2)	Luis Arroyo	12.00	6.00	3.50
(3)	Tony Bartirome	15.00	7.50	4.50
(4)	Jim Baumer	13.50	6.75	4.00
(5)	Bill Causion	12.00	6.00	3.50
(6)	Whammy Douglas	12.00	6.00	3.50
(7)	Joe Gibbon	12.00	6.00	3.50
(8)	Howie Goss	12.00	6.00	3.50
(9)	Spook Jacobs	15.00	7.50	4.50
(10)	Clyde King	12.00	6.00	3.50
(11)	Cholly Naranjo	12.00	6.00	3.50
(12)	George O'Donnell	12.00	6.00	3.50
(13)	Laurin Pepper	12.00	6.00	3.50
(14)	Dick Rand	12.00	6.00	3.50
(15)	Leo Rodriguez	12.00	6.00	3.50
(16)	Don Rowe	12.00	6.00	3.50
(17)	Art Swanson	12.00	6.00	3.50

1910 Contentnea First Series (T209)

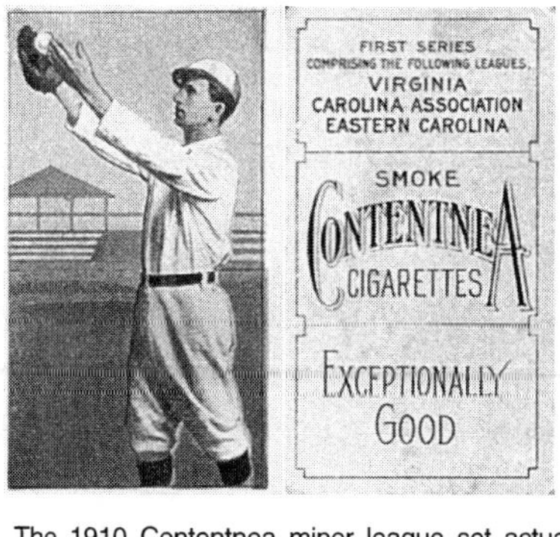

The 1910 Contentnea minor league set actually consists of two distinctively different series, both featuring players from the Virginia League, Carolina Association and Eastern Carolina League. The cards were distributed in packages of Contentnea cigarettes. The first series, featuring color photographs, consists of just 16 cards, each measuring 1-9/16" x 2-11/16". The front of the card has the player's last name and team printed at the bottom, while the back identifies the card as "First

Series" and carries an advertisement for Contentnea cigarettes. The second series, believed to have been issued later in 1910, is a massive 221-card set consisting of black-and-white player photos. The cards in this series are slightly larger, measuring 1-5/8" x 2-3/4". They carry the words "Photo Series" on the back, along with the cigarette advertisement. Only a handful of the players in the Contentnea set ever advanced to the major leagues and the set contains no major stars. Subsequently, it generally holds interest only to collectors who specialize in the old southern minor leagues.

		NM	EX	VG
Complete Set (16):		2000.	800.00	475.00
Common Player:		150.00	60.00	35.00
(1)	Armstrong	150.00	60.00	35.00
(2)	Booles	150.00	60.00	35.00
(3)	Bourquise (Bourquoise)	150.00	60.00	35.00
(4)	Cooper	150.00	60.00	35.00
(5)	Cowell	150.00	60.00	35.00
(6)	Crockett	150.00	60.00	35.00
(7)	Fullenwider	150.00	60.00	35.00
(8)	Gilmore	150.00	60.00	35.00
(9)	Hoffman	150.00	60.00	35.00
(10)	Lane	150.00	60.00	35.00
(11)	Martin	150.00	60.00	35.00
(12)	McGeehan	150.00	60.00	35.00
(13)	Pope	150.00	60.00	35.00
(14)	Sisson	150.00	60.00	35.00
(15)	Stubbe	150.00	60.00	35.00
(16)	Walsh	150.00	60.00	35.00

1910 Contentnea Photo Series (T209)

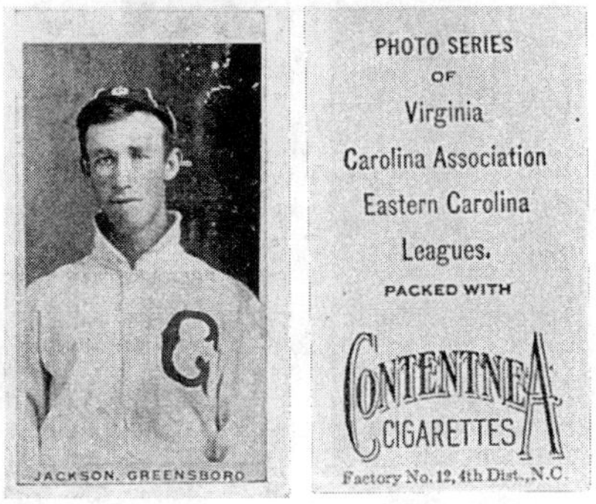

		NM	EX	VG
Complete Set (222):		12500.	5000.	3000.
Common Player:		75.00	30.00	20.00
(1)	Abercrombie	75.00	30.00	20.00
(2)	Andrada	75.00	30.00	20.00
(3)	Armstrong	75.00	30.00	20.00
(4)	Averett	75.00	30.00	20.00
(5)	Baker	75.00	30.00	20.00
(6)	Banner (Bonner)	75.00	30.00	20.00
(7)	Bausewein (Bansewein)	75.00	30.00	20.00
(8)	Beatty	75.00	30.00	20.00
(9)	Bentley	75.00	30.00	20.00
(10)	Beusse	75.00	30.00	20.00
(11)	Biel	75.00	30.00	20.00
(12)	Bigbie (Raleigh)	75.00	30.00	20.00
(13)	Bigbie (Richmond)	75.00	30.00	20.00
(14)	Blackstone	75.00	30.00	20.00
(15)	Bonner	75.00	30.00	20.00
(16)	Bourquin	75.00	30.00	20.00
(17)	Bowen	75.00	30.00	20.00
(18)	Boyle	75.00	30.00	20.00
(19)	Brandon	75.00	30.00	20.00
(20)	Brazelle (Brazell)	75.00	30.00	20.00
(21)	Brent	75.00	30.00	20.00
(22)	Brown	75.00	30.00	20.00
(23)	Busch	75.00	30.00	20.00
(24)	Bussey	75.00	30.00	20.00
(25)	Byrd	75.00	30.00	20.00
(26)	Cafalu (Cefalu)	75.00	30.00	20.00
(27)	Callahan	75.00	30.00	20.00
(28)	Chandler	75.00	30.00	20.00
(29)	Clapp	75.00	30.00	20.00
(30)	Clark (Clarke)	75.00	30.00	20.00
(31)	Clemens	75.00	30.00	20.00
(32)	Clunk	75.00	30.00	20.00
(33)	Cooper	75.00	30.00	20.00
(34)	Corbett	75.00	30.00	20.00
(35)	Cote	75.00	30.00	20.00
(36)	Coutts	75.00	30.00	20.00
(37)	Cowan (Cowen)	75.00	30.00	20.00
(38)	Cowells (Cowell)	75.00	30.00	20.00
(39)	Creagan (Cregan)	75.00	30.00	20.00
(40)	Crockett	75.00	30.00	20.00
(41)	Cross	75.00	30.00	20.00
(42)	Dailey	75.00	30.00	20.00
(43)	C. Derrck (Derrick)	75.00	30.00	20.00
(44)	F. Derrick	75.00	30.00	20.00
(45)	Doak (Greensboro)	75.00	30.00	20.00
(46)	Doak (Wilmington)	75.00	30.00	20.00
(47)	Dobard	75.00	30.00	20.00
(48)	Dobson	75.00	30.00	20.00
(49)	Doyle	75.00	30.00	20.00
(50)	Drumm	75.00	30.00	20.00
(51)	Duvie	75.00	30.00	20.00
(52)	Ebinger	75.00	30.00	20.00
(53)	Eldridge	75.00	30.00	20.00
(54)	Evans	75.00	30.00	20.00
(55)	Fairbanks	75.00	30.00	20.00
(56)	Farmer	75.00	30.00	20.00
(57)	Ferrell	75.00	30.00	20.00
(58)	Fisher	75.00	30.00	20.00
(59)	Flowers	75.00	30.00	20.00
(60)	Fogarty	75.00	30.00	20.00
(61)	Foltz	75.00	30.00	20.00
(62)	Foreman	75.00	30.00	20.00
(63)	Forque	75.00	30.00	20.00
(64)	Francis	75.00	30.00	20.00
(65)	Fulton	75.00	30.00	20.00
(66)	Galvin	75.00	30.00	20.00
(67)	Gardin	75.00	30.00	20.00
(68)	Garman	75.00	30.00	20.00
(69)	Gastmeyer	75.00	30.00	20.00
(70)	Gaston	75.00	30.00	20.00
(71)	Gates	75.00	30.00	20.00
(72)	Gehring	75.00	30.00	20.00
(73)	Gillespie	75.00	30.00	20.00
(74)	Gorham	75.00	30.00	20.00
(75)	Griffin (Danville)	75.00	30.00	20.00
(76)	Griffin (Lynchburg)	75.00	30.00	20.00
(77)	Guiheen	75.00	30.00	20.00
(78)	Gunderson	75.00	30.00	20.00
(79)	Hale	75.00	30.00	20.00
(80)	Halland (Holland)	75.00	30.00	20.00
(81)	Hamilton	75.00	30.00	20.00
(82)	Hammersley	75.00	30.00	20.00
(83)	Handiboe	75.00	30.00	20.00
(84)	Hannifen (Hannifan)	75.00	30.00	20.00
(85)	Hargrave	75.00	30.00	20.00
(86)	Harrington	75.00	30.00	20.00
(87)	Harris	75.00	30.00	20.00
(88)	Hart	75.00	30.00	20.00
(89)	Hartley	75.00	30.00	20.00
(90)	Hawkins	75.00	30.00	20.00
(91)	Hearne (Hearn)	75.00	30.00	20.00
(92)	Hicks	75.00	30.00	20.00
(93)	Hobbs	75.00	30.00	20.00
(94)	Hoffman	75.00	30.00	20.00
(95)	Hooker	75.00	30.00	20.00
(96)	Howard	75.00	30.00	20.00
(97)	Howedel (Howedell)	75.00	30.00	20.00
(98)	Hudson	75.00	30.00	20.00
(99)	Humphrey	75.00	30.00	20.00
(100)	Hyames	75.00	30.00	20.00
(101)	Irvine	75.00	30.00	20.00
(102)	Irving	75.00	30.00	20.00
(103)	Jackson (Greensboro)	75.00	30.00	20.00
(104)	Jackson (Spartanburg)	75.00	30.00	20.00
(105)	Jenkins (Greenville)	75.00	30.00	20.00
(106)	Jenkins (Roanoke)	75.00	30.00	20.00
(107)	Jobson	75.00	30.00	20.00
(108)	Johnson	75.00	30.00	20.00
(109)	Keating	75.00	30.00	20.00
(110)	Kelley	75.00	30.00	20.00
(111)	Kelly (Anderson)	75.00	30.00	20.00
(112)	Kelly (Goldsboro)	75.00	30.00	20.00
(113)	"King" Kelly	75.00	30.00	20.00
(114)	King	75.00	30.00	20.00
(115)	Kite	75.00	30.00	20.00
(116)	Kunkle	75.00	30.00	20.00
(117)	Landgraff	75.00	30.00	20.00
(118)	Lane	75.00	30.00	20.00
(119)	Lathrop	75.00	30.00	20.00
(120)	Lavoia	75.00	30.00	20.00
(121)	Levy	75.00	30.00	20.00
(122)	Lloyd	75.00	30.00	20.00
(123)	Loval	75.00	30.00	20.00
(124)	Lucia	75.00	30.00	20.00
(125)	Luyster	75.00	30.00	20.00
(126)	MacConachie	75.00	30.00	20.00
(127)	Malcolm	75.00	30.00	20.00
(128)	Martin	75.00	30.00	20.00
(129)	Mayberry	75.00	30.00	20.00
(130)	A. McCarthy	75.00	30.00	20.00
(131)	J. McCarthy	75.00	30.00	20.00
(132)	McCormick	75.00	30.00	20.00
(133)	McFarland	75.00	30.00	20.00
(134)	McFarlin	75.00	30.00	20.00
(135)	C. McGeehan	75.00	30.00	20.00
(136)	Dan McGeehan	75.00	30.00	20.00
(137)	McHugh	75.00	30.00	20.00
(138)	McKeavitt (McKevitt)	75.00	30.00	20.00
(139)	Merchant	75.00	30.00	20.00
(140)	Midkiff	75.00	30.00	20.00
(141)	Miller	75.00	30.00	20.00
(142)	Missitt	75.00	30.00	20.00
(143)	Morgan	75.00	30.00	20.00
(144)	Morrissey (Morrisey)	75.00	30.00	20.00
(145)	Mullany (Mullaney)	75.00	30.00	20.00
(146)	Mullinix	75.00	30.00	20.00
(147)	Mundell	75.00	30.00	20.00
(148)	Munsen (Munson)	75.00	30.00	20.00
(149)	Murdock (Murdoch)	75.00	30.00	20.00
(150)	Newton	75.00	30.00	20.00
(151)	Noojin	75.00	30.00	20.00
(152)	Novak	75.00	30.00	20.00
(153)	Ochs	75.00	30.00	20.00
(154)	Painter	75.00	30.00	20.00
(155)	Peloquin	75.00	30.00	20.00
(156)	Phealean (Phelan)	75.00	30.00	20.00
(157)	Phoenix	75.00	30.00	20.00
(158)	Powell	75.00	30.00	20.00
(159)	Presley (Pressley), Pritchard	75.00	30.00	20.00
(160)	Priest	75.00	30.00	20.00
(161)	Prim	75.00	30.00	20.00
(162)	Pritchard	75.00	30.00	20.00
(163)	Rawe (Rowe)	75.00	30.00	20.00
(164)	Redfern (Redfearn)	75.00	30.00	20.00
(165)	Reggy	75.00	30.00	20.00
(166)	Richardson	75.00	30.00	20.00
(167)	Rickard	75.00	30.00	20.00
(168)	Rickert	75.00	30.00	20.00
(169)	Ridgeway (Ridgway)	75.00	30.00	20.00
(170)	Roth	75.00	30.00	20.00
(171)	Salve	75.00	30.00	20.00
(172)	Schmidt	75.00	30.00	20.00
(173)	Schrader	75.00	30.00	20.00
(174)	Schumaker	75.00	30.00	20.00
(175)	Sexton	75.00	30.00	20.00
(176)	Shanghnessy (Shaughnessy)	75.00	30.00	20.00
(177)	Sharp	75.00	30.00	20.00
(178)	Shaw	75.00	30.00	20.00
(179)	Simmons	75.00	30.00	20.00
(180)	A. Smith	75.00	30.00	20.00
(181)	D. Smith	75.00	30.00	20.00
(182)	Smith (Portsmouth)	75.00	30.00	20.00
(183)	Spratt	75.00	30.00	20.00
(184)	Springs	75.00	30.00	20.00
(185)	Stewart	75.00	30.00	20.00
(186)	Stoehr	75.00	30.00	20.00
(187)	Stouch	75.00	30.00	20.00
(188)	Sullivan	75.00	30.00	20.00
(189)	Swindell	75.00	30.00	20.00
(190)	Taxis	75.00	30.00	20.00
(191)	Templin	75.00	30.00	20.00
(192)	Thompson	75.00	30.00	20.00
(193)	B.E. Thompson	75.00	30.00	20.00
(194)	Tiedeman	75.00	30.00	20.00
(195)	Titman	75.00	30.00	20.00
(196)	Toner	75.00	30.00	20.00
(197)	Turner	75.00	30.00	20.00
(198)	Tydeman	75.00	30.00	20.00
(199)	Vail	75.00	30.00	20.00
(200)	Verbout	75.00	30.00	20.00
(201)	Vickery	75.00	30.00	20.00
(202)	Walker (Norfolk)	75.00	30.00	20.00
(203)	Walker (Spartanburg)	75.00	30.00	20.00
(204)	Wallace	75.00	30.00	20.00
(205)	Walsh	75.00	30.00	20.00
(206)	Walters	75.00	30.00	20.00
(207)	Waters	75.00	30.00	20.00
(208)	Waymack	75.00	30.00	20.00
(209)	Webb	75.00	30.00	20.00
(210)	Wehrell	75.00	30.00	20.00
(211)	Weldon	75.00	30.00	20.00
(212)	Welsher	75.00	30.00	20.00
(213)	Westlake	75.00	30.00	20.00
(214)	Williams	75.00	30.00	20.00
(215)	Willis	75.00	30.00	20.00
(216)	Wingo	75.00	30.00	20.00
(217)	Wolf	75.00	30.00	20.00
(218)	Wood	75.00	30.00	20.00
(219)	Woolums	75.00	30.00	20.00
(220)	Workman	75.00	30.00	20.00
(221)	Wright	75.00	30.00	20.00
(222)	Wynne	75.00	30.00	20.00

1940 Crowley's Milk

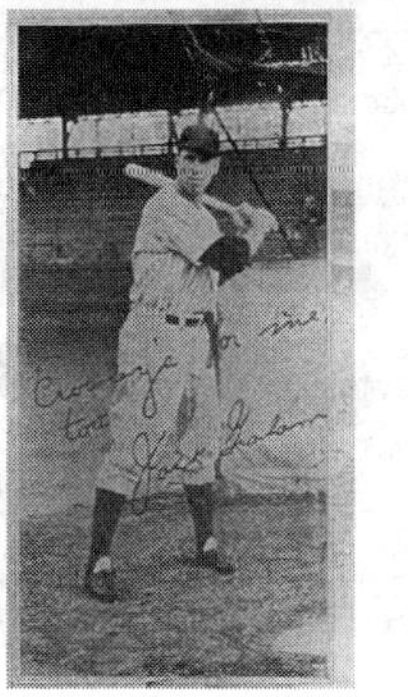

Members of the Binghampton, N.Y., Eastern League team are known in this set of 3" x 5" cards. Some have been seen with stamped postcard backs. Blue-and-white player photos are framed by a red rendition of a ballpark scene on the front of the unnumbered cards. Each card has a facsimile autograph ostensibly written by the pictured player. It is unknown whether the checklist below is complete. Several of the players later appeared with the N.Y. Yankees and other teams.

		NM	EX	VG
Complete Set (16):		1000.	500.00	300.00
Common Player:		150.00	75.00	45.00
(1)	Jimmy Adlam	150.00	75.00	45.00
(2)	Russ Bergman	150.00	75.00	45.00
(3)	Bill Bevens	180.00	90.00	54.00
(4)	Johnny Bianco	150.00	75.00	45.00
(5)	Fred Collins	150.00	75.00	45.00
(6)	Billie O'Donnell (trainer)	120.00	60.00	36.00
(7)	Jack Graham	150.00	75.00	45.00
(8)	Randy Gumpert	150.00	75.00	45.00
(9)	Al Gurske	150.00	75.00	45.00
(10)	Mike Milosevich	150.00	75.00	45.00
(11)	Earl Reid	150.00	75.00	45.00
(12)	Aaron Robinson	150.00	75.00	45.00
(13)	Frankie Silvanic	150.00	75.00	45.00
(14)	Pete Suder	150.00	75.00	45.00
(15)	Ray Volps	150.00	75.00	45.00
(16)	Herb White	150.00	75.00	45.00

Vintage cards in Good condition are valued at about 50% of the Very Good values shown here. Cards in Fair condition are valued at 25% or less of VG.

D

1959 Darigold Farms Spokane Indians

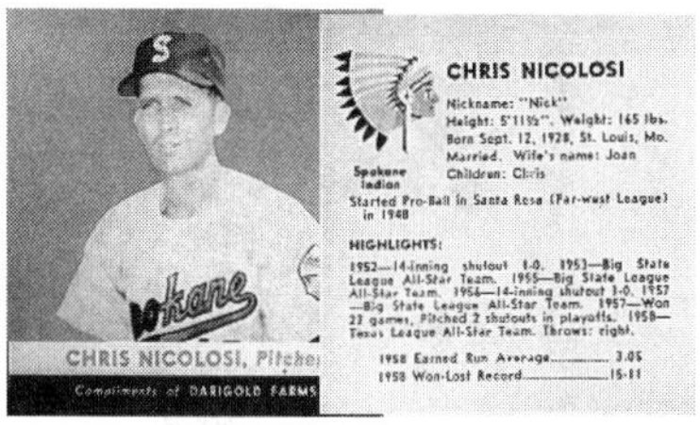

The 22 unnumbered cards in this set were glued to milk cartons by a folded tab at the top of each card. The basic card measures 2-1/2" x 2-3/8", with a 2-1/2" x 2-1/8" tab. Black-and-white player photos are set against colored backgrounds of yellow (1-8), red (9-16) and blue (17-22). Player biographical details and stats are printed in black on the back.

		NM	EX	VG
Complete Set (22):		700.00	350.00	210.00
Common Player:		30.00	15.00	9.00
(1)	Facundo Barragan	30.00	15.00	9.00
(2)	Steve Bilko	35.00	17.50	10.50
(3)	Bobby Bragan	40.00	20.00	12.00
(4)	Chuck Churn	30.00	15.00	9.00
(5)	Tom Davis	60.00	30.00	18.00
(6)	Dom Domenichelli	30.00	15.00	9.00
(7)	Bob Giallombardo	30.00	15.00	9.00
(8)	Connie Grob	30.00	15.00	9.00
(9)	Fred Hatfield	30.00	15.00	9.00
(10)	Bob Lillis	35.00	17.50	10.50
(11)	Lloyd Merritt	30.00	15.00	9.00
(12)	Larry Miller	30.00	15.00	9.00
(13)	Chris Nicolosi	30.00	15.00	9.00
(14)	Allen Norris	30.00	15.00	9.00
(15)	Phil Ortega	30.00	15.00	9.00
(16)	Phillips Paine	30.00	15.00	9.00
(17)	Bill Parsons	30.00	15.00	9.00
(18)	Hisel Patrick	30.00	15.00	9.00
(19)	Tony Roig	30.00	15.00	9.00
(20)	Tom Saffell	30.00	15.00	9.00
(21)	Norm Sherry	35.00	17.50	10.50
(22)	Ben Wade	30.00	15.00	9.00

1960 Darigold Farms Spokane Indians

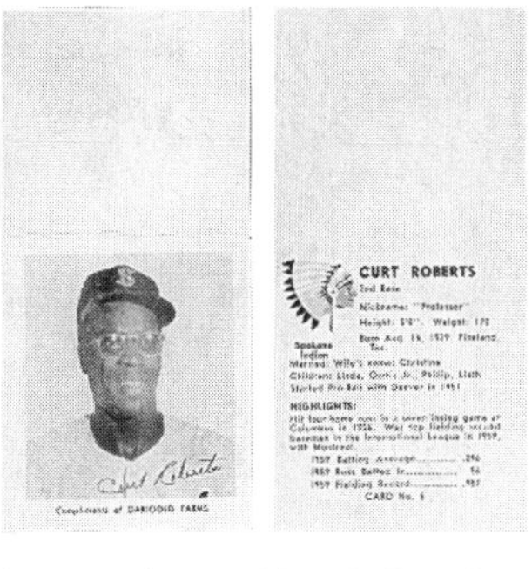

For its second annual baseball card set, the dairy added two cards, for a total of 24, and numbered the issue on the back. Card fronts were black-and-white photos against colored backgrounds of yellow (1-8), green (9-16) and red (17-24). A facsimile autograph appears on the front, as well. The basic card measures 2-3/8" x 2-11/16", with a folded 2-3/8" x 2-1/16" tab at the top, by which the card was glued to a milk carton. Backs are black-and-white.

		NM	EX	VG
Complete Set (24):		800.00	400.00	240.00
Common Player:		27.00	13.50	8.00
1	Chris Nicolosi	27.00	13.50	8.00
2	Jim Pagliaroni	27.00	13.50	8.00
3	Roy Smalley	27.00	13.50	8.00
4	Bill Bethel	27.00	13.50	8.00
5	Joe Liscio	27.00	13.50	8.00
6	Curt Roberts	27.00	13.50	8.00
7	Ed Palmquist	27.00	13.50	8.00
8	Willie Davis	75.00	37.00	22.00
9	Bob Giallombardo	27.00	13.50	8.00
10	Pedro Gomez	27.00	13.50	8.00
11	Mel Nelson	27.00	13.50	8.00
12	Charley Smith	27.00	13.50	8.00
13	Clarence Churn	27.00	13.50	8.00
14	Ramon Conde	27.00	13.50	8.00
15	George O'Donnell	27.00	13.50	8.00
16	Tony Roig	27.00	13.50	8.00
17	Frank Howard	80.00	40.00	24.00
18	Billy Harris	27.00	13.50	8.00
19	Mike Brumley	27.00	13.50	8.00
20	Earl Robinson	27.00	13.50	8.00
21	Ron Fairly	45.00	22.00	13.50
22	Joe Frazier	27.00	13.50	8.00
23	Allen Norris	27.00	13.50	8.00
24	Ford Young	27.00	13.50	8.00

The election of former players to the Hall of Fame does not always have an immediate upward effect on card values. The hobby market generally has done a good job of predicting those inductions and adjusting values over the course of several years.

E

1928 Pacific Coast League Exhibits

This regional series of 32 cards pictures players from the six California teams in the Pacific Coast League. Like the 1928 major league Exhibits, the PCL cards have a blue tint and are not numbered. They are blank-backed and measure 3-3/8" x 5-3/8". The set includes several misspellings. Cards are occasionally found with a corner clipped, the card corner to be used as a coupon with redemption value.

		NM	EX	VG
Complete Set (32):		3000.	1500.	900.00
Common Player:		80.00	40.00	24.00
1	Buzz Arlett	140.00	70.00	42.00
2	Earl Averill	300.00	150.00	90.00
3	Carl Berger (Walter)	140.00	70.00	42.00
4	"Ping" Bodie	120.00	60.00	36.00
5	Carl Dittmar	80.00	40.00	24.00
6	Jack Fenton	80.00	40.00	24.00
7	Neal "Mickey" Finn (Cornelius)	80.00	40.00	24.00
8	Ray French	80.00	40.00	24.00
9	Tony Governor	80.00	40.00	24.00
10	"Truck" Hannah	80.00	40.00	24.00
11	Mickey Heath	80.00	40.00	24.00
12	Wally Hood	80.00	40.00	24.00
13	"Fuzzy" Hufft	80.00	40.00	24.00
14	Snead Jolly (Smead Jolley)	80.00	40.00	24.00
15	Bobby "Ducky" Jones	80.00	40.00	24.00
16	Rudy Kallio	80.00	40.00	24.00
17	Ray Keating	80.00	40.00	24.00
18	Johnny Kerr	80.00	40.00	24.00
19	Harry Krause	80.00	40.00	24.00
20	Lynford H. Larry (Lary)	80.00	40.00	24.00
21	Dudley Lee	80.00	40.00	24.00
22	Walter "Duster" Mails	80.00	40.00	24.00
23	Jimmy Reese	100.00	50.00	30.00
24	"Dusty" Rhodes	80.00	40.00	24.00
25	Hal Rhyne	80.00	40.00	24.00
26	Hank Severied (Severeid)	80.00	40.00	24.00
27	Earl Sheely	80.00	40.00	24.00
28	Frank Shellenback	80.00	40.00	24.00
29	Gordon Slade	80.00	40.00	24.00
30	Hollis Thurston	80.00	40.00	24.00
31	"Babe" Twombly	80.00	40.00	24.00
32	Earl "Tex" Weathersby	80.00	40.00	24.00

1953 Montreal Royals Exhibits

Twenty-four Montreal Royals, including many future Brooklyn and L.A. Dodgers and Hall of Fame managers Walt Alston Tommy Lasorda, were included in a 64-card Canadian issue by Exhibit Supply Co., of Chicago. The cards are slightly smaller, at 3-1/4" x 5-1/4", than standard Exhibits and printed - blank-backed - on gray stock. Numbered on front, cards of the Montreal players can be found in either blue or reddish-brown tint. Only the Royals players from the issue are checklisted here.

		NM	EX	VG
Complete Set (24):		240.00	120.00	72.50
Common Player:		9.00	4.50	2.75
33	Don Hoak	11.00	5.50	3.25
34	Bob Alexander	9.00	4.50	2.75
35	John Simmons	9.00	4.50	2.75
36	Steve Lembo	9.00	4.50	2.75
37	Norm Larker	11.00	5.50	3.25
38	Bob Ludwick	9.00	4.50	2.75
39	Walt Moryn	11.00	5.50	3.25
40	Charlie Thompson	9.00	4.50	2.75
41	Ed Roebuck	11.00	5.50	3.25
42	Russell Rose	9.00	4.50	2.75
43	Edmundo (Sandy) Amoros	12.50	6.25	3.75
44	Bob Milliken	9.00	4.50	2.75
45	Art Fabbro	9.00	4.50	2.75
46	Spook Jacobs	9.00	4.50	2.75
47	Carmen Mauro	9.00	4.50	2.75
48	Walter Fiala	9.00	4.50	2.75
49	Rocky Nelson	9.00	4.50	2.75
50	Tom La Sorda (Lasorda)	50.00	25.00	15.00
51	Ronnie Lee	9.00	4.50	2.75
52	Hampton Coleman	9.00	4.50	2.75
53	Frank Marchio	9.00	4.50	2.75
54	William Sampson	9.00	4.50	2.75
55	Gil Mills	9.00	4.50	2.75
56	Al Ronning	9.00	4.50	2.75
61	Walt Alston	25.00	12.50	7.50

F

1953 Fargo-Moorhead Twins team issue

This set of team-issued cards includes the first of future home-run king Roger Maris (spelled Maras in the traditional family manner). The cards are about 3-1/4" x 5-5/16" with a white border surrounding a black-and-white posed photo. Player identification is in three lines of white type at lower-left. Backs are blank, except some cards which bear a rubber-stamped promotional message from the "Red River Scenes" newspaper. The unnumbered cards are checklisted here in alphabetical order. Three of the players are known in two or more poses.

		NM	EX	VG
Complete Set (21):		2000.	1000.	600.00
Common Player:		35.00	17.50	10.00
(1)	Zeke Bonura	50.00	25.00	15.00
(2)	Bob Borovicka	35.00	17.50	10.00
(3)	Ken Braeseke	35.00	17.50	10.00
(4)	Joe Camacho	35.00	17.50	10.00
(5)	Galen Fiss	35.00	17.50	10.00
(6)	Frank Gravino (batting follow-through)	35.00	17.50	10.00
(7)	Frank Gravino (hands on hips)	35.00	17.50	10.00
(8)	Frank Gravino (hands on knees)	35.00	17.50	10.00
(9)	Santo Luberto (fielding)	35.00	17.50	10.00
(10)	Roger Maras (fielding)	800.00	400.00	240.00
(11)	Roger Maras (batting)	800.00	400.00	240.00
(12)	Jerry Mehlish (Mehlisch)	35.00	17.50	10.00
(13)	Bob Melton	35.00	17.50	10.00
(14)	Ray Mendoza (stretching at 1B, ball in glove)	35.00	17.50	10.00
(15)	Ray Mendoza (stretching at 1B, no ball)	35.00	17.50	10.00
(16)	John Morse	35.00	17.50	10.00
(17)	Don Nance	35.00	17.50	10.00
(18)	Ray Seif	35.00	17.50	10.00
(19)	Will Sirois	35.00	17.50	10.00
(20)	Dick Wegner	35.00	17.50	10.00
(21)	Don Wolf	35.00	17.50	10.00

1966 Foremost Milk St. Petersburg Cardinals

Cardinals
Foremost
MILK
GEORGE "Sparky" ANDERSON
ST. PETERSBURG CARDINALS 1966

This 20-card black-and-white set includes players and the manager, Sparky Anderson, of the Florida State League farm club of the St. Louis Cardinals. The unnumbered, blank-backed cards measure 3-1/2" x 5-1/2".

		NM	EX	VG
Complete Set (20):		120.00	60.00	35.00
Common Player:		5.00	2.50	1.50
(1)	George "Sparky" Anderson	35.00	17.50	10.50
(2)	Dave Bakenhaster	5.00	2.50	1.50
(3)	Leonard Boyer	8.00	4.00	2.50
(4)	Ron Braddock	5.00	2.50	1.50
(5)	Thomas "Chip" Coulter	5.00	2.50	1.50
(6)	Ernest "Sweet Pea" Davis	5.00	2.50	1.50
(7)	Phil Knuckles	5.00	2.50	1.50
(8)	Doug Lukens	5.00	2.50	1.50
(9)	Terry Milani	5.00	2.50	1.50
(10)	Tim Morgan	5.00	2.50	1.50
(11)	Harry Parker	5.00	2.50	1.50
(12)	Jerry Robertson	5.00	2.50	1.50
(13)	Francisco Rodriguez	5.00	2.50	1.50
(14)	John "Sonny" Ruberto	5.00	2.50	1.50
(15)	Charlie Stewart	5.00	2.50	1.50
(16)	Gary L. Stone	5.00	2.50	1.50
(17)	Charles "Tim" Thompson	5.00	2.50	1.50
(18)	Jose Villar	5.00	2.50	1.50
(19)	Archie L. Wade	5.00	2.50	1.50
(20)	Jim Williamson	5.00	2.50	1.50

1952 Frostade

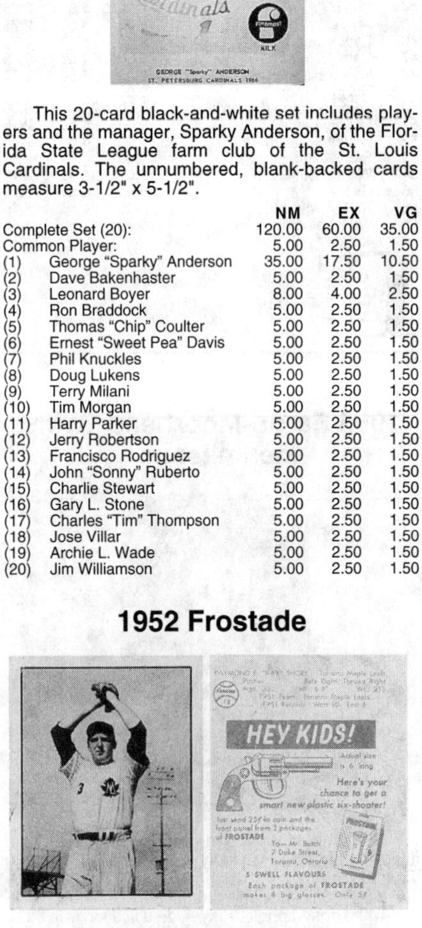
HEY KIDS!
Here's your chance to get a smart new plastic six-shooter!
5 SWELL FLAVOURS
FROSTADE

(See 1952 Parkhurst)

Suffix letters following a card number indicate a variation card.

1954 Fruiterie Saint Louis Tommy Lasorda

Royals

The date of issue attributed is only a best guess. It is also unknown how many other Montreal Royals players may be found in this issue. Printed in black-and-white on fairly thick 5-1/2" x 7" cardboard, this card features a portrait photo of the Royals' pitcher and future Hall of Fame manager along with a facsimile autograph on the borderless front. Rubber-stamped at top of the otherwise blank back is: "Fruiterie / Saint Louis De Franos / 515 RUE ROY PL. 1729", presumably identification of a Montreal business which distributed the card.

	NM	EX	VG
Tommy Lasorda	200.00	100.00	60.00

G

1956-57 Gil's Drive-Ins Seattle Rainiers

By presenting any nine of these pictures to either of GIL'S DRIVE-INS you will receive FREE an 8"x 10" player picture of your choice and you still keep your nine small pictures.
Two locations to serve you
GIL'S DRIVE-IN
4406 Rainier Avenue
1 mile south of Sicks' Stadium
—and—
3500 Avalon Way
35th S. W. and Avalon Way
West Seattle

(See 1956-57 Seattle Popcorn for checklist and values.)

1951 Globe Printing Fresno Cardinals

These 2-1/4" x 3-1/2" black-and-white, unnumbered, blank-backed cards were one of many minor league team sets issued by Globe Printing of San Jose, Calif., in the early 1950s. Cards were usually given away at the ballpark on a one-per-week or one-per-homestand basis, accounting for the rarity of surviving sets. The team was a California League (Class C) affiliate of the St. Louis Cardinals.

		NM	EX	VG
Complete Set (17):		500.00	250.00	150.00
Common Player:		30.00	15.00	9.00
(1)	Hal Atkinson	30.00	15.00	9.00
(2)	Larry Barton	30.00	15.00	9.00
(3)	Charlie Brooks	30.00	15.00	9.00
(4)	Bill Burton	30.00	15.00	9.00
(5)	Ray Herrera	30.00	15.00	9.00
(6)	Earl Jones	30.00	15.00	9.00
(7)	Jim King	30.00	15.00	9.00
(8)	Whitey Lageman	30.00	15.00	9.00
(9)	Wally Lamers	30.00	15.00	9.00
(10)	John McNamara	50.00	25.00	15.00
(11)	Gerry Mertz	30.00	15.00	9.00
(12)	Frank Olasin	30.00	15.00	9.00
(13)	Howie Phillips	30.00	15.00	9.00
(14)	Jack Ramsey	30.00	15.00	9.00
(15)	Tony Stathos	30.00	15.00	9.00
(16)	Whit Ulrich	30.00	15.00	9.00
(17)	Pete Younie	30.00	15.00	9.00

1951 Globe Printing San Jose Red Sox

RED SOX
MARVIN OWEN

These 2-1/4" x 3-1/2" black-and-white, unnumbered, blank-backed cards were one of many minor league team sets issued by Globe Printing of San Jose, Calif., in the early 1950s. Cards were usually given away at the ballpark on a one-per-week or one-per-homestand basis, accounting for the rarity of surviving sets. The team was a Class C farm club for the Boston Red Sox in the California League.

		NM	EX	VG
Complete Set (18):		500.00	250.00	150.00
Common Player:		30.00	15.00	9.00
(1)	Ken Aspromonte	50.00	25.00	15.00
(2)	Joe Buck	30.00	15.00	9.00
(3)	Harold Buckwalter	30.00	15.00	9.00
(4)	Al Curtis	30.00	15.00	9.00
(5)	Marvin Eyre	30.00	15.00	9.00
(6)	Jack Heinen	30.00	15.00	9.00
(7)	John Kinney	30.00	15.00	9.00
(8)	Walt Lucas	30.00	15.00	9.00
(9)	Syl McNinch	30.00	15.00	9.00
(10)	Stan McWilliams	30.00	15.00	9.00
(11)	Marvin Owen	30.00	15.00	9.00
(12)	Dick Piedrotti	30.00	15.00	9.00
(13)	Al Schroll	30.00	15.00	9.00
(14)	Ed Sobczak	30.00	15.00	9.00
(15)	Joe Stephenson	30.00	15.00	9.00
(16)	George Storti	30.00	15.00	9.00
(17)	Allan Van Alstyne	30.00	15.00	9.00
(18)	Floyd Warr	30.00	15.00	9.00

1952 Globe Printing Baltimore Orioles

ROY WEATHERLY

While most of the company's issues were for minor league teams in the lower classifications, Globe also did a set for the International League Baltimore Orioles. Similar to the company's other issues, the black-and-white cards measure about 2-1/4" x 3-3/8". The checklist here is obviously incomplete.

		NM	EX	VG
Common Player:		40.00	20.00	12.00
(1)	Al Cihocki	40.00	20.00	12.00
(2)	Blix Donnelly	40.00	20.00	12.00
(3)	Bob Greenwood	40.00	20.00	12.00
(4)	Don Heffner	40.00	20.00	12.00
(5)	Russ Kerns	40.00	20.00	12.00
(6)	Howie Moss	40.00	20.00	12.00
(7)	Dee Phillips	40.00	20.00	12.00
(8)	Jerry Scala	40.00	20.00	12.00
(9)	Danny Schell	40.00	20.00	12.00
(10)	Paul Stuffel	40.00	20.00	12.00
(11)	Roy Weatherly	40.00	20.00	12.00

1952 Globe Printing Colorado Springs Sky Sox

From the Class A Western League runners-up, this is one of many minor league sets issued in the early 1950s by the Globe Printing Co., of San Jose, Calif. The '52 Sky Sox were a farm team of the Chicago White Sox. Players included former Negro Leaguers and future major leaguers Connie Johnson and Sam Hairston, plus bonus-baby bust Gus Keriazakos. Cards are about 2-1/4" x 3-1/4", printed in black-and-white with blank backs. An album with die-cut pages to allow the corners of the cards to be slipped in was also available. Cards were likely given away one or two at a time at home games.

		NM	EX	VG
Complete Set (19):		600.00	300.00	180.00
Common Player:		30.00	15.00	9.00
Album:		50.00	25.00	15.00
(1)	Jerry Crosby	30.00	15.00	9.00
(2)	Vic Fucci	30.00	15.00	9.00
(3)	Don Gutteridge	30.00	15.00	9.00
(4)	Sam Hairston	45.00	22.00	13.50
(5)	Al Jacinto	30.00	15.00	9.00
(6)	Connie Johnson	35.00	17.50	10.50
(7)	Bob Kellogg	30.00	15.00	9.00
(8)	Gus Keriazakos	30.00	15.00	9.00
(9)	Ken Landenberger	30.00	15.00	9.00
(10)	George Noga	30.00	15.00	9.00
(11)	Floyd Penfold	30.00	15.00	9.00
(12)	Bill Pope	30.00	15.00	9.00
(13)	J.W. Porter	30.00	15.00	9.00
(14)	Bill (Red) Rose	30.00	15.00	9.00
(15)	Don Rudolph	30.00	15.00	9.00
(16)	Andy Skurski	30.00	15.00	9.00
(17)	Dick Strahs	30.00	15.00	9.00
(18)	Bill Wells	30.00	15.00	9.00
(19)	Dick Welteroth	30.00	15.00	9.00

1952 Globe Printing Columbus Cardinals

This set of 17 cards was given away at Golden Park during the 1952 season. The cards measure 2-1/8" x 3-3/8" and have black-and-white photos of players with the player's name in a white box in the left bottom corner of the photograph. The backs are blank. The cards are unnumbered and listed in alphabetical order.

		NM	EX	VG
Complete Set (17):		500.00	250.00	150.00
Common Player:		30.00	15.00	9.00
(1)	Chief Bender	30.00	15.00	9.00
(2)	Bob Betancourt	30.00	15.00	9.00
(3)	Tom Burgess	30.00	15.00	9.00
(4)	Jack Byers	30.00	15.00	9.00
(5)	Mike Curnan	30.00	15.00	9.00
(6)	Gil Daley	30.00	15.00	9.00
(7)	Bill Harris	30.00	15.00	9.00
(8)	Ev Joyner	30.00	15.00	9.00
(9)	Bob Kerce	30.00	15.00	9.00
(10)	Ted Lewandowski	30.00	15.00	9.00
(11)	John Mackey	30.00	15.00	9.00
(12)	Bill Paolisso	30.00	15.00	9.00
(13)	Dennis Reeder	30.00	15.00	9.00
(14)	Whit Ulrich	30.00	15.00	9.00
(15)	Norman Shope	30.00	15.00	9.00
(16)	Don Swartz	30.00	15.00	9.00
(17)	Len Wile	30.00	15.00	9.00

1952 Globe Printing Dallas Eagles

A Class AA farm team of the Cleveland Indians, the Eagles were one of the higher minor league teams chronicled by Globe Printing in its series of 2-1/4" x 3-3/8" blank-back, black-and-white cards sets of the early 1950s. The checklist here is not complete.

		NM	EX	VG
Common Player:		30.00	15.00	9.00
(1)	Dick Aylward	30.00	15.00	9.00
(2)	Bob Bundy	30.00	15.00	9.00
(3)	Dave Hoskins	30.00	15.00	9.00
(4)	Edward Knoblauch (Chuck Knoblauch's uncle)	30.00	15.00	9.00
(5)	Joe Kotrany	30.00	15.00	9.00
(6)	Peter Mazar	30.00	15.00	9.00
(7)	Edward Varhely	30.00	15.00	9.00

1952 Globe Printing Great Falls Electrics

Formatted like the other known minor league issues from Globe, this set chronicles the 1952 version of the Class C (Pioneer League) Great Falls (Montana) Electrics, a farm club of the Brooklyn Dodgers. The blank-backed cards are black-and-white and measure about 2-1/4" x 3-3/8". An album was issued with the cards.

		NM	EX	VG
Complete Set (16):		400.00	200.00	120.00
Common Player:		30.00	15.00	9.00
(1)	Don Bricker	30.00	15.00	9.00
(2)	Larry Hampshire	30.00	15.00	9.00
(3)	Ernie Jordan	30.00	15.00	9.00
(4)	Lou Landini	30.00	15.00	9.00
(5)	Danny Lastres	30.00	15.00	9.00
(6)	Joe Oliffe	30.00	15.00	9.00
(7)	Len Payne	30.00	15.00	9.00
(8)	Lou Rochelli	30.00	15.00	9.00
(9)	Earl Silverthorn	30.00	15.00	9.00
(10)	Eddie Serrano	30.00	15.00	9.00
(11)	Rick Small	30.00	15.00	9.00
(12)	Dick Smith	30.00	15.00	9.00
(13)	Hal Snyder	30.00	15.00	9.00
(14)	Armando Suarez	30.00	15.00	9.00
(15)	Emy Unzicker	30.00	15.00	9.00

1952 Globe Printing Jamestown Falcons

This Class D farm club of the Detroit Tigers won the 1952 Pony (Pennsylvania-Ontario-New York) League playoffs. Like other issues of Globe Printing, the roughly 2-1/4" x 3-3/8" 2cards are black-and-white with blank backs and the player name in a white strip at bottom-front. A light green album slotted to hold the cards is known for this issue.

		NM	EX	VG
Complete Set (16):		400.00	200.00	120.00
Common Player:		30.00	15.00	9.00
Album:		50.00	25.00	15.00
(1)	Jerry Davie	30.00	15.00	9.00
(2)	John Fickinger	30.00	15.00	9.00
(3)	Paul Franks	30.00	15.00	9.00
(4)	Red Gookin	30.00	15.00	9.00
(5)	Bill Harbour	30.00	15.00	9.00
(6)	Dick Hatfield	30.00	15.00	9.00
(7)	Charley Lau	45.00	22.00	13.50
(8)	Dick Lisiecki	30.00	15.00	9.00
(9)	Joe Melago	30.00	15.00	9.00
(10)	Claude Mitschele	30.00	15.00	9.00
(11)	Bob Neebling	30.00	15.00	9.00
(12)	Frank Oneto	30.00	15.00	9.00
(13)	George Risley	30.00	15.00	9.00
(14)	Bob Szabo	30.00	15.00	9.00
(15)	Ken Walters	30.00	15.00	9.00
(16)	Gabby Witucki	30.00	15.00	9.00

1952 Globe Printing Miami Beach Flamingos

These 2-1/4" x 3-1/2" black-and-white, unnumbered, blank-backed cards were one of many minor league team sets issued by Globe Printing of San Jose, Calif., in the early 1950s. Cards were usually given away at the ballpark on a one-per-week or one-per-homestand basis, accounting for the rarity of surviving sets. An embossed album is known for most of the team sets issued in 1952 or later. The Flamingos were an unaffiliated team in the Class B Florida International League.

		NM	EX	VG
Complete Set (25):		500.00	250.00	150.00
Common Player:		30.00	15.00	9.00
Album:		50.00	25.00	15.00
(1)	Billy Barrett	30.00	15.00	9.00
(2)	Art Bosch	30.00	15.00	9.00
(3)	Jack Caro	30.00	15.00	9.00
(4)	Chuck Ehlman	30.00	15.00	9.00
(5)	Oscar Garmendia	30.00	15.00	9.00
(6)	George Handy	30.00	15.00	9.00
(7)	Clark Henry	30.00	15.00	9.00
(8)	Dario Jiminez	30.00	15.00	9.00
(9)	Jesse Levan	30.00	15.00	9.00
(10)	Bobby Lyons	30.00	15.00	9.00
(11)	Pepper Martin	65.00	32.00	19.50
(12)	Dick McMillin	30.00	15.00	9.00
(13)	Pete Morant	30.00	15.00	9.00
(14)	Chico Morilla	30.00	15.00	9.00
(15)	Ken Munroe	30.00	15.00	9.00
(16)	Walt Nothe	30.00	15.00	9.00
(17)	Marshall O'Coine	30.00	15.00	9.00
(18)	Whitey Platt	30.00	15.00	9.00
(19)	Johnny Podgajny	30.00	15.00	9.00
(20)	Knobby Rosa	30.00	15.00	9.00
(21)	Harry Raulerson	30.00	15.00	9.00
(22)	Mort Smith	30.00	15.00	9.00
(23)	Tommy Venn	30.00	15.00	9.00
(24)	George Wehmeyer	30.00	15.00	9.00
(25)	Ray Williams	30.00	15.00	9.00

1952 Globe Printing Ogden Reds

These 2-1/4" x 3-1/2" black-and-white, unnumbered, blank-backed cards were one of many minor league team sets issued by Globe Printing of San Jose, Calif., in the early 1950s. Cards were usually given away at the ballpark on a one-per-week or one-per-homestand basis, accounting for the rarity of surviving sets. An embossed album is known for some of the team sets issued in 1952 or later. At least 10 O-Reds were issued in this set, though only one has been checklisted to date. The team was a Class C Pioneer League farm club of the Cincinnati Reds. The complete set price is not available.

		NM	EX	VG
Common Player:		30.00	15.00	9.00
(1)	Dave Bristol	30.00	15.00	9.00

1952 Globe Printing Oshkosh Giants

These 2-1/4" x 3-1/2" black-and-white, unnumbered, blank-backed cards were one of many minor league team sets issued by Globe Printing of San Jose, Calif., in the early 1950s. Cards were usually given away at the ballpark on a one-per-week or one-per-homestand basis, accounting for the rarity of surviving sets. An embossed album is known for most of the team sets issued in 1952 or later. The O-Giants were the Wisconsin State League affiliate of the N.Y. Giants. For a Class D team, a surprising number of the Oshkosh players graduated to the major leagues.

		NM	EX	VG
Complete Set (19):		500.00	250.00	150.00
Common Player:		30.00	15.00	9.00
Album:		50.00	25.00	15.00
(1)	Dan Banaszak	30.00	15.00	9.00
(2)	Paul Bentley	30.00	15.00	9.00
(3)	Joe Berke	30.00	15.00	9.00
(4)	Joe DeBellis	30.00	15.00	9.00
(5)	Ron Edwards	30.00	15.00	9.00
(6)	Dave Garcia	30.00	15.00	9.00
(7)	Weldon Grimesley	30.00	15.00	9.00
(8)	Cam Lewis	30.00	15.00	9.00
(9)	Paul McAuley	30.00	15.00	9.00
(10)	Don Mills	30.00	15.00	9.00
(11)	Ed Opich	30.00	15.00	9.00
(12)	John Practico	30.00	15.00	9.00
(13)	Rob R. Schmidt	30.00	15.00	9.00
(14)	Rob W. Schmidt	30.00	15.00	9.00
(15)	Frank Szekula	30.00	15.00	9.00
(16)	Victor Vick	30.00	15.00	9.00
(17)	Donald Wall	30.00	15.00	9.00
(18)	Ken Whitehead	30.00	15.00	9.00
(19)	Gordon Windhorn	30.00	15.00	9.00

1952 Globe Printing San Diego Padres

The Padres were one of the highest classification minor league teams for which Globe produced baseball cards in the early 1950s. Like other sets from the San Jose, Calif., printer, the 2-1/4" x 3-1/2" cards are black-and-white, blank-backed and feature the player's name on a white strip on front. It is likely an embossed album was also issued with the set. Because the Padres are quite often found as a team set, it's likely they were not distributed a card at a time as seems to have been the case with other sets.

		NM	EX	VG
Complete Set (18):		500.00	250.00	150.00
Common Player:		30.00	15.00	9.00
(1)	Al Benton	30.00	15.00	9.00
(2)	Dain Clay	30.00	15.00	9.00
(3)	John Davis	30.00	15.00	9.00
(4)	Dick Faber	30.00	15.00	9.00
(5)	Ben Flowers	30.00	15.00	9.00
(6)	Murray Franklin	30.00	15.00	9.00
(7)	Herb Gorman	30.00	15.00	9.00
(8)	Jack Graham	30.00	15.00	9.00
(9)	Memo Luna	30.00	15.00	9.00
(10)	Lefty O'Doul (Portrait to waist)	50.00	25.00	15.00
(11)	Lefty O'Doul (second pose unknown)	50.00	25.00	15.00
(12)	Al Olsen	30.00	15.00	9.00
(13)	Jimmie Reese	30.00	15.00	9.00
(14)	Al Richter	30.00	15.00	9.00
(15)	Jack Salveson	30.00	15.00	9.00
(16)	Lou Stringer	30.00	15.00	9.00
(17)	Lonnie Summers	30.00	15.00	9.00
(18)	Jack Tobin	30.00	15.00	9.00

1952 Globe Printing Syracuse Chiefs

Like the other contemporary issues of Globe Printing, the cards of the '52 Chiefs (International League) share a blank-back, black-and-white format. Player names are in black in a white strip on front. Cards measure about 2-1/4" x 3-3/8". The checklist here is incomplete.

		NM	EX	VG
Common Player:		30.00	15.00	9.00
(1)	Bruno Betzel	30.00	15.00	9.00
(2)	Johnny Blatnick	30.00	15.00	9.00
(3)	Charles Eisenmann	30.00	15.00	9.00
(4)	Myron Hayworth	30.00	15.00	9.00
(5)	John Welaj	30.00	15.00	9.00

The ratio of Excellent and Very Good prices to Near Mint can vary depending on relative collectibility for each grade in a specific set. Current listings reflect such adjustments.

1952 Globe Printing Ventura Braves

These 2-1/4" x 3-1/2" black-and-white, unnumbered, blank-backed cards were one of many minor league team sets issued by Globe Printing of San Jose, Calif., in the early 1950s. Cards were usually given away at the ballpark on a one-per-week or one-per-homestand basis, accounting for the rarity of surviving sets. An embossed album is known for most of the team sets issued in 1952 or later. It is known that 18 V-Braves were issued in this set, though only six have been checklisted to date. The team was a Class C California League farm club of the Boston Braves. The complete set price is not available.

		NM	EX	VG
Common Player:		30.00	15.00	9.00
Album:		50.00	25.00	15.00
(1)	Al Aguilar	30.00	15.00	9.00
(2)	Bud Belardi	30.00	15.00	9.00
(3)	Lee Kast	30.00	15.00	9.00
(4)	Richie Morse	30.00	15.00	9.00
(5)	Bob Sturgeon	30.00	15.00	9.00
(6)	Billy Wells	30.00	15.00	9.00

1957 Golden State Dairy S.F. Seals Stickers

There are 23 stickers known in this set, featuring the last minor league team in San Francisco. Virtually every player who appeared in more than 10 games for the Seals that season is included in the set. The stickers measure approximately 2" x 2-1/2", are printed in black-and-white, and blank-backed. They are checklisted here alphabetically, as the stickers are unnumbered.

		NM	EX	VG
Complete Set (23):		450.00	225.00	130.00
Common Player:		24.00	12.00	7.25
(1)	William "Bill" Abernathie	24.00	12.00	7.25
(2)	Kenneth "Chip" Aspromonte	24.00	12.00	7.25
(3)	Harry "Fritz" Dorish	24.00	12.00	7.25
(4)	Joe "Flash" Gordon	24.00	12.00	7.25
(5)	Grady Hatton Jr.	24.00	12.00	7.25
(6)	Thomas "Tommy" Hurd	24.00	12.00	7.25
(7)	Frank Kellert	24.00	12.00	7.25
(8)	Richard "Marty" Keough	24.00	12.00	7.25
(9)	Leo "Black Cat" Kiely	24.00	12.00	7.25
(10)	Harry William Malmberg	24.00	12.00	7.25
(11)	John McCall	24.00	12.00	7.25
(12)	Albert "Albie" Pearson	28.00	14.00	8.50
(13)	Jack Phillips	24.00	12.00	7.25
(14)	William "Bill" Renna	24.00	12.00	7.25
(15)	Edward "Ed" Sadowski	24.00	12.00	7.25
(16)	Robert W. Smith	24.00	12.00	7.25
(17)	Jack Spring	24.00	12.00	7.25
(18)	Jospeh H. Tanner	24.00	12.00	7.25
(19)	Salvador "Sal" Taormina	24.00	12.00	7.25
(20)	Maynard "Bert" Thiel	24.00	12.00	7.25
(21)	Anthony "Nini" Tornay	24.00	12.00	7.25
(22)	Thomas "Tommy" Umphlett	24.00	12.00	7.25
(23)	Glenn "Cap" Wright	24.00	12.00	7.25

1943 Grand Studio Milwaukee Brewers

It's unknown how these blank-backed, black-and-white, 3-1/2" x 5-1/2" pictures were distributed. The only identification is "PHOTO BY GRAND STUDIO" in the lower-right corner. It's likely the pictures were sold as a set at Borchert Field.

		NM	EX	VG
Complete Set (22):		500.00	250.00	150.00
Common Player:		30.00	15.00	9.00
(1)	Joe Berry	30.00	15.00	9.00
(2)	Bob Bowman	30.00	15.00	9.00
(3)	Earl Caldwell	30.00	15.00	9.00
(4)	Grey Clarke	30.00	15.00	9.00
(5)	Merv Conner	30.00	15.00	9.00
(6)	Paul Erickson	30.00	15.00	9.00
(7)	Charlie Grimm	30.00	15.00	9.00
(8)	Hank Helf	30.00	15.00	9.00
(9)	Don Johnson	30.00	15.00	9.00
(10)	Wes Livengood	30.00	15.00	9.00
(11)	Hershell Martin	30.00	15.00	9.00
(12)	Tommy Nelson	30.00	15.00	9.00
(13)	Ted Norbert	30.00	15.00	9.00
(14)	Bill Norman	30.00	15.00	9.00
(15)	Henry Oana	30.00	15.00	9.00
(16)	Jimmy Pruett	30.00	15.00	9.00
(17)	Bill Sahlin	30.00	15.00	9.00
(18)	Frank Secroy	30.00	15.00	9.00
(19)	Red Smith	30.00	15.00	9.00
(20)	Charles Sproull	30.00	15.00	9.00
(21)	Hugh Todd	30.00	15.00	9.00
(22)	Tony York	30.00	15.00	9.00

1888 Gypsy Queen California League

If or until further specimens are reported, the date of issue is speculative between about 1887-89. Undiscovered until 1998 was the fact that Gypsy Queen, a cigarette manufactured by Goodwin & Co. (Old Judge, etc.) had issued minor league cards, presumably of the relatively new California League. Like some contemporary issues, the card is a stiff piece of cardboard with a sepia-toned player photo glued to it. Size is about 1-1/2" x 2-1/2".

(1) Jas McDonald

The election of former players to the Hall of Fame does not always have an immediate upward effect on card values. The hobby market generally has done a good job of predicting those inductions and adjusting values over the course of several years.

H

1949 Hage's Dairy

"Red" Adams
SAN DIEGO

Hage's Dairy of California began a three-year run of regional baseball cards featuring Pacific Coast League players in 1949. Despite being produced by the local dairy, the cards were actually distributed inside popcorn boxes at the concession stand in Lane Field Park, home of the P.C.L. San Diego Padres. The 1949 set, like the following two years, was printed on a thin stock measuring 2-5/8" x 3-1/8". The checklist consists of 105 different cards, including several different poses for some of the players. Cards were continually being added or withdrawn to reflect roster changes on the minor league clubs. The Hage's sets were dominated by San Diego players, but also included representatives from the seven other P.C.L. teams. The 1949 cards can be found in four different tints - sepia, green, blue, and black and white. The unnumbered cards have blank backs. The player's name and team appear inside a box on the front of the card, and the 1949 cards can be dated by the large (quarter-inch) type used for the team names, which are sometimes referred to by city and other times by nickname.

		NM	EX	VG
	Complete Set (105):	2500.	1000.	600.00
	Common Player:	30.00	12.00	7.50
(1)	"Buster" Adams	30.00	12.00	7.50
(2)	"Red" Adams	30.00	12.00	7.50
(3)	Lee Anthony	30.00	12.00	7.50
(4)	Rinaldo Ardizoia	30.00	12.00	7.50
(5)	Del Baker	30.00	12.00	7.50
(6)	Ed Basinski	30.00	12.00	7.50
(7)	Jim Baxes	30.00	12.00	7.50
(8)	Heinz Becker	30.00	12.00	7.50
(9)	Herman Besse	30.00	12.00	7.50
(10)	Tom Bridges	30.00	12.00	7.50
(11)	Gene Brocker	30.00	12.00	7.50
(12)	Ralph Bucton	30.00	12.00	7.50
(13)	Mickey Burnett	30.00	12.00	7.50
(14)	Dain Clay (pose)	30.00	12.00	7.50
(15)	Dain Clay (batting)	30.00	12.00	7.50
(16)	Dain Corriden, Jim Reese	30.00	12.00	7.50
(17)	Pete Coscarart	30.00	12.00	7.50
(18)	Dom Dallessandro	30.00	12.00	7.50
(19)	Con Dempsey	30.00	12.00	7.50
(20)	Vince DiBiasi	30.00	12.00	7.50
(21)	Luke Easter (batting stance)	30.00	15.00	9.00
(22)	Luke Easter (batting follow thru)	30.00	15.00	9.00
(23)	Ed Fernandez	30.00	12.00	7.50
(24)	Les Fleming	30.00	12.00	7.50
(25)	Jess Flores	30.00	12.00	7.50
(26)	Cecil Garriott	30.00	12.00	7.50
(27)	Charles Gassaway	30.00	12.00	7.50
(28)	Mickey Grasso	30.00	12.00	7.50
(29)	Will Hafey (pitching)	30.00	12.00	7.50
(30)	Will Hafey (pose)	30.00	12.00	7.50
(31)	"Jeep" Handley	30.00	12.00	7.50
(32)	"Bucky" Harris (pose)	40.00	16.00	10.00
(33)	"Bucky" Harris (shouting)	40.00	16.00	10.00
(34)	Roy Helser	30.00	12.00	7.50
(35)	Lloyd Hittle	30.00	12.00	7.50
(36)	Ralph Hodgin	30.00	12.00	7.50
(37)	Leroy Jarvis	30.00	12.00	7.50
(38)	John Jensen	30.00	12.00	7.50
(39)	Al Jurisich	30.00	12.00	7.50
(40)	Herb Karpel	30.00	12.00	7.50
(41)	Frank Kelleher	30.00	12.00	7.50
(42)	Bill Kelly	30.00	12.00	7.50
(43)	Bob Kelly	30.00	12.00	7.50
(44)	Frank Kerr	30.00	12.00	7.50
(45)	Thomas Kipp	30.00	12.00	7.50
(46)	Al Lien	30.00	12.00	7.50
(47)	Lyman Linde (pose)	30.00	12.00	7.50
(48)	Lyman Linde (pitching)	30.00	12.00	7.50
(49)	Dennis Luby	30.00	12.00	7.50
(50)	"Red" Lynn	30.00	12.00	7.50
(51)	Pat Malone	30.00	12.00	7.50
(52)	Billy Martin	80.00	32.00	20.00
(53)	Joe Marty	30.00	12.00	7.50
(54)	Cliff Melton	30.00	12.00	7.50
(55)	Steve Mesner	30.00	12.00	7.50
(56)	Leon Mohr	30.00	12.00	7.50
(57)	"Butch" Moran	30.00	12.00	7.50
(58)	Glen Moulder	30.00	12.00	7.50
(59)	Steve Nagy	30.00	12.00	7.50
(60)	Roy Nicely	30.00	12.00	7.50
(61)	Walt Nothe	30.00	12.00	7.50
(62)	John O'Neill	30.00	12.00	7.50
(63)	"Pluto" Oliver	30.00	12.00	7.50
(64)	Al Olsen (pose)	30.00	12.00	7.50
(65)	Al Olsen (throwing)	30.00	12.00	7.50
(66)	Johnny Ostrowski	30.00	12.00	7.50
(67)	Ray Partee	30.00	12.00	7.50
(68)	Bill Raimondi	30.00	12.00	7.50
(69)	Bill Ramsey	30.00	12.00	7.50
(70)	Len Ratto	30.00	12.00	7.50
(71)	Xavier Rescigno	30.00	12.00	7.50
(72)	John Ritchey (batting)	30.00	12.00	7.50
(73)	John Ritchey (catching)	30.00	12.00	7.50
(74)	Mickey Rocco	30.00	12.00	7.50
(75)	John Rucker	30.00	12.00	7.50
(76)	Clarence Russell	30.00	12.00	7.50
(77)	Jack Salverson	30.00	12.00	7.50
(78)	Bill Schuster	30.00	12.00	7.50
(79)	Tom Seats	30.00	12.00	7.50
(80)	Neil Sheridan	30.00	12.00	7.50
(81)	Vince Shupe	30.00	12.00	7.50
(82)	Joe Sprinz	30.00	12.00	7.50
(83)	Chuck Stevens	30.00	12.00	7.50
(84)	Harvey Storey	30.00	12.00	7.50
(85)	Jim Tabor (Sacramento)	30.00	12.00	7.50
(86)	Jim Tabor (Seattle)	30.00	12.00	7.50
(87)	"Junior" Thompson	30.00	12.00	7.50
(88)	Arky Vaughn	40.00	16.00	10.00
(89)	Jackie Wagner	30.00	12.00	7.50
(90)	Jim Warner	30.00	12.00	7.50
(91)	Dick Wenner	30.00	12.00	7.50
(92)	Max West (pose)	30.00	12.00	7.50
(93)	Max West (batting swing)	30.00	12.00	7.50
(94)	Max West (batting follow-thru)	30.00	12.00	7.50
(95)	Hank Weyse	30.00	12.00	7.50
(96)	"Fuzzy" White	30.00	12.00	7.50
(97)	Jo Jo White	30.00	12.00	7.50
(98)	Artie Wilson	30.00	15.00	9.00
(99)	Bill Wilson	30.00	12.00	7.50
(100)	Bobbie Wilson (pose)	30.00	12.00	7.50
(101)	Bobbie Wilson (pitching)	30.00	12.00	7.50
(102)	"Pinky" Woods	30.00	12.00	7.50
(103)	Tony York	30.00	12.00	7.50
(104)	Del Young	30.00	12.00	7.50
(105)	Frank Zak	30.00	12.00	7.50

1950 Hage's Dairy

Padres
George Zuverink
SAN DIEGO

Perfect team
for every taste
Hage's
ICE CREAM
+
MILK
GEORGE ZUVERINK . . . Playing his first season of Triple A baseball, Zuverink already is one of the mainstays of the San Diego Padre mound staff. Is with the Padres on option from Cleveland and is expected to be in the major leagues before long.

The 1950 P.C.L. set from Hage's Dairy was similar in design and size (2-5/8" x 3-1/8") to the previous year and was again distributed in popcorn boxes at the San Diego stadium. The 1950 set is found with either a blank back or a back containing an advertisement for Hage's Ice Cream, "Your Favorite Brand". The advertising backs also contain the player's name and brief 1949 statistics at the bottom. There are 126 different cards in the 1950 set, including different poses for some of the players. Again, Padres dominate the unnumbered set with lesser representation from the other P.C.L. clubs. For the 1950 edition all team names are referred to by city (no nicknames) and the typeface is smaller.

		NM	EX	VG
	Complete Set (127):	2500.	1000.	600.00
	Common Player:	25.00	10.00	6.00
(1)	"Buster" Adams (kneeling)	25.00	10.00	6.00
(2a)	"Buster" Adams (batting follow-thru, with inscription)	25.00	10.00	6.00
(2b)	"Buster" Adams (batting follow-thru, no inscription)	25.00	10.00	6.00
(2c)	"Buster" Adams (batting follow-thru, body to left)	25.00	10.00	6.00
(3a)	"Buster" Adams (batting stance, caption box touching waist)	25.00	10.00	6.00
(3b)	"Buster" Adams (batting stance, caption box not ouching waist)	25.00	10.00	6.00
(4)	"Red" Adams	25.00	10.00	6.00
(5)	Dewey Adkins (photo actually Albie Glossop)	25.00	10.00	6.00
(6)	Rinaldo Ardizoia	25.00	10.00	6.00
(7)	Jose Bache	25.00	10.00	6.00
(8a)	Del Baker, Jim Reese (bat visible at lower right)	25.00	10.00	6.00
(8b)	Del Baker, Jim Reese (no bat visible)	25.00	10.00	6.00
(9)	George Bamberger	25.00	10.00	6.00
(10)	Richard Barrett	25.00	10.00	6.00
(11)	Frank Baumholtz	25.00	10.00	6.00
(12)	Henry Behrman	25.00	10.00	6.00
(13)	Bill Bevens	24.00	12.00	7.25
(14)	Ernie Bickhaus	25.00	10.00	6.00
(15)	Bill Burgher (pose)	25.00	10.00	6.00
(16)	Bill Burgher (catching)	25.00	10.00	6.00
(17)	Mark Christman	25.00	10.00	6.00
(18)	Clint Conaster	25.00	10.00	6.00
(19)	Herb Conyers (fielding)	25.00	10.00	6.00
(20)	Herb Conyers (batting)	25.00	10.00	6.00
(21)	Jim Davis	25.00	10.00	6.00
(22)	Ted Del Guercio	25.00	10.00	6.00
(23)	Vince DiBiasi	25.00	10.00	6.00
(24)	Jess Dobernic	25.00	10.00	6.00
(25)	"Red" Embree (pose)	25.00	10.00	6.00
(26)	"Red" Embree (pitching)	25.00	10.00	6.00
(27)	Elbie Fletcher	25.00	10.00	6.00
(28)	Guy Fletcher	25.00	10.00	6.00
(29)	Tony Freitas	25.00	10.00	6.00
(30)	Denny Galehouse	25.00	10.00	6.00
(31)	Jack Graham (pose, looking to left)	25.00	10.00	6.00
(32)	Jack Graham (pose, looking straight ahead)	25.00	10.00	6.00
(33)	Jack Graham (batting swing)	25.00	10.00	6.00
(34)	Jack Graham (batting stance)	25.00	10.00	6.00
(35)	Orval Grove	25.00	10.00	6.00
(36)	Lee Handley	25.00	10.00	6.00
(37)	Ralph Hodgin	25.00	10.00	6.00
(38)	Don Johnson	25.00	10.00	6.00
(39)	Al Jurisich (pose)	25.00	10.00	6.00
(40)	Al Jurisich (pitching wind-up)	25.00	10.00	6.00
(41)	Al Jurisich (pitching follow-thru)	25.00	10.00	6.00
(42)	Bill Kelly	25.00	10.00	6.00
(43)	Frank Kerr	25.00	10.00	6.00
(44)	Tom Kipp (pose)	25.00	10.00	6.00
(45)	Tom Kipp (pitching)	25.00	10.00	6.00
(46)	Mel Knezovich	25.00	10.00	6.00
(47)	Red Kress	25.00	10.00	6.00
(48)	Dario Lodigiani	25.00	10.00	6.00
(49)	Dennis Luby (pose)	25.00	10.00	6.00
(50)	Dennis Luby (throwing)	25.00	10.00	6.00
(51)	Al Lyons	25.00	10.00	6.00
(52)	Clarence Maddern	25.00	10.00	6.00
(53)	Joe Marty	25.00	10.00	6.00
(54)	Bob McCall	25.00	10.00	6.00
(55)	Cal McIrvin	25.00	10.00	6.00
(56)	Orestes Minoso (batting follow-thru)	50.00	20.00	12.00
(57)	Orestes Minoso (bunting)	50.00	20.00	12.00
(58)	Leon Mohr	25.00	10.00	6.00
(59)	Dee Moore (batting)	25.00	10.00	6.00
(60)	Dee Moore (catching)	25.00	10.00	6.00
(61)	Jim Moran	25.00	10.00	6.00
(62)	Glen Moulder	25.00	10.00	6.00
(63)	Milt Neilsen (pose)	25.00	10.00	6.00
(64)	Milt Neilsen (batting)	25.00	10.00	6.00
(65)	Milt Neilsen (throwing)	25.00	10.00	6.00
(66)	Rube Novotney	25.00	10.00	6.00
(67)	Al Olsen	25.00	10.00	6.00
(68)	Manny Perez	25.00	10.00	6.00
(69)	Bill Raemondi (Raimondi)	25.00	10.00	6.00
(70)	Len Ratto	25.00	10.00	6.00
(71)	Mickey Rocco	25.00	10.00	6.00
(72)	Marv Rotblatt	25.00	10.00	6.00
(73)	Lynwood Rowe (pose)	24.00	12.00	7.25
(74)	Lynwood Rowe (pitching)	24.00	12.00	7.25
(75)	Clarence Russell	25.00	10.00	6.00
(76)	Hal Saltzman (pitching follow-thru)	25.00	10.00	6.00
(77)	Hal Saltzman (pitching wind-up)	25.00	10.00	6.00
(78)	Hal Saltzman (pitching, leg in air)	25.00	10.00	6.00
(79)	Bob Savage (pose)	25.00	10.00	6.00
(80)	Bob Savage (pitching)	25.00	10.00	6.00
(81)	Charlie Schanz	25.00	10.00	6.00
(82)	Bill Schuster	25.00	10.00	6.00
(83)	Neil Sheridan	25.00	10.00	6.00
(84)	Harry Simpson (batting swing)	25.00	10.00	6.00
(85)	Harry Simpson (batting stance)	25.00	10.00	6.00
(86)	Harry Simpson (batting stance, close up)	25.00	10.00	6.00
(87)	Harry Simpson (batting follow-thru)	25.00	10.00	6.00
(88)	Elmer Singleton	25.00	10.00	6.00
(89)	Al Smith (pose)	25.00	10.00	6.00
(90)	Al Smith (batting stance)	25.00	10.00	6.00
(91)	Al Smith (fielding)	25.00	10.00	6.00
(92)	Alphonse Smith (glove above knee)	25.00	10.00	6.00
(93)	Alphonse Smith (glove below knee)	25.00	10.00	6.00
(94)	Steve Souchock	25.00	10.00	6.00
(95)	Jim Steiner	25.00	10.00	6.00
(96)	Harvey Storey (batting stance)	25.00	10.00	6.00
(97)	Harvey Storey (swinging bat)	25.00	10.00	6.00
(98)	Harvey Storey (throwing)	25.00	10.00	6.00
(99)	Harvey Storey (fielding, ball in glove)	25.00	10.00	6.00
(100)	Max Surkont	25.00	10.00	6.00
(101)	Jim Tabor	25.00	10.00	6.00
(102)	Forrest Thompson	25.00	10.00	6.00
(103)	Mike Tresh (pose)	25.00	10.00	6.00
(104)	Mike Tresh (catching)	25.00	10.00	6.00
(105)	Kenny Washington	25.00	10.00	6.00

(106)	Bill Waters (pose)	25.00	10.00	6.00
(107)	Bill Waters (pitching)	25.00	10.00	6.00
(108)	Roy Welmaker (pose)	25.00	10.00	6.00
(109)	Roy Welmaker (pitching)	25.00	10.00	6.00
(110)	Max West (pose)	25.00	10.00	6.00
(111)	Max West (batting stance)	25.00	10.00	6.00
(112)	Max West (kneeling)	25.00	10.00	6.00
(113)	Max West (batting follow-thru)	25.00	10.00	6.00
(114)	Al White	25.00	10.00	6.00
(115)	"Whitey" Wietelmann (pose)	25.00	10.00	6.00
(116)	"Whitey" Wietelmann (bunting)	25.00	10.00	6.00
(117)	"Whitey" Wietelmann (batting stance)	25.00	10.00	6.00
(118)	"Whitey" Wietelmann (throwing)	25.00	10.00	6.00
(119)	Bobbie Wilson	25.00	10.00	6.00
(120)	Bobby Wilson	25.00	10.00	6.00
(121)	Roy Zimmerman	25.00	10.00	6.00
(122)	George Zuverink	25.00	10.00	6.00

1951 Hage's Dairy

The final year of the Hage's P.C.L. issues saw the set reduced to 52 different unnumbered cards, all but 12 of them Padres. The set also includes six cards of Cleveland Indians players, which were issued during an exhibition series with the major league club, and six cards picturing members of the Hollywood Stars. No other P.C.L. teams are represented. The cards maintained the same size and style of the previous two years but were printed in more color tints, including blue, green, burgundy, gold, gray and sepia (but not black-and-white). The 1951 cards have blank backs and were again distributed in popcorn boxes at the San Diego stadium. The 1951 cards are the most common of the three sets issued by Hage's Dairy. The Indians and Stars players were issued in lesser quantities than the Padres, however, and command a higher value.

		NM	EX	VG
Complete Set (52):		1250.	625.00	375.00
Common Player:		25.00	10.00	6.00
(1)	"Buster" Adams	25.00	10.00	6.00
(2)	Del Baker	25.00	10.00	6.00
(3)	Ray Boone	50.00	20.00	12.00
(4)	Russ Christopher	25.00	10.00	6.00
(5)	Allie Clark	50.00	20.00	12.00
(6)	Herb Conyers	25.00	10.00	6.00
(7)	"Red" Embree (pitching, foot in air)	25.00	10.00	6.00
(8)	"Red" Embree (pitching, hands up)	25.00	10.00	6.00
(9)	Jess Flores	50.00	20.00	12.00
(10)	Murray Franklin	30.00	12.00	7.50
(11)	Jack Graham (portrait)	25.00	10.00	6.00
(12)	Jack Graham (batting)	25.00	10.00	6.00
(13)	Gene Handley	30.00	12.00	7.50
(14)	Charles Harris	25.00	10.00	6.00
(15)	Sam Jones (pitching, hands back)	25.00	10.00	6.00
(16)	Sam Jones (pitching, hands up)	25.00	10.00	6.00
(17)	Sam Jones (pitching, leg in air)	25.00	10.00	6.00
(18)	Al Jurisich	25.00	10.00	6.00
(19)	Frank Kerr (batting)	25.00	10.00	6.00
(20)	Frank Kerr (catching)	25.00	10.00	6.00
(21)	Dick Kinaman	25.00	10.00	6.00
(22)	Clarence Maddern (batting)	25.00	10.00	6.00
(23)	Clarence Maddern (fielding)	25.00	10.00	6.00
(24)	Harry Malmberg (bunting)	25.00	10.00	6.00
(25)	Harry Malmberg (batting follow-thru)	25.00	10.00	6.00
(26)	Harry Malmberg (fielding)	25.00	10.00	6.00
(27)	Gordon Maltzberger	30.00	12.00	7.50
(28)	Al Olsen (Cleveland)	50.00	20.00	12.00
(29)	Al Olsen (San Diego)	25.00	10.00	6.00
(30)	Jimmy Reese (clapping)	30.00	12.00	7.50
(31)	Jimmy Reese (hands on knees)	30.00	12.00	7.50
(32)	Al Rosen	60.00	24.00	12.50
(33)	Joe Rowell	25.00	10.00	6.00
(34)	Mike Sandlock	30.00	12.00	7.50
(35)	George Schmees	30.00	12.00	7.50
(36)	Charlie Sipple	25.00	10.00	6.00
(37)	Harvey Storey (batting follow-thru)	25.00	10.00	6.00
(38)	Harvey Storey (batting stance)	25.00	10.00	6.00
(39)	Harvey Storey (fielding)	25.00	10.00	6.00
(40)	Jack Tobin	25.00	10.00	6.00
(41)	Frank Tornay	25.00	10.00	6.00
(42)	Thurman Tucker	25.00	10.00	6.00
(43)	Ben Wade	30.00	12.00	7.50
(44)	Roy Welmaker	25.00	10.00	6.00
(45)	Leroy Wheat	25.00	10.00	6.00
(46)	Don White	25.00	10.00	6.00
(47)	"Whitey" Wietelman (batting)	25.00	10.00	6.00
(48)	"Whitey" Wietelman (fielding)	25.00	10.00	6.00
(49)	Bobby Wilson (batting)	25.00	10.00	6.00
(50)	Bobby Wilson (fielding)	25.00	10.00	6.00
(51)	Tony York	25.00	10.00	6.00
(52)	George Zuverink	50.00	20.00	12.00

1886 Hancock's Syracuse Stars

Currently representing the earliest known minor league baseball cards is this issue by a Syracuse department store's menswear department. The 1-5/8" x 3-3/16" cards feature sepia photos glued to a stiff black card-board backing with a gilt edge. The photos show the players in suits, presumably from the sponsor's racks. Backs have the player name and position printed at top. At center is an ad for Hancock's. At bottom is a credit line to "Goodwin" as photographer. It is likely other players of the International League Stars may yet be discovered.

		NM	EX	VG
Common Player:		10000.	5000.	3000.
(1)	Richard D. Buckley	10000.	5000.	3000.
(2)	Douglas Crothers	10000.	5000.	3000.
(3)	Philip H. Tomney	10000.	5000.	3000.

1960 Henry House Wieners Seattle Rainiers

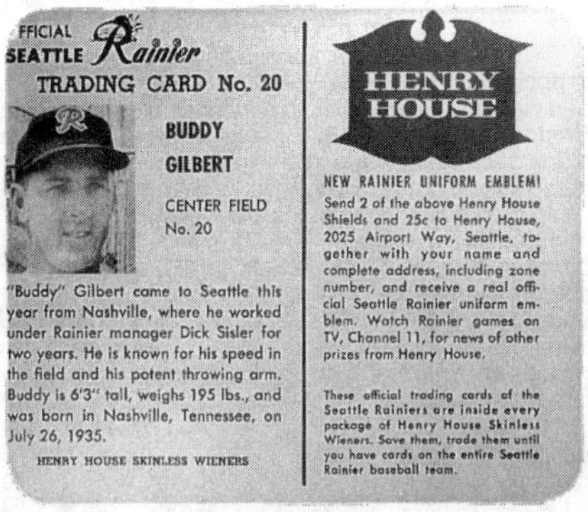

Eighteen different cards are known in this hot dog set; most players played major league baseball prior to their appearance with the Pacific Coast League Seattle Rainiers in 1960. Printed in red, the 4-1/2" x 3-3/4" cards are skip-numbered by player uniform number.

		NM	EX	VG
Complete Set (21):		3750.	1850.	1100.
Common Player:		150.00	37.50	22.50
2	Harry Malmberg	150.00	75.00	45.00
3	Francisco Obregon	150.00	75.00	45.00
4	Johnny O'Brien	175.00	87.00	52.00
5	Gordon Coleman	175.00	87.00	52.00
6	Bill Hain	150.00	75.00	45.00
8	Dick Sisler	175.00	87.00	52.00
9	Jerry Zimmerman	150.00	75.00	45.00
10	Hal Bevan	150.00	75.00	45.00
14	Rudy Regalado	150.00	75.00	45.00
15	Paul Pettit	150.00	75.00	45.00
20	Buddy Gilbert	150.00	75.00	45.00
21	Erv Palica	150.00	75.00	45.00
22	Joe Taylor	150.00	75.00	45.00
25	Bill Kennedy	150.00	75.00	45.00
26	Dave Stenhouse	150.00	75.00	45.00
28	Ray Ripplemeyer	150.00	75.00	45.00
30	Charlie Beamon	150.00	75.00	45.00
33	Don Rudolph	150.00	75.00	45.00

1888 S.F. Hess California League (N321)

One of several tobacco card sets produced by S.F. Hess & Co. of Rochester, this rare 40-card issue features players from the California League. The cards measure 2-7/8" x 1-1/2" and feature color drawings of players. The player's name and team are printed along the top margin of the card, while the words "S.F. Hess and Co.'s/Creole Cigarettes" appear at the bottom. "California League" is also printed in large capital letters above the player drawing, while the 1888 copyright date appears below. There are 35 players (including one umpire) in the set, and five players are pictured on two cards each, resulting in 40 different cards.

		NM	EX	VG
Complete Set (40):		140000.	70000.	42500.
Common Player:		4000.	2000.	1500.
(1)	Bennett	4000.	2000.	1500.
(2)	Borchers	4000.	2000.	1500.
(3)	Buckley	4000.	2000.	1500.
(4)	Burke (batting)	4000.	2000.	1500.
(5)	Burke (ready to pitch)	4000.	2000.	1500.
(6)	Burnett	4000.	2000.	1500.
(7)	Carroll	4000.	2000.	1500.
(8)	Donohue	4000.	2000.	1500.
(9)	Donovan	4000.	2000.	1500.
(10)	Finn	4000.	2000.	1500.
(11)	Gagus	4000.	2000.	1500.
(12)	Hanley	4000.	2000.	1500.
(13)	Hardie (C., wearing mask)	4000.	2000.	1500.
(14)	Hardie (C.F., with bat)	4000.	2000.	1500.
(15)	Hayes	4000.	2000.	1500.
(16)	Lawton	4000.	2000.	1500.
(17)	Levy	4000.	2000.	1500.
(18)	Long	4000.	2000.	1500.
(19)	McCord	4000.	2000.	1500.
(20)	Meegan	4000.	2000.	1500.
(21)	Moore	4000.	2000.	1500.
(22)	Mullee	4000.	2000.	1500.
(23)	Newhert	4000.	2000.	1500.
(24)	Noonan	4000.	2000.	1500.
(25)	O'Day	4000.	2000.	1500.
(26)	Perrier	4000.	2000.	1500.
(27)	Powers (1st B., catching)	4000.	2000.	1500.
(28)	Powers (1st B. & Capt., with bat)	4000.	2000.	1500.
(29)	Ryan	4000.	2000.	1500.
(30)	Selna	4000.	2000.	1500.
(31)	Shea	4000.	2000.	1500.
(32)	J. Sheridan (umpire)	4000.	2000.	1500.
(33)	"Big" Smith	4000.	2000.	1500.
(34)	H. Smith	4000.	2000.	1500.
(35)	J. Smith	4000.	2000.	1500.
(36)	Smett	4000.	2000.	1500.
(37)	Stockwell (throwing)	4000.	2000.	1500.
(38)	Stockwell (with bat)	4000.	2000.	1500.
(39)	Sweeney	4000.	2000.	1500.
(40)	Whitehead	4000.	2000.	1500.

Near Mint-Mint examples of vintage cards carry a significant premium over the Near Mint values shown here. This premium reflects limited availability of the highest-grade cards as well as demand for particular cards or sets in the best possible condition. Premiums of 2X-3X are not uncommon and many are even higher.

1888 S.F. Hess California League (N338-1)

This tobacco card set picturing players from the California League is one of the rarest of all 19th century issues. Issued in the late 1880s by S.F. Hess & Co. of Rochester, these 2-7/8" x 1-1/2" cards are so rare that only several examples are known to exist. Some of the photos in the N338-1 set are identical to the drawings in the N321 set, issued by S.F. Hess in 1888. The N338-1 cards are found with the words "California League" printed in an arc either above or below the player photo. The player's name appears below the photo. At the bottom of the card the words "S.F. Hess & Co.'s Creole Cigarettes" are printed in a rolling style.

		NM	EX	VG
Complete Set (16):		60000.	30000.	18000.
Common Player:		4000.	2000.	1250.
(1)	Borsher	4000.	2000.	1250.
(2)	Buckley	4000.	2000.	1250.
(3)	Carroll	4000.	2000.	1250.
(4)	C. Ebright	4000.	2000.	1250.
(5)	P. Incell	4000.	2000.	1250.
(6)	C.F. Lawton	4000.	2000.	1250.
(7)	C.F. Levy (throwing)	4000.	2000.	1250.
(8)	C.F. Levy (with bat)	4000.	2000.	1250.
(9)	C. McDonald	4000.	2000.	1250.
(10)	P. Meegan	4000.	2000.	1250.
(11)	S.S. Newhert	4000.	2000.	1250.
(12)	P. Noonan	4000.	2000.	1250.
(13)	R.F. Perrier	4000.	2000.	1250.
(14)	Perrier, H. Smith	4000.	2000.	1250.
(15)	Ryan	4000.	2000.	1250.
(16)	J. Smith, N. Smith	4000.	2000.	1250.
(17)	P. Sweeney	4000.	2000.	1250.

1888 S.F. Hess Newsboys League (N333)

Although not picturing actual baseball players, this 44-card set issued by S.F. Hess and Co. has a baseball theme. Cards measure 2-7/8" x 1-1/2" and feature pictures of newspaper boys from eight different papers in eight different cities (Rochester, Cleveland, Philadelphia, Boston, Albany, Detroit, New York and Syracuse). The boys are pictured in a portrait photo wearing a baseball-style shirt bearing the name of their newspaper. The boy's name, position and newspaper are printed below, while the words "Newsboys League" appears in capital letters at the top of the card. No identification is provided for the four Philadelphia newsboys, so a photo description is provided in the checklist that follows.

		NM	EX	VG
Complete Set (45):		31000.	15500.	9300.
Common Player:		775.00	375.00	225.00
(1)	R.J. Bell	775.00	375.00	225.00
(2)	Binden	775.00	375.00	225.00
(3)	Bowen	775.00	375.00	225.00
(4)	Boyle	775.00	375.00	225.00
(5)	Britcher	775.00	375.00	225.00
(6)	Caine	775.00	375.00	225.00
(7)	I. Cohen	775.00	375.00	225.00
(8)	R. Cohen	775.00	375.00	225.00
(9)	Cross	775.00	375.00	225.00
(10)	F. Cuddy	775.00	375.00	225.00
(11)	E. Daisey	775.00	375.00	225.00
(12)	Davis	775.00	375.00	225.00
(13)	B. Dinsmore	775.00	375.00	225.00
(14)	Donovan	775.00	375.00	225.00
(15)	A. Downer	775.00	375.00	225.00
(16)	Fanelly	775.00	375.00	225.00
(17)	J. Flood	775.00	375.00	225.00
(18)	C. Gallagher	775.00	375.00	225.00
(19)	M.H. Gallagher	775.00	375.00	225.00
(20)	D. Galligher	775.00	375.00	225.00
(21)	J. Galligher	775.00	375.00	225.00
(22)	Haskins	775.00	375.00	225.00
(23)	Herze	775.00	375.00	225.00
(24)	F. Horan	775.00	375.00	225.00
(25)	Hosler	775.00	375.00	225.00
(26)	Hyde	775.00	375.00	225.00
(27)	Keilty	775.00	375.00	225.00
(28)	C. Kellogg	775.00	375.00	225.00
(29)	Mahoney	775.00	375.00	225.00
(30)	Mayer	775.00	375.00	225.00
(31)	I. McDonald	775.00	375.00	225.00
(32)	McDowell (Rochester)	775.00	375.00	225.00
(33)	McGrady	775.00	375.00	225.00
(34)	O'Brien	775.00	375.00	225.00
(35)	E.C. Murphy	775.00	375.00	225.00
(36)	Sabin	775.00	375.00	225.00
(37)	Shedd	775.00	375.00	225.00
(38)	R. Sheehan	775.00	375.00	225.00
(39)	Smith	775.00	375.00	225.00
(40)	Talbot	775.00	375.00	225.00
(41)	Walsh	775.00	375.00	225.00
(42)	Philadelphia newsboy (hair parted on right side)	775.00	375.00	225.00
(43)	Philadelphia newsboy (hair parted on left side)	775.00	375.00	225.00
(44)	Philadelphia newsboy (no part in hair)	775.00	375.00	225.00
(45)	Philadelphia newsboy (head shaved)	775.00	375.00	225.00

1949 Hollywood Stars Team Issue

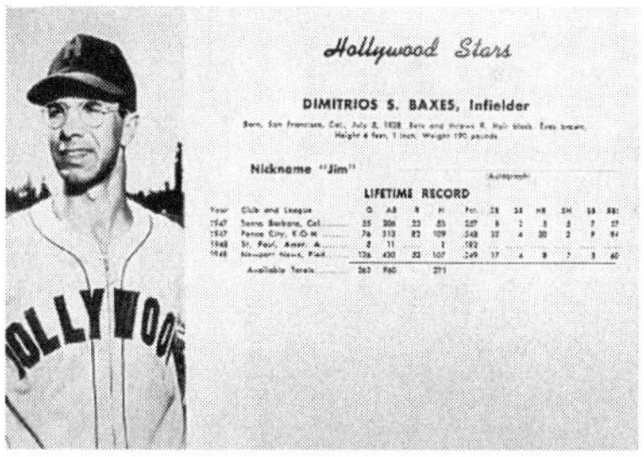

A team issue probably related to similar 1948-49 cards produced by Pacific Coast League crosstown rivals the L.A. Angels, these cards were likely produced by the publisher of the teams' yearbooks and sold at stadium souvenir stands. The cards are blank-backed, printed in black-and-white on thin semi-gloss cardboard, measuring 7-1/16" x 4-7/8". Portrait or posed action photos appear at left with complete major and minor league stats at right. A space for an autograph appears beneath the player's biographical data. The unnumbered cards are checklisted here in alphabetical order.

		NM	EX	VG
Complete Set (24):		450.00	225.00	135.00
Common Player:		22.00	11.00	6.50
(1)	Jim Baxes	22.00	11.00	6.50
(2)	George Fallon	22.00	11.00	6.50
(3)	John Fitzpatrick	22.00	11.00	6.50
(4)	George Genovese	22.00	11.00	6.50
(5)	Herb Gorman	22.00	11.00	6.50
(6)	Gene Handley	22.00	11.00	6.50
(7)	Fred Haney	22.00	11.00	6.50
(8)	Jim Hughes	22.00	11.00	6.50
(9)	Frank Kelleher	22.00	11.00	6.50
(10)	Gordy Maltzberger	22.00	11.00	6.50
(11)	Glen Moulder	22.00	11.00	6.50
(12)	Irv Noren	22.00	11.00	6.50
(13)	Ed Oliver	22.00	11.00	6.50
(14)	Karl Olsen	22.00	11.00	6.50
(15)	John O'Neil	22.00	11.00	6.50
(16)	Jack Paepke	22.00	11.00	6.50
(17)	Willard Ramsdell	22.00	11.00	6.50
(18)	Jack Salveson	22.00	11.00	6.50
(19)	Mike Sandlock	22.00	11.00	6.50
(20)	Art Shallock	22.00	11.00	6.50
(21)	Andy Skurski	22.00	11.00	6.50
(22)	Chuck Stevens	22.00	11.00	6.50
(23)	Al Unser	22.00	11.00	6.50
(24)	George Woods	22.00	11.00	6.50

Checklists with card numbers in parentheses ( ) indicates the numbers do not appear on the cards.

1950 Hollywood Stars Team Issue

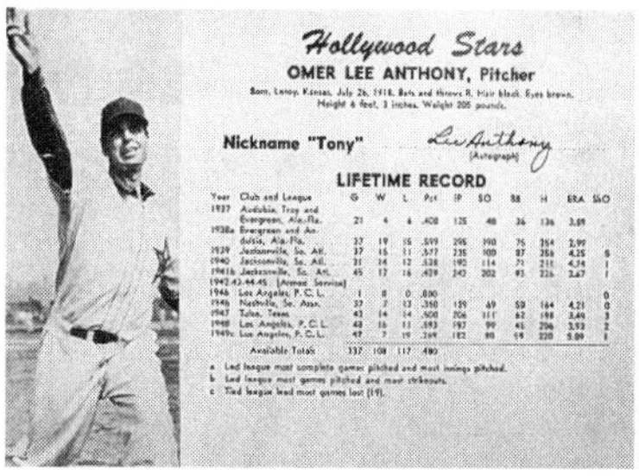

Virtually identical in format to the previous year's issue, the 1950 set differs principally in the inclusion of a facsimile autograph on front. In 1950 the Hollywood Stars were the PCL affiliate of the Brooklyn Dodgers. Both sets were listed in "The American Card Catalog" as W720.

		NM	EX	VG
Complete Set (32):		475.00	240.00	140.00
Common Player:		18.00	9.00	5.50
(1)	Lee Anthony	18.00	9.00	5.50
(2)	Bill Antonello	18.00	9.00	5.50
(3)	Dick Barrett	18.00	9.00	5.50
(4)	Jim Baxes	18.00	9.00	5.50
(5)	Clint Conaster	18.00	9.00	5.50
(6)	Cliff Dapper	18.00	9.00	5.50
(7)	George Fallon	18.00	9.00	5.50
(8)	John Fitzpatrick	18.00	9.00	5.50
(9)	Murray Franklin	18.00	9.00	5.50
(10)	Herb Gorman	18.00	9.00	5.50
(11)	Gene Handley	18.00	9.00	5.50
(12)	Fred Haney	18.00	9.00	5.50
(13)	Clarence Hicks	18.00	9.00	5.50
(14)	Herb Karpel	18.00	9.00	5.50
(15)	Frank Kelleher	18.00	9.00	5.50
(16)	Ken Lehman	18.00	9.00	5.50
(17)	Johnny Lindell	18.00	9.00	5.50
(18)	Gordy Maltzberger	18.00	9.00	5.50
(19)	Dan Menendez	18.00	9.00	5.50
(20)	Pershing Mondroff	18.00	9.00	5.50
(21)	Glen Moulder	18.00	9.00	5.50
(22)	John O'Neil	18.00	9.00	5.50
(23)	Jack Paepke	18.00	9.00	5.50
(24)	Jean Roy	18.00	9.00	5.50
(25)	Jack Salveson	18.00	9.00	5.50
(26)	Mike Sandlock	18.00	9.00	5.50
(27)	Ed Saver	18.00	9.00	5.50
(28)	George Schmees	18.00	9.00	5.50
(29)	Art Shallock	18.00	9.00	5.50
(30)	Chuck Stevens	18.00	9.00	5.50
(31)	Ben Wade	18.00	9.00	5.50
(32)	George Woods	18.00	9.00	5.50

1957 Hollywood Stars Team Issue

Presumably issued by the team, which had a working relationship with the Pittsburgh Pirates, this 23-card set features black-and-white blank-backed photos in a 4-1/8" x 6-3/16" format. Each picture has a facsimile autograph printed in black across the front. The unnumbered cards are checklisted here alphabetically.

		NM	EX	VG
Complete Set (23):		300.00	150.00	90.00
Common Player:		15.00	7.50	4.50
(1)	Jim Baumer	15.00	7.50	4.50
(2)	Carlos Bernier	15.00	7.50	4.50
(3)	Bill Causion	15.00	7.50	4.50
(4)	Chuck Churn	15.00	7.50	4.50
(5)	Bennie Daniels	15.00	7.50	4.50
(6)	Joe Duhem	15.00	7.50	4.50
(7)	John Fitzpatrick	15.00	7.50	4.50
(8)	Bob Garber	15.00	7.50	4.50
(9)	Bill Hall	15.00	7.50	4.50
(10)	Forrest "Spook" Jacobs	17.50	8.75	5.25
(11)	Clyde King	15.00	7.50	4.50

(12)	Nick Koback	15.00	7.50	4.50
(13)	Pete Naton	15.00	7.50	4.50
(14)	George O'Donnell	15.00	7.50	4.50
(15)	Paul Pettit	15.00	7.50	4.50
(16)	Curt Raydon	15.00	7.50	4.50
(17)	Leo Rodriguez	15.00	7.50	4.50
(18)	Don Rowe	15.00	7.50	4.50
(19)	Dick Smith	15.00	7.50	4.50
(20)	R.C. Stevens	15.00	7.50	4.50
(21)	Ben Wade	15.00	7.50	4.50
(22)	Fred Waters	15.00	7.50	4.50
(23)	George Witt	15.00	7.50	4.50

1912 Home Run Kisses (E136)

This 90-card set of Pacific Coast League players was produced in 1912 by the San Francisco candy company of Collins-McCarthy. Each card measures a large 2-1/4" x 4-1/4" and features sepia-toned player photos surrounded by an ornate frame. The front of the card has the words "Home Run Kisses" above the player's name. Most cards found are blank-backed, but others exist with a back that advises "Save Home Run Kisses Pictures for Valuable Premiums" along with other details of the Collins-McCarthy promotion.

		NM	EX	VG
Complete Set (90):		28000.	10000.	6250.
Common Player:		500.00	200.00	125.00
(1)	Ables	500.00	200.00	125.00
(2)	Agnew	500.00	200.00	125.00
(3)	Altman	500.00	200.00	125.00
(4)	Arrelanes	500.00	200.00	125.00
(5)	Auer	500.00	200.00	125.00
(6)	Bancroft	600.00	240.00	150.00
(7)	Bayless	500.00	200.00	125.00
(8)	Berry	500.00	200.00	125.00
(9)	Boles	500.00	200.00	125.00
(10)	Brashear	500.00	200.00	125.00
(11)	Brooks (Los Angeles)	500.00	200.00	125.00
(12)	Brooks (Oakland)	500.00	200.00	125.00
(13)	Brown	500.00	200.00	125.00
(14)	Burrell	500.00	200.00	125.00
(15)	Butler	500.00	200.00	125.00
(16)	Carlisle	500.00	200.00	125.00
(17)	Carson	500.00	200.00	125.00
(18)	Castleton	500.00	200.00	125.00
(19)	Chadbourne	500.00	200.00	125.00
(20)	Check	500.00	200.00	125.00
(21)	Core	500.00	200.00	125.00
(22)	Corhan	500.00	200.00	125.00
(23)	Coy	500.00	200.00	125.00
(24)	Daley	500.00	200.00	125.00
(25)	Dillon	500.00	200.00	125.00
(26)	Doane	500.00	200.00	125.00
(27)	Driscoll	500.00	200.00	125.00
(28)	Fisher	500.00	200.00	125.00
(29)	Flater	500.00	200.00	125.00
(30)	Gaddy	500.00	200.00	125.00
(31)	Gregg	500.00	200.00	125.00
(32)	Gregory	500.00	200.00	125.00
(33)	Harkness	500.00	200.00	125.00
(34)	Heitmuller	500.00	200.00	125.00
(35)	Henley	500.00	200.00	125.00
(36)	Hiester	500.00	200.00	125.00
(37)	Hoffman	500.00	200.00	125.00
(38)	Hogan	500.00	200.00	125.00
(39)	Hosp	500.00	200.00	125.00
(40)	Howley	500.00	200.00	125.00
(41)	Ireland	500.00	200.00	125.00
(42)	Johnson	500.00	200.00	125.00
(43)	Kane	500.00	200.00	125.00
(44)	Klawitter	500.00	200.00	125.00
(45)	Kreitz	500.00	200.00	125.00
(46)	Krueger	500.00	200.00	125.00
(47)	Leard	500.00	200.00	125.00
(48)	Leverencz	500.00	200.00	125.00
(49)	Lewis	500.00	200.00	125.00
(50)	Lindsay	500.00	200.00	125.00
(51)	Litschi	500.00	200.00	125.00
(52)	Lober	500.00	200.00	125.00
(53)	Malarkey	500.00	200.00	125.00
(54)	Martinoni	500.00	200.00	125.00
(55)	McArdle	500.00	200.00	125.00
(56)	McCorry	500.00	200.00	125.00
(57)	McDowell	500.00	200.00	125.00
(58)	McIver	500.00	200.00	125.00
(59)	Metzger	500.00	200.00	125.00
(60)	Miller	500.00	200.00	125.00
(61)	Mundorf	500.00	200.00	125.00
(62)	Nagle	500.00	200.00	125.00
(63)	Noyes	500.00	200.00	125.00
(64)	Olmstead	500.00	200.00	125.00
(65)	O'Rourke	500.00	200.00	125.00
(66)	Page	500.00	200.00	125.00
(67)	Parkins	500.00	200.00	125.00
(68)	Patterson (Oakland)	500.00	200.00	125.00
(69)	Patterson (Vernon)	500.00	200.00	125.00
(70)	Pernoll	500.00	200.00	125.00
(71)	Powell	500.00	200.00	125.00
(72)	Price	500.00	200.00	125.00
(73)	Raftery	500.00	200.00	125.00
(74)	Raleigh	500.00	200.00	125.00
(75)	Rogers	500.00	200.00	125.00
(76)	Schmidt	500.00	200.00	125.00
(77)	Schwenk	500.00	200.00	125.00
(78)	Sheehan	500.00	200.00	125.00
(79)	Shinn	500.00	200.00	125.00
(80)	Slagle	500.00	200.00	125.00
(81)	Smith	500.00	200.00	125.00
(82)	Stone	500.00	200.00	125.00
(83)	Swain	500.00	200.00	125.00
(84)	Taylor	500.00	200.00	125.00
(85)	Tiedeman	500.00	200.00	125.00
(86)	Toner	500.00	200.00	125.00
(87)	Tozer	500.00	200.00	125.00
(88)	Van Buren	500.00	200.00	125.00
(89)	Williams	500.00	200.00	125.00
(90)	Zacher	500.00	200.00	125.00

1940 Hughes Frozen Confections Sacramento Solons

These borderless 2 x 3" black-and-white cards of the Sacramento Solons can be found in two versions, either blank-backed or with the 1940 Solons Pacific Coast League schedule printed on back. Fronts featured action poses with a facsimile autograph.

		NM	EX	VG
Complete Set (20):		1500.	750.00	450.00
Common Player:		75.00	37.00	22.00
(1)	Mel Almada	75.00	37.00	22.00
(2)	Frank Asbell	75.00	37.00	22.00
(3)	Larry Barton	75.00	37.00	22.00
(4)	Robert Blattner	75.00	37.00	22.00
(5)	Bennie Borgmann	75.00	37.00	22.00
(6)	Tony Freitas	75.00	37.00	22.00
(7)	Art Garibaldi	75.00	37.00	22.00
(8)	Jim Grilk	75.00	37.00	22.00
(9)	Gene Handley	75.00	37.00	22.00
(10)	Oscar Judd	75.00	37.00	22.00
(11)	Lynn King	75.00	37.00	22.00
(12)	Norbert Kleinke	75.00	37.00	22.00
(13)	Max Marshall	75.00	37.00	22.00
(14)	William McLaughlin	75.00	37.00	22.00
(15)	Bruce Ogrodowski	75.00	37.00	22.00
(16)	Franich Riel	75.00	37.00	22.00
(17)	Bill Schmidt	75.00	37.00	22.00
(18)	Melvin Wasley	75.00	37.00	22.00
(19)	Chet Wieczorek	75.00	37.00	22.00
(20)	Deb Williams	75.00	37.00	22.00

1957 Hygrade Meats Seattle Rainiers

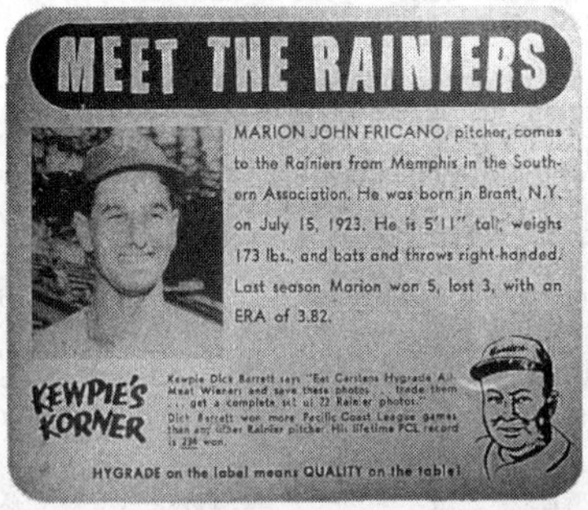

While the front of the cards mentions a complete set of 22 cards, only a dozen have been checklisted to date. The round-cornered cards measure 4-1/2 x 3-3/4" and are printed in red on white. Backs are blank. The cards feature only players of the Pacific Coast League Seattle Rainiers. The cards are unnumbered.

		NM	EX	VG
Common Player:		150.00	75.00	45.00
(1)	Dick Aylward	150.00	75.00	45.00
(2)	Bob Balcena	150.00	75.00	45.00
(3)	Jim Dyck	150.00	75.00	45.00
(4)	Marion Fricano	150.00	75.00	45.00
(5)	Bill Glynn	150.00	75.00	45.00
(6)	Larry Jansen	150.00	75.00	45.00
(7)	Bill Kennedy	150.00	75.00	45.00
(8)	Jack Lohrke	150.00	75.00	45.00
(9)	Frank O'Doul	200.00	100.00	60.00
(10)	Ray Orteig	150.00	75.00	45.00
(11)	Joe Taylor	150.00	75.00	45.00
(12)	Morrie (Maury) Wills	250.00	125.00	75.00

I

1912 Imperial Tobacco (C46)

This minor league set, issued in 1912 by the Imperial Tobacco Company, is the only tobacco baseball set issued in Canada. Designated as C46 in the American Card Catalog, each sepia-toned card measures 1-1/2" x 2-5/8" and features a distinctive card design that pictures the player inside an oval surrounded by a simulated woodgrain background featuring a bat, ball and glove in the borders. The player's last name appears in capital letters in a panel beneath the oval. (An exception is the card of James Murray, whose caption includes both first and last names.) The backs include the player's name and team at the top, followed by a brief biography. The 90 subjects in the set are members of the eight teams in the Eastern League (Rochester, Toronto, Buffalo, Newark, Providence, Baltimore, Montreal and Jersey City), even though the card backs refer to it as the International League. The set contains many players with major league experience, including Hall of Famers Joe Kelley and Joe "Iron Man" McGinnity.

		NM	EX	VG
Complete Set (90):		7425.	2975.	1850.
Common Player:		75.00	30.00	20.00
1	William O'Hara	160.00	50.00	30.00
2	James McGinley	105.00	42.00	26.00
3	"Frenchy" LeClaire	75.00	30.00	20.00
4	John White	75.00	30.00	20.00
5	James Murray	75.00	30.00	20.00
6	Joe Ward	75.00	30.00	20.00
7	Whitey Alperman	75.00	30.00	20.00
8	"Natty" Nattress	75.00	30.00	20.00
9	Fred Sline	75.00	30.00	20.00
10	Royal Rock	75.00	30.00	20.00
11	Ray Demmitt	75.00	30.00	20.00
12	"Butcher Boy" Schmidt	75.00	30.00	20.00
13	Samuel Frock	75.00	30.00	20.00
14	Fred Burchell	75.00	30.00	20.00
15	Jack Kelley	75.00	30.00	20.00
16	Frank Barberich	75.00	30.00	20.00
17	Frank Corridon	75.00	30.00	20.00
18	"Doc" Adkins	75.00	30.00	20.00
19	Jack Dunn	75.00	30.00	20.00
20	James Walsh	75.00	30.00	20.00
21	Charles Hanford	75.00	30.00	20.00
22	Dick Rudolph	75.00	30.00	20.00
23	Curt Elston	75.00	30.00	20.00
24	Silton	75.00	30.00	20.00
25	Charlie French	75.00	30.00	20.00
26	John Ganzel	75.00	30.00	20.00
27	Joe Kelley	325.00	130.00	80.00
28	Benny Meyers	75.00	30.00	20.00
29	George Schirm	75.00	30.00	20.00
30	William Purtell	75.00	30.00	20.00
31	Bayard Sharpe	75.00	30.00	20.00
32	Tony Smith	75.00	30.00	20.00
33	John Lush	75.00	30.00	20.00
34	William Collins	75.00	30.00	20.00
35	Art Phelan	75.00	30.00	20.00
36	Edward Phelps	75.00	30.00	20.00
37	"Rube" Vickers	75.00	30.00	20.00
38	Cy Seymour	75.00	30.00	20.00
39	"Shadow" Carroll	75.00	30.00	20.00
40	Jake Gettman	75.00	30.00	20.00
41	Luther Taylor	115.00	45.00	30.00
42	Walter Justis	75.00	30.00	20.00
43	Robert Fisher	75.00	30.00	20.00
44	Fred Parent	75.00	30.00	20.00
45	James Dygert	75.00	30.00	20.00
46	Johnnie Butler	75.00	30.00	20.00
47	Fred Mitchell	75.00	30.00	20.00
48	Heinie Batch	75.00	30.00	20.00
49	Michael Corcoran	75.00	30.00	20.00
50	Edward Doescher	75.00	30.00	20.00
51	Wheeler	75.00	30.00	20.00
52	Elijah Jones	75.00	30.00	20.00
53	Fred Truesdale	75.00	30.00	20.00
54	Fred Beebe	75.00	30.00	20.00

55	Louis Brockett	75.00	30.00	20.00
56	Wells	75.00	30.00	20.00
57	"Lew" McAllister	75.00	30.00	20.00
58	Ralph Stroud	75.00	30.00	20.00
59	Manser	75.00	30.00	20.00
60	"Ducky" Holmes	75.00	30.00	20.00
61	Rube Dessau	75.00	30.00	20.00
62	Fred Jacklitsch	75.00	30.00	20.00
63	Graham	75.00	30.00	20.00
64	Noah Henline	75.00	30.00	20.00
65	"Chick" Gandil	260.00	105.00	65.00
66	Tom Hughes	75.00	30.00	20.00
67	Joseph Delehanty	75.00	30.00	20.00
68	Pierce	75.00	30.00	20.00
69	Gaunt	75.00	30.00	20.00
70	Edward Fitzpatrick	75.00	30.00	20.00
71	Wyatt Lee	75.00	30.00	20.00
72	John Kissinger	75.00	30.00	20.00
73	William Malarkey	75.00	30.00	20.00
74	William Byers	75.00	30.00	20.00
75	George Simmons	75.00	30.00	20.00
76	Daniel Moeller	75.00	30.00	20.00
77	Joseph McGinnity	325.00	130.00	80.00
78	Alex Hardy	75.00	30.00	20.00
79	Bob Holmes	75.00	30.00	20.00
80	William Baxter	75.00	30.00	20.00
81	Edward Spencer	75.00	30.00	20.00
82	Bradley Kocher	75.00	30.00	20.00
83	Robert Shaw	75.00	30.00	20.00
84	Joseph Yeager	75.00	30.00	20.00
85	Carlo	75.00	30.00	20.00
86	William Abstein	75.00	30.00	20.00
87	Tim Jordan	75.00	30.00	20.00
88	Dick Breen	75.00	30.00	20.00
89	Tom McCarty	90.00	36.00	22.00
90	Ed Curtis	155.00	40.00	25.00

1923 Indianapolis Indians Foldout

Twenty-one players and staff are featured in this black-and-white accordian-fold souvenir. Each of the cards measures about 2" x 3".

	NM	EX	VG
Complete Foldout:	650.00	325.00	195.00
(Checklist not available)			

J

1967 Jones Dairy Buffalo Bison All-Stars

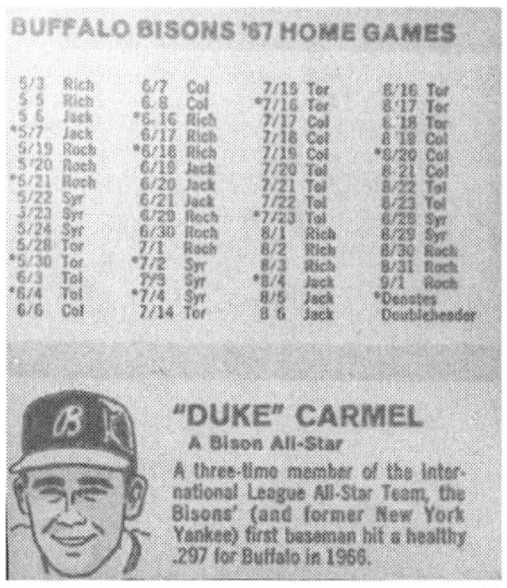

Apparently printed as part of a milk carton, only a single player is known for this issue. Printed in red and yellow, the piece includes a 1967 team home schedule, a player drawing and career highlights in a 2-3/4" x 3-1/8" format. Other players may yet surface.

		NM	EX	VG
(1)	"Duke" Carmel	40.00	20.00	12.00

The election of former players to the Hall of Fame does not always have an immediate upward effect on card values. The hobby market generally has done a good job of predicting those inductions and adjusting values over the course of several years.

K

1962 Kahn's Wieners Atlanta Crackers

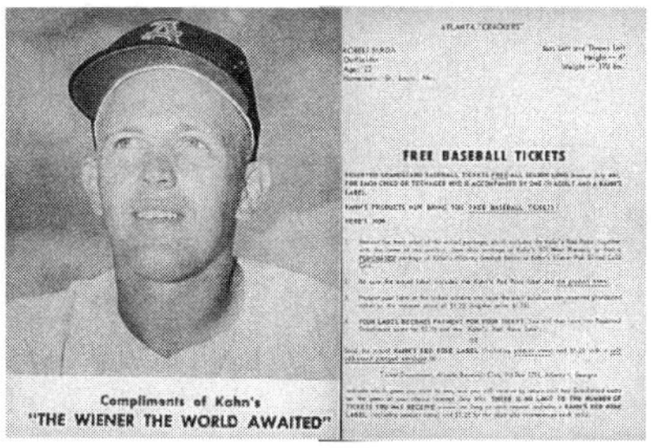

Kahn's made a single foray into the minor league market in 1962 with a separate 24-card set of Atlanta Crackers. The cards feature the same basic format, 3-1/4" x 4", borderless black-and-white photos with a Kahn's ad message in a white panel below the picture, as the major league issue. The backs are slightly different, having a free ticket offer in place of the player stats. Atlanta was the top farm club of the St. Louis Cardinals in 1962. The most famous alumnus in the set is Tim McCarver.

		NM	EX	VG
Complete Set (24):		400.00	200.00	120.00
Common Player:		17.00	8.50	5.00
(1)	James (Jimmy) Edward Beauchamp	17.00	8.50	5.00
(2)	Gerald Peter Buchek	17.00	8.50	5.00
(3)	Robert Burda	17.00	8.50	5.00
(4)	Hal Deitz	17.00	8.50	5.00
(5)	Robert John Duliba	17.00	8.50	5.00
(6)	Harry Michael Fanok	17.00	8.50	5.00
(7)	Phil Gagliano	17.00	8.50	5.00
(8)	John Glenn	17.00	8.50	5.00
(9)	Leroy Gregory	17.00	8.50	5.00
(10)	Richard (Dick) Henry Hughes	17.00	8.50	5.00
(11)	John Charles Kucks, Jr.	17.00	8.50	5.00
(12)	Johnny Joe Lewis	17.00	8.50	5.00
(13)	James (Mac - Timmie) Timothy McCarver	40.00	20.00	12.00
(14)	Robert F. Milliken	17.00	8.50	5.00
(15)	Joe Morgan	17.00	8.50	5.00
(16)	Ronald Charles Plaza	17.00	8.50	5.00
(17)	Bob Sadowski	17.00	8.50	5.00
(18)	Jim Saul	17.00	8.50	5.00
(19)	Willard Schmidt	17.00	8.50	5.00
(20)	Joe Schultz	17.00	8.50	5.00
(21)	Thomas Michael (Mike) Shannon	24.00	12.00	7.25
(22)	Paul Louis Toth	17.00	8.50	5.00
(23)	Andrew Lou Vickery	17.00	8.50	5.00
(24)	Fred Dwight Whitfield	17.00	8.50	5.00

1939 Kimball Automobile Trois-Rivieres Photocards

This set of 18 postcards and an accompanying envelope features the player of the Trois-Rivieres (Three Rivers) club of the Quebec Provincial League. Until 1940, the six-team QPL was not a part of organized baseball's minor league system. Several of the players were either former or future minor leaguers within OB. Paul "Pepper" Martin in the set is not the Pepper Martin of the contemporary, Gas House Gang St. Louis Cardinals. The black-and-white cards are about postcard-size and blank-backed, printed on sturdy card stock.

		NM	EX	VG
Complete Set (18):		150.00	75.00	45.00
Common Player:		12.00	6.00	3.50
(1)	George Andrews	12.00	6.00	3.50
(2)	Norm Bell	12.00	6.00	3.50
(3)	Henry Block	12.00	6.00	3.50
(4)	Addie Copple	12.00	6.00	3.50
(5)	Phil Corrigan	12.00	6.00	3.50
(6)	Joe Dickinson	12.00	6.00	3.50
(7)	Bill Hoffner	12.00	6.00	3.50
(8)	Jack Leroy	12.00	6.00	3.50
(9)	Leo Maloney	12.00	6.00	3.50
(10)	Martin	12.00	6.00	3.50
(11)	McGurk	12.00	6.00	3.50
(12)	Connie O'Leary	12.00	6.00	3.50
(13)	James Pickens	12.00	6.00	3.50
(14)	Dutch Prather	12.00	6.00	3.50
(15)	Jamie Skelton	12.00	6.00	3.50
(16)	Byron Speece	12.00	6.00	3.50
(17)	Gene Sullivan	12.00	6.00	3.50
(18)	Grover Wearshing	12.00	6.00	3.50

1952 Knowles Service Stations Stockton Ports

Contemporary, and sharing a format with, the many Globe minor league issues of the early '50s, this set of Stockton Ports (Class C California League) cards carries the advertising of Knowles Service Stations. The blank-backed, black-and-white cards measure 2-1/4" x 3-1/2" and are unnumbered. It is likely the checklist here is incomplete, so no complete set price is given. Among the players is a Japanese national whose card is in strong demand.

		NM	EX	VG
Common Player:		50.00	25.00	15.00
Album:		150.00	75.00	45.00
(1)	Wayne Clary	50.00	25.00	15.00
(2)	Harry Clements	50.00	25.00	15.00
(3)	John Crocco	50.00	25.00	15.00
(4)	Tony Freitas	50.00	25.00	15.00
(5)	Fibber Hirayama	250.00	125.00	75.00
(6)	Dave Mann	50.00	25.00	15.00
(7)	Larry Mann	50.00	25.00	15.00
(8)	Hank Moreno	50.00	25.00	15.00
(9)	Frank Romero	50.00	25.00	15.00
(10)	Chuck Thomas	50.00	25.00	15.00
(11)	Bud Watkins	50.00	25.00	15.00

1922-23 Kolb's Mothers' Bread Pins

Over a two-year period, Kolb's bakery sponsored a series of pins featuring members of the Reading (Pa.) Aces of the International League. The pins are 7/8" in diameter with black-and-white portraits on a white background. The player name (last name only, usually) and position are indicated beneath the photo. Above the photo, in red, is the sponsor's identification. The pins issued in 1922 have "MOTHERS'" in all capital letters; the 1923 pins have "Mothers'" in upper and lower case.

		NM	EX	VG
Complete Set (32):		800.00	400.00	240.00
Common Player:		60.00	30.00	18.00
(1)	Spencer Abbott	60.00	30.00	18.00
(2)	Charlie Babington	60.00	30.00	18.00
(3)	Bill Barrett	60.00	30.00	18.00
(4)	R. Bates	60.00	30.00	18.00
(5)	Chief Bender	90.00	45.00	27.00
(6)	Myrl Brown	60.00	30.00	18.00
(7)	Fred Carts	60.00	30.00	18.00
(8)	Nig Clarke	60.00	30.00	18.00
(9)	Tom Connelly	60.00	30.00	18.00
(10)	Gus Getz	95.00	47.00	28.00
(11)	Frank Gilhooley	60.00	30.00	18.00
(12)	Ray Gordonier	60.00	30.00	18.00
(13)	Hinkey Haines	75.00	37.00	22.00
(14)	Francis Karpp	60.00	30.00	18.00
(15)	Joseph Kelley	60.00	30.00	18.00
(16)	Andrew Kotch	60.00	30.00	18.00
(17)	William Lightner	60.00	30.00	18.00
(18)	Byrd Lynn	60.00	30.00	18.00
(19)	Al Mamaux	60.00	30.00	18.00
(20)	Martin	60.00	30.00	18.00
(21)	Ralph Miller	60.00	30.00	18.00
(22)	Otto Pahlman	60.00	30.00	18.00
(23)	Sam Post	60.00	30.00	18.00

(24)	Al Schact	75.00	37.00	22.00
(25)	John Scott	60.00	30.00	18.00
(26)	Walt Smallwood	60.00	30.00	18.00
(27)	Ross Swartz	60.00	30.00	18.00
(28)	Fred Thomas	60.00	30.00	18.00
(29)	Myles Thomas	60.00	30.00	18.00
(30)	Walt Tragesser	60.00	30.00	18.00
(31)	Washburn	60.00	30.00	18.00
(32)	Walter Wolfe	60.00	30.00	18.00

L

1952 La Patrie Album Sportif

Ballplayers from Montreal of the International League and several of the teams from the Class C Provincial (Quebec) League were featured in a series of colorized photos printed in the Sunday rotogravure section of "La Patrie newspaper. The photos are approximately 11" x 15-3/8" with red left and bottom trim and a vertical blue stripe at far left. Player information is printed in black and is in French. A number of the players went on to stardom with the Brooklyn and/or Los Angeles Dodgers.

		NM	EX	VG
Complete Set (20):		650.00	325.00	195.00
Common Player:		24.00	12.00	7.25
(1)	Bob Alexander	24.00	12.00	7.25
(2)	Herbie Bush	24.00	12.00	7.25
(3)	Georges Carpentier	24.00	12.00	7.25
(4)	Hampton Coleman	24.00	12.00	7.25
(5)	Walter Fiala	24.00	12.00	7.25
(6)	Jim Gilliam	36.00	18.00	11.00
(7)	Tom Hackett	24.00	12.00	7.25
(8)	Don Hoak	36.00	18.00	11.00
(9)	Herbie Lash	24.00	12.00	7.24
(10)	Tommy Lasorda	150.00	75.00	45.00
(11)	Mal Mallette	24.00	12.00	7.25
(12)	Georges Maranda (Aug. 17)	24.00	12.00	7.25
(13)	Carmen Mauro	24.00	12.00	7.25
(14)	Solly Mohn	24.00	12.00	7.25
(15)	Jacques Monette	24.00	12.00	7.25
(16)	Johnny Podres	75.00	37.00	22.00
(17)	Ed Roebuck	28.00	14.00	8.50
(18)	Charlie Thompson	28.00	14.00	8.50
(19)	Don Thompson	28.00	14.00	8.50
(20)	John Wingo	24.00	12.00	7.25

1928-32 La Presse Rotos

Players from Montreal's team in the International League (and occasionally other major and minor league teams' stars) were featured in a series of photos between 1928-32 in the Saturday rotogravure section of Montreal's "La Presse" newspaper. The format remained fairly consistent over the years. Large hand-tinted player photos were featured on the approximately 11" x 17-3/4" pages, with a French writeup below. On back was whatever features and ads happened to appear on the following page. The known player list is presented here in chronological order, but is not yet complete. Other athletes were also included in the series and are listed here to preserve date continuity. Gaps have been left in the numbering to better accomodate future additions to this list.

		NM	EX	VG
Common Player:		60.00	30.00	18.00
	1927			
(1)	(Nels Stewart) (hockey) (Dec. 10)	75.00	37.00	22.00
(2)	(Jimmy Ward) (hockey) (Dec. 24) 1928	60.00	30.00	18.00
(1)	(George Hainsworth) (hockey) (Jan. 7)	60.00	30.00	18.00
(2)	(Art Gagne) (hockey) (Jan. 14)	60.00	30.00	18.00
(3)	(Herb Gardiner) (hockey) (Jan. 21)	60.00	30.00	18.00
(4)	(Joseph Albert Leduc) (hockey) (Jan. 28)	60.00	30.00	18.00
(6)	Leonard Gaudreault (hockey) (Feb. 11)	60.00	30.00	18.00
(7)	Pit Lepine (hockey) (Feb. 18)	60.00	30.00	18.00
(9)	Georges Vezina (hockey) (March 3)	150.00	75.00	45.00
(13)	Cecil Hart et. al. (hockey) (March 31)	60.00	30.00	18.00
(15)	Lionel Conacher (hockey) (Apr. 14)	60.00	30.00	18.00
(16)	Red Porter (hockey) (Apr. 21)	60.00	30.00	18.00
(19)	Oliva Bourassa (jockey) (May 12)	60.00	30.00	18.00
(20)	Aldrick Gaudette (May 19)	60.00	30.00	18.00
(22)	Bob Shawkey (June 2)	80.00	40.00	24.00
(23)	Lachine team photo, portraits of starting nine (June 9)	60.00	30.00	18.00
(24)	Roy Buckalew, Frank Dunagan, Chester Fowler, Thomas Gulley, Peter Radwan, Richard Smith (June 16)	60.00	30.00	18.00
(25)	Seymour Edward Bailey (June 23)	60.00	30.00	18.00
(26)	Wilson F. Fewster (June 30)	60.00	30.00	18.00
(28)	Tom Daly (July 14)	60.00	30.00	18.00
(32)	Red Holt (Aug. 11)	60.00	30.00	18.00
(33)	Johnny Farrell (golf) (Aug. 18)	100.00	50.00	30.00
(34)	Pete Sanstol (boxer) (Aug. 25)	60.00	30.00	18.00
(37)	Vladek Zbysko, three other wrestlers (Sept. 15)	50.00	25.00	15.00
(38)	George Young (swimming) (Sept. 22)	60.00	30.00	18.00
(40)	George Herman Ruth (Oct. 13)	600.00	300.00	180.00
(41)	Henri Cochet (tennis) (Oct. 20)	70.00	35.00	21.00
(42)	Jos Laporte (cycling) (Oct. 27)	60.00	30.00	18.00
(43)	Johnny Prud'homme (Nov. 3)	60.00	30.00	18.00
(44)	Daisy King Shaw (swimming) (Nov. 10)	60.00	30.00	18.00
(49)	Martin Burke (hockey) (Dec. 15)	60.00	30.00	18.00
(50)	Nelson Stewart (hockey) (Dec. 22)	75.00	37.00	22.00
(51)	John Chevigny (football) (Dec. 29)	60.00	30.00	18.00
	1929			
(2)	("Happy" Day) (hockey) (Jan. 12)	60.00	30.00	18.00
(3)	(Clint Benedict) (hockey) (Jan. 19)	60.00	30.00	18.00
(4)	("Red" Dutton) (hockey) (Jan. 26)	60.00	30.00	18.00
(5)	(Jimmy Ward) (hockey) (Feb. 2)	60.00	30.00	18.00
(6)	(Bill Phillips) (hockey) (Feb. 9)	60.00	30.00	18.00
(7)	(Frank Boucher) (hockey) (Feb. 16)	75.00	37.00	22.00
(8)	(Lucien Brunet) (hockey) (Feb. 23)	60.00	30.00	18.00
(9)	(Georges Boucher) (hockey) (March 2)	60.00	30.00	18.00
(11)	(Armand Mondou) (hockey) (March 16)	60.00	30.00	18.00
(12)	(Bunny Cook) (hockey) (March 23)	60.00	30.00	18.00
(13)	(Georges Mantha) (hockey) (April 6)	60.00	30.00	18.00
(14)	Walter Paul Gautreau (April 13)	60.00	30.00	18.00
(16)	Herb Thormahlen (April 27)	60.00	30.00	18.00
(19)	Percy Williams (track) (May 18)	40.00	20.00	12.00
(23)	Harry Hill (boxing) (June 15)	60.00	30.00	18.00
(24)	Tommy Heeney (boxing) (June 22)	60.00	30.00	18.00
(25)	Bobby Walthour (bicycling) (June 29)	50.00	25.00	15.00
(27)	Elon Hogsett (July 13)	60.00	30.00	18.00
(28)	Andre Routis (boxing) (July 20)	60.00	30.00	18.00
(29)	Mlle. Pauline Gadbois (tennis) (July 27)	60.00	30.00	18.00
(30)	Helen Willis (tennis) (Aug. 3)	80.00	40.00	24.00
(31)	Tommy Loughran (boxer) (Aug. 10)	80.00	40.00	24.00
(32)	Vital Jacmain (bowling) (Aug. 17)	60.00	30.00	18.00
(36)	Max Schmeling (boxing) (Sept. 14)	125.00	62.00	37.00
(37)	Rolland Longtin (tennis) (Sept. 21)	60.00	30.00	18.00
(38)	Vittorio Campolo (boxer) (Sept. 28)	60.00	30.00	18.00
(39)	Martha Norelius (swimming) (Oct. 5)	60.00	30.00	18.00
(40)	Harrison R. Johnston (golf) (Oct. 12)	100.00	50.00	30.00
(41)	Robert M. "Lefty" Grove (Oct. 19)	200.00	100.00	60.00
(42)	Christopher Battalino (boxing) (Oct. 26)	50.00	25.00	15.00
(43)	Clarence Ross (swimmer) (Nov. 2)	35.00	17.50	10.00
(45)	Philadelphia A's Stars (Mickey Cochrane, Jimmie Foxx, Connie Mack, Al Simmons, Rube Walberg,Bing	90.00	45.00	27.00
(47)	(Gordon Fraser) (hockey) (Nov. 30)	60.00	30.00	18.00
(48)	(Jimmy Carlson) (hockey) (Dec. 7)	60.00	30.00	18.00
(51)	Leonard Seppala (sled-dog racing) (Dec. 21)	60.00	30.00	18.00
(52)	Hec Kilrea (hockey) (Dec. 28)1930	60.00	30.00	18.00
(2)	(King Clancy) (hockey) (Jan. 11)	75.00	37.00	22.00
(3)	(John Ross Roach) (hockey) (Jan. 18)	60.00	30.00	18.00
(4)	(Leo Bourgeault) (hockey) (Jan. 25)	60.00	30.00	18.00
(5)	(Raymond Boulanger) (hockey) (Feb. 1)	60.00	30.00	18.00
(6)	(Lionel Hitchman) (hockey) (Feb. 8)	60.00	30.00	18.00
(7)	(Joe Primeau) (hockey) (Feb. 15)	70.00	35.00	21.00
(8)	(Dutch Gainor) (hockey) (Feb. 22)	60.00	30.00	18.00
(9)	(Cecil "Tiny" Thompson) (hockey) (March 1)	60.00	30.00	18.00
(10)	(Gus Rivers) (hockey) (March 8)	60.00	30.00	18.00
(11)	Emil St-Goddard (sled-dog racing) (March 15)	60.00	30.00	18.00
(12)	Edouard Fabre (snow shoeing) (March 22)	60.00	30.00	18.00
(13)	Hooley Smith (hockey) (March 29)	70.00	35.00	21.00
(14)	"Flat" Walsh (hockey) (April 5)	60.00	30.00	18.00
(15)	Ed "Strangler" Lewis (wrestler) (April 12)	50.00	25.00	15.00
(19)	C. Ross Somerville (golf) (May 10)	125.00	62.00	37.00
(20)	Clarence De Mar (marathoner) (May 17)	50.00	25.00	15.00
(22)	Martin Griffin, John Pomorski, Arthur Smith, Herb Thormahlen (May 31)	60.00	30.00	18.00
(23)	James Calleran, Edward Conley, Lee Head, Jimmy Ripple (June 7)	60.00	30.00	18.00
(24)	Le Shamrock V.H. Lipton (sailing) (June 14)	50.00	25.00	15.00
(25)	(Joe Scalfaro) (boxer) (June 21)	50.00	25.00	15.00
(26)	Del Bissonette (June 28)	60.00	30.00	18.00
(27)	Gagnant (racehorse) (July 5)	50.00	25.00	15.00
(28)	Joe Hauser (July 12)	75.00	37.00	22.00
(29)	Gallant Fox (racehorse) (July 19)	50.00	25.00	15.00
(31)	(Jack Guest) (rowing) (Aug. 2)	50.00	25.00	15.00
(32)	(Joe Wright) (rowing) (Aug. 9)	50.00	25.00	15.00
(35)	(Peter Galuzzi, Anton Newton) (track) (Aug. 30)	50.00	25.00	15.00
(36)	(George A. Morin) (track) (Sept. 6)	50.00	25.00	15.00
(37)	Gowell Sylvester Claset (Sept. 13)	60.00	30.00	18.00
(40)	Mercedes Glotiz (swimmer) (Oct. 4)	50.00	25.00	15.00
(41)	Hack Wilson (Oct. 11)	200.00	100.00	60.00
(43)	Peggy Duncan (swimmer) (Oct. 25)	50.00	25.00	15.00
(46)	Nap. Bourdeal (track) (Nov. 15)	50.00	25.00	15.00
(47)	Enterprise - Harold Vanderbilt (yachting) (Nov. 22)	50.00	25.00	15.00
(50)	(Earl Miller) (hockey) (Dec. 13)	60.00	30.00	18.00
(51)	(Johnny Gagnon) (hockey) (Dec. 20)	60.00	30.00	18.00
(52)	(Art Somers) (hockey) (Dec. 27)	60.00	30.00	18.00
	1931			
(1)	(Johnny Gottselig) (hockey) (Jan. 3)	60.00	30.00	18.00
(3)	(Johnny Gallagher) (hockey) (Jan. 17)	60.00	30.00	18.00
(4)	(Earl Roche) (hockey) (Jan. 24)	60.00	30.00	18.00
(5)	(Jack McVicar) (hockey) (Jan. 31)	60.00	30.00	18.00
(6)	(Dave Kerr) (hockey) (Feb. 7)	60.00	30.00	18.00
(7)	(Jesse Roache) (hockey) (Feb. 14)	60.00	30.00	18.00

(8)	Paul Haynes (hockey) (Feb. 21)	60.00	30.00	18.00
(9)	Al Huggins (hockey) (Feb. 28)	60.00	30.00	18.00
(10)	Red Horner(hockey) (March 7)	60.00	30.00	18.00
(11)	Frank Hoey (winter sports) (Mar. 14)	50.00	25.00	15.00
(12)	Harvey Jackson (hockey) (March 21)	65.00	32.00	19.50
(13)	Charlie Conacher (hockey) (March 28)	75.00	37.00	22.00
(14)	Ralph Saint-Germain (hockey) (April 4)	60.00	30.00	18.00
(15)	Ebbie Goodfellow (hockey) (April 11)	60.00	30.00	18.00
(16)	Reggie McNamara (bicycling) (Apr. 25)	50.00	25.00	15.00
(17)	Erwin Rudolph (billards) (May 2)	50.00	25.00	15.00
(18)	Marcel Rainville (tennis) (May 9)	50.00	25.00	15.00
(19)	Johnny Risko (boxing) (May 16)	50.00	25.00	15.00
(20)	Laurent Gadou (bicycling) (May 23)	50.00	25.00	15.00
(21)	Chuck Klein (May 30)	175.00	87.00	52.00
(22)	Jocko Conlan (June 6)	100.00	50.00	30.00
(23)	Twenty Grand (racehorse) (June 13)	50.00	25.00	15.00
(25)	Lee Head (June 20)	60.00	30.00	18.00
(26)	Francis X. Shields (tennis) (June 27)	50.00	25.00	15.00
(27)	Jimmy Ripple (July 4)	60.00	30.00	18.00
(29)	Sol Mishkin (July 18)	60.00	30.00	18.00
(31)	Reggie Cooper (jockey) (Aug. 1)	50.00	25.00	15.00
(32)	Zenon Saint-Laurent (bicycling) (Aug. 8)	50.00	25.00	15.00
(33)	Walter Brown (Aug. 15)	60.00	30.00	18.00
(34)	Bunny Austin (tennis) (Aug. 22)	50.00	25.00	15.00
(38)	Eva Coleman (swimming) (Sept. 19)	60.00	30.00	18.00
(39)	Eileen Bennett Whittingstall (tennis) (Sept. 26)	50.00	25.00	15.00
(42)	Kaye Don (speedboat) (Oct. 17)	50.00	25.00	15.00
(43)	(Francis Ouimet) (golf) (Oct. 24)	50.00	25.00	15.00
(47)	Johnny Allen, Frank Barnes, Guy Cantrell, Ken Strong (Nov. 14)	60.00	30.00	18.00
(48)	John Pepper Martin (Nov. 21)	80.00	40.00	24.00
(51)	Gordie Perry (football) (Dec. 12)	50.00	25.00	15.00
(53)	Lola Couture (hockey) (Dec. 26)	60.00	30.00	18.00
	1932			
(3)	(J. Landry) (skiing) (Jan. 23)	50.00	25.00	15.00
(4)	(Anton Lekang) (skiing) (Jan. 30)	50.00	25.00	15.00
(5)	(Howard Boderay) (skiing) (Feb. 6)	50.00	25.00	15.00
(21)	(Billy Bartush) (wrestling) (May 21)	60.00	30.00	18.00
(22)	Johnny Grabowski (May 28)	60.00	30.00	18.00
(23)	Charles Sullivan (June 4)	60.00	30.00	18.00
(24)	Paul De Bruyn (marathoner) (June 11)	50.00	25.00	15.00
(25)	Walter "Doc" Gautreau (June 18)	60.00	30.00	18.00
(26)	John Clancy (June 25)	60.00	30.00	18.00
(27)	Buck Walters (July 2)	75.00	37.00	22.00
(28)	Bill McAfee (July 9)	60.00	30.00	18.00
(29)	George Puccinelli (July 16)	60.00	30.00	18.00
(30)	Freddie Frams (auto racer) (July 23)	50.00	25.00	15.00
(32)	Buck Crouse (Aug. 6)	60.00	30.00	18.00
(33)	Ollie Carnegie (Aug. 13)	60.00	30.00	18.00
(34)	Leo Mangum (Aug. 20)	60.00	30.00	18.00
(35)	Pete DeGrasse (boxer) (Aug. 27)	60.00	30.00	18.00
(42)	Roy Parmelee (Nov. 19)	60.00	30.00	18.00
	(Dates of issue not confirmed)			
	Dan Howley	60.00	30.00	18.00
	Richard Lesage (canoeing)	50.00	25.00	15.00
	Stanislaus Zbysko (wrestler)	50.00	25.00	15.00
	Ernie Jarvis (rowing)	50.00	25.00	15.00

1952 Laval Dairy Provincial League

This scarce Canadian minor league issue includes only players from the Class C Provincial League, centered in Quebec. The black-and-white cards are blank-backed and measure 1-3/4" x 2-1/2". The player name, position, date and place of birth and card number is in French. Teams represented in the set are Quebec (Braves), St. Jean (Pirates), Three Rivers (independent), Drummondville (Senators), Granby (Phillies) and Ste. Hyacinthe (Philadelphia A's).

		NM	EX	VG
Complete Set (114):		1995.	995.00	595.00
Common Player:		24.00	12.00	7.25
1	Georges McQuinn	24.00	12.00	7.25
2	Cliff Statham	24.00	12.00	7.25
3	Frank Wilson	24.00	12.00	7.25
4	(Frank Neri)	24.00	12.00	7.25
5	Georges Maranda	24.00	12.00	7.25
6	Richard "Dick" Cordeiro	24.00	12.00	7.25
7	Roger McCardell	24.00	12.00	7.25
8	Joseph Janiak	24.00	12.00	7.25
9	Herbert Shankman	24.00	12.00	7.25
10	Joe Subbiondo	24.00	12.00	7.25
11	Jack Brenner	24.00	12.00	7.25
12	Donald Buchanan	24.00	12.00	7.25
13	Robert Smith	24.00	12.00	7.25
14	Raymond Lague	24.00	12.00	7.25
15	Mike Fandozzi	24.00	12.00	7.25
16	Dick Moler	24.00	12.00	7.25
17	Edward Bazydio	24.00	12.00	7.25
18	(Danny Mazurek)	24.00	12.00	7.25
19	Edwin Charles	24.00	12.00	7.25
20	Jack Nullaney	24.00	12.00	7.25
21	Bob Bolan	24.00	12.00	7.25
22	Bob Long	24.00	12.00	7.25
23	Cleo Lewright	24.00	12.00	7.25
24	Herb Taylor	24.00	12.00	7.25
25	Frankie Gaeta	24.00	12.00	7.25
26	Bill Truitt	24.00	12.00	7.25
27	Jean Prats	24.00	12.00	7.25
28	Tex Taylor	24.00	12.00	7.25
29	Ron Delbianco	24.00	12.00	7.25
30	Joe DiLorenzo	24.00	12.00	7.25
31	Johnny Paszek	24.00	12.00	7.25
32	Ken Suess	24.00	12.00	7.25
33	Harry Sims	24.00	12.00	7.25
34	William Jackson	24.00	12.00	7.25
35	Jerry Mayers	24.00	12.00	7.25
36	Gordon Maltzberger	24.00	12.00	7.25
37	Gerry Cabana	24.00	12.00	7.25
38	Gary Rutkey	24.00	12.00	7.25
39	Ken Hatcher	24.00	12.00	7.25
40	Vincent Cosenza	24.00	12.00	7.25
41	Edward Yaeger	24.00	12.00	7.25
42	Jimmy Orr	24.00	12.00	7.25
43	Johnny Di Matino	24.00	12.00	7.25
44	Lenny Wisneski	24.00	12.00	7.25
45	Pete Caniglia	24.00	12.00	7.25
46	Guy Coleman	24.00	12.00	7.25
47	Herb Fleischer	24.00	12.00	7.25
48	Charles Yahrling	24.00	12.00	7.25
49	Roger Bedard	24.00	12.00	7.25
50	Al Barillari	24.00	12.00	7.25
51	Hugh Mulcahy	24.00	12.00	7.25
52	Vincent Canepa	24.00	12.00	7.25
53	Bob Loranger	24.00	12.00	7.25
54	Georges Carpentier	24.00	12.00	7.25
55	Bill Hamilton	24.00	12.00	7.25
56	Hector Lopez	24.00	12.00	7.25
57	Joel Taylor	24.00	12.00	7.25
58	Alonzo Brathwaite	24.00	12.00	7.25
59	Carl McQuillen	24.00	12.00	7.25
60	Robert Trice	24.00	12.00	7.25
61	John Dworak	24.00	12.00	7.25
62	Al Pinkston	24.00	12.00	7.25
63	William Shannon	24.00	12.00	7.25
64	Stanley Wotychowisz	24.00	12.00	7.25
65	Roger Herbert	24.00	12.00	7.25
66	Troy Spencer	24.00	12.00	7.25
67	Johnny Rohan	24.00	12.00	7.25
68	(John Sosh)	24.00	12.00	7.25
69	Ramon Mason	24.00	12.00	7.25
70	Tom Smith	24.00	12.00	7.25
71	Douglas McBean	24.00	12.00	7.25
72	Bill Babik	24.00	12.00	7.25
73	Dante Cozzi	24.00	12.00	7.25
74	Melville Doxtater	24.00	12.00	7.25
75	William Gilray	24.00	12.00	7.25
76	Armando Diaz	24.00	12.00	7.25
77	Ackroyd Smith	24.00	12.00	7.25
78	Germain Pizarro	24.00	12.00	7.25
79	Jim Heap	24.00	12.00	7.25
80	Herbert Crompton	24.00	12.00	7.25
81	Howard Bodell	24.00	12.00	7.25
82	Andre Schreiser	24.00	12.00	7.25
83	John Wingo	24.00	12.00	7.25
84	Salvatore Arduini	24.00	12.00	7.25
85	Fred Pallito	24.00	12.00	7.25
86	Aaron Osofsky	24.00	12.00	7.25
87	Jack DiGrace	24.00	12.00	7.25
88	Alphonso Chico Girard	24.00	12.00	7.25
89	Manuel Trabous	24.00	12.00	7.25
90	Tom Barnes	24.00	12.00	7.25
91	Humberto Robinson	24.00	12.00	7.25
92	Jack Bukowatz	24.00	12.00	7.25
93	Marco Mainini	24.00	12.00	7.25
94	Claude St. Vincent	24.00	12.00	7.25
95	Fernand Brosseau	24.00	12.00	7.25
96	John Malangone	24.00	12.00	7.25
97	Pierre Nantel	24.00	12.00	7.25
98	Donald Stevens	24.00	12.00	7.25
99	Jim Prappas	24.00	12.00	7.25
100	Richard Fitzgerald	24.00	12.00	7.25
101	Yves Aubin	24.00	12.00	7.25
102	Frank Novosel	24.00	12.00	7.25
103	Tony Campos	24.00	12.00	7.25
104	Gelso Oviedo	24.00	12.00	7.25
105	Guly Becker	24.00	12.00	7.25
106	Aurelio Ala	24.00	12.00	7.25
107	Orlando Andux	24.00	12.00	7.25
108	Tom Hackett	24.00	12.00	7.25
109	Guillame Vargas	24.00	12.00	7.25
110	Fransisco Salfran	24.00	12.00	7.25
111	Jean-Marc Blais	24.00	12.00	7.25
112	Vince Pizzitola	24.00	12.00	7.25
113	John Olsen	24.00	12.00	7.25
114	Jacques Monette	24.00	12.00	7.25

1948 Los Angeles Angels team issue

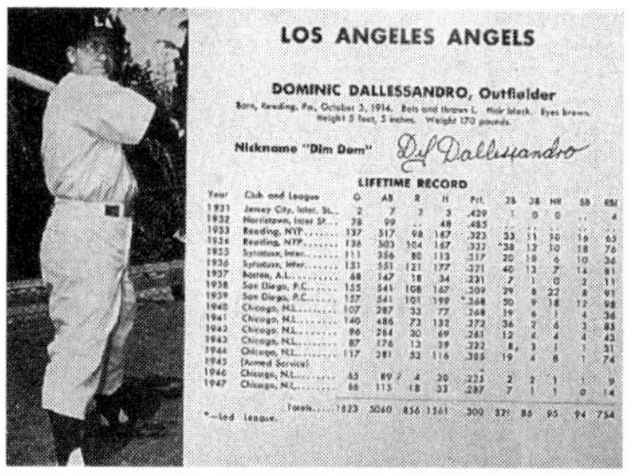

A team-issued set sold in a paper envelope for $1 at the ballpark, these cards were produced by the same firm which published the team's yearbook, Pacific Coast Sports Publishing Co., of Los Angeles. The blank-backed cards measure 6-3/4" x 4-3/4" and are printed in black-and-white on thin cardboard with a semi-gloss front surface. Cards feature a facsimile player autograph on front, along with a posed action or portrait photo and complete major and minor league stats. The cards are listed in the American Card Catalog, along with the subsequent year's issue, as W725. Many of the players on this Pacific Coast League team were former or future Chicago Cubs. The unnumbered cards are checklisted here alphabetically.

		NM	EX	VG
Complete Set (26):		300.00	150.00	90.00
Common Player:		22.00	11.00	6.50
(1)	Cliff Aberson	22.00	11.00	6.50
(2)	Red Adams	22.00	11.00	6.50
(3)	John Adkins	22.00	11.00	6.50
(4)	Lee Anthony	22.00	11.00	6.50
(5)	Russ Bauers	22.00	11.00	6.50
(6)	Ora Burnett	22.00	11.00	6.50
(7)	Donald Carlsen	22.00	11.00	6.50
(8)	Dom Dallessandro	22.00	11.00	6.50
(9)	Cecil Garriott	22.00	11.00	6.50
(10)	Paul Gillespie	22.00	11.00	6.50
(11)	Al Glossop	22.00	11.00	6.50
(12)	Tom Hafey	22.00	11.00	6.50
(13)	Don Johnson	22.00	11.00	6.50
(14)	Bill Kelly	22.00	11.00	6.50
(15)	Hal Kleine	22.00	11.00	6.50
(16)	Walt Lanfranconi	22.00	11.00	6.50
(17)	Ed Lukon	22.00	11.00	6.50
(18)	Red Lynn	22.00	11.00	6.50
(19)	Eddie Malone	22.00	11.00	6.50
(20)	Len Merullo	22.00	11.00	6.50
(21)	Ralph Novotney	22.00	11.00	6.50
(22)	John Ostrowski	22.00	11.00	6.50
(23)	John Sanford	22.00	11.00	6.50
(24)	Ed Sauer	22.00	11.00	6.50
(25)	Bill Schuster	22.00	11.00	6.50
(26)	John Warner	22.00	11.00	6.50

1949 Los Angeles Angels team issue

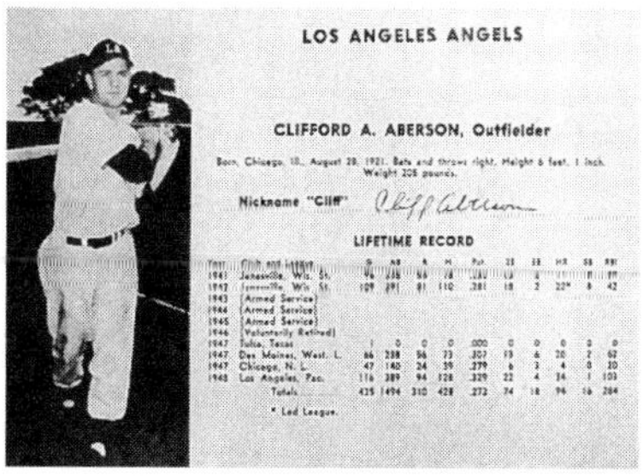

Little changed in the second year of this team issue. Cards remained at 6-3/4" x 4-3/4" in format, printed black-and-white on semi-gloss cardboard with a blank back. Many of the players (and even some of the photos) were repeated from the previous year. The unnumbered cards are checklisted here in alphabetical order.

		NM	EX	VG
Complete Set (39):		400.00	200.00	125.00
Common Player:		18.00	9.00	5.50
(1)	Cliff Aberson	18.00	9.00	5.50
(2)	Donald Alfano	18.00	9.00	5.50
(3)	Quentin Altizer	18.00	9.00	5.50
(4)	Lee Anthony	18.00	9.00	5.50
(5)	Nels Burbrink	18.00	9.00	5.50
(6)	Smoky Burgess	30.00	15.00	9.00
(7)	Don Carlsen	18.00	9.00	5.50
(8)	Joe Damato	18.00	9.00	5.50
(9)	Bill Emmerich	18.00	9.00	5.50
(10)	Ken Gables	18.00	9.00	5.50
(11)	Cecil Garriott	18.00	9.00	5.50
(12)	Al Glossop	18.00	9.00	5.50
(13)	Gordon Goldsberry	18.00	9.00	5.50
(14)	Frank Gustine	18.00	9.00	5.50
(15)	Lee Handley	18.00	9.00	5.50
(16)	Alan Ihde	18.00	9.00	5.50
(17)	Bob Kelley (announcer)	18.00	9.00	5.50
(18)	Bill Kelly	18.00	9.00	5.50
(19)	Bob Kelly	18.00	9.00	5.50
(20)	Walt Lanfranconi	18.00	9.00	5.50
(21)	Red Lynn	18.00	9.00	5.50
(22)	Clarence Maddern	18.00	9.00	5.50
(23)	Eddie Malone	18.00	9.00	5.50
(24)	Carmen Mauro	18.00	9.00	5.50
(25)	Booker McDaniels	18.00	9.00	5.50
(26)	Cal McLish	18.00	9.00	5.50
(27)	Butch Moran	18.00	9.00	5.50
(28)	Ralph Novotney	18.00	9.00	5.50
(29)	John Ostrowski	18.00	9.00	5.50
(30)	Bobby Rhawn	18.00	9.00	5.50
(31)	Bill Schuster	18.00	9.00	5.50
(32)	Pat Seerey	18.00	9.00	5.50
(33)	Bryan Stephens	18.00	9.00	5.50
(34)	Bob Sturgeon	18.00	9.00	5.50
(35)	Wayne Terwilliger	18.00	9.00	5.50
(36)	Gordon Van Dyke	18.00	9.00	5.50
(37)	John Warner	18.00	9.00	5.50
(38)	Don Watkins	18.00	9.00	5.50
(39)	Trainers, bat boys (Dickie Evans, Joe Liscio, Dave Flores,) (Billy Lund)	18.00	9.00	5.50

M

1954 MD Super Service Sacramento Solons

HANK SCHENZ
M D Super Service
16th and T Streets

This issue features only players of the Pacific Coast League Sacramento Solons. The unnumbered cards are printed in black-and-white and carry an ad for a local gas station. The borderless, blank-backed cards measure 2-1/8" x 3-3/8".

		NM	EX	VG
Complete Set (6):		400.00	200.00	120.00
Common Player:		75.00	37.00	22.00
(1)	Joe Brovia	75.00	37.00	22.00
(2)	Al Cicotte	75.00	37.00	22.00
(3)	Nippy Jones	75.00	37.00	22.00
(4)	Richie Meyers	75.00	37.00	22.00
(5)	Hank Schenz	75.00	37.00	22.00
(6)	Bud Sheeley	75.00	37.00	22.00

1963 Milwaukee Sausage Seattle Rainiers

MEL PARNELL
Rainiers

Inserted into meat packages by a Seattle sausage company, the 11 cards known in this set are all Seattle Rainiers players, several of whom had big league experience. Cards measure approximately 4-1/4"-square and are printed in blue, red and yellow. The unnumbered cards are checklisted in alphabetical order.

		NM	EX	VG
Complete Set (11):		3000.	1500.	900.00
Common Player:		300.00	150.00	90.00
(1)	Dave Hall	300.00	150.00	90.00
(2)	Bill Harrell	300.00	150.00	90.00
(3)	Pete Jernigan	300.00	150.00	90.00
(4)	Bill McLeod	300.00	150.00	90.00
(5)	Mel Parnell	350.00	175.00	105.00
(6)	Elmer Singleton	300.00	150.00	90.00
(7)	Archie Skeen	300.00	150.00	90.00
(8)	Paul Smith	300.00	150.00	90.00
(9)	Pete Smith	300.00	150.00	90.00
(10)	Bill Spanswick	300.00	150.00	90.00
(11)	George Spencer	300.00	150.00	90.00

1909 Minneapolis Tribune/ St. Paul Pioneer Press Mirrors

BEST SPORTING NEWS IN THE PIONEER PRESS
Oh, you Mike Kelly!
MANAGER MIKE

From the few players known, it is apparent these mirrors were issued in 1909 by two of the Twin Cities' daily newspapers. Each mirror is 2-1/8" diameter with a celluloid back. At center is a black-and-white player photo. All typography is in b/w, as well. A pair of concentric circles around the photo contain the player's name and a short description of his prowess. Olmstead's reads, "Unhittable in the Pinches"; Carisch's reads, "Nails 'em to the Cross Every Time". The outer circle contains an ad for the newspaper. This checklist is probably incomplete.

		NM	EX	VG
Common Player:		200.00	100.00	60.00
(1)	Fred Carisch	200.00	100.00	60.00
(2)	Michael Kelly	200.00	100.00	60.00
(3)	Fred Olmstead	200.00	100.00	60.00

1911 Mono Cigarettes (T217)

Chadbourn, Port.

As was common with many tobacco issues of the period, the T217 set - distributed on the West Coast by Mono Cigarettes - feature both baseball players and "Leading Actresses." The 23 baseball players in the Mono set are all from the Pacific Coast League. Two of the players (Delhi and Hughie Smith) are shown in two poses, resulting in a total of 25 different cards. The players are pictured in black-and-white photos on a card that measures approximately 1-1/2" x 2-5/8", the standard size of a tobacco card. The player's name and team appear at the bottom, while the back of the card carries an advertisement for Mono Cigarettes. The Mono set, which can be dated to the 1909-1911 period, is among the rarest of all tobacco cards.

		NM	EX	VG
Complete Set (25):		20000.	8000.	2500.
Common Player:		1000.	400.00	250.00
(1)	Aiken	1000.	400.00	250.00
(2)	Curtis Bernard	1000.	400.00	250.00
(3)	L. Burrell	1000.	400.00	250.00
(4)	Chadbourn	1000.	400.00	250.00
(5)	R. Couchman	1000.	400.00	250.00
(6)	Elmer Criger	1000.	400.00	250.00
(7)	Pete Daley	1000.	400.00	250.00
(8)	W. Delhi (glove at chest level)	1000.	400.00	250.00
(9)	W. Delhi (glove at shoulder level)	1000.	400.00	250.00
(10)	Bert Delmas	1000.	400.00	250.00
(11)	Ivan Howard	1000.	400.00	250.00
(12)	Kitty Knight	1000.	400.00	250.00
(13)	Gene Knapp (Krapp)	1000.	400.00	250.00
(14)	Metzger	1000.	400.00	250.00
(15)	Carl Mitze	1000.	400.00	250.00
(16)	J. O'Rourke	1000.	400.00	250.00
(17)	R. Peckinpaugh	1000.	400.00	250.00
(18)	Walter Schmidt	1000.	400.00	250.00
(19)	Hughie Smith (batting)	1000.	400.00	250.00
(20)	Hughie Smith (fielding)	1000.	400.00	250.00
(21)	Wm. Stein	1000.	400.00	250.00
(22)	Elmer Thorsen	1000.	400.00	250.00
(23)	Oscar Vitt	1000.	400.00	250.00
(24)	Clyde Wares	1000.	400.00	250.00
(25)	Geo. Wheeler	1000.	400.00	250.00

1947 Morley Studios Team Cards

Besides issuing individual player cards of the Tacoma team, Morley Studios also issued postcard-size pictures of the teams in the Class B Western International League of 1947. The 3-1/2" x 5-1/2" cards are blank-backed and carry a "Morley Studios / 1947" imprint on front.

		NM	EX	VG
Complete Set (8):		450.00	225.00	135.00
Common Player:		60.00	30.00	18.00
(1)	Bremerton Bluejackets	60.00	30.00	18.00
(2)	Salem Senators	60.00	30.00	18.00
(3)	Spokane Indians	60.00	30.00	18.00
(4)	Tacoma Tigers	60.00	30.00	18.00
(5)	Vancouver Capilanos	60.00	30.00	18.00
(6)	Victoria Athletics	60.00	30.00	18.00
(7)	Yakima Stars	60.00	30.00	18.00
(8)	Wenatchee Chiefs	60.00	30.00	18.00

1947 Morley Studios Tacoma Tigers

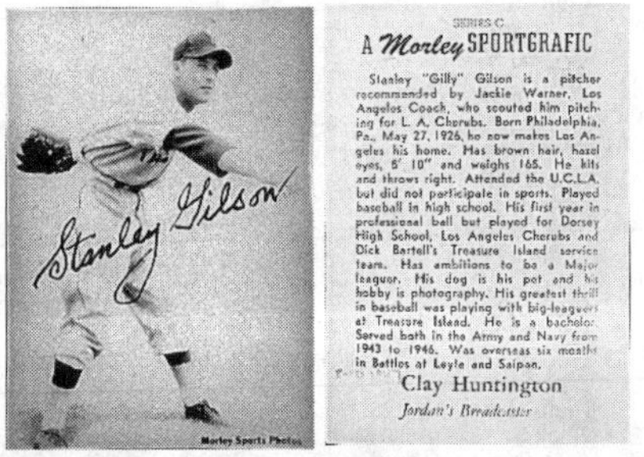
Stanley Gilson
Morley Sports Photos
SERIES C
A Morley SPORTGRAFIC
Stanley "Gilly" Gilson is a pitcher recommended by Jackie Warner, Los Angeles Coach, who scouted him pitching for L. A. Cherubs. Born Philadelphia, Pa., May 27, 1926, he now makes Los Angeles his home. Has brown hair, hazel eyes, 5' 10" and weighs 165. He hits and throws right. Attended the U.C.L.A. but did not participate in sports. Played baseball in high school. His first year in professional ball but played for Dorsey High School, Los Angeles Cherubs and Dick Bartell's Treasure Island service team. Has ambitions to be a Major leaguer. His dog is his pet and his hobby is photography. His greatest thrill in baseball was playing with big-leaguers at Treasure Island. He is a bachelor. Served both in the Army and Navy from 1943 to 1946. Was overseas six months in Battles at Leyte and Saipan.
Clay Huntington
Jordan's Broadcaster

This set of Tacoma Tigers (Western International League) features borderless black-and-white posed action photos with a facsimile autograph on front. A "Morley Sports Photos" or "Morley Studios" credit line appears at the bottom. Backs of the first seven cards are blank, while the others feature player biographies credited to "Jordan's (bread sponsor) Broadcaster" Clay Huntington and a Series A through F designation (though some cards lack the letter code). The unnumbered cards measure 2-1/2" x 3-1/2".

		NM	EX	VG
Complete Set (28):		2200.	1100.	650.00
Common Player:		80.00	40.00	24.00
	Blank-backed			
(1)	Hank Bartolomei	80.00	40.00	24.00
(2)	Rod Belcher (broadcaster)	80.00	40.00	24.00
(3)	Tip Berg (trainer)	80.00	40.00	24.00
(4)	Gene Clough	80.00	40.00	24.00
(5)	Clay Huntington (broadcaster)	80.00	40.00	24.00
(6)	Donald Mooney (bat boy)	80.00	40.00	24.00
(7)	Buck Tinsley	80.00	40.00	24.00
	Series A			
(8)	Richard A. Greco	80.00	40.00	24.00
(9)	Cy Greenlaw	80.00	40.00	24.00
(10)	Bob Joratz	80.00	40.00	24.00
(11)	Earl Kuper	80.00	40.00	24.00
	Series B			
(12)	(Neil Clifford)	80.00	40.00	24.00
(13)	Red Harvel	80.00	40.00	24.00
(14)	Julian Morgan	80.00	40.00	24.00
(15)	Pete Tedeschi	80.00	40.00	24.00

	Series C			
(16)	Stanley Gilson	80.00	40.00	24.00
(17)	Harry Nygard	80.00	40.00	24.00
(18)	Cleve Ramsey	80.00	40.00	24.00
(19)	Pete Sabutis	80.00	40.00	24.00
	Series D			
(20)	Mitch Chetkovich	80.00	40.00	24.00
(21)	Leroy Paton	80.00	40.00	24.00
(22)	Carl Shaply	80.00	40.00	24.00
(23)	Glenn Stetter	80.00	40.00	24.00
	Series E			
(24)	Bob Hedington	80.00	40.00	24.00
(25)	Ed Keehan	80.00	40.00	24.00
(26)	Gordon Walden	80.00	40.00	24.00
	Series F			
(27)	Maury Donovan	80.00	40.00	24.00
(28)	Guy Miller	80.00	40.00	24.00

1952 Mother's Cookies

This is one of the most popular regional minor league sets ever issued. Cards of Pacific Coast League players were included in packages of cookies. Distribution was limited to the West Coast. The 64 cards feature full color photos on a colored background, with player name and team. The cards measure 2-13/16" x 3-1/2", though the cards' rounded corners cause some variation in listed size. Card backs feature a very brief player statistic, card numbers and an offer for purchasing postage stamps. Five cards (11, 16, 29, 37 and 43) are considered scarce, while card #4 (Chuck Connors) is the most popular.

		NM	EX	VG
Complete Set (64):		2495.	1250.	750.00
Common Player:		40.00	20.00	12.00
1a	Johnny Lindell (regular back)	55.00	27.00	16.50
1b	Johnny Lindell ('52 Hollywood schedule on back)	55.00	27.00	16.50
2	Jim Davis	40.00	20.00	12.00
3	Al Gettle (Gettel)	40.00	20.00	12.00
4	Chuck Connors	350.00	175.00	105.00
5	Joe Grace	40.00	20.00	12.00
6	Eddie Basinski	40.00	20.00	12.00
7a	Gene Handley (regular back)	40.00	20.00	12.00
7b	Gene Handley (schedule back)	40.00	20.00	12.00
8	Walt Judnich	40.00	20.00	12.00
9	Jim Marshall	40.00	20.00	12.00
10	Max West	40.00	20.00	12.00
11	Bill MacCawley	80.00	40.00	24.00
12	Moreno Peiretti	40.00	20.00	12.00
13a	Fred Haney (regular back)	48.00	24.00	14.50
13b	Fred Haney ('52 Hollywood schedule on back)	48.00	24.00	14.50
14	Earl Johnson	40.00	20.00	12.00
15	Dave Dahle	40.00	20.00	12.00
16	Bob Talbot	80.00	40.00	24.00
17	Smokey Singleton	40.00	20.00	12.00
18	Frank Austin	40.00	20.00	12.00
19	Joe Gordon	48.00	24.00	14.50
20	Joe Marty	40.00	20.00	12.00
21	Bob Gillespie	40.00	20.00	12.00
22	Red Embree	40.00	20.00	12.00
23a	Lefty Olsen (brown belt)	40.00	20.00	12.00
23b	Lefty Olsen (black belt)	40.00	20.00	12.00
24a	Whitey Wietelmann (large photo, much of bat missing)	40.00	20.00	12.00
24b	Whitey Wietelmann (small photo, more bat shows)	40.00	20.00	12.00
25	Frank O'Doul	60.00	30.00	18.00
26	Memo Luna	40.00	20.00	12.00
27	John Davis	40.00	20.00	12.00
28	Dick Faber	40.00	20.00	12.00
29	Buddy Peterson	200.00	100.00	60.00
30	Hank Schenz	40.00	20.00	12.00
31	Tookie Gilbert	40.00	20.00	12.00
32	Mel Ott	100.00	50.00	30.00
33	Sam Chapman	40.00	20.00	12.00
34a	John Ragni (outfielder)	40.00	20.00	12.00
34b	John Ragni (pitcher)	40.00	20.00	12.00
35	Dick Cole	40.00	20.00	12.00
36	Tom Saffell	40.00	20.00	12.00
37	Roy Welmaker	80.00	40.00	24.00
38	Lou Stringer	40.00	20.00	12.00
39a	Chuck Stevens (team on back Hollywood)	40.00	20.00	12.00
39b	Chuck Stevens (team on back Seattle)	40.00	20.00	12.00
39c	Chuck Stevens (no team on back)	40.00	20.00	12.00
40	Artie Wilson	48.00	24.00	14.50
41	Charlie Schanz	40.00	20.00	12.00
42	Al Lyons	40.00	20.00	12.00
43	Joe Erautt	200.00	100.00	60.00
44	Clarence Maddern	40.00	20.00	12.00
45	Gene Baker	40.00	20.00	12.00
46	Tom Heath	40.00	20.00	12.00
47	Al Lien	40.00	20.00	12.00
48	Bill Reeder	40.00	20.00	12.00
49	Bob Thurman	40.00	20.00	12.00
50	Ray Orteig	40.00	20.00	12.00
51	Joe Brovia	40.00	20.00	12.00
52	Jim Russell	40.00	20.00	12.00
53	Fred Sanford	40.00	20.00	12.00
54	Jim Gladd	40.00	20.00	12.00
55	Clay Hopper	40.00	20.00	12.00
56	Bill Glynn	40.00	20.00	12.00
57	Mike McCormick	40.00	20.00	12.00
58	Richie Myers	40.00	20.00	12.00
59	Vinnie Smith	40.00	20.00	12.00
60a	Stan Hack (brown belt)	55.00	27.00	16.50
60b	Stan Hack (black belt)	55.00	27.00	16.50
61	Bob Spicer	40.00	20.00	12.00
62	Jack Hollis	40.00	20.00	12.00
63	Ed Chandler	40.00	20.00	12.00
64	Bill Moisan	55.00	27.00	16.50

1953 Mother's Cookies

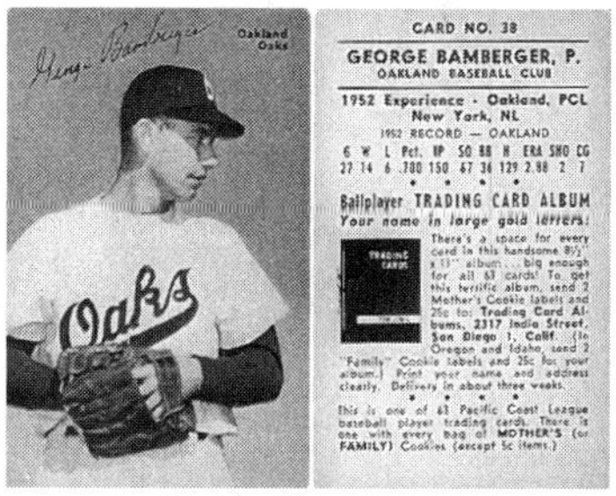

The 1953 Mother's Cookies cards are again 2-3/16" x 3-1/2", with rounded corners. There are 63 players from Pacific Coast League teams included. The full-color fronts have facsimile autographs rather than printed player names, and card backs offer a trading card album. Cards are generally more plentiful than in the 1952 set, with 11 of the cards apparently double printed.

		NM	EX	VG
Complete Set (63):		1100.	550.00	325.00
Common Player:		28.00	14.00	8.50
1	Lee Winter	35.00	17.50	10.50
2	Joe Ostrowski	28.00	14.00	8.50
3	Will Ramsdell	28.00	14.00	8.50
4	Bobby Bragan	35.00	17.50	10.50
5	Fletcher Robbe	28.00	14.00	8.50
6	Aaron Robinson	28.00	14.00	8.50
7	Augie Galan	28.00	14.00	8.50
8	Buddy Peterson	28.00	14.00	8.50
9	Frank Lefty O'Doul	45.00	22.00	13.50
10	Walt Pocekay	28.00	14.00	8.50
11	Nini Tornay	28.00	14.00	8.50
12	Jim Moran	28.00	14.00	8.50
13	George Schmees	28.00	14.00	8.50
14	Al Widmar	28.00	14.00	8.50
15	Ritchie Myers	28.00	14.00	8.50
16	Bill Howerton	28.00	14.00	8.50
17	Chuck Stevens	28.00	14.00	8.50
18	Joe Brovia	28.00	14.00	8.50
19	Max West	28.00	14.00	8.50
20	Eddie Malone	28.00	14.00	8.50
21	Gene Handley	28.00	14.00	8.50
22	William D. McCawley	28.00	14.00	8.50
23	Bill Sweeney	28.00	14.00	8.50
24	Tom Alston	28.00	14.00	8.50
25	George Vico	28.00	14.00	8.50
26	Hank Arft	28.00	14.00	8.50
27	Al Benton	28.00	14.00	8.50
28	"Pete" Milne	28.00	14.00	8.50
29	Jim Gladd	28.00	14.00	8.50
30	Earl Rapp	28.00	14.00	8.50
31	Ray Orteig	28.00	14.00	8.50
32	Eddie Basinski	28.00	14.00	8.50
33	Reno Cheso	28.00	14.00	8.50
34	Clarence Maddern	28.00	14.00	8.50
35	Marino Pieretti	28.00	14.00	8.50
36	Bill Raimondi	28.00	14.00	8.50
37	Frank Kelleher	28.00	14.00	8.50
38	George Bamberger	35.00	17.50	10.50
39	Dick Smith	28.00	14.00	8.50
40	Charley Schanz	28.00	14.00	8.50
41	John Van Cuyk	28.00	14.00	8.50
42	Lloyd Hittle	28.00	14.00	8.50
43	Tommy Heath	28.00	14.00	8.50
44	Frank Kalin	28.00	14.00	8.50
45	Jack Tobin	28.00	14.00	8.50
46	Jim Davis	28.00	14.00	8.50
47	Claude Christie	28.00	14.00	8.50
48	Elvin Tappe	28.00	14.00	8.50
49	Stan Hack	35.00	17.50	10.50
50	Fred Richards	28.00	14.00	8.50
51	Clay Hopper	28.00	14.00	8.50
52	Roy Welmaker	28.00	14.00	8.50
53	Red Adams	28.00	14.00	8.50
54	Piper Davis	28.00	14.00	8.50
55	Spider Jorgensen	28.00	14.00	8.50
56	Lee Walls	28.00	14.00	8.50
57	Jack Phillips	28.00	14.00	8.50
58	Red Lynn	28.00	14.00	8.50
59	Eddie Beckman	28.00	14.00	8.50
60	Gene Desautels	28.00	14.00	8.50
61	Bob Dillinger	28.00	14.00	8.50
62	Al Federoff	75.00	37.00	22.00
63	Bill Boemler	28.00	14.00	8.50

1920 Mrs. Sherlock's Bread Pins

Members of the Toledo Mud Hens of the American Association are featured on this set of pins sponsored by Mrs. Sherlock's Bread. The 7/8" celluloid pins have a player portrait in black-and-white at center, with his name and position indicated below. At top, in either red or black type is, "Mrs. Sherlock's Home Made Bread". The unnumbered pins are checklisted here alphabetically.

		NM	EX	VG
Complete Set (19):		900.00	450.00	275.00
Common Player:		60.00	30.00	18.00
(1)	Brady	60.00	30.00	18.00
(2)	Roger Bresnahan	90.00	45.00	27.00
(3)	Jean Dubuc	60.00	30.00	18.00
(4)	Dyer	60.00	30.00	18.00
(5)	Fox	60.00	30.00	18.00
(6)	Ham Hyatt	60.00	30.00	18.00
(7)	Jones	60.00	30.00	18.00
(8)	Joe Kelly	60.00	30.00	18.00
(9)	M. Kelly	60.00	30.00	18.00
(10)	Art Kores	60.00	30.00	18.00
(11)	McColl	60.00	30.00	18.00
(12)	Norm McNeill (McNeil)	60.00	30.00	18.00
(13)	Middleton	60.00	30.00	18.00
(14)	Murphy	60.00	30.00	18.00
(15)	Nelson	60.00	30.00	18.00
(16)	Dutch Stryker	60.00	30.00	18.00
(17)	Thompson	60.00	30.00	18.00
(18)	Al Wickland	60.00	30.00	18.00
(19)	Joe Wilhoit	60.00	30.00	18.00

1922 Mrs. Sherlock's Bread Pins

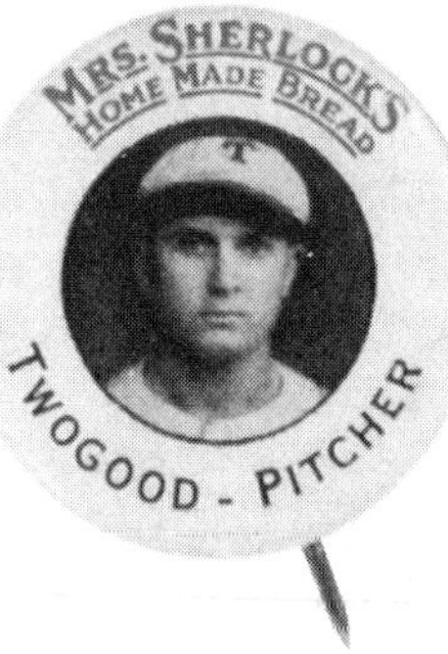

Members of the Toledo Mud Hens of the American Association are featured on this set of pins sponsored by Mrs. Sherlock's Bread. The 5/8"celluloid pins have a player portrait in brown or green at center, with his name and position indicated below. At top, in either brown or green type is, "Eat Mrs. Sherlock's Bread". The pins are numbered at lower-left.

		NM	EX	VG
Complete Set (21):		1000.	500.00	300.00
Common Player:		60.00	30.00	18.00
1	Roger Bresnahan	90.00	45.00	27.00
2	Brad Kocher	60.00	30.00	18.00

		NM	EX	VG
3	Hill	60.00	30.00	18.00
4	Huber	60.00	30.00	18.00
5	Doc Ayers	60.00	30.00	18.00
6	Parks	60.00	30.00	18.00
7	Giard	60.00	30.00	18.00
8	Grimes	60.00	30.00	18.00
9	McCullough	60.00	30.00	18.00
10	Shoup	60.00	30.00	18.00
11	Al Wickland	60.00	30.00	18.00
12	Baker	60.00	30.00	18.00
13	Schauffle	60.00	30.00	18.00
14	Wright	60.00	30.00	18.00
15	Lamar	60.00	30.00	18.00
16	Sallee	60.00	30.00	18.00
17	Fred Luderus	60.00	30.00	18.00
18	Walgomat	60.00	30.00	18.00
19	Ed Konetchy	60.00	30.00	18.00
20	O'Neill	60.00	30.00	18.00
21	Hugh Bedient	60.00	30.00	18.00

1933 Mrs. Sherlock's Bread Pins

Members of the Toledo Mud Hens of the American Association are featured on this set of pins sponsored by Mrs. Sherlock's Bread. The 7/8" celluloid pins have a player portrait in black-and-white at center, with his name and position indicated below. At top, in red type, is "Mrs. Sherlock's Home Made Bread" in two lines. The unnumbered pins are checklisted here alphabetically.

		NM	EX	VG
Complete Set (18):		750.00	375.00	225.00
Common Player:		50.00	25.00	15.00
(1)	LeRoy Bachman	50.00	25.00	15.00
(2)	George Detore	50.00	25.00	15.00
(3)	Frank Doljack	50.00	25.00	15.00
(4)	Milt Galatzer	50.00	25.00	15.00
(5)	Walter Henline	50.00	25.00	15.00
(6)	Roxie Lawson	50.00	25.00	15.00
(7)	Thornton Lee	50.00	25.00	15.00
(8)	Ed Montague	50.00	25.00	15.00
(9)	Steve O'Neill	50.00	25.00	15.00
(10)	Monte Pearson	50.00	25.00	15.00
(11)	Bob Reis	50.00	25.00	15.00
(12)	Scott	50.00	25.00	15.00
(13)	Bill Sweeney	50.00	25.00	15.00
(14)	Hal Trosky	50.00	25.00	15.00
(15)	Pete Turgeon	50.00	25.00	15.00
(16)	Forrest Twogood	50.00	25.00	15.00
(17)	Max West	50.00	25.00	15.00
(18)	Ralph Winegarner	50.00	25.00	15.00

N

1960 National Bank of Washington Tacoma Giants

These 3" x 5" unnumbered cards have color photos on front and are usually found with black-and-white backs with the bank's advertising. Uncut sheets of the cards were sold at Cheney Stadium in Tacoma either blank-backed or with a message from the Tacoma Athletic Commission. Only members of the Pacific Coast League Tacoma Giants are included in the set. The set contains the first card issued of Hall of Fame pitcher Juan Marichal. Unfortunately, fellow Hall of Famer Willie McCovey who played in 17 games for Tacoma in 1960 is not included in the set.

		NM	EX	VG
Complete Set (21):		900.00	450.00	275.00
Common Player:		25.00	12.50	7.50
(1)	Matty Alou	75.00	37.00	22.00
(2)	Ossie Alvarez	25.00	12.50	7.50
(3)	Don Choate	25.00	12.50	7.50
(4)	Red Davis	25.00	12.50	7.50
(5)	Bob Farley	25.00	12.50	7.50
(6)	Eddie Fisher	25.00	12.50	7.50
(7)	Tom Haller	25.00	12.50	7.50
(8)	Sherman Jones	25.00	12.50	7.50
(9)	Juan Marichal	400.00	200.00	120.00
(10)	Ray Monzant	25.00	12.50	7.50
(11)	Danny O'Connell	25.00	12.50	7.50
(12)	Jose Pagan	25.00	12.50	7.50
(13)	Bob Perry	25.00	12.50	7.50
(14)	Dick Phillips	25.00	12.50	7.50
(15)	Bobby Prescott	25.00	12.50	7.50
(16)	Marshall Renfroe	25.00	12.50	7.50
(17)	Frank Reveira	25.00	12.50	7.50
(18)	Dusty Rhodes	30.00	15.00	9.00
(19)	Sal Taormina	25.00	12.50	7.50
(20)	Verle Tiefenthaler	25.00	12.50	7.50
(21)	Dom Zanni	25.00	12.50	7.50

1961 National Bank of Washington Tacoma Giants

These 3" x 4" cards feature borderless sepia photos on the front. Backs have a sponsor's ad and a few player stats printed in dark blue. The unnumbered cards are checklisted here in alphabetical order.

		NM	EX	VG
Complete Set (21):		600.00	300.00	180.00
Common Player:		25.00	12.50	7.50
(1)	Rafael Alomar	40.00	20.00	12.00
(2)	Ernie Bowman	25.00	12.50	7.50
(3)	Bud Byerly	25.00	12.50	7.50
(4)	Ray Daviault	25.00	12.50	7.50
(5)	Red Davis	25.00	12.50	7.50
(6)	Bob Farley	25.00	12.50	7.50
(7)	Gil Garrido	25.00	12.50	7.50
(8)	John Goetz	25.00	12.50	7.50
(9)	Bill Hain	25.00	12.50	7.50
(10)	Ronald Herbel	25.00	12.50	7.50
(11)	Lynn Lovenguth	25.00	12.50	7.50
(12)	Georges H. Maranda	25.00	12.50	7.50
(13)	Manuel Mota	90.00	45.00	27.00
(14)	John Orsino	25.00	12.50	7.50
(15)	Bob Perry	25.00	12.50	7.50
(16)	Gaylord Perry	150.00	75.00	45.00
(17)	Dick Phillips	25.00	12.50	7.50
(18)	Frank Reveira	25.00	12.50	7.50
(19)	Dusty Rhodes	30.00	15.00	9.00
(20)	Verle Tiefenthaler	25.00	12.50	7.50
(21)	Dom Zanni	25.00	12.50	7.50

1907 Newark Evening World Supplements

The Newark Sailors of the Class A Eastern League are featured in this set of supplements from a local newspaper. The 7-1/2" x 10-15/16" pieces are printed in either sepia or black-and-white. An ornate border surrounds a player pose on a plain background. In a box beneath is player identification. Backs are blank. The unnumbered supplements are checklisted here in alphabetical order, though the list may not yet be complete.

		NM	EX	VG
Common Player:		400.00	200.00	120.00
(1)	William Carrick	400.00	200.00	120.00
(2)	James Cockman	400.00	200.00	120.00
(3)	Clyde Engle	400.00	200.00	120.00
(4)	James Jones	400.00	200.00	120.00
(5)	Paul Krichell	400.00	200.00	120.00
(6)	Henry LaBelle	400.00	200.00	120.00
(7)	William Mahling	400.00	200.00	120.00
(8)	Chas. McCafferty	400.00	200.00	120.00
(9)	Thomas McCarthy	400.00	200.00	120.00
(10)	James Mullen (Mullin)	400.00	200.00	120.00
(11)	Al Pardee	400.00	200.00	120.00
(12)	Bayard Sharpe	400.00	200.00	120.00
(13)	John E. Shea	400.00	200.00	120.00
(14)	Oscar Stanage	400.00	200.00	120.00
(15)	Elmer Zacher	400.00	200.00	120.00

O

1909 Obak (T212)

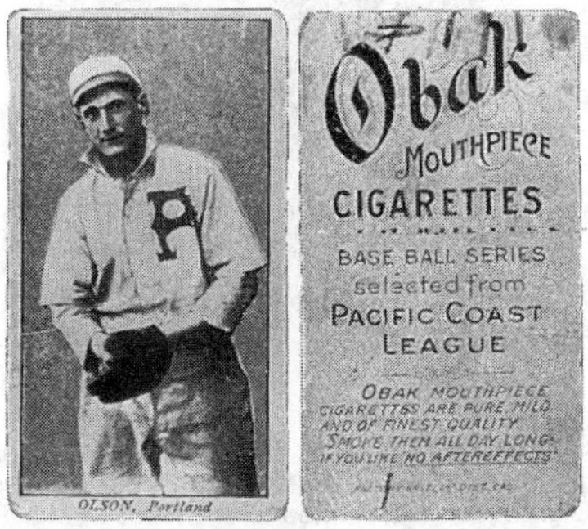

Collectors of early Pacific Coast League memorabilia consider the Obak Cigarette cards to be among the most significant of all the 20th Century minor league tobacco issues. Produced annually from 1909 to 1911, the Obak cards were actually three separate and distinct sets, but because they were all grouped together under a single T212 designation in the American Card Catalog, they are generally collected that way today. The Obak sets are closely related in style to the more popular T206 "White Border" set issued over the same three-year period, and, in fact, were produced by the California branch of the same American Tobacco Company conglomerate. The Obaks are the standard tobacco card size, 1-1/2" x 2-5/8" and feature a colored lithograph, along with the player's name and team, on the front of the card. The year of issue can easily be determined by examing the back. The 1909 issue has blue printing with the name "Obak" appearing in an "Old English" type style; for 1910 the type face was changed to straight block letters; and in 1911 the backs were printed in red and included a brief biography and player statistics. There are 269 different players in the three issues, but, because many of the subjects appeared in more than one year, Obak collectors generally consider the set complete at 426 different cards. The 1909 edition featured only teams from the Pacific Coast League, while the 1910 and 1911 sets were expanded to also include players from the Northwestern League. The Obak sets offer advanced collectors a challenging number of variations, and they have additional appeal because about 40 percent of the checklisted players had Major League experience.

		NM	EX	VG
Complete Set (75):		7150.	2850.	1775.
Common Player:		110.00	44.00	27.00
(1)	Baum	110.00	44.00	27.00
(2)	Bernard	110.00	44.00	27.00
(3)	Berry	110.00	44.00	27.00
(4)	Bodie	110.00	44.00	27.00
(5)	Boyce	110.00	44.00	27.00
(6)	Brackenridge	110.00	44.00	27.00
(7)	N. Brashear	110.00	44.00	27.00
(8)	Breen	110.00	44.00	27.00
(9)	Brown	110.00	44.00	27.00
(10)	D. Brown	110.00	44.00	27.00
(11)	Browning	110.00	44.00	27.00
(12)	Byrnes	110.00	44.00	27.00
(13)	Cameron	110.00	44.00	27.00
(14)	Carroll	110.00	44.00	27.00
(15)	Carson	110.00	44.00	27.00
(16)	Christian	110.00	44.00	27.00
(17)	Coy	110.00	44.00	27.00
(18)	Delmas	110.00	44.00	27.00
(19)	Dillon	110.00	44.00	27.00
(20)	Eagan	110.00	44.00	27.00
(21)	Easterly (Eastley)	110.00	44.00	27.00
(22)	Flannagan	110.00	44.00	27.00
(23)	Fisher	110.00	44.00	27.00

(24)	Fitzgerald	110.00	44.00	27.00
(25)	Gandil	750.00	300.00	187.00
(26)	Garrett	110.00	44.00	27.00
(27)	Graham	110.00	44.00	27.00
(28)	Graney	110.00	44.00	27.00
(29)	Griffin	110.00	44.00	27.00
(30)	Guyn	110.00	44.00	27.00
(31)	Haley	110.00	44.00	27.00
(32)	Harkins	110.00	44.00	27.00
(33)	Henley	110.00	44.00	27.00
(34)	Hitt	110.00	44.00	27.00
(35)	Hogan	110.00	44.00	27.00
(36)	W. Hogan	110.00	44.00	27.00
(37)	Howard	110.00	44.00	27.00
(38)	Howse	110.00	44.00	27.00
(39)	Jansing	110.00	44.00	27.00
(40)	LaLonge	110.00	44.00	27.00
(41)	C. Lewis	110.00	44.00	27.00
(42)	D. Lewis	110.00	44.00	27.00
(43)	J. Lewis	110.00	44.00	27.00
(44)	Martinez	110.00	44.00	27.00
(45)	McArdle	110.00	44.00	27.00
(46)	McCredie	110.00	44.00	27.00
(47)	McKune	110.00	44.00	27.00
(48)	Melchoir	110.00	44.00	27.00
(49)	Mohler	110.00	44.00	27.00
(50)	Mott	110.00	44.00	27.00
(51)	Mundorff	110.00	44.00	27.00
(52)	Murphy	110.00	44.00	27.00
(53)	Nagle	110.00	44.00	27.00
(54)	Nelson	110.00	44.00	27.00
(55)	Olson	110.00	44.00	27.00
(56)	Ornsdorff	110.00	44.00	27.00
(57)	Ort	110.00	44.00	27.00
(58)	Ragan	110.00	44.00	27.00
(59)	Raymer	110.00	44.00	27.00
(60)	Raymond	110.00	44.00	27.00
(61)	Reidy	110.00	44.00	27.00
(62)	Ryan	110.00	44.00	27.00
(63)	Shinn	110.00	44.00	27.00
(64)	Smith	110.00	44.00	27.00
(65)	Speas	110.00	44.00	27.00
(66)	Stoval (Stovall)	110.00	44.00	27.00
(67)	Tennant	110.00	44.00	27.00
(68)	Whalen	110.00	44.00	27.00
(69)	Wheeler	110.00	44.00	27.00
(70)	Wiggs	110.00	44.00	27.00
(71)	Willett	110.00	44.00	27.00
(72)	J. Williams	110.00	44.00	27.00
(73)	R. Williams	110.00	44.00	27.00
(74)	Willis	110.00	44.00	27.00
(75)	Zeider	110.00	44.00	27.00

1910 Obak (T212)

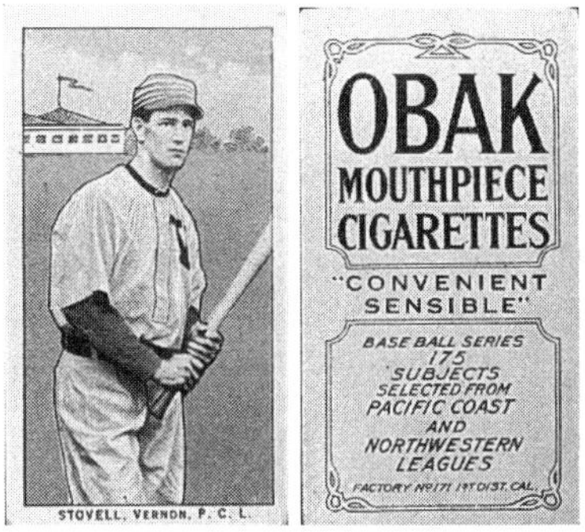

		NM	EX	VG
Complete Set (175):		10625.	4250.	2650.
Common Player:		75.00	30.00	18.50
(1)	Agnew	75.00	30.00	18.50
(2)	Akin	75.00	30.00	18.50
(3)	Ames	75.00	30.00	18.50
(4)	Annis	75.00	30.00	18.50
(5a)	Armbuster (Armbruster) ("150 subjects" back)	75.00	30.00	18.50
(5b)	Armbuster (Armbruster) ("175 subjects" back)	75.00	30.00	18.50
(6)	Baker	75.00	30.00	18.50
(7)	Bassey	75.00	30.00	18.50
(8)	Baum	75.00	30.00	18.50
(9)	Beall	75.00	30.00	18.50
(10)	Bennett	75.00	30.00	18.50
(11)	Bernard	75.00	30.00	18.50
(12a)	Berry ("150 subjects" back)	75.00	30.00	18.50
(12b)	Berry ("175 subjects" back)	75.00	30.00	18.50
(13)	Blankenship	75.00	30.00	18.50
(14)	Boardman	75.00	30.00	18.50
(15)	Bodie	75.00	30.00	18.50
(16)	Bonner	75.00	30.00	18.50
(17a)	Brackenridge ("150 subjects" back)	75.00	30.00	18.50
(17b)	Brackenridge ("175 subjects" back)	75.00	30.00	18.50
(18a)	N. Brashear ("150 subjects" back)	75.00	30.00	18.50
(18b)	N. Brashear ("175 subjects" back)	75.00	30.00	18.50
(19)	R. Brashear	75.00	30.00	18.50
(20)	Breen	75.00	30.00	18.50
(21a)	Briggs ("150 subjects" back)	75.00	30.00	18.50
(21b)	Briggs ("175 subjects" back)	75.00	30.00	18.50
(22)	Brinker	75.00	30.00	18.50
(23)	Briswalter	75.00	30.00	18.50
(24)	Brooks	75.00	30.00	18.50
(25)	Brown (Sacramento)	75.00	30.00	18.50
(26)	Brown (Vernon)	75.00	30.00	18.50
(27)	D. Brown	75.00	30.00	18.50
(28)	Browning	75.00	30.00	18.50
(29)	Burrell	75.00	30.00	18.50
(29.5)	Byrd	75.00	30.00	18.50
(30)	Byrnes	75.00	30.00	18.50
(31a)	Cameron ("150 subjects" back)	75.00	30.00	18.50
(31b)	Cameron ("175 subjects" back)	75.00	30.00	18.50
(32)	Capren (Capron)	75.00	30.00	18.50
(33)	Carlisle	75.00	30.00	18.50
(34)	Carroll	75.00	30.00	18.50
(35)	Cartwright	75.00	30.00	18.50
(36)	Casey	75.00	30.00	18.50
(37)	Caslleton (Castleton)	75.00	30.00	18.50
(38)	Chenault	75.00	30.00	18.50
(39)	Christian	75.00	30.00	18.50
(40)	Coleman	75.00	30.00	18.50
(41)	Cooney	75.00	30.00	18.50
(42a)	Coy ("150 subjects" back)	75.00	30.00	18.50
(42b)	Coy ("175 subjects" back)	75.00	30.00	18.50
(43a)	Criger ("150 subjects" back)	75.00	30.00	18.50
(43b)	Criger ("175 subjects" back)	75.00	30.00	18.50
(44)	Custer	75.00	30.00	18.50
(45)	Cutshaw	75.00	30.00	18.50
(46)	Daley	75.00	30.00	18.50
(47a)	Danzig ("150 subjects" back)	75.00	30.00	18.50
(47b)	Danzig ("175 subjects" back)	75.00	30.00	18.50
(48)	Daringer	75.00	30.00	18.50
(49)	Davis	75.00	30.00	18.50
(50)	Delhi	75.00	30.00	18.50
(51)	Delmas	75.00	30.00	18.50
(52a)	Dillon ("150 subjects" back)	75.00	30.00	18.50
(52b)	Dillon ("175 subjects" back)	75.00	30.00	18.50
(53)	Dretchko	75.00	30.00	18.50
(54)	Eastley	75.00	30.00	18.50
(55)	Erickson	75.00	30.00	18.50
(56)	Flannagan	75.00	30.00	18.50
(57)	Fisher (Portland)	75.00	30.00	18.50
(58a)	Fisher (Vernon, "150 subjects" back)	75.00	30.00	18.50
(58b)	Fisher (Vernon, "175 subjects" back)	75.00	30.00	18.50
(59)	Fitzgerald	75.00	30.00	18.50
(60)	Flood	75.00	30.00	18.50
(61)	Fournier	75.00	30.00	18.50
(62)	Frisk	75.00	30.00	18.50
(63)	Gaddy	75.00	30.00	18.50
(64)	Gardner	75.00	30.00	18.50
(65)	Garrett	75.00	30.00	18.50
(66)	Greggs (Gregg)	75.00	30.00	18.50
(67a)	Griffin ("150 subjects" back)	75.00	30.00	18.50
(67b)	Griffin ("175 subjects" back)	75.00	30.00	18.50
(68)	Gurney	75.00	30.00	18.50
(69)	Hall (Seattle)	75.00	30.00	18.50
(70)	Hall (Tacoma)	75.00	30.00	18.50
(71)	Harkins	75.00	30.00	18.50
(72)	Hartman	75.00	30.00	18.50
(73)	Hendrix	75.00	30.00	18.50
(74a)	Henley ("150 subjects" back)	75.00	30.00	18.50
(74b)	Henley ("175 subjects" back)	75.00	30.00	18.50
(75)	Hensling	75.00	30.00	18.50
(76)	Hetling	75.00	30.00	18.50
(77)	Hickey	75.00	30.00	18.50
(78a)	Hiester ("150 subjects" back)	75.00	30.00	18.50
(78b)	Hiester ("175 subjects" back)	75.00	30.00	18.50
(79)	Hitt	75.00	30.00	18.50
(80)	Hogan (Oakland)	75.00	30.00	18.50
(81a)	Hogan (Vernon, "150 subjects" back)	75.00	30.00	18.50
(81b)	Hogan (Vernon, "175 subjects" back)	75.00	30.00	18.50
(82)	Hollis	75.00	30.00	18.50
(83)	Holm	75.00	30.00	18.50
(84a)	Howard ("150 subjects" back)	75.00	30.00	18.50
(84b)	Howard ("175 subjects" back)	75.00	30.00	18.50
(85)	Hunt	75.00	30.00	18.50
(86)	James	75.00	30.00	18.50
(87)	Jansing	75.00	30.00	18.50
(88)	Jensen	75.00	30.00	18.50
(89)	Johnston	75.00	30.00	18.50
(90)	Keener	75.00	30.00	18.50
(91)	Killilay	75.00	30.00	18.50
(92)	Kippert	75.00	30.00	18.50
(93)	Klein	75.00	30.00	18.50
(94a)	Krapp ("150 subjects" back)	75.00	30.00	18.50
(94b)	Krapp ("175 subjects" back)	75.00	30.00	18.50
(95)	Kusel	75.00	30.00	18.50
(96a)	LaLonge ("150 subjects" back)	75.00	30.00	18.50
(96b)	LaLonge ("175 subjects" back)	75.00	30.00	18.50
(97)	Lewis	75.00	30.00	18.50
(98)	J. Lewis	75.00	30.00	18.50
(99)	Lindsay	75.00	30.00	18.50
(100)	Lively	75.00	30.00	18.50
(101)	Lynch	75.00	30.00	18.50
(102a)	Manush ("150 subjects" back)	75.00	30.00	18.50
(102b)	Manush ("175 subjects" back)	75.00	30.00	18.50
(103)	Martinke	75.00	30.00	18.50
(104a)	McArdle ("150 subjects" back)	75.00	30.00	18.50
(104b)	McArdle ("175 subjects" back)	75.00	30.00	18.50
(105a)	McCredie ("150 subjects" back)	75.00	30.00	18.50
(105b)	McCredie ("175 subjects" back)	75.00	30.00	18.50
(106a)	Melchoir ("150 subjects" back)	75.00	30.00	18.50
(106b)	Melchoir ("175 subjects" back)	75.00	30.00	18.50
(107)	Miller (San Francisco)	75.00	30.00	18.50
(108)	Miller (Seattle)	75.00	30.00	18.50
(109)	Mitze	75.00	30.00	18.50
(110a)	Mohler ("150 subjects" back)	75.00	30.00	18.50
(110b)	Mohler ("175 subjects" back)	75.00	30.00	18.50
(111a)	Moser ("150 subjects" back)	75.00	30.00	18.50
(111b)	Moser ("175 subjects" back)	75.00	30.00	18.50
(112)	Mott	75.00	30.00	18.50
(113a)	Mundorf (name incorrect, "150 subjects" back)	125.00	50.00	31.00
(113b)	Mundorff (name correct, "175 subjects" back)	75.00	30.00	18.50
(114a)	Murphy ("150 subjects" back)	75.00	30.00	18.50
(114b)	Murphy ("175 subjects" back)	75.00	30.00	18.50
(115)	Nagle	75.00	30.00	18.50
(116)	Nelson	75.00	30.00	18.50
(117)	Netzel	75.00	30.00	18.50
(118)	Nourse	75.00	30.00	18.50
(119)	Nordyke	75.00	30.00	18.50
(120)	Olson	75.00	30.00	18.50
(121)	Orendorff (Orsnsdorff)	75.00	30.00	18.50
(122a)	Ort ("150 subjects" back)	75.00	30.00	18.50
(122b)	Ort ("175 subjects" back)	75.00	30.00	18.50
(123)	Ostdiek	75.00	30.00	18.50
(124)	Pennington	75.00	30.00	18.50
(125)	Perrine	75.00	30.00	18.50
(126a)	Perry ("150 subjects" back)	75.00	30.00	18.50
(126b)	Perry ("175 subjects" back)	75.00	30.00	18.50
(127)	Persons	75.00	30.00	18.50
(128a)	Rapps ("150 subjects" back)	75.00	30.00	18.50
(128b)	Rapps ("175 subjects" back)	75.00	30.00	18.50
(129)	Raymer	75.00	30.00	18.50
(130)	Raymond	75.00	30.00	18.50
(131)	Rockenfield	75.00	30.00	18.50
(132)	Roth	75.00	30.00	18.50
(133)	D. Ryan	75.00	30.00	18.50
(134)	J. Ryan	75.00	30.00	18.50
(135)	Scharnweber	75.00	30.00	18.50
(136)	Schmutz	75.00	30.00	18.50
(137)	Seaton (Portland)	75.00	30.00	18.50
(138)	Seaton (Seattle)	75.00	30.00	18.50
(139)	Shafer	75.00	30.00	18.50
(140)	Shaw	75.00	30.00	18.50
(141)	Shea	75.00	30.00	18.50
(142)	Shinn	75.00	30.00	18.50
(143)	Smith	75.00	30.00	18.50
(144a)	H. Smith ("150 subjects" back)	75.00	30.00	18.50
(144b)	H. Smith ("175 subjects" back)	75.00	30.00	18.50
(145a)	J. Smith ("150 subjects" back)	75.00	30.00	18.50
(145b)	J. Smith ("175 subjects" back)	75.00	30.00	18.50
(146)	Speas	75.00	30.00	18.50
(147)	Spiesman	75.00	30.00	18.50
(148)	Starkell	75.00	30.00	18.50
(149a)	Steen ("150 subjects" back)	75.00	30.00	18.50
(149b)	Steen ("175 subjects" back)	75.00	30.00	18.50
(150)	Stevens	75.00	30.00	18.50
(151a)	Stewart ("150 subjects" back)	75.00	30.00	18.50
(151b)	Stewart ("175 subjects" back)	75.00	30.00	18.50
(152)	Stovell (Stovall)	75.00	30.00	18.50
(153)	Streib	75.00	30.00	18.50
(154)	Sugden	75.00	30.00	18.50
(155)	Sutor	75.00	30.00	18.50
(156)	Swain	75.00	30.00	18.50
(157a)	Swander ("150 subjects" back)	75.00	30.00	18.50
(157b)	Swander ("175 subjects" back)	75.00	30.00	18.50
(158)	Tennant	75.00	30.00	18.50
(159)	Thomas	75.00	30.00	18.50
(160)	Thompson	75.00	30.00	18.50
(161)	Thorsen	75.00	30.00	18.50
(162a)	Tonnesen ("150 subjects" back)	75.00	30.00	18.50
(162b)	Tonnesen ("175 subjects" back)	75.00	30.00	18.50
(163)	Tozer	75.00	30.00	18.50
(164)	Van Buren	75.00	30.00	18.50
(165)	Vitt	75.00	30.00	18.50
(166)	Wares	75.00	30.00	18.50
(167)	Waring	75.00	30.00	18.50
(168)	Warren	75.00	30.00	18.50
(169)	Weed	75.00	30.00	18.50
(170a)	Whalen ("150 subjects" back)	75.00	30.00	18.50
(170b)	Whalen ("175 subjects" back)	75.00	30.00	18.50
(171a)	Willett ("150 subjects" back)	75.00	30.00	18.50
(171b)	Willett ("175 subjects" back)	75.00	30.00	18.50
(172a)	Williams ("150 subjects" back)	75.00	30.00	18.50
(172b)	Williams ("175 subjects" back)	75.00	30.00	18.50
(173a)	Willis ("150 subjects" back)	75.00	30.00	18.50
(173b)	Willis ("175 subjects" back)	75.00	30.00	18.50
(174a)	Wolverton ("150 subjects" back)	75.00	30.00	18.50
(174b)	Wolverton ("175 subjects" back)	75.00	30.00	18.50
(175)	Zackert	75.00	30.00	18.50

Near Mint-Mint examples of vintage cards carry a significant premium over the Near Mint values shown here. This premium reflects limited availability of the highest-grade cards as well as demand for particular cards or sets in the best possible condition. Premiums of 2X-3X are not uncommon and many are even higher.

1911 Obak (T212)

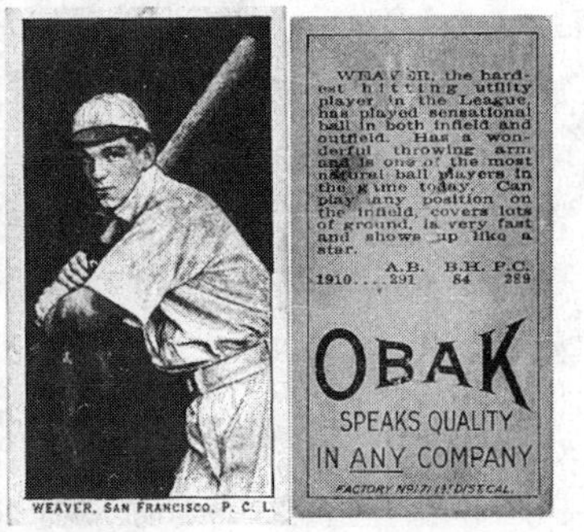

		NM	EX	VG
Complete Set (175):		10750.	4300.	2700.
Common Player:		75.00	30.00	18.50
(1)	Abbott	75.00	30.00	18.50
(2)	Ables	75.00	30.00	18.50
(3)	Adams	75.00	30.00	18.50
(4)	Agnew	75.00	30.00	18.50
(5)	Akin	75.00	30.00	18.50
(6)	Annis	75.00	30.00	18.50
(7)	Arrelanes (Arellanes)	75.00	30.00	18.50
(8)	Barry	75.00	30.00	18.50
(9)	Bassey	75.00	30.00	18.50
(10)	Baum	75.00	30.00	18.50
(11)	Bennett	75.00	30.00	18.50
(12)	Bernard	75.00	30.00	18.50
(13)	Berry	75.00	30.00	18.50
(14)	Bloomfield	75.00	30.00	18.50
(15)	Bonner	75.00	30.00	18.50
(16)	Brackenridge	75.00	30.00	18.50
(17)	Brashear	75.00	30.00	18.50
(18)	R. Brashear	75.00	30.00	18.50
(19)	Brinker	75.00	30.00	18.50
(20)	Brown	75.00	30.00	18.50
(21)	Browning	75.00	30.00	18.50
(22)	Bues	75.00	30.00	18.50
(23)	Burrell	75.00	30.00	18.50
(24)	Burns	75.00	30.00	18.50
(25)	Butler	75.00	30.00	18.50
(26)	Byram	75.00	30.00	18.50
(27)	Carlisle	75.00	30.00	18.50
(28)	Carson	75.00	30.00	18.50
(29)	Cartwright	75.00	30.00	18.50
(30)	Casey	75.00	30.00	18.50
(31)	Castleton	75.00	30.00	18.50
(32)	Chadbourne	75.00	30.00	18.50
(33)	Christian	75.00	30.00	18.50
(34)	Coleman	75.00	30.00	18.50
(35)	Cooney	75.00	30.00	18.50
(36)	Coy	75.00	30.00	18.50
(37)	Criger	75.00	30.00	18.50
(38)	Crukshank	75.00	30.00	18.50
(39)	Cutshaw	75.00	30.00	18.50
(40)	Daley	75.00	30.00	18.50
(41)	Danzig	75.00	30.00	18.50
(42)	Dashwood	75.00	30.00	18.50
(43)	Davis	75.00	30.00	18.50
(44)	Delhi	75.00	30.00	18.50
(45)	Delmas	75.00	30.00	18.50
(46)	Dillon	75.00	30.00	18.50
(47)	Engel	75.00	30.00	18.50
(48)	Erickson	75.00	30.00	18.50
(49)	Fitzgerald	75.00	30.00	18.50
(50)	Flater	75.00	30.00	18.50
(51)	Frisk	75.00	30.00	18.50
(52)	Fullerton	75.00	30.00	18.50
(53)	Garrett	75.00	30.00	18.50
(54)	Goodman	75.00	30.00	18.50
(55)	Gordon	75.00	30.00	18.50
(56)	Grindle	75.00	30.00	18.50
(57)	Hall	75.00	30.00	18.50
(58)	Harris	75.00	30.00	18.50
(59)	Hasty	75.00	30.00	18.50
(60)	Henderson	75.00	30.00	18.50
(61)	Henley	75.00	30.00	18.50
(62)	Hetling	75.00	30.00	18.50
(63)	Hiester	75.00	30.00	18.50
(64)	Higgins	75.00	30.00	18.50
(65)	Hitt	75.00	30.00	18.50
(66)	Hoffman	75.00	30.00	18.50
(67)	Hogan	75.00	30.00	18.50
(68)	Holm	75.00	30.00	18.50
(69)	Householder	75.00	30.00	18.50
(70)	Hosp	75.00	30.00	18.50
(71)	Howard	75.00	30.00	18.50
(72)	Hunt	75.00	30.00	18.50
(73)	James	75.00	30.00	18.50
(74)	Jensen	75.00	30.00	18.50
(75)	Kading	75.00	30.00	18.50
(76)	Kane	75.00	30.00	18.50
(77)	Kippert	75.00	30.00	18.50
(78)	Knight	75.00	30.00	18.50
(79)	Koestner	75.00	30.00	18.50
(80)	Krueger	75.00	30.00	18.50
(81)	Kuhn	75.00	30.00	18.50
(82)	LaLonge	75.00	30.00	18.50
(83)	Lamline	75.00	30.00	18.50
(84)	Leard	75.00	30.00	18.50
(85)	Lerchen	75.00	30.00	18.50
(86)	Lewis	75.00	30.00	18.50
(87)	Madden	75.00	30.00	18.50
(88)	Maggert	75.00	30.00	18.50
(89)	Mahoney	75.00	30.00	18.50
(90)	McArdle	75.00	30.00	18.50
(91)	McCredie	75.00	30.00	18.50
(92)	McDonnell	75.00	30.00	18.50
(93)	Meikle	75.00	30.00	18.50
(94)	Melchoir	75.00	30.00	18.50
(95)	Mensor	75.00	30.00	18.50
(96)	Metzger	75.00	30.00	18.50
(97)	Miller (Oakland)	75.00	30.00	18.50
(98)	Miller (San Francisco)	75.00	30.00	18.50
(99)	Ten Million	75.00	30.00	18.50
(100)	Mitze	75.00	30.00	18.50
(101)	Mohler	75.00	30.00	18.50
(102)	Moore	75.00	30.00	18.50
(103)	Morse	75.00	30.00	18.50
(104)	Moskiman	75.00	30.00	18.50
(105)	Mundorff	75.00	30.00	18.50
(106)	Murray	75.00	30.00	18.50
(107)	Netzel	75.00	30.00	18.50
(108)	Nordyke	75.00	30.00	18.50
(109)	Nourse	75.00	30.00	18.50
(110)	O'Rourke	75.00	30.00	18.50
(111)	Ostdiek	75.00	30.00	18.50
(112)	Patterson	75.00	30.00	18.50
(113)	Pearce	75.00	30.00	18.50
(114)	Peckinpaugh	75.00	30.00	18.50
(115)	Pernoll	75.00	30.00	18.50
(116)	Pfyl	75.00	30.00	18.50
(117)	Powell	75.00	30.00	18.50
(118)	Raleigh	75.00	30.00	18.50
(119)	Rapps	75.00	30.00	18.50
(120)	Raymer	75.00	30.00	18.50
(121)	Raymond	75.00	30.00	18.50
(122)	Reddick	75.00	30.00	18.50
(123)	Roche	75.00	30.00	18.50
(124)	Rockenfield	75.00	30.00	18.50
(125)	Rogers	75.00	30.00	18.50
(126)	Ross	75.00	30.00	18.50
(127)	Ryan	75.00	30.00	18.50
(128)	J. Ryan	75.00	30.00	18.50
(129)	Scharnweber	75.00	30.00	18.50
(130)	Schmidt	75.00	30.00	18.50
(131)	Schmutz	75.00	30.00	18.50
(132)	Seaton (Portland)	75.00	30.00	18.50
(133)	Seaton (Seattle)	75.00	30.00	18.50
(134)	Shaw	75.00	30.00	18.50
(135)	Shea	75.00	30.00	18.50
(136)	Sheehan (Portland)	75.00	30.00	18.50
(137)	Sheehan (Vernon)	75.00	30.00	18.50
(138)	Shinn	75.00	30.00	18.50
(139)	Skeels	75.00	30.00	18.50
(140)	H. Smith	75.00	30.00	18.50
(141)	Speas	75.00	30.00	18.50
(142)	Spencer	75.00	30.00	18.50
(143)	Spiesman	75.00	30.00	18.50
(144)	Starkel	75.00	30.00	18.50
(145)	Steen	75.00	30.00	18.50
(146)	Stewart	75.00	30.00	18.50
(147)	Stinson	75.00	30.00	18.50
(148)	Stovall	75.00	30.00	18.50
(149)	Strand	75.00	30.00	18.50
(150)	Sutor	75.00	30.00	18.50
(151)	Swain	75.00	30.00	18.50
(152)	Tennant	75.00	30.00	18.50
(153)	Thomas (Sacramento)	75.00	30.00	18.50
(154)	Thomas (Victoria)	75.00	30.00	18.50
(155)	Thompson	75.00	30.00	18.50
(156)	Thornton	75.00	30.00	18.50
(157)	Thorsen	75.00	30.00	18.50
(158)	Tiedeman	75.00	30.00	18.50
(159)	Tozer	75.00	30.00	18.50
(160)	Van Buren	75.00	30.00	18.50
(161)	Vitt	75.00	30.00	18.50
(162)	Ward	75.00	30.00	18.50
(163)	Wares	75.00	30.00	18.50
(164)	Warren	75.00	30.00	18.50
(165)	Weaver	750.00	300.00	187.00
(166)	Weed	75.00	30.00	18.50
(167)	Wheeler	75.00	30.00	18.50
(168)	Wiggs	75.00	30.00	18.50
(169)	Willett	75.00	30.00	18.50
(170)	Williams	75.00	30.00	18.50
(171)	Wolverton	75.00	30.00	18.50
(172)	Zacher	75.00	30.00	18.50
(173)	Zackert	75.00	30.00	18.50
(174)	Zamlock	75.00	30.00	18.50
(175)	Zimmerman	75.00	30.00	18.50

1911 Obak Cabinets (T4)

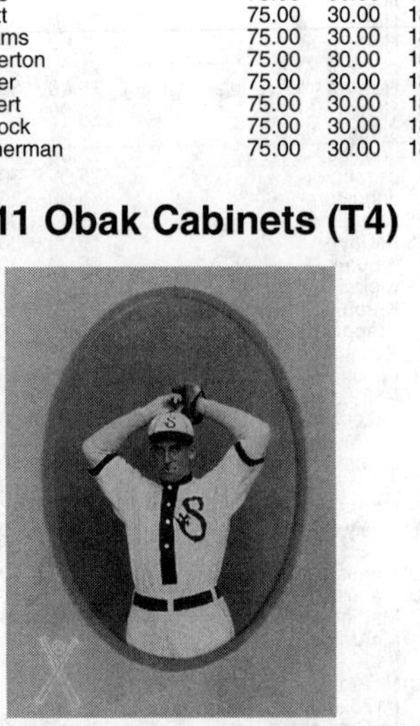

Among the scarcest of all the 20th Century tobacco issues, the T4 Obak Premiums were cabinet-sized cards distributed in conjunction with the more popular and better-known Obak T212 card set. Both sets were issued in 1911 by Obak "mouthpiece" cigarettes and featured players from the Pacific Coast League. The Obak Premiums measured a large 5" x 7" and are printed on a cardboard-like paper. The attractive cards featured a greyish monochome player photo inside a 3-1/2" x 5" oval. There was no printing on the front of the card to identify the player or indicate the Manufacturer, and the backs of the cards were blank. In most cases the photos used for the premiums were identical to the T212 photos, except for some cropping differences. Under the Obak mail-in promotion, 50 coupons from cigarette packages were required to obtain just one premium card, which may explain their extreme scarcity today. According to the coupon, all 175 players pictured in the regular T212 set were available as premium cards, but todate 30 different players have been found in the larger cabinet size. Most of the Obak premiums that exist in original condition contain a number, written in pencil on the back of the card, that corresponds to the checklist printed on the coupon. Because of their extreme scarcity, these cards are quite expensive and generally appeal only to the very advanced Pacific Coast League collectors.

		NM	EX	VG
Common Player:		3000.	1500.	900.00
3	Howard	3000.	1500.	900.00
22	Christian	3000.	1500.	900.00
24	Maggert	3000.	1500.	900.00
33	Flater	3000.	1500.	900.00
34	Zacher	3000.	1500.	900.00
37	Ryan	3000.	1500.	900.00
46	Bill Rodgers	3000.	1500.	900.00
49	Kuhn	3000.	1500.	900.00
59	Baum	3000.	1500.	900.00
71	Melchoir	3000.	1500.	900.00
72	Vitt	3000.	1500.	900.00
74	Berry	3000.	1500.	900.00
75	Miller	3000.	1500.	900.00
76	Tennant	3000.	1500.	900.00
77	Mohler	3000.	1500.	900.00
79	Sutor	3000.	1500.	900.00
80	Browning	3000.	1500.	900.00
81	Ryan	3000.	1500.	900.00
82	Powell	3000.	1500.	900.00
83	Schmidt	3000.	1500.	900.00
84	Meikle	3000.	1500.	900.00
85	Madden	3000.	1500.	900.00
86	Buck Weaver	12000.	6000.	4000.
87	Moskiman	3000.	1500.	900.00
88	Zamlock	3000.	1500.	900.00
92	Carlisle	3000.	1500.	900.00
97	Stewart	3000.	1500.	900.00
111	Mundorff	3000.	1500.	900.00
140	Annis	3000.	1500.	900.00
159	Dashwood	3000.	1500.	900.00
167	Spencer	3000.	1500.	900.00

1959 O'Keefe Ale Montreal Royals

This set of large (3" x 4") player stamps was issued in conjunction with an album as a promotion by O'Keefe Ale in Quebec. The pictures are black-and-white with player identification in the bottom border. Backs are blank and the edges are perforated. Many former Brooklyn Dodgers are included in the issue. The unnumbered stamps are listed here in alphabetical order.

		NM	EX	VG
Complete Set (24):		350.00	175.00	100.00
Common Player:		8.00	4.00	2.50
Album:		80.00	40.00	24.00
(1)	Edmundo Amoros	12.00	6.00	3.50
(2)	Bob Aspromonte	10.00	5.00	3.00
(3)	Batters Records	4.00	2.00	1.25
(4)	Babe Birrer	8.00	4.00	2.50
(5)	Clay Bryant	8.00	4.00	2.50
(6)	Mike Brumley	8.00	4.00	2.50
(7)	Yvon Dunn (trainer)	6.00	3.00	1.75
(8)	Bill George	8.00	4.00	2.50
(9)	Mike Goliat	8.00	4.00	2.50
(10)	John Gray	8.00	4.00	2.50
(11)	Billy Harris	8.00	4.00	2.50
(12)	Jim Koranda	8.00	4.00	2.50
(13)	Paul LaPalme	8.00	4.00	2.50
(14)	Tom Lasorda	60.00	30.00	18.00
(15)	Bob Lennon	9.00	4.50	2.75

		NM	EX	VG
(16)	Clyde Parris	8.00	4.00	2.50
(17)	Pitchers Records	4.00	2.00	1.25
(18)	Ed Rakow	8.00	4.00	2.50
(19)	Curt Roberts	8.00	4.00	2.50
(20)	Freddy Rodriguez	8.00	4.00	2.50
(21)	Harry Schwegman	8.00	4.00	2.50
(22)	Angel Scull	8.00	4.00	2.50
(23)	Dick Teed	8.00	4.00	2.50
(24)	Rene Valdes (Valdez)	8.00	4.00	2.50

1955 Old Homestead Franks Des Moines Bruins

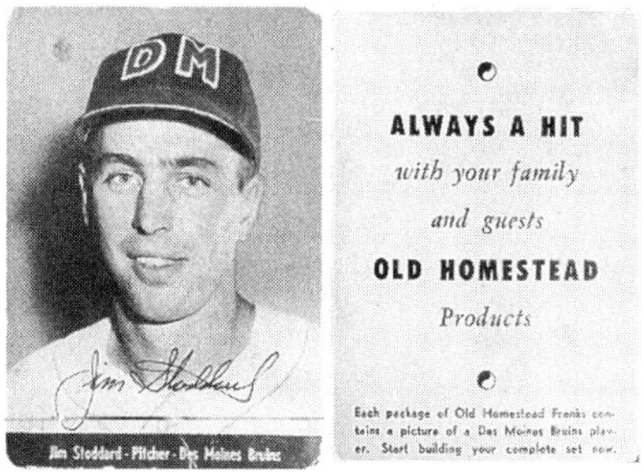

A very rare minor league issue, this set features players of the Class A Western League farm team of the Chicago Cubs. Many of the players were future major leaguers. Cards measure about 2-1/2" x 3-3/4" and have black-and-white portrait photos of the players with a facsimile autograph across the jersey. A black strip at the bottom of the card has the player and team name, and the position. Backs have an ad for the issuing hot dog company.

		NM	EX	VG
Complete Set (21):		850.00	425.00	250.00
Common Player:		55.00	26.00	16.00
(1)	Bob Anderson	55.00	26.00	16.00
(2)	Ray Bellino	55.00	26.00	16.00
(3)	Don Biebel	55.00	26.00	16.00
(4)	Bobby Cooke	55.00	26.00	16.00
(5)	Dave Cunningham	55.00	26.00	16.00
(6)	Bert Flammini	55.00	26.00	16.00
(7)	Gene Fodge	55.00	26.00	16.00
(8)	Eddie Haas	55.00	26.00	16.00
(9)	Paul Hoffmeister	55.00	26.00	16.00
(10)	Pepper Martin	70.00	35.00	21.00
(11)	Jim McDaniel	55.00	26.00	16.00
(12)	Bob McKee	55.00	26.00	16.00
(13)	Paul Menking	55.00	26.00	16.00
(14)	Vern Morgan	55.00	26.00	16.00
(15)	Joe Pearson	55.00	26.00	16.00
(16)	John Pramesa	55.00	26.00	16.00
(17)	Joe Stanka	55.00	26.00	16.00
(18)	Jim Stoddard	55.00	26.00	16.00
(19)	Bob Thorpe	55.00	26.00	16.00
(20)	Burdy Thurlby	55.00	26.00	16.00
(21)	Don Watkins	55.00	26.00	16.00

1910 Old Mill Cigarettes Series 1 (S. Atlantic League)

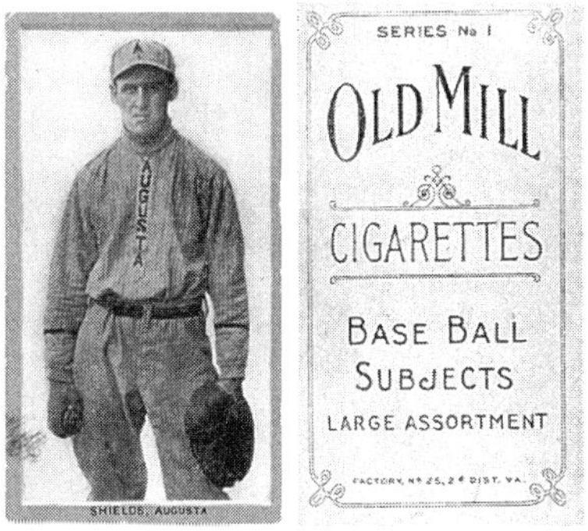

Because of their distinctive red borders, this 1910 minor league tobacco issue is often called the Red Border set by collectors. It's ACC designation is T210. A massive set, it consists of some 640 cards, each measuring 1-1/2" x 2-5/8". Fronts feature a glossy black-and-white photo, while the backs carry an ad for Old Mill Cigarettes. Each of the eight series is devoted to a different minor league. Series 1 features players from the South Atlantic League; Series 2 pictures players from the Virginia League; Series 3 is devoted to the Texas League; Series 4 features the Virginia Valley League; Series 5 pictures players from the Carolina Associations; Series 6 spotlights the Blue Grass League; Series 7 is devoted to the Eastern Carolina League; and Series 8 show players from the Southern Association. The various series are identified by a number along the top on the back of the cards. Collectors generally agree that Series 7 cards (Eastern Carolina League players) are the most difficult to find, while Series 2 cards (Virginia League) are the most common. The relative scarcity of the various series is reflected in the prices listed. Collectors should be aware that some Series 3 cards (Texas League) can be found with orange, rather than red, borders - apparently because not enough red ink was used during part of the print run.

		NM	EX	VG
Complete Set (75):		3200.	1250.	765.00
Common Player:		50.00	20.00	12.50
(1)	Bagwell	50.00	20.00	12.50
(2)	Balenti	50.00	20.00	12.50
(3)	Becker	50.00	20.00	12.50
(4)	Bensen	50.00	20.00	12.50
(5)	Benton	50.00	20.00	12.50
(6)	Bierkortte	50.00	20.00	12.50
(7)	Bierman	50.00	20.00	12.50
(8)	Breitenstein	50.00	20.00	12.50
(9)	Bremmerhof	50.00	20.00	12.50
(10)	Carter	50.00	20.00	12.50
(11)	Cavender	50.00	20.00	12.50
(12)	Collins	50.00	20.00	12.50
(13)	DeFraites	50.00	20.00	12.50
(14)	Dudley	50.00	20.00	12.50
(15)	Dwyer	50.00	20.00	12.50
(16)	Edwards	50.00	20.00	12.50
(17)	Enbanks	50.00	20.00	12.50
(18)	Eubank	50.00	20.00	12.50
(19)	Fox	50.00	20.00	12.50
(20)	Hannifan	50.00	20.00	12.50
(21)	Hartley	50.00	20.00	12.50
(22)	Hauser	50.00	20.00	12.50
(23)	Hille	50.00	20.00	12.50
(24)	Howard	50.00	20.00	12.50
(25)	Hoyt	50.00	20.00	12.50
(26)	Hubner	50.00	20.00	12.50
(27)	Ison	50.00	20.00	12.50
(28)	Jones	50.00	20.00	12.50
(29)	Kalkhoff	50.00	20.00	12.50
(30)	Krebs	50.00	20.00	12.50
(31)	Lawrence	50.00	20.00	12.50
(32)	Lee (Jacksonville)	50.00	20.00	12.50
(33)	Lee (Macon)	50.00	20.00	12.50
(34)	Lewis (Columbia)	50.00	20.00	12.50
(35)	Lewis (Columbus)	50.00	20.00	12.50
(36)	Lipe (batting)	50.00	20.00	12.50
(37)	Lipe (portrait)	50.00	20.00	12.50
(38)	Long	50.00	20.00	12.50
(39)	Magoon	50.00	20.00	12.50
(40)	Manion	50.00	20.00	12.50
(41)	Marshall	50.00	20.00	12.50
(42)	Martin	50.00	20.00	12.50
(43)	Martina	50.00	20.00	12.50
(44)	Massing	50.00	20.00	12.50
(45)	McLeod	50.00	20.00	12.50
(46)	McMahon	50.00	20.00	12.50
(47)	Morse	50.00	20.00	12.50
(48)	Mullane	50.00	20.00	12.50
(49)	Mulldowney	50.00	20.00	12.50
(50)	Murch	50.00	20.00	12.50
(51)	Norcum	50.00	20.00	12.50
(52)	Pelkey	50.00	20.00	12.50
(53)	Petit	50.00	20.00	12.50
(54)	Pierce	50.00	20.00	12.50
(55)	Pope	50.00	20.00	12.50
(56)	Radebaugh	50.00	20.00	12.50
(57)	Raynolds	50.00	20.00	12.50
(58)	Reagan	50.00	20.00	12.50
(59)	Redfern (Redfearn)	50.00	20.00	12.50
(60)	Reynolds	50.00	20.00	12.50
(61)	Schulz	50.00	20.00	12.50
(62)	Schulze	50.00	20.00	12.50
(63)	Schwietzka	50.00	20.00	12.50
(64)	Shields	50.00	20.00	12.50
(65)	Sisson	50.00	20.00	12.50
(66)	Smith	50.00	20.00	12.50
(67)	Sweeney	50.00	20.00	12.50
(68)	Taffee	50.00	20.00	12.50
(69)	Toren	50.00	20.00	12.50
(70)	Viola	70.00	28.00	17.50
(71)	Wagner	50.00	20.00	12.50
(72)	Wahl	50.00	20.00	12.50
(73)	Weems	50.00	20.00	12.50
(74)	Wells	50.00	20.00	12.50
(75)	Wohlleben	50.00	20.00	12.50

1910 Old Mill Cigarettes Series 2 (Virginia League)

		NM	EX	VG
Complete Set (87):		2950.	1175.	700.00
Common Player:		40.00	15.00	9.00
(1)	Andrada	40.00	15.00	9.00
(2)	Archer	40.00	15.00	9.00
(3)	Baker	40.00	15.00	9.00
(4)	Beham	40.00	15.00	9.00
(5)	Bonner	40.00	15.00	9.00
(6)	Bowen	40.00	15.00	9.00
(7)	Brandon	40.00	15.00	9.00
(8)	Breivogel	40.00	15.00	9.00
(9)	Brooks	40.00	15.00	9.00
(10)	Brown	40.00	15.00	9.00
(11)	Busch	40.00	15.00	9.00
(12)	Bussey	40.00	15.00	9.00
(13)	Cefalu	40.00	15.00	9.00
(14)	Chandler	40.00	15.00	9.00
(15)	Clarke	40.00	15.00	9.00
(16)	Clunk	40.00	15.00	9.00
(17)	Cote	40.00	15.00	9.00
(18)	Cowan	40.00	15.00	9.00
(19)	Decker	40.00	15.00	9.00
(20)	Doyle	40.00	15.00	9.00
(21)	Eddowes	40.00	15.00	9.00
(22)	Fisher	40.00	15.00	9.00
(23)	Fox	40.00	15.00	9.00
(24)	Foxen	40.00	15.00	9.00
(25)	Gaston	40.00	15.00	9.00
(26)	Gehring	40.00	15.00	9.00
(27)	Griffin (Danville)	40.00	15.00	9.00
(28)	Griffin (Lynchburg)	40.00	15.00	9.00
(29)	Hale	40.00	15.00	9.00
(30)	Hamilton	40.00	15.00	9.00
(31)	Hanks	40.00	15.00	9.00
(32)	Hannafin	40.00	15.00	9.00
(33)	Hoffman	40.00	15.00	9.00
(34)	Holland	40.00	15.00	9.00
(35)	Hooker	40.00	15.00	9.00
(36)	Irving	40.00	15.00	9.00
(37)	Jackson (Lynchburg)	40.00	15.00	9.00
(38)	Jackson (Norfolk)	40.00	15.00	9.00
(39)	Jackson (Portsmouth)	40.00	15.00	9.00
(40)	Jackson (Richmond)	40.00	15.00	9.00
(41)	Jenkins	40.00	15.00	9.00
(42)	Keifel	40.00	15.00	9.00
(43)	Kirkpatrick	40.00	15.00	9.00
(44)	Kunkel	40.00	15.00	9.00
(45)	Landgraff	40.00	15.00	9.00
(46)	Larkins	40.00	15.00	9.00
(47)	Laughlin	40.00	15.00	9.00
(48)	Lawlor	40.00	15.00	9.00
(49)	Levy	40.00	15.00	9.00
(50)	Lloyd	40.00	15.00	9.00
(51)	Loos	40.00	15.00	9.00
(52)	Lovell	40.00	15.00	9.00
(53)	Lucia	40.00	15.00	9.00
(54)	MacConachie	40.00	15.00	9.00
(55)	Mayberry	40.00	15.00	9.00
(56)	McFarland	40.00	15.00	9.00
(57)	Messitt	40.00	15.00	9.00
(58)	Michel	40.00	15.00	9.00
(59)	Mullaney	40.00	15.00	9.00
(60)	Munson	40.00	15.00	9.00
(61)	Neuton	40.00	15.00	9.00
(62)	Nimmo	40.00	15.00	0.00
(63)	Norris	40.00	15.00	9.00
(64)	Peterson	40.00	15.00	9.00
(65)	Powell	40.00	15.00	9.00
(66)	Pressly (Pressley)	40.00	15.00	9.00
(67)	Pritchard	40.00	15.00	9.00
(68)	Revelle	40.00	15.00	9.00
(69)	Rowe	40.00	15.00	9.00
(70)	Schmidt	40.00	15.00	9.00
(71)	Schrader	40.00	15.00	9.00
(72)	Sharp	40.00	15.00	9.00
(73)	Shaw	40.00	15.00	9.00
(74)	Smith (Lynchburg, batting)	40.00	15.00	9.00
(75)	Smith (Lynchburg, catching)	40.00	15.00	9.00
(76)	Smith (Portsmouth)	40.00	15.00	9.00
(77)	Spicer	40.00	15.00	9.00
(78)	Titman	40.00	15.00	9.00
(79)	Toner	40.00	15.00	9.00
(80)	Tydeman	40.00	15.00	9.00
(81)	Vail	40.00	15.00	9.00
(82)	Verbout	40.00	15.00	9.00
(83)	Walker	40.00	15.00	9.00
(84)	Wallace	40.00	15.00	9.00
(85)	Waymack	40.00	15.00	9.00
(86)	Woolums	40.00	15.00	9.00
(87)	Zimmerman	40.00	15.00	9.00

1910 Old Mill Cigarettes Series 3 (Texas League)

		NM	EX	VG
Complete Set (95):		4000.	1600.	950.00
Common Player:		50.00	20.00	12.00
(1)	Alexander	50.00	20.00	12.00
(2)	Ash	50.00	20.00	12.00
(3)	Bandy	50.00	20.00	12.00
(4)	Barenkemp	50.00	20.00	12.00
(5)	Belew	50.00	20.00	12.00
(6)	Bell	50.00	20.00	12.00
(7)	Bennett	50.00	20.00	12.00
(8)	Berlck	50.00	20.00	12.00
(9)	Billiard	50.00	20.00	12.00
(10)	Blanding	50.00	20.00	12.00
(11)	Blue	50.00	20.00	12.00
(12)	Burch	50.00	20.00	12.00
(13)	Burk	50.00	20.00	12.00
(14)	Carlin	50.00	20.00	12.00
(15)	Conaway	50.00	20.00	12.00
(16)	Corkhill	50.00	20.00	12.00
(17)	Cowan	50.00	20.00	12.00
(18)	Coyle	50.00	20.00	12.00
(19)	Crable	50.00	20.00	12.00
(20)	Curry	50.00	20.00	12.00
(21)	Dale	50.00	20.00	12.00
(22)	Davis	50.00	20.00	12.00
(23)	Deardorff	50.00	20.00	12.00
(24)	Donnelley	50.00	20.00	12.00
(25)	Doyle	50.00	20.00	12.00
(26)	Druke	50.00	20.00	12.00
(27)	Dugey	50.00	20.00	12.00
(28)	Ens	50.00	20.00	12.00
(29)	Evans	50.00	20.00	12.00
(30)	Fillman	50.00	20.00	12.00
(31)	Firestine	50.00	20.00	12.00
(32)	Francis	50.00	20.00	12.00
(33)	Galloway	50.00	20.00	12.00
(34)	Gardner	50.00	20.00	12.00
(35)	Gear	50.00	20.00	12.00
(36)	Glawe	50.00	20.00	12.00
(37)	Gordon	50.00	20.00	12.00
(38)	Gowdy	50.00	20.00	12.00

		NM	EX	VG
(39)	Harbison	50.00	20.00	12.00
(40)	Harper	50.00	20.00	12.00
(41)	Hicks	50.00	20.00	12.00
(42)	Hill	50.00	20.00	12.00
(43)	Hinninger	50.00	20.00	12.00
(44)	Hirsch	50.00	20.00	12.00
(45)	Hise	50.00	20.00	12.00
(46)	Hooks	50.00	20.00	12.00
(47)	Hornsby	50.00	20.00	12.00
(48)	Howell	50.00	20.00	12.00
(49)	Johnston	50.00	20.00	12.00
(50)	Jolley	50.00	20.00	12.00
(51)	Jones	50.00	20.00	12.00
(52)	Kaphan	50.00	20.00	12.00
(53)	Kipp	50.00	20.00	12.00
(54)	Leidy	50.00	20.00	12.00
(55)	Malloy	50.00	20.00	12.00
(56)	Maloney	50.00	20.00	12.00
(57)	Meagher	50.00	20.00	12.00
(58)	Merritt	50.00	20.00	12.00
(59)	McKay	50.00	20.00	12.00
(60)	Mills	50.00	20.00	12.00
(61)	Morris	50.00	20.00	12.00
(63)	Munsell	50.00	20.00	12.00
(64)	Nagel	50.00	20.00	12.00
(65)	Northen	50.00	20.00	12.00
(66)	Ogle	50.00	20.00	12.00
(67)	Onslow	50.00	20.00	12.00
(68)	Pendleton	50.00	20.00	12.00
(69)	Powell	50.00	20.00	12.00
(70)	Riley	50.00	20.00	12.00
(71)	Robertson	50.00	20.00	12.00
(72)	Rose	50.00	20.00	12.00
(73)	Salazor	50.00	20.00	12.00
(74)	Shindel	50.00	20.00	12.00
(75)	Shontz	50.00	20.00	12.00
(76)	Slaven	50.00	20.00	12.00
(77)	Smith (bat over shoulder)	50.00	20.00	12.00
(78)	Smith (bat at hip level)	50.00	20.00	12.00
(79)	Spangler	50.00	20.00	12.00
(80)	Stadeli	50.00	20.00	12.00
(81)	Stinson	50.00	20.00	12.00
(82)	Storch	50.00	20.00	12.00
(83)	Stringer	50.00	20.00	12.00
(84)	Tesreau	50.00	20.00	12.00
(85)	Thebo	50.00	20.00	12.00
(86)	Tullas	50.00	20.00	12.00
(87)	Walsh	50.00	20.00	12.00
(88)	Watson	50.00	20.00	12.00
(89)	Weber	50.00	20.00	12.00
(90)	Weeks	50.00	20.00	12.00
(91)	Wertherford	50.00	20.00	12.00
(92)	Wickenhofer	50.00	20.00	12.00
(93)	Williams	50.00	20.00	12.00
(94)	Woodburn	50.00	20.00	12.00
(95)	Yantz	50.00	20.00	12.00

1910 Old Mill Cigarettes Series 4 (Va. Valley League)

		NM	EX	VG
Complete Set (49):		2000.	835.00	500.00
Common Player:		50.00	20.00	12.00
(1)	Aylor	50.00	20.00	12.00
(2)	Benney	50.00	20.00	12.00
(3)	Best	50.00	20.00	12.00
(4)	Bonno	50.00	20.00	12.00
(5)	Brown	50.00	20.00	12.00
(6)	Brumfield	50.00	20.00	12.00
(7)	Campbell	50.00	20.00	12.00
(8)	Canepa	50.00	20.00	12.00
(9)	Carney	50.00	20.00	12.00
(10)	Carter	50.00	20.00	12.00
(11)	Cochrane	50.00	20.00	12.00
(12)	Coller	50.00	20.00	12.00
(13)	Connolly	50.00	20.00	12.00
(14)	Davis	50.00	20.00	12.00
(15)	Connell	50.00	20.00	12.00
(16)	Doshmer	50.00	20.00	12.00
(17)	Dougherty	50.00	20.00	12.00
(18)	Erlewein	50.00	20.00	12.00
(19)	Farrell	50.00	20.00	12.00
(20)	Geary	50.00	20.00	12.00
(21)	Halterman	50.00	20.00	12.00
(22)	Headly	50.00	20.00	12.00
(23)	Hollis	50.00	20.00	12.00
(24)	Hunter	50.00	20.00	12.00
(25)	Johnson	50.00	20.00	12.00
(26)	Kane	50.00	20.00	12.00
(27)	Kuehn	50.00	20.00	12.00
(28)	Leonard	50.00	20.00	12.00
(29)	Lux	50.00	20.00	12.00
(30)	McClain	50.00	20.00	12.00
(31)	Mollenkamp	50.00	20.00	12.00
(32)	Moore	50.00	20.00	12.00
(33)	Moye	50.00	20.00	12.00
(34)	O'Connor	50.00	20.00	12.00
(36)	Pick	50.00	20.00	12.00
(37)	Pickels	50.00	20.00	12.00
(38)	Schafer	50.00	20.00	12.00
(39)	Seaman	50.00	20.00	12.00
(40)	Spicer	50.00	20.00	12.00
(41)	Stanley	50.00	20.00	12.00
(42)	Stockum	50.00	20.00	12.00
(43)	Titlow	50.00	20.00	12.00
(44)	Waldron	50.00	20.00	12.00
(45)	Wills	50.00	20.00	12.00
(46)	Witter	50.00	20.00	12.00
(47)	Womach	50.00	20.00	12.00
(48)	Young	50.00	20.00	12.00
(49)	Zurlage	50.00	20.00	12.00

1910 Old Mill Cigarettes Series 5 (Carolina Assn.)

		NM	EX	VG
Complete Set (87):		3700.	1450.	900.00
Common Player:		50.00	20.00	12.00
(1)	Abercrombie	50.00	20.00	12.00
(2)	Averett	50.00	20.00	12.00
(3)	Bansewein	50.00	20.00	12.00
(4)	Bentley	50.00	20.00	12.00
(5)	C.G. Beusse	50.00	20.00	12.00
(6)	Fred Beusse	50.00	20.00	12.00
(7)	Bigbie	50.00	20.00	12.00
(8)	Bivens	50.00	20.00	12.00
(9)	Blackstone	50.00	20.00	12.00
(10)	Brannon	50.00	20.00	12.00
(11)	Brazell	50.00	20.00	12.00
(12)	Brent	50.00	20.00	12.00
(13)	Bullock	50.00	20.00	12.00
(14)	Cashion	50.00	20.00	12.00
(15)	Corbett	50.00	20.00	12.00
(16)	Corbett	50.00	20.00	12.00
(17)	Coutts	50.00	20.00	12.00
(18)	Lave Cross	50.00	20.00	12.00
(19)	Crouch	50.00	20.00	12.00
(20)	C.L. Derrick	50.00	20.00	12.00
(21)	F.B. Derrick	50.00	20.00	12.00
(22)	Dobard	50.00	20.00	12.00
(23)	Drumm	50.00	20.00	12.00
(24)	Duvie	50.00	20.00	12.00
(25)	Ehrhardt	50.00	20.00	12.00
(26)	Eldridge	50.00	20.00	12.00
(27)	Fairbanks	50.00	20.00	12.00
(28)	Farmer	50.00	20.00	12.00
(29)	Ferrell	50.00	20.00	12.00
(30)	Finn	50.00	20.00	12.00
(31)	Flowers	50.00	20.00	12.00
(32)	Fogarty	50.00	20.00	12.00
(33)	Francisco	50.00	20.00	12.00
(34)	Gardin	50.00	20.00	12.00
(35)	Gilmore	50.00	20.00	12.00
(36)	Gorham	50.00	20.00	12.00
(37)	Gorman	50.00	20.00	12.00
(38)	Guss	50.00	20.00	12.00
(39)	Hammersley	50.00	20.00	12.00
(40)	Hargrave	50.00	20.00	12.00
(41)	Harrington	50.00	20.00	12.00
(42)	Harris	50.00	20.00	12.00
(43)	Hartley	50.00	20.00	12.00
(44)	Hayes	50.00	20.00	12.00
(45)	Hicks	50.00	20.00	12.00
(46)	Humphrey	50.00	20.00	12.00
(47)	Jackson	50.00	20.00	12.00
(48)	James	50.00	20.00	12.00
(49)	Jenkins	50.00	20.00	12.00
(50)	Johnston	50.00	20.00	12.00
(51)	Kelly	50.00	20.00	12.00
(52)	Laval	50.00	20.00	12.00
(53)	Lothrop	50.00	20.00	12.00
(54)	MacConachie	50.00	20.00	12.00
(55)	Mangum	50.00	20.00	12.00
(56)	A. McCarthy	50.00	20.00	12.00
(57)	J. McCarthy	50.00	20.00	12.00
(58)	McEnroe	50.00	20.00	12.00
(59)	McFarlin	50.00	20.00	12.00
(60)	McHugh	50.00	20.00	12.00
(61)	McKevitt	50.00	20.00	12.00
(62)	Midkiff	50.00	20.00	12.00
(63)	Moore	50.00	20.00	12.00
(64)	Noojin	50.00	20.00	12.00
(65)	Ochs	50.00	20.00	12.00
(66)	Painter	50.00	20.00	12.00
(67)	Redfern (Redfearn)	50.00	20.00	12.00
(68)	Reis	50.00	20.00	12.00
(69)	Rickard	50.00	20.00	12.00
(70)	Roth (batting)	50.00	20.00	12.00
(71)	Roth (fielding)	50.00	20.00	12.00
(72)	Smith	50.00	20.00	12.00
(73)	Springs	50.00	20.00	12.00
(74)	Stouch	50.00	20.00	12.00
(75)	Taxis	50.00	20.00	12.00
(76)	Templin	50.00	20.00	12.00
(77)	Thrasher	50.00	20.00	12.00
(78)	Trammell	50.00	20.00	12.00
(79)	Walker	50.00	20.00	12.00
(80)	Walters	50.00	20.00	12.00
(81)	Wehrell	50.00	20.00	12.00
(82)	Weldon	50.00	20.00	12.00
(83)	Williams	50.00	20.00	12.00
(84)	Wingo	50.00	20.00	12.00
(85)	Workman	50.00	20.00	12.00
(86)	Wynne	50.00	20.00	12.00
(87)	Wysong	50.00	20.00	12.00

1910 Old Mill Cigarettes Series 6 (Blue Grass League)

		NM	EX	VG
Complete Set (66):		4500.	1800.	1100.
Common Player:		55.00	22.00	13.50
(1)	Angermeier (fielding)	55.00	22.00	13.50
(2)	Angermeir (portrait)	55.00	22.00	13.50
(3)	Atwell	55.00	22.00	13.50
(4)	Badger	55.00	22.00	13.50
(5)	Barnett	55.00	22.00	13.50
(6)	Barney	55.00	22.00	13.50
(7)	Beard	55.00	22.00	13.50
(8)	Bohannon	55.00	22.00	13.50
(9)	Callahan	55.00	22.00	13.50
(10)	Chapman	55.00	22.00	13.50
(11)	Chase	55.00	22.00	13.50
(12)	Coleman	55.00	22.00	13.50
(13)	Cornell (Frankfort)	55.00	22.00	13.50
(14)	Cornell (Winchester)	55.00	22.00	13.50
(15)	Creager	55.00	22.00	13.50
(16)	Dailey	55.00	22.00	13.50
(17)	Edington	55.00	22.00	13.50
(18)	Elgin	55.00	22.00	13.50
(19)	Ellis	55.00	22.00	13.50
(20)	Everden	55.00	22.00	13.50
(21)	Gisler	55.00	22.00	13.50
(22)	Goodman	55.00	22.00	13.50
(23)	Goostree (hands behind back)	55.00	22.00	13.50
(24)	Goostree (leaning on bat)	55.00	22.00	13.50
(25)	Haines	55.00	22.00	13.50
(26)	Harold	55.00	22.00	13.50
(27)	Heveron	55.00	22.00	13.50
(28)	Hicks	55.00	22.00	13.50
(29)	Hoffmann	55.00	22.00	13.50
(30)	Horn	55.00	22.00	13.50
(31)	Kaiser	55.00	22.00	13.50
(32)	Keifel	55.00	22.00	13.50
(33)	Kimbrough	55.00	22.00	13.50
(34)	Kirchen	55.00	22.00	13.50
(35)	Kircher	55.00	22.00	13.50
(36)	Kuhlman	55.00	22.00	13.50
(37)	Kuhlmann	55.00	22.00	13.50
(38)	L'Heureux	55.00	22.00	13.50
(39)	Mulvain	55.00	22.00	13.50
(40)	McKernan	55.00	22.00	13.50
(41)	Meyers	55.00	22.00	13.50
(42)	Moloney	55.00	22.00	13.50
(43)	Mullin	55.00	22.00	13.50
(44)	Olson	55.00	22.00	13.50
(45)	Oyler	55.00	22.00	13.50
(46)	Reed	55.00	22.00	13.50
(47)	Ross	55.00	22.00	13.50
(48)	Scheneberg (fielding)	55.00	22.00	13.50
(49)	Scheneberg (portrait)	55.00	22.00	13.50
(50)	Schultz	55.00	22.00	13.50
(51)	Scott	55.00	22.00	13.50
(52)	Sinex	55.00	22.00	13.50
(53)	Stengel	3500.	1750.	1050.
(54)	Thoss	55.00	22.00	13.50
(55)	Tilford	55.00	22.00	13.50
(56)	Toney	55.00	22.00	13.50
(57)	Van Landingham (Valladingham) (Lexington)	55.00	22.00	13.50
(58)	Van Landingham (Valladingham) (Shelbyville)	55.00	22.00	13.50
(59)	Viox	55.00	22.00	13.50
(60)	Walden	55.00	22.00	13.50
(61)	Whitaker	55.00	22.00	13.50
(62)	Wills	55.00	22.00	13.50
(63)	Womble	55.00	22.00	13.50
(64)	Wright	55.00	22.00	13.50
(65)	Yaeger	55.00	22.00	13.50
(66)	Yancey	55.00	22.00	13.50

1910 Old Mill Cigarettes Series 7 (E. Carolina League)

		NM	EX	VG
Complete Set (67):		3100.	1250.	750.00
Common Player:		55.00	22.00	13.50
(1)	Armstrong	55.00	22.00	13.50
(2)	Beatty	55.00	22.00	13.50
(3)	Biel	55.00	22.00	13.50
(4)	Bonner	55.00	22.00	13.50
(5)	Brandt	55.00	22.00	13.50
(6)	Brown	55.00	22.00	13.50
(7)	Cantwell	55.00	22.00	13.50
(8)	Carrol	55.00	22.00	13.50
(9)	Cooney	55.00	22.00	13.50
(10)	Cooper	55.00	22.00	13.50
(11)	Cowell	55.00	22.00	13.50
(12)	Creager (Cregan)	55.00	22.00	13.50
(13)	Crockett	55.00	22.00	13.50
(14)	Dailey	55.00	22.00	13.50
(15)	Dobbs	55.00	22.00	13.50
(16)	Dussault	55.00	22.00	13.50
(17)	Dwyer	55.00	22.00	13.50
(18)	Evans	55.00	22.00	13.50
(19)	Forgue	55.00	22.00	13.50
(20)	Fulton	55.00	22.00	13.50
(21)	Galvin	55.00	22.00	13.50
(22)	Gastmeyer (batting)	55.00	22.00	13.50
(23)	Gastmeyer (fielding)	55.00	22.00	13.50
(24)	Gates	55.00	22.00	13.50
(25)	Gillespie	55.00	22.00	13.50
(26)	Griffin	55.00	22.00	13.50
(27)	Gunderson	55.00	22.00	13.50
(28)	Ham	55.00	22.00	13.50
(29)	Handibe (Handiboe)	55.00	22.00	13.50
(30)	Hart	55.00	22.00	13.50
(31)	Hartley	55.00	22.00	13.50
(32)	Hobbs	55.00	22.00	13.50
(33)	Hyames	55.00	22.00	13.50
(34)	Irving	55.00	22.00	13.50
(35)	Kaiser	55.00	22.00	13.50
(36)	Kelley	55.00	22.00	13.50

		NM	EX	VG
(37)	Kelly	55.00	22.00	13.50
(38)	Kelly (mascot)	55.00	22.00	13.50
(39)	Luyster	55.00	22.00	13.50
(40)	MacDonald	55.00	22.00	13.50
(41)	Malcolm	55.00	22.00	13.50
(42)	Mayer	55.00	22.00	13.50
(43)	McCormac (McCormick)	55.00	22.00	13.50
(44)	McGeeham (McGeehan)	55.00	22.00	13.50
(45)	Merchant	55.00	22.00	13.50
(46)	Mills	55.00	22.00	13.50
(47)	Morgan	55.00	22.00	13.50
(48)	Morris	55.00	22.00	13.50
(49)	Munson	55.00	22.00	13.50
(50)	Newman	55.00	22.00	13.50
(51)	Noval (Novak)	55.00	22.00	13.50
(52)	O'Halloran	55.00	22.00	13.50
(53)	Phelan	55.00	22.00	13.50
(54)	Prim	55.00	22.00	13.50
(55)	Reeves	55.00	22.00	13.50
(56)	Richardson	55.00	22.00	13.50
(57)	Schumaker	55.00	22.00	13.50
(58)	Sharp	55.00	22.00	13.50
(59)	Sherrill	55.00	22.00	13.50
(60)	Simmons	55.00	22.00	13.50
(61)	Steinbach	55.00	22.00	13.50
(62)	Stohr	55.00	22.00	13.50
(63)	Taylor	55.00	22.00	13.50
(64)	Webb	55.00	22.00	13.50
(65)	Whelan	55.00	22.00	13.50
(66)	Wolf	55.00	22.00	13.50
(67)	Wright	55.00	22.00	13.50

1910 Old Mill Cigarettes Series 8 (Southern Assn.)

		NM	EX	VG
Complete Set (114):		25000.	12500.	7500.
Common Player:		55.00	22.00	13.50
(1)	Allen (Memphis)	55.00	22.00	13.50
(2)	Allen (Mobile)	55.00	22.00	13.50
(3)	Anderson	55.00	22.00	13.50
(4)	Babb	55.00	22.00	13.50
(5)	Bartley	55.00	22.00	13.50
(6)	Bauer	55.00	22.00	13.50
(7)	Bay	55.00	22.00	13.50
(8)	Bayliss	55.00	22.00	13.50
(9)	Berger	55.00	22.00	13.50
(10)	Bernhard	55.00	22.00	13.50
(11)	Bitroff	55.00	22.00	13.50
(12)	Breitenstein	55.00	22.00	13.50
(13)	Bronkie	55.00	22.00	13.50
(14)	Brooks	55.00	22.00	13.50
(15)	Burnett	55.00	22.00	13.50
(16)	Cafalu	55.00	22.00	13.50
(17)	Carson	55.00	22.00	13.50
(18)	Case	55.00	22.00	13.50
(19)	Chappelle	55.00	22.00	13.50
(20)	Cohen	55.00	22.00	13.50
(21)	Collins	55.00	22.00	13.50
(22)	Crandall	55.00	22.00	13.50
(23)	Cross	55.00	22.00	13.50
(24)	Jud. Daly	55.00	22.00	13.50
(25)	Davis	55.00	22.00	13.50
(26)	Demaree	55.00	22.00	13.50
(27)	DeMontreville	55.00	22.00	13.50
(28)	E. DeMontreville	55.00	22.00	13.50
(29)	Dick	55.00	22.00	13.50
(30)	Dobbs	55.00	22.00	13.50
(31)	Dudley	55.00	22.00	13.50
(32)	Dunn	55.00	22.00	13.50
(33)	Elliot	55.00	22.00	13.50
(34)	Emery	55.00	22.00	13.50
(35)	Erloff	55.00	22.00	13.50
(36)	Farrell	55.00	22.00	13.50
(37)	Fisher	55.00	22.00	13.50
(38)	Fleharty	55.00	22.00	13.50
(39)	Flood	55.00	22.00	13.50
(40)	Foster	55.00	22.00	13.50
(41)	Fritz	55.00	22.00	13.50
(42)	Greminger	55.00	22.00	13.50
(43)	Gribbon	55.00	22.00	13.50
(44)	Griffin	55.00	22.00	13.50
(45)	Gygli	55.00	22.00	13.50
(46)	Hanks	55.00	22.00	13.50
(47)	Hart	55.00	22.00	13.50
(48)	Hess	55.00	22.00	13.50
(49)	Hickman	55.00	22.00	13.50
(50)	Hohnhorst	55.00	22.00	13.50
(51)	Huelsman	55.00	22.00	13.50
(52)	Jackson	22500.	11250.	6750.
(53)	Jordan	55.00	22.00	13.50
(54)	Kane	55.00	22.00	13.50
(55)	Kelly	55.00	22.00	13.50
(56)	Kerwin	55.00	22.00	13.50
(57)	Keupper	55.00	22.00	13.50
(58)	LaFitte	55.00	22.00	13.50
(59)	Larsen	55.00	22.00	13.50
(60)	Lindsay	55.00	22.00	13.50
(61)	Lynch	55.00	22.00	13.50
(62)	Manuel	55.00	22.00	13.50
(63)	Manush	55.00	22.00	13.50
(64)	Marcan	55.00	22.00	13.50
(65)	Maxwell	55.00	22.00	13.50
(66)	McBride	55.00	22.00	13.50
(67)	McCreery	55.00	22.00	13.50
(68)	McGilvray	55.00	22.00	13.50
(69)	McLaurin	55.00	22.00	13.50
(70)	McTigue	55.00	22.00	13.50
(71)	Miller (Chattanooga)	55.00	22.00	13.50
(72)	Miller (Montgomery)	55.00	22.00	13.50
(73)	Molesworth	55.00	22.00	13.50
(74)	Moran	55.00	22.00	13.50
(75)	Newton	55.00	22.00	13.50
(76)	Nolley	55.00	22.00	13.50
(77)	Osteen	55.00	22.00	13.50
(78)	Owen	55.00	22.00	13.50
(79)	Paige	55.00	22.00	13.50
(80)	Patterson	55.00	22.00	13.50
(81)	Pepe	55.00	22.00	13.50
(82)	Perdue	55.00	22.00	13.50
(83)	Peters	55.00	22.00	13.50
(84)	Phillips	55.00	22.00	13.50
(85)	Pratt	55.00	22.00	13.50
(86)	Rementer	55.00	22.00	13.50
(87)	Rhodes	55.00	22.00	13.50
(88)	Rhoton	55.00	22.00	13.50
(89)	Robertson	55.00	22.00	13.50
(90)	Rogers	55.00	22.00	13.50
(91)	Rohe	55.00	22.00	13.50
(92)	Seabough (Seabaugh)	55.00	22.00	13.50
(93)	Seitz	55.00	22.00	13.50
(94)	Schlitzer	55.00	22.00	13.50
(95)	Schopp	55.00	22.00	13.50
(96)	Siegle	55.00	22.00	13.50
(97)	Smith	55.00	22.00	13.50
(98)	Sid. Smith	55.00	22.00	13.50
(99)	Steele	55.00	22.00	13.50
(100)	Swacina	55.00	22.00	13.50
(101)	Sweeney	55.00	22.00	13.50
(102)	Thomas (fielding)	55.00	22.00	13.50
(103)	Thomas (portrait)	55.00	22.00	13.50
(104)	Vinson	55.00	22.00	13.50
(105)	Wagner (Birmingham)	55.00	22.00	13.50
(106)	Wagner (Mobile)	55.00	22.00	13.50
(107)	Walker	55.00	22.00	13.50
(108)	Wanner	55.00	22.00	13.50
(109)	Welf	55.00	22.00	13.50
(110)	Whiteman	55.00	22.00	13.50
(111)	Whitney	55.00	22.00	13.50
(112)	Wilder	55.00	22.00	13.50
(113)	Wiseman	55.00	22.00	13.50
(114)	Yerkes	55.00	22.00	13.50

1910 Old Mill Cabinets

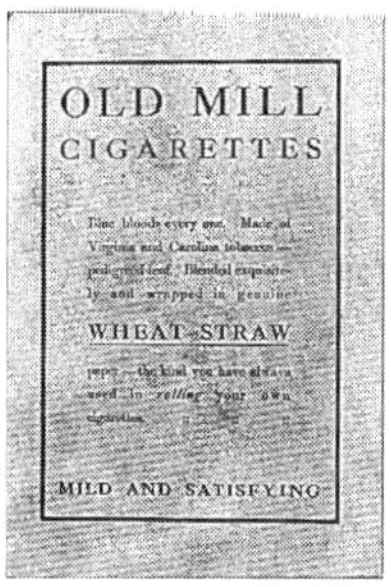

Similar in size and style to the more popular T3 Turkey Red cabinet cards of the same period, the Old Mill cabinets are much scarcer and picture fewer players. Issued in 1910 as a premium by Old Mill Cigarettes, these minor league cards measure approximately 5-3/8" x 7-5/8". Unlike the Turkey Reds, which feature full-color lithographs, the Old Mill cabinet cards picture the players in black-and-white photos surrounded by a wide tan border. The player's last name is printed in black in the lower-left corner, while his team designation appears in the lower-right. Backs carry an advertisement for Old Mill. There are currently 29 known subjects in the set, all players from the old Virginia League. Only two of them (Enos Kirkpatrick and Clarence Munson) ever reached the major leagues. Twenty-five of the 29 players were also featured in the second series of the T-210 set, a massive 640-card set also issued by Old Mill Cigarettes the same year. The Old Mill cabinet cards carry the ACC designation H801-7.

		NM	EX	VG
Common Player:		1000.	500.00	300.00
(1)	Bentley	1000.	500.00	300.00
(2)	Bowen	1000.	500.00	300.00
(3)	Brazille (Brazell)	1000.	500.00	300.00
(4)	Bush (Busch)	1000.	500.00	300.00
(5)	Bussey	1000.	500.00	300.00
(6)	Cross	1000.	500.00	300.00
(7)	Derrick	1000.	500.00	300.00
(8)	Doane	1000.	500.00	300.00
(9)	Doyle	1000.	500.00	300.00
(10)	Fox	1000.	500.00	300.00
(11)	Griffin	1000.	500.00	300.00
(12)	Hearn	1000.	500.00	300.00
(13)	Hooker	1000.	500.00	300.00
(14)	Kirkpatrick	1000.	500.00	300.00
(15)	Laughlin	1000.	500.00	300.00
(16)	McKevitt	1000.	500.00	300.00
(17)	Munson	1000.	500.00	300.00
(18)	Noojn (Noojin)	1000.	500.00	300.00
(19)	O'Halloran	1000.	500.00	300.00
(20)	Pressly	1000.	500.00	300.00
(21)	Revelle	1000.	500.00	300.00
(22)	A. Smith	1000.	500.00	300.00
(23)	Spratt	1000.	500.00	300.00
(24)	Simmons	1000.	500.00	300.00
(25)	Titman	1000.	500.00	300.00
(26)	Walters	1000.	500.00	300.00
(27)	Wallace	1000.	500.00	300.00
(28)	Weherell (Wehrell)	1000.	500.00	300.00
(29)	Woolums	1000.	500.00	300.00

1957 Omaha Cardinals Picture-Pak

These 3-3/8" x 4-3/8" black-and-white, blank-back photos were sold in a team picture pack. Fronts have a facsimile autograph. The unnumbered cards are checklisted here in alphabetical order.

		NM	EX	VG
Complete Set (24):		450.00	225.00	135.00
Common Player:		22.00	11.00	6.50
(1)	Frank Barnes	22.00	11.00	6.50
(2)	Bill Bergesch	22.00	11.00	6.50
(3)	Dick Brown	22.00	11.00	6.50
(4)	Tom Cheney	22.00	11.00	6.50
(5)	Nels Chittum	22.00	11.00	6.50
(6)	Jim Command	22.00	11.00	6.50
(7)	Chuck Diering	22.00	11.00	6.50
(8)	Sherry Dixon	22.00	11.00	6.50
(9)	Glen Gorbous	22.00	11.00	6.50
(10)	Johnny Keane	22.00	11.00	6.50
(11)	Jim King	22.00	11.00	6.50
(12)	Paul Kippels	22.00	11.00	6.50
(13)	Don Lassetter	22.00	11.00	6.50
(14)	Don Liddle	22.00	11.00	6.50
(15)	Lou Limmer	22.00	11.00	6.50
(16)	Boyd Linker	22.00	11.00	6.50
(17)	Bob Mabe	22.00	11.00	6.50
(18)	Herb Moford	22.00	11.00	6.50
(19)	Rance Pless	22.00	11.00	6.50
(20)	Kelton Russell	22.00	11.00	6.50
(21)	Barney Schultz	22.00	11.00	6.50
(22)	Milt Smith	22.00	11.00	6.50
(23)	Glen Stabelfeld	22.00	11.00	6.50
(24)	Header card	22.00	11.00	6.50

1958 Omaha Cardinals Picture-Pak

This rare late-1950s minor league issue contains the first card of Hall of Fame pitcher Bob Gibson. Probably sold as a complete set in format similar to major league picture packs of the era, there are 23 player cards and a header card. Cards measure 3-3/8" x 4-3/8", have a black-and-white player picture and facsimile autograph. They are blank-backed. The checklist of the unnumbered cards is printed here in alphabetical order.

		NM	EX	VG
Complete Set (24):		450.00	225.00	135.00
Common Player:		10.00	5.00	3.00
(1)	Tony Alomar	15.00	7.50	3.00
(2)	Dave Benedict	10.00	5.00	3.00
(3)	Bill Bergesch	10.00	5.00	3.00
(4)	Bob Blaylock	10.00	5.00	3.00
(5)	Prentice "Pidge" Browne	10.00	5.00	3.00
(6)	Chris Cannizzaro	10.00	5.00	3.00
(7)	Nels Chittum	10.00	5.00	3.00
(8)	Don Choate	10.00	5.00	3.00
(9)	Phil Clark	10.00	5.00	3.00
(10)	Jim Frey	20.00	10.00	6.00
(11)	Bob Gibson	200.00	100.00	60.00
(12)	Ev Joyner	10.00	5.00	3.00
(13)	Johnny Keane	10.00	5.00	3.00
(14)	Paul Kippels	10.00	5.00	3.00

		NM	EX	VG
(15)	Boyd Linker	10.00	5.00	3.00
(16)	Bob Mabe	10.00	5.00	3.00
(17)	Bernard Mateosky	10.00	5.00	3.00
(18)	Ronnie Plaza	10.00	5.00	3.00
(19)	Bill Queen	10.00	5.00	3.00
(20)	Bill Smith	10.00	5.00	3.00
(21)	Bobby G. Smith	10.00	5.00	3.00
(22)	Lee Tate	10.00	5.00	3.00
(23)	Benny Valenzuela	10.00	5.00	3.00
(24)	Header card	10.00	5.00	3.00

1962 Omaha Dodgers

This unnumbered black-and-white set measures 3-3/8" x 4-1/4" and is blank-backed. It was produced by photographer/collector Mel Bailey in an edition of 1,000 sets, sold for 50 cents by mail and at the stadium concession stand. Cards bear a facsimile autograph.

		NM	EX	VG
Complete Set (22):		200.00	100.00	60.00
Common Player:		10.00	5.00	3.00
(1)	Joe Altobelli	12.50	6.25	3.75
(2)	Jim Barbieri	10.00	5.00	3.00
(3)	Scott Breeden	10.00	5.00	3.00
(4)	Mike Brumley	10.00	5.00	3.00
(5)	Jose Cesar	10.00	5.00	3.00
(6)	Bill Hunter	10.00	5.00	3.00
(7)	Don LeJohn	10.00	5.00	3.00
(8)	Jack Lutz	10.00	5.00	3.00
(9)	Ken McMullen	10.00	5.00	3.00
(10)	Danny Ozark	10.00	5.00	3.00
(11)	Curt Roberts	10.00	5.00	3.00
(12)	Ernie Rodriguez	10.00	5.00	3.00
(13)	Dick Scarbrough	10.00	5.00	3.00
(14)	Bart Shirley	10.00	5.00	3.00
(15)	Dick Smith	10.00	5.00	3.00
(16)	Jack Smith	10.00	5.00	3.00
(17)	Nate Smith	10.00	5.00	3.00
(18)	Gene Snyder	10.00	5.00	3.00
(19)	Burbon Wheeler	10.00	5.00	3.00
(20)	Nick Wilhite (Willhite)	10.00	5.00	3.00
(21)	Jim Williams	10.00	5.00	3.00
(22)	Larry Williams	10.00	5.00	3.00

P

1911 Pacific Coast Biscuit (D310)

A dozen players each from six Pacific Coast League teams are represented in this set. Cards are about 2-1/2" x 4-1/4" with either black-and-white or sepia pictures on front. Backs have a checklist arranged by team.

		NM	EX	VG
Complete Set (72):		11750.	550.00	325.00
Common Player:		200.00	100.00	60.00
(1)	Ables	200.00	100.00	60.00
(2)	Agnew	200.00	100.00	60.00
(3)	Akin	200.00	100.00	60.00
(4)	Arrelanes	200.00	100.00	60.00
(5)	Baum	200.00	100.00	60.00
(6)	Bernard	200.00	100.00	60.00
(7)	Berry	200.00	100.00	60.00
(8)	Brashear	200.00	100.00	60.00
(9)	Browning	200.00	100.00	60.00
(10)	Burrell	200.00	100.00	60.00
(11)	Byram	200.00	100.00	60.00
(12)	Carlisle	200.00	100.00	60.00
(13)	Chadbourne	200.00	100.00	60.00
(14)	Christian	200.00	100.00	60.00
(15)	Cutshaw	200.00	100.00	60.00
(16)	Daley	200.00	100.00	60.00
(17)	Danzig	200.00	100.00	60.00
(18)	Delhi	200.00	100.00	60.00
(19)	Delmas	200.00	100.00	60.00
(20)	Dillon	200.00	100.00	60.00
(21)	Fitzgerald	200.00	100.00	60.00
(22)	Gipe	200.00	100.00	60.00
(23)	Heister	200.00	100.00	60.00
(24)	Henderson	200.00	100.00	60.00
(25)	Henley	200.00	100.00	60.00
(26)	Hitt	200.00	100.00	60.00
(27)	Hoffman	200.00	100.00	60.00
(28)	Hogan	200.00	100.00	60.00
(29)	Holland	200.00	100.00	60.00
(30)	Hosp	200.00	100.00	60.00
(31)	Howard	200.00	100.00	60.00
(32)	Kostner	200.00	100.00	60.00
(33)	Kuhn	200.00	100.00	60.00
(34)	LaLonge	200.00	100.00	60.00
(35)	Lewis	200.00	100.00	60.00
(36)	Maddern	200.00	100.00	60.00
(37)	Maggert	200.00	100.00	60.00
(38)	McArdle	200.00	100.00	60.00
(39)	McCredie	200.00	100.00	60.00
(40)	McDonnell	200.00	100.00	60.00
(41)	Metzger	200.00	100.00	60.00
(42)	Mitze	200.00	100.00	60.00
(43)	Mohler	200.00	100.00	60.00
(44)	Moore	200.00	100.00	60.00
(45)	Murray	200.00	100.00	60.00
(46)	Nourse	200.00	100.00	60.00
(47)	O'Rourke	200.00	100.00	60.00
(48)	Patterson	200.00	100.00	60.00
(49)	Peckinpaugh	225.00	112.00	67.00
(50)	Pernoll	200.00	100.00	60.00
(51)	Pfyl	200.00	100.00	60.00
(52)	Raleigh	200.00	100.00	60.00
(53)	Rapps	200.00	100.00	60.00
(54)	Ross	200.00	100.00	60.00
(55)	Ryan	200.00	100.00	60.00
(56)	Seaton	200.00	100.00	60.00
(57)	Sheehan	200.00	100.00	60.00
(58)	A. Smith	200.00	100.00	60.00
(59)	H. Smith	200.00	100.00	60.00
(60)	Steen	200.00	100.00	60.00
(61)	Stinson	200.00	100.00	60.00
(62)	Sutor	200.00	100.00	60.00
(63)	Tennant	200.00	100.00	60.00
(64)	Thompson	200.00	100.00	60.00
(65)	Tiedeman	200.00	100.00	60.00
(66)	Tozer	200.00	100.00	60.00
(67)	Van Buren	200.00	100.00	60.00
(68)	Witt	200.00	100.00	60.00
(69)	Wares	200.00	100.00	60.00
(70)	Weaver	600.00	300.00	180.00
(71)	Wolverton	200.00	100.00	60.00
(72)	Zacher	200.00	100.00	60.00

1911 Pacific Coast Biscuit (D311)

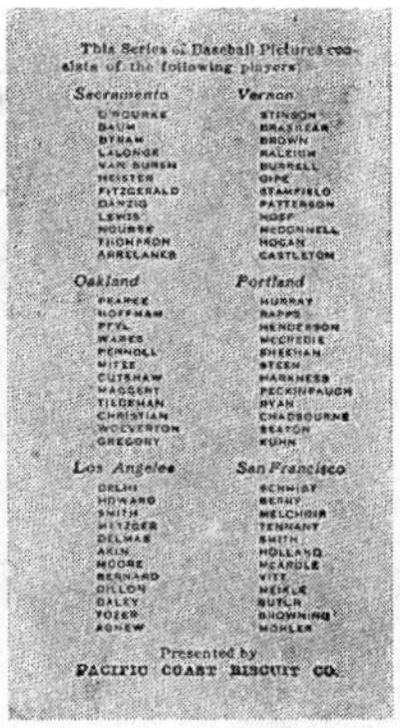

This Series of Baseball Pictures consists of the following players:

Sacramento: O'ROURKE, BAUM, BYRAM, LALONGE, VAN BUREN, HEISTER, FITZGERALD, DANZIG, LEWIS, NOURSE, THOMPSON, ARRELANES

Vernon: STINSON, BRASHEAR, BROWN, RALEIGH, BURRELL, GIPE, STAMFIELD, PATTERSON, HOSP, McDONNELL, HOGAN, CASTLETON

Oakland: PEARCE, HOFFMAN, PFYL, WARES, PERNOLL, MITZE, CUTSHAW, MAGGERT, TIEDEMAN, CHRISTIAN, WOLVERTON, GREGORY

Portland: MURRAY, RAPPS, HENDERSON, McCREDIE, SHEEHAN, STEEN, HARKNESS, PECKINPAUGH, RYAN, CHADBOURNE, SEATON, KUHN

Los Angeles: DELHI, HOWARD, SMITH, METZGER, DELMAS, AKIN, MOORE, BERNARD, DILLON, DALEY, TOZER, AGNEW

San Francisco: SCHMIDT, BERRY, MELCHOIR, TENNANT, SMITH, HOLLAND, McARDLE, VITT, MEIKLE, BUTLER, BROWNING, MOHLER

Presented by
PACIFIC COAST BISCUIT CO.

A dozen players each from six Pacific Coast League teams are represented in this set. Cards are about 1-1/2" x 2-5/8" with pastel colored pictures on front. Backs have a checklist arranged by team.

		NM	EX	VG
Complete Set (72):		8500.	4200.	2500.
Common Player:		150.00	75.00	45.00
(1)	Agnew	150.00	75.00	45.00
(2)	Akin	150.00	75.00	45.00
(3)	Arrelanes	150.00	75.00	45.00
(4)	Baum	150.00	75.00	45.00
(5)	Bernard	150.00	75.00	45.00
(6)	Berry	150.00	75.00	45.00
(7)	Brashear	150.00	75.00	45.00
(8)	Brown	150.00	75.00	45.00
(9)	Browning	150.00	75.00	45.00
(10)	Burrell	150.00	75.00	45.00
(11)	Byram	150.00	75.00	45.00
(12)	Castleton	150.00	75.00	45.00
(13)	Chadbourne	150.00	75.00	45.00
(14)	Christian	150.00	75.00	45.00
(15)	Cutshaw	150.00	75.00	45.00
(16)	Daley	150.00	75.00	45.00
(17)	Danzig	150.00	75.00	45.00
(18)	Delhi	150.00	75.00	45.00
(19)	Delmas	150.00	75.00	45.00
(20)	Dillon	150.00	75.00	45.00
(21)	Fitzgerald	150.00	75.00	45.00
(22)	Gipe	150.00	75.00	45.00
(23)	Gregory	150.00	75.00	45.00
(24)	Harkness	150.00	75.00	45.00
(25)	Heister	150.00	75.00	45.00
(26)	Henderson	150.00	75.00	45.00
(27)	Hoffman	150.00	75.00	45.00
(28)	Hogan	150.00	75.00	45.00
(29)	Holland	150.00	75.00	45.00
(30)	Hosp	150.00	75.00	45.00
(31)	Howard	150.00	75.00	45.00
(32)	Kuhn	150.00	75.00	45.00
(33)	LaLonge	150.00	75.00	45.00
(34)	Lewis	150.00	75.00	45.00
(35)	Maggert	150.00	75.00	45.00
(36)	McArdle	150.00	75.00	45.00
(37)	McCredie	150.00	75.00	45.00
(38)	McDonnell	150.00	75.00	45.00
(39)	Meikle	150.00	75.00	45.00
(40)	Melchoir	150.00	75.00	45.00
(41)	Metzger	150.00	75.00	45.00
(42)	Mitze	150.00	75.00	45.00
(43)	Mohler	150.00	75.00	45.00
(44)	Moore	150.00	75.00	45.00
(45)	Murray	150.00	75.00	45.00
(46)	Nourse	150.00	75.00	45.00
(47)	O'Rourke	150.00	75.00	45.00
(48)	Patterson	150.00	75.00	45.00
(49)	Pearce	150.00	75.00	45.00
(50)	Peckinpaugh	175.00	87.00	52.00
(51)	Pernoll	150.00	75.00	45.00
(52)	Pfyl	150.00	75.00	45.00
(53)	Raleigh	150.00	75.00	45.00
(54)	Rapps	150.00	75.00	45.00
(55)	Ryan	150.00	75.00	45.00
(56)	Schmidt	150.00	75.00	45.00
(57)	Seaton	150.00	75.00	45.00
(58)	Sheehan	150.00	75.00	45.00
(59)	A. Smith	150.00	75.00	45.00
(60)	H. Smith	150.00	75.00	45.00
(61)	Stamfield	150.00	75.00	45.00
(62)	Steen	150.00	75.00	45.00
(63)	Stinson	150.00	75.00	45.00
(64)	Sutor	150.00	75.00	45.00
(65)	Tennant	150.00	75.00	45.00
(66)	Thompson	150.00	75.00	45.00
(67)	Tiedeman	150.00	75.00	45.00
(68)	Tozer	150.00	75.00	45.00
(69)	Van Buren	150.00	75.00	45.00
(70)	Witt	150.00	75.00	45.00
(71)	Wares	150.00	75.00	45.00
(72)	Wolverton	150.00	75.00	45.00
(1)	Ables	150.00	75.00	45.00
(2)	Agnew	150.00	75.00	45.00
(3)	Akin	150.00	75.00	45.00
(4)	Arrelanes	150.00	75.00	45.00
(5)	Baum	150.00	75.00	45.00
(6)	Bernard	150.00	75.00	45.00
(7)	Berry	150.00	75.00	45.00
(8)	Brashear	150.00	75.00	45.00
(9)	Browning	150.00	75.00	45.00
(10)	Burrell	150.00	75.00	45.00
(11)	Byram	150.00	75.00	45.00
(12)	Carlisle	150.00	75.00	45.00
(13)	Chadbourne	150.00	75.00	45.00
(14)	Christian	150.00	75.00	45.00
(15)	Cutshaw	150.00	75.00	45.00
(16)	Daley	150.00	75.00	45.00
(17)	Danzig	150.00	75.00	45.00
(18)	Delhi	150.00	75.00	45.00
(19)	Delmas	150.00	75.00	45.00
(20)	Dillon	150.00	75.00	45.00
(21)	Fitzgerald	150.00	75.00	45.00
(22)	Gipe	150.00	75.00	45.00
(23)	Heister	150.00	75.00	45.00
(24)	Henderson	150.00	75.00	45.00
(25)	Henley	150.00	75.00	45.00
(26)	Hitt	150.00	75.00	45.00
(27)	Hoffman	150.00	75.00	45.00
(28)	Hogan	150.00	75.00	45.00
(29)	Holland	150.00	75.00	45.00
(30)	Hosp	150.00	75.00	45.00
(31)	Howard	150.00	75.00	45.00
(32)	Kostner	150.00	75.00	45.00
(33)	Kuhn	150.00	75.00	45.00
(34)	LaLonge	150.00	75.00	45.00
(35)	Lewis	150.00	75.00	45.00
(36)	Maddern	150.00	75.00	45.00
(37)	Maggert	150.00	75.00	45.00
(38)	McArdle	150.00	75.00	45.00
(39)	McCredie	150.00	75.00	45.00
(40)	McDonnell	150.00	75.00	45.00
(41)	Metzger	150.00	75.00	45.00
(42)	Mitz	150.00	75.00	45.00
(43)	Mohler	150.00	75.00	45.00
(44)	Moore	150.00	75.00	45.00
(45)	Murray	150.00	75.00	45.00
(46)	Nourse	150.00	75.00	45.00
(47)	O'Rourke	150.00	75.00	45.00
(48)	Patterson	150.00	75.00	45.00
(49)	Peckinpaugh	150.00	75.00	45.00
(50)	Pernoll	150.00	75.00	45.00
(51)	Pfyl	150.00	75.00	45.00
(52)	Raleigh	150.00	75.00	45.00
(53)	Rapps	150.00	75.00	45.00
(54)	Ross	150.00	75.00	45.00

		NM	EX	VG
(55)	Ryan	150.00	75.00	45.00
(56)	Seaton	150.00	75.00	45.00
(57)	Sheehan	150.00	75.00	45.00
(58)	A. Smith	150.00	75.00	45.00
(59)	H. Smith	150.00	75.00	45.00
(60)	Steen	150.00	75.00	45.00
(61)	Stinson	150.00	75.00	45.00
(62)	Sutor	150.00	75.00	45.00
(63)	Tennant	150.00	75.00	45.00
(64)	Thompson	150.00	75.00	45.00
(65)	Tiedeman	150.00	75.00	45.00
(66)	Tozer	150.00	75.00	45.00
(67)	Van Buren	150.00	75.00	45.00
(68)	Witt	150.00	75.00	45.00
(69)	Wares	150.00	75.00	45.00
(70)	Weaver	150.00	75.00	45.00
(71)	Wolverton	150.00	75.00	45.00
(72)	Zacher	150.00	75.00	45.00

1943-47 Parade Sportive

Over a period of years in the mid-1940s, Montreal sports radio personality Paul Stuart's Parade Sportive program issued a series of baseball player pictures of Montreal Royals and occasional other International League stars. The pictures were issued in 5" x 9-1/2"and 7" x 10" black-and-white, blank-back format. Each picture carries the name of the radio station on which Stuart's program was broadcast, along with and ad at the bottom for one of his sponsors. The unnumbered pictures are listed here alphabetically; it is unknown whether this list constitutes the complete issue.

		NM	EX	VG
Common Player:		20.00	10.00	6.00
(1)	Jack Banta	20.00	10.00	6.00
(2)	Stan Briard	20.00	10.00	6.00
(3)	Les Burge	20.00	10.00	6.00
(4)	Paul Calvert	20.00	10.00	6.00
(5)	Al Campanis	35.00	17.50	10.50
(6)	Red Durrett	20.00	10.00	6.00
(7)	Herman Franks	25.00	12.50	7.50
(8)	John Gabbard	20.00	10.00	6.00
(9)	Roland Gladu	20.00	10.00	6.00
(10)	Ray Hathaway	20.00	10.00	6.00
(11)	Clay Hopper	20.00	10.00	6.00
(12)	John Jorgensen	25.00	12.50	7.50
(13)	Paul "Pepper" Martin	20.00	10.00	6.00
(14)	Steve Nagy	20.00	10.00	6.00
(15)	Marv Rackley	20.00	10.00	6.00
(16)	Jackie Robinson	300.00	150.00	90.00
(17)	Jean-Pierre Roy	20.00	10.00	6.00
(18)	1944 Montreal Royals team photo	30.00	15.00	9.00
(19)	1945 Montreal Royals team photo	30.00	15.00	9.00
(20)	1946 Montreal Royals team photo	125.00	62.00	37.00
(21)	Stan Briard, Roland Gladu, Jean-Pierre Roy	20.00	10.00	6.00

1952 Parkhurst

Produced by a Canadian competitor to Kool-Aid, this 100-card set features players from three International League teams, the Toronto Maple Leafs, Montreal Royals and Ottawa Athletics, along with cards featuring baseball playing tips and quizzes. Measuring 2" x 2-1/2", the cards feature black-and-white player photos on front. Backs are printed in red and have a few biographical details, 1951 stats and an ad for Frostade.

		NM	EX	VG
Complete Set (100):		1950.	975.00	575.00
Common Player (1-25, 49-100):		25.00	12.50	7.50
Common Player (26-48):		10.00	5.00	3.00
1	Joe Becker	80.00	15.00	9.00
2	Bobby Rhawn	25.00	12.50	7.50
3	Aaron Silverman	25.00	12.50	7.50
4	Russ Bauers	25.00	12.50	7.50
5	Bill Jennings	25.00	12.50	7.50
6	Grover Bowers	25.00	12.50	7.50
7	Vic Lombardi	25.00	12.50	7.50
8	Billy DeMars	25.00	12.50	7.50
9	Frank Colman	25.00	12.50	7.50
10	Charley Grant	25.00	12.50	7.50
11	Irving Medlinger	25.00	12.50	7.50
12	Burke McLaughlin	25.00	12.50	7.50
13	Lew Morton	25.00	12.50	7.50
14	Red Barrett	25.00	12.50	7.50
15	Leon Foulk	25.00	12.50	7.50
16	Neil Sheridan	25.00	12.50	7.50
17	Ferrell Anderson	25.00	12.50	7.50
18	Roy Shore	25.00	12.50	7.50
19	Duke Markell	25.00	12.50	7.50
20	Bobby Balcena	25.00	12.50	7.50
21	Wilmer Fields	25.00	12.50	7.50
22	Charlie White	25.00	12.50	7.50
23	Red Fahr	25.00	12.50	7.50
24	Jose Bracho	25.00	12.50	7.50
25	Ed Stevens	25.00	12.50	7.50
26	Maple Leaf Stadium	25.00	12.50	7.50
27	Throwing Home	10.00	5.00	3.00
28	Regulation Baseball Diamond	10.00	5.00	3.00
29	Gripping the Bat	10.00	5.00	3.00
30	Hiding the Pitch	10.00	5.00	3.00
31	Catcher's Stance	10.00	5.00	3.00
32	Quiz: "How long does..."	10.00	5.00	3.00
33	Finger and Arm Exercises	10.00	5.00	3.00
34	First Baseman	10.00	5.00	3.00
35	Pitcher's Stance	10.00	5.00	3.00
36	Swinging Bats	10.00	5.00	3.00
37	Quiz: "Can a player advance..."	10.00	5.00	3.00
38	Watch the Ball	10.00	5.00	3.00
39	Quiz: "Can a team..."	10.00	5.00	3.00
40	Quiz: "Can a player put ..."	10.00	5.00	3.00
41	How to Bunt	10.00	5.00	3.00
42	Wrist Snap	10.00	5.00	3.00
43	Pitching Practice	10.00	5.00	3.00
44	Stealing Bases	10.00	5.00	3.00
45	Pitching 1	10.00	5.00	3.00
46	Pitching 2	10.00	5.00	3.00
47	Signals	10.00	5.00	3.00
48	Regulation baseballs	10.00	5.00	3.00
49	Al Ronning	25.00	12.50	7.50
50	Bill Lane	25.00	12.50	7.50
51	Will Sampson	25.00	12.50	7.50
52	Charlie Thompson	25.00	12.50	7.50
53	Ezra McGlothin	25.00	12.50	7.50
54	Spook Jacobs	24.00	12.00	7.25
55	Art Fabbro	25.00	12.50	7.50
56	Jim Hughes	25.00	12.50	7.50
57	Don Hoak	60.00	30.00	18.00
58	Tommy Lasorda	150.00	75.00	45.00
59	Gil Mills	25.00	12.50	7.50
60	Malcolm Mallette	25.00	12.50	7.50
61	Rocky Nelson	22.00	11.00	6.50
62	John Simmons	25.00	12.50	7.50
63	Bob Alexander	25.00	12.50	7.50
64	Dan Bankhead	35.00	17.50	10.50
65	Solomon Coleman	25.00	12.50	7.50
66	Walt Alston	150.00	75.00	45.00
67	Walt Fiala	25.00	12.50	7.50
68	Jim Gilliam	50.00	25.00	15.00
69	Jim Pendleton	25.00	12.50	7.50
70	Gino Cimoli	24.00	12.00	7.25
71	Carmen Mauro	25.00	12.50	7.50
72	Walt Moryn	25.00	12.50	7.50
73	Jim Romano	25.00	12.50	7.50
74	Joe Lutz	25.00	12.50	7.50
75	Ed Roebuck	25.00	12.50	7.50
76	Johnny Podres	50.00	25.00	15.00
77	Walter Novik	25.00	12.50	7.50
78	Lefty Gohl	25.00	12.50	7.50
79	Tom Kirk	25.00	12.50	7.50
80	Bob Betz	25.00	12.50	7.50
81	Bill Hockenbury	25.00	12.50	7.50
82	Al Rubeling	25.00	12.50	7.50
83	Julius Watlington	25.00	12.50	7.50
84	Frank Fanovich	25.00	12.50	7.50
85	Hank Foiles	25.00	12.50	7.50
86	Lou Limmer	25.00	12.50	7.50
87	Ed Hrabcsak	25.00	12.50	7.50
88	Bob Gardner	25.00	12.50	7.50
89	John Metkovich	25.00	12.50	7.50
90	Jean-Pierre Roy	25.00	12.50	7.50
91	Frank Skaff	25.00	12.50	7.50
92	Harry Desert	25.00	12.50	7.50
93	Stan Jok	25.00	12.50	7.50
94	Russ Swingle	25.00	12.50	7.50
95	Bob Wellman	25.00	12.50	7.50
96	John Conway	25.00	12.50	7.50
97	George Maskovich	25.00	12.50	7.50
98	Charlie Bishop	25.00	12.50	7.50
99	Joe Murray	25.00	12.50	7.50
100	Mike Kume	25.00	12.50	7.50

1935 Pebble Beach Clothiers

This series of black-and-white postcards includes only members of the three Bay area Pacific Coast League teams - the Oakland Oaks, Mission Reds and San Francisco Seals. The 3-1/2" x 5-3/8" cards have player identification at left in the bottom white border. The logotype of the clothier which sponsored the issued is at lower-right. The cards - each authentically autographed - were distributed by an area radio station. Backs have typical post-card indicia. This checklist may not be complete.

		NM	EX	VG
Common Player:		600.00	300.00	175.00
(1)	Leroy Anton	600.00	300.00	175.00
(2)	Joe DiMaggio	7500.	3750.	2250.
(3)	Wee Ludolph	600.00	300.00	175.00
(4)	Walter "The Great" Mails	600.00	300.00	175.00
(5)	Lefty O'Doul	900.00	450.00	270.00
(6)	Gabby Street	750.00	375.00	225.00
(7)	Oscar Vitt	600.00	300.00	175.00

1962 Pepsi-Cola Tulsa Oilers

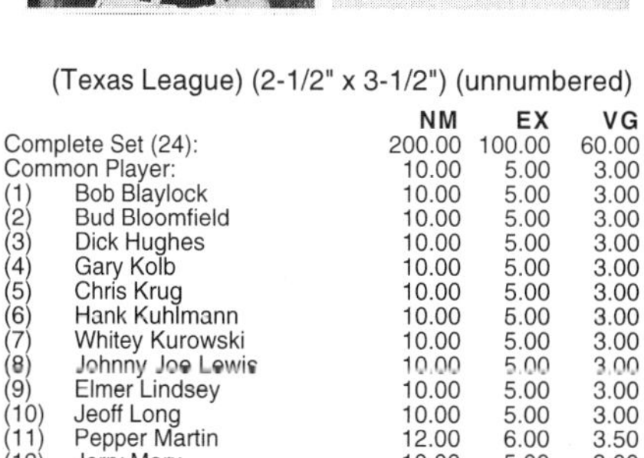

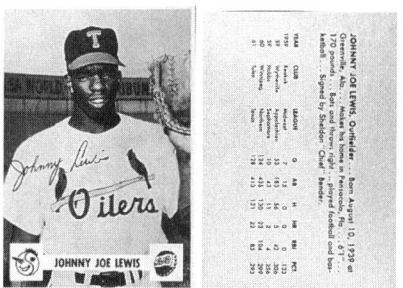

(Texas League) (2-1/2" x 3-1/2") (unnumbered)

		NM	EX	VG
Complete Set (24):		200.00	100.00	60.00
Common Player:		10.00	5.00	3.00
(1)	Bob Blaylock	10.00	5.00	3.00
(2)	Bud Bloomfield	10.00	5.00	3.00
(3)	Dick Hughes	10.00	5.00	3.00
(4)	Gary Kolb	10.00	5.00	3.00
(5)	Chris Krug	10.00	5.00	3.00
(6)	Hank Kuhlmann	10.00	5.00	3.00
(7)	Whitey Kurowski	10.00	5.00	3.00
(8)	Johnny Joe Lewis	10.00	5.00	3.00
(9)	Elmer Lindsey	10.00	5.00	3.00
(10)	Jeoff Long	10.00	5.00	3.00
(11)	Pepper Martin	12.00	6.00	3.50
(12)	Jerry Marx	10.00	5.00	3.00
(13)	Weldon Maudin	10.00	5.00	3.00
(14)	Dal Maxvill	12.00	6.00	3.50
(15)	Bill McNamee	10.00	5.00	3.00
(16)	Joe Patterson	10.00	5.00	3.00
(17)	Gordon Richardson	10.00	5.00	3.00
(18)	Daryl Robertson	10.00	5.00	3.00
(19)	Tom Schwaner	10.00	5.00	3.00
(20)	Joe Shipley	10.00	5.00	3.00
(21)	Jon Smith	10.00	5.00	3.00
(22)	Clint Stark	10.00	5.00	3.00
(23)	Terry Tucker	10.00	5.00	3.00
(24)	Bill Wakefield	10.00	5.00	3.00

1963 Pepsi-Cola Tulsa Oilers

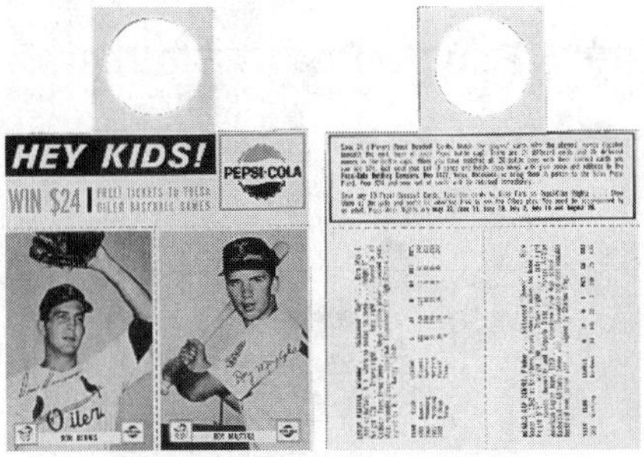

(Texas League) (2-1/2" x 3-1/2", unnumbered, issued in two-card panels with a holed top panel to hang on bottle)

		NM	EX	VG
Complete Set, Singles (24):		160.00	80.00	48.00
Complete Set, Panels (12):		220.00	110.00	65.00
Common Player:		9.00	4.50	2.75
(1)	Dennis Aust	9.00	4.50	2.75
(2)	Jim Beauchamp	9.00	4.50	2.75
(3)	Bud Bloomfield	9.00	4.50	2.75
(4)	Felix DeLeon	9.00	4.50	2.75
(5)	Don Dennis	9.00	4.50	2.75
(6)	Lamar Drummonds	9.00	4.50	2.75
(7)	Tom Hilgendorf	9.00	4.50	2.75
(8)	Gary Kolb	9.00	4.50	2.75
(9)	Chris Krug	9.00	4.50	2.75
(10)	Bee Lindsey	9.00	4.50	2.75
(11)	Ray Majtyka	9.00	4.50	2.75
(12)	Pepper Martin	11.00	5.50	3.25
(13)	Jerry Marx	9.00	4.50	2.75
(14)	Hunkey Mauldin	9.00	4.50	2.75
(15)	Joe Paterson	9.00	4.50	2.75
(16)	Grover Resinger	9.00	4.50	2.75
(17)	Gordon Richardson	9.00	4.50	2.75
(18)	Jon Smith	9.00	4.50	2.75
(19)	Chuck Taylor	9.00	4.50	2.75
(20)	Terry Tucker	9.00	4.50	2.75
(21)	Lou Vickery	9.00	4.50	2.75
(22)	Bill Wakefield	9.00	4.50	2.75
(23)	Harry Watts	9.00	4.50	2.75
(24)	Jerry Wild	9.00	4.50	2.75

1964 Pepsi-Cola Tulsa Oiler Autograph Cards

These unusual baseball cards - they don't have pictures! - were one of several 1960s issues by Pepsi in conjunction with the Tulsa Oilers. Apparently carton stuffers (they measure 2-3/16" x 9"), the cards provided free children's admission on special Pepsi-Oiler nights. The cards are printed in red, white and blue and have short player biographies under the baseball containing the facsimile autograph. The unnumbered cards are listed here in alphabetical order.

		NM	EX	VG
Complete Set (8):		40.00	20.00	12.00
Common Player:		6.00	3.00	1.80
(1)	Bob Blaylock	6.00	3.00	1.80
(2)	Nellie Briles	6.00	3.00	1.80
(3)	Bobby Dews	6.00	3.00	1.80
(4)	Roy Majtyka	6.00	3.00	1.80
(5)	Otto Meischner	6.00	3.00	1.80
(6)	Rogers Robinson	6.00	3.00	1.80
(7)	Jerry Wild	6.00	3.00	1.80
(8)	Lou Vickery	6.00	3.00	1.80

1966 Pepsi-Cola Tulsa Oilers

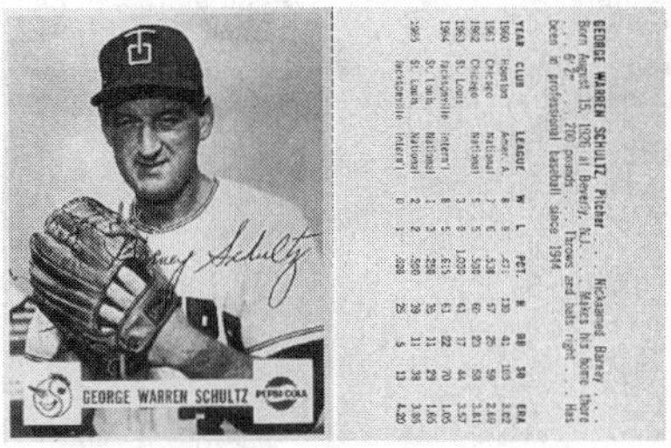

(Pacific Coast League) (2-1/2" x 3-1/2") (unnumbered)

		NM	EX	VG
Complete Set (24):		200.00	100.00	60.00
Common Player:		10.00	5.00	3.00
(1)	Florian Ackley	10.00	5.00	3.00
(2)	Dennis Aust	10.00	5.00	3.00
(3)	Elio Chacon	10.00	5.00	3.00
(4)	James Cosman	10.00	5.00	3.00
(5)	Mack Creager	10.00	5.00	3.00
(6)	Robert Dews	10.00	5.00	3.00
(7)	Harold Gilson	10.00	5.00	3.00
(8)	Larry Jaster	10.00	5.00	3.00
(9)	Alex Johnson	10.00	5.00	3.00
(10)	George Kernek	10.00	5.00	3.00
(11)	Jose Laboy	10.00	5.00	3.00
(12)	Richard LeMay	10.00	5.00	3.00
(13)	Charles Metro	10.00	5.00	3.00
(14)	David Pavlesic	10.00	5.00	3.00
(15)	Robert Pfeil	10.00	5.00	3.00
(16)	Ronald Piche	10.00	5.00	3.00
(17)	Robert Radovich	10.00	5.00	3.00
(18)	David Ricketts	10.00	5.00	3.00
(19)	Theodore Savage	10.00	5.00	3.00
(20)	George Schultz	10.00	5.00	3.00
(21)	Edward Spiezio	10.00	5.00	3.00
(22)	Clint Stark	10.00	5.00	3.00
(23)	Robert Tolan	10.00	5.00	3.00
(24)	Walter Williams	10.00	5.00	3.00

1956 Portland Beaver All-Star Pins

Stars of the Pacific Coast League Portland Beavers, all former and/or future major leaguers, are featured on these 1" black-and-white celluloid pins.

		NM	EX	VG
Complete Set (8):		450.00	225.00	135.00
Common Player:		75.00	37.50	22.00
(1)	Jim Baxes	75.00	37.50	22.00
(2)	Bob Borkowski	75.00	37.50	22.00
(3)	Sam Calderone	75.00	37.50	22.00
(4)	Jack Littrell	75.00	37.50	22.00
(5)	Luis Marquez	75.00	37.50	22.00
(6)	Ed Mickelson	75.00	37.50	22.00
(7)	Tom Saffell	75.00	37.50	22.00
(8)	Rene Valdez	75.00	37.50	22.00

R

1958 Ralph's Thriftway Seattle Rainiers

(See 1958 Seattle Popcorn for checklist and values.)

1968 Red Barn Memphis Blues

A regional issue of a Memphis chain of fast-food restaurants, these 2-1/2" x 3-3/4" cards feature members of the New York Mets' Class AA farm team. Cards have a blue-tinted player photo within an orange barn design. Player information in printed below. Backs are blank. The cards are checklisted here by uniform number.

		NM	EX	VG
Complete Set (8):		200.00	100.00	60.00
Common Player:		30.00	15.00	9.00
3	Mike "Spider" Jorgensen	30.00	15.00	9.00
6	Joe Moock	30.00	15.00	9.00
9	Rod Gaspar	30.00	15.00	9.00
16	Barry "Chief" Raziano	30.00	15.00	9.00
17	Curtis "Bubba" Brown	30.00	15.00	9.00
18	Roger Stevens	30.00	15.00	9.00
19	Ron Paul	30.00	15.00	9.00
24	Steve "Teddy" Christopher	30.00	15.00	9.00

1910 Red Sun (T211)

The 1910 minor league tobacco set issued by Red Sun Cigarettes features 75 players from the Southern Association. The Red Sun issue is similar in size and and style to the massive 640-card Old Mill set (T210) issued the same year. Cards in both sets measure 1-1/2" x 2-5/8" and feature glossy black-and-white player photos. Unlike the Old Mill set, however, the Red Sun cards have a green border surrounding the photograph and a bright red and white advertisement for Red Sun cigarettes on the back. A line at the bottom promotes the cards as "First Series 1 to 75." implying that additional sets would follow, but apparently none ever did. Each of the 75 subjects in the Red Sun set was also pictured in Series Eight of the Old Mill set. Because of the "Glossy" nature of the photographs, cards in both the Old Mill and Red Sun sets are susceptible to cracking, making condition and proper grading of these cards especially important to collectors.

		NM	EX	VG
Complete Set (75):		6750.	2700.	1600.
Common Player:		110.00	45.00	26.00
(1)	Allen	110.00	45.00	26.00
(2)	Anderson	110.00	45.00	26.00
(3)	Babb	110.00	45.00	26.00
(4)	Bartley	110.00	45.00	26.00
(5)	Bay	110.00	45.00	26.00
(6)	Bayliss	110.00	45.00	26.00
(7)	Berger	110.00	45.00	26.00
(8)	Bernard	110.00	45.00	26.00
(9)	Bitroff	110.00	45.00	26.00
(10)	Breitenstein	110.00	45.00	26.00
(11)	Bronkie	110.00	45.00	26.00
(12)	Brooks	110.00	45.00	26.00
(13)	Cafalu	110.00	45.00	26.00
(14)	Case	110.00	45.00	26.00
(15)	Chappelle	110.00	45.00	26.00
(16)	Cohen	110.00	45.00	26.00
(17)	Cross	110.00	45.00	26.00
(18)	Jud. Daly	110.00	45.00	26.00
(19)	Davis	110.00	45.00	26.00
(20)	DeMontreville	110.00	45.00	26.00
(21)	E. DeMontreville	110.00	45.00	26.00
(22)	Dick	110.00	45.00	26.00
(23)	Dunn	110.00	45.00	26.00
(24)	Erloff	110.00	45.00	26.00
(25)	Fisher	110.00	45.00	26.00
(26)	Flood	110.00	45.00	26.00
(27)	Foster	110.00	45.00	26.00
(28)	Fritz	110.00	45.00	26.00
(29)	Greminger	110.00	45.00	26.00
(30)	Gribbon	110.00	45.00	26.00
(31)	Griffin	110.00	45.00	26.00
(32)	Gygli	110.00	45.00	26.00
(33)	Hanks	110.00	45.00	26.00
(34)	Hart	110.00	45.00	26.00
(35)	Hess	110.00	45.00	26.00
(36)	Hickman	110.00	45.00	26.00
(37)	Hohnhorst	110.00	45.00	26.00
(38)	Huelsman	110.00	45.00	26.00
(39)	Jordan	110.00	45.00	26.00
(40)	Kane	110.00	45.00	26.00
(41)	Kelly	110.00	45.00	26.00

		NM	EX	VG
(42)	Kerwin	110.00	45.00	26.00
(43)	Keupper	110.00	45.00	26.00
(44)	LaFitte	110.00	45.00	26.00
(45)	Lindsay	110.00	45.00	26.00
(46)	Lynch	110.00	45.00	26.00
(47)	Manush	110.00	45.00	26.00
(48)	McCreery	110.00	45.00	26.00
(49)	Miller	110.00	45.00	26.00
(50)	Molesworth	110.00	45.00	26.00
(51)	Moran	110.00	45.00	26.00
(52)	Nolley	110.00	45.00	26.00
(53)	Paige	110.00	45.00	26.00
(54)	Pepe	110.00	45.00	26.00
(55)	Perdue	110.00	45.00	26.00
(56)	Pratt	110.00	45.00	26.00
(57)	Rhoton	110.00	45.00	26.00
(58)	Robertson	110.00	45.00	26.00
(59)	Rogers	110.00	45.00	26.00
(60)	Rohe	110.00	45.00	26.00
(61)	Seabaugh	110.00	45.00	26.00
(62)	Seitz	110.00	45.00	26.00
(63)	Siegle	110.00	45.00	26.00
(64)	Smith	110.00	45.00	26.00
(65)	Sid. Smith	110.00	45.00	26.00
(66)	Steele	110.00	45.00	26.00
(67)	Swacina	110.00	45.00	26.00
(68)	Sweeney	110.00	45.00	26.00
(69)	Thomas	110.00	45.00	26.00
(70)	Vinson	110.00	45.00	26.00
(71)	Wagner	110.00	45.00	26.00
(72)	Walker	110.00	45.00	26.00
(73)	Welf	110.00	45.00	26.00
(74)	Wilder	110.00	45.00	26.00
(75)	Wiseman	110.00	45.00	26.00

1946 Remar Bread Oakland Oaks

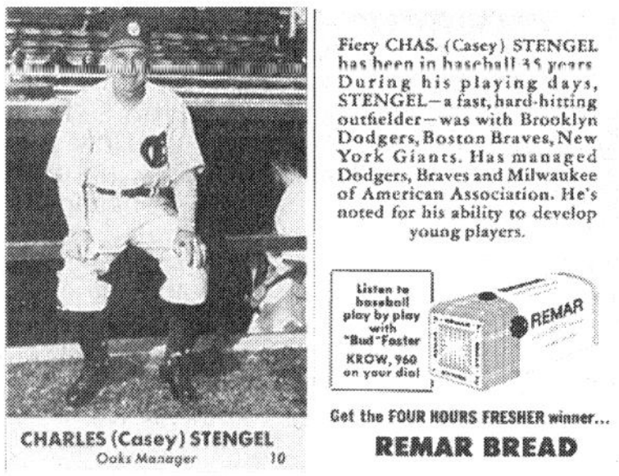
Fiery CHAS. (Casey) STENGEL has been in baseball 35 years. During his playing days, STENGEL—a fast, hard-hitting outfielder—was with Brooklyn Dodgers, Boston Braves, New York Giants. Has managed Dodgers, Braves and Milwaukee of American Association. He's noted for his ability to develop young players.
Listen to baseball play by play with "Bud" Foster KROW, 960 on your dial
REMAR
Get the FOUR HOURS FRESHER winner...
REMAR BREAD
CHARLES (Casey) STENGEL
Oaks Manager 10

Remar Baking Company issued several baseball card sets in the northern California area from 1946-1950, all picturing members of the Oakland Oaks of the Pacific Coast League. The 1946 set consists of 23 cards (five unnumbered, 18 numbered). Measuring 2" x 3", the cards were printed on heavy paper and feature black and white photos with the player's name, team and position at the bottom. The backs contain a brief write-up plus an ad for Remar Bread printed in red. The cards were distributed one per week. The first five cards were unnumbered. The rest of the set is numbered on the front, but begins with number "5", rather than "6".

		NM	EX	VG
Complete Set (23):		350.00	175.00	100.00
Common Player:		15.00	7.50	4.50
5	Hershell Martin (Herschel)	15.00	7.50	4.50
6	Bill Hart	15.00	7.50	4.50
7	Charlie Gassaway	15.00	7.50	4.50
8	Wally Westlake	15.00	7.50	4.50
9	Mickey Burnett	15.00	7.50	4.50
10	Charles (Casey) Stengel	75.00	37.00	22.00
11	Charlie Metro	15.00	7.50	4.50
12	Tom Hafey	15.00	7.50	4.50
13	Tony Sabol	15.00	7.50	4.50
14	Ed Kearse	15.00	7.50	4.50
15	Bud Foster (announcer)	15.00	7.50	4.50
16	Johnny Price	15.00	7.50	4.50
17	Gene Bearden	15.00	7.50	4.50
18	Floyd Speer	15.00	7.50	4.50
19	Bryan Stephens	15.00	7.50	4.50
20	Rinaldo (Rugger) Ardizoia	15.00	7.50	4.50
21	Ralph Buxton	15.00	7.50	4.50
22	Ambrose (Bo) Palica	15.00	7.50	4.50
----	Brooks Holder	15.00	7.50	4.50
----	Henry (Cotton) Pippen	15.00	7.50	4.50
----	Billy Raimondi	60.00	30.00	18.00
----	Les Scarsella	15.00	7.50	4.50
----	Glen (Gabby) Stewart	15.00	7.50	4.50

The ratio of Excellent and Very Good prices to Near Mint can vary depending on relative collectibility for each grade in a specific set. Current listings reflect such adjustments.

1947 Remar Bread Oakland Oaks

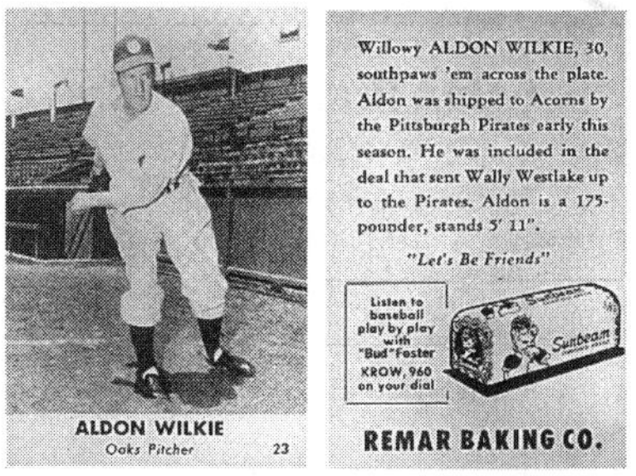
Willowy ALDON WILKIE, 30, southpaws 'em across the plate. Aldon was shipped to Acorns by the Pittsburgh Pirates early this season. He was included in the deal that sent Wally Westlake up to the Pirates. Aldon is a 175-pounder, stands 5' 11".
"Let's Be Friends"
Listen to baseball play by play with "Bud" Foster KROW, 960 on your dial
Sunbeam
ALDON WILKIE
Oaks Pitcher 23
REMAR BAKING CO.

Remar's second set consisted of 25 numbered cards, again measuring 2" x 3". The cards are nearly identical to the previous year's set, except the loaf of bread on the back is printed in blue, rather than red.

		NM	EX	VG
Complete Set (25):		350.00	175.00	105.00
Common Player:		15.00	7.50	4.50
1	Billy Raimondi	15.00	7.50	4.50
2	Les Scarsella	15.00	7.50	4.50
3	Brooks Holder	15.00	7.50	4.50
4	Charlie Gassaway	15.00	7.50	4.50
5	Mickey Burnett	15.00	7.50	4.50
6	Ralph Buxton	15.00	7.50	4.50
7	Ed Kearse	15.00	7.50	4.50
8	Charles (Casey) Stengel	65.00	32.00	19.50
9	Bud Foster (announcer)	15.00	7.50	4.50
10	Ambrose (Bo) Palica	15.00	7.50	4.50
11	Tom Hafey	15.00	7.50	4.50
12	Hershel Martin (Herschel)	15.00	7.50	4.50
13	Henry (Cotton) Pippen	15.00	7.50	4.50
14	Floyd Speer	15.00	7.50	4.50
15	Tony Sabol	15.00	7.50	4.50
16	Will Hafey	15.00	7.50	4.50
17	Ray Hamrick	15.00	7.50	4.50
18	Maurice Van Robays	15.00	7.50	4.50
19	Dario Lodigiani	15.00	7.50	4.50
20	Mel (Dizz) Duezabou	15.00	7.50	4.50
21	Damon Hayes	15.00	7.50	4.50
22	Gene Lillard	15.00	7.50	4.50
23	Aldon Wilkie	15.00	7.50	4.50
24	Dewey Soriano	15.00	7.50	4.50
25	Glen Crawford	15.00	7.50	4.50

1948 Remar Bread Oakland Oaks

(3-1/4" x 5-1/2") (the set is one team picture card) (black and white) (PCL)

	NM	EX	VG
1948 Oakland Oaks team photo	1200.	600.00	350.00

1949 Remar Bread Oakland Oaks

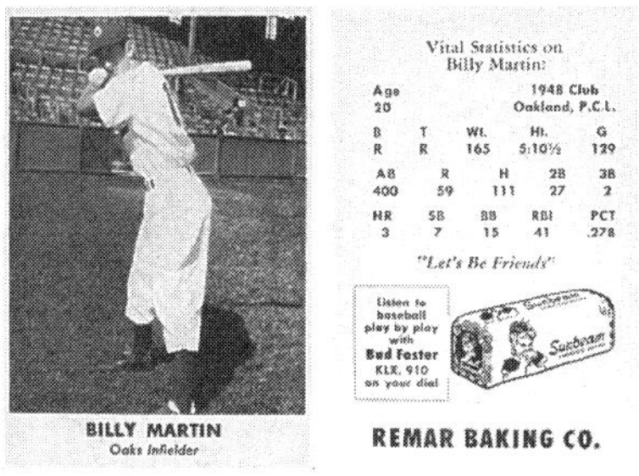
Vital Statistics on Billy Martin:
Age 20
1948 Club Oakland, P.C.L.
B T Wt. Ht. G
R R 165 5:10½ 129
AB R H 2B 3B
400 59 111 27 2
HR SB BB RBI PCT
3 7 15 41 .278
"Let's Be Friends"
Listen to baseball play by play with Bud Foster KLX, 910 on your dial
Sunbeam
BILLY MARTIN
Oaks Infielder
REMAR BAKING CO.

The 1949 Remar Bread issue was increased to 32 cards, again measuring 2" x 3". Unlike the two earlier sets, photos in the 1949 Remar set are surrounded by a thin, white border and are unnumbered. The player's name, team and position appear below the black and white photo. The backs are printed in blue and include the player's 1948 statistics and the distinctive loaf of bread.

		NM	EX	VG
Complete Set (32):		325.00	160.00	100.00
Common Player:		15.00	7.50	4.50
(1)	Ralph Buxton	15.00	7.50	4.50
(2)	Milo Candini	15.00	7.50	4.50
(3)	Rex Cecil	15.00	7.50	4.50
(4)	Loyd Christopher (Lloyd)	15.00	7.50	4.50
(5)	Charles Dressen	17.50	8.75	5.25
(6)	Mel Duezabou	15.00	7.50	4.50
(7)	Bud Foster (sportscaster)	15.00	7.50	4.50
(8)	Charlie Gassaway	15.00	7.50	4.50
(9)	Ray Hamrick	15.00	7.50	4.50
(10)	Jack Jensen	20.00	10.00	6.00
(11)	Earl Jones	15.00	7.50	4.50
(12)	George Kelly	18.00	9.00	5.50
(13)	Frank Kerr	15.00	7.50	4.50
(14)	Richard Kryhoski	15.00	7.50	4.50
(15)	Harry Lavagetto	15.00	7.50	4.50
(16)	Dario Lodigiani	15.00	7.50	4.50
(17)	Billy Martin	80.00	40.00	24.00
(18)	George Metkovich	15.00	7.50	4.50
(19)	Frank Nelson	15.00	7.50	4.50
(20)	Don Padgett	15.00	7.50	4.50
(21)	Alonzo Perry	15.00	7.50	4.50
(22)	Bill Raimondi	15.00	7.50	4.50
(23)	Earl Rapp	15.00	7.50	4.50
(24)	Eddie Samcoff	15.00	7.50	4.50
(25)	Les Scarsella	15.00	7.50	4.50
(26)	Forest Thompson (Forrest)	15.00	7.50	4.50
(27)	Earl Toolson	15.00	7.50	4.50
(28)	Lou Tost	15.00	7.50	4.50
(29)	Maurice Van Robays	15.00	7.50	4.50
(30)	Jim Wallace	15.00	7.50	4.50
(31)	Arthur Lee Wilson	18.00	9.00	5.50
(32)	Parnell Woods	15.00	7.50	4.50

1950 Remar Bread Oakland Oaks

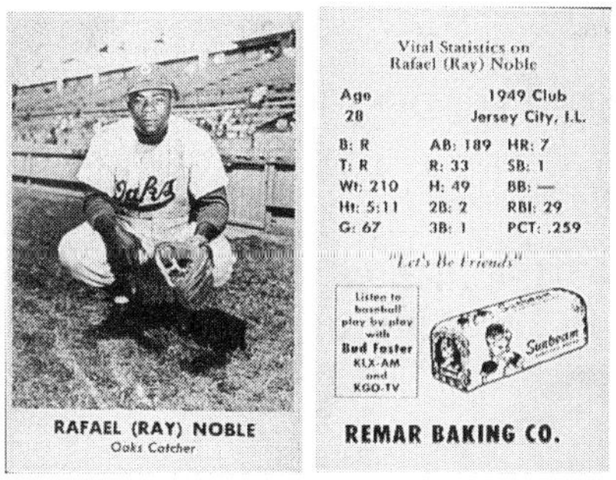
Vital Statistics on Rafael (Ray) Noble
Age 28
1949 Club Jersey City, I.L.
B: R AB: 189 HR: 7
T: R R: 33 SB: 1
Wt: 210 H: 49 BB: —
Ht: 5:11 2B: 2 RBI: 29
G: 67 3B: 1 PCT: .259
"Let's Be Friends"
Listen to baseball play by play with Bud Foster KLX-AM and KGO-TV
Sunbeam
RAFAEL (RAY) NOBLE
Oaks Catcher
REMAR BAKING CO.

The most common of the Remar Bread issues, the 1950 set contains 27 unnumbered cards, again measuring 2" x 3" and featuring members of the Oakland Oaks. The cards are nearly identical to the previous year's set but can be differentiated by the 1949 statistics on the back.

		NM	EX	VG
Complete Set (27):		200.00	100.00	60.00
Common Player:		15.00	7.50	4.50
(1)	George Bamberger	15.00	7.50	4.50
(2)	Hank Behrman	15.00	7.50	4.50
(3)	Loyd Christopher (Lloyd)	15.00	7.50	4.50
(4)	Chuck Dressen	15.00	7.50	4.50
(5)	Mel Duezabou	15.00	7.50	4.50
(6)	Augie Galan	15.00	7.50	4.50
(7)	Charlie Gassaway	15.00	7.50	4.50
(8)	Allen Gettel	15.00	7.50	4.50
(9)	Ernie W. Groth	15.00	7.50	4.50
(10)	Ray Hamrick	15.00	7.50	4.50
(11)	Earl Harrist	15.00	7.50	4.50
(12)	Billy Herman	18.00	9.00	5.50
(13)	Bob Hofman	15.00	7.50	4.50
(14)	George Kelly	18.00	9.00	5.50
(15)	Harry Lavagetto	15.00	7.50	4.50
(16)	Eddie Malone	15.00	7.50	4.50
(17)	George Metkovich	15.00	7.50	4.50
(18)	Frank Nelson	15.00	7.50	4.50
(19)	Rafael (Ray) Noble	15.00	7.50	4.50
(20)	Don Padgett	15.00	7.50	4.50
(21)	Earl Rapp	15.00	7.50	4.50
(22)	Clyde Shoun	15.00	7.50	4.50
(23)	Forrest Thompson	15.00	7.50	4.50
(24)	Louis Tost	15.00	7.50	4.50
(25)	Dick Wakefield	15.00	7.50	4.50
(26)	Artie Wilson	15.00	7.50	4.50
(27)	Roy Zimmerman	15.00	7.50	4.50

1959 Richmond Virginians

Photos of half a dozen local favorites of the International League Richmond Virginians were featured on ticket stubs during the 1959 season. The black-and-white player portions of the stub measure 2" x 3"and are blank-backed. The unnumbered cards are listed here alphabetically. Richmond was a farm club of the N.Y. Yankees.

		NM	EX	VG
Complete Set (6):		160.00	80.00	48.00
Common Player:		30.00	15.00	9.00
(1)	Clete Boyer	45.00	22.00	13.50
(2)	Jim Coates	30.00	15.00	9.00
(3)	Eli Grba	30.00	15.00	9.00
(4)	John James	30.00	15.00	9.00
(5)	Dick Sanders	30.00	15.00	9.00
(6)	Bill Short	30.00	15.00	9.00

1960 Richmond Virginians

In 1960 the Richmond Virginians of the International League continued the practice of using player photos on their game tickets. Black-and-white with a blank-back, the player portions of the tickets can be found in two sizes. Unnumbered cards are checklisted here alphabetically. The Richmond team was a farm club of the N.Y. Yankees.

		NM	EX	VG
Complete Set (6):		150.00	75.00	45.00
Common Player:		30.00	15.00	9.00
SMALL SIZE (2" x 2-3/4")				
(1)	Bob Martyn	30.00	15.00	9.00
(2)	Jack Reed	30.00	15.00	9.00
LARGE SIZE (2-3/8" x 2-7/8")				
(1)	Tony Asaro	30.00	15.00	9.00
(2)	Bill Shantz	30.00	15.00	9.00
(3)	Jerry Thomas	30.00	15.00	9.00
(4)	Bob Weisler	30.00	15.00	9.00

1966 Royal Crown Cola Columbus Yankees

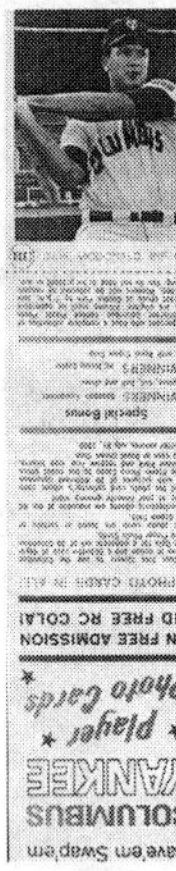

This set of 20 cards was distributed in eight packs of Royal Crown Cola, then based in Columbus, Ga. They were part of a strip measuring 2-1/4" wide. The first 3" of the 9-1/2" strip has a black-and-white photo of the player with his name, position and other biographical data, along with an RC logo in blue and red. The bottom of the strip has a promotion sponsored by the ball club and RC, offering a case of cola for turning in a complete set in an album provided for the cards. Those who turned in the cards were also eligible to win baseball equipment or picnic coolers in a giveaway at a July 31 game that year. Most cards have the advertisement removed. Strips that include the advertisement should be valued at 130-150% of values shown. The cards are unnumbered and listed in alphabetical order.

		NM	EX	VG
Complete Set (20):		450.00	225.00	140.00
Common Player:		25.00	12.50	7.50
(1)	Gil Blanco	25.00	12.50	7.50
(2)	Ronnie Boyer	30.00	15.00	9.00
(3)	Jim Brenneman	25.00	12.50	7.50
(4)	Butch Cretara	25.00	12.50	7.50
(5)	Bill Henry	25.00	12.50	7.50
(6)	Joe Jeran	25.00	12.50	7.50
(7)	Jerry Kenney	25.00	12.50	7.50
(8)	Ronnie Kirk	25.00	12.50	7.50
(9)	Tom Kowalski	25.00	12.50	7.50
(10)	Jim Marrujo	25.00	12.50	7.50
(11)	Dave McDonald	25.00	12.50	7.50
(12)	Ed Merritt	25.00	12.50	7.50
(13)	Jim Palma	25.00	12.50	7.50
(14)	Cecil Perkins	25.00	12.50	7.50
(15)	Jack Reed	25.00	12.50	7.50
(16)	Ellie Rodriguez	30.00	15.00	9.00
(17)	John Schroeppel	25.00	12.50	7.50
(18)	Dave Truelock	25.00	12.50	7.50
(19)	Steve Whitaker	25.00	12.50	7.50
(20)	Earl Willoughby	25.00	12.50	7.50

S

1950 San Francisco Seals Popcorn

These 3-1/4" x 4-1/2" black-and-white cards were issued with the purchase of caramel corn at Sicks Stadium.

		NM	EX	VG
Complete set:		150.00	75.00	45.00
Common player:		15.00	7.50	4.50
(1)	Dick Briskey	15.00	7.50	4.50
(2)	Ralph Buxton	15.00	7.50	4.50
(3)	Harry Feldman	15.00	7.50	4.50
(4)	Chet Johnson	15.00	7.50	4.50
(5)	Al Lien	15.00	7.50	4.50
(6)	Dario Lodigiani	15.00	7.50	4.50
(7)	Cliff Melton	15.00	7.50	4.50
(8)	Roy Nicely	15.00	7.50	4.50
(9)	Roy Partee	15.00	7.50	4.50
(10)	Manny Perez	15.00	7.50	4.50
(11)	Neill Sheridan	15.00	7.50	4.50
(12)	Elmer Singleton	15.00	7.50	4.50
(13)	Jack Tobin	15.00	7.50	4.50

1953 San Francisco Seals team issue

This set of 24 cards was sold at Seals Stadium and by mail for 25 cents. Fronts of the 4" x 5" black-and-white cards contain a player photo with facsimile autograph. The player's name, team and position are printed in the white bottom border. Backs of the unnumbered cards are blank.

		NM	EX	VG
Complete Set (24):		700.00	350.00	210.00
Common Player:		30.00	15.00	9.00
(1)	Bill Boemler	30.00	15.00	9.00
(2)	Bill Bradford	30.00	15.00	9.00
(3)	Reno Cheso	30.00	15.00	9.00
(4)	Harlond Clift	30.00	15.00	9.00
(5)	Walt Clough	30.00	15.00	9.00
(6)	Cliff Coggin	30.00	15.00	9.00
(7)	Tommy Heath	30.00	15.00	9.00
(8)	Leo Hughes (Trainer)	30.00	15.00	9.00
(9)	Frank Kalin	30.00	15.00	9.00
(10)	Al Lien	30.00	15.00	9.00
(11)	Al Lyons	30.00	15.00	9.00
(12)	John McCall	30.00	15.00	9.00
(13)	Bill McCawley	30.00	15.00	9.00
(14)	Jim Moran	30.00	15.00	9.00
(15)	Bob Muncrief	30.00	15.00	9.00
(16)	Leo Righetti	30.00	15.00	9.00
(17)	Ted Shandor	30.00	15.00	9.00
(18)	Elmer Singleton	30.00	15.00	9.00
(19)	Lou Stringer	30.00	15.00	9.00
(20)	Sal Taormina	30.00	15.00	9.00
(21)	Will Tiesiera	30.00	15.00	9.00
(22)	Nini Tornay	30.00	15.00	9.00
(23)	George Vico	30.00	15.00	9.00
(24)	Jerry Zuvela	30.00	15.00	9.00

1963 Scheible Press Rochester Red Wings

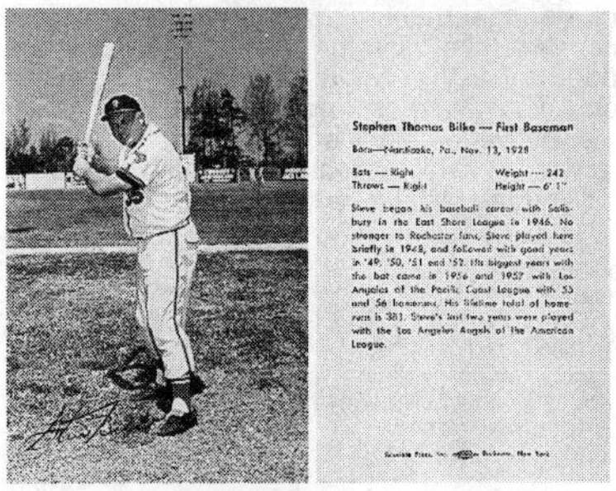

Apparently sold as a stadium concession stand item in a paper and cellophane envelope, the full-color 3-13/16" x 5-7/8" cards are found printed on either a heavy paper stock or thin cardboard stock, each with identical black-and-white back. Two blank-backed cards in slightly larger (4" x 5-7/8") format are checklisted here, although their relationship to the other photos is unknown. The '63 Red Wings were the International League affiliate of the Baltimore Orioles.

		NM	EX	VG
Complete Set (11):		225.00	112.50	67.50
Common Player:		20.00	10.00	6.00
(1)	Joe Altobelli	25.00	12.50	7.50
(2)	Steve Bilko	20.00	10.00	6.00
(3)	Sam E. Bowens	20.00	10.00	6.00
(4)	Don Brummer	20.00	10.00	6.00
(5)	Nelson Chittum (cardboard only)	20.00	10.00	6.00
(6a)	Luke Easter (small format)	30.00	15.00	9.00
(6b)	Luke Easter (large format)	30.00	15.00	9.00
(7)	Darrell Johnson, Chris Krug (paper only)	25.00	12.50	7.50
(8)	Ron Kabbes (large format)	20.00	10.00	6.00
(9)	Fred Valentine	20.00	10.00	6.00
(10)	Ozzie Virgil	20.00	10.00	6.00
(11)	Ray Youngdahl	20.00	10.00	6.00

1954-1968 Seattle Rainiers/Angels Popcorn

One of the longest-running minor league baseball card promotions was the 1954-68 Seattle popcorn cards. The principal sponsor was Centennial Mills, which had issued cards in the 1940s. Similar in format throughout their period of issue, the cards are 2" x 3"in size, black-and-white, usually featuring portrait photos on the front with the player's name or name and position below. In some years the cards were printed on semi-glossy stock. Some years' card backs are blank, in other years, backs feature ads for various local businesses; in a few years, cards could be found with both blank and printed backs. Many photo and spelling variations are known throughout the series; most are noted in the appropriate checklists. The unnumbered cards are checklisted alphabetically. It is possible a few stragglers will be added to these checklists in the future. In most years a group of 20 cards was released early in the year, supplemented later in the season as roster changes dictated. The cards were given away with the purchase of a box of popcorn sold at Seattle's Sicks stadium. During the card-issuing era, Seattle was an independent team in the Pacific Coast League in 1954-55. From 1956-60 they were a top farm team in the Reds system. They were a Red Sox affiliate from 1961-64, before tying up with the California Angels in 1965.

(Consult checklists for attribution of) (blank-back cards.)

1954 Seattle Rainiers Popcorn

(Blank-back. Most players photographed in dark cap with light "S".)

		NM	EX	VG
Complete Set (26):		350.00	175.00	100.00
Common Player:		15.00	7.50	4.50
(1)	Gene Bearden	15.00	7.50	4.50
(2)	Al Brightman	15.00	7.50	4.50
(3)	Jack Burkowatz	15.00	7.50	4.50
(4)	Tommy Byrne (photo reversed, backwards "S" on cap)	15.00	7.50	4.50
(5)	Joe Erautt	15.00	7.50	4.50
(6)	Bill Evans	15.00	7.50	4.50
(7)	Van Fletcher	15.00	7.50	4.50
(8)	Bob Hall	15.00	7.50	4.50
(9)	Pete Hernandez	15.00	7.50	4.50
(10)	Lloyd Jenney	15.00	7.50	4.50
(11)	Joe Joshua	15.00	7.50	4.50
(12)	Vern Kindsfather	15.00	7.50	4.50
(13)	Tom Lovrich	15.00	7.50	4.50
(14)	Clarence Maddern	15.00	7.50	4.50
(15)	Don Mallott	15.00	7.50	4.50
(16)	Loren Meyers	15.00	7.50	4.50
(17)	Steve Nagy	15.00	7.50	4.50
(18)	Ray Orteig	15.00	7.50	4.50
(19)	Gerry Priddy	15.00	7.50	4.50
(20)	George Schmees	15.00	7.50	4.50
(21)	Bill Schuster	15.00	7.50	4.50
(22)	Leo Thomas	15.00	7.50	4.50
(23)	Jack Tobin	15.00	7.50	4.50
(24)	Al Widmer	15.00	7.50	4.50
(25)	Artie Wilson	18.00	9.00	5.50
(26)	Al Zarilla	15.00	7.50	4.50

Suffix letters following a card number indicate a variation card.

1955 Seattle Rainiers Popcorn

(Blank-back. All players wearing light caps with "R" logo.)

		NM	EX	VG
Complete Set (22):		300.00	150.00	90.00
Common Player:		15.00	7.50	4.50
(1)	Bob Balcena	15.00	7.50	4.50
(2)	Monty Basgall	15.00	7.50	4.50
(3)	Ewell Blackwell	22.00	11.00	6.50
(4)	Bill Brenner	15.00	7.50	4.50
(5)	Jack Burkowatz	15.00	7.50	4.50
(6)	Van Fletcher	15.00	7.50	4.50
(7)	Joe Ginsberg	15.00	7.50	4.50
(8)	Jehosie Heard	15.00	7.50	4.50
(9)	Fred Hutchinson	20.00	10.00	6.00
(10)	Larry Jansen	15.00	7.50	4.50
(11)	Bob Kelly	15.00	7.50	4.50
(12)	Bill Kennedy	15.00	7.50	4.50
(13)	Lou Kretlow	15.00	7.50	4.50
(14)	Rocco Krsnich	15.00	7.50	4.50
(15)	Carmen Mauro	15.00	7.50	4.50
(16)	John Oldham	15.00	7.50	4.50
(17)	George Schmees	15.00	7.50	4.50
(18)	Elmer Singleton	15.00	7.50	4.50
(19)	Alan Strange	15.00	7.50	4.50
(20)	Gene Verble	15.00	7.50	4.50
(21)	Marv Williams	15.00	7.50	4.50
(22)	Harvey Zernia	15.00	7.50	4.50

1956 Seattle Rainiers Popcorn

(Blank-back or Gil's Drive-Ins (two locations) ad on back. Players wearing light cap with white "R".)

		NM	EX	VG
Complete Set (27):		350.00	175.00	100.00
Common Player:		15.00	7.50	4.50
(1)	Fred Baczewski	15.00	7.50	4.50
(2)	Bob Balcena	15.00	7.50	4.50
(3)	Bill Brenner	15.00	7.50	4.50
(4)	Sherry Dixon	15.00	7.50	4.50
(5)	Don Fracchia	15.00	7.50	4.50
(6)	Bill Glynn	15.00	7.50	4.50
(7)	Larry Jansen	15.00	7.50	4.50
(8)	Howie Judson	15.00	7.50	4.50
(9)	Bill Kennedy	15.00	7.50	4.50
(10)	Jack Lohrke	15.00	7.50	4.50
(11)	Vic Lombardi	15.00	7.50	4.50
(12)	Carmen Mauro	15.00	7.50	4.50
(13)	Ray Orteig	15.00	7.50	4.50
(14)	Bud Podbielan	15.00	7.50	4.50
(15)	Leo Righetti	15.00	7.50	4.50
(16)	Jim Robertson	15.00	7.50	4.50
(17)	Art Shallock (Schallock)	15.00	7.50	4.50
(18)	Art Schult	15.00	7.50	4.50
(19)	Luke Sewell	20.00	10.00	6.00
(20)	Elmer Singleton	15.00	7.50	4.50
(21a)	Milt Smith (action)	15.00	7.50	4.50
(21b)	Milt Smith (portrait)	15.00	7.50	4.50
(22)	Vern Stephens	15.00	7.50	4.50
(23)	Alan Strange	15.00	7.50	4.50
(24)	Joe Taylor	15.00	7.50	4.50
(25)	Artie Wilson	20.00	10.00	6.00
(26)	Harvey Zernia	15.00	7.50	4.50

1957 Seattle Rainiers Popcorn

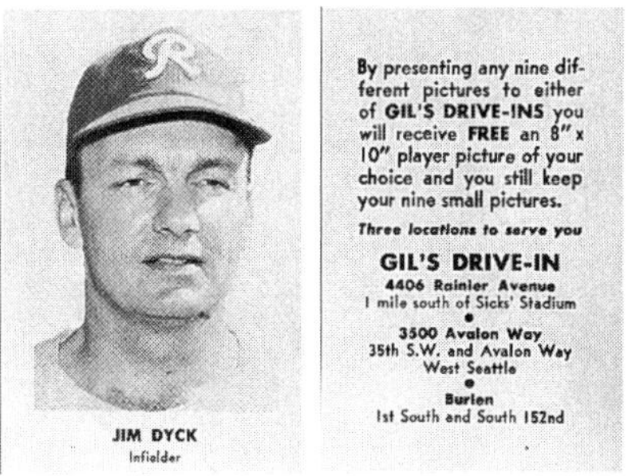

By presenting any nine different pictures to either of GIL'S DRIVE-INS you will receive FREE an 8" x 10" player picture of your choice and you still keep your nine small pictures.
Three locations to serve you
GIL'S DRIVE-IN
4406 Rainier Avenue
1 mile south of Sicks' Stadium
3500 Avalon Way
35th S.W. and Avalon Way
West Seattle
Burien
1st South and South 152nd
JIM DYCK
Infielder

(Blank-back or Gil's Drive-Ins (three locations) ad on back. Players wearing lighter caps with white "R". No base on letter "T" on outfielders or pitchers cards.)

		NM	EX	VG
Complete Set (24):		350.00	175.00	100.00
Common Player:		15.00	7.50	4.50
(1)	Dick Aylward	15.00	7.50	4.50
(2)	Bob Balcena	15.00	7.50	4.50
(3)	Eddie Basinki	15.00	7.50	4.50
(4)	Hal Bevan	15.00	7.50	4.50
(5)	Joe Black	24.00	12.00	7.25
(6)	Juan Delis	15.00	7.50	4.50
(7)	Jim Dyck	15.00	7.50	4.50
(8)	Marion Fricano	15.00	7.50	4.50
(9)	Bill Glynn	15.00	7.50	4.50
(10)	Larry Jansen	15.00	7.50	4.50
(11)	Howie Judson	15.00	7.50	4.50
(12)	Bill Kennedy	15.00	7.50	4.50
(13)	Jack Lohrke	15.00	7.50	4.50
(14)	Carmen Mauro	15.00	7.50	4.50
(15)	George Munger	15.00	7.50	4.50
(16)	Lefty O'Doul	25.00	12.50	7.50
(17)	Ray Orteig	15.00	7.50	4.50
(18)	Duane Pillette	15.00	7.50	4.50
(19)	Bud Podbielan	15.00	7.50	4.50
(20)	Charley Rabe	15.00	7.50	4.50
(21)	Leo Righetti	15.00	7.50	4.50
(22)	Joe Taylor	15.00	7.50	4.50
(23)	Edo Vanni	15.00	7.50	4.50
(24)	Morrie Wills (Maury)	55.00	27.00	16.50

1958 Seattle Rainiers Popcorn

(All cards have Ralph's Thriftway Market ad on back.)

		NM	EX	VG
Complete Set (19):		225.00	110.00	65.00
Common Player:		12.00	6.00	3.50
(1)	Bob Balcena	12.00	6.00	3.50
(2)	Ed Basinki	12.00	6.00	3.50
(3)	Hal Bevan	12.00	6.00	3.50
(4)	Jack Bloomfield	12.00	6.00	3.50
(5)	Juan Delis	12.00	6.00	3.50
(6)	Dutch Dotterer	12.00	6.00	3.50
(7)	Jim Dyck	12.00	6.00	3.50
(8)	Al Federoff	12.00	6.00	3.50
(9)	Art Fowler	12.00	6.00	3.50
(10)	Bill Kennedy	12.00	6.00	3.50
(11)	Marty Kutyna	12.00	6.00	3.50
(12)	Ray Orteig	12.00	6.00	3.50
(13)	Duane Pillette	12.00	6.00	3.50
(14)	Vada Pinson	35.00	17.50	10.50
(15)	Connie Ryan	12.00	6.00	3.50
(16)	Phil Shartzer	12.00	6.00	3.50
(17)	Max Surkont	12.00	6.00	3.50
(18)	Gale Wade	12.00	6.00	3.50
(19)	Ted Wieand	12.00	6.00	3.50

1959 Seattle Rainiers Popcorn

(Blank-back. First printing cards have players in lighter cap with white "R". Second printing cards have darker caps with shadow around "R".)

		NM	EX	VG
Complete Set (37):		400.00	200.00	120.00
Common Player:		12.00	6.00	3.50
(1)	Bobby Adams	12.00	6.00	3.50
(2)	Frank Amaya	12.00	6.00	3.50
(3)	Hal Bevan	12.00	6.00	3.50
(4)	Jack Bloomfield	12.00	6.00	3.50
(5)	Clarence Churn	12.00	6.00	3.50
(6)	Jack Dittmer	12.00	6.00	3.50
(7)	Jim Dyck	12.00	6.00	3.50
(8)	Dee Fondy	12.00	6.00	3.50
(9)	Mark Freeman	12.00	6.00	3.50
(10)	Dick Hanlon	12.00	6.00	3.50
(11)	Carroll Hardy	12.00	6.00	3.50
(12)	Bobby Henrich	12.00	6.00	3.50
(13)	Jay Hook	12.00	6.00	3.50
(14)	Fred Hutchinson	18.00	9.00	5.50
(15)	Jake Jenkins	12.00	6.00	3.50
(16)	Eddie Kazak	12.00	6.00	3.50
(17)	Bill Kennedy	12.00	6.00	3.50
(18)	Harry Lowrey	12.00	6.00	3.50
(19a)	Harry Malmbeg (Malmberg)	12.00	6.00	3.50
(19b)	Harry Malmberg	12.00	6.00	3.50
(20)	Bob Mape (Mabe)	12.00	6.00	3.50
(21)	Darrell Martin	12.00	6.00	3.50
(22)	John McCall	12.00	6.00	3.50
(23)	Claude Osteen	15.00	7.50	4.50
(24)	Paul Pettit	12.00	6.00	3.50
(25)	Charley Rabe	12.00	6.00	3.50
(26)	Rudy Regalado	12.00	6.00	3.50
(27)	Eric Rodin	12.00	6.00	3.50
(28)	Don Rudolph	12.00	6.00	3.50
(29)	Lou Skizas	12.00	6.00	3.50
(30)	Dave Stenhouse	12.00	6.00	3.50
(31)	Alan Strange	12.00	6.00	3.50
(32)	Max Surkont	12.00	6.00	3.50
(33)	Ted Tappe	12.00	6.00	3.50
(34)	Elmer Valo	12.00	6.00	3.50
(35)	Gale Wade	12.00	6.00	3.50
(36)	Bill Wight	12.00	6.00	3.50
(37)	Ed Winceniak	12.00	6.00	3.50

1960 Seattle Rainiers Popcorn

(Blank-back. All players posed against outfield fence wearing dark caps with shadowed "R".)

		NM	EX	VG
Complete Set (18):		200.00	100.00	60.00
Common Player:		12.00	6.00	3.50
(1)	Charlie Beamon	12.00	6.00	3.50
(2)	Hal Bevan	12.00	6.00	3.50
(3)	Whammy Douglas	12.00	6.00	3.50
(4)	Buddy Gilbert	12.00	6.00	3.50
(5)	Hal Jeffcoat	12.00	6.00	3.50
(6)	Leigh Lawrence	12.00	6.00	3.50
(7)	Darrell Martin	12.00	6.00	3.50
(8)	Francisco Obregon	12.00	6.00	3.50
(9)	Johnny O'Brien	12.00	6.00	3.50
(10)	Paul Pettitt	12.00	6.00	3.50
(11)	Ray Ripplemeyer	12.00	6.00	3.50
(12)	Don Rudolph	12.00	6.00	3.50
(13)	Willard Schmidt	12.00	6.00	3.50
(14)	Dick Sisler	12.00	6.00	3.50
(15)	Lou Skizas	12.00	6.00	3.50
(16)	Joe Taylor	12.00	6.00	3.50
(17)	Bob Thurman	12.00	6.00	3.50
(18)	Gerald Zimmerman	12.00	6.00	3.50

1961 Seattle Rainiers Popcorn

(Blank-back. New uniforms: dark cap with stylized "S", "Rainiers" on chest. Many players have both portrait and action poses. Tough to distinguish from 1962 set; names on '61s are more compact, bold than on '62 which has taller, lighter names.)

		NM	EX	VG
Complete Set (29):		325.00	160.00	97.00
Common Player:		12.00	6.00	3.50
(1)	Galen Cisco	12.00	6.00	3.50
(2)	Marlan Coughtry (batting)	12.00	6.00	3.50
(3)	Marlin Coughtry (portrait)	12.00	6.00	3.50
(4)	Pete Cronin	12.00	6.00	3.50
(5)	Arnold Earley	12.00	6.00	3.50
(6)	Bob Heffner (pitching)	12.00	6.00	3.50
(7)	Bob Heffner (portrait)	12.00	6.00	3.00
(8)	Curt Jensen (action)	12.00	6.00	3.50
(9)	Curt Jensen (portrait)	12.00	6.00	3.50
(10)	Harry Malmberg (coach)	12.00	6.00	3.50
(11)	Harry Malmberg (player-coach)	12.00	6.00	3.50
(12)	Dave Mann	12.00	6.00	3.50
(13)	Darrell Martin	12.00	6.00	3.50
(14)	Erv Palica (pitching)	12.00	6.00	3.50
(15)	Ervin Palica (portrait)	12.00	6.00	3.50
(16)	Johnny Pesky (action)	15.00	7.50	4.50
(17)	Johnny Pesky (portrait)	15.00	7.50	4.50
(18)	Dick Radatz	12.00	6.00	3.50
(19)	Ted Schreiber (batting)	12.00	6.00	3.50
(20)	Ted Shreiber (portrait)	12.00	6.00	3.50
(21)	Paul Smith (action)	12.00	6.00	3.50
(22)	Paul Smith (portrait)	12.00	6.00	3.00
(23)	John Tillman (infielder)	12.00	6.00	3.50
(24)	Bob Tillman (catcher)	12.00	6.00	3.50
(25)	Bo Toft	12.00	6.00	3.50
(26)	Tom Umphlett (action)	12.00	6.00	3.50
(27)	Tom Umphlett (portrait)	12.00	6.00	3.00
(28)	Earl Wilson	12.00	6.00	3.50
(29)	Ken Wolfe	12.00	6.00	3.50

1962 Seattle Rainiers Popcorn

(Blank-back. Nearly identical to '61s except for player name. On 1961 cards, name is compact and bold; on '62s the name is taller, lighter. Some photos repeated from 1961.)

		NM	EX	VG
Complete Set (19):		225.00	110.00	65.00
Common Player:		12.00	6.00	3.50
(1)	Dave Hall	12.00	6.00	3.50
(2)	Billy Harrell	12.00	6.00	3.50
(3)	Curt Jensen (Jenson)	12.00	6.00	3.50
(4)	Stew MacDonald	12.00	6.00	3.50
(5)	Bill MacLeod	12.00	6.00	3.50
(6)	Dave Mann (action)	12.00	6.00	3.50
(7)	Dave Mann (portrait)	12.00	6.00	3.00
(8)	Dave Morehead	12.00	6.00	3.50
(9)	John Pesky	15.00	7.50	4.50
(10)	Ted Schreiber (second baseman)	12.00	6.00	3.50
(11)	Ted Schreiber (infielder)	12.00	6.00	3.50
(12)	Elmer Singleton	12.00	6.00	3.50
(13)	Archie Skeen	12.00	6.00	3.50
(14)	Pete Smith	12.00	6.00	3.50
(15)	George Spencer	12.00	6.00	3.50
(16)	Bo Toft (1961 photo)	12.00	6.00	3.50
(17)	Bo Toft (new photo)	12.00	6.00	3.00
(18)	Tom Umphlett	12.00	6.00	3.50
(19)	Ken Wolfe	12.00	6.00	3.50

1963 Seattle Rainiers Popcorn

(Blank-back. No positions stated on cards except for manager and coach. Impossible to differentiate 1963 issue from 1964 except by player selection.)

		NM	EX	VG
Complete Set (15):		150.00	75.00	45.00
Common Player:		10.00	5.00	3.00
(1)	Don Gile	10.00	5.00	3.00
(2)	Dave Hall	10.00	5.00	3.00
(3)	Billy Harrell	10.00	5.00	3.00
(4)	Pete Jernigan	10.00	5.00	3.00
(5)	Stan Johnson	10.00	5.00	3.00
(6)	Dalton Jones	10.00	5.00	3.00
(7)	Mel Parnell	10.00	5.00	3.00
(8)	Joe Pedrazzini	10.00	5.00	3.00
(9)	Elmer Singleton	10.00	5.00	3.00
(10)	Archie Skeen	10.00	5.00	3.00
(11)	Rac Slider	10.00	5.00	3.00
(12)	Pete Smith	10.00	5.00	3.00
(13)	Bill Spanswick	10.00	5.00	3.00
(14)	George Spencer	10.00	5.00	3.00
(15)	Wilbur Wood	20.00	10.00	6.00

1964 Seattle Rainiers Popcorn

(Blank-back. Impossible to differentiate between 1963 and 1964 issues except by player selection.)

		NM	EX	VG
Complete Set (18):		150.00	75.00	45.00
Common Player:		10.00	5.00	3.00
(1)	Earl Averill	10.00	5.00	3.00
(2)	Billy Gardner	10.00	5.00	3.00
(3)	Russ Gibson	10.00	5.00	3.00
(4)	Guido Grilli	10.00	5.00	3.00
(5)	Bob Guindon	10.00	5.00	3.00
(6)	Billy Harrell	10.00	5.00	3.00
(7)	Fred Holmes	10.00	5.00	3.00
(8)	Stan Johnson	10.00	5.00	3.00
(9)	Hal Kolstad	10.00	5.00	3.00
(10)	Felix Maldonado	10.00	5.00	3.00
(11)	Gary Modrell	10.00	5.00	3.00
(12)	Merlin Nippert	10.00	5.00	3.00
(13)	Rico Petrocelli	16.00	8.00	4.75
(14)	Jay Ritchie	10.00	5.00	3.00
(15)	Barry Shetrone	10.00	5.00	3.00
(16)	Pete Smith	10.00	5.00	3.00
(17)	Bill Tuttle	10.00	5.00	3.00
(18)	Edo Vanni	10.00	5.00	3.00

1965 Seattle Angels Popcorn

(Back has cartoon angel batting. Several cards, issued prior to the season, have blank-backs.)

		NM	EX	VG
Complete Set (22):		200.00	100.00	60.00
Common Player:		10.00	5.00	3.00
(1)	Earl Averill	10.00	5.00	3.00
(2)	Tom Burgmeier	10.00	5.00	3.00
(3)	Bob Guindon	10.00	5.00	3.00
(4)	Jack Hernandez	10.00	5.00	3.00
(5)	Fred Holmes	10.00	5.00	3.00
(6)	Ed Kirkpatrick	10.00	5.00	3.00
(7)	Hal Kolstad	10.00	5.00	3.00
(8)	Joe Koppe	10.00	5.00	3.00
(9)	Les Kuhnz	10.00	5.00	3.00
(10)	Bob Lemon	18.00	9.00	5.50
(11)	Bobby Locke	10.00	5.00	3.00
(12)	Jim McGlothlin	10.00	5.00	3.00
(13a)	Bob Radovich (blank-back)	10.00	5.00	3.00
(13b)	Bob Radovich (ad-back)	10.00	5.00	3.00
(14)	Merritt Ranew	10.00	5.00	3.00
(15)	Jimmie Reese (blank-back)	12.50	6.25	3.75
(16a)	Rick Reichardt (blank-back)	10.00	5.00	3.00
(16b)	Rick Reichardt (ad-back)	10.00	5.00	3.00
(17)	Tom Satriano	10.00	5.00	3.00
(18)	Dick Simpson	10.00	5.00	3.00
(19)	Jack Spring (blank-back)	10.00	5.00	3.00
(20)	Ed Sukla	10.00	5.00	3.00
(21)	Jackie Warner	10.00	5.00	3.00
(22)	Stan Williams	10.00	5.00	3.00

Suffix letters following a card number indicate a variation card.

1966 Seattle Angels Popcorn

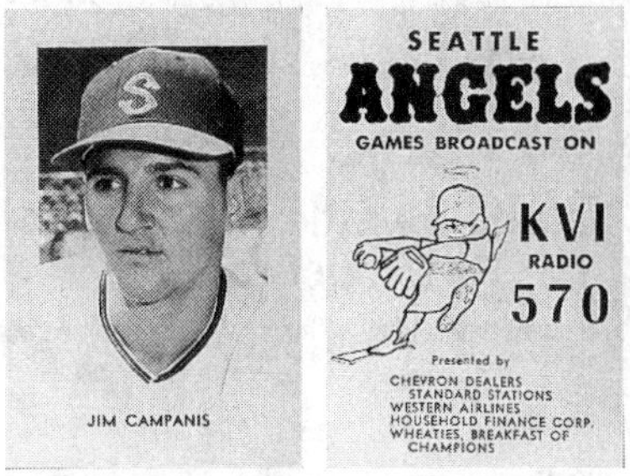

(Cartoon angel pitching on back, first "Presented by" advertiser at bottom is Chevron Dealers.)

		NM	EX	VG
Complete Set (29):		250.00	125.00	75.00
Common Player:		10.00	5.00	3.00
(1)	Del Bates	10.00	5.00	3.00
(2)	Tom Burgmeier	10.00	5.00	3.00
(3)	Jim Campanis	12.50	6.25	3.75
(4)	Jim Coates	10.00	5.00	3.00
(5)	Tony Cortopassi	10.00	5.00	3.00
(6)	Chuck Estrada	10.00	5.00	3.00
(7)	Ray Hernandez	10.00	5.00	3.00
(8)	Jay Johnstone	15.00	7.50	4.50
(9)	Bill Kelso	10.00	5.00	3.00
(10)	Vic LaRose	10.00	5.00	3.00
(11)	Bobby Locke	10.00	5.00	3.00
(12)	Rudy May	10.00	5.00	3.00
(13)	Andy Messersmith	12.50	7.50	4.50
(14)	Bubba Morton	10.00	5.00	3.00
(15)	Cotton Nash	10.00	5.00	3.00
(16)	John Olerud	16.00	8.00	4.75
(17)	Marty Pattin	10.00	5.00	3.00
(18)	Merritt Ranew	10.00	5.00	3.00
(19)	Minnie Rojas	10.00	5.00	3.00
(20)	George Rubio	10.00	5.00	3.00
(21)	Al Spangler	10.00	5.00	3.00
(22)	Ed Sukla	10.00	5.00	3.00
(23)	Felix Torres	10.00	5.00	3.00
(24)	Hector Torres	10.00	5.00	3.00
(25)	Ken Turner	10.00	5.00	3.00
(26)	Chuck Vinson	10.00	5.00	3.00
(27)	Don Wallace	10.00	5.00	3.00
(28)	Jack D. Warner	10.00	5.00	3.00
(29)	Mike White	10.00	5.00	3.00

1967 Seattle Angels Popcorn

(Cartoon angel pitching on back, first "Presented by" advertiser is Western Airlines.)

		NM	EX	VG
Complete Set (19):		175.00	85.00	50.00
Common Player:		9.00	4.50	2.75
(1)	George Banks	9.00	4.50	2.75
(2)	Tom Burgmeier	9.00	4.50	2.75
(3)	Jim Coates	9.00	4.50	2.75
(4)	Chuck Cottier	12.00	6.00	3.50
(5)	Tony Curry	9.00	4.50	2.75
(6)	Vern Geishert	9.00	4.50	2.75
(7)	Jesse Hickman	9.00	4.50	2.75
(8)	Bill Kelso	9.00	4.50	2.75
(9)	Ed Kirkpatrick	9.00	4.50	2.75
(10)	Chris Krug	9.00	4.50	2.75
(11)	Bobby Locke	9.00	4.50	2.75
(12)	Bill Murphy	9.00	4.50	2.75
(13)	Marty Pattin	9.00	4.50	2.75
(14)	Merritt Ranew	9.00	4.50	2.75
(15)	Bob Sadowski	9.00	4.50	2.75
(16)	Ed Sukla	9.00	4.50	2.75
(17)	Hector Torres	9.00	4.50	2.75
(18)	Chuck Vinson	9.00	4.50	2.75
(19)	Don Wallace	9.00	4.50	2.75

1968 Seattle Angels Popcorn

(Blank-back)

		NM	EX	VG
Complete Set (18):		150.00	75.00	45.00
Common Player:		9.00	4.50	2.75
(1)	Ethan Blackaby	9.00	4.50	2.75
(2)	Jim Coates	9.00	4.50	2.75
(3)	Tom Egan	9.00	4.50	2.75
(4)	Larry Elliott (Elliot)	9.00	4.50	2.75
(5)	Jim Englehardt	9.00	4.50	2.75
(6)	Gus Gil	9.00	4.50	2.75
(7)	Bill Harrelson	9.00	4.50	2.75
(8)	Steve Hovley	9.00	4.50	2.75
(9)	Jim Mahoney	9.00	4.50	2.75
(10)	Mickey McGuire	9.00	4.50	2.75
(11)	Joe Overton	9.00	4.50	2.75
(12)	Marty Pattin	9.00	4.50	2.75
(13)	Larry Sherry	9.00	4.50	2.75
(14)	Marv Staehle	9.00	4.50	2.75
(15)	Ed Sukla	9.00	4.50	2.75
(16)	Jarvis Tatum	9.00	4.50	2.75
(17)	Hawk Taylor	9.00	4.50	2.75
(18)	Chuck Vinson	9.00	4.50	2.75

1960 Shopsy's Frankfurters Toronto Maple Leafs

Only the Toronto Maple Leafs of the International League - including many former and future major leaguers - are included in this set. The cards are about 2-1/4" x 3-1/4", blank-back and printed in black-and-white. The unnumbered cards are checklisted here alphabetically.

		NM	EX	VG
Complete Set (23):		500.00	250.00	150.00
Common Player:		30.00	15.00	9.00
Album:		75.00	37.00	22.00
(1)	George Anderson (Sparky)	60.00	30.00	18.00
(2)	Bob Chakales	30.00	15.00	9.00
(3)	Al Cicotte	30.00	15.00	9.00
(4)	Rip Coleman	30.00	15.00	9.00
(5)	Steve Demeter	30.00	15.00	9.00
(6)	Don Dillard	30.00	15.00	9.00
(7)	Frank Funk	30.00	15.00	9.00
(8)	Russ Heman	30.00	15.00	9.00
(9)	Earl Hersh	30.00	15.00	9.00
(10)	Allen Jones	30.00	15.00	9.00
(11)	Jim King	30.00	15.00	9.00
(12)	Jack Kubiszyn	30.00	15.00	9.00
(13)	Mel McGaha	30.00	15.00	9.00
(14)	Bill Moran	30.00	15.00	9.00
(15)	Ron Negray	30.00	15.00	9.00
(16)	Herb Plews	30.00	15.00	9.00
(17)	Steve Ridzik	30.00	15.00	9.00
(18)	Pat Scantlebury	30.00	15.00	9.00
(19)	Bill Smith (trainer)	30.00	15.00	9.00
(20)	Bob Smith	30.00	15.00	9.00
(21)	Tim Thompson	30.00	15.00	9.00
(22)	Jack Waters	30.00	15.00	9.00
(23)	Archie Wilson	45.00	22.00	13.50

1947 Signal Gasoline Pacific Coast League

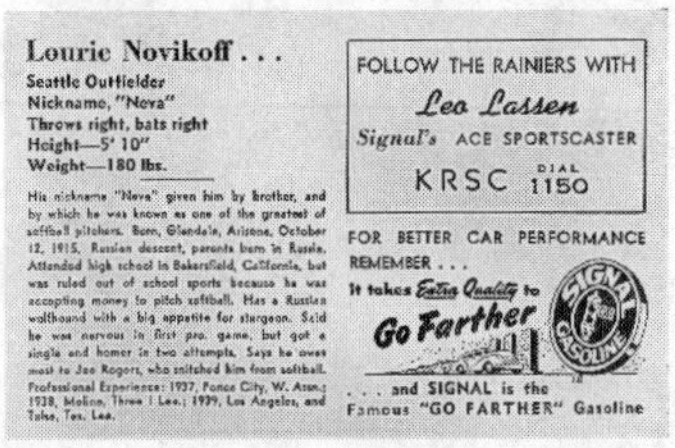

Five of the eight PCL teams participated in this baseball card promotion, giving away cards of home-team players. Because of vagaries of local distribution, some teams, notably Sacramento and Seattle, are scarcer than others, and there are specific player rarities among other teams. The black-and-white cards are 5-9/16"x 3-1/2" and feature on the front a drawing of the player and several personal or career highlights in cartoon form. The artwork was done by former N.Y. Giants pitcher Al Demaree. On the backs are player biographical details, an ad for Signal Gas and an ad for the co-sponsoring radio station in each locale. Cards are unnumbered.

	NM	EX	VG
Complete Set (89):	3575.	1775.	1075.
Common Player:	21.00	10.50	6.25

(Team sets listed below)

1947 Signal Gasoline Hollywood Stars

		NM	EX	VG
Complete Set (20):		525.00	260.00	155.00
Common Player:		21.00	10.50	6.25
(1)	Ed Albosta	21.00	10.50	6.25
(2)	Carl Cox	21.00	10.50	6.25
(3)	Frank Dasso	21.00	10.50	6.25
(4)	Tod Davis	21.00	10.50	6.25
(5)	Jim Delsing	21.00	10.50	6.25
(6)	Jimmy Dykes	26.00	13.00	7.75
(7)	Paul Gregory	21.00	10.50	6.25
(8)	Fred Haney	26.00	13.00	7.75
(9)	Frank Kelleher	21.00	10.50	6.25
(10)	Joe Krakauskas	21.00	10.50	6.25
(11)	Al Libke	21.00	10.50	6.25
(12)	Tony Lupien	21.00	10.50	6.25
(13)	Xaiver Rescigno	21.00	10.50	6.25
(14)	Jack Sherman	21.00	10.50	6.25
(15)	Andy Skurski	21.00	10.50	6.25
(16)	Glen (Glenn) Stewart	21.00	10.50	6.25
(17)	Al Unser	21.00	10.50	6.25
(18)	Fred Vaughn	21.00	10.50	6.25
(19)	Woody Williams	250.00	125.00	75.00
(20)	Dutch (Gus) Zernial	32.00	16.00	9.50

1947 Signal Gasoline Los Angeles Angels

		NM	EX	VG
Complete Set (18):		290.00	145.00	88.00
Common Player:		21.00	10.50	6.25
(1)	Red Adams	21.00	10.50	6.25
(2)	Larry Barton	21.00	10.50	6.25
(3)	Cliff Chambers	21.00	10.50	6.25
(4)	Lloyd Christopher	21.00	10.50	6.25
(5)	Cece Garriott	21.00	10.50	6.25
(6)	Al Glossop	21.00	10.50	6.25
(7)	Bill Kelly	21.00	10.50	6.25
(8)	Red Lynn	21.00	10.50	6.25
(9)	Eddie Malone	21.00	10.50	6.25
(10)	Dutch McCall	21.00	10.50	6.25
(11)	Don Osborne	21.00	10.50	6.25
(12)	John Ostrowski	21.00	10.50	6.25
(13)	Reggie Otero	21.00	10.50	6.25
(14)	Ray Prim	21.00	10.50	6.25
(15)	Ed Sauer	21.00	10.50	6.25
(16)	Bill Schuster	21.00	10.50	6.25
(17)	Tuck Stainback	21.00	10.50	6.25
(18)	Lou Stringer	21.00	10.50	6.25

1947 Signal Gasoline Oakland Oaks

		NM	EX	VG
Complete Set (19):		525.00	260.00	155.00
Common Player:		21.00	10.50	6.25
(1)	Vic Buccola	21.00	10.50	6.25
(2)	Mickey Burnett	21.00	10.50	6.25
(3)	Ralph Buxton	21.00	10.50	6.25
(4)	Vince DiMaggio	95.00	47.00	28.00
(5)	Dizz Duezabou	21.00	10.50	6.25
(6)	Bud Foster	21.00	10.50	6.25
(7)	Sherriff Gassaway	21.00	10.50	6.25
(8)	Tom Hafey	21.00	10.50	6.25
(9)	Brooks Holder	21.00	10.50	6.25
(10)	Gene Lillard	21.00	10.50	6.25
(11)	Dario Lodigiani	21.00	10.50	6.25
(12)	Hershel Martin	21.00	10.50	6.25
(13)	Cotton Pippen	21.00	10.50	6.25
(14)	Billy Raimondi	21.00	10.50	6.25
(15)	Tony Sabol	21.00	10.50	6.25
(16)	Les Scarsella	21.00	10.50	6.25
(17)	Floyd Speer	21.00	10.50	6.25
(18)	Casey Stengel	100.00	50.00	30.00
(19)	Maurice Van Robays	21.00	10.50	6.25

1947 Signal Gasoline Sacramento Solons

		NM	EX	VG
Complete Set (16):		1300.	650.00	390.00
Common Player:		45.00	22.00	13.50
(1)	Bud Beasley	45.00	22.00	13.50
(2)	Frank Dasso	45.00	22.00	13.50
(3)	Ed Fitzgerald (Fitz Gerald)	45.00	22.00	13.50
(4)	Guy Fletcher	45.00	22.00	13.50
(5)	Tony Freitas	45.00	22.00	13.50
(6)	Red Mann	45.00	22.00	13.50
(7)	Joe Marty	45.00	22.00	13.50
(8)	Steve Mesner	45.00	22.00	13.50
(9)	Bill Ramsey	45.00	22.00	13.50
(10)	Charley Ripple	195.00	97.00	58.00
(11)	John Rizzo	195.00	97.00	58.00
(12)	Al Smith	195.00	97.00	58.00
(13)	Ronnie Smith	195.00	97.00	58.00
(14)	Tommy Thompson	195.00	97.00	58.00
(15)	Jim Warner	85.00	42.00	25.00
(16)	Ed Zipay	85.00	42.00	25.00

1947 Signal Gasoline Seattle Rainiers

		NM	EX	VG
Complete Set (16):		1050.	525.00	310.00
Common Player:		55.00	27.50	16.50
(1)	Kewpie Barrett	70.00	35.00	21.00
(2)	Herman Besse	55.00	27.50	16.50
(3)	Guy Fletcher	55.00	27.50	16.50
(4)	Jack Jakucki	55.00	27.50	16.50
(5)	Bob Johnson	75.00	37.00	22.00
(6)	Pete Jonas	200.00	100.00	60.00
(7)	Hillis Layne	75.00	37.00	22.00
(8)	Red Mann	75.00	37.00	22.00
(9)	Lou Novikoff	75.00	37.00	22.00
(10)	John O'Neill	75.00	37.00	22.00
(11)	Bill Ramsey	75.00	37.00	22.00
(12)	Mickey Rocco	75.00	37.00	22.00
(13)	George Scharein	75.00	37.00	22.00
(14)	Hal Sueme	75.00	37.00	22.00
(15)	Jo Jo White	75.00	37.00	22.00
(16)	Tony York	75.00	37.00	22.00

1948 Signal Gasoline Oakland Oaks

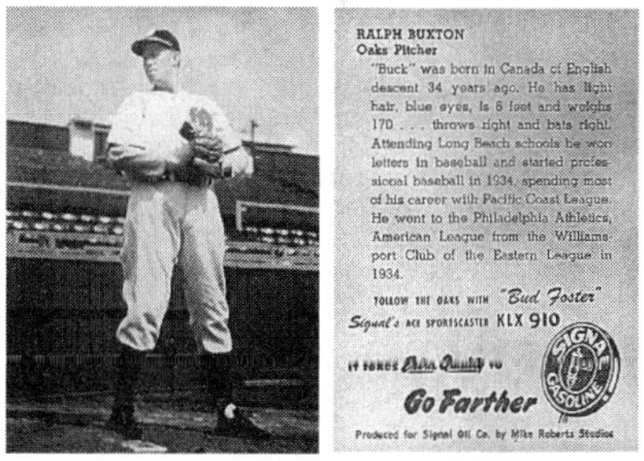

Issued by Signal Oil in the Oakland area in 1948, this 24-card set features members of the Oakland Oaks of the Pacific Coast League. The unnumbered cards, measuring 2-3/8" x 3-1/2", were given away at gas stations. The front consists of a color photo, while the backs (printed in either blue or black) contain a brief player write-up along with a Signal Oil ad and logo.

		NM	EX	VG
Complete Set (24):		585.00	290.00	175.00
Common Player:		22.00	11.00	6.50
(1)	John C. Babich	22.00	11.00	6.50
(2)	Ralph Buxton	22.00	11.00	6.50
(3)	Loyd E. Christopher (Lloyd)	22.00	11.00	6.50
(4)	Merrill Russell Combs	22.00	11.00	6.50
(5)	Melvin E. Deuzabou	22.00	11.00	6.50
(6)	Nicholas ("Nick") Etten	25.00	12.50	7.50
(7)	Bud Foster (announcer)	22.00	11.00	6.50
(8)	Charles Gassaway	22.00	11.00	6.50
(9)	Will Hafey	22.00	11.00	6.50
(10)	Ray Hamrick	22.00	11.00	6.50
(11)	Brooks Richard Holder	25.00	12.50	7.50
(12)	Earl Jones	22.00	11.00	6.50
(13)	Harry "Cookie" Lavagetto	22.00	11.00	6.50
(14)	Robert E. Lillard	22.00	11.00	6.50
(15)	Dario Lodigiani	22.00	11.00	6.50
(16)	Ernie Lombardi	40.00	20.00	12.00
(17a)	Alfred Manuel Martin (born 1921)	110.00	55.00	33.00
(17b)	Alfred Manuel Martin (born 1928)	110.00	55.00	33.00
(18)	George Michael Metkovich	22.00	11.00	6.50
(19)	William L. Raimondi	22.00	11.00	6.50
(20)	Les George Scarsella	22.00	11.00	6.50
(21)	Floyd Vernie Speer	22.00	11.00	6.50
(22)	Charles "Casey" Stengel	115.00	57.00	34.00
(23)	Maurice Van Robays	22.00	11.00	6.50
(24)	Aldon Jay Wilkie	22.00	11.00	6.50

1947 Smith's Oakland Oaks

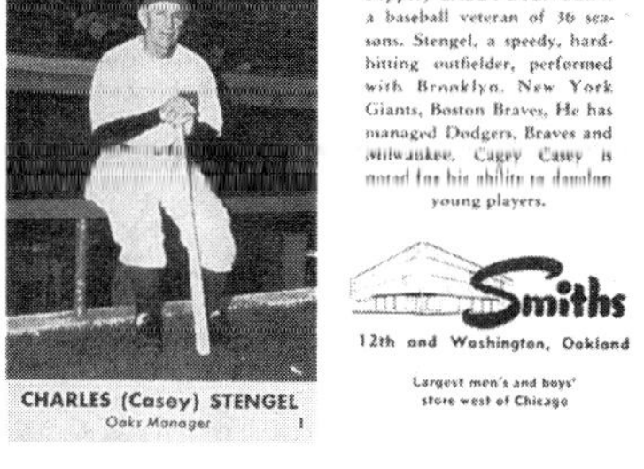

This regional set of Oakland Oaks (Pacific Coast League) cards was issued in 1947 by Smith's Clothing stores and is numbered in the lower right corner. The card fronts include a black and white photo with the player's name, team and position below. The backs carry a brief player write-up and an advertisement for Smith's Clothing. The cards measure 2" x 3" The Max Marshall card was apparently short-printed and is much scarcer than the rest of the set.

		NM	EX	VG
Complete Set (25):		750.00	375.00	225.00
Common Player:		22.00	11.00	6.50
1	Charles (Casey) Stengel	115.00	57.00	34.00
2	Billy Raimondi	22.00	11.00	6.50
3	Les Scarsella	22.00	11.00	6.50
4	Brooks Holder	22.00	11.00	6.50
5	Ray Hamrick	22.00	11.00	6.50
6	Gene Lillard	22.00	11.00	6.50
7	Maurice Van Robays	22.00	11.00	6.50
8	Charlie (Sheriff) Gassaway	22.00	11.00	6.50
9	Henry (Cotton) Pippen	22.00	11.00	6.50
10	James Arnold	22.00	11.00	6.50
11	Ralph (Buck) Buxton	22.00	11.00	6.50
12	Ambrose (Bo) Palica	22.00	11.00	6.50
13	Tony Sabol	22.00	11.00	6.50
14	Ed Kearse	22.00	11.00	6.50
15	Bill Hart	22.00	11.00	6.50
16	Donald (Snuffy) Smith	22.00	11.00	6.50
17	Oral (Mickey) Burnett	22.00	11.00	6.50
18	Tom Hafey	22.00	11.00	6.50
19	Will Hafey	22.00	11.00	6.50
20	Paul Gillespie	32.00	16.00	9.50
21	Damon Hayes	32.00	16.00	9.50
22	Max Marshall	160.00	80.00	48.00
23	Mel (Dizz) Duezabou	22.00	11.00	6.50
24	Mel Reeves	22.00	11.00	6.50
25	Joe Faria	32.00	16.00	9.50

1948 Smith's Oakland Oaks

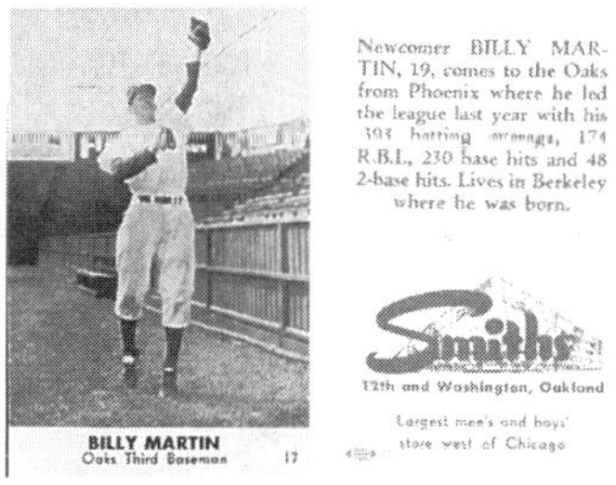

The 1948 Smith's Clothing issue was another 25-card regional set featuring members of the Oakland Oaks of the Pacific Coast League. Almost identical to the 1947 Smith's issue, the black and white cards again measure 2" x 3" but were printed on heavier, glossy stock. The player's name, team and position appear below the photo with the card number in the lower right corner. The back has a brief player write-up and an ad for Smith's Clothing.

		NM	EX	VG
Complete Set (25):		650.00	325.00	195.00
Common Player:		22.00	11.00	6.50
1	Billy Raimondi	22.00	11.00	6.50
2	Brooks Holder	22.00	11.00	6.50
3	Will Hafey	25.00	12.50	7.50
4	Nick Etten	22.00	11.00	6.50
5	Lloyd Christopher	22.00	11.00	6.50
6	Les Scarsella	22.00	11.00	6.50
7	Ray Hamrick	22.00	11.00	6.50
8	Gene Lillard	22.00	11.00	6.50
9	Maurice Van Robays	22.00	11.00	6.50
10	Charlie Gassaway	22.00	11.00	6.50
11	Ralph (Buck) Buxton	22.00	11.00	6.50
12	Tom Hafey	22.00	11.00	6.50
13	Damon Hayes	22.00	11.00	6.50
14	Mel (Dizz) Duezabou	22.00	11.00	6.50
15	Dario Lodigiani	22.00	11.00	6.50
16	Vic Buccola	22.00	11.00	6.50
17	Billy Martin	115.00	57.00	34.00
18	Floyd Speer	22.00	11.00	6.50
19	Eddie Samcoff	22.00	11.00	6.50
20	Charles (Casey) Stengel	115.00	57.00	34.00
21	Lloyd Hittle	22.00	11.00	6.50
22	Johnny Babich	22.00	11.00	6.50
23	Merrill Combs	22.00	11.00	6.50
24	Eddie Murphy	22.00	11.00	6.50
25	Bob Klinger	22.00	11.00	6.50

1948 Sommer & Kaufmann San Francisco Seals

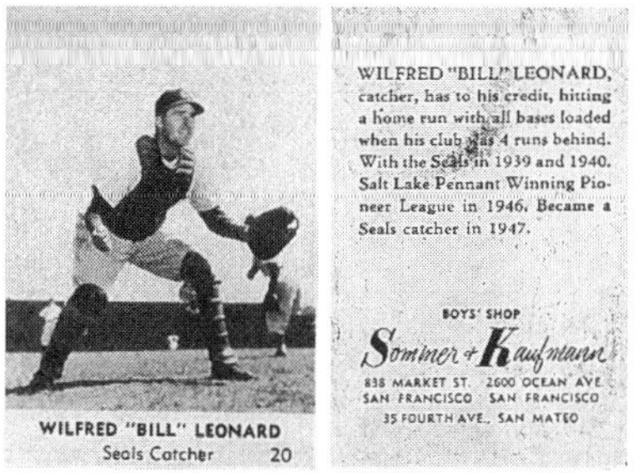

One of the more common of the many Pacific Coast League issues of the late 1940s, this emission from the San Francisco boys' clothier features 30 black-and-white 2" x 3" cards. Fronts have a player photo, name, position and card number. Backs have a few biographical details and stats, along with an ad. The 1948 issue can be differentiated from the 1949 issue by the words "BOYS SHOP" above the company logo on back.

		NM	EX	VG
Complete Set (30):		975.00	485.00	290.00
Common Player:		32.00	16.00	9.50
1	Lefty O'Doul	50.00	25.00	15.00
2	Jack Brewer	32.00	16.00	9.50
3	Con Dempsey	32.00	16.00	9.50
4	Tommy Fine	32.00	16.00	9.50
5	Kenneth Gables	32.00	16.00	9.50
6	Robert Joyce	32.00	16.00	9.50
7	Al Lien	32.00	16.00	9.50
8	Cliff Melton	32.00	16.00	9.50
9	Frank Shofner	32.00	16.00	9.50
10	Don Trower	32.00	16.00	9.50
11	Joe Brovia	32.00	16.00	9.50
12	Dino Paul Restelli	32.00	16.00	9.50
13	Gene Woodling	40.00	20.00	12.00
14	Ben Guintini	32.00	16.00	9.50
15	Felix Mackiewicz	32.00	16.00	9.50
16	John Patrick Tobin	32.00	16.00	9.50
17	Manuel Perez	32.00	16.00	9.50
18	Bill Werle	32.00	16.00	9.50
19	Homer Howell	32.00	16.00	9.50
20	Wilfred Leonard	32.00	16.00	9.50
21	Bruce Ogrodowski	32.00	16.00	9.50
22	Dick Lajeskie	32.00	16.00	9.50
23	Hugh Luby	32.00	16.00	9.50
24	Roy Nicely	32.00	16.00	9.50
25	Ray Orteig	32.00	16.00	9.50
26	Michael Rocco	32.00	16.00	9.50
27	Del Young	32.00	16.00	9.50
28	Joe Sprinz	32.00	16.00	9.50
29	Doc Hughes	32.00	16.00	9.50
30	Batboys	32.00	16.00	9.50

1949 Sommer & Kaufmann San Francisco Seals

JACK NICHOLAS BACCIOCCO, outfielder, Born, San Francisco, Feb. 10, 1925. Height 6', weight 185. Throws and bats right. Italian-Swedish descent. With Salt Lake and Reno in 1947. With Salt Lake in 1948. Hit .277.
Sommer & Kaufmann
838 MARKET ST. 2600 OCEAN AVE. SAN FRANCISCO
25 FOURTH AVE., SAN MATEO
Famous for Boys' "Hot Rod" Shoes
JACK NICHOLAS BACCIOCCO
Seals Outfielder 19

Twenty-eight black-and-white cards numbered 1-29 (#24 unknown) make up the second and final card issue of the "Frisco area clothier". Measuring 2" x 3", the cards are nearly identical to the '48 issue. The '49s can be identified by the mention of "Hot Rod" shoes on the back. Fronts feature a borderless player photo with a panel at the bottom giving name, position and card number. Backs have the ad for the boy's shop and a brief biographical player sketch.

		NM	EX	VG
Complete Set (29):		900.00	450.00	275.00
Common Player:		32.00	16.00	9.50
1	Lefty O'Doul	50.00	25.00	15.00
2	Jack Brewer	32.00	16.00	9.50
3	Kenneth Gables	32.00	16.00	9.50
4	Con Dempsey	32.00	16.00	9.50
5	Al Lien	32.00	16.00	9.50
6	Cliff Melton	32.00	16.00	9.50
7	Steve Nagy	32.00	16.00	9.50
8	Manny Perez	32.00	16.00	9.50
9	Roy Jarvis	32.00	16.00	9.50
10	Roy Partee	32.00	16.00	9.50
11	Reno Cheso	32.00	16.00	9.50
12	Dick Lajeskie	32.00	16.00	9.50
13	Roy Nicely	32.00	16.00	9.50
14	Mickey Rocco	32.00	16.00	9.50
15	Frank Shofner	32.00	16.00	9.50
16	Richard Holder	32.00	16.00	9.50
17	Dino Restelli	32.00	16.00	9.50
18	Floyd J. "Arky" Vaughan	65.00	32.00	19.50
19	Jackie Baccioccu	32.00	16.00	9.50
20	Bob Drilling	32.00	16.00	9.50
21	Del Young	32.00	16.00	9.50
22	Joe Sprinz	32.00	16.00	9.50
23	Doc Hughes	32.00	16.00	9.50
24	Unknown			
25	Bert Singleton	32.00	16.00	9.50
26	John Brocker	32.00	16.00	9.50
27	Jack Tobin	32.00	16.00	9.50
28	Walt Judnich	32.00	16.00	9.50
29	Hal Feldman	32.00	16.00	9.50

Checklists with card numbers in parentheses ( ) indicates the numbers do not appear on the cards.

1946 Sunbeam Bread Sacramento Solons

STEVE "LITTLE GOLIATH" MESNER, 28, born Los Angeles, Calif.; second season with Solons. Greatest baseball thrill: hitting three home runs in one game. Played in majors with Chicago White Sox, St. Louis Cards, Cincinnati Reds. Hobby: collecting all articles pertaining to baseball.
Listen to Baseball Play by Play With "Tony" Koester KFBK
Sunbeam BREAD
STEVE MESNER
1946 Solons Third Baseman
Photo by Joe Benetti

The 21 unnumbered cards in this Pacific Coast League team set are printed with black-and-white fronts containing a borderless player photo with a panel beneath containing name, position and a photo credit. Backs are printed in blue, red and yellow and contain a brief career summary and an ad for the bread brand. Each card can be found with two versions of the ad on back. One has a smaller loaf of bread and the word "Sunbeam" in blue, the other has a larger picture and "Sunbeam" in red. The cards measure approximately 2" x 3". Players are checklisted here in alphabetical order.

		NM	EX	VG
Complete Set (21):		425.00	210.00	125.00
Common Player:		16.00	8.00	4.75
(1)	Bud Beasley	16.00	8.00	4.75
(2)	Jack Calvey	16.00	8.00	4.75
(3)	Gene Crobett	16.00	8.00	4.75
(4)	Bill Conroy	16.00	8.00	4.75
(5)	Guy Fletcher	16.00	8.00	4.75
(6)	Tony Freitas	16.00	8.00	4.75
(7)	Ted Greenhalgh	16.00	8.00	4.75
(8)	Al Jarlett	16.00	8.00	4.75
(9)	Jesse Landrum	16.00	8.00	4.75
(10)	Gene Lillard	16.00	8.00	4.75
(11)	Garth Mann	16.00	8.00	4.75
(12)	Lilo Marcucci	16.00	8.00	4.75
(13)	Joe Marty (SP)	130.00	65.00	39.00
(14)	Steve Mesner	16.00	8.00	4.75
(15)	Herm Pillette	16.00	8.00	4.75
(16)	Earl Sheely	16.00	8.00	4.75
(17)	Al Smith	16.00	8.00	4.75
(18)	Gerald Staley	16.00	8.00	4.75
(19)	Averett Thompson	16.00	8.00	4.75
(20)	Jo Jo White	16.00	8.00	4.75
(21)	Bud Zipay	16.00	8.00	4.75

1947 Sunbeam Bread Sacramento Solons

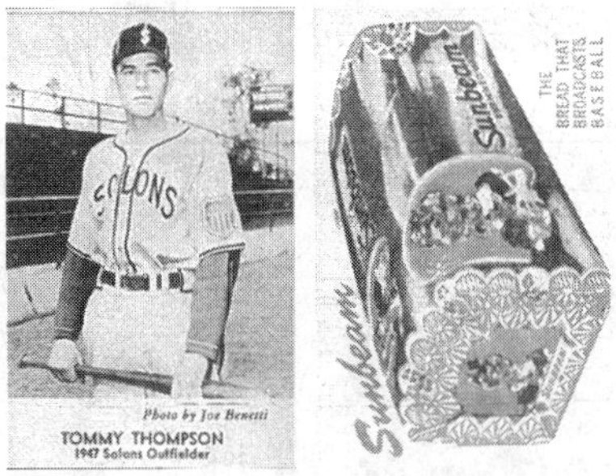

Similar in format to the 1946 issue, the 26 cards in the '47 set again featured black-and-white player photos on front, with a panel beneath giving player name, position and photo credit. Backs of the 2" x 3" cards had a color depiction of a loaf of the sponsoring company's bread. The unnumbered cards are alphabetically checklisted here.

		NM	EX	VG
Complete Set (26):		400.00	200.00	120.00
Common Player:		16.00	8.00	4.75
(1)	Gene Babbit	16.00	8.00	4.75
(2)	Bob Barthelson	16.00	8.00	4.75
(3)	Bud Beasley	16.00	8.00	4.75
(4)	Chuck Cronin	16.00	8.00	4.75
(5)	Eddie Fernandes	16.00	8.00	4.75
(6)	Ed Fitzgerald (Fitz Gerald)	16.00	8.00	4.75
(7)	Guy Fletcher	16.00	8.00	4.75
(8)	Tony Freitas	16.00	8.00	4.75
(9)	Garth Mann	16.00	8.00	4.75
(10)	Joe Marty	16.00	8.00	4.75
(11)	Lou McCollum	16.00	8.00	4.75
(12)	Steve Mesner	16.00	8.00	4.75
(13)	Frank Nelson	16.00	8.00	4.75
(14)	Tommy Nelson	16.00	8.00	4.75
(15)	Joe Orengo	16.00	8.00	4.75
(16)	Hugh Orphan	16.00	8.00	4.75
(17)	Nick Pesut	16.00	8.00	4.75
(18)	Bill Ramsey	16.00	8.00	4.75
(19)	Johnny Rizzo	16.00	8.00	4.75
(20)	Mike Schemer	16.00	8.00	4.75
(21)	Al Smith	16.00	8.00	4.75
(22)	Tommy Thompson	16.00	8.00	4.75
(23)	Jim Warner	16.00	8.00	4.75
(24)	Mel Wasley	16.00	8.00	4.75
(25)	Leo Wells	16.00	8.00	4.75
(26)	Eddie Zipay	16.00	8.00	4.75

1949 Sunbeam Bread Stockton Ports

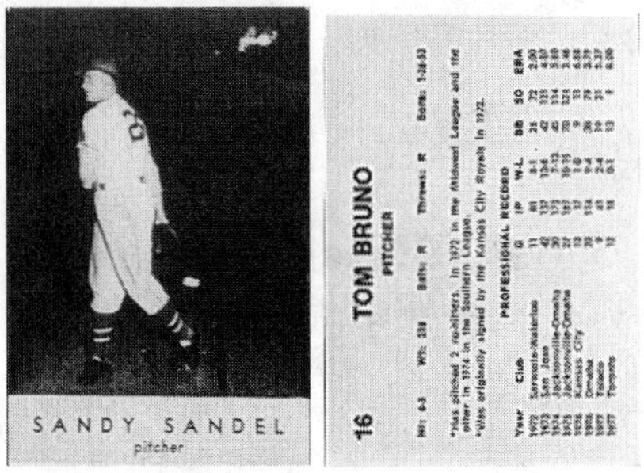

(California League) (2" x 3", unnumbered, b/w or blue tinted)

		NM	EX	VG
Complete Set (12):		2100.	1050.	625.00
Common Player:		175.00	90.00	50.00
(1)	Lou Bronzan	175.00	90.00	50.00
(2)	Jimmie Brown	175.00	90.00	50.00
(3)	Rocco Cardinale	175.00	90.00	50.00
(4)	Harry Clements	175.00	90.00	50.00
(5)	Nino Bongiovanni	175.00	90.00	50.00
(6)	Norm Grabar	175.00	90.00	50.00
(7)	Bud Guldborg	175.00	90.00	50.00
(8)	Carl Hoberg	175.00	90.00	50.00
(9)	Eddie Murphy	175.00	90.00	50.00
(10)	Sandy Sandel	175.00	90.00	50.00
(11)	Dick Stone	175.00	90.00	50.00
(12)	Matt Zidich	175.00	90.00	50.00

1949 Sunbeam/Pureta Sacramento Solons

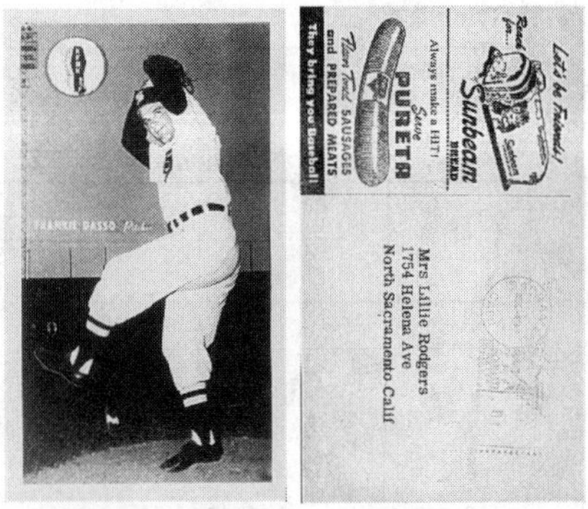

Players of the Pacific Coast League's Sacramento Solons were featured in this postcard-size (3-1/4" x 5-1/2") set. Fronts featured black-and-white player photos and the logo of the team's radio broadcaster. Backs feature ads for Sunbeam Bread and Pureta meats.

		NM	EX	VG
Complete Set (12):		900.00	450.00	270.00
Common Player:		110.00	55.00	35.00
(1)	Del Baker	110.00	55.00	33.00
(2)	Frankie Dasso	110.00	55.00	33.00
(3)	Walt Dropo	135.00	67.00	40.00
(4)	Joe Grace	110.00	55.00	33.00
(5)	Bob Gillespie	110.00	55.00	33.00
(6)	Ralph Hodgin	110.00	55.00	33.00
(7)	Freddie Marsh	110.00	55.00	33.00
(8)	Joe Marty	110.00	55.00	33.00
(9)	Len Ratto	110.00	55.00	33.00
(10)	Jim Tabor	110.00	55.00	33.00
(11)	Al White	110.00	55.00	33.00

		NM	EX	VG
(12)	Bill Wilson	110.00	55.00	33.00

1950 Sunbeam Bread Stockton Ports

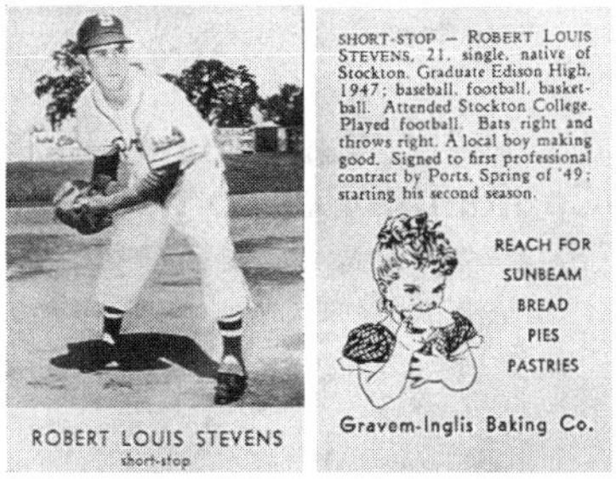

SHORT-STOP — ROBERT LOUIS STEVENS, 21, single, native of Stockton. Graduate Edison High, 1947; baseball, football, basket-ball. Attended Stockton College. Played football. Bats right and throws right. A local boy making good. Signed to first professional contract by Ports, Spring of '49; starting his second season.
REACH FOR SUNBEAM BREAD PIES PASTRIES
Gravem-Inglis Baking Co.
ROBERT LOUIS STEVENS
short-stop

(California League) (2" x 3") (black and white) (unnumbered)

		NM	EX	VG
Complete Set (13):		1100.	550.00	330.00
Common Player:		90.00	45.00	25.00
(1)	Richard L. Adams	90.00	45.00	25.00
(2)	James Edward Brown	90.00	45.00	25.00
(3)	Harry Clements	90.00	45.00	25.00
(4)	John Burton Goldborg	90.00	45.00	25.00
(5)	Gerald Lee Haines	90.00	45.00	25.00
(6)	Alfred Michael Heist	90.00	45.00	25.00
(7)	Don Masterson	90.00	45.00	25.00
(8)	Lauren Hugh Monroe	90.00	45.00	25.00
(9)	Frank E. Murray	90.00	45.00	25.00
(10)	Lauren Keith Simon Jr.	90.00	45.00	25.00
(11)	George Anthony Stanich	90.00	45.00	25.00
(12)	Robert Louis Stevens	90.00	45.00	25.00
(13)	Harold Lee Zurcher	90.00	45.00	25.00

1969 Syracuse Chiefs Postcard

Thurman Munson and a number of other future and former Yankees are featured on this 7" x 5-1/2" team-issued postcard. Front has a borderless color photo. On back, besides standard postcard indicia, are credits for the photography and printing and a key to the players in the picture.

	NM	EX	VG
1700021969 Syracuse Chiefs	45.00	22.00	13.50

T

1966 Toledo Mud Hens team issue

(3-1/4" x 5-1/2")(unnumbered)

		NM	EX	VG
Complete Set (25):		400.00	200.00	120.00
Common Player:		15.00	7.50	4.50
(1)	Loren Babe	15.00	7.50	4.50
(2)	Stan Bahnsen	15.00	7.50	4.50
(3)	Bill Bethea	15.00	7.50	4.50
(4)	Wayne Comer	15.00	7.50	4.50
(5)	Jack Cullen	15.00	7.50	4.50
(6)	Jack Curtis	15.00	7.50	4.50
(7)	Gil Downs	15.00	7.50	4.50
(8)	Joe Faroci	15.00	7.50	4.50
(9)	Frank Fernandez	15.00	7.50	4.50
(10)	Mike Ferraro	15.00	7.50	4.50
(11)	Doc Foley	15.00	7.50	4.50
(12)	Mike Hegan	15.00	7.50	4.50
(13)	Jim Horsford	15.00	7.50	4.50
(14)	Dick Hughes	15.00	7.50	4.50
(15)	Elvio Jiminez	15.00	7.50	4.50
(16)	Bob Lasko	15.00	7.50	4.50
(17)	Jim Merritt	15.00	7.50	4.50
(18)	Archie Moore	15.00	7.50	4.50
(19)	Bobby Murcer	35.00	17.50	10.50
(20)	Tony Preybycian	15.00	7.50	4.50
(21)	Bob Schmidt	15.00	7.50	4.50
(22)	Charlie Senger, Loren Babe, Bill Shantz	15.00	7.50	4.50
(23)	Bill Shantz	15.00	7.50	4.50
(24)	Paul Toth	15.00	7.50	4.50
(25)	Jerry Walker	15.00	7.50	4.50

1964 True-Aid Buffalo Bisons

(International League) (2-1/4" x 5-1/2") (unnumbered)

		NM	EX	VG
Complete Set (3):		150.00	75.00	45.00
(1)	Ed Bauta	40.00	20.00	12.00
(2)	Choo Choo Coleman	60.00	30.00	18.00
(3)	Cleon Jones	60.00	30.00	18.00

1960 Tulsa Oilers team issue

		NM	EX	VG
Complete Set (12):		240.00	120.00	72.50
Common Player:		25.00	12.50	7.50
(1)	Bob Blaylock	25.00	12.50	7.50
(2)	Artie Burnett	25.00	12.50	7.50
(3)	Bill Carpenter	25.00	12.50	7.50
(4)	Julio Gotay	25.00	12.50	7.50
(5)	Ray Katt	25.00	12.50	7.50
(6)	Harry Keister	25.00	12.50	7.50
(7)	Fred Koenig	25.00	12.50	7.50
(8)	Rich Rogers	25.00	12.50	7.50
(9)	Lynn Rube	25.00	12.50	7.50
(10)	Jim Schaffer	25.00	12.50	7.50
(11)	Ted Thiem	25.00	12.50	7.50
(12)	Dixie Walker	25.00	12.50	7.50

1910 T210

(See Old Mill (minor league) for) (checklist and values.)

1958 Union Oil Sacramento Solons

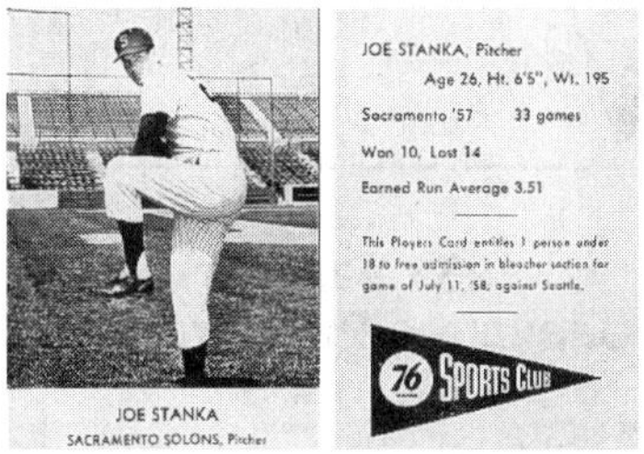

JOE STANKA, Pitcher
Age 26, Ht. 6'5", Wt. 195
Sacramento '57 33 games
Won 10, Lost 14
Earned Run Average 3.51
This Players Card entitles 1 person under 18 to free admission in bleacher section for game of July 11, '58, against Seattle.
SPORTS CLUB
JOE STANKA
SACRAMENTO SOLONS, Pitcher

Ten members of the independent Pacific Coast League team were included in a black-and-white card set distributed at Union 76 gas stations in that locale. Fronts feature borderless player photos with a wide white strip at the bottom on which is printed the player, team name and the position. Backs have brief stats, a "76 Sports Club" pennant and information about a specific game for which the card can be exchanged for admission by a child. Cards measure approximately 2-1/2" x 3-1/4".

		NM	EX	VG
Complete Set (10):		200.00	100.00	60.00
Common Player:		16.50	8.25	5.00
(1)	Marshall Bridges	30.00	15.00	9.00
(2)	Dick Cole	16.50	8.25	5.00
(3)	Jim Greengrass	16.50	8.25	5.00
(4)	Al Heist	16.50	8.25	5.00
(5)	Nippy Jones	16.50	8.25	5.00
(6)	Carlos Paula	16.50	8.25	5.00
(7)	Kal Segrist	16.50	8.25	5.00
(8)	Sibbi Sisti	20.00	10.00	6.00
(9)	Joe Stanka	30.00	15.00	9.00
(10)	Bud Watkins	16.50	8.25	5.00

The ratio of Excellent and Very Good prices to Near Mint can vary depending on relative collectibility for each grade in a specific set. Current listings reflect such adjustments.

U

1960 Union Oil Seattle Rainiers

Given away at Union 76 gas stations in the Seattle area, this set of nine full-color cards measure approximately 3-1/8" x 4". Backs have brief biographical data, a career summary and a large Union 76 logo. The cards are skip-numbered.

		NM	EX	VG
Complete Set (9):		175.00	87.50	50.00
Common Player:		10.00	5.00	3.00
4	Francisco Obregon	20.00	10.00	6.00
6	Drew Gilbert	10.00	5.00	3.00
7	Bill Hain	10.00	5.00	3.00
10	Ray Ripplemeyer	75.00	37.50	22.50
13	Joe Taylor	10.00	5.00	3.00
15	Lou Skizas	10.00	5.00	3.00
17	Don Rudolph	10.00	5.00	3.00
19	Gordy Coleman	15.00	7.50	4.50
22	Hal Breven	10.00	5.00	3.00

1961 Union Oil Pacific Coast League

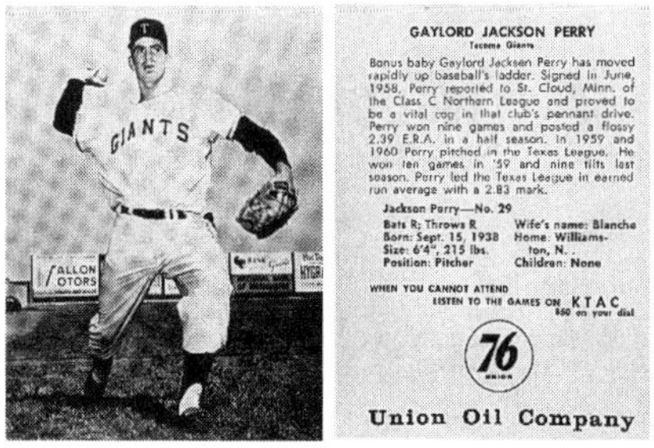

The last of three Union Oil PCL issues, the 67 cards in this set feature sepia-toned borderless photos on front in a 3" x 4" format. Backs are printed in blue and feature biographical data, a career summary, and ads by the issuing oil company and participating radio station co-sponsors. Six of the eight teams in the '61 PCL are featured, with Salt Lake City and Vancouver not participating in the promotion. Presumably because of smaller print runs, the cards distributed in Hawaii and Spokane bring a premium price. Hall of Fame pitcher Gaylord Perry is featured on his first baseball card in this set. Only the Tacoma cards are numbered and they are skip-numbered.

	NM	EX	VG
Complete Set (67):	750.00	375.00	225.00
Common Player:	8.00	4.00	2.40

(Team sets listed below)

1961 Union Oil Hawaii Islanders

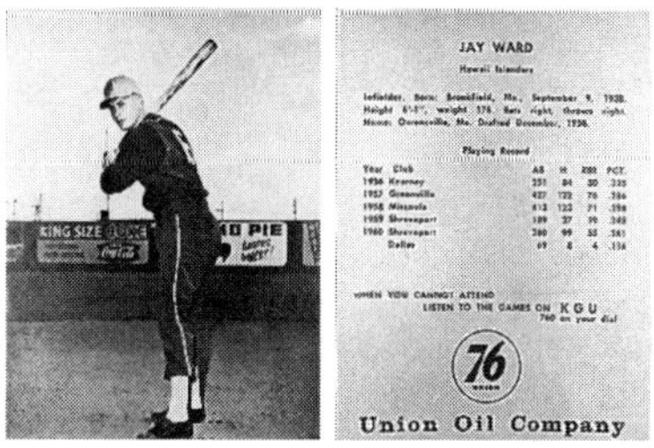

		NM	EX	VG
Complete Set (10):		200.00	100.00	60.00
Common Player:		20.00	10.00	6.00
(1)	Ray Jablonski	20.00	10.00	6.00
(2)	Jim McManus	20.00	10.00	6.00
(3)	George Prescott	50.00	25.00	15.00
(4)	Diego Segui	25.00	12.50	7.50
(5)	Rachel Slider	20.00	10.00	6.00
(6)	Jim Small	20.00	10.00	6.00
(7)	Milt Smith	20.00	10.00	6.00
(8)	Dave Thies	20.00	10.00	6.00
(9)	Jay Ward	20.00	10.00	6.00
(10)	Bill Werle	20.00	10.00	6.00

1961 Union Oil Portland Beavers

		NM	EX	VG
Complete Set (13):		100.00	50.00	30.00
Common Player:		10.00	5.00	3.00
(1)	Ed Bauta	10.00	5.00	3.00
(2)	Vern Benson	10.00	5.00	3.00
(3)	Jerry Buchek	10.00	5.00	3.00
(4)	Bob Burda	10.00	5.00	3.00
(5)	Duke Carmel	10.00	5.00	3.00
(6)	Don Choate	10.00	5.00	3.00
(7)	Phil Gagliano	10.00	5.00	3.00
(8)	Jim Hickman	10.00	5.00	3.00
(9)	Ray Katt	10.00	5.00	3.00
(10)	Mel Nelson	10.00	5.00	3.00
(11)	Jim Shaffer	10.00	5.00	3.00
(12)	Mike Shannon	15.00	7.50	4.50
(13)	Clint Stark	10.00	5.00	3.00

1961 Union Oil San Diego Padres

		NM	EX	VG
Complete Set (12):		125.00	62.00	37.00
Common Player:		10.00	5.00	3.00
(1)	Dick Barone	10.00	5.00	3.00
(2)	Jim Bolger	10.00	5.00	3.00
(3)	Kent Hadley	10.00	5.00	3.00
(4)	Mike Hershberger	13.00	6.50	4.00
(5)	Stan Johnson	10.00	5.00	3.00
(6)	Dick Lines	10.00	5.00	3.00
(7)	Jim Napier	10.00	5.00	3.00
(8)	Tony Roig	10.00	5.00	3.00
(9)	Herb Score	40.00	20.00	12.00
(10)	Harry Simpson	12.00	6.00	3.50
(11)	Joe Taylor	10.00	5.00	3.00
(12)	Ben Wade	10.00	5.00	3.00

1961 Union Oil Seattle Rainiers

		NM	EX	VG
Complete Set (11):		75.00	37.50	22.00
Common Player:		8.00	4.00	2.50
(1)	Galen Cisco	8.00	4.00	2.50
(2)	Lou Clinton	8.00	4.00	2.50
(3)	Marlan Coughtry	8.00	4.00	2.50
(4)	Harry Malmberg	8.00	4.00	2.50
(5)	Dave Mann	8.00	4.00	2.50
(6)	Derrell Martin	8.00	4.00	2.50
(7)	Erv Palica	8.00	4.00	2.50
(8)	Johnny Pesky	8.00	4.00	2.50
(9)	Bob Tillman	8.00	4.00	2.50
(10)	Marv Toft	8.00	4.00	2.50
(11)	Tom Umphlett	8.00	4.00	2.50

1961 Union Oil Spokane Indians

		NM	EX	VG
Complete Set (11):		100.00	50.00	30.00
Common Player:		10.00	5.00	3.00
(1)	Doug Camilli	10.00	5.00	3.00
(2)	Ramon Conde	10.00	5.00	3.00
(3)	Bob Giallombardo	10.00	5.00	3.00
(4)	Mike Goliat	10.00	5.00	3.00
(5)	Preston Gomez	40.00	20.00	12.00
(6)	Rod Graber	10.00	5.00	3.00
(7)	Tim Harkness	10.00	5.00	3.00
(8)	Jim Harwell	10.00	5.00	3.00
(9)	Howie Reed	10.00	5.00	3.00
(10)	Curt Roberts	10.00	5.00	3.00
(11)	Rene Valdes (Valdez)	10.00	5.00	3.00

1961 Union Oil Tacoma Giants

		NM	EX	VG
Complete Set (10):		150.00	75.00	45.00
Common Player:		10.00	5.00	3.00
10	Red Davis	10.00	5.00	3.00
12	Dick Phillips	10.00	5.00	3.00
17	Gil Garrido	10.00	5.00	3.00
20	Georges Maranda	10.00	5.00	3.00
25	John Orsino	10.00	5.00	3.00
26	Dusty Rhodes	15.00	7.50	4.50
28	Ron Herbel	10.00	5.00	3.00
29	Gaylord Perry	80.00	40.00	24.00
30	Rafael Alomar	15.00	7.50	4.50
34	Bob Farley	10.00	5.00	3.00

1961 Union Oil Taiyo Whales

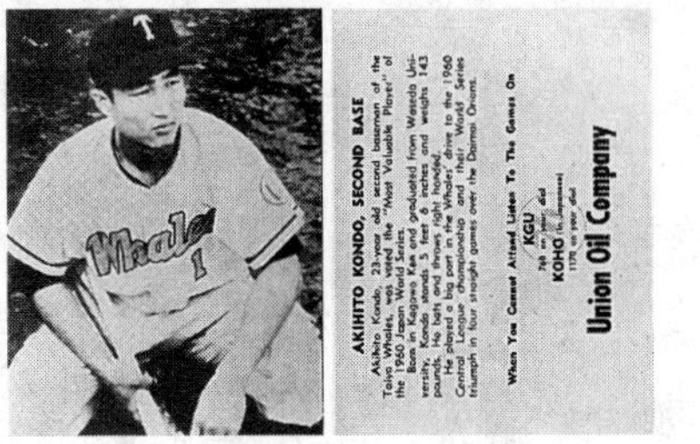

This three-card set was produced in conjunction with an exhibition series played in October, 1961, between the Taiyo Whales of Japan's Central League, and the Hawaii Islanders, a Class AAA Pacific Cost League farm club of the K.C. Athletics. The player cards measure just over 3" x 4", while the team photo card is 5" x 3-3/4". Cards are black-and-white and have some player biography and ads for Union Oil Co., and the English - and Japanese - language radio stations that carried the games.

		NM	EX	VG
Complete Set (3):		175.00	87.00	52.00
(1)	Akihito Kondo	50.00	25.00	15.00
(2)	Gentaro Shimada	50.00	25.00	15.00
(3)	Taiyo Whales Team	75.00	37.00	22.00

V

1951 Vancouver Capilanos Popcorn Issue

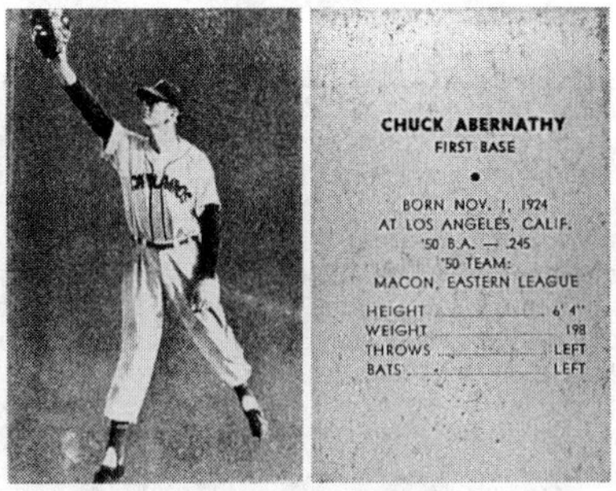

(1-7/8" x 2-7/8", black-and-white, 1950 stats on back. Names may appear in slightly different form than checklisted here) (Western International League)

		NM	EX	VG
Complete Set (24):		465.00	230.00	140.00
Common Player:		20.00	10.00	6.00
(1)	Chuck Abernathy	20.00	10.00	6.00
(2)	Jerry Barta	20.00	10.00	6.00
(3)	Bud Beasley	20.00	10.00	6.00
(4)	Gordy Brunswick	20.00	10.00	6.00
(5)	Reno Cheso	20.00	10.00	6.00
(6)	Ken Chorlton	20.00	10.00	6.00
(7)	Carl Gunnarson	20.00	10.00	6.00
(8)	Pete Hernandez	20.00	10.00	6.00
(9)	Vern Kindsfather	20.00	10.00	6.00
(10)	Bobby McGuire	20.00	10.00	6.00
(11)	Bob McLean	20.00	10.00	6.00
(12)	Charlie Mead	20.00	10.00	6.00
(13)	Jimmy Moore	20.00	10.00	6.00
(14)	George Nicholas	20.00	10.00	6.00
(15)	John Ritchey	20.00	10.00	6.00
(16)	Sandy Robertson	20.00	10.00	6.00
(17)	Bill Schuster	20.00	10.00	6.00
(18)	Dick Sinovic	20.00	10.00	6.00
(19)	Ron Smith	20.00	10.00	6.00
(20)	Bob Snyder	20.00	10.00	6.00
(21)	Don Tisnerat	20.00	10.00	6.00
(22)	Ray Tran	20.00	10.00	6.00
(23)	Reg Wallis (trainer)	20.00	10.00	6.00
(24)	Bill Whyte	20.00	10.00	6.00

1952 Vancouver Capilanos Popcorn Issue

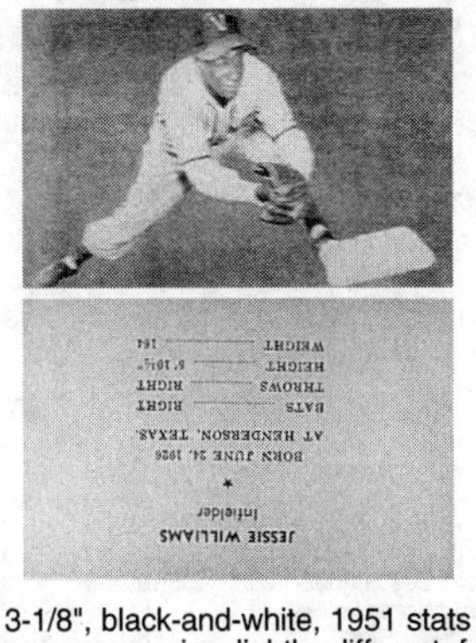

(2" x 3-1/8", black-and-white, 1951 stats on back. Names may appear in slightly different form than checklisted here.) (Western International League)

		NM	EX	VG
Complete Set (20):		400.00	200.00	120.00
Common Player:		20.00	10.00	6.00
(1)	Gordie Brunswick	20.00	10.00	6.00
(2)	Bob Duretto	20.00	10.00	6.00
(3)	Van Fletcher	20.00	10.00	6.00
(4)	John Guldborg	20.00	10.00	6.00
(5)	Paul Jones	20.00	10.00	6.00
(6)	Eddie Locke	20.00	10.00	6.00
(7)	Tom Lovrich	20.00	10.00	6.00
(8)	Jimmy Moore	20.00	10.00	6.00
(9)	George Nicholas	20.00	10.00	6.00
(10a)	John Ritchey	20.00	10.00	6.00
(10b)	Johnny Ritchie	20.00	10.00	6.00
(11)	Bill Schuster	20.00	10.00	6.00
(12)	Bob Snyder	20.00	10.00	6.00
(13)	Len Tran	20.00	10.00	6.00
(14)	Ray Tran	20.00	10.00	6.00
(15)	Edo Vanni	20.00	10.00	6.00
(16)	Jim Wert	20.00	10.00	6.00
(17)	Bill Whyte	20.00	10.00	6.00
(18a)	Jessie Williams	20.00	10.00	6.00
(18b)	Jesse Williams	20.00	10.00	6.00

1953 Vancouver Capilanos Popcorn Issue

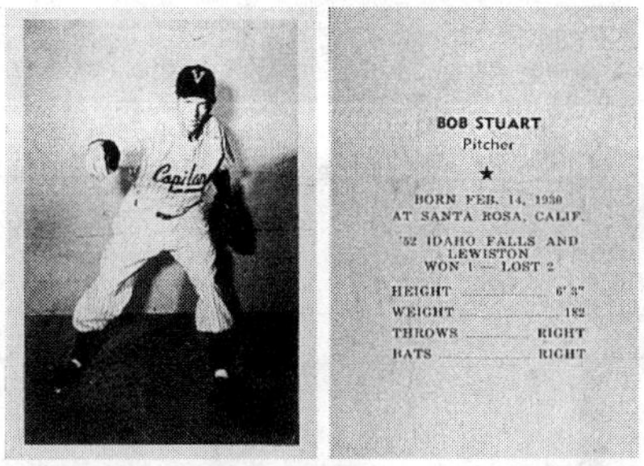

(2-3/16" x 3-3/16", black-and-white, 1952 stats on back. Names may appear in slightly different form than checklisted here.) (Western International League)

		NM	EX	VG
Complete Set (18):		330.00	165.00	100.00
Common Player:		20.00	10.00	6.00
(1)	Dick Briskey	20.00	10.00	6.00
(2)	Jack Bukowatz	20.00	10.00	6.00
(3)	Ken Chorlton	20.00	10.00	6.00
(4)	Van Fletcher	20.00	10.00	6.00
(5)	John Guldborg	20.00	10.00	6.00
(6)	Carl Gunnerson	20.00	10.00	6.00
(7)	Jim Hedgecock	20.00	10.00	6.00
(8)	Gordon Hernandez	20.00	10.00	6.00
(9)	Pete Hernandez	20.00	10.00	6.00
(10)	Jim Leavitt	20.00	10.00	6.00
(11)	Rod MacKay	20.00	10.00	6.00
(12)	Frank Mascaro	20.00	10.00	6.00
(13)	Lonnie Myers	20.00	10.00	6.00
(14)	Rod Owen	20.00	10.00	6.00
(15)	Harvey Storey	20.00	10.00	6.00
(16)	Bob Stuart	20.00	10.00	6.00
(17)	Dale Thomason	20.00	10.00	6.00
(18)	Jim Wert	20.00	10.00	6.00

1954 Vancouver Capilanos Popcorn Issue

(2-3/16" x 3-5/16", black-and-white, blank-back. Names may appear slightly different than checklisted here.) (Western International League)

		NM	EX	VG
Complete Set (14):		265.00	130.00	80.00
Common Player:		20.00	10.00	6.00
(1)	Bill Brenner	20.00	10.00	6.00
(2)	Ken Chorlton	20.00	10.00	6.00
(3)	John Cordell	20.00	10.00	6.00
(4)	Bob Duretto	20.00	10.00	6.00
(5)	Dick Greco	20.00	10.00	6.00
(6)	Arnie Hallgren	20.00	10.00	6.00
(7)	Danny Holden	20.00	10.00	6.00
(8)	Rod McKay	20.00	10.00	6.00
(9)	George Nicholas	20.00	10.00	6.00
(10)	Nick Pesut	20.00	10.00	6.00
(11)	Ken Richardson	20.00	10.00	6.00
(12)	Bob Roberts	20.00	10.00	6.00
(13)	Bob Wellman	20.00	10.00	6.00
(14)	Marvin Williams	20.00	10.00	6.00

1954 Veltex Lewiston Broncs

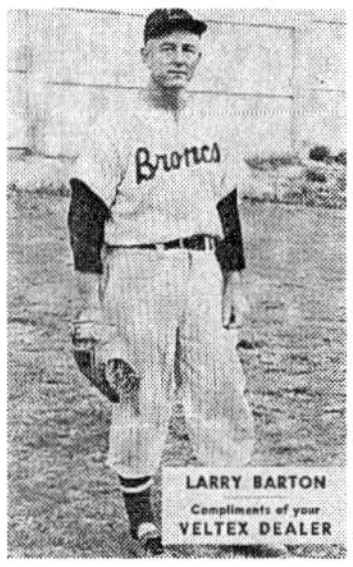

It is evident from the format of the card and of the accompanying album that this is a product of Globe Printing, which produced many minor league sets in the early 1950s. What makes this set of the 1954 Class A (Western International League) affiliate of the Baltimore Orioles unusual among Globe issues is the mention of a sponsor. The blank-back, black-and-white cards measure 2-3/16" x 3-3/8". The checklist below is obviously incomplete.

		NM	EX	VG
Common player:		40.00	20.00	12.00
Album:		50.00	25.00	15.00
(1)	Larry Barton	40.00	20.00	12.00

W

1911 Western Playground Association

Stars from around the Pacific Coast League are featured on this rare and unusual issue. The 2-1/4" x 3-1/2"cards have a front design similar to contemporary Zee Nuts cards: A dark brown border surrounding a sepia posed action photo of the player. Printed in white to one side of the player are "WESTERN PLAYGROUND ASSOCIATION / P.C. LEAGUE" and the player's last name. Backs are a "Membership Certificate" indicating the cards could be redeemed for 5% of their seven-cent "face value" toward the purchase of school playground apparatus or supplies. The cards were received with the purchase of writing tablet or "bank stock books." The alphabetized checklist here may be incomplete.

		NM	EX	VG
Complete Set (35):		17000.	8500.	5100.
Common Player:		700.00	350.00	210.00
(1)	Berry	700.00	350.00	210.00
(2)	Brashear	700.00	350.00	210.00
(3)	Carlisle	700.00	350.00	210.00
(4)	Castleton	700.00	350.00	210.00
(5)	Chadbourne	700.00	350.00	210.00
(6)	Christian	700.00	350.00	210.00
(7)	Coy	700.00	350.00	210.00
(8)	Daley	700.00	350.00	210.00
(9)	Dillon	700.00	350.00	210.00
(10)	French	700.00	350.00	210.00
(11)	Gregory	700.00	350.00	210.00
(12)	Harkness	700.00	350.00	210.00
(13)	Heitmuller	700.00	350.00	210.00
(14)	Henderson	700.00	350.00	210.00
(15)	Hoffman	700.00	350.00	210.00
(16)	Hogan	700.00	350.00	210.00
(17)	Kane	700.00	350.00	210.00
(18)	Lewis	700.00	350.00	210.00
(19)	Madden	700.00	350.00	210.00
(20)	Mahoney	700.00	350.00	210.00
(21)	Metzger	700.00	350.00	210.00
(22)	Miller	700.00	350.00	210.00
(23)	Mohler	700.00	350.00	210.00
(24)	Patterson	700.00	350.00	210.00
(25)	Peckinpaugh	700.00	350.00	210.00
(26)	Rapps	700.00	350.00	210.00
(27)	Rodgers	700.00	350.00	210.00
(28)	Ryan	700.00	350.00	210.00
(29)	Seaton	700.00	350.00	210.00
(30)	Sheehan	700.00	350.00	210.00
(31)	Stewart	700.00	350.00	210.00
(32)	Stinson	700.00	350.00	210.00
(33)	Suter	700.00	350.00	210.00
(34)	Wolverton	700.00	350.00	210.00
(35)	Zacher	700.00	350.00	210.00

1932 Wheaties Minneapolis Millers

Because of their similarity to the 1933 issue which carried Wheaties advertising on the back, these postcard-size photos of the 1932 Millers are believed to also have been issued by the Minneapolis-based cereal company. The 3-1/2" x 5-1/2" cards have black-and-white portraits or posed action photos on front. The checklist is presented here in alphabetical order and may not be complete.

		NM	EX	VG
Complete Set (14):		365.00	180.00	110.00
Common Player:		25.00	12.50	7.50
(1)	Rube Benton	25.00	12.50	7.50
(2)	Andy Cohen	27.50	13.50	8.25
(3)	Ray Fitzgerald	25.00	12.50	7.50
(4)	Babe Ganzel	25.00	12.50	7.50
(5)	Wes Griffin	25.00	12.50	7.50
(6)	Spencer Harris	25.00	12.50	7.50
(7)	Joe Hauser	40.00	20.00	12.00
(8)	Dutch Henry	25.00	12.50	7.50
(9)	Joe Mowry	25.00	12.50	7.50
(10)	Paul Richards	30.00	15.00	9.00
(11)	Bill Rodda	25.00	12.50	7.50
(12)	Art Ruble	25.00	12.50	7.50
(13)	Al Sheehan	25.00	12.50	7.50
(14)	Hy Vandenberg	25.00	12.50	7.50

Suffix letters following a card number indicate a variation card.

1933 Wheaties Minneapolis Millers

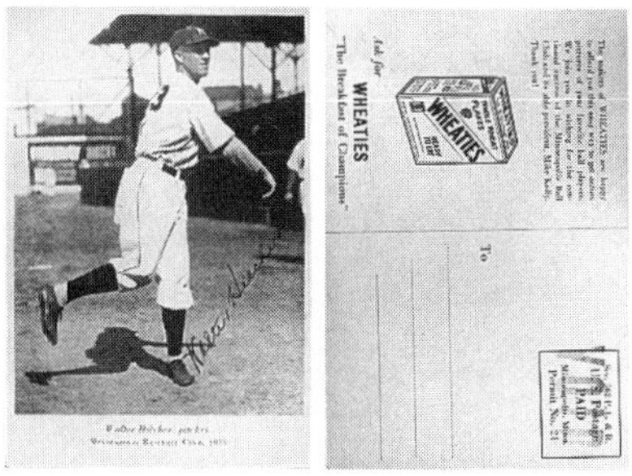

Prior to printing their first major league baseball cards on the backs of cereal boxes in 1935, Wheaties sponsored a minor league set for the hometown Minneapolis Millers in 1933. The 4" x 5-3/4" cards have a sepia-toned posed action photo on front, along with a facsimile autograph. The player's name, position, team and year are printed in the bottom border. The postcard back, printed in black-and-white, has a drawing of a Wheaties box and an ad for the cereal. The unnumbered cards are checklisted here alphabetically; it is possible this list is incomplete.

		NM	EX	VG
Complete Set (24):		865.00	430.00	255.00
Common Player:		40.00	20.00	12.00
(1)	Dave Bancroft	60.00	30.00	18.00
(2)	Rube Benton	40.00	20.00	12.00
(3)	Andy Cohen	45.00	22.00	13.50
(4)	Bob Fothergill	40.00	20.00	12.00
(5)	Babe Ganzel	40.00	20.00	12.00
(6)	Joe Glenn	40.00	20.00	12.00
(7)	Wes Griffin	40.00	20.00	12.00
(8)	Jack Hallet	40.00	20.00	12.00
(9)	Jerry Harrington (announcer)	40.00	20.00	12.00
(10)	Spencer Harris	60.00	30.00	18.00
(11)	Joe Hauser	80.00	40.00	24.00
(12)	Butch Henline	40.00	20.00	12.00
(13)	Walter Hilcher	40.00	20.00	12.00
(14)	Dutch Holland	40.00	20.00	12.00
(15)	Harry Holsclaw	40.00	20.00	12.00
(16)	Wes Kingdon	40.00	20.00	12.00
(17)	George Murray	40.00	20.00	12.00
(18)	Leo Norris	40.00	20.00	12.00
(19)	Jess Petty	40.00	20.00	12.00
(20)	Art Ruble	40.00	20.00	12.00
(21)	Al Sheehan (announcer)	40.00	20.00	12.00
(22)	Ernie Smith	40.00	20.00	12.00
(23)	Wally Tauscher	40.00	20.00	12.00
(24)	Hy Vandenburg	40.00	20.00	12.00

1933 Wheaties Seattle Indians

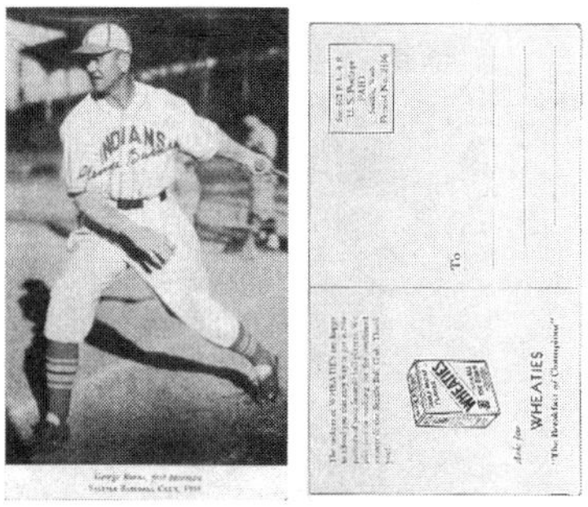

Prior to printing their first major league baseball cards on the backs of cereal boxes in 1935, Wheaties sponsored a minor league set for the Seattle Indians in 1933. The 4-1/8" x 7" cards have a sepia-toned posed action photo on front, along with a facsimile autograph. The player's name, position, team and year are printed in the bottom border. The postcard back, printed in black-and-white, has a drawing of a Wheaties box and an ad for the cereal. The unnumbered cards are checklisted here alphabetically; it is likely this list is incomplete.

		NM	EX	VG
(1)	George Burns	350.00	200.00	120.00
(2)	Joe Coscarart	350.00	200.00	120.00
(3)	"Junk" Walters	350.00	200.00	120.00

1912 Whitehead & Hoag P.C.L. Pins

A paper insert originally in the back of these pins identifies the maker as Whitehead & Hoag of San Francisco. The 7/8" diameter celluloid pins are printed in either black or blue on a white background. A player portrait photo is at center, with his last name below. Above is the city of his team and the Pacific Coast League initials. Listed in the "American Card Catalog" as PM5, the unnumbered pins are checklisted here alphabetically; it's possible additional pins in the issue remain to be reported. All pins seen are Oakland players except McCredie (Portland) and Berry (San Francisco).

		NM	EX	VG
Complete Set (26):		3200.	1600.	960.00
Common Player:		150.00	75.00	45.00
(1)	Harry Ables	150.00	75.00	45.00
(2)	Claude Berry	150.00	75.00	45.00
(3)	Tyler Christian	150.00	75.00	45.00
(4)	Cook	150.00	75.00	45.00
(5)	Bert Coy	150.00	75.00	45.00
(6)	Jack Flater	150.00	75.00	45.00
(7)	Gregory	150.00	75.00	45.00
(8)	Hamilton	150.00	75.00	45.00
(9)	Gus Hetling	150.00	75.00	45.00
(10a)	Hille	150.00	75.00	45.00
(10b)	Mgr. Hille	150.00	75.00	45.00
(11)	Izzy Hoffman	150.00	75.00	45.00
(12)	Bill Leard	150.00	75.00	45.00
(13)	Malarkey	150.00	75.00	45.00
(14)	Martinoni	150.00	75.00	45.00
(15)	Walter McCredie	150.00	75.00	45.00
(16)	Honus Mitze	150.00	75.00	45.00
(17)	Parkins	150.00	75.00	45.00
(18)	Pope	150.00	75.00	45.00
(19)	Bill Rapp (Rapps)	150.00	75.00	45.00
(20)	Tom Seaton	150.00	75.00	45.00
(21a)	Sharpe	150.00	75.00	45.00
(21b)	Mgr. Sharpe	150.00	75.00	45.00
(22)	Tommy Sheehan	150.00	75.00	45.00
(23)	Smith	150.00	75.00	45.00
(24)	John Tiedeman (Tiedemann)	150.00	75.00	45.00
(25)	Wilkinson	150.00	75.00	45.00
(26)	Elmer Zacher	150.00	75.00	45.00

1933 Worch Cigar American Association

Though the issuer is not identified anywhere on these blank-backed, 3-7/16" x 5-7/16" black-and-white cards, the individual player photos were available as premiums for redemption of cigar bands by the Worch Cigar Co., of St. Paul, Minn. The issue is similar in format to the major league cards of the same era, and indeed the cards were offered together. Most collectors prefer to chase either the major leaguers or the minor leaguers independently, so they are cataloged in that fashion. The set encompasses players from the 1932-33 Minneapolis Millers, the 1933 St. Paul Saints and a handful from the Columbus Redbirds and Kansas City Blues. The unnumbered cards are checklisted below alphabetically.

		NM	EX	VG
Complete Set (60):		1250.	625.00	375.00
Common Player:		35.00	17.50	10.50
(1)	Dave Bancroft	50.00	25.00	15.00
(2)	Clyde Beck	35.00	17.50	10.50
(3)	Rube Benton	35.00	17.50	10.50
(4)	W. Berger	35.00	17.50	10.50
(5)	Brannon	35.00	17.50	10.50
(6)	Andy Cohen	35.00	17.50	10.50
(7)	Nick Cullop	35.00	17.50	10.50
(8)	Day	35.00	17.50	10.50
(9)	Bob Fenner	35.00	17.50	10.50
(10)	Fischall	35.00	17.50	10.50
(11)	Fitzgerald	35.00	17.50	10.50
(12)	Gaffke	35.00	17.50	10.50
(13)	Foster Ganzel	35.00	17.50	10.50
(14)	Louis Garland	35.00	17.50	10.50
(15)	Joe Glenn	35.00	17.50	10.50
(16)	Wesley Griffin	35.00	17.50	10.50
(17)	Angelo Guiliani	35.00	17.50	10.50
(18)	Slim Harriss	35.00	17.50	10.50
(19)	Spencer Harris	35.00	17.50	10.50
(20)	Joe Hauser	40.00	20.00	12.00
(21)	Walter Henline	35.00	17.50	10.50
(22)	Frank "Dutch" Henry	35.00	17.50	10.50
(23)	Phil Hensick	35.00	17.50	10.50
(24)	Walter Hilcher	35.00	17.50	10.50
(25)	Hill	35.00	17.50	10.50
(26)	Jesse Hill	35.00	17.50	10.50
(27)	Bob Holand	35.00	17.50	10.50
(28)	Harry Holsclaw	35.00	17.50	10.50
(29)	Meredith Hopkins	35.00	17.50	10.50
(30)	Irvine Jeffries	35.00	17.50	10.50
(31)	Fred Koster	35.00	17.50	10.50
(32)	Walter Mails	35.00	17.50	10.50
(33)	Emmett McCann	35.00	17.50	10.50
(34)	Joe Mowry	35.00	17.50	10.50
(35)	Les Munns	35.00	17.50	10.50
(36)	George Murray	35.00	17.50	10.50
(37)	Floyd Newkirk	35.00	17.50	10.50
(38)	Leo Norris	35.00	17.50	10.50
(39)	Frank Packard	35.00	17.50	10.50
(40)	Ben Paschal	35.00	17.50	10.50
(41)	Jess Petty	35.00	17.50	10.50
(42)	Ray Radcliff	35.00	17.50	10.50
(43)	Paul Richards	37.50	18.50	11.00
(44)	Rodda	35.00	17.50	10.50
(45)	Rose	35.00	17.50	10.50
(46)	Larry Rosenthal	35.00	17.50	10.50
(47)	Art Ruble	35.00	17.50	10.50
(48)	Rosy Ryan	35.00	17.50	10.50
(49)	Al Sheehan (Millers announcer)	35.00	17.50	10.50
(50)	Art Shires	35.00	17.50	10.50
(51)	Ed Sicking	35.00	17.50	10.50
(52)	Ernest Smith	35.00	17.50	10.50
(53)	Walter Tauscher	35.00	17.50	10.50
(54)	Myles Thomas	35.00	17.50	10.50
(55)	Phil Todt	35.00	17.50	10.50
(56)	Gene Trow	35.00	17.50	10.50
(57)	Hy Van Denburg	35.00	17.50	10.50
(58)	Elam Van Gilder	35.00	17.50	10.50
(59)	Charles Wilson	35.00	17.50	10.50
(60)	Emil Yde	35.00	17.50	10.50

Z

1911 Zeenut Pacific Coast League

Produced for 28 straight years, these Pacific Coast League cards were among the longest-running and most popular baseball issues ever to appear on the West Coast. Issued by the Collins-McCarthy Candy Co. (later known as the Collins-Hencke Candy Co. and then simply the Collins Candy Co.) of San Francisco, Zeenut cards were inserted in boxes of the company's products: Zeenuts, Ruf-Neks and Home Run Kisses. All Zeenut cards issued from 1913 to 1938 included a half-inch coupon at the bottom that could be redeemed for various prizes. Since most of these coupons were removed (and many not too carefully) Zeenuts are difficult to find in top condition today, and only a very small percentage survived with the coupon intact. (The sizes listed in the following descriptions are for cards without coupons.) Over the 28-year span, it is estimated that nearly 3,700 different cards were issued as part of the Zeenuts series, but new discoveries are still being made, and the checklist continues to grow. It is sometimes difficult to differentiate one year from another after 1930. Because it is so rare to find Zeenuts cards with the coupon still attached, values listed are for cards without the coupon. Cards with the coupon still intact will generally command an additional 25-35 percent premium. The first Zeenut cards measure 2-1/8" x 4" and feature a sepia-toned photo on a brown background surrounded by an off-white border. The backs of the cards are blank. Although the 1911 cards did not include the coupon bottom, some cards have been found with punch holes, indicating they may have also been used for premiums. A total of 122 different players have been found.

		NM	EX	VG
Complete Set (123):		6500.	2800.	1950.
Common Player:		55.00	22.00	13.50
(1)	Abbott	55.00	22.00	13.50
(2)	Ables	55.00	22.00	13.50
(3a)	Agnew (large pose)	55.00	22.00	13.50
(3b)	Agnew (small pose)	55.00	22.00	13.50
(4a)	Akin (large pose)	55.00	22.00	13.50
(4b)	Akin (small pose)	55.00	22.00	13.50
(5)	Arellanes	55.00	22.00	13.50
(6a)	Arlett (large pose)	55.00	22.00	13.50
(6b)	Arlett (middle size pose)	55.00	22.00	13.50
(6c)	Arlett (small pose)	55.00	22.00	13.50
(7)	Barry	55.00	22.00	13.50
(8)	Baum	55.00	22.00	13.50
(9)	Bernard	55.00	22.00	13.50
(10)	Berry	55.00	22.00	13.50
(11)	Bohen	55.00	22.00	13.50
(12)	Brackenridge	55.00	22.00	13.50
(13)	Brashear	55.00	22.00	13.50
(14a)	Brown (large pose)	55.00	22.00	13.50
(14b)	Brown (small pose)	55.00	22.00	13.50
(15)	Browning	55.00	22.00	13.50
(16a)	Burrell (large pose)	55.00	22.00	13.50
(16b)	Burrell (small pose)	55.00	22.00	13.50
(17)	Byram	55.00	22.00	13.50
(18)	Carlisle	55.00	22.00	13.50
(19)	Carman	55.00	22.00	13.50
(20a)	Carson (large pose)	55.00	22.00	13.50
(20b)	Carson (middle size pose)	55.00	22.00	13.50
(20c)	Carson (small pose)	55.00	22.00	13.50
(21)	Castleton	55.00	22.00	13.50
(22)	Chadbourne	55.00	22.00	13.50
(23)	Christian	55.00	22.00	13.50
(24)	Couchman	55.00	22.00	13.50
(25)	Coy	55.00	22.00	13.50
(26)	Criger	55.00	22.00	13.50
(27)	Cutshaw	55.00	22.00	13.50
(28)	Daley	55.00	22.00	13.50
(29)	Danzig	55.00	22.00	13.50
(30)	Delhi	55.00	22.00	13.50
(31a)	Delmas (large pose)	55.00	22.00	13.50
(31b)	Delmas (small pose)	55.00	22.00	13.50
(32)	Dillon	55.00	22.00	13.50
(33a)	Discoll (name incorrect)	55.00	22.00	13.50
(33b)	Driscoll (name correct)	55.00	22.00	13.50
(34)	Dulin	55.00	22.00	13.50
(35)	Fanning	55.00	22.00	13.50
(36)	Fitzgerald	55.00	22.00	13.50
(37)	Flater	55.00	22.00	13.50
(38)	French	55.00	22.00	13.50
(39)	Fullerton	55.00	22.00	13.50
(40)	Gleason	55.00	22.00	13.50
(41)	Gregory	55.00	22.00	13.50
(42)	Halla	55.00	22.00	13.50
(43)	Harkness	55.00	22.00	13.50
(44a)	Heitmuller (large pose)	55.00	22.00	13.50
(44b)	Heitmuller (small pose)	55.00	22.00	13.50
(45)	Henley	55.00	22.00	13.50
(46)	Hetling	55.00	22.00	13.50
(47)	Hiester	55.00	22.00	13.50
(48a)	Hitt (large pose)	55.00	22.00	13.50
(48b)	Hitt (small pose)	55.00	22.00	13.50
(50)	Hoffman	55.00	22.00	13.50
(51)	Hogan	55.00	22.00	13.50
(52a)	Holland (large pose)	55.00	22.00	13.50
(52b)	Holland (small pose)	55.00	22.00	13.50
(53)	Hosp	55.00	22.00	13.50
(54a)	Howard (large pose)	55.00	22.00	13.50
(54b)	Howard (small pose)	55.00	22.00	13.50
(55)	Kane	55.00	22.00	13.50
(56)	Kerns	55.00	22.00	13.50
(57)	Kilroy	55.00	22.00	13.50
(58)	Knight	55.00	22.00	13.50
(59)	Koestner	55.00	22.00	13.50
(60)	Krueger	55.00	22.00	13.50
(61)	Kuhn	55.00	22.00	13.50
(62)	LaLonge	55.00	22.00	13.50
(63)	Lerchen	55.00	22.00	13.50
(64)	Leverenz	55.00	22.00	13.50
(65)	Lewis	55.00	22.00	13.50
(66)	Lindsay	55.00	22.00	13.50
(67)	Lober	55.00	22.00	13.50
(68)	Madden	55.00	22.00	13.50
(69)	Maggert	55.00	22.00	13.50
(70)	Mahoney	55.00	22.00	13.50
(71)	Martinoni	55.00	22.00	13.50
(72)	McArdle	55.00	22.00	13.50
(73)	McCredie	55.00	22.00	13.50
(74)	McDonnell	55.00	22.00	13.50
(75a)	McKune (large pose)	55.00	22.00	13.50
(75b)	McKune (middle size pose)	55.00	22.00	13.50
(75c)	McKune (small pose)	55.00	22.00	13.50
(76)	Meikle	55.00	22.00	13.50

(77)	Melchoir	55.00	22.00	13.50
(78)	Metzger	55.00	22.00	13.50
(79)	Miller	55.00	22.00	13.50
(80)	Mitze	55.00	22.00	13.50
(81)	Mohler	55.00	22.00	13.50
(82a)	Moore (large pose)	55.00	22.00	13.50
(82b)	Moore (small pose)	55.00	22.00	13.50
(83a)	Moskiman (lettering size large)	55.00	22.00	13.50
(83b)	Moskiman (lettering size small)	55.00	22.00	13.50
(84)	Murray	55.00	22.00	13.50
(85)	Naylor	55.00	22.00	13.50
(86)	Nebinger	55.00	22.00	13.50
(87)	Nourse	55.00	22.00	13.50
(88a)	Noyes (large pose)	55.00	22.00	13.50
(88b)	Noyes (small pose)	55.00	22.00	13.50
(89)	O'Rourke	55.00	22.00	13.50
(90)	Patterson (Oakland)	55.00	22.00	13.50
(91)	Patterson (Vernon)	55.00	22.00	13.50
(92)	Pearce	55.00	22.00	13.50
(93)	Peckinpaugh	48.00	19.00	12.00
(94)	Pernoll	55.00	22.00	13.50
(95)	Pfyl	55.00	22.00	13.50
(96)	Powell	55.00	22.00	13.50
(97a)	Raleigh (large pose)	55.00	22.00	13.50
(97b)	Raleigh (small pose)	55.00	22.00	13.50
(98)	Rapps	55.00	22.00	13.50
(99)	Rodgers	55.00	22.00	13.50
(100a)	Ryan (Portland, box around name and team)	70.00	28.00	17.50
(100b)	Ryan (Portland, no box around name and team)	55.00	22.00	13.50
(101)	Ryan (San Francisco)	55.00	22.00	13.50
(102)	Seaton	55.00	22.00	13.50
(103)	Shaw	55.00	22.00	13.50
(104)	Sheehan	55.00	22.00	13.50
(105)	Shinn	55.00	22.00	13.50
106a	Smith (Los Angeles, large pose)	55.00	22.00	13.50
(106b)	Smith (Los Angeles, small pose)	55.00	22.00	13.50
(107a)	Smith (San Francisco, large pose)	55.00	22.00	13.50
(107b)	Smith (San Francisco, small pose)	55.00	22.00	13.50
(108)	Steen	55.00	22.00	13.50
(109)	Stewart	55.00	22.00	13.50
(110a)	Stinson (large pose)	55.00	22.00	13.50
(110b)	Stinson (small pose)	55.00	22.00	13.50
(111)	Sutor	55.00	22.00	13.50
(112)	Tennant	55.00	22.00	13.50
(113)	Thomas	55.00	22.00	13.50
(114)	Thompson	55.00	22.00	13.50
(115)	Thornton	55.00	22.00	13.50
(116)	Tiedeman	55.00	22.00	13.50
(117)	Van Buren	55.00	22.00	13.50
(118)	Vitt	55.00	22.00	13.50
(119)	Wares	55.00	22.00	13.50
(120)	Buck Weaver	750.00	300.00	185.00
(121)	Wolverton	55.00	22.00	13.50
(122)	Zacher	55.00	22.00	13.50
(123)	Zamloch	55.00	22.00	13.50

1912 Zeenut Pacific Coast League

The second series of Zeenut cards measure 2-1/8" x 4-1/8" and featured sepia-toned photographs on a brown background with no border. Most cards have blank backs, but some have been found with printing advising collectors to "Save Zeenut pictures for valuable premiums." The checklist consists of 158 subjects, but more cards are still being discovered.

		NM	EX	VG
Complete Set (159):		6000.	2400.	1400.
Common Player:		48.00	24.00	14.50
(1)	Abbott	48.00	24.00	14.50
(2)	Ables	48.00	24.00	14.50
(3)	Agnew	48.00	24.00	14.50
(4)	Altman	48.00	24.00	14.50
(5)	Arellanes	48.00	24.00	14.50
(6)	Auer	48.00	24.00	14.50
(7)	Baker (horizontal pose)	48.00	24.00	14.50
(8)	Baker (vertical pose)	48.00	24.00	14.50
(9)	Bancroft	84.00	42.00	25.00
(10)	Baum	48.00	24.00	14.50
(11)	Bayless	48.00	24.00	14.50
(12)	Berger	48.00	24.00	14.50
(13)	Berry	48.00	24.00	14.50
(14)	Bohen	48.00	24.00	14.50
(15)	Boles	48.00	24.00	14.50
(16)	Bonner	48.00	24.00	14.50
(17)	Boone	48.00	24.00	14.50
(18)	Brackenridge	48.00	24.00	14.50
(19)	Brashear	48.00	24.00	14.50
(20)	Breen	48.00	24.00	14.50
(21)	Brooks (Los Angeles)	48.00	24.00	14.50
(22)	Brooks (Oakland)	48.00	24.00	14.50
(23)	Brown	48.00	24.00	14.50
(24)	Burch	48.00	24.00	14.50
(25)	Burrell	48.00	24.00	14.50
(26)	Butcher	48.00	24.00	14.50
(27)	Butler	48.00	24.00	14.50
(28)	Byram	48.00	24.00	14.50
(29)	Carlisle	48.00	24.00	14.50
(30)	Carson	48.00	24.00	14.50
(31)	Castleton	48.00	24.00	14.50
(32)	Chadbourne	48.00	24.00	14.50
(33)	Chech	48.00	24.00	14.50
(34)	Cheek	48.00	24.00	14.50
(35)	Christian	48.00	24.00	14.50
(36)	Cook	48.00	24.00	14.50
(37)	Core	48.00	24.00	14.50
(38)	Corhan	48.00	24.00	14.50
(39)	Coy	48.00	24.00	14.50
(40)	Daley	48.00	24.00	14.50
(41)	Delhi	48.00	24.00	14.50
(42)	Dillon	48.00	24.00	14.50
(43)	Doane	48.00	24.00	14.50
(44)	Driscoll	48.00	24.00	14.50
(45)	Durbin	48.00	24.00	14.50
(46)	Fanning	48.00	24.00	14.50
(47)	Felts	48.00	24.00	14.50
(48)	Fisher	48.00	24.00	14.50
(49)	Fitzgerald	48.00	24.00	14.50
(50)	Flater	48.00	24.00	14.50
(51)	Frick	48.00	24.00	14.50
(52)	Gaddy	48.00	24.00	14.50
(53)	Gedeon	48.00	24.00	14.50
(54)	Gilligan	48.00	24.00	14.50
(55)	Girot	48.00	24.00	14.50
(56)	Gray	48.00	24.00	14.50
(57)	Gregg	48.00	24.00	14.50
(58)	Gregory	48.00	24.00	14.50
(59)	Halla	48.00	24.00	14.50
(60)	Hamilton (Oakland)	48.00	24.00	14.50
(61)	Hamilton (San Francisco)	48.00	24.00	14.50
(62)	Harkness	48.00	24.00	14.50
(63)	Hartley	48.00	24.00	14.50
(64)	Heitmuller	48.00	24.00	14.50
(65)	Henley	48.00	24.00	14.50
(66)	Hetling (glove open)	48.00	24.00	14.50
(67)	Hetling (glove closed)	48.00	24.00	14.50
(68)	Hiester	48.00	24.00	14.50
(69)	Higginbottom	48.00	24.00	14.50
(70)	Hitt	48.00	24.00	14.50
(71)	Hoffman	48.00	24.00	14.50
(72)	Hogan	48.00	24.00	14.50
(73)	Hosp	48.00	24.00	14.50
(74)	Howard	48.00	24.00	14.50
(75)	Howley	48.00	24.00	14.50
(76)	Ireland	48.00	24.00	14.50
(77)	Jackson	48.00	24.00	14.50
(78)	Johnson	48.00	24.00	14.50
(79)	Kane	48.00	24.00	14.50
(80)	Killilay	48.00	24.00	14.50
(81)	Klawitter	48.00	24.00	14.50
(82)	Knight	48.00	24.00	14.50
(83)	Koestner ("P" visible)	48.00	24.00	14.50
(84)	Koestner (no "P" visible)	48.00	24.00	14.50
(85)	Kreitz	48.00	24.00	14.50
(86)	Krueger	48.00	24.00	14.50
(87)	LaLonge	48.00	24.00	14.50
(88)	Leard	48.00	24.00	14.50
(89)	Leverenz	48.00	24.00	14.50
(90)	Lewis	48.00	24.00	14.50
(91)	Lindsay	48.00	24.00	14.50
(92)	Litschi	48.00	24.00	14.50
(93)	Lober	48.00	24.00	14.50
(94)	Madden	48.00	24.00	14.50
(95)	Mahoney	48.00	24.00	14.50
(96)	Malarkey	48.00	24.00	14.50
(97)	Martinoni	48.00	24.00	14.50
(98)	McArdle	48.00	24.00	14.50
(99)	McAvoy	48.00	24.00	14.50
(100)	McCorrey	48.00	24.00	14.50
(101)	McCredie	48.00	24.00	14.50
(102)	McDonald	48.00	24.00	14.50
(103)	McDowell	48.00	24.00	14.50
(104)	McIver	48.00	24.00	14.50
(105)	Meikle	48.00	24.00	14.50
(106)	Metzger	48.00	24.00	14.50
(107)	Miller (Sacramento)	48.00	24.00	14.50
(108)	Miller (San Francisco)	48.00	24.00	14.50
(109)	Mitze	48.00	24.00	14.50
(110)	Mohler	48.00	24.00	14.50
(111)	Moore	48.00	24.00	14.50
(112)	Mundorf (batting)	48.00	24.00	14.50
(113)	Mundorf (fielding)	48.00	24.00	14.50
(114)	Nagle	48.00	24.00	14.50
(115)	Noyes	48.00	24.00	14.50
(116)	O'Rourke	48.00	24.00	14.50
(117)	Olmstead	48.00	24.00	14.50
(118)	Orr	48.00	24.00	14.50
(119)	Page	48.00	24.00	14.50
(120)	Parkins	48.00	24.00	14.50
(121)	Patterson (Oakland)	48.00	24.00	14.50
(122)	Patterson (Vernon)	48.00	24.00	14.50
(123)	Pernol	48.00	24.00	14.50
(124)	Pope	48.00	24.00	14.50
(125)	Powell	48.00	24.00	14.50
(126)	Price	48.00	24.00	14.50
(127)	Raftery	48.00	24.00	14.50
(128)	Raleigh	48.00	24.00	14.50
(129)	Rapps ("P" visible)	48.00	24.00	14.50
(130)	Rapps (no "P" visible)	48.00	24.00	14.50
(131)	Reidy	48.00	24.00	14.50
(132)	Rodgers	48.00	24.00	14.50
(133)	Rohrer	48.00	24.00	14.50
(134)	Schmidt	48.00	24.00	14.50
(135)	Schwenk	48.00	24.00	14.50
(136)	Sharpe	48.00	24.00	14.50
(137)	Sheehan	48.00	24.00	14.50
(138)	Shinn	48.00	24.00	14.50
(139)	Slagle	48.00	24.00	14.50
(140)	Smith	48.00	24.00	14.50
(141)	Stewart	48.00	24.00	14.50
(142)	Stinson	48.00	24.00	14.50
(143)	Stone	48.00	24.00	14.50
(144)	Sullivan	48.00	24.00	14.50
(145)	Swain	48.00	24.00	14.50
(146)	Taylor	48.00	24.00	14.50
(147)	Temple	48.00	24.00	14.50
(148)	Tiedeman	48.00	24.00	14.50
(149)	Toner	48.00	24.00	14.50
(150)	Tozer	48.00	24.00	14.50
(151)	Van Buren	48.00	24.00	14.50
(152)	Wagner	48.00	24.00	14.50
(153)	Whalen	48.00	24.00	14.50
(154)	Williams (Sacramento)	48.00	24.00	14.50
(155)	Williams (San Francisco)	48.00	24.00	14.50
(156)	Joe Williams	48.00	24.00	14.50
(157)	Wuffli	48.00	24.00	14.50
(158)	Zacher	48.00	24.00	14.50
(159)	Zimmerman	48.00	24.00	14.50

1913 Zeenut Pacific Coast League

		NM	EX	VG
Complete Set (148):		4750.	1900.	1150.
Common Player:		40.00	16.00	10.00
(1)	Abbott	40.00	16.00	10.00
(2)	Ables	40.00	16.00	10.00
(3)	Arelanes	40.00	16.00	10.00
(4)	Arlett	40.00	16.00	10.00
(5)	Baker	40.00	16.00	10.00
(6)	Baum	40.00	16.00	10.00
(7)	Bayless	40.00	16.00	10.00
(8)	Becker	40.00	16.00	10.00
(9)	Berry	40.00	16.00	10.00
(10)	Bliss	40.00	16.00	10.00
(11)	Boles	40.00	16.00	10.00
(12)	Brackenridge	40.00	16.00	10.00
(13)	Brashear	40.00	16.00	10.00
(14)	Brooks	40.00	16.00	10.00
(15)	Byrnes	40.00	16.00	10.00
(16)	Cadreau	40.00	16.00	10.00
(17)	Carlisle	40.00	16.00	10.00
(18)	Carson	40.00	16.00	10.00
(19)	Cartwright	40.00	16.00	10.00
(20)	Chadbourne	40.00	16.00	10.00
(21)	Charles	40.00	16.00	10.00
(22)	Cheek	40.00	16.00	10.00
(23)	Christian	40.00	16.00	10.00
(24)	Clarke	40.00	16.00	10.00
(25)	Clemons	40.00	16.00	10.00
(26)	Cook	40.00	16.00	10.00
(27)	Corhan	40.00	16.00	10.00
(28)	Coy	40.00	16.00	10.00
(29)	Crabb	40.00	16.00	10.00
(30)	Crisp	40.00	16.00	10.00
(31)	Derrick	40.00	16.00	10.00
(32)	DeCanniere	40.00	16.00	10.00
(33)	Dillon	40.00	16.00	10.00
(34)	Doane	40.00	16.00	10.00
(35)	Douglass	40.00	16.00	10.00
(36)	Downs	40.00	16.00	10.00
(37)	Driscoll	40.00	16.00	10.00
(38)	Drucke	40.00	16.00	10.00
(39)	Elliott	40.00	16.00	10.00
(40)	Ellis	40.00	16.00	10.00
(41)	Fanning	40.00	16.00	10.00
(42)	Fisher	40.00	16.00	10.00
(43)	Fitzgerald	40.00	16.00	10.00
(44)	Gardner	40.00	16.00	10.00
(45)	Gill	40.00	16.00	10.00
(46)	Goodwin	40.00	16.00	10.00
(47a)	Gregory (large pose)	40.00	16.00	10.00
(47b)	Gregory (small pose)	40.00	16.00	10.00
(48)	Grey	40.00	16.00	10.00
(49)	Guest	40.00	16.00	10.00
(50)	Hagerman	40.00	16.00	10.00
(51)	Halla	40.00	16.00	10.00
(52)	Hallinan	40.00	16.00	10.00
(53)	Harry Heilmann	250.00	125.00	75.00
(54)	Henley	40.00	16.00	10.00
(55)	Hetling	40.00	16.00	10.00
(56)	Higginbotham	40.00	16.00	10.00
(57)	Hitt	40.00	16.00	10.00

(58)	Hoffman	40.00	16.00	10.00
(59)	Hogan (San Francisco)	40.00	16.00	10.00
(60)	Hogan (Vernon)	40.00	16.00	10.00
(61)	Hosp	40.00	16.00	10.00
(62)	Howard (Los Angeles)	40.00	16.00	10.00
(63)	Howard (San Francisco)	40.00	16.00	10.00
(64)	Hughes	40.00	16.00	10.00
(65)	Jackson	40.00	16.00	10.00
(66)	James	40.00	16.00	10.00
(67)	Johnson	40.00	16.00	10.00
(68)	Johnston	40.00	16.00	10.00
(69)	Kane	40.00	16.00	10.00
(70)	Kaylor	40.00	16.00	10.00
(71)	Kenworthy	40.00	16.00	10.00
(72)	Killilay	40.00	16.00	10.00
(73)	Klawitter	40.00	16.00	10.00
(74)	Koestner	40.00	16.00	10.00
(75)	Kores	40.00	16.00	10.00
(76)	Krapp	40.00	16.00	10.00
(77)	Kreitz	40.00	16.00	10.00
(78)	Krause	40.00	16.00	10.00
(79)	Krueger	40.00	16.00	10.00
(80)	Leard	40.00	16.00	10.00
(81)	Leifield	40.00	16.00	10.00
(82)	Lewis	40.00	16.00	10.00
(83)	Lindsay	40.00	16.00	10.00
(84)	Litschi	40.00	16.00	10.00
(85)	Lively	40.00	16.00	10.00
(86)	Lober	40.00	16.00	10.00
(87)	Lohman	40.00	16.00	10.00
(88)	Maggart	40.00	16.00	10.00
(89)	Malarky	40.00	16.00	10.00
(90)	McArdle	40.00	16.00	10.00
(91)	McCarl	40.00	16.00	10.00
(92)	McCormick	40.00	16.00	10.00
(93)	McCorry	40.00	16.00	10.00
(94)	McCredie	40.00	16.00	10.00
(95)	McDonnell	40.00	16.00	10.00
(96)	Meloan	40.00	16.00	10.00
(97)	Metzger	40.00	16.00	10.00
(98)	Miller	40.00	16.00	10.00
(99)	Mitze	40.00	16.00	10.00
(100)	Moore	40.00	16.00	10.00
(101)	Moran	40.00	16.00	10.00
(102)	Mundorf	40.00	16.00	10.00
(103)	Munsell	40.00	16.00	10.00
(104)	Ness	40.00	16.00	10.00
(105)	O'Rourke	40.00	16.00	10.00
(106)	Overall	40.00	16.00	10.00
(107)	Page	40.00	16.00	10.00
(108)	Parkin	40.00	16.00	10.00
(109)	Patterson	40.00	16.00	10.00
(110)	Pearce	40.00	16.00	10.00
(111)	Pernoll	40.00	16.00	10.00
(112)	Perritt	40.00	16.00	10.00
(113)	Pope	40.00	16.00	10.00
(114)	Pruitt	40.00	16.00	10.00
(115)	Raleigh	40.00	16.00	10.00
(116)	Reitmyer	40.00	16.00	10.00
(117)	Riordan	40.00	16.00	10.00
(118)	Rodgers	40.00	16.00	10.00
(119)	Rogers	40.00	16.00	10.00
(120)	Rohrer	40.00	16.00	10.00
(121)	Ryan	40.00	16.00	10.00
(122)	Schaller	40.00	16.00	10.00
(123)	Schirm	40.00	16.00	10.00
(124)	Schmidt	40.00	16.00	10.00
(125)	Schulz	40.00	16.00	10.00
(126)	Sepulveda	40.00	16.00	10.00
(127)	Shinn	40.00	16.00	10.00
(128)	Spenger	40.00	16.00	10.00
(129)	Stanley	40.00	16.00	10.00
(130)	Stanridge	40.00	16.00	10.00
(131)	Stark	40.00	16.00	10.00
(132)	Sterritt	40.00	16.00	10.00
(133)	Stroud	40.00	16.00	10.00
(134)	Tennant	40.00	16.00	10.00
(135)	Thomas	40.00	16.00	10.00
(136)	Todd	40.00	16.00	10.00
(137)	Tonneman	40.00	16.00	10.00
(138)	Tozer	40.00	16.00	10.00
(139)	Van Buren	40.00	16.00	10.00
(140)	Wagner	40.00	16.00	10.00
(141)	West	40.00	16.00	10.00
(142)	Williams	40.00	16.00	10.00
(143)	Wolverton	40.00	16.00	10.00
(144)	Wotell	40.00	16.00	10.00
(145)	Wuffli	40.00	16.00	10.00
(146)	Young	40.00	16.00	10.00
(147)	Zacher	40.00	16.00	10.00
(148)	Zimmerman	40.00	16.00	10.00

1914 Zeenut Pacific Coast League

The 1914 Zeenut cards measure 2" x 3-1/2" without the coupon, and feature black-and-white photos on a gray, borderless background. To date, 146 different poses have been found. The backs are blank.

		NM	EX	VG
Complete Set (145):		4000.	1625.	975.00
Common Player:		35.00	15.00	9.00
(1)	Ables	35.00	15.00	9.00
(2)	Abstein	35.00	15.00	9.00
(3)	Alexander	35.00	15.00	9.00
(4)	Arbogast	35.00	15.00	9.00
(5)	Arlett	35.00	15.00	9.00
(6)	Arrelanes	35.00	15.00	9.00
(7)	Bancroft	100.00	40.00	25.00
(8)	Barham	35.00	15.00	9.00
(9)	Barrenkamp	35.00	15.00	9.00
(10)	Barton	35.00	15.00	9.00
(11)	Baum	35.00	15.00	9.00
(12)	Bayless	35.00	15.00	9.00
(13a)	Bliss (large pose)	35.00	15.00	9.00
(13b)	Bliss (small pose)	35.00	15.00	9.00
(14)	Boles	35.00	15.00	9.00
(15)	Borton	35.00	15.00	9.00
(16)	Brashear	35.00	15.00	9.00
(17)	Brenegan	35.00	15.00	9.00
(18)	Brooks	35.00	15.00	9.00
(19)	Brown	35.00	15.00	9.00
(20)	Butler	35.00	15.00	9.00
(21)	Jacinto Calvo	100.00	50.00	30.00
(22)	Carlisle	35.00	15.00	9.00
(23)	Cartwright	35.00	15.00	9.00
(24)	Charles	35.00	15.00	9.00
(25)	Chech	35.00	15.00	9.00
(26)	Christian	35.00	15.00	9.00
(27)	Clarke	35.00	15.00	9.00
(28)	Colligan	35.00	15.00	9.00
(29)	Cook	35.00	15.00	9.00
(31)	Coy	35.00	15.00	9.00
(32)	Crabb	35.00	15.00	9.00
(33)	Davis	35.00	15.00	9.00
(34)	Derrick	35.00	15.00	9.00
(35)	Devlin	35.00	15.00	9.00
(36)	DeCannier	35.00	15.00	9.00
(37)	Dillon	35.00	15.00	9.00
(38)	Doane	35.00	15.00	9.00
(39)	Downs	35.00	15.00	9.00
(40)	Ehmke	35.00	15.00	9.00
(41)	Ellis	35.00	15.00	9.00
(42)	Evans	35.00	15.00	9.00
(43)	Fanning	35.00	15.00	9.00
(44)	Fisher	35.00	15.00	9.00
(45)	Fitzgerald	35.00	15.00	9.00
(46)	Fleharty	35.00	15.00	9.00
(47)	Frambach	35.00	15.00	9.00
(48)	Gardner	35.00	15.00	9.00
(49)	Gedeon	35.00	15.00	9.00
(50)	Geyer	35.00	15.00	9.00
(51)	Gianini	35.00	15.00	9.00
(52)	Gregory	35.00	15.00	9.00
(53)	Guest	35.00	15.00	9.00
(54)	Hallinan	35.00	15.00	9.00
(55)	Hannah	35.00	15.00	9.00
(56)	Harkness (batting)	35.00	15.00	9.00
(57)	Haworth (batting)	35.00	15.00	9.00
(58)	Haworth (catching)	35.00	15.00	9.00
(59)	Henderson	35.00	15.00	9.00
(60)	Henley	35.00	15.00	9.00
(61)	Hern	35.00	15.00	9.00
(62)	Hettling	35.00	15.00	9.00
(63)	Higginbotham	35.00	15.00	9.00
(64)	Hitt	35.00	15.00	9.00
(65)	Hogan	35.00	15.00	9.00
(66a)	Hosp (large pose)	35.00	15.00	9.00
(66b)	Hosp (small pose)	35.00	15.00	9.00
(67)	Howard	35.00	15.00	9.00
(68)	Hughes (Los Angeles)	35.00	15.00	9.00
(69)	Hughes (San Francisco)	35.00	15.00	9.00
(70)	Johnson	35.00	15.00	9.00
(71)	Kane	35.00	15.00	9.00
(72)	Kaylor	35.00	15.00	9.00
(73)	Killilay	35.00	15.00	9.00
(74)	Klawitter	35.00	15.00	9.00
(75)	Klepfler	35.00	15.00	9.00
(76)	Kores	35.00	15.00	9.00
(77)	Kramer	35.00	15.00	9.00
(78)	Krause	35.00	15.00	9.00
(79a)	Leard (large pose)	35.00	15.00	9.00
(79b)	Leard (small pose)	35.00	15.00	9.00
(80)	Liefeld	35.00	15.00	9.00
(81)	Litschi	35.00	15.00	9.00
(82)	Lober	35.00	15.00	9.00
(83)	Loomis	35.00	15.00	9.00
(84)	Love	35.00	15.00	9.00
(85)	Lynn	35.00	15.00	9.00
(86)	Maggart	35.00	15.00	9.00
(87)	Malarkey	35.00	15.00	9.00
(88)	Martinoni	35.00	15.00	9.00
(89)	McArdle	35.00	15.00	9.00
(90)	McCredie	35.00	15.00	9.00
(91)	McDonald	35.00	15.00	9.00
(92)	Meek	35.00	15.00	9.00
(93)	Meloan	35.00	15.00	9.00
(94)	Menges	35.00	15.00	9.00
(95)	Metzger	35.00	15.00	9.00
(96)	Middleton	35.00	15.00	9.00
(97)	Mitze	35.00	15.00	9.00
(98)	Mohler	35.00	15.00	9.00
(99)	Moore	35.00	15.00	9.00
(100)	Moran	35.00	15.00	9.00
(101)	Mundorf	35.00	15.00	9.00
(102)	Murphy	35.00	15.00	9.00
(103)	Musser	35.00	15.00	9.00
(104)	Ness	35.00	15.00	9.00
(105)	O'Leary	35.00	15.00	9.00
(106)	Orr	35.00	15.00	9.00
(107)	Page	35.00	15.00	9.00
(108)	Pape	35.00	15.00	9.00
(109)	Parkin	35.00	15.00	9.00
(110a)	Peet (large pose)	35.00	15.00	9.00
(110b)	Peet (small pose)	35.00	15.00	9.00
(111)	Perkins	35.00	15.00	9.00
(112)	Pernoll	35.00	15.00	9.00
(113)	Perritt	35.00	15.00	9.00
(114)	Powell	35.00	15.00	9.00
(115)	Prough	35.00	15.00	9.00
(116)	Pruiett	35.00	15.00	9.00
(117)	Quinlan	35.00	15.00	9.00
(118a)	Haney (incorrect spelling)	35.00	15.00	9.00
(118b)	Ramey (correct spelling)	35.00	15.00	9.00
(119)	Rieger	35.00	15.00	9.00
(120)	Rodgers	35.00	15.00	9.00
(121)	Rogers	35.00	15.00	9.00
(122)	Rohrer	35.00	15.00	9.00
(123)	Ryan	35.00	15.00	9.00
(124)	Ryan	35.00	15.00	9.00
(125)	Sawyer	35.00	15.00	9.00
(126)	Schaller	35.00	15.00	9.00
(127)	Schmidt	35.00	15.00	9.00
(128)	Sepulveda	35.00	15.00	9.00
(129)	Shinn	35.00	15.00	9.00
(130)	Slagle	35.00	15.00	9.00
(131)	Speas	35.00	15.00	9.00
(132)	Stanridge	35.00	15.00	9.00
(133)	Stroud	35.00	15.00	9.00
(134)	Tennant	35.00	15.00	9.00
(135)	Tobin	35.00	15.00	9.00
(136)	Tozer	35.00	15.00	9.00
(137)	Van Buren	35.00	15.00	9.00
(138)	West	35.00	15.00	9.00
(139)	White	35.00	15.00	9.00
(140)	Wolter	35.00	15.00	9.00
(141)	Wolverton	35.00	15.00	9.00
(142)	Yantz	35.00	15.00	9.00
(143)	Young	35.00	15.00	9.00
(144)	Zacher	35.00	15.00	9.00
(145)	Zumwalt	35.00	15.00	9.00

1915 Zeenut Pacific Coast League

The 1915 Zeenut cards are dated on the front, making identification very easy. They measure 2" x 3-1/8" without the coupon and feature a black-and-white photo on a light background. To date 141 different cards are known to exist. This year is among the toughest of all Zeenuts to find.

		NM	EX	VG
Complete Set (141):		5250.	2000.	1200.
Common Player:		45.00	18.00	11.00
(1)	Ables	45.00	18.00	11.00
(2)	Abstein	45.00	18.00	11.00
(3)	Alcock	45.00	18.00	11.00
(4)	Arbogast	45.00	18.00	11.00
(5)	Baerwald	45.00	18.00	11.00
(6)	Barbour	45.00	18.00	11.00
(7)	Bates	45.00	18.00	11.00
(8)	Baum	45.00	18.00	11.00
(9)	Bayless	45.00	18.00	11.00
(10)	Beatty	45.00	18.00	11.00
(11)	Beer	45.00	18.00	11.00
(12)	Benham	45.00	18.00	11.00
(13)	Berger	45.00	18.00	11.00
(14)	Beumiller	45.00	18.00	11.00
(15)	Blankenship	45.00	18.00	11.00
(16)	Block	45.00	18.00	11.00
(17)	Bodie	45.00	18.00	11.00
(18)	Boles	45.00	18.00	11.00
(19)	Boyd	45.00	18.00	11.00
(20)	Bromley	45.00	18.00	11.00
(21)	Brown	45.00	18.00	11.00
(22)	Burns	75.00	37.00	22.00
(23)	Carlisle	45.00	18.00	11.00
(24)	Carrisch	45.00	18.00	11.00
(25)	Charles	45.00	18.00	11.00
(26)	Chech	45.00	18.00	11.00
(27)	Christian	45.00	18.00	11.00
(28)	Clarke	45.00	18.00	11.00
(29)	Couch	45.00	18.00	11.00
(30)	Stan Covaleski (Coveleski)	250.00	125.00	75.00
(31)	Daniels	45.00	18.00	11.00
(32)	Davis	45.00	18.00	11.00
(33)	DeCanniere	45.00	18.00	11.00
(34)	Dent	45.00	18.00	11.00
(35)	Derrick	45.00	18.00	11.00
(36)	Dillon	45.00	18.00	11.00
(37)	Doane	45.00	18.00	11.00
(38)	Downs	45.00	18.00	11.00
(39)	Elliott	45.00	18.00	11.00
(40)	F. Elliott	45.00	18.00	11.00
(41)	Ellis	45.00	18.00	11.00
(42)	Evans	45.00	18.00	11.00
(43)	Fanning	45.00	18.00	11.00
(44)	Faye	45.00	18.00	11.00
(45)	Fisher	45.00	18.00	11.00
(46)	Fittery	45.00	18.00	11.00
(47)	Fitzgerald	45.00	18.00	11.00
(48)	Fromme	45.00	18.00	11.00
(49)	Gardiner	45.00	18.00	11.00
(50)	Gedeon	45.00	18.00	11.00
(51)	Gleischmann	45.00	18.00	11.00
(52)	Gregory	45.00	18.00	11.00
(53)	Guest	45.00	18.00	11.00
(54)	Hall	45.00	18.00	11.00
(55)	Halla	45.00	18.00	11.00
(56)	Hallinan	45.00	18.00	11.00
(57)	Hannah	45.00	18.00	11.00
(58)	Harper	45.00	18.00	11.00
(59)	Harry Heilmann	250.00	125.00	75.00
(60)	Henley	45.00	18.00	11.00
(61)	Hetling	45.00	18.00	11.00

(62)	Higginbotham	45.00	18.00	11.00
(63)	Hilliard	45.00	18.00	11.00
(64)	Hitt (winding up)	45.00	18.00	11.00
(65)	Hitt (throwing)	45.00	18.00	11.00
(66)	Hogan	45.00	18.00	11.00
(67)	Hosp	45.00	18.00	11.00
(68)	Howard	45.00	18.00	11.00
(69)	Hughes	45.00	18.00	11.00
(70)	Johnson	45.00	18.00	11.00
(71)	Jones	45.00	18.00	11.00
(72)	Kahler	45.00	18.00	11.00
(73)	Kane	45.00	18.00	11.00
(74)	Karr	45.00	18.00	11.00
(75)	Killilay	45.00	18.00	11.00
(76)	Klawitter	45.00	18.00	11.00
(77)	Koerner	45.00	18.00	11.00
(78)	Krause	45.00	18.00	11.00
(79)	Kuhn	45.00	18.00	11.00
(80)	LaRoy	45.00	18.00	11.00
(81)	Leard	45.00	18.00	11.00
(82)	Lindsay	45.00	18.00	11.00
(83)	Litschi	45.00	18.00	11.00
(84)	Lober	45.00	18.00	11.00
(85)	Love	45.00	18.00	11.00
(86)	Lush	45.00	18.00	11.00
(87)	Maggart	45.00	18.00	11.00
(88)	Malarkey	45.00	18.00	11.00
(89)	Manda	45.00	18.00	11.00
(90)	Marcan	45.00	18.00	11.00
(91)	Martinoni	45.00	18.00	11.00
(92)	McAvoy	45.00	18.00	11.00
(93)	McCredie	45.00	18.00	11.00
(94)	McDonell	45.00	18.00	11.00
(95)	McMullen	800.00	400.00	240.00
(96)	Meek	45.00	18.00	11.00
(97)	Meloan	45.00	18.00	11.00
(98)	Metzger	45.00	18.00	11.00
(99)	Middleton	45.00	18.00	11.00
(100)	Mitchell	45.00	18.00	11.00
(101)	Mitze	45.00	18.00	11.00
(102)	Morgan	45.00	18.00	11.00
(103)	Mundorff	45.00	18.00	11.00
(104)	Murphy	45.00	18.00	11.00
(105)	Ness	45.00	18.00	11.00
(106)	Nutt	45.00	18.00	11.00
(107)	Orr	45.00	18.00	11.00
(108)	Pernoll	45.00	18.00	11.00
(109)	Perritt	45.00	18.00	11.00
(110)	Piercey	45.00	18.00	11.00
(111)	Price	45.00	18.00	11.00
(112)	Prough	45.00	18.00	11.00
(113)	Prueitt	45.00	18.00	11.00
(114)	Purtell	45.00	18.00	11.00
(115)	Reed	45.00	18.00	11.00
(116)	Reisigl	45.00	18.00	11.00
(117)	Remneas	45.00	18.00	11.00
(118)	Swede Risberg	500.00	250.00	150.00
(119)	Rohrer	45.00	18.00	11.00
(120)	Russell	45.00	18.00	11.00
(121)	Ryan (Los Angeles)	45.00	18.00	11.00
(122)	Ryan	45.00	18.00	11.00
(123)	Schaller	45.00	18.00	11.00
(124)	Schmidt	45.00	18.00	11.00
(125)	Scoggins	45.00	18.00	11.00
(126)	Sepulveda	45.00	18.00	11.00
(127)	Shinn	45.00	18.00	11.00
(128)	Smith	45.00	18.00	11.00
(129)	Speas	45.00	18.00	11.00
(130)	Spencer	45.00	18.00	11.00
(132)	Tennant	45.00	18.00	11.00
(133)	Terry	45.00	18.00	11.00
(134)	Tobin	45.00	18.00	11.00
(135)	West	45.00	18.00	11.00
(136)	White	45.00	18.00	11.00
(137)	Claude Williams	350.00	140.00	90.00
(138)	Johnny Williams	75.00	37.00	22.00
(139)	Wolter	45.00	18.00	11.00
(140)	Wolverton	45.00	18.00	11.00
(141)	Zacher	45.00	18.00	11.00

1916 Zeenut Pacific Coast League

The 1916 Zeenuts measure 2" x 3-1/8" without the coupon and are dated on the front (some cards were misdated 1915, however). The card fronts feature black-and-white photos on a blue background. There are 144 known subjects. The 1916 series is among the more difficult.

		NM	EX	VG
Complete Set (142):		7500.	3700.	2200.
Common Player:		40.00	16.00	10.00
(1)	Autrey	40.00	16.00	10.00
(2)	Barbeau	40.00	16.00	10.00
(3)	Barry	40.00	16.00	10.00
(4)	Bassler	40.00	16.00	10.00
(5)	Bates	40.00	16.00	10.00
(6)	Baum	40.00	16.00	10.00
(7)	Bayless	40.00	16.00	10.00
(8)	Beer	40.00	16.00	10.00
(9)	Berg	40.00	16.00	10.00
(10)	Berger	40.00	16.00	10.00
(11)	Blankenship	40.00	16.00	10.00
(12)	Block	40.00	16.00	10.00
(13)	Bodie	40.00	16.00	10.00
(14)	Bohne	40.00	16.00	10.00
(15)	Boles	40.00	16.00	10.00
(16)	Boyd	40.00	16.00	10.00
(17)	Brief	40.00	16.00	10.00
(18)	Brooks	40.00	16.00	10.00
(19)	Brown	40.00	16.00	10.00
(20)	Butler	40.00	16.00	10.00
(21)	Callahan	40.00	16.00	10.00
(22)	Carrisch	40.00	16.00	10.00
(23)	Chance	250.00	100.00	60.00
(24)	Jimmy Claxton	3500.	1750.	1050.
(25)	Coffey	40.00	16.00	10.00
(26)	Cook	40.00	16.00	10.00
(27)	Corbett	40.00	16.00	10.00
(28)	Couch	40.00	16.00	10.00
(29)	Crandall	40.00	16.00	10.00
(30)	Dalton	40.00	16.00	10.00
(31)	Davis	40.00	16.00	10.00
(32)	Derrick	40.00	16.00	10.00
(33)	Doane	40.00	16.00	10.00
(34)	Downs	40.00	16.00	10.00
(35)	Dugan	40.00	16.00	10.00
(36)	Eldred	40.00	16.00	10.00
(37)	F. Elliott	40.00	16.00	10.00
(38)	H. Elliott	40.00	16.00	10.00
(39)	Ellis	40.00	16.00	10.00
(40)	Erickson	40.00	16.00	10.00
(41)	Fanning	40.00	16.00	10.00
(42)	Fisher	40.00	16.00	10.00
(43)	Fittery	40.00	16.00	10.00
(44)	Fitzgerald	40.00	16.00	10.00
(45)	Fromme	40.00	16.00	10.00
(46)	Galloway	40.00	16.00	10.00
(47)	Gardner	40.00	16.00	10.00
(48)	Gay	40.00	16.00	10.00
(49)	Gleischmann	40.00	16.00	10.00
(50)	Griffith	40.00	16.00	10.00
(51)	Griggs	40.00	16.00	10.00
(52)	Guisto	40.00	16.00	10.00
(53)	Hagerman	40.00	16.00	10.00
(54)	Hall	40.00	16.00	10.00
(55)	Hallinan	40.00	16.00	10.00
(56)	Hannah	40.00	16.00	10.00
(57)	Harstadt	40.00	16.00	10.00
(58)	Haworth	40.00	16.00	10.00
(59)	Hess	40.00	16.00	10.00
(60)	Higginbotham	40.00	16.00	10.00
(61)	Hitt	40.00	16.00	10.00
(62)	Hogg	40.00	16.00	10.00
(63)	Hollocher	40.00	16.00	10.00
(64)	Horstman	40.00	16.00	10.00
(65)	Houck	40.00	16.00	10.00
(66)	Howard	40.00	16.00	10.00
(67)	Hughes	40.00	16.00	10.00
(68)	E. Johnston	40.00	16.00	10.00
(69)	G. Johnston	40.00	16.00	10.00
(70)	Jones	40.00	16.00	10.00
(71)	Kahler	40.00	16.00	10.00
(72)	Kane	40.00	16.00	10.00
(73)	Kelly	40.00	16.00	10.00
(74)	Kenworthy	40.00	16.00	10.00
(75)	Klawitter	40.00	16.00	10.00
(76)	Klein	40.00	16.00	10.00
(77)	Koerner	40.00	16.00	10.00
(78)	Krause	40.00	16.00	10.00
(79)	Kuhn	40.00	16.00	10.00
(80)	Lane	40.00	16.00	10.00
(81)	Larsen	40.00	16.00	10.00
(82)	Lush	40.00	16.00	10.00
(83)	Machold	40.00	16.00	10.00
(84)	Maggert	40.00	16.00	10.00
(85)	Manser	40.00	16.00	10.00
(86)	Martin	40.00	16.00	10.00
(87)	Mattick	40.00	16.00	10.00
(88)	McCredie	40.00	16.00	10.00
(89)	McGaffigan	40.00	16.00	10.00
(90)	McLarry	40.00	16.00	10.00
(91)	Menges	40.00	16.00	10.00
(92)	Middleton	40.00	16.00	10.00
(93)	Mitchell	40.00	16.00	10.00
(94)	Mitze	40.00	16.00	10.00
(95)	Munsell	40.00	16.00	10.00
(96)	Murphy	40.00	16.00	10.00
(97)	Nixon	40.00	16.00	10.00
(98)	Noyes	40.00	16.00	10.00
(99)	Nutt	40.00	16.00	10.00
(100)	O'Brien	40.00	16.00	10.00
(101)	Oldham	40.00	16.00	10.00
(102)	Orr	40.00	16.00	10.00
(103)	Patterson	40.00	16.00	10.00
(104)	Perritt	40.00	16.00	10.00
(105)	Prough	40.00	16.00	10.00
(106)	Prueitt	40.00	16.00	10.00
(107)	Quinlan	40.00	16.00	10.00
(108)	Quinn (Portland)	40.00	16.00	10.00
(109)	Quinn (Vernon)	40.00	16.00	10.00
(110)	Rader	40.00	16.00	10.00
(111)	Randall	40.00	16.00	10.00
(112)	Rath	40.00	16.00	10.00
(113)	Reisegl	40.00	16.00	10.00
(114)	Reuther	40.00	16.00	10.00
(115)	Swede Risberg	250.00	125.00	75.00
(116)	Roche	40.00	16.00	10.00
(117)	Ryan	40.00	16.00	10.00
(118)	Ryan	40.00	16.00	10.00
(119)	Scoggins	40.00	16.00	10.00
(120)	Sepulveda	40.00	16.00	10.00
(121)	Schaller	40.00	16.00	10.00
(122)	Sheehan	40.00	16.00	10.00
(123)	Shinn	40.00	16.00	10.00
(124)	Smith	40.00	16.00	10.00
(125)	Sothoron	40.00	16.00	10.00
(126)	Southworth	40.00	16.00	10.00
(127)	Speas	40.00	16.00	10.00
(128)	Spencer	40.00	16.00	10.00
(129)	Standridge	40.00	16.00	10.00
(130)	Steen	40.00	16.00	10.00
(131)	Stumpf	40.00	16.00	10.00
(132)	Vann	40.00	16.00	10.00
(133)	Vaughn	40.00	16.00	10.00
(134)	Ward	40.00	16.00	10.00
(135)	Whalling	40.00	16.00	10.00
(136)	Wilie	40.00	16.00	10.00
(137)	Williams	40.00	16.00	10.00
(138)	Wolverton	40.00	16.00	10.00
(139)	Wuffli	40.00	16.00	10.00
(140)	Zabel	40.00	16.00	10.00
(141)	Zacher	40.00	16.00	10.00
(142)	Zimmerman	40.00	16.00	10.00

1917 Zeenut Pacific Coast League

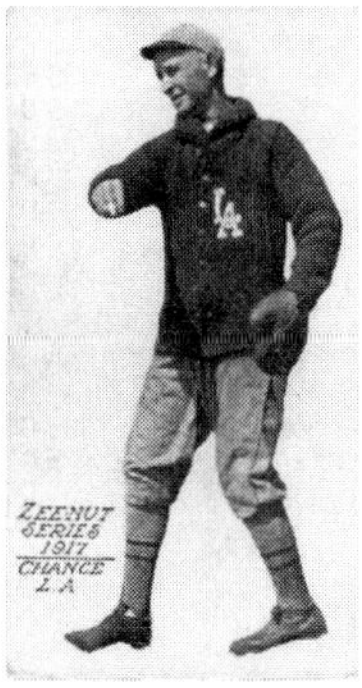

The 1917 Zeenuts measure 1-3/4" x 3-1/2" and feature black-and-white photos on a light background. They are dated on the front and have blank backs. An advertising poster has been found listing 119 players (two pose variations brings the total to 121), but to date, six players on the list have not been found.

		NM	EX	VG
Complete Set (121):		3700.	1450.	900.00
Common Player:		35.00	14.00	8.50
(1)	Arlett	35.00	14.00	8.50
(2)	Arrelanes	35.00	14.00	8.50
(3)	Baker (catching)	35.00	14.00	8.50
(4)	Baker (throwing)	35.00	14.00	8.50
(5)	Baldwin	35.00	14.00	8.50
(6)	Bassler	35.00	14.00	8.50
(7)	Baum	35.00	14.00	8.50
(8)	Beer	35.00	14.00	8.50
(9)	Bernhard	35.00	14.00	8.50
(10)	Bliss	35.00	14.00	8.50
(11)	Boles	35.00	14.00	8.50
(12)	Brenton	35.00	14.00	8.50
(13)	Brief	35.00	14.00	8.50
(14)	Brown	35.00	14.00	8.50
(15)	Burns	35.00	14.00	8.50
(16)	Callahan	35.00	14.00	8.50
(17)	Callan	35.00	14.00	8.50
(18)	Jacinto Calvo	100.00	40.00	25.00
(19)	Chadbourne	35.00	14.00	8.50
(20)	Frank Chance	400.00	160.00	95.00
(21)	Coltrin	35.00	14.00	8.50
(22)	Connifer	35.00	14.00	8.50
(23)	Corhan	35.00	14.00	8.50
(24)	Crandall (Los Angeles)	35.00	14.00	8.50
(25)	Crandall (Salt Lake)	35.00	14.00	8.50
(26)	Cress	35.00	14.00	8.50
(27)	Davis	35.00	14.00	8.50
(28)	DeCanniere	35.00	14.00	8.50
(29)	Doane	35.00	14.00	8.50
(30)	Dougan	35.00	14.00	8.50
(31)	Dougherty	35.00	14.00	8.50
(32)	Downs	35.00	14.00	8.50
(33)	Dubuc	35.00	14.00	8.50
(34)	Ellis	35.00	14.00	8.50
(35)	Erickson	35.00	14.00	8.50
(36)	Evans	35.00	14.00	8.50
(37)	Farmer	35.00	14.00	8.50
(38)	Fincher	35.00	14.00	8.50
(39)	Fisher	35.00	14.00	8.50
(40)	Fitzgerald	35.00	14.00	8.50
(41)	Fournier	35.00	14.00	8.50
(42)	Fromme	35.00	14.00	8.50
(43)	Galloway	35.00	14.00	8.50
(44)	Gislason	35.00	14.00	8.50
(45)	Goodbred	35.00	14.00	8.50
(46)	Griggs	35.00	14.00	8.50
(47)	Groehling	35.00	14.00	8.50
(48)	Hall (Los Angeles)	35.00	14.00	8.50
(49)	Hall (San Francisco)	35.00	14.00	8.50
(50)	Hannah	35.00	14.00	8.50

(51)	Harstad	35.00	14.00	8.50
(52)	Helfrich	35.00	14.00	8.50
(53)	Hess	35.00	14.00	8.50
(54)	Hitt	35.00	14.00	8.50
(55)	Hoff	35.00	14.00	8.50
(56)	Hollacher	35.00	14.00	8.50
(57)	Hollywood	35.00	14.00	8.50
(58)	Houck	35.00	14.00	8.50
(59)	Howard	35.00	14.00	8.50
(60)	Hughes	35.00	14.00	8.50
(61)	Johnson	35.00	14.00	8.50
(62)	Kilhullen	35.00	14.00	8.50
(63)	Killiffer (Killefer)	35.00	14.00	8.50
(64)	Koerner	35.00	14.00	8.50
(65)	Krause	35.00	14.00	8.50
(66)	Lane	35.00	14.00	8.50
(67)	Lapan	35.00	14.00	8.50
(68)	Leake	35.00	14.00	8.50
(69)	Lee	35.00	14.00	8.50
(70)	Leverenz	35.00	14.00	8.50
(71)	Maggert	35.00	14.00	8.50
(72)	Maisel	35.00	14.00	8.50
(73)	Mattick	35.00	14.00	8.50
(74)	McCreedie	35.00	14.00	8.50
(75)	McLarry	35.00	14.00	8.50
(76)	Mensor	35.00	14.00	8.50
(77)	Meusel	35.00	14.00	8.50
(78)	Middleton	35.00	14.00	8.50
(79)	Miller (batting)	35.00	14.00	8.50
(80)	Miller (throwing)	35.00	14.00	8.50
(81)	Mitchell	35.00	14.00	8.50
(82)	Mitze	35.00	14.00	8.50
(83)	Murphy	35.00	14.00	8.50
(84)	Murray	35.00	14.00	8.50
(85)	O'Brien	35.00	14.00	8.50
(86)	O'Mara	35.00	14.00	8.50
(87)	Oldham	35.00	14.00	8.50
(88)	Orr	35.00	14.00	8.50
(89)	Penelli	35.00	14.00	8.50
(90)	Penner	35.00	14.00	8.50
(91)	Pick	35.00	14.00	8.50
(92)	Prough	35.00	14.00	8.50
(93)	Pruiett	35.00	14.00	8.50
(94)	Quinlan	35.00	14.00	8.50
(95)	Quinn	35.00	14.00	8.50
(96)	Rath	35.00	14.00	8.50
(97)	Roche	35.00	14.00	8.50
(98)	Ryan (Los Angeles)	35.00	14.00	8.50
(99)	Ryan (Salt Lake)	35.00	14.00	8.50
(100)	Schaller	35.00	14.00	8.50
(101)	Schinkle	35.00	14.00	8.50
(102)	Schultz	35.00	14.00	8.50
(103)	Sheehan	35.00	14.00	8.50
(104)	Sheeley	35.00	14.00	8.50
(105)	Shinn	35.00	14.00	8.50
(106)	Siglin	35.00	14.00	8.50
(107)	Simon	35.00	14.00	8.50
(108)	Smith	35.00	14.00	8.50
(109)	Snyder	35.00	14.00	8.50
(110)	Stanridge	35.00	14.00	8.50
(111)	Steen	35.00	14.00	8.50
(112)	Stovall	35.00	14.00	8.50
(113)	Stumpf	35.00	14.00	8.50
(114)	Sullivan	35.00	14.00	8.50
(115)	Terry	35.00	14.00	8.50
(116)	Tobin	35.00	14.00	8.50
(117)	Valencia	35.00	14.00	8.50
(118)	Vaughn	35.00	14.00	8.50
(119)	Whalling	35.00	14.00	8.50
(120)	Wilie	35.00	14.00	8.50
(121)	Wolverton	35.00	14.00	8.50

1918 Zeenut Pacific Coast League

The 1918 Zeenuts are among the most distinctive because of their red borders surrounding the photos. They measure 1-3/4" x 3-1/8" and are among the more difficult years to find.

		NM	EX	VG
Complete Set (104):		3750.	1500.	900.00
Common Player:		45.00	16.00	11.00
(1)	Alcock	45.00	16.00	11.00
(2)	Arkenburg	45.00	16.00	11.00
(3)	A. Arlett	45.00	16.00	11.00
(4)	Baum	45.00	16.00	11.00
(5)	Boles	45.00	16.00	11.00
(6)	Borton	45.00	16.00	11.00
(7)	Brenton	45.00	16.00	11.00
(8)	Bromley	45.00	16.00	11.00
(9)	Brooks	45.00	16.00	11.00
(10)	Brown	45.00	16.00	11.00
(11)	Caldera	45.00	16.00	11.00
(12)	Camm (Kamm)	45.00	16.00	11.00
(13)	Chadbourne	45.00	16.00	11.00
(14)	Chappell	45.00	16.00	11.00
(15)	Codington	45.00	16.00	11.00
(16)	Conwright	45.00	16.00	11.00
(17)	Cooper	45.00	16.00	11.00
(18)	Cox	45.00	16.00	11.00
(19)	Crandall (Los Angeles)	45.00	16.00	11.00
(20)	Crandall (Salt Lake)	45.00	16.00	11.00
(21)	Crawford	45.00	16.00	11.00
(22)	Croll	45.00	16.00	11.00
(23)	Davis	45.00	16.00	11.00
(24)	DeVormer	45.00	16.00	11.00
(25)	Dobbs	45.00	16.00	11.00
(26)	Downs	45.00	16.00	11.00
(27)	Dubuc	45.00	16.00	11.00
(28)	Dunn	45.00	16.00	11.00
(29)	Easterly	45.00	16.00	11.00
(30)	Eldred	45.00	16.00	11.00
(31)	Elliot	45.00	16.00	11.00
(32)	Ellis	45.00	16.00	11.00
(33)	Essick	45.00	16.00	11.00
(34)	Farmer	45.00	16.00	11.00
(35)	Fisher	45.00	16.00	11.00
(36)	Fittery	45.00	16.00	11.00
(37)	Forsythe	45.00	16.00	11.00
(38)	Fournier	45.00	16.00	11.00
(39)	Fromme	45.00	16.00	11.00
(40)	Gardner (Oakland)	45.00	16.00	11.00
(41)	Gardner (Sacramento)	45.00	16.00	11.00
(42)	Goldie	45.00	16.00	11.00
(43)	Griggs	45.00	16.00	11.00
(44)	Hawkes	45.00	16.00	11.00
(45)	Hollander	45.00	16.00	11.00
(46)	Hosp	45.00	16.00	11.00
(47)	Howard	45.00	16.00	11.00
(48)	Hummel	45.00	16.00	11.00
(49)	Hunter	45.00	16.00	11.00
(50)	Johnson	45.00	16.00	11.00
(51)	G. Johnson	45.00	16.00	11.00
(52)	Kantlehner	45.00	16.00	11.00
(53)	Killefer	45.00	16.00	11.00
(54)	Koerner	45.00	16.00	11.00
(55)	Konnick	45.00	16.00	11.00
(56)	Kremer	45.00	16.00	11.00
(57)	Lapan	45.00	16.00	11.00
(58)	Leake	45.00	16.00	11.00
(59)	Leathers	45.00	16.00	11.00
(60)	Leifer	45.00	16.00	11.00
(61)	Leverenz	45.00	16.00	11.00
(62)	Llewlyn	45.00	16.00	11.00
(63)	Martin	45.00	16.00	11.00
(64)	McCabe	45.00	16.00	11.00
(65)	McCredie	45.00	16.00	11.00
(66)	McKee	45.00	16.00	11.00
(67)	McNulty	45.00	16.00	11.00
(68)	Mensor	45.00	16.00	11.00
(69)	Middleton	45.00	16.00	11.00
(70)	Miller (Oakland)	45.00	16.00	11.00
(71)	Miller (Salt Lake)	45.00	16.00	11.00
(72)	J. Mitchell	45.00	16.00	11.00
(73)	R. Mitchell	45.00	16.00	11.00
(74)	Mitze	45.00	16.00	11.00
(75)	Moore	45.00	16.00	11.00
(76)	Morton	45.00	16.00	11.00
(77)	Murray	45.00	16.00	11.00
(78)	O'Doul	80.00	48.00	20.00
(79)	Orr	45.00	16.00	11.00
(80)	Pepe	45.00	16.00	11.00
(81)	Pertica	45.00	16.00	11.00
(82)	Phillips	45.00	16.00	11.00
(83)	Pick	45.00	16.00	11.00
(84)	Pinelli	45.00	16.00	11.00
(85)	Prentice	45.00	16.00	11.00
(86)	Prough	45.00	16.00	11.00
(87)	Quinlan	45.00	16.00	11.00
(88)	Ritchie	45.00	16.00	11.00
(89)	Rogers	45.00	16.00	11.00
(90)	Ryan	45.00	16.00	11.00
(91)	Sand	45.00	16.00	11.00
(92)	Shader	45.00	16.00	11.00
(93)	Sheely	45.00	16.00	11.00
(94)	Siglin	45.00	16.00	11.00
(95)	Smale	45.00	16.00	11.00
(96)	Smith	45.00	16.00	11.00
(97)	Smith	45.00	16.00	11.00
(98)	Stanbridge	45.00	16.00	11.00
(99)	Terry	45.00	16.00	11.00
(100)	Valencia	45.00	16.00	11.00
(101)	West	45.00	16.00	11.00
(102)	Wilie	45.00	16.00	11.00
(103)	Williams	45.00	16.00	11.00
(104)	Wisterzill	45.00	16.00	11.00

Near Mint-Mint examples of vintage cards carry a significant premium over the Near Mint values shown here. This premium reflects limited availability of the highest-grade cards as well as demand for particular cards or sets in the best possible condition. Premiums of 2X-3X are not uncommon and many are even higher.

1919 Zeenut Pacific Coast League

The 1919-1921 Zeenuts cards were dated on the front and measure 1-3/4" x 3-1/8". They featured borderless, sepia-toned photos. To date, 144 subjects exist in the 1919 series; 151 have been found for 1920; and 168 different subjects have been discovered for 1921 (even though a promotional flier indicates 180 players).

		NM	EX	VG
Complete Set (144):		3100.	1250.	750.00
Common Player:		25.00	10.00	6.00
(1)	Ally	25.00	10.00	6.00
(2)	Fatty Arbuckle	350.00	140.00	85.00
(3)	A. Arlett	25.00	10.00	6.00
(4)	R. Arlett	24.00	12.00	7.25
(5)	Baker	25.00	10.00	6.00
(6)	Baldwin	25.00	10.00	6.00
(7)	Baum	25.00	10.00	6.00
(8)	Beck	25.00	10.00	6.00
(9)	Bigbee	25.00	10.00	6.00
(10)	Blue	25.00	10.00	6.00
(11)	Bohne	25.00	10.00	6.00
(12)	Boles	25.00	10.00	6.00
(13)	Borton	25.00	10.00	6.00
(14)	Bowman	25.00	10.00	6.00
(15)	Brooks	25.00	10.00	6.00
(16)	Brown	25.00	10.00	6.00
(17)	Byler	25.00	10.00	6.00
(18)	Caldera	25.00	10.00	6.00
(19)	Cavaney	25.00	10.00	6.00
(20)	Chadbourne	25.00	10.00	6.00
(21)	Chech	25.00	10.00	6.00
(22)	Church	25.00	10.00	6.00
(23)	Clymer	25.00	10.00	6.00
(24)	Coleman	25.00	10.00	6.00
(25)	Compton	25.00	10.00	6.00
(26)	Conkwright	25.00	10.00	6.00
(27)	Connolly	25.00	10.00	6.00
(28)	Cook	25.00	10.00	6.00
(29)	Cooper (Los Angeles)	25.00	10.00	6.00
(30)	Cooper (Oakland)	25.00	10.00	6.00
(31)	Cooper (Portland)	25.00	10.00	6.00
(32)	Corhan	25.00	10.00	6.00
(33)	Couch	25.00	10.00	6.00
(34)	Cox	25.00	10.00	6.00
(35)	Crandall (Los Angeles)	25.00	10.00	6.00
(36)	Crandall (San Francisco)	25.00	10.00	6.00
(37)	Crespi	25.00	10.00	6.00
(38)	Croll	25.00	10.00	6.00
(39)	Cunningham	25.00	10.00	6.00
(40)	Dawson	25.00	10.00	6.00
(41)	Dell	25.00	10.00	6.00
(42)	DeVormer	25.00	10.00	6.00
(43)	Driscoll	25.00	10.00	6.00
(44)	Eastley	25.00	10.00	6.00
(45)	Edington	25.00	10.00	6.00
(46)	Eldred	25.00	10.00	6.00
(47)	Elliott	25.00	10.00	6.00
(48)	Ellis	25.00	10.00	6.00
(49)	Essick	25.00	10.00	6.00
(50)	Fabrique	25.00	10.00	6.00
(51)	Falkenberg	25.00	10.00	6.00
(52)	Fallentine	25.00	10.00	6.00
(53)	Finneran	25.00	10.00	6.00
(54)	Fisher (Sacramento)	25.00	10.00	6.00
(55)	Fisher (Vernon)	25.00	10.00	6.00
(56)	Fitzgerald	25.00	10.00	6.00
(57)	Flannigan	25.00	10.00	6.00
(58)	Fournier	25.00	10.00	6.00
(59)	French	25.00	10.00	6.00
(60)	Fromme	25.00	10.00	6.00
(61)	Gibson	25.00	10.00	6.00
(62)	Griggs	25.00	10.00	6.00
(63)	Haney	25.00	10.00	6.00
(64)	Harper	25.00	10.00	6.00
(65)	Henkle	25.00	10.00	6.00
(66)	Herr	25.00	10.00	6.00
(67)	Hickey	25.00	10.00	6.00
(68)	High	25.00	10.00	6.00
(69)	Holling	25.00	10.00	6.00
(70)	Hosp	25.00	10.00	6.00
(71)	Houck	25.00	10.00	6.00
(72)	Howard	25.00	10.00	6.00
(73)	Kamm	25.00	10.00	6.00
(74)	Kenworthy	25.00	10.00	6.00
(75)	Killefer	25.00	10.00	6.00
(76)	King	25.00	10.00	6.00
(77)	Koehler	25.00	10.00	6.00
(78)	Koerner	25.00	10.00	6.00
(79)	Kramer (Oakland)	25.00	10.00	6.00
(80)	Kramer (San Francisco)	25.00	10.00	6.00

(81)	Land	25.00	10.00	6.00
(82)	Lane	25.00	10.00	6.00
(83)	Lapan	25.00	10.00	6.00
(84)	Larkin	25.00	10.00	6.00
(85)	Lee	25.00	10.00	6.00
(86)	Long	25.00	10.00	6.00
(87)	Mails	25.00	10.00	6.00
(88)	Mains	25.00	10.00	6.00
(89)	Maisel	25.00	10.00	6.00
(90)	Mathes	25.00	10.00	6.00
(91)	McCredie	25.00	10.00	6.00
(92)	McGaffigan	25.00	10.00	6.00
(93)	McHenry	25.00	10.00	6.00
(94)	McNulty	25.00	10.00	6.00
(95)	Meusel	25.00	12.50	7.50
(96)	Middleton	25.00	10.00	6.00
(97)	Mitchell	25.00	10.00	6.00
(98)	Mitze	25.00	10.00	6.00
(99)	Mulory	25.00	10.00	6.00
(100)	Murphy	25.00	10.00	6.00
(101)	Murray	25.00	10.00	6.00
(102)	Niehoff (Los Angeles)	25.00	10.00	6.00
(103)	Niehoff (Seattle)	25.00	10.00	6.00
(104)	Norse	25.00	10.00	6.00
(105)	Oldham	25.00	10.00	6.00
(106)	Orr	25.00	10.00	6.00
(107)	Penner	25.00	10.00	6.00
(108)	Pennington	25.00	10.00	6.00
(109)	Piercy	25.00	10.00	6.00
(110)	Pinelli	25.00	12.50	7.50
(111)	C. Prough	25.00	10.00	6.00
(112)	Rader	25.00	10.00	6.00
(113)	Reiger	25.00	10.00	6.00
(114)	Ritchie	25.00	10.00	6.00
(115)	Roach	25.00	10.00	6.00
(116)	Rodgers	25.00	10.00	6.00
(117)	Rumler	25.00	10.00	6.00
(118)	Sands	25.00	10.00	6.00
(119)	Schick	25.00	10.00	6.00
(120)	Schultz	25.00	10.00	6.00
(121)	Scott	25.00	10.00	6.00
(122)	Seaton	25.00	10.00	6.00
(123)	Sheely	25.00	10.00	6.00
(124)	Siglin	25.00	10.00	6.00
(125)	Smith	25.00	10.00	6.00
(126)	Bill Smith	25.00	10.00	6.00
(127)	Snell	25.00	10.00	6.00
(128)	Spangler	25.00	10.00	6.00
(129)	Speas	25.00	10.00	6.00
(130)	Spencer	25.00	10.00	6.00
(131)	Starasenich	25.00	10.00	6.00
(132)	Stumpf	25.00	10.00	6.00
(133)	Sutherland	25.00	10.00	6.00
(134)	Dazzy Vance	200.00	100.00	60.00
(135)	Walker	25.00	10.00	6.00
(136)	Walsh	25.00	10.00	6.00
(137)	Ware	25.00	10.00	6.00
(138)	Weaver	25.00	10.00	6.00
(139)	Westerzil	25.00	10.00	6.00
(140)	Wilhoit	25.00	10.00	6.00
(141)	Wilie	25.00	10.00	6.00
(142)	Willets	25.00	10.00	6.00
(143)	Zamloch	25.00	10.00	6.00
(144)	Zweifel	25.00	10.00	6.00

1920 Zeenut Pacific Coast League

		NM	EX	VG
Complete Set (152):		2650.	1000.	600.00
Common Player:		22.00	9.00	6.00
(1)	Adams	22.00	9.00	6.00
(2)	Agnew	22.00	9.00	6.00
(3)	Alcock	22.00	9.00	6.00
(4)	Aldrige	22.00	9.00	6.00
(5)	Andrews	22.00	9.00	6.00
(6)	Anfinson	22.00	9.00	6.00
(7)	A. Arlett	22.00	9.00	6.00
(8)	R. Arlett	20.00	10.00	6.00
(9)	Baker	22.00	9.00	6.00
(10)	Baldwin	22.00	9.00	6.00
(11)	Bassler	22.00	9.00	6.00
(12)	Baum	22.00	9.00	6.00
(13)	Blue	22.00	9.00	6.00
(14)	Bohne	22.00	9.00	6.00
(15)	Brenton	22.00	9.00	6.00
(16)	Bromley (dark hat)	22.00	9.00	6.00
(17)	Bromley (light hat)	22.00	9.00	6.00
(18)	Brown	22.00	9.00	6.00
(19)	Butler	22.00	9.00	6.00
(20)	Caveney	22.00	9.00	6.00
(21)	Chadbourne	22.00	9.00	6.00
(22)	Compton	22.00	9.00	6.00
(23)	Connolly	22.00	9.00	6.00
(24)	Cook	22.00	9.00	6.00
(25)	Corhan	22.00	9.00	6.00
(26)	Cox	22.00	9.00	6.00
(27)	K. Crandall	22.00	9.00	6.00
(28)	O. Crandall	22.00	9.00	6.00
(29)	Crawford	22.00	9.00	6.00
(30)	Cullop	22.00	9.00	6.00
(31)	Cunningham	22.00	9.00	6.00
(32)	DeVitalis	22.00	9.00	6.00
(33)	DeVormer	22.00	9.00	6.00
(34)	Dooley	22.00	9.00	6.00
(35)	Dorman	22.00	9.00	6.00
(36)	Dumovich	22.00	9.00	6.00
(37)	Dylar	22.00	9.00	6.00
(38)	Edington	22.00	9.00	6.00
(39)	Eldred	22.00	9.00	6.00
(40)	Ellis	22.00	9.00	6.00
(41)	Essick	22.00	9.00	6.00
(42)	Fisher	22.00	9.00	6.00
(43)	Fitzgerald	22.00	9.00	6.00
(44)	Fromme	22.00	9.00	6.00
(45)	Gardner	22.00	9.00	6.00
(46)	Ginglardi	22.00	9.00	6.00
(47)	Gough	22.00	9.00	6.00
(48)	Griggs	22.00	9.00	6.00
(49)	Guisto	22.00	9.00	6.00
(50)	Hamilton	22.00	9.00	6.00
(51)	Hanicy	22.00	9.00	6.00
(52)	Hartford	22.00	9.00	6.00
(53)	High	22.00	9.00	6.00
(54)	Hill	22.00	9.00	6.00
(55)	Hodges	22.00	9.00	6.00
(56)	Howard	22.00	9.00	6.00
(57)	James	22.00	9.00	6.00
(58)	Jenkins	22.00	9.00	6.00
(59)	Johnson (Portland)	22.00	9.00	6.00
(60)	Johnson (Salt Lake)	22.00	9.00	6.00
(61)	Jones	22.00	9.00	6.00
(62)	Juney	22.00	9.00	6.00
(63)	Kallio	22.00	9.00	6.00
(64)	Kamm	22.00	9.00	6.00
(65)	Keating	22.00	9.00	6.00
(66)	Kenworthy	22.00	9.00	6.00
(67)	Killeen	22.00	9.00	6.00
(68)	Killefer	22.00	9.00	6.00
(69)	Kingdon	22.00	9.00	6.00
(70)	Knight	22.00	9.00	6.00
(71)	Koehler	22.00	9.00	6.00
(72)	Koerner	22.00	9.00	6.00
(73)	Kopp	22.00	9.00	6.00
(74)	Kremer	22.00	9.00	6.00
(75)	Krug	22.00	9.00	6.00
(76)	Kunz	22.00	9.00	6.00
(77)	Lambert	22.00	9.00	6.00
(78)	Lane	22.00	9.00	6.00
(79)	Larkin	22.00	9.00	6.00
(80)	Leverenz	22.00	9.00	6.00
(81)	Long	22.00	9.00	6.00
(82)	Love	22.00	9.00	6.00
(83)	Maggart	22.00	9.00	6.00
(84)	Mails	22.00	9.00	6.00
(85)	Maisel	22.00	9.00	6.00
(86)	Matterson	22.00	9.00	6.00
(87)	Matteson	22.00	9.00	6.00
(88)	McAuley	22.00	9.00	6.00
(89)	McCredie	22.00	9.00	6.00
(90)	McGaffigan	22.00	9.00	6.00
(91)	McHenry	22.00	9.00	6.00
(92)	McQuaid	22.00	9.00	6.00
(93)	Miller	22.00	9.00	6.00
(94)	Mitchell	22.00	9.00	6.00
(95)	J. Mitchell	22.00	9.00	6.00
(96)	Mitchell	22.00	9.00	6.00
(97)	Mitze	22.00	9.00	6.00
(98)	Moffitt	22.00	9.00	6.00
(99)	Mollwitz	22.00	9.00	6.00
(100)	Morse	22.00	9.00	6.00
(101)	Mulligan	22.00	9.00	6.00
(102)	Murphy	22.00	9.00	6.00
(103)	Niehoff	22.00	9.00	6.00
(104)	Nixon	22.00	9.00	6.00
(105)	O'Shaughnessy	22.00	9.00	6.00
(106)	Orr	22.00	9.00	6.00
(107)	Paull	22.00	9.00	6.00
(108)	Penner	22.00	9.00	6.00
(109)	Pertica	22.00	9.00	6.00
(110)	Peterson	22.00	9.00	6.00
(111)	Polson	22.00	9.00	6.00
(112)	Prough	22.00	9.00	6.00
(113)	Reagan	22.00	9.00	6.00
(114)	Reiger	22.00	9.00	6.00
(115)	Reilly	22.00	9.00	6.00
(116)	Rheinhart	22.00	9.00	6.00
(117)	Rodgers	22.00	9.00	6.00
(118)	Ross	22.00	9.00	6.00
(119)	Rumler	22.00	9.00	6.00
(120)	Russell	22.00	9.00	6.00
(121)	Sands	22.00	9.00	6.00
(122)	Schaller	22.00	9.00	6.00
(123)	Schang	22.00	9.00	6.00
(124)	Schellenback	22.00	9.00	6.00
(125)	Schick	22.00	9.00	6.00
(126)	Schorr	22.00	9.00	6.00
(127)	Schroeder	22.00	9.00	6.00
(128)	Scott	22.00	9.00	6.00
(129)	Seaton	22.00	9.00	6.00
(130)	Sheely	22.00	9.00	6.00
(131)	Siebold	22.00	9.00	6.00
(132)	Siglin	22.00	9.00	6.00
(133)	Smith	22.00	9.00	6.00
(134)	G. Smith	22.00	9.00	6.00
(135)	Spellman	22.00	9.00	6.00
(136)	Spranger	22.00	9.00	6.00
(137)	Stroud	22.00	9.00	6.00
(138)	Stumpf	22.00	9.00	6.00
(139)	Sullivan	22.00	9.00	6.00
(140)	Sutherland	22.00	9.00	6.00
(141)	Thurston (dark hat)	22.00	9.00	6.00
(142)	Thurston (light hat)	22.00	9.00	6.00
(143)	Walsh	22.00	9.00	6.00
(144)	Wares	22.00	9.00	6.00
(145)	Weaver	22.00	9.00	6.00
(146)	Willie	22.00	9.00	6.00
(147)	Winn	22.00	9.00	6.00
(148)	Wisterzill	22.00	9.00	6.00
(149)	Worth	22.00	9.00	6.00
(150)	Yelle	22.00	9.00	6.00
(151)	Zamlock	22.00	9.00	6.00
(152)	Zeider	22.00	9.00	6.00

1921 Zeenut Pacific Coast League

		NM	EX	VG
Complete Set (169):		3000.	1200.	700.00
Common Player:		22.00	9.00	6.00
(1)	Adams	22.00	9.00	6.00
(2)	Alcock	22.00	9.00	6.00
(3)	Aldridge	22.00	9.00	6.00
(4)	Alton	22.00	9.00	6.00
(5)	Anfinson	22.00	9.00	6.00
(6)	Arlett	22.00	11.00	6.50
(7)	Baker	22.00	9.00	6.00
(8)	Baldwin	22.00	9.00	6.00
(9)	Bates	22.00	9.00	6.00
(10)	Berry	22.00	9.00	6.00
(11)	Blacholder	22.00	9.00	6.00
(12)	Blossom	22.00	9.00	6.00
(13)	Bourg	22.00	9.00	6.00
(14)	Brinley	22.00	9.00	6.00
(15)	Bromley	22.00	9.00	6.00
(16)	Brown	22.00	9.00	6.00
(17)	Brubaker	22.00	9.00	6.00
(18)	Butler	22.00	9.00	6.00
(19)	Byler	22.00	9.00	6.00
(20)	Carroll	22.00	9.00	6.00
(21)	Casey	22.00	9.00	6.00
(22)	Cather	22.00	9.00	6.00
(23)	Caveney	22.00	9.00	6.00
(24)	Chadbourne	22.00	9.00	6.00
(25)	Compton	22.00	9.00	6.00
(26)	Connel	22.00	9.00	6.00
(27)	Cook	22.00	9.00	6.00
(28)	Cooper	22.00	9.00	6.00
(29)	Couch	22.00	9.00	6.00
(30)	Cox	22.00	9.00	6.00
(31)	Crandall	22.00	9.00	6.00
(32)	Cravath	22.00	9.00	6.00
(33)	Crawford	90.00	35.00	20.00
(34)	Crumpler	22.00	9.00	6.00
(35)	Cunningham	22.00	9.00	6.00
(36)	Daley	22.00	9.00	6.00
(37)	Dell	22.00	9.00	6.00
(38)	Demaree	22.00	9.00	6.00
(39)	Douglas	22.00	9.00	6.00
(40)	Dumovich	22.00	9.00	6.00
(41)	Elliott	22.00	9.00	6.00
(42)	Ellis	22.00	9.00	6.00
(43)	Ellison	22.00	9.00	6.00
(44)	Essick	22.00	9.00	6.00
(45)	Faeth	22.00	9.00	6.00
(46)	Fisher	22.00	9.00	6.00
(47)	Fittery	22.00	9.00	6.00
(48)	Fitzgerald	22.00	9.00	6.00
(49)	Flaherty	22.00	9.00	6.00
(50)	Francis	22.00	9.00	6.00
(51)	French	22.00	9.00	6.00
(52)	Fromme	22.00	9.00	6.00
(53)	Gardner	22.00	9.00	6.00
(54)	Geary	22.00	9.00	6.00
(55)	Gennin	22.00	9.00	6.00
(56)	Gorman	22.00	9.00	6.00
(57)	Gould	22.00	9.00	6.00
(58)	Griggs	22.00	9.00	6.00
(59)	Hale	22.00	9.00	6.00
(60)	Hannah	22.00	9.00	6.00
(61)	Hansen	22.00	9.00	6.00
(62)	Hesse	22.00	9.00	6.00
(63)	High	22.00	9.00	6.00
(64)	Hughes	22.00	9.00	6.00
(65)	Hyatt	22.00	9.00	6.00
(66)	Jackson	22.00	9.00	6.00
(67)	Jacobs	22.00	9.00	6.00
(68)	Jacobs	22.00	9.00	6.00
(69)	Jenkins	22.00	9.00	6.00
(70)	Johnson	22.00	9.00	6.00
(71)	Jones	22.00	9.00	6.00
(72)	Jourden	22.00	9.00	6.00
(73)	Kallio	22.00	9.00	6.00
(74)	Kamm	22.00	9.00	6.00

(75)	Kearns	22.00	9.00	6.00
(76)	Kelly	22.00	9.00	6.00
(77)	Kersten	22.00	9.00	6.00
(78)	Kifer	22.00	9.00	6.00
(79)	Killefer	22.00	9.00	6.00
(80)	King	22.00	9.00	6.00
(81)	Kingdon	22.00	9.00	6.00
(82)	Knight	22.00	9.00	6.00
(83)	Koehler	22.00	9.00	6.00
(84)	Kopp	22.00	9.00	6.00
(85)	Krause	22.00	9.00	6.00
(86)	Kremer	22.00	9.00	6.00
(87)	Krug	22.00	9.00	6.00
(88)	Kunz	22.00	9.00	6.00
(89)	Lane	22.00	9.00	6.00
(90)	Leverenz	22.00	9.00	6.00
(91)	Lewis	22.00	9.00	6.00
(92)	Lindimore	22.00	9.00	6.00
(93)	Love	22.00	9.00	6.00
(94)	Ludolph	22.00	9.00	6.00
(95)	Lynn	22.00	9.00	6.00
(96)	Lyons	22.00	9.00	6.00
(97)	McAuley	22.00	9.00	6.00
(98)	McCredie	22.00	9.00	6.00
(99)	McGaffigan	22.00	9.00	6.00
(100)	McGraw	22.00	9.00	6.00
(101)	McQuaid	22.00	9.00	6.00
(102)	Merritt	22.00	9.00	6.00
(103)	Middleton	22.00	9.00	6.00
(104)	Miller	22.00	9.00	6.00
(105)	Mitchell	22.00	9.00	6.00
(106)	Mitze	22.00	9.00	6.00
(107)	Mollwitz	22.00	9.00	6.00
(108)	Morse	22.00	9.00	6.00
(109)	Murphy (Seattle)	22.00	9.00	6.00
(110)	Murphy (Vernon)	22.00	9.00	6.00
(111)	Mustain	22.00	9.00	6.00
(112)	Nickels	22.00	9.00	6.00
(113)	Niehaus	22.00	9.00	6.00
(114)	Niehoff	22.00	9.00	6.00
(115)	Nofziger	22.00	9.00	6.00
(116)	O'Connell	22.00	9.00	6.00
(117)	O'Doul	40.00	16.00	10.00
(118)	O'Malia	22.00	9.00	6.00
(119)	Oldring	22.00	9.00	6.00
(120)	Oliver	22.00	9.00	6.00
(121)	Orr	22.00	9.00	6.00
(122)	Paton	22.00	9.00	6.00
(123)	Penner	22.00	9.00	6.00
(124)	Pick	22.00	9.00	6.00
(125)	Pillette	22.00	9.00	6.00
(126)	Pinelli	22.00	9.00	6.00
(127)	Polson	22.00	9.00	6.00
(128)	Poole	22.00	9.00	6.00
(129)	Prough	22.00	9.00	6.00
(130)	Rath	22.00	9.00	6.00
(131)	Read	22.00	9.00	6.00
(132)	Reinhardt	22.00	9.00	6.00
(133)	Rieger	22.00	9.00	6.00
(134)	Rogers	22.00	9.00	6.00
(135)	Rose (Sacramento)	22.00	9.00	6.00
(136)	Rose (Salt Lake)	22.00	9.00	6.00
(137)	Ross (Portland)	22.00	9.00	6.00
(138)	Ross (Sacramento)	22.00	9.00	6.00
(139)	Ryan	22.00	9.00	6.00
(140)	Sand	22.00	9.00	6.00
(141)	Schick	22.00	9.00	6.00
(142)	Schneider	22.00	9.00	6.00
(143)	Scott	22.00	9.00	6.00
(144)	Shang	22.00	9.00	6.00
(145)	Sheehan	22.00	9.00	6.00
(146)	Shore	22.00	9.00	6.00
(147)	Shorr	22.00	9.00	6.00
(148)	Shultis	22.00	9.00	6.00
(149)	Siebold	22.00	9.00	6.00
(150)	Siglin	22.00	9.00	6.00
(151)	Smallwood	22.00	9.00	6.00
(152)	Smith	22.00	9.00	6.00
(153)	Spencer	22.00	9.00	6.00
(154)	Stanage	22.00	9.00	6.00
(155)	Statz	22.00	9.00	6.00
(156)	Stumph	22.00	9.00	6.00
(157)	Thomas	22.00	9.00	6.00
(158)	Thurston	22.00	9.00	6.00
(159)	Tyrrell	22.00	9.00	6.00
(160)	Van Osdoll	22.00	9.00	6.00
(161)	Walsh	22.00	9.00	6.00
(162)	White	22.00	9.00	6.00
(163)	Wilhoit	22.00	9.00	6.00
(164)	Wilie	22.00	9.00	6.00
(165)	Winn	22.00	9.00	6.00
(166)	Wolfer	22.00	9.00	6.00
(167)	Yelle	22.00	9.00	6.00
(168)	Young	22.00	9.00	6.00
(169)	Zeider	22.00	9.00	6.00

1922 Zeenut Pacific Coast League

The 1922 Zeenuts are dated on the front, measure 1-7/8" x 3-1/8" and feature black-and-white photos with sepia highlights. There are 162 subjects, and four of them (Koehler, Williams, Gregg and Schneider) have been found with variations in color tones.

		NM	EX	VG
Complete Set (162):		4800.	1900.	1150.
Common Player:		22.00	9.00	6.00
(1)	J. Adams	22.00	9.00	6.00
(2)	S. Adams	22.00	9.00	6.00
(3)	Agnew	22.00	9.00	6.00
(4)	Anfinson	22.00	9.00	6.00
(5)	Arlett	22.00	11.00	6.50
(6)	Baldwin	22.00	9.00	6.00
(7)	Barney	22.00	9.00	6.00
(8)	Bell	22.00	9.00	6.00
(9)	Blaeholder	22.00	9.00	6.00
(10)	Bodie	22.00	9.00	6.00
(11)	Brenton	22.00	9.00	6.00
(12)	Bromley	22.00	9.00	6.00
(13)	Brovold	22.00	9.00	6.00
(14)	Brown	22.00	9.00	6.00
(15)	Brubaker	22.00	9.00	6.00
(16)	Burger	22.00	9.00	6.00
(17)	Byler	22.00	9.00	6.00
(18)	Canfield	22.00	9.00	6.00
(19)	Carroll	22.00	9.00	6.00
(20)	Cartwright	22.00	9.00	6.00
(21)	Chadbourne	22.00	9.00	6.00
(22)	Compton	22.00	9.00	6.00
(23)	Connolly	22.00	9.00	6.00
(24)	Cook	22.00	9.00	6.00
(25)	Cooper	22.00	9.00	6.00
(26)	Coumbe	22.00	9.00	6.00
(27)	Cox	22.00	9.00	6.00
(28)	Crandall	22.00	9.00	6.00
(29)	Crumpler	22.00	9.00	6.00
(30)	Cueto	60.00	24.00	15.00
(31)	Dailey	22.00	9.00	6.00
(32)	Daly	22.00	9.00	6.00
(33)	Deal	22.00	9.00	6.00
(34)	Dell	22.00	9.00	6.00
(35)	Doyle	22.00	9.00	6.00
(36)	Dumovich	22.00	9.00	6.00
(37)	Eldred	22.00	9.00	6.00
(38)	Eller	22.00	9.00	6.00
(39)	Elliott	22.00	9.00	6.00
(40)	Ellison	22.00	9.00	6.00
(41)	Essick	22.00	9.00	6.00
(42)	Finneran	22.00	9.00	6.00
(43)	Fittery	22.00	9.00	6.00
(44)	Fitzgerald	22.00	9.00	6.00
(45)	Freeman	22.00	9.00	6.00
(46)	French	22.00	9.00	6.00
(47)	Gardner	22.00	9.00	6.00
(48)	Geary	22.00	9.00	6.00
(49)	Gibson	22.00	9.00	6.00
(50)	Gilder	22.00	9.00	6.00
(51)	Gould	22.00	9.00	6.00
(52)	Gregg	22.00	9.00	6.00
(53)	Gressett	22.00	9.00	6.00
(54)	Griggs	22.00	9.00	6.00
(55)	Hampton	22.00	9.00	6.00
(56)	Hannah	22.00	9.00	6.00
(57)	Hawks	22.00	9.00	6.00
(58)	Henke	22.00	9.00	6.00
(59)	High (Portland)	22.00	9.00	6.00
(60)	High (Vernon)	22.00	9.00	6.00
(61)	Houck	22.00	9.00	6.00
(62)	Howard	22.00	9.00	6.00
(63)	Hughes	22.00	9.00	6.00
(64)	Hyatt	22.00	9.00	6.00
(65)	Jacobs	22.00	9.00	6.00
(66)	James	22.00	9.00	6.00
(67)	Jenkins	22.00	9.00	6.00
(68)	Jones	22.00	9.00	6.00
(69)	Kallio	22.00	9.00	6.00
(70)	Kamm	22.00	9.00	6.00
(71)	Keiser	22.00	9.00	6.00
(72)	Kelly	22.00	9.00	6.00
(73)	Kenworthy	22.00	9.00	6.00
(74)	Kilduff	22.00	9.00	6.00
(75)	Killefer	22.00	9.00	6.00
(76)	Killhullen	22.00	9.00	6.00
(77)	King	22.00	9.00	6.00
(78)	Knight	22.00	9.00	6.00
(79)	Koehler	22.00	9.00	6.00
(80)	Kremer	22.00	9.00	6.00
(81)	Kunz	22.00	9.00	6.00
(82)	Lafayette	22.00	9.00	6.00
(83)	Lane	22.00	9.00	6.00
(84)	Tony Lazzeri	200.00	100.00	60.00
(85)	Lefevre	22.00	9.00	6.00
(86)	D. Lewis	22.00	9.00	6.00
(87)	S. Lewis	22.00	9.00	6.00
(88)	Lindimore	22.00	9.00	6.00
(89)	Locker	22.00	9.00	6.00
(90)	Lyons	22.00	9.00	6.00
(91)	Mack	22.00	9.00	6.00
(92)	Marriott	22.00	9.00	6.00
(93)	May	22.00	9.00	6.00
(94)	McAuley	22.00	9.00	6.00
(95)	McCabe	22.00	9.00	6.00
(96)	McCann	22.00	9.00	6.00
(97)	McCredie	22.00	9.00	6.00
(98)	McNeely	22.00	9.00	6.00
(99)	McQuaid	22.00	9.00	6.00
(100)	Miller	22.00	9.00	6.00
(101)	Mitchell	22.00	9.00	6.00
(102)	Mitze	22.00	9.00	6.00
(103)	Mollwitz	22.00	9.00	6.00
(104)	Monahan	22.00	9.00	6.00
(105)	Murphy (Seattle)	22.00	9.00	6.00
(106)	Murphy (Vernon)	22.00	9.00	6.00
(107)	Niehaus	22.00	9.00	6.00
(108)	O'Connell	22.00	9.00	6.00
(109)	Orr	22.00	9.00	6.00
(110)	Owen	22.00	9.00	6.00
(111)	Pearce	22.00	9.00	6.00
(112)	Pick	22.00	9.00	6.00
(113)	Ponder	22.00	9.00	6.00
(114)	Poole	22.00	9.00	6.00
(115)	Prough	22.00	9.00	6.00
(116)	Read	22.00	9.00	6.00
(117)	Richardson	22.00	9.00	6.00
(118)	Rieger	22.00	9.00	6.00
(119)	Ritchie	22.00	9.00	6.00
(120)	Ross	22.00	9.00	6.00
(121)	Ryan	22.00	9.00	6.00
(122)	Sand	22.00	9.00	6.00
(123)	Sargent	22.00	9.00	6.00
(124)	Sawyer	22.00	9.00	6.00
(125)	Schang	22.00	9.00	6.00
(126)	Schick	22.00	9.00	6.00
(127)	Schneider	22.00	9.00	6.00
(128)	Schorr	22.00	9.00	6.00
(129)	Schulte (Oakland)	22.00	9.00	6.00
(130)	Schulte (Seattle)	22.00	9.00	6.00
(131)	Scott	22.00	9.00	6.00
(132)	See	22.00	9.00	6.00
(133)	Shea	22.00	9.00	6.00
(134)	Sheehan	22.00	9.00	6.00
(135)	Siglin	22.00	9.00	6.00
(136)	Smith	22.00	9.00	6.00
(137)	Soria	22.00	9.00	6.00
(138)	Spencer	22.00	9.00	6.00
(139)	Stanage	22.00	9.00	6.00
(140)	Strand	22.00	9.00	6.00
(141)	Stumpf	22.00	9.00	6.00
(142)	Sullivan	22.00	9.00	6.00
(143)	Sutherland	22.00	9.00	6.00
(144)	Thomas	22.00	9.00	6.00
(145)	Jim Thorpe	2500.	1000.	600.00
(146)	Thurston	22.00	9.00	6.00
(147)	Tobin	22.00	9.00	6.00
(148)	Turner	22.00	9.00	6.00
(149)	Twombly	22.00	9.00	6.00
(150)	Valla	22.00	9.00	6.00
(151)	Vargas	22.00	9.00	6.00
(152)	Viveros	22.00	9.00	6.00
(153)	Wallace	22.00	9.00	6.00
(154)	Walsh	22.00	9.00	6.00
(155)	Wells	22.00	9.00	6.00
(156)	Westersil	22.00	9.00	6.00
(157)	Wheat	22.00	9.00	6.00
(158)	Wilhoit	22.00	9.00	6.00
(159)	Wilie	22.00	9.00	6.00
(160)	Williams	22.00	9.00	6.00
(161)	Yelle	22.00	9.00	6.00
(162)	Zeider	22.00	9.00	6.00

1923 Zeenut Pacific Coast League

This is the only year that Zeenuts cards were issued in two different sizes. Cards in the "regular" series measure 1-7/8" x 3", feature black-and-white photos and are dated 1923. A second series, containing just 24 cards (all San Francisco and Oakland players), were actually re-issues of the 1922 series with a "1923" date.

		NM	EX	VG
Complete Set (196):		3500.	1400.	825.00
Common Player:		22.00	9.00	6.00
(1)	Agnew (1923 photo)	22.00	9.00	6.00
(2)	Agnew (1922 photo re-dated)	20.00	10.00	6.00
(3)	Alten	22.00	9.00	6.00
(4)	Anderson	22.00	9.00	6.00
(5)	Anfinson	22.00	9.00	6.00
(6)	Arlett	22.00	11.00	6.50
(7)	Baker	22.00	9.00	6.00
(8)	Baldwin	22.00	9.00	6.00
(9)	Barney	22.00	9.00	6.00
(10)	Blake	22.00	9.00	6.00
(11)	Bodie	22.00	9.00	6.00
(12)	Brazil	22.00	9.00	6.00
(13)	Brenton	22.00	9.00	6.00
(14)	Brown (Oakland)	22.00	9.00	6.00
(15)	Brown (Sacramento)	22.00	9.00	6.00
(16)	Brubaker	22.00	9.00	6.00
(17)	Buckley	22.00	9.00	6.00
(18)	Canfield	22.00	9.00	6.00
(19)	Carroll	22.00	9.00	6.00
(20)	Cather	22.00	9.00	6.00
(21)	Chadbourne	22.00	9.00	6.00
(22)	Charvez	22.00	9.00	6.00
(23)	Cochrane	22.00	9.00	6.00
(24)	Colwell	22.00	9.00	6.00

(25)	Compton	22.00	9.00	6.00
(26)	Cook	22.00	9.00	6.00
(27)	Cooper (1923 photo)	22.00	9.00	6.00
(28)	Cooper (1922 photo re-date)	20.00	10.00	6.00
(29)	Coumbe	22.00	9.00	6.00
(30)	Courtney	22.00	9.00	6.00
(31)	Crandall	22.00	9.00	6.00
(32)	Crane	22.00	9.00	6.00
(33)	Crowder	22.00	9.00	6.00
(34)	Crumpler	22.00	9.00	6.00
(35)	Daly (Los Angeles)	22.00	9.00	6.00
(36)	Daly (Portland)	22.00	9.00	6.00
(37)	Deal	22.00	9.00	6.00
(38)	Doyle	22.00	9.00	6.00
(39)	Duchalsky	22.00	9.00	6.00
(40)	Eckert	22.00	9.00	6.00
(41)	Eldred	22.00	9.00	6.00
(42)	Eley	22.00	9.00	6.00
(43)	Eller	22.00	9.00	6.00
(44)	Ellison (1923 photo)	22.00	9.00	6.00
(45)	Ellison (1922 photo re-dated)	20.00	10.00	6.00
(46)	Essick	22.00	9.00	6.00
(47)	Fittery	22.00	9.00	6.00
(48)	Flashkamper	22.00	9.00	6.00
(49)	Frederick	22.00	9.00	6.00
(50)	French	22.00	9.00	6.00
(51)	Geary (1923 photo)	22.00	9.00	6.00
(52)	Geary (1922 photo re-dated)	20.00	10.00	6.00
(53)	Gilder	22.00	9.00	6.00
(54)	Golvin	22.00	9.00	6.00
(55)	Gorman	22.00	9.00	6.00
(56)	Gould	22.00	9.00	6.00
(57)	Gressett	22.00	9.00	6.00
(58)	Griggs	22.00	9.00	6.00
(59)	Hannah (Los Angeles)	22.00	9.00	6.00
(60)	Hannah (Vernon)	22.00	9.00	6.00
(61)	Hemingway	22.00	9.00	6.00
(62)	Hendryx	22.00	9.00	6.00
(63)	High	22.00	9.00	6.00
(64)	H. High	22.00	9.00	6.00
(65)	Hodge	22.00	9.00	6.00
(66)	Hood	22.00	9.00	6.00
(67)	Houghs	22.00	9.00	6.00
(68)	Howard (1923 photo)	22.00	9.00	6.00
(69)	Howard (1922 photo re-date)	20.00	10.00	6.00
(70)	Del Howard	22.00	9.00	6.00
(71)	Jacobs	22.00	9.00	6.00
(72)	James	22.00	9.00	6.00
(73)	Johnson	22.00	9.00	6.00
(74)	Johnston	22.00	9.00	6.00
(75)	Jolly (Jolley)	22.00	9.00	6.00
(76)	Jones (Los Angeles)	22.00	9.00	6.00
(77)	Jones (Oakland)	22.00	9.00	6.00
(78)	Jones (Portland)	22.00	9.00	6.00
(79)	Kallio	22.00	9.00	6.00
(80)	Kearns	22.00	9.00	6.00
(81)	Keiser	22.00	9.00	6.00
(82)	Keller	22.00	9.00	6.00
(83)	Kelly (San Francisco)	22.00	9.00	6.00
(84)	Kelly (Seattle)	22.00	9.00	6.00
(85)	Kenna	22.00	9.00	6.00
(86)	Kilduff	22.00	9.00	6.00
(87)	Killifer	22.00	9.00	6.00
(88)	King	22.00	9.00	6.00
(89)	Knight (1923 photo)	22.00	9.00	6.00
(90)	Knight (1922 photo re-dated)	20.00	10.00	6.00
(91)	Koehler	22.00	9.00	6.00
(92)	Kopp	22.00	9.00	6.00
(93)	Krause	22.00	9.00	6.00
(94)	Kremer	22.00	9.00	6.00
(95)	Krug	22.00	9.00	6.00
(96)	Lafayette (1923 photo)	22.00	9.00	6.00
(97)	Lafayette (1922 photo re-dated)	20.00	10.00	6.00
(98)	Lane	22.00	9.00	6.00
(99)	Lefevre	22.00	9.00	6.00
(100)	Leslie	22.00	9.00	6.00
(101)	Levere	22.00	9.00	6.00
(102)	Leverenz	22.00	9.00	6.00
(103)	Lewis	22.00	9.00	6.00
(104)	Lindimore	22.00	9.00	6.00
(105)	Locker	22.00	9.00	6.00
(106)	Lyons	22.00	9.00	6.00
(107)	Maderas	22.00	9.00	6.00
(108)	Mails	22.00	9.00	6.00
(109)	Marriott	22.00	9.00	6.00
(110)	Matzen	22.00	9.00	6.00
(111)	McAuley	22.00	9.00	6.00
(112)	McAuliffe	22.00	9.00	6.00
(113)	McCabe (Los Angeles)	22.00	9.00	6.00
(114)	McCabe (Salt Lake)	22.00	9.00	6.00
(115)	McCann	22.00	9.00	6.00
(116)	McGaffigan	22.00	9.00	6.00
(117)	McGinnis	22.00	9.00	6.00
(118)	McNeilly	22.00	9.00	6.00
(119)	McWeeney	22.00	9.00	6.00
(120)	Middleton	22.00	9.00	6.00
(121)	Miller	22.00	9.00	6.00
(122)	Mitchell (1923 photo)	22.00	9.00	6.00
(123)	Mitchell (1922 photo re-date)	20.00	10.00	6.00
(124)	Mitze	22.00	9.00	6.00
(125)	Mulligan	22.00	9.00	6.00
(126)	Murchio	22.00	9.00	6.00
(127)	D. Murphy	22.00	9.00	6.00
(128)	R. Murphy	22.00	9.00	6.00
(129)	Noack	22.00	9.00	6.00
(130)	O'Brien	22.00	9.00	6.00
(131)	Onslow	22.00	9.00	6.00
(132)	Orr	22.00	9.00	6.00
(133)	Pearce	22.00	9.00	6.00
(134)	Penner	22.00	9.00	6.00
(135)	Peters	22.00	9.00	6.00
(136)	Pick	22.00	9.00	6.00
(137)	Pigg	22.00	9.00	6.00
(138)	Plummer	22.00	9.00	6.00
(139)	Ponder	22.00	9.00	6.00
(140)	Poole	22.00	9.00	6.00
(141)	Ramage	22.00	9.00	6.00
(142)	Read (1923 photo)	22.00	9.00	6.00
(143)	Read (1922 photo re-dated)	20.00	10.00	6.00
(144)	Rhyne	22.00	9.00	6.00
(145)	Ritchie	22.00	9.00	6.00
(146)	Robertson	22.00	9.00	6.00
(147)	Rohwer (Sacramento)	22.00	9.00	6.00
(148)	Rohwer (Seattle)	22.00	9.00	6.00
(149)	Ryan	22.00	9.00	6.00
(150)	Sawyer	22.00	9.00	6.00
(151)	Schang	22.00	9.00	6.00
(152)	Schneider	22.00	9.00	6.00
(153)	Schroeder	22.00	9.00	6.00
(154)	Scott	22.00	9.00	6.00
(155)	See	22.00	9.00	6.00
(156)	Shea	22.00	9.00	6.00
(157)	M. Shea	22.00	9.00	6.00
(158)	Spec Shea	22.00	9.00	6.00
(159)	Sheehan	22.00	9.00	6.00
(160)	Shellenback	22.00	9.00	6.00
(161)	Siglin	22.00	9.00	6.00
(162)	Singleton	22.00	9.00	6.00
(163)	Smith	22.00	9.00	6.00
(164)	M.H. Smith	22.00	9.00	6.00
(165)	Stanton	22.00	9.00	6.00
(166)	Strand	22.00	9.00	6.00
(167)	Stumpf	22.00	9.00	6.00
(168)	Sutherland	22.00	9.00	6.00
(169)	Tesar	22.00	9.00	6.00
(170)	Thomas (Los Angeles)	22.00	9.00	6.00
(171)	Thomas (Oakland)	22.00	9.00	6.00
(172)	Tobin	22.00	9.00	6.00
(173)	Twombly	22.00	9.00	6.00
(174)	Valla	22.00	9.00	6.00
(175)	Vargas	22.00	9.00	6.00
(176)	Vitt	22.00	9.00	6.00
(177)	Wallace	22.00	9.00	6.00
(178)	Walsh (San Francisco)	22.00	9.00	6.00
(179)	Walsh (Seattle)	22.00	9.00	6.00
(180)	Paul Waner	150.00	60.00	35.00
(181)	Wells (Oakland)	22.00	9.00	6.00
(182)	Wells (San Francisco)	22.00	9.00	6.00
(183)	Welsh	22.00	9.00	6.00
(184)	Wilhoit	22.00	9.00	6.00
(185)	Wilie (1923 photo)	22.00	9.00	6.00
(186)	Wilie (1922 photo re-dated)	20.00	10.00	6.00
(187)	Williams	22.00	9.00	6.00
(188)	Witzel	22.00	9.00	6.00
(189)	Wolfer	22.00	9.00	6.00
(190)	Wolverton	22.00	9.00	6.00
(191)	Yarrison	22.00	9.00	6.00
(192)	Yaryan	22.00	9.00	6.00
(193)	Yelle (1923 photo)	22.00	9.00	6.00
(194)	Yelle (1922 photo re-dated)	20.00	10.00	6.00
(195)	Moses Yellowhorse	75.00	37.00	22.00
(196)	Zeider	22.00	9.00	6.00

1924 Zeenut Pacific Coast League

Zeenut cards in 1924 and 1925 measure 1-3/4" x 2-7/8" and display the date on the front. The cards include a full photographic background. There are 144 subjects known in the 1924 series and 162 known for 1925.

		NM	EX	VG
Complete Set (144):		2500.	1000.	600.00
Common Player:		20.00	8.00	5.00
(1)	Adams	20.00	8.00	5.00
(2)	Agnew	20.00	8.00	5.00
(3)	Arlett	18.00	9.00	5.50
(4)	Baker	20.00	8.00	5.00
(5)	E. Baldwin	20.00	8.00	5.00
(6)	T. Baldwin	20.00	8.00	5.00
(7)	Beck	20.00	8.00	5.00
(8)	Benton	20.00	8.00	5.00
(9)	Bernard	20.00	8.00	5.00
(10)	Bigbee	20.00	8.00	5.00
(11)	Billings	20.00	8.00	5.00
(12)	Blakesly	20.00	8.00	5.00
(13)	Brady	20.00	8.00	5.00
(14)	Brazil	20.00	8.00	5.00
(15)	Brown	20.00	8.00	5.00
(16)	Brubaker	20.00	8.00	5.00
(17)	Buckley	20.00	8.00	5.00
(18)	Burger	20.00	8.00	5.00
(19)	Byler	20.00	8.00	5.00
(20)	Cadore	20.00	8.00	5.00
(21)	Cather	20.00	8.00	5.00
(22)	Chadbourne	20.00	8.00	5.00
(23)	Christian	20.00	8.00	5.00
(24)	Mickey Cochrane (Portland)	250.00	125.00	75.00
(25)	Cochrane (Sacramento)	20.00	8.00	5.00
(26)	Cooper	20.00	8.00	5.00
(27)	Coumbe	20.00	8.00	5.00
(28)	Cox	20.00	8.00	5.00
(29)	Crandall	20.00	8.00	5.00
(30)	Daly	20.00	8.00	5.00
(31)	Deal	20.00	8.00	5.00
(32)	Distel	20.00	8.00	5.00
(33)	Durst	20.00	8.00	5.00
(34)	Eckert	20.00	8.00	5.00
(35)	Eldred	20.00	8.00	5.00
(36)	Ellison	20.00	8.00	5.00
(37)	Essick	20.00	8.00	5.00
(38)	Flashkamper	20.00	8.00	5.00
(39)	Foster	20.00	8.00	5.00
(40)	Fredericks	20.00	8.00	5.00
(41)	Geary	20.00	8.00	5.00
(42)	Goebel	20.00	8.00	5.00
(43)	Golvin	20.00	8.00	5.00
(44)	Gorman	20.00	8.00	5.00
(45)	Gould	20.00	8.00	5.00
(46)	Gressett	20.00	8.00	5.00
(47)	Griffin (San Francisco)	20.00	8.00	5.00
(48)	Griffin (Vernon)	20.00	8.00	5.00
(49)	Guisto	20.00	8.00	5.00
(50)	Gunther	20.00	8.00	5.00
(51)	Hall	20.00	8.00	5.00
(52)	Hannah	20.00	8.00	5.00
(53)	Hendryx	20.00	8.00	5.00
(54)	High	20.00	8.00	5.00
(55)	Hodge	20.00	8.00	5.00
(56)	Hood	20.00	8.00	5.00
(57)	Ivan Howard	20.00	8.00	5.00
(58)	Hughes (Los Angeles)	20.00	8.00	5.00
(59)	Hughes (Sacramento)	20.00	8.00	5.00
(60)	Jacobs	20.00	8.00	5.00
(61)	James	20.00	8.00	5.00
(62)	Jenkins	20.00	8.00	5.00
(63)	Johnson	20.00	8.00	5.00
(64)	Jones	20.00	8.00	5.00
(65)	Keck	20.00	8.00	5.00
(66)	Kelley	20.00	8.00	5.00
(67)	Kenworthy	20.00	8.00	5.00
(68)	Kilduff	20.00	8.00	5.00
(69)	Killifer	20.00	8.00	5.00
(70)	Kimmick	20.00	8.00	5.00
(71)	Kopp	20.00	8.00	5.00
(72)	Krause	20.00	8.00	5.00
(73)	Krug	20.00	8.00	5.00
(74)	Kunz	20.00	8.00	5.00
(75)	Lafayette	20.00	8.00	5.00
(76)	Lennon	20.00	8.00	5.00
(77)	Leptich	20.00	8.00	5.00
(78)	Leslie	20.00	8.00	5.00
(79)	Leverenz	20.00	8.00	5.00
(80)	Lewis	20.00	8.00	5.00
(81)	Maderas	20.00	8.00	5.00
(82)	Mails	20.00	8.00	5.00
(83)	McAuley	20.00	8.00	5.00
(84)	McCann	20.00	8.00	5.00
(85)	McDowell	20.00	8.00	5.00
(86)	McNeely	20.00	8.00	5.00
(87)	Menosky	20.00	8.00	5.00
(88)	Meyers	20.00	8.00	5.00
(89)	Miller	20.00	8.00	5.00
(90)	Mitchell	20.00	8.00	5.00
(91)	Mulligan	20.00	8.00	5.00
(92)	D. Murphy	20.00	8.00	5.00
(93)	R. Murphy	20.00	8.00	5.00
(94)	Osborne	20.00	8.00	5.00
(95)	Paynter	20.00	8.00	5.00
(96)	Penner	20.00	8.00	5.00
(97)	Peters (Sacramento)	20.00	8.00	5.00
(98)	Peters (Salt Lake)	20.00	8.00	5.00
(99)	Pick	20.00	8.00	5.00
(100)	Pillette	20.00	8.00	5.00
(101)	Poole	20.00	8.00	5.00
(102)	Prough	20.00	8.00	5.00
(103)	Querry	20.00	8.00	5.00
(104)	Read	20.00	8.00	5.00
(105)	Rhyne	20.00	8.00	5.00
(106)	Ritchie	20.00	8.00	5.00
(107)	Root	18.00	9.00	5.50
(108)	Rowher	20.00	8.00	5.00
(109)	Schang	20.00	8.00	5.00
(110)	Schneider	20.00	8.00	5.00
(111)	Schorr	20.00	8.00	5.00
(112)	Schroeder	20.00	8.00	5.00
(113)	Scott	20.00	8.00	5.00
(114)	Sellers	20.00	8.00	5.00
(115)	"Speck" Shay	20.00	8.00	5.00
(116)	Shea (Sacramento)	20.00	8.00	5.00
(117)	Shea (San Francisco)	20.00	8.00	5.00
(118)	Shellenback	20.00	8.00	5.00
(119)	Siebold	20.00	8.00	5.00
(120)	Siglin	20.00	8.00	5.00
(121)	Slade	20.00	8.00	5.00
(122)	Smith (Sacramento)	20.00	8.00	5.00
(123)	Smith (San Francisco)	20.00	8.00	5.00
(124)	Stanton	20.00	8.00	5.00
(125)	Tanner	20.00	8.00	5.00
(126)	Twomley	20.00	8.00	5.00
(127)	Valla	20.00	8.00	5.00
(128)	Vargas	20.00	8.00	5.00
(129)	Vines	20.00	8.00	5.00
(130)	Vitt	20.00	8.00	5.00
(131)	Wallace	20.00	8.00	5.00
(132)	Walsh	20.00	8.00	5.00
(133)	Paul Waner	125.00	50.00	30.00
(134)	Warner (fielding)	20.00	8.00	5.00
(135)	Warner (throwing)	20.00	8.00	5.00
(136)	Welsh	20.00	8.00	5.00
(137)	Wetzel	20.00	8.00	5.00
(138)	Whalen	20.00	8.00	5.00
(139)	Wilhoit	20.00	8.00	5.00
(140)	Williams (San Francisco)	20.00	8.00	5.00
(141)	Williams (Seattle)	20.00	8.00	5.00
(142)	Wolfer	20.00	8.00	5.00
(143)	Yelle	20.00	8.00	5.00

(144)	Moses Yellowhorse	75.00	37.00	22.00

1925 Zeenut Pacific Coast League

		NM	EX	VG
Complete Set (164):		2600.	1050.	625.00
Common Player:		20.00	8.00	5.00
(1)	Adeylatte	20.00	8.00	5.00
(2)	Agnew	20.00	8.00	5.00
(3)	Arlett	18.00	9.00	5.50
(4)	Bagby	20.00	8.00	5.00
(5)	Bahr	20.00	8.00	5.00
(6)	Baker	20.00	8.00	5.00
(7)	E. Baldwin	20.00	8.00	5.00
(8)	Barfoot	20.00	8.00	5.00
(9)	Beck	20.00	8.00	5.00
(10)	Becker	20.00	8.00	5.00
(11)	Blakesley	20.00	8.00	5.00
(12)	Boehler	20.00	8.00	5.00
(13)	Brady	20.00	8.00	5.00
(14)	Brandt	20.00	8.00	5.00
(15)	Bratcher	20.00	8.00	5.00
(16)	Brazil	20.00	8.00	5.00
(17)	Brower	20.00	8.00	5.00
(18)	Brown	20.00	8.00	5.00
(19)	Brubaker	20.00	8.00	5.00
(20)	Bryan	20.00	8.00	5.00
(21)	Canfield	20.00	8.00	5.00
(22)	W. Canfield	20.00	8.00	5.00
(23)	Cather	20.00	8.00	5.00
(24)	Chavez	20.00	8.00	5.00
(25)	Christain	20.00	8.00	5.00
(26)	Cochrane	20.00	8.00	5.00
(27)	Connolly	20.00	8.00	5.00
(28)	Cook	20.00	8.00	5.00
(29)	Cooper	20.00	8.00	5.00
(30)	Coumbe	20.00	8.00	5.00
(31)	Crandall	20.00	8.00	5.00
(32)	Crane	20.00	8.00	5.00
(33)	Crockett	20.00	8.00	5.00
(34)	Crosby	20.00	8.00	5.00
(35)	Cutshaw	20.00	8.00	5.00
(36)	Daly	20.00	8.00	5.00
(37)	Davis	20.00	8.00	5.00
(38)	Deal	20.00	8.00	5.00
(39)	Delaney	20.00	8.00	5.00
(40)	Dempsey	20.00	8.00	5.00
(41)	Dumovich	20.00	8.00	5.00
(42)	Eckert	20.00	8.00	5.00
(43)	Eldred	20.00	8.00	5.00
(44)	Elliott	20.00	8.00	5.00
(45)	Ellison	20.00	8.00	5.00
(46)	Emmer	20.00	8.00	5.00
(47)	Ennis	20.00	8.00	5.00
(48)	Essick	20.00	8.00	5.00
(49)	Finn	20.00	8.00	5.00
(50)	Flowers	20.00	8.00	5.00
(51)	Frederick	20.00	8.00	5.00
(52)	Fussell	20.00	8.00	5.00
(53)	Geary	20.00	8.00	5.00
(54)	Gorman	20.00	8.00	5.00
(55)	Griffin (San Francisco)	20.00	8.00	5.00
(56)	Griffin (Vernon)	20.00	8.00	5.00
(57)	Grimes	20.00	8.00	5.00
(58)	Guisto	20.00	8.00	5.00
(59)	Hannah	20.00	8.00	5.00
(60)	Haughy	20.00	8.00	5.00
(61)	Hemingway	20.00	8.00	5.00
(62)	Hendryx	20.00	8.00	5.00
(63)	Herman	25.00	10.00	6.00
(64)	High	20.00	8.00	5.00
(65)	Hoffman	20.00	8.00	5.00
(66)	Hood	20.00	8.00	5.00
(67)	Horan	20.00	8.00	5.00
(68)	Horton	20.00	8.00	5.00
(69)	Howard	20.00	8.00	5.00
(70)	Hughes	20.00	8.00	5.00
(71)	Hulvey	20.00	8.00	5.00
(72)	Hunnefield	20.00	8.00	5.00
(73)	Jacobs	20.00	8.00	5.00
(74)	James	20.00	8.00	5.00
(75)	Keating	20.00	8.00	5.00
(76)	Keefe	20.00	8.00	5.00
(77)	Kelly	20.00	8.00	5.00
(78)	Kilduff	20.00	8.00	5.00
(79)	Kohler	20.00	8.00	5.00
(80)	Kopp	20.00	8.00	5.00
(81)	Krause	20.00	8.00	5.00
(82)	Krug	20.00	8.00	5.00
(83)	Kunz	20.00	8.00	5.00
(84)	Lafayette	20.00	8.00	5.00
(85)	Tony Lazzeri	200.00	100.00	60.00
(86)	Leslie	20.00	8.00	5.00
(87)	Leverenz	20.00	8.00	5.00
(88)	Duffy Lewis	20.00	8.00	5.00
(89)	Lindemore	20.00	8.00	5.00
(90)	Ludolph	20.00	8.00	5.00
(91)	Makin	20.00	8.00	5.00
(92)	Martin (Sacramento)	20.00	8.00	5.00
(93)	Martin (Portland)	20.00	8.00	5.00
(94)	McCabe	20.00	8.00	5.00
(95)	McCann	20.00	8.00	5.00
(96)	McCarren	20.00	8.00	5.00
(97)	McDonald	20.00	8.00	5.00
(98)	McGinnis (Portland)	20.00	8.00	5.00
(99)	McGinnis (Sacramento)	20.00	8.00	5.00
(100)	McLaughlin	20.00	8.00	5.00
(101)	Milstead	20.00	8.00	5.00
(102)	Mitchell	20.00	8.00	5.00
(103)	Moudy	20.00	8.00	5.00
(104)	Mulcahy	20.00	8.00	5.00
(105)	Mulligan	20.00	8.00	5.00
(106)	Lefty O'Doul	75.00	37.00	22.00
(107)	O'Neil	20.00	8.00	5.00
(108)	Ortman	20.00	8.00	5.00
(109)	Pailey	20.00	8.00	5.00
(110)	Paynter	20.00	8.00	5.00
(111)	Peery	20.00	8.00	5.00
(112)	Penner	20.00	8.00	5.00
(113)	Pfeffer	20.00	8.00	5.00
(114)	Phillips	20.00	8.00	5.00
(115)	Pickering	20.00	8.00	5.00
(116)	Piercy	20.00	8.00	5.00
(117)	Pillette	20.00	8.00	5.00
(118)	Plummer	20.00	8.00	5.00
(119)	Ponder	20.00	8.00	5.00
(120)	Pruett	20.00	8.00	5.00
(121)	Rawlings	20.00	8.00	5.00
(122)	Read	20.00	8.00	5.00
(123)	Jimmy Reese	60.00	30.00	18.00
(124)	Rhyne	20.00	8.00	5.00
(125)	Riconda	20.00	8.00	5.00
(126)	Ritchie	20.00	8.00	5.00
(127)	Rohwer	20.00	8.00	5.00
(128)	Rowland	20.00	8.00	5.00
(129)	Ryan	20.00	8.00	5.00
(130)	Sandberg	20.00	8.00	5.00
(131)	Schang	20.00	8.00	5.00
(132)	Shea	20.00	8.00	5.00
(133)	M. Shea	20.00	8.00	5.00
(134)	Shellenbach	20.00	8.00	5.00
(135)	Sherling	20.00	8.00	5.00
(136)	Siglin	20.00	8.00	5.00
(137)	Slade	20.00	8.00	5.00
(138)	Spencer	20.00	8.00	5.00
(139)	Steward	20.00	8.00	5.00
(140)	Stivers	20.00	8.00	5.00
(141)	Suhr	20.00	8.00	5.00
(142)	Sutherland	20.00	8.00	5.00
(143)	Thomas (Portland)	20.00	8.00	5.00
(144)	Thomas (Vernon)	20.00	8.00	5.00
(145)	Thompson	20.00	8.00	5.00
(146)	Tobin	20.00	8.00	5.00
(147)	Twombly	20.00	8.00	5.00
(148)	Valla	20.00	8.00	5.00
(149)	Vinci	20.00	8.00	5.00
(150)	O. Vitt	20.00	8.00	5.00
(151)	Wachenfeld	20.00	8.00	5.00
(152)	Paul Waner	100.00	40.00	24.00
(153)	Lloyd Waner	125.00	50.00	30.00
(154)	Warner	20.00	8.00	5.00
(155)	Watson	20.00	8.00	5.00
(156)	Weinert	20.00	8.00	5.00
(157)	Whaley	20.00	8.00	5.00
(158)	Whitney	20.00	8.00	5.00
(159)	Williams	20.00	8.00	5.00
(160)	Winters	20.00	8.00	5.00
(161)	Wolfer	20.00	8.00	5.00
(162)	Woodring	20.00	8.00	5.00
(163)	Yeargin	20.00	8.00	5.00
(164)	Yelle	20.00	8.00	5.00

1926 Zeenut Pacific Coast League

Except for their slightly smaller size (1-3/4" x 2-3/4"), the 1926 Zeenut cards are nearly identical to the previous two years. Considered more difficult than other Zeenuts series of this era, the 1926 set consists of more than 170 known subjects.

		NM	EX	VG
Complete Set (172):		4100.	1650.	1000.
Common Player:		24.00	9.00	6.00
(1)	Agnew	24.00	9.00	6.00
(2)	Allen	24.00	9.00	6.00
(3)	Alley	24.00	9.00	6.00
(4)	Averill	100.00	40.00	24.00
(5)	Bagwell	24.00	9.00	6.00
(6)	Baker	24.00	9.00	6.00
(7)	T. Baldwin	24.00	9.00	6.00
(8)	Berry	24.00	9.00	6.00
(9)	Bool	24.00	9.00	6.00
(10)	Boone	24.00	9.00	6.00
(11)	Boyd	24.00	9.00	6.00
(12)	Brady	24.00	9.00	6.00
(13)	Brazil	24.00	9.00	6.00
(14)	Brower	24.00	9.00	6.00
(15)	Brubaker	24.00	9.00	6.00
(16)	Bryan	24.00	9.00	6.00
(17)	Burns	24.00	9.00	6.00
(18)	C. Canfield	24.00	9.00	6.00
(19)	W. Canfield	24.00	9.00	6.00
(20)	Carson	24.00	9.00	6.00
(21)	Christian	24.00	9.00	6.00
(22)	Cole	24.00	9.00	6.00
(23)	Connolly	24.00	9.00	6.00
(24)	Cook	24.00	9.00	6.00
(25)	Couch	24.00	9.00	6.00
(26)	Coumbe	24.00	9.00	6.00
(27)	Crockett	24.00	9.00	6.00
(28)	Cunningham	24.00	9.00	6.00
(29)	Cutshaw	24.00	9.00	6.00
(30)	Daglia	24.00	9.00	6.00
(31)	Danning	24.00	9.00	6.00
(32)	Davis	24.00	9.00	6.00
(33)	Delaney	24.00	9.00	6.00
(34)	Eckert	24.00	9.00	6.00
(35)	Eldred	24.00	9.00	6.00
(36)	Elliott	24.00	9.00	6.00
(37)	Ellison	24.00	9.00	6.00
(38)	Ellsworth	24.00	9.00	6.00
(39)	Elsh	24.00	9.00	6.00
(40)	Fenton	24.00	9.00	6.00
(41)	Finn	24.00	9.00	6.00
(42)	Flashkamper	24.00	9.00	6.00
(43)	Fowler	24.00	9.00	6.00
(44)	Frederick	24.00	9.00	6.00
(45)	Freeman	24.00	9.00	6.00
(46)	French	24.00	9.00	6.00
(47)	Garrison	24.00	9.00	6.00
(48)	Geary	24.00	9.00	6.00
(49)	Gillespie	24.00	9.00	6.00
(50)	Glazner	24.00	9.00	6.00
(51)	Gould	24.00	9.00	6.00
(52)	Governor	24.00	9.00	6.00
(53)	Griffin (Missions)	24.00	9.00	6.00
(54)	Griffin (San Francisco)	24.00	9.00	6.00
(55)	Guisto	24.00	9.00	6.00
(56)	Hamilton	24.00	9.00	6.00
(57)	Hannah	24.00	9.00	6.00
(58)	Hansen	24.00	9.00	6.00
(59)	Hasty	24.00	9.00	6.00
(60)	Hemingway	24.00	9.00	6.00
(61)	Hendryx	24.00	9.00	6.00
(62)	Hickok	24.00	9.00	6.00
(63)	Hillis	24.00	9.00	6.00
(64)	Hoffman	24.00	9.00	6.00
(65)	Hollerson	24.00	9.00	6.00
(66)	Holmes	24.00	9.00	6.00
(67)	Hood	24.00	9.00	6.00
(68)	Howard	24.00	9.00	6.00
(69)	Hufft	24.00	9.00	6.00
(70)	Hughes	24.00	9.00	6.00
(71)	Hulvey	24.00	9.00	6.00
(72)	Hurst	24.00	9.00	6.00
(73)	R. Jacobs	24.00	9.00	6.00
(74)	Jahn	24.00	9.00	6.00
(75)	Jenkins	24.00	9.00	6.00
(76)	Johnson	24.00	9.00	6.00
(77)	Jolly (Jolley)	24.00	9.00	6.00
(78)	Jones	24.00	9.00	6.00
(79)	Kallio	24.00	9.00	6.00
(80)	Keating	24.00	9.00	6.00
(81)	Kerr (Hollywood)	24.00	9.00	6.00
(82)	Kerr (San Francisco)	24.00	9.00	6.00
(83)	Kilduff	24.00	9.00	6.00
(84)	Killifer	24.00	9.00	6.00
(85)	Knight	24.00	9.00	6.00
(86)	Koehler	24.00	9.00	6.00
(87)	Kopp	24.00	9.00	6.00
(88)	Krause	24.00	9.00	6.00
(89)	Krug	24.00	9.00	6.00
(90)	Kunz	24.00	9.00	6.00
(91)	Lafayette	24.00	9.00	6.00
(92)	Lane	24.00	9.00	6.00
(93)	Lang	24.00	9.00	6.00
(94)	Lary	24.00	9.00	6.00
(95)	Leslie	24.00	9.00	6.00
(96)	Lindemore	24.00	9.00	6.00
(97)	Ludolph	24.00	9.00	6.00
(98)	Makin	24.00	9.00	6.00
(99)	Mangum	24.00	9.00	6.00
(100)	Martin	24.00	9.00	6.00
(101)	McCredie	24.00	9.00	6.00
(102)	McDowell	24.00	9.00	6.00
(103)	McKenry	24.00	9.00	6.00
(104)	McLoughlin	24.00	9.00	6.00
(105)	McNally	24.00	9.00	6.00
(106)	McPhee	24.00	9.00	6.00
(107)	Meeker	24.00	9.00	6.00
(108)	Metz	24.00	9.00	6.00
(109)	Miller	24.00	9.00	6.00
(110)	Mitchell (Los Angeles)	24.00	9.00	6.00
(111)	Mitchell (San Francisco)	24.00	9.00	6.00
(112)	Monroe	24.00	9.00	6.00
(113)	Moudy	24.00	9.00	6.00
(114)	Mulcahy	24.00	9.00	6.00
(115)	Mulligan	24.00	9.00	6.00
(116)	Murphy	24.00	9.00	6.00
(117)	Lefty O'Doul	80.00	40.00	24.00
(118)	O'Neill	24.00	9.00	6.00
(119)	Oeschger	24.00	9.00	6.00

(120)	Oliver	24.00	9.00	6.00
(121)	Ortman	24.00	9.00	6.00
(122)	Osborn	24.00	9.00	6.00
(123)	Paynter	24.00	9.00	6.00
(124)	Peters	24.00	9.00	6.00
(125)	Pfahler	24.00	9.00	6.00
(126)	Pillette	24.00	9.00	6.00
(127)	Plummer	24.00	9.00	6.00
(128)	Prothro	24.00	9.00	6.00
(129)	Pruett	24.00	9.00	6.00
(130)	Rachac	24.00	9.00	6.00
(131)	Ramsey	24.00	9.00	6.00
(132)	Rathjen	24.00	9.00	6.00
(133)	Read	24.00	9.00	6.00
(134)	Redman	24.00	9.00	6.00
(135)	Jimmy Reese	24.00	12.00	7.25
(136)	Rodda	24.00	9.00	6.00
(137)	Rohwer	24.00	9.00	6.00
(138)	Ryan	24.00	9.00	6.00
(139)	Sandberg	24.00	9.00	6.00
(140)	Sanders	24.00	9.00	6.00
(141)	E. Shea	24.00	9.00	6.00
(142)	M. Shea	24.00	9.00	6.00
(143)	Sheehan	24.00	9.00	6.00
(144)	Shellenbach	24.00	9.00	6.00
(145)	Sherlock	24.00	9.00	6.00
(146)	Siglin	24.00	9.00	6.00
(147)	Slade	24.00	9.00	6.00
(148)	E. Smith	24.00	9.00	6.00
(149)	M. Smith	24.00	9.00	6.00
(150)	Staley	24.00	9.00	6.00
(151)	Statz	24.00	9.00	6.00
(152)	Stroud	24.00	9.00	6.00
(153)	Stuart	24.00	9.00	6.00
(154)	Suhr	24.00	9.00	6.00
(155)	Swanson	24.00	9.00	6.00
(156)	Sweeney	24.00	9.00	6.00
(157)	Tadevich	24.00	9.00	6.00
(158)	Thomas	24.00	9.00	6.00
(159)	Thompson	24.00	9.00	6.00
(160)	Tobin	24.00	9.00	6.00
(161)	Valla	24.00	9.00	6.00
(162)	Vargas	24.00	9.00	6.00
(163)	Vinci	24.00	9.00	6.00
(164)	Walters	24.00	9.00	6.00
(165)	Waner	80.00	35.00	20.00
(166)	Weis	24.00	9.00	6.00
(167)	Whitney	24.00	9.00	6.00
(168)	Williams	24.00	9.00	6.00
(169)	Wright	24.00	9.00	6.00
(170)	Yelle	24.00	9.00	6.00
(171)	Zaeffel	24.00	9.00	6.00
(172)	Zoellers	24.00	9.00	6.00

1927 Zeenut Pacific Coast League

The 1927 Zeenuts are the same size and color as the 1926 issue, except the year is expressed in just two digits (27), a practice that continued through 1930. There are 144 subjects known.

		NM	EX	VG
Complete Set (144):		2000.	1000.	600.00
Common Player:		20.00	8.00	5.00
(1)	Agnew	20.00	8.00	5.00
(2)	Arlett	25.00	10.00	6.00
(3)	Averill	80.00	35.00	20.00
(4)	Backer	20.00	8.00	5.00
(5)	Bagwell	20.00	8.00	5.00
(6)	Baker	20.00	8.00	5.00
(7)	D. Baker	20.00	8.00	5.00
(8)	Ballenger	20.00	8.00	5.00
(9)	Baumgartner	20.00	8.00	5.00
(10)	Bigbee	20.00	8.00	5.00
(11)	Boehler	20.00	8.00	5.00
(12)	Bool	20.00	8.00	5.00
(13)	[illegible]	20.00	8.00	5.00
(14)	Brady	20.00	8.00	5.00
(15)	Bratcher	20.00	8.00	5.00
(16)	Brett	20.00	8.00	5.00
(17)	Brown	20.00	8.00	5.00
(18)	Brubaker	20.00	8.00	5.00
(19)	Bryan	20.00	8.00	5.00
(20)	Callaghan	20.00	8.00	5.00
(21)	Caveney	20.00	8.00	5.00
(22)	Christian	20.00	8.00	5.00
(23)	Cissell	20.00	8.00	5.00
(24)	Cook	20.00	8.00	5.00
(25)	Cooper (Oakland)	20.00	8.00	5.00
(26)	Cooper (Sacramento)	20.00	8.00	5.00
(27)	Cox	20.00	8.00	5.00
(28)	Cunningham	20.00	8.00	5.00
(29)	Daglia	20.00	8.00	5.00
(30)	Dickerman	20.00	8.00	5.00
(31)	Dumovitch	20.00	8.00	5.00
(32)	Eckert	20.00	8.00	5.00
(33)	Eldred	20.00	8.00	5.00
(34)	Ellison	20.00	8.00	5.00
(35)	Fenton	20.00	8.00	5.00
(36)	Finn	20.00	8.00	5.00
(37)	Fischer	20.00	8.00	5.00
(38)	Frederick	20.00	8.00	5.00
(39)	French	20.00	8.00	5.00
(40)	Fullerton	20.00	8.00	5.00
(41)	Geary	20.00	8.00	5.00
(42)	Gillespie	20.00	8.00	5.00
(43)	Gooch	20.00	8.00	5.00
(44)	Gould	20.00	8.00	5.00
(45)	Governor	20.00	8.00	5.00
(46)	Guisto	20.00	8.00	5.00
(47)	Hannah	20.00	8.00	5.00
(48)	Hasty	20.00	8.00	5.00
(49)	Hemingway	20.00	8.00	5.00
(50)	Hoffman	20.00	8.00	5.00
(51)	Hood	20.00	8.00	5.00
(52)	Hooper	80.00	35.00	20.00
(53)	Hudgens	20.00	8.00	5.00
(54)	Hufft	20.00	8.00	5.00
(55)	Hughes	20.00	8.00	5.00
(56)	Jahn	20.00	8.00	5.00
(57)	Johnson (Portland)	20.00	8.00	5.00
(58)	Johnson (Seals)	20.00	8.00	5.00
(59)	Jolly (Jolley)	20.00	8.00	5.00
(60)	Jones	20.00	8.00	5.00
(61)	Kallio	20.00	8.00	5.00
(62)	Keating	20.00	8.00	5.00
(63)	Keefe	20.00	8.00	5.00
(64)	Killifer	20.00	8.00	5.00
(65)	Kimmick	20.00	8.00	5.00
(66)	Kinney	20.00	8.00	5.00
(67)	Knight	20.00	8.00	5.00
(68)	Koehler	20.00	8.00	5.00
(69)	Kopp	20.00	8.00	5.00
(70)	Krause	20.00	8.00	5.00
(71)	Krug	20.00	8.00	5.00
(72)	Kunz	20.00	8.00	5.00
(73)	Lary	20.00	8.00	5.00
(74)	Leard	20.00	8.00	5.00
(75)	Lingrel	20.00	8.00	5.00
(76)	Ludolph	20.00	8.00	5.00
(77)	Mails	20.00	8.00	5.00
(78)	Makin	20.00	8.00	5.00
(79)	Martin	20.00	8.00	5.00
(80)	May	20.00	8.00	5.00
(81)	McCabe	20.00	8.00	5.00
(82)	McCurdy	20.00	8.00	5.00
(83)	McDaniel	20.00	8.00	5.00
(84)	McGee	20.00	8.00	5.00
(85)	McLaughlin	20.00	8.00	5.00
(86)	McMurtry	20.00	8.00	5.00
(87)	Metz	20.00	8.00	5.00
(88)	Miljus	20.00	8.00	5.00
(89)	Mitchell	20.00	8.00	5.00
(90)	Monroe	20.00	8.00	5.00
(91)	Moudy	20.00	8.00	5.00
(92)	Mulligan	20.00	8.00	5.00
(93)	Murphy	20.00	8.00	5.00
(94)	O'Brien	20.00	8.00	5.00
(95)	Lefty O'Doul	80.00	40.00	24.00
(96)	Oliver	20.00	8.00	5.00
(97)	Osborn	20.00	8.00	5.00
(98)	Parker (Missions, batting)	20.00	8.00	5.00
(99)	Parker (Missions, throwing)	20.00	8.00	5.00
(100)	Parker (Portland)	20.00	8.00	5.00
(101)	Peters	20.00	8.00	5.00
(102)	Pillette	20.00	8.00	5.00
(103)	Ponder	20.00	8.00	5.00
(104)	Prothro	20.00	8.00	5.00
(105)	Rachac	20.00	8.00	5.00
(106)	Ramsey	20.00	8.00	5.00
(107)	Read	20.00	8.00	5.00
(108)	Jimmy Reese	60.00	30.00	18.00
(109)	Rodda	20.00	8.00	5.00
(110)	Rohwer	20.00	8.00	5.00
(111)	Rose	20.00	8.00	5.00
(112)	Ryan	20.00	8.00	5.00
(113)	Sandberg	20.00	8.00	5.00
(114)	Sanders	20.00	8.00	5.00
(115)	Severeid	20.00	8.00	5.00
(116)	Shea	20.00	8.00	5.00
(117)	Sheehan (Hollywood)	20.00	8.00	5.00
(118)	Sheehan (Seals)	20.00	8.00	5.00
(119)	Sherlock	20.00	8.00	5.00
(120a)	Shinners (date is "1927")	25.00	10.00	6.00
(120b)	Shinners (date is "27")	20.00	8.00	5.00
(121)	Singleton	20.00	8.00	5.00
(122)	Slade	20.00	8.00	5.00
(123)	E. Smith	20.00	8.00	5.00
(124)	Sparks	20.00	8.00	5.00
(125)	Stokes	20.00	8.00	5.00
(126)	J. Storti	20.00	8.00	5.00
(127)	L. Storti	20.00	8.00	5.00
(128)	Strand	20.00	8.00	5.00
(129)	Suhr	20.00	8.00	5.00
(130)	Sunseri	20.00	8.00	5.00
(131)	Swanson	20.00	8.00	5.00
(132)	Tierney	20.00	8.00	5.00
(133)	Valla	20.00	8.00	5.00
(134)	Vargas	20.00	8.00	5.00
(135)	Vitt	20.00	8.00	5.00
(136)	Weinert	20.00	8.00	5.00
(137)	Weis	20.00	8.00	5.00
(138)	Wendell	20.00	8.00	5.00
(139)	Whitney	20.00	8.00	5.00
(140)	Williams	20.00	8.00	5.00
(141)	Guy Williams	20.00	8.00	5.00
(142)	Woodson	20.00	8.00	5.00
(143)	Wright	20.00	8.00	5.00
(144)	Yelle	20.00	8.00	5.00

1928 Zeenut Pacific Coast League

Zeenut cards from 1928 through 1930 maintain the same size and style as the 1927 series. The 1928 and 1929 series consist of 168 known subjects, while the 1930 series has 186. There are some lettering variations in the 1930 series.

		NM	EX	VG
Complete Set (168):		2200.	1100.	650.00
Common Player:		20.00	8.00	5.00
(1)	Agnew	20.00	8.00	5.00
(2)	Earl Averill	80.00	35.00	20.00
(3)	Backer	20.00	8.00	5.00
(4)	Baker	20.00	8.00	5.00
(5)	Baldwin	20.00	8.00	5.00
(6)	Barfoot	20.00	8.00	5.00
(7)	Bassler	20.00	8.00	5.00
(8)	Berger	20.00	8.00	5.00
(9)	Bigbee (Los Angeles)	20.00	8.00	5.00
(10)	Bigbee (Portland)	20.00	8.00	5.00
(11)	Bodie	20.00	8.00	5.00
(12)	Boehler	20.00	8.00	5.00
(13)	Bool	20.00	8.00	5.00
(14)	Boone	20.00	8.00	5.00
(15)	Borreani	20.00	8.00	5.00
(16)	Bratcher	20.00	8.00	5.00
(17)	Brenzel	20.00	8.00	5.00
(18)	Brubaker	20.00	8.00	5.00
(19)	Bryan	20.00	8.00	5.00
(20)	Burkett	20.00	8.00	5.00
(21)	Camilli	20.00	8.00	5.00
(22)	W. Canfield	20.00	8.00	5.00
(23)	Caveney	20.00	8.00	5.00
(24)	Cohen	20.00	8.00	5.00
(25)	Cook	20.00	8.00	5.00
(26)	Cooper	20.00	8.00	5.00
(27)	Craghead	20.00	8.00	5.00
(28)	Crosetti	30.00	12.00	8.00
(29)	Cunningham	20.00	8.00	5.00
(30)	Daglia	20.00	8.00	5.00
(31)	Davis	20.00	8.00	5.00
(32)	Dean	20.00	8.00	5.00
(33)	Dittmar	20.00	8.00	5.00
(34)	Donovan	20.00	8.00	5.00
(35)	Downs	20.00	8.00	5.00
(36)	Duff	20.00	8.00	5.00
(37)	Eckert	20.00	8.00	5.00
(38)	Eldred	20.00	8.00	5.00
(39)	Ellsworth	20.00	8.00	5.00
(40)	Fenton	20.00	8.00	5.00
(41)	Finn	20.00	8.00	5.00
(42)	Fitterer	20.00	8.00	5.00
(43)	Flynn	20.00	8.00	5.00
(44)	Frazier	20.00	8.00	5.00
(45)	French (Portland)	20.00	8.00	5.00
(46)	French (Sacramento)	20.00	8.00	5.00
(47)	Fullerton	20.00	8.00	5.00
(48)	Gabler	20.00	8.00	5.00
(49)	Gomes	20.00	8.00	5.00
(50)	Gooch	20.00	8.00	5.00
(51)	Gould	20.00	8.00	5.00
(52)	Governor	20.00	8.00	5.00
(53)	Graham ("S" on uniform)	20.00	8.00	5.00
(54)	Graham (no "S" on uniform)	20.00	8.00	5.00
(55)	Guisto	20.00	8.00	5.00
(56)	Hannah	20.00	8.00	5.00
(57)	Hansen	20.00	8.00	5.00
(58)	Harris	20.00	8.00	5.00
(59)	Hasty	20.00	8.00	5.00
(60)	Heath	20.00	8.00	5.00
(61)	Hoffman	20.00	8.00	5.00
(62)	Holling	20.00	8.00	5.00
(63)	Hood	20.00	8.00	5.00
(64)	House	20.00	8.00	5.00
(65)	Howard	20.00	8.00	5.00
(66)	Hudgens	20.00	8.00	5.00
(67)	Hufft	20.00	8.00	5.00
(68)	Hughes	20.00	8.00	5.00
(69)	Hulvey	20.00	8.00	5.00
(70)	Jacobs	20.00	8.00	5.00
(71)	Johnson (Portland)	20.00	8.00	5.00
(72)	Johnson (San Francisco)	20.00	8.00	5.00
(73)	Jolley	20.00	8.00	5.00
(74)	Jones (batting)	20.00	8.00	5.00
(75)	Jones (throwing)	20.00	8.00	5.00
(76)	Kallio	20.00	8.00	5.00
(77)	Keating	20.00	8.00	5.00
(78)	Keefe	20.00	8.00	5.00
(79)	Keesey	20.00	8.00	5.00
(80)	Kerr	20.00	8.00	5.00
(81)	Killifer	20.00	8.00	5.00

(82)	Kinney	20.00	8.00	5.00
(83)	Knight	20.00	8.00	5.00
(84)	Knothe	20.00	8.00	5.00
(85)	Koehler	20.00	8.00	5.00
(86)	Kopp	20.00	8.00	5.00
(87)	Krause	20.00	8.00	5.00
(88)	Krug	20.00	8.00	5.00
(89)	Lary	20.00	8.00	5.00
(90)	LeBourveau	20.00	8.00	5.00
(91)	Lee	20.00	8.00	5.00
(92)	Ernie Lombardi	100.00	40.00	24.00
(93)	Mails	20.00	8.00	5.00
(94)	Martin (Missions)	20.00	8.00	5.00
(95)	Martin (Seattle)	20.00	8.00	5.00
(96)	May	20.00	8.00	5.00
(97)	McCabe	20.00	8.00	5.00
(98)	McCrea	20.00	8.00	5.00
(99)	McDaniel	20.00	8.00	5.00
(100)	McLaughlin	20.00	8.00	5.00
(101)	McNulty	20.00	8.00	5.00
(102)	Mellano	20.00	8.00	5.00
(103)	Muesel (Meusel)	20.00	10.00	6.00
(104)	Middleton	20.00	8.00	5.00
(105)	Mishkin	20.00	8.00	5.00
(106)	Mitchell	20.00	8.00	5.00
(107)	Monroe	20.00	8.00	5.00
(108)	Moudy	20.00	8.00	5.00
(109)	Mulcahy	20.00	8.00	5.00
(110)	Muller	20.00	8.00	5.00
(111)	Mulligan	20.00	8.00	5.00
(112)	W. Murphy	20.00	8.00	5.00
(113)	Nance	20.00	8.00	5.00
(114)	Nelson	20.00	8.00	5.00
(115)	Osborn	20.00	8.00	5.00
(116)	Osborne	20.00	8.00	5.00
(117)	Parker	20.00	8.00	5.00
(118)	Peters	20.00	8.00	5.00
(119)	Pillette	20.00	8.00	5.00
(120)	Pinelli	20.00	8.00	5.00
(121)	Plitt	20.00	8.00	5.00
(122)	Ponder	20.00	8.00	5.00
(123)	Rachac	20.00	8.00	5.00
(124)	Read	20.00	8.00	5.00
(125)	Reed	20.00	8.00	5.00
(126)	Jimmy Reese	25.00	10.00	6.00
(127)	Rego	20.00	8.00	5.00
(128)	Rhodes	20.00	8.00	5.00
(129)	Rhyne	20.00	8.00	5.00
(130)	Rodda	20.00	8.00	5.00
(131)	Rohwer	20.00	8.00	5.00
(132)	Rose	20.00	8.00	5.00
(133)	Roth	20.00	8.00	5.00
(134)	Ruble	20.00	8.00	5.00
(135)	Ryan	20.00	8.00	5.00
(136)	Sandberg	20.00	8.00	5.00
(137)	Schulmerich	20.00	8.00	5.00
(138)	Severeid	20.00	8.00	5.00
(139)	Shea	20.00	8.00	5.00
(140)	Sheely	20.00	8.00	5.00
(141)	Shellenback	20.00	8.00	5.00
(142)	Sherlock	20.00	8.00	5.00
(143)	Sigafoos	20.00	8.00	5.00
(144)	Singleton	20.00	8.00	5.00
(145)	Slade	20.00	8.00	5.00
(146)	Smith	20.00	8.00	5.00
(147)	Sprinz	20.00	8.00	5.00
(148)	Staley	20.00	8.00	5.00
(149)	Suhr	20.00	8.00	5.00
(150)	Sunseri	20.00	8.00	5.00
(151)	Swanson	20.00	8.00	5.00
(152)	Sweeney	20.00	8.00	5.00
(153)	Teachout	20.00	8.00	5.00
(154)	Twombly	20.00	8.00	5.00
(155)	Vargas	20.00	8.00	5.00
(156)	Vinci	20.00	8.00	5.00
(157)	Vitt	20.00	8.00	5.00
(158)	Warhop	20.00	8.00	5.00
(159)	Weathersby	20.00	8.00	5.00
(160)	Weiss	20.00	8.00	5.00
(161)	Welch	20.00	8.00	5.00
(162)	Wera	20.00	8.00	5.00
(163)	Wetzel	20.00	8.00	5.00
(164)	Whitney	20.00	8.00	5.00
(165)	Williams	20.00	8.00	5.00
(166)	Wilson	20.00	8.00	5.00
(167)	Wolfer	20.00	8.00	5.00
(168)	Yerkes	20.00	8.00	5.00

1929 Zeenut Pacific Coast League

		NM	EX	VG
Complete Set (168):		2700.	1100.	650.00
Common Player:		20.00	8.00	5.00
(1)	Albert	20.00	8.00	5.00
(2)	Almada	20.00	8.00	5.00
(3)	Anderson	20.00	8.00	5.00
(4)	Anton	20.00	8.00	5.00
(5)	Backer	20.00	8.00	5.00
(6)	Baker	20.00	8.00	5.00
(7)	Baldwin	20.00	8.00	5.00
(8)	Barbee	20.00	8.00	5.00
(9)	Barfoot	20.00	8.00	5.00
(10)	Bassler	20.00	8.00	5.00
(11)	Bates	20.00	8.00	5.00
(12)	Berger	20.00	8.00	5.00
(13)	Boehler	20.00	8.00	5.00
(14)	Boone	20.00	8.00	5.00
(15)	Borreani	20.00	8.00	5.00
(16)	Brenzel	20.00	8.00	5.00
(17)	Brooks	20.00	8.00	5.00
(18)	Brubaker	20.00	8.00	5.00
(19)	Bryan	20.00	8.00	5.00
(20)	Burke	20.00	8.00	5.00
(21)	Burkett	20.00	8.00	5.00
(22)	Burns	20.00	8.00	5.00
(23)	Bush	20.00	8.00	5.00
(24)	Butler	20.00	8.00	5.00
(25)	Camilli	18.00	9.00	5.50
(26)	Carlyle	20.00	8.00	5.00
(27)	Carlyle	20.00	8.00	5.00
(28)	Cascarella	20.00	8.00	5.00
(29)	Caveney	20.00	8.00	5.00
(30)	Childs	20.00	8.00	5.00
(31)	Christensen	20.00	8.00	5.00
(32)	Cole	20.00	8.00	5.00
(33)	Collard	20.00	8.00	5.00
(34)	Cooper	20.00	8.00	5.00
(35)	Couch	20.00	8.00	5.00
(36)	Cox	20.00	8.00	5.00
(37)	Craghead	20.00	8.00	5.00
(38)	Crandall	20.00	8.00	5.00
(39)	Cronin	20.00	8.00	5.00
(40)	Crosetti	25.00	10.00	6.00
(41)	Daglia	20.00	8.00	5.00
(42)	Davis	20.00	8.00	5.00
(43)	Dean	20.00	8.00	5.00
(44)	Dittmar	20.00	8.00	5.00
(45)	Donovan	20.00	8.00	5.00
(46)	Dumovich	20.00	8.00	5.00
(47)	Eckardt	20.00	8.00	5.00
(48)	Ellsworth	20.00	8.00	5.00
(49)	Fenton	20.00	8.00	5.00
(50)	Finn	20.00	8.00	5.00
(51)	Fisch	20.00	8.00	5.00
(52)	Flynn	20.00	8.00	5.00
(53)	Frazier	20.00	8.00	5.00
(54)	Freitas	20.00	8.00	5.00
(55)	French	20.00	8.00	5.00
(56)	Gabler	20.00	8.00	5.00
(57)	Glynn	20.00	8.00	5.00
(58)	Lefty Gomez	300.00	150.00	90.00
(59)	Gould	20.00	8.00	5.00
(60)	Governor	20.00	8.00	5.00
(61)	Graham	20.00	8.00	5.00
(62)	Hand	20.00	8.00	5.00
(63)	Hannah	20.00	8.00	5.00
(64)	Harris	20.00	8.00	5.00
(65)	Heath	20.00	8.00	5.00
(66)	Heatherly	20.00	8.00	5.00
(67)	Hepting	20.00	8.00	5.00
(68)	Hillis	20.00	8.00	5.00
(69)	Hoffman	20.00	8.00	5.00
(70)	Holling	20.00	8.00	5.00
(71)	Hood	20.00	8.00	5.00
(72)	House	20.00	8.00	5.00
(73)	Howard	20.00	8.00	5.00
(74)	Hubbell	20.00	8.00	5.00
(75)	Hufft	20.00	8.00	5.00
(76)	Hurst	20.00	8.00	5.00
(77)	Jacobs (Los Angeles)	20.00	8.00	5.00
(78)	Jacobs (San Francisco)	20.00	8.00	5.00
(79)	Jahn	20.00	8.00	5.00
(80)	Jeffcoat	20.00	8.00	5.00
(81)	Johnson	20.00	8.00	5.00
(82)	Jolley	20.00	8.00	5.00
(83)	Jones	20.00	8.00	5.00
(84)	Jones	20.00	8.00	5.00
(85)	Kallio	20.00	8.00	5.00
(86)	Kasich	20.00	8.00	5.00
(87)	Keane	20.00	8.00	5.00
(88)	Keating	20.00	8.00	5.00
(89)	Keesey	20.00	8.00	5.00
(90)	Killifer	20.00	8.00	5.00
(91)	Knight	20.00	8.00	5.00
(92)	Knothe	20.00	8.00	5.00
(93)	Knott	20.00	8.00	5.00
(94)	Koehler	20.00	8.00	5.00
(95)	Krasovich	20.00	8.00	5.00
(96)	Krause	20.00	8.00	5.00
(97)	Krug (Hollywood)	20.00	8.00	5.00
(98)	Krug (Los Angeles)	20.00	8.00	5.00
(99)	Kunz	20.00	8.00	5.00
(100)	Langford	20.00	8.00	5.00
(101)	Lee	20.00	8.00	5.00
(102)	Ernie Lombardi	200.00	100.00	60.00
(103)	Mahaffey	20.00	8.00	5.00
(104)	Mails	20.00	8.00	5.00
(105)	Maloney	20.00	8.00	5.00
(106)	McCabe	20.00	8.00	5.00
(107)	McDaniel	20.00	8.00	5.00
(108)	McEvoy	20.00	8.00	5.00
(109)	McIssacs	20.00	8.00	5.00
(110)	McQuaid	20.00	8.00	5.00
(111)	Miller	20.00	8.00	5.00
(112)	Monroe	20.00	8.00	5.00
(113)	Muller	20.00	8.00	5.00
(114)	Mulligan	20.00	8.00	5.00
(115)	Nance	20.00	8.00	5.00
(116)	Nelson	20.00	8.00	5.00
(117)	Nevers	20.00	8.00	5.00
(118)	Oana	75.00	37.00	22.00
(119)	Olney	20.00	8.00	5.00
(120)	Ortman	20.00	8.00	5.00
(121)	Osborne	20.00	8.00	5.00
(122)	Ostenberg	20.00	8.00	5.00
(123)	Peters	20.00	8.00	5.00
(124)	Pillette	20.00	8.00	5.00
(125)	Pinelli	20.00	8.00	5.00
(126)	Pipgras	20.00	8.00	5.00
(127)	Plitt	20.00	8.00	5.00
(128)	Polvogt	20.00	8.00	5.00
(129)	Rachac	20.00	8.00	5.00
(130)	Read	20.00	8.00	5.00
(131)	Reed	20.00	8.00	5.00
(132)	Jimmy Reese	25.00	10.00	6.00
(133)	Rego	20.00	8.00	5.00
(134)	Ritter	20.00	8.00	5.00
(135)	Roberts	20.00	8.00	5.00
(136)	Rodda	20.00	8.00	5.00
(137)	Rodgers	20.00	8.00	5.00
(138)	Rohwer	20.00	8.00	5.00
(139)	Rollings	20.00	8.00	5.00
(140)	Rumler	20.00	8.00	5.00
(141)	Ryan	20.00	8.00	5.00
(142)	Sandberg	20.00	8.00	5.00
(143)	Schino	20.00	8.00	5.00
(144)	Schmidt	20.00	8.00	5.00
(145)	Schulmerich	20.00	8.00	5.00
(146)	Scott	20.00	8.00	5.00
(147)	Severeid	20.00	8.00	5.00
(148)	Shanklin	20.00	8.00	5.00
(149)	Sherlock	20.00	8.00	5.00
(150)	Slade	20.00	8.00	5.00
(151)	Staley	20.00	8.00	5.00
(152)	Statz	20.00	8.00	5.00
(153)	Steinecke	20.00	8.00	5.00
(154)	Suhr	20.00	8.00	5.00
(155)	Taylor	20.00	8.00	5.00
(156)	Thurston	20.00	8.00	5.00
(157)	Tierney	20.00	8.00	5.00
(158)	Tolson	20.00	8.00	5.00
(159)	Tomlin	20.00	8.00	5.00
(160)	Vergez	20.00	8.00	5.00
(161)	Vinci	20.00	8.00	5.00
(162)	Volkman	20.00	8.00	5.00
(163)	Walsh	20.00	8.00	5.00
(164)	Warren	20.00	8.00	5.00
(165)	Webb	20.00	8.00	5.00
(166)	Weustling	20.00	8.00	5.00
(167)	Williams	20.00	8.00	5.00
(168)	Wingo	20.00	8.00	5.00

1930 Zeenut Pacific Coast League

		NM	EX	VG
Complete Set (186):		3100.	1250.	750.00
Common Player:		20.00	8.00	5.00
(1)	Allington	20.00	8.00	5.00
(2)	Almada	20.00	8.00	5.00
(3)	Andrews	20.00	8.00	5.00
(4)	Anton	20.00	8.00	5.00
(5)	Arlett	20.00	10.00	6.00
(6)	Backer	20.00	8.00	5.00
(7)	Baecht	20.00	8.00	5.00
(8)	Baker	20.00	8.00	5.00
(9)	Baldwin	20.00	8.00	5.00
(10)	Ballou	20.00	8.00	5.00
(11)	Barbee	20.00	8.00	5.00
(12)	Barfoot	20.00	8.00	5.00
(13)	Bassler	20.00	8.00	5.00
(14)	Bates	20.00	8.00	5.00
(15)	Beck	20.00	8.00	5.00
(16)	Boone	20.00	8.00	5.00
(17)	Bowman	20.00	8.00	5.00
(18)	Brannon	20.00	8.00	5.00
(19)	Brenzel	20.00	8.00	5.00
(20)	Brown	20.00	8.00	5.00
(21)	Brubaker	20.00	8.00	5.00
(22)	Brucker	20.00	8.00	5.00
(23)	Bryan	20.00	8.00	5.00
(24)	Burkett	20.00	8.00	5.00
(25)	Burns	20.00	8.00	5.00
(26)	Butler	20.00	8.00	5.00
(27)	Camilli	20.00	8.00	5.00
(28)	Carlyle	20.00	8.00	5.00
(29)	Caster	20.00	8.00	5.00
(30)	Caveney	20.00	8.00	5.00
(31)	Chamberlain	20.00	8.00	5.00
(32)	Chatham	20.00	8.00	5.00
(33)	Childs	20.00	8.00	5.00

(34)	Christensen	20.00	8.00	5.00
(35)	Church	20.00	8.00	5.00
(36)	Cole	20.00	8.00	5.00
(37)	Coleman	20.00	8.00	5.00
(38)	Collins	20.00	8.00	5.00
(39)	Coscarart	20.00	8.00	5.00
(40)	Cox	20.00	8.00	5.00
(41)	Coyle	20.00	8.00	5.00
(42)	Craghead	20.00	8.00	5.00
(43)	Cronin	20.00	8.00	5.00
(44)	Crosetti	25.00	10.00	6.00
(45)	Daglia	20.00	8.00	5.00
(46)	Davis	20.00	8.00	5.00
(47)	Dean	20.00	8.00	5.00
(48)	DeViveiros	20.00	8.00	5.00
(49)	Dittmar	20.00	8.00	5.00
(50)	Donovan	20.00	8.00	5.00
(51)	Douglas	20.00	8.00	5.00
(52)	Dumovich	20.00	8.00	5.00
(53)	Edwards	20.00	8.00	5.00
(54)	Ellsworth	20.00	8.00	5.00
(55)	Falk	20.00	8.00	5.00
(56)	Fisch	20.00	8.00	5.00
(57)	Flynn	20.00	8.00	5.00
(58)	Freitas	20.00	8.00	5.00
(59)	French (Portland)	20.00	8.00	5.00
(60)	French (Sacramento)	20.00	8.00	5.00
(61)	Gabler	20.00	8.00	5.00
(62)	Gaston	20.00	8.00	5.00
(63)	Gazella	20.00	8.00	5.00
(64)	Gould	20.00	8.00	5.00
(65)	Governor	20.00	8.00	5.00
(66)	Green	20.00	8.00	5.00
(67)	Griffin	20.00	8.00	5.00
(68)	Haney	20.00	8.00	5.00
(69)	Hannah	20.00	8.00	5.00
(70)	Harper	20.00	8.00	5.00
(71)	Heath	20.00	8.00	5.00
(72)	Hillis	20.00	8.00	5.00
(73)	Hoag	20.00	8.00	5.00
(74)	Hoffman	20.00	8.00	5.00
(75)	Holland	20.00	8.00	5.00
(76)	Hollerson	20.00	8.00	5.00
(77)	Holling	20.00	8.00	5.00
(78)	Hood	20.00	8.00	5.00
(79)	Horn	20.00	8.00	5.00
(80)	House	20.00	8.00	5.00
(81)	Hubbell	20.00	8.00	5.00
(82)	Hufft	20.00	8.00	5.00
(83)	Hurst	20.00	8.00	5.00
(84)	Jacobs (Los Angeles)	20.00	8.00	5.00
(85)	Jacobs (Oakland)	20.00	8.00	5.00
(86)	Jacobs	20.00	8.00	5.00
(87)	Jahn	20.00	8.00	5.00
(88)	Jeffcoat	20.00	8.00	5.00
(89)	Johns	20.00	8.00	5.00
(90)	Johnson (Portland)	20.00	8.00	5.00
(91)	Johnson (Seattle)	20.00	8.00	5.00
(92)	Joiner	20.00	8.00	5.00
(93)	Kallio	20.00	8.00	5.00
(94)	Kasich	20.00	8.00	5.00
(95)	Keating	20.00	8.00	5.00
(96)	Kelly	20.00	8.00	5.00
(97)	Killifer	20.00	8.00	5.00
(98)	Knight	20.00	8.00	5.00
(99)	Knothe	20.00	8.00	5.00
(100)	Koehler	20.00	8.00	5.00
(101)	Kunz	20.00	8.00	5.00
(102)	Lamanski	20.00	8.00	5.00
(103)	Lawrence	20.00	8.00	5.00
(104)	Lee	20.00	8.00	5.00
(105)	Leishman	20.00	8.00	5.00
(106)	Lelivelt	20.00	8.00	5.00
(107)	Lieber	20.00	8.00	5.00
(108)	Ernie Lombardi	200.00	100.00	60.00
(109)	Mails	20.00	8.00	5.00
(110)	Maloney	20.00	8.00	5.00
(111)	Martin	20.00	8.00	5.00
(112)	McDougal	20.00	8.00	5.00
(113)	McLaughlin	20.00	8.00	5.00
(114)	McQuaide	20.00	8.00	5.00
(115)	Mellana	20.00	8.00	5.00
(116)	Miljus ("S" on uniform)	20.00	8.00	5.00
(117)	Miljus ("Seals" on uniform)	20.00	8.00	5.00
(118)	Monroe	20.00	8.00	5.00
(119)	Montgomery	20.00	8.00	5.00
(120)	Moore	20.00	8.00	5.00
(121)	Mulana	20.00	8.00	5.00
(122)	Muller	20.00	8.00	5.00
(123)	Mulligan	20.00	8.00	5.00
(124)	Nelson	20.00	8.00	5.00
(125)	Nevers	200.00	80.00	50.00
(126)	Odell	20.00	8.00	5.00
(127)	Olney	20.00	8.00	5.00
(128)	Osborne	20.00	8.00	5.00
(129)	Page	20.00	8.00	5.00
(130)	Palmisano	20.00	8.00	5.00
(131)	Parker	20.00	8.00	5.00
(132)	Pasedel	20.00	8.00	5.00
(133)	Pearson	20.00	8.00	5.00
(134)	Penebskey	20.00	8.00	5.00
(135)	Perry	20.00	8.00	5.00
(136)	Peters	20.00	8.00	5.00
(137)	Petterson	20.00	8.00	5.00
(138)	H. Pillette	20.00	8.00	5.00
(139)	T. Pillette	20.00	8.00	5.00
(140)	Pinelli	20.00	8.00	5.00
(141)	Pipgrass	20.00	8.00	5.00
(142)	Porter	20.00	8.00	5.00
(143)	Powles	20.00	8.00	5.00
(144)	Read	20.00	8.00	5.00
(145)	Reed	20.00	8.00	5.00
(146)	Rehg	20.00	8.00	5.00
(147)	Ricci	20.00	8.00	5.00
(148)	Roberts	20.00	8.00	5.00
(149)	Rodda	20.00	8.00	5.00
(150)	Rohwer	20.00	8.00	5.00
(151)	Rosenberg	20.00	8.00	5.00
(152)	Rumler	20.00	8.00	5.00
(153)	Ryan	20.00	8.00	5.00
(154)	Schino	20.00	8.00	5.00
(155)	Severeid	20.00	8.00	5.00
(156)	Shanklin	20.00	8.00	5.00
(157)	Sheely	20.00	8.00	5.00
(158)	Sigafoos	20.00	8.00	5.00
(159)	Statz	20.00	8.00	5.00
(160)	Steinbacker	20.00	8.00	5.00
(161)	Stevenson	20.00	8.00	5.00
(162)	Sulik	20.00	8.00	5.00
(163)	Taylor	20.00	8.00	5.00
(164)	Thomas (Sacramento)	20.00	8.00	5.00
(165)	Thomas (San Francisco)	20.00	8.00	5.00
(166)	Trembly	20.00	8.00	5.00
(167)	Turner	20.00	8.00	5.00
(168)	Turpin	20.00	8.00	5.00
(169)	Uhalt	20.00	8.00	5.00
(170)	Vergez	20.00	8.00	5.00
(171)	Vinci	20.00	8.00	5.00
(172)	Vitt	20.00	8.00	5.00
(173)	Wallgren	20.00	8.00	5.00
(174)	Walsh	20.00	8.00	5.00
(175)	Ward	20.00	8.00	5.00
(176)	Warren	20.00	8.00	5.00
(177)	Webb	20.00	8.00	5.00
(178)	Wetzell	20.00	8.00	5.00
(179)	F. Wetzel	20.00	8.00	5.00
(180)	Williams	20.00	8.00	5.00
(181)	Wilson	20.00	8.00	5.00
(182)	Wingo	20.00	8.00	5.00
(183)	Wirts	20.00	8.00	5.00
(184)	Woodall	20.00	8.00	5.00
(185)	Zamlack	20.00	8.00	5.00
(186)	Zinn	20.00	8.00	5.00

1931 Zeenut Pacific Coast League

Beginning in 1931, Zeenuts cards were no longer dated on the front, and cards without the coupon are very difficult to date. The words "Zeenuts Series" was also dropped from the front and replaced with just the words "Coast League." Zeenut cards in 1931 and 1932 measure 1-3/4" x 2-3/4".

		NM	EX	VG
Complete Set (120):		1900.	750.00	450.00
Common Player:		20.00	8.00	5.00
(1)	Abbott	20.00	8.00	5.00
(2)	Andrews	20.00	8.00	5.00
(3)	Anton	20.00	8.00	5.00
(4)	Backer	20.00	8.00	5.00
(5)	Baker	20.00	8.00	5.00
(6)	Baldwin	20.00	8.00	5.00
(7)	Barbee	20.00	8.00	5.00
(8)	Barton	20.00	8.00	5.00
(9)	Bassler	20.00	8.00	5.00
(10)	Berger (Missions)	20.00	8.00	5.00
(11)	Berger (Portland)	20.00	8.00	5.00
(12)	Biggs	20.00	8.00	5.00
(13)	Bowman	20.00	8.00	5.00
(14)	Brenzel	20.00	8.00	5.00
(15)	Bryan	20.00	8.00	5.00
(16)	Burns	20.00	8.00	5.00
(17)	Camilli	20.00	8.00	5.00
(18)	Campbell	20.00	8.00	5.00
(19)	Carlyle	20.00	8.00	5.00
(20)	Caveney	20.00	8.00	5.00
(21)	Chesterfield	20.00	8.00	5.00
(22)	Cole	20.00	8.00	5.00
(23)	Coleman	20.00	8.00	5.00
(24)	Coscarart	20.00	8.00	5.00
(25)	Crosetti	20.00	10.00	6.00
(26)	Davis	20.00	8.00	5.00
(27)	DeBerry	20.00	8.00	5.00
(28)	Demaree	20.00	8.00	5.00
(29)	Dean	20.00	8.00	5.00
(30)	Delaney	20.00	8.00	5.00
(31)	Dondero	20.00	8.00	5.00
(32)	Donovan	20.00	8.00	5.00
(33)	Douglas	20.00	8.00	5.00
(34)	Ellsworth	20.00	8.00	5.00
(35)	Farrell	20.00	8.00	5.00
(36)	Fenton	20.00	8.00	5.00
(37)	Fitzpatrick	20.00	8.00	5.00
(38)	Flagstead	20.00	8.00	5.00
(39)	Flynn	20.00	8.00	5.00
(40)	Frazier	20.00	8.00	5.00
(41)	Freitas	20.00	8.00	5.00
(42)	French	20.00	8.00	5.00
(43)	Fullerton	20.00	8.00	5.00
(44)	Gabler	20.00	8.00	5.00
(45)	Gazella	20.00	8.00	5.00
(46)	Hale	20.00	8.00	5.00
(47)	Hamilton	20.00	8.00	5.00
(48)	Haney	20.00	8.00	5.00
(49)	Hannah	20.00	8.00	5.00
(50)	Harper	20.00	8.00	5.00
(51)	Henderson	20.00	8.00	5.00
(52)	Herrmann	20.00	8.00	5.00
(53)	Hoffman	20.00	8.00	5.00
(54)	Holland	20.00	8.00	5.00
(55)	Holling	20.00	8.00	5.00
(56)	Hubbell	20.00	8.00	5.00
(57)	Hufft	20.00	8.00	5.00
(58)	Hurst	20.00	8.00	5.00
(59)	Jacobs	20.00	8.00	5.00
(60)	Kallio	20.00	8.00	5.00
(61)	Keating	20.00	8.00	5.00
(62)	Keesey	20.00	8.00	5.00
(63)	Knothe	20.00	8.00	5.00
(64)	Knott	20.00	8.00	5.00
(65)	Kohler	20.00	8.00	5.00
(66)	Lamanski	20.00	8.00	5.00
(67)	Lee	20.00	8.00	5.00
(68)	Lelivelt	20.00	8.00	5.00
(69)	Lieber	20.00	8.00	5.00
(70)	Lipanovic	20.00	8.00	5.00
(71)	McDonald	20.00	8.00	5.00
(72)	McDougall	20.00	8.00	5.00
(73)	McLaughlin	20.00	8.00	5.00
(74)	Monroe	20.00	8.00	5.00
(75)	Moss	20.00	8.00	5.00
(76)	Mulligan	20.00	8.00	5.00
(77)	Ortman	20.00	8.00	5.00
(78)	Orwoll	20.00	8.00	5.00
(79)	Parker	20.00	8.00	5.00
(80)	Penebskey	20.00	8.00	5.00
(81)	H. Pillette	20.00	8.00	5.00
(82)	T. Pillette	20.00	8.00	5.00
(83)	Pinelli	20.00	8.00	5.00
(84)	Pool	20.00	8.00	5.00
(85)	Posedel	20.00	8.00	5.00
(86)	Powers	20.00	8.00	5.00
(87)	Read	20.00	8.00	5.00
(88)	Jimmy Reese	25.00	10.00	6.00
(89)	Rhiel	20.00	8.00	5.00
(90)	Ricci	20.00	8.00	5.00
(91)	Rohwer	20.00	8.00	5.00
(92)	Ryan	20.00	8.00	5.00
(93)	Schino	20.00	8.00	5.00
(94)	Schulte	20.00	8.00	5.00
(95)	Severeid	20.00	8.00	5.00
(96)	Sharpe	20.00	8.00	5.00
(97)	Shellenback	20.00	8.00	5.00
(98)	Simas	20.00	8.00	5.00
(99)	Steinbacker	20.00	8.00	5.00
(100)	Summa	20.00	8.00	5.00
(101)	Tubbs	20.00	8.00	5.00
(102)	Turner	20.00	8.00	5.00
(103)	Turpin	20.00	8.00	5.00
(104)	Uhalt	20.00	8.00	5.00
(105)	Vinci	20.00	8.00	5.00
(106)	Vitt	20.00	8.00	5.00
(107)	Wade	20.00	8.00	5.00
(108)	Walsh	20.00	8.00	5.00
(109)	Walters	20.00	8.00	5.00
(110)	Wera	20.00	8.00	5.00
(111)	Wetzel	20.00	8.00	5.00
(112)	Williams (Portland)	20.00	8.00	5.00
(113)	Williams (San Francisco)	20.00	8.00	5.00
(114)	Wingo	20.00	8.00	5.00
(115)	Wirts	20.00	8.00	5.00
(116)	Wise	20.00	8.00	5.00
(117)	Woodall	20.00	8.00	5.00
(118)	Yerkes	20.00	8.00	5.00
(119)	Zamlock	20.00	8.00	5.00
(120)	Zinn	20.00	8.00	5.00

1932 Zeenut Pacific Coast League

		NM	EX	VG
Complete Set (120):		1550.	750.00	450.00
Common Player:		20.00	8.00	5.00
(1)	Abbott	20.00	8.00	5.00
(2)	Almada	20.00	8.00	5.00
(3)	Anton	20.00	8.00	5.00
(4)	Babich	20.00	8.00	5.00
(5)	Backer	20.00	8.00	5.00
(6)	Baker	20.00	8.00	5.00
(7)	Ballou	20.00	8.00	5.00
(8)	Bassler	20.00	8.00	5.00
(9)	Berger	20.00	8.00	5.00
(10)	Blackerby	20.00	8.00	5.00

(11)	Bordagaray	20.00	8.00	5.00
(12)	Brannon	20.00	8.00	5.00
(13)	Briggs	20.00	8.00	5.00
(14)	Brubaker	20.00	8.00	5.00
(15)	Callaghan	20.00	8.00	5.00
(16)	Camilli	20.00	8.00	5.00
(17)	Campbell	20.00	8.00	5.00
(18)	Carlyle	20.00	8.00	5.00
(19)	Caster	20.00	8.00	5.00
(20)	Caveney	20.00	8.00	5.00
(21)	Chamberlain	20.00	8.00	5.00
(22)	Cole	20.00	8.00	5.00
(23)	Collard	20.00	8.00	5.00
(24)	Cook	20.00	8.00	5.00
(25)	Coscarart	20.00	8.00	5.00
(26)	Cox	20.00	8.00	5.00
(27)	Cronin	20.00	8.00	5.00
(28)	Daglia	20.00	8.00	5.00
(29)	Dahlgren	25.00	10.00	6.00
(30)	Davis	20.00	8.00	5.00
(31)	Dean	20.00	8.00	5.00
(32)	Delaney	20.00	8.00	5.00
(33)	Demaree	20.00	8.00	5.00
(34)	Devine	20.00	8.00	5.00
(35)	DeViveiros	20.00	8.00	5.00
(36)	Dittmar	20.00	8.00	5.00
(37)	Donovan	20.00	8.00	5.00
(38)	Ellsworth	20.00	8.00	5.00
(39)	Fitzpatrick	20.00	8.00	5.00
(40)	Frazier	20.00	8.00	5.00
(41)	Freitas	20.00	8.00	5.00
(42)	Garibaldi	20.00	8.00	5.00
(43)	Gaston	20.00	8.00	5.00
(44)	Gazella	20.00	8.00	5.00
(45)	Gillick	20.00	8.00	5.00
(46)	Hafey	20.00	8.00	5.00
(47)	Haney	20.00	8.00	5.00
(48)	Hannah	20.00	8.00	5.00
(49)	Henderson	20.00	8.00	5.00
(50)	Herrmann	20.00	8.00	5.00
(51)	Hipps	20.00	8.00	5.00
(52)	Hofman	20.00	8.00	5.00
(53)	Holland	20.00	8.00	5.00
(54)	House	20.00	8.00	5.00
(55)	Hufft	20.00	8.00	5.00
(56)	Hunt	20.00	8.00	5.00
(57)	Hurst	20.00	8.00	5.00
(58)	Jacobs	20.00	8.00	5.00
(59)	Johns	20.00	8.00	5.00
(60)	Johnson (Missions)	20.00	8.00	5.00
(61)	Johnson (Portland)	20.00	8.00	5.00
(62)	Johnson (Seattle)	20.00	8.00	5.00
(63)	Joiner	20.00	8.00	5.00
(64)	Kallio	20.00	8.00	5.00
(65)	Kasich	20.00	8.00	5.00
(66)	Keesey	20.00	8.00	5.00
(67)	Kelly	20.00	8.00	5.00
(68)	Koehler	20.00	8.00	5.00
(69)	Lee	20.00	8.00	5.00
(70)	Lieber	20.00	8.00	5.00
(71)	Mailho	20.00	8.00	5.00
(72)	Martin (Oakland)	20.00	8.00	5.00
(73)	Martin (San Francisco)	20.00	8.00	5.00
(74)	McNeely	20.00	8.00	5.00
(75)	Miljus	20.00	8.00	5.00
(76)	Monroe	20.00	8.00	5.00
(77)	Mosolf	20.00	8.00	5.00
(78)	Moss	20.00	8.00	5.00
(79)	Muller	20.00	8.00	5.00
(80)	Mulligan	20.00	8.00	5.00
(81)	Oana	20.00	8.00	5.00
(82)	Osborn	20.00	8.00	5.00
(83)	Page	20.00	8.00	5.00
(84)	Penebsky	20.00	8.00	5.00
(85)	H. Pillette	20.00	8.00	5.00
(86)	Pinelli	25.00	12.50	7.50
(87)	Poole	20.00	8.00	5.00
(88)	Quellich	20.00	8.00	5.00
(89)	Read	20.00	8.00	5.00
(90)	Ricci	20.00	8.00	5.00
(91)	Salvo	20.00	8.00	5.00
(92)	Sankey	20.00	8.00	5.00
(93)	Sheehan	20.00	8.00	5.00
(94)	Shellenback	20.00	8.00	5.00
(95)	Sherlock (Hollywood)	20.00	8.00	5.00
(96)	Sherlock (Missions)	20.00	8.00	5.00
(97)	Shores	20.00	8.00	5.00
(98)	Simas	20.00	8.00	5.00
(99)	Statz	20.00	8.00	5.00
(100)	Steinbacker	20.00	8.00	5.00
(101)	Sulik	20.00	8.00	5.00
(102)	Summa	20.00	8.00	5.00
(103)	Thomas	20.00	8.00	5.00
(104)	Uhalt	20.00	8.00	5.00
(105)	Vinci	20.00	8.00	5.00
(106)	Vitt	20.00	8.00	5.00
(107)	Walsh (Missions)	20.00	8.00	5.00
(108)	Walsh (Oakland)	20.00	8.00	5.00
(109)	Walters	20.00	8.00	5.00
(110)	Ward	20.00	8.00	5.00
(111)	Welsh	20.00	8.00	5.00
(112)	Wera	20.00	8.00	5.00
(113)	Williams	20.00	8.00	5.00
(114)	Willoughby	20.00	8.00	5.00
(115)	Wirts	20.00	8.00	5.00
(116)	Wise	20.00	8.00	5.00
(117)	Woodall	20.00	8.00	5.00
(118)	Yde	20.00	8.00	5.00
(119)	Zahniser	20.00	8.00	5.00
(120)	Zamloch	20.00	8.00	5.00

1933 Zeenut Pacific Coast League (sepia)

This is the most confusing era for Zeenut cards. The cards of 1933-36 are nearly identical, displaying the words, "Coast League" in a small rectangle (with rounded corners), along with the player's name and team. The photos were black-and-white (except 1933 Zeenuts have also been found with sepia photos). Because no date appears on the photos, cards from these years are impossible to tell apart without the coupon bottom that lists an expiration date. To date over 161 subjects have been found, with some known to exist in all four years. There are cases where the exact same photo was used from one year to the next (sometimes with minor cropping differences). All cards of Joe and Vince DiMaggio have their last name misspelled "DeMaggio."

		NM	EX	VG
Complete Set (48):		850.00	345.00	200.00
Common Player:		20.00	8.00	5.00
(1)	L. Almada	18.00	9.00	5.50
(2)	Anton	20.00	8.00	5.00
(3)	Bassler	20.00	8.00	5.00
(4)	Bonnelly	20.00	8.00	5.00
(5)	Bordagary	20.00	8.00	5.00
(6)	Bottarini	20.00	8.00	5.00
(7)	Brannan	20.00	8.00	5.00
(8)	Brubaker	20.00	8.00	5.00
(9)	Bryan	20.00	8.00	5.00
(10)	Burns	20.00	8.00	5.00
(11)	Camilli	20.00	8.00	5.00
(12)	Chozen	20.00	8.00	5.00
(13)	Cole	20.00	8.00	5.00
(14)	Cronin	20.00	8.00	5.00
(15)	Dahlgren	18.00	9.00	5.50
(16)	Donovan	20.00	8.00	5.00
(17)	Douglas	20.00	8.00	5.00
(18)	Flynn	20.00	8.00	5.00
(19)	French	20.00	8.00	5.00
(20)	Frietas	20.00	8.00	5.00
(21)	Galan	20.00	8.00	5.00
(22)	Hofmann	20.00	8.00	5.00
(23)	Kelman	20.00	8.00	5.00
(24)	Lelivelt	20.00	8.00	5.00
(25)	Ludolph	20.00	8.00	5.00
(26)	McDonald	20.00	8.00	5.00
(27)	McNeely	20.00	8.00	5.00
(28)	McQuaid	20.00	8.00	5.00
(29)	Moncrief	20.00	8.00	5.00
(30)	Nelson	20.00	8.00	5.00
(31)	Osborne	20.00	8.00	5.00
(32)	Petersen	20.00	8.00	5.00
(33)	Reeves	20.00	8.00	5.00
(34)	Scott	20.00	8.00	5.00
(35)	Shellenback	20.00	8.00	5.00
(36)	J. Sherlock	20.00	8.00	5.00
(37)	V. Sherlock	20.00	8.00	5.00
(38)	Steinbacker	20.00	8.00	5.00
(39)	Stine	20.00	8.00	5.00
(40)	Strange	20.00	8.00	5.00
(41)	Sulik	20.00	8.00	5.00
(42)	Sweetland	20.00	8.00	5.00
(43)	Uhalt	20.00	8.00	5.00
(44)	Vinci	20.00	8.00	5.00
(45)	Vitt	20.00	8.00	5.00
(46)	Wetzel	20.00	8.00	5.00
(47)	Woodall	20.00	8.00	5.00
(48)	Zinn	20.00	8.00	5.00

The ratio of Excellent and Very Good prices to Near Mint can vary depending on relative collectibility for each grade in a specific set. Current listings reflect such adjustments.

1933-36 Zeenut Pacific Coast League (black and white)

		NM	EX	VG
Complete Set (159):		7500.	3000.	1800.
Common Player:		20.00	8.00	5.00
(1a)	Almada (large pose)	18.00	9.00	5.50
(1b)	Almada (small pose)	18.00	9.00	5.50
(2a)	Anton (large pose)	20.00	8.00	5.00
(2b)	Anton (small pose)	20.00	8.00	5.00
(3)	Babich	20.00	8.00	5.00
(4)	Backer	20.00	8.00	5.00
(5)	Ballou (black stockings)	20.00	8.00	5.00
(6a)	Ballou (stockings with band, large pose)	20.00	8.00	5.00
(6b)	Ballou (stockings with band, small pose)	20.00	8.00	5.00
(7)	Barath	20.00	8.00	5.00
(8)	Beck	20.00	8.00	5.00
(9)	C. Beck	20.00	8.00	5.00
(10)	W. Beck	20.00	8.00	5.00
(11)	Becker	20.00	8.00	5.00
(12)	Biongovanni	20.00	8.00	5.00
(13)	Blackerby	20.00	8.00	5.00
(14)	Blakely	20.00	8.00	5.00
(15)	Borja (Sacramento)	20.00	8.00	5.00
(16)	Borja (Seals)	20.00	8.00	5.00
(17)	Brundin	20.00	8.00	5.00
(18)	Carlyle	20.00	8.00	5.00
(19a)	Caveney (name incorrect)	20.00	8.00	5.00
(19b)	Cavaney (name correct)	20.00	8.00	5.00
(20)	Chelini	20.00	8.00	5.00
(21)	Cole (with glove)	20.00	8.00	5.00
(22)	Cole (no glove)	20.00	8.00	5.00
(23)	Connors	20.00	8.00	5.00
(24)	Coscarart (Missions)	20.00	8.00	5.00
(25)	Coscarart (Seattle)	20.00	8.00	5.00
(26)	Cox	20.00	8.00	5.00
(27)	Davis	20.00	8.00	5.00
(28)	J. DeMaggio (DiMaggio) (batting)	4000.	2000.	1200.
(29)	J. DeMaggio (DiMaggio) (throwing)	4000.	2000.	1200.
(30)	V. DeMaggio (DiMaggio)	350.00	150.00	90.00
(31)	DeViveiros	20.00	8.00	5.00
(32)	Densmore	20.00	8.00	5.00
(33)	Dittmar	20.00	8.00	5.00
(34)	Donovan	20.00	8.00	5.00
(35)	Douglas (Oakland)	20.00	8.00	5.00
(36)	Douglas (Seals)	20.00	8.00	5.00
(37a)	Duggan (large pose)	20.00	8.00	5.00
(37b)	Duggan (small pose)	20.00	8.00	5.00
(38)	Durst	20.00	8.00	5.00
(39a)	Eckhardt (large pose)	20.00	8.00	5.00
(39b)	Eckhardt (small pose)	20.00	8.00	5.00
(40)	Ellsworth	20.00	8.00	5.00
(41)	Fenton	20.00	8.00	5.00
(42)	Fitzpatrick	20.00	8.00	5.00
(43)	Francovich	20.00	8.00	5.00
(44)	Funk	20.00	8.00	5.00
(45a)	Garibaldi (large pose)	20.00	8.00	5.00
(45b)	Garibaldi (small pose)	20.00	8.00	5.00
(46)	Gibson (black sleeves)	20.00	8.00	5.00
(47)	Gibson (white sleeves)	20.00	8.00	5.00
(48)	Gira	20.00	8.00	5.00
(49)	Glaister	20.00	8.00	5.00
(50)	Graves	20.00	8.00	5.00
(51a)	Hafey (Missions, large pose)	20.00	8.00	5.00
(51b)	Hafey (Missions, middle-size pose)	20.00	8.00	5.00
(51c)	Hafey (Missions, small pose)	20.00	8.00	5.00
(52)	Hafey (Sacramento)	20.00	8.00	5.00
(53)	Haid (Oakland)	20.00	8.00	5.00
(54)	Haid (Seattle)	20.00	8.00	5.00
(55)	Haney	20.00	8.00	5.00
(56a)	Hartwig (Sacramento, large pose)	20.00	8.00	5.00
(56b)	Hartwig (Sacramento, small pose)	20.00	8.00	5.00
(57)	Hartwig (Seals)	20.00	8.00	5.00
(58)	Henderson	20.00	8.00	5.00
(59)	Herrmann	20.00	8.00	5.00
(60)	B. Holder	20.00	8.00	5.00
(61)	Holland	20.00	8.00	5.00
(62)	Horne	20.00	8.00	5.00
(63)	House	20.00	8.00	5.00
(64)	Hunt	20.00	8.00	5.00
(65)	A.E. Jacobs	20.00	8.00	5.00
(66)	Johns	20.00	8.00	5.00
(67)	D. Johnson	20.00	8.00	5.00
(68)	L. Johnson	20.00	8.00	5.00
(69)	Joiner	20.00	8.00	5.00

(70)	Jolley	20.00	8.00	5.00
(71)	Joost	20.00	8.00	5.00
(72)	Jorgensen	20.00	8.00	5.00
(73)	Kallio	20.00	8.00	5.00
(74)	Kamm	20.00	8.00	5.00
(75)	Kampouris	20.00	8.00	5.00
(76)	E. Kelly (Oakland)	20.00	8.00	5.00
(77)	E. Kelly (Seattle)	20.00	8.00	5.00
(78)	Kenna	20.00	8.00	5.00
(79)	Kintana	20.00	8.00	5.00
(80)	Lahman	20.00	8.00	5.00
(81)	Lieber	20.00	8.00	5.00
(82)	Ludolph	20.00	8.00	5.00
(83)	Mailho	20.00	8.00	5.00
(84a)	Mails (large pose)	20.00	8.00	5.00
(84b)	Mails (small pose)	20.00	8.00	5.00
(85)	Marty (black sleeves)	20.00	8.00	5.00
(86)	Marty (white sleeves)	20.00	8.00	5.00
(87)	Massuci (different pose)	20.00	8.00	5.00
(88)	Masucci (different pose)	20.00	8.00	5.00
(89a)	McEvoy (large pose)	20.00	8.00	5.00
(89b)	McEvoy (small pose)	20.00	8.00	5.00
(90)	McIsaacs	20.00	8.00	5.00
(91)	McMullen (Oakland)	20.00	8.00	5.00
(92)	McMullen (Seals)	20.00	8.00	5.00
(93)	Mitchell	20.00	8.00	5.00
(94a)	Monzo (large pose)	20.00	8.00	5.00
(94b)	Monzo (small pose)	20.00	8.00	5.00
(95)	Mort (throwing)	20.00	8.00	5.00
(96)	Mort (batting)	20.00	8.00	5.00
(97a)	Muller (Oakland, large pose)	20.00	8.00	5.00
(97b)	Muller (Oakland, small pose)	20.00	8.00	5.00
(98)	Muller (Seattle)	20.00	8.00	5.00
(99)	Mulligan (hands showing)	20.00	8.00	5.00
(100)	Mulligan (hands not showing)	20.00	8.00	5.00
(101)	Newkirk	20.00	8.00	5.00
(102)	Nicholas	20.00	8.00	5.00
(103)	Nitcholas	20.00	8.00	5.00
(103a)	Norbert (large pose)	20.00	8.00	5.00
(103b)	Norbert (small pose)	20.00	8.00	5.00
(105)	O'Doul (black sleeves)	40.00	16.00	10.00
(106)	O'Doul (white sleeves)	40.00	16.00	10.00
(107)	Oglesby	20.00	8.00	5.00
(108)	Ostenberg	20.00	8.00	5.00
(109)	Outen (throwing)	20.00	8.00	5.00
(110)	Outen (batting)	20.00	8.00	5.00
(111)	Page (Hollywood)	20.00	8.00	5.00
(112)	Page (Seattle)	20.00	8.00	5.00
(113)	Palmisano	20.00	8.00	5.00
(114)	Parker	20.00	8.00	5.00
(115)	Phebus	20.00	8.00	5.00
(116)	T. Pillette	20.00	8.00	5.00
(117)	Pool	20.00	8.00	5.00
(118)	Powers	20.00	8.00	5.00
(119)	Quellich	20.00	8.00	5.00
(120)	Radonitz	20.00	8.00	5.00
(121a)	Raimondi (large pose)	20.00	8.00	5.00
(121b)	Raimondi (small pose)	20.00	8.00	5.00
(122a)	Jimmy Reese (large pose)	60.00	30.00	18.00
(122b)	Jimmy Reese (small pose)	60.00	30.00	18.00
(123)	Rego	20.00	8.00	5.00
(124)	Rhyne (front)	20.00	8.00	5.00
(125)	Rosenberg	20.00	8.00	5.00
(126)	Salinsen	20.00	8.00	5.00
(127)	Salkeld	20.00	8.00	5.00
(128)	Salvo	20.00	8.00	5.00
(129)	Sever	20.00	8.00	5.00
(130)	Sheehan (black sleeves)	20.00	8.00	5.00
(131)	Sheehan (white sleeves)	20.00	8.00	5.00
(132a)	Sheely (large pose)	20.00	8.00	5.00
(132b)	Sheely (small pose)	20.00	8.00	5.00
(134)	Sprinz	20.00	8.00	5.00
(135)	Starritt	20.00	8.00	5.00
(136)	Statz	20.00	8.00	5.00
(137a)	Steinbacker (large pose)	20.00	8.00	5.00
(137b)	Steinbacker (small pose)	20.00	8.00	5.00
(138)	Stewart	20.00	8.00	5.00
(139)	Stitzel (Los Angeles)	20.00	8.00	5.00
(140)	Stitzel (Missions)	20.00	8.00	5.00
(141)	Stitzel (Seals)	20.00	8.00	5.00
(142)	Stoneham	20.00	8.00	5.00
(143)	Street	20.00	8.00	5.00
(144)	Stroner	20.00	8.00	5.00
(145)	Stutz	20.00	8.00	5.00
(146)	Sulik	20.00	8.00	5.00
(147a)	Thurston (Mission)	20.00	8.00	5.00
(147b)	Thurston (Missions)	20.00	8.00	5.00
(148)	Vitt (Hollywood)	20.00	8.00	5.00
(149)	Vitt (Oakland)	20.00	8.00	5.00
(150)	Wallgren	20.00	8.00	5.00
(151)	Walsh	20.00	8.00	5.00
(152)	Walters	20.00	8.00	5.00
(153)	West	20.00	8.00	5.00
(154a)	Wirts (large pose)	20.00	8.00	5.00
(154b)	Wirts (small pose)	20.00	8.00	5.00
(155)	Woodall (batting)	20.00	8.00	5.00
(156)	Woodall (throwing)	20.00	8.00	5.00
(157)	Wright (facing to front)	20.00	8.00	5.00
(158)	Wright (facing to left)	20.00	8.00	5.00
(159)	Zinn	20.00	8.00	5.00

1937-38 Zeenut Pacific Coast League

The 1937 and 1938 Zeenuts are similar to the 1933-1936 issues, except the black rectangle containing the player's name and team has square (rather than rounded) corners. Again, it is difficult to distinguish between the two years. In 1938, Zeenuts eliminated the coupon bottom and began including a separate coupon in the candy package along with the baseball card. The final two years of the Zeenuts issues, the 1937 and 1938 cards, are among the more difficult to find.

		NM	EX	VG
Complete Set (99):		3400.	1350.	825.00
Common Player:		40.00	16.00	10.00
(1)	Annunzio	40.00	16.00	10.00
(2)	Baker	40.00	16.00	10.00
(3)	Ballou	40.00	16.00	10.00
(4)	C. Beck	40.00	16.00	10.00
(5)	W. Beck	40.00	16.00	10.00
(6)	Bolin	40.00	16.00	10.00
(7)	Bongiavanni	40.00	16.00	10.00
(8)	Boss	40.00	16.00	10.00
(9)	Carson	40.00	16.00	10.00
(10)	Clabaugh	40.00	16.00	10.00
(11)	Clifford	40.00	16.00	10.00
(12)	B. Cole	40.00	16.00	10.00
(13)	Coscarart	40.00	16.00	10.00
(14)	Cronin	40.00	16.00	10.00
(15)	Cullop	40.00	16.00	10.00
(16)	Daglia	40.00	16.00	10.00
(17)	D. DeMaggio (DiMaggio)	350.00	150.00	85.00
(18)	Douglas	40.00	16.00	10.00
(19)	Frankovich	40.00	16.00	10.00
(20)	Frazier	40.00	16.00	10.00
(21)	Fredericks	40.00	16.00	10.00
(22)	Freitas	40.00	16.00	10.00
(23)	Gabrielson (Oakland)	40.00	16.00	10.00
(24)	Gabrielson (Seattle)	40.00	16.00	10.00
(25)	Garibaldi	40.00	16.00	10.00
(26)	Gibson	40.00	16.00	10.00
(27)	Gill	40.00	16.00	10.00
(28)	Graves	40.00	16.00	10.00
(29)	Guay	40.00	16.00	10.00
(30)	Gudat	40.00	16.00	10.00
(31)	Haid	40.00	16.00	10.00
(32)	Hannah	40.00	16.00	10.00
(33)	Hawkins	40.00	16.00	10.00
(34)	Herrmann	40.00	16.00	10.00
(35)	Holder	40.00	16.00	10.00
(36)	Jennings	40.00	16.00	10.00
(37)	Judnich	40.00	16.00	10.00
(38)	Klinger	40.00	16.00	10.00
(39)	Koenig	40.00	16.00	10.00
(40)	Koupal	40.00	16.00	10.00
(41)	Koy	40.00	16.00	10.00
(42)	Lamanski	40.00	16.00	10.00
(43)	Leishman (Oakland)	40.00	16.00	10.00
(44)	Leishman (Seattle)	40.00	16.00	10.00
(45)	G. Lillard	40.00	16.00	10.00
(46)	Mann	40.00	16.00	10.00
(47)	Marble (Hollywood)	40.00	16.00	10.00
(49)	Miller	40.00	16.00	10.00
(50)	Mills	40.00	16.00	10.00
(51)	Monzo	40.00	16.00	10.00
(52)	B. Mort (Hollywood)	40.00	16.00	10.00
(53)	B. Mort (Missions)	40.00	16.00	10.00
(54)	Muller	40.00	16.00	10.00
(55)	Murray	40.00	16.00	10.00
(56)	Newsome	40.00	16.00	10.00
(57)	Nitcholas	40.00	16.00	10.00
(58)	Olds	40.00	16.00	10.00
(59)	Orengo	40.00	16.00	10.00
(60)	Osborne	40.00	16.00	10.00
(61)	Outen	40.00	16.00	10.00
(62)	C. Outen (Hollywood)	40.00	16.00	10.00
(63)	C. Outen (Missions)	40.00	16.00	10.00
(64)	Pippin	40.00	16.00	10.00
(65)	Powell	40.00	16.00	10.00
(66)	Radonitz	40.00	16.00	10.00
(67)	Raimondi (Oakland)	40.00	16.00	10.00
(68)	Raimondi (San Francisco)	40.00	16.00	10.00
(69)	A. Raimondi	40.00	16.00	10.00
(70)	W. Raimondi	40.00	16.00	10.00
(71)	Rhyne	40.00	16.00	10.00
(72)	Rosenberg (Missions)	40.00	16.00	10.00
(73)	Rosenberg (Portland)	40.00	16.00	10.00
(74)	Sawyer	40.00	16.00	10.00
(75)	Seats	40.00	16.00	10.00
(76)	Sheehan (Oakland)	40.00	16.00	10.00
(77)	Sheehan (San Francisco)	40.00	16.00	10.00
(78)	Shores	40.00	16.00	10.00
(79)	Slade (Hollywood)	40.00	16.00	10.00
(80)	Slade (Missions)	40.00	16.00	10.00
(81)	Sprinz (Missions)	40.00	16.00	10.00
(82)	Sprinz (San Francisco)	40.00	16.00	10.00
(83)	Statz	40.00	16.00	10.00
(84)	Storey	40.00	16.00	10.00
(85)	Stringfellow	40.00	16.00	10.00
(86)	Stutz	40.00	16.00	10.00
(87)	Sweeney	40.00	16.00	10.00
(88)	Thomson	40.00	16.00	10.00
(89)	Tost (Hollywood)	40.00	16.00	10.00
(90)	Tost (Missions)	40.00	16.00	10.00
(91)	Ulrich	40.00	16.00	10.00
(92)	Vergez	40.00	16.00	10.00
(93)	Vezelich	40.00	16.00	10.00
(94)	Vitter (Hollywood)	40.00	16.00	10.00
(95)	Vitter (San Francisco)	40.00	16.00	10.00
(96)	West	40.00	16.00	10.00
(97)	Wilson	40.00	16.00	10.00
(98)	Woodall	40.00	16.00	10.00
(99)	Wright	40.00	16.00	10.00

Minor League Team Sets and Singles (1970-2000)

By 1970, the issue of minor league baseball cards as premiums with another product had virtually ceased. Since that time, the vast majority of cards issued each year have been in the form of team sets and, since 1989, wax- or foil-packed singles.

In exchange for the rights to sell card sets within the hobby, various card manufacturers and other sponsors have printed sets for the teams to sell at their concession stand, or give away at promotional games. Most card companies in recent years have not been able to make a profit on such an arrangement because of the relatively small print runs for each team set and the recent licensing fees required by Major League Baseball Properties.

Also listed in this section are miscellaneous sets of draft picks, pre-professional summer amateur leagues and Team USA, along with independent profesional teams which are not part of Organized Baseball's National Association of professional Baseball Leagues.

Since minor league team sets of the era are rarely broken up, and since the presence of a superstar player can represent virtually all of a set's value, only complete set prices are listed.

1970 McDonald's Wichita Aeros

(Cleveland Indians, AAA)(black and white) (2-1/2" x 3-14")(Card backs are blank)

NM

Complete Set (18): 300.00

(1) Ken Aspromonte
(2) Frank Baker
(3) Larry Burchard
(4) Lou Camilli
(5) Mike Carruthers
(6) Chris Chambliss
(7) Ed Farmer
(8) Pedro Gonzales
(9) Jerry Hinsley
(10) Luis Isaac
(11) John Lowenstein
(12) Cap Peterson
(13) Jim Rittwage
(14) Bill Rohr
(15) Richie Scheinblum
(16) John Scruggs
(17) Ken Suarez
(18) Dick Tidrow

1971 Currie Press Richmond Braves

(Atlanta Braves, AAA) (black and white) (3-3/8" x 5-5/16")

NM

Complete Set (18): 160.00

(1) Tommie Aaron
(2) Sam Ayoub
(3) Dusty Baker
(4) Jim Breazeale
(5) Jack Crist
(6) Shaun Fitzmaurice
(7) Jim French
(8) Larry Jaster
(9) Van Kelly
(10) Rich Kester
(11) Clyde King
(12) Dave Lobb
(13) Larry Maxie
(14) Hank McGraw
(15) Gary Neibauer
(16) Guy Rose
(17) Fred Velazquez
(18) Bobby Young

1971 Jeff Morey Syracuse Chiefs

(New York Yankees, AAA) (black and white) (3-1/2" x5-1/2")

NM

Complete Set (8): 125.00

(1) Len Boehmer
(2) Ossie Chavarria
(3) Alan Closter
(4) Fred Frazier
(5) Rob Gardner
(6) George Pena
(7) Rusty Torres
(8) Danny Walton

1972 TCMA Cedar Rapids Cardinals

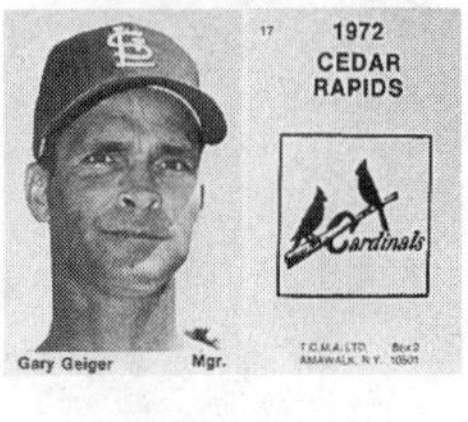

(St. Louis Cardinals, A) (a scarce 3-1/4" x 5" team photo was issued as part of the set, but is not often seen today)

NM

Complete Set, w/ team photo (30):325.00

Complete Set, no team photo (29): 175.00

1 Bill Pinkham
2 Mark Hale
3 Tom Zimmer
4 Don Buchheister
5 Jethro Mills
6 John Sawatski
7 Jim Gregory
8 Duke Wheeler
9 Victor Diaz
10 Jim Dunham
11 Mike Carmuso
12 Bruce Henderson
13 Manny Abreu
14 Luis Gonzales
15 Gary Trumbauer
16 Randy Rencor
17 Gary Geiger
18 Burt Nordstrom
19 Mike Proffitt
20 Milo Voskovitch
21 Jim Silvey
22 Joe Mazzella
23 Craig Burns
24 Leon Lee
25 Larry Aubel
26 Mark Mueller
27 Tony Velasquez
28 Bill Poe
29 Monte Bolinger
30 Team Photo

1972 Seattle Rainiers team issue

(Co-op, A) (black & white) (issued as 4-player 8-1/2"x 11" sheets; single cardsare 3-1/16" x 4-5/8")

NM

Complete Set (24): 45.00

(1) Rafael Amiami
(2) Greg Brust
(3) Wade Carpenter
(4) Mike Peters
(5) Jose Gomez
(6) Gene Lanthorn
(7) Jeff McKay
(8) Jay Tatar
(9) Rocky Hernandez
(10) Tony Pepper
(11) Roger Rasmussen
(12) Jack Winchester
(13) Wes Dixon
(14) Ray Ewing
(15) Ken Roll
(16) Rich Thompson
(17) Willy Adams
(18) Bill Kindoll
(19) Kevin Kooyman
(20) Wendell Stephens
(21) Steve Mezich
(22) John Ownes
(23) Jose Sencion
(24) Ray Washburn

Value of modern team sets is often predicated as much on inclusion of star player's early cards as on scarcity of the issue.

1972 Tacoma Twins team issue

(Minnesota Twins, AAA) (black & white, 2-3/8" x 3-1/8", blank-back)

NM

Complete Set (16): 27.50

(1) Mike Adams
(2) Glen Borgmann
(3) Mike Brooks
(4) Ezell Carter
(5) Mike Derrick
(6) Glenn Ezell
(7) Ken Gill
(8) Hal Haydel
(9) Ron Herbel
(10) Jim Holt
(11) Tom Kelly
(12) Steve Luebber
(13) Cap Peterson
(14) Dennis Saunders
(15) Jim Strickland
(16) Jerry Terrell

1972 Virginian-Pilot Tidewater Tides

During the 1972 baseball season, radio station WTAR sponsored a series of ads in the Virginian-Pilot (morning) and Ledger-Star (evening) newspapers in Norfolk. The 3-1/2" x 4" ads promoted an upcoming Tides game and each had a photo of a player or announcer and a thumbnail sketch. The unnumbered clippings are checklisted here alphabetically. The Tides were the N.Y. Mets, AAA farm club in 1972.

NM

Complete Set (22): 150.00

(1) Lute Barnes
(2) Hank Bauer
(3) Marty Brennaman (broadcaster)
(4) Chip Coulter
(5) Bill Dillman
(6) Bobby Etheridge
(7) Dick Fraim (broadcaster)
(8) John Glass
(9) Jim Gosger
(10) Jim Kennedy
(11) Tommy Moore
(12) Jose Morales
(13) Harry Parker
(14) Jerry Perkins
(15) Bob Rauch
(16) Fred Reahm
(17) Barry Raziano
(18) Billy Scripture
(19) Gary Sprague
(20) George Spriggs
(21) Brent Strom
(22) George Theodore

1973 TCMA Cedar Rapids Astros

(Houston Astros, A) (cards are slightly smaller than standard 2-1/2" x 3-1/2")

NM

Complete Set, w/ team photo (28): 150.00

Complete Set, no team photo (27) : 100.00

1 Arturo Gonzales (Gonzalez)
2 Ramon Perez
3 Al Williams
4 Guillermo Foster
5 Bob Dean
6 Fred Mims
7 Art Gardner
8 Jesus Reyes
9 Don Buchheister
10 Neil Rasmussen
11 Luis Pujols
12 George Vasquez
13 Paulo DeLeon
14 Mike Stanton
15 Luis Sanchez
16 Jose Sosa
17 Luis Melendez
18 Steve Englishby
19 Rafael Tatis
20 Richard Williams
21 Alfredo Javier
22 Romaldo Blanco
23 Bob Youse
24 Eleno Cuen
25 Leo Posada
26 Team Photo
27 Pancho Lopez
28 Jorge Moreno

1973 Sherbrooke Pirates team issue

(Pittsburgh Pirates, AA) (black & white, 3-1/4" x 4-1/4", blank-back)

	NM
Complete Set (18):	200.00

(1) Tony Armas
(2) David Arrington
(3) Mel Civil
(4) Pablo Cruz
(5) Frank Frontive
(6) Brad Gratz
(7) Roberto Guenns
(8) Juan Jiminez
(9) Ken Macha
(10) Mario Mendoza
(11) Jim Minshall
(12) Ron Mitchell
(13) Luther Quinn
(14) Jim Sadowski
(15) Kent Tekulve
(16) John Vance
(17) Bud Whileyman
(18) Alfredo Zavala

1973 Syracuse Chiefs team issue

(N.Y. Yankees, AAA) (black & white) (includes late-issue Pazik card)

	NM
Complete Set (30):	200.00

(1) Felipe Alou
(2) Matty Alou
(3) Ron Blomberg
(4) John Callison
(5) Horace Clark
(6) Alan Closter
(7) Joe DiMaggio
(8) Lou Gehrig
(9) Larry Gowell
(10) Ralph Houk
(11) Mike Kekich
(12) Ron Klimkowski
(13) Steve Kline
(14) Sparky Lyle
(15) Mickey Mantle
(16) Lindy McDaniel
(17) George Medich
(18) Gene Michael
(19) Thurman Munson
(20) Bobby Murcer
(21) Graig Nettles
(22) Mike Pazik
(23) Fritz Peterson
(24) Babe Ruth
(25) Cellie Sanchez
(26) Mel Stottlemyre
(27) Frank Tepedino
(28) Otto Velez
(29) Roy White
(30) George Zeber

1973 Caruso Tacoma Twins

(Minnesota Twins, AAA) (black and white, 2-3/8" x 3-1/8", blank backs)

	NM
Complete Set (21):	19.00

(1) Vic Albury
(2) Glen Borgmann
(3) Mike Brooks
(4) Bill Campbell
(5) Glenn Ezell
(6) Kerby Ferrell
(7) Dan Fife
(8) Bob Gebhard
(9) Ken Gill
(10) Bucky Guth
(11) Jim Hoppe
(12) Tom Kelly
(13) Craig Kusick
(14) John Matias
(15) Mike McCormick
(16) Jim Nettles
(17) Tim Norton
(18) Rick Renick
(19) Eric Soderholm
(20) Bob Storm
(21) Jim Strickland

1973 Click-Click Three Rivers Eagles photo pack

(Cincinnati Reds, AA) (7" x 8-3/4," blank-back, b&w)

	NM
Complete Set (18):	150.00

(1) Santo Alcala
(2) Jack Anduyar (Joaquin Andujar)
(3) Marc Bombard
(4) Eric Boyd
(5) Kent Durdick
(6) Art Cover
(7) Arturo De Freites (DeFreitas)
(8) Darrell Devitt
(9) Doug Flinn (Flynn)
(10) Ken Hansen
(11) Mike Heintz
(12) Tom Hume
(13) Ray Knight
(14) Gary Polczynski
(15) Greg Sinatro
(16) Tom Spencer
(17) Don Werner
(18) Pat Zachry

1973 Kansas State Bank Wichita Aeros

(Chicago Cubs, AAA) (black & white, 3-1/2" x 5") (reported production, 500; Porter card often found trimmed short)

	NM
Complete Set, w/variations (21):	165.00
Complete Set, no variations (19):	80.00

(1) Matt Alexander
(2) Tom Badcock
(3) Clinton Compton
(4a) Jim Hibbs (name/position on same line)
(4b) Jim Hibbs (name/position on two lines)
(5) Pete LaCock
(6) Tony LaRussa
(7) Tom Lundstedt
(8) Jim Marshall
(9) J.C. Martin
(10) Al Montreuil
(11) Joe Ortiz
(12) Griggy Porter
(13) Paul Reuschel
(14) Ralph Rickey
(15) Dave Rosello
(16) Jim Todd
(17) Chris Ward
(18a) Ron Tompkins (name/position on one line)
(18b) Ron Tompkins (name/position on two lines)
(19) Floyd Weaver

1974 Caruso Albuquerque Dukes

(L.A. Dodgers, AAA) (blue, red & orange, 2-3/4" x 3-5/8", blank-back)

	NM
Complete Set (16):	25.00

64 Henry Cruz
65 Tom Tischinski
66 Orlando Alvarez
67 Terry McDermott
68 Ivan DeJesus
69 Kevin Pasley
70 Phil Keller
71 Eddie Solomon
72 Charlie Manuel
73 Greg Shanahan
74 Lee Robinson
75 P.R. Powell
76 Jerry Royster
77 Stan Wasiak
78 Bobby Randall
79 Jim Allen

1974 Albuquerque Dukes team issue

(L.A. Dodgers, AAA) (blue and white, 2-1/2" x 4-1/8", blank-back) (edition of 2,000)

	NM
Complete Set (23):	350.00

(1) Orlando Alvarez
(2) Bernie Beckman
(3) Wayne Burney
(4) Henry Cruz
(5) Ivan De Jesus
(6) Greg Heydeman
(7) Rex Hudson
(8) Phil Keller
(9) Charlie Manuel
(10) Terry McDermott
(11) Rick Nitz
(12) Kevin Pasley
(13) P.R. Powell
(14) Bobby Randall
(15) Rick Rhoden
(16) Lee Robinson
(17) Jerry Royster
(18) Greg Shanahan
(19) Eddie Solomon
(20) Mike Strahler
(21) Tom Tischinski
(22) Stan Wall
(23) Stan Wasiak

1974 TCMA Cedar Rapids Astros

(Houston Astros, A)

	NM
Complete Set (28):	100.00

1 Bob Renninger
2 Bob Youse
3 Jesus Reyes
4 Arturo Gonzalez
5 Tom Rima
6 Joe Sambito
7 Dave Aloi
8 Mike Jones
9 Calvin Partley
10 Alejandro Taveras
11 Luis Pujols
12 Eric Brown
13 Luis Sanchez
14 Jose Alfaro
15 Jorge Moreno
16 Fred Mims
17 Fernando Tatis
18 Tom Tellman (Tellmann)
19 Kevin Drake
20 Guillermo Foster
21 Pastor Perez
22 Bob Cluck
23 Larry Elenes
24 Jose Sosa
25 Leo Posada
26 Mike Holland
27 Pablo DeLeon
28 Don Buchheister

1974 TCMA Gastonia Rangers

(Texas Rangers, A)

	NM
Complete Set (24):	150.00

(1) Curt Arnett
(2) Jon Astroth
(3) Mike Bacsik
(4) Len Barker
(5) Don Bodenhamer
(6) Don Bright
(7) Gary Cooper
(8) Rich Donnelly
(9) Dan Duran
(10) Dave Fendrick
(11) Lindsey Graham
(12) Tim Murphy
(13) Fred Nichols
(14) Drew Nickerson
(15) Ed Nottle
(16) Wally Pontiff
(17) Ray Rainbolt
(18) Rich Shubert
(19) Rick Simon
(20) Keith Smith
(21) John Sutton
(22) Mark Tanner
(23) Don Thomas
(24) Bobby Thompson

1974 Caruso Hawaii Islanders

(San Diego Padres, AAA) (black & red, 2-3/4" x 3-5/8", blank-back)

	NM
Complete Set (8):	18.00

101 Gene Locklear
102 Gary Jestadt
103 Hector Torres
104 Ed Acosta
105 Pat Corrales
106 Bill Almon
107 Rich Chiles
108 Roy Hartsfield

1974 Falstaff Beer Omaha Royals

OMAHA ROYALS
SPOTLIGHT
JIM CLARK
Outfielder
Because we're all in this together

(K.C. Royals, AAA) (black & white, 8-1/4" x 11", blank-back)

	NM
Complete Set (10):	165.00

(1) Jose Arcia
(2) Ed Bernard
(3) Jim Clark
(4) Jim Foor
(5) Tom Harmon
(6) Dennis Leonard
(7) Jose Martinez
(8) Dennis Paepke
(9) Paul Peiz
(10) Tom Poquette

1974 Caruso Phoenix Giants

(S.F. Giants, AAA) (blue, red & orange, 2-3/4" x 3-5/8", blank-back)

	NM
Complete Set (11):	18.00

80 Skip James
81 Mike Sadek
82 Leon Brown
83 Glenn Redmon
84 Ed Sukla
85 Glenn Adams
86 Bruce Christiansen
87 Jimmy Rosario
88 Frank Johnson
89 Glenn Ezell
90 Rocky Bridges

1974 Caruso Sacramento Solons

(Milwaukee Brewers, AAA) (blue & yellow, 2-3/4" x 3-5/8", blank-back)

	NM
Complete Set (18):	20.00

46 Tom Reynolds
47 Art Kusnyer
48 Gorman Thomas
49 Bill McNulty
50 Tom Bianco
51 Gary Cavallo
52 Tom Hausman
53 Roger Miller
54 Tom King
55 Craig Glassco
56 Jose Salado
57 Sixto Lezcano
58 Steve McCartney
59 Juan Lopez
60 Jack Lind
61 Rob Ellis
62 Bob Lemon
63 Bob Sheldon

1974 Caruso Salt Lake City Angels

(California Angels, AAA) (brown & red, 2-3/4" x 3-5/8", blank-back)

	NM
Complete Set (10):	18.00

91 Rudy Meoli
92 Bob Marcano
93 Frankie George
94 Dave Chorley
95 Morrie Nettles
96 Bruce Bochte
97 Norm Sherry
98 Jerry Bell
99 Paul Dade
100 Danny Briggs

1974 Seattle Rainiers team issue

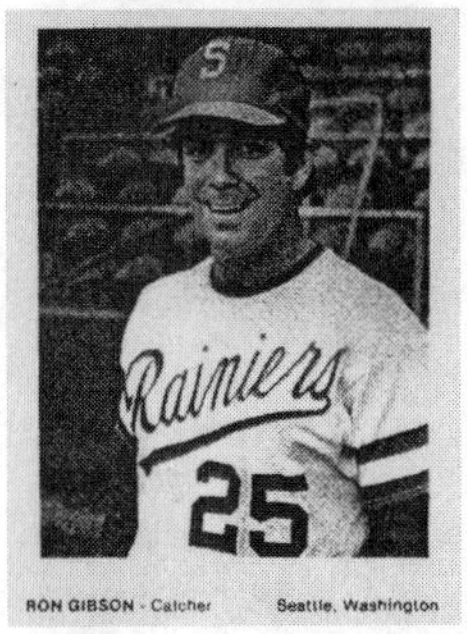

(Co-op, A) (black & white, blank-back) (printed four cards per 8-1/2" x 11" sheet; 300 sets produced plus 100 extra cards of four local favorites, designated with *)

	NM
Complete Set (20):	150.00

(1) Mike Armstrong
(2) Keith Halgerson
(3) Sam Hessley
(4) Rick Kuhn
(5) Carl Christiansen
(6) Bob Cummings
(7) Lynn Jones
(8) Jerry Rogers
(9) Tim Doerr
(10) Steve Meade
(11) Peter Savute
(12) Jim Turner
(13) Mike McNiel
(14) Steve Moore
(15) John Underwood
(16) Alan Viebrock
(17) Ron Gibson (*)
(18) Doug Peterson (*)
(19) Greg Riddock (*)
(20) Bill Taoukalas (*)

1974 Caruso Spokane Indians

(Texas Rangers, AAA) (brown & orange, 2-3/4" x 3-5/8", blank-back)

	NM
Complete Set (18):	19.00

28 Steve Dunning
29 Bob Johnson
30 Rick Henninger
31 Jim Schellenback
32 Rick Waits
33 Dave Driscione
34 Bill Fahey
35 Don Castle
36 Bob Jones
37 Dave Moates
38 Tom Robson
39 Mike Cubbage
40 Steve Greenberg
41 Roy Howell
42 Pete Mackanin
43 Vern Wilkens
44 Marty Martinez
45 Del Wilber

Values shown are a national average. Some teams and players enjoy regional popularity which may affect market prices.

1974 Syracuse Chiefs team issue

(N.Y. Yankees old-timers) (black-and-white, blank-back) (Some cards found with blue Indian-head logo on back, indicative of prize-winning status. Frazier's card is extremely scarce because it could be redeemed for a bicycle.)

	NM
Complete Set (30):	225.00

(1) Rich Bladt
(2) Ron Blomberg
(3) Tom Buskey
(4) Rick Dempsey
(5) Joe DiMaggio
(6) Pat Dobson
(7) Fred Frazier
(8) Whitey Ford
(9) Lou Gehrig
(10) Roger Hambright
(11) Mike Hegan
(12) Elston Howard
(13) Steve Kline
(14) Sparky Lyle
(15) Mickey Mantle
(16) Sam McDowell
(17) George Medich
(18) Gene Michael
(19) Thurman Munson
(20) Bobby Murcer
(21) Graig Nettles
(22) Dave Paga
(23) Fritz Peterson
(24) Babe Ruth
(25) Celerino Sanchez
(26) Fred Stanley
(27) Mel Stottlemyre
(28) Otto Velez
(29) Bill Virdon
(30) Roy White

1974 Caruso Tacoma Twins

(Minnesota Twins, AAA) (black & red on white, 2-3/4" x 3-5/8", blank-back)

	NM
Complete Set (27):	20.00

1 Jim Obradovich
2 Dale Soderholm
3 Craig Kusick
4 Cal Ermer
5 Eddie Bane
6 Dan Fife
7 Jim Hughes
8 Mike Pazik
9 Frank Schuster
10 Coley Smith
11 Earl Stephenson
12 Juan Vientidos
13 Dan Vossler
14 Mark Wiley
15 Sam Ceci
16 George Pena
17 Sergio Ferrer
18 Doug Howard
19 Bill Ralston
20 Rick Renick
21 Jim Van Wyck
22 Mike Adams
23 Lyman Bostock
24 Jim Fairey
25 Tom Kelly
26 Ed Palat
27 Danny Walton

1974 TCMA Tri-Valley Highlanders

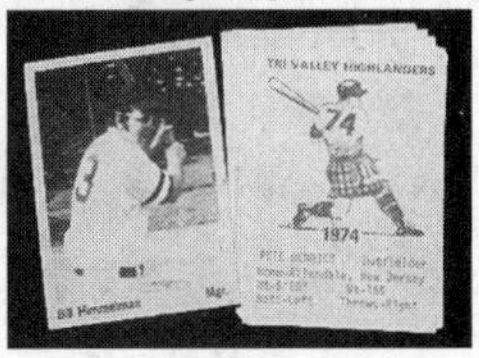

(New Jersey semi-pro Metropolitan Baseball League team) (black-and-white; 750 sets reported produced)

	NM
Complete Set (25):	125.00

(1) Bruce Atkins
(2) Tom Bangs
(3) Mike Burke
(4) Tom Butler
(5) Tom Butti
(6) Joe Chirico
(7) Bart Conners
(8) Pete Corigliano
(9) Ernie Doherty
(10) Keith Duncan
(11) Dan Esposito
(12) Bruce Garofalo
(13) John Guglielmotti
(14) Jim Hagman
(15) Keith Hagman
(16) Pete Henrici
(17) Bill Himmelman
(18) Pete Loyka
(19) Steve Loyka
(20) Clint Lynch
(21) Chip Muse
(22) Chip O'Neill
(23) Mark Palermo
(24) Kevin Stewart
(25) Bob Vanderclock

1974 One Day Film Wichita Aeros

(Chicago Cubs, AAA) (2-1/4" x 3-1/4" black & white; set price includes scarce Babcock card.)

	NM
Complete Set (28):	140.00

101 Francisco Lopez
102 Paul Zahn
103a Walter Babcock Jr. (W. Thomas Badcock)
103b Tom Badcock
104 Roberto Rodriguez
105 George Manz
106 Tom Dettore Jr.
107 David LaRoche
108 Daniel Corder
109 Mike Roarke
110 James Todd Jr.
111 Wilford Prail
112 Paul Reuschel
113 Cleo James
114 Al Montreuil
115 Ron Matney
116 Robert Sperring
117 Jack Hiatt
118 Griggy Porter Jr.
119 Ron Dunn
120 Gene Hiser
121 Alfredo Zavala
122 Dave Arrington
123 Steven Swisher
124 Pete LaCock
125 Scipio R. Spinks
126 Bob Drew (business mgr.)
127 John Wallenstein (gm)
128 Paul "Doc" St. Onge (trainer)

1975 Caruso Albuquerque Dukes

(L.A. Dodgers, AAA) (black & white, 2-3/4" x 3-7/8", blank-back)

	NM
Complete Set (21):	25.00

1 Orlando Alvarez
2 Joe Simpson
3 Jerry Royster
4 Lee Robinson
5 John Hale
6 Bobby Randall
7 Terry McDermott
8 Terry Collins
9 Cleo Smith
10 Wayne Burney
11 Dick Selma
12 Greg Shanahan
13 Rex Hudson
14 Stan Wasiak
15 Pablo Peguero
16 Rick Nitz
17 Stan Wall
18 Jim Allen
19 Jim Haller
20 Dennis Lewallyn
21 Wayne Miller

1975 TCMA Anderson Rangers

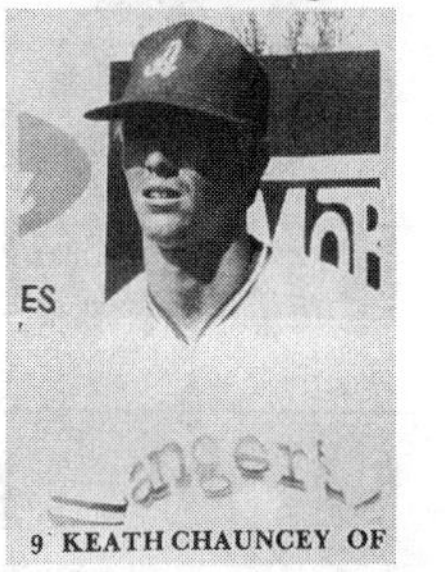

(Texas Rangers, A) (black and white)

	NM
Complete Set (25):	45.00

1 Tommy Smith
2 Rick Lisi
3 Mark Miller
8 Tim Brookens
9 Keath Chauncey
10 Glenn Purvis
15 Gary Grey
16 Curt Runyon
17 Terry Olson
18 Jim Crall
20 Dave McCarthy
23 Kerry Gettery
25 Danny Tidwell
28 Wes Goodale
29 Jeff Byrd
32 Jim Clancy (no picture on card)
37 Bob Carroll
39 Bill Patten
42 Freeman Evans
43 Don Bright
46 Joe Russell
47 Ward Smith
57 Drew Nickerson
67 Darrel Frolin
---- Ed Nottle

1975 TCMA Appleton Foxes

(Chicago White Sox, A) (b/w, facsimile signature on front)

	NM
Complete Set (29):	30.00

(1) Fred Anyzeski
(2) Kevin Bell
(3) Robert Bianco
(4) Paul Bock
(5) Bobby Combs
(6) Roy Coulter
(7) Bob Flynn (trainer)
(8) Bill Kautzer
(9) Tom King
(10) Bob Klein
(11) Odie Koehnke (batboy)
(12) Tony Komadina
(13) Juan Leonardo
(14) Ted Loehr
(15) Gordon Lund
(16) Bobby McClellan
(17) Candy Mercado
(18) Larry Monroe
(19) Johnny Narron
(20) Phil Nerone
(21) Ed Olszta
(22) Bob Palmer
(23) Harris Price
(24) Scott Richartz
(25) Silvano Robles
(26) Eric Thomas
(27) Tom Toman
(28) Ed Wheeler
(29) Batboys (Brian Garvey, Greg Mielke, Fred Holtz)

1975 TCMA Burlington Bees

(Milwaukee Brewers, A) (black and white)

	NM
Complete Set (29):	45.00

(1) John Buffamoyer
(2) Gary Conn
(3) Barry Cort
(4) Marty DeMerritt
(5) Butch Edge
(6) Terry Erwin
(7) Matt Galante
(8) Miguel Garcia
(9) Frank Gaton
(10) "Moose" Hass (Haas)
(11) Dennis Holmberg
(12) Sam Jones
(13) Sam Killingsworth
(14) Esteban Maria
(15) Victor Marichal
(16) Marcos Majias
(17) Sam Monteau
(18) Willie Mueller
(19) Abelino Pena
(20) Neil Rasmussen
(21) Alex Rodriquez
(22) Sal Rosario
(23) Pedro Sanchez
(24) Carey Scarborough
(25) Joe Slaymaker
(26) Ron Smith
(27) Gil Stafford
(28) Dave Sylvia
(29) John Whiting

1975 TCMA Cedar Rapids Giants

(S.F. Giants, A) (black and white)

	NM
Complete Set (32):	45.00

1 Tom Hughes
2 Mike Wilbins
3 Steve Cline

4 Joe Heinen
5 German de los Santos
6 John Riddle
7 Bob Thompson
8 Jeff Yurak
9 Terry Lee
10 Dan Beitey
11 John Nix
12 Don Sasser
13 Brian Felda
14 John Johnson
15 Mike Cash
16 Jim Ray
17 Dan Smith
18 Don Buchheister
19 Bob Hartsfield
20 Barney Wilson
21 Frank Ferrell
22 Mike Dodd
23 Jim Ayers
24 Jerry Stamps
25 Mark Woodbrey
26 Don Benedetti
27 Ron Hodges
28 Wayne Bradley
29 Calvin Moore
30 Garet Strong
31 Terry Kenny
32 Ernie Young

1975 TCMA Clinton Pilots

(Detroit Tigers, A) (black and white)

NM
Complete Set (31): 80.00
1 Jim Leyland
2 Dave Rozema
3 Dwight Carter
4 Brian Kelly
5 Grog Klino
6 Steve Gamby
7 Bill Michael
8 Randy Haas
9 Issac Gimenez
10 Ray Gimenez
11 Jim Murray
12 John Dinkelmeyer
13 Larry Feola
14 Tom Lantz
15 Not issued
16 Mike Uremovich
17 Kevin Slattery
18 Mark Wagner
19 Ben Hunt
20 Greg Shippy
21 Luis Atilano
22 Tom Perkins
23 Al Baker
24 Steve Trella
24a Jose Centeno
24b Steve Trella
25 Harry Schulz
26 Not issued
27 Mike Bartell
28 Al Callis
29 Venoy Garrison
30 Jeff Reinke
---- Dave Holm

1975 TCMA Dubuque Packers

(Houston Astros, A) (black and white)

NM
Complete Set (32): 40.00
1 Clancy (Mascot)
2 Terry Puhl
3 Jeff Smith
4 Tom Rima
5 Arnaldo Alvarado
6 Fay Thompson
7 Bob Dean
8 Mike Mendoza
9 John McLaren
10 Bob Cluck
11 Romo Blanco
12 Roger Polanco
13 Eleno Cuen
14 Rick Haynes
15 J.J. Cannon
16 Fernando Tatis
17 Mike Weeber
18 Alan Knicely
19 Tom Dixon
20 Paulo DeLeon
21 Luis Pujols
22 Jose Alfaro
23 Gordon Pladson
24 Dave Aloi
25 Jorge Moreno
26 Tom Twellman
27 George Lazarique (Lauzerique)
28 Arnie Costell
29 Kevin Drake
30 Mike Hasley
31 Jack Goetz
32 Alvin Osofsky

1975 Sussman Ft. Lauderdale Yankees

(N.Y. Yankees, A) (black & white, 2-1/2" x 3-1/2", blank-back) (Price includes the scarce Figueroa card; fewer than 20 were reported released due to its use in a prize redemption program)

NM
Complete Set (30): 80.00
1 Scott Norris
2 Mike Ferraro
3 Benny Perez
4 Neil Liebovitz
5 Dave Wright
6 Rich Meltz
7 Dave Rajsick
8 Greg Diehl
9 Tony Derosa
10 Rick Fleshman
11 Pat Peterson
12 Jim Sullivan
13 Marv Thompson
14 Joe Alvarez
15 Ken Kruppa
16 Jim Bierman
17 Doug Melvin
18 Joe Kwasny
19 Mike Heath
20 Sheldon Gill
21 Dennis Werth
22 Jesus Figueroa
23 Wilson Plunkett
24 Jose Alcantara
25 Leo Pasada
26 Garth Iorg
27 Scott Delgatti
28 Mike Rusk
29 Team Photo
30 Jerry Narron

1975 Caruso Hawaii Islanders

(San Diego Padres, AAA) (black & white, 2-7/8" x 3-7/8", blank-back)

NM
Complete Set (21): 25.00
1 Gus Gil
2 Steve Huntz
3 Bob Davis
4 Randy Elliott
5 Dave Roberts
6 Rod Gaspar
7 Jim Fairey
8 Jerry Turner
9 Marv Galliher
10 Sonny Jackson
11 Bill Almon
12 Brent Strom
13 Frank Linzy
14 Jim Shellenback
15 Larry Hardy
16 Gary Ross
17 Bob Strampe
18 Jerry Johnson
19 Butch Metzger
20 Dave Wehrmeister
21 Bob Miller

Value of modern team sets is often predicated as much on inclusion of star player's early cards as on scarcity of the issue.

1975 TCMA International League

(AAA) (black and white) (The value of this set has been depressed because of an apparent reprinting of the issue several years after its original release)

NM
Complete Set (31): 25.00
1 Jerry White
2 Dyar Miller
3 Mike Krizmanich
4 Earl Stephenson
5 Mike Reinbach
6 Jerry White
7 John Stearns
8 Lee Elia
9 Dave Pagan
10 Rob Andrews
11 Jim Hutto
12 Chris Coletta
13 Ron Clark
14 Bill Kirkpatrick
15 Fred Frazier
16 Joe Altobelli
17 Jim Hutto
18 Mike Willis
19 Glenn Stitzel
20 Fred Frazier
21 Gary Carter
22 Steve Dillard
23 Mike Krizmanich
24 Hank Webb
25 Karl Kuehl
26 Lee Elia
27 Chris Coletta
28 Mike Willis
29 Bob Gebhard
30 Dick Wissel
31 Dick Wissel

1975 TCMA Iowa Oaks

(Houston Astros, AAA)

NM
Complete Set (21): 125.00
(1) Carlos Alfonso
(2) Ron Boone
(3) Ray Busse
(4) Mike Cosgrove
(5) Jerry Davannon (DaVanon)
(6) Bob Didier
(7) Mike Easler
(8) Art Gardner
(9) Alfredo Javier
(10) Jesus de la Rosa
(11) Ramon de los Santos
(12) Joe Niekro
(13) George Pena
(14) Ramon Perez
(15) Russ Rothermal
(16) Ron Roznovsky
(17) Paul Siebert
(18) Joe Sparks
(19) Scipio Spinks
(20) Mike Stanton
(21) Alejandro Taveras

1975 TCMA Lafayette Drillers

(San Francisco, AA)

NM
Complete Set (32): 125.00
1 Chico Del Orbe
2 Wendell Kim
3 Joey Martin
4 Scott Wolfe
5 Tommy Smith
6 Jake Brown
7 Gary Atwell
8 Ernie Young
9 Craig Barnes
10 John Yeglinski
11 Tom Stedman
12 Gary Alexander
13 Jack Clark
14 Reggie Walton
15 Frank Riccelli
16 Rob Dressler
17 Kyle Hypes
18 Jay Dillard
19 Jeff Little
20 Julio Divison
21 Silvano Quezada
22 David Fuqua
23 Terry Cornutt
24 John Steigerwald
25 Bob Drew
26 Don Steele
27 Al Stuckeman
28 Dan Adams
29 Ducky Crandall
30 Denny Sommers
31 Clark Field
32 Batboys

1975 TCMA Lynchburg Rangers

(Texas Rangers, A)

NM
Complete Set (26): 40.00
(1) Rich Albert
(2) Curt Arnett
(3) George Ban
(4) Mel Barrow
(5) Larry Bradford
(6) Bobby Buford
(7) Bobby Cuellar
(8) Amado Dinzey
(9) Brian Doyle
(10) Dan Duran
(11) Chuck Hammond
(12) Eddie Holman
(13) William Johnson
(14) Jerome Johnson
(15) Robert Long
(16) Ken Miller
(17) Brian Nakamoto
(18) Pat Putnam
(19) Ray Rainbolt
(20) Ron Rockhill
(21) Jeff Scott
(22) Glenn Smith
(23) Mark Tanner
(24) Wayne Terwilliger
(25) Don Thomas
(26) Bobby Thompson

1975 Doug McWilliams 1955 Oakland Oaks

The Oakland Oaks team of 1955 is featured in this set, a collector's issue from baseball photographer Doug McWilliams, who shot the photos when he was 17 years old. The set commemorates the 20th anniversary of the city's last team in the Pacific Coast League. The 2-1/4" x 3-1/4" cards are printed in black-and-white on front and in blue on back. The unnumbered cards are checklisted here alphabetically. Sets originally sold for about $3.

NM
Complete Set (36): 65.00
(1) George Bamberger
(2) Jojo Barnes
(3) Charlie Beamon
(4) Fred Besana
(5) Bill (Bud) Black
(6) Tom Borland
(7) Ernie Broglio
(8) Joe Brovia
(9) Hal Brown
(10) Bob Cain
(11) Bill Consolo
(12) Art Cuitti
(13) Karl Drews
(14) Don Ferrarese
(15) Allen Gettel
(16) Pumpsie Green
(17) Clint Hartung
(18) John Jorgensen
(19) Joe Kirrene
(20) Brooks Lawrence
(21) Jim Marshall
(22) George Metkovich
(23) Don Moitoza
(24) Tom Munoz
(25) Bob Murphy
(26) Len Neal
(27) Lefty O'Doul
(28) Duane Pillette
(29) Tony Rivas
(30) Russell Rose
(31) Bill Serena
(32) Dick Strahs
(33) Bob Swift
(34) Eddie Taylor
(35) Chris Van Cuyk
(36) Wally Westlake

1975 Oklahoma City 89ers team issue

(Cleveland Indians, AAA) (black & white) (5,000 sets reported issued with 4,500 given to fans on baseball card nights)

NM
Complete Set (24): 35.00
1 Robert Grossman
2 Barry Lersch
3 Thomas Mc Gough
4 Richard Henninger
5 Thomas Brennan
6 Bruce Ellingsen
7 Larry Andersen
8 James Kern
9 James Strickland
10 Rick Waits
11 John Siracusa
12 Benjamin Heise
13 Orlando Gonzalez
14 Brian Ostrosser
15 Tommy Smith
16 Thomas Mc Millan
17 James Norris
18 Mike Hannah
19 Nelson Garcia
20 Joseph Lis
21 Gene Dusan
22 Michael Brooks
23 John Davis
24 Rex Rosser

1975 Top Trophies Omaha Royals

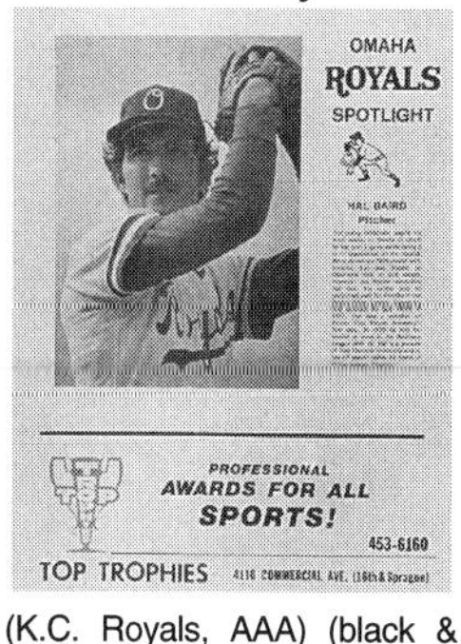

(K.C. Royals, AAA) (black & white, 8-1/2" x 11")

NM
Complete Set (18): 95.00
(1) Norm Angelini
(2) Al Autry

(3) Hal Baird
(4) Greg Chlan
(5) Mickey Cobb
(6) Bobby Floyd
(7) Ruppert Jones
(8) Gary Lance
(9) Mark Littell
(10) Keith Marshall
(11) Gary Martz
(12) Frank Ortenzio
(13) Craig Perkins
(14) Jamie Quirk
(15) Steve Staggs
(16) George Throop
(17) U. L. Washington
(18) Duke (John Wathan)

> The election of former players to the Hall of Fame does not always have an immediate upward effect on card values. The hobby market generally has done a good job of predicting those inductions and adjusting values over the course of several years.

1975 TCMA 1950's PCL

Former and future major leaguers who passed through the Pacific Coast League in the mid-1950s are featured in this collectors issue. The cards, printed in black-and-white on front and back, are an unusual 2-3/8" x 4-5/8" format. Fronts have mostly full-length action poses, shot in PCL parks of the era. An oval at bottom identifies the player, team and year. Horizontal backs have the player's major league affiliations and career stats, along with a card number, TCMA copyright and "1950's PCL" logo.

N17M
Complete Set (18): 250.00
1 Ernie Broglio
2 Karl Drews
3 Cal McLish
4 Art Schallock
5 Elmer Singleton
6 Chuck Dressen
7 George Bamberger
8 Charlie Beamon
9 Billy Consolo
10 Jim Atkins
11 Jack Lohrke
12 Carmen Mauro
13 Sam Chapman
14 George Metkovich
15 Lee Walls
16 Ron Jackson
17 Leo Thomas
18 Jim Walsh

1975 Broder Pacific Coast League All Stars

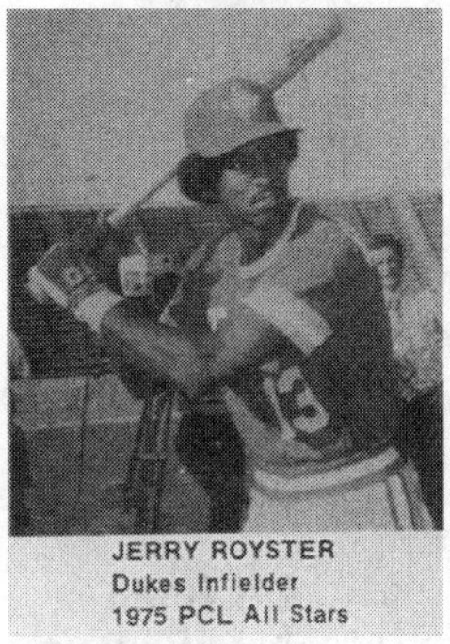

(black-and-white) (2" x 3", blank-back)

NM
Complete Set (37): 125.00
(1) Orlando Alvarez
(2) Ed Bane
(3) Charlie Chant
(4) Tommy Cruz
(5) Bob Davis
(6) Rob Dressler
(7) Bob Hansen
(8) Chuck Hartenstein
(9) Roy Hartsfield
(10) Leon Hooten
(11) Steve Huntz
(12) Ron Jackson
(13) Jerry Johnson
(14) Bob Jones
(15) Art Kusnyer
(16) John LeMaster
(17) Dave McKay
(18) Sid Monge
(19) Buzz Nitschke
(20) Rick Nitz
(21) Kevin Pasley
(22) Tony Pepper
(23) Stan Perzanowski
(24) Bobby Randall
(25) Barry Raziano
(26) Tommy Reynolds
(27) Dave Roberts
(28) Tom Robson
(29) Gary Ross
(30) Jerry Royster
(31) Norm Sherry
(32) Joe Simpson
(33) Horace Speed (action)
(34) Horace Speed (portrait)
(35) Rocky Stone
(36) Jerry Turner
(37) Stan Wall

1975 Caruso Phoenix Giants

(S.F. Giants, AAA) (black & white, 2-7/8" x 3-7/8", blank-back)

NM
Complete Set (21): 25.00
1 Leon Brown
2 Jim Williams
3 Horace Speed
4 Tony Pepper
5 Skip James
6 Jack Mull
7 Rick Bradley
8 Glenn Redmon
9 Larry Herndon
10 Bruce Christensen
11 Mike Edan
12 John LeMaster
13 Tom Heintzelman
14 Rod Dressler
15 Greg Minton
16 Bob Knepper
17 Tommy Toms
18 Ed Sulka
19 Tony Gonzalez
20 Kyle Hydes
21 Don Rose

> Checklists with card numbers in parentheses ( ) indicates the numbers do not appear on the cards.

1975 Circle K Foods Phoenix Giants

(S.F. Giants, AAA) (black & white)

NM
Complete Set (26): 9.00
1 Rocky Bridges
2 Jack Mull
3 Mike Sadek
4 Bob Nolan
5 Tony Gonzalez
6 Ed Sukla
7 Don Rose
8 Greg Minton
9 Tom Bradley
10 Bob Knepper
11 Rob Dressler
12 John Le Master
13 Glen Redmon
14 Skip James
15 Bruce Christiansen
16 Mike Eden
17 Tom Heintzelman
18 Tony Pepper
19 Jim Williams
20 Larry Herndon
21 Leon Brown
22 Horace Speed
23 Frank Johnson
24 Henry K Jordan
25 Ethan Blackaby
26 Michael J. Cramer

1975 TCMA Quad City Angels

(California Angels, A)

NM
Complete Set (34): 40.00
1 Rick Young
2 Ralph Botting
3 Willie Aikens
4 Bryant Fahrow
5 Stan Cliburn
6 Bobby Knoop
7 Jim Dorsey
8 Julio Cruz
9 Carl Person
10 Steve Mulliniks
11 Alex Guerrero
12 Manuel Jiminez
13 Rafael Kelly
14 Mike Howard
15 Carl Meche
16 Carlos Perez
17 Pat Kelly
18 John Hund
19 Mark Wulfemeyer
20 Steve Powers
21 John Roslund
22 Doug Slettvet
23 Billy Taylor
24 Mal Washington
25 Paul Hartzell
26 Steve Kelley
27 Andy Castillo
28 Danny Miller
29 Thad Bosley
30 Steve Brisbin
31 Kim Allen
32 Mark Stipetich
33 Mike Martinson
34 John Caneira

1975 TCMA 1961 Rochester Red Wings

This retroactive team set of the 1961 Rochester Red Wings features many former and future major leaguers, several of whom played with the team's Baltimore Orioles parent team. The set includes a card of Boog Powell. The card of Bob Johnson uses the same photo found of him on the 1968 Topps deckle edge test proof sheets. While there is some variation in size due to cutting, the cards measure about 3-1/4" x 4-3/16", and are printed in black-and-white. Fronts have player poses with the name in an oval at bottom and a white border around. Backs have major league record and stats, along with player identification and TCMA copyright line. The unnumbered cards are checklisted here alphabetically.

NM
Complete Set (11): 165.00
(1) Jim Finigan
(2) Frank House
(3) Bob Johnson
(4) Ron Kabbes
(5) John Kucks
(6) Boog Powell
(7) Art Quirk
(8) Ron Samford
(9) Barry Shetrone
(10) Bob Trowbridge
(11) Fred Valentine

1975 Caruso Sacramento Solons

(Milwaukee Brewers, AAA) (black & white, 2-3/4" x 3-7/8", blank-back)

NM
Complete Set (22): 25.00
1 Bob Hansen
2 Dave Lindsey
3 Tommie Reynolds
4 Jack Lind
5 Toby Bianco
6 Bill Mc Nulty
7 Duane Espy
8 Bob Sheldon
9 George Vasquez
10 Art Kusnyer
11 Rob Ellis
12 Jimmy Rosario
13 Steve Bowling
14 Rick Austin
15 Tom Widmar
16 Carl Austerman
17 Carlos Velasquez
18 Gordy Crane
19 Roger Miller
20 Bill Travers
21 Pat Osburn
22 Juan Lopez

1975 Caruso Salt Lake City Gulls

(California Angels, AAA) (black & white, 2-3/4" x 3-7/8", blank-back)

NM
Complete Set (20): 20.00
1 Rusty Torres
2 Dave Collins
3 John Balaz
4 Ron Jackson
5 Dan Briggs
6 John Doherty
7 Frankie George
8 Mike Miley
9 Darrell Darrow
10 Rocky Jordan
11 Ike Hampton
12 Gary Wheelock
13 Charlie Hockenberry
14 Gary Ryerson
15 Barry Raziano
16 Louis Quintana
17 Sid Monge
18 Charlie Hudson
19 Steve Blateric
20 Norm Sherry

1975 TCMA San Antonio Brewers

(Cleveland Indians, AA) (black and white)

NM
Complete Set (22): 25.00
(1) Wil Aaron
(2) Ed Arsenault
(3) Jerry Bell
(4) Mike Brooks
(5) Gary Cleverly
(6) Joe Garcia (gm)
(7) Bob Grossman
(8) Rich Guerra
(9) Mike Hannah
(10) Bob Hickey
(11) Bill Hiss
(12) Dennis Kinney
(13) Manny Lantigua
(14) Tom Linnert
(15) Tony Manning
(16) Steve Rametta
(17) Andy Rodriguez
(18) Ron Salyer
(19) Woody Smith
(20) Paul Starkovich
(21) Gary Weese
(22) Norm Werd

1975 TCMA Shreveport Captains

(Pittsburgh Pirates, AA) (black and white)

NM
Complete Set (23): 45.00
(1) Paul Djakonow
(2) Mike Edwards
(3) Mike Gonzalez
(4) Frank Grundler
(5) Randy Hopkins
(6) Tim Jones
(7) Mike Kavanagh
(8) Rick Langford
(9) Don Leshnock
(10) Ken Melvin
(11) Ron Mitchell
(12) Tim Murtaugh
(13) Dave Nelson
(14) Doug Nelson
(15) Steve Nicosa (Nicosia)
(16) Max Oliveras
(17) Mitchell Page
(18) Harry Saferight
(19) Randy Sealy
(20) Jim Sexton
(21) Rich Standart
(22) Tom Thomas
(23) Steve Williams

1975 Caruso Spokane Indians

(Milwaukee Brewers, AAA) (black & white, 2-3/4" x 3-7/8", blank-back)

NM
Complete Set (21): 21.00
1 Tom Robson
2 Dave Moates
3 Rudy Kinard
4 Charlie Bordes
5 Rick Guarnera
6 Roy Smalley
7 Ken Pape
8 Tommy Cruz
9 Bob Jones
10 Doug Ault
11 Ron Pruitt
12 Dave Criscione
13 John Astroth
14 Mike Cubbage
15 Rick Kemp
16 Rick Waits
17 Jerry Bostic
18 Mike Bacsik
19 Dave Moharter
20 Art De Filippis
21 Ron Norman

1975 Syracuse Chiefs team issue

(N.Y. Yankees, AAA) (black-and-white) (Issued as score-card inserts. Complete sets exchangeable for bicycle. Only six cards of Bladt released.)

NM
Complete Set (25): 225.00
(1) Rick Bladt
(2) Ron Blomberg
(3) Bobby Cox
(4) Rick Dempsey
(5) Pat Dobson
(6) Whitey Ford
(7) Elston Howard
(8) Gerry Kenney
(9) Sparky Lyle
(10) Mickey Mantle
(11) Tippy Martinez
(12) Scott McGregor
(13) George Medich
(14) Thurman Munson
(15) Graig Nettles
(16) Dave Pagan
(17) Billy Parker
(18) Babe Ruth
(19) Rick Sawyer
(20) Fred Stanley
(21) Mel Stottlemyre
(22) Otto Velez
(23) Bill Virdon
(24) Roy White
(25) Terry Whitfield

1975 KMO Radio Tacoma Twins

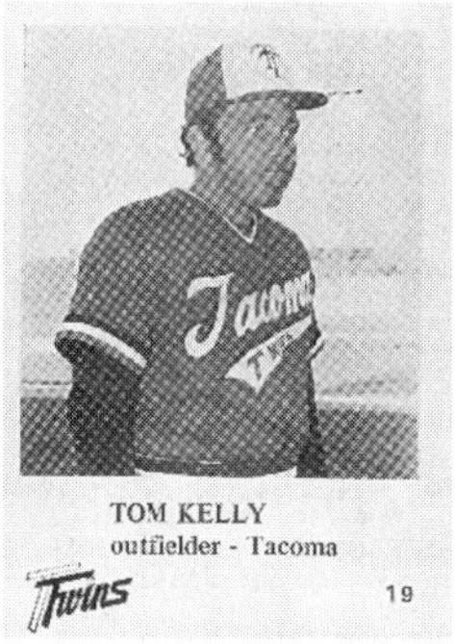

(Minnesota Twins, AAA) (black & white, 2-3/4" x 3-7/8")

NM
Complete Set (21): 20.00
1 Mark Wiley
2 Dave Mc Kay
3 Jerry Terrell
4 Tom Lunstedt
5 Bill Ralston
6 Randy Beach
7 Randy Bass
8 Rick Renick
9 Bob Gorinski
10 Cal Ermer
11 Tom Johnson
12 Rocky Stone
13 Eddie Bane
14 Mike Pazik
15 Greg Thayer
16 Brad Cutler
17 Coley Smith
18 Juan Vientidos
19 Tom Kelly
20 Ed Palat
21 Mike Poepping

1975 Stewart Sandwiches Tidewater Tides

(N.Y. Mets, AAA) (black-and-white) (300 sets available to hobby)

NM
Complete Set (24): 125.00
(1) Benny Ayala
(2) Bob Bartlett
(3) Dwight Bernard
(4) Kent Biggerstaff
(5) Bruce Boisclair
(6) Nardi Contreras
(7) Jerry Cram
(8) Mark De John
(9) Ron Diggle
(10) Nino Espinosa
(11) Leo Foster
(12) Joe Frazier
(13) Ron Hodges
(14) Jay Kleven
(15) Bill Laxton
(16) Gary Manderbach
(17) Brock Pemberton
(18) Terry Senn
(19) Roy Staiger
(20) Randy Sterling
(21) Craig Swan
(22) George Theodore
(23) Mike Vail
(24) Mike Wegener

1975 Caruso Tucson Toros

(Oakland A's, AAA) (black & white, 2-7/8" x 3-7/8", blank-back)

NM
Complete Set (21): 30.00
1 Bill Grabarkewitz
2 Tom Sandt
3 Ramon Webster
4 Gaylen Pitts
5 Buzz Nitschke
6 Mike Weathers
7 Dale Sanner
8 Charlie Chant
9 Ike Blessitt
10 Keith Lieppman
11 Rich McKinney
12 Juan Gomez
13 Lew Krausse
14 Craig Mitchell
15 Leo Mazzone
16 Skip Lockwood
17 Leon Hooten
18 Alan Griffin
19 Skip Pitlock
20 Roger Nelson
21 Hank Aguirre

1975 Tucson Toros team issue

(Oakland A's, AAA) (black & white)

NM
Complete Set (23): 40.00
Autograph Card
1 Hank Aguirre
2 Charlie Chant
3 Juan Gomez
4 Bill Grabarkewitz
5 Alan Griffin
6 Leon Hooten
7 Lew Krausse
8 Chester Lemon
9 Skip Lockwood
10 Leo Mazzone
11 Rich Mc Kinney
12 Craig Mitchell
13 Roger Nelson
14 Buzz Nitschke
15 Orlando Pena
16 Gaylen Pitts
17 Charlie Sands
18 Tom Sandt
19 Dale Sanner
20 Mike Weathers
21 Ramon Webster
22 Larry Davis
23 Freddie The Toro

1975 7-11 Tulsa Oilers

(St. Louis Cardinals, AAA) (black & white)

NM
Complete Set (24): 80.00
1 Hector Cruz
2 Leon Lee
3 Kenton "Ken" Boyer
4 Kenneth Reynolds
5 Richard Leon
6 Kenneth Crosby
7 Michael Kelleher
8 Harold Lanier
9 James Willoughby
10 William Parsons
11 Harold Rasmussen
12 Larry Herndon
13 Douglas Howard
14 Michael Proly
15 Gregory Terlecky
16 Jerry Mumphrey
17 Randall Wiles
18 Joseph Lindsey
19 John Johnson
20 James Foor
21 Sergio Robles
22 Thomas Harmon
23 Mario Guerreo
24 Richard Billings

1975 TCMA Waterbury Dodgers

(L.A. Dodgers, AA) (black and white)

NM
Complete Set (22): 60.00
(1) Tom Badcock
(2) Jose Baez
(3) Glenn Burke
(4) Larry Corrigan
(5) Bob Detherage
(6) Mike Dimmel
(7) Art Fischetti
(8) Dewey Forry
(9) Rafael Landestoy
(10) Dave Lanfair
(11) Don LeJohn
(12) Bob Lesslie
(13) Rich Magner
(14) Barney Mestek
(15) Steve Patchin
(16) Thad Philyaw
(17) Lance Rautzhan
(18) Jim Riggleman
(19) Don Standley
(20) Tim Steele
(21) Jim Van Der Beck
(22) Marvin Webb

1975 TCMA Waterloo Royals

(Kansas City Royals, A) (complete set price includes both Barranca variations)

NM
Complete Set, w/Barranca error (34): 135.00
Complete Set, no Barranca error (33): 75.00
(1a) German Barranca (Waterloo Royals logo on back)
(1b) German Barranca (Dubuque Packers logo and #17 on back)
(2) Al Bartlinski
(3) John Bass
(4) Charlie Beamon
(5) Roy Branch
(6) Brenda Brunk, Dave Brunk
(7) Willie Clark
(8) Pat Curran
(9) Karel Deleeuw
(10) Bobby Edmonson
(11) Bobby Falcon
(12) Craig Flanders
(13) Joe Gates
(14) Luis Gonzalez
(15) John Hart
(16) Dave Hrovat
(17) Steve Lacy
(18) Kevin Lahey
(19) Tom Laseter
(20) Manuel Moreta
(21) Lou Olsen
(22) Darrell Parker
(23) Jerry Peterson
(24) Dan Quisenberry
(25) Ed Sempsprott
(26) Luis Silverio
(27) Dick Smotherman
(28) Mark Souza
(29) John Sullivan
(30) Roy Tanner
(31) Hal Thomasson
(32) Gary Williams
(33) Mike Williams
(34) Willie Wilson

1975 Sussman West Palm Beach Expos

(Montreal Expos) (black & white, 2-1/2" x 3-1/2", blank-back) (Price includes late-issue Whitacre, Krause and Bernazard cards)

NM
Complete Set (32): 32.00
1 Julio Perez
2 Gary Gingrich
3 Jim Baby
4a Team photo (Fred Whitacre) (GM)
4b (Fred Whitacre) (GM)
5 Mark Ewell
6 Jose Bastian
7 Roberto Ramos
8 Carlos Ledezma
9 Joe Kerrigan
10 Hal Dues
11 Marcel Lacheman
12 Godfrey Evans
13 Jerry Fry
14 Ron Staggs
15 Mike Curran
16 William Welsh
17 Gordon Mac Kenzie
18 Chris Wood
19 Mike Grabowski
20 Bob Woodland
21 Shane Rawley
22 Gary Horstmann
23 Mike Finlayson
24 Dave Mac Quarrie
25 Larry Horn
26 Mark Knose
27 Ron Sorey
28 Guy Krause
29a Antonio Bernazard
29b Guy Krause
30 Antonio Bernazard

Checklists with card numbers in parentheses ( ) indicates the numbers do not appear on the cards.

1976 TCMA Appleton Foxes

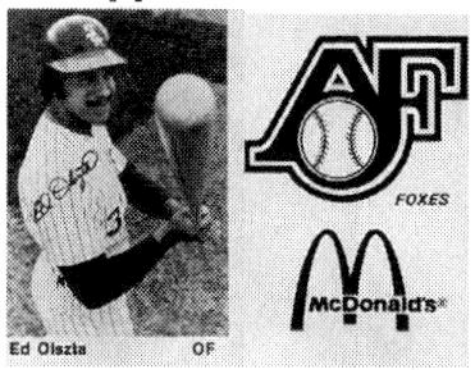

(Chicago White Sox, A) (b/w; facsimile autographs on front 1,000 sets produced)

NM
Complete Set (29): 40.00
(1) Jay Attardi
(2) Roy Coulter
(3) Curt Etchandy
(4) Rick "Bubba" Evans
(5) Mike Farrell
(6) Bob Flynn (trainer)
(7) Jim Handley
(8) Marshal Harper
(9) Tom Joyce
(10) Bill Kautzer
(11) Bill Lehman
(12) Mitch Lukevics
(13) Bob Madden
(14) Pete Maropis
(15) Candy Mercado
(16) Phil Nerone
(17) Mike Nored
(18) Ed Olszta
(19) Harris Price
(20) Curt Ramstack
(21) Scott Richartz
(22) Silvano Robles
(23) Ted Schultz
(24) Randy Seltzer
(25) Mike Smith
(26) Tommy Toman
(27) Ed Yesenchak
(28) Ed Holtz (gm), Jim Napier (manager)
(29) Batboys

1976 TCMA Arkansas Travelers

(St. Louis Cardinals, AA) (cards slightly larger than standard 2-1/2" by 3-1/2") (black and white) (1,000 sets produced)

NM
Complete Set (12): 150.00
(1) Cardell Camper
(2) Manny Castillo
(3) Bill Caudill
(4) Jack Krol
(5) Ryan Kurosaki
(6) Terry Landrum
(7) Ken Oberkfell
(8) Mike Ramsey
(9) John Urrea
(10) Bill Valentine
(11) Randy Wiles
(12) John Young

1976 TCMA Asheville Tourists

(Texas Rangers, A) (black & white) (1,000 sets produced)

NM
Complete Set (25): 60.00
1 Joe Russell
2 Randy Reynolds
3 Paul Mirabella
4 David Rivera
5 Bob Carroll
6 Bill Stone
7 Riccardo Lisi
8 Ward Smith
9 Harold Kelly
10 David McCarthy
11 Wayne Pinkerton
12 Richard Couch
13 Mike Arrington
14 Jerry Gaines
15 Patrick Putnam
16 Patrick Moock
17 Mark Miller
18 Larue Washington
19 Danny Tidwell
20 Wayne Terwilliger
21 Glenn Furvis
22 Len Glowzenski
23 Mark Soroko
24 Edward Miller
25 Joseph Stewart

1976 Batavia Trojans team issue

(Cleveland Indians, A) (black & white)

NM
Complete Set (29): 145.00
(1) Ron Arp
(2) John Brown
(3) Rocky Bullard
(4) John Buszka
(5) Al Cajide
(6) Jack Cassini
(7) Denny Doss
(8) Dave Fowlkes
(9) Ray Gault
(10) Tim Glass
(11) Larry Harmon
(12) Craig Harvey
(13) Kevin Jeansonne
(14) Bill Mitchell
(15) Steve Narleski
(16) Ken Preseren
(17) Nate Puryear
(18) Julian Rodriguez
(19) Mike Rowe
(20) Reggie Smith
(21) John Spence
(22) Sam Spence
(23) Paul Tasker
(24) John Teising
(25) Jeff Tomski
(26) Tony Toups
(27) Terry Tyson
(28) Troy Wilder
(29) Bubba Wilson

1976 TCMA Baton Rouge Cougars

(Independent, A) (black & white) (1,000 sets produced)

NM
Complete Set (21): 50.00
(1) Sterling Allen
(2) Nick Baltz
(3) Matt Batts
(4) Randy Benson
(5) Mike Brooks
(6) Tom Brown
(7) Jim Carruth (trainer)
(8) Winston Cole
(9) Robbie Cox
(10) Kevin Fogg
(11) Gary Grunsky
(12) Larry Keenum
(13) Paul Kennemur
(14) Terry Leach
(15) Mickey Miller
(16) Dave Obal
(17) Ken Palmer
(18) Gerry Poche (announcer)
(19) Ed Stephenson
(20) Bob Taylor
(21) Curtis Wallace

1976 TCMA Burlington Bees

(Milwaukee Brewers, A) (black & white) (1,000 sets produced)

NM
Complete Set (33): 35.00
(1) Greg Anderson
(2) Gary Conn
(3) Roger Danson
(4) John Dempsey
(5) Bill Dick
(6) Alvin Edge
(7) Butch Edge
(8) Miguel Encarcion
(9) Adalberto Flores
(10) Rich Ford
(11) Elliott Franklin
(12) George Frazier
(13) Matt Galante
(14) Frank Gaton
(15) Gary Gingrich
(16) Dave Globig
(17) John Hannon
(18) Dennis Holmberg
(19) Sam Jones
(20) Gary Larocque
(21) Shawn McCarthy
(22) Sam Monteau
(23) Willie Mueller
(24) Rick O'Keefe (O'Keeffe)
(25) Jay Passmore
(26) Abelino Pena
(27) Eric Restin
(28) Edgardo Romero
(29) Chuck Ross
(30) Dave Smith
(31) Ron Smith
(32) Talmage Tanks
(33) Ron Wrona

1976 TCMA Cedar Rapids Giants

(San Francisco Giants, A) (complete set price includes all variations) (black and white) (1,000 sets produced)

NM
Complete Set (37): 50.00
(1) Terry Adams
(2) Dave Anderson
(3) Ted Barnicle
(4) Jose Barrios
(5) Ken Barton
(6) Bryan Boyne
(7) Don Buchheister
(8) Ken Burton
(9) Wayne Cato
(10) Mike Glinatsis
(11a) Steve Grimes (Woodbrey back)
(11b) Steve Grimes (correct back)
(12) Ron Hodges
(13) John Johnson
(14) Steven McKown
(15) Dave Mendoza
(16) Stan Moline
(17) Dick Murray
(18) Billy Ray Parker (Prather)
(19) Francis Parker
(20) Wayne Pechek
(21) Tim Peterson
(22) Jim Pryor
(23) Mike Rex
(24) Pat Roy
(25) German de los Santos
(26) Don Sasser
(27) Ted Schoenhaus
(28) Steve Sherman
(29) Bill Tullish
(30) Lozando Washington
(31) Steve Watson
(32) Steve Wilkins
(33) Barney Wilson
(34a) Mark Woodbrey (Grimes back)
(34b) Mark Woodbrey (correct back)
(35) Ernie Young
(36) Jeff Yurak
(37) Team Photo

1976 TCMA Clinton Pilots

(Detroit Tigers, A) (complete set price includes scarce Kline and Robles cards) (black and white) (1,000 sets produced)

NM
Complete Set (37): 135.00
(1) Phil Bauer
(2) Mike Bigusiak
(3) Ken Bokek
(4) Bobby Buford
(5) Dave Burress
(6) Felan Byrd
(7) Tom Carlson
(8) George David
(9) Fred DePietro
(10) Julian Ditto
(11) Tim Doerr
(12) Mike Elders
(13) Freeman Evans
(14) Popilio Fermin
(15) Don Fletcher
(16) Miguel Garcia
(17) Kerry Getter
(18) Juan Gonzalez
(19) Bob Hartsfield
(20) Kent Hunziker
(21) Joe Jackson
(22) Tom King
(23) Greg Kline
(24) Willie Mueller
(25) Denzil Palmer
(26) Jack Parish
(27) Gene Quick
(28) Silvano Robles
(29) Phil Trucks
(30) Jackie Uhey
(31) Mike Vaughn
(32) Paul Vavruska
(33) Larry Walbring
(34) Mal Washington
(35) Ward Wilson
(36) Dave Wood
(37) Donna Colschen, Fritz Colschen

1976 TCMA Dubuque Packers

(Houston Astros, A) (black & white) (1,000 sets produced)

NM
Complete Set (40): 55.00
(1) Jose Alvarez
(2) Edward Anderson
(3) Reno Aragon
(4) Bruce Boehy
(5) Leroy Clark
(6) John Clothery
(7) Robert Cluck
(8) Neal Cooper
(9) Martin DeMerritt
(10) Jeff Ellison
(11) Larry Eubanks
(12) Barry Glabman
(13) Larry Green
(14) Robert Hallgren
(15) Michael Hasley
(16) Ray Hutchinson
(17) Alan Knicely
(18) Kenneth Lahonta
(19) George Lauzerique
(20) John Lee
(21) William Melendez
(22) Michael Mendoza
(23) Richard Miller
(24) Raul Nieves
(25) Martin Perez
(26) Donald Pisker
(27) Joseph Pittman
(28) Gordon Pladson
(29) Pedro Prieto
(30) Bill Roberts
(31) Alberto Rondon
(32) Simon Rosario
(33) Randy Rouse
(34) Jeffrey Smith
(35) Fay Thompson
(36) Tom Twellman
(37) Michael Tyler
(38) Jerry Willeford
(39) Gary Wilson
(40) Robert Cluck, Steve Greenberg, George Lauzerique

1976 Sussman Ft. Lauderdale Yankees

(N.Y. Yankees, A) (black & white, 2-1/2" x 3-1/2", blank-back)

NM
Complete Set (30): 70.00
1 Jesus Figueroa
2 Duke Drawdy
3 Jerry Narron
4 Joe Alcantara
5 Jim Mc Donald
6 Tom Davis
7 Bernardo Estevez
8 Jim Lysgaard
9 Domingo Ramos
10 Ken Kruppa
11 Nate Chapman
12 Antonio Bautista
13 Darnell Waters
14 Mike Heath
15 Damaso Garcia
16 Marty Caffrey
17 Mike Ferraro
18 Orlando Pena
19 Dave Wright
20 Greg Diehl
21 Willie Upshaw
22 Roger Slagle
23 Rick Stenholm
24 Benny Perez
25 Tim Lewis
26 Bevan Luis
27 Doug Melvin
28 Randy Niemann
29 Juan Espino
30 Sandy Valdespino

1976 Caruso Hawaii Islanders

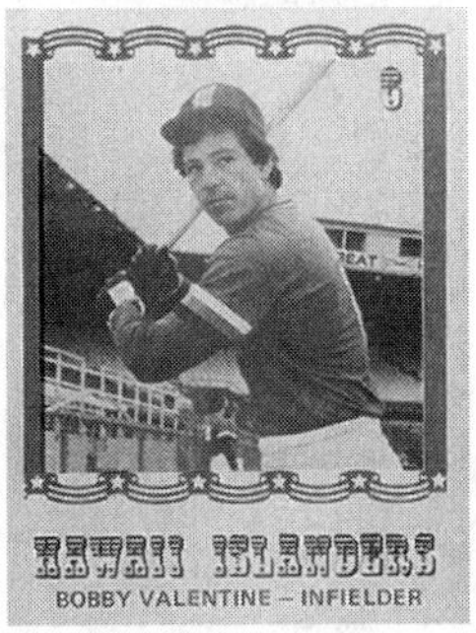

(San Diego Padres, AAA) (red and blue on white card stock, approximately 2-3/4" x 3-9/16")

NM
Complete Set (21): 30.00
1 Chuck Hartenstein
2 Jim Shellenback
3 Eddie Watt
4 Roy Hartsfield
5 Dave Roberts
6 Bobby Valentine
7 John Scott
8 Jerry Stone
9 Dave Hilton
10 Bill Almon
11 Joe Pepitone
12 Gaylen Mc Spadden
13 Gene Richards
14 Ken Reynolds
15 Jim Fairey
16 Dave Freisleben
17 Kala Kaaihue
18 Rod Gaspar
19 Jerry Johnson
20 Steve Huntz
21 Mike Champion

1976 Indianapolis Indians team issue

(Cincinnati Reds, AAA) (color)

NM
Complete Set (25): 45.00
Checklist
1 Jim Snyder
2 Larry Payne
3 Ray Knight
4 Arturo De Freites
5 Joe Henderson
6 Tom Spencer
7 Dave Revering
8 Jeff Sovern
9 Tom Hume
10 Rudy Meoli
11 Sonny Ruberto
12 Tom Carroll
13 Junior Kennedy
14 Lorin Grow
15 Dave Schneck
16 Manny Sarmiento
17 Don Werner
18 Mike Thompson
19 Keith Marshall
20 Rich Hinton
21 John Knox
22 Carlos Alfonso
23 Tony Franklin
24 Mac Scarce
25 Ron Mc Clain

1976 Oklahoma City 89ers team issue

(Philadelphia Phillies, AAA) (black & white) (sets given to first 2,000 fans attending July 26 game)

NM
Complete Set (30): 90.00
1 Terry R. Jones
2 Sergio Ferrer
3 Ronald B. Clark
4 Lonnie Smith
6 James F. Morrison
7 Mickael T. Buskey
8 Dane C. Iorg
10 Richard A. Bosetti
12 Fred Andrews
14 James Bunning
15 Randy L. Lerch
16 Danny J. Boitano
18 Willie Hernandez
19 William G. Nahorodny
20 Ruben Amaro
21 David Wallace
22 Wayne O. Nordhagen
23 Quency Hill
24 John M. Bastable
25 John E. Montague Jr.
26 Manuel M. Seoane
28 Larry G. Kiser
30 Robert L. Oliver

1976 Top Trophies Omaha Royals

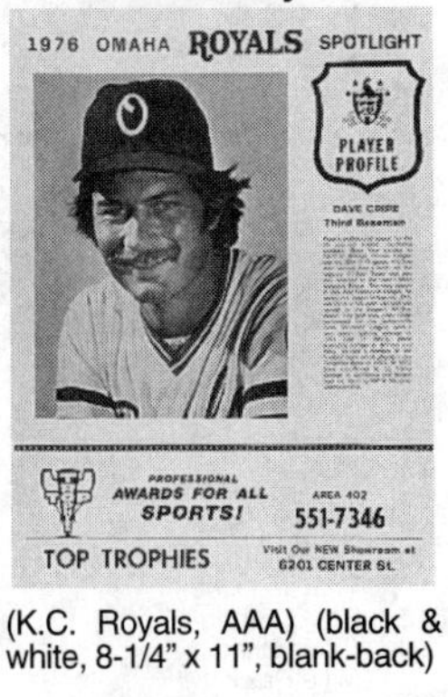

(K.C. Royals, AAA) (black & white, 8-1/4" x 11", blank-back)

NM
Complete Set (27): 135.00
(1) Hall Of Fame Members
(2) Hal Baird
(3) Cowboy (Mark Ballinger)

(4) Tom Bruno
(5) Jerry Cram
(6) Dave Cripe
(7) Dave Hasbach
(8) Bob Johnson
(9) Ruppert Jones
(10) Gary Lance
(11) Sheldon Mallory
(12) Gary Martz
(13) Bob Mc Clure
(14) Lynn Mc Kinney
(15) Brian Murphy
(16) Roger Nelson
(17) Lew Olsen
(18) Moose (Frank Ortenzio)
(19) Steve Patchin
(20) Max Patkin
(21) Craig Perkins
(22) Steve Staggs
(23) Bill Sudakis
(24) George Throop
(25) U. L. Washington
(26) Duke (John Wathan)
(27) Joe Zdeb

1976 Caruso Phoenix Giants

(S.F. Giants, AAA) (brown & red on yellow card stock, approximately 2-3/4" x 3-9/16")

		NM
Complete Set (20):		32.00
1	John Le Master	
2	Bruce Christensen	
3	Kyle Hypes	
4	Silvano Quezada	
5	Skip James	
6	Rocky Bridges	
7	Frank Riccelli	
8	Horace Speed	
9	Terry Cornutt	
10	Mike Wegener	
11	Gary Alexander	
12	Tommy Toms	
13	Bob Gallagher	
14	Mike Eden	
15	Bob Knepper	
16	Tom Heintzelman	
17	Joey Martin	
18	Ed Plank	
19	Jack Clark	
20	Bruce Miller	

1976 Valley Nat'l Bank Phoenix Giants

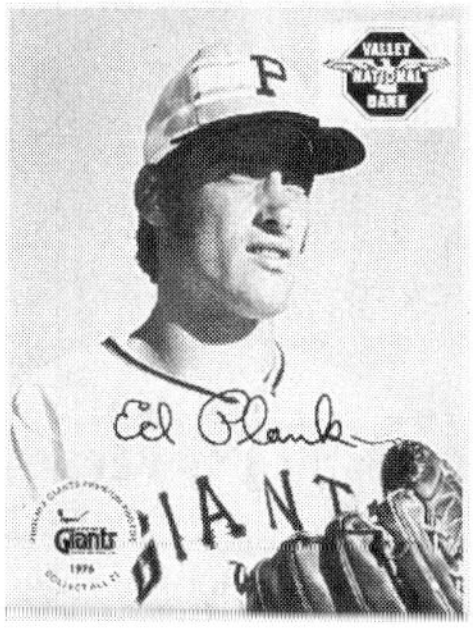

(S.F. Giants, AAA) (black & white, approximately 4-3/8" x 3-3/8", blank-back)

		NM
Complete Set (26):		15.00
(1)	Gary Alexander	
(2)	Rocky Bridges (in dugout)	
(3)	Rocky Bridges (on field)	
(4)	Bruce Christiansen	
(5)	Jack Clark	
(6)	Terry Cornutt	

(7) Jay Dillard
(8) Bob Gallagher
(9) Don Hahn
(10) Tom Heintzelman
(11) Kyle Hypes
(12) Skip James (fielding)
(13) Skip James (throwing)
(14) Harry Jordan
(15) Bob Knepper
(16) Johnny Le Master
(17) Joey Martin
(18) Bruce Miller
(19) Greg Minton
(20) Jack Mull
(21) Ed Plank
(22) Silvano Quezada
(23) Frank Ricelli
(24) Horace Speed
(25) Tommy Toms
(26) Mike Wegener

1976 Cramer Phoenix Giants

(S.F. Giants, AAA)

		NM
Complete Set (23):		25.00
2	Johnnie LeMaster	
10	Jack Mull	
11	Larry Herndon	
14	Bruce Miller	
15	Skip James	
17	Bruce Christensen	
18	Bob Gallagher	
19	Mike Eden	
20	Horace Speed	
22	Jack Clark	
23	Tom Heintzelman	
25	Gary Alexander	
26	Rocky Bridges	
28	Ed Plank	
30	Frank Ricelli (Riccelli)	
32	Silvano Quezoda (Quezada)	
33	Tommy Toms	
34	Bob Knepper	
35	Mike Wegener	
36	Kyle Hypes	
37	Rob Dressler	
38	Terry Cornutt	
----	Stadium Super Card (Ethan Blackaby)	

1976 Coke Phoenix Giants Premiums

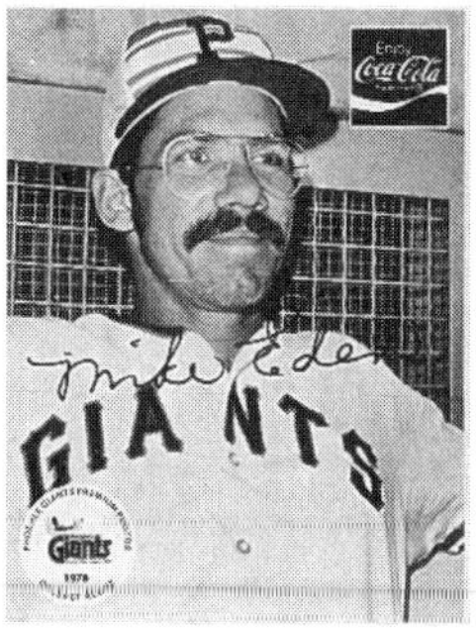

(S.F. Giants, AAA) (black & white, approximately 3-1/2" x 4-3/8", blank-back)

		NM
Complete Set (24):		18.00
(1)	Gary Alexander	
(2)	Bruce Christensen	
(3)	Jack Clark	
(4)	Terry Cornutt	
(5)	Rob Dressler	
(6)	Mike Eden	
(7)	Bob Gallagher	

(8) Tom Heintzelman
(9) Larry Herndon
(10) Kyle Hypes
(11) Bob Knepper
(12) Johnnie Lemaster
(13) Bruce Miller
(14) Jack Mull
(15) Ed Plank
(16) Silvano Quezada
(17) Frank Riccelli
(18) Horace Speed
(19) Tommy Toms
(20) Mike Wegener
(21a) Rocky Bridges
(21b) Rocky Bridges
(22a) Skip James
(22b) Skip James

1976 TCMA Quad City Angels

(California Angels, A) (black & white) (1,000 sets produced) (Mercedes is scarce late-issue card)

		NM
Complete Set, w/Mercedes (40):		205.00
Partial Set, no Mercedes (39):		135.00
(1)	Dan Beerbrower	
(2)	Ned Bergert	
(3)	Ralph Botting	
(4)	Bob Boyd	
(5)	Gary Boyle	
(6)	Rich Brewster	
(7)	Jim Brown	
(8)	Jerry Brust	
(9)	Bob Clark	
(10)	Mark Clear	
(11)	Stan Cliburn	
(12)	Steve Eddy	
(13)	Bill Ewing	
(14)	Bob Ferris	
(15)	John Flannery	
(16)	David Hollifield	
(17)	Rafael Kelly	
(18)	Corney (Carney) Lansford	
(19)	Joe Maddon	
(20)	Mike Martinson	
(21)	Manuel Mercedes	
(22)	Scott Moffit	
(23)	Don Mraz	
(24)	"Mystery Infielder"	
(25)	Jim Officer	
(26)	Harry Pells	
(27)	Charles Porter	
(28)	Jerry Quigley	
(29)	John Ricanelli	
(30)	Bob Slater	
(31)	Doug Slettvet	
(32)	Randy Smith	
(33)	Bob Starks	
(34)	Dave Steck	
(35)	Larry Stubing	
(36)	Billy Taylor	
(37)	Steve Tebbetts	
(38)	Richard Thon	
(39)	Steve Whitehead	
(40)	Ken Wright	

1976 Caruso Sacramento Solons

(Texas Rangers, AAA) (black & white)

		NM
Complete Set (23):		30.00
1	Dave Criscione	
2	Keith Smith	
3	Dave Moharter	
4	Craig Skok	
5	Bob Jones	
6	Mike Bacsik	
7	Tommy Cruz	
8	Tommy Boggs	
9	Doug Ault	
10	Greg Pryor	
11	Charlie Bordes	
12	Art De Filippis	
13	John Sutton	
14	Ed Nottle	
15	Jim Gideon	
16	Don Thomas	
17	Bump Wills	
18	Lew Beasley	
19	Jerry Bostic	
20	Len Barker	
21	David Clyde	
22	Rick Donnelly	
23	Greg Mohlberg	

1976 Caruso Salt Lake City Gulls

(California Angels, AAA) (black & white)

		NM
Complete Set (22):		18.00
1	Darrell Darrow	
2	Gary Wheelock	
3	Mike Overy	
4	Frankie George	
5	Carlos Lopez	
6	Mike Miley	
7	Mike Martinson	
8	Ed Kurpici	
9	Billy Smith	
10	Pat Cristelli	
11	Orlando Alvarez	
12	Ike Hampton	
13	Chuck Hockenbery	
14	Wayne Simpson	
15	Dick Lange	
16	Skip Pitlock	
17	Luis Quintana	
18	Paul Dade	
19	Dave Collins	
20	Dan Briggs	
21	Charlie Hudson	
22	Gil Flores	

1976 Knowlton's Dairy San Antonio Brewers

(Milwaukee Brewers, AA) (black & white, 2-1/2" x 3-1/2")

		NM
Complete Set (26):		45.00
(1)	Mel Barrow	
(2)	Frank Bolick	
(3)	Don Bright	
(4)	Mike Bucci	
(5)	Jeffrey Byrd	
(6)	Keith Chauncey	
(7)	Jim Clancy	
(8)	Bobby Cuellar	
(9)	Doug Duncan	
(10)	Dan Duran	
(11)	Gary Gray	
(12)	Ed Holman	
(13)	Rudy Jaramillo	
(14)	Marty Martinez	
(15)	Brian Nakamoto	
(16)	Ron Norman	
(17)	Wayne Pinkerton	
(18)	John Poloni	
(19)	Ray Rainbolt	
(20)	Rich Shubert	
(21)	Mike Steen	
(22)	Blair Stouffer	
(23)	Don G. Thomas	
(24)	Jim Thomas	
(25)	Bobby Thompson	
(26)	Dan Wheat	

Checklists with card numbers in parentheses ( ) indicates the numbers do not appear on the cards.

1976 Cramer Seattle Rainiers

(Independent, A) (black & white, 2" x 3")

		NM
Complete Set (20):		22.00
2	Steve Stillwell	
5	Doug Peterson	
6	Steve Watson	
7	Bob Kraft	
8	Russ Attebery	
9	Terry Sheehan	
11	George Benson	
12	Dave Stewart	
14	Paul Gilmartin	
17	Ken May	
18	Kevin Gilmartin	
19	Ken Kanikeberg	
20	Xavier Dixon	
21	Vince Barbisan	
23	Ken Peters	
26	Dave Sloan	
27	Jimmy Williams	
30	Danny Miller	
35	Art Peterson	
37	Dennis Peterson	

1976 TCMA Shreveport Captains

(Pittsburgh Pirates, AA) (Weinberg, team cards were scarce late issues) (black & white) (1,000 sets produced)

		NM
Complete Set, no Weinberg, team (23):		40.00
Complete Set, w/ Weinberg, team (25):		175.00
1	Gary Hargis	
2	Rich Standart	
3	Rich Anderson	
4	Doug Nelson	
5	Luke Wrenn	
6	Mike Gonzalez	
7	Rod Scurry	
8	Jim Sexton	
9	Paul Djakonow	
10	Dave Nelson	
11	Mike Edwards	
12	Randy Sealy	
13	John Lipon	
14	Albert Louis	
15	Silvio Martinez	
16	Steve Blomberg	
17	Frank Grundler	
18	Harry Saferight	
19	Chet Gunter	
20	Rafael Cariel	
21	Ron Mitchell	
22	Randy Hopkins	
23	Barry Weinberg	
----	Tim Murtaugh	
----	Team card (5-3/8" x 3-1/2")	

1976 Caruso Spokane Indians

(Milwaukee Brewers, AAA) (brown & orange on white card stock, 2-3/4" x 3-9/16")

NM
Complete Set (21): 25.00
1 Bobby Sheldon
2 Jimy Rosario
3 Sam Ceci
4 Tom Widmar
5 Ron Jacobs
6 Bob Ellis
7 Juan Lopez
8 Kevin Kobel
9 Bob Stampe
10 Moose Haas
11 Perry Danforth
12 Art Kuysner
13 Frank Howard
14 Gary Beare
15 Kurt Bevacqua
16 Tommie Reynolds
17 Bob Hansen
18 Steve Bowling
19 Lenn Sakata
20 Toby Bianco
21 Rick Austin

1976 Dairy Queen Tacoma Twins

(Minnesota Twins, AAA) (black & white)

NM
Complete Set (24): 27.50
(1) Paul Ausman
(2) Randy Bass
(3) Bill Butler
(4) Larry Cox
(5) Tom Epperly
(6) Cal Ermer
(7) Jim Gideon
(8) Bob Gorinski
(9) Tom Johnson
(10) Jack Maloof
(11) Bob Maneely
(12) Davis May
(13) Dave Mc Kay
(14) Willie Norwood
(15) Mike Pazik
(16) Mike Peopping
(17) Rick Rennick
(18) Tommy Sain
(19) Dale Solderholm
(20) Jim Van Wyck
(21) Juan Vientidos
(22) Mark Wiley
(23) Rob Wilfong
(24) Al Woods

1976 Caruso Tucson Toros

(Texas Rangers, AAA) (black & red on green card stock, 2-3/4" x 3-9/16")

NM
Complete Set (20): 22.00
1 Bob Picciolo
2 Don Hopkins
3 Keith Lieppman
4 Gary Woods
5 Mike Weathers
6 Angel Manguel
7 Bob Lacey
8 Rich McKinney
9 Harry Bright
10 Wayne Gross
11 Jim Holt
12 Leon Hooten
13 Alan Griffin
14 Gaylen Pitts
15 Craig Mitchell
16 Tom Bradley
17 Rick Lysander
18 Charlie Hudson
19 Jeff Newman
20 Charlie Sands

1976 Cramer Tucson Toros

(Texas Rangers, AAA) (black & white, 2-3/8" x 3-1/2")

NM
Complete Set (24): 17.00
2 Mike Weathers
3 Gary Woods
6 Keith Lieppman
8 Angel Manguel (Mangual)
9 Rob Picciolo
10 Chris Batton
11 Don Hopkins
12 Jeff Newman
14 Dale Sanner
15 Wayne Kirby
16 Leon Hooten
19 Bob Lacey
22 Rich McKinney
23 Harry Bright
25 Wayne Gross
28 Rick Lysander
32 Craig Mitchell
33 Juan Gomez
34 Alan Griffin
35 Tom Bradley
37 Jim Holt
39 Charlie Sands
42 Gaylen Pitts
44 Skip Pitlock

1976 Goof's Pants Tulsa Oilers

(St. Louis Cardinals, AAA) (black & white, 2-1/2" x 3-3/8") (Most sets are found with authentically autographed cards of coach Satchel Paige and Oilers Boys Baseball Camp Director Paul Dean.)

NM
Complete Set (26): 200.00
1 Ken Boyer
2 Lloyd Allen
3 Tom Harmon
4 Stan Butkus
5 Doug Clary (Clarey)
6 Mike Easler
7 Doug Capilla
8 Stan Mejias
9 Ed Crosby
10 Jimmy Freeman
11 John Tamargo
12 Leon Lee
13 Leron Lagrow
14 Luis Alvarado
15 Mike Potter
16 Mike Proly
17 Bill Rothan
18 Garry Templeton
19 Tom Walker
20 Charlie Chant
21 Steve Waterbury
22 Randy Wiles
23 Satchel Paige (autographed)
24 Paul Dean (autographed)
25 Earl Bass
26 Lee Landers

1976 TCMA Waterloo Royals

(K.C. Royals, A) (black & white) (1,000 sets produced)

NM
Complete Set (33): 70.00
(1) Bob Barr
(2) German Barranca
(3) Steve Beene
(4) Kent Cvejdlik
(5) Karel De Leeuw
(6) Rich Dubee
(7) Craig Eaton
(8) Richard Gale
(9) Danny Garcia
(10) Kevin Gillen
(11) Dale Hrovat
(12) Jack Hudson
(13) Clint Hurdle
(14) Bryan Jones
(15) Ron Kainer
(16) Steve Lacy
(17) Tom Laseter
(18) Fernando Llodrat
(19) Manuel Moreta
(20) Darrell Parker
(21) Ricky Passalacqua
(22) Jerry Peterson
(23) Ken Phelps
(24) Dan Quisenberry
(25) Ed Sempsrott
(26) Luis Silverio
(27) Ron Smith
(28) Mark Souza
(29) John Sullivan
(30) Roy Tanner
(31) Hal Thomasson
(32) Alan Viebrock
(33) Mike Williams

1976 TCMA Wausau Mets

(N.Y. Mets, A) (black & white) (1,000 sets produced)

NM
Complete Set (25): 70.00
(1) Gene Bardot
(2) Bob Barger
(3) Dave Bedrosian
(4) Butch Benton
(5) Keith Bodie
(6) Randy Brown
(7) Paul Cacciatore
(8) Larry Calufetti
(9) Ed Cipot
(10) Russell Clark
(11) Steve Darnell
(12) Tony Echols
(13) Ed Hicks
(14) Steve Kessels
(15) "Doc" Love (trainer)
(16) Luis Lunar
(17) Jeryl McIves
(18) Jim Mills
(19) Juan Monasterio
(20) Bill Monbouquette
(21) Ted O'Neill
(22) Mario Ramirez
(23) Willie Simon
(24) Fred Westfall
(25) Jim Brown (gm), Mike Feder (personnel)

1976 TCMA Williamsport Tomahawks

(Cleveland Indians, AA) (black & white) (1,000 sets produced)

NM
Complete Set (23): 50.00
(1) Wil Aaron
(2) Ed Arsenault
(3) Stan Bockewitz
(4) Wayne Cage
(5) Red Davis
(6) Bob Grossman
(7) Rich Guerra
(8) Mike Hannah
(9) Tom Linnert
(10) Tom McGough
(11) Mike Dolf
(12) Lou Isaac
(13) Pete Ithier
(14) Dennis Kinney
(15) George Mahan
(16) Tim Norrid
(17) Rick Oliver
(18) Bob Servoss
(19) Glenn Redmon
(20) Pat Wasko
(21) Gary Weese
(22) Kris Yoder
(23) Checklist

1977 TCMA Appleton Foxes

(Chicago White Sox, A) (facsimile autographs on front)

NM
Complete Set, both Minosi/Minoso (29): 120.00
Complete Set, "Minosi" only (28): 55.00
(1) Tim Bright
(2) Brad Calhoun
(3) Bobby Combs
(4) Marvis Foley
(5) Lorenzo Gray
(6) Marshal Harper
(7) Greg Herman
(8) Clay Hicks
(9) A.J. Hill
(10) Fred Howard
(11) Kent Hunziker
(12) Bob Madden
(13) John Martin
(14) Candy Mercado
(15a) Orestes Minosi, Jr. (name incorrect)
(15b) Orestes Minoso, Jr. (name correct)
(16) Ed Olszta
(17) Andy Pasillas
(18) Joel Perez
(19) Carlos Rios
(20) Keith Rokosz
(21) Randy Seltzer
(22) Michael Sivik
(23) Paul Soth
(24) Leo Sutherland
(25) Rick Thoren
(26) Steve Trout
(27) Mike Tulacz
(28) Ed Yesenchak
(29) Appleton Foxes Staff

1977 TCMA Arkansas Travelers

(St. Louis Cardinals, AA) (set price includes all late-issue variations) (black & white)

NM
Complete Set, all variations: 195.00
Complete Set, no "b" variations: 85.00
(1a) Carlton Roy Keller (team logo right)
(1b) Carlton Roy Keller (team logo left)
(2a) Ryan Kurosaki (logo right)
(2b) Ryan Kurosaki (logo left)
(3a) Teto Landrum (first name incorrect)
(3b) Terry Landrum (first name corrected)
(4a) Nick Leyva (logo right)
(4b) Nick Leyva (logo left)
(5) Mike Murphy
(6a) Mike Ramsey (logo right)
(6b) Mike Ramsey (logo left)
(7a) Andy Replogle (logo right)
(7b) Andy Replogle (logo left)
(8a) Jim Riggleman (logo right)
(8b) Jim Riggleman (logo left)
(9) Steve Staniland
(10a) John Yeglinski (logo right)
(10b) John Yeglinski (logo left)
(11a) John Young (logo right)
(11b) John Young (logo left)
(12) Ray Winder Field

1977 TCMA Asheville Tourists

(Texas Rangers, A) (black & white)

NM
Complete Set (29): 35.00
(1) Bryan Allard (Brian)
(2) Steve Bianchi
(3) Richard Couch
(4) Dennis Doyle
(5) Steve Finch
(6) Jerry Gaines
(7) Mike Griffin
(8) Mike Hicks
(9) Mike Jaccar
(10) Stan Jakubowski
(11) Greg Jemison
(12) Kerry Keenan
(13) Vic Mabee
(14) Dave McCarthy
(15) Arnold McCrary
(16) Ron Patrick
(17) Scott Peterson
(18) Dave Rivera
(19) Phil Roddy
(20) Jeff Scott
(21) Bill Simpson
(22) John Takas
(23) Wayne Terwilliger
(24) Al Thomson
(25) Phil Watson
(26) Len Whitehouse
(27) Wayne Wilkerson
(28) Glenn Williams
(29) Mike Williamson

1977 TCMA Bristol Red Sox

(Boston Red Sox, A) (black & white)

NM
Complete Set (20): 160.00
(1) Erwin Bryant
(2) Mark Buba
(3) Jose Caldera
(4) Tom Farias
(5) Joel Finch
(6) Glenn Fisher
(7) Otis Foster
(8) Ken Huizenga
(9) Ed Jurak
(10) Dave Koza
(11) Joe Kranich
(12) Dave Labossiere
(13) Breen Newcomer
(14) Mike O'Berry
(15) Gary Purcell
(16) Win Remmerswael (Remmerswaal)
(17) Burke Suter
(18) Steve Tarbell
(19) John Tudor
(20) Rich Waller

1977 TCMA Burlington Bees

(Milwaukee Brewers, A) (black & white) (Halls and Mercado are scarce late-issue cards)

NM
Complete Set, w/Halls, Mercado (27): 70.00
Partial Set, no Halls, Mercado (25): 60.00
(1) Daryl Bailey
(2) Tim Bannister
(3) Mike Dempsey
(4) Bill Dick
(5) Gary Donovan
(6) Larry Edwards
(7) Bert Flores
(8) Richard Ford

(9) Gary Gingerich
(10) Steve Greene
(11) Gary Halls
(12) Dave Hersh
(13) Al Manning
(14) Brad Meagher
(15) Candy Mercado
(16) Dennis Menke
(17) Larry Montgomery
(18) Willie Mueller
(19) Jose Oppenheimer
(20) Glenn Partridge
(21) Jay Passmore
(22) Rene Quinones
(23) Eric Restin
(24) Chuck Ross
(25) Terry Shoebridge
(26) Steve Splitt
(27) Jesus Vega

1977 TCMA Cedar Rapids Giants

(S.F. Giants, A) (complete set price includes scarce Laubhan card)

NM
Complete Set (25): 160.00
Partial Set, no Lubhan (24): 40.00
1 Rich Murray
2 Bob Brenly
3 Dave Anderson
4 John Sylvester
5 Ken Feinburg
6 Brian Moulton
7 Phil Nastu
8 Henry Marcias
9 Gary Ledbetter
10 Ken Barton
11 Jack Mull
12 Drew Nickerson
13 Jim Pryor
14 Mike Wardlow
15 Dave Myers
16 Bart Bass
17 Steve Sherman
18 Jon Harper
19 Don Buchheister
20 Mark Kuecker
21 Dan Hartwig
22 Chris Bourjos
23 Jeff Shourds
24 Steve Pearce
-- John Laubhan

1977 TCMA Charleston Patriots

(Pittsburgh Pirates, A) (black & white)

NM
Complete Set (25): 45.00
(1) Tom Burke III
(2) Jorge Carty
(3) Arcadio Cruz
(4) Bienvenido de la Rosa
(5) Rick Evans
(6) Stan Floyd
(7) Skip Leech
(8) Jim Mahoney
(9) Jim Miller
(10) Adalberto Ortiz
(11) Jim Parke
(12) Pascual Perez
(13) Eric Peterson
(14) Fred Rein
(15) Martin Rivas
(16) Bob Rock
(17) Richard Rodriquez
(18) Chuck Rouse
(19) Simon Santana
(20) Brian Schwerman
(21) Bob Semerano
(22) Jim Smith
(23) Alfredo Torres
(24) Candido Ventura
(25) Jerry Yandrick

1977 TCMA Clinton Dodgers

(L.A. Dodgers, A) (black & white) (production reported as 1,100 sets)

NM
Complete Set (29): 130.00
(1) Paul Bain
(2) Paul Bock
(3) Dave Cohea
(4) Gerry de la Cruz
(5) Jim Del Vecchio
(6) Charles Dorgan
(7) Jim Evans
(8) Chuck Gardner
(9) Rich Goulding
(10) Dan Henry
(11) Tim Jones
(12) George Kaage
(13) Ron Kittle
(14) Mark Kryka
(15) Mickey Lashley
(16) Don LeJohn, Jr.
(17) Dick McLaughlin
(18) Damon Middleton
(19) Jim Peterson
(20) Jose Reyes
(21) Tim Roche
(22) Eric Schmidt
(23) Mike Scioscia
(24) Hilario Soriano
(25) Dave Stewart
(26) Bill Swoope
(27) Ken Townsend
(28) Max Venable
(29) Mike Wilson

1977 TCMA Cocoa Astros

(Houston Astros, A) (black & white)

NM
Complete Set (25): 40.00
(1) Ed Anderson
(2) Reno Aragon
(3) Bruce Bochy
(4) Jeff Ellison
(5) Larry Eubanks
(6) Bob Hallgren
(7) Don Harkness
(8) Phil Klimas
(9) Randy Lamb
(10) Ramon Leader
(11) Diago Melendez
(12) Mark Miggins
(13) Dennis Miscik
(14) Jose Mota
(15) Jim Pankovits
(16) Gordy Pladson
(17) George Ploucher
(18) Pete Prieto
(19) Gary Rajsich
(20) Bert Roberge
(21) Simon Rosario
(22) Randy Rouse
(23) Dave Smith
(24) Tom Wiedenbauer
(25) Cocoa Astros Staff

1977 TCMA Columbus Clippers

(Pittsburgh Pirates, AAA) (black & white) (wrong-photo errors of Lois and Palmer were later corrected) (production reported of 1,100 sets)

NM
Complete Set, error photos (22): 275.00
Complete Set, w/correct photos (24): 350.00
(1) Dave Augustine
(2) Chris Batton
(3) Dale Berra
(4) Mike Easler
(5) Mike Edwards
(6) Gary Hargis
(7) Red Hartman
(8) Randy Hopkins
(9) Tim Jones
(10a) Alberto Lois (photo actually Lowell Palmer, white man)
(10b) Alberto Lois (correct photo, black man)
(11) Ken Macha
(12) Ron Mitchell
(13) Tim Murtaugh
(14) Doug Nelson
(15) Jim Nettles
(16) Steve Nicosa (Nicosia)
(17) Bob Oliver
(18a) Lowell Palmer (photo actually Alberto Lois, black man)
(18b) Lowell Palmer (correct photo, white man)
(19) Ray Price
(20) Fred Scherman
(21) Rich Standart
(22) Ed Whitson

1977 Life Insurance Co. of the Southwest Dallas Rangers

Former Dallas Rangers minor leaguers are featured in this collectors set issued in conjunction with the 1977 Dallas Sports Collectors Convention. The 2-3/4" x 3-3/4" cards are printed in black-and-white and sponsored by the Life Insurance Company of the Southwest in Dallas. Some cards have facsimile autographs or player names on front. Backs feature career highlights.

NM
Complete Set (9): 18.00
(1) Paul Aube
(2) Jodie Beeler
(3) Edward (Red) Borom
(4) Sal Gliatto
(5) Richard Herrscher
(6) Joe Kotrany
(7) Joe Macko
(8) Frank Murray
(9) Ron Samford

1977 TCMA Daytona Beach Islanders

(K.C. Royals, A) (black & white)

NM
Complete Set (27): 35.00
(1) Steve Beene
(2) Ed Cowan
(3) Rich Dubee
(4) Craig Eaton
(5) Bob Engelmeyer
(6) Jack Fleming
(7) Henry Greene
(8) Ben Grzybeck
(9) John Hoscheidt
(10) Sam Jones
(11) Tom Krattli
(12) Steve Lacey
(13) Mel Lowman
(14) Jose Martinez
(15) Ken Phelps
(16) Ray Prince
(17) Phil Pulido
(18) Tim Riley
(19) Cliff Roberts
(20) Juan Rodriquez
(21) Ed Sempsrott
(22) Marty Serrano
(23) Brad Simmons
(24) Paul Stevens
(25) Roy Tanner
(26) Hal Thomasson
(27) Buddy Yarbrough

1977 TCMA Evansville Triplets

(Detroit Tigers, AAA) (black & white)

NM
Complete Set (25): 375.00
(1) Bob Adams
(2) Julio Alonso
(3) Tom Bianco
(4) Tom Brookens
(5) George Cappuzzello
(6) Tim Corcoran
(7) Charles Day
(8) Pio DiSalva
(9) Jim Eschen
(10) Gary Geiger
(11) Eddie Glynn
(12) Dan Gonzales (Gonzalez)
(13) Glenn Gulliver
(14) Frank Harris
(15) Roric Harrison
(16) Artie James
(17) Marvin Lane
(18) Jerry Manuel
(19) Bob Molinaro
(20) Jack Morris
(21) Len Moss
(22) Lance Parrish
(23) Bruce Taylor
(24) John Valle
(25) Milt Wilcox

1977 Sussman Ft. Lauderdale Yankees

(New York Yankees, A) (black & white, 2-1/2" x 3-1/2", blank-back)

NM
Complete Set (31): 95.00
1 Pat Callahan
2 Woody Keys
3 Johnny Crawford
4 Jose Alcantara
5 Mark Theil
6 Joe Le Febvre
7 Beban Luis
8 Ted Wilborn
9 Gerry Gaube
10 Nat Showalter
11 Mark Softy
12 Jose Paulino
13 Roger Holt
14 Jim Mc Donald
15 Tim Kibbee
16 Tim Guess
17 Sam Ellis
18 Pat Tabler
19 Dave Wright
20 Steve Peters
21 Don Hogestyn
22 Scott Delgatti
23 Don Fisk
24 Stan Saleski
25 Jimmy De Paola
26 Mark Burlingame
27 Gus Gil
28 Butch Riggar
29 Juan Espino
30 Tony Cameron
31 Eddie Napoleon

1977 Caruso Hawaii Islanders

(San Diego Padres, AAA) (black & white)

NM
Complete Set (30): 24.00
1 Manny Estrada
3 Jim Wilhelm
4 Lin Hamilton
5 Luis Melendez
7 Pedro Garcia
8 Warren Hacker
9 Kala Kaaihu
10 Chuck Baker
11 Jerry Stone
12 Jim Fairey
14 John D'Acquisto
15 Jay Franklin
16 Dick Phillips
17 Bob Kammeyer
18 Rick Sweet
20 John Mc Allen
21 Mike Du Pree
22 Steve Mura
23 Vic Bernal
24 Clay Kirby
25 Mark Wiley
28 Steve Huntz
29 Eddie Watt
30 Chris Ward

1977 TCMA Holyoke Millers

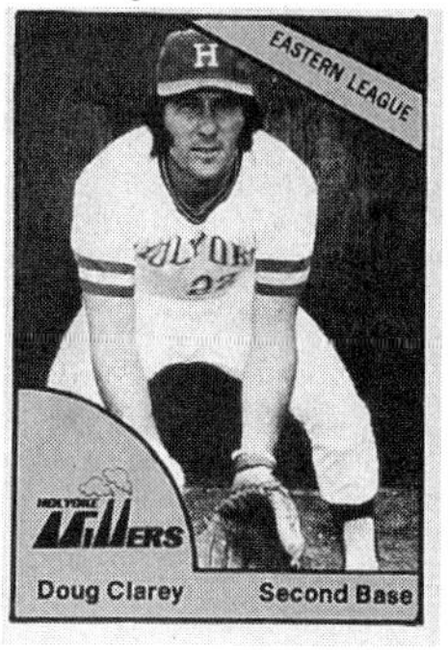

(Milwaukee Brewers, AA) (black & white)

NM
Complete Set (26): 27.50
(1) Ike Blessitt
(2) Mark Bomback
(3) John Buffamoyer
(4) Doug Clarey
(5) Garry Conn
(6) Gene Delyon
(7) Bill Dick
(8) Greg Erardi
(9) Rick Ford
(10) George Frazier
(11) Matt Galante
(12) John Hannon
(13) Lynn B. Herzig (president)
(14) Gary Holle
(15) Dale Hrovat
(16) Ron Jacobs
(17) Tom Kayser (gm)
(18) Gary LaRocque
(19) Lanny Phillips
(20) Neil Rasmussen
(21) Ed Rasmussen
(22) Ed Romero
(23) Bill Severns
(24) Rich Shubert
(25) Dave Smith
(26) Ron Wrona
(27) Jeff Yurak

1977 Indianapolis Indians team issue

(Cincinnati Reds, AAA) (color)

	NM
Complete Set (27):	20.00

2 Roy Majtyka
3 Joe Henderson
4 Dave Revering
5 Tom Hume
6 Ron Oester
7 Larry Payne
8 Don Werner
9 Paul Moskau
10 Dan Norman
11 Mike LaCoss
12 Mike Grace
13 Dan Dumoulin
14 Steve Henderson
15 Mac Scarce
16 Tommy Mutz
17 Larry Rothschild
18 Rudy Meoli
19 Raul Ferreyra
20 Arturo DeFreites
21 Mario Soto
22 Hugh Yancy
23 Barry Moss
24 Jack Maloof
25 Manny Sarmiento
26 Ron McClain
---- Team Photo
---- Checklist

1977 TCMA Jacksonville Suns

(K.C. Royals, AA) (black & white)

	NM
Complete Set (22):	80.00

(1) Mark Ballanger
(2) German Barranca
(3) Steve Burke
(4) Mike Denevi
(5) Rich Gale
(6) Joe Gates
(7) Jim Gaudet
(8) Kevin Gillen
(9) Bobby Glass
(10) Tim Ireland
(11) Dennis Kaspryzak
(12) Pete Koegel
(13) Gordon MacKenzie
(14) Frank McCann
(15) Randy McGilberry
(16) Lew Olsen
(17) Darrell Parker
(18) Bill Paschall
(19) Ken Phelps
(20) Dan Quisenberry
(21) Luis Silverio
(22) Gary Williams

1977 TCMA Lodi Dodgers

(L.A. Dodgers, A) (black & white)

	NM
Complete Set (25):	77.00

(1) Charles Barrett
(2) Mark Bradley
(3) Merv Garrison
(4) Brad Gulden
(5) Dan Henry
(6) Ubaldo Heredia
(7) Hank Jones
(8) Mike Lake
(9) Rudy Law
(10) Tony Martin
(11) Dave Patterson
(12) Pable Peguero
(13) Jack Perconte
(14) Charlie Phillips
(15) Don Ruzek
(16) Rick Sander
(17) Ed Santos
(18) Rod Scheller
(19) Steve Shirley
(20) Kelly Snider
(21) Mike Tennant
(22) Miguel Vallaran
(23) Stan Wasiak
(24) Myron White
(25) Mike Williams

1977 TCMA Lynchburg Mets

(New York Mets, A) (black & white) (Reardon is scarce late-issue card; Allen, Benton and Greenstein can be found with variations)

	NM
Complete Set, "a" variations, no Reardon (30):	115.00
Complete Set, Greenstein "a", Allen and Benton "b", no Reardon (30):	150.00
Complete Set, w/Reardon, all "b" variations (31):	350.00
Complete Set, w/Reardon and all variations (35):	1000.

(1) Jack Aker
(2a) Neil Allen (Pirates logo)
(2b) Neil Allen (Mets Logo)
(3) Gene Bardot
(4a) Butch Benton (knee showing)
(4b) Butch Benton (ankle showing)
(5) George Bradbury
(6) Mike Brown
(7) Randy Brown
(8) Robert Bryant
(9) Russell Clark
(10) Carmen Coppol
(11) Dave Covert
(12) Curt Fisher
(13) Ron Gill
(14) Scott Goodfarb
(15) Bob Grant
(16a) Stu Greenstein (knee to head photo)
(16b) Stu Greenstein (waist to head photo)
(17) Bob Healy
(18) Steve Keesses
(19) Jerry McIver
(20) Juan Monasterio
(21) Ted O'Neill
(22) Pacho Perez
(23) Mario Ramirez
(24) Jeff Reardon
(25) Bob Rossen
(26) Cliff Speck
(27) Randy Tate
(28) David Von Ohlen
(29) Fred Westfall
(30) Ward Wilson
(31) Steve Yost

1977 Chong Modesto A's

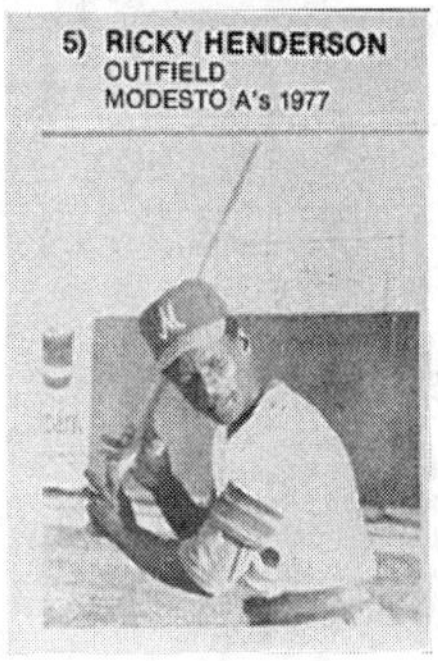

(Oakland A's, A) (black & white) (400 sets reported issued)

	NM
Complete Set (23):	1150.

1 Ted Smith
2 Barry Wright
3 Craig Minetto
4 Dominic Scala
5 Rickey Henderson
6 Jesse Wright
7 Mike Rodriguez
8 Ernie Camacho
9 Pat Dempsey
10 Randy Green
11 Mike Patterson
12 Mace Harrison
13 Rod Patterson
14 Monte Bothwell
15 Bart Braun
16 Rich Oziomiela
17 Tom Trebelhorn
18 Rod Mc Neely
19 Ron Beaurivage
20 Brian Meyl
21 John Eisinger
22 Juan Gomez, Tom Trebelhorn
---- Chong Distributor Card

1977 TCMA Newark Co-Pilots

(Milwaukee Brewers, A) (black & white)

	NM
Complete Set (29):	45.00

(1) Kevin Bass
(2) Manuel Betemit
(3) Rick Broas
(4) Ronald Buggs
(5) Chris Carstensen
(6) Pablo Cauallo
(7) Stan Davis
(8) Steve Day
(9) Tom DeRosa
(10) Ron Driver
(11) Gerry Erb
(12) Brian Fisher
(13) Adalberto Flores
(14) Bill Foley
(15) Eric Frey
(16) Jeff Harryman
(17) Dennis Holmberg
(18) Gary House
(19) Jerry Jenkins
(20) Tim Jordan
(21) David LaPoint
(22) Joe Mitchell
(23) Steve Manderfield
(24) Chester Nelson
(25) Rick Nicholson
(26) Joe Polese
(27) James Quinn
(28) John Roesch
(29) John Skorockocki

1977 Top Trophies Omaha Royals

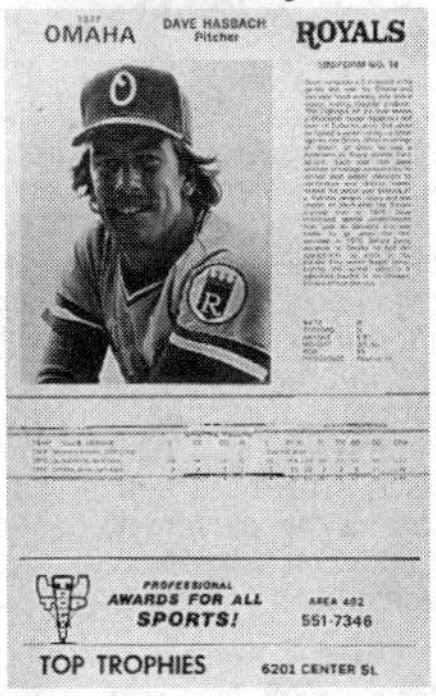

(K.C. Royals, AAA) (black & white with blue highlights, blank-backed, 7" x 10-3/4")

	NM
Complete Set (19):	115.00

(1) Mark Ballinger
(2) Steve Barr
(3) Charlie Beamon
(4) Jerry Cram
(5) Dave Cripe
(6) Rich Gale
(7) Dave Hasbach
(8) Clint Hurdle
(9) Rudy Kinard
(10) Pete Koegel
(11) Joe Lahoud
(12) Gary Lance
(13) Lynn Mc Kinney
(14) Ken Melvin
(15) Brian Murphy
(16) Greg Shanahan
(17) John Sullivan
(18) U. L. Washington
(19) Gary Wright

1977 TCMA Orlando Twins

(Minnesota Twins, AA) (black & white) (Felton is a scarce late-issue card)

	NM
Complete Set, w/Felton (23):	90.00
Partial Set, no Felton (22):	80.00

(1) Archie Amerson
(2) Paul Ausman
(3) Terry Bulling
(4) John Castino
(5) Wayne Caughey
(6) Julian Ditto
(7) Tom Epperly
(8) Frank Estes
(9) John Felton
(10) Greg Field
(11) Mike Gatlin
(12) John Goryl
(13) Bill Harris
(14) Bruce MacPherson
(15) Dennis Mattick
(16) Johnny Pittman
(17) Brian Rothrock
(18) Gary Serum
(19) Dale Soderholm
(20) Mark Souza
(21) Greg Thayer
(22) Steve Wagner
(23) Jeff Youngbauer

1977 Valley Nat'l Bank Phoenix Giants

(S.F. Giants, AAA) (black & white, approximately 4-3/8" x 3-3/8", with a blue bottom border) (all cards have facsimile autographs except Rick Bradley)

	NM
Complete Set (24):	27.50

(1) Chris Arnold
(2) Rick Bradley
(3) Rocky Bridges
(4) Terry Cornutt
(5) Rob Dressler
(6) Monroe Greenfield
(7) Don Hahn
(8) Randy Hammon
(9) Tom Heintzelman
(10) Kyle Hypes
(11) Skip James
(12) Garry Jestadt
(13) Harry Jordan
(14) Junior Kennedy
(15) Wendell Kim
(16) Bob Knepper
(17) Joey Martin
(18) Greg Minton
(19) Ed Plank
(20) Frank Riccelli
(21) Rick Sanderlin
(22) Horace Speed
(23) Tommy Toms
(24) Mike Wegener

1977 Cramer Phoenix Giants

(S.F. Giants, AAA) (color, 2-3/8" x 3-1/2")

	NM
Complete Set (24):	9.00

2 Wendell Kim
4 Vic Harris
6 Junior Kennedy
7 Greg Minton
9 Garry Jestadt
10 Rick Sanderlin
11 Don Hahn
12 Frank Riccelli
15 Skip James
16 Rob Dressler
17 Chris Arnold
18 Rick Bradley
20 Horace Speed
21 Bob Knepper
22 Michael Wegener
23 Tommy Toms
24 Dave Heaverlo
25 Gary Alexander
26 Rocky Bridges
27 Joey Martin
28 Ed Plank
29 Kyle Hypes
--- Ethan Blackaby (gm)
--- Harry Jordan (trainer)

1977 Coke Phoenix Giants Premiums

(S.F. Giants, AAA) (black & white, approximately 3-3/8" x 4-1/4") (all cards except Rick Bradley have facsimile autograph on front)

	NM
Complete Set (24):	24.00

(1) Gary Alexander
(2) Chris Arnold
(3) Rick Bradley
(4) Rocky Bridges
(5) Rob Dressler
(6) Don Hahn
(7) Vic Harris
(8) Dave Heaverlo
(9) Kyle Hypes
(10) Skip James
(11) Skip James
(12) Garry Jestadt
(13) Harry Jordan
(14) Junior Kennedy
(15) Wendell Kim
(16) Bob Knepper
(17) Joey Martin
(18) Greg Minton
(19) Ed Plank
(20) Frank Riccelli
(21) Rick Sanderlin
(22) Horace Speed
(23) Tommy Toms
(24) Mike Wegener

1977 TCMA Quad City Angels

(California Angels, A) (black & white)

	NM
Complete Set (29):	50.00

(1) Jim Ball
(2) Gary Balla
(3) Ned Bergert
(4) Mike Bishop
(5) Arturo Bonitto
(6) Bob Boyd
(7) Rich Brewster
(8) Scott Carnes
(9) Mark Clear
(10) Keith Comstock
(11) Frank Coppenbarger
(12) Chuck Cottier
(13) Joel Crisler
(14) John Harris
(15) Bob Healy
(16) John Henderson
(17) Craig Hendrickson
(18) Dave Hollifield
(19) Greg Johnson
(20) Donny Jones
(21) Scott Moffitt
(22) Steve Oliva
(23) Harry Pells
(24) Ken Schrom
(25) Rick Sentlinger
(26) Doug Slettvet
(27) Fernando Tarin
(28) Steve Tebbetts
(29) Ken Wright

1977 TCMA Reading Phillies

(Philadelphia Phillies, AA) (black & white)

	NM
Complete Set (23):	295.00

(1) Gary Begnaud

(2) George Benson
(3) Todd Brenizer
(4) Franco Ciammachilli
(5) Narda Contreras
(6) Rafael Contreras
(7) Phil Convertino
(8) Todd Cruz
(9) Bobby Demeo
(10) Lee Elia
(11) Dan Greenhalgh
(12) Glenn Gregson
(13) John Guarnaccia
(14) Jesus Hernaiz
(15) Mark Klein
(16) Pete Manos
(17) Jose Moreno
(18) Ed Olivaros
(19) Mel Roberts
(20) Kevin Saucier
(21) Tom Siliacato
(22) Rocky Skalisky
(23) Tom White

1977 McCurdy's Rochester Red Wings

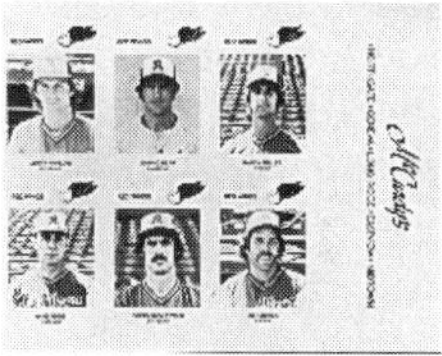

(Baltimore Orioles, AAA) (black & white set produced in form of four uncut sheets measuring 8-1/2" x 11", six players per sheet)

NM
Complete Set, Sheets (4): 175.00
Complete Set, Singles (24): 220.00
(1) David Criscione
(2) Pedro Liranzo
(3) Michael Parrott
(4) Taylor Duncan
(5) David Ford
(6) Earl Stephenson
(7) Blake Doyle
(8) Richard Bladt
(9) Terry Crowley
(10) Tony Chavez
(11) John Flinn
(12) Larry Harlow
(13) John O'Rear
(14) Randy Miller
(15) Mike Fiore
(16) Creighton Tevlin
(17) Ed Farmer
(18) John McCall
(19) Myrl Smith
(20) Gersan Jarquin
(21) Dave Harper
(22) Dennis Blair
(23) Kevin Kennedy
(24) Ken Boyer

1977 TCMA Salem Pirates

(Pittsburgh Pirates, A) (black & white) (Variations exist for several cards. Rein, Rodgers and Young are scarce late-issue cards.)

NM
Complete Set, "a" variations, no late-issues (25): 150.00
Complete Set, b" variations, with late issues (28): 250.00
(1) Paul Anthony
(2) Jim Brady
(3) Randy Bryandt
(4) Bryan Clark
(5) Casey Clark
(6) Stewart Cliburn
(7) Wink Cole
(8) Eugenio Cotes
(9a) Pablo Cruz (no shadow on face)
(9b) Pablo Cruz (shadow on face)
(10) Dennis Davis
(11a) John Dean (waist to cap photo)
(11b) John Dean (chest to cap photo)
(12) Dan DeBattista
(13) Steve Demeter
(14) Bob Mazur
(15a) Jerry McDonald (waist to cap photo)
(15b) Jerry McDonald (chest to cap photo)
(16a) Ossie Oliveras (portrait)
(16b) Ossie Oliveras (batting)
(17) Tony Pena
(18) Alphie Perdue
(19) Jeff Pinkus
(20a) Steve Powers (logo on left)
(20b) Steve Powers (logo on right)
(21) Fred Rein
(22) Dave Rodgers
(23) Luis Salazar
(24) Chuck Valley
(25) Rafael Vasquez
(26a) Dick Walterhouse (portrait)
(26b) Dick Walterhouse (batting)
(27a) Bob Weismiller (logo on left)
(27b) Bob Weismiller (logo on right)
(28) Ernie Young

1977 Cramer Salt Lake City Gulls

(California Angels, AAA) (color, 2-3/8" x 3-1/2")

NM
Complete Set (26): 10.00
1 Jimy Williams
2 Fred Frazier
4 Rance Mulliniks
5 Gilberto Flores
6 Chuck Dobson
7 Danny Goodwin
8 Tom Donohue
9 Thad Bosley
10 Pat Cristelli
11 Dave Machemer
12 Fred Kuhaulua
13 Orlando Alvarez
14 Frankie George
15 Bob Nolan
16 Luis Quintana
17 Stan Perzanowski
18 John Caneira
19 Frank Panick
20 Dick Lange
21 Mike Barlow
22 Willie Aikens
24 Mike Overy
25 Butch Alberts
---- Leonard Garcia

1977 Mr. Chef's San Jose Missions

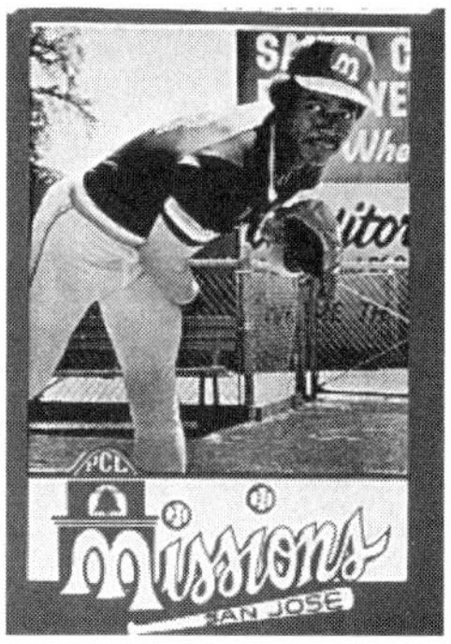

(Oakland A's, AAA) (black & white, blue borders)

NM
Complete Set (25): 15.00
1 Team Card/Checklist
2 Rene Lachemann
3 Blue Moon Odom
4 Derek Bryant
5 Milt Ramirez
6 Mark Williams
7 Jim Tyrone
8 Greg Sinatro
9 Charlie Beamon
10 Tim Hosley
11 Denny Haines
12 Mike Weathers
13 Don Hopkins
14 Bob Lacey
15 Craig Mitchell
16 Randy Boyd
17 Denny Walling
18 Randy Scarbery
19 Brian Kingman
20 Ron Bell
21 Randy Taylor
22 Jimmy Sexton
23 Brian Abraham
24 Dave Johnson
25 Paul Mitchell

1977 TCMA Shreveport Captains

(Pittsburgh Pirates, AA) (black & white)

NM
Complete Set (23): 95.00
(1) Doe Boyland
(2) Fred Breining
(3) Jim Busby
(4) Juan Deliza
(5) Paul Djakonow
(6) Chet Gunter
(7) Al Holland
(8) Rick Honeycutt
(9) Rusty Johnston
(10) Mike Kavanagh
(11) Jim Kidder
(12) John Lipon
(13) Larry Littleton
(14) Tim Murtaugh
(15) Doug Nelson
(16) Nelson Norman
(17) Leo Ortiz
(18) Don Robinson
(19) Felix Rodriquez
(20) Harry Saferight
(21) Rod Scurry
(22) Tommy Thomas
(23) Luke Wrenn

1977 TCMA Spartanburg Phillies

(Philadelphia Phillies, A) (black & white)

NM
Complete Set (24): 125.00
1 Pablo Minier
2 Tom Brunswick
3 Marty Bystrom
4 Jim Nickerson
5 Jarrell Whaley
6 Wally Nunn
7 Henry Mack
8 Jim Lasek
9 Joe Jones
10 Nick Popovich
11 Ricky Burdette
12 Armand Abreu
13 Ronnie Mattson
14 Glenn Ballard
15 Tony Gonzalez
16 Brian Watts
17 Elijah Bonaparte
18 Jeff Kraus
19 Mike Comptom
20 Bob Roman
21 Ozzie Virgil
22 Barry Janney
23 Sam Welborn
24 Ken Berger

1977 Cramer Spokane Indians

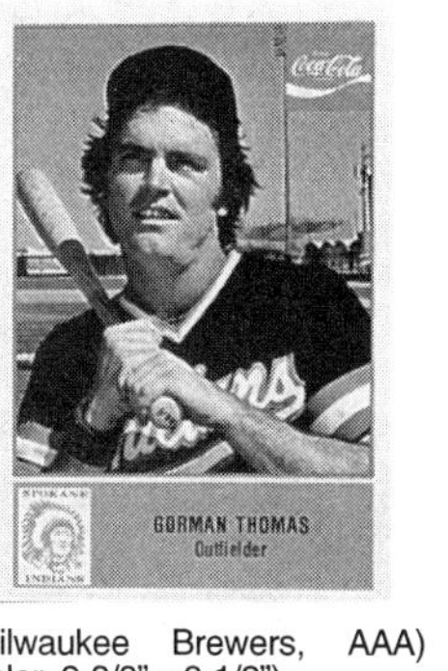

(Milwaukee Brewers, AAA) (color, 2-3/8" x 3-1/2")

NM
Complete Set (24): 13.00
1 Duane Espy
2 Bill McLaurine
4 Jim Gantner
6 Bill Sharp
7 Perry Danforth
8 Steve Ruling
10 Art Kusnyer
11 Lenn Sakata
12 Bob Sheldon
13 Gorman Thomas
14 Juan Lopez
15 Tommie Reynolds
16 Ron Diggle
17 Sam Hinds
18 Tom Hausman
19 Lary Sorensen
20 Ken Sanders
21 Dick Davis
22 Kevin Kobel
24 Bob Ellis
25 Roger Miller
26 John Felske
28 Rich Folkers
---- Mark Voorhees

1977 TCMA St. Petersburg Cardinals

(St. Louis Cardinals, A) (black & white) (Nagle is scarce late-issue card)

NM
Complete Set, w/Nagle (26): 80.00
Partial Set, no Nagle (25): 55.00
1 Kelly Paris
2 William Bowman
3 Felipe Zayas
4 John Littlefield
5 Denzel Martindale
6 John Fulgham
7 Raymond Searage
8 Frank Hundsacker
9 Michael Stone
10 Terry Gray
11 Daniel O'Brien
12 Jorge Arazamendi
13 Hub Kittle
14 Thomas Herr
15 Raymond Donaghue
16 Henry Mays
17 Scott Boras
18 Claude Crockett
19 Michael Pisarkiewicz
20 Robert Harrison
21 Hector Eduardo
22 Alfred Meyer
23 David Pennial
24 Benny Joe Edelen
25 Ralph Miller, Jr. (gm)
--- Mike Nagle

1977 Dairy Queen Tacoma Twins

(Minnesota Twins, AAA) (black & white)

NM
Complete Set (30): 30.00
1 Jim Van Wyck
2a Luis Gomez
2b Wayne Caughey
3 Dave Edwards
4 Sam Perlozzo
5 Sal Butera
6 Hosken Powell
7 Tommy Sain
8 Willie Norwood
9 John Lonchar
10 Tom Kelly
11 Eddie Bane
12 Davis May
13 Tom Hall
14 Gregg Bemis
15 Gary Ward
16 Gary Serum
17 Mike Proly
18 Steve Luebber
19 Art DeFillippis
20 Jim Gideon
21 Jim Hughes
22 Juan Veintidos
23 Randy Bass
24 Bill Butler
25 Dan Graham
26 Del Wilber
---- Tim Loberg
---- Rob Wilfong
---- Jeff Holly

1977 Cramer Tucson Toros

(Texas Rangers, AAA) (color, 2-3/8" x 3-1/2")

NM
Complete Set (24): 10.00
2 Dave Moates
4 Lew Beasley
5 Ken Pape
6 Wayne Pinkerton
7 Larue Washington
8 Greg Mahlberg
11 Keith Smith
12 Keathel Chauncey
13 David Moharter
14 Rich Donnelly
17 Rick Stelmaszek
19 Gary Gray
20 Bob Babcock
27 Ed Nottle
32 David Clyde
33 Kurt Bevacqua
35 John Poloni
40 Len Barker
45 Mark Soroko
51 Pat Putnam
52 Mike Bacsik
53 Bobby Cuellar
59 David Harper
---- Chip Steger

1977 TCMA Visalia Oaks

(Minnesota Twins, A) (black & white)

NM
Complete Set (17): 35.00
(1) John Altman
(2) Leland Byrd
(3) Bob Carroll
(4) Tim Costello
(5) Doug Duncan
(6) Rick Green
(7) James LaFountain
(8) Roy McMillan
(9) Dean Olson
(10) Glenn Purvis
(11) Frank Quintero
(12) Charlie Renneau
(13) Ray Smith
(14) Rick Sofield
(15) Kevin Stanfield
(16) Joe Stewart
(17) Bill Stone

1977 TCMA Waterloo Indians

(Cleveland Indians, A) (black & white) (Arnold and Strickfaden cards are scarce late-issues; Brennan can be found with error "Texas League" strip on front or corrected "Midwest League.)

NM
Partial Set, w/error Brennan, no late-issues (29): 65.00
Complete Set, w/error Brennan, Stickfaden with cap, late-issues (31): 125.00
Complete Set, w/correct Brennan, Stickfaden no cap, late-issues (31): 150.00
(1) Craig Adams
(2) John Arnold
(3a) Thomas Brennan (Texas League on front)
(3b) Thomas Brennan (Midwest League on front)
(4) John Buszka
(5) Norman Churchhill
(6) Dennis Doss

(7) Gene Dusan
(8) David Fowlkes
(9) Pedro Garcia
(10) Raymond Gault
(11) Craig Harvey
(12) William Hiss
(13) Rick Howerton
(14) Kevin Jeansonne
(15) Steven Narleski
(16) Thomas Pulchinski
(17) Nathaniel Puryear
(18) Junior Roman
(19) David Schuler
(20) Daniel Skiba
(21) Forest Smith
(22) Samuel Spence
(23a) Dave Strickfaden (trainer) (wearing cap)
(23b) Dave Strickfaden (trainer) (no cap)
(24) Jeffery Tomski
(25) Tony Toups
(26) Terry Tyson
(27) Michael Vaughn
(28) Patrick Washko
(29) Steven Widner
(30) Al Wihtal (Whitol)
(31) Dwain Wilson

1977 TCMA Wausau Mets

(N.Y. Mets, A) (black & white)

	NM
Complete Set (24):	60.00

(1) Kevan Aman
(2) Rick Armer
(3) Paul Cacciatore
(4) Buddy Cardwell
(5) Kelvin Chapman
(6) Alexander Coghan
(7) Gary Corrado
(8) Tom Egan
(9) Bob Grant
(10) James Hammer
(11) Randy Holman
(12) Luis Lunar
(13) Bill Muth
(14) Bob Pappageorgas
(15) Rick Patterson
(16) Don Pearson
(17) Dennis Sandoval
(18) Kim Seaman
(19) Keith Shermeyer
(20) Tony Thomas
(21) Tom Thurberg
(22) Alex Trevino
(23) Charlie Warren
(24) Rick Wolf

1977 TC7MA West Haven Yankees

(N.Y. Yankees, AA) (black & white)

	NM
Complete Set (25):	165.00

(1) Richard Anderson
(2) Antonie Bautista
(3) Jim Beattie
(4) Donald Castle
(5) Steven Coulson
(6) Duke Drawdy
(7) Michael Ferraro
(8) Jesus Figueroa
(9) Richard Fleshman
(10) Damaso Garcia
(11) Michael Heath
(12) Lloyd Kern
(13) Timothy Lewis
(14) Jim Lysgaard
(15) Douglas Melvin
(16) Carl Merrill
(17) Jerry Narron
(18) Nelson Pichardo
(19) Domingo Ramos
(20) Roger Slagle
(21) Garry Smith
(22) Richard Stenholm
(23) Sandy Valdespino
(24) Will Verhoeff
(25) Bob Zeig

1978 Cramer Albuquerque Dukes

(L.A. Dodgers, AAA) (color, 2-3/8" x 3-1/2")

	NM
Complete Set (20):	35.00

1 Dell Crandall (Del)
2 Terry Collins
3 Rudy Law
4 Enzo Hernandez
5 Ron Washington
6 Joe Simpson
7 Rafael Landestoy
9 Pablo Peguero
11 Bob Welch
12 John O'Rear
13 Hank Webb
14 Dennis Lewallyn
16 Pedro Guerrero
17 Joe Beckwith
19 Claude Westmoreland
20 Brad Gulden
21 Rick Sutcliffe
24 Kevin Keefe
29 Bill Butler
--- Team Logo & Schedule

1978 TCMA Appleton Foxes

(Chicago White Sox, A) (black and white)

	NM
Complete Set (25):	40.00

(1) Rod Allen
(2) Edward Bahns
(3) Phil Bauer
(4) Ross Baumgarten
(5) Harry Chappas
(6) Roy Coulter
(7) David Daniels
(8) Mark Esser
(9) Curt Etchandy
(10) Lorenzo Gray
(11) John Hanely
(12) Dave Hersh
(13) Clay Hicks
(14) Lamar Hoyt (LaMarr)
(15) Dewey Robinson
(16) Mike Sivik
(17) Jackie Smith
(18) Paul Soth
(19) Leo Sutherland
(20) Richard Thoren
(21) Tom Toman
(22) Phil Trucks
(23) Michael Tulacz
(24) Jeffery Vuksan
(25) Victor Walters

1978 TCMA Arkansas Travelers

(St. Louis Cardinals, AA) (black & white) (production reported as 1,100 sets)

	NM
Complete Set (23):	200.00

(1) Jose Aranzamendi
(2) Earl Bass
(3) Dave Boyer
(4) Glenn Brummer
(5) Mike Calise
(6) Roy Donaghue
(7) Gene Dotson
(8) Leon Durham
(9) Joe Edelen
(10) John Fulgham
(11) Nelson Garcia
(12) R.J. Harrison
(13) Terry Herr (Tommy)
(14) Terry Kennedy
(15) Ryan Kurosaki
(16) Jim Lentine
(17) John Littlefield
(18) Dan O'Brien
(19) Dave Penniall
(20) Len Strelitz
(21) Randy Thomas
(22) Tommy Thompson
(23) Fred Tisdale

1978 TCMA Asheville Tourists

(Texas Rangers, A) (black and white)

	NM
Complete Set (29):	42.00

(1) Jim Barbe
(2) John Butch
(3) Jim Capowski
(4) Ron Carney
(5) Joe Carrol
(6) Ted Davis
(7) Luis Gonzalez
(8) Issie Gutierrez
(9) Bob Hallgren
(10) Dave Hibner
(11) Mike Jirschele
(12) Bobby Johnson
(13) Chuck Lamson
(14) Bill LaRosa
(15) Ed Lynch
(16) Jim Mathews
(17) Arnold McCrary
(18) Mark Mercer
(19) Linvel Mosby
(20) Pat Nelson
(21) Steve Nielsen
(22) Scott Peterson
(23) Miguel Pizarro
(24) Steve Righetti
(25) Bill Simpson
(26) Mike Vickers
(27) Len Whitehouse
(28) Arnold Wilhoite
(29) George Wright

1978 TCMA Burlington Bees

(Milwaukee Brewers, A) (black and white)

	NM
Complete Set (28):	45.00

(1) John Adam
(2) Daryl Bailey
(3) Tim Bannister
(4) Kevin Bass
(5) Manuel Betemit
(6) Terry Bevington
(7) Chris Cartensen
(8) Tom DeRosa
(9) Bill Dick
(10) Frank DiPino
(11) Alvin Edge
(12) Larry Edwards
(13) Bill Foley
(14) Ed Gilliam
(15) Jeff Harryman
(16) Jerry Jenkins
(17) Jim Jordan
(18) David LaPoint
(19) Doug Loman
(20) Melvin Manning
(21) Larry Montgomery
(22) Steve Reed
(23) Ivan Rodriguez
(24) Terry Shoebridge
(25) Lee Sigman
(26) John Skorochocki
(27) Bob Smith
(28) Weldon Swift

1978 TCMA Cedar Rapids Giants

(S.F. Giants, A) (black and white)

	NM
Complete Set (29):	125.00

(1) Pat Alexander
(2) Darnell Baker
(3) Jeff Borruel
(4) De Wayne Buice
(5) Don Buchheister
(6) Raymondo Cosio
(7) Charles (Chili) Davis
(8) Ken Feinberg
(9) Rob Henderson
(10) Craig Hedrick
(11) Steve Holman
(12) Bob Kearney
(13) Craig Landis
(14) Doug Landuyt
(15) Javier Lopez
(16) Henry Macias
(17) Louis Marietta
(18) Jack Mull
(19) Venice Murray
(20) Bob Omo
(21) Juan Oppenheimer
(22) Ron Pisel
(23) Francisco Rojas
(24) Alfonso Rosario
(25) John Smith
(26) Jeff Stadler
(27) Jeff Stember
(28) Frankie Thon
(29) Veterans Memorial Stadium

1978 TCMA Charleston Charlies

(Houston Astros, AAA) (black & white)

	NM
Complete Set (20):	20.00

(1) Dave Augustine
(2) Jim Beauchamp
(3) Craig Cacek
(4) Joe Cannon
(5) Bob Coluccio
(6) Keith Drumright
(7) Mike Fischlin
(8) Larry Hardy
(9) Bo McLaughton (McLaughlin)
(10) Jim O'Bradovich
(11) Ramon Perez
(12) Don Pisker
(13) Luis Pujols
(14) Vern Ruhle
(15) Jose Sosa
(16) Rob Sperring
(17) Roy Thomas
(18) Mike Tyler
(19) Randy Wiles
(20) Rick Williams

1978 TCMA Charleston Pirates

(Pittsburgh Pirates, A) (black & white)

	NM
Complete Set (24):	27.50

(1) Doug Britt
(2) Bryan Clark
(3) Casey Clark
(4) Steve Farr
(5) Rick Federici
(6) Doug Frobel
(7) Tim Ganch
(8) Gene Gentile
(9) Luis Giminez
(10) Wendell Hihhett
(11) Woody Huyke
(12) Jean Leduc
(13) Brian Lucas
(14) Ed Lynch
(15) Vic Marte
(16) Tony Nicely
(17) Adalberto Ortiz
(18) Mike Pill
(19) Charlie Powell
(20) Wascar Reyes
(21) Carlos Rios
(22) Brian Schwerman
(23) Billy Scripture
(24) Ed Vargas

> The election of former players to the Hall of Fame does not always have an immediate upward effect on card values. The hobby market generally has done a good job of predicting those inductions and adjusting values over the course of several years.

1978 TCMA Clinton Dodgers

(L.A. Dodgers, A) (black & white)

	NM
Complete Set (33):	50.00

(1) Jan Bach, Rich Bach (owners)
(2) Jerry Bass
(3) Rocky Cordova
(4) Dean Craig
(5) Mark Elliott
(6) Larry Ferst
(7) Rick Ford
(8) Doug Foster
(9) Miguel Franjul
(10) Doug Harrison
(11) Leonardo Hernandez
(12) Mike Holt
(13) Mike Howard
(14) Tim Jones
(15) Kevin Joyce
(16) Mark Kryka
(17) Don LeJohn
(18) Jack Littrell
(19) Evon Martinson
(20) Rusty McDonald
(21) Dick McLaughlin
(22) Chris Mulden
(23) Rick Ollar
(24) Joe Purpura
(25) German Rivera
(26) Mike Stone
(27) Steve Sunker
(28) Bill Swoope
(29) Mark Van Bever
(30) Mitch Webster
(31) Larry Wright
(32) Batboys
(33) Riverview Stadium

1978 TCMA Columbus Clippers

(Pittsburgh Pirates, AAA) (color)

	NM
Complete Set (27):	30.00

(1) Dale Berra
(2) Dorian Boyland
(3) Fred Breining
(4) Cot Deal
(5) Mike Easler
(6) Mike Fiore
(7) Jim Fuller
(8) Fernando Gonzales (Gonzalez)
(9) Gary Hargis
(10) Al Holland
(11) Randy Hopkins
(12) Odell Jones
(13) John Lipon
(14) Alberto Lois
(15) Ken Macha
(16) Ron Mitchell
(17) Roger Nelson
(18) Steve Nicosia
(19) Ossie Olivares
(20) Dave Pagan
(21) Harry Saferight
(22) Mickey Scott
(23) Rod Scurry
(24) Tom Shopay
(25) Randy Tate
(26) Tom Walker
(27) Ed Whitson

1978 TCMA Daytona Beach Astros

(Houston Astros, A) (black & white)

	NM
Complete Set (26):	25.00

(1) Ricky Adams
(2) Rick Aponte
(3) Julio Beltran

(4) Al Cajide
(5) John Cloherty
(6) Paul Cooper
(7) Steve Englishby
(8) George Gross
(9) Don Harkness
(10) Pete Hernandez
(11) Kevin Houston
(12) Doug Jackson
(13) Ramon Leader
(14) Del Leatherwood
(15) Stan Leland
(16) Scott Loucks
(17) Jim MacDonald
(18) Diego Melendez
(19) Fred Morris
(20) Jose Mota
(21) Leo Posada
(22) Simon Rosario
(23) Randy Rouse
(24) Billy Smith
(25) Jose Turnes
(26) Randy Walraven

1978 Tiefel & Associates Denver Bears

(Montreal Expos, AAA) (color)

	NM
Complete Set (25):	25.00

1 Tony Bernazard
2 Tony Bernazard ("6 for 6")
3 Ossie Blanco
4 Leonel Carrion
5 Joe Carroll
6 Ed Creech
7 Don Demola
8 Doc Edwards
9 Jerry Fry
10 Dave Gronlund
11 Mike Hart
12 Tim Jones
13 Joe Keener
14 Larry Landreth
15 Pete Mackanin
16 Randy Miller
17 Frank Ortenzio
18 Bob Pate
19 Roberto Ramos
20 Steve Ratzer
21 Rick Resnick
22 Ken Rushing
23 Dan Schatzeder
24 Bryn Smith
25 Frank Orenzio, Bobby Pate, Rick Resnick

1978 TCMA Dunedin Blue Jays

(Toronto Blue Jays, A) (black & white)

	NM
Complete Set (27):	130.00

(1) Jesse Barfield
(2) Larry Bullard
(3) Jeff Carsley
(4) Rick Counts
(5) Tom Dejak
(6) Eduardo Dennis
(7) Wayne DeWright
(8) Roberto Galvez
(9) Miguel Gomez
(10) Scott Gregory
(11) Rick Hertel
(12) Darryl Hill
(13) Jack Hollis
(14) Dennis Homberg
(15) Mike Lebo
(16) Denis Menke
(17) Benny Perez
(18) Jay Robertson
(19) Dave Rohm
(20) Jose Rosario
(21) Pete Rowe
(22) Ron Sorey
(23) Fay Thompson
(24) Greg Wells
(25) Ralph Wheeler
(26) Randy Wiens
(27) Andre Wood

1978 Geneva Cubs team issue

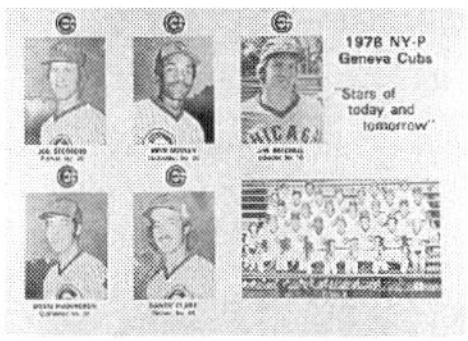

(Chicago Cubs, A) (black & white, blank-backed, issued on four 11" x 7-1/2" uncut sheets)

	NM
Complete Set (24):	225.00

4 Jeff Doyle
7 Bob Hartsfield
8 Mike Turgeon
10 Bill Morgan
11 Jerry Ahlert
14 Bubba Kizer
18 J.W. Mitchell
21 Joe Cole
22 Bill Ross
25 Joe Hicks
26 Mike Godley (photo reversed)
27 Mark Parker
28 Ted Trevino
29 Mark Gilbert
30 Lou Whetstone
31 Ted May
37 Joe McClain
39a Lamont Ennis
39b Doug McCracken
41 Tom Spino
44 Bill Earley
45 Randy Clark
49 Joe Stethers
---- Team card

1978 TCMA Greenwood Braves

(Atlanta Braves, A) (black & white)

	NM
Complete Set (29):	27.50

(1) Terry Abbot
(2) Tom Ballard
(3) "Space Man" Barr
(4) Clete Boyer
(5) Smokey Burgess
(6) Tim Cole
(7) Joe Cowley
(8) "Big John" Dyer
(9) Andre Forbes
(10) "Dirty Al" Gallagher
(11) Bill Haley
(12) Steve Hammond
(13) Bill Haslerig
(14) Danny Lucia
(15) Jeff Matthews
(16) Tommy Mee
(17) Alvin Moore
(18) "Big Ike" Pettaway
(19) Bob Porter
(20) "Raffie" Ramirez
(21) George Ramos
(22) Andre Sams
(23) "Snits" Snitker
(24) Scott Thayer
(25) Bruce Tonascia
(26) Wyatt "Tonk" Tonkin
(27) William Tucker
(28) Bob Veale
(29) Richard Wieters

Checklists with card numbers in parentheses ( ) indicates the numbers do not appear on the cards.

1978 TCMA Holyoke Millers

(Milwaukee Brewers, AA) (color)

	NM
Complete Set (24):	17.50

(1) Jeff Barker
(2) Ken Biggerstaff
(3) Ed Carroll
(4) Mike Dempsey
(5) Bill Dick
(6) Ronnie Driver
(7) Marshall Edwards
(8) George Farson
(9) Steve Green
(10) Steve Grimes
(11) Mike Henderson
(12) Lynn B. Herzig
(13) Gary Holle
(14) Ron Jacobs
(15) Bernado Leonard
(16) Willie Mueller
(17) Rick Nicholson
(18) Neil Rasmussen
(19) Chuck Ross
(20) Dave Smith
(21) Steve Splitt
(22) Esteban Texidor
(23) Don Whiting
(24) Jeff Yurak

1978 Indianapolis Indians team issue

(Cincinnati Reds, AAA) (color)

	NM
Complete Set (27):	30.00

1 Team Photo
2 Roy Majtyka
3 Paul Moskau
4 Harry Spilman
5 Mike LaCoss
6 Ron Oester
7 Dan Dumoulin
8 Ed Armbrister
9 Mario Soto
10 Tommy Mutz
11 Dave Moore
12 John Summers
13 Larry Payne
14 John Valle
15 George Cappuzzello
16 Mike Grace
17 Rafael Santo Domingo
18 Angel Torres
19 Vic Correll
20 Lynn Jones
21 Raul Ferreyra
22 Arturo Defreites
23 Frank Pastore
24 Randy Davidson
25 Jeff Sovern
26 Ron McClain
27 Checklist

1978 Sertoma 1950 Indianapolis Indians

The 1950 Indians are featured in this collectors issue by the Southside Indianapolis Sertoma service club. Numbered from 26-56 in continuation of the club's 1977 issue, the set features black-and-white player poses on the 2-1/2" x 3-1/2" cards. Facsimile autographs on the semi-gloss fronts identify the players. Backs have the player's 1950 Indianapolis stats and major league record, if any. Sets were originally sold for $3.50.

	NM
Complete Set (31):	24.00

26 Al Lopez
27 Bob Friend
28 Forrest Main
29 John McCall
30 Fred Strobel
31 Elmer Riddle
32 Johnny Hutchings
33 Frank Papish
34 Royce Lint
35 Hal Gregg
36 Bill Pierro
37 Joe Muir
38 Del Ballinger
39 Ed Fitz Gerald
40 Earl Turner
41 Dale Coogan
42 Eddie Stevens
43 Monty Basgall
44 Nanny Fernandez
45 Danny O'Connell
46 Leo Wells
47 Eddie Bockman
48 Russ Peters
49 Don Gutteridge
50 Frank Kalin
51 Culley Rikard
52 Dom Dellessandro
53 Ted Beard
54 Mizell Platt
55 Gus Bell
56 Tom Saffell

1978 TCMA Knoxville Knox Sox

(Chicago White Sox, AA) (black & white) (production reported as 1,100 sets)

	NM
Complete Set (25):	250.00

(1) Harold Baines
(2) Richard Barnes
(3) Richard Dotson
(4) Marvis Foley
(5) Ken Frailing
(6) Fred Frazier
(7) Joe Gates
(8) Quency Hill
(9) Fred Howard
(10) Rusty Kuntz
(11) Tony LaRussa
(12) Mitch Lukevics
(13) Larry Monroe
(14) Bill Moran
(15) Mark Naehring
(16) Chris Nyman
(17) Andy Pasillas
(18) Donn Seidholz
(19) Duane Shaffer
(20) Ken Silvestri
(21) Tom Spencer
(22) Willie Thompson
(23) Tommy Toman
(24) Steve Trout
(25) Mike Wolf

1978 TCMA Lodi Dodgers

(L.A. Dodgers, A) (black & white) (Scheller card is found with Charles Barrett back, or correct back)

	NM
Complete Set, w/Scheller error (25):	35.00
Complete Set, w/both Schellers (26):	60.00

(1) Paul Bain
(2) Bobby Brown
(3) H.P. Drake
(4) Larry Fobbs
(5) Marv Garrison
(6) Rick Goulding
(7) Brian Hayes
(8) Ubalso Heredia
(9) Hank Jones
(10) George Kaage
(11) Mike Lake
(12) Mickey Lashley
(13) Dave Richards
(14) Tim Roche
(15) Ron Roenicke
(16) Don Ruzek
(17a) Rod Scheller (Charles Barrett back)
(17b) Rod Scheller (corrected)
(18) Eric Schmidt
(19) Steve Shirley
(20) John Shoemaker
(21) Mike Stone
(22) Ken Townsend
(23) Max Venable
(24) John Walker
(25) Stan Wasiak

1978 Brittling's Memphis Chicks

(Montreal Expos, AA) (red and blue, 3-7/8" x 2-13/16")

	NM
Complete Set (10):	25.00

(1) Felipe Alou
(2) Ray Crowley
(3) Godfrey Evans
(4) Larry Goldetsky
(5) Warren Hemm
(6) Dale McMullen
(7) Julio Perez
(8) Joe Pettini
(9) John Scoras
(10) Rick Williams

1978 Olde Cards Minneapolis Millers/ St. Paul Saints

This collectors' set features players from the 1930s-1950s Minnesota Millers and St. Paul Saints of the American Association. It is often called among collectors the "Halsey Hall recalls" set because of the back commentaries written by the dean of Twin Cities baseball broadcasters in their minor league hey day. Fronts feature black-and-white line drawings of the players with a large color circle behind. Backs have Halsey Hall's reminisences of the player and are printed in black and orange on white. Sets originally sold for $3.

	NM
Complete Set (21):	32.00

1 Halsey Hall
2 Ray Dandridge
3 Bruno Haas
4 Fabian Gaffke
5 George Stumph
6 Herb Barna
7 Roy Campanella

8 Tom Sheehan
9 Ray Moore
10 Ted Williams
11 Harley Davidson
12 Jack Cassini
13 Pea Ridge Day
14 Oscar Roettger
15 Buzz Arlett
16 Joe Hauser
17 Rube Benton
18 Dave Barnhill
19 Hoyt Wilhelm
20 Willie Mays
21 Nicollett Park

1978 Chong Modesto A's

(Oakland A's, A) (black & white)

	NM
Complete Set (26):	85.00

1 Pat Dempsey
2 Ed Nottle
3 Mike Davis
4 Bruce Fournier
5 Dana Berry
6 Dave Mc Carthy
7 Doug Hunt
8 Dave Beard
9 Shooty Babbit
10 Dennis Wysznski
11 Mike Mc Lellan
12 Don Van Marter
13 Don Schubert
14 Craig Harris
15 Paul Mize
16 Chip Kniss
17 Tom Eagan
18 Jim Bennett
19 Robert Moore
20 John Lavery
21 Ken Palmer
22 Eric Attaway
23 Bob Markham
24 Dan Darichuk
25 Ted Nowakowski
26 Gaylen Pitts

1978 TCMA Newark Wayne Co-Pilots

(Milwaukee Brewers, A) (black & white)

	NM
Complete Set (45):	27.50

(1) Bert Acosta
(2) Sally Beal
(3) Randy Boyce
(4) Eddie Brunson
(5) Ron Bugga
(6) Pablo Cavallo
(7) Rafael Cuevas
(8) Stan Davis
(9) Greg Dellart
(10) Jorge DeJesus
(11) Roberto Diaz
(12) Duke Duncan
(13) Lance Ediger
(14) Willie Flowers
(15) Steve Gibson
(16) Sam Gierhan
(17) Dan Gilmartin
(18) Dean Hall
(19) Rocky Hall
(20) Nick Hernandez
(21) Doug Jones
(22) Tim Jordan
(23) Eliqio Kelly
(24) Harvey Kuenn
(25) David Lebron
(26) Jerry Lewis
(27) Steve Manderfield
(28) Ray Manship
(29) Dan Maxson
(30) Tom McLish
(31) Steve Norwood
(32) Rick Olsen
(33) Jim Padula
(34) Vince Pone
(35) Luis Ramirez
(36) Russell Ramirez
(37) Kenny Richardson
(38) Jim Robinson
(39) John Roesch
(40) Pat Seegers
(41) Tom Soto
(42) John Stevenson
(43) Al Wesolowski
(44) Nick Willhite
(45) Porter Wyatt

1978 Oklahoma City 89ers team issue

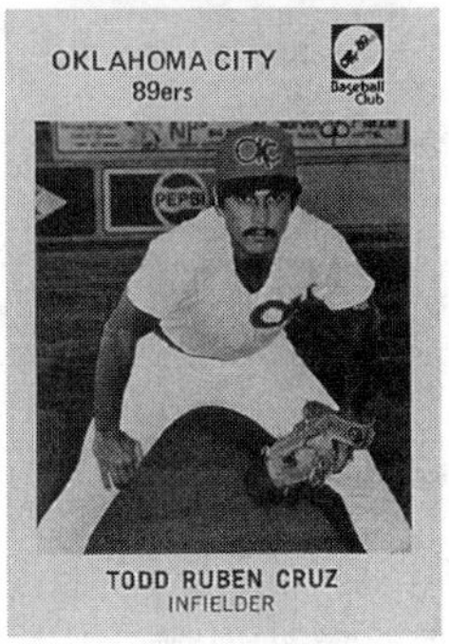

(Philadelphia Phillies, AAA) (black & white) (Wright is scarce late-issue card)

	NM
Complete Set, w/Wright (30):	150.00
Partial Set, no Wright (29):	55.00

1 Fred Ray Beene
3 Ramon Aviles
4 Lonnie Smith
5 Robert Michael DeMeo
6 James Forrest Morrison
7 Michael T. Buskey
8 Kerry Michael Dineen
9 Rogers Lee Brown
10 Steven Craig Waterbury
11 Orlando Alvarez
12 Todd Ruben Cruz
14 Kevin Andrew Saucier
15 Mike Anderson
16 Danny Jon Boitano
17 Charles Edward Kniffin
18 Daniel Dean Warthen
19 Bobby Keith Moreland
20 Orlando Gonzalez
21 Michael Sherman Wallace
22 John C. Vuckovich
23 John William Poff
25 Jackson A. Todd
26 Arnaldo Contreras Jr.
27 Michael James Ryan
28 Tom Harmon
29 William Connors
30 James L. Wright Jr.

1978 TCMA Orlando Twins

(Minnesota Twins, AA) (black & white)

	NM
Complete Set (23):	25.00

(1) Terry Bulling
(2) John Castino
(3) Mark Clapham
(4) Rich Dalton
(5) Rick Duncan
(6) Frank Estes
(7) John Goryl
(8) Jeff Holly
(9) Darrell Jackson
(10) Curt Lewis
(11) Bruce MacPherson
(12) Dennis Mantick
(13) Marty Maxwell
(14) Kevin McWhinter
(15) Warren Mertens
(16) Frank Quintero
(17) Tom Sain
(18) Terry Sheehan
(19) Ray Smith
(20) Dan Spain
(21) Jesus Vega
(22) Steve Wagner
(23) Kurt Whittmayer

1978 Cramer Phoenix Giants

(S.F. Giants, AAA) (color, 2-3/8" x 3-1/2")

	NM
Complete Set (25):	8.00

2 Wendell Kim
3 Greg Johnston
5 Howie Mitchell
6 Joe Strain
7 Greg Minton
10 Rick Sanderlin
11 Guy Sularz
12 Phil Nastu
13 Rocky Bridges
14 Mike Rowland
15 Mike Cash
16 Rob Dressler
17 Casey Parsons
18 Randy Hammon
19 Terry Cornutt
21 Jeff Little
22 Rich Murray
23 Don Carrithers
24 Art Gardner
25 Rick Bradley
27 Dennis Littlejohn
28 Ed Plank
29 Kyle Hypes
---- Ethan Blackaby
---- Harry Jordan

1978 TCMA Quad City Angels

(California Angels, A) (black & white)

	NM
Complete Set (30):	80.00

(1) Gary Balla
(2) Ned Bergert
(3) Jeff Bertoni
(4) Joe Blyleven
(5) Arturo Bonnitto
(6) Bob Border
(7) Jeff Connor
(8) Brian Harper
(9) Brad Havens
(10) Mike Heaton
(11) Don Jones
(12) Guy Jones
(13) Monte Mendenhall
(14) Mark Miller
(15) Charles Nash
(16) Steve Oliva
(17) Harry Pells
(18) John Pound
(19) Melvin Quarles
(20) Bran Riffle (Riffel)
(21) Greg Ris
(22) Andy Rodriguez
(23) Wade Schexnayder
(24) Darryl Sconiers
(25) Mike Stover
(26) Doug Thompson
(27) Jim Vallone
(28) Steve Van Deren
(29) Alan Wiggins
(30) Waterloo Municipal Stadium

1978 TCMA Richmond Braves

(Atlanta Braves, AAA) (color)

	NM
Complete Set (20):	20.00

(1) Tommie Aaron
(2) James Arline
(3) Bruce Benedict
(4) Larry Bradford
(5) Glenn Hubbard
(6) Frank LaCorte
(7) Michael Macha
(8) Jerry Maddox
(9) Richard Mahler
(10) Joey McLaughlin
(11) Edward Miller
(12) Jon Richardson (gm)
(13) Chico Ruiz
(14) John Sain
(15) Hank Small
(16) Duane Theiss
(17) Larry Whisenton
(18) Kris Yoder
(19) Front Office
(20) Chief Powa Hitta, Seymore Baseball (mascots)

1978 TCMA Rochester Red Wings

(Baltimore Orioles, AAA) (color)

	NM
Complete Set (17):	30.00

(1) Ray Bare
(2) Tom Bianco
(3) Don Cardoza
(4) Tony Chevez
(5) Tom Chism
(6) Dave Criscione
(7) Mike Dimmel
(8) Blake Doyle
(9) Skeeter Jarquin
(10) Kevin Kennedy
(11) Wayne Krenchicki
(12) Rafael Liranzo
(13) Marty Parrill
(14) Jeff Rineer
(15) Frank Robinson
(16) Earl Stephenson
(17) Tim Stoddard

1978 TCMA Salem Pirates

(Pittsburgh Pirates, A) (black & white)

	NM
Complete Set (20):	30.00

(1) Juan Arias
(2) Pablo Cruz
(3) Phil Cyburt
(4) Rickey Evans
(5) Marc Gelinas
(6) Sandy Hill
(7) Rick Lancelotti
(8) Robert Long
(9) Jim Mahoney
(10) Frank Miloszewski
(11) Bob Parsons
(12) Rick Peterson
(13) Luis Salazar
(14) Dean Rick
(15) Bob Rock
(16) Luis Salazar
(17) Rick Peterson
(18) Alfredo Torres
(19) Chich Valley
(20) Ben Wiltbank

1978 Cramer Salt Lake City Gulls

(California Angels, AAA) (color, 2-3/8" x 3-1/2")

	NM
Complete Set (27):	10.00

1 Tommy Smith
2 Jim Anderson
3 Dave Machemer
4 Dickie Thon
5 Kim Allen
6 Gil Flores
7 Deron Johnson
8 Tom Donohue
9 Steve Stroughter
10 Pat Cristelli
11 John Racanelli
14 Stan Cliburn
15 Bobby Jones
16 Gil Kubski
17 Chuck Porter
18 John Caneira
19 Bob Ferris
20 Dave Schuler
21 Mike Barlow
22 Willie Aikens
24 Mike Overy
25 Dave Frost
26 Carlos Perez
---- Leonard Garcia

Suffix letters following a card number indicate a variation card.

1978 Mr. Chef's San Jose Missions

(Seattle Mariners, AAA) (color)

	NM
Complete Set (24):	42.00

1 Team logo & checklist
2 Rene Lachemann
3 Greg Biercevicz
4 Frank Mac Cormack
5 Ed Crosby
6 Joe Decker
7 Jose Elguezabal
8 Gary Wheelock
9 Alan Griffin
10 Pete Ithier
11 Rick Baldwin
12 Charlie Beamon
13 Juan Berhnardt
14 Luis Delgado
15 Steve Hamrick
16 Tom Brown
17 Byron Mc Laughlin
18 Tommy Mc Millan
19 Bill Plummer
20 George Mitterwald
21 Archie Amerson
22 Manny Estrada
23 Jack Pierce
24 Mike Kekich

1978 Cramer Spokane Indians

(Milwaukee Brewers, AAA) (black & white, 2-3/8" x 3-1/2")

	NM
Complete Set (24):	10.00

1 Duane Espy
2 William L. McLaurine
3 Ronnie Jay "Ron" Diggle
4 Dale M. Hrovat
5 James P. Quirk
6 Lanny A. Phillips
7 Billy E. Severns
8 Tony Muser
9 Jack S. Heidemann
10 Edgardo Romero
11 Stephen M. Ruling
12 Creighton J. Tevlin
13 (I.) Juan Lopez
14 Not Issued
15 Tommie D. Reynolds
16 Not Issued
17 Ron R. Wrona
18 Barry L. Cort
19 Samuel H. Hinds
20 John A. Buffamoyer
21 Robert J. Galasso, Jr.
22 Edward J. Farmer
23 Not Issued
24 Lynn E. McKinney
25 Not Issued
26 John F. Felske
27 Gary R. Beare
28 Edgar F. "Ned" Yost

1978 Weiner King Springfield Redbirds

(St. Louis Cardinals, AAA) (black and white) (set price includes late-issue Oberkfell and Frazier cards)

NM
Complete Set (24): 80.00
1 Ken Oberkfell
2 Ron Farkas
3 Mike Potter
4 John Scott
5 Mike Ramsey
6 Nyls Nyman
7 David Bialas
8 Benny Ayala
9 Manny Castillo
10 John Tamargo
11 Eddie Daves
12 Lee Landers
13 Jimy Williams
14 Tommy Toms
15 Al Autry
16 Tom Bruno
17 Frank Riccelli
18 Silvio Martinez
19 Bill Rothan
20 Gregory Terlecky
21 Ron Selak
22 Aurelio Lopez
23 George Frazier
24 Ken Rudolph

1978 TCMA St. Petersburg Cardinals

(St. Louis Cardinals, A) (black & white)

NM
Complete Set (29): 40.00
(1) Fulvio Bertolotti
(2) Jack Boag (trainer)
(3) Mark Bumstead
(4) Tom Chamberlain
(5) Donnie Chesire
(6) Dennis Cirbo
(7) Glenn Comoletti
(8) Chris Davis
(9) Hector Eduardo
(10) Neil Fiala
(11) Julian Gutierrez
(12) Brett Houser
(13) Dave Johnson
(14) Dave Jorn
(15) Arno Kirchenwitz
(16) Terry Landrum
(17) Hal Lanier
(18) Chris Lombardo
(19) Ralph Miller, Jr. (gm)
(20) Kelly Paris
(21) Mike Pisarkiewicz
(22) Mike Pope
(23) Jim Reeves
(24) Gene Roof
(25) Larry Silver
(26) Elliot Waller
(27) Ray Williams
(28) Hal Witt
(29) Felipe Zayas

1978 TCMA Syracuse Chiefs

(Toronto Blue Jays, AAA) (color)

NM
Complete Set (22): 45.00
(1) Danny Ainge
(2) Butch Alberts
(3) Vern Benson
(4) Jeff Byrd
(5) Victor Cruz
(6) Mike Darr
(7) Andy Dyes
(8) Butch Edge
(9) Sam Ewing
(10) Chuck Fore
(11) Steve Grilli
(12) Pat Kelly
(13) Sheldon Mallory
(14) Luis Melendez
(15) Ken Pape
(16) Ken Reynolds
(17) Tom Sandt
(18) Mike Stanton
(19) Hector Torres
(20) Ernie Whitt
(21) Alvis Woods
(22) Gary Woods

1978 Cramer Tacoma Yankees

(N.Y. Yankees, AAA) (color, 2-3/8" x 3-1/2")

NM
Complete Set (24): 9.00
1 Mike Ferraro
8 Ed Napoleon
9 Dennis Werth
10 Roger Slagle
14 Dennis Irwin
15 Darryl Jones
17 Domingo Ramos
18 Jim Lysgaard
19 Jim Curnal
20 George Zeber
21 Bob Kammeyer
22 Marv Thompson
23 Roy Staiger
25 Steve Taylor
27 Dell Alston (Del)
28 Dave Rajsich
29 Larry McCall
38 Jerry Narron
39a Brian Doyle
39b Garry Smith
42 Damaso Garcia
43 Bob Polinsky
44 Tommy Cruz
47 Hoyt Wilhelm
54 Neal Mersch

1978 TCMA Tidewater Tides

(N.Y. Mets, AAA) (color) (complete set price includes scarce Verdi card)

NM
Complete Set (27): 25.00
(1) Neil Allen
(2) Fred Andrews
(3) Juan Berenguer
(4) Dwight Bernard
(5) Marshall Brant
(6) Mike Bruhart
(7) Ed Cipot
(8) Mardie Cornejo
(9) Sergio Ferrer
(10) Tom Hausman
(11) Roy Lee Jackson
(12) Ed Kurpiel
(13) Pepe Mangual
(14) Rich Miller
(15) Bob Myrick
(16) Dan Norman
(17) John Pacella
(18) Greg Pavlick
(19) Marty Perez
(20) Mario Ramirez
(21) Randy Rogers
(22) Luis Rosado
(23) Mike Scott
(24) Dan Smith
(25) Alex Trevino
(26) Mike Van De Casteele
(27) Frank Verdi

1978 Cramer Tucson Toros

(Texas Rangers, AAA) (color, 2-3/8" x 3-1/2") (co-sponsored by Orange Crush)

NM
Complete Set (25): 10.00
2 Larue Washington
4 Nelson Norman
9 Wayne Pinkerton
10 Paul Mirabella
12 Keathel Chauncey
13 David Moharter
14 Bill Fahey
15a Mike Bucci
15b Keith Smith
19 Bill Sample
20 Bob Babcock
21 Don Bright
22 Stan Thomas
24 Greg Mahlberg
27 Gary Gray
28 Danny Darwin
32 Pat Putnam
35 Rusty Torres
39 Jackie Brown
42 Rich Donnelly
45 Mike Bacsik
46 Bobby Cuellar
48 Jerry Reedy
59a David Harper
59b Jim Hughes

1978 TCMA Waterloo Indians

(Cleveland Indians, A) (black & white)

NM
Complete Set (26): 15.00
(1) Tom Anderson
(2) Ken Bolek
(3) Juan Bonilla
(4) Tim Brill
(5) John Buszka
(6) Bob Conley
(7) Sammy Davis
(8) Jack DuBeau
(9) Jerry Dybzinski
(10) Robin Fuson
(11) Tim Glass
(12) Vic Homstedt
(13) Don Hubbard
(14) Angelo Lo Grande
(15) Carl Nicholson
(16) Thomas Pulchinski (gm)
(17) Al Rauch
(18) Kevin Rhomberg
(19) Ramon Romero
(20) Ed Saavedra
(21) Forest Smith
(22) Sam Spence
(23) John Teising
(24) Lloyd Turner
(25) Glenn Wendt
(26) Troy Wilder

1978 TCMA Wausau Mets

(N.Y. Mets, A) (black & white)

NM
Complete Set (25): 55.00
(1) Curt Baker
(2) Don Brazell
(3) Stewart Bringhurst
(4) Greg Brown
(5) Bill Chamberlain
(6) Al Coghen
(7) Ed Cuervo
(8) Bruce Ferguson
(9) Jeff Franklin
(10) Brent Gaff
(11) John Hinkel
(12) Chris Jones
(13) Ken Jones
(14) Chris Kirby
(15) Randy Lamb
(16) Steve "Doc" Lowe (trainer)
(17) Mike Lowry
(18) Dan Monzon
(19) Jim Noonan
(20) Darryl Paquette
(21) Don Pearson
(22) Junior Roman
(23) Frank Sanchez
(24) Keith Shermeyer
(25) John McDonnell Stadium

1978 TCMA Wisconsin Rapids Twins

(Minnesota Twins, A) (black & white)

NM
Complete Set (18): 28.00
(1) Greg Allen
(2) Paul Croft
(3) George Dierburger
(4) Gary Dobbs
(5) Mark Funderburk
(6) Michael Gustave
(7) Lance Hallberg
(8) Elmore Hill
(9) Joe Keith Isaac
(10) Abner Johnson
(11) Elmer Lingerman
(12) Ronnie Mears
(13) John Minarcin
(14) Dean Moranda
(15) Eric Prevost
(16) Clyde Reichard
(17) Harold Rowe
(18) Richard Stelmaszek

1979 TCMA Albuquerque Dukes

(L.A. Dodgers, AAA) (color)

NM
Complete Set (23): 90.00
1 Pablo Peguero
2 Mike Tennent
3 Mike Williams
4 Bill Swiacki
5 Dave Stewart
6 Dave Patterson
7 Dennis Lewallyn
8 Kevin Keefe
9 Gerry Hannahs
10 Mike Scioscia
11 Mickey Hatcher
12 John O'Rear
13 Jack Perconte
14 Kelly Snider
15 Alex Taveras
16 Pedro Guerrero
17 Rich Magner
18 Bobby Mitchell
19 Rudy Law
20 Joe Beckwith
21 Claude Westmoreland
22 Bobby Castillo
23 Bobby Padilla

1979 University Volkswagen Albuquerque Dukes

(L.A. Dodgers, AAA)

NM
Complete Set (23): 175.00
(1) Joe Beckwith
(2) Robert Castillo
(3) Del Crandall
(4) Pedro Guerrero
(5) Gerald Hannahs
(6) Mickey Hatcher
(7) Kevin Keefe
(8) Rudy Law
(9) Dennis Lewallyn
(10) Rich Magner
(11) Bobby Mitchell
(12) John O'Rear
(13) Dave Patterson
(14) Pablo Peguero
(15) Jack Perconte
(16) Mike Scioscia
(17) Kelly Snider
(18) Dave Stewart
(19) Bill Swiacki
(20) Alex Taveras
(21) Mike Tennant
(22) Claude Westmoreland
(23) Mike Williams

1979 TCMA Appleton Foxes

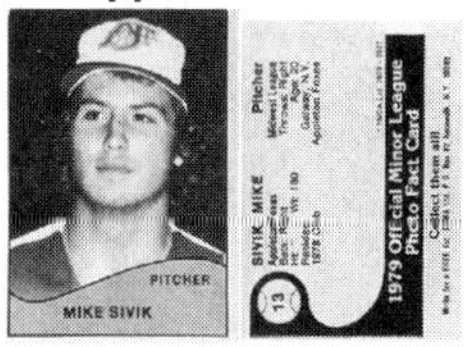

(Chicago White Sox, A) (black & white)

NM
Complete Set (25): 45.00
1 Paul Soth
2 Dennis Keating
3 Vito Lucarelli
4 Ed Bahns
5 Dave White
6 Kevin Hickey
7 Clancy Woods
8 Jeff Vuksan
9 Lorenzo Gray
10 Mike Johnson
11 Dave Daniels
12 Ivan Mesa
13 Mike Sivik
14 Phil Bauer
15 Mart Teutsch
16 Luis Estrada
17 Jim Breazeale
18 Vince Bienek
19 Bob Umdenstock
20 Mike Maitland
21 Duane Shaffer
22 Mark Platel
23 Don Kraeger (trainer)
24 Vic Walters
25 Paul Gbur

1979 TCMA Arkansas Travelers

(St. Louis Cardinals, AA) (color)

NM
Complete Set (23): 21.00
1 Arno Kirchenwitz
2 Len Strelitz
3 Raymond Williams
4 Terry Landrum
5 Jim Riggleman
6 John Littlefield
7 Thomas N. Thompson
8 Joseph Dotson
9 Elliott Waller
10 Joseph DeSa
11 Fred Tisdale
12 Jorge Aranzamendi
13 Neil Fiala
14 Mike McCormick
15 Fulvio Bertolotti
16 Dennis Delany
17 Chris Davis
18 Randy Thomas
19a Tom Chamberlain
19b Hector Eduardo
20 Ray Searage
21 David Johnson
22 Gene Roof

1979 TCMA Asheville Tourists

(Texas Rangers, A) (black & white)

	NM
Complete Set (28):	115.00

1 Luis Gonzalez
2 Tracy Cowger
3 Tom McGivney
4 Lynvel Mosby
5 Wayne Terwilliger
6 Jim Farr
7 Dave Chapman
8 Andy Tam
9 Jeff Zitek
10 George Wright
11 Dave Miller
12 Wes Williams
13 Jim McWilliams
14 Al Ortiz
15 Steve Righetti
16 Bobby Tanzi
17 Amos Lewis
18 Arnold Wilhoite
19 Pat Nelson
20 Mike Childs
21 Mike Vickers
22 Jeff Scott
23 Dan Dixon
24 Chuck Kwolek
25 Dave Hibner
26 Mike Richardt
27 Stan Reese
28 Gene Nelson

1979 TCMA Buffalo Bisons

(Pittsburgh Pirates, AA) (black and white)

	NM
Complete Set (21):	105.00

1 Dave Dravecky
2 Stu Cliburn
3 Rick Lancellotti
4 Joe Galante
5 Tony Pena
6 Jerry McDonald
7 Steve Demeter
8 Ernie Young
9 Bubba Evans
10 Marc Galinas
11 Juan Arias
12 Harry Dorish, Bob Weismiller
13 Fred Breining
14 Chick Valley
15 Tom McMillan
16 Luis Salazar
17 Jim Smith
18 Al Torres
19 Dick Walterhouse
20 Robert Long
21 Paul Djakonow

1979 TCMA Burlington Bees

(Milwaukee Brewers, A) (black & white)

	NM
Complete Set (25):	24.00

1 Larry Edwards
2 Russell Ramirez
3 Pat Seegers
4 Jim Robinson
5 Sam Gierham
6 Rocky Hall
7 Willie Lozado
8 Nick Hernandez
9 Ron Buggs
10 Dan Gilmartin
11 Mark Lepson
12 Doug Jones
13 Steve Gibson
14 Bob Gibson
15 Johnny Evans
16 Roberto Diaz
17 Duane Espy
18 Vince Bailey
19 Randy Boyce
20 Greg DeHart
21 Stan Davis
22 Vince Pone
23 Jim Padula
24 Steve Norwood
25 Steve Manderfield

1979 TCMA Cedar Rapids Giants

(S.F. Giants, A) (black & white)

	NM
Complete Set (32):	80.00

1 Steve Duckhorn
2 Jesus Cruz
3 Mark Benson
4 Jorge Mundroig
5 John Rabb
6 Robbie Henderson
7 Jeff Stadler
8 Matt Sutherland
9 Francisco Rojas
10 Rick Doss
11 Bruce Oliver
12 Bill Bellomo
13 Glenn Fisher
14 Bud Curran
15 Wayne Cato
16 Jeff Stember
17 Paul Plinski
18 Jose Chue
19 Rick Kean
20 George Torassa
21 Ned Raines
22 Lou Merietta
23 Craig Hedrick
24 Kelly Anderson
25 Harry Wing
26 Juan Oppenhiemer
27 Ray Cosio
28 Bob Deer (Rob)
29 Don Buchheister
30 Phil Sutton
31 Doug Linduyt
32 Bob Cummins

1979 TCMA Charleston Charlies

(Houston Astros, AAA) (color)

	NM
Complete Set, w/corrected photos (21):	40.00
Complete Set, no corrections (19):	20.00

1 Keith Drumright
2 Jim Beauchamp
3 Russ Rothermel
4 Reggie Baldwin
5 Gary Woods
6 Mike Fischlin
7 Mike Tyler
8 Dave Bergman
9 Ramon Perez
10a Mark Miggins (Dave Smithphoto, no mustache)
10b Mark Miggins (correct photo, with mustache)
11a David Smith (Mark Miggins photo, with mustache)
11b David Smith (correct photo, no mustache)
12 Dave Augustine
13 Gordy Pladson
14 Luis Pujols
15 Larry Hardy
16 Rob Sperring
17 Wilbur Howard
18 Gary Wilson
19 Mike Mendoza

1979 TCMA Clinton Dodgers

(L.A. Dodgers, A) (black & white)

	NM
Complete Set (28):	75.00

1 Mark Eliott
2 Clay Smith
3 Johnny Lee Robbins
4 Roberto Alexander
5 Matt Reeves
6 Alan Wiggins
7 Otis Bradley
8 Paul Popovich
9 Alejandro Pena
10 Steve Sax
11 Mitch Webster
12 Eric Schmidt
13 Chris Gancy
14 Kent Johnson
15 Marcos Rodriguez
16 Leonardo Hernandez
17 Dick McLaughlin
18 Dave Sax
19 Dave LaPointe
20 Rod Nelson
21 Bob Giesecke
22 Larry Wright
23 Steve Maples
24 Kevin Joyce
25 Bob White
26 Candido Maldonado
27 Frank Wilczewski
28 Larry Ferst

1979 TCMA Columbus Clippers

(N.Y. Yankees, AAA) (color)

	NM
Complete Set (29):	18.00

1 Brad Gulden
2 Roy Staiger
3 Paul Semall
4 Damaso Garcia
5 Garry Smith
6 Stan Williams
7 Gene Michael
8 Jim Beattie
9 Gerry McNertney
10 Dennis Werth
11 Mark Letendre (trainer)
12 Marvin Thompson
13 Tommy Cruz
14 Ron Davis
15 Bob Polinsky
16 Bruce Robinson
17 Greg Cochran
18 Rodger Holt
19 Dennis Sherrill
20 Steve Taylor
21 Rich Anderson
22 Nathan Chapman
23 Bob Kammeyer
24 Chris Welsh
25 Howard "Hopalong" Cassidy
26 Paul Mirabella
27 Bobby Brown
28 Daryl Jones
29 Mickey Vernon

1979 TCMA Elmira Pioneers

(Boston Red Sox, A) (black & white)

	NM
Complete Set (28):	90.00

1 Lloyd Bessard
2 Jay Fredlund
3 Ken Hagemann
4 Danny Huffstickler
5 Arturo Samaniego
6 Glenn Eddins, Jr.
7 Joaquin Gutierrez
8 Tom McCarthy
9 Steve Fortune
10 Don Hayford
11 Eddie Lee
12 Russell Lee Pruitt
13 Scott Gering
14 Dave Holt
15 Steve Schaefer
16 Tony Cleary
17 Andy Serrano
18 Francisco Vasquez
19 Gus Malespin
20 Hal Natupsky
21 Dick Berardino
22 Ed Berroa
23 Bill Limoncelli
24 Bob Birrell
25 Wayne Tremblay
26 Tom Brunner
27 Tom DeSanto
28 Mark Saunders

1979 TCMA Hawaii Islanders

(San Diego Padres, AAA) (color)

	NM
Complete Set (24):	15.00

1 Bob Mitchell
2 Lynn McKinney
3 Rick Sweet
4 Craig Stimac
5 Andy Dyes
6 Dick Phillips
7 Jim Wilhelm
8 Vic Bernal
9 Gary Lucas
10 Jim Beswick
11 Sam Perlozzo
12 Steve Brye
13 Don Reynolds
14 Steve Smith
15 Al Zarilla
16 Chuck Baker
17 Alan Fitzmorris
18 Dennis Kinney
19 Mike Dupree
20 Fred Kuhaulua
21 Juan Eichelberger
22 Dennis Blair
23 Tom Tellmann
24 Tony Castillo

1979 Cramer Hawaii Islanders

(San Diego Padres, AAA) (color, 2-3/8" x 3-1/2")

	NM
Complete Set (24):	7.50

3 Al Zarilla
5 Sam Perlozzo
8 Tucker Ashford
9 Steve Brye
10 Vic Bernal
11 Chuck Baker
12 Bob Mitchell
13 Juan Eichelberger
14 Craig Stimac
16 Tom Tellmann
17 Dennis Kinney
18 Rick Sweet
19 Al Fitzmorris
20 Lynn McKinney
21 Jim Beswick
22 Randy Fierbaugh
23 Fred Kuhaulua
24 Dick Phillips
25 Jim Wilhelm
26 Gary Lucas
27 Tony Castillo
28 Andy Dyes
29 Dave Wehrmeister
---- Team Logo & Schedule

1979 TCMA Holyoke Millers

(Milwaukee Brewers, AA) (color)

	NM
Complete Set (30):	15.00

1 Rene Quinones
2 Terry Bevington
3 Bill Foley
4 Ed Carroll
5 Kevin Bass
6 Bobby Smith
7 Mark Schuster
8 George Farson
9 Rick Olsen
10 Tom Soto
11 Ron Driver
12 Tom Cook
13 Gersan Jarquin
14 Rick Duran
15 Don Whiting
16 Brian Thorson
17 Mike Henderson
18 Butch Riggar
19 Steve Splitt
20 Larry Rush
21 Steve Reed
22 Darryl Bailey
23 Weldon Swift
24 Rocky Hall
25 Lance Rautzhan
26 Barry Cort
27 "Duke" Duncan
28 Jeff Yurak
29 Sam Hinds
30 Tom Kayser

1979 Indianapolis Indians team issue

(Cincinnati Reds, AAA) (color)

	NM
Complete Set (32):	24.00

1 Team Photo
2 Roy Majtyka
3 Ron Oester
4 Dave Moore
5 Harry Spilman
6 The Outfielders
7 Charlie Leibrandt
8 Tommy Mutz
9 Larry Rothschild
10 Eddie Milner
11 The Infielders
12 Doug Corbett
13 Randy Davidson
14 Bruce Berenyl
15 Don Lyle
16 George Cappuzzello
17 The Catchers
18 Mike Grace
19 Geoff Combe
20 Steve Bowling
21 Manny Sarmiento
22 Don Werner
23 The Relievers
24 Jay Howell
25 John Valle
26 Dan Dumoulin
27 Mickey Duval
28 Mario Soto
29 The Starters
30 Ron McClain
31 Bush Stadium
32 Checklist

1979 Iowa Oaks Police Set

(Chicago White Sox, AAA) (black and white)

	NM
Complete Set (14):	275.00

(1) Lloyd Allen
(2) Harold Baines
(3) Kevin Bell
(4) Harry Chappas
(5) Mike Colbern
(6) Fred Frazier
(7) Guy Hoffman
(8) Dewey Hoyt
(9) Art Kusnyer
(10) Tony LaRussa
(11) Bob Molinaro
(12) Chris Nyman
(13) Dewey Robinson
(14) John Sutton

1979 TCMA Jackson Mets

(N.Y. Mets, AA) (color) (Front office staff card is scarce)

NM
Complete Set, w/staff (25): 22.00
Partial Set, no staff (24): 16.00
1 "Paco" Perez
2 Wally Backman
3 Hubie Brooks
4 Wayne Sexton
5 Paul Wiener
6 Bob Wellman
7 Jodie Davis
8 Bob Grote
9 Sergio Beltre
10 Paul Cacciatore
11 Keith Bodie
12 Pete Hamner
13 Luis Lunar
14 Mike Howard
15 Dave Von Ohlen
16 Rick Anderson
17 Dan Smith
18 Rich Miller, Jr.
19 Bobby Bryant
20 Russell Clark
21 Greg Harris
22a Front Office Staff
22b Stan Hough
23 Ronald MacDonald
24 Fred Martinez

1979 TCMA Knoxville White Sox

(Chicago White Sox, AA) (black & white)

NM
Complete Set (26): 70.00
1 Mark Naehring
2 Phil Trucks
3 Luis Guzman
4 Gordy Lund
5 Richard Barnes
6 Britt Burns
7 Leo Sutherland
8 Richard Dotson
9 Don Seidholz
10 John Flannery
11 Mitch Lukevics
12 Ron Kittle
13 Willie Gutierrez
14 Larry Monroe
15 John Hanley
16 Joel Perez
17 Jackie Smith
18 Bruce Dal Canton
19 Ray Murillo
20 Andy Pasillas
21 Ted Barnicle
22 A.J. Hill
23 Ray Torres
24 Rod Allen
25 Tom Spencer
26 Willie Thompson

1979 TCMA Lodi Dodgers

(L.A. Dodgers, A) (black & white)

NM
Complete Set (21): 100.00
1 Rod Kemp
2 Augie Ruiz
3 Paul Bain
4 Alfredo Mejia
5 Skip Mann
6 Mike Marshall
7 Rocky Cordova
8 Steve Perry
9 Jesse Baez
10 Jim Nobles
11 Larry Powers
12 Johnny Walker
13 Bill Swoope
14 Stan Wasiak
15 Miguel Franjul
16 Jerry Bass
17 Bob Foster
18 Chris Malden
19 Brian Hayes
20 Hank Jones
21 Evon Martinson

1979 TCMA Memphis Chicks

(Montreal Expos, AA) (black & white) (production reported as 1,500 sets)

NM
Complete Set (24): 275.00
1 Steve Lovins
2 Steve Michael
3 Bill Armstrong
4 Julio Perez
5 Bryn Smith
6 Larry Goldetsky
7 Doug Simunic
8 Charlie Lea
9 Dave Hostetler
10 Anthony Johnson
11 Randy Schafer
12 Mike Finlayson
13 Rick Williams
14 Rick Engle
15 Bob Teneini
16 Ray Crowley
17 John Scoras
18 Jeff Gingrich
19 Dennis Sherow
20 Tim Raines
21 Billy Gardner
22 Pat Rooney
23 Warren Hemm
24 Godfrey Evans

1979 Chong Modesto A's

(Oakland A's, A) (black & white with gold on front, blank-back)

NM
Complete Set (24): 65.00
-- Logo Card
1 Gaylen Pitts
2 Rich Morales
3 Frank Kneuer
4 Pat Dempsey
5 Fred Devito
6 Dana Berry
7 Paul Stevens
8 Mike Woodard
9 Jay Greb
10 Kelvin Moore
11 Mike Davis
12 Bob Markham
13 Don Morris
14 Don Schubert
15 Craig Harris
16 Mike Yesenchak
17 Chuck Dougherty
18 Don Van Marter
19 Walt Bigos
20 John Gosse
21 Fritz Lund
22 Dave Mc Carthy
23 Ron Jensen

1979 Nashville Sounds team issue

(Cincinnati Reds, AA) (color)

NM
Complete Set (25): 24.00
(1) Mike Armstrong
(2) Skeeter Barnes
(3) Scott Brown
(4) Geoff W. Combe
(5) Bill Dawley
(6) Rick Duncan
(7) Rayl Ferreyra
(8) Bob Hamilton
(9) Paul Householder
(10) Greg Hughes
(11) Bill Kelly
(12) Bob Mayer
(13) Gene Menees
(14) Mark Miller
(15) Eddie Milner
(16) Farrell Owens
(17) Joe Price
(18) R. Santo Domingo
(19) George R. Scherger
(20) Larry Schmittou
(21) Tom Sohns
(22) Dave Van Gorder
(23) Duane Walker
(24) Team Photo
(25) 1979 Soundettes

1979 TCMA Newark Co-Pilots

(Independent, A) (black & white)

NM
Complete Set (24): 22.00
1 Tom Dann
2 Steve Nicastro
3 Joe Rigoli
4 Bob Bill
5 Mike Overton
6 Mike Fichman
7 Steve Dembowski
8 Mal Oleksak
9 Don Clatterbuck
10 Michael LaCasse
11 Kevin MacDonald
12 Joe McCann
13 Harry White
14 Mark Grier
15 Carl Adams
16 Bob Cross
17 Billy Clay
18 Keith Gainer
19 Richard Block
20 Kevin Rose
21 Mitch Wright
22 Len Spicer
23 Lance Viola
24 Andy Pascarella

1979 TCMA Ogden A's

(Oakland A's, AAA) (color)

NM
Complete Set (26): 165.00
1 Terry Enyart
2 Tim Hosley
3 Mike Morgan
4 Mike Rodriguez
5 Craig Mitchell
6 Jose Pagan
7 Mack Harrison
8 Dennis Haines
9 Rickey Henderson
10 Brian Abraham
11 Richard Lysander
12 Jeff Cox
13 Brian Kingman
14 Royle Stillman
15 Danny Goodwin
16 Rya Cosey
17 Mark Souza
18 Mark Budaska
19 Frank Kolarek
20 Pat Dempsey
21 Craig Mitchell
22 Allen Wirth
23 Jeff Jones
24 Mike Patterson
25 Bob Grandas
26 Keith Liepman

1979 Oklahoma City 89ers team issue

(Philadelphia Phillies, AAA) (b/w)

NM
Complete Set (24): 150.00
1 Fred Beene
2 Not Issued
3 Ramon Aviles
4a Lee Elia
4b Lonnie Smith
5 Robert DeMeo
6 James Morrison
7 Orlando Isales
8 Kerry Dineen
9 Bobby Moreland
10 Luis Aguayo
11 Jose Martinez
12 Not Issued
13 Not Issued
14 Kevin Saucier
15 Not Issued
16 Carlos Arroyo
17 Dickie Noles
18 Dan Larson
19 Not Issued
20 Orlando Gonzalez
21 Don McCormack
22 John Vukovich
23 John Poff
24 Jack Kucek
25 Pete Manos
26 Marty Bystrom
27 Not Issued
28 Ellis Deal
29 Gary Beare

1979 Trackle Pawtucket Red Sox Postcards

(Boston Red Sox, AAA) (3-1/2" x 5-3/8", b/w, postcard back, players unidentified)

NM
Complete Set (16): 25.00
(1) Barry Butera
(2) Bucky Denton
(3) Otis Foster
(4) Garry Hancock
(5) Glenn Hoffman
(6) Ken Huizenga
(7) Buddy Hunter
(8) Dave Koza
(9) Roger LaFrancois
(10) Andy Merchant
(11) Joe Morgan
(12) Win Remmerswaal
(13) Allen Ripley
(14) Steve Schneck
(15) Dave Stapleton
(16) Julio Valdez

1979 Cramer 1970s P.C.L. All-Stars

(AAA)

NM
Complete Set (160): 75.00
(1) Brian Abraham
(2) Willie Mays Aikens
(3) Gary Alexander
(4) Dell Alston
(5) Orlando Alvarez
(6) Chris Arnold
(7) Gerry Augustine
(8) Doug Ault
(9) Rick Austin
(10) Chuck Baker
(11) Eddie Bane
(12) Len Barker
(13) Mike Barlow
(14) Randy Bass
(15) Charlie Beamon, Jr.
(16) Lew Beasley
(17) Joe Beckwith
(18) Ron Bell
(19) Juan Berenguer
(20) Vic Bernal
(21) Dale Berra
(22) Kurt Bevacqua
(23) Dan Boone
(24) Jerry Bostic
(25) Steve Bowling
(26) Rocky Bridges
(27) Derek Bryant
(28) Mark Budaska
(29) Steve Burke
(30) Bill Butler
(31) Keathel Chauncey
(32) Jack Clark
(33) Stan Cliburn
(34) David Clyde
(35) Terry Cornutt
(36) Ray Cosey
(37) Jeff Cox
(38) Del Crandell
(39) Ed Crosby (Spokane)
(40) Ed Crosby (San Jose)
(41) Tommy Cruz
(42) Darrell Darrow
(43) Rich Donnelly
(44) Jim Dorsey
(45) Brian Doyle
(46) Rob Dressler
(47) Andy Dyes
(48) Rob Ellis
(49) Terry Enyart
(50) Cal Ermer
(51) Manny Estrada
(52) Greg Field
(53) Randy Fierbaugh
(54) Rick Foley
(55) Jay Franklin
(56) Pedro Garcia
(57) Mike Garman
(58) Jerry Garvin
(59) Pedro Guerrero
(60) Moose Haas
(61) Tom Hall
(62) Bob Hansen
(63) Vic Harris
(64) Tom Heinzelman
(65) Enzo Hernandez
(66) Frank Howard
(67) Phil Huffman
(68) Jim Hughes
(69) Skip James
(70) Garry Jestadt
(71) Bobby Jones
(72) Bob Kammeyer
(73) Kevin Keefe
(74) Wendall Kim
(75) Kevin Kobel
(76) Gil Kubski
(77) Fred Kuhaulua
(78) Craig Kusick
(79) Art Kusnyer
(80) Rafael Lanestoy
(81) Rudy Law
(82) Vance Law
(83) John Lemaster
(84) Jeff Leonard
(85) Sixto Lezcano
(86) Jack Lind
(87) Larry Lintz
(88) Jeff Little
(89) Dennis Littlejohn
(90) Juan Lopez
(91) Steve Luebber
(92) Greg Mahlberg
(93) Sheldon Mallory
(94) Jack Maloof
(95) Davis May
(96) Steve McCatty
(97) Dave McKay
(98) Lynn McKinney
(99) Tom McMillan
(100) Bill McNulty
(101) Luis Melendez
(102) Greg Minetto
(103) Craig Mitchell
(104) Dave Moharter
(105) Rance Mulliniks
(106) Steve Mura
(107) Larry Murray
(108) Tony Muser
(109) Phil Natsu
(110) Mike Norris
(111) Willie Norwood
(112) Kunio Ogawa

(113) Oswaldo Olivares
(114) Dan Osborn
(115) Tom Paciorek
(116) Ken Pape
(117) Dave Patterson
(118) Mike Pazik
(119) Sammy Perlozzo
(120) Ed Plank
(121) Bill Plummer
(122) John Poloni
(123) Mike Potter
(124) Hoskin Powell
(125) Mike Proly
(126) Pat Putnam
(127) Gus Quiros
(128) Milt Ramirez
(129) Barry Raziano
(130) Rick Rennick
(131) Tommie Reynolds
(132) Frank Ricelli
(133) Bruce Robinson
(134) Craig Ryan
(135) Lenn Sakata
(136) Mike Scioscia
(137) Bill Severns
(138) Rob Sheldon
(139) Joe Simpson
(140) Wayne Simpson
(141) Coley Smith
(142) Keith Smith
(143) Royle Stillman
(144) Craig Stok
(145) Jerry Stone
(146) Joe Strain
(147) Brent Strom
(148) Steve Strougher
(149) Rick Sutcliffe
(150) John Sutton
(151) Rick Sweet
(152) Danny Walton
(153) Mark Weathers
(154) Dave Wehrmeister
(155) Claude Westmorland
(156) Mark Wiley
(157) Rob Wilfong
(158) Bump Wills
(159) Dick Woodson
(160) Jeff Yurak

1979 Trackle Peninsula Pilots Postcards

(Philadelphia Phillies, A) (3-1/2" x 5-3/8", b/w, postcard back, players unidentified)

NM
Complete Set (19): 27.50
(1) Oscar Acosta
(2) Daryl Adams
(3) Butch Ballard
(4) Jose Castro
(5) Ron Clark
(6) Wil Culmer
(7) Bob Dernier
(8) Ernie Gause
(9) Marco Gonzalez
(10) Jim Lasek
(11) Tom Lombarski
(12) Bob Neal (gm)
(13) Ken Rowe
(14) Mike Ryan
(15) Ron Smith
(16) Steve Swain
(17) Phil Teston
(18) Greg Walker
(19) Wayne Williams

1979 Cramer Phoenix Giants

(S.F. Giants, AAA) (color, 2-7/16" x 3-1/2")

NM
Complete Set (26): 9.00
1 Doug Schafer
2 Kyle Hypes
3 Mike Rowland
4 Jeff Little
5 Rocky Bridges
6 Phil Nastu
7 Bill Bordley
8 Ed Plank
9 Joe Strain
10 Greg Johnston
11 Don Carrithers
12 Tom Heintzelman
13 Randy Harmon
14 Rick Bradley
15 Terry Cornutt
16 Chris Bourjos
17 Casey Parsons
18 Rich Murray
19 Dennis Littlejohn
20 Mark Kuecker
21 Rick Sanderlin
22 Guy Sularz
23 Mike Rex
24 Ethan Blackaby
---- Tommy Gonzales
---- Harry Jordan

1979 TCMA Portland Beavers

(Pittsburgh Pirates, AAA) (color)

NM
Complete Set (24): 19.00
1 Al Holland
2 Ossie Oliveras
3 Greg Field
4 Ben Wiltbank
5 Vance Law
6 Tom Sandt
7 Dorian Boyland
8 Ron Mitchell
9 John Lipon
10 Gene Cotes
11 Joe Coleman
12 Gene Pentz
13 Gary Hargis
14 Alberto Lois
15 Mike Garman
16 Manny Lantigua
17 Dan Warthen
18 Craig Cacek
19 Larry Littleton
20 Pascual Perez
21 Harry Saferight
22 Rod Scurry
23 Rick Jones
24 Rod Gilbreath

1979 TCMA Quad City Cubs

(Chicago Cubs, A) (black & white)

NM
Complete Set (27): 45.00
1 Mike Wright
2 Ed Mohr
3 Ed Moore
4 Roger Crow
5 Bill Morgan
6 Wayne Rohlfing
7 Ted May
8 Joe McClain
9 Rich McClure
10 J.W. Mitchell
11 Joe Hicks
12 Mark Gilbert
13 Joey Cole
14 Randy Clark
15 Hal Kizer
16 Craig Kornfeld
17 Bob Maddon
18 Gordon Hodgson
19 John Bargfeldt
20 Andy Walker
21 Freddy Forgeur
22 Jim Napier
23 Tom Spino
24 Mike Shepston
25 Steve Viskas
26 Bob Oliver
27 Norm Churchill

1979 TCMA Richmond Braves

(Atlanta Braves, AAA) (color)

NM
Complete Set (25): 15.00
1 Joey McLaughlin
2 Mike Reynolds
3 John Sain
4 Larry Whisenton
5 Larry Owen
6 Jerry Maddox
7 Jon Richardson (gm)
8 Seymour Baseball, Chief Powa-Hitta (mascots)
9 Radio Voices
10 Front Office
11 Jamie Easterly
12 Roger Alexander
13 Chico Ruiz
14 Terry Harper
15 Tom Burgess
16 Duane Thesis
17 Larry Bradford
18 Dan Morogiello
19 Jerry Keller
20 Pat Rockett
21 Rick Camp
22 Tommy Boggs
23 Jim Arline
24 Ed Miller
25 Tony Brizzolara

1979 TCMA Rochester Red Wings

(Baltimore Orioles, AAA) (color)

NM
Complete Set (20): 14.00
1 Jeff Youngbauer
2 Joe Kerrigan
3 Kevin Kennedy
4 Blake Doyle
5 Willie Royster
6 Art James
7 Tony Franklin
8 Carlos Lopez
9 Mike Eden
10 Howard Edwards
11 Tom Bianco
12 Gerry Pirtle
13 Jim Smith
14 Ken Diggle
15 Mark Corey
16 Jeff Rineer
17 Jose Bastian
18 Tom Chism
19 Tony Chevez
20 Dave Ford

1979 TCMA Salt Lake City Gulls

(California Angels, AAA) (color)

NM
Complete Set (23): 15.00
9 Mike Overy
10 Bob Ferris
11 Rance Mulliniks
12 Bob Clark
13 Bill Ewing
14 Jim Dorsey
15 Joel Crisler
16a John Harris
16b Gil Kubski
17a Darrell Darrow
17b Dave Schuler
18a Rick Foley
18b Carlos Perez
19a Chuck Porter
19b Dan Whitmer
20a Jay Peters
20b Floyd Rayford
21a Bobby Ramos
21b Bob Slater
22a Pepe Manguel
22b Jim Williams
23a Daniel Boone
23b Leonard Garcia

1979 TCMA Savannah Braves

(Atlanta Braves, AA) (color) (card #3 not issued)

NM
Complete Set (27): 25.00
1 Dom Chiti
2 Gary Cooper
4 Bill Haslerig
5 Brian Snitker
6 Tim Brill
7 Tim Graven
8 Sonny Jackson
9 Mike Shields
10 Greg Johnson
11 Clay Elliott
12 Jose Alvarez
13 Kris Yoder
14 Steve Bedrosian
15 Joe Cowley
16 Richard Witers (correct picture, wrong name & stats)
17 Leo Mazzone
18 Eddie Hass (correct picture, wrong name & stats)
19 Terry Leach
20 Tim Cole
21 Louis A. "A1" Pratt
22 Bob Porter
23 Rafael Ramirez
24 Kenny Smith
25 Mike Miller
26 Jim Wessinger
--- Rufino Linares

1979 TCMA Spokane Indians

(Seattle Mariners, AAA) (color)

NM
Complete Set (25): 12.50
1 Ed Crosby
2 Royle Stillman
3 Mike Potter
4 Danny Walton
5 Rod Craig
6 Charlie Beamon
7 Jack L. Pierce
8 Ken Pape
9 Reggie Walton
10 Bill Plummer
11 Gary Lance
12 George Decker
13 Jim Lewis
14 Mike Davey
15 Jack Heidemann
16 Rene Lachemann
17 Gary Wheelock
18 Rob Pietroburgo
19 Rob Dressler
20 Karl Anderson
21 Greg Biercevicz
22 Steve Burke
23 Terry Bulling
24 Moncho Berhardt
25 Manny Estrada

1979 TCMA Syracuse Chiefs

(Toronto Blue Jays, AAA) (color)

NM
Complete Set (20): 25.00
1 Greg Wells
2 Vern Benson
3 Ernie Whitt
4 Willie Upshaw
5 Mark Wiley
6 Domingo Ramos
7 Joe Cannon
8 Don Pisker
9 Butch Edge
10 Mike Sember
11 Dave Baker
12 Garth Iorg
13 Jackson Todd
14 Chuck Fore
15 Doug Ault
16 Davis May
17 Steve Grilli
18 Luis Rosado
19 Ken Raynolds
20 Steve Luebber

1979 Syracuse Chiefs team issue

(Toronto Blue Jays, AAA) (black & white, 4" x 6", blank-back)

NM
Complete Set (24): 125.00
1 Domingo Ramos
2 Papo Rosado
3 Chuck Scrivener
4 Dan Ainge
5 Dave Baker
6 Pat Kelly
7 Don Pisker
8 Vern Benson
9 Garth Iorg
10 Mike Sember
12 Ernie Whitt
14 Butch Alberts
15 Ken Reynolds
16 Jackson Todd
17 Doug Ault
19 Butch Edge
21 Steve Grilli
22 Davis May
23 Joe Cannon
25 Jerry Garvin
26 Willie Upshaw
27 Mark Wiley
29 Tom Buskey
31 Steve Luebber

1979 TCMA Tacoma Tugs

(Cleveland Indians, AAA) (color)

NM
Complete Set (26): 20.00
1 Ron Hassey
2 Tom Brown
3 Rick Borchers
4 Larry Andersen
5 Tom Brennan
6 Juan Berenguer
7 Bobby Cuellar
8 Todd Heimer
9 Gary Melson
10 Hugh Yancy
11 Sal Rende
12 Dave Oliver
13 Jerry Dybzinski
14 Mike Champion
15 Bob Allietta
16 Sandy Whitol
17 Nate Puryear
18 Carl Nicholson
19 Del Alston
20 Rich Chiles
21 Sheldon Mallory
22 Tim Norrid
23 Rob Ellis
24 Gene Dusan
25 Fred Gladding
26 Wayne Cage

1979 Tampico Alijadores team issue

(Class AAA, Mexcian League) (One of the few Mexican minor league card issues, this set features 2-3/4" x 4-1/4" printed on heavy stock. Player photos appear on front within a wide blue border with the team name at top, player name at bottom and a baseball at lower-right with the position. Backs have player data and stats and elements for playing a baseball card game. An album was available to house the cards. The cards are checklisted here alphabetically.)

NM
Complete Set (27): 45.00
Album: 12.00
(1) Robert Alsup
(2) Alejandro Alvarado
(3) Randy Brand
(4) Ernesto Cordoba

(5) Jose Luis de los Santos
(6) Ernesto Espinosa
(7) Baldemar Figueroa
(8) Raul Gamez
(9) Ramon Garcia
(10) Ricardo Gaytan
(11) Horacio Guzman
(12) Bart Johnson
(13) Felipe Leal
(14) Manuel Lugo
(15) Felizardo Martinez
(16) Raul Martinez
(17) Roberto Morales
(18) Cesar Moreno
(19) Arturo Orozco
(20) Daniel Rios
(21) Rigoberto Robles
(22) Arturo Rubio
(23) Reggie J. Sanders
(24) Aristeo Sauceda
(25) Jesus Sommers
(26) Cleo Smith
(27) Carlos Trevino

1979 TCMA Tidewater Tides

(N.Y. Mets, AAA) (color, edition of 4,000)

	NM
Complete Set (25):	65.00

1 Roy Lee Jackson
2 John Pacella
3 Jose Moreno
4 Frank Verdi
5 Jeff Reardon
6 Dwight Bernard
7 Mookie Wilson
8 Butch Benton
9 Ron Washington
10 Jim Buckner
11 Dan Norman
12 Mario Ramirez
13 Marshall Brant
14 Ed Cipot
15 Mike Scott
16 Stan Hough
17 Scott Holman
18 Kelvin Chapman
19 Mike Van De Casteele
20 Greg Pavlick
21 Bobby Bryant
22 Russell Clark
23 Jesse Orosco
24 Bob Gorinski
25 Earl Stephenson

1979 TCMA Toledo Mud Hens

(Minnesota Twins, AAA) (color)

	NM
Complete Set (22):	12.50

1 Gary Ward
2 Paul Thormodsgard
3 Cal Ermer
4 Archie Amerson
5 Kevin Stanfield
6 Dan Graham
7 Dave Engle
8 Sal Butera
9 Terry Felton
10 Terry Sheehan
11 Wayne Caughey
12 John Verhoeven
13 Buck Chamberlin
14 Jim Buckner
15 Tom Sain
16 Greg Thayer
17 Dave Coleman
18 Darrell Jackson
19 Frank Vilorio
20 Jesus Vega
21 Dennis Mantick
22 Ray Smith

1979 TCMA Tucson Toros

(Texas Rangers, AAA) (color)

	NM
Complete Set (24):	15.00

1 Gary Gray
2 Myrl Smith
3 Mike Bruhardt
4 Brian Allard
5 Mike Bucci
6 Stan Jakubowski
7 Ron Gooch
8 Rich Donnelly
9 Steve Bianchi
10 Marty Scott
11 Don Kainer
12 Wayne Pinkerton
13 Fla Strawn
14 Tom Grieve
15 Greg Mahlberg
16 Dave Moharter
17 Mike Hart
18 Odie Davis
19 Keathel Chauncey
20 Ed Lynch
21 Bob Myrick
22 Mel Barrow
23 Larry McCall
24 Jim Umbarger

1979 TCMA Tulsa Drillers

(Texas Rangers, AA) (color)

	NM
Complete Set (24):	20.00

1 Wayne Tolleson
2 Joe Russell
3 Len Whitehouse
4 Jim Capowski
5 Fla Strawn
6 Steve Finch
7 Dan Dixon
8 Ray Rainbolt
9 Steve Nielsen
10 Mark Mercer
11 Ron Gooch
12 Jack Ramirez
13 Jim Schaffer
14 Rick Lisi
15 Terry Bogener
16 John Butcher
17 Jim Barbe
18 Ron Carney
19 Dave Crutcher
20 Nick Capra
21 Mel Barrow
22 Hal Kelly
23 Bill Rollings
24 Roy Clark (country singer) (owner)

1979 TCMA Vancouver Canadians

(Milwaukee Brewers, AAA) (color)

	NM
Complete Set (25):	15.00

1 Skip James
2 Vic Harris
3 Ron Jacobs
4 Marshall Edwards
5 Craig Ryan
6 Tim Nordbrook
7 Mark Bomback
8 Andy Replogle
9 Danny Boitano
10 Rickey Keeton
11 Gus Quiros
12 Juan Lopez
13 Ned Yost
14 Clay Carroll
15 Kuni Ogawa
16 Randy Stein
17 Ed Romero
18 Jeff Yurak
19 Sam Hinds
20 John Felske
21 Billy Severns
22a Kent Biggerstaff (trainer)
22b Lenn Sakata
23a Willie Mueller
23b Creighton Tevlin

1979 TCMA Waterbury A's

(Oakland A's, AA) (black & white)

	NM
Complete Set (25):	85.00

1 Dennis DeBarr
2 Rick Tronerud
3 Walt Horn
4 Bart Braun
5 Dennis Wysznaski
6 Keith Atherton
7 Leroy Robbins
8 Frank Kolarek
9 Ed Nottle
10 Al Armstead
11 Shooty Babitt
12 Randy Green
13 Bob Klebba
14 Mike Patterson
15 Mike Davis
16 Al Minker
17 Larry Groover
18 Paul Mize
19 Bruce Fournier
20 Bob Grandas
21 Ron McNeely
22 Tim Conroy
23 Scott Meyer
24 Dave Beard
25 Robert Moore

1979 TCMA Waterloo Indians

(Cleveland Indians, A) (black & white)

	NM
Complete Set (32):	90.00

1a Matt Bullinger
1b Lynn Garrett
2a Lou Ganci
2b Tim Glass
3a Bill Hallstrom
3b Ron Linfonte
4a Keith Hendry
4b Jeff Klein
5 Troy Wilder
6 Jerry Stuzrien
7 Frank Regan
8 Gary Hinson
9 Steve McMurray
10 Sammy Davis
11 Rick Barnhart
12 John Asbell
13 Tom Anderson
14 Dane Anthony
15 Reid Cassidy
16 Scott Dwyer
17 Randy Rambis
18 Marcus Clark
19 Carmelo Castello (Castillo)
20 Rick Colzie
21 Ed Saavedra
22 Bob Diering
23 Mel Queen
24 Cal Emory
25 Peter Peltz
26 Tommy Martinez
27 Robbie Alvarez
28 John Walters
29 Dave Hudgins
30 Greg Johnson
31 Rod Hudson
32 Ray Richard

1979 TCMA Wausau Timbers

(Co-op, A) (black & white)

	NM
Complete Set (25):	25.00

1 Brent Gaff
2 Jerry Stutzriem
3 Todd Winterfeldt
4 Kerry Keenan
5 Dave Stockstill
6 Vic Mabee
7 Israel Gutierrez
8 Wally Goff
9 Joe Nemeth
10 Lloyd Turner
11 John Zisk
12 Bob Johnson
13 Rick Barnhart
14 Ramon Romero
15 Jack Littrell
16 Tom Robson
17 Donald Lowe
18 Dean Craig
19 Alex Christianson
20 Ted Davis
21 Mike Jirschele
22 Cameron Killebrew
23 Arnold McCrary
24 Jim Payne
25 Tom Owens

1979 TCMA West Haven Yankees

(N.Y. Yankees, AA) (color, edition of 2,000)

	NM
Complete Set (30):	60.00

1 Mark Johnston
2 Ed Napoleon
3 Don Cooper
4 Brian Dayett
5 Dan Schmitz
6 Pat Callahan
7 Nat Showalter
8 Carl Merrill
9 Dan Ledduke
10 Jim McDonald
11 Tom Filer
12 Kenny Baker
13 Willie McGee
14 Andy McGaffigan
15 Greg Jemison
16 Mark Softy
17 Mike Griffin
18 Tim Lewis
19 Steve Donohue
20 Tim Lollar
21 Dave Righetti
22 Batboys
23 Robert Zeig
24 Juan Espino
25 Joe Lefebvre
26 Mark Harris
27 Hoyt Wilhelm
28 Lloyd Kern
29 Front Office Staff
30 Neal Mersch

1979 TCMA Wisconsin Rapids Twins

(Minnesota Twins, A) (black & white)

	NM
Complete Set (23):	45.00

1 Antonio Lopez
2 Mike Ungs
3 Mike Riley
4 George Dierberger
5 Bob Blake
6 Alex Dovalis
7 Ron Grout
8 Matt Henderson
9 Steve Mapel
10 John Minarcin
11 Kim Nelson
12 Scott Stoltenberg
13 Bob Bohnet
14 Tarry Boelter
15 Gary Dobbs
16 Stan Cannon
17 Luis Bravo
18 Rubio Malone
19 Ted Kromy
20 Chuck Belk
21 Jose Rodriques
22 Jack Schumate
23 Rich Stelmaszek

Value of modern team sets is often predicated as much on inclusion of star player's early cards as on scarcity of the issue.

1980 TCMA Albuquerque Dukes

(L.A. Dodgers, AAA) (color)

	NM
Complete Set (27):	50.00

1 Dave Stewart
2 Joe Beckwith
3 Pablo Peguero
4 Kelly Snider
5 Bill Swiacki
6 Ron Roenicke
7 John O'Rear
8 Dennis Lewallyn
9 Doug Harrison
10 Dave Patterson
11 Claude Westmoreland
12 Myron White
13 Gary Weiss
14 Teddy Martinez
15 Mike Wilson
16 Jack Perconte
17 Kevin Keefe
18 Wayne Caughey
19 Terry Collins
20 Bobby Mitchell
21 Mark Nipp
22 Ted Power
23 Del Crandall
24 Paul Padilla
25 Gerald Hannahs
26 Mike Scioscia
27 Don Crow

1980 TCMA Anderson Braves

(Atlanta Braves, A) (color)

	NM
Complete Set (29):	32.00

1 Dan Church
2 Arcilio Castaigne
3 Duane Theiss
4 Tim Fuller
5 Larry Edwards
6 Tim Alexander
7 Dave Coghill
8 Sonny Jackson
9 Scott Patterson
10 Ken Ames
11 Felipe Arroyo
12 Dave Chase
13 Mark Moses
14 Bill Nice
15 Mike Payne
16 Carlos Rymer
17 Buddy Bailey
18 Roy North
19 Randy Whistler
20 Eric Ayala
21 Mike Koperda
22 Mike Garcia
23 Ken Scanlon
24 Miguel Sosa
25 Harold Williams
26 Brett Butler
27 Brook Jacoby
28 Brad Komminsk
29 Rafael Quezada

1980 TCMA Appleton Foxes

(Chicago White Sox, A) (black & white)

	NM
Complete Set (30):	125.00

1 Luis Estrada
2 Bob Fallon
3 Diego Melendez
4 William Mills
5 Rick Naumann
6 J.B. Brown
7 Jeff Vuksan
8 Vito Lucarelli
9 Ron Kittle
10 Larry Wright

11 Dennis Vasquez
12 Nelson Rodreguez
13 Steve Pastrovich
14 Daniel Ortega
15 Keith Brown
16 Jim English
17 A.J. Hill
18 Mitch Olson
19 Greg Stewart
20 Greg Walker
21 David White
22 Tim Carroll
23 Dave Daniels
24 Dennis Keatting
25 Bill Luzinski
26 Larry Doby
27 Larry Hall
28 Mike Maitland
29 Gordy Lund
30 Ron Wollenhaupt

1980 TCMA Arkansas Travelers

(St. Louis Cardinals, AA) (color)

NM
Complete Set (25): 17.50
1 Benny (Joe) Edelen
2 George Bjorkman
3 Jorge Aranzamendi
4 James Riggleman
5 John Ruberto
6 Mike Calise
7 Luis DeLeon
8 Mike Dimmel
9 Andrew Rincon
10 Dave Penniall
11 Alan Olmsted
12 James McIntyre
13 Ryan Kurosaki
14 David Johnson
15 Frank Hunsaker
16 Julian Gutierrez
17 Nelson Garcia
18 Freddie Tisdale
19 Felipe Zayas
20 Ray Williams
21 John Murphy
22 Kelly Paris
23 Bill Valentine
24 Mike McCormick
25 David Jorn

1980 TCMA Asheville Tourists

(Texas Rangers, A) (color, edition of 2,500)

NM
Complete Set (28): 30.00
1 Billy Goodman
2 Tom Robson
3 George Gomez
4 Melvin Gilliam
5 Andy Hancock
6 Jim Schaefer
7 Toni Fossas
8 Dave Hibner
9 Ron McKee
10 Bobby Ball
11 Jimmy Tjader
12 Joe Nemeth
13 Pete O'Brien
14 Ron Carney
15 Kerry Kenan
16 Jim Maxwell
17 Jay Pettibone
18 Bill Taylor
19 Daryl Smith
20 Linvel Mosby
21 Donnie Scott
22 Larry Donofrio
23 Frank Garcia
24 Rick Burdette
25 Dave Schmidt
26 Greg Eason
27 Shelton McMath
28 Mike Jirschele

1980 TCMA Batavia Trojans

(Cleveland Indians, A) (black & white)

NM
Complete Set (30): 110.00
1 Angelo Gilbert
2 Terry Norman
3 Mark Bajus
4 Todd Richards
5 Mike Kolodny
6 Kirk Jones
7 Tom Blackmon
8 Tom Burns
9 Monty Holland
10 Mike Schwarber
11 Orestes Moldes
12 Chuck Hollowell
13 Tom Stiboro
14 Brian Meier
15 Rick Elkin
16 Luis Duarte
17 Chuck Melito
18 Darold Ellison
19 Kevin Malone
20 Andy Alvis
21 Kelly Gruber
22 Rick Colzie
23 Justo Saavedra
24 Matt Minium
25 Dave Gallagher
26 Pat Grady
27 Chris Rehbaum
28 Jeff Moronko
29 Nelson Ruiz
30 Mark Wright

1980 TCMA Buffalo Bisons

(Pittsburgh Pirates, AA) (color)

NM
Complete Set (16): 28.00
1 Mike Barnes
2 Ron Mitchell
3 Rick Federici
4 Dave Dravecky
5 Jim Buckner
6 Drew Macauley
7 Steve Farr
8 Rick Evans
9 Not issued
10 Paul Djakonow
11 Mike Allen
12 Bob Rock
13 Al Torres
14 Larry Nicholson
15 Ed Vargas
16 Steve Demeter
---- Al Ortiz, Jr.

1980 TCMA Burlington Bees

(Milwaukee Brewers, A) (black & white)

NM
Complete Set (29): 40.00
1 Steve Gibson
2 Kevin McCoy
3 Mike Donovan
4 Mark Lepson
5 Dave Grier
6 Greg Dehart
7 Orlando Gonzalez
8 Steve Manderfield
9 Brian Thorson
10 Duane Espy
11 Vince Pone
12 Jesse Vasquez
13 Al Walker
14 Ty Coleman
15 Steve Norwood
16 Rich Bach
17 Greg Cicotte
18 Mike Anderson
19 Kurt Kingsolver
20 Walt Steele
21 Jorge DeJesus
22 Juan Castillo
23 Mark Higgins
24 Kirk Downs
25 John Evans
26 Curt Watanabe
27 Stan Levi
28 Karl McKay
29 Bengie Biggus

1980 TCMA Cedar Rapids Reds

(Cincinnati Reds, A) (color)

NM
Complete Set (26): 12.00
1 Mark Moore
2 Newt Box
3 Dave Hoenstine
4 Emil Drzayich
5 Larry Buckle
6 Carlos Porte
7 Eski Viltz
8 Steve Hughes
9 Tony Masone
10 Bob Lapple
11 Rick Jendra
12 Charlie McKinney
13 Jose Mota
14 Steve Skaggs
15 Frank DeJulio
16 Mark Miller
17 Les Straker
18 Paul Gibson
19 Jeff Jones
20 Mike Messaros
21 Don "Bucky" Buchheister
22 Jim Lett
23 Mike Kripner
24 Steve Daniels
25 Kevin Waller
26 Wayne Guinn

1980 TCMA Charleston Charlies

(Texas Rangers, AAA) (color)

NM
Complete Set (17): 15.00
1 Tom Burgess
2 Mark Scott
3 Wayne Pinkerton
4 Nelson Norman
5 Brian Allard
6 Greg Mahlberg
7 Dave Moharter
8 Mike Richardt
9 Richard Lisi
10 Mike Hart
11 Mark Mercer
12 Dan Duran
13 John Butcher
14 Fla Strawn
15 Odie Davis
16 Tucker Ashford
17 Bob Babcock

1980 WBTV Charlotte O's

(Baltimore Orioles, AA)

NM
Complete Set (27): 1500.
1 John Shelby
3 John Buffamoyer
4 Tommy Eaton
6 Cat Whitfield
9 Tommy Smith
11 Curt Fabrizio
13 Willie Royster
14 Drungo Hazewood
16 Cal Ripken Jr.
17 John Denman
18 Larry Anderson
19 David Huppert
20 Billy Presley
21 Brooks Carey
22 Russ Pensiero
24 Dan Ramierz
25 Jose Gonzales
27 Luis Quintana
30 Don Welchel
31 Will George
32 Edwin Neal
--- Logo Card
--- Team Photo
--- The Pepper Girls
--- Minnie Mendoza
--- Doc Cole
--- Marshall Hester

1980 Charlotte O's team issue

(Baltimore Orioles, AA) (set is bordered in orange)

NM
Complete Set (24): 2100.
(1) Larry Anderson
(2) John Buffamoyer
(3) Brooks Carey
(4) John Denman
(5) Tommy Eaton
(6) Kurt Fabrizio
(7) Will George
(8) Jose Gonzales
(9) Drungo Hazewood
(10) Dave Huppert
(11) Minnie Mendoza
(12) Edwin Neal
(13) Russ Pensiero
(14) Billy Presley
(15) Luis Quintana
(16) Dan Ramirez
(17) Cal Ripken, Jr.
(18) Willie Royster
(19) John Shelby
(20) Tommy Smith
(21) Don Welchel
(22) Cat Whitfield
(23) Jimmy Williams
(24) "The Pepper Girls"

1980 TCMA Clinton Giants

(S.F. Giants, A) (black & white)

NM
Complete Set (27): 90.00
1 Dave Wilhelmi
2 Dennis Rathjen
3 Jose Chue
4 Ramon Bautista
5 Jerry Stoval (Stovall)
6 Chris Goodchild
7 Ron Matrisciano
8 Ken Schwab
9 Tim Hagemann
10 Scott Garrelts
11 Art Maebe
12 Kevin Johnson
13 David Fonseca
14 Randy Kutcher
15 Tim Painton
16 Chris Brown
17 Frank Thon
18 Rafael Estepan
19 Glen Moon
20 Rob Deer
21 Ron Perodin
22 Stan Morton
23 Richard Figueroa
24 Bob Cummings
25 Gilbert Albright
26 Wayne Cato
27 Tommy Jones

1980 TCMA Columbus Astros

(Houston Astros, AA) (black & white)

NM
Complete Set (22): 45.00
1 Greg Cypret
2 Val Primmante
3 Tim Tolman
4 Stan Leland
5 Del Letherwood
6 Chick Valley
7 Johnny Ray
8 Bert Pena
9 Doug Stokke
10 Matt Galante
11 Greg Dahl
12 Rod Boxberger
13 John Hessler
14 Simone Rosario
15 Reggie Waller
16 Riccardo Aponte
17 Scott Loucks
18 Keith Bodie
19 Ron Meredith
20 Jim MacDonald
21 Mark Miggins
22 Rex Jones

1980 Columbus Clippers team issue

(N.Y. Yankees, AAA)

NM
Complete Set (25): 15.00
(1) Joe Altibelli (Altobelli)
(2) Marshall Brandt
(3) Ken Clay
(4) Greg Cochan
(5) Dave Coleman
(6) Brian Doyle
(7) Brad Gulden
(8) Roger Holt
(9) Bob Kammeyer
(10) Joe Lefebvre
(11) Jim Lewis
(12) Tim Lollar
(13) Jim McDonald
(14) Jim Nettles
(15) Dave Righetti
(16) Bruce Robinson
(17) Dennis Sherrill
(18) George H. Sisler Jr.
(19) Roger Slagle
(20) Roy Staiger
(21) Marv Thompson
(22) Dave Wehrmeister
(23) Chris Welsh
(24) Coaches/trainer card (Jerry McNertney, Sammy Ellis, Mark Letendre)
(25) Garry Smith

1980 Police Columbus Clippers

(N.Y. Yankees, AAA) (color, 2-3/8" x 3-3/4")

NM
Complete Set (25): 27.50
2 Brian Doyle
11 Roger Holt
12 Dennis Sherrill
14 Joe Lefebvre
15 Garry Smith
16 Joe Altibelli (Altobelli)
17 Dave Coleman
18 Roger Slagle
20 Brad Gulden
21 Jim Lewis
22 Marv Thompson
23 Tim Lollar
24 Dave Righetti
25 Roy Staiger
26 Bruce Robinson
27 Greg Cochran
28 Jim Nettles
29 Bob Kammeyer
30 Dave Wehrmeister
31 Jim McDonald
33 Marshall Brandt (Brant)
34 Chris Welsh
36 Ken Clay
---- George H. Sisler Jr. (general manager)
---- Coaches/Trainer Card (Sammy Ellis, Mark Letendre, Jerry McNertney)

1980 TCMA Columbus Clippers

(N.Y. Yankees, AAA) (color)

NM
Complete Set (28): 45.00
1 Tim Lollar
2 Roger Stagle
3 Chris Welsh
4 Wayne Harer
5 Garry Smith
6 Brad Gulden
7 Roger Holt
8 Joe Altobelli
9 Roy Staiger
10 Bob Kammeyer
11 Jim McDonald
12 Jim Nettles
13 Brian Doyle
14 Sammy Ellis
15 Bruce Robinson
16 Jim Lewis
17 Dave Righetti
18 Mark Letendre
19 Dave Coleman
20 Marshall Brant
21 Greg Cochran
22 Jerry McNertney
23 Dennis Sherrill
24 Marv Thompson
25 Dave Wehrmeister
26 Joe Lefebvre
27 George Sisler, Jr.
28 Juan Espino

1980 TCMA Elmira Pioneers

(Boston Red Sox, A) (black & white, edition of 1,100)

NM
Complete Set (44): 105.00
1 Alan Banes
2 Tom Bolton
3 Allan Bowlin
4 Dennis Boyd
5 Brice Cote
6 Steve Garrett
7 George Greco
8 Ty Herman

9 Ron Hill
10 Kevin Keenan
11 Jeff Hall
12 John Ackley
13 Mark Weinbrecht
14 Bob Sandling
15 Brandon Plainte
16 George Mecerod
17 Tom McCarthy
18 Mitch Johnson
19 Don Leach
20 Tim Duncan
21 Jeff Hunter
22 Tony Stevens
23 Ron Oddo
24 Wolf Ramos
25 Mike Bryant
26 Gus Burgess
27 Mike Ciampa
28 Simon Glenn
29 Dick Berardino
30 Parker Wilson
31 Brian Zell
32 Gilberto Gonzalez
33 Bob Crandall
34a Marve Handler
34b Bill Limoncelli
35 Brian Butera
36 Sam Mele
37 Frank Malzone
38 Charlie Wagner
39 Jay La Bare
40 Charlie Lynch
41 Alan Mintz
42 Rodolfo Santana
43 Miguel Valdez

1980 TCMA El Paso Diablos

(California Angels, AA) (color)

NM
Complete Set (20): 20.00
1 Brandt Humphrey
2 Dennis Gilbert
3 Scott Garnes
4 Rick Steirer
5 Tom Chevolek
6 Rich Rommel
7 Jim Saul
8 Mark Miller
9 Brian Harper
10 Bob Border
11 Joel Crisler
12 Mike Bishop
13 Tom Bhagwat
14 Daryl Sconiers
15 Don Smelser
16 Steve Brown
17 Tom Brunansky
18 Donny Jones
19 Perry Morrison
20 Rich Brewster
21 Rick Adams
22 Mike Walters
23 Jamie Hamilton
24 Charlie Phillips

1980 TCMA Evansville Triplets

(Detroit Tigers, AAA) (color)

NM
Complete Set (24): 15.00
1 Roger Weaver
2 Mark DeJohn
3 James Gaudet
4 David Steffen
5 Michael Chris
6 Mark Fidrych
7 Ed Putnam
8 Altar Greene
9 David Rucker
10 Gerald Ujdur
11 Darrell Brown
12 Steve Baker
13 Go Giannotta
14 John Martin
15 Ralph Treuel
16 David Machemer
17 Jim Leyland
18 Bruce Robbins
19 Martin Castillo
20 Dan Gonzales (Gonzalez)
21 Glenn Gulliver
22 Steve Patchin
23 Juan Lopez
24 Richard Leach

1980 TCMA Glens Falls White Sox (b/w)

(Chicago White Sox, AA) (black & white, edition of 1,100)

NM
Complete Set (29): 135.00
1 Steve Pastrovich
2 Len Bradley
3 Tom Johnson
4 Randy Evans
5 Mark Platel
6 Luis Rois
7 Rick Seilheimer
8 Ray Torres
9 Reggie Patterson
10 Kevin Hickey
11 Ted Barnicle
12 Rick Wieters
13 Mark Teutsch
14 Mark Esser
15 Andy Pasillas
16 Julio Perez
17 Ron Perry
18 Randy Johnson
19 Dom Fucci
20 Vince Bienek
21 A.J. Hill
22 Lorenzo Gray
23 Fran Mullins
24 Mike Pazik
25 Duane Shaffer
26 Orlando Cepeda
27 Allan Haines
28 Batboys
29 Bob Bolster

1980 TCMA Glens Falls White Sox (color)

(Chicago White Sox, AA) (color, edition of 2,500)

NM
Complete Set (30): 20.00
1 Ron Porry
2 Len Bradley
3 Mark Teutsch
4 Randy Johnson
5 Mark Esser
6 Andy Pasillas
7 Kevin Hickey
8 Rick Seilheimer
9 Mark Platel
10 Julio Perez
11 Vince Bienek
12 Fran Mullins
13 Rick Wieters
14 Dom Fucci
15 Randy Evans
16 Steve Pastrovich
17 Luis Rois
18 Reggie Patterson
19 Ted Barnicle
20 Sox Infield (Dom Fucci, Lorenzo Gray, A.J. Hill)
21 Mike Pazik
22 Allan Haines
23 Bob Bolster
24 Duane Shaffer
25 Orlando Cepeda
26 Lorenzo Gray
27 Ray Torres
28 Tom Johnson
29 Batboys
30 A.J. Hill

"1980" Greensboro Hornets Don Mattingly

Don Mattingly (Unauthorized issue produced in late 1980s; no collector value)

Suffix letters following a card number indicate a variation card.

1980 TCMA Hawaii Islanders

(San Diego Padres, AAA) (color)

NM
Complete Set (25): 15.00
1 Chuck Baker
2 Doug Rader
3 Bob Duensing
4 Juan Eichelberger
5 Eric Mustad
6 Craig Stimac
7 Graig Kusick
8 Jim Beswick
9 Dennis Blair
10 Bobby Mitchell
11 Chuck Hartenstein
12 John Yandle
13 Greg Wilkes
14 Tom Tellmann
15 George Stablein
16 Mike Armstrong
17 Mark Lee
18 Steve Smith
19 Tim Flannery
20 Rick Sweet
21 Tony Castillo
22 Broderick Perkins
23 Don Reynolds
24 Andy Dyes
25 Fred Kuhaulua

1980 TCMA Holyoke Millers

(Milwaukee Brewers, AA) (color)

NM
Complete Set (25): 15.00
1 Rick Kranitz
2 John Skorochocki
3 Mark Schuster
4 Barry Cort
5 Frank Thomas
6 Ivan Rodriguez
7 Eddie Brunson
8 Kuni Ogawa
9 Terry Shoebridge
10 Tom Kayser
11 Weldon Swift
12 Frank DiPino
13 Kevin Bass
14 David Green
15 Doug Loman
16 John Adams
17 Steve Lake
18 Steve Reed
19 Ed Carroll
20 Larry Montgomery
21 Terry Lee
22 Dave Curran
23 Gerald Ako
24 Tony Torres
25 Lee Stigman

1980 Indianapolis Indians team issue

(Cincinnati Reds, AAA) (color)

NM
Complete Set (32): 30.00
1 Team Photo
2 Jim Beauchamp
3 Sheldon Burnside
4 Mike Grace
5 Joe Price
6 John Hale
7 Geoff Combe
8 Dave Van Gorder
9 Bruce Berenyi
10 Eddie Milner
11 Jay Howell
12 Paul O'Neill
13 The Braintrust
14 Larry Rothschild
15 Paul Householder
16 The Relievers
17 Scott Brown
18 Mark Milner
19 The Starters
20 Blake Doyle
21 Gene Menees
22 Rafael Santo Domingo
23 Bill Kelly
24 Don Lyle
25 Bill Dawley
26 Duane Walker
27 Angel Torres
28 The Catchers
29 The Infielders
30 The Outfielders
31 John Young
32 Checklist

1980 Iowa Oaks Police Set

(Chicago White Sox, AAA) (set price includes all variations)

NM
Complete Set (16): 300.00
(1) Richard Barnes
(2) Nardi Contreras
(3) Henry Cruz
(4) Fred Frazier
(5) Joe Gates
(6) Guy Hoffman
(7) Lamar Hoyt
(8) Chris Nyman
(9) Dewey Robinson
(10) Leo Sutherland
(11) Pete Ward
(12) Mike Wolf
(13a) Mike Colbern (A Walk)
(13b) Mike Colbern (Rhubarb)
(14a) Raymundo Torres (Rhubarb)
(14b) Raymundo Torres (A Walk)

1980 TCMA Knoxville Blue Jays

(Toronto Blue Jays, AA) (black & white)

NM
Complete Set (28): 115.00
1 Chuck Fore
2 Gene Petralli
3 John Poloni
4 Pete Rowe
5 Paul Hodgson
6 Mark Stober
7 Davis May
8 Jesse Flores
9 Bob Silverman
10 Shaun McCarthy
11 Ralph Santana
12 Mike Cuellar, Jr.
13 Jesse Barfield
14 Ed Donnic
15 Tim Thompson
16 Tom Dejak
17 Pedro Hernandez
18 Larry Hardy
19 Dave Gibson
20 Jesus de la Rosa
21 Charlie Puelo
22 Andre Wood
23 Keith Walker
24 "Rocket" Wheeler
25 Bob Humphreys
26 Rick Morgan
27 Duane Larson
28 Ed Holtz

1980 TCMA Lynn Sailors

(Seattle Mariners, AA) (color)

NM
Complete Set (23): 15.00
1 Mike Moore
2 Larry Patterson
3 Rodney Hobbs
4 Bobby Floyd
5 Chuck Lindsay
6 Rob Simond
7 Mike Hart
8 Don Minnick
9 Orlando Mercado
10 Miguel Negron
11 Karl Best
12 Jeff Cary
13 Manny Estrada
14 Gary Pellant
15 Mickey Bowers
16 Tom Hunt
17 Joe Georger
18 Jammie Allen
19 R.J. Harrison
20 Roy Clark
21 Sam Welborn
22 Lloyd Kern
23 Ron Musselman

1980 TCMA Memphis Chicks

(Montreal Expos, AA) (black & white)

NM
Complete Set (30): 45.00
1 Steve Lovins
2 Charlie Lea
3 Anthony Johnson
4 Tom Gorman
5 Greg Bargar
6 Joe Abone
7 Larry Goldetsky
8 Larry Bearnarth
9 Mike Gates
10 Glen Franklin
11 Ray Crowley
12 Leonel Carrion
13 Terry Francona
14 Kevin Mendon
15 Brad Mills
16 Tony Phillips
17 Pat Rooney
18 Dennis Sherow
19 Tommy Joe Shimp
20 Bryn Smith
21 Chris Smith
22 Doug Simunic
23 Bob Tenenini
24 Grayling Tobias
25 Tom Wieghaus
26 Rick Williams
27 Steve Winfield
28 Frank Wren
29 Bud Yanus
30 Audie Thor

1980 Chong Modesto A's

(Oakland A's, A)

NM
Complete Set (29): 65.00
1 Don Schubert
2 Steve Gelfarb
3 Mike Woodard
4 Paul Stockley
5 Gordon Eakin
6 Kevin Jacobson
7 Al Armstead
8 Jim Bennett
9 Lynn Garrett
10 Bob Garrett
11 Rich Hatcher
12 Jim Durrman
13 Frank Kneuer
14 Frank Kolarek
15 John Gosse

16 Ron Mantsch
17 Rick Holloway
18 Ken Corzel
19 Don Van Marter
20 Chuck Dougherty
21 Tom Brunswick
22 Ed Retzer
23 Mark Ferguson
24 Roy Moretti
25 Keith Call
26 Bob Wood
27 Keith Lieppman
28 Brad Fischer
29 Dan Kiser

1980 Nashville Sounds team issue

(N.Y. Yankees, AA)

	NM
Complete Set (25):	12.50

(1) Ken Baker
(2) Steve Balboni
(3) Paul Boris
(4) Pat Callahan
(5) Nate Chapman
(6) Don Cooper
(7) Brian Dayett
(8) Pat Dobson
(9) Tom Filer
(10) Brad Gulden
(11) Greg Jemison
(12) Dan Ledduke
(13) Andy McGaffigan
(14) Willie McGee
(15) Stump (Carl Merrill)
(16) Eddie Napoleon
(17) Brian Ryder, Brian Ryder
(18) Rafel Santana
(19) Danny Schmitz
(20) Buck Showalter
(21) Roger Slagle
(22) Pat Tabler
(23) Steve Taylor
(24) James Werly
(25) Ted Wilborn

1980 TCMA Ogden A's

(Oakland A's, AAA) (color)

	NM
Complete Set (23):	15.00

1 Tim Hosley
2 Ray Cosey
3 Craig Minetto
4 Derek Bryant
5 Randy Green
6 Rich Lysander
7 Mark Busaska
8 Terry Enyart
9 Brian Abraham
10 Mark Souza
11 Bob Grandas
12 Frank Harris
13 John Sutton
14 Milt Ramirez
15 David Beard
16 Bruce Fournier
17 Allen Wirth
18 Royle Stillman
19 Jeff Cox
20 Kelvin Moore
21 Shooty Babbitt (Babitt)
22 Pat Dempsey
23 Jose Pagan

Values shown are a national average. Some teams and players enjoy regional popularity which may affect market prices.

1980 Oklahoma City 89ers team issue

(Philadelphia Phillies, AAA)

	NM
Complete Set (28):	40.00

1 John Loviglio
3 Luis Aguayo
4 Mike Anderson
6 Jim Snyder
7 Orlando Isales
8 Billy Smith
9 Luis Rodriguez
10 Ramon Lora
11 Jose Martinez
12 Leonard Matuszek
14 Orlando Sanchez
15 Elijah B. Bonaparte
16 Ruben Arroyo
17 Paul G. Thormodsgard
18 Scott A. Munninghoff
19 Porfirio Altamirano
20 Orlando E. Gonzalez
21 Donald McCormack
22 Robert Speck
23 John Poff
24 James L. Wright Jr.
25 William Suter Jr.
26 Martin Bystrom
28 Jerry Reed

1980 Police Omaha Royals

(K.C. Royals, AAA)

	NM
Complete Set (24):	75.00

(1) Dave Augustine
(2) German Barranca
(3) Leon Brown
(4) Steve Busby
(5) Manny Castillo
(6) Craig Chamberlain
(7) Jerry Cram
(8) Ken Cvejdlik
(9) Bob Detherage
(10) Keith Drumright
(11) Dan Fischer
(12) Danny Garcia
(13) Jim Gaudet
(14) Kelly Heath
(15) Tim Ireland
(16) Bill Laskey
(17) Randy McGilberry
(18) Mike Morley
(19) Tom Mutz
(20) Bill Paschall
(21) Ken Phelps
(22) Jeff Schattinger
(23) Joe Sparks
(24) Jeff Twitty

1980 TCMA Orlando Twins

(Minnesota Twins, AA) (black & white)

	NM
Complete Set (22):	110.00

1 Wade Adamson
2 Tim Barr
3 Tom Biko
4 Steve Green
5 Eddie Hodge
6 Steve Mapel
7 Jose Reyes
8 Lance Hallberg
9 Frank Estes
10 Lenny Faedo
11 Steve Benson
12 Tim Laudner
13 A. Cadahia
14 G. Ballard
15 Mike Ungs
16 Terry Sheehan
17 Steve McManaman
18 Alex Ramirez
19 Mark Funderburk
20 Kevin McWhirter
21 Scott Ullger
22 Roy McMillan

1980 TCMA Peninsula Pilots (b/w)

(Philadelphia Phillies, A) (black & white, edition of 1,100)

	NM
Complete Set (27):	65.00

1 Phil Teston
2 Daryl Adams
3 Carlos Cabassa
4 Miguel Alicea
5 Fred Warner
6 Kelly Faulk
7 Wally Goff
8 Wil Culmer
9 Keith Washington
10 Bob Tiefenauer
11 Don Carman
12 Roy Smith
13 Jim Wright
14 Randy Greer
15 Joe Bruno
16 Al White
17 Paul Kiess
18 Russ Hamric
19 Ray Borucki
20 Ron Smith
21 Julio Franco
22 Jeff Ulrich
23 Herb Orensky
24 John Fierro
25 Bob Neal
26 Frank Funk
27 Bill Dancy

1980 TCMA Peninsula Pilots (color)

(Philadelphia Phillies, A) (color, edition of 2,500)

	NM
Complete Set (27):	50.00

1 Phil Teston
2 Daryl Adams
3 Carlos Cabassa
4 Roy Smith
5 Don Carman
6 Miguel Alicea
7 Jim Wright
8 Fred Warner
9 Bob Neal
10 John Fierro
11 George Farson
12 Bill Dancy
13 Kelly Faulk
14 Wally Goff
15 Herb Orensky
16 Jeff Ulrich
17 Julio Franco
18 Keith Washington
19 Wil Culmer
20 Randy Greer
21 Joe Bruno
22 Al White
23 Paul Kiess
24 Russ Hamric
25 Ray Borucki
26 Ron Smith
27 Bob Tiefenauer

1980 Valley Nat'l Bank Phoenix Giants

P.C.L.
SEASON 1980
FRED BREINING
Pitcher
Phoenix
See back for Team Picture Premium Offer

(S.F. Giants, AAA) (2" x 5")

	NM
Complete Set (26):	8.00

1 Mike Williams
2 Bob Tufts
3 Doug Schaefer
4 Mike Rowland
5 Larry Prewitt
6 Ed Plank
7 Phil Nastu
8 Terry Cornutt
9 Fred Breining
10 Bill Bordley
11 Chris Bourjos
12 Max Venable
13 Casey Parsons
14 Craig Landis
15 Bob Kearney
16 Dennis Littlejohn
17 Jose Barrios
18 Mike Rex
19 Rich Murray
20 Joe Pettini
21 Guy Sularz
22 Rocky Bridges
23 Jim Duffalo
24 Ethan Blackaby
25 Tommy Gonzales
26 Harry Jordan

1980 TCMA Portland Beavers

(Pittsburgh Pirates, AAA) (color) (#16 not issued)

	NM
Complete Set (26):	18.00

1 Mike Tyler
2 Dorian Boyland
3 Craig Cacek
4 Jerry McDonald
5 Rob Ellis
6 Jim Mahoney
7 Pascual Perez
8 Tommy Sandt
9 Vance Law
10 Mickey Mahler
11 Dick Pole
12 Bill Fortinberry
13 Stewart Cliburn
14 Harry Dorish
15 Gary Hargis
17 Odell Jones
18 Tom Trebelhorn
19 Mike Davey
20 Rick Lancellotti
21 Robert Long
22 Rod Gilbreath
23 Larry Anderson (Andersen)
24 Tony Pena
25 Gene Pentz
26 Dan Warthen
27 Rick Rhoden

1980 TCMA Quad Cities Cubs

(Chicago Cubs, A) (black & white)

	NM
Complete Set (32):	85.00

1 Mike Thompson
2 Gerry Mims
3 Tim Millner
4 Ed Moore
5 Tom Morris
6 Glenn Swaggerty
7 Ray Soff
8 Carlos Gil
9 Richard Renwick
10 Mark Wilkins
11 Bob Maddon
12 Norm Churchill
13 Mike Diaz
14 Pete Bazan
15 Ted Trevino
16 Jack Upton
17 Craig Kornfeld
18 Jim Payne
19 Glenn Millhauser
20 Bruce Compton
21 Mike Kelley
22 Dennis Mork
23 Gordy Hodgson
24 Wayne Rohlfing
25 Phil Belmonte
26 Mike Wilson
27 Rich DeLoach
28 John Stockstill
29 Carmelo Martinez
30 Jim Napier
31 Davey Nesmoe
32 Roger Crow

1980 TCMA Reading Phillies

(Philadelphia Phillies, AA) (black and white) (1,100 sets produced)

	NM
Complete Set (24):	985.00

1 Wayne Williams
2 Jose Castro
3 Ozzie Virgil
4 Mark Davis
5 Don Fowler
6 Miguel Ibarra
7 Joe Jones
8 Jeff Kraus
9 Tommy Hart
10 Ernie Gause
11 Darren Burroughs
12 Tom Lombarski
13 Jorge Bell
14 John Devincenzo
15 Bob Dernier
16 Manny Abreu
17 Ron Clark
18 Rollie Dearmas
19 Cliff Speck
20 Dan Prior
21 Tony McDonald
22 Ryne Sandberg
23 Jesus Herniz
24 Steve Curry

1980 TCMA Richmond Braves

(Atlanta Braves, AAA) (color)

	NM
Complete Set (23):	15.00

1 Danny Morogiello
2 Rafael Ramirez
3 Butch Edge
4 Larry Whisenton
5 Fred Hatfield
6 Steve Hammond
7 Tony Brizzolara
8 Gary Melson
9 John Sain
10 Danny O'Brien
11 Rick Mahler
12 Charlie Keller
13 Butch Metzger
14 Horace Speed
15 Glenn Hubbard
16 Harry Saferight
17 Terry Harper
18 Ken Smith
19 Bob Beall
20 Craig Skok
21 Jim Wessinger
22 Eddie Miller
23 Bo McLaughlin

1980 TCMA Rochester Red Wings

(Baltimore Orioles, AAA) (color)

	NM
Complete Set (21):	17.50

1 Bob Bonner
2 Dallas Williams
3 Vern Thomas
4 Dan Logan
5 Mark Corey
6 Mike Boddicker
7 Larry Jones
8 Jeff Rineer
9 Tom Rowe
10 Jeff Schneider
11 Kevin Kennedy
12 Mike Eden
13 Doc Edwards
14 John Valle
15 Steve Luebber
16 Wayne Krenchicki
17 Jim Smith
18 Floyd Rayford
19 Tom Smith
20 Larry Johnson
21 Pete Torrez

1980 TCMA Salt Lake City Gulls

(California Angels, AAA) (color) (Set price includes scarce cards #18-21)

	NM
Complete Set (26):	12.00

1 Ralph Botting
2 Dan Whitmer
3 Craig Eaton
4 Scott Moffitt
5 Mark Nocciolo
6 Dave Schuler
7 Ken Schrom
8 Charlie Phillips
9 Jeff Bertoni
10 Rick Oliver
11 Jay Peters
12 John Harris
13 Carlos Perez
14 Steve Lubratich
15 Rick Foley
16 Jim Dorsey
17 Steve Eddy
18 Moose Stubing
19 Leonard Garcia
20 Sterling Gull
21 Gil Kubski
22 Pete Mangual
23 Bob Clark
24 Bob Ferris
25 Fernando Gonzalez
26 Mike Overy

1980 Jack In The Box San Jose Missions

(Seattle Mariners, A) (color, 2" x 3")

	NM
Complete Set (21):	50.00

1 Bill Plummer
2 Ed Aponte
3 Mark Batten
4 Bud Black
5 Mark Chellette
6 Ramon Estepa
7 Chris Flammang
8 Bill Gaffney
9 Rick Graser
10 Tim Hallgren
11 Tracy Harris
12 Steve Knight
13 Chris Krajewski
14 Jed Murray
15 Tito Nanni
16 Brian Snyder
18 Jeff Stottlemyre
19 Scott Stranski
20 Dave Valle
21 Checklist

1980 TCMA Spokane Indians

(Seattle Mariners, AAA) (color) (3,000 sets produced)

	NM
Complete Set (24):	22.00

1 Bob Stoddard
2 Dave Smith
3 Greg Biercevicz
4 Carlos Diaz
5 Joe Coleman
6 Ron McGee
7 Roy Branch
8 Bryan Clark
9 Vance McHenry
10 Terry Bulling
11 Kip Young
12 Manny Sarmiento
13 Randy Stein
14 Jim Maler
15 Dave Elder
16 Dave Henderson
17 Gary Wheelock
18 Rene Lachemann
19 Kim Allen
20 Rich Anderson
21 Reggie Walton
22 Dan Firova
23 Steve Stroughter
24 Charlie Beamon

1980 TCMA Syracuse Chiefs

(Toronto Blue Jays, AAA) (color)

	NM
Complete Set (23):	30.00

1 Garth Iorg
2 Doug Ault
3 Kevin Pasley
4 Jackson Todd
5 Pat Rockett
6 Jay Robertson
7 Mike Willis
8 Tom Brown
9 Phil Huffman
10 Butch Alberts
11 Jack Kucek
12 Mitchell Webster
13 Mike Barlow
14 Greg Wells
15 Pat Kelly
16 Lloyd Moseby
17 Dave Baker
18 Randy Benson
19 Harry Warner
20 Danny Ainge
21 Willie Upshaw
22 Domingo Ramos
23 Don Pisker

1980 Syracuse Chiefs team issue

(Toronto Blue Jays, AAA) (black & white, 3-1/4" x 5", blank-back)

	NM
Complete Set (24):	125.00

4 Don Pisker
5 Dave Baker
9 Garth Iorg
11 Kevin Pasley
12 Steve Davis
14 Butch Alberts
15 Lloyd Moseby
16 Jackson Todd
17 Mitchell Webster
18 Pat Rockett
19 Tom Brown
20 Jack Kucek
21 Steve Grilli
22 Phil Huffman
23 Mike Willis
24 Harry Warner
25 Doug Ault
26 Pat Kelly
27 Randy Benson
28 Luis Leal
29 Mike Barlow
30 Jay Robertson
32 Greg Wells
---- Tony DeRosa (Trainer)

1980 TCMA Tacoma Tigers

(Cleveland Indians, AAA) (color) (#1 not issued)

	NM
Complete Set (28):	15.00

2 Tim Norrid
3 Larry Littleton
4 Wayne Cage
5 Don Collins
6 Bobby Cuellar
7 Mel Queen
8 Larry McCall
9 Raphael Vasquez
10 Sandy Whitol
11 Bob Allietta
12 Tom Brennan
13 Mike Bucci
14 Sal Rende
15 Dave Oliver
16 Mike Champion
17 Gary Gray
18 Todd Heimer
19 John Bonilla
20 Kevin Rhomberg
21 Rick Borchers
22 Art Popham
23 Gene Dusan
24 Del Alston
25 Eric Wilkins
26 Steve Ciszczon
27a Louis DeLeon
27b Mike Paxton
---- Rob Pietroburgo

1980 TCMA Tidewater Tides

(N.Y. Mets, AAA) (color) (#16 not issued)

	NM
Complete Set (24):	35.00

1 Dave Von Ohlen
2 Jose Moreno
3 Juan Berenguer
4 Wally Backman
5 Sergio Ferrer
6 Gil Flores
7 Ed Cipot
8 Butch Benton
9 Ron MacDonald
10 Dyar Miller
11 Greg Harris
12 Tom Dixon
13 Reggie Baldwin
14 Fred Beene
15 Hubie Brooks
17 Mookie Wilson
18 Kelvin Chapman
19 Roy Lee Jackson
20 Jimmy Smith
21 Ed Lynch
22 Papo Rosado
23 Mike Scott (photo actually Joe Zdeb)
24 Frank Verdi
25 Randy McGilberry

1980 TCMA Toledo Mud Hens

(Minnesota Twins, AAA) (color)

	NM
Complete Set (20):	16.00

1 Steve Mapel
2 Bob Randall
3 Cal Ermer
4 Bruce MacPherson
5 Gary Sorum
6 Ron Washington
7 Terry Felton
8 Randy Bush
9 John Walker
10 Willie Norwood
11 Jesus Vega
12 Wilfredo Sarmiento
13 Steve Herz
14 Buck Chamberlin
15 Dave Engle
16 Ray Smith
17 Al Williams
18 Jeff Brueggemann
19 Bob Veselic
20 Kurt Seibert

1980 TCMA Tucson Toros

(Houston Astros, AAA) (color)

	NM
Complete Set (24):	12.00

1 Danny Heep
2 Jimmy Sexton
3 Joe Pittman
4 Rick Williams
5 Gary Wilson
6 Bob Sprowl
7 Jack Fleming
8 Tom Wiedenbauer
9 Jimmy Johnson
10 George Gross
11 Billy Smith
12 Dave LaBossiere
13 Dennis Miscik
14 Alan Knicely
15 Tom Spencer
16 Gary Rajsich
17 Mike Fischlin
18 Gordy Pladson
19 Jim Pankovits
20 Brent Strom
21 Mike Mendoza
22 Gary Woods
23 Bert Roberge
24 Doug Stokke

1980 TCMA Tulsa Drillers

(Texas Rangers, AA) (color)

	NM
Complete Set (26):	10.00

1 Jerry Gleaton
2 Dave Crutcher
3 Tony Hudson
4 Ted Davis
5 Mike Roberts
6 Jack Lozorko
7 Jim Farr
8 Nick Capra
9 Larry Reynolds
10 George Wright
11 Mel Barrow
12 Frank Garcia
13 Phil Klimas
14 Luis Gonzalez
15 Mike Jirschele
16 Wayne Tolleson
17 Ronnie Gooch
18 Tracy Cowger
19 Steve Nielsen
20 Chuck Lamson
21 Bobby Johnson
22 Dave Schmidt
23 Darrell Ortiz
24 Wayne Terwilliger
25 Mike Vickers
26 Mitch Fletcher

1980 TCMA Utica Blue Jays

(Toronto Blue Jays, A) (black & white)

	NM
Complete Set (33):	55.00

1 Larry Hardy
2 Rich White
3 Carlos Cabrera
4 Jim Baker
5 Felix Feliciano
6 Rafael Harris
7 Tom Norko
8 Silverio Valdez
9 Jon Woodworth
10 Bob Wilbur
11 Hector Torres
12 Tomas Castillo
13 Juan Castillo
14 Roberto Cerrud
15 Jose Escobar
16 Tony Gilmore
17 Luis Guzman
18 Toby Hernandez
19 Mark Holton
20 Dennis Howard
21 Miguel Ortiz
22 Tom O'Dowd
23 Al Montgomery
24 Bob McNair
25 Tom Lukish
26 Herman Lewis
27 Carlos Leal
28 Paul Langfield
29 Mike Hurdle
30 Bill Reade
31 Rafael Rivas
32 Miguel Rodriguez
33 Rico Sutton

Suffix letters following a card number indicate a variation card.

1980 TCMA Vancouver Canadians

(Milwaukee Brewers, AAA) (color)

	NM
Complete Set (22):	12.00

1 Lawrence Rush
2 Willie Mueller
3 Ned Yost
4 Gus Quiros
5 Bobby Glen Smith
6 Terry Bevington
7 Dave LaPoint
8 Billy Severns
9 Lance Rautzhan
10 Tim Nordbrook
11 Bob Didier
12 Kent Biggerstaff
13 Ed Romero
14 Dan Boitano
15 Craig Ryan
16 Rene Quinones
17 Mike Henderson
18 Fred Holdsworth
19 Marshall Edwards
20 Bob Galasso
21 Vic Harris
22 Rick Olsen

1980 TCMA Waterbury Reds

(Cincinnati Reds, AA) (black & white)

	NM
Complete Set (22):	100.00

1 Nick Fiorillo
2 Jeff Lahti
3 Steve Christmas
4 Doug Neuenschwander
5 Paul Herring
6 Randy Town
7 Bill Scherer (Scherrer)
8 Scott Dye
9 Lee Garrett
10 Mike Compton
11 Rick O'Keefe
12 Jose Brito
13 Bob Hamilton
14 Mark Gilbert
15 Skeeter Barnes
16 Tom Sohns
17 Dan Sarrett
18 Tom Lawless
19 Tom Foley
20 Russ Aldrich
21 Nick Esasky
22 Greg Hughes

1980 TCMA Waterloo Indians

(Cleveland Indians, A) (black & white)

	NM
Complete Set (35):	125.00

1 John Hoban
2 Dane Anthony
3 Ron Leach
4 Larry White
5 Tim Glass
6 Ramon Romero
7 Alan Willis
8 Jack Nuismer
9 John Bohnet
10 John Asbell
11 Larry Hrynko
12 Kirk Jones
13 Rick Barnhart
14 Daryl Fazzio
15 Bryan Meier
16 Chris Rehbaum
17 Sammy Torres
18 Bruce Chaney
19 Erik Peterson
20 George Cechetti
21 Robert Bohnet
22 Don Nicolet
23 Gary Hinson
24 Frank Regan
25 Everett Rey
26 Rick Baker
27 Carmelo Castillo
28 Tommy Martinez
29 Mike Taylor
30 Cal Emery
31 Chuck Stobbs
32 Bob Gariglio
33 Rich Blumeyer
34 Wes Mitchell
35 Von Hayes

1980 TCMA Wausau Timbers

(Seattle Mariners, A) (black & white)

		NM
Complete Set (23):		65.00
1	Tom Brennan	
2	John Burden	
3	Mark Cahill	
4	Tony Jordan	
5	Martin Little	
6	Edwin Nunez	
7	Steve Roche	
8	Elias Salva	
9	Mark Softy	
10	John Zisk	
11	Takashi Upshur	
12	Bobby Tanzi	
13	Jimmy Presley	
14	Mario Diaz	
15	Enrique Diaz	
16	Mike Hood	
17	Chris Henry	
18	Rick Graser	
19	Mike Frierson	
20	Kevin King	
21	Werner Lajszky	
22	Arnie McCrary	
23	Orlando Martinez	

1980 TCMA West Haven White Caps

(Oakland A's, AA) (color)

		NM
Complete Set (31):		13.00
1	Al Minker	
2	Dennis Wyszynski	
3	Leroy Robbins	
4	Don Morris	
5	Bruce Fournier	
6	Rob Klebba	
7	Paul Stevens	
8	Paul Mize	
9	Scott Meyer	
10	Bert Bradley	
11	Craig Harris	
12	Bobby Markham	
13	Fred Devito	
14	Darryl Ciaz	
15	Mike Patterson	
16	Keith Atherton	
17	Shooty Babbitt (Babitt)	
18a	Nick Beamon	
18b	Staff	
19a	Keith Comstock	
19b	John Gosse	
20a	David Goldstein	
20b	Ed Nottle	
21a	Keathel Chauncey	
21b	Rich Lynch	
21c	Bob Moore	
22a	Tim Conroy	
22b	Aggie Maggio	
23a	Benson	
23b	Randy Sealy	
24	Rick Tronerud	

1980 TCMA Wichita Aeros

(Chicago Cubs, AAA) (color)

		NM
Complete Set (22):		80.00
1	Karl Pagel	
2	Jim Tracy	
3	Kim Buettemeyer	
4	Mark Parker	
5	Bill Hayes	
6	Danny Rohn	
7	Randy Martz	
8	Jack Hiatt	
9	Jesus Figeroa	
10	Ignacio Javier	
11	Mike Turgeon	
12	Lee Smith	
13	Mike Allen	
14	Jesus Alfaro	
15	Paul Semall	
16	Jared Martin	
17	Brian Rosinski	
18	Steve Macko	
19	Vince Valentini	
20	George Riley	
21	Manny Seoane	
22	Mark Lemongello	

Checklists with card numbers in parentheses ( ) indicates the numbers do not appear on the cards.

1980 TCMA Wisconsin Rapids Twins

(Minnesota Twins, A) (black & white)

		NM
Complete Set (27):		150.00
1	Sam Arrington	
2	Luis Santos	
3	Robert Mulilgan	
4	Larry May	
5	Manuel Lunar	
6	William Lamkey	
7	Bob Konepa	
8	Hal Jackson	
9	Ken Francingues	
10	Conrad Everett	
11	Chris Thomas	
12	Paul Voight	
13	Richard Ray Austin	
14	Glenn Ballard	
15	James Christensen	
16	Manuel Colletti	
17	Gary Gaetti	
18	Kent Hrbek	
19	Kevin Miller	
20	Norberto Molina	
21	Brad Carlson	
22	Matt Henderson	
23	Joe Kubit	
24	Bruce Stocker	
25	Ray Stein	
26	Rich Stelmaszek	
27	Tony Oliva	

1981 TCMA Albuquerque Dukes

(L.A. Dodgers, AAA) (color) (Koufax was a scarce, withdrawn card)

		MT
Complete Set (26):		60.00
1	Dave Moore	
2	Dave Patterson	
3	Steve Shirley	
4	Alejandro Pena	
5	Ted Power	
6	Bill Swiacki	
7	Ricky Wright	
8	Dave Richards	
9	Ron Roenicke	
10	Brian Holton	
11	Kevin Keefe	
12	Brent Strom	
13	Don Crow	
14	Wayne Caughey	
15	Larry Fobbs	
16	Mike Marshall	
17	Jack Perconte	
18	Alex Taveras	
19	Gary Weiss	
20	Rudy Law	
21	Candy Maldonado	
22	Bobby Mitchell	
23a	Sandy Koufax	
23b	Tack Wilson	
24	Del Crandall	
25	Dick McLaughlin	

1981 Albuquerque Dukes team-issue photos

(L.A. Dodgers, AAA) (4" x 5" color photo prints, sold singly at stadium for $2 each)

		MT
Complete Set (20):		80.00
(1)	Wayne Causey	
(2)	Dave Cohea (trainer)	
(3)	Del Crandall	
(4)	Don Crow	
(5)	Larry Fobbs	
(6)	Brian Holton	
(7)	Kevin Keefe	
(8)	Dick McLaughlin	
(9)	Bobby Mitchell	
(10)	Dave Moore	
(11)	Dave Patterson	
(12)	Alejandro Pena	
(13)	Ted Power	
(14)	Dave Richards	
(15)	Ron Roenicke	
(16)	Steve Shirley	
(17)	Brent Strom	
(18)	Bill Swiacki	
(19)	Gary Weiss	
(20)	Ricky Wright	

1981 Trackle Alexandria Dukes Postcards

(Pittsburgh Pirates, A) (3-1/2" x 5-3/8", b/w, postcard back, players unidentified)

		MT
Complete Set (15):		25.00
(1)	Rafael Belliard	
(2)	Geronimo Blanco	
(3)	Benny de la Rosa	
(4)	Lance Dodd	
(5)	Jim Felts	
(6)	Joe Fiori	
(7)	Ken Ford	
(8)	Mike Johnson	
(9)	Scott Kuvinka	
(10)	Connor McGehee	
(11)	Art Ray	
(12)	Angel Rodriguez	
(13)	John Schaive	
(14)	Mike Toomey	
(15)	Ron Wotus	

1981 TCMA Appleton Foxes

(Chicago White Sox, A) (color)

		MT
Complete Set (29):		
1	Jesse Anderson	
2	Jeff Barnard	
3	Keith Desjarlais	
4	Kevin Flannery	
5	Tom Mullen	
6	Rick Naumann	
7	Dan Ortega	
8	Steve Pastrovich	
9	Mark Platel	
10	Jim Siwy	
11	Roy Schumacher	
12	Wayne Schukert	
13	Larry Donofrio	
14	Cecil Espy	
15	Leo Garcia	
16	Ike Golden	
17	John Hanley	
18	A.J. Hill	
19	Scott Meier	
20	Mike Morse	
21	Dave Nix	
22	Gary Robinette	
23	Ramon Romero	
24	Mark Seeger	
25	Ray Torres	
26	Wes Kent	
27	Dave Wall	
28	Sam Ewing	
29	Doug Wiesner	

1981 TCMA Arkansas Travelers

(St. Louis Cardinals, AA) (black & white)

		MT
Complete Set (23):		25.00
1	Felipe Zayas	
2	Steve Turco	
3	Donald Moore	
4	Dennis Delany	
5	Fred Tisdale	
6	Rhadames Mills	
7	Jeffrey Doyle	
8	Jorge Aranzamendi	
9	David Kable	
10	Kerry Burchett	
11	Jerry Johnson	
12	David Jorn	
13	Rafael Pimentel	
14	Mark Riggins	
15	Daniel Winslow	
16	Kevin Hagen	
17	James Gott	
18	Ralph Citarella	
19	James Riggleman	
20	Louis Pratt	
21	Gaylen Pitts	
22	Jerry McKune	
23	Arkansas Travelerettes	

1981 TCMA Batavia Trojans

(Cleveland Indians, A) (black & white, edition of 1,100)

		MT
Complete Set (30):		20.00
1	Mark Bajus	
2	Tom Burns	
3	Jose Roman	
4	Steve Cushing	
5	Mike Poindexter	
6	Todd Richard	
7	Brian Silvas	
8	Phil Deriso	
9	Bart Mackie	
10	Adalberto Nieves	
11	Rick Elkin	
12	Arnold Cochran	
13	Ray Martinez	
14	Jerry Nalley	
15	Junior Noboa	
16	Ed Tanner	
17	Sam Martin	
18	John Merchant	
19	Scott Collins	
20	Bernardo Brito	
21	Gary Holden	
22	Eric Jones	
23	Chris Rehbaum	
24	Randy Washington	
25	George Alpert	
26	Miguel Roman	
27	Dave Oliver	
28	Luis Isaac	
29	Paul Seymour	
30	John Jakubowski	

1981 TCMA Birmingham Barons

(Detroit Tigers, AA) (black & white)

		MT
Complete Set (25):		65.00
1	John Lackey	
2	Roy Majtyka	
3	Dwight Lowry	
4	Manny Seoane	
5	Ron Mathis	
6	Bruce Robbins	
7	Mark Dacko	
8	Mike Laga	
9	Frank Hunsaker	
10	Glenn Wilson	
11	Gary Bozich	
12	Howard Johnson	
13	Jeff Kenaga	
14	Bob Nandin	
15	Jack Smith	
16	Bruce Chaney	
17	Stan Younger	
18	Nick O'Connor	
19	Dick Pole	
20	Stine Poole	
21	Darrell Woodard	
22	Barbaro Garbey	
23	Augie Ruiz	
24	Paul Josephson	
25	Mike Beecroft	

1981 TCMA Bristol Red Sox

(Boston Red Sox, AA) (color)

		MT
Complete Set (22):		19.00
1	Craig Brooks	
2	Bill Moloney	
3	Kevin Kane	
4	Gene Gentile	
5	Reggie Whittemore	
6	Jim Wilson	
7	Brian Denman	
8	Tony Torchia	
9	Dave Schoppee	
10	Rick Colbert	
11	Chuck Sandberg	
12	Ed Jurak	
13	Jerry King	
14	Kenny Young	
15	Jay Fredlund	
16	Erwin Bryant	
17	Steve Shields	
18	Glenn Eddins	
19	Dave Tyler	
20	Clint Johnson	
21	Dennis Burtt	
22	Jim Watkins	

1981 TCMA Buffalo Bisons

(Pittsburgh Pirates, AA) (color)

		MT
Complete Set (25):		15.00
1	John Lipon	
2	John Holland	
3	Doug Britt	
4	Jose DeLeon	
5	Ben Wiltbank	
6	Benny de la Rosa	
7	Drew Macauley	
8	Carlos Ledezema	
9	Stew Cliburn	
10	Bob Rock	
11	Rafael Vasquez	
12	Dan Wortham	
13	Jose Rodriguez	
14	Billy Waag	
15	Gary Hargis	
16	Jose Calderon	
17	Angel Barez	
18	Steve Farr	
19	Carlos Rios	
20	Tony Incavigua	
21	Terry Salazar	
22	Doug Frobel	
23	Eddie Vargas	
24	Frank Riccelli	
25	Reggie Buchanan	

1981 TCMA Burlington Bees

(Milwaukee Brewers, A) (black & white) (#8 not issued)

		MT
Complete Set (29):		32.50
1	Dave Morris	
2	Vince Pone	
3	Kevin McCoy	
4	Steve Noewood	
5	Gene Smith	
6	Raymond Gallo	
7	Craig Herberholz	
9	Mark Lepson	
10	Tim Crews	
11	Steve Gibson	
12	Johnson Wood	
13	Murphy Susa	
14	Angel Morris	
15	Henry Contreras	
16	Steve Jordan	
17	Randy Ready	
18	Butch Kirby	
19	Mike Samuel	
20	Juan Castillo	
21	Brad DeKraai	
22	Carlos Ponce	
23	Mark Higgins	
24	Gerry Miller	
25	Ronnie Jones	
26	Karl McKay	
27	Joel Parker	
28	Bill Nowlan	
29	Lawrence Avery	
30	Terry Bevington	

1981 TCMA Cedar Rapids Reds

(Cincinnati Reds, A) (color)

		MT
Complete Set (26):		30.00

1 Larry Jackson
2 Kurt Kepshire
3 Brad Lesley
4 Rick Myles
5 Mike Raines
6 Ron Robinson
7 Mark Rothey
8 Ray Corbett
9 Dave Miley
10 Emil Drzavich
11 Kevin Hinds
12 Dave Hoenstine
13 Dean Seats
14 Mike Sorel
15 Tom Wesley
16 Jeff Jones
17 Ken Scarpace
18 Scott Terry
19 Randy Davidson
20 Don Buchheister
21 Jeff Clay
22 Mark Bowden
23 Bob Buchanan
24 Scott Ender
25 Greg McKinney
26 Dave Hall

1981 TCMA Charleston Charlies

(Cleveland Indians, AAA) (color)

	MT
Complete Set (24):	25.00

1 Tom Brennan
2 Bobby Cuellar
3 Gordy Glaser
4 Ed Glynn
5 Mike Paxton
6 Eric Wilkins
7 Sandy Whitol
8 Chris Bando
9 Tim Norrid
10 Kenny Barton
11 Mike Bucci
12 Len Faedo
13 Mike Fischlin
14 Angelo Logrande
15 Von Hayes
16 Odie Davis
17 Jim Lentine
18 Karl Pagel
19 Rodney Craig
20 Vassie Gardner
21 Mel Queen
22 Nate Puryear
23 Rob Petroburgo
24 Cal Emery

1981 TCMA Charleston Royals

(K.C. Royals, A) (black & white)

	MT
Complete Set (26):	15.00

1 Greg Jonson
2 Hector Arroyo
3 David W 23........ Rick Rizzo
24 Tad Venger
25 Willie Neal
26 Rick Mathews

1981 Charlotte O's team issue

(Baltimore Orioles, AA)

	MT
Complete Set (25):	90.00

(1) Juan Arias
(2) Don Bowman
(3) Scott Budner
(4) Storm Davis
(5) John Denman
(6) Tim Derryberry
(7) Allen Edwards
(8) Will George
(9) Tim Graven
(10) Drungo Hazewood
(11) Ricky Jones
(12) Mark Naehring
(13) Earl Neal
(14) Paul O'Neill
(15) Victor Rodriguez
(16) Willie Royster
(17) John Shelby
(18) Mark Smith
(19) Cliff Speck
(20) Bill Swaggerty
(21) Don Welchel
(22) Cat Whitfield
(23) Mark Wiley
(24) "The Pepper Girls"
(25) Team Logo

1981 TCMA Chattanooga Lookouts

(Cleveland Indians, AA) (black & white)

	MT
Complete Set (25):	20.00

1 Robert Gariglio
2 John Burden
3 Robbie Alvarez
4 Luis DeLeon
5 Steve Narleski
6 Matt Bullinger
7 Jack Nuismer
8 Steve Roche
9 Everett Rey
10 Todd Heimer
11 Tim Glass
12 Jeff Moronko
13 John Bohnet
14 George Cecchetti
15 Ricky Baker
16 Carmelo Castillo
17 Sal Rende
18 Rick Burchers
19 Chuck Stobbs
20 Craig Adams
21 Larry White
22 Jeff Tomski
23 Kevin Rhomberg
24 Woody Smith
25 Bud Anderson

1981 TCMA Clinton Giants

(S.F. Giants, A) (black & white)

	MT
Complete Set (29):	27.50

1 Joe Banach
2 Wendell Kim
3 Steve Cline
4 Dave Wilhelmi
5 Bruce Oliver
6 Ben Callo
7 Jose Chue
8 Art Gomez
9 Kevin Smay
10 Greg Bangert
11 Mark O'Connell
12 Matt Young
13 Dennis Schafer
14 Louis D'Amore
15 Gus Stokes
16 Kirk Ortega
17 John Taylor
18 Ken Frazier
19 James Johnson
20 Sean Toerner
21 Dave Wilson
22 Joe Henderson
23 Mike Lenti
24 Tom McLaughlin
25 Greg McSparron
26 Rolloa Adams
27 Lance Junker
28 Rich Figueroa
29 Mark Tudor

1981 Police Columbus Clippers

(N.Y. Yankees, AAA) (color, 2-3/8" x 3-3/4")

	MT
Complete Set (25):	17.50

(1) Tucker Ashford
(2) Steve Balboni
(3) Paul Boris
(4) Marshall Brant
(5) Pat Callahan
(6) Greg Cochran
(7) Dave Coleman
(8) Juan Espino
(9) Mike Griffin
(10) Wayne Harer
(11) Jim Lewis
(12) John Pacella
(13) Dave Righetti
(14) Andre Robertson
(15) Brian Ryder
(16) Dan Schmitz
(17) Buck Showalter
(18) George H. Sisler Jr.
(19) Garry Smith
(20) Rick Stenholm
(21) Pat Tabler
(22) Frank Verdi
(23) Dave Wehrmeister
(24) Coaches/Trainer (Jerry McNertney, Sammy Ellis, Mark Letendre)
(25) Sgt. Dick Hoover (Columbus Police Dept.)

1981 TCMA Columbus Clippers

(N.Y. Yankees, AAA) (color)

	MT
Complete Set (28):	40.00

1 Dick Stenholm
2 Tucker Ashford
3 Andre Robertson
4 Pat Callahan
5 Danny Schmitz
6 Jim Lewis
7 Paul Boris
8 Andy McGaffigan
9 Dave Righetti
10 Mike Griffin
11 Steve Balboni
12 Greg Cochran
13 Marshall Bryant
14 Brian Ryder
15 Juan Espino
16 Pat Tabler
17 Frank Verdi
18 Dave Coleman
19 Wayne Harer
20 Bill Showalter
21 Gary Smith
22 John Pacella
23 Dave Wehrmister (Wehrmeister)
24 Tom Filer
25 Mark Letenore (trainer)
26 Sam Ellis
27 George H. Sisler (gm)
28 Jerry McNertney

1981 TCMA Durham Bulls

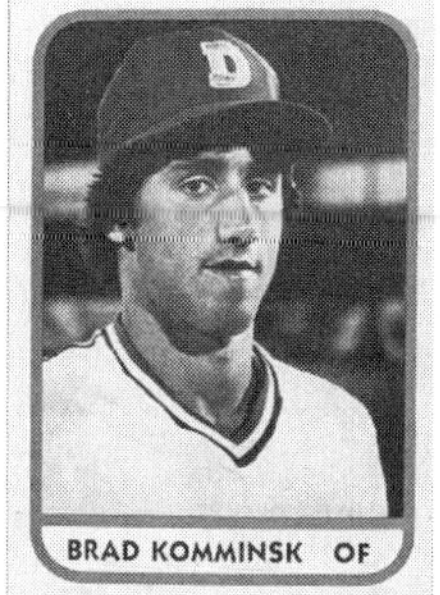

(Atlanta Braves, A) (black & white)

	MT
Complete Set (24):	25.00

1 Miguel Sosa
2 Mike Garcia
3 Kevin Rigby
4 Ken Scanlon
5 Tommy Thompson
6 Gary Cooper
7 Tom Hayes
8 Harold Williams
9 Keith Hagman
10 Brad Komminsk
11 Glen Bockhorn
12 Jeff Vuksan
13 Alvin Moore
14 Alan Gallagher
15 Rick Behenna
16 Rick Coatney
17 Jeff Dedmon
18 Glen Germer
19 Hoot Gibson
20 Danny Lucia
21 Roy North
22 Scott Patterson
23 Mike Payne
24 Gary Reiter

1981 Red Rooster Edmonton Trappers

(Chicago White Sox, AAA)

	MT
Complete Set (24):	20.00

1 Gary Holle
2 John Poff
3 Dan Williams
4 Nardi Contreras
5 Juan Agosto
6 Guy Hoffman
7 Chris Nyman
8 Gord Lund
9 Vern Thomas
10 Rich Barnes
11 John Flannery
12 Bill Atkinson
13 Hector Eduardo
14 Leo Sutherland
15 Ray Murillo
16 Joe Gates
17 Julio Perez
18 Marv Foley
19 Mike Colbern
20 Fran Mullins
21 Rod Allen
22 Reggie Patterson
23 Jay Loviglio
24 Mark Teutsch

1981 TCMA El Paso Diablos

(Milwaukee Brewers, AA) (color)

	MT
Complete Set (24):	18.00

1 Ed Irvine
2 Willie Lozado
3 Al Manning
4 John Skorochocki
5 Terry Showbridge
6 Stan Davis
7 Jerry Lane
8 Doug Loman
9 Gerry Ako
10 Jim Koontz
11 Doug Jones
12 Larry Motgomery
13 Bill Schroeder
14 Mike Madden
15 Bob Skubbe (Skube)
16 Chick Valley
17 Rick Krantiz
18 Tony Torres
19 Weldon Swift
20 Tim Cook
21 Johnny Evans
22 Tom Candiotti
23 Tony Muser
24 Al Price

1981 TCMA Evansville Triplets

(Detroit Tigers, AAA) (color)

	MT
Complete Set (22):	15.00

1 Jim Leyland
2 George Cappuzzello
3 Mike Chris
4 Mark Fidrych
5 Larry Pashnick
6 Larry Rothschild
7 Manny Seoane
8 Jerry Ujdur
9 Pat Underwood
10 Roger Weaver
11 Marty Castillo
12 Larry Johnson
13 Mark DeJohn
14 Vern Followell
15 Glenn Gulliver
16 Craig Kusick
17 Juan Lopez
18 Tim Corcoran
19 Les Filkins
20 Eddie Gates
21 Ken Houston
22 Dennis Kinney

1981 TCMA Glens Falls White Sox

(Chicago White Sox, AA) (color)

	MT
Complete Set (24):	40.00

1 Luis Estrada
2 Randy Evans
3 Robert Fallon
4 Chuck Johnson
5 Mickey Maitland
6 Tom Mullen
7 Dennis Vasquez
8 Richard Wieters
9 Ricky Seilheimer
10 Andy Pasillas
11 Dom Fucci
12 Tim Hulett
13 Ivan Mesa
14 Peter Peltz
15 Ron Perry
16 Greg Walker
17 Vince Bienek
18 Randy Johnson
19 Ron Kittle
20 Luis Rois
21 Raymundo Torres
22 Jim Mahoney
23 Len Bradley
24 Larry Edwards

1981 Trackle Hagerstown Suns Postcards

(Baltimore Orioles, A) (3-1/2" x 5-3/8", b/w, postcard back, players unidentified)

	MT
Complete Set (34):	40.00

(1) Dane Anthony
(2) Bill Butler
(3) Dave Corman
(4) Paul Croft
(5) Greg Dees
(6) Kenny Dixon
(7) Allen Edwards
(8) Kurt Fabrizio
(9) Dave Falcone
(10) Michael Frierson
(11) Neal Herrick
(12) Leon Hoke
(13) Ed Hook
(14) John Huey
(15) Scott Kuvinka
(16) Ron Leach
(17) Grady Little
(18) Ears McNeal

(19) Don Minnick
(20) John Mitcheltree
(21) Carl Nichols
(22) Bob Palmer
(23) Al Pardo
(24) John Pavlik
(25) Todd Richard
(26) David Rivera
(27) Ramon Romero
(28) Ronnie Rudd
(29) John Stefero
(30) Keith Thibodeaux
(31) Andy Timko
(32) Matt Tyner
(33) Ron Wotus
(34) Mike Wright

1981 TCMA Hawaii Islanders

(San Diego Padres, AAA) (color)

MT
Complete Set (23): 12.50
1 Tim Flannery
2 Jose Moreno
3 Gary Ashby
4 Steve Smith
5 Doug Gwosdz
6 Tony Castillo
7 Jim Beswick
8 Alan Wiggins
9 Rick Lancellotti
10 Curtis Reed
11 Mike Armstrong
12 Steve Fireovid
13 Alan Olmsted
14 George Stablein
15 Tom Tellmann
16 Kim Seaman
17 Fred Kuhualua
18 Floyd Chiffer
19 Eric Show
20 Larry Duensing
21 Doug Rader
22 Chuck Hartenstein
23 Mario Ramirez

1981 TCMA Holyoke Millers

(California Angels, AA) (color)

MT
Complete Set (26): 16.00
1 Ed Rodriguez
2 Jim Saul
3 Tom Kayser
4 T.J. Byrne
5 D. Comforti, D. Thomas
6 John Yandle
7 Ricky Adams
8 Mike Brown
9 Chris Clark
10 Dennis Gilbert
11 Curt Brown
12 Jeff Connor
13 Lonnie Dugger
14 Dave Duran
15 Rick Foley
16 Pat Keedy
17 Darrell Miller
18 Mark Nocciolo
19 Les Pearsey
20 Gary Pettis
21 Gustavo Polidor
22 Brandt Humphry
23 Bill Mooneyham
24 Perry Morrison
25 Dennis Rasmussen
26 Rick Rommell

1981 Holyoke Millers team issue

(California Angels, AA) (Black & white with blue highlights, 2" x 3", blank-back; also produced in the form of an uncut poster.)

MT
Complete Set (25): 80.00
(1) Rick Adams
(2) Mike Brown
(3) T.J. Byrne
(4) Chris Clark
(5) Jeff Connor
(6) Lonnie Dugger
(7) Dave Duran
(8) Rick Foley
(9) Dennis Gilbert
(10) Brandt Humphry
(11) Tom Kayser
(12) Pat Keedy
(13) Darrell Miller
(14) Bill Mooneyham
(15) Jerry Morrison
(16) Mark Nocciolo
(17) Les Pearsey
(18) Gary Pettis
(19) Gustavo Polidor
(20) Dennis Rasmussen
(21) Ed Rodriguez
(22) Rich Rommel
(23) Jim Saul
(24) Dave Thomas
(25) John Yandle

1981 Indianapolis Indians team issue

(Cincinnati Reds, AAA) (color)

MT
Complete Set (32): 27.50
1 Team Photo
2 Jim Beauchamp
3 Geoff Combe
4 Paul Householder
5 Charlie Leibrandt
6 Dave Van Gorder
7 Tom Foley
8 Kip Young
9 Eddie Milner
10 The Relievers
11 Jose Brito
12 Greg Mahlberg
13 Bill Bonham
14 The Teachers
15 Nick Esasky
16 Jeff Lahti
17 The Lightening Squad
18 Gene Menees
19 Scott Brown
20 The Outfielders
21 Duane Walker
22 Bill Kelly
23 The Infielders
24 Joe Kerrigan
25 German Barranca
26 The Starters
27 Paul Herring
28 Bill Dawley
29 Skeeter Barnes
30 The Catchers
31 Sergio Ferrer
32 John Young

1981 Trackle Kinston Eagles Postcards

(Toronto Blue Jays, A) (3-1/2" x 5-3/8", b/w, postcard back, players unidentified)

MT
Complete Set (23): 45.00
(1) Bernie Beckman
(2) Ty Carter
(3) Juan Castillo
(4) Sam Crafort
(5) Willie Ereu
(6) Tony Fernandez
(7) Randy Ford
(8) Toby Hernandez
(9) Dennis Howard
(10) Phil Lansford
(11) Mike Lebo
(12) John McLaren
(13) Carlos Neal
(14) Tom Norko
(15) Julio Paula
(16) Benji Perez
(17) Marty Pulley
(18) Terry Raley
(19) Ron Shepherd
(20) Bob Silverman
(21) Brian Stemberger
(22) Rico Sutton
(23) Tim Thompson

"1981" Las Vegas Stars Kevin McReynolds

Kevin McReynolds (Purports to be a card supporting Special Olympics; actually a late-1980s unauthorized issue with

1981 Trackle Lynchburg Mets Postcards

(N.Y. Mets, A) (3-1/2" x 5-3/8", b/w, postcard back, players unidentified)

MT
Complete Set (10): 50.00
(1) Mike Anicich
(2) Al DeLano
(3) David Duff
(4) Gene Dusan
(5) Roger Frash
(6) Lloyd McClendon
(7) Jose Oquendo
(8) Bill Rittweger
(9) Darryl Strawberry
(10) John Violette

1981 TCMA Lynn Sailors

(Seattle Mariners, AA) (color)

MT
Complete Set (28): 24.00
1 Karl Best
2 Bud Black
3 Mark Cahill
4 Joe Georger
5 Tracy Harris
6 R.J. Harrison
7 Steve Krueger
8 Jed Murray
9 Dave Sheriff
10 Rob Simond
11 Dave Smith
12 Matt Young
13 Jim Nelson
14 Dave Valle
15 Edwin Aponte
16 Billy Crone
17 Mario Diaz
18 Paul Serna
19 Mike White
20 Al Chambers
21 Ramon Estepa
22 Rodney Hobbs
23 Tito Nanni
24 Bobby Floyd
25 Mickey Bowers
26 Bob Randolph, Lloyd D. Kern
27 Jeff Stottlemyre
28 Clark Crist

1981 TCMA Miami Orioles

(Baltimore Orioles, A) (black & white)

MT
Complete Set, w/ scarce Willsher, Young: 135.00
Complete Set, no Willsher, Young : 15.00
1 Ron Dillard
2 Al Pardo
3 Freddie Smith
4 Mark Brown
5 Don Murelli
6 Minnie Mendoza
7 John DeLeon
8 Pat Dumouchelle
9 Satch Sanders
10 Francisco Oliveras
11 Mike Alvarez
12 Skip Clark
13 Andy Timko
14 Frank Ferroni
15 Lonnie Ivie
16 Neal Herrick
17 Leon Hoke
18 Tim Maples
19 Jeff Williams
20 Bret Gold
21 Scott Johnson
22 Chris Willsher
23 Mike Young

1981 Chong Modesto A's

(Oakland A's, A)

MT
Complete Set (30): 50.00
1 Rick Arnold
2 Ron Mantsch
3 Robert Moore
4 Ed Retzer
5 Don Van Marter
6 Robert Wood
7 Mark Ferguson
8 Ron Jensen
9 Bill Kreuger
10 Greg Mine
11 Mike Altobelli
12 Gordon Eakin
13 Terry Byrum
14 Paul Stockley
15 Monte Mc Abee
16 Selwyn Young
17 Kevin Jacobson
18 Joe Williams
19 Tom Colburn
20 Terry Harper
21 Jay Schellin
22 Dennis Stowe
23 Joe Soprano
24 Wayne Rudolph
25 Frank Harris
26 Keith Lieppman
27 Brad Fischer
28 Dwight Adams
29 Phil Danielson
30 Rod Murphy

Values shown are a national average. Some teams and players enjoy regional popularity which may affect market prices.

1981 Nashville Sounds team issue

(N.Y. Yankees, AA) (In the early 1990s, the team reprinted this set from original negatives, virtually impossible to differentiate from the original issue. This reprinting effectively killed the value of the set.)

MT
Complete Set (25): 20.00
(1) Manager, Trainer & Coaches
(2) Team Photo
(3) Rod Boxberger
(4) Pat Callahan
(5) Nate Chapman
(6) Brian Dayett
(7) Dan Hanggie
(8) Bob Jamison
(9) Curt Kaufman
(10) Dan Led Duke
(11) Don Mattingly
(12) Willie Mc Gee
(13) Mike Morgan
(14) Otis Nixon
(15) Erik Peterson
(16) Brian Poldberg
(17) Frank Ricci
(18) Wes Robbins
(19) Buck Showalter
(20) Roger Slagle
(21) Jeff Taylor
(22) Steve Taylor
(23) Rafael Villaman
(24) Jamie Werly
(25) Ted Wilborn

"1981" Nashville Sounds Don Mattingly

Don Mattingly (Unauthorized issue produced in late 1980s; no collector value)

1981 TCMA Oklahoma City 89'ers

(Philadelphia Phillies, AAA) (color)

MT
Complete Set (26): 120.00
1 Porfirio Altamirano
2 Carlos Arroyo
3 Eli Bonaparte
4 Warren Brusstar
5 Bob Dernier
6 Mark Davis
7 Dan Larsen
8 Orlando Isales
9 Don McCormack
10 Lenny Matuszek
11 Dennis Miscik
12 Manny McDonald
13 Scott Munninghoff
14 Dickie Noles
15 Jon Reelhorn
16 Luis Rodriguez
17 Ryne Sandberg
18 Bill Suter
19 Osvaldo (Ozzie) Virgil
20 George Vukovich
21 Bob Demeo
22 Ellis Deal
23 Jim Snyder
24 Jose Castro
25 Jim Rasmussen
26 Jeff Ulrich

1981 TCMA Omaha Royals

(K.C. Royals, AAA) (color)

	MT
Complete Set (24):	18.00

1 Joe Sparks
2 Jerry Cram
3 Paul McGannon
4 Craig Chamberlain
5 Gary Christenson
6 Atlee Hammaker
7 Dan Fischer
8 Don Hood
9 Mike Jones
10 Bill Laskey
11 Bill Paschall
12 Jeff Schattinger
13 Jim Gaudet
14 Greg Keatley
15 Manny Castillo
16 Onix Concepcion
17 Kelly Heath
18 Tim Ireland
19 Ron Johnson
20 Jim Buckner
21 Bob Detherage
22 Darryl Motley
23 Bombo Rivera
24 Pat Sheridan

1981 TCMA Pawtucket Red Sox

(Boston Red Sox, AAA) (color)

	MT
Complete Set (24):	125.00

1 Joel Finch
2 Mike Howard
3 Bruce Hurst
4 Keith MacWhorther
5 Bob Ojeda
6 Danny Parks
7 Win Remmerswaal
8 Luis Aponte
9 Jim Dorsey
10 Manny Sarmiento
11 Mike Smithson
12 Joe Morgan
13 Dale Robertson
14 Marty Barrett
15 Wade Boggs
16 Dave Koza
17 Julio Valdez
18 Sam Bowen
19 Lee Graham
20 Russ Laribee
21 Mike Ongarato
22 Chico Walker
23 Roger LaFrancois
24 Rich Gedman

"1981" Pawtucket Red Sox Wade Boggs

Wade Boggs
(Unauthorized issue produced in late 1980s; no collector value.)

1981 Trackle Peninsula Pilots Postcards

(Philadelphia Phillies, A) (3-1/2" x 5-3/8", b/w, postcard back, players unidentified)

	MT
Complete Set (39):	40.00

(1) Felix Agapay
(2) Jay Baller
(3) Dean Baugh
(4) Rafael Cepeda
(5) J.D. Crawford
(6) Bill Dancy
(7) Willie Darkis
(8) Rollie DeArmas
(9) Marty Decker
(10) Kelly Downs
(11) Steve Dunnegan
(12) Dave Enos
(13) John Fierro (trainer)
(14) Paul Fryer
(15) Goose Gregson
(16) Dave Harrigan
(17) Steve Harvey
(18) Ed Hearn
(19) Steve Jeltz
(20) Jon Lindsey
(21) Francisco Melendez
(22) David Mitchell
(23) Kyle Money
(24) Bob Neal (gm)
(25) Joe Nemeth
(26) Zeke Palmieri
(27) Dan Prior
(28) Mel Roberts
(29) Larry Rojas
(30) Randy Salava
(31) Vince Soreca
(32) Tony Taylor
(33) Denny Thomas
(34) Jeff Ulrich
(35) Fred Warner
(36) Mark Warren (business mgr.)
(37) Keith Washington
(38) Jerry Willard
(39) Phillie Phanatic (mascot)

1981 Valley Nat'l Bank Phoenix Giants

(S.F. Giants, AAA) (color, 3-3/8" x 2-1/4")

	MT
Complete Set (27):	12.00

1 Phoenix Booster Rooster/Checklist
2 Harry Jordan
3 Bob Tufts
4 Bob Brenly
5 Jeff Stember
6 Max Venable
7 Doug Shaefer
8 Mike Williams
9 Mark Clavert
10 Mike Rowland
11 Mike Rex
12 Jose Barrios
13 Al Hargesheimer
14 Dave Wiggins
15 Guy Sularz
16 Tommy Jones
17 Phil Hinrichs
18 Dennis Littlejohn
19 Wayne Pechek
20 Gene Pentz
21 Joe Pettini
22 Jeff Ransom
23 Tom Runnells
24 Rich Murray
25 Rocky Bridges
26 Tommy Gonzales
27 Ethan Blackaby

Checklists with card numbers in parentheses ( ) indicates the numbers do not appear on the cards.

1981 TCMA Portland Beavers

(Pittsburgh Pirates, AAA) (color)

	MT
Complete Set (27):	15.00

1 Pete Ward
2 Tom Trebelhorn
3 Santo Alcala
4 Matt Alexander
5 Mike Anderson
6 Dave Augustine
7 Bob Beall
8 Doe Boyland
9 Craig Cacek
10 Cecilio Guante
11 Dave Hilton
12 Willie Horton
13 Odell Jones
14 Vance Law
15 Mark Lee
16 Robert Long
17 Dale Mohorcic
18 Bobby Mitchell
19 Junior Ortiz
20 Pascual Perez
21 Tommy Sandt
22 Jimmy Smith
23 Luis Tiant
24 Alfredo Torres
25 Rusty Torres
26 Eleno Cuen
27 Kent Biggerstaff

1981 TCMA Quad City Cubs

(Chicago Cubs, A) (black & white)

	MT
Complete Set (33):	18.00

1 Dave Pagel
2 Don Hyman
3 Greg Tarnow
4 Rusty Piggot
5 Fritz Connally
6 Mike Buckley
7 Shane Allen
8 Mickey Tenney
9 Dennis Webb
10 Kevin Schoendienst
11 Jim Walsh
12 Terry Austin
13 Tom Johnson
14 Gary Monroe
15 Henry Cotto
16 Dan Cataline
17 Mike King
18 Tom Smith
19 Stan Kyles
20 Joe Housey
21 John Miglio
22 Ken Pryce
23 Ray Soff
24 Mark Vaji
25 Glenn Swaggerty
26 Craig Weissman
27 Jim Gerlach
28 Mark Wilkins
29 Don Schultze
30 Rich Morales
31 Gene Oliver
32 Roger Crow
33 Mike Palmer

1981 TCMA Reading Phillies

(Philadelphia Phillies, AA) (black & white)

	MT
Complete Set (24):	120.00

1 Jerry Reed
2 Kelly Faulk
3 Tom Hart
4 Darren Burroughs
5 Dan Prior
6 Miguel Alicea
7 Leroy Smith
8 Don Carman
9 Carlos Cabassa
10 Wally Goff
11 Herb Orensky
12 Miguel Ibarra
13 Jim Wright
14 Russ Hamric
15 Ron Smith
16 Tom Lombarski
17 Julio Franco
18 Ray Borucki
19 Keith Washington
20 Joe Bruno
21 Wil Culmer
22 Al Sanchez
23 Ron Clark
24 George Culver

1981 TCMA Redwood Pioneers

(California Angels, A) (black & white)

	MT
Complete Set (30):	16.00

1 Robert Bastian
2 Brian Buckley
3 Tom Crisler
4 Jay Kibbe
5 Ron Romanick
6 Jeff Smith
7 Ron Sylvia
8 Mike Venezia
9 Doug Rau
10 Aldo Bagiotti
11 Duffy Ryan
12 Wade Schexnayder
13 Harry Francis
14 Matt Gundelfinger
15 Ron Hunt
16 Marion Hunter
17 Tim Krauss
18 Mark Sproesser
19 Leo Lemon
20 Ken Tillman
21 Luis Zambrana
22 Warren Spahn
23 Tom Leonard
24 Kathy Leonard
25 David Levinson
26 Ralph Hartman
27 Chris Bankowski
28 Chris Cannizzaro
29 Barton Braun
30 Steve Levinson

1981 TCMA Richmond Braves

(Atlanta Braves, AAA) (color)

	MT
Complete Set (25):	30.00

1 John Sain
2 Tony Brizzolara
3 Jerry Keller
4 Ken Smith
5 Cragi Landis
6 Larry Whisenton
7 Bob Porter
8 Brett Butler
9 Chico Ruiz
10 Paul Runge
11 Butch Edge
12 Steve Bedrosian
13 Carlos Diaz
14 Larry McWilliams
15 Jose Alvarez
16 Steve Hammond
17 Steve Curry
18 Dan O'Brien
19 Ken Dayley
20 Matt Sinatro
21 Eddie Haas
22 Randy Johnson
23 Craig Robinson
24 Harry Saferight
25 Sam Ayoub

1981 TCMA Rochester Red Wings

(Baltimore Orioles, AAA) (color)

	MT
Complete Set (23):	450.00

1 Mike Boddicker
2 Bill Bonner
3 Brooks Carey
4 Tom Chism
5 Tom Eaton
6 Johnny Hale
7 Mike Hart
8 Drungo Hazewood
9 Dave Huppert
10 Kevin Kennedy
11 Dan Logan
12 Steve Luebber
13 Ed Putnam
14 Floyd Rayford
15 Cal Ripken, Jr.
16 Tom Rowe
17 John Valle
18 Don Welchel
19 Larry Jones
20 Richie Bancells
21 Chris Bourjos
22 Doc Edwards
23 Dallas Williams

1981 WTF Co. Rochester Red Wings

(Baltimore Orioles, AAA) (reported production of 1,800)

	MT
Complete Set (25):	450.00

1 Calvin Ripken Jr.
2 Dallas Williams
3 Chris Bourjos
4 Mark Corey
5 Doc Edwards
6 Thomas Rowe
7 Jeffrey Schneider
8 James Umbarger
9 Don Welchel
10 Larry Jones
11 Dan Logan
12 Steve Luebber
13 Eddy Putman
14 Floyd Rayford
15 David Huppert
16 Drungo Hazewood
17 James Hart
18 John Hale
19 Tom Eaton
20 Checklist
21 Bob Bonner
22 Brooks Carey
23 Mike Boddicker
24 Thomas Chism
25 Silver Stadium

1981 Trackle Salem Redbirds Team Issue

(S.D. Padres, A) (4" x 6" color photographs, blank-back; players not identified.)

	MT
Complete Set (16):	20.00

(1) Jerry Davis
(2) Ray Etchebarren

(3) Glenn Ezell
(4) Ismael Figueroa
(5) Billy Gerhardt
(6) Brian Greer
(7) Lin Hamilton
(8) Andy Krzanik
(9) Bill Long
(10) Steve Murray
(11) Mark Parent
(12) George Perez
(13) Luis Quinones
(14) Jeff Ronk
(15) Raymie Styons
(16) Phil Wilson

1981 TCMA Salt Lake City Gulls

(California Angels, AAA) (color)

MT
Complete Set (26): 15.00
1 Leonard Garcia
2 Ralph Botting
3 Steve Brown
4 Craig Eaton
5 Bob Ferris
6 Dave Frost
7 Christian Knapp
8 Mike Mahler
9 Alfredo Martinez
10 Carlos Perez
11 Dave Schuler
12 Ricky Steirer
13 Mike Walters
14 Mike Bishop
15 Brian Harper
16 Jeff Bertoni
17 Scott Carnes
18 Fernando Gonzalez
19 Steve Lubratich
20 Daryl Sconier
21 Tom Brunansky
22 Pepe Mangual
23 Scott Moffitt
24 Don Pisker
25 Moose Stubing
26 Bob Davis

1981 TCMA Shreveport Captains

(Pittsburgh Pirates, AA) (black & white)

MT
Complete Set (23): 25.00
1 Jack Mull
2 John Rabb
3 Jim Dunn
4 Tom O'Malley
5 Jim Wojcik
6 Glenn Fisher
7 Alan Fowlkes
8 Mike Tucker
9 Dan Gladden
10 Brad Bauman
11 Mark Dempsey
12 Paul Szymarek
13 Jim Duffalo
14 Doug Landuyt
15 Doran Perdue
16 Greg Baker
17 Ron Quick
18 Doug Wabeke
19 Jim Rothford
20 Scott Garrelts
21 Mark Lohuis
22 Greg Moyer
23 Pat Alexander

1981 TCMA Spokane Indians

(Seattle Mariners, AAA) (color)

MT
Complete Set (32): 14.00
1 Chris Flammang
2 Manny Estrada
3 Scott Stranski
4 Sam Welborn
5 Orlando Mercado
6 Roy Clark
7 Mike Hart
8 Greg Biercevicz
9 Bob Galasso
10 Brian Allard
11 Steve Finch
12 Doug Merrifield
13 Rene Lachemann
14 Reggie Walton
15 Ed Vande Berg
16 Ted Cox
17 Ron Musselman
18 Bob Stoddard
19 Joe Coleman
20 Vance McHenry
21 Ken Pape
22 Jim Mahler
23 Larry Patterson
24 Randy Stein
25 Allen Wirth
26 Casey Parsons
27 Kim Allen
28 Rich Anderson
29 Jim Beattie
30 Brad Gulden
31 Jamie Allen
32 Marty Martinez

1981 TCMA Syracuse Chiefs

(Toronto Blue Jays, AAA) (color)

MT
Complete Set (24): 12.00
1 Steve Baker
2 Tom Brown
3 Chuck Fore
4 Steve Grilli
5 Phil Huffman
6 Jack Kucek
7 Dale Murray
8 Kevin Pasley
9 Gene Petralli
10 Ramon Lora
11 Dave Baker
12 Charlie Beamon
13 Keith Chapman
14 Mike Davis
15 Pedro Hernandez
16 Greg Wells
17 Joe Cannon
18 Gil Kubski
19 Creighton Tevlin
20 Marv Thomson
21 Ken Schrom
22 Dave Tomlin
23 Bob Humphreys
24 Tony DeRosa

1981 Syracuse Chiefs team issue

(Toronto Blue Jays, AAA) (approximately 3-1/2" x 5-1/2", blank-back)

MT
Complete Set (24): 120.00
2 Pedro Hernandez
3 Kelvin Chapman
5 Dave Baker
6 Domingo Ramos
8 Dan Whitmer
9 Gene Petralli
10 Charlie Beamon
12 Steve Davis
14 Paul Mirabella
15 Ramon Lora
16 Dave Tomlin
17 Creighton Tevlin
19 Tom Brown
20 Jack Kucek
22 Marv Thompson
23 J.J. Cannon
24 Phil Huffman
25 Bob Humphreys
26 Jim Wright
27 Dale Murray
28 Steve Baker
29 Ken Schrom
31 Chuck Fore
32 "Boomer" Wells

1981 TCMA Tacoma Tigers

(Oakland A's, AAA) (color)

MT
Complete Set (32): 13.00
1 Larry Davis
2 Rick Randahl
3 Art Popham
4 Eric Mustad
5 Bob Kearney
6 Ed Nottle
7 Pat Dempsey
8 Dave Hamilton
9 Derek Bryant
10 Rich Bordi
11 Mike Davis
12 Jim Nettles
13 Mark Budaska
14 Don Fowler
15 Jim Sexton
16 Paul Mize
17 Keith Drumright
18 Kelvin Moore
19 Jeff Cox
20 Roy Thomas
21 Fred Holdsworth
22 Mark Souza
23 Rick Lysander
24 Dave Beard
25 Kevin Bell
26 Dave Heaverlo
27 Bob Grandas
28 Tigers Mascot
29 Batboys
30 Stan Naccarato
31 Jim Perry
32 Ed Figueroa

1981 TCMA Tidewater Tides

(N.Y. Mets, AAA) (color)

MT
Complete Set (29): 20.00
1 Ricky Sweet
2 Bruce Bochy
3 Ronald McDonald
4 Brian Giles
5 Ron Gardenhire
6 Phil Mankowski
7 Todd Winterfeldt
8 Wally Backman
9 Gary Rajsich
10 Sergio Beltre
11 Gil Flores
12 Mike Howard
13 Charlie Puleo
14 Tom Dixon
15 Scott Dye
16 Ed Lynch
17 Brent Gaff
18 Dave Von Ohlen
19 Mike Mendoza
20 Jesse Orosco
21 Jack Aker
22 Sam Perlozzo
23 Greg Harris
24 Ray Searage
25 Mark Daly
26 Rick Anderson
27 Danny Boitano
28 Dan Norman
29 Terry Leach

1981 TCMA Toledo Mud Hens

(Minnesota Twins, AAA) (color)

MT
Complete Set (22): 12.00
1 Cal Ermer
2 Buck Chamberlin
3 Jose Bastian
4 Terry Felton
5 Gerry Hannahs
6 Mike Kinnunen
7 Buce MacPherson
8 Wally Sarmiento
9 Bob Veselic
10 Ric Williams
11 Aurelio Cadahia
12 Steve Herz
13 Dave Machemer
14 Kurt Seibert
15 Kelly Snider
16 Jesus Vega
17 John Walker
18 Ron Washington
19 Keathel Chauncey
20 Ed Cipot
21 Frank Estes
22 Steve Stroughter

1981 TCMA Tucson Toros

(Houston Astros, AAA) (color)

MT
Complete Set (26): 20.00
1 Greg Cypret
2 Dell Leayherwood
3 Joe Pittman
4 Alan Knicely
5 Bob Cluck
6 Tom Vessey
7 Bert Pena
8 Simon Rosario
9 Mark Miggins
10 Johnny Ray
11 Scott Loucks
12 Jimmy Johnson
13 Tom Spencer
14 Dave Labossiere
15 Stan Leland
16 Ron Meredith
17 Jim Pankovits
18 Gordon Pladson
19 Pete Ladd
20 Tim Tolman
21 Bert Roberge
22 George Gross
23 Jim MacDonald
24 Billy Smith
25 Jack Donovan
26 Tom Wiedenbauer

1981 TCMA Tulsa Drillers

(Texas Rangers, AA) (color)

MT
Complete Set (30): 18.00
1 George Wright
2 Tracy Cowger
3 Phil Klimas
4 Marty Scott
5 Dave Stockstill
6 Mel Barrow
7 Larry Reynolds
8 Ted Davis
9 Steve Nielsen
10 Ron Carney
11 Joe Nemeth
12 Walt Terrell
13 Don Scott
14 Dennis Long
15 Dave Crutcher
16a Tony Fossas
16b Pete O'Brien
17 Mike Roberts
18 Ron Darling
19 Jack Lazorko
20 Tom Burgess
21 Tony Hudson
22 Kevin Richards
23 Greg Hughes
24 Brooks Wallace
25 Lindy Duncan
26 Bobby Ball
27 Joe Russell
28 Ron Gooch
29 Mike Jirschele

1981 TCMA Vancouver Canadians

(Milwaukee Brewers, AAA) (color)

MT
Complete Set (25): 14.00
1 Jamie Cocanower
2 Chuck Porter
3 Doug Wanz
4 Dwight Bernard
5 Mark Schuster
6 Frank Thomas
7 Brian Thorson
8 Ivan Rodriguez
9 Gil Kubski
10 Baylor Moore
11 Gus Quiros
12 Larry Rush
13 Rich Olsen
14 Terry Lee
15 Willie Mueller
16 Andy Replogle
17 Frank DiPino
18 Rene Quinones
19 Bobby Smith
20 Lee Stigman
21 John Flinn
22 Gerry Ako
23 Tom Soto
24 Kevin Bass
25 Steve Lake

1981 TCMA Vero Beach Dodgers

(L.A. Dodgers, A) (black & white)

MT
Complete Set (27): 15.00
1 Ed Amelung
2 Paul Bard
3 Frank Bryant
4 John Debus
5 Dan Forer
6 Art Hammond
7 Bobby Kenyon
8 Tony Lachowetz
9 Dave Lanning
10 Skip Mann
11 Holly Martin
12 Mike O'Malley
13 Felix Oroz
14 Steve Perry
15 Pat Raimondo
16 Curtis Reade
17 R.J. Reynolds
18 Greg Smith
19 Bill Sobbe
20 Terry Sutcliffe
21 Ricky Thomas
22 Brad Thorp
23 Juan Villaescusa
24 Brett Wise
25 David Wallace
26 John Shoemaker
27 Stan Wasiak

1981 TCMA Waterbury Reds

(Cincinnati Reds, AA) (black & white)

MT
Complete Set (23): 40.00
1 Rich Carlucci
2 Keefe Cato
3 Mike Dowless
4 Ken Jones
5 Doug Neuenschwander
6 Rick O'Keefe
7 Bill Scherrer
8 Lester Straker
9 Mike Sullivan
10 Randy Town
11 Anthony Walker
12 Steve Christmas
13 Adolfo Feliz
14 Tom Lawless
15 Gary Redus
16 Hector Rincones
17 Eski Viltz
18 Russ Aldrich
19 Mark Gilbert
20 Dave Bisceglia
21 Tony Walker
22 George Scherger
23 Lee Garrett

1981 TCMA Waterloo Indians

(Cleveland Indians, A) (black & white) (#17 not issued)

MT
Complete Set (34): 35.00

1 Gomer Hodge
2 Rick Colzie
3 Dennis Brogna
4 Larry Hrynko
5 John Asbell
6 Mark Bajus
7 Tom Burns
8 Mike Dixon
9 John Hoban
10 Mike Jeffcoat
11 Ricky Lintz
12 Tom Owens
13 Greg Pope
14 Ramon Romero
15 Mike Schwarber
16 Rich Thompson
18 Jack Fimple
19 John Malkin
20 Arnold Cochran
21 Shanie Dugas
22 Kelly Gruber
23 Marlin Methven
24 Juan Pacho
25 Larry Dotson
26 Dave Gallagher
27 Ed Saavedra
28 Mike Taylor
29 Winston Ficklin
30 Adalberto Nieves
31 Bernardo Brito
32 Steve Cushing
33 Ralph Elpin
34 Bob Feller
---- Louis Duarte

1981 TCMA Wausau Timbers

(Seattle Mariners, A) (black & white)

	MT
Complete Set (29):	35.00

1 Kevin Steger
2 Jeff Stottlemyre
3 Bob Hudson
4 Edwin Nunez
5 Tom Brennan
6 Mark Pedersen
7 Brian Snyder
8 Mark Batten
9 Chris Hunger
10 Don McKenzie
11 David Blume
12 Eddie Yampierre
13 Jesse Baez
14 Rick Adair
15 Jeff Cary
16 Enrique Diaz
17 Donnell Nixon
18 Harold Reynolds
19 Darnell Coles
20 Jimmy Presley
21 Clark Crist
22 Omar Minaya
23 Mark Chelette
24 Glenn Walker
25 John Moses
26 Ivan Calderon
27 Kevin King
28 Tom Hunt
29 Bill Plummer

1981 TCMA West Haven A's

(Oakland A's, AA) (color)

	MT
Complete Set (23):	27.50

1 Robert Didier
2 Keith Atherton
3 Bert Bradley
4 DeWayne Buice
5 Darryl Cias
6 Keith Comstock
7 Tim Conroy
8 Jim Durrman
9 Bobby Garrett
10 Bruce Fournier
11 Lynn Garrett
12 Steve Gelfarb
13 Rick Holloway
14 Tony Phillips
15 Ricky Tronerud
16 Don Morris
17 Mike Woodard
18 Alan Abraham
19 Dennis Sherow
20 Gorman Heimueller
21 Scott Meyer
22 Dick Lynch
23 Scott Pyle

> Value of modern team sets is often predicated as much on inclusion of star player's early cards as on scarcity of the issue.

1981 Trackle Winston-Salem Red Sox Postcards

(Boston Red Sox, A) (3-1/2" x 5-3/8", b/w, postcard back, players unidentified)

	MT
Complete Set (25):	35.00

(1) John Ackley
(2) Allan Bowlin
(3) Mike Brown
(4) Tom Brummer
(5) Kevin Clinton
(6) Scott Gering
(7) Frank Gill
(8) Jackie Gutierrez
(9) Ronnie Hill
(10) Al Hulbert
(11) Buddy Hunter
(12) Jeff Hunter
(13) Eddy Lee
(14) Steve Lyons
(15) Tom McCarthy
(16) Ron Oddo
(17) Keith Pecka
(18) Lee Pruitt
(19) Rolf Ramos
(20) Jack Sauer
(21) Tony Stevens
(22) Marc Sullivan
(23) Jim Teller
(24) Dave Tyler
(25) Parker Wilson

1981 TCMA Wisconsin Rapids Twins

(Minnesota Twins, A) (black & white)

	MT
Complete Set (23):	25.00

1 Ken Staples
2 Tom Leix
3 Smokey Everett
4 Tony Guerrero
5 Larry Harris
6 Kirby Krueger
7 Jeorge Ortiz
8 Adriano Pena
9 Luis Suarez
10 Mike Ungs
11 Mark Wright
12 Richard Yett
13 Ken Chandler
14 Jeff Reed
15 Michael Cole
16 Ken Foster
17 Jim Payne
18 Bill Price
19 Mandy Smith
20 Talbot Aiello
21 Jim Eisenreich
22 John Palica
23 Nelson Suarez

1982 TCMA Albuquerque Dukes

(L.A. Dodgers, AAA) (color)

	MT
Complete Set (27):	50.00

1 Joe Beckwith
2 John Franco
3 Burt Geiger
4 Orel Hershiser
5 Brian Holton
6 Dave Moore
7 Tom Niedenfuer
8 Steve Shirley
9 Rick Rodas
10 Larry White
11 Rick Wright
12 Don Crow
13 Dave Sax
14 Dave Anderson
15 Greg Brock
16 Larry Fobbs
17 Ross Jones
18 Alex Taveras
19 Mark Bradley
20 Dave Holman
21 Candy Maldonado
22 Mike Marshall
23 Tack Wilson
24 Del Crandall
25 Dave Cohea
26 Dick McLaughlin
27 Brent Strom

1982 Albuquerque Dukes team-issue photos

(L.A. Dodgers, AAA) (4" x 5" color photo prints, sold singly at stadium for $2 each)

	MT
Complete Set (28):	120.00

(1) Dave Anderson
(2) Joe Beckwith
(3) Mark Bradley
(4) Greg Brock
(5) Dave Cohea (trainer)
(6) Del Crandall
(7) Don Crow
(8) Sid Fernandez
(9) John Franco
(10) Bert Geiger
(11) Dale Holman
(12) Brian Holton
(13) Ross Jones
(14) Kevin Kennedy
(15) Candy Maldonado
(16) Mike Marshall
(17) Dick McLaughlin
(18) Dave Moore
(19) Alejandro Pena
(20) Ted Power
(21) Rich Rodas
(22) Dave Sax
(23) Steve Shirley
(24) Brent Strom
(25) Alex Taveras
(26) Larry D. White
(27) Tack Wilson
(28) Ricky Wright

1982 TCMA Alexandria Dukes

(Pittsburgh Pirates, A) (black & white)

	MT
Complete Set (27):	30.00

1 Johnny Taylor
2 Lee Marcheskie
3 Larry Lamonde
4 Ray Krawczyk
5 Jeffrey Horne
6 Christopher Green
7 Fernando Gonzales
8 Lance Dodd
9 Wilfrido Cordoba
10 Mike Quade
11 Brad Garnett
12 Marvin Clack
13 Nick Castaneda
14 Pete Rowe
15 Burk Goldthorn
16 James Churchill
17 Jeffrey Zaske
18 Timothy Wheeler
19 Brian McCann
20 Dan Warthen
21 John Lipon
22 Joe Orsulak
23 Ken Ford
24 Jim Felt
25 Nelson de la Rosa
26 Andy Smith
27 Rick Renteria

1982 TCMA Amarillo Gold Sox

(San Diego Padres, AA) (black & white)

	MT
Complete Set (25):	27.50

1 George Hinshaw
2 Brian Greer
3 John Stevenson
4 Joe Scherger
5 Gerry Davis
6 Bob Macias
7 Jeff Ronk
8 Don Purpura
9 Mike Martin
10 Mark Parent
11 James Steels
12 Jim Coffman
13 John White
14 Tom Biko
15 Neil Bryant
16 Mike Couchee
17 Steve Stone
18 Bill Long
19 Willie Hardwick
20 Marty Kain
21 Randy Kaczmarski
22 Rick Shaw
23 Glen Ezell
24 Mike Hebrard
25 Tom House

1982 Fritsch Appleton Foxes

(Chicago White Sox, A) (7a and 21a are sample cards, not issued with or included in the set price)

	MT
Complete Set (31):	10.00

1 Team Logo/Checklist
2 Jeff Overton
3 Leo Garcia
4 Jim Sutton
5 Wade L. Rowdon
6 Ramon Rosario
7a Al Jones (leg showing) (sample card)
7b Al Jones (no leg showing) (regular issue)
8 John Taylor
9 Scott Meier
10 Jess Anderson
11 Steve Pastrovich
12 Curt Reed
13 Wes Kent
14 John Skinner
15 Dave Nix
16 Joseph J. Paglino
17 Don Koch
18 Wayne Schuckert
19 Bill Babcock
20 Eddie Miles
21a Kevin Flannery (elbow showing) (sample card)
21b Kevin Flannery (elbow not showing) (regular issue)
22 Scott Gibson
23 Art Niemann
24 Daryl Boston
25 Michael J. Tanzi
26 Michael J. Buggs
27 Pat Adams
28 Al Heath
29 Doug Wiesner
30 Mike Pazik
31 Adrian Garrett

1982 TCMA Arkansas Travelers

(St. Louis Cardinals, AA) (black & white)

	MT
Complete Set (24):	100.00

1 Scott Arigoni
2 Kevin Hagen
3 Rickey Horton
4 Jeff Keener
5 Rafael Pimentel
6 Gerry Perry
7 Mark Riggins
8 Ed Sanford
9 Buddy Schultz
10 Tom Thurberg
11 Mark Salas
12 Tom Nieto
13 Jose Gonzales
14 Greg Guin
15 Peachy Guiterrez
16 Luis Ojeda
17 Don Moore
18 Jim Adduci
19 Andy Van Slyke
20 Jack Ayer
21 Larry Reynolds
22 Gaylen Pitts
23 Dave England
24 Jorge Aranzamendi

1982 TCMA Auburn Astros

(Houston Astros, A) (black & white)

	MT
Complete Set (19):	16.00

1 Tom Roarke
2 Bob Hartsfield
3 Jeff Jacobson
4 Mike Stellern
5 Ray Perkins
6 Eric Anderson
7 Jeff Meadows
8 Mike Hogan
9 Larry McIver
10 Bob Hinson
11 Jeff Datz
12 Tracy Dophied
13 Rich Bombard
14 Craig Kizer
15 Tom Riewerts
16 Steve Swain
17 Ricardo Rivera
18 Carlos Alfonso
19 Rick Thompson

1982 Fritsch Beloit Brewers

(Milwaukee Brewers, A) (2a and 27a are sample cards, not issued with or included in the set price)

	MT
Complete Set (27):	12.00

1 Team Logo/Checklist
2a Joe Henderson (catching) (sample card)
2b Joe Henderson (batting) (regular issue)
3 Gerry Miller
4 Bill Wegman
5 Johnson C. Wood
6 Ty Van Burkleo
7 John Hoban
8 John Gibbons
9 Fritz Fedor
10 Marcos Gomez
11 Dewey James
12 Mike Myerchin
13 Collin Tanabe
14 Kenny Clayton
15 Butch Kirby
16 Joe Edwin Morales
17 Gary Evans
18 Danny Gilmartin
19 Mike Samuel
20 Bryan Clutterbuck
21 Bill Max
22 Brad DeKraai
23 Martin Antunez
24 Terry Bevington
25 Bill Nowlan
26 Angel Morris Jr.
27a Ted Pallas (glove above head) (sample card)
27b Ted Pallas (glove at waist) (regular issue)

1982 TCMA Birmingham Barons

(Detroit Tigers, AA) (color)

	MT
Complete Set (24):	15.00

1 Stan Younger
2 Barbaro Garbey
3 Darrell Woodard
4 Homer Moncrief
5 Dave Gumpert
6 Mike Boocroft
7 Bob Melvin
8 Randy O'Neal
9 Chuck Cary
10 Kenny Baker
11 Bruce Fields
12 Randy Harvey
13 Rondal Rollins
14 Gary Hinson
15 John Flannery
16 Dave Hawarney
17 Kevin Pasley
18 Jerry Bass
19 Frank McCann
20 Steve Quealey
21 Charlie Nail

22 Emilio Carrasquel
23 Paul Gibson
24 Ed Brinkman

1982 TCMA Buffalo Bisons

(Pittsburgh Pirates, AA) (color)

	MT
Complete Set (18):	21.00

1 Rich Leggat
2 Bob Misak
3 Connor McGeehee
4 Drew McCauley
5 Greg Pastors
6 John Schaive
7 Al Torres
8 Keith Thibodeaux
9 Tim Wheeler
10 Kevin Houston
11 Ron Wotus
12 John Holland
13 Steve Farr
14 Eleno Cuen
15 Tim Burke
16 Mike Bielecki
17 Rick Peterson
18 Tom Sandt

1982 TCMA Burlington Rangers

(Texas Rangers, A) (black & white) (Avery is scarce late-issue card)

	MT
Complete Set, w/Avery (27):	80.00
Partial Set, no Avery (26):	24.00

1 Timothy Henry
2 Rodney Hodde
3 Anthony Hudson
4 James Jeffries
5 Keith Jones
6 Timothy Maki
7 Larry McLane
8 Michael Schmid
9 Gary Sharp
10 Gregory Tabor
11 Antonio Triplett
12 Raymond Warren
13 Curtis Wilkerson
14 Frank Brosiuos
15 Kevin Buckley
16 Chuckie Canady
17 Glen Cook
18 Douglas Davis
19 Mark Gammage
20 Jorge Gomez
21 Otto Gonzalez
22 Whitney Harry
23 Albert Hartman
24 Dwayne Henry
25 Martin Scott
26 Steven Nielsen
27 Larry Avery (G.M.)

1982 Fritsch Burlington Rangers

(Texas Rangers, A)

	MT
Complete Set (30):	9.00

1 Team Logo/Checklist
2 Lawrence Avery
3 Kevin Buckley
4 Dwayne Henry
5 Al Hartman
6 Tony Triplett
7 Ray Warren
8 Frank Brosious
9 Garry Venner
10 Keith Jones
11 Rod Hodde
12 Jorge Gomez
13 Curtis Wilkerson
14 Tim Henry
15 Greg Tabor
16 Chuckie Canady
17 Mark Gammage
18 Mike Schmid
19 Gary Sharp
20 Larry McLane
21 Tony Hudson
22 Doug Davis
23 Glen Cook
24 Whitney Harry
25 Jim Jeffries
26 Greg Campbell
27 Otto Gonzalez
28 Marty Scott
29 Tim Maki
30 Steve Nielsen

Suffix letters following a card number indicate a variation card.

1982 TCMA Cedar Rapids Reds

(Cincinnati Reds, A) (color)

	MT
Complete Set (27):	60.00

1 Mark Rothey
2 Rob Murphy
3 Curt Heidenreich
4 Steve Lowrey
5 Kurt Kepshire
6 Mike Riley
7 Freddie Toliver
8 Mike Ferguson
9 Mike Hennessy
10 Jim Pettibone
11 Larry Freeburg
12 Danny Lamar
13 Mark Matzen
14 Paul Kirsch
15 Adolfo Feliz
16 Tony Burley
17 Byron Peyton
18 Bill Metil
19 Dave Hall
20 Eric Davis
21 Paul O'Neill
22 Tim Stout
23 Scott Terry
24 Jeff Jones
25 Randy Davidson
26 David Clay
27 Don Buchheister

1982 TCMA Charleston Charlies

(Cleveland Indians, AAA) (color)

	MT
Complete Set (24):	12.00

1 Bud Anderson
2 John Bohnet
3 Gordy Glaser
4 Ed Glynn
5 Neal Heaton
6 Larry Hrynko
7 Silvio Martinez
8 Jack Nuismer
9 Rob Pietroburgo
10 Ray Searage
11 Bill Nahorodny
12 Tim Norrid
13 Craig Stimac
14 Luis DeLeon
15 Angelo LoGrande
16 Rich Murray
17 Kevin Rhomberg
18 Dave Rosello
19 Carmelo Castillo
20 Larry Littleton
21 Karl Pagel
22 Dave Riviera
23 Doc Edwards
24 Chuck Estrada

1982 TCMA Charleston Royals

(K.C. Royals, A) (black & white) (Cone and Psaltis cards have transposed backs)

	MT
Complete Set (24):	70.00

1 Jim Miner
2 Roger Hausen
3 Mike Sorrel
4 Tom McHugh
5 John Bryant
6 Danny Jackson
7 Mitch Ashmore
8 Perry Swanson
9 Bert Johnson
10 Chris Bryeans
11 Bob Umdenstock
12 Mike Kingery
13 Tim Ballard
14 Dick Vitato
15 Ron Krauss
16 Ken Patterson
17 Roland Oruna
18 Den Swank
19 Spiro Psaltis (Dave Cone name & bio on card)
20 Dave Cone (Spiro Psaltis name & bio on card)
21 Cliff Pastornicky
22 Willie Neal
23 Mark Farnsworth
24 Roy Tanner

1982 Charlotte O's team issue

(Baltimore Orioles, AA) (orange & blue border)

	MT
Complete Set (31):	80.00

(1) The Heroes
(2) Jesus Alfaro
(3) Juan Arias
(4) Tony Arnold
(5) Chris Bourjos
(6) Don Bowman
(7) Randy Boyd
(8) Mark Brown
(9) Carlos Cabassa
(10) Mark Corey
(11) Dan Craven
(12) John Denman
(13) H. Shelton Drum
(14) Drungo Hazewood
(15) Leo Hernandez
(16) Eddie Hook
(17) Dave Huppert
(18) Bruce Mac Pherson
(19) Minnie Mendoza
(20) Mark Naehring
(21) Phil Nastu
(22) Paul O'Neill
(23) Francisco Oliveras
(24) Russ Pensiero
(25) Julio Perez
(26) Tom Rowe
(27) Jeff Schaeffer (Schaefer)
(28) Mark Smith
(29) John Stefero
(30) Matt Tyner
(31) Mark Wiley

1982 TCMA Chattanooga Lookouts

(Cleveland Indians, AA) (black & white)

	MT
Complete Set (25):	45.00

1 Nate Puryear
2 Scott Munninghoff
3 Everett Rey
4 Ed Saavedra
5 Richard Thompson
6 Tim Glass
7 Ricky Baker
8 Dane Anthony
9 Tom Owens
10 Mike Schwarber
11 Sal Rende
12 Marlin Methvin
13 Shanie Dugas
14 George Cecchetti
15 Steve Roche
16 Kelly Gruber
17 Dave Gallagher
18 Robin Fuson
19 Steve Narleski
20 Rick Borchers
21 Jeff Moronko
22 Craig Adams
23 Al Gallagher
24 Chuck Stobbs
25 Hank Gaughan

1982 Fritsch Clinton Giants

(S.F. Giants, A)

	MT
Complete Set (32):	16.00

1 Team Logo/Checklist
2 Wendell Kim
3 Steve Cline
4 Matt Nokes
5 Phil Ouellette
6 Glenn Barling
7 Michael Jones
8 Todd Zacher
9 David Nenad
10 Everett Graham
11 Steve Wilcox
12 Randy Saunier
13 Ramon Bautista
14 Mike Dunn
15 Marty Baier
16 Kernan Ronan
17 Gene Lambert
18 Allen Smoot
19 Larry Crews
20 Brian Murtha
21 Glenn Jones
22 Eric Erickson
23 Mark Grant
24 Randy Ebersberger
25 Bob O'Connor
26 Mark Tudor
27 Gus Stokes
28 John Marks
29 Jim Weir
30 Mickey Swenson
31 Mark Swenson
32 Mark Swenson, Mickey Swenson

"1982" Columbus Clippers Don Mattingly

This fantasy issue was designed in rough similitude of the 1982 TCMA minor league cards. Black-and-white, and blank-backed, it shows Mattingly in action during a Columbus Clippers game in which the team wore circa 1884 uniforms.

(No collector value)

1982 Police Columbus Clippers

(N.Y. Yankees, AAA) (color, 2-3/8" x 3-3/4")

	MT
Complete Set (25):	42.00

(1) Tucker Ashford
(2) Steve Balboni
(3) Marshall Brant
(4) Mike Bruhert
(5) Greg Cochran
(6) Juan Espino
(7) Pete Filson
(8) Wayne Harper
(9) Curt Kaufman
(10) Jim Lewis
(11) Don Mattingly
(12) John Pacella
(13) Mike Patterson
(14) Scott Patterson
(15) Bobby Ramos
(16) Andre Robertson
(17) Dan Schmitz
(18) George H. Sisler Jr.
(19) Garry Smith
(20) Dave Stegman
(21) Bob Sykes
(22) Frank Verdi
(23) Dave Wehrmeister
(24) Jamie Werly
(25) Coaches/trainer card (Sammy Ellis, Jerry McNertney, Steve Donohue)

1982 TCMA Columbus Clippers

(N.Y. Yankees, AAA) (color) (3,500 sets reported issued)

	MT
Complete Set (26):	250.00

1 John Pacella
2 Tucker Ashford
3 Wayne Harer
4 Steve Balboni
5 Curt Kaufman
6 Marshall Brant
7 Mike Bruhert
8 Greg Cochran
9 Pete Filson
10 Jamie Werley
11 Dave Wehrmeister
12 Bob Sykes
13 David Stegman
14 Garry Smith
15 Dick Scott
16 Dan Schmitz
17 Andre Robertson
18 Bobby Ramos
19 Scott Patterson
20 Mike Patterson
21 Don Mattingly
22 Jim Lewis
23 Juan Espino
24 Steve Donohue, Sammy Ellis, Jerry McNertney
25 Frank Verdi
26 George H. Sisler, Jr.

1982 Fritsch Danville Suns

(California Angels, A) (7a is a sample card, not issued with or included in the set price)

	MT
Complete Set (28):	20.00

1 Team Logo/Checklist
2 Gus Gil
3 Jeff Ahern
4 T.R. Bryden
5 Mark Bingham
6 Bill White
7a Rick Turner (no glove) (sample card)
7b Rick Turner (with glove) (regular issue)
8 Jack Crawford
9 Kevin Price
10 Butch Dowies
11 Carlos Matos
12 Doug Lindsey
13 Tony Gonzalez
14 Marcel Lachemann
15 Richard Zaleski
16 Scott Oliver
17 Ellie Barros

18 Willie D. Williams
19 Freddy Machuca
20 Bill Worden
21 Devon White
22 Joe King
23 Mike Saverino
24 Brian Hartsock
25 Mark Bonner
26 Rafel Lugo
27 Dick Schofield
28 Norman Carrasco

1982 TCMA Daytona Beach Astros

(Houston Astros, A) (black & white)

Complete Set (25): MT 27.50
1 Guillermo Castro
2 Mitch Coplon
3 Joe Ferrante
4 Scott Gardner
5 Manny Hernandez
6 Uvaldo Regalado
7 Rex Schimpf
8 Ben Snyder
9 Roberto Yan
10 Doug Britt
11 Steve Dunnegan
12 Eric Bullock
13 Ty Gainey
14 Ira Lane
15 Neil Simons
16 Eric Swanson
17 Mark Campbell
18 Robbie McGorkle
19 Jamie Williams
20 Glenn Davis
21 Jim McKnight
22 Val Medina
23 Larry Simcox
24 Phil Smith
25 Mark Strucher

1982 TCMA Durham Bulls

(Atlanta Braves, A) (black & white)

Complete Set (25): MT 70.00
1 Mike Garcia
2 Keith Hagman
3 Scott Hood
4 Joe Lorenz
5 Bob Luzon
6 Bryan Neal
7 Ken Scanlon
8 Rick Siriano
9 Miguel Sosa
10 Jim Stefanski
11 Tommy Thompson
12 Freddy Tiburcio
13 Bob Tumpane
14 Dave Clay
15 Rick Coatney
16 Jeff Dedmon
17 Brian Fisher
18 Rick Hatcher
19 Mike Payne
20 Gary Reiter
21 Andre Treadway
22 Bruce Dal Canton
23 Buddy Bailey
24 Gene Lane
25 Bob Dews

1982 TCMA Edmonton Trappers

(Chicago White Sox, AAA) (color)

Complete Set (25): MT 27.50
1 Carlos Ibarra
2 Jose Castro
3 Jim Siwy
4 Steve Dillard
5 Chris Nyman
6 Guy Hoffman
7 Keith Desjarlais
8 Jay Loviglio
9 Fran Mullins
10 Lorenzo Gray
11 Leo Sutherland
12 Woody Agosto
13 Ron Kittle
14 Nardi Contreras
15 Reggie Patterson
16 David Hogg
17 Len Bradley
18 Dom Fucci
19 Rich Barnes
20 Rusty Kuntz
21 Rick Seilheimer
22 Gordy Lund
23 Geoff Combe
24 Dave Grossman
25 Jeff Schattinger

1982 TCMA El Paso Diablos

(Milwaukee Brewers, AA) (color)

Complete Set (24): MT 18.00
1 Eric Peyton
2 Dion James
3 Ron Koenigsfeld
4 Kurt Kingsolver
5 Dan Davidsmeier
6 Bill Foley
7 Randy Ready
8 Mark Schuster
9 Don Whiting
10 Mark Johnston
11 Joe Hansen
12 Steve Michael
13 Jerry Jenkins
14 Andy Beene
15 Steve Manderfield
16 Bob Schroeck
17 Dave Grier
18 Jack Uhey
19 Steve Parrott
20 Jim Koontz
21 Bob Gibson
22 Derek Tatsuno
23 Tony Muser
24 Al Price

1982 TCMA Evansville Triplets

(Detroit Tigers, AAA) (color)

Complete Set (25): MT 12.50
1 Howard Bailey
2 Juan Berenguer
3 Mark Dacko
4 Mark Lee
5 Rick Matula
6 Bruce Robbins
7 Larry Rothschild
8 Dave Rucker
9 Augie Ruez
10 Gerald Ujdur
11 Marty Castillo
12 Don McCormack
13 Stine Poole
14 Jeff Cox
15 Paul Djakonow
16 Mike Laga
17 Juan Lopez
18 Vern Followell
19 Les Filkins
20 Eddie Gates
21 Ray Hampton
22 Jeff Kenaga
23 Mark Corey
24 Ken Houston
25 Roy Majtyka

1982 TCMA Ft. Myers Royals

(K.C. Royals, A) (black & white)

Complete Set (23): MT 25.00
1 Rick Rizzo
2 Hal Hatcher
3 Tommy Thompson
4 Benny Gadahia
5 Warren Oliver
6 Greg Jonson
7 Nick Harsh
8 Mickey Palmer
9 Rick Plautz
10 Duane Gustavson
11 Tony Ferreira
12 Mike Alvarez
13 Jeff Gladden
14 Dave Wong
15 Fran Cutty
16 Mark Huismann
17 James Gleissner
18 Bill Best
19 Lester Strode
20 Mark Newman
21 Bill Pecota
22 Rick Mathews
23 Steve Morrow

1982 TCMA Glens Falls White Sox

(Chicago White Sox, AA) (black & white) (#14-15 not issued)

Complete Set (23): MT 125.00
1 Vince Bienek
2 J.B. Brown
3 Ed Cipot
4 Larry Donofrid
5 Dom Fucci
6 Tim Hulett
7 Phil Klimas
8 Mike Morse
9 Pete Peltz
10 Joel Skinner
11 Vern Thomas
12 Dan Williams
13 Dave Yobs
16 Larry Edwards
17 Bob Fallopn
18 Jack Hardy
19 Chuck Johnson
20 John Lackey
21 Mike Maitland
22 Tom Mullen
23 Mark Teutsch
24 Mike Withrow
25 Jim Mahoney

1982 Trackle Hagerstown Suns

(Baltimore Orioles, A) (3-1/2" x 5-3/8", b/w, postcard back, players unidentified)

Complete Set (21): MT 32.50
(1) Bill Butler
(2) Dave Corman
(3) Greg Dees
(4) Pat Dumouchelle
(5) Dave Falcone
(6) Charlie Guinn
(7) Neal Herrick
(8) Chris Holmes
(9) Joe Kucharski
(10) Grady Little
(11) Tim Maples
(12) Alec McCullough
(13) Tim Norris
(14) Al Pardo
(15) Jim Rooney
(16) Ken Rowe
(17) Larry Sheets
(18) Jeff Summers
(19) Andy Timko
(20) Johnny Tutt
(21) Jeff Williams

1982 TCMA Hawaii Islanders

(San Diego Padres, AAA) (color)

Complete Set (25): MT 300.00
1 Ron Tingley
2 Dave Richards
3 Steve Smith
4 Jim Pankovits
5 Jerry Johnson
6 Joe Lansford
7 Jerry De Simone
8 Dan Gausepohl
9 Aaron Cain
10 Tony Gwynn
11 Rick Lancellotti
12 Jeff Pyburn
13 Steve Fireovid
14 Andy Hawkins
15 George Stablein
16 Ron Meredith
17 Fred Kuhaulua
18 Tim Hamm
19 Tom Tellmann
20 Dave Dravecky
21 Mark Thurmond
22 Kim Seaman
23 Doug Rader
24 Chuck Hartenstein
25 Larry Duensing

1982 TCMA Holyoke Millers

(California Angels, AA) (color)

Complete Set (26): MT 12.00
1 Michael Barba
2 Brian Buckely
3 Jeff Conner
4 Lonnie Dugger
5 Dave Duran
6 Bill Mooneyham
7 Perry Morrison
8 Ron Romanick
9 David A. Smith
10 David W. Smith
11 Bob Palmer
12 Larry Patterson
13 Rick Adams
14 Bob Bohnet
15 Ron Hunt
16 Pat Keedy
17 Tim Krauss
18 Gus Polidor
19 Chris Clark
20 Harry Francis
21 Dennis Gilbert
22 Darrell Miller
23 Jack Hiatt
24 Marc Terrazas
25 George Como
26 Ben Surner

1982 Holyoke Millers team issue

(California Angels, AA) (This set was also produced in the form of a poster. Single cards measure approximately 1-7/8" x 2-7/8".)

Complete Set (29): MT 75.00
(1) Mike Barba
(2) Jim Beswick
(3) Bob Bohnet
(4) Rod Boxberger
(5) Brian Buckley
(6) Chris Clark
(7) Jeff Conner
(8) Harry Francis
(9) Dennis Gilbert
(10) Mike Gordon
(11) Jack Hiatt
(12) Pat Keedy
(13) Jay Kibbe
(14) Tim Krauss
(15) Steve Liddle
(16) Mark McCormack
(17) Darrell Miller
(18) Bill Mooneyham
(19) Bob Palmer
(20) Larry Patterson
(21) Gustavo Polidor
(22) Ron Romanick
(23) David A. Smith
(24) D.W. Smith
(25) Mark Sproesser
(26) Marc Terrazas
(27) Craig Thomas
(28) Mike Venezia
(29) Matt Wroth

1982 TCMA Idaho Falls Athletics

(Oakland A's, A) (black & white)

Complete Set (33): MT 20.00
1 Dave Baehr
2 Jim Bailey
3 Mark Border
4 Eric Brown
5 Tom Conquest
6 Doug Farrow
7 Todd Fischer
8 Angelo Gilbert
9 Mark Kochanski
10 Tim Lambert
11 Dave Leiper
12 Tenoa Stevenson
13 Steve Travers
14 Shawn Gill
15 Russ Wortmann
16 Leon Baham
17 Bill Davis
18 Mark Dye
19 John Michel
20 Clemente Oropeza
21 Greg Robles
22 Kenny Clayton
23 Steve Campbell
24 Rob Loscalzo
25 Eddie Malone
26 Gary McGraw
27 Jorge Oquendo
28 Ricky Thomas
29 Dave Wilder
30 Keith Lieppman
31 Grady Fuson
32 Mark Doberenz
33 Dave Sheriff

1982 Indianapolis Indians team issue

(Cincinnati Reds, AAA) (color)

Complete Set (32): MT 22.00
1 Team Photo
2 George Scherger
3 Kip Young
4 Nick Esasky
5 Brad Lesley
6 Duane Walker
7 Bill Dawley
8 The Instructors
9 Brooks Carey
10 Orlando Isales
11 Brian Ryder
12 Dave Van Gorder
13 Greg Harris
14 The Bullpen
15 Tom Lawless
16 Mike Dowless
17 Gary Redus
18 The Catchers
19 Rich Carlucci
20 Tom Foley
21 Ben Hayes
22 Steve Christmas
23 The Outfielders
24 Ron Farkas
25 Dave Tomlin
26 Dallas Williams
27 The Infielders
28 Gil Kubski
29 Neil Fiala
30 The Starting Pitchers
31 Lee Garrett
32 Behind The Scenes

1982 TCMA Iowa Cubs

(Chicago Cubs, AAA) (color)

Complete Set (32): MT 25.00
1 Alfred Benton
2 Scott Fletcher
3 Tom Grant
4 Mel Hall
5 Bill Hayes
6 Randy LaVigne
7 Jared Martin
8 Danny Rohn
9 Joe Strain
10 Pat Tabler
11 Scot Thompson
12 Jack Upton
13 Elliott Waller
14 Robert Blyth
15 Tom Filer

16 Jay Howell
17 Larry Jones
18 Chris Knapp
19 Ken Kravec
20 Craig Lefferts
21 Mark Parker
22 Mike Proly
23 Herman Segelke
24 Randy Stein
25 Jim Napier
26 Scott Breeden
27 Ken Grandquist
28 Bob Reynolds
29 Tom Butts
30 Frank Macy
31 Kim Hart
32 Dr. Richard Evans

1982 TCMA Jackson Mets

(N.Y. Mets, AA) (color)

MT
Complete Set (25): 70.00
1 Jeff Bittiger
2 Matt Bullinger
3 Ted Davis
4 Scott Dye
5 Steve Ibarguen
6 Jody Johnston
7 Brain Kolbe
8 Jose Rodriguez
9 John Semprini
10 Doug Sisk
11 Ronn Reynolds
12 Dave Duff
13 Rick Poe
14 Mike Anicich
15 Rick McMullen
16 Al Pedrique
17 Jim Woodward
18 Bill Rittweger
19 Billy Beane
20 Terry Blocker
21 Darryl Strawberry
22 Gene Dusan
23 Bob Apodaca
24 Bob Sikes
25 Bill Walberg

1982 Trackle Kinston Blue Jays Postcards

(Toronto Blue Jays, A) (3-1/2" x 5-3/8", b/w, postcard back, players unidentified)

MT
Complete Set (20): 25.00
(1) Kevin Aitcheson
(2) Bernie Beckman
(3) Ty Carter
(4) Steve Erickson
(5) Jose Escobar
(6) Garry Harris
(7) Toby Hernandez
(8) Herman Lewis
(9) Jack McKnight
(10) John McLaren
(11) Bob McNair
(12) Bob Nandin
(13) Jose Paulino
(14) Benjy Perez
(15) Bill Pinkham
(16) Terry Raley
(17) Augie Schmidt
(18) Jay Schroeder
(19) Rico Sutton
(20) Jim Wahlif

1982 TCMA Knoxville Blue Jays

(Toronto Blue Jays, AA) (black & white)

MT
Complete Set (23): 16.00
1 Team Photo
2 Scott Elam
3 Randy Ford
4 Dennis Howard
5 Tom Lukish
6 Colin McLaughlin
7 Keith Walker
8 Matt Williams
9 Brian Stemberger
10 Brian Milner
11 Dan Whitmer
12 Tim Thompson
13 Paul Hodgson
14 Andre Wood
15 Carlos Rios
16 Ed Dennis
17 Vern Ramie
18 J.J. Cannon
19 Vassie Gardner
20 Ron Shepherd
21 Larry Hardy
22 Hector Torres
23 John Woodworth

1982 Ehrler's Dairy Louisville Redbirds

(St. Louis Cardinals, AAA)

MT
Complete Set (30): 28.00
(1) George A. Bjorkman
(2) Jose Oscar Brito
(3) Glen E. Brummer
(4) Michael S. Calise
(5) Ralph A. Citarella
(6) Joseph De Sa
(7) Jeffrey D. Doyle
(8) Joseph F. Frazier
(9) John T. Fulgham
(10) David A. Green
(11) Ricky N. Horton
(12) David B. Kable
(13) Jeffrey Allen Lahti
(14) William Allen Lyons
(15) John R. Martin
(16) Willie D. McGee
(17) Jerry McKune
(18) Dyar K. Miller
(19) Gotay Mills
(20) Daniel J. Morogiello
(21) Alan R. Olmsted
(22) Kelly J. Paris
(23) Gaylen R. Pitts
(24) Andrew J. Rinson
(25) Gene (Eugene L. Roof)
(26) Orlando Sanchez
(27) Rafael Santana
(28) Jed Smith
(29) John A. Stuper
(30) Steven W. Winfield

1982 TCMA Lynchburg Mets

(N.Y. Mets, A) (black & white) (Webster, Johnston and Raeside are scarce late-issue cards)

MT
Complete Set, w/late issues (23): 60.00
Partial Set, no late issues (20): 50.00
1 Danny Monzon
2 Laschelle Tarver
3 Herman Winningham
4 John De Imonte
5 Bruce Kastelic
6 Kevin Mitchell
7 DeWayne Vaughn
8 Ed Rech
9 Jeff Sunderlage
10 Paul Wilmet
11 Tom Miller
12 Roger Frash
13 Duane Evans
14 Chuck Schonoor
15 Randy Milligan
16 Lloyd McClendon
17 Rick Myles
18 Roger Begue
19 Jay Tibbs
20 Bill Fultz
21 Rich Webster
22 Jody Johnston
23 John Raeside

Suffix letters following a card number indicate a variation card.

1982 TCMA Lynn Sailors

(Seattle Mariners, AA) (black & white)

MT
Complete Set (18): 35.00
1 Rick Adair
2 Carl Best (Karl)
3 Kevin Dukes
4 Joe Georger
5 Steve Krueger
6 Jed Murray
7 Jeff Stottlemyre
8 Scott Stranski (photo actually Jeff Stottlemyre)
9 Jim Nelson
10 Clark Crist
11 Bill Crone (photo actually John Moses)
12 Mario Diaz
13 Jim Presley
14 Ramon Estepa (photo acutally Tito Nanni)
15 Tito Nanni
16 Glenn Walker
17 Harold Reynolds
18 Mickey Bowers

1982 Fritsch Madison Muskies

(Oakland A's, A) (27a is a sample card, not issued with or included in the set price)

MT
Complete Set (34): 9.00
1 Team Logo/Checklist
2 Joel Boni
3 Steve Kiefer
4 Mike Flinn
5 John "Duke" Smith
6 Chuck Kolotka
7 Kevin Coughlon
8 Tom Heckman
9 Gene Ransom
10 Scott Anderson
11 Scot Mitchell
12 Mark Jarrett
13 Jeff Tipton
14 Mark Fellows
15 Monte R. McAbee
16 Ron Wilkinson
17 Allen Edwards
18 Frank Harris
19 Brad Fischer
20 James Feeley
21 Ron Harrison
22 Kevin D. Waller
23 Mike Ashman
24 Rob Vavrock
25 Jeff Kobernus
26 Keith Call
27a Pat O'Hara (batting) (sample card)
27b Pat O'Hara (catching) (regular issue)
28 Thomas Romano
29 Mark "Mac" McDonald
30 Bruce Amador
31 Jeff Cary
32 Hector Perez
33 Ed Janus
34 Bob Drew, Michael Duval

1982 TCMA Miami Marlins

(Baltimore Orioles, A) (black & white)

MT
Complete Set (22): 12.50
1 Will George
2 Mike Glinatsis
3 Marcos Gonzalez
4 Brian McDonough
5 Carlos Moreno
6 Joel Pyfrom
7 Tony Wadley
8 Jose Caballero
9 Ron Cardieri
10 Jorge Curbelo
11 Jorge Llano
12 Robbie Alvarez
13 Julio Beltran
14 Bob Boyce
15 Edgar Castro
16 Rick Rembielak
17 Angel Valdez
18 Raul Tovar
19 Lee Granger
20 Mike Kutner
21 Frank Contreras
22 John Tamargo

1982 Chong Modesto A's

(Oakland A's, A)

MT
Complete Set (27): 55.00
1 Dave Hudgens
2 Rod Murphy
3 Selwyn Young
4 Tom Copeland
5 Thad Reece
6 Rick Tronerud
7 Terry Harper
8 John Hotchkiss
9 Jimmy Camacho
10 Aurdie Colbert
11 Mickey Tettleton
12 Curt Young
13 Wayne Palicia
14 Ed Retzer
15 Paul Josephson
16 Mike Lynes
17 Mark Ferguson
18 Tony Herron
19 Gary Dawson
20 Tim Conroy
21 Rick Rodriguez
22 Don Van Marter
23 Wayne Rudolph
24 Pete Whisenant
25 Jim Durrman
26 Phil Danielson
27 Dan Kiser

1982 Nashville Sounds team issue

(N.Y. Yankees, AA)

MT
Complete Set (28): 9.50
1 Dave Banes
2 Mike Browning
3 Brian Butterfield
4 Ben Callahan
5 Pat Callahan
6 Nate Chapman
7 Clay Christiansen
8 Dean Craig
9 Brian Dayett
10 Tommie Dodd
11 Guy Elston
12 Ray Fontenot
13 Paul Grayner
14 Rex Hudler
15 Tim Knight
16 Chris Lein
17 Erik Peterson
18 Brian Poldberg
19 Frank Ricci
20 Mark Salas
21 Dan Schmitz
22 Buck Showalter
23 Roger Slagle
24 Garry Smith
25 Bob Sykes
26 Rafael Villaman
27 Stefan Wever
--- Manager/coaches (Hoyt Wilhelm, John Oates, Eddie Napoleon)

1982 TCMA Oklahoma City 89'ers

(Philadelphia Phillies, AAA) (color)

MT
Complete Set (25): 45.00
1 Mike Willis
2 Rowland Office
3 Tim Corcoran
4 Ramon Aviles
5 Ellis Deal
6 Ron Clark
7 Al Sanchez
8 Len Matuszek
9 Jerry Reed
10 Rusty Hamric
11 Julio Franco
12 Mark Davis
13 Joe Kerrigan
14 Tom Lombarski
15 Tony McDonald
16 Luis Rodriguez
17 Jeff Ulrich
18 Jim Rasmussen
19 Jon Reelhorn
20 Herb Orensky
21 Kelly Downs
22 Marty Decker
23 Darren Burroughs
24 Don Carman
25 Wil Culmer

1982 TCMA Omaha Royals

(K.C. Royals, AAA) (color)

MT
Complete Set w/photo variations (29): 75.00
Complete Set, no variations (27): 17.50
1 Mike Armstrong
2 Ralph Botting
3 Keith Creel
4 Dan Fischer
5 Don Hood
6 Phil Huffman
7 Bill Kelly
8 Dave Schuler
9 Bob Tufts
10 Frank Wills
11 Greg Keatley
12 Don Slaught
13 Mitch Ashmore
14 Buddy Biancalana
15 Manuel Colletti
16 Dave Edler
17a Ron Johnson (blue uniform, photo actually Dan Weiser)
17b Ron Johnson (white uniform, correct photo)
18a Dan Weiser (white uniform, photo actually Ron Johnson)
18b Dan Weiser (blue uniform, correct photo)
19 Darryl Motley
20 Bombo Rivera
21 Mark Ryal
22 Pat Sheridan
23 Luis Silverio
24 Bill Gorman
25 Joe Sparks
26 Jerry Cram
27 Paul McGannon

1982 TCMA Oneonta Yankees

(N.Y. Yankees, A) (black & white) (Elway card counterfeited circa 1987; recommend purchase only as complete set)

	MT
Complete Set (17):	500.00

1 Orestes Destrade
2 Jim Riggs
3 Brent Giesdal
4 Ken Berry
5 Dan O'Regan
6 Q.V. Lowe
7 Stan Sanders
8 Tim Birtsas
9 Steve Campagno
10 Pat Bone
11 Tim Byron
12 Jesus Alcala
13 John Elway
14 Mike Fennell
15 Jim Ferguson
16 Mike Gatlin
17 Pedro Medina

1982 TCMA Orlando Twins

(Minnesota Twins, AA) (black & white)

	MT
Complete Set (24):	35.00

1 Kevin Williams
2 Lee Belanger
3 Eric Broersma
4 Smokey Everett
5 Jack Hobbs
6 Bob Konopa
7 Mark Funderburk
8 Greg Gagne
9 Dave Meier
10 Mike McCain
11 Tony Pilla
12 Tim Teufel
13 Tom Kelly
14 Rick Austin
15 Chino Cadahia
16 Andre David
17 Steve Douglas
18 Ken Foster
19 Ted Kromy
20 Larry May
21 Bob Mulligan
22 Jay Pettibone
23 Sam Arrington
24 Eddie Hodge

1982 TCMA Orlando Twins Southern League Champions

(Minnesota Twins, AA) (black & white) (set features players from 1981 championship season)

	MT
Complete Set (24):	50.00

1 Rod Booker
2 Randy Bush
3 Chino Cadahia
4 Manny Colletti
5 Andre David
6 Steve Douglas
7 Gary Gaetti
8 Tim Laudner
9 Tim Teufel
10 Scott Ulger
11 Lance Hallberg
12 Tom Kelly
13 Eric Broersma
14 Scott Gleckel
15 Steve Green
16 Brad Havens
17 Jack Hobbs
18 Bob Konopa
19 Ted Kromy
20 Steve Mapel
21 Bob Mulligan
22 Jose Reyes
23 Gary Serum
24 Frank Viola

1982 Trackle Pawtucket Red Sox Postcards

(Boston Red Sox, AAA) (3-1/2" x 5-3/8", b/w, postcard back, players unidentified)

	MT
Complete Set (18):	32.50

(1) Marty Barrett
(2) Sam Bowen
(3) Craig Brooks
(4) Dennis Burtt
(5) Juan Bustabad
(6) Jim Dorsey
(7) Mark Fidrych
(8) Lee Graham
(9) Garry Hancock
(10) John Henry Johnson
(11) Dave Koza
(12) John Lickert
(13) Keith MacWhorter
(14) Bill Moloney
(15) Joe Morgan
(16) Dave Schmidt
(17) Dave Schoppee
(18) Jim Wilson

1982 Trackle Peninsula Pilots Postcards

(Philadelphia Phillies, A) (3-1/2" x 5-3/8", b/w, postcard back, players unidentified)

	MT
Complete Set (38):	60.00

(1) Mark Adamiak
(2) Buddy Bartholow
(3) George Culver
(4) Bill Currier
(5) Bill Dancy
(6) Willie Darkis
(7) Jimmy Darnell
(8) Darren Daulton
(9) Cot Deal
(10) Matt Dorin
(11) Ken Dowell
(12) Dave Enos
(13) John Fierro (trainer)
(14) Richie Gaynor
(15) Tony Ghelfi
(16) Wally Goff
(17) Frankie Griffin
(18) Steve Harvey
(19) Ed Hearn
(20) Charlie Hudson
(21) Bill Johnson
(22) Kent Keiser
(23) Mike Lavalliere
(24) Alan LeBoeuf
(25) Greg Legg
(26) Jon Lindsey
(27) Francisco Melendez
(28) Spider Reynolds
(29) Ron Richardson
(30) Mel Roberts
(31) Tony Roig
(32) Juan Samuel
(33) Gib Seibert
(34) Jeff Stone
(35) Steve True
(36) Harold Warner
(37) Mel Williams
(38) Ed Wojna

1982 Valley Nat'l Bank Phoenix Giants

(S.F. Giants, AAA) (color)

	MT
Complete Set (27):	15.00

1 Team Photo
2 Mike Chris
3 Ted Wilborn
4 Mike Rowland
5 John Rabb
6 Paul Szymarek
7 Rocky Bridges
8 Dave Roberts
9 Tommy Gonzales, Harry Jordan
10 Mike Tucker
11 Ethan Blackaby
12 Craig Chamberlain
13 Ron Pruitt
14 Mark Dempsey
15 Dorian Boyland
16 Jeff Stember
17 Mike Turgeon
18 Giantettes
19 Andy Mc Gaffigan
20 Kelly Smith
21 Tom Runnells
22 Dan Gladden
23 Tom O'Malley
24 Jose Barrios
25 Bill Martin
26 Mike Rex
27 Al Hergesheimer

1982 TCMA Portland Beavers

(Pittsburgh Pirates, AAA) (color) (#25 not issued)

	MT
Complete Set (25):	17.50

1 Jose DeLeon
2 Butch Edge
3 Cecilio Guante
4 Odell Jones
5 Robert Long
6 Randy Nieman
7 Pasqual Perez (Pascual)
8 Manny Sarmiento
9 Lee Tunnell
10 Stan Cliburn
11 Junior Ortiz
12 Wayne Caughey
13 Denny Gonzalez
14 Willie Horton
15 Bobby Mitchell
16 Nelson Norman
17 Eddie Vargas
18 Dave Augustine
19 Trench Davis
20 Doug Frobel
21 Jose Rodriguez
22 Reggie Walton
23 Jim Saul
24 Vern Law, Jim Saul
25 Not issued
26 Carlos Lezedma

1982 TCMA Quad City Cubs

(Chicago Cubs, A) (black & white)

	MT
Complete Set (28):	20.00

1 Darryl Banks
2 Allen Black
3 Russ Brahms
4 Rich Buonantony
5 Jorge Carpio
6 Tim Clarke
7 Mitch Cooke
8 Jeff Fruge
9 Ron Kaufman
10 Vance Lovelace
11 Mike Shulleetta
12 Roger Crow
13 Craig Weissman
14 Lee George
15 Wendell Henderson
16 Jeff Remo
17 James Allen
18 Ken Arnerich
19 Jeff Rutledge
20 Otis Tramble
21 Antonio Cordova
22 Darrin Jackson
23 Scott Miller
24 Rolando Roomes
25 Jim Walsh
26 George Enright
27 Quency Hill
28 Randy Roetter

1982 TCMA Reading Phillies

(Philadelphia Phillies, AA) (black & white)

	MT
Complete Set (22):	32.00

1 Jay Baller
2 Kelly Faulk
3 Butch Hughes
4 Kyle Money
5 John Palmieri
6 Dan Prior
7 Jim Rasmussen
8 Leroy Smith
9 Dennis Thomas
10 Richard Wortham
11 Gerry Willard
12 Al Velasquez
13 Dave Enos
14 Paul Fryer
15 Steve Jeltz
16 Jon Lindsey
17 Joe Nemeth
18 Randy Salava
19 Keith Washington
20 Steve Harvey
21 Tony McDonald
22 John Felske

1982 TCMA Redwood Pioneers

(California Angels, A) (black & white)

	MT
Complete Set (27):	18.00

1 Michael Brooks
2 Steven Eakes
3 Craig Gerber
4 Kevin Halicki
5 Gordon Jones
6 Tim Kammeyer
7 Steve Liddle
8 James Randall
9 Esmyel Romero
10 Michael Saatzer
11 Mark Smelko
12 Jeff Smith
13 Mark Sproesser
14 Darryl Stephens
15 Richard Sundberg
16 Ronald Sylvia
17 Paul Wright
18 Luis Zambrana
19 Harry Oliver
20 Glen Fisher
21 Ronald Hunt
22 Terry Harper
23 Kevin Jacobson
24 Barton Barun
25 Chris Cannizzaro
26 Brian Parfrey
27 Ralph Hartman

1982 TCMA Richmond Braves

(Atlanta Braves, AAA) (color) (Brizzolara can be found in either a catcher's pose - he's a pitcher - or portrait)

	MT
Complete Set, Both Brizzolara (32):	100.00
Complete Set, Brizzolara portrait (31):	32.00

1 Jose Alvarez
2a Tony Brizzolara (catching)
2b Tony Brizzolara (portrait)
3 Tim Cole
4 John D'Acquisto
5 Carlos Diaz
6 Craig McMurtry
7 Donnie Moore
8 Jeff Twitty
9 Roger Weaver
10 Jerry Keller
11 Larry Owen
12 Matt Sinatro
13 Brook Jacoby
14 Gerald Perry
15 Chico Ruiz
16 Paul Runge
17 Paul Zuvella
18 Mike Reynolds
19 Albert Hall
20 Leonel Vargas
21 Bob Porter
22 Mike Colbern
23 Ken Smith
24 Terry Harper
25 Ken Dayley
26 Mike Smith
27 Eddie Haas
28 Johnny Sain
29 Craig Robinson
30 Sam Ayoub
31 Albert Hall, Terry Harper, Brook Jacoby, Gerald Perry, Roger Weaver

1982 TCMA Rochester Red Wings

(Baltimore Orioles, AAA) (color)

	MT
Complete Set (22):	18.00

1 Mike Boddicker
2 John Flinn
3 Bruce MacPherson
4 Craig Minetto
5 Allan Ramirez
6 Cliff Speck
7 Bill Swaggerty
8 Don Welchel
9 Tim Derryberry
10 Dan Graham
11 Willie Royster
12 Glenn Gulliver
13 Rick Jones
14 Rick Lisi
15 Dan Logan
16 Vic Rodriguez
17 John Shelby
18 John Valle
19 Mike Young
20 Lance Nichols
21 Tom Chism
22 Ken Rowe

1982 Trackle Salem Redbirds Postcards

(S.D. Pades, A) (3-1/2" x 5-3/8", b/w, postcard back, players unidentified)

MT
Complete Set (21): 27.50
(1) Tom Brassil
(2) Paul Cacciatore
(3) Tim "Toy" Cannon
(4) Dave Christianson
(5) Rickey Coleman
(6) Steve Garcia
(7) Billy Gerhardt
(8) Rusty Gerhardt
(9) Mark Gillaspie
(10) Bob Klusacek
(11) Andy Krzanik
(12) Paul Noce
(13) Mark Parent
(14) Scott Parsons
(15) George Perez
(16) Steve Stone
(17) Raymie Styons
(18) Scott Thompson
(19) Joe Wood
(20) Jim Zerilla
(21) The Chicken (mascot)

1982 TCMA Salt Lake City Gulls

(Seattle Mariners, AAA) (color)

MT
Complete Set (25): 15.00
1 Doug Merrifield
2 Jamie Allen
3 Rod Allen
4 Rich Bordi
5 Al Chambers
6 Bryan Clark
7 Roy Clark
8 Steve Finch
9 Gary Gray
10 Tracy Harris
11 Mike Hart
12 Vance McHenry
13 Orlando Mercado
14 Ron Musselman
15 Casey Parsons
16 Domingo Ramos
17 Brian Snyder
18 Bob Stoddard
19 Roy Thomas
20 Dave Valle
21 Sammye Welborn
22 Matt Young
23 Manny Estrada
24 Bobby Floyd
25 Joe Decker

1982 TCMA Spokane Indians

(California Angels, AAA) (color)

MT
Complete Set (26): 14.00
1 Steve Brown
2 Craig Eaton
3 Rick Foley
4 Mickey Mahler
5 Fred Martinez
6 Paul Olden
7 Jeff Schneider
8 Rick Steirer
9 Mike Walters
10 Mike Bishop
11 Steve Herz
12 Jerry Narron
13 Jeff Bertoni
14 Craig Cacek
15 Scott Carnes
16 John Harris
17 Steve Lubratich
18 Les Pearsey
19 Mike Brown
20 Tom Brunansky
21 Ron Jackson
22 Pepe Mangual
23 Gary Pettis
24 Moose Stubing
25 Joe Coleman
26 Leonard Garcia

1982 Fritsch Springfield Cardinals

(St. Louis Cardinals, A) (9a is a sample card, not issued with or included in the set price)

MT
Complete Set (24): 10.00
1 Team Logo/Checklist
2 Dave Bialas
3 Bruce "Pic" Miller
4 Bill Lyons
5 Mike Pittman
6 Freddie Silva
7 Robert Hicks
8 Tom Epple
9a Dan Stryffeler (bat on shoulder) (sample card)
9b Dan Stryffeler (bat off shoulder) (regular issue)
10 Gus Malespin
11 Steve Winfield
12 Danny Cox
13 Greg Dunn
14 Bobby Kish
15 Tom Dozier
16 Marty Mason
17 Alan Hunsinger
18 Don Collins
19 Mike Harris
20 Randy Hunt
21 Deron Thomas
22 Harry McCulla
23 Brad Bennett
24 Francisco Batista

1982 TCMA Syracuse Chiefs

(Toronto Blue Jays, AAA) (color) (Larson, O'Keefe and Whitmer are scarce late-issue cards)

MT
Complete Set, w/late-issues (29): 75.00
Partial Set, no late-issues (26): 30.00
1 Mike Barlow
2 Tom Dixon
3 Mark Eichhorn
4 Mark Geisel
5 John Littlefield
6 Frank Ricelli
7 Ken Schrom
8 Steve Senteney
9 Jackson Todd
10 Jim Wright
11 Jim Gaudet
12 Ramon Lora
13 Gene Petralli
14 Dave Baker
15 Charlie Beamon
16 Brian Doyle
17 Tony Fernandez
18 Fred Manrique
19 Glenn Adams
20 George Bell
21 Pedro Hernandez
22 Creighton Tevlin
23 Mitch Webster
24 Doug Ault
25 Tom Craig
26 Jim Beauchamp
27a Duane Larson
27b Rick O'Keefe
28 Dan Whitmer

1982 Syracuse Chiefs team issue

(Toronto Blue Jays, AAA) (black & white, 3-1/4" x 5", blank-back)

MT
Complete Set (24): 150.00
1 Tony Fernandez
2 Fred Manrique
5 Dave Baker
6 Brian Doyle
8 Jim Beauchamp
10 Charlie Beamon
11 George Bell
12 Gino Petralli
14 Tom Dixon
16 Jackson Todd
17 Creighton Tevlin
18 Pedro Hernandez
20 Pete Dempsey
21 Steve Senteney
22 Ken Schrom
23 Mitch Webster
24 Glenn Adams
25 Doug Ault
26 John Littlefield
28 Mark Eichhorn
29 Dan Whitmer
30 Mike Barlow
31 Rick O'Keeffe (O'Keefe)
32 Dave Geisel

1982 TCMA Tacoma Tigers

(Oakland A's, AAA) (color) (Comstock and Sexton are scarce late-issue cards)

MT
Complete Set, w/Comstock, Sexton (39): 80.00
Partial Set, no Comstock, Sexton (37): 15.00
1 DeWayne Bruce
2 Don Fowler
3 Dave Heaverlo
4 Bill Castro
5 Gorman Heimueller
6 Dennis Kinney
7 Eric Mustad
8 Dave Patterson
9 Bill Swiacki
10 Ed Figueroa
11 Darryl Cias
12 Tim Hosley
13 Kevin Bell
14 Danny Goodwin
15 Paul Mize
16 Johnny Evans
17 Jim Nettles
18 Dennis Sherow
19 Ed Nottle
20 Larry Davis
21 Art Popham
22 Stan Naccarato
23 Keith Atherton
24 Jeff Jones
25 Brian Kingman
26 Pat Dempsey
27 Robert Kearney
28 Mack Babitt
29 Keith Drumright
30 Mike Gallego
31 Kelvin Moore
32 Tony Phillips
33 Rick Bosetti
34 Michael Davis
35 Bob Grandas
36 Mitchell Page
37 Tigers Mascot
38 Johnny Sexton
39 Keith Comstock

1982 TCMA Tidewater Tides

(N.Y. Mets, AAA) (color) (Cubbage card is scarce late-issue)

MT
Complete Set, w/Cubbage (26): 55.00
Partial Set, no Cubbage (25): 26.00
1 Rick Ownbey
2 Kelvin Chapman
3 Mike Davis
4 Mike Fitzgerald
5 Mike Howard
6 Bruce Bochy
7 Gil Flores
8 Brian Giles
9 Phil Mankowski
10 Ronald MacDonald
11 Rusty Tillman
12 Rick Anderson
13 Ron Darling
14 Terry Leach
15 Jose Oquendo
16 Marvell Wynne
17 Greg Biercevicz
18 Scott Holman
19 Jack Aker
20 Brent Gaff
21 Steve Ratzer
22 Bob Schaefer
23 Dave Von Ohlen
24 Walt Terrell
25 Mike Anicich
26 Mike Cubbage

1982 TCMA Toledo Mud Hens

(Minnesota Twins, AAA) (color) (#26-28 are scarce late-issue cards; #25 not issued)

MT
Complete Set, w/#26-28 (27): 75.00
Partial Set, no #26-28 (24): 32.00
1 Don Cooper
2 Glenn Dooner
3 Steve Korczyk
4 Jeff Little
5 Jack O'Connor
6 Bob Veselic
7 Frank Viola
8 Mike Walters
9 Rick Williams
10 Harry Saferight
11 Ray Smith
12 Rod Booker
13 Jim Christensen
14 Dave Machemer
15 Ivan Mesa
16 Kelly Snider
17 Greg Wells
18 Mike Sodders
19 Elijah Bonaparte
20 Randy Bush
21 Rick Sofield
22 Scott Ulger
23 Cal Ermer
24 Buck Chamberlin
26 Pete Filson
27 Doug Fregin
28 Bob Mitchell

1982 TCMA Tucson Toros

(Houston Astros, AAA) (color)

MT
Complete Set (28): 20.00
1 Bert Pena
2 Chris Jones
3 Mark Ross
4 Tom Vessey
5 Steve Lake
6 Greg Cypret
7 Billy Doran
8 Tim Tolman
9 Jim Tracy
10 Larry Ray
11 Harry Spillman (Spilman)
12 Jim McDonald
13 Rickey Keeton
14 Zacarias Paris
15 Bert Roberge
16 Rick Lysander
17 Mark Miggins
18 Billy Smith
19 Bobby Sprowl
20 George Cappuzzello
21 Gordy Pladson
22 Bill Wood
23 James Hand
24 Jim Johnson
25 Gary Tuck
26 Dennis Menke (Denis)
27 Dave Labossiere
28 Batboys

1982 TCMA Tulsa Drillers

(Texas Rangers, AA) (color) (#25-28 are scarce late-issue cards)

MT
Complete Set, w/#25-28 (28): 75.00
Partial Set, no #25-28 (25): 30.00
1 Tom Henke
2 Brad Mengwasser
3 Martin Leach
4 Dennis Long
5 Mike Mason
6 Tim Henry
7 Al Lachowicz
8 Kevin Richards
9 Jim Gideon
10 Tom Dunbar
11 Don Scott
12 Tracy Cowger
13 Steve Moore
14 Carmelo Aguayo
15 Dave Stockstill
16 Oscar Majia
17 Dan Murphy
18 Ron Dillard
19 Mike Jirschele
20 Gerry Neutang
21 Robert Ball
22 Tom Burgess
23 Orlando Gomez
24 Joe Nemeth
25 Curtis Wilkerson
26 Brett Benza
27 Steve Buechele
28 Mike Rubel

1982 TCMA Vancouver Canadians

(Milwaukee Brewers, AAA) (color)

MT
Complete Set (24): 15.00
1 Bob Skube
2 Frank Thomas
3 Bill Schroder (Schroeder)
4 Kevin Bass
5 Willie Lozada (Lozado)
6 John Skorochocki
7 Lawrence Rush
8 Ed Irvine
9 Stan Davis
10 Doug Loman
11 Steve Herz
12 Tim Cook
13 Doug Jones
14 Mike Madden
15 Rich Olsen
16 Frank DiPino
17 Pete Ladd
18 Chuck Valley
19 Rick Kranitz
20 Jaimie Cocanower (Jamie)
21 Chuck Porter
22 Mike Anderson
23 Eli Grba
24 Brian Thorson

1982 TCMA Vero Beach Dodgers

(L.A. Dodgers, A) (black & white)

MT
Complete Set (29): 50.00
1 Roberto Alexandro
2 Ernie Borbon
3 Paul Cozzolino
4 Dave Daniel
5 Rich Felt
6 Sid Fernandez
7 Robert Kenyon
8 Steve Martin
9 Peyton Mosher
10 Matt Reeves
11 Robert Slezak
12 Paul Bard
13 Steve Boncore
14 Jack Fimple
15 Robert Allen
16 Carmelo Alvarez
17 Jerry Bendorf
18 Sid Bream
19 Harold Perkins
20 Larry See
21 Ralph Bryant
22 Cecil Espy
23 Tony Lachowetz
24 Stu Pederson
25 Bob Seymour
26 Terry Collins
27 Rob Giesecke
28 Dave Wallace
29 John Shoemaker

1982 TCMA Waterbury Reds

(Cincinnati Reds, AA) (color)

MT
Complete Set (23): 35.00
1 Bill Landrum
2 Larry Buckle
3 Keefe Cato
4 Kenneth Jones

5 Gene Menees
6 Clem Freeman
7 Bob Buchanan
8 Jeff Russell
9 Ronald Robinson
10 Nicholas Fiorillo
11 Raymond Corbett
12 Michael Kripner
13 Skeeter Barnes
14 Danny Tartabull
15 Eski Viltz
16 Paul Herring
17 Glen Franklin
18 Mark Gilbert
19 Kenneth Scarpace
20 Tony Walker
21 Ronald Little
22 Crestwell Pratt
23 Jim Lett

1982 TCMA Waterloo Indians

(Cleveland Indians, A) (black & white) (#26-28 are scarce late-issue cards)

MT
Complete Set, w/#26-28 (28): 100.00
Partial Set, no #26-28 (25): 15.00
1 Steve Cushing
2 Rich Doyle
3 Ralph Elpin
4 Mike Jeffcoat
5 Wayne Johnson
6 Ricky Lintz
7 Rodney McDonald
8 John Miglio
9 Ramon Romero
10 David Wick
11 Alan Willis
12 John Malkin
13 Phillip Wilson
14 Rod Carraway
15 Winston Ficklin
16 Mike Gertz
17 Sam Martin
18 Junior Noboa
19 Ed Tanner
20 George Albert
21 Jerry Nalley
22 Chris Rehbaum
23 Dwight Taylor
24 Mike Taylor
25 Randy Washington
26 Gomer Hodge
27 Vic Albury
28 Ron Wollenhaupt

1982 Fritsch Waterloo Indians

(Cleveland Indians, A) (5a is a sample card, not issued with or included in the set price)

MT
Complete Set (28): 8.00
1 Team Logo/Checklist
2 Gomer Hodge
3 Vic Albury
4 Ron Wollenhaupt
5a Rickey Lintz (left wrist not showing) (sample card)
5b Rickey Lintz (left wrist showing) (regular issue)
6 Jerry Nalley
7 Phil Wilson
8 Rod McDonald
9 Rod Carraway
10 Steve Roche
11 Dave Gallagher
12 Ralph Elpin
13 Dave Wick
14 Mike Gertz
15 Steve Cushing
16 John Miglio
17 Chris Rehbaum
18 Marlin Methven
19 Winston Ficklin
20 John Malkin
21 Sammy Martin
22 Ed Tanner
23 Rich Doyle
24 Jose Roman
25 Wayne Johnson
26 Randy Washington
27 George Alpert
28 Junior Noboa

Value of modern team sets is often predicated as much on inclusion of star player's early cards as on scarcity of the issue.

1982 Fritsch Wausau Timbers

(Seattle Mariners, A)

MT
Complete Set (31): 10.00
1 Team Logo/Checklist
2 Team Photo
3 Jack Roeder
4 Stan Edmonds
5 Curtis Kouba
6 Bart Mackie
7 Joe Benes
8 Randy Meier
9 Donell Nixon
10 Ivan Calderon
11 Eric Parent
12 Mike Bucci
13 Bret McAfee
14 Ronn Dixon
15 Martin O. Enriquez
16 Luis Trinidad H. Castillo
17 R.J. Harrison
18 Mike Johnson
19 Mitch Zwolensky
20 Donny Holland
21 Jay Michael Erdahl
22 Mike Evans
23 Gary Pellant
24 Don Diego Pierce
25 Angel Vicente Fonseca
26 Bill Taylor
27 Ric Wilson
28 Chip Conklin
29 Terry Hayes
30 Tom Hunt
31 Bob Gisselman

1982 TCMA West Haven A's

(Oakland A's, AA) (black & white)

MT
Complete Set (29): 18.00
1 Brian Abraham
2 Bert Bradley
3 Jeff Carey
4 Chris Codiroli
5 Keith Comstock
6 Chuck Hensley
7 Bill Krueger
8 Lou Marietta
9 Jack Smith
10 Bill Bathe
11 Chuck Fick
12 Mike Gallego
13 Steve Gelfarb
14 Donnie Hill
15 Monte McAbee
16 Paul Mize
17 Tim Pyznarski
18 Ron Wilkerson
19 Mike Woodard
20 Jim Bennett
21 Lynn Garrett
22 Rodney Hobbs
23 Rusty McNealy
24 Luis Rojas
25 Dennis Sherow
26 Bob Didier
27 Keith Lieppman
28 Scot Pyle
29 Walt Horn

1982 Wichita Aeros team issue

(Montreal Expos, AAA) (color)

MT
Complete Set (21): 25.00
(1) Joseph Abone
(2) Felipe Alou
(3) Douglas Capilla
(4) Michael Gates
(5) Thomas Gorman
(6) Batting Leaders (Roy Johnson)
(7) Roy Johnson
(8) Wally Johnson
(9) Richard Little
(10) Willard Mueller
(11) Richard Murray
(12) Batting Leaders (Ken Phelps)
(13) Kenneth Phelps
(14) Luis Quintana
(15) Richard Ramos
(16) Pat Rooney
(17) William Sattler
(18) Kim Seaman
(19) Christopher Smith
(20) Michael Stenhouse
(21) Thomas Weighaus

1982 Trackle Winston-Salem Red Sox Postcards

(Boston Red Sox, A) (3-1/2" x 5-3/8", b/w, postcard back, players unidentified)

MT
Complete Set (14): 20.00
(1) John Ackley
(2) Tony Beal
(3) Todd Benzinger
(4) Kevin Clinton
(5) Charles Fisher
(6) Scott Gering
(7) Jeff Hunter
(8) Jeff Ledbetter
(9) Dave Malpeso
(10) Tom McCarthy
(11) Mark Meleski
(12) Brandon Plainte
(13) David Scheller
(14) Miguel Valdez

1982 Fritsch Wisconsin Rapids Twins

(Minnesota Twins, A)

MT
Complete Set (27): 10.00
1 Team Logo/Checklist
2 Greg Kipfer
3 Ken Staples
4 Mike Weiermiller
5 Dave Hoyt
6 Mark Wright
7 Alvaro "Espi" Espinoza
8 Paul Fleming
9 Johnny Salery
10 Herbert Carter
11 Rick Scheetz
12 Larry James Mikesell
13 Sebby Borriello
14 Mark Portugal
15 Jose Gil
16 Barry "B.C." Houston
17 Dick Henkemeyer
18 Phil Franko
19 John Foster
20 Eric Porter
21 Willi Flores
22 Mark Larcom
23 Steve Aragon
24 Marc J. Page
25 Jeff Arney
26 Craig Henderson
27 Rhett Whisman

1983 TCMA Albany-Colonie A's

(Oakland A's, AA) (black & white)

MT
Complete Set (20): 75.00
1 Jesse Anderson
2 Allen Edwards
3 Mark Fellows
4 Mark Ferguson
5 Paul Josephson
6 Mike Lynes
7 Steve Ontiveros
8 Gary Wex
9 Jim Durrman
10 Charlie O'Brien
11 Mike Ashman
12 Steve Kiefer
13 Tim Pyznarski
14 Luis Quinones
15 Phil Stephenson
16 Sly Young
17 Luis Bravo
18 Ron Harrison
19 Tom Romano
20 Pete Whisenant

1983 TCMA Albuquerque Dukes

(L.A. Dodgers, AAA) (color)

MT
Complete Set (25): 45.00
1 Franklin Stubbs
2 Bert Geiger
3 Orel Hershiser
4 Brian Holton
5 Dean Rennicke
6 Rich Rodas
7 Paul Voigt
8 Larry White
9 Steve Perry
10 Alex Taveras
11 Jack Fimple
12 Scotti Madison
13 Brent Strom
14 Candy Maldonado
15 Sid Bream
16 Ross Jones
17 German Rivera
18 Greg Schultz
19 Ed Amelung
20 Tony Brewer
21 Ernesto Borbon
22 Lemmie Miller
23 Del Crandall
24 Dave Cohea
25 Dick McLaughlin

1983 Albuquerque Dukes team-issue photos

(L.A. Dodgers, AAA) (Color photo prints sold singly at stadium for $2 each)

MT
Complete Set (16): 65.00
(1) Ed Amelung
(2) Ernesto Borbon
(3) Sid Bream
(4) Tony Brewer
(5) Terry Collins
(6) Jack Fimple
(7) John Franco
(8) Orel Hershiser
(9) Scotti Madison
(10) Lemmie Miller
(11) Steve Perry
(12) Dean Rennicke
(13) German Rivera
(14) Rick Rodas
(15) Franklin Stubbs
(16) Paul Voight

1983 TCMA Alexandria Dukes

(Pittsburgh Pirates, A) (black & white)

MT
Complete Set (31): 85.00
1 Bobby Lyons
2 Sam Khalifa
3 Chuck Meadows
4 Scott Borland
5 Nick Castaneda
6 Jim Opie
7 Marvin Clack
8 Pete Rice
9 Art Ray
10 Scott Bailes
11 John Lipon
12 Johnny Taylor
13 Jim Aulenback
14 Chris Lein
15 David Tumbas
16 Roberto Bonilla
17 Thomas Martinez
18 Sean Faherty
19 Craig Brown
20 David Johnson
21 Steve Susce
22 Jim Felt
23 Nelson de la Russa (de la Rosa)
24 Eric Zimmerman
25 Steve Lewis
26 Rubin Rodriguez
27 Ravelo Manzanillo
28 Mike Quade
29 Jim Buckmier
30 Dorn Taylor
31 Lorenzo Bundy

1983 TCMA Anderson Braves

(Atlanta Braves, A) (color)

MT
Complete Set (33): 20.00
1 Bill MacKay
2 Rick Albert
3 Skip Weisman
4 Randy Ingle
5 Dave May
6 Buzz Capra
7 John Baker
8 Jose Cano
9 Al Candelaria
10 Chip Reese
11 Ken Lynn
12 Charlie Morelock
13 John Mortillaro
14 Jim Rivera
15 Randy Rogers
16 Maximo Rosario
17 Rudy Torres
18 Sylverio Valdez
19 Ramon Vargas
20 Dave Griffin
21 Ralph Giansanti
22 Jay Palma
23 Andres Thomas
24 Dave Van Horn
25 Russ Anglin
26 Clint Brill
27 Jerry Ragsdale
28 Paul Llewellyn
29 Dave Morris
30 Larry Moser
31 Jay Roberts
32 Rich Thompson
33 Jeff Wagner

1983 Fritsch Appleton Foxes

(Chicago White Sox, A)

MT
Complete Set (30): 10.00
1 Bill Smith
2 Mike Trujillo
3 Dave McLaughlin
4 Kim Christensen
5 Joel Mc Keon
6 Jim Best
7 Rich DeVincenzo
8 Pat Adams
9 Steve Noworyta
10 Craig Smajstrla
11 Mike Henley
12 Rolando Pino
13 John Cangelosi
14 Ken Williams
15 Team Photo
16 Team Photo
17 Edwin Correa
18 Ed Sedar
19 Bill Atkinson
20 Al Jones
21 Greg Tarnow
22 Ron Karkovice
23 David Kinsel
24 Johnny Moses
25 John Boles
26 Garry Keeton
27 Don Ruzek
28 Bill Sandry
29 Al Heath
30 Team Logo/Checklist

1983 TCMA Arkansas Travelers

(St. Louis Cardinals, AA) (black & white)

MT
Complete Set (25): 70.00
1 Mike Rhodes
2 Ruben Gotay
3 Terry Clark
4 Kurt Kepshire
5 Walter Pierce
6 Mike Barba
7 Bill Thomas
8 Steve Winfield
9 Jerry Johnson
10 John Adams

11 Randy Hunt
12 Mark Salas
13 Mike Harris
14 Mike Wolters
15 Terry Pendelton
16 Luis Ojeda
17 Greg Guin
18 Alan Hunsinger
19 Rod Booker
20 Fran Batista
21 Gotay Mills
22 Larry Reynolds
23 Nick Leyva
24 Jorge Aranzamendi
25 Dave England

1983 TCMA Beaumont Golden Gators

(San Diego Padres, AA) (black & white) (card #3 of Steve Johnson is rarely found in Mint condition)

MT
Complete Set (23): 75.00
1 Mike Martin
2 Ozzie Guillen
3 Steve Johnson
4 Randy Kaczmarski
5 Walt Vanderbush
6 Jim Leopold
7 Bob Patterson
8 Mark Williamson
9 Marty Lain
10 Dan Purpura
11 John Kruk
12 Steve Garcia
13 Mark Parent
14 Jeff Ronk
15 Mark Gillaspie
16 Pat Casey
17 Frank Ricci
18 Willie Hardwick
19 Ray Haywood, Jr.
20 James Steels
21 Jack Maloof
22 Allen Gerhardt
23 Gene Confreda

1983 Fritsch Beloit Brewers

(Milwaukee Brewers, A)

MT
Complete Set (30): 12.50
1 Butch Kirby
2 Woolsey Rice
3 Dewey James
4 Jeff Gyarmati
5 John Mitchell
6 John Antonelli
7 Hank Landers
8 Jay Aldrich
9 Bruce Williams
10 Mark Johnston
11 Doug Norton
12 Steve Anderson
13 Bill Nowlan
14 Don Whiting
15 Team Logo/Checklist
16 Tim Nordbrook
17 Dave Tarrolly
18 Brian Finley
19 Jim Teahan
20 Tim Utecht
21 Billy Joe Robidoux
22 Chuck Crim
23 Edgar Diaz
24 Fritz Fedor
25 Dan Scarpetta
26 Hector Quinones
27 Chris Bosio
28 Stan Boroski
29 Joel Weatherford
---- Team Logo

1983 TCMA Birmingham Barons

(Detroit Tigers, AA) (color)

MT
Complete Set (25): 12.50
1 Raul Tovar
2 Don Gordon
3 Dan Williams
4 Dwight Lowry
5 Stan Younger
6 Dave Hawarny
7 Mark Smith
8 Doug Baker
9 Don Heinkel
10 Bruce Robbins
11 George Foussianes
12 Bob Melvin
13 Greg Norman
14 Chuck Cary
15 Scott Tabor
16 Nelson Simmons
17 Scottie Earl
18 Ted Davis
19 Colin Ward
20 Jon Furman
21 Pedro Chavez
22 Keith Comstock
23 Troy Dixon
24 Roger Mason
25 Roy Majtyka

1983 TCMA Buffalo Bisons

(Cleveland Indians, AA) (color)

MT
Complete Set (25): 27.50
1 Robin Fuson
2 Wayne Johnson
3 Rich Doyle
4 Gordie Glaser
5 Rod McDonald
6 Tom Owens
7 Rich Thompson
8 Jeff Green
9 Ramon Romero
10 John Malkin
11 Tim Glass
12 Everett Rey
13 Sal Rende
14 Jim Wilson
15 Shanie Dugas
16 Kelly Gruber
17 Jeff Moronko
18 Rene Quinones
19 Dave Gallagher
20 Ed Saavedra
21 Dwight Taylor
22 George Cecchetti
23 Joe Charboneau
24 Al Gallagher
25 Jack Aker

1983 TCMA Burlington Rangers

(Texas Rangers, A) (color)

MT
Complete Set (28): 16.00
1 Barry Bass
2 John Buckley
3 Glenn Cook
4 Jose Guzman
5 Dave Hopkins
6 Terry Johnson
7 Chris Joslin
8 Randy Kramer
9 Tim Maki
10 Todd Schulte
11 Mike Soper
12 Elijah Ben
13 Bob Brower
14 George Crum
15 Ron Dillard
16 Bob Gergen
17 Otto Gonzales
18 Whitney Harry
19 Bob Hausladen
20 Brendan Hennessey
21 Jeff Mace
22 Sam Sorce
23 Kevin Stock
24 Mark Sutton
25 Tony Triplett
26 Orlando Gomez
27 Greg Jemison
28 Greg Campbell

1983 Fritsch Burlington Rangers

(Texas Rangers, A)

MT
Complete Set (30): 12.50
1 Bob Hausladen
2 Todd Schulte
3 Sam Sorce
4 George Crum
5 Randy Kramer
6 Antonio Triplett
7 Jose Guzman
8 Elijah Ben
9 Barry Bass
10 Terry Johnson
11 Bobby Brower
12 Glen Cook
13 Bob Gergen
14 Ron Dillard
15 Whitney J. Harry
16 Chris Joslin
17 Otto Gonzalez
18 Brendan Hennessy
19 Tim Maki
20 John Buckley
21 Mark Sutton
22 Kevin Stock
23 David Hopkins
24 Jeff Mace
25 Greg Campbell
26 Greg Jemison
28 Team Logo/Checklist
29 Team Logo/Fritsch Ad
30 Sponsor Card

1983 TCMA Butte Copper Kings

(K.C. Royals, Rookie) (black & white)

MT
Complete Set (33): 32.00
1 Dennis Boatright
2 Dan Chelini
3 Dave Digirolama
4 Tom Edens
5 Phil George
6 Gary Klein
7 Stefan Lipson
8 Charley Luman
9 Randy Robinson
10 John Serritella
11 Jose Torres
12 Rob Vodvarka
13 Dave Landrith
14 Tom Niemann
15 Stan Oxner
16 Jim Bagnall
17 Vic Davila
18 Jere Longenecker
19 Mike Miller
20 Kevin Seitzer
21 Kevin Stanley
22 Mark Van Blaricom
23 Edward Allen
24 John Devich
25 Tommy Mohr
26 Dave Rooker
27 John Rubel
28 Jeff Schulz
29 Joe Kasunick
30 Tommy Jones
31 Guy Hansen
32 Bruce Platt
33 Tom Osowski

1983 TCMA Cedar Rapids Reds

(Cincinnati Reds, A) (color)

MT
Complete Set (28): 35.00
1 Bruce Kimm
2 Scott Jones
3 Dave Lochner
4 Mike Knox
5 Glenn Spagnola
6 Billy Hawley
7 Mike Konderla
8 Tim Scott
9 Tim Reynolds
10 Joe Stalp
11 Louie Trujillo
12 Steve Padia
13 Rob Murphy
14 Buddy Pryor
15 Scott Radloff
16 Tom Riley
17 Delwyn Young
18 Dave Haberle
19 Terry Lee
20 Mike Manfre
21 Vince Rover
22 Kal Daniels
23 Orsino Hill
24 Jeff Rhodes
25 Jay Munson
26 Don Buchheister
27 Batboys
28 Wayne Harmon

1983 Fritsch Cedar Rapids Reds

(Cincinnati Reds, A)

MT
Complete Set (26): 10.00
1 Tim Reynolds
2 Buddy Pryor
3 Tim Scott
4 Joe Stalp
5 Tom Riley
6 Wayne Harmon
7 Jay Munson
8 Dave Lochner
9 Mike Knox
10 Billy Hawley
11 Dave Haberle
12 Louie Trujillo
13 Terry Lee
14 Mike Konderla
15 Jeff Rhodes
16 Glenn Spagnola
17 Kal Daniels
18 Scott Jones
19 Vin Rover
20 Mike Manfre
21 Scott Radloff
22 Bruce Kimm
23 Orsino Hill
24 Rob Murphy
25 Steve Padia
26 Team Logo/Checklist

1983 TCMA Charleston Charlies

(Cleveland Indians, AAA) (color)

MT
Complete Set (22): 10.00
1 Jay Baller
2 Mike Jeffcoat
3 Larry Hrynko
4 Jerry Reed
5 Roy Smith
6 Sandy Whitol
7 Doug Simunic
8 Jerry Willard
9 Luis DeLeon
10 Angelo Logrande
11 Juan Pacho
12 Karl Pagel
13 Jack Perconte
14 Tim Norrid
15 Rodney Craig
16 Wil Culmer
17 Kevin Rhomberg
18 Otto Velez
19 Ed Glynn
20 Vic Albury
21 Steve Cisczon
22 Doc Edwards

1983 TCMA Charleston Royals

(K.C. Royals, A) (black & white)

MT
Complete Set (26): 18.00
1 Mark Pirruccello
2 Nicky Richards
3 Joe Szekely
4 Jim Bagnall
5 Chris Bryeans
6 Craig Goodin
7 Keith Hempfield
8 Bill Phillips
9 Rich Vitato
10 Edward Allen
11 Roland Oruna
12 Jack Shuffield
13 Van Snider
14 Richard Aube
15 John Bryant
16 Doug Cook
17 John Davis
18 Bob De Bord
19 Tom Drizmala
20 Rich Goodin
21 Ron McCormack
22 Israel Sanchez
23 John Serritella
24 Roy Tanner
25 Duane Gustavson
26 Mark Farnsworth

1983 TCMA Chattanooga Lookouts

(Seattle Mariners, AA) (black & white)

MT
Complete Set (28): 170.00
1 Darnell Coles
2 Paul Serna
3 Chris Hunger
4 Joe Whitmer
5 Ramon Estepa
6 Danny Tartabull
7 Vic Martin
8 Alvin Davis
9 Mike Bucci
10 Miguel Negron
11 Mark Langston
12 Mickey Bowers
13 Bob Randolph
14 Robert Hudson
15 Don (Clay) Hill
16 Jeff Stottlemyre
17 Tracy Harris
18 Kevin King
19 Kevin Dukes
20 John Burden
21 Mark Cahill
22 Kevin Steger
23 Tom Hunt
24 Chief Lookout
25 Harry Landreth
26 Dave Valle
27 Ivan Calderon
---- Team Photo

1983 Fritsch Clinton Giants

(S.F. Giants, A)

MT
Complete Set (30): 10.00
1 Bill Kuehn, Gus Stokes
2 Eric Halberg
3 Scott Norman
4 Billy Cabell
5 Jim Weir
6 Greg Lynn
7 Marty Baier
8 Ramon Bautista
9 Scott Rainey
10 Gene Lambert
11 Orlando Blackwell
12 Davis Tavarez
13 Bob Naber
14 Alonzo Powell
15 Mike Empting
16 John Hughes
17 Brian Bargerhuff
18 Alan Marr
19 Ken Mills
20 Kelvin Smith
21 Van Sowards
22 Kurt Mattson
23 Ed Stewart
24 Dennie Taft
25 Marty DeMerritt
26 Scott Blanke
27 Randy Weibel
28 Jeff Gladden
29 Bill Lachemann
30 Team Logo/Checklist

1983 TCMA Columbus Astros

(Houston Astros, AA) (black & white)

MT
Complete Set (24): 45.00
1 George Bjorkman
2 Ed Cuervo
3 John Csefalvay
4 Mike Grace
5 Jim Sherman
6 Mark Strucher
7 Larry Simcox
8 Steve Benson
9 Eric Bullock
10 Ty Gainey
11 Glenn Davis
12 Fransisco Jabalera
13 Jeff Calhoun
14 Jeff Heathcock
15 Jim MacDonald
16 Tim Meckes
17 Zac Paris
18 Pat Perry
19 Ben Snyder
20 Jack Smith
21 Bob Sprowl
22 Jack Hiatt
23 Ken Bolek
24 Rex Jones

Values shown are a national average. Some teams and players enjoy regional popularity which may affect market prices.

1983 TCMA Columbus Clippers

(N.Y. Yankees, AAA) (color)

	MT
Complete Set (27):	22.50

1 Johnny Oates
2 Coaching Staff
3 Juan Espino
4 Bradley Gulden
5 Silton Fontenot
6 David Wehrmeister
7 Timothy Burke
8 Dennis Rasmussen
9 Clay Christiansen
10 Stefan Wever
11 Curt Kaufman
12 Jesus Hernaiz
13 Guy Elston
14 Benjamin Callahan III
15 Stephen Balboni
16 Marshall Brant
17 Bert Campaneris
18 Edwin Rodriguez
19 Barry Evans
20 Robert Meacham
21 Clell Hobson, Jr.
22 Michael Patterson
23 Matthew Winters
24 James Hart
25 Otis Nixon
26 Brian Dayett
27 Rowland Office

1983 TCMA Daytona Beach Astros

(Houston Astros, A) (black & white)

	MT
Complete Set (27):	16.00

1 Dave Cripe
2 Stan Hough
3 Rich Bombard
4 Mike Callahan
5 Guillermo Castro
6 Manny Hernandez
7 Mark Knudson
8 Mike Hogan
9 Uvaldo Regaldo
10 Ed Reilly
11 Rex Schimpf
12 Jamey Shouppe
13 Tom Wiedenbauer
14 Don Berti
15 Jeff Datz
16 Jamie Williams
17 Randy Braun
18 Glenn Carpenter
19 Juan Delgado
20 Gary D'Onofrio
21 Steve McAllister
22 Ricardo Rivera
23 Jim Thomas
24 Mike Botkin
25 Curtis Burke
26 Louie Meadows
27 Tony Walker

1983 TCMA Durham Bulls

(Atlanta Braves, A) (color)

	MT
Complete Set (29):	22.00

1 Chip Childress
2 Steve Chmil
3 Terry Cormack
4 Inocencio Guerrero
5 Johnny Hatcher
6 Pat Hodge
7 Scott Hood
8 Mike Knox
9 Bob Luzon
10 Bryan Neal
11 Tony Neuendorff
12 Ken Scanlon
13 Rick Siriano
14 Freddy Tiburcio
15 Bob Tumpane
16 Mike Bormann
17 Dave Clay
18 Tim Cole
19 Mark Lance
20 Rich Leggatt
21 Dennis Lubert
22 Ike Pettaway
23 Allen Sears
24 Zane Smith
25 Duane Ward
26 Matt West
27 Tim Alexander
28 Brian Snitker
29 Leo Mazzone

1983 TCMA El Paso Diablos

(Milwaukee Brewers, AA) (color)

	MT
Complete Set (25):	12.00

1 Dan Burns
2 Eric Peyton
3 Joe Henderson
4 Jim Paciorek
5 Bryan Duquette
6 Stan Davis
7 Mark Effrig
8 Rene Quinones
9 Mike Felder
10 Juan Castillo
11 Stan Levi
12 Garrett Nago
13 Bill Max
14 Ray Gallo
15 Bryan Clutterbuck
16 Steve Parrott
17 Tim Crews
18 Al Price
19 Carlos Ponce
20 Kevin McCoy
21 Earnest Riles
22 Frank Thomas
23 Jack Lazorko
24 Bob Schroeck
25 Lee Sigman

1983 TCMA Erie Cardinals

(St. Louis Cardinals, A) (color)

	MT
Complete Set (25):	24.00

1 Paul Mangiardi
2 Joe Rigoli
3 John Rigos
4 Jim ReBoulet
5 Wilfredo Martinez
6 Bill Packer
7 Mark Dougherty
8 Keith Turnbull
9 Jamie Brisco
10 Brian Farley
11 Mike Behrend
12 Mark Angelo
13 Jeff Pasquali
14 Scott Pleis
15 Chuck McGrath
16 Jeff Gass
17 Phil Burwell
18 John Costello
19 Tim Kavanaugh
20 Tom Pagnozzi
21 Tom Rossi
22 Ernie Carrasco
23 Tom Caulfield
24 Mike Robinson
25 Kurt Kaull

1983 TCMA Evansville Triplets

(Detroit Tigers, AAA) (color)

	MT
Complete Set (25):	10.00

1 Mark Dacko
2 Craig Eaton
3 David Gumpert
4 Bryan Kelly
5 Steven Luebber
6 Charles Nall
7 Randall O'Neill
8 Larry Pashnick
9 Davis Rucker
10 Patrick Underwood
11 Martin Castillo
12 Willie Royster
13 Jeffery Bertoni
14 Julio Gonzales
15 Mike Laga
16 Juan Lopez
17 Kenneth Baker
18 Barbaro Garbey
19 Bob Grandas
20 Jeffrey Kenaga
21 Darryl Motley
22 Gordon MacKenzie
23 William Armstrong
24 Mark DeJohn
25 German Barranca

1983 TCMA Glens Falls White Sox

(Chicago White Sox, AA) (black & white)

	MT
Complete Set (24):	50.00

1 Darryl Boston
2 J.B. Brown
3 Wes Kent
4 Monte McAbee
5 Scott Meier
6 Ed Miles
7 Mike Morse
8 Dave Nix
9 Curt Reed
10 Ramon Romero
11 Pat Kelly
12 Tom Brennan
13 Keith Desjarlais
14 Mike Maitland
15 Homer Moncrief
16 Robert Moore
17 Tom Mullen
18 Steve Pastrovich
19 Wayne Schuckert
20 Mike Tanzi
21 Mike Withrow
22 Adrian Garrett
23 Lori Corcoran
24 Dick Manning

1983 TCMA Greensboro Hornets

(N.Y. Yankees, A) (color)

	MT
Complete Set (30):	35.00

1 Johnny Baldwin
2 Scott Beahan
3 Ozzie Canseco
4 Jim Corsi
5 Logan Easley
6 John Caston
7 Steve George
8 Randy Graham
9 Rich Gumbert
10 Daryl Humphrey
11 Steve Ray
12 Dick Seidel
13 Randy White
14 Fredi Gonzalez
15 Phil Lombardi
16 Mark Blaser
17 Maurice Ching
18 Mike Fennell
19 Roberto Kelly
20 Pedro Medina
21 Felix Perdomo
22 Jim Riggs
23 Jose Rivera
24 Stan Javier
25 Joe MacKay
26 Tony Russell
27 Carlos Tosca
28 Bill Evers
29 Q.V. Lowe
30 Don McGann

1983 Trackle Hagerstown Suns Postcards

(Baltimore Orioles, A) (3-1/2" x 5-3/8", b/w, postcard back, players unidentified)

	MT
Complete Set (16):	25.00

(1) Tommy Alexander
(2) Paul Bard
(3) Mark Butler
(4) Carlos Cabassa
(5) Carlos Concepcion
(6) Rick Cratch
(7) Jeff Doerr
(8) Pat Dumouchelle
(9) Kenny Gearhart
(10) Mark Leiter
(11) Ears McNeal
(12) Gerry Melillo
(13) Ron Salcedo
(14) Jeff Tipton
(15) Pete Torrez
(16) Jim Traber

1983 TCMA Idaho Falls Athletics

(Oakland A's, A) (black & white)

	MT
Complete Set (34):	16.00

1 Steve Bowens
2 Steve Chasteen
3 Oscar DeChavez
4 Wayne Giddings
5 Dave Hanna
6 Darel Hansen
7 Perry Johnson
8 Mark Leonette
9 Wade Mangum
10 Camilo Pascual
11 Larry Smith
12 Bob Vantrease
13 Tony Wadley
14 Joe Law
15 Eric Garrett
16 Matt Held
17 Mike Rojas
18 Steve Chumas
19 Darrell Dull
20 Rich Borowski
21 Twayne Harris
22 Rob Nelson
23 Felix Pagan
24 Mike Rantz
25 Mike Wilder
26 Maurice Castain
27 Steve Howard
28 Sly Humphrey
29 Tony Moncrief
30 Jim Nettles
31 Grady Fuson
32 Gary Lance
33 Mark Doberenz
34 Dave Sheriff

1983 Indianapolis Indians team issue

(Cincinnati Reds, AAA)

	MT
Complete Set (32):	16.00

1 Indians Team
2 "Last Season We Won It All"
3 Roy Hartsfield
4 Charlie Leibrandt
5 Nick Esasky
6 Greg Harris
7 Dallas Williams
8 Joe Edelen
9 The Starters (Mike Dowless, Greg Harris, Charlie Leibrandt, Jeff Russell, Freddie Toliver)
10 Willie Lozado
11 Brian Ryder
12 Tom Lawless
13 The Bullpen (Bob Buchanan, Rich Carlucci, Joe Edelen, Brad Lesley, Brian Ryder)
14 Jeff Russell
15 Ray Corbett
16 Rich Carlucci
17 The Infielders (Skeeter Barnes, Nick Esasky, Glen Franklin, John Harris, Tom Lawless, Willie
18 Orlando Isales
19 Freddie Toliver
20 Ron Little
21 The Catchers (Ray Corabett, Dave Van Gorder)
22 Mark Gilbert
23 Mike Dowless
24 Glen Franklin
25 The Outfielders (Mark Gilbert, Orlando Isales, Ron Little, Dallas Williams)
26 Brad Lesley
27 Dave Van Gorder
28 Bob Buchanan
29 John Harris
30 The Instructors (Ted Kluszewski, Fred Norman)
31 Skeeter Barnes
32 Lee Garrett

1983 TCMA Iowa Cubs

(Chicago Cubs, AAA) (color) (Mascot card can be found with #30 or a slightly different pose and no card number)

	MT
Complete Set, w/#30 Cubby (30):	110.00
Complete Set, #30 and no# Cubby (31):	145.00

1 Rich Bordi
2 Bill Earley
3 Tom Filer
4 Alan Hargesheimer
5 Larry Jones
6 Dan Larson
7 Reggie Patterson
8 John Perlman (Jon)
9 Don Schulze
10 Randy Stein
11 Mike Diaz
12 Bill Hayes
13 Fritz Connally
14 Joe Hicks
15 Jay Loviglio
16 Carmelo Martinez
17 Jerry Manuel
18 Dave Owen
19 Dan Rohn
20 Joe Carter
21 Henry Cotto
22 Tom Grant
23 Carlos Lezcano
24 Steve Carroll
25 Front Office Team
26 Jim Narier
27 Scott Breeden
28 Kim Hart
29 Ken Grandquist
30 Cubby (mascot)
--- Cubby (mascot)

1983 Kelly Studios Kinston Blue Jays

(Toronto Blue Jays, A)

	MT
Complete Set (29):	65.00

(1) Jim Bishop
(2) J.J. Cannon
(3) Ron Clark
(4) Scot Elam
(5) Jose Escobar
(6) Keith Gilliam
(7) Devallon Harper
(8) Moe Hazelette
(9) Ken Kinnard
(10) Chris Knapp
(11) Tom Layton
(12) Tom Layton
(13) Perry Lychak
(14) Peery Mader
(15) Alex Marte
(16) Mark Poole
(17) Joe Pursell
(18) Steve Reish
(19) Derrick Reutter
(20) Ralph Rivas
(21) Tim Rodgers
(22) Randy Romagna
(23) Eddie Santos
(24) Jay Schroeder
(25) Mike Sharperson
(26) Rico Sutton
(27) Bernie Tatis
(28) Guillermo Valenzuela
(29) Dave Wells

1983 TCMA Knoxville Blue Jays

(Toronto Blue Jays, AA) (black & white)

	MT
Complete Set (22):	18.00

1 Tom Blackmon
2 Stan Clarke
3 John Cerutti
4 Mercedes Esquer
5 Jack McKnight
6 Chris Phillips
7 Dave Shipanoff
8 Bill Pinkham
9 Dan Whitmer
10 Carry Harris
11 Chris Johnston
12 Augie Schmidt
13 Andre Wood
14 Chris Shaddy
15 Kevin Aitcheson
16 Eddie Dennis
17 Greg Griffin
18 Paul Hodgson
19 John McLaren
20 Doug Ault
21 John Woodworth
22 Gary McCune

1983 Baseball Hobby News Las Vegas Stars

(San Diego Padres, AAA) (color)

	MT
Complete Set (22):	20.00

(1) Greg Booker
(2) Bobby Brown
(3) Larry Brown
(4) Tim Cook
(5) Gerry Davis
(6) Gerry De Simone
(7) Harry Dunlop
(8) Steve Fireovid
(9) Larry Harlow
(10) Geroge Hinshaw
(11) Tom House
(12) Jerry Johnson
(13) Joe Lansford
(14) Bill Long
(15) Kevin Mc Reynolds
(16) Felix Oroz
(17) Joe Pittman
(18) Larry Rothschild
(19) Cecilio Ruiz
(20) James Steels
(21) Mark Thurmond
(22) Ron Tingley

1983 Riley's Louisville Redbirds

(St. Louis Cardinals, AAA)

	MT
Complete Set (30):	22.00

1 Jim Fregosi
2 Gaylen Pitts
3 Jerry Mc Kune
4 Dyar Miller
5 Gene Roof
6 Kevin Hagen
7 Joe De Sa
8 David Von Ohlen
9 Tom Nieto
10 Jeff Keener
11 Jeff Doyle
12 Tito Landrum
13 Jose Gonzalez
14 Jose Brito
15 Gene Dotson
16 Ralph Citarella
17 Andy Rincon
18 Andy Van Slyke
19 Jim Adduci
20 John Fulgham
21 Mike Calise
22 Dennis Werth
23 Ricky Horton
24 Orlando Sanchez
25 Tom Thurberg
26 Todd Worrell
27 Bill Lyons
28 Dave Kable
29 Doyle Harris
30 Jed Smith

1983 TCMA Lynchburg Mets

(N.Y. Mets, A) (black & white) (#12 not issued)

	MT
Complete Set (23):	65.00

1 Reggie Jackson
2 Larry McNutt
3 Bill Latham
4 Jeff Bettendorf
5 Bill Fultz
6 Darryl Denby
7 Randy Milligan
8 Greg Olson
9 Bruce Morrison
10 Dwight Gooden
11 Sam Perlozzo
13 John Cumberland
14a Mark Carreon
14b Dave Cochrane
15 Lenny Dykstra
16 Jay Tibbs
17 John Heller
18 Jeff Sunderlage
19 Dave Wyatt
20 Joe Graves
21 Rich Pickett
22 Ed Hearn
23 Wes Gardner

1983 TCMA Lynn Pirates

(Pittsburgh Pirates, AA) (black & white)

	MT
Complete Set (28):	45.00

1 Mike Bielecki
2 Wilfredo Cordoba
3 Fernando Gonzalez
4 John Lackey
5 Lee Marcheskie
6 Dale Mahorcic
7 Craig Pippin
8 Keith Thibodeaux
9 Tim Wheeler
11 Stan Cliburn
12 Burke Goldthorn
13 Peter Rowe
14 Rafael Belliard
15 Nelson Norman
16 Greg Pastors
17 Rich Renteria
18 John Schaive
19 Benny Distefano
20 Ken Ford
21 Connor McGeehee
22 Jose Rodriguez
23 Tommy Sandt
24 Frank Leger
25 Brian McCann
26 Thomas Lynn
27 Gary Fitzpatrick
28 Jay Walsh

1983 Fritsch Madison Muskies

(Oakland A's, A)

	MT
Complete Set (32):	35.00

1 B. Drew, E. Janus
2 S. Charry, M. Du Val
3 Dave Collins
4 Todd Fischer
5 Dave Wilder
6 Ray Alonzo
7 Dennis Gonsalves
8 Jorge Diaz
9 Thad Reece
10 Ed Retzer
11 Shawn Gill
12 Tom Conquest
13 Jose Canseco
14 Keith Call
15 Bob Loscalzo
16 Bob Hallas
17 Eddie Escribano
18 Gene Ransom
19 John Michel
20 Mikki Jackson
21 Juan Cruz
22 Greg Robles
23 Pete Kendrick
24 Gary Dawson
25 Glenn Godwin
26 John Huey
27 Dave Leiper
28 Brian Graham
29 Hector Perez
30 Frank Trucchio
31 Brad Fischer
32 Team Logo/Checklist

1983 TCMA Memphis Chicks

(Montreal Expos, AA) (black & white)

	MT
Complete Set (24):	30.00

1 Shooty Babitt
2 George Cruz
3 Rene Gonzales
4 John Damon
5 Jeff Carl
6 Larry Goldetsky
7 Don Carter
8 Nelson Santovenia
9 Dave Hoeksema
10 Tommy Joe Shimp
11 Tim Cates
12 Bud Yanus
13 Rod Nealeigh
14 Jeff Taylor
15 Leonel Carrion
16 Jim Auten
17 Bob Tenenini
18 Larry Glasscock
19 Joe Hesketh
20 Greg Bargar
21 Razor Shines
22 Jeff Porter
23 Rick Renick
24 Mike Kinnvnen

1983 TCMA Miami Marlins

(San Diego Padres, A) (black & white)

	MT
Complete Set (28):	80.00

1 Will George
2 Mike McClain
3 Scott Gardner
4 Francisco Cota
5 Gene Walter
6 Sergio Del Rosario
7 Bill Gerhardt
8 Chuck Kolotka
9 Greg Raymer
10 Kevin Rhodas
11 Jeff Dean
12 Ray Nodell
13 Billy Ireland
14 Jose Gomez
15 Dan Jones
16 Al Simmons
17 Paul Noce
18 Manny Del Rosario
19 John Frierson
20 Benito Santiago
21 Bob Allinger
22 Tim Cannon
23 Tommy Francis
24 Steve Sayles
25 Jim Breazeale
26 Mark Miggins
27 Dennis Maley
28 Todd Hutcheson

1983 TCMA Midland Cubs

(Chicago Cubs, AA) (black & white)

	MT
Complete Set (26):	25.00

1 Bill Schammel
2 Tommy Harmon
3 Glen Gregson
4 Jim Walsh
5 Neil Bryant
6 Dennis Brogna
7 Carlos Gil
8 Doug Weleno
9 Tim Millner
10 Bruce Chanye
11 Ken Pryce
12 Darrel Banks
13 Bill Hatcher
14 Tom Lombarski
15 George Borges
16 Trey Brooks
17 Don Hyman
18 Ron Richardson
19 Stan Kyles
20 Mike Anicich
21 Jim Gerlach
22 Ray Soff
23 Tom Johnson
24 Randy LaVigne
25 Rick Baker
26 A.J. Hill

1983 Chong Modesto A's

(Oakland A's, A)

	MT
Complete Set (30):	40.00

1 Bruce Amador
2 Eric Barry
3 Bob Bathe
4 Tommy Copeland
5 Kevin Coughlon
6 James Eppard
7 Charles Fick
8 Mike Gorman
9 Tony Herron
10 Rodney Hobbs, Mark Jarrett
11 Mark Jarrett
12 Jeff Kaiser
13 Jeff Kobernus
14 Tim Lambert
15 Rod Murphy
16 Ed Myers
17 Davis Peterson
18 Tab Rojas
19 Phil Strom
20 Mickey Tettleton
21 Raymond Thoma
22 Ricky Thomas
23 Robert Vavrock
24 Thomas Zmudosky
25 George Mitterwald
26 Rick Tronerud
27 Keith Lieppman
28 Phil Danielson
29 Dan Kiser
30 Davis Fry

1983 TCMA Nashua Angels

(California Angels, AA) (black & white) (Mint cards of Cliburn and Connor are scarce)

	MT
Complete Set (27):	15.00

1 Bob Bastian
2 Rod Boxberger
3 Stewart Cliburn
4 Jeff Connor
5 Bill Mooneyham
6 Ron Romanick
7 Mickey Saatzer
8 D.W. Smith
9 Ron Sylvia
10 Steve Liddle
11 Larry Patterson
12 Harry Francis
13 Craig Gerber
14 Gustavo Polidor
15 Darryl Stephens
16 Frank Vilorio
17 Jim Beswick
18 Sap Randall
19 Al Romero
20 Winston Llenas
21 Frank Reberger
22 Richard Zaleski
23 Mark McCormack
24 Ben Surner
25 Jerry Mileur
26 George Como
27 Nashua Angels Chicken

1983 Nashville Sounds team issue

(N.Y. Yankees, AA)

	MT
Complete Set (25):	12.00

(1) Scott Bradley
(2) Mike Browning
(3) Tim Burke
(4) Ben Callahan
(5) Pete Dalena
(6) Matt Gallegos
(7) Paul Grayner
(8) Doug Holmquist
(9) Frank Kneuer
(10) Tim Knight
(11) Vic Mata
(12) Derwin Mc Nealy
(13) Ed Olwine
(14) Mike Pagliarulo
(15) Scott Patterson
(16) Erik Peterson
(17) Mike Reddish
(18) Jim Saul
(19) Kelly Scott
(20) Mark Shifflett
(21) Buck Showalter
(22) Mark Silva
(23) Keith Smith
(24) Dave Szymczak
(25) Hoyt Wilhelm

1983 TCMA Oklahoma City 89'ers

(Texas Rangers, AAA) (color)

	MT
Complete Set (24):	25.00

1 Bill Stearns
2 Tommy Burgess
3 Terry Bogener
4 Nick Capra
5 Tracy Cowger

6 Victor Cruz
7 Tommy Dunbar
8 Mike Griffin
9 Thomas Henke
10 Michael Jirschele
11 Robert Jones
12 Peter MacKanin
13 Mark Mercer
14 Ron Musselman
15 David Rajsich
16 Paul Semall
17 David Stockstill
18 Don Werner
19 Curt Wilkerson
20 Mike Mason
21 Joe Strain
22 Jim Farr
23 Don Scott
24 Danny Wheat

1983 TCMA Omaha Royals

(K.C. Royals, AAA) (color)

	MT
Complete Set (26):	30.00

1 Mike Alvarez
2 Bud Black
3 Derek Botelho
4 Scott Brown
5 Keith Creel
6 Danny Jackson
7 Mike Parrott
8 Dan St. Clair
9 Dave Schuler
10 Vince Yuhas
11 Brian Poldberg
12 Russ Stephans
13 Buddy Biancalana
14 Jeff Cox
15 Mark Funderburk
16 Kelly Heath
17 Cliff Pastornicky
18 Steve Hammond
19 Bombo Rivera
20 Mark Ryal
21 Pat Sheridan
22 Dave Leeper
23 Bill Gorman
24 Joe Sparks
25 Jerry Cram
26 Paul McCannon

1983 TCMA Orlando Twins

(Minnesota Twins, AA) (Carroll is scarce late-issue card; #23-24 not issued)

	MT
Complete Set, w/Carroll (23):	65.00
Partial Set, no Carroll (22):	15.00

1 Phil Roof
2 Tony Pilla
3 Jim Weaver
4 Kevin Williams
5 Jeff Reed
6 Steve Lombardozzi
7 Mike McCain
8 John Palica
9 Mike Sodders
10 Chino Cadahia
11 Ken Foster
12 Jerry Lomastro
13 Manny Pena
14 Jay Pettibone
15 Rich Yett
16 Jack Hobbs
17 Ted Kromy
18 Kirby Krueger
19 Eric Broersma
20 Paul Gibson
21 Mike Giordano
22 Tony Guerrero
23 Not issued
24 Not issued
25 Carson Carroll

1983 TCMA Pawtucket Red Sox

(Boston Red Sox, AAA) (color)

	MT
Complete Set (26):	40.00

1 Bob Birrell
2 Dennis Boyd
3 Dennis Burtt
4 Steve Crawford
5 Brian Denman
6 Jim Dorsey
7 Mark Fidrych
8 Keith MacWhorter
9 Bill Moloney
10 Dave Schoppee
11 Steve Shields
12 Roger LaFrancois
13 John Lickert
14 Marty Barrett
15 Juan Bustabad
16 Mike Davis
17 Dave Koza
18 Jim Wilson
19 Reggie Whittemore
20 Gus Burgess
21 Geno Gentile
22 Lee Graham
23 Juan Pautt
24 Chico Walker
25 Tony Torchia
26 Mike Roarke

1983 Trackle Peninsula Pilots Postcards

(Philadelphia Phillies, A) (3-1/2" x 5-3/8", b/w, postcard back, players unidentified)

	MT
Complete Set (40):	50.00

(1) Jerry Arnold
(2) Bud Bartholow
(3) Tony Brown
(4) Marty Bystrom
(5) Rocky Childress
(6) Joe Cipolloni
(7) Rodgers Cole
(8) Will Currier
(9) Frankie Griffin
(10) Granny Hamner
(11) Bryan Hoppie
(12) Brian Hunter
(13) Jo-Jo Jones
(14) Kent Keiser
(15) Dave Kennard
(16) Alan LeBoeuf
(17) Ed Lowery
(18) John Machin
(19) Mike Maddux
(20) Barney Nugent (trainer)
(21) Jim Olander
(22) Jim Reilly
(23) Spider Reynolds
(24) Mel Roberts
(25) Yonis Rodriguez
(26) Larry Rojas
(27) Rick Schu
(28) Gib Seibert
(29) Dave Seiler
(30) Vince Soreca
(31) Brian Suarez
(32) Rick Surhoff
(33) Tony Taylor
(34) Kevin Walters
(35) Harold Warner
(36) Mark Warren (gm)
(37) Ed Watt
(38) Mel Williams
(39) Rick Young (business mgr.)
(40) Sergio Ysambert

1983 Fritsc Peoria Suns

(California Angels, A)

	MT
Complete Set (30):	12.50

1 Ray Jimenez
2 Joe King
3 Kevin Davis
4 Scott Glanz
5 Donald Groh
6 Dave Heath
7 Kris Kline
8 Doug McKenzie
9 Mark McLemore
10 Tom Smith
11 Rick Stromer
12 Jose Valdez
13 Don Timberlake
14 Mike Rizzo
15 Jack Crawford
16 Tom Rentschler
17 Jeff Salazar
18 Jay Lewis
19 Al Cristy
20 Rafael Lugo
21 Scott Suehr
22 Devon White
23 Julian Gonzalez
24 Brian Hartsock
25 Bob Kipper
26 Ron Phipps
27 Mike Saverino
28 Eddie Rodriguez
29 Joe Coleman
30 Team Logo/Checklist

1983 Baseball Hobby News Phoenix Giants

(S.F. Giants, AAA) (color)

	MT
Complete Set (28):	20.00

1 John Rabb
2 Mark Calvert
3 Scott Garrelts
4 Brian Asselstine
5 Jeff Ransom
6 Rich Murray
7 Jeff Cornell
8 Dan Gladden
9 Tom Runnells
10 Kernan Ronan
11 Phil Hinrichs
12 Kelvin Torve
13 Herman Segelke
14 Guy Sularz
15 Randy Kutcher
16 Ted Wilborn
17 Mike Brecht
18 Butch Hughes
19 Ron Pisel
20 Mark Davis
21 Mark Dempsey
22 Chris Smith
23 Craig Chamberlain
24 Jack Mull
25 Doug Landuyt
26 Ethan Blackaby
27 Phoenix Giants Rooster
28 Tommy Gonzalez

1983 TCMA Portland Beavers

(Philadelphia Phillies, AAA) (black & white) (#23-25 are scarce late-issue cards)

	MT
Complete Set, w/#23-25 (25):	150.00
Partial Set, no #23-25 (22):	90.00

1 Luis Aguayo
2 Juan Samuel
3 Larry Andersen
4 Kyle Money
5 Kevin Gross
6 Steve Jeltz
7 Jerry Keller
8 Len Matuszek
9 Kelly Downs
10 Ramon Aviles
11 Tim Corcoran
12 George Culver
13 John Felske
14 Chris Bourjos
15 Porfi Altamirano
16 Dick Davis
17 John Russell
18 Marty Decker
19 Charlie Hudson
20 Ed Miller
21 Ron Pruitt
22 Alejandro Sanchez
23 Stan Bahnsen
24 Larry Bradford
25 Kiko Garcia

1983 TCMA Quad City Cubs

(Chicago Cubs, A) (black & white)

	MT
Complete Set (27):	35.00

1 Roger Crow
2 Larry Cox
3 Dick Pole
4 Mario Panetta
5 David Barber, Kyle Benjamin
6 Mark Baker
7 Steve Balmer
8 Brad Blevins
9 Mitch Cook
10 Jeff Fruge
11 Rene German
12 Tim Grachen
13 Randy Lockie
14 Rudy Serafini
15 Brian Tuller
16 Steven Roadcap
17 Juan Velazquez
18 Jim Allen
19 Steve Cordner
20 Shawon Dunston
21 Gary Jones
22 Tony Woods
23 Jose Rivera
24 Stan Boderick
25 Damon Farmar
26 Dave Martinez
27 Rolando Roomes

1983 TCMA Reading Phillies

(Philadelphia Phillies, AA) (black & white)

	MT
Complete Set (24):	150.00

1 Bud Bartholow
2 Darren Burroughs
3 Don Carman
4 Jay Davisson
5 Rich Gaynor
6 Frankie Griffin
7 Bill Johnson
8 George Riley
9 Denny Thomas
10 Ed Wojna
11 Darren Daulton
12 Mike LaValliere
13 Den Dowell
14 Greg Legg
15 Francisco Melendez
16 Julio Perez
17 Juan Samuel
18 Willie Darkis
19 Randy Salava
20 Jeff Stone
21 Keith Washington
22 Mel Williams
23 Bill Dancy
24 Bob Tiefenauer

1983 TCMA Redwood Pioneers

(California Angels, A) (color)

	MT
Complete Set (32):	16.00

1 Jeff Ahern
2 Ken Angulo
3 Kris Bankowski
4 Mark Bonner
5 Norman Carrasco
6 Dave Brady
7 T.R. Bryden
8 Kevin Davis
9 Steve Enkes
10 Lonnie Garza
11 Dennis Gilbert
12 Terry Harper
13 Lee Jones
14 Lance Junker
15 Tim Kammeyer
16 Greg Key
17 Tony Mack
18 Mike Madril
19 Kirk McCaskill
20 Scott Oliver
21 Kevin Price
22 Tom Rentschuler
23 Mark Smelko
24 Rick Turner
25 Bill Worden
26 Goldie Wright
27 Luis Zambrana
28 Don Rowe
29 Bernie Smith
30 Jack Lind
31 Mark Terrazas
32 Pioneer Pete (team mascot)

1983 TCMA Richmond Braves

(Atlanta Braves, AAA) (color)

	MT
Complete Set (25):	20.00

1 Jose Alvarez
2 Tony Brizzolara
3 Joe Cowley
4 Ken Daley
5 Greg Field
6 Chuck Fore
7 Sam Ayoub
8 Gary Reiter
9 Augie Ruiz
10 Bob Walk
11 Matt Sinatro
12 Steve Swisher
13 Brook Jacoby
14 Gerald Perry
15 Chico Ruiz
16 Paul Runge
17 Paul Zuvella
18 Albert Hall
19 Brad Komminsk
20 Bob Porter
21 Leonel Vargas
22 Larry Whisenton
23 Eddie Haas
24 Craig Robinson
25 Johnny Sain

1983 TCMA Rochester Redwings

(Baltimore Orioles, AAA) (color)

	MT
Complete Set (25):	20.00

1 Lance Nichols
2 Mark Brown
3 John Flinn
4 Dave Ford
5 Craig Minetto
6 Dan Morogiello
7 Allan Ramirez
8 Mark Smith
9 Cliff Speck
10 Bill Swaggerty
11 Dave Huppert
12 Al Pardo
13 Floyd Rayford
14 Bob Bonner
15 Glenn Gulliver
16 Rick Jones
17 Dan Logan
18 John Valle
19 Elijah Bonaparte
20 Drungo Hazewood
21 Ric Lisi
22 Mike Young
23 Tom Chism
24 Richie Bancells
25 Mark Wiley

1983 Trackle Salem Redbirds Postcards

(S.D. Padres, A) (3-1/2" x 5-3/8", b/w, postcard back, players unidentified)

	MT
Complete Set (13):	25.00

(1) Frank Brosious

(2) Barry Brunenkant
(3) Billy Gerhardt
(4) Jerry Johnson
(5) Keith Jones
(6) Louis Langie
(7) Oscar Mejia
(8) Jaime Moreno
(9) Bruce Oliver
(10) Mark Poston
(11) Steve Smith
(12) John Westmoreland
(13) Kevin Wiggins

1983 TCMA Salt Lake City Gulls

(Seattle Mariners, AAA) (color)

MT
Complete Set (26): 24.00
1 Edwin Nunez
2 Jerry Gleaton
3 Robert Babcock
4 Brian Snyder
5 Karl Best
6 Brian Allard
7 Mike Moore
8 Rick Adair
9 Jed Murray
10 Joe Decker
11 Phil Bradley
12 Mark Woodmansee
13 Tito Nanni
14 Rod Allen
15 Bud Bulling
16 Jamie Nelson
17 Jim Maler
18 Bill Crone
19 John Moses
20 Glen Walker
21 Al Chambers
22 Harold Reynolds
23 Spike Owen
24 Bobby Floyd
25 Doug Merrifield
26 Manny Estrada

1983 Colla San Jose Bees

(Independent, A)

MT
Complete Set (26): 20.00
1 Frank Verdi
2 Hiromi Wada
3 Charlie Bertucio
4 Lee Granger
5 Brian Mc Donough
6 Gary Springer
7 Dan Mc Inerny
8 Osamu Abe
9 Yukiichi Komazaki
10 Hiro Shirahata
11 Mark Butler
12 Mark Jacob
13 Kerry Cook
14 Bruce Fields
15 Gary Legumina
16 Sadahito Ueda
17 Kraig Priessman
18 Katsuya Soma
19 Mike Daughtery
20 Carl Nichols
21 Jeff Gilbert
22 Jeff Summers
23 Leon Hoke
24 Kurt Leiter
25 Greg Dehart
26 Harry Steve

1983 Fritsch Springfield Cardinals

(St. Louis Cardinals, A)

MT
Complete Set (26): 10.00
1 Pete Stoll
2 David Clements
3 Paul Cherry
4 Sammy Martin
5 Dave Droschak
6 Curtis Ford
7 Marty Mason
8 Ed Tanner
9 Scott Arigoni
10 Brett Benza
11 Mick Shade
12 Joe Silkwood
13 Bob Geren
14 Greg Dunn
15 John Young
16 Dave Hoyt
17 Harry McCulla
18 Matt Gundelfinger
19 Randy Martinez
20 Mike Pittman
21 Dan Stryffeler
22 Dave Bialas
23 Mike Gambeski
24 Allen Morlock
25 Gus Malespin
26 Team Logo/Checklist

1983 TCMA St. Petersburg Cardinals

(St. Louis Cardinals, A) (black & white)

MT
Complete Set (30): 32.00
1 Joseph Boever
2 Javier Carranza
3 Henry Carson
4 Danny Cox
5 Thomas Dozier
6 Thomas Epple
7 Michael Hartley
8 Robert Kish
9 John Martin
10 Christian Martinez
11 Mark Riggins
12 Freddie Silva
13 Scott Young
14 Randall Champion
15 Timothy Wallace
16 James Burns
17 Frank Garcia
18 Brad Luther
19 Deron Thomas
20 Francisco Batista
21 Robert Helsom
22 Richard James
23 Jose Rodriguez
24 Barry Sayler
25 Steve F. Turco
26 Stephen Turgion
27 Ralph Miller, Jr.
28 Karl Rogozenski
29 James Riggleman
30 Dave Link

1983 TCMA Syracuse Chiefs

(Toronto Blue Jays, AAA) (color)

MT
Complete Set (26): 45.00
1 Jim Beauchamp
2 Bernie Beckman
3 Tommy Craig
4 Jim Baker
5 Mark Bomback
6 Don Cooper
7 Mark Eichhorn
8 Dennis Howard
9 Tom Lukish
10 Colin McLaughlin
11 Jeff Schneider
12 Keith Walker
13 Matt Williams
14 Toby Hernandez
15 Geno Petralli
16 Tony Fernandez
17 Fred Manrique
18 Bob Nandin
19 Jeff Reynolds
20 Tim Thompson
21 George Bell
22 Anthony Johnson
23 Vern Ramie
24 Ron Shepherd
25 Mitch Webster
26 Bob Humphreys

Values shown are a national average. Some teams and players enjoy regional popularity which may affect market prices.

1983 Syracuse Chiefs team issue

(Toronto Blue Jays, AAA) (black & white, 3-1/4" x 5", blank-back)

MT
Complete Set (25): 75.00
1 Tony Fernandez
2 Fred Manrique
4 Andre Wood
5 Jim Beauchamp
6 George Bell
7 Bob Nandin
9 Toby Hernandez
11 A.J. Johnson
12 Geno Petralli
14 Jeff Reynolds
15 Don Cooper
16 Bernie Beckman
17 Dennis Howard
19 Tim Thompson
21 Ron Shepherd
23 Mitch Webster
24 Tom Lukish
25 Vern Ramie
26 Mark Bomback
27 Jeff Schneider
29 Keith Walker
30 Chris Knapp
31 Colin McLaughlin
32 Matt Williams
33 Jim Baker

1983 TCMA Tacoma Tigers

(Oakland A's, AAA) (color) (McKay, Moore, Perry, Retzer and Rodriquez are scarce late-issue cards)

MT
Complete Set, w/late-issues (36): 110.00
Partial Set no late-issues (31): 12.00
1 Keith Atherton
2 Bert Bradley
3 DeWayne Buice
4 Gorman Heimueller
5 Chuck Hensley
6 Jerome King
7 Russ McDonald
8 Curt Young
9 Daryl Cias
10 Bill Bathe
11 Donnie Hill
12 John Hotchkiss
13 Mike Woodard
14 Jim Bennett
15 Lynn Garrett
16 Dave Hudgens
17 Rusty McNealy
18 Bob Didier
19 Stan Naccarato
20 Jim Nettles
21 Dave Heaverlo
22 Larry Davis
23 Art Popham
24 Tigers Mascot
25a Bob Christofferson
25b Danny Goodwin
26 Scott Pyle
27 Dennis Sherow
28 Jeff Jones
29a Dave McKay
29b Rickey Peters
30a Jim Christiansen
30b Dave Rodriguez
31 Ed Retzer
32 Kelvin Moore
33 Shawn Perry

1983 TCMA Tampa Tarpons

(Cincinnati Reds, A) (black & white) (set usually includes many miscut cards)

MT
Complete Set (30): 55.00
1 Tony Burley
2 Virg Conley
3 L.C. Culver
4 Tony Evans
5 Tom Browning
6 Not issued
7 Tim Dodd
8 Jason Felice
9 Adolfo Feliz
10 Fergy Ferguson
11 Jack Foley
12 Clem Freeman, Jr.
13 Orlando Gonzalez
14 Dave Hall
15 Ty Hubbard, III
16 Danny LaMar
17 Ted Langdon
18 Terrence McGriff
19 Paul O'Neil
20 Cressy Pratt
21 Kevin Steinmetz
22 Allen Swindle
23 Scott Terry
24 Tony Threatt
25 Steve Watson
26 Tracy Jones
27 Nick Fiorillo
28 Jim Hoff
29 Mike Sims
30 Bull Norman

1983 TCMA Tidewater Tides

(N.Y. Mets, AAA) (color)

MT
Complete Set (29): 40.00
1 Ron Darling
2 Mike Fitzgerald
3 Wally Backman
4 Clint Hurdle
5 Terry Leach
6 Mike Bishop
7 Kelvin Chapman
8 Gary Rajsich
9 Tim Leary
10 Steve Senteney
11 Tom Gorman
12 Walt Terrell
13 Jeff Bittiger
14 Scott Dye
15 Greg Biercevicz
16 Brent Gaff
17 Dan Schmitz
18 Mike Howard
19 Rusty Tillman
20 Ron Gardenhire
21 Marvell Wynne
22 Gil Flores
23 Davey Johnson
24 Al Jackson
25 Josh Wakana
26 Tucker Ashford
27 Bob Sikes
28 Darryl Strawberry
29 Jose Oquendo

1983 TCMA Toledo Mud Hens

(Minnesota Twins, AAA) (color)

MT
Complete Set w/scarce #26-29: 110.00
Partial Set #1-25: 18.00
1 Paul Boris
2 Terry Felton
3 Kevin Flannery
4 Ed Hodge
5 Steve Korczyk
6 Jim Lewis
7 Jeff Little
8 Bob Mulligan
9 Ken Schrom
10 Mike Walters
11 Rick Austin
12 Stine Poole
13 Dave Baker
14 Greg Gagne
15 Houston Jimenez
16 Tim Teufel
17 Jesus Vega
18 Michael Wilson
19 Andre David
20 Mike Hart
21 Randy Johnson
22 Dave Meier
23 Cal Ermer
24 Tim Agan, Kevin Flannery
25 Scott Tellgren
26 Eric Broersma
27 Mike McCain
28 Bryan Oelkers
29 Jack O'Conner

1983 TCMA Tri-Cities Triplets

(Texas Rangers, A) (black & white)

MT
Complete Set (28): 13.00
1 Bob Sebra
2 Steve Kordish
3 Bruce Kipper
4 Kerry Burns
5 Dennis Knight
6 Mark Cipres
7 John Munley
8 Robin Keathley
9 Nick Esposito
10 John Fryhoff
11 Dan Lindquist
12 Jim Allison
13 Bill Hance
14 Tony Carlucci
15 Reggie Mosley
16 Mark Gile
17 Ron Hansen
18 Mike Keehn
19 Vince Sakowski
20 Bert Martinez
21 Greg Bailey
22 Danny Simpson
23 Jim Cesario
24 Brendan Hennessy
25 Clint Curry
26 Dave Oliver
27 Gary Venner
28 Bob Bill

1983 TCMA Tucson Toros

(Houston Astros, AAA) (color) (Robles is scarce late-issue card)

MT
Complete Set, w/Robles (26): 60.00
Partial Set, no Robles (25): 15.00
1 Ed Bonine
2 Dan Boone
3 Buster Keeton
4 Ron Mathis
5 Ron Meredith
6 Jeff Morris
7 Gordie Pladson
8 Bert Roberge
9 Bob Veselic
10 Sam Welborn
11 Julio Solano
12 Steve Christmas
13 Luis Pujols
14 Wes Clements
15 Greg Cypret
16 Jim Pankovits
17 Bert Pena
18 Cliff Wherry
19 Chris Jones
20 Larry Ray
21 Bob Pate
22 Scott Loucks
23 Matt Galante
24 Gary Tuck
25 Dave Labossiere
26 Ruben Robles

1983 TCMA Tulsa Drillers

(Texas Rangers, AA) (color)

MT
Complete Set (25): 20.00
1 Jorge Gomez

2 Glen Cook
3 Tony Fossas
4 Rob Clark
5 Billy Taylor
6 Larry McLane
7 Daryl Smith
8 Dennis Long
9 Mitch Zwolensky
10 Tim Henry
11 Dwayne Henry
12 Kirk Killingsworth
13 Bob Brower
14 Chuckie Canady
15 Mike Rubel
16 John Buckley
17 Tracy Cowger
18 Steve Nielsen
19 Joe Nemeth
20 Jim Foit
21 Dan Murphy
22 Steve Buechele
23 Jerry Neufang
24 Terry Johnson
25 Marty Scott

1983 TCMA Vero Beach Dodgers

(L.A. Dodgers, A) (black & white)

MT
Complete Set (29): 30.00
1 Mike Beuder
2 Tom Duffy
3 Rick Felt
4 Mike Gentile
5 Brian Innis
6 Charlie Jones
7 Vance Lovelace
8 Morris Madden
9 Rafael Montalvo
10 Bill Scudder
11 Chris Thomas
12 Rob Slezak
13 Luis Rivera
14 Steve Boncore
15 Bob Gilles
16 Mariano Duncan
17 John Gregory
18 Hector Guzman
19 Gary Newsom
20 Harold Perkins
21 Billy White
22 Ralph Bryant
23 Jerald Cain
24 Dan Cataline
25 Reggie Williams
26 John Shoemaker
27 Rob Giesecke
28 Stan Wasiak
29 Dennis Lewallyn

1983 Fritsch Visalia Oaks

(Minnesota Twins, A)

MT
Complete Set (25): 245.00
1 Lee Belanger
2 Jeff Arney
3 Steve Aragon
4 Sam Arrington
5 Phil Franko
6 Kirby Puckett
7 Frank Ramppen
8 Bob DeCosta
9 Jack McMahon
10 Stan Holmes
11 Frank Eufemia
12 Ron McKelvie
13 Harry Warner
14 Jeff Brueggemann
15 Erez Borowsky
16 Mark Cartwright
17 Joe Kubit
18 Curt Wardle
19 Bennie Richie
20 Craig Henderson
21 Greg Howe
22 Curt Kindred
23 Alvaro Espinoza
24 Mark Portugal
25 Brian Rupe

1983 TCMA Waterbury Reds

(Cincinnati Reds, AA) (black & white)

MT
Complete Set (19): 40.00
1 Keefe Cato
2 Bryan Funk
3 Curt Heidenreich
4 Ken Jones
5 Bill Landrum
6 Jim Pettibone
7 Mark Rothey
8 Lester Straker
9 Lloyd McClendon
10 Dave Miley
11 Adolfo Feliz
12 Carlos Porte
13 Hector Rincones
14 Wade Rowdon
15 Eric Davis
16 Dexter Day
17 Leo Garcia
18 Ruben Guzman
19 Jim Lett

1983 Fritsch Waterloo Indians

(Cleveland Indians, A)

MT
Complete Set (29): 8.00
1 Randy Washington
2 Edwin Aponte
3 Ben Piphus
4 Eddie Diaz
5 Andy Ortiz
6 Juan Lopez
7 Nelson Pedraza
8 Junior Noboa
9 Jay Keeler
10 Wilson Valera
11 John Miglio
12 Jose Roman
13 Miguel Roman
14 Phil Wilson
15 Reggie Ritter
16 Pookie Bernstine
17 Bernardo Brito
18 Winston Ficklin
19 Ray Martinez
20 Jeff Barkley
21 Dane Anthony
22 Mike Gertz
23 Wes Pierorazio
24 Mike Poindexter
25 Rich Diaz
26 Rick Henke
27 Vic Albury
28 Gomer Hodge
29 Team Logo/Checklist Card

1983 Fritsch Wausau Timbers

(Seattle Mariners, A)

MT
Complete Set (31): 8.00
1 K.R. Houston
2 John Poloni
3 Gary Pellant
4 Tom Burns
5 Martin Enriquez
6 Brian David
7 Ronn Dixon
8 Tim Slavin
9 Terry Taylor
10 Eric Parent
11 Chip Conklin
12 David Myers
13 Kevin Roy
14 Todd Francis
15 Randy Meier
16 Robby Vollmer
17 Jesse Baez
18 Scott Barnhouse
19 Paul Schneider
20 Scott Roebuck
21 Tom Duggan
22 Bob Baldrick
23 Sam Haley
24 Ron Sismondo
25 Randy Newman
26 John Duncan
27 Dave Smith
28 Wray Begendahl
29 Kenny Briggs
30 R.J. Harrison
31 Team Logo/Checklist Card

1983 Dog-N-Shake Wichita Aeroes

(Montreal Expos, AAA)

MT
Complete Set (24): 28.00
1 Checklist
2 Felipe Alou
3 Shooty Babitt
4 Greg Bargar
5 Butch Benton
6 Tom Dixon
7 Mike Fuentes
8 Mike Gates
9 Gene Glynn
10 Dick Grapenthin
11 Bob James
12 Roy Johnson
13 Brad Mills
14 Eric Mustad
15 Luis Quintana
16 Rick Ramos
17 Bob Reece
18 Pat Rooney
19 Angel Salazar
20 Bill Sattler
21 Mike Stenhouse
22 Rennie Stennett
23 Tom Wieghaus
24 1982 Batting Title (Roy Johnson)

1983 Trackle Winston-Salem Red Sox Postcards

(Boston Red Sox, A) (3-1/2" x 5-3/8", b/w, postcard back, players unidentified)

MT
Complete Set (19): 25.00
(1) John Ackley
(2) Luis Alomar
(3) Kevin Burrell
(4) Tim Gordon
(5) Kevin Grubbs
(6) Sam Horn
(7) Mitch Johnson
(8) Manny Jose
(9) Tony Latham
(10) Mike Mesh
(11) Joe Morgan
(12) Sam Nattile
(13) David Oliva
(14) Luis Olmedo
(15) Mike Rochford
(16) Danny Sheaffer
(17) Bill Slack
(18) Craig Walck
(19) Mark Weinbrecht

1983 Fritsch Wisconsin Rapids Twins

(Minnesota Twins, A)

MT
Complete Set (28): 8.00
1 Coe Brier
2 Ronnie Scheer
3 Allan Anderson
4 Jeff Wilson
5 Joe Sain
6 Paul Felix
7 Carson Carroll
8 David Steinberg
9 Tim Graupmann
10 John Kearns
11 Bob Ferro
12 Mark Larcom
13 Johnny Salery
14 Bob Costello
15 Leo Cardenas, Jr.
16 Danny Clay
17 Brian Hobaugh
18 Mike Maack
19 Luis Cruz
20 Jim Burnos
21 Ken Klump
22 Paul Mancuso
23 Brad Skoglund
24 Michael Moreno
25 David Baehr
26 John Marks
27 Charlie Manuel
28 Team Logo/Checklist

1984 TCMA Albany-Colonie A'S

(Oakland A's, AA)

MT
Complete Set (26): 32.00
1 Jim Bennett
2 Ron Arnold
3 Gene Gentile
4 Rodney Hobbs
5 Thad Reece
6 Brian Graham
7 Keith Lieppman
8 Rick Tronerud
9 Brian Thorson
10 John Liburdi
11 Tom Dozier
12 Todd Fischer
13 Bob Hallas
14 Pete Kendrick
15 Stan Kyles
16 Erik Bernard
17 Tim Lambert
18 Ed Myers
19 Les Straker
20 Tom Zmudosky
21 Mike Ashman
22 Mickey Tettleton
23 Bob Bathe
24 Jim Eppard
25 Greg Robles
26 Ray Thoma

1984 Cramer Albuquerque Dukes

(L.A. Dodgers, AAA) (A limited-edition glossy set was also produced)

MT
Complete Set (26): 9.00
146 Jack Fimple
147 Rich Rodas
148 R.J. Reynolds
149 Sid Bream
150 Lemmie Miller
151 Franklin Stubbs
152 Dave Sax
153 Alex Taveras
154 Steve Perry
155 Don Smith
156 Robbie Allen
157 Greg Schultz
158 Larry White
159 Ernesto Borbon
160 Dean Rennicke
161 Tony Brewer
162 Larry See
163 Ed Amelung
164 John Debus
165 Ken Howell
166 Roberto Alexander
167 Terry Collins
168 Brian Holton
169 Dick McLaughlin
245 Dave Wallace
246 Mark Sheehy

1984 Albuquerque Dukes team-issue photos

(L.A. Dodgers, AAA) (3-1/2" x 5" color photo prints, sold at stadium for $2 each)

MT
Complete Set (27): 100.00
(1) Roberto Alexander
(2) Robbie Allen
(3) Ed Amelung
(4) Ernesto Borbon
(5) Sid Bream
(6) Tony Brewer
(7) Terry Collins
(8) Jon Debus
(9) Jack Fimple
(10) Brian Holton
(11) Ken Howell
(12) Dick McLaughlin
(13) Lemmie Miller
(14) Rafael Montalvo
(15) Steve Perry
(16) German Rivera
(17) Rick Rodas
(18) Dave Sax
(19) Greg Schultz
(20) Larry See
(21) Mark Sheehy
(22) Don Smith
(23) Charlie Strasser (trainer)
(24) Alex Taveras
(25) Paul Voight
(26) Dave Wallace
(27) Larry White

1984 TCMA Arkansas Travelers

(St. Louis Cardinals, AA)

MT
Complete Set (26): 20.00
1 Eddie Tanner
2 Dave Clements
3 Dan Stryffeler
4 Deron Thomas
5 Tim Wallace
6 Todd Worrell
7 Bob Helson
8 Al Morlock
9 Larry Reynolds
10 Greg Guin
11 Bob Geren
12 John Adams
13 Mark Schulte
14 Dave Bialas
15 Willie Hardwick
16 Curt Ford
17 John Martin
18 Pat Perry
19 Marty Mason
20 Joe Silkwood
21 Gotay Mills
22 John Young
23 Pete Stoll
24 Walt Pierce
25 Andy Hassler
26 Mike Harris

1984 TCMA Beaumont Golden Gators

(San Diego Padres, AA)

MT
Complete Set (25): 12.00
1 Jimmy Jones
2 Pete Kutsukos
3 James Steels
4 Al Newman
5 Mark Gillaspie
6 Ed Vosberg
7 Steve Murray
8 Mark Parent
9 Gene Walter
10 Kevin Towers
11 Bill Long
12 Tim Cook
13 Steve Schefsky
14 Jim Leopold
15 Jimmy Thomas
16 Pat Casey
17 Mark Wasinger
18 Steve Garcia
19 Jerry Johnson
20 Steve Johnson
21 Bobby Tolan
22 Chuck Kolotka
23 Todd Hutcheson
24 Ray Etchebarren
25 Jeff Ronk

1984 TCMA Buffalo Bisons

(Cleveland Indians, AA)

	MT
Complete Set (25):	12.00

1 Jeff Moronko
2 George Cecchetti
3 Tim Glass
4 "Junior" Naboa
5 Rene Quinones
6 Doug Simonic
7 Andy Allanson
8 Jose Roman
9 Jay Baller
10 Alec McCullock
11 Rich Doyle
12 Rich Thompson
13 Dave Szymczak
14 John Bohnet
15 Andy Ortiz
16 Ramon Romero
17 Steve Mardsen
18 Jack Aker
19 Ed Aponte
20 Randy Washington
21 Don Carter
22 Ed Saavedra
23 Pookie Bernstine
24 Robin Fuson
25 Doug Helmquist

1984 TCMA Butte Copper Kings

(Seattle Mariners, A)

	MT
Complete Set (27):	17.50

1 Manny Estrada
2 John Anderson
3 James Bowden
4 Dan Clark
5 Mike Wood
6 Tom Osowski
7 Carl Moesche
8 Greg Brinkman
9 Tony Diaz
10 Charlie Fonville
11 Steve French
12 Richard Hayden
13 Brad Kinney
14 Dan Larson
15 Mark Machalec
16 Rafael Matos
17 Pablo Monceratt
18 Arvid Morfin
19 Kevin Ochs
20 Bill O'Leary
21 Bregg Ray
22 Paul Steinert
23 Gregg Thienpont
24 George Uribe
25 Nestor Valiente
26 Lazaro Vilella
27 Logan White

1984 TCMA Cedar Rapids Reds

(Cincinnati Reds, A)

	MT
Complete Set (28):	20.00

1 Robbie Phillips
2 Ted Langdon
3 Jim Pettibone
4 Doug Barba
5 Paul Kirsch
6 Brian Funk
7 Hugh Kemp
8 Virgil Conley
9 Mike Konderla
10 Jordan Berge
11 Tim Dodd
12 Jim Lett
13 Dexter Day
14 Joe Oliver
15 Tom Riley
16 Lanell Culver
17 Kurt Stillwell
18 Danny LaMar
19 Don Buchheister
20 Ronnie Giddens
21 Mike Manfre
22 Scott Loseke
23 Rod Lich
24 Mike Dowless
25 Lenny Harris
26 Gary Denbo
27 Ron Henika
28 Dave Haberle

1984 TCMA Charlotte O'S

(Baltimore Orioles, AA)

	MT
Complete Set (27):	15.00

1 Bob Hice
2 Terry Mauney
3 Charlie Frederick
4 Ronni Salcedo
5 Paul Cameron
6 Carlos Concepcion
7 Al Pardo
8 Jeff Kenaga
9 Peter Torrez
10 Grady Little
11 Chris Willsher
12 Bobby Mariano
13 Pat Dumouchelle
14 Jamie Reed
15 Bob Konopa
16 Dave Falcone
17 Kenny Dixon
18 Jeff Gilbert
19 Jesus Alfaro
20 Jeff Williams
21 Paul Bard
22 Ken Gerhart
23 Kurt Leiter
24 John Tutt
25 Jeff Summers
26 Tony Arnold
27 Herbie Oliveras

1984 TCMA Chattanooga Lookouts

(Seattle Mariners, AA) (#17 not issued)

	MT
Complete Set (29):	12.50

1a Mike Evans
1b Kevin King
2 Ramon Estepa
3 Dan Hanggie
4 Brick Smith
5 Ed Holtz
6 Clark Crist
7 Ross Grimsley
8 Bill Plummer
9 Tom Hunt
10 Donnell Nixon (Donell)
11 John Semprini
12 Paul Serna
13 Mike Johnson
14 Harry Landreth
15 Lee Guetterman
16 Joe Whitmer
18 Rick Luecken
19 Tom Rowe
20 A.J. Hill
21 Randy Ramirez
22 Ric Wilson
23 Rick Adair
24 John Moses
25 Mario Diaz
26 Mickey Brantley
27 Don Clay Hill
28 Jeff McDonald
29 Greg Bartley

1984 Police Columbus Clippers

(N.Y. Yankees, AAA) (color, 2-3/8" x 3-3/4")

	MT
Complete Set (25):	10.00

2 Andre Robertson
4 Kelly Heath
12 Rex Hudler
14 Victor Mata
15 Mike O'Berry
17 Butch Hobson
19 Kelly Scott
20 Curt Brown
21 Brian Dayett
23 Dan Briggs
24 Mike Pagliarulo
25 Don Fowler
27 Don Cooper
29 Pat Rooney
31 Scott Patterson
32 Matt Winters
34 George Cappuzzello
36 Joe Cowley
38 Clay Christiansen
39 Dennis Rasmussen
40 Scott Bradley
42 Pete Dalena
--- "Stump" Merrill (manager)
--- George H. Sisler Jr. (general manager)
--- Coaches/trainer card (Mark Connor, Steve Donohue, Gil Patterson, Mickey Vernon)

1984 TCMA Columbus Clippers

(N.Y. Yankees, AAA)

	MT
Complete Set (25):	20.00

1 Mike Pagliarulo
2 Kelly Heath
3 Pat Rooney
4 Brian Dayett
5 Dan Briggs
6 Don Fowler
7 George Cappuzzello
8 Rex Hudler
9 Andre Robertson
10 Victor Mata
11 Scott Bradley
12 Clay Christianson
13 Joe Cowley
14 Scott Patterson
15 Curt Brown
16 Butch Hobson
17 Don Cooper
18 Pete Dalena
19 Kelly Scott
20 Mike O'Berry
21 Coach, Trainer & Manager
22 Matt Winters
23 Stump Merrill
24 George Sisler, Jr.
25 Dennis Rasmussen

1984 Daytona Beach Astros team issue

(Houston Astros, A)

	MT
Complete Set (25):	40.00

1 Dave Cripe
2 Stan Hough
3 Rich Bombard
4 Mik Crefin
5 Mike Friederich
6 Chuck Mathews
7 Greg Mize
8 Raynor Noble
9 Ray Perkins
10 Uvaldo Reglado
11 Doug Shaab
12 Don Berti
13 Jeff Datz
14 Robbie Wine
15 Glenn Carpenter
16 Bobby Falls
17 Ramon Rodriguez
18 Nelson Rood
19 Jim Sherman
20 Mike Botkin
21 Curtis Burke
22 Juan Delgado
23 Louis Meadows
24 Mike Stellern
25 Larry Lasky

1984 TCMA Durham Bulls

(Atlanta Braves, A)

	MT
Complete Set (30):	17.50

1 Simon Rosario
2 Mark Lance
3 Mike Yastrzemski
4 Pat Hodge
5 Johnny Hatcher
6 Terry Cormack
7 Jeff Wagner
8 Dave Griffin
9 Leo Mazzone
10 Tim Alexander
11 Rafael Barbosa
12 Bob Tumpane
13 Chip Childress
14 Andres Thomas
15 Mike Knox
16 Tony Neuendorff
17 Scott Hood
18 Rich Leggatt
19 Todd Lamb
20 Paul Assenmacher
21 Paul Josephson
22 Jose Cano
23 Steve Ziem
24 John Mortillaro
25 Brian Aviles
26 Jim Rivera
27 Marty Schreiber
28 Brian Snitker
29 Randy Ingle
30 Sonny Jackson

1984 Cramer Edmonton Trappers

(California Angels, AAA) (A limited-edition glossy set was also produced)

	MT
Complete Set (26):	7.00

97 Moose Stubing
98 Tim Krauss
99 Angel Moreno
100 Marty Kain
101 Sap Randall
102 Rick Steirer
103 Dave W. Smith
104 Rick Adams
105 Craig Gerber
106 Steve Finch
107 Steve Liddle
108 Chris Clark
109 Darrell Miller
110 Bill Mooneyham
111 Doug Corbett
112 Steve Lubratich
113 Stu Cliburn
114 Mike Browning
115 Joe Simpson
116 Reggie West
117 Mike Brown
118 Pat Keedy
119 Jay Kibbe
120 Ed Ott
242 Frank Reberger
249 Steve Lubratich

1984 TCMA El Paso Diablos

(Milwaukee Brewers, AA)

	MT
Complete Set (25):	20.00

1 Mark Effrig
2 Johnson Wood
3 Bob Schroeck
4 Steve Michael
5 Bryan Clutterbuck
6 Chuck Grim
7 Doug Jones
8 Mike Villegas
9 Mike Samuel
10 Tim Crews
11 Bryan Duquette
12 Terry Bevington
13 Kelvin Moore
14 Stan Davis
15 Ted Higuera
16 Juan Castillo
17 Dan Plante
18 Dave Klipstein
19 Alan Cartwright
20 Paul Hartzell
21 Joe Morales
22 Cam Walker
23 Mike Felder
24 Dale Sveum
25 Garrett Nago

1984 TCMA Evansville Triplets

(Detroit Tigers, AAA)

	MT
Complete Set (22):	18.00

1 Juan Lopez
2 Howard Bailey
3 Rondal Rollin
4 Gordon McKenzie
5 Pat Larkin
6 Mark Dacko
7 Stan Younger
8 Dave Gumpert
9 Nelson Simmons
10 Len Faedo
11 Bob Melvin
12 Dallas Williams
13 Doug Baker
14 Scotty Earl
15 John Harris
16 Mike Laga
17 Randy O'Neal
18 Jeff Conner
19 Don Heinkel
20 Bill Armstrong
21 Roger Mason
22 Carl Willis

1984 Cramer Everett Giants

(S.F. Giants, Rookie) (black & white) (James, Ewing, both Rush, #19, 20, 22 and 24 McDonald, #26 and #28 Perezchica are scarce late-issue cards)

	MT
Complete Set, w/late issues (42):	35.00
Partial Set, no late issues (35):	25.00

1 Greg Litton
2 Lyle Swepson
3a Mike Cicione
3b Darin James
4 Joe Olker
5 Harry Davis
6 a Greg Gilbert
6 b Daren James
7 Kent Cooper
8 Steve Cottrell
9 Kevin Woodhouse
10 Keith Silver
11 Dave Hornsby
12 a Stuart Tate
12 b Jim Ewing
13 a Rob Cosby
13 b Rod Rush
14 a Sixto Martes
14 b Rod Rush
15 Loren Hibbs
16 Dave Hinnrichs
17 Francisco Echevarria
18 Chris Stangel
19 a Paul Blair
19 b T.J. McDonald
20 a Terry Mulholland
20 b T.J. McDonald
21 Davis Tavarez
22 a Brad Porter
22 b T.J. McDonald
23 Francis Calzado
24 a Jim Wasem
24 b T.J. McDonald
25 John Grimes
26 a Todd Moriaty
26 b Tony Perezchica
27a John Ackerman
27b Tony Perezchica
28 a Rocky Bridges
28 b Tony Perezchica
29 Tom Wetzel
30 Tom Messier

1984 TCMA Greensboro Hornets

(N.Y. Yankees, A)

	MT
Complete Set (26):	25.00

1 Carlos Tosca
2 Ray Fortaleza
3 Brad Winler
4 Roberto Kelly
5 Jeff Horne
6 Fredi Gonzalez
7 Nattie George
8 Joey MacKay
9 Doug Carpenter
10 Brad Arnsberg
11 Chris Fedor

12 Bill Bulton
13 Dave Smalley
14 Tim Williams
15 Chuck Mathison
16 Eric Parent
17 Ricky Torres
18 Steve George
19 Mark Ferguson
20 Jonis Rodriguez
21 Bob Devlin
22 Moe Ching
23 Pedro Medina
24 Rich Mattocks
25 Mitch Seoane
26 Bill Englehart

1984 Pizza Hut Greenville Braves

(Atlanta Braves, AA) (Issued as unperforated 17" x 20-1/2" poster.)

		MT
Complete Set, Sheet (25):		80.00
1	Mike Cole	
2	Freddie Tiburcio	
5	Carlos Rios	
6	Joe Johnson	
9	Steve Chmil	
10	Marty Clary	
11	Randy Ingle	
12	Glen Bockhorn	
14	Augie Ruiz	
15	Matt Sinatro	
16	Rich Leggett	
18	Matt West	
19	Doc Estes	
20	Bobby Dews	
22	Steve Curry	
23	Roy North	
24	Tommy Thompson	
25	Inocencio Guerrero	
26	Bob Luzon	
27a	Leo Mazzone	
27b	Duane Ward	
28	Tim Cole	
29	Mike Bormann	
30	Andre Treadway	
---	David Clay	

1984 Trackle Hagerstown Suns Postcards

(Baltimore Orioles, A) (3-1/2" x 5-3/8", b/w, postcard back, players unidentified)

		MT
Complete Set (20):		35.00
(1)	Juan Arias	
(2)	Ben Bianchi	
(3)	Angelo Bruno	
(4)	Dom Chiti	
(5)	Carlos Concepcion	
(6)	Rick Cratch	
(7)	Rocky Cusack	
(8)	Tim Derryberry	
(9)	Glenn Dooner	
(10)	Fran Fitzgerald	
(11)	Lee Granger	
(12)	Len Johnston	
(13)	Jeff Kenaga	
(14)	Bill Lavelle	
(15)	Jeff Leriger	
(16)	Gerry Melillo	
(17)	Rick Rembielak	
(18)	Billy Ripken	
(19)	Ken Rowe	
(20)	Mike Vanderburg	

1984 Cramer Hawaii Islanders

(Pittsburgh Pirates, AAA) (A limited-edition glossy set was also produced)

		MT
Complete Set (25):		8.00
121	Al Pulido	
122	Jeff Zaske	
123	Kelly Paris	
124	Larry Lamonde	
125	Paul Semall	
126	Dave Tomlin	
127	Lorenzo Bundy	
128	Ron Wotus	
129	Ray Krawczyk	
130	Denny Gonzales (Gonzalez)	
131	Mike Bielecki	
132	Stan Cliburn	
133	Nelson Norman	
134	Chuck Hartenstein	
135	Mike Howard	
136	Bob Miscik	
137	Tom Sandt	
138	Jim Winn	
139	Trench Davis	
140	Tim Wheeler	
141	Bob Walk	
142	Steve Herz	
143	Carlos Ledezma	
144	Benny Distefano	
145	John Malkin	

1984 Idaho Falls A's team issue

(Oakland A's, A)

		MT
Complete Set (30):		40.00
(1)	Russ Applegate	
(2)	Eldridge Armstrong	
(3)	Darren Balsley	
(4)	Mickey Boyer	
(5)	Adan Brito	
(6)	Antonio Cabrera	
(7)	Mike Cupples	
(8)	Arturo Ferreira	
(9)	Mark Gillespie	
(10)	John Gonzalez	
(11)	Bob Hassel	
(12)	Jesus Hernaiz	
(13)	James Jackson	
(14)	Tony Johnson	
(15)	Felix Jose	
(16)	Mark Leonette	
(17)	Scott LeVander	
(18)	Jim Nettles	
(19)	Ramon Nunez	
(20)	Ken Patterson	
(21)	Ted Polakowski	
(22)	Basilio Reyes	
(23)	Kevin Russ	
(24)	Scott Sabo	
(25)	David Sheriff	
(26)	Bob Vantrease	
(27)	Camilo Veras	
(28)	Mike Walker	
(29)	Mark Warren	
(30)	James Wilridge	

1984 Indianapolis Indians team issue

(Montreal Expos, AAA)

		MT
Complete Set (32):		14.00
1	1984 Indianapolis Indians	
2	Bob Rodgers	
3	Leonel Carrion	
4	Chris Welsh	
5	Sal Butera	
6	Joe Hesketh	
7	Roy Johnson	
8	Craig Eaton	
9	Brad Mills	
10	The Catchers (George Bjorkman, Sal Butera)	
11	Eric Mustad	
12	Mike Fuentes	
13	Greg Bargar	
14	Shooty Babitt	
15	The Outfielders (Shooty Babitt, Mike Fuentes, Roy Johnson, Max Venable)	
16	Dick Grapenthin	
17	Razor Shines	
18	The Starting Pitchers (Greg Bargar, Tim Burke, Joe Hesketh, Eric Mustad, Chris Welsh)	
19	Bill Sattler	
20	George Bjorkman	
21	The Relief Pitchers (Darren Dilks, Craig Eaton, Dick Grapenthin, Bill Sattler)	
22	Gene Glynn	
23	Tim Burke	
24	Ron Johnson	
25	Rene Gonzales	
26	The Infielders (Mike Gates, Gene Glynn, Rene Gonzales, Ron Johnson, Brad Mills, Razor Shines)	
27	Darren Dilks	
28	Max Venable	
29	Mike Gates	
30	Mike Stenhouse	
31	Jeff Porter	
32	Bush Stadium	

1984 TCMA Iowa Cubs

(Chicago Cubs, AAA) (#26 not issued)

		MT
Complete Set (31):		80.00
1	Ken Pryce	
2	Bill Earley	
3	Cubby (team mascot)	
4	Dick Easter	
5	Ken Grandquist	
6	Jon Perlman	
7	Thad Bosley	
8	Don Rohn	
9	Joe Hicks	
10	B. Holden, F. Macy	
11	Jim Napier	
12	Pete Mackanin	
13	S. Bernabe, M. Schimming	
14	Trey Brooks	
15	Bill Hayes	
16	Don Werner	
17	Tom Lombarski	
18	Dave Owen	
19	B. Bielenberg, C. McCullough	
20	Gil Carlos	
21	Dick Cummings	
22	Don Schulze	
23	Porfirio Altamirano	
24	Billy Hatcher	
25	Joe Carter	
27	Ron Meredith	
28	Tom Filer	
29	Bill Johnson	
30	Tom Grant	
31	Reggie Patterson	
----	Derek Botelho	

1984 TCMA Jackson Mets

(N.Y. Mets, AA) (#13-14 not issued)

		MT
Complete Set (25):		40.00
1	DeWayne Vaughn	
2	Rick Myles	
3	Mark Lockenmeyer	
4	Calvin Schiraldi	
5	Reggie Jackson	
6	Jeff Innis	
7	Bill Fultz	
8	Joe Graves	
9	Jeff Bettendorf	
10	Greg Pavlick	
11	Staff (B. Hetrick, S. Massengale, R. Rainer)	
12	Bill Max	
15	Floyd Youmans	
16	Sam Perlozzo	
17	Billy Beane	
18	Lenny Dykstra	
19	Daryl Denby	
20	Mark Carreon	
21	Dave Cochran	
22	Steve Springer	
23	Al Pedrique	
24	Fermin Ubri	
25	Randy Milligan	
----	Ed Hearn	
----	Greg Olson	

1984 Smokey Bear Jackson Mets alumni

(N.Y. Mets, AA) (3" x 4")

		MT
Complete Set (15):		65.00
(1)	Neil Allen (Cardinals)	
(2)	Wally Backman (Mets)	
(3)	Hubie Brooks (Mets)	
(4)	Jody Davis (Cubs)	
(5)	Brian Giles (Mets)	
(6)	Tim Leary (Mets)	
(7)	Lee Mazzilli (Pirates)	
(8)	Jesse Orosco (Mets)	
(9)	Jeff Reardon (Expos)	
(10)	Doug Sisk (Mets)	
(11)	Darryl Strawberry (Mets)	
(12)	Mookie Wilson (Mets)	
(13)	Marvel Wynne (Pirates)	
(14)	Ned Yost (Rangers)	
(15)	Davey Johnson (Mets)	

1984 Trackle Kinston Blue Jays Postcards

(Toronto Blue Jays, A) (3-1/2" x 5-3/8", b/w, postcard back, players unidentified)

		MT
Complete Set (31):		35.00
(1)	Kevin Aitcheson	
(2)	Luis Aquino	
(3)	Doug Ault	
(4)	Kash Beauchamp	
(5)	J.J. Cannon	
(6)	Eddie Castro	
(7)	Mark Clemons	
(8)	Jeff DeWillis	
(9)	Cecil Fielder	
(10)	Greg Griffin	
(11)	Rob Holbrook	
(12)	John Holland	
(13)	Tom Linkmeyer	
(14)	Nelson Liriano	
(15)	Perry Lychak	
(16)	Omar Malave	
(17)	Alan McKay	
(18)	Jose Mesa	
(19)	Ralph Rivas	
(20)	Ronnie Robbins	
(21)	Drex Roberts	
(22)	Jose Segura	
(23)	Chris Shaddy	
(24)	Kevin Sliwinski	
(25)	Hilario Soriano	
(26)	Bobby Sprowl	
(27)	Rico Sutton	
(28)	Bernie Tatis	
(29)	Johnny Taylor	
(30)	Guillermo Valenzuela	
(31)	David Wells	

1984 Cramer Las Vegas Stars

(San Diego Padres, AAA) (A limited-edition, glossy set was also made)

		MT
Complete Set (25):		7.50
218	Greg Booker	
219	Ray Hayward	
220	Joe Lansford	
221	Bob Patterson	
222	Jerry Davis	
223	Jerry DeSimone	
224	Fritz Connally	
225	Bruce Bochy	
226	Marty Decker	
227	Mike Martin	
228	John Kruk	
229	Walt Vanderbush	
230	Rick Lancellotti	
231	Ed Wojna	
232	Tom House	
233	Felix Oroz	
234	George Hinshaw	
235	Darren Burroughs	
236	Ozzie Guillen	
237	Ron Roenicke	
238	Larry Brown	
239	Bob Cluck	
240	Ed Rodriguez	
244	Larry Duensing	
250	John Kruk	

Modern cards in Near Mint condition are generally valued at about 75% of the Mint values shown here. Excellent-condition cards are worth about 40% of the value shown. Cards in lower grades are generally not collectible.

1984 TCMA Little Falls Mets

(N.Y. Mets, A)

	MT
Complete Set (26):	32.00

1 Will Stiles
2 Keith Belcik
3 Mike Westbrook
4 Scott Little
5 Chuck Friedel
6 Ralph Adams
7 Jeff Karr
8 Ray Pereira
9 Keith Traylor
10 Shane Young
11 Owen Moreland,III
12 Jeff Howes
13 Bud Harrelson
14 Terence Johnson
15 Craig Kiley
16 Jeff Ciszkowski
17 Hector Perez
18 Bucky Autry
19 Kevin Elster
20 Alan Wilson
21 Mauro Gozzo
22 Mark Davis
23 Lew Graham
24 David West
25 Rich Rodriguez
26 Ron Dominco

1984 Riley's Louisville Redbirds

(St. Louis Cardinals, AAA)

	MT
Complete Set (30):	20.00

1 Jim Fregosi
2 Gaylen Pitts
3 Jerry Mc Kune
4 Dyar Miller
5 Gene Roof
6 Gary Rajsich
7 Doyle Harris
8 Tom Nieto
9 Dave Von Ohlen
10 Jed Smith
11 Kevin Hagen
12 Rod Booker
13 Jose Gonazlez
14 Bill Lyons
15 Terry Pendleton
16 Ralph Citarella
17 Kurt Kenshire
18 Vic Harris
19 Jim Aducci
20 Vince Coleman
21 Jack Ayer
22 Jeff Keener
23 Rick Ownbey
24 Terry Clark
25 Steve Baker
26 Jerry Johnson
27 Mark Salas
28 Mickey Mahler
29 Dave Kable
30 Dennis Werth

1984 Trackle Lynchburg Mets Postcards

(N.Y. Mets, A) (3-1/2" x 5-3/8", b/w, postcard back, players unidentified)

	MT
Complete Set (12):	25.00

(1) Mike Cubbage
(2) Jason Felice
(3) John Heller
(4) Paul Hollins
(5) Stan Jefferson
(6) Dave Jensen
(7) Barry Lyons
(8) Dave Magadan
(9) Randy Myers
(10) Julio Paula
(11) Wade Schexnayder
(12) Lou Thornton

1984 T&J Sportscards Madison Muskies

(Oakland A's, A) (black & white)

	MT
Complete Set (25):	15.00

1 Darrel Akerfelds
2 Larry Beardman
3 Rich Borowski
4 Maurice Castain
5 Kevin Coughlon
6 Mike Fulmer
7 Eric Garrett
8 Wayne Giddings
9 Shawn Gill
10 Dennis Gonsalves
11 Darel Hansen
12 Jim Jones
13 Bob Loscalzo
14 John Marquardt
15 Rob Nelson
16 Terry Steinbach
17 Tim Belcher
18 Al Heath
19 Luis Polonia
20 Joe Odom
21 Scotty Lee Whaley
22 Mike Wilder
23 Dave Schober
24 Gary Lance
25 Brad Fischer

1984 TCMA Maine Guides

(Cleveland Indians, AAA)

	MT
Complete Set (23):	10.00

1 Ramon Romero
2 Jerry Reed
3 Roy Smith
4 Steve Farr
5 Doug Simunic
6 Richard Barnes
7 Dave Gallagher
8 Bud Anderson
9 Vic Albury
10 Doc Edwards
11 Picky DeLeon
12 Lorenzo Gray
13 Guy Elston
14 Wil Culmer
15 Jeff Barkley
16 Karl Pagel
17 Juan Espino
18 Dwight Taylor
19 Rod Craig
20 Luis Quinones
21 Keith MacWhorter
22 Ed Glynn
23 Shanie Dugas

1984 TCMA Memphis Chicks

(K.C. Royals, AA)

	MT
Complete Set (25):	45.00

1 Rick Mathews
2 Rich Dubee
3 Rick Rizzo
4 Art Hartinez
5 Billy Best
6 Reggie Wyatt
7 Mike Kingery
8 Mitch Ashmore
9 Van Snider
10 Jeff Neuzil
11 Bill Wilder
12 Doug Cook
13 Bob Hegman
14 Lester Strode
15 Vinnie Yuhas
16 Jim Miner
17 Steve Reish
18 Roger Hansen
19 Doug Gilcrease
20 Hal Hatcher
21 Jose Reyes
22 Steve Morrow
23 Mark Pirruccello
24 Bill Pecota
25 Dave Cone

1984 TCMA Midland Cubs

(Chicago Cubs, AA)

	MT
Complete Set (24):	30.00

1 Joe Henderson
2 Antonio Cordova
3 Don Hyman
4 Jim Boudreau
5 John Huey
6 Jorge Carpio
7 Joe Housey
8 Darryl Banks
9 Ray Soff
10 Mike Capel
11 Jeff Moscaret
12 Doug Potestio
13 Dennis Brogna
14 Glenn Gregson
15 George Enright
16 Darrin Jackson
17 Danny Norman
18 Ricky Baker
19 Jim Auten
20 Jeff Jones
21 Paul Noce
22 Shawon Dunston
23 Gary Varsho
24 Tony Woods

1984 Chong Modesto A's

(Oakland A's, A)

	MT
Complete Set (28):	250.00

1 Eric Barry
2 Mark Bauer
3 Paul Bradley
4 Greg Cadaret
5 Jose Canseco
6 Chip Conklin
7 Ron Cummings
8 Rocky Coyle
9 Oscar De Chavez
10 Brian Dorsett
11 Mark Ferguson
12 Eric Garret
13 Mike Gorman
14 Juan Cruz
15 Brian Guinn
16 Stan Hilton
17 Joe Law
18 Dave Leiper
19 Tony Moncrief
20 Doug Scherer
21 Keith Thrower
22 Jose Tolentino
23 George Mitterwald
24 Jeff Kobernus
25 Mark Doberenz
26 Dan Kiser
27 Dave Fry
28 Tom Zmudosky

1984 Nashville Sounds team issue

(N.Y. Yankees, AA)

	MT
Complete Set (24):	11.00

(1) Johnny Baldwin
(2) Ben Callahan
(3) John Csefalvay
(4) Pete Dalena
(5) Pat Dempsey
(6) Don Fowler
(7) Randy Graham
(8) Johnny Hawkins
(9) Stan Javier
(10) Mike King
(11) Tim Knight
(12) Jim Marshall
(13) Don Mc Gann
(14) Scott Nielsen
(15) Dan Pasqua
(16) Erik Peterson
(17) Jim Rasmussen
(18) Jim Saul
(19) Mark Shiflett
(20) Keith Smith
(21) Bob Tewksbury
(22) Chuck Tomaselli
(23) Hoyt Wilhelm
(24) Bill Worden

1984 TCMA Newark Orioles

(Baltimore Orioles, A) (Arnold is scarce late-issue card)

	MT
Complete Set, w/Arnold (25):	32.00
Partial Set, no Arnold (24):	14.00

1 Randy Riley
2 Eric Bell
3 Troy Howerton
4 David Dahse
5 Dan Mickan
6 Wayne Wilson
7 Dan Fizpatrick
8 Alan Ennis
9 Rich Bair
10 Greg Wirth
11 David Smith
12 Mike Whalen
13 Dan Hayes
14 Tim Smith
15 Frank Velleggia
16 Jim Rooney
17 Rich Caldwell
18 Henry Gonzales
19 Larry Heise
20 Gerry Adams
21 Bob Gutierrez
22 Randy Wilson
23 Jim Hutto
24 Bob Kline
25 Jeff Arnold (bat boy)

1984 TCMA Oklahoma City 89'ers

(Texas Rangers, AAA)

	MT
Complete Set (24):	20.00

1 Al Lachowicz
2 Rob Clark
3 Tommy Burgess
4 Cliff Wherry
5 Rusty Gerhardt
6 Dan Larson
7 Mike Griffin
8 Dave Stockstill
9 Mike Jirschele
10 Tom Henke
11 Nick Capra
12 Tony Fossas
13 Steve Buechele
14 Mike Rubel
15 Barry Brunkenkant
16 Kevin Buckley
17 Chuckie Canady
18 Tommy Dunbar
19 Don Scott
20 Victor Cruz
21 Mitch Zwolensky
22 Glenn Cook
23 Dan Murphy
24 German Barranca

1984 TCMA Omaha Royals

(K.C. Royals, AAA)

	MT
Complete Set (30):	15.00

1 Charlie Leibrandt
2 Gene Lamont
3 Tony Ferreira
4 Al Hargesheimer
5 Frank Wills
6 Rickey Keeton
7 Nick Swartz
8 John Morris
9 Mike Brewer
10 Steve Hammond
11 Mike Parrott
12 Marty Wilkerson
13 Jerry Cram
14 Bill Gorman
15 Keith Creel
16 Vinnie Yuhas
17 Theo Shaw
18 Dan St. Clair
19 Mike Alvarez
20 Mike Jones
21 Cliff Pastornicky
22 Dave Leeper
23 Brian Poldberg
24 Mark Ryal
25 Rondin Johnson
26 Russ Stephens
27 Jim Scranton
28 Frank Mancuso
29 Matt Bassett
30 Terry Wendlandt

1984 TCMA Pawtucket Red Sox

(Boston Red Sox, AAA) ("b" variations and #26 Mike Davis are late-issue cards)

	MT
Complete Set, corrected (26):	250.00
Partial Set, w/errors (25):	225.00

1 Charlie Mitchell
2 Lee Graham
3a Tony Torcia (name incorrect)
3b Tony Torchia (name correct)
4 Dale Robertson
5 Dennis Burtt
6 Jim Dorsey

7 Chuck Davis (photo actually Mike Davis)
8 Paul Gnacinski
9 Gus Burgess
10a Paul Hundhammer (incorrect name on back)
10b Paul Hundhammer (correct name on back)
11a Tony Herron (incorrect name on back)
11b Tony Herron (correct name on back)
12 Juan Pautt
13 Kevin Romine
14 Steve Crawford
15 Reggie Whittemore
16 Chico Walker
17 Dave Malpeso
18 Steve Lyons
19 Pat Dodson
20 Marc Sullivan
21 Mike Rochford
22 Roger Clemens
23 Rich Gale
24 Brian Denman
25 Juan Bustabad
26 Mike Davis

1984 Trackle Peninsula Pilots Postcards

(Philadelphia Phillies, A) (3-1/2" x 5-3/8", b/w, postcard back, players unidentified)

	MT
Complete Set (48):	35.00

(1) Carlos Arroyo
(2) Tony Brown
(3) David Bulls
(4) Mitch Callis (trainer)
(5) Ramon Caraballo
(6) P.J. Carey
(7) Ron Clark
(8) Kevin Coker
(9) Randy Day
(10) Gralyn Engram
(11) Tony Evetts
(12) Billy Ferguson
(13) Mark Frishman
(14) Granny Hamner
(15) Ramon Henderson
(16) John Q. Hill
(17) Ken Jackson
(18) John Kanter
(19) Dave Kennard
(20) Steve Labay
(21) Jose Leiva
(22) Bruce Long
(23) Darren Loy
(24) John Machin
(25) Darryl Menard
(26) Keith Miller
(27) Nelson Morel
(28) Billy Morton
(29) Luis Mota
(30) Ray Ortega
(31) Jim Reilly
(32) Mel Roberts
(33) Ramon Roman
(34) David Rowan (gm)
(35) Dave Seiler
(36) Todd Soares
(37) Wayne Stewart
(38) Tony Taylor
(39) Wil Tejada
(40) Del Unser
(41) Jim Vest
(42) Kevin Walters
(43) Kevin Ward
(44) Harold Warner
(45) Brant Weatherford
(46) Mike Willis
(47) Steve Witt
(48) Scott Wright

1984 Cramer Phoenix Giants

(S.F. Giants, AAA) (A limited-edition, glossy set was also produced)

	MT
Complete Set (25):	12.00

1 Phil Oullette
2 Mark Calvert
3 Mark Grant
4 Rob Deer
5 Scott Garrelts
6 Rich Murray
7 Mark Schuster
8 Alejandro Sanchez
9 Jim Farr
10 Herman Segelke
11 Tom O'Malley
12 Jeff Cornell
13 Joe Pettini
14 Tip Lefebvre
15 Brian Kingman
16 Alan Fowlkes
17 Dan Gladden
18 Randy Kutcher
19 Jeff Blobaum
20 Randy Gomez
21 Colin Ward
22 Guy Sularz
23 Chris Brown
24 Jack Mull
241 Tim Blackwell

1984 Cramer Portland Beavers

(Philadelphia Phillies, AAA) (A limited-edition glossy set was also produced)

	MT
Complete Set (22):	20.00

195 Dave Wehrmeister
196 Stephen Mura
197 Jeff Stone
198 Darren Daulton
199 Francisco Melendez
200 Lee Elia
201 Kelly Downs
202 Bobby Mitchell
203 Randy Salava
204 Don Carman
205 Steve Jeltz
206 George Riley
207 Jose Calderon
208 John Russell
209 Rick Schu
210 Ken Dowell
211 Willie Darkis
212 Richard Gaynor
213 Jay Davisson
214 Steve Fireovid
215 George Culver
216 Russ Hamric

1984 TCMA Prince William Pirates

(Pittsburgh Pirates, A)

	MT
Complete Set (34):	14.00

1 Leon Roberts
2 Jim Buckmier
3 Sean Faherty
4 Shawn Holman
5 Jim Felt
6 Dorn Taylor
7 Mike Berger
8 Pete Piskol
9 John Pavlik
10 Brian Buckley
11 Eric Fink
12 Dorley Downs
13 Wilfredo Cordoba
14 Jim Aulenback
15 Joe Charboneau
16 Felix Fermin
17 Jeff Patton
18 Scott Borland
19 Steve Lewis
20 Don Williams
21 Shawn Stone
22 Sam Haro
23 Rich Sauveur
24 Mitch McKelvey
25 Kim Christenson
26 Craig Brown
27 David Tumbas
28 Leo Sanchez
29 John Lipon
30 Dave Johnson
31 Nick Castaneda
32 Kerry Baker
33 George Borges
34 Stacy Pettis

1984 TCMA Richmond Braves

(Atlanta Braves, AAA)

	MT
Complete Set (27):	10.00

1 Mike Reynolds
2 Rufino Linares
3 Ken Smith
4 Paul Boris
5 Larry Whisenton
6 Tom Hayes
7 Vic Lisi
8 Larry Owen
9 Tony Brizzolara
10 Brad Komminsk, Leo Vargas
11 Brad Komminsk
12 Leo Vargas
13 Craig Jones
14 Roger LaFrancois
15 Gary Reiter
16 Bob Galasso
17 Steve Shields
18 Randy Martz
19 Terry Leach
20 Brian Fisher
21 Joe Johnson
22 Sam Ayoub
23 Paul Zuvella
24 Paul Runge
25 Milt Thompson
26 Johnny Sain
27 Eddie Haas

1984 TCMA Rochester Red Wings

(Baltimore Orioles, AAA)

	MT
Complete Set (19):	16.00

1 Larry Sheets
2 Rich Carlucci
3 Mark Wiley
4 Jim Hutto
5 Mike Calise
6 John Valle
7 Lee Granger
8 Ismael Oquendo
9 Frank Verdi
10 Jeff Shaefer
11 Glenn Gulliver
12 Luis Rosado
13 Bob Bonner
14 Don Welchel
15 Leo Hernandez
16 Allan Ramirez
17 Bill Swaggerty
18 Joe Kucharski
19 Mike Young

1984 Trackle Salem Redbirds Postcards

(S.D. Padres, A) (3-1/2" x 5-3/8", b/w, postcard back, players unidentified)

	MT
Complete Set (27):	25.00

(1) Regan Bass
(2) Eli Ben
(3) Chino Cadahia
(4) Tony Carlucci
(5) Edgar Castro
(6) Rick Coatney
(7) George Crum
(8) Doug Davis
(9) Jaime Doughty
(10) Ron Dillard
(11) Jim Foit
(12) Mark Gile
(13) Otto Gonzalez
(14) Tony Hudson
(15) Chris Joslin
(16) Kirk Killingsworth
(17) Randy Kramer
(18) Marty Leach
(19) Jeff Mace
(20) Jerry Neufang
(21) Clyde Reichard
(22) Vinnie Sakowski
(23) Dan Scarpetta
(24) Daryl Smith
(25) Bill Stearns
(26) Kevin Stock
(27) Tony Triplett

1984 Cramer Salt Lake City Gulls

(Seattle Mariners, AAA) (A limited-edition glossy set was also produced)

	MT
Complete Set (24):	18.00

170 Danny Tartabull
171 Brian Allard
172 Bill Crone
173 Ivan Calderon
174 Tito Nanni
175 Dave Geisel
176 Dave Valle
177 Jed Murray
178 Brian Snyder
179 Robert Long
180 Jim Lewis
181 Bill Nahorodny
182 Jamie Allen
183 Edwin Nunez
184 Jim Presley
185 Harold Reynolds
186 Jerry Gleaton
187 Glen Walker
188 Al Chambers
189 Karl Best
190 Darnell Coles
191 Bobby Floyd
192 Bobby Cuellar
193 Brad Boylan

1984 TCMA Savannah Cardinals

(St. Louis Cardinals, A)

	MT
Complete Set (26):	15.00

1 Sonny James
2 Jeff Lauck
3 Barry McPherson
4 John Costello
5 Kurt Kaull
6 Chuck McGrath
7 Ken Huth
8 Hans Herzog
9 Ted Milner
10 Jim Reboulet
11 Mark Angelo
12 Bob Kish
13 Jamie Brisco
14 Jeff Perry
15 Ernie Carrasco
16 Harry McCulla
17 Bill Packer
18 Glenn Harris
19 Victor Paulino
20 George Vogel
21 Lloyd Merritt
22 Sal Agostinelli
23 Ted Carson
24 Miguel Soto
25 Ken Sinclair
26 Mike Behrend

Modern cards in Near Mint condition are generally valued at about 75% of the Mint values shown here. Excellent-condition cards are worth about 40% of the value shown. Cards in lower grades are generally not collectible.

1984 1st Base Sports Shreveport Captains

(S.F. Giants, AA)

	MT
Complete Set (24):	25.00

(1) Kevin Bates
(2) Orlando Blackwell
(3) Randy Bockus
(4) Steve Cline
(5) Larry Crews
(6) Bob Cumming
(7) Duane Espy
(8) Bob Gendron
(9) Mike Jones
(10) Chuck Lusted
(11) Kurt Mattson
(12) Bobby Moore
(13) Randy Morse
(14) Matt Nokes
(15) Bob O'Connor
(16) Jessie Reid
(17) Kernan Ronan
(18) Steve Smith
(19) Bryan Snyder
(20) Van Sowards
(21) Steve Stanicek
(22) John Stevenson
(23) Kelvin Torve
(24) Dave Wilhelmi

1984 Spokane Indians team issue

(San Diego Padres, A) (black-and-white photos)

	MT
Complete Set (23):	22.00

1 Rodney McCray
5 Trace Czyzewski
7 Eric Varoz
8 Larry Martin Jr.
9 Jose Lora
10 Jack Maloof
11 Mick Kelleher
14 Mike DeButch
15 Mike Costello
16 Brad Pounders
17 Efrain Valdez
18 Greg Sparks
20 Steve Luebber
23 Robert Perkins
25 John Carlson
26 Mick Gildehaus
27 Joe Filandino
30 Terry Forbes
32 Rusty Ford
34 Rich Scales
42 Joe Bitker
44 Jorge Suris
48 Randell Byers

1984 TCMA Syracuse Chiefs

(Toronto Blue Jays, AAA)

	MT
Complete Set (32):	35.00

1 Jim Beauchamp
2 Larry Hardy

3 Tommy Craig
4 Dennis Howard
5 Ron Shephard
6 Rick Leach
7 Anthony Johnson
8 Augie Schmidt
9 Tony Fernandez
10 Jerry Keller
11 Matt Williams
12 Fred Manrique
13 Bobby Nandin
14 Al Woods
15 Toby Hernandez
16 Mike Proly
17 Tim Rodgers
18 Mark Eichhorn
19 Stan Clarke
20 Tom Lukish
21 David Walsh
22 Mike Morgan
23 Mark Bomback
24 Manny Castillo
25 Dave Shipanoff
26 Dave Stenhouse
27 Kelly Gruber
28 Dale Holman
29 Jim Baker
30 Tim Thompson
31 John Cerutti
32 Batboys

1984 Cramer Tacoma Tigers

(Oakland A's, AAA) (A limited-edition glossy set was also made)

MT
Complete Set (25): 7.50
73 Bruce Robinson
74 Dave Hudgens
75 Ron Arnold
76 Ramon de los Santos
77 Tom Romano
78 Steve Kiefer
79 Carlos Lezcano
80 Bill Bathe
81 Mike Gallego
82 Jeff Jones
83 Steve Ontiveros
84 Bill Krueger
85 Curt Young
86 Chuck Hensley
87 Tim Pyznarski
88 Phil Stephenson
89 Mark Wagner
90 Ed Nottle
91 Danny Goodwin
92 Bert Bradley
93 John Hotchkiss
94 Dave Ford
95 Gorman Heimueller
96 Dan Meyer
247 Ed Farmer

1984 TCMA Tidewater Tides

(N.Y. Mets, AAA)

MT
Complete Set (28): 35.00
1 Scott Holman
2 Sid Fernandez
3 Wes Gardner
4 John Christensen
5 Herman Winningham
6 Bill Latham
7 Gil Flores
8 Brent Gaff
9 Rusty Tillman
10 Bob Schaefer
11 Ed Olwine
12 Rich Pickett
13 Jeff Bittiger
14 Tom Gorman
15 Jay Tibbs
16 Rafael Santana
17 Bob Sikes
18 Ross Jones
19 Rick Anderson
20 Terry Blocker
21 Laschelle Tarver
22 Al Jackson
23 Kevin Mitchell
24 Brian Giles
25 Ronn Reynolds
26 Terry Leach
27 Kelvin Chapman
28 Clint Hurdle

Value of modern team sets is often predicated as much on inclusion of star player's early cards as on scarcity of the issue.

1984 TCMA Tidewater Tides Darryl Strawberry

(N.Y. Mets, AAA)

MT
Darryl Strawberry 25.00
(Reportedly issued by TCMA as a promotion for its 1984 team-set line-up. Blank backed.)

1984 TCMA Toledo Mud Hens

(Minnesota Twins, AAA)

MT
Complete Set (24): 14.00
1 Steve Lombardozzi
2 Jeffrey Reed
3 Alvaro Espinoza
4 Ray Smith
5 Rich Yett
6 Cal Ermer
7 Dan Schmitz
8 Brad Havens
9 Bob Mulligan
10 Bob Mitchell
11 Andre David
12 Scott Ulger
13 James Weaver
14 Tom Klawitter
15 Jack O'Connor
16 Keith Comstock
17 Eric Broersma
18 Greg Field
19 Tim Agan
20 Dave Baker
21 Jim Shellenback
22 Tack Wilson
23 Rick Lysander
24 Jay Pettibone

1984 Cramer Tucson Toros

(Houston Astros, AAA) (A limited-edition glossy set was also made)

MT
Complete Set (25): 9.00
49 Eric Rasmussen
50 Matt Galante
51 Jose Alvarez
52 Chris Jones
53 Wes Clements
54 Greg Cypert
55 Dwight Bernard
56 Rex Jones
57 Tim Tolman
58 Jaime Williams
59 Manny Hernandez
60 Tye Waller
61 Jim Pankovits
62 Glenn Davis
63 Julio Solano
64 Eddie Bonine
65 Jeff Heathcock
66 Ruben Robles
67 Bert Pena
68 Mark Ross
69 Craig Minetto
70 Larry Ray
71 Luis Pujols
72 Ron Mathis
248 Gary Tuck

1984 Tulsa Drillers team issue

(Texas Rangers, AA)

MT
Complete Set (22): 18.00
4 Jorge Gomez
6 Keith Jones
7 Oscar Mejia
14 Greg Jemison
16 Dan Murphy
18 Randy Asadoor
19 Greg Tabor
20 Whitney Harry
22 Barry Bass
23 Orlando Gomez
24 Tim Meckes
26 Bob Gergen
27 John Buckley
28 Bill Hance
29 Jose Guzman
30 Steve Kordish
31 Javier Ortiz
32 Billy Taylor
34 Terry Johnson
36 Dwayne Henry
37 Tommy Joe Shimp
---- Greg Campbell

1984 Cramer Vancouver Canadians

(Milwaukee Brewers, AAA) (A limited-edition glossy set was also produced)

MT
Complete Set (25): 14.00
25 Ron Koenigsfeld
26 Andy Beene
27 Tony Muser
28 Doug Loman
29 Dan Davidsmeier
30 Ray Searage
31 Kelvin Moore
32 Tom Candiotti
33 Frankie Thomas
34 Carlos Ponce
35 Earnie Riles
36 Dan Boone
37 Dave Huppert
38 Hoskin Powell
39 Doug Jones
40 Bob Gibson
41 Eric Peyton
42 Scott Roberts
43 Jamie Nelson
44 Ed Irvine
45 Jim Koontz
46 Mike Anderson
47 Marshall Edwards
48 Jack Lazorko
243 Don Rowe

1984 TCMA Visalia Oaks

(Minnesota Twins, A)

MT
Complete Set (25): 16.00
1 Bennie Richie
2 Curt Kindred
3 Erez Borowsky
4 Alexis Marte
5 Vincent Ferraro
6 Osvaldo Alfonzo
7 Corey Elliot
8 Phillip Sheppard
9 Leonard Braddy
10 John Hilton
11 Timothy Thompson
12 Brian Hobaugh
13 Tom Reed
14 Jeffrey Schugel
15 Carson Carroll
16 Tim Graupmann
17 Matthew Butcher
18 Paul Mancuso
19 Antonio Codinach
20 Allan Anderson
21 Ronald Scheer
22 Scott Gibson
23 Joseph Tarangelo
---- Steven Aragon
---- Dan Lindquist

1984 Rock's Wichita Aeros

(Cincinnati Reds, AAA)

MT
Complete Set (23): 45.00
1 Charlie Puleo
2 Dave Miley
3 Hector Rincones
4 Leo Garcia
5 Tom Browning
6 Charlie Nail
7 Wayne Krenchicki
8 Ron Robinson
9 Curt Heidenrich
10 Dave Van Gorder
11 Tom Runnells
12 Mark Gilbert
13 Terry Bogener
14 Keefe Cato
15 Eric Davis
16 Skeeter Barner
17 Bill Landrum
18 Alan Knicely
19 John Franco
20 Fred Toliver
21 Wade Rowdon
22 Gene Dusan
---- Checklist

1984 Rock's Wichita Aeros Posters

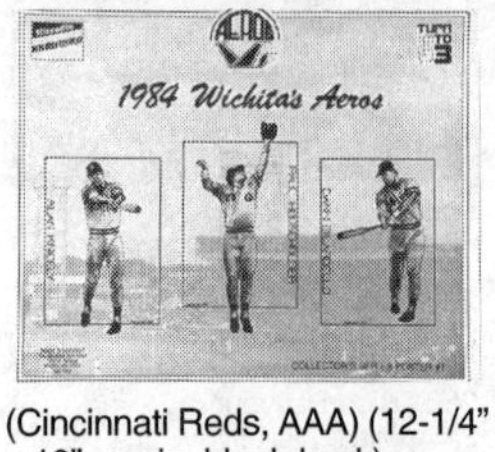

(Cincinnati Reds, AAA) (12-1/4" x 10", sepia, blank-back)

MT
Complete Set (3): 100.00
1 Alan Knicely, Paul Householder, Dann Bilardello
2 Tom Browning, Fred Toliver, Ron Robinson
3 Wade Rowdon, Tom Runnells, Terry Bogener

1984 Trackle Winston-Salem Spirits

(Boston Red Sox, A) (3-1/2" x 5-3/8", color photographs, blank-back, players unidentified)

MT
Complete Set (26): 50.00
(1) Andy Araujo
(2) Tony Cappadonna
(3) Tim Corder
(4) Jim Dennett
(5) Steve Ellsworth
(6) Edward Estrada
(7) Tim Gordon
(8) George Greco
(9) Mike Greenwell
(10) Kevin Grubbs
(11) Demarlo Hale
(12) Sam Horn
(13) Pat Jelks
(14) Manny Jose
(15) Dana Kiecker
(16) Bruce Lockhart
(17) Dave Oliva
(18) Luis Olmedo
(19) Robert Parkins
(20) David Peterson
(21) Rey Quinonez
(22) Billy Joe Richardson
(23) Bill Slack
(24) Tito Stewart
(25) Paul Thoutsis
(26) Gary Trembley

1985 TCMA Albany-Colonie Yankees

(N.Y. Yankees, AA) (Lindsey and Hughes are scarce late-issue cards)

MT
Complete Set, w/Lindsey and Hughes (35): 50.00
Partial Set, no Lindsey, Hughes (33): 40.00
1 Brad Arnsberg
2 Tim Byron
3 Darin Cloninger
4 Doug Drabek
5 Logan Easley
6 Mark Ferguson
7 Steve Frey
8 Randy Graham
9 Scott Nielsen
10 Scott Patterson
11 Bob Tewksbury
12 Bill Lindsey
13 Phil Lombardi
14 Mark Blaser
15 Ron Chapman
16 Orestes Destrade
17 Rafael Landestoy
18 Jim Riggs
19 Dick Scott
20 Doug Carpenter
21 Tony Russell
22 Brad Winkler
23 Barry Foote
24 Dave LaRoche
25 Jim Saul
26 Mike Fennell
27 Kevin Rand
28 Bernard Bremer
29 Erik Bernard
30 S. Hayes, J. Lemperle
31 Phil Pivnick
32 John Hawkins
33 Tim Knight
34 John Liburdi
35 Keith Hughes

1985 Cramer Albuquerque Dukes

(L.A. Dodgers, AAA) (color)

MT
Complete Set (25): 6.00
151 Dean Rennicke
152 Tony Brewer
153 Joe Vavra
154 Dennis Powell
155 Craig Shipley
156 Terry Collins
157 Hector Rincones
158 Ed Amelung
159 Erik Sonberg
160 Dick McLaughlin
161 Ralph Bryant
162 German Rivera
163 Jack Fimple
164 Brian Holton
165 Lemmie Miller
166 Bill Scudder
167 Stu Pederson
168 Larry White
169 Tim Meeks
170 Gil Reyes
171 Don Smith
172 Steve Martin
173 Rafael Montalvo
174 Rich Rodas
175 Franklin Stubbs

1985 Anchorage Glacier Pilots

(Summer Amateur) (Black, white & blue, 2-1/2" x 3-3/8")

MT
Complete Set (43): 7.50
(1) Bud Aufdermauer
(2) Billy Bartels
(3) Mike Beavers
(4) Barry Blackwell
(5) Dan Boone
(6) Jeff Brown
(7) Todd Credeur
(8) Bret Davis
(9) John Eccles
(10) Andrew Fava
(11) Eric Fox
(12) Amy Gills (trainer)
(13) Dan Grunhard
(14) Mark Haley
(15) Darryl Hamilton
(16) Dan Henley
(17) Steve Hill
(18) Brent Kemnitz (coach)
(19) Dan Lake
(20) Jamie Larson (bat boy)
(21) Miami Maniac (mascot)
(22) Dustin McFarland (mascot)
(23) Steve McFarland (manager)
(24) Dan McKeown (bat boy)
(25) Guy Normand
(26) Mike Oglesbee
(27) Ron Okerlund (general mgr.)
(28) John Orton
(29) Jack O'Toole (coach)
(30) Young Park
(31) Bob Reeve
(32) Kevin Ryan
(33) Lou Sinnett (operations mgr.)
(34) Matt Siuda
(35) Bobbie Taylor
(36) Fiona Taylor (bat girl)
(37) Doug Torborg
(38) Lefty Van Brunt (coach)
(39) Brett Varoz
(40) Alex Wallace
(41) Colby Ward
(42) Eric Wilner
(43) Eric Yaeger

1985 TCMA Beaumont Golden Gators

(San Diego Padres, AA)

MT
Complete Set (25): 25.00
1 Jeffrey Childers
2 Rickey Coleman
3 Mark Williamson
4 Shane Mack
5 Edward Vosberg
6 Gregory Smith
7 Peter Kutsukos
8 Jimmy Jones
9 Ulises Sierra
10 Rigo Rodriguez
11 Steven Schefsky
12 Michael McClain
13 Edward Miller
14 Thomas Brassil
15 Frank Castro
16 Mark Poston
17 Michael Mills
18 Gary Green
19 Mark Wasinger
20 David Corman
21 Benito Santiago
22 John Tutt
23 Todd Hutcheson
24 Jack Lamabe
25 Bobby Tolan

1985 TCMA Beloit Brewers

(Milwaukee Brewers, A)

MT
Complete Set (26): 10.00
1 Mike Samuel
2 Walt Pohle
3 Joe Mitchell
4 Jim Rowe
5 Mike Coin
6 Bob Simonson
7 Rob Dewolf
8 Mike Gobbo
9 Tom Steinbach
10 Angel Rodriguez
11 Frank Mattox
12 Bernard Kent
13 Darryel Walters
14 Wes Clements
15 Dean Freeland
16 Mike Frew
17 Greg Simmons
18 Alex Madrid
19 John Ludy
20 Gary Kanwisher
21 Alan Sadler
22 Martin Montano
23 Derek Diaz
24 Miguel Alicea
25 Rob Derksen
26 Dave Machemer

1985 Cramer Bend Phillies

(Philadelphia Phillies, A) (black & white, 2" x 3")

MT
Complete Set (24): 16.00
(1) Dion Beck
(2) Ben Blackmun
(3) Steve Bowden
(4) Rodney Brunelle
(5) Tim Collins
(6) Luis Faccio
(7) Kenley Graves
(8) Nat Green
(9) Jason Grimsley
(10) Steve Harris
(11) Vince Holyfield
(12) John Hurtado
(13) Ron Jones
(14) Bruce Luttrull
(15) Trey McCall
(16) John McKinney
(17) Robert Nazabal
(18) Rick Parker
(19) Mario Perez
(20) Ernie Rodriguez
(21) Floyd Rossum
(22) Steve Sharts
(23) Clifton Walker
(24) Carlos Zayas

1985 Birmingham Barons team issue

(Detroit Tigers, AA)

MT
Complete Set (25): 60.00
(1) Ricky Barlow
(2) Cary Golbert
(3) Curt Cornwell
(4) Mark Dejohn
(5) Steve Eagar
(6) Bruce Fields
(7) Paul Gibson
(8) Mike Henneman
(9) William Hinz
(10) John Hotchkiss
(11) Duane James
(12) Al Labozzetta
(13) Gordon Mackenzie
(14) Scotti Madison
(15) Steve McInnery
(16) Craig Mills
(17) Dan Norman
(18) Ramon Pena
(19) Joe Perrotte
(20) Jeff Robinson
(21) Ronald Rollin (Rondal)
(22) Benny Ruiz
(23) Gary Springer
(24) Dan St. Clair
(25) Reggie Thomas

1985 TCMA Buffalo Bisons

(Chicago White Sox, AAA)

MT
Complete Set (26): 9.00
1 John Boles
2 Nardi Contreras
3 Greg Latta
4 Steve Christmas
5 Rick Seltheimer
6 Joel Skinner
7 Nelson Barrera
8 Jose Castro
9 Bryan Little
10 Kelvin Moore
11 Ramon Romero
12 Alex Taveras
13 Mark Gilbert
14 Randy Johnson
15 Mark Ryal
16 Dave Yobs
17 Bob Fallon
18 Steve Fireovid
19 Jerry Gleaton
20 Jim Hickey
21 Bill Long
22 Joel McKeon
23 Tom Mullen
24 Scott Stranski
25 Bruce Tanner
26 Dave Wehrmeister

1985 TCMA Burlington Rangers

(Texas Rangers, A)

MT
Complete Set (28): 9.00
1 Joe Grayston
2 Mike Page
3 Larry Klein
4 Brad Hill
5 Steve Cullers
6 Neil Reilly
7 Dale Lanok
8 George Threadgill
9 Dave Darretta
10 Mike Bucci
11 Steve Neilsen
12 Sid Akins
13 Angelo Vasquez
14 Tim Owen
15 Jim St. Laurent
16 Bob O'Hearn
17 Jim Jagnow
18 Mark Kramer
19 Carlos Hernandez
20 Bryan Dial
21 Ty Harden
22 Robin Keathley
23 Stu Rogers
24 Darrell Whitaker
25 Steve Daniel
26 Ross Jones
27 Jim Allison
28 Jim Bridges

1985 Cramer Calgary Cannons

(Seattle Mariners, AAA)

MT
Complete Set (25): 17.50
76 Karl Best
77 Jim Lewis
78 Bobby Floyd
79 Paul Serna
80 Al Chambers
81 Don Scott
82 Roy Thomas
83 John Moses
84 Bobby Cuellar
85 Frank Wills
86 Pat Casey
87 Dave Tobik
88 Mickey Brantley
89 Paul Mirabella
90 Bob Stoddard
91 Ricky Nelson
92 Brian Snyder
93 Bill Crone
94 Danny Tartabull
95 Bob Long
96 Darnell Coles
97 Ron Tingley
98 Rick Luecken
99 Joe Whitmer
100 Clay Hill

1985 TCMA Cedar Rapids Reds

(Cincinnati Reds, A)

MT
Complete Set (32): 30.00
1 John Boyles
2 Mark Cieslak
3 Mike Coffey
4 Virgil Conley
5 Clay Daniel
6 Rob Dibble
7 Barry Fick
8 Mike Goedde
9 Doug Kampsen
10 Steve Oliverio
11 Jim Pettibone
12 Danny Smith
13 Ozzie Soto
14 Mark Berry
15 Greg Toler
16 Gary Denbo
17 Greg Monda
18 Carlos Porte
19 Brian Robinson
20 Eddie Williams
21 Dan Boever
22 Elvin Fulgencio
23 Tubby Pace
24 Darren Riley
25 Allen Sigler
26 Paul Kirsch
27 Jay Ward
28 Don Buchheister
29 Rod Licht
30 Bud Curren
31 Tom Riley
32 Scott Breeden

1985 TCMA Charlotte O'S

(Baltimore Orioles, A) (Nichols and Gilbert are scarce late-issue cards)

MT
Complete Set, w/Nichols, Gilbert (31): 17.50
Partial Set, no Nichols, Gilbert (29): 10.00
1 Kenny Gerhart
2 Lee Granger
3 Jeff Jacobson
4 Rick Lockwood
5 John Stefero
6 Dave Thielker
7 Kelvin Torve
8 Tony Arnold
9 Carl Nichols
10 Mike Reddish
11 Ron Salcedo
12 Jeff Schaefer
13 Dom Chiti
14 John Hart
15 Francisco Oliveras
16 Jeff Summers
17 Jeff Wood
18 Bobby Mariano
19 Rich Caldwell
20 Jeff Gilbert
21 John Babyan
22 John Hoover
23 Ricky Jones
24 John Flinn
25 Alan Ramirez
26 Jose Brito
27 Bob Hice
28 Terry Mauney
29 Charlie Frederick
30 Paul Cameron
31 Mike Couche

1985 Chattanooga Lookouts team issue

(Seattle Mariners, AAA) (blank-back)

MT
Complete Set (26): 90.00
(1) Rick Adair
(2) Brian Bargerhuff
(3) Greg Bartley
(4) Randy Braun
(5) Renard Brown
(6) Jim Bryant
(7) Clark Crist
(8) Brian David
(9) Mario Diaz
(10) Mike Evans
(11) Dan Firova
(12) Ross Grimsley
(13) Dave Hengel
(14) Paul Hollins
(15) Tom "Radar" Hunt
(16) Ken Jones
(17) Vic Martin
(18) Jeff McDonald
(19) Rusty McNealy
(20) Jed Murray
(21) Dave Myers
(22) Randy Newman
(23) Bill Plummer
(24) Brick Smith
(25) Terry Taylor
(26) Ric Wilson

1985 Police Columbus Clippers

(N.Y. Yankees, AAA) (color, 2-3/8" x 3-3/4")

MT
Complete Set (25): 8.00
1 Kelly Heath
3 Tom Barrett
5 Kelly Scott
11 Alphonso Pulido (Alfonso)
12 Rex Hudler
14 Pete Dalena
15 Tim Knight
16 Bert Bradley
17 Butch Hobson

18 Matt Winters
19 Keith Smith
20 Curt Brown
21 Dan Pasqua
23 Dan Briggs
26 Al Williams
27 Don Cooper
29 Juan Espino
37 Brian Fisher
38 Jim Deshaies
39 Clay Christiansen
42 Mark Silva
44 Kelly Faulk
--- Carl "Stump" Merrill (manager)
--- Coaches/trainer card (Steve Donohue, Q.V. Lowe, Jerry McNertney, Mickey Vernon)
---- George H. Sisler Jr. (general manager)

1985 TCMA Columbus Clippers

(N.Y. Yankees, AAA) (set price includes scarce Bonilla and Mata cards)

	MT
Complete Set (28):	18.00

1 Vic Mata
2 Bert Bradley
3 Curt Brown
4 Clay Christiansen
5 Don Cooper
6 Kelly Faulk
7 Brian Fisher
8 Alphonso Pulido
9 Kelly Scott
10 Al Williams
11 Juan Espino
12 Mike O'Berry
13 Tom Barrett
14 Dan Briggs
15 Pete Dalena
16 Kelly Heath
17 Butch Hobson
18 Rex Hudler
19 Keith Smith
20 Tim Knight
21 Dan Pasqua
22 Matt Winters
23 Jim Deshaies
24 Mark Silva
25 Doug Holmquist
26 Juan Bonilla
29 George Sisler
---- Coaches (Steve Donohue, Q.V. Lowe, Jerry McNertney, Mickey Vernon)

1985 Daytona Beach Islanders team issue

(Cleveland Indians, A)

	MT
Complete Set (30):	55.00

1 Tim Haller
2 Michael Holm
3 Dave Murray
4 Mike Halasaz
5 Ray Corbett
6 Jeff Hubbard
7 Perry Hill
8 Kurt Beamesderfer
10 Rick Poznanski
11 Tony Triplett
12 Bill Ripken
14 Pat Vanheyningen
15 Dan Van Cleve
16 Larry Heise
17 Jim Hutto
18 Tim Smith
19 Robert Gutierrez
20 Rob Amble
22 Chris Willsher
23 Eric Dersin
24 Rich Rice
25 Jeff Melrose
26 Carm Lo Sauro
27 Edward Rohan
28 Ben Bianchi
29 Justin Gannon
30 Bruce Kipper
31 Ron Johnson
---- Brian Robinson
---- Thomas Petrizzo

1985 TCMA Durham Bulls

(Atlanta Braves, A)

	MT
Complete Set (32):	15.00

1 Paul Assenmacher
2 Vince Barger
3 Kevin Blankenship
4 Mike Bormann
5 Kevin Coffman
6 Maximo Del Rosario
7 David Jones
8 Dave Morris
9 Mac Rogers
11 Mike Santiago
12 Marty Schrieber
13 Troy Tomsick
14 Harry Bright
15 Jim Grant
16 Bob Porter
17 Mike Delao
18 Flavio Alfaro
19 Chris Baird
20 Chip Childress
21 Terry Cormack
22 Sal D'Alessandro
23 Juan Fredymond
24 Dave Griffin
25 Wayne Harrison
26 Johnny Hatcher
27 Roger LaFrancois
28 Mike Nipper
29 Bob Posey
30 Mike Reynolds
31 Jeff Wagner
32 Mike Yastrzemski

1985 Cramer Edmonton Trappers

(California Angels, AAA)

	MT
Complete Set (25):	16.00

1 Pat Keedy
2 Wally Joyner
3 Mike Madril
4 Don Groh
5 Scott Oliver
6 Tony Mack
7 Kirk McCaskill
8 Reggie West
9 Rafael Lugo
10 James Randall
11 Marty Kain
12 Gus Polidor
13 Steve Liddle
14 Winston Llenas
15 Bob Ramos
16 Dave Smith
17 Tim Krauss
18 Chris Clark
19 Stewart Cliburn
20 Curt Kaufman
21 Bob Bastian
22 Norman Carrasco
23 Frank Reberger
24 Jack Howell
25 Al Romero

1985 TCMA Elmira Pioneers

(Boston Red Sox, A)

	MT
Complete Set (25):	70.00

1 John Abbot (Abbott)
2 Brady Anderson
3 Mike Carista
4 Dell Carter
5 Jim Cox
6 Roberto Fuentes
7 Dan Gabriele
8 Gary Gouldrup
9 Brock Knight
10 Eric Laseke
11 Derek Livernois
12 Greg Lotzar
13 Greg Magistri
14 Josias Manzanillo
15 Donnie McGowan
16 Bill Plante
17 Todd Pratt
18 Carlos Quintana
19 Marte Rogers
20 Victor Rosario
21 Tim Speakman
22 John Toale
23 Luis Vasquez
24 Kerman Williams
25 Bill Zupka

1985 Cramer Everett Giants Series I

(S.F. Giants, A) (black & white, 2" x 3")

	MT
Complete Set (24):	7.50

(1) David Blakely
(2) George Bonilla (pitching)
(3) George Bonilla (portrait)
(4) Ty Dabney
(5) Tom Ealy
(6) Kim Flowers (portrait)
(7) Kim Flowers (with glove)
(8) George Jones (portrait)
(9) George Jones (with bat)
(10) Joe Kmak
(11) Alan Marr
(12) Willie Mijares
(13) Todd Miller
(14) Rick Nelson (holding bat)
(15) Rick Nelson (swinging bat)
(16) Tom Osowski
(17) Darren Pearson (standing in shadow)
(18) Darren Pearson (sunlight on right side)
(19) Brian Petty
(20) Steve Santora
(21) Howard Townsend (portrait)
(22) Howard Townsend (with glove)
(23) John Verducci
(24) Mike Whitt

1985 Cramer Everett Giants Series II

(S.F. Giants, A) (black & white, 2" x 3")

	MT
Complete Set (24):	15.00

1 Jeff Carter
2 Mike Dandos
3 Bruce Graham
4 Dave Hornsby
5 Lloyd Jackson
6 Robert Jackson
7 Darrin James
8 Joe Jordan
9 Randy McCament
10 Timber Mead
11 Dave Morris
12 Curt Motton
13 Brian Ohnoutka
14 Doug Robertson
15 Darrell Rodgers
16 Steve Santora
17 Billy Smith
18 Joe Strain
19 Jack Uhey
20 John Van Kempen
21 Paul Van Stone
22 Mike Whitt
23 Rick Wilson
24 Trevor Wilson

Suffix letters following a card number indicate a variation card.

1985 Smokey Bear Fresno Giants

(S.F. Giants, A) (2-5/8" x 4", black-and-white photos, orange borders) (1,000 sets reported produced)

	MT
Complete Set (31):	90.00

1 Wendell Kim
2 Marty De Merritt
3 Charles Culberson
4 Angel Escobar
5 Dave Allen
6 Mike Jones
7 Jim Wasem
8 Mackey Sasser
9 Deron McCue
10 Greg Gilbert
11 Charlie Hayes
12 Greg Litton
13 Romy Cucjen
14 John Grimes
15 Ed Puikunas
16 Dan Winters
17 Charlie Corbell
18 Jay Reid
19 Stuart Tate
20 Al Candelaria
21 Todd Kuhn
22 John Burkett
23 Steve Smith
24 Rich Henning
25 Tommy Alexander
26 Todd Oakes
27 Don Wolfe
28 Paul Neff, Paul Reyne
29 Bill Thompson
30 Curt Goldgrabe
31 Mary Driscoll

1985 TCMA Ft. Myers Royals

(K.C. Royals, A)

	MT
Complete Set (30):	25.00

1 Ed Bass
2 Todd Mabe
3 Brad Davis
4 Craig Walter
5 Don Sparling
6 Tom Niemann
7 Angel Morris
8 Jeff Hull
9 Kevin Seitzer
10 Mark Van Blaricom
11 Phil George
12 Jose DeJesus
13 Jose Nunez
14 Jeff Brown
15 Israel Sanchez
16 Chito Martinez
17 Doug Gilcrease
18 Gary Thurman
19 Tommy Mohr
20 Theo Shaw
21 Mark Farnsworth
22 Steve DeSalvo
23 Mike Keckler
24 Jackie Blackburn
25 Jim Moore
26 Duane Gustavson
27 Mike Alvarez
28 Luis Santos
29 Derek Vanacore
30 Jose Rodiles

1985 TCMA Greensboro Hornets

(Boston Red Sox, A)

	MT
Complete Set (28):	10.00

1 Doug Camilli
2 Alan Ashikinazy
3 Tary Scott
4 Manuel Jose
5 Thomas Bonk
6 Bruce Lockhart
7 Christopher Moritz
8 Joseph Skripko
9 Zachary Crouch
10 Roberto Zambrano
11 Joseph Stephenson
12 Wayne Tremblay
13 Eduardo Zambrano
14 Pat Dewechter
15 Roy Hall
16 James Corsi
17 Daryl Irvine
18 Eric Hetzel
19 David Peterson
20 Daniel Cakeler
21 Ernest Abril
22 Patrick Jelks
23 Jose Flores
24 Eugene Barrios
25 Anthony DeFrancesco
26 Leverne Jackson
27 Bradley Mettler
28 John DePrimo

1985 Pizza Hut Greenville Braves

(Atlanta Braves, AA) (Set issued in form of 16-1/2" x 21" poster.)

	MT
Complete Set (26):	60.00

4a Bob Luzon
4b Bill Slack
5 Mike Knox
6 Maximo Rosario
7 Tom Hayes
8 Andres Thomas
11 Jeff Ransom
12 Glen Bockhorn
14 Randy Ingle
15 Rich Leggatt
16 Paul Assenmacher
17 Rick Albert
19 Todd Lamb
20 Tommy Thompson
22 Leo Vargas
25 Inocencio Guerrero
27 Steve Ziem
30 Andre Treadway
31 Larry Bradford
32 Jim Beauchamp
40 Ben Callahan
55 Luke Appling
--- Bob Tumpane
--- Ken Smith
--- Team logo card (in white)
--- Team logo card (in navy blue)

1985 Greenville Braves team issue

(Atlanta Braves, AA)

	MT
Complete Set (26):	65.00

(1) Rick Albert
(2) Brian Aviles
(3) Jim Beauchamp
(4) Glen Bockhorn
(5) Larry Bradford
(6) Inocencio Guerrero
(7) Tom Hayes
(8) Randy Ingle
(9) Joe Johnson
(10) Mike Knox
(11) Todd Lamb
(12) Rich Leggatt
(13) Bob Luzon
(14) Simon Rosario
(15) Matt Sinatro
(16) Bill Slack
(17) Jeff Taylor
(18) Andre Thomas
(19) Tommy Thompson
(20) Freddie Tiburcio
(21) Andre Treadway
(22) Bob Tumpane
(23) Leo Vargas
(24) Duane Ward
(25) Larry Whisenton
(26) Steve Ziem

1985 Trackle Hagerstown Suns Postcards

(Baltimore Orioles, A) (3-1/2"x 5-3/8", b/w, postcard back, players unidentified)

	MT
Complete Set (15):	25.00

(1) Greg Biagini
(2) Eric Bell
(3) Bob Bellini
(4) Edgar Castro
(5) Glenn Dooner
(6) Alan Hixon
(7) Jerry Holtz
(8) Gerry Melillo
(9) Keith Mucha
(10) Chris Padget
(11) Dana Smith
(12) D.L. Smith
(13) Frank Velleggia
(14) Jeff Williams
(15) Roger Wilson

1985 Cramer Hawaii Islanders

(Pittsburgh Pirates, AAA)

	MT
Complete Set (25):	7.50

226 Jim Opie
227 Sam Khalifa
228 Scott Loucks
229 Denio Gonzalez
230 Rick Reuschel
231 Benny Distefano
232 Paul Semall
233 Tommy Sandt
234 Mitchell Page
235 Steve Shirley
236 Hedi Vargas
237 Jim Winn
238 Trench Davis
239 Bobby Miscik
240 Chris Green
241 Dave Tomlin
242 Stan Cliburn
243 Bob Walk
244 Steve Herz
245 Ray Krawczyk
246 John Henry Johnson
247 John Malkin
248 Manny Sarmiento
249 Jeff Zaske
250 Jerry Dybzinski

1985 Huntsville Stars team issue

(Oakland A's, AA)

	MT
Complete Set (25):	11.00
Uncut Sheet:	25.00

Brian Thorson
11 Luis Polonia
14 Brian Graham
15 Tom Dozier
16 Terry Steinbach
17 Chip Conklin
18 John Marquardt
19 Ray Thoma
20 Stan Javier
21 Bill Monneyham
22 Brian Dorsett
23 Scott Whaley
24 Gary lance
25 Brad Fischer
26 Mark Bauer
30 Larry Smith
31 Tim Belcher
32 Darrel Akerfelds
33 Eric Plunk
34 Greg Cadaret
40 Joe Law
41 Rob Nelson
42 Wayne Giddings
43 Rick Stromer
44 Jose Canseco

1985 Indianapolis Indians team issue

(Montreal Expos, AAA)

	MT
Complete Set (36):	50.00

1 Team photo
2 Felipe Alou
3 Andres Galarraga
4 Rich Stoll
5 Roy Johnson
6 Steve Baker
7 Mike Fuentes
8 Tim Cates
9 Max Venable
10 Fred Breining
11 Rene Gonzales
12 Fred Manrique
13 Greg Bargar
14 Al Newman
15 Sal Butera
16 Mickey Mahler
17 Dave Hostetler
18 Paul Hertzler
19 Randy St. Claire
20 George Bjorkman
21 Wally Johnson
22 Jack O'Connor
23 Dave Hocksema
24 Steve Brown
25 Casey Candaele
26 Coaches/Trainer Card
27 The Broadcasters
28 Ray Knight (Indianapolis alumni)
29 Dave Revering (Indianapolis alumni)
30 Ron Oester (Indianapolis alumni)
31 Mario Soto (Indianapolis alumni)
32 Bruce Berenyi (Indianapolis alumni)
33 Charlie Leibrandt (Indianapolis alumni)
34 Gary Redus (Indianapolis alumni)
35 Nick Esasky (Indianapolis alumni)
36 Bob Rodgers (Indianapolis alumni)

1985 TCMA International League All-Stars

(Class AAA) (Greenwell, Mitchell and Slider are scare late-issue cards)

	MT
Complete Set , w/late-issues (45):	65.00
Partial Set, no late-issues (42):	40.00

1 Bob Shaffer
2 Bob Tumpane
3 Miguel Sosa
4 Kevin Mitchell
5 Carlos Rios
6 Lasbelle Tarver
7 Billy Beane
8 Doc Estes
9 Larry Owen
10 Ed Hearn
11 Tony Brizzolara
12 John Rabb
13 Billy Springer (Steve Springer)
14 Al Pedrique
15 John Gibbons
16 Terry Blocker
17 Joe Johnson
18 Charlie Mitchell (withdrawn from set - scarce)
19 Rick Anderson
20 Jeff Bittiger
21 Wes Gardner
22 Roy Majtyka
23 Bruce Dal Canton
24 Doc Edwards
25 Jim Wilson
26 Juan Bonilla
27 Scott Ullger
28 Kelly Paris
29 Rick Leach
30 Mike Hart
31 Kelly Heath
32 Juan Espino
33 Dan Briggs
34 Jim Deshaies
35 Dave Gallagher
36 Dan Rohn
37 Kelly Gruber
38 Jeff Reed
39 Dennis Burtt
40 Brad Havens
41 Tom Henke
42 Tom Rowe
43 Brian Allard
44 Mike Greenwell (withdrawn from set - scarce)
45 Rac Slider (withdrawn from set - scarce)

1985 TCMA Iowa Cubs

(Chicago Cubs, AAA)

	MT
Complete Set (34):	15.00

1 Tony Castillo
2 Bill Hayes
3 Trey Brooks
4 Tom Lombarski
5 Paul Noce
6 Dave Owen
7 Julio Valdez
8 Brian Dayett
9 Tom Grant
10 Billy Hatcher
11 Chico Walker
12 Jay Baller
13 Derek Botelho
14 Dave Gumpert
15 Scott Holman
16 Bill Johnson
17 Ron Meridith
18 Sam Bernabe
19 Jon Perlman
20 Ken Pryce
21 Larry Rothschild
22 Mark Gillaspie
23 Dave Hostetler
24 Greg Hoffmann
25 Dick Cummings
26 Ken Grandquist
27 Don Silverman
28 Larry Cox
29 Jim Colborn
30 Steve Carroll
31 Steve Weck
33 Bruce Bielenberg
35 Cubby (mascot) (Del Roy Smith (batboy), Danny Woolis (batboy))
36 Steve Rodiles

1985 TCMA Kinston Blue Jays

(Toronto Blue Jays, A)

	MT
Complete Set (26):	30.00

1 Mark Clemons
2 Omar Bencomo
3 Tony Castillo
4 Mike Cullen
5 Mark Dickman
6 Perry Lychak
7 Alan McKay
8 Jose Mesa
9 Pablo Reyes
10 Jose Segura
11 Willie Shanks
12 Mark Cooper
13 Nelson Liriano
14 Randy Romagna
15 Pat Borders
16 Webster Garrison
17 Omar Malave
18 Joselito Reyes
19 Glen-Allen Hill
20 Drex Roberts
21 Geronimo Berroa
22 Ken Whitfield
23 Eric Yelding
24 Grady Little
25 Rocket Wheeler
26 Tex Drake

1985 Cramer Las Vegas Stars

(San Diego Padres, AAA)

	MT
Complete Set (25):	20.00

101 Victor Rodriguez
102 Rusty Tillman
103 John Kruk
104 Ray Hayward
105 Mark Parent
106 Steve Lubratich
107 Marty Decker
108 Ed Rodriguez
109 Lance McCullers
110 Bob Cluck
111 Walt Vanderbush
112 Gene Walter
113 George Hinshaw
114 Ray Smith
115 Steve Garcia
116 Randy Asadoor
117 Bob Patterson
118 Keefe Cato
119 Jim Leopold
120 Ed Wojna
121 Sonny Siebert
122 Tim Pyznarski
123 Mike Couchee
124 Kevin Kristan
125 James Steels

1985 TCMA Little Falls Mets

(N.Y. Mets, A)

	MT
Complete Set (27):	10.00

1 Mike Anderson
2 Kevin Armstrong
3 Steve Brueggemann
4 Ron Dominico
5 Brian Givens
6 Lorin Jundy
7 Kelvin Page
8 Chris Rauth
9 Jeff Richardson
10 John Touzzo
11 Tom Wachs
12 Todd Welborn
13 Mark Brunswick
14 Ron Narcisse
15 Rob Colescott
16 Kurt DeLuca
17 Andres Espinoza
18 Dave Gelatt
19 T.J. Johnson
20 Luis Natera
21 Craig Repoz
22 Joaquin Contreras
23 Cliff Gonzalez
24 Maury Gooden
25 Dean Johnson
26 Johnny Monell
27 Bryant Robertson

1985 Riley's Louisville Redbirds

(St. Louis Cardinals, AAA)

	MT
Complete Set (30):	14.00

1 Jim Fregosi
2 Joe Rigoli
3 Frank Evans
4 Jerry Mc Kune
5 Vince Coleman
6 Andy Hassler
7 Kevin Hagen
8 Jeff Keener
9 Dave Kable
10 Jed Smith
11 Randy Hunt
12 Joe Pettini
13 Curt Ford
14 Dave Clements
15 Jose Oquendo
16 Matt Keough
17 Bill Lyons
18 Pat Perry
19 Willie Lozado
20 Fred Martinez
21 Jack Ayer
22 Mike Lavalliere
23 John Morris
24 Mick Shade
25 Ben Hayes
26 Rick Ownby (Ownbey)
27 Casey Parsons
28 Todd Worrell
29 Mike Anderson
30 Ron Jackson

1985 TCMA Lynchburg Mets

(N.Y. Mets, A)

	MT
Complete Set (27):	14.00
1 Mike Cubbage	
2 Jim Bibby	
3 Dave Tresch	
4 Jeff Innis	
5 Reggie Dobie	
6 Mickey Weston	
7 Wray Bergendahl	
8 Dave Jensen	
9 Jose Bautista	
10 David Wyatt	
11 Tom Burns	
12 Kyle Hartshorn	
13 Joe Klink	
14 Kevin Burrell	
15 Al Carmichael	
16 Steve Philips	
17 Chris Maloney	
18 Keith Miller	
19 Kevin Elster	
20 Frank Moscat	
21 Wilmer Caraballo	
22 Andy Lawrence	
23 Rey Martinez	
24 John Wilson	
25 Shawn Abner	
26 George Doggett	
27 Scott Little	

1985 TCMA Madison Muskies

(Oakland A's, A)

	MT
Complete Set (25):	18.00
1 Scott Sabo	
2 Faustoe Santos	
3 Scott Whaley	
4 Roy Anderson	
5 Russell Appletgate	
6 Antionio Arlas	
7 Gregory Brake	
8 Todd Burns	
9 Brian Criswell	
10 Michael Cupples	
11 Brian Dorsett	
12 Patrick Dietrick	
13 Jose Ferreira	
14 Robert Gould	
15 Darel Hansen	
16 Mark Howie	
17 Domingo Jose	
18 John Kanter	
19 Russell Kibler	
20 Joseph Kramer	
21 Andrew Krause	
22 Mark Leonette	
23 James Nettles	
24 Richard Wise	
25 David Schober	

1985 T&J Sportscards Madison Muskies

(Oakland A's, A)

	MT
Complete Set (25):	22.00
1 Roy Anderson	
2 Russ Applegate	
3 Tony Arias	
4 Greg Brake	
5 Todd Burns	
6 Brian Criswell	
7 Mike Cupples	
8 Brian Dorsett	
9 P.J. Dietrick	
10 Arturo Ferreira	
11 Bob Gould	
12 Darel Hansen	
13 Mark Howie	
14 Felix Jose	
15 John Kanter	
16 Russ Kibler	
17 Joe Kramer	
18 Andy Krause	
19 Mark Leonette	
20 Jim Nettles	
21 Scott Sabo	
22 Faustoe Santos	
23 Dave Schober	
24 Scotty Lee Whaley	
25 Rick Wise	

1985 TCMA Maine Guides

(Cleveland Indians, AAA)

	MT
Complete Set (32):	10.00
1 Jeff Barkley	
2 Dave Beard	
3 Jose Calderon	
4 Mark Calvert	
5 Bryan Clark	
6 Keith Creel	
8 Jerry Reed	
9 Tommy Rowe	
10 Roy Smith	
11 Rich Thompson	
12 Jim Siwy	
13 Jose Roman	
14 Pat Dempsey	
15 Kevin Buckley	
16 Geno Petralli	
17 Shanie Dugas	
18 Barry Evans	
19 Jeff Moronko	
20 Junior Noboa	
21 Luis Quinones	
22 Danny Rohn	
23 Orlando Sanchez	
24 Jim Wilson	
26 Mike Brewer	
27 Dave Gallagher	
28 Dwight Taylor	
29 Doc Edwards	
30 Brian Allard	
31 Steve Ciszczon	
32 Scott Tellgren	

1985 TCMA Mexico City Tigers

(Independent, AAA)

	MT
Complete Set (29):	10.00
1 Jesus Rios	
2 Roberto Mendez	
3 Maurillo Arangure	
4 Oswaldo Alvarez	
5 Martin Buitimea	
6 Ramon Villegas	
7 Rodolfo Dimas	
8 Francisco Montano	
9 Ildefonso Velazquel	
10 Lorenzo Retes	
11 Francisco Coto	
12 Juan Palafox	
13 Martin Torres	
14 Jose Aguilar	
15 Jose Alvarado	
16 Ismael Jaime	
17 Homar Rojas	
18 Adulfo Camacho	
19 Jose De Jesus	
20 Manuel Morales	
21 Amado Peralta	
22 Ricardo Renteria	
23 Nicolas Castaneda	
24 Antionio Castro	
25 Matias Caprillo	
26 Javier Cruz	
27 Juan Bellacetin	
28 Luis Ibarra	
29 "Chano" & The Chicken	

1985 TCMA Midland Angels

(California Angels, AA)

	MT
Complete Set (25):	25.00
1 Tito Nanni	
2 Bryan Price	
3 Greg Key	
4 Fred Wilburn	
5 Mark Bonner	
6 David Heath	
7 Doug McKenzie	
8 Devon White	
9 Dan Murphy	
10 Joe Maddon	
11 Tom Bryden	
12 Don Timberlake	
13 Steve Finch	
14 Doug Davis	
15 Ken Angulo	
16 Spiro Psaltis	
17 Mark McLemore	
18 Kevin Davis	
19 Billie Merrifield	
20 Aurelio Monteagudo	
21 Scott Suehr	
22 Ed Delzer	
23 Juan Cruz	
24 Reggie Montgomery	
25 Julian Gonzalez	

1985 Chong Modesto A's

(Oakland A's, A) (Sets can be found with six misspelled names, "McGuire," etc., - reportedly only 200 made - or corrected names, "McGwire", etc.)

	MT
Complete Error Set, "McGuire" (28):	1350.
Complete Corrected Set, "McGwire" (28):	800.00
1a Kelvin Stock (error)	
1b Kevin Stock (correct)	
2 Paul Bradley	
3 Antonio Cabrera	
4 Twayne Harris	
5 Oscar De Chavez	
6 Eric Garrett	
7 Brian Guinn	
8a Allan Health (error)	
8b Allan Heath (correct)	
9 Joe Strong	
10 Mike Fulmer	
11 Randy Harvey	
12 Kevin Coughlon	
13 Jim Eppard	
14 Pete Kendrick	
15 Jim Jones	
16 Steve Howard	
17a Mark McGuire (error)	
17b Mark McGwire (correct)	
18a Rick Rodriquez (error)	
18b Rick Rodriguez (correct)	
19 Mark Bauer	
20a Damon Farmer (error)	
20b Damon Farmar (correct)	
21 Dave Wilder	
22 Stan Hilton	
23 Doug Scherer	
24 Bob Loscalzo	
25 Joe Odom	
26 George Mitterwald	
27a Rick Traverud (error)	
27b Rick Tronerud (correct)	
28 John Cartelli	

1985 TCMA Nashua Pirates

(Pittsburgh Pirates, AA)

	MT
Complete Set (29):	18.00
1 Scott Bailes	
2 Kerry Baker	
3 Mike Berger	
4 Craig Brown	
5 Kim Christenson	
6 Nelson de la Rosa	
7 Dorley Downs	
8 Stan Fansler	
9 Felix Fermin	
10 Ken Ford	
11 Sam Haro	
12 Dave Johnson	
13 Tony Laird	
14 Larry Lamonde	
15 Ravelo Manzanillo	
16 Lee Marcheskie	
17 Steve McAllister	
18 Mitch McKelvy	
19 Pete Rice	
20 Leon Roberts	
21 Ruben Rodriguez	
22 Leo Sanchez	
23 Rich Sauveur	
24 Don Taylor	
25 Dave Tumbas	
26 Donald Williams	
27 John Lipon	
28 George Como	
29 Jerome Mileur	

1985 Nashville Sounds team issue

(Detroit Tigers, AAA)

	MT
Complete Set (25):	8.00
(1) Doug Baker	
(2) Darrell Brown	
(3) Chuck Cary	
(4) Jeff Conner	
(5) Brian Denman	
(6) Scott Earl	
(7) Bryan Kelly	
(8) Rusty Kuntz	
(9) Mike Laga	
(10) Dwight Lowry	
(11) Scotti Madison	
(12) Don McGann	
(13) Gordy McKenzie	
(14) Dan Meyer	
(15) Bobby Mitchell	
(16) Rich Monteleone	
(17) John Pacella	
(18) Chris Pittaro	
(19) Joe Pittman	
(20) Leon Roberts	
(21) Steve Shirley	
(22) Nelson Simmons	
(23) Robert Stoddard	
(24) Paul Voight	
(25) Don Werner	

1985 TCMA Newark Orioles

(Baltimore Orioles, A)

	MT
Complete Set (25):	10.00
1 Scott Williams	
2 Randy King	
3 Ty Nichols	
4 Greg Talamantez	
5 Jeff Tackett	
6 Hemmy McFarlane	
7 Tony Rohan	
8 Mike Holm	
9 Gerald Adams	
10 Henry Gonzalez	
11 Wayne Wilson	
12 Benny Bautista	
13 Sherwin Cijntje	
14 Rico Rossy	
15 Robert Gutierrez	
16 Mark Schockman	
17 Rob Dromerhauser	
18 Ray Crone	
19 Chris Gaeta	
20 Pat Van Heyningen	
21 Pete Mancini	
22 Jesse Vazquez	
23 Matt Skinner	
24 Kevin Burke	
25 Frank Bellino	

1985 TCMA Oklahoma City 89'ers

(Texas Rangers, AAA)

	MT
Complete Set (30):	24.00
1 Orlando Mercado	
2 Mitch Zwolensky	
3 Jeff Kunkel	
4 Mike Jirchele	
5 Geno Petralli	
6 Jim Anderson	
7 Tommy Boggs	
8 Glen Cook	
9 Ricky Wright	
10 Tony Fossas	
11 Jose Guzman	
12 Mike Parrott	
13 Tommy Shimp	
14 Greg Cambell	
15 Dave Oliver	
16 George Wright	
17 Steve Buechele	
18 Oddibie McDowell	
19 Bob Sebra	
20 Jim Maler	
21 Bob Brower	
22 Mike Rubel	
23 Dave Stockstill	
24 Rusty Gerhardt	
25 Nick Capra	
26 Dale Mohorcic	
27 Dale Murray	
28 Greg Tabor	
29 Chuckie Canady	
30 Bill Earley	

1985 TCMA Omaha Royals

(K.C. Royals, AAA)

	MT
Complete Set (31):	32.00
1 Bil Gorman	
2 Matt Bassett	
3 Nick Swartz	
4 Frank Mancuso	
5 Terry Wendlandt	
6 Gus Cherry	
7 Les Strode	
8 Rich Murray	
9 Pat Putnam	
10 Tony Ferreira	
11 Rich Dubee	
12 Butch Davis	
13 Mike Griffin	
14 Renie Martin	
15 Mark Huismann	
16 Jamie Quirk	
17 Jim Scranton	
18 Mike Kinnunen	
19 John Morris	
20 Marty Wilkerson	
21 Rondin Johnson	
22 Gene Lamont	
23 Mike Kingery	
24 Dave Leeper	
25 Dave Cone	
26 Al Hargesheimer	
27 Kenny Baker	
28 Buster Keeton	
29 Bill Pecota	
30 Bob Hegman	
31 Brian Pohlberg	

1985 TCMA Orlando Twins

(Minnesota Twins, AA)

	MT
Complete Set (26):	10.00
1 Steve Aragon	
2 Erez Borowsky	
3 Mark Davison	
4 Paul Felix	
5 Mark Funderburk	
6 Dan Hanggie	
7 Alexis Marte	
8 Mike Moreno	
9 Greg Morhardt	
10 Bobby Ralston	
11 Sam Sorce	
12 Jeff Trout	
13 Mike Verkuilen	
14 Ossie Alfonzo	
15 Al Cardwood	
16 Danny Clay	
17 Ken Klump	
18 Paul Mancuso	
19 Bob Mulligan	
20 Les Straker	
21 Tim Wiseman	
22 Charlie Manuel	
23 Wayne Hattaway	
24 Dave Williams	
25 Gorman Heimueller	
26 Craig Henderson	

1985 Osceola Astros team issue

(Houston Astros, A)

MT
Complete Set (30): 110.00
(1) Troy Afenir
(2) Karl Allaire
(3) Mark Baker
(4) Curtis Burke
(5) Ken Caminiti
(6) Earl Cash
(7) Mike Cerefin
(8) Dave Cripe
(9) Greg Dube
(10) Mike Friederich
(11) Tony Hampton
(12) Scott Houp
(13) Ryan Job
(14) Kevin Jones
(15) Kirk Jones
(16) Clarke Lange
(17) Larry Lasky
(18) Arbrey Lucas
(19) Rob Mallicoat
(20) Mark Mangham
(21) Chuck Mathews
(22) Jim O'Dell
(23) Bob Parker
(24) Mark Reynolds
(25) David Rosen
(26) Doug Shaab
(27) Glenn Sherlock
(28) Mike Stellern
(29) Charley Taylor
(30) Gerald Young

1985 TCMA Pawtucket Red Sox

(Boston Red Sox, AAA) (#6 not issued)

MT
Complete Set (20): 30.00
1 Gus Burgess
2 Juan Bustabad
3 Pat Dodson
4 Mike Greenwell
5 Paul Hundhammer
7 Dave Malpeso
8 Mike Mesh
9 Garry Miller-Jones
10 Sam Nattile
11 Kevin Romine
12 Danny Sheaffer
13 Robin Fuson
14 Rac Slider
15 Dave Sax
16 Tony Herron
17 Tom McCarthy
18 Kevin Kane
19 Mitch Johnson
20 Charlie Mitchell
21 George Mercerod

1985 Trackle Peninsula Pilots Postcards

(Philadelphia Phillies, A) (3-1/2" x 5-3/8", b/w, postcard back, players unidentified)

MT
Complete Set (40): 35.00
(1) Shawn Barton
(2) Eric Bennett
(3) Mark Bowden
(4) Travis Chambers
(5) Ron Clark
(6) Pat Coveney
(7) Wayne Dannenberg
(8) Lee Davis
(9) Damon Dombek
(10) Gralyn Engram
(11) Todd Frohwirth
(12) Roberto Giansiracusa
(13) Ron Gideon
(14) Ramon Henderson
(15) Robert Hicks
(16) Brian Householder
(17) Michael Jackson
(18) Todd Johnson
(19) Bart Kaiser
(20) Dave Kennard
(21) Jeff Knox
(22) Ken Kraft
(23) Jose Leiva
(24) Ray Lloyd
(25) Bruce Long
(26) Tom Magrann
(27) Scott McClanahan
(28) Steve McDevitt
(29) John McLarnon
(30) Billy Morton
(31) Howard Nichols
(32) Dan Odgers
(33) Sergio Perez
(34) Bud Ray
(35) Ray Roman
(36) Fernando Soto
(37) Steve True
(38) Ed Watt
(39) Brant Weatherford
(40) Carlos Zayas

1985 Cramer Phoenix Giants

(S.F. Giants, AAA)

MT
Complete Set (25): 7.50
176 Jack Lazorko
177 Randy Kutcher
178 Larry Crews
179 Randy Gomez
180 Fran Mullins
181 Mike Woodard
182 Phil Oullette
183 John Rabb
184 Jeff Robinson
185 Mark Schuster
186 Pat Adams
187 Jim Lefebvre
188 Ricky Adams
189 Kelly Downs
190 Roger Mason
191 Bob Lacey
192 Doug Mansalino
193 Kevin Rhomberg
194 Augie Schmidt
195 Tack Wilson
196 Greg Schultz
197 Bobby Cummings
198 Colin Ward
199 Mark Grant
200 Jeff Cornell

1985 Cramer Portland Beavers

(Philadelphia Phillies, AAA)

MT
Complete Set (25): 25.00
26 David Rucker
27 Gib Seibert
28 Dave Shipanoff
29 Chris James
30 Steve Moses
31 Rocky Childress
32 Alan LeBoeuf
33 Arturo Gonzalez
34 Rick Schu
35 Bill Dancy
36 Jim Olander
37 Randy Salava
38 Mike Maddux
39 Bill Nahorodny
40 Tony Ghelfi
41 Jay Davisson
42 Darren Daulton
43 Francisco Melendez
44 Ralph Citarella
45 Rodger Cole
46 Ken Dowell
47 Bob Tiefenauer
48 Greg Legg
49 Rick Surhoff
50 Mike Diaz

1985 TCMA Prince Williams Pirates

(Pittsburgh Pirates, A)

MT
Complete Set (31): 18.00
1 Orlando Lind
2 Scott Neal
3 Barry Jones
4 Jose Melendez
5 Chip Cunningham
6 Terry Adkins
7 Robby Russell
8 Dimas Gutierrez
9 Steve Lewis
10 Jim Neidlinger
11 Steve Barnard
12 Mike Folga
13 Chris Lein
14 Lance Belen
15 Scott Borland
16 Shawn Holman
17 Jose Lind
18 Tony Blasucci
19 Gary Grudzinski
20 Reggie Barringer
21 Kevin Gordon
22 John Smiley
23 Ed Ott
24 Mike Stevens
25 Van Evans
26 Frank Klopp
27 J.B. Moore
28 Dave Butters
29 Scott Knox
30 Burk Goldthorn
31 Brian Jones

1985 ProCards Reading Phillies

(Philadelphia Phillies, AA)

MT
Complete Set (25): 6.00
1 George Culver
2 Randy Day
3 Marvin Freeman
4 Bruce Long
5 Ramon Caraballo
6 Kevin Ward
7 Keith Miller
8 Jose Escobar
9 Ken Kinnard
10 Todd Soares
11 Greg Jelks
12 Ken Jackson
13 Tony Brown
14 Joe Cipolloni
15 Wilfredo Tejada
16 Rob Hicks
17 Scott Wright
18 Bryan Hobbie
19 Mark Bowden
20 Jim Olson
21 Steve Labay
22 Tony Evetts
23 Darryl Menard
24 Rich Gaynor
25 Barney Nugent

1985 TCMA Richmond Braves

(Atlanta Braves, AAA)

MT
Complete Set (26): 12.50
1 Tony Brizzolara
2 Marty Clary
3 David Clay
4 Jeff Dedmon
5 Dan Morogiello
6 Mike Payne
7 Gary Reiter
8 Dave Schuler
9 Steve Shields
10 Matt West
11 John Lickert
12 Larry Owen
13 Glenn Gulliver
14 Randy Johnson
15 Carlos Rios
16 Ken Smith
17 Miguel Sosa
18 Doc Estes
19 Lee Graham
20 Gene Roof
21 Milt Thompson
22 John Rabb
23 Bruce Dal Canton
24 Sam Ayoub
25 Sonny Jackson
26 Roy Majtyka

1985 TCMA Rochester Red Wings

(Baltimore Orioles, AAA) (set price includes scarce Biercevicz and Bjorkman cards)

MT
Complete Set (31): 16.00
1 Raymond Corbett
2 Al Pardo
3 Luis Rosado
4 Dave Falcone
5 Leonardo Hernandez
6 Ricky Jones
7 Nelson Norman
8 Kelly Paris
9 James Traber
10 Roderick Allen
11 Darrel Brown
12 Robert Molinaro
13 John Shelby
14 Gerald Augustine
15 Jose Brito
16 Bradley Havens
17 Phillip Huffman
18 Jerry Johnson
19 Odell Jones
20 Joseph Kucharski
21 David Rajsich
22 William Swaggerty
23 Donald Welchel
24 Frank Verdi
25 Sandy Valdespino
26 "The Braintrust"
27 D. Gordon, J. Kurcharski
28 Jamie Reed
29 Mark Wiley
30 Greg Biercevicz
31 George Bjorkman

1985 Rochester Red Wings Cal Ripken picture ticket

(Baltimore Orioles, AAA) (Color photo of Ripken on individual game tickets)

MT
Cal Ripken Jr. 6.00

1985 Trackle Salem Redbirds Postcards

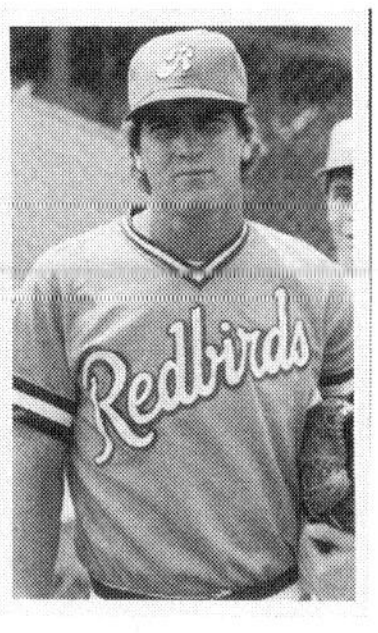

(Texas Rangers, A) (3-1/2" x 5-3/8", b/w, postcard back, players unidentified)

MT
Complete Set (23): 25.00
(1) Greg Bailey
(2) Regan Bass
(3) Marty Blair
(4) Kevin Bootay
(5) Jerry Browne
(6) Benny Cadahia
(7) Chino Cadahia
(8) Tony Carlucci
(9) Rick Coatney
(10) Riley Epps
(11) Al Farmer
(12) Don Freeman
(13) Dave Harman
(14) Al Hartman
(15) Ricky Hester
(16) Paul Kilgus
(17) Ronnie King
(18) Rick Knapp
(19) Bert Martinez
(20) Joe Morales
(21) Bill Stearns
(22) Mike Winbush
(23) Mitch Williams

1985 Cramer Spokane Indians

(San Diego Padres, A) (black & white, 2" x 3")

MT
Complete Set (24): 12.00
(1) Eric Bauer
(2) Bill Blount
(3) Jerald Clark
(4) Joey Cora
(5) Adam Ging
(6) Greg Hall
(7) Greg Harris
(8) Nate Hill
(9) Chris Knabenshue
(10) Glen Kulper
(11) Joe Lynch
(12) Jack Maloof
(13) Matt Maysey
(14) Tom Meagher
(15) Maurice Morton
(16) Jay Nieporte
(17) Eric Nolte
(18) Juan Paris
(19) Jeff Parks
(20) Ramon Rodriguez
(21) Norm Sherry
(22) Bill Stevenson
(23) Jorge Suris
(24) Jim Tatum

1985 Cramer Spokane Indians All-Time Greats

(black & white, 2" x 3")

MT
Complete Set (24): 10.00
(1) Doyle Alexander
(2) John Billingham
(3) Bill Buckner
(4) Willie Crawford
(5) Jim Fairey
(6) Alan Foster
(7) Steve Garvey
(8) Charlie Hough
(9) Tommy Hutton
(10) Von Joshua
(11) Ray Lamb
(12) Tom Lasorda
(13) Dave Lopes
(14) Joe Moeller
(15) Tom Paciorek
(16) John Purdin
(17) Bill Russell
(18) Ted Sizemore
(19) Gus Sposito
(20) Jack Spring
(21) Bob Stinson
(22) Bob Valentine
(23) Sandy Vance
(24) Geoff Zahn

1985 TCMA Springfield Cardinals

(St. Louis Cardinals, A)

	MT
Complete Set (25):	12.50

1 John Rigos
2 Rich Embser
3 Jim Fregosi
4 Jim Van Houten
5 John Costello
6 Todd Demeter
7 John Digioia
8 Greg Dunn
9 John Fassero
10 Lloyd Merrit
11 Mike Fitzgerald
12 Craig Wilson
13 Mike Hartley
14 Matt Kinzer
15 Ron Leon
16 Brad Luther
17 Harry McCulla
18 Steve Turco
19 Steve Turgeon
20 Charles McGrath
21 Jay North
22 Angelo Nunley
23 Pete Stoll
25 Mike Robinson
30 Paul Wilmet

1985 TCMA Syracuse Chiefs

(Toronto Blue Jays, AAA)

	MT
Complete Set (31):	165.00

1 Gibson Alba
2 Fred McGriff
3 Gary Allenson
4 Stan Clark (Clarke)
5 Dale Holman
6 Tom Filer
7 Keith Gilliam
8 Tom Henke
9 Dennis Howard
10 John Woodworth
11 Rick Leach
12 Matt Williams
13 Don Gordon
14 Alex Infante
15 Colin McLaughlin
16 Pat Rooney
17 Mark Poole
18 Jerry Keller
19 Mike Sharperson
20 John Mayberry
21 Doug Ault
22 Kelly Gruber
23 Vance McHenry
24 Red Coughlin
25 Dale Holman, Fred McGriff
26 Batboys
27 John Cerutti
28 Dennis Homberg
29 Derwin McNealy
30 Cloyd Boyer
31 Dave Stegman

1985 Cramer Tacoma Tigers

(Oakland A's, AAA)

	MT
Complete Set (25):	15.00

126 Keith Lieppman
127 Jose Tolentino
128 Keith Thrower
129 Chuck Estrada
130 Ricky Peters
131 Tom Romano
132 Phil Stephenson
133 Jose Rijo
134 Danny Goodwin
135 Thad Reece
136 Mike Ashman
137 Ron Harrison
138 Stan Kyles
139 Steve Kiefer
140 Tim Lambert
141 Doug Scherer
142 Steve Ontiveros
143 Bob Bathe
144 Bob Owchinko
145 Tom Dozier
146 Joe Lansford
147 Steve Mura
148 Bill Bathe
149 Mike Chris
150 Tom Tellman (Tellmann)

1985 TCMA Tidewater Tides

(N.Y. Mets, AAA) (#16, Springer corrected card is a scarce late-issue)

	MT
Complete Set, w/#16 (28):	70.00
Partial Set, no #16 (27):	55.00

1 Rick Lancellotti
2 Terry Leach
3 Sid Fernandez
4 Jeff Bettendorf
5 Calvin Schiraldi
6 Rick Anderson
7 Randy Niemann
8 Jeff Bittiger
9 Wes Gardner
10 Bill Latham
11 Rick Aguilera
12 Ed Olwine
13 Laschelle Tarver
14 Billy Beane
15 John Gibbons
16 Steve Springer (black bat, photo actually Ed Hearn)
17 Steve Springer (white bat, correct photo)
18 Kevin Mitchell
19 Terry Blocker
20 Len Dykstra
21 Ed Hearn
22 Ross Jones
23 Mike Davis
24 Alfredo Pedrique
25 Mark Carreon
26 John Cumberland
27 Bob Schaefer
28 Rick Rainer

1985 TCMA Toledo Mud Hens

(Minnesota Twins, AAA) (Chiffer is scarce late-issue card)

	MT
Complete Set w/Chiffer (26):	18.00
Partial Set, no Chiffer (25):	12.00

1 Allan Anderson
2 Eric Broersma
3 Mark Brown
4 Dennis Burtt
6 Frank Eufemia
8 Ed Hodge
10 Mark Portugal
11 Mike Walters
12 Len Whitehouse
13 Toby Hernandez
14 Jeff Reed
15 Alvaro Espinoza
16 Houston Jiminez
17 Steve Lombardozzi
18 Scott Ullger
19 Reggie Whittemore
20 Andre David
21 Mike Hart
22 Stan Holmes
23 Greg Howe
24 Jerry Lomastro
25 Al Woods
26 Cal Ermer
27 Jim Shellenback
30 Rich Yett
32 Floyd Cliffer

1985 Cramer Tucson Toros

(Houston Astros, AAA)

	MT
Complete Set (25):	11.00

51 Chris Jones
52 Eric Bullock
53 Jimmy Johnson
54 Mark Ross
55 Larry Acker
56 Manny Hernandez
57 Vern Followell
58 Larry Montgomery
59 Rick Colbert
60 Mark Knudson
61 Rafael Landestoy
62 Stan Hough
63 Mike Calise
64 Tye Waller
65 Glenn Davis
66 Randy Martz
67 Chuck Jackson
68 John Mizerock
69 Ty Gainey
70 Eddie Bonine
71 Pedro Hernandez
72 James Miner
73 Charlie Kerfeld
74 Rex Jones
75 Brad Mills

1985 Tulsa Drillers team issue

(Texas Rangers, AA) (Sierra is scarce late-issue card)

	MT
Complete Set, w/Sierra (28):	90.00
Partial Set, no Sierra (27):	80.00

1 Ken Reitz
4 George Crum
6 George Foussianes
7 Oscar Mejia
9 Jamie Doughty
10 Mark Gile
12 Ruben Sierra
14 Barry Brunenkant
17 Larry Pott
18 Bobby Witt
19 Duane James
20 Tony Hudson
22 Jeff Moronko
23 Orlando Gomez
24 Jeff Mace
25 Bob Gergen
26 Barry Bass
27 Rob Clark
28 Bill Fahey
29 Dwayne Henry
30 Terry Johnson
31 Javier Ortiz
32 Kirk Killingsworth
33 Scott Anderson
34 Bill Taylor
35 Otto Gonzalez
36 Al Lachowicz
37 Clyde Reichard

1985 TCMA Utica Blue Sox

(Independent, A)

	MT
Complete Set (26):	45.00

1 Jim Allison
2 Ross Jones
3 Dave Linton
4 Paulino Paixao
5 Bob Sudo
6 Darren Travels
7 Sergio Valdez
8 Rob Williams
9 Roger Dean
10 Pancho Hedfelt
11 Al Hibbs
12 Esteban Beltre
13 Rodney Clark
14 Jeff Scheaffer
15 Alfonso Traverez
16 Larry Walker
17 Bob Brown
18 Andy Donatelli
19 Ray Garcia
20 Raymond Noble
21 Fred Perez
22 Troy Ricker
23 Steve St. Claire
24 Ken Brett
25 Gene Glynn
26 Dan Gazzilli

1985 Cramer Vancouver Canadians

(Milwaukee Brewers, AAA)

	MT
Complete Set (25):	9.00

201 Dan Davidsmeier
202 Brad Lesley
203 Tim Leary
204 Bobby Clark
205 Juan Castillo
206 Jim Aducci
207 Earnie Riles
208 Mike Paul
209 Dale Sveum
210 Jaime Cocanower
211 Mike Felder
212 Brian Duquette
213 Jim Paciorek
214 Bob Skube
215 Tom Trebelhorn
216 Bill Wegman
217 Mike Martin
218 Scott Roberts
219 Rick Waits
220 Chuck Crim
221 Jaime Nelson
222 Brian Clutterbuck
223 Garret Nago
224 Carlos Ponce
225 Al Price

1985 TCMA Vero Beach Dodgers

(L.A. Dodgers, A)

	MT
Complete Set (27):	14.00

1 Bobby Hamilton
2 Tracy Woodson
3 John Schlichting
4 Gary Newsom
5 Manuel Francois
6 Joe Szekley
7 Felipe Gutierrez
8 Wayne Kirby
9 Gary Legumina
10 Ed Jacobo
11 Henry Gatewood
12 Norberto Flores
13 Harry Ritch
14 Joe Karmeris
15 William Brennan
16 Bob Jacobsen
17 Vince Beringhele
18 Mike Schweignoffer
19 Bary Wohler
20 Greg Mayberry
21 Luis Lopez
22 Mike Pesavento
23 Mike Cherry
24 Rob Giesecke
25 Dennis Lewallyn
26 Stan Wasiak
27 John Shoemaker

1985 TCMA Visalia Oaks

(Minnesota Twins, A)

	MT
Complete Set (25):	18.00

1 Phil Wilson
2 Doug Palmer
3 Perry Husband
4 Bill O'Connor
5 Sal Nicolosi
6 Jeff Schugel
7 Brad Bierley
8 Jay Bell
9 Chris Forgione
10 Robert Calley
11 Tom DiCeglio
12 Chris Calvert
13 Dave Vetsch
14 Gene Larkin
15 Bob Lee
16 Ray Velasquez
17 Todd Budke
18 Jeff Rojas
19 Wes Pierorazio
20 Neil Landmark
21 Tony Guerrero
22 Jose Dominguez
23 Scott Klingbell
24 Troy Galloway
25 Danny Schmitz

1985 TCMA Waterbury Indians

(Cleveland Indians, AA)

	MT
Complete Set (25):	21.00

1 Nelson Pedraza
2 Wilson Valera
3 Randy Washington
4 Winston Ficklin
5 Glenn Edwards
6 Richard Doyle
7 Mickey Street
8 John Miglio
9 Cal Santarelli
10 Wayne Johnson
11 Reggie Ritter
12 Doug Jones
13 Marty Leach
14 Jeff Arney
15 Dave Clark
16 Ron Wallenhaupt
17 German Barranca
18 Tim Glass
19 Jim Driscoll
20 George Cecchetti
21 John Farrell
22 Jack Aker
23 Cory Snyder
24 Andy Allanson
25 Dain Syverson

1985 Trackle Winston-Salem Spirits Postcards

(Chicago Cubs, A) (3-1/2" x 5-3/8", b/w, postcard back, players unidentified)

	MT
Complete Set (23):	50.00

(1) Rich Amaral
(2) Greg Bell
(3) Damon Berryhill
(4) Don Bethel
(5) Jim Boudreau
(6) Luis Cruz
(7) Jim Dickerson
(8) Cal Emery
(9) Hector Freytes
(10) Drew Hall
(11) Rick Hopkins
(12) Dave Martinez
(13) Dave Masters
(14) Steve Maye
(15) Simon Mejias
(16) Jamie Moyer
(17) Jim Phillips
(18) Rick Rembielak
(19) Steve Roadcap
(20) Rolando Roomes
(21) Erskine Thomason
(22) Mike Tullier
(23) Rick Wrona

1986 TCMA Albany-Colonie Yankees

(N.Y. Yankees, AA)

	MT
Complete Set (23):	15.00

1 Jim Riggs
2 Roberto Kelly
3 Carson Carroll
4 Miguel Sosa
5 Tom Barrett
6 Ferdi Gonzalez
7 Keith Hughes
8 Bill Monobouquette
9 Carlos Martinez
10 Tony Russell

11 Mike Heifferon
12 Eric Bernard
13 John Liburdi
14 Eric Dersin
15 Jeff Pries
16 Jim Saul
17 Logan Easley
18 Mo Ching
19 John Lemperie
20 Chuck Yaeger
21 Eric Schmidt
22 Bill Lindsey
23 Darren Reed
24 John Kennedy
25 Aris Tirado
26 Bill Fulton
27 Joe Impagliazzo
28 Clay Christensen
29 Steve George
30 Brent Blum
31 Bob Davidson
32 Bullpen Action (Brent Blum, Logan Easley, Bill Monobouquette)

1986 ProCards Albuquerque Dukes

(L.A. Dodgers, AAA)

MT
Complete Set (28): 6.00
(1) Ed Amelung
(2) Ralph Bryant
(3) Terry Collins
(4) Lenny Currier
(5) Jon Debus
(6) Dave Eichhorn
(7) Jack Fimple
(8) Balvino Galvez
(9) Jose Gonzalez
(10) Jeff Hamilton
(11) Mark Heuer
(12) Brian Holton
(13) Dennis Livingston
(14) Scott May
(15) Dick McLaughlin
(16) Adrian Meagher
(17) Tim Meeks
(18) Gary Newsom
(19) Stu Pederson
(20) Gil Reyes
(21) Mike Schweighoffer
(22) Larry See
(23) Craig Shipley
(24) Steve Shirley
(25) Joe Vavra
(26) Dave Wallace
(27) Mike Watters
(28) Reggie Williams

1986 Albuquerque Dukes team-issue photos

(L.A. Dodgers, AAA) (3-3/8" x 5" color photo prints, sold at stadium for $2 each)

MT
Complete Set (28): 100.00
(1) Ed Amelung
(2) Ralph Bryant
(3) Terry Collins
(4) Lenny Currier (trainer)
(5) Jon Debus
(6) Dave Eichhorn
(7) Jack Fimple
(8) Balvino Gonzalez
(9) Jose Gonzalez
(10) Jeff Hamilton
(11) Mark Heuer
(12) Brian Holton
(13) Dennis Livingston
(14) Scott May
(15) Dick McLaughlin
(16) Adrian Meagher
(17) Tim Meeks
(18) Gary Newsom
(19) Stu Pederson
(20) Gil Reyes
(21) Mike Schweighoffer
(22) Larry See
(23) Craig Shipley
(24) Steve Shirley
(25) Joe Vavra
(26) Dave Wallace
(27) Mike Watters
(28) Reggie Williams

Values shown are a national average. Some teams and players enjoy regional popularity which may affect market prices.

1986 Anchorage Glacier Pilots

(Summer Amateur) (Black, white & blue, 2-1/2" x 3-1/4")

MT
Complete Set (42): 18.00
(1) Steve Bates
(2) Lyle BeFort
(3) David Bettendorf
(4) Todd Bunge
(5) Wes Chamberlain
(6) Steve Chitren
(7) Scott Davenport
(8) Rob DeYoung
(9) Terry Elliot
(10) Ken Garcia
(11) Bryan Gates (bat boy)
(12) Shawn Gilbert
(13) Amy Gills (trainer)
(14) Kip Gross
(15) Kyle Harris (bat boy)
(16) Ray Harris
(17) Adam Hilpert
(18) Terry Jorgenson (Jorgensen)
(19) Brent Kemnitz (coach)
(20) Joe Klancnik
(21) Jamie Larson (bat boy)
(22) Dave Lucas (coach)
(23) Dustin McFarland (mascot)
(24) Kelly McFarland (SP, staff)
(25) Steve McFarland (manager)
(26) Rich McIntyre
(27) Allen Meyer
(28) Rick Olivas
(29) Joe Ortiz
(30) Jack O'Toole (coach)
(31) Bob Parry
(32) Tim Peters
(33) Matt Puetz
(34) Bud Rostel
(35) Mike Schambaugh
(36) Deon Simmons (bat boy)
(37) Mark Standiford
(38) Derek Stroud
(39) Lefty Van Brunt (coach)
(40) Steve Wapnick
(41) Eric Yeager
(42) Andy Woods (mascot)

1986 ProCards Appleton Foxes

(Chicago White Sox, A)

MT
Complete Set (28): 6.00
(1) Tony Bartolomucci
(2) John Boling
(3) Glen Braxton
(4) Kurt Brown
(5) Buzz Capra
(6) Tony Cento
(7) William Eveline
(8) James Filippi
(9) Cornelio Garcia
(10) Tom Hartley
(11) Richard Issac
(12) Scott Kershaw
(13) William Magallanes
(14) Steve McLaughlin
(15) Eric Milholand
(16) Steve Moran
(17) Donn Pall
(18) Luis Peraza
(19) David Reynolds
(20) Jesus Sandoval
(21) Ron Scruggs
(22) Dave Sheldon
(23) Duke Sims
(24) John Stein
(25) George Stone
(26) Randy Velarde
(27) Aubrey Waggoner
(28) Marty Warren

1986 ProCards Arkansas Travelers

(St. Louis Cardinals, AA)

MT
Complete Set (26): 14.00
(1) Tom Almante
(2) Rod Booker
(3) Ernie Carrasco
(4) Paul Cherry
(5) Dave Clements
(6) Mark Dougherty
(7) Rich Embser
(8) Lance Johnson
(9) Dave Kable
(10) Jeff Kenner
(11) Jeff Ledbetter
(12) Joe Magrane
(13) John Martin
(14) Henry McCulla
(15) Curt Metzger
(16) Allen Morlock
(17) Mike Rhodes
(18) Mark Riggins
(19) James Riggleman
(20) Mike Robinson
(21) Jose Rodriguez
(22) Mark Schulte
(23) Ray Soff
(24) Eddie Tanner
(25) Tim Wallace
(26) Scott Young

1986 ProCards Ashville Tourists

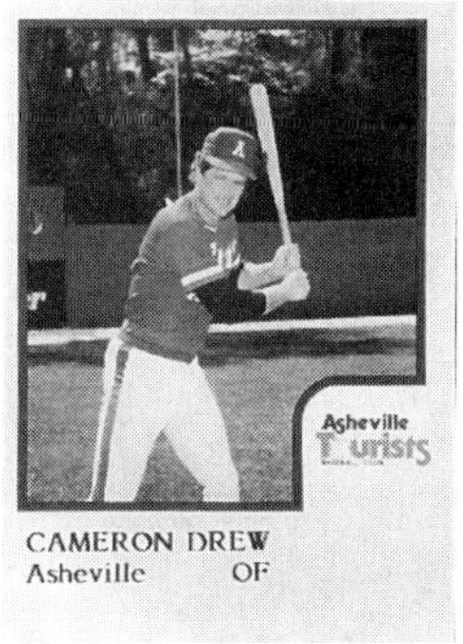

(Houston Astros, A)

MT
Complete Set (29): 6.00
(1) Tim Arnsburg
(2) Jeff Baldwin
(3) Ken Bolek
(4) Chris Clawson
(5) Carlo Colombino
(6) Todd Credeur
(7) Pedro DeLeon
(8) Cameron Drew
(9) Jeff Edwards
(10) John Elliot
(11) Stan Fascher
(12) Fred Gladding
(13) Neder Horta
(14) Bert Hunter
(15) Blaise Ilsley
(16) Richard Johnson
(17) Larry Lasky
(18) Scott Markley
(19) David Meads
(20) Tony Metoyer
(21) Gary Murphy
(22) Carlos Reyes
(23) A. Rodriguez
(24) Ron Roebuck
(25) Wayne Rogalski
(26) Joe Schulte
(27) Shawn Talbott
(28) Dan Walters
(29) Terry Wells

1986 ProCards Auburn Astros

(Houston Astros, A)

MT
Complete Set (27): 6.00
(1) Troy Aleshire
(2) Dave Banks
(3) Keith Bodie
(4) Daven Bond
(5) Bill Bonham
(6) Damon Brooks
(7) Gary Cooper
(8) Jeff Edwards
(9) Joel Estes
(10) Scott Gray
(11) Carl Grovom
(12) Trent Hubbard
(13) Bert Hunter
(14) Gayron Jackson
(15) Rusty Kryzanowski
(16) Brian Meyer
(17) Guy Nomrand
(18) Jimmy Olson
(19) Dave Potts
(20) Ron Roebuck
(21) Dave Rohde
(22) Pedro Sanchez
(23) Richie Simon
(24) Matt Stennett
(25) Jim Vike
(26) Kevin Wasilewski
(27) Ed Whited

1986 ProCards Bakersfield Dodgers

(L.A. Dodgers, A)

MT
Complete Set (29): 17.50
(1) Dave Alarid
(2) Mike Batesole
(3) Manuel Benitez
(4) Mike Burke
(5) Dave Carlucci
(6) Jovon Edwards
(7) Mike Fiala
(8) Bert Flores
(9) Rick Gahbrielson
(10) Rene Garcia
(11) Darryl Gilliam
(12) Anthony Hardwick
(13) Ted Holcomb
(14) Jay Hornacek
(15) Ron Jackson
(16) Stan Jonston
(17) Tim Kelly
(18) Brian Kopetsky
(19) Don "Ducky" LeJohn
(20) Ramon Martinez
(21) Andy Naworski
(22) Jeff Nelson
(23) Jay Ray
(24) Jack Savage
(25) Bryan Smith
(26) Dan Smith
(27) Walt Stull
(28) John Wetteland
(29) Mike White

1986 ProCards Beaumont Golden Gators

(Houston Astros, AA)

MT
Complete Set (25): 15.00
(1) Santos Alomar
(2) Joe Bitker
(3) Tom Brassil
(4) Randy Byers
(5) Frank Castro
(6) Joe Chavez
(7) Joey Cora
(8) Mike Costello
(9) Mike Debutch
(10) Rich Doyle
(11) Rusty Ford
(12) Brent Gjesdal
(13) Eric Hardgrave
(14) Steve Lubratich
(15) Steve Luebber
(16) Shane Mack
(17) Paul Mancuso
(18) Mike McClain
(19) Mike Mills
(20) Mark Poston
(21) Candy Sierra
(22) Todd Simmons
(23) Steve Smith
(24) Eric Varoz
(25) Bill Wrona

1986 Cramer Bellingham Mariners

(Seattle Mariners, Rookie)

MT
Complete Set (29): 6.00
101 David Hartnett
102 Jim Bowie Jr.
103 Michael McDonald
104 Jose Bennet
105 Deron Johnson, Jr.
106 Wendell Bolar
107 Gregory Briley
108 Jose Tartabull, Jr.
109 Thomas Little
110 Jerry Goff
111 Michael Thorpe
112 Brad Rohde
113 James Pritikin
114 Bret Simmermacher
115 Tim Fortugno
116 Arvid Morfin
117 Jody Ryan
118 Troy Williams
119 Randy Little
120 James Blueberg
121 Richard DeLuca
122 Daniel Disher
123 Ted Williams
124 Raul Mendez
125 Fausto Ramirez
126 Clay Gunn
127 Rudy Webster
128 Patrick Lennon
129 Mark Wooden

1986 ProCards Beloit Brewers

(Milwaukee Brewers, A)

MT
Complete Set (26): 5.00
(1) Shon Ashley
(2) Rich Bosley
(3) Bob Caci
(4) Isaiah Clark
(5) Carlos Escalera
(6) Frank Fazzini
(7) Dan Fitzpatrick
(8) Ed Greene
(9) Joe Haney
(10) Doug Henry
(11) Gomer Hodge
(12) Tom Kleean
(13) Lance Lincoln
(14) Rusty McGinnis
(15) Charlie McGrew
(16) Carl Moraw
(17) Ray Ojeda
(18) Warren Olson
(19) Juan Reyes
(20) Jim Rowe
(21) Greg Simmons
(22) Bob Simonson
(23) Jeff Smith
(24) Jose Ventura
(25) Randy Veres
(26) Larry Whitford

1986 Cramer Bend Phillies

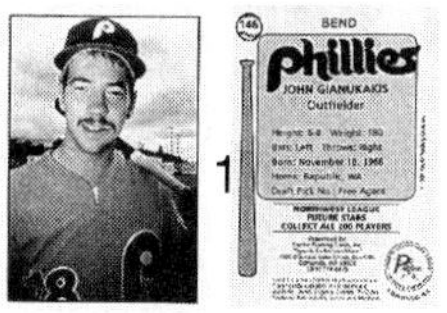

(Philadelphia Phillies, A)

MT
Complete Set (25): 12.00
130 Roderick Robertson
131 Quinn Williams
132 Al Hibbs
133 Scott Ruckman
134 Doug Hodo
135 Stephen Scarsone
136 Charles Malone
137 Keith Greene
138 Donald Church
139 Andrew Ashby
140 Elvis Romero
141 Glen Anderson
142 Kenny Miller
143 Fred Christopher
144 Brad Moore
145 Leroy Ventress
146 John Gianukakis
147 Chris Limbach
148 Tim Sossamon
149 Ryan Silva
150 Gary Berman
151 Bubba Allison
152 Juan Ascencio
153 Jeff Myaer
154 Garland Kiser

1986 Birmingham Barons team issue

(Chicago White Sox, AA)

	MT
Complete Set (28):	60.00

1 Steve Oswald
2 Manny Salinas
3 Ken Reed
4 Dave White
5 Troy Thomas
6 Tony Menendez
7 Tom Moritz
8 Ron Karkovice
9 John Johnson
10 Mike Harris
11 Dave Cochrane
12 Rolando Pino
13 Mike Taylor
14 Rick Seilheimer
15 Tom Forrester
16 Jack Hardy
17 Mike Yastrzemski
18 Jim Hickey
19 Bobby Thigpen
20 Bob Bolin
21 Mark Williams
22 Kurt Walker
23 Marv Foley
24 Ken Koch
25 Tom Haller
26 Sam Hairston
27 Rich DeVincenzo
28 Rondal Rollin

1986 ProCards Buffalo Bisons

(Chicago White Sox, AAA)

	MT
Complete Set (26):	6.00

(1) Glen Bockhorn
(2) Dick Bosman
(3) Daryl Boston
(4) Scott Bradley
(5) Tony Brizzolara
(6) Darren Burroughs
(7) Nick Capra
(8) Bryan Clark
(9) Joe Cowley
(10) Joe Desa
(11) Pete Filson
(12) Jerry Don Gleaton
(13) Al Jones
(14) Tim Krauss
(15) Greg Latta
(16) Bill Long
(17) Jim Marshall
(18) Steve McCatty
(19) Russ Morman
(20) Chris Nyman
(21) Bruce Tanner
(22) Tom Thomson
(23) Dave Wehrmeister
(24) Ken Williams
(25) Matt Winters
(26) Dave Yobs

1986 ProCards Burlington Expos

(Montreal Expos, K.C. Royals, A)

	MT
Complete Set (28):	25.00

(1) Tom Arrington
(2) Daryl Asbe
(3) Luis Corcino
(4) Matt Crouch
(5) Geff Davis
(6) Pat Dougherty
(7) Fritz Fedor
(8) Cesar Hernandez
(9) Jim Hunter
(10) Jeff Huson
(11) Juan Jimenez
(12) Tom Johnson
(13) Frank Laureano
(14) Tim Lemons
(15) Andy Leonard
(16) J.R. Miner
(17) Melido Perez
(18) Jose Rodriguez
(19) Brad Shores
(20) Joe Slotnick
(21) Stuart Stauffacher
(22) Bob Sudo
(23) Scott Sundgren
(24) Alfonso Tavarez
(25) Larry Walker
(26) Bob Williams
(27) John Williams
(28) Team Photo

1986 ProCards Calgary Cannons

(Seattle Mariners, AAA)

	MT
Complete Set (26):	6.00

(1) Greg Bartley
(2) Mickey Brantley
(3) Randy Braun
(4) Pat Casey
(5) Bill Crone
(6) Mario Diaz
(7) Jerry Dybzinski
(8) Steve Fireovid
(9) Dan Firova
(10) Ross Grimsley
(11) Dave Hengel
(12) Clay Hill
(13) Vic Martin
(14) Doug Merrifield
(15) Rich Montelone
(16) John Moses
(17) Jed Murray
(18) Ricky Nelson
(19) Randy Newman
(20) Jack O'Conner
(21) Bill Plummer
(22) Jerry Reed
(23) Harold Reynolds
(24) Dave Valle
(25) Bill Wilkinson
(26) Joe Witmer

1986 TCMA Cedar Rapids Reds

(Cincinnati Reds, A)

	MT
Complete Set (28):	7.00

1 Dan Belinskas
2 Brad Brusky
3 Mike Converse
4 Mike Campbell
5 Tim Deltz
6 Curt Kindred
7 Gino Mintelli
8 Mike Roesler
9 Greg Simpson
10 Mike Smith
11 Greg Toler
12 Mike Vincent
13 Rod Zeratsky
14 Marty Brown
15 Joe Dunlap
16 Mark Germann
17 Scott Hilgenberg
18 Randy Hindman
19 Cal Cain
20 Mark Jackson
21 Chris Jones
22 Allen Sigler
23 John Bryant
24 Paul Kirsch
25 Gene Dusan
26 Neal Davenport
27 "Bucky" Buchheister
28 Lamar the Dog (mascot)

Checklists with card numbers in parentheses ( ) indicates the numbers do not appear on the cards.

1986 ProCards Charleston Rainbows

(San Diego Padres, A)

	MT
Complete Set (29):	30.00

(1) Carlos Baerega (Baerga)
(2) Miguel Batista (with bat)
(3) Miguel Batista (with glove)
(4) Billy Blount
(5) Victor Cabrera
(6) Rafael Chaves
(7) Jeff Cisco
(8) Roberto Clemente, Jr.
(9) Jim Daniel
(10) Carl Ferraro
(11) Greg Harris
(12) Pat Kelly
(13) Chris Knabenshue
(14) Jim Lewis
(15) Bill Marx
(16) Matt Maysey
(17) Rod McCray
(18) Tom Meagher
(19) Jaime Moreno
(20) Eric Nolte
(21) Juan Paris
(22) Joe Pleasac
(23) Ramon Rodriguez
(24) Greg Sparks
(25) Bill Stevenson
(26) Jim Tatum
(27) Kevin Towers
(28) Rafael Valez
(29) Jim Wasem

1986 WBTV Charlotte O's

(Baltimore Orioles, AA)

	MT
Complete Set (30):	35.00

(1) Kurt Beamesderfer
(2) Eric Bell
(3) Greg Biagini
(4) Terry Bogner
(5) Jim Boudreau
(6) Mark Brown
(7) Paul Cameron (sportscaster)
(8) Tom Dodd
(9) Dave Falcone
(10) John Flinn
(11) Charlie Frederick (sportscaster)
(12) Lee Granger
(13) Bob Hice (sportscaster)
(14) Jerry Holtz
(15) John Hoover
(16) Joe Kucharski
(17) Terry Mauney (sportscaster)
(18) Carl Nichols
(19) Francisco Oliveras
(20) Chris Padget
(21) Mike Raczka
(22) Joe Redfield
(23) Rich Rice
(24) Billy Ripken
(25) Rico Rossy
(26) Ron Salcedo
(27) Dave Smith
(28) Scott Stranski
(29) Jeff Wood
(30) O's Fans

1986 ProCards Chattanooga Lookouts

(Seattle Mariners, AA)

	MT
Complete Set (25):	15.00

(1) Ben Amaya
(2) Bob Baldrick
(3) Brian Bargerhuff
(4) Terry Bell
(5) Jim Bryant
(6) John Burden
(7) Scott Buss
(8) Brian David
(9) John Duncun (photo actually Mike Campbell)
(10) Bob Gunnarson
(11) Matt Hall
(12) R.J. Harrison
(13) Paul Hollins
(14) Tom Hunt
(15) Ross Jones
(16) Rick Luecken
(17) Edgar Martinez
(18) Jeff McDonald
(19) Rusty McNealy
(20) Rick Moore
(21) Dave Myers
(22) Paul Schneider
(23) Brick Smith
(24) Terry Taylor
(25) Mike Wishnevski

1986 ProCards Clearwater Phillies

(Philadelphia Phillies, A)

	MT
Complete Set (26):	6.00

(1) Carlos Arroyo
(2) Bruce Carter
(3) Travis Chambers
(4) Ron Clark
(5) Pat Coveney
(6) Shawn Dantzler
(7) Greg Edge
(8) Jim Fortenberry
(9) Todd Frohwirth
(10) Billy Jester
(11) Ronald Jones
(12) Bart Kaiser
(13) Jeff Kaye
(14) Jeff Knox
(15) Ken Kraft
(16) Scott Madden
(17) Mike Miller
(18) Tom Newell
(19) Segio Perez
(20) Mark Pottinger
(21) Walley Ritchie
(22) Bob Scanlan
(23) Scott Steen
(24) Rodney Wheeler
(25) Steven Williams
(26) Ted Zipeto

1986 ProCards Clinton Giants

(S.F Giants, A) (set price includes the scarce Hutchins card)

	MT
Complete Set (30):	6.00

(1) John Barry
(2) Dave Blakely
(3) George Bonilla
(4) Jeff Carter
(5) Todd Cash
(6) Tom Ealy
(7) Bill Evers
(8) Perry Flowers
(9) Dean Freeland
(10) Dave Hornsby
(11) Lance Hutchins
(12) Lloyd Jackson
(13) Timber Mead
(14) Todd Miller
(15) Dave Morris
(16) Jack Mull
(17) Rick Nelson
(18) Eric Pawling
(19) Darren Pearson
(20) Jose Pena
(21) C.L. Penigar
(22) Eric Pilkington
(23) Doug Robertson
(24) Dobie Swepson
(25) Howard Townsend
(26) Paul Van Stone
(27) Matt Walker
(28) Mike Whitt
(29) Trevor Wilson
(30) Team Photo

1986 ProCards Columbia Mets

(N.Y. Mets, AA)

	MT
Complete Set (28):	25.00

(1) Bob Apodaca
(2) Jaime Archibald
(3) Kevin Armstrong
(4) Brandon Bailey
(5) Chris Bayer
(6) Mark Brunswick
(7) Joaquin Contreras
(8) Kurt Deluca
(9) Tom Doyle
(10) Dave Gelatt
(11) Brian Givens (blue jersey)
(12) Brian Givens (white jersey)
(13) Alan Hayden
(14) Barry Hightower
(15) Troy James
(16) Scott Jaster
(17) Greg Jeffries (Jefferies)
(18) Geary Jones
(19) Johnny Monell
(20) Felix Perdomo
(21) Chris Rauth
(22) Craig Repoz
(23) Robert Rinehart, Jr.
(24) Daniel Siblerud
(25) William Stiles
(26) John Thozzo
(27) Thomas Wachs
(28) Mark Willoughby

1986 ProCards Columbus Astros

(Houston Astros, AA)

	MT
Complete Set (25):	20.00

(1) Troy Afenir
(2) Karl Allaire
(3) Mark Baker
(4) Jeff Bettendorf
(5) Rich Bombard
(6) Ken Caminiti
(7) Mitch Cook
(8) Dave Cripe
(9) Jeff Datz
(10) Juan Delgado
(11) Ed Duke
(12) Bobby Falls
(13) Mike Friederich
(14) Tom Funk
(15) Ryan Job
(16) Tony Kelley
(17) Rob Mallicoat
(18) Chuck Mathews
(19) Joe Mikulik
(20) Jim O'Dell
(21) Bob Parker
(22) Larry Ray
(23) Roger Samuels
(24) Chuck Taylor
(25) Gerald Young

1986 Police Columbus Clippers

(New York Yankees, AAA)

	MT
Complete Set (25):	11.00

(1) Mike Armstrong
(2) Brad Arnsberg
(3) Clay Christiansen
(4) Pete Dalena

(5) Orestes Destrade
(6) Doug Drabek
(7) Juan Espino
(8) Kelly Faulk
(9) Randy Graham
(10) Leo Hernandez
(11) Al Holland
(12) Phil Lombardi
(13) Victor Mata
(14) Derwin McNealy
(15) Dan Pasqua
(16) Scott Patterson
(17) Jeff Pries
(18) Alfonso Pulido
(19) Andre Robertson
(20) Mark Silva
(21) Keith Smith
(22) Mike Soper
(23) Dave Stegman
(24) Manager Card (George Sisler, Jr., Barry Foote) (George Sisler Jr., Barry Foote)
(25) Coaches/trainer card (Dave LaRoche, Brian Butterfield, Kevin Rand)

1986 ProCards Columbus Clippers

(N.Y. Yankees, AAA)

	MT
Complete Set (26):	9.00

(1) Mike Armstrong
(2) Brad Arnsburg
(3) Clay Christiansen
(4) Pete Dalena
(5) Orestes Destrade
(6) Doug Drabek
(7) Juan Espino
(8) Kelly Faulk
(9) Barry Foote
(10) Randy Graham
(11) Leo Hernandez
(12) Al Holland
(13) Brian Butterfield, Dave LaRoche, Kevin Rand
(14) Phil Lombardi
(15) Victor Mata
(16) Derwin McNealy
(17) Dan Pasqua
(18) Scott Patterson
(19) Jeff Pries
(20) Alfonso Pulido
(21) Andre Robertson
(22) Mark Silva
(23) Keith Smith
(24) Mike Soper
(25) Miguel Sosa
(26) Dave Stegman

1986 ProCards Daytona Beach Islanders

(Independent, A)

	MT
Complete Set (28):	6.00

(1) Jim Allison
(2) Regan Bass
(3) Warren Busick
(4) Chino Cadihia
(5) Tony Clark
(6) Rafael Cruz
(7) Mike Dotzler
(8) Darrin Garner
(9) Otto Gonzalez
(10) Ty Harden
(11) David Hausterman
(12) Perry W. Hill
(13) Paul James
(14) Ross Jones
(15) Mark Kramer
(16) Dave Linton
(17) Carmen Losauro
(18) Jimmy Meadows
(19) Jeff Melrose
(20) Tim Owen
(21) Larry Pardo
(22) Dave Rolland
(23) Ron Russell
(24) Travis Sheffield
(25) Ed Soto
(26) Jim St. Laurent
(27) George Threadgill
(28) Tom West

1986 ProCards Durham Bulls

(Atlanta Braves, A)

	MT
Complete Set (27):	22.00

(1) Buddy Bailey
(2) Jeff Blauser
(3) Johnny Cash
(4) Bill Clossen
(5) Kevin Coffman
(6) Tim Criswell
(7) Chris Cron
(8) Maximo Del Rosario
(9) Drew Denson
(10) Todd Dewey
(11) Juan Fredymond
(12) Ronnie Gant
(13) Wayne Harrison
(14) Larry Jaster
(15) Cesar Jiminez
(16) John Kilner
(17) Todd Lamb
(18) Mike Merrill
(19) Charlie Morelock
(20) Mike Nipper
(21) Bob Posey
(22) Mike Reynolds
(23) Jim Rockey
(24) Mac Rogers
(25) Rick Siebert
(26) Gerald Wagner
(27) Phil Wellman

1986 ProCards Edmonton Trappers

(California Angels, AAA)

	MT
Complete Set (27):	9.00

(1) Robert Bastien
(2) Norman Carrasco
(3) Ray Chadwick
(4) Bobby Clark
(5) The Cliburns (Stan Cliburn, Stewart Cliburn)
(6) Stan Cliburn
(7) Stewart Cliburn
(8) Steven Finch
(9) Todd Fischer
(10) Tony Fossas
(11) Alan Kim Fowlkes
(12) Leonard Garcia
(13) Craig Gerber
(14) Chris Green
(15) Jack Howell
(16) Pat Keedy
(17) Steven Liddle
(18) Rufino Linares
(19) Winston Llenas
(20) Tony Lynn Mack
(21) Reggie Montgomery
(22) Gus Polidor
(23) Frank Reberger
(24) Al Romero
(25) Mark Ryal
(26) David Wayne Smith
(27) Devon White

1986 ProCards Elmira Pioneers

(Boston Red Sox, A)

	MT
Complete Set (30):	20.00

(1) Mike Baker
(2) Steve Bast
(3) Ken Bourne
(4) Tim Buheller
(5) Mike Coffey
(6) Scott Cooper
(7) Roger Haggerty
(8) Bart Haley
(9) Keith Harrison
(10) Tony Hill
(11) Joe Marchese
(12) Dave Milstien
(13) Jim Morrison
(14) Glen O'Donnell
(15) Lem Pilkinton
(16) Chris Rawdon
(17) Julio Rosario
(18) Ken Ryan
(19) Ed Sardinha
(20) Curt Schilling
(21) Thom Sepela
(22) Scott Sommers
(23) Joaquin Tejada
(24) Al Thorton
(25) David Walters
(26) Ron Warren
(27) Stuart Weidie
(28) Mike Whiting
(29) Kerman Williams
(30) Paul Williams

Value of modern team sets is often predicated as much on inclusion of star player's early cards as on scarcity of the issue.

1986 ProCards El Paso Diablos

(Milwaukee Brewers, AA)

	MT
Complete Set (23):	6.00

(1) Jay Aldrich
(2) Robby Allen
(3) Jesus Alfaro
(4) Bill Bates
(5) Alan Cartwright
(6) Dave Clay
(7) Tim Crews
(8) Derek Diaz
(9) Duffy Dyer
(10) Brian Finley
(11) Lavell Freeman
(12) John Gibbons
(13) Dave Huppert
(14) Pete Hendrick
(15) Pete Kolb
(16) Dan Murphy
(17) Garrett Nago
(18) Bob Nandin
(19) Steve Stanicek
(20) Dave Stapleton
(21) John Thorton
(22) Jackson Todd
(23) Cam Walker

1986 ProCards Erie Cardinals

(St. Louis Cardinals, A) (Hershman is scarce card)

	MT
Complete Set, w/Hershman (31):	35.00
Partial Set, no Hershman (30):	14.00

(1) Luis Alicea
(2) Tom Baine
(3) Mark Behny
(4) Brad Bluestone
(5) Randy Butts
(6) Rick Christain
(7) Bien Figueroa
(8) Robert Glisson
(9) Stephen Graff
(10) Kerry Griffith
(11) John Hackett
(12) Scott Hamilton
(13) William Hershman
(14) Eric Hohn
(15) Joe Hollinshed
(16) David Horton
(17) Glen Kuiper
(18) Scott Lawrence
(19) Roberto Marte
(20) Steve Meyer
(21) Carey Nemeth
(22) Robert Nettles
(23) Carrol Parker
(24) Francisco Perez
(25) Kyle Reese
(26) Joe Rigoli
(27) Steve Shade
(28) Greg Smith
(29) Steve Turgeon
(30) Stanley Zaltsman
(31) Todd Zeile

1986 Cramer Eugene Emeralds

(K.C. Royals, A)

	MT
Complete Set (25):	12.00

26 Rob Wolkoys
27 David Tinkle
28 Brian McRae
29 Mike Oblesbee
30 Carlos Escalera
31 Pat Bailey
32 Tim Goff
33 Ondra Ford
34 Robert Bell
35 John Larios
36 Jim Larsen
37 Kenny Jackson
38 Sean Berry
39 Randy Goodenough
40 Mike Butcher
41 Kevin Karcher
42 Chuck Mount
43 Greg Hibbard
44 Boo Champagne
45 Gary Blouin
46 Ken Adams
47 Gus Jones
48 Joe Skodny
49 Mike Tresmer
50 Dennis Moeller

1986 Cramer Everett Giants (b/w)

(S.F. Giants, A) (2" x 3")

	MT
Complete Set (36):	9.00

(1) James "Earl" Averill
(2) Brock Birch
(3) Andrew Dixon
(4) Kevin Fitzgerald
(5) Ricky Fleming
(6) Brad Gambee
(7) Bruce Graham
(8) Chuck Higson
(9) James Jones
(10) Keith Krafve
(11) Mark Leonard
(12) Shaun MacKenzie
(13) Jim Massey
(14) Paul McClellan
(15) Tim McCoy
(16) Jim McNamara
(17) Willie Mijares
(18) Dave Nash
(19) Marty Newton
(20) Dave Patterson
(21) James Pena
(22) John Rannow
(23) Kevin Redick
(24) Drew Ricker
(25) Robin Reimer
(26) Gregg Ritchie
(27) Tod Ronson
(28) Chris Shultis
(29) Damon Skyta
(30) Joe Strain
(31) Chris Stubberfield
(32) Chuck Tate
(33) John Toal
(34) Jack Uhey
(35) Matt Walker
(36) Todd Wilson

1986 Cramer Everett Giants (color)

(S.F. Giants, A) (color)

	MT
Complete Set (32):	42.00

1 Kevin Fitzgerald
2 Paul McClellan
3 Matt Williams
4 Brad Gambee
5 Gregg Ritchie
6 Kevin Redick
7 John Toal
8 Russ Swan
9 Drew Ricker
10 Jim McNamara
11 Andrew Dixon
12 David Patterson
13 Tim McCoy
14 James Pena
15 Marty Newton
16 Chuck Tate
17 Jim Massey
18 Chris Stubberfield
19 John Rannow
20 Shaun MacKenzie
21 Tod Ronson
22 Chris Shultis
23 Brock Birch
24 Keith Krafve
25 James Jones
180 Joe Strain
181 Todd Wilson
182 Mark Leonard
183 Robin Riemer
184 David Nash
185 Chuck Higson
186 Matt Walker

1986 ProCards Florida State League All-Stars

(Class A)

	MT
Complete Set (50):	75.00

(1) Odie Abril
(2) Julio Alcala
(3) Chris Alvarez
(4) Brady Anderson
(5) Scott Arnold
(6) Tim Arnold
(7) Mark Berry
(8) Dave Bialas
(9) Marc Bombard
(10) Norman Brock
(11) Alex Cole
(12) Rufus Ellis
(13) Jeff Fassero
(14) Jeff Fischer
(15) John Fishel
(16) Jim Fortenberry
(17) Pete Geist
(18) Otto Gonzalez
(19) Maurice Guercio
(20) Matt Harrison
(21) John Hawkins
(22) Brad Henderson
(23) Ted Higgins
(24) Dave Holt
(25) Jim Jefferson
(26) Ron Johns
(27) Ron Jones
(28) Dan Juenke
(29) Tim Leiper
(30) Joel Lono
(31) Luis Lopez
(32) Rob Lopez
(33) Greg Lotzar
(34) Walt McConnell
(35) Jim Meadows
(36) Chris Morgan
(37) Max Oliveras
(38) Ray Perkins
(39) Dody Rather
(40) Jim Reboulet
(41) Darren Riley
(42) Don Rowland
(43) Tary Scott
(44) Mike Sears
(45) Doug Strange
(46) George Threadgill
(47) Shane Turner
(48) Luis Vasquez
(49) Tom West
(50) John Wockenfuss

1986 Smokey Bear Fresno Giants

(S.F. Giants, A)

	MT
Complete Set (32):	40.00

1 Tim Blackwell (manager)
2 Gary Davenport (coach)
3 Vince Sferrazza (trainer)
4 Gary Jones
5 Felipe Gonzalez
6 Joe Kmak
7 Greg Gilbert
8 Sam Moore
9 Mike Villa
10 Tom Messier
11 Randy McCament
12 Joe Olker
13 Dave Hinnrichs
14 Eric Erickson
15 Darrell Rodgers
16 Dennis Cook
17 Steve Smith

18 Hector Quinones
19 Ty Dabney
20 Tony Perezchica
21 Scott Thompson
22 Tom Mathews
23 John Skurla
24 T.J. McDonald
25 Charles Culberson
26 Harry Davis
27 Kenny Compton (batboy)
28 Tony Vitale (groundskeeper)
29 Smokey Bear (batting)
30 Smokey Bear (throwing)
31 Smokey Bear (saluting)
---- Introductory Card

1986 ProCards Ft. Lauderdale Yankees

(N.Y. Yankees, A)

	MT
Complete Set (23):	7.00

(1) Chris Alverez
(2) Anthony Balabon
(3) Douglas Carpenter
(4) Chris Carroll
(5) Gary Cathcart
(6) Mike Christopher
(7) Ysidro Giron
(8) Fred Gonzalez
(9) Robert Green
(10) Maurice Guerico
(11) Mathew Harrison
(12) Johnny Hawkins
(13) Theodore Higgins
(14) Harvey Lee
(15) Jason Maas
(16) Michael McClear
(17) Kenneth Patterson
(18) Johnnie Pleicones
(19) Norman Santiago
(20) Robert Sepanek
(21) Scott Shaw
(22) Aristarco Tirado
(23) Shane Turner

1986 ProCards Ft. Myers Royals

(K.C. Royals, A)

	MT
Complete Set (29):	6.00

(1) Julio Alcala
(2) Mike Alvarez
(3) Jeff Bedell
(4) Stan Boroski
(5) Pete Carey
(6) Bob Davis
(7) Jose DeJesus
(8) Rafael DeLeon
(9) Rufus Ellis
(10) Mark Farnsworth
(11) Phil George
(12) Carlos Gonzalez
(13) Duane Gustavson
(14) Jeff Hull
(15) Chris Jelic
(16) Kevin Koslofski
(17) Deric Ladnier
(18) Mike Loggins
(19) Mitch McKelvey
(20) Bill Mulligan
(21) Geoff Peterson
(22) Henry Robinson
(23) Ricky Rojas
(24) Gregg Schmidt
(25) Mark Van Blaricom
(26) Bob Van Vuren
(27) Troy Watkins
(28) Dejon Watson
(29) Don Woyce

1986 ProCards Geneva Cubs

(Chicago Cubs, A)

	MT
Complete Set (27):	6.00

(1) Jim Bullinger
(2) Todd Cloninger
(3) Tony Collins
(4) Mike Curtis
(5) Sergio Espinal
(6) Jimmie Gardner
(7) John Green
(8) Tony Hamza
(9) Derrick Hardamon
(10) Phil Harrison
(11) Clint Harwick
(12) Joe Housey
(13) Ced Landrum
(14) Jerry Lapenta
(15) Tony LaPoint
(16) Jay Loviglio
(17) Kelly Mann
(18) Jim Matas
(19) Steve Melendez
(20) Chuck Oertli
(21) Brian Otten
(22) Randy Penvose
(23) Parnell Perry
(24) Harry Shelton
(25) Jose Soto
(26) Bob Strickland
(27) Fernando Zarranz

1986 ProCards Glens Falls Tigers

(Detroit Tigers, AAA)

	MT
Complete Set (24):	6.00

(1) Ricky Barlow
(2) Willie Darkins
(3) Allen Duffy
(4) Paul Felix
(5) Marty Freeman
(6) Paul Gibson
(7) Mike Gorman
(8) Ruben Guzman
(9) Jeff Herman
(10) John Hiller
(11) Al Labozzetta
(12) Scott Lusader
(13) Morris Madden
(14) Frank Masters
(15) Steve McInerney
(16) Craig Mills
(17) Rey Palacios
(18) Roman Pena
(19) Benny Ruiz
(20) Bob Schaefer
(21) Steve Searcy
(22) Max Soto
(23) James Walewander
(24) Craig Weissmann

1986 ProCards Greensboro Hornets

(Boston Red Sox, A)

	MT
Complete Set (27):	7.00

(1) John Abbott
(2) Alan Ashkinazy
(3) Doug Camilli
(4) Kevin Camilli
(5) Jose Flores
(6) Dan Gabriele
(7) Chris Gaeckle
(8) Dan Gakeler
(9) Mike Goff
(10) Dan Hale
(11) Ray Hansen
(12) Tom Kane
(13) Derek Livernois
(14) Don McGowan
(15) Jim Orsag
(16) Billy Plante
(17) Todd Pratt
(18) Carlos Quintana
(19) Ray Revak
(20) John Roberts
(21) Victor Rosario
(22) Larry Shikles
(23) John Toale
(24) Paul Toutsis
(25) Pete Youngman
(26) Eddie Zambrano
(27) Bill Zupka

1986 ProCards Greenville Braves

(Atlanta Braves, AA) (Set also produced as 16" x 20" poster with a logo card added)

	MT
Complete Set (24):	48.00

(1) Rick Albert
(2) Jose Alvarez
(3) Jim Beauchamp
(4) Kevin Blankenship
(5) Chip Childress
(6) Steve Curry
(7) Sal D'Alessandro
(8) Darryl Denby
(9) Tom Glavine
(10) Paul Gnacinski
(11) Dave Griffin
(12) Jeff Groves
(13) Inocencio Guerrero
(14) Randy Ingle
(15) Carlos Rios
(16) Mike Scott
(17) Bill Slack
(18) Pete Smith
(19) Thornton Stringfellow
(20) Freddy Tiburcio
(21) Greg Tubbs
(22) Bob Tumpane
(23) Steve Ziem
(24) Logo card (poster set only)

1986 ProCards Hagerstown Suns

(Baltimore Orioles, A)

	MT
Complete Set (29):	6.00

(1) Jeff Ballard
(2) Frank Bellino
(3) Mickey Billmeyer
(4) Sherwin Clintje
(5) Brian Dudois
(6) Chris Eagelston
(7) Glenn Gulliver
(8) Scott Khoury
(9) Tom Magrann
(10) Paul McNeal
(11) Bob Milacki
(12) Bob Molinaro
(13) Ty Nichols
(14) Pete Palermo
(15) Tim Richardson
(16) Norman Roberts
(17) Geraldo Sanchez
(18) Dana Smith
(19) Chuck Stanhope
(20) Pete Stanicek
(21) Earl Stephenson
(22) Scott Stranski
(23) Craig Strobel
(24) Greg Talamantez
(25) Paul Thorpe
(26) Jesse Vasquez
(27) Ted Wilborn
(28) Wayne Wilson
(29) Craig Worthington

1986 ProCards Hawaii Islanders

(Pittsburgh Pirates, AAA)

	MT
Complete Set (23):	6.00

(1) Jackie Brown
(2) Glenn Brummer
(3) Trench Davis
(4) Benny Distefano
(5) Cecil Espy
(6) Tom Fandt
(7) Stan Fansler
(8) Ed Farmer
(9) Felix Fermin
(10) Burk Goldthorn
(11) Sam Haro
(12) Dave Johnson
(13) Barry Jones
(14) Ray Krawczyk
(15) Carlos Ledezma
(16) Dave Leeper
(17) Bobby Miscik
(18) Scott Neal
(19) Bob Patterson
(20) Rick Renteria
(21) Lee Tunnell
(22) Ron Wotus
(23) Jeff Zaske

1986 Huntsville Stars team issue

(Oakland A's, AA)

	MT
Complete Set (25):	80.00
Uncut Sheet:	95.00

10 Amin David
11 Gary Jones
12 Dave Nix
14 Dave Wilder
15 Rocky Coyle
16 Terry Steinbach
18 Damon Farmar
19 Ray Thoma
20 Brian Guinn
21 Todd Burns
22 Stan Hilton
23 Wally Whitehurst
24 Jose Tolentino
25 Brad Fischer
26 Mark Leonette
30 Stan Kyles
31 Tim Belcher
32 Scott Whaley
33 Mark McGwire
34 Greg Cadaret
40 Doug Scherer
41 John Cox
42 Kirk McDonald
44 Rick Tronerud
45 Roy Johnson

1986 Indianapolis Indians team issue

(Montreal Expos, AAA)

	MT
Complete Set (36):	15.00

1 Team logo
2 Owen J. Bush
3 Joe Sparks
4 Rich Stoll
5 Jack Glasscock
6 Randy Hunt
7 Tom Romano
8 Amos Rusie
9 Bob Owchinko
10 Rene Gonzales
11 Authentic document
12 John Dopson
13 Derrell Baker
14 1928 Indianapolis team photo
15 Randy St. Claire
16 "Skeeter" Barnes
17 Rodger Cole
18 "Lefty Bob" Logan
19 Wally Johnson
20 Len Barker
21 Al Lopez
22 Mike Hocutt
23 Bob Sebra
24 Herb Score
25 Curt Brown
26 Dallas Williams
27 Larry Groves
28 Luis Rivera
29 Don Buford
30 Tom Nieto
31 Dave Tomlin
32 "Champ" Summers
33 Casey Candaele
34 Tim Barrett
35 Billy Moore
36 Coaches/trainer (Jerry Manuel, Lee Garrett, Rick Williams)

1986 ProCards Iowa Cubs

(Chicago Cubs, AAA)

	MT
Complete Set (26):	6.00

(1) Johnny Abrego
(2) Bob Bathe
(3) Pookie Berustine
(4) Trey Brooks
(5) Mike Brumley
(6) Steve Christmas
(7) Jim Colborn
(8) Jeff Cornell
(9) Larry Cox
(10) Steve Engel
(11) Terry Francona
(12) Dave Grossman
(13) Dave Gumpert
(14) Steve Hammond
(15) Joe Hicks
(16) Guy Hoffman
(17) Dave Martinez
(18) Ron Meridith
(19) Brad Mills
(20) Paul Noce
(21) Gary Parmenter
(22) Doug Potestio
(23) Ken Pryce
(24) Bobby Ramos
(25) Julio Valdez
(26) Chico Walker

1986 TCMA Jackson Mets

(N.Y. Mets, AA)

	MT
Complete Set (27):	8.00

1 Jim Adamczak
2 Reggie Dobie
3 Wray Bergendahl
4 Tom Edens
5 Kyle Hartshorn
6 Jeff Innis
7 Kurt Lundgren
8 Ed Pruitt
9 Mike Santiago
10 Mickey Weston
11 Doug Gwosdz
12 Greg Olson
13 Kevin Elster
14 Dennis Glynn
15 Paul Hertzler
16 Andy Lawrence
17 Jeff McKnight
18 Rick Lockwood
19 Shawn Abner
20 Jason Felice
21 Scott Little
22 Johnny Wilson
23 Sam McCrary
24 Mike Cubbage
25 Glenn Abbott
26 Randy Milligan
27 Keith Miller

1986 TCMA Jacksonville Expos

(Montreal Expos, AA)

	MT
Complete Set (26):	8.00

1 Tony Nicometi
2 Johnny Paredes
3 Jim Cecchini
4 Armando Moreno
5 Tom Traen
6 Peter Camelo
7 John Trautwein
8 Nelson Santovenia
9 Leonel Carrion
10 Q.V. Lowe
11 Joe Graves
12 Greg Raymer
13 Matt Sferrazza
14 Kevin Price
15 Mark Gardner
16 Troy McKay
17 Gary Weinberger
18 Wilfredo Tejada
19 Tommy Thompson
20 Mark Corey
21 Jeff Reynolds
22 Norman Nelson
23 Brian Holman
24 Bill Cutshall
25 Jack Daugherty
26 Tim McCormack

1986 ProCards Jamestown Expos

(Montreal Expos, A)

	MT
Complete Set (30):	7.00

(1) Michael Blowers
(2) Don Burke
(3) C. Scott Clemo
(4) William D'Boever
(5) Kody Duey
(6) Jerome Duke
(7) Kenneth Fox
(8) Paul Frye
(9) Chan Galbato
(10) Robert Gaylor
(11) Michael Haines
(12) Mark Hardy
(13) Gene Harris
(14) Steven King
(15) Paul Peter Martineau
(16) James McDonald
(17) David Morrow
(18) Jeffrey Oller
(19) Troy Ricker
(20) Michael Robertson
(21) Dean Rockweiler
(22) Robert Shannon
(23) Steve St. Claire
(24) Joe Beely Sims
(25) Jeffrey Tabaka
(26) Darren Travels
(27) Sal Vaccaro
(28) Jeffrey Wedvick
(29) Frank Welborn
(30) Yippee (team mascot)

1986 ProCards Kenosha Twins

(Minnesota Twins, A)

	MT
Complete Set (25):	6.00

(1) Paul Abbott
(2) Larry Blackwell
(3) Jeff Bumgarner
(4) James Cook
(5) Mark Davis
(6) Tom DiCeglio
(7) Julio Delancer
(8) Rafael DeLima
(9) Tom Fiore
(10) Steven Gasser
(11) Marty Lanoux
(12) Bob Lee
(13) Don Leppert
(14) Jerry Mack
(15) Howard Manzon
(16) Ted Miller
(17) Edgar Naveda
(18) Tim O'Conner
(19) Yorkis Perez
(20) Bob Perry
(21) Mike Redding
(22) Bob Strube
(23) Luis Tapais
(24) Gary Thomason
(25) Leonard Webster

1986 ProCards Kinston Eagles

(Independent, A)

	MT
Complete Set (24):	6.00

(1) Howard Akers
(2) Bubba Brevell
(3) Scott Cannon
(4) Ed Delzer
(5) Van Evans
(6) Bruce Fischback
(7) Gene Gentile
(8) Al Heath
(9) Mike Ingle
(10) Lindsey Johnson
(11) Roger Johnson
(12) Randy Kramer
(13) Dan Larsen
(14) Perry Lychak
(15) Scott Melvin
(16) Paul Moralez
(17) Marty Reed
(18) Emmett Robinson
(19) Gabriel Robles
(20) Randy Romagna
(21) Melvin Rosario
(22) John Schofield
(23) Dave Trembley
(24) Ken Whitfield

1986 ProCards Knoxville Blue Jays

(Toronto Blue Jays, AA)

	MT
Complete Set (27):	7.00

(1) Kash Beauchamp
(2) Jim Bishop
(3) Pat Borders
(4) Sal Campusano (Sil)
(5) J.J. Cannon
(6) Eddie Dennis
(7) Tim Englund
(8) Keith Gilliam
(9) Larry Hardy
(10) Glenallen Hill
(11) Randy Holland
(12) Jim Howard
(13) Tony Hudson
(14) Manny Lee
(15) Nelson Liriano
(16) Colin McLaughlin
(17) Greg Moore
(18) Oswald Peraza
(19) Jose Segura
(20) Chris Shaddy
(21) Kevin Sliwinski
(22) Matt Stark
(23) Bernie Tatis
(24) Norm Tonnucci
(25) Dave Walsh
(26) Mike Yearout
(27) Cliff Young

1986 ProCards Lakeland Tigers

(Detroit Tigers, A)

	MT
Complete Set (25):	35.00

(1) Jeff Agar
(2) Bernie Anderson
(3) Tommy Burgess
(4) Bill Cooper
(5) Steve Eagar
(6) Ken Gohmann
(7) Keith Hoskinson
(8) Mark Lee
(9) Tim Leiper
(10) Al Liebert
(11) Tony Long
(12) Porfi Martinez
(13) Chip McHugh
(14) Jeff Minick
(15) Dave Minnema
(16) Chris Morgan
(17) Rod Poissant
(18) Laney Prioleau
(19) Art Raubolt
(20) Donnie Rowland
(21) Joseph Slavic
(22) Terry Smith
(23) John Smoltz
(24) Doug Strange
(25) Mike York

1986 ProCards Las Vegas Stars

(San Diego Padres, AAA) (Larry Bowa is scarce card found only in sets distrbuted at ballpark)

	MT
Complete Set, w/Bowa, Hutcheson (26):	18.00
Partial Set, w/Hutcheson, no Bowa (25):	10.00
Partial Set, no Bowa or Hutcheson (24):	7.00

(1) Randy Asadoor
(2) Greg Booker
(3) Steve Garcia
(4) Dick Grapenthin
(5) Gary Green
(6) Ray Hayward
(7) Todd Hutcheson (trainer)
(8) Jimmy Jones
(9) Steve Kemp
(10) Steve Lubratich
(11) Mark Parent
(12) Tim Pyznarski
(13) Edwin Rodriguez
(14) Benito Santiago
(15) James Siwy
(16) Gregory Smith
(17) Brian Snyder
(18) James Steels
(19) Bob Stoddard
(20) John Tutt
(21) Ed Vosberg
(22) Mark Wasinger
(23) Mark Williamson
(24) Ed Wojna
(25) Gary Woods
(26) Larry Bowa (included only in ballpark giveaway sets)

1986 ProCards Little Falls Mets

(N.Y. Mets, A)

	MT
Complete Set (29):	6.00

(1) Mike Anderson
(2) Pete Bauer
(3) Lou Berge
(4) Rick Brown
(5) Genaro Castro
(6) Rob Colescott
(7) Pat Crosby
(8) Mark DiVincenzo
(9) Rick Duant
(10) Ken Farmer
(11) Mark Fiedler
(12) Cliff Gonzalez
(13) Ceoric Hawkins
(14) Rob Hernandez
(15) Alex Jiminez
(16) Lorin Jundy
(17) Rich Lundahl
(18) Dan McMurtrie
(19) Rich Miller
(20) Rodney Murrel
(21) Ron Narcisse
(22) Luis Natera
(23) Fritz Polka
(24) Jaime Roseboro
(25) Joel Sklar
(26) Heath Slocumb
(27) Andy Taylor
(28) Tony Thompson
(29) Todd Welborn

1986 Louisville Redbirds team issue

(St. Louis Cardinals, AAA)

	MT
Complete Set (30):	12.00

1 Jim Fregosi
2 Dyar Miller
3 David Hudson
4 Jack Ayer
5 Steve Braun
6 Joe Boever
7 Rod Booker
8 Rich Buonantony
9 Ralph Citarella
10 Greg Dunn
11 Mike Dunne
12 Bill Farley
13 Curt Ford
14 Kurt Kepshire
15 Alan Knicely
16 Jim Lindeman
17 Bill Lyons
18 Fred Manrique
19 Fred Martinez
20 John Morris
21 Tom Pagnozzi
22 Casey Parsons
23 Joe Pettini
24 Marty Pevey
25 Dave Rajsich
26 Ray Soff
27 Dan Stryffeler
28 Tim Wallace
29 Jed Smith
30 Mascots (B. Johnson & D. Harris)

1986 ProCards Lynchburg Mets

(N.Y. Mets, A)

	MT
Complete Set (28):	6.00

(1) Ralph Adams
(2) Jim Bibby
(3) Desi Brooks
(4) Kevin Brown
(5) Wilmer Caraballo
(6) Al Carmichael
(7) Jeff Ciszkowski
(8) Angelo Cuevas
(9) Bobby Floyd
(10) Jeff Gardner
(11) Steve Gay
(12) Ronnie Gideon
(13) Mauro Gozzo
(14) Marcus Lawton
(15) Chuck Lynn
(16) Hector Perez
(17) Steve Phillips
(18) Jeff Richardson
(19) Rich Rodriguez
(20) Zoilo Sanchez
(21) Eric Stampel
(22) Dave Tresch
(23) Wilson Valera
(24) Juan Villanueva
(25) Dave West
(26) Mike Westbrook
(27) Dan Winters
(28) Shane Young

1986 ProCards Macon Pirates

(Pittsburgh Pirates, A)

	MT
Complete Set (27):	10.00

(1) Ben Abner
(2) Kevin Andersh
(3) Kirk Berry
(4) Dwight Bernard
(5) Octavio Cepeda
(6) Tony Chance
(7) Jim Davins
(8) Dorley Downs
(9) Kevin Franchi
(10) Ron Giddens
(11) Andy Hall
(12) Todd Hansen
(13) Rob Hatfield
(14) Guillermo Mercedes
(15) Orlando Merced
(16) Douglas Moreno
(17) Rafael Muratti
(18) Luis Pena
(19) Julio Perez
(20) Mike Quade
(21) Gilbert Roca
(22) Jeff Satzinger
(23) Brian Stackhouse
(24) Mike Stevanus
(25) Keith Swartzlander
(26) Jay Wollenburg
(27) Joey Zellner

1986 T&J Sportscards Madison Muskies

(Oakland A's, A)

	MT
Complete Set (27):	10.00

1 Doug Ames
2 Tony Arias
3 Larry Arndt
4 Tony Cabrera
5 Ron Carter
6 Brian Criswell
7 Mike Cupples
8 Pat Dietrick
9 Bobby Gould
10 Marty Hall
11 Mark Howie
12 Andre Jacas
13 Russ Kibler
14 Kirk McDonald
15 Dave Nix
16 Dave Otto
17 Scott Sabo
18 Jeff Shaver
19 Nelson Silverio
20 Bob Stocker
21 Camilo Veras
22 Walt Weiss
23 Wally Whitehurst
24 Jim Nettles
25 Dave Schober
26 Dave Schillinglaw
27 Rick Wise

1986 ProCards Madison Muskies

(Oakland A's, A)

	MT
Complete Set (28):	6.00

(1) Douglas Ames
(2) Tony Arias
(3) Larry Arnot
(4) Antonio Cabrera
(5) Ron Carter
(6) Brian Criswell
(7) Michael Cupples
(8) Patrick Dietrick
(9) Bobby Gould
(10) Marty Hall
(11) Mark Howie
(12) Andre Jacas
(13) Russell Kibler
(14) Kirk McDonald
(15) James Nettles
(16) Dave Nix
(17) David Otto
(18) Kevin Russ
(19) Scott Sabo
(20) Dave Schober
(21) Jeffrey Shaver
(22) Dave Shillinglaw
(23) Nelson Silverio
(24) Robert Stocker
(25) Camilo Veras
(26) Walter Weiss
(27) Walter Whitehurst
(28) Rick Wise

1986 ProCards Maine Guides

(Cleveland Indians, AAA)

	MT
Complete Set (26):	6.00

(1) Barry Bruenkant
(2) Kevin Buckley
(3) George Cecchetti
(4) Steve Ciszczon
(5) Dave Clark
(6) Steve Commer
(7) Keith Creel
(8) Barry Evans
(9) Dave Gallagher
(10) Kevin Hagen
(11) Doug Jones
(12) Jim Napier
(13) Junior Noboa
(14) Bryan Oelkers
(15) Craig Pippen
(16) Reggie Ritter
(17) Scott Roberts
(18) Jose Roman
(19) Tommy Rowe
(20) Cory Snyder
(21) Curt Wardle
(22) Randy Washington
(23) Jim Weaver
(24) Frank Wills
(25) Jim Wilson
(26) Rich Yett

1986 Cramer Medford A's

(Oakland A's, A)

	MT
Complete Set (25):	8.00

51 William Savarino
52 James Reiser
53 David Veres
54 Mark Stancel
55 Mark Beavers
56 William Reynolds
57 Luis Martinez
58 Bill Coonan
59 Pat Gilbert
60 Larry Ritchey
61 Glenn Hoffinger
62 Robbie Gilbert
63 Todd Hartley
64 Kevin Tapani
65 Weston Weber
66 Jeff Kopyta
67 Dann Howitt
68 Jeff Glover
69 Lance Blankenship
70 Kevin Kunkel
71 James Carroll
72 Darrin Duffy
73 John Kent
74 Vincent Teixeira
75 Keith Wentz

1986 Time Out Sports Memphis Chicks

(Kansas City Royals, AA) (Production reported as 10,000 gold sets, 5,000 silver.)

	MT
Complete Set, Gold (26):	16.00
Complete Set, Silver (26):	35.00

1 Tommy Jones
3 Gary Thurman
5 Gene Morgan
6 Mike Miller
7 Hector Rincones
9 Van Snider
10 Chito Martinez
11 Phil George
12 Art Martinez
14 Israel Sanchez
15 Doug Gilcrease
16 Jere Longenecker
18 Joe Jarrell
20 Angel Morris

21 Mitch McKelvey
23 Rick Goodin
24 Jimmy Daniel
25 Rich Dubee
26 Ken Crew
27 Terry Bell
28 Bo Jackson
29 John Davis
32 Jose Rodiles
33 Luis De Los Santos
35 Mike McFarlane
---- Steve Morrow

1986 ProCards Miami Marlins

(Baltimore Orioles, A)

	MT
Complete Set (29):	6.00

(1) German Bautista
(2) Juan Bellver
(3) Mike Browning
(4) Rick Carrano
(5) Tim Dulin
(6) Todd Edwards
(7) Marc Estes
(8) John Harrington
(9) Fred Hatfield
(10) Tommy Hearn
(11) Alan Hixon
(12) Lance Hudson
(13) Dan Juenke
(14) Bob Latmore
(15) Kurt Leiter
(16) Pedro Llanes
(17) Jerry Miller
(18) Curt Morgan
(19) Luis Ojeda
(20) Ray Perkins
(21) Eric Rasmussen
(22) Elem Rossy
(23) Todd Smith
(24) Phil Taylor
(25) Dave Van Ohlen
(26) Greg Wallace
(27) Phil Wielegman
(28) Roger Wilson
(29) John Wockenfuss

1986 ProCards Midland Angels

(California Angels, AA)

	MT
Complete Set (26):	6.00

(1) Doug Banning
(2) Brian Brady
(3) DeWayne Buice
(4) Vinicio Cedeno
(5) Terry Clark
(6) Mike Cook
(7) Sherman Corbett
(8) Doug Davis
(9) Brian Hartsock
(10) Dave Heath
(11) John Hotchkiss
(12) Kevin King
(13) Vance Lovelace
(14) Joe Maddon
(15) Mike Madril
(16) Mark McLemore
(17) Bill Merriefield
(18) Aurelio Monteagudo
(19) Rafael Pimental
(20) James Randall
(21) Jeff Schaffer
(22) Don Timberlake
(23) Raul Tovar
(24) Phil Venturino
(25) Glen Walker
(26) Richard Zaleski

1986 Chong Modesto A's

(Oakland A's, A)

	MT
Complete Set (27):	17.50

1 Roy Anderson
2 Russ Applegate
3 Darren Baisley
4 Bo Kent
5 Tyler Brilinski
6 Pat Dietrick
7 Mike Duncan
8 Darel Hansen
9 Twayne Harris
10 Steve Howard
11 James Jones
12 Felix Jose
13 Lance Blankenship
14 Richard Martig
15 Shannon Mendenhall
16 Jerome Nelson
17 Jose Peguero
18 Bob Sharpnack
19 Mark Tortorice
20 Bruce Walton
21 Joe Xavier
22 Kevin Tapani
23 Mark Beavers
24 Butch Hughes
25 Tommie Reynolds
26 John Cartelli
27 Jeff Koryta

1986 ProCards Modesto A's

(Oakland A's, A) (Anderson in catching pose is a scarce card)

	MT
Complete Set, Anderson catching (26):	6.00
Complete Set, two Andersons (27):	15.00

(1a) Roy Anderson (catching)
(1b) Roy Anderson (with bat)
(2) Russell Applegate
(3) Darren Balsley
(4) Tyler Brilinski
(5) John "Doc" Cartelli
(6) Jerry Deguero
(7) Mike Duncan
(8) Vic Figueroa
(9) Steve Gorey
(10) Darel Hansen
(11) Twayne Harris
(12) Mike Hogan
(13) Steve Howard
(14) Butch Hughes
(15) Jim Jones
(16) Felix Jose
(17) John Kanter
(18) Joe Kramer
(19) Rich Martig
(20) Jerome Nelson
(21) Tommie Reynolds
(22) Bob Sharpnack
(23) Jim Strichek
(24) Joe Strong
(25) Mark Tortorice
(26) Bruce Walton

1986 ProCards Nashua Pirates

(Pittsburgh Pirates, AA)

	MT
Complete Set (28):	6.00

(1) Mike Ashman
(2) Kerry Baker
(3) Mike Berger
(4) Craig Brown
(5) Matias Carrillo
(6) Scott Fiepke
(7) Ken Ford
(8) Kevin Gordon
(9) Tommy Gregg
(10) Dimas Gutierrez
(11) Reggie Hammonds
(12) Martin Hernandez
(13) Shawn Holman
(14) Tony Laird
(15) Jim Leopold
(16) Jose Lind
(17) Orlando Lind
(18) Steve McAllister
(19) Jim Neidlinger
(20) Jim Opie
(21) Hipolito Pena
(22) Pete Rice
(23) Ruben Rodriguez
(24) Dennis Rogers
(25) Rich Sauveur
(26) Dorn Taylor
(27) Spin Williams
(28) "H" Williams

Suffix letters following a card number indicate a variation card.

1986 Nashville Sounds team issue

(Detroit Tigers, AAA)

	MT
Complete Set (24):	10.00

(1) Doug Baker
(2) Fred Breining
(3) Chuck Cary
(4) Pedro Chavez
(5) Jeff Conner
(6) Brian Denman
(7) Scott Earl
(8) Bruce Fields
(9) Paul Gibson
(10) Brian Harper
(11) Don Heinkel
(12) Mike Henneman
(13) Rodney Hobbs
(14) Bryan Kelly
(15) Jack Lazorko
(16) Scotti Madison
(17) Don McGann
(18) Matt Nokes
(19) Chris Nyman
(20) German Rivera
(21) Leon Roberts
(22) Jeff Robinson
(23) Gene Roof
(24) Tim Tolman

1986 ProCards New Britain Red Sox

(Boston Red Sox, AA)

	MT
Complete Set (25):	18.00

(1) Andy Araujo
(2) Tony Beal
(3) Jose Birriel
(4) Ellis Burks
(5) Pete Cappadona
(6) Robert Chadwick
(7) Jim Corsi
(8) Steve Curry
(9) Chuck Davis
(10) Steve Ellsworth
(11) Eduardo Estrada
(12) Demarlo Hale
(13) Sam Horn
(14) Pat Jelks
(15) Dana Kiecker
(16) John Marzano
(17) Bill McInnis
(18) Mark Meleski
(19) Sam Nattile
(20) Dave Peterson
(21) Jody Reed
(22) Paul Slifko
(23) Hector Steward
(24) Tony Torchia
(25) Scott Wade

1986 ProCards Oklahoma City 89'ers

(Texas Rangers, AAA)

	MT
Complete Set (26):	8.00

(1) Bob Brower
(2) Greg Campbell
(3) Rob Clark
(4) Glen Cook
(5) Tommy Dunbar
(6) Dave Geisel
(7) Rusty Gerhardt
(8) Bobby Jones
(9) Jeff Kunkel
(10) Willie Lozado
(11) Jim Maler
(12) Orlando Mercado
(13) Dale Mohoric (Mohorcic)
(14) Jeff Moronko
(15) Dave Oliver
(16) Dave Owen
(17) Mike Parrott
(18) Luis Pujols
(19) Jeff Russell
(20) Tommy Joe Shimp
(21) Ruben Sierra (photo actually Orlando Merced)
(22) Rick Surhoff
(23) Greg Tabor
(24) Don Welchel
(25) Don Werner
(26) Matt Williams

1986 TCMA Omaha Royals

(K.C. Royals, AA)

	MT
Complete Set (25):	18.00

1 Bill Hayes
2 Ron Johnson
3 Kevin Seitzer
4 Mike Kingery
5 Roger Hansen
6 Jeff Schultz
7 Jim Scranton
8 Bob Hegman
9 Marty Wilkerson
10 Russ Stephans
11 Dwight Taylor
12 Bill Pecota
13 Mike Brewer
14 Joe Citari
15 Mike Griffin
16 Dave Cone
17 Scott Tabor
18 Jim Strode
19 Dave Schuler
20 Theo Shaw
21 Alan Hargesheimer
22 Tom Mullen
23 John Boles
24 Frank Funk
25 Scott Bankhead

1986 ProCards Omaha Royals

(K.C. Royals, AAA)

	MT
Complete Set (29):	18.00

(1) Scott Bankhead
(2) John Boles
(3) Mike Brewer
(4) Keefe Cato
(5) Joe Citari
(6) David Cone
(7) Frank Funk
(8) Mike Griffin
(9) Roger Hansen
(10) Bill Hayes
(11) Bob Hegman
(12) Rondin Johnson
(13) Mike Kingery
(14) Renie Martin
(15) Mike Miller
(16) Tom Mullen
(17) Bill Pecota
(18) Jose Reyes
(19) Dave Schuler
(20) Jeff Schulz
(21) Jim Scranton
(22) Kevin Seitzer
(23) Theo Shaw
(24) Russ Stephans
(25) Lester Strode
(26) Nick Swartz
(27) Scott Taber
(28) Mike Warren
(29) Marty Wilkerson

1986 ProCards Orlando Twins

(Minnesota Twins, AA)

	MT
Complete Set (24):	6.00

(1) Steve Aragon
(2) Brad Bierley
(3) Todd Budke
(4) Mark Clemons
(5) Jose Dominguez
(6) Troy Galloway
(7) Steve Gomez
(8) Stan Holmes
(9) Joe Klink
(10) Gene Larkin
(11) John Marquardt
(12) George Mitterwald
(13) Greg Morhardt
(14) Steve Padia
(15) Doug Palmer
(16) Ray Ramirez
(17) Robbie Smith
(18) Alan Sontag
(19) Sam Sorce
(20) Jeff Taylor
(21) Jeff Trout
(22) Dave Vetsch
(23) Kevin Wiggins
(24) Phil Wilson

1986 ProCards Osceola Astros

(Houston Astros, A)

	MT
Complete Set (29):	6.00

(1) Norman Brock
(2) Mike Brown
(3) Scott Camp
(4) Jesus Carrion
(5) Earl Cash
(6) Don Dunster
(7) Francois Durocher
(8) John Fishel
(9) Terry Green
(10) Anthony Hampton
(11) Geysi Heredia
(12) Stan Hough
(13) Ken Houston
(14) Chris Huchingson
(15) Calvin James
(16) Joe Kwolek
(17) Jeff Livin
(18) Darryl Menard
(19) Pete Mueller
(20) Randy Randle
(21) Dody Rather
(22) Marty Schreiber
(23) Glenn Sherlock
(24) Doug Snyder
(25) Mel Stottlemyre
(26) Gary Tuck
(27) Jose Vargas
(28) Tom Wiedenbauer
(29) Jamie Williams

1986 ProCards Palm Springs Angels

(California Angels, A)

	MT
Complete Set (29):	22.00

(1) Kent Anderson
(2) Bobby Bell
(3) Dante Bichette
(4) Paul Bilak
(5) Mike Butler
(6) Richie Carter
(7) Pete Coachman
(8) Larry Cook
(9) Barry Dacus
(10) John DiGioia
(11) Mark Doran
(12) Todd Eggertsen
(13) William Fraser
(14) Miguel Garcia
(15) Billy Geivett
(16) Bryan Harvey
(17) Chuck Hernandez
(18) Doug Jennings
(19) Tom Kotchman
(20) Reggie Lambert
(21) Scott Marrott
(22) David Martinez
(23) Dave Montanari
(24) Dario Nunez
(25) Erik Pappas
(26) Stacey Pettis
(27) Bryan Price
(28) Mike Romanovsky
(29) Ty Van Burkleo

1986 Smokey Bear Palm Springs Angels

(California Angels, A) (2-13/16" x 3-3/4", blue-and-white photos, red, white and blue borders)

	MT
Complete Set (28):	30.00

1 Tom Osowski (general manager)
2 Tom Kotchman (manager)
3 Chuck Hernandez (coach)
4 Paul Bilak (trainer)
5 Bobby Bell
6 Eric Pappas
7 John DiGioia
8 Miguel Garcia
9 William Fraser
10 Mike Romanovsky
11 Larry Cook
12 Bryan Harvey
13 Scott Marrett
14 Richie Carter
15 Bryan Price
16 Todd Eggertson
17 Mick Butler
18 Phil Venturino
19 Barry Dacus
20 Ty Van Burkleo
21 David Montanari
22 Pete Coachman
23 Billy Geivett
24 Mitch Seoane
25 Dario Nunez
26 Doug Jennings
27 Reggie Lambert
---- Introductory Card

1986 ProCards Pawtucket Red Sox

(Boston Red Sox, AAA)

	MT
Complete Set (28):	15.00

(1) Todd Benzinger
(2) Dick Berardino
(3) Mike Brown
(4) Chris Cannizzaro
(5) John Christensen (glove on right hand)
(6) John Christensen (glove on left hand)
(7) Tony Cleary
(8) Mike Dalton
(9) Pat Dodson
(10) Mike Greenwell
(11) Mitch Johnson
(12) John Leister
(13) George Mecerod
(14) Mike Mesh
(15) Gary Miller-Jones
(16) Ed Nottle
(17) Rey Quinonez
(18) Mike Rochford
(19) Kevin Romine
(20) Calvin Schiraldi
(21) Jeff Sellers
(22) Danny Sheaffer
(23) Mike Stenhouse
(24) Laschelle Tarver
(25) Gary Tremblay
(26) Mike Trujillo
(27) Dana Williams
(28) Rob Woodard

1986 ProCards Peninsula White Sox

(Chicago White Sox, A)

	MT
Complete Set (28):	6.00

(1) Jorge Alcazar
(2) Larry Allen
(3) Jeff Anderson
(4) Bob Bailey
(5) Jerry Bertolani
(6) Virgil Conley
(7) Dan Cronkright
(8) Tom Drees
(9) Wayne Edwards
(10) Duane Engram
(11) Chuck Hartenstein
(12) Mark Henry
(13) Tom Hildebrand
(14) Chris Jefts
(15) Tom Lahrman
(16) Jim Markert
(17) Glen McElroy
(18) Mike Moore
(19) John Pawlowski
(20) Adam Peterson
(21) Darrell Pruitt
(22) Kevin Renz
(23) Ron Scheer
(24) Ed Sedar
(25) Pete Venturini
(26) Dave Wallwork
(27) Eric Wilson
(28) Jim Winters

1986 ProCards Peoria Chiefs

(Chicago Cubs, A)

	MT
Complete Set (27):	50.00

(1) Scott Anders
(2) Dick Canan
(3) Tony Collins
(4) Leonard Damian
(5) Bill Danek
(6) John Fierro
(7) Jim Gardner
(8) Mark Grace
(9) John Green
(10) Tony Hamza
(11) Jeff Hirsch
(12) Greg Kallevig
(13) Joe Kraemer
(14) John Lewis
(15) Dave Liddell
(16) Tom Lombarski
(17) Pete Mackanin
(18) Bob Mandeville
(19) Bill Phillips
(20) Kris Roth
(21) Tad Scowik
(22) Jeff Small
(23) Dwight Smith
(24) John Turner
(25) Tim Wallace
(26) Jim Wright
(27) Fernando Zarranz

1986 ProCards Phoenix Firebirds

(S.F. Giants, AAA)

	MT
Complete Set (26):	6.00

(1) Rick Adams
(2) Mike Aldrete
(3) Randy Bockus
(4) Kelly Downs
(5) Duane Espy
(6) Randy Gomez
(7) Everett Graham
(8) Mark Grant
(9) Chuck Hensley
(10) Mike Jeffcoat
(11) Randy Johnson
(12) Cris Jones
(13) Randy Kutcher
(14) Rick Lancellotti
(15) Jim Lefebvre
(16) Jack McNight
(17) Bob Moore
(18) Terry Mulholland
(19) Phil Ouellette
(20) Jon Perlman
(21) Luis Quinones
(22) Jesse Reid
(23) Cliff Shidawara
(24) Frank Williams
(25) Jack Wilson
(26) Mike Woodard

1986 ProCards Pittsfield Cubs

(Chicago Cubs, AA)

	MT
Complete Set (25):	250.00

(1) Rich Amaral
(2) Damon Berryhill
(3) Mike Capel
(4) Bruce Crabbe
(5) Luis Cruz
(6) Jackie Davidson
(7) Jim Dickerson
(8) Drew Hall
(9) Carl Hamilton
(10) Darrin Jackson
(11) Dave Kopf
(12) Mike Lacer
(13) Dave Lenderman
(14) Greg Maddux
(15) Mike Martin
(16) Allen McKay
(17) Jamie Moyer
(18) Rafael Palmeiro
(19) Dick Pole
(20) Steve Roadcap
(21) Jeff Rutledge
(22) Tom Spencer
(23) Phil Stephenson
(24) Gary Varsho
(25) Tony Woods

1986 Pittsfield Cubs team poster

(Chicago Cubs, AA) (10-7/8" x 16-3/4")

	MT
Poster:	85.00

(1) Rich Amaral
(2) Damon Berryhill
(3) Brad Blevins
(4) Mike Capel
(5) Troy Chestnut
(6) Bruce Crabbe
(7) Luis Cruz
(8) Jackie Davidson
(9) Drew Hall
(10) Carl Hamilton
(11) Darrin Jackson
(12) Dave Kopf
(13) Tom Layton
(14) Dave Lenderman
(15) Mike Martin
(16) Alan McKay
(17) Paul Noce
(18) Rafael Palmeiro
(19) Rolando Roomes
(20) Phil Stephenson
(21) Gary Varsho
(22) Tony Woods

1986 ProCards Portland Beavers

(Philadelphia Phillies, AAA) (Miller's card was withdrawn from distribution and is scarce)

	MT
Complete Set, w/Miller (23):	20.00
Partial Set, no Miller (22):	6.00

(1) Jeff Bittiger
(2) Dave Bulls
(3) Joe Cipolloni
(4) Randy Day
(5) Ken Dowell
(6) Arturo Gonzalez
(7) Tom Gorman
(8) Kevin Hickey
(9) Rob Hicks
(10) Chris James
(11) Greg Jelks
(12) Tim Knight
(13) Alan LeBoeuf
(14) Randy Lerch
(15) Mike Maddux
(16) Francisco Melendez
(17) Keith Miller
(18) Kyle Money
(19) Ronn Reynolds
(20) Dave Shipanoff
(21) Jeff Stone
(22) Bobby Tiefenauer
(23) Fred Toliver

1986 ProCards Prince William Pirates

(Pittsburgh Pirates, A)

	MT
Complete Set (27):	7.00

(1) Reggie Barringer
(2) Lance Belen
(3) Tony Blasucci
(4) Rocky Bridges
(5) Tony Chance
(6) Carey Cheek
(7) Jeff Cook
(8) Ron Delucchi
(9) Tim Drummond
(10) Sal Ferreiras
(11) Brett Gideon
(12) Mike Goodwin
(13) Brian Jones
(14) Bob Koopman
(15) Tim McMillan
(16) Jose Melendez
(17) Larry Melton
(18) Page Odle
(19) Chris Pierce
(20) Tom Prince
(21) Chris Ritter
(22) Dave Rooker
(23) Rob Russell
(24) John Smiley
(25) Greg Stading
(26) Mike Stevens
(27) Kyle Todd

1986 ProCards Quad Cities Angels

(California Angels, A)

	MT
Complete Set (33):	10.00

(1) Edgar Alfonso
(2) Tom Alfredson
(3) Bob Auth
(4) Gerald Baker
(5) Mark Ban
(6) Tim Burcham
(7) Chris Collins
(8) Frank DiMichele
(9) Santiago Espinosa
(10) Andres Esponisa (Espinoza)
(11) Chuck Finley
(12) Ken Grant
(13) Dan Grunard
(14) Randy Harvey
(15) Dave Johnson
(16) Sam Joseph
(17) Scott Kannenberg
(18) Bill Lachemann
(19) Jeff Manto
(20) Mark Marino
(21) Ed Marquez
(22) Steve McGuire
(23) Glenn Meyers
(24) Richerd Morehouse
(25) Gary Nalls
(26) Giovanny Reyes
(27) Edwin Rivera
(28) Ed Rodriguez
(29) Robert Rose
(30) Mickey Saatzer
(31) Glenn Washington
(32) Roger Zottneck
(33) Team Card

1986 ProCards Reading Phillies

(Philadelphia Phillies, AA)

	MT
Complete Set (26):	6.00

(1) Ramon Aviles
(2) Shawn Barton
(3) Mark Bowden
(4) Tony Brown
(5) Jose Cecena
(6) George Culver
(7) Steve DeAngelis
(8) Marvin Freeman
(9) Ramon Henderson
(10) Ken Jackson
(11) Michael Jackson
(12) Ricky Jordan
(13) Steve Labay
(14) Jose Leiva
(15) Bruce Long
(16) Darren Loy
(17) Keith Miller
(18) Steve Moses
(19) Howard Nichols, Jr.
(20) Barney Nugent
(21) Jim Olander
(22) Ray Ramon
(23) Bruce Ruffin
(24) Mike Shelton
(25) Kevin Ward
(26) Lenny Watts

1986 ProCards Richmond Braves

(Atlanta Braves, AAA)

	MT
Complete Set (26):	6.00

(1) Sam Ayoub
(2) Dave Beard
(3) Steve Curry
(4) Bruce Dal Canton
(5) Juan Eichelberger
(6) Doc Estes
(7) Lee Graham
(8) Al Hall
(9) Kelly Heath
(10) Mike Jones
(11) Brad Komminsk
(12) Robert Long
(13) Roy Majtyka
(14) Ed Olwine
(15) Larry Owen
(16) Gerald Perry
(17) Charlie Puleo
(18) John Rabb
(19) Paul Runge
(20) Steve Shields
(21) Cliff Speck
(22) Mark Strucher
(23) Ron Tingley
(24) Andre Treadway
(25) Matt West
(26) Paul Zuvella

1986 ProCards Rochester Red Wings

(Baltimore Orioles, AAA)

	MT
Complete Set (26):	6.00

(1) Tony Arnold
(2) Dom Chiti
(3) Ken Gerhart
(4) Glenn Gulliver
(5) John Habyan
(6) John Hart
(7) Mike Hart
(8) Rex Hudler
(9) Phil Hoffman
(10) Odell Jones
(11) Rick Jones
(12) Mick Kinnunen
(13) Curt Motton
(14) Tom O'Malley
(15) Al Pardo
(16) Kelly Paris
(17) Eric Rasmussen
(18) Mike Reddish
(19) Don Scott
(20) Nelson Simmons
(21) Mike Skinner
(22) Ken Smith
(23) Kelvin Torve
(24) Jim Traber
(25) Jeff Williams
(26) Silver Stadium

1986 Cramer Salem Angels

(California Angels, A)

	MT
Complete Set (25):	7.00

76 Colin Charland
77 Giovanny Reyes
78 Jeff Gay
79 Julio Granco
80 Brandy Vann
81 Alan Mills
82 Gary Gorski
83 Bobby Cabello
84 Bill Vanderwel
85 Greg Jackson
86 Scott Cerny
87 Michael Knapp
88 Daryl Green
89 Colby Ward
90 James Bisceglia
91 Greg Fix
92 Luis Merejo
93 Tony Bonura
94 David Grilione
95 Terence Carr
96 Lee Stevens
97 Michael Fetters
98 Santiago Espinosa
99 Mike Spearnock
100 Roberto Hernandez

1986 ProCards Salem Red Birds

(Texas Rangers, A)

	MT
Complete Set (29):	6.00

(1) Kevin Bootay
(2) Mike Bucci
(3) Joel Cartaya
(4) Jeff Clay
(5) Bryan Dial
(6) Tom Duggan
(7) Riley Epps
(8) Al Farmer
(9) Greg Ferlenda
(10) Stephen Glasker
(11) Tim Hallgren
(12) Brad Hill
(13) Duane James
(14) Ron King
(15) Steve Kordish
(16) Chad Kreuter
(17) Steve Lankard
(18) Jeff Mays
(19) Tim McLoughlin
(20) Bob Mortimer
(21) Dave Murray
(22) Bob O'Hearn
(23) Kevin Reimer
(24) Dave Satnat
(25) Mitch Thomas
(26) Jose Vargas
(27) Jim Vlcek
(28) Darrell Whitaker
(29) Mike Winbush

1986 ProCards San Jose Bees

(Independent, A)

	MT
Complete Set (25):	6.00

(1) Freddie Arroyo
(2) Shawn Barton
(3) Mike Bigusiak
(4) Randy Bispo
(5) James Bolt
(6) Darryl Cias
(7) Ken Foster
(8) Darren Garrick
(9) Lorenzo Gray
(10) Steven Howe
(11) Brian Kubala
(12) Edward McCarter
(13) Ted Milner
(14) Yoshi Nakashima
(15) Mike Nittoli
(16) Dave Okubo
(17) Ken Reitz
(18) Daryl Sconiers
(19) Harry Steve
(20) Nori Tanabe
(21) Jim Tinkey
(22) Mike Verdi
(23) Hank Wada
(24) Mickey Yamano
(25) George Yokota

1986 ProCards Shreveport Captains

(S.F. Giants, AA)

MT
Complete Set (28): 9.00
(1) Jeff Brantley
(2) John Burkett
(3) Kevin Burrell
(4) Alan Cockrell
(5) Charlie Corbell
(6) Marty Demerritt
(7) Angel Escobar
(8) George Ferran
(9) John Grimes
(10) Dean Hummel
(11) Charlie Hayes
(12) Mike Jones
(13) Wendell Kim
(14) Marty Demerritt
(15) Greg Litton
(16) Daryl Masuyama
(17) Deron McCue
(18) Scott Medvin
(19) Steve Miller
(20) Brian Ohnoutka
(21) Ed Phikunas
(22) Mackey Sasser
(23) Keith Silver
(24) Stu Tate
(25) Todd Thomas
(26) John Verducci
(27) Colin Ward
(28) Team Card

1986 Donn Jennings Southern League All-Stars

(AA)

MT
Complete Set (25): 90.00
Uncut Sheet: 250.00
1 Bill Ripken
2 Mike Yastrzemski
3 Mark McGwire
4 Gary Thurman
5 Karkovice Ron
6 Jose Tolentino
7 Chris Padget
8 Brian Guinn
9 Luis De Los Santos
10 Terry Steinback
11 Larry Ray
12 Tom Dodd
13 Bo Jackson (Future Star)
14 Jose Canseco (1985 MVP)
15 Alonzo Powell
16 Glenallen Hill
17 Brick Smith
18 Todd Burns
19 Dave White
20 Paul Schneider
21 Brian Holman
22 Anthony Kelly
23 Tom Glavine
24 Cliff Young
25 Kevin Price

1986 Cramer Spokane Indians

(San Diego Padres, A)

MT
Complete Set (25): 30.00
155 Brian Wood
156 Bob Lutticken
157 Jim Navilliat
158 Carl Holmes
159 Ronald Moore
160 George Brett
161 Greg Harris
162 Dave Brockil
163 Ricky Bones
164 Brian Harrison
165 Paul Quinzer
166 Mark Sampson
167 Mike Basso
168 Craig Cooper
169 Tom Levasseur
170 Terry McDevitt
171 Thomas Howard
172 Tony Pellegrino
173 Keith Harrison
174 Warren Newson
175 Kevin Coentopp
176 Jeff Yurtin
177 Rob Picciolo
178 James Austin
179 William Taylor

1986 University City Spokane Indians

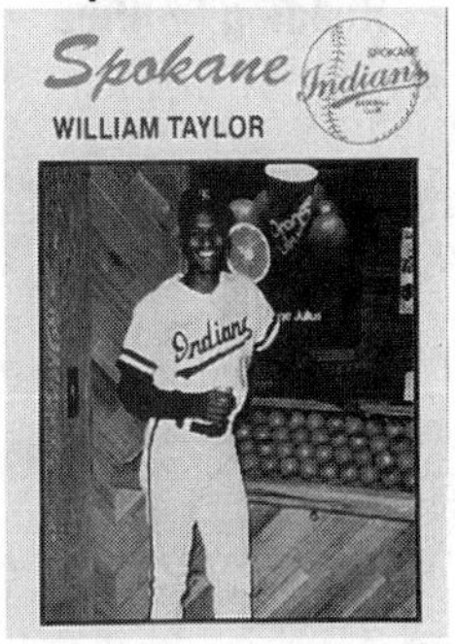

(San Diego Padres, A) (color)

MT
Complete Set (24): 65.00
6 James Austin
7 Terry McDevitt
8 Bob Picciolo
9 Tommy LeVasseur
10 Rickey Bones
11 Brian Harrison
12 Bob Lutticken
14 William Taylor
15 Jeff Yurtin
16 Tony Pellegrino
17 Greg Harris
20 Kevin Koentopp
21 Thomas Howard
22 Brian Wood
23 Sonny Siebert
24 Keith Harrison
25 Doug Brucail
26 Mike Basso
27 Paul Quinzer
28 Jim Navilliat
30 Craig Cooper
31 Warren Newson
32 Dave Collinshaw
34 Mark Sampson

The election of former players to the Hall of Fame does not always have an immediate upward effect on card values. The hobby market generally has done a good job of predicting those inductions and adjusting values over the course of several years.

1986 TCMA Stars Of The Future Post Card Set

(AAA)

MT
Complete Set (40): 30.00
1 Cooper Stadium - Home of the Clippers
2 Team/manager (Barry Foote)
3 Pitchers (Alfonso Pulido, Doug Drabek, Mike Armstrong, Brad Arnsberg)
4 Catchers (Juan Espino, Phil Lombardi, Darwin McNeely, Dave Stegman)
5 First base, Second base, shortstop (Orestes Destrade, Andre Robertson, Mike Soper, Leo Hernandez)
6 Doug Potestio
7 Julio Valdez
8 Dave Martinez, Steve Hammond, Mike Brumley
9 Dave Gumpert, Ken Price
10 Trey Brooks
11 Joe Hicks
12 Pookie Bernstine
13 Johnny Abrego
14 Dennis Livingston
15 Mike Watters
16 Stu Pederson
17 Ralph Bryant
18 Jeff Hamilton
19 Balvino Galvez
20 Ed Amelung
21 Alvis Woods
22 Scott Ullger
23 Andre David
24 Dennis Burtt
25 Geraldo "Jerry" Lomastro
26 Fred McGriff
27 Alex Infante
28 Stan Clarke, Rondal Rollin
29 Chris Johnston
30 Jeff Hearron
31 Stan Jefferson
32 Dave Magadan
33 John Gibbons
34 John Mitchell
35 Tony Ferreira
36 Jesse Reid
37 Jim Lefebvre
38 Mike Aldrete
39 Terry Mulholland
40 Mark Grant

1986 ProCards St. Petersburg Cards

(St. Louis Cardinals, A)

MT
Complete Set (29): 8.00
(1) Sal Agostinelli
(2) Scott Arnold
(3) Richard Arzola
(4) David Bilalis
(5) Henry Carson
(6) Alex Cole
(7) John Costello
(8) Jeff Fassero
(9) Jim Fregosi, Jr.
(10) Brad Henderson
(11) Hans Herzog
(12) Stephen Hill
(13) Howard Hilton
(14) Ken Infante
(15) Ronald Johns
(16) Bill Jones
(17) Matt Kinzer
(18) Martin Mason
(19) Charles McGrath
(20) Jesus Mendez
(21) Scott Murray
(22) Jay North
(23) Mauricio Nunez
(24) Steven Petitt
(25) Jim Puzey
(26) Jim Reboulet
(27) John Rigos
(28) Roy Silver
(29) Mike Theisen

1986 ProCards Stockton Ports

(Milwaukee Brewers, A)

MT
Complete Set (26): 6.00
(1) John Beuerlein
(2) Jamie Brisco
(3) Todd Brown
(4) Tim Casey
(5) Rob Derksen
(6) Rob DeWolf
(7) Todd France
(8) Mike Frew
(9) Mike Fulmer
(10) Mike Gobbo
(11) Gary Kanwisher
(12) Matt Kent
(13) John Ludy
(14) Dave Machaemer
(15) Joe Mitchell
(16) Mario Monico
(17) Martin Montano
(18) Frank Mattox
(19) Doug Norton
(20) Jeff Peterek
(21) Walter Pohle
(22) Danny Ratliff
(23) Jeff Reece
(24) Alan Sadler
(25) Darryel Walters
(26) Fred Williams

1986 ProCards Sumter Braves

(Atlanta Braves, A)

MT
Complete Set (30): 30.00
(1) Tom Abrell
(2) John Alva
(3) Ron Bianco
(4) Johnny Cuevas
(5) Shawn Frazier
(6) Jeff Greene
(7) Tom Greene
(8) Kevin Harmon
(9) Mike Hennessy
(10) Dennis Hood
(11) Dodd Johnson
(12) Barry Jones
(13) Clarence Jones
(14) David Jones
(15) Dave Justice
(16) Mark Lemke
(17) Al Martin
(18) Ed Mathews
(19) Leo Mazzone
(20) Bob McNally
(21) Bob Pfaff
(22) Ellis Roby
(23) Matt Rowe
(24) Jim Salisbury
(25) David Seitz
(26) Brian Snitker
(27) Andy Tomberlain
(28) Rob Tomberlain
(29) Danny Weems
(30) Jeff Wetherby

1986 ProCards Syracuse Chiefs

(Toronto Blue Jays, AAA)

MT
Complete Set (27): 35.00
(1) Gibson Alba
(2) Luis Aquino
(3) Doug Ault
(4) Joe Beckwith
(5) Stan Clarke
(6) Rich Carlucci
(7) Jose Castro
(8) John Cerutti
(9) Don Cooper
(10) Red Coughlin
(11) Otis Green
(12) Dale Holman
(13) Dennis Howard
(14) Alex Infante
(15) Joe Johnston
(16) Luis Leal
(17) Manny Lee
(18) Fred McGriff
(19) Steve Mingori
(20) Ron Musselman
(21) Mark Poole
(22) Mike Sharperson
(23) Ron Shepherd
(24) Dave Stenhouse
(25) Lou Thornton
(26) Rockett Wheeler
(27) John Woodworth

1986 ProCards Tacoma Tigers

(Oakland A's, AAA)

MT
Complete Set (25): 7.00
(1) Darrel Ackerfelds
(2) Ralph Citarella
(3) Brian Dorsett
(4) Tom Dozier
(5) Jim Eppard
(6) Chuck Estrada
(7) Mike Gallego
(8) Walt Horn
(9) Brian Javier
(10) Jeff Kaiser
(11) Tim Lambert
(12) Dave Leiper
(13) Keith Lieppman
(14) Joey McLaughlin
(15) Rob Nelson
(16) Eric Plunk
(17) Luis Polonia
(18) Thad Reece
(19) Rick Rodriguez
(20) Lenn Sakata
(21) Ray Smith
(22) Keith Thrower
(23) Rusty Tillman
(24) Jerry Willard
(25) Curt Young

1986 ProCards Tampa Tarpons

(Cincinnati Reds, A)

MT
Complete Set (27): 6.00
(1) Carlos Acosta
(2) Tim Barker
(3) Mark Berry
(4) Phil Dale
(5) Chuck Donahue
(6) Jeff Hayward
(7) Jim Jefferson
(8) Dave Keller
(9) Ted Langdon
(10) Rod Lich
(11) Joel Lond
(12) Rob Lopez
(13) Tim Mirabito
(14) Angelo Nunley
(15) Mike Ramsey
(16) Darren Riley
(17) Dusty Rogers
(18) Isidro Rondon
(19) Francisco Silverio
(20) Jack Smith
(21) Ozzie Soto
(22) Tom Summer
(23) Francisco Tenacen
(24) Don Wakamatsu
(25) Brant Weatherford
(26) Jeff Wilson
(27) Tom Wilson

1986 ProCards Tidewater Tides - Tides Emblem

(N.Y. Mets, AAA)

MT
Complete Set (29): 9.00
(1) Rick Anderson
(2) Terry Blocker

(3) Tom Burns
(4) Mark Carreon
(5) Tim Corcoran
(6) John Cumberland
(7) Mike Davis
(8) Tony Ferreira
(9) Doug Frobel
(10) Ron Gardenhire
(11) John Gibbons
(12) Ed Glynn
(13) Ed Hearn
(14) Stan Jefferson
(15) Terry Leach
(16) Barry Lyons
(17) Dave Magadan
(18) Tom McCarthy
(19) Marlin McPhail
(20) Randy Milligan
(21) John Mitchell
(22) Randy Myers
(23) Alfredo Pedrique
(24) Sam Perlozzo
(25) Rick Rainer
(26) Doug Sisk
(27) Steve Springer
(28) DeWayne Vaughn
(29) Dave Wyatt

1986 ProCards Tidewater Tides - Mets Emblem

(N.Y. Mets, AAA)

	MT
Complete Set (29):	9.00

(1) Richard Anderson
(2) Terry Blocker
(3) Tom Burns
(4) Mark Carreon
(5) Tim Corcoran
(6) John Cumberland
(7) Michael Davis
(8) Tony Ferreira
(9) Doug Frobel
(10) Ronald Gardenhire
(11) John Gibbons
(12) Edward Glynn
(13) Edward Hearn
(14) Stanley Jefferson
(15) Terry Leach
(16) Barry Lyons
(17) David Magadan
(18) Marlin McPhail
(19) Tom McCarthy
(20) Randy Milligan
(21) John Mitchell
(22) Randy Myers
(23) Sam Perlozzo
(24) Alfredo Pedrique
(25) Rick Rainer
(26) Doug Sisk
(27) Steven Springer
(28) DeWayne Vaughn
(29) David Wyatt

1986 ProCards Toledo Mud Hens

(Minnesota Twins, AAA)

	MT
Complete Set (24):	6.00

(1) Allen Anderson
(2) Brad Boylan
(3) Eric Broersma
(4) Mark Brown
(5) Danny Clay
(6) Mark Davidson
(7) Andre David
(8) Pat Dempsey
(9) Alvaro Espinosa
(10) Frank Eufemia
(11) Mark Funderburk
(12) Gorman Heimueller
(13) Richard Leggatt
(14) Jerry Lomastro
(15) Charlie Manuel
(16) Alex Morte
(17) Charlie Mitchell
(18) Bob Ralston
(19) Mario Ramirez
(20) Ramon Romero
(21) Les Straker
(22) Scott Ullger
(23) Ron Washington
(24) Al Woods

1986 Cramer Tri-Cities Triplets

(Co-op, A)

	MT
Complete Set (21):	9.00

180 Joe Strain
181 Tod Wilson
182 Mark Leonard
183 Robin Riomer
184 David Nash
185 Chuck Higso
186 Matt Walker
187 Andy Naworski
188 Kevin Brockway
189 Bruce Carter
190 Dan Adriance
191 Tony Rasmus
192 Kendall Walling
193 Eric Pawling
194 Joe Giola
195 John Jaha
196 Daron Connelly
197 David Connelly
198 Andy Hall
199 Darryl Gilliam
200 Thomas Ealy

1986 ProCards Tucson Toros

(Houston Astros, AAA)

	MT
Complete Set (26):	6.00

(1) Larry Acker
(2) Carlos Alfonso
(3) Don August
(4) Glen Carpenter
(5) Ty Gainey
(6) Jeff Heathcock
(7) Manny Hernandez
(8) Chuck Jackson
(9) Rex Jones
(10) Mark Knudson
(11) Rob Mallicoat
(12) Ron Mathis
(13) Louie Meadows
(14) Jim Miner
(15) John Mizerock
(16) Rafael Montalvo
(17) Ray Noble
(18) Bert Pena
(19) Nelson Rood
(20) Mark Ross
(21) Jim Sherman
(22) Jim Thomas
(23) Duane Walker
(24) Ty Waller
(25) Eddie Watt
(26) Robbie Wine

1986 Tulsa Drillers team issue

(Texas Rangers, AA)

	MT
Complete Set (27):	20.00

1 Mark Poole
2 Tony Triplett
3 Kirk Killingsworth
4 Mike Couchee
5 Art Gardner
6 Bill Stearns
7 Tim Rodgers
8 Mike Loynd
9a Jerry Browne
9b Rick Knapp
10 Steve Wilson
11 Jamie Doughty
12 Benny Cadahia
14 Bob Gergen
15 Greg Ferlenda
16 Kevin Bootay
17 Javier Ortiz
18 Greg Bailey
19 Dan Olsson
20 Paul Kilgus
21 Jeff Melrose
22 Rick Raether
23 Randy Kramer
24 Larry Klein
25 Mike Stanley
26 Bob Bill
27 Jose Mota

1986 ProCards Vancouver Canadians

(Milwaukee Brewers, AAA)

	MT
Complete Set (27):	9.00

(1) Jim Adduci
(2) Terry Bevington
(3) Mike Birkbeck
(4) Chris Bosio
(5) Glenn Braggs
(6) Mark Ciardi
(7) Bryan Clutterbuck (photo actually Bob Gibson)
(8) Chuck Crim
(9) Dan Davidsmeier
(10) Ed Diaz
(11) Bryan Duquette
(12) Bob Gibson (photo actually Bryan Clutterbuck)
(13) Dion James
(14) John Johnson
(15) Steve Kiefer
(16) Dave Klipstein
(17) Joe Meyer
(18) Ed Myers
(19) Charlie O'Brien
(20) Jim Paciorek
(21) Mike Paul
(22) Chuck Porter
(23) Ray Searage
(24) B.J. Surhoff
(25) Dale Sveum
(26) Rich Thompson
(27) Rick Waits

1986 ProCards Ventura Gulls

(Toronto Blue Jays, A)

	MT
Complete Set (28):	8.00

(1) Geronimo Berroa
(2) Hugh Brinson
(3) Francisco Cabrera
(4) Mark Dickmon
(5) Rob Ducey
(6) Oscar Escobar
(7) Glenn Ezell
(8) Sandy Guerrero
(9) Mike Jones
(10) Ken Kinnard
(11) Darryl Landrum
(12) Omar Malave
(13) Domingo Martinez
(14) Jose Mesa
(15) Steve Mumaw
(16) Jeff Musselman
(17) Greg Myers
(18) Al Olsen
(19) Alfredo Ortiz
(20) Zack Paris
(21) Todd Provence
(22) Pablo Reyes
(23) Luis Reyna
(24) Willie Shanks
(25) Todd Stottlemyre
(26) Tom Wasilewski
(27) Dave Wells
(28) Eric Yelding

1986 ProCards Vermont Reds

(Cincinnati Reds, AA)

	MT
Complete Set (24):	7.00

(1) Jordan Berge
(2) John Boyles
(3) Norm Charlton
(4) Jeff Cox
(5) Clay Daniel
(6) Gary Denbo
(7) Rob Dibble
(8) Jeff Gray
(9) Lenny Harris
(10) Billy Hawley
(11) Ron Henika
(12) Mike Manfre
(13) Greg Monda
(14) Steve Oliverio
(15) Buddy Pryor
(16) Brian Robinson
(17) Jim Scott
(18) Brooks Shumake
(19) Mike Sims
(20) Danny Smith
(21) Glen Spagnola
(22) Jeff Treadway
(23) Jay Ward
(24) Delwyn Young

1986 ProCards Vero Beach Dodgers

(L.A. Dodgers, A)

	MT
Complete Set (27):	9.00

(1) Andy Anthony
(2) Kevin Ayers
(3) Michael Cherry
(4) Carl Cox
(5) Kevin Devine
(6) Peter Geist
(7) Rob Giesecke
(8) Juan Guzman
(9) Jeff Hartman
(10) Darren Holmes
(11) Michael Hoff
(12) Ed Jacobo
(13) Robert Jacobsen
(14) Wayne Kirby
(15) Ken Lampert
(16) Luis Lopez
(17) Walt McConnell
(18) Domingo Michel
(19) Jon Pequignot
(20) Rod Rochie
(21) John Schlichting
(22) Jorge Sepulveda
(23) John Shoemaker
(24) Felix Tejeda
(25) Bob Tucker
(26) Jesus Vila
(27) Stan Wasiak

1986 ProCards Visalia Oaks

(Minnesota Twins, A)

	MT
Complete Set (24):	6.00

(1) Mike Adams
(2) Joey Aragon
(3) Ben Bianchi
(4) Gary Borg
(5) Bob Callfy
(6) Alfredo Cardwood
(7) DeWayne Coleman
(8) Rob Cramer
(9) Chris Forgione
(10) Henry Gatewood
(11) Donnie Iasparro
(12) Chris Kroener
(13) Sal Nicolosi
(14) Bill O'Conner
(15) Wes Pierorazio
(16) Shannon Raybon
(17) Scott Rohlof
(18) Danny Schmitz
(19) Tom Schwarz
(20) Tim Senne
(21) Bob Tabeling
(22) Tom Thomas
(23) Ray Velasquez
(24) Eddie Yanes

1986 ProCards Waterbury Indians

(Cleveland Indians, AA)

	MT
Complete Set (26):	7.50

(1) Jeff Arney
(2) Chris Beasley
(3) Mike Bellaman
(4) Jay Bell
(5) Bernardo Brito
(6) George Crum
(7) Jim Driscoll
(8) Luis Encarnacion
(9) John Farrell
(10) Winston Ficklin
(11) Orlando Gomez
(12) Milt Harper
(13) Rick Henke
(14) Bob Link
(15) Don Lovell
(16) Oscar Mejia
(17) Kent Murphy
(18) Michael Murphy
(19) Cliff Pastornicky
(20) Miguel Roman
(21) Cal Santarelli
(22) Craig Smajstra
(23) Daryl Smith
(24) Dain Syverson
(25) Steve Whitmyer
(26) Bill Worden

1986 ProCards Waterloo Indians

(Cleveland Indians, A)

	MT
Complete Set (32):	6.00

(1) Brian Allard
(2) David Alvis
(3) Keith Bennett
(4) Dave Bresnahan
(5) Claudio Carrasco
(6) Glen Fairchild
(7) Mike Farr
(8) Myron Gardner
(9) Andy Ghelfi
(10) John Githens
(11) Mark Higgins
(12) Trey Hillman
(13) Steve Johnson
(14) Scott Jordan
(15) Greg Karpuk
(16) Lee Kuntz
(17) Greg LaFever
(18) Luis Medina
(19) Manny Mercado
(20) Rod Nichols
(21) Mike Poehl
(22) John Power
(23) Mike Rountree
(24) Don Santo
(25) Charles Scott
(26) Rob Swain
(27) Steve Swisher
(28) Chuck Todd
(29) Kevin Trudeau
(30) Casey Webster
(31) Greg Williamson
(32) Mike Workman

1986 ProCards Watertown Pirates

(Pittsburgh Pirates, A)

	MT
Complete Set (27):	25.00

(1) Steve Adams
(2) Moises Alou
(3) Jeff Banister
(4) Daryl Boyd
(5) Lawrence Brady
(6) Guy Conti
(7) Bill Copp
(8) Jeff Gurtcheff
(9) Craig Heakins
(10) Mike Khoury
(11) Tim Kirk
(12) Blaine Lockley
(13) Dino Moran
(14) Douglas Moreno
(15) Steve Moser
(16) Ed Ott
(17) Al Quintana
(18) Randy Robicheaux
(19) Carl Rose
(20) Scott Runge
(21) Bill Sampen
(22) Butch Schlopy
(23) Tom Shields
(24) Tracy Toy
(25) Glenn Trudo
(26) Miguel Varverde
(27) Mike Walker

1986 ProCards Wausau Timbers

(Seattle Mariners, A)

	MT
Complete Set (29):	8.00

(1) Robert Bernardo
(2) Fremio Cabrera
(3) John Clem
(4) Don Cohoon
(5) Bobby Cuellar
(6) Mike Darby
(7) Bret Davis
(8) William Diaz
(9) Tom Eccleston
(10) Joe Georger
(11) Bob Gibree
(12) Dan Larson
(13) Benito Malave
(14) Brian McCann
(15) Dave McCorkle
(16) Tim McLain
(17) Pablo Moncerratt
(18) Clay Parker
(19) Jeff Roberts
(20) Brad Rohde
(21) Mike Schooler
(22) Rich Slominski
(23) Paul Serna
(24) Bob Siegel
(25) Dave Snell
(26) Jorge Uribe
(27) Omar Visquel
(28) Anthony Woods
(29) Clint Zavaras

1986 ProCards West Palm Beach Expos

(Montreal Expos, A)

	MT
Complete Set (28):	37.50

(1) Felipe Alou
(2) Tim Arnold
(3) Scott Ayers
(4) Kent Bachman
(5) Esteban Beltre
(6) Mark Blaser
(7) Edgar Caceres
(8) Allen Collins
(9) Kerry Cook
(10) Bill Cunningham
(11) Mike Day
(12) Bob Devlin
(13) Eddie Dixon
(14) Kevin Dunton
(15) Jeff Fischer
(16) George Flower
(17) Keith Foley
(18) Gene Glynn
(19) Sam Haley
(20) Melvin Houston
(21) Randy Johnson
(22) Jim Kahmann
(23) Scott Mann
(24) Alonzo Powell
(25) Iggy Rodriguez
(26) Tim Thiessen
(27) Gary Wayne
(28) Bud Yanus

1986 ProCards Winston-Salem Spirits

(Chicago Cubs, A)

	MT
Complete Set (29):	6.00

(1) Bob Bafia
(2) Greg Bell
(3) Brent Casteel
(4) Doug Dacenzo (Dascenzo)
(5) Jim Essian
(6) Ron Ewart
(7) Rick Hopkins
(8) Brian House
(9) Rick Krantiz
(10) Lester Lancaster
(11) Dave Masters
(12) Steve Maye
(13) Julius McDougal
(14) Mark McMorris
(15) William Menendez
(16) David Pavlas
(17) Jim Phillip
(18) Jeff Pico
(19) Cohen Renfroe
(20) Tim Rice
(21) Don Richardson
(22) Rolando Roomes
(23) Mike Tullier
(24) Hector Villanueva
(25) Darcy Walker
(26) Rick Wrona
(27) Ernie Shore Stadium
(28) Ernie Shore Stadium
(29) Team Photo

1986 ProCards Winter Haven Red Sox

(Boston Red Sox, A)

	MT
Complete Set (27):	20.00

(1) Odie Abril
(2) Brady Anderson
(3) Gregg Barrios
(4) Greg Bochesa
(5) Mike Carista
(6) Mike Clarkin
(7) Tony DeFrancesco
(8) Robert Fuentes
(9) Angel Gonzalez
(10) Dave Holt
(11) Daryl Irvine
(12) Laverne Jackson
(13) Manny Jose
(14) Eric Laseke
(15) Bruce Lockhart
(16) Greg Lotzar
(17) Tim McGee
(18) Chris Moritz
(19) Rob Parkins
(20) John Sanderski
(21) Tary Scott
(22) Mike Sears
(23) Scott Skripko
(24) Jim Snediker
(25) Dan Sullivan
(26) Luis Vasquez
(27) Robert Zambrano

1987 ProCards Albany-Colonie Yankees

(N.Y. Yankees, AA)

	MT
Complete Set (23):	7.00

739 Steve Rosenberg
740 Tony Russell
741 Bob Barker
742 Eric Schmidt
743 Robert Geren
744 Maurice Guercio
745 Randy Velarde
746 Ted Higgins
747 Gary Cathcart
749 Tim Layana
750 Jim Howard
751 Matthew Harrison
752 Carson Carroll
753 Chris Alvarez
754 Darren Reed
755 Jeff Knox
756 Jeffrey Pries
757 Tommy Jones
758 Fredi Gonzalez
759 Hal Morris
760 Brent Blum
761 Steve Frey
762 Jerry McNertney

1987 Albuquerque Dukes team issue

(L.A. Dodgers, AAA)

	MT
Complete Set (30):	8.00

1 Terry Collins
2 Ben Hines
3 Brent Strom
4 Lenny Currier
5 William Brennan
6 Dennis Burtt
7 Jaime Cocanower
8 Tim Crews
9 Jeff Edwards
10 Hector Heredia
11 Shawn Hillegas
12 Pete Ladd
13 Dennis Livingston
14 Tim Meeks
15 Jon Debus
16 Orlando Mercado
17 Gilberto Reyes
18 Shanie Dugas
19 Jeff Hamilton
20 Jack Perconte
21 Larry See
22 Craig Shipley
23 Brad Wellman
24 Tracy Woodson
25 Ralph Bryant
26 Jose Gonzalez
27 Chris Gwynn
28 George Hinshaw
29 Stu Pederson
30 Mike Ramsey

1987 Albuquerque Dukes team-issue photos

(L.A. Dodgers, AAA) (3" x 5" color photo prints, sold singly at stadium for $2 each)

	MT
Complete Set (35):	135.00

(1) William Brennan
(2) Dennis Burtt
(3) Ralph Bryant
(4) Terry Collins
(5) Jaime Cocanower
(6) Tim Crews
(7) Lenny Currier (trainer)
(8) Ron Davis
(9) Jon Debus
(10) Shanie Dugas
(11) Mariano Duncan
(12) Jeff Edwards
(13) Jose Gonzalez
(14) Jeff Hamilton
(15) Hector Heredia
(16) Shawn Hillegas
(17) Ben Hines
(18) George Hinshaw
(19) Ken Howell
(20) Bill Krueger
(21) Pete Ladd
(22) Dennis Livingston
(23) Tim Meeks
(24) Orlando Mercado
(25) Stu Pederson
(26) Jack Perconte
(27) Mike Ramsey
(28) Gil Reyes
(29) Jack Savage
(30) Larry See
(31) Craig Shipley
(32) Brent Strom
(33) Brad Wellman
(34) Tracy Woodson
(35) Reggie Williams

1987 Anchorage Glacier Pilots

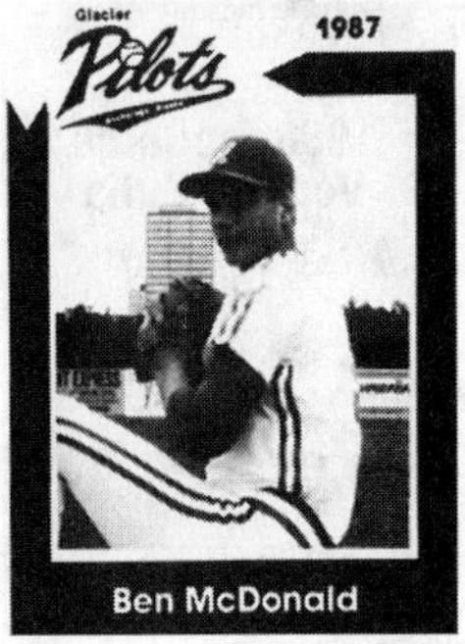

(Summer Amateur) (Black, white & blue 2-1/2" x 3-1/4")

	MT
Complete Set (41):	25.00

(1) Phillip Bieger
(2) Mike Bishop
(3) Jeff Bonacquista
(4) Steve Chitren
(5) Adell Davenport, Jr.
(6) Tom Deller
(7) Shane Durham
(8) Brad Eagar
(9) Phillip Espinosa
(10) Chris Estep
(11) Joe Federico
(12) Jim Foley
(13) Dave Foreman (statistician)
(14) Bryan Gates (bat boy)
(15) Greg Gilbert
(16) Amy Gills (trainer)
(17) Michael Grace
(18) David Haas
(19) Kwang Ung Kim (coach)
(20) Brent Kemnitz (coach)
(21) Jeff Livesey
(22) Dick Lobdell (announcer)
(23) Ben McDonald
(24) Dustin McFarland (mascot)
(25) Steve McFarland (manager)
(26) Kourtney McPheeters (bat boy)
(27) Darren Moss (bat boy)
(28) Jack O'Toole (coach)
(29) Mark Razook
(30) Dennis Reed
(31) Bud Rostel
(32) Russell Springer
(33) Mark Standiford
(34) Tim Stanley
(35) Kelly Thompson (announcer)
(36) Jim Van Brunt (bat boy)
(37) Lefty Van Brunt (coach)
(38) Steve Willis
(39) Larry Woods (announcer)
(40) Eric Yaeger
(41) Mark Zappelli

1987 ProCards Appleton Foxes

(K.C. Royals, A)

	MT
Complete Set (30):	5.00

513 Chuck Mount
514 Bill Gilmore
515 John Larios
516 Pete Capello
517 D.J. Watson
518 Carlos Escalera
519 Frank Laureano
520 Deric Ladnier
521 Mike Tresemer
522 Mike Butcher
523 Joe Skodny
524 Darren Watkins
525 Ben Lee
526 Carlos Gonzalez
527 Charlie Eisenreich
528 Tom Gilles
529 Brian Poldberg
530 Mike Alvarez
531 Pat Bailey
532 Jose Rodriquez
533 Rob Wolkovs
534 Mike Leon
535 Tony Pickett
536 Ken Barry
537 Luke Nocas
538 Dennis Moeller
539 Greg Hibbard
540 Kenny Jackson
541 Phil McKinzie
542 Jim Willis

1987 ProCards Arkansas Travelers

(St. Louis Cardinals, AA)

	MT
Complete Set (25):	8.00

570 Dennis Carter
571 Mike Robinson
572 Charles McGrath
573 Jose Calderon
574 Kennedy Infante
575 Jeff Passero
576 James Riggleman
577 Randall Champion
578 Steven Peters
579 Paul Wilmet
580 James Fregosi
581 Roy Silver
582 Scott Arnold
583 Tim Jones
584 Sal Agostinelli
585 Luis Alicea
586 Craig Weissmann
587 Jeff Oyster
588 Kenneth Hill
589 Alex Cole
590 Mike Fitzgerald
591 Ray Stevens
592 James Reboult
593 Brad Henderson
594 John Costello

1987 ProCards Asheville Tourists

(Houston Astros, A)

	MT
Complete Set (28):	5.00

1818 Karl Rhodes
1819 Trent Hubbard
1820 Gene Confreda
1821 Keith Bodie
1822 Ryan Bowen
1823 Daven Bond
1824 Lou Frazier
1825 Doug Gonring
1826 Jim Olson
1827 Marty Hall
1828 Charlie Taylor
1829 Kevin Wasilewski
1830 Guy Normand
1831 Mike Stoker
1832 Nedar Horta
1833 Bert Hunter
1834 Mike Simms
1835 Shawn Talbott
1836 Victor Hithe
1837 Sam August
1838 Todd McClure
1839 Mike Oglesbee
1840 Lou Deiley
1841 Ed Whited
1842 Jeff Edwards
1843 Gorky Perez
1844 Pedro Sanchez
1845 John Sheehan

1987 ProCards Auburn Astros

(Houston Astros, A) (#2449 not issued)

	MT
Complete Set (25):	6.00

2446 John Massarelli
2447 Rusty Harris
2448 Todd McClure
2450 Damon Brooks
2451 Billy Paul Carver
2452 Andres Mota
2453 Dan Lewis
2454 Steve Polverini
2455 Randy Hennis
2456 Chris Hawkins
2457 Gary Tuck
2458 Dan Nyssen
2459 Carlos Laboy
2460 Gorky Perez
2461 Robert Romo
2462 Todd Newman
2463 Greg Johnson
2464 Rick Aponte
2465 Hector Herrera
2466 Ken Dickson
2467 Al Osuna
2468 Edison Renteria
2469 Dean Hartgraves
2470 Richie Simon
2471 Douglas Royalty

1987 ProCards Bakersfield Dodgers

(L.A. Dodgers, A)

	MT
Complete Set (29):	6.00

1406 Mike Hartley
1407 Dan Montgomery
1408 Macario Gastelum
1409 Miguel Mota
1410 Juan Guzman
1411 Billy Brooks
1412 Juan Bell
1413 Todd Kroll
1414 John Stein
1415 Luis Lopez
1416 Jim Kating
1417 Mike White
1418 Doug Cox
1419 Stan Johnston
1420 Kevin Kennedy
1421 Mark Sheehy
1422 Rod Roche
1423 Ted Holcomb
1424 Eric Managham
1425 Fred Farwell
1426 Dave Hansen
1427 Tim Anderson
1428 Wayne Kirby
1429 Paul Moralez
1430 Carlos Hernandez
1431 Mike Siler
1432 Mike Munoz
1433 Mike Pitz
1434 Willie Pinelli

1987 Baseball USA - Pan-Am Games (blue)

The amateur players who represented the USA in international competition are featured in this set. While 36 numbered and unnumbered cards comprise the complete set, most sets are found without the portrait photo of Carpenter. Standard 2-1/2" x 3-1/2" format cards have black-and-white photos bordered in blue. In the upper-left corner is a "BASEBALL USA 1987" script logo. At bottom center is the Plymouth sponsor's logo. Backs are printed in blue on white and feature player data and stats. Frank Thomas made his first baseball card appearance in this set.

	MT
Complete Set (35):	200.00
Partial Set (34):	175.00

2 Larry Lamphere
4 Clyde Keller
5 Dave Silvestri

8 Jeff Mutis 175.00
9 Rick Hirtensteiner
10 Don Guillot
11 Ted Wood
14 Ty Griffin
15 Steve Hecht
18 Larry Gonzales
19 Tino Martinez
20 Mike Fiore
21 Longo Garcia
22 Bert Heffernan
23 Jim Poole
24 Joe Slusarski
25 Pat Combs
27 Chris Nichting
28 Scott Servais
30 Scott Livingstone
31 Gregg Olson
33 Ed Sprague
34a Cris Carpenter (portrait)
34b Cris Carpenter (w/ glove)
36 Frank Thomas
38 Jim Abbott
--- Bob Bensch
--- Ken Dominguez
--- Ron Fraser
--- Brad Kelley
--- Jim Morris
--- Vinny Scavo
--- Jerry Weinstein
--- Millington Legion Field
--- Checklist

1987 Bellingham Mariners team issue

(Seattle Mariners, A) (15,000 sets including 100 uncut sheets reported produced)

MT
Complete Set (35): 350.00
1 Jeffrey Hooper
2 Erick Bryant
3 Brian Wilkerson
4 Dorian Daughtry
5 Kevin Reichardt
6 Keith Helton
7 John Hoffman
8 Victor Manguel
9 Chuck Carr
10 Tom Peters
11 Todd Haney
12 Joe Georger
13 Jeff Morrison
14 Wade Taylor
15 Ken Griffey, Jr.
16 Spyder Webb
17 Otis Patrick
18 Mike Goff
19 Brian Baldwin
20 Tony Cayson
21 Mike Sisco
22 Mike McGuire
23 Ruben Gonzalez
24 Rick Sweet
25 Daryl Burrus
26 Scott Stoerck
27 Fausto Ramirez
28 Salty Parker
29 Steve Bieksha
30 Paul Togneri
31 Corey Paul
32 Batboys
33 Team Photo
---- Marty Reese
---- Team Logo Card

1987 ProCards Beloit Brewers

(Milwaukee Brewers, A)

MT
Complete Set (26): 9.00
1266 Randy Veres
1267 Greg Vaughn
1268 John Jaha
1269 Shon Ashley
1270 Steve Monson
1271 Steve Kostichka 9.00
1272 Jamie Cangemi
1273 Robert Jones
1274 Brian Stone
1275 Brian Drahman
1276 Jim Rowe
1277 Doug Henry
1278 Rusty McGinnis
1279 Lance Lincoln
1280 Terry Brown
1281 Ron Harrison
1282 Tim Barker
1283 Gomer Hodge
1284 Dave Carley
1285 Hector Alberro
1286 Tim Watkins
1287 Ray Ojeda
1288 Dan Adriance
1289 Manny Chireno
1290 Dave Taylor
1291 Tim McIntosh

1987 Best Birmingham Barons

(Chicago White Sox, AA)

MT
Complete Set (28): 7.00
1 Rico Petrocelli
2 Sam Hairston, Sr.
3 Moe Drabowsky
4 James Wesley (Jim) O'Dell
5 Marlin McPhail
6 Wil Caraballo
7 Rondal Rollin
8 Larry Acker
9 Jeff Bettendorf
10 Antonio G. (Tony) Menendez
11 Richard Kent (Rich) Gaynor
12 John Robert Boling
13 Adam Charles Peterson
14 Gardner C. (Grady) Hall
15 Donn Steven Pall
16 James Joseph (Jim) Hickey
17 John Pawlowski
18 John Graydon (Jack) Hardy
19 Rolando Pino
20 Kenton Craig (Kent) Torve
21 Darrell Ray Pruitt
22 Peter Paul Venturini
23 Manual Victor Salinas
24 James A. (Jim) Winters
25 Troy Gene Thomas
26 William Donald (Bill) Lindsey
27 Jorge Enrique Alcazar
28 Rick DeHart (trainer)

1987 Buffalo Bisons team issue

(Cleveland Indians, AAA)

MT
Complete Set (29): 9.00
1 Don Lovell
2 Kent Murphy
3 Andy Allanson
4 Jay Bell
5 Barry Brunkenkant
6 Dave Clark
7 Doug Frobel
8 Junior Noboa
9 Casey Parsons
10 Craig Smajstria
11 Ron Tingley
12 Randy Washington
13 Eddie Williams
14 Gibson Alba
15 John Farrell
16 Jeff Kaiser
17 Mike Murphy
18 Bryan Oelkers
19 Reggie Ritter
20 Scott Roberts
21 Jose Roman
22 Don Shulze
23 Frank Wills
24 Rod Allen
25 Orlando Gomez
26 Mike Bucci, Rick Peterson
27 Mike Billoni
28 Donald "Butcher" Palmer
29 John Murphy, Pete Weber

1987 ProCards Burlington Expos

(Montreal Expos, A)

MT
Complete Set (29): 6.00
1067 Leonard Kelly
1068 James Vincent Olson
1069 Nels Jacobsen
1070 Tony Welborn
1071 Kent Bottenfield
1072 Sal Vaccaro
1073 Doug Duke
1074 Jeff Oller
1075 Mike Dull
1076 Jose Alou
1077 Steven St. Claire
1078 Ben Spitale
1079 Kevin Finigan
1080 Russ Schueler
1081 Delwyn Young
1082 Jeff Wedvick
1083 David Morrow
1084 Bobby Gaylor
1085 Mike Ishmael
1086 Mark Hardy
1087 Buzz Capra
1088 John Howes
1089 Bobby Pate
1090 J.R. Miner
1091 Sean Cunningham
1092 Dan Larson
1093 Mel Rojas
1094 Robin DeYoung
1095 Doug Vontz

1987 ProCards Calgary Cannons

(Seattle Mariners, AAA)

MT
Complete Set (24): 10.00
2309 Edgar Martinez
2310 Mike Watters
2311 Jim Weaver
2312 Bill Plummer
2313 Ross Grimsley
2314 Dennis Powell
2315 Mike Brown
2316 Paul Schneider
2317 Dave Hengel
2318 Karl Best
2319 Mario Diaz
2320 Brick Smith
2321 Roy Thomas
2322 Mike Campbell
2323 Randy Braun
2324 Mike Wishnevski
2325 Terry Taylor
2326 Stan Clarke
2327 Donell Nixon
2328 Tony Ferreira
2329 Jerry Narron
2330 Dave Gallagher
2331 Doug Gwosdz
2332 Rich Monteleone

1987 ProCards Cedar Rapids Reds

(Cincinnati Reds, A)

MT
Complete Set (28): 6.00
1010 Al Lobozzetta
1011 Phil Dale 6.00
1012 Scott Willis
1013 Curt Kindred
1014 Joe Lazor
1015 Joel Lono
1016 Scott Scudder
1017 Ron Mullins
1018 Mendy Espinal
1019 Keith Brown
1020 Dusty Rogers
1021 Joe Bruno
1022 Keith Lockhart
1023 Reggie Jefferson
1024 Greg Lonigro
1025 Don Wakamatsu
1026 Brian Robinson
1027 Cal Cain
1028 Mike Vincent
1029 Ted Wilborn
1030 John Stewart
1031 Don Brown
1032 Francisco Silverio
1033 Paul Kirsch
1034 Bernie Walker
1035 Rich Bombard
1036 Jim Knudtson
1037 Lamar (mascot)

1987 ProCards Charleston Rainbows

(San Diego Padres, A)

MT
Complete Set (23): 24.00
1984 Brian Brooks
1985 Carlos Baerga
1986 Gregg S. Harris
1987 Michael J. King
1988 Gregory Hall
1989 William Taylor
1990 James P. Austin
1991 Brian Lee Harrison
1992 Gary Lance
1993 Mike Young
1994 James Navilliat
1995 Terry McDevitt
1996 Omar Olivares
1997 Matt Maysey
1998 Rafael Valdez
1999 Warren Newson
2000 Tony Torchia
2001 Jamie Norena
2002 Jimmy Tatum, Jr.
2003 Michael A. Basso
2004 Ricardo Bones
2005 Keith Harrison
2006 Doug Brocail

1987 ProCards Charleston Wheelers

(Independent, A)

MT
Complete Set (28): 5.00
2135 William Melvin
2136 James Hendrix
2137 Gilbert Villaueva
2138 Alan Wilson
2139 Steven Scarsone
2140 Peter Callas
2141 Rodney Brunelle
2142 Bob Gsellman
2143 Steven Mehl
2144 Gary Pifer
2145 Larry Allen
2146 John Knapp
2147 Danny Weems
2148 Hal Dyer
2149 Carl Grovom
2150 Kevin Main
2151 Timothy McMillian
2152 Robert Strickland
2153 J. Anthony LaPoint
2154 Jimmie Gardiver
2155 Steven O'Quinn
2156 Christopher Keshock
2157 L. Timothy Sossamon
2158 Jack Peel
2159 Norberto Martin
2160 Thomas Abrell
2161 Randall Robinson
2162 Doyle Balthazar

Modern cards in Near Mint condition are generally valued at about 75% of the Mint values shown here. Excellent-condition cards are worth about 40% of the value shown. Cards in lower grades are generally not collectible.

1987 Charlotte O's team issue

(Baltimore Orioles, AA)

MT
Complete Set (30): 10.00
(1) Miguel Alicea
(2) Kurt Beamesderfer
(3) Greg Biagini
(4) Paul Cameron
(5) Sherwin Cijntle
(6) Matt Cimo
(7) Jim Daniel
(8) Tom Dodd
(9) Dave Falcone
(10) John Flinn
(11) Charlie Frederick
(12) Bob Hice
(13) Jerry Holtz
(14) John Hoover
(15) Paul Householder
(16) Joe Jarrell
(17) Ricky Jones
(18) Joe Kucharski
(19) Robert Long
(20) Terry Mauney
(21) Bob Milacki
(22) Francisco Javier Oliveras
(23) Mike Raczka
(24) Rico Rossy
(25) Chester Durwood Stanhope
(26) Pete Stanicek
(27) Jack Tackett
(28) Greg Talamantez
(29) Jeff Wood
(30) Crockett Park

1987 Best Chattanooga Lookouts

(Seattle Mariners, AA) (A second version of this set was printed in a quantity of 1,000 with the cards featuring a Coca-Cola logo on front.)

MT
Complete Set, no Coke logo (26): 8.00
Complete Set, w/Coke logo (26): 16.00
1 Sal Rende
2 Dan Warthen
3 Gregory Bartley
4 James Parker
5 James Walker
6 Calvin Jones
7 James Bryant
8 Michael Schooler
9 Douglas Givler
10 Erik Hanson
11 Michael Christ
12 Kenneth Spratke
13 Robert Gunnarson
14 Roger Hansen
15 Bill McGuire
16 Eric Fox
17 Greg Briley
18 Gregory Fulton
19 Nesi Balelo
20 David Myers
21 Matthew Hall
22 John Gibbons
23 Brian David
24 William Mendek
25 Andre Robertson
26 Tom Hunt (trainer)

1987 ProCards Clearwater Phillies

(Philadelphia Phillies, A)

MT
Complete Set (27): 6.00
1521 Rick Parker
1522 Brad Moore
1523 Curt Befort

1524 Chuck Malone
1525 Olen Parker
1526 Carlos Zayas
1527 Bobby Behnsch
1528 Jeff Kaye
1529 Harvey Brumfield
1530 Shawn Dantzier
1531 Ramon Caraballo
1532 Eric Boudreaux
1533 Garry Clark
1534 Warren Magec
1535 Carlos Arroyo
1536 Steve Sharts
1537 Gary White
1538 Gary Berman
1539 Rollie DeArmas
1540 Dave Brundage
1541 Julio Machado
1542 Juan Sanchez
1543 Brad Brink
1544 Allen Wisdom
1545 Bart Kaiser
1546 Todd Howey
1547 Travis Warren

1987 ProCards Clinton Giants

(S.F. Giants, A)

MT
Complete Set (29): 6.00
981 Doug Robertson
982 John Toal
983 Dave Patterson
984 Gregg Ritchie
985 Jim Anderson
986 Willie Mijares
987 Felipe Gonzales
988 Tod Ronson
989 Jim McNamara
990 John Rannow
991 Bill Carlson
992 Tom Ealy
993 Kevin Redick
994 Mark Leonard
995 Dee Dixon
996 Kim Flowers
997 Bill Evers
998 Todd Oakes
999 Jim Pena
1000 Brock Birch
1001 Paul McClellan
1002 Drew Ricker
1003 Sam Moore
1004 Daron Connelly
1005 Bob Richmond
1006 Ray Velasquaz
1007 Trevor Wilson
1008 Bryan Hickerson
1009 Team Photo

1987 ProCards Columbia Mets

(N.Y. Mets, AA)

MT
Complete Set (29): 6.00
1623 Barry Hightower
1624 Bob Apodaca
1625 Brandon Bailey
1626 Cliff Gonzalez
1627 David Lau
1628 Jaime Roseboro
1629 Rich Lundahl
1630 Adam Ging
1631 Johnny Monell
1632 Butch Hobson
1633 Steve Kennelley
1634 Rick Brown
1635 David Liddell
1636 Luis Natera
1637 Bobby Hernandez
1638 Victor Garcia
1639 Scott Henion
1640 Juan Marina
1641 Dan McMurtrie
1642 Mike Anderson
1643 Fritz Polka
1644 Rodney Murrell
1645 Tom Doyle
1646 Danny Naughton
1647 Rick Durant
1648 Julio Valera
1649 Rob Colescott
1650 Alex Jiminez
1651 Todd Welborn

1987 ProCards Columbus Astros

(Houston Astros, AA)

MT
Complete Set (25): 10.00
841 Al Chambers
842 Jeff Datz
843 Fred Gladding
844 Troy Afenir
845 Jim Thomas
846 Mel Stottlemyre
847 Cameron Drew
848 Blaise Isley
849 Mitch Cook
850 Rob Parker
851 Jim Van Houten
852 John Fishel
853 Mark Baker
854 Karl Allaire
855 Joe Mikulik
856 Tom Wiedenbauer
857 Dody Rather
858 Jose Rodiles
859 Earl Cash
860 Jeff Livin
861 Larry Lasky
862 Rob Mallicoat
863 Rich Johnson
864 Norman Brock
865 Ken Caminiti

1987 Police Columbus Clippers

(N.Y. Yankees, AAA) (Lombardi and Moronko cards were withdrawn from distribution and are scarce)

MT
Complete Set w/Lombardi, Moronko (26): 17.50
Complete Set, no Lombardi, Moronko (24): 15.00
(1) Mike Armstrong
(2) Brad Arnsberg
(3) Rich Bordi
(4) Jay Buhner
(5) Pete Dalena
(6) Bucky Dent
(7) Orestes Destrade
(8) Juan Espino
(9) Pete Filson
(10) Bill Fulton
(11) Randy Graham
(12) Al Holland
(13) Keith Hughes
(14) Roberto Kelly
(15) Al Leiter
(16) Bryan Little
(17) Phil Lombardi (withdrawn from set)
(18) Mitch Lyden
(19) Bobby Meacham
(20) Jeff Moronko (withdrawn)
(21) Alfonso Pulido
(22) Ron Romanick
(23) Glenn Sherlock
(24) George Sisler
(25) Shane Turner
(26) Coaches (Clete Boyer, John Summers, Jerry McNertney, Ken Rowe)

1987 ProCards Columbus Clippers

(N.Y. Yankees, AAA)

MT
Complete Set (27): 15.00
24 Bucky Dent
25 Clete Boyer, Jerry McNertney, Kevin Rand, Ken Rowe, Champ Summers
26 Glenn Sherlock
27 Juan Espino
28 Mitch Lyden
29 Bobby Meacham
30 Pete Dalena
31 Orestes Destrade
32 Shane Turner
33 Bryan Little
34 Jeff Moronko
35 Phil Lombardi
36 Dick Scott
37 Roberto Kelly
38 Jay Buhner
39 Henry Cotto
40 Keith Hughes
41 Rich Bordi
42 Randy Graham
43 Alfonso Pulido
44 Mike Armstrong
45 Al Holland
46 Ron Romanick
47 Brad Arnsberg
48 Pete Filson
49 Al Leiter
50 Bill Fulton

1987 TCMA Columbus Clippers

(N.Y. Yankees, AAA)

MT
Complete Set (25): 10.00
1 Brad Arnsberg
2 Rich Bordi
3 Pete Filson
4 Bill Fulton
5 Randy Graham
6 Al Holland
7 Alfonso Pulido
8 Ron Romanick
9 Bob Tewksbury
10 Juan Espino
11 Mitch Lyden
12 Pete Dalena
13 Orestes Destrade
14 Bryan Little
15 Phil Lombardi
16 Bobby Meacham
17 Jeff Moronko
18 Shane Turner
19 Jay Buhner
20 Henry Cotto
21 Keith Hughes
22 Roberto Kelly
23 Bucky Dent
24 Jerry McNertney, Kevin Rand, Ken Rowe, Champ Summers (coaches)
25 Glenn Sherlock

1987 ProCards Daytona Beach Admirals

(Chicago White Sox, A)

MT
Complete Set (26): 6.00
2283 Todd Trafton
2284 Carl Sullivan
2285 Eric Milholland
2286 Tom Drees
2287 Tony Blasucci
2288 Carlos de la Cruz
2289 Ken Reed
2290 Doug Little
2291 James Brennen
2292 Mark Henry
2293 Francisco Abreu
2294 Conde Cortez
2295 Patrick Coveny
2296 Matt Merculio
2297 Wayne Edwards
2298 Chris Jefts
2299 Frank Potesto
2300 Billy Eveline
2301 Ed Sedar
2302 Chris Cota
2303 Gralyn Engram
2304 Jerry Bertolani
2305 Andy Nieto
2306 Dan Cronkright
2307 Mike Gellinger
2308 Glen McElroy

1987 ProCards Denver Zephyrs

(Milwaukee Brewers, AAA)

MT
Complete Set (27): 5.00
212 David Clay
213 Tim Pyznarski
214 Al Price
215 Jay Aldrich
216 Joey Meyer
217 Brad Komminsk
218 Billy Bates
219 Ron Harrison
220 Paul Mirabella
221 Alex Madrid
222 Dave Schuler
223 Dave Klipstein
224 Terry Bevington
225 John Beuerlein
226 Dan Scarpetta
227 Jim Adduci
228 Don August
229 Steve Kiefer
230 Alan Cartwright
231 Mark Knudson
232 Jackson Todd
233 David Davidsmeier
234 Bryan Clutterbuck
235 Charlie O'Brien
236 Keith Smith
237 Al Jones
238 Steve Stanicek

1987 ProCards Dunedin Blue Jays

(Toronto Blue Jays, A)

MT
Complete Set (29): 6.00
923 Carlos Diaz
924 Steve Cummings
925 Bob Watts
926 Mike Jones
927 Hugh Brinson
928 Bob Bailor
929 Dennis Holmberg
930 Dana Johnson
931 Darren Baisley
932 Steve Mumaw
933 Daryl Landrum
934 Tony Castillo
935 Steve Mingori
936 Ric Moreno
937 Webster Garrison
938 Hector de la Cruz
939 Chris Jones
940 Ray Young
941 Kevin Batiste
942 Greg David
943 Shawn Jeter
944 Willie Blair
945 Domingo Martinez
946 Earl Sanders
947 Jerry Schunk
948 Pedro Munoz
949 Ken Rivers
950 Derek Ware
951 Pat Saitta

1987 ProCards Durham Bulls

(Atlanta Braves, A)

MT
Complete Set (28): 6.00
1652 Cesar Jimenez
1653 Barry Jones
1654 Jeff Weiss
1655 Bob Pfaff
1656 Sid Akins
1657 Brian G. Smitker
1658 Tim Criswell
1659 Johnny Cuevas
1660 Gary Newsom
1661 Ellis Roby
1662 Dave Miller
1663 Kent Mercker
1664 John Stewart
1665 Alex Smith
1666 Bill Slack
1667 Eddie Matthews (Mathews)
1668 Mike Merrill
1669 Rick Siebert
1670 Gary Eave
1671 Rick Morris
1672 Juan Fredymond
1673 Jeff Greene
1674 D.J. Jones
1675 Jim Salisbury
1676 John Alva
1677 Mark Lemke
1678 Dennis Hood
1679 Dodd Johnson

1987 ProCards Edmonton Trappers

(California Angels, AAA)

MT
Complete Set (23): 6.00
2061 Jim Eppard
2062 Jack Lazorko
2063 David Heath
2064 Bobby Misick
2065 Dave Shippanoff (Shipanoff)
2066 Michael Ramsey
2067 Doug Banning
2068 Kevin King
2069 Allen Morelock
2070 Tack Wilson
2071 Ed Amelung
2072 Tom Kotchman
2073 Pete Coachman
2074 Bill Merrifield
2075 Richard Zaleski
2076 James Randall
2077 Frank Reberger
2078 Sherman Corbett
2079 Norm Carrasco
2080 Tony Fossas
2081 T.R. Bryden
2082 Terry Clark
2083 Jack Fimple

1987 Elmira Pioneers team issue - black

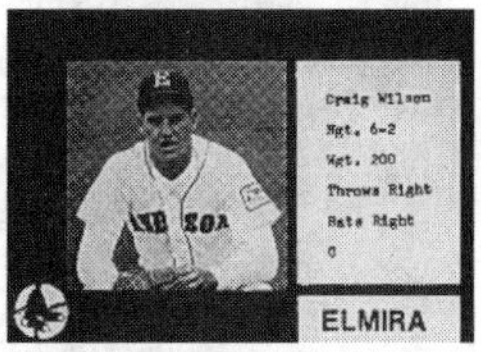

(Boston Red Sox, A)

MT
Complete Set (34): 6.00
1 Clyde Smoll
2 Bill Limoncelli
3 Dave Sullivan
4 Miguel Monegro
5 Larry Scanneli
6 Kendrick Bourne
7 Robert Echevarria
8 Julio Rosario
9 Brian Warfel
10 Terry Marrs
11 Sam Melton
12 Scott Powers
13 Al Thornton
14 Luis Dorante
15 Mike Kelly
16 Vincent Degifico
17 Tony Mosley
18 Craig Wilson
19 Steve Michael
20 Thom Sepela
21 Tony Romero
22 Johnny Diaz
23 Greg McCollum
24 Edward Banasiak
25 Joaquin Tejeda
26 Jose Pemberton
27 Ronnie Richardson
28 Bernie Stento
29 Al Bumbry
30 Felix Maldonado
31 Frank Malzone
32 Eddie Popowski
33 Charlie Wagner
34 Paul Brown

1987 Elmira Pioneers team issue - red

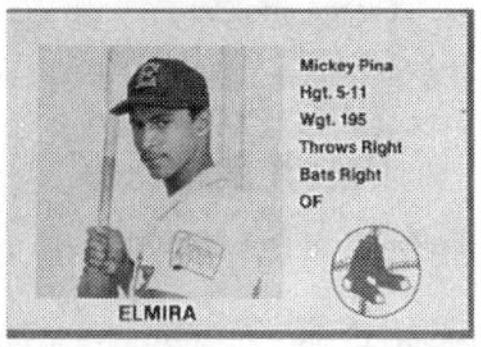

(Boston Red Sox, A)

MT
Complete Set (36): 70.00
1 Clyde Smoll

2 Bill Limoncelli
3 Dave Sullivan
4 Miguel Monegro
5 Larry Scanneli
6 Kendrick Bourne
7 Robert Echevarria
8 Julio Rosario
9 Brian Warfel
10 Terry Marrs
11 Sam Melton
12 Scott Powers
13 Al Thornton
14 Luis Dorante
15 Mike Kelly
16 Vincent Degifico
17 Tony Mosley
18 Craig Wilson
19 Steve Michael
20 Thom Sepela
21 Tony Romero
22 Johnny Diaz
23 Greg McCollum
24 Edward Banasiak
25 Joaquin Tejada
26 Jose Pemberton
27 Ronnie Richardson
28 Bernie Stento
29 Al Bumbry
30 Reggie Harris
31 Bob Zupcic
32 Mike Dillard
33 Mickey Pina
34 Phillip Plantier
35 Checklist
36 Checklist

1987 ProCards El Paso Diablos

(Milwaukee Brewers, AA)

	MT
Complete Set (27):	5.00

1548 Lavell Freeman
1549 Joseph Mitchell
1550 Donald Scott
1551 Peter Kendrick
1552 Garrett Nago
1553 Robert DeWolf
1554 Eric Hardgrave
1555 Frank Mattox
1556 Pete Kolb
1557 Jamie Brisco
1558 Mark Ambrose
1559 John Miglio
1560 Tim Casey
1561 Duffy Dyer
1562 Jesus Alfaro
1563 Derek Diaz
1564 Todd Brown
1565 Cameron Walker
1566 Walter Pohle
1567 Paul Lindblad
1568 Darryel Walters
1569 Daniel Murphy, Jr.
1570 Jeffrey Peterek
1571 Alan Sadler
1572 Ramon Serna
1573 Michael Gobbo
1574 Barry Bass

1987 ProCards Erie Cardinals

(St. Louis Cardinals, A)

	MT
Complete Set (29):	6.00

2566 Rick Christian
2567 Opie Moran
2568 Joe Rigoli
2569 Reed Olmstead
2570 Ron Leon
2571 Steve Jeffers
2572 Eddie Carter
2573 Steve Jongewaard
2574 Ernie Radcliffe
2575 Roberto Marte
2576 Gregg Smith
2577 Antron Grier
2578 Keith Bennett
2579 Tim Meamber
2580 Scott Broadfoot
2581 Tony Russo
2582 Mike Evans
2583 Orlando Thomas
2584 Brad Harvick
2585 Kevin Robinson
2586 Dave Payton
2587 Scott Halama
2588 Jerry Daniels
2589 Chris Houser
2590 Darren Nelson
2591 Jeremy Hernandez
2592 Pat Moore
2593 Mike Hinkle
2594 Tim Redman

1987 ProCards Eugene Emeralds

(K.C. Royals, A)

	MT
Complete Set (30):	15.00

2648 Darryl Robinson
2649 Antoine Pickett
2650 Doug Hupke
2651 Erv Houston
2652 Stu Cole
2653 Bob Moore
2654 James Campbell
2655 Archie Smith
2656 Doug Bock
2657 Doug Nelson
2658 Ben Pierce
2659 Keith Shibata
2660 Pete Alborano
2661 Brian McCormack
2662 Trey Gainous
2663 Derek Sholl
2664 Darren Watkins
2665 Bud Adams
2666 Luis Mallea
2667 Tony Clements
2668 Jorge Pedre
2669 Juan Berrios
2670 Montie Phillips
2671 Jim Hudson
2672 Kevin Appier
2673 Tom Gordon
2674 Terry Shumpert
2675 Don Wright
2676 Kevin Pickens
2677 Dennis Studeman

1987 Cramer Everett Giants

(S.F. Giants, A)

	MT
Complete Set (34):	6.50

1 Matt Walker
2 Gilbert Heredia
3 Scott Goins
4 Anthony Piazza
5 Lonnie Phillips
6 Richard Aldrete
7 Andy Rohn
8 Kip Southland
9 Jamie Cooper
10 Glenn Abraham
11 Randy Lind
12 Joe Strain
13 Eric Gunderson
14 Chris Kocman
15 Tony Michalak
16 Tom Hostetler
17 Michael Ham
18 Todd Hawkins
19 Jimmy Terrill
20 Shaun MacKenzie
21 Jim Massey
22 Rob Wilson
23 Donn Perno
24 Gary Geiger
25 Bill Bluhm
26 Jeff Morris
27 Brad Comstock
28 Dickens Benoit
29 Brad Gambee
30 Mark Owens
31 Mike Remlinger
32 Mark Dewey
33 Bruce Graham
34 Checklist

1987 ProCards Fayetteville Generals

(Detroit Tigers, A)

	MT
Complete Set (27):	6.00

1292 Hector Berrios
1293 Jose Ramos
1294 Dan O'Neill
1295 Steve Parascand
1296 Basilio Cabrera
1297 Ramon Solano
1298 Zach Doster
1299 Milt Cuyler
1300 Wade Phillips
1301 Darryl Martin
1302 Scott Aldred
1303 Manny Mantrana
1304 Darren Hursey
1305 Carlos Rivera
1306 Allen Liebert
1307 Paul Foster
1308 John Lipon
1309 Juan Lopez
1310 Arnie Beyeler
1311 Marcos Gonzalez
1312 Liliano Castro
1313 Luis Melendez
1314 Phil Clark
1315 Ron Rightnowar
1316 Ken Williams
1317 Rob Friesen
1318 Glenn Belcher

1987 ProCards Ft. Lauderdale Yankees

(N.Y. Yankees, A)

	MT
Complete Set (30):	32.00

669 Jose Laboy
680 Tim Becker
681 Marty Bystrom
682 Steve Frey
683 Troy Evers
684 Chris Carroll
685 Bob Green
686 Scott Shaw
687 Mike Christopher
688 Dana Ridenour
689 Andy Stankiewicz
690 George Berube
691 Max Ward
692 Dan Arendas
693 Paul Lassard
694 Ron Rub
695 Bill Voeltz
696 Scott Gay
697 Rich Scheid
698 Kevin Mass (Maas)
700 Bernie Williams
701 Steve Adkins
702 John Johnson
703 Jim Leyritz
704 Jeff Hellman
705 Mel Rosario
706 Mark Manering
707 Steve Brow
708 Fred Carter
709 Ken Patterson

1987 ProCards Ft. Myers Royals

(K.C. Royals, A)

	MT
Complete Set (34):	16.00

2220 Bill Mulligan
2221 Stan Boroski
2222 Gary Blouin
2223 Mike Trapp
2224 David Tinkle
2225 Greg Hibbard
2226 Sean Berry
2227 Boo Champagne
2228 Andy Naworski
2229 Tim Odom
2230 Jesus DeLeon
2231 Mark Schulte
2232 Dennis Studeman
2233 Gus Jones
2234 Charles Culberson
2235 Vasquez Aquedo
2236 Tim Goff
2237 Rufus Ellis
2238 Tom Johnson
2239 Ricky Rojas
2240 Terry Jones
2241 Luis Corcino
2242 Randy Goodenough
2243 Kevin Koslofski
2244 Tom Gordon
2245 Brian McRae
2246 Kyle Reese
2247 Ken Kravec
2248 Jerry Terrell
2249 Angel Morris
2250 Mark Farnsworth
2251 David Howard
2252 Jacob Brumfield
2253 Ron Johnson

1987 ProCards Gastonia Rangers

(Texas Rangers, A)

	MT
Complete Set (29):	375.00

1761 Felipe Castillo
1762 Glenn Patterson
1763 Aurelio Cadania
1764 Juan Gonzalez
1765 Bob Gross
1766 Saul M. Barretto
1767 Phil Bryant
1768 Dean Palmer
1769 Rivert (Ortiz) Lino
1770 Allen Gerhardt
1771 Bob Malloy
1772 Gus Meizosa
1773 Raphael Cruz
1774 Ed Soto
1775 Roger Pavlik
1776 Paul Postier
1777 Ross Jones
1778 Wayne Rosenthal
1779 Michael Scanlin
1780 Ronald Jackson
1781 James McCutcheon
1782 Darrin Garner
1783 Richard Ramirez
1784 Art Gardner
1785 Jose Velez
1786 Darrell Whitaker
1787 John Burgos
1788 Francisco Sanchez
1789 Samuel Sosa

1987 ProCards Geneva Cubs

(Chicago Cubs, A)

	MT
Complete Set (26):	12.00

2622 Mike Aspray
2623 Brett Robinson
2624 Mark North
2625 Tom Spencer
2626 Steve Melendez
2627 Ken Reynolds
2628 Rick Wilkins
2629 Herberto Andrade
2630 Ray Mullino
2631 Fernando Ramsey
2632 Derrick Moore
2633 Mike Boswell
2634 Marty Rivero
2635 Mike Reeder
2636 Gabby Rodriguez
2637 Bill Melvin
2638 Henry Gomez
2639 Ed Caballero
2640 Jeff Massicotte
2641 Simeon Mejias
2642 Kevin Main
2643 Phil Mannion
2644 Eddie Williams
2645 Vaughn Williams
2646 Glenn Sullivan
2647 Steve Owens

1987 ProCards Glens Falls Tigers

(Detroit Tigers, AA)

	MT
Complete Set (25):	24.00

349 Ruben Guzman
350 Chris Hoiles
351 Tom Burgess
352 Jeff Jones
353 Wes Clements
354 Kevin Ritz
355 Steve McInerney
356 Bill Cooper
357 Tim Leiper
358 Doug Strange
359 Ron Marigny
360 Jeff Agar
361 Matt Sferrazza
362 Benny Ruiz
363 Mark Lee
364 Rod Poissant
365 Chris Morgan
366 Jeff Hermann
367 Paul Felix
368 Ramon Pena
369 Pedro Chavez
370 Dan DiMascio
371 John Duffy
372 John Smoltz
373 Chip McHugh

1987 ProCards Greensboro Hornets

(Boston Red Sox, A)

	MT
Complete Set (26):	6.00

1704 Tom Kane
1705 Curt Schilling
1706 Dick Bererdino
1707 Pete Youngman
1708 Mike Carista
1709 Ken Ryan
1710 Chuck Wacha
1711 John Roberts
1712 Scott Summers
1713 Scott Cooper
1714 Joe Marchese
1715 Juan Paris
1716 Juan Molero
1717 Tony Hill
1718 Gilberto Martinez
1719 Tim McGee
1720 Ray Hansen
1721 Alex Flores
1722 Victor Rosario
1723 Dan Hale
1724 Mike Baker
1725 Jim Morrison
1726 Lem Pilkinton
1727 John Sanderski
1728 Chris Gaeckle
1729 David Walters

1987 Best Greenville Braves

(Atlanta Braves, AA)

	MT
Complete Set (28):	28.00

1 James Beauchamp
2 Leo D. Mazzone
3 Roland T. Jackson
4 Randy Ingle
5 Carlos Rafael Rios
6 Ronald Nipper
7 Andrew Denson
8 Adrian Charles Wills
9 David Justice
10 Todd Alan Dewey
11 Willie John Childress
12 Edgar Yost
13 Ronald Edwin Gant
14 John Steven Kilner
15 Brian Keith Aviles
16 Bryan Pierce Farmer
17 Inocencio Guerrero
18 Maximo Del Rosario
19 Kevin Blankenship
20 Kevin Reese Coffman
21 Jeffrey Wetherby
22 Larry Wayne Heise
23 Ira Thomas Greene
24 Peter John Smith
25 Johnny Hatcher
26 Gregory Alan Tubbs
27 Kenneth Joe Kinnard
28 Michael William Scott

The election of former players to the Hall of Fame does not always have an immediate upward effect on card values. The hobby market generally has done a good job of predicting those inductions and adjusting values over the course of several years.

1987 ProCards Hagerstown Suns

(Baltimore Orioles, A)

	MT
Complete Set (29):	5.00
1465 Mike Borgatti	
1466 Paul McNeal	
1467 Will George	
1468 Brian Dubois	
1469 Leo Gomez	
1470 Benny Bautista	
1471 Gerry Lomastro	
1472 Craig Strobel	
1473 Randy Struek	
1474 Tim Dulin	
1475 Glenn Gulliver	
1476 Blaine Beatty	
1477 John Posey	
1478 Louie Paulino	
1479 Steve Bowden	
1480 Wayne Wilson	
1481 Pete Palermo	
1482 Rick Carriger	
1483 Tim Richardson	
1484 Kevin Burke	
1485 Frank Bellino	
1486 Rafael Skeetl	
1487 Paul Thorpe	
1488 Mel Mallinak	
1489 Gordon Dillard	
1490 Scott Khoury	
1491 Ernie Young	
1492 Geraldo Sanchez	
1493 Doug Cinnella	

1987 ProCards Harrisburg Senators

(Pittsburgh Pirates, AA)

	MT
Complete Set (26):	7.00
374 Shawn Holman	
375 Dave Trembley	
376 Tom Prince	
377 David Rooker	
378 Jose Melendez	
379 Felix Fermin	
380 Phillip Wellman	
381 Craig Brown	
382 Scott Neal	
383 Jeff Cook	
384 Lance Belen	
385 Rob Russell	
386 Kyle Todd	
387 Orlando Lind	
388 Don Williams	
389 Dave Douglas	
390 Brian Jones	
391 Brett Gideon	
392 Tommy Gregg	
393 Jim Neidlinger	
394 Gino Gentile	
395 Dimas Gutierrez	
396 Mike Walker	
397 Rich Sauveur	
398 Chris Ritter	
399 Ben Abner	

1987 ProCards Hawaii Islanders

(Chicago White Sox, AAA)

	MT
Complete Set (27):	6.00
185 Mike Yastrzemski	
186 Ken Williams	
187 Jack Hardy	
188 David White	
189 Derek Tatsuno	
190 Ralph Citarella	
191 Tom Forrester	
192 Brian Giles	
193 Tommy Thompson	
194 Don Rowe	
195 Jim Rasmussen	
196 Mike Taylor	
197 Dave Cochrane	
198 Tim Scott	
199 Scott Nielson	
200 Bill Long	
201 Ray Krawczyk	
202 Kevin Hickey	
203 Joey McLaughlin	
204 Kala Kaaihue	
205 Carlos Martinez	
206 Russ Norman	
207 Tim Krauss	
208 Randy Gomez	
209 Greg Latta	
210 Bob Bailey	
211 Pat Keedy	

Suffix letters following a card number indicate a variation card.

1987 Huntsville Stars team issue

(Oakland A's, AA)

	MT
Complete Set (25):	6.00
1 Roy Anderson	
2 Larry Arndt	
3 Tim Birtsas	
4 Lance Blankenship	
5 Tyler Brilinski	
6 Todd Burns	
7 Jim Corsi	
8 Brian Criswell	
9 Pat Dietrick	
10 Darrin Duffy	
11 Brad Fischer	
12 Scott Hemond	
13 Steve Howard	
14 Mark Howie	
15 Jimmy Jones	
16 Felix Jose	
17 Russ Kibler	
18 Joe Kramer	
19 Reese Lambert	
20 Doug Scherer	
21 Jeff Shaver	
22 Jose Tolentino	
23 Walt Weiss	
24 Wally Whitehurst	
25 Joe Xavier	

1987 ProCards Idaho Falls Braves

(Atlanta Braves, A)

	MT
Complete Set (27):	5.00
2595 Mike Wilson	
2596 Anthony Ferrebee	
2597 Phillip Maldonado	
2598 Mark Martin	
2599 Jeff Allison	
2600 Richard Duke	
2601 Chuck Lavrusky	
2602 Kevin McNees	
2603 Rod Gilbreath	
2604 Teddy Williams	
2605 Walter Hawkins	
2606 Chris Bryant	
2607 A.J. Waznik	
2608 Mike Lomeli	
2609 Gregg Gilbert	
2610 Jim Procopio	
2611 Bill Wright	
2612 Herb Hippauf	
2613 Matthew Williams	
2614 Joe Koh	
2615 Daerren Cox	
2616 Steve Glass	
2617 Frank Ramirez	
2618 John Mitchell	
2619 Jeff Dodig	
2620 Pat Abbatiello	
2621 Greg Ziegler	

1987 Indianapolis Indians team issue

(Montreal Expos, AAA)

	MT
Complete Set (36):	16.00
1 Team Photo	
2 It Was Magic	
3 The Magic Continues	
4 Joe Sparks	
5 Jerry Manuel	
6 Luis Pujols	
7 Dave Tomlin	
8 Razor Shines	
9 Tim Barrett	
10 Jack Daugherty	
11 Ubaldo Heredia	
12 Ron Shepherd	
13 Curt Brown	
14 Tom Romano	
15 Jeff Fischer	
16 Jeff Reynolds	
17 Jeff Parrett	
18 Billy Moore	
19 Mark Gardner	
20 Johnny Paredes	
21 Sergio Valdez	
22 Dallas Williams	
23 Mike Smith	
24 Kelly Faulk	
25 Wilfredo Tejada	
26 Pascual Perez	
27 Luis Rivera	
28 Scott Clemo	
29 Nelson Norman	
30 Mark Corey	
31 Dennis Martinez	
32 Tim McCormack (trainer)	
33 Alonzo Powell	
34 The Voices of the Indians (Tom Akins, Howard Kellman)	
35 The Bat Boys (Kenny Akins, Sean Schnaiter, Mark Schumacher)	
36 Bill Rowley	

1987 TCMA International League All-Stars

(AAA) (2-1/2" x 3-3/4")

	MT
Complete Set:	8.00
1 Jeff Moronko	
2 Jay Buhner	
3 Brad Arnsberg	
4 Roberto Kelly	
5 Randy Milligan	
6 Kevin Elster	
7 Sam Horn	
8 Nelson Liriano	
9 Ed Nottle	
10 Don Gordon	
11 Rey Palacios	
12 Mark Carreon	
13 Randy Velarde	
14 Bruce Fields	
15 Mike Henneman	
16 Scott Lusader	
17 Jim Walewander	
18 Keith Miller	
19 John Marzano	
20 Todd Benzinger	
21 Jody Reed	
22 Tom Bolton	
23 Orestes Destrade	
24 Sylvester Campusano	
25 Todd Stottlemyre	
26 Rob Ducey	
27 Bill Ripken	
28 Jeff Ballard	
29 Pete Stanicek	
30 Craig Worthington	
31 Chris Padget	
32 Tom Glavine	
33 Jeff Blauser	
34 Marty Clary	
35 David Griffin	
36 Keith Miller	
37 Travis Chambers	
38 Al Leiter	
39 Columbus Clippers Team	
40 Tidewater Tides Team	
41 Pawtucket Red Sox Team	
42 Syracuse Chiefs Team	
43 Toledo Mud Hens Team	
44 Rochester Red Wings Team	
45 Maine Guides Team	

1987 Iowa Cubs team issue

(Chicago Cubs, AAA)

	MT
Complete Set (25):	29.00
1 Carl Hamilton	
2 Drew Hall	
3 Jackie Davidson	
4 Mike Capel	
5 Jay Baller	
6 Doug Potestio	
7 Gary Parmenter	
8 Tom Layton	
9 Joe Kraemer	
10 Dave Kopf	
11 Paul Noce	
12 Bruce Crabbe	
13 Mike Brumley	
14 Bill Hayes	
15 Damon Berryhill	
16 Pookie Bernstine	
17 Julio Valdez	
18 Phil Stephenson	
19 Wade Rowdon	
20 Luis Quinones	
21 Dick Pole	
22 Larry Cox	
23 Gary Varsho	
24 Rafael Palmeiro	
25 Darrin Jackson	

1987 Jackson Mets team issue

(N.Y. Mets, AA)

	MT
Complete Set (25):	11.00
1 Dan Winters	
2 Jeff McKnight	
3 Jose Bautista	
4 Tucker Ashford	
5 Tom McCarthy	
6 Zoilo Sanchez	
7 Shane Young	
8 Kurt Lundgren	
9 Jeff Gardner	
10 Mike Hocutt	
11 Mickey Weston	
12 Al Carmichael	
13 Sam McCrary	
14 Ed Pruitt	
15 Joaquin Contreras	
16 Marcus Lawton	
17 Johnny Wilson	
18 Steve Phillips	
19 Kyle Hartshorn	
20 Glenn Abbott	
21 Tom Burns	
22 Alan Hayden	
23 Dave West	
24 Gregg Jefferies	
25 Mike Santiago	

1987 ProCards Jacksonville Expos

(Montreal Expos, AA)

	MT
Complete Set (29):	22.00
429 Larry Walker	
430 Tim Arnold	
431 Norm Santiago	
432 Pete Camelo	
433 Nelson Santovenia	
434 Mike Berger	
435 Andy Lawrence	
436 Scott Mann	
437 Edgar Caceres	
438 Gary Weinberger	
439 Esteban Beltre	
440 Armando Moreno	
441 James Opie	
442 Mike Shade	
443 Dave Graybill	
444 Mike Payne	
445 Bill Cunningham	
446 Bob Devlin	
447 Bob Sudo	
448 Kevin Price	
449 John Trautwein	
450 Gary Wayne	
451 Randy Johnson	
452 Brian Holman	
453 Tommy Thompson	
454 Joe Kerrigan	
455 Mike Quade	
456 Jim Kahmann	
457 Team Photo	

1987 ProCards Jamestown Expos

(Montreal Expos, A) (#2542 not issued)

	MT
Complete Set (29):	6.00
2538 Russ Martin	
2539 Angelo Cianfrocco	
2540 Michael Ishmael	
2541 Scott McHugh	
2543 Jesus Paredes	
2544 F. Boi Rodriguez	
2545 Joe B. Sims	
2546 Larry Doss	
2547 Terrel E. Hansen	
2548 Jorge Mitchell	
2549 Kelvin Shephard	
2550 Troy Landon Ricker	
2551 John Vander Wal	
2552 Corey Viltz	
2553 Gene Glynn	
2554 Brian Braden	
2555 Bob Natal	
2556 Scott Ayers	
2557 Mario Brito	
2558 Bob Kerrigan	
2559 Gilles Bergeron	
2560 Danilo Leon	
2561 Howard Earl Farmer	
2562 Matt Shiflett	
2563 Kevin Cavalier	
2564 Jeff Carter	
2565 Chris Marchok	
2678 Q.V. Lowe	
2679 Jeff Wedrick	

1987 ProCards Kenosha Twins

(Minnesota Twins, A)

	MT
Complete Set (29):	5.00
1155 Jim Davins	
1156 Robert Hernandez	
1157 Michael Randle	
1158 Kendall Snyder	
1159 Edgar Naveda	
1160 Rafael DeLima	
1161 Buddy Buzzard	
1162 Burt Beattie	
1163 Rusty Kryzanowski	
1164 Michael Lexa	
1165 Mike Dyer	
1166 David Jacas	
1167 Robert Tinkey	
1168 Jarvis Brown	
1169 Dana Heinle	
1170 Dwight Bernard	
1171 Jeff Satzinger	
1172 Carl Thomas	
1173 Derek Parks	
1174 Lenny Webster	
1175 Scott Leius	
1176 Chris Forgione	
1177 Elvis Romero	

1178 Paul Abbott
1179 Miguel Murphy
1180 German Gonzalez
1181 Don Leppert
1182 John Skelton
1183 Enrique Rios

1987 ProCards Kinston Indians

(Cleveland Indians, A)

	MT
Complete Set (24):	5.00

1680 Bill Shamblin
1681 Kevin Wickander
1682 Mark Gilles
1683 Charles Soos
1684 Scott Buss
1685 Phillip Dillmore
1686 Lewis Kent
1687 Jim Grossman
1688 Michael Poehl
1689 Fritz Fedor
1690 Brian Graham
1691 Scott Jordan
1692 Casey Webster
1693 Michael Workman
1694 Michael Farr
1695 Andrew Ghelfi
1696 James Bruske
1697 Robert Swain
1698 Trey Hillman
1699 Doyle Wilson
1700 Thomas Hinzo
1701 Milton Harper
1702 Kerry Richardson
1703 Rodney Nichols

1987 ProCards Knoxville Blue Jays

(Toronto Blue Jays, AA)

	MT
Complete Set (27):	6.00

1494 Jose Mesa
1495 Chris Shaddy
1496 Mike Yearout
1497 Omar Malave
1498 Aurelio Monteagudo
1499 Rocky Coyle
1500 Troy Chestnut
1501 Tim Englund
1502 Luis Reyna
1503 Kevin Silwinski
1504 Todd Provence
1505 Eric Yelding
1506 Keith Gilliam
1507 Omar Bencomo
1508 Geronimo Berroa
1509 Bernie Tatis
1510 Enrique Burgos
1511 Oswald Peraza
1512 Dave Walsh
1513 Pat Borders
1514 Jeff Hearron
1515 Randy Holland
1516 Glenn Ezell
1517 Kevin Kierst
1518 Norm Tomucci
1519 J.J. Cannon
1520 Cliff Young

1987 ProCards Lakeland Tigers

(Detroit Tigers, A)

	MT
Complete Set (26):	5.00

2333 Wayne Housie
2334 Keith Nicholson
2335 Craig Mills
2336 Rich Wieligman
2337 Scott Schultz
2338 Donnie Rowland
2339 Kevin Bradshaw
2340 Doyle Balthazar
2341 Ron Marigny
2342 Bernie Anderson
2343 Terry Smith
2344 Rocky Cusack
2345 Richard Carter
2346 Rich Lacko
2347 Wade Phillips
2348 Mike Hansen
2349 Mark Lee
2350 Pat Austin
2351 Bob Thomson
2352 Mark Pottinger
2353 Robinson Garces
2354 Blane Fox
2355 Dave Cooper
2356 Adam Dempsay
2357 Paul Wenson
2358 Ken Gohmann

1987 ProCards Las Vegas Stars

(San Diego Padres, AAA)

	MT
Complete Set (24):	5.00

106 Joe Bitker
107 Shawn Abner
108 Jack Kroll
109 Joe Lansford
110 Scott Parsons
111 Sonny Seibert
112 Randy Asadoor
113 Kevin John Buckley
114 Rusty Ford
115 Mark Poston
116 Todd Simmons
117 Ray Hayward
118 Todd Hutcheson
119 Randell Byers
120 Brian Snyder
121 Bill Blount
122 Jimmy Jones
123 Shane Mack
124 Edwin Rodriguez
125 Steve Garcia
126 Craig Wiley
127 Gary Green
128 Leon Roberts
129 Ed Vosberg
130 James Siwy
131 Rob Piccolo
132 Mark Wasinger

1987 ProCards Little Falls Mets

(N.Y. Mets, A)

	MT
Complete Set (30):	30.00

2382 Terry Bross
2383 Pat Disabato
2384 Terry Griffin
2385 Eric Hillman
2386 Lorin Jundy
2387 Steve LaRose
2388 Jim McAnarney
2389 Mike Miller
2390 Steve Newton
2391 Jeff Smith
2392 Dave Trautwein
2393 Butch Wallen
2394 Anthony Young
2395 Javier Gonzalez
2396 Todd Hundley
2397 Tim Bogar
2398 Ron Height
2399 Alex Jiminez (Jimenez)
2400 Dave Joiner
2401 Bob Olah
2402 Radhames Polanco
2403 Rob Lemle
2404 Terry McDaniel
2405 Danny Naughton
2406 Titi Roche
2407 Jim Tesmer
2409 Rich Miller
2410 Al Jackson
2411 Rick McWane

1987 Louisville Redbirds team issue

(St. Louis Cardinals, AAA)

	MT
Complete Set (30):	12.00

1 Mike Jorgensen
2 Joe Pettini
3 Jack Ayer
4 Greg Bargar
5 Joe Boever
6 Rod Booker
7 Rich Buontatony
8 Jose Calderon
9 Paul Cherry
10 Rick Colbert
11 Mark Dougherty
12 Dan Driessen
13 Bill Earley
14 Dick Grapenthin
15 David Green
16 Lance Johnson
17 Tim Jones
18 Mickey Mahler
19 John A. Martin
20 John Morris
21 John Murphy
22 Tom Pagnozzi
23 Mike Laga
24 Bill Lyons
25 Joe Magrane
26 Victor Rodriguez
27 Ray Soff
28 Duane Walker
29 David "Hap" Hudson
30 Billy Johnson

1987 ProCards Lynchburg Mets

(N.Y. Mets, A)

	MT
Complete Set (28):	5.00

2163 Craig Repoz
2164 Juan Villanueva
2165 Tom Wachs
2166 Chris Jelic
2167 Kip Gross
2168 Desi Brooks
2169 Eric Erickson
2170 Ron Gideon
2171 James Archibald
2172 Hector Perez
2173 Alan Hayden
2174 Felix Perdomo
2175 Jeff Ciszkowski
2176 Pete Bauer
2177 Chris Rauth
2178 Bill Stiles
2179 Geary Jones
2180 Dave Gelatt
2181 Rich Rodriguez
2182 Jim Bibby
2183 Scott Jaster
2184 John Tamargo
2185 Troy James
2186 Jeff Richardson
2187 Mark Brunswick
2188 Wilson Valera
2189 Scott Lawrenson
2190 Brian Givens

1987 ProCards Macon Pirates

(Pittsburgh Pirates, A)

	MT
Complete Set (25):	6.00

1184 Ernesto Santana
1185 Tracy Toy
1186 Joel Forrest
1187 Jeff Banister
1188 Tony Mealy
1189 John Love
1190 Mike York
1191 Tony Longmire
1192 Tim Vaughn
1193 Richard Reed
1194 Pete Murphy
1195 Blane Lockley
1196 Steve Adams
1197 Julio Perez
1198 Doug Ellis
1199 Julio Peguero
1200 Stan Belinda
1201 Damon Hansel
1202 Craig Heakins
1203 Ed Yacopino
1204 Glenn Trudo
1205 Scott Ruskin
1206 Tonny Cohen
1207 Dennis Rogers
1208 Dave Moharter

Values shown are a national average. Some teams and players enjoy regional popularity which may affect market prices.

1987 T&J Sportscards Madison Muskies

(Oakland A's, A)

	MT
Complete Set (23):	9.00

1 Gerry Barragan
2 Mark Beavers
3 Ozzie Canseco
4 Jim Carroll
5 Mike Cupples
6 Blaine Deabenberfer
7 Pat Gilbert
8 Jeff Glover
9 Scott Hemond
10 Jeff Kopyta
11 Kevin Kunkel
12 Luis Martinez
13 Doug Ortman
14 Dave Otto
15 Jamie Reiser
16 Luis Salcedo
17 Bob Sharpnack
18 Bob Stocker
19 Vinnie Teixeira
20 Camilo Veras
21 Wes Weber
22 Jim Nettles
23 Dave Schober

1987 ProCards Madison Muskies

(Oakland A's, A)

	MT
Complete Set (25):	6.00

488 Bert Bradley
489 David D. Schober
490 Scott Hemond
491 James Nettles
492 Vince Teixeira
493 Ozzie Canseco
494 Pat Gilbert
495 Luis Martinez
496 Doug Ortman
497 Jamie Reiser
498 Weston Weber
499 Gerry Barragan
500 Leland Maddox
501 Ken Jones
502 Camilo Veras
503 Mike Cupples
504 Jeffrey Glover
505 Jeff Kopyta
506 Kevin Kunkel
507 Mark Beavers
508 Jim Carroll
509 Blaine Deabenderfer, Jr.
510 Reese Lambert
511 Luis Salcedo
512 Bob Sharpnack

1987 TCMA Maine Guides

(Philadelphia Phillies, AAA) (Cards #26-27 were withdrawn; "Maine" was misspelled as "Main" on card fronts. Only 800 of the error sets were reported sold.)

	MT
Complete Set, w/26-27 (27):	30.00
Partial Set, no #26-27 (25):	10.00

1 Shawn Barton
2 Jeff Calhoun
3 Travis Chambers
4 Marvin Freeman
5 Mike Maddux
6 Tom Newell
7 Fred Toliver
8 Joe Cipolloni
9 Darren Loy
10 Ken Dowell
11 Ken Jackson
12 Greg Jelks
13 Alan LeBoeuf
14 Greg Legg
15 Keith Miller
16 Gib Seibert
17 Ron Jones
18 Jim Olander
19 Jeff Stone
20 Len Watts
21 Darren Daulton
22 Kevin Ward
23 Bill Dancy
24 Tim Corcoran
25 Mike Willis
26 Barney Nugent (trainer)
27 Mike Mixon (announcer)

1987 ProCards Maine Guides

(Philadelphia Phillies, AAA)

	MT
Complete Set (23):	5.00

1 Jim Olander
2 Doug Bair
3 Len Watts
4 Greg Legg
5 Fred Tolliver (Toliver)
6 Shawn Barton
7 Ken Jackson
8 Keith Miller
9 Greg Jelks
10 Barney Nugent
11 Jeff Stone
12 Marvin Freeman
13 Steve DeAngelis
14 Jeff Calhoun
15 Gib Seibert
16 Ken Dowell
17 Wally Ritchie
18 Joe Cipolloni
19 Travis Chambers
20 Tom Newell
21 Darren Loy
22 Alan LeBoeuf
23 Ron Jones

1987 ProCards Memphis Chicks

(K.C. Royals, AA)

	MT
Complete Set (27):	6.00

625 Mike Fuentes
626 Phil George
627 Mauro Gozzo
628 Mike Loggins
629 Jose DeJesus
630 Mark Shiflett
631 Matt Winters
632 Jamie Nelson
633 Jere Longenecker
634 Bob Schafer
635 Rich Dubee
636 Mark Van Blaricom
637 Tim Lambert
638 Scott Stranski
639 Theo Shaw
640 Gene Morgan
641 Terry Bell
642 Rick Luecken
643 Don Sparling
644 Ken Crew
645 Duane Gustavson
646 Mike Miller
647 Jose Rivera
648 Julio Alcala
649 Jim Bennett
650 Steve Morrow
651 Jim Eisenreich

1987 Best Memphis Chicks

(K.C. Royals, AA)

	MT
Complete Set (27):	7.00

1 Bob Schaefer
2 Duane Gustavson
3 Rich Dubee
4 Jose Rivera
5 Julio Alcala
6 Mark Van Blaricom
7 Jim Bennett
8 Ken Crew
9 Jose DeJesus
10 Scott Stranski
11 Phil George
12 Theo Shaw
13 Mark Shiflett
14 Don Sparling
15 Mike Miller
16 Tim Lambert
17 Gene Morgan
18 Mike Loggins
19 Jere Longenecker
20 Mauro Gozza

21 Jim Eisenreich
22 Rick Luecken
23 Terry Bell
24 Matt Winters
25 Mike Fuentes
26 Jamie Nelson
27 Steve Morrow (trainer)

1987 ProCards Miami Marlins

(Baltimore Orioles, A) (#715, 726 not issued)

	MT
Complete Set (25):	5.00

710 Kenny King
711 Jim Falzone
712 Stacey Burdick
713 Scott Evans
714 Tony Woods
716 Doug Carpenter
717 Rick Richardi
718 Tony Rohan
719 Bobby Latmore
720 Mickey Billmeyer
721 Masahito Watanabe
722 Shuji Inagaki
723 Scott Diez
724 Mike Browning
725 Frank Colston
727 Ken Adderly
728 Greg Daniels
729 John Harrington
730 Fred de la Mata
731 Hideharu Matsuo
732 Larry Mims
733 Tom Magrann
734 Toshimitsu Suetsugu
735 Luis Ojeda
---- Mamoru Sugiura

1987 ProCards Midland Angels

(California Angels, AA)

	MT
Complete Set (30):	5.00

595 Miguel Garcia
596 David Martinez
597 Bill Geivett
598 Chris Collins
599 Brian Brady
600 Doug Banning
601 Ty Van Burkleo
602 Vinicio Cedeno
603 Al Olson
604 Doug Davis
605 John Hotchkiss
606 Edwin Marquez
607 Joe Redfield
608 Damon Farmar
609 Max Oliveras
610 Doug Jennings
611 Stan Holmes
612 Chuck Hernandez
613 Toby Mack
614 Mitch Seoane
615 Mark Doran
616 Mike Romanovsky
617 Robbie Allen
618 Vance Lovelace
619 Brian Harvey
620 Steve McGuire
621 Marty Reed
622 Barry Dacus
623 Phil Venturino
624 Team Photo

1987 Chong Modesto A's

(Oakland A's, A) (edition of 1,000)

	MT
Complete Set (32):	9.00

1 Mike Bordick
2 Pat Britt
3 Jim Corsi
4 David Gavin
5 Robert Gould
6 Scott Holcomb
7 Dann Howitt
8 Steve Iannini
9 Bo Kent
10 Joe Law
11 John Minch
12 Jerome Nelson
13 Jose Peguero
14 Bill Savarino
15 Kevin Tapini
16 David Veres
17 Bruce Walton
18 Kevin Williamson
19 Chris Hayes
20 Frank Masters
21 Jeff Whitney
22 Drew Stratton
23 Tommie Reynolds
24 Butch Huges
25 John Cartelli
26 Bob Fingers
27 Gary Gorski
28 The Pro Sportsworld Team
1 Tony LaRussa
2 Joe Rudi
3 Dave Duncan
4 Dave Leiper

1 Tony LaRussa
2 Joe Rudi
3 Dave Duncan
4 Dave Leiper

1987 ProCards Modesto A's

(Oakland A's, A)

	MT
Complete Set (25):	6.00

266 John Kent
267 William Savarino III
268 David Veres
269 Michael Duncan
270 Jerome Nelson
271 Michael Bordick
272 John Minch
273 Steve Gokey
274 Butch Hughes
275 Lance Blankenship
276 Robert Gould
277 Kevin Tapani
278 Chris Hayes
279 Bruce Walton
280 Steve Iannini
281 Kevin Williamson
282 Jerry Peguero
283 Bob Fingers
284 Joseph Law
285 Dann Howitt
286 Patrick Britt
287 John Cartelli
288 Tommie D. Reynolds
289 Scott Holcomb
290 Jim Corsi

"1987" Moeller High School Ken Griffey Jr.

These cards are unauthorized collectors' issues purporting to date from 1987, when Junior was a student at Moeller High School in Cincinnati. In reality, the cards were not seen until many years later, perhaps as recently as 1999. Fronts have a color photo with a blue border. Back of the "regular" card has biographical data and information and may be found with or without vertical colored stripes; back of the "All-American" bannered card has a photo of Griffey in Seattle uniform. Because the cards are unauthorized, they have no collector value.

Ken Griffey, Jr.
Ken Griffey, Jr. (High School All-American banner)

1987 ProCards Myrtle Beach Blue Jays

(Toronto Blue Jays, A)

	MT
Complete Set (30):	18.00

1435 Julian Yan
1436 Oscar Escobar
1437 Jose Diaz
1438 Darren Hall
1439 Doug Linton
1440 Vince Horsman
1441 Barry Foote
1442 Mike Murray
1443 Leroy Stanton
1444 Patrick Hentgen
1445 Tom Quinlan
1446 Randy Knorr
1447 Dennis Jones
1448 Cesar Mejia
1449 Lindsay Foster
1450 Jim Tracy
1451 John Poloni
1452 John Shea
1453 Rocket Wheeler
1454 Wayne Davis
1455 Junior Felix
1456 Rich Depastino
1457 Victor Diaz
1458 Mark Whiten
1459 Joe Humphries
1460 Bob Guehther
1461 Andy Dziadkowiec
1462 Francisco Cabrera
1463 Luis Sojo
1464 Paul Rodgers

1987 Nashville Sounds team issue

(Cincinnati Reds, AAA) (set price includes the scarce Hill card)

	MT
Complete Set (26):	6.00

(1) Mark Berry
(2) Norm Charlton
(3) Bill Cutshall
(4) Rob Dibble
(5) Leo Garcia
(6) Wayne Garland
(7) Orlando Gonzalez
(8) Jeff Gray
(9) Lenny Harris
(10) Ron Henika
(11) Bob Jamison
(12) Duncan Stewart
(13) Hugh Kemp
(14) Mike Konderla
(15) Jack Lind
(16) Mike Manfre
(17) Jeff Montgomery
(18) Pat Pacillo
(19) Buddy Pryor
(20) Chris Sabo
(21) Eddie Tanner
(22) Scott Terry
(23) Jeff Treadway
(24) Max Venable
(25) Carl Willis
(26) John Young

1987 Nashville Sounds Don Mattingly picture ticket

(Cincinnati Reds, AAA) (Color photo on individual game tickets)

	MT
Don Mattingly	6.00

1987 ProCards Newark Orioles

(Baltimore Orioles, A)

	MT
Complete Set (29):	7.00

2769 David Esquer
2770 Mike Lehman
2771 Mike Hart
2772 Earl Stephenson
2773 John Oliphant
2774 Gary Arnold
2775 Jack Voigt
2776 Tom Michno
2777 Frank Bryan
2778 Craig Lopez
2779 Steve Culkar
2780 Mike Sander
2781 Bob Shoulders
2782 Joe Gast
2783 Bob Williams
2784 Mike Elmore
2785 Chaun Wilson
2786 Danny Hartline
2787 Don Buford, Jr.
2788 Jeff Ahr
2789 Steven Finley
2790 Dickie Winzenread
2791 Scott Evans
2792 Mike Eberle
2793 Ernie Young
2794 Thomas Shannon
2795 Randy Strijek
2796 Tom Harms
2797 Luis Pena

1987 ProCards New Britain Red Sox

(Boston Red Sox, AA)

	MT
Complete Set (25):	12.00

763 Mike Clarkin
764 Zach Crouch
765 Bill Zupka
766 Angel Gonzalez
767 Luis Vasquez
768 Greg Lotzar
769 Brady Anderson
770 Bill McInnis
771 Bob Chadwick
772 Scott Skripko
773 Steve Bast
774 Carlos Quintana
775 Greg Bochesa
776 Daryl Irvine
777 Tony DeFrancesco
778 Dana Williams
779 Dana Kiecker
780 Dave Holt
781 Dan Gakeler
782 Roberto Zambrano
783 Josias Manzanillo
784 Tary Scott
785 Chris Mortiz
786 Jose Birriel
787 Ed Estrada

1987 ProCards Oklahoma City 89'ers

(Texas Rangers, AAA)

	MT
Complete Set (27):	8.00

133 Paul Kilgus
134 Gary Wheelock
135 Dave Owen
136 Frank Pastore
137 Don Werner
138 Dave Meier
139 Keith Creel
140 Mike Stanley
141 Kirk Killingsworth
142 Mike Jeffcoat
143 Steve Kemp
144 Toby Harrah
145 Ron Meridith
146 Glen Cook
147 Javier Ortiz
148 Cecil Espy
149 Tim Rodgers
150 Dwayne Henry
151 Greg Smith
152 Tom O'Malley
153 Greg Tabor
154 Alan Knicely
155 Nick Capra
156 Ray Ramirez
157 Bill Taylor
158 Jeff Zaske
159 Dave Rucker

1987 ProCards Omaha Royals

(K.C. Royals, AAA)

	MT
Complete Set (26):	6.00

2084 Frank Funk
2085 Jose Angero
2086 John Wathan
2087 Van Snider
2088 Nick Swartz
2089 Gary Thurman
2090 Chito Martinez
2091 Dwight Taylor
2092 Joe Citari
2093 Derek Botelho
2094 Rondin Johnson
2095 Bob Stoddard
2096 Al Hargesheimer
2097 Steve Shirley
2098 Craig Pippin
2099 Adrian Garrett
2100 Scott Madison
2101 Israel Sanchez
2102 John Davis
2103 Ron Wotus
2104 Bobby Ramos
2105 Rick Anderson
2106 Jeff Schulz
2107 Mike MacFarlane (Macfarlane)
2108 Luis de las Santos (de los Santos)
2109 Tom Muller

1987 ProCards Oneonta Yankees

(N.Y. Yankees, A)

	MT
Complete Set (33):	32.00

2505 Lew Hill
2506 Anthony Morrison
2507 Darrel Tingle
2508 Bernie Williams
2509 Hector Vargas
2510 Gerald Williams
2511 Dan Roman
2512 Steve Erickson
2513 Tom Popplewell
2514 Doug Gogolewski
2515 Bill DaCoste
2516 David Turgeon
2517 Tom Weeks
2518 Brian Butterfield
2519 Freddie Hailey
2520 Julio Ramon
2521 Dave Eiland
2522 Jay Makemson
2523 Bill Voeltz
2524 Chris Byrnes
2525 Randy Foster
2526 Mark Mitchell
2527 Rod Ehrhard
2528 Gary Allenson
2529 Rod Imes
2530 Mark Marris
2531 Bobby Dickerson
2532 Tim Bishop
2533 Dean Kelley
2534 Ed Martel
2535 Luc Berube
2536 Jack Gills
2537 Tom Cloninger

1987 ProCards Orlando Twins

(Minnesota Twins, AA) (#885 not issued)

	MT
Complete Set (26):	5.00

866 Jeff Bumgarner
867 Robbie Smith
868 Dan Smith
869 John Eccles
870 Henry Gatewood
871 Bobby Ralston
872 Jim Shellenback
873 Ken Koch
874 George Mitterwald
875 Mark Clemons
876 Steve Gasser
877 Toby Nivens
878 Steve Gomez
879 Brad Bierley
880 Jeff Reboulet
881 Gary Borg
882 Doug Palmer
883 Tom Schwarz

884 Eddie Yanes
886 Jeff Bronkey
887 Wes Pierorazio
888 Allan Sontag
889 Darrell Higgs
890 Mark Funderburk
891 Larry Blackwell
892 Dave Vetsch

1987 ProCards Osceola Astros

(Houston Astros, A)

	MT
Complete Set (29):	5.00

952 Terry Wells
953 Juan Lopez
954 Mike Brown
955 Carlo Colobino
956 Randy Randle
957 Ken Bolek
958 Calvin James
959 Dan Walters
960 Doug Snyder
961 Jeff Baldwin
962 Stan Fascher
963 Tony Metoyer
964 Brian Meyer
965 Joe Schulte
966 Jose Vargas
967 David Potts
968 John Elliott
969 Jack Billingham
970 Don Dunster
971 Joel Estes
972 Gary Cooper
973 Juan Delgrado
974 Scott Markley
975 Ken Houston
976 Terry Green
977 Tim Arnsberg
978 Jose Cano
979 Todd Credeur
980 David Rohde

1987 ProCards Palm Springs Angels

(California Angels, A)

	MT
Complete Set (31):	7.00

291 Mike Spearnock
292 Al Heath
293 David Johnson
294 Jeff Manto
295 Reggie Lambert
296 Paul Bilak
297 Kenny Grant
298 Dan Grunhard
299 Colin Charland
300 Mike Shull
301 Paul Sorrento
302 Lee Stevens
303 Bill Vanderwel
304 Colby Ward
305 Glenn Washington
306 Roger Zottneck
307 Bill Lachemann
308 Tim Kelly
309 Tom Alfredson
310 Edgar Alfonso
311 Tim Burham
312 Dario Nunez
313 Erik Pappas
314 Michael Anderson
315 Bobby Bell
316 Mike Fetters
317 Frank DiMichele
318 Richard Morehouse
319 Todd Eggertsen
320 Mark Marino
321 Andres Espinoza
322 Gary Nalls

1987 BDK 1987 Pan-Am Team USA

(Black-and-white with red borders.)

	MT
Complete Set: (26):	10.00

1 Tino Martinez
2 Ty Griffin
3 Scott Servais
4 Scott Livingston (Livingstone)
5 Pat Combs
6 Mike Fiore
7 Steve Hecht
8 Chris Nichting
9 Don Guillot
10 Larry Gonzales
11 Larry Lamphere
12 Gregg Olson
13 Jim Poole
14 Longo Garcia
15 Ted Wood
16 Jeff Mutis
17 Rick Hirtensteiner
18 Bert Heffernan
19 Cris Carpenter
20 Joe Slusarski
21 Clyde Keller
22 Ed Sprague
23 Frank Thomas
24 Dave Silvestri
25 Jim Abbott
--- Millington Legion Field/checklist

1987 TCMA Pawtucket Red Sox

(Boston Red Sox, AAA)

	MT
Complete Set:	5.00

1 Andy Araujo
2 Chris Cannizzaro
3 Steve Curry
4 Mike Dalton
5 Chuck Davis
6 Steve Ellsworth
7 Mitch Johnson
8 Danny Sheaffer
9 Mike Rochford
10 Hector Stewart
11 John Marzano
12 Gary Tremblay
13 Todd Benzinger
14 Sam Horn
15 Mike Mesh
16 Gary Miller-Jones
17 Jody Reed
18 Kevin Romine
19 LaSchelle Tarver
20 Scott Wade
21 Ed Nottle
22 Ellis Burks
23 Rob Woodard
24 Pat Dodson
25 Dave Sax
26 John Leister
27 Tom Bolton
28 Mark Meleski

1987 ProCards Pawtucket Red Sox

(Boston Red Sox, AAA)

	MT
Complete Set (27):	5.00

51 John Marzano
52 Sam Horn
53 Stephen Curry
54 Kevin Romine
55 John Leister
56 Jody Reed
57 Todd Benzinger
58 Mitchell Johnson
59 Mike Rochford
60 LaSchelle Tarver
61 Hector Stewart
62 Tom Bolten
63 Glenn Hoffman
64 Andy Araujo
65 Tony Cleary
66 Mike Dalton
67 Steve Ellsworth
68 Mike Mesh
69 Gary Miller-Jones
70 Gary Tremblay
71 Scott Wade
72 Ed Nottle
73 Ellis Burks
74 Chuck Davis
75 Mark Meleski
76 Dana Williams
77 Chris Cannizzaro

1987 ProCards Peninsula White Sox

(Chicago White Sox, A)

	MT
Complete Set (29):	5.00

1872 Mark Davis
1873 Kevin Renz
1874 Chet Diemidc
1875 Mark Foley
1876 Daniel Tauken
1877 Joe Singley
1878 Dewey Robinson
1879 Aubrey Waggoner
1880 Mike Ollom
1881 Craig Grebeck
1882 Dave Reynolds
1883 Scott Radinsky
1884 Miguel Audain
1885 Bruce Hulstrom
1886 Tom Sutryk
1887 Glenn Braxton
1888 Ron Scheer
1889 Dave Wallwork
1890 Tom Reichel
1891 Jeff Greene
1892 Kelsey Isa
1893 Tom Lahrman
1894 Bo Kennedy
1895 Todd Hall
1896 Ron Scruggs
1807 Kurt Brown
1898 Virgil Conley
1899 Tony Cento
1900 Dan Wagner

1987 ProCards Peoria Chiefs

(Chicago Cubs, A)

	MT
Complete Set (28):	7.50

400 Ray Mullino
401 Butch Garcia
402 John Green
403 Sergio Espinal
404 Dick Canan
405 Jerry Lapenta
406 Steve Hill
407 Shawn Boskie
408 Greg Iaverone
409 John Berringer
410 Joe Housey
411 Derrick May
412 Pat Gomez
413 Greg Smith
414 Brian Otten
415 David Rosario
416 Elvin Paulino
417 Edwards Williams
418 Harry Shelton
419 Jerome Walton
420 Simeon Mejias
421 Parnell Perry
422 Phil Harrison
423 Steve Parker
424 Kelly Mann
425 Mike Folga
426 Jim Tracy
427 William Kazmierczak
428 Fernando Zarranz

1987 Pizza World Peoria Chiefs

(Chicago Cubs, A) (4-1/4" x 5-1/2", black & white)

	MT
Complete Set (6):	75.00

(1) Butch Garcia
(2) Pat Gomez
(3) John Green
(4) Steve Hill
(5) Jerome Walton
(6) Chief Rainout

1987 ProCards Phoenix Firebirds

(S.F. Giants, AAA)

	MT
Complete Set (28):	10.00

78 Chris Jones
79 Matt Williams
80 Randy Bockus
81 George Ferran
82 Terry Mulholland
83 Charlie Corbell
84 Angel Escobar
85 Kevin Burrell
86 Colin Ward
87 Mike Woodard
88 Larry Hardy
89 Randy Kutcher
90 Jon Perlman
91 Jack McKnight
92 Alan Cockrell
93 Jessie Reid
94 Joe Price
95 John Verducci
96 Cliff Shidawara
97 Mackey Sasser
98 Pat Adams
99 Duane Espy
100 Wendell Kim
101 Atlee Hammaker
102 Francisco Melendez
103 Steve Miller
104 Mike Rubel
105 Jeff Brantly

1987 ProCards Pittsfield Cubs

(Chicago Cubs, A)

	MT
Complete Set (26):	20.00

323 Ray Thoma
324 Greg Bell
325 Hector Villanueva
326 Jim Essian
327 Jim Wright
328 Brian McCann
329 Brian House
330 Laddy Renfroe
331 Mike Miller
332 Mark Grace
333 Brian Guinn
334 Jim Phillips
335 Leonard Damian
336 Dave Masters
337 Dave Pavlas
338 Mark Leonette
339 Rick Wrona
340 David Wilder
341 Jeff Pico
342 Rick Hopkins
343 Roger Williams
344 Rich Amaral
345 Doug Dascenzo
346 Tim Rice
347 Rolando Roomes
348 Dwight Smith

1987 Pittsfield Cubs team poster

(Chicago Cubs, AA) (10-7/8" x 16-3/4")

	MT
Complete Poster:	40.00

(1) Rick Amaral
(2) Greg Bell
(3) Leonard Damian
(4) Doug Dascenzo
(5) Jim Essian
(6) Mark Grace
(7) Rick Hopkins
(8) Brian House
(9) Dave Masters
(10) Brian McCann
(11) Dave Pavlas
(12) Jim Phillips
(13) Jeff Pico
(14) Laddie Renfroe
(15) Tim Rice
(16) Rolando Roomes
(17) Dwight Smith
(18) Ray Thomas
(19) Hector Villanueva
(20) Ben Webber
(21) Roger Williams
(22) Jim Wright
(23) Rick Wrona

1987 The Bon Pocatello Giants

(S.F. Giants, R)

	MT
Complete Set (32):	65.00

1 Doug Messer
2 Rafael Landestoy
3 Brett Lewis
4 Steve Connolly
5 Steve Lienhard
6 Kevin Meier
7 Jim Jones
8 Reid Gunter
9 Mike Greenwood
10 Jim Malseed
11 Domingo DeLaRosa
12 Matt Williams
13 Bill Carlson
14 John Vuz
15 Dominick Johnson
16 Jim Myers
17 Dave Edwards
18 Ron McLintock
19 Mike Williams
20 Mike Wandler
21 Karl Breitenbucher
22 Keith James
23 Andres Santana
24 Rocco Bofolino
25 Jesus Figueroa
26 Francisco Arias
27 Juan Guerrero
28 Jesus Laya
29 Erik Johnson
30 Diego Segui
31 Glenn Abraham
32 Jose Linarez

1987 ProCards Port Charlotte Rangers

(Texas Rangers, A)

	MT
Complete Set (27):	5.00

2034 Ken Clawson
2035 John Schofield
2036 Steve Lankard
2037 Scott Morse
2038 John Barfield
2039 Mitch Thomas
2040 Marty Cerny
2041 Edwin Morales
2042 Rick Raether
2043 Steve Wilson
2044 Jeff Mays
2045 Jeff Andrews
2046 Greg Harrell
2047 Fred Samson
2048 Stephen Glasker
2049 Mick Billmeyer
2050 Jose Vargas
2051 Rick Bernardo
2052 Mark Kramer
2053 Julio DeLeon
2054 Joel Cartaya
2055 Chris Colon
2056 Gar Millay
2057 Jim Skaalen
2058 Chad Kreuter
2059 Kevin Reimer
2060 Joe Pearn

1987 ProCards Portland Beavers

(Minnesota Twins, AAA)

	MT
Complete Set (24):	5.00

160 Jeff Bittiger
161 Pat Dempsey
162 Randy Niemann
163 Allan Anderson
164 Billy Beane
165 Chris Pittaro
166 Pat Casey
167 Roy Smith
168 Phil Wilson
169 Steve Liddle
170 Danny Clay
171 Julius McDougal
172 Kevin Hagen
173 Alvaro Espinosa
174 Kevin Trudeau
175 Ben Bianchi
176 Alex Marte
177 Bill Latham
178 Gene Larkin
179 Greg Morhardt
180 Ron Musselman
181 Charlie Manuel
182 Ken Silvestri
183 Brad Boylan
184 Ron Gardenhire

1987 ProCards Prince William Yankees

(N.Y. Yankees, A)

	MT
Complete Set (29):	6.00

2254 Hensley Meulens
2255 Yanko Hauradou
2256 Bob Davidson
2257 Ricky Torres
2258 Ralph Kraus
2259 Scott Kamieniecki
2260 Alan Mills
2261 Art Calvert
2262 Rick Balabon
2263 Rob Sepanek, Jr.
2264 Chris Howard
2265 Mickey Tresh
2266 Chris Lombardozzi
2267 Mike Heifferon
2268 Bill Clossen
2269 Bill Voeltz
2270 Ysidro Giron
2271 Aris Tirado
2272 Amalio Carreno
2273 Steve Adkins
2274 Hector Vargas
2275 Fernando Figuerda (Figueroa)
2276 Ramon Manon
2277 Jason Maas
2278 Rob Lambert
2279 Joe Hicks
2280 Tony Gwinn
2281 John Ramos
2282 William Morales

1987 ProCards Quad City Angels

(California Angels, A)

	MT
Complete Set (30):	6.00

1096 Terrence Carr
1097 Troy Giles
1098 Edgar Rodriguez
1099 Santiago Espinosa
1100 Giovanny Reyes
1101 Lawrence Pardo
1102 Jose Tapia
1103 Roberto Hernandez
1104 Scott Kannenberg
1105 Daryl Green
1106 Luis Merejo
1107 Brandy Vann
1108 Mike Kelser
1109 Jim Bisceglia
1110 Rafael Pineda
1111 Elvin Rivera
1112 Greg Fix
1113 Eddie Rodriguez
1114 Don Long
1115 Gary Ruby
1116 Jim McCollom
1117 Chris Graves
1118 Chris Cron
1119 Scott Cerney
1120 Kendall Walling
1121 Jeff Gay
1122 Michael Knapp
1123 Ken Bandy
1124 Dave Grilione
1125 Greg Jackson
1126 Luis Gallardo

1987 ProCards Reading Phillies

(Philadelphia Phillies, AA)

	MT
Complete Set (26):	5.00

788 George Culver
789 Tony Brown
790 Joe Lefebvre
791 Greg Edge
792 Miguel Vargas
793 Dan Giesen
794 Tom Barrett
795 Dion Beck
796 Mike Shelton
797 Bruce Long
798 Ray Roman
799 Kevin Ward
800 Rick Lundblade
801 Howard Nichols
802 Ramon Henderson
803 Ricky Jordan
804 Mark Bowden
805 Steve Blackshear
806 Todd Frohwirth
807 Bob Scanlon
808 Jim Fortenberry
809 Jose Leiva
810 John McLarnan
811 Steve Williams
812 Michael Miller
813 Rob Hicks

1987 TCMA Richmond Braves

(Atlanta Braves, AAA)

	MT
Complete Set:	18.00

1 Chuck Cary
2 Floyd Chiffer
3 Marty Clary
4 Juan Eichelberger
5 Tom Glavine
6 Chuck Hensley
7 Bean Stringfellow
8 Matt West
9 Steve Ziem
10 John Mizerock
11 Jeff Blauser
12 Mike Fischlin
13 David Griffin
14 Paul Runge
15 Mark Strucher
16 Bob Tumpane
17 Trench Davis
18 Kelly Heath
19 Darryl Motley
20 John Rabb
21 Roy Majtyka
22 Nardi Contreras
23 Dale Holman
24 Jim McManus
25 Cliff Speck
26 Rich Albert
27 Mike Brown
28 Stan Cliburn
29 Sam Ayoub

1987 Bob's Cameras Richmond Braves

(Atlanta Braves, AAA) (3-7/8" x 5" color photo prints)

	MT
Complete Set (23):	90.00

(1) Chuck Cary
(2) Floyd Chiffer
(3) Marty Clary
(4) Sal D'Alessandro
(5) Trench Davis
(6) Juan Eichelberger
(7) Mike Fischlin
(8) Tom Glavine
(9) Dave Griffin
(10) Inocencio Guerrero
(11) Kelly Heath
(12) Chuck Hensley
(13) Dale Holman
(14) John Mizerock
(15) Darryl Motley
(16) Ed Olwine
(17) John Rabb
(18) Paul Runge
(19) Cliff Speck
(20) Mark Strucher
(21) Bob Tumpane
(22) Matt West
(23) Steve Ziem

1987 Crown Oil Richmond Braves

(Atlanta Braves, AAA) (Issued in form of perforated 11" x 28-1/2" sheet.)

	MT
Complete Set (29):	30.00

1 Kelly Heath
2 Jeff Blauser
5 Mark Strueher
6 Roy Majtyka
8 John Mizerock
9 Bob Tumpane
10 Sal D'Alessandro
12 Paul Runge
14 Tom Glavine
15 Juan Eichelberger
18 Mike Fischlin
19 Steve Ziem
20 John Rabb
24 David Griffin
25 Dale Holman
26 Rick Albert
28 Floyd Chiffer
29 Stan Cliburn
30 Darryl Motley
31 Bean Stringfellow
32 Trench Davis
34 Marty Clary
37 Chuck Hensley
39 Cliff Speck
42 Mike Brown
43 Nardi Contreras
45 Matt West
47 Chuck Cary
--- Sam Ayoub

1987 TCMA Rochester Red Wings

(Baltimore Orioles, AAA)

	MT
Complete Set:	5.00

1 Jeff Ballard
2 Luis DeLeon
3 Mike Griffin
4 John Habyan
5 Brad Havens
6 Phil Huffman
7 Jack O'Connor
8 Eric Rasmussen
9 Mike Skinner
10 Carl Nichols
11 Dave Van Gorder
12 Chris Padget
13 Bill Ripken
14 David Lee Smith
15 Kelvin Torve
16 Ron Washington
17 Craig Worthington
18 Mike Hart
19 Ron Salcedo
20 Jim Traber
21 Scott Ullger
22 Chris Green
23 Curt Motton
24 John Hart
25 Dom Chiti
26 Jerry Lomastro
27 Joe Kucharski
28 Rex Mudler
29 Don Gordon, Joe Kucharski

Checklists with card numbers in parentheses ( ) indicates the numbers do not appear on the cards.

1987 ProCards Rochester Red Wings

(Baltimore Orioles, AAA)

	MT
Complete Set (27):	5.00

1901 Phil Hoffman
1902 Dave Van Gorder
1903 John Hart
1904 Ron Salcedo
1905 Mike Skinner
1906 Chris Padget
1907 Scott Ullger
1908 Eric Rasmussen
1909 Mike Griffin
1910 Mike Hart
1911 Carl Nichols
1912 Bill Ripken
1913 Curt Motton
1914 D.L. Smith
1915 Dom Chiti
1916 Luis DeLeon
1917 Brad Havens
1918 Nelson Simmons
1919 Ron Washington
1920 Jack O'Connor
1921 Kelvin Torve
1922 Jamie Reed
1923 Craig Worthington
1924 John Habyan
1925 Jeff Ballard
1926 Jim Traber
1927 Bob Molinaro

1987 ProCards Salem Angels

(California Angels, A)

	MT
Complete Set (34):	6.00

2412 Edgar Rodriguez
2413 Gary Buckels
2414 Jay Bobel, Jr.
2415 Troy Giles
2416 Robert Wassenaar
2417 John Orton
2418 Mario Molina
2419 Bill Robinson
2420 Greg Jackson
2421 Eric Reinholtz
2422 Jorge Montero
2423 Ramon Martinez
2424 Reed Peters
2425 Tony Rasmus
2426 Jim Townsend
2427 Frnak Mutz
2428 Ruben Amaro
2429 Santiago Espinosa
2430 Wiley Lee, Jr.
2431 Paul List
2432 Rafael Pineda
2433 Kevin Flora
2434 Mikael Musolino
2435 Mike Erb
2436 Luis Gallardo
2437 Cary Grubb
2438 Lanny Abshier
2439 Freddie Davis, Jr.
2440 Scott Randolph
2441 Jeff Goettsch
2442 Jesse Flores
2443 Mark Weidemaier
2444 Chris Smith
2445 Derek Winchell

1987 ProCards Salem Buccaneers

(Pittsburgh Pirates, A)

	MT
Complete Set (30):	11.00

1236 Kevin Franchi
1237 Mike Stevens
1238 Larry Melton
1239 Rob Hatfield
1240 Octavio Cepeda
1241 Greg Stading
1242 Pete Rice
1243 Tim Kirk
1244 Ben Morrow
1245 Matias Carrillo
1246 Martin Hernandez
1247 Mike Dotzher
1248 Steve Moser
1249 John Rigos
1250 Harold Williams
1251 Gilberto Roca
1252 Rafael Muratti
1253 Jim Thrift
1254 Bill Copp
1255 Bob Koopmann
1256 Bill Sampen
1257 Mike Stevanus
1258 Reggie Barringer
1259 Jeff King
1260 Tony Chance
1261 Todd Smith
1262 Doug Pittman
1263 Chris Lein
1264 Steve Demeter
1265 Kevin Davis

1987 Smokey Bear Salinas Spurs

(Seattle Mariners, A)

	MT
Complete Set (32):	90.00

1 Keith Foley
2 Jorge Uribe
3 Dave Snell
4 Maryann Hudson
5 Mike Brants
6 William Diaz
7 Andrea Fine
8 Dave "Doc" Mosley
9 John Clem
10 Rick Moore
11 Greg Brinkman
12 Dave McCorkle
13 Bob Bernardo
14 Tom Eccelston
15 Danny Larson
16 Jovan Edwads
17 Michael Darby
18 Buddy Meacham
19 Omar Visquel
20 Robert Gibree
21 Tom Krause
22 Steve Murray
23 Pablo Moncerratt
24 Tom Newberg
25 Jeff Hull
26 Tim Fortugno
27 Jeff Nelson
28 Mike Kolovitz
29 John Burden
30 Clint Zavaras
31 Smokey Bear
32 Greg Mahlberg

1987 Salt Lake City Trappers team issue

(Independent, R)

	MT
Complete Set (30):	8.00

1 Kurt Strange
2 Michael Malinak
3 Kent Hetrick
4 Jon Beuder
5 Neil Reynolds
6 James Ferguson
7 Coach/Bat Boys (Lance Bagshaw, Ryan Bagshaw, Andy Iacona, Reuben Rodriguez) (coach)
8 John Groennert
9 Isaac Alleyne
10 Todd Noonan
11 Jim Gilligan
12 David Ward
13 Ed Citronnelli
14 General Manager/ Public Relations (Steve Pearson, Glenn Seninger)
15 Kouichi Ikeue
16 Mike Humphrey
17 Niles Creekmore
18 Frank Colston

19 Adam Casillas
20 Yasuhiro Hiyama
21 Trainer/Announcer (Steve Fong, Randy Kerdoon)
22 Anthony Blackmon
23 Matt Huff
24 Jon Leake
25 Tim Peters
26 Steve Scott
27 David Poss
28 Team Photo/ Checklist
--- Barry Moss
--- Kim Casey, Joie Casey

1987 San Antonio Dodgers team issue

(L.A. Dodgers, AA) (Sets sold at the ballpark did not include logo cards.)

MT
Complete Set, no logo card (24): 8.00
Complete Set w/ logo card (25): 10.00
1 Jeff Schaefer
2 Andres Mena
3 Manager/Coaches (Gary LaRocque, Dennis Lewallyn, Jim Stoeckel)
4 Tim Scott
5 Alonzo Tellez
6 Rob Rowen
7 Domingo Michel
8 Barry Wohler
9 Juan Bustabad
10 Mike Devereaux
11 Scott May
12 Jeff Brown
13 Mike Schweighoffer
14 Walt McConnell
15 Felix Tejeda
16 Mike Huff
17 Joe Szekely
18 Bob Hamilton
19 Jon Pequignot
20 Dave Eichhorn
21 Homar Rojas
22 Jack Savage
23 Ken Harvey
24 Mark Heuer
--- Team logo card

1987 ProCards San Bernardino Spirits

(Independent, A)

MT
Complete Set (23): 5.00
2359 Steve Walker
2360 Larry Smith
2361 Jeff Edwards
2362 Don Stearns
2363 Randy Harvey
2364 Stan Sanchez
2365 Rich Dauer
2366 Ron Carter
2367 Mark Combs
2368 James Filippi
2369 Delwyn Young
2370 Vince Shinholster
2371 Brian Hartsock
2372 Leon Baham
2373 Scott Marrett
2374 Mike Brocki
2375 Brian Morrison
2376 Walt Stull
2377 Robert Greenlee
2378 Todd Cruz
2379 Tony Triplett
2380 Todd Hayes
2381 Tom Thompson

1987 ProCards San Jose Bees

(Independent, A)

MT
Complete Set (30): 5.00
2191 Sam Hirose
2192 Hector Nakamura
2193 Ken Reitz
2194 Sal Vaccaro
2195 Harvey Lee
2196 Charlie Moore
2197 Rocky Osaka
2198 Kat Kamei
2199 Frank Bryan
2200 Ted Haraguchi
2201 Mickey Yamano
2202 Dan Mori
2203 Tom Nabekawa
2204 Rattoo Akimoto
2205 David Rolland
2206 Mark Seay
2207 Paco Burgos
2208 Elias Sosas
2209 Mike Verdi
2210 Rick Tracy
2211 Warren Brusstar
2212 Lawrence Feola
2213 Roger Erickson
2214 Julian Gonzales
2215 Eddie Gonzales
2216 Steve McCatty
2217 Rusty McNealy
2218 Daryl Sconiers
2219 Shawn Barton
----- Brian Kubala

1987 ProCards Savannah Cardinals

(St. Louis Cardinals, A)

MT
Complete Set (26): 5.00
1846 Bobby DeLoach
1847 Chuck Johnson
1848 David Krebs
1849 Geronimo Pena
1850 Eric Hahn
1851 Scott Nichols
1852 Jay Martel
1853 Greg Ward
1854 Pat Hewes
1855 Mike Henry
1856 Mark Grater
1857 Mark Davis
1858 Pedro Llanes
1859 Carroll Parker
1860 Chico Singletary
1861 Carey Nemeth
1862 Reed Olmstead
1863 Eddie Looper
1864 Julian Martinez
1865 Franklin Abreu
1866 Don Dumas
1867 Stan Zaltsman
1868 Lenny Picota
1869 Mark Behny
1870 Scott Lawrence
1871 Mark DeJohn

1987 ProCards Shreveport Captains

(S.F. Giants, AA)

MT
Complete Set (25): 8.00
458 Everett Graham
459 Paul Meyers
460 Ty Dabney
461 Dennis Cook
462 Dean Freeland
463 Tony Perezchica
464 Scott Medvin
465 Greg Litton
466 Romy Cucjen
467 Kirt Manwaring
468 Todd Thomas
469 Brian Ohnoutka
470 Jeff Brantley
471 John Burkett
472 Ed Puikunas
473 Randy McCament
474 Charlie Hayes
475 T.J. McDonald
476 Deron McCue
477 Stuart Tate
478 Tom Wasilewski
479 John Grimes
480 Vince Sferazza
481 Marty DeMerritt
482 Jack Mull

The election of former players to the Hall of Fame does not always have an immediate upward effect on card values. The hobby market generally has done a good job of predicting those inductions and adjusting values over the course of several years.

1987 Donn Jennings Southern League All-Stars

(AA)

MT
Complete Set (25): 6.00
1 Dave Falcone
2 Rondal Rollin
3 Geronimo Berroa
4 Bernie Tatis
5 Nelson Santovenia
6 Tom Dodd
7 Cameron Drew
8 Larry Walker
9 Matt Winters
10 Ken Caminiti
11 Dave Myers
12 Jimmy Jones
13 Ronnie Gant
14 John Trautwein
15 Rob Mallicoat
16 Randy Johnson
17 Kevin Price
18 Steve Gasser
19 Kevin Coffman
20 Adam Peterson
21 Jeff Bettendorf
22 Jim Beauchamp (manager)
23 Rico Petrocelli (coach)
24 Greg Biagini (coach)
25 Leo Mazzone (coach)

1987 ProCards Spartanburg Phillies

(Philadelphia Phillies, A)

MT
Complete Set (28): 6.00
1790 Jim Platts
1791 Peter Maldonado
1792 Gene Bierscheid
1793 Jeff Stark
1794 Charles McElroy
1795 Mark Sims
1796 Garry Clark
1797 Keith Greene
1798 Kenny Miller
1799 Michel Lamarche
1800 Ramon Aviles
1801 Ron Nelson
1802 Andy Ashby
1803 Trey McCall
1804 Todd Crosby
1805 Cliff Walker
1806 Martin Foley
1807 Luis Iglesias
1808 Elbi Romero
1809 Vince Holyfield
1810 Jeff Grotewald
1811 Bob Tiefanauer
1812 Vladimir Perez
1813 Cesar Delrosa
1814 Phillip Price
1815 Scott Hufford
1816 Fred Christopher
1817 Mike Colpitt

1987 ProCards Spokane Indians

(San Diego Padres, A)

MT
Complete Set (25): 7.50
2680 Osvaldo Sanchez
2681 Darrin Reichle
2682 Tony Lewis
2683 Saul Soltero
2684 Jay Estrada
2685 Rich Holsman
2686 Andy Skeels
2687 David Hollins
2688 Charles Hilleman
2689 Steve Lubratich
2690 Reggie Farmer
2691 Monte Brooks
2692 Bobby Sheridan
2693 Kevin Farmer
2694 Francisco de la Cruz
2695 David Bond
2696 Paul Faries
2697 Bob Lutticken
2698 Terry Gilmore
2699 Pedro Aquino
2700 Todd Torchia
2701 Steve Hendricks
2702 Jose Valentin
2703 Mike Myers
2704 Dustin Picciolo, Rob Picciolo (Mgr., son)

1987 Best Springfield Cardinals

(St. Louis Cardinals, A)

MT
Complete Set (28): 15.00
1 Gaylen Pitts
2 Mark A. Riggins
3 Alexander Ojea
4 Stephen W. Meyer
5 James W. Puzey
6 Ronald M. Johns
7 Tim Lemons
8 John T. Baine
9 Jeffrey L. Graham
10 William E. Bivens
11 Robert J. Faron
12 Stephen F. Hill
13 Howard Hilton
14 David Takach
15 Michael I. Perez
16 David J. Sala
17 Scott W. Hamilton
18 Robert A. Glisson
19 Michael S. Raziano
20 Brian Farley
21 Larry R. Breedlove
22 Bienvendo Figueroa
23 Vincent L. Kindred
24 Scott Melvin
25 Otis B. Gilkey
26 Todd E. Zeile
27 Bluestone Brad
28 Scott Norman

1987 ProCards St. Petersburg Cardinals

(St. Louis Cardinals, A)

MT
Complete Set (27): 5.00
2007 Dave Osteen
2008 Craig Wilson
2009 Jesus Mendez
2010 Mike Sassone
2011 Mike Robertson
2012 Mauricio Nunez
2013 Brett Harrison
2014 Joe Cunningham
2015 Michael Senne
2016 Tom Amante
2017 Mike Fox
2018 Dave Horton
2019 John Murphy
2020 David DeCordova
2021 Chris Forrest
2022 Hans Herzog
2023 Tom Mauch
2024 Dave Bialas
2025 Marty Mason
2026 Crucito Lara
2027 William Hershmann
2028 Benito Malave
2029 Gregory Becker
2030 Randy Butts
2031 Jay North
2032 Pete Fagan
2033 Rob Livchak

1987 ProCards Stockton Ports

(Milwaukee Brewers, A)

MT
Complete Set (27): 18.00
239 Gary Sheffield
240 Rob Derksen
241 Dave Machemer
242 Sandy Guerrero
243 Todd France
244 Danny Fitzpatrick
245 Mario Monico
246 Daryl Hamilton
247 Renard Brown
248 Angel Rodriguez
249 Isaiah Clark
250 Charley McGrew
251 Martin Montano
252 Ruben Escalera
253 Mike Frew
254 John Ludy
255 Luis Castillo
256 George Canale
257 Jim Hunter
258 Keith Fleming
259 Carl Moraw
260 Tim Torricelli
261 Jim Morris
263 Gary Kanwisher
264 Fred Williams
265 Ed Puig

1987 ProCards Sumter Braves

(Atlanta Braves, A)

MT
Complete Set (30): 7.00
1349 Jerald Frost
1350 William Turner
1351 Miguel Sabino
1352 Walt Williams
1353 Bob McNally
1354 Clarence Jones
1355 Kevin Brown
1356 Rusty Richards
1357 Paul Marak
1358 Buddy Bailey
1359 Mark Clark
1360 Kevin Harmon
1361 David Plumb
1362 Carl Jones
1363 Rich Longuil
1364 Mike Bell
1365 Jesse Minton
1366 Rich Maloney
1367 Jim Czajkowski
1368 Jim Lemasters
1369 Larry Jaster
1370 Danny Rogers
1371 Ken Pennington
1372 Al Martin
1373 James Nowlin
1374 Brian Deak
1375 Sean Ross
1376 Gerald Wagner
1377 David Butts
1378 Jay Johnson

1987 TCMA Syracuse Chiefs

(Toronto Blue Jays, AAA)

MT
Complete Set: 8.00
1 Luis Aquino
2 Steve Davis
3 Jeff Hearron
4 Don Gordon
5 Odell Jones
6 Colin McLaughlin
7 Jose Segura
8 Todd Stottlemyre
9 David Wells
10 Greg Myers
11 Dave Stenhouse
12 Jose Castro
13 Jose Escobar
14 Otis Green
15 Alex Infante
16 Manny Lee
17 Nelson Liriano
18 Silvester Campusano
19 Rob Ducey
20 Glenallen Hill
21 Lou Thornton
22 Doc Estes
23 Doug Ault
24 Dave LaRoche
25 Hector Torres
26 Don Gordon, Joe Kucharski
27 Joseph Coyle
28 Mel Queen
29 Kash Beauchamp
30 Steve Fireovid
31 Randy Day
32 Eddie Mahar
33 Red Coughlin

1987 ProCards Syracuse Chiefs

(Toronto Blue Jays, AAA)

MT
Complete Set (23): 6.00
1928 Silve Campusano
1929 Nelson Liriano
1930 Lou Thornton
1931 Greg Myers
1932 Don Gordon
1933 Steve Fireovid
1934 Doug Ault
1935 Alex Infante
1936 Jose Segura
1937 Luis Aquino

1938 Todd Stottlemyre
1939 Tony Hudson
1940 Dave Stenhouse
1941 Manny Lee
1942 Otis Green
1943 Rob Ducey
1944 Jose Escobar
1945 Jose Castro
1946 Dave LaRoche
1947 Hector Torres
1948 Steve Davis
1949 Doc Estes
1950 Glenallen Hill

1987 Syracuse Chiefs Souvenir Tickets

To mark the 10th anniversary of the team's association with the Toronto Blue Jays, the Chiefs issued a set of souvenir tickets picturing Blue Jays players in their stint with Syracuse. The issue is in the form of two sheets, about 10-1/2" x 6-1/2". One sheet has five player-photo tickets and a double-wide logo/checklist panel. The other sheet has seven tickets. Each 1-1/2" x 6-1/2" ticket has a color player photo at top center and a "VOID" notice where the seat assignment would be. The sheets were originally sold for $4.

	MT
Complete Set, sheets (2):	12.00
Complete Set, singles (12):	8.00

1 Ernie Whitt
2 Garth Iorg
3 Dave Steib
4 Willie Upshaw
5 Lloyd Mosbey (Moseby)
6 Tony Fernandez
7 Mark Eichhorn
8 George Bell
9 John Cerutti
10 Jimmy Key
11 Rick Leach
12 Tom Henke

1987 ProCards Tacoma Tigers

(Oakland A's, AAA)

	MT
Complete Set (23):	5.00

1575 Tim Dozier
1576 Darrel Akerfelds
1577 Stan Kyles
1578 Bobby Clark
1579 Gary Jones
1580 Wayne Krenchicki
1581 Dave Van Ohlen
1582 Bruce Tanner
1583 Matt Sinatro
1584 Thad Reece
1585 Eric Broersma
1586 Chuck Estrada
1587 Steve Henderson
1588 Keith Lieppman
1589 Roy Johnson
1590 Dan Rohn
1591 Jose Tolentino
1592 Bill Mooneyham
1593 Jerry Willard
1594 Alejandro Sanchez
1595 Tim Belcher
1596 Brian Dorsett
1597 Tim Birtsas

1987 ProCards Tampa Tarpons

(Cincinnati Reds, A)

	MT
Complete Set (30):	6.00

1319 Gary Denbo
1320 Pete Carey
1321 Mike Converse
1322 Ken Huseby
1323 Mike Roesler
1324 Kevin Pearson
1325 Juan Pinol
1326 Marc Bombard
1327 Tim Swob
1328 Dwayne Williams
1329 Tom Novak
1330 Jeff Richardson
1331 Bret Williamson
1332 Jack Smith
1333 Chris Hammond
1334 Timber Mead
1335 Kent Willis
1336 Mark Jackson
1337 Steve Davis
1338 Gino Minutelli
1339 Mike Campbell
1340 Chris Fernandez
1341 Neal Davenport
1342 Scott Hilgenberg
1343 Jeff Forney
1344 Billy Hawley
1345 Pete Beeler
1346 Rod Zeratsky
1347 Rich Sapienza
1348 Mike Villa

1987 Texas League All-Stars

(AA)

	MT
Complete Set (35):	20.00

1 Mike Debutch
2 Roy Silver
3 Joe Lynch
4 Doug Jennings
5 Brad Pounders
6 Jack Mull
7 Jeff Gardner
8 Roberto Alomar
9 Ed Jurak
10 Sandy Alomar, Jr.
11 Gregg Jefferies
12 Joe Redfield
13 Steve Smith
14 Shane Young
15 Marty Reed
16 Joaquin Contreras
17 Jim St. Laurent
18 Thomas Howard
19 Steve Peters
20 John Miglio
21 Scott Arnold
22 Kirt Manwaring
23 Greg Harris
24 Marcus Lawton
25 Lavel Freeman
26 Mike Fitzgerald
27 Charlie Hayes
28 Mike Devereaux
29 David West
30 Jesus Alfaro
31 Ray Stephens
32 Ty Dabney
33 John Burkett
34 Jack Savage
35 Joe Szckely

1987 TCMA Tidewater Tides

(N.Y. Mets, AAA)

	MT
Complete Set:	7.00

1 Reggie Dobie
2 Tom Edens
3 Bob Gibson
4 Ed Glynn
5 Jeff Innis
6 Tom McCarthy
7 John Mitchell
8 DeWayne Vaughn
9 Dave Wyatt
10 John Gibbons
11 Greg Olson
12 Andre David
13 Kevin Elster
14 Tom Lombarski
15 Jeff McKnight
16 Keith Miller
17 Randy Milligan
18 Steve Springer
19 Terry Blocker
20 Mark Carreon
21 Gene Walter
22 Clint Hurdle
23 Mike Cubbage
24 John Cumberland
25 Rick Rainer
26 Don Schulze
27 Bob Buchanan
28 Bill Latham
29 Jose Roman
30 Dwight Gooden

1987 ProCards Tidewater Tides

(N.Y. Mets, AAA)

	MT
Complete Set (33):	7.00

2472 Clint Hurdle
2473 DeWayne Vaugh
2474 Reggie Dobie
2475 Jeff McKnight
2476 Terry Blocker
2477 John Gibbons
2478 Jason Felice
2479 Jeff Innis
2480 Tom Edens
2481 Keith Miller
2482 Steve Springer
2483 Mike Cubbage
2484 Tom McCarthy
2485 Dave Wyatt
2486 Ed Glynn
2487 Ricky Nelson
2488 Tom Lombarski
2489 John Cumberland
2490 Greg Olson
2491 John Mitchell
2492 Mark Carreon
2493 Bill Latham
2494 Jose Roman
2495 Andre David
2496 Don Schulze
2497 Bob Buchanan
2498 Gene Walter
2499 Randy Milligan
2500 Rob Evans
2501 Rick Rainer
2502 Dwight Gooden
2503 Kevin Elster
2504 Bob Gibson

1987 TCMA Toledo Mud Hens

(Detroit Tigers, AAA)

	MT
Complete Set:	6.00

1 Rey Palacios
2 Don Heinkel
3 German Rivera
4 Bill Laskey
5 Mike Stenhouse
6 Fred Tiburcio
7 Jim Walewander
8 Scott Lusader
9 Bruce Fields
10 Scott Earl
11 Jeff Ransom
12 James R. Wright
13 Mike Henneman
14 John Pacella
15 Morris Madden
16 Steve Searcy
17 Paul Gibson
18 Jed Murray
19 Ricky Barlow
20 Doug Baker
21 Leon Roberts
22 Gene Roof
23 Tim Tolman
24 Jerry Davis
25 Dwight Lowry

1987 ProCards Toledo Mud Hens

(Detroit Tigers, AAA)

	MT
Complete Set (30):	6.00

1954 Scott Earl
1955 Steve Searcy
1956 Scott Lusader
1957 German Rivera
1958 Jim Walewander
1959 Ricky Wright
1960 Don Heinkel
1961 John Pacella
1962 Ricky Barlow
1963 Paul Gibson
1964 Fred Tiburcio
1965 Tim Tolman
1966 Jed Murray
1967 Bruce Fields
1968 Rey Palacios
1969 Mike Henneman
1970 Doug Baker
1971 Morris Madden
1972 Mike Stenhouse
1973 Leon Roberts
1974 Bill Laskey
1975 Gene Roof
1976 Don McGann
1977 Jeff Ransom
1978 John Hiller
1979 Billy Bean
1980 Willie Hernandez
1981 Kirk Gibson
1982 Bryan Kelly
1983 Jerry Davis

1987 ProCards Tucson Toros

(Houston Astros, AAA)

	MT
Complete Set (25):	5.00

2110 Juan Agosto
2111 Glenn Carpenter
2112 Robbie Wine
2113 Bill Crone
2114 Rafael Montalvo
2115 Tye Waller
2116 Manny Hernandez
2117 Dale Berra
2118 Louie Meadows
2119 Rocky Childress
2120 Gerald Young
2121 Ray Fontenot
2122 Jim Miner
2123 Ron Mathis
2124 Nelson Rood
2125 Bert Pena
2126 Kevin Hagen
2127 Jeff Heathcock
2128 Eric Bullock
2129 Ronn Reynolds
2130 Anthony Kelley
2131 Eddie Watt
2132 Ty Gainey
2133 Bob Didier
2134 Tom Funk

1987 Jones Photo Tucson Toros

(Houston Astros, AAA) (3" x 5-1/8")

	MT
Complete Set (24):	45.00

(1) Dale Berra
(2) Eric Bullock
(3) Glenn Carpenter
(4) Bill Crone
(5) Bob Dider
(6) Jeff Edwards
(7) Tom Funk
(8) TY Gainey
(9) Jeff Heathcock
(10) Manny Hernandez
(11) Paul Householder
(12) Chuck Jackson
(13) Anthony Kelley
(14) Ron Mathis
(15) Louie Meadows
(16) Jim Miner
(17) Rafael Montaivo
(18) Raynor Noble
(19) Ronn Reynolds
(20) Nelson Rood
(21) Tye Waller
(22) Ed Watt
(23) Robbie Wine
(24) Gerald Young

1987 Tulsa Drillers team issue

(Texas Rangers, AA)

	MT
Complete Set (28):	8.00

1 Dave Murray
2 Brad Hill
3 Mike Jirschele
4 Bobby Jones
5 Mike Couchee
6 Bill Stearns
7 Dave Harman
8 Greg Ferlenda
9 Jeff Melrose
10 Otto Gonzalez
11 Eddie Jurak
12 Jim St. Laurent
13 Howard Hilton, Dave Pavlas
14 Ruben Guzman
15 Tom Duggan
16 George Threadgill
17 Ken Rogers
18 Rick Knapp
19 Jose Cecena
20 Bob Malloy
21 Darrell Whitaker
22 Rick Odekirk
23 Larry Klein
24 Tommy West
25 Jose Mota
26 Gary Mielke
27 Rob Bill
28 Rod Lung

1987 ProCards Utica Blue Sox

(Philadelphia Phillies, A)

	MT
Complete Set (33):	6.00

2705 Manlio Perez
2706 Leroy Ventress
2707 Rafael Bustamante
2708 Kim Batiste
2709 Scott Ruckman
2710 Shelby McDonald
2711 Troy Zerb
2712 Robert Jones
2713 Jim Vatcher
2714 Doug Lindsey
2715 Jeffrey Scott
2716 Gary White
2717 Mark Cobb
2718 Bob Chadwick
2719 David Monterio
2720 Marc Lopez
2721 Rick Trlicek
2722 Steve Kirkpatrick
2723 Darrell Coulter
2724 Scott Reaves
2725 Joe Williams
2726 Royal Thomas
2727 John LaRosa
2728 Timothy Peek
2729 Andy Ashby
2730 Matt Rambo
2731 Jaime Barragan
2732 Robert Hurta
2733 Phil Fagnano
2734 Corey Smith
2735 Ike Galloway
2736 Dave Allen
2737 Greg McCarthy

1987 ProCards Vancouver Canadians

(Pittsburgh Pirates, AAA)

	MT
Complete Set (25):	5.00

1598 Mike Bielecki
1599 Jackie Brown
1600 Jeff Cox
1601 Carlos LeDezma
1602 Mark Ross
1603 Tommy Dunbar
1604 Stan Fansler
1605 Rocky Bridges
1606 Dave Johnson
1607 Sammy Haro
1608 Sammy Khalifa
1609 Houston Jimenez
1610 Tim Drummond
1611 Dave Leeper
1612 Mike Dunne
1613 Randy Kramer
1614 Butch Davis
1615 Hipolito Pena
1616 Jose Lind
1617 Larry Ray
1618 Danny Bilardello
1619 Vincente Palacios
1620 Ruben Rodriquez
1621 Dorn Taylor
1622 U.L. Washington

1987 ProCards Vermont Reds

(Cincinnati Reds, A) (#836 not issued)

	MT
Complete Set (26):	5.00
814 Brad Brusky	
815 Jim Jefferson	
816 Ted Langdon	
817 Francisco Tenacen	
818 Marty Brown	
819 Greg Simpson	
820 Ramon Sambo	
821 Tim Mirabito	
822 Rob Lopez	
823 Joe Dunlap	
824 Tom Dietz	
825 Mike Smith	
826 Angelo Nunley	
827 Steve Oliverio	
828 John Bryant	
829 Tom Runnells	
830 Dave Miley	
831 Glenn Spagnolia	
832 Joe Oliver	
833 Mark Germann	
834 Greg Monita	
835 Chris Jones	
837 Mark Berry	
838 Darren Riley	
839 Marvin Haynes	
840 Rod Lich	

1987 ProCards Vero Beach Dodgers

(L.A. Dodgers, A)

	MT
Complete Set (31):	8.00
1730 John Wetteland	
1731 Jose Tapia	
1732 Joe Spagnuolo	
1733 Dan Pena	
1734 Darren Holmes	
1735 Pete Feist	
1736 Ramon Martinez	
1737 Pat Zachry	
1738 Fred Gegan	
1739 Ken Lambert	
1740 Manny Francois	
1741 Mancy Benitez	
1742 Mike Garner	
1743 Tom Thomas	
1744 Mike Batesole	
1745 Jeff Brown	
1746 Kevin Campbell	
1747 Rob Giesecke	
1748 Joe Kesselmark	
1749 Jay Hornacek	
1750 Felipe Esteban	
1751 Tom Beyers	
1752 Kevin Devine	
1753 Bryan Smith	
1754 Mike Burke	
1755 Bill Bartels	
1756 Rene Garcia	
1757 Lee Langley	
1758 Kevin Shea	
1759 John Shoemaker	
1760 Phil Torres	

1987 ProCards Visalia Oaks

(Minnesota Twins, A)

	MT
Complete Set (27):	5.00
543 Jamie Williams	
544 Glen Myers	
545 Kenny Morgan	
546 Tim Cota	
547 Bob Strube	
548 Bob Lee	
549 Jeff Perry	
550 Kurt Walker	
551 Troy Galloway	
552 Dave Blakely	
553 Park Pittman	
554 Ike Goldstein	
555 Chris Calvert	
556 Tim Senne	
557 Kenny Davis	
558 Mike Redding	
559 Tim O'Connor	
560 Todd Burke	
561 Joey Aragon	
562 Joey Zellner	
563 John Pust	
564 Mike Adams	
565 Marty Lanoux	
566 Gordon Heimueller	
567 Dan Schmitz	
568 Clark Lange	
569 Shannon Raybon	

1987 ProCards Waterloo Indians

(Cleveland Indians, A)

	MT
Complete Set (29):	5.00
1038 Fidel Compres	
1039 Manny Mercado	
1040 Jim Richardson	
1041 Steve Johnigan	
1042 Brad Wolten	
1043 Mark Pike	
1044 Dave Alvis	
1045 Tom Gamba	
1046 Scott Johnson	
1047 Glenn Adams	
1048 Todd Gonzales	
1049 Kevin Kuykendall	
1050 John Githens	
1051 Mike Walker	
1052 Bruce Egloff	
1053 Jeff Shaw	
1054 Carl Chambers	
1055 Rudy Seanez	
1056 Paul Kuzniar	
1057 Don Santos	
1058 Keith Seifert	
1059 Ray Williamson	
1060 Tom Lampkin	
1061 Riley Polk	
1062 Glenn Fairchild	
1063 Claudio Carrasco	
1064 Lenny Randle	
1065 Dan Redmond	
1066 Rick Adair	

1987 ProCards Watertown Pirates

(Pittsburgh Pirates, A)

	MT
Complete Set (31):	14.00
2798 Ben Webb	
2799 Rodger Castner	
2800 Robert Harris	
2801 Ed Shea	
2802 Scott Runge	
2803 Chip Duncan	
2804 Scott Barczi	
2805 Keith Raisanen	
2806 Pete Freeman	
2807 Steve Carter	
2808 Kevin Burdick	
2809 Wesley Chamberlain	
2810 Domingo Merejo	
2811 Junior Vizcaino	
2812 Keith Shepherd	
2813 Ed Hartman	
2814 Jose Acosta	
2815 Jim Garrison	
2816 Jody Williams	
2817 Mark Thomas	
2818 Rob Barnwell	
2819 Jeff Griffith	
2820 Joe Pacholec	
2821 Pete Murphy	
2822 Mark Koller	
2823 Joe Macavage	
2824 Moises Alou	
2825 Doug Torberg	
2826 Charlie Green	
2827 Jeff Cox	
2828 Mike Sandoval	

1987 ProCards Wausau Timbers

(Seattle Mariners, A) (Price includes the scarce #1152 card)

	MT
Complete Set (28):	5.00
1127 Bobby Cuellar	
1128 Jim Blueberg	
1129 Jody Ryan	
1130 Dan Disher	
1131 Howard Townsend	
1132 Troy Williams	
1133 Patrick Lennon	
1134 Jose Tartabull	
1135 Wendell Bolar	
1136 Clay Gunn	
1137 Jose Bennett	
1138 Ted Williams	
1139 Anthony Woods	
1140 Drew Kosco	
1141 Jim Bowie	
1142 Mark Wooden	
1143 Jerry Goff	
1144 Deron Johnson	
1145 Mike Thorpe	
1146 Michael McDonald	
1147 Trent Intorcia	
1148 Dave Hartnott	
1149 Mark Gold	
1150 Pat Rice	
1151 Rudy Webster	
1152 Unidentified Player	
1153 Ric Wilson	
1154 Tim Erickson	

1987 ProCards West Palm Beach Expos

(Montreal Expos, A)

	MT
Complete Set (28):	6.00
652 Rob Leary	
653 Tim Touma	
654 Paul Frye	
655 Alfredo Cardwood	
656 Jeff Tabaka	
657 Rob Williams	
658 Derrell Baker	
659 Pat Sipe	
660 Kevin Dean	
661 Bob Caffrey	
662 Bud Yanus	
663 Don Burke	
664 Mike Blowers	
665 Cesar Hernandez	
666 Al Collins	
667 Yorkis Perez	
668 Charlie Lea	
669 Omer Munoz	
670 Mel Houston	
671 Tommy Traen	
672 Eddie Dixon	
673 Kevin Kristan	
674 Jeff Huson	
675 Don Burke	
676 Steve Rousey	
677 Gene Harris	
678 Geff Davis	
679 John Spinosa	

1987 Rock's Wichita Pilots

(San Diego Padres, AA)

	MT
Complete Set (25):	60.00
10 Mike Debutch	
11 Kevin Armstrong	
12 Tommy Alexander	
14 Roberto Alomar	
15 Sandy Alomar, Jr.	
17 Nate Colbert	
18 Chris Knabenshue	
19 Brad Pounders	
20 Steve Smith	
21 Joe Lynch	
22 Greg Harris	
23 Eric Nolte	
24 Thomas Howard	
25 Jeff Reece	
26 Mike Costello	
27 Scott Rainey	
28 Jeff Stewart	
29 Dave Cortez	
30 Tom Brassil	
31 Candy Sierra	
32 Kevin Brown	
33 Eric Bauer	
42 Steve Luebber	
43 Jerald Clark	
44 Cam Walker	

1987 ProCards Williamsport Bills

(Cleveland Indians, AA)

	MT
Complete Set (27):	5.00
1379 Dain Syverson	
1380 Keith Bennett	
1381 Winston Ficklin	
1382 Oscar Mejia	
1383 Luis Encarnacion	
1384 Steve Moses	
1385 Bobby Link	
1386 Jim Bishop	
1387 Mark Higgins	
1388 Mike Bellaman	
1389 Ivan Murrell	
1390 Daryl Smith	
1391 Miguel Roman	
1392 Dave Bresnahan	
1393 Rick Henke	
1394 Brian Allard	
1395 Greg LaFever	
1396 Steve Swosher	
1397 Greg Dube	
1398 Scott Sabo	
1399 Roger Wilson	
1400 Chris Beasley	
1401 Bernardo Brito	
1402 Luis Medina	
1403 Turner Gill	
1404 Greg Karpuk	
1405 Joe Skalski	

1987 ProCards Winston-Salem Spirits

(Chicago Cubs, A)

	MT
Complete Set (27):	5.00
1209 Mark McMorris	
1210 Greg Kallevig	
1211 Todd Cloninger	
1212 Cedric Landrum	
1213 Bill Danek	
1214 Phil Hannon	
1215 Heath Slocumb	
1216 Bob Bafia	
1217 Luis Cruz	
1218 Jim Bullinger	
1219 Tad Slowik	
1220 Glenn Gregson	
1221 Jay Loviglio	
1222 Lee Grimes	
1223 Tim Wallace	
1224 John Lewis	
1225 Joe Girardi	
1226 Gabby Robles	
1227 Mike Tullier	
1228 Mike Miller	
1229 Chuck Oertli	
1230 Kris Roth	
1231 Jeff Hirsch	
1232 Jeff Small	
1233 DeWayne Coleman	
1234 Jim Matas	
1235 Mike Curtis	

1987 ProCards Winter Haven Red Sox

(Boston Red Sox, A)

	MT
Complete Set (30):	5.00
893 Tim Buheller	
894 Felix Dedos	
895 Livio Padilla	
896 Larry Shikles	
897 Ronnie McGowan	
898 Bart Haley	
899 Erik Laseke	
900 Leverne Jackson	
901 Daniel Sullivan	
902 Dan Gabrielle	
903 Mike Coffey	
904 Stuart Weidie	
905 Bruce Lockhart	
906 David Milstein	
907 Odie Abril	
908 John Toale	
909 Manny Jose	
910 Wayne Murphy	
911 Mike Sears	
912 Paul Slifko	
913 Eduardo Zambrano	
914 Eric Hetzel	
915 Derek Livernois	
916 Doug Camilli	
917 Mike Ickes	
918 Roger Haggerty	
919 Paul Thoutsis	
920 Jim Orsag	
921 Todd Pratt	
922 Dana Gomez	

1987 ProCards Wytheville Cubs

(Chicago Cubs, A)

	MT
Complete Set (31):	6.00
2738 Anthony Whitson	
2739 Matt Walbeck	
2740 Horace Tucker	
2741 Scott Taylor	
2742 Derek Stroud	
2743 Dave Sommer	
2744 Jossy Rosario	
2745 Victor Quiles	
2746 Eric Perry	
2747 Elvin Paulino	
2748 Nelson Nunex	
2749 Greg Jackson	
2750 John Gardner	
2751 Edger Galarza	
2752 Henry Fleming	
2753 Matthew Franco	
2754 Francisco Espino	
2755 Darren Eggleston	
2756 Jay Eddings	
2757 Braz Davis	
2758 Frank Castillo	
2759 Danny Carpenter	
2760 Carlos Canino	
2761 Frank Campos	
2762 Matt Cakora	
2763 Warren Arrington	
2764 Alex Arias	
2765 Tom King	
2766 Rick Kranitz	
2767 Brad Mills	
2768 Team Photo	

1988 ProCards Triple-A All-Stars

(AAA)

		MT
Complete Set (45):		12.00
1	Mike Devereaux	
2	Chris Gwynn	
3	Tracy Woodson	
4	Benny Distefano	
5	Tom Prince	
6	Eddie Jurak	
7	Phil Ouellette	
8	Luis Medina	
9	Bob Geren	
10	Mike Kinnunen	
11	Scott Nielsen	
12	Lavell Freeman	
13	Tim Pyznarski	
14	German Rivera	
15	Urbano Lugo	
16	Bill Bathe	
17	Bob Sebra	
18	Mike Bielecki	
19	Dwight Smith	
20	Sandy Alomar	
21	Mike Brumley	
22	Joey Cora	
23	Greg Harris	
24	Dick Grapenthin	
25	Mike Shelton	
26	Marty Brown	
27	Hugh Kemp	
28	Tom O'Malley	
29	Steve Finley	
30	Luis de los Santos	
31	Steve Curry	
32	Tony Perezchica	
33	Roy Smith	
34	Joe Boever	
35	Bob Milacki	
36	Geronimo Berroa	
37	Eric Yelding	
38	Lance Blankenship	
39	Mark Carreon	
40	Gregg Jefferies	
41	David West	
42	Mark Huismann	
43	Rey Palacios	
44	Cameron Drew	
45	Donn Pall	
46	Sap Randall	
47	Terry Collins	
48	Carlos Ledezma	
49	Bill Plummer	
50	Joe Sparks	
51	Toby Harrah	
52	Ed Nottle	
53	Randy Holland	
54	Mike Cubbage	
----	Checklist	

1988 CMC (TCMA) AAA All-Stars

(AAA)

		MT
Complete Set (55):		12.00
1	Bill Bathe (Iowa)	
2	Luis De Los Santos (Omaha)	12.00

3 Johnny Paredes (Indianapolis)
4 Tom O'Malley (Oklahoma City)
5 Felix Fermin (Buffalo)
6 Billy Moore (Indianapolis)
7 Ronaldo Roomes (Iowa)
8 Van Snider (Nashville)
9 German Rivera (Denver)
10 Lavell Freeman (Denver)
11 Dorn Taylor (Buffalo)
12 Norm Charlton (Nashville)
13 Randy Johnson (Indianapolis)
14 Gary Sheffield (Denver)
15 Mike Harkey (Iowa)
16 Bob Geren (Columbus)
17 Dave Griffin (Richmond)
18 Tom Barrett (Maine)
19 Craig Worthington (Rochester)
20 Randy Velarde (Columbus)
21 Steve Finley (Rochester)
22 Carlos Quintana (Pawtucket)
23 Mark Carreon (Tidewater)
24 Lonnie Smith (Richmond)
25 Steve Searcy (Toledo)
26 Mark Huismann (Toledo)
27 Gregg Jefferies (Tidewater)
28 Ricky Jordan (Maine)
29 Dave West (Tidewater)
30 John Smoltz (Richmond)
31 Sandy Alomar Jr. (Las Vegas)
32 Francisco Melendez (Phoenix)
33 Mike Woodard (Vancouver)
34 Edgar Martinez (Calgary)
35 Mike Brumley (Las Vegas)
36 Mike Deveraux (Albuquerque)
37 Cameron Drew (Tucson)
38 Luis Medina (Colorado Springs)
39 Rod Allen (Colorado Springs)
40 George Henshaw (Albuquerque)
41 Bill Brenna (Albuquerque)
42 Bill Krueger (Albuquerque)
43 Karl Best (Portland)
44 Juan Bell (Albuquerque)
45 Ramon Martinez (Albuquerque)

1988 Star Company

Many of the team sets issued by Star Co. in its years in the minor league card business can be found in two versions. An early-season issue, generally provided to the hobby market, and a late-season issue usually offered for sale only at the ballpark. Many of the late-issue cards were of potential stars who joined the clubs after the initial sets were released. The late-issue cards may be printed with border colors at odds with the rest of the team set and are often unnumbered. Other late-issue cards corrected glaring errors, such as wrong photos.

(See Star Co. listings under individual cities for checklists, values)

1988 ProCards Albany-Colonie Yankees

(N.Y. Yankees, AA)

	MT
Complete Set (27):	5.00

1329 Amalio Carreno
1330 Andy Stankiewicz
1331 Bob Green
1332 Rob Sepanek
1333 Tim Layana
1334 Bobby Davidson
1335 Gary Cathcart
1336 Dave Eiland
1337 Mike Christopher
1338 Rick Torres
1339 Tony Ferreira
1340 Troy Evers
1341 Tim Becker
1342 Dana Ridenour
1343 Melvin Rosario
1344 Jim Leyritz
1345 Scott Shaw
1346 Jason Mass (Maas)
1347 Oscar Azocar
1348 Aris Tirado
1349 Hensley Meulens
1350 Dickie Scott
1351 Deron Johnson
1352 Tommy Jones
1353 Tony Cloninger
1354 Mike Heifferon
---- Checklist

1988 ProCards Albuquerque Dukes

(L.A. Dodgers, AAA)

	MT
Complete Set (29):	5.00

249 Steve Garcia
250 Bill Brennan
251 Brent Strom
252 Mike Devereaux
253 Mike Sharperson
254 Von Joshua
255 Mariano Duncan
256 Tracy Woodson
257 Gilberto Reyes
258 Jose Gonzalez
259 Chris Gwynn
260 John Gibbons
261 Tony Arnold
262 Ray Searage
263 Mike Hartley
264 Tim Crews
265 Shawn Hillegas
266 Shanie Dugas
267 Mike Ramsey
268 George Hinshaw
269 Jon Debus
270 Terry Collins
271 Bill Krueger
272 Lenny Currier
273 Chuck Hensley
274 Hector Heredia
275 Stan Kyles
276 Dennis Burtt
---- Checklist

1988 CMC (TCMA) Albuquerque Dukes

(L.A. Dodgers, AAA)

	MT
Complete Set (25):	5.00

1 Shawn Hillegas
2 Stan Kyles
3 Bill Krueger
4 Ray Searage
5 Tony Arnold
6 Bill Brennan
7 Dennis Burtt
8 Tim Crews
9 Mike Hartley
10 Chuck Hensley
11 Hector Heredia
12 Chris Gwynn
13 Hinshaw George
14 Mike Ramsey
15 Jon Debus
16 Mike Sharperson
17 Tracy Woodson
18 Mike Devereaux
19 Jose Gonzalez
20 John Gibbons
21 Gil Reyes
22 Shanie Dugas
23 Mariano Duncan
24 Steve Garcia
25 Terry Collins

1988 Albuquerque Dukes team-issue photos

(L.A. Dodgers, AAA) (3-1/2" x 5" color photo prints, sold at stadium for $2 each)

	MT
Complete Set (35):	135.00

(1) Tony Arnold
(2) Randy Asadoor
(3) Juan Bell
(4) Bill Brennan
(5) Dennis Burtt
(6) Terry Collins
(7) Steve Crawford
(8) Tim Crews
(9) Lenny Currier (trainer)
(10) Jon Debus
(11) Mike Devereaux
(12) Shanie Dugas
(13) Mariano Duncan
(14) Steve Garcia
(15) John Gibbons
(16) Jose Gonzalez
(17) Chris Gwynn
(18) Mike Hartley
(19) Chuck Hensley
(20) Hector Heredia
(21) Shawn Hillegas
(22) George Hinshaw
(23) Ken Howell
(24) Von Joshua
(25) Bill Krueger
(26) Stan Kyles
(27) Ramon Martinez
(28) Ron Mathis
(29) Jose Mota
(30) Mike Ramsey
(31) Gil Reyes
(32) Ray Searage
(33) Mike Sharperson
(34) Brent Strom
(35) Tracy Woodson

"1982" Anchorage Glacier Pilots

While carrying a 1982 date on front, this card was actually issued in 1988, after McGwire had established himself as a slugging major league star. While he had played in the Alaskan summer league in 1992 - as a pitcher and first baseman - the team had issued no contemporary cards. This one-card set was issued in an edition of 10,000 with an original selling price of about $6. Front of the standard size card has a blue frame around a black-and-white photo of McGwire on the mound. Back has biographical and college ball data, along with the logo of the team. A similar card exists of Casey Candaele.

	MT
Mark McGwire	250.00
Casey Candaele	2.00

1988 ProCards Appleton Foxes

(K.C. Royals, A)

	MT
Complete Set (30):	5.00

137 Jorge Pedre
138 Luis Mallea
139 Brian Meyers
140 Kevin Shaw
141 Doug Nelson
142 Terry Shumpert
143 Linton Dyer
144 Darryl Robinson
145 Dave Howard
146 Don Wright
147 Bill Stonikas
148 Karl Drezek
149 Tom Gordon
150 Tim Odom
151 Trey Gainous
152 Brian McCormack
153 Keith Shibata
154 Frank Henderson
155 Jesus DeLeon
156 Chris Gurchiek
157 Doug Bock
158 Jeff Baum
159 Andre Rabouin
160 Dennis Moeller
161 Bobby Knecht
162 Brian Poldberg
163 Mike Leon
164 Larry Dawson
165 Team photo
---- Checklist

1988 Grand Slam Arkansas Travelers

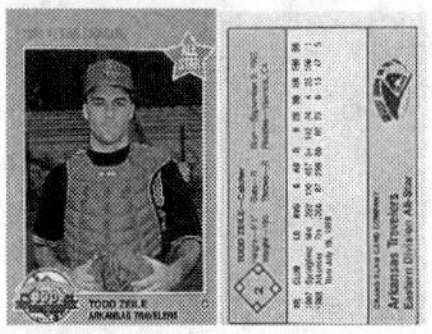

(St. Louis Cardinals, AA) (6,000 sets)

	MT
Complete Set (25):	6.00

1 Rick Colbert
2 Brad Henderson
3 Steve Engel
4 Jim Riggleman
5 Jeff Fassero
6 Bien Figueroa
7 Todd Zeile
8 Tom Baine
9 Bob Faron
10 Mauricio Nunez
11 Ken Infante
12 Howard Hilton
13 Brett Harrison
14 Matt Kinzer
15 Jesus Mendez
16 Jim Fregosi
17 Benito Malave
18 Mike Sassone
19 Mike Robinson
20 Mike Robertson
21 Mike Perez
22 Jim Puzey
23 Dave Osteen
24 Jeff Oyster
25 Mike Senne

1988 ProCards Asheville Tourists

(Houston Astros, A)

	MT
Complete Set (31):	5.00

1049 Billy Carver
1050 Kenny Dickson
1051 Greg Johnson
1052 Andy Harter
1053 Ramon Cedeno
1054 Mike Beams
1055 Joe Charno
1056 Carlos Laboy
1057 Neder Horta
1058 Ed Renteria
1059 Chris Lee
1060 Harold Allen
1061 Dan Lewis
1062 Gorky Perez
1063 Fred Costello
1064 Joe Locke
1065 Doug Royalty
1066 Joe Ortiz
1067 Charley Taylor
1068 Gary Tuck
1069 Richie Simon
1070 Dennis Tafoya
1071 Danny Newman
1072 Dean Hartgraves
1073 Mike Hook
1074 Carlos Henry
1075 Dave Cunningham
1076 Gene Confreda
1077 Ron McKee
1078 Todd Weber
---- Checklist

1988 ProCards Auburn Astros

(Houston Astros, A)

	MT
Complete Set (29):	40.00

1947 Larry Lamphere
1948 Scott Spurgeon
1949 Chris Small
1950 Wally Trice
1951 Dennis Tafoya
1952 Pat Penafeather
1953 Kenny Lofton
1954 Ron Porterfield
1955 Rodney Windes
1956 Harry Fuller
1957 Ken Morris
1958 Dave Shermet
1959 Bernie Jenkins
1960 Rod Scheckla
1961 John Massarelli
1962 Mike Beams
1963 Rick Wise
1964 Bob Neal
1965 Neder Horta
1966 Andy Mota
1967 Frank Cacciatore
1968 Jim DeSapio
1969 Rick Dunnum
1970 Gordy Farmer
1971 John Graham
1972 David Klinefelter
1973 Luis Gonzalez
1974 Mica Lewis
---- Checklist

1988 ProCards Augusta Pirates

(Pittsburgh Pirates, A)

	MT
Complete Set (33):	12.00

359 Wes Chamberlain
360 Moises Alou
361 Miguel Valverde
362 Mickey Peyton
363 Jeff Griffith
364 Orlando Merced
365 Carlos Garcia
366 Eddie Hartman
367 Pete Freeman
368 Scott Barczi
369 Jimmy Garrison
370 Ben Shelton
371 Jose Acosta
372 Joe Macavage
373 Joe Pacholec
374 Butch Schlopy
375 Keith Shepherd
376 Scott Runge
377 Willie Smith
378 Ron Downs
379 Tracy Toy
380 Tonny Cohen
381 Joel Forrest
382 Jeff Cox
383 Dave Moharter
384 Glenn Trudo
385 S. Carter
386 Robert Harris
387 Jmaes Rhoades
388 Paul Day
389 Len Monheimer
1576 Mark Merchant
---- Checklist

1988 Cal Cards Bakersfield Dodgers

(L.A. Dodgers, A)

	MT
Complete Set (34):	5.00

234 Jeff Brown
235 Dan Henley
236 John Knapp
237 Alan Lewis
238 Dan Montgomery
239 Jose Munoz

240 Jose Vizcaino
241 Amilcar Valdez
242 Adam Brown
243 Carlos Hernandez
244 Billy Argo
245 Jay Hornacek
246 John Beuder
247 Bruce Dostal
248 Steve Green
249 Wayne Kirby
250 Billy Brooks
251 Carlos Carrasco
252 Chris Cerny
253 Chris Gettler
254 Ken King
255 Todd Kroll
256 Lee Langley
257 Dan Pena
258 Tim Scott
259 Zak Shinall
260 Dennis Springer
261 John Wanish
262 Gary La Rogue
263 Guy Conti
264 Stan Johnston
265 Tommy Davis
266 Jack Patton
267 Rick Smith

1988 Baseball America AA Top Prospects

(Class AA) (All cards have "AA-" prefix to card number)

		MT
Complete Set (30):		17.50
1	Hensley Meulens	
2	Mike Harkey	
3	Rob Ritchie	
4	Omar Vizquel	
5	Jerome Walton	
6	Chuck Malone	
7	Tom Lampkin	
8	Joe Girardi	
9	Kevin Wickander	
10	Bill McGuire	
11	Pete Harnisch	
12	Derek Park	
13	Alex Sanchez	
14	Jose DeJesus	
15	Rafael DeLima	
16	Mark Lemke	
17	Chris Hammond	
18	German Gonzalez	
19	Dennis Jones	
20	Francisco Cabrera	
21	Ramon Martinez	
22	Gary Sheffield	
23	Juan Bell	
24	Greg Vaughn	
25	Kevin Brown	
26	Mike Munoz	
27	Trevor Wilson	
28	John Wetteland	
29	Jeff Manto	
30	Buddy Bailey	

1988 Star Baseball City Royals

(K.C. Royals, A) (Vasquez and Walker cards originally issued with transposed photos, later corrected.)

		MT
Complete Set: w/variations (27):		27.50
Partial Set: no variations (25):		15.00
1	Bud Adams	
2	Ken Adams	
3	Jon Alexander	
4	Jose Anglero	
5	Kevin Appier	
6	Sean Berry	
7	Mike Butcher	
8	Dera Clark	
9	Tony Bridges-Clements	
10	Jeff Conine	
11	Carlos Escalera	
12	Carlos Gonzalez	
13	Dan Harlan	
14	Kenny Jackson	
15	Kevin Koslofski	
16	Richie LeBlanc Jr.	
17	Brian McRae	
18	Bobby Moore	
19	Harvey Pulliam Jr.	
20	Tom Rice	
21	Joe Skodny	
22	Mike Tresemer	
23a	Aguedo Vasquez (wrong photo - pitching)	
23b	Aguedo Vasquez (corrected - portrait photo)	
24a	Steve Walker wrong photo - portrait)	
24b	Steve Walker (corrected - pitching photo)	
25	DeJon Watson	

1988 ProCards Batavia Clippers

(Philadelphia Phillies, A)

		MT
Complete Set (31):		5.00
1662	Bob Tiefenauer	
1663	Dave Cash	
1664	Don McCormack	
1665	Tony Trevino	
1666	Leroy Ventress	
1667	Nicio Martinez	
1668	Scott Drury	
1669	Wayne Fuller	
1670	Rick Trlicek	
1671	Eric Enos	
1672	Mark Bradford	
1673	Erik Bratlien	
1674	Tim Dell	
1675	Mike Owens	
1676	Tom Marsh	
1677	Chris Walker	
1678	Nick Santa Cruz	
1679	Joe Tenhunfeld	
1680	Ike Galloway	
1681	Rich Walker	
1682	Todd Elam	
1683	Matt Viggiano	
1684	Dave Allen	
1685	Rich Tracy	
1686	Fred Felton III	
1687	Andy Barrick	
1688	Gary Wilson	
1689	Brian Cummings	
1690	Troy Zerb	
1691	Brad Rogers	
----	Checklist	

1988 Legoe Bellingham Mariners

(Seattle Mariners, A)

		MT
Complete Set (32):		6.00
1	Ricky Candelari	
2	Dorian Daughtry	
3	Tony Cayson	
4	Ellerton Maynard	
5	Mike McLaughlin	
6	Tom McNamara	
7	Greg Prikl	
8	Julio Reyan	
9	Jeff Miller	
10	Pete Schmidt	
11	Tim Stargell	
12	Gary Wheelock	
13	Brian Wilkinson	
14	Lee Hancock	
15	John Kohli	
16	Jim Kosnik	
17	Tom Liss	
18	Victor Mangual	
19	Scott Pitcher	
20	Keith Barrett	
21	Scott Stoerck	
22	Nick Felix	
23	Ted Eldredge	
24	Chris Doll	
25	Erick Bryant	
26	Mike Beiras	
27	Otis Patrick	
28	P.J. Carey	
29	Donnie Reynolds	
30	Batboys (Jeff Crnich, Mike Thompson)	
31	Spyder Webb	
----	Mariners logo	

1988 Bellingham Mariners team issue

(Seattle Mariners, A)

		MT
Complete Set (33):		12.00
1	Jeff Hooper	
2	Erick Bryant	
3	Brian Wilkinson	
4	Dorian Daughty	
5	Kevin Reichardt	
6	Keith Helton	
7	John Hoffman	
8	Victor Mangual	
9	Chuck Carr	
10	Tom Peters	
11	Todd Haney	
12	Joe Georger	
13	Jeff Morrison	
14	Wade Taylor	
15	Ken Griffey, Jr.	
16	Spyder Webb	
17	Otis Patrick	
18	Mike Goff	
19	Brian Baldwin	
20	Tony Cayson	
21	Mike Sisco	
22	Mike McGuire	
23	Ruben Gonzalez	
24	Rick Sweet	
25	Daryl Burrus	
26	Scott Stoerck	
27	Fausto Ramirez	
28	Salty Parker	
29	Steve Beiksha	
30	Paul Togneri	
31	Corey Paul	
32	Chris Van Buren	
33	Team Photo/ Checklist	

1988 Grand Slam Beloit Brewers

(Milwaukee Brewers, A) (5,000 sets)

		MT
Complete Set (25):		6.00
1	Gomer Hodge	
2	Gary Robson	
3	Jim Poulin	
4	Frank Bolick	
5	Tim Raley	
6	Dan Adriance	
7	Charlie McGrew	
8	Juan Uribe	
9	Bob Simonson	
10	Mark Chapman	
11	Bob Sobczyk	
12	Bryan Foster	
13	Kent Hetrick	
14	Torricelli Tim	
15	Mike Guerrero	
16	Curt Krippner	
17	Tim Wahl	
18	Leonardo Perez	
19	Dave Nilsson	
20	Dan Peters	
21	Randy Moore	
22	Mike Whitlock	
23	Chris Cassels	
24	Steve Sparks	
25	Chris Johnson	

1988 Legoe Bend Bucks

(California Angels, A)

		MT
Complete Set (36):		16.00
1	Angel Carrasquillo	
2	Jeff Kipila	
3	Shawn Cunningham	
4	Jeff Oberdank	
5	Ramon Martinez	
6	Frank Brito	
7	Gary DiSarcina	
8	Steve Kirwin	
9	Jeff Kelso	
10	Jim Edmonds	
11	Dave Patrick	
12	Chris Threadgill	
13	Huascar Mateo	
14	Tim Taft	
15	Dave Sturdivant	
16	Enrique Tejeda	
17	Miguel Batista	
18	Bruce Vegely	
19	Dave Neal	
20	John Fritz	
21	Glenn Carter	
22	Mark Holzemer	
23	Todd James	
24	John Marchese	
25	Justin Martin	
26	Don Vidmar	
27	Don Long	
28	Howie Gershberg	
29	Rick Ingalls	
30	Derek Winchell	
31	Gary Murphy	
32	Paul List	
33	Shawn Cunningham, Gary DiSarcina, Jeff Oberdank	
34	Bucky Buck (Mascot/checklist on back)	
35	Charles Phillips	
----	Bucks logo	

1988 ProCards Billings Mustangs

(Cincinnati Reds, A)

		MT
Complete Set (31):		12.00
1802	David Keller	
1803	John Groninger	
1804	Jim Brune	
1805	Duane Mulville	
1806	Glenn Sutko	
1807	Scott Sellner	
1808	Michael Mulvaney	
1809	Doug Bond	
1810	Steve Reyes	
1811	Tony Terzariel	
1812	Dante Johnson	
1813	Danny Perozo	
1814	Scott Economy	
1815	John Groennert	
1816	Tomas Rodriguez	
1817	Steve McCarthy	
1818	Steve Foster	
1819	Brian Nichols	
1820	Brian Landy	
1821	Jerry Spradlin	
1822	Reggie Sanders	
1823	C.L. Thomas	
1824	Vicente Javier	
1825	Johnny Almaraz	
1826	Carl Stewart	
1827	Jim Hoff	
1828	Kurt Dempster	
1829	Michael Songini	
1830	Benny Colvard	
1831	Carl Nordstrom	
----	Checklist	

1988 Best Birmingham Barons

(Chicago White Sox, AA)

		MT
Complete Set (29):		5.00
1	Wayne Edwards	
2	Tony Biasucci	
3	Tom Drees	
4	Ray Chadwick	
5	Jim Markert	
6	Dave Wallwork	
7	Moe Drabowsky	
8	Rico Petrocelli	
9	Todd Trafton	
10	Tommy Tompson	
11	Pete Venturini	
12	Tom Forrester	
13	Dan Wagner	
14	Mark Davis	
15	Rick Pollack	
16	Carlos Martinez	
17	Rich Gaynor	
18	John Boling	
19	Daryl Smith	
20	Tony Menedez	
21	Dan Cronkright	
22	Matt Merullo	
23	Jerry Bertolani	
24	Craig Grebeck	
25	Willie Magallanes	
26	Doug Little	
27	Chuck Mount	
28	Kevin Renz	
29	Checklist/Hoover Metro Stadium	

1988 ProCards Boise Hawks

(Independent, A)

		MT
Complete Set (29):		5.00
	Checklist	
1605	John Bilello	
1606	Michael Tate	
1607	Wendell Bolar	
1608	Michael Moore	
1609	Christopher Gurchiek	
1610	James Qualls	
1611	Mike Shambaugh	
1612	Edward Holub	
1613	Christopher Shultis	
1614	Barry Griffin	
1615	Larry Lundeen	
1616	Jeff Mace	
1617	Earl Malone	
1618	Jerry Backus	
1619	Randy Janikowski	
1620	Michael Larson	
1621	Chuck Lavrusky	
1622	Michael Lomeli	
1623	Bill Wenrick	
1624	Charles Douglas	
1625	Mark Krumback	
1626	Joseph Mancini	
1627	Daren De Pew	
1628	Keven Bottenfield	
1629	Tim MacKinnon	
1630	Frank Jury	
1631	Robert Winterburn	
1632	Mal Fichman	

1988 ProCards Bristol Tigers

(Detroit Tigers, A)

		MT
Complete Set (32):		8.00
1862	Rick Mag	
1863	Carlos Maldonado	
1864	Doug Biggs	
1865	Tim Brader	
1866	Juan Estevez	
1867	Bob Frassa	
1868	Rusty Meacham	
1869	Julio Rosa	
1870	Ron Howard	
1871	Mike Davidson	
1872	Rich Rowland	
1873	Freddy Padilla	
1874	Jimmy Hayes	
1875	Chris Gollehon	
1876	Eric Shoup	
1877	Mike Rendina	
1878	Duane Walker	
1879	Blaine Rudolph	
1880	Mike Koller	
1881	Tom Aldrich	
1882	Marcos Bentances	
1883	Mick Delas	
1884	Bret Roach	
1885	Rico Brogna	
1886	Ed Ferm	
1887	Kurt Shea	
1888	Rob Thomas	
1889	Mike Jones	
1890	Paul Nozling	
1891	Tookie Spann	
1892	Benny Castillo	
----	Checklist	

The election of former players to the Hall of Fame does not always have an immediate upward effect on card values. The hobby market generally has done a good job of predicting those inductions and adjusting values over the course of several years.

1988 Buffalo Bisons team issue

(Pittsburgh Pirates, AAA) (Set issued as 14" x 23" perforated sheet. Blank-back single cards measure 3-1/2" x 4-1/4", production reported as 5,000)

	MT
Complete Set (8):	24.00

(1) Rocky Bridges
(2) Benny Distefano
(3) Dave Johnson
(4) Bryan Little
(5) Morris Madden
(6) Jim Reboulet
(7) Tom Romano
(8) Dorn Taylor

1988 ProCards Buffalo Bisons

(Pittsburgh Pirates, AAA)

	MT
Complete Set (31):	5.00

1464 Randy Kramer
1465 Felix Fermin
1466 Morris Madden
1467 Bob Patterson
1468 Dorn Taylor
1469 Stan Fansler
1470 Jim Reboulet
1471 Rico Rossy
1472 Dave Rucker
1473 Denny Gonzalez
1474 Tommy Gregg
1475 Bernie Tatis
1476 Dave Johnson
1477 Donald Palmer
1478 Rocky Bridges
1479 Jackie Brown
1480 Stan Cliburn
1481 Carlos Ledezma
1482 Kevin Hodge
1483 Dave Sax
1484 Scott Medvin
1485 Tom Romano
1486 Orestes Destrade
1487 Skeeter Barnes
1488 Tom Prince
1489 Benny Distefano
1490 Logan Easley
1491 Bryan Little
1492 Brett Gideon
1493 Pilot Field
---- Checklist

1988 CMC (TCMA) Buffalo Bisons

(Pittsburgh Pirates, AAA)

	MT
Complete Set (25):	5.00

1 Logan Easley
2 Stan Fansler
3 Brett Gideon
4 Dave Johnson
5 Randy Kramer
6 Morris Madden
7 Bob Patterson
8 Dave Rucker
9 Dorn Taylor
10 Scott Medvin
11 Benny Distefano
12 Tommy Gregg
13 Tom Romano
14 Bernie Tatis
15 Denny Gonzalez
16 Bryan Little
17 Jim Reboulet
18 Rico Rossy
19 Tom Prince
20 Orestes Destrade
21 Felix Fermin
22 Dave Sax
23 Skeeter Barnes
24 Stan Cliburn
25 Rocky Bridges

1988 ProCards Burlington Braves

(Atlanta Braves, A)

	MT
Complete Set (31):	6.00

1106 Lynn Robinson
1107 Carl Pointer-Jones
1108 Mike Stanton
1109 Chad Smith
1110 Matt Turner
1111 Pat Tilman
1112 Brian Murphy
1113 Jerald Frost
1114 Steve Glass
1115 Brian Champion
1116 Grady Little
1117 Brian Cummings
1118 Jim Lemasters
1119 Jeff Greene
1120 Jim Nowlin
1121 Dave Karasinski
1122 Jaime Cuesta
1123 Dave Grilone
1124 Albert Martin
1125 Sean Ross
1126 Rich Casarotti
1127 Rick Berg
1128 Eduardo Perez
1129 Andy Tomberlin
1130 Brian Hunter
1131 Gil Garrido, Jr.
1132 Brian Deak
1133 John Mitchell
1134 Jack Aker
1135 Paul Egins III (trainer)
---- Checklist

1988 ProCards Burlington Indians

(Cleveland Indians, A)

	MT
Complete Set (31):	9.00

1772 Brent Roberts
1773 Rick Falkner
1774 Lenny Gilmore
1775 Martin Eddy
1776 Randy Mazey
1777 Vince Barranco
1778 Sean Baron
1779 Jeff Bonchek
1780 Rouglas Odor
1781 Axel Castillo
1782 Todd Butler
1783 Carlos Mota
1784 Scott Allen
1785 Charles Alexander
1786 Mike Bucci
1787 Pedro Arias
1788 Pablo Gomez
1789 David Oliveras
1790 Doug Piatt
1791 Barry Blundin
1792 Jeff Mutis
1793 Mike Ashworth
1794 Bob Kairls
1795 Brett Merriman
1796 Greg McMichael
1797 Andre Halle
1798 Brian Johnson
1799 Dan Williams
1800 Mark Lewis
1801 Ray Borowicz
---- Checklist

Values shown are a national average. Some teams and players enjoy regional popularity which may affect market prices.

1988 Sport Pro Butte Copper Kings

(Texas Rangers, A)

	MT
Complete Set (29):	7.50

1 Mike Hamilton
2 Jim Hivizda
3 Greg Kuzman
4 Tim MacNeil
5 Robb Nen
6 Ken Penland
7 Carl Randle
8 Bill Schorr
9 Cedrick Shaw
10 Kyle Spencer
11 Kenny Shiozaki
12 Denny Tomori
13 Bill Losa
14 Jeff Frye
15 Rob Maurer
16 Dom Pierce
17 Joe Wardlow
18 Trey McCoy
19 Rod Morris
20 Mike Spear
21 Thayer Swain
22 Monty Farriss
23 Travis Law
24 Brad Fontes
25 Jeff Hainline
26 Steve Allen
27 Ev Cunningham
28 Ernie Rodriquez
29 Bump Wills

1988 ProCards Calgary Cannons

(Seattle Mariners, AAA)

	MT
Complete Set (28):	7.50

779 Rod Scurry
780 Darren Burroughs
781 Terry Taylor
782 Edgar Martinez
783 Mike Wishnevski
784 Brian Giles
785 Dave Cocrane
786 Erik Hanson
787 Doug Merrifield
788 Matt West
789 Dan Warthen
790 Roger Hansen
791 Jim Walker
792 Jay Baller
793 Paul Schneider
794 John Christensen
795 Mike Schooler
796 Dennis Powell
797 Rich Monteleone
798 Mike Watters
799 Greg Briley
800 Bill Plummer
801 Phil Ouellette
802 Nelson Simmons
803 Brick Smith
804 Mario Diaz
1550 Dave Hengel
---- Checklist

1988 CMC (TCMA) Calgary Cannons

(Seattle Mariners, AAA)

	MT
Complete Set (25):	6.00

1 Darren Burroughs
2 Paul Schneider
3 Rich Monteleone
4 Dennis Powell
5 Jay Baller
6 Mike Christ
7 Jim Walker
8 Matt West
9 Mike Schooler
10 Rod Scurry
11 Donell Nixon
12 Phil Ouellette
13 Greg Briley
14 Dave Cochrane
15 Brian Giles
16 Edgar Martinez
17 John Christensen
18 Dave Hengel
19 Nelson Simmons
20 Mike Wishnevski
21 Roger Hansen
22 Doug Merrifield
23 Mike Watters
24 Bill Plummer
25 Dan Warthen

1988 Cal League All-Stars

(Class A)

	MT
Complete Set (50):	100.00

1 Dave Patterson
2 Gil Heredia
3 Mark Leonard
4 Paul Blair
5 Eric Gunderson
6 Doug Robertson
7 Rich Aldrete
8 Montie Phillips
9 Ron Coomer
10 David Veres
11 Danny Fitzpatrick
12 Tim McIntosh
13 Robert Jones
14 Shon Ashley
15 Sandy Guerrero
16 Charlie Montoyo
17 Ruben Escalera
18 Rob Derksen
19 Dave Huppert
20 Joe Strong
21 Jim Allison
22 Joe Ortiz
23 Matt Bohn (umpire)
24 Dick Fossa (umpire)
25 Joe Gagliardi (League president)
26 Ken Griffey Jr.
27 Jim Bowie
28 Ted Williams
29 Keith Helton
30 Jim Blueberg
31 Colin Charland
32 Ruben Amaro, Jr.
33 Scott Cerny
34 Chris Cron
35 Bill Lachemann (Manager)
36 Gary Ruby (Coach)
37 Mike Randle
38 John Eccles
39 Marty Lanoux
40 Jim Williams
41 Ricky Bones
42 Rafael Chavez
43 Paul Faries
44 Dave Hollins
45 Warren Newson
46 Jeff D. Brown
47 Jose Vizcaino
48 Adam Brown
49 Ken Franek (umpire)
50 Red Morrow (umpire)

1988 Cal Cards California League All-Stars

(A)

	MT
Complete Set (56):	17.50

1 Jose Offerman
2 Eric Karros
3 Mark Merchant
4 Willie Banks
5 Lance Rice
6 Carlos Capellan
7 Jose Valentin
8 Dave Jacas
9 Braulio Castillo
10 Mike Humphreys
11 Wiley Lee
12 Ruben Gonzalez
13 Johnny Ard
14 Mike Goff
15 Jeff Hartsock
16 James Wray
17 Doug Simons
18 Jerry Brooks
19 Eddie Pye
20 Andy Skeels
21 Sean Snedeker
22 Steve Finken
23 Tim Johnson
24 Guy Conti
25 Scott Ullger
26 Tim Terrio
27 Bill Weiss
28 Don Drysdale
29 Charlie Montoyo
30 Jim Jones
31 Stan Royer
32 Bobby Jones
33 Darren Lewis
34 Gary Borg
35 Steve Hecht
36 Gary Nalls
37 John Dalfanz
38 Chris George
39 Mike Ignasiak
40 Kevin Meier
41 Joe Strong
42 Shawn Barton
43 Mark Dewey
44 Bill Savarino
45 John Jaha
46 Joe Kmak
47 Steve Lienhard
48 Greg Sparks
49 Duane Espy
50 Todd Oakes
51 Scott Wilson
52 Brent Howard
53 Erik DeSonnaville
54 Bob Brooks
55 George Ulrich
56 Joe Gagliardi

1988 Ballpark Cape Cod Prospects

(Summer amateur league for college prospects) (6,500 sets reported produced)

	MT
Complete Set (30):	135.00

1 Tom Drell
2 Mark Johnson
3 Jimmie Jones
4 Jeff Bagwell
5 Robert Gralewski
6 Dennis Burbank
7 Brian Shabosky
8 Jeff Litzinger
9 Thomas Raffo
10 Bob Kiser
11 John Valentin
12 Kevin Morton
13 Jesse Lewis
14 Frank Thomas
15 Chuck Knoblauch
16 Maurice Vaughn
17 Mike Mordecai
18 Stephen P. O'Donnell
19 Harry Ball
20 Brian Turang
21 Brewster Whitecaps team card
22 Orleans Cardinals team card
23 Chatham A's team card
24 Cotuit Kettleers team card
25 Wareham Gatemen team card
26 Bourne Braves team card
27 Falmouth Commodores team card
28 Yarmouth-Dennis Red Sox team card
29 Harwich Mariners team card
30 Hyannis Mets

1988 P & L Cape Cod League

The summer league for college stars spawned this 186-card issue which featured some of the 1990s hottest stars in their pre-professional days. The 2-1/2" x 3-1/2" cards feature color player poses on front, with Cape Cod League in red at top. The player's name and team are in black at bottom. Backs are printed in black-and-white and have biographical data, college highlights and a card number. Cards are arranged numerically by team, with between 16 and 20 cards per team. Production was reported as 5,000 sets.

MT
Complete Set (186): 120.00
BOURNE BRAVES
1 Mark Johnson
2 John Valente
3 Warren Sawkiw
4 Ed Therrien
5 Lenny Richardson
6 Paul Ciaglo
7 Alejandro Alvarez
8 Rich Cordani
9 Chris Snyder
10 Mike Kelly
11 Keith Wiley
12 Brian Moure
13 David Flynn
14 Ed Cooney
15 Joe Conti
16 Joe Delli Carri
17 Eamon Kingman
18 Tom Drell
19 Joe Logan
20 Jeff Borgese
HARWICH MARINERS
21 John Byington
22 Brian Turang
23 Travis Tarchione
24 Mike Turschke
25 Rick Hirtensteiner
26 Pete Tsotsos
27 Harrison Ball
28 Larry Russell
29 Alan Zinter
30 Brian Ahern
31 Chris Schaefer
32 Mike McNary
33 Chris Ebright
34 Darryl Scott
35 Russell Springer
36 Rafael Nova
YARMOUTH-DENNIS RED SOX
37 Ron Raper
38 Brian Shehan
39 Dave Wrona
40 Doug Shields
41 Stephen O'Donnell
42 Mike Mordecai
43 Steve Parris
44 Mike Zimmerman
45 Mitch Hannahs
46 Nolan Lane
47 Kurt Olson
48 Peter Altenberger
49 Rick Strickland
50 Bill Klenoshek
51 Eric Wedge
52 Larry Owens
53 Denny Neagle
54 Preston Woods
55 Jim Dougherty
56 John Davis (Chatam Athletics on card front)
CHATHAM ATHLETICS
57 Jeff Bagwell
58 John Riginos
59 Mark Sweeney
60 Scott Odierno
61 Michael LeBlanc
62 Mike Hinde
63 Scott Shockey
64 Brian Dour
65 Matt Dunbar
66 Dave Swartzbaugh
67 Curry Harden
68 Don Hutchinson
69 Mike Gardella
70 James Jones
71 Colin Ryan
72 Bob Rivell
FALMOUTH COMMODORES
73 Duane O'Hara
74 Bobby Kiser
75 Mike Trombley
76 Jon Farrell
77 Mark LaRosa
78 Scott Erwin
79 Tom Raffo
80 George Tsamis
81 Alan Botkin
82 Bob McCreary
83 Jeff Cerqueira
84 Jim Jimaki
85 Mike McNamara
86 Tom Hickox
87 Scott Miller
88 Gary Scott
89 Brian Specyalski
90 Ron Frazier
91 Marcelino Sellas
92 Craig Cala
WAREHAM GATEMEN
93 Mo Vaughn
94 Chuck Knoblauch
95 Dana Brown
96 Mike Weimerskirch
97 Darron Cox
98 Kevin Long
99 Kevin King
100 Dan Arendas
101 Burke Masters
102 Pat Leinan
103 Troy Bradford
104 Rich Samplinski
105 Sam Colarusso
106 John Thoden
107 Randy Pryor
108 John Kosenski
109 Keith Langston
110 Jody Hurst
111 Kevin Castleberry
112 Kyle Sanborn
ORLEANS CARDINALS
113 Casey Waller
114 Brian Bark
115 Chris Barnes
116 Jesse Levis
117 George Sells
118 Tom Williams
119 Todd Mayo
120 Mathew Howard
121 Sam Taylor
122 Mike Grimes
123 Scott Centala
124 Drew Comeau
125 J.T. Snow
126 Frank Thomas
127 Jason Klonoski
128 Marty Durkin
129 Tim Lata
130 Brian Barnes
131 Sam Drake
HYANNIS METS
132 Tom Hardgrove
133 Lance Jones
134 Kirk Dressendorfer
135 Brad Myers
136 Gordon Tipton
137 Terry Taylor
138 John Valentin
139 Kevin Morton
140 Ed Horowitz
141 Dave Tollison
142 Ricky Kimball
143 Tim Williams
144 Tony Kounas
145 Jeromy Burnitz
146 Mark Smith
147 Brad Beanblossom
148 Stewart Keyes
149 Will Vespe
BREWSTER WHITECAPS
150 Henry Manning
151 Dennis Burbank
152 Darryl Vice
153 Erik Bennett
154 Bob Gralewski
155 Michael Boyan
156 F.P. Santangelo
157 Bob Allen
158 Michael Myers
159 Andrew Albrecht
160 Bob Fazekas
161 Chris Slattery
162 Scott Morehouse
163 Robbie Katzaroff
164 Chris Jones
165 Bret Donovan
166 Tucker Hammagren
167 Dave Staton
COUIT KETTLEERS
168 J.T. Bruett
169 Jeff Kent
170 Troy Buckley
171 Garrett Teel
172 Mark Carper
173 Joe Kelly
174 Michael Wiseman
175 Howard Prager
176 Tim Salmon
177 Dan Wilson
178 James Hoog
179 Trent Turner
180 David Krol
181 Steven Treadway
182 Pat Varni
183 Troy Chacon
184 Roger Miller
185 Jeff Litzinger
186 Brian Shabosky

1988 Star Carolina League ad card

League logo on front, backs advertises Star sets

MT
8.00
(unclear distribution)

1988 Star Carolina League All-Stars

(Class A)

MT
Complete Set (40): 9.00
1 Jay Ward
2 Mike Hart
3 Stan Belinda
4 Royal Clayton
5 Scott Cooper
6 Brian DuBois
7 Mike Eberle
8 Andy Hall
9 Chris Howard
10 Dean Kelley
11 Tim Kirk
12 Joe Marchese
13 Jim Orsag
14 Julio Peguero
15 John Ramos
16 Enrique Rios
17 Randy Strijek
18 Junior Vizcaino
19 Bernie Williams
20 Bob Zupcic
21 Glenn Adams
22 Pete Alborano
23 Beau Allred
24 Kevin Bearse
25 Mike Bell
26 Luis Cruz
27 Butch Garcia
28 Phil Harrison
29 Allen Liebert
30 Kelly Mann
31 Kent Mercker
32 Rick Morris
33 Charles Ogden
34 Dave Plumb
35 Greg Smith
36 Rob Swain
37 Theron Todd
38 Mike Twardoski
39 Danny Weems
40 Mike Westbrook

Suffix letters following a card number indicate a variation card.

1988 ProCards Cedar Rapids Reds

(Cincinnati Reds, A)

MT
Complete Set (31): 5.00
1136 Don Buchheister
1137 Greg Simpson
1138 Bill Dodd
1139 Mike Moscrey
1140 Sandy Krume
1141 Chico Fernandez
1142 Freddy Benavides
1143 Gary Denbo
1144 Marc Bombard
1145 Bruce Colson
1146 Reggie Jefferson
1147 Pete Beeler
1148 Rich Sapienza
1149 Ramon Sambo
1150 Steve Davis
1151 Jeff Forney
1152 Greg Lonigro
1153 Doug Eastman
1154 Jim Brune
1155 Eddie Rush
1156 Brad Brusky
1157 Scott Scudder
1158 Carl Nordstrom
1159 Butch Henry
1160 Sam Chavez
1161 Bud Curran
1162 Darrell Rodgers
1163 Milton Hill
1164 Mike Malinak
1165 Jim Bishop
---- Checklist

1988 ProCards Charleston Rainbows

(San Diego Padres, A)

MT
Complete Set (30): 5.00
1193 Willie Forbes
1194 Tony Pellegrino
1195 Jim Wasem
1196 David Bond
1197 Charles Hillemann
1198 Jose Valentin
1199 Mike Myers
1200 Osvaldo Sanchez
1201 Rafael Valdez
1202 Mike King
1203 Guillermo Velazquez
1204 Monte Brooks
1205 Mark Kleven
1206 Todd Hansen
1207 Keith Harrison
1208 Darrin Reichle
1209 Todd Torchia
1210 Omar Olivares
1211 Doug Brocail
1212 Gary Lance
1213 Jay Estrada
1214 Tony Lewis
1215 Saul Soltero
1216 Reggie Farmer
1217 Bob Lutticken
1218 Jaime Moreno
1219 Jack Krol
1220 Nelson Silverio
1221 Tim Barker
---- Checklist

1988 Best Charleston Wheelers

(Chicago Cubs, A)

MT
Complete Set (28): 5.00
1 Matt Walbeck
2 Brad Mills
3 Greg Mahlberg
4 Scott Taylor
5 Mike Reeder
6 Lee Grimes
7 Eric Perry
8 Steve Owens
9 Alex Arias
10 Darren Eggleston
11 Tony Duenas
12 Jay Eddings
13 Patrick Gomez
14 Henry Gomez
15 John Gardner
16 Marcus Lopez
17 Matt Cakora
18 Don Cohoon
19 DeWayne Coleman
20 Braz Davis
21 Harry Shelton
22 Fernando Ramsey
23 Elio Jose
24 Frank Campos
25 Ray Mullino
26 Nick Rameriez
27 Bob Grimes
28 Checklist/Wheelers Stadium

1988 Star Charlotte Rangers

(Texas Rangers, A) (Rey Sanchez is scarce late-issue card)

MT
Complete Set, w/Sanchez (24): 140.00
Partial Set, no Sanchez (23): 90.00
1 Rick Bernardo
2 Brian Bohanon
3 Omar Brewer
4 Phil Bryant
5 Paco Burgos
6 Rufus Ellis
7 Darrin Garner
8 Juan Gonzalez
9 Bill Haselman
10 Jonathan Hurst
11 Mark Kramer
12 Adam Lamle
13 Darren Loy
14 Barry Manuel
15 Terry Mathews
16 Jeff Mays
17 Darren Niethammer
18 Dean Palmer
19 Mark Petkovsek
20 Lino Rivera
21 Wayne Rosenthal
22 Tony Scruggs
23 Sammy Sosa
---- Rey Sanchez

1988 Charlotte Knights team issue

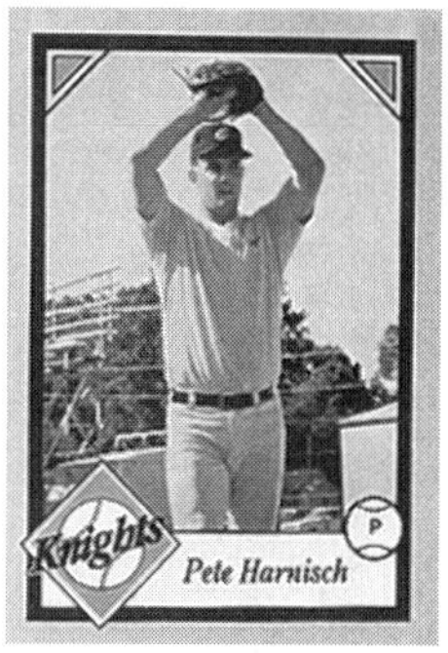

(Baltimore Orioles, AA)

MT
Complete Set (25): 10.00
1 Brian Householder
2 Bob Williams
3 Butch Davis
4 Kevin Price
5 Tim Dulin
6 Rob Walton
7 Jim O'Dell
8 Jeff Tackett
9 Joe Jarrell
10 Jeff Wood
11 John Posey
12 Craig Chamberlain
13 Rocky Cusak
14 Mike Pazik
15 Rafel Skeete
16 Jim Daniel
17 Paul Thorpe
18 Pete Harnisch
19 Jerry Holtz
20 Gordon Dillard
21 Dana Smith
22 Ty Nichols
23 Greg Biagini
24 Curt Brown
25 Sherwin Cijntje

1988 Best Chattanooga Lookouts

(Cincinnati Reds, AA)

MT
Complete Set (26): 5.00
1 Timber Mead
2 Chris Hammond
3 Keith Brown
4 Joe Lazor
5 Rich Bombard
6 Chris Jones
7 Tony DeFrancasco
8 Hedi Vargas
9 Keith Lockhart
10 Mark Germann
11 Darrell Pruitt
12 Don Wakamatsu
13 Brian Finley
14 Tom Runnells
15 Tim Deitz
16 Gino Minutelli
17 Joe Bruno
18 Phil Dale
19 Jim Jefferson
20 Lary Sorenson
21 Mike Smith
22 Jeff Richardson
23 Bernie Walker
24 Darren Riley
25 Angelo Nunley
26 Logo/checklist

1988 Chattanooga Lookouts Legends #1 team issue

MT
Complete Set (32): 28.00
(1) Chris Bando
(2) Juan Bonilla
(3) Joe Charboneau
(4) Pat Corrales
(5) Ellis Clary
(6) Gil Coan
(7) Jeff Cox
(8) Sonny Dixon
(9) Lee Elia
(10) Joe Engel
(11) Engel Stadium
(12) Cal Ermer
(13) Don Grate
(14) Roy Hawes
(15) "Spook" Jacobs
(16) Jim Kaat
(17) Matt Keough
(18) Harmon Killebrew
(19) Rene Lacheman
(20) Hillis Layne
(21) Jesse Levan
(22) Frank Lucchesi
(23) Jackie Mitchell
(24) Louis "Bobo" Newsom
(25) Sal Rende
(26) Kevin Rhomberg
(27) Costen Shockley
(28) Al Sima
(29) Buck Varner
(30) Gene Verble
(31) Junior Wooten
(32) Checklist

1988 Star Clearwater Phillies

(Philadelphia Phillies, A) (#15 not issued)

MT
Complete Set (27): 5.00
1 Steve Bates
2 Cliff Brantley
3 Rod Brunelle
4 Pete Callas
5a Chris Calvert
5b Luis Iglesias (misnumbered)
6 Ramon Caraballo
7 Fred Christopher
8 Garry Clark
9 Todd Crosby
10 Shawn Dantzler
11 Kevin Fynan
12 Jason Grimsley
13 Jeff Grotewold
14 Todd Howey
16 Steve Kirkpatrick
17 Chris Limbach
18 Pete Maldonado
19 Trey McCall
20 Scott Reaves
21 Mark Sims
22 Steve Scarsone
23 Brad Smith
24 Tim Taft
25 Royal Thomas
26 Travis Walden

1988 ProCards Clinton Giants

(S.F. Giants, A)

MT
Complete Set (29): 6.00
693 John Vuz
694 Steve Lienhard
695 Rod Beck
696 Steve Connelly
697 Tom Hostetler
698 Scott Nelson
699 Mark Poling
700 Bill Carlson
701 Juan Guerrero
702 Jimmy Terrill
703 Jim Anderson
704 Mark Owens
705 Andres Santana
706 Todd Miller
707 Craig Colbert
708 Erik Johnson
709 Mike Ham
710 Tony Michalak
711 Mark Dewey
712 Bill Evers
713 Mike Stanfield
714 Robert Lucero
715 Jamie Cooper
716 Elanis Westbrooks
717 Jeff Morris
718 Tom Ealy
719 Mike Villa
720 Lonnie Phillips
---- Checklist

1988 ProCards Colorado Springs Sky Sox

(Cleveland Indians, AAA)

MT
Complete Set (25): 5.00
1522 John Stefero
1523 Don Lovell
1524 Reggie Williams
1525 Randy Washington
1526 Mike Brown
1527 Tommy Hinzo
1528 Paul Zuvella
1529 Charles Scott
1530 Rick Peterson
1531 Jeff Kaiser
1532 Ron Tingley
1533 Joe Skalski
1534 Domingo Ramos
1535 Keith Bennett
1536 Aurelio Rodriguez
1537 Darrel Akerfelds
1538 Don Gordon
1539 Steve Ciszczon
1540 Reggie Ritter
1541 Terry Francona
1542 Jon Perlman
1543 Luis Medina
1544 Mark Higgins
1545 Rod Allen
1546 Steve Swisher
1547 Eddie Williams
1548 Ron Mathis
1549 Rick Rodriguez
---- Checklist

1988 CMC (TCMA) Colorado Springs Sky Sox

(Cleveland Indians, AAA)

MT
Complete Set (29): 5.00
1 Darrel Akerfelds
2 MIke Brown
3 Don Gordon
4 Jeff Kaiser
5 Ron Mathis
6 Jon Perlman
7 Reggie Ritter
8 Rick Rodrigez
9 Charlie Scott
10 Joe Skalski
11 John Stefano
12 Ron Tingley
13 Mark Higgins
14 Tommy Hinzo
15 Don Lovell
16 Domingo Ramos
17 Eddie Williams
18 Paul Zuvella
19 Rod Allen
20 Terry Francona
21 Luis Medina
22 Randy Washington
23 Reggie Williams
24 Steve Swisher
25 Aurelio Rodriguez

1988 Grand Slam Columbia Mets

(N.Y. Mets, A) (5,000 sets)

MT
Complete Set (28): 5.00
1 Butch Hobson
2 Pete Bauer
3 Rick Durant
4 Rocky Elli
5 Eric Hillman
6 Steve Larose
7 Juan Marina
8 James McAnarney
9 Mike Miller
10 Kevin Ponder
11 Julio Valera
12 Javier Gonzalez
13 David Lau
14 Alex Diaz
15 Alex Jimenez
16 David Joiner
17 Rodney Murrell
18 Fred Hina
19 Manny Mantrana
20 Scott Spoolstra
21 Rob Lemle
22 Terry McDaniel
23 Danny Naughton
24 Jaime Roseboro
25 Scott Jaster
26 Chris Donnels
28 Joel Horlen

1988 Best Columbus Astros

(Houston Astros, AA)

MT
Complete Set (28): 5.00
1 Charlie Kerfeld
2 Don Dunster
3 Terry Wells
4 Glenn Spagnola
5 Brian Meyer
6 Ken Crew
7 Doug Givler
8 Jose Vargas
9 Kyle Todd
10 Juan Lopez
11 David Rohde
12 Dan Walters
13 John Elliott
14 Rich Johnson
15 Larry Lasky
16 Jeff Edwards
17 Blaise Ilsley
18 Tom Funk
19 Carlo Colombino
20 Fred Gladding
21 Gary Cooper
22 Terry Green
23 Troy Afenir
24 Dayton Preston
25 Tom Wiedenbauer
26 Clavin James
27 Norman Brock
28 Team photo/checklist

1988 Police Columbus Clippers

(N.Y. Yankees, AAA)

MT
Complete Set (25): 9.00
(1) Chris Alvarez
(2) Jay Buhner
(3) Pat Clements
(4) Casey Close
(5) Pete Dalena
(6) Alvaro Espinoza
(7) Bill Fulton
(8) Bob Geren
(9) Matt Harrison
(10) Mike Kinnunen
(11) Rick Langford
(12) Jeff Moronko
(13) Hal Morris
(14) Jamie Nelson
(15) Scott Nielson
(16) Clay Parker
(17) Bert Pena
(18) Hipolito Pena
(19) Eric Schmidt
(20) Steve Shields
(21) Cliff Speck
(22) Randy Velarde
(23) Turner Ward
(24) Coaches/trainer (Champ Summers, Kevin Rand, Don Rowe)
(25) Managers (George Sisler, Bucky Dent)

1988 ProCards Columbus Clippers

(N.Y. Yankees, AAA)

MT
Complete Set (29): 8.00
303 Bob Geren
304 Glenn Sherlock
305 Jamie Nelson
306 Bucky Dent
307 Field staff
308 Rick Langford
309 Clay Parker
310 Scott Nielsen
311 Cliff Speck
312 Bill Fulton
313 Eric Schmidt
314 Steve Shields
315 Hipolito Pena
316 Mike Kinnunen
317 Matt Harrison
318 Pat Clements
319 Rob Lambert
320 Alvaro Espinoza
321 Pete Dalena
322 Berto Pena
323 Chris Alvarez
324 Randy Velarde
325 Casey Close
326 Max Ward
327 Hal Morris
328 Jeff Moronko
329 Jay Buhner
330 Team photo
---- Checklist

1988 CMC (TCMA) Columbus Clippers

(N.Y. Yankees, AAA)

MT
Complete Set (26): 5.00
1 Pat Clements
2 Clay Parker
3 Scott Nielsen
4 Bill Fulton
5 Matt Harrison
6 Steve Shields
7 Hipolito Pena
8 Eric Schmidt
9 Mike Kinnuenen
10 Rick Langford
11 Bob Geren
12 Jamie Nelson
13 Berton Pena
14 Rob Lambert
15 Alvaro Espinoza
16 Pete Dalena
17 Randy Velarde
18 Jeff Moronko
19 Turner Ward
20 Hal Morris
21 Casey Close
22 Cliff Speck
23 Jay Buhner
24 Chris Alvarez
25 Bucky Dent
26 Governor's Cup

1988 ProCards Denver Zephyrs

(Milwaukee Brewers, AAA)

MT
Complete Set (30): 5.00
1250 Todd Jackson
1251 Alex Madrid
1252 Peter Kolb
1253 German Rivera
1254 Bill Mooneyham
1255 Darryel Walters
1256 Kiki Diaz
1257 Tom Filer
1258 Paul Mirabella
1259 Don August
1260 John Miglio
1261 Keith Smith
1262 Ronn Reynolds
1263 Brad Komminsk
1264 Duffy Dyer
1265 Tim Watkins
1266 Steve Stanicek
1267 Billy Jo Robidoux
1268 Charlie O'Brien
1269 Pete Kendrick
1270 Jay Aldrich
1271 Billy Bates
1272 Mark Ciardi
1273 Tim Pyznarski
1274 Darryl Hamilton
1275 Mark Knudson
1276 Mike Konderla
1277 Lavell Freeman
1278 Todd Brown
---- Checklist

1988 CMC (TCMA) Denver Zephyrs

(Milwaukee Brewers, AAA)

MT
Complete Set (25): 5.00
1 Mark Knudson
2 Mike Konderla

3 Alex Madrid
4 John Miglio
5 Paul Mirabella
6 Tim Watkins
7 Jay Aldrich
8 Don August
9 Mark Ciardi
10 Tom Filer
11 Tim Pyznarski
12 German Rivera
13 Billy Jo Robidoux
14 Keith Smith
15 Charlie O'Brien
16 Ronn Reynolds
17 Billy Bates
18 Kiki Diaz
19 Todd Brown
20 Lavell Freeman
21 Brad Komminsk
22 Steve Stanicek
23 Darryel Walters
24 Darryl Hamilton
25 Duffy Dyer

1988 Star Dunedin Blue Jays

(Toronto Blue Jays, A)

	MT
Complete Set (25):	10.00

1 Francisco Cabrera
2 Tony Castillo
3 Wayne Davis
4 Jose Diaz
5 Richard DePastino
6 Lindsay Foster
7 Peter Geist
8 Darren Hall
9 Pat Hentgen
10 Vince Horsman
11 Shawn Jeter
12 Steve Mumaw
13 Pedro Munoz
14 Paul Rodgers
15 Earl Sanders
16 Jerry Schunk
17 Jason Townley
18 James Tracy
19 Darrin Wade
20 Bob Watts
21 Mark Whiten
22 Bob Wishnevski
23 Julian Yan
24 Mark Young

1988 Star Durham Bulls (Blue)

(Atlanta Braves, A) (The no-number Costner blue card was issued late at the request of the ball club and sold as singles.)

	MT
Complete Set, no Costner (24):	10.00
Complete Set, blue Costner (25):	15.00

1 Michael Bell
2 Scott Bohlke
3 David Butts
4 Jim Czajowski
5 Jeff Dodig
6 Mike Fowler
7 Ted Holcomb
8 Cesar Jimenez
9 Dodd Johnson
10 Rich Longuil
11 Phil Maldinado
12 Rich Maloney
13 Paul Marak
14 Kent Mercker
15 Rick Morris
16 Kenneth Pennington
17 Dave Plumb
18 Ellis Roby
19 Doug Stockam
20 Mike Stoker
21 Theron Todd
22 Lee Upshaw
23 Danny Weems
24 Walt Williams
---- Kevin Costner (blue)

1988 Star Durham Bulls (Orange)

(Atlanta Braves, A)

	MT
Complete Set (26):	10.00

1 Michael Bell
2 Scott Bohlke
3 David Butts
4 Jim Czajowski
5 Jeff Dodig
6 Mike Fowler
7 Ted Holcomb
8 Cesar Jimenez
9 Dodd Johnson
10 Rich Longuil
11 Phil Maldonado
12 Rich Maloney
13 Paul Marak
14 Kent Mercker
15 Rick Morris
16 Kenneth Pennington
17 Dave Plumb
18 Ellis Roby
19 Doug Stockam
20 Mike Stoker
21 Theron Todd
22 Lee Upshaw
23 Danny Weems
24 Walt Williams
25 Buddy Bailey
26 Kevin Costner

1988 ProCards Eastern League All-Stars

(Class AA)

	MT
Complete Set (52):	7.00

1 Dave Eiland
2 Kevin Maas
3 Hensley Meulens
4 Dana Ridenour
5 Andy Stankiewicz
6 Dan Dimascio
7 Shawn Holman
8 Tobey Lovullo
9 Julius McDougal
10 Cesar Mejia
11 Rob Richie
12 Delwyn Young
13 Jeff Cook
14 Kevin Davis
15 Dimas Gutierrez
16 Jeff King
17 Larry Melton
18 Paul Wilmet
19 Jose Birriel
20 Mike Carista
21 Ed Estrada
22 Todd Pratt
23 John Roberts
24 Luis Vasquez
25 Joe Girardi
26 Mike Harkey
27 Bryan House
28 Hector Villanueva
29 Jerome Walton
30 Dean Wilkins
31 Tony Brown
32 Greg Edge
33 Warren Magee
34 Chuck Malone
35 Jeff Hull
36 Ricky Rojas
37 Omar Vizquel
38 Jim Wilson
39 Mark Howie
40 Scott Jordan
41 Tom Lampkin
42 Mike Poehl
43 Casey Webster
44 Kevin Wickander
45 Dave Trembley
46 Harold Williams
47 Jim Essian
48 Grant Jackson
49 Brian McCann
50 Brian Allard
51 Brian Graham
52 Mike Hargrove

1988 ProCards Edmonton Trappers

(California Angels, AAA)

	MT
Complete Set (31):	9.00

555 Joe Redfield
556 Jack Lazorko
557 Vance Lovelace
558 Jim Eppard
559 Doug Davis
560 Joe Johnson
561 Chico Walker
562 Marty Reed
563 Chuck Hernandez
564 Junior Noboa
565 Frank Dimichele
566 Phil Venturino
567 Mike Cook
568 Barry Dacus
569 Terry Clark
570 Mark Doran
571 Stan Holmes
572 Brian Brady
573 Kevin King
574 Kent Anderson
575 Edwin Marquez
576 Dante Bichette
577 Bobby Miscik
578 Pete Coachman
579 Darrell Miller
580 Tom Kotchman
581 Urbano Lugo
582 Miguel Alicea
583 Craig Gerber
584 Al Olson
---- Checklist

1988 CMC (TCMA) Edmonton Trappers

(California Angels, AAA)

	MT
Complete Set (25):	9.00

1 Terry Clark
2 Mike Cook
3 Jack Lazorko
4 Vance Lovelace
5 Bryan Harvey
6 Urbano Lugo
7 Joe Johnson
8 Philip Venturino
9 Marty Reed
10 Barry Dacus
11 Miguel Alicea
12 Darrell Miller
13 Pete Coachman
14 Stan Holmes
15 Bob Miscik
16 Brian Brady
17 Kent Anderson
18 Doug Davis
19 Edwin Marquez
20 Joe Redfield
21 Jim Eppard
22 Tom Kotchman
23 Dante Bichette
24 Mark Doran
25 Kevin King

1988 Elmira Pioneers team issue - red

(Boston Red Sox, A)

	MT
Complete Set (30):	7.00

1 Pioneers logo
2 Alberto Pratts
3 Steve Michael
4 Scott Taylor
5 Bernie Dzafic
6 Dan Kite
7 John Dolan
8 Peter Estrada
9 Tim Stange
10 Al Sanders
11 Carlos Rivera
12 Luis Dorante
13 John Flaherty
14 Pedro Matilla
15 David Monegro
16 Lou Munoz
17 Tim Naehring
18 Julio Rosario
19 Willie Tatum
20 Al Thornton
21 Chris Whitehead
22 Terry Marrs
23 Mickey Rivers Jr.
24 Larry Scannell
25 John Spencer
26 Brian Warfel
27 Bill Limoncelli
28 John Post
29 Dennis Robarge
30 Clyde Smoll

1988 Elmira Pioneers team issue - blue

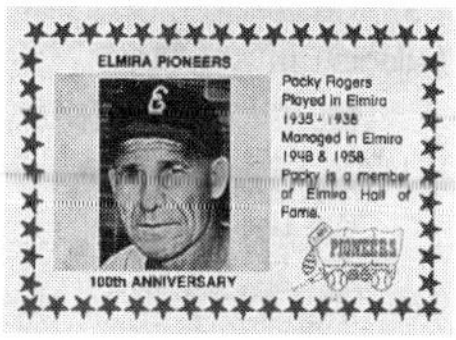

(Boston Red Sox, A) (Reported 2,000 sets produced)

	MT
Complete Set (12):	95.00

(1) Reggie Harris
(2) Tony Mosley
(3) Mickey Pina
(4) Ronnie Richardson
(5) Packy Rogers
(6) Tony Romero
(7) Julio Rosario
(8) Brian Warfel
(9) Bob Zupcic
(10) Team Photo (1941)
(11) Team photo (1967)
(12) Team photo (1979)

1988 Best El Paso Diablos

(Milwaukee Brewers, AA) (Besides the regular issue this set was also produced in a "Platinum" edition of 1,300 numbered sets. The limited edition cards have silver and black fronts and blue backs.)

	MT
Complete Set (30):	20.00
Complete Set, Platinum:	40.00

1 Gary Sheffield
2 Donald Scott
3 Daniel Scarpetta
4 Jamie Brisco
5 George Canale
6 Dave Machemer
7 Ramon Serna
8 Luis Castillo
9 Bill Mooneyham
10 Paul Lindblad
11 Jim Rowe
12 Matias Carrillo
13 Alan Cartwright
14 Robert DeWolf
15 Mark Ambrose
16 Andy Anderson
17 Barry Bass
18 Bradley Wheeler
19 Fred Williams
20 Gregory Vaughn
21 Jeffrey Peterek
22 Edward Puig
23 Angel Rodriguez
24 Adrian Meagher
25 Joseph Mitchell
26 Mario Monico
27 Rob Hicks
28 James Hunter
29 Frankie Mattox
30 Checklist/Dudley Dome

1988 Best Eugene Emeralds

(K.C. Royals, A)

	MT
Complete Set (30):	6.00

1 Bob Hamblin (Hamelin)
2 Steve Hoeme
3 Greg Harvey
4 Steve Otto
5 Bill Drohan
6 Hector Wagner
7 Kyle Irvin
8 Jim Smith
9 Brad Hopper
10 Randy Vaughn
11 Joel Johnston
12 David Rolls
13 Rob Buchanan
14 Jeff Hulse
15 Fred Russell
16 Jeff Garber
17 Kelvin Davis
18 Ron Collins
19 Bill Gardner
20 Steve Preston
21 Karl Drezek
22 Bobby Holley
23 Frank Henderson
24 John Gilcrist
25 Derek Sholl
26 Gerald Ingram
27 Milt Richardson
28 Frankie Watson
29 Keith Shibata
30 Logo/checklist

1988 ProCards Fayetteville Generals

(Detroit Tigers, A)

	MT
Complete Set (28):	22.00

1079 Keith Nicholson
1080 Glenn Belcher
1081 Steve Pegues
1082 Andy Toney
1083 Luis Melendez
1084 Larry Coker
1085 Mark Adler
1086 Jose Ramos
1087 Robinson Garces
1088 Steve Parascand
1089 Chuck Duquette
1090 Zack Doster
1091 Duben Bello
1092 Charles Steward
1093 Felix Liriano
1094 Travis Fryman
1095 Dave Richards
1096 Ron Cook
1097 Chris Schnurbursh
1098 Randy Luciani
1099 Kevin Camilli
1100 Miguel Murphy
1101 Liliano Castro
1102 Bill Henderson
1103 Michael Wilkins
1104 Leon Roberts
1105 Mike DeLao
---- Checklist

1988 Star Florida State League All-Stars

(Class A)

	MT
Complete Set (52):	10.00

1 John Shoemaker
2 Felipe Alou
3 Keith Bodie
4 Doug Cinnella
5 Scott Diez
6 Kip Gross
7 Dave Hansen
8 Randy Hennis
9 Nels Jacobsen
10 Chris Limbach
11 Luis Martinez
12 Todd McClure
13 Brian Morrison
14 Bob Natal
15 Chris Nichting
16 Geronimo Pena
17 Fritz Polka
18 Karl Rhodes
19 Homar Rojas
20 Miguel Santana
21 Mike Simms
22 Greg Talamantez
23 John Vander Wal
24 Juan Villaneuva
25 Mike White
26 Masahiro Yamaoto
27 Buck Showalter
28 John Lipon
29 Russ Meyer
30 Luis Silverio
31 Phil Clark
32 Milt Cuyler
33 Jose Diaz
34 Carlos Escalera
35 Greg Everson
36 Blame Fox
37 Cornelio Garcia
38 Darrin Garner
39 Mike Hansen
40 Brent Knackert
41 Adam Lamle
42 Richie LeBlanc
43 Ravelo Manzanillo
44 Kevin Mmahat
45 Tony Morrison
46 Livio Padilla
47 Dean Palmer
48 Dan Rohrmeier
49 Carl Sullivan
50 Aquedo Vasquez
51 Don Vesling
52 Julian Yan

1988 ProCards Fresno Suns

(Independent, A)

	MT
Complete Set (29):	6.00

1222 Frank Bryan
1223 Kim Flowers
1224 John Bilello
1225 Chuck Higson

1226 Brad Comstock
1227 John Barry
1228 Dave Nash
1229 Gary Geiger
1230 Dan Simonds
1231 Rocco Buffolino
1232 Jim Malseed
1233 Hector Miyauchi
1234 Antony Tagi
1235 Bullet Manabe
1236 Dean Treanor
1237 Jon Hobbs
1238 Joe Ueda
1239 Richard Yagi
1240 Tracey Pancoski
1241 Ernie Young
1242 Todd Hawkins
1243 Tony Triplett
1244 Rob Rowen
1245 Marty Montano
1246 George Omachi
1247 Joe Mancini
1248 Tom Bell
1249 Donna Van Duzer
---- Checklist

1988 Cal Cards Fresno Suns

(Independent, A)

MT
Complete Set (27): 5.00
1 Tony Triplett
2 Marc Combs
3 Joe Mancini
4 Jon Hobbs
5 Ernie Young
6 Dan Simonds
7 Tracy Pancoski
8 Frank Bellino
9 Todd Hawkins
10 John Barry
11 Kim Flowers
12 Jim Malseed
13 Dave Nash
14 Richard Yagi
15 Hector Miyauchi
16 Steve Bowden
17 Frank Bryan
18 John Bilello
19 Rob Rowen
20 Anthony Tagi
21 Bullet Manabe
22 Chuck Higson
23 Gary Geiger
24 Rocco Buffalino
25 Brad Comstock
26 Dean Treanor
27 Tom Bell

1988 Star Ft. Lauderdale Yankees

(N.Y. Yankees, A)

MT
Complete Set (25): 5.00
1 Dan Arendas
2 Luc Berube
3 Art Calvert
4 Darrin Chapin
5 Bob Dickerson
6 Jim Ehrhard
7 Steve Erickson
8 Fernando Figueroa
9 Scott Gay
10 Doug Gogolewski
11 Fred Hailey
12 Rodney Imes
13 Scott Kamieniecki
14 Ralph Kraus
15 Mark Mitchell
16 Kevin Mmahat
17 Tony Morrison
18 Carlos Rodriguez
19 Gabriel Rodriguez
20 Dan Roman
21 Wade Taylor
22 David Turgeon
23 Bill Voeltz
24 Thomas Weeks

1988 ProCards Gastonia Rangers

(Texas Rangers, A)

MT
Complete Set (30): 10.00
995 Marv Rockman
996 Bob Lavender
997 Bill Findlay
998 Mike Taylor
999 Jay Baker
1000 Rick Knapp
1001 Chris Shiflett
1002 Luke Sable
1003 Robb Nan (Nen)
1004 Jim McCutcheon
1005 Cris Colon
1006 Joe Pearn
1007 Brant Alyea
1008 Felipe Castillo
1009 Orlando Gomez
1010 Kevin Belcher
1011 Jose Velez
1012 Jeff Melrose
1013 Bill Losa
1014 Pat Garman
1015 Brad Meyer
1016 Marty Cerny
1017 Wilson Alvarez
1018 Brian Steiner
1019 Spencer Wilkinson
1020 Roger Pavlik
1021 Glenn Patterson
1022 Saul Barretto
1023 Chuck Marguardt
---- Checklist

1988 ProCards Geneva Cubs

(Chicago Cubs, A)

MT
Complete Set (30): 5.00
1633 Eric Perry
1634 Nick Ramirez
1635 Eric Williams
1636 Gary Arnold
1637 Ray Figueroa
1638 Jim Murphy
1639 Skip Eggleston
1640 Rick Mundy
1641 Dave Goodwin
1642 Mike Sodders
1643 Tim Ellis
1644 Dan Johnston
1645 Matt Leonard
1646 Eligio Rodriguez
1647 Tracy Smith
1648 Francisco Espino
1649 Derrick Stroud
1650 Bill St. Peter
1651 Scott Taylor
1652 Ben Shreve
1653 Chris Lutz
1654 Bill Hayes
1655 Carlos Canino
1656 Ken Shepard
1657 George Brzezinski
1658 Marty Owens
1659 Dave Oster
1660 Sheila Arnold
1661 Quinn's Cards
---- Checklist

1988 ProCards Glens Falls Tigers

(Detroit Tigers, AA)

MT
Complete Set (27): 5.00
913 Wayne Housie
914 Pat Austin
915 Eric Hardgrave
916 Delwyn Young
917 John Wockenfuss
918 Ken Williams
919 Julius McDougal
920 Rich Lacko
921 Paul Wenson
922 Rich Wieligman
923 Torey Lovullo
924 Cesar Mejia
925 Rob Richie
926 Kevin Ritz
927 Mike Schwabe
928 Bernie Anderson
929 Shawn Holman
930 Ken Gotmann
931 Dan Dimascio
932 Adam Dempsay
933 Bill Cooper
934 Kevin Bradshaw
935 Hector Berrios
936 Jeff Jones
937 Robert Link
938 Tim Leiper
---- Checklist

The election of former players to the Hall of Fame does not always have an immediate upward effect on card values. The hobby market generally has done a good job of predicting those inductions and adjusting values over the course of several years.

1988 Sport Pro Great Falls Dodgers

(L.A. Dodgers, R)

MT
Complete Set (27): 22.00
1 Bill Bene
2 Eric Karros
3 Brett Magnusson
4 Ernie Carr
5 Chris Morrow
6 Mike McHugh
7 Lance Rice
8 Jeff Castillo
9 Eddie Pye
10 Dan Opperman
11 Jerry Brooks
12 Don Carroll
13 Jim Wray
14 John Braase
15 Steve Finken
16 Brock McMurray
17 Bill Wengert
18 John Huebner
19 Bryan Beals
20 Sean Snedeker
21 Jeff Hartsock
22 Jose Offerman
23 Mike James
24 Cam Biberdorf
25 Ramon Valdes
26 Tim Johnson
27 Goose Gregson

1988 ProCards Greensboro Hornets

(Cincinnati Reds, A)

MT
Complete Set (26): 5.00
1551 Bill Risley
1552 Quinn Marsh
1553 Scott Jeffery
1554 Keith Thomas
1555 Brian Lane
1556 Shane Letterio
1557 Brad Robinson
1558 Eddie Taubenese
1559 Joe Turek
1560 Kevin Pearson
1561 Ron Mullins
1562 Adam Casillias
1563 Tony Mealy
1564 Ken Huseby
1565 Scott Westermann
1566 Mack Jenkins
1567 Rosario Rodriguez
1568 Andy Rickman
1569 Jack Smith
1570 Steve Hester
1571 Jimmy Mee
1572 Don Brown
1573 Keith Kaiser
1574 Joey Vierra
1575 Mark Berry
---- Checklist

1988 Best Greenville Braves

(Atlanta Braves, AA)

MT
Complete Set (24): 5.00
1 Ed Whited
2 Terry Bell
3 Sal D'Alessandro
4 Inocencio Guerrero
5 Dennis Hood
6 John Alva
7 Miguel Sabino
8 Barry Jones
9 Drew Denson
10 Mark Lemke
11 Jim Lovell
12 Dale Polley
13 Bryan Farmer
14 Dave Miller
15 Steve Ziem
16 Kevin Blankenship
17 Maximo Del Rosario
18 Tom Dozier
19 Andy Nezelek
20 John Kilner
21 Tom Dunbar
22 Eddie Mathews
23 Mike Fischlin
24 Logo/checklist

1988 Star Hagerstown Suns

(Baltimore Orioles, AA)

MT
Complete Set, w/varitions (27): 10.00
Partial Set, no Variations(25): 6.00
1 Jeff Ahr
2 Dave Bettendorf
3 Don Buford Jr.
4 Mike Eberle
5 Scott Evans
6 Craig Faulkner
7 Steve Finley
8 Tom Harms
9 Walt Harris
10 Bob Latmore
11 Kevin McNees
12 Larry Mims
13 Chris Myers
14 Matt Nowak
15 Louie Paulino
16a Pete Palermo (correct name and stats, wrong picture)
16b Pete Palermo (corrected picture, however listed as Carolina League rather than Hagerstown)
17a Chris Pinder (correct name and stats, wrong picture)
17b Chris Pinder (corrected picture, however listed as Carolina League rather than Hagerstown)
18 Mike Sander
19 David Segui (Segui)
20 Steve Sonneberger
21 Randy Strijek
22 Anthony Telford
23 Jack Voigt
24 Bob Williams
25 Chaun Wilson

1988 ProCards Hamilton Redbirds

(St. Louis Cardinals, A)

MT
Complete Set (30): 5.00
1719 Chris Houser
1720 Scott Halama
1721 John Cebuhar
1722 Brad Duvall
1723 Antron Grier
1724 Rick Christian
1725 Mark Battell
1726 Lee Plemel
1727 Mike Ross
1728 Dale Kisten
1729 Tim Redman
1730 Kevin Robinson
1731 Cory Saterfield
1732 Dan Radison
1733 Luis Melendez
1734 Mike Evans
1735 Randy Butts
1736 Mark Clark
1737 John Lepley
1738 Joe Federico
1739 Steve Fanning
1740 Rodney Brooks
1741 Tom Malchesky
1742 Ed Lampe
1743 J.P. Gentleman
1744 Dean Weese
1745 Steve Graham
1746 Frank Moran
1747 Joe Hall
---- Checklist

1988 ProCards Harrisburg Senators

(Pittsburgh Pirates, AA)

MT
Complete Set (30): 6.00
834 John Rigos
835 Jeff Cook
836 Tommy Shields
837 Kevin Davis
838 Scott Little
839 Spin Williams
840 Rick Reed
841 Dimas Gutierrez
842 Jim Neidlinger
843 Mike Curtis
844 Lance Belen
845 Chris Ritter
846 Dave Trembley
847 Orlando Lind
848 Jose Melendez
849 Ron Johns
850 Mike Walker
851 Gilberto Roca
852 Paul Wilmet
853 Bill Copp
854 Tony Chance
855 Jeff Banister
856 Gino Gentile
857 Larry Melton
858 Robby Russell
859 Jeff King
860 Clay Daniel
861 Harold Williams
862 Scott Kautz
---- Checklist

1988 Huntsville Stars team issue

(Oakland A's, A)

MT
Complete Set (25): 5.00
(1) Mike Bordick
(2) Scott Chiamparino
(3) Brian Criswell
(4) Pat Dietrick
(5) DeMarlo Hale
(6) Scott Hemond
(7) Scott Holcomb
(8) Steve Howard
(9) Jimmy Jones
(10) Bo Kent
(11) Kirk McDonald
(12) John Minch
(13) Jerome Nelson
(14) Jerry Peguero
(15) Tommie Reynolds
(16) Andre Robertson
(17) Will Schock
(18) Bob Sharpnack
(19) Dave Shotkoski
(20) Kevin Sliwinski
(21) Greg Sparks
(22) Bruce Tanner
(23) Camilo Veras
(24) Dave Veres
(25) Bruce Walton

1988 ProCards Idaho Falls Braves

(Atlanta Braves, A)

MT
Complete Set (31): 5.00
1832 The Clubhouse
1833 Team photo/checklist
1834 Daryl Blanks
1835 Marco Paddy
1836 Gary Schoonover
1837 Glenn Mitchell
1838 Rodney Richey
1839 John Albertson
1840 Lamar Hall
1841 Dave Monteiro
1842 Matthew Williams
1843 Chris Jones
1844 Ramces Guerrero
1845 Donovan Campbell
1846 Kevin Henry
1847 Greg Harper
1848 Al Bacosa
1849 Pat Stivers
1850 Keith LeClair
1851 Eric Kuhlman
1852 Rai Henninger
1853 Jim Procopio
1854 Paul Opdyke
1855 Rudy Gardey
1856 Mark Eskins
1857 Daniel Lehnerz
1858 Jim Kortright
1859 Steve Lopez
1860 Herb Hippauf
1861 Rich Pohle
---- Checklist

1988 ProCards Indianapolis Indians

(Montreal Expos, AAA)

	MT
Complete Set (31):	10.00

496 Joe Sparks
497 Billy Moore
498 Tim McCormack
499 Mike Colbern, Joe Kerrigan
500 Nelson Santovenia
501 Sergio Valdez
502 Tim Barrett
503 Jeff Fischer
504 Brian Holman
505 Steve Shirley
506 Kurt Kepshire
507 Mel Houston
508 Gary Wayne
509 Mike Smith
510 Randy Johnson
511 Bob Sebra
512 Joe Hesketh
513 Rex Hudler
514 Razor Shines
515 Garrett Nago
516 Johnny Paredes
517 Nelson Norman
518 Otis Nixon
519 Mike Berger
520 Alonzo Powell
521 Jack Daugherty
522 Tim Hulett
523 Wil Tejada
524 Ron Shepherd
525 Tom Akins, Howard Kellman
---- Checklist

1988 CMC (TCMA) Indianapolis Indians

(Montreal Expos, AAA)

	MT
Complete Set (25):	6.00

1 Randy Johnson
2 Kurt Kepshire
3 Bob Sebra
4 Steve Shirley
5 Tim Barrett
6 Jeff Fischer
7 Mike Smith
8 Sergio Valdez
9 Brian Holman
10 Rex Hudler
11 Johnny Paredes
12 Razor Shines
13 Billy Moore
14 Otis Nixon
15 Alonzo Powell
16 Ron Shepherd
17 Tim Hulett
18 Nelson Santovenia
19 Wilfredo Tejada
20 Mike Berger
21 Jack Daugherty
22 Garrett Nago
23 Mel Houston
24 Joe Sparks
25 Mike Colbern, Joe Kerrigan, Nelson Norman

1988 ProCards Iowa Cubs

(Chicago Cubs, AAA)

	MT
Complete Set (30):	9.00

526 Brian Guinn
527 Bill Bathe
528 Doug Dascenzo
529 Rick Surhoff
530 Dwight Smith
531 Dave Grossman
532 Jeff Hirsch
533 Dave Masters
534 Bob Tewksbury
535 Gary Varsho
536 Dave Meier
537 Damon Berryhill
538 Paul Noce
539 Mark Grace
540 Phil Stephenson
541 Bill Landrum
542 Jim Wright
543 Pete Mackanin
544 Leonard Damian
545 Roger Williams
546 Jeff Pico
547 Mike Capel
548 Greg Tabor
549 Joe Kraemer
550 Bruce Crabbe
551 Laddie Renfroe
552 Front office
553 More Front Office
554 Cubbie Bear (mascot)
---- Checklist

1988 CMC (TCMA) Iowa Cubs

(Chicago Cubs, AAA)

	MT
Complete Set (25):	7.00

1 Mike Capel
2 Len Damian
3 Jeff Pico
4 Laddie Renfroe
5 Bob Tewksbury
6 Jeff Hirsch
7 Joe Kraemer
8 Bill Landrum
9 Dave Masters
10 Rich Surhoff
11 Roger Williams
12 Damon Berryhill
13 Bruce Crabbe
14 Mark Grace
15 Brian Guinn
16 Paul Noce
17 Phil Stephenson
18 Greg Tabor
19 Doug Dascenzo
20 Dave Meier
21 Dwight Smith
22 Gary Varsho
23 Bill Bathe
24 Pete Mackanin
25 Jim Wright

1988 Grand Slam Jackson Mets

(N.Y. Mets, AA) (10,000 sets)

	MT
Complete Set (25):	5.00

1 Ron Gideon
2 Zoilo Sanchez
3 Geary Jones
4 Tucker Ashford
5 Glenn Abbott
6 Kyle Hartshorn
7 Tom Doyle
8 Chris Jelic
9 Mike Santiago
10 Jeff Gardner
11 Virgil Conley
12 Craig Shipley
13 Rich Rodriguez
14 Brian Given
15 Blaine Beatty
16 Todd Welborn
17 Miguel Roman
18 Manny Salinas
19 Shawn Barton
20 Joaquin Contreras
21 Angelo Cuevas
22 Mickey Weston
23 Kevin Tapani
24 Felix Perdomo
25 Alan Hayden

1988 ProCards Jacksonville Expos

(Montreal Expos, AA)

	MT
Complete Set (32):	5.00

964 Scott Mann
965 Orsino Hill
966 Jeffrey Huson
967 Eddie Dixon
968 Derrell Baker
969 Nardi Contreras
970 Doug Duke
971 Tommy Thompson
972 Andy Lawrence
973 Yorkis Perez
974 Jim Kahmann
975 Mike Blowers
976 Randy Braun
977 Mark Clemons
978 Todd Soares
979 Bob Caffrey
980 Gene Harris
981 Pat Sipe
982 Tommy Alexander
983 Armando Moreno
984 Kevin Dean
985 Mike Shade
986 Rich Sauver
987 Mark Gardner
988 Rick Carriger
989 John Hoover
990 Gary Engelkin
991 Esteban Belter
992 Richie Lewis
993 Team Photo
994 Sam Molfson Park
---- Checklist

1988 Best Jacksonville Expos

(Montreal Expos, AA)

	MT
Complete Set (29):	5.00

1 Rick Carriger
2 Mike Shade
3 Rich Sauver
4 John Hoover
5 Gene Harris
6 Eddie Dixon
7 Mark Gardner
8 Mark Clemons
9 Tommy Alexander
10 Richie Lewis
11 Yorkis Perez
12 Orsino Hill
13 Kevin Dean
14 Derrell Baker
15 Bill Mann
16 Mike Blowers
17 Esteban Beltre
18 Jeff Huson
19 Andy Lawrence
20 Pat Sipe
21 Randy Braun
22 Doug Duke
23 Nardi Contreras
24 Tommy Thompson
25 Bob Caffrey
26 Jim Yalmann
27 Armando Moreno
28 Gary Engelkin
29 Checklist/Sam W. Wolfson Stadium

1988 ProCards Jamestown Expos

(Montreal Expos, A)

	MT
Complete Set (30):	20.00

1893 Kevin P. Malone
1894 Roger LaFrancois
1895 Wilfredo Nieva
1896 Bryn Kosco
1897 Bret Davis
1898 Rob Kerrigan
1899 Daniel Freed
1900 Angel Rivera
1901 Jeff Atha
1902 Tim Piechowski
1903 Isaac Alleyne
1904 Tim Laker
1905 Rodney Boddie
1906 Idaiberto Echemendia
1907 Brian Sajonia
1908 Joe Siddall
1909 Joe Klancnik
1910 Marquis Grissom
1911 Keith Kaub
1912 Jose Solarte
1913 Danilo Leon
1914 Steve Overeem
1915 Kevin Finigan
1916 Jorge Mitchell
1917 Javan Reagans
1918 Darrin Winston
1919 Tim Stanley
1920 Dan Archibald
1921 Martin Robitaille
2039 Q.V. Lowe
---- Checklist

1988 ProCards Kenosha Twins

(Minnesota Twins, A)

	MT
Complete Set (29):	5.00

1379 Bob Tinkey
1380 Willie Banks
1381 Dwight Bernard
1382 Fred White
1383 Rusty Kryzanowski
1384 Steve Stowell
1385 Alex Perez
1386 Chad Swanson
1387 Tom Gilles
1388 Doug Pittman
1389 Dave Jacas
1390 Jarvis Brown
1391 David Smith
1392 Lenny Webster
1393 Frank Valdez
1394 Mark Ericson
1395 Michael Lexa
1396 Carlos Capellan
1397 Chris Martin
1398 Pete Delkus
1399 Don Leppert
1400 John Skelton
1401 Shane Jenny
1402 Ron Gardenhire
1403 Bob Lee
1404 Basil Meyer
1405 Tom Marten
1406 Pat Bangtson
---- Checklist

1988 Star Kinston Indians

(Cleveland Indians, A)

	MT
Complete Set (24):	45.00

1 Beau Allread
2 Kevin Bearse
3 Joey Belle (Albert)
4 Steven Bird
5 Glenn Fairchild
6 Greg Ferlinda
7 Mark Gilles
8 John Githens
9 Todd Gonzales
10 David Harwell
11 Christopher Isaacson
12 Scott Johnson
13 Carl Kelipuleole
14 Lewis Kent
15 Allen Liebert
16 Everado Magallanes
17 Mark Maloney
18 Charles Ogden
19 James Richardson
20 Charles Soos
21 Robert Swain
22 Michael Twardoski
23 Michael Westbrook
24 Raymond Williamson

1988 Best Knoxville Blue Jays

(Toronto Blue Jays, AA)

	MT
Complete Set (26):	5.00

1 Alex Sanchez
2 Sanchez Felix
3 John Shea
4 Mike Jones
5 Jimy Kelly
6 Domingo Martinez
7 Kevin Batiste
8 Hector Delacruz
9 Kash Beauchamp
10 Darren Balsley
11 Doug Scherer
12 Carlos Diaz
13 Jose Escobar
14 Ken Rivers
15 Doug Linton
16 Chris Jones
17 Omar Bencomo
18 Correa Guzman
19 Dennis Jones
20 Steve Cummings
21 Gary McCune
22 Tim Ringler
23 John Poloni
24 Hugh Brinson
25 Tom Quinlan
26 Logo/checklist

1988 Star Lakeland Tigers

(Detroit Tigers, A)

	MT
Complete Set (25):	5.00

1 Scott Aldred
2 Doyle Balthazar
3 Arnie Beyeler
4 Basilio Cabrera
5 Luis Galindo
6 Richard Carter
7 Phil Clark
8 Milt Cuyler
9 Dean Decillis
10 Gregory Everson
11 Paul Foster
12 Blane Fox
13 Mike Hansen
14 Lance Hudson
15 Scott Hufford
16 Darren Hursey
17 Mark Lee
18 Randy Nosek
19 Dan O'Neill
20 Wade Phillips
21 Gary Pifer
22 Ron Rightnowar
23 Joseph Slavik
24 Bob Thomson
25 Donald Vesling

1988 ProCards Las Vegas Stars

(San Diego Padres, AAA)

	MT
Complete Set (28):	12.00

222 Edward Vosberg
223 Joe Lynch
224 Randall Byers
225 Joel McKeon
226 Todd Hutcheson
227 Greg Harris
228 Pete Roberts
229 Jerald Clark
230 Joe Bitker
231 Roberto Alomar
232 Gary Green
233 Shane Mack
234 Joey Cora
235 Mike Brumley
236 Sandy Alomar
237 Rob Nelson
238 Tom Brassil

239 Thomas Howard
240 Todd Simmons
241 Bruce Bochy
242 Kevin Towers
243 Steve Lubratich
244 Steve Smith
245 Bip Roberts
246 Keith Comstock
247 Brad Pounders
248 Sonny Siebert
---- Checklist

1988 CMC (TCMA Las Vegas Stars

(San Diego Padres, AAA)

	MT
Complete Set (25):	9.00

1 Joe Bitker
2 Keith Comstock
3 Greg Harris
4 Joel McKeon
5 Pete Roberts
6 Todd Simmons
7 Ed Vosberg
8 Kevin Towers
9 Joe Lynch
10 Shane Mack
11 Thomas Howard
12 Jerald Clark
13 Randy Byers
14 Bip Roberts
15 Brad Pounders
16 Rob Nelson
17 Gary Green
18 Joey Cora
19 Mike Brumley
20 Roberto Alomar
21 Bruce Bochy
22 Sandy Alomar, Jr.
23 Tom Brassil
24 Steve Smith
25 Sonny Siebert

1988 Little Sun Legends of Minor League Baseball

	MT
Complete Set (11):	15.00

(1) Header card
2 Pete Gray
3 Ike Boone
4 Lou Novikoff
5 Luke Easter
6 Steve Bilko
7 Frank Shellenback
8 Smead Jolley
9 Jigger Statz
10 Joe Hauser
11 Fidel Castro

1988 Pucko Little Falls Mets

(N.Y. Mets, A) (4,000 sets produced)

	MT
Complete Set (29):	12.50

1 Lee May
2 Kevin Baez
3 Tom Bales
4 Tom Becker
5 Ron Height
6 Todd Hundley
7 Michael Noelke
8 Bob Olah
9 Steve Piskor
10 Radhames Polanco
11 Titi Roche
12 Sammye Sanchez
13 Greg Turtletaub
14 Lonnie Walker
15 Terry Bross
16 Terry Griffin
17 Chris Hill
18 Steve Newton
19 Vladimir Perez
20 Dale Plummer
21 Dave Proctor
22 Pete Schourek
23 John Wenrick
24 Anthony Young
25 Brian Zimmerman
26 Bill Stein
27 Al Jackson
28 Rick McWane
29 Frenk Minnissale

1988 ProCards Louisville Redbirds

(st. Louis Cardinals, AAA)

	MT
Complete Set (26):	5.00

421 David Green
422 Carl Ray Stephens
423 John Martin
424 Sal Agostinelli
425 Duane Walker
426 Dick Grapenthin
427 Mike Fitzgerald
428 Chris Carpenter (Cris)
429 John Murphy
430 Randy O'Neal
431 Roy Silver
432 Bill Lyons
433 Tim Jones
434 David Hudson
435 Joe Pettini
436 Luis Alicea
437 Jim Leopold
438 Alex Cole
439 Craig Wilson
440 John Costello
441 Mike Jorgenson (Jorgensen)
442 Gibson Alba
443 Dave Rajsich
444 Mark Dougherty
445 Rich Bounantony
---- Checklist

1988 CMC (TCMA) Louisville Redbirds

(St Louis Cardinals, AAA)

	MT
Complete Set (25):	5.00

1 John Costello
2 Dick Grapenthin
3 John Martin
4 Randy O'Neal
5 Tim Conroy
6 Gibson Alba
7 Rich Buonantony
8 Chris Carpenter (Cris)
9 Dave Rajsich
10 Jim Leopold
11 Alex Cole
12 Bill Lyons
13 Tim Jones
14 David Green
15 Craig Wilson
16 John Murphy
17 Duane Walker
18 Mike Fitzgerald
19 Carl Ray Stephens
20 Luis Alicea
21 Sal Agostinelli
22 Roy Silver
23 Mark Dougherty
24 Joe Pettini
25 Mike Jorgenson (Jorgensen)

Value of modern team sets is often predicated as much on inclusion of star player's early cards as on scarcity of the issue.

1988 Louisville Redbirds team issue

(St. Louis Cardinals, AAA)

	MT
Complete Set (55):	9.00

1 Mike Jorgensen
2 Joe Pettini
3 Darold Knowles
4 Steve Braun
5 Sal Agostinelli
6 Gibson Alba
7 Luis Alicea
8 Scott Arnold
9 Greg Bargar
10 Rod Booker
11 Derek Botelho
12 Rich Buonantony
13 Cris Carpenter
14 Alex Cole
15 Tim Conroy
16 John Costello
17 Danny Cox
18 Mark Dougherty
19 Mike Fitzgerald
20 Dick Grapenthin
21 David Green
22 Mike Hocutt
23 Tim Jones
24 Matt Kinzer
25 Wayne Krenchicki
26 Mike Laga
27 Jim Leopold
28 Jim Lindeman
29 Rick Lockwood
30 Bill Lyons
31 Joe Magrane
32 John A. Martin
33 Greg Mathews
34 Ron Meridith
35 John Morris
36 John V. Murphy
37 Randy O'Neal
38 Jeff Oyster
39 Steve Peters
40 Jim Puzey
41 Dave Rajsich
42 Mike Robinson
43 Mark Ryal
44 Roy Silver
45 Carl Ray Stephens
46 Lester Strode
47 Scott Terry
48 Lee Tunnell
49 Duane Walker
50 Craig Wilson
51 David "Hap" Hudson
52 Billy "Bird" Johnson
53 Billings & Burnett
54 Checklist
---- Redbirds logo

1988 Star Lynchburg Red Sox

(Boston Red Sox, A)

	MT
Complete Set (27):	6.00

1 Billy Bartels
2 Paul Brown
3 Tim Buheller
4 Randy Cina
5 Scott Cooper
6 Paul Devlin
7 David Gray
8 Bart Haley
9 Reggie Harris
10 Joseph Marchese
11 Gilberto Martinez
12 Gregory McCollum
13 Timothy McGee
14 Shannon Mendenhall
15 Juan Molero
16 Jim Orsag
17 Mickey Pina
18 Jeffrey Plympton
19 Scott Powers
20 Ronnie Richardson
21 Enrique Rios
22 Kenneth Ryan
23 Scott Sommers
24 David Walters
25 Stuart Weidie
26 Craig Wilson
27 Robert Zupcic
--- Team logo/sponsor card

1988 T&J Sportscards Madison Muskies

(Oakland A's, A) (color, 2-3/8" x 3-3/8")

	MT
Complete Set (25):	10.00

1 Rob Alexander
2 Bruce Arola
3 Pedro Baez
4 Bert Bradley
5 Scott Brosius
6 Nasusel Cabrera
7 Ozzie Canseco
8 Felix Caraballo
9 Jim Carroll
10 Jim Chenevey
11 Dave Gavin
12 Chris Gust
13 Demarlo Hale
14 Fred Hanker
15 Frank Masters
16 Jim Nettles
17 Bob Parry
18 Jamie Reiser
19 Dion Reyna
20 Marteese Robinson
21 Will Schock
22 Matt Siuda
23 Bob Stocker
24 Brian Thorson
25 Pat Wernig

1988 ProCards Maine Phillies

(Philadelphia Phillies, AAA)

	MT
Complete Set (27):	5.00

277 Jim Olander
278 Kevin Ward
279 Marvin Freeman
280 Ron Jones
281 John McLarnan
282 Mike Shelton
283 Travis Chambers
284 Tom Barrett
285 John Russell
286 Ricky Jordan
287 Ken Jackson
288 Shane Turner
289 Brad Brink
290 Keith Miller
291 Rick Lundblade
292 Marty Bystrom
293 Tom Newell
294 Bob Scanlan
295 Ramon Henderson
296 Todd Frohwirth
297 Danny Clay
298 Greg Jelks
299 Barney Nugent
300 George Culver
301 Joe Lefebvre
302 Ramon Aviles
---- Checklist

1988 CMC (TCMA) Maine Phillies

(Phildelphia Phillies, AAA)

	MT
Complete Set (25):	5.00

1 Marty Bystrom
2 Travis Chambers
3 Barney Nugent
4 Marvin Freeman
5 Brad Brink
6 John McLarnan
7 Mike Shelton
8 Tom Newell
9 Bob Scanlan
10 Todd Frohwirth
11 Ricky Jordon (Jordan)
12 John Russell
13 Shane Turner
14 Ron Jones
15 Rick Lundblade
16 Tommy Barrett
17 Kenny Jackson
18 Greg Jelks
19 Ramon Henderson
20 Keith Miller
21 Jim Olander
22 Kevin Ward
23 George Culver
24 Ramon Aviles
25 Joe Lefebvre

1988 Star Managers/Costner

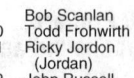

This set featuring 20 managers and a card of actor Kevin Costner was produced as an incentive for dealers to buy complete minor league runs from Star. The cards have gold borders which do not match the borders on their respective team sets. Team sets sold at stadiums around the minors do not have the manager's card. Some hobby dealers included the manager's card in sets which they sold.

	MT
Complete Set (21):	15.00

1 Glenn Adams (Kinston)
2 Felipe Alou (West Palm Beach)
3 Doug Ault (Dunedin)
4 Buddy Bailey (Durham)
5 Dick Berardino (Lynchburg)
6 Dave Bialas (St. Petersburg)
7 Keith Bodie (Osceola)
8 Joe Breeden (Virginia)
9 Kevin Costner (actor)
10 Marv Foley (Tampa)
11 Mike Hart (Hagerstown)
12 Granny Hamner (Clearwater)
13 Clint Hurdle (St. Lucie)
14 Bobby Jones (Charlotte)
15 John Lipon (Lakeland)
16 Jay Loviglio (Winston-Salem)
17 Jose Santiago (Miami)
18 John Shoemaker (Vero Beach)
19 Buck Showalter (Ft. Lauderdale)
20 Luis Silverio (Baseball City)
21 Jay Ward

1988 Star Martinsville Phillies

(Philadelphia Phillies, R) (Red- and blue-bordered sets were issued; only 700 of the latter)

	MT
Complete Set, Red (32):	10.00
Complete Set, Blue (32):	5.00

1 John Anderson
2 Kenneth Bean
3 Al Bennett

4 Toby Borland
5 Greg Breaux
6 Tim Churchill
7 Dan Coccia
8 Matt Current
9 Mike Dafforn
10 Rollie DeArmas
11 Tom Doyle
12 Donnie Elliot
13 John Escobar
14 Paul Fletcher
15 Reggie Garcia
16 Brian Harper
17 Dennis Hoffman
18 Luther Johnson
19 Craig Johnston
20 Troy Kent
21 Darrell Lindsey
22 Antonio Linares
23 Aurelio Llanos
24 Chris Lowe
25 Nick Macaluso
26 John Marshall
27 Eulogio Perez
28 Edwin Rosado
29 Victor Rosario
30 Francisco Tejada
31 Chris Toney
32 Ray Walker

1988 Best Memphis Chicks

(K.C. Royals, AA)

MT
Complete Set (28): 5.00
1 Mel Stottlemyre
2 Rich Thompson
3 Mark Van Blaricom
4 Steve Morrow
5 Ken Bowen
6 Jacob Brumfield
7 Larry Acker
8 Matt Crouch
9 Casey Parson
10 Jim Campbell
11 Kevin Burrell
12 Luis Encarnacion
13 Mark Gillaspie
14 Ken Kravec
15 Randy Hunt
16 Mauro Gozzo
17 Charlie Culberson
18 Jose DeJesus
19 Matt Winters
20 Rick Lueken
21 Chito Martinez
22 Mike Miller
23 Ken Spratke
24 Thad Reece
25 Jose Rivera
26 Sal Rende
27 Tim McCarver Stadium
28 Checklist

1988 Star Miami Marlins

(Independent, A)

MT
Complete Set (24): 5.00
1 Jeff Allison
2 Mick Billmeyer
3 Ron Brevell
4 Mike Browning
5 Hector Cotto
6 Tony Diaz
7 Scott Diez
8 Orlando Gonzalez
9 Clay Hill
10 Matt Huff
11 Kanenori Tarumi
12 Shuji Inagaki
13 Trent Intorcia
14 Masao Kida
15 Brian Morrison
16 Rafael Muratti
17 Mitsuru Ogiwara
18 Julio Perez
19 Arnie Prieto
20 Rick Richardi
21 Sal Roldan
22 Tony Rohan
23 Motokuni Sano
24 Dave Von Ohlen

1988 Grand Slam Midland Angels

(California Angels, AA) (6,000 sets)

MT
Complete Set (25): 5.00
1 Max Oliveras
2 Kurt Walker
3 Tim Kelly
4 Vinicio Cedeno
5 Shane Young
6 Tim Burcham
7 Chris Collins
8 Frank Dimichelle
9 Todd Eggertsen
10 Mike Fetters
11 Colby Ward
12 Steve McGuire
13 Mike Knapp
14 Erik Pappas
15 Tom Alfredson
16 Danny Grunhard
17 C.L. Penigar
18 Lee Stevens
19 Jesus Alfaro
20 David Martinez
21 Jeff Manto
22 Jim McCollom
23 Jim Thomas
24 Craig Gerber
25 Norm Carrasco

1988 Grand Slam Midwest League All-Stars

(Class A) (10,000 sets)

MT
Complete Set (59): 11.00
1 Mark Owens (Clinton)
2 Andres Santana (Clinton)
3 Erik Johnson (Clinton)
4 Jamie Cooper (Clinton)
5 Rod Beck (Clinton)
6 Stephen Connolly (Clinton)
7 Tom Hostetler (Clinton)
8 Pete Beeler (Cedar Rapids)
9 Greg Lonigro (Cedar Rapids)
10 Jeff Forney (Cedar Rapids)
11 Bill Dodd (Cedar Rapids)
12 Butch Henry (Cedar Rapids)
13 Darrell Rodgers (Cedar Rapids)
14 Scott Scudder (Cedar Rapids)
15 Marc Bombard (Cedar Rapids)
16 Brian Deak (Burlington)
17 Rich Casarotti (Burlington)
18 Brian Hunter (Burlington)
19 Al Martin (Burlington)
20 Jim Lemasters (Burlington)
21 Troy Neel (Waterloo)
22 Tommy Kramer (Waterloo)
23 Bob Rose (Quad City)
24 Wiley Lee (Quad City)
25 Gary Buckels (Quad City)
26 Ray Lankford (Springfield)
27 Greg Becker (Springfield)
28 Greg Kallevig (Peoria)
29 Fernando Zarranz (Peoria)
30 Steve Olin (Waterloo)
31 Lenny Webster (Kenosha)
32 Shawn Gilbert (Kenosha)
33 Jarvis Brown (Kenosha)
34 Pat Bangston (Kenosha)
35 Pete Delkus (Kenosha)
36 Ron Gardenhire (Kenosha)
37 Jorge Pedre (Appleton)
38 Darryl Robinson (Appleton)
39 Jesus Deleon (Appleton)
40 Tom Gordon (Appleton)
41 Bobby Knecht (Appleton)
42 Greg Colbrunn (Rockford)
43 John Mello (Rockford)
44 Delino DeShields (Rockford)
45 Mario Brito (Rockford)
46 Howard Farmer (Rockford)
47 Tim Peters (Rockford)
48 Mike Maksudian (S. Bend)
49 Ray Payton (S. Bend)
50 Scott Brosius (Madison)
51 Ozzie Canseco (Madison)
52 Jim Chenevey (Madison)
53 Pat Wernig (Madison)
54 Will Schock (Madison)
55 Mike McDonald (Wausau)
56 Chuck Carr (Wausau)
57 Mike Goff (Wausau)
58 Kurt Stange (Wausau)
59 Mark Chapman (Beloit)

1988 Chong Modesto A's

(Oakland A's, A) (black & white)

MT
Complete Set (36): 5.00
1 Jeff Newman
2 Pete Richert
3 Dave Hollenback
4 Rich Berg
5 Felix Caraballo
6 Jim Carroll
7 Jeff Childers
8 Scott Chiamparino
9 Jim Foley
10 Jeff Glover
11 Gary Gorski
12 Jeff Kopta
13 Steve Maye
14 Mark Stancel
15 Weston Weber
16 Ray Young
17 Jorge Brito
18 Francis Ciprian
19 Tony Arias
20 Isaiah Clark
21 Ron Coomer
22 Darrin Duffy
23 Dave Finley
24 Angel Martinez
25 Dan Russell
26 Pat Gilbert
27 Dann Howitt
28 Antoine Pickett
29 Drew Stratton
30 Steve Gokey
31 Dave Shotkoski
32 David Veres
33 Mike Gallego
34 Walt Weiss
35 Greg Cadaret
36 Checklist

1988 Cal Cards Modesto A's

(Oakland A's, A)

MT
Complete Set (28): 6.00
56 David Veres
57 David Shotkoski
58 Ray Young
59 Kevin Williamson
60 Jeff Glover
61 Mark Beavers
62 Gary Gorski
63 Jeff Kopyta
64 Scott Chiamparino
65 Mark Stancel
66 Steve Maye
67 Dann Howitt
68 Jorge Brito
69 Drew Stratton
70 David Finley
71 Keith Watkins
72 Ron Coomer
73 Gerry Barragan
74 Luis Martinez
75 Bill Savarino
76 Heriberto Done
77 Randy Randle
78 Francis Ciprian
79 Patrick Gilbert
80 Vince Teixeira
81 Jeff Newman
82 Pete Richert
83 Dave Hollenback

1988 ProCards Myrtle Beach Blue Jays

(Toronto Blue Jays, A)

MT
Complete Set (28): 10.00
1166 Steve Wapnick
1167 Graeme Lloyd
1168 Denis Boucher
1169 Bernardino Nunez
1170 Edgar Marquez
1171 Derek Bell
1172 Steve Woide
1173 Chris Floyd
1174 Nate Cromwell
1175 Juan de la Rosa
1176 Greg David
1177 Dan Etzweiler
1178 Xavier Hernandez
1179 Mike Murray
1180 Leroy Stanton
1181 Omar Malave
1182 Randy Knorr
1183 Greg Vella
1184 Mike Timlin
1185 Steve Towey
1186 Williams Suero
1187 Allan Silverstein
1188 Richard Hebner
1189 Luis Sojo
1190 Jimmy Rogers
1191 Rob MacDonald
1192 Todd Provence
---- Checklist

1988 ProCards Nashville Sounds

(Cincinnati Reds, AAA)

MT
Complete Set (26): 5.00
471 Scott Earl
472 Pat Pacillo
473 Van Snider
474 Dave Klipstein
475 Ron Roenicke
476 Dan Boever
477 Tim Birtsas
478 Jeff Gray
479 Hugh Kemp
480 Doug Gwosdz
481 Marty Brown
482 Steve Oliverio
483 Joe Oliver
484 Jack Armstrong
485 Mike Jones
486 Jack Lind
487 Rob Lopez
488 Norm Charlton
489 Lenny Harris
490 Luis Quinones
491 Greg Monda
492 Mike Roesler
493 Robbie Dibble
494 Wayne Garland
495 John R. Young
---- Checklist

1988 CMC (TCMA) Nashville Sounds

(Cincinnati Reds, AAA)

MT
Complete Set (25): 5.00
1 Jack Armstrong
2 Tim Birtsas
3 Norm Charlton
4 Rob Dibble
5 Jeff Gray
6 Mike Jones
7 Hugh Kemp
8 Rob Lopez
9 Steve Oliverio
10 Pat Pacillo
11 Mike Roesler
12 Lenny Harris
13 Greg Monda
14 Luis Quinones
15 Dan Boever
16 Doug Gwosdz
17 Joe Oliver
18 Marty Brown
19 Scott Earl
20 Dave Klipstein
21 Ron Roenicke
22 Van Snider
23 Jack Lind
24 Wayne Garland
25 John Young

1988 Nashville Sounds team issue

(Cincinnati Reds, AAA)

MT
Complete Set (24): 5.00
(1) Jack Armstrong
(2) Skeeter Barnes
(3) Dan Boever
(4) Marty Brown
(5) Norm Charlton
(6) Tony DeFrancesco
(7) Rob Dibble
(8) Scottie Earl
(9) Jeff Gray
(10) Doug Gwosdz
(11) Lenny Harris
(12) Jim Jefferson
(13) Mike Jones
(14) Hugh Kemp
(15) Terry McGriff
(16) Charlie Mitchell
(17) Steve Oliverio
(18) Luis Quinones
(19) Ron Roenicke
(20) Candy Sierra
(21) Van Snider
(22) Eddie Tanner
(23) Hedi Vargas
(24) Manager/coach/trainer (John Young, Frank Luchessi, Wayne Garland)

1988 ProCards New Britain Red Sox

(Boston Red Sox, AA)

MT
Complete Set (25): 12.50
889 Luis Vasquez
890 Daryl Irvine
891 Mike Clarkin
892 Doug Palmer
893 Bob Chadwick
894 John Roberts
895 Eduardo Zambrano
896 Mike Dalton
897 Manny Jose
898 Dan Gabriollo
899 Larry Shikles
900 Greg Bochesa
901 Tim McGee
902 Jose Birriel
903 Ed Estrada
904 Dan Gakeler
905 Tito Stewart
906 Todd Pratt
907 Chris Moritz
908 Curt Schilling
909 Mike Carista
910 Angel Gonzalez
911 Roberto Zambrano
912 Jason Jackson
---- Checklist

1988 ProCards Oklahoma City 89'ers

(Texas Rangers, AAA)

	MT
Complete Set (27):	5.00

27 Scott May
28 Bill Taylor
29 Rick Odekirk
30 Jeff Kunkel
31 Dan Rohn
32 Larry Klein
33 Dwayne Henry
34 Tony Fossas
35 Gary Mielke
36 Bill Merrifield
37 Don Werner
38 James Steels
39 Jim St. Laurent
40 Gar Millay
41 Jose Tolentino
42 Robbie Wine
43 Darrell Whitaker
44 Craig McMurtry
45 Barbaro Garbey
46 Toby Harrah
47 Otto Gonzalez
48 Tom O'Malley
49 Ray Hayward
50 Ferguson Jenkins
51 Ray Ramirez
52 Ed Vande Berg
---- Checklist

1988 CMC (TCMA) Oklahoma City 89'ers

(Texas Rangers, AAA)

	MT
Complete Set (25):	5.00

1 Scott Anderson
2 Dwayne Henry
3 Scott May
4 Craig McMurtry
5 Gary Mielke
6 Ferguson Jenkins
7 Ray Hayward
8 Ed Vande Berg
9 Tony Fossas
10 Rick Odekirk
11 Darrell Whitaker
12 Otto Gonzalez
13 Gar Millay
14 Jose Tolentino
15 Bill Merrifield
16 Barbaro Garbey
17 Larry Klein
18 Jeff Kunkel
19 Tom O'Malley
20 Dan Rohn
21 Don Werner
22 Robby Wine
23 Jim St. Laurent
24 James Steels
25 Toby Harrah

1988 ProCards Omaha Royals

(K.C. Royals, AAA)

	MT
Complete Set (29):	5.00

1494 Rich Dubee
1495 Tom Poquette
1496 Israel Sanchez
1497 Jerry Gleaton
1498 Bill Swaggerty
1499 Nick Capra
1500 Nick Swartz
1501 Jeff Montgomery
1502 Buddy Biancalana
1503 Glenn Ezell
1504 Mike Loggins
1505 Tom Dodd
1506 Luis de los Santos
1507 Tom Mullen
1508 Jeff Schulz
1509 Jose Castro
1510 Dave Owen
1511 Don Welchel
1512 Rick Anderson
1513 Steve Fireovid
1514 Bob Buchanan
1515 Ron Johnson
1516 Larry Owen
1517 Al Hargesheimer
1518 Dann Bilardello
1519 Joe Citari
1520 Luis Aquino
1521 Gary Thurman
---- Checklist

1988 CMC (TCMA) Omaha Royals

(K.C. Royals, AAA)

	MT
Complete Set (25):	5.00

1 Rick Anderson
2 Luis Aquino
3 Bob Buchanan
4 Steve Fireovid
5 Jerry Don Gleaton
6 Al Hargesheimer
7 Jeff Montgomery
8 Tom Mullen
9 Bill Swaggerty
10 Rondin Johnson
11 Israel Sanchez
12 Nick Capra
13 Mike Loggins
14 Gary Thurman
15 Jeff Schulz
16 Dave Owen
17 Dann Bilardello
18 Larry Owen
19 Tom Dodd
20 Buddy Biancalana
21 Joe Citari
22 Luis de los Santos
23 Rich Dubee
24 Jose Castro
25 Glenn Ezell

1988 ProCards Oneonta Yankees

(N.Y. Yankees, A)

	MT
Complete Set (34):	5.00

Checklist
2040 Ed Martel
2041 Andy Cook
2042 Todd Brill
2043 Pat Kelly
2044 Bob DeJardin
2045 Jason Bridges
2046 Herb Erhardt
2047 Ken Greer
2048 Skip Nelloms
2049 Hector Vargas
2050 John Seeburger
2051 Craig Brink
2052 Jeff Livesey
2053 Rey Fernandez
2054 Miguel Torres
2055 Jorge Candelaria
2056 Bob Hunter
2057 Jeff Hoffman
2058 Bob Zeihen
2059 Mike Draper
2060 Art Canestro
2061 Bruce Prybylinski
2062 Jerry Nielsen
2063 Jay Makemson
2064 Gary Allenson, Kelvin Allenson
2065 Tim Weston
2066 Alan Warren
2067 Jay Knoblauh
2068 Mark Martin
2069 Jeff Johnson
2070 Jeff Taylor
2071 Frank Seminara
2072 Rod Ehrhard

1988 Best Orlando Twins

(Minnesota Twins, AA)

	MT
Complete Set (29):	5.00

1 Derek Parks
2 Tim O'Connor
3 Duane Gustavson
4 Eddie Yanes
5 Mark Funderburk
6 Toby Nivens
7 Steven Comer
8 James Pittman
9 Mike Dyer
10 Jaime Williams
11 Joey Aragon
12 Gary Borg
13 Jeff Satzinger
14 Kevin Trudeau
15 Terry Jorgensen
16 Chris Forgione
17 German Gonzalez
18 Chip Hale
19 Jeff Reboulet
20 Larry Casian
21 Mike Dotzler
22 Rafael DeLima
23 Steve Gasser
24 Francisco Oliveras
25 Shannon Raybon
26 Wayne Hattaway
27 Bill Cutshall
28 Bernardo Brito
29 Checklist/Tinker Field

1988 Star Osceola Astros

(Houston Astros, A)

	MT
Complete Set (25):	5.00

1 Manuel Acta
2 Samuel August
3 Jeff Baldwin
4 Daven Bond
5 Ryan Bowen
6 Todd Credeur
7 Louis Deiley
8 Pedro DeLeon
9 Tony Eusebio
10 Lou Frazier
11 Carl Grovom
12 Rusty Harris
13 Randall Hennis
14 Victor Hithe
15 Trent Hubbard
16 Bert Hunter
17 Todd McClure
18 Guy Normand
19 Dan Nyssen
20 Alfonso Osuna
21 David Potts
22 Karl Rhodes
23 Pedro Sanchez
24 John Sheenan
25 Mike Simms

1988 ProCards Palm Springs Angels

(California Angels, A)

	MT
Complete Set (32):	5.00

1433 John Orton
1434 Ruben Amaro
1435 J. Gary Ruby
1436 Bill Lacheman
1437 Luis Merejo
1438 Mike Anderson
1439 Reed Peters
1440 Scott Cerny
1441 Chris Cron
1442 Dan Ward
1443 Mike Erb
1444 Scott Kannenberg
1445 John Fritz
1446 Jose Tapia
1447 Colin Charland
1448 Dario Nunez
1449 Richard Morehouse
1450 Paul Sorrento
1451 Jeff Barns
1452 Jim McAnany
1453 Tim Dyson
1454 Gary Nalls
1455 Glenn Washington
1456 Mark Baca
1457 Bill Vanderwel
1458 Jim Bisceglia
1459 Bobby Bell
1460 Jimmy Long
1461 Reggie Lambert
1462 Bill Durney
1463 Jeff Richardson
---- Checklist

1988 Cal Cards Palm Springs Angels

(California Angels, A)

	MT
Complete Set (31):	5.00

85 Colin Charland
86 Mike Erb
87 John Fritz
88 Scott Kannenberg
89 Jim Long
90 Luis Merejo
91 Rich Morehouse
92 Jeff Richardson
93 Jose Tapia
94 Bill Vanderwel
95 Dan Ward
96 Edgar Alfonzo
97 Ruben Amaro
98 Mike Anderson
99 Mark Baca
100 Jeff Barns
101 Scott Cerny
102 Cris Cron
103 Ted Dyson
104 Jim McAnany
105 Mike Musolino
106 Gary Nalls
107 John Orton
108 Reed Peters
109 Giovanny Reyes
110 Paul Sorrento
111 Glenn Washington
112 Bill Lachemann
113 Reggie Lambert
114 Gary Ruby
115 Bill Durney

1988 ProCards Pawtucket Red Sox

(Boston Red Sox, AAA)

	MT
Complete Set (26):	5.00

446 Andy Araujo
447 Mike Rochford
448 Rob Woodward
449 Eric Hetzel
450 Gary Tremblay
451 Chris Cannizzaro
452 Tom Bolton
453 Carlos Quintana
454 Mark Meleski
455 Mitch Johnson
456 Bill McInnis
457 Zack Crouch
458 Scott Wade
459 Gary Miller-Jones
460 Dana Williams
461 Dana Kiecker
462 Angel Gonzalez
463 Mike Mesh
464 Randy Kutcher
465 Glenn Hoffman
466 Pat Dodson
467 Tony Cleary
468 Steve Curry
469 Ed Nottie
470 John Leister
---- Checklist

1988 CMC (TCMA) Pawtucket Red Sox

(Boston Red Sox, AAA)

	MT
Complete Set (25):	5.00

1 Rob Woodward
2 Mike Rochford
3 Mitch Johnson
4 John Leister
5 Andy Araujo
6 Zack Crouch
7 Steve Curry
8 Eric Hetzel
9 Tom Bolton
10 Dana Kiecker
11 Randy Kutcher
12 Bill McInnis
13 Glenn Hoffman
14 Tony Cleary
15 Chris Cannizzaro
16 Pat Dodson
17 Angel Gonzalez
18 Mike Mesh
19 Gary Miller-Jones
20 Carlos Quintana
21 Dana Williams
22 Gary Tremblay
23 Scott Wade
24 Ed Nottie
25 Mark Meleski

1988 Peoria Chiefs team issue

(Chicago Cubs, A) (production reported as 5,000 sets)

	MT
Complete Set (35):	65.00

(1) Herbie Andrade
(2) Warren Arrington
(3) Mike Aspray
(4) Lenny Bell
(5) Pookie Bernstine
(6) Mike Boswell
(7) Ed Caballero
(8) Chiefs' Alumni
(9) Rusty Crockett
(10) Sergio Espinal
(11) Mark Grace
(12) Carl Hamilton
(13) Phil Hannon
(14) Hersey Hawkins
(15) Greg Kallevig
(16) Rick Kranitz
(17) Jerry Lapenta
(18) Greg Maddux
(19) Jeff Massicotte
(20) Steve Melendez
(21) Bill Melvin
(22) Mark North
(23) Rafael Palmeiro
(24) Elvin Pulino
(25) Pete & Harry
(26) Jeff Pico
(27) Marty Rivero
(28) Brett Robinson
(29) Gabby Rodriguez
(30) Stars of the Future
(31) Jim Tracy
(32) Rick Wilkins
(33) Eddie Williams
(34) Jerome Walton
(35) Fernando Zarranz

1988 ProCards Phoenix Firebirds

(S.F. Giants, AAA)

	MT
Complete Set (29):	10.00

53 Tim Blackwell
54 Mark Wasinger
55 Randy Bockus
56 Matt Williams
57 Charlie Hayes
58 Deron McCue
59 Rusty Tillman
60 Everett Graham
61 Kirt Manwaring
62 Roger Mason
63 Angel Escobar
64 Francisco Melendez
65 Wendell Kim
66 Cliff Shidawara
67 Marty DeMerritt
68 Alan Cockrell
69 Bobby Ramos
70 Roger Samuels
71 Randy McCament
72 Ty Dabney
73 Mike Hogan
74 Ed Puikunas
75 Tony Perezchica
76 John Burkett
77 Terry Mulholland
78 Jeff Brantley
79 Brian Ohnoutka
80 Dennis Cook
---- Checklist

1988 CMC (TCMA) Phoenix Firebirds

(S.F. Giants, AAA)

	MT
Complete Set (25):	10.00

1 Randy Bockus
2 John Burkett
3 Dennis Cook
4 Roger Mason
5 Jeff Brantley
6 Mike Hogan
7 Brian Ohnoutka
8 Roger Samuels
9 Randy McCament
10 Terry Mullholland
11 Ed Puikunas
12 Kirt Manwaring
13 Bobby Ramos
14 Angel Escobar
15 Charlie Hayes
16 Tony Perezchica
17 Mark Wasinger
18 Matt Williams
19 Alan Cockrell
20 Everett Graham
21 Rusty Tillman
22 Ty Dabney
23 Deron McCue
24 Wendell Kim
25 Tim Blackwell, Marty DeMarrite

1988 ProCards Pittsfield Cubs

(Chicago Cubs, AA)

	MT
Complete Set (25):	5.00

1355 Hector Villanueva

1356 Mitch Zwolensky
1357 Julio Valdez
1358 Ray Thoma
1359 Joe Girardi
1360 Jim Essian
1361 Bryan House
1362 Rich Amaral
1363 Bob Bafia
1364 Brian McCann
1365 Mike Tullier
1366 Jerry Lapenta
1367 Jim Bullinger
1368 Dean Wilkins
1369 Steve Parker
1370 Ced Landrum
1371 Mark Leonette
1372 Rich Scheid
1373 Dave Kopf
1374 Jerome Walton
1375 Jackie Davidson
1376 Kris Roth
1377 Mike Harkey
1378 Gary Parmenter
---- Checklist

1988 Pittsfield Cubs team poster

(Chicago Cubs, AA) (Set issued as 10-7/8" x 16-3/4" poster.)

MT
Complete Poster: 21.00
(1) Rich Amaral
(2) Bob Bafia
(3) Jim Bullinger
(4) Jackie Davidson
(5) Jim Essian
(6) Joe Girardi (not pictured)
(7) Mike Harkey
(8) Bryan House
(9) Grant Jackson (not pictured)
(10) Dave Kopf
(11) Cedric Landrum
(12) Jerry LaPenta
(13) Mark Leonette
(14) Brian McCann
(15) Alan McKay
(16) E.J. Narcise (not pictured)
(17) Steve Parker
(18) Gary Parmenter
(19) Kris Roth
(20) Rich Scheid
(21) Jeff Small
(22) Ray Thoma
(23) Mike Tullier (not pictured)
(24) Hector Villanueva
(25) Robin Wadsworth (not pictured)
(26) Jerome Walton (not pictured)
(27) Matt Webber, Ben Webber
(28) Dean Wilkens
(29) Rick Wrona
(30) Mitch Zwolensky

1988 ProCards Pocatello Giants

(S.F. Giants, R)

MT
Complete Set (31): 5.00
--- Checklist
2073 Don Brock
2074 David Wuthrich
2075 Andre George
2076 Jim Myers
2077 Carlos Sanchez
2078 Francisco (Arias)
2079 Sean Thompson
2080 Scott Ebert
2081 Adam Hilpert
2082 Steve Reed
2083 Lance Burnett
2084 Dave Edwards
2085 Marino Hernandez
2086 Greg Lee
2087 Reuben Smiley
2088 Dario Toussaint
2089 Victor Cruz
2090 Brett Hewatt
2091 Kevin Rodgers
2092 Adam Smith
2093 Kevin Hall
2094 David Slavin
2095 Dobie (Swepson)
2096 Jesus Laya
2097 Joey Speaks
2098 David Booth
2099 Carl Hanselman
2100 Diego Segui
2101 Jack Hiatt
2102 Jack Penrod

1988 ProCards Portland Beavers

(Minnesota Twins, AAA)

MT
Complete Set (25): 5.00
639 Brad Bierley
640 Eric Bullock
641 Kelvin Torve
642 Jim Winn
643 John Moses
644 Jim Shellenback
645 Roy Smith
646 Karl Best
647 Doug Baker
648 Brad Boylan
649 Vic Rodrigeuz
650 Jim Mahoney
651 Brian Harper
652 Winston Ficklin
653 Chris Pittaro
654 Allan Anderson
655 Steve Liddle
656 Ricky Jones
657 Bobby Ralston
658 Mark Portugal
659 Jeff Bumgarner
660 Jim Davins
661 Phil Wilson
662 Ray Soff
663 T.R. Bryden
664 Fred Toliver
---- Checklist

1988 CMC (TCMA) Portland Beavers

(Minnesota Twins, AAA)

MT
Complete Set (25): 5.00
1 Andy Anderson
2 Karl Best
3 T.R. Bryden
4 Jeff Bumgarner
5 Mark Portugal
6 Roy Smith
7 Ray Soff
8 Freddie Toliver
9 Jim Winn
10 Jim Davins
11 Brian Harper
12 Steve Liddle
13 Doug Baker
14 Ricky Jones
15 Kelvin Torve
16 Brad Bierly
17 Eric Bullock
18 Winston Ficklin
19 Chris Pittaro
20 Vic Rodriguez
21 Robby Ralston
22 John Moses
23 Phil Wilson
24 Jim Mahoney
25 Jim Shellenback

1988 Star Prince William Yankees

(N.Y. Yankees, A)

MT
Complete Set (25): 17.50
1 Steve Adkins
2 Tim Bishop
3 Brent Blum
4 Dennis Brow
5 Ken Brown
6 Royal Clayton
7 Bill Dacosta
8 Luis Faccio
9 Reynaldo Fernandez
10 Randy Foster
11 Victor Garcia
12 Chris Howard
13 Dean Kelly
14 Jose Laboy
15 Kevin Maas
16 Mark Marris
17 Alan Mills
18 William Morales
19 Tom Popplewell
20 John Ramos
21 Jerry Hub
22 Darrell Tingle
23 Mickey Tresh
24 Bernie Williams
25 Gerald Williams

1988 ProCards Pulaksi Braves

(Atlanta Braves, R)

MT
Complete Set (25): 6.00
1748 Phillip Wellman
1749 Fred Koenig
1750 Smoky Burgess
1751 Scott Goselin
1752 Scott Grove
1753 John Greenwood
1754 Tom Rizzo
1755 Steve Wendell
1756 Glen Gardner
1757 David Reis
1758 Errol Flynn
1759 Paul Reis
1760 Calvain Culberson
1761 Ricky Rigsby
1762 Brent McCoy
1763 Chris Mitta
1764 Mike Urman
1765 David Piela
1766 Roger Hailey
1767 Robert Minaya
1768 Randy Simmons
1769 Ron Thomas
1770 Cloyd Boyer
1771 Don Bowman
---- Checklist

1988 Grand Slam Quad City Angels

(California Angels, A) (5,000 sets)

MT
Complete Set (30): 5.00
1 Eddie Rodriguez
2 Mike Couchee
3 Bill Zick
4 Wiley Lee
5 Kevin Flora
6 Larry Pardo
7 Edgal Rodriguez
8 Bill Robinson
9 Terence Carr
10 Steve Dunn
11 David Holdridge
12 Frank Mutz
13 Daryl Green
14 Bob Rose
15 Troy Giles
16 Rod Lung
17 Jim Townsend
18 Mario Molina
19 Edgar Alfonzo
20 Roberto Hernandez
21 Kenny Grant
22 Jim Aylward
23 Cesar DeLaRosa
24 Charlie Romero
25 Rob Wassenaar
26 Tim McKinnis
27 Chris Graves
28 Gary Buckels
29 Brandy Vann
30 Mike Musolino

1988 ProCards Reading Phillies

(Philadelphia Phillies, AA)

MT
Complete Set (27): 5.00
863 Tom Schwarz
864 Alan Leboeuf
865 Steve Sharts
866 Brad Moore
867 Tony Brown
868 Scott Service
869 Chuck Malone
870 Tim Sossamon
871 Warren Magee
872 Jeff Kaye
873 Gary Berman
874 Dan Giesen
875 Chuck McElroy
876 Tim Fortugno
877 Steve Deangelis
878 Rick Parker
879 Howard Nichols
880 Greg Edge
881 Harvey Brumfield
882 Greg Legg
883 Vince Holyfield
884 Jose Leiva
885 Ray Roman
886 Chris Calvert
887 Tim Corcoran
888 Carlos Arroyo
---- Checklist

1988 Cal Cards Reno Silver Sox

(Independent, A)

MT
Complete Set (24): 5.00
268 Alan Fowlkes
269 Elvin Rivera
270 Tony LaCerra
271 Reggie Glover
272 Bill Shamblin
273 Scott Madden
274 Joe Strong
275 John Savage
276 Frank Mutz
277 Mike Garner
278 Kinney Sims
279 Jamie Allison
280 Jim Aylward
281 Cary Grubb
282 Chris Holmes
283 Robbie Rogers
284 Mike Rountree
285 Joe Ortiz
286 Gregg Ward
287 Dave Liddell
288 Jim Pace
289 Pete Houston
290 Fred Carter
291 Nate Oliver

1988 ProCards Richmond Braves

(Atlanta Braves, AAA)

MT
Complete Set (27): 22.00
1 Lonnie Smith
2 Tommy Greene
3 Ronnie Gant
4 Todd Dewey
5 Greg Tubbs
6 Sam Ayoub
7 Juan Espino
8 Carlos Rios
9 Jeff Wetherby
10 Juan Eichelberger
11 Marty Clary
12 Jose Alvarez
13 Bean Stringfellow
14 Sid Akins
15 Jim Beauchamp
16 Leo Mazzone
17 Clarence Jones
18 Jeff Blauser
19 John Mizerock
20 Dave Griffin
21 Derek Lilliquist
22 Joe Boever
23 John Smoltz
24 Dave Justice
25 Alex Smith
26 Gary Eave
---- Checklist

1988 Bob's Cameras Richmond Braves

(Atlanta Braves, AAA) (3-7/8" x 5" color photo prints)

MT
Complete Set (25): 95.00
1 Joe Boever
2 Bean Stringfellow
3 Carlos Rios
4 Sid Akins
5 Lonnie Smith
6a Jeff Blauser
6b Todd Dewey
7 Derek Lilliquist
8 John Smoltz
9 Juan Espino
10 John Mizerock
11 Marty Clary
12 Mike Fischlin
13 David Justice
14 Dave Griffin
15 Tommy Greene
16 Alex Smith
17 Jeff Wetherby
18 Gary Eave
19 Greg Tubbs
20 Dave Miller
21 Kevin Coffman
22 Tommy Dunbar
23 John Grubb
24 Barry Jones

1988 CMC (TCMA) Richmond Braves

(Atlanta Braves, AAA)

MT
Complete Set (25): 10.00
1 Tommy Green
2 Derek Lilliquist
3 John Smoltz
4 Bean Stringfellow
5 Gary Eave
6 Juan Eichelberger
7 Sid Akins
8 Jose Alvarez
9 Joe Boever
10 Marty Clary
11 Todd Dewey
12 Ron Gant
13 Alex Smith
14 Lonnie Smith
15 Greg Tubbs
16 Jeff Wetherby
17 David Justice
18 Carlos Rios
19 Dave Griffin
20 Juan Espino
21 John Mizerock
22 Jeff Blauser
23 Jim Beauchamp
24 Leo Mazzone
25 Clarence Jones

1988 Richmond Braves team issue foldout

(Atlanta Braves, AAA) (Set issued as 11" x 28-3/4" perforated sheet.)

MT
Complete Foldout: 25.00
1 Sam Ayoub
2 Jeff Blauser
4 Mike Fischlin
5 Lonnie Smith
6 Carlos Rios
9 Jim Beauchamp
14 Terry Bell
15 Greg Tubbs
16 Sid Akins
18 Dave Justice
19 Bean Strinfellow
20 Dave Miller
22 Jeff Wetherby
24 Derek Lilliquist
25 John Mizerock
26 John Smoltz
27 Johnny Grubb
28 Steve Ziem
29 Juan Espino
30 Alex Smith
31 Gary Eave
32 Marty Clary
33 Tommy Greene
34 Dave Griffin
36 Joe Boever
---- Team photo

1988 ProCards Riverside Red Wave

(San Diego Padres, A)

MT
Complete Set (27): 5.00
1407 Ron Oglesby
1408 Kevin Farmer
1409 Steve Hendricks
1410 Brian Brooks
1411 Pat Jelks
1412 Jim Daniel
1413 Tony Torchia
1414 Tye Waller
1415 Greg Hall
1416 Warren Newson
1417 Tom Levasseur
1418 Dave Hollins
1419 Bill Taylor
1420 Brian Wood
1421 Bill Blount
1422 Paul Faries
1423 Jim Lewis
1424 Bill Marx
1425 Andy Skeels
1426 Ricky Bones
1427 Rich Holsman
1428 Brian Harrison
1429 Rafel Chavez

1430 Terry McDevitt
1431 Kevin Garner
1432 Steve Loubier
---- Checklist

1988 Cal Cards Riverside Red Wave

(San Diego Padres, A)

MT
Complete Set (28): 5.00
206 Kevin Armstrong
207 James Austin
208 Ricky Bones
209 Rafael Chaves
210 Brian Harrison
211 Richard Holsman
212 James Lewis
213 Steve Loubier
214 Bill Marx
215 Brian Wood
216 Brian Brooks
217 Paul Faries
218 Kevin Farmer
219 Greg Hall
220 Kevin Garner
221 Steve Hendricks
222 Dave Hollins
223 Tom Levasseur
224 Terry McDevitt
225 Warren Newsom
226 Andy Skeels
227 Bill Taylor
228 Pat Jelks
229 Tony Torchia
230 William Blount
231 Jim Danile
232 Ron Oglesby
233 Tye Waller

1988 ProCards Rochester Red Wings

(Baltimore Orioles, AAA)

MT
Complete Set (30): 5.00
193 Dale Berra
194 Eric Bell
195 Dave Smith
196 Bob Gibson
197 Vic Mata
198 Sherwin Cinjntje
199 Jeff Ballard
200 Ron Salcedo
201 Jay Tibbs
202 Mickey Tettleton
203 Matt Cimo
204 Chris Padget
205 Pete Stanicek
206 Jose Mesa
207 Reg Montgomery
208 Mark Bowden
209 Bill Scherrer
210 Mike Griffin
211 Johnny Oates
212 Dom Chiti
213 Keith Hughes
214 Jamie Reed
215 John Habyan
216 Jerry Narron
217 Craig Worthington
218 Curt Motton
219 Dickie Noles
220 Jay Colley
221 Silver Stadium
---- Checklist

1988 CMC (TCMA) Rochester Red Wings

(Baltimore Orioles, AAA)

MT
Complete Set (25): 5.00
1 Jeff Ballard
2 Eric Bell
3 Jose Mesa
4 Mark Bowden
5 Bob Gibson
6 John Habyan
7 Mike Griffin
8 Dickie Noles
9 Bill Scherrer
10 Jay Tibbs
11 Matt Cimo
12 Dale Berra
13 Chris Padget
14 Jerry Narron
15 Keith Hughes
16 Ron Salcedo
17 David Lee Smith
18 Pete Stanicek
19 Craig Worthington
20 Sherwin Cinjtje
21 Mickey Tettleton
22 Tito Landrum
23 Vic Mata
24 Johnny Oates
25 Curt Motton

1988 Pucko Rochester Red Wings

(Baltimore Orioles, AAA)

MT
Complete Set (36): 12.00
1 Rochester Red Wings
2 Mark Bowden
3 Dale Berra
4 Curt Brown
5 Matt Cimo
6 Gordon Dillard
7 Steve Finley
8 Mike Griffin
9 John Habyan
10 Pete Harnisch
11 Kevin Hickey
12 Gerry Holtz
13 Keith Hughes
14 Ken Landreaux
15 Vic Mata
16 Bob Milacki
17 Jerry Narron
18 Carl Nichols
19 Dickie Noles
20 Chris Padget
21 Tim Pyznarski
22 Mike Raczka
23 Wade Rowdon
24 Ron Salcedo
25 Chuck Stanhope
26 Jeff Stone
27 Craig Worthington
28 Dom Chiti
29 Curt Motton
30 Johnny Oates
31 Jamie Reed
32 Bob Goughan
33 Rochester Red Wings
34 Rochester Red Wings
35 Rochester Red Wings
36 Rochester Red Wings

1988 Rochester Red Wings team issue

(Baltimore Orioles, AAA)

MT
Complete Set (26): 14.00
(1) Jeff Ballard
(2) Eric Bell
(3) Dale Berra
(4) Mark Bowden
(5) Dom Chiti
(6) Sherwin Cijntje
(7) Matt Cimo
(8) Bob Gibson
(9) Mike Griffin
(10) John Habyan
(11) Keith Hughes
(12) Vic Mata
(13) Jose Mesa
(14) Curt Motton
(15) Jerry Narron
(16) Dickie Noles
(17) Johnny Oates
(18) Chris Padget
(19) Ron Salcedo
(20) Bill Scherrer
(21) Dave (D.L.) Smith
(22) Pete Stanicek
(23) Mickey Tettleton
(24) Jay Tibbs
(25) Jim Traber
(26) Craig Worthington

1988 Rockford Expos team issue

(Montreal Expos, A)

MT
Complete Set (34): 9.00
1 Alan Bannister
3 Gene Glynn
4 Trevor Penn
6 Steve Pearse
9 Jesus Paredes
13 Arci Cianfrocco
14 Delino DeShields
15 Kent Willis
17 Paul Frye
20 Mike Parrott
22 Kevin Sheary
23 Rob Kerrigan
27 Greg Colburn (Colbrunn)
28 Mario Brito
33 James Faulk
35 John Mello
39 Chris Pollack
41 Dave Clark
42 Chris Lariviere
44 Troy Ricker
45 Jeff Carter
46 Chris Marchok
47 Cesar Hernandez
48 Howard Farmer
49 Rob Leary
51 Scott Bromby
55 Nate Minchey
---- John Cain
---- Sean Cunningham
---- Jeff Hauser
---- Scott Lane
---- Bill Larsen
---- Thomas Shannon
---- Dan Deweerdt

1988 Star Salem Buccaneers

(Pittsburgh Pirates, A)

MT
Complete Set (25): 5.00
1 Steve Adams
2 Stan Belinda
3 Kevin Burdick
4 Terry Crowley
5 Chip Duncan
6 Oscar Escobar
7 Andy Hall
8 Scott Henion
9 Tim Kirk
10 Tony Longmire
11 John Love
12 Tim McKinley
13 Tim McMillan
14 Pete Murphy
15 Julio Peguero
16 Keith Raisnen
17 Richard Reed
18 Scott Ruskin
19 Mike Stevanus
20 Dave Takach
21 Doug Torborg
22 Junior Vizcaino
23 Ben Webb
24 Ed Yacopino
25 Mike York

1988 Salt Lake City Trappers team issue

(Independent, R)

MT
Complete Set (30): 9.00
1 Patrick Waid
2 Murray Brothers
3 Coaches
4 Front office and announcer
5 Chris Sloniger
6 Bullpen coach and batboys
7 Ray Karczewski
8 Kelly Zane
9 Jeff Allison
10 Tommy Boyce
11 Bobby Edwards
12 Rick L. Hurni
13 Will Ambos
14 Greg "Tank" Ehmig
15 Michael Gibbons
16 Promo/business manager and scout
17 Kerry Shaw
18 Barry Moss
19 Doug Howard
20 Myron "Pops" Gardner
21 Fred Riscen
22 Martin Peralta
23 Terence "T-Can" Glover
24 Tim McKercher
25 Mando Verdugo
26 Bill Wenrick
27 Sal Roldan
28 Lee Carballo
29 Sean Johnson
30 Bill Murray

1988 Best San Antonio Missions

(L.A. Dodgers, AA) (Besides the regular issue, this set was also produced in a numbered "Platinum" edition of 1,300. The premium cards feature silver and black fronts and blue backs.)

MT
Complete Set (28): 9.00
Complete Set, Platinum: 18.00
1 Ramon Martinez
2 Barry Wohler
3 Michael Pitz
4 Greg LaFever
5 Tony Mack
6 Domingo Michel
7 Michael Munoz
8 Wayne Kirby
9 Jim Kating
10 Mike Schweighoffer
11 Joe Kesselmark
12 Juan Bustabad
13 David Eichhorn
14 Manuel Francois
15 Darrin Fletcher
16 Walter McConnell
17 Phil Torres
18 Jose Mota
19 Mike Huff
20 Joe Humphries
21 John Wetteland
22 Javier Ortiz
23 Kevin Kennedy
24 Juan Bell
25 Mark Sheehy
26 Luis Lopez
27 Pat Zachry
28 Logo/checklist

1988 Best San Bernardino Spirit

(Seattle Mariners, A) (In addition to the regular issue, a premium "Platinum" edition of 1,300 numbered sets was also produced, featuring silver and black fronts and blue backs.)

MT
Complete Set (28): 250.00
Complete Set, Platinum: 650.00
Complete Platinum Set, Unopened: 1000.
1 Ken Griffey Jr.
2 Don Reynolds
3 Lee Townsend
4 Ted Williams
5 Anthony Woods
6 Pat Rice
7 Jody Ryan
8 Rich DeLucia
9 William Diaz
10 Dan Disher
11 Ted Eldredge
12 Jerry Goff
13 Jose Tartabull
14 Ralph Dick
15 Jim Blueburg
16 Jim Bowie Jr.
17 Dave Burba
18 Clay Gunn
19 Keith Helton
20 Steve Hisey
21 Joe Kemp
22 Bryan King
23 Jeff Nelson
24 Rich Doyle
25 Todd Hayes
26 Mike Brocki
27 Bobby Cuellar
28 Checklist/Fiscalini Field

1988 Cal Cards San Bernardino Spirit

(Seattle Mariners, A)

MT
Complete Set (28): 30.00
28 Bryan King
29 Steve Murray
30 Jim Bowie Jr.
31 Dan Disher
32 Clay Gunn
33 Jerry Goff
34 Ken Griffey Jr.
35 Joe Kemp
36 Jose Tartabull
37 William Diaz
38 Ted Williams
39 Steve Hisey
40 Mike Brocki
41 Ted Eldredge
42 Jody Ryan
43 Pat Rice
44 Keith Helton
45 Howard Townsend
46 Tim McLain
47 Jim Blueberg
48 Jeff Nelson
49 David Burba
50 Rich DeLucia
51 Todd Hayes
52 Rich Doyle
53 Ralph Dick
54 Bobby Cuellar
55 Don Reynolds

1988 ProCards San Jose Giants

(S.F. Giants, A)

MT
Complete Set (30): 5.00
108 Koli Maeda
109 Paul Blair
110 Willie Mijares
111 Dave Peterson
112 Gary Jones
113 Scott Murray
114 Eric Gunderson
115 Doug Robertson
116 Ray Velasquez
117 Masa Yamamoto
118 Russ Swan
119 Rich Aldrete
120 Tom Meagher
121 Ken Suzuki
122 Todd Oakes
123 Sam Hirose
124 Lance Hutchins
125 Duane Espy
126 Tod Ronson
127 Eric Pilkington
128 Tad Hanyuda
129 Greg Conner
130 Gil Heredia
131 Gregg Ritchie
132 Kevin Meier
133 Jim McNamara
134 Mark Leonard
135 Daron Connelly
136 Joe Johdo
---- Checklist

1988 Cal Cards San Jose Giants

(S.F. Giants, A)

MT
Complete Set (29): 5.00
116 Rich Aldrete
117 Paul Blair
118 Greg Conner
119 Tad Hanyuda
120 Joe Jodo
121 Gary Jones
122 Mark Leonard
123 Jim McNamara
124 William Mijares
125 Scott Murray
126 Dave Patterson
127 Gregg Ritchie
128 Tod Ronson
129 Ken Suzuki
130 Daron Connelly
131 Eric Gunderson
132 Gil Heredia
133 Koji Maeda
134 Tom Meagher
135 Kevin Meier
136 Eric Pilkington
137 Doug Robertson
138 Russ Swan
139 Ray Velasquez
140 Masa Yamamoto
141 Duane Espy
142 Sam Hirose
143 Todd Oakes
144 Lance Hutchins

1988 ProCards Savannah Cardinals

(St. Louis Cardinals, A)

MT
Complete Set (29): 5.00
331 Mike Hinkle
332 Ken Smith
333 Tony Russo
334 Tim Sherrill
335 Rob Colescott
336 Martin Mason
337 Keith Champion
338 Dave Krebs
339 Mark Behny
340 Bill Hershman
341 Roberto Marte
342 Hal Hempen
343 Clint Horsley
344 Tim Meamber
345 Brad Harvick
346 Reed Olmstead
347 John Sellick
348 Jim Ferguson
349 Stan Barrs
350 Eddie Looper
351 Kris Huffman
352 Ryan Johnston
353 Mike Alvarez
354 Eddie Carter
355 Antron Grier
356 Jean Gentleman
357 Greg Doss
358 Francisco Rosario
---- Checklist

1988 ProCards Shreveport Captains

(S.F. Giants, AA)

MT
Complete Set (25): 5.00
Complete Set, Taco Bell (25): 45.00
1279 Jack Mull
1280 Joe Kmak
1281 Jose Dominguez
1282 Joe Olker
1283 Mike Benjamin
1284 Vince Sferrazza
1285 Dean Freeland
1286 Steve Cline
1287 Andy Dixon
1288 Paul Meyers
1289 George Bonilla
1290 Paul McClellan
1291 Jeff Carter
1292 Jose Pena
1293 Romy Cucjen
1294 Rick Nelson
1295 Stuart Tate
1296 Mike Remlinger
1297 John Skurla
1298 Trevor Wilson
1299 Harry Davis
1300 Tim McCoy
1301 Ed Puikunas
1302 T.J. McDonald
---- Checklist

1988 Grand Slam South Atlantic League All-Stars

(Class A) (8,000 sets, 2-3/8" x 3-1/2")

MT
Complete Set (28): 7.00
1 Richie Hebner (Myrtle Beach)
2 Mel Roberts (Spartanburg)
3 Ned Yost (Sumter)
4 Bill Paul Carver (Asheville)
5 Ron Downs (Augusta)
6 Eddie Taubensee (Greensboro)
7 Brian Lane (Greensboro)
8 Joe Turek (Greensboro)
9 Ron Mullins (Greensboro)
10 Omar Olivares (Charleston)
11 Darrin Reichle (Charleston)
12 Guillermo Velazquez
13 Alex Arias (Charleston)
14 Mike Miller (Columbia)
15 Anthony Toney (Fayetteville)
16 Brant Alyea (Gastonia)
17 Williams Suero (Myrtle Beach)
18 Luis Sojo (Myrtle Beach)
19 Greg Vella (Myrtle Beach)
20 Derek Bell (Myrtle Beach)
21 Xavier Hernandez (Myrtle Beach)
22 Jimmy Rogers (Myrtle Beach)
23 Denis Boucher (Myrtle Beach)
24 Rob Colescott (Savannah)
25 John Sellick (Sumter)
26 James Vatcher (Spartanburg)
27 Andy Carter (Spartanburg)
28 Dennis Burlingame (Sumter)

1988 Grand Slam South Bend White Sox

(Chicago White Sox, A) (5,000 sets)

MT
Complete Set (28): 5.00
1 Cesar Bernhardt
2 Larry Allen
3 Javier Ocasio
4 Kevin Murdock
5 Ed Smith
6 Ray Payton
7 Dwayne Hosey
8 Rod McCray
9 Kinnis Pledger
10 Mike Maksudian
11 Wilson Valera
12 Bernando Cruz
13 Kurt Brown
14 Don Cooper
15 Steve Dillard
16 Jim Reinebold
17 Ed Sedar
18 Argenis Conde
19 Mike Girouard
20 Julian Gonzalez
21 Curt Hasler
22 John Hudek
23 Bo Kennedy
24 Rob Resnikoff
25 Randy Robinson
26 Steve Schrenik
27 Mark Tortorice
28 Stanley Coveleski

1988 Donn Jennings Southern League All-Stars

(AA)

MT
Complete Set (40): 5.00
1 Matt Winters
2 Kevin Burrell
3 Steve Howard
4 Mike Bordick
5 Keith Lockhart
6 Darrell Pruitt
7 Matt Merullo
8 Jerry Bertolani
9 Tim Dulin
10 Carlo Columbino
11 Rafael Delima
12 Derek Parks
13 Bernardo Brito
14 Barry Jones
15 Mark Lemke
16 Ed Whited
17 Drew Denson
18 Jeff Huson
19 Bob Caffrey
20 Randy Braun
21 Armando Moreno
22 Frrancisco Cabreba
23 Webster Garrison
24 Junior Felix
25 Domingo Martinez
26 Alex Sanchez
27 Steve Cummings
28 Kevin Blankenship
29 Larry Casian
30 German Gonzales
31 Brian Meyer
32 Pete Harnisch
33 Brian Householder
34 Tom Drees
35 Joe Lazor
36 Chris Hammond
37 Joe Bruno
38 Rico Petrocelli
39 Tommy Thompson
40 Nardi Contreres

1988 ProCards Southern Oregon A's

(Oakland A's, A)

MT
Complete Set (28): 5.00
1692 Jim Buccheri
1693 Tim Vannaman
1694 Richard Rozman
1695 Nick Venuto
1696 Tony Ariola
1697 Joel Smith
1698 DeWayne Jones
1699 Tom Carcione
1700 Josue Espinal
1701 Stan Royer
1702 Rod Correia
1703 Joel Chimelis
1704 Mike Messerly
1705 Dean Borelli
1706 Lee Tinsley
1707 Tony Floyd
1708 Greg Ferguson
1709 Kevin MacLeod
1710 Mike Mungin
1711 Dan Eskew
1712 Jim Lawson
1713 Ray Harris
1714 J.P. Ricciardi
1715 Jerry Rizza
1716 Joe Hillman
1717 Lenny Sakata
1718 Jesus Hernaiz
---- Checklist

1988 ProCards Spartanburg Phillies

(Philadelphia Phillies, A)

MT
Complete Set (26): 5.00
1024 Jeff Stark
1025 Matt Rambo
1026 Bob Hurta
1027 Tim Peek
1028 Greg McCarthy
1029 Darrell Coulter
1030 Shelby McDonald
1031 John Larosa
1032 Phil Fagnano
1033 Mel Roberts
1034 Rod Robertson
1035 Kim Batista
1036 Jaime Barragan
1037 Scott Ruckman
1038 Marty Foley
1039 Carlos Zayas
1040 Tony Trevino
1041 Gary Maasberg
1042 Doug Lindsey
1043 Todd Felton
1044 Gary White
1045 Jim Vatcher
1046 Bob Britt
1047 Buzz Capra
1048 Jim Platts
---- Checklist

1988 Star Spartanburg Phillies

(Philadelphia Phillies, A) (Both red- and blue-bordered versions were issued; only 700 of the latter)

MT
Complete Set, red (25): 5.00
Complete Set, blue (25): 13.00
1 Jimmy Barragan
2 Kim Batiste
3 Andy Carter
4 Mark Cobb
5 Darrell Coulter
6 Paul Ellison
7 Martin Foley
8 Bobby Hurta
9 Stephen Kirkpatrick
10 John Larosa
11 Doug Lindsey
12 Tim Mauser
13 Greg McCarthy
14 Sheebie McDonald
15 Timothy Peek
16 Matt Rambo
17 Scott Reaves
18 Rod Robertson
19 Scott Ruckman
20 Royal Thomas Jr.
21 James Vatcher
22 Mel Roberts
23 Buzz Capra
24 Brett Massie (trainer)

1988 ProCards Spokane Indians

(San Diego Padres, A)

MT
Complete Set (26): 5.00
1922 Greg Conley
1923 Tye Waller
1924 Rob Cantwell
1925 Kelly Lifgren
1926 Mike Humphreys
1927 Squeezer Thompson
1928 Steve Lubratich
1929 Pedro Aquino
1930 Luis Lopez
1931 Craig Bigham
1932 Greg Smith
1933 A.J. Sager
1934 John Kuehl
1935 Chad Kuhn
1936 Nicko Riesgo
1937 Brad Hoyer
1938 David Briggs
1939 Bob Curnow
1940 Brian Cisarik
1941 Renay Bryand
1942 Barry Hightower
1943 Mark Verstandig
1944 Craig Proctor
1945 Chris Haslock
1946 Ron Morton
---- Checklist

1988 Best Springfield Cardinals

(St. Louis Cardinals, A)

MT
Complete Set (28): 21.00
1 Robert Glisson
2 Mark Grater
3 Jeremy Hernandez
4 Michael Henry
5 Gregory Becker
6 Shawn Hathaway
7 William Bivens
8 Andrew Taylor
9 James Gibbs
10 Frank Postio
11 Bob Sudo
12 Charles Johnson
13 Bernard Gilkey
14 Raymond Lankford
15 David Payton
16 Michael Raziano
17 Alex Ojea
18 Stephen Meyer
19 Rodney Brewer
20 Steven Jeffers
21 Franklin Abreu
22 John Murphy
23 Gary Nichols
24 Ed Fulton
25 Chris Maloney
26 Mark De John
27 Brad Bluestone
28 Logo/checklist

1988 ProCards Stockton Ports

(Milwaukee Brewers, A)

MT
Complete Set (33): 6.00
721 Rob Derkson
722 Steve Monson
723 Mark Aguilar
724 Shon Ashley
725 Keith Fleming
726 Alan Sadler
727 Sandy Guerrero
728 Gil Villanueva
729 Dave Taylor
730 Randy Veres
731 Ron Romanick
732 Bobby Jones
733 Tim McIntosh
734 Brian Drahman
735 Ruben Escalera
736 Jaime Navarro
737 Charlie Montoyo
738 Bill Spiers
739 Brian Stone
740 Dave Hoppert
741 Rob Smith
742 Angel Rodriguez
743 John Jaha
744 Jay Williams
745 Danny Fitzpatrick
746 Carl Moraw
747 Doug Henry
748 Narcisso Elvira
749 Angel Miranda
750 Don Miller
751 Dan Chapman
752 Mike Conroy, Mark Marine
---- Checklist

1988 Star St. Lucie Mets

(N.Y. Mets, A)

MT
Complete Set (25): 5.00
1 Brandon Bailey
2 Chris Bayer
3 Kevin Brown
4 Rick Brown
5 Jeff Ciszkowski
6 Chris Donnels
7 Jovon Edwards
8 Dave Gelatt
9 Adam Ging
10 Kip Gross
11 Rob Hernandez
12 Andre Jacas
13 Scott Jaster
14 Geary Jones
15 Manny Mantrana
16 Gus Meizoso
17 Doug Myres
18 Hector Perez
19 Fritz Polka
20 Craig Repoz
21 Bill Stiles
22 Greg Talamantez
23 John Toale
24 Dave Trautwein
25 Juan Villanueva

1988 Cal Cards Stockton Ports

(Milwaukee Brewers, A)

MT
Complete Set (31): 5.00
175 Steve Monson
176 Ron Romanick

177 Doug Henry
178 Brian Stone
179 Randy Veres
180 Angel Miranda
181 Alan Sadler
182 Jaime Navarro
183 Narcisco Elvira
184 Carl Moraw
185 Keith Fleming
186 Brian Drahman
187 Danny Fitzpatrick
188 Gil Villanueva
189 Tim McIntosh
190 Robert Jones
191 Mark Aguilar
192 Robert Smith
193 John Jaha
194 Shon Ashley
195 Dave Taylor
196 Sandy Guerrero
197 Bill Spiers
198 Angel Rodriguez
199 Charlie Montoyo
200 Ruben Escalera
201 Rob Derksen
202 Dave Huppert
203 Jay Williams
204 Don Miller
205 Dan Chapman

1988 Star St. Petersburg Cardinals

(St. Louis Cardinals, A) (Scarce late-issue cards are Fagan and Riggins)

	MT
Complete, w/Riggins, Fagan (27):	15.00
Partial, no Riggins, Fagan (25):	5.00

1 John Balfanz
2 Scott Braodfoot
3 Dennis Carter
4 Joseph Cunningham
5 Jerry Daniels
6 Terry Elliot
7 James Fernandez
8 Scott Hamilton
9 Patrick Hews
10 Stephen Hill
11 Crucito Lara
12 Scott Lawrence
13 Robert Livchak
14 Lonnie Maclin
15 Julian Martinez
16 Thomas Mauch
17 Kevin Maxey
18 Scott Melvin
19 Darren Nelson
20 Jay North
21 Geronimo Pena
22 Lenin Picota
23 Larry Pierson
24 Terrence Thomas
25 Stanley Zaltsman
26 Mark Riggins (late issue)
27 Pete Fagan (late issue)

1988 ProCards St. Catharines Blue Jays

(Toronto Blue Jays, A)

	MT
Complete Set (35):	6.00

2005 Armando Pagliari
2006 Luis Salazar
2007 Timothy Brown
2008 Jose Villa
2009 Benigno Placeres
2010 Brad Evaschuk
2011 Jose Guarache
2012 Pablo Castro
2013 Donn Wolfe
2014 Eddie Dennis
2015 Mike McAlpin
2016 Timothy Hodge
2017 Nigel Wilson
2018 Daniel Dodd
2019 Greg Williams
2020 Greg McCutcheon
2021 Robert Montalvo
2022 Curtis Johnson
2023 David Weathers
2024 Jose Martinez
2025 Edgar Marquez
2026 Rafael Martinez
2027 Jason Townley
2028 Marcos Tavaras
2029 Greg Harding
2030 Bryan Dixon
2031 Mike Jockish
2032 Mike Taylor
2033 Rick Vaughn
2034 Anthony Ward
2035 Ryan Thompson
2036 Darrin Wade
2037 Armando Serra
2038 Patrick Guerrero
---- Checklist

1988 ProCards Sumter Braves

(Atlanta Braves, A)

	MT
Complete Set (32):	6.00

390 Keith Mitchell
391 Tony Baldwin
392 Bob Cole
393 Dennis Burlingame
394 John Reilley
395 Wes Currin
396 Mark Davis
397 Johnny Cuevas
398 Jesus Mendoza
399 Jose Valencia
400 Winnie Relaford
401 Greg Harper
402 Rick Siebert
403 Marcos Vezquez
404 Skipper Wright
405 Gregg Gilbert
406 Greg Cloninger
407 A J Waznik
408 Glenn Mitchell
409 Juan Fredymond
410 Ben Rivera
411 David Colon
412 Tom Redington
413 Dave Nied
414 Ned Yost
415 Larry Jaster
416 Rick Albert
417 Willy Johnson
418 Ralph Meister
419 Teddy Williams
420 Ed Holtz
---- Checklist

1988 ProCards Syracuse Chiefs

(Toronto Blue Jays, AAA)

	MT
Complete Set (30):	5.00

805 Jack O'Connor
806 Luis Leal
807 Cliff Young
808 Geronimo Berroa
809 Norm Tonucci
810 Luis Reyna
811 Kelly Hetah
812 Glenallen Hill
813 Alexis Infante
814 Steve Davis
815 Enrique Burgos
816 Doug Bair
817 Bob Bailor
818 Galen Cisco
819 Red Coughlin
820 Jose Nunez
821 Greg Myers
822 Hector Torres
823 Colin McLaughlin
824 Mark Ross
825 Rob Ducey
826 Sal Butera
827 Bob Shirley
828 Marc DeBottis
829 Randy Holland
830 Frank Wills
831 Otis Green
832 Eric Yelding
833 Chris Shaddy
---- Checklist

1988 CMC (TCMA) Syracuse Chiefs

(Toronto Blue Jays, AAA)

	MT
Complete Set (25):	5.00

1 Steve Davis
2 Randy Holland
3 Colin McLaughlin
4 Jose Nunez
5 Mark Ross
6 Norm Tonucci
7 Bob Shirley
8 Cliff Young
9 Doug Bair
10 Jack O'Connor
11 Frank Wills
12 Luis Reyna
13 Geronimo Berroa
14 Rob Ducey
15 Glenallen Hill
16 Sal Butera
17 Eric Yelding
18 Greg Myers
19 Otis Green
20 Kelly Heath
21 Alexis Infante
22 Chris Shaddy
23 Hector Torres
24 Bob Bailor
25 Galen Cisco

1988 Syracuse Chiefs Souvenir Tickets

Commemorating its 11th anniversary as the top farm club of the Toronto Blue Jays, the Syracuse Chiefs produced a set of souvneir tickets in 1988 picturing Blue Jays stars in their days with the Chiefs. Besides being issued as individual tickets for the season's first dozen home games, the tickets were also issued as a pair of unperforated 10-1/2" x 6-1/2" uncut sheets. Individual tickets measure 1-1/2" x 6-1/2" and feature a color photo at center with a blue border. Backs are printed in black.

	MT
Complete Set, souvenir sheets (2):	12.00
Complete Set, single tickets (12):	8.00

1 George Bell
2 Silvestre Campusano
3 John Cerutti
4 Rob Ducey
5 Mark Eichhorn
6 Tony Fernandez
7 Jimmy Key
8 Nelson Liriano
9 Lloyd Moseby
10 Mel Stottlemyre, Jr.
11 Willie Upshaw
12 David Wells

1988 ProCards Tacoma Tigers

(Oakland A's, AAA)

	MT
Complete Set (28):	5.00

612 Gary Jones
613 Joe Xavier
614 Felix Jose
615 Eddie Jurak
616 Matt Sinatro
617 Tyler Brilinski
618 Jim Jones
619 Jeff Shaver
620 Stan Naccarato
621 Roy Johnson
622 Brad Fischer
623 Chuck Estrada
624 Orlando Mercado
625 Jim Corsi
626 Kevin Sliwinski
627 Rich Bordi
628 Bob Stoddard
629 Brian Snyder
630 Lance Blankenship
631 Reese Lambert
632 Todd Burns
633 Tim Meeks
634 Andre Robertson
635 Wayne Krenchicki
636 Charlie Corbell
637 Alex Sanchez
638 Luis Polonia
---- Checklist

1988 CMC (TCMA) Tacoma Tigers

(Oakland A's, AAA)

	MT
Complete Set (25):	5.00

1 Rich Bordi
2 Todd Burns
3 Charlie Corbell
4 Reese Lambert
5 Tim Meeks
6 Jeff Zaske
7 Jim Corsi
8 Jeff Shaver
9 Brian Snyder
10 Bob Stoddard
11 Lance Blakenship
12 Tyler Brilinski
13 Ed Jurak
14 Wayne Krenchicki
15 Roy Johnson
16 Luis Polonia
17 Alex Sanchez
18 Matt Sinatro
19 Andre Robertson
20 Kevin Sliwinski
21 Jimmy Jones
22 Orlando Mercado
23 Gary Jones
24 Felix Jose
25 Joe Xavier

1988 Tacoma Tigers team issue McGwire photo

(5-1/8" x 8-3/8", black-and-white, blank-back)

	MT
Mark McGwire (5-1/8" x 8-1/2" b/w photo)	50.00

1988 Star Tampa Tarpons

(Chicago White Sox, A)

	MT
Complete Set (24):	5.00

1 Hernan Adames
2 Leon Baham
3 Kurt Brown
4 Chris Cauley
5 Brian Davis
6 Bill Eveline
7 Cornelio Garcia
8 Jeff Greene
9 Buddy Groom
10 Todd Hall
11 Brent Knackert
12 Jerry Kutzler
13 Tom Lahrman
14 Ravelo Manzanillo
15 Norberto Martin
16 Pat Mehrtens
17 Eric Milholland
18 Kevin Murdock
19 Mike Ollom
20 Jack Peel
21 Dave Reynolds
22 Dan Rohrmeier
23 Carl Sullivan
24 Tony Woods
---- Team logo

Value of modern team sets is often predicated as much on inclusion of star player's early cards as on scarcity of the issue.

1988 Grand Slam Texas League All-Stars

(Class AA) (12,000 sets)

	MT
Complete Set (39):	11.00

1 Jack Mull (Shreveport)
2 Todd Zeile (Arkansas)
3 Chad Kreuter (Tulsa)
4 Gary Alexander (Tulsa)
5 Steve Wilson (Tulsa)
6 Dan Scarpetta (El Paso)
7 John Wetteland (San Antonio)
8 Joe Olker (Shreveport)
9 Kevin Bootay (Tulsa)
10 Angelo Cuevas (Jackson)
11 Mike Benjamin (Shreveport)
12 Scott Coolbaugh (Tulsa)
13 Brett Harrison (Arkansas)
14 Manny Salinas (Jackson)
15 John Skurla (Shreveport)
16 Tom Baine (Arkansas)
17 John Barfield (Tulsa)
18 Blaine Beatty (Jackson)
19 Jose Dominguez (Shreveport)
20 Scott Arnold (Arkansas)
21 Dave Pavlas (Tulsa)
22 Kevin Kennedy (San Antonio)
23 Mike Basso (Wichita)
24 Mario Monico (El Paso)
25 Fred Williams (El Paso)
26 Gary Sheffield (El Paso)
27 Jim McCollom (Midland)
28 Ramon Martinez (San Antonio)
29 Terry Gilmore (Wichita)
30 Mike Munoz (San Antonio)
31 Ed Puig (El Paso)
32 Carlos Baerga (Wichita)
33 Mike Huff (San Antonio)
34 Chris Knabenshue (Wichita)
35 Greg Vaughn (El Paso)
36 Mike Knapp (Midland)
37 Luis Lopez (San Antonio)
38 Frank Mattox (El Paso)
39 Jeff Manto (Midland)

1988 ProCards Tidewater Tides

(N.Y. Mets, AAA)

	MT
Complete Set (29):	9.00

1577 John Mitchell
1578 Phil Lombardi
1579 John Cumberland
1580 Sam McCrary
1581 Tom Edens
1582 Jeff Innis
1583 Jack Savage

1584 Tim Tolman
1585 Rich Miller
1586 Mike Cubbage
1587 Jeff McKnight
1588 Mark Carren
1589 Wally Whitehurst
1590 Reggie Dobie
1591 Marcus Lawton
1592 Dave West
1593 Tim Drummond
1594 Al Pardo
1595 Ken Dowell
1596 Andre David
1597 Greg Olson
1598 Steve Springer
1599 Tom McCarthy
1600 Gregg Jefferies
1601 Jose Roman
1602 Steve Frey
1603 Darren Reed
1604 Keith Miller
---- Checklist

1988 Tidewater Tides team issue foldout

(N.Y. Mets, AAA) (This set was issued as a foldout poster with a team photo and individual 2-1/4" x 3" color cards perforated for easy removal.)

	MT
Complete Foldout:	18.00

4 Steve Frey
5 Ken Dowell
9 Gregg Jeffries
10 Steve Springer
11 Darren Reed
16 Tim Tolman
17 Andre David
18 Jeff McKnight
19 Jose Roman
21 Wally Whitehurst
22 Joaquin Contreras
23 Jack Savage
25 Keith Miller
26 Mike Cubbage
27 John Miller
28 Tom Edens
29 Greg Olson
30 Dave West
31 Mark Carreon
33 Phil Lombardi
34 John Cumberland
35 Tim Drummond
36 Tom McCarthy
37 Rich Miller
39 Randy Niemann
40 Jeff Innis
---- Sam McCrary
---- Dave Rosenfield
---- R.C. Reuteman
---- Tony Mercurio
---- Team photo

1988 CMC (TCMA) Tidewater Tides

(N.Y. Mets, AAA)

	MT
Complete Set, "Jeffries" (26):	13.00
Complete Set, "Jefferies" (26):	10.00

1 Jack Savage
2 David West
3 Jeff Innis
4 Tim Drummond
5 Tom Edens
6 Steve Frey
7 Tom McCarthy
8 John Mitchell
9 Jose Roman
10 Randy Niemann
11 Wally Whitehurst
12 Phil Lombardi
13 Greg Olson
14 Ken Dowell
15a Gregg Jeffries (name incorrect)
15b Gregg Jefferies (name correct)
16 Darren Reed
17 Joaquin Contreas
18 Andre David
19 Jeff McKnight
20 Keith Miller
21 Steve Springer
22 Mark Carreon
23 Tim Tolman
24 Mike Cubbage
25 John Cumberland
26 Rich Miller

1988 ProCards Toledo Mud Hens

(Detroit Tigers, AAA)

	MT
Complete Set (28):	6.00

585 Jeff Reynolds
586 Dave Beard
587 Doug Strange
588 Mark Huismann
589 Donnie Rowland
590 Pat Corrales
591 Paul Cherry
592 Eric King
593 Mike Trujillo
594 Scott Lusader
595 Billy Bean
596 John Duffy
597 Chris Hoiles
598 Pete Rice
599 Gene Roof
600 Paul Felix
601 Pedro Chavez
602 Benny Ruiz
603 Tim Leiper
604 Don Schulze
605 Rey Palacios
606 Don McGann
607 Stan Clarke
608 Dave Cooper
609 Steve Searcy
610 Ramon Pena
611 Mike Brown
---- Checklist

1988 CMC (TCMA) Toledo Mud Hens

(Detroit Tigers, AAA)

	MT
Complete Set (25):	5.00

1 Dave Beard
2 Stan Clarke
3 Don Schulze
4 Steve Searcy
5 Eric King
6 Roman Pena
7 Mike Trujillo
8 Dave Cooper
9 Paul Cherry
10 John Duffy
11 Mark Huisman
12 Billy Bean
13 Scott Lusader
14 Doug Strange
15 Jeff Reynolds
16 Benny Ruis
17 Pedro Chavez
18 Rey Palacios
19 Chris Hoiles
20 Paul Felix
21 Tim Leiper
22 Donnie Rowland
23 Pete Rice
24 Mike Brown
25 Pat Corrales

1988 ProCards Tucson Toros

(Houston Astros, AAA)

	MT
Complete Set (28):	10.00

166 Craig Biggio
167 Karl Allaire
168 Craig Smajstrla
169 Manny Hernandez
170 Rafael Montalvo
171 Jose Cano
172 Jim Weaver
173 Glenn Carpenter
174 Luis DeLeon
175 Pat Keedy
176 Joe Mikulik
177 Louie Meadows
178 John Fishel
179 Clay Christiansen
180 Kevin Hagen
181 Rocky Childress
182 Ken Caminiti
183 Dave Meads
184 Eddie Watt
185 Mike Loynd
186 Anthony Kelley
187 Jeff Datz
188 Cameron Drew
189 Ernie Camacho
190 Bob Didier
191 Nelson Rood
192 Rex Jones
---- Checklist

1988 Jones Photo Tucson Toros

(Houston Astros, AAA) (3" x 5-1/8", 500 sets produced, each set comes in a protective miniature binder.)

	MT
Complete Set (24):	95.00

(1) Karl Allaire
(2) Craig Biggio
(3) Ken Caminiti
(4) Jose Cano
(5) Glenn Carpenter
(6) Rocky Childress
(7) Jeff Datz
(8) Luis DeLeon
(9) Bob Didier
(10) Drew Cameron
(11) John Fishel
(12) Kevin Hagen
(13) Manny Hernandez
(14) Pat Keedy
(15) Anthony Kelley
(16) Dave Meads
(17) Joe Mikulik
(18) Rafael Montalvo
(19) Nelson Rood
(20) Joe Sambito
(21) Alex Trevino
(22) Eddie Watt
(23) Jim Weaver
(24) Craig Smajstria

1988 CMC (TCMA) Tucson Toros

(Houston Astros, AAA)

	MT
Complete Set (25):	6.00

1 Manny Hernandez
2 Anthony Kelley
3 Mike Loynd
4 Dave Meads
5 Kevin Hagen
6 Rafael Montalvo
7 Jose Cano
8 Rocky Childress
9 Jeff Datz
10 Luis DeLeon
11 Ken Caminiti
12 Glenn Carpenter
13 Nelson Rood
14 Cameron Drew
15 Craig Biggio
16 Alex Trevino
17 Karl Allaire
18 Joe Mikulik
19 John Fishel
20 Louie Meadows
21 Jim Weaver
22 Pat Keedy
23 Craig Smajstrla
24 Bob Didier
25 Eddie Watt

1988 Tulsa Drillers team issue

(Texas Rangers, AA)

	MT
Complete Set (28):	25.00

1 Mike Scanlin
2 George Threadgill
3 Monty Fariss
4 Mitch Thomas
5 Efrain Valdez
6 Darrell Whitaker
7 Jose Vargas
8 Steve Wilson
9 Jeff Andrews
10 Jim Skaalen
11 Stan Hough
12 Gary Alexander
13 Kevin Bootay
14 John Barfield
15 Kevin Brown
16 Joel Cartaya
17 Bubba Jackson
18 Scott Coolbaugh
19 Chad Kreuter
20 Steve Lankard
21 Gar Millay
22 Bob Malloy
23 Dave Pavlas
24 Paul Fostier
25 Kevin Reimer
26 Rick Raether
27 Greg Harrel
28 Kenny Rogers

1988 Pucko Utica Blue Sox

(Chicago White Sox, A) (3,500 sets produced)

	MT
Complete Set (29):	6.00

1 Rob Lukachyk
2 Clemente Alvarez
3 Brett Berry
4 Mark Chasey
5 Paul Fuller
6 Vince Harris
7 Derek Lee
8 Steve Mehl
9 Jesus Merejo
10 Eugenio Tejada
11 Marcus Trammell
12 Randy Warren
13 John Zaksek
14 John Chafin
15 Virgil Cooper
16 Fred Dabney
17 Carlos de la Cruz
18 Keith Felden
19 Scott Fuller
20 Mike Galvan
21 Pat Mehrtens
22 Frank Merigliano
23 Jose Pena
24 Ron Stephens
25 Ed Walsh
26 Rick Patterson
27 Preston Douglas
28 Steve Jessup
29 Joanne Gerace

1988 ProCards Vancouver Canadians

(Chicago White Sox, AAA)

	MT
Complete Set (27):	5.00

753 Jeff Schaefer
754 Steve Rosenberg
755 Jack Hardy
756 Edward Wojna
757 Ken Patterson
758 Bill Lindsey
759 Donn Pall
760 Russ Morman
761 Grady Hall
762 Carl Willis
763 Joel Davis
764 Santiago Garcia
765 James Randall
766 Daryl Sconiers
767 Mike Woodard
768 Ron Jackson
769 Eli Grba
770 Greg Hibbard
771 Dave Gallagher
772 Jorge Alcazar
773 Ron Karkovice
774 Mike Yastrzemski
775 Troy Thomas
776 Adam Peterson
777 Marlin McPhail
778 Terry Bevington
---- Checklist

1988 CMC (TCMA) Vancouver Canadians

(Chicago White Sox, AAA)

	MT
Complete Set (25):	5.00

1 Jeff Bittiger
2 Joel Davis
3 Steve Rosenberg
4 Carl Willis
5 Ed Wojna
6 Ken Patterson
7 Adam Peterson
8 Grady Hall
9 Donn Pall
10 Jack Hardy
11 Greg Hibbard
12 Kelly Paris
13 Santiago Garcia
14 Mike Woodwood
15 Ron Karkovice
16 Bill Lindsey
17 Russ Morman
18 Troy Thomas
19 Mike Yastrzemski
20 James Randall
21 Jeff Schafer (Schaefer)
22 Daryl Sconiers
23 Jorge Alcazar
24 Dave Gallagher
25 Marlin McPhail

1988 ProCards Vermont Mariners

(Seattle Mariners, AA) (Griffey card was issued long after his 17-game stint with Vermont was ended. Counterfeit Griffey cards exist; well-centered Griffey cards should be viewed with suspicion.)

	MT
Complete Set, no Griffey (26):	5.00
Late-issue Ken Griffey Jr.:	100.00

939 Mark Wooden
940 Bryan Price
941 Dave Schuler
942 Greg Fulton
943 Bill McGuire
944 Jim Wilson
945 Eric Fox
946 Omar Vizquel
947 Pat Lennon
948 Keith Foley
949 Nezi Balelo
950 John Gibbons
951 Dave Brundage
952 Dave Myers
953 Jorge Uribe
954 Rich Morales
955 Tom Newberg
956 Dave Snell
957 Greg Brinkman
958 Bill Mendek
959 Ricky Rojas
960 Clint Zavaras
961 Jeff Hull
962 Calvin Jones
963 Dave McCorkle
---- Checklist

1988 Star Vero Beach Dodgers

(L.A. Dodgers, A)

	MT
Complete Set (26):	5.00

1 Michael Batesole
2 Kevin Campbell
3 Timothy Cash
4 Doug Cox
5 Thomas DeMerit
6 Felipe Esteban
7 Howard Freiling
8 Henry Goshay
9 David Hansen
10 Jeffrey Hartman
11 Gordon Hershiser
12 Carl Johnson
13 Eric Mangham
14 Angel Martinez
15 Gregory Mayberry
16 Frank Mustari
17 Jeffrey Mons
18 Christopher Nichting
19 Hidetsugu Nishimura
20 Douglas Noch
21 Jay Ray
22 Homar Rojas
23 Miguel Santana
24 Mike White
25 Stephen Wood
26 Masahiro Yamamoto

1988 Star Virginia Generals

(Independent, A) (Ford and Phillippe are scarce late-issue cards, as is corrected Joslyn card)

MT
Complete Set w/late-issues (24): 10.00
Partial Set, no late issues (22): 5.00
1 Pete Alborano
2 Mike Borgatti
3 Kevin Brooks
4 Pete Capello
5 Lee Carballo
6 Luis Corcino
7 Steve Culkaf
8 Brian Dubois
9 Kent Headley
10 Jimi Hendrix
11 Tom Johnson
12a John Joslyn (correct name & stats, wrong picture)
12b John Joslyn (corrected)
13 Frank Laureano
14 Carmelo Losauro
15 Pat McKinley
16 Angel Morris
17 Gregory Papageorge
18 Phil Price
19 Ruben Pujols
20 Ernest Radcliffe Jr.
21 Kyle Reese
22 Kent Willis
23 Ondra Ford (late issue)
--- Team logo/ad card
--- Gilinda Phillippe (late issue - very scarce)

1988 ProCards Visalia Oaks

(Minnesota Twins, A)

MT
Complete Set (28): 5.00
81 Kenny Davis
82 Dana Heinle
83 Larry Blackwell
84 John Eccles
85 Mike Randle
86 Kenny Grant
87 A.J. Richardson
88 Troy James
89 Jose Marzan
90 Kenny Morgan
91 Shawn Gilbert
92 Paul Abbott
93 Mike Redding
94 Steve Scanlon
95 Jeff Bronkey
96 Slim Williams
97 Tim Arnold
98 Joey Zellner
99 Scott Ullger
100 Doug Snyder
101 Bob Strube
102 Scott Leius
103 Edgar Naveda
104 Marty Lanoux
105 Gorman Heimueller
106 Andy Seidensticker
107 Doug Kline
---- Checklist

1988 Cal Cards Visalia Oaks

(Minnesota Twins, A)

MT
Complete Set (30): 5.00
145 Kenny Davis
146 Ken Morgan
147 Mike Randle
148 Joey Zellner
149 Tim Arnold
150 John Eccles
151 Shawn Gilbert
152 Kenny Grant
153 Marty Lanoux
154 Scott Leius
155 Jose Marzan
156 Ed Naveda
157 A.J. Richardson
158 Doug Snyder
159 Larry Blackwell
160 Mike Reddings
161 Steve Scanlon
162 Bob Strube
163 Jim Williams
164 Troy James
165 Paul Abbott
166 Jeff Bronkey
167 Mark Guthrie
168 Dana Heinle
169 Doug Kline
170 Scott Ullger
171 Bruce Bucz
172 Andy Seidensticker
173 Mark Jones
174 Gorman Heimueller

1988 ProCards Waterloo Indians

(Cleveland Indians, A)

MT
Complete Set (29): 5.00
665 Tommy Kurczewski
666 Andy Casano
667 Angel Ortiz
668 Bill Bluhm
669 John Stutz
670 Willie Garza
671 Jim Baxter
672 Scott Khoury
673 T.J. Gamba
674 Bill Narleski
675 Julio Liriano
676 Ramon Bautista
677 Ivan McBride
678 Keith Seifert
679 Steve Colavito
680 Sam Ferretti
681 Troy Neel
682 Peter Kuld
683 Mark Pike
684 Keith Bennett
685 Roger Hill
686 Eric Rasmussen
687 Ken Bolek
688 Steve Olin
689 Tom Kramer
690 Tony Scaglione
691 Greg Roscoe
692 Rudy Seanez
---- Checklist

1988 Pucko Watertown Pirates

(Pittsburgh Pirates, A) (3,500 sets produced)

MT
Complete Set (35): 6.00
1 Keith Richardson
2 Joe Ausanio
3 Steve Buckholz
4 Rodger Castner
5 Joel Forrest
6 Tim Holmes
7 Mark Koller
8 Craig Lewis
9 Dan Nielson
10 Ernesto Santana
11 Mike Stevanus
12 Randy Tomlin
13 Bobby Underwood
14 Bryan Arnold
15 Jay Bluthardt
16 Ken Buksa
17 Ralph Denkenberger
18 Chris Estep
19 Mike Huyler
20 Deron Johnson
21 Domingo Merejo
22 Steve Montejo
23 Darwin Pennye
24 Paul Spalt
25 Dave Stone
26 Mike Valla
27 Tim Wakefield
28 John Wehner
29 Flavio Williams
30 John Young
31 Stan Cliburn
32 Tom Barnard
33 Robert Bill
34 Gene Sunnen
35 Bob Burgess, Bob Morgia

1988 Grand Slam Wausau Timbers

(Seattle Mariners, A) (5,000 sets)

MT
Complete Set (28): 5.00
1 Rick Sweet
2 Chuck Kniffen
3 Fausto Ramirez
4 Chris Doll
5 Lorenzo Sisney
6 Ruben Gonzalez
7 Keith Frink
8 Chuck Carr
9 John Hoffman
10 Kurt Stange
11 Mike McDonald
12 Jim Pritikin
13 Ray Williams
14 Todd Haney
15 Todd Azar
16 Jeff Hooper
17 Rudy Webster
18 Steve Bieksha
19 Chuck Webb
20 Mike McGuire
21 Brian Baldwin
22 Tony Woods
23 Scott Stoerick
24 Frank Colston
25 Mike Gardiner
26 Dru Kosco
27 Mike Goff
28 Randy Roetter

1988 Star West Palm Beach Expos

(Montreal Expos, A)

MT
Complete Set (26): 5.00
1 Pat Adams
2 Jose Alou
3 Kent Bottenfield
4 Kevin Cavalier
5 Doug Cinnella
6 Scott Clemo
7 Al Collins
8 Rob DeYoung
9 Mike Dull
10 Bobby Gaylor
11 John Howes
12 Nels Jacobsen
13 Ross Jones
14 Tyrone Kingwood
15 Danilo Leon
16 Guinn Mack
17 Rob Mason
18 Omer Munoz
19 Bob Natal
20 Jeff Oller
21 Boi Rodriguez
22 Norm Santiago
23 Jeff Tabaka
24 John Vanderwal
25 Corey Viltz
26 Tony Welborn

1988 Rock's Wichita Pilots

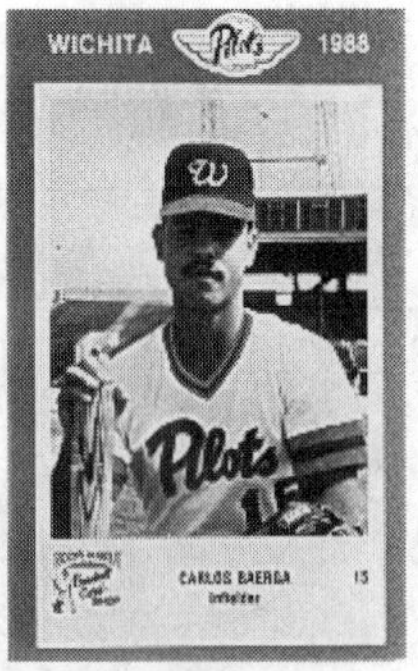

(San Diego Padres, AA)

MT
Complete Set (29): 27.50
10 Mike DeButch
11 Jeff Yurtin
12 Craig Wiley
14 Chris Knabenshue
15 Carlos Baerga
16 Mike Basso
17 Nate Colbert
18 Jim Tatum
19 Gregg Harris
20 Terry Gilmore
21 Bill Wrona
22 Jimmy Lester
23 Paul Quinzer
24 Craig Cooper
25 James Austin
26 Mike Costello
27 Jeff Hermann
28 Pat Jelks
29 Bill Stevenson
30 Jeff Childers
31 Mike Mills
32 Kevin Brown
33 Eric Bauer
40 Pat Kelly
41 Rusty Ford
42 Steve Luebber
43 Matt Maysey
---- Joe Chavez
---- Pilots logo

1988 ProCards Williamsport Bills

(Cleveland Indians, AA)

MT
Complete Set (27): 5.00
1303 Lee Kuntz
1304 Tom Lampkin
1305 Kent Murphy
1306 Mike Hargrove
1307 Mike Farr
1308 Andy Ghelfi
1309 Jeff Shaw
1310 Mike Walker
1311 Brian Allard
1312 Turner Gill
1313 Brian Graham
1314 Tony Ghelfi
1315 Kevin Wickander
1316 Stan Hilton
1317 Casey Webster
1318 Theo Shaw
1319 Darryl Landrum
1320 Claudio Carrasco
1321 Paul Kuzniar
1322 Mark Howie
1323 Jim Bruske
1324 Doyle Wilson
1325 Mike Poehl
1326 Scott Jordan
1327 Milt Harper
1328 Kerry Richardson
---- Checklist

1988 Star Winston-Salem Spirits

(Chicago Cubs, A)

MT
Complete Set (22): 5.00
1 John Berringer
2 Luis Cruz
3 Victor Garcia
4 Henry Gatewood
5 Phil Harrison
6 Steve Hill
7 Bill Kazmierczak
8 John Lewis
9 Kelly Mann
10 Jim Matas
11 Derrick May
12 Tom Michno
13 Brian Otten
14 Gregg Patterson
15 David Rosario
16 Heath Slocumb
17 Greg Smith
18 Glen Sullivan
19 Jeff Schwarz
20 Francisco Tenacen
21 Tim Wallace
22 Eric Woods

1988 Star Winter Haven Red Sox

(Boston Red Sox, A)

MT
Complete Set (27): 8.00
1 John Abbott
2 Odie Abril
3 Mike Baker
4 Eddie Banasiak
5 Ken Bourne
6 Dale Burgo
7 Johnny Diaz
8 Donald Florence
9 Roger Haggerty
10 Michael Kelly
11 Jorge Kuilan
12 Donnie McGowan
13 David Milstien
14 Miguel Monegro
15 Tony Mosley
16 Luis Munoz
17 Warren Olson
18 Livio Padilla
19 Juan Paris
20 Phil Plantier
21 Carlos Rivera
22 Julio Rosario
23 Michael Thompson
24 Doug Treadway
25 Leslie Wallin
26 Brian Warfel
27 Paul Williams Jr.

1988 ProCards Wytheville Cubs

(Chicago Cubs, A)

MT
Complete Set (31): 5.00
1975 Milciades Uribe
1976 Rob Bonneau
1977 Wayne Weinheimer
1978 Kevin Roberson
1979 Brad Huff
1980 Victor Cancel
1981 Sean Reed
1982 Marvin Cole
1983 Bill Paynter
1984 Tony Whitson
1985 Daren Burns
1986 Roberto Smalls
1987 Bubba Browder
1988 Julio Valdez
1989 Bill Earley
1990 Woody Smith
1991 Steve Roadcap
1992 Benny Shreve
1993 Mike Galdu
1994 Kenny Holley
1995 Ivan Marteniz
1996 Matt Leonard
1997 Juan Adams
1998 Jason Doss
1999 Marc Caosielli
2000 Billy Gamble
2001 Ronnie Rasp
2002 Jerome Williams
2003 Troy Bailey
2004 Team Photo
---- Checklist

1989 Star Minor League Baseball

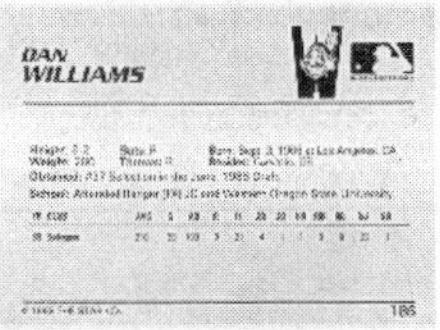

In 1989, Star became the first minor league card producer to venture into the wax pack market when it issued a 100-card set. A second series was issued later, numbered 101-200. There were no factory sets issued, nor was there a checklist available to the collector. Unlike its predecessor, which had borders of various colors, the second series all sport red borders. A total of 10,000 cases of 288 packs each was issued for Series 1.

MT
Complete Set (200): 18.00
Common Player: .05
1 Eric Anthony .50
2 David Rohde (Photo of Karl Rhodes) .10
3 Mike Simms .05
4 John Faccio .05
5 Oreste Marrero .05
6 Troy O'Leary .10
7 Rob Maurer .05
8 Rod Morris .05
9 Ed Ohman .05
10 Jim Byrd .05

11	Mark Cobb	.05
12	Pat Combs	.10
13	Tim Mauser	.05
14	Jim Vatcher	.05
15	Luis Gonzalez	.25
16	Andres Mota	.05
17	Scott Servais	.10
18	David Silvestri	.05
19	Kevin Burdick	.05
20	Tommy Shields	.05
21	Mike York	.05
22	Mike Anaya	.05
23	Dale Plummer	.05
24	Titi Roche	.05
25	Vincent Zawaski	.05
26	Anthony Barron	.05
27	Rafael Bournigal	.10
28	Albert Bustillos	.05
29	Mark Griffin	.05
30	Brett Magnusson	.05
31	Mike Jones	.05
32	Bret Barberie	.10
33	Bert Echemendia	.05
34	Mike Bell	.15
35	Brian Hunter	.10
36	Jim LeMasters	.05
37	Rick Morris	.05
38	Dominic Pierce	.05
39	Joey Wardlow	.05
40	Dera Clark	.05
41	Stu Cole	.05
42	Bob Hamelin	.20
43	Deric Ladnier	.05
44	Brian McRae	.35
45	Mike Tresemer	.05
46	Steve Walker	.05
47	Greg Becker	.05
48	Art Calvert	.05
49	Todd Crosby	.05
50	Shawn Hathaway	.05
51	Rich Garces	.10
52	Todd McClure	.05
53	Steve Morris	.05
54	Tim Dell	.05
55	Antonio Linares	.05
56	John Marchall	.06
57	Mike Morandini	.10
58	Paul Fuller	.05
59	John Hudek	.10
60	Ron Stephens	.05
61	Scott Tedder	.05
62	Pete Alborano	.05
63	Kevin Shaw	.05
64	Anthony Ariola	.05
65	James Buccheri	.05
66	William Love	.05
67	Steve Avery	.25
68	Rich Casarotti	.05
69	Brian Champion	.05
70	Wes Currin	.05
71	Brian Deak	.05
72	Ken Pennington	.05
73	Theron Todd	.05
74	Andy Tomberlin	.05
75	Richard Falkner	.05
76	Tommy Kramer	.05
77	Charles Nagy	.75
78	Chris Howard	.05
79	Mike Rhodes	.05
80	Gabriel Rodriguez	.05
81	Bob Zeihen	.05
82	Rod Beck	.50
83	Jamie Cooper	.05
84	Steve Decker	.10
85	Mark Dewey	.05
86	Juan Guerrero	.05
87	Andres Santana	.05
88	Pedro DeLeon	.05
89	Pat Kelly	.10
90	Bill Masse	.05
91	Jerry Nielson	.05
92	Mark Ohims	.05
93	Moises Alou	2.50
94	Ed Hartman	.05
95	Keith Richardson	.05
96	Royal Clayton	.05
97	Bobby Davidson	.05
98	Mitch Lyden	.05
99a	Hensley Meulens, Hensley Meulens (error - St. Petersburg)	5.00
99b	Hensley Meulens (correct - Albany)	.10
100	John Ramos	.05
101	Robin Ventura	3.00
102	Luis Mercedes	.05
103	Dave Miller	.05
104	Randy Berlin	.05
105	Mike Campas	.05
106	Jose Trujillo	.05
107	Lem Pikenton	.05
108	Frank Bolick	.05
109	Bert Heffernan	.05
110	Chris Czarnik	.05
111	Andy Benes	.75
112	Skipper Wright	.05
113	Eric Alexander	.05
114	Manny Alexander	.10
115	Jimmy Roso	.05
116	Chris Donnels	.10
117	Jaime Roseboro	.05
118	Julian Yan	.05
119	Vincent Degifico	.05
120	Mike Morandini	.15
121	Goose Gozzo	.05
122	Pedro Munoz	.10
123	Keith Helton	.05
124	Tino Martinez	2.50
125	Sandy Alomar	2.50
126	Scott Cooper	.10
127	Daryl Irvine	.05
128	Jim Orsag	.05
129	Mickey Pina	.05
130	Scott Sommers	.05
131	Ed Zambrano	.05
132	Dave Bettendorf	.05
133	Steve Allen	.05
134	Kevin Belcher	.05
135	Doug Cronk	.05
136	Tito Stewart	.05
137	Jeff Frye	.05
138	Trey McCoy	.05
139	Robb Nen	.10
140	Jim Hvizda	.05
141	Tommy Boyce	.05
142	Michael Maksudian	.05
143	Matt Current	.05
144	Tom Hardgrove	.05
145	Julio Vargas	.05
146	Dan Welch	.05
147	Steve Dunn	.10
148	Mike Musuraca	.05
149	Mike House	.05
150	Deion Sanders	3.00
151	Willie Mota	.05
152	Tim Nedin	.05
153	Kerry Taylor	.05
154	Beau Alred	.05
155	Troy Neel	.10
156	Shawn Hare	.10
157	Chris Butterfield	.05
158	Tim Hines	.05
159	Pat Howell	.05
160	Paul Johnson	.05
161	Ryan Richmond	.05
162	Ernie Baker	.05
163	Pedro Castellano	.05
164	Eric Jaques	.05
165	Mark Willoughby	.05
166	Dan Segui	.05
167	Richard Skackle	.05
168	Mark Lewis	.30
169	John Johnstone	.05
170	Phil Plantier	.10
171	Wes Chamberlain	.10
172	James Harris	.05
173	Felix Antigua	.05
174	Bruce Schreiber	.05
175	Pete Rose Jr.	.50
176	Kelly Woods	.05
177	Anthony DeLaCruz	.05
178	Charles Nagy	.75
179	Nolan Lane	.05
180	Fabio Gomez	.05
181	Chris Butler	.05
182	Brett Merriman	.05
183	Carlos Mota	.05
184	Doug Piatt	.05
185	Marc Tepper	.05
186	Dan Williams	.05
187	Maximo Aleys	.05
188	Ken Lewis	.05
189	Joey Vierra	.05
190	Ron Morton	.05
191	Brook Fordyce	.05
192	Steve McCarthy	.05
193	Steve Hosey	.05
194	Steve Foster	.05
195	Ron Crowe	.05
196	Steve Callahan	.05
197	Benny Colvard	.05
198	Adam Casillas	.05
199	Joey Belle	6.00
200	Ben McDonald	.25

1989 Minor League Team Sets

For the first time in several years, no major new producers entered the minor league team set market in 1989. That didn't diminish the number of sets, however, as more than 350 basic sets and variations were issued; the largest number to that date. Some teams had as many as three different sets, not counting variations. Most of the variations were again the result of Star adding late cards to previously issued sets. Abbreviations used in these listings include: Cal (California League), CMC (Collector's Marketing Corp./TCMA), DD (Dunkin' Donuts), DJ (Donn Jennings), GS (Grand Slam), PC (ProCards), and SP (Sport Pro).

	MT
356 team sets and variations	
CMC AAA All-Stars (45)	8.00
PC AAA All-Stars (55)	9.00
Best Albany Yankees (30)	17.50
Best Albany Yankees - platinum (30)	30.00
Best Albany Yankees All-Decade (36)	8.00
PC Albany Yankees (29)	12.00
Star Albany-Colonie Yankees (22)	5.00
Star Albany-Colonie Yankees (23)	12.00
CMC Albuquerque Dukes (25)	5.00
PC Albuquerque Dukes (30)	6.00
Team Albuquerque Dukes (45)	175.00
Tribune Albuquerque Dukes (29)	25.00
Team Anchorage Glacier Pilots (35)	14.00
PC Appleton Foxes (31)	5.00
GS Arkansas Travelers (25)	11.00
PC Asheville Tourists (30)	4.00
PC Auburn Astros (31)	18.00
PC Auburn Astros poster	30.00
PC Augusta Pirates (32)	5.00
Cal Bakersfield Dodgers (29)	5.00
Baseball America AA Top Prospects (31)	39.00
Star Baseball City Royals (24)	9.00
Star Baseball City Royals - glossy (24)	40.00
Star Baseball City Royals (26)	11.00
PC Batavia Clippers (31)	4.00
Legoe Bellingham Mariners (36)	6.00
Star Beloit Brewers 1 (26)	6.00
Star Beloit Brewers 1 - glossy (26)	30.00
Star Beloit Brewers 2 (25)	6.00
Legoe Bend Bucks (30)	18.00
PC Billings Mustangs (31)	5.00
SP Billings Mustangs (30)	5.00
Best Birmingham Barons (30)	15.00
Best Birmingham Barons - platinum (30)	24.00
Best Birmingham Barons All-Decade (34)	9.00
PC Birmingham Barons (31)	8.50
Star Bluefield Orioles (25)	5.00
Star Bluefield Orioles - glossy (25)	25.00
Star Bluefield Orioles (30)	8.00
PC Boise Hawks (31)	5.00
Star Bristol Tigers (27)	5.00
Star Bristol Tigers (31)	7.00
CMC Buffalo Bisons (25)	6.00
PC Buffalo Bisons (27)	6.00
PC Burlington Braves (32)	5.00
Star Burlington Braves (25)	4.00
Star Burlington Braves - glossy (25)	20.00
Star Burlington Braves (29)	8.00
Star Burlington Indians (25)	4.00
Star Burlington Indians - glossy (25)	20.00
Star Burlington Indians (30)	8.00
SP Butte Copper Kings (30)	7.50
CMC Calgary Cannons (25)	7.00
PC Calgary Cannons (24)	7.00
Cal League All-Stars (56)	5.00
Best Canton-Akron Indians (28)	5.00
PC Canton-Akron Indians (28)	4.00
Star Canton-Akron Indians (25)	20.00
Star Canton-Akron Indians - glossy (25)	100.00
Best Cedar Rapids Reds (30)	6.00
Best Cedar Rapids Reds All-Decade (36)	7.00
PC Cedar Rapids Reds (29)	5.00
Star Cedar Rapids Reds (29)	4.00
Star Cedar Rapids Reds - glossy (29)	20.00
Star Cedar Rapids Reds (30)	8.00
PC Charleston Rainbows (28)	5.00
Best Charleston Wheelers (27)	5.00
PC Charleston Wheelers (28)	5.00
Team Charlotte Knights (25)	8.00
Star Charlotte Rangers (28)	7.00
Star Charlotte Rangers - glossy (28)	35.00
Star Charlotte Rangers (31)	11.00
Best Chattanooga Lookouts (26)	5.00
GS Chattanooga Lookouts (25)	5.00
Team Chattanooga Lookouts Legends (29)	16.00
Star Clearwater Phillies (25)	4.00
Star Clearwater Phillies - glossy (25)	20.00
Star Clearwater Phillies (28)	9.00
PC Clinton Giants (31)	9.00
CMC Colorado Spring Sky Sox (25)	5.00
PC Colorado Springs Sky Sox (28)	5.00
Best Columbia Mets (30)	15.00
GS Columbia Mets (29)	15.00
CMC Columbus Clippers (30)	9.00
PC Columbus Clippers (28)	8.00
Police Columbus Clippers (25)	6.00
Best Columbus Mudcats (28)	8.00
Best Columbus Mudcats - platinum (28)	11.00
PC Columbus Mudcats (31)	6.00
Star Columbus Mudcats (23)	5.00
Star Columbus Mudcats - glossy (23)	25.00
Star Columbus Mudcats (24)	9.00
CMC Denver Zyphers (25)	5.00
PC Denver Zephyrs (28)	5.00
Star Dunedin Blue Jays (25)	7.00
Star Dunedin Blue Jays - glossy (25)	35.00
Star Dunedin Blue Jays (26)	11.00
Star Durham Bulls (25)	11.00
Star Durham Bulls orange/blue (29)	14.00
Star Durham Bulls blue/orange (29)	14.00
Star Durham Bulls - glossy (28)	35.00
Team Durham Bulls (29)	19.00
PC Eastern League All-Stars (26)	12.00
PC Eastern League Diamond Diplomacy (50)	7.50
CMC Edmonton Trappers (25)	5.00
PC Edmonton Trappers (25)	5.00
Star Elizabethton Twins (31)	20.00
Star Elizabethtown Twins - glossy (31)	95.00
Pucko Elmira Pioneers (32)	5.00
GS El Paso Diablos (30)	5.00
Star Erie Orioles (25)	8.00
Star Erie Orioles - glossy (25)	35.00
Star Erie Orioles (29)	9.00
Best Eugene Emeralds (25)	5.00
Star Everett Giants (32)	5.00
Star Everett Giants - glossy (32)	35.00
PC Fayetteville Generals (29)	5.00
Team Fayetteville Generals (10)	5.00
Star Frederick Keys (24)	8.00
Star Frederick Keys - glossy (24)	40.00
Star Frederick Keys (28)	12.00
Star Ft. Lauderdale Yankees (25)	6.00
Star Ft. Lauderdale Yankees (29)	10.00
PC Gastonia Rangers (30)	70.00
Star Gastonia Rangers (26)	60.00
Star Gastonia Rangers - glossy (26)	150.00
PC Geneva Cubs (31)	5.00
SP Great Falls Dodgers (33)	7.00
PC Greensboro Hornets (29)	9.00
Best Greenville Braves (29)	12.00
Best Greenville Braves - platinum (29)	24.00
PC Greenville Braves (30)	6.00
Star Greenville Braves (25)	5.00
Star Greenville Braves - glossy (25)	25.00
Best Hagerstown Suns (29)	6.00
Best Hagerstown Suns All-Decade (36)	7.00
PC Hagerstown Suns (26)	5.00
Star Hagerstown Suns (22)	4.00
Star Hagerstown Suns - glossy (22)	20.00
Star Hamilton Redbirds (23)	5.00
Star Hamilton Redbirds - glossy (23)	25.00
Star Hamilton Redbirds (29)	11.00
PC Harrisburg Senators (26)	7.00
Star Harrisburg Senators (23)	6.00
Star Harrisburg Senators - glossy (23)	30.00
SP Helena Brewers (27)	7.00
Little Sun High School Prospects (23)	20.00
Best Huntsville Stars (29)	5.50

PC Idaho Falls Braves (31)	5.00
CMC Indianapolis Indians (25)	7.50
PC Indianapolis Indians (32)	7.50
CMC Iowa Cubs (25)	5.00
PC Iowa Cubs (28)	5.00
GS Jackson Mets (30)	4.00
Best Jacksonville Expos (29)	11.00
Best Jacksonville Expos - platinum (29)	27.50
PC Jacksonville Expos (29)	10.00
PC Jamestown Expos (30)	5.00
Star Johnson City Cardinals (26)	4.00
Star Johnson City Cards - glossy (26)	20.00
PC Kenosha Twins (29)	5.00
Star Kenosha Twins (25)	5.00
Star Kenosha Twins (27)	9.00
Star Kingsport Mets (25)	5.00
Star Kingsport Mets - glossy (25)	25.00
Star Kingsport Mets (30)	9.00
Star Kinston Indians (25)	11.00
Star Kinston Indians - glossy (25)	50.00
Star Kinston Indians (27)	16.00
Best Knoxville Blue Jays (31)	9.00
Best Knoxville Blue Jays (33)	12.00
PC Knoxville Blue Jays (31)	9.00
Star Knoxville Blue Jays (25)	9.00
Star Knoxville Blue Jays - glossy (25)	45.00
Star Lakeland Tigers (25)	5.00
Star Lakeland Tigers - glossy (25)	25.00
Star Lakeland Tigers (28)	9.00
CMC Las Vegas Stars (25)	12.00
PC Las Vegas Stars (29)	12.00
PC London Tigers (32)	18.00
CMC Louisville Red Birds (25)	5.00
PC Louisville Redbirds (28)	7.00
Team Louisville Redbirds (38)	10.00
Team Louisville Redbirds - glossy (38)	25.00
Star Lynchburg Red Sox (25)	6.00
Star Lynchburg Red Sox (30)	9.00
Star Madison Muskies (22)	5.00
Star Madison Muskies - glossy (22)	25.00
Star Madison Muskies (26)	12.00
Star Martinsville Phillies (35)	5.00
Star Martinsville Phillies - glossy (35)	25.00
Best Medford A's (31)	5.00
Best Memphis Chicks (28)	8.00
PC Memphis Chicks (28)	7.50
Star Memphis Chicks (24)	7.00
Star Memphis Chicks - glossy (24)	35.00
Star Miami Miracle 1 (25)	6.00
Star Miami Miracle 1 - glossy (25)	30.00
Star Miami Miracle 2 (22)	4.00
GS Midland Angels (30)	5.00
Cal Modesto A's (25)	5.00
Chong Modesto A's (36)	42.00
PC Myrtle Beach Blue Jays (30)	5.00
CMC Nashville Sounds (25)	5.00
PC Nashville Sounds (28)	5.00
Team Nashville Sounds (30)	12.00
PC New Britain Red Sox (27)	7.00
Star New Britain Red Sox (25)	6.00
Star New Britain Red Sox - glossy (25)	30.00
Pucko Niagara Falls Rapids (29)	4.00
CMC Oklahoma City 89ers (25)	5.00
PC Oklahoma City 89ers (29)	6.00
CMC Omaha Royals (25)	7.00
PC Omaha Royals (27)	8.00
PC Oneonta Yankees (32)	11.00
Best Orlando Twins (31)	6.00
PC Orlando Twins (30)	5.00
Star Osceola Astros (25)	6.00
Star Osceola Astros - glossy (25)	30.00
Star Osceola Astros (27)	10.00
Cal Palm Springs Angels (32)	4.00
PC Palm Springs Angels (28)	5.00
CMC Pawtucket Red Sox (25)	5.00
DD Pawtucket Red Sox foldout	45.00
PC Pawtucket Red Sox (28)	5.00
Team Peninsula Oilers (28)	7.50
Star Peninsula Pilots (25)	4.00
Star Peninsula Pilots - glossy (25)	20.00
Star Peninsula Pilots (26)	7.00
Team Peoria Chiefs (35)	11.00
CMC Phoenix Firebirds (25)	12.00
PC Phoenix Firebirds (29)	11.00
Star Pittsfield Mets (25)	5.00
Star Pittsfield Mets - glossy (25)	25.00
Star Pittsfield Mets (29)	9.00
CMC Portland Beavers (25)	5.00
PC Portland Beavers (26)	5.00
Star Princeton Pirates (25)	4.00
Star Princeton Pirates - glossy (25)	20.00
Star Princeton Pirates (28)	8.00
Star Prince Williams Cannons (25)	5.00
Star Prince Williams Cannons (29)	9.00
PC Pulaski Braves (28)	27.50
Best Quad City Angels (31)	12.00
GS Quad City Angels (30)	14.00
Best Reading Phillies (27)	5.00
PC Reading Phillies (27)	5.00
Star Reading Phillies (26)	5.00
Star Reading Phillies - glossy (26)	25.00
Star Reading Phillies (29)	9.00
Cal Reno Silver Sox (27)	5.00
Bob's Richmond Braves (29)	70.00
CMC Richmond Braves (25)	11.00
PC Richmond Braves (31)	14.00
Team Richmond Braves foldout	15.00
Best Riverside Red Wave (30)	5.00
Cal Riverside Red Wave (31)	5.00
PC Riverside Red Wave (31)	5.00
CMC Rochester Red Wings (25)	5.00
PC Rochester Red Wings (30)	6.00
Team Rockford Expos (31)	7.00
Star Salem Buccaneers (25)	7.00
Star Salem Buccaneers - glossy (25)	35.00
Star Salem Buccaneers (28)	10.00
Team Salem Dodgers (30)	57.00
Cal Salinas Spurs (27)	4.00
PC Salinas Spurs (30)	5.00
Team Salt Lake City Trappers (30)	9.50
Best San Antonio Missions (28)	6.00
Best S.A. Missions - platinum (28)	9.00
Best San Bernadino Spirit (29)	5.00
Cal San Bernadino Spirit (31)	4.00
Best San Jose Giants (31)	5.00
Cal San Jose Giants (30)	5.00
PC San Jose Giants (30)	5.00
Star San Jose Giants (25)	5.00
Star San Jose Giants - glossy (25)	25.00
Star San Jose Giants (28)	9.00
Star Sarasota White Sox (25)	5.00
Star Sarasota White Sox - glossy (25)	25.00
PC Savannah Cardinals (30)	5.00
CMC Scranton Red Barons (25)	5.00
PC Scranton Red Barons (28)	5.00
PC Shreveport Captains (27)	5.00
GS South Atlantic League A-S (46)	13.00
GS South Bend White Sox (30)	5.00
DJ Southern League All-Stars (25)	6.00
PC Spartanburg Phillies (30)	4.00
Star Spartanburg Phillies (25)	5.00
Star Spartanburg Phillies (26)	9.00
SP Spokane Indians (26)	6.00
Best Springfield Cardinals (30)	5.00
Best Springfield All-Decade (36)	7.00
PC St. Catharines Blue Jays (28)	30.00
Star St. Lucie Mets (25)	4.00
Star St. Lucie Mets - glossy (25)	20.00
Star St. Lucie Mets (27)	8.00
Star St. Petersburg Cardinals (25)	5.00
Star St. Pete Cardinals - glossy (25)	25.00
Star St. Petersburg Cardinals (29)	9.00
Best Stockton Ports (32)	6.00
Cal Stockton Ports (30)	5.00
PC Stockton Ports (31)	5.00
Star Stockton Ports (28)	6.00
Star Stockton Ports - glossy (28)	30.00
PC Sumter Braves (33)	5.00
CMC Syracuse Chiefs (25)	5.00
PC Syracuse Chiefs (27)	5.00
Team Syracuse Chiefs foldout	17.50
CMC Tacoma Tigers (25)	5.00
PC Tacoma Tigers (32)	45.00
GS Texas League All-Stars (40)	16.00
Candl Tidewater Tides foldout	10.00
CMC Tidewater Tides (29)	5.00
PC Tidewater Tides (30)	5.00
CMC Toledo Mud Hens (25)	5.00
PC Toledo Mud Hens (30)	5.00
CMC Tucson Toros (25)	5.00
Jones Tucson Toros (26)	70.00
PC Tucson Toros (28)	5.00
Best Tulsa Drillers Decade Greats (36)	45.00
GS Tulsa Drillers (26)	40.00
Team Tulsa Drillers (27)	75.00
Pucko Utice Blue Sox (34)	5.00
CMC Vancouver Canadians (25)	11.00
PC Vancouver Canadians (27)	11.00
Star Vero Beach Dodgers (25)	9.00
Star Vero Beach Dodgers - glossy (25)	45.00
Star Vero Beach Dodgers (39)	18.00
Cal Visalia Oaks (29)	4.00
PC Visalia Oaks (31)	5.00
PC Waterloo Diamonds (28)	5.00
Star Waterloo Diamonds (32)	4.00
Star Waterloo Diamonds - glossy (32)	20.00
Star Watertown Indians (25)	5.00
Star Watertown Indians - glossy (25)	25.00
Star Watertown Indians (29)	9.00
GS Wausau Timbers (28)	5.00
Pucko Welland Pirates (35)	6.00
Star West Palm Beach Expos (24)	7.00
Star West Palm Beach Expos - glossy (24)	35.00
Star West Palm Beach Expos (31)	12.00
Rock's Wichita Wranglers (30)	10.00
Rock's Wichita Wrangers - Bonus Set (2)	6.00
Rock's Wichita Wranglers - Stadium (30)	12.00
Rock's Wranglers - Highlight (20)	7.00
Rock's Wichita Wranglers - Update (20)	8.00
PC Williamsport Bills (25)	10.00
Star Williamsport Bills (24)	10.00
Star Williamsport Bills - glossy (24)	60.00
Star Williamsport Bills (25)	15.00
Star Winston-Salem Spirits (22)	5.00
Star Winston-Salem Spirits (26)	9.00
Star Winter Haven Red Sox (25)	11.00
Star Winter Haven Red Sox - glossy (25)	55.00
Star Winter Haven Red Sox (29)	12.00
Star Wytheville Cubs (25)	4.00
Star Wytheville Cubs - glossy (25)	20.00
Star Wytheville Cubs (30)	8.00

1990 Best

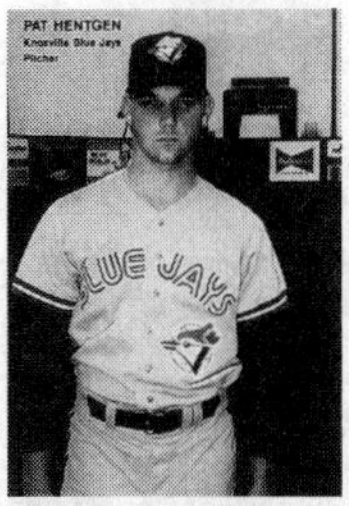

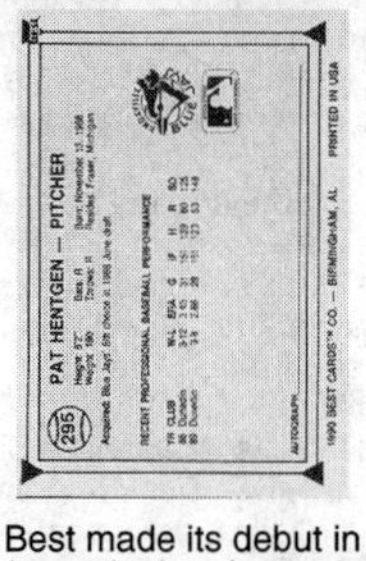

Best made its debut in the single-card minor league market in 1990 with a 324-card set. The cards were issued in foil packs and were not available as a complete set.

		MT
Complete Set (324):		90.00
Common Player:		.15
1	Frank Thomas	24.00
2	Eric Wedge	.15
3	Willie Ansley	.15
4	Mark Lewis	.45
5	Greg Colbrunn	.15
6	David Staton	.15
7	Ben McDonald	.15
8	Brent Mayne	.15
9	Ray Holbert	.15
10	T.R. Lewis	.15
11	Willie Banks	.15
12	Steve Dunn	.15
13	Juan Andujar	.15
14	Roger Salkeld	.20
15	Steve Hosey	.15
16	Tyler Houston	.15
17	David Holdridge	.15
18	Todd Malone	.15
19	Tony Scruggs	.15
20	Darron Cox	.15
21	Mike Linskey	.15
22	Darren Lewis	.25
23	Eddie Zosky	.25
24	Ramser Correa	.15
25	Lee Upshaw	.15
26	Bernie Williams	4.00
27	Brian Harrison	.15
28	Len Brutcher	.15
29	Scott Centala	.15
30	Kenny Morgan	.15
31	Pedro Borbon	.15
32	Lee Hancock	.15
33	Clay Bellinger	.15
34	Chris Meyers	.15
35	Russ Garside	.15
36	Ron Plemmons	.15
37	Jose LeBron	.15
38	Tom Hardgrove	.15
39	Alan Newman	.15
40	Ramon Jimenez	.15
41	Ezequiel Herrera	.15
42	Jason Satre	.15
43	Bob Malloy	.15
44	William Suero	.15
45	Lenny Webster	.15
46	Andy Ashby	.25
47	Darren Ritter	.15
48	Andy Mota	.15
49	Pat Gomez	.15
50	Ron Stephens	.15
51	Daniel Eskew	.15
52	Joe Andrzejewski	.15
53	Doug Robbins	.15
54	Noel Velez	.15
55	Dana Ridenour	.15
56	Luis Martinez	.15
57	Dave Fleming	.15
58	Adell Davenport	.15
59	Brent McCoy	.15
60	Johnny Ard	.15
61	Cal Eldred	.40
62	Tab Brown	.15
63	Scott Kamieniecki	.25
64	Scott Bryant	.15
65	Brad Pennington	.25
66	Bernie Jenkins	.15
67	Frank Carey	.15
68	Matt Witkowski	.15
69	Checklist 1-48	.15
70	Josias Manzanillo	.25
71	Checklist 49-96	.15
72	Andujar Cedeno	.15
73	Rick Rojas	.15
74	Scott Brosius	.30
75	Tom Redington	.15
76	Kevin Rogers	.15
77	Jerry Wolak	.15
78	Rick Davis	.15
79	Juan Guzman	.45
80	Cesar Bernhardt	.15
81	Randy Simmons	.15
82	Clyde Keller	.15
83	Anthony Manahan	.15
84	Tom Maynard	.15
86	Sean Berry	.30
87	Brian Boltz	.15
88	Shawn Gilbert	.15
89	Rafael Novoa	.15
90	John Vander Wal	.30
91	Scott Pose	.25
92	Don Stanford	.15
93	Joe Federico	.15
94	Todd Watson	.15
95	Luis Gonzalez	.25
96	Pat Leinen	.15
97	Joel Estes	.15
98	Troy O'Leary	.15
99	Matt Stark	.15
100	Tony Tarasco	.15
101	Marc Lipson	.15
102	Kevin Higgins	.15
103	Jack Voight	.15
104	Steve Schrenk	.15
105	Jonathan Hurst	.15
106	Scott Erickson	.65
107	Javier Lopez	4.00
108	Bob Zupcic	.15
109	Edwin Marquez	.15
110	Shawn Heiden	.15

111 Mike Maksudian .15
112 Tony Eusebio .25
113 Chris Hancock .15
114 Royce Clayton .45
115 Tim Mauser .15
116 Ckecklist 97-144 .15
117 Carlos Maldonado .15
118 Rex DeLa Nuez .15
119 Mike Curtis .15
120 Roger Miller .15
121 Daryl Moore .15
122 Turk Wendell .20
123 Dan Rambo .15
124 Scott Kimball .15
125 Willie Magallanes .15
126 Dannie Harris .15
127 Joey James .15
128 Wil Cordero .75
129 Rob Taylor .15
130 Bryce Florie .15
131 Mike Mitchner .15
132 Jeff Bagwell 12.00
133 Caesar Devares .15
134 Tim Gillis .15
135 Victor Hithe .15
136 Earl Steinmetz .15
137 Carl Keliipuleole .15
138 Ted Williams .15
139 Jorge Pedre .15
140 Amalio Carreno .15
141 Chris Gill .15
142 Dennis Wiseman .15
143 Checklist 145-192 .15
144 Derek Lee .20
145 Brett Snyder .15
146 Chuck Knoblauch 4.00
147 Rafael Quirico .15
148 Julian Yan .15
149 John Thelen .15
150 Checklist 193-240 .15
151 Darrin Reichle .15
152 John Ramos .15
153 Patrick Lennon .15
154 Wade Taylor .25
155 Mike Twardoski .15
156 Jeff Conine 1.00
157 Kelly Mann .15
158 Gary Wilson .15
159 Chris Frye .15
160 Roger Hailey .15
161 Harold Allen .15
162 Ozzie Canseco .20
163 Checklist 241-288 .15
164 Rudy Seanez .20
165 John Zaksek .15
166 Roberto DeLeon .15
167 Matt Merullo .15
168 Checklist 289-324 (Wrong numbers listed on checklist.) .15
169 Terrell Hansen .15
170 Ron Crowe .15
171 Luis Galindez .15
172 Vilato Marrero .15
173 Scott Cepicky .15
174 Gary Resetar .15
175 Rich Scheid .15
176 Jimmy Rogers .15
177 Ken Pennington .15
178 Tom Martin .15
179 Mitch Lyden .15
180 Jorge Brito .15
181 Chris Gorton .15
182 Mark Sims .15
183 Jose Olmeda .15
184 Ed Taubensee .25
185 Steve Morris .15
186 Tim Pugh .20
187 Barry Winford .15
188 Allen Leibert .15
189 Kurt Brown .15
190 Kelly Lifgren .15
191 Mike Kelly .15
192 Robert Munoz .15
193 Judd Johnson .15
194 Hector Wagner .15
195 Dave Reis .15
196 Isaiah Clark .15
197 William Schock .15
198 Ruben Gonzalez .15
199 Mike Eberle .15
200 Michael Arner .15
201 Raphael Bustamante .15
202 John Patterson .15
203 Joe Slusarski .15
204 Rodney McCray .15
205 Wally Trice .15
206 Edgar Caceres .15
207 Eugene Jones .15
208 Joey Wardlow .15
209 Steven Martin .15
210 Woody Williams .15
211 Kevin Morton .15
212 Bobby DeJardin .15
213 Chris Bennett .15
214 Brian Johnson .15
215 Randy Snyder .15
216 Roberto Hernandez .35
217 Glen Gardner .15
218 Fred Costello .15
219 Melvin Nieves .15
220 Al Martin .35
221 Kerry Knox .15
222 Mike Eatinger .15
223 Jim Myers .15
224 Jay Owens .15
225 Jayson Best .15
226 Mike McDonald .15
227 Kim Batiste .15
228 Rich Delucia .20
229 Chris Delarwelle .15
230 Jeff Hoffman .15
231 Bobby Moore .20
232 Dan Wilson .30
233 Greg Pirkl .15
234 Craig Newkirk .15
235 Mike Hensley .15
236 Ryan Klesko 4.00
237 Donald Sparks .15
238 J.D. Noland .15
239 Chris Howard .15
240 Stan Royer .30
241 Manuel Alexander .25
242 Jeff Plympton .15
243 Jeff Juden .50
244 Charles Nagy 1.00
245 Ryan Bowen .35
246 Scott Taylor .15
247 Tom Quinlan .15
248 Royal Thomas .15
249 Ricky Rhodes .15
250 Alex Fernandez 1.50
251 Bruce Egloff .15
252 Greg Sparks .15
253 Brian Dour .15
254 John Byington .15
255 Stacey Burdick .15
256 Danny Matznick .15
257 Reed Olmstead .15
258 Jim Bowie .15
259 Jim Newlan .15
260 Ramon Caraballo .15
261 Brian Barnes .15
262 Mike Gardiner .15
263 Andy Fox .20
264 Brian McKeon .15
265 Andy Tomberlin .15
266 Frank Bellino .15
267 Tim Lata .15
268 Mike Burton .15
269 Jim Orsag .15
270 Scott Romano .15
271 Leon Glenn .15
272 Mike Misuraca .15
273 Randy Knorr .15
274 Eddie Tucker .15
275 Ken Powell .15
276 Brian McRae .35
277 Mark Merchant .15
278 Vinny Castilla 2.00
279 Stephen Chitren .15
280 Marteese Robinson .15
281 Osvaldo Sanchez .15
282 Mike Mongiello .15
283 John Valentin .75
284 Timmie Morrow .15
285 Matt Murray .15
286 Darrell Sherman .15
287 Royal Clayton .15
288 Jason Robertson .15
289 John Kilner .15
290 Jeff Mutis .15
291 Gary Alexander .15
292 Oreste Marrero .15
293 Melvin Wearing .15
294 Scott Meadows .15
295 Pat Hentgen 1.25
296 John Hudek .20
297 Tim Stargell .15
298 Tony Brown .15
299 Scott Plemmons .15
300 Chris Nabholz .15
301 Brian Romero .15
302 Vince Kindred .15
303 Robert Ayrault .20
304 Steve Stowell .15
305 Don Strange .15
306 Tim Nedin .15
307 Derek Livernois .15
308 Kerry Woodson .15
309 Sam Ferretti .15
310 Reuben Smiley .15
311 Jim Campbell .15
312 Al Osuna .15
313 Luis Mercedes .15
314 Billy Reed .15
315 Vince Harris .15
316 Jeff Carter .15
317 Dave Riddle .15
318 Frank Thomas (Bonus Card) 12.00
319 Eric Wedge (Bonus Card) .15
320 Mark Lewis (Bonus Card) .15
321 Alex Fernandez (Bonus Card) .50
322 Chuck Knoblauch (Bonus Card) 2.50
323 Charles Nagy (Bonus Card) .75
324 Tyler Houston (Bonus Card) .20

1990 Classic #1 Draft Picks

The first-round draft picks of each team are featured in this issue. Reported production was 150,000 sets, including 2,500 uncut 100-card (four sets) sheets originally retailed within the hobby for $59. A certificate of authenticity accompanies each individually numbered set or sheet. Unlike other Classic issues, this set is not designed for use with the trivia board game. Cards #2 and 22 were not issued.

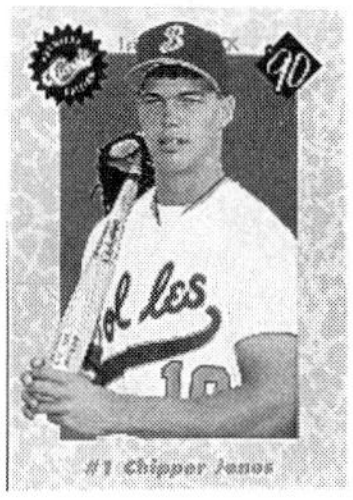

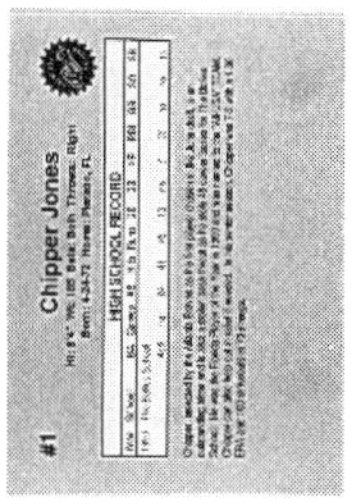

		MT
Complete Set (27):		6.00
Common Player:		.10
Uncut Sheet:		25.00
1	Chipper Jones	3.00
2	Not Issued	
3	Mike Lieberthal	.30
4	Alex Fernandez	.75
4P	Alex Fernandez (promo card)	.50
5	Kurt Miller	.10
6	Marc Newfield	.35
7	Dan Wilson	.20
8	Tim Costo	.10
9	Ron Walden	.10
10	Carl Everett	.25
11	Shane Andrews	.25
12	Todd Ritchie	.10
13	Donovan Osborne	.10
14	Todd Van Poppel	.25
14P	Todd Van Poppel (promo card)	.50
15	Adam Hyzdu	.10
16	Dan Smith	.10
17	Jeromy Burnitz	.75
18	Aaron Holbert	.10
19	Eric Christopherson	.10
20	Mike Mussina	2.00
21	Tom Nevers	.10
22	Not Issued	
23	Lance Dickson	.10
24	Rondell White	1.50
25	Robbie Beckett	.10
26	Don Peters	.10
---	Future Stars-Checklist Chipper Jones, Rondell White	1.50

1990 Collectors Marketing Corp. Pre-Rookie

This set combines CMC team sets with cards produced by ProCards and purchased by CMC. The ProCards were given a glossy facing and randomly inserted in wax packs along with CMC cards. The cards are numbered at bottom-right on back. These numbers were not coordinated with the original CMC team sets, and therefore many team sets were separated with ProCards cards between them. The CMC cards in this set differ from the original CMC team sets by the color of their backs (yellow in lieu of green) and the players are pictured in place of the team logos. A checklist was available through the company. Shortly after the cards hit the market, the CMC company was sold to Impel Marketing. Since the original CMC team sets were issued as one complete AAA set in a special wooden box, there were packaging problems with duplicates and/or missing cards.

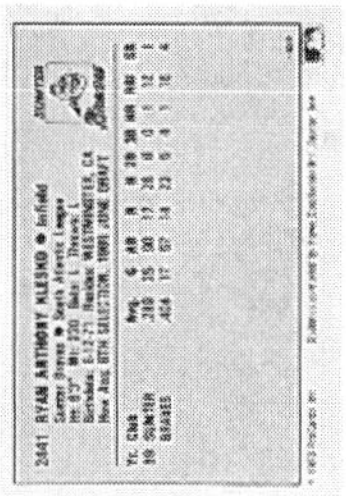

		MT
Complete Set (880):		60.00
Common Player:		.05
1	Stan Belinda	.10
2	Gordon Dillard	.05
3	Torry Collinc	.05
4	Mark Huisman	.05
5	Hugh Kemp	.05
6	Scott Medvin	.05
7	Vincente Palacios	.05
8	Rick Reed	.05
9	Mark Ross	.05
10	Dorn Taylor	.05
11	Mike York	.05
12	Jeff Richardson	.05
13	Dann Bilardello	.05
14	Tom Prince	.05
15	Danny Sheaffer	.10
16	Kevin Burdick	.05
17	Steve Kiefer	.05
18	Orlando Merced	.30
19	Armando Moreno	.05
20	Mark Ryal	.05
21	Tommy Shields	.05
22	Steve Carter	.05
23	Wes Chamberlain	.10
24	Jeff Cook	.05
25	Scott Little	.05
26	Jeff Peterek	.05
27	Ed Puig	.05
28	Tim Watkins	.05
29	Tom Edens	.05
30	Mike Capel	.05
31	Darryel Walters	.05
32	Joe Xavier	.05
33	Tim Torricelli	.05
34	Joe Redfield	.05
35	D.L. Smith	.05
36	Billy Moore	.05
37	Joe Mitchell	.05
38	Mario Monico	.05
39	Frank Mattox	.05
40	Tim McIntosh	.05
41	Mark Higgins	.05
42	George Canale	.05
43	Don Grodon	.05
44	Al Sadler	.05
45	Don August	.05
46	Mike Birkbeck	.05
47	Dennis Powell	.05
48	Chuck McGrath	.05
49	Ruben Escalera	.05
50	Dave Machemer	.05
51	Steve Fireovid	.05
52	Danny Clay	.05
53	Howard Farmer	.05
54	Travis Chambers	.05
55	Chris Marchok	.05
56	Dan Gakeler	.05
57	Scott Anderson	.05
58	Dale Mohorcic	.05
59	Richard Thompson	.05
60	Eddie Dixon	.05
61	Jim Davins	.05
62	Edwin Marquez	.05
63	Jerry Goff	.05
64	Dwight Lowery	.05
65	Jim Steels	.05
66	Quinn Mack	.05
67	Eric Bullock	.05
68	Otis Green	.05
69	Randy Braun	.05
70	Mel Houston	.05
71	Johnny Paredes	.05
72	Romy Cucjen	.05
73	Jose Castro	.05
74	Esteban Beltre	.05
75	Tim Johnson	.05
76	Shawn Boskie	.10
77	Dave Masters	.05
78	Kevin Blankenship	.05
79	Greg Kallevig	.05
80	Steve Parker	.05
81	David Pavlas	.05
82	Jeff Pico	.05
83	Laddie Renfroe	.05
84	Dean Wilkins	.05
85	Paul Wilmet	.05
86	Bob Bafia	.05
87	Brian Guinn	.05
88	Greg Smith	.05
89	Derrick May	.15
90	Glenn Sullivan	.05
91	Bill Wrona	.05
92	Eric Pappas	.05
93	Hector Villanueva	.05
94	Ced Landrum	.05
95	Jeff Small	.05
96	Gary Varsho	.05
97	Brad Bierly	.05
98	Jeff Hearron	.05
99	Jim Essian	.05
100	Brian McCann	.05
101	Scott Arnold	.05
102	Gibson Alba	.05
103	Cris Carpetner	.05
104	Stan Clarke	.05
105	Mike Hinkle	.05
106	Howard Hilton	.05
107	Dave Osteen	.05
108	Mike Perez	.05
109	Bernard Gilkey	.75
110	Dennis Carter	.05
111	Julian Martinez	.05
112	Rod Brewer	.05
113	Ray Stephens	.05
114	Ray Lankford	.75
115	Craig Wilson	.05
116	Roy Silver	.05
117	Bien Figueroa	.05
118	Jesus Mendez	.05
119	Geronimo Pena	.05
120	Omar Olivares	.10
121	Mark Grater	.05
122	Tim Sherrill	.05
123	Pat Austin	.05
124	Todd Crosby	.05
125	Scott Nichols	.05
126	Milt Hill	.05
127	Robert Moore	.10
128	Joey Vierra	.05
129	Terry McGriff	.05
130	Chris Hammond	.15
131	Charlie Mitchell	.05
132	Rodney Imes	.05
133	Rob Lopez	.05
134	Keith Brown	.05
135	Scott Scudder	.10
136	Bob Sebra	.05
137	Donnie Scott	.05
138	Skeeter Barnes	.05
139	Paul Noce	.05
140	Leo Garcia	.05
141	Chris Jones	.05
142	Kevin Pearson	.05
143	Darryl Motley	.05
144	Keith Lockhart	.10
145	Brian Lane	.05
146	Eddie Tanner	.05
147	Reggie Jefferson	.15
148	Neil Allen	.05
149	Pete Mackanin	.05
150	Ray Ripplemeyer	.05
151	Jack Hardy	.05
152	Steve Lankard	.05
153	John Hoover	.05
154	David Lynch	.05
155	Mark Petkovsek	.10
156	David Miller	.05
157	Brad Arnsberg	.05
158	Jeff Satzinger	.05
159	John Barfield	.05
160	Mike Berger	.05
161	John Russell	.05
162	Pat Garman	.05
163	Gary Green	.05
164	Bryan House	.05
165	Ron Washington	.05
166	Nick Capra	.05
167	Juan Gonzalez	11.00
168	Gar Millay	.05
169	Kevin Reimer	.05
170	Bernie Tatis	.05
171	Steve Smith	.05
172	Dick Egan	.05
173	Stan Hough	.05
174	Ray Ramirez	.05
175	Moc Drabowcky	.10
176	Jay Baller	.05
177	Ray Chadwick	.05
178	Dera Clark	.05
179	Luis Encarnacion	.05
180	Jim LeMasters	.05
181	Mike Magnante	.05
182	Mel Stottlemyre	.05
183	Tony Ferreira	.05
184	Pete Filson	.05
185	Andy McGaffigan	.05
186	Luis DeLos Santos	.05
187	Mike Loggins	.05
188	Chito Martinez	.05
189	Bobby Meacham	.05
190	Russ Morman	.05
191	Bill Pecota	.05

192	Harvey Pulliam	.05
193	Jeff Schulz	.05
194	Gary Thurman	.05
195	Thad Reece	.05
196	Tim Spehr	.05
197	Paul Zuvella	.05
198	Not issued	
199a	Tom Poquette, Rich Dubee	.05
199b	Bob Hamelin	.10
200	Sal Rende	.05
201	Steve Adkins	.05
202	Dave Eiland	.05
203	John Habyan	.05
204	Mark Leiter	.05
205	Kevin Mmahat	.05
206	Hipolito Pena	.05
207	Willie Smith	.05
208	Rich Monteleone	.05
209	Hensley Meulens	.05
210	Andy Stankiewicz	.10
211	Jim Leyritz	.35
212	Jim Walewander	.05
213	Oscar Azocar	.05
214	John Fishel	.05
215	Jason Maas	.05
216	Van Snider	.05
217	Kevin Maas	.05
218	Ricky Torres	.05
219	Dave Sax	.05
220	Darrin Chapin	.05
221	Rob Sepanek	.05
222	Mark Wasinger	.05
223	Jimmy Jones	.05
224	Clippers Coaches	.05
225	Stump Merrill	.05
226	Bob Davidson	.05
227	Eric Boudreaux	.05
228	Marvin Freeman	.05
229	Jason Grimsley	.05
230	Chuck Malone	.05
231	Dickie Moles	.05
232	Wally Ritchie	.05
233	Bob Scanlan	.05
234	Scott Service	.05
235	Steve Sharts	.05
236	John Gibbons	.05
237	Sal Agostinelli	.05
238	Jim Adduci	.05
239	Kelly Heath	.05
240	Mickey Morandini	.20
241	Victor Rosario	.05
242	Steve Stanicek	.05
243	Jim Vatcher	.05
244	Bill Dancy	.05
245	Ron Jones	.05
246	Chris Knabenshue	.05
247	Keith Miller	.05
248	Floyd Rayford	.05
249	Jim Wright	.05
250	Todd Frohwirth	.05
251	Barney Nugent	.05
252	Tito Stewart	.05
253	John Trautwein	.05
254	Mike Rochford	.05
255	Larry Shikles	.05
256	Daryl Irvine	.05
257	John Leister	.05
258	Joe Johnson	.05
259	Mark Meleski	.05
260	Steven Bast	.05
261	Ed Nottle	.05
262	John Flaherty	.05
263	John Marzano	.05
264	Gary Tremblay	.05
265	Scott Cooper	.10
266	Angel Gonzalez	.05
267	Julius McDougal	.05
268	Tim Naehring	.10
269	Jim Pankovits	.05
270	Rick Lancelotti	.05
271	Mickey Pina	.05
272	Phil Plantier	.10
273	Jeff Stone	.05
274	Scott Wade	.05
275	Mike Dalton	.05
276	Jeff Gray	.05
277	Steve Avery	.25
278	Braves Coaches	.05
279	Dale Polley	.05
280	Rusty Richards	.05
281	Andy Nezelek	.05
282	Ed Olwine	.05
283	Jim Beauchamp	.05
284	Paul Marak	.05
285	Dave Justice	5.00
286	Jimmy Kremers	.05
287	Drew Denson	.05
288	Barry Jones	.05
289	Francisco Cabrera	.05
290	Bruce Crabbe	.05
291	Dennis Hood	.05
292	Geronimo Berroa	.10
293	Ed Whited	.05
294	Sam Ayoub	.05
295	Brian Hunter	.10
296	Tommy Green	.10
297	John Mizerock	.05
298	Ken Dowell	.05
299	John Alva	.05
300	Bill Lasky	.05
301	Brian Snyder	.05
302	Ben McDonald	.20
303	Rob Woodward	.05
304	Mickey Weston	.05
305	Mike Jones	.05
306	Curtis Schilling	.60
307	Jay Aldrich	.05
308	Paul Blair	.05
309	Mike Smith	.05
310	Jeff Tackett	.05
311	Leo Gomez	.10
312	Juan Bell	.10
313	Chris Hoiles	.15
314	Donell Nixon	.05
315	Steve Stanicek	.05
316	Tim Dulin	.05
317	Chris Padget	.05
318	Greg Walker	.05
319	Tony Chance	.05
320	Jeff McKnight	.05
321	J.J. Bautista	.05
322	John Mitchell	.05
323	Vic Hithe	.05
324	Darrell Miller	.05
325	Shane Turner	.05
326	Greg Biagini	.05
327	Alex Sanchez	.10
328	Mauro Gozzo	.05
329	Steven Cummings	.05
330	Tom Gilles	.05
331	Douglas Linton	.05
332	Mike Loynd	.05
333	Bob Shirley	.05
334	John Shea	.05
335	Paul Kilgus	.05
336	Carlos Diaz	.05
337	Joe Szekely	.05
338	Rick Lysander	.05
339	Jim Eppard	.05
340	Derek Bell	.65
341	Jose Escobar	.05
342	Webster Garrison	.05
343	Paul Runge	.05
344	Luis Sojo	.10
345	Ed Sprague	.15
346	Hector Delacruz	.05
347	Rob Ducey	.05
348	Ozzie Virgil	.05
349	Stu Pederson	.05
350	Mark Whiten	.20
351	Andy Dziadkowiec	.05
352	Shawn Barton	.05
353	Kevin Brown	.05
354	Rocky Childress	.05
355	Brian Givens	.05
356	Manny Hernandez	.05
357	Jeff Innis	.05
358	Cesar Mejia	.05
359	Scott Nielson	.05
360	Dale Plummer	.05
361	Ray Soff	.05
362	Lou Thornton	.05
363	Dave Trautwein	.05
364	Julio Valera	.05
365	Tim Bogar	.10
366	Mike DeButch	.05
367	Jeff Gardner	.05
368	Denny Gonzalez	.05
369	Chris Jelic	.05
370	Roger Samuels	.05
371	Dave Liddell	.05
372	Orlando Mercado	.15
373	Kelvin Torva	.05
374	Alex Diaz	.05
375	Keith Hughes	.05
376	Darren Reed	.05
377	Zolio Sanchez	.05
378	Do Vesling	.05
379	Scott Aldred	.05
380	Dennis Burtt	.05
381	Shawn Holman	.05
382	Matt Kinzer	.05
383	Randy Mosek	.05
384	Jose Ramos	.05
385	Kevin Ritz	.05
386	Mike Schwabe	.05
387	Steve Searcy	.05
388	Eric Stone	.05
389	Domingo Michel	.05
390	Phil Ouellette	.05
391	Shawn Hare	.10
392	Jim Lindeman	.05
393	Scott Livingstone	.15
394	Lavel Freeman	.05
395	Travis Fryman	.50
396	Scott Lusader	.05
397	Dean Decillis	.05
398	Milt Cuyler	.10
399	Not issued	
400	Phil Clark	.05
401	Torey Lovullo	.05
402	Aurelio Rodriguez	.05
403	Mike Christopher	.05
404	Jeff Bittiger	.05
405	Jeff Fischer	.05
406	Steve Davis	.05
407	Morris Madden	.05
408	Darren Holmes	.15
409	Greg Mayberry	.05
410	Mike Maddux	.05
411	Tim Scott	.05
412	Jim Neidlinger	.05
413	Dave Walsh	.05
414	Dennis Springer	.05
415	Terry Wells	.05
416	Adam Brown	.05
417	Darrin Fletcher	.20
418	Carlos Hernandez	.10
419	Dave Hansen	.10
420	Dan Henley	.05
421	Jose Offerman	.25
422	Jose Vizcaino	.15
423	Luis Lopez	.05
424	Butch Davis	.05
425	Wayne Kirby	.10
426	Mike Huff	.10
427	Billy Bean	.05
428	Pat Pacillo	.05
429	Tony Blasucci	.05
430	Mike Walker	.05
431	Pat Rice	.05
432	Terry Taylor	.05
433	David Burba	.05
434	Vance Lovelace	.05
435	Ed Vande Berg	.05
436	Greg Fulton	.05
437	Ed Jurak	.05
438	Dave Cochrane	.05
439	Edgar Martinez	.90
440	Matt Sinatro	.05
441	Bill McGuire	.05
442	Mickey Brantley	.05
443	Tom Dodd	.05
444	Jim Weaver	.05
445	Todd Haney	.05
446	Casey Close	.05
447	Theo Shaw	.05
448	Keith Helton	.05
449	Jose Melendez	.05
450	Tom Jones	.05
451	Dan Warthen	.05
452	Randy Roetter	.05
453	Mike Walker	.05
454	Colby Ward	.05
455	Joe Skalski	.05
456	Efrain Valdez	.05
457	Doug Robertson	.05
458	Jeff Edwards	.05
459	Greg McMichael	.05
460	Carl Willis	.05
461	Beau Allred	.05
462	Jeff Kaiser	.05
463	Ty Gainey	.05
464	Tom Lampkin	.05
465	Ever Magallanes	.05
466	Tom Magrann	.05
467	Jeff Manto	.05
468	Luis Medina	.05
469	Troy Neel	.20
470	Steve Springer	.05
471	Not issued	
472	Turner Ward	.10
473	Casey Webster	.05
474	Jeff Weatherly	.05
475	Alan Cockrell	.05
476a	Rick Adair	.05
476b	Steve McInerney (trainer)	.05
477	Bobby Molinaro	.05
478	Cliff Young	.05
479	Michael Arner	.05
480	Gary Buckels	.05
481	Timothy Burcham	.05
482	Sherman Corbett	.05
483	Mike Erb	.05
484	Mike Fetters	.05
485	Chuck Hernandez	.05
486	Jeff Heathcock	.05
487	Scott Lewis	.05
488	Rafael Montalvo	.05
489	John Skuria	.05
490	Lee Stevens	.05
491	Nelson Rood	.05
492	Bobby Rose	.05
493	Dan Grunhard	.05
494	Reed Peters	.05
495	Doug Davis	.05
496	Gary DiSarcina	.15
497	Pete Coachman	.05
498	Chris Cron	.05
499	Karl Allaire	.05
500	Ron Tingley	.05
501	Chris Beasley	.05
502	Max Oliveras	.05
503	Roger Smithberg	.05
504	Steve Peters	.05
505	Matt Maysey	.10
506	Terry Gilmore	.05
507	Jeff Datz	.05
508	Eric Nolte	.05
509	Jim Lewis	.05
510	Pete Roberts	.05
511	Dan Murphy	.05
512	Rich Rodriguez	.05
513	Joe Lynch	.05
514	Mike Basso	.05
515	Ronn Reynolds	.05
516	Jose Mota	.05
517	Paul Faries	.05
518	Warren Newson	.10
519	Alex Cole	.10
520	Tom Levasseur	.05
521	Charles Hillemann	.05
522	Jeff Yurtin	.05
523	Rafael Valdez	.05
524	Brian Ohnoutka	.05
525	Pat Kelley	.05
526	Gary Lance	.05
527	Tony Torchia	.05
528	Paul McClellan	.05
529	Randy McCament	.05
530	Gil Heredia	.10
531	George Bonilla	.05
532	Russ Swan	.05
533	Ed Vosberg	.05
534	Eric Gunderson	.05
535	Trevor Wilson	.10
536	Greg Booker	.05
537	Kirt Manwaring	.10
538	Mike Kingery	.05
539	Brian Brady	.05
540	Mark Bailey	.05
541	Gregg Ritchie	.05
542	George Hinshaw	.05
543	Craig Colbert	.05
544	Kash Beauchamp	.05
545	Jeff Carter	.05
546	Mark Leonard	.05
547	Tony Perezchica	.05
548	Mike Laga	.05
549	Mike Benjamin	.10
550	Timber Mead	.05
551	Duane Espy	.05
552	Tim Ireland	.05
553	Paul Abbott	.05
554	Pat Bangston	.05
555	Larry Casian	.05
556	Mike Cook	.05
557	Pete Delkus	.05
558	Mike Dyer	.05
559	Charlie Scott	.05
560	Francisco Oliveras	.05
561	Park Pittman	.05
562	Jimmy Williams	.05
563	Rich Yett	.05
564	Vic Rodriguez	.05
565	Jamie Nelson	.05
566	Derek Parks	.10
567	Ed Naveda	.05
568	Scott Leius	.10
569	Terry Jorgensen	.05
570	Doug Baker	.05
571	Chip Hale	.05
572	Dave Jacas	.05
573	Jim Shellenback	.05
574	Rafael DeLima	.05
575	Bernardo Brito	.05
576	J.T. Bruett	.05
577	Paul Sorrento	.15
578	Ray Young	.05
579	Dave Veres	.05
580	Scott Chiamparino	.05
581	Tony Ariola	.05
582	Weston Weber	.05
583	Bruce Walton	.05
584	Dave Otto	.05
585	Reese Lambert	.05
586	Joe Bitker	.05
587	Joe Law	.05
588	Ed Wojna	.05
589	Timothy Casey	.05
590	Patrick Dietrick	.05
591	Bruce Fields	.05
592	Eric Fox	.10
593	Scott Hemond	.10
594	Steve Howard	.05
595	Doug Jennings	.05
596	Al Pedrique	.05
597	Dann Howitt	.05
598	Russ McGinnis	.05
599	Troy Afenir	.05
600	Larry Arndt	.05
601	Dickie Scott	.05
602	Kevin Ward	.05
603	Ryan Bowen	.15
604	Brian Meyer	.05
605	Terry Clark	.05
606	Darryl Kile	.25
607	Randy St. Claire	.05
608	Randy Hennis	.05
609	Lee Tunnell	.05
610	Bill Brennan	.05
611	Craig Smajstrla	.05
612	Gary Cooper	.05
613	Carl Nichols	.05
614	Louie Meadows	.05
615	Jose Tolentino	.05
616	Harry Spillman	.05
617	Javier Ortiz	.05
618	Doug Strange	.10
619	Jim Olander	.05
620	Karl Rhodes	.15
621	David Rohde	.05
622	Mike Simms	.05
623	Scott Servais	.15
624	Pedro Sanchez	.05
625	Kevin Dean	.05
626	Brian Fisher	.05
627	Bob Skinner	.05
628	Wilson Alvarez	.35
629	Adam Peterson	.05
630	Tom Drees	.05
631	Ravelo Manzanillo	.05
632	Marv Foley	.05
633	Grady Hall	.05
634	Mike Campbell	.05
635	Shawn Hillegas	.05
636	C.L. Penigar	.05
637	John Pawlowski	.05
638	Steve Rosenberg	.05
639	Jose Segura	.05
640	Rich Amaral	.10
641	Pete Dalena	.05
642	Ramon Sambo	.05
643	Marcus Lawton	.05
644	Orsino Hill	.05
645	Marlin McPhail	.05
646	Keith Smith	.05
647	Todd Trafton	.05
648	Norberto Martin	.05
649	Don Wakamatsu	.05
650	Jerry Willard	.05
651	Dana Williams	.05
652	Tracy Woodson	.05
653	Glenn Hoffman	.05
654	Anthony Scruggs	.05
655	Reggie Sanders	.40
656	Rick Lueken	.05
657	Kent Mercker	.10
658	Dukes Coaches	.05
659	Richard Shockey (photo is Mo Sanford)	.15
660a	Brian Barnes	.05
660b	Mario Brito	.05
661	Not issued	
662	Ed Quijada	.05
663	Steve Wapnick	.05
664	Kevin Tahan	.05
665	Johnny Guzman	.10
666	Bronswell Patrick	.05
667	Kevin Kennedy	.05
668	Orlando Miller	.20
669	Mauricio Nunez	.05
670	Hector Rivera	.05
671	Roger LaFrancois	.05
672	Jackson Todd	.05
673	John Young	.05
674	Bob Bailor	.05
675	David Hajeck	.05
676	Ralph Wheeler	.05
677	Anthony Gutierrez	.05
678	Gaylen Pitts	.05
679	Mark Riggins	.05
680	Brad Bluestone	.05
681	Dick Bosman	.05
682	Wil Cordero	.55
683	Todd Hutcheson	.05
684	Steve Swisher	.05
685	John Cumberland	.05
686	Rich Miller	.05
687	Scott Lawrenson	.05
688	Larry Hardy	.05
689	Danny Boone	.05
690	Terrel Hansen	.05
691a	Tom Gamboa	.05
691b	Jeff Jones	.05
692	Gavin Osteen	.05
693	Dave Riddle	.05
694	Tim Pugh	.15
695	Eugene Jones	.05
696	Scott Pose	.10
697	Ramon Jimenez	.05
698	Fred Russell	.05
699	Louis Talbert	.05
700	J.D. Noland	.05
701	Osvaldo Sanchez	.05
702	David Colon	.05
703	Jeff Hart	.05
704	Jeff Hoffman	.05
705	Sean Gilliam	.05
706	Al Pacheco	.05
707	Jason Satre	.05
708	Tim Cecil	.05
709	Phil Wiese	.05
710	Larry Pardo	.05
711	Clemente Acosta	.05
712	Chris Johnson	.05
713	Frank Bolick	.10
714	Jose Garcia	.05
715	Adell Davenport	.05
716	Kevin Rogers	.10
717	Dan Rambo	.05
718	Vince Harris	.05
719	Darrell Sherman	.10
720	Isaiah Clark	.05
721	Miguel Sabino	.05
722	Frank Valdez	.05
723	Giovanni Miranda	.05
724	Daryl Ratliff	.05
725	Mike Brewinton	.05
726	Eric Parkinson	.05
727	Vin Castilla	.40
728	Roger Hailey	.10
729	Earl Steinmetz	.05
730	Doug Gogolewski	.05
731	Andy Cook	.05
732	John Toale	.05
733	Mike Curtis	.05
734	Delwyn Young	.05
735	Scott Meadows	.05
736	Don Sparks	.05
737	Gary Wilson	.05
738	Blas Minor	.10
739	Jeff Bagwell	12.00
740	Phil Bryant	.05
741	Felipe Castillo	.05
742	Craig Faulkner	.05
743	Jeff Conine	.75
744	Kevin Belcher	.05
745	Bill Haselman	.05
746	Matt Stark	.05
747	Todd Hall	.05
748	Scott Centala	.05
749	Doug Simons	.05
750	Shawn Gilbert	.05
751	Kenny Morgan	.05
752	Andy Mota	.05
753	Jeff Baldwin	.05
754	Reed Olmstead	.10
755	Basil Meyer	.05
756	Mark Razook	.05
757	Ken Pennington	.05
758	Shane Letterio	.05
759	Ted Williams	.05
760	Luis Gonzalez	.25
761	Carlos Garcia	.15
762	Terry Crowley	.05
763	Julio Peguero	.05
764	Francisco Delarosa	.05
765	Rodney Lofton	.05
766	Eric McCray	.05
767	Mike Wilkins	.05
768	John Kiely	.05
769	Derek Lee	.20
770	Bo Kennedy	.05
771	John Hudek	.10
772	Bernie Nunez	.05

773 Tom Quinlan .05
774 Jim Tatum .05
775 Casey Waller .05
776 Doug Lindsey .05
777 Roberto Zambrano .05
778 Wade Taylor .10
779 Carlos Maldonado .05
780 Brent Mayne .10
781 Jerry Rub .05
782 Vincent Phillips .05
783 Eric Wedge .05
784 Andrew Ashby .20
785 Royal Clayton .05
786 Jeffrey Osbourne .05
787 Pat Kelly .10
788 John Wehner .05
789 Bernie Williams 4.00
790 Moises Alou .90
791 Mark Merchant .05
792 Chris Myers .05
793 Donald Harris .10
794 Michael McDonald .05
795 Jim Blueberg .05
796 James Bowie .05
797 Ruben Gonzalez .05
798 Rob Maurer .05
799 Monty Farris .05
800 Bob Ayrault .10
801 Tim Mauser .05
802 David Holdridge .05
803 Kim Batiste .05
804 Dan Peltier .10
805 Derek Livernois .05
806 Thomas Fischer .05
807 Chuck Knoblauch 3.00
808 Willie Banks .10
809 Johnny Ard .05
810 Willie Ansley .05
811 Andujar Cedeno .10
812 Eddie Zosky .10
813 Randy Knorr .05
814 Juan Guzman .50
815 Jimmy Rogers .05
816 Nate Cromwell .05
817 Aubrey Waggoner .05
818 Frank Thomas 15.00
819 Matt Merullo .05
820 Roberto Hernandez .30
821 Cesar Bernhardt .05
822 Sterling Hitchcock .30
823 Ricky Rhodes .05
824 Todd Malone .05
825 Andy Fox .05
826 Ryan Klesko 3.00
827 Tyler Houston .15
828 Tab Brown .05
829 Brian McRae .45
830 Victor Cole .05
831 Mark Lewis .25
832 Rudy Seanez .10
833 Charles Nagy .25
834 Jeff Mutis .10
835 Carl Keliipuleole .05
836 Steve Pegues .05
837 Mike Lumley .05
838 Tim Leiner .05
839 Dave Evans .05
840 Darron Cox .05
841 Tony Ochs .05
842 Paul Coleman .05
843 Rafael Novoa .05
844 Clay Bellinger .05
845 Jason McFarlin .05
846 Craig Paquette .05
847 Timmie Morrow .05
848 Brian Hunter .25
849 Willie Greene .10
850 Austin Manahan .05
851 Rich Aude .05
852 Luis Lopez .05
853 Darrin Reichle .05
854 Tim Salmon 5.00
855 Royce Clayton .50
856 Steve Hosey .15
857 Kerry Woodson .05
858 Roger Salkeld .25
859 Tim Stargell .05
860 Greg Pirkl .05
861 Pat Mahomes .10
862 Denny Naegle .50
863 Troy Buckley .05
864 Ray Ortiz .05
865 Leo Perez .05
866 Cal Eldred .25
867 Darin Kracl .05
868 Lee Tinsley .10
869 T.R. Lewis .10
870 Jim Roso .05
871 Tom Taylor .05
872 Matt Anderson .05
873 Kerwin Moore .05
874 Rich Tunison .05
875 Brian Ahern .05
876 Eddie Taubensee .10
877 Scott Bryant .05
878 Steve Martin .05
879 Josias Mazanillo .05
880 Bob Zupcic .05

1990 ProCards A & AA Minor League Stars

This set was originally marketed for ProCards in wax packs by Progressive Sports Images in 1991 and, later, was distributed as a complete set.

MT
Complete Set (200): 15.00
Common Player: .05
1 Mike Linskey .05
2 Ben McDonald .10
3 Francisco DeLaRosa .05
4 Jose Mesa .15
5 Kevin Morton .10
6 Dan O'Neill .05
7 Dave Owen .05
8 Jeff Plympton .05
9 Charles Nagy .30
10 Rudy Seanez .10
11 Bruce Egloff .05
12 Joe Ausanio .05
13 Jim Tracy .05
14 Randy Tomlin .10
15 Jim Campbell .05
16 Mike Gardiner .05
17 Rusty Meacham .05
18 John Kiely .10
19 Darrin Chapin .05
20 Wade Taylor .05
21 Don Stanford .05
22 Andy Ashby .25
23 Bob Ayrault .10
24 Luis Mercedes .05
25 Scott Meadows .05
26 Jeff Bagwell 4.00
27 Mark Lewis .15
28 Carlos Garcia .10
29 Moises Alou 1.00
30 Rico Brogna .10
31 Bernie Williams 3.00
32 Pat Kelly .10
33 Mitch Lyden .05
34 Hector Wagner .05
35 Carlos Maldonado .05
36 Brian Barnes .10
37 Chris Nabholz .05
38 Jeff Carter .05
39 Johnny Ard .05
40 Willie Banks .10
41 Scott Erickson .30
42 Greg Johnson .05
43 Al Osuna .05
44 Bob MacDonald .05
45 Pat Hentgen .50
46 Frank Thomas 8.00
47 Matt Stark .05
48 Jeff Conine .75
49 Sean Berry .15
50 Brian McRae .35
51 Bobby Moore .10
52 Brent Mayne .10
53 Greg Colbrunn .10
54 Terrel Hansen .05
55 Lenny Webster .05
56 Chuck Knoblauch 2.00
57 Willie Ansley .05
58 Andujar Cedeno .05
59 Luis Gonzalez .20
60 Eddie Zosky .15
61 William Suero .05
62 Tom Quinlan .05
63 Kelly Mann .05
64 Mike Bell .05
65 Mark Dewey .05
66 Tom Hostetler .05
67 Kevin Belcher .05
68 Bill Haselman .05
69 Bob Maurer .05
70 Dan Rohrmeier .05
71 Dan Peltier .05
72 Steven Decker .05
73 Dave Patterson .05
74 Ed Zinter .05
75 David Bird .05
76 Willie Espinal .05
77 Dennis Fletcher .05
78 Travis Buckley .05
79 Brian Romero .05
80 Mike Arner .05
81 Brian Evans .05
82 John Graves .05
83 Randy Marshall .05
84 Mike Garcia .05
85 Jeff Braley .05
86 Ricky Rhodes .05
87 Jim Haller .05
88 Sterling Hitchcock .15
89 Rob Blumberg .05
90 Mike Ogliaruso .05
91 Gregg Martin .05
92 Tim Pugh .10
93 Roger Hailey .05
94 Don Strange .05
95 Robert Gaddy .05
96 Willie Greene .15
97 Austin Manahan .05
98 Tony Scruggs .05
99 Mike Burton .05
100 Shawn Holtzclaw .05
101 Orlando Miller .10
102 David Hajek .05
103 Scott Pose .10
104 Tyler Houston .10
105 Melvin Nieves .10
106 Ryan Klesko 2.00
107 Daryl Moore .05
108 Skip Wiley .05
109 Brian McKeon .05
110 Rusty Kilgo .05
111 Chris Bushing .05
112 Alan Newman .05
113 Marc Lipson .05
114 Darin Kracl .05
115 Matt Grott .05
116 Rafael Novoa .05
117 Pat Rapp .10
118 Ed Gustafson .05
119 Chris Hancock .05
120 Mo Sanford .10
121 Bill Risley .05
122 Victor Garcia .05
123 Dave McAuliffe .05
124 Pedro Borbon .05
125 Rich Tunlson .05
126 Fred Cooley .05
127 Joey James .05
128 Reggie Sanders .75
129 Scott Bryant .05
130 Brent McCoy .05
131 Ramon Caraballo .05
132 Javier Lopez 2.00
133 Brian Harrison .05
134 Rich DeLucia .10
135 Roger Salkeld .10
136 Kerry Woodson .05
137 Chris Johnson .05
138 Cal Eldred .15
139 Angel Miranda .05
140 Richard Garces .05
141 Pat Mahomes .05
142 Denny Neagle .20
143 George Tsamis .05
144 Johnny Guzman .05
145 Dan Rambo .05
146 Jim Myers .05
147 Darrell Sherman .05
148 Dave Staton .10
149 Brian Turang .05
150 Bo Dodson .05
151 Dave Nilsson .20
152 Frank Bolick .05
153 Ray Ortiz .05
154 J.T. Bruett .05
155 John Patterson .10
156 Royce Clayton .35
157 Hilly Hathaway .05
158 Phil Leftwich .05
159 Randy Powers .05
160 Todd Van Poppel .10
161 Don Peters .05
162 Dave Zancanaro .05
163 Kirk Dressendorfer .05
164 Curtis Shaw .05
165 Joe Rosselli .05
166 Mark Dalesandro .05
167 Eric Helfand .05
168 Eric Booker .05
169 Adam Hyzdu .05
170 Eric Christopherson .05
171 Marcus Jensen .05
172 Derek Reid .05
173 Lance Dickson .05
174 Tim Parker .05
175 Jessie Hollins .05
176 Sam Militello .05
177 Darren Hodges .05
178 Kirt Ojala .05
179 Steve Karsay .10
180 Andrew Hartung .05
181 Kevin Jordan .10
182 Robert Eenhoorn .05
183 Jalal Leach .05
184 Carlos Delgado 1.50
185 Sean Cheetham .05
186 J.J. Munoz .05
187 Jim Thome 1.50
188 Tracy Sanders .05
189 Tony Clark 1.50
190 Jose Viera .05
191 Pat Dando .05
192 Brian Kowitz .05
193 Mike Lieberthal .20
194 Jeff Borgese .05
195 Mike Ferry .05
196 K.C. Gillum .05
197 Elliott Quinones .05
198 Grant Brittain .05
199 Checklist 1-100 .05
200 Checklist 101-200 .05

1990 ProCards Future Stars AAA Baseball

This series was the second produced for ProCards by Progressive Sports Images. The 1989 issue had simply been AAA players from the regular ProCards team sets with 1989 stats added. The 1990 series, complete with 1990 stats, features cards from all AAA teams in a completely different format from the '90 team sets. Although the cards were numbered consecutively 1-700, an attempt was made to maintain team integrity. The series was later issued in complete sets. Due to scarcity of certain cards in inventory and additional labor costs to dealers, the consumer can expect to pay a minimum of $3-6 for team sets from this product.

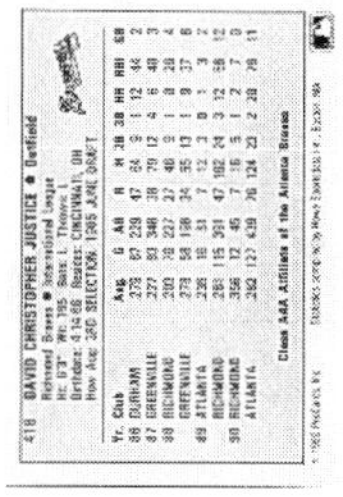

MT
Complete Set (700): 24.00
Common Player: .05
1 Terry Gilmore .05
2 Jim Lewis .05
3 Joe Lynch .05
4 Matt Maysey .10
5 Dan Murphy .05
6 Eric Nolte .05
7 Brian Ohnoutka .05
8 Steve Peters .05
9 Paul Quinzer .05
10 Pete Roberts .05
11 Rich Rodriguez .05
12 Roger Smithberg .05
13 Rafael Valdez .05
14 Mike Basso .05
15 Ronn Reynolds .05
16 Paul Faries .05
17 Tom LeVasseur .05
18 Jose Mota .05
19 Eddie Williams .05
20 Jeff Yurtin .05
21 Alex Cole .10
22 Charles Hillemann .05
23 Thomas Howard .10
24 Warren Newson .10
25 Pat Kelly .10
26 Gary Lance .05
27 Tony Torchia .05
28 George Bonilla .05
29 Greg Booker .05
30 Rich Bordi .10
31 John Burkett .35
32 Gil Heredia .05
33 Bob Knepper .05
34 Randy McCament .05
35 Paul McClellan .05
36 Timber Mead .05
37 Ed Vosberg .05
38 Trevor Wilson .20
39 Mark Bailey .05
40 Kirt Manwaring .10
41 Mike Benjamin .10
42 Brian Brady .05
43 Jeff Carter .05
44 Craig Colbert .05
45 Erik Johnson .05
46 Greg Litton .05
47 Kash Beauchamp .05
48 George Hinshaw .05
49 Mike Kingery .05
50 Mark Leonard .05
51 Gregg Ritchie .05
52 Rick Parker .05
53 Duane Espy .05
54 Tim Ireland .05
55 Larry Hardy .05
56 Jeff Bittiger .05
57 Mike Christopher .05
58 Steve Davis .05
59 Jeff Fischer .05
60 Darren Holmes .15
61 Morris Madden .05
62 Mike Maddux .05
63 Greg Mayberry .05
64 Jim Neidlinger .05
65 Tim Scott .05
66 Dave Walsh .05
67 Terry Wells .05
68 Adam Brown .05
69 Darrin Fletcher .20
70 Carlos Hernandez .10
71 Dave Hansen .10
72 Dan Henley .05
73 Glenn Hoffman .05
74 Walt McConnell .05
75 Jose Offerman .10
76 Jose Vizcaino .15
77 Billy Bean .05
78 Butch Davis .05
79 Mike Huff .05
80 Wayne Kirby .10
81 Luis Lopez .05
82 Kevin Kennedy .05
83 Claude Osteen .05
84 Von Joshua .05
85 Chris Beasley .05
86 Gary Buckels .05
87 Tim Burcham .05
88 Sherman Corbett .05
89 Mike Erb .05
90 Mike Fetters .05
91 Jeff Heathcock .05
92 Scott Lewis .05
93 Rafael Montalvo .05
94 Cliff Young .05
95 Doug Davis .05
96 Ron Tingley .05
97 Karl Allaire .05
98 Pete Coachman .05
99 Chris Cron .05
100 Gary DiSarcina .15
101 Nelson Rood .05
102 Bobby Rose .05
103 Lee Stevens .10
104 Dan Grunhard .05
105 Reed Peters .05
106 John Skurla .05
107 Max Oliveras .05
108 Chuck Hernandez .05
109 Tony Blasucci .05
110 Dave Burba .10
111 Keith Helton .05
112 Vance Lovelace .05
113 Jose Melendez .05
114 Pat Pacillo .05
115 Pat Rice .05
116 Terry Taylor .05
117 Mike Walker .05
118 Bill McGuire .05
119 Matt Sinatro .05
120 Mario Diaz .05
121 Greg Fulton .05
122 Todd Haney .10
123 Ed Jurak .05
124 Tino Martinez 2.00
125 Jeff Schaefer .10
126 Casey Close .05
127 Tom Dodd .05
128 Jim Weaver .05
129 Tommy Jones .05
130 Dan Warthen .05
131 Tony Ariola .05
132 Joe Bitker .05
133 Scott Chiamparino .05
134 Reese Lambert .05
135 Joe Law .05
136 Dave Otto .05
137 Dave Veres .05
138 Bruce Walton .05
139 Weston Weber .05
140 Ed Wojna .05
141 Ray Young .05
142 Troy Afenir .05
143 Russ McGinnis .05
144 Larry Arndt .05
145 Mike Bordick .15
146 Scott Hemond .05
147 Dann Howitt .05
148 Doug Jennings .05
149 Al Pedrique .05
150 Dick Scott .05
151 Tim Casey .05
152 Pat Dietrick .05
153 Bruce Fields .05
154 Eric Fox .05
155 Steve Howard .05
156 Kevin Ward .05
157 Brad Fischer .05
158 Chuck Estrada .05
159 Wilson Alvarez .50
160 Mike Campbell .05
161 Tom Drees .05
162 Grady Hall .05
163 Shawn Hillegas .05
164 Ravelo Manzanillo .05
165 John Pawlowski .05
166 Adam Peterson .05
167 Steve Rosenberg .05
168 Jose Segura .05
169 Don Wakamatsu .05
170 Jerry Willard .05
171 Rich Amaral .10
172 Pete Dalena .05
173 Norberto Martin .10
174 Keith Smith .05
175 Todd Trafton .05
176 Tracy Woodson .05
177 Orsino Hill .05
178 Marcus Lawton .05
179 Marlin McPhail .05
180 C.L. Penigar .05
181 Ramon Sambo .05
182 Dana Williams .05
183 Marv Foley .05
184 Moe Drabowsky .10
185 Roger LaFrancois .05
186 Ryan Bowen .15
187 William Brennan .05
188 Terry Clark .05
189 Brian Fisher .05
190 Randy Hennis .05
191 Darryl Kile .25
192 Brian Meyer .05
193 Randy St. Claire .05

194 Lee Tunnell .05
195 Carl Nichols .05
196 Scott Servais .10
197 Pedro Sanchez .05
198 Mike Simms .05
199 Criag Smajstria .05
200 Harry Spilman .05
201 Doug Strange .10
202 Jose Tolentino .05
203 Gary Cooper .05
204 Kevin Dean .05
205 Louie Meadows .05
206 Jim Olander .05
207 Javier Ortiz .05
208 Karl Rhodes .10
209 Bob Skinner .05
210 Brent Strom .05
211 Tim Tolman .05
212 Greg McMichael .10
213 Doug Robertson .05
214 Jeff Shaw .05
215 Joe Skalski .05
216 Efrain Valdez .05
217 Mike Walker .05
218 Colby Ward .05
219 Carl Willis .05
220 Tom Lampkin .05
221 Tom Magrann .05
222 Juan Castillo .05
223 Ever Magallanes .05
224 Jeff Manto .10
225 Luis Medina .05
226 Troy Neel .15
227 Steve Springer .05
228 Casey Webster .05
229 Beau Allred .05
230 Alan Cockrell .05
231 Ty Gainey .05
232 Dwight Taylor .05
233 Turner Ward .10
234 Jeff Wetherby .05
235 Bobby Molinaro .05
236 Buddy Bell .10
237 Rick Adair .05
238 Paul Abbott .05
239 Pat Bangston .05
240 Larry Casian .05
241 Mike Cook .05
242 Pete Delkus .05
243 Mike Dyer .05
244 Mark Guthrie .05
245 Orlando Lind .05
246 Francisco Oliveras .05
247 Park Pittman .05
248 Charles Scott .05
249 Jimmy Williams .05
250 Jamie Nelson .05
251 Derek Parks .05
252 Doug Baker .05
253 Chip Hale .10
254 Terry Jorgensen .05
255 Scott Leius .10
256 Marty Lanoux .05
257 Ed Naveda .05
258 Victor Rodriguez .05
259 Paul Sorrento .08
260 Bernardo Brito .05
261 Rafael Delima .05
262 David Jacas .05
263 Alonzo Powell .05
264 Jim Shellenback .05
265 Shawn Barton .05
266 Kevin Brown .05
267 Rocky Childress .05
268 Brian Givens .05
269 Manny Hernandez .05
270 Jeff Innis .05
271 Cesar Mejia .05
272 Scott Nielsen .05
273 Dale Plummer .05
274 Rogre Samuels .05
275 Ray Soff .05
276 Dave Trautwein .05
277 Julio Valera .05
278 Dave Liddell .05
279 Orlando Mercado .15
280 Tim Bogar .10
281 Mike DeButch .05
282 Jeff Gardner .10
283 Denny Gonzalez .05
284 Chris Jelic .05
285 Kelvin Torve .05
286 Alex Diaz .05
287 Keith Hughes .05
288 Darren Reed .10
289 Zollo Sanchez .05
290 Lou Thornton .05
291 Steve Swisher .05
292 John Cumberland .05
293 Rich Miller .05
294 Jose DeJesus .05
295 Marvin Freeman .05
296 Todd Frohwirth .05
297 Jason Grimsley .10
298 Chuck Malone .05
299 Brad Moore .05
300 Wally Ritchie .05
301 Bob Scanlan .10
302 Scott Service .05
303 Steve Sharts .05
304 John Gibbons .05
305 Tom Nieto .05
306 Jim Adduci .05
307 Kelly Heath .05
308 Mickey Morandini .20
309 Victor Rosario .05
310 Steve Stanicek .05
311 Greg Legg .05
312 Ron Jones .05
313 Chris Knabenshue .05
314 Keith Miller .05
315 Jim Vatcher .05
316 Jim Wright .05
317 Steve Adkins .05
318 Darrin Chapin .05
319 Bob Davidson .05
320 Dave Eiland .05
321 John Habyan .05
322 Jimmy Jones .05
323 Mark Leiter .05
324 Kevin Mmahat .05
325 Rich Monteleone .05
326 Willie Smith .05
327 Ricky Torres .05
328 Jeff Datz .05
329 Brian Dorsett .05
330 Dave Sax .05
331 Jim Leyritz .15
332 Hensley Meulens .05
333 Carlos Rodriguez .05
334 Rob Sepanek .05
335 Andy Stankiewicz .10
336 Jim Walewander .05
337 Mark Wasinger .05
338 Oscar Azocar .05
339 John Fishel .05
340 Jason Maas .05
341 Kevin Maas .05
342 Van Snider .05
343 Field Staff .05
344 Tom Gilles .05
345 Mauro Gozzo .05
346 Paul Kilgus .05
347 Doug Linton .05
348 Mike Loynd .05
349 Rick Lysander .05
350 Alex Sanchez .05
351 John Shea .05
352 Steve Wapnick .05
353 Andy Dziadkowiec .05
354 Joe Szekely .05
355 Ozzie Virgil .05
356 Jim Eppard .05
357 Jose Escobar .05
358 Webster Garrison .05
359 Paul Runge .05
360 Luis Sojo .10
361 Ed Sprague .15
362 Derek Bell .60
363 Hector DeLaCruz .05
364 Rob Ducey .10
365 Pedro Munoz .15
366 Stu Pederson .05
367 Mark Whiten .25
368 Bob Bailor .05
369 Bob Shirley .05
370 Rocket Wheeler .05
371 Scott Aldred .05
372 Dennis Burtt .05
373 Shawn Holman .05
374 Matt Kinzer .05
375 Randy Nosek .05
376 Jose Ramos .05
377 Kevin Ritz .10
378 Mike Schwabe .05
379 Steve Searcy .05
380 Eric Stone .05
381 Don Vesling .05
382 Phil Clark .05
383 Phil Ouellette .05
384 Dean DeCillis .05
385 Travis Fryman .75
386 Jim Lindeman .05
387 Scott Livingstone .10
388 Torey Lovullo .05
389 Domingo Michel .05
390 Milt Cuyler .10
391 Lavell Freeman .05
392 Shawn Hare .10
393 Scott Lusader .05
394 Tom Gamboa .05
395 Jeff Jones .05
396 Aurelio Rodriguez .05
397 Steve Avery .10
398 Tommy Greene .15
399 Bill Laskey .05
400 Paul Marak .05
401 Andy Nezelek .05
402 Ed Olwine .05
403 Dale Polley .05
404 Rusty Richards .05
405 Brian Snyder .05
406 Jimmy Kremers .05
407 John Mizerock .05
408 John Alva .05
409 Francisco Cabrera .05
410 Bruce Crabbe .05
411 Drew Denson .05
412 Ken Dowell .05
413 Ed Whited .05
414 Geronimo Berroa .10
415 Dennis Hood .05
416 Brian Hunter .10
417 Barry Jones .05
418 Dave Justice 4.00
419 Jim Beauchamp .05
420 John Grubb .05
421 Leo Mazzone .05
422 Sonny Jackson .05
423 Rick Berg .05
424 Steve Bast .05
425 Tom Bolton .05
426 Steve Curry .05
427 Mike Dalton .05
428 Jeff Gray .05
429 Daryl Irvine .05
430 Joe Johnson .05
431 John Leister .05
432 Mike Rochford .05
433 Larry Shikles .05
434 Tito Stewart .05
435 John Trautwein .05
436 John Flaherty .10
437 John Marzano .05
438 Gary Tremblay .05
439 Scott Cooper .10
440 Angel Gonzalez .05
441 Tim Naehring .05
442 Jim Pankovits .05
443 Mo Vaughn 4.00
444 Rick Lancellotti .05
445 Mickey Pina .05
446 Phil Plantier .05
447 Jeff Stone .05
448 Scott Wade .05
449 Ed Nottle .05
450 Mark Meleski .05
451 Lee Stange .05
452 Jay Aldrich .05
453 Jose Bautista .05
454 Eric Bell .05
455 Dan Boone .05
456 Ben McDonald .10
457 John Mitchell .05
458 Curt Schilling .65
459 Mike Smith .05
460 Rob Woodward .05
461 Chris Hoiles .10
462 Darrell Miller .05
463 Jeff Tackett .10
464 Juan Bell .05
465 Tim Dullin .05
466 Leo Gomez .10
467 Jeff McKnight .05
468 Shane Turner .05
469 Greg Walker .05
470 Tony Chance .05
471 Victor Hithe .05
472 Donnell Nixon .05
473 Chris Padget .05
474 Pete Stanicek .05
475 Mike Linskey .05
476 Joaquin Contreras .05
477 Greg Biagini .05
478 Dick Bosman .05
479 Paul Blair .05
480 Stan Belinda .10
481 Gordon Dillard .05
482 Mark Huismann .05
483 Hugh Kemp .05
484 Scott Medvin .05
485 Vincente Palacios .05
486 Rick Reed .05
487 Mark Ross .05
488 Dorn Taylor .05
489 Mike York .05
490 Dann Bilardello .05
491 Tom Prince .05
492 Danny Sheaffer .10
493 Kevin Burdick .05
494 Steve Kiefer .05
495 Orlando Merced .20
496 Armando Moreno .05
497 Jeff Richardson .05
498 Mark Ryal .05
499 Tommy Shields .05
500 Steve Carter .05
501 Wes Chamberlain .10
502 Jeff Cook .05
503 Scott Little .05
504 Terry Collins .05
505 Jackie Brown .05
506 Steve Henderson .05
507 Gibson Alba .05
508 Scott Arnold .05
509 Cris Carpenter .05
510 Stan Clarke .05
511 Mark Grater .05
512 Howard Hilton .05
513 Mike Hinkle .05
514 Omar Olivares .10
515 Dave Osteen .05
516 Mike Perez .05
517 Tim Sherrill .05
518 Scott Nichols .05
519 Ray Stephens .05
520 Pat Austin .05
521 Rod Brewer .05
522 Todd Crosby .05
523 Bien Figueroa .05
524 Julian Martinez .05
525 Jesus Mendez .05
526 Geronimo Pena .10
527 Craig Wilson .05
528 Dennis Carter .05
529 Bernard Gilkey 1.00
530 Ray Lankford 1.00
531 Mauricio Nunez .05
532 Roy Silver .05
533 Gaylen Pitts .05
534 Mark Riggins .05
535 Neil Allen .05
536 Keith Brown .05
537 Chris Hammond .15
538 Milton Hill .05
539 Rodney Imes .05
540 Rob Lopez .05
541 Charlie Mitchell .05
542 Bobby Moore .05
543 Rosario Rodriguez .05
544 Scott Scudder .05
545 Bob Sebra .05
546 Joey Vierra .05
547 Tony DeFrancesco .05
548 Terry McGriff .05
549 Donnie Scott .05
550 Reggie Jefferson .15
551 Brian Lane .05
552 Chris Lombardozzi .05
553 Paul Noce .05
554 Kevin Pearson .05
555 Eddie Tanner .05
556 Skeeter Barnes .05
557 Leo Garcia .05
558 Chris Jones .05
559 Keith Lockhart .10
560 Darryl Motley .05
561 Pete Mackanin .05
562 Ray Ripplemeyer .05
563 Scott Anderson .05
564 Esteban Beltre .10
565 Travis Chambers .05
566 Randy Braun .05
567 Danny Clay .05
568 Eric Bullock .05
569 Jim Davins .05
570 Jose Castro .05
571 Eddie Dixon .05
572 Romy Cucjen .05
573 Howard Farmer .05
574 Jerry Goff .05
575 Steve Fireovid .05
576 Otis Green .05
577 Dan Gakeler .05
578 Mel Houston .05
579 Balvino Galvez .05
580 Dwight Lowery .05
581 Dale Mohorcic .05
582 Quinn Mack .05
583 Chris Marchok .05
584 Edwin Marquez .05
585 Mel Rojas .15
586 Johnny Paredes .05
587 Rich Thompson .05
588 German Rivera .05
589 James Steels .05
590 Tim Johnson .05
591 Gomer Hodge .05
592 Joe Kerrigan .05
593 Ray Chadwick .05
594 Dera Clark .05
595 Luis Encarnacion .05
596 Tony Ferreira .05
597 Pete Filson .05
598 Jim LeMasters .05
599 Mike Magnante .05
600 Mike Tresemer .05
601 Mel Stottlemyre .05
602 Bill Wilkinson .05
603 Kevin Burrell .05
604 Tim Spehr .05
605 Luis DeLosSantos .05
606 Bob Hamelin .10
607 Bobby Meacham .05
608 Russ Morman .05
609 Thad Reece .05
610 Paul Zuvella .05
611 Mike Loggins .05
612 Chito Martinez .05
613 Harvey Pulliam .05
614 Jeff Schulz .05
615 Sal Rende .05
616 Tom Poquette .05
617 Rich Dubee .05
618 Kevin Blankenship .05
619 Shawn Boskie .10
620 Mark Bowden .05
621 Greg Kallevig .05
622 Dave Masters .05
623 Steve Parker .05
624 Dave Pavlas .05
625 Laddie Renfroe .05
626 Paul Wilmet .05
627 Jeff Hearron .05
628 Erik Pappas .05
629 Hector Villanueva .05
630 Bob Bafia .05
631 Brian Guinn .05
632 Jeff Small .05
633 Greg Smith .05
634 Glenn Sullivan .05
635 Bill Wrona .05
636 Brad Bierley .05
637 Cedric Landrum .05
638 Derrick May .10
639 Gary Varsho .05
640 Jim Essian .05
641 Don August .05
642 Mike Birkbeck .05
643 Mike Capel .05
644 Logan Easley .05
645 Tom Edens .05
646 Don Gordon .05
647 Chuck McGrath .05
648 Jeff Peterek .05
649 Dennis Powell .05
650 Ed Puig .05
651 Alan Sadler .05
652 Tim Watkins .05
653 Tim McIntosh .05
654 Tim Torricelli .05
655 George Canale .05
656 Mark Higgins .05
658 Joe Mitchell .05
659 Joe Redfield .05
660 D.L. Smith .05
661 Joe Xavier .05
662 Ruben Escalera .05
663 Mario Monico .05
664 Billy Moore .05
665 Darryel Walters .05
666 Dave Machemer .05
667 Jackson Todd .05
668 Gerald Alexander .05
669 Brad Arnsberg .05
670 John Barfield .05
671 Jack Hardy .05
672 Ray Hayward .05
673 John Hoover .05
674 Steve Lankard .05
675 David Lynch .05
676 Craig McMurtry .05
677 David Miller .05
678 Mark Petkovsek .10
679 Jeff Satzinger .05
680 Mike Berger .05
681 Dave Engle .05
682 John Russell .05
683 Pat Dodson .05
684 Pat Garman .05
685 Gary Green .05
686 Bryan House .05
687 Dean Palmer .50
688 Ron Washington .05
689 Nick Capra .05
690 Juan Gonzalez 7.50
691 Gar Millay .05
692 Kevin Reimer .05
693 Bernie Tatis .05
694 Checklist 1-100 .05
695 Checklist 101-200 .05
696 Checklist 201-300 .05
697 Checklist 301-400 .05
698 Checklist 401-500 .05
699 Checklist 501-600 .05
700 Checklist 601-700 .05

1990 Star Minor League Baseball Wax

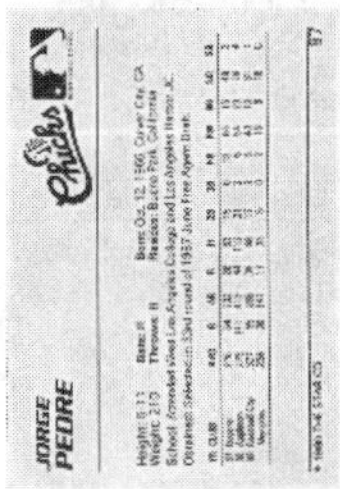

Star finished the 1990 season with another 100-card wax series. This series was closely akin in makeup to its 1989 predecessor. The set features yellow borders around color photos. There was no checklist and the cards were not available as a complete set. A second series was planned, but never materialized.

		MT
Complete Set (100):		15.00
Common Player:		.05
1	Bruce Schreiber	.05
2	Jeff Juden	.20
3	Kenny Lofton	4.00
4	Scott Makarewicz	.05
5	Al Sanders	.05
6	Rod Boddie	.05
7	Jim Faulk	.05
8	Dan Freed	.05
9	D.J. Dozier	.05
10	Nicko Riesgo	.05
11	Alan Zinter	.05
12	Jim Bruske	.05
13	Mark Lewis	.15
14	Willie Ansley	.05
15	Tony Eusebio	.10
16	Luis Gonzalez	.15
17	Andy Mota	.05
18	Tony Barron	.05
19	Kevin Maas	.05
20	Anthony Collier	.05
21	Ramon Taveras	.05
22	Eric Young	.25
23	Everett Cunningham	.05
24	Barry Manuel	.05
25	David Perez	.05
26	Ivan Rodriguez	4.00
27	Fred Samson	.05
28	Ben McDonald	.10
29	Blas Minor	.05

30	Jeff Bagwell	6.00
31	Mike Twardoski	.05
32	T.R. Lewis	.05
33	Ron Cook	.05
34	Ivan Cruz	.05
35	Jody Hurst	.05
36	Keith Kimberlin	.05
37	Lino Rivera	.05
38	Mike Tresh	.05
39	Hernan Cortes	.05
40	Jay Knoblauch	.05
41	Larry Stanford	.05
42	Hector Vargas	.05
43	Jacob Brumfield	.05
44	Mark Parnell	.05
45	Willie Banks	.10
46	Reed Olmstead	.05
47	Mike Redding	.05
48	Rich DeLucia	.10
49	Mike Gardiner	.05
50	Royal Clayton	.05
51	Darrin Chapin	.05
52	Mitch Lyden	.05
53	Don Sparks	.05
54	Bernie Williams	3.00
55	Steve Dunn	.05
56	Alan Newman	.05
57	Brent McCoy	.05
58	Mike Galvan	.05
59	Greg Perschke	.05
60	Rob Resnikoff	.05
61	Sammy Sosa	12.00
62	Bobby DeLoach	.05
63	Jesse Cross	.05
64	Ray Giannelli	.05
65	Jeff Kent	.50
66	Greg O'Halloran	.05
67	Mike Timlin	.10
68	Brian McRae	.25
69	Anthony Ward	.05
70	Toby Borland	.05
71	Joe Millette	.05
72	Tony Trevino	.05
73	Anthony Kelley	.05
74	George Kerfut	.05
75	Scott Meadows	.05
76	Luis Mercedes	.05
77	Dan Barbara	.05
78	Rod Poissant	.05
79	Gary Alexander	.05
80	Bob Ayrault	.10
81	Kim Batiste	.05
82	Pete Alborano	.05
83	Scott Centala	.05
84	Stu Cole	.05
85	Jeff Conine	.75
86	Bobby Moore	.10
87	Jorge Pedre	.05
88	Mike Maksudian	.05
89	Jerry Schunk	.05
90	William Suero	.05
91	Eddie Zosky	.10
92	Jeff Hoffman	.05
93	Ramon Jimenez	.05
94	Michael Bell	.05
95	Thomas Redington	.05
96	Michael Arner	.05
97	Brian Romero	.05
98	Tony Scruggs	.05
99	James Harris	.05
100	Tito Navarro	.05

1990 Minor League Team Sets

The number of minor league team sets and variations declined a bit from the peak year of 1989. Sportsprint entered the field with eight sets, while CMC-TCMA issued its final minor league team sets. Abbreviations used in these listings include: Cal (California League), CMC (Collector's Marketing Corp./TCMA), DD (Dunkin' Donuts), DJ (Donn Jennings), GS (Grand Slam), PC (ProCards) and SP (Sport Pro).

	MT
292 team sets and variations	
1990 PC AAA All-Stars (54)	15.00
1990 Best Albany-Colonie Yankees (26)	7.00
1990 PC Albany-Colonie Yankees (29)	7.00
1990 Star Albany-Colonie Yankees (28)	5.00
1990 CMC Albuquerque Dukes (28)	6.00
1990 PC Albuquerque Dukes (30)	7.00
1990 Team Albuquerque Dukes (35)	135.00
1990 Box Appleton Foxes (30)	3.00
1990 Diamond Appleton Foxes (29)	4.00
1990 PC Appleton Foxes (29)	3.00
1990 GS Arkansas Travelers (30)	9.00
1990 PC Asheville Tourists (28)	9.00
1990 Best Auburn Astros (25)	4.00
1990 PC Auburn Astros (26)	3.00
1990 PC Augusta Pirates (27)	7.00
1990 Cal Bakersfield Dodgers (32)	4.00
1990 Star Baseball City Royals (31)	4.00
1990 PC Batavia Clippers (30)	3.00
1990 Legoe Bellingham Mariners (38)	7.50
1990 Best Beloit Brewers (27)	5.00
1990 Star Beloit Brewers (27)	5.00
1990 Legoe Bend Bucks (32)	3.00
1990 PC Billings Mustangs (30)	3.00
1990 Best Birmingham Barons (30)	65.00
1990 Best Birmingham All-Decade (34)	7.50
1990 PC Birmingham Barons (28)	40.00
1990 Star Bluefield Orioles (22)	8.00
1990 PC Boise Hawks (33)	8.00
1990 PC Bristol Tigers (29)	18.00
1990 Star Bristol Tigers (30)	18.00
1990 CMC Buffalo Bisons (25)	7.00
1990 PC Buffalo Bisons (28)	8.00
1990 Team Buffalo Bisons (28)	10.00
1990 Best Burlington Braves (30)	14.00
1990 PC Burlington Braves (30)	13.00
1990 Star Burlington Braves (31)	15.00
1990 PC Burlington Indians (29)	24.00
1990 SP Butte Copper Kings (30)	13.00
1990 CMC Calgary Cannons (25)	9.00
1990 PC Calgary Cannons (23)	7.00
1990 Cal League All-Stars (56)	7.00
1990 Best Canton-Akron Indians (28)	8.00
1990 PC Canton-Akron Indians (27)	8.00
1990 Star Canton-Akron Indians (21)	8.00
1990 Sportsprint Carolina League A-S (52)	7.00
1990 Best Cedar Rapids Reds (27)	6.00
1990 PC Cedar Rapids Reds (27)	6.00
1990 Best Charleston Rainbows (28)	4.00
1990 PC Charleston Rainbows (28)	3.00
1990 Best Charleston Wheelers (29)	5.00
1990 PC Charleston Wheelers (28)	4.00
1990 Team Charlotte Knights (25)	9.00
1990 Star Charlotte Rangers (30)	17.50
1990 GS Chattanooga Lookouts (27)	4.00
1990 Diamond Clearwater Phillies (9)	10.00
1990 Star Clearwater Phillies (27)	4.00
1990 Best Clinton Giants (29)	4.00
1990 PC Clinton Giants (29)	3.00
1990 Team Clinton Giants Update (12)	5.50
1990 CMC Colorado Springs Sky Sox (24)	5.00
1990 PC Colorado Springs Sky Sox (27)	5.00
1990 GS Columbia Mets (30)	4.00
1990 Play II Columbia Mets (27)	4.00
1990 Play II Columbia Mets postcards (27)	18.00
1990 CMC Columbus Clippers (26)	6.00
1990 Police Columbus Clippers (25)	7.00
1990 PC Columbus Clippers (28)	5.00
1990 Team Columbus Clippers foldout	12.00
1990 Best Columbus Mudcats (29)	8.00
1990 PC Columbus Mudcats (27)	8.00
1990 Star Columbus Mudcats (29)	8.00
1990 CMC Denver Zephyrs (26)	5.00
1990 PC Denver Zephyrs (28)	4.00
1990 Star Dunedin Blue Jays (28)	6.00
1990 Sportsprint Durham Bulls (29)	7.50
1990 Sportsprint Durham Bulls update (8)	24.00
1990 PC Eastern League All-Stars (48)	14.00
1990 CMC Edmonton Trappers (23)	6.00
1990 PC Edmonton Trappers (25)	4.00
1990 Star Elizabethton Twins (26)	5.00
1990 Pucko Elmira Pioneers (27)	6.00
1990 GS El Paso Diablos (25)	4.00
1990 Team El Paso Diablos All-Time (45):	35.00
1990 Star Erie Sailors (31)	3.00
1990 GS Eugene Emeralds (30)	4.00
1990 Best Everett Giants (28)	7.50
1990 PC Everett Giants (32)	7.50
1990 PC Fayetteville Generals (28)	3.00
1990 Star Florida State League All-Stars (50)	30.00
1990 Sportsprint Frederick Keys (30)	6.00
1990 Star Ft. Lauderdale Yankees (29)	4.00
1990 Best Gastonia Rangers (30)	5.00
1990 PC Gastonia Rangers (29)	5.00
1990 Star Gastonia Rangers (29)	4.00
1990 PC Gate City Pioneers (27)	5.00
1990 SP Gate City Pioneers (24)	4.00
1990 PC Geneva Cubs (27)	3.00
1990 Star Geneva Cubs (32)	5.00
1990 SP Great Falls Dodgers (30)	125.00
1990 Best Greensboro Hornets (30)	6.00
1990 PC Greensboro Hornets (31)	6.00
1990 Star Greensboro Hornets (26)	6.00
1990 Best Greenville Braves (22)	5.00
1990 PC Greenville Braves (26)	5.00
1990 Star Greenville Braves (24)	4.00
1990 Best Hagerstown Suns (30)	5.00
1990 PC Hagerstown Suns (32)	6.00
1990 Star Hagerstown Suns (28)	4.00
1990 Best Hamilton Redbirds (28)	5.00
1990 Star Hamilton Redbirds (29)	4.00
1990 PC Harrisburg Senators (26)	8.00
1990 Star Harrisburg Senators (25)	7.00
1990 SP Helena Brewers (29)	6.00
1990 Little Sun High School Prospects (24)	7.00
1990 PC Huntington Cubs (33)	5.00
1990 Best Huntsville Stars (27)	5.00
1990 PC Idaho Falls Braves (31)	3.00
1990 CMC Indianapolis Indians (25)	5.00
1990 PC Indianapolis Indians (31)	4.00
1990 CMC Iowa Cubs (25)	5.00
1990 PC Iowa Cubs (24)	5.00
1990 GS Jackson Mets (28)	8.00
1990 Best Jacksonville Expos (31)	7.00
1990 PC Jacksonville Expos (29)	8.00
1990 Pucko Jamestown Expos (34)	5.00
1990 Star Johnson City Cardinals (30)	3.00
1990 Best Kenosha Twins (30)	4.00
1990 PC Kenosha Twins (27)	3.00
1990 Star Kenosha Twins (29)	3.00
1990 Best Kingsport Mets (28)	9.00
1990 Star Kingsport Mets (30)	12.00
1990 Sportsprint Kinston Indians (31)	8.00
1990 Diamond Kissimmee Dodgers (29)	3.00
1990 Best Knoxville Blue Jays (28)	7.00
1990 PC Knoxville Blue Jays (25)	7.00
1990 Star Knoxville Blue Jays (26)	6.00
1990 Star Lakeland Tigers (28)	5.00
1990 Star Lakeland Tigers (31)	12.00
1990 CMC Las Vegas Stars (25)	7.00
1990 PC Las Vegas Stars (28)	5.00
1990 PC London Tigers (22)	6.00
1990 CMC Louisville Redbirds (29)	7.00
1990 PC Louisville Redbirds (29)	8.00
1990 Team Louisville Redbirds (42)	13.50
1990 Sportsprint Lynchburg Red Sox (27)	5.00
1990 Best Madison Muskies (29)	5.00
1990 PC Madison Muskies (26)	5.00
1990 PC Martinsville Phillies (34)	4.00
1990 Best Medicine Hat Blue Jays (28)	5.00
1990 Best Memphis Chicks (29)	7.00
1990 PC Memphis Chicks (28)	7.00
1990 Star Memphis Chicks (27)	7.00
1990 Star Miami Miracle I (31)	3.00
1990 Star Miami Miracle II (31)	3.00
1990 GS Midland Angels (28)	4.00
1990 1 Hour Midland Angels (35)	50.00
1990 GS Midwest League All-Stars (58)	10.00
1990 Cal Modesto A's (25)	3.00
1990 Chong Modesto A's (36)	7.50
1990 PC Modesto A's (29)	3.00
1990 PC Myrtle Beach Blue Jays (29)	3.00
1990 CMC Nashville Sounds (26)	6.50
1990 PC Nashville Sounds (29)	5.00
1990 Team Nashville Sounds (30)	6.00
1990 Best New Britain Red Sox (29)	35.00
1990 PC New Britain Red Sox (26)	22.00
1990 Star New Britain Red Sox (27)	22.00
1990 Pucko Niagara Falls Rapids (33)	5.00
1990 CMC Oklahoma City 89ers (24)	35.00
1990 PC Oklahoma City 89ers (30)	27.50
1990 CMC Omaha Royals (25)	7.00
1990 PC Omaha Royals (26)	6.00
1990 PC Oneonta Yankees (29)	6.50
1990 Best Orlando Sun Rays (30)	19.00
1990 PC Orlando Sun Rays (27)	17.50
1990 Star Orlando Sun Rays (28)	20.00
1990 Star Osceola Astros (30)	12.00
1990 Cal Palm Springs Angels (26)	7.00
1990 PC Palm Springs Angels (28)	10.00
1990 CMC Pawtucket Red Sox (25)	19.00
1990 DD Pawtucket Red Sox foldout	60.00
1990 PC Pawtucket Red Sox (29)	18.00
1990 Team Peninsula Oilers (24)	7.00
1990 Star Peninsula Pilots (27)	3.00
1990 Team Peoria Chiefs (38)	10.00
1990 Team Peoria Chiefs sheet (30)	20.00
1990 Team Peoria Chiefs update (7)	6.00
1990 Team Peoria Chiefs Carl Cunningham (4)	10.00
1990 CMC Phoenix Firebirds (26)	6.50
1990 PC Phoenix Firebirds (29)	6.00
1990 Pucko Pittsfield Mets (32)	7.50
1990 CMC Portland Beavers (25)	6.00
1990 PC Portland Beavers (28)	5.00
1990 Diamond Princeton Patriots (30)	5.00
1990 Sportsprint Prince William Cannons (30)	6.00
1990 Best Pulaski Braves (29)	4.00
1990 PC Pulaski Braves (31)	4.00
1990 GS Quad City Angels (30)	5.50
1990 Best Reading Phillies (26)	4.00
1990 PC Reading Phillies (27)	5.00
1990 Star Reading Phillies (28)	4.00
1990 Cal Reno Silver Sox (31)	3.00
1990 Bob's Richmond Braves (21)	55.00
1990 Bob's Richmond Braves (22)	60.00
1990 CMC Richmond Braves (27)	10.00
1990 PC Richmond Braves (28)	13.00
1990 Team Richmond Braves foldout	25.00
1990 Team Richmond 25th Anniversary (23)	27.50
1990 Best Riverside Red Wave (27)	4.00
1990 Cal Riverside Red Wave (27)	4.00
1990 PC Riverside Red Wave (28)	4.00
1990 CMC Rochester Red Wings (27)	9.00
1990 PC Rochester Red Wings (29)	8.00
1990 Team Rochester Red Wings (36)	37.50
1990 PC Rockford Expos (29)	3.00
1990 Team Rockford Expos (28)	10.00
1990 Star Salem Buccaneers (27)	4.00
1990 Cal Salinas Spurs (32)	3.00
1990 PC Salinas Spurs (26)	3.00
1990 BBC Etc. Salt Lake City Trappers (30)	6.00
1990 GS San Antonio Missions (30)	9.00
1990 Best San Bernardino Spirit (28)	5.00

1990 Cal San Bernardino Spirit (32)	4.00
1990 PC San Bernardino Spirit (28)	4.00
1990 Best San Jose Giants (30)	7.00
1990 Cal San Jose Giants (28)	7.00
1990 PC San Jose Giants (29)	7.00
1990 Star San Jose Giants (30)	7.00
1990 Star Sarasota White Sox (30)	4.00
1990 PC Savannah Cardinals (28)	4.00
1990 CMC Scranton Red Barons (25)	5.00
1990 PC Scranton Red Barons (24)	5.00
1990 PC Shreveport Captains (27)	5.00
1990	5.00
1990 Star Shreveport Captains (27)	5.00
1990 Star South Atlantic League A-S (48)	9.00
1990 Best South Bend White Sox (29)	4.00
1990 GS South Bend White Sox (30)	3.00
1990 DJ Southern League A-S (50)	10.00
1990 Best Southern Oregon Athletics (30)	5.00
1990 PC Southern Oregon Athletics (29)	5.00
1990 Best Spartanburg Phillies (30)	4.00
1990 PC Spartanburg Phillies (28)	3.00
1990 Star Spartanburg Phillies (29)	3.00
1990 SP Spokane Indians (28)	6.00
1990 Best Springfield Cardinals (29)	4.00
1990 PC St. Catharines Blue Jays (34)	14.00
1990 Stearns St. Cloud Rox (9)	35.00
1990 Star St. Lucie Mets (31)	4.00
1990 Star St. Lucie Mets (33)	6.00
1990 Star St. Petersburg Cardinals (26)	3.00
1990 Best Stockton Ports (29)	6.00
1990 Cal Stockton Ports (29)	5.00
1990 PC Stockton Ports (29)	5.00
1990 Best Sumter Braves (30)	25.00
1990 PC Sumter Braves (30)	22.00
1990 CMC Syracuse Chiefs (28)	9.00
1990 PC Syracuse Chiefs (28)	7.00
1990 Team Syracuse Chiefs (30)	22.00
1990 CMC Tacoma Tigers (25)	6.50
1990 PC Tacoma Tigers (29)	5.00
1990 Diamond Tampa Yankees (28)	16.00
1990 GS Texas League A-S (38)	10.00
1990 CMC Tidewater Tides (30)	7.00
1990 PC Tidewater Tides (30)	5.00
1990 Team Tidewater Tides foldout	5.00
1990 CMC Toledo Mud Hens (27)	13.00
1990 PC Toledo Mud Hens (27)	8.00
1990 CMC Tucson Toros (25)	5.00
1990 PC Tucson Toros (27)	5.00
1990 PC Tulsa Drillers (28)	7.00
1990 Team Tulsa Drillers (28)	7.00
1990 Smokey USC alumni (12)	250.00
1990 Pucko Utica Blue Sox (30)	4.00
1990 CMC Vancouver Canadians (28)	7.50
1990 PC Vancouver Canadians (28)	7.00
1990 Star Vero Beach Dodgers (32)	80.00
1990 Cal Visalia Oaks (31)	5.00
1990 PC Visalia Oaks (26)	6.00
1990 Best Waterloo Diamonds (28)	4.00
1990 PC Waterloo Diamonds (27)	3.00
1990 Star Watertown Indians (28)	3.00
1990 Best Wausau Timbers (28)	4.00
1990 PC Wausau Timbers (32)	3.00
1990 Star Wausau Timbers (29)	3.00
1990 Pucko Welland Pirates (36)	5.00
1990 Star West Palm Beach Expos (31)	4.00
1990 Rock's Wichita Wranglers (28)	5.00
1990 Best Williamsport Bills (27)	4.00
1990 PC Williamsport Bills (26)	3.00
1990 Star Williamsport Bills (27)	3.00
1990 Sportsprint Winston-Salem Spirits (30)	4.00
1990 Star Winter Haven Red Sox (28)	4.00
1990 Golden Yakima Bears (36)	9.00

1991 Impel/Line Drive Previews

To introduce its forthcoming series of Class AA and Class AAA minor league wax product, Impel sent dealers this six-card set. Numbered the same as the player's cards in either the AA or AAA issue, the previews differ from the issued versions only in slight variations in photo cropping.

		MT
Complete Set (6):		5.00
Common Player:		.50
47	Greg Tubbs (AAA)	.50
79	Tim Costo (AA)	.75
167	Reggie Sanders (AA)	1.50
221	Rick Wilkins (AAA)	1.00
422	Hugh Walker (AA)	.50
573	Anthony Young (AAA)	.75

1991 Impel/Line Drive Pre-Rookie AA

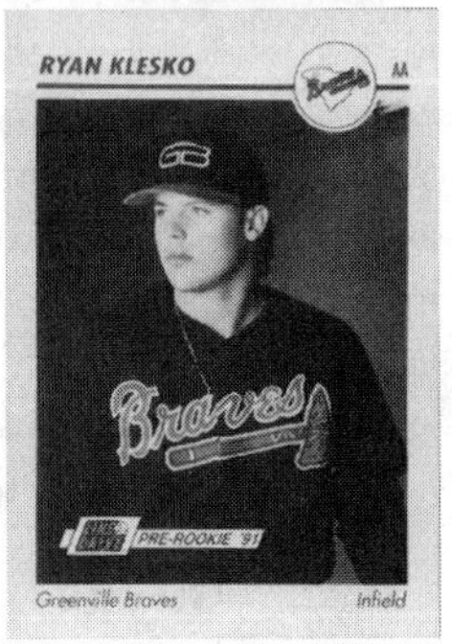

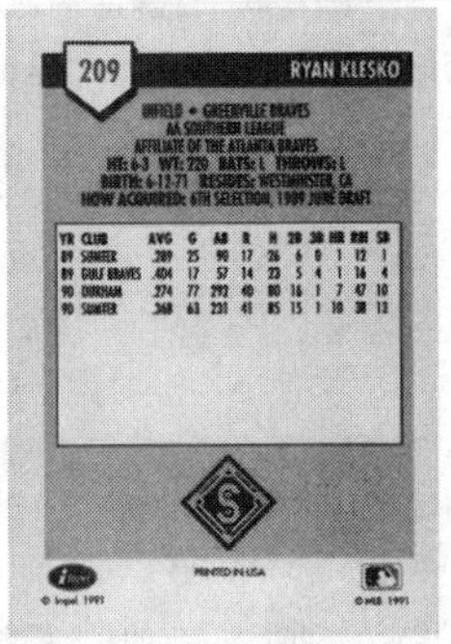

Impel followed its successful AAA wax series with a 650-card AA wax series consisting of 25 players from each team. Like the AAA series, a checklist for the AA series was available from the company. Due to a scarcity of certain cards in inventory and additional labor costs to dealers, consumer can be expected to pay a minimum of $4-6 for team sets made from this product. Line Drive team sets sold at the stadiums included team checklist cards.

		MT
Complete Set (650):		15.00
Common Player:		.05
1	Andy Cook	.05
2	Russell Davis	.35
3	Bobby DeJardin	.05
4	Mike Draper	.05
5	Victor Garcia	.05
6	Mike Gardella	.05
7	Cullen Hartzog	.05
8	Jay Knoblauh	.05
9	Billy Masse	.05
10	Jeff Livesey	.05
11	Edward Martel	.05
12	Vince Phillips	.05
13	Tom Popplewell	.05
14	Jerry Rub	.05
15	Dave Silvestri	.05
16	Tom Newell	.05
17	Willie Smith	.05
18	J.T. Snow	.60
19	Don Stanford	.05
20	Larry Stanford	.05
21	John Toale	.05
22	Hector Vargas	.05
23	Gerald Williams	.25
24	Dan Radison	.05
25	Dave Jorn, Bob Mariano (Coaches)	.05
26	Frank Abreu	.05
27	Cliff Brannon	.05
28	Greg Carmona	.05
29	Ric Christian	.05
30	John Ericks	.05
31	Steve Fanning	.05
32	Joey Fernandez	.05
33	Jose Fernandez	.05
34	Mike Flore	.05
35	David Grimes	.05
36	Dale Kisten	.05
37	John Lepley	.05
38	Luis Martinez	.05
39	Mike Milchin	.05
40	Donovan Osborne	.10
41	Gabriel Ozuna	.05
42	Lee Plemel	.05
43	Don Prybylinski	.05
44	John Sellick	.05
45	Jeff Shireman	.05
46	Brian Stone	.05
47	Charlie White	.05
48	Dennis Wiseman	.05
49	Joe Pettini	.05
50	Scott Melvin, Marty Mason	.05
51	Wilson Alvarez	.50
52	Wayne Busby	.05
53	Darrin Campbell	.05
54	Mark Chasey	.05
55	Ron Coomer	.05
56	Argenis Cortez	.05
57	Mike Davino	.05
58	Lindsay Foster	.05
59	Ramon Garcia	.05
60	Kevin Garner	.05
61	Jeff Gay	.05
62	Chris Howard	.05
63	John Hudek	.10
64	Scott Jaster	.05
65	Bo Kennedy	.05
66	Derek Lee	.10
67	Frank Merigliano	.05
68	Scott Middaugh	.05
69	Javier Ocasio	.05
70	Kinnis Pledger	.05
71	Greg Roth	.05
72	Aubrey Waggoner	.05
73	Jose Ventura	.05
74	Tony Franklin	.05
75	Rick Peterson, Pat Roessler, Sam Hairston	.05
76	Ramon Bautista	.05
77	Eric Bell	.05
78	Jim Bruske	.05
79	Tim Costo	.10
80	Mike Curtis	.05
81	Jerry DiPoto	.05
82	Daren Epley	.05
83	Sam Ferrelli	.05
84	Garland Kiser	.05
85	Ty Kovach	.05
86	Tom Kramer	.05
87	Molan Lane	.05
88	Jesse Levis	.05
89	Carlos Martinez	.10
90	Jeff Mutis	.10
91	Rouglas Odor	.05
92	Gary Resetar	.05
93	Greg Roscoe	.05
94	Miguel Sabino	.05
95	Bernie Tatis	.05
96	Jim Thome	3.00
97	Ken Ramos	.05
98	Ken Whitfield	.05
99	Ken Bolek	.05
100	Dave Keller	.05
101	Steve Adams	.05
102	Stan Fansler	.05
103	Mandy Romero	.05
104	Terry Crowley Jr.	.05
105	Chip Duncan	.05
106	Greg Edge	.05
107	Chris Estep	.05
108	Carl Hamilton	.05
109	Lee Hancock	.05
110	Tim Hines	.05
111	Mike Huyler	.05
112	Paul Miller	.05
113	Pete Murphy	.05
114	Darwin Pennye	.05
115	Mike Roesler	.05
116	Bruce Schreiber	.05
117	Greg Sparks	.05
118	Dennis Tafoya	.05
119	Tim Wakefield	.10
120	Ben Webb	.05
121	John Wehner	.05
122	Ed Yacopino	.05
123	Eddie Zambrano	.05
124	Marc Bombard	.05
125	Trent Jewett, Spin Williams	.05
126	Alex Arias	.10
127	Paul Blair	.05
128	Jim Bullinger	.05
129	Dick Canan	.05
130	Rusty Crockett	.05
131	Steve DiBartolomeo	.05
132	John Gardner	.05
133	Henry Gomez	.05
134	Ty Griffin	.05
135	Shannon Jones	.05
136	Mike Knapp	.05
137	Tim Parker	.05
138	Elvin Paulino	.05
139	Fernando Ramsey	.05
140	Kevin Roberson	.10
141	John Salles	.05
142	Mike Sodders	.05
143	Bill St. Peter	.05
144	Julio Strauss	.05
145	Scott Taylor	.05
146	Tim Watkins	.05
147	Doug Welch	.05
148	Billy White	.05
149	Jay Loviglio	.05
150	Rick Kranitz	.05
151	Rick Allen	.05
152	Mike Anderson	.05
153	Bobby Ayala	.10
154	Pete Beeler	.05
155	Jeff Branson	.10
156	Scott Bryant	.05
157	Bill Dodd	.05
158	Steve Foster	.05
159	Victor Garcia	.05
160	Frank Kremblas	.05
161	Greg Lonigro	.05
162	Dave McAuliffe	.05
163	Steve McCarthy	.05
164	Scott Pose	.10
165	Tim Pugh	.10
166	Bill Risley	.05
167	Reggie Sanders	.45
168	Mo Sanford	.10
169	Scott Sellner	.05
170	Jerry Spradlin	.05
171	Glenn Sutko	.05
172	Todd Trafton	.05
173	Bernie Walker	.05
174	Jim Tracy	.05
175	Mike Griffin	.05
176	Shon Ashley	.05
177	John Byington	.05
178	Mark Chapman	.05
179	Jim Czajkowski	.05
180	Ruben Escalera	.05
181	Craig Faulkner	.05
182	Tim Fortugno	.05
183	Don Gordon	.05
184	Mitch Hannahs	.05
185	Steve Lienhard	.05
186	Dave Jacas	.05
187	Kenny Jackson	.05
188	John Jaha	.20
189	Chris Johnson	.05
190	Mark Kiefer	.05
191	Pat Listach	.05
192	Tom McGraw	.05
193	Angel Miranda	.10
194	Dave Nilsson	.10
195	Jeff Schwarz	.05
196	Steve Sparks	.05
197	Jim Tatum	.05
198	Brandy Vann	.05
199	Dave Huppert	.05
200	Paul Lindblad	.05
201	Rich Casarotti	.05
202	Vinnie Castilla	1.00
203	Brian Champion	.05
204	Popeye Cole	.05
205	Johnny Cuevas	.05
206	Brian Deak	.05
207	Pat Gomez	.05
208	Judd Johnson	.05
209	Ryan Klesko	2.00
210	Rich Maloney	.05
211	Al Martin	.30
212	Keith Mitchell	.05
213	Rick Morris	.05
214	Ben Rivera	.05
215	Napoleon Robinson	.05
216	Boi Rodriguez	.05
217	Sean Ross	.05
218	Earl Sanders	.05
219	Scott Taylor	.05
220	Lee Upshaw	.05
221	Preston Watson	.05
222	Turk Wendell	.10
223	Mark Wohlers	.20
224	Chris Chambliss	.05
225	Terry Harper, Bill Slack, Randy Ingle	.05
226	Jeff Bumgarner	.05
227	Stacey Burdick	.05
228	Paul Carey	.05
229	Bobby Dickerson	.05
230	Roy Gilbert	.05
231	Ricky Gutierrez	.10
232	Tim Holland	.05
233	Stacy Jones	.05
234	Tyrone Kingwood	.05
235	Mike Lehman	.05
236	Rod Lofton	.05
237	Kevin Hickey	.05
238	Joel McKeon	.05
239	Scott Meadows	.05
240	Steve Luebber	.05
241	Mike Oquist	.05
242	Ozzie Peraza	.05
243	Tim Raley	.05
244	Arthur Rhodes	.10
245	Doug Robbins	.05
246	Ken Shamburg	.05
247	Todd Stephan	.05
248	Jack Voight	.05
249	Jerry Narron	.05
250	Joe Durham	.05
251	Chris Cassels	.05
252	Archie Clanfrocco (Archi)	.05
253	Dan Freed	.05
254	Greg Fulton	.05
255	Chris Haney	.05
256	Cesar Hernandez	.05
257	Richard Holsman	.05
258	Rob Katzaroff	.05
259	Bryan Kosco	.05
260	Ken Lake	.05
261	Hector Rivera	.05
262	Chris Marchok	.05
263	Chris Martin	.05
264	Matt Maysey	.15
265	Omer Munoz	.05
266	Bob Natal	.05
267	Chris Pollack	.05
268	F.P. Santangelo	.15
269	Joe Siddall	.05
270	Stan Spencer	.05
271	Matt Stairs	.50
272	David Wainhouse	.10
273	Pete Young	.05
274	Mike Quade	.05
275	Joe Kerrigan, Pete Dalena	.05
276	Marco Armas	.05
277	Bob Bafia	.05
278	Dean Borrelli	.05
279	John Briscoe	.05
280	James Buccheri	.05
281	Tom Carcione	.05
282	Joel Chimelis	.05
283	Fred Cooley	.05
284	Russ Cormier	.05
285	Matt Grott	.05
286	Dwayne Hosey	.10
287	Chad Kuhn	.05
288	Dave Latter	.05
289	Francisco Matos	.05
290	Gavin Osteen	.05
291	Tim Peek	.05
292	Don Peters	.05
293	Scott Shockey	.05
294	Will Tejada	.15
295	Lee Tinsley	.10
296	Todd Van Poppel	.10
297	Darryl Vice	.05
298	Dave Zancanaro	.05
299	Casey Parsons	.05
300	Bert Bradley	.05
301	Frank Carey	.05
302	Larry Carter	.05
303	Royce Clayton	.40
304	Tom Ealy	.05
305	Juan Guerrero	.05
306	Bryan Hickerson	.05
307	Steve Hosey	.10
308	Tom Hostetler	.05
309	Erik Johnson	.05
310	Dan Lewis	.05
311	Paul McClellan	.05
312	Jim McNamara	.05
313	Kevin Meier	.05
314	Jim Myers	.05
315	Dave Patterson	.05
316	John Patterson	.10
317	Jim Pena	.05
318	Dan Rambo	.05
319	Steve Reed	.05
320	Kevin Rogers	.10
321	Reuben Smiley	.05
322	Scooter Tucker	.05
323	Pete Weber	.05
324	Bill Evers	.05
325	Tony Taylor, Todd Oakes	.05
326	Fernando Arguelles	.05
327	Shawn Barton	.05
328	Jim Blueberg	.05
329	Frank Bolick	.05
330	Bret Boone	.75
331	Jim Bowie	.05
332	Jim Campanis	.05
333	Gary Eave	.05
334	David Evans	.05
335	Fernando Figueroa	.05
336	Dave Fleming	.10

337	Ruben Gonzalez	.05
338	Mike McDonald	.05
339	Jeff Nelson	.05
340	Jim Newlin	.05
341	Ken Pennington	.05
342	Mike Pitz	.05
343	Dave Richards	.05
344	Roger Salkeld	.25
345	Jack Smith	.05
346	Tim Stargell	.05
347	Brian Turang	.10
348	Ted Williams	.05
349	Jim Nettles	.05
350	Bobby Cuellar, Lem Pilkinton	.05
351	Pete Blohm	.05
352	Domingo Cedeno	.05
353	Nate Cromwell	.05
354	Jesse Cross	.05
355	Juan De La Rosa	.05
356	Bobby LeLoach	.05
357	Ray Giannelli	.05
358	Darren Hall	.05
359	Mark Young	.05
360	Jeff Kent	.75
361	Randy Knorr	.10
362	Jose Monzon	.05
363	Bernie Nunez	.05
364	Paul Rodgers	.05
365	Jimmy Rogers	.05
366	Mike Taylor	.05
367	Ryan Thompson	.10
368	Jason Townley	.05
369	Rick Trlicek	.05
370	Anthony Ward	.05
371	Dave Weathers	.05
372	Woody Williams	.05
373	Julian Yan	.05
374	John Stearns	.05
375	Mike McAlpin, Steve Mingori	.05
376	Doyle Balthazar	.05
377	Basilio Cabrera	.05
378	Ron Cook	.05
379	Ivan Cruz	.10
380	Dean DeCillis	.05
381	John DeSilva	.05
382	John Doherty	.05
383	Lou Frazier	.05
384	Luis Galindo	.05
385	Greg Gohr	.05
386	Bud Groom	.05
387	Darren Hursey	.05
388	Ricardo Ingram	.10
389	Keith Kimberlin	.05
390	Todd Krumm	.05
391	Randy Marshall	.05
392	Domingo Michel	.05
393	Steve Pegues	.05
394	Jose Ramos	.05
395	Bob Reimink	.05
396	Ruben Rodriguez	.05
397	Eric Stone	.05
398	Marty Willis	.05
399	Gene Roof	.05
400	Jeff Jones, Dan Raley	.05
401	Pete Alborano	.05
402	Jim Baxter	.05
403	Tony Clements	.05
404	Archie Corbin	.05
405	Andres Cruz	.05
406	Jeff Garber	.05
407	David Gonzalez	.05
408	Kevin Koslofski	.05
409	Deric Ladnier	.05
410	Mark Parnell	.05
411	Jorge Pedre	.05
412	Doug Peters	.05
413	Hipolito Pichardo	.10
414	Eddie Pierce	.05
415	Mike Poehl	.05
416	Darryl Robinson	.05
417	Steve Shifflett	.05
418	Jim Smith	.05
419	Lou Talbert	.05
420	Terry Taylor	.05
421	Rich Tunison	.05
422	Hugh Walker	.05
423	Darren Watkins	.05
424	Jeff Cox	.05
425	Brian Peterson, Mike Alvarez	.05
426	Clemente Acosta	.05
427	Jeff Barns	.05
428	Mike Butcher	.05
429	Glenn Carter	.05
430	Marvin Cobb	.05
431	Sherman Corbett	.05
432	Kevin Davis	.05
433	Damlon Easley	.15
434	Kevin Flora	.05
435	Larry Gonzales	.05
436	Mark Howie	.05
437	Todd James	.05
438	Bobby Jones	.30
439	Steve King	.05
440	Marcus Lawton	.05
441	Ken Rivers	.05
442	Doug Robertson	.05
443	Tim Salmon	4.00
444	Ramon Sambo	.05
445	Daryl Sconiers	.05
446	Dave Shotkoski	.05
447	Terry Taylor	.05
448	Mark Zappelli	.05
449	Don Long	.05
450	Kernan Ronan, Gene Richards	.05
451	Michael Beams	.05
452	Greg Blosser	.05
453	Brian Conroy	.05
454	Freddie Davis	.05
455	Colin Dixon	.05
456	Peter Estrada	.05
457	Ray Fagnant	.05
458	Tom Fischer	.05
459	John Flaherty	.05
460	Donald Florence	.05
461	Blane Fox	.05
462	Steve Hendricks	.05
463	Wayne Housie	.05
464	Peter Hoy	.05
465	Thomas Kane	.05
466	David Milstien	.05
467	Juan Paris	.05
468	Scott Powers	.05
469	Paul Quantrill	.10
470	Randy Randle	.05
471	Al Sanders	.05
472	Scott Taylor	.05
473	John Valentin	.50
474	Gary Allenson	.05
475	Rick Wise	.05
476	Pat Bangtson	.05
477	Carlos Capellan	.05
478	Rafael DeLima	.05
479	Frank Valdez	.05
480	Cheo Garcia	.05
481	Shawn Gilbert	.05
482	Greg Johnson	.05
483	Jay Kvasnicka	.05
484	Orlando Lind	.05
485	Pat Mahomes	.05
486	Jose Marzan	.05
487	Dan Masteller	.05
488	Bob McCreary	.05
489	Steve Muh	.05
490	Reed Olmstead	.05
491	Ray Ortiz	.05
492	Derek Parks	.05
493	Joe Siwa	.05
494	Steve Stowell	.05
495	Mike Trombley	.05
496	Jim Shellenback	.05
497	Rob Wassenaar	.05
498	Phil Wiese	.05
499	Scott Ullger	.05
500	Mark Funderbuck	.05
501	Jason Backs	.05
502	Toby Borland	.10
503	Cliff Brantley	.10
504	Dana Brown	.05
505	John Burgos	.05
506	Andy Carter	.05
507	Bruce Dostal	.05
508	Rick Dunnum	.05
509	John Martin	.05
510	David Holdridge	.05
511	Darrell Lindsey	.05
512	Doug Lindsey	.05
513	Tony Longmire	.10
514	Tom Marsh	.05
515	Rod Robertson	.05
516	Edwin Rosado	.05
517	Sean Ryan	.05
518	Steve Scarsone	.05
519	Mark Sims	.05
520	Jeff Tabaka	.05
521	Tony Trevino	.05
522	Casey Waller	.05
523	Cary Williams	.05
524	Don McCormack	.05
525	Al LeBoeuf	.05
526	Steve Allen	.05
527	Jorge Alvarez	.05
528	Bryan Baar	.05
529	Tim Barker	.05
530	Tony Barron	.05
531	Cam Biberdorf	.05
532	Jason Brosnan	.05
533	Braulio Castillo	.10
534	Steve Finken	.05
535	Freddy Gonzalez	.05
536	Mike James	.05
537	Brett Magnusson	.05
538	Jose Munoz	.05
539	Lance Rice	.05
540	Zak Shinall	.05
541	Dennis Springer	.05
542	Ramon Taveras	.05
543	Jimmy Terrill	.05
544	Brian Traxler	.05
545	Jody Treadwell	.05
546	Mike White	.05
547	Mike Wilkins	.05
548	Eric Young	.10
549	John Shoemaker	.05
550	James Wray	.05
551	Willie Ansley	.05
552	Sam August	.05
553	Jeff Baldwin	.05
554	Pete Bauer	.05
555	Kevin Coffman	.05
556	Kevin Dean	.05
557	Tony Eusebio	.10
558	Dean Freeland	.05
559	Rusty Harris	.05
560	Dean Hartgraves	.05
561	Trent Hubbard	.05
562	Bert Hunter	.05
563	Bernie Jenkins	.05
564	Jeff Juden	.15
565	Keith Kalser	.05
566	Steve Larose	.05
567	Lance Madsen	.05
568	Scott Makarewicz	.05
569	Rob Mallicoat	.05
570	Joe Mikulik	.05
571	Orlando Miller	.10
572	Shane Reynolds	.15
573	Richie Simon	.05
574	Rick Sweet	.05
575	Don Reynolds, Charlie Taylor	.05
576	Rob Brown	.05
577	Mike Burton	.05
578	Evertt Cunningham	.05
579	Jeff Frye	.10
580	Pat Garman	.05
581	Bryan Gore	.05
582	David Green	.05
583	Donald Harris	.10
584	Jose Hernandez	.10
585	Greg Iavarone	.05
586	Barry Manuel	.05
587	Trey McCoy	.05
588	Rod Morris	.05
589	Robb Nen	.10
590	David Perez	.05
591	Bobby Reed	.05
592	Ivan Rodriguez	4.00
593	Dan Rohrmeier	.05
594	Brian Romero	.05
595	Luke Sable	.05
596	Frederic Samson	.05
597	Cedric Shaw	.05
598	Chris Shiflett	.05
599	Bobby Jones	.10
600	Oscar Acosta, Jeff Hubbard	.05
601	Mike Basso	.05
602	Doug Brocail	.10
603	Rafael Chavez	.05
604	Brian Cisarik	.05
605	Greg David	.05
606	Rick Davis	.05
607	Vince Harris	.05
608	Charles Hillemann	.05
609	Kerry Knox	.05
610	Pete Kuld	.05
611	Jim Lewis	.05
612	Luis Lopez	.10
613	Pedro Martinez	.35
614	Tim McWilliam	.05
615	Tom Redington	.05
616	Darrin Reichle	.05
617	A.J. Sager	.05
618	Frank Seminara	.05
619	Darrell Sherman	.10
620	Jose Valentin	.10
621	Guillermo Velasquez	.05
622	Tim Wallace	.05
623	Brian Wood	.05
624	Steve Lubratich	.05
625	John Cumberland, Jack Maloof	.05
626	Tim Bogar	.10
627	Jeromy Burnitz	.15
628	Hernan Cortez	.05
629	Steve Davis	.05
630	Joe Delli Carri	.05
631	D.J. Dozier	.05
632	Javier Gonzalez	.05
633	Rudy Hernandez	.05
634	Chris Hill	.05
635	John Johnstone	.05
636	Doug Kline	.05
637	Loy McBride	.05
638	Joel Horlen	.05
639	Tito Navarro	.05
640	Toby Nivens	.05
641	Bryan Rogers	.05
642	David Sommer	.05
643	Greg Talamantez	.05
644	Dave Telgheder	.10
645	Jose Vargas	.05
646	Aguedo Vasquez	.05
647	Paul Williams	.05
648	Alan Zinter	.05
649	Clint Hurdle	.05
650	Jim Eschen	.05

1991 Impel/Line Drive

Pre-Rookie AAA

Impel made its maiden voyage into the minor league market in 1991 with this set of AAA cards issued in poly packs. Unlike its predecessor (see CMC 1990 Pre-Rookie) of 1990, this set featured complete team sets of 25 cards each within the overall issue, with no other company's product mixed in. Cards were numbered consecutively with all cards of a particular team kept together. The cards were issued only in poly packs and not as a complete set. A checklist was available from the company. Impel is the third company to handle this line. It all started with TCMA in 1972; CMC took over in 1988 and Impel bought out CMC in 1990. Due to a scarcity of certain cards in inventory and additional labor costs to dealers, the consumer can be expected to pay a minimum of $3-6 for team sets from this product. Line Drive team sets sold at the stadiums included team checklist cards.

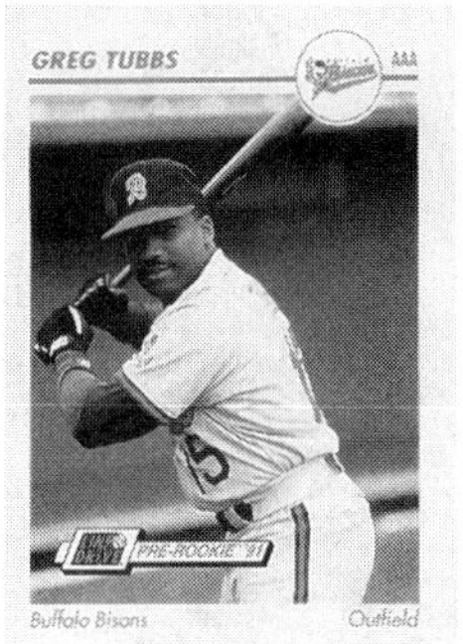

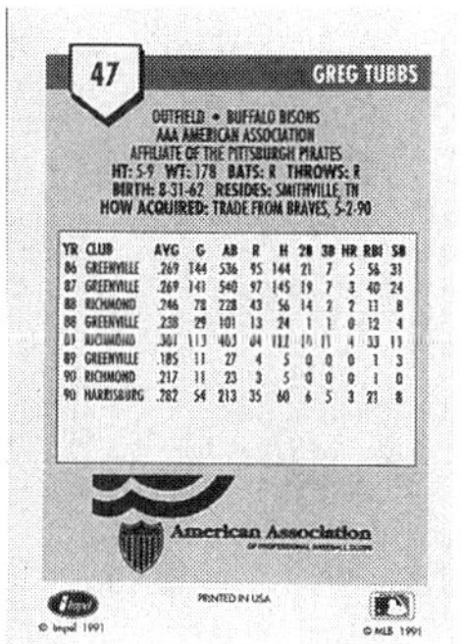

		MT
Complete Set (650):		20.00
Common Player:		.05
1	Billy Bean	.05
2	Jerry Brooks	.05
3	Mike Christopher	.05
4	Dennis Cook	.10
5	Butch Davis	.05
6	Tom Goodwin	.10
7	Dave Hansen	.05
8	Jeff Hartsock	.05
9	Bert Heffernan	.05
10	Carlos Hernandez	.05
11	Chris Jones	.05
12	Eric Karros	1.50
13	Dave Lynch	.05
14	Luis Martinez	.05
15	Jamie McAndrew	.05
16	Jim Neidlinger	.05
17	Jose Offerman	.20
18	Eddie Pye	.05
19	Henry Rodriguez	.20
20	Greg Smith	.05
21	Dave Veres	.05
22	Dave Walsh	.05
23	John Wetteland	.20
24	Kevin Kennedy	.05
25	Von Joshua, Claude Osteen	.05
26	Jeff Banister	.05
27	Cecil Espy	.05
28	Steve Fireovid	.05
29	Carlos Garcia	.10
30	Mark Huismann	.05
31	Scott Little	.05
32	Tom Magrann	.05
33	Roger Mason	.05
34	Tim Meeks	.05
35	Orlando Merced	.20
36	Joey Meyer	.05
37	Keith Miller	.05
38	Blas Minor	.05
39	Armando Moreno	.05
40	Jeff Neely	.10
41	Joe Redfield	.05
42	Rick Rood	.05
43	Jeff Richardson	.05
44	Rosario Rodriguez	.05
45	Jeff Schulz	.05
46	Jim Tracy	.05
47	Greg Tubbs	.05
48	Mike York	.05
49	Terry Collins	.05
50	Jackie Brown	.05
51	Rich Amaral	.10
52	Rick Balabon	.05
53	Dave Brundage	.05
54	Dave Burba	.10
55	Dave Cochrane	.05
56	Alan Cockrell	.05
57	Mike Cook	.05
58	Keith Helton	.05
59	Dennis Hood	.05
60	Chris Howard	.05
61	Chuck Jackson	.05
62	Calvin Jones	.05
63	Pat Lennon	.05
64	Shane Letterio	.05
65	Vance Lovelace	.05
66	Tino Martinez	1.50
67	John Mitchell	.05
68	Dennis Powell	.05
69	Alonzo Powell	.05
70	Pat Rice	.05
71	Ricky Rojas	.05
72	Steve Springer	.05
73	Ed VandeBerg	.05
74	Keith Bodie	.05
75	Ross Grimsley	.05
76	Eddie Taubensee	.10
77	Jeff Bittiger	.05
78	Willie Blair	.05
79	Marty Brown	.05
80	Kevin Burdick	.05
81	Steve Cummings	.05
82	Mauro Gozzo	.05
83	Ricky Horton	.05
84	Stan Jefferson	.05
85	Brian Johnson	.05
86	Barry Jones	.05
87	Wayne Kirby	.10
88	Mark Lewis	.15
89	Rudy Seanez	.10
90	Luis Lopez	.10
91	Ecer Magallanes	.05
92	Luis Medina	.05
93	Dave Otto	.05
94	Roberto Zambrano	.05
95	Jeff Shaw	.05
96	Efrain Valdez	.05
97	Sergio Valdez	.05
98	Kevin Wickander	.05
99	Charlie Manuel	.05
100	Rick Adair, Jim Gabella	.05
101	Steve Adkins	.05
102	Daven Bond	.05
103	Darrin Chapin	.05
104	Royal Clayton	.05
105	Steve Howe	.15
106	Keith Hughes	.05
107	Mike Humphreys	.05
108	Jeff Johnson	.05
109	Scott Kamieniecki	.10
110	Pat Kelly	.10
111	Jason Maas	.05
112	Alan Mills	.05
113	Rich Monteleone	.05
114	Hipolito Pena	.05
115	John Ramos	.05
116	Carlos Rodriguez	.05
117	Dave Sax	.05
118	Van Snider	.05
119	Don Sparks	.05
120	Andy Stankiewicz	.10
121	Wade Taylor	.05
122	Jim Walewander	.05
123	Bernie Williams	3.00
124	Rick Down	.05
125	Denbo, Boyer, Meyer	.05
126	D.L. Smith	.05
127	James Austin	.05
128	Esteban Beltre	.10
129	Mickey Brantley	.05
130	George Canale	.05
131	Matias Carrillo	.05
132	Juan Castillo	.05
133	Jim Davins	.05
134	Carlos Diaz	.05
135	Cal Eldred	.20
136	Narciso Elvira	.05
137	Brian Fisher	.05
138	Chris George	.05
139	Sandy Guerrero	.05
140	Doug Henry	.10
141	Darren Holmes	.10
142	Mike Ignasiak	.05
143	Jeff Kaiser	.05
144	Joe Kmak	.05
145	Tim McIntosh	.05
146	Charlie Montoyo	.05
147	Jim Olander	.05
148	Ed Puig	.05
149	Tony Muser	.05
150	Lamar Johnson, Don Rowe	.05
151	Kyle Abbott	.10
152	Ruben Amaro	.10
153	Kent Anderson	.05
154	Mike Erb	.05
155	Randy Bockus	.05
156	Gary Buckels	.05
157	Tim Burcham	.05
158	Chris Cron	.05
159	Chad Curtis	.40
160	Doug Davis	.05
161	Mark Davis	.05
162	Gary DiSarcina	.15
163	Mike Fetters	.05
164	Joe Grahe	.05
165	Dan Grunhard	.05
166	Dave Leiper	.05
167	Rafael Montalvo	.05
168	Reed Peters	.05
169	Bobby Rose	.05
170	Lee Stevens	.10
171	Ron Tingley	.05
172	Ed Vosberg	.05

173	Mark Wasinger	.05
174	Max Oliveras	.05
175	Lenn Sakata, Gary Ruby	.05
176	Bret Barbarie	.10
177	Kevin Bearse	.05
178	Kent Bottenfield	.10
179	Wil Cordero	.50
180	Mike Davis	.05
181	Alex Diaz	.05
182	Eddie Dixon	.05
183	Jeff Fassero	.10
184	Jerry Goff	.05
185	Todd Haney	.05
186	Steve Hecht	.05
187	Jimmy Kremers	.05
188	Quinn Mack	.05
189	David Masters	.05
190	Marlin McPhall	.05
191	Doug Piatt	.05
192	Dana Ridenour	.05
193	Scott Service	.05
194	Razor Shines	.05
195	Tito Stewart	.05
196	Mel Houston	.05
197	John Vander Wal	.10
198	Darrin Winston	.05
199	Jerry Manuel	.05
200	Gomer Hodge, Nardi Contreras	.05
201	Brad Bierley	.05
202	Steve Carter	.05
203	Frank Castillo	.05
204	Lance Dickson	.10
205	Craig Smajstrla	.05
206	Brian Guinn	.05
207	Joe Kraemer	.05
208	Cedric Landrum	.05
209	Derrick May	.10
210	Scott May	.05
211	Ryss McGinnis	.05
212	Chuck Mount	.05
213	Dave Pavlas	.05
214	Laddie Renfroe	.05
215	David Rosario	.05
216	Rey Sanchez	.10
217	Dan Simonds	.05
218	Jeff Small	.05
219	Doug Strange	.10
220	Glenn Sullivan	.05
221	Rick Wilkins	.25
222	Steve Wilson	.05
223	Bob Scanlan	.10
224	Jim Essian	.05
225	Grant Jackson	.05
226	Luis Alicea	.10
227	Rod Brewer	.05
228	Nick Castaneda	.05
229	Stan Clarke	.05
230	Marty Clary	.05
231	Fidel Compres	.05
232	Todd Crosby	.05
233	Bob Davidson	.05
234	Bien Figueroa	.05
235	Ed Fulton	.05
236	Mark Grater	.05
237	Omar Olivares	.10
238	Brian Jordan	1.50
239	Lonnie Maclin	.05
240	Julian Martinez	.05
241	Al Nipper	.05
242	Dave Osteen	.05
243	Leny Picota	.05
244	Dave Richardson	.05
245	Mike Ross	.05
246	Stan Royer	.15
247	Tim Sherrill	.05
248	Carl Ray Stephens	.05
249	Mark DeJohn	.05
250	Mark Riggins	.05
251	Billy Bates	.05
252	Freddie Benavides	.05
253	Keith Brown	.05
254	Adam Casillas	.05
255	Tony DeFrancesco	.05
256	Leo Garcia	.05
257	Angel Gonzalez	.05
258	Denny Gonzalez	.05
259	Kip Gross	.05
260	Charlie Mitchell	.05
261	Milton Hill	.05
262	Rodney Imes	.05
263	Reggie Jefferson	.10
264	Keith Lockhart	.10
265	Manny Jose	.05
266	Terry Lee	.05
267	Rob Lopez	.05
268	Gino Minutelli	.05
269	Kevin Pearson	.05
270	Ross Powell	.05
271	Donnie Scott	.05
272	Luis Vasquez	.05
273	Joey Vierra	.05
274	Pete Mackanin	.05
275	Don Gullett, Jim Lett	.05
276	Oscar Azocar	.05
277	Dann Bilardello	.05
278	Ricky Bones	.10
279	Brian Dorsett	.05
280	Scott Coolbaugh	.05
281	John Costello	.05
282	Terry Gilmore	.05
283	Jeremy Hernandez	.05
284	Kevin Higgins	.05
285	Chris Jelic	.05
286	Dean Kelley	.05
287	Derek Lilliquist	.05
288	Jose Meledez	.05
289	Jose Mota	.05
290	Adam Peterson	.05
291	Ed Romero	.05
292	Steven Rosenberg	.05
293	Tim Scott	.05
294	Dave Staton	.10
295	Will Taylor	.05
296	Jim Vatcher	.05
297	Dan Walters	.05
298	Kevin Ward	.05
299	Jim Riggleman	.05
300	Jon Matlack, Tony Torchia	.05
301	Gerald Alexander	.05
302	Kevin Belcher	.05
303	Jeff Andrews	.05
304	Tony Scruggs	.05
305	Jeff Bronkey	.05
306	Paco Burgos	.05
307	Nick Capra	.05
308	Monty Fariss	.05
309	Darrin Garner	.05
310	Bill Haselman	.05
311	Terry Mathews	.05
312	Rob Maurer	.05
313	Gar Millay	.05
314	Dean Palmer	.75
315	Roger Pavlik	.10
316	Dan Peltier	.05
317	Steve Peters	.05
318	Mark Petkovsek	.10
319	Jim Poole	.05
320	Paul Postier	.05
321	Wayne Rosenthal	.05
322	Dan Smith	.10
323	Terry Wells	.05
324	Tommy Thompson	.05
325	Stan Hough	.05
326	Sean Berry	.10
327	Jacob Brumfield	.10
328	Bob Buchanan	.05
329	Kevin Burrell	.05
330	Stu Cole	.05
331	Victor Cole	.05
332	Jeff Conine	.60
333	Tommy Dunbar	.05
334	Luis Encarnacion	.05
335	Greg Everson	.05
336	Bob Hamelin	.15
337	Joel Johnston	.05
338	Frank Laureano	.05
339	Jim LeMasters	.05
340	Mike Magnante	.05
341	Carlos Maldonado	.05
342	Andy McGaffigan	.05
343	Bobby Moore	.05
344	Harvey Pulliam	.05
345	Daryl Smith	.05
346	Tim Spehr	.05
347	Hector Wagner	.05
348	Paul Zuvella	.05
349	Sal Rende	.05
350	Brian Poldberg, Guy Hansen	.05
351	Luis Aguayo	.05
352	Tom Barrett	.05
353	Mike Brumley	.05
354	Scott Cooper	.05
355	Mike Gardiner	.05
356	Eric Hetzel	.05
357	Mike Twardoski	.05
358	Rick Lancellotti	.05
359	Derek Livernois	.05
360	Mark Meleski	.05
361	Kevin Morton	.05
362	Dan O'Neill	.05
363	Jim Pankovits	.05
364	Mickey Pina	.05
365	Phil Plantier	.05
366	Jeff Plympton	.05
367	Todd Pratt	.10
368	Larry Shikles	.05
369	Jeff Stone	.05
370	Mo Vaughn	4.00
371	David Walters	.05
372	Eric Wedge	.05
373	Bob Zupcic	.05
374	Butch Hobson	.05
375	Rich Gale	.05
376	Rich Aldrete	.05
377	Mark Bailey	.05
378	Rod Beck	.15
379	Jeff Carter	.05
380	Craig Colbert	.05
381	Darnell Coles	.05
382	Mark Dewey	.05
383	Gil Heredia	.10
384	Darren Lewis	.25
385	Johnny Ard	.05
386	Rafael Novoa	.05
387	Francisco Oliveras	.05
388	Tony Perezchica	.05
389	Mark Thurmond	.05
390	Mike Remlinger	.05
391	Greg Ritchie	.05
392	Rick Rodriguez	.05
393	Andres Santana	.05
394	Jose Segura	.05
395	Stuart Tate	.05
396	Jimmy Williams	.05
397	Jim Wilson	.05
398	Ted Wood	.05
399	Duane Espy	.05
400	Alan Bannister, Larry Hardy	.05
401	Paul Abbott	.05
402	Willie Banks	.10
403	Bernardo Brito	.05
404	Jarvis Brown	.05
405	J.T. Bruett	.05
406	Tim Drummond	.05
407	Tom Edens	.05
408	Rich Garces	.10
409	Chip Hale	.05
410	Terry Jorgensen	.05
411	Kenny Morgan	.05
412	Pedro Munoz	.10
413	Edgar Naveda	.05
414	Denny Naegle	.25
415	Jeff Reboulet	.10
416	Victor Rodriguez	.05
417	Jack Savage	.05
418	Dan Sheaffer	.05
419	Charles Scott	.05
420	Paul Sorrento	.10
421	George Tsamis	.05
422	Lenny Webster	.05
423	Carl Willis	.05
424	Russ Nixon	.05
425	Jim Dwyer, Gordon Heimueller, Paul Kirsch	.05
426	John Alva	.05
427	Mike Bell	.05
428	Tony Castillo	.05
429	Bruce Crabbe	.05
430	John Davis	.05
431	Brian Hunter	.10
432	Randy Kramer	.05
433	Mike Loggins	.05
434	Kelly Mann	.05
435	Tom McCarthy	.05
436	Yorkis Perez	.05
437	Dale Polley	.05
438	Armando Reynoso	.10
439	Rusty Richards	.05
440	Victor Rosario	.05
441	Mark Ross	.05
442	Rico Rossy	.05
443	Randy St. Claire	.05
444	Joe Szekely	.05
445	Andy Tomberlin	.05
446	Matt Turner	.05
447	Glenn Wilson	.05
448	Tracy Woodson	.05
449	Phil Niekro	.75
450	Bruce Del Canton, Sonny Jackson	.05
451	Tony Chance	.05
452	Joaquin Contreras	.05
453	Francisco DeLaRosa	.05
454	Benny Distefano	.05
455	Mike Eberle	.05
456	Todd Frohwirth	.05
457	Steve Jeltz	.05
458	Chito Martinez	.05
459	Dave Martinez	.10
460	Jeff McKnight	.05
461	Luis Mercedes	.05
462	Mike Mussina	3.00
463	Chris Myers	.05
464	Joe Price	.05
465	Israel Sanchez	.05
466	David Segui	.35
467	Tommy Shields	.05
468	Mike Linskey	.05
469	Jeff Tackett	.05
470	Anthony Telford	.05
471	Shane Turner	.05
472	Jeff Wetherby	.05
473	Rob Woodward	.05
474	Greg Biagini	.05
475	Mike Young, Dick Bosman	.05
476	Sal Agostinelli	.05
477	Gary Alexander	.05
478	Andy Ashby	.20
479	Bob Ayrault	.10
480	Kim Batiste	.10
481	Amalio Carreno	.05
482	Rocky Elli	.05
483	Darrin Fletcher	.10
484	Jeff Grotewold	.05
485	Chris Knabenshue	.05
486	Greg Legg	.05
487	Jim Lindeman	.05
488	Chuck Malone	.05
489	Tim Mauser	.05
490	Louie Meadows	.05
491	Mickey Morandini	.15
492	Julio Peguero	.05
493	Wally Ritchie	.05
494	Bruce Ruffin	.05
495	Rick Schu	.05
496	Ray Searage	.05
497	Scott Wade	.05
498	Gary Wilson	.05
499	Bill Dancy	.05
500	Floyd Rayford, Jim Wright	.05
501	Derek Bell	.75
502	Rob Ducey	.10
503	Julius McDougal	.05
504	Juan Guzman	.75
505	Pat Hentgen	.50
506	Shawn Jeter	.05
507	Doug Linton	.05
508	Bob MacDonald	.05
509	Mike Maksudian	.05
510	Ravelo Manzanillo	.05
511	Domingo Martinez	.05
512	Stu Pederson	.05
513	Marty Pevey	.05
514	Tom Quinlan	.05
515	Alex Sanchez	.05
516	Jerry Schunk	.05
517	John Shea	.05
518	Ed Sprague	.15
519	William Suero	.05
520	Steve Wapnick	.05
521	Mickey Weston	.05
522	John Poloni	.05
523	Eddie Zosky	.10
524	Bob Bailor	.05
525	Rocket Wheeler	.05
526	Troy Afenir	.05
527	Mike Bordick	.15
528	Jorge Brito	.05
529	Scott Brosius	.15
530	Kevin Campbell	.05
531	Pete Coachman	.05
532	Dan Eskew	.05
533	Eric Fox	.05
534	Apolinar Garcia	.05
535	Webster Garrison	.05
536	Johnny Guzman	.05
537	Jeff Pico	.05
538	Dann Howitt	.05
539	Doug Jennings	.05
540	Brad Komminsk	.05
541	Tim McCoy	.05
542	Jeff Musselman	.05
543	Troy Neel	.25
544	Will Schock	.05
545	Nelson Simmons	.05
546	Bruce Walton	.05
547	Pat Wernig	.05
548	Ron Witmeyer	.05
549	Jeff Newman	.05
550	Glenn Abbott	.05
551	Kevin Baez	.05
552	Blaine Beatty	.05
553	Doug Cinnella	.05
554	Chris Donnels	.05
555	Jeff Gardner	.05
556	Terrel Hansen	.05
557	Manny Hernandez	.05
558	Eric Hillman	.05
559	Todd Hundley	1.00
560	Alex Jimenez	.05
561	Tim Leiper	.05
562	Lee May	.05
563	Orlando Mercado	.15
564	Brad Moore	.05
565	Al Pedrique	.05
566	Dale Plummer	.05
567	Rich Saveur	.05
568	Ray Soff	.05
569	Kelvin Torve	.05
570	Dave Trautwein	.05
571	Julio Valera	.05
572	Robbie Wine	.05
573	Anthony Young	.05
574	Steve Swisher	.05
575	Ron Washington, Bob Apodaca	.05
576	Scott Aldred	.05
577	Karl Allaire	.05
578	Skeeter Barnes	.05
579	Arnie Beyeler	.05
580	Rico Brogna	.10
581	Phil Clark	.05
582	Mike Dalton	.05
583	Curt Ford	.05
584	Dan Gakeler	.05
585	David Haas	.05
586	Shawn Hare	.15
587	John Kiely	.10
588	Mark Leiter	.05
589	Scott Livingstone	.10
590	Mitch Lyden	.05
591	Eric Mangham	.05
592	Rusty Meacham	.10
593	Mike Munoz	.05
594	Randy Nosek	.05
595	Johnny Paredes	.05
596	Kevin Ritz	.05
597	Rich Rowland	.10
598	Don Vesling	.05
599	Joe Sparks	.05
600	Mark Wagner, Ralph Treuel	.05
601	Harold Allen	.05
602	Eric Anthony	.10
603	Doug Baker	.05
604	Ryan Bowen	.10
605	Mike Capel	.05
606	Andujar Cedeno	.10
607	Terry Clark	.05
608	Carlo Colombino	.05
609	Gary Cooper	.05
610	Calvin Schiraldi	.05
611	Randy Hennis	.05
612	Butch Henry	.05
613	Blaise Isley	.05
614	Kenny Lofton	4.00
615	Terry McGriff	.05
616	Andy Mota	.05
617	Javier Ortiz	.05
618	Scott Servais	.10
619	Mike Simms	.05
620	Jose Tolentino	.05
621	Lee Tunnell	.05
622	Brent Strom	.05
623	Gerald Young	.05
624	Bob Skinner	.05
625	Dave Engle	.05
626	Cesar Bernhardt	.05
627	Mario Brito	.05
628	Kurt Brown	.05
629	John Cangelosi	.05
630	Jeff Carter	.05
631	Tom Drees	.05
632	Grady Hall	.05
633	Joe Hall	.05
634	Curt Hasler	.05
635	Danny Heep	.05
636	Dan Henley	.05
637	Roberto Hernandez	.30
638	Orsino Hill	.05
639	Jerry Kutzler	.05
640	Noberto Martin	.05
641	Rod McCray	.05
642	Bob Nelson	.05
643	Warren Newsom	.10
644	Greg Perschke	.05
645	Rich Scheid	.05
646	Matt Stark	.05
647	Ron Stephens	.05
648	Don Wakamatsu	.05
649	Marv Foley	.05
650	Roger LaFrancois, Moe Drabowsky	.05

1991 Classic Best Promo Sheet

Four of the year's brightest minor league stars, along with spokesman Mike Schmidt are featured on this promo sheet for Classic Best's minor league singles set. The sheet measures 7-1/2" x 7-1/8". The back is printed in black-and-white.

	MT
Uncut Sheet: Todd Van Poppel, Ryan Klesko, Tim Costo, Mike Schmidt, D.J. Dozier	15.00

1991 Classic Best

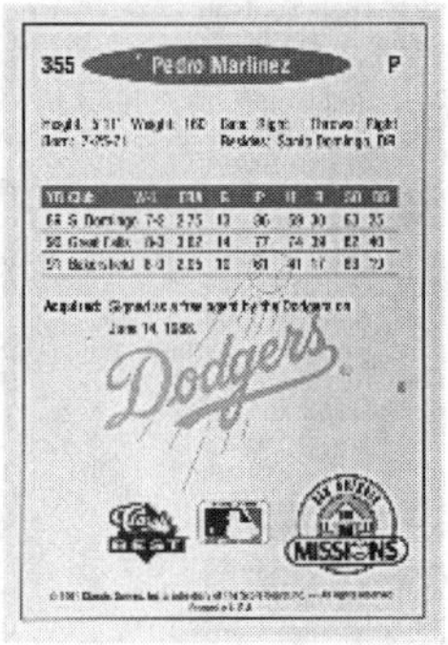

Classic Best entered the single-card minor league market in 1991 with a 450-card set. The first 396 cards were issued in poly packs and later available in factory sets. Cards numbered 397-450

were only available in the factory sets. Hall of Famer Mike Schmidt, who is card #1 in the set, personally autographed 2,100 of his cards, which were inserted at the rate of one per 8,000 packs.

		MT
Complete Wax Set (396):		12.50
Complete Factory Set (450):		15.00
Common Player:		.05
1	Mike Schmidt	.50
1a	Mike Schmidt (autographed edition of 2,100)	150.00
2	Kevin Roberson	.10
3	Paul Rodgers	.05
4	Marc Newfield	.10
5	Marc Ronan	.05
6	Marty Willis	.05
7	Jason Hardtke	.05
8	Matt Mieske	.10
9	Brian Johnson	.05
10	Alex Arias	.10
11	Eric Young	.10
12	Donald Harris	.10
13	Bruce Chick	.05
14	Brian Williams	.05
15	Brian Cornelius	.05
16	Brian Giles	.05
17	Brad Ausmus	.10
18	Ivan Cruz	.05
19	Keven Flora	.05
20	Robbie Katzaroff	.05
21	Randy Knorr	.05
22	Micky Henson	.05
23	Chris Haney	.05
24	Jeff Mutis	.05
25	Barry Winford	.05
26	Ray Giannelli	.05
27	Donovan Osborne	.05
28	Ruben Gonzalez	.05
29	Howard Battle	.10
30	Greg O'Halloran	.05
31	Ben Van Ryn	.05
32	Rick Hulsman	.05
33	Jose Valentin	.05
34	Jose Zambrano	.05
35	John Gross	.05
36	Jessie Hollins	.05
37	Kevin Scott	.05
38	Kerwin Moore	.05
39	Eric Albright	.05
40	Ernesto Rodriguez	.05
41	Reggie Sanders	.25
42	Henry Werland	.05
43	Boo Moore	.05
44	Mike Messerly	.05
45	Mike Lansing	.30
46	Mike Gardella	.05
47	Mo Sanford	.10
48	Tavo Alvarez	.05
49	Nick Davis	.05
50	Charlie Hillemann	.05
51	Jeff Darwin	.05
52	Reid Cornelius	.05
53	Matt Rambo	.05
54	Rich Batchelor	.05
55	Ricky Gutierrez	.10
56	Rod Bolton	.05
57	Pat Bryant	.05
58	Hugh Walker	.05
59	Keith Schmidt	.05
60	Ceasar Morillo	.05
61	Gabe White	.25
62	Javy Lopez	2.00
63	Carlos Delgado	.75
64	John Johnstone	.05
65	Andres Berumen	.05
66	Brian Kowitz	.05
67	Shane Reynolds (photo actually Orlando Miller)	.15
68	Jeromy Burnitz	.25
69	Scott Bryant	.05
70	Jason McFarlin	.05
71	John Conner	.05
72	Garrett Jenkins	.05
73	Greg Kobza	.05
74	Mark Swope	.05
75	Jerome Williams	.05
76	Jeff Bonner	.05
77	Jermaine Swinton	.05
78	John Cohen	.05
79	Johnny Calzado	.05
80	Juan Andujar	.05
81	Paul Ellis	.05
82	Paul Gonzalez	.05
83	Scott Taylor	.05
84	Stan Spencer	.05
85	Steve Martin	.05
86	Scott Cepicky	.05
87	Max Aleys	.05
88	Michael Brown (Photo actually Matt Brown)	.05
89	Jim Waggoner	.05
90	Mickey Rivers Jr.	.05
91	Nate Crowmwell	.05
92	Carlos Perez	.15
93	Matt Brown (Photo actually Michael Brown)	.05
94	Jose Hernandez	.05
95	Johnny Ruffin	.10
96	Kevin Jordan	.10
97	Manny Alexander	.10
98	Tony Longmire	.10
99	Lonell Roberts	.05
100	Doug Lindsey	.05
101	Al Harley	.05
102	Jerry Thurston	.05
103	Mike Williams	.05
104	David Bell	.05
105	Greg Johnson	.05
106	Roger Salkeld	.10
107	Mike Milchin	.05
108	Jeff Kent	.35
109	Tim Stargell	.05
110	Miah Bradbury	.05
111	Paul Fletcher	.05
112	Steven Rolen	.05
113	Tony Spires	.05
114	Kevin Tolar	.05
115	Kevin Dattola	.05
116	Sherman Obando	.10
117	Sean Ryan	.05
118	Carlos Mota	.05
119	Steve Karsay	.25
120	Kelly Lifgren	.05
121	Damion Easley	.20
122	Fred Russell	.05
123	Freddie Davis Jr.	.05
124	Dave Zancanaro	.05
125	Jeff Jackson	.05
126	Steve Pegues	.05
127	Gerald Williams	.10
128	Eric Helfand	.10
129	Gary Painter	.05
130	Colin Ryan	.05
131	Randy Brown	.05
132	Andy Fox	.05
133	Mike Ogliaruso	.05
134	Matt Franco	.05
135	Willie Ansley	.05
136	Ivan Rodriguez	3.00
137	Anthony Lewis	.05
138	Bill Wertz	.05
139	Tom Kinney	.05
140	Brad Hassinger	.05
141	Elliot Gray	.05
142	Clemente Alvarez	.05
143	Mike Hankins	.05
144	Jim Haller	.05
145	Manuel Martinez	.05
146	Nilson Robledo	.05
147	Rex DeLa Nuez	.05
148	Steve Bethea	.05
149	Oscar Munoz	.05
150	Sam Militello	.05
151	Phil Hiatt	.05
152	Alberto de los Santos	.05
153	Darrell Sherman	.05
154	Henry Mercedes	.05
155	David Holdridge	.05
156	Sean Ross	.05
157	Brandon Wilson	.05
158	William Pennyfeather	.05
159	Derek Parks	.05
160	Troy O'Leary	.08
161	Genaro Campusano	.05
162	Robbie Beckett	.08
163	Chris Burton	.05
164	Jeff Williams	.05
165	John Massarelli	.05
166	John Kelly	.05
167	Jim Wiley	.05
168	Mark Mitchelson	.05
169	Jeff McNeely	.10
170	Keith Kimberlin	.05
171	Mike DeKneef	.05
172	Rusty Greer	.25
173	Pete Castellano	.05
174	Paul Torres	.05
175	Rod McCall	.05
176	Jim Bullinger	.05
177	Brian Champion	.05
178	Greg Hunter	.05
179	Luis Galindez	.05
180	Rodney Eldridge	.05
181	Rudy Pemberton	.05
182	Russ Davis	.20
183	Cristobal Colon	.05
184	Scott Bream	.05
185	Tim Nedin	.05
186	Joe Ausanio	.05
187	Shanhon Withem	.05
188	Mike Oquist	.05
189	Pete Young	.05
190	Paul Carey	.05
191	Chris Gies	.05
192	Gar Finnvold	.05
193	Greg Martin	.05
194	Oreste Marrero	.05
195	Jim Thome	3.00
196	Bill Ostermeyer	.05
197	David Hulse	.05
198	Damon Buford	.05
199	Jonathan Hurst	.05
200	Rich Tunison	.05
201	Tom Nevers	.05
202	Tracy Sanders	.05
203	Troy Buckley	.05
204	Todd Gugglana	.05
205	Tim Laker	.05
206	Dean Locklear	.05
207	Lee Tinsley	.05
208	Jose Velez	.05
209	Greg Zaun	.10
210	Bill Ashley	.10
211	Gary Caraballo	.05
212	Kiki Jones	.05
213	Dave Wrona	.05
214	Michael Carter	.05
215	Leon Glenn Jr.	.05
216	Glenn Sutko	.05
217	Pat Howell	.05
218	Austin Manahan	.05
219	Jon Jenkins	.05
220	Brook Fordyce	.05
221	Kevin Rodgers	.05
222	David Allen	.05
223	Kurt Archer	.05
224	Keith Mitchell	.05
225	Bruce Schreiber	.05
226	Greg Blosser	.05
227	Dave Nilsson	.20
228	Fred Colley	.05
229	Marc Lipson	.05
230	Jay Gainer	.05
231	Sean Cheetham	.05
232	Tim Howard	.05
233	Steve Hosey	.10
234	Javier Ocasio	.05
235	Ricky Rhodes	.05
236	Mark Griffin	.05
237	Scott Shockey	.05
238	T.R. Lewis	.10
239	Kevin Young	.20
240	Robb Nen	.10
241	Steve Dunn	.05
242	Tommy Taylor	.05
243	Keith Valrie	.05
244	Mateo Ozuna	.05
245	Scott Bullett	.10
246	Anthony Brown	.05
247	Phil Leftwich	.10
248	Cliff Garrett	.05
249	Wade Fyock	.05
250	Shayne Rea	.05
251	Royce Clayton	.25
252	Martin Martinez	.05
253	Dave Patterson	.05
254	Robert Fitzpatrick	.05
255	John Jackson	.05
256	Enoch Simmons	.05
257	Dave Proctor	.05
258	Garret Anderson	.60
259	Mark Delesandro	.05
260	Ken Edenfield	.05
261	Tom Raffo	.05
262	Tim Cecil	.05
263	Bobby Magallanes	.05
264	Vince Castaldo	.05
265	Terry Burrows	.05
266	Victor Madrigal	.05
267	Tyler Houston	.10
268	Chipper Jones	6.00
269	Terry Bradshaw	.08
270	Jalal Leach	.05
271	Jose Ventura	.05
272	Derek Lee	.10
273	Derek Reld	.05
274	David Wilson	.05
275	Patrick Rapp	.10
276	John Roper	.10
277	Rogello Nunez	.05
278	Fred White	.05
279	J.T. Snow	.50
280	Pedro Astacio	.15
281	Corey Thomas	.05
282	Chris Johnson	.05
283	Ignacio Duran	.05
284	Dave Fleming	.10
285	Wilson Alvarez	.30
286	Eric Booker	.05
287	John Ericks	.05
288	Don Peters	.05
289	Ed Ferm	.05
290	Mike Lieberthal	.10
291	John Jaha	.15
292	Bryan Baar	.05
293	Archie Corbin	.05
294	Kevin Tatar	.05
295	Shea Wardwell	.05
296	Hipilito Pichardo	.08
297	Curtis Leskanic	.10
298	Sam August (photo actually Jeff Juden)	.05
299	Tim Pugh	.15
300	Mike Huyler	.05
301	Mark Parnell	.05
302	Jeff Juden (photo actually Shane Reynolds)	.60
303	Carl Sullivan	.05
304	Tyrone Kingwood	.05
305	Glenn Carter	.05
306	Tom Fischer	.05
307	Braulio Castillo	.05
308	Bob McCreary	.05
309	Ty Kovach	.05
310	Troy Salvior	.05
311	Mike Weimerskirch	.05
312	Chistopher Hatcher	.05
313	Bryan Smith	.05
314	John Patterson	.05
315	Scooter Tucker	.05
316	Ray Callari	.05
317	Mike Moberg	.05
318	Midre Cummings	.10
319	Todd Ritchie	.08
320	Eric Christopherson	.10
321	Adam Hyzdu	.05
322	Andres Duncan	.05
323	Mike Myers	.05
324	Salomon Torres	.05
325	Tony Gilmore	.05
326	Walter Trice	.05
327	Tom Redington	.05
328	Terry Taylor	.05
329	Tim Salmon	1.50
330	Dan Masteller	.05
331	Mark Wohlers	.15
332	Willie Smith	.05
333	Todd Jones	.08
334	Alan Zinter	.05
335	Arthur Rhodes	.10
336	Toby Borland	.05
337	Shawn Whalen	.05
338	Scott Sanders	.05
339	Bill Meury	.05
340	Amadoz Arias	.05
341	Denny Hoppe	.05
342	Dave Telgheder	.05
343	Paul Bruno	.05
344	Paul Russo	.05
345	Rich Becker (Photo actually Tim Persing)	.10
346	Steve Vondran	.05
347	Rich Langford	.05
348	Ron Lockett	.05
349	Sam Taylor	.05
350	Willie Greene	.10
351	Tom Houk	.05
352	Lance Painter	.05
353	Dan Wilson	.10
354	John Kuehl	.05
355	Pedro Martinez	1.50
356	John Byington	.05
357	Scott Freeman	.05
358	Bo Dodson	.05
359	Julian Vasquez	.05
360	Rondell White	1.50
361	Aaron Small	.05
362	Doug Fitzer	.05
363	Billy White	.05
364	Jeff Tuss	.05
365	Jeff Barry	.05
366	Craig Pueschner	.05
367	Julio Bruno	.05
368	Jamie Dismuke	.05
369	K.C. Gillium	.05
370	Jason Klonoski	.05
371	Tim Persing (Photo actually Rich Becker)	.05
372	Mark Borcherding	.05
373	Larry Luebbers	.05
374	Carlos Fermin	.05
375	Charlie Rogers	.05
376	Ramon Caraballo	.05
377	Orlando Miller (photo actually Sam August)	.10
378	Joey James	.05
379	Dan Rogers	.05
380	Jon Shave	.05
381	Frank Bolick	.05
382	Frank Seminara	.05
383	Mel Wearing Jr.	.05
384	Zak Shinall	.05
385	Sterling Hitchcock	.30
386	Todd Van Poppel	.10
387	D.J. Dozier	.05
388	Ryan Klesko	2.00
389	Tim Costo	.10
390	Brad Pennington	.10
391	Checklist 1-66	.05
392	Checklist 67-132	.05
393	Checklist 133-198	.05
394	Checklist 199-264	.05
395	Checklist 265-330	.05
396	Checklist 331-396	.05
397	Frank Rodriguez	.20
398	Frank Jacons	.05
399	Mike Kelly	.10
400	David McCarty	.10
401	Scott Stahoviak	.10
402	Doug Glanville	.10
403	Curt Krippner	.05
404	Joe Vitiello	.15
405	Justin Thompson	.35
406	Trevor Miller	.10
407	Tarrick Brock	.05
408	Eddie Williams	.05
409	Scott Ruffcorn	.10
410	Chris Durkin	.05
411	Jim Kewis	.05
412	Calvin Reese	.10
413	Toby Rumfield	.05
414	Brent Gates	.15
415	Mike Neill	.05
416	Tyler Green	.20
417	Ron Allen	.05
418	Larry Thomas Jr.	.05
419	Chris Weinke	.25
420	Matt Brewer	.05
421	Dax Jones	.05
422	Jon Farrell	.05
423	Dan Jones	.05
424	Eduardo Perez	.10
425	Rodney Pedraza	.05
426	Tom McKinnon	.05
427	Al Watson	.05
428	Herbert Perry	.05
429	Shawn Estes	.10
430	Tommy Adams	.05
431	Mike Grace	.05
432	Tyson Godfrey	.05
433	Andy Hartung	.05
434	Shawn Livsey	.05
435	Earl Cunningham	.05
436	Scott Lydy	.10
437	Aaron Sele	.25
438	Tim Costo	.10
439	Tanyon Sturtze	.05
440	Ed Ramos	.05
441	Buck McNabb	.05
442	Scott Hatteberg	.10
443	Brian Barber	.10
444	Julian Heredia	.05
445	Chris Pritchett	.10
446	Bubba Smith	.05
447	Shawn Purdy	.05
448	Jeff Borski	.05
449	Jamie Gonzalez	.05
450	Checklist 397-450	.05

1991 Classic Best Gold Bonus

Each jumbo pack of Classic Best cards contains one Gold Bonus card of a top prospect. The cards are virtually identical to the regular-issue version except for the use of a gold-foil oval for the player's name. Backs have a "BC" prefix to the card number.

		MT
Complete Set (20):		12.00
Common Player:		.25
1	Mike Schmidt	1.50
2	Marc Newfield	.35
3	Matt Mieske	.25
4	Reggie Sanders	.75
5	Jeromy Burnitz	2.00
6	Todd Van Poppel	.25
7	Ivan Rodriguez	5.00
8	Sam Militello	.25
9	Jim Thome	5.00
10	Brook Fordyce	.25
11	Dave Nilsson	.25
12	Royce Clayton	.40
13	Mark Wohlers	.25
14	Arthur Rhodes	.25
15	Ryan Klesko	3.00
16	Mike Kelly	.25
17	Frankie Rodriguez	.25
18	David McCarty	.25
19	Tyler Green	.35
20	Eduardo Perez	.25

1991 Classic Draft Picks Promos

Multi-colored backs marked "For Promotional Purposes Only" differentiate the promos for Classic's second annual baseball draft picks set from the regularly issued cards.

		MT
Complete Set (4):		2.00
Common Player:		.50
(1)	Tyler Green	.50
(2)	Mike Kelly	.50

(3) Brien Taylor .50
(4) Dmitri Young .50

1991 Classic Draft Picks

After releasing a 26-card draft pick set in 1990, Classic returned with a 50-card issue for 1991. A reported 330,000 hobby sets were produced, along with 165,000 sets for the retail market. Card fronts feature gray and maroon borders surrounding full-color photos and the Classic logo in the upper-left corner. A special bonus card of Frankie Rodriguez is also included with the set. Each set includes a certificate of authenticity.

		MT
Complete Set (50):		3.00
Common Player:		.03
1	Brien Taylor	.10
2	Mike Kelly	.05
3	David McCarty	.05
4	Dmitri Young	.15
5	Joe Vitiello	.05
6	Mark Smith	.05
7	Tyler Green	.05
8	Shawn Estes	.25
9	Doug Glanville	.05
10	Manny Ramirez	1.00
11	Cliff Floyd	.50
12	Tyrone Hill	.05
13	Eduardo Perez	.10
14	Al Shirley	.03
15	Benji Gil	.10
16	Calvin Reese	.10
17	Allen Watson	.05
18	Brian Barber	.03
19	Aaron Sele	.20
20	Jon Farrell	.03
21	Scott Ruffcorn	.05
22	Brent Gates	.10
23	Scott Stahoviak	.03
24	Tom McKinnon	.03
25	Shawn Livsey	.03
26	Jason Pruitt	.03
27	Greg Anthony	.03
28	Justin Thompson	.25
29	Steve Whitaker	.03
30	Jorge Fabregas	.10
31	Jeff Ware	.05
32	Bobby Jones	.15
33	J.J. Johnson	.03
34	Mike Rossiter	.03
35	Dan Chowlowsky	.03
36	Jimmy Gonzalez	.03
37	Trevor Miller	.03
38	Scott Hatteberg	.03
39	Mike Groppuso	.03
40	Ryan Long	.03
41	Eddie Williams	.03
42	Mike Durant	.03
43	Buck McNabb	.03
44	Jimmy Lewis	.03
45	Eddie Ramos	.03
46	Terry Horn	.03
47	Jon Barnes	.03
48	Shawn Curran	.03
49	Tommy Adams	.03
50	Trevor Mallory	.03
---	Frankie Rodriguez (Bonus Card)	.15

1991 Classic Four Sport (Baseball)

Late in 1991 Classic released a four-sport draft picks set of 230 base cards, 10 foil "Limited Print" cards and more than 60,000 autographed cards seeded one per 260 packs. Cards have color photos on front with wide mottled blue-gray borders. A "wax seal" in red at upper-left carries the set's logo. Player name and position are in black at the bottom. Backs are printed in color with biographical data, high school or college stats and career highlights. Twenty percent of the 25,000 cases printed were an English-French version, which carries a premium of about a 50% premium. Only the cards featuring baseball players are checklisted here.

		MT
Common Card:		.05
1	Future Stars Russell Maryland, Brien Taylor, Larry Johnson, Eric Lindros	.10
51	Brien Taylor	.10
52	Mike Kelly	.05
53	David McCarty	.10
54	Dmitri Young	.20
55	Joe Vitiello	.05
56	Mark Smith	.05
57	Tyler Green	.10
58	Shawn Estes (photo reversed)	.40
59	Doug Glanville	.10
60	Manny Ramirez	1.00
61	Cliff Floyd	.50
62	Tyrone Hill	.05
63	Eduardo Perez	.10
64	Al Shirley	.05
65	Benji Gil	.10
66	Calvin Reese	.10
67	Allen Watson	.10
68	Brian Barber	.05
69	Aaron Sele	.25
70	John Farrell	.05
71	Scott Ruffcorn	.05
72	Brent Gates	.10
73	Scott Stahoviak	.05
74	Tom McKinnon	.05
75	Shawn Livsey	.05
76	Jason Pruitt	.05
77	Greg Anthony	.05
78	Justin Thompson	.40
79	Steve Whitaker	.05
80	Jorge Fabregas	.10
81	Jeff Ware	.05
82	Bobby Jones	.10
83	J.J. Johnson	.05
84	Mike Rossiter	.05
85	Dan Chowlowsky	.05
86	Jimmy Gonzalez	.05
87	Trever Miller	.05
88	Scott Hatteberg	.05
89	Mike Groppuso	.05
90	Ryan Long	.05
91	Eddie Williams	.05
92	Mike Durant	.05
93	Buck McNabb	.05
94	Jimmy Lewis	.05
95	Eddie Ramos	.05
96	Terry Horn	.05
97	John Barnes	.05
98	Shawn Curran	.05
99	Tommy Adams	.05
100	Trevor Mallory	.05
101	Frankie Rodriguez	.15
218	Joe Hamilton	.25
219	Marc Kroon	.05
225	Shawn Green	.25
LP7	Brien Taylor (Limited Print silver foil)	1.50

1991 Classic Four Sport (Baseball) Autographed

Approximately 60 of the more than 200 players in the 1991 Classic Four Sport draft picks issue autographed as many as 2,600 cards apiece for insertion as random foil-pack inserts; in all more than 60,000 autographed cards were distributed. The number in parentheses in the listings here indicates the number of cards reportedly signed by each player. Only the baseball players are listed here.

		MT
Common Player:		3.00
51	Brien Taylor (2600)	15.00
52	Mike Kelly (2600)	6.00
53	David McCarty (2450)	6.00
54	Dmitri Young (2600)	15.00
55	Joe Vitiello (1900)	5.00
56	Mark Smith (1700)	3.00
58	Shawn Estes (2000) (photo reversed)	10.00
59	Doug Glanville (2000)	6.00
61	Cliff Floyd (2000)	24.00
62	Tyrone Hill (1000)	3.00
63	Eduardo Perez (950)	6.00
101	Frankie Rodriguez	12.00
218	Joe Hamilton (2000)	24.00

1991 Front Row Draft Picks Promos

These cards were issued to introduce and advertise the premier edition of Front Row draft picks. They are similar in format to the regular-issue cards except for the promo notice/ad on back.

		MT
Complete Set (5):		1.00
Common Player:		.25
(1)	Chris Durkin	.25
(2)	John Farrell	.25
(3)	Mike Neill	.25
(4)	Scott Ruffcorn	.25
(5)	Chad Schoenvogel	.25

1991 Front Row Draft Picks

A total of 240,000 of these sets were produced. The bonus card in the set was redeemable by Front Row for a special Frankie Rodriguez card. The first 120,000 collectors returning bonus cards also received Front Row's mini-update set. The cards feature full-color photos on both sides. Each set includes a numbered certificate of authenticity.

		MT
Complete Set (50):		2.00
Common Player:		.10
1	Frankie Rodriguez	.50
2	Aaron Sele	.50
3	Chad Schoenvogel	.10
4	Scott Ruffcorn	.10
5	Dan Chowlowski	.10
6	Gene Schall	.10
7	Trever Miller	.10
8	Chris Durkin	.10
(8p)	Chris Durkin (promo)	.25
9	Mike Neill	.10
10	Kevin Stocker	.15
11	Bobby Jones	.25
12	Jon Farrell	.10
13	Ronnie Allen	.10
14	Mike Rossiter	.10
15	Scott Hatteberg	.15
16	Rodney Pedraza	.10
17	Mike Durant	.10
18	Ryan Long	.10
19	Greg Anthony	.10
20	Jon Barnes	.10
21	Brian Barber	.10
22	Brent Gates	.20
23	Calvin Reese	.15
24	Terry Horn	.10
25	Scott Stahoviak	.10
26	Jason Pruitt	.10
27	Shawn Curran	.10
28	Jimmy Lewis	.10
29	Alex Ochoa	.25
30	Joe Deberry	.10
31	Justin Thompson	.15
32	Jimmy Gonzalez	.10
33	Eddie Ramos	.10
34	Tyler Green	.25
35	Toby Rumfield	.10
36	Dave Doorneweerd	.10
37	Jeff Hostetler	.10
38	Shawn Livsey	.10
39	Mike Groppuso	.10
40	Steve Whitaker	.10
41	Tom McKinnon	.10
42	Buck McNabb	.10
43	Al Shirley	.10
44	Allan Watson	.15
45	Bill Bliss	.10
46	Todd Hollandsworth	.50
47	Manny Ramirez	1.50
48	J.J. Johnson	.10
49	Cliff Floyd	.75
50a	Bonus card	.25
50 (b)	Benji Gil	.25
51	Herb Perry	.10
52	Terrik Brock	.10
53	Trevor Mallory	.10
54	Chris Pritchett	.15
FR1	Frank Rodriguez (pitching)	.25
FR2	Frank Rodriguez (pitching)	.25
FR3	Frank Rodriguez (batting)	.25
FR4	Frank Rodriguez (pitching)	.25
FR5	Frank Rodriguez (batting)	.25

1991 Front Row Draft Picks Update

These five cards were distributed to the first 120,000 collectors redeeming a bonus card from the 1991 draft picks set. Fronts have color photos with metallic silver-foil borders. Backs have a color photo of the player as a boy, plus personal data, high school and/or college stats and career achievements.

		MT
Complete Set (5):		1.00
Common Player:		.25
50	Benji Gil	.25
51	Herb Perry	.25
52	Terrik Brock	.25
53	Trevor Mallory	.25
54	Chris Pritchett	.25

1991 Front Row Frankie Rodriguez Signature Cards

This series of five cards was sold in both autographed and unautographed sets, complete with certificates of authenticity, each with an individual serial number from within an edition of 10,000. The 2-1/2" x 3-1/2" cards are UV coated front and back. Fronts have color pitching and batting game-action photos. Backs of cards #1-4 have information on Rodriguez' junior college career, the back of card #5 has another action photo.

		MT
Complete Set (5):		1.00
Complete Set, w/Autograph (5):		3.00
1-5	Frankie Rodriguez	

Player names in *Italic* type indicate a rookie card.

1991 ProCards Tomorrow's Heroes

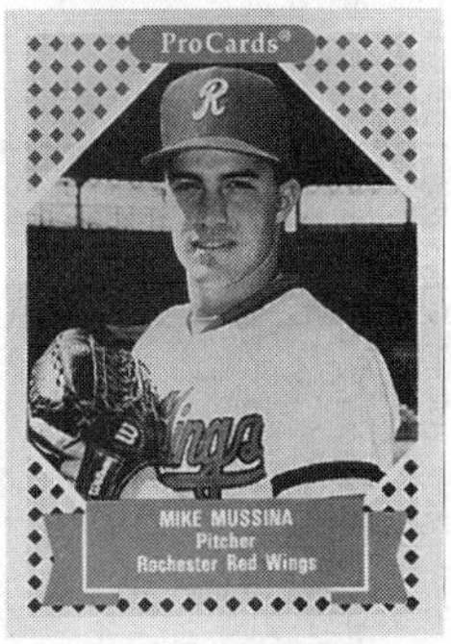

This Procards issue is comprised of an assortment of AAA, AA and A classification players representing all 26 contemporary Major League organizations. Cards are numbered beginning with Baltimore of the American League and concluding with San Francisco of the National League. Each of the Major League segments then has representation of the best players within their minor league organization; example: BALTIMORE ORIOLES AAA - Mussina, Mercedes, Frowirth, Martinez, Sequi AA - Rhodes, Jones A - Moore, Alexander, Williams, Anderson, Lemp, Krivda. "Tomorrow's Heroes" in a great title since there are dozens of prospects in the set; many of whom would soon be mainstays on big league rosters. Cards were only available in foil packs. Cards are bordered in white with a prominent pink and gray checkered interior pattern. Card manufacturer, player's name, position, and team are lettered in white and bordered in red. Original plans reportedly called for production of 10,000 cases, but those plans were changed dramatically to a limited production run of 1,007 cases upon the acquisition of ProCards by Fleer; thereby resulting in this product becoming a scarce commodity.

		MT
Complete Set (360):		45.00
Common Player:		.10
1	Mike Mussina	3.00
2	Luis Mercedes	.15
3	Todd Frohwirth	.10
4	Chito Martinez	.10
5	David Sequi	.20
6	Arthur Rhodes	.10
7	Stacy Jones	.10
8	Daryl Moore	.10
9	Manny Alexander	.15
10	Jeff Williams	.10
11	Matt Anderson	.10
12	Chris Lemp	.10
13	Rick Krivda	.10
14	Phil Plantier	.10
15	Mo Vaughn	4.00
16	Scott Cooper	.10
17	Mike Gardiner	.10
18	Kevin Morton	.15
19	Jeff Plympton	.10
20	Jeff McNeely	.15
21	Willie Tatum	.10
22	Tim Smith	.10
23	Frank Rodriguez	.25
24	Chris Davis	.10
25	Cory Bailey	.10
26	Rob Henkel	.10
27	Kyle Abbott	.15
28	Lee Stevens	.10
29	Chad Curtis	.50
30	Ruben Amaro	.15
31	Mark Howie	.10
32	Tim Salmon	4.00
33	Kevin Flora	.10
34	Garret Anderson	.50
35	Darryl Scott	.10
36	Don Vidmar	.10
37	Korey Keling	.10
38	Troy Percival	.15
39	Eduardo Perez	.15
40	Julian Heredia	.10
41	Wilson Alvarez	.50
42	Ramon Garcia	.10
43	Johnny Ruffin	.15
44	Scott Cepicky	.10
45	Rod Bolton	.10
46	Rogelio Nunez	.10
47	Brandon Wilson	.10
48	Marc Kubicki	.10
49	Mark Lewis	.25
50	Jim Thome	3.00
51	Tim Costo	.15
52	Jeff Mutis	.10
53	Tracy Sanders	.10
54	Mike Soper	.10
55	Miguel Flores	.10
56	Brian Giles	.15
57	Curtis Leskanic	.15
58	Kyle Washington	.10
59	Jason Hardtke	.10
60	Albie Lopez	.10
61	Oscar Resendez	.10
62	Manny Ramirez	4.00
63	Rico Brogna	.20
64	Scott Livingstone	.15
65	Greg Gohr	.10
66	Scott Aldred	.10
67	Brian Warren	.10
68	Bob Undorf	.10
69	Rob Grable	.10
70	Tom Mezzanotte	.10
71	Justin Thompson	.20
72	Trever Miller	.25
73	Joel Johnston	.10
74	Kevin Koslofski	.10
75	Archie Corbin	.10
76	Phil Hiatt	.10
77	Danny Miceli	.15
78	Joe Randa	.15
79	Mark Johnson	.20
80	Joe Vitiello	.20
81	Cal Eldred	.25
82	Doug Henry	.10
83	Dave Nilsson	.25
84	John Jaha	.30
85	Shon Ashley	.10
86	Jim Tatum	.10
87	Bo Dodson	.10
88	Otis Green	.10
89	Denny Neagle	.30
90	Checklist 1-90	.10
91	Pedro Munoz	.10
92	Jarvis Brown	.10
93	Pat Mahomes	.10
94	Cheo Garcia	.10
95	David McCarty	.10
96	Chris Delarwelle	.10
97	Scott Stahoviak	.15
98	Midre Cummings	.15
99	Todd Ritchie	.10
100	Dave Sartain	.10
101	Pedro Grifol	.10
102	Eddie Guardado	.10
103	Bob Carlson	.10
104	Sandy Diaz	.10
105	John Ramos	.10
106	Bernie Williams	4.00
107	Wade Taylor	.10
108	Pat Kelly	.10
109	Jeff Johnson	.10
110	Scott Kamieniecki	.15
111	Dave Silvestri	.10
112	Ed Maritel	.10
113	Willie Smith	.10
114	J.T. Snow	.50
115	Gerald Williams	.25
116	Larry Stanford	.10
117	Bruce Prybylinski	.10
118	Rey Noriega	.10
119	Rich Batchelor	.10
120	Brad Ausmus	.15
121	Robert Eenhoorn	.10
122	Sam Militello	.10
123	Jason Robertson	.10
124	Carl Everett	.25
125	Kiki Hernandez	.10
126	Rafael Quirico	.10
127	Lyle Mouton	.10
128	Tim Flannelly	.10
129	Todd Van Poppel	.15
130	Tim Peek	.10
131	Henry Mercedes	.10
132	Todd Smith	.10
133	Brent Gates	.15
134	Gary Hust	.10
135	Mike Neill	.10
136	Russ Brock	.10
137	Ricky Kimball	.10
138	Tino Martinez	2.50
139	Calvin Jones	.10
140	Roger Salkeld	.15
141	Dave Fleming	.15
142	Bret Boone	.75
143	Jim Campanis	.10
144	Marc Newfield	.10
145	Mike Hampton	.10
146	Shawn Estes	.45
147	David Lisiecki	.10
148	Dean Palmer	.65
149	Rob Maurer	.10
150	Jim Poole	.10
151	Terry Mathews	.10
152	Monty Fariss	.10
153	Ivan Rodriguez	4.00
154	Barry Manuel	.10
155	Donald Harris	.10
156	Rusty Greer	.25
157	Matt Whiteside	.10
158	Derek Bell	.60
159	Eddie Zosky	.15
160	Domingo Martinez	.10
161	Juan Guzman	.45
162	Ed Sprague	.20
163	Rob Ducey	.15
164	Vince Horsman	.10
165	Darren Hall	.10
166	Rick Trlicek	.10
167	Dave Weathers	.10
168	Robert Perez	.10
169	Nigel Wilson	.10
170	Carlos Delgado	1.00
171	Steve Karsay	.15
172	Howard Battle	.15
173	Huck Fiener	.10
174	Robert Butler	.10
175	Giovanni Carrara	.10
176	Michael Taylor	.10
177	Brian Hunter	.15
178	Turk Wendell	.15
179	Mark Wohlers	.30
180	Checklist 91-180	.10
181	Ryan Klesko	3.00
182	Keith Mitchell	.10
183	Vinny Castilla	.35
184	Napoleon Robinson	.10
185	Mike Kelly	.10
186	Javy Lopez	3.00
187	Ramon Caraballo	.10
188	David Nied	.10
189	Don Strange	.10
190	Chipper Jones	6.00
191	Troy Hughes	.10
192	Don Robinson	.10
193	Lance Marks	.10
194	Manuel Jimenez	.10
195	Tony Graffagnino (Graffanino)	.10
196	Brad Woodall	.10
197	Kevin Grijak	.10
198	Darin Paulino	.10
199	Lance Dickson	.15
200	Rey Sanchez	.10
201	Elvin Paulino	.10
202	Alex Arias	.15
203	Fernando Ramsey	.10
204	Pete Castellano	.10
205	Ryan Hawblitzel	.10
206	John Jensen	.10
207	Jerrone Williams	.10
208	Earl Cunningham	.10
209	Phil Dauphin	.10
210	Doug Glanville	.15
211	Jim Robinson	.10
212	Ken Arnold	.10
213	Reggie Jefferson	.10
214	Reggie Sanders	.50
215	Mo Sanford	.30
216	Steve Foster	.10
217	Dan Wilson	.15
218	John Roper	.10
219	Trevor Hoffman	.35
220	Calvin Reese	.15
221	John Hrusovsky	.10
222	Andy Mota	.10
223	Kenny Lofton	4.00
224	Andujar Cedeno	.10
225	Ryan Bowen	.15
226	Jeff Juden	.20
227	Chris Gardner	.10
228	Brian Williams	.10
229	Ed Ponte	.10
230	Chris Hatcher	.10
231	Fletcher Thompson	.10
232	Wally Trice	.10
233	Donne Wall	.10
234	Tom Nevers	.10
235	Jim Daugherty	.10
236	Mark Loughlin	.10
237	Jose Offerman	.15
238	Dave Hansen	.15
239	Carlos Hernandez	.10
240	Eric Karros	1.00
241	Henry Rodriguez	.30
242	Jamie McAndrew	.10
243	Tom Goodwin	.20
244	Pedro Martinez	1.00
245	Braulio Castillo	.15
246	Matt Howard	.10
247	Michael Mimbs	.10
248	Murph Proctor	.10
249	Vernon Spearman	.10
250	Jason Kerr	.10
251	Mike Sharp	.10
252	Pedro Osuna	.10
253	Doug Piatt	.10
254	Wil Cordero	.45
255	John VanderWal	.10
256	Bret Barberie	.10
257	Todd Haney	.10
258	Chris Haney	.10
259	Matt Stairs	.50
260	David Wainhouse	.10
261	Bob Natal	.10
262	Rob Katzaroff	.10
263	Willie Greene	.15
264	Reid Cornelius	.10
265	Glenn Murray	.10
266	Rondell White	1.50
267	Tavo Alvarez	.10
268	Gabe White	.15
269	Brian Looney	.10
270	Checklist 181-270	.10
271	Derrick White	.10
272	Heath Haynes	.10
273	Mike Daniel	.10
274	Jim Austin	.10
275	Chris Donnels	.10
276	Julio Valera	.10
277	Todd Hundley	.75
278	Anthony Young	.10
279	Jeff Gardner	.10
280	Jeromy Burnitz	.20
281	Tito Navarro	.10
282	D.J. Dozier	.10
283	Julian Vasquez	.10
284	Pat Howell	.10
285	Brook Fordyce	.10
286	Todd Douma	.10
287	Jose Martinez	.10
288	Ricky Otero	.20
289	Quilvio Veras	.20
290	Joe Crawford	.10
291	Todd Fiegel	.10
292	Jason Jacome	.10
293	Kim Batiste	.15
294	Andy Ashby	.30
295	Wes Chamberlain	.15
296	Dave Hollins	.40
297	Tony Longmire	.15
298	Nikco Riesgo	.10
299	Cliff Brantley	.15
300	Troy Paulsen	.10
301	Elliott Gray	.10
302	Mike Lieberthal	.20
303	Tyler Green	.20
304	Dan Brown	.10
305	Carlos Garcia	.20
306	John Wehner	.15
307	Paul Miller	.10
308	Tim Wakefield	.15
309	Kurt Miller	.10
310	Joe Sondrini	.10
311	Hector Fajardo	.10
312	Scott Bullett	.10
313	Jon Farrell	.10
314	Marc Pisciotta	.10
315	Rheal Cormier	.10
316	Omar Olivares	.10
317	Donovan Osborne	.10
318	Clyde Keller	.10
319	John Kelly	.10
320	Terry Bradshaw	.10
321	Brian Eversgerd	.10
322	Dmitri Young	.30
323	Eddie Williams	.10
324	Brian Barber	.15
325	Andy Bruce	.10
326	Tom McKinnon	.10
327	Jamie Cochran	.10
328	Steve Jones	.10
329	Jerry Santos	.10
330	Allen Watson	.15
331	John Mabry	.15
332	Jose Melendez	.10
333	Dave Staton	.20
334	Frank Seminara	.10
335	Matt Mieske	.15
336	Jay Gaines	.10
337	J.D. Noland	.10
338	Roberto Arredondo	.10
339	Lance Painter	.10
340	Darren Lewis	.40
341	Ted Wood	.10
342	Johnny Ard	.10
343	Royce Clayton	.35
344	Paul McClellan	.10
345	John Patterson	.10
346	Steve Hosey	.10
347	Larry Carter	.10
348	Juan Guerrero	.10
349	Bryan Hickerson	.10
350	Rich Huisman	.10
351	Kevin McGehee	.10
352	Gary Sharko	.10
353	Salomon Torres	.10
354	Eric Christopherson	.10
355	Rod Huffman	.10
356	Bill VanLandingham	.10
357	Frank Charles	.10
358	Ken Grundt	.10
359	Matt Brewer	.10
360	Checklist 271-360	.10

1991 Minor League Team Sets

The number of independently (team, or card dealer) sponsored team sets continued to decline in 1991, leaving ProCards to slug it out with Classic Best, the new kid on the block created when Best sold out to Classic Games. In these listings, abbreviations include: BK (Burger King), Cal (California League), CB (Classic Best), DD (Dunkin' Donuts), MB (Merchants Bank), PC (ProCards), and SP (Sport Pro).

	MT
280 team sets and variations	
1991 PC AAA All-Stars (55)	11.00
1991 Kraft Albany Yankees (6)	12.50
1991 PC Albany Yankees (28)	5.00
1991 PC Albuquerque Dukes (27)	9.00
1991 Team Albuquerque Dukes (41)	165.00
1991 CB Appleton Foxes (30)	6.00
1991 PC Appleton Foxes (28)	3.00
1991 PC Arkansas Travelers (29)	3.00
1991 CB Asheville Tourists (30)	6.00
1991 PC Asheville Tourists (29)	3.00
1991 CB Auburn Astros (30)	5.00
1991 PC Auburn Astros (26)	6.00
1991 CB Augusta Pirates (30)	6.00
1991 PC Augusta Pirates (31)	3.00
1991 Cal Bakersfield Dodgers (32)	35.00
1991 CB Baseball City Royals (30)	5.00
1991 PC Baseball City Royals (29)	6.00
1991 CB Batavia Clippers (30)	5.00
1991 PC Batavia Clippers (30)	5.00
1991 CB Bellingham Mariners (30)	6.00
1991 PC Bellingham Mariners (32)	3.00
1991 CB Beloit Brewers (30)	6.00
1991 PC Beloit Brewers (28)	3.00
1991 CB Bend Bucks (29)	6.00
1991 PC Bend Bucks (29)	3.00
1991 PC Billings Mustangs (28)	3.00
1991 SP Billings Mustangs (30)	5.00
1991 PC Birmingham Barons (28)	6.00
1991 CB Bluefield Orioles (30)	6.00
1991 PC Bluefield Orioles (26)	5.00
1991 CB Boise Hawks (30)	6.00
1991 PC Boise Hawks (35)	3.00
1991 CB Bristol Tigers (30)	6.00
1991 PC Bristol Tigers (30)	3.00
1991 PC Buffalo Bisons (26)	3.00
1991 Team Buffalo Bisons (27)	6.00
1991 CB Burlington Astros (30)	6.00
1991 PC Burlington Astros (28)	6.00
1991 PC Burlington Indians (34)	20.00
1991 SP Butte Copper Kings (30)	8.00
1991 SP Butte Copper Kings update (2)	2.00
1991 PC Calgary Cannons (25)	6.00
1991 Cal League All-Stars (56)	12.00
1991 PC Canton-Akron Indians (28)	8.00
1991 PC Carolina League A-S (47)	8.50
1991 PC Carolina Mudcats (26)	6.00
1991 CB Cedar Rapids Reds (30)	3.00
1991 PC Cedar Rapids Reds (30)	6.00
1991 CB Charleston Rainbows (30)	6.00
1991 PC Charleston Rainbows (27)	3.00
1991 CB Charleston Wheelers (30)	6.00
1991 PC Charleston Wheelers (27)	6.00
1991 PC Charlotte Knights (26)	6.00
1991 CB Charlotte Rangers (30)	6.50
1991 PC Charlotte Rangers (28)	6.50
1991 PC Chattanooga Lookouts (27)	5.50
1991 CB Clearwater Phillies (30)	6.00
1991 PC Clearwater Phillies (29)	3.00
1991 CB Clinton Giants (30)	5.00
1991 PC Clinton Giants (29)	5.00
1991 PC Colorado Springs Sky Sox (28)	6.00
1991 Play II Columbia Mets (32)	17.50
1991 Play II Columbia Mets postcards (28)	24.00
1991 PC Columbus Clippers (29)	6.00

1991 Police Columbus Clippers (24)	6.50
1991 CB Columbus Indians (30)	5.00
1991 PC Columbus Indians (32)	3.00
1991 PC Denver Zephyrs (27)	6.00
1991 CB Dunedin Blue Jays (30)	5.00
1991 PC Dunedin Blue Jays (29)	5.00
1991 CB Durham Bulls (30)	10.00
1991 PC Durham Bulls (33)	9.00
1991 PC Durham Bulls update (9)	6.00
1991 PC Edmonton Trappers (28)	5.00
1991 PC Elizabethton Twins (26)	3.00
1991 CB Elmira Pioneers (30)	7.50
1991 PC Elmira Pioneers (29)	5.00
1991 PC El Paso Diablos (26)	5.00
1991 Team El Paso Diablos All-Time (45)	35.00
1991 CB Erie Sailors (30)	6.00
1991 PC Erie Sailors (30)	3.00
1991 CB Eugene Emeralds (30)	5.00
1991 PC Eugene Emeralds (30)	5.00
1991 CB Everett Giants (30)	6.00
1991 PC Everett Giants (33)	6.00
1991 CB Fayetteville Generals (30)	6.00
1991 PC Fayetteville Generals (29)	6.00
1991 PC Florida State League A-S (46)	6.00
1991 CB Frederick Keys (30)	6.00
1991 PC Frederick Keys (29)	5.00
1991 CB Ft. Lauderdale Yankees (30)	6.00
1991 PC Ft. Lauderdale Yankees (31)	3.00
1991 CB Gastonia Rangers (30)	7.50
1991 PC Gastonia Rangers (31)	6.00
1991 CB Geneva Cubs (30)	5.00
1991 PC Geneva Cubs (30)	6.00
1991 SP Great Falls Dodgers (30)	7.50
1991 PC Greensboro Hornets (29)	7.50
1991 CB Greenville Braves (30)	10.00
1991 PC Greenville Braves (27)	9.00
1991 SP Gulf Coast Rangers (30)	5.00
1991 PC Hagerstown Suns (28)	6.00
1991 CB Hamilton Redbirds (30)	7.50
1991 PC Hamilton Redbirds (33)	7.00
1991 PC Harrisburg Senators (29)	5.00
1991 SP Helena Brewers (30)	9.00
1991 CB High Desert Mavericks (30)	6.00
1991 PC High Desert Mavericks (32)	6.00
1991 Little Sun High School Prospects (36)	12.00
1991 LS High School Prospects - gold (36)	22.00
1991 CB Huntington Cubs (30)	6.00
1991 PC Huntington Cubs (32)	3.00
1991 BK Huntsville Stars (26)	5.00
1991 CB Huntsville Stars (30)	6.00
1991 PC Huntsville Stars (26)	6.00
1991 PC Idaho Falls Braves (29)	5.00
1991 SP Idaho Falls Braves (30)	6.00
1991 PC Indianapolis Indians (28)	6.00
1991 PC Iowa Cubs (26)	5.00
1991 PC Jackson Generals (28)	5.00
1991 PC Jacksonville Suns (29)	6.00
1991 CB Jamestown Expos (30)	9.00
1991 PC Jamestown Expos (29)	7.00
1991 CB Johnson City Cardinals (30)	12.00
1991 PC Johnson City Cardinals (29)	9.00
1991 CB Kane County Cougars (30)	7.50
1991 PC Kane County Cougars (28)	3.00
1991 Team Kane County Cougars (27)	6.00
1991 CB Kenosha Twins (30)	5.00
1991 PC Kenosha Twins (28)	5.00
1991 CB Kingsport Mets (30)	5.00
1991 PC Kingsport Mets (28)	6.00
1991 CB Kinston Indians (31)	6.00
1991 PC Kinston Indians (31)	6.00
1991 PC Kissimmee Dodgers (32)	7.00
1991 PC Knoxville Blue Jays (28)	6.00
1991 CB Lakeland Tigers (30)	6.00
1991 PC Lakeland Tigers (29)	3.00
1991 PC Las Vegas Stars (31)	5.00
1991 PC London Tigers (26)	3.00
1991 PC Louisville Redbirds (29)	7.00
1991 Team Louisville Redbirds (34)	9.00
1991 CB Lynchburg Red Sox (30)	6.00
1991 PC Lynchburg Red Sox (28)	3.00
1991 CB Macon Braves (30)	50.00
1991 PC Macon Braves (31)	20.00
1991 CB Madison Muskies (30)	6.00
1991 PC Madison Muskies (27)	3.00
1991 CB Martinsville Phillies (30)	6.00
1991 PC Martinsville Phillies (31)	3.00
1991 PC Medicine Hat Blue Jays (31)	6.00
1991 SP Medicine Hat Blue Jays (30)	7.00
1991 SP Memphis Chicks (27)	6.00
1991 CB Miami Miracle (30)	6.00
1991 PC Miami Miracle (30)	3.00
1991 GS Midland Angels (1)	3.00
1991 1 Hour Midland Angels (32)	65.00
1991 PC Midland Angels (27)	8.00
1991 PC Midwest League A-S (51)	8.00
1991 CB Modesto A's (28)	6.00
1991 Chong Modesto A's (35)	6.00
1991 PC Modesto A's (30)	3.00
1991 CB Myrtle Beach Hurricanes (30)	10.00
1991 PC Myrtle Beach Hurricanes (30)	7.50
1991 PC Nashville Sounds (27)	6.00
1991 Team Nashville Sounds (34)	7.00
1991 PC New Britain Red Sox (26)	6.00
1991 CB Niagara Falls Rapids (30)	9.00
1991 PC Niagara Falls Rapids (30)	6.00
1991 PC Oklahoma City 89ers (27)	5.00
1991 PC Omaha Royals (26)	7.00
1991 PC Oneonta Yankees (27)	6.00
1991 PC Orlando Sun Rays (28)	6.00
1991 CB Osceola Astros (30)	7.50
1991 PC Osceola Astros (29)	6.00
1991 PC Palm Springs Angels (30)	5.00
1991 DD Pawtucket Red Sox foldout	60.00
1991 PC Pawtucket Red Sox (27)	8.00
1991 Team Peninsula Oilers (30)	7.00
1991 CB Peninsula Pilots (29)	6.00
1991 PC Peninsula Pilots (28)	3.00
1991 CB Peoria Chiefs (30)	6.00
1991 PC Peoria Chiefs (29)	6.00
1991 Team Peoria Chiefs (34)	6.00
1991 PC Phoenix Firebirds (29)	6.00
1991 CB Pittsfield Mets (29)	6.00
1991 PC Pittsfield Mets (28)	5.00
1991 PC Pocatello Pioneers (31)	3.00
1991 SP Pocatello Pioneers (30)	6.00
1991 PC Portland Beavers (28)	6.00
1991 CB Princeton Reds (30)	6.00
1991 PC Princeton Reds (30)	6.00
1991 CB Prince Williams Cannons (30)	5.00
1991 PC Prince Williams Cannons (29)	5.00
1991 CB Pulaski Braves (30)	6.00
1991 PC Pulaski Braves (31)	3.00
1991 CB Quad City Angels (30)	9.00
1991 PC Quad City Angels (31)	8.00
1991 PC Reading Phillies (27)	3.00
1991 Cal Reno Silver Sox (29)	3.00
1991 Bob's Richmond Braves (42)	75.00
1991 PC Richmond Braves (30)	4.50
1991 Ukrop's Richmond Braves (28)	22.00
1991 PC Rochester Red Wings (27)	6.00
1991 Team Rochester Red Wings foldout	60.00
1991 CB Rockford Expos (30)	6.00
1991 PC Rockford Expos (29)	3.00
1991 CB Salem Buccaneers (27)	6.00
1991 PC Salem Buccaneers (27)	3.00
1991 CB Salinas Spurs (30)	6.00
1991 PC Salinas Spurs (31)	3.00
1991 PC Salt Lake City Trappers (30)	6.00
1991 SP Salt Lake City Trappers (30)	6.50
1991 HEB San Antonio Missions (32)	65.00
1991 PC San Antonio Missions (30)	7.00
1991 CB San Bernardino Spirit (29)	8.00
1991 PC San Bernardino Spirit (29)	7.00
1991 CB San Jose Giants (30)	6.00
1991 PC San Jose Giants (30)	3.00
1991 CB Sarasota White Sox (30)	5.00
1991 PC Sarasota White Sox (30)	6.00
1991 CB Savannah Cardinals (30)	6.00
1991 PC Savannah Cardinals (29)	6.00
1991 PC Scranton Red Barons (29)	7.00
1991 PC Shreveport Captains (28)	6.00
1991 PC South Atlantic League A-S (48)	15.00
1991 CB South Bend White Sox (30)	6.00
1991 PC South Bend White Sox (30)	5.00
1991 CB Southern Oregon A's (30)	5.00
1991 PC Southern Oregon A's (37)	6.00
1991 PC Southern Oregon's A's Alumni (36)	7.00
1991 CB Spartanburg Phillies (30)	6.00
1991 PC Spartanburg Phillies (30)	3.00
1991 CB Spokane Indians (30)	6.00
1991 PC Spokane Indians (31)	3.00
1991 CB Springfield Cardinals (30)	6.00
1991 PC Springfield Cardinals (31)	3.00
1991 CB St. Catherines Blue Jays (30)	6.00
1991 PC St. Catherines Blue Jays (28)	6.00
1991 CB St. Lucie Mets (30)	6.00
1991 PC St. Lucie Mets (28)	5.00
1991 CB St. Petersburg Cardinals (30)	6.00
1991 PC St. Petersburg Cardinals (30)	6.00
1991 CB Stockton Ports (30)	6.00
1991 PC Stockton Ports (27)	3.00
1991 CB Sumter Flyers (30)	10.00
1991 PC Sumter Flyers (31)	7.50
1991 Kraft Syracuse Chiefs (5)	15.00
1991 MB Syracuse Chiefs foldout	22.00
1991 PC Syracuse Chiefs (25)	6.00
1991 PC Tacoma Tigers (29)	6.00
1991 Team Tampa Yankees (33)	5.00
1991 PC Tidewater Tides (30)	5.00
1991 PC Toledo Mudhens (28)	6.00
1991 PC Tucson Toros (28)	8.00
1991 PC Tulsa Drillers (27)	8.00
1991 Team Tulsa Drillers (30)	20.00
1991 CB Utica Blue Sox (30)	9.00
1991 PC Utica Blue Sox (29)	5.00
1991 PC Vancouver Canadians (27)	6.00
1991 CB Vero Beach Dodgers (30)	7.50
1991 PC Vero Beach Dodgers (33)	7.00
1991 CB Visalia Oaks (28)	8.00
1991 PC Visalia Oaks (25)	5.00
1991 CB Waterloo Diamonds (30)	6.00
1991 PC Waterloo Diamonds (29)	3.00
1991 CB Watertown Indians (30)	6.00
1991 PC Watertown Indians (31)	3.00
1991 CB Welland Pirates (30)	6.00
1991 PC Welland Pirates (31)	3.00
1991 CB West Palm Beach Expos (30)	5.00
1991 PC West Palm Beach Expos (30)	6.00
1991 PC Wichita Wranglers (28)	6.00
1991 Rock's Wichita Wranglers - hor. (27)	6.00
1991 Rock's Wichita Wranglers - vert. (29)	6.00
1991 PC Williamsport Bills (27)	5.00
1991 CB Winston-Salem Spirits (30)	5.00
1991 PC Winston-Salem Spirits (28)	6.00
1991 CB Winter Haven Red Sox (30)	6.00
1991 PC Winter Haven Red Sox (27)	3.00
1991 CB Yakima Bears (30)	6.00
1991 PC Yakima Bears (30)	3.00

1992 Classic Best

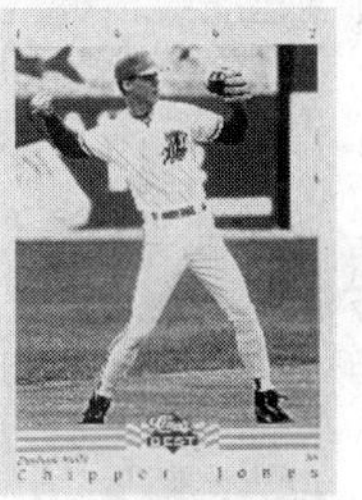

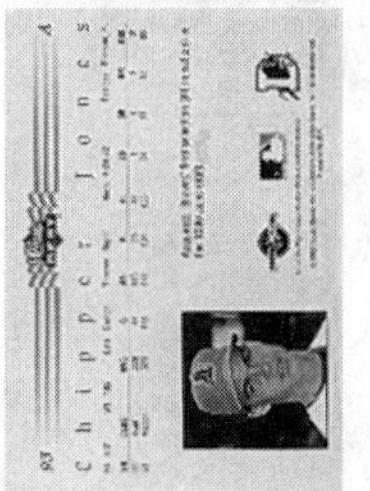

This 400-card wax pack set has an All-American look, with a red, white and blue card design. A banner beneath the photo has the player's name, team and position. On back the player's name is stretched horizontally near the top, and there is a portrait photo. A factory set was issued which includes 50 cards not found in wax packs. Autographed cards of five stars and prospects were included as random wax pack inserts, while the Clayton autograph card was found exclusively in jumbo packs.

		MT
Complete Set (400):		15.00
Complete Factory Set (450):		20.00
Common Player:		.05
1	Nolan Ryan	3.00
2	Darius Gash	.05
3	Brad Ausmus	.10
4	Mike Gardella	.05
5	Mark Hutton	.05
6	Bobby Munoz	.10
7	Don Sparks	.05
8	Shane Andrews	.15
9	Gary Hymel	.05
10	Roberto Arredondo	.05
11	Joe Randa	.10
12	Pedro Grifol	.05
13	Steve Dixon	.05
14	John Thomas	.05
15	Chris Durkin	.05
16	Jeff Conger	.05
17	Jon Farrell	.05
18	Antonio Mitchell	.05
19	Matt Ruebel	.05
20	Darren Burton	.05
21	Lance Jennings	.05
22	Kerwin Moore	.05
23	Julio Bruno	.05
24	Joe Vitiello	.15
25	Brook Fordyce	.05
26	Rob Katzaroff	.05
27	Julian Vasquez	.05
28	Alan Zinter	.05
29	Clemente Alvarez	.05
30	Scott Cepicky	.05
31	Mike Mongiello	.05
32	Tom Redington	.05
33	Johnny Ruffin	.10
34	Eric Booker	.05
35	Manny Martinez	.05
36	Mike Grimes	.05
37	Paul Byrd	.10
38	Brian Giles	.10
39	David Mlicki	.10
40	Tracy Sanders	.05
41	Kyle Washington	.05
42	Scott Bullett	.10
43	Steve Cooke	.15
44	Austin Manahan	.05
45	Ben Shelton	.10
46	Joe DeBerry	.05
47	Steve Gibralter	.10
48	Willie Greene	.20
49	Brian Koelling	.05
50	Larry Luebbers	.05
51	Greg "Pepper" Anthony	.05
52	Homer Bush	.10
53	Manny Cora	.05
54	Joey Hamilton	.40
55	David Mowry	.05
56	Bobby Perna	.05
57	Jamie Dismuke	.05
58	Kenneth Gillum	.05
59	Calvin Reese	.15
60	Phil Dauphin	.10
61	Ryan Hawblitzel	.10
62	Tim Parker	.05
63	Dave Swartzbaugh	.05
64	Billy White	.05
65	Terry Burrows	.05
66	Chris Gies	.05
67	Kurt Miller	.05
68	Timmie Morrow	.05
69	Benny Colvard	.05
70	Tim Costo	.10
71	Mica Lewis	.05
72	John Roper	.10
73	Kevin Tatar	.05
74	Joel Adamson	.05
75	Mike Farmer	.05
76	Kevin Stocker	.10
77	David Tokheim	.05
78	Ray Jackson	.05
79	Dax Jones	.05
80	Randy Curtis	.05
81	Eric Reichenbach	.05
82	Jerome Tolliver	.05
83	Quilvio Veras	.15
84	George Evangelista	.05
85	Pat Bryant	.05
86	Willie Canate	.05
87	Brian Lane	.05
88	Howard Battle	.10
89	Rob Butler	.10
90	Carlos Delgado	1.00
91	Tyler Houston	.10

92	Troy Hughes	.05
93	Chipper Jones	4.00
94	Mel Nieves	.10
95	Jose Olmeda	.10
96	John Finn	.05
97	Mike Guerrero	.05
98	Troy O'Leary	.10
99	Ben Blomdahl	.05
100	Mike Schmidt	1.00
101	Carlos Burguillos	.05
102	Kiki Hernandez	.05
103	Brian Dubose	.05
104	Kevin Morgan	.05
105	Justin Thompson	.50
106	Jason Alstead	.05
107	Matt Anderson	.10
108	Brad Pennington	.10
109	Brad Tyler	.05
110	Jovino Carvajal	.05
111	Roger Luce	.05
112	Ken Powell	.05
113	Steve Sadecki	.05
114	Craig Clayton	.05
115	Russell Davis	.20
116	Mike Kelly	.10
117	Javier Lopez	1.50
118	Doug Piatt	.05
119	Manny Alexander	.10
120	Damon Buford	.10
121	Erik Schullstrom	.05
122	Mark Smith	.10
123	Jeff Williams	.05
124	Reid Cornelius	.10
125	Tim Laker	.10
126	Chris Martin	.05
127	Mike Mathile	.05
128	Derrick White	.05
129	Luis Galindez	.05
130	John Kuehl	.05
131	Ray McDavid	.10
132	Sean Mulligan	.05
133	Tookie Spann	.05
134	Marcos Armas	.05
135	Scott Erwin	.05
136	Johnny Guzman	.05
137	Mike Mohler	.05
138	Craig Paquette	.05
139	Dean Tatarian	.05
140	Orlando Miller	.15
141	Tow Maynard	.05
142	Marc Newfield	.10
143	Greg Pirkl	.05
144	Jesus Tavarez	.05
145	Tom Smith	.05
146	Brad Seitzer	.05
147	Brent Brede	.05
148	Elston Hansen	.05
149	Jamie Ogden	.05
150	Rogelio Nunez	.05
151	Manny Cervantes	.05
152	David Sartain	.05
153	Shawn Bryant	.05
154	Chad Ogea	.35
155	Manny Ramirez	4.00
156	Darrell Whitmore	.05
157	Greg O'Halloran	.05
158	Tim Brown	.05
159	Curtis Pride	.10
160	Marcus Moore	.05
161	Robert Perez	.05
162	Aaron Small	.05
163	David Tollison	.05
164	Nigel Wilson	.05
165	Jim Givens	.05
166	Dennis McNamara	.05
167	Kelley O'Neal	.05
168	Rudy Pemberton	.05
169	Joe Perona	.05
170	Brian Cornelius	.05
171	Ivan Cruz	.05
172	Frank Gonzales	.05
173	Mike Lumley	.05
174	Brian Warren	.05
175	Aaron Sele	.40
176	Gary Caraballo	.05
177	Creighton Gubanich	.05
178	Brad Parker	.05
179	Scott Sheldon	.15
180	Archie Corbin	.05
181	Phil Hiatt	.10
182	Domingo Mota	.05
183	Dan Carlson	.05
184	Hugh Walker	.05
185	Joe Ciccarella	.05
186	John Jackson	.05
187	Brent Gates	.20
188	Eric Helfand	.10
189	Damon Mashore	.10
190	Malcolm (Curtis) Shaw	.05
191	Jason Wood	.05
192	Terry Powers	.05
193	Steve Karsay	.15
194	Greg Blosser	.10
195	Gar Finnvold	.05
196	Scott Hatteberg	.10
197	Derek Livernois	.05
198	Jeff McNeely	.10
199	Rex DeLaNuez	.05
200	Ken Griffey Jr.	4.00
201	Pat Meares	.10
202	Alan Newman	.05
203	Paul Russo	.05
204	Anthony Collier	.05
205	Roberto Petagine	.05
206	Brian Hunter	.75
207	James Mouton	.05
208	Tom Nevers	.10
209	Garret Anderson	.30
210	Clifton Garrett	.05
211	Eduardo Perez	.10
212	Shawn Purdy	.05
213	Darren Bragg	.05
214	Glenn Murray	.05
215	Ruben Santana	.05
216	Bubba Smith	.05
217	Terry Adams	.05
218	William (Bill) Bliss	.05
219	German Diaz	.05
220	Willie Gardner	.05
221	Ed Larregui	.05
222	Tim Garland	.05
223	Kevin Jordan	.05
224	Tim Rumer	.05
225	Jason Robertson	.05
226	Todd Claus	.05
227	Julian Heredia	.05
228	Mark Sweeney	.10
229	Robert Eenhoorn	.05
230	Tyler Green	.15
231	Mike Lieberthal	.15
232	Ron Lockett	.05
233	Tom Nuneviller	.05
234	Sean Ryan	.05
235	Alvaro Benavides	.05
236	Kevin Bellomo	.05
237	Tony Bridges	.05
238	Eric Whitford	.05
239	James Bishop	.05
240	Midre Cummings	.15
241	Tom Green	.05
242	Marcus Hanel	.05
243	Billy Ashley	.10
244	Matt Howard	.05
245	Tommy Adams	.05
246	Craig Bryant	.05
247	Ron Pezzoni	.05
248	Barry Miller	.05
249	Jason McFarlin	.05
250	Joe Rosselli	.05
251	Billy Van Landingham	.10
252	Chris Seelbach	.05
253	Jason Bere	.20
254	Eric Christopherson	.05
255	Rick Huisman	.05
256	Kevin McGehee	.05
257	Salomon Torres	.05
258	Brian Boehringer	.05
259	Glenn DiSarcina	.05
260	Jason Schmidt	.05
261	Charles Poe	.05
262	Ricky Bottalico	.15
263	Tommy Eason	.05
264	Joel Gilmore	.05
265	Pat Ruth	.05
266	Gene Schall	.10
267	Jim Campbell	.05
268	Brian Barber	.05
269	Allen Battle	.05
270	Marc Ronan	.05
271	Scott Simmons	.05
272	Dmitri Young	.15
273	Butch Huskey	.20
274	Frank Jacobs	.05
275	Aaron Ledesma	.05
276	Jose Martinez	.05
277	Andy Beasley	.05
278	Paul Ellis	.05
279	John Kelly	.05
280	Jeremy McGarity	.05
281	Mateo Ozuna	.05
282	Allen Watson	.10
283	Francisco Gamez	.05
284	Leon Glenn	.05
285	Duane Singleton	.05
286	Andy Pettitte	3.00
287	Donald Harris	.10
288	Robb Nen	.10
289	Jose Oliva	.05
290	Keith Garagozzo	.05
291	Dan Smith	.05
292	Kiki Jones	.05
293	Rich Becker	.25
294	Mike Durant	.05
295	Denny Hocking	.05
296	Mike Lewis	.05
297	Troy Ricker	.05
298	Todd Ritchie	.10
299	Scott Stahoviak	.10
300	Brien Taylor	.10
301	Jim Austin	.05
302	Mike Daniel	.05
303	Joseph Eischen	.10
304	Ranbir Grewal	.05
305	Rondell White (photo actually Glenn Murray)	.75
306	Mark Hubbard	.05
307	Tate Seefried	.15
308	Tom Wilson	.05
309	Benji Gil	.15
310	Mike Edwards	.05
311	J.D. Noland	.05
312	Jay Gainer	.05
313	Lance Painter	.05
314	Tim Worell	.05
315	Sean Cheetham	.05
316	Earl Cunningham	.05
317	Brad Erdman	.05
318	Paul Torres	.05
319	Jose Vierra	.05
320	Chris Gambs	.05
321	Brandon Wilson	.05
322	Brett Donovan	.05
323	Larry Thomas	.05
324	Brian Griffiths	.05
325	Chad Schoenvogel	.05
326	Mandy Romero	.05
327	Chris Curtis	.05
328	Jim Campanis	.05
329	Anthony Manahan	.05
330	Jason Townley	.05
331	Fidel Compres	.05
332	John Ericks	.05
333	Don Prybylinski	.05
334	Jason Best	.05
335	Rob Wishnevski	.05
336	John Byington	.05
337	Omar Garcia	.05
338	Tony Eusebio	.10
339	Paul Swingle	.05
340	Mark Zappelli	.05
341	Bobby Jones	.50
342	J.R. Phillips	.10
343	Jim Edmonds	1.00
344	Greg Hansell	.05
345	Mike Piazza	4.00
346	Mike Busch	.05
347	Darrell Sherman	.10
348	Shawn Green	.10
349	Willie Mota	.05
350	David McCarty	.05
351	James Dougherty	.05
352	Fernando Vina	.20
353	Ken Huckaby	.05
354	Joe Vitko	.05
355	Roberto (Diaz) Mejia	.05
356	Willis Otanez	.05
357	Billy Lott	.05
358	Jason Pruitt	.05
359	Jorge Fabregas	.10
360	Mike Stefanski	.05
361	Robert Saitz	.05
362	Scott Talanoa	.05
363	LaRue Baber	.05
364	Tyrone Hill	.05
365	Rick Mediavilla	.05
366	Eddie Williams	.05
367	Rigo Beltran	.05
368	Doug VanderWeele	.05
369	Donnie Elliott	.05
370	Dan Cholowsky	.05
371	Derrell Rumsey	.05
372	Anthony Graffagnino (Graffanino)	.05
373	Scott Ruffcorn	.10
374	Mike Rossiter	.05
375	Mike Robertson	.05
376	P.J. Forbes	.05
377	Doug Brady	.05
378	Rick Clelland	.05
379	Ugueth Urbina	.25
380	Cliff Floyd	.45
381	Danny Young	.05
382	Eddie Ramos	.05
383	Bob Abreu	.75
384	Gary Mota	.05
385	Tony Womack	.45
386	Jeff Motuzas	.05
387	Desi Relaford	.10
388	John Elerman	.05
389	Walt McKeel	.05
390	Tim VanEgmond	.05
391	Frank Rodriguez	.15
392	Paul Carey	.10
393	Michael Matheny	.10
394	George Glinatsis	.05
395	Checklist (1-69)	.05
396	Checklist (70-138)	.05
397	Checklist (139-207)	.05
398	Checklist (208-276)	.05
399	Checklist (277-345)	.05
400	Checklist (346-400)	.05
401	Paul Shuey	.10
402	Derek Jeter	4.00
403	Derek Wallace	.10
404	Sean Lowe	.10
405	Jim Pittsley	.05
406	Shannon Stewart	.10
407	Jamie Arnold	.10
408	Jason Kendall	.50
409	Eddie Pearson	.05
410	Todd Steverson	.10
411	Dan Serafini	.10
412	John Burke	.05
413	Jeff Schmidt	.05
414	Sherard Clinkscales	.05
415	Shon Walker	.10
416	Brandon Cromer	.10
417	Johnny Damon	.50
418	Michael Moore	.05
419	Michael Matthews	.05
420	Brian Sackinsky	.05
421	Jon Lieber	.10
422	Danny Clyburn	.10
423	Chris Smith	.05
424	Dwain Bostic	.05
425	Bob Wolcott	.05
426	Mike Gulan	.05
427	Yuri Sanchez	.05
428	Tony Sheffield	.05
429	Ritchie Moody	.05
430	Andy Hartung	.05
431	Trey Beamon	.15
432	Tim Crabtree	.10
433	Mark Thompson	.05
434	John Lynch	.05
439	Tavo Alvarez	.10
441	Troy Penix	.05
442	Scott Pose	.10
447	Jesus Martinez	.05
449	Chad Fonville	.10

Autographs:

(1)	Ken Griffey, Jr. (edition of 3,100)	200.00
(2)	David McCarty (1,000)	15.00
(3)	Nolan Ryan (3,100)	200.00
(4)	Mike Schmidt (4,100)	75.00
(5)	Brien Taylor (3,100)	15.00
(6)	Royce Clayton (2,000)	15.00

1992 Classic Best Blue Bonus

These bonus cards were randomly inserted into 1992 Classic Best white jumbo packs, one per pack. Cards are numbered with a BC prefix. Format is similar to the regular cards, with the presence on front of blue foil.

		MT
Complete Set (30):		30.00
Common Player:		.25
1	Nolan Ryan	5.00
2	Mark Hutton	.25
3	Shane Andrews	.25
4	Scott Bullett	.25
5	Kurt Miller	.25
6	Carlos Delgado	1.00
7	Chipper Jones	8.00
8	Dmitri Young	.75
9	Mike Kelly	.25
10	Javy Lopez	3.00
11	Aaron Sele	.75
12	Ken Griffey, Jr.	6.00
13	Midre Cummings	.50
14	Salomon Torres	.25
15	Brien Taylor	.50
16	Mike Piazza	8.00
17	David McCarty	.25
18	Scott Ruffcorn	.25
19	Cliff Floyd	1.00
20	Frankie Rodriguez	.35
21	Paul Shuey	.25
22	Derek Jeter	8.00
23	Derek Wallace	.25
24	Shannon Stewart	.25
25	Jamie Arnold	.25
26	Jason Kendall	1.50
27	Todd Steverson	.25
28	Dan Serafini	.25
29	John Burke	.25
30	Michael Moore	.25
1	Royce Clayton (Autograph)	40.00

1992 Classic Best Red Bonus

The red bonus cards were randomly inserted in 1992 Classic Best black jumbo packs, one per pack. Cards are numbered with a BC prefix, and feature red-foil graphic highlights on front.

		MT
Complete Set (20):		15.00
Common Player:		.25
1	Nolan Ryan	3.00
2	Mark Hutton	.25
3	Shane Andrews	.25
4	Scott Bullett	.25
5	Kurt Miller	.25
6	Carlos Delgado	1.00
7	Chipper Jones	7.50
8	Dmitri Young	.50
9	Mike Kelly	.25
10	Javy Lopez	2.00
11	Aaron Sele	.60
12	Ken Griffey, Jr.	4.00
13	Midre Cummings	.35
14	Salomon Torres	.25
15	Brien Taylor	.45
16	Mike Piazza	7.50
17	David McCarty	.25
18	Scott Ruffcorn	.25
19	Cliff Floyd	.75
20	Frankie Rodriguez	.35

1992 Classic Draft Picks Previews

To introduce its coming baseball draft picks set, Classic inserted a series of preview cards in foil packs of its basketball draft picks product. Preview card fronts are similar to the issued version, with a large "PREVIEW" over the Classic logo at lower-left. Backs have a cartoon picture of a batter and an announcement that only 11,200 of each of the five preview cards were produced.

		MT
Complete Set (5):		7.50
Common Player:		1.50
BB1	Phil Nevin	1.50
BB2	Paul Shuey	1.50
BB3	B.J. Wallace	1.50
BB4	Jeffrey Hammonds	3.00
BB5	Chad Mottola	1.50

1992 Classic Draft Picks Promos

These promo cards were released in cello packs to premiere the '92 Classic Draft Picks issue. Cards are similar in design to the issued versions, with color photos front and back. Backs are marked "For Promotional Purposes Only".

		MT
Complete Set (3):		6.00
Common Player:		2.00
1	Jeffery Hammonds (Jeffrey)	2.00
2	Phil Nevin	2.00
3	Brien Taylor	3.00

1992 Classic Draft Picks

The top draft picks of 1992 are featured in this set, along with a Flashback subset (#86-95) of rising stars from the 1990-91 drafts. Cards were sold in 16-card foil packs including one foil bonus card. Fronts have a color action photo bordered in white with a dark green name stripe at bottom and the set logo at lower-left. Backs are in dark green with another photo and 1991-92 high school or college stats. Production was reported at 5,000 numbered cases.

		MT
Complete Set (125):		3.00
Common Player:		.05
1	Phil Nevin	.05
2	Paul Shuey	.05
3	B.J. Wallace	.05
4	Jeffrey Hammonds	.15
5	Chad Mottola	.05
6	Derek Jeter	2.00
7	Michael Tucker	.40
8	Derek Wallace	.05

9	Kenny Felder	.05
10	Chad McConnell	.05
11	Sean Lowe	.05
12	Ricky Greene	.05
13	Chris Roberts	.05
14	Shannon Stewart	.15
15	Benji Grigsby	.05
16	Jamie Arnold	.05
17	Rick Helling	.25
18	Jason Kendall	.50
19	Todd Steverson	.05
20	Dan Serafini	.05
21	Jeff Schmidt	.05
22	Sherard Clinkscales	.05
23	Ryan Luzinski	.05
24	Shon Walker	.05
25	Brandon Cromer	.10
26	Dave Landaker	.05
27	Michael Mathews	.05
28	Brian Sackinsky	.05
29	Jon Lieber	.05
30	Jim Rosenbohm	.05
31	De Shawn Warren	.05
32	Danny Clyburn	.05
33	Chris Smith	.05
34	Dwain Bostic	.05
35	Bobby Hughes	.25
36	Rick Magdellano	.05
37	Bob Wolcott	.05
38	Mike Gulan	.05
39	Yuri Sanchez	.05
40	Tony Sheffield	.05
41	Dan Melendez	.10
42	Jason Giambi	.25
43	Ritchie Moody	.05
44	Trey Beamon	.20
45	Tim Crabtree	.05
46	Chad Roper	.05
47	Mark Thompson	.10
48	Marquis Riley	.05
49	Tom Knauss	.05
50	Chris Holt	.05
51	Jonathan Nunnally	.15
52	Everett Stull	.05
53	Billy Owens	.05
54	Todd Etler	.05
55	Benji Simonton	.05
56	Dwight Maness	.05
57	Chris Eddy	.05
58	Brant Brown	.20
59	Trevor Humphrey	.05
60	Chris Widger	.05
61	Steve Montgomery	.05
62	Chris Gomez	.05
63	Jared Baker	.05
64	Doug Hecker	.05
65	David Spykstra	.05
66	Scott Miller	.05
67	Carey Paige	.05
68	Dave Manning	.05
69	James Keefe	.05
70	Levon Largusa	.05
71	Roger Bailey	.10
72	Rich Ireland	.05
73	Matt Williams	.05
74	Scott Gentile	.05
75	Hut Smith	.05
76	Rodney Henderson	.05
77	Mike Buddie	.05
78	Stephen Lyons	.05
79	John Burke	.05
80	Jim Pittsley	.05
81	Donnie Leshnock	.05
82	Cory Pearson	.05
83	Kurt Ehmann	.05
84	Bobby Bonds Jr.	.15
85	Steven Cox	.25
86	Brien Taylor (Flashback)	.10
87	Mike Kelly (Flashback)	.05
88	David McCarty (Flashback)	.05
89	Dmitri Young (Flashback)	.05
90	Joe Hamilton (Flashback)	.05
91	Mark Smith (Flashback)	.05
92	Doug Glanville (Flashback)	.05
93	Mike Lieberthal (Flashback)	.05
94	Joe Vitiello (Flashback)	.05
95	Mike Mussina (Flashback)	.25
96	Derek Hacopian	.05
97	Ted Corbin	.05
98	Carlton Fleming	.05
99	Aaron Rounsifer	.05
100	Chad Fox	.10
101	Chris Sheff	.05
102	Ben Jones	.05
103	David Post	.05
104	Jonnie Gendron	.05
105	Bob Juday	.05
106	David Becker	.05
107	Brandon Pico	.05
108	Tom Evans	.05
109	Jeff Faino	.05
110	Shawn Wills	.05
111	Derrick Cantrell	.05
112	Steve Rodriguez	.05
113	Ray Suplee	.05
114	Pat Leahy	.05
115	Matt Luke	.10
116	Jon McMullen	.05
117	Preston Wilson	.25
118	Gus Gandarillas	.05
119	Pete Janicki	.05
120	Byron Mathews	.05
121	Eric Owens	.05
122	John Lynch	.05
123	Mike Hickey	.05
124	Checklist 1	.05
125	Checklist 2	.05

1992 Classic Draft Picks Foil Bonus

Other than having their fronts printed on metallic foil and card numbers which are preceded by a "BC" prefix, these inserts are identical to the same players' cards in the regular Classic 1992 Draft Picks issue. One foil bonus card was included in each 16-card foil pack.

		MT
Complete Set (20):		8.00
Common Player:		.25
1	Phil Nevin	.25
2	Paul Shuey	.25
3	B.J. Wallace	.25
4	Jeffrey Hammonds	.50
5	Chad Mottola	.25
6	Derek Jeter	4.00
7	Michael Tucker	1.00
8	Derek Wallace	.25
9	Kenny Felder	.25
10	Chad McConnell	.25
11	Sean Lowe	.25
12	Chris Roberts	.25
13	Shannon Stewart	.25
14	Benji Grigsby	.25
15	Jamie Arnold	.25
16	Ryan Luzinski	.25
17	Bobby Bonds Jr.	.35
18	Brien Taylor	.40
19	Mike Kelly	.25
20	Mike Mussina	2.00

1992 Classic Four Sport Previews

Foil packs of Classic's baseball and hockey draft picks issues included randomly inserted previews of the Four Sport issue. Fronts of the promos are similar to the issued cards with full-bleed action photos and a vertical player identification strip at right. On these cards, a "PREVIEW" banner is printed above the Classic logo. Backs announce the debut of the Four Sport set and indicate the Preview card is one of an edition of 10,000 of each player. Only the single baseball player among the Preview cards is listed here.

		MT
4	Phil Nevin	1.00

1992 Classic Four Sport

The top draft picks of 1992 are featured in this set, along with a Flashback subset of rising stars. Fronts have a large borderless color action photo with a vertical strip at left featuring the player's name and position, with the Four Sport logo at top. Backs have another photo and 1991-92 high school or college stats. Production was reported at 40,000 cases. Only the baseball players are listed here.

		MT
Common Player:		.05
226	Phil Nevin	.10
227	Paul Shuey	.10
228	B.J. Wallace	.10
229	Jeffrey Hammonds	.25
230	Chad Mottola	.10
231	Derek Jeter	2.00
232	Michael Tucker	.75
233	Derek Wallace	.10
234	Kenny Felder	.05
235	Chad McConnell	.05
236	Sean Lowe	.05
237	Ricky Greene	.10
238	Chris Roberts	.05
239	Shannon Stewart	.10
240	Benji Grigsby	.05
241	Jamie Arnold	.05
242	Rick Helling	.10
243	Jason Kendall	.50
244	Todd Steverson	.10
245	Dan Serafini	.10
246	Jeff Schmidt	.05
247	Sherard Clinkscales	.05
248	Ryan Luzinski	.05
249	Shon Walker	.10
250	Brandon Cromer	.05
251	Dave Landaker	.05
252	Michael Mathews	.05
253	Brian Sackinsky	.05
254	Jon Lieber	.10
255	Jim Rosenbohm	.05
256	De Shawn Warren	.05
257	Danny Clyburn	.10
258	Chris Smith	.05
259	Dwain Bostic	.05
260	Bobby Hughes	.10
261	Rick Magdellano	.05
262	Bob Wolcott	.05
263	Mike Gulan	.05
264	Yuri Sanchez	.05
265	Tony Sheffield	.05
266	Dan Melendez	.05
267	Jason Giambi	.50
268	Ritchie Moody	.05
269	Trey Beamon	.10
270	Tim Crabtree	.10
271	Chad Roper	.05
272	Mark Thompson	.05
273	Marquis Riley	.05
274	Tom Knauss	.05
275	Chris Holt	.05
276	Jonathan Nunnally	.25
277	Everett Stull	.10
278	Billy Owens	.05
279	Todd Etler	.05
280	Benji Simonton	.05
281	Dwight Maness	.05
282	Chris Eddy	.05
283	Brant Brown	.40
284	Trevor Humphrey	.05
285	Chris Widger	.05
286	Steve Montgomery	.05
287	Chris Gomez	.15
288	Jared Baker	.05
289	Doug Hecker	.05
290	David Spykstra	.05
291	Scott Miller	.05
292	Carey Paige	.05
293	Dave Manning	.05
294	James Keefe	.05
295	Levon Largusa	.05
296	Roger Bailey	.10
297	Rich Ireland	.05
298	Matt Williams	.05
299	Scott Gentile	.05
300	Hut Smith	.05
301	Dave Brown	.05
302	Bobby Bonds Jr.	.35
303	Reggie Smith	.05
304	Preston Wilson	.25
305	John Burke	.05
306	Rodney Henderson	.10
307	Pete Janicki	.05
308	Brien Taylor (Flashback)	.10
309	Mike Kelly (Flashback)	.05
314	Jim Pittsley	.05

1992 Classic Four Sport Autographs

More than 50 of the draft picks from the four major team sports which appear in Classic's Four Sport issue can also be found in among randomly inserted autographed cards. Fronts are formatted like the base set, with full-bleed action photos and include a serial number from within the edition limit specified for each player. Backs have a congratulatory message for finding an autographed card. Only the baseball players from the issue are listed here, arranged by the numerical order of their cards in the base set; the autographed cards are not numbered.

	MT
Common Player:	8.00
(226) Phil Nevin (1,475)	12.00
(227) Paul Shuey (4,050)	12.00
(229) Jeffrey Hammonds (2,950)	15.00
(231) Derek Jeter (1,125)	95.00
(233) Derek Wallace (1,475)	8.00
(241) Jamie Arnold (1,575)	8.00
(242) Rick Helling (2,875)	15.00
(245) Dan Serafini (1,475)	8.00
(248) Ryan Luzinski (1,575)	8.00

1992 Classic Four Sport Bonus Cards

These bonus cards were issued on per jumbo pack. In format similar to the base set, they have a silver metallic foil strip vertically on front with player identification. Backs are numbered with a BC prefix. Only the baseball players among the 20 draft picks are listed here, along with a special Future Superstars multi-player card which was produced in an edition of 10,000.

		MT
Common Player:		.50
BC18	Phil Nevin	.50
BC19	Jeffrey Hammonds	.75
BC20	Michael Tucker	.75
FS1	Phil Nevin, Shaquille O'Neal, Desmond Howard, Roman Hamrlik	25.00

1992 Classic Four Sport LP

These "Limited Print" (46,080 of each) foil cards were random inserts in packs of '92 Classic Four Sport. Only the baseball players are listed here.

		MT
Common Player:		2.00
LP17	Phil Nevin	2.00
LP18	Jeffrey Hammonds	2.00
LP19	Paul Shuey	2.00
LP20	Ryan Luzinsky (Luzinski)	2.00
LP21	Brien Taylor	2.00

1992-93 Fleer Excel

Excel was Fleer's 1992 entry into minor league cards. The 250-card set features full-color photos inside a white border with the player's name, team, logo and Excel logo in gold-foil stamping. Backs have large photos, career statistics, team logos and biographical information. Cards are UV coated. Cards were intended to be sold in 14-card packs for a suggested retail price of $1.49 each. The Excel All-Stars are listed at the end of the 250-card checklist. Cards for these 10 players were randomly inserted into the foil packs.

		MT
Complete Set (250):		45.00
Common Player:		.10
Wax Box:		35.00
1	Mike D'Andrea	.10
2	Chipper Jones	6.00
3	Mike Kelly	.15
4	Brian Kowitz	.10
5	Napoleon Robinson	.10
6	Tony Tarasco	.10
7	Pedro Castellano	.10
8	Doug Glanville	.15
9	Andy Hartung	.10
10	Jay Hassel	.10
11	Ryan Hawblitzel	.15
12	Kevin Roberson	.15
13	Chad Tredaway	.10
14	Jose Vierra	.10
15	Matt Walbeck	.20
16	Tim Belk	.10
17	Jamie Dismuke	.10
18	Chad Fox	.20
19	Micah Franklin	.10
20	Dan Frye	.10
21	Steve Gibralter	.15
22	Demetrish Jenkins	.10
23	Jason Kummerfeidt	.10
24	Bob Loftin	.10
25	Chad Mottola	.25
26	Bobby Perna	.10
27	Scott Pose	.15
28	Calvin Reese	.20
29	John Roper	.10
30	Jerry Spradlin	.10
31	Roger Bailey	.15
32	Jason Bates	.15
33	John Burke	.10
34	Jason Hutchins	.10
35	Troy Ricker	.10
36	Mark Thompson	.10
37	Lou Lucca	.10
38	John Lynch	.10
39	Todd Pridy	.10
40	Gary Cooper	.10
41	Jim Dougherty	.10
42	Tony Eusebio	.15
43	Chris Hatcher	.15
44	Chris Hill	.10
45	Trent Hubbard	.10
46	Todd Jones	.10
47	Jeff Juden	.75
48	James Mouton	.15
49	Tom Nevers	.10
50	Jim Waring	.10
51	Chris Abbe	.10
52	Jay Kirkpatrick	.10
53	Raul Mondesi	2.50
54	Vernon Spearman	.10
55	Tavo Alvarez	.10
56	Shane Andrews	.30
57	Yamil Benitez	.10
58	Cliff Floyd	.75
59	Antonio Grissom	.10
60	Tyrone Horne	.10
61	Mike Lansing	.75
62	Edgar Tovar	.10
63	Ugueth Urbina	.50
64	David Wainhouse	.15
65	Derrick White	.10
66	Gabe White	.40
67	Rondell White	2.00
68	Edgar Alfonzo	.10
69	Jeromy Burnitz	.40
70	Jay Davis	.10
71	Cesar Diaz	.10
72	Todd Douma	.10
73	Brook Fordyce	.10
74	Butch Huskey	.50
75	Bobby Jones	.75
76	Jose Martinez	.15
77	Ricky Otero	.15

78	Jim Popoff	.10
79	Al Shirley	.10
80	Julian Vasquez	.10
81	Quilvio Veras	.15
82	Fernando Vina	.25
83	Ron Blazier	.10
84	Tommy Eason	.10
85	Tyler Green	.25
86	Mike Lieberthal	.15
87	Tom Nuneviller	.10
88	Matt Whisenant	.10
89	Jon Zuber	.10
90	Midre Cummings	.35
91	Jon Farrell	.10
92	Ramon Martinez	.15
93	Antonio Mitchell	.10
94	Keith Thomas	.10
95	Rene Arocha	.10
96	Brian Barber	.15
97	Jamie Cochran	.10
98	Mike Gulan	.10
99	Keith Johns	.10
100	John Kelly	.10
101	Anthony Lewis	.10
102	T.J. Mathews	.10
103	Kevin Meier	.10
104	David Oehrlein	.10
105	Gerry Santos	.10
106	Basil Shabazz	.10
107	Eddie Williams	.10
108	Dmitri Young	.50
109	Jay Gainer	.10
110	Pedro Martinez	2.00
111	Dave Staton	.15
112	Tim Worrell	.10
113	Dan Carlson	.10
114	Joel Chimelis	.10
115	Eric Christopherson	.10
116	Adell Davenport	.10
117	Ken Grundt	.10
118	Rick Huisman	.10
119	Andre Keene	.10
120	Kevin McGehee	.10
121	Salomon Torres	.10
122	Damon Buford	.10
123	Stanton Cameron	.10
124	Rick Krivda	.10
125	Alex Ochoa	.50
126	Brad Penington	.15
127	Mark Smith	.15
128	Mel Wearing	.10
129	Cory Bailey	.10
130	Greg Blosser	.10
131	Joe Caruso	.10
132	Jason Friedman	.10
133	Jose Malave	.10
134	Jeff McNeely	.15
135	Luis Ortiz	.10
136	Ed Riley	.10
137	Frank Rodriguez	.20
138	Aaron Sele	.50
139	Garret Anderson	.90
140	Ron Correia	.10
141	Jim Edmonds	2.00
142	John Fritz	.10
143	Brian Grebeck	.10
144	Jeff Kipila	.10
145	Orlando Palmeiro	.10
146	Eduardo Perez	.15
147	John Pricher	.10
148	Chris Pritchett	.10
149	James Baldwin	.35
150	Rodney Bolton	.10
151	Essex Burton	.10
152	Scott Cepicky	.10
153	Steve Olsen	.10
154	Scott Ruffcorn	.10
155	Scott Schrenk	.10
156	Larry Thomas	.10
157	Brandon Wilson	.15
158	Paul Byrd	.10
159	Willie Canate	.10
160	Marc Marini	.10
161	Jonathan Nunnally	.25
162	Chad Ogea	.25
163	Herb Perry	.10
164	Manny Ramirez	6.00
165	Omar Ramirez	.10
166	Ken Ramos	.10
167	Tracy Sanders	.10
168	Paul Shuey	.15
169	Kyle Washington	.10
170	Ivan Cruz	.10
171	Lou Frazier	.10
172	Brian Bevil	.10
173	Shane Halter	.10
174	Phil Hiatt	.10
175	Lance Jennings	.10
176	Les Norman	.10
177	Joe Randa	.20
178	Dan Rohrmeier	.10
179	Larry Sutton	.10
180	Joe Vitiello	.25
181	John Byington	.10
182	Edgar Caceres	.10
183	Jeff Cirillo	.50
184	Mike Farrell	.10
185	Kenny Felder	.10
186	Tyrone Hill	.15
187	Brian Hostetler	.10
188	Danan Hughes	.10
189	Scott Karl	.20
190	Joe Kmak	.10
191	Rob Lakachyk	.10
192	Matt Mieske	.20
193	Troy O'Leary	.15
194	Cecil Rodriques	.10
195	Tim Unroe	.10
196	Wes Weger	.10
197	Rich Becker	.20
198	Marty Cordova	.50
199	Steve Dunn	.10
200	Mike Durant	.10
201	Denny Hocking	.10
202	David McCarty	.15
203	Damian Miller	.10
204	Scott Stahoviak	.15
205	Russ Davis	.50
206	Mike Draper	.10
207	Carl Everett	.15
208	Lew Hill	.10
209	Mark Hutton	.10
210	Derek Jeter	8.00
211	Kevin Jordan	.15
212	Lyle Mouton	.10
213	Bobby Munoz	.25
214	Andy Pettitte	3.00
215	Brien Taylor	.20
216	Brent Gates	.35
217	Eric Helfand	.10
218	Curtis Shaw	.10
219	Todd Van Poppel	.15
220	Miah Bradbury	.10
221	Darren Bragg	.10
222	Jim Converse	.10
223	John Cummings	.10
224	Shawn Estes	.50
225	Mike Hampton	.10
226	Derek Lowe	.10
227	Ellerton Maynard	.10
228	Fred McNair	.10
229	Marc Newfield	.15
230	Desi Relaford	.15
231	Ruben Santana	.10
232	Bubba Smith	.10
233	Brian Turang	.10
234	Benji Gil	.15
235	Jose Oliva	.10
236	Jon Shave	.10
237	Travis Baptist	.15
238	Howard Battle	.15
239	Rob Butler	.10
240	Tim Crabtree	.15
241	Juan DeLaRosa	.10
242	Carlos Delgado	3.00
243	Alex Gonzalez	.75
244	Steve Karsay	.40
245	Paul Spoljaric	.15
246	Todd Steverson	.20
247	Nigel Wilson	.10
248	Checklist	.10
249	Checklist	.10
250	Checklist	.10

1992-93 Fleer Excel All-Stars

These 10 All-Star cards were randomly inserted in Fleer Excel's 1992-93 foil packs. Cards are UV coated and feature the Excel logo on the front, along with the player's name and All-Star status, stamped in gold foil.

		MT
Complete Set (10):		30.00
Common Player:		1.00
1	Brien Taylor	1.00
2	Chipper Jones	15.00
3	Rondell White	4.00
4	Mike Lieberthal	1.00
5	Bobby Jones	3.00
6	Carlos Delgado	4.00
7	Aaron Sele	1.50
8	Brent Gates	1.50
9	Phil Hiatt	1.00
10	Brandon Wilson	1.00

1992-93 Fleer Excel League Leaders

These randomly inserted cards feature 20 different Minor League league leaders. "League Leaders" and the player's name are stamped in gold foil on the front, which also has an Excel logo. The cards were random inserts in 1992-93 Fleer Excel jumbo packs.

		MT
Complete Set (20):		15.00
Common Player:		.75
1	Travis Baptist	1.00
2	Bubba Smith	.75
3	Rob Butler	.75
4	Marty Cordova	2.00
5	John Fritz	.75
6	Quilivio Veras	.75
7	Cliff Floyd	2.00
8	Denny Hocking	.75
9	Rich Becker	2.00
10	Jim Popoff	.75
11	John Kelly	.75
12	Tavo Alvarez	.75
13	Scott Pose	.75
14	Steve Gibralter	.75
15	Joe Caruso	.75
16	Chad Ogea	1.00
17	Troy O'Leary	.75
18	Russ Davis	1.50
19	John Cummings	.75
20	Ken Ramos	.75

1992 Front Row Draft Picks

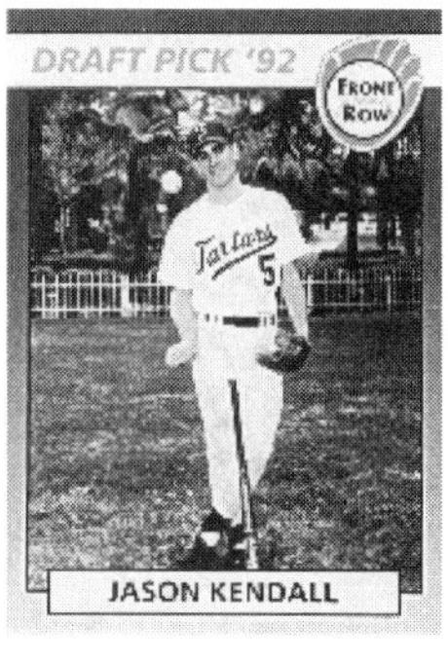

One hundred of the top players in the 1992 amateur draft are featured in this set. Sold in both wax packs and factory sets, the issue included a number of foil-stamped parallel cards, plus gold Frank Thomas and Ken Griffey, Jr., and autographed Whitey Ford, Brooks Robinson and Yogi Berra cards as random inserts. The basic cards are UV-coated front and feature posed or game-action color photos of the players in their high school or college uniforms with borders in graduated shades of blue. Backs have biographical data, stats and career highlights, plus another picture - generally a boyhood photo. According to released production figures, about 330,000 sets are possible.

		MT
Complete Set (100):		4.00
Common Player:		.05
Silver highlighted cards valued at 2X		
Gold highlighted cards valued at 3X-4X		
1	Dan Melendez	.05
2	Billy Owens	.05
3	Sherard Clinkscales	.05
4	Tim Moore	.05
5	Michael Hickey	.05
6	Kenny Carlyle	.05
7	Todd Steverson	.10
8	Ted Corbin	.05
9	Tim Crabtree	.10
10	Jason Angel	.05
11	Mike Gulan	.05
12	Jared Baker	.05
13	Mike Buddie	.05
14	Brandon Pico	.05
15	Jonathan Nunnally	.20
16	Scott Patton	.05
17	Tony Sheffield	.05
18	Danny Clyburn	.05
19	Tom Knauss	.05
20	Carey Paige	.05
21	Keith Johnson	.05
22	Larry Mitchell	.05
23	Tim Leger	.05
24	Doug Hecker	.05
25	Aaron Thatcher	.05
26	Marquis Riley	.05
27	Jamie Taylor	.05
28	Don Wengert	.10
29	Jason Moler	.10
30	Kevin Kloek	.05
31	Kevin Pearson	.05
32	David Mysel	.05
33	Chris Holt	.05
34	Chris Gomez	.25
35	Joe Hamilton	.10
36	Brandon Cromer	.10
37	Lloyd Peever	.05
38	Gordon Sanchez	.05
39	Bonus card	.05
40	Jason Giambi	.60
41	Sean Runyan	.05
42	Jamie Keefe	.05
43	Scott Gentile	.05
44	Michael Tucker	.30
45	Scott Klingenbeck	.05
46	Ed Christian	.05
47	Scott Miller	.05
48	Rick Navarro	.05
49	Bill Selby	.05
50	Chris Roberts	.25
51	John Dillinger	.05
52	Keith Johns	.05
53	Matthew Williams	.05
54	Garvin Alston	.05
55	Derek Jeter	1.00
56	Chris Eddy	.05
57	Jeff Schmidt	.05
58	Chris Petersen	.05
59	Chris Sheff	.05
60	Chad Roper	.10
61	Rich Ireland	.05
62	Tibor Brown	.05
63	Todd Etler	.05
64	John Turlais	.05
65	Shawn Holcomb	.05
66	Ben Jones	.05
67	Marcel Galligani	.05
68	Troy Penix	.05
69	Matt Luke	.10
70	David Post	.05
71	Michael Warner	.05
72	Alexis Aranzamendi	.05
73	Larry Hingle	.05
74	Shon Walker	.05
75	Mark Thompson	.10
76	Jon Lieber	.05
77	Wes Weger	.05
78	Mike Smith	.05
79	Ritchie Moody	.05
80	B.J. Wallace	.10
81	Rick Helling	.25
82	Chad Mottola	.10
83	Brant Brown	.10
84	Steve Rodriguez	.05
85	John Vanhof	.05
86	Brian Wolf	.05
87	Steve Montgomery	.10
88	Eric Owens	.20
89	Jason Kendall	.50
90	Bob Bennett	.05
91	Joe Petcka	.05
92	Jim Rosenbohm	.05
93	David Manning	.05
94	Dave Landaker	.05
95	Dan Kyslinger	.05
96	Roger Bailey	.20
97	Jon Zuber	.05
98	Steve Cox	.25
99	Chris Widger	.25
100	Checklist	.05
---	Ken Griffey Jr. (gold card)	15.00
---	Frank Thomas (gold card)	10.00
---	Yogi Berra (autographed)	15.00
---	Whitey Ford (autographed)	15.00
---	Brooks Robinson (autographed)	15.00

Checklists with card numbers in parentheses ( ) indicates the numbers do not appear on the card.

1992 SkyBox AA

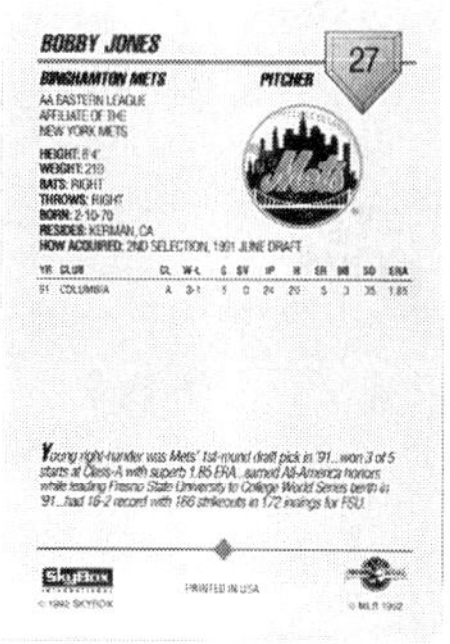

SkyBox Pre-Rookie 1992 baseball cards were released in two 310-card sets; one for Triple A and one for Double A. Each set includes 289 top prospects, plus subsets (1991 statistical leaders, players of the year and minor league stadiums) and checklist cards. Cards were intended to be sold in 15-card packs for a suggested retail price of 95 cents each. SkyBox also offered 25-card Pre-Rookie team sets which include all players and coaches on the opening day roster of each of the 52 AA and AAA teams, plus a team checklist. Sets were to be available at most of the teams' stadiums. The top prospects which appear in the 15-card packs are also depicted in the team sets, but the team cards use a different numbering system and delete the card back copy except for statistics.

		MT
Complete Set (310):		12.00
Common Player:		.05
1	Rich Batchelor	.05
2	Russ Davis	.35
3	Kiki Hernandez	.05
4	Sterling Hitchcock	.35
5	Darren Hodges	.05
6	Jeff Hoffman	.05
7	Mark Hulton	.05
8	Bobby Munoz	.10
9	Roy Noriega	.05
10	Sherman Obando	.10
11	John Viera	.05
12	Cliff Brannon	.05
13	Chuck Carr	.15
14	Fidel Compres	.05
15	Tripp Cromer	.10
16	John Ericks	.05
17	Gabby Ozuna	.05
18	Don Prybylinski	.05
19	John Sellick	.05
20	John Thomas	.05
21	Tom Urbani	.05
22	Chris Butterfield	.05
23	Todd Douma	.05
24	Brook Fordyce	.05
25	Tim Howard	.05
26	John Johnstone	.05
27	Bobby Jones	.20
28	Rob Katzaroff	.05
29	Gregg Langbehn	.05
30	Curtis Pride	.15
31	Julian Vasquez	.05
32	Joe Vitko	.05
33	Tom Wegmann	.05
34	Mike White	.05
35	Alan Zinter	.05

36 Clemente Alvarez .05
37 Cesar Bernhardt .05
38 Wayne Busby .05
39 Scott Cepicky .05
40 John Hudek .15
41 Scott Jaster .05
42 Bo Kennedy .05
43 Mike Mongiello .05
44 Kinnis Pledger .05
45 Johnny Ruffin .05
46 Jose Ventura .05
47 Paul Byrd .05
48 Colin Charland .05
49 Miguel Flores .05
50 Brian Giles .10
51 Jose Hernandez .05
52 Nolan Lene .05
53 David Mlicki .05
54 Tracy Sanders .05
55 Mike Soper .05
56 Kelly Stinnett .05
57 Joe Turek .05
58 Kyle Washington .05
59 Dave Bird .05
60 Scott Bullett .05
61 Steve Cooke .10
62 Alberto De Los Santos .05
63 Stan Fansier .05
64 Austin Manahan .05
65 Daryl Ratliff .05
66 Mandy Romero .05
67 Ben Shelton .05
68 Paul Wagner .05
69 Mike Zimmerman .05
70 Phil Dauphin .05
71 Chris Ebright .05
72 Mike Grace .05
73 Ryan Hawbitzel .05
74 Jessie Hollins .05
75 Tim Parker .05
76 Dave Swartzbaugh .05
77 Steve Trachsel .35
78 Billy White .05
79 Bobby Ayala .10
80 Tim Costa .05
81 Ty Griffin .05
82 Cesar Hernandez .05
83 Trevor Hoffman .25
84 Brian Lane .05
85 Scott Pose .10
86 Johnny Ray .05
87 John Roper .05
88 Glenn Sutko .05
89 Kevin Tatar .05
90 John Byington .05
91 Tony Diggs .05
92 Bo Dodson .05
93 Craig Faulkner .05
94 Jim Hunter .05
95 Oreste Marrero .05
96 Troy O'Leary .10
97 Brian Bark .05
98 Dennis Burlingame .05
99 Ramon Carabello .10
100 Mike Kelly .10
101 Javier Lopez 2.00
102 Don Strange .05
103 Tony Tarasco .10
104 Manny Alexander .15
105 Damon Buford .10
106 Cesar Devares .05
107 Rodney Lofton .05
108 Brent Miller .05
109 David Miller .05
110 Daryl Moore .05
111 John O'Donoghue .10
112 Erik Schulstrom .05
113 Mark Smith .10
114 Mel Wearing .05
115 Jeff Williams .05
116 Kip Yaughn .05
117 Doug Bochller .05
118 Travis Buckley .05
119 Reid Cornelius .10
120 Chris Johnson .05
121 Tim Laker .10
122 Chris Martin .05
123 Mike Mathile .05
124 Darwin Pennye .05
125 Doug Platt .05
126 Kurt Abbott .20
127 Marcos Amas .05
128 James Buccheri .05
129 Kevin Dettola .05
130 Scott Erwin .05
131 Johnny Guzman .05
132 David Jacas .05
133 Francisco Matos .05
134 Mike Mohler .05
135 Craig Paquette .10
136 Todd Revenig .05
137 Todd Smith .05
138 Ricky Strebeck .05
139 Sam August .05
140 Tony Eusebio .10
141 Brian Griffiths .05
142 Todd Jones .05
143 Orlando Miller .15
144 Howard Prager .05
145 Matt Rambo .05
146 Lee Sammons .05
147 Richie Simon .05
148 Frank Bolick .05
149 Jim Campanis .05
150 Jim Converse .05
151 Bobby Holley .05
152 Troy Kent .05
153 Brent Knackert .10
154 Anthony Manahan .05
155 Tow Maynard .05
156 Mike McDonald .05
157 Marc Newfield .10
158 Greg Pirkl .05
159 Jesus Tavarez .05
160 Kerry Woodson .05
161 Graeme Lloyd .10
162 Paul Menhart .05
163 Marcus Moore .05
164 Greg O'Halloran .05
165 Mark Ohlms .05
166 Robert Perez .05
167 Aaron Small .05
168 Nigel Wilson .05
169 Julian Yan .05
170 Jeff Braley .05
171 Brian Cornelius .05
172 Ivan Cruz .05
173 Lou Frazier .05
174 Frank Gonzales .05
175 Tyrone Kingwood .05
176 Leo Torres .05
177 Brien Warren .05
178 Brian Ahern .05
179 Tony Bridges .05
180 Paco Burgos .05
181 Adam Casillas .05
182 Archie Corbin .05
183 Phil Hiatt .10
184 Marcus Lawton .05
185 Domingo Mota .05
186 Mark Parnell .05
187 Ed Pierce .05
188 Rich Tunison .05
189 Hugh Walker .05
190 Skip Wiley .05
191 Dave Adams .05
192 Mick Billmeyer .05
193 Marvin Cobb .05
194 Jim Edmonds 1.50
195 Corey Kapano .05
196 Jeff Kiplia .05
197 Joe Kraemer .05
198 Ray Martinez .05
199 J.R. Phillips .10
200 Darryl Scott .05
201 Paul Swingle .05
202 Mark Zappelli .05
203 Greg Blosser .10
204 Bruce Chick .05
205 Colin Dixon .05
206 Gar Finnvold .05
207 Scott Hatteberg .10
208 Derek Livernois .05
209 Jeff McNeely .10
210 Tony Mosley .05
211 Bill Norris .05
212 Ed Riley .05
213 Ken Ryan .10
214 Tim Smith .05
215 Willie Tatum .05
216 Rex De La Nuez .05
217 Rich Garces .05
218 Curtis Leskanic .10
219 Mica Lewis .05
220 David McCarty .10
221 Pat Meares .10
222 Alan Newman .05
223 Jay Owens .10
224 Carlos Pulido .05
225 Rusty Richards .05
226 Paul Russo .05
227 Brad Brink .05
228 Andy Carter .05
229 Tyler Green .15
230 Mike Lieberthal .15
231 Chris Limbach .05
232 Ron Lockett .05
233 Tom Nuneviller .05
234 Troy Paulsen .05
235 Todd Pratt .05
236 Sean Ryan .05
237 Matt Stevens .05
238 Sam Taylor .05
239 Casey Waller .05
240 Mike Williams .05
241 Jorge Alvarez .05
242 Billy Ashley .05
243 Tim Barker .05
244 Bill Bene .05
245 John Deutsch .05
246 Greg Hansell .05
247 Matt Howard .05
248 Ron Maurer .05
249 Mike Mimbs .05
250 Chris Morrow .05
251 Mike Piazza 6.00
252 Dennis Springer .05
253 Clay Bellinger .05
254 Dan Carlson .05
255 Eric Christopherson .05
256 Adell Davenport .05
257 Steve Finken .05
258 Rick Huisman .05
259 Kevin McGehee .05
260 Don Rambo .05
261 Steve Reed .05
262 Kevin Rogers .05
263 Salomon Torres .05
264 Pete Weber .05
265 Brian Romero .05
266 Cris Colon .05
267 Rusty Greer .45
268 Donald Harris .10
269 David Hulse .10
270 Pete Kuld .05
271 Robb Nen .10
272 Jose Oliva .05
273 Steve Rowley .05
274 Jon Shave .10
275 Cedric Shaw .05
276 Dan Smith .10
277 Matt Whiteside .10
278 Scott Frederickson .05
279 Jay Gainer .05
280 Paul Gonzalez .05
281 Vince Harris .05
282 Ray Holbert .05
283 Dwayne Hosey .10
284 J.D. Noland .05
285 Lance Painter .10
286 Scott Sanders .05
287 Darrell Sherman .10
288 Brian Wood .05
289 Tim Worrell .10
290 John Jaha .15
291 Jim Bowie .05
292 Mark Howie .05
293 Matt Stairs .25
294 Larry Carter .05
295 Pat Mahomes .10
296 Jeff Mutis .10
297 Municipal Stadium .05
298 Knights Castle .05
299 Engel Stadium .05
300 Tim McCarver Stadium .05
301 Beehive Field .05
302 Tinker Field .05
303 Checklist Alpha 1 .05
304 Checklist Alpha 2 .05
305 Checklist Alpha 3 .05
306 Checklist Alpha 4 .05
307 Checklist Numeric 1 .05
308 Checklist Numeric 2 .05
309 Checklist Numeric 3 .05
310 Checklist Numeric 4 .05

The election of former players to the Hall of Fame does not always have an immediate upward effect on card prices. The hobby market generally has done a good job of predicting those inductions and adjusting values over the course of several years.

1992 SkyBox AAA

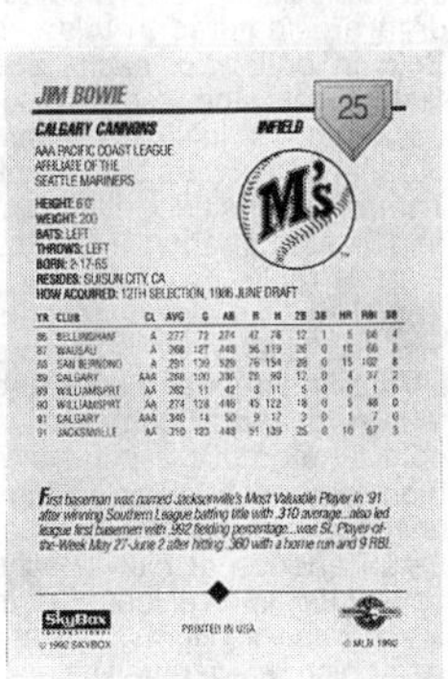

		MT
Complete Set (310):		15.00
Common Player:		.05

1 Pedro Astacio .20
2 Bryan Baar .05
3 Tom Goodwin .15
4 Jeff Hamilton .10
5 Pedro Martinez 2.00
6 Jamie McAndrew .10
7 Mark Mimbs .05
8 Raul Mondesi 2.50
9 Jose Munoz .05
10 Henry Rodriguez .25
11 Eric Young .15
12 Joe Ausanio .05
13 Victor Cole .05
14 Carlos Garcia .10
15 Blas Minor .05
16 William Pennyfeather .05
17 Mark Petkovsek .10
18 Jeff Richardson .05
19 Rosario Rodriguez .05
20 Tim Wakefield .15
21 John Wehner .10
22 Kevin Young .25
23 Mike Blowers .10
24 Bret Boone .90
25 Jim Bowie .05
26 Dave Brundage .05
27 Randy Kramer .05
28 Patrick Lennon .05
29 Jim Newlin .05
30 Jose Nunez .05
31 Mike Remlinger .05
32 Pat Rice .05
33 Roger Salkeld .15
34 Beau Allred .05
35 Denis Boucher .05
36 Mike Christopher .05
37 Daren Epley .05
38 Tom Kramer .05
39 Jerry DiPoto .05
40 Jeff Mutis .05
41 Jeff Shaw .05
42 Lee Tinsley .10
43 Kevin Wickander .05
44 Royal Clayton .05
45 Bobby Dejardin .05
46 Mike Draper .05
47 Mike Humphreys .05
48 Torey Lovullo .05
49 Ed Martel .05
50 Billy Masse .05
51 Hensley Meulens .05
52 Sam Militello .05
53 John Ramos .05
54 David Rosario .05
55 David Silvestri .10
56 J.T. Snow .50
57 Russ Springer .10
58 Jerry Stanford .05
59 Wade Taylor .10
60 Gerald Williams .10
61 Cal Eldred .15
62 Chris George .05
63 Otis Green .05
64 Mike Ignasiak .05
65 John Jaha .15
66 Mark Kiefer .05
67 Matt Mieske .10
68 Angel Miranda .05
69 Dave Nilsson .15
70 Jim Olander .05
71 Jim Tatum .05
72 Jose Valentin .05
73 Don Barbara .05
74 Chris Beasley .05
75 Mike Butcher .05
76 Damion Easley .15
77 Kevin Flora .05
78 Tim Fortugno .05
79 Larry Gonzales .05
80 Todd James .05
81 Tim Salmon 2.00
82 Don Vidmar .05
83 Cliff Young .05
84 Shon Ashley .05
85 Brian Barnes .05
86 Blaine Beatty .05
87 Kent Bottenfield .10
88 Wil Cordero .25
89 Jerry Goff .05
90 Jon Hurst .05
91 Jim Kremers .05
92 Matt Maysey .10
93 Rob Natal .05
94 Matt Stairs .25
95 David Wainhouse .10
96 Alex Arias .10
97 Scott Bryant .05
98 Jim Bullinger .10
99 Pedro Castellano .10
100 Lance Dickson .10
101 John Gardner .05
102 Jeff Hartsock .05
103 Elvin Paulino .05
104 Fernando Ramsey .05
105 Laddie Renfroe .05
106 Kevin Roberson .15
107 John Salles .05
108 Derrick May .10
109 Turk Wendell .15
110 Doug Brocail .10
111 Terry Bross .05
112 Scott Coolbaugh .05
113 Rick Davis .05
114 Jeff Gardner .05
115 Steve Pegues .05
116 Frank Seminara .05
117 Dave Staton .10
118 Will Taylor .05
119 Jim Vatcher .05
120 Guillermo Velasquez .05
121 Dan Walters .05
122 Rene Arocha .10
123 Rod Brewer .05
124 Ozzie Canseco .10
125 Mark Clark .15
126 Joey Fernandez .05
127 Lonnie Maclin .05
128 Mike Milchin .05
129 Stan Royer .10
130 Tracy Woodson .05
131 Bob Buchanan .05
132 Mark Howie .05
133 Tony Menendez .05
134 Gino Minutelli .05
135 Tim Pugh .10
136 Mo Sanford .10
137 Joey Vierra .05
138 Dan Wilson .10
139 Kevin Blankenship .05
140 Todd Burns .05
141 Tom Drees .05
142 Jeff Frye .05
143 Chuck Jackson .05
144 Rob Maurer .05
145 Russ McGinnis .05
146 Dan Peltier .05
147 Wayne Rosenthal .05
148 Bob Sebra .05
149 Sean Berry .10
150 Stu Cole .05
151 Jeff Conine .50
152 Kevin Koslovski .05
153 Kevin Long .05
154 Carlos Maldonado .05
155 Dennis Moeller .05
156 Harvey Pulliam .05
157 Luis Medina .05
158 Steve Shifflett .05
159 Tim Spehr .05
160 Brian Conroy .05
161 Wayne Housie .05
162 Daryl Irvine .05
163 Dave Milstien .05
164 Jeff Plympton .05
165 Paul Quantrill .10
166 Larry Shikles .05
167 Scott Taylor .05
168 Mike Twardoski .05
169 John Valentin .40
170 David Walters .05
171 Eric Wedge .05
172 Bob Zupcic .05
173 Johnny Ard .05
174 Larry Carter .05
175 Steve Decker .05
176 Steve Hosey .15
177 Paul McClellan .05
178 Jim Myers .05
179 Jamie Cooper .05
180 Pat Rapp .10
181 Ted Wood .05
182 Willie Banks .10
183 Bernardo Brito .05
184 J.T. Bruett .05
185 Larry Casian .05
186 Shawn Gilbert .05
187 Greg Johnson .05
188 Terry Jorgensen .05
189 Edgar Naveda .05
190 Derek Parks .10
191 Danny Sheaffer .10
192 Mike Trombley .10
193 George Tsamis .05
194 Rob Waseenaar .05
195 Vinny Castilla .40
196 Pat Gomez .15
197 Ryan Klesko 1.50
198 Keith Mitchell .05
199 Bobby Moore .10
200 David Nied .05
201 Amando Reynoso .05
202 Napoleon Robinson .05
203 Boi Rodriguez .05
204 Randy St. Claire .05
205 Mark Wohlers .15
206 Ricky Gutierrez .15
207 Mike Lehman .05
208 Richie Lewis .05
209 Scott Meadows .05
210 Mike Oquist .05
211 Arthur Rhodes .10
212 Ken Shamburg .05
213 Todd Stephan .05
214 Anthony Telford .10
215 Jack Voight .05
216 Bob Ayrault .10
217 Toby Borland .10
218 Braulio Castillo .10
219 Darrin Chapin .05
220 Bruce Dostal .05
221 Tim Mauser .05
222 Steve Scarsone .10
223 Rick Schu .05
224 Butch Davis .05
225 Ray Giannelli .05
226 Randy Knorr .10
227 Al Leiter .25
228 Doug Linton .05
229 Domingo Martinez .05
230 Tom Quinlan .05
231 Jerry Schunk .05
232 Ed Sprague .10
233 David Weathers .10
234 Eddie Zosky .10
235 John Briscoe .05
236 Kevin Campbell .05
237 Jeff Carter .05
238 Steve Chitren .05
239 Reggie Harris .05
240 Dann Howitt .05
241 Troy Neel .20
242 Gavin Osteen .05

243	Tim Peek	.05
244	Todd Van Poppel	.10
245	Ron Witmeyer	.05
246	David Zancanaro	.05
247	Kevin Baez	.05
248	Jeromy Burnitz	.20
249	Chris Donnels	.10
250	D.J. Dozier	.05
251	Terrel Hansen	.05
252	Eric Hillman	.05
253	Pat Howell	.05
254	Lee May	.05
255	Pete Schourek	.15
256	David Telgheder	.10
257	Julio Valera	.05
258	Rico Brogna	.15
259	Steve Carter	.05
260	Steve Cummings	.10
261	Greg Gohr	.05
262	David Haas	.05
263	Shawn Hare	.10
264	Riccardo Ingram	.05
265	John Kiely	.10
266	Kurt Knudsen	.05
267	Victor Rosario	.05
268	Rich Rowland	.10
269	John DeSilva	.05
270	Gary Cooper	.05
271	Chris Gardner	.05
272	Jeff Juden	.10
273	Rob Mallicoat	.05
274	Andy Mota	.05
275	Shane Reynolds	.10
276	Mike Simms	.05
277	Scooter Tucker	.05
278	Brian Williams	.05
279	Rod Bolton	.05
280	Ron Coomer	.05
281	Chris Cron	.05
282	Ramon Garcia	.05
283	Chris Howard	.05
284	Roberto Hernandez	.15
285	Derek Lee	.10
286	Ever Magallanes	.05
287	Norberto Martin	.10
288	Greg Perschke	.05
289	Ron Stephens	.05
290	Derek Bell	.40
291	Rich Amaral	.10
292	Derek Bell	.40
293	Jim Olander	.05
294	Gil Heredia	.10
295	Rick Reed	.05
296	Amando Reynoso	.10
297	Charlotte, N.C.	.05
298	Ottawa, Ontario	.05
299	Pilot Field	.05
300	Harold Cooper Stadium	.05
301	Bush Stadium	.05
302	Silver Stadium	.05
303	Checklist Alpha 1	.05
304	Checklist Alpha 2	.05
305	Checklist Alpha 3	.05
306	Checklist Alpha 4	.05
307	Checklist Numeric 1	.05
308	Checklist Numeric 2	.05
309	Checklist Numeric 3	.05
310	Checklist Numeric 4	.05

1992 Upper Deck Minor League Promos

This two-card promo set was distributed at FanFest, the National Sports Collectors Convention and a number of minor league ballgames. Similar in format to Upper Deck's regular minor league issue, the promos feature a star-shaped hologram on back.

		MT
Complete Set (2):		8.00
1	Brien Taylor	3.00
350	Frank Rodriguez	5.00

Player names in *Italic* type indicate a rookie card.

1992 Upper Deck Minor League

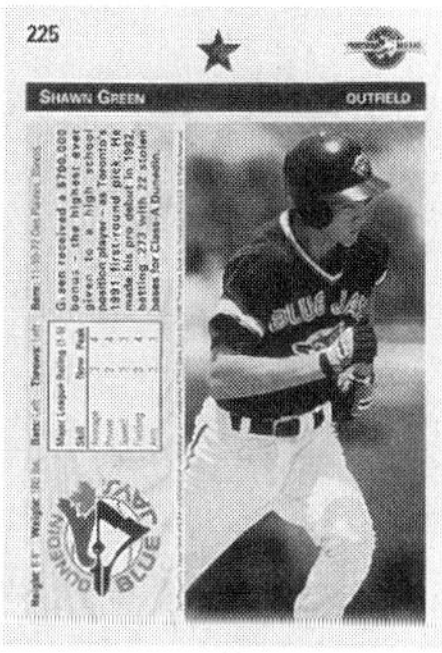

For the first time in 1992, Upper Deck entered the minor league card market with a set of 330 base cards plus several inserts. The UD minor league cards are very similar in format to the company's 1992 major league issue, including UV-coating front and back and the use of color player photos on both sides. UD adopted a star-shaped foil hologram on back as an anti-counterfeiting device for its minor league issues.

		MT
Complete Set (330):		75.00
Common Player:		.10
Wax Box:		120.00
1	Draft Pick checklist Johnny Damon, Michael Tucker	.50
2	B.J. Wallace	.25
3	Jeffrey Hammonds	.50
4	Chad Mottola	.25
5	Derek Jeter	7.50
6	Michael Tucker	2.00
7	Derek Wallace	.20
8	Chad McConnell	.30
9	Rick Greene	.10
10	Shannon Stewart	.20
11	Benji Grigsby	.20
12	Jamie Arnold	.15
13	Rick Helling	.15
14	Jason Kendall	2.00
15	Eddie Pearson	.10
16	Todd Steverson	.30
17	John Burke	.10
18	Brandon Cromer	.10
19	Johnny Damon	2.00
20	Jason Giambi	2.00
21	John Lynch	.10
22	Jared Baker	.10
23	Roger Bailey	.15
24	Angels checklist	.15
25	Astros checklist	.10
26	Athletics checklist	.10
27	Blue Jays checklist	.10
28	Braves checklist	.25
29	Brewers checklist	.10
30	Cardinals checklist	.10
31	Cubs checklist	.10
32	Dodgers checklist	.25
33	Expos checklist	.25
34	Giants checklist	.10
35	Indians checklist	.30
36	Mariners checklist	.10
37	Mets checklist	.10
38	Orioles checklist	.10
39	Padres checklist	.10
40	Phillies checklist	.10
41	Pirates checklist	.10
42	Rangers checklist	.10
43	Red Sox checklist	.20
44	Reds checklist	.10
45	Royals checklist	.15
46	Tigers checklist	.15
47	Twins checklist	.15
48	White Sox checklist	.10
49	Yankees checklist	.50
50	Diamond Skills checklist	.40
51	Damon Buford	.15
52	Mike Nell	.10
53	Carlos Delgado	.75
54	Frank Rodriguez	.75
55	Manny Ramirez	6.00
56	Carl Everett	.30
57	Brien Taylor	.20
58	Kurt Miller	.10
59	Alex Ochoa	.40
60	Alex Gonzalez	.75
61	Darrell Sherman	.15
62	Dmitri Young	.50
63	Cliff Floyd	.75
64	Ray McDavid	.30
65	Rondell White	2.00
66	Chipper Jones	7.50
67	Allen Watson	.30
68	Tyler Green	.25
69	Steve Gibralter	.10
70	Calvin Reese	.25
71	Scott Burrell	.10
72	Julian Vasquez	.10
73	Juan Delarosa	.10
74	Lance Dickson	.10
75	Todd Van Poppel	.20
76	Joey Hamilton	.40
77	Mark Mimbs	.10
78	Austin Manahan	.10
79	Mike Milchin	.10
80	David Bell	.10
81	Terrell Lowery	.10
82	Tony Tarasco	.10
83	Shon Walker	.10
84	Robb Nen	.15
85	Turk Wendell	.20
86	John Byington	.10
87	Derek Reid	.10
88	Lee Heath	.10
89	Matt Anderson	1.50
90	Joe Perona	.10
91	Tito Navarro	.10
92	Scott Erwin	.10
93	Jim Pittsley	.10
94	Chris Seelbach	.10
95	Skeets Thomas	.10
96	Kevin Flora	.10
97	Scott Pose	.15
98	Jason Hardtke	.10
99	Joe Ciccarella	.10
100	Les Norman	.10
101	Joe Calder	.10
102	Willie Otanez	.15
103	Ray Holbert	.10
104	Dan Serafini	.15
105	Trevor Hoffman	.50
106	Todd Ritchie	.10
107	Lance Jennings	.10
108	Jon Farrell	.10
109	Rick Gorecki	.10
110	Kevin Stocker	.20
111	Joe Caruso	.10
112	Tom Nuneviller	.10
113	Matt Mieske	.25
114	Luis Ortiz	.10
115	Marty Cordova	.75
116	Rikkert Faneyte	.10
117	Rodney Bolton	.10
118	Steve Trachsel	.60
119	Sean Lowe	.10
120	Sean Ryan	.10
121	Tim Vanegmond	.10
122	Craig Paquette	.10
123	Andre Keene	.10
124	Kevin Roberson	.15
125	Mark Anthony	.10
126	Joe DeBerry	.10
127	Tracy Sanders	.10
128	Eric Christopherson	.10
129	Steve Dreyer	.10
130	Jeromy Burnitz	.40
131	Mike Lansing	.50
132	Russ Davis	.75
133	Pedro Castellano	.15
134	Troy Percival	.25
135	Tyrone Hill	.15
136	Rene Arocha	.15
137	John DeSilva	.10
138	Donnie Wall	.10
139	Justin Mashore	.10
140	Miguel Flores	.10
141	John Finn	.10
142	Paul Shuey	.15
143	Gabby Martinez	.10
144	Ryan Luzinski	.10
145	Brent Gates	.50
146	Manny Ramirez	5.00
147	Mark Hutton	.10
148	Derek Lee	.20
149	Marc Pisciotta	.15
150	Greg Hansell	.10
151	Tyler Houston	.15
152	Chris Pritchett	.15
153	Allen Watson	.15
154	Steve Karsay	.25
155	Carl Everett	.45
156	Mike Robertson	.10
157	Fausto Cruz	.10
158	Kiki Hernandez	.10
159	Bill Bliss	.10
160	Todd Hollandsworth	.75
161	Justin Thompson	.60
162	Ozzie Timmons	.15
163	Raul Mondesi	4.00
164	Shawn Estes	.40
165	Chipper Jones	7.50
166	Kurt Miller	.15
167	Tyler Green	.20
168	Jimmy Haynes	.10
169	David Doorneweerd	.10
170	Bubba Smith	.10
171	Scott Lydy	.15
172	Aaron Holbert	.10
173	Doug Glanville	.15
174	Benji Gil	.20
175	Eddie Williams	.10
176	Phil Hiatt	.15
177	Chris Durkin	.15
178	Brian Barber	.15
179	John Cummings	.10
180	Frank Campos	.10
181	Tim Worrell	.10
182	Tony Clark	5.00
183	T.R. Lewis	.10
184	Mike Lieberthal	.25
185	Keith Mitchell	.10
186	Rick Huisman	.10
187	Quilvio Veras	.20
188	Brian Hancock	.10
189	Tarrik Brock	.10
190	Herbert Perry	.10
191	Dave Staton	.15
192	Derek Lowe	.10
193	Joel Wolfe	.10
194	Lyle Mouton	.15
195	Greg Gohr	.10
196	Duane Singleton	.25
197	Jamie McAndrew	.20
198	Brad Pennington	.15
199	Pork Chop Pough	.25
200	Boo Moore	.10
201	Henry Blanco	.10
202	Gabe White	.30
203	Manny Cora	.15
204	Keith Gordon	.10
205	John Jackson	.10
206	Mike Hostetler	.10
207	Jeff McCurry	.10
208	Steve Olsen	.10
209	Roberto Mejia	.10
210	Ramon Caraballo	.15
211	Matt Whisenant	.15
212	Mike Bovee	.10
213	Riccardo Ingram	.15
214	Mike Rossiter	.10
215	Andres Duncan	.10
216	Steve Dunn	.15
217	Mike Grace	.10
218	Tim Howard	.10
219	Todd Jones	.15
220	Tyrone Kingwood	.10
221	Damon Buford	.15
222	Bobby Munoz	.15
223	Jim Campanis	.10
224	Johnny Ruffin	.15
225	Shawn Green	.75
226	Calvin Reese	.30
227	Kevin McGehee	.10
228	J.R. Phillips	.15
229	Rafael Quirico	.10
230	Mike Zimmerman	.10
231	Ron Lockett	.10
232	Bobby Reed	.10
233	John Roper	.15
234	John Mabry	.45
235	Chris Martin	.10
236	Ricky Otero	.15
237	Orlando Miller	.25
238	Scott Hatteberg	.20
239	Toby Borland	.25
240	Alan Newman	.10
241	Ivan Cruz	.10
242	Paul Byrd	.15
243	Daryl Henderson	.10
244	Adam Hyzdu	.15
245	Rich Becker	.25
246	Scott Ruffcorn	.10
247	Tommy Adams	.10
248	Jose Martinez	.10
249	Darrell Sherman	.15
250	Tom Nevers	.10
251	Brandon Wilson	.10
252	Mike Hampton	.10
253	Mo Sanford	.15
254	Alex Ochoa	.50
255	David McCarty	.15
256	Ray McDavid	.20
257	Roger Salkeld	.20
258	Jeff McNeely	.20
259	Jim Converse	.10
260	Greg Blosser	.10
261	Salomon Torres	.10
262	Tavo Alvarez	.10
263	Marc Newfield	.20
264	Carlos Delgado	3.00
265	Brien Taylor	.15
266	Frank Rodriguez	.60
267	Cliff Floyd	.50
268	Troy O'Leary	.15
269	Butch Huskey	.75
270	Michael Carter	.15
271	Eduardo Perez	.15
272	Gary Mota	.10
273	Mike Neill	.10
274	Dmitri Young	.75
275	Mike Kelly	.20
276	Rondell White	1.50
277	Midre Cummings	.25
278	Kerwin Moore	.15
279	Derrick White	.10
280	Howard Battle	.20
281	Mark Smith	.20
282	Ben Shelton	.15
283	Jose Oliva	.10
284	Steve Gibralter	.10
285	Billy Hall	.10
286	Nigel Wilson	.10
287	Brook Fordyce	.10
288	Mike Durrant	.10
289	Gary Caraballo	.10
290	Shane Andrews	.40
291	Aaron Sele	.50
292	Garret Anderson	2.50
293	Oscar Munoz	.10
294	Bobby Jones	.75
295	Joe Rosselli	.10
296	Chad Ogea	.50
297	Ugueth Urbina	.50
298	Ryan Hawblitzel	.15
299	Dennis Burlingame	.10
300	Damon Mashore	.10
301	Jeff Jackson	.10
302	Glenn Murray	.10
303	Darren Burton	.10
304	Scott Cepicky	.10
305	Phil Dauphin	.10
306	Kevin Tatar	.10
307	Domingo Jean	.10
308	Darren Oliver	.10
309	Joe Vitiello	.15
310	John Johnstone	.10
311	Bo Dodson	.10
312	Jon Shave	.10
313	Roberto Petagine	.10
314	Clifton Garrett	.10
315	Rob Butler	.15
316	Jermaine Swinton	.10
317	Alex Gonzalez	.75
318	Jeff Williams	.10
319	James Baldwin	.60
320	Scott Stahoviak	.25
321	John Cotton	.10
322	Jim Wawruck	.10
324	Brian Hunter	2.50
325	Joe Randa	.15
326	Robert Eenhoorn	.10
327	Rod Lofton	.10
328	Buck McNabb	.15
329	Jorge Fabregas	.20
330	Brian Koelling	.10

1992 Upper Deck Minor League Player of the Year

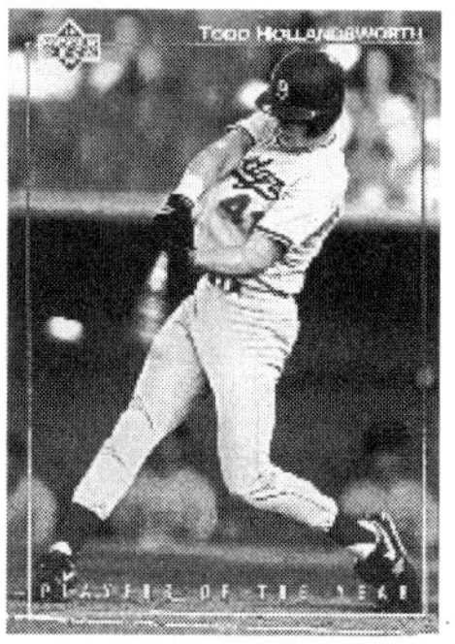

This 26-card insert set features players who are considered as the top minor league player for each major league team. Cards, which are numbered with a PY prefix, have full-bleed photos and gold foil stamping on the fronts.

		MT
Complete Set (26):		90.00
Common Player:		3.00
1	Garret Anderson	10.00
2	Gary Mota	3.00
3	Scott Lydy	3.00
4	Carlos Delgado	10.00
5	Chipper Jones	35.00
6	Troy O'Leary	3.00
7	Dmitri Young	8.00
8	Ozzie Timmons	3.00
9	Todd Hollandsworth	8.00
10	Cliff Floyd	8.00
11	Joe Rosselli	3.00
12	Chad Ogea	6.00
13	Tommy Adams	3.00
14	Bobby Jones	8.00
15	Mark Smith	4.00
16	Ray McDavid	4.00
17	Mike Lieberthal	6.00
18	Midre Cummings	4.00
19	Kurt Miller	3.00
20	Aaron Sele	6.00
21	Steve Gibralter	4.00
22	Phil Hiatt	3.00
23	Ivan Cruz	3.00
24	Marty Cordova	8.00
25	Brandon Taylor	3.00
26	Brien Taylor	6.00

1992 Upper Deck Minor League Top Prospect Holograms

These nine holograms were random inserts in Upper Deck's 1992 minor league packs. Cards, numbered with a TP prefix, feature nine of the top minor league prospects.

		MT
Complete Set (9):		48.00
Common Player:		3.00
(1)	Midre Cummings	3.00
(2)	Cliff Floyd	6.00
(3)	Chipper Jones	20.00
(4)	Mike Kelly	3.00
(5)	David McCarty	3.00
(6)	Frank Rodriguez	3.00
(7)	Rondell White	8.00
(8)	Dmitri Young	4.00
(9)	Brien Taylor	4.00

1992 Minor League Team Sets

While the number of minor league team sets issued in 1992 was much greater than the previous year, many of the small card-shop set makers left the field in favor of the Classic Best and Fleer/Pro-Cards combines. New to the team set market was Skybox (tracing its roots back to TC-MA) which issued team-set versions of its foil-pack AA and AAA cards. The only other new entity in the market was the Class A Midwest League which marketed an All-Star set. Abbreviations found in these listings are: BK (Burger King), Cal (California League), CB (Classic Best), DD (Dunkin' Donuts), FPC (Fleer/ProCards), SB (SkyBox) and SP (Sport Pro).

	MT
333 team sets and variations	
1992 SB AAA All-Stars (38)	15.00
1992 CB Albany Polecats (29)	10.00
1992 FPC Albany Polecats (27)	10.00
1992 FPC Albany Yankees (28)	4.00
1992 SB Albany Yankees (26)	5.50
1992 FPC Albuquerque Dukes (32)	17.50
1992 SB Albuquerque Dukes (26)	14.00
1992 Team Albuquerque Dukes (49)	190.00
1992 CB Appleton Foxes (30)	4.00
1992 FPC Appleton Foxes (32)	4.00
1992 FPC Arkansas Travelers (27)	3.00
1992 FPC Arkansas Travelers w/ Wendy's ad (28)	6.00
1992 SB Arkansas Travelers (26)	6.00
1992 CB Asheville Tourists (30)	8.00
1992 CB Auburn Astros (29)	4.00
1992 FPC Auburn Astros (31)	3.00
1992 CB Augusta Pirates (27)	3.00
1992 FPC Augusta Pirates (29)	3.00
1992 Cal Bakersfield Dodgers (33)	7.00
1992 CB Baseball City Royals (27)	6.00
1992 FPC Baseball City Royals (27)	5.00
1992 CB Batavia Clippers (29)	4.00
1992 FPC Batavia Cilppers (32)	3.00
1992 CB Bellingham Mariners (29)	6.50
1992 FPC Bellingham Mariners (33)	4.00
1992 CB Beloit Brewers (30)	5.00
1992 FPC Beloit Brewers (29)	5.00
1992 CB Bend Rockies (28)	5.00
1992 FPC Bend Rockies (27)	6.00
1992 FPC Billings Mustangs (30)	5.00
1992 SP Billings Mustangs (30)	8.00
1992 SB Binghampton Mets (26)	7.00
1992 FPC Binghampton Mets (28)	7.00
1992 SB Birmingham Barons (26)	6.00
1992 FPC Birmingham Barons (28)	3.00
1992 CB Bluefield Orioles (25)	4.00
1992 FPC Bluefield Orioles (26)	3.00
1992 CB Boise Hawks (30)	3.00
1992 FPC Boise Hawks (33)	3.00
1992 CB Bristol Tigers (29)	3.00
1992 FPC Bristol Tigers (33)	3.00
1992 FPC Buffalo Bisons (27)	6.00
1992 SB Buffalo Bisons (26)	5.50
1992 CB Burlington Astros (29)	3.00
1992 FPC Burlington Astros (30)	3.00
1992 CB Burlington Indians (30)	7.00
1992 FPC Burlington Indians (32)	3.00
1992 SP Butte Copper Kings (30)	6.00
1992 FPC Calgary Cannons (22)	6.50
1992 SB Calgary Cannons (26)	6.00
1992 Cal League All-Stars (53)	7.00
1992 FPC Canton-Akron Indians (28)	4.00
1992 SB Canton-Akron Indians (26)	6.00
1992 FPC Carolina Mudcats (26)	3.00
1992 SB Carolina Mud Cats (26)	5.50
1992 CB Cedar Rapids Reds (30)	5.00
1992 FPC Cedar Rapids Reds (30)	3.00
1992 CB Charleston Rainbows (24)	7.50
1992 FPC Charleston Rainbows (28)	5.00
1992 CB Charleston Wheelers (24)	6.00
1992 FPC Charleston Wheelers (25)	6.00
1992 FPC Charlotte Knights (25)	6.00
1992 SB Charlotte Knights (26)	5.50
1992 CB Charlotte Rangers (29)	4.00
1992 FPC Charlotte Rangers (27)	3.00
1992 FPC Chattanooga Lookouts (27)	4.00
1992 SB Chattanooga Lookouts (26)	5.50
1992 CB Clearwater Phillies (26)	4.00
1992 FPC Clearwater Phillies (32)	3.00
1992 CB Clinton Giants (30)	4.00
1992 FPC Clinton Giants (29)	3.00
1992 FPC Colorado Springs Sky Sox (28)	5.00
1992 SB Colorado Springs Sky Sox (26)	5.50
1992 CB Columbia Mets (29)	6.00
1992 FPC Columbia Mets (26)	6.00
1992 Play II Columbia Mets (42)	32.00
1992 Play II Columbia Mets inserts (9)	125.00
1992 FPC Columbus Clippers (28)	6.00
1992 Police Columbus Clippers (25)	7.50
1992 SB Columbus Clippers (26)	6.00
1992 CB Columbus Redstixx (29)	4.00
1992 FPC Columbus Redstixx (32)	5.00
1992 Team Columbus Redstixx (7)	4.00
1992 FPC Denver Zephyrs (28)	6.00
1992 Re/Max Denver Record Holders (20)	5.00
1992 SB Denver Zephyrs (26)	5.00
1992 CB Dunedin Blue Jays (30)	75.00
1992 FPC Dunedin Blue Jays (27)	12.00
1992 CB Durham Bulls (27)	30.00
1992 FPC Durham Bulls (28)	19.00
1992 Team Durham Bulls (29)	18.00
1992 FPC Edmonton Trappers (24)	8.00
1992 SB Edmonton Trappers (26)	8.00
1992 CB Elizabethton Twins (25)	5.00
1992 FPC Elizabethton Twins (28)	5.00
1992 CB Elmira Pioneers (26)	4.00
1992 FPC Elmira Pioneers (25)	5.00
1992 FPC El Paso Diablos (27)	3.00
1992 SB El Paso Diablos (26)	5.50
1992 CB Erie Sailors (30)	4.00
1992 FPC Erie Sailors (33)	3.00
1992 CB Eugene Emeralds (27)	13.00
1992 FPC Eugene Emeralds (26)	10.00
1992 CB Everett Giants (30)	4.00
1992 FPC Everett Giants (32)	4.00
1992 CB Fayetteville Generals (30)	7.00
1992 FPC Fayetteville Generals (29)	3.00
1992 CB Frederick Keys (28)	4.00
1992 FPC Frederick Keys (28)	4.00
1992 CB Ft. Lauderdale Yankees (25)	7.00
1992 FPC Ft. Lauderdale Yankees (31)	7.50
1992 Team Ft. Lauderdale Yankees (33)	7.00
1992 CB Ft. Myers Miracle (28)	4.00
1992 FPC Ft. Myers Miracle (27)	3.00
1992 CB Gastonia Rangers (27)	7.00
1992 FPC Gastonia Rangers (29)	7.00
1992 CB Geneva Cubs (29)	7.50
1992 FPC Geneva Cubs (28)	3.00
1992 SP Great Falls Dodgers (30)	9.00
1992 CB Greensboro Hornets (29)	22.00
1992 FPC Greensboro Hornets (30)	21.00
1992 FPC Greenville Braves (25)	8.00
1992 SB Greenville Braves (26)	9.00
1992 FPC Gulf Coast Dodgers (31)	10.00
1992 FPC Gulf Coast Mets (31)	15.00
1992 SP Gulf Coast Rangers (30)	6.00
1992 FPC Gulf Coast Yankees (30)	135.00
1992 FPC Hagerstown Suns (25)	4.00
1992 SB Hagerstown Suns (26)	6.00
1992 CB Hamilton Redbirds (30)	4.00
1992 FPC Hamilton Redbirds (32)	4.00
1992 FPC Harrisburg Senators (26)	4.00
1992 SB Harrisburg Senators (26)	6.50
1992 FPC Helena Brewers (27)	4.00
1992 SP Helena Brewers (27)	6.00
1992 CB High Desert Mavericks (30)	4.00
1992 Little Sun High School Prospects (30)	14.00
1992 CB Huntington Cubs (30)	8.50
1992 FPC Huntington Cubs (32)	6.00
1992 BK Huntsville Stars (26)	5.00
1992 SB Huntsville Stars (26)	5.50
1992 FPC Huntsville Stars (27)	5.00
1992 FPC Idaho Falls Gems (32)	5.00
1992 SP Idaho Falls Gems (29)	9.00
1992 FPC Indianapolis Indians (27)	6.00
1992 SB Indianapolis Indians (26)	6.00
1992 FPC Iowa Cubs (24)	5.00
1992 SB Iowa Cubs (26)	5.50
1992 FPC Jackson Generals (27)	4.00
1992 SB Jackson Generals (26)	6.00
1992 FPC Jacksonville Suns (26)	6.50
1992 SB Jacksonville Suns (26)	6.00
1992 CB Jamestown Expos (29)	7.00
1992 FPC Jamestown Expos (28)	5.00
1992 CB Johnson City Cardinals (28)	4.00
1992 FPC Johnson City Cardinals (31)	3.00
1992 CB Kane County Cougars (28)	10.00
1992 FPC Kane Couty Cougars (29)	11.00
1992 Team Kane County Cougars (30)	8.00
1992 CB Kenosha Twins (27)	6.00
1992 FPC Kenosha Twins (28)	3.50
1992 CB Kingsport Mets (26)	6.00
1992 FPC Kingsport Mets (31)	7.00
1992 CB Kinston Indians (29)	4.00
1992 FPC Kinston Indians (29)	22.00
1992 FPC Knoxville Blue Jays (29)	5.00
1992 SB Knoxville Blue Jays (26)	5.50
1992 CB Lakeland Tigers (30)	4.00
1992 FPC Lakeland Tigers (26)	3.00
1992 FPC Las Vegas Stars (24)	6.00
1992 SB Las Vegas Stars (26)	6.00
1992 SP Lethbridge Mounties (26)	6.00
1992 FPC London Tigers (29)	3.00
1992 SB London Tigers (26)	5.50
1992 FPC Louisville Redbirds (26)	6.00
1992 SB Louisville Redbirds (26)	5.50
1992 Team Louisville Redbirds (30)	8.00
1992 CB Lynchburg Red Sox (27)	7.00
1992 FPC Lynchburg Red Sox (26)	6.00
1992 CB Macon Braves (28)	6.50
1992 FPC Macon Braves (30)	5.00
1992 CB Madison Muskies (28)	4.00
1992 FPC Madison Muskies (29)	3.00
1992 CB Martinsville Phillies (30)	5.00
1992 FPC Martinsville Phillies (32)	3.00
1992 FPC Medicine Hat Blue Jays (24)	3.00
1992 SP Medicine Hat Blue Jays (30)	6.00
1992 FPC Memphis Chicks (29)	5.00
1992 SB Memphis Chicks (26)	6.00
1992 CB Miami Miracle (30)	6.00
1992 FPC Midland Angels (26)	6.00
1992 SB Midland Angels (26)	8.00
1992 1 Hour Midland Angels (28)	70.00
1992 Midwest League All-Stars (54)	13.00
1992 CB Modesto A's (27)	6.00
1992 Chong Modesto A's (26)	4.00
1992 FPC Modesto A's (22)	5.00
1992 CB Myrtle Beach Hurricanes (30)	8.50
1992 FPC Myrtle Beach Hurricanes (29)	7.00
1992 FPC Nashville Sounds (26)	6.00
1992 SB Nashville Sounds (26)	5.00
1992 Team Nashville Sounds (33)	7.00
1992 FPC New Britain Red Sox (27)	5.00
1992 SB New Britain Red Sox (26)	5.50
1992 CB Niagara Falls Rapids (29)	17.00
1992 FPC Niagara Falls Rapids (32)	12.00
1992 FPC Oklahoma City 89ers (28)	6.00
1992 SB Oklahoma City 89ers (26)	6.00
1992 FPC Omaha Royals (29)	5.00
1992 SB Omaha Royals (26)	6.00
1992 CB Oneonta Yankees (30)	6.00
1992 FPC Orlando Sunrays (26)	7.00
1992 SB Orlando Sunrays (26)	5.50
1992 CB Osceola Astros (29)	6.00
1992 FPC Osceola Astros (28)	6.00
1992 CB Palm Springs Angels (30)	7.00
1992 FPC Palm Springs Angels (29)	7.00
1992 DD Pawtucket Red Sox foldout	60.00
1992 FPC Pawtucket Red Sox (28)	10.00
1992 Fram Pawtucket Red Sox poster	50.00
1992 SB Pawtucket Red Sox (26)	6.00
1992 Team Peninsula Oilers (28)	7.00
1992 CB Peninsula Pilots (30)	4.00
1992 FPC Peninsula Pilots (28)	6.00
1992 CB Peoria Chiefs (30)	4.00
1992 Team Peoria Chiefs (31)	5.00
1992 FPC Phoenix Firebirds (26)	3.00
1992 SB Phoenix Firebirds (26)	5.00
1992 CB Pittsfield Mets (21)	14.00
1992 FPC Pittsfield Mets (28)	12.00
1992 FPC Portland Beavers (26)	5.00

1992 SB Portland Beavers (26)	5.50
1992 CB Princeton Reds (29)	4.00
1992 FPC Princeton Reds (29)	3.00
1992 CB Prince William Cannons (29)	5.00
1992 FPC Prince William Cannons (29)	3.00
1992 CB Pulaski Braves (29)	4.00
1992 FPC Pulaski Braves (32)	3.00
1992 CB Quad City Bandits (30)	4.00
1992 FPC Quad City Bandits (30)	4.00
1992 FPC Reading Phillies (29)	4.00
1992 SB Reading Phillies (26)	6.00
1992 Cal Reno Silver Sox (29)	3.00
1992 Bleacher Bums Richmond Braves (25)	19.00
1992 Bob's Richmond Braves (26):	70.00
1992 FPC Richmond Braves (28):	8.00
1992 Richmond Comix Richmond Braves (26)	24.00
1992 SB Richmond Braves (26)	7.50
1992 Ukrop's Richmond Braves (50)	30.00
1992 FPC Rochester Red Wings (26)	6.00
1992 SB Rochester Red Wings (26)	6.00
1992 CB Rockford Expos (30)	6.00
1992 FPC Rockford Expos (28)	6.00
1992 CB Salem Buccaneers (28)	5.00
1992 FPC Salem Buccaneers (28)	5.00
1992 CB Salinas Spurs (30)	4.00
1992 FPC Salinas Spurs (31)	3.00
1992 SP Salt Lake City Trappers (30)	6.00
1992 FPC San Antonio Missions (24)	14.00
1992 HEB San Antonio Missions (44)	70.00
1992 SB San Antonio Missions (26)	17.00
1992 CB San Bernardino Spirit (30)	4.00
1992 FPC San Bernardino Spirit (33)	3.00
1992 CB San Jose Giants (30)	5.00
1992 CB Sarasota White Sox (30)	6.00
1992 FPC Sarasota White Sox (30)	7.50
1992 CB Savannah Cardinals (25)	4.00
1992 FPC Savannah Cardinals (30)	3.00
1992 FPC Scranton Red Barons (27)	5.00
1992 SB Scranton Red Barons (26)	6.00
1992 Team Scranton Red Barons (30)	12.00
1992 FPC Shreveport Captains (27)	4.00
1992 SB Shreveport Captains (26)	6.00
1992 Play II South Atlantic League A-S (42)	20.00
1992 CB South Bend White Sox (27)	6.00
1992 FPC South Bend White Sox (30)	6.00
1992 CB Southern Oregon A's (30)	4.00
1992 FPC Southern Oregon A's (33)	3.00
1992 CB Spartanburg Phillies (25)	4.00
1992 FPC Spartanburg Phillies (29)	3.00
1992 CB Spokane Indians (30)	4.00
1992 FPC Spokane Indians (30)	3.00
1992 CB Springfield Cardinals (29)	6.00
1992 FPC Springfield Cardinals (29)	6.00
1992 CB St. Catharines Blue Jays (30)	5.00
1992 FPC St. Catharines Blue Jays (29)	6.00
1992 CB St. Lucie Mets (29)	6.00
1992 FPC St. Lucie Mets (30)	4.00
1992 CB St. Petersburg Cardinals (29)	4.00
1992 FPC St. Petersburg Cardinals (26)	3.00
1992 CB Stockton Ports (25)	4.00
1992 FPC Stockton Ports (28)	3.00
1992 FPC Syracuse Chiefs (31)	7.00
1992 MB Syracuse Chiefs foldout	20.00
1992 SB Syracuse Chiefs (26)	5.50
1992 Tallmadge Syracuse Chiefs foldout	15.00
1992 FPC Tacoma Tigers (26)	5.00
1992 SB Tacoma Tigers (26)	5.50
1992 FPC Tidewater Tides (28)	5.00
1992 SB Tidewater Tides (26)	6.00
1992 FPC Toledo Mud Hens (29)	5.00
1992 SB Toledo Mud Hens (26)	6.00
1992 FPC Tucson Toros (30)	6.00
1992 SB Tucson Toros (26)	6.00
1992 FPC Tulsa Drillers (27)	6.00
1992 FPC Tulsa Drillers w/ BBC Stores ad (28)	9.00
1992 SB Tulsa Drillers (26)	6.00
1992 Team Tulsa Drillers (30)	11.00
1992 CB Utica Blue Sox (26)	10.00
1992 FPC Vancouver Canadians (24)	5.00
1992 SB Vancouver Canadians (26)	5.50
1992 CB Vero Beach Dodgers (30)	5.00
1992 FPC Vero Beach Dodgers (32)	5.00
1992 CB Visalia Oaks (26)	11.00
1992 FPC Visalia Oaks (28)	10.00
1992 CB Waterloo Diamonds (30)	4.00
1992 FPC Waterloo Diamonds (27)	3.00
1992 CB Watertown Indians (29)	5.00
1992 FPC Watertown Indians (29)	3.00
1992 CB Welland Pirates (29)	4.00
1992 FPC Welland Pirates (30)	3.00
1992 CB West Palm Beach Expos (30)	8.00
1992 FPC West Palm Beach Expos (29)	7.50
1992 FPC Wichita Wranglers (21)	4.00
1992 SB Wichita Wranglers (26)	5.00
1992 CB Winston-Salem Spirits (28)	4.00
1992 FPC Winston-Salem Spirits (28)	3.00
1992 Team Winston-Salem Spirits (27)	4.00
1992 CB Winter Haven Red Sox (30)	4.00
1992 FPC Winter Haven Red Sox (30)	3.00
1992 CB Yakima Bears (26)	4.00
1992 FPC Yakima Bears (32)	3.00

1993 Classic Best Promos

These cards were distributed to dealers to preview the forthcoming Classic Best set.

		MT
	Complete Set (4):	5.00
	Common Player:	.50
PR1	Derek Jeter	4.00
PR2	Carlos Delgado (MVP)	2.00
PR3	Rick Helling	.50
PR4	Derek Wallace	.50

1993 Classic Best

Classic Best's 1993 Minor League series is 300 cards, plus four insert sets, a puzzle set and autographed cards from eight players. The set includes players from A, AA and AAA classifications. Autographed Carlos Delgado, Cliff Floyd, Jeffrey Hammonds, Derek Jeter, Mike Kelly, Phil Nevin, Paul Shuey and Dmitri Young cards (1,200 each) were randomly inserted into packs, as were puzzle contest pieces. By completing a nine-card puzzle, 500 collectors could win a plaque of the eight autographed cards featured in the series. The set's inserts are: Young Guns, Expansion #1 Picks, MVPs and Player and Manager of the Year.

		MT
	Complete Set (300):	15.00
	Common Player:	.05
1	Paul Shuey	.10
2	Brad Clontz	.10
3	Phil Dauphin	.05
4	Kevin Flora	.05
5	Doug Glanville	.15
6	Hilly Hathaway	.05
7	Scott Hatteberg	.15
8	Ryan Hawblitzel	.05
9	Bob Henkel	.05
10	Mike Kelly	.10
11	Jose Malave	.05
12	Jeff McNeely	.10
13	Roberto Mejia	.05
14	Kevin Roberson	.15
15	Chad Roper	.10
16	John Roper	.05
17	Pete Rose Jr.	.40
18	Paul Russo	.10
19	John Salles	.05
20	Tracy Sanders	.05
21	Chris Saunders	.05
22	Jason Schmidt	.10
23	Aaron Sele	.75
24	Bob Abreu	.45
25	Don Sparks	.05
26	Scott Stahoviak	.10
27	Matt Stairs	.20
28	Todd Steverson	.15
29	Ozzie Timmons	.10
30	Michael Tucker	.75
31	Jose Viera	.05
32	B.J. Wallace	.15
33	Mark Wohlers	.20
34	Gabe White	.25
35	Rick White	.05
36	Rondell White	1.00
37	Gerald Williams	.15
38	Mike Williams	.05
39	Todd Williams	.05
40	Desi Wilson	.10
41	Johnny Ard	.05
42	Jamie Arnold	.15
43	Howard Battle	.10
44	Greg Blosser	.10
45	Rob Butler	.05
46	Dan Carlson	.05
47	Joe Caruso	.05
48	Bobby Chouinard	.10
49	Adell Davenport	.05
50	Juan De La Rosa	.05
51	Alex Gonzalez	.60
52	Steve Hosey	.10
53	Rick Krivda	.05
54	T.R. Lewis	.10
55	Jose Mercedes	.10
56	Melvin Nieves	.10
57	Luis Ortiz	.05
58	Joe Rosselli	.10
59	Brian Sackinsky	.05
60	Salomon Torres	.10
61	James Baldwin	.20
62	Travis Baptist	.10
63	Bret Boone	.50
64	Mike Buddie	.05
65	Paul Carey	.05
66	Tim Crabtree	.10
67	Tony Longmire	.15
68	Robert Eenhoorn	.05
69	Paul Ellis	.05
70	Shawn Estes	.20
71	Andy Fox	.05
72	Shawn Green (photo actually Alex Gonzalez)	.15
73	Jimmy Haynes	.05
74	Sterling Hitchcock	.15
75	Mark Hutton	.05
76	Domingo Jean	.05
77	Kevin Jordan	.10
78	Steve Karsay	.25
79	Paul Fletcher	.05
80	Mike Milchin	.05
81	Lyle Mouton	.10
82	Bobby Munoz	.10
83	Alex Ochoa	.45
84	Steve Olsen	.05
85	Billy Owens	.05
86	Eddie Pearson	.05
87	Mike Robertson	.05
88	Johnny Ruffin	.15
89	Mark Smith	.15
90	Brandon Wilson	.05
91	Derek Jeter	4.00
92	Edgardo Alfonzo	.65
93	Jeff Alkire	.10
94	Roger Bailey	.10
95	Jeff Barry	.05
96	Terrell Buckley	.50
97	Hector Carrasco	.10
98	Danny Clyburn	.10
99	Darren Burton	.05
100	Scott Eyre	.05
101	Chad Fox	.10
102	Joe Hudson	.05
103	Jason Hutchins	.05
104	Bobby Jones	.50
105	Jason Kendall	.45
106	Rickey Magdaleno	.05
107	Buck McNabb	.10
108	Doug Mlicki	.05
109	Chris Eddy	.05
110	Jon Lieber	.10
111	Ken Powell	.05
112	Todd Pridy	.05
113	Marquis Riley	.05
114	Steve Rodriguez	.10
115	Brian Rupp	.05
116	Yuri Sanchez	.05
117	Al Shirley	.05
118	Paul Spoljaric	.10
119	Amaury Telemaco	.10
120	Shon Walker	.10
121	Tavo Alvarez	.10
122	Shane Andrews	.15
123	Billy Ashley	.10
124	Brian Barber	.10
125	Trey Beamon	.25
126	Scott Bryant	.05
127	Scott Bullett	.10
128	Ozzie Canseco	.10
129	Brian Carpenter	.10
130	Roger Cedeno (photos actually Dan Melendez)	.25
131	Randy Curtis	.05
132	Alberto De Los Santos	.05
133	Steve Dixon	.05
134	Joey Eischen	.10
135	Brook Fordyce	.10
136	Rick Gorecki	.05
137	Lee Hancock	.05
138	Todd Hollandsworth	.50
139	Frank Jacobs	.05
140	Mark Johnson	.25
141	Albie Lopez	.05
142	Dan Malendez	.05
143	William Pennyfeather	.05
144	Scott Lydy	.10
145	Chris Snopek	.15
146	Quilvio Veras	.15
147	Jose Vidro	.05
148	Allen Watson	.10
149	Matt Whisenant	.05
150	Craig Wilson	.05
151	Rich Becker	.20
152	Mike Durant	.05
153	Brad Ausmus	.10
154	Robbie Beckett	.10
155	Steve Dunn	.05
156	Paul Byrd	.05
157	Jason Bere	.35
158	Ben Blomdahl	.05
159	John Brothers	.05
160	Tim Costo	.10
161	Joel Chimelis	.05
162	Kenny Carlyle	.05
163	Garvin Alston	.10
164	Sean Bergman	.05
165	Marshall Boze	.10
166	Terry Burrows	.05
167	Danny Bautista	.10
168	Jason Bates	.15
169	Brent Bowers	.05
170	Rico Brogna	.15
171	Armann Brown	.05
172	Brant Brown	.25
173	Julio Bruno	.05
174	Mike DeJean	.05
175	Nick Delvecchio	.10
176	Bobby Bonds Jr.	.15
177	Miguel Castellano	.05
178	Tommy Adams	.10
179	Alan Burke	.05
180	John Burke	.10
181	Ivan Cruz	.05
182	Johnny Damon	.50
183	Carl Everett	.25
184	Jorge Fabregas	.15
185	John Fantauzzi	.05
186	Mike Farmer	.05
187	Mike Farrell	.05
188	Omar Garcia	.05
189	Brent Gates	.25
190	Jason Giambi	.75
191	K.C. Gullum	.05
192	Chris Gomez	.10
193	Ricky Greene	.10
194	Willie Greene	.15
195	Benji Grigsby	.10
196	Mike Groppuso	.05
197	Johnny Guzman	.10
198	Bob Hamelin	.20
199	Joey Hamilton	.25
200	Chris Haney	.10
201	Donald Harris	.10
202	Andy Hartung	.10
203	Chris Hatcher	.05
204	Rick Helling	.25
205	Edgar Herrera	.05
206	Aaron Holbert	.05
207	Ray Holbert	.05
208	Tyler Houston	.15
209	Brian Hunter	.35
210	Miguel Jiminez	.10
211	Charles Johnson	.75
212	Corey Kapano	.05
213	Tom Knauss	.05
214	Brian Koelling	.10
215	Brian Lane	.05
216	Kevin Legault	.05
217	Mark Lewis	.15
218	Luis Lopez	.10
219	Jose Martinez	.10
220	Mitch Meluskey	.25
221	Casey Mendenhall	.05
222	Danny Mitchell	.05
223	Tony Mitchell	.05
224	Ritchie Moody	.10
225	James Mouton	.10
226	Steve Murphy	.05
227	Mike Neill	.05
228	Tom Nevers	.10
229	Alan Newman	.05
230	Tom Nuneviller	.05
231	Jonathan Nunnally	.20
232	Chad Ogea	.20
233	Ray Ortiz	.05
234	Orlando Palmeiro	.10
235	Craig Paquette	.10
236	Troy Percival	.15
237	Bobby Perna	.05
238	John Pricher	.05
239	Ken Ramos	.05
240	Joe Randa	.15
241	Ron Blazier	.05
242	Terry Bradshaw	.10
243	Jason Hisey	.05
244	Sean Lowe	.05
245	Chad McConnell	.15
246	Jackie Nickell	.05
247	Pat Rapp	.10
248	Calvin Reese	.15
249	Desi Relaford	.15
250	Troy Ricker	.05
251	Todd Ritchie	.10
252	Chris Roberts	.10
253	Scott Sanders	.05
254	Ruben Santana	.10
255	Chris Seelbach	.05
256	Dan Serafini	.10
257	Curtis Shaw	.05
258	Kennie Steenstra	.10
259	Kevin Stocker	.15
260	Tanyon Sturtze	.05
261	Tim Stutheit	.05
262	Jamie Taylor	.10
263	Chad Townsend	.05
264	Steve Trachsel	.30
265	Jose Valentin	.10
266	K.C. Waller	.05
267	Chris Weinke	.15
268	Darrell Whitmore	.10
269	Juan Williams	.05
270	Tim Worrell	.10
271	Tim Belk	.05
272	London Bradley	.05
273	Tilson Brito	.05
274	Felipe Crespo	.05
275	Kenny Felder	.10
276	Billy Hall	.05
277	Terrell Hansen	.05
278	Rod Henderson	.10
279	Bobby Holley	.05
280	Bobby Hughes	.15
281	Rick Huisman	.05
282	Jack Johnson	.05
283	Gabby Martinez	.10
284	Jose Millares	.05
285	Jason Moler	.15
286	Willie Mota	.10
287	Marty Neff	.05

288	Eric Owens	.05
289	Daryl Ratliff	.05
290	Ozzie Sanchez	.05
291	Dave Silvestri	.10
292	Chris Stynes	.05
293	Aubrey Waggoner	.05
294	Jimmy White	.05
295	Jim Campanis	.10
296	Tony Womack	.50
297	Checklist 1	.05
298	Checklist 2	.05
299	Checklist 3	.05
300	Checklist 4	.05
----	Derek Wallace (Promo card, 1993 Nat'l Convention)	2.00

1993 Classic Best Ad Cards

Two of baseball's brightest prospects in 1993 are featured on this pair of advertising cards issued as "fillers" to round out 30-card team sets of Classic Best minor league baseball cards. The cards advertise the quartet of chase sets to be found in 1993 Classic Best foil packs. Backgrounds on front and back are black, with white type and color Classic Best logos. Color photos of the players appear on the right side of the front, though the players are not identified.

		MT
Complete Set (2):		7.00
(1)	Chipper Jones	6.00
(2)	Brien Taylor	1.00

1993 Classic Best Autographs

In its 1993 foil packs, Classic Best randomly included autographed cards of eight top prospects. Each player signd 1,200 cards.

		MT
Complete Set (8):		200.00
Common Player:		15.00
(1)	Carlos Delgado	35.00
(2)	Cliff Floyd	25.00
(3)	Jeffrey Hammonds	20.00
(4)	Derek Jeter	80.00
(5)	Mike Kelly	15.00
(6)	Phil Nevin	15.00
(7)	Paul Shuey	15.00
(8)	Dmitri Young	20.00

1993 Classic Best Expansion #1 Picks

These two cards, featuring the top picks by the Major League's two new expansion clubs (Colorado Rockies and Florida Marlins), were randomly inserted in 1993 Classic Best foil packs. The cards are numbered with an EP prefix.

		MT
Complete Set (2):		4.00
1	John Burke	1.00
2	Charles Johnson	3.00

1993 Classic Best MVPs

These 10 cards, numbered with an MVP prefix, were randomly inserted into 1993 Classic Best foil packs. The cards feature MVP-caliber prospects from the minors.

		MT
Complete Set (10):		10.00
Common Player:		.50
1	Bubba Smith	.50
2	Javy Lopez	4.00
3	Marty Cordova	1.50
4	Troy O'Leary	.50
5	Steve Gibralter	.50
6	Gary Mota	.50
7	Larry Sutton	.50
8	Dan Frye	.50
9	Russ Davis	1.50
10	Carlos Delgado	3.00

1993 Classic Best Player & Manager of the Year

This two-card set features Carlos Delgado as the player of the year and Marc Hill as the manager of the year. Cards, numbered with a PM prefix, were random inserts in 1993 Classic Best foil packs.

		MT
Complete Set (2):		3.00
1	Carlos Delgado	3.00
2	Marc Hill	.75

1993 Classic Best Young Guns

These 28 foil-printed cards were randomly inserted into Classic Best's 1993 foil packs. The cards are numbered with a YG prefix.

		MT
Complete Set (28):		12.50
Common Player:		.15
1	Midre Cummings	.20
2	Carlos Delgado	1.00
3	Cliff Floyd	.60
4	Jeffrey Hammonds	.25
5	Tyrone Hill	.15
6	Butch Huskey	.25
7	Chipper Jones	3.75
8	Mike Lieberthal	.20
9	David McCarty	.15
10	Ray McDavid	.15
11	Kurt Miller	.15
12	Raul Mondesi	2.00
13	Chad Mottola	.20
14	Calvin Murray	.20
15	Phil Nevin	.15
16	Marc Newfield	.20
17	Eduardo Perez	.20
18	Manny Ramirez	2.50
19	Edgar Renteria	1.00
20	Frank Rodriguez	.20
21	Scott Ruffcorn	.15
22	Brien Taylor	.20
23	Justin Thompson	.25
24	Mark Thompson	.15
25	Todd Van Poppel	.20
26	Joe Vitiello	.15
27	Derek Wallace	.20
28	Dmitri Young	.40

1993 Classic Best AA All-Star Game Souvenir Sheet

This 11" x 8-1/2" souvenir sheet was distributed at the 1993 Class AA All-Star Game in Memphis on July 12. Printed on glossy cardboard, the sheet features reproductions of the CB cards of five participants in the game. In the background is a ghost image of a collage of caps from more than a dozen AA teams. The back is blank and the sheet carries a seal at lower-left with a serial number from within an edition of 10,350.

	MT
Souvenir Sheet: Brian Barber, Carlos Delgado, Cliff Floyd, Manny Ramirez, Frank Rodriguez	6.00

1993 Classic Best/ Fisher Nuts Stars of the Future

Nineteen projected stars of the future were included in this set produced by Classic Best as a promotion for Fisher Nuts. Cards are similar in format to regular-issue Classic Best cards of 1992, but feature Fisher Nuts advertising on front and back.

		MT
Complete Set (20):		17.50
Common Player:		.50
1	Joe Vitiello	1.00
2	Steve Gibralter	.50
3	Rob Butler	.50
4	Carlos Delgado	2.00
5	Chipper Jones	8.00
6	Mike Kelly	.50
7	Marc Newfield	1.00
8	Aaron Sele	1.50
9	Brent Gates	1.00
10	Eduardo Perez	.50
11	Mike Lieberthal	.75
12	Midre Cummings	.75
13	Dmitri Young	1.00
14	Brien Taylor	.50
15	David McCarty	.50
16	Scott Ruffcorn	.50
17	Cliff Floyd	2.50
18	Rondell White	2.50
19	Paul Shuey	.50
---	Checklist	.10

1993 Classic Best Gold Promos

This three card set was distributed at Tri-Star Sports' 1993 spring training card show in Phoenix. Cards are virtually identical to the regular-issue Classic Best Gold except for a gold-foil Tri-Star show logo on front and numbering "X of 3" on back.

		MT
Complete Set (3):		3.00
Common Player:		1.00
1	David McCarty	1.00
2	Mike Kelly	1.00
3	Barry Bonds	2.00

1993 Classic Best Gold

The 1993 Classic Best Minor League Baseball Gold Premiere Edition cards feature three color photos of each player and are foil-stamped on both sides. Each card is color-coded using team colors and includes statistics through the 1992 season. The set includes 216 players from Double A, Single A and Rookie leagues, plus randomly inserted autographed cards of Barry Bonds and Gary Sheffield. No factory sets or jumbo packs were produced; cards are limited to 6,000 sequentially-numbered 10-box cases.

		MT
Complete Set (220):		24.00
Common Player:		.05
Barry Bonds Auto.:		100.00
Gary Sheffield Auto.:		40.00
1	Barry Bonds	1.00
2	Mark Hutton	.05
3	Lyle Mouton	.05
4	Don Sparks	.05
5	Joe Randa	.15
6	Dave Mlicki	.05
7	Ken Ramos	.05
8	Bill Wertz	.05
9	Jon Shave	.05
10	Dan Smith	.10
11	William Canate	.05
12	Albie Lopez	.05
13	Rod McCall	.05
14	Paul Shuey	.10
15	Ian Doyle	.05
16	Marc Marini	.05
17	Brien Taylor	.10
18	Mike Kelly	.10
19	Andy Nezelek	.05
20	Marcos Armas	.05
21	Chad Ogea	.25
22	Frank Rodriguez	.25
23	Aaron Sele	.40
24	Tim Vanegmond	.05
25	Phil Hiatt	.10
26	Dan Rohrmeir (Rohrmeier)	.05
27	Greg Blosser	.10
28	Scott Hatteberg	.10
29	Ed Riley	.05
30	Edgar Alfonzo	.05
31	Jorge Fabregas	.10
32	Eduardo Perez	.10
33	John Cummings	.10
34	Bubba Smith	.05
35	Kevin Jordan	.10
36	Tyler Green	.15
37	Heath Haynes	.05
38	Gabe White	.20
39	Doug Glanville	.10
40	Jose Viera	.05
41	Richie Becker	.25
42	Marty Cordova	.60
43	Mike Durant	.05
44	Todd Ritchie	.10
45	Scott Stahoviak	.10
46	Tavo Alvarez	.10
47	Chris Malinoski	.05
48	Rondell White	1.50
49	Tim Worrell	.05
50	Benji Gil	.10
51	Ben Blomdahl	.05
52	Rich Kelley	.05
53	Justin Thompson	.20
54	Scott Pose	.10
55	John Roper	.05
56	Rafael Chaves	.05
57	Billy Hall	.05
58	Ray McDavid	.10
59	Mark Smith	.20
60	Jeff Williams	.05

61	Bobby Jones	.35
62	Stanton Cameron	.05
63	Mike Lumley	.05
64	Troy Buckley	.05
65	James Dougherty	.10
66	Chris Hill	.05
67	Tom Nevers	.10
68	Joe Rosselli	.05
69	Steve Whitaker	.05
70	Butch Huskey	.50
71	Shane Andrews	.20
72	Cliff Floyd	.45
73	Alex Ochoa	.20
74	Brent Gates	.25
75	Curtis Shaw	.05
76	Midre Cummings	.25
77	Steve Olsen	.05
78	Mike Robertson	.05
79	Scott Ruffcorn	.10
80	Brandon Wilson	.10
81	Darren Burton	.05
82	Kerwin Moore	.05
83	Joe Vitiello	.15
84	Hugh Walker	.05
85	Howard Battle	.10
86	Rob Butler	.05
87	Carlos Delgado	1.50
88	Jeff Ware	.05
89	Mike Hostetler	.05
90	Brian Kowitz	.05
91	Ryan Hawblitzel	.05
92	Juan De La Rosa	.05
93	David McCarty	.15
94	Paul Russo	.05
95	Dan Cholowsky	.10
96	Dmitri Young	.40
97	Paul Ellis	.05
98	Jay Kirkpatrick	.05
99	Jeff Jackson	.05
100	Duane Singleton	.10
101	Kiki Hernandez	.05
102	Raul Hernandez	.05
103	Brian Bevil	.05
104	Mark Johnson	.10
105	Bob Abreu	.75
106	Gary Mota	.05
107	Jose Cabrera	.05
108	Jeff Runion	.05
109	B.J. Wallace	.15
110	Jim Arnold	.05
111	Dwight Maness	.05
112	Fernando DaSilva	.05
113	Chris Burr	.05
114	Dan Serafini	.10
115	Derek Jeter	4.00
116	Lew Hill	.05
117	Andy Pettitte	2.00
118	Keith John	.05
119	Sean Lowe	.10
120	T.J. Mathews	.10
121	Ricardo Medina	.05
122	Scott Gentile	.05
123	Everett Stull	.05
124	Manny Ramirez	3.00
125	Archie Corbin	.05
126	Matt Karchner	.05
127	Domingo Mota	.05
128	Alex Gonzalez	.75
129	Joe Lis	.05
130	Paul Spoljaric	.10
131	Clifton Garrett	.05
132	Marc Hill	.05
133	Jesus Martinez	.05
134	Salomon Torres	.05
135	Tommy Eason	.05
136	Matt Whisenant	.05
137	Jon Zuber	.05
138	Luis Martinez	.05
139	Glenn Murray	.05
140	John Saffer	.05
141	Tommy Adams	.10
142	Manny Cervantes	.05
143	George Glinatsis	.05
144	Chris Dessellier	.05
145	Joe Pomierski	.05
146	John Vanhof	.05
147	Matt Williams	.05
148	Maurice Christmas	.05
149	Damon Hollins	.20
150	Sean Smith	.05
151	Doug Hecker	.05
152	Jamie Sepeda	.05
153	Steve Solomon	.05
154	Jeff Tabaka	.05
155	Greg Elliott	.05
156	Jim Waring	.05
157	Omar Garcia	.05
158	Ricky Otero	.10
159	Jami Brewington	.05
160	Chad Fonville	.10
161	Sean Runyan	.05
162	Jim Givens	.05
163	Dennis McNamara	.05
164	Hudy Pemberton	.05
165	Brian Raabe	.05
166	Jeffrey Hammonds	.50
167	Chris Hatcher	.15
168	Chris Saunders	.05
169	Aaron Fultz	.05
170	Mike Freitas	.05
171	Tim Adkins	.05
172	Chipper Jones	4.00
173	Brandon Cromer	.10
174	Shannon Stewart	.20
175	David Tollison	.05
176	Rob Adkins	.05
177	Todd Steverson	.15
178	Dennis Konuszewski	.05
179	Marty Neff	.05
180	Vernon Spearman	.05
181	Don Wengert	.05
182	Alan Battle	.10
183	Michael Moore	.05
184	Sherard Clinkscales	.10
185	Jamie Dismuke	.10
186	Tucker Hammargren	.05
187	John Hrusovsky	.05
188	Elliott Quinones	.05
189	Calvin Reese	.20
190	Rich Ireland	.05
191	Shawn Estes	.10
192	Greg Shockey	.05
193	Mike Zimmerman	.05
194	Danny Clyburn	.15
195	Jason Kendall	.50
196	Shon Walker	.10
197	Gary Wilson	.05
198	John Dillinger	.05
199	Jim Keefe	.05
200	Eddie Pearson	.05
201	Johnny Damon	.40
202	Jim Pittsley	.05
203	Jason Bere	.25
204	James Baldwin	.30
205	John Burke	.15
206	Scot Sealy	.05
207	Ken Carlyle	.05
208	Tim Crabtree	.10
209	Quilvio Veras	.15
210	Edgardo Alfonzo	.35
211	Adell Davenport	.05
212	Dan Frye	.05
213	Derek Lowe	.10
214	Steve Gibralter	.10
215	Troy O'Leary	.10
216	Gary Sheffield	.45
217	Checklist 1-55	.05
218	Checklist 56-110	.05
219	Checklist 111-165	.05
220	Checklist 166-220	.05

1993 Classic Best Gold LPs

These Limited Print (LP) cards were random inserts in white jumbo packs of Classic Best, seeded on average about two per box. The LPs share the basic design of the Classic Best Gold set, but have on back a congratulatory message on receiving the LP insert.

		MT
Complete Set (5):		15.00
Common Player:		3.00
1	David McCarthy	3.00
2	Brien Taylor	4.00
3	Joe Vitiello	3.00
4	Mike Kelly	3.00
5	Carlos Delgado	4.00

Modern cards in Near Mint condition are valued at about 75% of the Mint value shown here. Excellent-condition cards are worth 50%. Cards in lower grades are not generally collectible.

1993 Classic 4 Sport

Fifty top players from the 1993 draft are featured among their counterparts in the other team sports in the base set, parallels and inserts of the '93 4 Sport issue. Only the baseball players are listed here.

		MT
Complete (Baseball) Set (50):		4.00
Common Player:		.05
260	Alex Rodriguez	2.00
PR4	Alex Rodriguez (promo card)	2.00
261	Darren Dreifort	.50
262	Matt Brunson	.15
263	Matt Drews	.10
264	Wayne Gomes	.10
265	Jeff Granger	.10
266	Steve Soderstrom	.05
267	Brooks Kieschnick	.15
268	Daron Kirkreit	.10
269	Billy Wagner	.50
270	Alan Benes	.25
271	Scott Christman	.05
272	Willie Adams	.10
273	Jermaine Allensworth	.15
274	Jason Baker	.05
275	Brian Banks	.05
276	Marc Barcelo	.05
277	Jeff D'Amico	.10
278	Todd Dunn	.10
279	Dan Ehler	.05
280	Tony Fuduric	.05
281	Ryan Hancock	.05
282	Vee Hightower	.05
283	Andre King	.10
284	Brett King	.05
285	Derrek Lee	.20
286	Andrew Lorraine	.05
287	Eric Ludwick	.05
288	Ryan McGuire	.50
289	Anthony Medrano	.05
290	Joel Moore	.05
291	Dan Perkins	.05
292	Kevin Pickford	.05
293	Jon Ratliff	.05
294	Bryan Rekar	.05
295	Andy Rice	.05
296	Carl Schulz	.05
297	Chris Singleton	.05
298	Cameron Smith	.05
299	Marc Valdes	.05
300	Joe Wagner	.05
301	John Wasdin	.10
302	Pat Watkins	.05
303	Dax Winslett	.05
304	Jamey Wright	.15
305	Kelly Wunsch	.15
306	Jeff D'Amico	.10
307	Brian Anderson	.15
308	Trot Nixon	.25
309	Kirk Presley	.05

1993 Classic 4 Sport Draft Stars

Top draft picks in all four major team sports are featured in this chrome-technology insert set, found one per jumbo pack of Classic 4 Sport. The cards feature action photos on a silver-metallic background with gold-foil graphics. At lower-left on each card is a notice that it is one of 80,000. Conventionally printed backs have another photo, personal data and career highlight. Only the baseball players are listed here.

		MT
Common Player:		.50
DS55	Alex Rodriguez	5.00
DS56	Brooks Kieschnick	1.00
DS57	Jeff Granger	.50

1993 Classic 4 Sport Gold

Fifty top baseball players from the 1993 draft are featured among their counterparts in the other major team sports in this factory set of gold edition parallel cards. Each set contains autographed cards of Alex Rodriguez, Jerome Bettis, Chris Gratton and Alonzo Mourning, in an edition of 3,900 each. Only the baseball players are listed here.

	MT
Complete (Baseball) Set (50):	20.00
Common Player:	.25
Gold stars valued at 5X regular version	
Alex Rodriguez (autographed edition of 3,900)	60.00

1993 Classic 4 Sport Inserts

A number of baseball players were featured among the draft picks of the major team sports in the many insert series of the '93 Classic 4 Sport issue. Only the baseball players are listed here.

		MT
	TRI-CARDS	
3/8/13	Jeff Granger, Brooks Kieschnick, Alex Rodriguez	5.00
5/10/15	Alex Rodriguez	10.00
	LIMITED PRINT	
LP18	Alex Rodriguez	6.00
LP19	Darren Dreifort	1.00
LP20	Jeff Granger	1.00
LP21	Brooks Kieschnick	1.00
	ACETATES	
9	Alex Rodriguez	6.00
10	Jeff Granger	1.00

1993 Classic 4 Sport McDonald's

These 4 Sport "Exclusive Collection" cards were distributed in portions of the Mid-Atlantic states and central Florida at McDonald's. Besides established stars and prospects in each of the major team sports, the five-card packs contained random LP (Limited Production) inserts, autographs and redemption cards for autographed memorabilia. Cards have action photos bordered at right by a forest green strip with the player name and position in gold-foil. A special logo is at upper-right. Backs repeat a portion of the photo along with personal data, stats and career highlights. A gold-foil McDonald's arches logo is at bottom. Only the baseball players among the 35 cards are listed here.

		MT
Common Player:		.25
11	Darren Daulton	.45
26	Bull and Baby Bull (Greg Luzinski, Ryan Luzinski)	.45
31	Chad McConnell	.25
32	Phil Nevin	.25
33	Paul Shuey	.35
34	Derek Wallace	.25

1993-94 Fleer Excel

Fleer's 1993-94 minor league set features players who have never appeared in a Major League game. The set of 300, up from 250 cards the previous year, uses UV coating for card fronts and backs, plus gold-foil stamping on the fronts. There are 297 players included in the regular issue, plus three checklists. Players are arranged alphabetically within their major league organization and league. Three insert sets were also available: Minor League All-Stars, League Leaders and "First Year Phenoms." Cards from the three insert sets were randomly included in foil packs.

	MT
Complete Set (300):	40.00
Common Player:	.10

1 Armando Benitez .20
2 Stanton Cameron .10
3 Eric Chavez 2.00
4 Rick Forney .10
5 Jim Foster .10
6 Curtis Goodwin .20
7 Jimmy Haynes .15
8 Scott Klingenbeck .10
9 Rick Krivda .10
10 T.R. Lewis .10
11 Brian Link .10
12 Scott McClain .10
13 Alex Ochoa .50
14 Jay Powell .15
15 Brian Sackinsky .10
16 Brad Tyler .10
17 Gregg Zaun .15
18 Joel Bennett .10
19 Felix Colon .10
20 Ryan McGuire 1.50
21 Frank Rodriguez .20
22 Tim Vanegmond .10
23 Garret Anderson 1.00
24 Jorge Fabregas .20
25 P.J. Forbes .10
26 John Fritz .10
27 Todd Greene .75
28 Jose Musset .10
29 Orlando Palmeiro .10
30 John Pricher .10
31 Chris Pritchett .15
32 Marquis Riley .10
33 Luis Andujar .10
34 James Baldwin .40
35 Brian Boehringer .10
36 Ron Coomer .10
37 Ray Durham .75
38 Robert Ellis .10
39 Jeff Pierce .10
40 Olmedo Saenz .10
41 Brandon Wilson .30
42 Ian Doyle .10
43 Jason Fronio .10
44 Derek Hacopian .10
45 Daron Kirkreit .25
46 Mike Neal .10
47 Chad Ogea .40
48 Cesar Perez .10
49 Omar Ramirez .10
50 J.J. Thobe .10
51 Casey Whitten .10
52 Eric Danapilis .10
53 Brian Edmondson .10
54 Tony Fuduric .10
55 Rick Greene .10
56 Bob Higginson 1.50
57 Felipe Lira .15
58 Joshua Neese .10
59 Shannon Penn .10
60 John Rosengren .10
61 Phil Stidham .10
62 Justin Thompson .75
63 Shawn Wooten .10
64 Brian Bevil .10
65 Mel Bunch .10
66 Johnny Damon 1.00
67 Chris Eddy .10
68 Jon Lieber .10
69 Les Norman .10
70 Jim Pittsley .10
71 Kris Ralston .10
72 Joe Randa .25
73 Kevin Rawitzer .10
74 Chris Sheehan .10
75 Robert Toth .10
76 Michael Tucker 1.00
77 Brian Banks .10
78 Marshall Boze .10
79 Jeff Cirillo .40
80 Bo Dodson .10
81 Bobby Hughes .20
82 Scott Karl .15
83 Mike Matheny .15
84 Kevin Riggs .10
85 Sid Roberson .10
86 Charlie Rogers .10
87 Mike Stefanski .10
88 Scott Talanoa .10
89 Derek Wachter .10
90 Wes Weger .10
91 Anthony Byrd .10
92 Marty Cordova .75
93 Steve Dunn .10
94 Gus Gandarillos .10
95 LaTroy Hawkins .40
96 Oscar Munoz .10
97 Dan Perkins .10
98 Ken Serafini .10
99 Ken Tirpack .10
100 Russ Davis .50
101 Nick Delvecchio .10
102 Robert Eenhoorn .10
103 Ron Frazier .10
104 Kraig Hawkins .10
105 Keith Heberling .10
106 Derek Jeter 4.00
107 Kevin Jordan .15
108 Ryan Karp .10
109 Matt Luke .15
110 Lyle Mouton .10
111 Andy Pettitte 2.50
112 Jorge Posada .20
113 Ruben Rivera 1.50
114 Tate Seefried .15
115 Brien Taylor .15
116 Mark Acre .15
117 Jim Bowie .10
118 Russ Brock .10
119 Fausto Cruz .15
120 Jason Giambi .75
121 Izzy Molina .10
122 George Williams .10
123 Joel Wolfe .10
124 Ernie Young .10
125 Tim Davis .10
126 Jackie Nickell .10
127 Ruben Santana .10
128 Makato Suzuki (Makoto) .20
129 Ron Villone .15
130 Rich Aurilia .10
131 John Detmer .10
132 Scott Eyre .10
133 Dave Geeve .10
134 Rick Helling .25
135 Kerry Lacy .10
136 Trey McCoy .10
137 Wes Shook .10
138 Howard Battle .15
139 D.J. Boston .10
140 Rich Butler .10
141 Brad Cornett .10
142 Jesse Cross .10
143 Alex Gonzalez .75
144 Kurt Heble .10
145 Jose Herrera .10
146 Ryan Jones .10
147 Robert Perez .10
148 Jose Silva .10
149 Shannon Stewart .20
150 Chris Weinke .25
151 Jamie Arnold .20
152 Chris Brock .10
153 Tony Graffagnino (Graffanino) .10
154 Damon Hollins .75
155 Mike Hostetler .10
156 Mike Kelly .25
157 Andre King .10
158 Darrell May .10
159 Vince Moore .10
160 Don Strange .10
161 Dominic Therrien .10
162 Terrell Wade .25
163 Brant Brown .25
164 Matt Franco .10
165 Brooks Kieschnick .50
166 Jon Ratliff .10
167 Kennie Steenstra .20
168 Amaury Telemaco .15
169 Ozzie Timmons .15
170 Hector Trinidad .10
171 Travis Willis .10
172 Tim Belk .10
173 Jamie Dismuke .10
174 Mike Ferry .10
175 Chris Hook .10
176 John Hrusovsky .10
177 Cleveland Ladell .10
178 Martin Lister .10
179 Chad Mottola .40
180 Eric Owens .10
181 Scott Sullivan .10
182 Pat Watkins .10
183 Jason Bates .40
184 John Burke .10
185 Quinton McCracken .15
186 Neifi Perez .75
187 Bryan Rekar .10
188 Mark Thompson .20
189 Tim Clark .10
190 Vic Darensbourg .10
191 Charles Johnson 1.50
192 Bryn Kosco .10
193 Reynol Mendoza .10
194 Kerwin Moore .10
195 John Toale .10
196 Bob Abreu 1.50
197 Jim Bruske .20
198 Jim Dougherty .10
199 Tony Eusebio .20
200 Kevin Gallaher .10
201 Chris Holt .10
202 Brian Hunter .75
203 Orlando Miller .20
204 Donovan Mitchell .10
205 Alvin Morman .10
206 James Mouton .15
207 Phil Nevin .25
208 Roberto Petagine .10
209 Billy Wagner .75
210 Mike Busch .10
211 Roger Cedeno .20
212 Chris Demetral .10
213 Rick Gorecki .10
214 Ryan Henderson .10
215 Todd Hollandsworth .75
216 Ken Huckaby .10
217 Rich Linares .10
218 Ryan Luzinski .10
219 Doug Newstrom .10
220 Ben Van Ryn .10
221 Todd Williams .10
222 Shane Andrews .40
223 Reid Cornelius .10
224 Joey Eischen .20
225 Heath Haynes .10
226 Rod Henderson .10
227 Mark LaRosa .10
228 Glenn Murray .10
229 Ugueth Urbina .30
230 B.J. Wallace .20
231 Gabe White .35
232 Edgardo Alfonzo 1.50
233 Randy Curtis .10
234 Omar Garcia .10
235 Jason Isringhausen .50
236 Eric Ludwick .10
237 Bill Pulsipher .50
238 Chris Roberts .15
239 Quilivio Veras .15
240 Pete Walker .10
241 Mike Welch .10
242 Preston Wilson .65
243 Ricky Bottalico .40
244 Alan Burke .10
245 Phil Geisler .15
246 Mike Lieberthal .20
247 Jason Moler .20
248 Gene Schall .40
249 Mark Tranberg .10
250 Jermaine Allensworth .25
251 Michael Brown .10
252 Jason Kendall .75
253 Jeff McCurry .10
254 Jeff Alkire .10
255 Mike Badorek .10
256 Brian Barber .20
257 Alan Benes 1.00
258 Jeff Berblinger .10
259 Joe Biasucci .10
260 Terry Bradshaw .10
261 Duff Brumley .10
262 Kirk Bullinger .10
263 Mike Busby .10
264 Jamie Cochran .10
265 Clint Davis .10
266 Mike Gulan .10
267 Aaron Holbert .20
268 John Kelly .10
269 John Mabry .25
270 Frankie Martinez .10
271 T.J. Mathews .10
272 Aldo Pecorilli .10
273 Doug Radziewicz .10
274 Brian Rupp .10
275 Gerald Witasick .10
276 Dmitri Young .50
277 Homer Bush .15
278 Glenn Dishman .10
279 Sean Drinkwater .10
280 Bryce Florie .15
281 Billy Hall .10
282 Jason Hardtke .20
283 Ray Holbert .15
284 Brian Johnson .10
285 Ray McDavid .15
286 Ira Smith .10
287 Steve Day .10
288 Kurt Ehmann .10
289 Chad Fonville .20
290 Kris Franko .10
291 Aaron Fultz .15
292 Marcus Jensen .10
293 Calvin Murray .10
294 Jeff Richey .10
295 Bill VanLandingham .10
296 Keith Williams .10
297 Chris Wimmer .10
298 Checklist .10
299 Checklist .10
300 Checklist .10

1993-94 Fleer Excel All-Stars

Fleer Excel All-Star cards, random inserts in foil packs, feature 10 Minor League All-Stars. A crown with the player's name and "All-Star" in gold foil on the front indicates the player's status. Backs, numbered 1 of 10, etc., give a career summary.

	MT
Complete Set (10):	15.00
Common Player:	1.00

1 Charles Johnson 3.00
2 Roberto Petagine 1.00
3 James Mouton 1.00
4 Russ Davis 2.00
5 Alex Gonzalez 2.00
6 Johnny Damon 2.00
7 Garret Anderson 2.00
8 Brian Hunter 2.00
9 D.J. Boston 1.00
10 Terrell Wade 1.00

> Player names in *Italic* type indicate a rookie card.

1993-94 Fleer Excel League Leaders

Fleer Excel's League Leader cards feature 10 players who have compiled league-best statistics. The player's name and "League Leader" are stamped in gold foil on the front; the back has a career summary. Cards, numbered 1 of 10, etc., were random inserts in foil packs.

	MT
Complete Set (20):	20.00
Common Player:	.75

1 James Baldwin 1.00
2 Joel Bennett .75
3 Ricky Bottalico 1.50
4 Mike Busch .75
5 Duff Brumley .75
6 Jamie Cochran .75
7 John Dettmer .75
8 Joey Eischen .75
9 LaTroy Hawkins 1.00
10 Derek Jeter 8.00
11 Ryan Karp .75
12 Rick Krivda .75
13 Trey McCoy .75
14 Jason Moler .75
15 Chad Mottola .75
16 Jose Silva .75
17 Brien Taylor 1.00
18 Michael Tucker 3.00
19 Ugueth Urbina 2.00
20 Ben Van Ryn .75

1993-94 Fleer Excel 1st Year Phenoms

"1st Year Phenoms" is stamped in gold foil on the front of each of the 10 different cards representing players who have made their minor league debuts in a grand fashion. The cards, random inserts in foil packs, are numbered 1 of 10, etc., and feature a summary of the player's minor league accomplishments.

	MT
Complete Set (10):	9.00
Common Player:	.75

1 Jim Foster .75
2 Brian Link .75
3 Jeff Berblinger .75
4 Doug Newstrom .75
5 Mike Neal .75
6 Jermaine Allensworth 1.50
7 Todd Greene 3.00
8 Keith Williams .75
9 Shawn Wooten .75
10 Joshua Neese .75

1993 Minor League Team Sets

While the number of team sets grew slightly in 1993, the number of issuers again declined. The market's two giants, Classic Best and Fleer/ProCards had the lion's share of production. Of the team sets issued, Classic Best had 33% and Fleer/ProCards 58% (with considerable duplication). Abbreviations used in these listings are: Cal (California League), CB (Classic

Best), DD (Dunkin' Donuts), FPC (Fleer/ProCards and SP (Sport Pro).

	MT
282 team sets and variations	
1993 FPC AAA All-Stars (55)	16.00
1993 CB Albany Polecats (30)	6.50
1993 FPC Albany Polecats (28)	5.00
1993 FPC Albany-Colonie Yankees (29)	6.00
1993 FPC Albuquerque Dukes (31)	11.00
1993 Team Albuquerque Dukes (40)	150.00
1993 CB Appleton Foxes (30)	6.50
1993 FPC Appleton Foxes (29)	5.00
1993 FPC Arkansas Travelers (27)	5.00
1993 CB Asheville Tourists (28)	10.00
1993 FPC Asheville Tourists (30)	8.00
1993 CB Auburn Astros (30)	12.00
1993 FPC Auburn Astros (30)	5.00
1993 CB Augusta Priates (28)	14.00
1993 FPC Augusta Pirates (27)	11.00
1993 Cal Bakersfield Dodgers (32)	10.00
1993 CB Batavia Clippers (30)	6.00
1993 FPC Batavia Clippers (30)	5.00
1993 CB Bellingham Mariners (30)	6.00
1993 FPC Bellingham Mariners (31)	5.00
1993 CB Beloit Brewers (29)	6.00
1993 FPC Beloit Brewers (30)	6.00
1993 CB Bend Rockies (30)	9.00
1993 FPC Bend Rockies (30)	5.00
1993 FPC Billings Mustangs (30)	5.00
1993 SP Billings Mustangs (28)	9.00
1993 FPC Binghampton Mets (26)	7.00
1993 FPC Birmingham Barons (27)	8.00
1993 CB Bluefield Orioles (30)	6.00
1993 FPC Bluefield Orioles (27)	5.00
1993 CB Boise Hawks (30)	12.00
1993 FPC Boise Hawks (30)	9.00
1993 FPC Bowie Bay Sox (24)	7.00
1993 CB Bristol Tigers (30)	6.00
1993 FPC Bristol Tigers (30)	5.00
1993 FPC Buffalo Bisons (27)	5.00
1993 CB Burlington Bees (29)	6.50
1993 FPC Burlington Bees (28)	5.00
1993 CB Burlington Indians (30)	12.00
1993 FPC Burlington Indians (31)	9.50
1993 SP Butte Copper Kings (24)	6.50
1993 FPC Calgary Cannons (29)	5.00
1993 FPC Canton-Akron Indians (26)	16.00
1993 CB Capital City Bombers (27)	6.50
1993 FPC Capital City Bombers (26)	6.50
1993 FPC Carolina League A-S (52)	12.50
1993 FPC Carolina Mudcats (29)	6.00
1993 Team Carolina Mudcats (24)	7.00
1993 CB Cedar Rapids Kernels (30)	6.50
1993 FPC Cedar Rapids Kernels (28)	5.00
1993 CB Central Valley Rockies (28)	6.00
1993 FPC Central Valley Rockies (29)	5.00
1993 CB Charleston Rainbows (30)	6.50
1993 FPC Charleston Rainbows (31)	5.00
1993 FPC Charlotte Knights (28)	8.00
1993 CB Charlotte Rangers (30)	6.50
1993 FPC Charlotte Rangers (28)	5.00
1993 FPC Chattanooga Lookouts (26)	5.00
1993 CB Clearwater Phillies (29)	6.50
1993 FPC Clearwater Phillies (27)	5.00
1993 CB Clinton Giants (29)	6.50
1993 FPC Clinton Giants (28)	5.00
1993 FPC Colorado Springs Sky Sox (25)	6.00
1993 FPC Columbus Clippers (27)	6.00
1993 Police Columbus Clippers (25)	6.00
1993 Team Columbus Clippers (26)	15.00
1993 CB Columbus Redstixx (30)	6.50
1993 FPC Columbus Redstixx (30)	6.50
1993 CB Danville Braves (30)	9.00
1993 FPC Danville Braves (31)	7.00
1993 CB Daytona Cubs (27)	5.00
1993 FPC Daytona Cubs (26)	4.00
1993 Team Duluth-Superior Dukes (31)	7.00
1993 CB Dunedin Blue Jays (30)	6.00
1993 FPC Duendin Blue Jays (27)	4.00
1993 Team Dunedin Blue Jays (30)	14.00
1993 CB Durham Bulls (30)	5.00
1993 FPC Durham Bulls (31)	4.00
1993 Team Durham Bulls (31)	7.00
1993 FPC Edmonton Trappers (27)	7.00
1993 CB Elizabethton Twins (30)	9.00
1993 FPC Elizabethton Twins (25)	5.00
1993 CB Elmira Pioneers (30)	6.50
1993 FPC Elmira Pioneers (29)	5.00
1993 FPC El Paso Diablos (30)	5.00
1993 CB Erie Sailors (30)	6.00
1993 FPC Erie Sailors (30)	5.00
1993 CB Eugene Emeralds (30)	6.00
1993 FPC Eugene Emeralds (29)	5.00
1993 CB Everett Giants (30)	6.00
1993 FPC Everett Giants (31)	5.00
1993 CB Fayetteville Generals (30)	5.00
1993 FPC Fayetteville Generals (29)	4.00
1993 FPC Florida State League A-S (51)	10.00
1993 CB Frederick Keys (30)	7.50
1993 FPC Frederick Keys (30)	7.50
1993 CB Ft. Lauderdale Red Sox (30)	4.00
1993 FPC Ft. Lauderdale Red Sox (30)	4.00
1993 CB Ft. Myers Miracle (29)	7.00
1993 FPC Ft. Myers Miracle (29)	5.00
1993 CB Ft. Wayne Wizards (30)	6.00
1993 FPC Ft. Wayne Wizards (28)	6.00
1993 CB Geneva Cubs (30)	6.00
1993 FPC Geneva Cubs (31)	5.00
1993 CB Glens Falls Redbirds (30)	6.00
1993 FPC Glens Falls Redbirds (31)	5.00
1993 SP Great Falls Dodgers (29)	16.00
1993 CB Greensboro Hornets (28)	150.00
1993 FPC Greensboro Hornets (31)	32.00
1993 FPC Greenville Braves (28)	5.00
1993 Team Greenville Braves foldout	24.00
1993 CB Hagerstown Suns (28)	5.00
1993 FPC Hagerstown Suns (30)	4.00
1993 FPC Harrisburg Senators (28)	9.00
1993 FPC Helena Brewers (31)	5.00
1993 SP Helena Brewers (28)	7.00
1993 CB Hickory Crawdads (30)	12.50
1993 FPC Hickory Crawdads (30)	16.00
1993 CB High Desert Mavericks (29)	9.00
1993 FPC High Desert Mavericks (30)	4.00
1993 CB Huntington Cubs (30)	9.00
1993 FPC Huntington Cubs (30)	5.00
1993 FPC Huntsville Stars (26)	5.00
1993 FPC Idaho Falls Braves (31)	5.00
1993 SP Idaho Falls Braves (30)	7.00
1993 FPC Indianapolis Indians (25)	5.00
1993 FPC Iowa Cubs (24)	5.00
1993 FPC Jackson Generals (27)	6.00
1993 FPC Jacksonville Suns (22)	6.00
1993 CB Jamestown Expos (30)	6.00
1993 FPC Jamestown Expos (28)	5.00
1993 CB Johnson City Cardinals (30)	6.00
1993 FPC Johnson City Cardinals (31)	5.00
1993 CB Kane County Cougars (30)	24.00
1993 FPC Kane County Cougars (28)	25.00
1993 Team Kane County Cougars (30)	25.00
1993 CB Kingsport Mets (31)	7.00
1993 FPC Kingsport Mets (27)	7.00
1993 CB Kinston Indians (30)	7.50
1993 FPC Kinston Indians (30)	6.00
1993 Team Kinston Indians (30)	15.00
1993 FPC Knoxville Smokies (29)	25.00
1993 CB Lakeland Tigers (29)	6.00
1993 FPC Lakeland Tigers (31)	5.00
1993 FPC Las Vegas Stars (29)	5.00
1993 FPC Lethbridge Mounties (26)	5.00
1993 SP Lethbridge Mounties (26)	6.00
1993 FPC London Tigers (29)	4.00
1993 FPC Louisville Redbirds (26)	6.00
1993 CB Lynchburg Red Sox (28)	6.50
1993 FPC Lynchburg Red Sox (29)	5.00
1993 CB Macon Braves (30)	7.00
1993 FPC Macon Braves (30)	6.00
1993 CB Madison Muskies (28)	6.50
1993 FPC Madison Muskies (27)	4.00
1993 CB Martinsville Phillies (30)	7.00
1993 FPC Martinsville Phillies (31)	6.00
1993 FPC Medicine Hat Blue Jays (27)	5.00
1993 SP Medicine Hat Blue Jays (25)	7.00
1993 FPC Memphis Chicks (25)	6.00
1993 FPC Midland Angels (27)	5.00
1993 FPC Midland w/bank, chemical ads (29)	10.00
1993 OHP Midland Angels (33)	42.00
1993 FPC Midwest League A-S (56)	13.00
1993 CB Modesto A's (28)	12.00
1993 FPC Modesto A's (28)	12.00
1993 FPC Nashville Sounds (25)	6.50
1993 FPC Nashville Xpress (27)	5.00
1993 FPC New Britain Red Sox (28)	5.00
1993 FPC New Orleans Zephyrs (26)	6.00
1993 CB Niagara Falls Rapids (30)	6.00
1993 FPC Niagara Fllas Rapids (31)	5.00
1993 FPC Norfolk Tides (27)	7.00
1993 FPC Oklahoma City 89ers (26)	5.00
1993 FPC Omaha Royals (29)	5.00
1993 TM Omaha Royals 25th Anniversary (18)	20.00
1993 CB Oneonta Yankees (30)	18.00
1993 FPC Oneonta Yankees (31)	18.00
1993 FPC Orlando Cubs (26)	6.00
1993 CB Osceola Astros (29)	7.00
1993 FPC Osceola Astros (27)	7.00
1993 FPC Ottawa Lynx (23)	5.00
1993 CB Palm Springs Angels (30)	6.50
1993 FPC Palm Springs Angels (29)	4.00
1993 DD Pawtucket Red Sox foldout	55.00
1993 FPC Pawtucket Red Sox (29)	7.00
1993 Team Pawtucket Red Sox (25)	7.50
1993 Team Peninsula Oilers (32)	7.00
1993 CB Peoria Chiefs (27)	6.50
1993 FPC Peoria Chiefs (27)	4.00
1993 Team Peoria Chiefs (30)	16.00
1993 FPC Phoenix Firebirds (29)	6.00
1993 CB Pittsfield Mets (30)	10.00
1993 FPC Pittsfield Mets (30)	7.00
1993 FPC Pocatello Posse (25)	4.00
1993 SP Pocatello Posse (26)	6.50
1993 FPC Portland Beavers (21)	6.00
1993 CB Princeton Reds (30)	6.00
1993 FPC Princeton Reds (31)	5.00
1993 CB Prince Williams Cannons (30)	7.50
1993 FPC Prince Williams Cannons (30)	4.00
1993 CB Quad City Bandits (27)	5.00
1993 FPC Quad City Bandits (29)	4.00
1993 CB Rancho Cucamonga Quakes (30)	7.00
1993 FPC Rancho Cucamonga Quakes (32)	7.00
1993 FPC Reading Phillies (26)	5.00
1993 Bleacher Bums Richmond Braves foldout	30.00
1993 Bleacher Bums Richmond foldout - gold	90.00
1993 FPC Richmond Braves (30)	16.00
1993 Pepsi Richmond Braves (25)	32.00
1993 Richmond Camera Richmond Braves (25)	85.00
1993 Richmond Comix Richmond Braves (30)	40.00
1993 Cal Riverside Pilots (31)	7.50
1993 FPC Rochester Red Wings (29)	7.50
1993 CB Rockford Royals (30)	16.00
1993 FPC Rockford Royals (31)	15.00
1993 CB Salem Buccaneers (30)	5.00
1993 FPC Salem Buccaneers (29)	4.00
1993 FPC San Antonio Missions (28)	8.00
1993 HEB San Antonio Missions (32)	65.00
1993 CB San Bernardino Spirit (26)	5.00
1993 FPC San Bernardino Spirit (26)	4.00
1993 CB San Jose Giants (30)	5.00
1993 FPC San Jose Giants (29)	4.00
1993 CB Sarasota White Sox (29)	6.00
1993 FPC Sarasota White Sox (30)	4.00
1993 CB Savannah Cardinals (29)	6.00
1993 FPC Savannah Cardinals (27)	4.00
1993 FPC Scranton Red Barons (25)	7.50
1993 Team Scranton Red Barons (30)	8.00
1993 FPC Shreveport Captains (27)	6.00
1993 Team Sioux Falls Canaries (28)	7.00
1993 FPC South Atlantic League A-S (57)	24.00
1993 Play II South Atlantic League A-S (42)	40.00
1993 Play II SAL All-Stars inserts (18)	115.00
1993 CB South Bend White Sox (29)	9.00
1993 FPC South Bend White Sox (30)	9.00
1993 CB Southern Oregon A's (30)	9.00
1993 FPC Southern Oregon A's (30)	7.00
1993 CB Spartanburg Phillies (28)	6.00
1993 FPC Spartanburg Phillies (29)	4.00
1993 CB Spokane Indians (30)	6.00
1993 FPC Spokane Indians (27)	5.00
1993 CB Springfield Cardinals (29)	6.00
1993 FPC Springfield Cardinals (29)	4.00
1993 CB St. Catherines Blue Jays (30)	9.00
1993 FPC St. Catharines Blue Jays (27)	6.00
1993 CB St. Lucie Mets (28)	7.00
1993 FPC St. Lucie Mets (28)	5.00
1993 Team St. Paul Saints (26)	7.00
1993 CB St. Petersburg Cardinals (30)	7.50
1993 FPC St. Petersburg Cardinals (30)	5.00
1993 CB Stockton Ports (30)	5.00
1993 FPC Stockton Ports (29)	4.00
1993 FPC Syracuse Chiefs (27)	6.00
1993 FPC Tacoma Tigers (27)	6.00
1993 FPC Toledo Mud Hens (28)	5.00
1993 FPC Tucson Toros (29)	6.00
1993 FPC Tulsa Drillers (27)	6.00
1993 FPC Tulsa Drillers w/ BBC Stores ad (27)	9.00
1993 Team Tulsa Drillers (30)	20.00
1993 CB Utica Blue Sox (30)	6.50
1993 FPC Utica Blue Sox (26)	5.00
1993 FPC Vancouver Canadians (28)	9.00
1993 CB Vero Beach Dodgers (30)	7.50
1993 FPC Vero Beach Dodgers (31)	6.00
1993 CB Waterloo Diamonds (30)	7.50
1993 FPC Waterloo Diamonds (29)	6.00
1993 CB Watertown Indians (30)	6.00
1993 FPC Watertown Indians (30)	5.00
1993 CB Welland Pirates (30)	6.00
1993 FPC Welland Pirates (31)	5.00
1993 CB West Palm Beach Expos (30)	6.00
1993 FPC West Palm Beach Expos (30)	4.00
1993 CB West Virginia Wheelers (27)	6.00
1993 FPC West Virginia Wheelers (27)	4.00
1993 FPC Wichita Wranglers (26)	6.00
1993 CB Wilmington Blue Rocks (30)	14.00
1993 FPC Wilmington Blue Rocks (30)	12.00
1993 CB Winston-Salem Spirits (27)	6.00
1993 FPC Winston-Salem Spirits (25)	4.00
1993 CB Yakima Bears (30)	6.00
1993 FPC Yakima Bears (31)	5.00

1994 Action Packed Scouting Report Prototype

Though he does not appear in the issued set, Blue Jays prospect Alex Gonzalez was pictured on a prototype card for Action Packed's first foray into the minor league card market. Two other cards, similar in format to the regularly issued version, were also issued. Each of the sample cards has a small gray "PROTOTYPE" on back, above the card number.

		MT
Complete Set (3):		8.00
Common Player:		3.00
1	Trot Nixon	3.00
2	Alex Gonzalez (Franchise Gem)	4.00
3	Russ Davis (Franchise Gem)	3.00

1994 Action Packed Scouting Report

Action Packed Scouting Report features a mix of top prospects from the Class A-AAA minor leagues. Cards feature the hallmark Action Packed technology of embossed, heavily lacquered player photos on front. Backs have the player name in a vertical gold-foil strip at top, and a "scouting report" and minor league stats beneath. A subset of 12 "Franchise Gem" players features a second player photo on back, along with a black diamond, which when activated by finger heat, reveals the players projected Major League debut season. A second subset of five cards honors the 40th anniversary of Roberto Clemente's debut in U.S. professional baseball. The final card in the set is a gold-foil version of MLB's 125th anniversary logo, which is also the set checklist card. Inserts offered 24-karat gold versions of the 12 "Franchise Gem" cards in the set, along with the MLB logo card, plus randomly packaged Franchise Gem cards which have a heat-and-reveal spot on the back with an "Exchange" notation. Those cards could be redeemed for diamond-studded versions of the Franchise Gem cards.

		MT
Complete Set (72):		25.00
Common Player:		.15
1	Alex Rodriguez	8.00
2	Trot Nixon	.40
3	Chan Ho Park	1.00
4	Brooks Kieshnick	.15
5	Matt Brunson	.10
6	Wayne Gomes	.10
7	Charles Johnson	1.00
8	Kirk Presley	.15
9	Daron Kirkriet	.15
10	Curtis Goodwin	.30
11	Alex Ochoa	.50
12	Midre Cummings	.30
13	Russ Davis	.50
14	Phil Nevin	.15
15	J.R. Phillips	.15
16	Jeff Granger	.15
17	Makato Suzuki (Makoto)	.15
18	Johnny Damon	1.00
19	Chad Mottola	.30
20	Scott Ruffcorn	.15
21	Brian Barber	.15
22	Frank Rodriguez	.35
22a	Frank Rodriguez (autographed edition of 2,500 foil-pack redemptions)	12.50
23	Michael Jordan	10.00
24	Michael Tucker	1.50
25	Rondell White	1.50
26	Ugueth Urbina	.40
27	Tyrone Hill	.15
28	Dmitri Young	.30
29	Marshall Boze	.10
30	Marc Newfield	.15
31	James Baldwin	.45
32	Terrell Wade	.10
33	Curtis Pride	.20
34	Gabe White	.35
35	Derrek Lee	.75
36	Bill Pulsipher	.30
37	Butch Huskey	.60
38	Nigel Wilson	.10
39	Tim Clark	.10
40	Ozzie Timmons	.10
41	Brien Taylor	.15
42	J.T. Snow	1.00
43	Derek Jeter	5.00
44	Rick Krivda	.10
45	Kevin Millar	.10
46	Matt Franco	.10
47	Jose Silva	.10
48	Benji Gil	.15
49	Pokey Reese	.25
50	Todd Hollandsworth	.75
51	Robert Ellis	.10
52	Brian L. Hunter	.75
53	Todd Ritchie	.10
54	Kurt Miller	.15
55	Alex Rodriguez (Franchise Gem)	8.00
56	Chan Ho Park (FG)	1.00
57	Brooks Kieschnick (FG)	.30
58	Charles Johnson (FG)	1.00
59	Alex Ochoa (FG)	.50
60	Midre Cummings (FG)	.30
61	Phil Nevin (FG)	.20
62	Jose Silva (FG)	.15
63	James Baldwin (FG)	.45
64	Rondell White (FG)	1.50
65	Trot Nixon (FG)	.40
66	Todd Hollandsworth (FG)	.75
67	Hidden Talent Roberto Clemente	.50
68	Four-Time Batting Champ Roberto Clemente	.50
69	1966 NL MVP Roberto Clemente	.50
70	3,000-Hit Club Roberto Clemente	.50
71	1973 Hall of Fame Roberto Clemente	.50
72	Gold-foil 125th Anniversary logo/ checklist	.15

1994 Action Packed SR Gold Franchise Gems

The 12 24-karat cards in this Action Packed insert set were randomly inserted in foil packs at an average rate of one per 96 packs. This roughly translates to a production figure of 1,850 each of the gold cards. Gold cards have a "24 KT Gold" notation above the Action Packed logo on front, have the player's name in gold on the back and are specially numbered with a "G" suffix.

		MT
Complete Set (12):		275.00
Common Player:		10.00
1G	Alex Rodriguez	125.00
2G	Chan Ho Park	40.00
3G	Brooks Kieschnick	15.00
4G	Charles Johnson	25.00
5G	Alex Ochoa	15.00
6G	Midre Cummings	10.00
7G	Phil Nevin	10.00
8G	Jose Silva	10.00
9G	James Baldwin	10.00
10G	Rondell White	30.00
11G	Trot Nixon	15.00
12G	Todd Hollandsworth	10.00

1994 Action Packed SR Diamond Franchise Gems

		MT
Complete Set (12):		800.00
Common Player:		40.00
1G	Alex Rodriguez	500.00
2G	Chan Ho Park	150.00
3G	Brooks Kieschnick	40.00
4G	Charles Johnson	60.00
5G	Alex Ochoa	50.00
6G	Midre Cummings	40.00
7G	Phil Nevin	40.00
8G	Jose Silva	40.00
9G	James Baldwin	50.00
10G	Rondell White	100.00
11G	Trot Nixon	60.00
12G	Todd Hollandsworth	40.00

1994 Classic All-Star Minor League

Classic's minor league wax issue for '94 features a 200-card base set with several chase sets and autograph inserts. Cards feature borderless action phtos on front. Graphics include the Classic logo (upper-left), MLB team logo (lower-right), and minor league team logo (lower-left). Backs have a large portrait photo with the bottom half "ghosted" to allow overprinting of stats and career data.

		MT
Complete Set (200):		25.00
Common Player:		.05
1	Michael Jordan	4.00
2	Felipe Lira	.05
3	Jose Silva	.05
4	Yuri Sanchez	.05
5	Marcus Jensen	.05
6	Julio Santana	.05
7	Angel Martinez	.05
8	Jose Herrera	.05
9	D.J. Boston	.05
10	Trot Nixon	.25
11	Trey Beamon	.10
12	Danny Clyburn	.10
13	John Wasdin	.05
14	Vince Moore	.05
15	Vic Darensbourg	.05
16	Kevin Gallaher	.05
17	Julio Bruno	.05
18	Terrell Lowery	.05
19	Phil Geisler	.05
20	Chan Ho Park	1.50
21	Chad McConnell	.05
22	Ricky Bottalico	.20
23	Jim Pittsley	.05
24	Gabe Martinez	.05
25	Johnny Damon	.35
26	Basil Shabazz	.10
27	Billy Ashley	.10
28	Andy Petitte	.50
29	Robert Ellis	.05
30	Mike Zolecki	.05
31	League All-Star #1	.05
32	John Burke	.05
33	Chris Snopek	.10
34	Mark Thompson	.10
35	Jimmy Haynes	.05
36	Ron Villone	.05
37	Curtis Goodwin	.05
38	Tim Belk	.05
39	Rod Henderson	.05
40	Butch Huskey	.15
41	Chris Smith	.05
42	B.J. Wallace	.15
43	Guillermo Mercedes	.05
44	Ugueth Urbina	.10
45	Fausto Cruz	.05
46	Julian Tavarez	.10
47	Scott Lydy	.10
48	Darren Burton	.05
49	Mac Suzuki	.15
50	Kirk Presley	.10
51	Checklist Alex Rodriguez	.25
52	Armando Benitez	.25
53	Rodney Pedraza	.05
54	LaTroy Hawkins	.15
55	Rick Forney	.05
56	Tripp Cromer	.10
57	Andres Berumen	.05
58	Terry Bradshaw	.05
59	Omar Ramirez	.05
60	Derek Jeter	3.00
61	Kerwin Moore	.05
62	Andy Larkin	.05
63	Neifi Perez	.50
64	Casey Whitten	.05
65	Jon Ratliff	.05
66	J.J. Johnson	.05
67	Preston Wilson	.25
68	Jason Isringhausen	.10
69	Adam Meinershagen	.05
70	Rondell White	.25
71	Shannon Stewart	.15
72	Keith Heberling	.05
73	Ruben Rivera	.10
74	Mike Lieberthal	.10
75	Damon Hollins	.15
76	Jason Jacome	.05
77	Amaury Telemaco	.05
78	Scott Talanoa	.05
79	Dave Stevens	.05
80	Brien Taylor	.20
81	League All-Stars #2	.05
82	Brian Barber	.10
83	Ray Durham	.15
84	Brent Bowers	.05
85	Shane Andrews	.15
86	Gabe White	.15
87	Midre Cummings	.15
88	Brad Radke	.15
89	Joe Randa	.10
90	Phil Nevin	.10
91	Joe Vitiello	.10
92	Ray McDavid	.05
93	Robbie Beckett	.10
94	Frank Rodriguez	.20
95	Marc Newfield	.10
96	Joey Eischen	.10
97	Manny Alexander	.15
98	Jeff McNeely	.10
99	Mark Smith	.10
100	Alex Rodriguez	3.00
101	Todd Hollandsworth	.50
102	Scott Ruffcorn	.15
103	Kurt Miller	.10
104	Justin Mashore	.05
105	Garret Anderson	.25
106	Nigel Wilson	.05
107	Howard Battle	.05
108	Calvin Reese	.15
109	Orlando Miller	.15
110	Bill Pulsipher	.10
111	Edgar Renteria	.25
112	Steve Gibraltar	.10
113	Gene Schall	.05
114	John Roper	.05
115	Alvin Morman	.05
116	Doug Glanville	.05
117	Mark Hutton	.05
118	Glenn Murray	.05
119	Curtis Shaw	.05
120	Alex Ochoa	.15
121	Michael Moore	.05
122	Joey Hamilton	.35
123	James Baldwin	.25
124	Chad Ogea	.15
125	Rikkert Faneyte	.05
126	Benji Gil	.10
127	Kenny Felder	.05
128	Brant Brown	.15
129	Eddie Pearson	.05
130	Derrek Lee	.10
131	League All-Stars #3	.05
132	Dan Serafini	.10
133	Ramon Caraballo	.05
134	Derek Wallace	.10
135	Jamie Arnold	.10
136	Domingo Jean	.05
137	Jose Malave	.05
138	Derek Lowe	.05
139	Marshall Boze	.05
140	Billy Wagner	.25
141	Matt Franco	.05
142	Roger Cedeno	.10
143	Russ Davis	.15
144	Kevin Flora	.05
145	Rick Gorecki	.05
146	Rick Greene	.05
147	Brian Hunter	.20
148	Rich Aurilla	.05
149	Jason Moller	.05
150	Michael Tucker	.25
151	Checklist Alex Rodriguez	.50
152	Chad Mottola	.25
153	Calvin Murray	.05
154	Melvin Nieves	.10
155	Luis Ortiz	.05
156	Chris Roberts	.05
157	Todd Williams	.05
158	Tony Phillips	.05
159	DeShawn Warren	.05
160	Paul Shuey	.10
161	Dmitri Young	.15
162	Jermaine Allensworth	.25
163	Daron Kirkreit	.05
164	Scott Christman	.05
165	Steve Soderstrom	.05
166	J.R. Phillips	.10
167	Karim Garcia	2.00
168	Mark Acre	.05
169	Jose Paniagua	.05
170	Terrell Wade	.05
171	Mike Bell	.25
172	Alan Benes	.25
173	Jeff D'Amico	.25
174	Tate Seefried	.10
175	Wayne Gomes	.15
176	Chris Singleton	.05
177	Marc Valdes	.05
178	Jamey Wright	.15
179	Jay Powell	.05
180	Charles Johnson	.75
181	Mitch House	.05
182	Torii Hunter	.05
183	Jeff Suppan	.20
184	Roberto Petagine	.05
185	Ryan McGuire	.75
186	Andrew Lorraine	.15
187	Matt Brunson	.05
188	Eduardo Perez	.10
189	Jay Witasick	.05
190	Shawn Green	.05
191	Cleveland Ladell	.05
192	Paul Bako	.05
193	Brook Fordyce	.05
194	Kym Ashworth	.05
195	Tony Mitchell	.05
196	Tony Clark	.75
197	Curtis Pride	.10
198	Arquimedez Pozo	.05
199	Rey Ordonez	.50
200	Brooks Kieschnick	.15
	AUTOGRAPHED CARDS	.05
1	Alex Rodriguez (edition of 2,100)	.05
2	Terrell Wade (2,080)	.05
3	Brooks Kieschnick (3,400)	.05
4	Rondell White (2,880)	.05
5	Michael Tucker (2,400)	.05
6	Kirk Presley (1,300)	.05

1994 Classic Bonus Baby

Five of the hottest prospects of the day are featured in this insert set. Fronts feature action photos which have been graphically enhanced to convey the image of speed. In the lower-right corner is a gold-foil box with "BONUS BABY," the Classic logotype and player name. Backs have another photo career highlights, appropriate logos and a serial number from within an edition of 9,994 of each card.

	MT
Complete Set (5):	15.00
Common Player:	1.00
BB1 Trot Nixon	1.50
BB2 Kirk Presley	1.00
BB3 Alex Rodriguez	12.00
BB4 Brooks Kieschnick	1.00
BB5 Michael Tucker	1.50

1994 Classic Cream of the Crop

These premium cards are a one-per-pack insert in Classic's All-Star minor league issue. Cards have player photos on a borderless "metallized" background. The player and insert set name are printed on black in orange blocks at bottom. Horizontally formatted backs are conventionally printed and include a large photo and career summary.

	MT
Complete Set (25):	12.00
Common Player:	.25
CC1 Trot Nixon	.50
CC2 Kirk Presley	.25
CC3 Mac Suzuki	.25
CC4 Brooks Kieschnick	.40
CC5 Johnny Damon	.50
CC6 Howard Battle	.25
CC7 Michael Tucker	.50
CC8 Todd Hollandsworth	.25
CC9 J.R. Phillips	.25
CC10Shannon Stewart	.50
CC11Alex Rodriguez	3.00
CC12Terrell Wade	.25
CC13Rondell White	.50
CC14James Baldwin	.25
CC15Shane Andrews	.35
CC16Chan Ho Park	1.00
CC17Derek Jeter	3.00
CC18Charles Johnson	.65
CC19Bill Pulsipher	.25
CC20Phil Nevin	.25
CC21Scott Ruffcorn	.25
CC22Midre Cummings	.35
CC23Frank Rodriguez	.25
CC24Dmitri Young	.25
CC25Shawn Green	.25

1994 Classic Cream of the Crop Update

Each pack of Classic Update contains one of these premium inserts. Cards have player photos set against a refractive foil background. The player's name and set logo are printed in white on dark blue panels at bottom. Backs are formatted horizontally, conventionally printed and include another photo, career highlights and appropriate team, licensor and licensee logos.

	MT
Complete Set (20):	16.00
Common Player:	.25
CC1 Paul Wilson	.25
CC2 Ben Grieve	6.00
CC3 Dustin Hermanson	.50
CC4 Antone Williamson	.25
CC5 Josh Booty	.25
CC6 Doug Million	.25
CC7 Todd Walker	2.00
CC8 C.J. Nitkowski	.25
CC9 Jaret Wright	1.00
CC10Mark Farris	.25
CC11Nomar Garciaparra	6.00
CC12Paul Konerko	2.00
CC13Jayson Peterson	.25
CC14Matt Smith	.25
CC15Ramon Castro	.25
CC16Cade Gaspar	.25
CC17Terrence Long	.45
CC18Hiram Bocachica	.25
CC19Dante Powell	.50
CC20Brian Buchanan	.25

1994 Classic Assets (Baseball)

A number of baseball players are featured in the five-sport lineup of the base set, inserts and phonecards in Assets' debut year. Parallel cards bearing a silver facsimile autograph on front are worth 4X-6X the values quoted.

	MT
Base Set/Inserts	
4 Nolan Ryan	1.00
4 Nolan Ryan (silver-foil signature)	5.00
13 Paul Wilson	.50
13 Paul Wilson (silver-foil signature)	3.00
18 Ben Grieve	1.00
18 Ben Grieve (silver-foil signature)	5.00
29 Nolan Ryan	1.00
38 Paul Wilson	.50
43 Ben Grieve	1.00
64 Doug Million	.25
65 Barry Bonds	.50
89 Doug Million	.25
90 Barry Bonds	.40
DC4 Nolan Ryan (diecut)	10.00
DC15Nomar Garciaparra (diecut)	6.00
DC17Barry Bonds (diecut)	4.00
DC18Paul Wilson (die-cut)	3.50

1994 Classic Assets Chrome

Technology similar to Topps "Finest" was used for the fronts of this four-sport 20-card insert series found in Classic Assets. The final four cards in the set are baseball players and are checklisted here. Fronts have gold-foil graphic highlights and a "1 of 9,750" notation. Backs are conventionally printed with a player portrait photo and career details. Cards are numbered with a "CC" prefix.

	MT
Complete (Baseball) Set (4):	20.00
Common Player:	2.00
CC17Alex Rodriguez	15.00
CC18Kirk Presley	2.00
CC19Trot Nixon	3.00
CC20Brooks Kieschnick	2.00

1994 Classic Assets (Baseball) Foncards

A number of baseball players are featured in the five-sport lineup of the base set, inserts and phonecards in Assets' debut year.

	MT
Complete (Baseball) Set (14): 135.00	
(1) Ben Grieve (1 min. Foncard)	2.00
(2) Ben Grieve ($2 Foncard)	3.50
(3) Nolan Ryan (1 min. Foncard)	4.00
(4) Nolan Ryan ($2 Foncard)	6.00
(5) Nolan Ryan ($5 Foncard)	7.50
(6) Nolan Ryan ($100 Foncard)	40.00
(7) Paul Wilson (1 min. Foncard)	1.50
(8) Paul Wilson ($2 Foncard)	1.50
(9) Doug Million (1 min. Foncard)	1.50
(10) Doug Million ($2 Foncard)	1.50
(11) Barry Bonds (1 min. Foncard)	2.00
(12) Barry Bonds ($2 Foncard)	3.00
(13) Barry Bonds ($5 Foncard)	5.00
(14) Barry Bonds ($200 Foncard)	20.00

1994 Classic Best Gold

This 200-card set features UV coating on both sides of the cards and foil stamping on the fronts. Virtually every level of minor league baseball is represented in this set. Insert sets highlight first-round draft picks and glow-in-the dark illustrated acetate cards.

	MT
Complete Set (200):	20.00
Common Player:	.05
1 Brien Taylor	.25
2 Jeff D'Amico	.75
3 Trot Nixon	.50
4 Clayton Byrne	.05
5 Eric Chavez	3.00
6 Matt Jarvis	.05
7 Billy Owens	.05
8 Jay Powell	.10
9 Robert Eenhoorn	.05
10 Trey Beamon	.20
11 Todd Williams	.05
12 Tim Davis	.05
13 Brian Barber	.10
14 Jeff Shireman	.05
15 Melvin Mora	.05
16 Phil Nevin	.10
17 Kendall Rhine	.05
18 Billy Wagner	.75
19 Jason Kendall	.30
20 Kelly Wunsch	.15
21 D.J. Boston	.05
22 Shannon Stewart	.15
23 Anthony Manahan	.05
24 Dwight Robinson	.05
25 Alan Benes	.50
26 Dennis Slininger	.05
27 John Burke	.05
28 Jamey Wright	.20
29 Scott Eyre	.05
30 Jack Kimel	.05
31 Kerry Lacy	.05
32 Rich Aurilia	.05
33 Dave Giberti	.05
34 Daryl Henderson	.05
35 Stanley Evans	.05
36 Wayne Gomes	.10
37 Rob Grable	.05
38 Mike Juhl	.05
39 Jason Moler	.15
40 Jon Zuber	.05
41 Chad Fonville	.15
42 Mark Thompson	.05
43 Billy Masse	.05
44 Derek Hacopian	.05
45 J.J. Thobe	.05
46 Charles York	.05
47 Jamie Howard	.05
48 Andre King	.10
49 Tim Delgado	.05
50 Mike Hubbard	.05
51 Bernie Nunez	.05
52 Jon Ratliff	.05
53 Pedro Valdez	.05
54 Rich Butler	.05
55 Felipe Crespo	.05
56 Randy Phillips	.05
57 Todd Steverson	.10
58 Chris Stynes	.05
59 Ben Weber	.05
60 Chris Weinke	.15
61 Rob Lukachyk	.05
62 Brett King	.05
63 Chris Singleton	.05
64 Brian Bright	.05
65 Brent Brede	.05
66 Steve Hazlett	.05
67 Dan Serafini	.10
68 Matt Farner	.05
69 Jeremy Lee	.05
70 Anthony Medrano	.05
71 Josue Estrada	.05
72 Martin Mainville	.05
73 Chris Schwab	.10
74 John Roskos	.05
75 Charles Peterson	.05
76 Kevin Pickford	.05
77 Charles Rice	.05
78 Mike Bell	.05
79 Ed Diaz	.05
80 Torii Hunter	.05
81 Kelcey Mucker	.05
82 Nick Delvecchio	.05
83 Derek Jeter	4.00
84 Ryan Karp	.05
85 Matt Luke	.10
86 Ray Suplee	.05
87 Tyler Houston	.15
88 Brad Cornett	.05
89 Kris Harmes	.05
90 Shane Andrews	.25
91 Ugueth Urbina	.30
92 Chris Mader	.05
93 Eddie Pearson	.05
94 Tim Clark	.05
95 Chris Malinoski	.05
96 John Toale	.05
97 Mark Acre	.10
98 Ernie Young	.05
99 Jeff Schmidt	.05
100 Roberto Petagine	.05
101 Eddy Diaz	.05
102 Ruben Santana	.05
103 Ron Villone	.05
104 Nate Dishington	.05
105 Charles Johnson	1.00
106 Preston Wilson	.50
107 Paul Shuey	.15
108 Howard Battle	.15
109 Tim Hyers	.05
110 Rick Greene	.10
111 Justin Thompson	.50
112 Frank Rodriguez	.25
113 Jamie Arnold	.10
114 Marty Malloy	.05
115 Darrell May	.05
116 Leo Ramirez	.05
117 Tom Thobe	.05
118 Terrell Wade	.15
119 Marc Valdes	.05
120 Scott Rolen	4.00
121 Les Norman	.05
122 Michael Tucker	1.00
123 Joe Vitiello	.15
124 Chris Roberts	.10
125 Jason Giambi	.50
126 Izzy Molina	.05
127 Scott Shockey	.05
128 John Wasdin	.05
129 Joel Wolfe	.05
130 Brooks Kieschnick	.35
131 Kennie Steenstra	.10
132 Hector Trinidad	.05
133 Derek Wallace	.05
134 Kevin Lane	.05
135 Buck McNabb	.05
136 James Mouton	.15
137 Joey Eischen	.10
138 Todd Haney	.05
139 John Pricher	.05
140 Jeff Brown	.05
141 Jason Hardtke	.05
142 Derrek Lee	1.00
143 Ira Smith	.05
144 Mike Kelly	.15
145 Mark Smith	.20
146 Sherard Clinkscales	.05
147 Ben VanRyn	.05
148 Tim Cooper	.05
149 Manny Martinez	.05
150 Kurt Ehmann	.05
151 Doug Mirabelli	.05
152 Chris Wimmer	.05
153 Scott Christman	.05
154 Kevin Coughlin	.05
155 Troy Fryman	.05
156 Sean Johnston	.05
157 Jeff Alkire	.05
158 Mike Busby	.05
159 John O'Brien	.05
160 Brian Rupp	.05
161 Steve Soderstrom	.05
162 Craig Wilson	.05
163 Alan Burke	.05
164 Mike Murphy	.05
165 T.J. Mathews	.05
166 Edgardo Alfonzo	1.00
167 Randy Curtis	.05
168 Bernie Millan	.05
169 Mike Cantu	.05
170 Clint Davis	.05
171 Jason Kisey	.05
172 Aldo Pecorilli	.05
173 Dmitri Young	.40
174 Marshall Boze	.10
175 Bill Hardwick	.05
176 Kevin Riggs	.05
177 Lee Stevens	.05
178 Webster Garrison	.05
179 Wally Ritchie	.05
180 Cris Colon	.05
181 Rick Helling	.25
182 Trey McCoy	.05
183 Marc Barcelo	.05
184 Chris Demetral	.05
185 Rick Linares	.05
186 Daron Kirkreit	.15
187 Casey Whitten	.05
188 Shon Walker	.10
189 Rod Henderson	.05
190 Tyrone Horne	.10
191 B.J. Wallace	.20
192 Louis Maberry	.05
193 Brian Boehringer	.05
194 Glenn DiSarcina	.05
195 Melvin Bunch	.05
196 Chad Mottola	.45
197 Ryan Luzinski	.05

198	Tom Wilson	.05
199	Checklist 1	.05
200	Checklist 2	.05

1994 Classic Best Gold #1 Picks

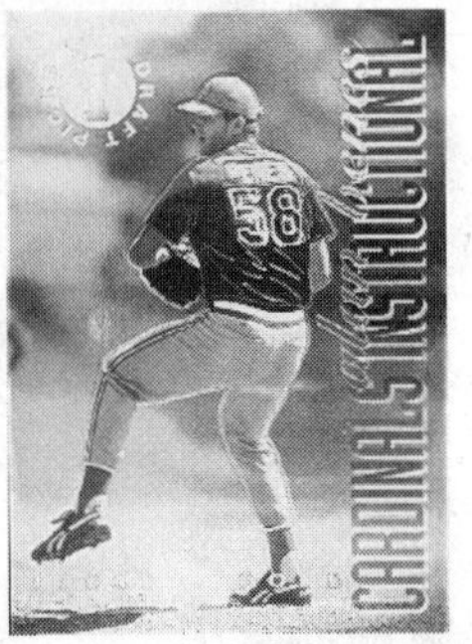

Classic Best's #1 Draft Pick insert cards feature 19 top picks. The cards, numbered with an LP prefix, utilize a chromium effect printing process that gives the cards a reflective textured effect. They are randomly inserted at an average rate of one per 12 foil packs.

		MT
Complete Set (19):		12.00
Common Player:		.50
1	Alan Benes	2.50
2	Scott Christman	.50
3	Jeff D'Amico	1.00
4	Wayne Gomes	.50
5	Torii Hunter	.50
6	Brooks Kieschnick	.75
7	Daron Kirkreit	.75
8	Derrek Lee	3.00
9	Trot Nixon	2.50
10	Charles Peterson	.50
11	Jay Powell	.50
12	Jon Ratliff	.50
13	Chris Schwabb	.50
14	Steve Soderstrom	.50
15	Marc Valdes	.50
16	Billy Wagner	2.50
17	John Wasdin	.50
18	Jamey Wright	.50
19	Kelly Wunsch	.50

1994 Classic Best Illustrated Acetate

Classic Best Gold's acetate insert cards feature illustrations of minor league stars by comic artist Neal Adams, printed on plastic. The glow-in-the-dark cards, are inserted at a rate of one per 90 packs. The unnumbered cards when laid in proper order from left to right share a contiguous background design and have typography which reads "1994 Minor League Gold" across the tops of the cards and "Superstars" in clear letters across the bottoms. Backs also share a cosmic art background, and include a small color player photo and career highlights.

		MT
Complete Set (5):		20.00
Common Player:		3.00
1	Brien Taylor	2.00
2	Dmitri Young	2.00
3	Derek Jeter	18.00
4	Phil Nevin	2.00
5	Frank Rodriguez	2.00

1994 Classic Best Gold David Justice Autograph

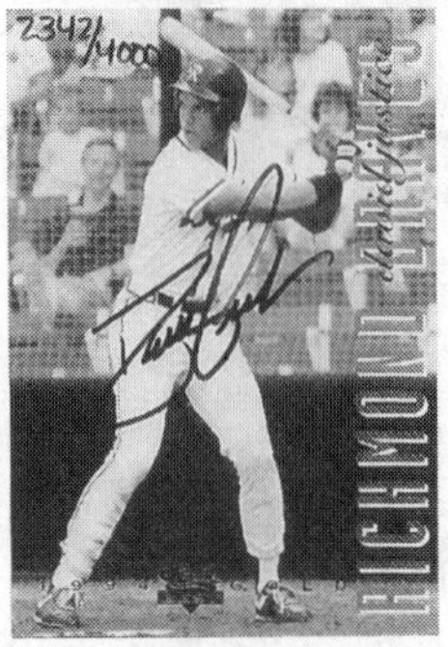

An authentically autographed card of David Justice was issued as an insert in 1994 Classic Best Gold. The gold-foil highlighted cards were inserted at the rate of about one per case (360 foil packs). Each card is serially numbered within an edition of 4,000.

	MT
David Justice	65.00

1994 Classic Best Gold Rookie Express

These chase cards are found only in Classic Best Gold jumbo packs at the rate of one per pack. The cards use the same chromium layered technolody as the #1 draft pick inserts and share an identical checklist. Card #20 is printed with glow in the dark ink.

		MT
Complete Set (20):		6.00
Common Player:		.25
1	Alan Benes	1.00
2	Scott Christman	.25
3	Jeff D'Amico	.50
4	Wayne Gomes	.25
5	Torii Hunter	.25
6	Brooks Kieschnick	.75
7	Daron Kirkreit	.25
8	Derrek Lee	.25
9	Trot Nixon	.50
10	Charles Peterson	.25
11	Jay Powell	.25
12	Jon Ratliff	.25
13	Chris Schwab	.25
14	Steve Soderstrom	.25
15	Marc Valdes	.25
16	Billy Wagner	1.00
17	John Wasdin	.25
18	Jamey Wright	.50
19	Kelly Wunsch	.25
20	Brooks Kieschnick	1.00

1994 Classic 4 Sport (Baseball)

A number of baseball players are included in the base-card set, parallels and chase cards in this issue.

	MT
Base set/inserts:	
Printer's Proofs #161-188: 15X-20X	
Gold card #161-188: 2X-3X	
161 Paul Wilson	.75
(161) Paul Wilson (autographed edition of 2,400)	10.00
162 Ben Grieve	2.00
(162) Ben Grieve (autographed edition of 2,500)	20.00
163 Doug Million	.10
164 C.J. Nitkowski	.10
165 Tommy Davis	.10
166 Dustin Hermanson	.15
167 Travis Miller	.10
168 McKay Christiansen	.10
169 Victor Rodriguez	.10
170 Jacob Cruz	.10
171 Rick Heiserman	.10
172 Mark Farris	.10
173 Nomar Garciaparra	3.00
(173) Nomar Garciaparra (autographed edition of 1,020)	30.00
174 Paul Konerko	.50
(174) Paul Konerko (autographed edition of 970)	15.00
175 Trey Moore	.10
176 Brian Stephenson	.10
177 Matt Smith	.10
178 Kevin Brown	.10
179 Cade Gaspar	.10
180 Bret Wagner	.10
(180) Bret Wagner (autographed edition of 970)	5.00
181 Mike Thurman	.10
182 Doug Webb	.10
183 Ryan Nye	.10
184 Brian Buchanan	.10
(184) Brian Buchanan (autographed edition of 950)	5.00
185 Scott Elarton	.10
186 Mark Johnson	.25
187 Jacob Shumate	.15
188 Kevin Witt	.10
HV3 Paul Wilson (High Voltage)	6.00
HV7 Ben Grieve (High Voltage)	12.00
HV11 Dustin Hermanson (High Voltage)	6.00
HV15 Doug Million (High Voltage)	.50
HV20 Nomar Garciaparra (High Voltage)	30.00
TC5 Paul Wilson, Doug Million, Cade Gaspar (Tricard)	3.00
16/25 Paul Wilson (Classic Picks)	2.50
17/25 Ben Grieve (Classic Picks)	5.00
18/25 Trey Moore (Classic Picks)	.50
19/25 Nomar Garciaparra (Classic Picks)	10.00
20/25 Doug Million (Classic Picks)	.50

The values of some parallel-card issues will have to be calculated based on figures presented in the heading for the regular-issue card set.

1994 Classic 4 Sport (Baseball) Foncards

A number of baseball players are included in the Sprint Foncard inserts in this issue.

		MT
(1)	Ben Grieve ($1 Foncard)	1.50
(2)	Ben Grieve ($2 Foncard)	3.00
(3)	Ben Grieve ($3 Foncard)	4.50
(4)	Ben Grieve ($4 Foncard)	6.00
(5)	Ben Grieve ($5 Foncard)	7.50
(6)	Paul Wilson ($1 Foncard)	.70
(7)	Paul Wilson ($2 Foncard)	1.50
(8)	Paul Wilson ($3 Foncard)	2.25
(9)	Paul Wilson ($4 Foncard)	3.00
(10)	Paul Wilson ($5 Foncard)	3.75

1994 Classic Images (Baseball)

Young players from the four major team sports are featured in the 1994 debut edition of Images. Only the baseball players are listed here.

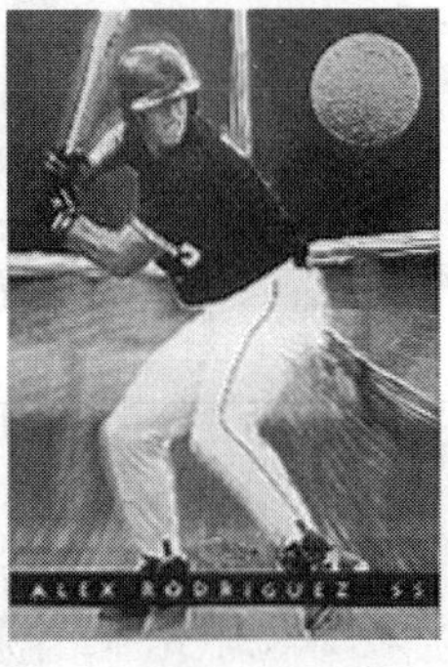

		MT
Complete (Baseball) Set (26):		3.00
3	Alex Rodriguez	1.50
7	Jeff D'Amico	.25
11	Alan Benes	.25
15	Jeff Granger	.10
19	Daron Kirkreit	.15
23	Billy Wagner	.35
31	Brian Anderson	.10
37	Matt Brunson	.10
42	Kirk Presley	.10
47	Chris Carpenter	.10
49	Kelly Wunsch	.10
51	Jon Ratliff	.10
52	Wayne Gomes	.10
54	Trot Nixon	.25
55	Andre King	.10
63	Darren Dreifort	.25
69	Brooks Kieschnick	.15
77	Torii Hunter	.10
80	Steve Soderstrom	.10
85	Derrek Lee	.25
93	Jay Powell	.10
105	Matt Drews	.15
115	Scott Christman	.10
131	Kirk Presley (b/w)	.10
139	Trot Nixon (b/w)	.25
143	Alex Rodriguez (b/w)	1.00

1994 Classic Images (Baseball) Sudden Impact

The young professionals who were believed to have the greatest chance for early stardom in the four major team sports were chosen for a 1-per-pack insert set called "Sudden Impact". The cards have fronts printed on gold foil. Only the baseball players are listed here.

		MT
Complete (baseball) Set (3):		3.00
SI1	Carlos Delgado	.50
SI3	Derek Jeter	1.00
SI4	Alex Rodriguez	2.00

1994 Classic Tri-Cards

An innovative concept which never caught on with collectors, these minor league "tri-cards" feature three different players in the standard 3-1/2" x 2-1/2" format. The complete set consists of 84 cards on 28 three-player panels. The panels are perforated to allow separation into three individual cards of about 1-1/8" x 2-1/2". Each panel features one prospect from the Class A, AA and AAA farm clubs of a major league team. Values shown are for complete three-player panels. Individual player cards have little or no collector value. Fronts feature action photos with a minor league team logo at lower-right. Backs have some career data, the major league team logo and a "1 of 8,000" notice.

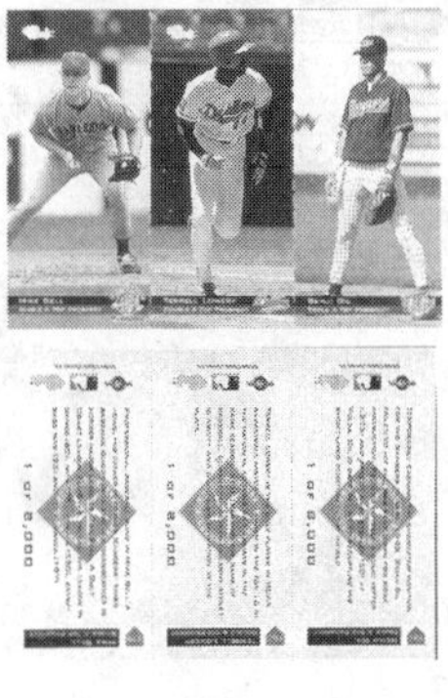

		MT
Complete Panel Set (28):		125.00
Common Panel:		2.50
	ATLANTA BRAVES	2.50
T1	Jamie Arnold	2.50
T2	Terrell Wade	2.50
T3	Ramon Caraballo	2.50
	BALTIMORE ORIOLES	3.00
T4	Jay Powell	2.50

T5	Alex Ochoa	2.50
T6	Manny Alexander	2.50
	BOSTON RED SOX	3.00
T7	Trot Nixon	2.50
T8	Jose Malave	2.50
T9	Frank Rodriguez	2.50
	CALIFORNIA ANGELS	2.50
T10	De Shawn Warren	2.50
T11	Chris Smith	2.50
T12	Andrew Lorraine	2.50
	CHICAGO CUBS	2.50
T13	Jon Ratliff	2.50
T14	Brooks Kieschnick	2.50
T15	Matt Franco	2.50
	CHICAGO WHITE SOX	2.50
T16	Eddie Pearson	2.50
T17	Chris Snopek	2.50
T18	James Baldwin	2.50
	CINCINNATI REDS	2.50
T19	Paul Bako	2.50
T20	Chad Mottola	2.50
T21	John Roper	2.50
	CLEVELAND INDIANS	2.50
T22	Daron Kirkreit	2.50
T23	Tony Mitchell	2.50
T24	Chad Ogea	2.50
	COLORADO ROCKIES	2.50
T25	Mike Zolecki	2.50
T26	Rodney Pedraza	2.50
T27	Mark Thompson	2.50
	DETROIT TIGERS	5.00
T28	Matt Brunson	2.50
T29	Tony Clark	2.50
T30	Felipe Lira	2.50
	FLORIDA MARLINS	7.00
T31	Edgar Renteria	2.50
T32	Charles Johnson	2.50
T33	Kurt Miller	2.50
	HOUSTON ASTROS	5.00
T34	Billy Wagner	2.50
T35	Kevin Gallaher	2.50
T36	Phil Nevin	2.50
	KANSAS CITY ROYALS	7.00
T37	Johnny Damon	2.50
T38	Darren Burton	2.50
T39	Michael Tucker	2.50
	LOS ANGELES DODGERS	9.00
T40	Kym Ashworth	2.50
T41	Chan Ho Park	2.50
T42	Todd Hollandsworth	2.50
	MILWAUKEE BREWERS	2.50
T43	Gabe Martinez	2.50
T44	Scott Talanoa	2.50
T45	Marshall Boze	2.50
	MINNESOTA TWINS	2.50
T46	LaTroy Hawkins	2.50
T47	Brad Radke	2.50
T48	Dave Stevens	2.50
	MONTREAL EXPOS	4.00
T49	Jose Paniagua	2.50
T50	Ugueth Urbina	2.50
T51	Rondell White	2.50
	NEW YORK METS	5.00
T52	Kirk Presley	2.50
T53	Bill Pulsipher	2.50
T54	Butch Huskey	2.50
	NEW YORK YANKEES	25.00
T55	Derek Jeter	2.50
T56	Brien Taylor	2.50
T57	Russ Davis	2.50
	OAKLAND A'S	2.50
T58	Jose Herrera	2.50
T59	Curtis Shaw	2.50
T60	Mark Acre	2.50
	PHILADELPHIA PHILLIES	2.50
T61	Wayne Gomes	2.50
T62	Jason Moler	2.50
T63	Phil Geisler	2.50
	PITTSBURGH PIRATES	4.00
T64	Mitch House	2.50
T65	Jermaine Allensworth	2.50
T66	Midre Cummings	2.50
	SAN DIEGO PADRES	2.50
T67	Derrek Lee	2.50
T68	Robbie Beckett	2.50
T69	Ray McDavid	2.50
	SAN FRANCISCO GIANTS	2.50
T70	Chris Singleton	2.50
T71	Calvin Murray	2.50
T72	J.R. Phillips	2.50
	SEATTLE MARINERS	25.00
T73	Alex Rodriguez	2.50
T74	Mac Suzuki	2.50
T75	Marc Newfield	2.50
	ST. LOUIS CARDINALS	5.00
T76	Basil Shabazz	2.50
T77	Dmitri Young	2.50
T78	Brian Barber	2.50
	TEXAS RANGERS	3.00
T79	Mike Bell	2.50
T80	Terrell Lowery	2.50
T81	Benji Gil	2.50
	TORONTO BLUE JAYS	3.00
T82	Jose Silva	2.50
T83	Brent Bowers	2.50
T84	Shawn Green	2.50

1994-95 Fleer Excel

Color-enhanced photos on both sides, gold-foil highlights and UV coating give a major league look to Fleer's set of prospects. Players are arranged alphabetically within the parent team and are chosen from all rungs of the minor league ladder from Short Season A clubs to AAA. Backs feature a second version of the front photo and complete career stats, along with the minor league team logo. Excel was sold in 14-card packs with a $1.49 retail price. Three insert sets included at random in packs were All-Stars, League Leaders and 1st Year Phenoms.

		MT
	Complete Set (300):	30.00
	Common Player:	.05
1	Kimera Bartee	.10
2	Harry Berrios	.05
3	Tommy Davis	.20
4	Cesar Devarez	.05
5	Curtis Goodwin	.15
6	Jimmy Haynes	.05
7	Chris Lemp	.05
8	Alex Ochoa	.25
9	B.J. Waszgis	.05
10	Nomar Garciaparra	6.00
11	Jose Malave	.05
12	Glenn Murray	.05
13	Trot Nixon	.25
14	Frank Rodriguez	.25
15	Bill Selby	.05
16	Jeff Suppan	.10
17	George Arias	.20
18	Todd Blyleven	.10
19	John Donati	.05
20	Todd Greene	.45
21	Bret Hemphill	.05
22	Michael Holtz	.05
23	Troy Percival	.15
24	Luis Raven	.05
25	James Baldwin	.20
26	Mike Bertotti	.05
27	Ben Boulware	.05
28	Ray Durham	.25
29	Jimmy Hurst	.05
30	Rich Pratt	.05
31	Mike Sirotka	.05
32	Archie Vazquez	.05
33	Harold Williams	.05
34	Chris Woodfin	.05
35	David Bell	.05
36	Todd Betts	.05
37	Jim Betzsold	.05
38	Einar Diaz	.05
39	Travis Driskill	.05
40	Damian Jackson	.05
41	Daron Kirkreit	.10
42	Steve Kline	.05
43	Tony Mitchell	.05
44	Enrique Wilson	.35
45	Jaret Wright	.75
46	Matt Brunson	.10
47	Tony Clark	2.00
48	Cade Gaspar	.05
49	John Grimm	.05
50	Bob Higginson	.45
51	Shannon Penn	.05
52	John Rosengren	.05
53	Jaime Bluma	.05
54	Mike Bovee	.05
55	Nevin Brewer	.05
56	Johnny Damon	.45
57	Lino Diaz	.05
58	Bart Evans	.05
59	Sal Fasano	.05
60	Tim Grieve	.10
61	Jim Pittsley	.10
62	Joe Randa	.15
63	Ken Ray	.05
64	Glendon Rusch	.05
65	Larry Sutton	.05
66	Dilson Torres	.05
67	Michael Tucker	.50
68	Joe Vitiello	.10
69	James Cole	.05
70	Danny Klassen	.10
71	Jeff Kramer	.05
72	Mark Loretta	.10
73	Danny Perez	.05
74	Sid Roberson	.05
75	Scott Talanoa	.05
76	Tim Unroe	.05
77	Antone Williamson	.15
78	Marc Barcelo	.05
79	Trevor Cobb	.05
80	Marty Cordova	.25
81	Darren Fidge	.05
82	Troy Fortin	.05
83	Gus Gandarillas	.05
84	Adrian Gordon	.05
85	LaTroy Hawkins	.20
86	Matt Lawton	.05
87	Jake Patterson	.05
88	Brad Radke	.05
89	Todd Walker	1.50
90	Brian Boehringer	.05
91	Brian Buchanan	.10
92	Andy Croghan	.05
93	Chris Cumberland	.10
94	Matt Drews	.05
95	Keith Heberling	.05
96	Jason Jarvis	.05
97	Derek Jeter	5.00
98	Ricky Ledee	1.50
99	Matt Luke	.10
100	James Musselwhite	.05
101	Andy Pettitte	1.50
102	Mariano Rivera	.50
103	Ruben Rivera	.75
104	Tate Seefried	.25
105	Scott Standish	.05
106	Jim Banks	.05
107	Tony Batista	.05
108	Ben Grieve	2.50
109	Jose Herrera	.05
110	Steve Lemke	.05
111	Eric Martins	.05
112	Scott Spiezio	.25
113	John Wasdin	.10
114	Scott Davison	.05
115	Chris Dean	.05
116	Giomar Guevara	.05
117	Tim Harikkala	.05
118	Brett Hinchliffe	.05
119	Matt Mantei	.05
120	Arquimedez Pozo	.05
121	Marino Santana	.05
122	John Vanhof	.05
123	Chris Widger	.10
124	Mike Bell	.05
125	Mark Brandenburg	.05
126	Kevin Brown	.05
127	Bucky Buckles	.05
128	Jaime Escamilla	.05
129	Terrell Lowery	.05
130	Jerry Martin	.05
131	Reid Ryan	.35
132	Julio Santana	.05
133	Howard Battle	.15
134	D.J. Boston	.10
135	Chris Carpenter	.25
136	Freddy Garcia	.10
137	Aaron Jersild	.05
138	Ricardo Jordan	.05
139	Angel Martinez	.05
140	Jose Pett	.05
141	Jose Silva	.05
142	David Sinnes	.05
143	Rob Steinert	.05
144	Chris Stynes	.05
145	Mike Toney	.05
146	Chris Weinke	.15
147	Kevin Witt	.05
148	Brad Clontz	.05
149	Jermaine Dye	.25
150	Tony Graffanino	.05
151	Kevin Grijak	.05
152	Damon Hollins	.25
153	Marcus Hostetler	.05
154	Darrell May	.05
155	Wonderful Monds	.10
156	Carl Schulz	.05
157	Chris Seelbach	.05
158	Jacob Shumate	.05
159	Terrell Wade	.10
160	Glenn Williams	.25
161	Alex Cabrera	.05
162	Gabe Duross	.05
163	Shawn Hill	.05
164	Mike Hubbard	.05
165	Dave Hutcheson	.05
166	Brooks Kieschnick	.15
167	Bobby Morris	.05
168	Jayson Peterson	.05
169	Jason Ryan	.05
170	Ozzie Timmons	.05
171	Cedric Allen	.05
172	Aaron Boone	.25
173	Ray Brown	.05
174	Damon Callahan	.05
175	Decomba Conner	.05
176	Emiliano Giron	.05
177	James Lofton	.05
178	Nick Morrow	.05
179	C.J. Nitkowski	.15
180	Eddie Priest	.05
181	Pokey Reese	.15
182	Jason Robbins	.05
183	Scott Sullivan	.05
184	Pat Watkins	.05
185	Juan Acevedo	.10
186	Derrick Gibson	1.50
187	Pookie Jones	.05
188	Terry Jones	.05
189	Doug Million	.05
190	Lloyd Peever	.05
191	Jacob Viano	.05
192	Mark Voisard	.05
193	Josh Booty	.10
194	Will Cunnane	.05
195	Andy Larkin	.05
196	Billy McMillon	.05
197	Kevin Millar	.05
198	Marc Valdes	.05
199	Bob Abreu	.50
200	Jamie Daspit	.05
201	Scott Elarton	.05
202	Kevin Gallaher	.05
203	Richard Hidalgo	.25
204	Chris Holt	.05
205	Rick Huisman	.05
206	Doug Mlicki	.05
207	Julien Tucker	.05
208	Billy Wagner	.25
209	Juan Castro	.10
210	Roger Cedeno	.15
211	Ron Coomer	.05
212	Karim Garcia	2.00
213	Todd Hollandsworth	.25
214	Paul Konerko	3.00
215	Antonio Osuna	.05
216	Willis Otanez	.10
217	Dan Ricabal	.05
218	Ken Sikes	.05
219	Yamil Benitez	.05
220	Geoff Blum	.05
221	Scott Gentile	.05
222	Mark Grudzielanek	.40
223	Kevin Northrup	.05
224	Carlos Perez	.25
225	Matt Raleigh	.05
226	Al Reyes	.05
227	Everett Stull	.05
228	Ugueth Urbina	.25
229	Neil Weber	.05
230	Edgardo Alfonzo	.40
231	Jason Isringhausen	.50
232	Terrence Long	.15
233	Rey Ordonez	.50
234	Ricky Otero	.15
235	Jay Payton	1.50
236	Kirk Presley	.10
237	Bill Pulsipher	.25
238	Chris Roberts	.05
239	Jeff Tam	.05
240	Paul Wilson	.40
241	David Doster	.05
242	Wayne Gomes	.05
243	Jeremy Kendall	.05
244	Ryan Nye	.05
245	Shane Pullen	.05
246	Scott Rolen	5.00
247	Gene Schall	.10
248	Brian Stumpf	.05
249	Jake Austin	.05
250	Trey Beamon	.25
251	Danny Clyburn	.10
252	Louis Collier	.05
253	Mark Farris	.05
254	Mark Johnson	.15
255	Jason Kendall	.50
256	Esteban Loaiza	.10
257	Joe Maskivish	.05
258	Ramon Morel	.05
259	Gary Wilson	.05
260	Matt Arrandale	.05
261	Allen Battle	.10
262	Alan Benes	.60
263	Jeff Berblinger	.05
264	Terry Bradshaw	.05
265	Darrell Deak	.05
266	Craig Grasser	.05
267	Yates Hall	.05
268	Kevin Lovingier	.05
269	Elieser Marrero	.05
270	Jeff Matulevich	.05
271	Joe McEwing	.05
272	Eric Miller	.05
273	Tom Minor	.05
274	Scott Simmons	.05
275	Chris Stewart	.05
276	Bret Wagner	.05
277	Travis Welch	.05
278	Jay Witasick	.05
279	Homer Bush	.15
280	Raul Casanova	.10
281	Glenn Dishman	.05
282	Gary Dixon	.05
283	Devohn Duncan	.05
284	Dustin Hermanson	.50
285	Earl Johnson	.05
286	Derrek Lee	.75
287	Todd Schmitt	.05
288	Ira Smith	.05
289	Jason Thompson	.10
290	Bryan Wolff	.05
291	Jeff Martin	.05
292	Dante Powell	.35
293	Jeff Richey	.05
294	Joe Rosselli	.10
295	Benji Simonton	.05
296	Steve Whitaker	.05
297	Keith Williams	.05
298	Checklist	.05
299	Checklist	.05
300	Checklist	.05

1994-95 Fleer Excel All-Stars

An all-star team of minor league prospects is presented in this chase set. Borderless color action photos of the players are surrounded with a colorful graphic "aura," while the player name is given in bold angled type. Fronts are gold-foil enhanced with the Excel and All-Star logos. Backs repeat the front photo in slightly larger size and include career highlights. All-Star inserts are found on an average of one per four packs.

		MT
	Complete Set (10):	11.00
	Common Player:	.50
1	Raul Casanova	.50
2	Tony Clark	2.00
3	Ray Durham	.75
4	Ron Coomer	.50
5	Derek Jeter	5.00
6	Trey Beamon	.75
7	Johnny Damon	.75
8	Ruben Rivera	.75
9	Todd Greene	.75
10	Alan Benes	1.00

1994-95 Fleer Excel League Leaders

Statistical leaders from all levels of minor league play are featured in this insert set. Front action photos are placed against a graphically enhanced background, with the player's name in gold foil at the bottom. Backs feature career summaries. League Leader inserts are found on an average of more than one per two packs.

		MT
Complete Set (20):		8.00
Common Player:		.25
1	Juan Acevedo	.25
2	James Baldwin	.50
3	Allen Battle	.25
4	Harry Berrios	.25
5	Brad Clontz	.25
6	Will Cunnane	.25
7	Glenn Dishman	.25
8	LaTroy Hawkins	.50
9	Jimmy Haynes	.25
10	Richard Hidalgo	2.00
11	Earl Johnson	.25
12	Jim Pittsley	.25
13	Bill Pulsipher	.75
14	Benji Simonton	.25
15	Larry Sutton	.25
16	Michael Tucker	1.50
17	Tim Unroe	.25
18	Joe Vitiello	.25
19	Billy Wagner	1.00
20	Harold Williams	.25

1994-95 Fleer Excel 1st Year Phenoms

Ten players who made an impact in their debut season of pro ball are highlighted in this chase set. Color action photos are set against a background that has been divided into colorized zones. The player's name and team are at bottom, with the card title and Excel logo enhanced in gold foil. Backs have a close-up version of the front photo and a career summary. The First Year Phenom cards are inserted at an average rate of one per 12 packs.

		MT
Complete Set (10):		20.00
Common Player:		1.00
1	Paul Konerko	5.00
2	Ray Brown	1.00
3	Chris Dean	1.00
4	Aaron Boone	1.50
5	Rey Ordonez	5.00
6	Decomba Conner	1.00
7	Ben Grieve	7.50
8	Jay Payton	3.00
9	Dante Powell	1.00
10	Dustin Hermanson	2.00

1994 Signature Rookies

This 50-card set features top prospects from the minor leagues. Cards are UV coated with gold foil highlights and full color backs and fronts with a borderless design. The issue was sold in packs of seven only through hobby dealers. The print run was limited to 45,000 of each card, as indicated on the fronts. Each pack includes an autographed card or certificate redeemable for an autograph. In addition to the autographed cards, Signature Rookies has a Hottest Prospects insert set, a five-card Bonus Signature insert set, and a five-card Cliff Floyd insert set. Because cards are licensed only by the individual players and not Major League Baseball, minor league uniform logos have been removed from the photos.

		MT
Complete Set (50):		6.00
Common Player:		.10
1	Russell Davis	.40
2	Brant Brown	.20
3a	Ricky Bottalico (photo actually Jamie Sepeda)	.25
3b	Ricky Bottalico (correct photo)	2.50
4	Brian Bevil	.10
5	Garret Anderson	.50
6	Rod Henderson	.10
7	Keith Heberling	.10
8	Scott Hatteberg	.15
9	Brook Fordyce	.10
10	Joey Eischen	.25
11	Orlando Miller	.20
12	Ray McDavid	.15
13	Andre King	.10
14	Todd Hollandsworth	.50
15	Tyrone Hill	.10
16	Paul Spoljaric	.10
17	Todd Ritchie	.10
18	Herbert Perry	.10
19	Alex Ochoa	.25
20	Mike Neill	.10
21	John Burke	.10
22	Alan Benes	.50
23	Robbie Beckett	.15
24	Brian Barber	.15
25	Justin Thompson	.20
26	Joey Hamilton	.25
27	Rick Greene	.10
28	Wayne Gomes	.10
29	Matthew "Big Bird" Drews	.20
30	Jeff D'Amico	.25
31	Bryn Kosco	.10
32	Brooks Kieschnick	.25
33	Jason Kendall	.50
34	Mike Kelly	.15
35	Derek Jeter	2.00
36	Jay Powell	.10
37	Phil Nevin	.15
38	Kurt Miller	.10
39	Chad McConnell	.10
40	Sean Lowe	.15
41	Michael Tucker	.75
42	Paul Shuey	.15
43	Dan Smith	.10
44	Calvin Reese	.20
45	Kirk Presley	.10
46	Jamey "Jamo" Wright	.15
47	Gabe White	.30
48	John Wasdin	.10
49	Billy Wagner	.40
50	Joe "Vit" Vitiello	.20

1994 Signature Rookies - Autographed

The autographed versions of the 1994 Signature Rookies set was a one-per-pack insert. Basically the same as the regular issue, each card is authentically autographed and numbered from within an edition of 8,650.

		MT
Complete Set (50):		200.00
Common Player:		1.00
1	Russell Davis	7.50
2	Brant Brown	2.00
3	Ricky Bottalico	5.00
4	Brian Bevil	1.00
5	Garret Anderson	10.00
6	Rod Henderson	3.00
7	Keith Heberling	1.00
8	Scott Hatteberg	1.00
9	Brook Fordyce	2.00
10	Joey Eischen	4.00
11	Orlando Miller	5.00
12	Ray McDavid	3.00
13	Andre King	3.00
14	Todd Hollandsworth	7.50
15	Tyrone Hill	5.00
16	Paul Spoljaric	3.00
17	Todd Ritchie	2.00
18	Herbert Perry	1.00
19	Alex Ochoa	5.00
20	Mike Neill	1.00
21	John Burke	1.00
22	Alan Benes	7.50
23	Robbie Beckett	2.00
24	Brian Barber	2.00
25	Justin "J.T." Thompson	5.00
26	Joey Hamilton	7.50
27	Rick Greene	1.00
28	Wayne Gomes	3.00
29	Matthew "Big Bird" Drews	5.00
30	Jeff D'Amico	2.00
31	Bryn Kosco	1.00
32	Brooks Kieschnick	5.00
33	Jason Kendall	10.00
34	Mike Kelly	3.00
35	Derek Jeter	35.00
36	Jay Powell	2.00
37	Phil Nevin	4.00
38	Kurt Miller	1.00
39	Chad McConnell	2.00
40	Sean Lowe	2.00
41	Michael Tucker	10.00
42	Paul Shuey	5.00
43	Dan Smith	1.00
44	Calvin Reese	5.00
45	Kirk Presley	3.00
46	Jamey "Jamo" Wright	4.00
47	Gabe White	5.00
48	John Wasdin	2.00
49	Billy Wagner	9.00
50	Joe "Vit" Vitiello	4.00

1994 Signature Rookies Bonus Signature Set

Signature Rookies packs had Bonus cards randomly inserted in them; there were 1,000 sets of the five-card set made. The cards are numbered with a P prefix.

		MT
Complete Set (5):		60.00
Common Player:		15.00
P1	Rick Helling	15.00
P2	Charles Johnson	20.00
P3	Chad Mottola	10.00
P4	J.R. Phillips	10.00
P5	Glen (Glenn) Williams	15.00

1994 Signature Rookies Cliff Floyd Set

Montreal Expos' top prospect Cliff Floyd is featured on this five-card Signature Rookies insert set. The cards, numbered with a B prefix, were limited to 10,000 complete sets. Cards were random inserts inside packs.

		MT
Complete Set (5):		4.00
Common Card:		1.00
B1	Cliff Floyd	1.00
B1a	Cliff Floyd (autograph)	10.00
B2	Cliff Floyd	1.00
B2a	Cliff Floyd (autograph)	10.00
B3	Cliff Floyd	1.00
B3a	Cliff Floyd (autograph)	10.00
B4	Cliff Floyd	1.00
B4a	Cliff Floyd (autograph)	10.00
B5	Cliff Floyd	1.00
B5a	Cliff Floyd (autograph)	10.00

1994 Signature Rookies Hottest Prospects

Signature Rookies' 12-card Hottest Prospects insert set cards are numbered with an S prefix. There were 5,000 complete sets made. Autographed sets, 1,000 of each card, were made available to dealers as an early-order incentive.

		MT
Complete Set (12):		4.00
Common Player:		.10
1	John Burke	.10
1a	John Burke (autographed)	2.00
2	Russ Davis	.25
2a	Russ Davis (autographed)	4.00
3	Todd Hollandsworth	.25
3a	Todd Hollandsworth (autographed)	4.00
4	Derek Jeter	3.00
4a	Derek Jeter (autographed)	60.00
5	Mike Kelly	.10
5a	Mike Kelly (autographed)	4.00
6	Ray McDavid	.10
6	Ray McDavid (autographed)	2.00
7	Kurt Miller	.10
7a	Kurt Miller (autographed)	2.00
8	Phil Nevin	.15
8a	Phil Nevin (autographed)	4.00
9	Alex Ochoa	.20
9a	Alex Ochoa (autographed)	4.00
10	Justin "J.T." Thompson	.75
10a	Justin "J.T." Thompson (autographed)	5.00
11	Michael Tucker	.75
11a	Michael Tucker (autographed)	5.00
12	Gabe White	.25
12a	Gabe White (autographed)	7.50

Player names in *Italic* type indicate a rookie card.

1994 Signature Rookies Gold Standard Promos

Thess gold-foil enhanced cards introduced SR's multi-sport Gold Standard brand. In the same format as the regular-issue cards, the promos have a "1 of 10,000" notice printed vertically on front, along with "PROMO". Backs have a "P" prefix to the card number. Only the baseball player from the promo issue is listed here.

	MT
James Mouton	2.00

1994 Signature Rookies Gold Standard (Baseball)

Twenty-five young players from each of the four major team sports were featured in the base set of Gold Standard. In addition, insert sets offered cards of "Legends," Hall of Famers (signed and unsigned) and a partial parallel set featuring gold facsimile autographs. Basic cards have an action photo on front and portrait photo with personal data and stats on back. There is a gold-foil Gold Standard logo on both front and back. Minor and major league uniform logos have been removed from the photos because the cards were only licensed by individual players and collegiate licensing authorities.

		MT
Complete (Baseball) Set (36):		30.00
Common Player:		.10
51	Josh Booty	.25
52	Roger Cedeno	.25
53	Cliff Floyd	.50
53 (p)	Cliff Floyd (promo, edition of 10,000)	2.00
54	Ben Grieve	.50
55	Joey Hamilton	.35
56	Todd Hollandsworth	.25
57	Brian Hunter	.35
58	Charles Johnson	.45
59	Brooks Kieschnick	.25
60	Mike Kelly	.10
61	Ray McDavid	.10
62	Kurt Miller	.10
63	James Mouton	.10
63 (p)	James Mouton (promo, edition of 10,000)	1.00
64	Phil Nevin	.15
65	Alex Ochoa	.25
66	Herbert Perry	.10
67	Kirk Presley	.15
68	Bill Pulsipher	.10
69	Scott Ruffcorn	.10
70	Paul Shuey	.10
71	Michael Tucker	.25
72	Terrell Wade	.10
73	Gabe White	.25
74	Paul Wilson	.25
75	Dmitri Young	.15
HOF15	Catfish Hunter	.25
HOF15	Catfish Hunter (autographed)	8.00
HOF20	Willie Stargell	.25

HOF20	Willie Stargell (autographed)	8.00
L3	"Pee Wee" Reese (Legends)	.50
L4	Nolan Ryan (Legends)	3.00
GS4	Josh Booty (Gold Signature)	1.00
GS6	Brooks Kieschnick (Gold Signature)	.50
GS8	Charles Johnson (Gold Signature)	1.00
GS10	Cliff Floyd (Gold Signature)	.50
GS15	James Mouton (Gold Signature)	.25

1994 Signature Rookies Draft Picks

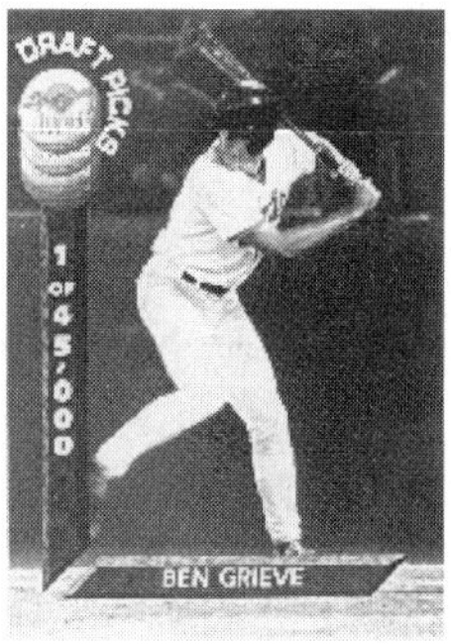

One hundred top players from the 1994 amateur draft are featured in this set. Most cards feature game-action, borderless color photos of the players in their college uniforms. At left is a vertical marbled panel with the SR Draft Picks logo on top and the edition number (45,000 for regular, 7,750 for parallel autographs) in gold foil. At bottom the player name is also in gold foil on a marbled panel. Backs have a small portrait photo, college stats and career notes, draft status and appropriate licensors' logos and copyright data.

		MT
	Complete Set (101):	12.50
	Common Player:	.10
1	Josh Booty	.15
2	Paul Wilson	.50
3	Ben Grieve	.75
4	Dustin Hermanson	.20
5	Antone Williamson	.15
6	McKay Christiansen	.10
7	Doug Million	.10
8	Todd Walker	.55
9	C.J. Nitkowski	.15
10	Jaret Wright	.35
11	Mark Farris	.10
12	Nomar Garciaparra	1.00
13	Paul Konerko	.35
14	Jason Varitek	.10
15	Jayson Peterson	.10
16	Matt Smith	.10
17	Ramon Castro	.15
18	Cade Gaspar	.10
19	Bret Wagner	.10
20	Terrence Long	.25
21	Hiram Bocachica	.10
22	Dante Powell	.15
23	Brian Buchanan	.15
24	Scott Elarton	.10
25	Mark Johnson	.15
26	Jacob Shumate	.10
27	Kevin Witt	.10
28	Jay Payton	.25
29	Mike Thurman	.10
30	Jacob Cruz	.15
31	Chris Clemons	.10
32	Travis Miller	.10
33	Shawn Johnston	.10
34	Brad Rigby	.10
35	Doug Webb	.10
36	John Ambrose	.10
37	Cleatus Davidson	.10
38	Tony Terry	.10
39	Jason Camilli	.10
40	Roger Goedde	.10
41	Corey Pointer	.10
42	Trey Moore	.10
43	Brian Stephenson	.10
44	Dan Lock	.10
45	Mike Darr	.10
46	Carl Dale	.10
47	Tommy Davis	.10
48	Kevin Brown	.10
49	Ryan Nye	.10
50	Rod Smith	.10
51	Andy Taulbee	.10
52	Jerry Whittaker	.10
53	John Crowther	.10
54	Bryon Gainey	.10
55	Bill King	.10
56	Heath Murray	.10
57	Larry Barnes	.10
58	Todd Cady	.10
59	Paul Failla	.10
60	Brian Meadows	.10
61	A.J. Pierzynski	.10
62	Aaron Boone	.15
63	Mike Metcalfe	.10
64	Matt Wagner	.10
65	Jaime Bluma	.10
66	Oscor Robles	.10
67	Greg Whiteman	.10
68	Roger Worley	.10
69	Paul Ottavinia	.10
70	Joe Giuliano	.10
71	Chris McBride	.10
72	Jason Beverlin	.10
73	Gordon Amerson	.10
74	Tom Mott	.10
75	Rob Welch	.10
76	Jason Kelley	.10
77	Matt Treanor	.10
78	Jason Sikes	.10
79	Steve Shoemaker	.10
80	Troy Brohawn	.10
81	Jeff Abbott	.10
82	Steve Woodard	.10
83	Greg Morris	.10
84	John Slamka	.10
85	John Schroeder	.10
86	Clay Carruthers	.10
87	Eddie Brooks	.10
88	Tim Byrdak	.10
89	Bobby Howry	.10
90	Vic Darensbourg	.10
91	Midre Cummings	.15
92	John Dettmer	.10
93	Gar Finnvold	.10
94	Dwayne Hosey	.10
95	Jason Jacome	.10
96	Doug Jennings	.10
97	Luis A. Lopez	.10
98	John Mabry	.35
99	Rondell White	.55
100	J.T. Snow	.50
101	Checklist	.05

1994 Signature Rookies Draft Picks - Autographed

A parallel set featuring the 100 players in the Signature Rookies Draft Pick set has each card authentically autographed. The only differences between the autographed cards and the regular version are the hand-numbered "X of 7,750" notation on the vertical marbled column at left, and the gold-foil "Authentic Signature" logo above that. Autographed cards were inserted on a one-per-pack basis.

		MT
	Complete Set (100):	300.00
	Common Player:	2.00
1	Josh Booty	5.00
2	Paul Wilson	10.00
3	Ben Grieve	30.00
4	Dustin Hermanson	4.00
5	Antone Williamson	5.00
6	McKay Christiansen	2.00
7	Doug Million	5.00
8	Todd Walker	10.00
9	C.J. Nitkowski	3.00
10	Jaret Wright	12.50
11	Mark Farris	2.00
12	Nomar Garciaparra	35.00
13	Paul Konerko	15.00
14	Jason Varitek	5.00
15	Jayson Peterson	2.00
16	Matt Smith	2.00
17	Ramon Castro	2.00
18	Cade Gaspar	2.00
19	Bret Wagner	2.00
20	Terrence Long	3.50
21	Hiram Bocachica	2.00
22	Dante Powell	3.00
23	Brian Buchanan	3.00
24	Scott Elarton	2.00
25	Mark Johnson	2.00
26	Jacob Shumate	2.00
27	Kevin Witt	2.00
28	Jay Payton	5.00
29	Mike Thurman	2.00
30	Jacob Cruz	3.00
31	Chris Clemons	2.00
32	Travis Miller	2.00
33	Shawn Johnston	2.00
34	Brad Rigby	2.00
35	Doug Webb	2.00
36	John Ambrose	2.00
37	Cleatus Davidson	2.00
38	Tony Terry	2.00
39	Jason Camilli	2.00
40	Roger Goedde	2.00
41	Corey Pointer	2.00
42	Trey Moore	2.00
43	Brian Stephenson	2.00
44	Dan Lock	2.00
45	Mike Darr	2.00
46	Carl Dale	2.00
47	Tommy Davis	2.00
48	Kevin Brown	2.00
49	Ryan Nye	2.00
50	Rod Smith	2.00
51	Andy Taulbee	2.00
52	Jerry Whittaker	2.00
53	John Crowther	2.00
54	Bryon Gainey	2.00
55	Bill King	2.00
56	Heath Murray	2.00
57	Larry Barnes	2.00
58	Todd Cady	2.00
59	Paul Failla	2.00
60	Brian Meadows	2.00
61	A.J. Pierzynski	2.00
62	Aaron Boone	5.00
63	Mike Metcalfe	2.00
64	Matt Wagner	2.00
65	Jaime Bluma	2.00
66	Oscor Robles	2.00
67	Greg Whiteman	2.00
68	Roger Worley	2.00
69	Paul Ottavinia	2.00
70	Joe Giuliano	2.00
71	Chris McBride	2.00
72	Jason Beverlin	2.00
73	Gordon Amerson	2.00
74	Tom Mott	2.00
75	Rob Welch	2.00
76	Jason Kelley	2.00
77	Matt Treanor	2.00
78	Jason Sikes	2.00
79	Steve Shoemaker	2.00
80	Troy Brohawn	2.00
81	Jeff Abbott	2.00
82	Steve Woodard	2.00
83	Greg Morris	2.00
84	John Slamka	2.00
85	John Schroeder	2.00
86	Clay Carruthers	2.00
87	Eddie Brooks	2.00
88	Tim Byrdak	2.00
89	Bobby Howry	2.00
90	Vic Darensbourg	2.00
91	Midre Cummings	3.00
92	John Dettmer	2.00
93	Gar Finnvold	2.00
94	Dwayne Hosey	2.00
95	Jason Jacome	2.00
96	Doug Jennings	2.00
97	Luis A. Lopez	2.00
98	John Mabry	9.00
99	Rondell White	9.00
100	J.T. Snow	7.50

1994 Signature Rookies Draft Picks Bonus Signatures

Ten players who do not otherwise appear in the Draft Picks set or inserts are featured in this special autographed chase card set. Between 3,250 and 3,350 of each card were signed by the respective player.

		MT
	Complete Set (10):	30.00
	Common Player:	3.00
1	Russ Johnson	3.00
2	Carlton Loewer	3.00
3	Matt Beaumont	4.00
4	Yates Hall	3.00
5	Jeremy Powell	3.00
6	Paul O'Malley	3.00
7	Scott Shores	3.00
8	Jed Hansen	3.00
9	Ryan Helms	3.00
10	Darrell Nicholas	3.00

1994 Signature Rookies Draft Picks Flip Cards

These "two-headed" cards have virtually identical fronts and backs with different player photos on each side. According to information provided at the time of issue, each of the featured players autographed 1,000 of the cards, with 250 of each bearing autographs on each side. Each side is highlighted with gold foil and features a notation that it is "1 of 15,000".

		MT
	Complete Set (5):	5.00
	Common Player:	.50
1	Ken Griffey Jr., Craig Griffey	2.00
1	Ken Griffey Jr., Craig Griffey (Ken autograph)	150.00
1	Ken Griffey Jr., Craig Griffey (Craig autograph)	10.00
1	Ken Griffey Jr., Craig Griffey (Both autographs)	200.00
2	Craig Griffey, Ken Griffey Sr.	.50
2	Craig Griffey, Ken Griffey Sr. (Craig autograph)	10.00
2	Craig Griffey, Ken Griffey Sr. (Ken autograph)	10.00
2	Craig Griffey, Ken Griffey Sr. (Both autographs)	20.00
3	Ken Griffey Jr., Ken Griffey Sr.	2.00
3	Ken Griffey Jr., Ken Griffey Sr. (Junior autograph)	150.00
3	Ken Griffey Jr., Ken Griffey Sr. (Senior autograph)	10.00
3	Ken Griffey Jr., Ken Griffey Sr. (Both autographs)	200.00
4	Nolan Ryan, Reid Ryan	2.00
4	Nolan Ryan, Reid Ryan (Nolan autograph)	150.00
4	Nolan Ryan, Reid Ryan (Reid autograph)	10.00
4	Nolan Ryan, Reid Ryan (Both autographs)	200.00
5	Paul Wilson, Phil Nevin	1.00
5	Paul Wilson, Phil Nevin (Wilson autograph)	20.00
5	Paul Wilson, Phil Nevin (Nevin autograph)	10.00
5	Paul Wilson, Phil Nevin (Both autographs)	40.00

1994 Signature Rookies Draft Picks Top Prospects

Five top young pitching prospects are featured in this insert set. Both regular and a parallel autographed edition (2,100 each) were found as pack inserts. Standard 2-1/2" x 3-1/2" cards are UV coated on both sides and gold-foil enhanced on front, including a notice the card is "1 of 20,000". Backs have a ghosted image of the front photo in the background, along with an enlargement of the player's portrait from that photo. Biological data, career highlights and professional career stats are overprinted.

		MT
	Complete Set (5):	1.50
	Common Player:	.50
T6	Scott Ruffcorn	.25
T6	Scott Ruffcorn (autographed)	10.00
T7	Brad Woodall	.40
T7	Brad Woodall (autographed)	10.00
T8	Andrew Lorraine	.25
T8	Andrew Lorraine (autographed)	10.00
T9	LaTroy Hawkins	.25
T9	LaTroy Hawkins (autographed)	10.00
T10	Alan Benes	.50
T10	Alan Benes (autographed)	15.00

1994 Signature Rookies Mail In Promos

This set parallels the Hottest Prospects insert set but was only available via a mail-in promotion. Where the pack-insert version has printed down the left side in gold foil, "1 of 5,000," the mail-in version reads, "Mail In Promo / 1 of 3,000". Cards are numbered with an "S" prefix.

		MT
	Complete Set (12):	15.00
	Common Player:	.25
S1	John Burke	.25
S2	Russ Davis	.50
S3	Todd Hollandsworth	1.25
S4	Derek Jeter	9.00
S5	Mike Kelly	.30
S6	Ray McDavid	.30
S7	Kurt Miller	.25
S8	Phil Nevin	.50
S9	Alex Ochoa	.50
S10	Justin "J.T." Thompson	.50
S11	Michael Tucker	2.50
S12	Gabe White	.60

1994 Signature Rookies Tetrad (Baseball)

Twenty of the 120 cards in the four-sport Tetrad issue, plus several of the inserts, feature baseball players. Fronts have a borderless color action photo with a classic marble column at left bearing the Signature Rookies and Tetrad logos. The player name and "1 of 45,000" notation on front are in gold foil. Backs have an ancient temple background design with player data, stats and career summary. Cards are numbered in Roman numerals at top. All but one of the baseball players' cards was also issued in an edition of 7,500 authentically autographed cards.

	MT
Complete (Baseball) Set (20):	2.50
Baseball Set, Autographed (20)	50.00
Common Player:	.10
Common Player, Autographed:	2.00
84 Edgardo Alfonzo	.25
84a Edgardo Alfonzo (autographed)	8.00
85 David Bell	.15
85a David Bell (autographed)	3.00
86 Christopher Carpenter	.10
86a Christopher Carpenter (autographed)	2.00
87 Roger Cedeno	.15
87a Roger Cedeno (autographed)	3.00
88 Phil Geisler	.10
88a Phil Geisler (autographed)	2.00
89 Curtis Goodwin	.20
89a Curtis Goodwin (autographed)	4.00
90 Jeff Granger	.10
90a Jeff Granger (autographed)	2.00
91 Brian Hunter	.20
91a Brian Hunter (autographed)	4.00
92 Adam Hyzdu	.10
92a Adam Hyzdu (autographed)	2.00
93 Scott Klingenbeck	.10
93a Scott Klingenbeck (autographed)	2.00
94 Derrek Lee	.15
94a Derrek Lee (autographed)	3.00
95 Calvin Murray	.10
95a Calvin Murray (autographed)	2.00
96 Roberto Petagine	.10
96a Roberto Petagine (autographed)	2.00
97 Bill Pulsipher	.15
97a Bill Pulsipher (autographed)	3.00
98 Marquis Riley	.10
98a Marquis Riley (autographed)	2.00
99 Frankie Rodriguez	.15
99a Frank Rodriguez (autographed)	3.00
100 Scott Ruffcorn	.10
100a Scott Ruffcorn (autographed)	2.00
101 Roger Salkeld	.10
101a Roger Salkeld (autographed)	2.00
102 Marc Valdes	.10
102a Marc Valdes (autographed)	2.00
103 Ernie Young	.10
103a Ernie Young (autographed)	2.00
134 Paul Wilson (Top Prospects)	1.00
134a Paul Wilson (Top Prospects) (autographed edition of 2,000)	12.50
FLIP1 Charles Johnson, Charles Johnson (edition of 7,500)	1.00
FLIP1a Charles Johnson, Charles Johnson (autographed) (edition of 275)	45.00
FLIP5 Glen Williams, Monty Williams (Glenn) (edition of 7,500)	1.50
FLIP5a Glen Williams, Monty Williams (Glenn) (autographed edition of 275)	25.00
PROMO 1 Paul Wilson (1 of 10,000)	1.00

1994 Upper Deck Minor League

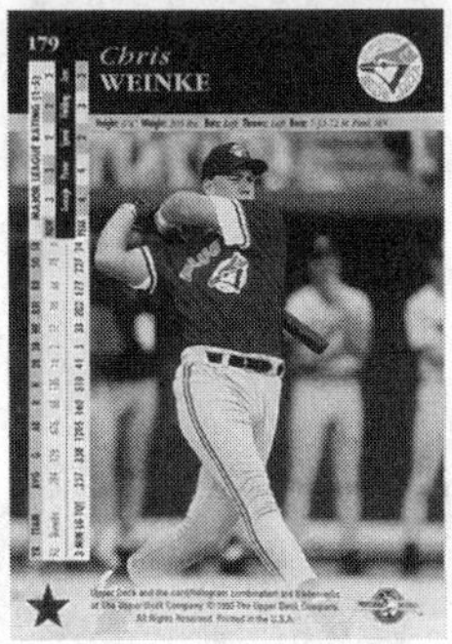

Upper Deck's 1994 minor league cards are similar in format to their major league counterparts. The super-premium set of 270 cards features the top professional players who had yet to appear in a Major League game. Cards have UV coating and foil accents, along with color photography on both sides of the card. The player's name is printed in silver foil, as is his Major League team affiliation. The regular player cards (225) have ratings by Baseball America on the back. Subsets include: Major League Evaluations (15), with backs done by noted statistical innovator Bill James; Star Potential (20), showcasing top young players; and Upper Deck All-Stars, one per position, as selected by experts at Baseball America. Insert series include Organizational Players of the Year (28); Trade Cards redeemable by mail for two top picks in the 1994 draft; and Top 10 Prospects (oversized cards), inserted in each box. These were also available as regular-sized cards through an on-pack offer.

	MT
Complete Set (270):	20.00
Common Player:	.10
1 Alex Gonzalez	.75
2 Brooks Kieschnick	.25
3 Michael Tucker	.75
4 Trot Nixon	.50
5 Brien Taylor	.20
6 Quinton McCracken	.15
7 Terrell Wade	.25
8 Brandon Wilson	.15
9 Roberto Petagine	.10
10 Chad Mottola	.40
11 T.R. Lewis	.10
12 Herbert Perry	.10
13 Bob Abreu	2.00
14 Jorge Fabregas	.15
15 Mike Kelly	.15
16 Ryan McGuire	.25
17 Alan Zinter	.10
18 Troy Hughes	.10
19 Brook Fordyce	.15
20 Alex Ochoa	.50
21 Chris Wimmer	.15
22 Jason Hardtke	.10
23 Ricardo Hildago	2.00
24 Greg Zaun	.15
25 Roger Cedeno	.20
26 Curtis Shaw	.15
27 Brian Giles	.35
28 Felix Rodriguez	.10
29 Motor-Boat Jones	.15
30 Dmitri Young	.50
31 Justin Mashore	.10
32 Curtis Goodwin	.15
33 Marquis Riley	.10
34 Les Norman	.10
35 Billy Hall	.10
36 Jamie Arnold	.15
37 Mike Farmer	.10
38 Brent Bowers	.10
39 Chad McConnell	.15
40 Mike Robertson	.10
41 Brent Cookson	.10
42 Dan Cholowsky	.10
43 Justin Thompson	.60
44 Joe Vitiello	.20
45 Todd Steverson	.25
46 Brian Bevil	.10
47 Paul Shuey	.10
48 Scott Eyre	.10
49 Rick Greene	.10
50 Jose Silva	.10
51 Kurt Miller	.10
52 Ron Villone	.10
53 Darren Bragg	.15
54 Mike Lieberthal	.15
55 Gabe White	.20
56 Vince Moore	.10
57 Tony Clark	2.00
58 Chris Eddy	.10
59 Ray Durham	.25
60 Todd Hollandsworth	.75
61 Andres Berumen	.10
62 Quilvio Veras	.15
63 Wayne Gomes	.15
64 Ryan Karp	.10
65 Randy Curtis	.10
66 Steve Rodriguez	.10
67 Jason Schmidt	.10
68 Mark Acre	.10
69 B.J. Wallace	.20
70 Alvin Morman	.10
71 Travis Baptist	.15
72 Jim Wawruck	.10
73 Marty Cordova	.40
74 Jamie Dismuke	.10
75 Joe Randa	.20
76 Danny Clyburn	.15
77 Joey Eischen	.15
78 Chris Seelbach	.10
79 Izzy Molina	.10
80 Chris Roberts	.10
81 Rod Henderson	.10
82 Kennie Steenstra	.10
83 Ugueth Urbina	.20
84 Stanton Cameron	.10
85 Doug Glanville	.20
86 Billy Wagner	.65
87 Tate Seefried	.10
88 Tyler Houston	.15
89 Derek Lowe	.15
90 Alan Benes	1.00
91 Terrell Wade	.15
92 Rod Henderson (All-Star)	.10
93 Charles Johnson (AS)	.60
94 D.J. Boston (AS)	.10
95 Ruben Santana (AS)	.10
96 Joe Randa (AS)	.10
97 Alex Gonzalez (AS)	.30
98 Tim Clark (AS)	.10
99 Randy Curtis (AS)	.10
100 Brian Hunter (AS)	.50
101 Jose Lima	.15
102 Ray Holbert	.10
103 Karim Garcia	3.00
104 Chris Martin	.10
105 David Bell	.10
106 Tim Clark	.10
107 Matt Drews	.15
108 Dan Serafini	.15
109 Demetrish Jenkins	.10
110 Charles Johnson	1.00
111 Jason Moler	.30
112 Brett Backlund	.10
113 Kevin Jordan	.15
114 Jesus Tavarez	.10
115 Frank Rodriguez	.35
116 Derrek Lee	1.00
117 Pokey Reese	.15
118 Dave Stevens	.10
119 Julio Bruno	.10
120 D.J. Boston	.15
121 Jim Dougherty	.15
122 Daron Kirkreit	.25
123 Kerwin Moore	.10
124 Jason Kendall	.60
125 Johnny Damon	.50
126 Andre King	.15
127 Raul Gonzalez	.20
128 Eddie Pearson	.10
129 Yuri Sanchez	.10
130 Russ Davis	.60
131 Arquimedez Pozo	.10
132 Jon Lieber	.10
133 Glenn Murray	.10
134 Brant Brown	.40
135 Brian Hunter	.40
136 Mike Gulan	.10
137 Tim Vanegmond	.10
138 Billy Vanlandingham	.15
139 Robert Ellis	.10
140 Calvin Murray	.10
141 Kurt Ehmann	.10
142 Brian DuBose	.10
143 Robert Eenhoorn	.10
144 Howard Battle	.10
145 Jason Giambi	.60
146 James Baldwin (Major League Evaluation)	.45
147 Rick Helling (MLE)	.25
148 Ricky Bottalico (MLE)	.25
149 Paul Spolijaric (Spoljaric) (MLE)	.15
150 Alex Gonzalez (MLE)	.50
151 Tavo Alvarez (MLE)	.10
152 Joey Eischen (MLE)	.15
153 Shane Andrews (MLE)	.25
154 James Mouton (MLE)	.40
155 Russ Davis (MLE)	.50
156 Phil Nevin (MLE)	.40
157 Garret Anderson (MLE)	1.00
158 Gabe White (MLE)	.30
159 Brian Hunter (MLE)	.35
160 Ray McDavid (MLE)	.10
161 Mike Durrant	.10
162 Eric Owens	.10
163 Rick Gorecki	.10
164 Lyle Mouton	.10
165 Ray McDavid	.10
166 Tony Graffagnino (Graffanino)	.10
167 Todd Ritchie	.15
168 Jose Herrera	.10
169 Steve Dunn	.10
170 Tavo Alvarez	.10
171 Jon Farrell	.10
172 Omar Ramirez	.10
173 Ruben Santana	.10
174 Tracy Sanders	.10
175 Shane Andrews	.15
176 Rob Henkel	.10
177 Joel Wolfe	.10
178 Chris Schwab	.10
179 Chris Weinke	.25
180 Ozzie Timmons	.10
181 Jason Bates	.20
182 Matt Brunson	.10
183 Garret Anderson	1.00
184 Brian Rupp	.10
185 Derek Jeter	5.00
186 Desi Relaford	.20
187 Darren Burton	.10
188 David Mysel	.10
189 Steve Soderstrom	.10
190 Steve Gibralter	.15
191 Brian Sackinsky	.10
192 Marc Pisciotta	.15
193 Gene Schall	.15
194 Jimmy Haynes	.10
195 Shannon Stewart	.20
196 Neifi Perez	1.00
197 Cris Colon	.10
198 Trey Beamon	.25
199 Jon Zuber	.10
200 John Burke	.10
201 Derek Wallace	.10
202 Chad Ogea	.30
203 Ernie Young	.10
204 Jose Malave	.10
205 Bill Pulsipher	.40
206 Leon Glenn	.10
207 Scott Sullivan	.10
208 Orlando Miller	.25
209 John Wasdin	.10
210 Paul Spoljaric	.20
211 Charles Peterson	.10
212 Ben Van Ryn	.10
213 Chris Sexton	.10
214 Bobby Bonds Jr.	.20
215 James Mouton	.40
216 Terrell Lowery	.10
217 Oscar Munoz	.10
218 Mike Bell	.10
219 Preston Wilson	.60
220 Mark Thompson	.15
221 Aaron Holbert	.10
222 Tommy Adams	.10
223 Ramon D. Martinez	.15
224 Tim Davis	.10
225 Ricky Bottalico	.15
226 Rick Krivda	.10
227 Troy Percival	.20
228 Mark Sweeney	.15
229 Joey Hamilton	.60
230 Phil Nevin	.10
231 John Ratliff	.10
232 Mark Smith	.15
233 Tyrone Hill	.15
234 Kevin Riggs	.10
235 John Dettmer	.15
236 Brian Barber	.15
237 Hector Trinidad	.10
238 Jeff Alkire	.10
239 Phil Geisler	.10
240 Rick Helling	.25
241 Edgardo Alfonzo	.50
242 Matt Franco	.10
243 Chad Roper	.15
244 Basil Shabazz	.10
245 James Baldwin	.40
246 Scott Hatteberg	.15
247 Glenn DiSarcina	.10
248 LaTroy Hawkins	.40
249 Marshall Boze	.10
250 Michael Moore	.10
251 Brien Taylor (Star Potential)	.15
252 Johnny Damon (SP)	.60
253 Curtis Goodwin (SP)	.60
254 Jose Silva (SP)	.10
255 Terrell Wade (SP)	.10
256 Dmitri Young (SP)	.35
257 Roger Cedeno (SP)	.25
258 Alex Ochoa (SP)	.40
259 D.J. Boston (SP)	.15
260 Michael Tucker (SP)	.75
261 Calvin Murray (SP)	.10
262 Frank Rodriguez (SP)	.35
263 Michael Moore (SP)	.10
264 Ugueth Urbina (SP)	.35
265 Chad Mottola (SP)	.60
266 Todd Hollandsworth (SP)	1.00
267 Rod Henderson (SP)	.15
268 Roberto Petagine (SP)	.10
269 Charles Johnson (SP)	.60
270 Trot Nixon (SP)	.50
MJ23 Michael Jordan (Silver)	20.00
MJ23 Michael Jordan (Gold)	60.00
TC1 Alex Rodriguez (trade card)	60.00
TC2 Kirk Presley (trade card)	5.00
---- Redemption card #1, expired 12/31/94	.50
---- Redemption card #2, expired 12/31/94	.50

1994 Upper Deck Michael Jordan Scouting Report Supers

Though all six of the cards in this set show Jordan in the uniform of the Chicago White Sox, the cards were available only in a combination buy with a pack of Upper Deck's 1994 minor league cards at Wal-Mart stores. Each of the cards measures 3-1/2" x 5" and features full-color photos on front and back. Five of the cards have a large "Scouting Report" logo vertically at left and the backs discuss Jordan's baseball tools. The sixth card is a super-size version of his '94 UD minor league card.

	MT
Complete Set (6):	20.00
Common Jordan:	3.00
SR1 Michael Jordan (Hitting)	3.00
SR2 Michael Jordan (Fielding)	3.00
SR3 Michael Jordan (Throwing)	3.00
SR4 Michael Jordan (Speed)	3.00
SR5 Michael Jordan (Summary)	3.00
MJ23 Michael Jordan (White Sox Top Prospects)	5.00

Checklists with card numbers in parentheses ( ) indicates the numbers do not appear on the card.

1994 Upper Deck Minor League Player of the Year

This 28-card insert set features one top prospect from each Major League organization. The cards, numbered with a PY prefix, were random inserts in 1994 Upper Deck Minor League foil packs.

		MT
Complete Set (28):		45.00
Common Player:		1.50
1	Marquis Riley	1.00
2	Roberto Petagine	1.00
3	Ernie Young	1.50
4	Alex Gonzalez	5.00
5	Hiawatha Wade	1.50
6	Marshall Boze	1.00
7	Mike Gulan	1.50
8	Brant Brown	4.00
9	Roger Cedeno	2.00
10	Rod Henderson	1.00
11	Calvin Murray	1.00
12	Omar Ramirez	1.00
13	Ruben Santana	1.00
14	Charles Johnson	6.00
15	Bill Pulsipher	2.00
16	Alex Ochoa	3.00
17	Ray McDavid	2.00
18	Jason Moler	2.00
19	Danny Clyburn	1.00
20	Rick Helling	2.00
21	Frank Rodriquez	3.00
22	Chad Mottola	3.00
23	John Burke	1.00
24	Michael Tucker	4.00
25	Brian DuBose	1.00
26	LaTroy Hawkins	1.00
27	James Baldwin	1.50
28	Ryan Karp	1.00

1994 Upper Deck Minor League Top 10 Prospects

Ten top Major League prospects are featured in two different size versions. A jumbo version of 5-1/4" x 8-1/2" cards was inserted one per foil box of 1994 Upper Deck Minor League baseball cards. The cards are numbered with a TP prefix. The Top 10 Prospects were also available in a standard-size version (2-1/2" x 3-1/2") available through an on-pack offer; collectors could receive a 10-card set by sending in 15 foil pack wrappers, plus $2 for shipping costs. Box-topper card #8 features only a game-action silhouettes; the mail-in offer card pictures Alex Rodriguez.

		MT
Complete Set (10):		30.00
Common Player:		3.00
Jumbo cards worth 50%		
1	Roger Cedeno	2.00
2	Johnny Damon	6.00
3	Alex Gonzalez	4.00
4	Charles Johnson	7.00
5	Chad Mottola	2.00
6	Phil Nevin	2.00
7	Alex Ochoa	3.00
8a	1993 No. 1 Draft Pick (silhouettes, jumbo)	2.00
8b	Alex Rodriguez (mail-in card, standard)	30.00
9	Jose Silva	2.00
10	Michael Tucker	6.00

1994 Minor League Team Sets

Largely through issues by teams in independent leagues, the number of minor league teams issuing sets and the number of sets issued climbed a bit in 1994 as Classic and Fleer/ProCards retained their grip on the marketplace for a final year, with shares of 33% and 57%, respectively. Abbreviations found in these listings are: DD (Dunkin' Donuts), FPC (Fleer/ProCards) and SP (Sport Pro).

	MT
295 team sets and variations	
1994 FPC AAA All-Stars (47)	14.00
1994 Classic Albany Polecats (30)	6.00
1994 FPC Albany Polecats (30)	6.00
1994 FPC Albany-Colonie Yankees (31)	8.00
1994 Team Albany-Colonie Yearbook w/cards (3)	80.00
1994 FPC Albuquerque Dukes (27)	6.00
1994 Team Albuquerque Dukes (28)	110.00
1994 Team Alexandria Aces (26)	7.00
1994 Team Amarillo Dillas (30)	7.00
1994 Classic Appleton Foxes (30)	250.00
1994 FPC Appleton Foxes (28)	70.00
1994 Arizona Fall League (21)	16.00
1994 FPC Arkansas Travelers (26)	6.00
1994 Classic Asheville Tourists (30)	17.50
1994 FPC Asheville Tourists (30)	14.00
1994 Classic Auburn Astros (30)	5.00
1994 FPC Auburn Astros (29)	4.00
1994 Classic Augusta Greenjackets (30)	6.00
1994 FPC Augusta Greenjackets (28)	5.00
1994 Classic Bakersfield Dodgers (30)	5.00
1994 Classic Batavia Clippers (30)	5.00
1994 FPC Batavia Clippers (31)	4.00
1994 Team Beaumont Bullfrogs (23)	7.00
1994 Classic Bellingham Mariners (30)	6.00
1994 FPC Bellingham Mariners (31)	5.00
1994 Classic Beloit Brewers (30)	6.00
1994 FPC Beloit Brewers (30)	5.00
1994 Classic Bend Rockies (30)	28.00
1994 FPC Bend Rockies (31)	14.00
1994 FPC Billings Mustangs (27)	8.00
1994 SP Billings Mustangs (30)	15.00
1994 FPC Binghampton Mets (28)	6.00
1994 Classic Birmingham Barons (30)	16.00
1994 FPC Birmingham Barons (28)	12.00
1994 Classic Bluefield Orioles (30)	10.00
1994 FPC Bluefield Orioles (30)	7.00
1994 Classic Boise Hawks (30)	6.00
1994 FPC Boise Hawks (31)	5.00
1994 FPC Bowie Baysox (27)	6.00
1994 Classic Brevard County Manatees (30)	12.00
1994 FPC Brevard County Manatees (30)	10.00
1994 Classic Bristol Tigers (30)	13.00
1994 FPC Bristol Tigers (30)	13.00
1994 FPC Buffalo Bisons (28)	6.00
1994 Classic Burlington Bees (30)	19.00
1994 FPC Burlington Bees (29)	15.00
1994 Classic Burlington Indians (30)	15.00
1994 FPC Burlington Indians (31)	11.00
1994 SP Butte Copper Kings (30)	7.00
1994 FPC Calgary Cannons (27)	6.00
1994 FPC Canton-Akron Indians (30)	6.00
1994 Classic Capital City Bombers (30)	6.00
1994 FPC Capital City Bombers (29)	5.00
1994 FPC Carolina League All-Stars (53)	13.00
1994 FPC Carolina Mudcats (28)	6.00
1994 Classic Cedar Rapids Kernels (30)	6.00
1994 FPC Cedar Rapids Kernels (27)	5.00
1994 Classic Central Valley Rockies (30)	9.00
1994 FPC Central Valley Rockies (30)	7.00
1994 Classic Charleston River Dogs (30)	10.00
1994 FPC Charleston Riverdogs (29)	6.00
1994 Classic Charleston Wheelers (30)	7.50
1994 FPC Charleston Wheelers (28)	5.00
1994 FPC Charlotte Knights (26)	5.00
1994 Classic Charlotte Rangers (30)	6.50
1994 FPC Charlotte Rangers (27)	5.00
1994 FPC Chattanooga Lookouts (27)	5.00
1994 Team Chillicothe Paints (22)	9.00
1994 Classic Clearwater Phillies (30)	6.00
1994 FPC Clearwater Phillies (30)	5.00
1994 Classic Clinton Lumberkings (30)	6.00
1994 FPC Clinton Lumberkings (30)	5.00
1994 FPC Colorado Springs Sky Sox (28)	6.00
1994 FPC Columbus Clippers (30)	6.00
1994 Police Columbus Clippers (25)	8.00
1994 Team Columbus Clippers (28)	12.00
1994 Classic Columbus Redstixx (30)	15.00
1994 FPC Columbus Redstixx (31)	12.00
1994 Team Corpus Christi Barracudas (28)	7.00
1994 Classic Danville Braves (30)	17.00
1994 FPC Danville Braves (30)	14.00
1994 Classic Daytona Cubs (30)	13.00
1994 FPC Daytona Cubs (29)	9.00
1994 Team Duluth-Superior Dukes (27)	7.00
1994 Classic Dunedin Blue Jays (30)	6.00
1994 FPC Dunedin Blue Jays (30)	6.00
1994 Team Dunedin Blue Jays (29)	70.00
1994 Classic Durham Bulls (30)	9.00
1994 FPC Durham Bulls (30)	7.00
1994 Team Durham Bulls (32)	9.00
1994 FPC Edmonton Trappers (27)	6.00
1994 Classic Elizabethton Twins (30)	9.00
1994 FPC Elizabethton Twins (29)	8.00
1994 Classic Elmira Pioneers (30)	12.00
1994 FPC Elmira Pioneers (27)	5.00
1994 FPC El Paso Diablos (28)	6.00
1994 Classic Eugene Emeralds (30)	8.00
1994 FPC Eugene Emeralds (28)	5.00
1994 Classic Everett Giants (30)	8.00
1994 FPC Everett Giants (31)	6.00
1994 Classic Fayetteville Generals (30)	12.00
1994 FPC Fayetteville Generals (29)	9.00
1994 FPC Florida State League A-S (52)	27.50
1994 Classic Frederick Keys (30)	6.00
1994 FPC Frederick Keys (29)	5.00
1994 Classic Ft. Myers Miracle (30)	6.00
1994 FPC Ft. Myers Miracle (28)	5.00
1994 Ft. Myers Diamond Girls (13)	6.00
1994 Classic Ft. Wayne Wizards (30)	6.00
1994 FPC Ft. Wayne Wizards (28)	5.00
1994 SP Great Falls Dodgers (30)	10.00
1994 Classic Greensboro Bats (30)	12.00
1994 FPC Greensboro Bats (31)	10.00
1994 FPC Greenville Braves (28)	6.00
1994 Team Greenville Braves foldout	24.00
1994 Classic Hagerstown Suns (30)	6.00
1994 FPC Hagerstown Suns (29)	5.00
1994 FPC Harrisburg Senators (29)	6.00
1994 FPC Helena Brewers (27)	5.00
1994 SP Helena Brewers (30)	7.00
1994 Classic Hickory Crawdads (30)	6.00
1994 FPC Hickory Crawdads (30)	5.00
1994 Classic High Desert Mavericks (30)	8.00
1994 FPC High Desert Mavericks (30)	5.00
1994 Classic Hudson Valley Renegades (30)	9.00
1994 FPC Hudson Valley Renegades (30)	7.00
1994 Classic Huntington Cubs (30)	6.00
1994 FPC Huntington Cubs (31)	5.00
1994 FPC Huntsville Stars (27)	6.00
1994 FPC Idaho Falls Braves (31)	5.00
1994 SP Idaho Falls Braves (30)	8.00
1994 FPC Indianapolis Indians (27)	5.00
1994 FPC Iowa Cubs (26)	5.00
1994 Team Iowa Cubs (9)	6.00
1994 FPC Jackson Generals (27)	6.00
1994 Smokey Bear Jackson Generals (27)	20.00
1994 FPC Jacksonville Suns (27)	6.00
1994 Classic Jamestown Jammers (30)	12.00
1994 FPC Jamestown Jammers (30)	8.00
1994 Classic Johnson City Cardinals (30)	7.00
1994 FPC Johnson City Cardinals (31)	6.00
1994 Classic Kane County Cougars (30)	7.50
1994 FPC Kane County Cougars (30)	5.00
1994 Team Kane County Cougars (30)	7.00
1994 Classic Kingsport Mets (30)	11.00
1994 FPC Kingsport Mets (29)	8.00
1994 Classic Kinston Indians (30)	8.00
1994 FPC Kinston Indians (29)	6.00
1994 FPC Knoxville Smokies (28)	6.00
1994 Classic Lake Elsinore Storm (30)	11.00
1994 FPC Lake Elsinore Storm (28)	10.00
1994 Classic Lakeland Tigers (30)	8.00
1994 FPC Lakeland Tigers (28)	5.00
1994 FPC Las Vegas Stars (25)	6.00
1994 FPC Lethbridge Mounties (30)	5.00
1994 SP Lethbridge Mounties (30)	7.00
1994 FPC Louisville Redbirds (29)	6.00
1994 Classic Lynchburg Red Sox (30)	7.00
1994 FPC Lynchburg Red Sox (29)	6.00
1994 Classic Macon Braves (30)	11.00
1994 FPC Macon Braves (31)	8.00
1994 Classic Madison Hatters (30)	6.00
1994 FPC Madison Hatters (30)	5.00
1994 Classic Martinsville Phillies (30)	6.00
1994 FPC Martinsville Phillies (31)	5.00
1994 FPC Medicine Hat Blue Jays (29)	7.50
1994 SP Medicine Hat Blue Jays (30)	14.00
1994 FPC Memphis Chicks (28)	6.00
1994 FPC Midland Angels (27)	5.00
1994 OHP Midland Angels (33)	42.00
1994 FPC Midwest League All-Stars (59)	30.00
1994 Team Minneapolis Loons (23)	6.00
1994 Team Mobile Bay Sharks (23)	7.00
1994 Classic Modesto A's (30)	6.00
1994 FPC Modesto A's (26)	5.00
1994 FPC Nashville Sounds (27)	6.00
1994 FPC Nashville Xpress (28)	5.00
1994 FPC New Britain Red Sox (27)	5.00
1994 FPC New Haven Ravens (29)	5.00
1994 Classic New Jersey Cardinals (30)	7.00
1994 FPC New Jersey Cardinals (31)	5.00
1994 FPC New Orleans Zephyrs (27)	6.00
1994 FPC Norfolk Tides (27)	6.00
1994 FPC Ogden Raptors (24)	5.00
1994 SP Ogden Raptors (30)	7.00
1994 FPC Oklahoma City 89ers (25)	6.00
1994 FPC Omaha Royals (27)	6.00
1994 Classic Oneonta Yankees (30)	10.00
1994 FPC Oneonta Yankees (31)	5.00
1994 FPC Orlando Cubs (26)	7.00
1994 Classic Osceola Astros (30)	6.00

1994 FPC Osecola Astros (30)	5.00
1994 FPC Ottawa Lynx (19)	7.00
1994 DD Pawtucket Red Sox foldout	50.00
1994 FPC Pawtucket Red Sox (25)	7.00
1994 Classic Peoria Chiefs (30)	6.00
1994 FPC Peoria Chiefs (29)	5.00
1994 FPC Phoenix Firebirds (27)	6.00
1994 Classic Pittsfield Mets (30)	18.00
1994 FPC Pittsfield Mets (27)	16.00
1994 FPC Portland Sea Dogs (27)	7.50
1994 Team Portland Sea Dogs (31)	10.00
1994 Classic Princeton Reds (30)	8.00
1994 FPC Princeton Reds (29)	5.00
1994 Classic Prince Williams Cannons (30)	10.00
1994 FPC Prince William Cannons (28)	6.00
1994 Classic Quad City River Bandits (30)	10.00
1994 FPC Quad City River Bandits (29)	7.00
1994 Classic Rancho Cucamonga Quakes (30)	19.00
1994 FPC Rancho Cucamonga Quakes (29)	15.00
1994 FPC Reading Phillies (27)	5.00
1994 FPC Richmond Braves (30)	5.00
1994 Richmond Camera Richmond Braves (28)	55.00
1994 Team Richmond Braves foldout	40.00
1994 Team Rio Grande White Wings (25)	7.00
1994 FPC Rochester Red Wings (27)	5.00
1994 Classic Rockford Royals (30)	8.00
1994 FPC Rockford Royals (31)	5.00
1994 Classic Salem Buccaneers (30)	9.00
1994 FPC Salem Buccaneers (28)	6.00
1994 FPC Salt Lake City Buzz (27)	5.00
1994 FPC San Antonio Missions (31)	9.00
1994 HEB San Antonio Missions (36)	65.00
1994 Team San Antonio Tejanos (28)	7.00
1994 Classic San Bernardino Spirit (30)	8.00
1994 FPC San Bernardino Spirit (28)	5.00
1994 Classic San Jose Giants (30)	7.50
1994 FPC San Jose Giants (29)	5.00
1994 Classic Sarasota Red Sox (30)	11.00
1994 FPC Sarasota Red Sox (30)	9.00
1994 Classic Savannah Cardinals (30)	13.50
1994 FPC Savannah Cardinals (31)	10.00
1994 FPC Scranton Red Barons (26)	6.00
1994 Team Scranton Red Barons (30)	7.50
1994 FPC Shreveport Captains (29)	5.00
1994 Team Sioux City Explorers (26)	7.00
1994 Team Sioux Falls Canaries (28)	7.00
1994 FPC South Atlantic League A-S (57)	19.00
1994 Classic South Bend Silver Hawks (30)	6.00
1994 FPC South Bend Silver Hawks (29)	5.00
1994 Classic Southern Oregon Athletics (30)	32.00
1994 FPC Southern Oregon Athletics (29)	20.00
1994 Classic Spartanburg Phillies (30)	40.00
1994 FPC Spartanburg Phillies (30)	25.00
1994 Classic Spokane Indians (30)	6.00
1994 FPC Spokane Indians (30)	5.00
1994 Classic Sultans of Springfield (30)	6.00
1994 FPC Springfield Sultans (27)	5.00
1994 Classic St. Catherines Blue Jays (30)	10.00
1994 FPC St. Catherines Blue Jays (30)	5.00
1994 Classic St. Lucie Mets (30)	13.00
1994 FPC St. Lucie Mets (29)	8.00
1994 Team St. Paul Saints (28)	7.00
1994 Classic St. Petersburg Cardinals (30)	13.00
1994 FPC St. Petersburg Cardinals (29)	9.00
1994 Classic Stockton Ports (30)	6.00
1994 FPC Stockton Ports (28)	5.00
1994 FPC Syracuse Chiefs (26)	5.00
1994 FPC Tacoma Tigers (28)	5.00
1994 Classic Tampa Yankees (30)	30.00
1994 FPC Tampa Yankees (32)	14.00
1994 Team Thunder Bay Whiskey Jacks (25)	7.50
1994 FPC Toledo Mud Hens (27)	5.00
1994 FPC Trenton Thunder (27)	5.00
1994 FPC Tucson Toros (29)	5.00
1994 FPC Tulsa Drillers (27)	5.00
1994 Team Tulsa Drillers (30)	10.00
1994 Team Tyler Wildcatters (25)	7.00
1994 Classic Utica Blue Sox (30)	7.00
1994 FPC Utica Blue Sox (29)	5.00
1994 FPC Vancouver Canadians (26)	9.00
1994 Classic Vermont Expos (30)	10.00
1994 FPC Vermont Expos (28)	5.00
1994 Classic Vero Beach Dodgers (30)	28.00
1994 FPC Vero Beach Dodgers (31)	16.00
1994 Classic Watertown Indians (30)	6.00
1994 FPC Watertown Indians (30)	5.00
1994 Classic Welland Pirates (30)	7.00
1994 FPC Welland Pirates (31)	5.00
1994 Classic West Michigan Whitecaps (30)	7.00
1994 FPC West Michigan Whitecaps (28)	5.00
1994 Classic West Palm Beach Expos (30)	7.00
1994 FPC West Palm Beach Expos (30)	5.00
1994 FPC Wichita Wranglers (26)	5.00
1994 Classic Williamsport Cubs (30)	6.00
1994 FPC Williamsport Cubs (30)	5.00
1994 Classic Wilmington Blue Rocks (30)	11.00
1994 FPC Wilmington Blue Rocks (29)	10.00
1994 Team Wilmington Blue Rocks	40.00
1994 Team Winnipeg Goldeyes (30)	11.00
1994 Classic Winston-Salem Spirits (30)	6.00
1994 FPC Winston-Salem Spirits (28)	5.00
1994 Classic Yakima Bears (30)	32.00
1994 FPC Yakima Bears (30)	25.00

1995 Action Packed Scouting Report

Action Packed's final minor league issue combines cards of baseball's best young prospects with cards honoring its oldest performer (#80-82 feature ballpark clown Max Patkin). The basic set features large player photos on front on which the player figure has been embossed. Cards #52-61 have a "#1 Draft Pick" logo in an upper corner. Cards #62-79 are "Franchise Gems" with an appropriate logo in an upper corner. Each of the "Franchise Gem" cards can also be found in a 24-karat gold stamped parallel edition, while card #1, Jeter's "Player of the Year" card can be found once every 480 packs in a diamond-chip encrusted, autographed version.

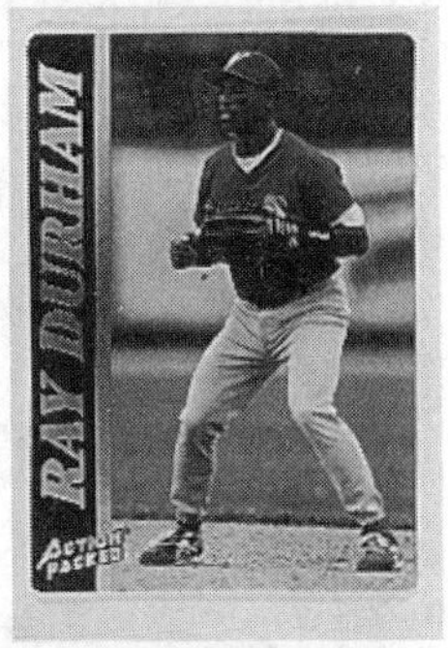

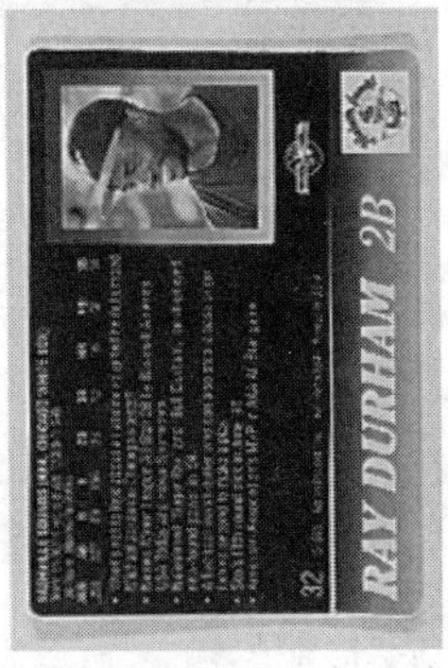

		MT
Complete Set (83):		20.00
Common Player:		.10
Derek Jeter Autographed (1G):		40.00
Derek Jeter Autographed (1D):		80.00
1	Derek Jeter (Player of the Year)	2.00
2	Trot Nixon	.25
3	Charles Johnson	.35
4	Chan Ho Park	.40
5	Terrell Wade	.10
6	Carlos Delgado	1.00
7	Brian Hunter	.35
8	Tony Clark	1.50
9	Russ Davis	.35
10	Derek Jeter	2.00
11	Alex Gonzalez	.15
12	Scott Ruffcorn	.10
13	Todd Hollandsworth	.30
14	Phil Nevin	.10
15	Marc Newfield	.10
16	Jose Silva	.10
17	Willie Greene	.10
18	Billy Ashley	.10
19	James Baldwin	.15
20	Jeff Granger	.10
21	Michael Tucker	.35
22	Johnny Damon	.35
23	Roger Cedeno	.10
24	Makoto Suzuki	.10
25	Curtis Goodwin	.25
26	Frankie Rodriguez	.15
27	Roberto Mejia	.10
28	LaTroy Hawkins	.10
29	Alex Ochoa	.25
30	Jose Oliva	.10
31	Ruben Rivera	.50
32	Ray Durham	.25
33	Eduardo Perez	.10
34	Jose Malave	.10
35	Jeromy Burnitz	.25
36	Brad Woodall	.10
37	Joe Vitiello	.15
38	Daron Kirkreit	.10
39	Jimmy Haynes	.10
40	Andrew Lorraine	.10
41	Arquimedez Pozo	.10
42	Armando Benitez	.10
43	Alan Benes	.50
44	Julian Tavarez	.10
45	Curtis Pride	.15
46	Homer Bush	.15
47	Pokey Reese	.10
48	Billy Wagner	.25
49	Richard Hidalgo	.30
50	Allen Battle	.10
51	Kevin Millar	.10
52	Paul Wilson (#1 Draft Pick)	.35
53	Ben Grieve (#1 Draft Pick)	4.00
54	Dustin Hermanson (#1 Draft Pick)	.50
55	Antone Williamson (#1 Draft Pick)	.10
56	Josh Booty (#1 Draft Pick)	.10
57	Doug Million (#1 Draft Pick)	.10
58	Jaret Wright (#1 Draft Pick)	2.50
59	Todd Walker (#1 Draft Pick)	1.00
60	Nomar Garciaparra (#1 Draft Pick)	5.00
61	C.J. Nitkowski (#1 Draft Pick)	.10
62	Charles Johnson (Franchise Gem)	.35
63	Marc Newfield (Franchise Gem)	.10
64	Ray Durham (Franchise Gem)	.25
65	Carlos Delgado (Franchise Gem)	.50
66	Alex Gonzalez (Franchise Gem)	.15
67	Derek Jeter (Franchise Gem)	2.00
68	Jose Oliva (Franchise Gem)	.10
69	Billy Ashley (Franchise Gem)	.10
70	Brian Hunter (Franchise Gem)	.35
71	Ruben Rivera (Franchise Gem)	.50
72	Alan Benes (Franchise Gem)	.50
73	Willie Greene (Franchise Gem)	.10
74	Russ Davis (Franchise Gem)	.35
75	Jose Malave (Franchise Gem)	.10
76	LaTroy Hawkins (Franchise Gem)	.10
77	Frankie Rodriguez (Franchise Gem)	.10
78	Scott Ruffcorn (Franchise Gem)	.10
79	Ben Grieve (Franchise Gem)	4.00
80	Max Patkin	.10
81	Max Patkin	.10
82	Max Patkin	.10
83	Checklist Derek Jeter	.35

1995 Action Packed 24KT Gold

Eighteen better-than-average prospects were selected for this random insert series. 24KT Gold Franchise Gem cards are die-cut in a tombstone shape with a large baseball at top on front. The front is highlighted by gold-foil graphics. Backs have a few stats and are numbered with a "G" suffix.

		MT
Complete Set (18):		175.00
Common Player:		6.00
1G	Charles Johnson	24.00
2G	Marc Newfield	6.00
3G	Ray Durham	12.00
4G	Carlos Delgado	24.00
5G	Alex Gonzalez	9.00
6G	Derek Jeter	60.00
7G	Jose Oliva	6.00
8G	Billy Ashley	6.00
9G	Brian L. Hunter	12.00
10G	Ruben Rivera	6.00
11G	Alan Benes	15.00
12G	Willie Greene	6.00
13G	Russ Davis	6.00
14G	Jose Malave	6.00
15G	LaTroy Hawkins	6.00
16G	Frank Rodriguez	6.00
17G	Scott Ruffcorn	6.00
18G	Ben Grieve	24.00

1995 Best Top 100

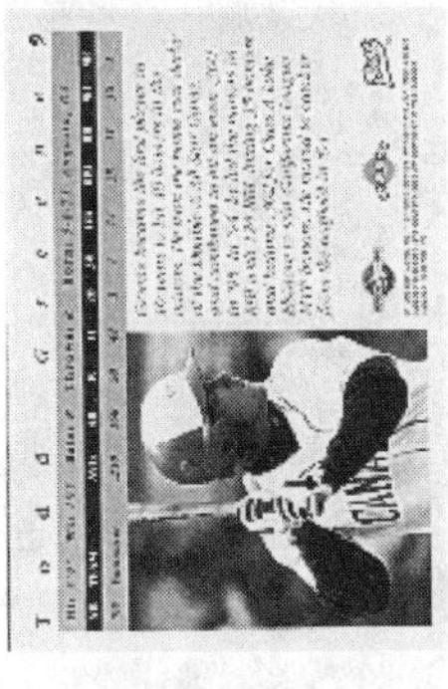

In mid-1995 some of the founding principals of Best re-acquired the brand name from Classic and began production of a new generation of minor league cards. Following the 1995 season, the company released a set of 100 top minor league players. White bordered card fronts feature team logos at upper-right. Backs have a portrait photo, 1995 stats and a scouting report on the player. The issue was sold in 12-card hobby foil packs and 16-card retail packs. Hobby packs included a special autographed edition card of four top prospects randomly inserted at an average rate of one per 18 packs. The retail packs had inserts of 23 First Round Draft Picks and 10 "Best of the Best" cards.

		MT
Complete Set (101):		20.00
Common Player:		.05
1	Rocky Coppinger	.25
2	Rafael Orellano	.05
3	Nomar Garciaparra	6.00
4	Ryan McGuire	.50
5	Pork Chop Pough	.15
6	Trot Nixon	.25
7	Donnie Sadler	.25
8	Chris Allison	.05
9	Todd Greene	.45
10	George Arias	.25
11	Matt Beaumont	.20
12	Jeff Abbott	.05
13	Tom Fordham	.05
14	Damian Jackson	.05
15	Richie Sexson	1.00
16	Bartolo Colon	.65
17	David Roberts	.05
18	Daryle Ward	.45
19	Brandon Reed	.05
20	Juan Encarnacion	.35
21	Eddy Gaillard	.05
22	Derek Hacopian	.05
23	Glendon Rusch	.25
24	Lino Diaz	.05
25	Tim Byrdak	.10
26	Antone Williamson	.25
27	Jonas Hamlin	.05
28	Todd Walker	.75
29	Dan Serafini	.10
30	Kimera Bartee	.10
31	Shane Bowers	.05
32	Tyrone Horne	.15
33	Nick Del Vecchio	.05
34	Mike Figga	.05

35	Matt Drews	.15
36	Ray Ricken	.05
37	Ben Grieve	4.00
38	Steve Cox	.35
39	Scott Spiezio	.20
40	Desi Relaford	.15
41	Matt Wagner	.10
42	James Bonnici	.05
43	Osvaldo Fernandez	.25
44	Marino Santana	.05
45	Julio Santana	.05
46	Jeff Davis	.05
47	Trey Beamon	.30
48	Jose Pett	.05
49	Chris Carpenter	.30
50	Andruw Jones	5.00
51	Damon Hollins	.25
52	Jermaine Dye	.50
53	Aldo Pecorilli	.05
54	Carey Paige	.05
55	Damian Moss	.30
56	Ron Wright	1.00
57	Brooks Kieschnick	.20
58	Pedro Valdes	.05
59	Scott Samuels	.05
60	Bobby Morris	.05
61	Amaury Telemaco	.10
62	Steve Gibralter	.10
63	Pokey Reese	.10
64	Pat Watkins	.05
65	Aaron Boone	.25
66	Jamey Wright	.25
67	Derrick Gibson	1.50
68	Brent Crowther	.05
69	Ralph Milliard	.05
70	Edgar Renteria	.45
71	Billy McMillon	.05
72	Clemente Nunez	.05
73	Bob Abreu	.40
74	Eric Ludwick	.05
75	Tony Mounce	.05
76	Chris Latham	.05
77	Wilton Guerrero	.25
78	Adam Riggs	.20
79	Paul Konerko	3.00
80	Vladimir Guerrero	5.00
81	Brad Fullmer	.50
82	Hiram Bocachica	.10
83	Paul Wilson	.65
84	Jay Payton	1.00
85	Rey Ordonez	.45
86	Wendell Magee	.20
87	Wayne Gomes	.05
88	Carlton Loewer	.10
89	Scott Rolen	5.00
90	Rich Hunter	.05
91	Jason Kendall	.50
92	Micah Franklin	.10
93	Elmer Dessens	.05
94	Matt Ruebel	.05
95	Mike Gulan	.05
96	Jay Witasick	.05
97	Bret Wagner	.05
98	Greg LaRocca	.05
99	Jason Thompson	.10
100	Derrek Lee	.75
----	Checklist	.05

Player names in *Italic* type indicate a rookie card.

1995 Best Top 100 Autographed

A special autographed edition of four of the top prospects from Best's Top 100 set was produced as a random insert. The autographed cards were inserted only in the 12-card hobby version foil packs, at an average rate of one per 18 packs (two per box). The autograph cards feature a vignetted photo of the player on front with his name printed in silver at lower-right and an authentic autograph on front. Backs have a ghost image of the front photo and a congratulatory message, along with appropriate logos and copyright notices.

		MT
Complete Set (4):		60.00
Common Player:		10.00
(1)	Todd Greene	12.00
(2)	Andruw Jones	40.00
(3)	Jay Payton	15.00
(4)	Paul Wilson	12.00

1995 Best Top 100 Best of the Best

Numbered contiguously from the regular set, but found only as one-per-pack inserts in 16-card retail foil packs, this chase set feature 10 of the brightest minor league stars of 1995. Fronts are in horizontal format with a color photo superimposed on a green background photo. Backs have 1995 and career stats along with career highlights.

		MT
Complete Set (10):		12.00
Common Card:		.25
101	Jason Kendall	.50
102	Derrek Lee	.75
103	Todd Walker	2.00
104	Edgar Renteria	.75
105	Scott Rolen	5.00
106	Andruw Jones	5.00
107	Jay Payton	.75
108	Derrick Gibson	.75
109	Paul Wilson	.50
110	Brandon Reed	.25

1995 Best Top 100 First Round Draft Picks

Another one-per-pack insert exclusive to 16-card retail foil packs of Best Top 100 is this set of first round picks from the June, 1995, amateur draft. Cards are similar in format to the regular-issue Top 100 but have the front photo background posterized. Backs have a short biography.

		MT
Complete Set (23):		12.00
Common Player:		.10
111	Ben Davis	1.00
112	Chad Hermansen	3.00
113	Corey Jenkins	.10
114	Geoff Jenkins	1.00
115	Ryan Jaroncyk	.10
116	Andy Yount	.10
117	Reggie Taylor	.25
118	Joe Fontenot	.10
119	Mike Drumright	.10
120	David Yokum	.10
121	Jonathan Johnson	.10
122	Jaime Jones	.75
123	Tony McKnight	.20
124	Michael Barrett	1.50
125	Roy Halladay	.50
126	Todd Helton	5.00
127	Juan LeBron	.25
128	Darin Erstad	5.00
129	Jose Cruz, Jr.	4.00
130	Kerry Wood	6.00
131	Shea Morenz	.10
132	Mark Redman	.10
133	Matt Morris	1.00

1995 Best Top 100 Franchise

A dozen projected franchise players of the future are included in this insert set. Cards F1-F6 are retail pack inserts, cards F7-F12 are hobby pack inserts. All cards have gold-foil highlights on front. Franchise inserts are found on average of one per three foil boxes.

		MT
Complete Set (12):		125.00
Common Player:		3.00
F1	Darin Erstad	30.00
F2	Nomar Garciaparra	35.00
F3	Rocky Coppinger	3.00
F4	Matt Drews	3.00
F5	Ben Grieve	20.00
F6	Todd Walker	15.00
F7	Edgar Renteria	12.00
F8	Derrick Gibson	12.00
F9	Andruw Jones	25.00
F10	Derrek Lee	8.00
F11	Jason Kendall	12.00
F12	Paul Wilson	6.00

1995 Classic Assets Gold (Baseball)

This super-premium five-sport set offers 50 base cards and a wide range of inserts with extremely limited production on some. The baseball players from the issue are listed here. Only 500 of each gold diecut were produced and 349 of each gold signature.

		MT
Base Set/Inserts:		
11	Nolan Ryan	1.00
11	Nolan Ryan (silver signature)	10.00
11	Nolan Ryan (gold signature)	35.00
SDC18	Nolan Ryan (silver diecut)	10.00
GDC18	Nolan Ryan (gold diecut)	45.00
12	Barry Bonds	.40
12	Barry Bonds (silver signature)	4.00
12	Barry Bonds (gold signature)	9.00
SDC9	Barry Bonds (silver diecut)	4.00
GDC9	Barry Bonds (gold diecut)	9.00
13	Ben Grieve	1.00
13	Ben Grieve (silver signature)	5.00
13	Ben Grieve (gold signature)	12.50
SDC1	Ben Grieve (silver diecut)	5.00
GDC1	Ben Grieve (gold diecut)	15.00
14	Dustin Hermanson	.25
14	Dustin Hermanson (silver signature)	2.50
14	Dustin Hermanson (gold signature)	6.00

Player names in *Italic* type indicate a rookie card.

1995 Classic Assets Gold (Baseball) Foncards

This super-premium five-sport set offers 50 base cards and a wide range of inserts with extremely limited production on some. The baseball player Foncards from Sprint are listed here.

		MT
Complete (Baseball) Set (8):		325.00
(1)	Barry Bonds ($2 Foncard)	1.00
(2)	Ben Grieve ($2 Foncard)	2.00
(3)	Dustin Hermanson ($2 Foncard)	1.00
(4)	Nolan Ryan ($2 Foncard)	2.00
(5)	Barry Bonds ($5 Foncard)	2.00
(6)	Nolan Ryan ($5 Foncard)	5.00
(7)	Barry Bonds, Nolan Ryan ($25 Foncard)	15.00
(8)	Nolan Ryan ($1,000 Foncard)	300.00

1995 Classic 5 Sport (Baseball)

Thirty-one baseball players are included in the 200 cards of this issue which covers the four major team sports plus auto racing, with the emphasis on up-and-coming youngsters. Fronts have color poses or action photos at left. Minor or major league uniform logos have been removed because the cards are licensed only by the individual players. At right is a stack of baseballs with the player's name in gold vertically and the city in which he plays and his position in white. Backs have another color photo at right with personal data and a career summary in a gold marbled panel at left. Professional stats are in a black box at bottom. Besides the standard format, each card can also be found in a die-cut and a printer's proof version as random pack inserts, as well as an autographed version.

		MT
Complete (Baseball) Set (31):		6.50
Common Player:		.10
93	Ben Grieve	.75
94	Roger Cedeno	.20
95	Michael Barrett	.50
96	Ben Davis	.40
97	Paul Wilson	.35
98	Calvin Reese	.10
99	Jermaine Dye	.15
100	Alvie Shepherd	.10
101	Ryan Jaroncyk	.10
102	Mark Farris	.10
103	Karim Garcia	.50
104	Rey Ordonez	.75
105	Jay Payton	.40
106	Dustin Hermanson	.15
107	Tommy Davis	.10
108	C.J. Nitkowski	.10
109	Todd Greene	.15
110	Billy Wagner	.25
111	Mark Redman	.10
112	Brooks Kieschnick	.15
113	Paul Konerko	.30
114	Brad Fullmer	.35
115	Vladimir Guerrero	.75
116	Bartolo Colon	.45
117	Doug Million	.10
118	Steve Gibraltar	.15
119	Tony McKnight	.20
120	Derrek Lee	.15
121	Nomar Garciaparra	1.00
122	Chad Hermansen	.50
193	Barry Bonds (Picture Perfect)	.40

1995 Classic 5 Sport (Baseball) Autographed

Autographed versions of each of the base cards in the 5 Sport set were available as random pack inserts.

		MT
Complete (Baseball) Set (31):		125.00
Common Player:		2.00
93	Ben Grieve	20.00
94	Roger Cedeno	6.00
95	Michael Barrett	8.00
96	Ben Davis	8.00
97	Paul Wilson	7.00
98	Calvin Reese	3.00
99	Jermaine Dye	6.00
100	Alvie Shepherd	2.00
101	Ryan Jaroncyk	2.00
102	Mark Farris	2.00
103	Karim Garcia	12.50
104	Rey Ordonez	15.00
105	Jay Payton	8.00
106	Dustin Hermanson	6.00
107	Tommy Davis	2.00
108	C.J. Nitkowski	2.00
109	Todd Greene	4.50
110	Billy Wagner	4.50
111	Mark Redman	2.00
112	Brooks Kieschnick	5.00
113	Paul Konerko	7.50
114	Brad Fullmer	4.50
115	Vladimir Guerrero	15.00
116	Bartolo Colon	12.50
117	Doug Million	15.00
118	Steve Gibraltar	3.00
119	Tony McKnight	3.00
120	Derrek Lee	3.00
121	Nomar Garciaparra	30.00
122	Chad Hermansen	15.00
193	Barry Bonds (Picture Perfect)	25.00

1995 Classic 5 Sport (Baseball) Die-cuts

Each of the 200 players in the 5 Sport set can also be found in a die-cut parallel version which was inserted at the rate of one per pack. Other than the die-cutting around the baseball at the right edge, and the player's name being printed in silver, rather than gold ink, the die-cuts are identical to the standard format.

	MT
Complete (Baseball) Set (31):	40.00
Common Player:	.25
(Stars valued 6-8X base cards)	

1995 Classic 5 Sport (Baseball) Printers Proofs

A random pack insert, this parallel set of all 200 cards in the 5 Sport set is printed in an edition of just 795 cards each. Identical in format to the standard issue, the cards feature a purple-foil notation on front.

	MT
Complete (Baseball) Set (31):	90.00
Common Player:	1.00
(Stars valued 8-10X base cards)	

1995 Classic 5 Sport (Baseball) Foncards

A single baseball player Foncard is included among the inserts in 1995 Classic 5 Sport.

		MT
(1)	C.J. Nitkowski ($3 Foncard)	4.00
(2)	Nomar Garciaparra ($4 Foncard)	8.00

1995 Classic 5 Sport (Baseball) Inserts

A number of the insert sets found with 5 Sports include baseball players.

		MT
	Complete (Baseball) Set (4):	40.00
SP5	Paul Wilson (5 Sport Preview, hockey pack insert)	5.00
RS7	Paul Wilson (Record Setters)	4.00
FT13	Ben Grieve (Fast Track)	4.00
1	Barry Bonds (Hot Box Autographs) (edition of 630)	35.00

1995 Classic 5 Sport (Baseball) Strive For Five

These interactive game cards were inserted approximately one per 10 packs by number and/or suit (sport) and redeemed for prizes ranging from autographed cards to $5,000 cash. The standard size cards have silver metallic foil borders and numbers on front. Player action photos are separated from the background by a large 5 Sport logo. Printed in fine white type on the green back are game rules and prize details. Only the baseball players among the issue's 65 cards are listed here.

		MT
	Common Player:	1.00
1	Paul Wilson	1.00
2	Billy Wagner	3.00
3	Ben Grieve	12.00
4	Bartolo Colon	2.50
5	Tommy Davis	1.00
6	C.J. Nitkowski	1.00
7	Mark Redman	1.00
8	Todd Greene	1.50
9	Jay Payton	1.00
10	Nomar Garciaparra	12.00
J	Ben Davis	1.00
Q	Doug Million	1.00
K	Dustin Hermanson	3.00

1995 Classic Images '95 (Baseball)

Eighteen of the 120 regular cards in this four-sport prospects collection feature baseball players. Cards feature a color action photo on an etched metallic foil background. Backs have another player photo, personal data, stats and a career summary.

		MT
	Complete (Baseball) Set (18):	3.00
	Common Player:	.10
76	Paul Wilson	.40
77	Ben Grieve	1.50
78	Doug Million	.10
79	Bret Wagner	.10
80	Dustin Hermanson	.15
81	Doug Webb	.10
82	Brian Stephenson	.10
83	Jacob Cruz	.10
84	Cade Gaspar	.10
85	Nomar Garciaparra	2.00
86	Mike Thurman	.10
87	Brian Buchanan	.10
88	Mark Johnson	.25
89	Jacob Shumate	.15
90	Kevin Witt	.10
91	Victor Rodriguez	.15
92	Trey Moore	.10
93	Barry Bonds	.50

1995 Classic Images '95 Classic Performances

This is the only one of the several Images '95 insert sets to include baseball players. Horizontal format cards feature color player photos on a background of etched gold metallic foil. Backs have another color photo and a description of the career highlight, along with a serial number from within an edition of 4,495. Stated odds of picking a Classic Performances card were one per 12 packs.

	MT
Complete (Baseball) Set (3):	15.00
CP16 Paul Wilson	2.00
CP17 Barry Bonds	4.00
CP18 Nolan Ryan	12.00

1995 Signature Rookies

Fifty top prospects are featured in the 1995 Signature Rookies base set, along with many types of insert cards at varying levels of scarcity.

		MT
	Complete Set (50):	3.00
	Common Player:	.05
1	Mark Acre	.10
2	Edgar Alfonzo	.05
3	Ivan Arteaga	.05
4	Rich Aude	.05
5	Joe Ausanio	.05
6	Marc Barcelo	.05
7	Allen Battle	.05
8	Rigo Beltran	.05
9	Darren Bragg	.15
10	Rico Brogna	.25
11	Mike Busch	.05
12	Juan F. Castillo	.05
13	Joe Ciccarella	.05
14	Darrel Deak	.05
15	Steve Dunn	.10
16	Vaughn Eshelman	.05
17	Bart Evans	.05
18	Rikkert Faneyte	.05
19	Kenny Felder	.05
20	Micah Franklin	.10
21	Brad Fullmer	.50
22	Willie Greene	.10
23	Greg Hansell	.05
24	Phil Hiatt	.10
25	Todd Hollandsworth	.25
26	Damon Hollins	.25
27	Chris Hook	.05
28	Kerry Lacy	.05
29	Todd LaRocca	.05
30	Sean Lawrence	.05
31	Aaron Ledesma	.05
32	Esteban Loaiza	.10
33	Albie Lopez	.05
34	Luis Lopez	.10
35	Marc Marini	.05
36	Nate Minchey	.05
37	Doug Mlicki	.05
38	Glenn Murray	.05
39	Troy O'Leary	.10
40	Eric Owens	.05
41	Orlando Palmeiro	.05
42	Todd Pridy	.05
43	Joe Randa	.10
44	Jason Schmidt	.10
45	Basil Shabazz	.05
46	Paul Spoljaric	.10
47	J.J. Thobe	.05
48	Sean Whiteside	.05
49	Gary Wilson	.05
50	Shannon Withem	.10

1995 Signature Rookies - Autographed

Each of the cards in the Signature Rookies set was also issued in an authentically-autographed edition of 5,750 as random pack inserts. Some cards were represented in packs by coupons redeemable for the cards. Cards of Kerry Lacy and Basil Shabazz were never autographed.

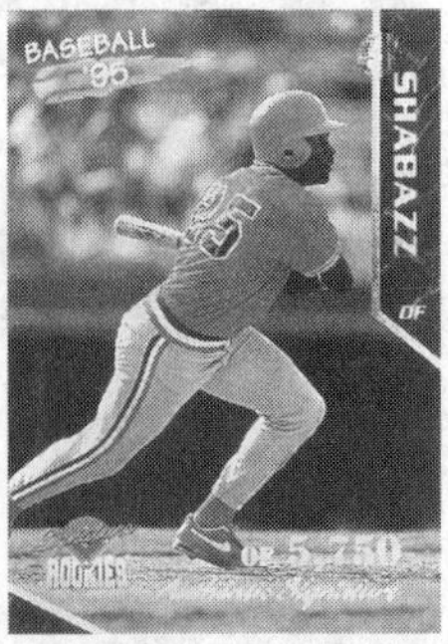

		MT
	Complete Set (48/50):	60.00
	Common Player:	1.00
1	Mark Acre	2.00
2	Edgar Alfonzo	1.00
3	Ivan Arteaga	1.00
4	Rich Aude	1.00
5	Joe Ausanio	1.00
6	Marc Barcelo	1.00
7	Allen Battle	2.00
8	Rigo Beltran	1.00
9	Darren Bragg	3.00
10	Rico Brogna	5.00
11	Mike Busch	1.00
12	Juan F. Castillo	1.00
13	Joe Ciccarella	1.00
14	Darrel Deak	1.00
15	Steve Dunn	2.00
16	Vaughn Eshelman	2.00
17	Bart Evans	1.00
18	Rikkert Faneyte	1.00
19	Kenny Felder	1.00
20	Micah Franklin	2.00
21	Brad Fullmer	12.00
22	Willie Greene	2.00
23	Greg Hansell	1.00
24	Phil Hiatt	2.00
25	Todd Hollandsworth	6.00
26	Damon Hollins	6.00
27	Chris Hook	1.00
28	Kerry Lacy (not signed)	.50
29	Todd LaRocca	1.00
30	Sean Lawrence	1.00
31	Aaron Ledesma	1.00
32	Esteban Loaiza	2.00
33	Albie Lopez	1.00
34	Luis Lopez	2.50
35	Marc Marini	1.00
36	Nate Minchey	1.00
37	Doug Mlicki	1.00
38	Glenn Murray	1.00
39	Troy O'Leary	2.00
40	Eric Owens	1.00
41	Orlando Palmeiro	1.00
42	Todd Pridy	1.00
43	Joe Randa	2.00
44	Jason Schmidt	2.00
45	Basil Shabazz (not signed)	.50
46	Paul Spoljaric	2.00
47	J.J. Thobe	1.00
48	Sean Whiteside	1.00
49	Gary Wilson	1.00
50	Shannon Withem	2.00

1995 Signature Rookies Draft Day Stars

Five hot picks from the 1994 amateur draft are featured in this insert set on both unsigned and authentically autographed cards. Fronts have a pair of photos on a background of bright colors. The player name, Draft Day Star logo and edition number (10,000 each plain, 2,000 autographed) are in gold foil. Backs repeat one of the front photos and have a few career notes and stats along with personal data.

		MT
	Complete Set (5):	2.00
	Complete Set, Autographed (5):	65.00
	Common Player:	.25
	Common Autograph:	8.00
DD1	Matt Beaumont	.25
DD1a	Matt Beaumont (autographed)	8.00
DD2	Josh Booty	.50
DD2a	Josh Booty (autographed)	10.00
DD3	Russ Johnson	.25
DD3a	Russ Johnson (autographed)	12.00
DD4	Todd Walker	.75
DD4a	Todd Walker (autographed)	15.00
DD5	Jaret Wright	1.00
DD5a	Jaret Wright (autographed)	25.00

1995 Signature Rookies Fame & Fortune Erstad!

This insert issue to the Fame & Fortune football/basketball set features University of Nebraska football/baseball star and 1995 #1 overall draft pick Darin Erstad. The cards have borderless color game-action (either baseball or football) photos of the player with his name repeated in varying sizes of gray letters in the background. Down one side in gold foil is "ERSTAD!", shadowed in red. The Fame & Fortune logo is in gold in a lower corner. Backs have a white background, another color photo, his college baseball stats and a few sentences about his career to date.

		MT
	Complete Set (5):	12.50
	Common Player:	2.50
E1	Darin Erstad (batting)	2.50
E2	Darin Erstad (batting)	2.50
E3	Darin Erstad (punting)	2.50
E4	Darin Erstad (batting)	2.50
E5	Darin Erstad (fielding)	2.50

1995 Signature Rookies Future Dynasty

A player action photo is set in a homeplate design on a garish background of tan, burgundy, blue and green waves on this insert series. The player name, edition limit (5,000 of each regular card, 1,000 of each autographed) and other graphic highlights are in gold foil. Backs have two more player photos, stats, personal data and career summary.

	MT
Complete Set (5):	3.00
Complete Set, Autographed (5):	80.00
Common Player:	.25
Common Autograph:	6.00
FD1 Billy Ashley	.25
FD1aBilly Ashley (autographed)	6.00
FD2 Ben Grieve	1.00
FD2aBen Grieve (autographed)	25.00
FD3 Derek Jeter	1.50
FD3aDerek Jeter (autographed)	40.00
FD4 Ruben Rivera	.25
FD4aRuben Rivera (autographed)	6.00
FD5 Antone Williamson	.50
FD5aAntone Williamson (autographed)	8.00
FD5pAntone Williamson (promo card)	1.50

1995 Signature Rookies Major Rookies

Five of 1995's top rookies are featured in this insert set. Cards come in both unsigned (edition of 10,000 each) and genuinely autographed (edition of 750 each). Fronts have player action photos with a huge green and orange "MAJOR ROOKIES" logo behind. The player name and edition number are in gold foil. Backs also feature the green and orange color scheme and have another color photo, stats and personal data, and a paragraph about the player.

	MT
Complete Set (5):	6.00
Complete Set, Autographed (5):	120.00
Common Player:	.50
Common Autograph:	8.00
MR1 Marty Cordova	.75
MR1aMarty Cordova (autographed)	12.00
MR2 Benji Gil	.50
MR2aBenji Gil (autographed)	12.00
MR3 Charles Johnson	1.00
MR3aCharles Johnson (autographed)	20.00
MR4 Manny Ramirez	2.00
MR4aManny Ramirez (autographed)	40.00
MR5 Alex Rodriguez	3.00
MR5aAlex Rodriguez (autographed)	50.00

1995 Signature Rookies Organizational Player/ Year

These inserts are found in both autographed (edition of 1,000) and unsigned (7,500) form. The design emphasizes the foundation nature of the players chosen, with a red brick wall at one side and an action photo at the other. The card title and player name are in gold foil. Backs repeat the brick wall background, have another color photo and the usual personal data, stats and career summary.

	MT
Complete Set (5):	1.50
Complete Set, Autographed (5):	27.50
Common Player:	.25
Common Autograph:	5.00
OP1 Juan Acevedo	.25
OP1aJuan Acevedo (autographed)	5.00
OP2 Johnny Damon	.50
OP2aJohnny Damon (autographed)	10.00
OP3 Ray Durham	.35
OP3aRay Durham (autographed)	6.00
OP4 LaTroy Hawkins	.25
OP4aLaTroy Hawkins (autographed)	5.00
OP5 Brad Woodall	.50
OP5aBrad Woodall (autographed)	5.00

1995 Signature Rookies Preview

Players who looked to be ready for the major leagues are the focus of this set. Large color action photos on front are surmounted by a red strip bearing the player's name in gold foil. Gold highlights at bottom have the SR Preview logo at lower-left and "1 of 25,000" at center. Backs have two more color photos of the player, with one of them ghosted in muted shades. The player's complete minor league record is included. Each of the cards in the set can also be found in an autographed version of 6,000. Minor and major league team logos have been removed from the player photos and, in some cases, replaced with unofficial logos to avoid licensing problems.

		MT
Complete Set (38):		2.00
Common Player:		.10
1	Tavo Alvarez	.10
2	Rich Batchelor	.10
3	Doug Bochtler	.10
4	Jerry Brooks	.10
5	Scott Bryant	.10
6	Mike Busby	.10
7	Fred Costello	.10
8	Glenn Dishman	.10
9	James Foster	.10
10	Webster Garrison	.10
11	Tony Graffanino	.10
12	Billy Hall	.10
13	Mike Hubbard	.10
14	Jason Hutchins	.10
15	Rick Kelley	.10
16	Jerry Koller	.10
17	Ryan Luzinski	.10
18	Anthony Manahan	.10
19	Mike Matthews	.10
20	Greg McCarty	.10
21	Jeff McCurry	.10
22	Gino Minutelli	.10
23	Izzy Molina	.25
24	Scott Moten	.10
25	Peter Munro	.10
26	Willis Otanez	.25
27	Rodney Pedraza	.10
28	Brandon Pico	.10
29	Brian Raabe	.10
30	Eddie Rios	.10
31	Toby Rumfield	.10
32	Andy Sheets	.10
33	Larry Sutton	.15
34	Brian Thomas	.10
35	Hector Trinidad	.20
36	Jim Waring	.10
37	Mike Welch	.10
38	Steve Wojciechowski	.10

1995 Signature Rookies Preview - Autographed

Each of the cards in the 1995 Signature Rookies Preview set can be found in an autographed edition. The cards are hand-signed and numbered within an edition of 6,000. The autographed cards have a gold-foil "1 of 6,000" notation at bottom-center on front.

		MT
Complete Set (38):		75.00
Common Player:		2.00
1	Tavo Alvarez	2.00
2	Rich Batchelor	2.00
3	Doug Bochtler	2.00
4	Jerry Brooks	2.00
5	Scott Bryant	2.00
6	Mike Busby	2.00
7	Fred Costello	2.00
8	Glenn Dishman	2.00
9	James Foster	2.00
10	Webster Garrison	2.00
11	Tony Graffanino	4.00
12	Billy Hall	2.00
13	Mike Hubbard	2.00
14	Jason Hutchins	2.00
15	Rick Kelley	2.00
16	Jerry Koller	2.00
17	Ryan Luzinski	4.00
18	Anthony Manahan	2.00
19	Mike Matthews	2.00
20	Greg McCarty	2.00
21	Jeff McCurry	2.00
22	Gino Minutelli	2.00
23	Izzy Molina	4.00
24	Scott Moten	2.00
25	Peter Munro	2.00
26	Willis Otanez	8.00
27	Rodney Pedraza	2.00
28	Brandon Pico	2.00
29	Brian Raabe	2.00
30	Eddie Rios	2.00
31	Toby Rumfield	2.00
32	Andy Sheets	2.00
33	Larry Sutton	2.00
34	Brian Thomas	2.00
35	Hector Trinidad	6.00
36	Jim Waring	2.00
37	Mike Welch	2.00
38	Steve Wojciechowski	2.00

Checklists with card numbers in parentheses ( ) indicates the numbers do not appear on the card.

1995 Signature Rookies Star Squad

Ten players who were already making their marks in the Major Leagues were featured in this insert set. The cards have player action photos on front with large red areas above and below containing a star and "STAR SQUAD" designation and the player's name and manufacturer's logo. A vertical gold-foil stamping notes, "1 of 10,000". Backs have another player photo along with a few stats, biographical bits and career summary. Uniform logos have been airbrushed away or replaced with unofficial logos since the cards are licensed only by the individual players and not Major League Baseball. An autographed edition of 525 cards of each player was also randomly inserted.

		MT
Complete Set (10):		22.00
Complete Autographed Set (10):		225.00
Common Player:		1.00
Common Autograph:		15.00
1	Ruben Rivera	2.00
1a	Ruben Rivera (autographed)	30.00
2	Charles Johnson	3.00
2a	Charles Johnson (autographed)	30.00
3	Derek Jeter	6.00
3a	Derek Jeter (autographed)	60.00
4	Todd Hollandsworth	2.00
4a	Todd Hollandsworth (autographed)	20.00
5	Billy Ashley	2.00
5a	Billy Ashley (autographed)	20.00
6	Benji Gil	2.00
6a	Benji Gil (autographed)	20.00
7	Vaughn Eshelman	1.00
7a	Vaughn Eshelman (autographed)	15.00
8	Ray Durham	2.00
8a	Ray Durham (autographed)	30.00
9	Marty Cordova	2.50
9a	Marty Cordova (autographed)	20.00
10	Manny Ramirez	4.00
10a	Manny Ramirez (autographed)	40.00

1995 Signature Rookies Tetrad (Baseball)

Thirty-one baseball players are featured among the young stars of the four major team sports in this issue. Fronts have a color action photo with the background muted in black-and-white. The player's name is in gold foil in a green marbled panel at bottom. Tetrad's "You Make the Call" logo is also in gold foil. Backs have two more photos, personal data and stats and repeated the green marbled motif.

		MT
Complete (Baseball) Set (31):		8.00
Common Player:		.10
31	Andy Yount	.10
32	Jose Cruz, Jr.	1.00
33	Dustin Hermanson	.15
34	David Yocum	.10
35	Dmitri Young	.15
36	Kerry Wood	1.50
37	Jonathan Johnson	.10
38	Shea Morenz	.10
39	Matt Morris	.10
40	Reggie Taylor	.25
41	Antone Williamson	.40
42	Derek Wallace	.15
43	Ben Grieve	1.00
44	Benji Gil	.20
45	Todd Walker	.60
46	Jason Thompson	.25
47	Scott Stahoviak	.15
48	Chris Roberts	.10
49	Dante Powell	.15
50	Torii Hunter	.10
56	Bryan Rekar	.10
57	Jaime Jones	.10
58	Todd Helton	1.00
59	Joe Fontenot	.10
60	Tony Clark	1.00
71	Tony McKnight	.20
72	Roy Halladay	.10
73	Mike Drumright	.10
74	Ben Davis	.35
75	Michael Barrett	.75
76	Sid Roberson	.10

1995 Signature Rookies Tetrad Autobilia (Baseball)

Thirty baseball players are included among the young stars of the four major team sports in this 100-card issue. Fronts have a background of greens and purples with three sizes of a player action photo muted in the background. In the foreground is a large color action photo. Graphic highlights are in gold foil, including a bar at bottom with the player name. Backs have a couple more color player photos on a yellow and magenta background. Stats, draft status and a few words about the player are included. Each of the cards could also be found in an autographed version as a random pack insert.

	MT
Complete (Baseball) Set (30):	24.00
Common Player:	.25

18	Juan Acevedo	.25
19	Trey Beamon	.25
20	Tim Belk	.25
21	Mike Bovee	.25
22	Brad Clontz	.25
23	Marty Cordova	.75
24	Johnny Damon	1.50
25	Jeff Darwin	.25
26	Nick Delvecchio	.25
27	Ray Durham	.50
28	Jermaine Dye	.75
29	Jimmy Haynes	.25
30	Mark Hubbard	.25
31	Russ Johnson	.25
32	Andy Larkin	.25
33	Kris Ralston	.25
34	Luis Raven	.25
35	Desi Relaford	.25
36	Jeff Suppan	.25
37	Brad Woodall	.25
72	Ruben Rivera	1.50
85	Jose Cruz, Jr.	3.00
86	Darin Erstad	5.00
87	Todd Helton	3.00
88	Chad Hermansen	1.00
89	Jonathan Johnson	.25
90	Manny Ramirez	3.00
91	Kerry Wood	4.00
92	Ben Davis	1.00
93	Jaime Jones	.25

1995 Signature Rookies Tetrad Auto-phonex Test Issue

One baseball player was included in this promo set for an SR Tetrad product. Standard-size cards are highlighted on front with gold foil. Backs have color portrait and action photos, player data and stats.

		MT
T4	Ruben Rivera	.50

1995 Signature Rookies Tetrad B-1 Bomber

The #1 overall pick in the 1995 amateur draft is honored on this five-card insert set recalling the college career of Darin Erstad. Fronts have various action photos of Erstad in his college uniform. Half of the background has been replaced with a vertical green area featuring a large purple "B-1 BOMBER" logo and a gold-foil notation that the card is "1 of 30,000". Erstad's name also appears in gold foil, along with Tetrad's "You Make the Call" logo. Backs have more photos of Erstad, some in his uniform as Big Red's punter/field goal specialist, along with biographical data, college stats and highlights. Cards are numbered B1-B5.

		MT
Complete Set (5):		5.00
Common Player:		.75
B1	Darin Erstad (batting)	.75
B2	Darin Erstad (fielding)	.75
B3	Darin Erstad (batting)	.75
B4	Darin Erstad (running)	.75
B5	Darin Erstad (batting)	.75

1995 Signature Rookies Tetrad SR Force (Baseball)

Ten of the top young players in each of the four major team sports were included in an SR Force insert set with Signature Rookies Tetrad. A color action photo on the white front background has had team logos removed to avoid licensing problems. Three inset photos repeat details from the large picture. "SR FORCE" in printed in purples and greens at top. Gold-foil highlights include the player name and "1 of 6,000" notation. Backs have a large ghosted photo in the background and three detail photos at left, along with personal data, stats and a few words about the player.

		MT
Complete Set (10):		7.50
Common Player:		.25
F11	Manny Ramirez	1.50
F12	Jaret Wright	1.00
F13	Ruben Rivera	.50
F14	Derek Jeter	1.50
F15	Monty Fariss	.25
F16	Jason Isringhausen	.50
F17	Marty Cordova	.75
F18	Garret Anderson	.75
F19	Alex Rodriguez	2.00
F20	Carlton Loewer	.25

1995 Signature Rookies T-95 Old Judge Series

In an unusual size (2-1/16" x 3-1/16") and in a format more reminiscent of the 1914-15 Cracker Jack cards than the original Old Judge issue of the 1880s, Signature Rookies produced a minor league issue for 1995. Cards have player photos set against bright solid-colored backgrounds. The player's last name and city of major league affiliation are printed in the white border at bottom. Backs have a few biographical details, 1994 stats and a paragraph about the prospect. Because the cards are licensed only by the individual players, and not Major League Baseball, uniform logos have been airbrushed off and unofficial cap logos and, in some cases, team names have been added. Each of the 35 regular cards in the set can also be found in an autographed version of 5,750. In addition 250 autographed cards of Joe DiMaggio were also randomly inserted. One autographed card or trade-in coupon was included in each pack. Several series of insert cards were issued, besides the autographs.

		MT
Complete Set (36):		4.00
Complete Autographed Set (35):		85.00
Common Player:		.05
Common Autograph:		1.00
1	Bob Abreu	.50
1a	Bob Abreu (autographed)	5.00
2	Kym Ashworth	.10
2a	Kym Ashworth (autographed)	2.00
3	Jared Baker	.05
3a	Jared Baker (autographed)	1.00
4	Paul Bako	.05
4a	Paul Bako (autographed)	1.00
5	Jason Bates	.10
5a	Jason Bates (autographed)	2.00
6	Yamil Benitez	.25
6a	Yamil Benitez (autographed)	2.00
7	Marshall Boze	.20
7a	Marshall Boze (autographed)	2.00
8	Rich Butler	.10
8a	Rich Butler (autographed)	2.00
9	John Carter	.05
9a	John Carter (autographed)	1.00
10	Jeff Cirillo	.35
10a	Jeff Cirillo (autographed)	5.00
11	Randy Curtis	.05
11a	Randy Curtis (autographed)	1.00
12	Sal Fasano	.05
12a	Sal Fasano (autographed)	1.00
13	Aaron Fultz	.05
13a	Aaron Fultz (autographed)	1.00
14	Karim Garcia	.75
14a	Karim Garcia (autographed)	7.50
15	Kevin Grijak	.05
15a	Kevin Grijak (autographed)	1.00
16	Wilton Guerrero	.20
16a	Wilton Guerrero (autographed)	2.00
17	Stacy Hollins	.05
17a	Stacy Hollins (autographed)	1.00
18	Bobby Hughes	.15
18a	Bobby Hughes (autographed)	3.00
19	Jimmy Hurst	.05
19a	Jimmy Hurst (autographed)	1.00
20	Jason Isringhausen	.50
20a	Jason Isringhausen (autographed)	9.00
21	Ryan Karp	.05
21a	Ryan Karp (autographed)	1.00
22	Derek Lowe	.10
22a	Derek Lowe (autographed)	2.00
23	Matt Luke	.10
23a	Matt Luke (autographed)	2.00
24	Lyle Mouton	.10
24a	Lyle Mouton (autographed)	2.00
25	Dave Mysel	.05
25a	Dave Mysel (autographed)	1.00
26	Marc Newfield	.20
26a	Marc Newfield (autographed)	3.00
27	Jim Pittsley	.10
27a	Jim Pittsley (autographed)	2.00
28	Chris Sheff	.05
28a	Chris Sheff (autographed)	1.00
29	Tate Seefried	.10
29a	Tate Seefried (autographed)	2.00
30	Shawn Senior	.05
30a	Shawn Senior (autographed)	1.00
31	Andy Stewart	.05
31a	Andy Stewart (autographed)	1.00
32	Ozzie Timmons	.05
32a	Ozzie Timmons (autographed)	1.00
33	Quilvio Veras	.15
33a	Quilvio Veras (autographed)	3.00
34	Donnie White	.05
34a	Donnie White (autographed)	1.00
35	Mike Zimmerman	.05
35a	Mike Zimmerman (autographed)	1.00
36	Checklist Ruben Rivera	.25

1995 Signature Rookies T-95 Hot Prospects

Five players judged destined for big league fame are featured in this insert set. Cards measure 2-1/16" x 3-1/16". Action photos on front have a large black vertical strip down one side with the player's name in red and gold. A gold-foil notation at bottom says each card is "1 of 7,500". Backs have another color photo and a vertically compressed black-and-white version of the front photo, along with a paragraph about the prospect and his '94 stats. Cards are licensed only by the individual players, so uniform logos have been replaced with unofficial lettering, or airbrushed completely away. Each of the Hot Prospects inserts can also be found in an autographed edition of 1,550. Insertion rates are one per 16 packs for the regular cards, one per 45 packs for the autographed cards.

		MT
Complete Set (5):		6.00
Complete Autographed Set (5):		50.00
Common Player:		1.00
Common Autograph:		10.00
HP1	Billy Ashley	1.00
HP1a	Billy Ashley (autographed)	15.00
HP2	Brad Clontz	1.00
HP2a	Brad Clontz (autographed)	10.00
HP3	Andrew Lorraine	1.00
HP3a	Andrew Lorraine (autographed)	10.00
HP4	Ruben Rivera	3.00
HP4a	Ruben Rivera (autographed)	20.00
HP5	Jason Thompson	2.00
HP5a	Jason Thompson (autographed)	15.00

1995 Signature Rookies T-95 Joe DiMaggio Bonus Cards

A classic photo of Joe DiMaggio, minus uniform logos, is featured in this, the scarcest of the T-95 inserts. There are 5,000 unsigned cards, inserted at the rate of one per 43 packs (about three boxes), and 250 autographed cards (one per three cases or 864 packs).

		MT
JD1	Joe DiMaggio	6.00
JD1a	Joe DiMaggio (autographed)	250.00
PROMO	Joe DiMaggio (marked PROMO on back)	2.00

1995 Signature Rookies T-95 Minor League All Stars

In the same 2-1/16" x 3-1/16" size as the regular-issue Old Judge T-95 cards and other inserts for 1995, this All-Star insert set was printed in an edition of 7,500 cards of each player (one per 20 packs, on average). Fronts have a borderless negative black-and-white player photo of which a 1" x 1-1/2" portion has been rendered in color. The player name is in gold foil in a black marbled panel at lower-right. Backs have a color dual-image player photo, a paragraph about his prospects and his 1994 stats. Uniform and cap logos have been removed and replaced with unofficial lettering because the cards are licensed only by the players and not by Major League Baseball. Each All-Star card can also be found in an autographed edition of 2,100 (one per 30 packs).

MT
Complete Set (5): 3.00
Complete Autographed Set (5): 24.00
Common Player: .50
Common Autograph: 3.00
AS1 Trey Beamon 1.00
AS1a Trey Beamon (autographed) 9.00
AS2 Tim Belk .50
AS2a Tim Belk (autographed) 3.00
AS3 Jimmy Haynes .50
AS3a Jimmy Haynes (autographed) 3.00
AS4 Mark Johnson 1.00
AS4a Mark Johnson (autographed) 12.00
AS5 Chris Stynes .50
AS5a Chris Stynes (autographed) 3.00

1995 Signature Rookies T-95 Preview '95

In the same size (2-1/16" x 3-1/16") as the Signature Rookies Old Judge T-95 Series with which they were issued as inserts (one per two packs, average), the Preview '95 cards offer action photos with gold-foil highlights set against black marbled panels at top-right and lower-left. A gold-foil notation at bottom indicates each card is "1 of 5,750". Backs have a close-up repeat of the front photo, a second photo, biographical notes, career summary and 1994 stats. Because the cards are licensed only by the individual players, and not Major League Baseball, uniform logos have been airbrushed off and unofficial cap logos and, in some cases, team names have been added. Each of the 35 regular cards in the set can also be found in an autographed version of 500, about once every 14 packs.

MT
Complete Set (35): 7.50
Complete Autographed Set (35): 200.00
Common Player: .10
Common Autograph: 5.50
1 Bob Abreu .50
1a Bob Abreu (autographed) 10.00
2 Kym Ashworth .10
2a Kym Ashworth (autographed) 2.00
3 Jared Baker .10
3a Jared Baker (autographed) 2.00
4 Paul Bako .10
4a Paul Bako (autographed) 2.00
5 Jason Bates .35
5a Jason Bates (autographed) 10.00
6 Yamil Benitez .25
6a Yamil Benitez (autographed) 5.00
7 Marshall Boze .15
7a Marshall Boze (autographed) 4.00
8 Rich Butler .15
8a Rich Butler (autographed) 4.00
9 John Carter .15
9a John Carter (autographed) 4.00
10 Jeff Cirillo .50
10a Jeff Cirillo (autographed) 10.00
11 Randy Curtis .10
11a Randy Curtis (autographed) 2.00
12 Sal Fasano .10
12a Sal Fasano (autographed) 2.00
13 Aaron Fultz .10
13a Aaron Fultz (autographed) 2.00
14 Karim Garcia 1.00
14a Karim Garcia (autographed) 25.00
15 Kevin Grijak .10
15a Kevin Grijak (autographed) 2.00
16 Wilton Guerrero .45
16a Wilton Guerrero (autographed) 8.00
17 Stacy Hollins .10
17a Stacy Hollins (autographed) 2.00
18 Bobby Hughes .10
18a Bobby Hughes (autographed) 2.00
19 Jimmy Hurst .10
19a Jimmy Hurst (autographed) 2.00
20 Jason Isringhausen .75
20a Jason Isringhausen (autographed) 15.00
21 Ryan Karp .10
21a Ryan Karp (autographed) 2.00
22 Derek Lowe .10
22a Derek Lowe (autographed) 2.00
23 Matt Luke .20
23a Matt Luke (autographed) 5.00
24 Lyle Mouton .10
24a Lyle Mouton (autographed) 2.00
25 Dave Mysel .10
25a Dave Mysel (autographed) 2.00
26 Marc Newfield .20
26a Marc Newfield (autographed) 5.00
27 Jim Pittsley .20
27a Jim Pittsley (autographed) 4.00
28 Chris Sheff .10
28a Chris Sheff (autographed) 2.00
29 Tate Seefried .20
29a Tate Seefried (autographed) 4.00
30 Shawn Senior .10
30a Shawn Senior (autographed) 2.00
31 Andy Stewart .10
31a Andy Stewart (autographed) 2.00
32 Ozzie Timmons .15
32a Ozzie Timmons (autographed) 3.00
33 Quilvio Veras .20
33a Quilvio Veras (autographed) 4.00
34 Donnie White .10
34a Donnie White (autographed) 2.00
35 Mike Zimmerman .10
35a Mike Zimmerman (autographed) 2.00

1995 Upper Deck Minor League

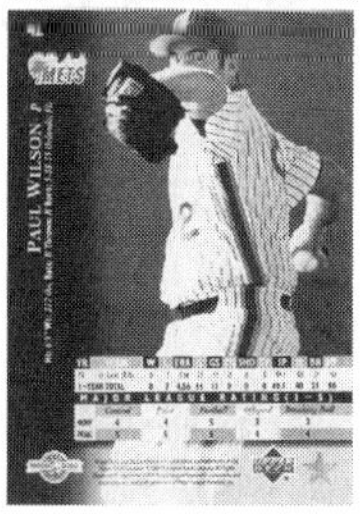

Superb borderless color photos front and back are featured in UD's 1995 minor league base set. A number of subsets within the 225-card issue allow the showcasing of top prospects on multiple cards. Still more cards of the same players are featured in the various chase sets randomly found in the foil packs. The player's name and UD logo are stamped in silver-foil on card fronts, while a star-shaped hologram is on back. As a dealer incentive for early orders, 10 players signed 1,000 cards each.

MT
Complete Set (225): 35.00
Common Player: .10
1 Derek Jeter 4.00
1a Derek Jeter (autographed) 100.00
2 Michael Tucker .25
3 Alex Ochoa .40
3a Alex Ochoa (autographed) 9.00
4 Bill Pulsipher .30
5 Terrell Wade .15
5a Terrell Wade (autographed) 9.00
6 Johnny Damon .75
6a Johnny Damon (autographed) 30.00
7 LaTroy Hawkins .15
7a LaTroy Hawkins (autographed) 7.50
8 Ruben Rivera .40
9 Jason Giambi .75
9a Jason Giambi (autographed) 15.00
10 Todd Hollandsworth .40
10a Todd Hollandsworth (autographed) 15.00
11 Alan Benes .50
11a Alan Benes (autographed) 12.00
12 John Wasdin .15
13 Roger Cedeno .75
14 Karim Garcia .25
15 Brooks Kieschnick .15
16 David Bell .10
17 Trot Nixon .75
18 Jose Malave .10
19 Rey Ordonez .75
20 Raul Casanova .20
21 Chad Mottola .25
22 Phil Nevin .50
23 Jim Pittsley .10
24 Frank Rodriguez .15
25 Todd Greene .25
26 Mike Bell .10
26a Mike Bell (autographed) 8.00
27 Jason Kendall 1.00
28 Pokey Reese 1.50
29 Jose Silva .10
30 Kirk Presley .15
31 Joe Randa .15
32 Shannon Stewart 1.00
33 Danny Clyburn .15
34 Glenn Williams .25
35 Terry Bradshaw .10
36 Jimmy Hurst .10
37 Scott Spiezio .40
38 Richard Hidalgo .50
39 Matt Brunson .10
40 Juan Acevedo .10
41 Trey Beamon .20
42 Kimera Bartee .15
43 James Baldwin .15
44 Matt Arrandale .10
45 Michael Jordan 5.00
46 Wonderful Terrific Monds .20
48 Bob Abreu 2.00
49 Edgardo Alfonzo 1.50
50 Damon Hollins .35
51 Marc Barcelo .10
52 D.J. Boston .10
53 Einar Diaz .10
54 Matt Drews .30
55 Benji Simonson .10
56 Bart Evans .10
57 Micah Franklin .10
58 Curtis Goodwin .20
59 Craig Griffey .25
60 Billy Wagner .40
61 Jimmy Haynes .10
62 Jose Herrera .10
63 Greg Keagle .10
64 Andy Larkin .10
65 Jason Isringhausen .25
66 Derrek Lee .50
67 Terrell Lowery .15
68 Ryan Luzinski .10
69 Angel Martinez .10
70 Tony Clark 1.00
71 Ryan McGuire .40
72 Damian Moss .25
73 Hugo Pivaral .10
74 Arquimedez Pozo .10
75 Daron Kirkreit .25
76 Luis Raven .10
77 Desi Relaford .25
78 Scott Rolen 4.00
79 Joe Rosselli .10
80 Chris Roberts .10
81 Giomar Guevara .10
82 Gene Schall .15
83 Jeff Suppan .25
84 Makato Suzuki (Makoto) .20
85 Jason Thompson .15
86 Marc Valdes .10
87 Pat Watkins .10
88 Jay Witasick .25
89 Ray Durham 1.00
90 Brad Fullmer 2.00
91 Roger Bailey .15
92 DeShawn Warren .15
93 Jermaine Dye 1.50
94 Scott Romano .10
95 Aaron Boone .50
96 Tate Seefried .15
97 Chris Stynes .10
98 Chris Widger .10
99 Desi Wilson .15
100 Dante Powell .25
101 Neifi Perez (Season Highlights) .25
102 Alex Ochoa (SH) .25
103 Kelly Wunsch (SH) .15
104 Jason Robbins (SH) .10
105 Kevin Coughlin (SH) .10
106 Bill Pulsipher (SH) .25
107 Roger Cedeno (International Flavor) .40
108 Jose Herrera (IF) .10
109 Andre King (IF) .15
110 Rey Ordonez (IF) .40
111 Jose Pett (IF) .10
112 Ruben Rivera (IF) .20
113 Jose Silva (IF) .10
114 Makato Suzuki (Makoto) (IF) .20
115 Glenn Williams (IF) .25
116 Wil Cunnane .10
117 Neifi Perez .75
118 Andre King .15
119 Quinton McCracken .15
120 Brian Giles 1.50
121 Kenny Felder .10
122 Jermaine Allensworth .20
123 Allen Battle .10
124 Howard Battle .10
125 Doug Million .10
126 Geoff Blum .10
127 Vladimir Guerrero 10.00
128 Torii Hunter .10
129 Doug Glanville .20
130 Dustin Hermanson 1.00
131 Mark Grudzielanek .50
132 Phil Geisler .10
133 Chris Carpenter .75
134 Brian Seckinsky .10
135 Josh Booty .25
136 Shane Andrews .25
137 Scott Eyre .10
138 Chad Fox .15
139 George Arias .20
140 Scott Sullivan .10
141 Todd Dunn .10
142 Nate Holdren .10
143 Gus Gandarillas .10
144 Scott Talanoa .10
145 Sal Fasano .10
146 Stoney Briggs .10
147 Yamil Benitez .10
148 Chris Wimmer .10
149 Mariano De Los Santos .10
150 Ben Grieve 4.00
151 Homer Bush .20
152 Wilton Guerrero .15
153 Benji Grigsby .10
154 Cade Caspar .10
155 Hiram Bocachica .15
156 Dave Vanhof .10
157 Frank Catalanotto .10
158 Marcus Jensen .10
159 Jamie Arnold .15
160 Cesar Devarez .10
161 Alan Benes (Road to the Show) .35
162 Johnny Damon (RS) .25
163 LaTroy Hawkins (RS) .15
164 Dustin Hermanson (RS) .20
165 Derek Jeter (RS) 2.00
166 Terrell Wade (RS) .15
167 Todd Walker (RS) .50
168 John Wasdin (RS) .15
169 Paul Wilson (RS) .20
170 Todd Walker .75
171 Danny Klassen .20
172 Bobby Morris .10
173 Kelly Wunsch .15
174 Fletcher Thompson .10
175 Terrence Long .25
176 Andy Petitte 1.00
177 Lou Pote .10
178 Steve Kline .10
179 Damian Jackson .50
180 Matt Smith .10
181 Tim Unroe .10
182 Jim Cole .10
183 Bill McMillon .10
184 Matt Luke .15
185 Sergio Nunez .10
186 Edgar Renteria 1.50
187 Bill Selby .10
188 Jamey Wright .20
189 Steve Whitaker .15
190 Joe Vitiello .15
191 Jacob Shumate .10
192 C.J. Nitkowski .15
193 Mark Johnson .40
194 Paul Konerko 2.50
195 Jay Payton .40
196 Jayson Peterson .10
197 Brian Buchanan .10
198 Ramon Castro .10
199 Antone Williamson .25
200 Paul Wilson .25
200a Paul Wilson (autographed) 10.00
201 Jaret Wright .75
202 Carlton Loewer .15
203 Jon Zuber .10
204 Ugueth Urbina .40
205 Nomar Garciaparra 6.00
206 Yuri Sanchez .10
207 Jason Moler .15
208 Lyle Mouton .10
209 Mark Johnson .40
210 Matt Raleigh .10
211 Julio Santana .10
212 Willie Ontafez .10
213 Ozzie Timmons .10
214 Victor Rodriguez .10
215 Paul Wilson (1994 Draft Class) .50
216 Ben Grieve (DC) 2.00
217 Dustin Hermanson (DC) .30
218 Antone Williamson (DC) .25
219 Josh Booty (DC) .15
220 Todd Walker (DC) .50
221 Jason Varitek (DC) .50
222 Paul Konerko (DC) 2.00
223 Doug Million (DC) .10
224 Hiram Bocachica (DC) .10
225 Durham Athletic Park .20

1995 Upper Deck Minor League Future Stock

Each card in the base set of 1995 Upper Deck minor league can also be found in a "Future Stock" parallel issue. The cards are identical except for the appearance of an FS shield in silver-foil in an upper corner of the card front.

MT
Complete Set (225): 95.00
Common Player: .25
(Star players valued at 3X-4X the same card in the regular issue.)

1995 Upper Deck Minor League Michael Jordan Highlights

This set of 3-1/2" x 5" cards was available only via a mail-in offer for $3 and 15 UD Minor League foil wrappers. Card fronts are printed on foil and feature highlights from Jordan's only season of professional baseball. Backs have a graduated yellow background with a color photo of

Jordan and a few words about the highlight, along with the logos of the Birmingham Barons, UD and the minor league licensing authority.

		MT
Complete Set (5):		25.00
Common Card:		5.00
MJ-1	Michael Jordan (White Sox Welcome)	5.00
MJ-2	Michael Jordan (Jordan Supplies Offense at Classic)	5.00
MJ-3	Michael Jordan (13-game Hitting Streak)	5.00
MJ-4	Michael Jordan (Jordan Hits First Home Run!)	5.00
MJ-5	Michael Jordan (Jordan Does Extracurricular Baseball)	5.00

1995 Upper Deck Minor League Michael Jordan One-On-One

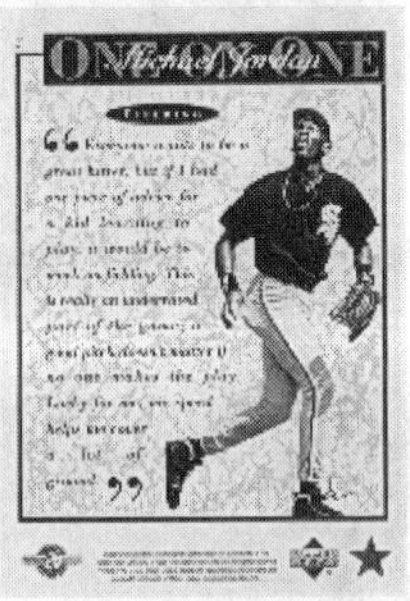

This 10-card set was produced for inclusion exclusively in mini-packs of Upper Deck Minor League baseball cards sold in Wal-Mart stores. The packs had three cards from the regular set plus one of the 10 One-On-One Jordan cards. Card fronts are in horizontal format and include a silver-foil "Michael Jordan / 95 / Retires" stamp on front. Backs have a color photo of Jordan and short text.

		MT
Complete Set (10):		5.00
Common Card:		.50
1	Michael Jordan (Throwing)	.50
2	Michael Jordan (Fielding)	.50
3	Michael Jordan (Hitting)	.50
4	Michael Jordan (Speed)	.50
5	Michael Jordan (Overall Report)	.50
6	Michael Jordan ('94 Spring Training)	.50
7	Michael Jordan ('94 Regular Season)	.50
8	Michael Jordan (1st Home Run)	.50
9	Michael Jordan ('94 Autumn)	.50
10	Michael Jordan (The Future)	.50

1995 Upper Deck Minor League Michael Jordan's Scrapbook

Printed on metallic-foil fronts, this 10-card chase series chronicles Michael Jordan's season of minor league baseball with the Birmingham Barons. Backs feature a continuing narrative.

		MT
Complete Set (10):		135.00
Common Card:		15.00
1	Decisions Michael Jordan	15.00
2	Practice Michael Jordan	15.00
3	Spring Training and Assignment Michael Jordan	15.00
4	Windy City Classic Michael Jordan	15.00
5	Firsts Michael Jordan	15.00
6	The Hitting Streak Michael Jordan	15.00
7	Struggles Michael Jordan	15.00
8	Life on the Road Michael Jordan	15.00
9	First Home Run Michael Jordan	15.00
10	Arizona Fall League Michael Jordan	15.00

1995 Upper Deck Minor League Organizational Pro-Files

Each team's top prospect is featured in this chase card set. Fronts are in horizontal format, printed on metallic foil. Backs have a checklist of that team's minor leaguers found in the regular UD minor league set.

		MT
Complete Set (28):		125.00
Common Player:		2.00
OP1	Terrell Wade	2.00
OP2	Alex Ochoa	3.00
OP3	Nomar Garciaparra	20.00
OP4	Todd Greene	6.00
OP5	Brooks Kieschnick	2.00
OP6	Michael Jordan	25.00
OP7	C.J. Nitkowski	3.00
OP8	Daron Kickreit	3.00
OP9	Juan Acevedo	2.00
OP10	Tony Clark	8.00
OP11	Josh Booty	3.00
OP12	Billy Wagner	4.00
OP13	Johnny Damon	4.00
OP14	Paul Konerko	12.00
OP15	Antone Williamson	2.00
OP16	Todd Walker	7.00
OP17	Ugueth Urbina	3.00
OP18	Bill Pulsipher	3.00
OP19	Ruben Rivera	4.00
OP20	John Wasdin	2.00
OP21	Scott Rolen	15.00
OP22	Trey Beamon	3.00
OP23	Alan Benes	6.00
OP24	Raul Casanova	2.00
OP25	Dante Powell	3.00
OP26	Arquimedez Pozo	2.00
OP27	Julio Santana	2.00
OP28	Jose Silva	2.00

1995 Upper Deck Minor League Top 10 Prospects

A copper "10" on a background of silver and purple metallic foil is featured on the front of these insert cards. Backs serve as a checklist for the regular UD minor league cards. Unlike the previous year, the Top 10 Prospects cards were issued only in 2-1/2" x 3-1/2" format in 1995.

		MT
Complete Set (10):		25.00
Common Player:		2.00
1	Derek Jeter	12.00
2	James Baldwin	2.00
3	Johnny Damon	4.00
4	Ruben Rivera	2.00
5	Bill Pulsipher	2.00
6	Jose Silva	2.00
7	Roger Cedeno	3.00
8	Alan Benes	3.00
9	Michael Tucker	2.00
10	Todd Hollandsworth	3.00

1995 Upper Deck/SP Top Prospects

Upper Deck brought its premium SP brand name to minor league cards in late 1995 with the issue of Top Prospects. Base cards all feature die-cut tops and have fronts with color player action photos printed on metallic foil backgrounds. Backs have another photo along with a few stats, personal data and career highlights. The set's first 10 cards are a Top 10 Prospects subset which have checklists on back and feature a different front design showing the player in a golden oval against a mauve textured background. Cards #100-115 are a subset titled "1995 Draft Class" and feature the player photos against a golden sunrise design. Insert cards found in foil packs include autographed cards of 26 players, "Destination the Show" cards of fast-track minor leaguers and Jordan Time Capsule cards. SP Top Prospects was sold in eight-card foil packs with a $4.19 suggested retail.

		MT
Complete Set (165):		120.00
Common Player:		.10
Wax Box:		300.00
1	Andruw Jones (Top 10 Prospect)	8.00
2	Brooks Kieschnick (Top 10 Prospect)	.25
3	Nomar Garciaparra (Top 10 Prospect)	12.00
4	Adam Riggs (Top 10 Prospect)	.25
5	Paul Wilson (Top 10 Prospect)	.40
6	Trey Beamon (Top 10 Prospect)	.35
7	Vladimir Guerrero (Top 10 Prospect)	20.00
8	Ben Grieve (Top 10 Prospect)	8.00
9	Jay Payton (Top 10 Prospect)	.75
10	Todd Walker (Top 10 Prospect)	2.00
11	Jermaine Dye	.25
12	Damon Hollins	.30
13	Wonderful Monds	.25
14	Damian Moss	.50
15	Andruw Jones	8.00
16	Danny Clyburn	.25
17	Billy Percibal	.10
18	Rocky Coppinger	.25
19	Tommy Davis	.15
20	Nomar Garciaparra	12.00
21	Trot Nixon	.75
22	Jose Malave	.10
23	Ryan McGuire	.35
24	Rafael Orellano	.10
25	Darin Erstad	4.00
26	George Arias	.35
27	Matt Beaumont	.15
28	Jason Dickson	1.00
29	Greg Shockey	.10
30	Brooks Kieschnick	.25
31	Jon Ratliff	.10
32	Amaury Telemaco	.10
33	Bob Morris	.10
34	Charles Poe	.15
35	Harold Williams	.10
36	Jeff Abbott	.10
37	Tom Fordham	.10
38	Pokey Reese	1.00
39	Pat Watkins	.10
40	Aaron Boone	.75
41	Chad Mottola	.40
42	Jason Robbins	.10
43	Jaret Wright	3.00
44	Casey Whitten	.10
45	Bartolo Colon	3.00
46	Richie Sexson	2.50
47	Enrique Wilson	1.00
48	Doug Million	.10
49	Joel Moore	.10
50	Derrick Gibson	1.00
51	Neifi Perez	1.00
52	Jamey Wright	.25
53	Juan Encarnacion	3.00
54	Cade Gaspar	.10
55	Justin Thompson	1.00
56	Bubba Trammell	.75
57	Daryle Ward	1.00
58	Clemente Nunez	.10
59	Will Cunnane	.10
60	Billy McMillon	.10
61	Matt Whisenant	.10
62	Edgar Renteria	1.50
63	Josh Booty	.30
64	Bob Abreu	4.00
65	Richard Hidalgo	2.50
66	Ramon Castro	.15
67	Scott Elarton	.50
68	Jhonny Perez	.10
69	Mendy Lopez	.10
70	Glendon Rusch	.15
71	Sal Fasano	.10
72	Sergio Nunez	.10
73	Matt Smith	.15
74	Chris Latham	.10
75	Adam Riggs	.25
76	Wilton Guerrero	.40
77	Paul Konerko	5.00
78	Gary Rath	.10
79	Jim Cole	.10
80	Jeff D'Amico	.35
81	Antone Williamson	.40
82	Todd Dunn	.10
83	Brian Banks	.10
84	Shane Bowers	.10
85	Todd Walker	2.00
86	Troy Carrasco	.10
87	Travis Miller	.10
88	Kimera Bartee	.15
89	Dan Serafini	.20
90	Vladimir Guerrero	20.00
91	Hiram Bocachica	.35
92	Brad Fullmer	2.50
93	Geoff Blum	.10
94	Israel Alcantara	.10
95	Jay Payton	1.00
96	Rey Ordonez	.75
97	Paul Wilson	.40
98	Preston Wilson	.25
99	Terrence Long	.25
100	Darin Erstad	4.00
101	Gabe Alvarez	.10
102	Jonathan Johnson	.15
103	Adam Benes	.20
104	Dennis Martinez, Jr.	.20
105	Jaime Jones	.35
106	Chad Hermansen	4.00
107	Geoff Jenkins	3.00
108	Juan LeBron	.30
109	Mark Redman	.10
110	Jose Cruz Jr.	3.00
111	Carlos Beltran	4.00
112	Todd Helton	6.00
113	Andy Yount	.10
114	Ryan Jaroncyk	.10
115	Sean Johnston	.10
116	Scott Romano	.10
117	Brian Buchanan	.15
118	Nick Delvecchio	.15
119	Ramiro Mendoza	.75
120	Matt Drews	.25
121	Shane Spencer	1.50
122	Jason McDonald	.50
123	Scott Spiezio	.50
124	Brad Rigby	.10
125	Ben Grieve	8.00
126	Steve Cox	.20
127	Willie Morales	.10
128	Wayne Gomes	.40
129	Larry Wimberly	.10
130	Scott Rolen	8.00
131	Carlton Loewer	.15
132	Wendell Magee	.25
133	Charles Peterson	.10
134	Lou Collier	.10
135	Trey Beamon	.40
136	Micah Franklin	.15
137	Jason Kendall	2.00
138	Homer Bush	.30
139	Dickie Woodridge	.10
140	Derrek Lee	.75
141	Raul Casanova	.40
142	Greg LaRocca	.10
143	Jason Thompson	.15
144	Jacob Cruz	1.00
145	Jesse Ibarra	.35
146	Jay Canizaro	.10
147	Steve Soderstrom	.10
148	Dante Powell	.75
149	James Bonnici	.10
150	Raul Ibanez	.40
151	Trey Moore	.10
152	Desi Relaford	.30
153	Jason Varitek	1.00
154	Jay Witasick	.10
155	Bret Wagner	.15
156	Aaron Holbert	.15
157	Fernando Tatis	5.00
158	Mike Bell	.15
159	Jeff Davis	.10
160	Julio Santana	.10
161	Kevin Brown	.35
162	Felipe Crespo	.15
163	Kevin Witt	.15
164	Mark Sievert	.10
165	Jose Pett	.10

Checklists with card numbers in parentheses ( ) indicates the numbers do not appear on the card.

1995 Upper Deck/SP Top Prospects Autographs

Similar in format to the rest of the SP Top Propects set, including the die-cut tops, the autograph insert cards have standard (non-metallized) printing on front and no UV coat, allowing the autograph to be more efficiently signed. Each card has a uniquely numbered hologram serial number attached and the back is a certificate of authenticity. Autograph cards were inserted at an average rate of once per 31 foil packs; about one per box. It is believed only 20 of the Michael Jordan card were printed.

	MT
Complete Set (26):	5500.
Common Player:	15.00
(1) Bob Abreu	40.00
(2) Gabe Alvarez	15.00
(3) George Arias	15.00
(4) Trey Beamon	15.00
(5) Aaron Boone	20.00
(6) Raul Casanova	15.00
(7) Bartolo Colon	30.00
(8) Jermaine Dye	35.00
(9) Nomar Garciaparra	150.00
(10) Todd Greene	20.00
(11) Ben Grieve	100.00
(12) Vladimir Guerrero	175.00
(13) Richard Hidalgo	30.00
(14) Andruw Jones	100.00
(15) Michael Jordan	4750.
(16) Jason Kendall	30.00
(17) Brooks Kieschnick	20.00
(18) Derrek Lee	20.00
(19) Wonderful Monds	15.00
(20) Rey Ordonez	20.00
(21) Jay Payton	20.00
(22) Adam Riggs	15.00
(23) Scott Rolen	100.00
(24) Jason Thompson	20.00
(25) Paul Wilson	15.00
(26) Jaret Wright	25.00

1995 Upper Deck/SP Top Prospects Destination the Show

Players deemed to be on the fast track to the majors are featured in this insert set. Like the rest of the SP Top Prospect cards, the tops are die-cut and the player photo is set against a metallic foil background. Tan borders and gold-foil graphic highlights complete the front design. Backs have another player photo and career highlights.

	MT
Complete Set (20):	750.00
Common Player:	15.00
DS1 Andruw Jones	75.00
DS2 Richard Hidalgo	25.00
DS3 Paul Wilson	15.00
DS4 Brooks Kieschnick	20.00
DS5 Ben Grieve	60.00
DS6 Adam Riggs	15.00
DS7 Vladimir Guerrero	150.00
DS8 Paul Konerko	50.00
DS9 Jose Cruz Jr.	40.00
DS10Todd Walker	20.00
DS11Darin Erstad	50.00
DS12Derrek Lee	20.00
DS13Scott Rolen	75.00
DS14Trey Beamon	15.00
DS15Nomar Garciaparra	125.00
DS16Jason Kendall	25.00
DS17Aaron Boone	25.00
DS18Matt Drews	15.00
DS19Derrick Gibson	15.00
DS20Jay Payton	15.00

1995 Upper Deck/SP Top Prospects Jordan Time Capsule

Taking full advantage of its license to produce Michael Jordan baseball cards, Upper Deck included a four-card Time Capsule chase set in its SP Top Prospects minor league set. Cards feature photos of Jordan in his minor league days, vignetted with a silver-foil effect around the borders. The Jordan cards are inserted at an average rate of about one per 19 packs.

	MT
Complete Set (4):	22.00
TC1 Michael Jordan	7.50
TC2 Michael Jordan	7.50
TC3 Michael Jordan	7.50
TC4 Michael Jordan	7.50

1995 Minor League Team Sets

A major change in the market for minor league team sets came in 1995 when the field's top two players, Classic and Fleer/Pro Cards dropped out. Classic was gone entirely in 1995 and Fleer was down to a handful of sets. Both of the major card companies had discovered the short press runs and high costs of production could not be recouped in a thin market. Teams desiring card sets were left to produce their own. A small group of regional graphics firms was able to sign a few or a dozen teams each. One such company, Grandstand (GS) remains active. For collectors, the big boys dropping out meant an end to easy availability of the annual issues. Some teams sold or gave away their entire production and a strong market arose of dealers who scoured the nation to pick up sets to serve the hobby market. Player selection no longer was the sole basis of value beginning in 1995, market availability became critical to price. When all was said and done, over 140 team sets were issued in 1995, compared to the 275 of the previous year.

	MT
142 team sets and variations	
1995 Team Abilene Prairie Dogs (30)	7.00
1995 Team Albany Diamond Dogs (26)	7.00
1995 Team Alexandria Aces (22)	7.00
1995 Team Amarillo Dillas (25)	7.00
1995 Arizona Fall League (22)	20.00
1995 Team Arkansas Travelers (30)	16.00
1995 Team Asheville Tourists (30)	14.00
1995 Team Asheville Tourists update (14)	24.00
1995 Team Auburn Astros (30)	14.00
1995 Team Bakersfield Blaze (32)	12.50
1995 Team Batavia Clippers (33)	17.50
1995 Team Bellingham Giants (36)	17.50
1995 Team Beloit Snappers (31)	19.00
1995 Team Billings Mustangs (29)	100.00
1995 Team Binghampton Mets (28)	12.50
1995 Team Boise Hawks (35)	13.00
1995 Team Bowie Baysox (31)	9.00
1995 Fleer/PC Brevard County Manatees (30)	8.00
1995 Team Burlington Bees (36)	15.00
1995 Team Butte Copper Kings (32)	7.00
1995 Fleer/PC Carolina Mudcats (30)	9.00
1995 Carolina League 50th Anniversary (35)	8.00
1995 Team Cedar Rapids Kernels (32)	12.50
1995 Team Charleston RiverDogs (30)	30.00
1995 Team Charleston RiverDogs update (9)	35.00
1995 Team Charlotte Knights (30)	12.50
1995 Team Chattanooga Lookouts (32)	10.00
1995 Fleer/PC Clearwater Phillies (30)	9.50
1995 Team Colorado Springs Sky Sox (34)	9.50
1995 Kroger Columbus Clippers panels (8)	30.00
1995 Police Columbus Clippers (32)	20.00
1995 Team Columbus Clippers (32)	16.00
1995 Team Corpus Christi Barracudas (24)	7.00
1995 Team Danville Braves (6 panels)	37.50
1995 Photostars USA Ben Davis (2)	6.00
1995 Team Dunedin Blue Jays (30)	85.00
1995 Team Durham Bulls (40)	9.00
1995 Team Edmonton Trappers (30)	12.50
1995 Team Elmira Pioneers (30)	20.00
1995 Team Elmira Pioneers update (31)	35.00
1995 Team El Paso Diablos (24)	12.00
1995 Team Eugene Emeralds (32)	25.00
1995 Team Evansville Otters (26)	7.00
1995 Team Evansville Otters update (26)	7.00
1995 Team Everett Aquasox (30)	30.00
1995 Team Fayetteville Generals (30)	32.50
1995 Team Ft. Myers Miracle (32)	12.00
1995 Team Ft. Wayne Wizards (32)	9.00
1995 GS Grays Harbor Gulls (31)	7.00
1995 Team Great Falls Dodgers (40)	65.00
1995 Team Greensboro Bats (33)	15.00
1995 Team Greenville Braves (28)	14.00
1995 Fleer/PC Hagerstown Suns (30)	8.50
1995 Team Hardware City Rock Cats (29)	29.50
1995 Team Harrisburg Senators (28)	11.00
1995 Team Helena Brewers (32)	13.00
1995 Team Hudson Valley Renegades (30)	10.00
1995 Team Huntsville Stars (29)	12.00
1995 Team Idaho Falls Braves (27)	16.50
1995 Fleer/PC Indianapolis Indians (30)	7.50
1995 Team Iowa Cubs (25)	12.50
1995 Smokey Bear Jackson Generals (26)	20.00
1995 Team Jackson Generals (27)	16.50
1995 Team Jacksonville Suns (28)	9.00
1995 Team Kane County Cougars (32)	14.00
1995 Kane Co. Cougars Legends (15)	11.00
1995 Team Kinston Indians (30)	17.50
1995 Fleer/PC Knoxville Smokies (30)	7.50
1995 Team Lake Elsinore Storm (30)	32.00
1995 Team Laredo Apaches (25)	7.00
1995 FPC Louisville Redbirds (30)	45.00
1995 Team Lubbock Crickets (25)	7.00
1995 Team Lynchburg Hillcats (30)	8.00
1995 Team Macon Braves (30)	135.00
1995 Team Macon Braves Update (6)	35.00
1995 Team Martinsville Phillies (6 panels)	125.00
1995 Team Memphis Chicks (27)	14.50
1995 Team Michigan Battle Cats (30)	15.00
1995 1 Hour Midland Angels (36)	75.00
1995 Team Midland Angels (30)	11.50
1995 Midwest League All-Stars (58)	12.50
1995 Team Minneapolis Loons (25)	6.00
1995 Team Mobile BaySharks (25)	7.00
1995 Team Modesto A's (32)	24.00
1995 Team Nashville Sounds foldout	35.00
1995 Team New Haven Ravens (33)	15.00
1995 Team New Jersey Cardinals (30)	15.00
1995 Team Norfolk Tides (30)	13.00
1995 Team Norwich Navigators (42)	9.00
1995 Team Norwich Navigators update (11)	7.50
1995 Team Ogden Raptors (30)	15.00
1995 Team Ogden Raptors poster	22.00
1995 Team Oklahoma City 89ers (27)	20.00
1995 Team Omaha Royals (29)	11.00
1995 Fleer/PC Orlando Cubs (30)	8.00
1995 DD Pawtucket Red Sox foldout	50.00
1995 Team Pawtucket Red Sox (30)	10.00
1995 Team Peoria Chiefs (31)	9.50
1995 Team Phoenix Firebirds (30)	8.00
1995 Fleer/PC Piedmont Phillies (30)	8.00
1995 Team Pittsfield Mets (32)	11.00
1995 Team Port City Roosters (29)	8.50
1995 Team Portland Sea Dogs (30)	9.00
1995 Team Prince William Cannons (30)	13.00
1995 Team Quad Cities River Bandits (30)	20.00
1995 Team Rancho Cucamonga Quakes (30)	32.00
1995 Team Reading Phillies (28)	32.00
1995 Team Reading Phillies E.L. Champs (36)	27.00
1995 Pepsi Richmond Braves POGs (27)	50.00
1995 Richmond Camera Richmond Braves (29)	60.00
1995 Team Richmond Braves (30)	8.00
1995 Team Rio Grande Valley White Wings (26)	7.00
1995 Team Rochester Red Wings (48)	8.50
1995 Team Rockford Cubbies (32)	13.50
1995 Team Salem Avalanche (30)	19.00
1995 HEB San Antonio Missions (32)	60.00
1995 Team San Antonio Missions (30)	14.00
1995 Team San Bernardino Spirit (32)	45.00
1995 Team Scranton Red Barons (30)	42.50
1995 Team Spokane Indians (32)	14.00
1995 Team Sultans of Springfield (30)	12.00
1995 Team St. Catherines Stompers (36)	100.00
1995 Team St. Lucie Mets (37)	14.50
1995 Team St. Paul Saints (29)	7.00
1995 Team Syracuse Chiefs (30)	9.50
1995 Team All-Time Syracuse Chiefs (72)	75.00
1995 Team Tacoma Rainiers (30)	45.00
1995 Team Tampa Yankees (30)	9.50
1995 Team Thunder Bay Whiskey Jacks (25)	7.00
1995 Team Toledo Mud Hens (30)	8.00
1995 Team Trenton Thunder (31)	125.00
1995 Team Trenton Thunder foldout	150.00
1995 Team Tucson Toros (29)	8.00
1995 Team Tulsa Drillers (30)	10.00
1995 Team Tyler Wildcatters (24)	7.00
1995 Team Vero Beach Dodgers (30)	25.00
1995 Team Watertown Indians (30)	85.00
1995 Team West Mighigan Whitecaps (30)	10.00
1995 Team Wichita Wranglers (30)	12.50
1995 Team Wilmington Blue Rocks (30)	17.50
1995 Team Yakima Bears (36)	17.50
1995 Team Zanseville Greys (xx)	7.00

1996 Best Autograph Series

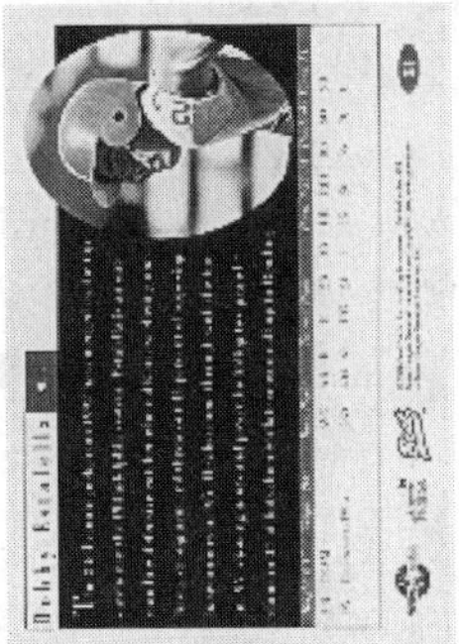

The basic set for this premiere edition consists of 99 of the top prospects from all levels of minor league baseball - from Instructional League through Class AAA. Released at the end of October, cards picture players with their 1996 teams, mostly in game-action photos on the fronts. The player's minor league team logo, name and position are at bottom. Backs have a portrait photo in an oval at top-right, with a career summary in the black box at left and 1995 stats at bottom. The cards were issued in foil packs of six, with one card being of the special autographed type. An insert set features 1996 first-round draft picks.

		MT
Complete Set (99):		10.00
Common Player:		.05
Wax Box:		45.00
1	Winston Abreu	.05
2	Antonio Alfonseca	.05
3	Richard Almanzar	.05
4	Gabe Alvarez	.05
5	Marlon Anderson	.05
6	Kym Ashworth	.05
7	Marc Barcelo	.05
8	Brian Barkley	.05
9	Mike Bell	.15
10	Carlos Beltran	.10
11	Shayne Bennett	.05
12	Jeremy Blevins	.05
13	Kevin Brown	.75
14	Ray Brown	.05
15	Homer Bush	.15
16	Jay Canizaro	.05
17	Troy Carrasco	.05
18	Raul Casanova	.10
19	Luis Castillo	.25
20	Ramon Castro	.15
21	Gary Coffee	.05
22	Decomba Conner	.05
23	Kevin Coughlin	.05
24	Jacob Cruz	1.50
25	Jeff D'Amico	.50
26	Tommy Davis	.10
27	Edwin Diaz	.05
28	Einar Diaz	.10
29	David Doster	.05
30	Derrin Ebert	.05
31	Bobby Estalella	.75
32	Alex Gonzalez	1.00
33	Kevin Grijak	.05
34	Jose Guillen	2.00
35	Tim Harkrider	.05
36	Dan Held	.05
37	Wes Helms	.75
38	Erik Hiljus	.05
39	Aaron Holbert	.05
40	Raul Ibanez	.20
41	Jesse Ibarra	.25
42	Marty Janzen	.05
43	Robin Jennings	.20
44	Shawn Johnston	.05
45	Randy Jorgensen	.05
46	Marc Kroon	.05
47	Mike Kusiewicz	.05
48	Carlos Lee	1.00
49	Brian Lesher	.05
50	George Lombard	1.50
51	Roberto Lopez	.05
52	Fernando Lunar	.05
53	Len Manning	.05
54	Eddy Martinez	.05
55	Jesus Martinez	.05
56	Onan Masaoka	.15
57	Joe Maskivish	.05
58	Jeff Matulevich	.05
59	Brian Meadows	.05
60	Mike Metcalfe	.05
61	Doug Mlicki	.05
62	Steve Montgomery	.05
63	Trey Moore	.05
64	Nick Morrow	.05
65	Bryant Nelson	.05
66	Sergio Nunez	.05
67	Hector Ortega	.05
68	Russell Ortiz	.05
69	Eric Owens	.05
70	Billy Percibal	.05
71	Charles Peterson	.05
72	A.J. Pierzynski	.05
73	Charles Poe	.10
74	Dante Powell	.40
75	Kenny Pumphrey	.05
76	Angel Ramirez	.05
77	Julio Ramirez	.05
78	Gary Rath	.05
79	Jon Ratliff	.05
80	Brad Rigby	.05
81	Benj Sampson	.05
82	Greg Shockey	.05
83	Steve Shoemaker	.05
84	Demond Smith	.05
85	Robert Smith	.05
86	Steve Soderstrom	.05
87	Fernando Tatis	2.50
88	Jose Texidor	.05
89	Brett Tomko	.05
90	Jose Valentin	.05
91	Jason Varitek	.25
92	Andrew Vessel	.05
93	Casey Whitten	.05
94	Enrique Wilson	.05
95	Preston Wilson	.45
96	Larry Wimberly	.05
97	Jaret Wright	.75
98	Dmitri Young	.25
99	Joe Young	.05

1996 Best Autograph Series Autographs

The top prospects in Class A, AA and AAA are featured on the autographed cards which are the heart of Best's premiere Autograph Series issue. One genuinely autographed card is included in each six-card foil pack. Autographed cards differ in design from the base set in the action photos on front are vignetted in an oval against a white background. The player name and minor league team logo are at bottom. Backs carry a congratulatory message over a large issuer logo. The unnumbered autographed cards are checklisted here in alphabetical order.

		MT
Complete Set (91):		500.00
Common Player:		3.00
(1)	Israel Alcantera	3.00
(2)	Richard Almanzar	3.00
(3)	Brian Banks	6.00
(4)	Marc Barcelo	3.00
(5)	Kimera Bartee	6.00
(6)	Jeremy Blevins	3.00
(7)	Jaime Bluma	3.00
(8)	D.J. Boston	3.00
(9)	Kevin Brown	12.00
(10)	Homer Bush	5.00
(11)	Jay Canizaro	6.00
(12)	Luis Castillo	8.00
(13)	Davey Coggin	3.00
(14)	Bartolo Colon	15.00
(15)	Jacob Cruz	15.00
(16)	Lino Diaz	3.00
(17)	Todd Dunn	6.00
(18)	Jermaine Dye	15.00
(19)	Bobby Estalella	10.00
(20)	Tom Fordham	3.00
(21)	Karim Garcia	20.00
(22)	Todd Greene	10.00
(23)	Ben Grieve	40.00
(24)	Mike Gulan	3.00
(25)	Derek Hacopian	3.00
(26)	Wes Helms	20.00
(27)	Brett Herbison	3.00
(28)	Chad Hermansen	25.00
(29)	Aaron Holbert	3.00
(30)	Damon Hollins	5.00
(31)	Ryan Jaroncyk	4.00
(32)	Geoff Jenkins	10.00
(33)	Earl Johnson	3.00
(34)	Andruw Jones	50.00
(35)	Jason Kendall	20.00
(36)	Brooks Kieschnick	4.00
(37)	Andre King	3.00
(38)	Paul Konerko	30.00
(39)	Todd Landry	3.00
(40)	Mendy Lopez	3.00
(41)	Roberto Lopez	3.00
(42)	Eric Ludwick	3.00
(43)	Mike Maurer	3.00
(44)	Brian Meadows	3.00
(45)	Ralph Milliard	3.00
(46)	Doug Mlicki	3.00
(47)	Julio Mosquera	3.00
(48)	Tony Mounce	3.00
(49)	Sergio Nunez	3.00
(50)	Russell Ortiz	3.00
(51)	Carey Paige	3.00
(52)	Jay Payton	15.00
(53)	Charles Peterson	4.00
(54)	Tommy Phelps	3.00
(55)	Hugo Pivaral	3.00
(56)	Dante Powell	4.00
(57)	Angel Ramirez	3.00
(58)	Gary Rath	3.00
(59)	Mark Redman	3.00
(60)	Adam Riggs	4.00
(61)	Lonell Roberts	3.00
(62)	Scott Rolen	40.00
(63)	Glendon Rusch	3.00
(64)	Matt Sachse	3.00
(65)	Donnie Sadler	8.00
(66)	William Santamaria	3.00
(67)	Todd Schmitt	3.00
(68)	Richie Sexson	15.00
(69)	Alvie Shepherd	3.00
(70)	Steve Shoemaker	3.00
(71)	Brian Sikorski	3.00
(72)	Randall Simon	12.00
(73)	Matt Smith	4.00
(74)	Scott Spiezio	10.00
(75)	Everett Stull, II	3.00
(76)	Jose Texidor	3.00
(77)	Mike Thurman	3.00
(78)	Brett Tomko	4.00
(79)	Hector Trinidad	3.00
(80)	Pedro Valdes	3.00
(81)	Andrew Vessel	3.00
(82)	Jacob Viano	3.00
(83)	Terrell Wade	4.00
(84)	Bret Wagner	3.00
(85)	Todd Walker	15.00
(86)	Travis Welch	3.00
(87)	Casey Whitten	4.00
(88)	Paul Wilson	8.00
(89)	Preston Wilson	9.00
(90)	Kevin Witt	4.00
(91)	Jamey Wright	6.00

1996 Best Autograph Series First Round Draft Picks

Besides the autographed cards, the only other inserts found in Best's '96 Autograph Series is this run of 16 first-round draft picks who made their pro debut in 1996. For some of the players it is their baseball card. Fronts have player poses against large minor league team logos. Backs repeat the front player photo in a subdued sepia image over which is printed the player biography. Cards are numbered with a "FR" prefix.

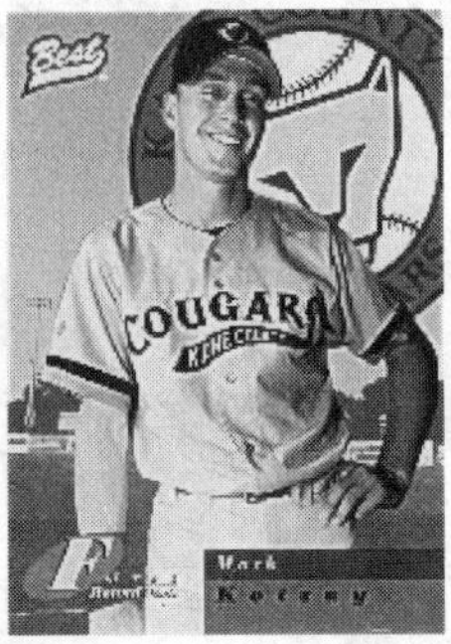

		MT
Complete Set (16):		32.00
Common Player:		1.50
1	Chad Green	6.00
2	Mark Kotsay	7.50
3	Robert Stratton	1.50
4	Dermal Brown	2.50
5	Matt Halloran	2.50
6	Joe Lawrence	1.50
7	Todd Noel	3.00
8	Jake Westbrook	2.50
9	Gil Meche	1.50
10	Damian Rolls	2.00
11	John Oliver	1.50
12	Josh Garrett	2.00
13	A.J. Zapp	3.00
14	Danny Peoples	2.50
15	Paul Wilder	2.50
16	Nick Bierbrodt	1.50

1996 Best Player of the Year

Budding Braves superstar Andruw Jones is featured in this late-season insert issue. Five hundred of each card were autographed and have a certificate of authenticity on back.

		MT
Complete Set (5):		20.00
Complete Set, Autographed (5):		200.00
Common Card:		4.00
Common Card, Autographed:		50.00
(1)	Andruw Jones (batting)	
(2)	Andruw Jones (running)	
(3)	Andruw Jones (seated w/bat)	
(4)	Andruw Jones (seated w/glove)	
(5)	Andruw Jones (in Bulls uniform)	

1996 Classic Assets (Baseball)

Issued in two series this five-sport card set provides the base set for a phone card chase program. Only the baseball players from the base set, inserts and phone cards are listed here.

		MT
Base Set/Inserts:		
4	Barry Bonds	.40
18	Jason Kendall	.40
33	Jay Payton	.45
39	Nolan Ryan	.75
48	Paul Wilson	.40
64	Doug Million	.25
64	Doug Million (silver signature)	1.50
65	Barry Bonds	.40
65	Barry Bonds (silver signature)	4.00
DC15	Nomar Garciaparra (diecut)	6.00
DC17	Barry Bonds (diecut)	4.00
DC18	Paul Wilson (diecut)	3.00
CA7	Cal Ripken Jr. (Cut Above)	15.00
CA10	Barry Bonds (Cut Above)	4.00
S1	Barry Bonds (Silksations)	12.00

1996 Classic Assets (Baseball) Foncards

Issued in two series these five-sport phone cards are the main chase-card element in Classic Assets. Only the baseball players are listed here.

		MT
Complete (Baseball) Set (22):		400.00
(1)	Barry Bonds (1 min. Foncard, Series I)	1.00
(2)	Barry Bonds ($2 Foncard, Series I)	2.00
(3)	Barry Bonds (1 min. Foncard, Series II)	1.00
(4)	Barry Bonds ($2 Foncard, Series II)	2.00
(5)	Doug Million (1 min. Foncard)	1.00
(6)	Doug Million ($2 Foncard)	1.50
(7)	Cal Ripken Jr. (1 min. Foncard)	2.50
(8)	Cal Ripken Jr. ($2 Foncard)	5.00
(9)	Cal Ripken Jr. (Cut Above Foncard)	5.00
(10)	Nolan Ryan (1 min. Foncard)	1.50
(11)	Nolan Ryan ($2 Foncard)	3.00
(12)	Barry Bonds ($5 Foncard, Series I)	2.50
(13)	Barry Bonds ($5 Foncard, Series II)	2.50
(14)	Cal Ripken Jr. ($5 Foncard)	7.50
(15)	Nolan Ryan ($5 Foncard)	4.50
(16)	Cal Ripken Jr. ($10 Foncard)	10.00
(17)	Jackie Robinson ($10 Foncard)	10.00
(18)	Cal Ripken Jr. ($100 Foncard)	50.00
(19)	Barry Bonds ($200 Foncard)	20.00
(20)	Cal Ripken Jr. ($1,000 Foncard)	225.00
(20p)	Cal Ripken Jr. ($1,000 Foncard promotional sample)	15.00
(21)	Cal Ripken Jr. ($5 Crystal Foncard)	15.00
(22)	Cal Ripken Jr. ($20 Crystal Foncard)	55.00

)

> The values of some parallel-card issues will have to be calculated based on figures presented in the heading for the regular-issue card set.

1996 Classic Clear Assets (Baseball)

A number of baseball players are featured in the base set, inserts and phone cards which make up the all-acetate Clear Assets set.

MT

Base Set/Inserts
52 Barry Bonds .60
53 Chad Hermansen .75
54 Ben Davis .50
55 Jay Payton .50
X4 Barry Bonds (3X) 20.00

1996 Classic Clear Assets (Baseball) Foncards

A number of baseball players are featured in the base set, inserts and phone cards which make up the all-acetate Clear Assets set.

MT

Complete (Baseball) Foncard Set (7): 230.00
6/30 Barry Bonds 1.50
($2 Foncard)
8/30 Nolan Ryan 3.00
($2 Foncard)
16/30 Cal Ripken Jr. 2.00
($2 Foncard)
5/20 Barry Bonds 2.50
($5 Foncard)
12/20 Cal Ripken Jr. 3.00
($5 Foncard)
5/10 Cal Ripken Jr. 7.50
($10 Foncard)
5/5 Cal Ripken Jr. 225.00
($1,000 Foncard)

1996 Classic 4 Sports McDonald's LP

Randomly inserted in the five-card packs of a special 4 Sport version issued regionally by McDonald's are these premium LP (Limited Production) cards. Format is similar to the base cards except for a gold-foil notation on front that the card is "1 of 16,750". Darren Daulton is the only baseball player among the LPs.

MT

LP1 Darren Daulton 1.00

1996 Classic Signings (Baseball)

Another five-sport card set with the lure of an autographed card in every pack and a chance to win autographed memorabilia, Signings includes the usual line-up of Classic spokesmen and baseball prospects among the 100-card base set, parallel editions and chase sets.

MT

Base Set/Inserts:
60 Ben Grieve 1.50
60 Ben Grieve (diecut) 6.00
60 Ben Grieve 20.00
(autographed)
61 Paul Wilson .75
61 Paul Wilson (diecut) 4.00
61 Paul Wilson 15.00
(autographed)
62 Calvin Reese .50
62 Calvin Reese (diecut) 2.50
62 Calvin Reese 8.00
(autographed)
63 Karim Garcia 1.00
63 Karim Garcia (diecut) 5.00
63 Karim Garcia 18.00
(autographed)
64 Mark Farris .50
64 Mark Farris (diecut) 2.50
64 Mark Farris 8.00
(autographed)
65 Jay Payton .75
65 Jay Payton (diecut) 4.00
65 Jay Payton 18.00
(autographed)
66 Dustin Hermanson .50
66 Dustin Hermanson 2.50
(diecut)
66 Dustin Hermanson 8.00
(autographed)
67 Michael Barrett 1.25
67 Michael Barrett 4.50
(diecut)
67 Michael Barrett 15.00
(autographed)
68 Ryan Jaroncyk .50
68 Ryan Jaroncyk 2.50
(diecut)
68 Ryan Jaroncyk 6.00
(autographed)
69 Ben Davis .65
69 Ben Davis (diecut) 4.00
69 Ben Davis 15.00
(autographed)
93 Barry Bonds .75
93 Barry Bonds (diecut) 5.00
93 Barry Bonds 20.00
(autographed)
21 Paul Wilson 4.50
(Freshly Inked)
22 Nomar Garciaparra 7.50
(Freshly Inked)
8 Barry Bonds 6.00
(Etched in Stone)

1996 Classic Visions (Baseball)

The usual prospects and Classic spokesmen are included in this five-sports issue printed on extra-thick card stock and highlighted with both silver- and gold-foil stamping.

MT

Complete (Baseball) Set (14): 3.00
Common Player: .10
95 Barry Bonds .35
96 Nolan Ryan .50
97 Ben Grieve .50
98 Ben Davis .40
99 Paul Wilson .25
100 C.J. Nitkowski .15
101 Chad Hermansen .40
102 Jason Kendall .35
103 Todd Greene .25
104 Dustin Hermanson .15
105 Karim Garcia .40
106 Doug Million .15
107 Jay Payton .30
130 Nolan Ryan .50
(Legendary Futures)

1996 Classic Visions Signings (Baseball)

A handful of baseball players is included among the five sports represented in this set, but only among the 100 base cards; none of the inserts are baseball players.

MT

Complete (Baseball) Set (8): 5.00
Complete (Baseball) Set, Autographed: 150.00
Common Player: .50
Common Player, Autographed: 10.00
80 Barry Bonds .50
(80) Barry Bonds 15.00
(autographed)
81 Nolan Ryan 1.00
(81) Nolan Ryan 60.00
(autographed)
82 Ben Davis .65
(82) Ben Davis 15.00
(autographed)
83 Chad Hermansen .50
(83) Chad Hermansen 15.00
(autographed)
84 Jason Kendall .50
(84) Jason Kendall 15.00
(autographed)
85 Todd Greene .50
(85) Todd Greene 15.00
(autographed)
86 Karim Garcia .75
(86) Karim Garcia 20.00
(autographed)
87 Jay Payton .75
(87) Jay Payton 15.00
(autographed)

1996 Fleer Excel

Major league quality in a minor league set was touted by Fleer for its 1996 Excel issue. Cards were printed on cardboard described as 40% thicker than typical minor league cards, with each card having copper-foil highlights on front. Each of the players in the basic 250-card set is depicted on front in a posed or game-action borderless photo. Backs have two more photos of the player, generally close-up action and portraits. Backs also provide full pro stats. The set is arranged alphabetically by player within organization and league. Each foil pack includes one card from among the five insert sets produced in conjunction with the Excel set.

MT

Complete Set (250): 35.00
Common Player: .05
1 Kimera Bartee .15
2 Carlos Chavez .05
3 Rocky Coppinger .25
4 Tommy Davis .10
5 Eddy Martinez .10
6 Billy Owens .05
7 Billy Percibal .05
8 Garrett Stephenson .05
9 Rachaad Stewart .05
10 Chris Allison .05
11 Virgil Chevalier .05
12 Nomar Garciaparra 7.50
13 Jose Malave .05
14 Ryan McGuire .75
15 Trot Nixon .20
16 Rafael Orellano .05
17 Pork Chop Pough .20
18 Donnie Sadler .40
19 Bill Selby .05
20 Nathan Tebbs .05
21 George Arias .10
22 Matt Beaumont .10
23 Danny Buxbaum .05
24 Jovino Carvajal .05
25 Geoff Edsell .05
26 Darin Erstad 6.00
27 Aaron Guiel .05
28 Mike Holtz .05
29 Ryan Kane .05
30 Jeff Abbott .05
31 Kevin Coughlin .05
32 Tom Fordham .05
33 Carlos Lee 2.00
34 Frank Menechino .05
35 Charles Poe .05
36 Nilson Robledo .05
37 Juan Thomas .05
38 Archie Vazouez .05
(Vazquez)
39 Bruce Aven .05
40 Russ Branyan 2.50
41 Bartolo Colon 1.50
42 Einar Diaz .05
43 Mike Glavine .25
44 Ricky Gutierrez .15
45 Rick Heiserman .05
46 Richie Sexson 1.25
47 Enrique Wilson .10
48 Jaret Wright 5.00
49 Bryan Corey .05
50 Mike Drumright .10
51 Juan Encarnacion 1.50
52 Brandon Reed .05
53 Bubba Trammell .75
54 Daryle Ward 1.00
55 Jaime Bluma .05
56 Tim Byrdak .05
57 Gary Coffee .05
58 Lino Diaz .05
59 Sal Fasano .05
60 Jed Hansen .05
61 Juan LeBron .10
62 Sean McNally .05
63 Anthony Medrano .05
64 Rodolfo Mendez .05
65 Sergio Nunez .05
66 Mandy Romero .05
67 Glendon Rusch .05
68 Brian Banks .05
69 Jeff D'Amico .60
70 Jonas Hamlin .05
71 Geoff Jenkins 1.25
72 Roberto Lopez .05
73 Gerald Parent .05
74 Doug Webb .10
75 Antone Williamson .40
76 Shane Bowers .05
77 Shane Gunderson .05
78 Corey Koskie .40
79 Jake Patterson .05
80 A.J. Pierzynski .05
81 Mark Redman .05
82 Dan Serafini .10
83 Todd Walker 1.50
84 Chris Corn .05
85 Nick Delvecchio .05
86 Dan Donato .05
87 Matt Drews .60
88 Mike Figga .05
89 Ben Ford .05
90 Marty Janzen .05
91 Shea Morenz .20
92 Ray Ricken .05
93 Shane Spencer 1.50
94 Bob St. Pierre .05
95 Jay Tessmer .15
96 Chris Wilcox .05
97 Steve Cox .25
98 Ben Grieve 6.00
99 Jason McDonald .05
100 Brad Rigby .05
101 Demond Smith .05
102 Jim Bonnici .05
103 Jose Cruz Jr. 5.00
104 Osvaldo Fernandez .15
105 Raul Ibanez .10
106 Desi Relaford .25
107 Marino Santana .05
108 Kevin Brown .50
109 Jeff Davis .05
110 Edwin Diaz .05
111 Jonathan Johnson .05
112 Fernando Tatis 2.00
113 Andrew Vessel .05
114 John Curl .05
115 Ryan Jones .05
116 Julio Mosquera .05
117 Jeff Patzke .05
118 Mike Peeples .05
119 Mark Sievert .05
120 Joe Young .05
121 Winston Abreu .05
122 Anthony Briggs .05
123 Matt Byrd .05
124 Jermaine Dye .25
125 Derrin Ebert .05
126 Wes Helms 1.00
127 Damon Hollins .40
128 Ryan Jacobs .05
129 Andruw Jones 7.50
130 Gus Kennedy .05
131 George Lombard 1.25
132 Damian Moss .75
133 Robert Smith .40
134 Pedro Swann .05
135 Ron Wright 2.00
136 Pat Cline .25
137 Robin Jennings .15
138 Brooks Kieschnick .20
139 Ed Larregui .05
140 Jason Maxwell .05
141 Bobby Morris .05
142 Amaury Telemaco .15
143 Pedro Valdes .05
144 Cedric Allen .05
145 Justin Atchley .05
146 Aaron Boone .40
147 Steve Goodhart .05
148 Chris Murphy .05
149 Christian Rojas .05
150 Terry Wright .05
151 Brent Crowther .05
152 Angel Echevarria .05
153 Derrick Gibson 1.50
154 Todd Helton 3.50
155 Terry Jones .05
156 David Kennedy .05
157 Mike Kusiewicz .05
158 Joel Moore .05
159 Jacob Viano .05
160 Jamey Wright .50
161 Todd Dunwoody 1.00
162 Ryan Jackson .05
163 Billy McMillon .05
164 Ralph Milliard .05
165 Clemente Nunez .10
166 Edgar Renteria .75
167 Chris Sheff .05
168 Matt Whisenant .10
169 Bob Abreu .75
170 Ramon Castro .15
171 Richard Hidalgo 1.25
172 Tony McKnight .20
173 Tony Mounce .05
174 Roberto Duran .05
175 Wilton Guerrero .30
176 Joe Jacobsen .05
177 Paul Konerko 3.50
178 Chris Latham .05
179 Onan Masaoka .50
180 Mike Metcalfe .05
181 Kevin Pincavitch .05
182 Adam Riggs .15
183 David Yocum .05
184 Jake Benz .05
185 Hiram Bocachica .40
186 Brad Fullmer 1.25
187 Vladimir Guerrero 5.00
188 Eric Ludwick .05
189 Carlos Mendoza .05
190 Jarrod Patterson .10
191 Jay Payton 1.25
192 Paul Wilson .40
193 Julio Zorrilla .05
194 Marlon Anderson .05
195 Ron Blazier .05
196 Steve Carver .05
197 Blake Doolan .05
198 David Doster .05
199 Tommy Eason .05
200 Zach Elliott .05
201 Bobby Estalella .75
202 Rob Grable .05
203 Bronson Heflin .05
204 Dan Held .05
205 Kevin Hooker .05
206 Rich Hunter .05
207 Carlton Loewer .15
208 Wendell Magee .25
SAMPLE Wendell Magee 2.00
(Different back design)
209 Len Manning .05
210 Fred McNair .05
211 Ryan Nye .05
212 Scott Rolen 5.00
213 Brian Stumpf .05
214 Reggie Taylor .35
215 Larry Wimberly .05
216 Micah Franklin .10
217 Chad Hermansen 3.00
218 Jason Kendall .50
219 Garrett Long .05
220 Joe Maskivish .05
221 Chris Peters .05
222 Charles Peterson .10
223 Charles Rice .05
224 Reed Secrist .05
225 Derek Swafford .05
226 Mike Busby .05
227 Mike Gulan .05
228 Chris Haas .05
229 Jeff Matulevich .05
230 Steve Montgomery .10
231 Matt Morris .50
232 Bret Wagner .05
233 Gabe Alvarez .15
234 Raul Casanova .15
235 Ben Davis .75
236 Bubba Dixon .05
237 Greg LaRocca .05
238 Derrek Lee 1.00
239 Jason Thompson .25
240 Darin Blood .20
241 Jay Canizaro .05
242 Edwin Corps .05
243 Jacob Cruz 1.00
244 Joe Fontenot .05
245 Jesse Ibarra .35

246	Dante Powell	.75
247	Keith Williams	.15
248	Checklist 1-103	.05
249	Checklist 104-213	.05
250	Checklist 214-250, inserts	.05

1996 Fleer Excel All-Stars

Labeled "can't miss" stars from all minor league levels, the players in this insert set are "up in lights" as the color action photo on front is repeated in the background as if being projected on a scoreboard. The player's name, team and the Fleer Excel All-Star logo are printed in silver holographic foil. Backs have a portrait photo at one side with career highlights on the other. All-Star cards are found, on average, once per 13 packs of Excel.

		MT
Complete Set (10):		25.00
Common Player:		.50
1	Jason Kendall	4.00
2	Steve Cox	1.00
3	Adam Riggs	.50
4	George Arias	.60
5	Wilton Guerrero	1.00
6	Vladimir Guerrero	10.00
7	Andruw Jones	15.00
8	Jay Payton	1.50
9	Raul Ibanez	1.00
10	Paul Wilson	1.00

1996 Fleer Excel Climbing

Players who are "Climbing" their organization's minor league ladder at a faster than usual pace are featured in this insert set. Against a background of colorful, out-of-focus A's (Fleer calls the background "pearlized") is a player action photo. The name and Excel Climbing logo are in gold-foil. On back is a large portrait photo and details of the player's rise through the classifications, printed on a background of green, blue and purple. Climbing inserts are found at an average rate of one per six packs.

		MT
Complete Set (10):		10.00
Common Player:		.50
1	Jeff Abbott	.50
2	Rocky Coppinger	.75
3	Brent Crowther	.50
4	Rich Hunter	.50
5	Chris Latham	.60
6	Wendell Magee	.75
7	Jay Payton	1.25
8	Ray Ricken	.50
9	Scott Rolen	6.00
10	Paul Wilson	1.00

1996 Fleer Excel First Year Phenoms

Potential future superstars in their first year of pro ball are featured in this chase set. Cards feature action photos on a background of garishly colored baseball equipment and silver-foil graphic highlights. Backs have subdued earth tones as a background with a haloed player portrait on one end and a necessarily short career summary at the other end. The First Year Phenoms cards are found, on average, once per three foil packs.

		MT
Complete Set (10):		30.00
Common Player:		.50
1	Gabe Alvarez	.50
2	Jose Cruz Jr.	6.00
3	Ben Davis	2.00
4	Darin Erstad	8.00
5	Todd Helton	6.00
6	Chad Hermansen	4.00
7	Geoff Jenkins	3.00
8	Carlton Loewer	.50
9	Shea Morenz	.50
10	Matt Morris	.50

1996 Fleer Excel Season Crowns

Statistical leaders and award winners from various minor leagues are featured in this chase set. Fronts feature a rich brown tapestry background, with player action photo superimposed. The player's name, Excel logo and large Season Crown title and crown are in silver-foil. Backs have a white version of the tapestry background over which are printed the details of the player's performance. A large color portrait photo on one end completes the design. Season Crown inserts are found at an average rate of one per four packs.

		MT
Complete Set (10):		24.00
Common Player:		.50
1	Matt Beaumont	.50
2	Bartolo Colon	5.00
3	Matt Drews	1.00
4	Derrick Gibson	2.00
5	Vladimir Guerrero	8.00
6	Andruw Jones	10.00
7	Brandon Reed	.50
8	Glendon Rusch	.50
9	Richie Sexson	3.00
10	Shane Spencer	4.00

1996 Fleer Excel Team Leaders

Team offensive statistical leaders are featured on this, the scarcest of the Excel chase sets. Printed on plastic, the cards feature player action poses on a background which includes portions of the team logo. Backs have a portrait photo and information the player's statistical feat. The plastic Team Leaders cards are seeded one per 35 packs, on average.

		MT
Complete Set (10):		25.00
Common Player:		2.00
1	George Arias	2.00
2	Kevin Coughlin	2.00
3	Wilton Guerrero	2.00
4	Dan Held	2.00
5	Brooks Kieschnick	2.00
6	Wendell Magee	3.00
7	Jason McDonald	2.00
8	Adam Riggs	3.00
9	Juan Thomas	2.00
10	Ron Wright	8.00

1996 Signature Rookies Old Judge T-96

Signature Rookies returned for a second year with a smaller than standard size minor league issue; all cards except the checklist are in 2" x 3" format. Because SR contracted with individual players and did not seek Major League Baseball licensing, neither team names nor logos appear on the cards. Most cards have had the major or minor league uniform logos airbrushed off, while some have a fantasy logo added in their place. The set was issued in seven-card foil packs which contain five regular cards, one autographed card and one card from the six insert series. Given the advertised print run, and equal production of each card, about 16,000 of each were available. Fronts of the regular issue cards have a player portrait against a solid color background. Stats on back are complete only through 1994, though some of the career highlights refer to the 1995 season. Fronts of the autographed cards have a line of print added in the top border: "Authentic Signature", and are UV coated. Besides the player autograph on those cards, there is a serial number from within an edition of 6,000.

		MT
Complete Set (38):		2.00
Common Player:		.10
1	Tommy Adams	.15
2	Travis Baptist	.15
3	Mike Birkbeck	.10
4	Jim Bowie	.10
5	Duff Brumley	.10
6	Scott Bullett	.10
7	Frank Catalanotto	.15
8	Chris Cumberland	.15
9	Travis Driskill	.10
10	John Frascatore	.15
11	Brian Giles	.15
12	Vladimir Guerrero	1.50
13	Butch Huskey	.40
14	Greg Keagle	.10
15	Jay Kirkpatrick	.10
16	Ed Larregui	.10
17	Mitch Lyden	.10
18	T.J. Mathews	.10
19	Brian Maxcy	.10
20	Jeff McNeely	.10
21	Tony Mitchell	.10
22	Kerwin Moore	.10
23	Oscar Munoz	.10
24	Les Norman	.10
25	Jayhawk Owens	.10
26	Mark Petkovsek	.15
27	Hugo Pivaral	.10
28	Chad Renfroe	.10
29	Victor Rodriguez	.10
30	Matt Rundels	.10
31	Willie Smith	.10
32	Amaury Telemaco	.10
33	Robert Toth	.10
34	Ben Van Ryn	.10
35	Wes Weger	.10
36	Don Wengert	.10
37	Kelly Wunsch	.10
---	Checklist	.10

1996 Signature Rookies Old Judge T-96 - Autographed

Each pack of SR's Old Judge T-96 Series includes an authentically autographed card. Almost identical to the regular-issue cards, fronts of the autographed cards have a line of print added in the top border: "Authentic Signature", and are UV coated. Besides the player autograph on those cards, there is a serial number from within an edition of 6,000.

		MT
Complete Set, Autographs (37):		125.00
Common Autograph:		2.00
1	Tommy Adams (autographed)	3.00
2	Travis Baptist (autographed)	2.00
3	Mike Birkbeck (autographed)	2.00
4	Jim Bowie (autographed)	2.00
5	Duff Brumley (autographed)	2.00
6	Scott Bullett (autographed)	4.00
7	Frank Catalanotto (autographed)	2.00
8	Chris Cumberland (autographed)	4.00
9	Travis Driskill (autographed)	2.00
10	John Frascatore (autographed)	3.00
11	Brian Giles (autographed)	6.00
12	Vladimir Guerrero (autographed)	24.00
13	Butch Huskey (autographed)	10.00
14	Greg Keagle (autographed)	2.00
15	Jay Kirkpatrick (autographed)	3.00
16	Ed Larregui (autographed)	2.00
17	Mitch Lyden (autographed)	2.00
18	T.J. Mathews (autographed)	2.00
19	Brian Maxcy (autographed)	2.00
20	Jeff McNeely (autographed)	3.00
21	Tony Mitchell (autographed)	2.00
22	Kerwin Moore (autographed)	2.00
23	Oscar Munoz (autographed)	2.00
24	Les Norman (autographed)	2.00
25	Jayhawk Owens (autographed)	4.00
26	Mark Petkovsek (autographed)	5.00
27	Hugo Pivaral (autographed)	2.00
28	Chad Renfroe (autographed)	2.00
29	Victor Rodriguez (autographed)	4.00
30	Matt Rundels (autographed)	2.00
31	Willie Smith (autographed)	2.00
32	Amaury Telemaco (autographed)	4.00
33	Robert Toth (autographed)	2.00
34	Ben Van Ryn (autographed)	2.00
35	Wes Weger (autographed)	2.00
36	Don Wengert (autographed)	3.00
37	Kelly Wunsch (autographed)	4.00

1996 Signature Rookies Old Judge T-96 Junior Hit Man

Ken Griffey, Jr., is the featured player in this insert set. Each card pictures him in action on the UV-coated borderless front photo. His name and the set logo are in gold foil. Backs, also UV coated, have a portrait photo, stats and a few words about Junior, all on a red and white bull's eye background. Cards are numbered with a "J" prefix. Each card can be found in a regular and an autographed version.

		MT
Complete Set (5):		15.00
Complete Set, Autographed (5):		400.00
Common Card:		3.00
Autographed Card:		75.00
1	Ken Griffey Jr.	3.00
1a	Ken Griffey Jr. (autographed)	75.00
2	Ken Griffey Jr.	3.00
2a	Ken Griffey Jr. (autographed)	75.00
3	Ken Griffey Jr.	3.00
3a	Ken Griffey Jr. (autographed)	75.00
4	Ken Griffey Jr.	3.00
4a	Ken Griffey Jr. (autographed)	75.00
5	Ken Griffey Jr.	3.00
5a	Ken Griffey Jr. (autographed)	75.00

1996 Signature Rookies Old Judge T-96 Major Respect

Five players whose major league careers began with a bang are the subject of this insert set. UV-coated cards have player action photos on a background of red rays with a purple "MAJOR RESPECT" logo at bottom. The player's name is in gold foil down the side. Backs have the standard stats, player data and career notes along with a portrait photo. All uniform logos have been airbrushed off since the cards are not licensed by Major League Baseball. Card numbers have an "M" prefix. Each card can be found in both an unautographed form and authentically signed.

		MT
	Complete Set (5):	3.00
	Complete Set, Autographed (5):	100.00
	Common Player:	.75
	Common Autograph:	30.00
1	Alex Rodriguez	1.50
1a	Alex Rodriguez (autographed)	45.00
2	Johnny Damon	.75
2a	Johnny Damon (autographed)	20.00
3	Karim Garcia	1.00
3a	Karim Garcia (autographed)	30.00
4	Garrett Anderson	.75
4a	Garrett Anderson (autographed)	20.00
5	Bill Pulsipher	.75
5a	Bill Pulsipher (autographed)	15.00

1996 Signature Rookies Old Judge T-96 Peak Picks

Some of the top picks of the 1995 draft are shown in this insert issue. Fronts have borderless action photos of the players in their college uniforms. "PEAK PICKS" and their names are in gold foil. Backs have a close-up picture, vital data, college and 1995 minor league stats and a few words about the player's college career. Cards are UV coated both front and back and carry a "P" prefix to the number. Each card can be found in an authentically autographed version, as well as unsigned.

		MT
	Complete Set (10):	10.00
	Complete Set, Autographed (10):	100.00
	Common Player:	.50
	Common Autograph:	10.00
1	Darin Erstad	3.00
1a	Darin Erstad (autographed)	30.00
2	Jose Cruz, Jr.	3.00
2a	Jose Cruz, Jr. (autographed)	20.00
3	Jonathan Johnson	.50
3a	Jonathan Johnson (autographed)	4.00
4	Todd Helton	2.00
4a	Todd Helton (autographed)	25.00
5	Matt Morris	.50
5a	Matt Morris (autographed)	8.00
6	Tony McKnight	.50
6a	Tony McKnight (autographed)	4.00
7	Reggie Taylor	.50
7a	Reggie Taylor (autographed)	4.00
8	David Yocum	.50
8a	David Yocum (autographed)	4.00
9	Shea Morenz	.50
9a	Shea Morenz (autographed)	6.00
10	Ben Davis	2.00
10a	Ben Davis (autographed)	20.00

1996 Signature Rookies Old Judge T-96 Rising Stars

Five players projected to be major league stars are the focus of this insert set. Cards are UV-coated on each side. Fronts have borderless color action photos with the player name and "Rising Stars" logo in gold foil. Backs have a portrait photo, biographical details and complete minor league stats through 1995. Because the cards are licensed only with individual players and collegiate authorities, minor and major league uniform logos have been removed from the photos. Each card can be found in both an autographed and unautographed version. Cards are numbered with a "R" prefix.

		MT
	Complete Set (5):	3.00
	Complete Set, Autographed (5):	50.00
	Common Player:	.25
	Common Autograph:	6.00
1	Jermaine Dye	.50
1a	Jermaine Dye (autographed)	8.00
2	Ben Grieve	2.00
2a	Ben Grieve (autographed)	35.00
3	Ryan Helms	.25
3a	Ryan Helms (autographed)	6.00
4	Jeff Darwin	.25
4a	Jeff Darwin (autographed)	6.00
5	Alan Benes	1.00
5a	Alan Benes (autographed)	10.00

1996 Signature Rookies Old Judge T-96 Rookie/Year

American League Rookie of the Year Marty Cordova is the focus of this insert set. Each card pictures him in a borderless game-action photo. His name and the set logo are in gold foil. Backs have another photo, full stats, vital data and a few words about the player. The card number is preceded by a "RY" prefix. Twins logos have been airbrushed off the photos. Besides the regular version, each card can be found authentically autographed.

		MT
	Complete Set (5):	2.00
	Complete Set, Autographed (5):	35.00
	Common Card:	.25
	Autographed Card:	8.00
1	Marty Cordoua	.50
1a	Marty Cordova (autographed)	8.00
2	Marty Cordova	.50
2a	Marty Cordova (autographed)	8.00
3	Marty Cordova	.50
3a	Marty Cordova (autographed)	8.00
4	Marty Cordova	.50
4a	Marty Cordova (autographed)	8.00
5	Marty Cordova	.50
5a	Marty Cordova (autographed)	8.00

1996 Signature Rookies Old Judge T-96 Top Prospect

Ten of the minor leagues' best players are featured in this insert set. UV-coated on both sides, fronts have an action photo on a white background with the player's name in gold foil. Backs have a portrait photo, complete pro stats through the 1995 season and a few personal details. Cards are numbered with a "T" prefix.

		MT
	Complete Set (10):	2.00
	Complete Autographed Set (10):	45.00
	Common Player:	.25
	Common Autograph:	4.00
1	Juan Acevedo	.50
1a	Juan Acevedo (autographed)	8.00
2	Mike Bovee	.25
2a	Mike Bovee (autographed)	4.00
3	Mark Hubbard	.25
3a	Mark Hubbard (autographed)	4.00
4	Luis Raven	.25
4a	Luis Raven (autographed)	4.00
5	Desi Relaford	.75
5a	Desi Relaford (autographed)	8.00
6	Antone Williamson	.50
6a	Antone Williamson (autographed)	6.00
7	Nick Delvecchio	.25
7a	Nick Delvecchio (autographed)	4.00
8	Andy Larkin	.25
8a	Andy Larkin (autographed)	4.00
9	Kris Ralston	.25
9a	Kris Ralston (autographed)	4.00
10	Jeff Suppan	.75
10a	Jeff Suppan (autographed)	8.00

1996 Signature Rookies Ken Griffey Jr.

This five-card set features logoless front and back photos of Ken Griffey Jr. Fronts have his name in both red ink and gold foil. Backs have personal data, stats and a few kind words.

		MT
	Common Card:	1.00
G1-G5	Ken Griffey Jr.	

1996 Minor League Team Sets

For 1996, Best leapt into the void created by the pull-back of Classic and Fleer from the minor league team set market, claiming a 75% share of the approximately 175 team sets issued. Many other teams issued their sets independently or with small regional graphics firms such as Grandstand (GS). Availability of many teams sets continued to outstrip player popularity as a factor in determining prices in the hobby market.

	MT
183 team sets and variations	
1996 Best AA All-Stars (56)	20.00
1996 GS Abilene Prairie Dogs (28)	7.00
1996 GS Alexandria Aces (26)	7.00
1996 GS Amarillo Dillas (19)	7.00
1996 Best Appalachian League Prospects (30)	13.00
1996 Best Arkansas Travelers (29)	20.00
1996 Best Asheville Tourists (30)	11.00
1996 Best Auburn Doubledays (30)	9.50
1996 Best Augusta Greenjackets (29)	75.00
1996 Team Batavia Clippers (34)	11.00
1996 Team Bellingham Giants (36)	13.50
1996 Team Beloit Snappers (36)	25.00
1996 Team Billings Mustangs (31)	65.00
1996 Best Binghampton Mets (30)	9.50
1996 Best Birmingham Barons (30)	8.00
1996 Best Bluefield Orioles (30)	16.00
1996 Best Boise Hawks (30)	12.00
1996 Best Bowie Baysox (27)	7.50
1996 Best Brevard County Manatees (30)	9.50
1996 Best Bristol White Sox (30)	9.00
1996 Best Buffalo Bisons (24)	9.00
1996 Team Burlington Bees (33)	35.00
1996 Best Burlington Indians (30)	9.50
1996 Best Butte Copper Kings (30)	8.00
1996 Best Canton-Akron Indians (30)	14.50
1996 Best Carolina Mudcats (30)	9.00
1996 Best Carolina League/Modesto A-S (26)	15.00
1996 Best Carolina/ Modesto sponsor's set (36)	45.00
1996 Best Carolina/ Modesto insert set (10)	100.00
1996 Team Cedar Rapids Kernels (34)	11.00
1996 Team Charleston RiverDogs (32)	45.00
1996 Best Charlotte Knights (29)	11.00
1996 Best Chattanooga Lookouts (30)	10.00
1996 Team Clinton Lumberkings (30)	37.50
1996 Team Colorado Springs Sky Sox (34)	11.00
1996 Best Columbus Clippers (30)	9.00
1996 Police Columbus Clippers (25)	9.00
1996 Team Columbus Clippers POGs (24)	35.00
1996 Best Danville Braves (30)	27.50
1996 Best Daytona Cubs (30)	60.00
1996 Best Delmarva Shorebirds (30)	60.00
1996 Best Dunedin Blue Jays (30)	15.00
1996 Team Dunedin Blue Jays (30)	36.00
1996 Team Dunedin Blue Jays update (18)	30.00
1996 Best Durham Bulls, blue (30)	45.00
1996 Best Durham Bulls update, brown (30)	30.00
1996 Team Edmonton Trappers (xx)	50.00
1996 Best El Paso Diablos (30)	12.00
1996 Best Erie Sea Wolves (25)	21.00
1996 Best Eugene Emeralds (27)	14.00
1996 Best Everett Aquasox (30)	9.00
1996 Best Fayetteville Generals (30)	45.00
1996 Best Frederick Keys (30)	11.00
1996 Best Ft. Myers Miracle (30)	14.00
1996 Best Ft. Wayne Wizards (31)	9.50
1996 Team Grays Harbor Gulls (26)	7.00

1996 Best Great Falls Dodgers (30)	20.00
1996 Team Great Falls Dodgers (35)	21.00
1996 Best Greensboro Bats (30)	32.00
1996 Best Greenville Braves (30)	25.00
1996 Team/Coke Greenville Braves (30)	47.00
1996 Best Hagerstown Suns (30)	10.00
1996 Best Hardware City Rock Cats (30)	10.00
1996 Best Harrisburg Senators (29)	35.00
1996 Team Helena Brewers (34)	42.50
1996 Best Hickory Crawdads (30)	24.00
1996 Best High Desert Mavericks (30)	9.00
1996 Police High Desert Mavericks (24)	20.00
1996 Team Hilo Stars (36)	15.00
1996 Team Honolulu Sharks (35)	19.00
1996 Best Hudson Valley Renegades (30)	9.50
1996 Burger King Huntsville Stars (28)	85.00
1996 BK Huntsville Stars uncut sheet	125.00
1996 Team Idaho Falls Braves (32)	10.00
1996 Best Indianapolis Indians (30)	7.50
1996 Best Iowa Cubs (30)	9.00
1996 Best Jackson Generals (27)	15.00
1996 Smokey Bear Jackson Generals (27)	17.50
1996 Best Jacksonville Suns (30)	17.50
1996 Best Johnson City Cardinals (35)	14.00
1996 Team Kane County Cougars (31)	11.00
1996 Team Kane Co. Cougars - Connie's (30)	28.00
1996 Team Kane County Cougars - gold (30)	16.00
1996 Team Kane County Cougars update (13)	32.00
1996 Best Kinston Indians (30)	24.00
1996 Best Kissimmee Cobras (30)	9.00
1996 Best Knoxville Smokies (25)	10.00
1996 Best Lake Elsinore Storm (30)	11.00
1996 Best Lakeland Tigers (30)	14.00
1996 Best Lancaster Jethawks (30)	17.00
1996 Best Lansing Lugnuts (30)	110.00
1996 Best Las Vegas Stars (30)	10.00
1996 Best Lethbridge Black Diamonds (33)	13.00
1996 Best Louisville Redbirds (29)	12.00
1996 Best Lowell Spinners (30)	10.00
1996 GS Lubbock Crickets (24)	6.50
1996 Best Lynchburg Hillcats (30)	29.00
1996 Best Lynchburg Hillcats update (1)	10.00
1996 Best Macon Braves (30)	14.00
1996 Best Martinsville Phillies (30)	10.00
1996 Mascots of the Midwest League (12)	6.00
1996 Team Maui Stingrays (36)	19.00
1996 Team Medicine Hat Blue Jays (33)	47.50
1996 Best Memphis Chicks (30)	18.00
1996 Team Meridian Brakemen (24)	8.00
1996 Best Michigan Battle Cats (30)	15.00
1996 Best Midland Angels (29)	9.50
1996 Team Midland Angels (24)	70.00
1996 Best Midwest League A-S (58)	10.00
1996 Best Modesto A's (30)	24.00
1996 Best Nashville Sounds (30)	8.00
1996 Team Nashville Sounds foldout	25.00
1996 Best New Haven Ravens (31)	18.00
1996 Best New Haven Ravens (32)	24.00
1996 Team New Haven Ravens raffle sheet	10.00
1996 Best New Jersey Cardinals (30)	9.00
1996 Best Norfolk Tides (30)	11.00
1996 Best Norwich Navigators (28)	7.50
1996 Team Norwich Navigators update (12)	23.00
1996 Team Ogden Raptors (39)	11.50
1996 Best Oklahoma City 89ers (28)	8.00
1996 Best Omaha Royals (30)	14.00
1996 Best Orlando Cubs (30)	9.00
1996 DD Pawtucket Red Sox foldout	47.50
1996 Best Peoria Chiefs (30)	17.50
1996 Best Phoenix Firebirds (30)	9.00
1996 Team Phoenix Firebirds (30)	9.00
1996 Best Piedmont Boll Weevils (30)	325.00
1996 Best Pittsfield Mets (30)	14.00
1996 Best Port City Roosters (29)	8.00
1996 Best Portland Rockies (30)	9.00
1996 Best Portland Sea Dogs (29)	67.50
1996 Best Prince William Cannons (30)	9.50
1996 Best Quad City River Bandits (29)	9.00
1996 Best Rancho Cucamonga Quakes (30)	9.50
1996 Best Reading Phillies (29)	25.00
1996 Best Richmond Braves (30)	9.50
1996 Best Richmond Braves update (30)	35.00
1996 Richmond Camera Richmond Braves (25)	110.00
1996 Team Richmond Braves alumni (6)	37.50
1996 GS Rio Grande Valley White Wings (23)	6.00
1996 Best Rochester Red Wings (30)	10.00
1996 Team Rockford Cubbies (32)	14.00
1996 Best Salem Avalanche (30)	9.00
1996 Best San Antonio Missions (30)	11.00
1996 HEB San Antonio Missions (32)	60.00
1996 Best San Bernardino Stampede (30)	8.00
1996 Best San Jose Giants (30)	9.50
1996 Best Sarasota Red Sox (30)	9.50
1996 Best Savannah Sandgnats (30)	80.00
1996 Best Scranton/W-B Red Barons (30)	9.50
1996 Team Sioux City Explorers (30)	7.50
1996 Best South Bend Silver Hawks (28)	12.00
1996 Team Southern Oregon Timberjacks (28)	65.00
1996 Best Spokane Indians (30)	22.00
1996 Best St. Catherines Stompers (30)	15.00
1996 Team St. Lucie Mets (36)	16.00
1996 Best St. Petersburg Cardinals (30)	9.00
1996 Best Stockton Ports (30)	10.00
1996 Team Syracuse Chiefs (30)	13.50
1996 Best Tacoma Rainiers (30)	8.00
1996 Best Tampa Yankees (29)	10.00
1996 Best Texas League All-Stars (36)	14.00
1996 Team Thunder Bay Whiskey Jacks (25)	7.00
1996 Best Toledo Mud Hens (30)	8.00
1996 Best Trenton Thunder (30)	17.50
1996 Best Tucson Toros (29)	9.00
1996 Team Tulsa Drillers (30)	10.00
1996 Team Tulsa 20th anniversary (32)	21.00
1996 GS Tyler Wildcatters (25)	6.50
1996 Best Vancouver Canadians (30)	19.00
1996 Best Vermont Expos (30)	10.00
1996 Best Vero Beach Dodgers (30)	50.00
1996 Team Watertown Indians (36)	12.50
1996 Best West Michigan Whitecaps (30)	12.50
1996 Team West Oahu Canefires (36)	20.00
1996 Best West Palm Beach Expos (31)	65.00
1996 Best Wichita Wranglers (30)	14.00
1996 Team Wichita Wranglers (18)	14.00
1996 Best Wilmington Blue Rocks (30)	9.50
1996 Best Wisconsin Timber Rattlers (30)	15.00
1996 Team Yakima Bears (35)	16.00
1996 Team Zanesville Greys (23)	6.00

1997 Best Autograph Series

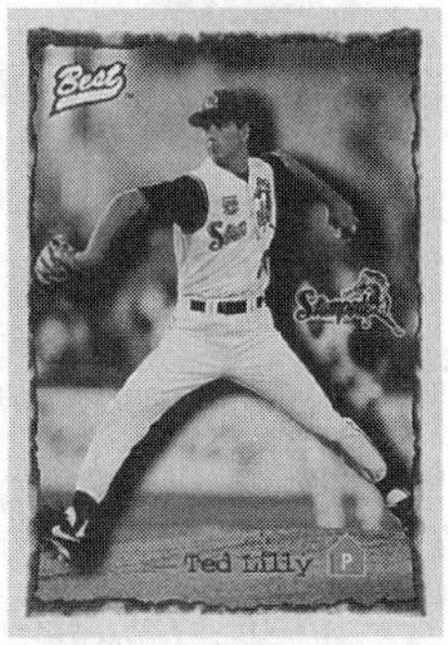

This end-of-year product showcases minor league talent which developed during the season including cards of 1997 draft picks and players who climbed their organizational ladder. The series is numbered 51-100 in continuation of the early-season Best Prospects issue. Cards were sold in foil packs with four regular cards and an autographed card. Fronts have action photos on a ragged-edged background with Best and team logos. Backs have a portrait photo, player data, highlights and stats.

		MT
Complete Set (50):		20.00
Common Player:		.25
51	Mike Stoner	.40
52	George Lombard	.50
53	Calvin Pickering	1.00
54	Antonio Armas	.50
55	John Barnes	.30
56	Russell Branyan	.75
57	Sean Casey	1.00
58	Edgard Velasquez	.35
59	Mike Vavrek	.25
60	Magglio Ordonez	1.50
61	Mike Caruso	.35
62	Pat Cline	.25
63	Courtney Duncan	.25
64	Juan Encarnacion	.75
65	Jason Varitek	.25
66	Alex Gonzalez	.75
67	Ryan Jackson	.25
68	Kevin Millar	.50
69	John Roskos	.25
70	Daryle Ward	.75
71	Dermal Brown	.75
72	Ted Lilly	.25
73	Chad Green	.50
74	David Ortiz	.50
75	Jacque Jones	.50
76	Luis Rivas	.25
77	Orlando Cabrera	.25
78	Javier Vazquez	.35
79	Jesus Sanchez	.25
80	Eric Milton	.50
81	Ricky Ledee	.75
82	Ramon Hernandez	.50
83	A.J. Hinch	.50
84	Marlon Anderson	.50
85	Ryan Brannan	.25
86	Abraham Nunez	.25
87	Matt Clement	.50
88	Kerry Robinson	.25
89	Cliff Politte	.35
90	Pablo Ortega	.25
91	Aramis Ramirez	.75
92	Eric Chavez	1.00
93	Brent Butler	.50
94	Cole Liniak	.50
95	Travis Lee	1.00
96	Adrian Beltre	1.50
97	Paul Konerko	.75
98	Brad Fullmer	.50
99	Jeremy Giambi	.50
100	Gil Meche	.35

1997 Best Autograph Series Autographs

Inserted one per pack, the 45 players in this series include two dozen of the first round draft picks of 1997. Each player autographed 250 cards, which are serially numbered on back. Autographed cards are listed here in alphabetical order.

		MT
Complete Set (44):		485.00
Common Player:		7.00
(1)	Richard Almanzar	7.00
(2)	Kris Benson	30.00
(3)	Darin Blood	11.00
(4)	Adrian Brown	7.00
(5)	Dermal Brown	25.00
(6)	Kevin Brown	24.00
(7)	Eric Chavez	40.00
(8)	D.T. Cromer	7.00
(9)	Lorenzo de la Cruz	7.00
(10)	Adam Eaton	7.00
(11)	Nelson Figueroa	7.00
(12)	Juan Gonzalez	7.00
(13)	Chad Green	15.00
(14)	Seth Greisinger	7.00
(15)	Ben Grieve	50.00
(16)	Matt Halloran	7.00
(17)	Chad Hermansen	35.00
(18)	Mark Johnson	7.00
(19)	Billy Koch	15.00
(20)	Paul Konerko	25.00
(21)	Mark Kotsay	25.00
(22)	Joe Lawrence	7.00
(23)	Braden Looper	7.00
(24)	Gil Meche	7.00
(25)	Eric Milton	15.00
(26)	Abraham Nunez	7.00
(27)	John Oliver	7.00
(28)	Russell Ortiz	11.00
(29)	John Patterson	7.00
(30)	Carl Pavano	17.50
(31)	Elvis Pena	7.00
(32)	Danny Peoples	7.00
(33)	Neifi Perez	18.50
(34)	Sidney Ponson	11.00
(35)	Aramis Ramirez	24.00
(36)	Britt Reames	7.00
(37)	Kerry Robinson	7.00
(38)	Bubba Trammell	12.00
(39)	Mike Villano	7.00
(40)	Jake Westbrook	15.00
(41)	Paul Wilder	15.00
(42)	Enrique Wilson	15.00
(43)	Kerry Wood	40.00
(44)	A.J. Zapp	18.50

1997 Best Autograph Series Cornerstone

A dozen of the biggest names in the minor leagues are featured in this insert set as future cornerstones of Major League teams. Backs have a close-up photo of that on front and typical player data, highlights and stats. Insertion rate was given as one per 49 packs.

		MT
Complete Set (12):		175.00
Common Player:		8.00
1	Travis Lee	30.00
2	Adrian Beltre	30.00
3	Ben Grieve	35.00
4	Paul Konerko	15.00
5	Ricky Ledee	15.00
6	Brad Fullmer	15.00
7	Alex Gonzalez	8.00
8	Russell Branyan	15.00
9	Eric Milton	15.00
10	Jaret Wright	12.00
11	Derrek Lee	15.00
12	Kris Benson	15.00

1997 Best Autograph Series Diamond Best II

Younger minor league stars are featured in this insert set carried over from the Best Prospects issue earlier in the year. Cards have action photos on a white background with a large team logo. Backs repeat the photo and logo in smaller size and provide player data and stats.

		MT
Complete Set (10):		60.00
Common Player:		5.00
11	Dermal Brown	10.00
12	Aramis Ramirez	8.00
13	Ramon Hernandez	8.00
14	Eric Chavez	12.00
15	A.J. Zapp	10.00
16	A.J. Hinch	5.00
17	Juan Melo	5.00
18	Cole Liniak	7.50
19	David Ortiz	5.00
20	Russell Branyan	8.00

1997 Best Autograph Series Premium Preview

These cards were inserted one per box as a box-topper to promote box purchases. Each card is numbered within an edition of 200. Fronts have color action photos against a ghost-image black-and-white photo.

Backs repeat the fronts' background photo and have a small close-up of the color picture. Personal data, stats and highlights are given on back, as well.

		MT
Complete Set (50):		300.00
Common Player:		4.00
1	Jaret Wright	12.00
2	Damian Jackson	4.00
3	Kerry Wood	25.00
4	Adrian Beltre	25.00
5	Sean Casey	25.00
6	Paul Konerko	15.00
7	Ben Grieve	30.00
8	Hideki Irabu	6.00
9	Rolando Arrojo	6.00
10	Robinson Checo	4.00
11	Donnie Sadler	4.00
12	Todd Helton	30.00
13	Jose Cruz Jr.	10.00
14	Ricky Ledee	15.00
15	Calvin Pickering	12.00
16	Alex Gonzalez	7.50
17	Alvie Shepherd	4.00
18	Michael Coleman	4.00
19	Derrick Lee	4.00
20	Brad Fullmer	10.00
21	Derrick Gibson	15.00
22	A.J. Hinch	5.00
23	Juan Melo	5.00
24	David Ortiz	10.00
25	Ramon Hernandez	15.00
26	Mike Stoner	10.00
27	George Lombard	10.00
28	Chad Hermansen	25.00
29	Mark Fischer	4.00
30	Trot Nixon	6.00
31	Kevin Nicholson	4.00
32	Kevin Millar	8.00
33	John Roskos	4.00
35	Randall Simon	15.00
36	Carl Pavano	10.00
37	Brian Rose	8.00
38	Enrique Wilson	6.00
39	Russell Branyan	15.00
40	Chan Perry	6.00
41	Juan Encarnacion	10.00
42	Grant Roberts	10.00
43	Marlon Anderson	4.00
44	Matt White	15.00
45	Jason Varitek	12.00
46	Cole Liniak	10.00
47	Roy Halladay	8.00
48	Magglio Ordonez	20.00
50	Travis Lee	20.00

1997 Best Prospects Promos

Some of the hottest players in the minor leagues at the start of 1997 were chosen by Best to showcase its 1997 "Prospects" issue. Fronts are virtually identical to the regular-issue cards, with action photos and team and Best logos. Backs of the 2-1/2" x 3-1/2" cards are in full color and include the issue's logo and a large team logo. A green strip at top center reads "FOR PROMOTIONAL PURPOSES ONLY". The unnumbered promo cards are checklisted here in alphabetical order.

		MT
Complete Set (5):		18.00
Common Player:		3.00
(1)	Kris Benson	3.00
(2)	Hideki Irabu	4.00
(3)	Travis Lee	5.00
(4)	Matt White	3.00
(5)	Kerry Wood	5.00

1997 Best Prospects

The basic set of minor league player cards from Best in 1997 includes 50 top prospects. Fronts of the 2-1/2" x 3-1/2" cards have action photos with Best and team logos superimposed. Player name is in typewriter style at bottom, with his position abbreviated in a red home plate. Backs have a close-up version of the front photo, a black box at top with personal data, an overall purple background and 1996 stats at bottom. Cards were issued in six-card foil packs with 18 packs per box. Several insert sets are included in the issue.

		MT
Complete Set (50):		10.00
Common Player:		.10
1	Kerry Wood	1.00
2	Matt White	.50
3	Travis Lee	1.00
4	Miguel Tejada	.75
5	Kris Benson	.30
6	Paul Konerko	.30
7	Jose Cruz, Jr.	.50
8	Derrek Lee	.15
9	Todd Helton	1.00
10	Carl Pavano	.30
11	Ben Grieve	.75
12	Richard Hidalgo	.20
13	Chad Hermansen	.50
14	Jaret Wright	.25
15	Roy Halladay	.25
16	Hideki Irabu	.50
17	Matt Morris	.10
18	Aramis Ramirez	.35
19	Robinson Checo	.10
20	Chris Carpenter	.20
21	Adrian Beltre	1.50
22	Braden Looper	.10
23	Luis Rolando Arrojo	.30
24	Juan Melo	.10
25	Elieser Marrero	.25
26	Kevin McGlinchy	.30
27	Sidney Ponson	.15
28	John Patterson	.30
29	Brian Rose	.30
30	Joe Fontonot	.10
31	Chris Reitsma	.10
32	Paul Wilder	.20
33	Ron Wright	.20
34	A.J. Zapp	.40
35	Donnie Sadler	.10
36	Valerio DeLosSantos	.10
37	Eric Chavez	.75
38	Jake Westbrook	.20
39	Seth Greisinger	.20
40	Derrick Gibson	.35
41	Ben Davis	.15
42	Rafael Medina	.10
43	Britt Reames	.10
44	Ben Petrick	.75
45	Josh Paul	.10
46	Brad Fullmer	.40
47	Jarrod Washburn	.25
48	Kevin Escobar	.20
49	Manuel Aybar	.25
50	Wes Helms	.25

1997 Best Prospects Autographs

Ten of the best prospects in the minor leagues are featured in this insert set. Fronts feature action photos vignetted against a white background. The Best logo is printed at top-left, while a holographic-foil "Best Prospects" logo is at upper-right. The player name and team logo are at bottom. Backs have a Best Autograph Series logo ghosted on a white background, and a congratulatory message in orange and black. Stated rate of insertion for the autographed cards is one per box (18 packs). The autographed cards are not numbered. An announced Jeff Liefer card was replaced by Wes Helms.

		MT
Complete Set (10):		70.00
Common Autograph:		4.00
(1)	Ben Grieve	25.00
(2)	Wes Helms	12.00
(3)	Brett Herbison	4.00
(4)	Chad Hermansen	20.00
(5)	Geoff Jenkins	12.00
(6)	Paul Konerko	20.00
(7)	Ben Petrick	10.00
(8)	Donnie Sadler	4.00
(9)	Randall Simon	10.00
(10)	Brett Tomko	8.00

1997 Best Prospects All Stars

		MT
Complete Set (15):		18.00
Common Player:		.50
1	Seth Greisinger	.50
2	Hideki Irabu	2.50
3	Josh Paul	.50
4	Jaret Wright	4.00
5	Norm Hutchins	.50
6	Miguel Tejada	2.50
7	Ruben Mateo	2.50
8	Matt White	1.50
9	Marc Lewis	.75
10	Jose Cruz	5.00
11	Quincy Carter	.50
12	Kris Benson	1.50
13	Ben Petrick	.50
14	Adrian Beltre	3.50
15	Travis Lee	5.00

1997 Best Prospects Best Bets Preview

With only 200 hand-numbered cards of each player issued, these are the toughest pull among the Best Prospects inserts, being found on average only one per 90 packs. Fronts have an action photo against a background of red bricks and green stripes. Team and manufacturer logos are also featured on front. Backs have a close-up version of the front photo on a background of green stripes and a black polygon. Cards are individually numbered at top-right.

		MT
Complete Set (10):		160.00
Common Player:		5.00
1	Miguel Tejada	40.00
2	Adrian Beltre	40.00
3	Hideki Irabu	15.00
4	Kris Benson	25.00
5	Matt White	10.00
6	Travis Lee	30.00
7	Corey Erickson	5.00
8	Jose Cruz	15.00
9	Marc Lewis	8.00
10	Luis Rolando Arrojo	10.00

1997 Best Prospects Best Five

The field of best minor leaguers is whittled to five for this insert set. Rather than being issued inside the foil packs, these cards are placed one per box as a dealer premium. A close-up baseball design is used for a background on both front and back. An action photo dominates the front with a "Best 5" logo at top and player ID at bottom, along with his team logo. Backs have personal data, career highlights and stats, along with a small detail of the front photo.

		MT
Complete Set (5):		10.00
Common Player:		1.00
1	Kris Benson	2.00
2	Kerry Wood	5.00
3	Travis Lee	4.00
4	Hideki Irabu	2.00
5	Matt White	1.50

1997 Best Prospects Best Guns

Top minor league pitchers are featured in this retail-only insert. One card was inserted atop the packs in each box.

		MT
Complete Set (10):		20.00
Common Player:		1.50
1	Robinson Checo	1.50
2	Rolando Arrojo	2.50
3	Clayton Bruner	1.50
4	Grant Roberts	2.50
5	Brian Rose	1.50
6	Carl Pavano	3.00
7	Kerry Wood	6.00
8	Kris Benson	2.50
9	Jaret Wright	4.00
10	Cliff Politte	1.50

1997 Best Prospects Best Lumber

The scarcest of three retail-only inserts in Best Prospects issue is this run of potentially big hitters. The Best Lumber cards are found only on average of one per five boxes.

		MT
Complete Set (10):		120.00
Common Player:		8.00
1	Paul Konerko	15.00
2	Derrick Lee	8.00
3	Ricky Ledee	12.00
4	Brad Fullmer	10.00
5	Ben Grieve	30.00
6	Russ Branyon	12.00
7	A.J. Hinch	8.00
8	Adrian Beltre	20.00
9	Mike Stoner	8.00
10	Travis Lee	25.00

1997 Best Prospects Best Wheels

The speed merchants of the minor leagues are featured in this retail-only Best Propsects insert. Cards are random pack inserts at a rate of one per box.

		MT
Complete Set (5):		20.00
Common Player:		2.00
1	Donnie Sadler	2.00
2	Juan Encarnacion	5.00
3	Damian Jackson	3.00
4	Chad Green	3.00
5	Mark Kotsay	8.00

1997 Best Prospects Diamond Best

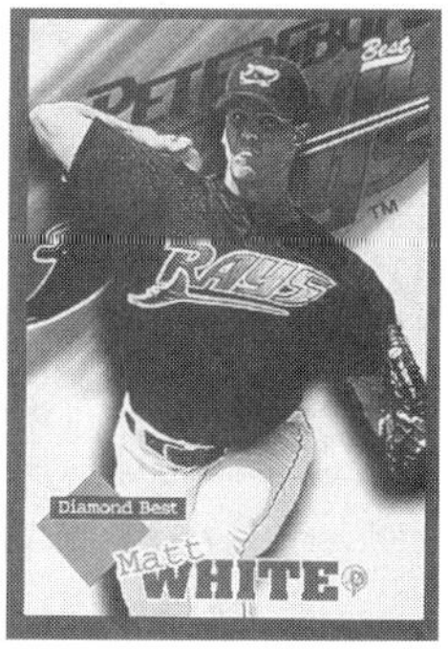

Seeded at a rate of fewer than one per box (about every 19 packs), this insert set features arguably the top 10 minor league players of 1996. Fronts of the 2-1/2" x 3-1/2" cards have a white background surrounded by a blue border. An action photo is superimposed on a large team logo. The "Diamond Best" logo, player name and position are in red, white and blue at bottom. Backs have a second version of the player photo on a white background streaked with gray. A red box has career highlights; personal data is at right.

		MT
Complete Set (10):		25.00
Common Player:		1.00
1	Hideki Irabu	2.00
2	Kerry Wood	5.00
3	Matt White	2.50
4	Travis Lee	5.00
5	Miguel Tejada	4.00
6	Kris Benson	2.00
7	Paul Konerko	2.00
8	Jose Cruz	2.00
9	Derrek Lee	1.00
10	Todd Helton	5.00

1997 Minor League Team Sets

The number of team sets increased a bit for 1997. Market leader Best again produced more than 100 teams' sets. A newcomer, Grandstand (GS in the listings), produced 17 team sets and updates, mostly for teams in the Western U.S. A developing trend in 1997 was the growth of formats other than single cards, such as strips and sheets, and the issue of late-season or post-season update sets.

	MT
199 team sets and variations	
1997 Team Aberdeen Pheasants (28)	8.00
1997 Team Abilene Prairie Dogs (30)	7.00
1997 Best Akron Aeros (31)	14.00
1997 GS Albuquerque Dukes (30)	12.00
1997 GS Albuquerque Dukes Update (5)	6.00
1997 GS Alexandria Aces (26)	7.00
1997 Team Amarillo Dillas (21)	7.00
1997 Best Appalachian League Propsects (30)	11.00
1997 Arizona Fall League (21)	12.50
1997 Best Arkansas Travelers (30)	9.00
1997 Best Asheville Tourists (30)	9.00
1997 Team Auburn Doubledays (30)	8.50
1997 Best Augusta Greenjackets (30)	9.00
1997 Team Bakersfield Blaze (30)	8.00
1997 Team Bakersfield Blaze w/Pepsi ads (30)	8.00
1997 Team Batavia Clippers (32)	9.00
1997 Best Beloit Snappers (30)	9.00
1997 GS Bend Bandits (27)	7.50
1997 Team Billings Mustangs (36)	75.00
1997 Best Binghampton Mets (32)	9.00
1997 Magic Prints Binghampton Mets (5)	18.00
1997 Best Birmingham Barons (30)	7.50
1997 GS Boise Hawks (32)	15.00
1997 Best Bowie Baysox (29)	35.00
1997 Best Brevard County Manatees (31)	9.00
1997 Best Bristol Sox (30)	8.00
1997 Best Buffalo Bisons (30)	9.00
1997 Best Burlington Bees (31)	14.00
1997 GS Burlington Indians (31)	11.00
1997 Best Butte Copper Kings (30)	8.00
1997 Best Butte C.K. w/ sponsors' ads (30)	8.00
1997 Best Calgary Cannons (30)	35.00
1997 Team Calgary Cannons (36)	75.00
1997 Best California League Prospects (31)	17.50
1997 Best California-Carolina League A-S (50)	16.00
1997 Best Capital City Bombers (30)	24.00
1997 Best Carolina Legue Prospects (31)	14.00
1997 Best Carolina Mudcats (29)	9.00
1997 GS Cedar Rapids Kernels (30)	17.00
1997 GS Charleston RiverDogs (29)	9.00
1997 Best Charlotte Knights (30)	9.00
1997 Best Chattanooga Lookouts (27)	8.00
1997 GS Chillicothe Paints (28)	8.50
1997 GS Clarksville Coyotes (25)	7.50
1997 Best Clearwater Phillies (30)	8.50
1997 GS Clinton Lumber Kings (30)	9.00
1997 Team Colorado Springs Sky Sox (29)	8.00
1997 Team Colorado Springs All-Time (32)	8.00
1997 Best Columbus Clippers (30)	9.00
1997 Police Columbus Clippers (29)	9.00
1997 Team Columbus Clippers 20th Anniv. (30)	10.00
1997 Best Danville Braves (30)	25.00
1997 Best Delmarva Shorebirds (30)	34.00
1997 GS Duluth-Superior Dukes (26)	7.00
1997 Team Dunedin Blue Jays (34)	7.50
1997 Team Dunedin Blue Jays Family Night (30)	19.00
1997 TM Durham Bulls (30)	20.00
1997 Team Durham Bulls "Bulls to Braves" (10)	17.50
1997 Best Eastern League Prospects (31)	11.00
1997 Team Edmonton Trappers (xx)	24.00
1997 Best El Paso Diablos (30)	7.50
1997 Best Erie Sea Wolves (30)	8.50
1997 Best Eugene Emeralds (30)	8.00
1997 GS Everett Aquasox (30)	10.00
1997 MA Fargo-Moorhead RedHawks (30)	8.50
1997 Best Florida State League Prospects (33)	12.00
1997 Best Frederick Keys (30)	8.00
1997 Best Ft. Myers Miracle (30)	9.00
1997 Best Ft. Wayne Wizards (29)	8.50
1997 GS Grand Forks Varmints (21)	7.00
1997	7.00
1997 GS Grays Harbor Gulls (27)	6.00
1997 Best Great Falls Dodgers (30)	13.00
1997 Best Greensboro Bats (30)	40.00
1997 GS Greenville Braves (28)	8.50
1997 Best Hagerstown Suns (30)	8.00
1997 Best Harrisburg Senators (28)	11.00
1997 Best Harrisburg w/ad logos (28)	17.50
1997 Best Helena Brewers (30)	16.00
1997 Best Hickory Crawdads (30)	9.50
1997 Best Hickory Crawdads update (30)	10.00
1997 GS High Desert Mavericks (30)	50.00
1997 GS High Desert Mavericks update (18)	21.00
1997 Best Hudson Valley Renegades (30)	10.00
1997 Burger King Huntsville Stars (27)	12.50
1997 Team Idaho Falls Braves (32)	8.00
1997 Best Indianapolis Indians (29)	9.00
1997 Best Iowa Cubs (29)	8.00
1997 Best Jackson Generals (28)	12.00
1997 Smokey Bear Jackson Generals (26)	16.00
1997 Best Jacksonville Suns (27)	8.50
1997 Team Johnson City Cardinals (37)	8.50
1997 Team Kane County Cougars (32)	12.00
1997 Connie's Pizza Kane County Cougars (32)	24.00
1997 Best Kinston Indians (30)	10.00
1997 Best Kissimee Cobras (30)	9.00
1997 Best Knoxville Smokies (28)	8.00
1997 GS Lafayette Leopards (26)	7.50
1997 Horizon Outlet Lake Elsinore Storm (20)	27.50
1997 GS Lake Elsinore Storm (30)	8.50
1997 Best Lakeland Tigers (30)	8.50
1997 Best Lancaster JetHawks (30)	8.00
1997 Team Lansing Lugnuts (30)	15.00
1997 Best Las Vegas Stars (30)	8.00
1997 Best Lethbridge Black Diamonds (30)	10.00
1997 Best Louisville Redbirds (30)	22.00
1997 Best Lowell Spinners (30)	8.50
1997 Best Lynchburg Hillcats (30)	27.50
1997 Best Macon Braves (30)	24.00
1997 Best Michigan Battle Cats (30)	14.50
1997 Best Midland Angels (29)	8.00
1997 Team Midland Angels (23)	50.00
1997 Best Midwest League Prospects (30)	11.00
1997 Best Mobile BayBears (30)	8.00
1997 GS Modesto A's (30)	10.00
1997 Team Nashville Sounds (32)	16.00
1997 Best New Britain Rock Cats (30)	8.00
1997 Best New Haven Ravens (30)	8.00
1997 Best New Jersey Cardinals (30)	8.00
1997 Best N.J. Cardinals Top Prospects (6)	9.00
1997 Best Norfolk Tides (34)	8.00
1997 Northern League All-Stars (42)	12.00
1997 Best Norwich Navigators (32)	8.00
1997 Team Norwich Navigators (30)	27.50
1997 Team Ogden Raptors (32)	9.00
1997 Best Oklahoma City 89ers (25)	8.00
1997 Best Omaha Royals (26)	8.00
1997 Best Orlando Rays (30)	25.00
1997 Denny's Orlando Rays (25)	50.00
1997 Best Pawtucket Red Sox (30)	9.00
1997 Dunkin' Donuts Pawtucket Red Sox foldout	40.00
1997 Team Pawtucket 25th Anniversary (31)	20.00
1997 Team Pawtucket 25th Anniversary foldout	60.00
1997 Best Peoria Chiefs (30)	8.00
1997 Team Phoenix Firebirds (30)	9.00
1997 All-Time Firebirds Dream Team (30)	8.50
1997 Best Piedmont Boll Weevils (30)	9.00
1997 Best Pittsfield Mets (30)	9.00
1997 GS Portland Rockies (30)	8.00
1997 Best Portland Sea Dogs (30)	12.50
1997 Best Prince William Cannons (30)	9.00
1997 Best Princeton Devil Rays (30)	12.00
1997 Best Quad City River Bandits (30)	24.00
1997 GS Rancho Cucamonga Quakes (30)	8.00
1997 GS Rancho Cucamonga Quakes update (7)	6.00
1997 Best Reading Phillies (27)	8.00
1997 GS Reno Chukars (27)	9.00
1997 Best Richmond Braves (30)	8.00
1997 Richmond Camera Richmond Braves (20)	52.00
1997 Team Rio Grande Valley White Wings (23)	7.00
1997 Best Rochester Red Wings (30)	8.00
1997 Best Rockford Cubbies (30)	60.00
1997 Team Salem Avalanche (38)	12.50
1997 Team Salem Avalanche update (10)	5.00
1997 Team Salem-Keizer Volcanoes (42)	11.00
1997 Best Salt Lake City Buzz (29)	8.00
1997 Best San Antonio Missions (30)	9.00
1997 Best San Bernardino Stampede (30)	8.00
1997 Best San Jose Giants (30)	9.00
1997 Best Sarasota Red Sox (30)	30.00
1997 Best Scranton Red Barons (30)	8.00
1997 Best Shreveport Captains (28)	10.00
1997 Best Shreveport w/ WK SportsCare ads (29)	10.00
1997 GS Sioux City Explorers (27)	7.00
1997 GS Sioux Falls Canaries (28)	7.00
1997 Best So. Atlantic League Prospects (31)	11.00
1997 Best South Bend Silver Hawks (30)	12.50
1997 Best Southern League Prospects (32)	12.00
1997 Best Southern Oregon Timberjacks (29)	12.00
1997 GS Spokane Indians (31)	12.00
1997 Best St. Catherines Stompers (30)	20.00
1997 Best St. Lucie Mets (30)	9.50
1997 Team St. Paul Saints (32)	110.00
1997 Best St. Petersburg Devil Rays (30)	10.00
1997 Best St. Pete Devil Rays update (30)	22.00
1997 Best Stockton Ports (30)	9.00
1997 Best Syracuse Chiefs (30)	9.00
1997 Best Tacoma Rainiers (30)	13.00
1997 Best Tampa Yankees (33)	11.00
1997 Best Texas League Prospects (31)	9.50
1997 Best Toledo Mud Hens (36)	9.00
1997 Best Trenton Thunder (30)	9.00
1997 Best Tucson Toros (29)	11.00
1997 Jones Photo Tucson Toros (5)	95.00
1997 Team Tulsa Drillers (30)	8.50
1997 GS Tyler Wildcatters (24)	7.00
1997 Best Vancouver Canadians (30)	9.50
1997 Best Vermont Expos (30)	8.00
1997 Best Vero Beach Dodgers (30)	35.00
1997 GS Visalia Oaks (30)	32.50
1997 Team Watertown Indians (36)	9.00
1997 Best West Michigan Whitecaps (30)	8.50
1997 Best Wichita Wranglers (30)	7.00
1997 Best Williamsport Cubs (29)	9.00
1997 Best Wilmington Blue Rocks (30)	8.00
1997 Best Wisconsin Timber Rattlers (29)	9.00
1997 GS Yakima Bears (36)	9.00

1998 Best Premium Preview Sean Casey Super

This 5" x 7" version of Casey's 1997 Best Premium Preview card was created as a giveaway for use at Jan. 9-11 Tuff Stuff Classic card show. The front has a large color pose of Casey against a black-and-white ghost-image portrait photo. Tuff Stuff and Best logos are in the upper corners. On back is a large show logo, Casey biographical data and a serial number from within an edition of 1,000.

	MT
Sean Casey	6.00

1998 Team Best Player of the Year Promos

This promo set was issued to preview Team Best's first 1998 minor league singles issue - Player of the Year. The promos feature the base card and four of the set's inserts. Fronts are nearly identical to the issued versions, except for the use of "Best" rather than "Team Best" logos. Promo card backs have the PoY logo in color at center. The unnumbered promo cards are checklisted here alphabetically.

		MT
Complete Set (5):		10.00
Common Player:		2.00
(1)	Todd Helton (Contender)	3.00
(2)	Paul Konerko (Player of the Year)	2.00
(3)	Mark Kotsay (Diamond Best)	2.00
(4)	Darnell McDonald (base card)	2.00
(5)	Kerry Wood (Possibilities)	1.50

1998 Team Best Player of the Year

The first product under the firm's new Team Best logo was this foil-pack series of 50 minor leaguers, many of whom began making their names in the big leagues in 1998. Fronts feature color action photos with tan borders. Manufacturer and minor league team logos appear in the upper corners. On back are a postage-stamp size repeat of the head portion of the player photo at upper-left. To the right are personal data. At lower-left are 1997 season stats, with career highlights to the right. Cards were sold in six-card packs.

	MT
Complete Set (50):	15.00
Common Player:	.10

Wax Box:		45.00
1	Ryan Anderson	2.00
2	Lorenzo Barcelo	.10
3	Hiram Bocachica	.25
4	David Borkowski	.10
5	Russ Branyan	.50
6	Dermal Brown	.50
7	Brent Butler	.25
8	Enrique Calero	.10
9	Bruce Chen	.50
10	Ryan Christenson	.25
11	Pat Cline	.15
12	Scott Elarton	.10
13	Juan Encarnacion	.75
14	Mark Fischer	.10
15	Troy Glaus	3.00
16	Alex Hernandez	.10
17	Norm Hutchins	.10
18	Geoff Jenkins	.35
19	Adam Kennedy	.40
20	Corey Koskie	.10
21	Mark Kotsay	1.00
22	Ricky Ledee	.25
23	Carlos Lee	.15
24	Corey Lee	.10
25	Mike Lowell	.10
26	T.R. Marcinczyk	.10
27	Willie Martinez	.10
28	Darnell McDonald	.50
29	Jackson Melian	1.00
30	Chad Meyers	.10
31	Ryan Minor	.50
32	Kenderick Moore	.10
33	Julio Moreno	.10
34	Rod Myers	.10
35	Abraham Nunez	.20
36	Vladimir Nunez	.10
37	Ramon Ortiz	.25
38	Chan Perry	.10
39	Ben Petrick	.25
40	Angel Ramirez	1.00
41	Grant Roberts	.10
42	Alex Sanchez	.10
43	Jared Sandberg	.25
44	Scott Schoeneweis	.10
45	Steve Shoemaker	.10
46	Matt White	.60
47	Paul Wilder	.10
48	Preston Wilson	.50
49	Kevin Witt	.10
50	Jay Yennaco	.10

1998 Team Best Player of the Year Autographs - Hobby

Nearly two dozen of the top minor leaguers provided autographed cards for this Team Best insert set. Cards feature vignetted action photos with the player's name in a bat at bottom. Team and manufacturer logos are in the top corners. Many of the autographed cards feature players who are not in the base set. Stated odds of pulling an autograph card are one per 19 packs.

		MT
Complete Set (22):		275.00
Common Player:		6.00
1	Kris Benson	20.00
2	Dermal Brown	15.00
3	Eric Chavez	30.00
4	Chad Green	6.00
5	Seth Greisinger	6.00
6	Ben Grieve	30.00
7	Chad Hermansen	20.00
8	Billy Koch	10.00
9	Paul Konerko	25.00
10	Braden Looper	6.00
11	Gil Meche	6.00
12	Eric Milton	15.00
13	John Patterson	10.00
14	Carl Pavano	15.00
15	Danny Peoples	10.00
16	Sidney Ponson	6.00
17	Brian Rose	6.00
18	Bubba Trammell	10.00
19	Jake Westbrook	6.00
20	Paul Wilder	10.00
21	Kerry Wood	40.00
22	A.J. Zapp	10.00

1998 Team Best Player of the Year Autographs - Retail

A completely different selection of players and design was presented in the autographed cards inserted into Team Best retail packs. Fronts have action photos with a large team logo in the background. In the top-right corner "Best Premium" appears in gold-foil script. Backs have a Best Premium logo and are hand-numbered from within an edition of 250 of each player.

		MT
Complete Set (49):		800.00
Common Player:		5.00
(1)	Richard Almanzar	8.00
(2)	Kris Benson	20.00
(3)	Darin Blood	5.00
(4)	Adrian Brown	5.00
(5)	Dermal Brown	15.00
(6)	Kevin Brown	15.00
(7)	Eric Chavez	30.00
(8)	D.T. Cromer	5.00
(9)	Lorenzo de la Cruz	5.00
(10)	Adam Eaton	5.00
(11)	Nelson Figueroa	5.00
(12)	Juan Gonzalez	5.00
(13)	Chad Green	8.00
(14)	Seth Greisinger	8.00
(15)	Ben Grieve	35.00
(16)	Matt Halloran	5.00
(17)	Chad Hermansen	15.00
(18)	Mark Johnson	15.00
(19)	Billy Koch	8.00
(20)	Paul Konerko	25.00
(21)	Mark Kotsay	15.00
(22)	Joe Lawrence	5.00
(23)	Braden Looper	10.00
(24)	Kevin McGlinchy	5.00
(25)	Gil Meche	5.00
(26)	Juan Melo	5.00
(27)	Eric Milton	15.00
(28)	John Nicholson	5.00
(29)	Todd Noel	10.00
(30)	Abraham Nunez	15.00
(31)	Russell Ortiz	5.00
(32)	Yudith Ozario	5.00
(33)	John Patterson	10.00
(34)	Carl Pavano	15.00
(35)	Elvis Pena	5.00
(36)	Danny Peoples	5.00
(37)	Neifi Perez	15.00
(38)	Sidney Ponson	15.00
(39)	Aramis Ramirez	15.00
(40)	Britt Reames	5.00
(41)	Kerry Robinson	5.00
(42)	Jeff Sexton	5.00
(43)	Bubba Trammell	10.00
(44)	Mike Villano	5.00
(45)	Jake Westbrook	5.00
(46)	Paul Wilder	10.00
(47)	Enrique Wilson	8.00
(48)	Kerry Wood	40.00
(49)	A.J. Zapp	15.00

1998 Team Best Player of the Year Contenders

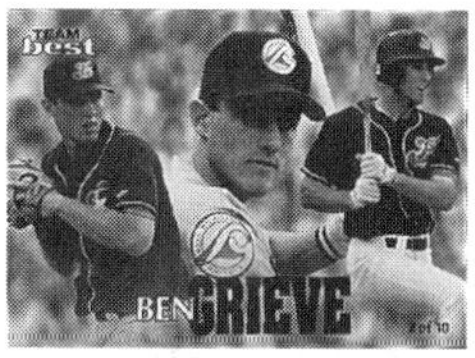

Candidates for minor league player of the year are featured in this scarce insert set. Six of the players are pictured on horizontal-format cards which have three photos on front showing the player in different uniforms on his road to the majors. Four of the players also have a vertical-format card with a single photo on front. Each card is serially numbered on the back from within an edition of 400 each. The background on back is a sepia version of the front photo and there is a PoY stamp logo at center. Stated odds of finding a Contender card are one per 90 packs.

		MT
Complete Set (10):		160.00
Common Player:		10.00
1	Derrick Gibson	15.00
2	Ben Grieve	30.00
3	Ben Grieve (vertical)	30.00
4	Todd Helton	25.00
5	Todd Helton (vertical)	25.00
6	Mark Kotsay	15.00
7	Mark Kotsay (vertical)	15.00
8	Carl Pavano	15.00
9	Brian Rose	10.00
10	Brian Rose (vertical)	10.00

1998 Team Best Player of the Year Young Guns

This is a retail-only insert, with each card individually serial numbered on back to a limit of 100. Cards share the photos used on the hobby-only Contenders insert set (edition of 400), except the Young Guns cards have a white background instead of the mottled brown of the Contenders. Insert ratio was reported at one per 90 packs on average.

		MT
Complete Set (10):		
Common Player:		30.00
1	Derrick Gibson	50.00
2	Ben Grieve	100.00
3	Ben Grieve (vertical)	100.00
4	Todd Helton	50.00
5	Todd Helton (vertical)	50.00
6	Mark Kotsay	40.00
7	Mark Kotsay (vertical)	40.00
8	Carl Pavano	50.00
9	Brian Rose	30.00
10	Brian Rose (vertical)	30.00

1998 Team Best Diamond Best

Red, white and blue typography and a team logo in the background mark this insert series. Backs have a smaller version of the front photo, biographical data, 1997 stats and appropriate logos. Odds of pulling a Diamond Best card are stated as one per 19 packs.

		MT
Complete Set (10):		55.00
Common Player:		3.00
1	Darnell McDonald	8.00
2	Adrian Beltre	15.00
3	Derrick Gibson	6.00
4	Mark Kotsay	6.00
5	Braden Looper	4.00
6	Carl Pavano	5.00
7	Brian Rose	4.00
8	Jared Sandberg	3.00
9	Vernon Wells	6.00
10	Sean Casey	6.00

Player names in *Italic* type indicate a rookie card.

1998 Team Best Diamond Best Autographs

Autographs of eight top prospects are featured on Diamond Best style inserts in this chase card set. Actual odds of finding one of the autographed cards is one in 180 packs. Konerko's and Patterson's cards were never released.

		MT
Complete Set (8):		200.00
Common Player:		10.00
1	Kris Benson	20.00
2	Dermal Brown	20.00
3	Eric Chavez	30.00
4	Todd Helton	35.00
5	Paul Konerko (Never released)	
6	John Patterson (Never released)	
7	Braden Looper	20.00
8	Juan Melo	17.50
9	Kerry Wood	40.00
10	A.J. Zapp	20.00

1998 Team Best Paul Konerko

Designated as Player of the Year, former Dodgers farmhand Paul Konerko was honored with a six-card insert issue. Found at the average rate of just one per two boxes (36 packs), the Konerko cards trace his rise through the minor leagues. Fronts have borderless photos and team logos of his minor league stops. Backs detail each season's stats and highlights on a background of a sepia version of the front photo.

		MT
Complete Set (6):		50.00
Common Card:		12.00
1	Paul Konerko (3-photo horizontal)	12.00
2	Paul Konerko (San Bernardino Stampede)	12.00
3	Paul Konerko (San Antonio Missions)	12.00
4	Paul Konerko (Albuquerque Dukes)	12.00
5	Paul Konerko (Yakima Bears)	12.00
6	Paul Konerko (PoY stamp)	12.00

1998 Team Best Possibilities

Two players each are featured in this insert card series. Both fronts and backs have action player photos set against a swirling blue background. Team and licensor logos are part of the design as well. Odds to pull this insert were stated as one per 19 packs.

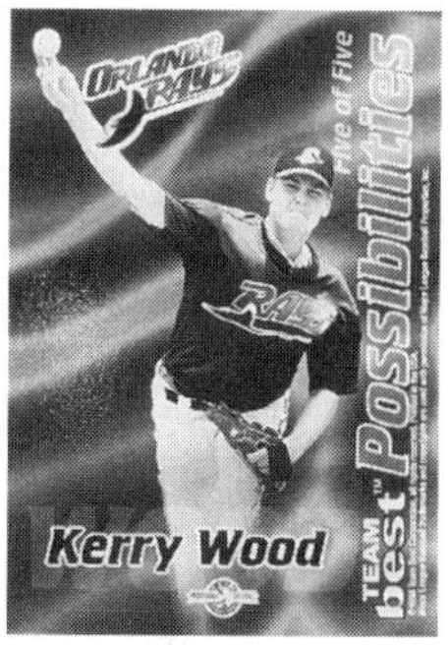

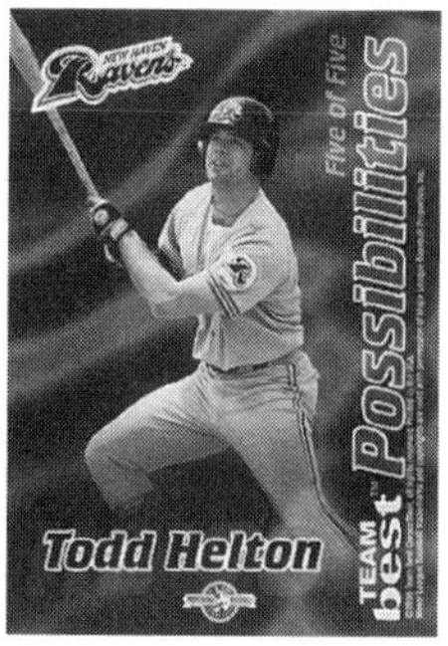

		MT
Complete Set (5):		40.00
Common Player:		5.00
1	Chris Benson, Mark Kotsay	5.00
2	Braden Looper, Sean Casey	5.00
3	Brian Rose, Dermal Brown	5.00
4	Matt White, Ben Grieve	7.50
5	Kerry Wood, Todd Helton	10.00

1998 Team Best Signature Series Promos

To introduce its Signature Series of minor league cards, Team Best created a group of promo cards featuring top players. The promo cards have fronts which are identical to the regular-issue versions. Backs have a blue background with a large Signature Series logo at center and a notice at bottom: "Promotional Purposes Only".

		MT
Complete Set (5):		17.50
Common Player:		2.00
(1)	Rich Ankiel (Diamond Best)	2.00
(2)	Bruce Chen (base set)	2.00
(3)	J.D. Drew (#1 Pick)	6.00
(4)	Troy Glaus (#1 Pick)	6.00
(5)	Ryan Minor (Cornerstone)	2.50

1998 Team Best Signature Series

In many ways Team Best's Signature Series minor league issue is a continuation of the company's Player of the Year series issued earlier in the year. For example, the base cards in the Signature Series retain the design and continue the card numbering of the earlier series. The Signature Series debuted in September, in six-card foil packs. Half a dozen insert sets were included among the base cards.

		MT
	Complete Set (50):	24.00
	Common Player:	.25
	Wax Box:	45.00
51	Matt Anderson	.50
52	Rich Ankiel	4.00
53	Tony Armas	.40
54	John Barnes	.25
55	Robbie Bell	.25
56	Kris Benson	.50
57	Lance Berkman	.50
58	Russell Branyon	.50
59	Brent Butler	.25
60	Troy Cameron	.25
61	Eric Chavez	1.50
62	Bruce Chen	.50
63	Matt Clement	.50
64	Ben Davis	.40
65	J.D. Drew	2.00
66	Tim Drew	.25
67	Derrick Gibson	.50
68	Troy Glaus	3.00
69	Chad Hermansen	.75
70	Ramon Hernandez	.25
71	Gabe Kapler	1.50
72	Mike Kinkade	.50
73	Scott Krause	.25
74	Mike Lowell	.50
75	Willie Martinez	.25
76	Donzell McDonald	.25
77	Gil Meche	.35
78	Juan Melo	.25
79	Wade Miller	.25
80	Ryan Minor	1.00
81	Abraham Nunez	.40
82	Pablo Ozuna	.50
83	John Patterson	.50
84	Josh Paul	.25
85	Ben Petrick	.25
86	Calvin Pickering	.50
87	Placido Polanco	.25
88	Aramis Ramirez	.75
89	Julio Ramirez	.25
90	Luis Rivas	.25
91	Luis Rivera	.25
92	Ruben Rivera	.25
93	Grant Roberts	.25
94	Jimmy Rollins	.25
95	Bobby Seay	.25
96	Jason Standridge	.50
97	Dernell Stenson	.50
98	Vernon Wells	.75
99	Matt White	.50
100	Ed Yarnall	.50
---	Special offer card, Kerry Wood autograph	
---	Special offer card, Team Best promos	
---	Special offer card - Sig. Series promos	

1998 Team Best Signature Series Autographs

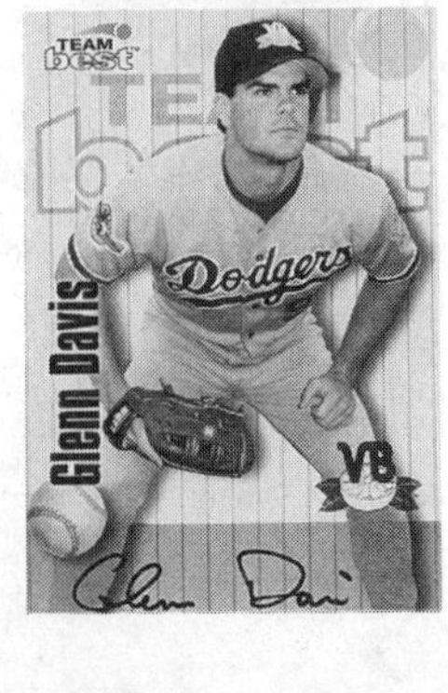

This series of authentically autographed insert cards was inserted at the rate of about five per box of Team Best Signature Series. Cards feature color photos on a beige pinstriped background. Backs repeat the background and have a large baseball with an authenticity notice overprinted. The unnumbered cards are listed here in alphabetical order. Autographed cards of Barrett, Colon, Teut and Westbrook were received too late to be inserted.

		MT
	Complete Set (53):	300.00
	Common Player:	4.00
(1)	John Bale	4.00
(2)	Kevin Barker	4.00
(3)	Not Issued Michael Barrett	
(4)	Todd Belitz	4.00
(5)	Aaron Bond	4.00
(6)	A.J. Burnett	8.00
(7)	Brent Butler	6.00
(8)	Buddy Carlyle	4.00
(9)	Ramon Castro	4.00
(10)	Frank Catalanotto	6.00
(11)	Giuseppe Chiaramonte	4.00
(12)	Not Issued Bartolo Colon	
(13)	Alex Cora	4.00
(14)	Francisco Cordero	4.00
(15)	David Cortes	6.00
(16)	Dean Crow	8.00
(17)	Doug Davis	4.00
(18)	Glenn Davis	4.00
(19)	Travis Dawkins	15.00
(20)	Matt DeWitt	4.00
(21)	Octavio Dotel	4.00
(22)	Mike Duvall	4.00
(23)	Troy Glaus	35.00
(24)	Geoff Goetz	4.00
(25)	Jason Grilli	4.00
(26)	Al Hawkins	4.00
(27)	Bryan Hebson	4.00
(28)	Alex Hernandez	4.00
(29)	Doug Johnston	4.00
(30)	Juan LeBron	12.50
(31)	John Leroy	4.00
(32)	Randi Mallard	4.00
(33)	Sam Marsonek	4.00
(34)	Ramon Martinez	4.00
(35)	Ruben Mateo	15.00
(36)	Joe Mays	4.00
(37)	David Melendez	4.00
(38)	Justin Miller	4.00
(39)	Ryan Minor	15.00
(40)	Warren Morris	8.00
(41)	Pablo Ozuna	6.00
(42)	Brian Passini	4.00
(43)	Santiago Perez	4.00
(44)	Marc Pisciotta	4.00
(45)	Rob Ramsey	4.00
(46)	Grant Roberts	8.00
(47)	John Roskos	4.00
(48)	Luis de los Santos	6.00
(49)	Brian Simmons	4.00
(50)	Reggie Taylor	4.00
(51)	Not Issued Nathan Teut	
(52)	Andy Thompson	4.00
(53)	Chris Tynan	4.00
(54)	Jose Vidro	8.00
(55)	Jayson Werth	4.00
(56)	Not Issued Jake Westbrook	
(57)	Ed Yarnall	10.00

1998 Team Best Signature Series Autographed Super

Each 10-box case of late-season Team Best Signature Series included one of 10 authentically autographed large-format (4" x 6") case topper cards. Fronts have a gold-foil Team Best logo at top and an Auto Best logo at bottom. Also on front is a serial number from within an edition of 500 of each player. Backs have a large notice of authenticity.

		MT
	Complete Set (12):	220.00
	Common Player:	10.00
1	Kris Benson	20.00
2	Sean Casey (Akron)	30.00
3	Sean Casey (Buffalo)	30.00
4	Seth Greisinger	10.00
5	Ben Grieve	30.00
6	Chad Hermansen	20.00
7	Paul Konerko	30.00
8	Britt Reames	10.00
9	Jake Westbrook	10.00
10	Paul Wilder	15.00
11	Kerry Wood	40.00
12	A.J. Zapp	15.00

1998 Team Best Signature Series Best Bets

This retail-exclusive insert set features the cream of the 1998 minor league crop. Fronts have player action photos separated from a white background by a colorful aura. A team logo appears at bottom. Backs repeat a close-up of the photo and have 1997 stats, biographical data and a few words about the player. The Best Bet cards use the same photos found on the hobby-only Cornerstone inserts. The unnumbered cards are checklisted here in alphabetical order.

		MT
	Complete Set (12):	300.00
	Common Player:	12.00
(1)	Matt Anderson	12.00
(2)	Lance Berkman	18.00
(3)	Eric Chavez	35.00
(4)	Bruce Chen	15.00
(5)	Matt Clement	24.00
(6)	J.D. Drew	60.00
(7)	Troy Glaus	70.00
(8)	George Lombard	18.00
(9)	Ryan Minor	24.00
(10)	Dernell Stenson	12.00
(11)	Jayson Werth	18.00
(12)	Ed Yarnall	18.00

1998 Team Best Signature Series Cornerstone

This retail-exclusive insert set features the cream of the 1998 minor league top and many of tomorrow's big league stars. Fronts have player action photos separated from a white background by a colored aura. A team logo also appears. Backs repeat the photo in a close-up format and have 1997 stats, biographical data and a few words about the player. The Best Bet cards use the same photos as those found on the Cornerstone insert issue. The unnumbered cards are checklisted here in alphabetical order.

		MT
	Complete Set (12):	250.00
	Common Player:	10.00
(1)	Matt Anderson	10.00
(2)	Lance Berkman	15.00
(3)	Eric Chavez	30.00
(4)	Bruce Chen	15.00
(5)	Matt Clement	20.00
(6)	J.D. Drew	50.00
(7)	Troy Glaus	60.00
(8)	George Lombard	15.00
(9)	Ryan Minor	20.00
(10)	Dernell Stenson	10.00
(11)	Jayson Werth	15.00
(12)	Ed Yarnall	15.00

1998 Team Best Signature Series Diamond Best

Another insert series which was continued from Team Best's Player of the Year series is Diamond Best. Cards in the Signature Series are numbered contiguously from the earlier series and have the same basic design of an action photo on a white background with a large minor league team logo. Backs have a smaller version of the front photo, a bit of personal data and a few words about the player. Diamond Best inserts are found on average of about one per 19 packs (just under one per box).

		MT
	Complete Set (10):	80.00
	Common Player:	3.00
11	Rich Ankiel	25.00
		3.00
12	Michael Barrett	6.00
13	Matt Clement	3.00
14	J.D. Drew	15.00
15	Bobby Estalella	8.00
16	Troy Glaus	20.00
17	Alex Gonzalez	6.00
18	George Lombard	6.00
19	Mike Lowell	8.00
20	Dernell Stenson	5.00

1998 Team Best Signature Series Full-Count Autographs

Utilizing the basic design of the company's inaugural minor league issue of 1997, Team Best created a chase set of authentically autographed cards under the title "Full Count". Each card carries a Full Count logo in gold foil on front. Backs have a statement of authentication overprinted on a stylized ball diamond.

		MT
	Complete Set (24):	300.00
	Common Player:	10.00
1	Kris Benson	15.00
2	Dermal Brown	10.00
3	Eric Chavez	25.00
4	Chad Green	10.00
5	Ben Grieve	30.00
6	Todd Helton	25.00
7	Chad Hermanson	10.00
8	Paul Konerko	25.00
9	Mark Kotsay	15.00
10	Braden Looper	10.00
11	Gil Meche	10.00
12	Juan Melo	10.00
13	Eric Milton	15.00
14	Abraham Nunez	10.00
15	John Patterson	10.00
16	Carl Pavano	15.00
17	Sidney Ponson	15.00
18	Aramis Ramirez	15.00
19	Britt Reames	10.00
20	Kerry Robinson	10.00
21	Jake Westbrook	10.00
22	Paul Wilder	15.00
23	Kerry Wood	40.00
24	A.J. Zapp	15.00

1998 Team Best Signature Series #1 Pick

This special series of chase cards was issued as a box-topper, one per 18-pack box. Card fronts feature both portrait and action photos. In a baseball at lower-right is a "#1 PICK" gold hologram. Backs have individual silver-foil serial numbers from within an edition of 900 each.

		MT
	Complete Set (42):	200.00
	Common Player:	4.00
1	Aaron Akin	4.00
2	Matt Anderson	6.00
3	Ryan Anderson	20.00
4	Shane Arthurs	4.00
5	Michael Barrett	6.00
6	Kris Benson	6.00
7	Lance Berkman	5.00
8	Rocky Biddle	4.00
9	Ryan Bradley	6.00
10	Dermal Brown	6.00
11	Troy Cameron	5.00
12	Brett Caradonna	4.00
13	Eric Chavez	10.00
14	Mike Cuddyer	4.00
15	John Curtice	4.00
16	Glenn Davis	4.00
17	J.J. Davis	5.00
18	Jason Dellaero	4.00
19	J.D. Drew	25.00
20	Tim Drew	4.00
21	Brian DuBose	4.00
22	Mark Fischer	4.00
23	Troy Glaus	20.00
24	Geoff Goetz	5.00
25	Jason Grilli	4.00
26	Nathan Haynes	4.00
27	Bryan Hebson	4.00
28	Geoff Jenkins	8.00
29	Adam Kennedy	8.00
30	Billy Koch	6.00
31	Matt LeCroy	4.00

32	Mark Mangum	4.00
33	Darnell McDonald	6.00
34	Kevin Nicholson	4.00
35	John Patterson	5.00
36	Danny Peoples	4.00
37	Dan Reichert	4.00
38	Jason Romano	4.00
39	Jason Standridge	6.00
40	Vernon Wells	8.00
41	Jayson Werth	4.00
42	Matt White	6.00

1998 Upper Deck SP Prospects

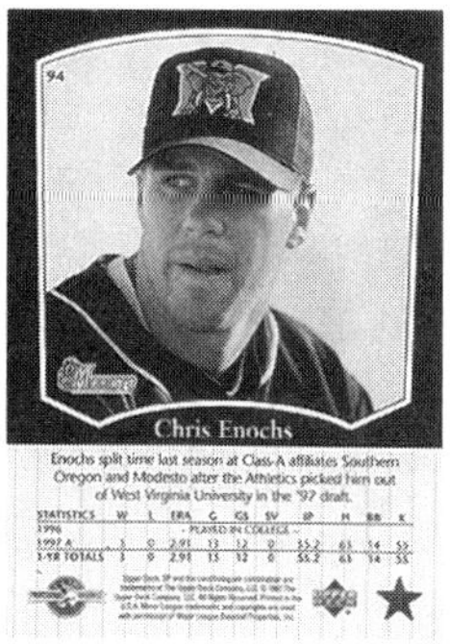

The best of the minor league class of 1997 are featured in this issue which marks Upper Deck's return to the minor league card market after a two-year layoff. All players, even the relatively few who have had major league experience, are featured in their minor league uniforms in the base set of 126 cards. There are three 30-card insert sets: Destination the Show (1:90 packs), Signature Cards (1:16) and Small Town Heroes (1:5). At the high end of the chase spectrum, a President's Edition parallel set of the regular, DS and STH cards was produced in an edition of just 10 cards each. Retail price at issue was $4.39 for an eight-card pack. Fronts are printed on a foiled background with a textured silver-foil border; team and SP logos are in the bottom corners. Backs are conventionally printed with another color photo and up to two years of stats. The first 10 cards in the set are a series of Top 10 prospects which have checklist backs. Production was reported to be 1,000 hobby-only cases.

		MT
Complete Set (126):		60.00
Common Player:		.50
Wax Box:		100.00
1	Travis Lee (Top 10 Prospects)	2.00
2	Paul Konerko (Top 10 Prospects)	2.00
3	Ben Grieve (Top 10 Prospects)	3.00
4	Kerry Wood (Top 10 Prospects)	3.00
5	Miguel Tejada (Top 10 Prospects)	2.00
6	Juan Encarnacion (Top 10 Prospects)	.50
7	Jackson Melian (Top 10 Prospects)	1.50
8	Chad Hermansen (Top 10 Prospects)	1.00
9	Aramis Ramirez (Top 10 Prospects)	1.00
10	Russell Branyan (Top 10 Prospects)	.75
11	Norm Hutchins	.50
12	Jarrod Washburn	.75
13	Larry Barnes	.50
14	Scott Schoeneweis	.50
15	Travis Lee	2.00
16	Mike Stoner	.50
17	Nick Bierbrodt	.50
18	Vladimir Nunez	.50
19	Wes Helms	.50
20	Jason Marquis	.75
21	George Lombard	.50
22	Bruce Chen	1.00
23	Rob Bell	1.00
24	Adam Johnson	.50
25	Ryan Minor	2.00
26	Sidney Ponson	.50
27	Calvin Pickering	1.00
28	Donnie Sadler	.75
29	Cole Liniak	.50
30	Carl Pavano	1.25
31	Kerry Wood	3.00
32	Pat Cline	.50
33	Jason Maxwell	.50
34	Jason Dellaero	.50
35	Mike Caruso	1.00
36	Jeff Liefer	.50
37	Brian Simmons	.50
38	Carlos Lee	3.00
39	Jeff Inglin	.50
40	Darron Ingram	.50
41	Justin Towle	.75
42	Pat Watkins	.50
43	Richie Sexson	2.00
44	Danny Peoples	.50
45	Russell Branyan	1.00
46	Scott Morgan	.50
47	Mike Glavine	.50
48	Willie Martinez	.50
49	Jake Westbrook	.50
50	Derrick Gibson	.75
51	Ben Petrick	1.00
52	Juan Encarnacion	1.50
53	Seth Greisinger	.50
54	Robert Fick	.75
55	Dave Borkowski	.50
56	Jesse Ibarra	.50
57	Nate Rolison	.50
58	Jaime Jones	.50
59	Aaron Akin	.50
60	Alex Gonzalez	.75
61	Richard Hidalgo	1.25
62	Scott Elarton	.75
63	Daryle Ward	2.00
64	Jeremy Giambi	2.00
65	Dermal Brown	1.00
66	Enrique Calero	.50
67	Glenn Davis	.50
68	Adrian Beltre	3.00
69	Alex Cora	.50
70	Paul Konerko	2.00
71	Mike Kincade	.50
72	Danny Klassen	.50
73	Chad Green	.50
74	Kevin Barker	.50
75	David Ortiz	.50
76	Jacque Jones	2.00
77	Luis Rivas	.50
78	Hiram Bocachica	.50
79	Javier Vazquez	1.00
80	Brad Fullmer	1.50
81	Preston Wilson	1.25
82	Octavio Dotel	.75
83	Fletcher Bates	.50
84	Grant Roberts	.75
85	Jackson Melian	2.50
86	Katsuhiro Maeda	1.00
87	Ricky Ledee	1.50
88	Eric Milton	1.50
89	Eric Chavez	2.50
90	Ben Grieve	2.50
91	Miguel Tejada	2.00
92	A.J. Hinch	1.00
93	Ramon Hernandez	1.50
94	Chris Enochs	.50
95	Marlon Anderson	1.50
96	Reggie Taylor	.50
97	Steve Carver	.50
98	Ron Wright	.50
99	Kris Benson	1.00
100	Chad Hermansen	1.00
101	Aramis Ramirez	1.00
102	Adam Kennedy	1.00
103	Braden Looper	.50
104	Cliff Politte	.50
105	Brent Butler	.50
106	Juan Melo	.50
107	Ben Davis	1.00
108	Kevin Nicholson	.50
109	Gary Matthews Jr.	.50
110	Matt Clement	1.50
111	Jason Brester	.50
112	Joe Fontenot	.50
113	Darin Blood	.50
114	Greg Wooten	.50
115	Jeff Farnsworth	.50
116	Robert Luce	.50
117	Rolando Arrojo	1.00
118	Doug Johnson	.75
119	James Manias	.50
120	Alex Sanchez	.75
121	Warren Morris	1.00
122	Ruben Mateo	3.00
123	Corey Lee	.50
124	Roy Halladay	1.50
125	Kevin Witt	.75
126	Tom Evans	.50

1998 Upper Deck SP Prospects President's Edition

Among the rarest minor league cards of the modern era are the foiled and die-cut version of SP Top Prospects known as the President's Edition. The set parallels the 126 cards of the base issue, plus the 30-card Destination the Show and Small Town Heroes inserts. Only 10 cards each exist in the parallel version.

	MT
Common Player: (President's Edition cards valued at 150X-200X regular versions.)	75.00

1998 Upper Deck SP Prospects Autographs

Authentically autographed cards of some of the minor leagues' top prospects are featured in this insert set found on average of once per 16 packs. The autograph cards have a player photo vignetted in a white panel at center, with his signature below. Backs have a printed certificate of authenticity. Cards of Wes Helms, Jackson Melian and David Ortiz, originally announced on UD's checklist, were never issued.

		MT
Complete Set (26):		475.00
Common Player:		10.00
AB	Adrian Beltre	40.00
KB	Kris Benson	25.00
RB	Russell Branyan	15.00
BB	Brent Butler	15.00
EC	Eric Chavez	30.00
RF	Robert Fick	15.00
DG	Derrick Gibson	20.00
BG	Ben Grieve	40.00
CH	Chad Hermansen	25.00
RH	Ramon Hernandez	20.00
JJ	Jacque Jones	20.00
PK	Paul Konerko	25.00
RL	Ricky Ledee	25.00
CL	Corey Lee	10.00
TL	Travis Lee	40.00
KM	Katsuhiro Maeda	15.00
GM	Gary Matthews Jr.	10.00
JMO	Juan Melo	10.00
SM	Scott Morgan	10.00
WM	Warren Morris	20.00
DP	Danny Peoples	10.00
GR	Grant Roberts	10.00
MT	Miguel Tejada	35.00
JT	Justin Towle	10.00
DW	Daryle Ward	25.00
KW	Kerry Wood	50.00

Player names in *Italic* type indicate a rookie card.

1998 Upper Deck SP Prospects Destination The Show

Thirty top minor leaguers who are likely to begin major leagues careers in 1998 are featured in this insert set. The chase cards are seeded on average of one per 90 packs.

		MT
Complete Set (30):		800.00
Common Player:		15.00
DS1	Travis Lee	40.00
DS2	Eric Chavez	40.00
DS3	Ramon Hernandez	40.00
DS4	Daryle Ward	40.00
DS5	Jackson Melian	40.00
DS6	Ben Grieve	50.00
DS7	Brent Butler	15.00
DS8	Rolando Arrojo	25.00
DS9	Ryan Minor	30.00
DS10	Adrian Beltre	40.00
DS11	Sidney Ponson	20.00
DS12	Gary Matthews Jr.	25.00
DS13	Ron Wright	15.00
DS14	Warren Morris	25.00
DS15	Russell Branyan	20.00
DS16	Paul Konerko	40.00
DS17	Mike Caruso	25.00
DS18	Jacque Jones	40.00
DS19	Preston Wilson	30.00
DS20	Chad Hermansen	25.00
DS21	Aramis Ramirez	30.00
DS22	Kerry Wood	70.00
DS23	Corey Lee	20.00
DS24	Carl Pavano	25.00
DS25	Kris Benson	40.00
DS26	Derrick Gibson	25.00
DS27	Mike Stoner	15.00
DS28	Juan Melo	15.00
DS29	Mike Kinkade	15.00
DS30	Alex Gonzalez	25.00

1998 Upper Deck SP Prospects Small Town Heroes

The small towns across America which are the roots of many pro ballplayers are featured in this chase set from Upper Deck's 1998 SP Top Prospects issue. The series focuses for the most part on players who are early in their minor league careers. These cards are inserted at an average rate of one per five packs.

		MT
Complete Set (30):		60.00
Common Player:		1.00
H1	Travis Lee	5.00
H2	Eric Chavez	4.00
H3	Mike Caruso	1.50
H4	Adrian Beltre	5.00
H5	Jackson Melian	5.00
H6	Adam Johnson	3.00
H7	Carlos Lee	4.00
H8	Kris Benson	3.00
H9	Jacque Jones	2.00
H10	Russell Branyan	2.50
H11	John Patterson	1.00
H12	Ryan Minor	2.50
H13	Dermal Brown	3.00
H14	Mike Stoner	1.50
H15	Derrick Gibson	2.00
H16	Ben Davis	3.00
H17	Kevin Witt	2.00
H18	Justin Towle	1.00
H19	Doug Johnson	2.00
H20	Chad Hermansen	4.00
H21	Sidney Ponson	2.00
H22	Marlon Anderson	1.00
H23	Kerry Wood	5.00
H24	Alex Gonzalez	1.00
H25	Carl Pavano	2.50
H26	A.J. Hinch	3.00
H27	Juan Melo	2.00
H28	Dave Borkowski	1.00
H29	Jake Westbrook	2.00
H30	Daryle Ward	3.00

1998 Minor League Team Sets

Besides Best (under the Multi-Ad Sports logo), which maintained the lion's share of the team-set market, several other companies - notably Grandstand (GS), Choice Marketing (CH), Blueline Communications (BL) and Warning Track Cards (WTC) - also produced sets for more than one team.

	MT
206 team sets and variations	8.00
MA AA All-Star Game (60)	11.00
Team Aberdeen Pheasants (25)	7.00
WTC Adirondack Lumberjacks (25)	6.50
MA Akron Aeros (30)	8.50
WTC Albany-Colonie Diamond Dogs (25)	6.50
GS Albuquerque Dukes (30)	9.00
WTC Allentown (25)	6.50
BL Appalachian League Top Prospects (31)	14.00
Arizona Fall League (25)	10.00
MA Arkansas Travelers (30)	8.00
Team Arkansas Travelers Highlights (10)	60.00

Team Arkansas Travelers Update (1)	30.00
MA Asheville Tourists (30)	9.00
Team Atlantic City Surf (31)	7.50
Team Auburn Doubledays (34)	9.50
MA Augusta Greenjackets (30)	8.00
Team Batavia Muckdogs (35)	37.50
MA Beloit Snappers (30)	22.00
Team Billings Mustangs (38)	20.00
BL Binghampton Mets (30)	8.00
TM Binghamton Mets "Jumbo" (12)	65.00
GS Birmingham Barons (30)	10.00
BL Bluefield Orioles (32)	9.00
GS Boise Hawks (34)	8.50
MA Bowie Baysox (30)	16.00
Team Bowie Nationals (31)	14.00
MA Bridgeport Bluefish (30)	7.50
BL Bristol White Sox (30)	9.00
GS Buffalo Bisons (30)	10.00
MA Burlington Bees (30)	12.50
GS Butte Copper Kings (34)	7.00
MA Cape Fear Crocs (30)	9.50
MA Capital City Bombers (30)	42.00
MA C.C. Bombers w/ Fox 57 ads (30)	45.00
Choice Carolina League All-Stars (42)	11.50
BL Carolina League Top Prospects (33)	25.00
MA Carolina Mudcats (30)	8.00
Team Cedar Rapids Kernels (31)	7.50
MA Charleston Alley Cats (31)	8.50
GS Charleston RiverDogs (30)	9.00
BL Charlotte Knights (30)	9.00
MA Charlotte Rangers (30)	30.00
GS Chattanooga Lookouts (30)	8.50
GS Chattanooga w/ Slush Puppy ads (31)	75.00
MA Clearwater Phillies (30)	7.50
MA Clearwater Phillies Update (30)	12.00
GS Clinton LumberKings (30)	7.50
Team Colorado Springs Sky Sox (31)	8.00
MA Columbus Clippers (30)	9.00
Police Columbus Clippers (25)	9.00
MA Columbus RedStixx (30)	15.00
BL Danville Braves (31)	27.50
BL Danville 97s (31)	17.50
GS Daytona Cubs (21)	9.00
Team Delaware Stars (28)	14.00
Team Delmarva Rockfish (32)	14.00
MA Delmarva Shorebirds (30)	19.00
Team Dunedin Blue Jays (33)	9.00
Team Dunedin Blue Jays stickers (24)	15.00
Durham Bulls (XX)	14.50
MA Eastern League Top Prospects (30)	8.50
Edmonton Trappers (XX)	60.00
GS El Paso Diablos (29)	8.00
MA Erie Seawolves (30)	8.00
GS Eugene Emeralds (32)	7.50
GS Everett Aquasox (30)	8.00
MA Fargo-Moorhead RedHawks (30)	8.50
MA Frederick Keys (30)	9.00
Team Frederick Regiment (32)	14.00
GS Fresno Grizzlies (30)	11.00
Team Ft. Myers Miracle (32)	9.00
BL Ft. Wayne Wizards (30)	9.00
GS Great Falls Dodgers (31)	9.50
MA Greensboro Bats (30)	16.00
GS Greenville Braves (28)	10.00
MA Hagerstown Suns (30)	11.00
MA Harrisburg Senators (30)	11.00
MA Harris. Senators w/WINK 104 ad (30)	16.00
MA Helena Brewers (33)	15.00
MA Hickory Crawdads (30)	8.00
Team Hickory Crawdads Update (30)	9.00
GS High Desert Mavericks (30)	15.00
Team Hudson Valley Renegades (30)	9.00
Team Huntsville Stars (26)	16.00
BL Indianapolis Indians (36)	8.00
BL Iowa Cubs (30)	12.00
MA Jackson Generals (28)	9.00
MA Jacksonville Suns (28)	8.50
Team Johnson City Cardinals (36)	8.50
WTC Johnstown Johnnies (25)	6.50
BL Jupiter Hammerheads (30)	9.50
Team Kane County Cougars (32)	8.50
Team Kane County Cougars, Connie's (32)	15.00
BL Kinston Indians (30)	8.50
BL Kissimmee Cobras (30)	8.00
GS Knoxville Smokies (27)	9.00
GS Lake Elsinore Storm (30)	8.50
MA Lakeland Tigers (30)	10.00
GS Lancaster JetHawks (30)	9.00
BL Lansing Lugnuts (31)	15.00
MA Las Vegas Stars (28)	9.00
GS Lethbridge Black Diamonds (30)	9.00
BL Louisville Redbirds (36)	22.50
MA Lowell Spinners (31)	8.50
BL Lynchburg HillCats (29)	8.50
MA Macon Braves (29)	20.00
MA Madison Black Wolf (25)	8.00
GS Martinsville Phillies (29)	9.50
GS Memphis Redbirds (25)	9.00
Team Memphis Redbirds Update (1)	25.00
MA Michigan Battle Cats (30)	9.00
GS Midland Angels (28)	14.50
GS Midland Angels Sponsor's Set (30)	20.00
Team Midland Angels, "Claus" (28)	75.00
Team Midland Angels, "Glaus" (28)	80.00
MA Midwest League Top Prospects (28)	15.00
GS Mobile BayBears S.L. Champs (25)	17.00
Team Mobile Bay Bears (31)	11.00
GS Modesto A's (30)	12.00
Team Nashville Sounds - numbered (33)	12.00
Team Nashville Sounds - unnumbered (31)	18.00
MA New Britain Rock Cats (27)	8.50
MA New Haven Ravens (31)	8.50
MA N.H. Ravens w/ Maritime ads (31)	8.50
MA New Jersey Cardinals (33)	9.00
WTC New Jersey Jackals (25)	6.50
MA New Orleans Zephyrs (28)	8.50
BL Norfolk Tides (36)	8.00
BL Norfolk Tides w/ Fox 33 ads (30)	8.00
BL Norwich Navigators (26)	8.00
Team Ogden Raptors (36)	15.00
MA Oklahoma City Redhawks (30)	8.00
MA Omaha Royals (30)	8.00
GS Oneonta Yankees (32)	10.00
MA Orlando Rays (29)	8.00
Ottawa Lynx (xx)	55.00
BL Pawtucket Red Sox (30)	9.00
DD Pawtucket Red Sox foldout	30.00
MA Peoria Chiefs (30)	60.00
MA Piedmont Boll Weevils (29)	8.50
MA Pittsfield Mets (34)	8.50
GS Portland Rockies (30)	8.00
BL Portland Sea Dogs (30)	11.00
BL Portland Sea Dogs 5th Anniv. (36)	15.00
BL Princeton Devil Rays (30)	10.00
BL Prince Williams Cannons (30)	40.00
MA Prince William Decade Greats (30)	9.00
GS Quad City River Bandits (30)	9.00
GS Rancho Cucamonga Quakes (31)	45.00
GS R.C. Quakes w/ GTE ads (31)	50.00
MA Reading Phillies (28)	9.00
MA Reading Phillies Update (30)	9.00
BL Richmond Braves (30)	7.50
Richmond Camera Richmond Braves (20)	55.00
BL Rochester Red Wings (30)	8.50
MA Rockford Cubbies (30)	12.00
Team Rockford Cubbies (30)	17.00
Choice Salem Avalanche (30)	8.00
GS Salem-Keizer Volcanoes (36)	8.00
MA Salt Lake City Buzz (30)	8.00
GS San Antonio Missions (30)	11.00
GS San Bernardino Stampede (32)	8.00
San Bernardino Stampede team issue (28)	32.50
BL San Jose Giants (30)	7.50
MA Savannah Sand Gnats (30)	8.00
BL Scranton/Wilkes-Barre Red Barons (30)	9.00
Team S/W-B Red Barons 10th Anniver. (20)	9.00
MA Shreveport Captains (29)	10.00
MA Shreveport w/WK SportsCare ads (30)	10.00
Team Sonoma County Crushers (28)	6.50
MA South Atlantic League Prospects (30)	11.00
MA South Bend Silver Hawks (27)	10.00
GS Southern League Top Prospects (32)	9.00
GS Southern Oregon Timberjacks (33)	12.50
GS Spokane Indians (33)	8.50
Team St. Catherines Stompers	9.00
MA St. Luice Mets (30)	15.00
Team St. Paul Saints, Wheaties logo (32)	55.00
Team St. Paul Saints, no logo (32)	35.00
MA St. Petersburg Devil Rays (30)	11.00
GS Stockton Ports (30)	9.50
GS Stockton Ports Update (6)	8.00
GS Syracuse SkyChiefs (31)	8.00
BL Tacoma Rainiers (30)	9.00
MA Tampa Yankees (30)	20.00
GS Texas League Top Prospects (30)	10.00
BL Toledo Mud Hens (33)	9.00
MA Trenton Thunder (30)	10.00
MA Tucson Sidewinders (29)	8.50
Team Tulsa Drillers (27)	9.00
Team Tulsa Texas League Champs (32)	10.00
GS Vancouver Canadians (30)	28.00
Team Vermont Expos (35)	8.50
MA Vero Beach Dodgers (31)	9.50
GS Visalia Oaks (31)	15.00
WTC Waterbury Spirit (25)	6.50
Team Watertown Indians (35)	9.50
MA West Michigan Whitecaps (30)	7.50
MA West Tennessee Diamond Jaxx (30)	7.50
MA Wichita Wranglers (30)	8.50
MA Williamsport Cubs (30)	8.00
Team Williamsport Cubs Jeremy Gonzalez	5.00
Team Williamsport Cubs Kerry Wood	9.50
Team W. Cubs Kerry Wood phone card	9.00
Choice Wilmington Blue Rocks (30)	25.00
BL Winston-Salem Warthogs (30)	10.00
MA Wisconsin Timber Rattlers (30)	11.50
GS Yakima Bears (34)	9.50

1999 Just Imagine Promos

These 10-card promo packs were issued to preview Just Minors second card issue of the season. All of the promo cards share a common back advertising the set and its inserts.

		MT
Complete Set (10):		12.00
Common Player:		1.00
(1)	Jeff Austin (Just Debuts)	1.00
(2)	Pat Burrell (Just 9)	2.50
(3)	Sean Casey (Just Longshots)	2.00
(4)	Sean Casey (Just Stars)	2.00
(5)	John Elway (vertical art)	2.00
(6)	John Elway (horizontal art)	2.00
(7)	Jody Gerut (Just Debuts)	1.00
(8)	Nick Johnson (Just Longshots)	2.50
(9)	Aramis Ramirez (Just 9)	1.00
(10)	Alfonso Soriano (Just Stars)	3.00

1999 Just Imagine

Contiguously numbered (#51-150) from where the company's earlier Just 99 series left off (#1-50), Just Imagine presents an almost entirely new checklist while retaining many of the design elements and insert series from the Just 99 issue. The main difference in the base cards is that the colored stripe presenting the player name is horizontal on Just Imagine, where it was vertical on Just 99 cards. Backs of the JI repeat a vertical slice of the front photo and offer previous year and career professional stats. Just Imagine was issued in six-card foil packs in which were seeded several insert series, including autographed cards.

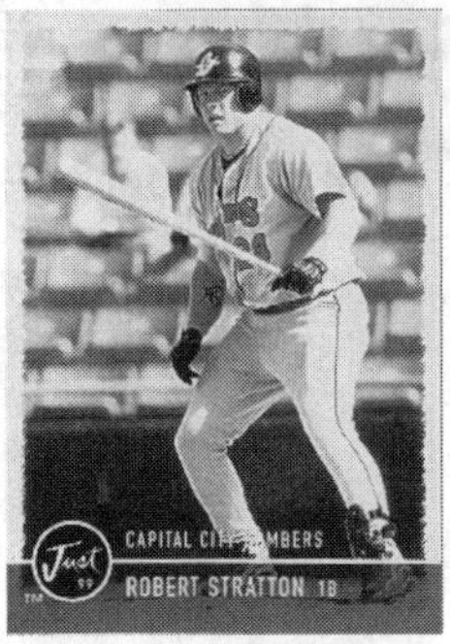

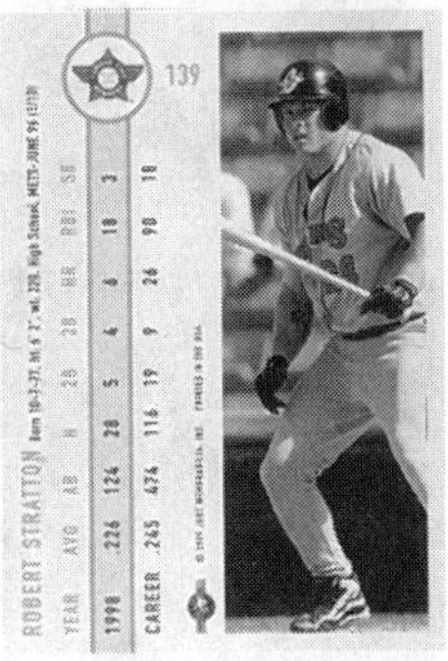

		MT
Complete Set (100):		15.00
Common Player:		.10
Wax Box:		25.00
51	Paul Ah Yat	.25
52	Israel Alcantara (team name in stripe)	.10
53	Erick Almonte	.10
54	Gabe Alvarez	.35
55	Tony Armas, Jr.	.25
56	Jeff Austin	.35
57	Benito Baez	.10
58	Kevin Beirne	.10
59	Ron Belliard	.45
60	Micah Bowie	.35
61	Russell Branyan	.50
62	Antone Brooks	.15
63	A.J. Burnett	.25
64	Pat Burrell	1.00
65	Brent Butler	.10
66	Troy Cameron	.75
67	Sean Casey	.75
68	Bruce Chen	.50
69	Chin-Feng Chen	.75
70	Jin Ho Cho	.65
71	Jesus Colome	.25
72	Carl Crawford	.25
73	Bubba Crosby	.10
74	Jack Cust	.25
75	Mike Darr	.10
76	Ben Davis	.30
77	Octavio Dotel	.25
78	Kelly Dransfeldt	.10
79	Adam Dunn	.10
80	Erubiel Durazo	.25
81	John Elway (Oneonta Yankees)	1.00
81a	John Elway (autographed edition of 100)	125.00
82	John Elway (Denver Broncos)	1.00
83	Mario Encarnacion	.15
84	Seth Etherton	.15
85	Adam Everett	.15
86	Franky Figueroa	.10
87	Mike Frank	.10
88	Jon Garland	.25
89	Chris George	.10
90	Jody Gerut	.25
91	Derrick Gibson	.45
92	Jerry Hairston Jr.	.40
93	Josh Hamilton	2.00
94	Jason Hart	.10
95	Chad Harville	.15
96	Nathan Haynes	.10
97	Junior Herndon	.10
98	Shea Hillenbrand	.10
99	Matt Holliday	.40
100	Brandon Inge	.10
101	Jacque Jones	.45
102	Gabe Kapler	.65
103	Austin Kearns	.10
104	Brandon Larson	.10

105	Jason LaRue	.75
106	Carlos Lee	.20
107	Corey Lee	.15
108	Donny Leon	.10
109	George Lombard	.55
110	Julio Lugo, Jr.	.15
111	Chris Magruder	.20
112	Mark Mangum	.10
113	Jason Marquis	.10
114	Ruben Mateo	.50
115	Luis Matos	.25
116	Gary Matthews Jr.	.25
117	Juan Melo	.30
118	Orber Moreno	.10
119	Mark Mulder	.40
120	Corey Patterson	.50
121	Angel Pena	.20
122	Elvis Pena	.20
123	Kyle Peterson	.15
124	Adam Piatt	.75
125	Calvin Pickering	.75
126	Jeremy Powell	.10
127	Luke Prokopec	.10
128	Aramis Ramirez	.45
129	Julio Ramirez	.10
130	Matt Riley	.25
131	Luis Rivera	.25
132	Grant Roberts	.15
133	Ryan Rupe	.20
134	C.C. Sabathia	.25
135	Luis Saturria	.10
136	Fernando Seguignol	.15
137	Alfonso Soriano	1.50
138	Patrick Strange	.10
139	Robert Stratton	.15
140	Reggie Taylor	.25
141	Jorge Toca	.10
142	Tony Torcato	.10
143	Bubba Trammell	.15
144	T.J. Tucker	.10
145	Juan Uribe	.10
146	Kip Wells	.40
147	Ricky Williams (Piedmont Boll Weevils)	1.50
148	Ricky Williams (Texas Longhorns)	1.50
149	Kevin Witt	.15
150	Ed Yarnall	.25

1999 Just Imagine Just Black

Issued at the rate of just one per case (240 packs), this set parallels the base issue, except for the presence of black borders on front and individual serial numbers within an edition of 50 cards each.

	MT
Common Player:	12.50
High-demand Players: 100X (See 1999 Just Imagine for checklist and base card values.)	

1999 Just Imagine Autographs - Base Set

Authentically autographed cards from Just Minors' Imagine issue were seeded at the average rate of two per 24-pack box. Autographed cards repeat the photo used in the base set but have the bottom portion ghosted to allow the autograph to appear more prominently. Backs have a congratulatory message.

		MT
Complete Set (46):		265.00
Common Player:		4.00
(1)	Israel Alcantara	4.00
(2)	Hector Almonte	4.00
(3)	Rick Ankiel	45.00
(4)	Jeff Austin	10.00
(5)	Benito Baez	4.00
(6)	Kevin Barker	4.00
(7)	Kevin Beirne	7.00
(8)	Micah Bowie	7.00
(9)	Antone Brooks	4.00
(10)	Sean Casey	25.00
(11)	Jesus Colome	4.00
(12)	Bubba Crosby	6.00
(13)	Jack Cust	8.00
(14)	Ben Davis	6.00
(15)	Seth Etherton	6.00
(16)	Mike Frank	6.00
(17)	Jon Garland	8.00
(18)	Chris George	7.00
(19)	Jason Grilli	6.00
(20)	Junior Herndon	6.00
(21)	Gabe Kapler	12.00
(22)	Corey Lee	8.00
(24)	Danny Leon	8.00
(25)	George Lombard	7.00
(26)	Julio Lugo, Jr.	4.00
(27)	Chris Magruder	6.00
(28)	Mark Mangum	4.00
(28)	Jason Marquis	6.00
(29)	Luis Matos	6.00
(30)	Juan Melo	12.00
(31)	Orber Moreno	8.00
(32)	Pablo Ozuna	12.00
(33)	Kyle Peterson	7.00
(34)	Ben Petrick	6.00
(35)	Calvin Pickering	12.00
(36)	Aramis Ramirez	8.00
(37)	Zach Sorensen	6.00
(38)	Alfonso Soriano	35.00
(39)	Patrick Strange	10.00
(40)	Reggie Taylor	5.00
(41)	Jorge Toca	6.00
(42)	Bubba Trammell	6.00
(43)	T.J. Tucker	7.00
(44)	Juan Uribe	4.00
(45)	Kip Wells	6.00
(46)	Randy Wolf	7.00

1999 Just Imagine Autographs - Die-cut

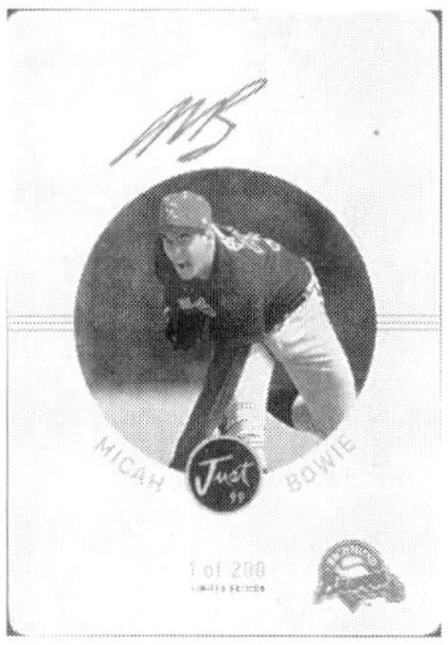

Some of the players who appear in the autographed card series (and a few who don't) can also be found in a much more limited autographed insert. Called die-cut autographs, these cards repeat in a circle at center the photo found on the base card. The background is white with the autograph at top; corners are rounded. On back, each die-cut autograph card is serially numbered from within an edition of 200.

		MT
Complete Set (17):		195.00
Common Player:		7.50
(1)	Rick Ankiel	50.00
(2)	Jeff Austin	12.00
(3)	Kevin Beirne	7.50
(4)	Micah Bowie	12.00
(5)	Troy Cameron	15.00
(6)	Seth Etherton	7.50
(7)	Mike Frank	7.50
(8)	Chris George	9.00
(9)	Gabe Kapler	25.00
(10)	George Lombard	15.00
(11)	Jason Marquis	9.00
(12)	Pablo Ozuna	12.00
(13)	Calvin Pickering	15.00
(14)	Zach Sorensen	7.50
(15)	Jorge Toca	7.50
(16)	T.J. Tucker	10.00
(17)	Randy Wolf	7.50

Player names in *Italic* type indicate a rookie card.

1999 Just Imagine Autographs - Just Imagine

Some of the players who appear in the base autographed card series (and a few who don't) can also be found in a much more limited insert, called Just Imagine Autographs. On back, each Just Imagine autograph card is serially numbered from within an edition of 200.

		MT
Complete Set (23):		300.00
Common Player:		6.00
(1)	Israel Alcantara	6.00
(2)	Rick Ankiel	40.00
(3)	Jeff Austin	8.00
(4)	Micah Bowie	10.00
(5)	Sean Casey	20.00
(6)	Jack Cust	6.00
(7)	John Elway	6.00
(8)	Mike Frank	9.00
(9)	Rafael Furcal	12.00
(10)	Jon Garland	9.00
(11)	Gabe Kapler	15.00
(12)	Julio Lugo, Jr.	6.00
(13)	Jason Marquis	9.00
(14)	Pablo Ozuna	15.00
(15)	Kyle Peterson	10.00
(16)	Julio Ramirez	9.00
(17)	Alfonso Soriano	35.00
(18)	Jorge Toca	9.00
(19)	T.J. Tucker	10.00
(20)	Kip Wells	6.00
(22)	Ricky Williams (Texas Longhorns)	35.00
(23)	Ricky Williams (Heisman Trophy)	40.00

1999 Just Imagine Just Debut

Inserted one per box as a box-topper and sealed inside a paper envelope, this insert set chronicles the professional debut of 10 top minor league prospects. Fronts have a color photo at center with a ticket design at bottom. Backs have two small black-and-white copies of the front photo, statistics from the debut game and career highlights. Numbered on front, cards have a "JD-0999-" prefix.

		MT
Complete Set (10):		12.00
Common Player:		1.00
01	Jeff Austin	2.50
02	Chin-Feng Chen	3.00
03	Erubiel Durazo	2.00
04	Jody Gerut	1.00
05	Josh Hamilton	3.00
06	Corey Patterson	1.50
07	Alfonso Soriano	4.00
08	Jorge Toca	1.00
09	Kip Wells	2.50
10	Brad Wilkerson	2.00

1999 Just Imagine Just Longshots

Seeded at the rate of about one per eight foil packs (three per box) these insert cards feature players who have overcome long odds as low picks in the amateur draft to arrive on the brink of major league stardom. Fronts have action photos on a white background. In the black data box at bottom along with player identification is information on the round in which he was drafted and his overall rank in the draft. Backs have a monocolor version of the photo in the background and a few words about the player and his career to date. Card numbers on back have an "LS" prefix and the player's initials as a suffix.

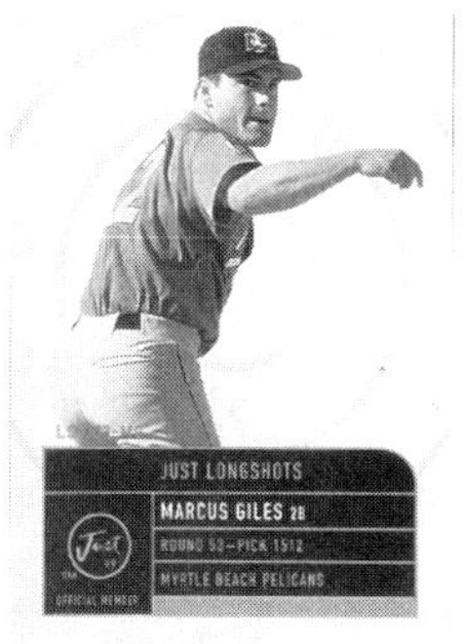

		MT
Complete Set (10):		7.00
Common Player:		.50
001	Wes Anderson	.50
002	David Eckstein	.50
003	Marcus Giles	1.00
004	Kevin Haverbusch	.75
005	Gabe Kapler	1.00
006	Julio Lugo, Jr.	.50
007	Gary Matthews Jr.	.80
008	Ryan Minor	.85
009	Jason Regan	.50
010	Daryle Ward	.75

1999 Just Imagine Just Nine

Top Prospects at each position are featured in this insert set. Fronts have a small player photo at top-center, which is repeated larger in the background in a single color. Backs repeat the front photo and have a few career highlights. Cards are inserted one per case (240 packs).

	MT
Complete Set (9):	135.00
Common Player:	12.50
JN-01Rick Ankiel	25.00
JN-02Ron Belliard	12.50
JN-03Pat Burrell	20.00
JN-04Lance Berkman	18.00
JN-05Ben Davis	12.50
JN-06Ruben Mateo	18.00
JN-07Corey Patterson	12.50
JN-08Aramis Ramirez	15.00
JN-09Alfonso Soriano	25.00

1999 Just Imagine Just Stars

Ten of the biggest names on 1999 minor league rosters are presented in this insert series which was seeded on the average of one per box (24 packs) in Just Imagine. Only the star-shaped central portion of the front photo is printed in color, the rest is black-and-white. Backs repeat a portion of the front photo in a colored star on a white background. A few career highlights and predictions are also included.

	MT
Complete Set (10):	15.00
Common Player:	1.00
JS-01Rick Ankiel	3.00
JS-02Pat Burrell	2.50
JS-03Sean Casey	1.50
JS-04Erubiel Durazo	2.00
JS-05Ben Davis	1.00
JS-06Jacque Jones	1.50
JS-07Ruben Mateo	2.00
JS-08Gary Matthews Jr.	1.50
JS-09Adam Piatt	2.00
JS-10Alfonso Soriano	3.00

1999 Just Justifiable '99 Promos

Top minor league stars are featured on the sample cards issued to promote Just's third issue of 1999. As was the case with the company's other promo cards, not all of the players seen on the samples were issued in the set. Backs of all the sample cards are identical, detailing the forthcoming Justifiable '99 issue.

		MT
Complete Set (5):		12.00
Common Player:		3.00
(1)	Pat Burrell (Just the Facts)	4.50
(2)	Sean Burroughs (base card)	3.50
(3)	Josh Hamilton (Just Debuts)	4.50
(4)	Adam Piatt (Just Spotlights)	3.00
(5)	Ben Sheets (Just Drafted)	3.00

1999 Just Justifiable

Numbered from 151-250, this minor league singles issue continues where Just's The Start (#1-50) and Imagine (#51-150) left off earlier in the year. Justifiable was sold in a 24-pack box (six cards per pack) which included one of five 6" player action figures. The Justifiable base cards are in the same basic format as the earlier issues, except the color strip which contains the player name is vertically on the right side of the card. Backs repeat a vertical slice of the front photo and include 1998 and career stats, along with a team logo.

		MT
Complete Set (100):		15.00
Common Player:		.10
Wax Box:		35.00
151	Winston Abreu	.10
152	Chris Aguila	.10
153	Bronson Arroyo	.15

154	Robert Averette	.10
155	Mike Bacsik	.10
156	Andrew Beinbrink	.10
157	Matt Belisle	.10
158	Matt Blank	.10
159	Jung Bong	.15
160	Milton Bradley	.25
161	Ryan Bradley	.10
162	Dee Brown	.25
163	Sean Burroughs	1.00
164	Chance Caple	.10
165	Hee Choi	2.00
166	Mike Christensen	.15
167	Doug Clark	.10
168	Javier Colina	.10
169	Brian Cooper	.10
170	Pat Daneker	.10
171	Randey Dorame	.10
172	Ryan Drese	.10
173	Chris Duncan	.10
174	Adam Dunn	.10
175	David Eckstein	.10
176	Alex Fernandez	.15
177	Choo Freeman	.35
178	Neil Friendling	.10
179	Eddy Furniss	.15
180	B.J. Garbe	.25
181	Yon German	.10
182	Esteban German	.20
183	Dan Gummitt	.10
184	Will Hartley	.10
185	Jesus Hernandez	.10
186	Alex Hernandez	.10
187	Jay Hood	.10
188	Aubrey Huff	.10
189	Chad Hutchinson	.10
190	Jason Jennings	.25
191	Jaime Jones	.10
192	David Kelton	.25
193	Michael Lamb	.15
194	Jacques Landry	.10
195	Ryan Langerhans	.50
196	Nelson Lara	.10
197	Nick Leach	.15
198	Steve Lomasney	.25
199	Felipe Lopez	.10
200	Ryan Ludwick	.10
201	Pat Manning	.20
202	T.R. Marcinczyk	.25
203	Hipolito Martinez	.10
204	Tony McKnight	.10
205	Tydus Meadows	.25
206	Corky Miller	.10
207	Frank Moore	.10
208	Scott Morgan	.10
209	Tony Mota	.10
210	Ntema Ndungidi	.10
211	David Noyce	.10
212	Franklin Nunez	.10
213	Jose Ortiz	.25
214	Jimmy Osting	.10
215	Jorge Padilla	.10
216	Mike Paradis	.10
217	Brandon Parker	.25
218	Jarrod Patterson	.10
219	John Patterson	.25
220	Jay Payton	.10
221	Juan Pena	.15
222	Brad Penny	.10
223	Danny Peoples	.25
224	Paul Phillips	.10
225	Josh Pressley	.10
226	Tim Raines, Jr.	.50
227	Paul Rigdon	.20
228	Jimmy Rollins	.10
229	J.C. Romero	.10
230	Marcos Scutaro	.10
231	Sammy Serrano	.10
232	Wascar Serrano	.15
233	Ben Sheets	.10
234	Carlos Silva	.10
235	Scott Sobkowiak	.10
236	Ramon Soler	.10
237	Shawn Sonnier	.10
238	Jovanny Sosa	.10
239	Jason Standridge	.30
240	Brent Stentz	.10
241	Seth Taylor	.20
242	Jason Tyner	.15
243	Brant Ust	.10
244	Eric Valent	.25
245	Ismael Villegas	.10
246	David Walling	.15
247	Rico Washington	.20
248	Brad Wilkerson	.10
249	Patrick Williams	.20
250	Barry Zito	.40

1999 Just Justifiable Just Black

Issued at the rate of just one per case (240 packs), this set parallels the base issue, except for the presence of black borders on front and individual serial numbers within an edition of 50 cards each.

	MT
Common Player:	12.50
High-demand Players: 100X	

(See 1999 Just Justifiable for checklist and base card values.)

1999 Just Justifiable Autographs - Base Set

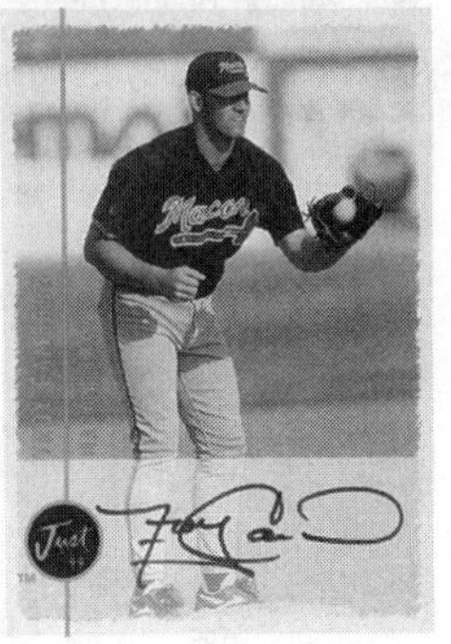

Base-set autographed cards from Just Minors' Justifiable issue were seeded at the average rate of two per 24-pack box. Autographed cards repeat the photo used in the base set but have the bottom portion ghosted to allow the autograph to appear more prominently. Backs have a congratulatory message.

		MT
Complete Set (18):		200.00
Common Player:		4.00
(1)	Rick Ankiel	45.00
(2)	Sean Burroughs	30.00
(3)	Eric Byrnes	4.00
(4)	Troy Cameron	20.00
(5)	Juan Dilone	4.00
(6)	Rafael Furcal	12.00
(7)	Jason Hart	4.00
(8)	Shea Hillenbrand	8.00
(9)	Nick Johnson	30.00
(10)	Adam Kennedy	12.00
(11)	Mark Mulder	8.00
(12)	Pablo Ozuna	9.00
(13)	Corey Patterson	15.00
(14)	Angel Pena	8.00
(15)	Julio Ramirez	6.00
(16)	Matt Riley	6.00
(17)	Grant Roberts	4.00
(18)	Tony Torcato	4.00

1999 Just Justifiable Autographs - Die-Cut

Some of the players who appear in the autographed card base set (and a few who don't) can also be found in a much more limited autographed insert. Called die-cut autographs, these cards repeat the photo found on the base card in a circle at center. The background is white with the autograph at top; corners are rounded. On back, each die-cut autograph card is serially numbered from within an edition of 200.

		MT
Complete Set (7):		160.00
Common Player:		8.00
(1)	Rick Ankiel	65.00
(2)	Matt Belisle	8.00
(3)	Sean Burroughs	50.00
(4)	Gil Meche	15.00
(5)	Mark Mulder	15.00
(6)	Corey Patterson	35.00
(7)	Matt Riley	8.00

1999 Just Justifiable Autographs - Just Diamonds

Some of the players who appear in the base autographed card series (and a few who don't) can also be found in a much more limited insert, called Just Diamonds Autographs. The cards have player pictures in a diamond frame at the center of a white background. A trapazoid at bottom has the signature. On back, each Just Diamonds autograph card is serially numbered from within an edition of 200.

		MT
Complete Set (11):		225.00
Common Player:		8.00
(1)_	Rick Ankiel	65.00
(2)	Matt Belisle	8.00
(3)	Sean Burroughs	50.00
(4)	Troy Cameron	30.00
(5)	Dionys Cesar	8.00
(6)	Rafael Furcal	15.00
(7)	Nick Johnson	30.00
(8)	Pablo Ozuna	12.00
(9)	Corey Patterson	35.00
(10)	Aramis Ramirez	12.00
(11)	Kip Wells	8.00

1999 Just Justifiable Just Debut

These are the rarest inserts in Justifiable, found only one per 240 packs. There is a horizontal color photo at center with black borders at top and bottom. Details of the player's first professional game are in the bottom border. Card numbers are prefixed with "JD".

		MT
Complete Set (10):		250.00
Common Player:		15.00
01	B.J. Garbe	15.00
02	Ben Sheets	20.00
03	Jeff Austin	25.00
04	Chin-Feng Chen	40.00
05	Jody Gerut	15.00
06	Josh Hamilton	40.00
07	Corey Patterson	35.00
08	Alfonso Soriano	75.00
09	Jorge Luis Toca	20.00
10	Kip Wells	15.00

1999 Just Justifiable Just Drafted

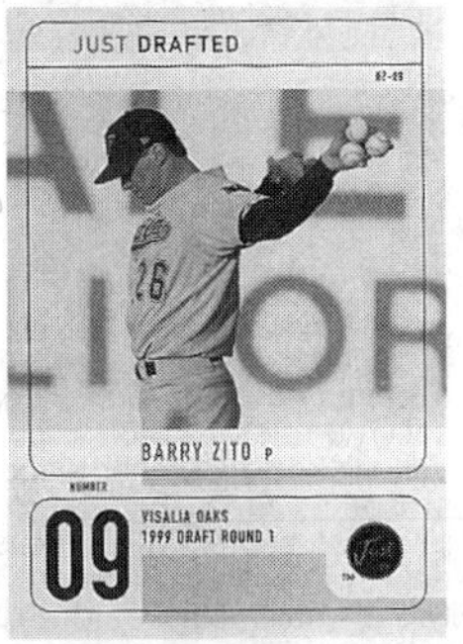

This insert of 1999 draftees was issued one per box sealed in a black paper envelope. Fronts have a horizontal color photo at center with draft details below. Backs have a few career numbers and a team logo. Cards are numbered with a "JD" prefix.

		MT
Complete Set (10):		3.00
Common Player:		3.00
01	Larry Bigbie	3.00
02	Chance Caple	3.00
03	Chris Duncan	4.00
04	B.J. Garbe	3.00
05	Josh Hamilton	6.00
06	Will Hartley	3.00
07	Mike Paradis	3.00
08	Ben Sheets	4.00
09	David Walling	3.00
10	Barry Zito	5.00

Checklists with card numbers in parentheses ( ) indicates the numbers do not appear on the card.

1999 Just Justifiable Just Figures

In the first-ever random pairing of baseball cards and action figures, each box of Just Justifiable included one of five action player figures along with 24 foil packs of minor league cards. About 6" tall, each figure has poseable arms and legs. Each player was issued in both fielding and batting versions. Certain figures, details of which were not released, were issued in more limited numbers in one or the other of their poses. Until that situation is clarified, only a common figure value will be shown in these listings. Besides the five players issued in boxes, a Rick Ankiel figure was available exclusive via mail-in offer for $13.

		MT
Common Figure:		8.00
(1a)	Hank Aaron (1974 Atlanta Braves, batting)	
(1b)	Hank Aaron (1974 Atlanta Braves, fielding)	
(2a)	Michael Barrett (1998 Harrisburg Senators, batting)	
(2b)	Michael Barrett (1998 Harrisburg Senators, fielding)	
(3a)	John Elway (1982 Oneonta Yankees, batting)	
(3b)	John Elway (1982 Oneonta Yankees, fielding)	
(4a)	Gabe Kapler 1998 Jacksonville Suns, batting)	
(4b)	Gabe Kapler (1998 Jacksonville Suns, fielding)	
(5a)	Ricky Williams (1996 Piedmont Boll Weevils, batting)	
(5b)	Ricky Williams (1996 Piedmont Boll Weevils, fielding)	
(6)	Rick Ankiel	

1999 Just Justifiable Just Spotlights

Seeded one per 24-pack box, these inserts feature top minor league stars. Fronts have a white background with spotlight beams and a color player photo in the center circle. Backs repeat the front photo in full-size format and have career highlights and biographical data. Cards numbers are prefixed with "JS".

		MT
Complete Set (10):		
Common Player:		2.00
01	Dee Brown	2.00
02	Pat Burrell	12.00
03	Josh Hamilton	6.00
04	Nick Johnson	12.00
05	Jason Marquis	2.00
06	Pablo Ozuna	2.00
07	John Patterson	9.00
08	Adam Piatt	6.00
09	Matt Riley	4.00
10	Alfonso Soriano	12.00

1999 Just Justifiable Just the Facts

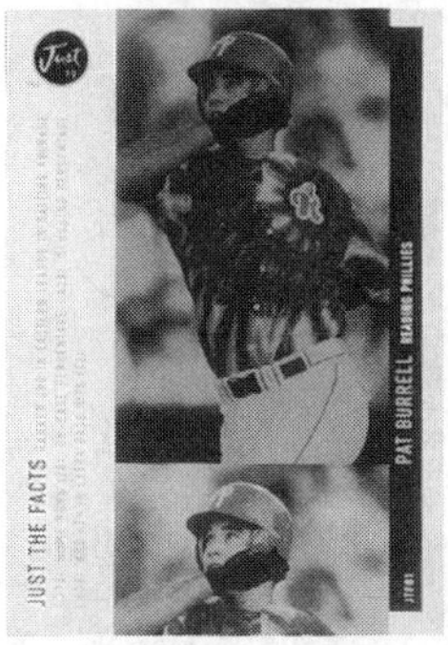

Top talent in the minor leagues is featured in this insert set found on average of one per 24 packs. Cards have monochromatic versions of the same photo on front, along with a few player details and career highlights. Backs have the full-color version of the photo vertically and a bit more personal detail. Card numbers have a "JTF" prefix.

		MT
Complete Set (10):		50.00
Common Player:		2.00
01	Pat Burrell	12.00
02	Sean Burroughs	9.00
03	Adam Eaton	2.00
04	Marcus Giles	4.00
05	Josh Hamilton	6.00
06	Nick Johnson	12.00
07	Corey Patterson	6.00
08	Jason Standridge	3.00
09	Jorge Luis Toca	3.00
10	Eric Valent	2.00

1999 Just The Start Promos

To introduce its premiere minor league issue, Just Minors produced a set of five promotional cards typifying its base set and four inserts. Fronts are virtually identical to the issued versions. Backs are generic with manufacturer and minor league association logo, copyright information, promotional notice and "1 of 5".

		MT
Complete Set (5):		15.00
Common Player:		3.00
(1)	Ryan Anderson (base set)	3.00
(2)	Lance Berkman (Just Nine)	3.00
(3)	Pat Burrell (Just News)	6.00
(4)	Gabe Kapler (Just Power)	5.00
(5)	Ruben Mateo (Just Due)	4.50

1999 Just The Start

The Just 99 base set features a large color photo on front with white borders at top, bottom and right. At left is a 1/2" vertical color strip in which the player's name and position appears; his team name is vertically to the right of that strip. The Just 99 logo is at bottom. Backs repeat a portion of the front photo on the right. Horizontally at left are personal data, 1998 and pro career stats. A team logo and card number are at top center. The issue was sold in six-card foil packs and 24-pack boxes.

		MT
Complete Set (50):		12.50
Common Player:		.10
Wax Box:		25.00
1	Hector Almonte	.30
2	Wes Anderson	.10
3	Ryan Anderson	.75
4	Clayton Andrews	.15
5	Rick Ankiel	2.00
6	Brad Baisley	.25
7	Kevin Barker	.65
8	Michael Barrett	.50
9	Kris Benson	.65
10	Peter Bergeron	.55
11	Lance Berkman	.25
12	Nate Bump	.50
13	Eric Byrnes	.35
14	Giuseppe Chiaramonte	.50
15	Glenn Davis	1.00
16	Juan Dilone	.15
17	Eric DuBose	.10
18	Rick Elder	.25
19	Alex Escobar	.65
20	Rafael Furcal	.65
21	Shawn Gallagher	.50
22	Marcus Giles	1.50
23	Geoff Goetz	.25
24	Jason Grilli	.45
25	Cristian Guzman	.35
26	Mark Harriger	.10
27	Nick Johnson	.75
28	Gabe Kapler	1.25
29	Kenny Kelly	.30
30	Adam Kennedy	.75
31	Corey Lee	.25
32	Kevin McGlinchy	.50
33	Gil Meche	.40
34	Jackson Melian	.75
35	Warren Morris	.60
36	Ricky Williams (baseball)	2.50
37	Pablo Ozuna	.35
38	Ben Petrick	.25
39	Scott Pratt	.20
40	Chris Reinike	.15
41	Zach Sorenson	.30
42	Dernell Stenson	.75
43	Andy Thompson	.10
44	Luis Vizcaino	.25
45	Daryle Ward	.50
46	Vernon Wells	.75
47	Jayson Werth	.50
48	Jake Westbrook	.35
49	Ricky Williams (football)	3.00
50	Randy Wolf	.65

1999 Just The Start Just Black

Issued at the rate of just one per case (240 packs), this set parallels the base issue, except for the presence of black borders on front and individual serial numbers within an edition of 50 cards each.

	MT
Common Player:	12.50
High-demand Players: 100X	

(See 1999 Just the Start for checklist and base card values.)

1999 Just The Start Autographs

Authentically autographed cards from Just Minors debut issue were seeded at the average rate of two per 24-pack box. Autographed cards repeat the photo used in the base set but have the bottom portion ghosted to allow the autograph to appear more prominently. Backs have a congratulatory message.

		MT
Complete Set (25):		150.00
Common Player:		3.00
(1)	Hector Almonte	3.00
(2)	Brad Baisley	4.50
(3)	Michael Barrett	8.00
(4)	Kris Benson	6.00
(5)	Brent Billingsley	3.00
(6)	Casey Blake	3.00
(7)	Glenn Davis	7.50
(8)	Juan Dilone	5.00
(9)	Rick Elder	6.00
(10)	Mark Fischer	4.00
(11)	Rafael Furcal	7.50
(12)	Geoff Goetz	4.50
(13)	Jason Grilli	4.50
(14)	Mark Harriger	3.00
(15)	Heath Honeycutt	4.50
(16)	Gabe Kapler	8.00
(17)	Adam Kennedy	5.00
(18)	Juan Melo	9.00
(19)	Mark Mulder	6.00
(20)	Andy Thompson	3.00
(21)	Peter Tucci	5.00
(22)	Luis Vizcaino	6.00
(23)	Jayson Werth	6.00
(24)	Jake Westbrook	7.50
(25)	Ricky Williams	60.00

1999 Just The Start Autographs - Die-cut

Some of the players who appear in the autographed card series can also be found in a much more limited autographed insert. Called die-cut autographs, these cards repeat in a circle at center the photo found on the base card. The background is white with the autograph at top; corners are rounded. On back, each die-cut autograph card is serially numbered from within an edition of 200.

		MT
Complete Set (15):		200.00
Common Player:		7.50
(1)	Hector Almonte	7.50
(2)	Brad Baisley	9.00
(3)	Michael Barrett	15.00
(4)	Kris Benson	12.00
(5)	Casey Blake	7.50
(6)	Glenn Davis	15.00
(7)	Rick Elder	9.00
(8)	Geoff Goetz	10.00
(9)	Jason Grilli	7.50
(10)	Mark Harriger	7.50
(11)	Gabe Kapler	25.00
(12)	Mark Mulder	12.00
(13)	Jayson Werth	7.50
(14)	Jake Westbrook	15.00
(15)	Ricky Williams	125.00

1999 Just The Start Just Due

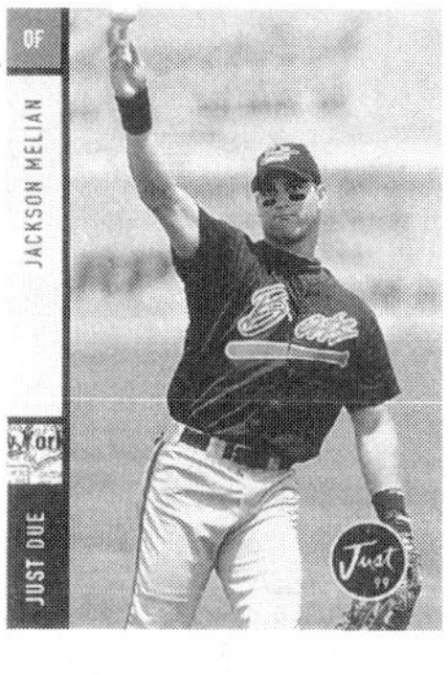

Players on the brink of their major league careers and projected stardom are featured in this insert series. Cards have large color action photos on front and a tiny map at left specifying the city where their parent major league team plays. Backs have a repeat of the front elements, with a small photo and larger map, along with personal data and career highlights. Stated odds of insertion are one per six packs.

	MT
Complete Set (10):	7.50
Common Player:	.50
Jd-01Michael Barrett	1.00
Jd-02Kris Benson	1.00
Jd-03Peter Bergeron	.50
Jd-04Lance Berkman	2.00
Jd-05Nick Johnson	2.00
Jd-06Gabe Kapler	1.75
Jd-07Corey Lee	.50
Jd-08Jackson Melian	1.00
Jd-09Dernell Stenson	.75
Jd-10Randy Wolf	.50

1999 Just The Start Just News

The scarcest of the Just 99 inserts, found at the rate of just one per 240 packs.

	MT
Complete Set (6):	125.00
Common Player:	12.50
Jn-01Rick Ankiel, Alex Escobar	30.00
Jn-02Marcus Giles, Mark Harriger	12.50
Jn-03Gabe Kapler, Kevin McGlinchy	25.00
Jn-04Jackson Melian, Warren Morris	12.50
Jn-05Dernell Stenson, Vernon Wells	20.00
Jn-06Ricky Williams, Ricky Williams	40.00

1999 Just The Start Just Nine

Top Prospects at each position are featured in this insert set. Fronts have a small player photo at top-center, which is repeated larger in the background in a single color. Backs repeat the front photo and have a few career highlights. Cards are inserted one per box as a box-topper in a sealed paper envelope.

	MT
Complete Set (9):	17.50
Common Player:	1.00
J9-01Rick Ankiel	5.00
J9-02Michael Barrett	3.00
J9-03Lance Berkman	2.00
J9-04Alex Escobar	3.00
J9-05Nick Johnson	2.50
J9-06Gabe Kapler	3.00
J9-07Warren Morris	1.00
J9-08Pablo Ozuna	1.50
J9-09Ben Petrick	1.00

1999 Just The Start Just Power

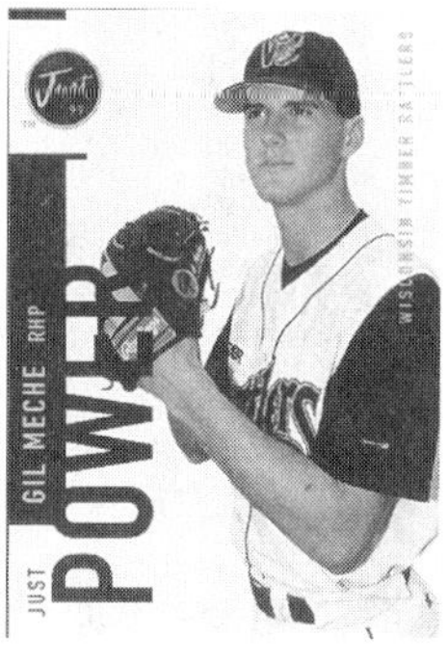

Some of the hardest hitters and throwers in the minor leagues are included in this chase set. Seeded one per 24-pack box, the cards have player action photos on front on a white background. The photo is repeated on back with its full background, but only in one color. A few career highlights also appear on back.

	MT
Complete Set (10):	18.00
Common Player:	1.00
Jp-01Ryan Anderson	2.00
Jp-02Wes Anderson	1.00
Jp-03Lance Berkman	2.00
Jp-04Juan Dilone	1.00
Jp-05Marcus Giles	4.00
Jp-06Gabe Kapler	3.00
Jp-07Kevin McGlinchy	2.00
Jp-08Gil Meche	1.00
Jp-09Dernell Stenson	2.00
Jp-10Ricky Williams	7.50

1999 SP Top Prospects

The projected stars of the new millenium were previewed in Upper Deck's SP Top Prospects minor league set issued in the 1999 preseason. The 126 cards in the base set have player photos surrounded by gold refractive-foil borders. The player's major league parent team is named at top and the logo of his 1998 minor league team is at lower-right. Backs have another color photo, a few words about the player and his minor league career stats. A parallel President's Edition set, with only 10 numbered cards of each player, was also released. The President's Edition cards replace the gold front borders with silver. The issue was sold in eight-card packs with a suggested retail price of $4.99.

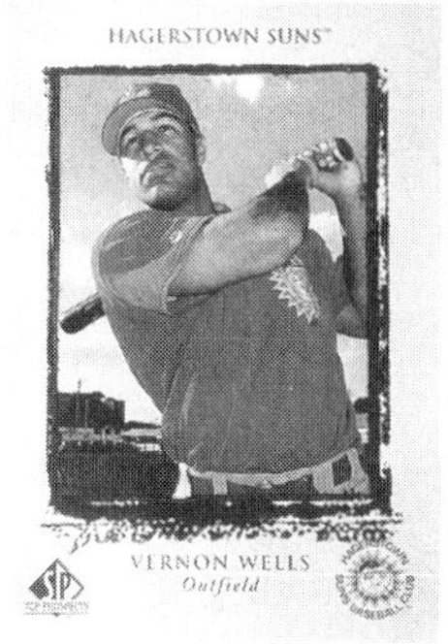

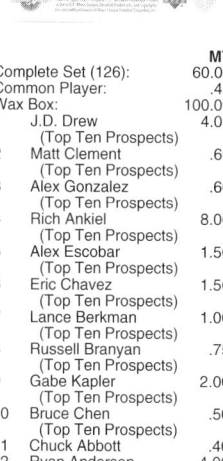

		MT
Complete Set (126):		60.00
Common Player:		.40
Wax Box:		100.00
1	J.D. Drew (Top Ten Prospects)	4.00
2	Matt Clement (Top Ten Prospects)	.60
3	Alex Gonzalez (Top Ten Prospects)	.60
4	Rich Ankiel (Top Ten Prospects)	8.00
5	Alex Escobar (Top Ten Prospects)	1.50
6	Eric Chavez (Top Ten Prospects)	1.50
7	Lance Berkman (Top Ten Prospects)	1.00
8	Russell Branyan (Top Ten Prospects)	.75
9	Gabe Kapler (Top Ten Prospects)	2.00
10	Bruce Chen (Top Ten Prospects)	.50
11	Chuck Abbott	.40
12	Ryan Anderson	4.00
13	Rick Ankiel	10.00
14	Michael Barrett	.75
15	Carlos Beltran	.75
16	Buck Jacobsen	.75
17	Kris Benson	.75
18	Lance Berkman	1.00
19	Ryan Brannan	.40
20	Russell Branyan	.75
21	Dermal Brown	.75
22	Roosevelt Brown	.40
23	Juan LeBron	.40
24	Brent Butler	.75
25	Ross Gload	.75
26	Eric Chavez	1.50
27	Bruce Chen	.50
28	Matt Clement	.60
29	Adonis Harrison	.75
30	Francisco Cordero	.40
31	David Cortes	1.50
32	Paxton Crawford	.75
33	Joe Crede	.40
34	Bobby Cripps	.40
35	Mike Cuddyer	2.00
36	John Curtice	.75
37	Mike Darr	.40
38	Ben Davis	.40
39	Glenn Davis	.40
40	Matt DeWitt	.40
41	Shea Hillenbrand	.40
42	Adam Eaton	.40
43	Mario Encarnacion	1.00
44	Chris Enochs	.75
45	Pat Burrell	5.00
46	Kyle Farnsworth	.75
47	Nelson Figueroa	.40
48	Shawn Gallagher	.75
49	Chad Hutchinson	.75
50	Marcus Giles	.40

51	J.D. Drew	4.00
52	Alex Gonzalez	.40
53	Chad Green	.40
54	Jason Grilli	.75
55	Seth Etherton	.75
56	Roy Halladay	.75
57	*Tyson Hartshorn*	.75
58	Al Hawkins	.40
59	Chad Hermansen	1.00
60	Ramon Hernandez	.75
61	Mark Johnson	.40
62	Doug Johnston	.40
63	Jacque Jones	.75
64	Adam Kennedy	.75
65	Cesar King	.75
66	Brendan Kingman	.40
67	Mike Kinkade	.75
68	Corey Koskie	.75
69	Mike Kusiewicz	.40
70	Mike Colangelo	.40
71	Jason LaRue	.40
72	Joe Lawrence	.40
73	Carlos Lee	1.00
74	Jeff Liefer	.40
75	Mike Lincoln	.40
76	George Lombard	.40
77	Mike Lowell	.75
78	Alex Escobar	2.50
79	Sam Marsonek	.40
80	Ruben Mateo	1.50
81	Brian Benefield	.40
82	Gary Matthews Jr.	.40
83	Joe Mays	.40
84	Jackson Melian	2.00
85	Juan Melo	.40
86	Chad Meyers	.40
87	Matt Miller	.40
88	Damon Minor	.40
89	Ryan Minor	.75
90	Mike Mitchell	.40
91	Shea Morenz	.40
92	Warren Morris	.40
93	Drew Henson	10.00
94	Todd Noel	.40
95	Pablo Ozuna	1.50
96	John Patterson	.75
97	Josh Paul	.40
98	Angel Pena	.40
99	Juan Pena	2.00
100	Danny Peoples	.40
101	Santiago Perez	.40
102	Tommy Peterman	.40
103	Ben Petrick	.40
104	Calvin Pickering	.75
105	John Powers	.40
106	Gabe Kapler	5.00
107	Rob Ramsey	.40
108	Luis Figueroa	.40
109	Grant Roberts	.40
110	Fernando Seguignol	2.00
111	Juan Sosa	.40
112	Dernell Stenson	1.50
113	John Stephens	.40
114	Mike Stoner	.75
115	Reggie Taylor	.40
116	Justin Towle	.40
117	Carlos Villalobos	.75
118	Vernon Wells	1.00
119	Jason Werth	.40
120	Jake Westbrook	.40
121	Matt White	.60
122	Ricky Williams	10.00
123	Kevin Witt	.40
124	Dewayne Wise	.50
125	Ed Yarnall	.75
126	Mike Zywica	.40

1999 SP Top Prospects President's Edition

The use of silver prismatic foil borders on front is the key visual difference on this parallel issue. Also on the front, the notation "President's Edition" is printed at top. On back the cards have a silver-foil serial number from within an edition of just 10 pieces each.

	MT
Common Player:	40.00
Stars: 100X	
(See 1999 SP Top Prosepcts for checklist and base card values.)	

1999 SP Top Prospects Chirography

Top draft picks are featured in this set of autographed insert cards. Fronts have player photos framed in gold foil on a white border. At bottom is the player's authentic autograph. Backs have a congratulatory notice from Upper Deck CEO Richard McWilliam. Cards are "numbered" with player initials. Insertion rate is one per 10 packs.

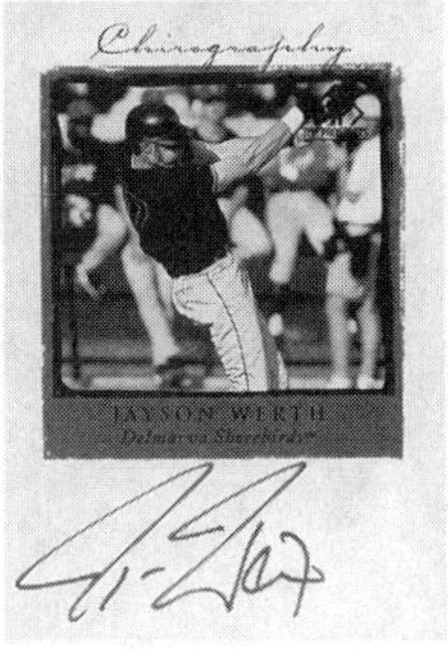

		MT
Complete Set (30):		
Common Player:		10.00
RA	Ryan Anderson	25.00
RiA	Rick Ankiel	40.00
LB	Lance Berkman	17.50
DB	Dermal Brown	10.00
BB	Brent Butler	10.00
EC	Eric Chavez	20.00
BC	Bruce Chen	15.00
MC	Matt Clement	17.50
FC	Francisco Cordero	10.00
DC	David Cortes	15.00
MD	Mike Darr	10.00
CE	Chris Enochs	15.00
CH	Chad Hermansen	15.00
RH	Ramon Hernandez	15.00
CK	Cesar King	15.00
MK	Mike Kinkade	15.00
CL	Carlos Lee	15.00
GL	George Lombard	15.00
ML	Mike Lowell	17.50
RM	Ruben Mateo	30.00
GM	Gary Matthews Jr.	17.50
JaM	Jackson Melian	22.00
JM	Juan Melo	10.00
RyM	Ryan Minor	20.00
WM	Warren Morris	17.50
JP	John Patterson	12.50
BP	Ben Petrick	15.00
JW	Jayson Werth	12.50
MW	Matt White	10.00
EY	Eddie Yarnell	17.50

1999 SP Top Prospects Destination the Show

The top names in minor league baseball are found in the checklist of this insert set. Cards have player photos on a silver-foil background. On back is an individual serial number from within an edition of 100 of each card.

		MT
Common Player:		12.50
D1	Ryan Anderson	62.00
D2	Rick Ankiel	60.00
D3	Lance Berkman	20.00
D4	Russell Branyan	12.50
D5	Juan Melo	12.50
D6	Alex Gonzalez	12.50
D7	Eric Chavez	50.00
D8	Bruce Chen	20.00
D9	Matt Clement	25.00
D10	Eddie Yarnell	25.00
D11	Dernell Stenson	40.00
D12	Corey Koskie	20.00
D13	J.D. Drew	120.00
D14	Chad Hermansen	30.00
D15	Ramon Hernandez	12.50
D16	Cesar King	20.00
D17	Mike Kinkade	25.00
D18	Carlos Lee	35.00
D19	George Lombard	25.00
D20	Ruben Mateo	40.00
D21	Gary Matthews Jr.	20.00
D22	Pat Burrell	65.00
D23	Ryan Minor	25.00
D24	Warren Morris	12.50
D25	Gabe Kapler	75.00
D26	Mike Lowell	20.00
D27	Jason Werth	12.50
D28	Matt White	12.50
D29	Pablo Ozuna	30.00
D30	Mike Stoner	20.00

The values of some parallel-card issues will have to be calculated based on figures presented in the heading for the regular-issue card set.

1999 SP Top Prospects Great Futures

Minor league players deemed to have especially "Great Futures" are featured in this insert set. Fronts have action photos on gold refractive-foil backgrounds. Backs repeat a detail of the front photo and offer a few career highlights and stats. Cards are numbered with a "GF" prefix. Stated rate of insertion was one per five packs.

		MT
Complete Set (30):		65.00
Common Player:		1.50
GF1	Ryan Anderson	8.00
GF2	Rick Ankiel	3.00
GF3	Lance Berkman	3.00
GF4	Russell Branyan	1.50
GF5	Dermal Brown	1.50
GF6	Brent Butler	1.50
GF7	Eric Chavez	4.00
GF8	Bruce Chen	2.50
GF9	Matt Clement	1.50
GF10	Eddie Yarnell	3.00
GF11	Mike Darr	1.50
GF12	Chris Enochs	1.50
GF13	J.D. Drew	15.00
GF14	Chad Hermansen	4.00
GF15	Ramon Hernandez	3.00
GF16	Cesar King	1.50
GF17	Mike Kinkade	1.50
GF18	Carlos Lee	3.00
GF19	George Lombard	1.50
GF20	Ruben Mateo	1.50
GF21	Gary Matthews Jr.	3.00
GF22	Jackson Melian	3.00
GF23	Ryan Minor	4.00
GF24	Warren Morris	1.50
GF25	John Patterson	1.50
GF26	Ben Petrick	1.50
GF27	Jason Werth	1.50
GF28	Matt White	2.00
GF29	Francisco Cordero	1.50
GF30	Mike Stoner	3.00

1999 SP Top Prospects Retrospectives

The minor league careers of two of the 20th Century's greatest athletes are recalled in this insert set. Fronts have player photos with a gold-foil frame on a white background. The regular inserts are inserted at an announced rate of one per 13 packs. Additionally, each player autographed 10 of the his cards.

	MT
Complete Set (10):	25.00
Common Griffey (R1-R5):	3.00
Common Jordan (R6-R10):	5.00
Griffey Autographed Card:	450.00
Jordan Autographed Card:	650.00

1999 Team Best Baseball America's Top Prospects Promos

Team Best partnered with baseball's best publication for minor league coverage to create a top prospects' card set. To debut the concept, this series of promo cards was issued. Fronts are virtually identical to the later-issued versions while all of the sample cards have an identical back. The back has a green baseball background with Team Best, Baseball America's Top Prospects, and National Association of Professional Baseball League's logos. A red strip at bottom has "Promotional Purposes Only" printed in white.

		MT
Complete Set (5):		10.00
Common Player:		2.00
(1)	Rick Ankiel (regular)	2.00
(2)	Lance Berkman (regular)	2.00
(3)	Pat Burrell (Possibilities)	5.00
(4)	Marcus Giles (MVP)	2.00
(5)	Ryan Minor (Scout's Choice)	3.50

1999 Team Best Baseball America's Top Prospects

The editors of "Baseball America" selected 100 top prospects for inclusion in this Team Best minor league issue which debuted in June. Cards have action photos on front which are bordered at top and right in red. BA's logotype appears at top. The player's minor league team logo is at bottom-right. Backs have biographical data, draft details and career highlights along with appropriate logos. Cards were sold in six-card foil packs.

		MT
Complete Set (100):		12.50
Common Player:		.10
Wax Box:		24.00
1	Paul Ah Yat	.15
2	Efrain Alamo	.10
3	Chip Alley	.15
4	Ryan Anderson	.25
5	Rick Ankiel	.75
6	Tony Armas, Jr.	.15
7	Bronson Arroyo	.20
8	Mike Bacsik	.10
9	Kevin Barker	.10
10	Fletcher Bates	.15
11	Rob Bell	.20
12	Ron Belliard	.25
13	Peter Bergeron	.25
14	Lance Berkman	.45
15	Nick Bierbrodt	.10
16	Milton Bradley	.10
17	Russell Branyan	.25
18	Pat Burrell	1.50
19	Sean Burroughs	.50
20	Brent Butler	.10
21	Bruce Chen	.25
22	Chin-Feng Chen	.75
23	Giuseppe Chiaramonte	.35
24	Jin Ho Cho	.50
25	Francis Collins	.10
26	Joe Crede	.15
27	Cesar Crespo	.10
28	Bubba Crosby	.10
29	Michael Cuddyer	.45
30	Ben Davis	.25
31	Tim DeCinces	.10
32	Tomas de la Rosa	.10
33	Octavio Dotel	.35
34	Kelly Dransfeldt	.10
35	Tim Drew	.25
36	Matt Drews	.15
37	Mike Drumright	.15
38	Todd Dunn	.25
39	Chad Durham	.10
40	Alex Eckelman	.10
41	Chris Enochs	.10
42	Cordell Farley	.10
43	Frankie Figueroa	.10
44	Joe Fontenot	.10
45	Eric Gillespie	.10
46	Mike Glavine	.15
47	Jason Grote	.10
48	Jerry Hairston	.25
49	Toby Hall	.10
50	Chad Harville	.10
51	Alex Hernandez	.10
52	Junior Herndon	.10
53	Mike Huelsmann	.10
54	Aubrey Huff	.10
55	Chad Hutchinson	.20
56	Jamie Jones	.15
57	Kenny Kelly	.10
58	Scott Krause	.15
59	Jason LaRue	.10
60	Carlos Lee	.20
61	Corey Lee	.20
62	Willie Martinez	.25
63	Ruben Mateo	.90
64	Darnell McDonald	.35
65	Cody McKay	.10
66	Dan McKinley	.10
67	Jackson Melian	.75
68	Jason Middlebrook	.15
69	Ryan Minor	.65
70	Mark Mulder	.25
71	Vladimir Nunez	.15
72	Pablo Ozuna	.15
73	Corey Patterson	.75
74	John Patterson	.15
75	Josh Paul	.15
76	Angel Pena	.20
77	Carlos Pena	.10
78	Juan Pena	.20
79	Brad Penny	.25
80	Kyle Peterson	.10
81	Ben Petrick	.30
82	Calvin Pickering	.45
83	Arquimedez Pozo	.10
84	Paul Rigdon	.10
85	Grant Roberts	.10
86	Nate Rolison	.10
87	Damian Rolls	.30
88	Ryan Rupe	.20
89	Jose Santos	.15
90	Todd Sears	.10
91	Fernando Seguignol	.25
92	Brett Taft	.10
93	Chris Truby	.10
94	Jayson Werth	.15
95	Matt White	.25
96	Todd Williams	.10
97	Cliff Wilson	.10
98	Randy Wolf	.15
99	Kelly Wunsch	.10
100	Mike Zwicka	.10
---	Promo set/autograph card offer	
---	Promo set/1996-1997 pack offer	
---	Promo set offer	

1999 Team Best BA's Top Prospects Box-Toppers

Bell has a major league fa
pitch is his hard curveball.
097 / 150
©1999 Team Best Corporation, all rights reserved.
Printed in the USA. Minor League Baseball trademarks
and copyrights are used with permission of
Major League Baseball Properties, Inc.

Each 18-pack box of Team Best Baseball America's Top Prospects includes one individually sleeved parallel card of the base set. Silver parallels are individually serial numbered to 150; gold parallels to 50.

	MT
Complete Set, Silver (100):	250.00
Common Player, Silver:	6.00
Common Player, Gold:	15.00

(See checklist for base values; silvers valued at 35X, golds at 100X.)

1999 Team Best BA's Top Prospects Autographs

Sharing the format used in Team Best's earlier 1999 issue, the two-per-box autograph inserts in Baseball America's Top Prospects issue features virtually an entirely new line-up. Fronts have color photos with a diffused background. The Team Best logo is at top-left, the minor league team logo at bottom-left. Backs have an authentication statement overprinted on a baseball diamond photo. The autograph cards are not numbered and are listed here alphabetically. Insert signature cards of Mike Darr, Kevin McGlinchy and Tony Torcato which had been announced for this product were late in being returned to Team Best and were inserted into Player of the Year packs in the post-season.

		MT
Complete Set (44):		250.00
Common Player:		3.00
(1)	Rick Ankiel	20.00
(2)	Michael Barrett	10.00
(3)	Lance Berkman	10.00
(4)	A.J. Burnett	6.00
(5)	Steve Carver	3.00
(6)	Bruce Chen	12.50
(7)	Michael Cuddyer	5.00
(8)	J.D. Drew	75.00
(9)	Tim Drew	3.00
(10)	Alex Escobar	25.00
(11)	Seth Etherton	3.00
(12)	Brian Falkenborg	3.00
(13)	Robert Fick	3.00
(14)	Mark Fischer	5.00
(15)	Eddy Furniss	6.00
(16)	Troy Glaus	25.00
(17)	Nathan Haynes	3.00
(18)	Chad Hermansen	4.50
(19)	Shea Hillenbrand	3.00
(20)	Mark Johnson	3.00
(21)	Adam Kennedy	6.00
(22)	Jason LaRue	3.00
(23)	Matt LeCroy	3.00
(24)	Carlos Lee	4.50
(25)	Corey Lee	7.50
(26)	Felipe Lopez	3.00
(27)	Darnell McDonald	6.00
(28)	Mark Mulder	7.50
(29)	Trot Nixon	6.00
(30)	Todd Noel	4.00
(31)	Pablo Ozuna	9.00
(32)	Brad Penny	7.50
(33)	Calvin Pickering	6.00
(34)	Matt Riley	3.00
(35)	Jason Romano	3.00
(36)	Ryan Rupe	15.00
(37)	Randall Simon	7.50
(38)	Jason Standridge	5.00
(39)	Nathan Teut	3.00
(40)	Pete Tucci	5.00
(41)	Eric Valent	10.00
(42)	Vernon Wells	6.00
(43)	Jake Westbrook	7.50
(44)	Randy Wolf	7.50

1999 Team Best BA's Top Prospects Best Possibilities

Two players each are feature on these double-front cards. Inserted at the rate of about one per 18-pack box, the inserts feature action photos against a pastel swirling background.

		MT
Complete Set (5):		45.00
Common Player:		6.00
1	Ryan Anderson, Calvin Pickering	15.00
2	Rick Ankiel, Chad Hermansen	15.00
3	Ryan Bradley, Ryan Minor	10.00
4	John Patterson, Lance Berkman	6.00
5	Brad Penny, Pat Burrell	20.00

1999 Team Best BA's Top Prospects League MVP

MVPs of various minor leagues are featured in this one-per-box insert set. Fronts have portrait photos on a blurred background. BA's logotype is in a blue stripe at top, player name and position are in an orange stripe at bottom. Team logos appear at lower-right. On back is a large Baseball America Top Prospects logo and a summary of the player's MVP season. The same cards were inserted into TB's Baseball America's Diamond Best edition at the rate of one per 19 packs.

		MT
Complete Set (10):		20.00
Common Player:		2.00
1	Brian August	2.00
2	Joe Crede	2.00
3	Shawn Gallagher	2.00
4	Jay Gibbons	2.00
5	Marcus Giles	4.50
6	Jason Hart	2.00
7	Tyrone Horne	4.00
8	Pablo Ozuna	3.50
9	Brad Penny	4.00
10	Calvin Pickering	4.50

1999 Team Best BA's Top Prospects Scout's Choice

The "Scout's Choice" for major league stardom are presented in the scarcest (one per 90 packs) of the BA's Top Prospects insert sets. Cards have a simulated Polaroid photo of the player on a wood-look background with a paper-clip and team logo at upper-right and a gold seal at lower-right. Backs repeat some of the front details and have a scouting report and previous season stats.

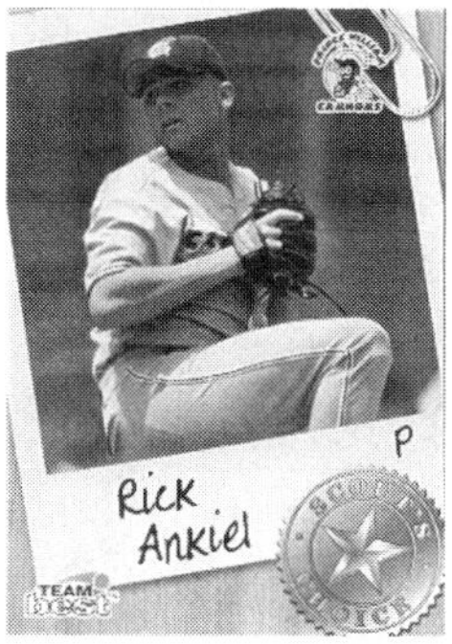

		MT
Complete Set (10):		150.00
Common Player:		12.50
1	Rick Ankiel	25.00
2	Lance Berkman	12.50
3	Pat Burrell	35.00
4	Octavio Dotel	20.00
5	Alex Escobar	20.00
6	George Lombard	15.00
7	Ruben Mateo	15.00
8	Ryan Minor	15.00
9	Pablo Ozuna	12.50
10	Dernell Stenson	12.50

1999 Team Best Baseball America's Diamond Best Edition

The use on front of a gold- or silver-foil (each card can be found both ways) Team Best logo surmounted by a quartet of diamonds is all that differentiates the base cards in this issue from TB's earlier Baseball America Top Prospects issue. Diamond Best cards were issued six cards per pack, six packs per box along with a Team Best/Salvino Rookie Bammer stuffed bear representing one of five top minor league stars. Each bear is accompanied by a special "Card of Authenticity" serially numbered within an edition of 10,000 each.

		MT
Complete Set (100):		20.00
Common Player:		.10
1	Paul Ah Yat	.15
2	Efrain Alamo	.10
3	Chip Alley	.15
4	Ryan Anderson	1.00
5	Rick Ankiel	2.50
6	Tony Armas, Jr.	.40
7	Bronson Arroyo	.20
8	Mike Bacsik	.10
9	Kevin Barker	.10
10	Fletcher Bates	.15
11	Rob Bell	.40
12	Ron Belliard	.40
13	Peter Bergeron	.25
14	Lance Berkman	.25
15	Nick Bierbrodt	.10
16	Milton Bradley	.10
17	Russell Branyan	.25
18	Pat Burrell	2.00
19	Sean Burroughs	2.00
20	Brent Butler	.10
21	Bruce Chen	.25
22	Chin-Feng Chen	.75
23	Giuseppe Chiaramonte	.35
24	Jin Ho Cho	.25
25	Francis Collins	.10
26	Joe Crede	.15
27	Cesar Crespo	.10
28	Bubba Crosby	.10
29	Michael Cuddyer	.20
30	Ben Davis	.25
31	Tim DeCinces	.10
32	Tomas de la Rosa	.10
33	Octavio Dotel	.25
34	Kelly Dransfeldt	.10
35	Tim Drew	.25
36	Matt Drews	.15
37	Mike Drumright	.15
38	Todd Dunn	.25
39	Chad Durham	.10
40	Alex Eckelman	.10
41	Chris Enochs	.10
42	Cordell Farley	.10
43	Frankie Figueroa	.10
44	Joe Fontenot	.10
45	Eric Gillespie	.10
46	Mike Glavine	.15
47	Jason Grote	.10
48	Jerry Hairston	.25
49	Toby Hall	.10
50	Chad Harville	.10
51	Alex Hernandez	.10
52	Junior Herndon	.10
53	Mike Huelsmann	.10
54	Aubrey Huff	.10
55	Chad Hutchinson	.20
56	Jamie Jones	.15
57	Kenny Kelly	.10
58	Scott Krause	.15
59	Jason LaRue	.10
60	Carlos Lee	.75
61	Corey Lee	.20
62	Willie Martinez	.25
63	Ruben Mateo	1.00
64	Darnell McDonald	.50
65	Cody McKay	.10
66	Dan McKinley	.10
67	Jackson Melian	.75
68	Jason Middlebrook	.15
69	Ryan Minor	.50
70	Mark Mulder	.40
71	Vladimir Nunez	.15
72	Pablo Ozuna	.15
73	Corey Patterson	2.50
74	John Patterson	.15
75	Josh Paul	.15
76	Angel Pena	.20
77	Carlos Pena	.10
78	Juan Pena	.20
79	Brad Penny	.75
80	Kyle Peterson	.10
81	Ben Petrick	.30
82	Calvin Pickering	.25
83	Arquimedez Pozo	.10
84	Paul Rigdon	.10
85	Grant Roberts	.10
86	Nate Rolison	.10
87	Damian Rolls	.30
88	Ryan Rupe	.40
89	Jose Santos	.15
90	Todd Sears	.10
91	Fernando Seguignol	.50
92	Brett Taft	.10
93	Chris Truby	.10
94	Jayson Werth	.15
95	Matt White	.25
96	Todd Williams	.10
97	Cliff Wilson	.10
98	Randy Wolf	.15
99	Kelly Wunsch	.10
100	Mike Zwicka	.10

1999 Team Best BA's Diamond Best Inserts

Player action photos and team logos on a white background are the front design for this insert set. Backs have a small copy of the front photo, a few biographical notes and career highlights. Cards are found on an average of one per 30 packs (five boxes) of Team Best Baseball America's Diamond Best Edition.

		MT
Complete Set (10):		125.00
Common Player:		10.00
1	Ryan Anderson	25.00
2	Pat Burrell	45.00
3	Bruce Chen	15.00
4	Mike Darr	10.00
5	Octavio Dotel	12.00
6	Jason LaRue	10.00
7	Damon Minor	12.00
8	Kyle Peterson	10.00
9	Fernando Seguignol	10.00
10	Alfonso Soriano	50.00

1999 Team Best Player of the Year

Team Best post-season card set features top stars at all stops on road to the big leagues. The 50-card base set offers color action photos on which the background has been muted in shades of blue. Backs have season stats, a few biographical data, a career highlight or two and a color team logo. Player of the Year was sold in six-card foil packs.

		MT
Complete Set (50):		15.00
Common Player:		.10
1	Ryan Anderson	.25
2	Rick Ankiel	.75
3	Jeff Austin	.50
4	Kurt Bierek	.10
5	Jung Bong	.15
6	Dee Brown	.15
7	Nate Bump	.15
8	Pat Burrell	1.50
9	Sean Burroughs	.50
10	Brent Butler	.10
11	Chin-Feng Chen	.75
12	Hee Seop Choi	.75
13	Joe Crede	.15
14	Jack Cust	.10
15	Travis Dawkins	.10
16	Trent Durrington	.10
17	Seth Etherton	.10
18	Vince Faison	.15
19	Choo Freeman	.25
20	Rafael Furcal	.50
21	Jay Gibbons	.10
22	Marcus Giles	.50
23	J.M. Gold	.30
24	Jeff Goldbach	.10
25	Josh Hamilton	.60
26	Kevin Haverbusch	.25
27	D'Angelo Jiminez	.25
28	Nick Johnson	.50
29	Adam Kennedy	.25
30	Steve Lomasney	.25
31	George Lombard	.15
32	Felipe Lopez	.20
33	Jason Marquis	.10
34	Tydus Meadows	.15
35	Aaron Myette	.15
36	Corey Patterson	.75
37	Carlos Pena	.10
38	Adam Piatt	.35
39	Julio Ramirez	.10
40	Matt Riley	.15
41	Juan Rivera	.10
42	Jason Romano	.10
43	Aaron Rowand	.10
44	C.C. Sabathia	.25
45	Alfonso Soriano	1.50
46	Jason Standridge	.35
47	Dernell Stenson	.25
48	Jorge Toca	.25
49	Eric Valent	.10
50	Jayson Werth	.10

1999 Team Best Player of the Year Silver/Gold

Each of the 50 base cards in Player of the Year was paralleled in silver- and gold-foil enhanced editions. Fronts have a foil company logo at upper-right, while each card is serially numbered on back; the silvers to 150, the golds to 50.

	MT
Common Silver:	6.00
Silver Stars: 35X	
Common Gold:	15.00
Gold Stars: 100X	
(See 1999 Team Best Player of the Year for checklist and base card values.)	

1999 Team Best Player of the Year Autographs

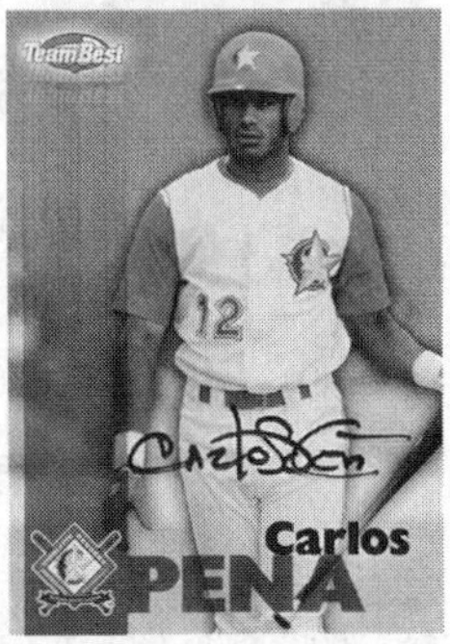

The authentically autographed cards which drive the sale of most minor league singles products were inserted about one per three packs of Player of the Year. Besides 26 autograph cards specifically designated for the POY issue, cards of Mike Darr, Kevin McGlinchy and Tony Torcato which were received too late for inclusion in TB's Baseball America's Top Prospects issue were also inserted. The POY autographs have player photos on a linen-look background with a graduated purple band vertically at left. Backs have a congratulatory message of authenticity from TB's chairman. The unnumbered cards are checklisted here alphabetically.

		MT
Complete Set (29):		200.00
Common Player:		4.00
(1)	Rick Ankiel	35.00
(2)	Tony Armas, Jr.	8.00
(3)	Nick Bierbrodt	4.00
(4)	Jamie Brown	4.00
(5)	Jesus Colome	4.00
(6)	Mike Darr	6.00
(7)	Octavio Dotel	8.00
(8)	Kelly Dransfeldt	6.00
(9)	Adam Everett	6.00
(10)	Vince Faison	6.00
(11)	Troy Glaus	15.00
(12)	Junior Herndon	4.00
(13)	Aubrey Huff	6.00
(14)	Corey Lee	12.00
(15)	Jason Marquis	4.00
(16)	Willie Martinez	4.00
(17)	Ruben Mateo	12.00
(18)	Kevin McGlinchy	10.00
(19)	Ryan Minor	12.00
(20)	Warren Morris	8.00
(21)	Corey Patterson	15.00
(22)	Carlos Pena	4.00
(23)	Ben Petrick	6.00
(24)	Paul Rigdon	4.00
(25)	Grant Roberts	6.00
(26)	C.C. Sabathia	6.00
(27)	Tony Torcato	4.00
(28)	Jason Tyner	4.00
(29)	Ed Yarnall	12.00

1999 Team Best Player of the Year Ankiel/Piatt

Two top candidates for Player of the Year honors, pitcher Rick Ankiel and third baseman Adam Piatt are featured in this insert set. Cards have player photos on a sepia background with a pair of TB POY logos. Backs repeat the front photo in a muted image and have stats, biographical data and career highlights.

		MT
Complete Set (10):		7.00
Common Card:		.50
1-6	Rick Ankiel	1.00
7-10	Adam Piatt	.50

1999 Team Best Player of the Year Contenders

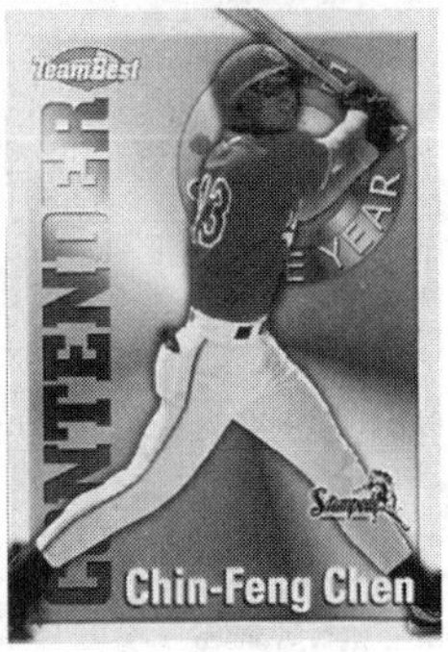

The scarcest inserts in the set are these top candidates for Minor League Player of the Year honors. Fronts have action photos set on a silver foil-look background with a large POY logo. Backs have a smaller version of the front photo, personal data, season stats and the players credentials for the honor. Contenders were seeded on average of one per 90 packs.

		MT
Complete Set (10):		150.00
Common Player:		12.50
1	Dee Brown	12.50
2	Pat Burrell	35.00
3	Chin-Feng Chen	25.00
4	Rafael Furcal	15.00
5	Nick Johnson	25.00
6	Ramon Ortiz	12.50
7	Aramis Ramirez	12.50
8	Matt Riley	15.00
9	Jason Standridge	15.00
10	Vernon Wells	20.00

Checklists with card numbers in parentheses ( ) indicates the numbers do not appear on the card.

1999 Team Best Player of the Year Past POY Autographs

Autographed cards of past Team Best Players of the Year were a special insert in the '99 issue. No average insertion rate was given.

		MT
Complete Set (3):		
(1)	Andruw Jones	35.00
(2)	Paul Konerko	15.00
(3)	Eric Chavez	20.00

1999 Team Best Rookie Promos

This quartet of sample cards was issued to introduce Team Best's 1999 Rookie edition. Fronts of the cards are identical to the issued versions. Backs have a red background with large Team Bets Rookie logo and promo notice.

		MT
Complete Set (5):		12.00
Common Player:		3.00
(1)	Ryan Bradley (Best Guns)	3.00
(2)	Alex Escobar (Best Wheels)	3.00
(3)	Adam Everett	3.00
(4)	Marcus Giles (Best Lumber)	3.00
(5)	Pablo Ozuna, J.D. Drew (1999 Future Stars)	4.00

1999 Team Best Rookie

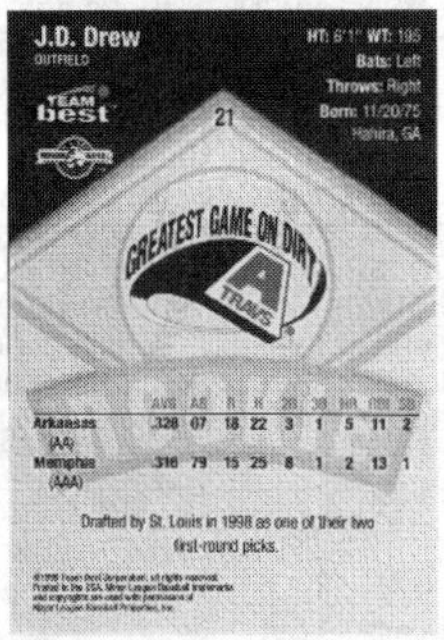

Top prospects at all levels of the minor leagues going into the 1999 season are featured in the base set and insert series of Team Best Rookie. Regular cards have action photos set against a woven-look background with a large baseball, diamond diagram and "ROOKIE" banner. The issuer's logo is at upper-left, the player's minor league team logo from the previous season is at upper-right. Backs have a large team logo at center and 1998 stats. Each box of 18 foil packs included one individually sleeved gold (edition of 50) or silver (edition of 125) parallel of a base-set card.

		MT
Complete Set (100):		15.00
Common Player:		.10
1	Chip Ambres	.25
2	Scott Barrett	.10
3	Todd Bellhorn	.10
4	Darren Blakely	.10
5	Matt Borne	.10
6	Nate Bump	.25
7	Ryan Bundy	.10
8	Eric Byrnes	.20
9	David Callahan	.10
10	Rob Castelli	.10
11	Doug Clark	.10
12	Greg Clark	.10
13	Darryl Conyer	.10
14	Jeremy Cotten	.10
15	Bubba Crosby	.10
16	Mike Curry	.10
17	Mike Dean	.10
18	David Diaz	.10
19	Jeremy Dodson	.10
20	Ryan Drese	.10
21	J.D. Drew	2.00
22	Morgan Ensberg	.10
23	Adam Everett	.50
24	Mike Fischer	.20
25	Pete Fisher	.10
26	Josh Fogg	.10
27	Brad Freeman	.15
28	Nate Frese	.10
29	Eddy Furniss	.15
30	Keith Ginter	.10
31	Eric Good	.10
32	Josh Hancock (error, blue cap)	.25
32	Josh Hancock (correct, red cap)	.25
33	Ryan Harber	.10
34	Jason Hart	.10
35	Jason Hill	.10
36	Heath Honeycutt	.15
37	Aubrey Huff	.10
38	Chad Hutchinson	.35
39	Brandon Inge	.20
40	Brett Jodie	.10
41	Gabe Johnson	.15
42	Clint Johnston	.10
43	Jesse Joyce	.10
44	Randy Keisler	.10
45	Jarrod Kingrey	.10
46	Craig Kuzmic	.10
47	Tim Lemon	.10
48	Ryan Lentz	.10
49	Neil Longo	.10
50	Felipe Lopez	.45
51	Javier Lopez	.10
52	Phil Lowery	.20
53	Chris Magruder	.10
54	Mike Maroth	.10
55	Kennon McArthur	.10
56	Shawn McCorkle	.25
57	Arturo McDowell	.10
58	Josh McKinley	.10
59	Jason Michaels	.10
60	Ryan Moskau	.25
61	Mark Mulder	.35
62	Will Ohman	.10
63	Todd Ozias	.25
64	Matt Padgett	.20
65	Corey Patterson	.75
66	Adam Pettyjohn	.10
67	Brad Piercy	.15
68	Scott Pratt	.10
69	Kris Rayborn	.10
70	Chris Reinike	.15
71	Billy Rich	.10
72	Ryan Ridenour	.20
73	Brian Rogers	.25
74	Aaron Rowand	.30
75	Ryan Rupe	.20
76	C.C. Sabathia	.15
77	Jason Saenz	.15
78	Aaron Sams	.10
79	Sammy Serrano	.15
80	Clint Smith	.25
81	Pat Burrell	2.50
82	Zach Sorensen	.15
83	Steve Stemle	.10
84	John Stewart	.10
85	Tyler Thompson	.15
86	Matt Thornton	.15
87	Tony Torcato	.20
88	Keola de la Tori	.20
89	Andres Torres	.10
90	Jason Tyner	.10
91	Jeff Urban	.10
92	Eric Valent	.50
93	Derek Wathan	.15
94	Jeff Weaver	.25
95	Jake Weber	.25
96	Ken Westmoreland	.25
97	Brad Wilkerson	.15
98	Clyde Williams	.15
99	Jeff Winchester	.10
100	Mitch Wylie	.10
		.10
	INSERTED OFFER CARDS	.10
	'95 First Round Picks Set	.10
	Baseball America Subscription	.10
	Promo card set	.10
	Promo card set plus packs and autograph	.10

1999 Team Best Rookie Gold/Silver Parallels

Each 18-pack box of Team Best Rookie includes as a box-topper an individually sleeved silver- or gold-foil parallel to one of the base cards. Except for the metallic foil on front and the serial number on back, the parallels are identical to the issued cards. Silver parallels are numbered within an edition of 125; golds in an edition of 50.

	MT
Common Silver:	5.00
Common Gold:	12.00
(High-demand cards valued at multipliers of base cards: Silver - 35X; Gold - 100X)	

1999 Team Best Rookie Autographs

The best of the Best Rookie series is featured in this insert set. Cards have authentic autographs across the front and have an authenticity notice on back. Two dozen of the featured players were inserted at the average rate of two per box (about one per nine packs) while autographed cards of J.D. Drew were seeded at one per case (180 packs).

		MT
Complete Set (25):		200.00
Common Player:		3.00
1	Rick Ankiel	20.00
2	Michael Barrett	8.00
3	Lance Berkman	6.00
4	A.J. Burnett	5.00
5	Bruce Chen	10.00
6	Michael Cuddyer	5.00
7	J.D. Drew	60.00
8	Alex Escobar	15.00
9	Seth Etherton	3.00
10	Mark Fischer	5.00
11	Troy Glaus	25.00
12	Nathan Haynes	3.00
13	Shea Hillenbrand	3.00
14	Matt LeCroy	5.00
15	Corey Lee	4.00

16	Trot Nixon	6.00
17	Todd Noel	2.00
18	Pablo Ozuna	7.50
19	Brad Penny	7.50
20	Calvin Pickering	6.00
21	Matt Riley	6.00
22	Jason Romano	3.00
23	Pete Tucci	5.00
24	Eric Valent	8.00
25	Jake Westbrook	5.00

1999 Team Best Rookie Best Guns

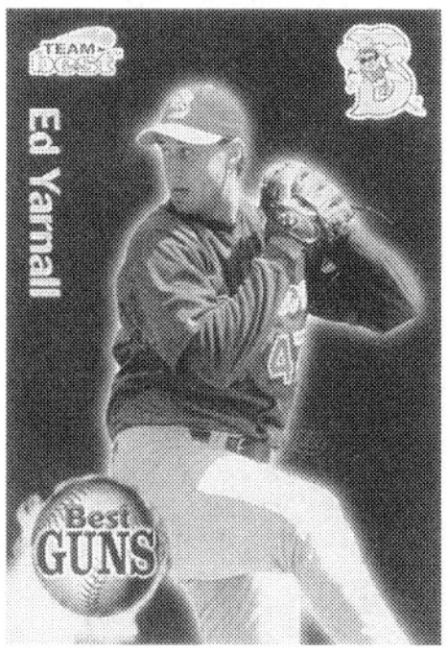

Inserted at an announced rate of about one per box, this chase set features the hardest-throwing prospects in the minor leagues. Fronts have photos showing the awesome arms in action. A baseball trailing flames appears at lower-left, the player's minor league team logo at upper-right. Backs repeat part of the front photo within the flaming fastball motif and offer previous season's stats and a few words about the pitcher.

		MT
Complete Set (10):		15.00
Common Player:		1.00
1	Ryan Anderson	3.00
2	Rick Ankiel	7.50
3	Ryan Bradley	2.00
4	Bruce Chen	5.00
5	Matt Clement	3.00
6	Octavio Dotel	3.00
7	John Patterson	3.00
8	Matt Riley	5.00
9	Brent Stentz	1.00
10	Ed Yarnall	1.50

1999 Team Best Rookie Best Lumber

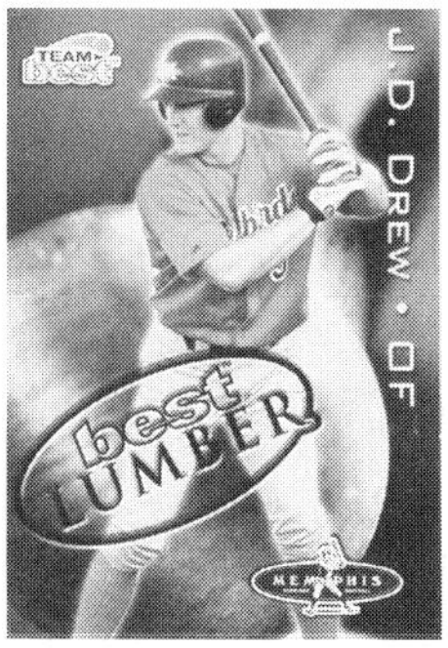

Projected heavy hitters on their way to the major leagues are featured in this hobby-only chase set. The players' power swings are shown on front photos superimposed over a bat knob and overprinted with a "best LUMBER" logo in the style of a bat's label. Average rate of insertion was announced as one per 90 packs. Backs repeat the front motif and part of the front photo, adding some biographical and career details, along with 1998 stats.

		MT
Complete Set (10):		100.00
Common Player:		5.00
1	Michael Barrett	10.00
2	Lance Berkman	10.00
3	J.D. Drew	30.00
4	Marcus Giles	15.00
5	Troy Glaus	15.00
6	George Lombard	5.00
7	Doug Mientkiewicz	5.00
8	Trot Nixon	5.00
9	Calvin Pickering	5.00
10	Pete Tucci	5.00

1999 Team Best Rookie Best Wheels

The projected base-stealing and ball-hawking kings of the future are presented in this insert set. Stated insertion rate is one per 19 packs. Fronts have a portrait photo. Backs repeat part of the photo and offer biographical data, 1998 stats and a few words about the player.

		MT
Complete Set (5):		5.00
Common Player:		.50
1	Alex Escobar	2.50
2	Cordell Farley	.50
3	Carlos Febles	1.00
4	Nathan Haynes	.50
5	Pablo Ozuna	1.00

1999 Team Best Rookie Future Stars

With two players per card, the odds are doubled that one will be a major league superstar of the future. Fronts have a pair of portrait photos. Backs have a large Team Best Rookie logo and a serial number from within an edition of 900 per card. Stated odds of finding a Future Stars card are one per box.

		MT
Complete Set (25):		75.00
Common Player:		2.50
1	Darryl Conyer, Javier Lopez	2.50
2	Troy Cameron, Luis Rivera	2.50
3	Troy Glaus, Darren Blakely	5.00
4	Jayson Werth, Darnell McDonald	10.00
5	Adam Everett, Mike Maroth	2.50
6	Aaron Rowand, Josh Fogg	3.50
7	Corey Patterson, Aaron Sams	6.00
8	C.C. Sabathia, Zach Sorensen	2.50
9	Jeff Weaver, Brandon Inge	7.50
10	Chip Ambres, Derek Wathan	4.00
11	Bubba Crosby, Ryan Moskau	2.50
12	Josh McKinley, Brad Wilkerson	2.50
13	Randy Keisler, Ryan Bradley	2.50
14	Jason Tyner, Jason Saenz	2.50
15	Mark Mulder, Jason Hart	4.50
16	Eric Valent, Jason Michaels	4.00
17	Clint Johnston, Eddy Furniss	4.00
18	Pablo Ozuna, J.D. Drew	10.00
19	Rick Ankiel, Chad Hutchinson	20.00
20	J.D. Drew, Tim Drew	9.00
21	Darnell McDonald, Donzell McDonald	3.00
22	Tony Torcato, Nate Bump	2.50
23	Matt Thornton, Ryan Anderson	5.00
24	Felipe Lopez, Vernon Wells	5.00
25	Ryan Bundy, Jarrod Kingrey	2.50

1999 Team Best Rookie League Leaders

Projected league leaders on their way to the major leagues are featured in this retail-only chase set which is virtually identical to the Best Lumber hobby insert. The players' power swings are shown on front photos superimposed on a plain blue background with a "League Leaders" logo in the style of a bat's label. Backs repeat the front motif and part of the front photo, adding some biographical and career details, along with 1998 stats.

		MT
Complete Set (10):		100.00
Common Player:		5.00
1	Michael Barrett	10.00
2	Lance Berkman	10.00
3	J.D. Drew	50.00
4	Marcus Giles	15.00
5	Troy Glaus	10.00
6	George Lombard	5.00
7	Doug Mientkiewicz	5.00
8	Trot Nixon	5.00
9	Calvin Pickering	5.00
10	Pete Tucci	5.00

1999 Team Best Salvino Rookie Bammers Card/ Authenticity

Each of the "Rookie Bammer" stuffed bears issued with the Baseball America's Diamond Best Edition card set was accompanied by a "Card of Authenticity." Fronts have action photos with three stars in the background and a minor league team logo at lower-right. Backs repeat the front photo in a ghosted image and have a notice of authenticity from Team Best CEO Don White. Each card is serially numbered from within an edition of 10,000 each. Sample versions of each card were also produced, marked with a strip on back, "Promotional Purposes Only" and numbered "10000/10000"; they are valued at $2-3 apiece.

		MT
Complete Set (6):		30.00
Common Player:		5.00
(1)	Ryan Anderson	5.00
(2)	Rick Ankiel	7.50
(3)	Lance Berkman	5.00
(4)	Pat Burrell	10.00
(5)	J.D. Drew (Arkansas Travelers)	10.00
(6)	J.D. Drew (Memphis Redbirds)	10.00

1999 Minor League Team Sets

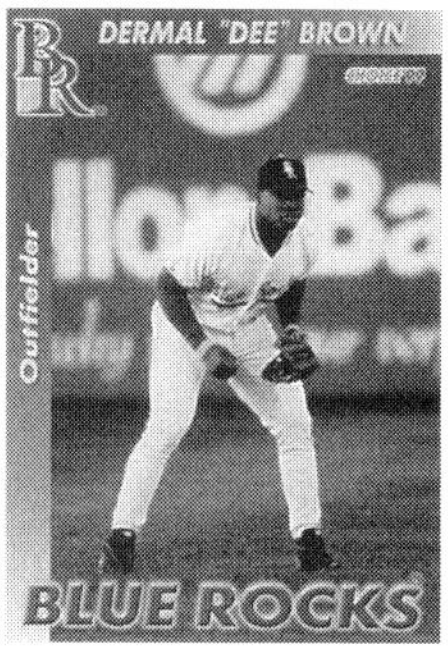

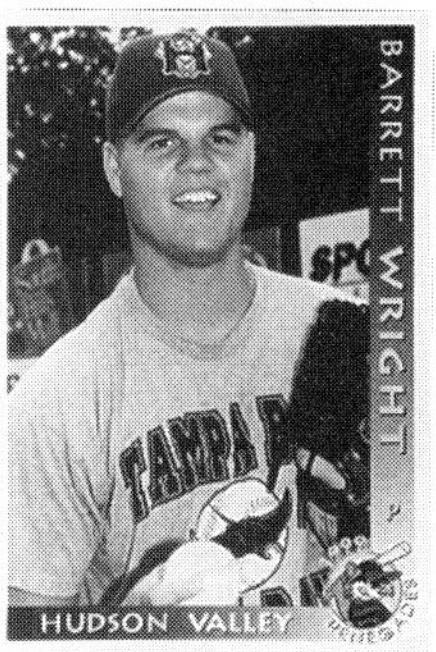

(Manufacturers abbreviations used include: BL - Blueline Communications; GS - Grandstand; MA - Multi-Ad Services; TM - team issued; CH - Choice Marketing.)

	MT
187 team sets and variations	8.50
MA Akron Aeros (30)	8.50
GS Albuquerque Dukes (30)	9.75
GS Albuquerque Dukes Sponsor's Set (31)	11.00
GS Altoona Curve (31)	9.00
MA Appalachian League Top Prospects (30)	20.00
MA Arkansas Travelers (30)	45.00
Arizona Fall League (30)	20.00
MA Asheville Tourists (30)	17.50
GS Asheville Tourists Update (10)	15.00
GS Auburn Doubledays (33)	8.50
MA Augusta Greenjackets (30)	9.50
TM Bakersfield Blaze (30)	9.50
TM Batavia Muckdogs (41)	10.50
MA Beloit Snappers (29)	12.00
GS Billings Mustangs (32)	11.00
BL Binghampton Mets (30)	8.50
TM Binghampton Mets "Jumbo" (12)	50.00
GS Birmingham Barons (30)	8.50
GS Bluefield Orioles (32)	9.00
GS Boise Hawks (34)	9.50
MA Bowie Baysox (30)	10.00
MA Brevard County Manatees (30)	8.50
GS Bristol Sox (30)	8.50
GS Bristol Sox Update (6)	5.00
BL Buffalo Bisons (30)	9.50
MA Burlington Bees (33)	11.00
GS Burlington Indians (32)	11.50
GS Butte Copper Kings (33)	8.50
TM Cape Fear Crocs (30)	15.00
MA Capital City Bombers (30)	11.00
MA Capital City '98 SAL Champs (31)	27.50
CH Carolina League Prospects (30)	10.50
TM Carolina Mudcats (31)	8.50
MA Cedar Rapids Kernels (34)	8.50
MA Charleston Alley Cats (30)	9.00
TM Charleston River Dogs (32)	8.50
BL Charlotte Knights (30)	8.50
GS Chattanooga Lookouts (30)	8.50
GS Chico Heat (27)	9.00
GS Chillicothe Paints (26)	7.00
MA Clearwater Phillies (30)	8.50
GS Clinton LumberKings (32)	11.00
TM Colorado Springs Sky Sox (30)	8.50
BL Columbus Clippers (31)	8.50
MA Columbus Red Stixx (30)	12.00
GS Danville Braves (30)	11.00
Roox Daytona Cubs (30)	12.00
MA Delmarva Shorebirds (29)	11.00
MA Dunedin Blue Jays (30)	8.50
BL Durham Bulls (30)	12.00
TM Edmonton Trappers (25)	12.50
TM Elizabethtown Twins (32)	20.00
GS El Paso Diablos (30)	8.50
MA Erie Seawolves (28)	8.50
GS Eugene Emeralds (30)	8.50
GS Everett Aqua Sox (31)	9.50
GS Frederick Keys (28)	11.00
GS Fresno Grizzlies (30)	8.50
TM Ft. Myers Miracle (31)	8.50
MA Ft. Wayne Wizards (30)	30.00
MA Great Falls Dodgers (30)	9.00
MA Greensboro Bats (30)	10.00
GS Greenville Braves (28)	9.50
MA Hagerstown Suns (30)	9.50
MA Harrisburg Senators (30)	11.00
MA Helena Brewers (30)	13.00

MA Hickory Crawdads (30)	9.50
MA Hickory Crawdads Update (30)	10.00
GS High Desert Mavericks (27)	14.00
GS H.D. Mavericks Sponsor's Set (27)	14.00
GS Hudson Valley Renegades (32)	11.00
GS Hudson Valley Renegades Update (1)	5.00
GS H.V. Renegades Update, Autographed	17.50
TM Huntsville Stars (30)	8.50
BL Indianapolis Indians (31)	8.50
International League Top Prospects (30)	11.00
MA Iowa Cubs (30)	10.00
MA Jackson Generals (30)	9.50
GS Jacksonville Suns (28)	8.50
GS Jacksonville Suns Update (5)	20.00
TM Johnson City Cardinals (36)	8.50
TM Kane County Cougars (31)	8.50
CH Kinston Indians (30)	9.50
MA Kissimmee Cobras (30)	8.50
GS Knoxville Smokies (27)	8.50
GS Lake Elsinore Land Sharks (33)	9.00
GS Lake Elsinore Storm (30)	8.00
MA Lakeland Tigers (30)	8.50
GS Lancaster JetHawks (30)	9.00
GS Lancaster JetHawks (Valley Press) (30)	13.00
GS Lancaster Stealth (34)	10.00
GS Lansing Lugnuts (29)	25.00
MA Las Vegas Stars (30)	9.00
BL Louisville RiverBats (34)	20.00
MA Lowell Spinners (32)	9.50
CH Lynchburg Hillcats (30)	9.50
MA Macon Braves (30)	11.50
MA Mahoning Valley Scrappers (30)	10.00
GS Martinsville Astros (30)	10.00
TM Memphis Redbirds (30)	13.50
MA Michigan Battle Cats (30)	8.50
GS Midland Rockhounds (30)	9.50
TM Midland Rockhounds (25)	65.00
MA Midwest League Prospects (29)	15.00
GS Missoula Osprey (31)	9.00
TM Mobile Baybears (32)	14.00
GS Modesto A's (30)	9.50
MA Myrtle Beach Pelicans (30)	10.50
TM Nashville Sounds (30)	8.50
MA New Britain Rock Cats (29)	9.50
BL New Haven Ravens (30)	8.50
MA New Jersey Cardinals (32)	8.50
TM N.J. Cardinals Top Prospects (6)	15.00
MA New Orleans Zephyrs (28)	9.50
BL Norfolk Tides (36)	9.50
BL Norwich Navigators (30)	10.00
TM Ogden Raptors (37)	8.50
MA Oklahoma Redhawks (30)	8.50
MA Omaha GoldenSpikes (30)	8.50
MA Orlando Rays (30)	9.50
BL Pawtucket Red Sox (30)	11.00
DD Pawtucket Red Sox foldout	35.00
MA Peoria Chiefs (30)	8.50
MA Piedmont Boll Weevils (30)	8.50
MA Pittsfield Mets (30)	8.50
GS Portland Sea Dogs (30)	11.50
CH Potomac Cannons (30)	10.00
GS Princeton Devil Rays (30)	35.00
GS Princeton Devil Rays Update (30)	20.00
GS Pulaski Rangers (30)	8.50
TM Quad City River Bandits (31)	11.00
GS Rancho Cucamonga Surfers (31)	13.00
GS Rancho Cucamonga Quakes (30)	12.00
MA Reading Phillies (28)	9.50
MA Reading Phillies Update (30)	10.00
BL Richmond Braves (30)	8.50
Richmond Camera Richmond Braves (20)	50.00
GS Rio Grand Valley WhiteWings (25)	8.50
CH Rochester Red Wings (30)	8.50
TM Rockford Reds (28)	12.00
CH Salem Avalanche (30)	9.50
MA Salem-Keizer Volcanoes (36)	8.50
GS San Antonio Missions (31)	9.50
GS San Bernardino Stampede (31)	8.50
BL San Jose Giants (30)	9.50
TM Sarasota Red Sox (29)	8.50
MA Savannah Sand Gnats (29)	9.50
BL Scranton/Wilkes-Barre Red Barons (32)	8.50
MA Shreveport Captains (28)	8.50
GS Sioux City X's (30)	8.50
MA South Atlantic League Prospects (30)	11.00
MA South Bend Silver Hawks (31)	9.50
GS Southern League Top Prospects (31)	10.00
GS Southern Oregon Timberjacks (29)	10.00
Wonder Bread So. Oregon Timberjacks (10)	45.00
GS So. Oregon Timberjacks Update (8)	7.50
GS Spokane Indians (35)	10.00
MA Staten Island Yankees (33)	12.00
GS Stockton Ports (30)	8.50
MA St. Catherines Stompers	8.50
GS St. Lucie Mets (31)	12.00
TM St. Paul Saints (32)	9.00
MA St. Petersburg Devil Rays (29)	11.00
BL Syracuse SkyChiefs (28)	9.50
BL Tacoma Rainiers (30)	9.50
MA Tampa Yankees (28)	8.50
MA Tampa Yankees Update (30)	10.00
GS Texas League Top Prospects (32)	10.00
BL Toledo Mud Hens (32)	8.50
MA Trenton Thunder (30)	9.75
MA Tucson Sidewinders (29)	9.50
TM Tulsa Drillers (30)	9.50
GS Vancouver Canadians (30)	10.00
GS Vermont Expos (35)	9.50
MA Vero Beach Dodgers (30)	11.00
GS Visalia Oaks (27)	8.50
MA West Michigan Whitecaps (30)	8.50
MA West Michigan Whitecaps Update (12)	17.00
MA W. Mich. Whitecaps '94-'98 Stars (30)	9.50
GS West Tennessee Diamond Jaxx (30)	8.50
CH Wichita Wranglers (30)	8.50
CH Wichita Wranglers/ Sedgwick Zoo (30)	15.00
MA Williamsport Crosscutters (34)	9.50
Choice Wilmington Blue Rocks (30)	9.50
CH Winston-Salem Warthogs (30)	9.50
MA Wisconsin Timber Rattlers (35)	8.50
GS Yakima Bears (31)	9.50

2000 SP Top Prospects

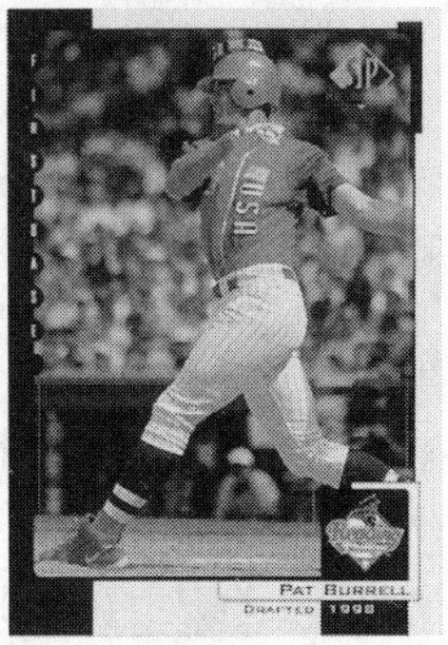

As the brand name implies, only the minor leaguers with the brightest futures are featured in the 135-card base set of this Upper Deck specialty issue. The first 10 cards in the set are checklists featuring the biggest names. Nearly a dozen parallel and insert sets are found in the eight-card, $4.99 foil packs. Besides the "regular" version, the base set can be found in a Premium Edition parallel of 175 each and a President's Edition of just 10 each, utilizing holo-patterned foil technology.

		MT
Complete Set (135):		40.00
Common Player:		.40
1	Rick Ankiel (Top 10 Checklist)	3.00
2	Brad Penny (Top 10 Checklist)	2.00
3	Ryan Anderson (Top 10 Checklist)	.75
4	Pablo Ozun (Top 10 Checklist)	.40
5	Alex Escobar (Top 10 Checklist)	.40
6	John Patterson (Top 10 Checklist)	.40
7	Corey Patterson (Top 10 Checklist)	1.50
8	Nick Johnson (Top 10 Checklist)	1.50
9	Pat Burrell (Top 10 Checklist)	1.00
10	Matt Riley (Top 10 Checklist)	.75
11	Larry Barnes	.40
12	Brian Cooper	.40
13	E.J. t'Hoen	.40
14	Oscar Salazar	.40
15	Mark Mulder	.40
16	Roberto Vaz	.40
17	Eric DuBose	.40
18	Jacques Landry	.40
19	Adam Piatt	.60
20	Josue Espada	.40
21	Jesus Colome	.40
22	Barry Zito	.60
23	Eric Byrnes	.40
24	Jason Hart	.40
25	Felipe Lopez	.50
26	Pascual Coco	.40
27	Vernon Wells	.90
28	John Sneed	.40
29	Jorge Nunez	.40
30	Cameron Reimers	.40
31	Jung Bong	.50
32	Rafael Furcal	.75
33	Jason Marquis	.40
34	Derrin Ebert	.40
35	Troy Cameron	.40
36	Chad Green	.40
37	Rick Ankiel	5.00
38	Chad Hutchinson	.65
39	Chris Haas	.40
40	Brent Butler	.40
41	Adam Kennedy	.40
42	Donovan Graves	.40
43	Ben Christiansen	.40
44	Corey Patterson	4.00
45	Eric Hinske	.40
46	Tydus Meadows	.40
47	Micah Bowie	.50
48	Todd Belitz	.40
49	Matt White	.40
50	Kenny Kelly	.40
51	Josh Hamilton	2.50
52	Aubrey Huff	.60
53	Abraham Nunez	.40
54	John Patterson	.40
55	Bubba Crosby	.40
56	Chin-Feng Chen	1.50
57	David Ross	.40
58	Guillermo Mota	.40
59	Milton Bradley	.50
60	Peter Bergeron	.75
61	Josh McKinley	.50
62	Tony Armas, Jr.	.50
63	Josh Reding	.40
64	Tony Torcato	.40
65	Mike Glendenning	.40
66	Jesus Hernandez	.40
67	C.C. Sabathia	.40
68	Mike Edwards	.40
69	Kevin Gryboski	.40
70	Harvey Hargrove	.40
71	Ryan Anderson	.50
72	Peanut Williams	.40
73	Brad Penny	1.00
74	Pablo Ozuna	.80
75	Jason Grilli	.50
76	Julio Ramirez	.50
77	A.J. Burnett	.50
78	Nate Bump	.40
79	Wes Anderson	.40
80	Grant Roberts	.40
81	Alex Escobar	.60
82	Jason Tyner	.40
83	Jorge Toca	.50
84	Robert Stratton	.40
85	Rick Elder	.40
86	Keith Reed	.40
87	Darnell McDonald	.50
88	Jayson Werth	.60
89	Matt Riley	.75
90	Wascar Serrano	.40
91	Vince Faison	.40
92	Omar Ortiz	.40
93	Junior Herndon	.40
94	Sean Burroughs	2.00
95	Eric Valent	.75
96	Pat Burrell	1.50
97	Reggie Taylor	.65
98	Eddy Furniss	.50
99	Chad Hermansen	.50
100	Kevin Haverbusch	.40
101	Carlos Pena	.40
102	Adam Everett	.40
103	Dernell Stenson	.50
104	David Eckstein	.40
105	John Curtice	.40
106	Travis Dawkins	.90
107	Jacobo Sequea	.40
108	Eric LeBlanc	.40
109	Rob Bell	.40
110	Austin Kearns	.40
111	Jeff Winchester	.40
112	Choo Freeman	.40
113	Ben Petrick	.50
114	Jody Gerut	.40
115	Josh Kalinowski	.40
116	Travis Thompson	.40
117	Jeff Austin	.40
118	Junior Guerrero	.40
119	Eric Munson	.65
120	Eric Gillespie	.40
121	Michael Cuddyer	.50
122	Jason Ryan	.40
123	Luis Rivas	.40
124	Ryan Mills	.40
125	Michael Restovich	.40
126	Josh Fogg	.40
127	Luis Raven	.40
128	Joe Crede	.40
129	Aaron Rowand	.40
130	Kip Wells	.40
131	Nick Johnson	1.50
132	Ryan Bradley	.75
133	Andy Brown	.40
134	Donny Leon	.40
135	Jackson Melian	.50

2000 SP Top Prospects Premium Edition

Each of the 135 cards in the base set were also issued in this parallel edition numbered on front to just 175 each. Cards fronts have a metallic-foil background.

	MT
Common Player:	4.00
Stars: VALUE UNDETERMINED (See 2000 SP Top Prospects for checklist and base card values.)	

2000 SP Top Prospects President's Edition

Utilizing holo-patterned foil technology, each of the 135 base cards in SP Top Prospects was also issued in this numbered edition of just 10 pieces each.

	MT
Common Player:	45.00
Stars: 75-150X (See 2000 SP Top Prospects for checklist and base card values.)	

2000 SP Top Prospects Big Town Dreams

Premium holo-foil technology is showcased on this insert issue inserted at an average rate of one per 11 packs.

		MT
Complete Set (10):		40.00
Common Player:		3.00
1	Jorge Toca	4.50
2	Josh Hamilton	6.00
3	Alex Escobar	4.50
4	Joe Crede	3.00
5	Eric Munson	4.50
6	Chin-Feng Chen	6.00
7	Dernell Stenson	3.00
8	Pat Burrell	5.00
9	Corey Patterson	7.50
10	Donny Leon	3.00

2000 SP Top Prospects Chirography

For 2000, Upper Deck improved the odds of finding an autographed card to one per eight packs. Cards feature 34 top prospects in a horizontal format which uses a ghosted minor league logo on a white background to host the signature. A gold version parallels the Chirography inserts, with cards numbered to 25 apiece.

		MT
Complete Set (45):		550.00
Common Player:		6.00
RA	Rick Ankiel	60.00
TA	Tony Armas, Jr.	15.00
Rob	Rob Bell	6.00
PBe	Peter Bergeron	15.00
RB	Ryan Bradley	12.00
AJ	A.J. Burnett	12.00
PB	Pat Burrell	35.00
SB	Sean Burroughs	35.00
Ben	Ben Christiansen	9.00
PC	Pascual Coco	12.00
JC	Joe Crede	6.00
BC	Bubba Crosby	6.00
MC	Michael Cuddyer	6.00

ED	Eric DuBose	6.00
AE	Alex Escobar	15.00
AEv	Adam Everett	20.00
JG	Jody Gerut	6.00
JGr	Jason Grilli	7.50
JH	Josh Hamilton	40.00
CH	Chad Hermansen	15.00
JHe	Junior Herndon	6.00
AH	Aubrey Huff	7.50
CHu	Chad Hutchinson	6.00
NJ	Nick Johnson	45.00
AK	Austin Kearns	9.00
FL	Felipe Lopez	15.00
JMA	Jason Marquis	7.50
JM	Josh McKinley	15.00
RM	Ryan Mills	6.00
MM	Mark Mulder	15.00
EM	Eric Munson	20.00
PO	Pablo Ozuna	12.00
Cpa	Corey Patterson	45.00
CP	Carlos Pena	7.50
BP	Brad Penny	25.00
JR	Julio Ramirez	9.00
MR	Matt Riley	15.00
GR	Grant Roberts	12.00
AS	Alfonso Soriano	30.00
DS	Dernell Stenson	9.00
RT	Reggie Taylor	12.00
Jto	Jorge Toca	15.00
TT	Tony Torcato	12.00
JT	Jason Tyner	6.00
JW	Jayson Werth	7.50

2000 SP Top Prospects Chirography Gold

This parallel of the 34-player Chirography insert series is highlighted on front with gold graphics. Each card is serially numbered within an edition of 25.

	MT
Common Player:	25.00
Stars: 4X	
(See 2000 SP Top Prospects Chirography for checklist and base card values.)	

2000 SP Top Prospects Destination the Show

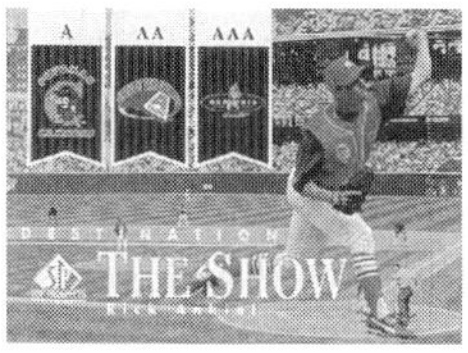

A horizontal format with a black-and-white backdrop to the color action photo is found on this top of the line insert series featuring 20 players who are most likely to be seen in the major leagues. Stated insertion rate was one per 92 packs.

		MT
Complete Set (20):		550.00
Common Player:		15.00
1	Rick Ankiel	150.00
2	Brad Penny	75.00
3	John Patterson	35.00
4	Rob Bell	15.00
5	Mark Mulder	20.00
6	Corey Patterson	95.00
7	Eric Munson	45.00
8	Nick Johnson	95.00
9	Dernell Stenson	25.00
10	Ryan Bradley	15.00
11	Alex Escobar	35.00
12	Matt White	30.00
13	Michael Cuddyer	15.00
14	Ryan Anderson	25.00
15	Pablo Ozuna	20.00
16	Pat Burrell	45.00
17	A.J. Burnett	25.00
18	Josh Hamilton	55.00
19	Jason Grilli	15.00
20	Matt Riley	35.00

Misspellings of names are not uncommon on modern minor league cards. Unless a corrected version was issued, such errors have no effect on value.

2000 SP Top Prospects Game-Used Bats

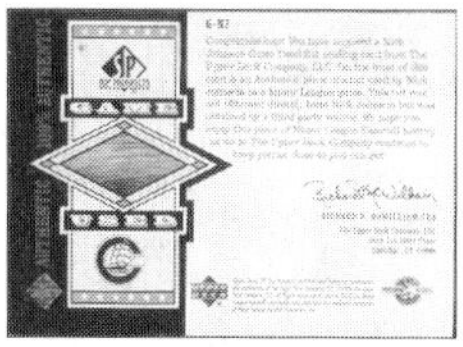

Slices of minor-league lumber wielded by top minor league stars of 1999, plus Ken Griffey Jr. and Michael Jordan are the "holy grail" for pack busters of SP Top Prospects. The horizontal-format cards have a diamond-shaped piece of game-used bat along with a color photo. Besides the regular version, Junior and Jordan also autographed a limited number of the cards, 24 and 45, respectively. The stated overall insertion rate for the bat cards is one per 288 packs (about one per 12 boxes).

		MT
Complete Set (13):		650.00
Common Player:		40.00
Pbe	Peter Bergeron	40.00
PB	Pat Burrell	125.00
RF	Rafael Furcal	75.00
JR	Ken Griffey Jr.	250.00
JR	Ken Griffey Jr. (autographed edition of 24)	
JH	Josh Hamilton	60.00
NJ	Nick Johnson	90.00
MJ	Michael Jordan	500.00
MJ	Michael Jordan (autographed edition of 45)	
EM	Eric Munson	40.00
PO	Pablo Ozuna	45.00
CP	Corey Patterson	75.00
AS	Alfonso Soriano	90.00
JT	Jorge Toca	40.00
JW	Jayson Werth	45.00

2000 SP Top Prospects Great Futures

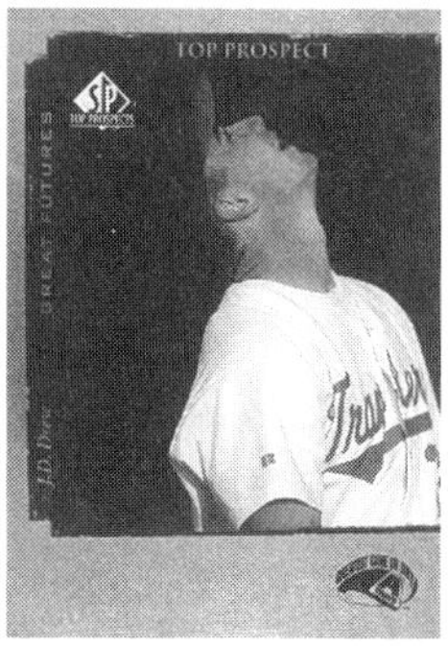

Twenty top minor league stars destined for big-league futures are the content of this insert set, found on average of one per four packs.

		MT
Complete Set (20):		45.00
Common Player:		.75
1	Jorge Toca	.75
2	Ryan Anderson	1.25
3	Eric Munson	1.25
4	Rick Ankiel	7.00
5	Rob Bell	.75
6	Matt Riley	3.00
7	Pat Burrell	6.00
8	Nick Johnson	7.00
9	Jody Gerut	.75
10	Sean Burroughs	4.50
11	Austin Kearns	1.25
12	Corey Patterson	7.00
13	Josh Hamilton	4.50
14	Rafael Furcal	2.50
15	Donny Leon	.75
16	Peter Bergeron	1.50
17	A.J. Burnett	1.25
18	Alex Escobar	1.25
19	Brad Penny	1.25
20	Chin-Feng Chen	2.50

2000 SP Top Prospects Minor Memories

The minor league careers of Ken Griffey Jr. and Michael Jordan are traced in this series. Stated odds of pulling one of the inserts are one per 11 packs.

		MT
Complete Set (10):		15.00
Common Player:		1.50
MJ01	Michael Jordan	2.50
MJ02	Michael Jordan	2.50
MJ03	Michael Jordan	2.50
MJ04	Michael Jordan	2.50
MJ05	Michael Jordan	2.50
Jr01	Ken Griffey Jr.	1.50
Jr02	Ken Griffey Jr.	1.50
Jr03	Ken Griffey Jr.	1.50
Jr04	Ken Griffey Jr.	1.50
Jr05	Ken Griffey Jr.	1.50

2000 SP Top Prospects Prospective Superstars

Upper Deck labled the dozen players in this insert set as "can't-miss super prospects" and inserted these cards one per 24 packs of SP Top Prospects.

		MT
Complete Set (12):		165.00
Common Player:		5.00
1	Pat Burrell	25.00
2	Eric Munson	10.00
3	Rick Ankiel	45.00
4	Brad Penny	10.00
5	Ben Petrick	5.00
6	Josh Hamilton	25.00
7	Adam Piatt	10.00
8	A.J. Burnett	5.00
9	Rafael Furcal	7.50
10	Sean Burroughs	20.00
11	Chin-Feng Chen	15.00
12	Nick Johnson	35.00

2000 SP Top Prospects Small Town Heroes

Capturing the feel of minor league baseball across the nation, this insert series showcases players whose 1999 season were spent in places like Princeton and Norwich. Insertion rate was announced as one per 11 packs.

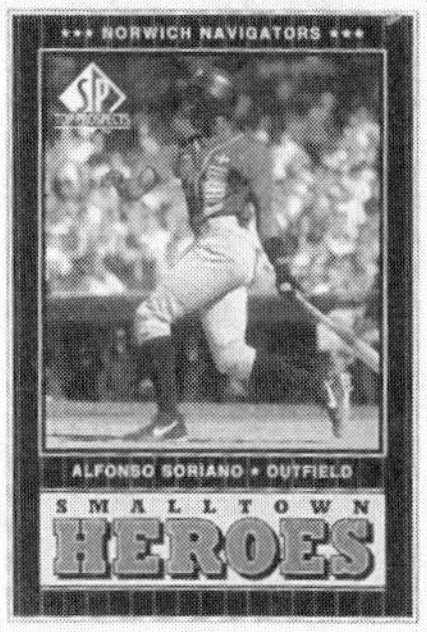

		MT
Complete Set (12):		30.00
Common Player:		3.00
1	Josh Hamilton	6.00
2	Jorge Toca	3.00
3	John Patterson	3.00
4	Jacques Landry	3.00
5	Felipe Lopez	4.50
6	Choo Freeman	3.00
7	Eric Valent	3.00
8	Jody Gerut	3.00
9	Michael Restovich	3.00
10	Pablo Ozuna	4.50
11	Kip Wells	3.00
12	Michael Cuddyer	3.00

2000 Team Best Rookies 2000 Promos

These cards introduced both TB's Rookies 2000 and Baseball Fanatics Trading Card Game issues. Fronts are virtually identical to the issued versions of the cards. Backs have a large Rookies 2000 or Baseball Fanatics logo at center.

		MT
Complete Set (5):		12.00
Common Player:		3.00
(1)	Baseball Fanatics header card	.50
(2)	Pat Burrell (Babbitt's Bombers)	5.00
(3)	Sean Burroughs	4.00
(4)	Corey Myers	3.00
(5)	Corey Patterson (#1 Pick)	5.00

2000 Team Best Rookies 2000

Significant problems with numbering of cards in the range #3-99 plagued this otherwise attractive minor league presentation. Corrected versions, which were available only by mail-in exchange, had to be issued for some 20 cards. They are marked with an SP in the checklist here. All but one (Ben Broussard) of the players in the base set is presented in two different formats. A few can also be found in the "Babbitt's Bombers" insert sets and the autographed cards. Cards #1-100 have player photos surrounded with a frame resembling cut stone. A Rookies 2000 logo is at upper-right. On most cards there is a Team Best logo at lower-left and a minor league team logo at lower-right. On some cards the team logo is replaced with the TB logo. Cards #101-112 are similar in design though the color of stone borders is brown, rather than gray; these player's represent #1 draft picks. Backs repeat a portion of the front photo in tight vertical format at left, and offer personal data and career highlights. Cards #113-213 feature the same line-up as #1-100, and most use the same photo on front, though in a borderless design. Their backs are similar in format to the low-numbers. Cards #214-225 repeat the checklist of #1 picks on a "two-headed" borderless format. All "b" version cards in the checklist represent the originally printed error cards which have the correct photos on front and back, but have the "a" player's biographical data and career highlights. Eight "Babbitt's Bombers" (named for the photographer) cards are inserted at a 1:72 pack rate with parallels in gold numbered to 100 and silver to 150. Also found as inserts at a rate of about one per three packs are authentically autographed cards. Team Best Rookie 2000 cards were sold in a basic six-card foil pack with 18 packs per box.

		MT
Complete Set (225):		20.00
Common Player:		.10
Wax Box:		45.00
1	Kurt Ainsworth	.15
2	Travis Anderson	.10
3a	Ryan Baerlocher	.10
3b	Chris Sampson	.10
4	Andrew Beinbrink (SP)	.25
5	Jonathan Berry	.10
6	Larry Bigbie	.10
7	Josh Bonifay	.10
8	Casey Burns	.10
9	Mike Bynum (SP)	.25
10	Marlon Byrd	.15
11	Terry Byron (SP)	.25
12	Chance Caple	.10
13	Matt Cepicky	.25
14a	Ryan Christianson	.25
14b	Joe Thurston	.10
15	B.R. Cook	.10
16	Carl Crawford	.15
17	Chuck Crowder	.10
18	Jeremy Cunningham	.10
19a	Chris Curry	.10
19b	Mike Bynum	.10
20a	Phil Devey	.10
20b	Andrew Beinbrink	.10
21a	Grant Dorn	.10

21b Chris Testa .10
22 Mike Dwyer (SP) .25
23a Mike Dzurilla .15
23b Barry Zito .20
24 Vince Faison .20
25 Carlos Figueroa .10
26 Aaron Franke .10
27 Charlie Frazier .10
28 B.J. Garbe .10
29 Curtis Gay .10
30 Jay Gehrke .15
31 Scott Goodman .10
32 Alex Graman .10
33a Ryan Gripp .15
33b Robb Quinlan .10
34 Josh Hamilton (SP) 3.00
35 Ken Harvey .25
36 Jeff Heaverlo .10
37 Ben Hickman .10
38 Mike Hill (SP) .25
39 Josh Holliday .10
40 Kevin Hooper .10
41a Ryan Jamison .10
41b Josh Hamilton 1.00
42 Eric Johnson .15
43 Jake Joseph .10
44 Ryan Kibler (SP) .25
45 John Lackey .10
46 Jake Laidlaw .10
47 Jay Landreth (SP) .25
48 Jason Lane .10
49 Jay Langston .10
50 Peyton Lewis .10
51a Robert MacDougal .10
51b Ben Sheets .15
52 Mike Mallory .20
53 Justin Martin .10
54 Lamont Matthews .10
55 Matt McClendon .10
56 Sean McGowan .10
57a Todd Mitchell .10
57b Terry Byron .10
58a Matt Mize .10
58b Matt Watson .10
59 Jason Moore .10
60 Corey Myers .10
61 Derrick Nunley .10
62 Rodney Nye .10
63a Mike Paradis .10
63b Mike Dwyer .10
64 Tino Pascucci .10
65 Dustin Pate .10
66 Mike Patten .10
67 Brad Pautz .10
68a Josh Pearse .10
68b Ryan Kibler .10
69 Andy Phillips .15
70 Robb Quinlan (SP) .25
71a G.J. Raymundo .10
71b Dominic Woody .10
72a Justin Reid .10
72b Mike Rosamond .10
73 Nate Robertson .10
74 Mike Rosamond (SP) .25
75 Chris Sampson (SP) .25
76 Matt Schneider .10
77 Sean Schumacher .10
78 Ben Sheets (SP) .50
79 Jeremy Sickles .10
80a Kyle Snyder .10
80b Mike Hill .10
81 Jack Taschner .10
82a Seth Taylor .10
82b Charles Williams .10
83 Chris Testa (SP) .25
84 Mike Thompson (SP) .25
85 Joe Thurston (SP) .25
86a Jon Topolski .10
86b Jerome Williams .10
87a Dan Tosca .10
87b Jay Landreth .10
88 Nick Trzeniak .10
89 Brant Ust .10
90 Josh Vitek .10
91 David Walling .10
92 Jeremy Ward .10
93 Anthony Ware .10
94 Matt Watson (SP) .25
95 Charles Williams (SP) .25
96 Jerome Williams (SP) .25
97 Dominic Woody (SP) .25
98 Shane Wright .10
99 Barry Zito (SP) .50
100 Alec Zumwalt .10
101 Chip Ambres (#1 Pick) .20
102 Jeff Austin (#1 Pick) .10
103 Pat Burrell (#1 Pick) .50
104 Sean Burroughs (#1 Pick) 1.00
105 Bubba Crosby (#1 Pick) .10
106 Choo Freeman (#1 Pick) .25
107 Josh Hamilton (#1 Pick) 1.00
108 Mark Mulder (#1 Pick) .15
109 Corey Patterson (#1 Pick) 1.00
110 Carlos Pena (#1 Pick) .20
111 Eric Valent (#1 Pick) .35
112 Kip Wells (#1 Pick) .50
113 Kurt Ainsworth (#1 on front) .15
114 Travis Anderson .10
115 Ryan Baerlocher (#3 on front) .10
116 Andrew Beinbrink .10
117 Jonathan Berry .10
118 Larry Bigbie .10
119 Josh Bonifay .10
120 Ben Broussard .10
121 Casey Burns (#8 on front) .10
122 Mike Bynum .10
123 Marlon Byrd .15
124 Terry Byron .10
125 Chance Caple .10
126 Matt Cepicky .25
127 Ryan Christianson .25
128 B.R. Cook .10
129 Carl Crawford .15
130 Chuck Crowder .10
131 Jeremy Cunningham .10
132 Chris Curry .10
133 Phil Devey .10
134 Grant Dorn .10
135 Mike Dwyer .10
136 Mike Dzurilla .15
137 Vince Faison .20
138 Carlos Figueroa .10
139 Aaron Franke .10
140 Charlie Frazier .10
141 B.J. Garbe .10
142 Curtis Gay .10
143 Jay Gehrke .15
144 Scott Goodman .10
145 Alex Graman .10
146 Ryan Gripp .15
147 Josh Hamilton 1.00
148 Ken Harvey .25
149 Jeff Heaverlo .10
150 Ben Hickman .10
151 Mike Hill .10
152 Josh Holliday .10
153 Kevin Hooper .10
154 Ryan Jamison .10
155 Eric Johnson .15
156 Jake Joseph .10
157 Ryan Kibler .10
158 John Lackey .10
159 Jake Laidlaw .10
160 Jay Landreth .10
161 Jason Lane .10
162 Jay Langston .10
163 Peyton Lewis .10
164 Robert MacDougal .10
165 Mike Mallory .20
166 Justin Martin .10
167 Lamont Matthews .10
168 Matt McClendon .10
169 Sean McGowan .10
170 Todd Mitchell .10
171 Matt Mize .10
172 Jason Moore .10
173 Corey Myers .10
174 Derrick Nunley .10
175 Rodney Nye .10
176 Mike Paradis .10
177 Tino Pascucci .10
178 Dustin Pate .10
179 Mike Patten .10
180 Brad Pautz .10
181 Josh Pearse .10
182 Andy Phillips .15
183 Robb Quinlan .10
184 G.J. Raymundo .10
185 Justin Reid .10
186 Nate Robertson .10
187 Mike Rosamond .10
188 Chris Sampson .10
189 Matt Schneider .10
190 Sean Schumacher .10
191 Ben Sheets .15
192 Jeremy Sickles .10
193 Kyle Snyder .10
194 Jack Taschner .10
195 Seth Taylor .10
196 Chris Testa .10
197 Mike Thompson .10
198 Joe Thurston .10
199 Jon Topolski .10
200 Dan Tosca .10
201 Nick Trzeniak .10
202 Brant Ust .10
203 Josh Vitek .10
204 David Walling .10
205 Jeremy Ward .10
206 Anthony Ware .10
207 Matt Watson .10
208 Charles Williams .10
209 Jerome Williams .10
210 Dominic Woody .10
211 Shane Wright .10
212 Barry Zito .20
213 Alec Zumwalt .10
214 Chip Ambres (#1 Pick) .20
215 Jeff Austin (#1 Pick) .10
216 Pat Burrell (#1 Pick) .50
217 Sean Burroughs (#1 Pick) 1.00
218 Bubba Crosby (#1 Pick) .10
219 Choo Freeman (#1 Pick) .25
220 Josh Hamilton (#1 Pick) 1.00
221 Mark Mulder (#1 Pick) .15
222 Corey Patterson (#1 Pick) 1.00
223 Carlos Pena (#1 Pick) .20
224 Eric Valent (#1 Pick) .35
225 Kip Wells (#1 Pick) .50
Autograph Contest card .05
Baseball Fanatcs preview card .05
Babbitt's Bomber's offer card .05

2000 Team Best Rookies 2000 Autographs

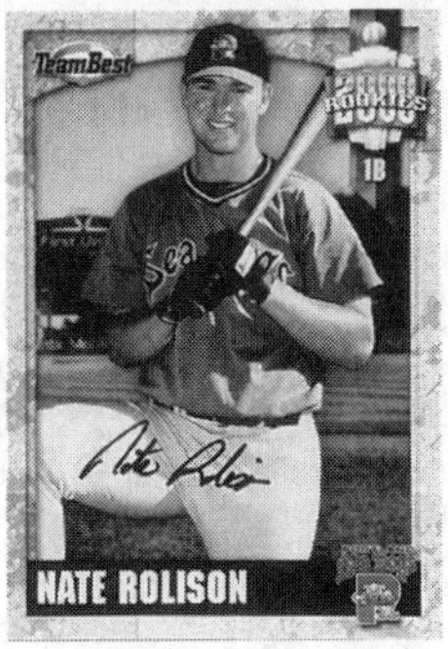

A mixed line-up of first-year pros and established minor league stars is featured in the autographed inserts seeded in TB Rookies 2000 at a rate of about one per three packs. Autograph cards follow the format of the low-number cards in the base set. Backs have a "Declaration of Authenticity" from TB chairman/CEO Dan R. White, Jr. The unnumbered autograph cards are listed here alphabetically.

MT
Complete Set (25): 125.00
Common Player: 4.00
(1) Kurt Ainsworth 6.00
(2) Chad Allen 4.00
(3) Chip Ambres 6.00
(4) Ryan Anderson 15.00
(5) Andy Brown 4.00
(6) Sean Burroughs 15.00
(7) Francisco Cordero 4.00
(8) Bubba Crosby 4.00
(9) Jack Cust 6.00
(10) Rick Elder 4.00
(11) Choo Freeman 4.00
(12) Jeff Goldbach 4.00
(13) Josh Hamilton 20.00
(14) Chad Harville 4.00
(15) Jeff Heaverlo 4.00
(16) Cesar Izturis 6.00
(17) Austin Kearns 6.00
(18) Mike Lincoln 6.00
(19) George Lombard 4.00
(20) Julio Lugo 4.00
(21) Jim Morris 4.00
(22) Nate Rolison 4.00
(23) B.J. Ryan 4.00
(24) Pat Strange 4.00
(25) Tyler Walker 4.00

2000 Team Best Rookies 2000 Babbitt's Bombers

While most of the players in the base set were first year pros in 1999, the selection of players in the Rookie 2000 set leans to established minor league (and future Major League) stars. Seeded only one per 72 foil packs, the Bombers cards feature top sluggers in a format similar to the low-number cards in the base set. The silhouette of a four-engine bomber appears at upper-left on front. Backs have multiple copies of the bomber symbol, along with personal data and career highlights. Parallels of the insert are a silver version, numbered to 150, and a gold version, numbered to 100.

MT
Complete Set (8): 45.00
Common Player: 5.00
Silver: 1.5X
Gold: 2X
1 Russell Branyan 6.00
2 Morgan Burkhart 5.00
3 Pat Burrell 10.00
4 Josh Hamilton 15.00
5 Nick Johnson 10.00
6 George Lombard 7.50
7 Carlos Pena 5.00
8 Dernell Stenson 5.00

GLOSSARY OF HOBBY TERMS

ACC: Acronym for the American Card Catalog. This catalog, written by Jefferson Burdick and last published in 1960, uses numerical and alphabetical designations for identifying and cataloging card sets. The letter used in the ACC designation refers to the generic type of card: B = blankets; D = bakery inserts, including bread; E = early candy and gum; F = food inserts; H = advertising; M = periodicals; N = 19th century U.S. tobacco; PC = postcards; R = recent candy and gum cards, 1930 to present; T = 20th century U.S. tobacco; UO = gas and oil inserts; V = Canadian candy; W = Exhibits, strip cards, team-issued cards. A one-, two- or three-digit number follows the letter prefix. The numbers represent the company or entity which issued the cards.

Acetate: Plastic or acrylic card stock, usually clear.

Action Packed: A football card manufacturer which produced its first set in 1989. The company has also done basketball and baseball sets, too. Sold to Pinnacle in 1996.

Airbrushing: The touching up of a photo by an artist. Usually done on trading cards to show a player, who has changed teams, in his new uniform. Often used to remove team logos from players' uniforms on card sets which are not licensed by Major League Baseball Properties.

All-Star card: A special card identifying a player as a member of a National League, American League or unofficial other all-star team. Players shown on all-star cards may or may not be members of their league's official All-Star team. All-star cards can be part of a regular set or issued as an independent or insert set.

Artist's Proof: An insert card type introduced in the mid1990s. Usually in the form of a parallel set, and limited to the first 1,000 or 2,000 of each card, they are marked with a special metallic-foil logo on front or other indicator. The theory behind artist's proof cards is that the first impressions off the new printing plates will have the sharpest detail and most accurate color.

Ask price: The price at which a dealer, investor or collector offers to sell his cards.

Assorted: A term used in ads to indicate a lot of cards which may contain multiples of one or more cards. Lots which do not contain doubles are labeled "different."

Autographed card: A card that has actually been signed by the player pictured, as opposed to the facsimile signatures that are sometimes printed on cards as part of the design. The value of an autographed card is generally greater than that same card would be if it were unautographed. The use of autographed cards as pack inserts was pioneered in 1990 by Upper Deck and is now a staple in most companies' chase card programs.

Autograph guest: A current or former player or other celebrity who attends a card convention to sign autographs for fans. A fee, which can range from a few dollars to more than $100 for a player such as Joe DiMaggio, is usually charged for the autograph.

Baseball's Best: A season-end glossy set made by Donruss in 1988 and 1989. Also the name of a boxed set made by Fleer in 1987 and 1988, and the name of a set of insert cards made by Baseball Cards magazine in 1989 and 1990.

Bazooka: The best-known bubble gum brand name from Topps. Various on-box and inserted baseball card issues were given away with multi-piece Bazooka packages from 1959-71 and again beginning in 1988.

Beckett: The trademarked name for the hobby's largest circulation line of sportscard periodical and book price guides. Named for founder and price guide pioneer Dr. Jim Beckett. Among novice collectors the term is sometimes incorrectly used as a generic term for a price guide magazine.

Bid board: An area at a card shop where customers can place their cards to be bid on by other customers over a specific period. The highest bid buys the card and the collector pays a percentage of the sale price or a fixed fee to the store owner.

Bid price: The price an investor, dealer, etc., offers to pay for cards.

Big cards: The trade name for Topps' oversized, glossyfinish card issues produced from 1988-1990. The cards are reminiscent of Topps cards from the 1950s. While most Topps and other cards were produced in the nowstandard 2-1/2" x 3-1/2" size, the Big cards measure 3-3/4" x 2-5/8".

Black Gold: A parallel set for Leaf Baseball in 1992, or an insert in Topps sets from 1993-1994.

Blank-back: Usually refers to a card that has no printing on the back because of a manufacturing mistake. As with most printing errors on cards, premium value usually attaches only to cards of superstar players. Cards that were intentionally issued without printing on the back are also known as blank-backed.

Blanket: An early 20th-century collectible consisting of a square piece of felt or other fabric which came wrapped around a package of cigarettes. Baseball players were one of the several subjects found on blankets. Most popular are the 5-1/4" x 5-1/4" B18 blankets from 1914, so-called because they were sometimes sewn together to form a blanket.

Blazer: A good with extraordinary eye appeal. Usually refers to an older card with exceptionally fresh color and white borders.

Bleached: A card which has had bleach applied to its borders or other white surfaces to remove signs of aging. Bleached cards are considered to have been unethically altered and are worth much less than a card in the same grade with natural surfaces.

Blister pack: A method of card packaging in which cards are packaged in hard plastic on a cardboard backing, with three or four pockets of cards. Best known as Donruss and Topps issues of the late 1980s.

Book price: The retail selling price which appears in a price guide. Frequently used as a verb, as in "This card books for $8, but I'll let you have it for $6."

Borders: The portion of a card which surrounds the picture. Borders are usually white but are sometimes colored. The condition of a card's borders is one of the vital components in determining a card's grade. As techniques of card printing and cutting became more sophisticated in the late 1980s, various card brands began to appear with borderless photos on front.

Bowman: A Philadelphia card company which made baseball cards from 1948-55, football cards from 1948-55, basketball cards in 1948, and various entertainment cards in the same era. It was Topps' principal competitor in that era. Bowman was bought by Topps in 1956 and card production ceased. Topps revived the Bowman name in 1989 for new series of low-priced cards in baseball and other sports.

Bowman's Best: A premium priced, high-tech brand name for one of Topps' niche products.

Box-bottom cards: Cards printed on the bottom and/or sides of wax-or foil-pack boxes. Box-bottom cards are not considered to be part of the regular set and generally are not valuable unless kept intact as a panel.

Boxed set: A set of cards, usually consisting of either 33 or 44 cards, issued as a complete set and sold in its own box at a large chain or discount store. Boxed sets are usually made under contract by one of the major manufacturers and contain cards of only the biggest names or hottest rookies.

Brick: A wrapped lot of cards, usually all from one year. See "starter set."

Burger King cards (BK): Cards issued in conjunction with Burger King products, 1977-1987. For most of those years the cards were produced by Topps, often using the same photos as contemporary Topps cards, though with different card numbers.

Buy price: The price which a dealer is willing to pay for cards or memorabilia. A dealer's buy price is usually 50% or less than that item's catalog or retail price to allow the dealer a profit margin.

Cabinet card: A large card, typically 4" x 6" to 5" x 7", from the late 19th or early 20th Century. Generally an actual photograph mounted on a heavy cardboard matte bearing the issuers advertising, the cards were often given away as premiums by tobacco companies or periodicals. The name "cabinet" derives from how they were often displayed - inside curio cabinets.

Caption: The title on a card which identifies or describes the subject pictured, but may also be a line of dialogue. It generally appears under the illustration and/or on the back.

Card lot: A) A quantity of the same card, usually sold at a discounted price. B) A mixture of cards, exact contents usually unspecified, sold as a group.

Card stock: The paper, cardboard or other material on which baseball cards are printed.

Case: The basic wholesale packaging for trading cards when sold from manufacturer to dealer or retail store. A case contains wax-pack boxes or other product units. For instance, a 1990 Topps "wax case" is made up of 20 "wax boxes." By the early 1990s different types of case configurations for the same product destined for different sales outlets became common.

Cello box: A retail display box of cello packs, usually, but not always, containing 24 packs.

Cello case: A wholesale unit of cello boxes, usually, but not always, containing 16 boxes.

Cello pack: A cellophane-wrapped pack of cards. A cello pack usually contains more cards than a wax pack. Depending on how the cards are packaged, the top and bottom card of a cello pack may or may not be easily visible through the cellophane. Many collectors will pay a premium for a cello pack with a card of a star player or hot rookie showing on the top or bottom. Since the mid-1990s some manufacturers' cello packs are also known as "magazine" or "jumbo" packs.

Centering: The positioning of a card picture between its borders. A well-centered card has even borders, an important factor in grading and/or pricing a card. Centering is described as a ratio of the amount of one border to the border opposite it, either "S/S" (side-to-side) or "T/B" (top-to-bottom). A perfectly centered cards borders are described as "50/50". A card with noticeably unequal borders might be described as "70/30".

Chase card: A pack insert card, usually produced in very limited quantities relative to the set in which it is inserted. Originated because collectors often buy multiple packs "chasing" the scarce inserts.

Checklist: A list of every card in a particular set, usually with a space allowing the collector to check whether he has the card. A checklist can appear on a card, in a book or elsewhere. Checklists on cards are worth more if they're left unchecked. In sets issued prior to the mid1970s, checklist cards are often scarcer than others in the issue because they were saved less often than favorite players' cards.

Cherry pick: A) To use superior knowledge to buy a card for much less than its true value. B) To pick and choose among cards when buying so as to acquire the best and leave the rest.

Chipping: A card-grading term referring to a condition in which a portion of a card's dark-colored border is worn away. Chipping is a real problem, for instance, with 1953 and 1971 Topps cards, and more recent issues with colored borders or borderless photos.

Classic cards: Cards made by Game Time Ltd. to go with its Classic Baseball trivia game. The cards were first made in 1987 and sold only in complete sets. The company was sold to The Score Board in 1988 and the brand name was continued on the several sets a year usually produced.

Clear Cut Finest: A card printed on clear or tinted acetate utilizing Topps' Finest technology.

Coin: A metal or plastic coin-sized disc which depicts a player. It can also refer to an actual coin or a coin-sized silver piece which commemorates an actual event.

Collation: The act of putting cards in order, usually numerical order. Sometimes used as a noun to describe the relative ratio of different cards within a pack, box or other sales unit.

Collectible: Something worth collecting. Baseball cards, programs, pennants, uniforms, and autographs are all examples of collectibles.

Collector issue: A set of cards produced primarily to be sold to collectors and not issued as a premium to be given away or sold with a commercial product. Collector issues fall into two categories: authorized (meaning the issue was made with the approval of professional sports and the players' association) or unauthorized (meaning the issue was made without approval).

Combination card: A single card which depicts two or more players, but is not a team card.

Common card: A card picturing a "common" or ordinary player-that is, not a star or superstar. "Commons" are the lowest-priced cards in a given series or set.

Condition: One of the major factors in determining the value of a card; describes its state of preservation.

Convention: Also known as a baseball card show or trading card show. A gathering of anywhere from one to 600 or more card dealers at a single location (convention center, hotel ballroom, school auditorium or mall) for the purpose of buying, selling or trading cards. A convention is open to the public, and often times a fee is required to attend the show. Many conventions feature a player or several players to sign autographs.

Counterfeit card: A reproduction made to look like a real card for the purpose of selling it to an unsuspecting buyer as the genuine article, Counterfeit cards have no collector value and in most cases are illegal to buy and sell, even without intention to defraud.

Crash card: An interactive "You Crash the Game" card from Upper Deck's Collectors Choice brand. If the pictured player accomplished a specific goal-such as a home run-on a specific date, the card could be redeemed for a special set. Issued in silver and gold versions beginning in 1994.

Crease: Damage to the surface and/or core of a card, usually due to mishandling, but sometimes a result of the printing/packaging process. Creases substantially lower a card's grade and value, depending on their number and severity.

CY: Cy Young Award. Top award given my each major league annually to the pitcher judged to be the year's best by the baseball writers. Named after the major leagues' winningest pitcher of all time.

Dealer: A person who buys, sells and trades baseball cards and other memorabilia for profit. A dealer may be full-time, part-time, own a shop, operate a mail-order business from his home, deal at baseball card shows on weekends or do any combination of the above.

Decollation: The act of putting cards in random order, usually for packaging.

Diamond King: A Donruss card featuring the artwork produced by Perez-Steele Galleries. Issued as part of the regular baseball series from 1982-1991, thereafter as random pack inserts. Diamond King Supers are 5" x 7" versions of the 1985-1991 DK cards available via mailorder offer on Donruss wax packs.

Die-cut card: A) A baseball card in which the player's outline or other design/graphic element has been partially separated from the background, enabling the card to be folded into a "stand-up" figure. Die-cut cards that have never been folded are worth more to collectors. B) A card on which part of the background has been cut away, usually to create a parallel set. Upper Deck made this process popular beginning with its 1993 SP product, by cutting the top of a card in a crown-type fashion, not the traditional squared corners. By 1996 some companies were using laser technology to create complex cutouts as part of card designs.

Ding: Slight damage to the corner or edge of a card.

Disc: A round card, usually showing head-and-shoulder shots of players, printed on paper or thin cardboard, as opposed to a plastic or metal "coin", or a thick-cardboard "POG".

Distributor: Persons or companies which buy cards directly from the card manufacturers or from other sources and resell them on a large scale, usually to retailers. Sometimes distributors receive exclusive products, and thus are the only source of distribution for the product.

Donruss: A baseball-card manufacturer and candy company subsidiary of the Leaf Corp. Donruss began issuing baseball cards in 1981, but had produced nonsports sets prior to that. The company was sold to Pinnacle in 1996.

Double embossed: Photos raised on front and back of a card to give it a 3D effect; an innovation introduced by Topps.

Double-print: An individual card that, because of a particular printing configuration, appears twice on the same press sheet and is, therefore, twice as common as the other cards. Topps commonly double-printed cards of the big-name stars in the late-1960s and 1970s.

Doubles: A duplicate of a card in your collection. A card which, since you retain one for your set, can be traded or sold.

Drake's: An Ohio-based bakery that made baseball cards in 1950 and again from 1981-88; most of the latter series being printed directly on the bottom and sides of snack product boxes.

Dufex: Pinnacle's brand name for card-printing technology in which transparent inks are applied to a textured metallic foil background. First used on a baseball card in 1993.

Electric Diamond: A parallel set used in Upper Deck products. Generally includes the use of prismatic silver or gold foil in place of the regular foil highlights on card fronts, plus a special logo.

Embossed: Raised photos on a card to make it appear 3D. Probably first used on a baseball card in Topps' 1965 insert set, then on large-format plastic cards in 1985-86. Most widely used by Action Packed in its various sportscard issues beginning in 1988.

Error card: A card that contains a mistake, including wrong photos, misspelled words, incorrect statistics, and so forth. Usually error cards have no extra value unless they have been corrected, resulting in a "variation" card.

Exclusive: In hobby terms usually refers to availability from a single source. Certain card sets are made for exclusive sale through hobby stores, others for the large retail chains, etc. Some insert cards are also exclusive to one type or other of packaging.

Exhibit cards: Postcard-size cards picturing baseball players and other celebrities and sold in penny-arcade machines. Exhibit cards were produced from the 1920s to the 1960s and then certain cards were reprinted or rereleased in the early 1980s.

Extended set: A term used to describe a late-season series of cards added on to and numbered after a regular set. Also known as an extended series, update set or traded set.

Facsimile autograph: A reproduced autograph. Facsimile autographs are often found on sports cards as part of the card's design.

Factory set: A complete set of cards collated and packaged by the card company. A factory set may or may not be packaged in a special box. Usually factory sets are sealed or have sealed inner packs as an added security measure. Factory sets with intact seals or inner packs command a slight premium over hand-collated sets. Many factory sets now offer exclusive insert cards to entice collectors who may have already completed a set from pack purchases.

Felt: A baseball item consisting of a felt pennant, usually 'with a photograph or likeness of the player attached. Felts were made in 1916 and again from 1936-37.

Finest: Super-premium brand by Topps utilizing chromium technology and enhanced color quality, which provides added depth and dimension through the use of multi-color metallization. First used in 1993 Topps Finest Baseball.

First card: Once used to indicate the first card of a player by a major manufacturer. A first card may or may not be a player's rookie card; for instance, if a player appeared in a Fleer set one year and a Score set the next, the Fleer card would be that player's rookie card and his first Fleer card, while the Score card would be his first Score card but not his rookie card. The term has fallen out of favor with the flood of new cards and companies since the early 1990s.

First Day Issue: A parallel set used in Topps Stadium Club products and elsewhere, similar in concept to Artist's Proofs, supposedly signifying a card of superior technical reproduction.

Flannel: A uniform jersey made of a cotton or wool material. Most flannels were discontinued and replaced by knit jerseys in the early 1970s.

Fleer: A Philadelphia manufacturer of baseball, football, basketball and entertainment cards. Fleer made baseball cards annually from 1959-63 and again from 1981 to the present,

Fleer Glossy Tin: Limited-edition set produced by Fleer, which features the year's regular issue set and update with a high-gloss UV finish on front. These sets take their name from the colorful lithographed tin box in which they were sold from 1987-1989.

Fleer Update (FU): A 132-to200-card post-season set from Fleer which includes players traded to other teams during the season, and rookies (1984-1994). Sold exclusively through hobby dealers in its own separate box. Called Final Edition in 1993.

Foil: Thin metallic layer used either as a background for printing or die-stamped onto a card as a graphic enhancement. Can be gold, silver, bronze, prismatic or any color.

Foil box: A retail display box of foil packs, usually, but not always, containing 36 packs.

Foil case: A wholesale unit of foil boxes, usually, but not always, containing 24 boxes.

Foil pack: A pack of baseball cards packaged in a tamper-proof, shiny foil. Upper Deck debuted the use of foil packaging with its 1989 baseball cards to prevent various pack-searching abuses. Since then the use of foil has replaced waxed paper for card packs in many applications.

Foil-Tech: SkyBox's high-tech printing process for a chromium card with enhanced color, similar to Topps' Finest.

Food set: A set either inserted in packages of food (hot dogs, cereal, popcorn, potato chips, candy, cookies, etc.) or offered as a send-in offer by a food company. Examples of food sets include Kahn's Wieners, Mother's Cookies, etc.

Full-bleed: A card on which the front and/or back features a photo extending to all edges of the card with no contrasting border.

Full sheet: A full press sheet of cards that has never been cut; sometimes referred to as an "uncut" sheet. The number of cards on a sheet varies with the printing process, but most often contains 100 or 132 cards.

Gallery of Champions: Trade name for a set of miniature metallic reproductions of Topps cards made and sold by Topps from 1986-90. Gallery of Champions ingots were made in bronze, aluminum, silver and pewter.

Gem: Usually seen as an adjective describing a Mint card. A Gem Mint card usually exhibits extraordinary brightness of color, whiteness of borders and perfect centering.

Gloss: The amount of surface shine on a card. Most baseball cards are made with some surface gloss which is subject to scuffing as the card is handled. Cards that keep more of their gloss keep more of their value.

Glossy card: A card with a special, extra-shiny finish, usually the result of a coating of ultraviolet film during the printing process.

Glossy set: A set of glossy cards. Glossy sets can be either small and common (Topps' sendaway all-star sets) or large and scarce. Fleer, Topps, Score and Bowman have made glossy versions of their regular baseball card sets.

Gold: A parallel set used in Topps products on which some of the graphic elements of the card design are replaced with gold foil.

Gold Medallion: A parallel set used in Fleer Ultra products. Gold Medallions run parallel to the regular set and inserts and feature a special foil logo on front. Said to number less than 10% the print run of the cards they parallel.

Gold Rush: A parallel set used in Score products, usually found one per pack. On these cards the background behind the player photo has been printed on gold foil.

Gold Signature: A parallel set used in Upper Deck Collector's Choice products. Usually found one per box, these cards feature a facsimile autograph in gold ink on the front of the card and, sometimes, gold instead of white borders.

Goudey: A famous maker of baseball cards. The Goudey Gum Co. of Boston made baseball cards and non-sport cards from 1933-39.

Grade: The state of preservation of a card or piece of memorabilia. An item's value is based in large part on its grade (condition).

Grading service: A company that charges a fee to provide an independent judgment of a card's grade. After a card is graded, it is placed in a tamper-proof plastic holder. Card grading services are a recent innovation, patterned after similar services in the coin collecting hobby. The basic appeal of third-party graded cards is believed to be to investors who do not want to take the time or make the effort to learn to grade, or who do not trust the word of a seller concerning the condition of a card they are buying.

Hall of Fame Postcard: A long-running series of postcards produced by several manufacturers and sold by the National Baseball Hall of Fame. Popular among autograph collectors.

Hall of Famer (HOFer): A member of the Baseball Hall of Fame in Cooperstown, N.Y., but also used to refer to a baseball card picturing a member of the Hall of Fame. Hall of Famer cards almost always command a premium over other cards.

Hand-collated set: A set assembled card-by-card by hand, usually by a collector or dealer putting the set together out of packs or vending boxes.

Hartland: A statue produced by a Wisconsin plastics company in the late 1950s and early 1960s. Eighteen major league baseball players were models for Hartlands. The company also produced football player statues and a long line of Western and historical figures, horses and farm animals. Hartland baseball figures were reissued in 1989 along with new statues of players not in the original series.

High numbers: Usually the final series in a particular set of cards. High numbers were generally produced in smaller quantities than other series and are, therefore, scarcer and more valuable.

Hologram: The silvery, laser-etched trademark printed as an anti-counterfeiting device on Upper Deck cards. Also, a card printed wholly with holographic technology.

Holoview: Acetate card with a hologram on the front. First used in Upper Deck's 1993 Football Pro Bowl inserts.

In-action card: A card showing a ballplayer in action, as opposed to posed.

Insert: A collectible included inside a regular pack of baseball cards to boost sales. Inserts have included posters, baseball player stamps, coins, stickers, comic books, special cards, and tattoos. Since 1990 it has been popular for card companies to create special very limited edition series of cards for random insertion to enhance sales of their packs, essentially creating a legal lottery.

Interactive card: A card, usually an insert of limited production, which can be traded in for special prizes if the player, team etc., pictured thereon accomplishes a specific goal.

Jell-O cards: Cards printed on the backs of Jell-O packages 1962-1963.

Jogo: A Canadian card manufacturer that has been producing card sets picturing players from the Canadian Football League (CFL) for the past decade.

Jumbo: An oversized card; see "Super'.

Jumbo pack: A cello or foil pack containing more cards than the same issue's hobby or retail packaging. Sometimes contains special inserts not found in other types of packs, Usually reserved for sale in large retail chains.

Kellogg's: A cereal company which packaged and/or offered by mail three-dimensional baseball cards in its cereal from 1970-83, 1991-92.

Key cards: The most important or valuable cards in a set.

Last card: The final card issued of a ballplayer (or the final card of any particular set).

Layering: A term used in card grading to describe the separation of the layers of paper that make up the cardboard stock. Layering is a sign of wear that is first noticeable at the corners of the card.

Leaf: Donruss' parent firm. Donruss issued baseball cards in Canada under the Leaf name from 1985-88, then used the name for an upscale brand of baseball cards beginning in 1990. The sportscard division of Leaf was sold to Pinnacle in 1996.

Legitimate issue: A licensed card set issued as a premium with a commercial product to increase sales; not a collector issue.

Letter of authenticity: A letter stating that a certain piece of memorabilia, such as a uniform, is authentic. Issued by the seller to the buyer and often containing a guarantee.

Lenticular motion: A card production process who gives the picture on the finished product the illusion of motion when the viewing angle is changed.

Light F/X: Foil-etched background cards. Used in rookie subsets of SP Products beginning with 1993 Upper Deck SP Baseball.

Limited edition: A term often used by makers of cards and memorabilia to indicate scarcity. A limited edition means just that-production of the item in question will be limited to a certain number. However, that number may be large or small and is no guarantee of current or future value.

Lithograph: An art print made by a specific process that results in a print of outstanding clarity. Most lithographs are limited editions-though, as always, some lithographs are more limited than others.

Logo sticker: A peel-off, adhesive-backed reproduction of a team's symbol. Logo stickers were inserted in Fleer wax packs from the 1970s through the 1980s.

Mail-bid auction: A form of auction where all bids are sent in through the mail. The person who sends in the highest bid gets the merchandise.

Magazine pack: A special pack configuration, often containing different insert series, meant to be sold through magazine distributors to certain types of retail outlets.

Major set: A large, nationally-distributed set produced by a major card manufacturer, such as Topps, Fleer, Donruss, Pinnacle or Upper Deck.

Master set: A set containing not only one of each card number, but one of each variation which might exist in the set, as well as all insert series issued with that set.

Megalot: A card investor's term referring to a very large (normally 1,000 or more) group of cards of one player, purchased as an investment.

Memorabilia: Usually used in sports collecting to refer to items other than cards which mark or commemorate a player and his career, a team or an event.

Micro-lined foil board: Technology used on Classic's Images product line. First used in Classic Images Football.

Mini: Small-size cards, sometimes miniature reproductions of regular cards (1975 Topps mini) and sometimes independent issues (1986-90 Topps Mini League Leaders).

Minor leaguer: A card depicting a player from the minor leagues.

Miscut: A card that has been cut incorrectly from a press sheet during the manufacturing process and decreases in value as a result.

Mother's: An Oakland, Calif.-based cookie company which has issued high-quality glossy-finish team sets since 1982.

Multi-player card: A card picturing more than one player. Multi-player cards often show rookies or stars.

Museum Collection: A parallel set, used in Pinnacle products, using Dufex foil-printing technology to reproduce the base cards in a set in a limited-edition, high-tech format.

MVP: Most Valuable Player award winner, awarded annual by each major league.

MVP Contenders: An interactive set in Leaf products. Insert cards which could be traded in for special sets if the pictured player won his league's MVP.

Mylar: Trade name for a type of inert plastic used to make supplies for the protection of cards and memorabilia.

Nine-pocket sheet: The most common type of plastic sheet. A nine-pocket sheet is about the size of a sheet of typing paper and is designed to fit into a standard three-ring binder. The sheet has nine pockets to hold most normal-sized modern cards.

Non-sports card: A card picturing a subject other than sports. Non-sports cards have depicted movie stars, television shows, U.S. presidents, moments in history, entertainers and other subjects. Now often being referred to as "entertainment cards."

Notching: A card-grading term used to describe indentations along the edge of a card, sometimes caused by a rubber band. Notching decreases a card's value.

Obverse: The front of the card displaying the picture.

Off-center: A term used in card grading to describe a card that has uneven borders.

Old Judge: A brand of cigarettes which was popular in the late 1800s. Also the name given to the huge set of baseball cards issued as a premium with that brand of cigarettes. The cards, issued from 1887-90, carried advertisements for Old Judge cigarettes.

100-percent etched foil: Metallic-foil background over which the player photo is printed. Used in Fleer Ultra inserts.

O-Pee-Chee: Topps' Canadian licensee. O-Pee-Chee made and sold a baseball card set that resembled Topps' set but usually had fewer cards, and a hockey card set that resembled Topps but had more cards. O-Pee-Chee cards can sometimes be distinguished from Topps cards by the bilingual (French-English) backs. OPC ceased production of baseball cards after the 1994 issue.

Out of register: A term used to describe a poorly printed card on which the various colors are not correctly superimposed upon one another, creating a "fuzzy" picture thereby decreasing the value of the card.

Own The Game: Interactive inserts in Topps products.

Panel: A strip of two or more uncut cards. Some card sets are issued in panels.

Panini: An Italian sticker manufacturer which came into the U.S. baseball sticker market in 1988 with a large and attractive set of baseball stickers. Panini also makes hockey, basketball and football stickers. The company was purchased by Fleer in 1994.

Parkhurst: A Canadian card manufacturer that produced NHL hockey sets in the 1950s and 1960s. Collectors often refer to Parkhurst cards as "Parkies." The company produced a minor league baseball set in 1952.

Perez-Steele: Usually used as a term to refer to an ongoing set of Hall of Fame postcards issued by the Perez-Steele Galleries of Fort Washington, Pa. The company has made a number of artistic card sets, including the Celebration and Greatest Moments sets. Popular with autograph collectors.

Phone auction: An auction where bids for baseball cards or other memorabilia are taken over the phone. The highest bidder gets the merchandise.

Pinnacle: A top-of-the-line brand name originated in 1992 from Score. In 1994 Score changed the name of its "umbrella" organization to Pinnacle Brands.

Plastic sheet: A polyethylene or polyvinyl sheet designed to store baseball cards, the most common being the ninepocket sheet (which fits today's standard-sized cards). The sheets have prepunched holes on the left side which allows them to be placed in a three-ring binder.

Platinum: A parallel set used in 1995 Score baseball which was available only by mail in a trade for complete Gold Rush team sets.

Play Ball: The brand name of baseball cards produced by Gum Inc. (1939-1941).

POG: Brand name for a thick, round cardboard, plastic or metal card, about silver dollar size (1-5/8") used to play a game. Originated in away as the tops of glass containers of pineapple-orange-guava fruit drink. Playing and collecting POGs was a fad which lasted about five minutes on the Mainland in 1994.

Police set: A regional card set made for a police department and given away to kids, usually one card at a time, to promote friendly relations. Police cards often carry a safety or anti-drug message on the back. Baseball, football, basketball and hockey police sets have been made of major league, minor league and college teams. Similar sets issued by fire departments are also generically called "police sets" or "safety sets."

Polyethylene: A type of plastic used to make card sheets and other collectors' supplies. Very flexible, but not as clear as other types of plastic. Safer than PVC for very long-term card storage.

Post: A cereal company which printed baseball and football cards from 1960-63 on the backs of its cereal boxes. Today the most valuable Post cards are uncut panels found on boxes. In 1990, the company returned with an annual baseball card set inserted into its cereal boxes, with separate versions for the U.S. and Canada.

PPD: Postage paid.

Power Matrix: An intensely bright, almost glowing, foil printing technology first used on special Topps Stadium Club cards, then in the base brand sets as an insert.

Predictor: Interactive inserts in Upper Deck products that pick winners for certain statistical and individual leaders. Redeemable for special sets.

Premium: An extra. In terms of cards, this can either refer to a card inserted in a package of some other product or something extra inserted in a package of cards. "Premium" can also refer to the extra money a high-series or star card commands.

Pre-rookie: Term sometimes used to refer to any card of a player issued before his rookie card-a minor league card, for example, or a high school, college or Olympic team card.

Press Proof: A parallel set used in Donruss products, usually the first 2,000 printed of any card. Conveys the notion of especially sharp detail and colors from new printing plates. Usually designated by a small metallic foil seal on the card front.

Press run: The total number of any one set of cards printed.

Price guide: A periodical or book which contains checklists of cards, sets and other memorabilia and their values in varying conditions.

Price on request (P.O.R.): A dealer will advertise a card P.O.R. if he believes the card will fluctuate in price from the time he places his ad until the time the ad is seen by the public.

Printer's Proof: A parallel set used in Classic products; see also Artist's Proof and Press Proof.

Prism: Metallic background with various backgrounds, like squares. Used in Pacific products. The variously angled geometric shapes reflect light and color differently as the viewing angle changes. Also a brand name for premium line of Pacific's cards, sold one per pack.

ProCards: A large and important maker of minor league cards between 1986-1991. ProCards revolutionized the minor league card business in 1986 when it issued around 100 different minor league team sets. The company was sold to Fleer in 1992.

Promo card: A card made for promotional purposes. Promo cards generally have very relatively limited distribution and can be quite valuable. They are often marked with a large overprint on front and back.

Proof card: A card made not to be sold but to test the card presses, the card design, photography, colors, paper, statistical accuracy and so forth.

Prototype: Technically a card made to demonstrate a new product in an effort to win licensing approval from leagues and players' unions. Term is often used incorrectly as interchangeable with "promo card."

Puzzle piece, poster piece: The back of a card containing a partial design which, when pieced together with corresponding pieces, forms a large picture or poster. Also, the three-piece jigsaw puzzle panel which was inserted with Donruss cards from 1982-91.

PVC: Shortened name of a chemical compound (polyvinylchloride), sometimes used to make plastic sheets and other card collectors' supplies. PVC plastic is generally clearer and stiffer than other types of plastic sheets but may have a shorter safe life.

Rack box: A retail display box of rack packs. There are usually 24 rack packs to a rack box.

Rack case: A wholesale case of rack boxes. There are usually three or six rack boxes in a rack case.

Rack pack: A cellophane-wrapped pack of cards, usually having three compartments, designed to be hung from a peg in a retail store. Rack packs vary in the number of cards in each pack; also, some rack packs consist of nothing but cello-wrapped wax packs.

Rare: Difficult to obtain and limited in number. See "Scarce."

Rated Rookie (RR): A Donruss subset featuring young players the company thinks are the top rookie players from a particular year (1984-present).

Record Breaker card: A special Topps card found in a regular issue set which commemorates a record-breaking performance by a player from the previous season.

Regional set: A card set limited in distribution to one geographical area. Regional sets often depict players from one team.

Refractor: A special version of a Finest or other Topps' brand high-tech card featuring a shiny, rainbow effect when viewed under proper conditions. Usually issued as a parallel set. First used in 1993 Topps Finest baseball.

Reprint: A reproduction of a previously-issued sports card or set. Generally produced to satisfy collector demand, they usually-but not always-are labeled "reprint" and have little collector value.

Restored card: A card which has had "cosmetic surgery"-that is, a card which has had its imperfections fixed long after the card was issued. A card restorer can rebuild corners, remove creases, gum or other stains and restore gloss to card stock. Restored cards should be clearly labeled as such by whoever is selling them, and should be priced much less than unrestored cards in the same apparent condition.

Reverse: The back of a card.

Reversed negative: A common error in which the picture negative is flip-flopped so the picture is printed backward, or reversed.

Rookie card: A player's first card issued by a major card producer. It may or may not be issued during the player's actual rookie season. In the years prior to promo-and insert-card mania, a rookie card was often a player's most valuable card.

ROY: Rookie of the Year award given annually by each major league.

SASE: A term used in hobby advertisements and elsewhere to indicate a "self-addressed, stamped envelope" should be provided for reply.

Scarce: Not easily obtainable. A relative term.

SCD: Sports Collectors Digest, the hobby's oldest and largest magazine.

Score: Brand name of sports cards originated by Major League Marketing, manufactured by Optigraphics and distributed by Amurol in 1988. Score cards are distinguished by high-quality photos and graphics and the first use of full-color backs. Since 1992 it has been the base-brand product for the Pinnacle family since 1992.

Scuff: A rub or abrasion on a card which removes a portion of its gloss or printing. Scuffed cards are worth less than non-scuffed cards.

Sell price: The price at which a dealer will sell cards, generally the retail or "book" price of a card.

Sepia: A reddish-brown coloration used in some card sets instead of traditional black-and-white. In the 19th Century it was the result of the chemicals used to create certain photographic images. Provides an antique look.

Series: A group of cards that is part of a set and was issued at one time. The term is usually applied to Topps sets from 1952 through 1973, when sets were issued in various series.

Set: A complete run of cards, including one number of each card issued by a particular manufacturer in a particular year; for example, a 1985 Fleer set.

Short-print: A card that, for whatever reason, is not printed in as great a quantity as other cards in the set. The opposite of a double-print.

Silver Signature: A parallel set used in Upper Deck Collector's Choice products, usually inserted one per pack. Features a facsimile autograph in silver ink on the card front.

Skip-numbered: A set of cards not numbered in exact sequence, with some numbers missing. Some manufacturers have issued skip-numbered sets to trick collectors into buying more cards, looking for card numbers that didn't exist. Other sets became skip-numbered when one or more players were dropped from the set at the last minute and were not replaced.

Slab: Slang for the sealed, hard-plastic holder in which cards graded by a grading service are encased. Graded cards are said to be "slabbed."

Sleeve: A soft plastic envelope, sealed on three sides, used to house and protect individual baseball cards.

Special card: A card in a set that depicts something other than a single player without mention of any special event that may involve that player; for example, a checklist card, All-Star card, team card or team leaders card.

Spectralight: Parallel set used in Topps products, having a posterized, shiny color-foil background.

Sportflics/Sportflix: Brand name of a baseball card made by Major League Marketing and Optigraphics and distributed by Amurol. Sportflics, which use an exclusive three-dimensional process to put several images on one card, were first made from 1986-1990 in various sizes and formats of cards and discs. Score reintroduced the brand name in 1994 as Sportflics 2000, changing it again to Sportflix in 1995.

S/S or S-to-S: Side-to-side. Expressed as a ratio to describe the centering within a card's vertical borders.

Stamp: An adhesive-backed paper which depicts a player. When the stamp, which can be an individual or a sheet of many stamps, is moistened, it can be attached to another surface or corresponding stamp album.

Standard size card: A card which measures 2-1/2" by 3-1/2". In 1957, Topps baseball cards were produced in the 2-1/2" by 3-1/2" size, which set the standard for modern trading cards.

Star card: A designation used to describe a player of better-than-average skill and performance who isn't of "superstar' caliber. The term "minor star" may also be used to differentiate between various levels of skill and popularity. In terms of value, star cards fall between commons and superstars.

Starter kit: A prepackaged kit for new collectors. Often it contains a binder and plastic sheets, individual card protectors, plastic holders, a book or magazine on collecting or a price guide, and cards.

Starter set: A less-than-complete set of cards meant to give beginning collectors a start towards completing a certain set.

Starting Lineup: A line of plastic action figures with accompanying cards produced by Kenner since 1988. Also, the trademark for a computer-based baseball game with cards produced by Parker Brothers.

Sticker: An adhesive-backed card. Stickers can either be card-size or smaller. Topps, Fleer and Panini have issued major sports sticker sets in the last several years. Stickers are not tremendously popular with collectors in the U.S.

Stock: The cardboard or other substance on which a card is printed.

Subset: A set of cards with the same theme within a larger set. Examples: Donruss Diamond Kings are a "subset" of the Donruss set; or Topps All-Star cards are a subset of the Topps set.

Super card: A designation referring to the physical size of a card. Generally, any card postcard size or larger is referred to as a super. Also called jumbos.

Superstar card: A card picturing a player of Hall-of-Fame (current or future) caliber.

Super Team: Interactive inserts in Stadium Club products that pick divisional, conference and championship teams and are redeemable for special card sets in the depicted team wins.

Tab: A portion of a card, usually perforated, which can be removed from the card without damaging the central part of the card. Often used in redemption programs in earlier years.

Tattoos: Transfers showing ballplayers and/or team logos. Tattoos were a popular wax-pack premium 'in 1960s Topps wax packs; later Topps launched them as a stand-alone product, with little success.

T/B or T-to-B: Top-to-bottom. Describes the ratio of a card's centering between its horizontal borders.

Team card: A card picturing an entire team.

Team set: All the cards from a particular set showing members of a particular team. Team set collecting is becoming a very popular type of collecting as the cost and/or number of complete sets increases.

Team-issued set: A set given away or sold by an individual team.

Test issue: A set of cards distributed on a limited basis to test its marketability. Topps issued a variety of test products in the 1960s, 1970s and 1980s.

3-D card: Term used to refer to various types of cards and issues. A 3-D card may have a diffused background that lets the foreground image stand out (Kellogg's), multiple images (Sportflics) or a raised image (Topps 3-D).

Tiffany: Name given by collectors to Topps' glossy versions of its regular and traded sets issued between 1984-1991.

Tin: Slang for a Fleer glossy set (1987-89), which are packaged in colorful, numbered tin boxes.

Tobacco cards: Cards issued in the late 19th and early 20th Centuries as a premium with cigarettes or other tobacco products. The first tobacco cards were issued around 1886; the last tobacco baseball cards were issued with Red Man chewing tobacco in the mid-1950s.

Topps: The major figure in sportscard making for the last 45 years, Topps began issuing sports card sets in 1951 and has issued them every year since.

Traded set: An auxiliary set of cards issued toward the end of the season to reflect trades that were made after the printing of the regular set. Sometimes called "Update" sets, they also usually feature rookies not included in the regular set. The first stand-alone traded set was a baseball traded set issued by Topps in 1981.

Trimmed card: A card that has been cut down from its original size, greatly reducing its value.

Two-way mirror: Process that pictures a silver, see-through mirror on the front, with a player photo on the back that can be seen through the front. First used in 1994-95 Donruss Hockey Masked Marvels.

Uncut sheet: A full press sheet of cards that has never been cut into individual cards.

UV: Ultraviolet. Usually refers to a glossy coating applied to front (and sometimes back) of cards to impart a shiny surface.

Update set: See "Traded set."

Upper Deck: A California-based company which introduced a line of ultra-high-quality, expensive baseball cards in 1989, essentially beginning the high-tech card era.

Variation: A card that exists in two different forms within the same set. A "variation" frequently occurs when an error card has been corrected. Some variations are worth more than others, based on the quantity of each variation produced.

Vending case: A wholesale package containing nothing but cards, originally intended to be used to fill card-vending machines. Most often a vending case contains 24 boxes of 500 cards each.

Vending set: A set put together from cards in vending boxes. Such sets will not have cards that exhibit wax or gum stains.

Want list: A collector's or dealer's list of items he wishes to buy. Often, a collector will send a dealer a "want list," and the dealer will try to locate the items on the list.

Wax box: A retail box of wax packs. There are usually 36 wax packs in a wax box.

Wax case: A wholesale case of wax boxes. There are usually 20 wax boxes in a wax case. Often the term is shortened to "wax."

Wax pack: The basic unit of retail baseball card packaging until the early 1990s. A specific number of baseball cards, packaged with a premium (bubble gum, puzzle pieces, logo stickers and so forth) in a wax-coated wrapper. By 1991 the premiums had disappeared and the wax was being replaced by tamperproof plastic or foil.

Wax stain: A condition caused by wax from the pack wrapper melting onto a card. Wax stains lower the value of a card, but can often be removed by rubbing with a pair of pantyhose or using a commercial wax-removal solution.

Wrapper: What card packs are packaged in. A collectible item in itself.

Wrong backs: A card with the wrong back (the player on the front does not match the biography/statistics on the back). Most collectors think these cards are damaged and are worth less than a correctly-printed card, although some collectors will pay premiums on superstars or hot rookies.

ALPHABETICAL INDEX

A

B

C

D

E

F

G

H

I

J

K

L

M

N

O

P

Q

R

S

T

U

V

W

Y

Z

CHRONOLOGICAL INDEX

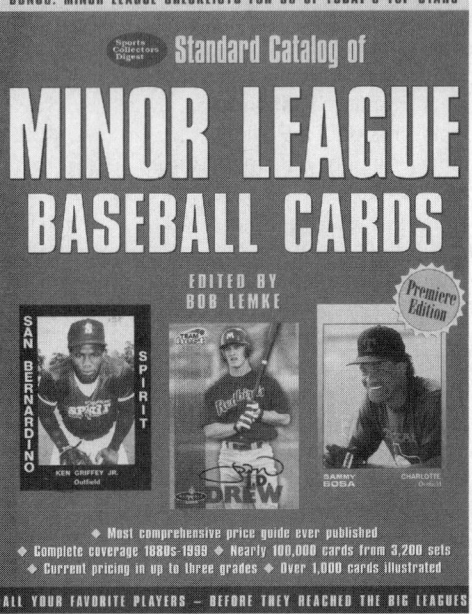

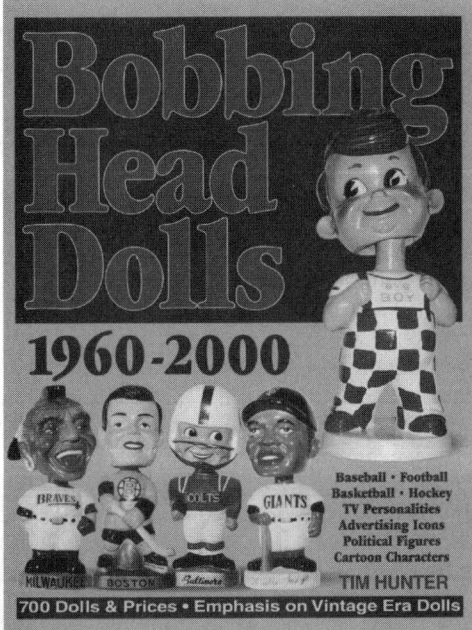

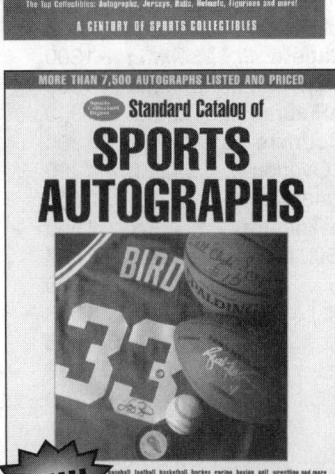

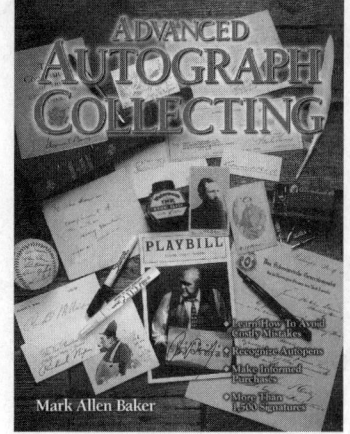

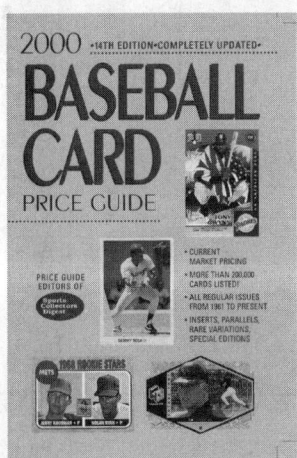

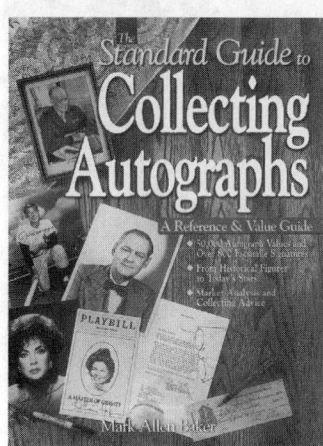

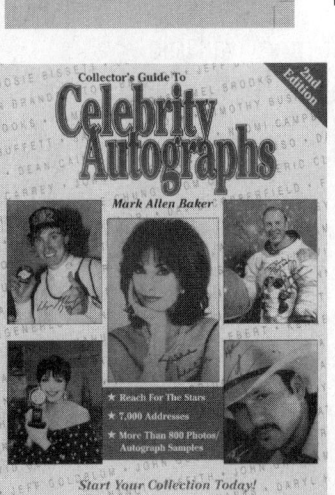